COLLINS
COBUILD
LEARNER'S
DICTIONARY

**THE UNIVERSITY
OF BIRMINGHAM**

**COLLINS
COBUILD**

HarperCollins*Publishers*

HarperCollins Publishers
77-85 Fulham Palace Road
London   W6 8JB

COBUILD is a trademark of William Collins, Sons & Co Ltd
This edition first published in Great Britain 1996
© HarperCollins Publishers 1996

2 4 6 8 1 0 9 7 5 3 1

ISBN 0 00 375058 2 paperback
ISBN 0 00 375057 4 hardback
Norway ISBN 0 00 375072 8 PLC

Computer typeset by
Morton Word Processing Ltd.
Scarborough
England

Printed in Great Britain.

Corpus Acknowledgements

We would like to acknowledge the assistance of the many hundreds of individuals
and companies who have kindly given permission for copyright material to be
used in The Bank of English. The written sources include many national and
regional newspapers in Britain and overseas; magazine and periodical publishers;
and book publishers in Britain, the United States, and Australia. Extensive spoken
data has been provided by radio and television broadcasting companies; research
workers at many universities and other institutions; and numerous individual contributors. We are grateful to them all.

Note

Contents

The COBUILD Series

Founding Editor in Chief
John Sinclair

Publishing Director
Gwyneth Fox

EDITORIAL TEAM

Editorial Manager
Stephen Bullon

Editors

Christina Rammell   Laura Wedgeworth
Catherine Brown   Rosalind Combley
Ceri Hewitt   Heather Raybould
John Todd   John Williams

Editorial Assistance
Michael Lax
Miranda Timewell

Computing Staff	Secretarial Staff	Publishing Manager
Tim Lane	Sue Crawley	Debbie Seymour
Andrea Lewis	Michelle Devereux	

Production Manager	Design	Illustrations
Gillian McNair	Ray Barnett	Ela Bullon
	Ted Carden	Anthony Boswell
	Lynsey Roxburgh	

We would like to thank Dr Julia Penelope for her advice on American English. We also gratefully acknowledge the invaluable contribution of all those who compiled and edited the Collins COBUILD English Dictionary, whose work provided the basis for this book.

Introduction

COBUILD has been in existence for more than 16 years, collecting and analysing increasingly large quantities of written and spoken English. All the statements that COBUILD makes are based on an examination of the English language in use, as represented in The Bank of English - our present collection, which now stands at over 250 million words.

This dictionary continues the established tradition of COBUILD Dictionaries in providing clear and detailed information about the English language. The explanations are all written in full sentences, and are based on the information we have derived from The Bank of English. The examples are all taken from this corpus, and represent *real* language in use; that is to say, each example is a chunk of language that served a purpose in a real text or conversation, and is not made up.

The Bank of English

The Bank of English is a computer-held store of thousands of texts of English, known as a *corpus*. These texts range from serious novels, through popular fiction, newspapers, magazines and junk mail, to informal spoken conversations. About 25% of the texts are American, and a further 5% come from varieties of English such as Australian and Singaporean. At the time of writing, this corpus stands at over 250 million words, of which 20 million words have been transcribed from spontaneous speech.

The corpus is a rich store of information about the language. It enables dictionary writers to examine how words have been used, and to write dictionary entries which reflect the central and typical uses of the language. Every entry in this dictionary is based on the evidence of the corpus.

By using the corpus, we are able to establish which are the common and important meanings of a word, and which are the main grammatical patterns. This information is then carefully assembled by the editors and presented in a clear and detailed way.

The entries

As with all COBUILD dictionaries, explanations of meaning are presented in full sentences. This style of explanation enables us to present words in their typical context, and to show the typical grammatical patterns associated with them. The direct and informal style of the explanations is similar to the way in which teachers in a classroom would explain what a word means.

The way the explanations are written shows you what the typical contexts, typical collocates, and typical structures are. For example, the explanation of meaning 1 of *sanction* says:

> If someone in authority **sanctions** an action or practice, they officially approve of it and allow it to be done.

This shows that the subject of the verb *sanction* is normally a person, and that it must be a person in authority. This information is important if you have to make a choice between the words *sanction* or *allow*, for example, because it shows you the sort of context in which the word will typically occur.

The explanation of meaning 21 of *run* says:

> When you say that vehicles such as trains and buses **run** from one place to another, you mean they regularly travel along that route.

This shows that this meaning of *run* is used only of vehicles, and so you would not say of your regular journey to school or work that you 'run' there.

Typical grammatical structures are also given in the explanations. For example, verbs which typically occur in the passive voice are defined in the passive. The first meaning of *reserve* says:

> If something **is reserved** for a particular person or purpose, it is kept specially for that person or purpose.

This use of the passive in the explanation reflects the most typical usage in the language, and is supported by the grammar note in the extra column, which says: *usu passive*.

The explanations are often illustrated by examples, which are taken directly from The Bank of English. The examples have been carefully chosen to reflect typical collocations and structural patterns, and to show the word being used in a natural context.

The Extra Column

Information about frequency, grammar, register, and pragmatics is provided in the extra column, enabling you to find this information at a glance, separately from the main column of explanations and examples. This means that you will always know where to find information: explanations and examples for each meaning in the main column, with the other information laid out alongside it.

Frequency

The corpus also enables us to provide information about frequency, so that whenever you look up a word you can see immediately if it is a very common word or not. About half the entries in the dictionary have a frequency marker in the extra column. They work on a scale from 5 black diamonds down to one black diamond.

Words with five black diamonds are the common grammar words, such as **the**, **with**, **also** and so on, as well as the more common vocabulary items such as **stand**, **sit**, and **think**. This is the smallest group of words, but because they are the most frequent words, they form a huge proportion of the language.

Words with four black diamonds are also very common words, and together with the five-diamond words account for 75% of all English usage.

Words with three, with two, and with one black diamond are progressively less frequent. And finally, about half the entries in the dictionary have no frequency band marker at all. These are words which you are more likely to read or hear than use regularly.

At the back of the book, we have listed all the words in the top four frequency bands.

Grammar

Grammar information is provided for all meanings, starting with a basic word class such as VERB, N-COUNT, and so on. If there is something important to say about restrictions, or about typical patterns, this information is provided after a colon (:). In the case of verbs, every example has a corresponding pattern spelled out in the extra column. There is a list of abbreviations used in the grammar notations inside the front cover, and an explanation of the word classes and patterns on pages xi - xxii.

Pragmatics

In some entries, you will see in the extra column a box with the word `pragmatics' inside it. This box indicates that a particular explanation is doing more than explaining straightforward meaning. There are several areas of language behaviour that are signalled by this box:

Functions: such as inviting, agreeing, advising, and so on.
Discourse organizing: commenting on the structure of what you are saying while you are saying it. For example, if you introduce a reason for something with the phrase *for a start*, you are indicating that there are further reasons that you might or could mention.
Expressing attitudes: some words make clear what the speaker's attitude is as well as describing or naming a person or object. For example, if you use the verb *deign*, you are expressing quite strongly the fact that you do not approve of the way in which someone agreed to do something.
Emphasizing: certain words and phrases are used to emphasize what is being said. For example, if someone says 'It's mighty hot', they are emphasizing how hot they think it is.

All these types of behaviour are indicated in the extra column by the pragmatics box.

Style and Register

The final category of information in the extra column is style, register, and regional variation. Vocabulary items that are used in British English and not American English are labelled BRITISH in the extra column; and similarly American vocabulary items are labelled AMERICAN. In many cases, the explanations will tell you what the equivalent word or expression is in the other region. Other labels indicate formal and informal language, spoken language, and so on.

The appendices

This book does not quite finish at the end of the dictionary text. There are several appendices, listed on the contents page, which provide information on geographical place names in English, compass points, numbers, dates, time, and weights and measures. The words in the top four frequency bands are listed here too, and finally, there are 20 pages of illustrations, all specially drawn for this book.

As with all COBUILD Dictionaries, it is our aim to provide information clearly and precisely. We welcome feedback from users, and are always pleased to hear your views. If you have any comments or criticisms of this dictionary, please write to us.

COBUILD
Institute of Research and Development
University of Birmingham Research Park
Vincent Drive
Birmingham B15 2SQ
Great Britain

e-mail: editors@cobuild.collins.co.uk

Guide to the Dictionary Entries

'ghost town
'ghost-write
ghoul
GHQ
GI

ORDER OF ENTRIES: headwords in alphabetical order, taking no notice of capital letters, hyphens, apostrophes, accents, or spaces between words.

gan·der /'gændə/ **ganders**. A gander is a male goose.

gab·ar·dine /ˌgæbə'diːn/ **gabardines**; also spelled **gaberdine**.

HEADWORDS: the main form of the headword appears in large bold face letters, starting in the left hand margin.

Hyphenation points are included, telling you where it is acceptable to hyphenate the headword.

Variant forms or alternative spellings of a headword are given at the end of information about the headword.

gher·kin /'gɜːkɪn/ **gherkins**.

glit·ter /'glɪtə/ **glitters, glittering, glittered**.

gloomy /'gluːmi/ **gloomier, gloomiest**.

ghet·to /'getəʊ/ **ghettos** or **ghettoes**.

gam·bol /'gæmbəl/ **gambols, gambolling, gam-bolled**; spelled **gamboling, gamboled** in American English.

INFLECTED FORMS: given in smaller bold face letters, for noun, verb, adjective, and adverb forms.

Notes about inflected forms.

gey·ser /'giːzə/ **geysers**.

gradu·ate, **graduates, graduating, graduated**. The noun is pronounced /'grædʒʊət/. The verb is pronounced /'grædʒʊeɪt/.

PRONUNCIATION: See guide inside the back cover.

Notes about pronunciation.

gilt /gɪlt/ **gilts**. **1** A gilt object is covered with a thin layer of gold or gold paint. **2** Gilts are the same as gilt-edged stocks or securities.

MEANING NUMBERS: for words with more than one meaning or use.

DEFINITIONS: written in full sentences, using common words and showing the common ways in which the headword is used.

For example, the definition of a verb can tell you what kinds of subject and object are used with the verb in that meaning, and whether the verb is typically used in a particular structure.

The definition of an adjective can tell you what other words are commonly used with it in that meaning, and whether it is more often used before a noun or after a verb.

EXAMPLES: are all genuine examples of real language, taken from the Bank of English. They are carefully selected to show typical contexts in which the word or expression is found, and the grammatical patterns in which it most often occurs.

In some cases where a word has several possible structures and collocates, the definition shows the most frequent usage, and the examples illustrate other possibilities.

DERIVED WORDS: other words formed from the headword with a closely linked meaning are given after the diamond symbol ♦.

Changes in word class where the meaning is very closely linked are introduced by a triangle symbol ►.

8 If you **guide** a vehicle somewhere, you control it carefully to make sure that it goes in the right direction. *Captain Shelton guided his plane down the runway.*

grad·ual /ˈɡrædʒuəl/. A **gradual** change or process occurs in small stages over a long period of time, rather than suddenly. *You can expect her progress at school to be gradual rather than brilliant.*

5 If you describe someone or something as **great**, you approve of them or admire them. *Arturo has this great place in Cazadero… I think she's great.*

give /ɡɪv/ **gives, giving, gave, given**. **1** You can use **give** with nouns that refer to physical actions. The whole expression refers to the performing of the action. For example, 'She gave a smile' means almost the same as 'She smiled'. *She stretched her arms out and gave a great yawn… He reached for her hand and gave it a reassuring squeeze.*

gripe /ɡraɪp/ **gripes, griping, griped**. If you say that someone is griping, you mean they are complaining about something in an annoying way. *I am sick of hearing motorists griping about the state of the roads.*

groomed /ɡruːmd/. You use **groomed** in expressions such as **well groomed** and **badly groomed** to say how neat, clean, and smart a person is. *She always appeared perfectly grooomed.*

glib /ɡlɪb/. If you describe what someone says as **glib**, you disapprove of it because it suggests that something is simple or easy when this is not the case at all. ♦ **glib·ly** *We talk glibly of equality of opportunity.*

glid·er /ˈɡlaɪdə/ **gliders**. A **glider** is an aircraft without an engine, which flies by floating on air currents. ♦ **glid·ing**. **Gliding** is the sport or activity of flying in a glider.

glare /ɡleə/ **glares, glaring, glared**. **1** If you glare at someone, you look at them with an angry expression on your face. *Jacob glared and muttered something.* ► Also a noun. *His glasses magnified his irritable glare.*

grouse, /ɡraʊs/ **grouses, grousing, groused**. The form **grouse** is used as the plural for meaning 1. **1 Grouse** are small fat birds which are often shot for sport and can be eaten. ► **Grouse** is the flesh of this bird eaten as food. *… roast grouse.*

5 If you say that a child is being **as good as gold**, you are emphasizing that they are behaving very well. **6** If you say that someone has **a heart of gold**, you are emphasizing that they are very good and kind.

PHRASE
PRAGMATICS
PHRASE

PHRASES: are highlighted in bold type and marked PHRASE in the extra column.

---

6 Gas is the fuel which is used to drive motor vehicles. The British word is petrol. *...a tank of gas. ...gas stations.* • If you **step on the gas** when you are driving a vehicle, you go faster.

N-UNCOUNT
AMERICAN

PHRASE

If a phrase is very closely connected with another use or meaning, it may be included within the same meaning number after the symbol •.

---

grind down. If you say that someone **grinds you down**, you mean that they treat you very harshly and cruelly, reducing your confidence or your will to resist.

PHRASAL VB
V n P
PRAGMATICS

grind on. If you say that something **grinds on**, you disapprove of the fact that it continues to happen in the same way for a long time.

PHRASAL VB
V P
PRAGMATICS

PHRASAL VERBS: in alphabetical order at the end of an entry.

---

5 When you **gather** something such as your strength, courage, or thoughts, you make an effort to prepare yourself to do something. *You must gather your strenght for the journey.* ▶ **Gather up** means the same as **gather**. *She was gathering up her courage to approach him.*

VERB
V n

PHRASAL VB
V P noun
also V n P

Sometimes phrasal verbs are explained earlier in the entry, after the symbol ▶.

---

gaol.er /'dʒeɪlə/**gaoler.** See **jailer.**

CROSS REFERENCES: indicating that relevant information can be found at another entry.

---

7 See also **greenhouse gas, natural gas, tear gas, gas chamber, gas mask.**

---

9 General workers do a variety of jobs which require no special skill or training. *...a tractor driver and two general labourers.* **10** See also **generally.**

ADJ:ADJ n

---

8 • to **gather dust:** see **dust.**

Cross references to phrases follow the symbol •.

---

gas mask, gas masks. A **gas mask** is a device worn over someone's face in order to protect them from poisonous gases.

◆◇◇◇◇
N-COUNT

EXTRA COLUMN

gereral e'lection, general elections. A **general election** is an election at which all the citizens of a country vote for people to represent them in the national parliament.

◆◆◆◇◇
N-COUNT

FREQUENCY: information from the Bank of English about how important a word is. See Page 1316

---

gain·ful /'geɪnfʊl/. If you are in **gainful** employment, you have a job for which you are paid and which is not against the law. *...lack of opportunities for gainful employment.* ✦ **gain·ful·ly** *Both parents were gainfully employed.*

ADJ:ADJ n
FORMAL

ADV:
ADV -ed

GRAMMAR: see pages xi – xxii where the structural patterns are explained.

2 When you **gasp**, you take a short quick breath through your mouth, especially when you are surprised, shocked, or in pain. *She gasped for air... 'Stop!' he gasped.*

VERB:V
V for n
V with quote

The extra column also contains information about pragmatics and about style and register; this is explained on the next page.

Pragmatics

In this dictionary the word PRAGMATICS is shown in the extra column next to words and expressions which are used by speakers of English to do more than simply convey meaning. People often use language to do things such as invite friends to parties, compliment someone on their appearance, promise to do something, insult someone, or express their disapproval of something. Many words and expressions in English, as in other languages, therefore 'do' something as well as 'mean' something.

In order to be successful in this area of communication, learners of English need to know which words and expressions do which things. We have analyzed the data and found, for example, the ways in which English speakers invite, persuade, give advice, or express annoyance. In this dictionary we draw attention to those words and expressions, so that learners can get as much information as possible about communicating clearly and effectively in English.

For every word meaning where there is information which is important for correct use, or which may be confusing for the learner, we show this in the extra column with the word PRAGMATICS, and include additional information in the definition about how, when, and why the word or expression is used.

For example, the entry for the word *grotty* has a pragmatics box in the extra column. The explanation begins:

If you describe something as **grotty**

this shows that the speaker is expressing a subjective judgement. The explanation continues:

you dislike it and think that it is unpleasant or of poor quality.

this shows the speaker's feelings about something.

Finally, there is an example showing a typical use in context:

...a grotty little flat in Camden.

Style and Register

Some words or meanings are used mainly by particular groups of people, or in particular social contexts. In this dictionary, when this is true of a particular word or expression, we mention it in the extra column using the following labels:

Geographical labels

AMERICAN: used mainly by speakers and writers in the USA, and in other places where American English is used or taught. e.g. *gasoline, gearshift.*

BRITISH: used mainly by speakers and writers in Britian, and in other places where British English is used or taught. e.g. *gazump, geezer.*

Style labels

DATED: generally considered to be old-fashioned, and no longer in common use. e.g. *gallant, gosh.*

FORMAL: used mainly in official situations, or by political and business organizations, or when speaking or writing to people in authority. e.g. *generality, germane.*

INFORMAL: used mainly in informal situations, conversations, and personal letters. e.g. *gig, gigantic.*

JOURNALISM: used mainly in newspapers, and in television and radio broadcasts. e.g. *game plan.*

LITERARY: used mainly in novels, poetry, and other forms of literature. e.g. *gladden, gossamer.*

RUDE: likely to offend people, or insult them; words labelled RUDE should usually be avoided.

SPOKEN: used mainly in speech rather than in writing. e.g. *get up to* .

TECHNICAL: used mainly when talking or writing about objects, events, or processes in a specialist subject, such as business, music, or medicine. e.g. *gunnery, generic.*

WRITTEN: used mainly in writing rather than in speech. e.g. *gingerly.*

Grammar

Introduction

Nearly all the words that are explained in the dictionary have grammar information given about them in the extra column. For each word or meaning, its primary word class, or part of speech, is shown in capital letters. Examples of word classes are N-COUNT, VERB, ADJ-GRADED, PRON, and PHRASE. In many cases, the primary word class is followed by one or more patterns which extend or restrict the use of the word. The patterns are introduced by a colon. Examples of primary word classes followed by patterns are:

N-COUNT: also *by/with* N
N-UNCOUNT: also N *in* pl
ADJ-GRADED: ADJ n

In the patterns, the primary word class (N, ADJ,) is shown in capital letters, other English words *(by/with)* associated with the pattern are shown in italics, and other information (passive, pl) is shown in ordinary type. Alternative patterns may be shown using a slash (/). For example, a noun which has the pattern N *between/to/of* n is always followed by one of the prepositions 'between', 'to', or 'of'. In the patterns, word class abbreviations in capitals refer to the word that is being explained, and word class abbreviations in small letters refer to other elements in the pattern.

For verbs, the information about patterns is presented in a slightly different way. Instead of all the patterns being shown immediately after the primary word class, each pattern associated with that meaning of the verb is shown separately, one after the other, in the extra column. The order of the patterns corresponds to the order of the examples. However, in some cases, the first pattern, instead of having an example, is illustrated by the way the verb is used in the definition. In addition, some less common patterns may be shown in the extra column without any examples being given. These additional patterns are introduced by the word Also.

The entry for encroach, meaning 2, illustrates all three types of pattern:

2 If something **encroaches** on a place, it spreads and takes over more and more of that place. *I turned into the dirt road and followed it through encroaching trees and bushes.*

VERB:
V *on* n
V-ing
Also V prep/adv
FORMAL

The primary word-class VERB is followed by a colon (:) and then the first pattern, V *on* n. The colon indicates that the first pattern is illustrated in the definition (If something

encroaches on a place...) rather than in the examples.

The second pattern, V-ing, corresponds to the example, in which the present participle of the verb is used as an adjective (...*encroaching trees and bushes*).

The final pattern, V prep/adv, is introduced by the word Also. This means that, although the pattern can be found in The Bank of English, it is not shown in the definition or the examples. In this case, the pattern shows that *encroach* can be followed by a range of different prepositions, adverbs, and adverbial phrases:

Thickets and woodland encroach to the water's edge.

The inky clouds encroached further and a clap of thunder echoed around the valley.

Heat encroaches from the outer shell towards the inside.

Individual word classes and patterns

In showing the grammar patterns, we have used abbreviations and conventions which the user will find relatively easy to interpret.

The sections below contain further information about the more frequent patterns. This material will enable you to understand the meaning of those less common patterns which we have not had the space to cover here. A full list of abbreviations can be found on the inside front cover of the dictionary.

Verbs

VERB, VB
mean an ordinary verb. All verb entries provide further information, as described below.

V
means that the word is used as a simple intransitive verb. That is, it does not have an object.

fail 7 *Many food crops **failed** because of the drought.*
film 2 *A South African television crew **has been filming** recently in Budapest.*
think 4 *She closed her eyes for a moment, trying to **think**.*

V prep/adv, V adv/prep
mean that the verb is intransitive, and also has an adjunct of some sort with it. The adjunct can be a prepositional phrase, an adverb, or an

adverbial phrase. Both patterns mean the same thing: if prep is given first, the first example of the pattern shows a prepositional phrase, and if adv is given first, the first example shows an adverb or adverbial phrase.

arrive 1 *The Princess Royal **arrived at Gatwick** this morning.* (V prep/adv)
circle 6 *There were two helicopters **circling around**.* (V adv/prep)

V prep
means that the verb is intransitive and is followed by a prepositional phrase. Many verbs with this pattern can be followed by a range of different prepositions.

lie 1 7 *His country's economy **lies in** ruins.*
nod 2 *'Does it work?' he asked, **nodding at** the piano.*

V adv
means that the verb is intransitive and is followed by an adverb or adverbial phrase.

score 3 *Congress as an institution **scores low** in public opinion polls.*
wheel 7 *He **wheeled around** to face her.*

V *with* n, V *to* n, V *for* n, etc
mean that the verb is intransitive and is followed by the specified preposition and then a noun or noun group.

accord 3 *Such an approach **accords with the principles** of socialist ideology.* (V *with* n)
tread 1 *Oh, sorry, I didn't mean to **tread on your foot**.* (V *on* n)
change 3 *The mood gradually **changed from resignation to rage**.* (V *from* n *to* n)

V *together*, V *away*, V *out*, etc
mean that the verb is intransitive and is followed by the specified adverb.

group 6 *We want to encourage them to **group together**.* (V *together*)
billow 1 *Her pink dress **billowed out** around her.* (V *out*)

V-ing
means that the present participle of the verb is being used as an adjective.

fade 1 *...**fading** portraits of the Queen.*
holiday 2 *Vacant rooms on the campus were being used by **holidaying** families.*

V -ing
means that the verb is followed by another verb,

and that the second verb is in the '-ing' form.

mind 2 2 *Would you **mind waiting** outside ?*
stop 1 *He can't **stop thinking** about it.*

V to-inf
means that the verb is followed by another verb, and that the second verb is in the infinitive form with 'to'.

afford 1 *We couldn't **afford to buy** a new rug.*
want 1 *People **wanted to know** who this talented designer was.*

V inf
means that the verb is followed by another verb, and that the second verb is in the infinitive form without 'to'.

dare 1 *...problems in our family that I didn't **dare tell** Uncle.*

V that
means that the verb introduces a 'that'-clause. The clause may begin with the word 'that' but does not necessarily do so.

specify 2 *One rule **specifies that learner drivers must be supervised by adults**.*
tell 10 *You can **tell he's joking**.*

V wh
means that the verb introduces a clause beginning with a 'wh'-word such as 'what', 'why', and 'when'. 'How' and 'if' are also 'wh'-words.

analyse 1 ***Analyse what is causing the stress in your life**.*
care 1 *...young men who did not **care whether they lived or died**.*
decide 5 *The results will **decide if he will win a place at a good university**.*

V with quote
means that the verb is used to introduce or indicate direct speech, that is, the precise words that someone said or wrote.

continue 5 *'Anyway, that was what gave us the idea,' she **continued** after a pause.*
whisper 1 *'Keep your voice down,' I **whispered**.*

V adj
means that the verb is followed by an adjective complement. This pattern is often associated with link verbs.

escape 4 *The man's girlfriend managed to **escape unhurt**.*
feel 1 *I **am feeling** very **depressed**.*

V *as* n, **V** *as* adj
means that the verb is intransitive and is followed by a noun or adjective complement introduced by 'as'.

practise 3 *He was born in Hong Kong where he subsequently* **practised as a lawyer** *until his retirement.*
rank 5 *St Petersburg's night life* **ranks as more exciting** *than the capital's.*

V amount
means that the verb is followed by a word or phrase indicating an amount of something, such as 'a lot', 'nothing', or 'four hundred pounds'.

fall 6 *Oil product prices* **fell 0.2 per cent.**
weigh 1 *You always* **weigh less** *in the morning.*

V n
means that the word is used as a simple transitive verb in the active voice. That is, it occurs in clauses containing only a subject, a verb, and an object. The object is usually a noun group.

crush 1 *Andrew* **crushed his empty can.**
revitalize *This hair conditioner is excellent for* **revitalizing dry, lifeless hair.**

V n prep/adv, **V** n adv/prep
mean that the verb is transitive, and also has an adjunct of some sort with it. The adjunct can be a prepositional phrase, an adverb, or an adverbial phrase. Both these patterns mean the same thing.

scatter 1 *She tore the rose apart and* **scattered the petals over the grave.**
wave 2 *Leshka* **waved him away** *with a show of irritation.*

V n *with* n, **V** n *to* n, **V** n *from* n, etc
mean that the verb is transitive and that the object is followed by the specified preposition and then another noun or noun group.

alternate 1 *He went to the gym six days a week,* **alternating weight training with aerobics.** (V n *with* n)
compensate 1 *...the official promise to* **compensate people for the price rise.** (V n *for* n)

V n with adv
means that the verb is transitive, and that an adverb or adverbial phrase can come between the verb and the object.

pare 1 *He took out a slab of cheese,* **pared off a slice** *and ate it hastily.*
move 9 *The band* **have moved forward their**

Leeds date *to October 27.*

V n -ing
means that the verb is transitive, and that the object is followed by another verb in the '-ing'-form.

prevent 1 *We recognized the possibility and took steps to* **prevent it happening.**
remember 1 *I* **remember her being** *a dominant figure.*

V n to-inf
means that the verb is transitive, and that the object is followed by another verb in the infinitive form with 'to'.

enable 1 *The new test should* **enable doctors to detect** *the disease early.*
incite *He* **incited his fellow citizens to take** *their revenge.*

V n that
means that the verb is transitive, and that the object is followed by a 'that'-clause. The clause may begin with the word 'that' but does not necessarily do so.

reassure *She just* **reassured me that everything was fine.**
promise 1 **Promise me you will not waste your time.**

V n wh
means that the verb is transitive and is followed by a clause beginning with a question word such as 'what', 'why', 'how', or 'if'.

remind 2 *Need I* **remind you who the enemy is?**
teach 1 *George* **had taught him how to ride.**

V n adj
means that the verb is transitive and that the object is followed by an adjective complement.

call 2 *She* **calls me lazy.**
find 10 *We're sure you'll* **find it exciting!**

V n with adj
means that the verb is transitive and is used with an adjective complement which can come before the object.

kick 1 *He escaped by* **kicking open the window.**
shoot 1 *Gunmen* **shot dead the brother of the minister.**

V n *as* n, **V** n *as* adj
mean that the verb is transitive and that the

object is followed by a noun or adjective complement introduced by 'as'.

hail 1 *US magazines **hailed her as the greatest rock'n'roll singer in the world**.*
describe 2 *Even his closest allies **describe him as forceful, aggressive and determined**.*

V n n
means that the verb must have two objects.

pay 10 *Do **pay us a visit** next time you're in Birmingham.*
name 5 *My mother insisted on **naming me Horace**.*

V-ed
means that the past participle of the verb is used without an auxiliary verb, for example as an adjective or in an implied passive relative clause.

deflate 2 *...a **deflated** balloon.*
accompany 1 *The Prime Minister, **accompanied** by the governor, led the President up to the house.*

be V-ed
means that the verb is transitive and is used in the passive voice. This pattern is not shown if the previous example shows the pattern V n.

educate 1 *He **was educated** at Haslingden Grammar School.*
eat 1 *The bananas should **be eaten** within two days.*

be V-ed prep/adv, be V-ed with n, etc
mean that the verb is in the passive voice and is followed by an adjunct or clause of the specified kind. These patterns are not shown if the previous example shows an active pattern of the same type.

spare 6 *Northern Somalia **was** largely **spared** from the famine.* (be V-ed from n)
allege *The accused **is alleged to have killed** a man.* (be V-ed to-inf)

have n V-ed
means that the past participle of the verb is used in a causative construction with the verb 'have'. The subject of the verb 'have' causes the action indicated by the past participle to be done by another person or thing.

cut 3 *You've **had your hair cut**, it looks great.*
decorate 2 *I **had the flat decorated**.*

get V-ed
means that the past participle of the verb is used after the verb 'get', usually to indicate that someone or something enters into the state indicated by the past participle.

change 7 *I've got to **get changed** first.*
separate 6 *But a group of six women and 23 children **got separated** from the others.*

it V
means that the verb is used as an intransitive, impersonal verb, with 'it' as its subject.

rain 3 *When they got there on the Saturday **it was raining**.*

it V n, it V n to-inf, it V n that
mean that the verb is used as a transitive, impersonal verb with 'it' as its subject.

embarrass 1 ***It embarrassed him that he had no idea of what was going on**.* (it V n that)
grieve 2 ***It grieved me to see** the poor man in such distress.* (it V n to-inf)

V way prep/adv, V way adv/prep
mean that the verb is followed by an adverbial adjunct which is introduced by the noun 'way', and that 'way' is preceded by a possessive determiner.

fight 2 *The team **has fought its way to the cup final**.*
wing 9 *A few moments later they were airborne and **winging their way south**.*

V pron-refl
means that the verb is transitive, and that the object is a reflexive pronoun.

enjoy 2 *I **am** really **enjoying myself** at the moment.*
repeat 5 *The UN will have to work hard to stop history **repeating itself**.*

pl-n V, pl-n V n
mean that the verb has a plural noun as its subject.

balance 5 ***Supply and demand** on the currency market will generally **balance**.* (pl-n V)
share 2 ***Two Americans** will **share this year's Nobel Prize for Medicine**.* (pl-n V n)

V pl-n
means that the verb is transitive and has a plural noun as its object.

balance 5 *The state has got to find some way to **balance these two needs**.*
compare 1 ***Compare the two illustrations** in Fig 60.*

Some verb entries contain information in the basic code for the verb: this basic code appears at the start of the entry, and examples are then accompanied by patterns in the extra column in the usual way.

V-LINK

means a link verb such as *be, become, taste,* or *feel*. Link verbs connect a subject and a complement. The most common patterns with link verbs are V n and V adj.

be 2 1 *My grandfather was a butcher.*
smell 3 *It smells delicious.*

V-ERG

means an ergative verb. An ergative verb is used both in the pattern V and in the pattern V n. The noun group that is the subject of the V pattern refers to the same kind of thing as the noun group n in the V n pattern. Ergative verbs allow you to describe an action from the point of view of the performer of the action or from the point of view of something which is affected by the action.

close 1 3 *Let your eyes close gently... Bess closed her eyes and fell asleep.*
escalate *The dispute could escalate... Defeat could cause one side or other to escalate the conflict.*

V-RECIP

means a reciprocal verb. Reciprocal verbs describe processes in which two or more people, groups, or things interact mutually: they do the same thing to each other, or participate jointly in the same action or event. Reciprocal verbs are used in the pattern pl-n V, where the subject consists of two or more participants. The participants can also be referred to separately in other patterns such as V n and V *with* n. Note that the subject can change places with the object of the verb or preposition without any change of meaning.

feud *Their families had feuded since their teenage daughters quarrelled two years ago... He feuded with his ex-wife.*
meet 1 *We met by chance... He's the kindest and sincerest person I've ever met.*

V-RECIP-ERG

means an ergative reciprocal verb. Like an ergative verb, it occurs in the patterns V and V n. Like a reciprocal verb, it occurs in patterns which include pl-n V and V with n. The typical ergative-reciprocal patterns are therefore pl-n V, V *with* n, V pl-n, and V n *with* n.

entwine 1 *His dazed eyes stare at the eels, which still writhe and entwine... The giraffes were managing to entwine their necks in the most astonishing manner... He entwined his fingers with hers.*
integrate 2 *Ann wanted the conservatory to integrate with the kitchen... Little attempt was made to integrate the parts into a coherent whole... It believes that by integrating the rail lines with its buses it can make them pay.*

V-PASSIVE

means a verb that occurs in the passive voice and never in the active voice.

orphan 2 *Jones was orphaned at the age of ten.*
rumoured *Her parents are rumoured to be on the verge of splitting up.*

VB: usu passive

means that the verb is transitive and is usually used in the passive voice. Verbs used in this way typically occur in the pattern *be* V-ed.

penalize *Some of the players may, on occasion, break the rules and be penalized.*
overlay 1 *The floor was overlaid with rugs of oriental design.*

VB: no passive

means that the verb is transitive but cannot be used in the passive voice. Verbs used in this way typically occur in the pattern V n.

flee *Thousands have been compelled to flee the country.*
hold 2 2 *Death doesn't hold any fear for me.*

VB: no cont

means that the verb is not used in the continuous tenses.

confirm 1 *These new statistics confirm our worst fears.*
need 1 *He desperately needed money.*

VB: only cont

means that the verb is used only in the continuous tenses (the auxiliary 'be' followed by the 'ing'-form).

crawl 4 *This place is crawling with police.*
keep 22 *She hasn't been keeping too well lately.*

VB: only imper

means that the verb is used only in the imperative.

let 4 *Let me tell you what I saw last night.*
look 1 10 *Look what a mess you've made of your life.*

VERB: with brd-neg
means a verb that always occurs in a broad negative construction, that is, in a clause which is negative in meaning. The clause may contain a negative element such as 'no-one', 'never', or 'hardly', or may show that it is negative in some other way.

abide *I can't abide people who can't make up their minds.*
wish 7 *Without wishing to be unkind, she's not the most interesting company.*

AUX
means an auxiliary verb, such as some meanings of *be, have, get,* and *do.* An auxiliary verb is used with another verb to modify the grammar of that verb, for example, to form the continuous tenses or the passive voice, or to form negatives and interrogatives.

be 1 1 *This is happening in every school.*
get 1 7 *Does she ever get asked for her autograph?*
do 1 1 *They don't want to work.*

MODAL
means a modal verb such as *may, must,* or *would.* Most modal verbs are used before the infinitive form of a verb without 'to'. Modal verbs do not inflect, for example, they do not have an '-s' in the third person singular.

must 2 ... *Candidates must satisfy the general conditions for admission.*
can 1 9 ... *Can I help you?*
will 1 3 ... *If she refuses to follow rules about car safety, she won't be allowed to use the car.*

Phrasal Verbs

PHRASAL VB
means a verb that consists of a verb and one or more particles, e.g. *look after, look back, look down on.* The combination of verb and particle often has a very different meaning from that of the verb used on its own.
In the extra column patterns describing phrasal verb behaviour V refers to the verb, and P to the particle or particles.

V P
means that the phrasal verb is used intransitively, with the particle coming after the verb.

fall apart 1 *Bit by bit the building fell apart.*
keep up 1 *Things are changing so fast, it's hard to keep up.*

V P n
means that the phrasal verb is followed by a noun, pronoun, or noun group. In this pattern, the particle behaves as a preposition, and has an object.

make of *Nancy wasn't sure what to make of Mick's apology.*
sit through *...movies so bad you can hardly bear to sit through them.*

V P with n, V P to n, V P on n, etc
mean that the phrasal verb is intransitive and is followed by the specified preposition and then a noun or noun group.

blend in 1 *The toad had changed its colour to blend in with its new environment.* (V P with n)
wait around *The attacker may have been waiting around for an opportunity to strike.* (V P for n)

V P noun
means that the phrasal verb is used transitively, with the object coming after the particle. The object can be any noun group except a personal pronoun such as 'him' or 'it'.

open up 5 *The postmaster and his wife arrived to open up the shop.*
hand in *All eighty opposition members of parliament have handed in their resignation.*

V n P
means that the phrasal verb is used transitively, and that the object can come between the verb and the particle. The object is usually a pronoun or a short noun group.

phone up *Phone him up and tell him to come and have dinner with you.*
cut off 1 *He threatened to cut my hair off.*

V n P n
means that the phrasal verb is transitive, and also that the phrasal particle is followed by another noun, pronoun, or noun group. In this pattern, the phrasal particle can usually be regarded as a preposition.

hold against *Bernstein lost the case, but never held it against Grundy.*
keep to 3 *Keep costs to a minimum.*

V n P to n, V n P of n, V P noun with n, etc
mean that the phrasal verb is used transitively, with the object between the verb and the particle, and that it is followed by a phrase introduced by the specified preposition.

give back *I **gave the textbook back** to him.* (V n P to n)
take away 1 *'Give me the knife,' he said softly, 'or I'll **take it away from you.'** (V n P from n)
marry off *He had the good fortune to **marry off his daughter to the local chief**.* (V P noun *to* n)

V-ed P

means that the past participle of the phrasal verb is used without an auxiliary verb, for example as an adjective.

play back *Ted might benefit from hearing his own voice recorded and **played back**.*
rope off *...a large **roped-off** area.*

be V-ed P

means that the phrasal verb is transitive and is used in the passive voice. This pattern is not shown if the previous example shows the pattern V P noun or V n P.

set up 7 *He claimed yesterday that **he had been set up** after drugs were discovered at his home.*
take over 2 *The republic of Byelorussia **was taken over** by the Soviet Union at the end of World War II.*

V P P n

means that the phrasal verb is followed by two fixed phrasal particles, and then a noun, pronoun, or noun group.

do away with *The long-range goal must be to **do away with** nuclear weapons.*
look down on *I wasn't successful, so they **looked down on** me.*

V n P P n

means that the phrasal verb is transitive, and includes two phrasal particles. The second particle is followed by another noun, pronoun, or noun group.

turn over to *When he first leased the land in the late 1970s, he planned to **turn it over to cereal production**.*
worm out of *It took me weeks to **worm the facts out of** him.*

Nouns

N-COUNT

means an ordinary count noun. Count nouns have both a singular and a plural form. When a count noun is used in the singular, it must have a determiner such as 'a', 'an', 'the', or 'my' in front of it.

head 1 *She turned her **head** away from him.*
germ 1 *Chlorine is widely used to kill **germs**.*

N-UNCOUNT

means an uncount noun. Uncount nouns refer to things that are not normally counted or considered to be individual items. Uncount nouns do not have a plural form, and are used with a singular verb.

dampness 1 *The tins had to be kept away from **dampness**, soot and cooking fumes.*
influence 1 *As Hugh grew older, she had less **influence** and couldn't control him.*

N-VAR

means a variable noun. A variable noun typically combines the behaviour of both count and uncount nouns in the same sense. The singular form occurs freely with and without determiners. Variable nouns also have a plural form.

Some variable nouns refer to abstract things, such as 'hardship', or to individual instances of that abstract thing.

Other variable nouns refer to substances: with count noun behaviour, they refer to a mass of the substance, and with uncount noun behaviour, they refer to types or brands.

fire 1 2 *... A family of four has died in a **fire**... Much of historic Rennes was destroyed by **fire** in 1720.*
legend 1 *...the **legends** of ancient Greece...Irish **legend**.*
injustice 1 *They'll continue to fight **injustice**... They resented the **injustices** of the system.*
detergent *Rinse in cold water to remove any remaining **detergent**... We used several different **detergents** in our stain-removal tests.*

N-SING

means a singular noun. A singular noun is always singular, and needs a determiner.

mockery 2 *The present system is a **mockery** of justice.*
march 5 *...the relentless **march** of technology.*

N-PLURAL

means a plural noun. A plural noun is always plural and is used with plural verbs. If a pronoun is used to stand for the noun, it is a plural pronoun such as 'they' or 'them'.

people 1 *Millions of **people** have lost their homes.*
grocery 2 *...two bags of **groceries**.*

N-PROPER

means a proper noun. A proper noun refers to one person, place, thing, or institution, and begins with a capital letter. Many proper nouns are used without a determiner.

Fleet Street *He was the highest-paid sub-editor in Fleet Street.*
god 1 *He believes in God.*

N-TITLE

means a noun that is used to refer to someone who has a particular role or position. Titles come before the name of the person and begin with a capital letter. Many N-TITLEs are also N-COUNTs.

Reverend *...the Reverend Jim Simons.*
constable *...Constable Stuart Clark.*

N-VOC

means a vocative noun, that is, a noun which is used when speaking directly to someone or writing to them. Vocative nouns do not need a determiner, but some may be used with a possessive determiner.

constable *Thanks for your help, Constable.*
dearest 1 *What's wrong, my dearest? You look tired.*

N-FAMILY

means a noun which refers to a member of a family. Family nouns behave like count nouns, typically in the singular following a possessive determiner. They are also used like vocative nouns and proper nouns, with no determiner.

dad *He's living with his mum and dad.*
daddy *Look at me, Daddy!*
mommy *Mommy and I went in an aeroplane.*

N-COLL-COUNT, N-COLL-UNCOUNT, N-COLL-SING, etc

mean a collective noun of the specified type. Collective nouns refer to a group of people or things. In the singular, they can be used with either a singular or plural verb.

couple 2 *The couple have no children.*
press 12 *Today the British press is full of articles on India's new prime minister.*

N-COUNT: with supp, N-UNCOUNT: with supp, N-SING: with supp, etc

mean a noun that is not used on its own, but always with other supporting words, such as a preceding noun or adjective, or a following phrase introduced by a preposition.

sanction 1 *The king could not enact laws without*

the sanction of Parliament.
speed 2 *Each learner can proceed at his own speed.*
feel 15 *The room has a warm, cosy feel.*

N-SING: the N, N-PLURAL: the N, N-PROPER: the N, etc

mean a noun which always has the definite article 'the' in front of it. Other words can sometimes come between the definite article and the noun.

dying 2 *By the time our officers arrived, the dead and the dying were everywhere.*
level 2 *The water level of the Mississippi River is already 6.5 feet below normal.*

N-SING: a N

means a singular noun that is always preceded by the indefinite article 'a' or 'an'.

think 4 *I'll have a think about that.*
time 7 *He stayed for quite a time.*

N-SING: also no det

means a singular noun that is sometimes used without a determiner, rather like an uncount noun.

affray *Barnstaple crown court was told he caused an affray... They were convicted of affray.*

N-UNCOUNT: also a N

means a noun which is typically uncount, but which is sometimes immediately preceded by the indefinite article 'a' or 'an'. There is no corresponding plural form.

torture 3 *The friction of the sheets against his skin was torture... Learning - something she had always loved - became a torture.*

N-UNCOUNT: also N in pl

means an uncount noun which also has a plural form. However, there is no corresponding singular form which can be immediately preceded by 'a' or 'an'.

research *...cancer research ...his researches into which kinds of flowers bees get their best honey from.*

N-COUNT: also by N, N-COUNT: also in N, etc

mean that the noun is typically a count noun, but that it can also be used in the singular without a determiner when it is preceded by the preposition that is specified.

ticket 1 *I queued for two hours to get a ticket to see the football game... Entrance is free, but by ticket only.* (N-COUNT: also by N)

siege 1 *We must do everything possible to lift the siege ...a city virtually under siege.* (N-COUNT: also *under* N)

N-COUNT: N *of* n, **N-UNCOUNT: N** *of* n, etc
mean that the noun is always followed by a prepositional phrase introduced by 'of'.

piece 9 *It is a highly complex piece of legislation.*
cloak 2 *Today most of England will be under a cloak of thick mist.*

N-COUNT: with poss, N-UNCOUNT: with poss, N-SING: with poss
mean that the noun is typically preceded by a possessive determiner, or that it is followed by a phrase indicating possession, introduced by 'of'.

history 6 *He couldn't get a new job because of his medical history.*
accession at **accede** 2 *...the 40th anniversary of the Queen's accession to the throne.*
brainchild *The record was the brainchild of rock star Bob Geldof.*

N-COUNT: n N, N-UNCOUNT: n N, etc
mean that the noun is typically modified by another noun or noun group before it.

house 6 *She was fired from her job at a publishing house.*
hunting 2 *Job hunting should be approached as a job in itself.*

Adjectives

ADJ-GRADED
means a graded adjective, that is, an adjective which is sometimes used with an adverb or phrase indicating degree, such as 'very', 'too', or 'less'. Many graded adjectives have comparative and superlative forms, usually made by adding '-er' and '-est' to the base form.

bad 1 *The pain is often so bad she wants to scream.*
clear 1 *The space telescope has taken the clearest pictures ever of Pluto.*

ADJ
means an ungraded adjective. An ungraded adjective is not used with an adverb indicating degree.

absent 1 *He has been absent from his desk for two weeks.*
cellular *...molecular and cellular mechanisms.*

ADJ-GRADED: ADJ n, **ADJ: ADJ** n
mean that the adjective comes only in front of a noun or noun group.

wide 8 *He emphasised the wider issue of superpower cooperation.*
facial 1 *His facial expression didn't change.*

ADJ: n ADJ
means that the adjective is preceded by the noun or noun group that it modifies. This pattern is rather unusual in English.

proper 4 *A distinction must be made between archaeology proper and science-based archaeology.*
thick 2 *The folder was two inches thick.*

ADJ-GRADED: det ADJ, ADJ: det ADJ
mean that the adjective is always preceded by a determiner.

bare 7 *The army would try to hold the western desert with a bare minimum of forces.*
last 2 *Much has changed since my last visit.*

ADJ-GRADED: v-link ADJ, ADJ: v-link ADJ
mean that the adjective is used after a link verb such as 'be' or 'feel', but never before a noun.

daunted at **daunt** *It is hard to pick up such a book and not to feel a little daunted.*
afoot *Everybody knew that something awful was afoot.*

ADJ/ADJ-GRADED: v-link ADJ *to* n
ADJ/ADJ-GRADED: v-link ADJ *with* n, etc
mean that the adjective is typically used after a link verb, and is followed by a phrase introduced by the specified preposition.

true 9 *India has remained true to democracy.*
inconsistent 4 *The outburst was inconsistent with the image he has cultivated.*

ADJ-GRADED: v-link ADJ to-inf, ADJ: v-link ADJ to-inf
mean that the adjective is typically used after a link verb, and is followed by a verb in the infinitive with 'to'.

pleased 2 *We will be pleased to answer any questions you may have.*
likely 2 *Once people have seen that something actually works, they are much more likely to accept change.*

Adverbs

ADV-GRADED
means a graded adverb, that is, an adverb which

is sometimes used with an adverb or phrase indicating degree.

happily at **happy** 1*Albert leaned back **happily**.*
long 1 6 *He has been on a diet for as **long** as any of his friends can remember.*

ADV
means an ungraded adverb. An ungraded adverb is not used with another adverb indicating degree.

biologically at **biological** 1 *Much of our behaviour is **biologically** determined.*
lately 1 *Dad's health hasn't been too good **lately**.*

ADV-GRADED: ADV with v, ADV: ADV with v
mean that the adverb typically modifies a verb. It can come before or after the verb without any change of meaning.

methodically at **methodical** *She **methodically** put the things into her suitcase.*
posthumously at **posthumous** *She was **posthumously** awarded the George Cross.*

ADV-GRADED: ADV after v, ADV: ADV after v
mean that the adverb typically modifies a verb, and must come later than the verb in the sentence or clause.

peacefully at **peaceful** 4 *Except for traffic noise the night **passed peacefully**.*
aboard *It had taken two hours to **load** all the people **aboard**.*

ADV-GRADED: ADV before v, ADV: ADV before v
mean that the adverb typically modifies a verb. If the verb consists of one word, the adverb comes before it. If there is an auxiliary with the verb, the adverb comes between them.

richly 3 *He achieved the success he so **richly** deserved.*
just 1 1 *I've **just** bought a new house.*

ADV-GRADED: ADV with cl/group, ADV: ADV with cl/group
mean that the adverb typically modifies a whole sentence, clause, or phrase.

admittedly *It's only a theory, **admittedly**, but the pieces fit together.*
probably 1 *Van Gogh is **probably** the best-known painter in the world.*

ADV-GRADED: ADV adj/adv, ADV: ADV adj/adv
mean that the adverb typically modifies an adjective or adverb.

equally at **equal** 1 *All these techniques are **equally effective**.*
reasonably at **reasonable** 4 *I can dance **reasonably well**.*

ADV: ADV prep
means that the adverb typically modifies a prepositional phrase.

all 4 *...universities **all round the world**.*
full 16 *The burning liquid hit him **full in the right eye**.*

Other word classes

COLOUR
means a word referring to a colour. These words can behave like adjectives, and also like nouns.

blue 1 *...her pale **blue** eyes.*
black 1 *He was dressed all in **black**.*

COMB
means a combining form. A combining form is a word which is joined with another word, usually with a hyphen, to form compounds.

-day *...a two-**day** visit to Zambia.*
-haired at **hair** 1 *...a small, dark-**haired** man.*

CONJ
means a conjunction. Conjunctions are used to link grammatical elements of the same type, such as two clauses or two words.

although 2 ***Although** I was only six, I can remember seeing it on TV.*
and 1 *I'm going to write good jokes **and** become a good comedian.*
nor 1 *I can give you neither an opinion **nor** any advice.*

CONVENTION
means a word or fixed phrase which is used in conversation, for example when greeting someone, apologizing, or replying, e.g. *hello, sorry, no comment.*

DET
means a determiner. A determiner is a word that is used at the beginning of a noun group.

the 2 *...a slight increase in **the** consumption of meat.*
both 1 *He gripped her suddenly by **both** arms.*

DET-POSS
means a possessive determiner, which is used to

say who or what something belongs or relates to.

my 1 *John's **my** best friend.*
its *The Labour Party concludes **its** annual conference today.*

EXCLAM
means an exclamation. An exclamation is a word or phrase which is spoken suddenly, loudly, or emphatically in order to express a strong emotion such as shock or anger. Exclamations are often followed by exclamation marks.

oh 2 *'**Oh!**' Kenny blinked. 'Has everyone gone?'*
heaven 8 ***Good Heavens!** That explains a lot!*

NUMBER
means a word such as *three* or *hundred*. Numbers are typically used like determiners, adjectives, pronouns, and quantifiers. Some numbers, such as *hundred*, *thousand*, and *million*, always follow a determiner or another number.

eighteen *He was employed by them for **eighteen** years.*
billion 1 *...3 **billion** dollars.*
nil 1 *They beat the defending champions, Argentina, one-**nil** in the final.*

ORDINAL
means a type of number that is used like an adjective or an adverb.

hundredth 1 *...the **hundredth** anniversary of his birth.*
first 1 *Johnson came **first** in the one hundred metres.*

PHRASE
means a group of words which are used together with little variation. Phrases have a meaning of their own, which is not always understandable from their component parts.

ice 3 *I do want to get closer to them. How can I **break the ice**?*
kind 1 4 *She's a very unusual woman, **one of a kind**.*

PHR-CONJ
means a phrasal conjunction. A phrasal conjunction is a phrase which behaves like a conjunction.

as 2 4 *He burst into a high-pitched laugh, **as though** he'd said something funny.*
else 4 *Make sure you are strapped in very well, **or else** you will fall out.*

PHR-MODAL
means a phrasal modal. Phrasal modals are phrases which, like modals, occur before the infinitive form of a verb. Most phrasal modals beginning with *be* or *have* inflect; the other phrasal modals do not.

ought 2 *You **ought to** ask a lawyer's advice.*
better 9 *I think we **had better** go home.*
going 2 *I was not **going to** compromise.*

PHR-PREP
means a phrasal preposition. A phrasal preposition is a phrase which behaves like a preposition.

according to 1 *Philip stayed at the hotel, **according to** Mr Hemming.*
front 14 *She sat down **in front of** her dressing-table mirror.*

PREDET
means a predeterminer. A predeterminer is used in a noun group before a determiner.

double 3 *The offer was to start a new research laboratory at **double** the salary he was then getting.*
all 2 *She's worked **all** her life.*

PREFIX
means a letter or group of letters, such as *un-* or *multi-*, which is added to the beginning of a word in order to form another word. For example, the prefix *un-* is added to *happy* to form *unhappy*.

PREP
means a preposition. A preposition is followed by a noun group or the '-ing'-form of a verb.

on 1 *He is sitting beside her **on** the sofa.*
about 1 *Helen's told me **about** you.*
of 2 *He had little chance **of** winning.*

PRON
means a pronoun. Pronouns are used like noun groups, to refer to someone or something that has already been mentioned or whose identity is already known.

her 1 *I went in the room and told her I had something to say to **her**.*
all 1 *I'd spent **all** I had, every last penny.*

PRON-INDEF
means an indefinite pronoun. Indefinite pronouns are words like *anyone*, *everything*, *everyone*, and *something*.

PRON-REFL

means a reflexive pronoun. Reflexive pronouns are pronouns which are used as the object of a verb or preposition when they refer to the same person or thing as the subject of the verb.

yourself 1 *Have the courage to be honest with yourself.*
ourselves 1 *We sat round the fire to keep ourselves warm.*

PRON-REL

means a relative pronoun like *which* or *who*. Relative pronouns can be the subject or the object of a verb in a relative clause, or the object of a preposition.

whom 3 *One writer in whom I had taken an interest was Immanuel Velikovsky.*
where 2 *Conditions which apply to your flight are available at the travel agency where you book your holiday.*

PRON-POSS

means a possessive pronoun, which is used to say who or what something belongs or relates to.

hers 1 *His hand as it shook hers was warm and firm.*
yours 1 *I believe Paul was a friend of yours.*

QUANT

means a quantifier. A quantifier comes before 'of' and a noun group.

bit 1 *All it required was a bit of work.*
each 1 *He handed each of them a page of photos.*

QUESTION

means a 'wh'-word, or similar word, which is used to begin a question.

when 1 *When did you get married?*
how 1 *How do you manage to keep the place so tidy?*

SUFFIX

means a letter or group of letters, such as *-ly* or *-ness*, which is added to the end of a word in order to form a new word, usually of a different word class. For example, *-ly* is added to *quick* to form *quickly*.

A a

A, a /eɪ/ **A's, a's. 1 A** is the first letter of the English N-VAR alphabet. **2** In music, **A** is the sixth note in the scale N-VAR of C major. **3** If you get an **A** as a mark for a piece of N-VAR work or in an exam, your work is extremely good. **4 A** or **a** is used as an abbreviation for words beginning with a, such as 'acre' or 'answer'. **5** People talk about getting **from A to B** when they are PHRASE referring generally to journeys they need to make, without saying where the journeys will take them. *Cars are for getting people from A to B in maximum safety.*

a /ə, STRONG eɪ/ or **an** /ən, STRONG æn/. **A** or **an** is ♦♦♦♦♦ the indefinite article. It is used at the beginning of noun groups which refer to only one person or thing. The form **an** is used in front of words that begin with vowel sounds.

1 You use **a** or **an** when you are referring to someone DET or something for the first time and your listener or reader may not know which particular thing you mean. *A waiter entered with a tray... Today you've got a new teacher... I manage a hotel.* **2** You use **a** or **an** DET when you are referring to any person or thing of a particular type and do not want to be specific. *...expensive make-up that we saw being advertised by a beautiful model... Bring a sleeping bag. ...waiting for a bus.* **3** You use **a** or **an** in front of a noun when that noun DET follows an adjective, or when the noun is followed by words that describe it more fully. *The islanders exhibit a constant happiness with life... He did have a real knowledge of the country.* **4** You use **a** or **an** when you DET want to refer to a single type or brand of something. *Bollinger 'RD' is a rare, highly prized wine.* **5** You use **a** or **an** to refer to someone or something as DET a representative member of a group, class, or general type. *A boy must learn to stand up and fight like a man.* **6** You use **a** or **an** in front of the names of days, DET months, or festivals when you are referring to one particular instance of that day, month, or festival. *...a favorite present from a Christmas long ago.* **7** You use DET **a** or **an** when you are saying what someone is or what job they have. *I explained that I was an artist, but that I was sometimes a plumber as well.* **8** You use **a** or **an** in front of the names of people as a DET way of indicating that you do not know them or anything about them and you are saying their name for the first time. *...a Mrs P. R. Slater of Peterborough.* **9** You use **a** or **an** in front of the names of people when DET you want to refer to someone else who has the same qualities or character as the person named. *It would be wrong to see the Prime Minister as simply a Mrs Thatcher in disguise.* **10** You use **a** or **an** in front of a DET surname when you want to refer to someone who belongs to the family with that surname. *As far as I can recall, Patti was a Smith.* **11** You use **a** or **an** in front of DET the names of painters and sculptors to refer to one individual work of art created by them. *Most people have very little difficulty in seeing why a Van Gogh is a work of genius.* **12** You use **a** in quantifiers such as **a lot**, **a little**, and **a** DET **bit**. **13** You use **a** or **an** instead of the number 'one' in DET front of numbers and measurements such as 'thousand', 'hour', and 'half'. *...a hundred miles. ...a quarter of an hour.* **14** You use **a** or **an** in expressions such DET as **eight hours a day** to express a rate or ratio. *Prices start at £13.95 a metre for printed cotton.*

aah /ɑː/. See **ah**.

aback /əˈbæk/. If you are **taken aback** by some- ♦◊◊◊◊ thing, you are very surprised or shocked by it. PHRASE *Roland was taken aback by our strength of feeling.*

aba·cus /ˈæbəkəs/ **abacuses.** An **abacus** is a N-COUNT frame used for counting. It has rods with sliding beads on them.

aban·don /əˈbændən/ **abandons, abandoning,** ♦♦♦◊◊ **abandoned. 1** If you **abandon** a place, thing, or VERB person, you leave them forever or for a long time, V n especially when you should not do so. *He claimed that his parents had abandoned him.* ● See also **abandoned.** ◆ **aban·don·ment** /əˈbændənmənt/ N-UNCOUNT *...memories of her father's complete abandonment of her.* **2** If you **abandon** an activity or piece of work, VERB you stop doing it before it is finished. *The author-* V n *ities have abandoned any attempt to distribute food.* ◆ **abandonment** *Rain forced the abandonment of* N-UNCOUNT *the next day's competitions.* **3** If you **abandon** an VERB: V n idea or way of thinking, you stop having that idea or thinking in that way. ◆ **abandonment.** N-UNCOUNT **4** If people **abandon ship**, they get off a ship because PHRASE it is sinking. **5** If you **abandon** yourself to an emotion, you think VERB about it a lot and feel it strongly. *He abandoned him-* V pron-refl to *self to his suffering.* **6** If you say that someone does N-UNCOUNT something with **abandon**, you mean that they behave PRAGMATICS in a wild, uncontrolled way and do not care about how they should behave; used showing disapproval. *He has splashed dollars around with gay abandon.*

aban·doned /əˈbændənd/. An **abandoned** place or ♦♦♦◊◊ building is no longer used or occupied. *The river is* ADJ *threatened by pollution from abandoned mines.*

abashed /əˈbæʃt/. If you are **abashed**, you feel em- ADJ-GRADED barrassed and ashamed. *He seemed both abashed* WRITTEN *and secretly delighted at Dan's gift.*

abate /əˈbeɪt/ **abates, abating, abated.** If ◆◊◊◊◊ something **abates**, it becomes much less strong or VERB widespread. *The storms had abated by the time they* V *rounded Cape Horn.* FORMAL

abate·ment /əˈbeɪtmənt/. **Abatement** means a re- N-UNCOUNT: duction in the strength or level of something. *The* also a N *talks have produced little abatement of violence.* FORMAL

ab·at·toir /ˈæbətwɑː/ **abattoirs.** An **abattoir** is a N-COUNT place where animals are killed to provide meat.

ab·bey /ˈæbi/ **abbeys.** An **abbey** is a church with ♦♦◊◊◊ buildings attached to it in which monks or nuns live N-COUNT or used to live.

ab·bot /ˈæbət/ **abbots.** An **abbot** is the monk who N-COUNT is in charge of all the monks in a monastery or abbey.

ab·bre·vi·ate /əˈbriːvieɪt/ **abbreviates, abbre-** VERB **viating, abbreviated.** If you **abbreviate** some- V n to n thing, especially a word or a piece of writing, you Also V n make it shorter. *He persuaded his son to abbreviate his first name to Alec.* ◆ **ab·bre·viat·ed** *...an abbre-* ADJ-GRADED *viated document without detailed proposals.*

ab·bre·via·tion /ə,briːviˈeɪʃən/ **abbreviations.** An N-COUNT **abbreviation** is a short form of a word or phrase, made by leaving out some of the letters. *The postal abbreviation for Kansas is KS.*

ABC /,eɪ biː ˈsiː/ **ABCs.** The **ABC** of a subject or ac- ♦♦◊◊◊ tivity is the parts of it that you have to learn first be- N-COUNT cause they are the most important and basic. *...the ABC of Marxism.*

ab·di·cate /ˈæbdɪkeɪt/ **abdicates, abdicating,** **abdicated. 1** If a king or queen **abdicates**, he or VERB she resigns. *The last French king was Louis Philippe,* V *who abdicated in 1848.* ◆ **ab·di·ca·tion** Also V n /,æbdɪˈkeɪʃən/. **2** If you **abdicate** your responsibility N-UNCOUNT for something, you refuse to accept the responsibil- VERB ity for it any longer. *Many parents simply abdicate* V n

all responsibility for their children. ♦ **abdication** N-UNCOUNT
...a complete abdication of responsibility. N of n

ab·do·men /ˈæbdəmən/ **abdomens.** Your abdo- ◆◇◇◇◇
men is the part of your body below your chest N-COUNT
where your stomach and intestines are. ♦ **ab·domi-** FORMAL
·nal /æbˈdɒmɪnəl/ *...abdominal pain.* ADJ: ADJ n

ab·domi·nals /æbˈdɒmɪnəlz/. Your abdominal N-PLURAL
muscles can be referred to as your **abdominals.**

ab·duct /æbˈdʌkt/ **abducts, abducting, ab-** ◆◇◇◇◇
ducted. If someone **is abducted** by another per- VERB:
son, he or she is taken away illegally, usually by be V-ed
force. *A fourth man was charged with abducting the* V n
boy. ♦ **ab·duc·tion** /æbˈdʌkʃən/ **abductions** *...the* N-VAR
abduction of four black youths. ♦ **ab·duc·tor,**
abductors. N-COUNT

ab·er·rant /æˈberənt/. **Aberrant** means unusual ADJ-GRADED
and not socially acceptable. *...Ian's rages and aber-* FORMAL
rant behavior.

ab·er·ra·tion /ˌæbəˈreɪʃən/ **aberrations. 1** An ab- ◆◇◇◇◇
erration is an incident or way of behaving that is N-VAR
not typical. *In a moment of aberration he had*
dialled the wrong number. **2** If you describe a per- N-VAR
son or their behaviour as an **aberration**, you believe
that they are strange and not socially acceptable. *He*
considers David a terrible aberration among the
more respectable theorists. ...sexual aberration.

abet /əˈbet/ **abets, abetting, abetted.** If one per- VERB
son **abets** another person, they help or encourage V n
them to do something wrong. **Aiding and abetting** a
crime is itself a criminal offence. *We shall strike*
hard, without flinching, at terrorists and those who
abet them.

abey·ance /əˈbeɪəns/. If something is **in abeyance**, PHRASE
it is not operating or being used at present. *The* FORMAL
matter was left in abeyance until Haig saw French.

ab·hor /æbˈhɔː/ **abhors, abhorring, abhorred.** If VERB
you **abhor** something, you hate it very much, espe- V n
cially for moral reasons. *He was a man who ab-* FORMAL
horred violence. ♦ **ab·hor·rent** /æbˈhɒrənt/, AM ADJ-GRADED
-ˈhɔːr-/. *Racial discrimination is abhorrent to my*
council and our staff. ♦ **ab·hor·rence** /æbˈhɒrəns/, N-UNCOUNT
AM -ˈhɔːr-/ *...their abhorrence of racism.*

abide /əˈbaɪd/ **abides, abiding, abided.** If you ◆◇◇◇◇
can't **abide** someone or something, you dislike VB: no
them very much. *I can't abide people who can't* passive,
make up their minds. ● See also **law-abiding.** with brd-neg
V n

abide by. If you **abide by** a law, agreement, or deci- PHRASAL VB
sion, you do what it says you should do. *They have got* V P n
to abide by the rules.

abid·ing /əˈbaɪdɪŋ/. An **abiding** feeling, memory, ◆◇◇◇◇
or interest is one that you have for a very long time. ADJ-GRADED:
One of my abiding memories of him is of his singing. ADJ n

abil·ity /əˈbɪlɪti/ **abilities. 1** Your **ability** to do ◆◆◆◇
something is the fact that you can do it. *...the hu-* N-SING:
man ability to recognise complex sound patterns. N to-inf
2 Your **ability** is the quality or skill that you have N-VAR
which makes it possible for you to do something.
Her drama teacher spotted her ability... They repeat-
edly questioned his leadership abilities. **3** If you do PHRASE
something **to the best of** your **abilities** or **to the**
best of your **ability**, you do it as well as you can. *I*
take care of them to the best of my abilities.

ab·ject /ˈæbdʒekt/. **1** You use **abject** to emphasize ◆◇◇◇◇
that a situation or quality is shameful or depressing. ADJ-GRADED
Both of them died in abject poverty... This scheme PRAGMATICS
was an abject failure. **2** If you describe someone as ADJ-GRADED
abject, you think that they have no self-respect or
courage.

ab·jure /æbˈdʒʊə/ **abjures, abjuring, abjured.** If VERB
you **abjure** something such as a belief or way of life, V n
you state publicly that you will give it up or that you FORMAL
reject it. *He abjured the Protestant faith and became*
King in 1594.

ablaze /əˈbleɪz/. **1** Something that is **ablaze** is ◆◇◇◇◇
burning fiercely. *Shops, houses, and vehicles were set* ADJ:
ablaze. **2** If a place is **ablaze** with lights or colours, it v-link ADJ
is very bright because of them. *In spring, the valleys* ADJ:
are ablaze with colour. **3** If someone is **ablaze**, or if ADJ:
their eyes are **ablaze**, their expression shows that v-link ADJ

they are feeling a strong emotion. *Her voice is pas-*
sionate. Her eyes are ablaze.

able /ˈeɪbəl/ **abler** /ˈeɪblə/ **ablest** /ˈeɪblɪst/. **1** If ◆◆◆◆
someone or something **is able to** do something, PHR-MODAL
they have skills or qualities which make it possible
for them to do it. *The older child should be able to*
prepare a simple meal... They seemed able to work
together very efficiently. **2** If someone or something PHR-MODAL
is able to do something, they have enough freedom,
power, time, or money to do it. *You'll be able to*
read in peace... Men should be able to retire at 60.
3 Someone who is **able** is very clever or very good ADJ-GRADED
at doing something. *...one of the brightest and ablest*
members of the government.

-able /-əbəl/. **-able** combines with verbs to form ad- SUFFIX
jectives. Adjectives formed in this way describe
someone or something that can have a particular
thing done to them. For example, if something is
avoidable, it can be avoided.

able-bodied /ˌeɪbəl ˈbɒdid/. An **able-bodied** person ADJ-GRADED
is physically strong and healthy. *The gym can be*
used by both able-bodied and disabled people. ▶ **The** N-PLURAL:
able-bodied are people who are able-bodied. the N

ab·lu·tions /əˈbluːʃənz/. **Ablutions** is a formal or N-PLURAL
humorous word for the activity of washing yourself.
Manny was meticulous about his ablutions.

ably /ˈeɪbli/. **Ably** means skilfully and successfully. ADV-GRADED:
He was ably assisted by a number of members. ADV with v

ab·nor·mal /æbˈnɔːməl/. Someone or something ◆◇◇◇◇
that is **abnormal** is unusual, especially in a way that ADJ-GRADED
is worrying. *...a child with an abnormal fear of*
strangers. ♦ **ab·nor·mal·ly** *...abnormally high lev-* ADV
els of glucose.

ab·nor·mal·ity /ˌæbnɔːˈmælɪti/ **abnormalities.** ◆◇◇◇◇
An **abnormality** in something, especially in a per- N-VAR
son's body or behaviour, is an unusual part or feature of it that may be worrying or dangerous. *Fur-*
ther scans are required to confirm the diagnosis of
an abnormality.

aboard /əˈbɔːd/. If you are **aboard** a ship or plane, ◆◆◇◇◇
you are on it or in it. *No-one else was aboard the* PREP
plane. ▶ Also an adverb. *It had taken two hours to* ADV:
load all the people aboard. ADV after v

abode /əˈbəʊd/ **abodes. 1** Your **abode** is the place N-COUNT
where you live. *It is the abode of a domesticated* FORMAL
man. **2** The term **no fixed abode** is used to refer to PHRASE
people who are homeless. *30 per cent of psychiatric* LEGAL
beds are occupied by people of no fixed abode.

abol·ish /əˈbɒlɪʃ/ **abolishes, abolishing, abol-** ◆◇◇◇◇
ished. If someone in authority **abolishes** a system VERB
or practice, they formally put an end to it. *Parlia-* V n
ment voted to abolish the death penalty. ♦ **abo·li-**
·tion /ˌæbəˈlɪʃən/ *...President de Klerk's commitment* N-UNCOUNT:
to the abolition of apartheid. also a N

abo·li·tion·ist /ˌæbəˈlɪʃənɪst/ **abolitionists.** An N-COUNT
abolitionist is someone who campaigns for the
abolition of a particular system or practice. *Many*
southerners remained quiet abolitionists.

A-bomb /ˈeɪ bɒm/ **A-bombs.** An **A-bomb** is an N-COUNT
atomic bomb.

abomi·nable /əˈbɒmɪnəbəl/. Something that is ADJ-GRADED
abominable is very unpleasant or very bad. *The*
President described the killings as an abominable
crime... The normal English diet is abominable.
♦ **abomi·nably** /əˈbɒmɪnəbli/. *Chloe has behaved* ADV
abominably.

abom·ina·tion /əˌbɒmɪˈneɪʃən/ **abominations.** If N-COUNT
you say that something is an **abomination**, you PRAGMATICS
think that it is completely unacceptable. *What is* FORMAL
happening is an abomination.

abo·rigi·nal /ˌæbəˈrɪdʒɪnəl/ **aboriginals. 1** An ◆◇◇◇◇
Aboriginal is an Australian Aborigine. **2 Aboriginal** ADJ: ADJ n
means belonging or relating to the Australian Aborigines. *...Aboriginal art. ...a protest over aboriginal*
land rights. **3** The **aboriginal** people or animals of ADJ: ADJ n
a place are ones that have been there from the earli-
est known times or that were there before Europeans arrived.

Abo·rig·i·ne /ˌæbəˈrɪdʒini/ **Aborigines. Aborigines** N-COUNT are members of the tribes that were living in Australia when Europeans arrived there.

abort /əˈbɔːt/ **aborts, aborting, aborted. 1** If an ◆◇◇◇◇ unborn baby **is aborted**, the pregnancy is ended deliberately and the baby is not born alive. ...*the lover* V n *who walked out on her after she had aborted their* FORMAL *child.* **2** If someone **aborts** a process, plan, or activity, they stop it before it has been completed. *The* beV-ed *take-off was aborted.*

abor·tion /əˈbɔːʃən/ **abortions.** An **abortion** is a ◆◆◇◇◇ medical operation in which a pregnancy is deliberately ended by removing an unwanted baby from a woman's body.

abor·tion·ist /əˈbɔːʃənɪst/ **abortionists.** An **abor-** N-COUNT **tionist** is someone who performs abortions, usually illegally. ● See also **anti-abortionist**.

abor·tive /əˈbɔːtɪv/. An **abortive** attempt or action ◆◇◇◇◇ is unsuccessful. *An abortive attempt was made to* ADJ *assassinate Hitler.* FORMAL

abound /əˈbaʊnd/ **abounds, abounding,** ◆◇◇◇◇ **abounded.** If things **abound**, or if a place **abounds** VERB with things, there are very large numbers of them. V *Stories abound about when he was in charge... The* Also V in n *book abounds with close-up images from space.* FORMAL

about /əˈbaʊt/. **1** You use **about** to introduce who ◆◆◆◆◆ or what something relates to or concerns. *Helen's* PREP *told me about you... She knew a lot about food. ...advice about exercise, and diet.* **2** When you mention PREP the things that an activity or institution is **about**, you are saying what it involves or what its aims are. *Leadership is about the ability to implement change.* **3** You use **about** after some adjectives to indicate PREP the person or thing that a feeling or state of mind relates to. *I feel so guilty and angry about the whole issue.* **4** If you do something **about** a problem, you PREP take action in order to solve it. *He felt helpless to do anything about it.* **5** When you say that there is a PREP particular quality **about** someone or something, you mean that they have this quality but you can't specify it exactly. *There's something a little peculiar about the results of your test.* **6 About** is used in front of a number to show that the ADV: number is not exact. *Inflation is running at about 2.7* ADV num *percent... The child is about eight years old.* **7** If someone or something moves **about**, they keep ADV: moving in different directions. *The house isn't big,* ADV after v *what with three children running about.* ▶ Also a PREP preposition. *From 1879 to 1888 he wandered about Germany, Switzerland, and Italy.* **8** If someone or something is **about**, they are present ADJ: or available. *There's lots of money about these days for* v-link ADJ *schemes like this.* **9** If you are **about** to do something, you are going to ADJ: do it very soon. If something is **about** to happen, it will v-link ADJ to-happen very soon. *I think he's about to leave... The* inf *film was about to start.* **10** If someone gets **out and about**, they are able to PHRASE move or travel about outdoors. *Despite considerable pain she has been getting out and about almost as normal.* **11** ● **how about**: see **how**. ● **what about**: see **what**. ● **just about**: see **just**.

a,bout-'face, about-faces. An **about-face** is the N-COUNT same as an **about-turn**. *The about-face is a big embarrassment to the Prime Minister.*

a,bout-'turn, about-turns. An **about-turn** is a N-COUNT complete change of attitude or opinion. *The deci-* BRITISH *sion was seen as an about-turn for the Government.*

above /əˈbʌv/. **1** If one thing is **above** another one, ◆◆◆◆◇ it is directly over it or higher than it. *He lifted his* PREP *hands above his head... Apartment 46 was a quiet apartment, unlike the one above it.* ▶ Also an ad- ADV verb. *A long scream sounded from somewhere above.* **2** In writing, you use **above** to refer to something that ADV has already been mentioned or illustrated. *Several* PRAGMATICS *conclusions could be drawn from the results described above.* ▶ Also a noun. *For additional information,* N-COLL-SING: *contact any of the above.* ▶ Also an adjective. *I may be* theN *reached at the above address.* ADJ: ADJ n

3 If an amount or measurement is **above** a particular PREP level, it is greater than that level. *The temperature crept up to just above 40 degrees. ...above average levels of rainfall... Government spending is planned to rise 3 per cent above inflation.* ▶ Also an adverb. *Banks have* ADV: *been charging 25 percent and above for unsecured* amount and *loans.* **4** If you hear one sound **above** another, it is ADV louder or clearer than the second one. *...trying to talk* PREP *above the noise.* **5** If someone is **above** you, they are in a higher social PREP position than you or in a position of authority over you. *He was a notch or so above her in the social scale... Look at the people above you in the positions of power.* ▶ Also an adverb. *I had orders from above to get him* ADV: *dropped.* **6** If someone thinks that they are **above** from ADV something, they think that they are too good or too PREP important for it; used showing disapproval. *He was* PRAGMATICS *one of those men who live above their own rules.* **7** If someone is **above** criticism or suspicion, they PREP cannot be criticized or suspected because of their good qualities or their position. *He was a respected academic and above suspicion.* **8** If you value one per- PREP son or thing **above** any other, you value them more or consider that they are more important. *...his tendency to put the team above everything.* **9** ● **over and above**: see **over**. ● **above the law**: see **law**. ● **above board**: see **board**.

abrade /əˈbreɪd/ **abrades, abrading, abraded.** VERB If something rough **abrades** something else, it V n scratches it or wears it down by rubbing against it. FORMAL *The brutally rough rock has abraded the skin.*

abra·sion /əˈbreɪʒən/ **abrasions.** An **abrasion** is N-COUNT an area on a person's body where the skin has been FORMAL scraped.

abra·sive /əˈbreɪsɪv/ **abrasives. 1** Someone who ◆◇◇◇◇ has an **abrasive** manner is unkind and rude. ADJ-GRADED *...strong language and abrasive remarks.* **2** An **abra-** ADJ-GRADED **sive** substance is rough and can be used to clean hard surfaces. *...abrasive cleaners.* ▶ Also a noun. N-VAR *Avoid abrasives, which can damage the tiles.*

abreast /əˈbrest/. **1** If people or things walk or ◆◇◇◇◇ move **abreast**, they are side by side, and facing in ADV the same direction. *The steep pavement was too narrow for them to walk abreast.* **2** If you are **abreast of** PHR-PREP someone or something, you are level with them or in line with them. *As he drew abreast of the man he pretended to stumble.* **3** If you keep **abreast of** a PHR-PREP subject, you know all the most recent facts about it. *He will be keeping abreast of the news.*

abridge /əˈbrɪdʒ/ **abridges, abridging,** VERB: V n **abridged.** If a writer or editor **abridges** a book, play, or article, they make it shorter by removing some parts of it. ♦ **abridged** *...an abridged version* ADJ-GRADED *of her new novel.*

abroad /əˈbrɔːd/. If you go **abroad**, you go to a for- ◆◆◆◇◇ eign country. *I would love to go abroad this year.* ADV *...public opposition here and abroad... He will stand in for Mr Goh when he is abroad.*

ab·ro·gate /ˈæbrəgeɪt/ **abrogates, abrogating,** VERB **abrogated.** If someone in authority **abrogates** V n something such as a law or agreement, they put an FORMAL end to it. *The next prime minister could abrogate the treaty.* ♦ **ab·ro·ga·tion** /ˌæbrəˈgeɪʃən/ *...the abroga-* N-UNCOUNT: *tion of trade union rights.* N of n

ab·rupt /əˈbrʌpt/. **1** An **abrupt** change or action is ◆◇◇◇◇ very sudden, often in a way which is unpleasant. ADJ-GRADED *Rosie's idyllic world came to an abrupt end when her parents' marriage broke up.* ♦ **ab·rupt·ly** *He* ADV-GRADED: *stopped abruptly.* **2** Someone who is **abrupt** speaks ADV with v in a rather rude, unfriendly way. *He was abrupt to* ADJ-GRADED *the point of rudeness.* ♦ **abruptly** *'Good night, then,'* ADV-GRADED *she said abruptly.* ♦ **ab·rupt·ness** *Simon was hurt* N-UNCOUNT *by your abruptness.*

ab·scess /ˈæbses/ **abscesses.** An **abscess** is a N-COUNT painful swelling, containing pus. *I had an abscess at the base of my tooth.*

ab·scond /æbˈskɒnd/ **absconds, absconding,** ◆◇◇◇◇ **absconded. 1** If someone **absconds** from some- VERB where such as a prison, they escape from it or leave V it without permission. *Twice he absconded after less* Also V from n FORMAL

than an hour in the remand home. **2** If someone **ab-** `VERB` `V with n` `FORMAL`
sconds with something, they leave and take it with
them, although it does not belong to them. *His*
partners were crooks and absconded with the funds.

ab·seil /ˈæbseɪl/ **abseils, abseiling, abseiled.** If `VERB:` `V down n` `BRITISH`
mountain climbers **abseil** down a cliff or rock face,
they go down it by sliding in a controlled way down
a rope, with their feet against the cliff or rock. The
usual American word is **rappel.**

ab·sence /ˈæbsəns/ **absences. 1** Someone's **ab-** ◆◆◇◇ `N-VAR:` `with supp`
sence from a place is the fact that they are not
there. *...letters which had arrived for me in my ab-*
sence... Eleanor would later blame her mother-in-
law for her husband's frequent absences. **2** The **ab-** `N-SING:` `with supp`
sence of something from a place is the fact that it is
not there or does not exist. *The presence or absence*
of clouds can have an important impact on heat
transfer... In the absence of a will the courts decide
who the guardian is. **3** See also **leave of absence.**
● **conspicuous by** one's **absence:** see **conspicuous.**

ab·sent, absents, absenting, absented. The ◆◆◇◇
adjective and preposition are pronounced /ˈæbsənt/. `ADJ`
The verb is pronounced /æbˈsent/. **1** If someone or
something is **absent** from a place or situation, they
are not there. *He has been absent from his desk for*
two weeks... The pictures, too, were absent from the
walls. **2** If someone appears **absent**, they are not `ADJ-GRADED`
paying attention because they are thinking about
something else. *'Nothing,' Rosie said in an absent*
way. ♦ **ab·sent·ly** /ˈæbsəntli/ *He nodded absently.* `ADV-GRADED`
3 If someone **absents** themselves from a place, they `VERB` `V pron-refl`
do not go or stay there. *She was old enough to ab-* `from n`
sent herself from the lunch table if she chose. `FORMAL`

ab·sen·tee /ˌæbsənˈtiː/ **absentees. 1** An **absen-** ◆◇◇◇ `N-COUNT`
tee is a person who is expected to be in a particular
place but who is not there. *I was expecting far more*
in the classes but there are a lot of absentees. **2** **Ab-** `ADJ: ADJ n`
sentee is used to describe someone who is not there
to do a particular job in person. *Absentee fathers*
will be forced to pay child maintenance. **3** In the `ADJ: ADJ n`
United States, if you vote by **absentee** ballot, you
vote in advance because you will be away on the
day of an election.

ab·sen·tee·ism /ˌæbsənˈtiːɪzəm/. **Absenteeism** is `N-UNCOUNT`
the fact or habit of frequently being away from work
or school, usually without a good reason.

ab·sen·tia /æbˈsentiə, AM -ˈsenʃə/. If something is `PHRASE`
done to you **in absentia**, it is done to you when you `FORMAL`
are not present. *The other defendants were sen-*
tenced in absentia.

absent-'minded. Someone who is **absent-** `ADJ-GRADED`
minded forgets things or does not pay attention to
what they are doing. *Malcolm is a genius, but he's*
the absent-minded professor type. ♦ **absent-**
minded·ly *Elizabeth absent-mindedly picked a* `ADV-GRADED:` `ADV with v`
thread from his lapel. ♦ **absent-minded·ness** *You* `N-UNCOUNT`
will have to put up with Grace's absent-mindedness.

ab·sinthe /ˈæbsɪnθ/. **Absinthe** is a very strong alco- `N-UNCOUNT`
holic drink. It is green in colour and bitter in taste.

ab·so·lute /ˈæbsəluːt/ **absolutes. 1** Absolute ◆◆◇◇ `ADJ`
means total and complete. *It's not really suited to*
absolute beginners... A sick person needs absolute
confidence and trust in a doctor. ♦ **ab·so·lute·ly** `ADV`
/ˈæbsəluːtli/ *Jill is absolutely right... I absolutely ref-*
use to get married. **2** You use **absolute** to emphasize `ADJ: ADJ n`
something that you are saying. *About 12 inches wide* `PRAGMATICS`
is the absolute minimum you should consider... I
think it's absolute nonsense. **3** An **absolute** ruler has `ADJ: ADJ n`
complete power and authority over his or her coun-
try. *...the doctrine of absolute monarchy.*
4 Absolute is used to say that something is definite `ADJ`
and will not change even if circumstances change.
John brought the absolute proof that we needed... They
had given an absolute assurance that it would be kept
secret. **5** An amount that is expressed in **absolute** `ADJ: ADJ n`
terms is expressed as a fixed amount rather than be-
ing expressed with reference to variable factors such
as what you earn or the effects of inflation. *They might*
be just as badly in debt, both in absolute terms and as a
proportion of their incomes. **6** Absolute rules and `ADJ`

principles are believed to be true, right, or relevant in
all situations. *...certain assumptions which are accept-*
ed without question as absolute truths. ▶ Also a noun. `N-COUNT`
We tend to think in absolutes.
7 See also **decree absolute.**

ab·so·lute·ly /ˌæbsəˈluːtli/. **Absolutely** is an em- ◆◆◆◇
phatic way of saying yes or agreeing with someone. `ADV` `PRAGMATICS`
Absolutely not is an emphatic way of saying no or
disagreeing with someone. *'Was it worth it?'—*
'Absolutely.'... 'Did they approach you?'—'No, abso-
lutely not.'

absolute ma'jority, absolute majorities. If a `N-COUNT`
political party wins an **absolute majority** in an election, they obtain more seats or votes than the total
number gained by their opponents.

absolute 'zero. **Absolute zero** is a theoretical `N-UNCOUNT`
temperature that is thought to be the lowest possible temperature.

ab·so·lu·tion /ˌæbsəˈluːʃən/. If someone is given `N-UNCOUNT`
absolution, they are forgiven for their sins. *She felt* `FORMAL`
as if his words had granted her absolution.

ab·so·lut·ism /ˈæbsəluːtɪzəm/. **1 Absolutism** is a `N-UNCOUNT`
political system in which one ruler or leader has
complete power and authority over a country. *...the*
triumphal reassertion of royal absolutism. **2** You `N-UNCOUNT`
describe someone's beliefs as **absolutism** if they are `PRAGMATICS`
believed to be true, right, or relevant in all situations, without any allowances being made for different circumstances; used showing disapproval. *They*
are saying, with varying degrees of absolutism, that
animals should not be exploited at all. ♦ **ab·so·lut-**
·ist *This absolutist belief is replaced by an apprecia-* `ADJ`
tion that rules can vary.

ab·solve /æbˈzɒlv/ **absolves, absolving, ab-** `VERB`
solved. If a report or investigation **absolves** some- `V n of/from n` `Also V n`
one from blame or responsibility, it formally states
that he or she is not to blame. *...a police investiga-*
tion yesterday which absolved the police of all
blame.

ab·sorb /əbˈzɔːb/ **absorbs, absorbing, ab-** ◆◆◇◇
sorbed. 1 If an object **absorbs** something such as `VERB` `V n` `be V-ed into n`
liquid, gas, or heat, the liquid or heat enters the ob-
ject or is drawn into it. *Plants absorb carbon dioxide*
from the air... Refined sugars are absorbed into the
bloodstream very quickly. ♦ **ab·sorp·tion** `N-UNCOUNT`
/əbˈzɔːpʃən/ *Vitamin C increases the absorption of*
iron from food. **2** If a group **is absorbed** into a larg- `VERB` `be V-ed into n` `Also V n`
er group, it becomes part of the larger group. *The*
Colonial Office was absorbed into the Foreign Office.
♦ **absorption** *...East Germany's absorption into the* `N-UNCOUNT`
Federal Republic. **3** If you **absorb** information, you `VERB` `V n`
learn and understand it. *Too often he only absorbs*
half the information.
4 If something **absorbs** a force or shock, it reduces its `VERB` `V n`
effect. *...footwear which does not absorb the impact of*
the foot striking the ground. **5** If a system or society `VERB` `V n`
absorbs changes, effects, or costs, it is able to deal
with them without being badly affected. *The banks*
would be forced to absorb large losses. **6** If something `VERB` `V n`
absorbs something such as money, space, or time, it
uses up a great deal of it. *It might help if campaigning*
didn't absorb so much time and money.
7 If something **absorbs** you, it interests you a great `VERB` `V n`
deal and takes up all your attention and energy. *...a se-*
cond career which absorbed her more completely than
her acting ever had. ♦ **ab·sorbed** *He had discovered* `ADJ-GRADED:` `v-link ADJ`
politics and was rapidly becoming absorbed by it.
♦ **ab·sorp·tion** *He was struck by the artists' total ab-* `N-UNCOUNT:` `poss N in/with n`
sorption in their work. **8** See also **absorbing.**

ab·sor·bent /əbˈzɔːbənt/. **Absorbent** material soaks `ADJ-GRADED`
up liquid easily. *The towels are highly absorbent.*
♦ **ab·sor·ben·cy** /əbˈzɔːbənsi/. `N-UNCOUNT`

ab·sorb·er /əbˈzɔːbə/. See **shock absorber.**

ab·sorb·ing /əbˈzɔːbɪŋ/. An **absorbing** activity in- ◆◇◇◇
terests you a great deal and takes up all your atten- `ADJ-GRADED`
tion and energy. *'Two Sisters' is an absorbing read.*

ab·sorp·tion /əbˈzɔːpʃən/. See **absorb.**

ab·stain /æbˈsteɪn/ **abstains, abstaining, ab-** ◆◇◇◇
stained. 1 If you **abstain** from something, usually `VERB` `V from n` `FORMAL`
something you want to do, you deliberately do not

do it. *Abstain from sex or use condoms.* ♦ **ab·sten·** N-UNCOUNT
·tion /æbˈstenʃən/ *...abstention from alcohol.* **2** If VERB
you **abstain** during a vote, you do not use your vote. V
Six voted against and two abstained. ♦ **ab·sten·** N-VAR
·tion, abstentions *The number of abstentions is
likely to be crucial.*

ab·sti·nence /ˈæbstɪnəns/. **Abstinence** is the prac- ◆◇◇◇◇
tice of abstaining from something such as alcoholic N-UNCOUNT
drink or sex, often for health or religious reasons.

ab·stract, abstracts, abstracting, abstract- ◆◆◇◇◇
ed. The adjective and noun are pronounced
/ˈæbstrækt/. The verb is pronounced /æbˈstrækt/.
1 An **abstract** idea or way of thinking is based on ADJ-GRADED
general ideas rather than on real things and events.
*...starting with a few abstract principles. ...the facul-
ty of abstract reasoning.* ♦ **ab·stract·ly** *It is hard to* ADV-GRADED
think abstractly in these conditions. **2** When you talk PHRASE
or think about something **in the abstract**, you talk
or think about it in a general way, rather than considering particular things or events. *Money was a
commodity she never thought about except in the
abstract.*
3 In grammar, an **abstract** noun refers to a quality or ADJ: ADJ n
idea rather than to a physical object.
4 **Abstract** art makes use of shapes and patterns ra- ADJ-GRADED
ther than showing people or things as they actually
are. *...a modern abstract painting.* **5** An **abstract** is an N-COUNT
abstract work of art. *He persuaded her to change from
abstracts to portraits.*
6 An **abstract** of an article, document, or speech is a N-COUNT
short piece of writing that summarizes the main
points of it.
7 If you **abstract** something from somewhere, you VERB
take it from there. *The author has abstracted poems* V n from v
from earlier books. Also V n
FORMAL

ab·stract·ed /æbˈstræktɪd/. Someone who is **ab-** ADJ-GRADED
stracted is thinking so deeply that they are not fully WRITTEN
aware of what is happening around them. *The same
abstracted look was still on his face.*

ab·strac·tion /æbˈstrækʃən/ **abstractions. 1** An ◆◇◇◇◇
abstraction is a general idea rather than one relat- N-VAR
ing to a particular object, person, or situation. *Is it FORMAL
worth fighting a big war, in the name of an abstrac-
tion like sovereignty?* **2** **Abstraction** is the state of N-UNCOUNT
being very deep in thought. *Andrew noticed her ab- WRITTEN
straction and asked, 'What's bothering you?'*

ab·struse /æbˈstruːs/. If you describe something as ADJ-GRADED
abstruse, you mean that it is difficult to understand. FORMAL
...fruitless discussions about abstruse resolutions.

ab·surd /æbˈsɜːd/. If you say that something is **ab-** ◆◆◇◇◇
surd, you are criticizing it because you think that it PRAGMATICS
is ridiculous or that it does not make sense. *It is absurd to be discussing compulsory redundancy policies for teachers.* ▶ **The absurd** is something that is N-SING:
absurd. ♦ **ab·surd·ly** *Prices were still absurdly low,* theN
in his opinion. ♦ **ab·surd·ity** /æbˈsɜːdɪti/ **absurd-** ADV-GRADED
ities *...the absurdity of all wars.* N-VAR

ab·surd·ist /æbˈsɜːdɪst/. An **absurdist** play shows ADJ
the absurdity of some aspect of society or human
behaviour.

abun·dance /əˈbʌndəns/. An **abundance** of some- ◆◇◇◇◇
thing is a very large quantity of it. *This area of N-COLL-SING
France has an abundance of safe beaches... Food was
in abundance.*

abun·dant /əˈbʌndənt/. Something that is **abun-** ◆◇◇◇◇
dant is present in large quantities. *There is an abun- ADJ-GRADED
dant supply of cheap labour.* ♦ **abun·dant·ly** *All* ADV-GRADED
the pages are abundantly illustrated.

abun·dant·ly /əˈbʌndəntli/. If something is **abun-** ADV: ADV adj
dantly clear, it is extremely obvious. *He made abundantly clear his admiration for her work.*

abuse, abuses, abusing, abused. The noun is ◆◆◆◇
pronounced /əˈbjuːs/. The verb is pronounced
/əˈbjuːz/. **1** **Abuse** of someone is cruel and violent N-UNCOUNT:
treatment of them. *...investigation of alleged child also N in pl
abuse. ...controversy over human rights abuses.*
♦ **abu·sive** /əˈbjuːsɪv/ *...her cruel and abusive hus- ADJ-GRADED
band.* **2** If someone **is abused**, they are treated cru- VERB:
elly and violently. *...parents who feel they cannot beV-ed
V n

cope or might **abuse** their children.* ♦ **abus·er,** N-COUNT
abusers *...a convicted child abuser.*
3 **Abuse** consists of extremely rude and insulting N-UNCOUNT
things that people say when they are angry. *I was left
shouting abuse as the car sped off.* ♦ **abu·sive** *...abu- ADJ-GRADED
sive language.* **4** You can say that someone **is abused** VERB
if extremely rude and insulting things are said to beV-ed
them. *He was verbally abused by other soldiers.* Also V n
5 **Abuse** of something is the use of it in a wrong way or N-VAR:
for a bad purpose. *...an abuse of power. ...drug and al- with supp
cohol abuse.* **6** If you **abuse** something, you use it in a VERB
wrong way or for a bad purpose. *...how the rich and V n
powerful can abuse their position.* ♦ **abus·er** *...the* N-COUNT
treatment of alcohol and drug abusers.

abut /əˈbʌt/ **abuts, abutting, abutted.** When VERB
land or a building **abuts** something or **abuts on** V on n
something, it is next to it. *One edge of the garden FORMAL
abutted on an old entrance to the mine. ...the house
abutting our hotel.*

abuzz /əˈbʌz/. If someone says that a place is **abuzz** ADJ:
with rumours or plans, they mean that everyone v-link ADJ
there is excited about them. *Washington has been JOURNALISM
abuzz with stories.*

abys·mal /əˈbɪzməl/. If you describe a situation or ADJ-GRADED
the condition of something as **abysmal**, you think PRAGMATICS
that it is very bad. *The general standard of racing
was abysmal.* ♦ **abys·mal·ly** *Standards of hygiene* ADV-GRADED
*are abysmally low... As the chart shows, it has failed
abysmally.*

abyss /æˈbɪs/ **abysses. 1** An **abyss** is a very deep ◆◇◇◇◇
hole in the ground. *The wheels spun ominously close N-COUNT
to a vertical abyss.* **2** If someone is on the edge or LITERARY
brink of an **abyss**, they are about to enter into a N-COUNT
very frightening or threatening situation. **3** A very LITERARY
great difference between two people, things, or N-COUNT
groups can be referred to as an **abyss**. *...the abyss LITERARY
between what you think you are and what you actually are?*

AC /ˌeɪ ˈsiː/. **AC** is used to refer to an electric cur- ◆◇◇◇◇
rent that continually changes direction as it flows. N-UNCOUNT
AC is an abbreviation for 'alternating current'.

aca·cia /əˈkeɪʃə/ **acacias.** The form **acacia** can N-COUNT
also be used for the plural. An **acacia** or an **acacia
tree** is a tree which grows in warm countries and
which usually has small yellow or white flowers.

aca·deme /ˈækədiːm/. The academic world of uni- N-UNCOUNT
versities is sometimes referred to as **academe**. FORMAL

aca·demia /ˌækəˈdiːmiə/. **Academia** refers to all the N-UNCOUNT
academics in a particular country or region, the institutions they work in, and their work. *...links between industry and academia.*

aca·dem·ic /ˌækəˈdemɪk/ **academics. 1** Academ- ◆◆◆◇
ic is used to describe things that relate to the work ADJ: ADJ n
done in schools, colleges, and universities, especially work which involves studying and reasoning rather than practical or technical skills. *Their academic standards are high.* ♦ **aca·dem·ical·ly** ADV
/ˌækəˈdemɪkli/ *He is academically gifted.* **2** Academic ADJ: ADJ n
is used to describe things that relate to schools, colleges, and universities. *...the start of the last academic year.* **3** Academic is used to describe work, ADJ-GRADED
or a school, college, or university, that places emphasis on studying and reasoning rather than on
practical or technical skills. *The author has settled
for a more academic approach.* **4** Someone who is ADJ-GRADED
academic is good at studying. *...less academic children.* **5** An **academic** is a member of a university or N-COUNT
college who teaches or does research. *The move has
upset many prominent academics.*
6 You say that you think a particular point is **academ-** ADJ-GRADED
ic when you want to indicate that you think it has no
real relevance or effect. *This was not an academic exercise – soldiers' lives were at risk.*

acad·emi·cian /əˌkædəˈmɪʃən, AM ˌækədə-/ **acad-** N-COUNT
emicians. An **academician** is a member of an
academy which has been formed to promote and
maintain standards in a particular field.

acad·emy /əˈkædəmi/ **academies. 1** Schools and ◆◆◇◇◇
colleges, especially those specializing in particular N-COUNT

subjects or skills, sometimes have **academy** as part of their name. ...*the Royal Academy of Music.* **2** Academy appears in the names of some societies formed to promote and maintain standards in a particular field. ...*the American Academy of Psychotherapists.*

ac·cede /æk'si:d/ **accedes, acceding, acceded.** **1** If you **accede** to someone's request, you do what they ask. *I never understood why he didn't just accede to our demands at the outset.* **2** When a member of a royal family **accedes** to the throne, they become king or queen. ...*when Prince Charles accedes to the throne.* ♦ **ac·ces·sion** ...*the 40th anniversary of the Queen's accession to the throne.*
[VERB V to n FORMAL | VERB Also V FORMAL | N-UNCOUNT: with poss]

ac·cel·er·ate /æk'seləreɪt/ **accelerates, accelerating, accelerated.** **1** If someone or something **accelerates** a process or the rate of something, or if the process or rate **accelerates**, it gets faster and faster. *The government is to accelerate its privatisation programme... Growth will accelerate to 2.9 per cent next year.* ♦ **ac·cel·er·a·tion** /æk,selə'reɪʃən/ *He has also called for an acceleration of political reforms.* **2** When a moving vehicle **accelerates**, it goes faster and faster. ♦ **acceleration** *Acceleration to 60 mph takes a mere 5.7 seconds.*
[♦◇◇◇ | V-ERG V n V | N-UNCOUNT | N-UNCOUNT]

ac·cel·er·a·tion /æk,selə'reɪʃən/. In physics, **acceleration** is the rate at which the speed of an object is increasing.
[♦◇◇◇ N-UNCOUNT TECHNICAL]

ac·cel·er·a·tor /æk'seləreɪtə/ **accelerators.** The **accelerator** in a car or other vehicle is the pedal which you press with your foot in order to make the vehicle go faster. See picture headed **car and bicycle.**
[♦◇◇◇ N-COUNT]

ac·cent, accents, accenting, accented. The noun is pronounced /'æksənt/. The verb is pronounced /æk'sent/. **1** Someone who speaks with a particular **accent** pronounces the words of a language in a distinctive way that shows which country, region, or social class they come from. *He had developed a slight American accent.* **2** An **accent** is a short line or other mark which is written above certain letters in some languages and which indicates the way those letters are pronounced. **3** If you put the **accent** on a particular feature of something, you emphasize it or give it special importance. *He is putting the accent on military readiness.* **4** If something is **accented** by something else, it is emphasized by it. ...*a white dress accented by a ribbon... The classical choreography is accented by steps from Hungarian folk dances.*
[♦♦◇◇ | N-COUNT | N-COUNT | N-SING | VB: no cont V-ed be V-ed Also V n WRITTEN]

ac·cent·ed /'æksentɪd/. **Accented** language or speech is spoken with a particular accent. ...*heavily accented English. ...his soft, accented voice.* ● See also **accent.**
[ADJ-GRADED]

ac·cen·tu·ate /æk'sentʃueɪt/ **accentuates, accentuating, accentuated.** To **accentuate** something means to emphasize it or make it more noticeable. *His shaven head accentuates his large round face.*
[♦◇◇◇ VERB V n]

ac·cept /æk'sept/ **accepts, accepting, accepted.** **1** If you **accept** something that you have been offered, you say yes to it or agree to take it. *I accepted his offer of permanent employment... All those invited to next week's peace conference have accepted.* **2** If you **accept** an idea, statement, or fact, you believe that it is true or valid. *I do not accept that there is any kind of crisis in British science... I don't think they would accept that view... He did not accept this reply as valid.* **3** If you **accept** an unpleasant fact or situation, you get used to it or recognize that it cannot be changed. *Urban dwellers often accept noise as part of city life... I wasn't willing to accept that her leaving was a possibility.* **4** If you **accept** a plan or an intended action, you agree to it and allow it to happen. ...*Britain's reluctance to accept a proposal for a single European currency.* **5** If a person, company, or organization **accepts** something such as a document, they recognize that it is genuine or satisfactory, and agree to consider it or handle it. *Proof of postage will not be accepted as proof of receipt.*
[♦♦♦♦♦ | VERB V n V | VERB V that V n V n as adj/n | VERB: V n V n as n/adj V that | VERB V n | VERB: V n be V-ed as n Also V n as n/ adj]

6 If an organization or person **accepts** you, you are allowed to join the organization or use the services that are offered. *Should the British Army accept gays? ...incentives to private landlords to accept young people as tenants.*
[VERB V n V n as n Also V n into n]

7 If a person or a group of people **accepts** you, they begin to be friendly towards you or to think of you as part of the group. *Many men still have difficulty accepting a woman as a business partner... Stephen was accepted into the family like an adopted brother.*
[VERB: V n V n for/as n V into n]

8 If you **accept** the responsibility or blame for something, you recognize that you are responsible for it.
[VERB: V n]

9 If you **accept** someone's advice or suggestion, you agree to do what they say. *An older man, for instance, would never accept orders from a younger woman.*
[VERB V n]

10 If someone's body **accepts** a transplanted organ, the organ becomes part of the body and starts to function normally. **11** If a machine **accepts** a particular kind of thing, it is designed to take it and deal with it or process it. *The telephone booths accept 10 and 20 pence coins.*
[VERB: V n | VERB V n]

12 See also **accepted.**

ac·cept·able /æk'septəbəl/. **1** Acceptable activities and situations are those that most people approve of or consider to be normal. *It is becoming more acceptable for women to drink... The air pollution exceeds acceptable levels by 10 times or more.* ♦ **ac·cept·abil·ity** /æk,septə'bɪlɪti/ ...*increasing the social acceptability of divorce.* ♦ **ac·cept·ably** /æk'septəbli/ *The aim of discipline is to teach children to behave acceptably.* **2** If something is **acceptable** to you, you agree to consider it, use it, or allow it to happen. *They have thrashed out a compromise formula acceptable to Moscow. ...a mutually acceptable new contract.* **3** If you describe something as **acceptable,** you mean that it is good enough or fairly good. *We've made an acceptable start, but it could've been better.* ♦ **acceptably** ...*an acceptably accurate solution to a problem.*
[♦♦◇◇ ADJ-GRADED | N-UNCOUNT | ADV-GRADED | ADJ-GRADED | ADJ-GRADED | ADV-GRADED]

ac·cept·ance /æk'septəns/ **acceptances.** **1** Acceptance of an offer or a proposal is the act of saying yes to it or agreeing to it. *The Party is being degraded by its acceptance of secret donations... Several shareholders have withdrawn earlier acceptances of the offer. ...a letter of acceptance.* **2** If there is **acceptance** of an idea, most people believe or agree that it is true. ...*a theory that is steadily gaining acceptance.* **3** Your **acceptance** of a situation, especially an unpleasant or difficult one, is an attitude or feeling that you cannot change it and that you must get used to it. ...*his calm acceptance of whatever comes his way.* **4** If there is **acceptance** of a new product, people start to like it and get used to it. *Avant-garde music to this day has not found general public acceptance.* **5** Acceptance of someone into a group means beginning to think of them as part of the group and to act in a friendly way towards them. *A very determined effort by society will ensure that the disabled achieve real acceptance and integration.*
[♦♦◇◇ N-VAR | N-UNCOUNT | N-UNCOUNT | N-UNCOUNT | N-UNCOUNT]

ac·cept·ed /æk'septɪd/. **Accepted** ideas are agreed by most people to be correct or reasonable. *There is no generally accepted definition of life.* ● See also **accept.**
[♦♦♦◇ ADJ]

ac·cess /'ækses/ **accesses, accessing, accessed.** **1** If you have **access** to a building or other place, you are able or allowed to go into it. *The facilities have been adapted to give access to wheelchair users... Scientists have only recently been able to gain access to the area.* **2** If you have **access** to something such as information or equipment, you have the opportunity or right to see it or use it. ...*a Code of Practice that would give patients right of access to their medical records.* **3** If you have **access** to a person, you have the opportunity or right to see them or meet them. *My ex-wife deliberately sabotages my access to the children.* **4** If you **access** something, especially information held on a computer, you succeed in obtaining it. *You've illegally accessed and misused confidential security files.*
[♦♦◇◇ | N-UNCOUNT | N-UNCOUNT | N-UNCOUNT | VERB V n]

'access course, access courses. In Britain, an N-COUNT access course is an educational course which prepares adults with few or no qualifications for study at a university or other place of higher education.

ac·ces·sible /æk'sesɪbəl/. **1** If a place or building ◆◆◇◇◇ is accessible to people, it is easy for them to reach it ADJ-GRADED or get into it. If an object is accessible, it is easy to reach. ...a low cupboard that's easily accessible to your toddler... The premises are wheelchair accessible. ♦ **ac·ces·sibil·ity** /æk,sesɪ'bɪlɪti/ ...the easy N-UNCOUNT accessibility of Harare to the rest of the world. **2** If ADJ-GRADED something is accessible to people, they can easily use it or obtain it. ...to make the system accessible to more people. ♦ **accessibility** ...growing public N-UNCOUNT concern about the cost, quality and accessibility of health care. **3** If you describe a book, painting, or ADJ-GRADED other work of art as accessible, you approve of it PRAGMATICS because it is simple and accessible for people to understand and appreciate easily. ...literary books that are accessible to a general audience. ♦ **accessibility** N-UNCOUNT ...to increase the accessibility of the arts to the public.

ac·ces·sion /æk'seʃən/. A country's accession to a N-UNCOUNT group of countries or to an association is its joining FORMAL that group of countries or association. ...Namibia's accession to the Lome convention. ● See also accede.

ac·ces·so·rize /æk'sesəraɪz/ **accessorizes, ac-** VERB **cessorizing, accessorized;** also spelled **acces-** Also V n with n **sorise** in British English. To accessorize something WRITTEN such as a set of furniture or clothing means to add other things to it in order to make it look more attractive. Adding extra fabrics and linens is one of the easiest ways to accessorize your bedroom.

ac·ces·so·ry /æk'sesəri/ **accessories. 1** Acces- ◆◆◇◇◇ sories are items of equipment that are not essential, N-COUNT but which can be used with or added to something else in order to make it more efficient, useful, or decorative. ...hand-made bedroom and bathroom accessories. **2** Accessories are articles, such as belts N-COUNT and handbags, which you wear or carry but which are not part of your main clothing. ...clothing, shoes and accessories. **3** If someone is an accessory to a N-COUNT crime, they willingly help the person who commits LEGAL it, but do not take part in the crime itself. **4** You can ADJ use accessory to describe something which contrib- FORMAL utes to an activity or process, but is not the most essential or important part of it. ...the essentiality of minerals as accessory food factors required for maintaining life.

'access road, access roads. An access road is a N-COUNT road which enables traffic to reach a particular place or area.

ac·ci·dent /'æksɪdənt/ **accidents. 1** An accident ◆◆◆◇◇ happens when a vehicle hits a person, object, or N-COUNT other vehicle, causing injury or damage. ...a serious car accident. **2** If someone has an accident, some- N-COUNT thing unpleasant happens to them that was not intended, sometimes causing injury or death. I had an accident at work... The killing of the young man was an accident. **3** If something happens by accident, it happens com- N-VAR pletely by chance. She discovered the problem by accident... Like an accident of nature, this family has produced more talent than seems possible. **4** You begin a PHRASE sentence with 'It's no accident' if you want to suggest that something was done deliberately or has a logical explanation, although it might appear to have happened by chance. It is no accident that Justice is often pictured as blind.

ac·ci·den·tal /,æksɪ'dentəl/. An accidental event ◆◆◇◇◇ happens by chance or as the result of an accident, ADJ and is not deliberately intended. ...a verdict of accidental death... His hand brushed against hers; it could have been either accidental or deliberate. ♦ **ac·ci·den·tal·ly** /,æksɪ'dentli/. A special locking ADV: system means the door cannot be opened accidental- ADV with v ly... She had accidentally kicked me.

'accident prone; also spelled **accident-prone.** If ADJ-GRADED you describe someone or something as accident

prone, you mean that a lot of accidents or other unpleasant things happen to them.

ac·claim /ə'kleɪm/ **acclaims, acclaiming, ac-** ◆◆◇◇◇ **claimed. 1** If someone or something is acclaimed, VB: usu they are praised enthusiastically. She has been ac- passive claimed for the TV dramas 'Prime Suspect' and n/-ing 'Civvies'... He was acclaimed as England's greatest beV-ed as n modern painter... He too, had been acclaimed a FORMAL hero. ♦ **ac·claimed** ...six highly acclaimed novels. ADJ-GRADED **2** Acclaim is public praise for someone or something. N-UNCOUNT Angela Bassett has won critical acclaim for her excel- FORMAL lent performance.

ac·cla·ma·tion /,æklə'meɪʃən/. **1** Acclamation is a N-UNCOUNT noisy or enthusiastic expression of approval for FORMAL someone or something. The event went ahead to universal acclamation. **2** If someone is chosen or N-UNCOUNT elected by acclamation, they are elected as a result FORMAL of an oral vote. Al Gore was nominated by acclamation for vice president.

ac·cli·ma·tize /ə'klaɪmətaɪz/ **acclimatizes, ac-** V-ERG **climatizing, acclimatized;** also spelled **acclima-** V ton **tise** in British English. When you acclimatize or are V-ed **acclimatized** to a new situation, place, or climate, Also V, you become used to it. The athletes are acclimatis- V n ton ing to the heat... He has left for St Louis early to ac- FORMAL climatise himself... She figured that it would take her two years to get acclimatized. ♦ **ac·cli·ma·ti·za-** **·tion** /ə,klaɪmətaɪ'zeɪʃən/ Acclimatization to higher N-UNCOUNT altitudes may take several weeks.

ac·co·lade /'ækəleɪd/ **accolades.** An accolade is ◆◇◇◇◇ something that is done or said about someone N-COUNT which shows how much people admire them. To FORMAL ride for one's country is the ultimate accolade.

ac·com·mo·date /ə'kɒmədeɪt/ **accommodates,** ◆◆◇◇◇ **accommodating, accommodated. 1** If a VB: no cont building or space can accommodate someone or V n something, it has enough room for them. The school in Poldown was not big enough to accommodate all the children. **2** To accommodate someone means to VERB provide them with a place to stay. ...a hotel built to V n accommodate guests for the wedding of King beV-ed Alfonso... Students are accommodated in homes prep/adv nearby. **3** If something is planned or changed to accommo- VERB date a particular fact or situation, it is planned or V n changed to take it into account. The roads are built to accommodate gradual temperature changes. **4** If you VERB accommodate to something new, you change your V ton behaviour or ideas so that you are able to deal with it. FORMAL Some animal and plant species cannot accommodate to the rapidly-changing conditions. **5** If you do something to accommodate someone, VERB you do it with the main purpose of pleasing or satisfy- V n ing them. He has never put an arm around his wife to accommodate photographers. ♦ **ac·com·mo·dat-** **·ing** Lindi seemed a nice, accommodating girl. ADJ-GRADED

ac·com·mo·da·tion /ə,kɒmə'deɪʃən/ **accommo-** ◆◆◇◇◇ **dations. 1** Accommodation is used to refer to N-UNCOUNT: buildings or rooms where people live or stay. The also N in pl usual American word is **accommodations.** The gov- BRITISH ernment will provide temporary accommodation for up to three thousand people... Rates are higher for deluxe accommodations. **2** Accommodation is N-UNCOUNT space in buildings or vehicles that is available for FORMAL certain things, people, or activities. The school occupies split-site accommodation on the main campus. **3** An accommodation is an agreement or compro- N-COUNT mise between different people or groups which en- FORMAL ables them to exist together without trouble. Religions, to survive, must make accommodations with the larger political structures that nurture them.

ac·com·pa·ni·ment /ə'kʌmpnɪmənt/ **accompa-** ◆◇◇◇◇ **niments. 1** The accompaniment to a song or tune N-COUNT is the music that is played at the same time as it and forms a background to it. **2** An accompani- N-COUNT ment is something which goes with another thing. This recipe makes a good accompaniment to ice-cream. ● If one thing happens to the accompani- PHR-PREP ment of another, they happen at the same time. The

two teams took a lap of honour together to the accompaniment of fireworks.

ac·com·pa·nist /əˈkʌmpənɪst/ **accompanists.** N-COUNT
An **accompanist** is a musician, especially a pianist, who plays one part of a piece of music while someone else sings or plays the main tune.

ac·com·pa·ny /əˈkʌmpəni/ **accompanies, accompanying, accompanied. 1** If you accompany someone, you go somewhere with them. *Ken agreed to accompany me... The Prime Minister, accompanied by the governor, led the President up to the house.* **2** If one thing **accompanies** another, it happens or exists at the same time, or as a result of it. *This volume of essays was designed to accompany an exhibition... The proposal was instantly voted through with two to one in favour, accompanied by enthusiastic applause.* **3** If you **accompany** a singer or a musician, you play one part of a piece of music while they sing or play the main tune.   ◆◆◆◇◇ VERB V n V-ed FORMAL / VERB V n V-ed FORMAL / VERB: V n

ac·com·pli /æˈkɒmpliː/. See **fait accompli.**

ac·com·plice /əˈkʌmplɪs, AM əˈkɒm-/ **accomplices.** Someone's **accomplice** is a person who helps them to commit a crime.   ◆◇◇◇◇ N-COUNT

ac·com·plish /əˈkʌmplɪʃ, AM əˈkɒm-/ **accomplishes, accomplishing, accomplished.** If you **accomplish** something, you succeed in doing it. *If we'd all work together, I think we could accomplish our goal.* **⟐ ac·com·plish·ment** *He wished Mr Walesa success in the accomplishment of his highly important mission.*   ◆◆◇◇◇ VERB V n / N-UNCOUNT

ac·com·plished /əˈkʌmplɪʃt, AM əˈkɒm-/. If someone is **accomplished** at something, they are very good at it. *...one of the most accomplished composers of our time.*   ◆◆◇◇◇ ADJ-GRADED FORMAL

ac·com·plish·ment /əˈkʌmplɪʃmənt, AM əˈkɒm-/ **accomplishments.** Your **accomplishments** are the things that you have achieved, or the things that you have done well. *The list of her accomplishments is staggering... By any standards, the accomplishments of the past year are extraordinary.*   ◆◇◇◇◇ N-COUNT FORMAL

ac·cord /əˈkɔːd/ **accords, according, accorded. 1** An **accord** between countries or groups of people is a formal agreement, for example to end a war. *...UNITA, legalised as a political party under the 1991 peace accords.* **2** If you **are accorded** a particular kind of treatment, people treat you in that way. *His predecessor was accorded an equally tumultuous welcome... The government accorded him the rank of Colonel.* **3** If one fact, idea, or condition **accords with** another, there is no conflict between them. *Such an approach accords with the principles of socialist ideology.* **4** If one person, action, or fact is **in accord with** another, there is no conflict between them. You can also say that two people or things are **in accord.** *...this military action, taken in accord with United Nations resolutions.* **5** If something happens **of its own accord,** it seems to happen automatically, without anybody making it happen. *In many cases the disease will clear up of its own accord.* **6** If you do something **of your own accord,** you do it because you want to, without being asked or forced. **7** See also **according to.**   ◆◆◆◆◇ N-COUNT / VERB be V-ed n V n n Also V n to n FORMAL / V with n FORMAL PHRASE FORMAL / PHRASE / PHRASE

ac·cord·ance /əˈkɔːdəns/. If something is done **in accordance with** a particular rule or system, it is done in the way that the rule or system says that it should be done. *He must be treated in accordance with the rules of the Geneva Convention.*   ◆◇◇◇◇ PHR-PREP

ac·cord·ing·ly /əˈkɔːdɪŋli/. **1** You use **accordingly** to introduce a fact or situation which is a result or consequence of something that you have just referred to. *We have a different background, a different history. Accordingly, we have the right to different futures.* **2** If you consider a situation and then act **accordingly,** the way you act depends on the nature of the situation. *It is a difficult job and they should be paid accordingly.*   ◆◆◇◇◇ ADV PRAGMATICS / ADV: ADV after v

ac'cording to. 1 If someone says that something is true **according to** a particular person, book, or   ◆◆◆◆◇ PHR-PREP

other source of information, they are indicating where they got their information. *Philip stayed at the hotel, according to Mr Hemming.* **2** If something is done **according to** a particular set of principles, these principles are used as a basis for the way it is done. *They both played the game according to the rules.* **3** If something varies **according to** a changing or variable factor, it varies in a way that is determined by this factor. *Prices vary according to the quantity ordered.* **4** If something happens **according to plan,** it varies exactly in the way that it was intended to happen. *If all goes according to plan, the first concert will be Tuesday evening.*   PHR-PREP / PHR-PREP / PHRASE

ac·cor·di·on /əˈkɔːdiən/ **accordions.** An **accordion** is a musical instrument in the shape of a fairly large box which you play by pressing keys or buttons while moving the two sides of the box together and apart.   ◆◇◇◇◇ N-COUNT

ac·cost /əˈkɒst, AM əˈkɔːst/ **accosts, accosting, accosted.** If someone, especially a stranger, **accosts** you, they stop you or go up to you and speak to you, especially in the way that you do not want them to. *This man had accosted me in the street.*   VERB PRAGMATICS V n FORMAL

ac·count /əˈkaʊnt/ **accounts, accounting, accounted. 1** If you have an **account** with a bank or a similar organization, you have an arrangement to leave your money there and take some out when you need it. *...a savings account.* **2** In business, a regular customer of a company can be referred to as an **account,** especially when the customer is another company. *Biggart Donald, the Glasgow-based marketing agency, has won two Edinburgh accounts.* **3** **Accounts** are detailed records of all the money that a person or business receives and spends. *He kept detailed accounts. ...Rolls-Royce's profit and loss account. ...an account book.* **4** An **account** is a written or spoken report of something that has happened. *He gave a detailed account of what happened.* **5** An **account** of something is a theory which is intended to explain or describe it. *...a relatively unsophisticated account of human behaviour... Science, on Weber's account, is an essentially value-free activity.* **6** If you say that something **is accounted** a particular thing, you are reporting someone's judgment or opinion that it is that thing. *The opening day of the battle was, nevertheless, accounted a success. ...homosexuals, whose sexual behaviour is still accounted sinful by the church.* **7** If you say that something is true **by all accounts** or **from all accounts,** you believe it is true because other people say so. *He is, by all accounts, a superb teacher.* **8** If you say that someone **gave a good account of** themselves in a particular situation, you mean that they performed well, although they may not have been completely successful. **9** If you say that something concerning a particular person is true **by** his or her **own account,** you mean that you believe it because that person has said it is true. *He was by his own account an ambitious workaholic.* **10** If someone **is called, held,** or **brought to account** for something they have done wrong, they are made to explain why they did it, and are often criticized or punished for it. *Individuals who repeatedly provide false information should be called to account for their actions.* **11** If you say that something is of **no account** or of **little account,** you mean that it is very unimportant and is not worth considering. *These obscure groups were of little account in either national or international politics.* **12** If you **take** something **into account,** or **take account of** something, you consider it when you are thinking about a situation or deciding what to do. *The defendant asked for 21 similar offences to be taken into account.* **13** You use **on account of** to introduce the reason or explanation for something. *The President declined to deliver the speech himself, on account of a sore throat.* **14** Your feelings on someone's **account** are the feelings you have when you think about them or imagine yourself to be in their situation. *Mollie told me what she'd done and I was really scared on her account.* **15** If   ◆◆◆◆◆ N-COUNT / N-COUNT / N-COUNT / N-COUNT: with supp / N-COUNT FORMAL / VB: usu passive be V-ed n be V-ed adj FORMAL / PHRASE / PHRASE / PHRASE / PHRASE / PHRASE FORMAL / PHRASE / PHR-PREP PRAGMATICS / PHRASE / PHRASE

you tell someone not to do something **on** your **ac·count**, you mean that they should do it only if they want to, and not because they think it will please you. *Don't leave on my account.* **16** If you say that something should **on no account** be done, you are emphasizing that it should not be done under any circumstances. *On no account should finches and lovebirds be housed together.* **17** You can use **on that account** or **on this account** when you want to say that something happens for the reason you have just mentioned. *Wine is radioactive but few people stop drinking it on that account.* **18** If you do something **on your own account**, you do it because you want to and without being asked. *I told him if he withdrew it was on his own account.* **19** If you buy or pay for something **on account**, you pay nothing or only part of the cost at first, and pay the rest later. *He was ordered to pay the company £500,000 on account.* **20** If you take part in a business activity **on your own account**, you do it for yourself, and not as a representative or employee of a company. **21** If you **settle accounts**, or **settle** your **accounts**, with an enemy or opponent, you bring your conflict or quarrel to an end by defeating them. You can also say that two enemies or opponents **settle accounts**, or **settle** their **accounts**. **22** See also **accounting, bank account, current account, deposit account**.

account for. **1** If a particular thing **accounts for** a part or proportion of something, that part or proportion consists of that thing, or is used or produced by it. *Computers account for 5% of the country's commercial electricity consumption.* **2** If something **accounts for** a particular fact or situation, it causes or explains it. *The gene they discovered today doesn't account for all those cases.* **3** If you can **account for** something, you can explain it or give the necessary information about it. *How do you account for the company's alarmingly high staff turnover?* **4** If someone has to **account for** an action or policy, they may be required to explain it to other people and will be held responsible if it fails. *The President alone must account for his government's reforms.* **5** If a sum of money **is accounted for** in a budget, it has been included in that budget for a particular purpose. *The really heavy redundancy costs have been accounted for.*

ac·count·able /əˈkaʊntəbəl/. If you are **accountable** to someone for something that you do, you are responsible for it and must be prepared to justify your actions to that person. *Public officials can finally be held accountable for their actions.* ♦ **ac·count·abil·ity** /əˌkaʊntəˈbɪlɪti/ *...an impetus towards democracy and greater accountability.*

ac·count·an·cy /əˈkaʊntənsi/. **Accountancy** is the theory or practice of keeping financial accounts.

ac·count·ant /əˈkaʊntənt/ **accountants.** An **accountant** is a person whose job is to keep financial accounts.

ac·count·ing /əˈkaʊntɪŋ/. **Accounting** is the activity of keeping detailed records of the amounts of money a business or person receives and spends. *...allegations of theft, forgery and false accounting.* ● See also **account**.

ac·cou·tre·ment /əˈkuːtrəmənt/ **accoutrements.** **Accoutrements** are all the things you have with you when you travel or when you take part in a particular activity. *...stationery and all the accoutrements of writing.*

ac·cred·it /əˈkredɪt/ **accredits, accrediting, accredited.** **1** If an educational qualification or institution **is accredited**, it is officially declared to be of an approved standard. *The MSc is accredited by the British Computer Society.* ♦ **ac·cred·i·ta·tion** /əˌkredɪˈteɪʃən/ *...the Council for the Accreditation of Teacher Education.* **2** If someone such as a diplomat or journalist **is accredited** to a particular job or place, they are officially recognized as having that job, or the right to be in that place. *The President proposed that Russian diplomats could be accredited to NATO headquarters.* ♦ **accreditation** *Media*

representatives should arrive at the Press Centre by 11:40 to obtain accreditation.

ac·cre·tion /əˈkriːʃən/ **accretions.** **1** An **accretion** is an addition to something, usually one that has been added over a period of time. *...the mythical structure has been overlaid by literary accretions.* **2 Accretion** is the process of new layers or parts being added to something. *The question arises as to whether the accretion of more powers is the answer.*

ac·crue /əˈkruː/ **accrues, accruing, accrued.** **1** If money or interest **accrues** or if it **is accrued**, it gradually increases in amount over a period of time. *Affluent people never let interest charges accrue. ...a longer time in which to accrue profits.* **2** If profits or benefits **accrue** to someone or if they **are accrued**, they accumulate over a period of time. *Financial economies may accrue through more advantageous bulk-buying discounts... The fee structure alone will exceed the tax benefits accrued.*

ac·cu·mu·late /əˈkjuːmjʊleɪt/ **accumulates, accumulating, accumulated.** When you **accumulate** things or when they **accumulate**, they collect or are gathered over a period of time. *Households accumulate wealth across a broad spectrum of assets... Lead can accumulate in the body.* ♦ **ac·cu·mu·la·tion** *...the accumulation of capital.*

ac·cu·mu·la·tion /əˌkjuːmjʊˈleɪʃən/ **accumulations.** An **accumulation** of something is a large number of things which have been collected together or acquired over a period of time. *...a big table strewn with an accumulation of farm publications. ...accumulations of dirt.*

ac·cu·mu·la·tive /əˈkjuːmjʊlətɪv, AM -leɪtɪv/. If something is **accumulative**, it increases in amount or intensity over a period of time. *The consensus is that risk factors have an accumulative effect.*

ac·cu·mu·la·tor /əˈkjuːmjʊleɪtə/ **accumulators.** In horse racing an **accumulator** is a betting system in which any money won in one race is automatically bet on other races.

ac·cu·rate /ˈækjʊrət/. **1** Something that is **accurate** is correct to a very detailed level. An **accurate** instrument is able to give you information that is correct to a very detailed level. *This is the most accurate description of the killer to date... Quartz timepieces are very accurate.* ♦ **ac·cu·ra·cy** *The preceding text cannot be guaranteed as to the accuracy of speakers' words or spelling.* ♦ **ac·cu·rate·ly** *The test can accurately predict what a bigger explosion would do.* **2** An **accurate** statement or account gives a true or fair judgment of something. *Stalin gave an accurate assessment of the utility of nuclear weapons.* ♦ **accurately** *What many people mean by the word 'power' could be more accurately described as control.* **3** An **accurate** weapon or throw reaches the exact point or target that it was intended to reach. You can also describe a person as **accurate** if they fire a weapon or throw something in this way. *The rifle was extremely accurate... The pilots, however, were not as accurate as they should be.* ♦ **ac·cu·ra·cy** *...weapons that could fire with accuracy at targets 3,000 yards away.* ♦ **ac·cu·rate·ly** *The more accurately you can aim bombs from aircraft, the fewer civilians you will kill.*

ac·curs·ed /əˈkɜːsɪd, əˈkɜːst/. Some people use **accursed** to describe something which they are very annoyed with. *It was about time he left that accursed woman.*

ac·cu·sa·tion /ˌækjʊˈzeɪʃən/ **accusations.** If you make an **accusation** against someone, you criticize them or express the belief that they have done something wrong. *Serbia has rejected accusations that it was to blame... I am not worried about accusations of being 'soft'.* ● See also **accuse**.

ac·cu·sa·tive /əˈkjuːzətɪv/. In the grammar of some languages, **the accusative**, or the **accusative case**, is the case used for a noun when it is the direct object of a verb, or the object of some prepositions. In English, only the pronouns 'me', 'him',

[right column margin codes:]
PRAGMATICS SPOKEN
PHRASE
PRAGMATICS
PHRASE
PRAGMATICS
PHRASE
PHRASE
PHRASE
PHRASE
PHRASAL VB / V P n
V P n
V P n
be V-ed P / Also V P n
◆◇◇◇ ADJ-GRADED
N-UNCOUNT
◆◇◇◇ N-UNCOUNT
◆◇◇◇ N-COUNT
◆◇◇◇ N-UNCOUNT
N-COUNT DATED
◆◇◇◇ VB: usu be V-ed / N-UNCOUNT
VB: usu be V-ed to n / Also be V-ed FORMAL
N-UNCOUNT

N-COUNT FORMAL
N-UNCOUNT FORMAL
◆◇◇◇ V-ERG / V / Vn
V-ERG / V / Also V n, V to n FORMAL
◆◆◇◇ V-ERG / Vn / V
N-UNCOUNT
◆◇◇◇ N-COUNT
ADJ
N-COUNT BRITISH
◆◆◇◇ ADJ-GRADED
N-UNCOUNT
ADV-GRADED
ADJ-GRADED
ADV-GRADED: ADV with v
ADJ-GRADED
N-UNCOUNT
ADV-GRADED: ADV with v
ADJ: ADJ n PRAGMATICS DATED
◆◆◇◇ N-VAR
N-SING: the N

'her', 'us', and 'them' are in the accusative. Compare **nominative**.

ac·cu·sa·tory /ə'kjuːzətəri, AM -tɔːri/. An accusatory look, remark, or tone of voice suggests blame or criticism. ADJ-GRADED WRITTEN

ac·cuse /ə'kjuːz/ **accuses, accusing, accused. 1** If you **accuse** someone of doing something wrong or dishonest, you say or tell them that you believe that they did it. *He was accusing her of having an affair.* **2** If you **are accused** of a crime, a witness or someone in authority claims that you did it, and you may be formally charged with it and put on trial. *Her assistant was accused of theft... He faced a total of seven charges, all accusing him of lying in his testimony.* ♦ **ac·cu·sa·tion, accusations** The government denied the accusation that it was involved. ♦ **ac·cus·er, accusers** *Defendants have the right to confront their accusers.* **3** If someone **stands accused** of something, they have been accused of it. *Today, Rostov stands accused of extortion.* ◆◆◆◇◇ VERB V n of n/-ing Also V, V n VERB be V-ed of n V n of n Also V n N-COUNT N-COUNT PHRASE

ac·cused /ə'kjuːzd/; **accused** is both the singular and the plural form. You can use **the accused** to refer to a person or a group of people charged with a crime or on trial for it. *The accused is alleged to be a member of a right-wing gang.* ◆◇◇◇◇ N-COUNT: the N LEGAL

ac·cus·ing /ə'kjuːzɪŋ/. If you look at someone with an **accusing** expression or speak to them in an **accusing** tone of voice, it shows that you think that they have done something wrong. *The accusing look in her eyes conveyed her sense of betrayal.* ♦ **ac·cus·ing·ly** *'Where have you been?' he asked Blake accusingly.* ● See also **accuse**. ADJ-GRADED ADV-GRADED: ADV after v

ac·cus·tom /ə'kʌstəm/ **accustoms, accustoming, accustomed.** If you **accustom** yourself or someone else to something, you make yourself or them experience it or learn about it, so that it becomes familiar or natural. *...while his team accustoms itself to the pace and style of first division rugby... Shakespeare has accustomed us to a mixture of humor and tragedy.* ◆◇◇◇◇ VERB V pron-refl to n V n to n FORMAL

ac·cus·tomed /ə'kʌstəmd/. **1** If you are **accustomed to** something, you know it so well or have experienced it so often that it seems natural, unsurprising, or easy to deal with. *He was accustomed to hard work.* **2** When your eyes become **accustomed to** darkness or bright light, you start to be able to see things, after not being able to see properly at first. *My eyes were becoming accustomed to the gloom.* **3** You can use **accustomed** to describe an action that someone usually does, a quality that they usually show, or an object that they usually use. *He took up his accustomed position... Freed acted with his accustomed shrewdness.* ◆◇◇◇◇ ADJ-GRADED: v-link ADJ to n/-ing ADJ: v-link ADJ to n ADJ: poss ADJ n

ace /eɪs/ **aces. 1** An **ace** is a playing card with a single symbol on it. *...the ace of hearts.* **2** In tennis, an **ace** is a serve which is so fast that the other player cannot reach the ball. **3** If you describe someone such as a sports player as an **ace**, you mean that they are very good at their sport. *...former motor-racing ace Stirling Moss.* ► Also an adjective. *...ace horror-film producer Lawrence Woolsey.* **4** If you say that something is **ace**, you think that it is good and you like it a lot. *I enjoy going to see bands play. It's ace, isn't it?* **5** If you come **within an ace of** doing something, you very nearly do or experience it. *He came within an ace of succeeding.* ◆◆◇◇◇ N-COUNT N-COUNT N-COUNT JOURNALISM ADJ: ADJ n ADJ PRAGMATICS INFORMAL PHRASE

acer·bic /ə'sɜːbɪk/. If you describe someone's sense of humour or the things they say as **acerbic**, you approve of it because it is critical and direct. *...his acerbic wit and repartee.* ADJ-GRADED PRAGMATICS FORMAL

ac·etate /'æsɪteɪt/. **Acetate** is a shiny man-made material, sometimes used for making clothes or records. *The jacket is lined with acetate satin.* N-UNCOUNT

acetic acid /ə,siːtɪk 'æsɪd/. **Acetic acid** is a colourless acid. It is the main substance in vinegar. N-UNCOUNT

ac·etone /'æsɪtəʊn/. **Acetone** is a type of solvent. N-UNCOUNT

acety·lene /ə'setɪliːn/. **Acetylene** is a colourless gas which burns with a very hot bright flame. N-UNCOUNT

ache /eɪk/ **aches, aching, ached. 1** If you **ache** or a part of your body **aches**, you feel a steady, fairly strong pain. *His joints are aching.* **2** An **ache** is a steady, fairly strong pain in a part of your body. ● See also **backache, headache, heartache, stomach ache. 3** If you **ache** for something or your heart **aches**, you want something very much, and feel very unhappy because you cannot have it. *She still ached for the lost intimacy and sexual contact of marriage. ...a country aching to get away from its past.* ► Also a noun. *...an overwhelming ache for support from others.* **4** You can use **aches and pains** to refer in a general way to any minor pains that you feel in your body. ◆◆◇◇◇ VERB V N-COUNT VERB V for n V to-inf Also V WRITTEN N-SING N for n PHRASE

achieve /ə'tʃiːv/ **achieves, achieving, achieved.** If you **achieve** a particular aim or effect, you succeed in doing it or causing it to happen, usually after a lot of effort. *We have achieved what we set out to do.* ♦ **achiev·able** /ə'tʃiːvəbəl/ *Start with smaller, easily achievable goals.* ♦ **achieve·ment** *It is only the achievement of these goals that will finally bring lasting peace.* ◆◆◆◇◇ VERB V n ADJ-GRADED N-UNCOUNT

achieve·ment /ə'tʃiːvmənt/ **achievements.** An **achievement** is something which someone has succeeded in doing, especially after a lot of effort. *It was a great achievement. ...a celebration of women's achievements.* ◆◆◇◇◇ N-COUNT

achiev·er /ə'tʃiːvə/ **achievers.** An **achiever** is someone who is successful in their studies or their work, usually as a result of their efforts. A low **achiever** is someone who achieves less than those around them. *In school, he was not one of the achievers. ...a way to keep low achievers from dropping out.* ◆◇◇◇◇ N-COUNT

Achilles heel /ə,kɪliːz 'hiːl/. Someone's **Achilles heel** is the weakest point in their character or nature, where it is easiest for other people to attack or criticize them. *His Achilles heel is, he likes his food too much.* N-SING

Achilles ten·don /ə,kɪliːz 'tendən/ **Achilles tendons.** Your **Achilles tendon** or your **Achilles** is the tendon inside the back of your leg just above your heel. N-COUNT

ach·ing·ly /'eɪkɪŋli/. You can use **achingly** for emphasis when you are referring to things that inspire feelings of wanting something very much, but of not being able to have it. *...a passionate child achingly hungry for emotional experience.* ADV-GRADED: ADV adj/adv PRAGMATICS WRITTEN

achy /'eɪki/. If you feel **achy**, your body aches. ADJ-GRADED

acid /'æsɪd/ **acids. 1** An **acid** is a chemical substance, usually a liquid, which contains hydrogen and can react with other substances to form salts. *...citric acid... Acids in the stomach destroy the virus.* **2** An **acid** substance contains acid. *These shrubs must have an acid, lime-free soil.* ♦ **acid·ic** /ə'sɪdɪk/ *Dissolved carbon dioxide makes the water more acidic.* ♦ **acid·ity** /æ'sɪdɪti/ *...the acidity of rain-water.* **3** An **acid** fruit or drink has a sour or sharp taste. *These wines may taste rather hard and somewhat acid.* ♦ **acid·ic** *If the sprouts smell, or taste, mouldy or acidic do not eat them.* ♦ **acid·ity** *...a finely balanced wine with ripe acidity.* **4** An **acid** remark, or **acid** humour, is very unkind or critical. *She has an acid tongue. 'You don't know how to be a mother and you never did,' she said acidly.* **5** See also **amino acid, hydrochloric acid, nitric acid, nucleic acid, sulphuric acid.** ◆◆◇◇◇ N-VAR ADJ-GRADED ADJ-GRADED N-UNCOUNT ADJ-GRADED ADJ-GRADED N-UNCOUNT ADJ-GRADED ADV-GRADED

,acid 'rain. Acid rain is rain polluted by acid released into the atmosphere from factories and other industrial processes. ◆◇◇◇◇ N-UNCOUNT

,acid 'test. The **acid test** of something is an important aspect or result that it might have, which allows you to decide whether it is true or successful. *The case is an acid test of the justice system.* N-SING: the N

ac·knowl·edge /æk'nɒlɪdʒ/ **acknowledges, acknowledging, acknowledged. 1** If you **acknowledge** a fact or a situation, you accept or admit that it is true or that it exists. *Naylor acknowledged,* ◆◆◆◇◇ VERB V that V n Also V n to-inf,

A

in a letter to the judge, that he was a drug addict... *Belatedly, the government has acknowledged the problem.* ◆ **ac·knowl·edge·ment** *The President's resignation appears to be an acknowledgment that he has lost all hope.* **2** If someone's achievements, status, or qualities **are acknowledged**, they are known about and recognized by a lot of people, or by a particular group of people. *He is also acknowledged as an excellent goal-keeper... Some of the clergy refused to acknowledge the new king's legitimacy.* **3** If you **acknowledge** a message or letter, you write to the person who sent it to say that you have received it. *The army sent me a postcard acknowledging my request.* ◆ **ac·knowl·edge·ment.** *I have received neither an acknowledgment nor a reply.* **4** If you **acknowledge** someone, for example with a nod or a smile, you show that you have seen and recognized them. *She never even acknowledged the man who opened the door.* ◆ **ac·knowl·edge·ment** *Farling smiled in acknowledgement.*

V n as n/adj
FORMAL

N-SING
also no det

VERB
be V-ed as n
V n
Also V n to-inf

VERB
V n

N-COUNT

VERB
V n

N-UNCOUNT:
also a N

ac·knowl·edge·ment /ækˈnɒlɪdʒmənt/ **acknowledgements;** also spelled **acknowledgment**. **1** The **acknowledgements** in a book are the section in which the author thanks all the people who have helped him or her. **2** An **acknowledgement** is a published statement in which you express your gratitude for or appreciation of something. *...an acknowledgement of the donation in a printed bulletin... Grateful acknowledgment is made for permission to reprint.*

◆◇◇◇

N-PLURAL

N-VAR

acme /ˈækmi/. The **acme** of something is its highest point of achievement or excellence. *His work is considered the acme of cinematic art.*

N-SING
FORMAL

acne /ˈækni/. If someone has **acne**, they have a lot of spots on their face and neck.

◆◇◇◇
N-UNCOUNT

aco·lyte /ˈækəlaɪt/ **acolytes**. **1** An **acolyte** is a follower or assistant of an important person. *Richard Brome, an acolyte of Ben Jonson's, wrote 'The Jovial Crew'.* **2** An **acolyte** is someone who assists a priest in performing certain religious services.

N-COUNT
FORMAL

N-COUNT

acorn /ˈeɪkɔːn/ **acorns**. An **acorn** is a pale oval nut that is the fruit of an oak tree.

N-COUNT

acous·tic /əˈkuːstɪk/ **acoustics**. **1** An **acoustic** guitar or other instrument produces a natural sound which is not made louder by electrical apparatus. ◆ **acous·ti·cal·ly** /əˈkuːstɪkli/ *...acoustically based music.* **2** If you refer to the **acoustics** of a room or building, you are referring to the structural features which determine how well you can hear music or speech in it. *The acoustics of the theatre are still superb.* ◆ **acoustically** *The church is fully air-conditioned and acoustically perfect.* **3** **Acoustic** or **acoustical** means relating to sound or hearing. *...acoustic signals.* **4** **Acoustics** is the scientific study of sound.

◆◆◇◇
ADJ: ADJ n

ADV

N-PLURAL

ADV: ADV adj

ADJ: ADJ n
TECHNICAL

N-UNCOUNT
TECHNICAL

acous·ti·cal /əˈkuːstɪkəl/. **Acoustical** means relating to sound or hearing.

ADJ
TECHNICAL

ac·quaint /əˈkweɪnt/ **acquaints, acquainting, acquainted**. If you **acquaint** someone with something, you tell them about it so that they know it or become familiar with it. If you **acquaint** yourself with something, you become familiar with it. *Have steps been taken to acquaint breeders with their right to apply for licences?... I want to acquaint myself with your abilities.* ● See also **acquainted**.

◆◇◇◇
VERB
V n with n
V pron-refl
with n
FORMAL

ac·quaint·ance /əˈkweɪntəns/ **acquaintances**. **1** An **acquaintance** is someone who you have met and know slightly, but not well. *He exchanged a few words with the proprietor, an old acquaintance of his.* **2** If you have an **acquaintance** with someone, you have met them and you know them. *I struck up an acquaintance with a shopkeeper... On first acquaintance she is cool and slightly distant.* **3** A person of your **acquaintance** is someone who you have met and know. *...a highly cultivated woman of our acquaintance.* **4** When you **make** someone's **acquaintance**, you meet them for the first time and get to know them a little. *I am so pleased to make your acquaintance, Mr Tweed.* **5** Your **acquaintance** with a subject is your knowl-

◆◇◇◇
N-COUNT

N-VAR

PHRASE
FORMAL

PHRASE
FORMAL

N-UNCOUNT

edge or experience of it. *They had little or no acquaintance with Chinese philosophy or history.*

FORMAL

ac·quaint·ed /əˈkweɪntɪd/. **1** If you are **acquainted** with something, you know about it because you have learned it or experienced it. *He was well acquainted with the literature of France.* **2** If you are **acquainted** with someone, you have met them and you know them. You can also say that two people are **acquainted**. *No-one personally acquainted with the couple was permitted to talk to the Press.* **3** If you become **acquainted** with someone that you do not know, you talk to each other or do something together so that you get to know each other. You can also say that two people become **acquainted**. *At first the meetings were a way to get acquainted with each other.* **4** See also **acquaint**.

ADJ-GRADED:
v-link ADJ
with n
FORMAL

ADJ-GRADED:
v-link ADJ
FORMAL

ADJ-GRADED:
v-link ADJ

ac·qui·esce /ˌækwiˈes/ **acquiesces, acquiescing, acquiesced**. If you **acquiesce** to something, you agree to do what someone wants or to accept what they do. *Steve seemed to acquiesce in the decision... When her mother suggested that she should not go far from the hotel, Alice willingly acquiesced.*

VERB
V in/to n
V
FORMAL

ac·qui·es·cence /ˌækwiˈesəns/. **Acquiescence** is agreement to do what someone wants, or acceptance of what they do even though you do not agree with it. *Deirdre smiled her acquiescence.* ◆ **ac·qui·es·cent** /ˌækwiˈesənt/ *The other men were acquiescent, but Trevor had an independent streak.*

N-UNCOUNT:
with supp

ADJ-GRADED

ac·quire /əˈkwaɪə/ **acquires, acquiring, acquired**. **1** If you **acquire** something, you buy or obtain it for yourself, or someone gives it to you. *General Motors acquired a 50% stake in Saab... I recently acquired some wood from a holly tree which had been felled.* **2** If you **acquire** something such as a skill or a habit, you gradually learn or develop it. *I've never acquired a taste for wine... She will be able to pass on the acquired knowledge to trainee teachers.* **3** If someone or something **acquires** a certain reputation, they start to have that reputation. *...a city that has acquired a reputation for violence.* **4** If you describe something as an **acquired taste**, you mean that a lot of people do not like it when they first experience it, but often start to like it more when they get to know it.

◆◆◆◇◇
VERB
V n
V n from n
FORMAL

VERB
V n
V-ed

VERB
V n

PHRASE

ac·quired immune de·fi·ciency syndrome. **Acquired immune deficiency syndrome** is the same as **AIDS**.

N-UNCOUNT

ac·qui·si·tion /ˌækwɪˈzɪʃən/ **acquisitions**. **1** In business, if a company or business person makes an **acquisition**, they buy another company or part of a company. *...the acquisition of a profitable paper recycling company.* **2** If you make an **acquisition**, you buy or obtain something, often to add to things that you already have. *...the President's recent acquisition of a helicopter.* **3** You can use **acquisition** to refer to an object that you buy or obtain. *...his latest acquisition – a Georgian house in Dublin.* **4** The **acquisition** of a skill or a particular type of knowledge is the process of learning it or developing it. *...language acquisition.*

◆◆◇◇
N-VAR
TECHNICAL

N-COUNT

N-COUNT

N-UNCOUNT:
n N,
N of n

ac·quisi·tive /əˈkwɪzɪtɪv/. If you describe a person or an organization as **acquisitive**, you mean that they like getting new possessions; used showing disapproval. *We live in an acquisitive society.*

ADJ-GRADED
PRAGMATICS

ac·quit /əˈkwɪt/ **acquits, acquitting, acquitted**. **1** If someone **is acquitted** of a crime in a court of law, they are formally declared not to have committed the crime. *Mr Ling was acquitted of disorderly behaviour.* ◆ **ac·quit·tal** /əˈkwɪtəl/ **acquittals** *The judge ordered their acquittal.* **2** If you **acquit** yourself well or admirably in a particular situation, other people feel that you have behaved well or admirably. *Most officers and men acquitted themselves well throughout the action.*

◆◆◇◇
VB: usu
passive
be V-ed of n
Also be V-ed

N-VAR

VERB
V pron-refl
adv
FORMAL

acre /ˈeɪkə/ **acres**. An **acre** is an area of land measuring 4840 square yards or 4047 square metres.

◆◆◆◇◇
N-COUNT

acre·age /ˈeɪkərɪdʒ/ **acreages**. **Acreage** is a large area of agricultural land. *He has sown coffee on part of his acreage.*

N-VAR
FORMAL

ac·rid /'ækrɪd/. An **acrid** smell or taste is strong and sharp, and usually unpleasant. ...*the acrid smell of tobacco.* `ADJ-GRADED`

ac·ri·mo·ni·ous /ˌækrɪ'məʊniəs/. **Acrimonious** words or quarrels are bitter and angry. *The divorce was extremely acrimonious.* ♦ **ac·ri·mo·ni·ous·ly** *Our relationship ended acrimoniously.* ◆◇◇◇ `FORMAL` `ADJ-GRADED` `ADJ-GRADED:` `ADV with v`

ac·ri·mo·ny /'ækrɪməni, AM -məʊni/. **Acrimony** is bitter and angry words or quarrels. *The council's first meeting ended in acrimony.* `N-UNCOUNT` `FORMAL`

ac·ro·bat /'ækrəbæt/ **acrobats.** An **acrobat** is an entertainer who performs difficult jumps, somersaults, and balancing acts. ...*a circus acrobat.* `N-COUNT`

ac·ro·bat·ic /ˌækrə'bætɪk/. An **acrobatic** movement or display involves difficult jumps, somersaults, and balancing acts. ...*a sensational acrobatic feat.* ♦ **ac·ro·bat·ics** *A young girl performed acrobatics on a palomino horse.* `ADJ-GRADED` `N-PLURAL`

ac·ro·nym /'ækrənɪm/ **acronyms.** An **acronym** is a word made from the initial letters of the words in a phrase. For example NATO is made up of the first letters of 'the North Atlantic Treaty Organization'. ◆◇◇◇ `N-COUNT`

across /ə'krɒs, AM ə'krɔːs/. **1** If someone or something goes **across** a place or a boundary, they go from one side of it to the other. *She walked across the floor... He watched Karl run across the street.* ► Also an adverb. *Richard stood up and walked across to the window.* **2** If you look **across** at something or someone who is fairly distant from you, you look towards them. *He glanced across at his sleeping wife. ...breathtaking views across to the hills.* **3** Something that is **across** something such as a street, river, or area is on the other side of it. *I saw you across the room.* ► Also an adverb. *They parked across from the Castro Theatre.* **4** If something is situated or stretched **across** something else, it is situated or stretched from one side of it to the other. ...*the floating bridge across Lake Washington... She found her clothes lying across the chair... He scrawled his name across the bill.* **5** You use **across** to say that a particular expression is shown on someone's face. *An enormous grin spread across his face.* **6** If someone hits you **across** the face or head, they hit you on that part. *Graham hit him across the face.* **7** When something happens **across** a place or organization, it happens equally everywhere within it. *The film 'Hook' opens across America on December 11... 2,000 workers across all state agencies are to be fired.* **8** When something happens **across** a political, religious, or social barrier, it involves people in different groups. ...*parties competing across the political spectrum. ...cosmetics that appeal across the colour barrier.* ● **across the board**: see **board**. **9 Across** is used in measurements to show the width of something. *This hand-decorated plate measures 30cm across.* ◆◆◆◆◆ `PREP` `ADV:` `ADV after v` `ADV:` `ADV after v` `PREP` `ADV:` `ADV after v` `PREP` `PREP` `PREP` `PREP` `ADV:` `amount ADV`

acryl·ic /ə'krɪlɪk/ **acrylics. 1 Acrylic** fabrics and clothing are man-made and manufactured by a chemical process. **2 Acrylics** or **acrylic paint** is a type of paint used by artists. ◆◇◇◇ `N-UNCOUNT` `N-VAR`

act /ækt/ **acts, acting, acted. 1** When you **act**, you do something for a particular purpose. ...*when police acted to stop widespread looting... The bank acted properly in the best interests of the depositors.* **2** An **act** is a single thing that someone does. ...*the act of reading... My insurance excludes acts of sabotage.* **3** If you **act on** advice or information, you do what has been advised or suggested. *A patient will usually listen to the physician's advice and act on it.* **4** If someone **acts** in a particular way, they behave in that way. ...*a gang of youths who were acting suspiciously... He acted as if he hadn't heard.* **5** If someone or something **acts as** a particular thing, they have that role or function. *He acted both as the ship's surgeon and as chaplain for the men.* **6** If someone **acts** in a particular way, they pretend to be something that they are not. *Chris acted astonished as he examined the note... Kenworthy had tried not to act the policeman.* **7** If you say that someone's behaviour is ◆◆◆◆◆ `VERB` `V` `V adv/prep` `N-COUNT` `FORMAL` `VERB` `V on/upon n` `VERB` `V adv` `V as if` `Also V like n` `VERB` `V as/like n` `VERB` `V adj` `V n` `N-SING`

an **act**, you mean that it does not express their real feelings. *Did she do this on purpose, was it all just a game, an act?* **8** When professionals such as lawyers or estate agents **act for** you, or **act on** your **behalf**, they are employed by you to deal with a particular matter. *Daniel Webster acted for Boston traders... Sam and I asked a broker to act on our behalf.* `VERB` `V for n` `V prep`

9 An **Act** is a law passed by the government. *Until 1857 a woman could not sue for divorce except by an Act of Parliament.* `N-COUNT`

10 If a force or substance **acts on** someone or something, it has a certain effect on them. *He's taking a dangerous drug: it acts very fast on the central nervous system.* `VERB` `V on/upon n` `Also V`

11 If you **act**, or **act** a part in a play or film, you have a part in it. ...*Helen, whose husband was acting in Roberto's films.* **12** An **act** in a play, opera, or ballet is one of the main parts into which it is divided. *Act II contained one of the funniest scenes I have ever witnessed.* **13** An **act** in a show is a short performance which is one of several in the show. ...*the best new comedy acts.* `VERB: V` `V in n` `Also V n` `N-COUNT` `N-COUNT`

14 If you **catch** someone **in the act**, you discover them doing something wrong or committing a crime. *The men were caught in the act of digging up buried explosives.* **15** You say that someone was **in the act of** doing something to indicate what they were doing when they were seen or interrupted. *Ken was in the act of paying his bill when Neil came up behind him.* **16** If someone who has been behaving badly **cleans up** their **act**, they start to behave in a more acceptable or responsible way. *Advertisers need to clean up their act.* **17** If you **get** your **act together**, you organize your life or your affairs so that you are able to achieve what you want or to deal with something effectively. *We have to get our act together – we have to organize ourselves.* **18** If you **get in on the act**, you take part in or take advantage of something that was started by someone else. *Kodak, anxious to get in on the act, launched its own instant camera.* **19** ● **act the fool**: see **fool**. `PHRASE` `PHRASE` `PHRASE` `INFORMAL` `PHRASE` `INFORMAL` `PHRASE` `INFORMAL`

act out. If you **act out** an event which has happened, you copy the actions which took place and make them into a play. *The group acts out the stories in such a way that the members experience really being there.* `PHRASAL VB` `V P n` `Also V n P`

act up. 1 If something **is acting up**, it is not working properly. *She was messing with the coffee pot, which was acting up again.* **2** If a child **is acting up**, he or she is behaving badly. *I could hear Jonathan acting up downstairs.* `PHRASAL VB` `V P` `INFORMAL` `V P`

act·ing /'æktɪŋ/. **1 Acting** is the activity or profession of performing in plays or films. ...*her acting career.* **2** You use **acting** before the title of a job to indicate that someone is doing that job temporarily. ...*the new acting President.* ◆◆◇◇◇ `N-UNCOUNT` `ADJ: ADJ n`

ac·tion /'ækʃən/ **actions. 1 Action** is doing something for a particular purpose, or on a particular occasion. *She was anxious to avoid any action which might harm him... The government is taking emergency action to deal with a housing crisis... Peter had a reason for his action.* ◆◆◆◆◆ `N-VAR`

2 A legal **action** is an attempt to get a court order to stop someone doing something or to pay compensation for damage they have caused. `N-COUNT` `LEGAL`

3 The **action** of a chemical is the way in which it works, or the effects that it has. ...*the nature and action of poisons.* `N-UNCOUNT`

4 The **action** is all the important and exciting things that are happening in a situation. *Hollywood is where the action is now.* **5** If someone wants to have **a piece of the action** or **a slice of the action**, they want to be involved in an exciting activity or situation, for example in order to make money. `N-SING:` `the N` `PHRASE`

6 The fighting which takes place in a war can be referred to as **action**. *He'd been listed as missing in action.* `N-UNCOUNT`

7 If someone or something is **out of action**, they are injured or damaged and cannot work or be used. *He's been out of action for 16 months with a serious knee injury. ...the lifts went out of action.* **8** If you **put** an idea `PHRASE` `PHRASE`

or policy **into action**, you begin to use it or cause it to operate. *We are ready to put some of these recommendations into action.* ● **in actual fact**: see **fact**.

action 'replay, action replays. An action replay is a repeated showing, usually in slow motion, of an event that has just been on television. The usual American term is **instant replay**.   N-COUNT BRITISH

ac·ti·vate /'æktɪveɪt/ **activates, activating, activated.** If a device or process **is activated**, something causes it to start working. *Video cameras with night vision can be activated by movement.*   ◆◇◇◇◇ VB: usu passive be V-ed

ac·tive /'æktɪv/. **1** Someone who is **active** moves around a lot or does a lot of things. *How physically active are you?... Having an active youngster about the house can be quite wearing.* **2** If you have an **active** mind or imagination, you are always thinking of new things. **3** If someone is **active** in an organization, cause, or campaign, they do things for it rather than just give it their support. *...an active member of the Conservative Party... He is active on Tyler's behalf.* ♦ **ac·tive·ly** *They actively campaigned for the vote.* **4 Active** is used to emphasize that someone is taking action in order to achieve something, rather than just waiting for it to happen. *The engineers were prepared to take active steps to further their cause.* ♦ **actively** *They have never been actively encouraged to take such risks.* **5** If a person or animal is **active** in a particular place or at a particular time, they are performing their usual activities or performing a particular activity. *Guerrilla groups are active in the province. ...animals which are active at night.* **6** An **active** volcano has erupted recently or is expected to erupt quite soon. **7** An **active** substance has a chemical or biological effect on things. *The active ingredient in some of the mouthwashes was simply detergent.* **8** In grammar, **the active** or **the active voice** means the forms of a verb which are used when the subject refers to a person or thing that does something. For example, in 'I saw her yesterday', the verb is in the active. Compare **passive**.   ◆◆◆◇ ADJ-GRADED ... ADV ADJ: ADJ n PRAGMATICS ... ADV ... ADJ ... ADJ ... ADJ ... N-SING: the N

active 'duty. Active duty means the same as **active service**.   N-UNCOUNT

active 'service. Someone who is on **active service** is taking part in a war as a member of the armed forces. *He was killed on active service.*   N-UNCOUNT BRITISH

ac·tiv·ism /'æktɪvɪzm/. **Activism** is the process of campaigning in public or working for an organization in order to bring about political or social change. *He believed in political activism to achieve justice.* ♦ **ac·tiv·ist** /'æktɪvɪst/ **activists.** *...animal rights activists.*   ◆◆◇◇ N-UNCOUNT ... N-COUNT

ac·tiv·ity /æk'tɪvɪti/ **activities. 1 Activity** is a situation in which a lot of things are happening or being done. *We will see an extraordinary level of activity in the market for UK government bonds.* **2** An **activity** is something that you spend time doing. *Activities range from canoeing to bird watching.* **3** The **activities** of a group are the things that they do in order to achieve their aims. *...a jail term for terrorist activities.*   ◆◆◆◇ N-UNCOUNT ... N-COUNT ... N-PLURAL: with supp

act of 'God, acts of God. An act of God is an event that is beyond human control, especially one in which something is damaged or someone is hurt. *The President described the disaster as an act of God.*   N-COUNT

ac·tor /'æktə/ **actors.** An **actor** is someone whose job is acting in plays or films.   ◆◆◆◇ N-COUNT

ac·tress /'æktrəs/ **actresses.** An **actress** is a woman whose job is acting in plays or films.   ◆◆◆◇ N-COUNT

ac·tual /'æktʃuəl/. **1** You use **actual** to emphasize that you are referring to something real or genuine. *The segments are filmed using either local actors or the actual people involved... The actual number of AIDS victims is much higher than statistics reflect.* **2** You use **actual** to contrast the important aspect of something with a less important aspect. *She had compiled pages of notes, but she had not yet gotten down to doing the actual writing... The exercises in*   ◆◆◇◇ ADJ: ADJ n PRAGMATICS ... ADJ: ADJ n PRAGMATICS

this chapter can guide you, but it will be up to you to do the actual work. ● **in actual fact**: see **fact**.

ac·tu·al·ity /,æktʃu'ælɪti/ **actualities. 1** You can use **in actuality** to emphasize that what you are saying is true, when it contrasts with what you have previously said. *The woman he had seen shining onstage with such beauty and gracefulness was in actuality older than she had seemed.* **2 Actuality** is the state of really existing rather than being imagined. *It exists in dreams rather than actuality.* **3** An **actuality** is a fact or condition that really exists. *To stop the fighting there requires the threat and probably the actuality of military force.*   ◆◇◇◇ PHRASE PRAGMATICS ... N-UNCOUNT ... N-COUNT FORMAL

ac·tu·al·ly /'æktʃuəli/. **1** You use **actually** to indicate that a situation exists or happened, or to emphasize that it is true, especially when this is surprising. *I grew bored and actually fell asleep for a few minutes... Interest is only payable on the amount actually borrowed.* **2** You use **actually** when you are correcting or contradicting someone. *No, I'm not a student. I'm a doctor, actually... 'So it's not a family show then?'—'Well, actually, I think that's exactly what it is.'* **3** You can use **actually** when you are politely expressing an opinion that other people might not have expected from you. *'Do you think it's a good idea to socialize with one's patients?'— 'Actually, I do.'... I would be surprised, actually, if he left Birmingham.* **4** You use **actually** to introduce a new topic into a conversation. *Well actually, John, I rang you for some advice.*   ◆◆◆◆◆ ADV PRAGMATICS ... ADV: ADV with cl PRAGMATICS ... ADV: ADV with cl PRAGMATICS ... ADV: ADV with cl PRAGMATICS

ac·tu·ary /'æktʃuəri, AM -tʃueri/ **actuaries.** An **actuary** is a person who is employed by insurance companies to calculate how much they should charge their clients for insurance. ♦ **ac·tu·ari·al** /,æktʃu'eəriəl/ *...actuarial work.*   N-COUNT ... ADJ: ADJ n

ac·tu·ate /'æktʃueɪt/ **actuates, actuating, actuated.** If a person is **actuated** by an emotion, that emotion makes them act in a certain way. If something **actuates** a device, the device starts working. *They were actuated by desire... The engines overheated, actuating the fire extinguishers.*   VERB be V-ed V n FORMAL

acu·ity /ə'kjuːɪti/. **Acuity** is sharpness or quickness of vision, hearing, or thought. *Caffeine gives a boost of energy and temporarily sharpens mental acuity.*   N-UNCOUNT FORMAL

acu·men /'ækjumen, AM ə'kjuːmən/. **Acumen** is the ability to make good judgements and quick decisions. *His sharp business acumen meant he quickly rose to the top.*   N-UNCOUNT

acu·pres·sure /'ækjupreʃə/. **Acupressure** is the treatment of pain by a type of massage.   N-UNCOUNT

acu·punc·ture /'ækjupʌŋktʃə/. **Acupuncture** is the treatment of a person's illness or pain by sticking small needles into their body. ♦ **acu·punc·tur·ist** /'ækjupʌŋktʃərɪst/ **acupuncturists** *...a trained acupuncturist.*   ◆◇◇◇ N-UNCOUNT ... N-COUNT

acute /ə'kjuːt/. **1** An **acute** situation or feeling is very intense or unpleasant. *...acute embarrassment... The labour shortage is becoming acute.* ♦ **acute·ly** *It was an acutely uncomfortable journey.* **2** An **acute** illness becomes severe very quickly but does not last very long. Compare **chronic**. *...an acute case of dysentery.* **3** If a person's or animal's senses are **acute**, they are sensitive and powerful. *In the dark my sense of smell and hearing become so acute.* **4** If someone is **acute**, they are quick to notice things and understand them. *Into her nineties, her thinking remained acute and her character forceful.* **5** An **acute** angle is less than 90°. **6** An **acute** accent is a symbol that is placed over vowels in some languages in order to indicate how that vowel is pronounced or to show that the vowel is stressed.   ◆◆◇◇ ... ADV-GRADED ... ADJ: ADJ n MEDICAL ... ADJ-GRADED ... ADJ-GRADED ... ADJ-GRADED ... ADJ: ADJ n, n ADJ

acute·ly /ə'kjuːtli/. If you feel or notice something **acutely**, you feel or notice it very strongly. *He was acutely aware of the odour of cooking oil... Those tensions have been felt most acutely by women.*   ◆◇◇◇ ADV-GRADED

ad /æd/ **ads.** An **ad** is an advertisement. *...a full-page magazine ad.*   ◆◆◇◇ N-COUNT INFORMAL

AD /,eɪ 'diː/. You use **AD** in dates to indicate the number of years or centuries that have passed since   ◆◇◇◇

the year in which Jesus Christ is believed to have been born. ...*the Great Fire of 1136 AD.*

ad·age /'ædɪdʒ/ **adages.** An **adage** is something which people often say and which expresses a general truth. *The old adage 'Every baby brings its own love' usually turns out to be true.*
N-COUNT DATED

ada·mant /'ædəmənt/. If someone is **adamant** about something, they are determined not to change their mind about it. *The prime minister is adamant that he will not resign.* ♦ **ada·mant·ly** *She was adamantly opposed to her husband travelling to Brussels.*
◆◇◇◇◇ ADJ-GRADED

ADV-GRADED

Adam's apple /,ædəmz 'æpəl/ **Adam's apples.** A man's **Adam's apple** is the lump that sticks out of the front of his neck below his throat.
N-COUNT

a·dapt /ə'dæpt/ **adapts, adapting, adapted. 1** If you **adapt** to a new situation, you change your ideas or behaviour in order to deal with it successfully. *We will have to be prepared to adapt to the change... MPs have quickly adapted themselves to the cameras.* **2** If you **adapt** something, you change it to make it suitable for a new purpose or situation. *Shelves were built to adapt the library for use as an office.* **3** If you **adapt** a book or play, you change it so that it can be made into a film or a television programme. *The scriptwriter helped him to adapt his novel for the screen.* **4** See also **adapted**.
◆◆◇◇◇ VERB
V to n
V pron-refl to n
Also V

VERB
V n
Also V n to n

VERB
V n

adapt·able /ə'dæptəbəl/. If you describe a person or animal as **adaptable**, you mean that they are able to change their ideas or behaviour in order to deal with new situations. *Humans are infinitely adaptable.* ♦ **adapt·abil·ity** /ə,dæptə'bɪlɪti/ ...*this adaptability which many animals do indeed show.*
◆◇◇◇◇ ADJ-GRADED

N-UNCOUNT

ad·ap·ta·tion /,ædæp'teɪʃən/ **adaptations. 1** An **adaptation** of a novel or play is a play or film that is based on it. ...*his screen adaptation of Shakespeare's Henry the Fifth.* **2 Adaptation** is the act of changing something or changing your behaviour to make it suitable for a new purpose or situation. *Most living creatures are capable of adaptation.*
◆◇◇◇◇ N-COUNT

N-UNCOUNT

a·dapt·ed /ə'dæptɪd/. If something is **adapted** to a particular situation or purpose, it is especially suitable for it. *The camel's feet, well adapted for dry sand, are useless on mud.* ● See also **adapt**.
ADJ-GRADED
v-link ADJ to/for n

adap·tion /ə'dæpʃən/ **adaptions. Adaption** means the same as **adaptation**.
N-VAR

adap·tive /ə'dæptɪv/. **Adaptive** means having the ability to adapt to different situations. *Societies need to develop highly adaptive behavioural rules for survival.*
ADJ-GRADED FORMAL

adap·tor /ə'dæptə/ **adaptors;** also spelled **adapter**. An **adaptor** is a device for connecting two or more electrical plugs to the same socket or for connecting a device with a plug that does not fit into the socket.
N-COUNT

add /æd/ **adds, adding, added. 1** If you **add** numbers or amounts together, you calculate their total. *Banks add all the interest and other charges together... Two and three added together are five.* ▶ **Add up** means the same as **add**. *More than a quarter of seven year-olds cannot add up properly... We just added all the numbers up.* **2** If you **add** one thing to another, you put it in or on the other thing, to complete or improve it. *Add the grated cheese to the sauce... He wants to add a huge sports complex to Binfield Manor.* **3** If one thing **adds** to another, it increases it. *Cheerful faces added to the general gaiety.* **4** To **add** a particular quality to something means to cause it to have that quality. *A delicious blend of cider and delicate fruit juices adds a little sparkle to any occasion.* **5** You use **added to this** or **added to that** to introduce a fact that supports or expands what you are saying. *More than 750 commercial airliners were involved in fatal accidents last year. Added to that were the 1,550 smaller aircraft.* ● **add insult to injury:** see **insult**. **6** If you **add** something when you are speaking, you say something more. *'You can tell that he is extremely embarrassed,' Mr Brigden added... The Italian central bank added that the aim was to provide stability... Hunt added his congratulations.*
◆◆◆◆◆ V pl-n with together

PHRASAL VB
V P
V n P
Also V P noun

VERB
V n to n
Also V n

VERB
V to n

VERB
V n to n
Also V n

PHRASE
PRAGMATICS

VERB
V with quote
V that
V n

add in. If you **add in** something, you include it as a part of something else. *Once the vegetables start to cook add in a couple of tablespoons of water.*
PHRASAL VB
V P noun

add on. 1 If something **is added on**, it is attached to or made part of something else. *The colour is either drab or garish and is obviously added on.* **2** If you **add on** an extra amount or item to a list or total, you include it in the list or total. *Many loan application forms automatically add on insurance.* **3** If you **add on** to something, especially a building, you make it larger. *That's only a two bedroom home, so you might want to add on.*
PHRASAL VB
usu passive
be V-ed P
V P noun
Also V n P

V P
Also V P to n

add up. 1 See add 1. **2** If facts or events do not **add up**, they make you confused about a situation because they do not seem reasonable and sensible. *This charge of burglary just doesn't add up.* **3** If small amounts of something **add up**, they gradually increase. *It's the little minor problems that add up.*
PHRASAL VB
V P

V P

add up to. If amounts **add up to** a particular total, they result in that total when they are put together. *Profits can add up to millions of dollars.*
PHRASAL VB
V P P n

add·ed /'ædɪd/. You use **added** to say that something has more of a particular thing or quality than is usual. *For added protection choose moisturising lipsticks with a sun screen. ...new services which were sophisticated and had added value.*
◆◇◇◇◇ ADJ: ADJ n

ad·den·dum /ə'dendəm/ **addenda** /ə'dendə/. An **addendum** is an additional section at the end of a book or document.
N-COUNT

ad·der /'ædə/ **adders.** An **adder** is a small poisonous snake that has a black zigzag pattern on its back.
N-COUNT

ad·dict /'ædɪkt/ **addicts. 1** An **addict** is someone who cannot stop taking harmful drugs. ...*a drug addict.* ♦ **ad·dict·ed** /ə'dɪktɪd/ *Many of the women are addicted to heroin.* **2** If you say that someone is an **addict**, you mean that they like a particular activity very much and spend as much time doing it as they can. *She is a TV addict.* ♦ **addicted** *She had become addicted to golf.*
◆◆◇◇◇ N-COUNT

ADJ-GRADED

N-COUNT

ADJ-GRADED

ad·dic·tion /ə'dɪkʃən/ **addictions. 1 Addiction** is the condition of taking harmful drugs and being unable to stop taking them. ...*drug addiction.* **2** An **addiction** to something is a very strong desire or need for it. *He needed money to feed his addiction to gambling.*
◆◆◇◇◇ N-VAR

N-VAR

ad·dic·tive /ə'dɪktɪv/. **1** If a drug is **addictive**, people who take it cannot stop taking it. *Cigarettes are highly addictive.* **2** Something that is **addictive** is so enjoyable that it makes you want to do it or have it a lot. *Video movie-making can quickly become addictive.* **3** If someone has an **addictive** personality, they easily become addicted to something.
◆◇◇◇◇ ADJ-GRADED

ADJ-GRADED

ADJ-GRADED

ad·di·tion /ə'dɪʃən/ **additions. 1** You use **in addition** or **with the addition of** when you want to mention another item connected with the subject you are discussing. *There's a postage and packing fee in addition to the repair charge... It was completely refurbished in 1987, with the addition of a picnic site.* **2** An **addition** to something is a thing which is added to it. *This is a fine book; a worthy addition to the Cambridge Encyclopedia series.* ♦ **ad·di·tion·al** *The US is sending additional troops to the region.* **3 Addition** is the process of calculating the total of two or more numbers. ...*simple addition and subtraction problems.*
◆◆◆◇ PHRASE
PRAGMATICS

N-COUNT

ADJ

N-UNCOUNT

ad·di·tion·al·ly /ə'dɪʃənəli/. **1** You sometimes use **additionally** to introduce something extra such as an extra fact or reason. *All teachers are qualified to teach their native language. Additionally, we select our teachers for their engaging personalities.* **2 Additionally** is used to say that something happens to a greater extent than before. *He will sign a personal guarantee to additionally secure the loan.*
◆◇◇◇◇ ADV:
ADV with cl
PRAGMATICS
FORMAL

ADV:
ADV with v

ad·di·tive /'ædɪtɪv/ **additives.** An **additive** is a substance which is added in small amounts to foods or other things in order to make them look better, taste stronger, or last longer. *Strict safety tests are*
◆◇◇◇◇ N-COUNT

carried out on food additives. ...additive-free baby foods.

ad·dled /'ædəld/. If you describe someone as **ad-** ADJ-GRADED **dled**, you mean that they are confused or unable to think properly. *She wore a sweet and slightly addled expression.*

'add-on, add-ons. An **add-on** is an extra piece of N-COUNT equipment that can be added to a larger one which you already own in order to improve it. *Nintendo hopes to price the add-on modem at less than $200.*

ad·dress /ə'dres, AM 'ædres/ **addresses, ad-** ◆◆◆◇ **dressing, addressed. 1** Your **address** is the N-COUNT number of the house, and the name of the street and the town where you live or work. *The address is 2025 Main Street, Northwest, Washington, DC, 20036. ...your name and address.* **2** If a letter, en- VB: usu velope, or parcel **is addressed** to you, your name passive and address has been written on it. *Applications* be V-ed to n *should be addressed to the business affairs editor.* **3** If you **address** a group of people, you give a speech VERB to them. *Nelson Mandela is due to address a gathering* V n *of supporters here shortly.* ▶ Also a noun. *...an address* N-COUNT *to the American people.* **4** If you **address** someone or VERB **address** a remark to someone, you say something to V n them. *The two foreign ministers did not address each* V n to n *other directly... I will address this complaint to the bank concerned.* **5** If you **address** someone by a name VERB or a title such as 'sir', you call them that name or title. *I* V n as n *heard him address her as darling.* **6** If you **address** a problem or task or if you **address** VERB yourself to it, you try to understand it or deal with it. V n *Mr King sought to address those fears when he spoke at* V pron-refl to *the meeting... Throughout the book we have addressed ourselves to the problem of ethics.*

ad·dress book, address books. An **address** N-COUNT **book** is a book in which you write people's names and addresses.

ad·dressee /ˌædre'siː/ **addressees.** The **ad-** N-COUNT **dressee** of a letter or parcel is the person or compa- FORMAL ny that it is addressed to.

ad·duce /æ'djuːs, AM -'duːs/ **adduces, adducing,** VERB **adduced.** If you **adduce** a fact or reason, you V n mention it in order to support an argument. *...the* FORMAL *evidence we adduce to back up her arguments.*

ad·enoids /'ædɪnɔɪdz/. **Adenoids** are soft lumps of N-PLURAL flesh at the back and top of a person's throat.

adept, adepts. The adjective is pronounced ◆◇◇◇◇ /æ'dept/. The noun is pronounced /'ædept/. Some- ADJ-GRADED one who is **adept** at something can do it skilfully. *He's usually very adept at keeping his private life out of the media.* ▶ An **adept** is someone who is adept N-COUNT at something.

ad·equate /'ædɪkwət/. If something is **adequate**, ◆◆◇◇◇ there is enough of it or it is good enough to be used ADJ-GRADED or accepted. *...an amount adequate to purchase another house... The western diet should be perfectly adequate for most people.* ♦ **ad·equa·cy** *...concern* N-UNCOUNT *over the adequacy of the diet.* ♦ **ad·equate·ly** *I* ADV-GRADED: *speak the language adequately.* ADV with v

ad·here /æd'hɪə/ **adheres, adhering, adhered.** ◆◆◇◇◇ **1** If you **adhere** to a rule, you act in the way that it VERB says you should. *All members of the association ad-* V to n *here to a strict code of practice.* ♦ **ad·her·ence** N-UNCOUNT /æd'hɪərəns/. *...strict adherence to the constitution.* **2** If you **adhere** to an opinion or belief, you support VERB or hold it. *This newspaper does not adhere to the* V to n *view that justice is all about punishment.* ♦ **ad·her-** **·ent** /æd'hɪərənt/ **adherents.** *Communism was* N-COUNT *gaining adherents in Latin America.* **3** If something VERB **adheres** to something else, it sticks firmly to it. V to n *Small particles adhere to the seed... This sticky com-* V *pound adheres well on this surface.*

ad·he·sion /æd'hiːʒən/. **Adhesion** is the ability of N-UNCOUNT one thing to stick firmly to another. *Better driving* FORMAL *equipment will improve track adhesion in slippery conditions.*

ad·he·sive /æd'hiːsɪv/ **adhesives.** An **adhesive** is ◆◇◇◇◇ a substance which is used to make things stick firm- N-VAR ly together. *Glue the mirror in with a strong adhe-* *sive.* ▶ Also an adjective. *...adhesive tape.* ADJ-GRADED

ad hoc /ˌæd 'hɒk/. An **ad hoc** activity or organiza- ◆◇◇◇◇ tion is done or formed only because a situation has ADJ made it necessary and is not planned in advance. *I would accept opportunities in TV on an ad hoc basis. ...ad hoc committees.*

adieu /ə'djuː/. **Adieu** is a literary word which CONVENTION means the same as **goodbye**. LITERARY

ad in·fi·ni·tum /ˌæd ɪnfɪ'naɪtəm/. If something hap- ADV: pens **ad infinitum**, it is repeated again and again in ADV after v the same way. *This cycle repeats itself ad infinitum.*

adj. Adj is a written abbreviation for **adjective**.

ad·ja·cent /ə'dʒeɪsənt/. If one thing is **adjacent** to ◆◇◇◇◇ another, the two things are next to each other. *He* ADJ *sat in an adjacent room. ...offices adjacent to the museum.*

ad·jec·tive /'ædʒɪktɪv/ **adjectives.** An adjective ◆◇◇◇◇ is a word such as 'big', 'dead', or 'financial' that de- N-COUNT scribes a person or thing, or gives extra information about them. Adjectives usually come before nouns or after link verbs. ♦ **ad·jec·ti·val** /ˌædʒɪk'taɪvl/ *...an* ADJ *adjectival phrase.*

'adjective group, adjective groups. An **adjec-** N-COUNT **tive group** or **adjectival group** is a group of words based on an adjective, such as 'very nice' or 'interested in football'. An adjective group can also consist simply of an adjective.

ad·join /ə'dʒɔɪn/ **adjoins, adjoining, adjoined.** ◆◇◇◇◇ If one place or object **adjoins** another, they are next VERB to each other. *Fields adjoined the garden... We wait-* V n *ed in an adjoining office.* V-ing FORMAL

ad·journ /ə'dʒɜːn/ **adjourns, adjourning, ad-** ◆◇◇◇◇ **journed.** If a meeting or trial **is adjourned** or if it V-ERG **adjourns**, it is stopped for a short time. *The pro-* be V-ed *ceedings have now been adjourned until next week...* V *The court may not adjourn until three.* ♦ **ad·journ-** **·ment** /ə'dʒɜːnmənt/ **adjournments.** *The court or-* N-COUNT *dered a four month adjournment.*

ad·judge /ə'dʒʌdʒ/ **adjudges, adjudging, ad-** VERB **judged.** If someone **is adjudged** to be something, be V-ed to-inf they are judged or considered to be that thing. *He* be V-ed n *was adjudged to be guilty... At college he was ad-* FORMAL *judged the Best Speaker.*

ad·ju·di·cate /ə'dʒuːdɪkeɪt/ **adjudicates, adjudi-** VERB **cating, adjudicated.** If you **adjudicate** on a dis- V prep pute or problem, you make an official judgement V n about it. *...a commissioner to adjudicate on legal* Also V *rights. ...a suitable place to adjudicate claims.* ♦ **ad·ju·di·ca·tion** /ə,dʒuːdɪ'keɪʃən/ **adjudica-** N-VAR **tions** *...unbiased adjudication of cases of unfair dis-* *missal.* ♦ **ad·ju·di·ca·tor** /ə'dʒuːdɪkeɪtə/ **adjudi-** N-COUNT **cators.**

ad·junct /'ædʒʌŋkt/ **adjuncts. 1** An **adjunct** is N-COUNT something that is connected with a larger or more important thing. *Physical therapy is an important adjunct to drug treatments.* **2** In grammar, an **ad-** N-COUNT **junct** is a word or group of words which indicates the circumstances of an action, event, or situation. An adjunct is usually a prepositional phrase or an adverb group.

ad·just /ə'dʒʌst/ **adjusts, adjusting, adjusted.** ◆◆◆◇◇ **1** When you **adjust** to a new situation, you get used VERB to it by changing your behaviour or your ideas. *We* V n to n *have been preparing our fighters to adjust them-* V to n *selves to civil society... I felt I had adjusted to the* Also V *idea of being a mother very well.* ● See also **well-** **adjusted.** ♦ **ad·just·ment** /ə'dʒʌstmənt/ **adjust-** N-COUNT **ments.** *He will have to make major adjustments to his thinking.* **2** If you **adjust** something, you change VERB it so that it is more effective or appropriate. *Pana-* V n *ma has adjusted its tax and labour laws.* ♦ **adjustment** *Investment is up by 5.7% after ad-* N-COUNT *justment for inflation.* **3** If you **adjust** something VERB such as your clothing or a machine, you correct or V n alter its position or setting. *She adjusted her head scarf fussily.* ♦ **adjustment. 4** If you **adjust** your vi- N-COUNT sion or if your vision **adjusts**, the muscles of your V-ERG eye alter to cope with changes in light or distance. V *He stopped to try to adjust his vision to the faint starlight... We stood in the doorway until our eyes adjusted.*

ad·just·able /əˈdʒʌstəbəl/. If something is **adjustable**, it can be changed to different positions or sizes. *The bags have adjustable shoulder straps.* ◆◇◇◇◇ ADJ

ad·just·er /əˈdʒʌstə/ **adjusters.** An **adjuster** is someone who is employed by an insurance company to investigate claims. N-COUNT

ad·ju·tant /ˈædʒʊtənt/ **adjutants.** An **adjutant** is an officer in the army who deals with administrative work. N-COUNT

,ad·'lib, ad-libs, ad-libbing, ad-libbed; also spelled **ad lib.** If you **ad-lib** something in a play or a speech, you say something which has not been planned or written beforehand. *He began comically ad-libbing a script... He is rather disjointed when he ad-libs.* ▶ Also a noun. *...a brilliant ad-lib.* VERB / V n / V / N-COUNT

ad·man /ˈædmæn/ **admen.** An **adman** is someone who works in advertising. N-COUNT INFORMAL

ad·min /ˈædmɪn/. **Admin** is the activity or process of organizing an institution or organization. *...the prison's admin staff.* N-UNCOUNT INFORMAL

ad·min·is·ter /ædˈmɪnɪstə/ **administers, administering, administered. 1** If someone **administers** something such as a country, the law, or a test, they take responsibility for organizing and supervising it. *The plan calls for the UN to administer the country until elections can be held.* **2** If a doctor or a nurse **administers** a drug, they give it to a patient. *Sister came to watch the staff nurse administer the drugs.* **3** If someone **administers** a punch or a kick, they punch or kick someone. ◆◆◇◇◇ VERB / V n / Also V n to n / VERB / V n / Also V n to n / FORMAL / VERB: V n / FORMAL

ad·min·is·tra·tion /ædˌmɪnɪˈstreɪʃən/ **administrations. 1 Administration** is the range of activities connected with organizing and supervising the way that an organization functions. *Too much time is spent on administration. ...business administration.* **2** The **administration** of something is the process of organizing and supervising it. *...the administration of justice... The cost of administration is around £500.* **3** The **administration** of a company or institution is the group of people who organize and supervise it. *They would like the college administration to exert more control.* **4** You can refer to a country's government as the **administration.** *...the administration's handling of the post-Gulf War situation.* ◆◆◆◆◇ N-UNCOUNT / N-UNCOUNT / N-SING: the N / N-COUNT: AMERICAN

ad·min·is·tra·tive /ædˈmɪnɪstrətɪv, AM -streɪt-/. **Administrative** work involves organizing and supervising an organization. *...administrative costs.* ◆ **ad·min·is·tra·tive·ly** *Cuba is politically and administratively divided into 14 provinces.* ◆◆◇◇◇ ADJ / ADV

ad·min·is·tra·tor /ædˈmɪnɪstreɪtə/ **administrators.** An **administrator** is a person whose job involves helping to organize and supervise the way that an organization functions. ◆◆◇◇◇ N-COUNT

ad·mi·rable /ˈædmɪrəbəl/. An **admirable** quality or action is one that deserves to be praised and admired. *Beyton is an admirable character.* ◆ **ad·mi·rably** /ˈædmɪrəbli/ *Peter had dealt admirably with the sudden questions... Johnstone's research is admirably wide-ranging.* ◆◆◇◇◇ ADJ-GRADED / ADV-GRADED

ad·mi·ral /ˈædmərəl/ **admirals.** An **admiral** is a very senior officer in the Navy. ◆◆◇◇◇ N-COUNT

Ad·mi·ral·ty /ˈædmərəlti/. In Britain, the government department that is in charge of the navy used to be called the **Admiralty.** N-PROPER: the N

ad·mire /ədˈmaɪə/ **admires, admiring, admired. 1** If you **admire** someone or something, you like and respect them very much. *I admired her when I first met her... All those who knew him will admire him for his work.* ◆ **ad·mi·ra·tion** /ˌædmɪˈreɪʃən/. *I have always had the greatest admiration for him... Meg's eyes widened in admiration.* ◆ **ad·mir·er, admirers.** *He was an admirer of her grandfather's paintings.* **2** If you **admire** someone or something, you look at them with pleasure. *We took time to stop and admire the view.* **3** See also **admiring.** ◆◆◆◇◇ VERB / V n / V n for n/-ing / N-UNCOUNT / N-COUNT / VERB / V n

ad·mir·er /ədˈmaɪərə/ **admirers.** A woman's **admirers** are the men who are attracted to her. ● See also **admire.** N-COUNT

ad·mir·ing /ədˈmaɪərɪŋ/. An **admiring** expression indicates a person's liking and respect for someone or something. An **admiring** person is someone who likes or respects another person or thing. *He cast her admiring glances all the way down the stairs.* ◆ **ad·mir·ing·ly** *He glanced admiringly at the design.* ● See also **admire.** ADJ-GRADED / ADV-GRADED: ADV with v

ad·mis·sible /ædˈmɪsɪbəl/. If evidence is **admissible**, it is allowed in a court of law. ADJ

ad·mis·sion /ædˈmɪʃən/ **admissions. 1** If you gain **admission** to a place or organization, you are given permission to enter it or join it. *Students apply for admission to a particular college... There have been substantial increases in hospital admissions.* **2** Admission or an **admission** fee at a park, museum, or other place is the amount of money that you pay to enter it. **3** An **admission** is a statement that something bad or embarrassing is true. *By his own admission, he is not playing well... She wanted some admission of guilt from her father.* ◆◆◇◇◇ N-VAR / N-UNCOUNT / N-VAR

ad·mit /ædˈmɪt/ **admits, admitting, admitted. 1** If you **admit** that something bad or embarrassing is true, you agree, often reluctantly, that it is true. *Up to two thirds of 14 to 16 year olds admit to buying drink illegally... I'd be ashamed to admit feeling jealous... None of these people will admit responsibility... 'Most of my tennis is at club level,' he admitted.* **2** If someone **is admitted** to hospital, they are taken into hospital for treatment. *She was admitted to hospital with a soaring temperature... He was admitted yesterday for treatment.* **3** If someone **is admitted** to a place or organization, they are allowed to enter or join it. *He was admitted to university after the war... Embassy security personnel refused to admit him... Journalists are rarely admitted to the region.* ◆◆◆◆◇ VERB: / V that / V to -ing/n / V -ing / V n / V with quote / VB: usu passive / be V-ed to n / be V-ed / VERB / be V-ed to n / V n to n

ad·mit·tance /ædˈmɪtəns/. **Admittance** is the act of entering a place or institution or the right to enter it. *Dr Patel had a similar experience trying to gain admittance into medical school.* N-UNCOUNT

ad·mit·ted·ly /ædˈmɪtɪdli/. You use **admittedly** when you are saying something which weakens the force of your statement. *It's only a theory, admittedly, but the pieces fit together.* ◆◇◇◇◇ ADV: ADV with cl/-group / PRAGMATICS

ad·mon·ish /ædˈmɒnɪʃ/ **admonishes, admonishing, admonished.** If you **admonish** someone, you tell them sternly that they have done something wrong. *They told me I was a fool and admonished me for taking risks... She admonished him gently, 'You should rest, not talk.'* ◆ **ad·mon·ish·ment, admonishments** *The admonishment in his normally mild voice surprised his wife.* VERB / V n for n/-ing / V n with quote / Also V n, / V n to-inf / FORMAL / N-COUNT

ad·moni·tion /ˌædməˈnɪʃən/ **admonitions.** An **admonition** is a warning or criticism about someone's behaviour. *She is full of admonitions about smoking, now that she has given it up.* N-VAR FORMAL

ad nau·seam /ˌæd ˈnɔːziæm, AM -ziəm/. If someone does something **ad nauseam**, they do it repeatedly and over a long period of time so that it becomes annoying or boring. PHRASE

ado /əˈduː/. If you do something **without further ado**, you do it immediately. *'And now, without further ado, let me introduce our benefactor.'* PHRASE DATED

ado·be /əˈdəʊbi/. **Adobe** is a mixture of mud and straw that is dried into bricks in the sun and used for building in hot countries. N-UNCOUNT

ado·les·cence /ˌædəˈlesəns/. **Adolescence** is the period of your life in which you develop from being a child into being an adult. ◆◇◇◇◇ N-UNCOUNT

ado·les·cent /ˌædəˈlesənt/ **adolescents. Adolescent** is used to describe young people who are no longer children but who have not yet become adults. It also refers to their behaviour. *An adolescent boy should have an adult in whom he can confide. ...adolescent rebellion.* ▶ Also a noun. *Young adolescents are happiest with small groups of close friends.* ◆◆◇◇◇ ADJ / N-COUNT

adopt /əˈdɒpt/ **adopts, adopting, adopted. 1** If you **adopt** someone else's child, you take it into your own family and make it legally your child. ◆◆◆◇ VERB: / V n, / V

Compare **foster**. ♦ **adopt·er, adopters** *A social* N-COUNT *worker is appointed to interview the prospective adopters.* ♦ **adop·tion, adoptions** *They gave their* N-VAR *babies up for adoption.*
2 If you **adopt** a new attitude, plan, or way of behav- VERB ing, you begin to have it. *Pupils should be helped to* V n *adopt a positive approach to the environment.* Also V n as n
♦ **adop·tion** /ə'dɒpʃən/ *...the adoption of Japanese* N-UNCOUNT *management practices.* **3** If you **adopt** an accent or a VERB tone of voice, you speak differently from normal, es- V n pecially to create a particular effect. *He has adopted the accent of a Second World War newscaster.* **4** If you VERB **adopt** a physical position, you move yourself into it. *I* V n *tried to adopt a foetal position.* FORMAL
5 If you **adopt** a country, you choose it as a place to VERB live. *Podulski had joined the U.S. Navy as an aviator,* V n *adopting a new country and a new profession.*
ador·able /ə'dɔːrəbəl/. If you say that someone or ♦◇◇◇◇ something is **adorable**, you are emphasizing that ADJ-GRADED they are very attractive and that you feel great affec- PRAGMATICS tion for them. *We had three adorable children.*
adore /ə'dɔː/ **adores, adoring, adored. 1** If you ♦♦◇◇◇ **adore** someone, you feel great love and admiration VB: no cont for them. *She adored her parents.* ♦ **ado·ra·tion** N-UNCOUNT /ˌædɔː'reɪʃən/. *He had been used to female adora- tion.* ♦ **ador·ing** *...adoring audiences.* ♦ **ador·ing-** ADJ-GRADED **·ly** *She gazes adoringly at her husband.* **2** If you ADV-GRADED **adore** something, you like it very much. *My mother* VB: no cont *adores bananas.* INFORMAL
adorn /ə'dɔːn/ **adorns, adorning, adorned.** If ♦◇◇◇◇ something **adorns** a place or an object, it makes it VERB look more beautiful. *Several magnificent oil paint-* V n *ings adorn the walls.* ♦ **adorn·ment** /ə'dɔːnmənt/ N-VAR **adornments** *...a building without any adornment or decoration... Cosmetics are used for adornment.*
adrena·lin /ə'drenəlɪn/; also spelled **adrenaline.** ♦◇◇◇◇ **Adrenalin** is a substance which your body produces N-UNCOUNT when you are angry, scared, or excited. It makes your heart beat faster and gives you more energy.
adrift /ə'drɪft/. **1** If a boat is **adrift**, it is floating on ♦◇◇◇◇ the water and is not tied to anything or controlled ADJ: by anyone. *They were spotted after three hours adrift* v-link ADJ, *in a dinghy.* **2** If something or someone has gone ADJ-GRADED: **adrift**, they no longer seem to have any purpose or v-link ADJ direction. *...that plan that has gone adrift.* **3** In ADJ-GRADED: *growing sense that she was adrift and isolated.* **3** In v-link ADJ sport, if a team or a player is **adrift** of their rivals, BRITISH they are behind them. *Aberdeen are nine points adrift of Rangers.*
adroit /ə'drɔɪt/. Someone who is **adroit** is quick ADJ-GRADED and skilful in their thoughts or actions. *...a remark- ably adroit and determined politician.* ♦ **adroit·ly** ADV-GRADED *He drove adroitly.*
adu·la·tion /ˌædʒə'leɪʃən/. **Adulation** is uncritical N-UNCOUNT admiration and praise. *The book was received with adulation by critics.*
adult /'ædʌlt, AM ə'dʌlt/ **adults. 1** An **adult** is a ♦♦♦♦◇ mature, fully developed person. *Children under 14* N-COUNT *must be accompanied by an adult.* ♦ **adult·hood** N-UNCOUNT /'ædʌlthʊd, AM ə'dʌlt-/. **Adulthood** is the state of being an adult. *Few people nowadays are able to maintain friendships into adulthood.* **2** An **adult** is a N-COUNT fully developed animal. *...a pair of adult birds.*
3 Adult means relating to the time when you are an ADJ: ADJ n adult, or typical of adult people. *I've lived most of my adult life in London.* **4** If you say that someone is ADJ-GRADED **adult** about something, you think that they act in a mature, intelligent way. **5** You can describe things ADJ such as films or books as **adult** when they contain sex- ually explicit material. *...an adult movie.*
ˌ**adult edu'cation.** **Adult education** is education N-UNCOUNT for adults, for example at evening classes.
adul·ter·ate /ə'dʌltəreɪt/ **adulterates, adulter-** VB: usu **ating, adulterated.** If something such as food or passive drink **is adulterated**, it has had water or cheaper be V-ed products added to it. *The food had been adulterated to increase its weight.*
adul·ter·er /ə'dʌltərə/ **adulterers.** An **adulterer** is N-COUNT someone who commits adultery.

adul·ter·ous /ə'dʌltərəs/. An **adulterous** relation- ADJ ship is a sexual relationship between a married per- son and someone they are not married to.
adul·tery /ə'dʌltəri/. If a married person commits ♦◇◇◇◇ **adultery**, they have sex with someone that they are N-UNCOUNT not married to.
adult·hood. See **adult**.
adv. **Adv** is a written abbreviation for **adverb**.
ad·vance /æd'vɑːns, -'væns/ **advances, advanc-** ♦♦♦♦◇ **ing, advanced. 1** To **advance** means to move for- VERB ward, often in order to attack someone. *Rebel forces* V prep/adv *are advancing on the capital... The water is advanc-* V *ing at a rate of between 5cm and 7cm a day.* ► Also N-VAR a noun. *The defences are intended to obstruct any advance by tanks and other vehicles.* **2** To **advance** VERB means to make progress, especially in your knowl- V edge of something. *Japan has advanced from a ru- ral, feudal society to an urban, industrial power.*
3 An **advance** in a particular subject or activity is N-VAR progress in understanding it or in doing it well. *Air safety has not improved since the dramatic advances of the 1970s.* **4** If something is an **advance** on what N-SING was previously available or done, it is better in some way. *This could be an advance on the present situa- tion.* ● See also **advanced**.
5 If you make **advances** to someone, you try to start a N-PLURAL sexual relationship with them. *She rejected his* LITERARY *advances.*
6 If you **advance** someone a sum of money, you lend VERB: V n n it to them, or pay it to them earlier than arranged. *The* V n *bank advanced $1.2 billion to help Mexico with debt repayments.* **7** An **advance** is money which is lent or N-COUNT paid to someone before they have earned it. *She was paid a £100,000 advance for her next two novels.*
8 To **advance** an event, or its time or date, means to VERB bring it forward to an earlier time or date. *Too much* V n *protein in the diet may advance the ageing process.*
9 If you **advance** a cause, interest, or claim, you sup- VERB port it and help to make it successful. *When not pro-* V n *ducing art of his own, Oliver was busy advancing the work of others.* ♦ **ad·vance·ment** *...her work for the* N-UNCOUNT *advancement of the status of women.*
10 When a theory or argument **is advanced**, it is put VB: usu forward for discussion. *Many theories have been ad-* passive *vanced as to why some women suffer from depression.* be V-ed
11 Advance booking, notice, or warning is done or ADJ: ADJ n given before an event happens. *The event received lit- tle advance publicity.* **12** An **advance** party or group is ADJ: ADJ n a small group of people who go on ahead of the main group. *The United Nations has sent an advance party to Cambodia.*
13 If one thing happens or is done **in advance of** an- PHR-PREP other, it happens or is done before the other thing.
14 If you do something **in advance**, you do it before a PHRASE particular date or event. *The subject of the talk is an- nounced a week in advance.*
ad·vanced /æd'vɑːnst, -'vænst/. **1** An **advanced** ♦♦♦◇◇ system, method, or design is modern and has been ADJ-GRADED developed from an earlier version of the same thing. *...the most advanced optical telescope in the world.*
2 An **advanced** country has reached a high level of ADJ-GRADED industrial or technological development. *...the edu- cational levels reached in other advanced countries.*
3 An **advanced** student has already learned the ba- ADJ-GRADED sic facts of a subject and is doing more difficult work. An **advanced** course of study is designed for such students. **4** Something that is at an **advanced** ADJ-GRADED stage or level is at a late stage of development. *...vic- tims of advanced kidney disease... His ideas should be more advanced by the time the Committee meets.*
5 If you say that someone is of **advanced** years or is ADJ-GRADED **advanced** in age, you are saying in a polite way that PRAGMATICS they are old. FORMAL
ad·vance·ment /æd'vɑːnsmənt, -'væns-/. **Ad-** ♦◇◇◇◇ **vancement** is promotion in your job or to a higher N-UNCOUNT social class. *He cared little for social advancement.* ● See also **advance**.
ad·van·tage /æd'vɑːntɪdʒ, -'væn-/ **advantages.** ♦♦♦♦◇ **1** An **advantage** is something that puts you in a bet- N-COUNT ter position than other people. *A good crowd will be*

a definite advantage to me and the rest of the team.
2 Advantage is the state of being in a better position than others who are competing against you. *Men have created a social and physical position of advantage for themselves.* **3** An **advantage** is a way in which one thing is better than another. *The great advantage of home-grown oranges is their magnificent flavour.* **4** If you **take advantage** of something, you make good use of it while you can. *I intend to take full advantage of this trip to buy the things we need.* **5** If someone **takes advantage** of you, they treat you unfairly for their own benefit. **6** If you use or turn something **to** your **advantage**, you exploit it in order to benefit from it.

ad·van·taged /æd'vɑːntɪdʒd, -'væn-/. A person or place that is **advantaged** is in a better social or financial position than other people or places. *Some cities are always going to be more advantaged.* `ADJ-GRADED`

ad·van·ta·geous /ˌædvən'teɪdʒəs/. If something is **advantageous** to you, it is likely to benefit you. *...very advantageous prices... Free exchange of goods was advantageous to all.* `ADJ-GRADED`

ad·vent /'ædvent/. **1** The **advent** of an important event or invention is the fact of it starting or coming into existence. *The advent of war led to a greater austerity.* **2** The **advent** of a person at a place is their arrival there. *Deptford had come alive with the advent of the new priest at St Paul's.* `N-UNCOUNT FORMAL` `N-UNCOUNT LITERARY`

ad·ven·ture /æd'ventʃə/ **adventures. 1** If someone has an **adventure**, they become involved in an unusual, exciting, and rather dangerous journey or series of events. *I set off for a new adventure in the United States.* **2 Adventure** is excitement and willingness to do new, unusual, or rather dangerous things. *...a feeling of adventure and excitement.* `N-COUNT` `N-UNCOUNT`

ad,venture 'playground, adventure playgrounds. An **adventure playground** is an area of land with equipment for children to play on, usually in cities or in a park. `N-COUNT BRITISH`

ad·ven·tur·er /æd'ventʃərə/ **adventurers. 1** An **adventurer** is a person who enjoys going to new and exciting places. *...a true adventurer's paradise.* **2** If you describe someone as an **adventurer**, you disapprove of them because they are using dishonest or immoral methods to gain money or power. *...ambitious political adventurers.* `N-COUNT` `N-COUNT PRAGMATICS`

ad·ven·tur·ism /æd'ventʃərɪzəm/. If you refer to someone's actions, especially in politics, as **adventurism**, you disapprove of them because that person takes risks and acts unfairly to achieve what they want. *Lenin dismissed guerrilla warfare as 'left adventurism'.* ♦ **ad·ven·tur·ist** /æd'ventʃərɪst/ **adventurists** ...political adventurists. `N-UNCOUNT PRAGMATICS` `N-COUNT`

ad·ven·tur·ous /æd'ventʃərəs/. **1** Someone who is **adventurous** is willing to take risks and to try new methods. Something that is **adventurous** involves new things or ideas. *...an adventurous businessman... The menu seemed more adventurous before.* **2** Someone who is **adventurous** is eager to visit new places and have new experiences. *He had always wanted an adventurous life in the tropics.* `ADJ-GRADED` `ADJ-GRADED`

ad·verb /'ædvɜːb/ **adverbs.** An **adverb** is a word such as 'slowly', 'fortunately', 'very', or 'now' which adds information about the action or situation mentioned in a clause. `N-COUNT`

'adverb group, adverb groups. An **adverb group** or **adverbial group** is a group of words based on an adverb, such as 'very slowly' or 'fortunately for us'. An adverb group can also consist simply of an adverb. `N-COUNT`

ad·ver·bial /æd'vɜːbiəl/. In grammar, **adverbial** means relating to adverbs or like an adverb. *...an adverbial expression.* `ADJ`

ad·ver·sar·ial /ˌædvə'seəriəl/. If you describe something as **adversarial**, you mean that it involves two or more people or organizations which are opposing each other. *In our country there is an adversarial relationship between government and business.* `ADJ-GRADED FORMAL`

ad·ver·sary /'ædvəsəri, AM -seri/ **adversaries.** Your **adversary** is someone you are competing with or fighting against. *...political adversaries.* `N-COUNT`

ad·verse /'ædvɜːs, AM æd'vɜːrs/. **Adverse** conditions or effects are unfavourable to you. *The police said Mr Hadfield's decision would have no adverse effect on the progress of the investigation.* ♦ **ad·verse·ly** *Price changes must not adversely affect the living standards of the people.* `ADJ-GRADED` `ADV-GRADED: ADV with v`

ad·ver·sity /æd'vɜːsɪti/ **adversities. Adversity** is a very difficult or unfavourable situation. *He has not yet shown himself to be a really strong character in the face of adversity.* `N-VAR`

ad·vert /'ædvɜːt/ **adverts. 1** An **advert** is an announcement in a newspaper, on television, or on a poster about something such as a product, event, or job vacancy. *I saw an advert for a transport job with a large steel and engineering company.* **2** If you say that an example of something is an **advert** for that thing in general, you mean that it shows how good that thing is. *This courtroom battle has been a poor advert for English justice.* **3** The **adverts** can refer to the interval in a commercial television programme, or between programmes, during which advertisements are shown. `N-COUNT BRITISH` `N-COUNT BRITISH` `N-PLURAL: theN BRITISH, INFORMAL`

ad·ver·tise /'ædvətaɪz/ **advertises, advertising, advertised. 1** If you **advertise** something such as a product, event, or job, you tell people about it in newspapers, on television, or on posters in order to encourage them to buy the product, go to the event, or apply for the job. *Tourist offices displays advertise holidays in Greece... Religious groups are currently not allowed to advertise on television.* ♦ **ad·ver·tis·er, advertisers** *To reach the millions of people who watch television, advertisers are willing to pay big money.* ♦ **ad·ver·tis·ing** *The zoo launched an advertising campaign to attract more people.* **2** If you **advertise** for someone to do something for you, you announce it in a newspaper, on television, or on a notice board. *We advertised for staff in a local newspaper.* **3** If someone or something **advertises** a particular quality, they show it in their appearance or behaviour. *His hard sinewy body advertised his ruthlessness of purpose.* **4** If you do not **advertise** the fact that something is the case, you try not to let other people know about it. *I didn't want to advertise the fact that he hadn't driven me to the airport.* `VERB Vn V` `N-COUNT` `N-UNCOUNT` `VERB V forn` `VERB Vn LITERARY` `VERB Vn`

ad·ver·tise·ment /'ædvɜːtɪsmənt, AM ˌædvə'taɪz-/ **advertisements. 1** An **advertisement** is an announcement in a newspaper, on television, or on a poster about something such as a product, event, or job vacancy. *Miss Parrish recently placed an advertisement in the local newspaper.* **2** If you say that an example of something is an **advertisement** for that thing in general, you mean that it shows how good that thing is. *The Treviso team were an effective advertisement for the improving state of Italian club rugby.* `N-COUNT WRITTEN` `N-COUNT`

Ad·ver·tis·er /'ædvətaɪzə/. **Advertiser** is used in the name of some local newspapers. *Taylor became editor of the Croydon Advertiser in 1950.*

ad·ver·tor·ial /ˌædvɜː'tɔːriəl/ **advertorials.** An **advertorial** is an advertisement that uses the style of newspaper or magazine articles or television documentary programmes. `N-VAR`

ad·vice /æd'vaɪs/. **1** If you give someone **advice**, you tell them what you think they should do in a particular situation. *...advice on how to prevent crime in your area... Take my advice and stay away from him!* **2** If you **take legal advice**, you ask a lawyer for his or her professional opinion on a situation. *If you are prosecuted by the police, then it is essential that you take specialist legal advice.* `N-UNCOUNT` `PHRASE FORMAL`

ad·vis·able /æd'vaɪzəbəl/. If you tell someone that it is **advisable** to do something, you are suggesting that they should do it, because it is likely to achieve the result they want. *Because of the popularity of the region, it is advisable to book hotels or camp sites in advance.* ♦ **ad·vis·abil·ity** /æd,vaɪzə'bɪlɪti/ *Every-* `ADJ-GRADED: v-link ADJ PRAGMATICS FORMAL` `N-UNCOUNT:`

thing he said pointed to the advisability of her theN ofn
returning.

ad·vise /æd'vaɪz/ **advises, advising, advised.** ◆◆◆◇◇
1 If you **advise** someone to do something, you tell VERB
them what you think they should do. *The minister* V n to-inf
advised him to leave as soon as possible... Herbert V n wh
would surely advise her how to approach the bank... V against n
I would strongly advise against it... Doctors advise V that
that he should be transferred. **2** If an expert **advises** VERB
people on a particular subject, he or she gives them V n on n
help and information on that subject. *...an officer* V on n
who advises undergraduates from London's City
University on money matters... A family doctor will
be able to advise on suitable birth control.
3 If you **advise** someone of a fact or situation, you tell VERB
them the fact or explain what the situation is. *I think it* V n on n
best that I advise you of my decision to retire. **4** If an of- FORMAL
ficial document states that you **are advised** to do V-PASSIVE
something, it is telling you the correct or appropriate beV-ed to-inf
thing to do. *Residents are advised not to put their rub-* FORMAL
bish bags on the pavement outside their houses.
5 See also **ill-advised, well advised**.

ad·vis·ed·ly /æd'vaɪzɪdli/. If you say that you are ADV:
using a word or expression **advisedly**, you are indi- ADV after v
cating that you have deliberately chosen to use it, PRAGMATICS
even though it may sound unusual, wrong, or offensive. *We have to see him again (I say 'him' advisedly*
since most doctors are still men).

ad·vis·er /æd'vaɪzə/ **advisers;** also spelled **advi-** ◆◆◆◇◇
sor. An **adviser** is an expert whose job is to give ad- N-COUNT
vice to other people. *He became an adviser to the*
government on American affairs. ...a careers adviser.

ad·vi·so·ry /æd'vaɪzəri/ **advisories. 1** An **adviso-** ◆◆◇◇◇
ry group, or a group or person with an **advisory** ADJ
role, regularly gives suggestions and help to people FORMAL
or organizations. *...the advisory committee on the*
safety of nuclear installations. **2** An **advisory** is an N-COUNT
official announcement or report that warns people AMERICAN
about bad weather, diseases, or other dangers or
problems. *Both the Missouri and Kansas Highway*
Patrols have issued travel advisories for tonight.
...health advisories.

ad·vo·ca·cy /'ædvəkəsi/. **1** Someone's **advocacy** ◆◇◇◇◇
of a particular action or plan is their act of recom- N-SING
mending it publicly. *...the president's advocacy of* FORMAL
higher taxes. **2 Advocacy** is the way in which law- N-UNCOUNT
yers deal with cases in court. *...to seek to improve* FORMAL
the quality of advocacy in the criminal courts. **3** An N-UNCOUNT
advocacy group or organization is one that tries to AMERICAN
influence the decisions of a government or other
authority. *...the consumer advocacy group Public*
Voice for Food & Health Policy.

ad·vo·cate, **advocates, advocating, advo-** ◆◆◆◇◇
cated. The verb is pronounced /'ædvəkeɪt/. The
noun is pronounced /'ædvəkət/. **1** If you **advocate** a VERB
particular action or plan, you recommend it public- V n
ly. *Mr Williams is a conservative who advocates few-* FORMAL
er government controls on business. ► Also a noun. N-COUNT
He is a strong advocate of economic aid for develop-
ing countries. **2** An **advocate** is a lawyer who speaks N-COUNT
in favour of someone or defends them in a court of LEGAL
law. **3** An **advocate** for a particular group is a per- N-COUNT:
son who works for the interests of that group. *...ad-* with supp
vocates for the homeless. ...consumer advocates.
• See also **devil's advocate**.

aegis /'iːdʒɪs/. Something that is done **under the** PHR-PREP
aegis of a person or organization is done with their FORMAL
official support and backing. *The military space pro-*
gramme will continue under the aegis of the joint
strategic armed forces.

aeon /'iːɒn/ **aeons;** spelled **eon** in American Eng- N-COUNT
lish. An **aeon** is an extremely long period of time.
Aeons ago, there were deserts where there is now fer-
tile land.

aer·ate /'eəreɪt/ **aerates, aerating, aerated.** To VERB
aerate a substance means to cause air or gas to pass V n
through it. *Aerate the soil by spiking with a fork.*

aer·ial /'eəriəl/ **aerials. 1** You talk about **aerial** at- ◆◆◇◇◇
tacks and **aerial** photographs to indicate that peo- ADJ: ADJ n
ple or things on the ground are attacked or photo-

graphed by people in aeroplanes. *Weeks of aerial*
bombardment had destroyed factories and highways.
...an aerial view of the Great Basin of Nevada. **2** You ADJ: ADJ n
can use **aerial** to describe things that exist or happen above the ground or in the air. *The seagulls*
swirled in aerial combat. **3** An **aerial** is a device or a N-COUNT
piece of wire that receives television or radio signals BRITISH
and is usually attached to a radio, television, car, or
building. The usual American word is **antenna**. See
pictures headed **car and bicycle** and **house and**
flat.

aero- /'eərəʊ-/. **1 aero-** is used at the beginning of PREFIX
words, especially nouns, that refer to things or activities connected with air or movement through
the air. *...aero-dynamics.* **2 aero-** combines with COMB
nouns to form nouns relating to aeroplanes. *...the*
British aero-engine maker, Rolls-Royce.

aero·bat·ics /ˌeərə'bætɪks/; the form **aerobatic** N-PLURAL
used as a modifier. **Aerobatics** are skilful and spectacular movements made by aeroplanes, usually to
entertain people watching from the ground. *...one of*
the greatest aerobatic display pilots.

aero·bics /eə'rəʊbɪks/. **Aerobics** is a form of exer- ◆◇◇◇◇
cise which increases the amount of oxygen in your N-PLURAL
blood, and strengthens your heart and lungs. The
verb that follows **aerobics** may be either singular or
plural. *...an aerobics class.* ♦ **aero·bic** /eə'rəʊbɪk/ ADJ-GRADED
Aerobic exercise gets the heart pumping.

aero·drome /'eərədrəʊm/ **aerodromes.** An **aero-** N-COUNT
drome is an enclosed area where small aeroplanes BRITISH
can land and take off.

aero·dy·nam·ic /ˌeərəʊdaɪ'næmɪk/. If something ADJ-GRADED
such as a car has an **aerodynamic** shape or design,
it goes faster and uses less fuel than other cars because the air passes over it more easily.

aero·dy·nam·ics /ˌeərəʊdaɪ'næmɪks/; the form N-PLURAL
aerodynamic is used as a modifier. **Aerodynamics**
is the study of the way in which objects move
through the air. The verb that follows **aerodynamics**
may be either singular or plural. *The laws of aerody-*
namics. ...sound aerodynamic principles.

aero·naut·ics /ˌeərə'nɔːtɪks/. **Aeronautics** is the N-UNCOUNT
science of designing and constructing aeroplanes.
♦ **aero·nau·ti·cal** /ˌeərə'nɔːtɪkəl/ *...the biggest aero-* ADJ: ADJ n
nautical research laboratory in Europe.

aero·plane /'eərəpleɪn/ **aeroplanes.** An **aero-** ◆◆◇◇◇
plane is a vehicle with wings and one or more en- N-COUNT
gines that enable it to fly through the air. The usual BRITISH
American word is **airplane**.

aero·sol /'eərəsɒl, AM -sɔːl/ **aerosols.** An **aerosol** ◆◇◇◇◇
is a small container in which a liquid such as paint N-COUNT
or deodorant is kept under pressure. When you
press a button, the liquid is forced out as a fine
spray or foam.

aero·space /'eərəʊspeɪs/. **Aerospace** companies ◆◆◇◇◇
are involved in developing and making aircraft, mis- N-UNCOUNT
siles, and space vehicles.

aes·thete /'iːsθiːt, AM 'es-/ **aesthetes.** An **aes-** N-COUNT
thete is someone who loves and appreciates works
of art and beautiful things.

aes·thet·ic /iːs'θetɪk, AM es-/; also spelled **esthetic.** ◆◆◇◇◇
Aesthetic involves beauty or art, and people's ap- ADJ-GRADED
preciation of beautiful things. *...products chosen for*
their aesthetic appeal. ♦ **aes·theti·cal·ly** ADV-GRADED
/iːs'θetɪkli, AM es-/ *A statue which is aesthetically*
pleasing to one person, however, may be repulsive to
another.

aes·thet·ics /iːs'θetɪks, AM es-/. **Aesthetics** is a ◆◇◇◇◇
branch of philosophy concerned with the study of N-UNCOUNT
the concept of beauty.

aeti·ol·ogy /ˌiːti'ɒlədʒi/. See **etiology**.

afar /ə'fɑː/. **Afar** means a long way away. *Seen from* ADV
afar, its towering buildings beckon the visitor in. LITERARY

af·fable /'æfəbəl/. Someone who is **affable** is ◆◇◇◇◇
pleasant and friendly. *Mr Brooke is an extremely af-* ADJ-GRADED
fable and approachable man. ♦ **af·fably** 'Good ADV-GRADED
morning,' said Thorne affably.

af·fair /ə'feə/ **affairs. 1** If an event or a series of ◆◆◆◇◇
events has been mentioned and you want to talk N-SING:
theN

about it again, you can refer to it as **the affair**. *The government has mishandled the whole affair.*
2 Journalists often refer to an important or interesting event or situation as '**the ... affair**'. *...the Watergate affair.* N-SING the supp N
3 You can describe the main quality of an event by saying that it is a particular kind of **affair**. *Michael said that his planned 10-day visit would be a purely private affair.* N-SING
4 You can describe an object as a particular kind of **affair** when you want to draw attention to a particular feature, or indicate that it is unusual. *All their beds were distinctive; Mac's was an iron affair with brass knobs.* N-SING: supp N DATED
5 In politics and journalism, **affairs** is used to refer to a particular type of activity or to the activities in a particular place. *He does not want to interfere in the internal affairs of another country... With more details, here's our foreign affairs correspondent.* ● See also current affairs, state of affairs. **6** Your **affairs** are all the matters connected with your life which you consider to be private and normally deal with yourself. *The unexpectedness of my father's death meant that his affairs are not entirely in order.* N-PLURAL
7 If two people who are not married to each other have an **affair**, they have a sexual relationship. ● See also affair. N-COUNT
8 If you say that a decision or situation is someone's **affair**, you mean that it is their responsibility, and other people should not interfere. *If you wish to make a fool of yourself and damage your career here, that is your affair.* N-SING: poss N BRITISH, DATED

af·fect /əˈfekt/ **affects, affecting, affected.** **1** If something **affects** someone or something else, it influences them or causes them to change in some way. *More than seven million people have been affected by drought.* **2** If a disease **affects** someone, it causes them to become ill. *AIDS seems to affect men and women in equal numbers.* **3** If something or someone **affects** you, they make you feel a strong emotion, especially sadness or pity. *If Jim had been more independent, the divorce would not have affected him as deeply.* **♦ af·fect·ing** One of the most affecting pieces of film shows soldiers standing round a mass grave. ◆◆◆◆◇ VERB V n / VERB V n / VERB V n / ADJ-GRADED
4 If you **affect** a particular characteristic or way of behaving, you pretend that it is genuine, or natural for you. *He listened to them, affecting an amused interest.* VERB V n Also V to-inf LITERARY

af·fec·ta·tion /ˌæfekˈteɪʃən/ **affectations.** If you say that someone's attitude or behaviour is an **affectation**, you disapprove of the fact that it is not genuine or natural, but is intended to impress other people. *Lawson writes so well: in plain English, without fuss or affectation.* N-VAR PRAGMATICS

af·fect·ed /əˈfektɪd/. If you describe someone's behaviour as **affected**, you disapprove of the fact that they behave in an unnatural way that is intended to impress other people. *She passed along with an affected air and a disdainful look.* ADJ PRAGMATICS

af·fec·tion /əˈfekʃən/ **affections.** **1** If you regard someone or something with **affection**, you like them and are fond of them. *She thought of him with affection... She had developed quite an affection for the place.* **2** Your **affections** are your feelings of love or fondness for someone. *The distant object of his affections is Caroline.* ◆◆◇◇◇ N-UNCOUNT: also N in pl / N-PLURAL: with poss

af·fec·tion·ate /əˈfekʃənət/. If you are **affectionate**, you show your love or fondness for another person in the way that you behave towards them. *...an affectionate hug.* **♦ af·fec·tion·ate·ly** He looked affectionately at his niece. ◆◇◇◇◇ ADJ-GRADED / ADV-GRADED: ADV with v

af·fi·da·vit /ˌæfɪˈdeɪvɪt/ **affidavits.** An **affidavit** is a written statement which you swear is true and which may be used as evidence in a court of law. ◆◇◇◇◇ N-COUNT

af·fili·ate, affiliates, affiliating, affiliated. The noun is pronounced /əˈfɪliət/. The verb is pronounced /əˈfɪlieɪt/. **1** An **affiliate** is an organization which is officially connected with another, larger organization or is a member of it. *...twelve companies, including three affiliates of a Texas oil firm.* ◆◆◇◇◇ N-COUNT FORMAL
2 If an organization **affiliates to** or **with** another larg- VERB

er organization, it forms a close connection with the larger organization or becomes a member of it. *The Government will not allow the staff association to affiliate with outside unions.* **♦ af·fili·at·ed** *Their country is not affiliated to the Organisation of African Unity. ...the United Nations and its affiliated organisations.* **♦ -affiliated.** -affiliated combines with nouns to form adjectives that describe which organization something or someone is affiliated to. *...church-affiliated schools.* **♦ af·filia·tion** /əˌfɪliˈeɪʃən/ **affiliations.** *The group has no affiliation to any political party.* **3** If a professional person, such as a lawyer or doctor, **affiliates** with an organization, they become officially connected with that organization or do some official work for it. *He wanted to affiliate with a U.S. firm.* **♦ af·fili·at·ed** *He will remain affiliated with the 480-lawyer firm as a special associate director.* V to/with n Also V FORMAL / ADJ / COMB / N-VAR / VERB V with n AMERICAN, FORMAL / ADJ

af·fin·ity /əˈfɪnɪti/ **affinities.** **1** If you have an **affinity** with someone or something, you feel that you are similar to them or understand them very well. *He has a close affinity with the landscape he knew when he was growing up.* **2** If people or things have an **affinity** with each other, they are similar in some ways. *The festival has affinities with the Roman festival of Cybele.* ◆◇◇◇◇ N-SING: also no det, with supp / N-COUNT FORMAL

af·firm /əˈfɜːm/ **affirms, affirming, affirmed.** **1** If you **affirm** that something is true, you state firmly and publicly that it is true. *The European Community has repeatedly affirmed that it's in agreement with the Americans. ...a speech in which he affirmed a commitment to lower taxes.* **♦ af·fir·ma·tion** /ˌæfəˈmeɪʃən/ **affirmations** The ministers issued a robust affirmation of their faith in the European Monetary System. **2** If an event **affirms** something, it shows that it is true or exists. *Everything I had accomplished seemed to affirm that opinion.* **♦ affirmation** *...the youngsters' expression of violence, which he saw as the affirmation of their rebellion.* ◆◆◇◇◇ VERB V that Also V with quote, V n to-inf FORMAL / N-VAR / VERB V n FORMAL / N-UNCOUNT: also a N

af·firma·tive /əˈfɜːmətɪv/. **1** An **affirmative** word or gesture indicates that you agree with what someone has said or that the answer to a question is 'yes'. *Haig was desperately eager for an affirmative answer.* **♦ af·firma·tive·ly** *'Is that clear?' Bob nodded his head affirmatively.* **2** If you reply to a question **in the affirmative**, you say 'yes' or make a gesture that means 'yes'. **3** In grammar, an **affirmative** clause is positive and does not contain a negative word. ◆◇◇◇◇ ADJ FORMAL / ADV: ADV with v PHRASE FORMAL / ADJ

af·firmative 'action. **Affirmative action** means making sure that members of disadvantaged groups, such as racial minorities or women, get an appropriate share of the opportunities available. The British term is **positive discrimination**. *A growing number of whites are challenging affirmative action policies.* ◆◇◇◇◇ N-UNCOUNT AMERICAN

af·fix, affixes, affixing, affixed. The verb is pronounced /əˈfɪks/. The noun is pronounced /ˈæfɪks/. **1** If you **affix** one thing to another, you stick it or attach it to the other thing. *Complete the form and affix four tokens to its back... I covered the scroll in sealing wax, and affixed a red ribbon. ...storage racks affixed to the sides of buses.* **2** An **affix** is a letter or group of letters, for example 'un-' or '-y', which is added to either the beginning or the end of a word to form a different word with a different meaning. For example, 'un-' is added to 'kind' to form 'unkind'. Compare **prefix** and **suffix**. VERB V n to n / V n / V-ed FORMAL / N-COUNT

af·flict /əˈflɪkt/ **afflicts, afflicting, afflicted.** If you **are afflicted** by pain, illness, or disaster, it affects you badly and makes you suffer. *Italy has been afflicted by political corruption for decades... There are two main problems which afflict people with hearing impairments.* **♦ af·flic·tion** /əˈflɪkʃən/ **afflictions.** An **affliction** is something which afflicts someone. *Hay fever is an affliction which arrives at an early age.* VERB be V-ed by/ with n FORMAL / N-VAR

af·flu·ent /ˈæfluənt/. If you are **affluent**, you have a lot of money or a high standard of living. *Cigarette* ◆◇◇◇◇ ADJ-GRADED

smoking used to be commoner among affluent people. ◆ **af·flu·ence** /ˈæfluəns/ The postwar era was one of new affluence for the working class. `N-UNCOUNT`

af·ford /əˈfɔːd/ **affords, affording, afforded.** ◆◆◆◇◇
1 If you **cannot afford** something, you do not have enough money to pay for it. ...afford a new refrigerator... We couldn't afford to buy a new rug. **2** If you say that you cannot **afford** to do something or allow it to happen, you mean that you must not do it or must prevent it from happening because it would be harmful or embarrassing to you. We can't afford to wait... The country could not afford the luxury of an election. **3** If someone or something **affords** you an opportunity or advantage, they give it to you. This affords us the opportunity to ask questions about how the systems might change... It was a cold room, but it afforded a fine view of the Old City. `VERB V n` `V to-inf` `V n` `VERB V to-inf V n` `VERB V n n V n FORMAL`

af·ford·able /əˈfɔːdəbəl/. If something is **affordable**, people have enough money to buy it. ...affordable housing. ◆ **af·forda·bil·ity** /əˌfɔːdəˈbɪlɪti/ ...the affordability of highly sophisticated weapons. ◆◇◇◇◇ `ADJ-GRADED` `N-UNCOUNT`

af·fray /əˈfreɪ/. An **affray** is a noisy and violent fight, especially in a public place. Barnstaple crown court was told he caused an affray... They were convicted of affray. `N-SING: also no det FORMAL`

af·front /əˈfrʌnt/ **affronts, affronting, affronted. 1** If something **affronts** you, you feel insulted and hurt because of it. ...results which would affront the good sense of right-thinking persons. ◆ **af·front·ed** He pretended to be affronted, but inwardly he was pleased. **2** If something is an **affront** to you, it is an obvious insult to you. The prisons were overcrowded, a disgrace, an affront to civilised society... She has taken my enquiry as a personal affront. ◆◇◇◇◇ `VERB V n FORMAL` `ADJ-GRADED` `N-COUNT`

afi·cio·na·do /əˌfɪʃəˈnɑːdəʊ/ **aficionados.** If someone is an **aficionado** of something, they like it and know a lot about it. I happen to be an aficionado of the opera and symphony. `N-COUNT`

afield /əˈfiːld/. **Far afield**, **further afield**, or **farther afield** means in places or areas other than the nearest or most obvious one. ...courses and seminars for wine growers in the Rhône as well as from further afield. ◆◇◇◇◇ `PHRASE`

afire /əˈfaɪə/. If something is **afire** or is set **afire**, it is on fire or looks as if it is on fire. The houses were set afire but there were only minor injuries to seven personnel. `ADJ: v-link ADJ, v n ADJ`

aflame /əˈfleɪm/. If something is on fire, you can say it is **aflame**. Hundreds of rolled newspapers were set aflame among the 50,000 crowd. `ADJ: v-link ADJ, v n ADJ LITERARY`

afloat /əˈfləʊt/. **1** When someone or something is **afloat**, they remain partly above the surface of water and do not sink. ...their valiant efforts to keep the tanker afloat. **2** If a person, business, or country stays **afloat** or is kept **afloat**, they have just enough money to pay their debts and not become bankrupt. A number of efforts were being made to keep the company afloat. ◆◇◇◇◇ `ADJ: ADV after v, v-link ADJ` `ADJ: ADV after v, v-link ADV`

afoot /əˈfʊt/. If you say that a plan is **afoot**, it is already happening or being planned, but you do not know much about it. Everybody knew that something awful was afoot. ◆◇◇◇◇ `ADJ: v-link ADJ`

afore·men·tioned /əˈfɔːmenʃənd/. When you refer to **the aforementioned** person or subject, you mean the person or subject that has already been mentioned. The aforementioned Mr Boylett had been based on a real-life member of the staff at Radley. ◆◇◇◇◇ `ADJ: det ADJ FORMAL`

afore·said /əˈfɔːsed/. **Aforesaid** means the same as **aforementioned**. ...the aforesaid organizations and institutions. `ADJ: det ADJ FORMAL`

afoul /əˈfaʊl/. If you **run afoul of** someone or something, you do something which gets you into trouble with them. ...an otherwise law-abiding citizen who, if left to his own devices, would never have run afoul of the law. `PHRASE AMERICAN`

afraid /əˈfreɪd/. **1** If you are **afraid**, you are frightened because you think that something very unpleasant is going to happen to you. I was afraid of the other boys... I refuse to accept a local situation ◆◆◆◇◇ `ADJ-GRADED: v-link ADJ`

that makes women afraid to walk downtown. **2** If you are **afraid** for someone else, you are worried that something horrible is going to happen to them. She's afraid for her family in Somalia. **3** If you are **afraid** that something unpleasant will happen, you are worried that it may happen and you want to avoid it. I was afraid that nobody would believe me... The Government is afraid of losing the election. **4** When you want to apologize to someone or to disagree with them in a polite way, you can say **I'm afraid**. We don't have anything like that, I'm afraid... 'Bad news?'—'I'm afraid so.' `ADJ-GRADED: v-link ADJ` `ADJ-GRADED: v-link ADJ` `PHRASE` `PRAGMATICS` `SPOKEN`

afresh /əˈfreʃ/. If you do something **afresh**, you do it again in a different way. Only one expert source seemed prepared to analyse the problem afresh. `ADV: ADV after v`

Afro /ˈæfrəʊ/. **Afro** hair is very tightly curled and sticks out all around your head. She looks great in her Afro wig. ◆◇◇◇◇ `ADJ`

Afro- /ˈæfrəʊ-/. **Afro-** is used to form adjectives and nouns that describe something that is connected with Africa. ...very well known Afro-American family. ...an Afro-centric fashion show. `COMB`

Afro-Carib'bean, Afro-Caribbeans. Afro-Caribbean refers to people of African descent who come from the Caribbean. ...Britain's Afro-Caribbean community. ▶ An **Afro-Caribbean** is someone who is Afro-Caribbean. ◆◇◇◇◇ `ADJ` `N-COUNT`

aft /ɑːft, æft/. If you go **aft** in a boat or plane, you go to the back of it. If you are **aft**, you are in the back. Clark shook hands with the pilot and walked aft. ▶ Also an adjective. ...the aft cabin. ◆◇◇◇◇ `ADV: ADV after v` `ADJ: ADJ n`

af·ter /ˈɑːftə, ˈæftə/. **1** If something happens **after** a particular date or event, it happens during the period of time that follows it. After 19 May, strikes were occurring on a daily basis... It wasn't until after Christmas that I met Paul. ▶ Also a conjunction. After Don told me this, he spoke of his mother... Marina cared for him after he seriously injured his eye. **2** If you do something **after** doing something else, you do it during the period of time that follows it. After completing and signing it, please return the form to us. ...women who have changed their mind after deciding not to have children. **3** You use **after** when you are talking about time. For example, if something will happen during **the day after** or **the weekend after** a particular date or event, it will happen during the next day or during the next weekend. She's leaving the day after tomorrow. ▶ Also an adverb. Tomorrow. Or the next day. Or the day after. **4** In American English, **after** is used when telling the time. If it is, for example, **ten after six**, the time is ten minutes past six. **5** If you do several things **one after the other** or **one after another**, you do one thing, then the next, and so on, with no break between your actions. Sybil ate three ginger biscuits, one after the other, greedily. **6** If you go **after** someone, you follow or chase them. Why don't you go after him, he's your son. **7** If you call, shout, or stare **after** someone, you call, shout, or stare at them as they move away from you. 'Come back!' he called after me. **8** If you are **after** something, you are trying to get it. I did eventually find what I was after. **9** If you tell someone that one place is a particular distance **after** another, you mean that it is situated beyond the other place and further away from you. Turn south, and after 4 kilometres take the road to Collazzone. **10** If something is written **after** something else on a page, it is written following it or underneath it. **11** You use **after** in order to give the most important aspect of something when comparing it with another aspect. After Germany, America is Britain's second-biggest customer. **12** If you do something **after** someone, you do it for them, because they cannot or will not do it for themselves. She used to mess up the floor and I had to clean up after her. **13** To be named **after** someone means to be given the same name as them. Phillimore Island is named after Sir Robert Phillimore. ◆◆◆◆ `PREP` `CONJ` `PREP` `PREP` `ADV: ADV after v` `PREP` `PHRASE` `PREP` `PREP` `PREP` `PREP` `PREP` `PREP` `PREP`

14 If you say **after you** to someone, you are being polite and allowing them to go in front of you or through a doorway before you do. *CONVENTION PRAGMATICS*
15 ● **day after day**: see **day**. ● **year after year**: see **year**. ● **after all**: see **all**.
after- /'ɑːftə-, 'æftə-/. **After-** is added to nouns to form adjectives which indicate that something takes place or exists after an event or process. *...an after-dinner speech... After-tax profit fell by 28 percent.* *COMB*
'after-care. After-care is the nursing and care of people who have been treated in hospital, and who are now recovering. *As part of the treatment, he attended 15 weeks of after-care.* *N-UNCOUNT*
'after-effect, after-effects. The **after-effects** of an event, experience, or substance are the conditions which result from it. *...the after-effects of the world's worst nuclear accident.* *N-COUNT*
after·glow /'ɑːftəɡləʊ, 'æf-/. You can refer to the good feeling or effects that remain after an event as the **afterglow**. *...the afterglow of victory in war.* *N-UNCOUNT*
,after-'hours. You use **after-hours** to describe activities which happen after the end of the usual time at which peoiple do them. *...an after-hours drink. ...after-hours trading.* *ADJ: ADJ n* ◆◇◇◇◇
after·life /'ɑːftəlaɪf, 'æf-/ **afterlives;** also spelled **after-life.** The **afterlife** is a life that some people believe begins when you die, for example a life in heaven. *N-COUNT*
after·math /'ɑːftəmɑːθ, 'æftəmæθ/. The **aftermath** of an important event, especially a harmful one, is the situation that results from it. *In the aftermath of the coup, the troops opened fire on the demonstrators. ...the aftermath of the disaster.* *N-SING with supp* ◆◆◇◇◇
after·noon /,ɑːftə'nuːn, ,æf-/ **afternoons.** The **afternoon** is the part of each day which begins at lunchtime and ends at about six o'clock. *He's arriving in the afternoon... He had stayed in his room all afternoon. ...an afternoon news conference.* *N-VAR* ◆◆◆◇
,afternoon 'tea, afternoon teas. In Britain, **afternoon tea** is a light meal or snack that some people have in the afternoon. *N-VAR*
,after-'school. After-school activities are those that are organized for children in the afternoon or evening after they have finished school. *ADJ: ADJ n* ◆◇◇◇◇
after·shave /'ɑːftəʃeɪv, 'æf-/ **aftershaves;** also spelled **after-shave. Aftershave** is a liquid with a pleasant smell that men sometimes put on their faces after shaving. *N-VAR*
after·shock /'ɑːftəʃɒk, 'æf-/ **aftershocks. After-shocks** are smaller earthquakes which occur after a large earthquake. *Early this morning, a second strong aftershock struck Northern California.* *N-COUNT*
after·taste /'ɑːftəteɪst, 'æf-/; also spelled **after-taste.** An **aftertaste** is a taste that remains in your mouth after you have finished eating or drinking something. *It is very thick and creamy with no bitter aftertaste.* *N-SING*
after·thought /'ɑːftəθɔːt, 'æf-/ **afterthoughts.** If you do or say something as an **afterthought**, you do or say it after something else as an addition, perhaps without careful thought. *Almost as an afterthought he added that he missed her.* *N-COUNT*
after·wards /'ɑːftəwədz, 'æf-/. The form **afterward** is also used, mainly in American English. If you do something or if something happens **afterwards**, you do it or it happens after a particular event or time that has already been mentioned. *Shortly afterwards, police arrested four suspects... James was taken to hospital but died soon afterwards.* *ADV: ADV with cl* ◆◆◆◇◇
again /ə'ɡen, ə'ɡeɪn/. **1** You use **again** to indicate that something happens a second time, or after it has already happened before. *He kissed her again... I don't ever want to go through anything like that again.* **2** You can use **again and again** or **time and again** to emphasize that something happens many times. *He would go over his work again and again until he felt he had it right... Time and again political parties have failed to tackle this issue.* **3** You use **again** to indicate that something is now in a par- *ADV* ◆◆◆◆ *PHRASE PRAGMATICS* *ADV: ADV after v*

ticular state or place that it used to be in. *He opened his attache-case, removed a folder, then closed it again... I started to feel good about myself again.*
4 You can use **again** when you want to point out that there is a similarity between the subject that you are talking about now and a previous subject. *Again the pregnancy was very similar to my previous two.* **5** You can use **again** in expressions such as **but again, then again,** and **there again** when you want to introduce a remark which contrasts with or weakens something that you have just said. *You may be happy to buy imitation leather, and then again, you may wonder what you're getting for your money.* *ADV: ADV cl PRAGMATICS* *ADV: ADV with cl PRAGMATICS*
6 You use **again** in expressions such as **half as much again** when you are indicating how much greater one amount is than another amount that you have just mentioned or are about to mention. *Sherry is half as strong again as table wine.* **7** ● **now and again**: see **now**. ● **once again**: see **once**. *ADV: amount ADV PRAGMATICS*
against /ə'ɡenst, ə'ɡeɪnst/. **1** If something is leaning or pressing **against** something else, it is touching it. *She leaned against him. ...a table pushed against a wall. ...the rain beating against the window panes.* *PREP* ◆◆◆◆◆
2 If you are **against** something such as a plan, policy, or system, you think it is wrong, bad, or stupid. *Joan was very much against commencing drug treatment. ...a march to protest against job losses.* ► Also an adverb. *The vote for the suspension of the party was 283 in favour with 29 against.* **3** If you **have** something **against** someone, you dislike them. *PREP* *ADV: ADV after v* *PHRASE*
4 If you take action **against** someone or something, you try to harm them. *Security forces are still using violence against opponents of the government.* **5** If you take action **against** a possible future event, you try to prevent it. *...the fight against crime... They are arguing against hospital closures.* **6** If you do something **against** someone's wishes, advice, or orders, you do not do what they want you to do or tell you to do. *He didn't want to go against the wishes of the German government... He discharged himself from hospital against the advice of doctors.* **7** If you compete **against** someone in a game, you try to beat them. *The tour will include games against the Australian Barbarians.* *PREP* *PREP* *PREP* *PREP*
8 If you do something in order to protect yourself **against** something unpleasant or harmful, you do something which will make its effects on you less serious if it happens. *...insurance against ordinary risks such as fire, flood, and breakage... It has been claimed that wine helps protect against heart disease.* *PREP*
9 If something is **against** the law or **against** the rules, there is a law or a rule which says that you must not do it. *It is against the law to detain you against your will for any length of time.* *PREP*
10 If you are moving **against** a current, tide, or wind, you are moving in the opposite direction to it. *They were going to sail around the little island, against the tide.* *PREP*
11 If something happens or is considered **against** a particular background of events, it is considered in relation to those events, because those events are relevant to it. *The profits rise was achieved against a backdrop of falling metal prices.* **12** If something is measured or valued **against** something else, it is measured or valued by comparing it with the other thing. *Our policies have to be judged against a clear test: will it improve the standard of education?... The US dollar is down against most foreign currencies today.* **13** If you discuss a particular set of facts or figures **as against** another set, you are comparing or contrasting the two sets of facts or figures. *Only about 60% of voters were firm in their intention at the start of the campaign, as against 80% before.* *PREP* *PREP* *PHRASE*
14 The chances **against** something happening are the chances that it will not happen. *One's chances against cancer depend on smoking, obesity, and poor diet.* ► Also an adverb. *What were the odds against?* **15** ● **up against**: see **up**. ● **against the clock**: see **clock**. *PREP* *ADV: n ADV*

agape /əˈɡeɪp/. If someone has their mouth **agape**, their mouth is open very wide, often because they are very surprised. ADJ: v-link ADJ WRITTEN

ag·ate /ˈæɡɪt/ **agates.** Agate is a very hard, usually striped stone which is used to make jewellery. N-VAR

age /eɪdʒ/ **ages, ageing** or **aging, aged. 1** Your ◆◆◆◆ age is the number of years that you have lived. She N-VAR has a nephew who is just ten years of age... At the age of sixteen he qualified for a place at the University... I admired him for being so confident at his age. **2** The **age** of a thing is the number of years since it N-VAR was made. ...the age of the building. **3** Age is the N-UNCOUNT state of being old or the process of becoming older. This cologne, like wine, improves with age... At 67, he is showing signs of age. **4** When someone **ages**, V-ERG they seem much older and weaker or less alert. He V seemed to have aged in the last few months... Worry V-ing had aged him. ...his ageing mother. ♦ **age·ing** In- N-UNCOUNT adequate fluid intake and poor diet both contribute to ageing. **5** An **age** is a period in history. ...the age of steam and N-COUNT steel. ...Bronze Age pottery. **6** You can say **an age** or N-COUNT **ages** to mean a very long time. He waited what seemed INFORMAL an age... The bus took absolutely ages to arrive. **7** If something **comes of age**, it reaches an important PHRASE stage of development and is accepted by a large number of people. ...an issue that has come of age in Britain in the last decade. **8** When someone **comes of age**, PHRASE they legally become an adult. **9** Someone who is **un-** PHRASE **der age** is not legally old enough to do something, for example to buy an alcoholic drink. Because she was under age, her parents were still responsible for her. ...under age smoking. **10** See also **aged, coming of age, dark age, golden age, ice age, Iron Age, middle age, Stone Age.**

aged. Pronounced /eɪdʒd/ for meaning 1, and ◆◆◇◇◇ /ˈeɪdʒɪd/ for meaning 2. **1** You use **aged** followed by ADJ a number to say how old someone is. Alan has two children, aged eleven and nine. **2 Aged** means very ADJ: ADJ n old. She has an aged parent. ► You can refer to peo- N-PLURAL: ple who are very old as **the aged. 3** See also theN **middle-aged.**

'age group, age groups. An **age group** is the ◆◇◇◇◇ people in a place or organization who were born N-COUNT during a particular period of time, for example all the people aged between 18 and 25. ...a style that would appeal to all age groups.

age·ist /ˈeɪdʒɪst/. **Ageist** behaviour is based on the ADJ-GRADED belief that older people are of less value than PRAGMATICS younger people; used showing disapproval. ...ageist bias from employers. ♦ **age·ism** /ˈeɪdʒɪzəm/. N-UNCOUNT

age·less /ˈeɪdʒləs/. **1** If you describe someone as ADJ **ageless**, you mean that they never seem to look any LITERARY older. **2** If you describe something as **ageless**, you ADJ mean that it is impossible to tell how old it is, or LITERARY that it seems to have existed for ever. ...the ageless oceans.

'age limit, age limits. An **age limit** is the oldest or N-COUNT youngest age at which particular rules allow you to do something. There is a minimum age limit.

agen·cy /ˈeɪdʒənsi/ **agencies. 1** An **agency** is a ◆◆◆◇◇ business which provides a service on behalf of other N-COUNT businesses. We had to hire maids through an agency. ...a successful advertising agency. ● See also **em-** **ployment agency, press agency, travel agency.** **2** An **agency** is a government organization respon- N-COUNT sible for a certain area of administration. ...the Central Intelligence Agency.

agen·da /əˈdʒendə/ **agendas. 1** You can refer to ◆◆◆◇◇ the political issues which are important at a par- N-COUNT: ticular time as an **agenda**. Does television set the with supp agenda on foreign policy?... Many of the coalition members could have their own political agendas. ● See also **hidden agenda. 2** An **agenda** is a list of N-COUNT the items that have to be discussed at a meeting. This is sure to be an item on the agenda next week... High on the agenda is economic integration.

agent /ˈeɪdʒənt/ **agents. 1** An **agent** is a person ◆◆◆◇◇ who looks after someone else's business affairs or N-COUNT does business on their behalf. You are buying direct,

rather than through an agent. ● See also **estate agent, press agent, travel agent. 2** An **agent** in the N-COUNT arts world is a person who gets work for an actor or musician, or who sells the work of a writer to publishers. **3** An **agent** is a person who works for a N-COUNT country's secret service. **4** If you refer to someone N-COUNT: or something as the **agent of** a particular effect, you N of n mean that they cause this effect. He identifies Gorbachev as the key agent of change. **5** A chemical N-COUNT: that has a particular effect or is used for a particular supp N purpose can be referred to as a particular kind of **agent.** ...the bleaching agent in white flour.

agent pro·vo·ca·teur /ˌæʒɒn prɒvɒkəˈtɜː/ **agents** N-COUNT **provocateurs.** An **agent provocateur** is a person who is employed by a government or the police to encourage certain groups of people to break the law, because the government or police want to arrest them or want them to lose public support.

,age of con'sent. The age of consent is the age ◆◇◇◇◇ at which a person can legally marry or agree to have N-SING: a sexual relationship. theN

,age-'old. An **age-old** story, tradition, or problem ◆◇◇◇◇ has existed for many generations or centuries. ...this ADJ age-old struggle for control. WRITTEN

ag·glom·era·tion /əˌɡlɒməˈreɪʃən/ **agglomera-** N-VAR **tions.** An **agglomeration** of things is a lot of differ- FORMAL ent things gathered together, often in no particular order or arrangement. The album is a bizarre agglomeration of styles.

ag·gran·dize /əˈɡrændaɪz/ **aggrandizes, aggran-** VERB: V n **dizing, aggrandized;** also spelled **aggrandise** in PRAGMATICS British English. To **aggrandize** someone means to V pron-refl make them seem richer, more powerful, and more important than they really are. My father would go on and on, showing off, aggrandising himself. ♦ **ag-** **·gran·dize·ment** /əˈɡrændɪzmənt/ ...those who are N-UNCOUNT using the banking system for their own personal aggrandizement. ● See also **self-aggrandizement.**

ag·gra·vate /ˈæɡrəveɪt/ **aggravates, aggravat-** ◆◇◇◇◇ **ing, aggravated. 1** If someone or something **ag-** VERB **gravates** a situation, they make it worse. Stress and V n lack of sleep can aggravate the situation. **2** If some- VERB one or something **aggravates** you, they make you V n annoyed. What aggravates you most about this INFORMAL country? ♦ **ag·gra·vat·ing** You don't realise how ADJ-GRADED aggravating you can be. ♦ **ag·gra·va·tion** N-VAR /ˌæɡrəˈveɪʃən/ **aggravations** I just couldn't take the aggravation.

ag·gra·vat·ed /ˈæɡrəveɪtɪd/. **Aggravated** is used to ADJ: ADJ n describe a serious crime which involves violence. LEGAL Both were charged with aggravated burglary.

ag·gre·gate, aggregates, aggregating, ag- ◆◆◇◇◇ **gregated.** The adjective and noun are pronounced /ˈæɡrɪɡət/. The verb is pronounced /ˈæɡrɪɡeɪt/. **1** An **aggregate** amount or score is made up of sev- ADJ: ADJ n eral smaller amounts or scores added together. ...the TECHNICAL rate of growth of aggregate demand... The aggregate score of 707 runs was a world record for a one-day match. ► Also a noun. The highest aggregate came N-COUNT in the third round where Leeds and Middlesbrough drew 4-4. **2** An **aggregate** is a number of people or N-COUNT things that are being considered as a single thing. FORMAL ...society viewed as an aggregate of individuals. **3** If VERB amounts or things **are aggregated**, they are added beV-ed into n together and considered as a single amount or V pl-n thing. The results were to be aggregated into nation- FORMAL al league tables... We should never aggregate votes to predict results under another system. ♦ **ag·gre·ga-** **·tion** /ˌæɡrɪˈɡeɪʃən/ ...aggregation of the results in- N-UNCOUNT vites distortion. **4** If a number of different things or PHRASE amounts are considered **in aggregate**, they are con- FORMAL sidered as a single thing or total. In aggregate, such policies could reduce carbon dioxide emissions by about 25 per cent. **5** If one team beats another **on** PHRASE **aggregate**, it wins because it has a higher total score BRITISH than the other team after a series of games.

ag·gres·sion /əˈɡreʃən/ **aggressions. 1** Aggres- ◆◆◇◇◇ sion is a quality of anger and determination that N-UNCOUNT makes you ready to attack other people. Aggression is by no means a male-only trait. **2 Aggression** is N-VAR

violent and attacking behaviour. *The raid was an unjustifiable act of aggression.*

ag·gres·sive /ə'gresɪv/. **1** An **aggressive** person or animal has a quality of anger and determination that makes them ready to attack. *Some children are much more aggressive than others... Aggressive behaviour is a sign of emotional distress.* ♦ **ag·gres·sive·ly** *They'll react aggressively.* ♦ **ag·gres·sive·ness** *Her aggressiveness made it difficult for him to explain his own feelings.* **2** People who are **aggressive** in their activities behave in a forceful way because they are very eager to succeed. *...a very aggressive and competitive executive... The Zambian game is much more aggressive than European soccer.* ♦ **ag·gres·sive·ly** *...countries noted for aggressively pursuing energy efficiency.*
◆◆◇◇ ADJ-GRADED
ADV-GRADED
N-UNCOUNT
ADJ-GRADED
ADV-GRADED

ag·gres·sor /ə'gresə/ **aggressors.** The **aggressor** in a fight or battle is the person, group, or country that starts it.
◆◇◇◇◇ N-COUNT

ag·grieved /ə'gri:vd/. If you feel **aggrieved**, you feel upset and angry because of the way in which you have been treated.
◆◇◇◇◇ ADJ-GRADED

ag·gro /'ægrəʊ/. **1** **Aggro** is the difficulties and problems that are involved in something. *Simply phone the ticket hot-line and all that aggro will be a thing of the past.* **2** **Aggro** is aggressive or violent behaviour. *...hooliganism and racist aggro.*
N-UNCOUNT INFORMAL BRITISH
N-UNCOUNT BRITISH INFORMAL

aghast /ə'ɡɑːst, ə'ɡæst/. If you are **aghast**, you are filled with horror and surprise. *While she watched, aghast, his eyes glazed over... His colleagues were aghast at the sackings.*
ADJ-GRADED FORMAL

ag·ile /'ædʒaɪl, AM -dʒəl/. **1** Someone who is **agile** can move with great ease and speed. *He is very agile for a big man.* ♦ **agil·ity** /ə'dʒɪlɪti/. *The strength and agility of youth.* **2** If you have an **agile** mind, you think quickly and intelligently. ♦ **agility** *They are not mere exercises in mental agility.*
◆◇◇◇◇ ADJ-GRADED
N-UNCOUNT
ADJ-GRADED
N-UNCOUNT

ag·ing /'eɪdʒɪŋ/. See **age**.

agi·tate /'ædʒɪteɪt/ **agitates, agitating, agitated.** **1** If people **agitate** for something, they protest or take part in political activity in order to get it. *The women worked in these mills had begun to agitate for better conditions.* ♦ **agi·ta·tion** /ˌædʒɪ'teɪʃən/ *At least seventy students were injured in the continuing agitation against the decision.* **2** If you **agitate** something, you shake it so that it moves about. *Agitate the water with a finger.* ♦ **agitation** *Temperature is a measure of the agitation of the molecules of matter.*
◆◇◇◇◇
VERB V for n Also V, V for n to-inf
N-UNCOUNT
VERB V n FORMAL
N-UNCOUNT

agi·tat·ed /'ædʒɪteɪtɪd/. If someone is **agitated**, they are very worried or upset, and show this in their behaviour or voice. *Susan seemed agitated about something.* ♦ **agi·ta·tion** *Danny returned to Father's house in a state of intense agitation.* ● See also **agitate**.
ADJ-GRADED
N-UNCOUNT

agi·ta·tor /'ædʒɪteɪtə/ **agitators.** If you describe someone involved in politics as an **agitator**, you disapprove of them because of the trouble they cause in organizing campaigns and protests. *...a famous actress who was accused of being a Communist agitator.*
N-COUNT
PRAGMATICS

agit·prop /'ædʒɪtprɒp/. **Agitprop** is the use of artistic forms such as drama or posters to further political aims.
N-UNCOUNT

aglow /ə'ɡləʊ/. **1** If something is **aglow**, it is shining and bright with a soft, warm light. *The night skies will be aglow with fireworks.* **2** If someone is **aglow** or if their face is **aglow**, they look excited. *'It was incredible,' Kurt says, suddenly aglow.*
ADJ: v-link ADJ LITERARY
ADJ: v-link ADJ LITERARY

AGM /ˌeɪ dʒiː 'em/ **AGMs.** The **AGM** of a company or organization is a meeting which it holds once a year in order to discuss the previous year's activities and accounts. **AGM** is an abbreviation for 'Annual General Meeting'.
◆◇◇◇◇ N-COUNT BRITISH

ag·nos·tic /æɡ'nɒstɪk/ **agnostics.** An **agnostic** believes that it is not possible to know whether God exists or not. *You grew up in an agnostic household.* ♦ **ag·nos·ti·cism** /æɡ'nɒstɪsɪzəm/ *...scientific versions of scepticism and agnosticism.*
N-COUNT
N-UNCOUNT

ago /ə'ɡəʊ/. You use **ago** when you are referring to past time. For example, if something happened one year **ago** or a long time **ago**, it is one year or a long time since it happened. *He was killed a few days ago... She died long ago.*
◆◆◆◆◆ ADV: n ADV, long ADV

agog /ə'ɡɒɡ/. If you are **agog**, you are excited about something, and eager to know more about it. *The city was agog with rumours.*
ADJ

ago·nize /'ægənaɪz/ **agonizes, agonizing, agonized;** also spelled **agonise** in British English. If you **agonize** over something, you feel very anxious about it and spend a long time thinking about it. *He was agonizing over the moral issues involved.*
VERB V over/about n Also V

ago·nized /'ægənaɪzd/; also spelled **agonised**. **Agonized** describes something that you say or do when you are in great physical or mental pain. *He heard agonized sobs.*
ADJ-GRADED

ago·niz·ing /'ægənaɪzɪŋ/; also spelled **agonising**. **1** Something that is **agonizing** causes you to feel great physical or mental pain. *The wait was agonizing.* ♦ **ago·niz·ing·ly** *Progress was agonizingly slow.* **2** **Agonizing** decisions and choices are very difficult to make.
◆◇◇◇◇ ADJ-GRADED
ADV
ADJ-GRADED

ago·ny /'æɡəni/ **agonies.** **Agony** is great physical or mental pain. *She called out in agony... He suffered agonies of religious doubt.*
◆◆◇◇◇ N-COUNT: also N in pl

'agony aunt, agony aunts. An **agony aunt** is a person who writes a column in a newspaper or magazine in which they answer readers' letters about their personal problems. The usual American term is **advice columnist**.
N-COUNT BRITISH

'agony column, agony columns. In some newspapers and magazines, the **agony column** is the part where readers' letters about their personal problems are printed and answered. The usual American term is **advice column**.
N-COUNT BRITISH

ago·ra·pho·bia /ˌæɡərə'fəʊbiə/. **Agoraphobia** is the fear of open or public places. ♦ **ago·ra·pho·bic** /ˌæɡərə'fəʊbɪk/. Someone who is **agoraphobic** suffers from agoraphobia.
N-UNCOUNT MEDICAL
ADJ-GRADED

agrar·ian /ə'ɡreəriən/. In the social sciences, **agrarian** means relating to farming, the countryside, and the use of land. *...a highly developed agrarian economy.*
ADJ

agree /ə'ɡriː/ **agrees, agreeing, agreed.** **1** If people **agree** with each other about something, they have the same opinion about it or say that they have the same opinion. *If we agreed all the time it would be a bit boring... I'm not sure I agree with you... 'It's appalling.'—'It is. I agree.'... I agree that the demise of London Zoo would be terrible.* **2** If you **agree** to do something or **agree** to a proposal, you say that you will do what someone wants, or that you will let something be done. *He agreed to pay me for the drawings... Donna agreed to both requests.* **3** If people **agree** on something or **agree** something, they all decide to have or do something. *The warring sides have agreed on an unconditional ceasefire... We never agree a date... The court had given the unions until September 11 to agree terms with a buyer.* ● If two people who are arguing about something **agree to disagree** or **agree to differ**, they decide to stop arguing because neither of them is going to change their opinion. **4** If you **agree** with an action or suggestion, you approve of it. *He knew they'd agree with his stand.*
◆◆◆◆◆ V-RECIP pl-n V V with n
V that Also V with quote
VERB V to-inf V to n Also V
V-RECIP pl-n V on n pl-n V n V n with n V n with n to-inf
PHRASE
VERB V with n

5 If one account of an event or one set of figures **agrees** with another, the two accounts or sets of figures are the same or are consistent with each other. *His second statement agrees with facts as stated by the other witnesses.* ♦ **agree·ment** *Other surveys have produced results essentially in agreement with these figures.* **6** If some food that you eat **does not agree with** you, it makes you feel ill. *I don't think the food here agrees with me.* **7** In grammar, if a word **agrees** with a noun or pronoun, it has a form appropriate to the number or gender of the noun or pronoun. For example, in 'He hates it', the singular verb agrees with the singular pronoun 'he'. You can also say that two words **agree**. ♦ **agreement, agreements.**
V-RECIP V with n Also pl-n V
N-UNCOUNT
VB: with neg
V-RECIP: V with n, pl-n V
N-VAR

8 See also **agreed, agreement.**

agree·able /ə'griːəbəl/. **1** If something or someone is **agreeable**, they are pleasant and people like them. ...*an agreeable surprise... I've gone out of my way to be agreeable to his friends.* ♦ **agree·ably** *At first we chatted agreeably.* **2** If you are **agreeable** to something or if it is **agreeable** to you, you are willing to do it or to allow it to happen. ...*a solution that would be agreeable to all.* ◇◇◇◇ ADJ-GRADED · ADV-GRADED · ADJ-GRADED: v-link ADJ FORMAL

agreed /ə'griːd/. **1** If people are **agreed** on something, they have reached a joint decision on it or have the same opinion about it. *Okay, so are we agreed on going north?... All twelve member states are agreed that something needs to be done.* **2** When you are discussing something formally, you can say '**Agreed?**' to check whether the other people agree with what you have just said. You can say '**Agreed**' if you agree with what someone has just said. *'That means we move out today. Agreed?'—'Agreed.'* **3** See also **agree.** ◆◇◇◇◇ ADJ: v-link ADJ · CONVENTION PRAGMATICS

agree·ment /ə'griːmənt/ **agreements. 1** Agreement or an **agreement** is a joint decision that a particular course of action should be taken. ...*a new defence agreement between Greece and the United States... The two men had not reached agreement on the issues discussed.* **2** Agreement with someone means having the same opinion as they have. *There was general agreement.* ● If you are **in agreement** with someone, you have the same opinion as they have. *The judges were not all in agreement.* **3** Agreement to a course of action means allowing it to happen or giving it your approval. *The clinic doctor will then write to your GP to get his agreement.* ● If you are **in agreement** with a plan or proposal, you approve of it. *The president was in full agreement with the proposal.* **4** See also **agree.** ◆◆◆◇ N-VAR · N-UNCOUNT · PHRASE · N-UNCOUNT · PHRASE

ag·ri·busi·ness /'ægribɪznɪs/. **Agribusiness** consists of the various businesses that produce, sell, and distribute farm products on a large scale. N-UNCOUNT

ag·ri·cul·tur·al /ˌægrɪ'kʌltʃərəl/. **1** Agricultural means involving or relating to agriculture. ...*corn and other agricultural products.* **2** An **agricultural** place or society is one in which agriculture is important or highly developed. ◆◆◆◇◇ ADJ · ADJ

ag·ri·cul·tur·al·ist /ˌægrɪ'kʌltʃərəlɪst/ **agriculturalists. An agriculturalist** is an expert on agriculture who advises farmers. N-COUNT

ag·ri·cul·ture /'ægrɪkʌltʃə/. **Agriculture** is farming and the methods that are used to raise and look after crops and animals. ◆◆◆◇◇ N-UNCOUNT

agro- /'ægrəʊ-/. **Agro-** is used to form nouns and adjectives which refer to things relating to agriculture, or to agriculture combined with another activity. ...*agro-chemical residues.* PREFIX

agrono·mist /ə'grɒnəmɪst/ **agronomists.** An **agronomist** is someone who studies the cultivation of land in order to produce crops. N-COUNT

aground /ə'graʊnd/. If a ship runs **aground**, it touches the ground at the bottom of an area of water and gets stuck. ◆◇◇◇◇ ADV

ah /ɑː/. **Ah** is used in writing to represent a noise that people make in conversation, for example to acknowledge or draw attention to something, or to express surprise or disappointment. *Ah, this seems to be the train now.* ◆◆◆◇◇ EXCLAM PRAGMATICS

aha /ɑː'hɑː/. **Aha** is used in writing to represent a noise that people make in conversation, for example to acknowledge something, or to express satisfaction, triumph, or surprise. *'That's more than a half year away.'—'Aha, very true.'... Aha! Here at last, the answer to the question that has baffled scholars.* EXCLAM PRAGMATICS

ahead 1 adverb uses

ahead /ə'hed/. **1** Something that is **ahead** is in front of you. If you look **ahead**, you look directly in front of you. *Brett looked straight ahead... The road ahead was now blocked solid... Ahead, he saw the side railings of First Bridge.* **2** You use **ahead** with verbs such as 'push', 'move', and 'forge' to indicate that a plan, scheme, or organization is making fast progress. *Now BBC World Televi-* ◆◆◆◇ ADV · ADV: ADV after v

sion is forging ahead on its own. **3** If you are **ahead** in your work or achievements, you have made more progress than you expected and are performing well. *Troops are withdrawing from the country ahead of schedule... Children in small classes were 1.5 months ahead in reading.* **4** If a person or a team is **ahead** in a competition, they are winning. *A goal would have put Dublin 6-1 ahead... Clinton was ahead in the polls.* **5 Ahead** means in the future. *A much bigger battle is ahead for the president... Now I can remember without mourning, and begin to look ahead. ...the days ahead.* **6** If you prepare or plan something **ahead**, you do it some time before a future event so that everything is ready for that event to take place. *Book ahead as the restaurant is very popular.* **7** If you go **ahead**, or if you go on **ahead**, you go in front of someone who is going to the same place so that you arrive there some time before they do. *I'd have to send Tina on ahead with Rachael.* ADV · ADV · ADV: ADV after v · ADV: ADV after v

ahead 2 preposition uses

a'head of. 1 If someone or something is **ahead of** you, they are in front of you and often fairly distant from you. *I saw a man in a blue jacket thirty metres ahead of me... She walked ahead of Helene up the steps.* **2** If an event or period of time lies **ahead of** you, it is going to happen or come soon or in the future. *I tried to think about all the problems that were ahead of me... We have a very busy day ahead of us.* **3** If something happens **ahead of** an event or time, it happens before that event or time. *The Prime Minister was speaking ahead of today's meeting.* **4** If something happens **ahead of** schedule or **ahead of** time, it happens earlier than was planned. *The election was held six months ahead of schedule.* **5** In a competition, if a person or team does something **ahead of** someone else, they do it before the second person or team. *Robert Millar finished 1 minute and 35 seconds ahead of the Frenchman.* **6** If someone is **ahead of** someone else, they have made more progress and are more advanced in what they are doing. *Henry generally stayed ahead of the others in the academic subjects.* **7** ● **one step ahead**: see **step.** ● **ahead of** one's **time**: see **time.** ◆◆◇◇ PHR-PREP · PHR-PREP · PHR-PREP · PHR-PREP · PHR-PREP · PHR-PREP

ahem; usually pronounced as two short coughs. Writers put **ahem** to show that a speaker is about to say something difficult, embarrassing, or amusing, or something that is not exactly true or accurate. *It is not unknown for valuable display items to go, ahem, missing.* CONVENTION PRAGMATICS

ahold /ə'həʊld/. If you **get ahold of** someone or something, you manage to contact, find, or get them. *I tried again to get ahold of my cousin Joan, and I got her on the phone.* PHRASE AMERICAN

ahoy /ə'hɔɪ/. **Ahoy** is a call used to attract attention by people in boats. EXCLAM PRAGMATICS

AI /ˌeɪ 'aɪ/. **AI** is an abbreviation for **artificial intelligence**, or **artificial insemination**. N-UNCOUNT

aid /eɪd/ **aids, aiding, aided. 1** Aid is money, equipment, or services that are provided for people or countries who need them. ...*regular flights carrying humanitarian aid to Cambodia... They have already pledged billions of dollars in aid.* **2** To **aid** a country, organization, or person means to provide them with money, equipment, or services that they need. ...*US efforts to aid Kurdish refugees.* ♦ **-aided** ...*grant-aided factories. ...state-aided schools.* **3** To **aid** someone means to help or assist them. ...*a software system to aid managers in advanced decision-making.* ▶ Also a noun. *He was forced to turn for aid to his former enemy.* **4** If you perform a task with the **aid** of something, you use it to perform that task. *He succeeded with the aid of a completely new method... Gently raise your upper body to a sitting position, without the aid of your hands.* **5** An **aid** is an object, device, or technique that makes something easier to do. *The book is an invaluable aid to teachers of literature... The company specialises in computer aids for disabled people.* **6** If something **aids** a process, ◆◆◆◆ N-UNCOUNT · VERB: V n · COMB · VERB: V n · Also V n to-inf WRITTEN · N-UNCOUNT · N-UNCOUNT · N-COUNT · VERB

it makes it easier or more likely to happen. *The export sector will continue to aid the economic recovery... Calcium may aid in the prevention of colon cancer.* `V n` `V in n/-ing`

7 An activity or event **in aid of** a particular cause or charity is intended to raise money for that cause or charity. *...a charity performance in aid of Great Ormond Street Children's Hospital.* **8** If you **come** or **go to** someone's **aid**, you try to help them when they are in danger or difficulty. *Horrified neighbours rushed to his aid as he fell.* `PHRASE` `BRITISH` `PHRASE`

9 See also **Band-aid, first aid, hearing aid, legal aid**.

aide /eɪd/ **aides.** An **aide** is an assistant to someone who has an important job. *...a close aide to the Prime Minister.* `◆◇◇◇` `N-COUNT`

aide-de-camp /ˌeɪd də 'kɒm/ **aides-de-camp.** An **aide-de-camp** is an officer in the armed forces who helps an officer of higher rank. `N-COUNT`

aide-memoire /ˌeɪd 'memwaː/ **aide-memoires.** An **aide-memoire** is something such as a list that you use to remind you of something. `N-COUNT`

AIDS /eɪdz/. **AIDS** is a disease which destroys the natural system of protection that the body has against other diseases. **AIDS** is an abbreviation for **acquired immune deficiency syndrome**. `◆◆◆◇` `N-UNCOUNT`

ailer·on /'eɪlərɒn/ **ailerons.** An **aileron** is a flap on the back edge of the wing of an aeroplane that can be raised or lowered in order to control the plane's movement. `N-COUNT`

ail·ing /'eɪlɪŋ/. **1** An **ailing** organization is in difficulty and is becoming weaker. *...the ailing American economy.* **2** If someone is **ailing**, they are ill and are not getting better. `◆◇◇◇` `ADJ` `ADJ`

ail·ment /'eɪlmənt/ **ailments.** An **ailment** is an illness or disease. `◆◇◇◇` `N-COUNT`

aim /eɪm/ **aims, aiming, aimed. 1** If you **aim** for something or **aim** to do something, you plan or hope to achieve it. *He said he would aim for the 100 metres world record. ...an appeal which aims to raise funds for children with special needs.* **2** The **aim** of something that you do is the purpose for which you do it or the result that it is intended to achieve. *The aim of the festival is to increase awareness of Hindu culture. ...a research programme that has largely failed to achieve its principal aims.* **3** If an action or plan **is aimed** at achieving something, it is intended or planned to achieve it. *The new measures are aimed at tightening existing sanctions.* `◆◆◆◇` `VERB` `V for/at n/-ing` `V to-inf` `N-COUNT` `V-PASSIVE` `be V-ed at n/-ing`

4 If your actions or remarks **are aimed** at a particular person or group, you intend that the person or group should notice them and be influenced by them. *His message was aimed at the undecided middle ground of Israeli politics. ...advertising aimed at children.* **5** If you **aim** a weapon or object **at** something or someone, you point it towards them before firing or throwing it. *He was aiming the rifle at Wade... I was supposed to aim at the same spot all the time.* **6** Your **aim** is your skill or action in pointing a weapon or other object at its target. *The jerk of the rope altered his aim and the bullet missed.* **7** When you **take aim**, you point a weapon or object at someone or something, before firing or throwing it. `VERB` `be V-ed at n` `V-ed` `Also V n` `VERB` `V n at n` `V at n` `Also V` `N-SING` `PHRASE`

8 If you **take aim at** someone or something, you criticize them strongly. *Holden took particular aim at the Green Party candidate.* `PHRASE` `AMERICAN`

aim·less /'eɪmləs/. A person or activity that is **aimless** has no clear purpose or plan. *...several hours of aimless searching.* ◆ **aim·less·ly** *I wandered around aimlessly.* ◆ **aim·less·ness** *His sense of aimlessness increased.* `◆◇◇◇` `ADJ-GRADED` `ADV-GRADED:` `ADV after v` `N-UNCOUNT`

ain't /eɪnt/. **Ain't** is used in some dialects of English instead of 'am not', 'aren't', 'isn't', 'haven't', and 'hasn't'. *'It's obvious, ain't it?... I ain't got kids.* `◆◆◇◇` `SPOKEN`

air /eə/ **airs, airing, aired. 1** **Air** is the mixture of gases which forms the earth's atmosphere and which we breathe. *Draughts help to circulate air... Keith opened the window and leaned out into the cold air.* **2** If someone or something disappears **into thin air**, they disappear completely. If someone or something appears **out of thin air**, they appear suddenly and mysteriously. **3** If you say that you are `◆◆◆◆◆` `N-UNCOUNT` `PHRASE` `PHRASE`

walking on air, you mean that you feel extremely happy because of something. **4** **The air** is the space around things or above the ground. *Government troops broke up the protest by firing their guns in the air.* **5** If you do something to **clear the air**, you do it in order to get rid of any misunderstandings that there might be. *...an inquiry just to clear the air and settle the facts of the case.* **6** If something is **in the air** it is felt to be present, but it is not talked about. *There was great excitement in the air.* **7** If you say that a decision or a situation is **up in the air**, you mean that it has not yet been completely settled or planned. *The president's trip to Moscow is up in the air.* `N-SING:` `the N` `PHRASE` `PHRASE` `PHRASE`

8 **Air** is used to refer to travel in aircraft. *...air travel. ...a mysterious letter addressed to me and sent by air.* `N-UNCOUNT`

9 An **air** is a simple or traditional tune. `N-COUNT`

10 If someone or something has a particular **air**, they give this general impression. *...regarding him with an air of faint amusement... The meal gave the occasion an almost festive air.* `N-SING:` `with supp`

11 If a broadcasting company **airs** a television or radio programme, they show it on television or broadcast it on the radio. *TV station KCCO aired a story recently on teenage drinking.* ◆ **air·ing** *...his university could not tolerate the airing of this material.* **12** If you **air** your opinions, you make them known to people. *Both sides agreed they had aired all their differences.* ◆ **airing** *Their views would at long last get an airing.* `VERB` `V n` `AMERICAN` `N-SING` `VERB` `V n` `N-SING:` `a N` `PHRASE`

13 If someone is **on the air**, they are broadcasting on radio or television. If a programme is **on the air**, it is being broadcast on radio or television. If it is **off the air**, it is not being broadcast. *The programme went off the air.*

14 If you **air** a room or building, you let fresh air into it. *Her mother systematically cleaned and aired each room.* **15** If you **air** clothing, you put it somewhere warm to make sure that it is completely dry. `VERB` `V n` `VERB: V n`

16 If you refer to someone's **airs and graces**, you mean that they behave in a way that shows that they think they are more important than other people; used showing disapproval. *She lacks the airs and graces many successful actresses have.* `PHRASE` `PRAGMATICS` `BRITISH`

air·bag /'eəbæg/ **airbags;** also spelled **air bag**. An **airbag** is a safety device in a car which inflates automatically if the car crashes, to protect people who are thrown forward. `N-COUNT`

'air base, air bases; also spelled **airbase**. An **air base** is a centre where military aircraft take off or land, and where many of the centre's staff live. `◆◇◇◇` `N-COUNT`

air·borne /'eəbɔːn/. **1** If an aircraft is **airborne**, it is flying in the air. *The pilot did manage to get airborne.* **2** **Airborne** troops use parachutes to get into enemy territory. **3** **Airborne** means in the air or carried in the air. *...airborne pollutants such as pollen.* `◆◇◇◇` `ADJ:` `v-link ADJ` `ADJ: ADJ n` `ADJ`

air·brush /'eəbrʌʃ/ **airbrushes, airbrushing, airbrushed. 1** An **airbrush** is an artist's tool which sprays paint onto a surface. **2** To **airbrush** a photograph or other image means to make improvements to it using an airbrush. `N-COUNT` `VERB: V n`

Air·bus /'eəbʌs/ **Airbuses.** An **Airbus** is an aeroplane which is designed to carry a large number of passengers for fairly short distances. **Airbus** is a trademark. `N-COUNT`

,air-con'ditioned. If a room or vehicle is **air-conditioned**, the air in it is kept cool and dry by means of a special machine. `◆◇◇◇` `ADJ`

,air-con'ditioner, air-conditioners; also spelled **air conditioner**. An **air-conditioner** is a machine which keeps the air in a building cool and dry. `N-COUNT`

,air-con'ditioning; also spelled **air conditioning**. **Air-conditioning** is a method of providing buildings and vehicles with cool dry air. `◆◇◇◇` `N-UNCOUNT`

air·craft /'eəkrɑːft, -kræft/ **aircraft** is both the singular and the plural form. An **aircraft** is a vehicle which can fly, for example an aeroplane or a helicopter. *Three military aircraft were destroyed.* `◆◆◆◇` `N-COUNT`

'aircraft carrier, aircraft carriers. An **aircraft carrier** is a warship with a long, flat deck where aircraft can take off and land. `◆◇◇◇` `N-COUNT`

air·crew /ˈeəkruː/ **aircrews;** also spelled **air crew.** N-COLL-COUNT The **aircrew** on a plane are the pilot and other people who are responsible for flying it and for looking after any passengers who are on it.

air-drop, air-drops, air-dropping, air-dropped; also spelled **air drop.** When a country or organization **air-drops** supplies to an area that is hard to get to, it delivers supplies there by dropping them from aircraft. ...*plans to start air dropping food to rural villages.* ► Also a noun. ...*an air drop of relief supplies into Bosnia.* VERB V n to/into n Also V n / N-COUNT

air·fare /ˈeəfeə/ **airfares.** The **airfare** to a place is N-COUNT the amount it costs to fly there.

air·field /ˈeəfiːəld/ **airfields.** An **airfield** is an area of ground where aircraft take off and land. It is smaller than an airport. ◆◇◇◇◇ N-COUNT

air force, air forces; also spelled **airforce.** An **air force** is the part of a country's armed forces concerned with fighting in the air. ...*the United States Air Force.* ◆◆◆◇◇ N-COUNT

air·frame /ˈeəfreɪm/ **airframes.** The **airframe** of an aircraft is its body excluding the engines. N-COUNT

air freshener, air fresheners. An **air freshener** N-VAR is a product which makes rooms smell pleasant.

air·gun /ˈeəɡʌn/ **airguns;** also spelled **air gun.** An N-COUNT **airgun** is a gun which fires using air pressure.

air·head /ˈeəhed/ **airheads.** If you call someone an **airhead,** you are criticizing them because you think they are stupid and interested in unimportant things. N-COUNT PRAGMATICS INFORMAL

air hostess, air hostesses. An **air hostess** is a N-COUNT woman who looks after passengers in an aircraft. BRITISH

airing cupboard, airing cupboards. An **airing** N-COUNT **cupboard** is a warm cupboard where you put BRITISH clothes or towels, to make sure they are completely dry.

air·less /ˈeələs/. If a place is **airless,** there is no ADJ-GRADED fresh air in it. ...*a dark, airless room.*

air·lift /ˈeəlɪft/ **airlifts, airlifting, airlifted. 1** An **airlift** is an operation to move people, troops, or goods by air, especially in a war or when land routes are closed. ...*an airlift of food, medicines and blankets.* **2** If people, troops, or goods **are airlifted** somewhere, they are carried by air, especially in a war or when land routes are closed. *The injured were airlifted to hospital in Prestwick.* ◆◆◇◇◇ N-COUNT / VERB be V-ed adv/prep Also V n

air·line /ˈeəlaɪn/ **airlines.** An **airline** is a company which provides regular services carrying people or goods in aeroplanes. ◆◆◆◇ N-COUNT

air·lin·er /ˈeəlaɪnə/ **airliners.** An **airliner** is a large aeroplane that is used for carrying passengers. ◆◇◇◇◇ N-COUNT

air·lock /ˈeəlɒk/ **airlocks;** also spelled **air lock.** An **airlock** is a compartment between places which do not have the same air pressure, for example in a spacecraft or submarine. N-COUNT

air·mail /ˈeəmeɪl/. **Airmail** is the system of sending N-UNCOUNT letters, parcels, and goods by air. ...*an airmail letter...* *Goods are generally shipped by airmail.*

air·man /ˈeəmæn/ **airmen.** An **airman** is a man who serves in his country's air force. ◆◇◇◇◇ N-COUNT

air·plane /ˈeəpleɪn/ **airplanes.** An **airplane** is a vehicle with wings and one or more engines that enable it to fly through the air. The usual British word is **aeroplane.** ◆◆◇◇◇ N-COUNT AMERICAN

air·play /ˈeəpleɪ/. The **airplay** which a piece of N-UNCOUNT popular music receives is the number of times it is played on the radio.

air·port /ˈeəpɔːt/ **airports.** An **airport** is a place where aircraft land and take off, which has buildings and facilities for passengers. ◆◆◆◆◇ N-COUNT

air power; also spelled **airpower.** A nation's **air power** is the strength of its air force. *The U.S. says it will use air power to protect the peacekeepers.* ◆◇◇◇◇ N-UNCOUNT

air raid, air raids. An **air raid** is an attack by military aircraft in which bombs are dropped. *The war began with overnight air raids on Baghdad and Kuwait.* ...*an underground air raid shelter.* ◆◇◇◇◇ N-COUNT

air rifle, air rifles. An **air rifle** is a rifle which fires N-COUNT using air pressure.

air·ship /ˈeəʃɪp/ **airships.** An **airship** is an aircraft that consists of a large balloon filled with gas with a compartment underneath for passengers. ◆◇◇◇◇ N-COUNT

air·show /ˈeəʃəʊ/ **airshows;** also spelled **air show.** An **airshow** is an event at which pilots entertain spectators by performing skilful aeroplane manoeuvres in the sky. N-COUNT

air·space /ˈeəspeɪs/; also spelled **air space.** A country's **airspace** is the part of the sky that is over that country and is considered to belong to it. *They left Colombian airspace.* N-UNCOUNT

air·speed /ˈeəspiːd/ **airspeeds;** also spelled **air speed.** An aircraft's **airspeed** is the speed at which it travels through the air. N-COUNT

air strike, air strikes. An **air strike** is an attack by military aircraft in which bombs are dropped. *A senior defence official said last night that they would continue the air strikes.* ◆◇◇◇◇ N-COUNT

air·strip /ˈeəstrɪp/ **airstrips.** An **airstrip** is a stretch of land which has been cleared so that aircraft can take off and land. *We landed on a grass airstrip.* ◆◇◇◇◇ N-COUNT

air·tight /ˈeətaɪt/. If a container is **airtight,** its lid ADJ fits so tightly that no air can get in or out.

air time; also spelled **airtime.** The **air time** that N-UNCOUNT something gets is the amount of television or radio time that is spent on it. *Even the best women's teams get little air time... They devoted their entire airtime to covering the storm.*

air-to-air. Air-to-air combat is a battle between ADJ: ADJ n military aeroplanes where rockets or bullets are fired at one aeroplane from another. ...*air-to-air missiles.*

air traffic con'trol. 1 Air traffic control is the N-UNCOUNT activity of controlling aircraft by radio from the ground in order to avoid collisions, especially when the aircraft are landing or taking off. ...*the nation's overburdened air traffic control system.* **2 Air traffic control** is the group of people on the ground who control aircraft by radio in order to avoid collisions. N-COLL-UNCOUNT

air traffic con'troller, air traffic controllers. An **air traffic controller** is someone whose job is to control aircraft by radio from the ground in order to avoid collisions. ◆◇◇◇◇ N-COUNT

air·waves /ˈeəweɪvz/. If someone says something over the **airwaves** or on the **airwaves,** they say it on the radio or television. ◆◇◇◇◇ N-PLURAL JOURNALISM

air·way /ˈeəweɪ/ **airways. 1 Airways** is used in the name of some airlines. ...*British Airways.* **2** A person's **airways** are the passages from their nose and mouth down to their lungs, through which air enters and leaves their body. ◆◇◇◇◇ N-COUNT MEDICAL

air·woman /ˈeəwʊmən/ **airwomen.** An **airwoman** N-COUNT is a woman who serves in her country's air force.

air·worthy /ˈeəwɜːði/. If an aircraft is **airworthy,** it ADJ-GRADED is safe to fly. *The mechanics try to keep the helicopters airworthy.*

airy /ˈeəri/ **airier, airiest. 1** If a building or room is **airy,** it has plenty of fresh air inside. *The bathroom has a light and airy feel.* **2** You can use **airy** to describe someone's behaviour when they are lighthearted and casual about things which some people take seriously. ...*an airy wave of his hand.* ♦ **airi·ly** /ˈeərɪli/ *'It'll be all right,' he said airily.* ◆◇◇◇◇ ADJ-GRADED / ADJ-GRADED: ADJ n / ADV-GRADED: ADV with v

airy-'fairy. If you describe someone's ideas as **airy-fairy,** you are criticizing them because you think they are vague, impractical, and unrealistic. ADJ-GRADED PRAGMATICS BRITISH

aisle /aɪl/ **aisles. 1** An **aisle** is a long narrow gap that people can walk along between rows of seats in a public building such as a church, or between rows of shelves in a supermarket. ...*the frozen food aisle.* **2 The aisle** is used in expressions such as **walking down the aisle** to refer to the act of getting married. *He was in no hurry to walk down the aisle.* ◆◇◇◇◇ N-COUNT / N-SING: the N

ajar /əˈdʒɑː/. If a door is **ajar,** it is slightly open. *He left the door ajar.* ADJ: v-link ADJ

aka. aka is an abbreviation for 'also known as'; it is used especially when referring to a nickname or stage name. ...*Stuart Leslie Goddard, aka Adam Ant.* ◆◇◇◇◇

akim·bo /ə'kɪmbəʊ/. If you stand **arms akimbo**, PHRASE DATED
you stand with your hands on your hips and your
elbows pointing outwards.

akin /ə'kɪn/. If one thing is **akin** to another, it is ◆◇◇◇◇
similar to it in some way. *The journey will be more* v-link ADJ to n
akin to air travel than to a conventional train. FORMAL

à la /'ɑː lɑː/. If you do something **à la** a particular PHR-PREP
person, you do it in the style or in the way that they
would do it. *Choose a crisp, tailored dress à la*
Audrey Hepburn.

ala·bas·ter /'æləbɑːstə, -bæs-/. **Alabaster** is a white N-UNCOUNT
stone that is used for making statues, vases, and ornaments. *...alabaster figures of maidens.*

à la carte /ˌɑː lɑː 'kɑːt/. An **à la carte** menu in a ADJ: ADJ n
restaurant offers you a selection of individually
priced dishes for each course. ▶ Also an adverb. ADV:
When eating à la carte, expect to pay £60 for two. ADV after v

alac·rity /ə'lækrɪti/. If you do something with **alac-** N-UNCOUNT
rity, you do it quickly and eagerly. *I accepted with* FORMAL
alacrity.

alarm /ə'lɑːm/ **alarms, alarming, alarmed.** ◆◆◆◇◇
1 Alarm is a feeling of fear or anxiety that some- N-UNCOUNT
thing unpleasant or dangerous might happen. *She*
sat up in alarm... The moves reflect growing alarm
over recent events. **2** If something **alarms** you, it VERB: V n
makes you afraid or anxious that something un-
pleasant or dangerous might happen. ◆ **alarmed** ADJ-GRADED
They should not be too alarmed by the press re-
ports... The Americans are alarmed at this prospect.
◆ **alarm·ing** *...the alarming increase in crime.* ADJ-GRADED
◆ **alarm·ing·ly** *...the alarmingly high rate of heart* ADV-GRADED
disease.
3 An **alarm** is an automatic device that warns you of N-COUNT
danger, for example by ringing a bell. *He heard the*
alarm go off. ...an extremely sophisticated alarm sys-
tem. **4** An **alarm** is the same as an **alarm clock**. **5** See N-COUNT
also **burglar alarm, false alarm, fire alarm.**
6 If you say that something sets **alarm bells** ringing, PHRASE
you mean that it makes people feel worried or concerned about something. *Alarm bells are beginning to*
sound at Westminster. **7** If you **raise the alarm** or PHRASE
sound the alarm, you warn people of danger. *A neigh-*
bour raised the alarm after hearing the shots.

a'larm clock, alarm clocks. An **alarm clock** is a N-COUNT
clock that you can set to make a noise so that it
wakes you up at a particular time. *I set my alarm*
clock for 4.30.

alarm·ist /ə'lɑːmɪst/. You use **alarmist** to describe ADJ-GRADED
someone or something that causes unnecessary fear
or anxiety. *The change is not as dramatic as some of*
the more alarmist reports would have us believe.

alas /ə'læs/. You use **alas** to say that you think that ◆◇◇◇◇
the facts you are talking about are sad, unfortunate, ADV:
or regrettable. *Alas, it's not that simple.* ADV with cl
PRAGMATICS

al·ba·tross /'ælbətrɒs, AM -trɔːs/ **albatrosses.** ◆◇◇◇◇
1 An **albatross** is a very large black and white N-COUNT
seabird. **2** If you describe something or someone as N-COUNT
an **albatross** around your neck, you mean that they
cause you great problems from which you cannot
escape. *Privatization could become a political alba-*
tross for the ruling Tories.

al·be·it /ɔːl'biːɪt/. You use **albeit** to introduce a fact ◆◆◇◇◇
or comment which reduces the force or significance ADV:
of what you have just said. *Charles's letter was in-* ADV with cl/
deed published, albeit in a somewhat abbreviated group
form. PRAGMATICS
FORMAL

al·bi·no /æl'biːnəʊ, AM -'baɪn-/ **albinos.** An **albino** N-COUNT
is a person or animal with very white skin, white
hair, and pink eyes. ▶ Also an adjective. *...albino* ADJ: ADJ n
deer.

al·bum /'ælbəm/ **albums. 1** An **album** is a CD, rec- ◆◆◇◇◇
ord, or cassette with about an hour's worth of music N-COUNT
on it, usually in several different tracks. *...Terence*
Trent D'Arby's new album 'Symphony Or Damn'.
2 An **album** is a book in which you keep things N-COUNT
such as photographs or stamps that you have collected. *Theresa showed me her photo album.*

al·bu·min /'ælbjʊmɪn, AM æl'bjuːmɪn/. **Albumin** is a N-UNCOUNT
protein that is found in blood plasma, egg white,
and some other substances.

al·che·my /'ælkəmi/. **1 Alchemy** was a form of N-UNCOUNT
chemistry studied in the Middle Ages, which was
concerned with trying to discover ways to change
ordinary metals into gold. ◆ **al·chemi·cal** ADJ: ADJ n
/æl'kemɪkəl/ *...alchemical experiments.* ◆ **al·che-**
mist, /'ælkəmɪst/ **alchemists.** An **alchemist** was N-COUNT
a person who practised alchemy. **2 Alchemy** is the N-UNCOUNT
power to change or create things in a way which LITERARY
seems mysterious or magical. *By some mysterious*
alchemy it was hoped to fulfil all three objectives.

al·co·hol /'ælkəhɒl, AM -hɔːl/ **alcohols. 1** Drinks ◆◆◆◇◇
that can make people drunk, such as beer, wine, N-UNCOUNT
and whisky, can be referred to as **alcohol**. *Do either*
of you smoke cigarettes or drink alcohol? **2 Alcohol** N-VAR
is a colourless liquid that is found in drinks such as
beer, wine, and whisky. It is also used in products
such as perfumes and cleaning fluids.

al·co·hol·ic /ˌælkə'hɒlɪk, AM -'hɔːl-/ **alcoholics.** ◆◆◇◇◇
1 An **alcoholic** is someone who cannot stop drink- N-COUNT
ing large amounts of alcohol, even when this is
making them ill. ◆ **al·co·hol·ism** /'ælkəhɒlɪzəm/. N-UNCOUNT
His sister died two years ago as a result of alcohol-
ism. **2 Alcoholic** drinks contain alcohol. ADJ-GRADED

al·cove /'ælkəʊv/ **alcoves.** An **alcove** is a small ◆◇◇◇◇
area of a room which is formed by one part of a wall N-COUNT
being built further back than the rest of the wall.

al den·te /æl 'denteɪ/. If you cook pasta or a vegeta- ADJ
ble until it is **al dente**, you cook it just long enough
so that it is neither hard nor soft but is firm and
slightly chewy.

al·der /'ɔːldə/ **alders.** An **alder** is a tree or shrub N-VAR
that grows in Northern temperate areas, often in
damp places. It has cones, and its leaves have small
points along the edges.

al·der·man /'ɔːldəmən/ **aldermen. 1** In the United N-COUNT;
States and Canada, an **alderman** is a member of the N-TITLE
governing body of a city. **2** In England and Wales,
an **alderman** is a senior or honoured member of a N-TITLE
local council.

ale /eɪl/ **ales. Ale** is the same as **beer**. *...our selec-* ◆◇◇◇◇
tion of ales and spirits. ● See also **ginger ale, real** N-VAR
ale.

alec /'ælɪk/ **alecs.** See **smart alec.**

aleck /'ælɪk/ **alecks.** See **smart alec.**

alert /ə'lɜːt/ **alerts, alerting, alerted. 1** If you ◆◆◆◇◇
are **alert**, you are paying full attention to things ADJ-GRADED
around you and are able to deal with anything that
might happen. *We all have to stay alert... He had*
been spotted by an alert neighbour. ◆ **alert·ness** N-UNCOUNT
The drug improved mental alertness. **2** If you are ADJ-GRADED:
alert to something, you are fully aware of it. *The* v-link ADJ to n
bank is alert to the danger.
3 If you **alert** someone to a dangerous or unpleasant VERB
situation, you tell them about it. *He wanted to alert* V n to n
people to the activities of the group... I was hoping he'd V n
alert the police. **4** An **alert** is a situation in which peo- N-COUNT
ple prepare themselves for something dangerous that
might happen soon. *Due to a security alert, this train*
will not be stopping at Oxford Circus. **5** See also **red**
alert.
6 If soldiers or police are on **alert**, they are ready to PHRASE
deal with anything that may happen. *Police have been*
put on alert. **7** If you are on the **alert** for something, PHRASE
you are ready to deal with it if it happens. *They want to*
be on the alert for similar buying opportunities.

A lev·el /'eɪ levəl/ **A levels. A levels** are British ◆◆◇◇◇
educational qualifications which schoolchildren N-VAR
take when they are seventeen or eighteen years old.
He left school with four A levels.

al·fal·fa /æl'fælfə/. **Alfalfa** is a plant that is used for N-UNCOUNT
feeding farm animals. The shoots that develop from
its seeds are sometimes eaten as a vegetable.

al·fres·co /æl'freskəʊ/; also spelled **al fresco**. An **al-**
fresco activity, especially a meal, takes place in the ADJ: ADJ n
open air. *...a wonderful al fresco breakfast.* ▶ Also ADV:
an adverb. *He came across the man shaving alfresco.* ADV after v

al·gae /'ældʒiː, 'ælgaɪ/. **Algae** is a type of plant with ◆◇◇◇◇
no stems or leaves that grows in water or on damp N-COLL-
surfaces. UNCOUNT

al·gal /ˈælgəl/. **Algal** means relating to algae. *...algal growth in the harbour.* ADJ: ADJ n

al·ge·bra /ˈældʒɪbrə/. **Algebra** is a type of mathematics in which letters are used to represent quantities. ♦ **al·ge·bra·ic** /ˌældʒɪˈbreɪɪk/ *...algebraic equations.* N-UNCOUNT

ADJ: ADJ n

al·go·rithm /ˈælgərɪðəm/ **algorithms.** An **algorithm** is a series of mathematical steps, especially in a computer programme, which will give you the answer to a particular kind of problem or question. N-COUNT

alia /ˈeɪliə/. See **inter alia**.

ali·as /ˈeɪliəs/ **aliases. 1** An **alias** is a false name, especially one used by a criminal. **2** You use **alias** when you are mentioning another name that someone, especially a criminal or an actor, is known by. *...Richard Thorp, alias Alan Turner.* N-COUNT PREP

ali·bi /ˈælɪbaɪ/ **alibis.** If you have an **alibi**, you can prove that you were somewhere else when a crime was committed. *The police had a suspect but he later proved to have an alibi.* N-COUNT

al·ien /ˈeɪliən/ **aliens. 1 Alien** is used to describe someone or something that belongs to a different country, race, group, or culture. This use usually indicates disapproval, and is considered offensive by some people. *They were opposed to what he described as the presence of alien forces in the region. ...alone in an alien culture.* **2** An **alien** is someone who is not a legal citizen of the country in which they live. *When war broke out, he was interned as an enemy alien.* **3** If something is **alien** to you or to your normal feelings or behaviour, it is not the way you would normally feel or behave. *Such an attitude is alien to most businessmen.* **4** In science fiction, an **alien** is a creature from outer space.
ADJ PRAGMATICS
N-COUNT LEGAL
ADJ-GRADED: v-link ADJ to n
N-COUNT

al·ien·ate /ˈeɪliəneɪt/ **alienates, alienating, alienated.** If you **alienate** someone such as a friend or ally, you cause them to lose their friendly relationship or contact with you. *The government cannot afford to alienate either group... Gambling was alienating me from anyone who'd ever loved me.* ♦ **al·ien·at·ed** *He felt alienated from his peers.* ♦ **al·iena·tion** /ˌeɪliəˈneɪʃən/. *...her sense of alienation from the world.*
VERB
V n
V n from n
ADJ-GRADED
N-UNCOUNT

alight /əˈlaɪt/ **alights, alighting, alighted. 1** If something is **alight**, it is burning. *Several buildings were set alight.* **2** If someone's eyes are **alight** or if their face is **alight**, the expression in their eyes or on their face shows that they are feeling a strong emotion such as excitement or happiness. *Her eyes were alight with a girlish enjoyment of life.* **3** If a bird or insect **alights** somewhere, it lands there. *A thrush alighted on a branch of the pine tree. ...a bee alights on a flower.* **4** When you **alight** from a train, bus, or other vehicle, you get out of it after a journey. *Two men alighted from the vehicle.* **5** If someone **alights** on something, they suddenly see it, think of it, or take an interest in it. *He would then suddenly alight on the tune he really wanted to play.*
ADJ: v n ADJ, v-link ADJ
ADJ: v-link ADJ
VERB
V prep/adv
LITERARY
VERB
V prep/adv
FORMAL
VERB
V on/upon n
LITERARY

align /əˈlaɪn/ **aligns, aligning, aligned. 1** If you **align** yourself with a particular group, you support them because you have the same political aim. *There have been signs that the prime minister is aligning himself with the liberals.* ♦ **align·ment, alignments** *He refused to compromise the church by a particular political alignment.* **2** If you **align** something, you place it in a precise position in relation to something else. *Keep the rough edge of the fabric aligned with the raw edge of the piping.*
VERB
V pron-refl
prep
N-VAR
VERB
V-ed
Also V n prep

align·ment /əˈlaɪnmənt/. The **alignment** of something is its position in relation to something else or to its correct position. *...the belief that there is a link between the alignment of the planets and events on the Earth.* ● See also **align**.
N-UNCOUNT

alike /əˈlaɪk/. **1** If two or more things are **alike**, they are similar in some way. *We looked very alike.* ▶ Also an adverb. *...their assumption that all men and women think alike.* **2** You use **alike** after mentioning two or more people, groups, or things in order to emphasize that you are referring to both or
ADJ-GRADED:
v-link ADJ
ADV-GRADED
ADV after v
ADV:
n and n ADV
PRAGMATICS

all of them. *The techniques are being applied almost everywhere by big and small firms alike.* **3** See also **look-alike**.

ali·mo·ny /ˈælɪməni, AM -məʊni/. **Alimony** is money that a court of law orders someone to pay to their former wife or husband after they have got divorced. This money is sometimes paid in regular amounts and sometimes as a single large amount.
N-UNCOUNT

alive /əˈlaɪv/. **1** If people or animals are **alive**, they are living. *They kept her alive on a life support machine.* **2** If an activity, organization, or situation is **alive**, it continues to exist or function. *The big factories are trying to stay alive by cutting costs.* **3** If you say that someone or something is **alive and well**, you are emphasizing that they continue to survive. *A Yorkshire farmer who went missing yesterday during a blizzard has been found alive and well.* **4** If you say that someone or something is **alive and kicking**, you are emphasizing not only that they continue to survive, but also that they are very active. *There are growing worries that the secret police may still be alive and kicking.* **5** If you say that someone seems **alive**, you mean that they seem to be very lively and to enjoy everything that they do. *I never expected to feel so alive in my life again.* **6** If a place is **alive** with something, there are a lot of people or things there and it seems busy or exciting. *The street was alive with the sounds of the soldiers.* **7** If people, places, or events **come alive**, or something **brings** them **alive**, they start to be active or lively again after a quiet or dull period. *...the songs of birds that bring the garden alive.* **8** If a story or description **comes alive**, it becomes interesting, lively, or realistic. If someone or something **brings** it **alive**, they cause it to seem alive. **9** If you are **alive** to a situation or problem, you are aware of it and realize how important it is. *He was fully alive to the danger represented by the movement.* **10** If you say that someone **will be eaten alive**, you mean that they will find it very difficult to deal with a group of people because they lack experience or confidence. *Sid would be eaten alive by the hardened criminals in the jail.*
ADJ: v-link ADJ, ADJ-GRADED: v-link ADJ
PHRASE PRAGMATICS
PHRASE PRAGMATICS
ADJ-GRADED
ADJ
PHRASE
PHRASE
ADJ: v-link ADJ to n/wh
PHRASE INFORMAL

al·ka·li /ˈælkəlaɪ/ **alkalis.** An **alkali** is a substance with a pH value of more than 7. Alkalis form chemical salts when they are combined with acids. ♦ **al·ka·line** *Many shrubs prefer a neutral or alkaline soil.*
N-VAR
ADJ-GRADED

all /ɔːl/. **1** You use **all** to indicate that you are referring to the whole of a particular group or thing or to everyone or everything of a particular kind. *This anger twisted all his later relationships... President Bush will need all his skill in the coming weeks to carry American public opinion with him.* ▶ Also a determiner. *There is built-in storage space in all bedrooms.* ▶ Also a quantifier. *He was told to pack up all of his letters and personal belongings... He was talking to all of us.* ▶ Also a pronoun. *I'd spent all I had, every last penny... Milk, oily fish and egg all contain vitamin D... We all admire professionalism and dedication.* **2** You use **all** to refer to the whole of a period of time. *George had to cut grass all afternoon.* ▶ Also a predeterminer. *She's worked all her life... He was looking at me all the time.* **3** You use **all** to refer to a situation or to life in general. *All is silent on the island now... All has not been well of late.* **4** You use **all** to emphasize that something is completely true, or happens everywhere or always. *I got scared and I ran and left her all alone. ...universities all round the world.* **5** You use **all** at the beginning of a clause when you are emphasizing that something is the only thing that is important. *All you ever want to do is go shopping!... All I could say was, 'I'm sorry'.* **6** You use **all** in expressions such as **in all sincerity** and **in all probability** when you are emphasizing that you are being sincere or that something is very probable. *In all fairness he had to admit that she was neither dishonest nor lazy.* **7 All** is used in structures such as **all the more** or **all the better** to mean even more or
PREDET
DET
QUANT
PRON
DET
PREDET
PRON
PRON
ADV: ADV prep/adv PRAGMATICS
PRON PRAGMATICS
DET PRAGMATICS
ADV: ADV the adv/ adj-compar

even better than before. *The living room is decorated in pale colours that make it all the more airy.* **8** You use **all** in expressions such as **seen it all** and **done it all** to emphasize that someone has had a lot of experience of something. *Here's a man who has seen it all.* **9** You use **all** in front of an adjective when you want to emphasize a quality that affects someone or something temporarily. *You've gone all chatty... He came over all dizzy when he stood up.* PRON PRAGMATICS / ADV: v-link ADV adj-graded PRAGMATICS INFORMAL, BRITISH

10 You say **above all** to indicate that the thing you are mentioning is the most important point. *Above all, chairs should be comfortable.* **11** You use **after all** when introducing a statement which supports or helps to explain something that you have just said. *I thought you might know somebody. After all, you're the man with connections.* **12** You use **after all** when you are saying that something you thought might not be true is in fact true. *The Social Democrats say they are ready after all to begin talks on joining a coalition government.* PHRASE PRAGMATICS / PHRASE PRAGMATICS / PHRASE

13 You use **and all** when you want to emphasize that what you are talking about includes the thing mentioned, especially when this is surprising or unusual. *He dropped his sausage on the pavement and someone's dog ate it, mustard and all.* **14** You use **at all** at the end of a clause to give emphasis in negative statements, conditional clauses, and questions. *Robin never really liked him at all... Surely if the woman had any decency at all, she'd have withdrawn at once... Are you dizzy at all?* **15** You use **of all** to emphasize the words 'first' or 'last', or a superlative adjective or adverb. *First of all, answer these questions... Now she faces her toughest task of all.* **16** You use **of all** in expressions such as **of all people** or **of all things** when you want to emphasize someone or something surprising. *One group of women, sitting on the ground, was singing, of all things, 'Greensleeves'.* **17** You use **all** in expressions like **of all the cheek** or **of all the luck** to emphasize how angry or surprised you are at what someone else has done or said. *Of all the lazy, indifferent, unbusinesslike attitudes to have!* **18** You use **all** of before a number to emphasize how small or large an amount is. *It took him all of 41 minutes to score his first goal.* **19** You can say **that's all** at the end of a sentence when you are explaining something and want to emphasize how simple or brief your explanation is. *'Why do you want to know that?' he demanded.—'Just curious, that's all.'* PHRASE PRAGMATICS / PHRASE PRAGMATICS / PHRASE PRAGMATICS / PHRASE / PHRASE PRAGMATICS / PHRASE PRAGMATICS / PHRASE PRAGMATICS

20 In all means in total. *In all some 15 million people live in the selected areas... Thirteen people in all had taken part in planning the murder.* **21** You use **all in all** to introduce a summary or generalization. *All in all, it appeared that a pretty depressing summer awaited Jones.* PHRASE / PHRASE PRAGMATICS

22 All but a particular person or thing means everyone or everything except that person or thing. *The general was an unattractive man to all but his most ardent admirers... The plant will stand all but the worst winters out of doors.* **23** You use **all but** to say that something is almost the case. *The concrete wall that used to divide this city has now all but gone.* PHRASE / PHRASE

24 You use **for all** to indicate that the thing mentioned does not affect or contradict the truth of what you are saying. *For all its beauty, Prague could soon lose some of the individuality that the communist years helped to preserve.* **25** You use **for all** in phrases such as **for all I know**, and **for all he cares**, to emphasize that you don't know something or that something does not really matter to someone. *They chose to decide that Margaret was lying, and for all I know or care, they were right.* PHRASE / PHRASE PRAGMATICS

26 If you **give** your **all**, you make the maximum effort possible. PHRASE

27 If something such as an activity is a particular price **all in**, that price includes everything that is offered. *Dinner is about £25 all in.* PHRASE BRITISH

28 You use **all that** in statements with negative meaning when you want to weaken the force of what you are saying. *It doesn't work out to all that much per* PHRASE PRAGMATICS SPOKEN

hour... He said it would not be all that difficult to reach a peaceful conclusion to the conflict.

29 You use **all very well** in structures where you are suggesting that you do not really approve of something or think that it is unreasonable. *It is all very well to urge people to give more to charity when they have less, but is it really fair?* PHRASE PRAGMATICS

30 One and all means everyone present or everyone in a particular group. *Being in charge of the National Health Service reforms did not endear you to one and all.* PHRASE DATED

31 You use **all** when you are talking about an equal score in a game. For example, if the score is three **all**, both players or teams have three points. ADV: amount ADV

all- /ɔːl-/. **1 All-** is used to form adjectives which describe something as consisting only of the thing mentioned or as having only the quality indicated. *...an all-star cast... It is often very hard to compare all-male and all-female jobs.* **2 All-** is used to form adjectives which describe something as including or affecting everything or everyone. *Nursing a demented person is an all-consuming task... There are no all-embracing EC directives on race equality.* **3 All-** is used to form adjectives which describe something as being suitable for or including all types of a particular thing. *...an all-party government. ...jeans, the all-purpose denim trousers.* COMB / COMB / COMB

Allah /ˈælə, ˈælɑː/. **Allah** is the name of God in Islam. ◆◇◇◇◇ N-PROPER

all-A'merican. If you describe someone as an **all-American** boy or girl, you mean that they seem to have all the typical qualities that are valued by ordinary Americans, such as good looks and patriotism. *A wholesome all-American family.* ADJ: ADJ n

al·lay /əˈleɪ/ **allays, allaying, allayed.** If you **allay** someone's fears or doubts, you stop them feeling afraid or doubtful. ◆◇◇◇◇ VERB: V n FORMAL

all 'clear. 1 The all clear is a signal that a dangerous situation, for example an air raid, has ended. *The all clear was sounded about 10 minutes after the alert was given.* ► Someone can say '**all clear**' as a signal that a dangerous situation has ended. **2** If someone in authority gives you **the all clear**, they give you permission to continue with a plan or activity, usually after a problem has been sorted out. *I hope to be given the all clear to resume playing when I see the specialist in three weeks.* N-SING the N / CONVENTION / N-SING the N

'all-comers. See comer.

al·le·ga·tion /ˌælɪˈɡeɪʃən/ **allegations.** An allegation is a statement saying that someone has done something wrong. *The company has denied the allegations. ...allegations of brutality and theft.* ◆◆◆◇◇ N-COUNT

al·lege /əˈledʒ/ **alleges, alleging, alleged.** If you **allege** that someone has done something wrong, you say it but do not prove it. *She alleged that there was rampant drug use among the male members of the group... The accused is alleged to have killed a man... It was alleged that the restaurant discriminated against black customers.* ◆ **al·leged** *They have begun a hunger strike in protest at the alleged beating.* ◆ **al·leg·ed·ly** /əˈledʒɪdli/ *His van allegedly struck the two as they were crossing a street.* ◆◆◆◆◇ VERB V that be V-ed to-inf it be V-ed that Also V with quote FORMAL / ADJ: ADJ n / ADV

al·le·giance /əˈliːdʒəns/ **allegiances.** Your allegiance is your support for and loyalty to a particular group, person, or belief. *My allegiance to Kendall and his company ran deep.* ◆◇◇◇◇ N-VAR

al·le·go·ry /ˈælɪɡəri, AM -ɡɔːri/ **allegories.** An allegory is a story, poem, or painting in which the characters and events are symbols of something else. Allegories are often moral, religious, or political. *The book is a kind of allegory of Latin American history.* ◆ **al·le·gori·cal** /ˌælɪˈɡɒrɪkəl, AM -ˈɡɔːr-/ *...the allegorical interpretation of scripture.* N-COUNT / ADJ-GRADED

all-em'bracing. Something that is **all-embracing** includes or affects everyone or everything. *His hospitality was instantaneous and all-embracing.* ADJ-GRADED

al·ler·gen /ˈælədʒen/ **allergens.** An **allergen** is a substance that causes an allergic reaction. N-COUNT

al·ler·gic /ə'lɜːdʒɪk/. If you are **allergic** to something, or have an **allergic** reaction to something, you become ill or get a rash when you eat it, smell it, or touch it. ◆◇◇◇◇ ADJ

al·ler·gy /'ælədʒi/ **allergies.** If you have a particular **allergy**, you become ill or get a rash when you eat, smell, or touch something that does not normally make people ill. *Allergy to cats is one of the commonest causes of asthma. ...food allergies.* ◆◆◇◇◇ N-VAR

al·le·vi·ate /ə'liːviːeɪt/ **alleviates, alleviating, alleviated.** If you **alleviate** pain, suffering, or an unpleasant condition, you make it less intense or severe. *...the problem of alleviating mass poverty.* ◆◇◇◇◇ VERB V n FORMAL

♦ **al·le·vi·a·tion** /ə,liːviː'eɪʃən/ *...the alleviation of the refugees' misery.* N-UNCOUNT

al·ley /'æli/ **alleys.** An **alley** is a narrow passage or street with buildings or walls on both sides. ● See also **blind alley, bowling alley.** ◆◇◇◇◇ N-COUNT

alley·way /'æliweɪ/ **alleyways.** An **alleyway** is the same as an **alley.** ◆◇◇◇◇ N-COUNT

al·li·ance /ə'laɪəns/ **alliances.** An **alliance** is a relationship in which different countries, political parties, or organizations work together for some purpose. You can also refer to the group that is formed in this way as an **alliance.** *The two parties were still too much apart to form an alliance. ...a movement of professionals in alliance with progressive businessmen and politicians.* ◆◆◇◇◇ N-VAR

al·lied /'ælaɪd, AM ə'laɪd/. 1 **Allied** forces or troops are armies from different countries who are fighting on the same side in a war. *They're backed by allied warplanes and tanks.* 2 **Allied** countries, political parties, or groups are united by a formal agreement. *...forces from three allied nations. ...a think-tank allied to the right wing of the Democratic Party.* 3 If one thing or group is **allied** to another, it is related to it because the two things have particular qualities or characteristics in common. *...lectures on subjects allied to health, beauty and fitness. ...doctors, and allied medical professionals.* 4 Something that is **allied** to another thing occurs with the other thing. *...a disastrous rise in interest rates allied with a stock market slump.* 5 See also **ally.** ◆◆◇◇◇ ADJ: ADJ n / ADJ: ADJ n, v-link ADJ n / ADJ: v-link ADJ to/with n, ADJ n / ADJ: v-link ADJ to/with n

al·li·ga·tor /'ælɪgeɪtə/ **alligators.** 1 An **alligator** is a large reptile with short legs, a long tail and very powerful jaws. 2 **Alligator** boots and bags are made from the skin of an alligator. ◆◇◇◇◇ N-COUNT / ADJ

all-in'clusive. **All-inclusive** is used to indicate that a price, especially the price of a holiday, includes all the charges and all the services offered. *...an all-inclusive two-week holiday.* ADJ

al·lit·era·tion /ə,lɪtə'reɪʃən/ **alliterations.** **Alliteration** is the use in speech or writing of several words close together which all begin with the same letter or sound. N-VAR TECHNICAL

al·lo·cate /'æləkeɪt/ **allocates, allocating, allocated.** If one item or share of something is **allocated** to a particular person or for a particular purpose, it is given to that person or used for that purpose. *Tickets are limited and will be allocated to those who apply first... The 1985 federal budget allocated $7.3 billion for development programmes... Our plan is to allocate one member of staff to handle appointments.* ♦ **al·lo·ca·tion** /,ælə'keɪʃən/ **allocations.** *His sons quarrelled bitterly over the allocation of family resources... The allocation for Pakistan was still under review.* ◆◆◇◇◇ VERB be V-ed to n V n for/to n Also V n n, V n / N-VAR

al·lot /ə'lɒt/ **allots, allotting, allotted.** If something is **allotted** to someone, it is given to them as their share. *The seats are allotted to the candidates who have won the most votes... We were allotted half an hour to address the committee.* ♦ **al·lot·ment, allotments.** *His meager allotment of gas had to be saved for emergencies.* ◆◇◇◇◇ VB: usu passive be V-ed to n be V-ed to n / N-COUNT

al·lot·ment /ə'lɒtmənt/ **allotments.** 1 In Britain, an **allotment** is a small area of land which a person rents to grow vegetables on. 2 See also **allot.** ◆◇◇◇◇ N-COUNT

all-'out. You use **all-out** to describe actions that are carried out in a very energetic and determined way, using all the resources available. *...an all-out* ◆◇◇◇◇ ADJ: ADJ n

effort to bring the fire under control. ▶ Also an adverb. *We will be going all out to ensure it doesn't happen again.* ADV: ADV after v

al·low /ə'laʊ/ **allows, allowing, allowed.** 1 If someone **is allowed** to do something, it is all right for them to do it and they will not get into trouble. *The children are not allowed to watch violent TV programmes... They will be allowed home... Smoking will not be allowed.* 2 If you **are allowed** something, you are given permission to have it or are given it. *Gifts like chocolates or flowers are allowed... He should be allowed the occasional treat.* 3 If you **allow** something to happen, you do not prevent it. *He won't allow himself to fail... If the soil is allowed to dry out the tree could die.* 4 If something **allows** something to happen, it gives the opportunity for it to happen. *The compromise will allow him to continue his free market reforms... This would allow more effective planning.* 5 If you **allow** a particular length of time or a particular amount of something for a particular purpose, you include it in your planning. *Please allow 28 days for delivery... Allow about 75ml (3fl oz) per six servings.* 6 Some people say '**Allow me**' as a polite way of offering to do something for someone. *Allow me, Frau Bruckner.* 7 Some people use **Allow me to...** as a way of introducing something that they want to say. *Allow me to introduce Dr Amberg.* ◆◆◆◆◆ VERB be V-ed to-inf be V-ed adv/ prep be V-ed / VERB be V-ed n be V-ed n Also V n n / VERB V n to-inf / VERB V n to-inf . V n Also V n n / VERB V n for/per n Also V n / PHRASE PRAGMATICS FORMAL / PHRASE PRAGMATICS FORMAL

allow for. If you **allow for** certain problems or expenses, you include some extra time or money in your planning so that you can deal with them if they occur. *The Agency's budget simply did not allow for such a massive increase.* PHRASAL VB V P n

al·low·able /ə'laʊəbəl/. 1 If people decide that something is **allowable**, they let it happen without trying to stop it. 2 **Allowable** deductions or expenses are sums of money that are subtracted from your earnings before the amount of income tax that you have to pay is calculated. ADJ / ADJ TECHNICAL

al·low·ance /ə'laʊəns/ **allowances.** 1 An **allowance** is money that is given to someone, usually on a regular basis, in order to help them pay for the things that they need. *...the severe disablement allowance of £26.20 per week.* 2 A child's **allowance** is money that is given to him or her every week or every month by his or her parents. The usual British term is **pocket money.** 3 In Britain, your tax **allowance** is the amount of money that you are allowed to earn before you have to start paying income tax. 4 A particular type of **allowance** is an amount of something that you are allowed in particular circumstances. *Most of our flights have a baggage allowance of 44lbs per passenger.* 5 If you **make allowances** for something, you take it into account in your decisions, plans, or actions. *The raw exam results make no allowance for social background.* 6 If you **make allowances** for someone, you accept behaviour which you would not normally accept, or deal with them less severely than you would normally, because of a problem that they have. ◆◆◇◇◇ N-COUNT / N-COUNT AMERICAN / N-COUNT / N-COUNT: with supp / PHRASE / PHRASE

al·loy /'ælɔɪ/ **alloys.** An **alloy** is a metal that is made by mixing two or more types of metal together. *Bronze is an alloy of copper and tin.* ◆◇◇◇◇ N-VAR

all-'powerful. An **all-powerful** person or organization has the power to do anything they want. *...the all-powerful labour unions.* ADJ

all-'purpose. You use **all-purpose** to refer to things that have lots of different uses or can be used in lots of different situations. *You can substitute all-purpose flour if you cannot find pastry flour.* ADJ: ADJ n

all 'right; also spelled **alright.** 1 If you say that someone or something is **all right**, you mean that you find them satisfactory or acceptable. *I consider you a good friend, and if it's all right with you, I'd like to keep it that way... 'How was this school you attended?'—'It was all right.'* 2 If you say that something happens or goes **all right**, you mean that it happens in a satisfactory or acceptable manner. *Things have thankfully worked out all right... 'Can you walk all right?' the nurse asked him.* 3 If some- ◆◆◆◆◇ ADJ: v-link ADJ / ADV: ADV after v / ADJ:

one or something is **all right**, they are well or safe. *All she's worried about is whether he is all right... Are you feeling all right now?*

4 You say **'all right'** when you are agreeing to something. *'I think you should go now.'—'All right.'... 'I'll explain later.'—'All right then.'* **5** You say **'all right?'** after you have given an instruction or explanation to someone to check that they have understood what you have just said, or that they agree with or accept it. *Peter, you get half the fees. All right?... I'll see you tomorrow, all right?* **6** You say **'all right'** during a discussion to show that you understand something that someone has just said, and to introduce a statement that relates to it. *I said there was no room in my mother's house, and he said, 'All right, come to my studio and paint'.* **7** If someone in a position of authority says **'all right'**, and suggests talking about or doing something else, they are indicating that they want you to end one activity and start another. *All right, boys and girls, let's meet again next week.*

8 If you say that something is true **all right** or something will happen **all right**, you are emphasizing that there is no doubt that it is true or that it will happen. *It's an isolated spot all right... I remember him all right.*

,all-'rounder, all-rounders. Someone who is an **all-rounder** is good at a lot of different skills, academic subjects, or sports. *I class myself as an all-rounder and a team man at heart.*

,all-'seater. An **all-seater** stadium has enough seats for all the spectators who are in it, rather than having some areas where spectators stand to watch the match.

all-,singing, all-'dancing. If you describe something new as **all-singing, all-dancing**, you mean that it is very modern and advanced. *...an all-singing, all-dancing computer system.*

all·spice /'ɔːlspaɪs/. Allspice is a powder used as a spice in cooking.

'all-star. An **all-star** cast, performance, or game is one which contains only famous or extremely good performers or players.

,all-'time. **All-time** is used when you are comparing all the things of a particular type that there have ever been. For example, if you say that something is the **all-time** best, you mean that it is the best thing of its type that there has ever been. *The president's popularity nationally is at an all-time low.*

al·lude /ə'luːd/ **alludes, alluding, alluded.** If you **allude** to something, you mention it in an indirect way. *She sometimes alluded to a feeling that she herself was to blame.*

al·lure /ə'ljʊə, AM ə'lʊr/. The **allure** of something or someone is the pleasing or exciting quality that they have. *It's a game that has really lost its allure. ...the captivating allure of Isabelle Adjani.* ♦ **al·lur·ing** *...the most alluring city in South-East Asia.*

al·lu·sion /ə'luːʒən/ **allusions.** An **allusion** is an indirect reference to someone or something. *This last point was understood to be an allusion to the long-standing hostility between the two leaders.*

al·lu·sive /ə'luːsɪv/. **Allusive** speech, writing, or art is full of indirect references to people or things.

al·lu·vial /ə'luːviəl/. **Alluvial** soils are left behind on land which has been flooded or where a river once flowed.

ally, allies, allying, allied. The noun is pronounced /'ælaɪ/. The verb is pronounced /ə'laɪ/. **1** A country's **ally** is another country that has an agreement to support it, especially in war. *Washington would not take such a step without its allies' approval... Cuba has traditionally been a staunch ally of the Soviet Union.* **2** The **Allies** were the armed forces that fought against Germany and Japan in the Second World War.

3 If you describe someone as your **ally**, you mean that they help and support you, especially when other people are opposing you. *She will regret losing a close political ally.* **4** If you **ally** yourself with someone or

something, you give them your support. *He will have no choice but to ally himself with the new movement.* **5** See also **allied**.

alma ma·ter /ˌælmə 'mɑːtə, - 'meɪtə/ **alma maters.** Your **alma mater** is the school or university which you went to.

al·ma·nac /'ɔːlmənæk/ **almanacs;** also spelled **almanack.** An **almanac** is a book published every year which contains information about a variety of subjects, such as the dates of important events, or astronomical and astrological data.

al·ma·nack /'ɔːlmənæk/ **almanacks.** See **almanac.**

al·mighty /ɔːl'maɪti/. **1 The Almighty** is another name for God. You can also refer to **Almighty God. 2** People sometimes say **God Almighty** or **Christ Almighty** to express their surprise, anger, or horror. Some people are offended by this use. **3 Almighty** means very serious or great in extent. *I had the most almighty row with the waitress... I heard an almighty bang.*

al·mond /'ɑːmənd/ **almonds. Almonds** are pale oval nuts. They are often used in cooking.

al·most /'ɔːlməʊst/. You use **almost** to indicate that something is not completely the case but is nearly the case. *The couple had been dating for almost three years... He was almost as tall as Pete... He contracted Spanish flu, which almost killed him.*

alms /ɑːmz/. **Alms** are gifts of money, clothes, or food to poor people.

alms·house /'ɑːmzhaʊs/ **almshouses. Almshouses** are houses which were built and run by charities to provide accommodation for poor or old people who could not afford to pay rent.

aloe vera /ˌæləʊ 'vɪərə/. **Aloe vera** is a substance that contains a lot of vitamins and minerals and is often used in lotions, creams, and ointments. **Aloe vera** is also the name of the plant from which this substance is extracted.

aloft /ə'lɒft, AM ə'lɔːft/. Something that is **aloft** is in the air or off the ground. *They held their arms aloft before crowds of cheering well-wishers.*

alone /ə'ləʊn/. **1** When you are **alone**, you are not with any other people. *He was all alone in the middle of the hall.* ► Also an adverb. *She has lived alone in this house for almost five years now.* **2** If one person is **alone** with another person, or if two or more people are **alone**, they are together, without anyone else present. *I couldn't imagine why he would want to be alone with me... My brother and I were alone with Vincent.* **3** If you say that you are **alone** or feel **alone**, you mean that nobody is with you, or nobody at all cares about you. *Never in her life had she felt so alone, so abandoned.*

4 You say that one person or thing **alone** does something when you are emphasizing that only one person or thing is involved. *You alone should determine what is right for you.* **5** If you say that one person or thing **alone** is responsible for part of an amount, you are emphasizing the size of that part and the size of the total amount. *The BBC alone is sending 300 technicians, directors and commentators.* **6** If you say that someone or something is **alone** in doing something, you mean that they are the only person or thing that does it, and so are different from other people or things. *Am I alone in recognising that these two statistics have quite different implications?* ► Also an adverb. *Alone among the major candidates, Gaviria expressed a determination to continue the campaign.*

7 When someone does something **alone**, they do it without help from other people. *Bringing up a child alone should give you a sense of achievement.* **8** If you **go it alone**, you do something without any help from other people. *I missed the stimulation of working with others when I tried to go it alone.* ● **leave** someone or something **alone**: see **leave.** ● **let alone**: see **let.**

along /ə'lɒŋ, AM ə'lɔːŋ/. **1** If you move or look **along** something such as a road, you move or look towards one end of it. *Newman walked along the street alone... The young man led Mark Ryle along a*

corridor... I looked along the length of the building.
2 If something is situated **along** a road, river, or PREP
corridor, it is situated in it or beside it. ...houses
built on piles along the river... Along each wall
stretched green metal filing cabinets. **3** When some- ADV:
one or something moves **along**, they keep moving ADV after v
in a particular direction. He raised his voice a little,
talking into the wind as they walked along. ...traffic
that moved along sluggishly.
4 If you say that something is going **along** in a particu- ADV:
lar way, you mean that it is progressing in that way. ADV after v
...the negotiations which have been dragging along interminably... My life is going along nicely.
5 If you take someone or something **along** when you ADV:
go somewhere, you take them with you. This is open to ADV after v
women of all ages, so bring along your friends and colleagues... Wives will have to bring along their marriage
certificate. **6** If someone or something is coming ADV:
along or is sent **along**, they are coming or being sent ADV after v
to a particular place. She invited everyone she knew to
come along... He had the material tested and sent
along the results.
7 You use **along with** to mention someone or some- PHR-PREP
thing else that is also involved in an action or situation. The baby's mother escaped from the fire along
with two other children.
8 If something has been true or been present **all** PHRASE
along, it has been true or been present throughout a
period of time. I've been fooling myself all along... She
had been planning all along to leave Hungary.
9 • along the way: see way.
along·side /ə,lɒŋ'saɪd, AM -,lɔːŋ-/. **1** If something ♦♦♦◇◇
is **alongside** something else, it is next to it. He PREP
crossed the street and walked alongside Central
Park... Much of the industry was located alongside
rivers. ► Also an adverb. He waited several minutes ADV:
for a car to pull up alongside. **2** If you work along- ADV after v
side other people, you work in the same place and PREP
co-operate with them. **3** If one thing exists or devel- PREP
ops **alongside** another, the two things exist or
develop together at the same time. Her personal
self-confidence will develop alongside her technique.
aloof /ə'luːf/. **1** If you say that someone is **aloof**, ♦◇◇◇◇
you are criticizing them because they do not like to ADJ-GRADED
socialize and are not very friendly towards other PRAGMATICS
people. He seemed aloof and detached. ♦ **aloof-**
·ness He had an air of aloofness about him. **2** If N-UNCOUNT
someone stays **aloof** from something, they do not ADJ-GRADED:
become involved with it. The Government is keeping v-link ADJ
aloof from the controversy. from n
FORMAL
aloud /ə'laʊd/. **1** When you say something, read, or ♦◇◇◇◇
laugh **aloud**, you speak or laugh so that other peo- ADV:
ple can hear you. Our father read aloud to us. **2** If ADV after v
you **think aloud**, you express your thoughts as they PHRASE
occur to you, rather than thinking first and then
speaking.
al·paca /æl'pækə/. Alpaca is a type of soft wool. N-UNCOUNT
al·pha·bet /'ælfəbet/ **alphabets.** An **alphabet** is a ♦◇◇◇
set of letters, usually presented in a fixed order, N-COUNT
which is used for writing the words of a particular
language or group of languages. The modern Russian alphabet has 31 letters.
al·pha·beti·cal /,ælfə'betɪkəl/. **Alphabetical** means ADJ: ADJ n
arranged according to the normal order of the let-
ters in the alphabet. Their herbs and spices are arranged in alphabetical order. ♦ **al·pha·beti·cal·ly** ADV
/,ælfə'betɪkli/.
al·pine /'ælpaɪn/. **Alpine** means existing in or relat- ♦◇◇◇◇
ing to mountains, especially the Alps. ...grassy, al- ADJ
pine meadows.
al·pines /'ælpaɪnz/. **Alpines** are small flowering N-PLURAL
plants that grow high up on mountains and are
sometimes grown in gardens.
al·ready /ɔːl'redi/. **1** You use **already** to focus on ♦♦♦♦♦
the fact that something has happened, or that ADV:
something had happened before the moment you ADV before v,
are referring to. Speakers of British English use **al-** cl ADV
ready with a perfect tense. Some speakers of American English use **already** with the simple past tense.
They had already voted for him at the first ballot...

They've spent nearly a billion dollars on it already...
She says she already told the neighbors not to come
over. **2** You use **already** to focus on the fact that a ADV:
situation exists at this present moment or that it ADV before v,
exists at an earlier time than expected. You use **al-** ADV with
ready after the verb 'be' or an auxiliary verb, or be- group
fore a verb if there is no auxiliary. The authorities
believe those security measures are already paying
off... He was already late for his appointment... She
also tried to make a mockery of our already tarnished justice system... Already, he has a luxurious,
secluded villa.
al·right /,ɔːl'raɪt/. See **all right**. ♦◇◇◇◇
Al·sa·tian /æl'seɪʃən/ **Alsatians.** An **Alsatian** is a N-COUNT
large dog that is often used to guard buildings or by BRITISH
the police.
also /'ɔːlsəʊ/. **1** You can use **also** to give more in- ♦♦♦♦♦
formation about a person or thing, or to add anoth- ADV:
er relevant fact. ...Patricia Becker, an author who ADV before v,
also teaches macrobiotic cooking classes... He is an ADV with cl/
asthmatic who was also anaemic three months ago... group
She has a reputation for brilliance. Also, she is gor- PRAGMATICS
geous. **2** You can use **also** to indicate that some- ADV:
thing you have just said or implied about one per- ADV before v,
son or thing is true of someone or something else. ADV with
Two adults were also killed and at least ten more group
people were wounded... Not only cancer, but also PRAGMATICS
heart and lung disease are influenced by smoking.
'also-ran, also-rans. If you describe someone as N-COUNT
an **also-ran**, you mean that they have been or are PRAGMATICS
likely to be unsuccessful in a contest; used showing
disapproval.
al·tar /'ɔːltə/ **altars.** An **altar** is a holy table in a ♦◇◇◇◇
church or temple. N-COUNT
al·ter /'ɔːltə/ **alters, altering, altered.** If some- ♦♦◇◇◇
thing **alters** or if you **alter** it, it changes. Little had V-ERG: V
altered in the village. ...genetically altered human re- V-ed
productive cells. ♦ **al·tera·tion** /,ɔːltə'reɪʃən/ **al-** Also V n
terations ...the structural alterations made to the V-NAR
house.
al·ter·ca·tion /,ɔːltə'keɪʃən/ **altercations.** An **al-** N-COUNT
tercation is a noisy argument or disagreement. A FORMAL
doorman at the club was involved in an altercation
with a man.
alter 'ego, alter egos. 1 Your **alter ego** is the N-COUNT
other side of your personality from the one which
people normally see. **2** You can describe the char- N-COUNT
acter that an actor usually plays on television or in
films as his or her **alter ego**. **3** Your **alter ego** is a N-COUNT
very close and intimate friend whose character is
often the opposite of your own.
al·ter·nate, alternates, alternating, alternat- ♦♦◇◇◇
ed. The verb is pronounced /'ɔːltəneɪt/. The adjective is pronounced /ɔːl'tɜːnət/. **1** When you alter- V-RECIP-ERG
nate two things, you keep using one then the other. V between/
When one thing **alternates** with another, the first V pl n
regularly occurs after the other. I alternated between V n with n
feeling freezing cold and boiling hot... Alternate lay- Also pl-n V
ers of that mixture and eggplant... He went to the
gym six days a week, alternating weight training
with aerobics. ► Also an adjective. They were ADJ: ADJ n
streaked with alternate bands of colour. ♦ **al·ter-**
·nate·ly He could alternately bully and charm peo- ADV
ple. ♦ **al·ter·na·tion** /,ɔːltə'neɪʃən/ **alternations** N-VAR
The alternation of sun and snow continued for the
rest of our holiday. **2** If something happens on, for ADJ: ADJ n
example, **alternate** days, it happens every two days,
and does not happen on the days in between. Lesley
had agreed to Jim going skiing in alternate years.
3 You use **alternate** to describe a different plan, ADJ: ADJ n
idea, or system that can be used instead of the one AMERICAN
in operation. His group was forced to turn back and
take an alternate route.
alternating 'current, alternating currents. N-VAR
An **alternating current** is an electric current that
continually changes direction as it flows. The abbreviation 'AC' is also used.
al·ter·na·tive /ɔːl'tɜːnətɪv/ **alternatives. 1** If one ♦♦♦♦◇
thing is an **alternative** to another, the first can be N-COUNT
found, used, or done instead of the second. New

ways to treat arthritis may provide an alternative to painkillers. ▶ Also an adjective. *There were alternative methods of travel available.* **2 Alternative** is used to describe something that is very different from the usual things of its kind, especially when it contrasts with traditional things. *...alternative health care. ...alternative medicine.*   ADJ: ADJ n / ADJ: ADJ n

al·ter·na·tive·ly /ɔːlˈtɜːnətɪvli/. You use **alternatively** to introduce a suggestion or to mention something different from what has just been stated. *Allow about eight hours for the drive from Calais. Alternatively, you can fly to Brive.*   ◆◆◇◇◇ ADV: ADV with cl PRAGMATICS

al·ter·na·tor /ˈɔːltəneɪtə/ **alternators.** An **alternator** is a device that creates an electrical current that changes direction as it flows.   N-COUNT

al·though /ɔːlˈðəʊ/. **1** You use **although** to introduce a statement which contrasts with the statement in the main clause. *Although he is known to only a few, his reputation among them is very great... Although the shooting has stopped for now, the destruction left behind is enormous.* **2** You use **although** to introduce a statement which makes the main clause of the sentence seem surprising or unexpected. *Although I was only six, I can remember seeing it on TV.* **3** You use **although** to introduce a clause which gives some information that is relevant to the main clause but modifies the strength of that statement. *He was in love with her, although a man seldom puts that name to what he feels.* **4** You use **although** when admitting a fact about something which you regard as less important than a contrasting fact. *Although they're expensive, they last forever.*   ◆◆◆◆◆ CONJ PRAGMATICS / CONJ PRAGMATICS / CONJ PRAGMATICS / CONJ PRAGMATICS

al·time·ter /ˈæltɪmiːtə, AM ælˈtɪmɪtə/ **altimeters.** An **altimeter** is an instrument in an aircraft that shows the height of the aircraft above the ground.   N-COUNT

al·ti·tude /ˈæltɪtjuːd, AM -tuːd/ **altitudes.** If something is at a particular **altitude**, it is at that height above sea level. *The aircraft had reached its cruising altitude of about 39,000 feet.*   ◆◇◇◇◇ N-VAR

alto /ˈæltəʊ/ **altos. 1** In choral singing, an **alto** is a male or female singer whose voice is between the soprano and tenor ranges. **2** An **alto** musical instrument has a range of notes of medium pitch.   N-COUNT / ADJ: ADJ n

al·to·geth·er /ˌɔːltəˈgeðə/. **1** You use **altogether** to emphasize that something has stopped, been done, or finished completely. *Mr Kanemaru announced he was leaving politics altogether.* **2** You use **altogether** to emphasize that someone or something has more of a quality than other people or things. *The choice of language is altogether different... These people live, it seems, in an altogether more physically intense world than the rest of us.* **3** You use **altogether** to modify a negative statement and make it less forceful. *We were not altogether sure that the comet would miss the Earth.* **4** You can use **altogether** to introduce a summary or evaluation of what you have been saying. *Altogether, it was a delightful town garden.* **5** If several amounts add up to a particular amount **altogether**, that amount is their total. *Britain has a dozen warships in the area, with a total of five thousand military personnel altogether.*   ◆◆◆◇◇ ADV: ADV after v PRAGMATICS / ADV: ADV adj/adv PRAGMATICS / ADV: with neg, ADV group PRAGMATICS / ADV: ADV with cl PRAGMATICS / ADV: ADV with amount

al·tru·ism /ˈæltruɪzəm/. **Altruism** is unselfish concern for other people's happiness and welfare. ▶ **al·tru·is·tic** /ˌæltruˈɪstɪk/ *...motives and ambitions that are not entirely altruistic.*   N-UNCOUNT / ADJ-GRADED

alu·min·ium /ˌæluːˈmɪniəm/. **Aluminium** is a lightweight metal used, for example, for making cooking equipment and aircraft parts. The usual American word is **aluminum** /əˈluːmɪnəm/.   ◆◆◇◇◇ N-UNCOUNT BRITISH

alum·nus /əˈlʌmnəs/ **alumni** /əˈlʌmnaɪ/. The **alumni** of a school, college, or university are the people who used to be students there.   ◆◇◇◇◇ N-COUNT AMERICAN

al·ways /ˈɔːlweɪz/. **1** If you **always** do something, you do it whenever a particular situation arises. *Whenever I get into a relationship, I always fall madly in love... She's always late for everything.* **2** If something is **always** the case, it is the case all the time, continuously. *We will always remember his*   ◆◆◆◆◆ ADV / ADV

generous hospitality... He was always cheerful. **3** If you say that something is **always** happening, especially something which annoys you, you mean that it happens repeatedly. *She was always moving things around.* **4** You use **always** in expressions such as **can always** or **could always** when you are making suggestions. *If you can't find any decent apples, you can always try growing them yourself.* **5** You can say that someone **always** was, for example, awkward or lucky to indicate that you are not surprised about what they are doing or have just done. *You always were a good friend.*   ADV: ADV before v-cont / ADV: can/could ADV inf PRAGMATICS / ADV PRAGMATICS

Alzheimer's Dis·ease /ˈæltshaɪməz dɪsiːz/. **Alzheimer's Disease** is a disorder of the brain resulting in a gradual decline in mental abilities.   ◆◇◇◇◇ N-UNCOUNT

am /əm, STRONG æm/. **Am** is the first person singular of the present tense of **be**. **Am** is often contracted to **'m**. The negative of am is **am not**, which in questions and tags is usually abbreviated to **aren't**.

Am. **Am.** is a written abbreviation for **American**.

a.m. /ˌeɪ ˈem/. **a.m.** is used after a number to indicate a particular time between midnight and noon. *The program starts at 9 a.m.*   ◆◆◇◇◇

amalgam /əˈmælgəm/ **amalgams. 1** Something that is an **amalgam** of two or more things is a mixture of them. *Marlene Dietrich was a complex amalgam of a great number of women.* **2 Amalgam** is a mixture of mercury and another metal, usually silver, that is used in dentistry to make fillings.   ◆◇◇◇◇ N-COUNT / N-UNCOUNT

amal·gam·ate /əˈmælgəmeɪt/ **amalgamates, amalgamating, amalgamated.** When two or more things, especially organizations, **amalgamate** or **are amalgamated**, they become one large thing. *The firm has amalgamated with an American company... The Visitors' Centre amalgamates the traditions of the Old World with the technology of the New.* ♦ **amal·gama·tion** /əˌmælgəˈmeɪʃən/ **amalgamations** *Athletics South Africa was formed by an amalgamation of two organisations.*   ◆◇◇◇◇ V-RECIP-ERG V with/into n V n with/into n Also pl-n V, V pl-n / N-VAR

amass /əˈmæs/ **amasses, amassing, amassed.** If you **amass** something such as money or information, you gradually get a lot of it. *It was better not to enquire into how he had amassed his fortune.*   ◆◇◇◇◇ VERB V n

ama·teur /ˈæmətə, AM -tʃɜːr/ **amateurs.** An **amateur** is someone who does something as a hobby and not as a job. *Paul Weller's father boxed as an amateur.* ▶ Also an adjective. *...the local amateur dramatics society.*   ◆◆◆◇◇ N-COUNT / ADJ: ADJ n

ama·teur·ish /ˈæmətərɪʃ, AM -tʃɜːrɪʃ/. If you describe something as **amateurish**, you think that it is not skilfully made or done.   ADJ-GRADED PRAGMATICS

ama·teur·ism /ˈæmətərɪzəm, AM -tʃɜːr-/. **Amateurism** is the belief that people should take part in sports and other activities as a hobby, for pleasure, rather than as a job, for money.   N-UNCOUNT

amaze /əˈmeɪz/ **amazes, amazing, amazed.** If something **amazes** you, it surprises you very much. *He amazed us by his knowledge of Welsh history.* ♦ **amazed** *She is amazed that people still risk travelling without insurance.* ♦ **amaze·ment** /əˈmeɪzmənt/. *I stared at her in amazement.*   ◆◆◇◇◇ VERB: Also V, it V n / ADJ-GRADED / N-UNCOUNT

amaz·ing /əˈmeɪzɪŋ/. You say that something is **amazing** when it is very surprising and makes you feel pleasure, approval, or wonder. *It's amazing what we can remember. ...the most amazing stunts you're ever likely to see.* ♦ **amaz·ing·ly** *She was an amazingly good cook.*   ◆◆◆◇◇ ADJ-GRADED / ADV-GRADED

Ama·zon /ˈæməzən/ **Amazons. 1** In Greek mythology, the **Amazons** were a tribe of women warriors. **2** A tall, strong, assertive woman is sometimes referred to as an **Amazon**.   N-COUNT / N-COUNT

am·bas·sa·dor /æmˈbæsədə/ **ambassadors.** An **ambassador** is an important official who lives in a foreign country and represents his or her own country's interests there. *...the German ambassador to Poland.* ♦ **am·bas·sa·dor·ial** /æmˌbæsəˈdɔːriəl/ *His three ambassadorial posts were in Djakarta, Reykjavik and Dublin.*   ◆◆◇◇◇ N-COUNT / ADJ: ADJ n

am·ber /'æmbə/. **1 Amber** is a hard yellowish-brown substance used for making jewellery. **2 Amber** is used to describe things that are yellowish-brown in colour. *A burst of sunshine sent a beam of amber light through the window.* ◆◇◇◇◇ N-UNCOUNT COLOUR

am·bi·ance /'æmbiəns/. See **ambience**.

am·bi·dex·trous /ˌæmbi'dekstrəs/. Someone who is **ambidextrous** can use both their right hand and their left hand equally skilfully. ADJ

am·bi·ence /'æmbiəns/; also spelled **ambiance**. The **ambience** of a place is the character and atmosphere that it seems to have. *The overall ambience of the room is cosy.* ◆◇◇◇◇ N-SING: also no det LITERARY

am·bi·ent /'æmbiənt/. **1** The **ambient** temperature is the temperature of the air in a particular place. **2 Ambient** sound or light is the sound or light which is all around you. *...ambient sounds of children in the background.* ADJ: ADJ n ADJ-GRADED FORMAL

am·big·u·ous /æm'bɪɡjuəs/. **1** If you describe something as **ambiguous**, you mean that it is unclear or confusing because it can be understood in more than one way. *This agreement is very ambiguous and open to various interpretations.* ♦ **am·bi·gu·ity** /ˌæmbɪ'ɡjuːɪti/ **ambiguities** *...the ambiguities of language.* ♦ **am·bigu·ous·ly** *Zaire's national conference on democracy ended ambiguously.* **2** If you describe something as **ambiguous**, you mean that it contains several different ideas or attitudes that do not fit well together. *Students have ambiguous feelings about their role in the world.* ♦ **am·bi·gu·ity** *The author's style suggests a certain ambiguity in his moral view.* ◆◆◇◇◇ ADJ-GRADED N-VAR ADV-GRADED ADJ-GRADED N-VAR

am·bit /'æmbɪt/. The **ambit** of something is its range or extent. *Her case falls within the ambit of moral law.* N-SING FORMAL

am·bi·tion /æm'bɪʃən/ **ambitions**. **1** If you have an **ambition** to do or achieve something, you want very much to do it or achieve it. *His ambition is to sail round the world.* **2 Ambition** is the desire to be successful, rich, or powerful. *Even when I was young I never had any ambition.* ◆◆◆◇◇ N-COUNT N-UNCOUNT

am·bi·tious /æm'bɪʃəs/. **1** Someone who is **ambitious** has a strong desire to be successful, rich, or powerful. *He's a very ambitious lad and he wants to play at the highest level.* **2** An **ambitious** idea or plan is on a large scale and needs a lot of work to be carried out successfully. *The ambitious project was completed in only nine months.* ♦ **am·bi·tious·ly** *Trade and industrial policies should be used more ambitiously.* ◆◆◇◇◇ ADJ-GRADED ADJ-GRADED ADV-GRADED

am·biva·lent /æm'bɪvələnt/. If you say that someone is **ambivalent** about something, they seem to be uncertain whether they really want it, or whether they really approve of it. *She remained ambivalent about her marriage. ...an ambivalent attitude to the Church.* ♦ **am·biva·lence** /'æm'bɪvələns/ **ambivalences** *...my ambivalence about getting married again.* ◆◇◇◇◇ ADJ-GRADED N-VAR

am·ble /'æmbəl/ **ambles, ambling, ambled.** When you **amble**, you walk slowly and in a relaxed manner. *We ambled along in front of the houses.* ▶ Also a noun. *...an afternoon's amble around the oldest parts of Paris.* VERB V adv/prep N-SING

am·bu·lance /'æmbjuləns/ **ambulances.** An **ambulance** is a vehicle for taking people to and from hospital. *His wife called for an ambulance.* ◆◆◇◇◇ N-COUNT: also by N

am·bu·lance·man /'æmbjulənsmæn/ **ambulancemen.** An **ambulanceman** is a person who drives an ambulance or takes care of sick people in an ambulance on the way to hospital. N-COUNT BRITISH

am·bush /'æmbʊʃ/ **ambushes, ambushing, ambushed. 1** If a group of people **ambush** their enemies, they attack them after hiding and waiting for them. *Rebels ambushed and killed 10 patrolmen.* ▶ Also a noun. *Guerrillas also killed a Japanese policeman in an ambush.* **2** If someone is lying in **ambush**, they are hiding and waiting for someone, usually to attack them. ◆◆◇◇◇ VERB V n N-VAR PHRASE

ame·lio·rate /ə'miːliəreɪt/ **ameliorates, ameliorating, ameliorated.** If someone or something VERB V n

ameliorates a situation, they make it better or easier in some way. *He expected me to do something to ameliorate his depression.* ♦ **ame·lio·ra·tion** /əˌmiːliə'reɪʃən/ *...a demand for amelioration of conditions.* FORMAL N-UNCOUNT

amen /ˌɑː'men, ˌeɪ-/. **Amen** is said by Christians at the end of a prayer. CONVENTION

ame·nable /ə'miːnəbəl/. If you are **amenable** to something, you are willing to do it or accept it. *The Jordanian leader seemed amenable to attending a conference.* ADJ-GRADED

amend /ə'mend/ **amends, amending, amended. 1** If you **amend** something that has been written such as a law, you change it in order to improve it or make it more accurate. *Kaunda agreed to amend the constitution and allow multi-party elections.* **2** If you **make amends** when you have harmed someone, you show that you are sorry by doing something to please them. *He wanted to make amends for causing their marriage to fail.* ◆◆◇◇◇ VERB Also V with quote PHRASE

amend·ment /ə'mendmənt/ **amendments. 1** An **amendment** is a section that is added to a law or rule in order to change it. *...an amendment to the defense bill.* **2** An **amendment** is a change or correction to a piece of writing. *I showed him the script and he made loads of amendments and corrections.* ◆◆◆◇◇ N-VAR N-COUNT

amen·ity /ə'miːnɪti, AM -'men-/ **amenities. Amenities** are things such as shopping centres or sports facilities that are provided for people's convenience, enjoyment, or comfort. *The hotel amenities include health clubs, and conference facilities.* ◆◇◇◇◇ N-COUNT

Ameri·ca·na /əˌmerɪ'kɑːnə/. Objects that come from or relate to America are referred to as **Americana**. *...1950s Americana.* N-UNCOUNT

A,merican 'football, American footballs. 1 American football is a game similar to rugby that is played between two teams of eleven players. **2** An **American football** is an oval shaped ball used for playing American football. ◆◇◇◇◇ N-UNCOUNT N-COUNT BRITISH

A,merican 'Indian, American Indians. American Indian people or things belong to or come from one of the native peoples of America. ▶ An **American Indian** is someone who belongs to or comes from one of the native peoples of America. ADJ N-COUNT

Ameri·can·ism /ə'merɪkənɪzəm/ **Americanisms. 1** An **Americanism** is an expression that is typical of people living in the United States of America. *He was, to adopt an Americanism 'an empty suit'.* **2 Americanism** is the quality or state of being American. *I liked the film's Americanism.* N-COUNT N-UNCOUNT

Ameri·can·ize /ə'merɪkənaɪz/ **Americanizes, Americanizing, Americanized;** also spelled **Americanise** in British English. If someone **Americanizes** someone or something, they make them follow American customs and practice. *He hated the climate, the food, and the people, especially those who tried to Americanize him.* ♦ **ameri·cani·za·tion** /əˌmerɪkənaɪ'zeɪʃən/ **americanizations** *...the americanization of French culture.* VERB V n N-VAR

Am·er·in·dian /ˌæmə'rɪndiən/ **Amerindians. Amerindian** means the same as **American Indian**.

am·ethyst /'æməθɪst/ **amethysts. 1 Amethysts** are clear purple stones, sometimes used to make jewellery. **2 Amethyst** is used to describe things that are purple in colour. *...amethyst glass.* N-VAR COLOUR

ami·able /'eɪmiəbəl/. Someone who is **amiable** is friendly and pleasant to be with. *She had been surprised at how amiable and polite he had seemed.* ♦ **ami·ably** *We chatted amiably about old friends.* ◆◇◇◇◇ ADJ-GRADED WRITTEN ADV-GRADED

ami·cable /'æmɪkəbəl/. When people have an **amicable** relationship, they are pleasant to each other and solve their problems without quarrelling. *The meeting ended on reasonably amicable terms.* ♦ **ami·cably** /'æmɪkəbli/ *He hoped the dispute could be settled amicably.* ◆◇◇◇◇ ADJ-GRADED ADV-GRADED: ADV with v

amid /ə'mɪd/. The form **amidst** is also used, but is more literary. **1** If something happens **amid** noises or events of some kind, it happens while the other things are happening. *Children were changing classrooms amid laughter and shouts.* **2** If something is ◆◆◆◇◇ PREP PREP

amid other things, it is surrounded by them. *...a* LITERARY
tiny bungalow amid clusters of trees.

amid·ships /əˈmɪdʃɪps/. **Amidships** means halfway ADV:
along the length of a ship. *We'd hit a fishing boat* ADV after v
amidships, cutting it in half.

amidst /əˈmɪdst/. **Amidst** means the same as **amid**. PREP

ami·no acid /əˌmiːnəʊ ˈæsɪd/ **amino acids.** Ami- ◆◇◇◇◇
no acids are substances containing nitrogen and N-COUNT
hydrogen which are needed by the body to make TECHNICAL
protein. Some amino acids are produced naturally
in the body and others are obtained from food.

amiss /əˈmɪs/. **1** If you say that something is **amiss**, ADJ-GRADED:
you mean there is something wrong. *Something is* v-link ADJ
radically amiss in our health care system. **2** If you PHRASE
say that something **would not go amiss** or **would
not come amiss**, you mean that it would be pleasant and useful. *The cracks are showing in the walls
and a lick of paint would not come amiss.*

am·ity /ˈæmɪti/. **Amity** is peaceful, friendly relations N-UNCOUNT
between people or countries. *The two countries* FORMAL
have always lived in amity with each other.

ammo /ˈæməʊ/. **Ammo** is ammunition for guns and N-UNCOUNT
other weapons. INFORMAL

am·mo·nia /əˈməʊniə/. **Ammonia** is a colourless ◆◇◇◇◇
liquid or gas with a strong, sharp smell. It is used in N-UNCOUNT
making household cleaning substances.

am·mu·ni·tion /ˌæmjʊˈnɪʃən/. **1 Ammunition** is ◆◆◇◇◇
bullets and rockets that are made to be fired from N-UNCOUNT
guns. *He had only seven rounds of ammunition for
the revolver.* **2** You can describe information that N-UNCOUNT
you can use against someone in an argument or
discussion as **ammunition**. *The improved trade figures have given the government fresh ammunition.*

am·ne·sia /æmˈniːziə, -ʒə/. If someone is suffering N-UNCOUNT
from **amnesia**, they have lost their memory.

am·ne·si·ac /æmˈniːziæk/ **amnesiacs.** Someone ADJ
who is **amnesiac** has lost their memory. *Pat had
been found, wandering, apparently amnesiac and
shocked.* ▶ An **amnesiac** is someone who is amnesi- N-COUNT
ac. *...profound amnesiacs.*

am·nes·ty /ˈæmnɪsti/ **amnesties. 1** An **amnesty** ◆◆◇◇◇
is an official pardon granted to a group of prisoners N-VAR
by the state. *Activists who were involved in crimes of
violence will not automatically be granted amnesty.*
2 An **amnesty** is a period of time during which peo- N-COUNT
ple can confess to a crime or give up weapons without being punished. *The government has announced
an immediate amnesty for rebel fighters.*

am·nio·cen·tesis /ˌæmniəʊsenˈtiːsɪs/. If a preg- N-UNCOUNT
nant woman has an **amniocentesis**, fluid is removed from her womb in order to check that her
unborn baby is healthy.

amoe·ba /əˈmiːbə/ **amoebae** /əˈmiːbiː/ or **amoe-** N-COUNT
bas. An **amoeba** is the smallest kind of living creature, consisting of only one cell.

amok /əˈmʌk, əˈmɒk/. If a person, animal, or ma- PHRASE
chine **runs amok**, they behave in a violent and uncontrolled way. *A soldier was arrested after running
amok with a vehicle through Berlin.*

among /əˈmʌŋ/. The form **amongst** is also used, ◆◆◆◆◆
but is more literary. **1** Someone or something that PREP
is situated or moving **among** a group of things or
people are surrounded by them. *They walked among
the crowds in Red Square. ...a garden of semi-
tropical vegetation set among pools and waterfalls.*
2 If you are **among** people of a particular kind, you PREP
are with them. *I was brought up among people who
read and wrote a lot.*
3 If someone or something is **among** a group, they are PREP
a member of that group. *Also among the speakers was
the new American ambassador to Moscow.* **4** If you PREP
want to focus on something that is happening within
a particular group of people, you can say that it is happening **among** that group. *Homicide is the leading
cause of death among black men.* **5** If something hap- PREP
pens **among** a group of people, it happens within the
whole of that group or between the members of that
group. *Intense debate continues among the leadership... Much of the talk of political disaster had been
among intellectuals.* **6** If something such as a feeling, PREP

opinion, or situation exists **among** a group of people,
most of them have it or experience it. *There was some
concern among book and magazine retailers after last
Wednesday's news.* **7** You use **among** before a noun to PREP
mention a group when talking about a smaller group
within it. *Among those 18 and over, 510,000 benefit
claimants were not unemployed.*
8 If something applies to a particular person or thing PREP
among others, it also applies to other people or
things. *She had worked, among others, with George
Bernard Shaw.*
9 If something is shared **among** a number of people, PREP
some of it is given to all of them. *Her affection was
equally shared among all three children.*
10 If people talk, fight, or agree **among** themselves, PREP
they do it together. *The directors have been arguing
among themselves.*

amongst /əˈmʌŋst/. **Amongst** means the same as ◆◆◇◇◇
among. PREP

amor·al /ˌeɪˈmɒrəl, AM -ˈmɔːr-/. An **amoral** person ADJ-GRADED
does not care whether people consider that what PRAGMATICS
they do is right or wrong; used showing disapproval.
*...a society threatened by amoral and often random
violence.* ♦ **amo·ral·ity** /ˌeɪmɔːˈrælɪti/. N-UNCOUNT

amo·rous /ˈæmərəs/. If you describe someone's ADJ-GRADED
feelings or actions as **amorous**, you mean that they
involve sexual desire. *The object of his amorous intentions is Martina.*

amor·phous /əˈmɔːfəs/. Something that is **amor-** ADJ-GRADED
phous has no clear shape or structure. *A dark,
strangely amorphous shadow filled the room.*

amor·tize /əˈmɔːtaɪz, AM ˈæmər-/ **amortizes,** VERB: V n
amortizing, amortized; also spelled **amortise** in V n over n
British English. If you **amortize** a debt, you pay it TECHNICAL
back in regular instalments. *He may elect to amortize
the premium over the life of the bond.*

amount /əˈmaʊnt/ **amounts, amounting,** ◆◆◆◆◇
amounted. 1 The **amount** of something is how N-VAR
much there is, or how much you have, need, or get.
*He needs that amount of money to survive... I still do
a certain amount of work.* **2** If something **amounts** VERB
to a particular total, all the parts of it add up to that V to amount
total. *Spending on sports-related items amounted to
£9.75 billion.* **3** If you say that there are **any amount** PHRASE
of things or people, you mean that there are a lot of
them. *There are any amount of clubs you could join.*

amount to. If you say that one thing **amounts to** PHRASAL VB
something else, you consider the first thing to be the LINK
same as the second thing. *The banks have what* PRAGMATICS
amounts to a monopoly. V P n

amp /æmp/ **amps. 1** An **amp** is the same as an **am-** N-COUNT
père. *Use a 3 amp fuse for equipment up to 720
watts.* **2** An **amp** is the same as an **amplifier**. *I got* N-COUNT
my furniture and my guitar and amp from thrift INFORMAL
stores.

ampère /ˈæmpeə, AM -pɪə/ **ampères;** also spelled N-COUNT
ampere. An **ampère** is a unit which is used for
measuring electric current. The abbreviation **amp** is
also used.

am·pheta·mine /æmˈfetəmiːn/ **amphetamines.** ◆◇◇◇◇
Amphetamine is a drug which increases people's N-VAR
energy and reduces their appetite.

am·phib·ian /æmˈfɪbiən/ **amphibians. Amphib-** N-COUNT
ians are animals such as frogs and toads that can
live both on land and in water.

am·phibi·ous /æmˈfɪbiəs/. **1** In an **amphibious** ◆◇◇◇◇
military operation, army and navy forces attack a ADJ: ADJ n
place from the sea. **2** An **amphibious** vehicle is able ADJ
to move on both land and water. **3** Amphibious ADJ
animals are animals such as frogs and toads that
can live both on land and in water.

am·phi·thea·tre /ˈæmfɪθɪətə/ **amphitheatres;**
spelled **amphitheater** in American English. **1** An N-COUNT
amphitheatre is a large open area surrounded by
rows of seats sloping upwards. **2** You can describe N-COUNT
land which partly or completely surrounds an open
area as an **amphitheatre**. *...a natural amphitheatre
of mountains.*

am·ple /ˈæmpəl/ **ampler, amplest. 1** If there is ◆◆◇◇◇
an **ample** amount of something, there is enough of ADJ-GRADED

A

it and usually some extra. *There'll be ample opportunity to relax. ...ample space for a good-sized kitchen.* ◆ **am·ply** *His essays and journalism amply demonstrate his commitment to democracy.* **2** If you describe someone's figure as **ample**, you mean that they are large in a pleasant or attractive way. [ADV-GRADED] [ADJ-GRADED WRITTEN]

am·pli·fi·er /ˈæmplɪfaɪə/ **amplifiers.** An **amplifier** is an electronic device in a radio or stereo system which causes sounds or signals to get louder. [N-COUNT] ◆◇◇◇

am·pli·fy /ˈæmplɪfaɪ/ **amplifies, amplifying, amplified. 1** If you **amplify** a sound, you make it louder, usually by using electronic equipment. *The music was amplified with microphones.* ◆ **am·pli·fi·ca·tion** /ˌæmplɪfɪˈkeɪʃən/ *...a voice that needed no amplification.* **2** To **amplify** something means to increase its strength or intensity. *Her anxiety about the world was amplifying her personal fears.* [VERB: V n] [be V-ed] [N-UNCOUNT] [VERB V n] ◆◇◇◇

am·pli·tude /ˈæmplɪtjuːd, AM -tuːd/ **amplitudes. 1** In physics, the **amplitude** of a sound wave or electrical signal is its strength. **2 Amplitude** is the quality of being large in size or quantity. *...the time it takes a sound to reach full amplitude.* [N-VAR TECHNICAL] [N-UNCOUNT FORMAL]

am·poule /ˈæmpuːl/ **ampoules;** spelled **ampule** in American English. An **ampoule** is a small container, usually made of glass, that contains a drug or medicine which will be injected into someone. [N-COUNT]

am·pu·tate /ˈæmpjʊteɪt/ **amputates, amputating, amputated.** If a surgeon **amputates** someone's arm or leg, he or she cuts all or part of it off in an operation because it is diseased or badly damaged. *He had to have one leg amputated.* ◆ **am·pu·ta·tion** /ˌæmpjʊˈteɪʃən/ **amputations.** [VERB: V n] [have n V-ed] [Also V] [N-VAR] ◆◇◇◇

am·pu·tee /ˌæmpjʊˈtiː/ **amputees.** An **amputee** is someone who has had all or part of an arm or a leg amputated. [N-COUNT]

amu·let /ˈæmjʊlət/ **amulets.** An **amulet** is a small object that you wear or carry because you think it will bring you good luck and protect you from evil or injury. [N-COUNT]

amuse /əˈmjuːz/ **amuses, amusing, amused. 1** If something **amuses** you, it makes you want to laugh or smile. *The thought seemed to amuse him.* **2** If you **amuse** yourself, you do something in order to pass the time and not become bored. *I need to amuse myself so I won't keep thinking about things.* **3** See also **amused, amusing.** [VERB V n] [VERB V pron-refl] [Also V n] ◆◇◇◇

amused /əˈmjuːzd/. **1** If you are **amused** by something, it makes you want to laugh or smile. *Sara was not amused by Franklin's teasing... He was amused to learn that he and O'Brien had similar ideas.* **2** If you **keep** someone **amused**, you find things to do which stop them getting bored. *Having pictures to colour will keep children amused for hours.* [ADJ-GRADED] [PHRASE] ◆◇◇◇

amuse·ment /əˈmjuːzmənt/ **amusements. 1 Amusement** is the feeling that you have when you think that something is funny. *He stopped and watched with amusement.* **2 Amusement** is the pleasure that you get from being entertained or from doing something interesting. *She excelled at impersonations, which provided great amusement for him and his friends.* **3 Amusements** are ways of passing the time pleasantly. *People had very few amusements to choose from. There was no radio, few or television.* **4 Amusements** are games, rides on roundabouts, and other things that you can enjoy at a fairground or holiday resort. [N-UNCOUNT] [N-UNCOUNT] [N-COUNT] [N-PLURAL] ◆◇◇◇

a'musement arcade, amusement arcades. In Britain, an **amusement arcade** is a large room in which you can play games on machines which work when you put money in them. [N-COUNT]

a'musement park, amusement parks. An **amusement park** is the same as a **funfair.** [N-COUNT AMERICAN]

amus·ing /əˈmjuːzɪŋ/. Someone or something that is **amusing** makes you laugh or smile. *He had a terrific sense of humour and could be very amusing.* ◆ **amus·ing·ly** *Recline & Sprawl is an amusingly named furniture shop in London.* [ADJ-GRADED] [ADV-GRADED] ◆◆◇◇

an /ən, STRONG æn/. **an** is used instead of 'a', the indefinite article, in front of words that begin with vowel sounds: see **a.** [DET]

-an /-ən/ **-ans. 1 -an** is added to the names of some places in order to form adjectives or nouns that describe or refer to someone or something that comes from that place. *The Australian foreign minister... Glaswegians smoke more than people in Edinburgh.* **2 -an** is added to the names of famous people in order to form adjectives or nouns that describe or refer to something or someone that is connected with or typical of that person's work or the time at which they lived. *...a great Shakespearean actor. ...a tradition perfected by the Elizabethans.* [SUFFIX] [SUFFIX]

ana·bol·ic ster·oid /ˌænəˈbɒlɪk ˈstɛrɔɪd, ˈstɪər-/ **anabolic steroids. Anabolic steroids** are illegal drugs which people, especially athletes, take to make their muscles bigger and to give them more strength. [N-COUNT]

anach·ro·nism /əˈnækrənɪzəm/ **anachronisms. 1** You say that something is an **anachronism** when you think that it is out of date or old-fashioned. *The dowry with all its attendant cruelties is an anachronism.* ◆ **anach·ro·nis·tic** /əˌnækrəˈnɪstɪk/ *My children regard handwriting as some lost, anachronistic art.* **2** An **anachronism** is something in a book, play, or film that is wrong because it did not exist at the time the book, play, or film is set. *We had to stick to the period; any anachronisms, particularly in the dance, would be wrong.* [N-COUNT] [ADJ-GRADED] [N-COUNT]

anaemia /əˈniːmiə/; spelled **anemia** in American English. **Anaemia** is a medical condition in which there are too few red cells in your blood, so that you feel tired and look pale. [N-UNCOUNT] ◆◇◇◇

anaemic /əˈniːmɪk/; spelled **anemic** in American English. **1** Someone who is **anaemic** suffers from anaemia. *Losing a lot of blood makes you tired and anaemic.* **2** If you describe something as **anaemic**, you mean that it is not as strong or effective as you think it should be. *We will see some economic recovery, but it will be very anaemic.* [ADJ-GRADED] [ADJ-GRADED PRAGMATICS]

an·ae·robic /ˌænəˈrəʊbɪk/. **1 Anaerobic** activity is physical activity such as sprinting which can only be carried on for a short period of time, because it makes you out of breath. *Lactic acid can build up in the muscles with anaerobic exercise and make them feel stiff.* **2** An **anaerobic** creature is one which does not need oxygen in order to live. *...anaerobic micro-organisms.* [ADJ: ADJ n TECHNICAL] [ADJ: ADJ n TECHNICAL]

an·aes·the·sia /ˌænɪsˈθiːziə, -ʒə/; also spelled **anesthesia. Anaesthesia** is the use of anaesthetics in medicine and surgery. *The operation can be done under local anaesthesia.* [N-UNCOUNT]

an·aes·thet·ic /ˌænɪsˈθetɪk/ **anaesthetics;** also spelled **anesthetic. Anaesthetic** is a substance that doctors use to stop you feeling pain during an operation. [N-VAR] ◆◇◇◇

anaes·the·tist /əˈniːsθətɪst/ **anaesthetists;** also spelled **anesthetist. 1** An **anaesthetist** is a doctor who specializes in giving anaesthetics to patients. The usual American word is **anesthesiologist. 2** An **anesthetist** is a nurse or other person who gives an anaesthetic to a patient. [N-COUNT BRITISH] [N-COUNT AMERICAN]

anaes·the·tize /əˈniːsθətaɪz/ **anaesthetizes, anaesthetizing, anaesthetized;** also spelled **anaesthetise** in British English, and **anesthetize** in American English. **1** When a doctor or other trained person **anaesthetizes** a patient, they make the patient unconscious or unable to feel pain by giving them an anaesthetic. **2** If something such as a drug **anaesthetizes** part or all of your body, it makes you unable to feel anything in that part of your body. *...a potent drug that anaesthetizes the brain.* [VERB: V n] [VERB V n]

ana·gram /ˈænəɡræm/ **anagrams.** An **anagram** is a word or phrase formed by changing the order of the letters in another word or phrase. For example, 'tops' is an anagram of 'stop'. [N-COUNT]

anal /ˈeɪnəl/. **Anal** means relating to the anus of a person or animal. [ADJ] ◆◇◇◇

an·alge·sic /ˌænəlˈdʒiːzɪk/ **analgesics.** An **analgesic** drug lessens the effect of pain. *Aloe may have an analgesic effect on inflammation.* ▶ An **analgesic** is an analgesic drug. [ADJ-GRADED MEDICAL] [N-COUNT]

analo·gous /əˈnæləgəs/. If one thing is **analogous** ADJ-GRADED
to another, the two things are similar in some way. FORMAL
Hiring a new employee, at whatever level, is analo-
gous to choosing a business partner.

ana·logue /ˈænəlɒg, AM -lɔːg/ **analogues;** spelled ◆◇◇◇◇
analog in American English. British English also
uses the spelling **analog** for meaning 3. **1** If one N-COUNT
thing is an **analogue** of another, it is similar in some FORMAL
way. *No model can ever be a perfect analogue of na-*
ture itself.
2 An **analogue** watch or clock shows time by meas- ADJ
uring with a pointer on a dial rather than with a number display. Compare **digital**. **3 Analogue** technology ADJ
involves measuring, storing, or recording an infinitely
variable amount of information by using physical
quantities such as voltage. Compare **digital**. *The ana-*
logue signals from the video tape are converted into
digital code.

anal·ogy /əˈnælədʒi/ **analogies.** If you make or ◆◇◇◇
draw an **analogy** between two things, you show that N-COUNT
they are alike in some way. *...an analogy between*
teaching and industry.

ana·lyse /ˈænəlaɪz/ **analyses, analysing, ana-** ◆◆◇◇◇
lysed; spelled **analyze** in American English. **1** If VERB
you **analyse** something, you consider it carefully or V n
use statistical methods in order to fully understand V wh
it. *McCarthy was asked to analyse the data... Analyse*
what is causing the stress in your life. **2** If you **ana-** VERB: V n
lyse something, you examine it using scientific have n V-ed
methods in order to find out what it consists of.
They had their tablets analysed.

ana·lys·er /ˈænəlaɪzə/ **analysers;** spelled **analyzer** N-COUNT
in American English. An **analyser** is a piece of
equipment which is used to analyse the substances
that are present in something such as a gas.

analy·sis /əˈnæləsɪs/ **analyses** /əˈnæləsiːz/. **1** An ◆◆◇◇◇
analysis is the process or result of considering N-VAR
something carefully or using statistical methods in
order to understand or explain it. *We did an analy-*
sis of the way that government money has been
spent. **2 Analysis** is the scientific process of examin- N-VAR
ing something in order to find out what it consists
of. *They collect blood samples for analysis.*
3 You use the expression **in the final analysis** or **in** PHRASE
the last analysis to indicate that the statement you PRAGMATICS
are making is the most important or basic aspect of an FORMAL
issue. *They say that violence in the last analysis pro-*
duces more violence.

ana·lyst /ˈænəlɪst/ **analysts. 1** An **analyst** is a per- ◆◆◆◇
son whose job is to analyse a subject and give opin- N-COUNT
ions about it. *...a political analyst.* **2** An **analyst** is N-COUNT
someone, usually a doctor, who examines and treats
people who are emotionally disturbed.

ana·lyt·ic /ˌænəˈlɪtɪk/. **Analytic** means the same as ADJ-GRADED
analytical.

ana·lyti·cal /ˌænəˈlɪtɪkəl/. **1** An **analytical** way of ◆◇◇◇
doing something involves the use of logical reason- ADJ-GRADED
ing. *I have an analytical approach to every survey.*
◆ **ana·lyti·cal·ly** /ˌænəˈlɪtɪkli/ *A teacher can encour-* ADV-GRADED
age children to think analytically. **2 Analytical** re- ADJ: ADJ n
search involves using chemical analysis.

ana·lyze /ˈænəlaɪz/. See **analyse**.

an·ar·chic /æˈnɑːkɪk/. If you describe someone or ◆◇◇◇
something as **anarchic**, you disapprove of them be- ADJ-GRADED
cause they do not recognize or obey any rules or PRAGMATICS
laws. *...anarchic attitudes and complete disrespect*
for authority.

an·ar·chism /ˈænəkɪzəm/. **Anarchism** is the belief N-UNCOUNT
that the laws and power of governments should be
replaced by people working together freely.

an·ar·chist /ˈænəkɪst/ **anarchists. 1** An **anarchist** ◆◇◇◇
is a person who believes in anarchism. In the past, N-COUNT
anarchists often thought that governments should
be overthrown using violence. *West Berlin always*
had a large anarchist community. ◆ **an·ar·chis·tic** ADJ
/ˌænəˈkɪstɪk/ *Their political beliefs led them to anar-*
chistic revolt. **2** If you say that someone is an **anar-** N-COUNT
chist, you disapprove of them because they seem to PRAGMATICS
pay no attention to the rules or laws that everyone
else obeys. *He was a true misanthrope, a social*

anarchist. ◆ **anarchistic** *The Hells Angels were once* ADJ-GRADED
the most notorious and anarchistic of bike gangs.

an·ar·chy /ˈænəki/. If you describe a situation as ◆◇◇◇
anarchy, you mean that nobody seems to be paying N-UNCOUNT
any attention to rules or laws. *The school's liberal,* PRAGMATICS
individualistic traditions were in danger of slipping
into anarchy.

anath·ema /əˈnæθəmə/. If something is **anathema** ◆◇◇◇
to you, you strongly dislike it. *Violence was anath-* N-UNCOUNT
ema to them.

ana·tomi·cal /ˌænəˈtɒmɪkəl/. **Anatomical** means ADJ
relating to the structure of the bodies of people and
animals. *...minute anatomical differences between*
insects. ◆ **ana·tomi·cal·ly** /ˌænəˈtɒmɪkli/. *I need* ADV
my pictures to be anatomically correct.

anat·omy /əˈnætəmi/ **anatomies. 1 Anatomy** is ◆◇◇◇
the study of the structure of the bodies of people or N-UNCOUNT
animals. ◆ **anato·mist** /əˈnætəmɪst/ **anatomists.** N-COUNT
An **anatomist** is an expert in anatomy. **2** You can N-COUNT
refer to your body as your **anatomy**. *The ball hit*
him in the most sensitive part of his anatomy. **3** The N-SING
anatomy of a subject or an idea is an examination
or investigation of it. *This was a troubling essay on*
the anatomy of nationhood.

an·ces·tor /ˈænsestə/ **ancestors. 1** Your ances- ◆◆◇◇
tors are the people from whom you are descended. N-COUNT
...our daily lives, so different from those of our ances-
tors. **2** An **ancestor** of something modern is an N-COUNT
earlier thing from which it developed. *The direct an-*
cestor of the modern cat was the Kaffir cat.

an·ces·tral /ænˈsestrəl/. You use **ancestral** to refer ◆◇◇◇
to a person's family in former times. *...the family's* ADJ
ancestral home.

an·ces·try /ˈænsestri/ **ancestries.** Your ancestry ◆◇◇◇
is the fact that you are descended from certain peo- N-COUNT
ple. *...a family who could trace their ancestry back to*
the sixteenth century.

an·chor /ˈæŋkə/ **anchors, anchoring, an-** ◆◆◇◇
chored. 1 An **anchor** is a heavy hooked object that N-COUNT
is dropped from a boat into the water at the end of
a chain in order to make the boat stay in one place.
2 When a boat **anchors** or when you **anchor** it, its V-ERG
anchor is dropped into the water in order to make it V
stay in one place. *We could anchor off the pier.* **3** If Also V n
a boat is **at anchor**, it is floating in a particular PHRASE
place and is prevented from moving by its anchor.
4 When the people on a boat **drop anchor**, they PHRASE
drop the boat's anchor into the water in order to
prevent the boat from moving.
5 If you **anchor** an object somewhere, you fix it to VERB
something to prevent it moving from that place. *The* V n prep
roots anchor the plant in the earth. **6** If one thing is Also V n
anchor for something else, it makes that thing stable N-COUNT
and secure. *He provided an emotional anchor for*
her... Mr Deng remains the anchor of China's fragile
political balance. **7** If something **is anchored in** VB: usu
something or **to** something, it has strong links with it. passive
A united Germany must be firmly anchored in NATO. be V-ed in/to
8 The person who **anchors** a television or radio pro- VERB: V n
gramme presents it and acts as a link between interviews and reports which come from other places or
studios. **9** The **anchor** on a television or radio pro- N-COUNT
gramme, such as a news programme, is the person
who presents it.

an·chor·age /ˈæŋkərɪdʒ/ **anchorages.** An an- ◆◇◇◇
chorage is a place where a boat can anchor safely. N-VAR
The nearest safe anchorage was in Halifax.

anchor·man /ˈæŋkəmæn/ **anchormen;** also N-COUNT
spelled **anchor man**. The **anchorman** on a television or radio programme is the person who presents it.

anchor·woman /ˈæŋkəwʊmən/ **anchorwomen.** N-COUNT
The **anchorwoman** on a television or radio programme is the woman who presents it.

an·cho·vy /ˈæntʃəvi, AM -tʃoʊvi/ **anchovies. An-** ◆◇◇◇
chovies are very small fish with a strong salty taste. N-VAR
...a tin of anchovies. ...anchovy fillets.

an·cien re·gime /ˌɒnsjɒn reɪˈʒiːm/. The **ancien** N-SING
regime was the political and social system in France
before the revolution of 1789.

an·cient /'eɪnʃənt/ **ancients. 1 Ancient** means belonging to the distant past, especially to the period in history before the end of the Roman Empire. ...*ancient Greece and Rome.* **2 Ancient** means very old, or having existed for a long time. ...*ancient Jewish traditions.* ...*a few acres of ancient woodland.* **3 The ancients** are the people of an old civilization, especially classical Greece and Rome.

ancient 'history. 1 Ancient history is the history of ancient civilizations, especially Greece and Rome. **2** If you describe something as **ancient history**, you mean that it happened in the past and is no longer relevant to the present. *It does not bother me now at all. It is all ancient history.*

an·cil·lary /æn'sɪləri, AM 'ænsəleri/. **1** The **ancillary** workers in an institution are the people such as cleaners and cooks whose work supports the main work of the institution. **2 Ancillary** means additional to something else. *Ancillary charges are at least $30 per day.* ...*professions ancillary to medicine.*

and /ənd, STRONG ænd/. **1** You use **and** to link two or more words, groups, or clauses. *When he returned, she and Simon had already gone... I'm going to write good jokes and become a good comedian... I'm 53 and I'm very happy.* **2** You use **and** to link two identical words or phrases in order to emphasize the degree of something or to suggest that something continues or increases over a period of time. *Learning becomes more and more difficult as we get older... We talked for hours and hours.* **3** You use **and** to link two statements about events when one of the events follows the other. *I waved goodbye and went down the stone harbour steps.* **4** You use **and** to link two statements when the second statement continues the point that has been made in the first statement. *You could only really tell the effects of the disease in the long term, and five years wasn't long enough.* **5** You use **and** to link two clauses when the second clause is a result of the first clause. *All through yesterday crowds have been arriving and by midnight thousands of people packed the square.* **6** You use **and** at the beginning of a sentence to introduce something else that you want to add to what to have just said. Some people think that starting a sentence with **and** is incorrect. *Commuter airlines fly to out-of-the-way places. And business travelers are the ones who go to those locations.* **7** You use **and** to introduce a question which follows logically from what someone has just said. *'He used to be so handsome.'—'And now?'* **8 And** is used by broadcasters and people making announcements to change a topic or to start talking about a topic they have just mentioned. *And now the drought in Sudan... Football, and Aston Villa will reclaim their lead at the top of the English First Division.* **9** You use **and** to indicate that two numbers are to be added together. *What does two and two make?* **10 And** is used before a fraction that comes after a whole number. *McCain spent five and a half years in a prisoner of war camp.* **11** You use **and** in numbers larger than one hundred, after the words 'hundred' or 'thousand' and before other numbers. *We printed two hundred and fifty invitations.*

an·drogy·nous /æn'drɒdʒɪnəs/. **1** An **androgynous** person, animal, or plant has both male and female sexual characteristics. **2** If you describe someone or something as **androgynous**, you mean that they are not distinctly masculine or feminine in appearance or in behaviour. *Belinda was always attracted to men with an androgynous quality to them.*

an·drogy·ny /æn'drɒdʒɪni/. **Androgyny** is the state of being neither distinctly masculine nor distinctly feminine.

an·droid /'ændrɔɪd/ **androids.** In science fiction, an **android** is a robot that looks like a human being.

an·ec·do·tal /ˌænɪk'dəʊtəl/. **Anecdotal** evidence is based on individual accounts, rather than on reliable research or statistics. *Anecdotal evidence suggests that sales in Europe have slipped.*

an·ec·dote /'ænɪkdəʊt/ **anecdotes.** An anecdote is a short, amusing account of something that has happened. *Pete was telling them an anecdote about their mother.*

anemia /ə'niːmiə/. See anaemia.

anemic /ə'niːmɪk/. See anaemic.

anemo·ne /ə'nemənɪ/ **anemones.** An anemone is a garden plant with red, purple, or white flowers.

an·es·the·sia /ˌænɪs'θiːziə, -ʒə/. See anaesthesia.

an·es·thesi·olo·gist /ˌænɪsθiːzi'ɒlədʒɪst/ **anesthesiologists.** An anaesthesiologist is a doctor who specializes in giving anaesthetics to patients. The usual British word is **anaesthetist**.

an·es·thet·ic /ˌænɪs'θetɪk/. See anaesthetic.

anes·the·tist /ə'niːsθətɪst/. See anaesthetist.

anes·the·tize /ə'niːsθətaɪz/. See anaesthetize.

anew /ə'njuː, AM ə'nuː/. If you do something **anew**, you do it again, often in a different way from before. *She's ready to start anew... He began his work anew.*

an·gel /'eɪndʒəl/ **angels. 1 Angels** are spiritual beings that some people believe are God's messengers and servants in heaven. **2** You can call someone you like very much an **angel** in order to show affection, especially when they have been kind to you. *Thank you a thousand times, you're an angel.* **3** If you describe someone as an **angel**, you mean that they seem to be very kind and considerate. *He was such an angel to put up with it.*

an·gel·ic /æn'dʒelɪk/. **1** If you say that someone looks **angelic**, you mean that they appear to be very good, kind, and gentle. ...*an angelic face.* **2 Angelic** means like angels or relating to angels.

an·gel·ica /æn'dʒelɪkə/. **Angelica** is the candied stems of the angelica plant which can be used in making cakes or sweets.

an·ger /'æŋgə/ **angers, angering, angered. 1 Anger** is the strong emotion that you feel when you think that someone has behaved in an unfair, cruel, or unacceptable way. *He cried with anger and frustration... Ellen felt both despair and anger.* **2** If something **angers** you, it makes you feel angry. *The decision to allow more offshore oil drilling angered some Californians.*

an·gi·na /æn'dʒaɪnə/. **Angina** is severe pain in the chest and left arm, caused by heart disease.

an·gle /'æŋgəl/ **angles, angling, angled. 1** An **angle** is the difference in direction between two lines or surfaces. *The boat is now leaning at a 30 degree angle.* ● See also **right angle**. **2** An **angle** is the shape that is created where two lines or surfaces join together. ...*the angle of the blade.* **3** If you **angle** something or if it **angles** in a particular direction, it faces or points in that direction. *Open the slats for a bright light or angle them for more shade... The path angled downhill.* **4** An **angle** is the direction from which you look at something. *Thanks to the angle at which he stood, he could just see the sunset.* **5** If something is **at an angle**, it is leaning in a particular direction so that it is not straight, horizontal, or vertical. *An iron bar stuck out at an angle.* **6** You can refer to a way of presenting something or thinking about it as a particular **angle**. *He was considering the idea from all angles.* **7** If someone **is angling for** something, they are trying to make someone offer it to them without asking for it openly and directly. *It sounds as if he's just angling for sympathy.* **8** See also **angling**.

an·gler /'æŋglə/ **anglers.** An angler is someone who fishes with a fishing rod as a hobby.

An·gli·can /'æŋglɪkən/ **Anglicans.** An Anglican is a member of the Church of England. ...*an Anglican priest.*

An·gli·can·ism /'æŋglɪkənɪzəm/. **Anglicanism** refers to the beliefs and practices of the Church of England.

an·gli·cize /'æŋglɪsaɪz/ **anglicizes, anglicizing, anglicized;** also spelled **anglicise** in British English. If you **anglicize** something, you change it so that it resembles or becomes part of the English

language or English culture. *He had anglicized his surname... When Dutch colonial rule ended in the 19th century the civil service was anglicised.* ♦ **an‧gli‧cized** ...*an anglicised version of the continental street-side cafe.* ADJ-GRADED

an‧gling /ˈæŋglɪŋ/. Angling is the activity or sport of fishing with a fishing rod. ◆◇◇◇ N-UNCOUNT

Anglo- /ˈæŋgləʊ-/. 1 **Anglo-** combines with nationality adjectives to form adjectives which describe something connected with relations between Britain and another country. ...*Anglo-American relations. ...the Anglo-Irish Agreement.* 2 **Anglo-** combines with adjectives and nouns indicating nationality to form adjectives or nouns which describe a person who has one British parent and one non-British parent, who has non-British parents but lives in Britain, or who has British parents but lives in another country. ...*born of Anglo-American parentage. ...the Anglo-Asian community.* COMB

An‧glo‧phile /ˈæŋgləʊfaɪl/ **Anglophiles.** If you describe a non-British person as **Anglophile**, you mean that they are very interested in Britain and British culture. ...*the most Anglophile President ever to enter the Oval Office.* ▶ Also a noun. *He became a fanatical Anglophile.* ADJ-GRADED N-COUNT

An‧glo‧phone /ˈæŋgləfəʊn/ **Anglophones.** 1 **Anglophone** communities are English-speaking communities in areas where more than one language is commonly spoken. ...*anglophone Africa.* 2 **Anglophones** are people whose native language is English or who speak English because they live in a country where English is one of the official languages. ADJ: ADJ n N-COUNT

Anglo-'Saxon, Anglo-Saxons. 1 The **Anglo-Saxon** period is the period of English history from the fifth century A.D. to the Norman Conquest in 1066. ...*Roman and Anglo-Saxon remains. ...an early Anglo-Saxon king.* ▶ An **Anglo-Saxon** was someone who was Anglo-Saxon. 2 **Anglo-Saxon** is the language that was spoken in England between the fifth century A.D. and the Norman Conquest in 1066. 3 **Anglo-Saxon** people are members of or are descended from the English race. ...*white Anglo-Saxon Protestant men.* ▶ Also a noun. *You are Anglo-Saxons, we are Latins.* ADJ N-COUNT N-UNCOUNT N-COUNT

an‧go‧ra /æŋˈgɔːrə/. 1 An **angora** goat, rabbit, or cat has long silky hair. 2 **Angora** cloth or clothing is made from the hair of the angora goat or rabbit. ADJ: ADJ n N-UNCOUNT

an‧gry /ˈæŋgri/ **angrier, angriest.** 1 When you are **angry**, you feel strong dislike or impatience about something. *She had been very angry at the person who stole her new bike. ...an angry mob.* ♦ **an‧gri‧ly** /ˈæŋgrɪli/ *Officials reacted angrily to those charges.* 2 An **angry** wound or rash is inflamed and painful. 3 If you describe the sky or sea as **angry**, you mean that it is dark and stormy. ◆◆◆◇ ADJ-GRADED ADV with v ADJ-GRADED ADJ-GRADED LITERARY

angst /æŋst/. **Angst** is a feeling of anxiety and worry. *Many kids suffer from acne and angst.* ◆◇◇◇ N-UNCOUNT

an‧guish /ˈæŋgwɪʃ/. **Anguish** is great mental suffering or physical pain. *Mark looked at him in anguish.* ◆◇◇◇ N-UNCOUNT

an‧guished /ˈæŋgwɪʃt/. **Anguished** means showing or feeling great mental suffering or physical pain. *She let out an anguished cry.* ◆◇◇◇ ADJ-GRADED WRITTEN

an‧gu‧lar /ˈæŋgjʊlə/. **Angular** things have shapes that contain a lot of straight lines and sharp points. ...*an angular face with prominent cheekbones.* ◆◇◇◇ ADJ-GRADED

ani‧mal /ˈænɪməl/ **animals.** 1 Any living creature other than a human being can be referred to as an **animal**. *He was attacked by wild animals.* 2 Any living creature, including a human being, can be referred to as an **animal**. *Watch any young human being, or any other young animal.* 3 **Animal** products come from animals rather than from plants. ...*animal fats found in red meat, hard cheeses and so on.* 4 If you say that someone is an **animal**, you find their behaviour disgusting or very unpleasant. *This man is an animal, a beast.* 5 **Animal** qualities, feelings, or abilities relate to someone's physical nature and instincts rather than to their mind. ...*an animal panic to run and hide.* ◆◆◆◇ N-COUNT N-COUNT ADJ N-COUNT ADJ

6 You can refer to someone as a particular type of **animal** in order to say what their interests are or what their typical behaviour is. *You're quite a party animal aren't you?* N-COUNT: supp N

,**animal 'rights.** People who are concerned with **animal rights** believe very firmly that animals should not be exploited or abused by humans. ◆◇◇◇ N-UNCOUNT

ani‧mate, animates, animating, animated. The adjective is pronounced /ˈænɪmət/. The verb is pronounced /ˈænɪmeɪt/. 1 Something that is **animate** has life, in contrast to things like stones and machines which do not. ...*all aspects of the material world, animate and inanimate.* 2 To **animate** something means to make it lively or more cheerful. *The girls watched, little teasing smiles animating their faces.* ADJ VERB V n

ani‧mat‧ed /ˈænɪmeɪtɪd/. 1 Someone who is **animated** or who is having an **animated** conversation is lively and expressive. *She was seen in animated conversation with the singer.* ♦ **ani‧mat‧ed‧ly** *Sammy was standing close to Ned, talking animatedly with him.* ♦ **ani‧ma‧tion** /ˌænɪˈmeɪʃən/ *They both spoke with animation.* 2 An **animated** film is one in which puppets, models, or drawings appear to move. ...*Disney's animated film 'Lady and the Tramp.'* ♦ **ani‧ma‧tion, animations** ...*traditional cartoon animation. ...documentaries, animations, old classics.* ◆◆◇◇ ADJ-GRADED ADV with v N-UNCOUNT ADJ: ADJ n N-VAR

ani‧ma‧tion. See **animated**; see also **suspended animation.**

ani‧ma‧tor /ˈænɪmeɪtə/ **animators.** An **animator** is a person who makes films using animation. N-COUNT

ani‧mos‧ity /ˌænɪˈmɒsɪti/ **animosities. Animosity** is a strong feeling of dislike and anger. *He insisted that he had no personal animosity towards the Prime Minister.* ◆◇◇◇ N-UNCOUNT: also N in pl

ani‧mus /ˈænɪməs/. If a person has an **animus** against someone, they have a strong feeling of dislike for them, even when there is no reason for it. N-UNCOUNT WRITTEN

ani‧seed /ˈænɪsiːd/. **Aniseed** is a substance made from the seeds of the anise plant. It is used as a flavouring in sweets, drinks, and medicines. *Fennel and pernod add a sutble aniseed flavour.* N-UNCOUNT

an‧kle /ˈæŋkəl/ **ankles.** Your **ankle** is the joint where your foot joins your leg. See picture headed **human body**. *John twisted his ankle badly.* ◆◆◇◇ N-COUNT

an‧nals /ˈænəlz/. 1 If something is in the **annals** of a nation or field of activity, it is recorded as part of its history. ...*the annals of military history.* 2 You can refer to the journal of a particular field of academic research as its **annals**. ...*the 'Annals of Internal Medicine'.* N-PLURAL N-PLURAL: with supp

an‧nex, annexes, annexing, annexed; also spelled **annexe**. The verb is pronounced /æˈneks/. The noun is pronounced /ˈæneks/. 1 If a country **annexes** another country or an area of land, it seizes it and takes control of it. ...*the plan to invade and annex Kuwait. ...the idea of annexing Abkhazia to Russia.* ♦ **an‧nexa‧tion** /ˌænekˈseɪʃən/ **annexations** ...*Indonesia's annexation of East Timor.* 2 An **annexe** is a building which is joined to or is next to a larger main building. ...*setting up a museum in an annexe to the theatre.* 3 An **annexe** to a document is a section added to it at the end. *The Annex lists and discusses eight titles.* ◆◇◇◇ VERB V n V n to n N-COUNT N-COUNT N-COUNT

an‧ni‧hi‧late /əˈnaɪɪleɪt/ **annihilates, annihilating, annihilated.** 1 To **annihilate** something means to destroy it completely. *Laser weapons may not yet be powerful enough to annihilate enemy targets.* ♦ **an‧ni‧hi‧la‧tion** /əˌnaɪɪˈleɪʃən/ *Leaders fear the annihilation of their people.* 2 If you **annihilate** someone in a contest or argument, you totally defeat them. *Coetzer annihilated 12th seed Nathalie Tauziat 6-0, 6-0.* ◆◇◇◇ VERB V n N-UNCOUNT VERB V n

an‧ni‧ver‧sa‧ry /ˌænɪˈvɜːsəri/ **anniversaries.** An **anniversary** is a date which is remembered or celebrated because a special event happened on that date in a previous year. ...*the one hundredth anniversary of the birth of Ho Chi Minh.* ◆◆◆◇ N-COUNT

an·no·tate /'ænəυteɪt/ **annotates, annotating,** VERB: V n
annotated. If you **annotate** written work or a dia- V-ed
gram, you add notes to it. ...*an annotated bibliogra-*
phy. ♦ **an·no·ta·tion** *She retained a number of* N-UNCOUNT
copies for further annotation.

an·no·ta·tion /,ænəυ'teɪʃən/ **annotations.** An **an-** N-COUNT
notation is a note that is added to a text or diagram.

an·nounce /ə'naυns/ **announces, announcing,** ◆◆◆◆
announced. 1 If you **announce** something, you VERB
tell people about it publicly or officially. *He will an-* V that
nounce tonight that he is resigning... She was plan- V n
ning to announce her engagement... It was an- *it be* V-ed that
nounced that the groups have agreed to a cease-fire.
♦ **announcement** /ə'naυnsmənt/ ...*the announce-* N-SING
ment of the engagement... There has been no official
announcement of the arrests. **2** If you **announce** a VERB
piece of news or an intention, you say it loudly and V that
clearly, so that everyone you are with can hear it. V with quote
Peter announced that he had no intention of wasting
his time at any university... 'I'm having a bath and
going to bed,' she announced. **3** If an airport or rail- VERB: V n
way employee **announces** something, they tell the V that
public about it by means of a loudspeaker system.
They announced his plane was delayed. ♦ **an-**
·nounc·er, announcers *The announcer apolo-* N-COUNT
gised for the delay. **4** If a letter, sound, or sign **an-** VERB
nounces something, it informs people about it. *The* V n
next letter announced the birth of another boy.

an·nounce·ment /ə'naυnsmənt/ **announce-** ◆◆◆◇◇
ments. 1 An **announcement** is a statement made N-COUNT
to the public or to the media which gives information about something that has happened or that will
happen. *Mr Shevardnadze made the announcement*
that he was to step down. **2** An **announcement** in a N-COUNT
public place is a short piece of writing telling people
about something or asking for something. *He will*
place an announcement in the personal column of
The Daily Telegraph.

an·nounc·er /ə'naυnsə/ **announcers.** An **an-** ◆◆◇◇◇
nouncer is someone who introduces programmes N-COUNT
on radio or television or who reads the text of a radio or television advertisement. *The radio announc-*
er said it was nine o'clock.

an·noy /ə'nɔɪ/ **annoys, annoying, annoyed.** If ◆◇◇◇◇
someone or something **annoys** you, they make you VERB
fairly angry and impatient. *Try making a note of the* V n
things which annoy you... It annoyed me that I *it* V that
didn't have time to do more ironing... It just annoyed *it* V n to-inf
me to hear him go on. ● See also **annoyed,** Also V
annoying.

an·noy·ance /ə'nɔɪəns/ **annoyances. 1** Annoy- ◆◇◇◇◇
ance is the feeling that you get when someone N-UNCOUNT
makes you feel fairly angry or impatient. *To her an-*
noyance the stranger did not go away... He denied
there was any annoyance with the British. **2** An **an-** N-COUNT
noyance is something that makes you feel angry or
impatient. *Snoring can be more than an annoyance.*

an·noyed /ə'nɔɪd/. If you are **annoyed**, you are ◆◇◇◇◇
fairly angry about something. *She tapped her fore-* ADJ-GRADED
head and looked annoyed with herself... Syria is an-
noyed that the PLO called last month's Arab summit
in Baghdad. ● See also **annoy**.

an·noy·ing /ə'nɔɪɪŋ/. Someone or something that ◆◇◇◇◇
is **annoying** makes you feel fairly angry and impa- ADJ-GRADED
tient. *The annoying thing about the scheme is that*
it's confusing. ♦ **an·noy·ing·ly** *Alex looked annoy-* ADV-GRADED
ingly cheerful. ● See also **annoy**.

an·nual /'ænjυəl/ **annuals. 1** Annual events hap- ◆◆◆◇◇
pen once every year. ...*the annual conference of* ADJ: ADJ n
Britain's trade union movement. ...its annual report.
♦ **an·nual·ly** *Companies report to their share-* ADV:
holders annually. **2** Annual quantities or rates relate ADV with v
to a period of one year. ...*annual sales of about $80* ADJ: ADJ n
million. ♦ **annually** *El Salvador produces 100,000* ADV
tons of refined copper annually. **3** An **annual** is a N-COUNT
book or magazine that is published once a year. *I*
looked for Wyman's picture in my high-school an-
nual. **4** An **annual** is a plant that grows and dies N-COUNT
within one year.

an·nu·ity /ə'njuːɪti, AM ə'nuːɪti/ **annuities.** An an- ◆◇◇◇◇
nuity is an investment or insurance policy that pays N-COUNT
someone a fixed sum of money each year.

an·nul /ə'nʌl/ **annuls, annulling, annulled.** If an VB: usu
election or a contract **is annulled**, it is declared in- passive
valid, so that legally it is considered never to have *be* V-ed
existed. *The marriage was annulled last month.*
♦ **an·nul·ment** /ə'nʌlmənt/ **annulments** ...*the an-* N-VAR
nulment of the elections.

an·num /'ænəm/. See **per annum**.

An·nun·cia·tion /ə,nʌnsi'eɪʃən/. In Christian be- N-PROPER:
lief, **the Annunciation** was the announcement by *the* N
the Archangel Gabriel to Mary that she was going to
give birth to the son of God.

an·ode /'ænəυd/ **anodes.** An **anode** is the positive N-COUNT
electrode in a cell such as a battery. ● See also
cathode.

ano·dyne /'ænədaɪn/. Something that is **anodyne** is ADJ-GRADED
neutral and not dangerous or distressing. *Their* FORMAL
quarterly meetings were anodyne affairs.

anoint /ə'nɔɪnt/ **anoints, anointing, anointed.** VERB
1 If someone **anoints** a person, they put oil or an- V n
other liquid on a part of that person's body, usually V n as n
for religious or ceremonial reasons. *He anointed my*
forehead... The Pope has anointed him as Arch-
bishop. **2** If someone in a position of authority VERB
anoints someone as something, they choose that V n as n
person to do a particular important job. ...*anointing* Also V n n
Mr Wasmosy as the Colorado candidate... Mr. Olsen
has always avoided anointing any successor.

anoma·ly /ə'nɒməli/ **anomalies.** If something is ◆◇◇◇◇
an **anomaly**, it is different from what is usual or ex- N-COUNT
pected. *The British public's wariness of opera is an* FORMAL
anomaly in Europe. ♦ **anoma·lous** /ə'nɒmələs/. ADJ-GRADED
This anomalous behaviour has baffled scientists.

anon /ə'nɒn/. **Anon** means quite soon. *You shall see* ADV
him anon. LITERARY

anon. /ə'nɒn/. **Anon.** is often written after poems
or other writing to indicate that the author is not
known. **Anon.** is an abbreviation for 'anonymous'.

anony·mous /ə'nɒnɪməs/. **1** If you remain **anony-** ◆◆◇◇◇
mous when you do something, you do not let peo- ADJ
ple know that you were the person who did it.
Something that is **anonymous** does not reveal who
you are. *You can remain anonymous if you wish.*
...*anonymous phone calls.* ♦ **ano·nym·ity** N-UNCOUNT
/,ænə'nɪmɪti/ *Both mother and daughter, who have*
requested anonymity, are doing fine. ♦ **anony-**
·mous·ly *The latest photographs were sent anony-* ADV
mously to the magazine's Paris headquarters. **2** If ADJ-GRADED
you describe a place as **anonymous** you dislike it PRAGMATICS
because it has no unusual or interesting features.
...*an anonymous holiday villa.*

ano·rak /'ænəræk/ **anoraks. 1** An **anorak** is a ◆◇◇◇◇
warm waterproof jacket, usually with a hood. **2** If N-COUNT
you describe someone as an **anorak**, you are mak- N-COUNT
ing fun of them because they are very enthusiastic PRAGMATICS
about a particular activity, sport, or way of life, and BRITISH,
you think that this makes them very boring. *Most* INFORMAL
computer manuals appear to have been written by
anoraks from hell.

ano·rexia /,ænə'reksiə/. **Anorexia** or **anorexia ner-** ◆◇◇◇◇
vosa is an illness in which a person has an over- N-UNCOUNT
whelming fear of becoming fat, and so refuses to eat
enough and becomes thinner and thinner.

ano·rex·ic /,ænə'reksɪk/ **anorexics.** If someone is ADJ
anorexic, they are suffering from anorexia and so
are very thin. ...*an anorexic teenager.* ● Also a noun. N-COUNT
Not eating makes an anorexic feel in control.

an·oth·er /ə'nʌðə/. **1** Another thing or person ◆◆◆◆
means one more in addition to those that already DET
exist or are known about. *Another change that Sue*
made was to install central heating... We're going to
have another baby. ► Also a pronoun. *The demand* PRON
generated by one factory required the construction of
another. **2** You use **another** when you want to em- DET
phasize that an additional thing or person is differ- PRAGMATICS
ent from one that already exists. *The counsellor re-*
ferred her to another therapist. ► Also a pronoun. *He* PRON
said one thing and has done quite another. **3** You DET

use **another** before a word referring to a distance, length of time, or other amount, to indicate an additional amount. *Continue down the same road for another 2 kilometres.* **4** You use **another** in front of the name of a well-known person, place, or event to indicate that you think they are just like that person, place, or event. *There is another Maradona in this year's World Cup: Romania's 25-year old star midfielder Georghe Hagi.* [DET]

5 You use **one another** to indicate that each member of a group does something to or for the other members. *...women learning to help themselves and one another.* **6** If you talk about **one** thing **after another**, you are referring to a series of repeated or continuous events. *They kept going, destroying one store after another.* **7** You use **or another** in expressions such as **one kind or another** when you do not want to be precise about which of several alternatives or possibilities you are referring to. *All of these industries have at one time or another been linked to cancer.* [PRON] [PHRASE] [PHRASE]

an·swer /'ɑːnsə, 'æn-/ **answers, answering, answered.** **1** When you **answer** someone who has asked you something, you say something back to them. *Just answer the question... 'When?' asked Alba, calmly. 'Tonight', answered Hunter... Williams answered that he had no specific proposals yet.* **2** An **answer** is something that you say when you answer someone. *Without waiting for an answer, he turned and went in through the door... I don't quite know what to say in answer to your question.* **3** If you say that someone will not **take no for an answer**, you mean that they go on trying to make you agree to something even after you have refused. *She is tough, unwilling to take no for an answer.* [◆◆◆◆◇] [VERB] [V n] [V with quote] [V that] [Also V] [N-COUNT: also in N too] [PHRASE]

4 If you **answer** a letter or advertisement, you write to the person who wrote it. *She answered an advert for a job as a cook.* **5** An **answer** is a letter that you write to someone who has written to you. *I wrote to him but I never had an answer back... She wrote to Roosevelt's secretary in answer to his letter.* [VERB] [V n] [Also V] [N-COUNT: also in N too]

6 When you **answer** the telephone, you pick it up when it rings. When you **answer** the door, you open it when you hear a knock or the bell. *She answered her phone on the first ring.* ▶ Also a noun. *I knocked at the front door and there was no answer.* [VERB] [V n] [Also V] [N-COUNT]

7 Someone's **answer** to a question in a test or quiz is what they write or say in an attempt to give the facts that are asked for. The **answer** to a question is the fact that was asked for. *Simply marking an answer wrong will not help the pupil. ...the answers to the Brain of Soccer 1993 quiz.* **8** When you **answer** a question in a test or quiz, you write or say something in an attempt to give the facts that are asked for. *She answered 81 questions.* [N-COUNT] [VERB] [V n]

9 An **answer** to a problem is a solution to it. *There are no easy answers to the problems facing the economy... Legislation is only part of the answer.* **10** If something **answers** a need or purpose, it satisfies it, because it has the right qualities. *Would communism answer their needs?* [N-COUNT] [VERB] [V n]

11 Your **answer** to something that someone has said or done is what you say or do in response to it. *In answer to speculation that she wouldn't finish the race, she boldly declared her intention of winning it.* **12** If you **answer** something that someone has said or done, you respond to it. *He answered her smile with one of his own... That statement seemed designed to answer criticism of allied bombing missions.* [N-COUNT: also in N too] [VERB] [V n with n] [V n]

13 If you say that something is a place's **answer** to a famous thing, you mean that the first thing is the equivalent of the second in that place. *Cachaca is Brazil's answer to tequila.* [N-SING: poss N too]

14 If someone or something **answers** a particular description or **answers to** it, they have the characteristics described. *...two men answering the description.* [VERB] [V n] [Also V too n]

answer back. If someone **answers back**, they speak rudely to you when you speak to them. *She was beaten by teachers for answering back.* [PHRASAL VB] [V P] [Also V n P]

answer for. 1 If you have to **answer for** something bad or wrong you have done, you are punished for it. [PHRASAL VB] [V P n]

He must be made to answer for his terrible crimes. **2** If you say that someone **has a lot to answer for**, you are saying that their actions have led to problems which you think they are responsible for. [PHRASE]

an·swer·able /'ɑːnsərəbəl, 'æn-/. **1** If you are **answerable** to someone, you have to report to them and explain your actions. *Councils should be answerable to the people who elect them.* **2** If you are **answerable** for your actions or for someone else's actions, you are considered to be responsible for them and must be punished if it is justified. *He must be made answerable for these terrible crimes.* [ADJ: v-link ADJ to n] [ADJ: v-link ADJ]

'answering machine, answering machines. An **answering machine** is a device which you connect to your telephone and which records telephone messages while you are out. [◆◇◇◇◇] [N-COUNT]

an·swer·phone /'ɑːnsəfəʊn, 'æn-/ **answerphones.** An **answerphone** is the same as an answering machine. [N-COUNT] [BRITISH]

ant /ænt/ **ants.** Ants are small crawling insects that live in large groups. See picture headed **insects**. [◆◇◇◇◇] [N-COUNT]

ant·acid /ænt'æsɪd/ **antacids.** Antacid is a substance that reduces the level of acid in the stomach. [N-VAR]

an·tag·o·nism /æn'tægənɪzəm/ **antagonisms.** Antagonism between people is hatred or hostility between them. *There is still much antagonism between trades unions and the oil companies.* [◆◇◇◇◇] [N-UNCOUNT: also N in pl]

an·tag·o·nist /æn'tægənɪst/ **antagonists.** Your **antagonist** is your opponent or enemy. *Spassky had never previously lost to his antagonist.* [◆◇◇◇◇] [N-COUNT]

an·tag·o·nis·tic /æn,tægə'nɪstɪk/. If a person is **antagonistic** to someone or something, they show hatred or hostility towards them. *The women I interviewed were aggressively antagonistic to the idea.* [ADJ-GRADED]

an·tag·o·nize /æn'tægənaɪz/ **antagonizes, antagonizing, antagonized;** also spelled **antagonise** in British English. If you **antagonize** someone, you make them feel angry or hostile towards you. [◆◇◇◇◇] [VERB: V n]

Ant·arc·tic /ænt'ɑːktɪk/. The Antarctic is the area around the South Pole. [◆◇◇◇◇] [N-PROPER]

ante /'ænti/ **antes, anted.** If you **up the ante**, you increase your demands when you are in a dispute or fighting for something. [PHRASE] [JOURNALISM]

ante up. If you **ante up** an amount of money, you pay it, sometimes reluctantly. The usual British term is **cough up.** *Paul Reichmann offered to ante up $2 million.* [PHRASAL VB] [no cont] [V P n] [AMERICAN]

ant·eater /'ænti:tə/ **anteaters.** An **anteater** is an animal with a long snout that eats termites or ants. See picture headed **animals**. [N-COUNT]

ante·ced·ent /,ænti'si:dənt/ **antecedents. 1** An **antecedent** of something happened or existed before it and was similar to it in some way. *...the historical antecedents of this theory.* ▶ Also an adjective. *...antecedent legislation.* **2** Your **antecedents** are your ancestors. *Princess Grace, born Grace Kelly in Philadelphia, had Irish antecedents.* [N-COUNT] [FORMAL] [ADJ] [N-COUNT] [FORMAL]

ante·cham·ber /'æntɪʃeɪmbə/ **antechambers.** An **antechamber** is a small room leading into a larger room. *Her office was an antechamber to UNACO headquarters.* [N-COUNT]

ante·di·lu·vian /,æntɪdɪ'luːvɪən/. People sometimes describe old or old-fashioned things as **antediluvian.** *...those antediluvian days before telephone answering machines.* [ADJ] [PRAGMATICS] [LITERARY]

ante·lope /'æntɪləʊp/ **antelopes.** An **antelope** is an animal similar to a deer that lives in Africa or Asia. The plural is either 'antelope' or 'antelopes'. [N-COUNT]

ante·na·tal /,ænti'neɪtəl/; also spelled **ante-natal.** Antenatal means relating to the medical care of women when they are expecting a baby. The American word is **prenatal.** *...antenatal classes. ...antenatal care.* [ADJ: ADJ n] [BRITISH]

an·ten·na /æn'tenə/ **antennae** /æn'teni:/ or **antennas.** Antennas is the usual plural form for meaning 2. **1** The **antennae** of an insect are the two long thin parts attached to its head that it uses to feel things. See picture headed **insects.** **2** An **antenna** is a device that sends and receives television or radio signals. See pictures headed **car and bicycle** [◆◇◇◇◇] [N-COUNT] [N-COUNT]

and **house and flat**. ...*radio antennas for satellite communication.*

an·te·ri·or /æn'tɪərɪə/. **Anterior** describes a part of the body that is situated at or towards the front of another part. ...*the left anterior descending artery.* ADJ MEDICAL

ante·room /'æntɪruːm/ **anterooms;** also spelled **ante-room.** An **anteroom** is a small room leading into a larger room. *I was waiting in the anteroom of a BBC radio studio.* N-COUNT

an·them /'ænθəm/ **anthems.** An **anthem** is a song which is used to represent a particular nation, society, or group and which is sung on special occasions. ...*the Czech anthem.* ...*the Olympic anthem.* ● See also **national anthem.** ◆◇◇◇◇ N-COUNT

ant·hill /'ænthɪl/ **anthills.** An **anthill** is a mound of earth formed by ants when they are making a nest. N-COUNT

an·thol·ogy /æn'θɒlədʒi/ **anthologies.** An **anthology** is a collection of writings by different writers published in one book. ...*an anthology of poetry.* ◆◇◇◇◇ N-COUNT

an·thra·cite /'ænθrəsaɪt/. **Anthracite** is a type of very hard coal which burns slowly, producing a lot of heat and very little smoke. N-UNCOUNT

an·thrax /'ænθræks/. **Anthrax** is a disease of cattle and sheep, in which they get painful sores and a fever. N-UNCOUNT

an·thro·pol·ogy /ˌænθrə'pɒlədʒi/. **Anthropology** is the scientific study of people, society, and culture. ◆◇◇◇◇ N-UNCOUNT
♦ **an·thro·polo·gist** /ˌænθrə'pɒlədʒɪst/ **anthropologists** ...*an anthropologist who had been in China.* ♦ **an·thro·po·logi·cal** /ˌænθrəpə'lɒdʒɪkəl/ ...*anthropological research.* N-COUNT / ADJ: ADJ n

an·thro·po·mor·phic /ˌænθrəpə'mɔːfɪk/. **Anthropomorphic** means relating to the idea that an animal, a god, or an object has feelings or characteristics like those of a human being. ...*the anthropomorphic attitude to animals.* ADJ

anti /'ænti/ **antis. 1** You can refer to people who are opposed to a particular activity or idea as the **antis.** *These 'antis' are nothing more than paid troublemakers.* **2** If someone is opposed to something you can say that they are **anti** it. *That's why you're so anti other people smoking.* N-COUNT INFORMAL / ADJ-GRADED: v-link ADJ

anti- /'ænti-/. **Anti-** is used in front of nouns and adjectives to form other nouns and adjectives that describe someone or something that acts against or is opposed to someone or something. ...*anti-government demonstrations.* ...*anti-discrimination legislation.* ...*anti-inflammatory drugs.* PREFIX

anti-a'bortionist, anti-abortionists. An **anti-abortionist** is someone who wants to limit or prevent the legal availability of abortions. N-COUNT

anti·bi·ot·ic /ˌæntɪbaɪ'ɒtɪk/ **antibiotics.** Antibiotics are drugs that are used in medicine to kill bacteria and infections. ◆◆◇◇◇ N-COUNT

anti·body /'æntɪbɒdi/ **antibodies.** Antibodies are substances which a person's or an animal's body produces in their blood in order to destroy substances which carry disease. ◆◆◇◇◇ N-COUNT

an·tici·pate /æn'tɪsɪpeɪt/ **anticipates, anticipating, anticipated. 1** If you **anticipate** an event, you realize in advance that it may happen and you are prepared for it. *We couldn't have anticipated the result of our campaigning... It is anticipated that the equivalent of 192 full-time jobs will be lost.* **2** If you **anticipate** a question, request, or need, you do what is necessary or required before the question, request, or need occurs. *Do you expect your partner to anticipate your needs?* **3** If you **anticipate** something, you do it, think it, or say it before someone else does. *Rauschenberg anticipated the conceptual art movement of the 80s.* ◆◆◇◇◇ VERB V n / it be V-ed that Also V, V that / VERB V n / VERB V n

an·tici·pat·ed /æn'tɪsɪpeɪtɪd/. If an event is eagerly **anticipated**, people expect that it will be very good, exciting, or interesting. ...*one of the conference's most keenly anticipated debates.* ADJ-GRADED

an·tici·pa·tion /ænˌtɪsɪ'peɪʃən/. **1 Anticipation** is a feeling of excitement about something pleasant or exciting that you know is going to happen. *We await the next volume of this superb edition with keen anticipation.* **2** If something is done **in antici-** ◆◇◇◇◇ N-UNCOUNT / PHRASE

pation of an event, it is done because people believe that event is going to happen. *Troops in the Philippines have been put on full alert in anticipation of trouble.*

an·tici·pa·tory /ænˌtɪsɪ'peɪtəri, AM ænˈtɪsɪpətɔːri/. An **anticipatory** feeling or action is one that you have or do because you are expecting something to happen soon. ...*anticipatory excitement at the prospect of cooking and eating such delights.* ADJ FORMAL

anti·cli·max /ˌænti'klaɪmæks/ **anticlimaxes.** You can describe something as an **anticlimax** if it disappoints you because it happens after something that was very exciting, or because it is not as exciting as you expected. *It was sad that his international career should end in such anticlimax.* N-VAR

anti·clock·wise /ˌænti'klɒkwaɪz/; also spelled **anti-clockwise.** If something is moving **anticlockwise,** it is moving in the opposite direction to the direction in which the hands of a clock move. The usual American word is **counterclockwise.** ...*turning the knob anticlockwise.* ▶ Also an adjective. ...*an anticlockwise route around the coast.* ADV: ADV after v BRITISH / ADJ: ADJ n

an·tics /'æntɪks/. **Antics** are funny, silly, or unusual ways of behaving. *Elizabeth tolerated Sarah's antics.* ◆◇◇◇◇ N-PLURAL

anti·cy·clone /ˌænti'saɪkləʊn/ **anticyclones.** An **anticyclone** is an area of high atmospheric pressure which causes settled weather conditions. N-COUNT

anti·dote /'æntɪdəʊt/ **antidotes. 1** An **antidote** is a chemical substance that stops or controls the effect of a poison. **2** Something that is an **antidote** to a difficult or unpleasant situation helps you to overcome the situation. *Massage is a wonderful antidote to stress.* ◆◇◇◇◇ N-COUNT / N-COUNT

anti·freeze /'æntifriːz/. **Antifreeze** is a liquid which is added to water to stop it freezing. N-UNCOUNT: also a N

'anti-hero, anti-heroes. An **anti-hero** is the main character in a novel, play, or film who behaves completely differently to the way that people expect a hero to behave. ...*a tough, belligerent anti-hero.* N-COUNT

anti·his·ta·mine /ˌænti'hɪstəmɪn/ **antihistamines;** also spelled **anti-histamine.** An **antihistamine** is a drug that is used to treat illnesses that are caused by allergies. N-COUNT

anti·mat·ter /'æntimætə/. **Antimatter** is a form of matter whose particles have characteristics and properties opposite to those of ordinary matter. N-UNCOUNT TECHNICAL

an·tipa·thy /æn'tɪpəθi/. **Antipathy** is a strong feeling of dislike or hostility. ...*their patent antipathy to my smoking.* ◆◇◇◇◇ N-UNCOUNT

An·tipo·dean /ænˌtɪpə'diːən/. **Antipodean** describes people or things that come from or relate to Australia and New Zealand. ...*Antipodean wines.* ADJ BRITISH

Anti·podes /æn'tɪpədiːz/. People sometimes refer to Australia and New Zealand as the **Antipodes.** N-PROPER BRITISH

anti·quar·ian /ˌænti'kweəriən/ **antiquarians. 1 Antiquarian** means concerned with old and rare objects. ...*antiquarian and second-hand books.* **2** An **antiquarian** is the same as an **antiquary.** ADJ: ADJ n / N-COUNT

anti·quary /'æntɪkwəri, AM -kweri/ **antiquaries.** An **antiquary** is a person who studies the past, or who collects or buys and sells old and valuable objects. N-COUNT

anti·quat·ed /'æntɪkweɪtɪd/. If you describe something as **antiquated,** you disapprove of it because it is very old or old-fashioned. *Many factories are so antiquated they are not worth saving.* ◆◇◇◇◇ ADJ-GRADED PRAGMATICS

an·tique /æn'tiːk/ **antiques.** An **antique** is an old object such as a piece of china or furniture which is valuable because of its beauty or rarity. ...*a genuine antique.* ...*antique silver jewellery.* ◆◆◆◇◇ N-COUNT

an'tique shop, antique shops. An antique shop is a shop where antiques are sold. N-COUNT

an·tiq·uity /æn'tɪkwɪti/ **antiquities. 1 Antiquity** is the distant past, especially the time of the ancient Egyptians, Greeks, and Romans. *The town was famous in antiquity for its white bulls.* **2 Antiquities** are things such as buildings, statues, or coins that were made in ancient times and have survived to the present day. ◆◇◇◇◇ N-UNCOUNT / N-COUNT

anti-Semite /ˌænti 'siːmaɪt, AM - 'sem-/ **anti-Semites.** An **anti-Semite** is someone who strongly dislikes and is prejudiced against Jewish people. N-COUNT
♦ **anti-Semitic** /ˌænti səˈmɪtɪk/ ...*His anti-Semitic beliefs were well-known in America.* ADJ-GRADED

anti-Semitism /ˌænti ˈsemɪtɪzəm/. **Anti-Semitism** is hostility to and prejudice against Jewish people. ◆◇◇◇ N-UNCOUNT

anti·sep·tic /ˌæntiˈseptɪk/ **antiseptics. 1 Anti-septic** is a substance that kills germs and harmful bacteria. **2** Something that is **antiseptic** kills germs and harmful bacteria. *These vegetables and herbs have strong antiseptic qualities.* ◇◇◇◇ N-VAR / ADJ

anti·social; also spelled **antisocial. 1 Anti-social** people are unwilling to meet and be friendly with other people. **2 Anti-social** behaviour is annoying or upsetting to other people. ◆◇◇◇ ADJ-GRADED / ADJ-GRADED

an·tith·e·sis /ænˈtɪθəsɪs/ **antitheses** /ænˈtɪθəsiːz/. **1** The **antithesis** of something is its exact opposite. *He is the antithesis of the American superhero.* **2** If there is an **antithesis** between two things, there is a contrast between them. ...*the antithesis between instinct and reason.* N-COUNT FORMAL / N-COUNT FORMAL

anti·thet·i·cal /ˌæntɪˈθetɪkəl/. Something that is **antithetical** to something else is the opposite of it and is unable to exist with it. *The oppressive use of power is antithetical to our democratic ideals.* ADJ

anti·trust /ˌæntiˈtrʌst/. In the United States, **antitrust** laws are intended to stop large firms dominating the market. ◆◇◇◇ ADJ: ADJ n

ant·ler /ˈæntlə/ **antlers.** A male deer's **antlers** are the branched horns on its head. N-COUNT

an·to·nym /ˈæntənɪm/ **antonyms.** The **antonym** of a word is a word which means the opposite. N-COUNT FORMAL

anus /ˈeɪnəs/ **anuses.** A person's **anus** is the hole between their buttocks, from which faeces leave their body. N-COUNT

an·vil /ˈænvɪl/ **anvils.** An **anvil** is a heavy iron block on which hot metals are beaten into shape. N-COUNT

anxi·ety /æŋˈzaɪɪti/ **anxieties.** Anxiety is a feeling of nervousness or worry. *Her voice was full of anxiety.* ...*anxieties about the economic chaos in the country.* ◆◆◇◇ N-UNCOUNT: also N in pl

anx·ious /ˈæŋkʃəs/. **1** If you are **anxious** to do something or **anxious** that something should happen, you very much want to do it or very much want it to happen. *The Americans are anxious to avoid conflict in South Asia... He is anxious that there should be no delay... Those anxious for reform say that the present system is too narrow.* **2** If you are feeling **anxious,** you are nervous or worried about something. You can also use **anxious** to describe a time when someone feels anxious. *When did you start to feel anxious about looking older?... The Prime Minister faces anxious hours before the votes are counted.* ♦ **anx·ious·ly** *They waited anxiously for news of John's health.* ◆◆◇◇ ADJ-GRADED: v-link ADJ / ADJ-GRADED / ADV-GRADED: ADV with v

any /ˈeni/. **1** You use **any** in statements with negative meaning to indicate that no thing or person of a particular type exists, is present, or is involved in a situation. *I never make any big decisions... We are doing this all without any support from the hospital... Earlier reports were unable to confirm that there were any survivors... It is too early to say what effect, if any, there will be on the workforce.* ▶ Also a quantifier. *You don't know any of my friends... There was nothing any of us could do.* ▶ Also a pronoun. *The children needed new school clothes and Kim couldn't afford any.* **2** You use **any** to emphasize a comparative adjective or adverb in a negative statement. *I can't see things getting any easier.* **3** You use **any** in questions and conditional clauses to ask whether there is some of a particular thing or some of a particular group of people, or to suggest that there might be. *Do you speak any foreign languages?... Are there any ladies in the audience?... Have you got any cheese?* ▶ Also a quantifier. *Introduce foods one at a time and notice if you feel uncomfortable with any of them... Have you ever used a homeopathic remedy for any of the following reasons?* ▶ Also ◆◆◆◆ DET / QUANT / PRON / ADV: ADV compar PRAGMATICS / DET / QUANT / PRON

a pronoun. *The plants are inspected for insects and if I find any, they are squashed.* **4** You use **any** in positive statements when you are referring to someone or something of a particular kind that might exist, occur, or be involved in a situation, when their exact identity or nature is irrelevant. *Any actor will tell you that it is easier to perform than to be themselves... I'm prepared to take any advice.* ▶ Also a quantifier. *Nealy disappeared two days ago, several miles away from any of the fighting. ...the biggest mistake any of them could remember.* ▶ Also a pronoun. *Clean the mussels and discard any that do not close.* **5** If you say that someone or something is **not just any** person or thing, you mean that they are special in some way. *Finzer is not just any East Coast businessman.* **6** If something does not happen or is not true **any more** or **any longer,** it has stopped happening or is no longer true. *I don't want to see her any more... I couldn't keep the tears hidden any longer.* **7** ● **in any case:** see **case.** ● **by any chance:** see **chance.** ● **in any event:** see **event.** ● **by any means:** see **means.** ● **any old:** see **old.** ● **at any rate:** see **rate.** DET / QUANT / PRON / PHRASE / PHRASE

any·body /ˈenibɒdi/. **Anybody** means the same as **anyone.** ◆◆◇◇ PRON-INDEF

any·how /ˈenihaʊ/. **Anyhow** means the same as **anyway.** ◆◇◇◇ ADV

any·more /ˌeniˈmɔː/. If something does not happen or is not true **anymore,** it has stopped happening or is no longer true. Some people think this spelling is incorrect and prefer to use **any more.** *People are not interested in movies anymore.* ◆◇◇◇ ADV: ADV after v

any·one /ˈeniwʌn/. The form **anybody** is also used. **1** You use **anyone** or **anybody** in statements with negative meaning to indicate in a general way that nobody is present or involved in an action. *You needn't talk to anyone if you don't want to... He was far too scared to tell anybody... Presidents are not any different from anybody else.* **2** You use **anyone** or **anybody** in questions and conditional clauses to ask or talk about someone who might be involved in a particular situation or action. *Did you tell anyone where I was?... If anybody wants me, I'll be at the police station.* **3** You also use **anyone** and **anybody** before words which indicate the kind of person you are talking about. *It's not a job for anyone who is slow with numbers... Anybody interested in pop culture at all should buy 'Pure Cult'.* **4** You use **anyone** or **anybody** to say that a particular thing would be true of any person out of a very large number of people. *Anyone could be doing what I'm doing... Al Smith could make anybody laugh.* ◆◆◆◇ PRON-INDEF / PRON-INDEF / PRON-INDEF / PRON-INDEF

any·place /ˈenipleɪs/. **Anyplace** means the same as **anywhere.** *She didn't have anyplace to go.* ADV AMERICAN

any·thing /ˈeniθɪŋ/. **1** You use **anything** in statements with negative meaning to indicate in a general way that nothing is present or that an action or event does not or cannot happen. *She couldn't see or hear anything... I couldn't manage anything.* **2** You use **anything** in questions and conditional clauses to ask or talk about whether something is present or happening. *Did you find anything?... If there's anything I could do for him.* **3** You use **anything** before words which indicate the kind of thing you are talking about. *She collects anything that has charm. ...anything that's cheap.* **4** You use **anything** to say that a particular thing could be true about any one of a very large number of things. *Anything could happen... He just has to say 'please' and he can have anything.* **5** When you do not want to be exact, you use **anything** to talk about a particular range of things or quantities. ...*anything from 25 to 40 litres of milk per day... Fights with his father lasted anything between fifteen minutes and an hour.* **6** You use **anything** in expressions such as **anything near, anything close to,** and **anything like** to emphasize a statement that you are making. *The only way he can live anything near a normal life is to give him an operation... Plainer examples of the early period do not fetch anything like these sums.* **7** You use **anything but** ◆◆◆◆ PRON-INDEF / PRON-INDEF / PRON-INDEF / PRON-INDEF PRAGMATICS / PRON-INDEF / PRON-INDEF PRAGMATICS / PHRASE

to emphasize that something is not the case. *I will be anything but quiet on Saturday night!... What existed in central and eastern Europe was anything but democratic socialism... He was not always so insulated from politicians; anything but.* **8** You use **as anything** after an adjective to emphasize a quality that someone has. *He used to be as smart as anything... She opened the door and jumped out, quick as anything.* **9** If you say that you **would not** do something or be something **for anything**, you mean that you definitely would not want to do or be that thing. *I wouldn't take that job for anything.* **10** You use **if anything**, especially after a negative statement, to introduce a statement that adds to what you have just said. *I never had to clean up after him. If anything, he did most of the cleaning.* **11** You can add **or anything** to the end of a clause or sentence in order to refer vaguely to other things that are or may be similar to what has just been mentioned. *He didn't cry or scream or anything.*

any·time /ˌeniˈtaɪm/. You use **anytime** to mean at an unspecified point in time. *The college admits students anytime during the year... He can leave anytime he wants.*

any·way /ˈeniweɪ/. The form **anyhow** is also used. **1** You use **anyway** to indicate that a statement explains or supports a previous point. *I'm certain David's told you his business troubles. Anyway, it's no secret that he owes money... Mother certainly won't let him stay with her and anyhow he wouldn't.* **2** You use **anyway** to suggest that a statement is true or relevant in spite of other things that have been said. *I don't know why I settled on Aberdeen, but anyway I did... I wasn't qualified to apply for the job really but I got it anyhow.* **3** You use **anyway** to correct or modify a statement. *Mary Ann doesn't want to have children. Not right now, anyway.* **4** You use **anyway** to indicate that you are asking what the real situation is. *What do you want from me, anyway?* **5** You use **anyway** to indicate that you are missing out some details in a story and are passing on to the next main point or event. *I was told to go to Reading for this interview. It was a very amusing affair. Anyhow, I got the job.* **6** You use **anyway** to change the topic or return to a previous topic. *'I've got a terrible cold.'—'Have you? Oh dear. Anyway, so you're not going to go away this weekend?'* **7** You use **anyway** to indicate that you want to end the conversation. *'Anyway, give our love to Francis. Bye.'*

any·ways /ˈeniweɪz/. Some people use **anyways** instead of **anyway**.

any·where /ˈeniweə/. **1** You use **anywhere** in statements with negative meaning to indicate that a place of a particular kind does not exist, or that a thing or person does not exist. *I haven't got anywhere to live... There had never been such a beautiful woman anywhere in the world.* **2** You use **anywhere** in questions and conditional clauses to ask or talk about a place without saying exactly where you mean. *Did you try to get help from anywhere?* **3** You use **anywhere** to refer to a place when you are emphasizing that it could be any of a large number of places. *...jokes that are so funny they always work anywhere.* **4** You use **anywhere** before words that indicate the kind of place you are talking about. *He'll meet you anywhere you want. ...if you come across anywhere that has something special to offer.* **5** When you do not want to be exact, you use **anywhere** to refer to a particular range of things. *His shoes cost anywhere from $200 up... My visits lasted anywhere from three weeks to two months.* **6** You use **anywhere** in expressions such as **anywhere near** and **anywhere close to** to emphasize a statement that you are making. *There weren't anywhere near enough empty boxes... The only one who's anywhere close to the truth is my mother.* **7** If you say that someone or something **is not getting anywhere** or **is not going anywhere**, you mean that they are not making progress. *The conversation did*

not seem to be getting anywhere... I didn't see that my career as a film-maker was going anywhere.

aor·ta /eɪˈɔːtə/ **aortas**. Your **aorta** is the main artery through which blood leaves your heart before it flows through the rest of your body.

apace /əˈpeɪs/. If something develops or continues **apace**, it is developing or continuing quickly. *Land reclamation continues apace... Their plan is proceeding apace.*

apart 1 positions and states

apart /əˈpɑːt/. In addition to the uses shown below, **apart** is used in phrasal verbs such as 'grow apart', 'take apart', 'set apart', and 'tell apart'. **1** When someone or something is positioned **apart** from someone or something else, they are some distance from that person or thing. *He was standing a bit apart from the rest of us. ...standing some distance apart.* **2** If two people or things are positioned **apart**, there is a space or a distance between them. *Ray and sister Renee lived just 25 miles apart from each other. ...regions that were too far apart... He was standing, feet apart.* **3** If two people are **apart**, they are no longer living together or spending time together, either permanently or just for a short time. *It was the first time Jane and I had been apart... Mum and Dad live apart.* **4** If two people or things move **apart** or are pulled **apart**, they move away from each other. *He tried in vain to keep the two dogs apart.* **5** If something comes **apart**, its parts separate from each other. *The handles of two of Ivanisevic's new rackets came apart.* **6** If people or groups are a long way **apart**, they have completely different views about something and disagree about it. *They're so far apart on such a wide range of issues.*

apart 2 indicating exceptions and focusing

apart /əˈpɑːt/. **1** You use **apart from** when you are making an exception to a general statement. *The room was empty apart from one man seated beside the fire... She was the only British competitor apart from Richard Meade.* **2** You use **apart** when you are making an exception to a general statement. *This was, New York apart, the first American city I had ever been in.* **3** You use **apart from** to indicate that you are aware of one aspect of a situation, but that you are going to focus on another aspect. *Illiteracy threatens Britain's industrial performance. But, quite apart from that, the individual who can't read or write is unlikely to get a job.* **4** You use **apart** to indicate that you are aware of one aspect of a situation, but that you are going to focus on another aspect. *That argument apart, it is for the Germans themselves to work out how their forces should come together.*

apart·heid /əˈpɑːtheɪt/. **Apartheid** was a political system in South Africa in which people were divided into racial groups and kept apart by law.

apart·ment /əˈpɑːtmənt/ **apartments**. **1** An **apartment** is a set of rooms for living in, usually on one floor of a large building. The usual British word is **flat**. **2** The **apartments** of an important person such as a king, queen, or president are a set of large rooms which are used by them.

a'partment house, apartment houses. An **apartment house** is a tall building which contains different apartments on different floors. The British expression is **block of flats**.

apa·thet·ic /ˌæpəˈθetɪk/. If someone is **apathetic**, they are not interested in doing something or not interested in something that is happening; used showing disapproval. *Even the most apathetic students are beginning to sit up and listen... Others feel apathetic about the candidates.*

apa·thy /ˈæpəθi/. **Apathy** is a state of mind in which someone is not interested in anything; often used showing disapproval. *...the political apathy and emotional uncertainty of young Americans.*

ape /eɪp/ **apes, aping, aped**. **1 Apes** are chimpanzees, gorillas, and other animals in the same family. **2** If you **ape** someone's speech or behaviour,

you imitate it. ...*French films which merely aped* `V n`
Hollywood.

ape·ri·tif /æ,perɪ'tiːf/ **aperitifs.** An **aperitif** is an al- `N-COUNT`
coholic drink that you have before a meal.

ap·er·ture /'æpətʃə/ **apertures. 1** An **aperture** is ◆◇◇◇◇
a narrow hole or gap. *Through the aperture he could* `N-COUNT`
see daylight. **2** In photography, the **aperture** of a ca- `FORMAL`
mera is the size of the hole through which light `N-COUNT`
passes to reach the film.

apex /'eɪpeks/ **apexes. 1** The **apex** of an organiza- `N-SING`
tion or system is the highest and most important
position in it. *At the apex of the party was its central*
committee. **2** The **apex** of something such as a pyra- `N-COUNT`
mid is its pointed top or end.

Apex; also spelled APEX. In Britain, an **Apex** or an `N-SING`
Apex ticket is a ticket for a journey by air or rail
which costs less than the standard ticket, but which
you have to book in advance.

aphid /'eɪfɪd/ **aphids. Aphids** are very small in- ◆◇◇◇◇
sects which live on plants and suck their juices. `N-COUNT`

apho·rism /'æfərɪzəm/ **aphorisms.** An **aphorism** `N-COUNT`
is a short witty sentence which expresses a general `FORMAL`
truth or observation.

aph·ro·disi·ac /,æfrə'dɪziæk/ **aphrodisiacs.** An `N-COUNT`
aphrodisiac is a food, drink, or drug which is said to
make people want to have sex. ▶ Also an adjective. `ADJ-GRADED`
...plants with narcotic or aphrodisiac qualities.

apiece /ə'piːs/. **1** If people have a particular num- ◆◇◇◇◇
ber of things **apiece**, they have that number each. `ADV:`
He and I had two fish apiece... The World Series be- `amount ADV`
tween the Atlanta Braves and Toronto Blue Jays is
tied at one game apiece. **2** If a number of similar `ADV:`
things are for sale at a certain price **apiece**, that is `amount ADV`
the price for each one of them. *...shells at a yard sale*
priced at 35 cents apiece.

aplen·ty /ə'plenti/. If you have something **aplenty**, `ADV: n ADV`
you have plenty of it. *There were chances aplenty to* `LITERARY`
win the game.

aplomb /ə'plɒm/. If you do something with `N-UNCOUNT`
aplomb, you do it with confidence in a relaxed way. `FORMAL`
The whole cast executed the production with truly
professional aplomb.

apoca·lypse /ə'pɒkəlɪps/. The **apocalypse** is the ◆◇◇◇◇
total destruction and end of the world. *We live in* `N-SING`
the shadow of the apocalypse.

apoca·lyp·tic /ə,pɒkə'lɪptɪk/. **Apocalyptic** means ◆◇◇◇◇
relating to very great events or disasters in the fu- `ADJ-GRADED`
ture. *...an apocalyptic vision about the second com-*
ing of Christ.

apoc·ry·phal /ə'pɒkrɪfəl/. An **apocryphal** story is `ADJ`
one which is often told as if it were true, although it
is probably not true.

apo·gee /'æpədʒiː/. The **apogee** of something such `N-SING:`
as a culture or a business is its highest or its greatest `with supp`
point. *The Alliance for Progress reached its apogee* `FORMAL`
during the first half of the decade.

apo·liti·cal /,eɪpə'lɪtɪkəl/. **1** Someone who is **apo-** `ADJ-GRADED`
litical is not interested in politics. **2** If you describe `ADJ`
an organization or an activity as **apolitical**, you
mean that it is not linked to a particular political
party. *...the normally apolitical European Commis-*
sion. ...an apolitical campaign.

apolo·get·ic /ə,pɒlə'dʒetɪk/. If you are **apologetic**, ◆◇◇◇◇
you show or say that you are sorry for causing `ADJ-GRADED`
trouble for someone, for hurting them, or for
disappointing them. *The hospital staff were very*
apologetic but that couldn't really compensate.
♦ **apolo·geti·cal·ly** /ə,pɒlə'dʒetɪkli/ *'It's of no great* `ADV-GRADED:`
literary merit,' he said, almost apologetically. `ADV with v`

apo·lo·gia /,æpə'ləʊdʒiə/ **apologias.** An **apologia** `N-COUNT`
is a statement in which you defend something that `FORMAL`
you strongly believe in, for example a way of life, a
person's behaviour, or a philosophy. *The left have*
seen the work as an apologia for privilege.

apolo·gise /ə'pɒlədʒaɪz/. See **apologize**.

apolo·gist /ə'pɒlədʒɪst/ **apologists.** An **apologist** `N-COUNT`
is a person who writes or speaks in defence of a be- `FORMAL`
lief, a cause, or a person's life. *I am no apologist for*
Hitler.

apolo·gize /ə'pɒlədʒaɪz/ **apologizes, apologiz-** ◆◆◇◇◇
ing, apologized; also spelled **apologise** in British `VERB`
English. When you **apologize** to someone, you say `PRAGMATICS`
that you are sorry that you have hurt them or `V forn/-ing`
caused trouble for them. You can say **'I apologize'** `V ton`
as a formal way of saying sorry. *I apologize for being* `Also V`
late... He apologized to the people who had been
affected.

apol·ogy /ə'pɒlədʒi/ **apologies. 1** An **apology** is ◆◆◇◇◇
something that you say or write in order to tell `N-VAR`
someone that you are sorry that you have hurt them
or caused trouble for them. *...a letter of apology...*
He made a public apology for the team's perfor-
mance. **2** If you offer or make your **apologies**, you `N-PLURAL`
apologize. **3** If you say that you **make no apologies** `FORMAL`
for what you have done, you are emphasizing that `PHRASE`
you feel that you have done nothing wrong. *I make*
no apologies for the way we played.

apo·plexy /'æpəpleksi/. **1** **Apoplexy** is extreme an- `N-UNCOUNT`
ger. *He has already caused apoplexy with his books* `FORMAL`
on class and on war. ♦ **apo·plec·tic** /,æpə'plektɪk/ `ADJ`
My father was apoplectic when he discovered the
truth. **2** **Apoplexy** is a stroke. *His father died of* `N-UNCOUNT`
apoplexy. `DATED`

apos·ta·sy /ə'pɒstəsi/. If someone is accused of `N-UNCOUNT`
apostasy, they are accused of abandoning their reli- `FORMAL`
gious faith, political loyalties, or principles. ♦ **apos-**
·tate /ə'pɒsteɪt/ **apostates.** An **apostate** is some- `N-COUNT`
one who has abandoned their religious faith, politi-
cal loyalties, or principles.

apos·tle /ə'pɒsəl/ **apostles. 1** The **apostles** were `N-COUNT`
the followers of Jesus Christ who went from place to
place telling people about him and trying to per-
suade them to become Christians. **2** An **apostle** of a `N-COUNT`
particular idea or cause is someone who strongly
believes in it and works hard to promote it. *...even*
though we present ourselves as the apostles of free
trade.

Ap·os·tol·ic /,æpə'stɒlɪk/. **1** **Apostolic** means be- `ADJ`
longing or relating to a Christian religious leader,
especially the Pope, who is considered to inherit
authority from Christ's early followers. **2** **Apostolic** `ADJ`
means belonging or relating to the early followers of
Christ and to their teaching.

apos·tro·phe /ə'pɒstrəfi/ **apostrophes.** An **apos-** `N-COUNT`
trophe is the mark ', written to indicate that one or
more letters have been omitted from a word, as in
'isn't'. It is also added to nouns to form possessives,
as in 'Mike's car'; see also **'s**.

apoth·ecary /ə'pɒθɪkri, AM -keri/ **apothecaries.** `N-COUNT`
An **apothecary** was a person who prepared medi- `DATED`
cines for people.

apoth·eo·sis /ə,pɒθi'əʊsɪs/. **1** If something is the `N-SING`
apotheosis of something else, it is the ideal or best `FORMAL`
possible example of it. *The Oriental in Bangkok is*
the apotheosis of the grand hotel. **2** If you describe `N-SING:`
an event or a time as someone's **apotheosis**, you `with poss`
mean that it was the greatest point in their career or `FORMAL`
their life.

ap·pal /ə'pɔːl/ **appals, appalling, appalled;** ◆◆◇◇◇
spelled **appall** in American English. If something `VERB`
appals you, it shocks or disgusts you because it `V n`
seems so bad or unpleasant. *My wife now looks like*
her mother, which appals me. ♦ **ap·palled** *The* `ADJ-GRADED`
Americans are appalled at the statements made at
the conference. ♦ **ap·pal·ling** *They have been living* `ADJ-GRADED`
under the most appalling conditions. ♦ **ap·pal·ling-**
·ly *The detection rate for racial crimes is appallingly* `ADV-GRADED`
low.

ap·pal·ling /ə'pɔːlɪŋ/. **1** You can use **appalling** to ◆◇◇◇◇
emphasize that something is very great or severe. *I* `ADJ-GRADED`
developed an appalling headache. ♦ **ap·pal·ling·ly** `PRAGMATICS`
It's been an appallingly busy morning. **2** See also `ADV-GRADED`
appal.

ap·pa·rat·chik /,æpə'rætʃɪk/ **apparatchiks.** An `N-COUNT`
apparatchik is an active long-term member of a po- `PRAGMATICS`
litical party; used showing disapproval. *Political* `FORMAL`
party apparatchiks are appointed to every office of
social authority.

ap·pa·rat·us /ˌæpəˈreɪtəs, -ˈræt-/ **apparatuses.** ◆◇◇◇◇
1 The **apparatus** of an organization or system is its N-VAR: with supp
structure and method of operation. ...*a massive bu-*
reaucratic apparatus. **2 Apparatus** is the equip- N-VAR
ment, such as tools and machines, which is used to
do a particular job or activity. ...*firemen wearing*
breathing apparatus.

ap·par·el /əˈpærəl/. **Apparel** is clothes, especially ◆◇◇◇◇
formal clothes worn on an important occasion. N-UNCOUNT FORMAL, AMERICAN
Women's apparel is offered in petite, regular, and
tall models.

ap·par·ent /əˈpærənt/. **1** An **apparent** situation, ◆◆◇◇◇
quality, or feeling seems to exist, although you can- ADJ: ADJ n
not be certain that it does exist. *There is at last an*
apparent end to the destructive price war. **2** If you PHRASE
say that something happens **for no apparent rea-**
son, you cannot understand why it happens.
3 If something is **apparent** to you, it is clear and obvi- ADJ-GRADED: v-link ADJ
ous to you. *It has been apparent that in other areas*
standards have held up well.

ap·par·ent·ly /əˈpærəntli/. **1** You use **apparently** ◆◆◆◇
to indicate that the information you are giving is ADV PRAGMATICS
something that you have heard, but you are not certain that it is true. *Apparently the girls are not at all*
amused by the whole business. **2** You use **apparent-** ADV
ly to refer to something that the facts which are currently available suggest is the case. ...*an apparently*
endless recession.

ap·pa·ri·tion /ˌæpəˈrɪʃən/ **apparitions.** An appari- N-COUNT FORMAL
tion is someone you see or think you see but who is
not really there as a physical being. ...*these appari-*
tions of the Virgin.

ap·peal /əˈpiːl/ **appeals, appealing, appealed.** ◆◆◆◇
1 If you **appeal** to someone to do something, you VERB V to/for n to-inf
make a serious and urgent request to them. *Deng* V to n for n
Xiaoping recently appealed for students to return to V for n
China... He will appeal to the state for an extension
of unemployment benefits... The UN has appealed
for help from the international community. ► Also a N-COUNT
noun. *He has a message from King Fahd, believed to*
be an appeal for Arab unity. ...a last-minute appeal
to him to call off his trip.
2 An **appeal** is an attempt to raise money for a charity N-COUNT
or for a good cause. ...*an appeal to save a library con-*
taining priceless manuscripts.
3 If you **appeal** against a decision, you formally ask VERB V against n
someone in authority to change it. In American Eng- V to n to-inf
lish, you **appeal** a decision. *They would appeal* V n
against the decision... Maguire has appealed to the Su- BRITISH
preme Court to stop her extradition... We intend to ap-
peal the verdict. **4** An **appeal** is a formal request for a N-VAR
decision to be changed. *Heath's appeal against the*
sentence was later successful... She lost the case on ap-
peal. ● See also **court of appeal.**
5 If something **appeals** to you, you find it attractive or VERB
interesting. *The idea appealed to him... The range has* V to n Also V
long appealed to all tastes. **6** The **appeal** of something N-UNCOUNT: with supp
is a quality that it has which people find attractive or
interesting. *Its new title was meant to give the party*
greater public appeal... Johnson's appeal is to people in
all walks of life. ● See also **sex appeal.**

ap·peal·ing /əˈpiːlɪŋ/. **1** Someone or something ◆◇◇◇◇
that is **appealing** is pleasing and attractive. *There* ADJ-GRADED
was a sense of humour to what he did that I found
very appealing... That's a very appealing idea. ♦ **ap-**
·peal·ing·ly *Irish whiskeys, rather like the Irish* ADV-GRADED
themselves, have an appealingly direct charm. **2** An ADJ
appealing expression or tone of voice indicates to
someone that you want help, advice, or approval.
She gave him a soft appealing look. ♦ **appealingly** ADV: ADV after v
Dena looked appealingly at Blair, hoping to hear a
contrary opinion. **3** See also **appeal.**

ap·pear /əˈpɪə/ **appears, appearing, ap-** ◆◆◆◆
peared. 1 If you say that something **appears** to be V-LINK: no cont
the way you describe it, you are reporting what you PRAGMATICS
believe or what you have been told, though you *there* V to-inf
cannot be sure it is true. *There appears to be in-* *it* V that
creasing support for the leadership... The aircraft ap- *it* V adj that/ to-inf
pears to have crashed... It appears that some missiles to-inf
have been moved... It appears unlikely that the UN V adj/n

would consider making such a move... Those talks
appear as distant as ever. **2** If someone or some- V-LINK: no cont
thing **appears** to have a particular quality or charac- V adj
teristic, they give the impression of having that V n V to-inf
quality or characteristic. *She did her best to appear*
more self-assured than she felt... He is anxious to ap-
pear a gentleman... Under stress these people will
appear to be superficial, over-eager and manipula-
tive.
3 When someone or something **appears**, they move VERB
into a position where you can see them, for example V Also there V n
when they arrive somewhere. *A woman appeared at*
the far end of the street. **4** When something new **ap-** VERB
pears, it begins to exist or reaches a stage of develop- V Also there V n
ment where its existence can be noticed. ...*white flow-*
ers which appear in early summer. **5** When something VERB: V
such as a book **appears**, it is published or becomes
available for people to buy.
6 When someone **appears** in a play, a show, or a VERB
television programme, they take part in it. *Jill Bennett* V in n V on/at n
became John Osborne's fourth wife, and appeared in
several of his plays... Student leaders appeared on tele-
vision to ask for calm. **7** When someone **appears** be- VERB
fore a court of law or before an official committee, V in/at n Also V before n
they go there in order to answer charges or to give information as a witness. *Two other executives appeared*
at Worthing Magistrates' Court.

ap·pear·ance /əˈpɪərəns/ **appearances. 1** When ◆◆◆◆
someone makes an **appearance** in an event or in N-COUNT
in a broadcast, they take part in it. ...*the president's*
second public appearance... Keegan made 68 ap-
pearances in two seasons for Southampton. **2** If you PHRASE
put in an appearance at an event, you go to it for a
short time, but do not stay.
3 The **appearance** of someone or something in a N-SING: with supp
place is their arrival there, especially when it is unexpected. *The sudden appearance of a few bags of rice*
could start a riot. **4** The **appearance** of something N-SING: with supp
new is its coming into existence or use. *Flowering*
plants were making their first appearance... Fears are
growing of a cholera outbreak following the appear-
ance of a number of cases.
5 Someone's or something's **appearance** is what they N-SING: with supp
look like or how they present themselves. *She used to*
be so fussy about her appearance... A flat-roofed exten-
sion will add nothing to the value or appearance of the
house. **6** If something has the **appearance** of a quality, N-SING: with supp
it seems to have that quality. *We tried to meet both*
children's needs without the appearance of favorit-
ism... The US president risked giving the appearance
that the US was taking sides.
7 If something is true **to all appearances, from all ap-** PHRASE
pearances, or **by all appearances**, it seems from what
you observe or know about it that it is true. *He was to*
all appearances an unassuming man. **8** If you **keep up** PHRASE
appearances, you try to behave and dress in a way
that people expect of you, even if you can no longer
afford it.

ap'pearance money. Appearance money is N-UNCOUNT BRITISH
money paid to a famous person such as a sports
star or film star for taking part in a public event.

ap·pease /əˈpiːz/ **appeases, appeasing, ap-** ◆◇◇◇◇
peased. If you try to **appease** someone, you try to VERB PRAGMATICS
stop them being angry by giving them what they V n
want; often used showing disapproval. *Gandhi was*
accused by some of trying to appease both factions of
the electorate. ♦ **ap·peas·er, appeasers** *Not* N-COUNT
many such appeasers were left in 1941. ♦ **ap·pease-**
·ment *They have already been accused of appease-* N-UNCOUNT
ment by more militant organisations.

ap·pel·lant /əˈpelənt/ **appellants.** An appellant is N-COUNT LEGAL
someone who is appealing against a court's deci-
sion after they have been judged guilty of a crime.

ap·pel·late court /əˌpelɪt ˈkɔːt/ **appellate** N-COUNT
courts. In the United States, an **appellate court** is
a special court where people who have been convicted of a crime can appeal against their conviction. The usual British term is **court of appeal.**

ap·pel·la·tion /ˌæpəˈleɪʃən/ **appellations.** An ap- ◆◇◇◇◇
pellation is a name or title that a person, place, or N-COUNT FORMAL

thing is given. *His critics called him 'the King of Pork'. Burdick never minded the appellation.*

ap·pend /ə'pend/ **appends, appending, appended.** When you **append** something to something else, especially a piece of writing, you attach it or add it to the end of it. *Violet appended a note at the end of the letter... His real name hadn't been appended to the manuscript.*
VERB
V n
be V-ed to n
FORMAL

ap·pend·age /ə'pendɪdʒ/ **appendages.** An **appendage** is something that is joined to or connected with something larger or more important. *Upon marriage she automatically lost most of her legal rights and became an appendage of her husband.*
N-COUNT
FORMAL

ap·pen·di·ces /ə'pendɪsiːz/. **Appendices** is a plural of **appendix**.

ap·pen·di·ci·tis /ə,pendɪ'saɪtɪs/. **Appendicitis** is an illness in which a person's appendix is infected and painful.
N-UNCOUNT

ap·pen·dix /ə'pendɪks/ **appendices** /ə'pendɪsiːz/ or **appendixes. 1** Your **appendix** is a small closed tube inside your body which is attached to your digestive system. It has no particular function. **2** An **appendix** to a book is extra information that is placed after the end of the main text. *These data are elaborated upon in the Appendix.*
◆◇◇◇
N-COUNT
N-COUNT

ap·pe·tite /'æpɪtaɪt/ **appetites. 1** Your **appetite** is your desire to eat. *He has a healthy appetite... Symptoms are a slight fever, headache and loss of appetite.* **2** Someone's **appetite** for something is their strong desire for it. *...his appetite for success. ...just enough information to whet his appetite.*
◆◆◇◇
N-VAR
N-COUNT

ap·pe·tiz·er /'æpɪtaɪzə/ **appetizers;** also spelled **appetiser** in British English. An **appetizer** is the first course of a meal. It consists of a small amount of food.
N-COUNT

ap·pe·tiz·ing /'æpɪtaɪzɪŋ/; also spelled **appetising** in British English. **Appetizing** food looks and smells good, so that you want to eat it. *...the appetising smell of freshly baked bread.* ♦ **ap·pe·tiz·ing·ly** *It is simply and appetisingly laid out.*
ADJ-GRADED
ADV-GRADED:
ADV adj/-ed

ap·plaud /ə'plɔːd/ **applauds, applauding, applauded. 1** When a group of people **applaud**, they clap their hands in order to show approval, for example when they have enjoyed a play or concert. *The audience laughed and applauded... Every person stood to applaud his unforgettable act of courage.* **2** When an attitude or action **is applauded**, people praise it. *He should be applauded for his courage... This last move can only be applauded.*
◆◆◇◇
VERB
V
V n
VERB
be V-ed for n
be V-ed
Also V n

ap·plause /ə'plɔːz/. **Applause** is the noise made by a group of people clapping their hands to show approval. *They greeted him with thunderous applause. ...a round of applause.*
◆◆◇◇
N-UNCOUNT

ap·ple /'æpəl/ **apples. 1** An **apple** is a round fruit with smooth green, yellow, or red skin and firm white flesh. See picture headed **fruit.** ● See also **Adam's apple, Big Apple, crab apple. 2** If you say that someone is **the apple of** your **eye,** you mean that they are very important to you and you are extremely fond of them.
◆◆◇◇
N-VAR
PHRASE

apple·cart /'æpəlkɑːt/. If you **upset the applecart,** you do something which causes a plan, system, or arrangement to go wrong.
PHRASE
JOURNALISM

ap·pli·ance /ə'plaɪəns/ **appliances. 1** An **appliance** is a device or machine in your home that you use to do a job such as cleaning or cooking. Appliances are often electrical. *...the vacuum cleaner, the washing machine and other household appliances.* **2** The **appliance** of a skill or of knowledge is its use for a particular purpose. *They were the result of the intellectual appliance of science.*
◆◆◇◇
N-COUNT
FORMAL
N-SING

ap·pli·cable /'æplɪkəbəl, ə'plɪkə-/. Something that is **applicable** to a particular situation is relevant to it or can be applied to it. *What is a reasonable standard for one family is not applicable for another. ...a review of energy usage and, where applicable, the production and disposal of waste.* ♦ **ap·plic·abil·ity** /ə,plɪkə'bɪləti/ *...the applicability of his theories to education.*
◆◇◇◇
ADJ-GRADED
N-UNCOUNT

ap·pli·cant /'æplɪkənt/ **applicants.** An **applicant** for something such as a job or a place at a college is someone who makes a formal written request to be given it. *He is one of thirty applicants for the manager's job.*
◆◆◇◇
N-COUNT

ap·pli·ca·tion /,æplɪ'keɪʃən/ **applications. 1** Someone's **application** for something such as a job or membership of an organization is a formal written request to be allowed to have it. *His application for membership of the organisation was rejected. ...Turkey's application to join the European Community... Tickets are available on application.* **2** The **application** of a rule or piece of knowledge is the use of it in a particular situation. *...the practical application of the theory. ...artificial intelligence and its application to robotics.* **3** Application is hard work and concentration on what you are doing over a period of time. *...his immense talent, boundless energy and unremitting application.* **4** The **application** of something to a surface is the act or process of putting it on or rubbing it into the surface. *With repeated applications of weedkiller, the weeds were overcome.*
◆◆◇
N-COUNT:
also on N
N-VAR
N-UNCOUNT
N-VAR

ap·pli·ca·tor /'æplɪkeɪtə/ **applicators. 1** An **applicator** is something such as a brush or sponge which is used to apply make-up to the face, or powder or liquid to a surface. **2** An **applicator** is a tube or other device which is used to insert tampons or pessaries into the vagina.
N-COUNT
N-COUNT

ap·plied /ə'plaɪd/. An **applied** subject of study has a practical use, rather than being concerned only with theory. *...Applied Physics. ...applied research.*
ADJ: ADJ n

ap·pli·que /ə'pliːkeɪ, AM ,æplɪ'keɪ/ also spelled **appliqué. Applique** is the craft of sewing fabric shapes onto larger pieces of cloth. You can also use applique to refer to things you make using this craft.
N-UNCOUNT

ap·pli·qued /ə'pliːkeɪd, AM ,æplɪ'keɪd/; also spelled **appliquéd. Appliqued** shapes or fabric are formed from pieces of fabric which are sewn on to clothes or larger pieces of cloth. *...a magnificent appliqued bedspread.*
ADJ

ap·ply /ə'plaɪ/ **applies, applying, applied. 1** If you **apply** for something such as a job or membership of an organization, you write a letter or fill in a form in order to ask formally for it. *I am continuing to apply for jobs... They may apply to join the organization.* **2** If you **apply** yourself to something or **apply** your mind to something, you concentrate hard on doing it or on thinking about it. *Faulks has applied himself to this task with considerable energy... He applied his mind to how rockets could be used to make money.* **3** If something such as a rule or a remark **applies** to a person or in a situation, it is relevant to the person or the situation. *The convention does not apply to us... The rule applies where a person owns stock in a corporation.* **4** If you **apply** something such as a rule, system, or skill, you use it in a situation or activity. *The Government appears to be applying the same principle. ...applying the technology to practical business problems.* **5** A name that **is applied** to someone or something is used to refer to them. *...a biological term which cannot be applied to a whole culture.* **6** If you **apply** something to a surface, you put it on or rub it into the surface. *Apply direct pressure to the wound... Applying the dye can be messy.* **7** When the driver of a vehicle **applies** the brakes, he or she uses them to slow the vehicle down or to stop it from moving. **8** See also **applied.**
◆◆◆◇
VERB
V for n
V to-inf
VERB
V pron-refl to
n/-ing
V n to n/-ing
Also V pron-
refl
VB: no cont
V to n
V
VERB
V n ton
V n to n
VERB
be V-ed to n
VERB
V n ton
V n ton
VERB: V n
FORMAL

ap·point /ə'pɔɪnt/ **appoints, appointing, appointed.** If you **appoint** someone to a job or official position, you formally choose them for it. *It made sense to appoint a banker to this job... The Prime Minister has appointed a civilian as defence minister... She was appointed a US delegate to the United Nations.*
◆◆◇◇
VERB
V n to n
V n as n
VERB: V n
be V-ed n
Also V n n

ap·point·ed /ə'pɔɪntɪd/. If something happens at the **appointed** time, it happens at the time that was decided in advance. *The appointed hour of the ceremony was drawing nearer.*
ADJ: ADJ n
FORMAL

-appointed /-əˈpɔɪntɪd/. **-appointed** combines with adverbs to form adjectives such as **well-appointed** that describe a building or room that is equipped or furnished in the way that is mentioned. *...the well-appointed kitchen. ...a tastefully appointed sitting room.* • See also **self-appointed**. COMB WRITTEN

ap·poin·tee /əˌpɔɪnˈtiː/ **appointees.** An appointee is someone who has been chosen for a particular job or position of responsibility. *...a recent appointee to the Supreme Court.* ◆◇◇◇◇ N-COUNT FORMAL

ap·point·ment /əˈpɔɪntmənt/ **appointments.** **1** The **appointment** of a person to a particular job is the choice of that person to do it. *...his appointment as foreign minister.* **2** An **appointment** is a job or position of responsibility. *...an appointment as a researcher.* **3** If you have an **appointment** with someone, you have arranged to see them at a particular time, usually in connection with their work. *She has an appointment with her accountant. ...a dental appointment.* **4** If something can be done by **appointment**, people can arrange in advance to do it at a particular time. *Viewing is by appointment only.* ◆◆◇◇◇ N-VAR: with poss / N-COUNT / N-COUNT / PHRASE

ap·por·tion /əˈpɔːʃən/ **apportions, apportioning, apportioned.** When you apportion something such as blame, you decide how much of it different people deserve or should be given. *The experts are even-handed in apportioning blame.* VERB V n prep Also V n FORMAL

ap·po·site /ˈæpəzɪt/. Something that is **apposite** is suitable for or appropriate to what is happening or being discussed. *The events of recent days have made his central theme even more apposite.* ADJ-GRADED FORMAL

ap·po·si·tion /ˌæpəˈzɪʃən/. If two noun groups referring to the same thing are in **apposition**, one is placed immediately after the other, with no conjunction joining them, as in '...her father, Nigel'. N-UNCOUNT

ap·prais·al /əˈpreɪzəl/ **appraisals. 1** If you make an **appraisal** of something, you consider it carefully and form an opinion about it. *...a calm appraisal of the situation... Self-appraisal is never easy.* **2** **Appraisal** is an official or formal evaluation of the strengths and weaknesses of someone or something. *Appraisal is now a tool of management. ...an appraisal of your financial standing.* ◆◇◇◇◇ N-VAR / N-VAR

ap·praise /əˈpreɪz/ **appraises, appraising, appraised.** If you **appraise** something or someone, you consider them carefully and form an opinion about them. *This prompted many employers to appraise their selection and recruitment policies.* ◆◇◇◇◇ VERB V n FORMAL

ap·prais·er /əˈpreɪzə/ **appraisers.** An **appraiser** is someone whose job is to estimate the cost or value of something such as property. The usual British word is **valuer**. N-COUNT AMERICAN

ap·pre·ci·able /əˈpriːʃəbəl/. An **appreciable** amount or effect is large enough to be important or clearly noticed. *This has not had an appreciable effect on production.* ♦ **ap·pre·ci·ably** /əˈpriːʃəbli/ *Summer temperatures are appreciably more comfortable there.* ADJ-GRADED FORMAL / ADV

ap·pre·ci·ate /əˈpriːʃieɪt/ **appreciates, appreciating, appreciated. 1** If you **appreciate** something, for example a piece of music or good food, you like it because you recognize its good qualities. *Anyone can appreciate our music.* ♦ **ap·pre·cia·tion** /əˌpriːʃiˈeɪʃən/ *...children's understanding and appreciation of art.* **2** If you **appreciate** a situation or problem, you understand it and know what it involves. *She never really appreciated the depth and bitterness of the Irish conflict... He appreciates that co-operation with the media is part of his professional duties.* ♦ **appreciation** *They have a stronger appreciation of the importance of economic incentives.* **3** If you say that you **appreciate** something that someone does for you, you mean that you are grateful to them for it. *Peter stood by me when I most needed it. I'll always appreciate that... I'd appreciate it if you wouldn't mention it.* ♦ **appreciation** *...his appreciation for what he called Saudi Arabia's moderate and realistic oil policies. ...the gifts presented to them in appreciation of their work.* ◆◆◇◇ VERB V n / N-UNCOUNT / VERB V n V that / N-UNCOUNT / VERB PRAGMATICS V n V it if / N-UNCOUNT

4 If something that you own **appreciates** over a period of time, its value increases. *Houses will appreciate in value.* ♦ **appreciation** *...capital appreciation of the property.* VERB V / N-UNCOUNT

ap·pre·cia·tive /əˈpriːʃətɪv/. **1** An **appreciative** reaction shows the enjoyment that you are getting from something. *...appreciative laughter.* ♦ **ap·pre·cia·tive·ly** *She looked appreciatively at Blair's lovely pictures.* **2** If you are **appreciative** of something, you are grateful for it. *We have been very appreciative of their support.* ◆◇◇◇◇ ADJ-GRADED / ADV-GRADED: ADV with v ADJ-GRADED

ap·pre·hend /ˌæprɪˈhend/ **apprehends, apprehending, apprehended. 1** If the police **apprehend** someone, they catch them and arrest them. ♦ **ap·pre·hen·sion** /ˌæprɪˈhenʃən/ *...information leading to the apprehension of the alleged killer.* **2** If you **apprehend** something, you understand it. *Only now can I begin to apprehend the power of these forces.* ♦ **apprehension** *...the sudden apprehension of something familiar as something alien.* ◆◇◇◇◇ VERB: V n FORMAL / N-UNCOUNT / VERB V n FORMAL / N-UNCOUNT

ap·pre·hen·sive /ˌæprɪˈhensɪv/. Someone who is **apprehensive** is afraid that something bad may happen. *People are still terribly apprehensive about the future.* ♦ **ap·pre·hen·sive·ly** *I waited apprehensively.* ♦ **ap·pre·hen·sion** /ˌæprɪˈhenʃən/ **apprehensions.** *...real anger and apprehension about the future.* ◆◇◇◇◇ ADJ-GRADED / ADV-GRADED: ADV with v / N-VAR

ap·pren·tice /əˈprentɪs/ **apprentices, apprenticing, apprenticed. 1** An **apprentice** is a young person who works for someone in order to learn their skill. *...an apprentice carpenter.* **2** If a young person **is apprenticed** to someone, they go to work for them in order to learn their skill. *I was apprenticed to a builder when I was fourteen.* ◆◇◇◇◇ N-COUNT / VB: usu passive beV-ed to n

ap·pren·tice·ship /əˈprentɪsʃɪp/ **apprenticeships.** Someone who has an **apprenticeship** works for a fixed period of time for a person who has a particular skill in order to learn the skill. **Apprenticeship** is the system of learning a skill like this. ◆◇◇◇◇ N-VAR

ap·prise /əˈpraɪz/ **apprises, apprising, apprised.** When you **are apprised** of something, someone tells you about it. *Have these customers been fully apprised of the advantages?... I thought I needed to apprise the students of the dangers.* VERB beV-ed of n V n of n FORMAL

ap·proach /əˈprəʊtʃ/ **approaches, approaching, approached. 1** When you **approach** something, you get closer to it. *He didn't approach the front door at once... When I approached, they grew silent. ...the approaching car.* ▶ Also a noun. *At their approach the little boy ran away and hid. ...the approach of a low-flying helicopter.* **2** An **approach** to a place is a road, path, or other route that leads to it. *The path serves as an approach to the boat house.* **3** If you **approach** someone about something, you speak to them about it for the first time, often making an offer or request. *Anna approached several builders and was fortunate to come across Eddie. ...when Chappel approached me about the job.* ▶ Also a noun. *...approaches from buyers interested in the whole of the group.* ◆◆◆◇ VERB V n V / N-COUNT / N-COUNT / VB: no cont V n / N-COUNT

4 When you **approach** a task, problem, or situation in a particular way, you deal with it or think about it in that way. *The Bank has approached the issue in a practical way.* **5** Your **approach** to a task, problem, or situation is the way you deal with it or think about it. *...different approaches to gathering information. ...the adversarial approach of the British legal system.* VERB V n prep/adv / N-COUNT

6 As a future time or event **approaches**, or as you **approach** it, it gradually gets nearer as time passes. *As autumn approached, the plants and colours in the garden changed. ...the approaching crisis. ...as we approach the 21st century.* ▶ Also a noun. *...the approach of crucial elections.* **7** If something **approaches** a particular level or state, it almost reaches that level or state. *...speeds approaching 200mph.* V-ERG V-ing V n / N-SING / VERB V n

ap·proach·able /əˈprəʊtʃəbəl/. If you describe someone as **approachable**, you think that they are friendly and easy to talk to. ADJ-GRADED

ap·pro·ba·tion /ˌæprəˈbeɪʃən/. **Approbation** is approval of something or agreement to it. *The result has not met universal approbation.* N-UNCOUNT FORMAL

ap·pro·pri·ate, appropriates, appropriating, appropriated. The adjective is pronounced /əˈprəʊpriət/. The verb is pronounced /əˈprəʊprieɪt/. **1** Something that is **appropriate** is suitable or acceptable for a particular situation. *It is appropriate that Irish names dominate the list. ...an outfit appropriate to the job... The teacher can then take appropriate action.* ◆ **ap·pro·pri·ate·ly** *Dress appropriately... It's entitled, appropriately enough, 'Art for the Nation'.* ◆ **ap·pro·pri·ate·ness** *He wonders about the appropriateness of each move he makes.* **2** If someone **appropriates** something which does not belong to them, they take it, usually without the right to do so. *Several other newspapers have appropriated the idea.* ◆ **ap·pro·pria·tion.** /əˌprəʊpriˈeɪʃən/ *...illegal appropriation of land.* **3** If a government or organization **appropriates** an amount of money for a particular purpose, it reserves it for that purpose. *Congress will appropriate more funding for this purpose.* ◆ **ap·pro·pria·tion, appropria·tions.** An **appropriation** is an amount of money which is appropriated. *...defence appropriations.* ◆◆◇◇ ADJ-GRADED / ADV-GRADED / N-UNCOUNT / VERB V n FORMAL / N-UNCOUNT: also a N VERB V n FORMAL / N-COUNT

ap·prov·al /əˈpruːvəl/ **approvals. 1** If you win someone's **approval** for something that you ask for or suggest, they agree to it. *The chairman has also given his approval for an investigation... Mr Clinton could not change present policy without the approval of Congress.* **2 Approval** is a formal or official statement that something is acceptable. *...the testing and approval of new drugs.* **3** If someone or something has your **approval**, you like and admire them. *...an obsessive drive to gain his father's approval.* **4** If a person or organization gives something their **seal of approval** or their **stamp of approval**, they officially say that they admire or like it, or that they think it is acceptable. *Ministers have put their seal of approval on the proposal.* ◆◆◆◇◇ N-UNCOUNT / N-VAR / N-UNCOUNT / PHRASE

ap·prove /əˈpruːv/ **approves, approving, approved. 1** If you **approve** of something or someone, you like them or think they are good. *Not everyone approves of the festival... You've never approved of Henry.* ◆ **ap·prov·ing** *Helen got the benefit of an approving nod.* ◆ **ap·prov·ing·ly** *He nodded approvingly.* **2** If someone in authority **approves** something, they officially agree to it or state that they are satisfied with it. *The Russian Parliament has approved a program of radical economic reforms.* ◆◆◆◆◇ VERB V of n / ADJ-GRADED / ADV-GRADED / VERB V n

ap·proved /əˈpruːvd/. An **approved** method or course of action is officially recommended or acceptable. *The approved method of cleaning is industrial sand-blasting.* ADJ-GRADED

approx. Approx. is a written abbreviation for **approximately.** *Group Size: Approx. 12 to 16.*

ap·proxi·mate, approximates, approximating, approximated. The adjective is pronounced /əˈprɒksɪmət/. The verb is pronounced /əˈprɒksɪmeɪt/. **1 Approximate** quantities are close to the correct quantity, but are not exact. *...the approximate cost of a gasoline engine... The times are approximate only... They did not have even an approximate idea what the Germans really wanted.* ◆ **ap·proxi·mate·ly** *Approximately $150 million is to be spent on improvements.* **2** If something **approximates** to something else, it is similar to it but is not exactly the same. *...something approximating to a just outcome.* ◆◆◇◇◇ ADJ-GRADED / ADV: ADV num VERB V to n

ap·proxi·ma·tion, approxima·tions. 1 An **approximation** is a fact, object, or description which is similar to something else, but which is not exactly the same. *That is a fair approximation of the way in which the next boss is being chosen.* **2** An **approximation** is a number, calculation, or position that is close to a correct number, time, or position, but is not exact. *Clearly that's an approximation, but my guess is there'll be a reasonable balance.* N-COUNT / N-COUNT

Apr. Apr. is a written abbreviation for **April.** *An agreement was reached on Apr. 27.* ◆◆◇◇◇

apres-ski /ˈæpreɪ skiː/; also spelled **après-ski. Apres-ski** consists of evening entertainment and social activities which take place in ski resorts. N-UNCOUNT

apri·cot /ˈeɪprɪkɒt/ **apricots.** An **apricot** is a small, soft, fruit with orange flesh and a stone inside. ◆◇◇◇◇ N-VAR

April /ˈeɪprɪl/ **Aprils. April** is the fourth month of the year in the Western calendar. See Appendix headed **Dates.** ◆◆◆◇ N-VAR

April 'Fool, April Fools. 1 An **April Fool** is a trick that is played on April Fool's Day. **2** You say **'April Fool!'** to someone who has just been deceived by an April Fool's Day trick in order to tell them it was a trick and to make fun of them. N-COUNT / EXCLAM PRAGMATICS

April 'Fool's Day. April Fool's Day is the 1st of April, the day on which people traditionally play tricks on each other up until midday. N-UNCOUNT

a prio·ri /ˌeɪ praɪˈɔːraɪ/. An **a priori** argument, reason, or probability is based on an assumed principle or fact, rather than on actual observed facts. *In the absence of such evidence, there is no a priori hypothesis to work with.* ▶ Also an adverb. *One assumes, a priori, that a parent would be better at dealing with problems.* ADJ / ADV

apron /ˈeɪprən/ **aprons. 1** An **apron** is a piece of clothing that you put over the front of your normal clothes and tie round your waist, especially when you are cooking, in order to prevent your clothes from getting dirty. ● If you say that someone is tied to another person's **apron strings**, you mean that they are controlled or influenced too much by the other person. **2** At an airport, the **apron** is an area of concrete or tarmac where aircraft are parked. *The Lear jet was waiting on the apron.* ◆◇◇◇◇ N-COUNT / PHRASE / N-COUNT

ap·ro·pos /ˌæprəˈpəʊ/. **1** Something which is **apropos, or apropos of,** a subject or event, is connected with it or relevant to it. *...all my suggestions apropos the script... George Orwell once asked, apropos of publishers, 'Why don't they just say, "We don't want your poems"?'* **2** Something that is **apropos** is very suitable in a particular situation. *He said what he thought was apropos.* PREP FORMAL / ADJ-GRADED: v-link ADJ FORMAL

apt /æpt/. **1** An **apt** remark, description, or choice is especially suitable. *...a particularly apt logo for next year's festival.* ◆ **apt·ly** *...the beach in the aptly named town of Oceanside.* **2** If someone or something is **apt** to do something, they often do it and so it is likely that they will do it again. *She was apt to raise her voice.* ◆◆◇◇◇ ADJ-GRADED / ADV-GRADED / ADJ-GRADED: v-link ADJ to-inf

ap·ti·tude /ˈæptɪtjuːd, AM -tuːd/ **aptitudes.** Someone's **aptitude** for a particular kind of work or activity is their ability to learn it quickly and to do it well. *Some students have more aptitude for academic work than others.* ◆◇◇◇◇ N-VAR

'aptitude test, aptitude tests. An **aptitude test** is a test that is specially designed to find out how easily and how well you can do something. N-COUNT

aqua /ˈækwə/. **Aqua** is the same as the colour **aquamarine.** ◆◇◇◇◇ COLOUR

aqua·marine /ˌækwəməˈriːn/ **aquamarines. 1 Aquamarines** are clear greenish-blue stones, sometimes used to make jewellery. **2 Aquamarine** is used to describe things that are greenish-blue in colour. *...warm aquamarine seas.* N-VAR / COLOUR

aquar·ium /əˈkweəriəm/ **aquariums** or **aquaria** /əˈkweəriə/. **1** An **aquarium** is a place where fish and underwater animals are kept and displayed. **2** An **aquarium** is a glass tank filled with water, in which people keep fish. ◆◇◇◇◇ N-COUNT / N-COUNT

aquat·ic /əˈkwætɪk/. **1** An **aquatic** animal or plant lives or grows on or in water. *The pond is quite small but can support many aquatic plants.* **2 Aquatic** means relating to water. *...our aquatic resources.* ◆◇◇◇◇ ADJ / ADJ

aque·duct /ˈækwɪdʌkt/ **aqueducts. 1** An **aqueduct** is a long bridge with many arches, which carries a water supply or a canal over a valley. **2** An **aqueduct** is a large pipe or canal which carries a N-COUNT / N-COUNT

water supply to a city or a farming area. ...*a nation-wide system of aqueducts to carry water to the arid parts of this country.*

aque·ous /'eɪkwiəs/. An **aqueous** solution or cream has water as its base. ...*an aqueous solution containing various sodium salts.* ADJ: ADJ n TECHNICAL

aqui·fer /'ækwɪfə/ **aquifers.** An **aquifer** is rock beneath the earth's surface which absorbs and holds water, making it a valuable source of water. N-COUNT TECHNICAL

aqui·line /'ækwɪlaɪn/. If someone has an **aquiline** profile, their nose is large, thin, and usually curved. ADJ-GRADED FORMAL

Arab /'ærəb/ **Arabs.** **Arabs** are the major ethnic group in the Middle East and parts of North Africa. ▶ Also an adjective. *Little has changed in the Arab world.* N-COUNT / ADJ

ara·besque /ˌærə'besk/ **arabesques.** In art, an **arabesque** is an elaborate design of flowing lines. ...*a clay water jug decorated with painted arabesques.* N-COUNT

Ara·bian /ə'reɪbiən/. **Arabian** means belonging or relating to Arabia, especially to Saudi Arabia. ...*the Arabian Peninsula.* ◆◆◆◇ ADJ

Ara·bic /'ærəbɪk/. **1 Arabic** is a language that is spoken in the Middle East and North Africa. **2** Something that is **Arabic** belongs or relates to the language, writing, or culture of the Arabs. ...*swirling Arabic script.* ...*modern Arabic literature.* **3** An **Arabic** numeral is one of the written figures such as 1, 2, 3, or 4. N-UNCOUNT / ADJ / ADJ: ADJ n

ar·able /'ærəbəl/. **Arable** farming involves growing crops rather than keeping animals. **Arable** land is land that is used for arable farming. ADJ

ar·bi·ter /'ɑːbɪtə/ **arbiters. 1** An **arbiter** is a person or institution that judges and settles a quarrel between two other people or groups. *He was the ultimate arbiter on both theological and political matters.* **2** An **arbiter** of taste or style is someone who has a lot of influence in deciding what is fashionable or socially desirable. *Sequins have often aroused the scorn of arbiters of taste.* ◆◇◇◇ N-COUNT FORMAL / N-COUNT FORMAL

ar·bi·trage /'ɑːbɪtrɑːʒ/. In finance, **arbitrage** is the activity of buying shares or currency in one financial market and selling them at a profit in another. ◆◇◇◇ N-UNCOUNT

ar·bi·tra·ger /'ɑːbɪtrɑː'ʒɑː/ **arbitragers;** also spelled **arbitrageur.** In economics, an **arbitrager** is someone who buys currencies, securities, or commodities on one country's market in order to make money by immediately selling them at a profit on another's market. N-COUNT

ar·bi·trary /'ɑːbɪtri, AM -treri/. If you describe an action, rule, or decision as **arbitrary**, you think that it is not based on any principle, plan, or system. It often seems unfair because of this. ...*arbitrary arrests and detention without trial.* ♦ **ar·bi·trari·ly** /ˌɑːbɪ'treərɪli/ *The victims were not chosen arbitrarily.* ♦ **ar·bi·trari·ness** /'ɑːbɪtrərinəs, AM -trer-/ ...*the apparent arbitrariness by which she sets the prices.* ◆◇◇◇ ADJ-GRADED PRAGMATICS / ADV-GRADED: ADV with v / N-UNCOUNT

ar·bi·trate /'ɑːbɪtreɪt/ **arbitrates, arbitrating, arbitrated.** When someone in authority **arbitrates** between two people or groups who are in dispute, they consider all the facts and make an official decision about who is right. *He arbitrates between investors and members of the association.* ♦ **ar·bi·tra·tor** /'ɑːbɪtreɪtə/ **arbitrators** *He served as an arbitrator in a series of commercial disputes.* VERB V between pl-n Also V / N-COUNT

ar·bi·tra·tion /ˌɑːbɪ'treɪʃən/. **Arbitration** is the judging of a dispute between people or groups by someone who is not involved. ...*the independent arbitration service, ACAS... The matter is likely to go to arbitration.* ◆◇◇◇ N-UNCOUNT

ar·bo·re·tum /ˌɑːbə'riːtəm/ **arboretums.** An **arboretum** is a specially designed garden of different types of trees. N-COUNT

ar·bour /'ɑːbə/ **arbours;** spelled **arbor** in American English. An **arbour** is a shelter in a garden which is formed by leaves and stems of plants growing close together over a light framework. N-COUNT

arc /ɑːk/ **arcs, arcing, arced. 1** An **arc** is a smoothly curving line or movement. *His 71 offices are spread through the Thames Valley and in an arc* ◆◇◇◇ N-COUNT around north London. **2** In geometry, an **arc** is a part of the line that forms the outside of a circle. **3** If something **arcs** in a particular direction, it makes a smoothly curving line or movement. *A rainbow arced gracefully over the town.* N-COUNT / VERB V prep/adv LITERARY

ar·cade /ɑː'keɪd/ **arcades. 1** An **arcade** is a covered passage where there are shops or market stalls. **2** An **arcade** is the same as an **amusement arcade**. ◆◇◇◇ N-COUNT / N-COUNT

ar'cade game, arcade games. An **arcade game** is a computer game of the type that is often played in amusement arcades. N-COUNT

ar·cane /ɑː'keɪn/. Something that is **arcane** is secret or mysterious. ...*the arcane world of contemporary music.* ◆◇◇◇ ADJ-GRADED FORMAL

arch /ɑːtʃ/ **arches, arching, arched. 1** An **arch** is a structure that is curved at the top and is supported on either side by a pillar, post, or wall. *They walked through the arch.* ...*railway arches.* **2** The **arch** of your foot is the curved section of bone at the top. **3** If you **arch** a part of your body such as your back or if it **arches**, you bend it so that it forms a curve. *Don't arch your back.* **4** If something **arches** in a particular direction, it makes a curved line or movement. ...*the domed ceiling arching overhead.* If you **5 arch** your eyebrows, you raise them as a way of showing surprise or disapproval. *'Oh really?' he said, arching an eyebrow.* **6** See also **arched**. **7** If you describe someone's behaviour as **arch**, you mean that it is rather exaggerated or artificial, often in a way that is intended to be amusing or playful. ...*that curious, slightly amused and even arch expression.* ♦ **arch·ly** *'You can't fool me,' Shirley said archly.* ◆◇◇◇ N-COUNT / N-COUNT / V-ERG V n Also V / VERB V adv/prep / VERB V n / ADJ-GRADED / ADV-GRADED

arch- /ɑːtʃ-/. **Arch-** combines with nouns that refer to people, usually people who are opposed to something or who are considered bad, to emphasize that these people are extreme representatives of something. For example, your **arch-rival** is the rival you most want to beat. ...*his arch-enemy.* COMB

ar·chae·ol·ogy /ˌɑːki'ɒlədʒi/; also spelled **archeology. Archaeology** is the study of societies and people of the past, by examining the remains of their buildings, tools, and other artefacts. ♦ **ar·chaeo·logi·cal** /ˌɑːkiə'lɒdʒɪkəl/ ...*one of England's most important archaeological sites.* ♦ **ar·chae·olo·gist** /ˌɑːki'ɒlədʒɪst/ **archaeologists** *The archaeologists found a house built around 300 BC.* ◆◇◇◇ N-UNCOUNT / ADJ: ADJ n / N-COUNT

ar·cha·ic /ɑː'keɪɪk/. **Archaic** means extremely old or extremely old-fashioned. ...*archaic laws that are very seldom used.* ◆◇◇◇ ADJ-GRADED

arch·angel /'ɑːkeɪndʒəl/ **archangels.** An **archangel** is a high-ranking angel. ...*the Archangels Gabriel and Michael.* N-COUNT; N-TITLE: the N

arch·bishop /ˌɑːtʃ'bɪʃəp/ **archbishops.** In the Roman Catholic, Orthodox, and Anglican Churches, an **archbishop** is a bishop of the highest rank. N-COUNT; N-TITLE

arch·dio·cese /ˌɑːtʃ'daɪəsɪs/ **archdioceses** /ˌɑːtʃ'daɪəsiːz/. An **archdiocese** is the area over which an archbishop has control. N-COUNT

arched /ɑːtʃt/. **1** An **arched** window or doorway is curved at the top. **2** An **arched** bridge has arches as part of its structure. **3** You use **arched** to describe something that is curved like an arch. *A frown formed between her arched brows.* ◆◇◇◇ ADJ / ADJ / ADJ

ar·che·ol·ogy /ˌɑːki'ɒlədʒi/. See **archaeology.**

ar·chery /'ɑːtʃəri/. **Archery** is a sport in which people shoot arrows at a target using a bow. ♦ **arch·er,** **archers.** An **archer** is someone who does archery. N-UNCOUNT / N-COUNT

ar·che·type /'ɑːkitaɪp/ **archetypes.** An **archetype** is someone or something that is considered to be a perfect or typical example of a particular kind of person or thing, because it has all their most important characteristics. *He came to this country 20 years ago and is the archetype of the successful Asian businessman.* ♦ **ar·che·typ·al** /ˌɑːki'taɪpəl/ *Cricket is the archetypal English game.* ◆◇◇◇ N-COUNT FORMAL / ADJ-GRADED

ar·che·typi·cal /ˌɑːkɪ'tɪpɪkəl/. **Archetypical** means the same as **archetypal**. ...*an archetypical BBC voice.* ADJ

archi·pela·go /ˌɑːkɪpe'lægəʊ/ **archipelagos** or **archipelagoes.** An **archipelago** is a group of islands, especially small islands. N-COUNT

archi·tect /ˈɑːkɪtekt/ **architects. 1** An architect ◆◇◇◇◇ is a person who designs buildings. *...the American* N-COUNT *architect Michael Gabellini.* **2** A person who plans N-COUNT the design of large projects such as landscaping or with supp railways can be referred to as an **architect** of a particular kind. *...Paul Andreu, chief architect of French railways.* **3** The **architect** of an idea, event, or insti- N-COUNT tution is the person who invented it or made it hap- FORMAL pen. *...Russia's chief architect of economic reform.*

archi·tec·ture /ˈɑːkɪtektʃə/ **architectures.** ◆◆◇◇◇ **1** Architecture is the art of planning, designing, and N-UNCOUNT constructing buildings. *He studied classical architecture and design in Rome.* ♦ **archi·tec·tur·al** ADJ /ˌɑːkɪˈtektʃərəl/. *...Tibet's architectural heritage. ...the unique architectural style of towns like Lamu.* ♦ **archi·tec·tur·al·ly** *...the most architecturally* ADV *stunning hotels in India.* **2** The **architecture** of a N-UNCOUNT building is the style in which it is designed and con- with supp structed. *...a fine example of Moroccan architecture.* **3** The **architecture** of something is its structure. N-UNCOUNT *...the crumbling intellectual architecture of modern* also N in pl *society.* FORMAL

ar·chive /ˈɑːkaɪv/ **archives.** The **archive** or **ar-** N-COUNT **chives** are a collection of documents and records that contain historical information. You can also use **archives** to refer to the place where archives are stored. *...the archives of the Imperial War Museum. ...pieces of archive film.* ♦ **ar·chiv·al** /ɑːˈkaɪvəl/. ADJ *...his extensive use of archival material.*

archi·vist /ˈɑːkɪvɪst/ **archivists.** An **archivist** is a N-COUNT person whose job is to collect, sort, and preserve historical documents and records.

arch·way /ˈɑːtʃweɪ/ **archways.** An **archway** is a N-COUNT passage or entrance with a curved roof.

ˈarc light, arc lights. Arc lights are a type of very N-COUNT bright electric light.

arc·tic /ˈɑːktɪk/. **1** The **Arctic** is the area of the ◆◇◇◇◇ world around the North Pole. **2** If you describe a N-PROPER: place or the weather as **arctic**, you are emphasizing theN that it is extremely cold. *The bathroom, with its* ADJ-GRADED spartan pre-war facilities, is positively arctic. PRAGMATICS INFORMAL

ˌArctic 'Circle. The **Arctic Circle** is an imaginary N-PROPER: line drawn around the northern part of the world at theN approximately 66° North.

ar·dent /ˈɑːdənt/. **Ardent** is used to describe some- ◆◇◇◇◇ one who has extremely strong feelings about some- ADJ-GRADED thing or someone. *...one of the most ardent support-ers of the administration's policy.* ♦ **ar·dent·ly** *Why* ADV-GRADED *had Hilton defended him so ardently?*

ar·dour /ˈɑːdə/; spelled **ardor** in American English. N-UNCOUNT **Ardour** is an intense passionate feeling of love or also N in pl enthusiasm for someone or something. *The sexual* LITERARY *ardour had cooled. ...my ardor for football.*

ar·du·ous /ˈɑːdʒʊəs/. Something that is **arduous** is ◆◇◇◇◇ difficult and tiring, and involves a lot of effort. *...a* ADJ-GRADED *long, hot and arduous journey... The task was more arduous than he had calculated.*

are /ə, STRONG ɑː/. **Are** is the plural and the second person singular of the present tense of the verb **be**. **Are** is often abbreviated to **'re** after pronouns.

area /ˈeərɪə/ **areas. 1** An **area** is a particular part ◆◆◆◆◆ of a town, a country, a region, or the world. *...the* N-COUNT *large number of community groups in the area. ...if there is an election in your area... Half the French population still lived in rural areas.* **2** A particular N-COUNT: **area** is a piece of land or part of a building that is suppN used for a particular activity. *...a picnic area. ...the main check-in area located in Terminal 1.* **3** An N-COUNT **area** is a particular place on a surface or object, for with supp example an external part of your body. *Massage may help to increase blood flow to specific areas of the body.* **4** The **area** of a surface such as a piece of N-VAR land is the amount of flat space or ground that it covers, measured in square units. *The islands cover a total area of 625.6 square kilometers.* **5** You can N-COUNT use **area** to refer to a particular subject or topic, or to a particular part of a larger, more general situa-tion or activity. *...the politically sensitive area of old age pensions. ...all other areas of society... She wants to be involved in every area of your life.* **6** See

also **catchment area, disaster area, grey area, pen-alty area.**

ˈarea code, area codes. The **area code** for a par- N-COUNT ticular city or region is a series of numbers that you have to dial if you are making a telephone call to that place from a different area.

arena /əˈriːnə/ **arenas. 1** An **arena** is a place ◆◆◇◇◇ where sports, entertainments, and other public N-COUNT events take place. It has seats around it where peo-ple sit and watch. *...the largest indoor sports arena in the world.* **2** You can refer to a field of activity, N-COUNT especially one where there is a lot of conflict or ac-tion, as an **arena** of a particular kind. *...the political arena... Oil speculation proved a natural arena for his skills.*

aren't /ɑːnt, AM ˈɑːrənt/. **1** Are not is usually said ◆◆◆◆◇ or written as **aren't**. **2** Aren't is the form that is INFORMAL usually used instead of **am not** in negative question tags.

ar·gon /ˈɑːɡɒn/. **Argon** is an inert gas which occurs N-UNCOUNT in very small amounts in the atmosphere.

ar·got /ˈɑːɡəʊ/ **argots.** An **argot** is a special vo- N-VAR cabulary used by a particular group of people, FORMAL which other people find difficult to understand. *...the argot of the university campus.*

ar·gu·able /ˈɑːɡjʊəbəl/. **1** If you say that it is **argu-** ADJ-GRADED **able** that something is true, you believe that it can FORMAL be supported by evidence and that many people would agree with it. *It is arguable that this was not as grave a handicap as it might appear.* **2** An idea, ADJ-GRADED point, or comment that is **arguable** is not obviously FORMAL true or correct and should be questioned. *It is argu-able whether he ever had much control over the real economic power.*

ar·gu·ably /ˈɑːɡjʊəbli/. You can use **arguably** ◆◇◇◇◇ when you are stating your opinion or belief, as a ADV way of giving more authority to it. *They are arguably* PRAGMATICS *the most important band since The Rolling Stones.*

ar·gue /ˈɑːɡjuː/ **argues, arguing, argued. 1** If ◆◆◆◇◇ you **argue** that something is true, you state it and VERB give the reasons why you think it is true. If you **ar-** V that **gue for** or **against** an idea or policy, you state the V for/against reasons why you support or oppose it. *His lawyers* n *are arguing that he is unfit to stand trial... It could* V n *be argued that the British are not aggressive* Also V with *enough... The report argues against tax increases... I* quote, *argued the case for an independent central bank.* **2** If V you **argue** with someone about something, you dis- V-RECIP cuss or debate it with them, with each of you giving V with n your different or opposing opinions. *He was arguing* about/overn *with the King about the need to maintain the army* pl-n V about/ *at full strength... They are arguing over foreign poli-* overn *cy... The two of them sitting in their office were argu-* pl-n V n *ing this point.* **3** If one person **argues** with another, V-RECIP they speak angrily to each other about something V with n that they disagree about. *The committee is con-* pl-n V *cerned about players' behaviour, especially arguing* Also V about/ *with referees... They were still arguing.* **4** If you tell overn someone not to **argue** with you, you want them to VERB do or believe what you say without protest or dis- PRAGMATICS agreement. *Just get in and don't argue with me.* **5** If V with n you say that nobody can **argue** with a particular fact Also V or opinion, you are emphasizing that it is obviously VB: with brd-true and so everyone must accept it. *We produced* neg *the best soccer of the tournament. Nobody would ar-* PRAGMATICS *gue with that.* V with n Also V that SPOKEN

argue out. If two or more people **argue** something PHRASAL VB **out**, they discuss it thoroughly in order to reach a con- V n P clusion or decision. *If there's a dispute we argue it* Also V P noun *out... The question of divorce was discussed and ar-gued out.*

ar·gu·ment /ˈɑːɡjʊmənt/ **arguments. 1** An **argu-** ◆◆◆◆◇ **ment** is a statement or set of statements that you N-VAR use in order to try to convince people that your opinion about something is correct. *There's a strong argument for lowering the price... The doctors have set out their arguments against the proposals.* ● See also **counter-argument. 2** An **argument** is a discus- N-VAR sion or debate in which a number of people put for-ward different or opposing opinions. *...fresh argu-*

ments about the role of the extreme right in France... The issue has caused heated political argument. **3** An **argument** is a conversation in which people disagree with each other angrily or noisily. *She got into an argument with one of the marchers.* **4** If you accept something without **argument**, you do not question it or disagree with it. *He complied without argument.* — N-COUNT / N-UNCOUNT: with brd-neg

ar·gu·men·ta·tion /,ɑːgjumen'teɪʃən/. **Argumentation** is the process of arguing in a systematic or logical way, for example in philosophy. — N-UNCOUNT FORMAL

ar·gu·men·ta·tive /,ɑːgjʊ'mentətɪv/. If you describe someone as **argumentative**, you disapprove of them because they are always ready to disagree or start quarrelling with other people. *You're in an argumentative mood today!* — ADJ-GRADED PRAGMATICS

aria /'ɑːriə/ **arias**. An **aria** is a song for one of the leading singers in an opera or choral work. — ◆◇◇◇◇ N-COUNT

arid /'ærɪd/. **1 Arid** land is so dry that very few plants can grow on it. *...crops that can withstand arid conditions.* **2** If you describe something such as a period of your life or an academic subject as **arid**, you mean that it has so little interest, excitement, or purpose that it makes you feel bored or unhappy. *...the politically arid years of military dictatorship in the 1960s and '70s.* — ◆◇◇◇◇ ADJ-GRADED

arise /ə'raɪz/ **arises, arising, arose, arisen** /ə'rɪzən/. **1** If a situation or problem **arises**, it begins to exist or people start to become aware of it. *...when the opportunity arises.* **2** If something **arises from** a particular situation, or **arises out of it**, it is created or caused by the situation. *The charges arise out of a long-running fraud enquiry by Merseyside police.* **3** If something such as a new species, organization, or system **arises**, it begins to exist and develop. *New biological species arise only after the passage of millennia.* **4** When you **arise**, you get out of bed in the morning. *He arose at 6:30 a.m. as usual.* **5** When you **arise** from a chair or a kneeling position, you stand up. *When I arose from the chair, my father and Eleanor's father were in deep conversation.* **6** You can say that something tall such as a building or mountain **arises** from the ground around it. *...the flat terrace, from which arises the cubic volume of the house.* — ◆◆◇◇ / VERB V / VERB V from/out of n / VERB V / VERB: V FORMAL VERB: V FORMAL / VERB V from LITERARY

ar·is·toc·ra·cy /,ærɪ'stɒkrəsi/ **aristocracies**. The **aristocracy** is a class of people in some countries who have a high social rank and special titles. — ◆◇◇◇◇ N-COLL-COUNT

aris·to·crat /'ærɪstəkræt, ə'rɪst-/ **aristocrats**. An **aristocrat** is someone whose family has a high social rank, especially someone who has a title. ◆ **aris·to·crat·ic** /...a wealthy, aristocratic family.* — ◆◇◇◇◇ N-COUNT / ADJ-GRADED

arith·me·tic /ə'rɪθmɪtɪk/. **1 Arithmetic** is the part of mathematics that is concerned with adding, subtracting, multiplying, and dividing numbers. ◆ **arith·meti·cal** /,ærɪθ'metɪkəl/. *...arithmetical problems.* **2** If you refer to the **arithmetic** of a situation, you are concerned with those aspects of it that can be expressed in numbers. *The budgetary arithmetic for 1993 suggests that government borrowing is set to surge.* — ◆◇◇◇◇ N-UNCOUNT / ADJ / N-UNCOUNT

ark /ɑːk/. In the Bible, the **ark** was a large boat which Noah built in order to save his family and two of every kind of animal from a flood. — ◆◇◇◇◇ N-SING

arm 1 *part of your body or of something else*

arm /ɑːm/ **arms**. **1** Your **arms** are the two long parts of your body that are attached to your shoulders and that have your hands at the end. See picture headed **human body**. *He had a large parcel under his left arm.* ◆ **-armed** *...plump-armed women in cotton dresses.* **2** If two people are walking **arm in arm**, they are walking together with their arms linked. *He walked from the court arm in arm with his wife.* **3** If you hold something **at arm's length**, you hold it away from your body with your arm straight. **4** The **arm** of a piece of clothing is the part of it that covers your arm. **5** The **arm** of a chair is the part on which you rest your arm when you are sitting down. — ◆◆◆◆◆ N-COUNT / COMB / PHRASE / PHRASE / N-COUNT / N-COUNT

6 An **arm** of an object is a long thin part of it that sticks out from the main part. *...the arms of the doctor's spectacles.* **7** An **arm** of land or water is a long thin area of it that is joined to a broader area. *At the end of the other arm of Cardigan Bay is Bardsey Island.* **8** An **arm** of an organization is a section of it that operates in a particular country or that deals with a particular activity. *...the British arm of an American company.* — N-COUNT / N-COUNT / N-COUNT

9 If you say that something costs **an arm and a leg**, you mean that it is very expensive. **10** If you **keep** someone **at arm's length**, you avoid becoming too friendly or involved with them. *She had always kept the family at arm's length.* **11** If you say that a list is **as long as your arm**, you emphasize that it is very long. **12** If you welcome some action or change **with open arms**, you are very pleased about it. If you welcome a person **with open arms** you are very pleased about their arrival. *They would no doubt welcome the action with open arms.* **13** If you **twist** someone's **arm**, you persuade them to do something. *She had twisted his arm to get him to invite her.* — PHRASE INFORMAL / PHRASE / PHRASE PRAGMATICS / PHRASE INFORMAL / PHRASE PRAGMATICS / PHRASE INFORMAL

arm 2 *weapons*

arm /ɑːm/ **arms, arming, armed**. **1 Arms** are weapons, especially bombs and guns. *The IRA had extensive supplies of arms. ...arms control.* **2** If you **arm** someone with a weapon, you provide them with it. *She had armed herself with a loaded rifle.* ◆ **-armed** *...a nuclear-armed power.* **3** If a country has people **under arms**, it has people trained to use weapons and to fight a war. **4** If soldiers **lay down their arms**, they stop fighting and surrender. **5** If one group or country **takes up arms** against another, they prepare to attack and fight them. *They threatened to take up arms against the government if their demands were not met.* **6** If you **arm** someone with something that will be useful in a particular situation, you provide them with it. *If she armed herself with all the knowledge she could gather she could handle anything.* **7** The **arms** of a city or of a noble family are its coat of arms. **Arms** is often used in the names of pubs. *...the arms of Philippe V. ...his local pub, the Abercorn Arms.* **8** If people are **up in arms** about something, they are very angry about it and are protesting strongly against it. *Environmental groups are up in arms about plans to sink an oil well close to Hadrian's Wall.* **9** See also **armed, coat of arms, comrade-in-arms, small arms**. — ◆◆◆◆◆ N-PLURAL FORMAL VERB / V n with n Also V n / COMB PHRASE / PHRASE / PHRASE DATED PHRASE / VERB V n with n / N-PLURAL / PHRASE

ar·ma·da /,ɑː'mɑːdə/ **armadas**. An **armada** is a large fleet of warships. *An armada of U.S. Navy ships participated in the invasion.* — N-COUNT

ar·ma·dil·lo /,ɑːmə'dɪləʊ/ **armadillos**. An **armadillo** is a small animal whose body is covered with large bony scales. Armadillos live in South America and in southern parts of North America. — N-COUNT

Ar·ma·ged·don /,ɑːmə'gedən/. When people refer to **Armageddon**, they are referring to a terrible battle or war that will lead to the total destruction of the world or the human race. — N-UNCOUNT

Ar·ma·gnac /'ɑːmənjæk/ **Armagnacs**. Armagnac is a type of brandy from southern France. — N-VAR

ar·ma·ment /'ɑːməmənt/ **armaments**. **1 Armaments** are weapons and military equipment belonging to an army or country. *...nuclear and other armaments.* **2 Armament** is used to refer to weapons and bombs carried by an aircraft or other military vehicle. **3** A country's increase in the number and effectiveness of its weapons is its **armament**. *...the pursuit of national security through national armament.* — ◆◇◇◇◇ N-PLURAL / N-VAR TECHNICAL / N-UNCOUNT

arm·band /'ɑːmbænd/ **armbands**. An **armband** is a band of fabric that you wear round your arm in order to show that you have an official position or belong to a particular group. — N-COUNT

arm·chair /'ɑːmtʃeə/ **armchairs**. **1** An **armchair** is a big comfortable chair which has a support on each side for your arms. **2** An **armchair** critic, fan, or traveller knows about a particular subject from what he or she has read or heard about rather than from practical experience; sometimes used showing — ◆◇◇◇◇ N-COUNT / ADJ: ADJ n

disapproval. *This great book is ideal for both the travelling supporter and the armchair fan.* If **3 a bank or shop provides an armchair** service, their customers can carry out financial transactions or order goods from home, using the telephone, a computer, or the postal service, rather than having to go into the bank or shop.

armed /ɑːmd/. **1** Someone who is **armed** is carrying a weapon, usually a gun. You can also use **armed** to describe the actions or crimes that they carry out using their weapons. *Police believe he may be armed. ...armed guards. ...armed robbery.* **2** See also **arm**. ◆◆◆◇ ADJ

armed 'forces. The **armed forces** or the **armed services** of a country are its military forces, usually the army, navy, and air force. ◆◆◇◇ N-PLURAL

arm·ful /ˈɑːmful/ **armfuls.** An **armful** of something is the amount of it that you can carry fairly easily. *He hurried out with an armful of brochures.* N-COUNT

arm·hole /ˈɑːmhəʊl/ **armholes.** The **armholes** of something such as a shirt or dress are the openings through which you put your arms, or the places where the sleeves are attached. N-COUNT

ar·mi·stice /ˈɑːmɪstɪs/. An **armistice** is an agreement between countries who are at war with one another to stop fighting and to discuss ways of making a peaceful settlement. N-SING

arm·load /ˈɑːmləʊd/ **armloads.** An **armload** of something is the same as an **armful** of something. N-COUNT

ar·mor /ˈɑːmə/. See **armour**.

ar·mor·er /ˈɑːmərə/ **armorers.** See **armourer**.

ar·mo·ry /ˈɑːməri/ **armories.** See **armoury**.

ar·mour /ˈɑːmə/; spelled **armor** in American English. **1 Armour** consists of tanks and other military vehicles used in battle. *...the biggest movement of heavy British armour since the Second World War.* ◆ **ar·moured** *These front-line defences are backed up by armoured units in reserve.* **2 Armour** is a hard, usually metal, covering that protects a vehicle against attack. *...a formidable warhead that can penetrate the armour of most tanks.* ◆ **armoured** *...armoured vehicles carrying troops.* **3** In former times, **armour** was special metal clothing that soldiers wore for protection in battle. *...a medieval suit of armour.* **4** See also **body armour**. ● **a chink in someone's armour**: see **chink**. ● **a knight in shining armour**: see **knight**. ◆◆◇◇ N-UNCOUNT TECHNICAL; ADJ; N-UNCOUNT; ADJ; N-UNCOUNT

ar·mour·er /ˈɑːmərə/ **armourers**; spelled **armorer** in American English. An **armourer** is someone who makes or supplies weapons. N-COUNT

armour-'plating; spelled **armor-plating** in American English. The **armour-plating** on a vehicle or building is the hard metal covering which is intended to protect it from gunfire and other missiles. ◆ **armour-plated** *...an armour-plated car.* N-UNCOUNT; ADJ

ar·moury /ˈɑːməri/ **armouries**; spelled **armory** in American English. **1** You can refer to a large number of things which someone has available for a particular purpose as their **armoury**. *The strongest weapon in the government's armoury is the price cuts announced on Saturday.* **2** A country's **armoury** is all its weapons and military equipment. *...a treaty to reduce the armouries of conventional weapons in Europe.* **3** An **armoury** is a place where weapons, bombs, and other military equipment are stored. ◆◇◇◇ N-COUNT; N-COUNT; N-COUNT

arm·pit /ˈɑːmpɪt/ **armpits.** Your **armpits** are the areas of your body under your arms where your arms join your shoulders. See picture headed **human body**. ◆◇◇◇ N-COUNT

arm·rest /ˈɑːmrest/ **armrests.** The **armrests** on a chair are the two pieces on either side that support your arms when you are sitting down. N-COUNT

'arms race. An **arms race** is a situation in which two countries or groups of countries are continually trying to get more and better weapons than each other. ◆◇◇◇ N-SING

army /ˈɑːmi/ **armies.** **1** A country's **army** is a large organized group of its people who are armed and trained to fight on land in a war. *The army is about to launch a major offensive. ...a top-ranking army* ◆◆◆◆◆ N-COLL-COUNT officer. **2** An **army** of people, animals, or things is a large number of them, especially when they are regarded as a force of some kind. *...data collected by an army of volunteers. ...armies of ants.* N-COLL-COUNT: N of n

'A-road, A-roads. In Britain, an **A-road** is a major road. *Stick to the A-roads.* ◆◇◇◇ N-COUNT

aro·ma /əˈrəʊmə/ **aromas.** An **aroma** is a strong pleasant smell. *...the wonderful aroma of freshly baked bread.* ◆◇◇◇ N-COUNT

aroma·ther·a·py /əˌrəʊməˈθerəpi/. **Aromatherapy** is a type of treatment that is used especially to relieve tension, which involves massaging the body with special fragrant oils. ◆ **aroma·ther·a·pist** /əˌrəʊməˈθerəpɪst/ **aromatherapists.** An **aromatherapist** is a person who is qualified to practise aromatherapy. ◆◇◇◇ N-UNCOUNT; N-COUNT

aro·mat·ic /ˌærəˈmætɪk/. An **aromatic** plant or food has a strong pleasant smell of herbs or spices. *...an evergreen shrub with deep green, aromatic leaves. ...an aromatic beef stew.* ◆◇◇◇ ADJ-GRADED

arose /əˈrəʊz/. **Arose** is the past tense of **arise**.

around /əˈraʊnd/. **Around** is an adverb and a preposition. In British English, the word 'round' is often used instead. **Around** is often used with verbs of movement, such as 'walk' and 'drive', and also in phrasal verbs such as 'get around'. ◆◆◆◆◆

1 To be positioned **around** a place or object means to surround it or be on all sides of it. To move **around** a place means to go along its edge, back to your starting point. *She looked at the papers around her. ...a prosperous suburb built around a new mosque.* ▶ Also an adverb. *The Memorial seems almost ugly, dominating the landscape for miles around.* **2** If you move **around** a corner or obstacle, you move to the other side of it. If you look **around** a corner or obstacle, you look to see what is on the other side. *The photographer stopped clicking and hurried around the corner... I peered around the edge of the shed.* **3** If you turn **around**, you turn so that you are facing in the opposite direction. *I turned around and wrote the title on the blackboard.* **4** When you are giving measurements, you can use **around** to mention the circumference of something. *She was 5 foot 4 inches, 38 around the chest, 28 around the waist and 40 around the hips.* **5** If you move **around** a place, you travel through it, going to most of its parts. If you look **around** a place, you look at every part of it. *I've been walking around Moscow... He glanced discreetly around the room.* ▶ Also an adverb. *He backed away from the edge, looking all around at the flat horizon.* **6** If someone moves **around** a place, they move through various parts of that place without having any particular destination. *Much of my time is spent weaving my way around drinks parties... They milled around the ballroom with video cameras.* ▶ Also an adverb. *...a scruffy youth wandering around looking lost.* **7** If you go **around** to someone's house, you visit them. *We went around to see the other girls.* **8** You use **around** in expressions such as **hang around** when you are saying that someone is spending time in a place and not doing anything very important. *I'm just going to be hanging around twiddling my thumbs... They sat around for an hour discussing political affairs.* ▶ Also a preposition. *He used to skip lessons and hang around the harbor.* **9** If someone **has been around**, they have had a lot of experience of different people and situations. *He's been around a long time and has acquired a number of skills.* PREP; ADV: n ADV; PREP; ADV: ADV after v; PREP; ADV: ADV after v PREP; ADV: ADV after v PREP; ADV: ADV after v ADV: ADV after v ADV; PREP; PHRASE INFORMAL

10 If you move things **around**, you move them so that they are in different places. *She moved things around so the table was beneath the windows.* **11** If a wheel or object turns **around**, it turns on its axis. *The boat started to spin around in the water.* ADV: ADV after v; ADV: ADV after v

12 You use **around** to say that something happens in or relates to different parts of a place or area, or is near a place or area. *...scattered violence around the country... Elephants were often to be found in swamp in eastern Kenya around the Tana River. ...pests and diseases around the garden.* ▶ Also an adverb. *What the* PREP; ADV

hell do you think you're doing following me around? *...the best Parma ham for miles around.*

13 If someone or something is **around**, they exist or are present in a place. *...having lots of people around that you can talk to.* **14** The people **around** you are the people who you come into contact with, especially your friends, colleagues, and relatives. *We change our behaviour by observing the behaviour of those around us... Those around her would forgive her for weeping.* ADV — PREP

15 If something such as a film, a discussion, or a plan is based **around** something, that thing is its main theme. *...the gentle comedy based around the Larkin family... The discussion centered around four subjects.* PREP

16 You use **around** in expressions such as **this time around** or **to come around** when you are describing something that has happened before or things that happen regularly. *Senator Bentsen has declined to get involved this time around. ...when July Fourth comes around.* ADV

17 **Around** means approximately. *My salary was around £19,000... Rolls Royce produces around 1,000 extremely desirable cars a year.* ▶ Also a preposition. *He expects the elections to be held around November.* ADV — PREP

18 **Around about** means approximately. *He's charging you around about a hundred pounds an hour.* PHR-PREP SPOKEN

19 You say **all around** to indicate that something affects all parts of a situation or all members of a group. *He compared the achievements of the British and the French during 1916 and concluded that the latter were better all around.* PHRASE

20 • **the other way around:** see **way.** • **get your tongue around something:** see **tongue.**

a,round-the-'clock. See **clock.**

arouse /ə'raʊz/ **arouses, arousing, aroused.** **1** If something **arouses** a particular reaction or attitude in people, it causes them to have that reaction or attitude. *His revolutionary work in linguistics has aroused intense scholarly interest.* **2** If something **arouses** a particular feeling or instinct that exists in someone, it causes them to experience that feeling or instinct strongly. *There is nothing quite like a crisp, dry sherry to arouse the appetite.* ♦ **arous·al** *Thinking about thoughts can provoke strong physiological arousal.* **3** If you **are aroused** by something, it makes you feel sexually excited. *Some men are aroused when their partner says erotic words to them.* ♦ **arousal** *...feelings of sexual arousal.* ♦ **aroused** *They get most sexually aroused in the morning.* ♦ **arous·ing** **4** If something **arouses** you, it makes you feel angry. *He apologized, saying this subject always aroused him.* **5** If something **arouses** you from sleep, it wakes you up. ◆◆◇◇ VERB V n — VERB V n Also V n in n — N-UNCOUNT — VB: usu passive be V-ed — N-UNCOUNT — ADJ-GRADED ADJ-GRADED — VERB V n — VERB: V n WRITTEN

ar·raign /ə'reɪn/ **arraigns, arraigning, arraigned.** If someone **is arraigned** on a particular charge, they are brought before a court of law to answer that charge. *She was arraigned today on charges of assault and kidnapping.* ♦ **ar·raign·ment, arraignments** *Keating and his associates are scheduled for arraignment October 5th.* VB: usu passive be V-ed LEGAL — N-VAR

ar·range /ə'reɪndʒ/ **arranges, arranging, arranged.** **1** If you **arrange** an event or meeting, you make plans for it to happen. *She arranged an appointment for Friday afternoon. ...the carefully arranged welcome.* **2** If you **arrange** with someone to do something, you make plans with them to do it. *I've arranged to see him on Friday morning... He had arranged for the boxes to be stored until they could be collected.* **3** If you **arrange** something for someone, you make it possible for them to have it or to do it. *I will arrange for someone to take you round... The hotel manager will arrange for a baby-sitter... I've arranged your hotels for you.* ♦ **ar·rang·er, ar·rangers** *...a funeral arranger.* **4** If you **arrange** things somewhere, you place them in a particular position, usually to make them look attractive or tidy. *She enjoys arranging dried flowers... A number of seats have been arranged in front of the painting.* ♦ **ar·range·ment, arrangements** *...imaginative flower arrangements.* **5** If a piece of music **is ar-** ◆◆◆◇ VERB V n V-ed — VERB V to-inf V for n to-inf Also V that — VERB V to-inf V for n V n — N-COUNT — VERB V n V n prep — N-COUNT: with supp

ranged by someone, it is changed or adapted so that it is suitable for particular instruments or voices, or for a particular performance. *The songs were arranged by another well-known bass player, Ron Carter.* ♦ **ar·range·ment** *...an arrangement of a well-known piece by Mozart.* ♦ **ar·rang·er** *...the band's resident arranger.* VB: usu passive be V-ed — N-COUNT — N-COUNT

ar·ranged /ə'reɪndʒd/. If you say how things are **arranged**, you are talking about their position in relation to each other or to something else. *The house itself is three stories high and arranged around a courtyard. ...neatly-arranged little houses.* ADJ

ar,ranged 'marriage, arranged marriages. In an **arranged marriage**, the parents choose the person who their son or daughter will marry. N-COUNT

ar·range·ment /ə'reɪndʒmənt/ **arrangements.** **1 Arrangements** are plans and preparations which you make so that something will happen or be possible. *...final arrangements for the summit... She telephoned Ellen, but made no arrangements to see her.* **2** An **arrangement** is an agreement that you make with someone to do something. *The caves can be visited only by prior arrangement... Her class teacher made a special arrangement to discuss her progress at school.* **3** See also **arrange.** ◆◆◆◇ N-COUNT — N-COUNT: also by N

ar·rant /'ærənt/. **Arrant** is used to emphasize that something or someone is very bad in some way; used showing disapproval. *That's the most arrant nonsense I've ever heard. ...an arrant coward.* ADJ: ADJ n PRAGMATICS FORMAL

ar·ray /ə'reɪ/ **arrays. 1** An **array** of different things or people is a large number or wide range of them. *She experienced a bewildering array of emotions... A dazzling array of celebrities are expected at the Mayfair gallery.* **2** An **array** of objects is a collection of them that is displayed or arranged in a particular way. *...an impressive array of pill bottles stacked on top of the fridge.* **3** An **array** of instruments such as telescopes or solar panels is a number of them that are connected together to form a single unit. *The solar arrays are very fragile.* **4** In science and mathematics, an **array** of things such as atoms or numbers is a regular pattern or structure that is formed by them. *...an ordered array of molecules within materials.* ◆◆◇◇ N-COLL-COUNT — N-COUNT — N-COUNT — N-COUNT TECHNICAL

ar·rayed /ə'reɪd/. **1** If things are **arrayed** in a particular way, they are arranged or displayed in that way. *Cartons of Chinese food were arrayed on a large oak table.* **2** If something such as a military force is **arrayed against** someone, it is ready and able to be used against them. *...his plan to defeat the two armies arrayed against him.* ADJ: v-link ADJ FORMAL — ADJ: v-link ADJ against n FORMAL

ar·rears /ə'rɪəz/. **1 Arrears** are amounts of money that you owe, especially regular payments that you should have made earlier. *They have promised to pay the arrears over the next five years.* **2** If someone is **in arrears** with their payments, or has got **into arrears**, they have not paid the regular amounts of money that they should have paid. *...the 300,000 households who are more than six months in arrears with their mortgages.* ◆◇◇◇ N-PLURAL — PHRASE

ar·rest /ə'rest/ **arrests, arresting, arrested. 1** When the police **arrest** someone, they take charge of them and take them to a police station, because they believe they may have committed a crime. *Police arrested five young men in connection with one of the attacks... Seven people were arrested for minor offences.* ▶ Also a noun. *Police chased the fleeing terrorists and later made two arrests... Murder squad detectives approached the man and placed him under arrest.* **2** If something or someone **arrests** a process, they stop it continuing. *The sufferer may have to make major changes in his or her life to arrest the disease.* **3** If something **arrests** your attention, you suddenly notice it because it is striking or surprising. *The work of an architect of genius always arrests the attention.* ♦ **ar·rest·ing** *The most arresting feature is the painted wall decoration.* **4** See also **house arrest.** ◆◆◆◇ VERB V n be V-ed for n Also V n for n — N-VAR — VERB V n FORMAL — VERB V n FORMAL — ADJ-GRADED

ar·ri·val /əˈraɪvəl/ **arrivals.** **1** When a person or vehicle arrives at a place, you can refer to their **arrival**. ...*the day after his arrival in England... He was dead on arrival at the nearby hospital.* **2** When someone starts a new job, you can refer to their **arrival** in that job. ...*the arrival of a new president... The company had eight departures and 11 new arrivals on its management board in 1980-89.* **3** When something is brought to you or becomes available, you can refer to its **arrival**. ...*while awaiting the arrival of orange juice and coffee.* **4** When a particular time comes or a particular event happens, you can refer to its **arrival**. ...*the arrival of the New Year.* **5** You can refer to someone who has just arrived at a place as a new **arrival**. *A high proportion of the new arrivals are skilled professionals.* **6** When a baby is born, you can refer to its **arrival**. ...*the arrival of a new child.* **7** You can refer to a baby who has just been born as a new **arrival**.

ar·rive /əˈraɪv/ **arrives, arriving, arrived.** **1** When a person or vehicle **arrives** at a place, they come to it at the end of a journey. *Fresh groups of guests were... The Princess Royal arrived at Gatwick this morning.* **2** When you **arrive** at a place, you come to it for the first time in order to stay, live, or work there. ...*before the European settlers arrived in the country.* **3** When something such as letter or meal **arrives**, it is brought or delivered to you. *Breakfast arrived while he was in the bathroom.* **4** When something such as a new product or invention **arrives**, it becomes available. *Several long-awaited videos will finally arrive in the shops this month.* **5** When a particular moment or event **arrives**, it happens or comes. *The time has arrived when I need to give up smoking.* **6** When you **arrive at** something such as a decision or a conclusion, you decide or conclude something, after thinking about it or discussing it. ...*if the jury cannot arrive at a unanimous decision.* **7** When a baby **arrives**, it is born. **8** If you say that someone **has arrived**, you mean that they have become successful or famous. *You know you've arrived when you get your own logo at the end of your shows.*

ar·ro·gant /ˈærəgənt/. Someone who is **arrogant** behaves in a proud unpleasant way because they believe that they are more important than others. *He was so arrogant... That sounds arrogant, doesn't it? ...an air of arrogant indifference.* ♦ **ar·ro·gance** *At times the arrogance of those in power is quite blatant.* ♦ **ar·ro·gant·ly** *Simpson arrogantly claimed: 'We won't lose another game.'*

ar·ro·gate /ˈærəgeɪt/ **arrogates, arrogating, arrogated.** If someone **arrogates** to themselves something such as a responsibility or privilege, they claim or take it even though they have no right to do so; used showing disapproval. *The assembly arrogated to itself the right to alter the relationships within the Federation.*

ar·row /ˈærəʊ/ **arrows.** **1** An **arrow** is a long thin weapon which is sharp and pointed at one end and which often has feathers at the other end. An arrow is shot from a bow. ...*warriors armed with bows and arrows.* **2** An **arrow** is a written or printed sign that consists of a straight line with another line bent at a sharp angle at one end. This is a printed arrow: →. The arrow points in a particular direction to indicate where something is. **3** ● **slings and arrows**: see **sling**.

arrow·head /ˈærəʊhed/ **arrowheads;** also spelled **arrow-head.** An **arrowhead** is the sharp pointed part of an arrow.

arrow·root /ˈærəʊruːt/. **Arrowroot** is a starch obtained from a West Indian plant. It is used in cooking, for example for thickening sauces.

arse /ɑːs/ **arses.** Your **arse** is your bottom. Some people find this word offensive. The usual American word is **ass**.

ar·senal /ˈɑːsənəl/ **arsenals.** **1** An **arsenal** is a large collection of weapons and military equipment held by a country, group, or person. ...*their nuclear arsenals.* **2** You can use **arsenal** to refer to a large number of tools, methods, or resources that someone has available to help them achieve what they want to do. *Managers use a full arsenal of motivational techniques... He has more punches in his arsenal than other boxers.*

ar·senic /ˈɑːsənɪk/. **Arsenic** is a very strong poison which can kill people.

ar·son /ˈɑːsən/. **Arson** is the crime of deliberately setting fire to a building or vehicle. ♦ **ar·son·ist** /ˈɑːsənɪst/ **arsonists.** An **arsonist** is a person who commits arson.

art /ɑːt/ **arts.** **1** **Art** consists of paintings, sculpture, and other pictures or objects which are created for people to look at and admire or think deeply about. ...*contemporary American art. ...the first exhibition of such art in the West.* **2** **Art** is the activity or educational subject that consists of creating paintings, sculptures, and other pictures or objects for people to look at and admire or think deeply about. ...*Farnham College of Art and Design.* **3** The **arts** are activities such as music, painting, literature, cinema, and dance, which people can take part in for enjoyment, or to create works which express serious meanings or ideas of beauty. ...*a patron of the arts. ...the Arts Council of Great Britain. ...the art of cinema.* **4** **Arts** or **art** is used in the names of theatres or cinemas which show plays or films that are intended to make the audience think deeply about the content, and not simply to entertain them. ...*the Cambridge Arts Cinema.* **5** At a university or college, **arts** are subjects such as history, literature, or languages, in contrast to scientific subjects. **6** If you describe an activity as an **art**, you mean that it requires skill and that people learn to do it by instinct or experience, rather than by learning facts or rules. ...*pioneers who transformed clinical medicine from an art to a science.* **7** See also **fine art**, **martial art**, **state-of-the-art**, **work of art**.

8 **Art** is an old-fashioned form of the second person singular of the present tense of the verb **be**. *Father, I know thou art aware of me at all times.*

Art Deco /ˌɑːt ˈdekəʊ/; also spelled **art deco.** **Art Deco** is a style of decoration and architecture that was common in the 1920s and 30s. It is characterized by simple, bold, geometric designs and the use of plastic and glass.

ar·te·fact /ˈɑːtɪfækt/ **artefacts;** spelled **artifact** in American English. An **artefact** is an ornament, tool, or other object that is made by a human being, especially one that has archaeological or cultural interest.

ar·te·rio·scle·ro·sis /ɑːˌtɪəriəʊskleˈrəʊsɪs/. **Arteriosclerosis** is a medical condition in which the walls of your arteries become hard and thick, so your blood cannot flow through them properly.

ar·tery /ˈɑːtəri/ **arteries.** **1** Your **arteries** are the tubes in your body that carry blood from your heart to the rest of your body. ♦ **ar·te·rial** /ɑːˈtɪəriəl/ ...*arterial disease.* **2** An **artery** is an important main route within a complex road, railway, or river system. ♦ **arterial** ...*a major arterial road.*

'art form, art forms. If you describe an activity as an **art form**, you mean that it is concerned with creating things that are beautiful or have a serious meaning. *Graffiti is now an art form. ...Indian dance and related art forms.*

art·ful /ˈɑːtfʊl/. **1** If you describe someone as **artful**, you mean that they are clever and skilful at achieving what they want, especially by deceiving people. ♦ **art·ful·ly** ...*products that were well-made and artfully designed.* **2** If you use **artful** to describe the way someone has done or arranged something, you approve of it because it is clever or elegant. ...*an artful contrast of shapes... Despite some artful editing, the anthology is a weak one.* ♦ **artfully** ...*artfully arranged flowers.*

'art-house. An **art-house** film is an unusual experimental film that is intended to be a serious artistic work rather than popular entertainment.

ar·thri·tis /ɑːˈθraɪtɪs/. **Arthritis** is a medical condition in which the joints in someone's body are swollen and painful. See also **rheumatoid arthritis**. ◆◆◇◇◇ N-UNCOUNT

◆ **ar·thrit·ic** /ɑːˈθrɪtɪk/ ...*an elderly lady who suffered with arthritic hands. ...arthritic symptoms.* ADJ

ar·ti·choke /ˈɑːtɪtʃəʊk/ **artichokes**. **1** Artichokes or **globe artichokes** are round green vegetables that have fleshy leaves arranged like the petals of a flower. **2** Artichokes or **Jerusalem artichokes** are small yellowish-white vegetables that grow underground and look like knobbly potatoes. ◆◇◇◇◇ N-VAR / N-VAR

ar·ti·cle /ˈɑːtɪkəl/ **articles**. **1** An **article** is a piece of writing in a newspaper or magazine. ...*Canning's article about the Buxton Festival.* **2** An **article** of a formal agreement or document is a section of it which deals with a particular point. ...*Article 50 of the UN charter.* ◆◆◆◇ N-COUNT / N-COUNT

3 You can refer to objects as **articles** of some kind. ...*articles of clothing... He had stripped the house of all articles of value.* **4** If you describe something as **the genuine article**, you are emphasizing that it is genuine, and often that it is very good. *The vodka was the genuine article.* N-COUNT FORMAL / PRAGMATICS

5 In grammar, an **article** is a kind of determiner. In English, 'a' and 'an' are called **the indefinite article**, and 'the' is called **the definite article**. N-COUNT

ar·ti·cled /ˈɑːtɪkəld/. In Britain, someone who is **articled** to a firm of lawyers is employed by the firm and is training to become qualified. ...*an articled clerk.* ADJ: v-link ADJ to n, ADJ n

article of 'faith, articles of faith. If something is an **article of faith** for a person or group, they believe in it totally. *It used to be an article of faith that a man's career was more important than the convenience of his family.* N-COUNT

ar·ticu·late, articulates, articulating, articulated. The adjective is pronounced /ɑːˈtɪkjʊlət/. The verb is pronounced /ɑːˈtɪkjʊleɪt/. **1** If you describe someone as **articulate**, you mean that they are able to express their thoughts and ideas easily and well. *She is an articulate young woman... The child was unable to offer an articulate description of what she had witnessed.* ◆ **ar·ticu·la·cy** /ɑːˈtɪkjʊləsi/ *To start a revolution, you need discipline, incisiveness and articulacy.* **2** When you **articulate** your ideas or feelings, you express them clearly in words. *The president has been accused of failing to articulate an overall vision in foreign affairs.* ◆ **ar·ticu·la·tion** *This was seen as a way of restricting women's articulation of grievances.* ◆◆◇◇◇ ADJ-GRADED / N-UNCOUNT / VERB V n/wh FORMAL / N-UNCOUNT

ar·ticu·lat·ed /ɑːˈtɪkjʊleɪtɪd/. An **articulated** vehicle, especially a lorry, is made in two or more sections which are joined together by metal bars, so that the vehicle can turn more easily. ADJ BRITISH

ar·ticu·la·tion /ɑːˌtɪkjʊˈleɪʃən/. **Articulation** is the action of producing a sound or word clearly in speech or music. ...*a singer able to sustain a full tone and clear articulation.* ● See also **articulate**. N-UNCOUNT FORMAL

ar·ti·fact /ˈɑːtɪfækt/. See **artefact**.

ar·ti·fice /ˈɑːtɪfɪs/ **artifices**. **Artifice** is the clever use of tricks and devices. N-VAR FORMAL

ar·ti·fi·cial /ˌɑːtɪˈfɪʃəl/. **1** Artificial objects, materials, or processes do not occur naturally and are created by human beings, for example using science or technology. *The city is dotted with small lakes, natural and artificial... He did not want his life to be prolonged by artificial means.* ◆ **ar·ti·fi·cial·ly** ...*artificially sweetened lemonade.* **2** An **artificial** state or situation exists only because someone has created it, and therefore often seems unnatural or unnecessary. *He foresaw an open society without artificial barriers of background, religion or race.* ◆ **ar·ti·fi·ci·al·ity** /ˌɑːtɪfɪʃiˈælɪti/ ...*the capriciousness and artificiality of our adversarial system of justice.* ◆ **ar·ti·fi·cial·ly** ...*state subsidies that have kept retail prices artificially low.* **3** If you describe someone or their behaviour as **artificial**, you disapprove of them because they pretend to have attitudes and feelings which they do not really have. ◆ **ar·ti·fi·ci·al·ity** ...*the artificiality of the current agonising about the* ◆◆◇◇◇ ADJ / ADV / ADJ-GRADED / N-UNCOUNT / ADV-GRADED / ADJ-GRADED PRAGMATICS / N-UNCOUNT

relative merits of higher taxes and bigger spending cuts. **4** If you say that food tastes or looks **artificial**, you do not like it because its taste or appearance does not seem genuine, and seems to be created by added substances. ...*complaints that their tinned peas were an artificial shade of green.* ADJ-GRADED

artificial insemi'nation. Artificial insemination is a medical technique for making a woman or female animal pregnant by injecting previously stored sperm into her womb. N-UNCOUNT

artificial in'telligence. Artificial intelligence is a type of computer technology concerned with making machines work in an intelligent way, similar to the way that the human mind works. ◆◇◇◇ N-UNCOUNT

artificial respi'ration. Artificial respiration is the forcing of air into the lungs of someone who has stopped breathing, usually by blowing through their mouth or nose, in order to keep them alive and to help them to start breathing again. N-UNCOUNT

ar·til·lery /ɑːˈtɪləri/. **1 Artillery** consists of large powerful guns which are transported on wheels and used by an army. **2 The artillery** is the section of an army which is trained to use large powerful guns. *He left the Artillery to command a radar unit.* ◆◆◇◇◇ N-UNCOUNT / N-COLL-SING: the N

ar·ti·san /ˌɑːtɪˈzæn/ **artisans**. People who had jobs that required skill with their hands used to be referred to as **artisans**. ◆◇◇◇◇ N-COUNT

art·ist /ˈɑːtɪst/ **artists**. **1** An **artist** is someone who draws or paints pictures or creates sculptures as a job or a hobby. **2** An **artist** is a person who creates novels, poems, films, or other things which can be considered as works of art. *His books are enormously easy to read, yet he is a serious artist.* **3** An **artist** is a performer such as a musician, actor, or dancer. ...*a popular artist who has sold millions of records.* **4** If you say that someone is an **artist** at a particular activity, you mean that they are very skilled at it. *Jack is an outstanding barber, an artist with shears.* ◆◆◆◇ N-COUNT / N-COUNT / N-COUNT / N-COUNT

ar·tiste /ɑːˈtiːst/ **artistes**. An **artiste** is a professional entertainer, for example a singer or a dancer. ...*a Parisian cabaret artiste.* N-COUNT BRITISH

ar·tis·tic /ɑːˈtɪstɪk/. **1** Someone who is **artistic** is good at drawing or painting, or arranging things in a beautiful way. **2 Artistic** means relating to art or artists. ...*the campaign for artistic freedom.* ◆ **ar·tis·ti·cal·ly** /ɑːˈtɪstɪkli/ ...*artistically gifted children... Artistically, the photographs are stunning.* **3** An **artistic** design or arrangement is beautiful. ...*an artistic arrangement of stone paving.* ◆ **artistically** ...*artistically carved vessels. ...vegetarian dishes which can be presented artistically.* ◆◆◇◇◇ ADJ-GRADED / ADJ / ADV / ADJ-GRADED / ADV-GRADED

art·ist·ry /ˈɑːtɪstri/. **1 Artistry** is the creative skill of an artist, writer, actor, or musician. ...*his artistry as a cellist. ...portrait sculptors of considerable skill and artistry.* **2** You can use **artistry** to refer to a high level of skill in a profession or sport. ...*his dazzling contribution of pace and artistry which inspired the team.* N-UNCOUNT / N-UNCOUNT

art·less /ˈɑːtləs/. An **artless** person is simple and honest, and does not think of deceiving others. ...*Hemingway's artless air and charmings smile.* ADJ-GRADED

Art Nou·veau /ˌɑːt nuːˈvəʊ/; also spelled **art nouveau**. **Art Nouveau** is a style of decoration and architecture that was common in the 1890s. It is characterized by flowing lines and patterns of flowers and leaves. ...*the Art Nouveau posters of Alphonse Mucha.* N-UNCOUNT

arts·y /ˈɑːtsi/. **Artsy** means the same as **arty**. ...*all the middle-class artsy gang.* ADJ-GRADED INFORMAL

art·work /ˈɑːtwɜːk/ **artworks**. **1 Artwork** is drawings and photographs that are prepared in order to be included in something such as a book or advertisement. ...*the artwork for the LP.* **2 Artworks** are paintings or sculptures which are of high quality. ...*6,000 contemporary and modern artworks. ...a magnificent collection of artwork.* ◆◇◇◇◇ N-UNCOUNT / N-VAR

arty /ˈɑːti/. Someone who is **arty** seems very interested in the arts. You can describe a person or work of art as **arty** when you want to suggest that they are pretentious. ...*an arty French film.* ADJ-GRADED INFORMAL

as 1 conjunction and preposition uses

as /əz, STRONG æz/. **1** If something happens **as** ◆◆◆◆◆
something else happens, it happens at the same CONJ
time. *Another policeman has been killed as fighting
continued... All the jury's eyes were on him as he
continued.* **2** If you do something **as** a child or **as** a PREP
teenager, for example, you do it when you are a
child or a teenager. *She loved singing as a child.*
3 You use **as** when you are indicating what someone PREP
or something is or is thought to be, or what function
they have. *The news apparently came as a complete
surprise... He has worked as a diplomat.*
4 You use **as** when you are mentioning the way that CONJ
something happens or is done, or to indicate that
something happens or is done in the same way as
something else. *I'll behave toward them as I would like
to be treated... The book was banned in the US, as were
two subsequent books.*
5 You use the structure **as...as** when you are compar- PHR-CONJ
ing things. *I never went through a final exam that was
as difficult as that one... There was no obvious reason
why this could not be as good a film as the original.*
► Also a conjunction. *I've learned that being a mother* PHR-CONJ
isn't as bad as I thought at first! **6** You use **as...as** to PHR-CONJ
emphasize how large or small something is. *You can
look forward to a significant cash return by saving
from as little as £10 a month. ...as many as eight thousand letters.*
7 You can use **as** to mean 'because'. *This is important* CONJ
as it sets the mood for the rest of the day.
8 You use **as** in expressions like **as a result** and **as a** PREP
consequence to indicate how two situations or events
are related to each other. *As a result of the growing
fears about home security, more people are arranging
for someone to stay in their home when they're away...
Different demands are being placed on employees. As a
consequence, the education system needs to change.*
9 You use **as** to introduce short clauses which show CONJ
why you believe something to be true, or why someone else might believe something to be true. *We were
sitting, as I remember, in a riverside restaurant... As
you can see, we're still working.* **10** You say **as it were** PHRASE
in order to make what you are saying sound less defi- PRAGMATICS
nite. *I didn't, as it were, understand the question.*
11 You use expressions such as **as it is** and **as it turns** PHRASE
out when you are making a contrast between a pos- PRAGMATICS
sible situation and what actually happened or is the
case. *I want to work at home on a Tuesday but as it
turns out sometimes it's a Wednesday or a Thursday.*
12 As is used in a large number of expressions which
are explained under other words in this dictionary.
For example, **as against** is explained at **against**.

as 2 used with other prepositions and conjunctions

as /əz, STRONG æz/. **1** You use **as for** and **as to** at ◆◆◆◆◆
the beginning of a sentence in order to introduce a PHR-PREP
slightly different subject that is still connected to
the previous one. *I feel that there's a lot of pressure
put on policemen. And as for putting guns in their
hands, I don't think that's a very good idea at all.*
2 You use **as to** to indicate what something refers PHR-PREP
to. *They should make decisions as to whether the
student needs more help.* **3** If you say that some- PHR-PREP
thing will happen **as of** or **as from** a particular date
or time, you mean that it will happen from that
time onwards. *She is to retire as from 1 October.*
4 You use **as if** and **as though** when you are giving PHR-CONJ
a possible explanation for something or saying that
something appears to be true although it is not. *He
burst into a high-pitched laugh, as though he'd said
something funny.*

asap /ˌeɪ es eɪ 'piː/ or **ASAP.** asap is an abbrevia- ADV:
tion for 'as soon as possible'. *I want two good en-* ADV after v
gines down here asap.

as·bes·tos /æs'bestɒs/. Asbestos is a grey ma- ◆◇◇◇◇
terial which does not burn and which is used as a N-UNCOUNT
protection against fire or heat. *...asbestos gloves.*

as·cend /ə'send/ **ascends, ascending, as-** ◆◇◇◇◇
cended. 1 If you **ascend** a hill or staircase, you go VERB
up it. *Mrs Clayton had to hold Lizzie's hand as they* V n
ascended the steps... Then we ascend steeply through V prep/adv
                                    WRITTEN

forests of rhododendron. **2** If a staircase or path **as-** VERB
cends, it leads upwards to a higher place. *A number* V prep/adv
of staircases ascend from the cobbled streets onto the Also V n
ramparts. **3** If something **ascends**, it moves WRITTEN
upwards, usually vertically or into the air. *They as-* VERB: V
cended 55,900 feet in their balloon. V amount
                                    WRITTEN
4 If someone **ascends** to an important position, they VERB
achieve it or are appointed to it. When someone **as-** V to n
cends a throne, they become king, queen, or pope. V n
...the year he ascended to power... Sixtus V ascended FORMAL
the papal throne. **5** If you **ascend** in your career or in VERB
society, you gradually achieve success or a higher sta- V prep/adv
tus. *Mobutu ascended through the ranks, eventually* Also V n
becoming commander of the army. **6** When religious WRITTEN
people say a divine being or a person's soul **ascends** VERB:
to heaven, they mean it goes to heaven. **7** See also V to/into n
ascending.

as·cend·ancy /ə'sendənsi/; also spelled **ascend-** N-UNCOUNT
ency. If one group has **ascendancy** over another FORMAL
group, it has more power or influence than the other group. *The two provinces have long fought for political ascendancy... The extremists are gaining
ascendancy.*

as·cend·ant /ə'sendənt/. If a person or thing is **in** ◆◇◇◇◇
the ascendant, they have more power, influence, or PHRASE
popularity than other people or things, or their FORMAL
power, influence, or popularity is increasing. *Radical reformers are once more in the ascendant.*

as·cend·ency /ə'sendənsi/. See **ascendancy.**

as·cend·ing /ə'sendɪŋ/. If a group of things is ar- ADJ: ADJ n
ranged in **ascending** order, each thing is bigger,
greater, or more important than the thing before it.
● See also **ascend.**

as·cen·sion /ə'senʃən/. **1** In some religions, when N-SING:
someone is believed to go to heaven, people refer to with poss
this as their **ascension** to heaven. *...the crucifixion,
resurrection and ascension of Jesus Christ.* **2** When N-SING:
someone reaches a high rank or important position, with poss
you can call this their **ascension** to this rank or po- WRITTEN
sition. *...50 years after his ascension to the Cambodian throne.*

as·cent /ə'sent/ **ascents. 1** An **ascent** is an ◆◇◇◇◇
upward journey or slope, especially when you are N-COUNT
walking or climbing. *He led the first ascent of Kang-
chenjunga, the world's third highest mountain... It
was a tough course over a gradual ascent.* **2** An **as-** N-COUNT
cent is an upward vertical movement. *The elevator
began its slow ascent.* **3** The **ascent** of a person to a N-SING
more important or successful position is the pro- WRITTEN
cess of reaching this position. *...their ascent to power... His own career continues its inexorable ascent.*
4 In some religions, when someone is believed to N-COUNT
go to heaven, people refer to this as their **ascent** to
heaven.

as·cer·tain /ˌæsə'teɪn/ **ascertains, ascertain-** ◆◇◇◇◇
ing, ascertained. If you **ascertain** the truth about VERB
something, you find out what it is, especially by V n
making a deliberate effort. *The teacher will be able* V that
to ascertain the extent to which the child under- Also V wh
stands what he is reading. ...once they had ascer- FORMAL
tained that he was not a spy.

as·cet·ic /ə'setɪk/ **ascetics.** An ascetic person has ADJ-GRADED
a way of life that is simple and strict, usually because of their religious beliefs. *...priests practising
an ascetic life.* ● An **ascetic** is someone who is as- N-COUNT
cetic. ♦ **as·ceti·cism** /ə'setɪsɪzəm/. Asceticism is N-UNCOUNT
an ascetic way of life.

ascor·bic acid /æˌskɔːbɪk 'æsɪd/. Ascorbic acid is N-UNCOUNT
another name for vitamin C. TECHNICAL

as·cribe /ə'skraɪb/ **ascribes, ascribing, as-** ◆◇◇◇◇
cribed. 1 If you **ascribe** an event or condition to a VERB
particular cause, you say or consider that it was V n to n
caused by that thing. *An autopsy eventually ascribed* FORMAL
the baby's death to sudden infant death syndrome.
2 If you **ascribe** a quality **to** someone, you consider VERB
that they possess it. *We do not ascribe a superior* V n to n
wisdom to government or the state. **3** If you **ascribe** FORMAL
something such as a quotation or a work of art **to** V n to n
someone, you say that they said it or created it. *He* FORMAL
mistakenly ascribes the expression 'survival of the fit-

test' to Charles Darwin. **4** If you **ascribe to** a particular belief or opinion, you hold that belief or opinion. *He ascribes to a philosophy that permeates every part of his life.* — VERB, V ton, FORMAL

asexu·al /ˌeɪˈsekʃʊəl/. **1** Something that is **asexual** involves no sexual activity. *Their relationship was totally asexual. ...asexual reproduction.* **2** Someone who is **asexual** is not sexually attracted to other people. — ADJ, ADJ

ash /æʃ/ **ashes. 1** Ash is the grey or black powdery substance that is left after something is burnt. You can also refer to this substance as **ashes**. *...volcanic ash. ...cigarette ash... He ordered their villages burned to ashes.* **2** A dead person's **ashes** are their remains after their body has been cremated. **3** An **ash** is a tree that has smooth grey bark and winged seeds. — N-UNCOUNT: also N in pl; N-PLURAL; N-VAR

ashamed /əˈʃeɪmd/. **1** If someone is **ashamed**, they feel embarrassed or guilty because of something they do or have done, or because of their appearance. *I felt incredibly ashamed of myself for getting so angry... She was ashamed that she looked so shabby... I'm a lesbian and I'm not ashamed about it.* **2** If you are **ashamed of** someone, you feel embarrassed to be connected with them, often because of their appearance or because you disapprove of something they have done. **3** If someone is **ashamed** to do something, they do not want to do it because they feel embarrassed about it. *Women are often ashamed to admit they are being abused.* — ADJ-GRADED: v-link ADJ; ADJ-GRADED: v-link ADJ of n; ADJ-GRADED: v-link ADJ to-inf

ash·en /ˈæʃən/. If someone has an **ashen** face, they look very pale, especially because they are ill, shocked, or frightened. *He was ashen and trembling... 'We've got to make sure this doesn't happen again,' said an ashen-faced spokesman.* — ADJ

ashore /əˈʃɔː/. Someone or something that comes **ashore** comes from the sea onto the shore. *Oil has come ashore on a ten mile stretch to the east of Plymouth... Once ashore, the vessel was thoroughly inspected.* — ADV after v, be ADV

ash·tray /ˈæʃtreɪ/ **ashtrays.** An ashtray is a small dish in which smokers can put the ash from their cigarettes and cigars. — N-COUNT

Asian /ˈeɪʒən/ **Asians.** Someone or something that is **Asian** comes from or is associated with Asia. British people use this term especially when they are referring to people or things that come from India, Pakistan, and Bangladesh. Americans use this term especially when they are referring to people or things that come from China, Korea, Thailand, Japan, or Vietnam. *...Asian music. ...the Asian community in San Francisco.* ▶ An **Asian** is a person of Asian origin. *Many of the shops were run by Asians.* — ADJ; N-COUNT

Asi·at·ic /ˌeɪʒiˈætɪk/. **Asiatic** means belonging or relating to Asia or its people. — ADJ, DATED

aside /əˈsaɪd/ **asides.** In addition to the uses shown below, **aside** is used in phrasal verbs such as 'cast aside' and 'stand aside'. **1** If you move something **aside**, you move it to one side of you. *Sarah closed the book and laid it aside.* **2** If you move **aside**, you get out of someone's way. *She stepped aside to let them pass.* **3** If you take or draw someone **aside**, you take them a little way away from a group of people in order to talk to them in private. **4** If you set something such as time, money, or space **aside** for a particular purpose, you save it and do not use it for anything else. *She wants to put her pocket-money aside for holidays. ...the ground set aside for the new cathedral.* **5** If you brush or sweep **aside** a feeling or suggestion, you reject it. *Mr Major yesterday swept aside any doubts about a Tory victory.* **6** You use **aside** to indicate that you are excluding something from what you are saying, and not taking it into account. *Leaving aside the tiny minority who are clinically depressed, most people who have bad moods also have very good moods... Emotional arguments aside, here are the facts... Sunderland haven't made a particularly good start to the season, aside from their win over Charlton.* **7** An **aside** is a comment that a character in a play — ADV: ADV after v; ADV: ADV after v; ADV: ADV after v; ADV: ADV after v; ADV: ADV after v; ADV: ADV after v, ADV from n, PRAGMATICS; N-COUNT

makes to the audience, which the other characters are supposed not to be able to hear. **8** An **aside** is something that you say that is not directly connected with what you are talking about. *He'll begin one thought, inject several fascinating asides, then pick up his original idea minutes later.* — N-COUNT

asi·nine /ˈæsɪnaɪn/. If you describe something or someone as **asinine**, you are emphasizing that they are very foolish. *I have never heard such an asinine discussion.* — ADJ-GRADED, PRAGMATICS, FORMAL

ask /ɑːsk, æsk/ **asks, asking, asked. 1** If you ask someone something, you say it to them in the form of a question because you want to know the answer. *'How is Frank?' he asked... I asked him his name... I wasn't the only one asking questions... She asked me if I'd enjoyed my dinner... If Daniel asks what happened in court we will tell him... You will have to ask David about that.* **2** You can say **'may I ask'** as a way of asking a question, which shows you are annoyed or suspicious about something. *May I ask where you're going, sir?* **3** If you **ask** someone to do something, you tell them that you want them to do it. *She said she had been asked to take two suitcases to Africa by a man called Sean.* **4** If you **ask** to do something, you tell someone that you want to do it. *I asked to see the Director.* **5** If you **ask for** something, you say that you would like it. If you **ask for** someone, you say that you want to see them or speak to them. *I decided to go to the next house and ask for food... There's a man at the gate asking for you.* **6** If something is yours **for the asking**, you could get it very easily if you wanted it. *He knew the nomination was his for the asking.* **7** If you **ask** someone's permission, opinion, or forgiveness, you try to obtain it by putting a question to them. *Please ask permission from whoever pays the phone bill before making your call.* **8** If you say that someone **is asking for trouble** or **is asking for it**, you mean that they are behaving in a way that makes it very likely that they will get into trouble. **9** If you **ask** someone to an event or place, you invite them there. *Couldn't you ask Jon to the party?... She asked me back to her house.* **10** If someone **is asking** a particular price for something, they are selling it for that price. *Mr Pantelaras was asking £6,000 for his collection.* **11** You reply **'don't ask me'** when you do not know the answer to a question, usually when you are annoyed or surprised that you have been asked. *'She's got other things on her mind, wouldn't you think?' 'Don't ask me,' murmured Chris. 'I've never met her.'* **12** If you say **'I ask you'**, you are emphasizing how much you disapprove of someone or something. *That silly old bat. I ask you, who'd she think she was?* **13** You can say **'if you ask me'** to emphasize that you are stating your personal opinion. *He was nuts, if you ask me.* — VERB, V with quote, V n n, V n wh, V wh, V n wh, V n about n, Also V, V about n, PHRASE, PRAGMATICS, FORMAL; VERB, V n to-inf, be V-ed to-inf; VERB, V to-inf; VERB, V for n; PHRASE; VERB, V n; PHRASE; VERB, V n prep/adv; VERB, V n for n, Also V n; CONVENTION, PRAGMATICS; EXCLAM, PRAGMATICS; PHRASE, PRAGMATICS

ask after. If someone **asks after** you, they ask someone how you are. *I had a letter from Jane. She asks after you.* — PHRASAL VB, V P n

ask around or **ask round.** If you **ask around**, you ask several people the same question. *Ask around to see what others living in your area think about their doctors.* — PHRASAL VB, V P

askance /əˈskæns/. **1** If you **look askance** at someone or something, you have a doubtful or suspicious attitude towards them. *They have always looked askance at the western notion of democracy.* **2** If you **look askance** at someone, you look at them in a doubtful or suspicious way. — PHRASE; PHRASE

askew /əˈskjuː/. Something that is **askew** is not straight, or not level with what it should be level with. *Some of the doors hung askew.* — ADJ-GRADED: v-link ADJ

'asking price, asking prices. The **asking price** of something is the price which the person selling it says that they want for it, although they may accept less. *...offers 15% below the asking price.* — N-COUNT

asleep /əˈsliːp/. **1** Someone who is **asleep** is sleeping. *My four year-old daughter was asleep on the sofa.* **2** When you **fall asleep**, you start sleeping. — ADJ: v-link ADJ; PHRASE

3 Someone who is **fast asleep** or **sound asleep** is sleeping deeply. PHRASE

as·par·a·gus /ə'spærəgəs/. Asparagus is a long, green vegetable with small shoots at one end. It is cooked and served whole. ◆◇◇◇◇ N-UNCOUNT

as·pect /'æspekt/ **aspects. 1** An aspect of something is one of the parts of its character or nature. *Climate and weather affect every aspect of our lives... Monroe described the financial aspect as crucial.* **2** If something begins to have a new **aspect**, it begins to have a new appearance or quality. *Our journey had taken on a new aspect. The countryside was no longer familiar.* ◆◆◆◇ N-COUNT

N-SING: with supp

3 The **aspect** of a building or window is the direction in which it faces. *The house had a south-west aspect.* N-COUNT FORMAL

4 In grammar, **aspect** is the way that a verb group shows whether an activity is continuing, is repeated, or is completed. Compare **tense**. N-UNCOUNT

as·pen /'æspən/ **aspens.** An aspen is a tall kind of poplar tree. ◆◇◇◇◇ N-VAR

as·per·i·ty /æ'speriti/. Asperity is impatience and severity that you express in your tone of voice. *'I told you Preskel had no idea,' remarked Kemp with some asperity.* N-UNCOUNT FORMAL

as·per·sions /ə'spɜːʃənz, AM -ʒənz/. If you **cast aspersions** on someone or something, you suggest that they are not very good in some way. PHRASE FORMAL

as·phalt /'æsfælt, -fɔːlt/. Asphalt is a black substance used to make the surfaces of things such as roads and playgrounds. N-UNCOUNT

as·phyx·ia /æs'fɪksiə/. Asphyxia is death or loss of consciousness caused by being unable to breathe properly. *...asphyxia through smoke inhalation.* N-UNCOUNT MEDICAL

as·phyxi·ate /æs'fɪksieɪt/ **asphyxiates, asphyxiating, asphyxiated.** If someone **is asphyxiated**, they die or lose consciousness because they are unable to breathe properly. *Three people were asphyxiated in the crush for last week's train.* **♦ as·phyxia·tion** /æs,fɪksi'eɪʃən/ *She died from asphyxiation.* VB: usu passive be V-ed

N-UNCOUNT

as·pic /'æspɪk/. Aspic is a clear shiny jelly made from meat juices. It is used in making cold savoury meat dishes. N-UNCOUNT

as·pir·ant /ə'spaɪrənt, 'æspɪrənt/ **aspirants. 1** Someone who is an **aspirant** to political power or to an important job has a strong desire to achieve it. *Any aspirant to the presidency here must be seriously rich.* **2** Aspirant means the same as **aspiring**. *...aspirant politicians.* N-COUNT

ADJ: ADJ n

as·pi·ra·tion·al /,æspɪ'reɪʃənəl/. If you describe someone as **aspirational**, you mean that they have strong hopes of moving to a higher social status. If you describe a product as **aspirational**, you mean that it is bought or enjoyed by people who have strong hopes of moving to a higher social class. *...the typical tensions of an aspirational household... Fine music, particularly opera, has become aspirational, like fine wine or foreign travel.* ADJ-GRADED JOURNALISM

as·pire /ə'spaɪə/ **aspires, aspiring, aspired.** If you **aspire to** something such as an important job, you have an ambition to achieve it. *...people who aspire to public office... They aspired to be gentlemen.* **♦ as·pi·ra·tion, aspirations** *...the republic's aspiration to statehood. ...the needs and aspirations of our pupils.* ◆◆◇◇◇ VERB V to n/-ing V to-inf

N-VAR

as·pi·rin /'æspɪrɪn/ **aspirins; aspirin** can also be used for the plural. Aspirin is a mild drug which reduces pain and fever. *She took some aspirins.* ◆◇◇◇◇ N-VAR

as·pir·ing /ə'spaɪərɪŋ/. If you use **aspiring** to describe someone who is starting a particular career, you mean that they are trying to become successful in it. *...aspiring young artists.* ● See also **aspire**. ◆◇◇◇◇ ADJ: ADJ n

ass /æs/ **asses. 1** An ass is the same as a **donkey**. *...the Messiah-King, riding on an ass.* **2** If you call someone an **ass**, you mean that they are behaving in a silly way or saying silly things. *The two commanders made asses of themselves by absurd, panicky statements.* **3** Your **ass** is the part of your body that you sit down on. The equivalent informal British word is **arse**. ◆◆◇◇◇ N-COUNT DATED N-COUNT INFORMAL

N-COUNT INFORMAL, AMERICAN

4 To **kick ass** or to **kick** someone's **ass** means to let them know either by telling them or by using physical force that you are not pleased with them. *They've really been kicking ass lately – busting places up, harassing everybody.* PHRASE INFORMAL, AMERICAN

as·sail /ə'seɪl/ **assails, assailing, assailed. 1** If someone **assails** you, they criticize you strongly. *The opposition's newspapers assail the government each day.* **2** If someone **assails** you, they attack you violently. *Dividing his command, Morgan assailed both strongholds at the same time.* **3** If you **are assailed** by something unpleasant such as fears or problems, you are greatly troubled by a large number of them. *She is assailed by self-doubt and emotional insecurity.* ◆◇◇◇◇ VERB V n WRITTEN VERB V n WRITTEN VB: usu passive be V-ed WRITTEN

as·sail·ant /ə'seɪlənt/ **assailants.** Someone's **assailant** is a person who has physically attacked them. *Other party-goers rescued the injured man from his assailant.* ◆◇◇◇◇ N-COUNT FORMAL

as·sas·sin /ə'sæsɪn/ **assassins.** An assassin is a person who assassinates someone. ◆◇◇◇◇ N-COUNT

as·sas·si·nate /ə'sæsɪneɪt/ **assassinates, assassinating, assassinated.** If someone important **is assassinated**, they are murdered as a political act. *Would the USA be radically different today if Kennedy had not been assassinated?* **♦ as·sas·si·na·tion** /ə,sæsɪ'neɪʃən/ **assassinations** *She would like an investigation into the assassination of her husband.* ◆◆◇◇◇ VERB be V-ed Also V n

N-VAR

as·sault /ə'sɔːlt/ **assaults, assaulting, assaulted. 1** An **assault** by an army is a strong attack made on an area held by the enemy. *The rebels are poised for a new assault on the government garrisons.* **2** Assault weapons such as rifles are intended for soldiers to use in battle rather than for purposes such as hunting. *...AK-47 assault rifles.* **3** An **assault** on a person is a physical attack on them. *...one of a series of savage sexual assaults on women... At the police station, I was charged with assault.* **4** To **assault** someone means to physically attack them. *The gang assaulted him with iron bars.* **5** An **assault** on someone's beliefs is a strong criticism of them. *He leveled a verbal assault against his Democratic opponents.* ◆◆◆◇◇ N-COUNT

ADJ: ADJ n

N-VAR

VERB V n

N-COUNT

as'sault course, assault courses. An assault course is an area of land covered with obstacles such as walls or ditches, which people, especially soldiers, run over as an exercise to improve their skills and strength. The usual American term is **obstacle course**. N-COUNT BRITISH

as·say /æ'seɪ/ **assays.** An assay is a test to see how much metal there is in an ore, or to see to what extent a precious metal consists of impurities. N-COUNT TECHNICAL

as·sem·blage /ə'semblɪdʒ/ **assemblages.** An assemblage of people or things is a collection of them. *There is a rich assemblage of flora and fauna.* N-COUNT FORMAL

as·sem·ble /ə'sembəl/ **assembles, assembling, assembled. 1** When people **assemble** or when someone **assembles** them, they come together in a group. *...a convenient place for students to assemble between classes... The assembled multitude cheered and whistled.* **2** To **assemble** something means to fit the different parts of it together. *She had been trying to assemble the bomb when it went off.* **♦ as·sem·bler, assemblers** *The firm is an assembler of computers, not a manufacturer.* ◆◆◇◇◇ V-ERG V-ed

VERB V n

N-COUNT

as·sem·bly /ə'sembli/ **assemblies. 1** An **assembly** is a large group of people who meet regularly to make decisions or laws for a particular region or country. *...the National Assembly. ...an assembly of party members from the Russian republic.* **2** An **assembly** is a group of people gathered together for a particular purpose. *...an assembly of women Olympic gold-medal winners.* **3** When you refer to rights of **assembly** or restrictions on **assembly**, you are referring to the legal right that people have to gather together. *They were accused of unlawful assembly.* **4** In a school, **assembly** is a gathering of all the teachers and pupils at the beginning of the school day. *By 9, the juniors are in the hall for assembly.* ◆◆◇◇◇ N-COUNT

N-COUNT

N-UNCOUNT FORMAL

N-UNCOUNT: also N in pl

A

5 The **assembly** of a machine, device, or object is the process of fitting its different parts together. *...car assembly plants.*   N-UNCOUNT

as·sembly line, assembly lines. An **assembly line** is an arrangement of workers and machines in a factory where each worker makes only one part of a product. The product passes from one worker to another until it is finished.   ◆◇◇◇◇ N-COUNT

as·sembly·man /əˈsemblimən/ **assemblymen.** An **assemblyman** is an elected member of an assembly of people who make decisions and laws. *...a California state assemblyman from Los Angeles.*   N-COUNT; N-TITLE AMERICAN

as·sembly·woman /əˈsembliwʊmən/ **assemblywomen.** An **assemblywoman** is a female elected member of an assembly of people who make decisions and laws. *...state Assemblywoman Marguerite Hudson.*   N-COUNT; N-TITLE AMERICAN

as·sent /əˈsent/ **assents, assenting, assented.** **1** If someone gives their **assent** to something that has been suggested, they formally agree to it. *Both Denmark and Britain will give their final assent to the Maastricht treaty this summer... Mr Yeltsin will be unable to pass a new constitution without the assent of parliament.* **2** If you **assent** to something, you agree to it or agree with it. *I assented to the request of the American publishers to write this book.*   ◆◇◇◇◇ N-UNCOUNT   VERB V to n Also V

as·sert /əˈsɜːt/ **asserts, asserting, asserted.** **1** If someone **asserts** a fact or belief, they state it firmly. *Mr. Helm plans to assert that the bill violates the First Amendment. ...the defendants, who continue to assert their innocence... Altman asserted, 'We were making a political statement'.* ♦ **as·ser·tion** /əˈsɜːʃən/ **assertions** *There is no concrete evidence to support assertions that the recession is truly over.* **2** If you **assert** your authority, you make it clear by your behaviour that you have authority. *The army made an attempt to assert its authority in the south of the country.* ♦ **assertion** *The decision is seen as an assertion of his authority within the company.* **3** If you **assert** your right or claim to something, you insist that you have the right to it. *The republics began asserting their right to govern themselves.* ♦ **assertion** *These institutions have made the assertion of ethnic identity possible.* **4** If you **assert** yourself, you speak and act in a forceful way, so that people take notice of you.   VERB V that V n V with quote FORMAL   N-VAR   VERB V n   N-UNCOUNT   VERB V n   N-UNCOUNT   VERB V pron-refl

as·ser·tive /əˈsɜːtɪv/. Someone who is **assertive** states their needs and opinions clearly, so that people take notice. *Women have become more assertive in the past decade.* ♦ **as·ser·tive·ly** *'You don't need to do that,' said Pearl assertively.* ♦ **as·ser·tive·ness** *Clare's assertiveness stirred up his deep-seated sense of inadequacy.*   ◆◇◇◇◇ ADJ-GRADED   ADV-GRADED   N-UNCOUNT

as·sess /əˈses/ **assesses, assessing, assessed.** **1** If you **assess** a person, thing, or situation, you consider them in order to make a judgement about them. *Our correspondent has been assessing the impact of the sanctions... It would be a matter of assessing whether she was well enough to travel.* ♦ **as·sess·ment** /əˈsesmənt/ **assessments** *There is little assessment of the damage to the natural environment... Heggie was remanded to a mental hospital for assessment by doctors.* **2** If you **assess** the amount of money that something is worth or should be paid, you calculate or estimate it. *...how to assess the value of your belongings... What's the property's assessed value?* ♦ **assessment** *...income assessment.*   ◆◆◆◇ VERB V n V wh   N-VAR   VERB V-ed Also V wh   N-VAR

as·ses·sor /əˈsesə/ **assessors.** **1** An **assessor** is a person who is employed to calculate the value of something, for example the amount of taxes that should be paid by someone. **2** An **assessor** is a person who officially judges someone's performance, for example in an exam, at an interview or at a sporting event.   ◆◇◇◇◇ N-COUNT   N-COUNT BRITISH

as·set /ˈæset/ **assets. 1** Something or someone that is an **asset** is considered useful or helps a person or organization to be successful. *Her leadership qualities were the greatest asset of the Conservative Party.* **2** The **assets** of a company or a person are all   ◆◆◆◇ N-COUNT   N-PLURAL

the things that they own. *The group had assets of 3.5 billion francs.*

'asset-stripping. If you say that a person or company is involved in **asset-stripping**, you are criticizing them because they buy companies cheaply, sell off their assets to make a profit and then close the companies down.   N-UNCOUNT PRAGMATICS

as·sidu·ous /əˈsɪdʒuəs/. Someone who is **assiduous** works hard or does things with care and dedication. *...an assiduous student.* ♦ **as·sidu·ous·ly** *They planned their careers and worked assiduously to see them achieved.*   ◆◇◇◇◇ ADJ-GRADED   ADV-GRADED

as·sign /əˈsaɪn/ **assigns, assigning, assigned.** **1** If you **assign** a piece of work to someone, you give them the work to do. *I would assign a topic to children which they would write about... Later in the year, she'll assign them research papers. ...when teachers assign homework.* **2** If you **assign** something to someone, you say that it is for their use. *The selling broker is then required to assign a portion of the commission to the buyer broker... He assigned her all his land.* **3** If someone **is assigned** to a particular place, group, or person, they are sent there, usually in order to work at that place or for that person. *I was assigned to Troop A of the 10th Cavalry... Did you choose Russia or were you simply assigned there?... Each of us was assigned a minder.* **4** If you **assign** a particular function or value to something, you give it to them or decide that they have it. *Assign the letters of the alphabet their numerical values – A equals 1, B equals 2, etc.*   ◆◆◇◇◇ VERB V n to n V n n V n Also V n to-inf   VERB V n to n LEGAL   VB: usu passive be V-ed to n be V-ed adv be V-ed n   VERB: V n to n V n n

as·sig·na·tion /ˌæsɪgˈneɪʃən/ **assignations.** An **assignation** is a secret meeting with a lover.   N-COUNT FORMAL

as·sign·ment /əˈsaɪnmənt/ **assignments. 1** An **assignment** is a task or piece of work that you are given to do, especially as part of your job or studies. *The assessment for the course involves written assignments and practical tests.* **2** You can refer to someone being given a particular task or job as their **assignment** to the task or job. *...an Australian division scheduled for assignment to Greece... I hardly ever take photographs except on assignment.*   ◆◆◇◇◇ N-COUNT   N-UNCOUNT

as·simi·late /əˈsɪmɪleɪt/ **assimilates, assimilating, assimilated. 1** When people such as immigrants **assimilate** into a community or when that community **assimilates** them, they become an accepted part of it. *Asian-Americans are just as willing to assimilate... His family tried to assimilate into the white and Hispanic communities... The Vietnamese are trying to assimilate themselves and become Americans.* ♦ **as·simi·la·tion** /əˌsɪmɪˈleɪʃən/ *They promote social integration and assimilation of minority ethnic groups.* **2** If you **assimilate** new ideas, customs, or techniques, you learn them or adopt them. *My mind could only assimilate one impossibility at a time.* ♦ **assimilation** *This technique brings life to instruction and eases assimilation of knowledge.*   ◆◇◇◇◇ V-ERG V into/with n V pron-refl Also V n, V n into n   N-UNCOUNT   VERB V n   N-UNCOUNT

as·sist /əˈsɪst/ **assists, assisting, assisted. 1** If you **assist** someone, you help them to do a job or task by doing part of the work for them. *Julia was assisting him to prepare his speech... The family decided to assist me with my chores.* **2** If you **assist** someone, you give them information, advice, or money. *The public is urgently requested to assist police in tracing this man... Foreign Office officials assisted with transport and finance problems... The Authority will provide a welfare worker to assist you.* **3** If something **assists** in doing a task, it makes the task easier to do. *...a chemical that assists in the manufacture of proteins. ...some good sources of information to assist you in making the best selection.*   ◆◆◆◇◇ VERB V n to-inf V n with n   VERB V n in -ing V with n V n Also V n to-inf   VERB V in/with n /-ing V n in/with n/-ing

as·sis·tance /əˈsɪstəns/. **1** If you give someone **assistance**, you help them do a job or task by doing part of the work for them or by giving them information, advice, or money. *Any assistance you could give the police will be greatly appreciated... She can still come downstairs with assistance.* **2** If something is done with the **assistance** of a particular thing, that thing is helpful or necessary for doing it. *The*   ◆◆◆◇◇ N-UNCOUNT   N-UNCOUNT

translations were carried out with the assistance of a medical dictionary. **3** Someone or something that **is of assistance** to you is helpful or useful to you. *He was of great assistance to me in researches for my books... Can I be of any assistance?* **4** If you **come to** someone's **assistance**, you take action to help them. *They are appealing to the world community to come to Jordan's assistance.* PHRASE / PHRASE

as·sis·tant /əˈsɪstənt/ **assistants. 1** Assistant is used in front of titles or jobs to indicate a slightly lower rank. *...the assistant Secretary of Defense.* **2** Someone's **assistant** is a person who helps them in their work. *The salesman had been accompanied to the meeting by an assistant.* **3** An **assistant** is a person who works in a shop selling things to customers. *The assistant took the book and checked the price on the back cover. ...a sales assistant.* ADJ: ADJ n / N-COUNT / N-COUNT

as·so·ci·ate, associates, associating, associated. The verb is pronounced /əˈsəʊsieit/. The noun and adjective are pronounced /əˈsəʊsiət/. **1** If you **associate** someone or something with another thing, the two are connected in your mind. *People always associate that sort of blues music with sadness.* **2** If you **are associated with** a particular organization, cause, or point of view, you support it publicly. *I haven't been associated with the project over the last year... The press feels the need to associate itself with the green movement.* **3** If you say that someone **is associating** with another person or group of people, you mean they are spending a lot of time in the company of people you do not approve of. *What would they think if they knew that they were associating with a murderer?.* **4** Your **associates** are the people you are closely connected with, especially at work. *...the restaurant owner's business associates.* **5** Associate is used before a rank or title to indicate a slightly different or lower status. *Mr Lin is Associate Director of the Institute.* VERB V n with n / VERB be V-ed with n V pron-refl with n / VERB V with n / N-COUNT / ADJ: ADJ n

as·so·ci·at·ed /əˈsəʊsieitid/. **1** If one thing is **associated** with another, the two things are connected with each other. *These symptoms are particularly associated with migraine headaches.* **2** Associated is used in the names of some companies that are made up of a number of smaller companies which have joined together. *...the Associated Press.* ADJ / ADJ: ADJ n

as·so·ci·a·tion /əˌsəʊsiˈeɪʃən/ **associations. 1** An **association** is an official group of people who have the same occupation, aim, or interest. *...the British Olympic Association. ...research associations.* ● See also **housing association. 2** Your **association** with a person or a thing such as an organization is the connection that you have with them. If someone does something **in association with** someone else, they do it together. *...the company's six-year association with retailer J.C. Penney Co... The book is published by Headmain LTD in association with the Hardy Plant Society.* **3** If something has particular **associations** for you, it is connected in your mind with a particular memory, idea, or feeling. *Black was considered inappropriate because of its associations with death.* **4** If one thing is found **in association with** another, they are found together. *Bioflavonoids are found in association with vitamin C.* N-COUNT / N-COUNT / N-COUNT / PHRASE

as·so·cia·tive /əˈsəʊʃətɪv, AM -ʃiətɪv/. Associative thoughts are things that you think of because you see, hear, or think of something that reminds you of those things or which you associate with those things. *The associative guilt was ingrained in his soul.* ADJ FORMAL

as·sort·ed /əˈsɔːtɪd/. A group of **assorted** things is a group of similar things that are of different sizes or colours or have different qualities. *...swimsuits, sizes 12-18, in assorted colours.* ADJ

as·sort·ment /əˈsɔːtmənt/ **assortments.** An **assortment** is a group of similar things that are of different sizes or colours or have different qualities. *...an assortment of cheese.* N-COUNT

as·suage /əˈsweɪdʒ/ **assuages, assuaging, assuaged. 1** If you **assuage** an unpleasant feeling that someone has, you make them feel it less VERB V n LITERARY

strongly. *To assuage his wife's grief, he took her on a tour of Europe.* **2** If you **assuage** a need or desire for something, you satisfy it. *The meat they'd managed to procure assuaged their hunger.* VERB V n LITERARY

as·sume /əˈsjuːm, AM əˈsuːm/ **assumes, assuming, assumed. 1** If you **assume** that something is true, you imagine that it is true, sometimes wrongly. *If the package is wrapped well, we assume the contents are also wonderful... If mistakes occurred, they were assumed to be the fault of the commander... 'Today?'—'I'd assume so, yeah.'* **2** You can use **let us assume** when you are considering a possible situation or event, so that you can think about the consequences. *Let us assume those clubs actually win something. Then players will receive large bonuses.* ● See also **assuming.** **3** If someone **assumes** power or responsibility, they take power or responsibility. *Mr Cross will assume the role of Chief Executive.* **4** If something **assumes** a particular quality, it begins to have that quality. *In his dreams, the mountains assumed enormous importance.* **5** If you **assume** a particular expression or way of behaving, you start to look or behave in this way. *Prue assumed a placatory tone of voice.* VERB V that / be V-ed to-inf / V so / PHRASE PRAGMATICS / VERB V n / VERB V n / VERB V n

as,sumed 'name, assumed names. If you do something under an **assumed name**, you do it using a name that is not your real name. *The articles were published in San Francisco newspapers under the assumed name of Dorothy Dodge.* N-COUNT

as·sum·ing /əˈsjuːmɪŋ, AM -ˈsuːm-/. You use **assuming** or **assuming that** when you are considering a possible situation or event, so that you can think about the consequences. *Assuming you are a stone above your youthful weight, you probably do want to lose a few pounds... But assuming that the talks make progress, won't they do too little, too late?* CONJ PRAGMATICS

as·sump·tion /əˈsʌmpʃən/ **assumptions. 1** If you make an **assumption** that something is true or will happen, you accept that it is true or will happen, often without any real proof. *...their assumption that all men and women think alike... Economists are working on the assumption of an interest rate cut.* **2** Someone's **assumption of** power or responsibility is their taking of it. *The government have retained the support which greeted their assumption of power last March.* N-COUNT / N-UNCOUNT: N of n

as·sur·ance /əˈʃʊərəns/ **assurances. 1** If you give someone an **assurance** that something is true or will happen, you say that it is definitely true or will definitely happen, in order to make them feel less worried. *He would like an assurance that other forces will not move into the territory that his forces vacate.* **2** If you do something with **assurance**, you do it with a feeling of confidence and certainty. *Masur led the orchestra with assurance... The EC is now acquiring greater assurance and authority.* **3** Assurance is insurance that provides cover in the event of death. ● See also **life assurance.** N-VAR / N-UNCOUNT / N-UNCOUNT BRITISH

as·sure /əˈʃʊə/ **assures, assuring, assured. 1** If you **assure** someone that something is true or will happen, you tell them that it is definitely true or will definitely happen, often in order to make them less worried. *He hastened to assure me that there was nothing traumatic to report... 'Couldn't be safer,' Max assured her confidently... Government officials recently assured Hindus of protection.* ● See also **assured. 2** To **assure** someone of something means to make certain that they will get it. *Mr Mandela must assure himself of broad-based black support... Ways must be found to assure our children a decent start in life.* **3** You use **I can assure you, I assure you** or **let me assure you** when you want to emphasize the truth of what you are saying, especially when expressing your confidence or determination about something. *I can assure you that the animals are well cared for.* VERB V n that / V n with quote / V n of n / VERB V n of n / V n n / PHRASE PRAGMATICS

as·sured /əˈʃʊəd/. **1** Someone who is **assured** is very confident and feels at ease. *He was infinitely more assured than in his recent parliamentary appearances.* **2** If something is **assured**, it is certain to ADJ-GRADED / ADJ:

happen. *Our victory is assured; nothing can stop us.* v-link ADJ
3 If you **are assured of** something, you are certain ADJ-GRADED:
to get it or achieve it. *Laura Davies is assured of a* v-link ADJ of n
place in Europe's team. **4** If you say that someone PHRASE
can rest assured that something is true, you mean PRAGMATICS
that it is definitely true, so they do not need to worry about it. *Their parents can rest assured that their*
children's safety will be of paramount importance.
5 You use **rest assured** when you want to empha- PHRASE
size your determination to do something. *Rest as-* PRAGMATICS
sured I will tell them of your rudeness.

as·sur·ed·ly /ə'ʃʊərɪdli/. If something is **assuredly** ADV-GRADED
true, it is definitely true. *Competitiveness is, assured-*
ly, not going to happen by leaving events to market
forces alone.

as·ter·isk /'æstərɪsk/ **asterisks.** An **asterisk** is the N-COUNT
sign ✳. It is used especially to indicate important information in a text.

astern /ə'stɜːn/. **1** Something that is **astern** is at the ADV:
back of a ship or behind the back part of a ship. *The* be ADV
captain was astern, pretending he was sleeping. **2** A ADV:
ship that is moving **astern** is moving backwards. ADV after v
Steering gear comes under most severe test with the TECHNICAL
yacht going astern.

as·ter·oid /'æstərɔɪd/ **asteroids.** An **asteroid** is ◆◇◇◇◇
one of the very small planets that move around the N-COUNT
sun between the orbits of Mars and Jupiter.

asth·ma /'æsmə, AM 'æz-/. **Asthma** is a lung condi- ◆◆◇◇◇
tion often caused by allergies. Sufferers have sud- N-UNCOUNT
den attacks when they have difficulty breathing.

asth·mat·ic /æs'mætɪk, AM æz-/ **asthmatics.** Peo- N-COUNT
ple who suffer from asthma are sometimes referred
to as **asthmatics**. *I have been an asthmatic from*
childhood and was never able to play any sports.
► Also an adjective. *One child in ten is asthmatic.* ADJ-GRADED
...asthmatic breathing.

astig·ma·tism /ə'stɪgmətɪzəm/. If someone has N-UNCOUNT
astigmatism, the front of their eye has a slightly irregular shape, so they cannot see properly.

aston·ish /ə'stɒnɪʃ/ **astonishes, astonishing,** ◆◇◇◇◇
astonished. If something or someone **astonishes** VERB
you, they surprise you very much. *Her dedication* V n
constantly astonishes me.

aston·ished /ə'stɒnɪʃt/. If you are **astonished** by ◆◇◇◇◇
something, you are very surprised about it. *I was* ADJ-GRADED
astonished by his stupidity... They were astonished to
find the driver was a six-year-old boy.

aston·ish·ing /ə'stɒnɪʃɪŋ/. Something that is ◆◆◇◇◇
astonishing is very surprising. *...an astonishing dis-* ADJ-GRADED
play of physical strength. ♦ **aston·ish·ing·ly** *Isa-* ADV-GRADED
bella was an astonishingly beautiful young woman.

aston·ish·ment /ə'stɒnɪʃmənt/. **Astonishment** is ◆◇◇◇◇
a feeling of great surprise. *I spotted a shooting star* N-UNCOUNT
which, to my astonishment, was bright green in col-
our... 'What?' Meg asked in astonishment.

astound /ə'staʊnd/ **astounds, astounding,** VERB
astounded. If something **astounds** you, you are V n
very surprised by it. *He used to astound his friends* Also V
with feats of physical endurance.

astound·ed /ə'staʊndɪd/. If you are **astounded** by ◆◇◇◇◇
something, you are shocked or amazed that it could ADJ-GRADED
exist or happen. *I was astounded by its beauty... I*
am astounded at the comments made by the Chief.

astound·ing /ə'staʊndɪŋ/. If something is ◆◇◇◇◇
astounding, you are shocked or amazed that it ADJ-GRADED
could exist or happen. *The results are quite astound-*
ing. ♦ **astound·ing·ly** *Astoundingly, an American* ADV-GRADED
had won the Tour de France.

as·tral /'æstrəl/. **Astral** means relating to the stars. ◆◇◇◇◇
...a huge astral black hole. ADJ

astray /ə'streɪ/. **1** If you **are led astray** by someone ◆◇◇◇◇
or something, they make you behave badly or fool- PHRASE
ishly. *The judge thought he'd been led astray by older*
children. **2** If someone or something **leads** you PHRASE
astray, they make you believe something which is
not accurate or true, causing you to make a wrong
decision. *The testimony would inflame the jurors,*
and lead them astray from the facts of the case. **3** If PHRASE
something **goes astray**, it gets lost while it is being

taken or sent somewhere. *Many items of mail being*
sent to her have gone astray.

astride /ə'straɪd/. If you sit or stand **astride** some- ADV
thing, you sit or stand with one leg on each side of
it. *...three youths who stood astride their bicycles.*

as·trin·gent /ə'strɪndʒənt/ **astringents. 1** An **as-** ◆◇◇◇◇
tringent is a liquid that you put on your skin to N-COUNT
make it less greasy or to make cuts stop bleeding.
Using an astringent may be too drying for some
skins. ► Also an adjective. *...an astringent lotion.* ADJ: ADJ n
2 If something has an **astringent** taste, it is sharp or ADJ-GRADED
bitter. *The fruit has a tart and astringent flavour.* FORMAL

astro- /'æstrəʊ-/. **Astro-** is used to form words PREFIX
which refer to things relating to the stars or to outer
space. *...astro-navigation.*

as·trolo·ger /ə'strɒlədʒə/ **astrologers.** An **as-** ◆◇◇◇◇
trologer is a person who uses astrology in order to N-COUNT
try to tell you things about your character and your
future.

as·trol·ogy /ə'strɒlədʒi/. **Astrology** is the study of ◆◇◇◇◇
the movements of the planets, sun, moon, and stars N-UNCOUNT
in the belief that these movements can influence
people's lives. ♦ **as·tro·logi·cal** /,æstrə'lɒdʒɪkəl/ *He* ADJ: ADJ n
has had a lifelong interest in astrological research.

as·tro·naut /'æstrənɔːt/ **astronauts.** An **astro-** ◆◇◇◇◇
naut is a person who travels in or pilots a space- N-COUNT
craft.

as·trono·mer /ə'strɒnəmə/ **astronomers.** An **as-** ◆◆◇◇◇
tronomer is a scientist who studies the stars, plan- N-COUNT
ets, and other natural objects in space.

as·tro·nomi·cal /,æstrə'nɒmɪkəl/. If you describe ADJ
an amount, especially the cost of something as **as-** PRAGMATICS
tronomical, you are emphasizing that it is very
large indeed. *The cost will be astronomical.* ♦ **as-**
·tro·nomi·cal·ly /,æstrə'nɒmɪkli/ *House prices had* ADV
risen astronomically.

as·trono·my /ə'strɒnəmi/. **Astronomy** is the ◆◆◇◇◇
scientific study of the stars, planets, and other natu- N-UNCOUNT
ral objects in space. ♦ **as·tro·nomi·cal** *...the Brit-* ADJ
ish Astronomical Association.

as·tro·phys·ics /,æstrəʊ'fɪzɪks/. **Astrophysics** is N-UNCOUNT
the study of the physical and chemical structure of
the stars, planets, and other natural objects in
space. ♦ **as·tro·physi·cist** /,æstrəʊ'fɪzɪsɪst/ **astro-** N-COUNT
physicists *...the astrophysicists who study*
gamma-ray bursts.

as·tute /ə'stjuːt, AM ə'stuːt/. If you describe some- ◆◇◇◇◇
one as **astute**, you think they show an understand- ADJ-GRADED
ing of behaviour and situations, and are skilful at
using this knowledge to their own advantage. *She*
was politically astute. ...astute business decisions.
♦ **as·tute·ly** *Oxford, as Evelyn Waugh astutely ob-* ADV-GRADED
served, is a city best seen in early summer. ♦ **as-**
·tute·ness *...her political astuteness.* N-UNCOUNT

asun·der /ə'sʌndə/. If something is torn **asunder**, it ADV:
is violently separated into two or more parts or ADV after v
pieces. *The debate is tearing Wall Street asunder.* LITERARY

asy·lum /ə'saɪləm/ **asylums. 1** An **asylum** is a ◆◆◇◇◇
mental hospital. **2** If a government gives a person N-COUNT
from another country **asylum**, they allow them to N-UNCOUNT
stay, usually because they are unable to return
home safely for political reasons. *He applied for asy-*
lum in 1987 after fleeing the police back home. ...asy-
lum seekers.

asym·met·ric /,eɪsɪ'metrɪk/. **Asymmetric** means ADJ-GRADED
the same as **asymmetrical**.

asym·met·ri·cal /,eɪsɪ'metrɪkəl/. Something that is ADJ-GRADED
asymmetrical has two sides or halves that are different in shape, size, or style.

asym·me·try /,eɪ'sɪmətri/ **asymmetries.** Asym- N-VAR
metry is the appearance that something has when
its two sides or halves are different in shape, size, or
style. *...the asymmetry of Van de Velde's designs.*

at /ət, STRONG æt/. As well as the uses shown be- ◆◆◆◆◆
low, **at** is used after some verbs, nouns, and adjectives to introduce extra information. **At** is also used
in phrasal verbs such as 'keep on at' and 'play at'.
1 You use **at** to indicate the place or event where PREP
something happens or is situated. *We had dinner at a*
restaurant. ...muscles at the back of the thigh... Mr

Hurd was speaking at a news conference in Jordan. **2** If PREP
someone is **at** school or college, or **at** a particular
school or college, they go there regularly to study. *It
was at university that he first encountered Hopkins... I
majored in psychology at Hunter College.* **3** If you are PREP
at something such as a desk, a window, or someone's
side, you are next to it or them. *An assistant sat typing
away at a table beside him... Graham was already at
the door... At his side was a beautiful young woman.*
4 When you are describing where someone or some- PREP
thing is, you can say that they are **at** a certain distance,
or that they are **at** an angle in relation to something
else. *The two journalists followed at a discreet distance... The tree was leaning at a low angle from the
ground.*
5 You use **at** to indicate what someone or something PREP
is repeatedly doing something to. *...the handkerchief
with which she kept dabbing at her eyes... Miss Melville took a cookie and nibbled at it.*
6 If something happens **at** a particular time, that is PREP
the time when it happens or begins to happen. *The funeral will be carried out this afternoon at 3.00... He
only sees her at Christmas and Easter.* **7** If you do PREP
something at a particular age, you do it when you are
that age. *Mary Martin has died at her home in California at the age of seventy-six.*
8 You use **at** to express a rate, frequency, level, or PREP
price. *I drove back down the highway at normal
speed... Check the oil at regular intervals... The submarine lies at a depth of 6,000 feet in the Barents Sea.* **9** PREP
You use **at** before a number or amount to indicate a
measurement. *Weighing in at eighty tons, the B-19
was easily the largest and most sophisticated warplane. ...as unemployment stays pegged at three
million.*
10 If you look **at** someone or something, you look to- PREP
wards them. If you direct something such as an object
or a comment **at** someone, you direct it towards
them. *He looked at Michael and laughed... The crowds
became violent and threw petrol bombs at the police...
A couple of people started shouting abuse at them.*
11 You can use **at** after verbs such as smile or wave PREP
and before nouns referring to people to indicate that
you have put on an expression or made a gesture
which someone is meant to see or understand. *She
opened the door and stood there, frowning at me... We
waved at the staff.* **12** If you point or gesture **at** some- PREP
thing, you move your arm or head in its direction so
that it will be noticed by someone you are with. *He
pointed at the empty bottle... He gestured at the
shelves. 'I've bought many books from him.'*
13 If you are working **at** something, you are dealing PREP
with it. If you are aiming **at** something, you are trying
to achieve it. *She has worked hard at her marriage. ...a
$1.04m grant aimed at improving student perfor-
mance.* **14** You use **at** to indicate how well someone PREP
does an activity or task. *I'm good at my work... Robin is
an expert at cheesemaking... She excels at sport.*
15 If something is done **at** someone's invitation or re- PREP
quest, it is done as a result of it. *She left the light on in
the bathroom at his request... I visited Japan in 1987 at
the invitation of the Foreign Minister.*
16 You use **at** to indicate what someone is reacting to. PREP
*Eleanor was annoyed at having had to wait so long...
The British team did not disguise their delight at their
success... Six months ago she would have laughed at
the idea.*
17 You use **at** to say that someone or something is in a PREP
particular state or condition. *We are not at liberty to
disclose that information... Their countries had been
at war for nearly six weeks.*
18 You use **at** before a possessive pronoun and a PREP
superlative adjective to say that someone or something has more of a particular quality than at any other time. *He was at his happiest whilst playing cricket.*
19 You use **at** to say how something is being done. PREP
*...shots fired at random from a minibus... Mr Martin
was taken out of his car at gunpoint.*
20 ● **at all**: see **all**.

ata·vis·tic /ˌætə'vɪstɪk/. If you describe someone's ADJ-GRADED
feelings or behaviour as **atavistic**, you think they are FORMAL
like the feelings or behaviour of their primitive ancestors. *...an atavistic fear of thunder and lightning.*
ate /et, eɪt/. **Ate** is the past tense of **eat**.
at·el·ier /ə'telieɪ, AM ˌætə'ljeɪ/ **ateliers**. An **atelier** N-COUNT
is an artist's studio or workshop.
athe·ist /'eɪθiɪst/ **atheists**. An **atheist** is a person ◆◇◇◇◇
who believes that there is no God. Compare **agnos-** N-COUNT
tic. ♦ **athe·ism** /'eɪθiɪzəm/. *...his inclination toward* N-UNCOUNT
atheism. ♦ **athe·is·tic** /ˌeɪθi'ɪstɪk/. *...atheistic phi-* ADJ
losophers. ...an atheistic communist regime.
ath·lete /'æθliːt/ **athletes**. **1** An **athlete** is a per- ◆◆◇◇◇
son who takes part in athletics. *...American athlete* N-COUNT
and gold medallist Jesse Owens. **2** You can refer to N-COUNT
someone who is fit and athletic as an **athlete**. *I was
no athlete.*
,athlete's 'foot. **Athlete's foot** is an infection in N-UNCOUNT
which the skin between the toes peels off.
ath·let·ic /æθ'letɪk/. **1 Athletic** means relating to ◆◆◇◇◇
athletes and athletics. *...athletic ability. ...athletic* ADJ: ADJ n
activities. ♦ **ath·leti·cal·ly** /æθ'letɪkli/ *...academ-* ADV
ically able and athletically outstanding. **2** An **ath-** ADJ-GRADED
letic person is fit, and able to perform energetic
movements easily. *Xandra is an athletic 36-year-old
with a 21-year-old's body.* ♦ **athletically** When ADV
*Newman put in a header from 10 yards, the goal-
keeper athletically tipped it over.*
ath·leti·cism /æθ'letɪsɪzəm/. A person's **athleti-** N-UNCOUNT
cism is their fitness and ability to perform well at
sports or other physical activities.
ath·let·ics /æθ'letɪks/. **Athletics** refers to track and ◆◆◇◇◇
field sports such as running, the high jump, and the N-UNCOUNT
javelin. *As the modern Olympics grew in stature, so
too did athletics.*
-ation /-'eɪʃən/ **-ations**. **-ation** and **-tion** are added SUFFIX
to some verbs in order to form nouns. Nouns
formed in this way often refer to a state or process.
at·las /'ætləs/ **atlases**. An **atlas** is a book of maps ◆◇◇◇◇
of all the areas in the world. N-COUNT
ATM /ˌeɪ tiː 'em/ **ATMs**. An **ATM** is a machine built N-COUNT
into the wall of a bank or other building, which al- AMERICAN
lows people to take out money from their bank account by using a special card. ATM is an abbreviation for 'automated teller machine'. The usual British expression is **cash dispenser**.
at·mos·phere /'ætməsfɪə/ **atmospheres**. **1** A ◆◆◆◇◇
planet's **atmosphere** is the layer of air or other N-COUNT
gases around it. *The shuttle Columbia will re-enter
Earth's atmosphere tomorrow morning.* **2** The **at-** N-COUNT
mosphere of a place is the air that you breathe
there. *These gases pollute the atmosphere of towns
and cities.*
3 The **atmosphere** of a place is the general impres- N-SING
sion that you get of it. *Pale wooden floors and plenty of
natural light add to the relaxed atmosphere.* **4** If a N-UNCOUNT
place or an event has **atmosphere**, it is interesting.
The old harbour is still full of atmosphere.
at·mos·pher·ic /ˌætməs'ferɪk/. **1 Atmospheric** is ◆◇◇◇◇
used to describe something which relates to the ADJ
Earth's atmosphere. *...atmospheric pressure.* **2** If ADJ-GRADED
you describe a place or a piece of music as **atmos-** PRAGMATICS
pheric, you like it because it has a particular quality
which is interesting or exciting and makes you feel a
particular emotion. *One of the most atmospheric
corners of Prague is the old Jewish ghetto.*
at·mos·pher·ics /ˌætməs'ferɪks/. **Atmospherics** N-PLURAL
are elements in something such as a piece of music
or a story which create a certain atmosphere.
...Dickensian atmospherics.
at·oll /'ætɒl, AM -tɔːl/ **atolls**. An **atoll** is a crescent- N-COUNT
shaped coral island surrounding a lagoon.
atom /'ætəm/ **atoms**. An **atom** is the smallest pos- ◆◆◇◇◇
sible amount of a chemical element. *A methane* N-COUNT
*molecule is composed of one carbon atom attached
to four hydrogens.*
'atom bomb, atom bombs. An **atom bomb** or an N-COUNT
atomic bomb is a bomb that causes an explosion by
a sudden release of energy that results from splitting atoms.

atom·ic /ə'tɒmɪk/. **1 Atomic** means relating to power that is produced from the energy released by splitting atoms. ...*atomic energy.* ...*atomic weapons.* **2 Atomic** means relating to atoms.
◆◆◇◇◇ ADJ
ADJ: ADJ n

aton·al /ˌeɪ'təʊnəl/. **Atonal** music is not written or played in any key or system of scales.
ADJ

atone /ə'təʊn/ **atones, atoning, atoned.** If you **atone** for something that you have done, you do something to show that you are sorry you did it. *He felt he had atoned for what he had done to his son... He atoned by apologizing.* ♦ **atone·ment** True guilt is characterized by a readiness to make atonement for having done wrong.
VERB
V forn
V by-ing
Also V
FORMAL
N-UNCOUNT

atop /ə'tɒp/. If something is **atop** something else, it is on top of it. *Under the newspaper, atop a sheet of paper, lay an envelope.*
◆◇◇◇ PREP LITERARY

A to Z /ˌeɪ tə 'zed, AM - 'ziː/. **A to Zs. 1** In Britain, an **A to Z** is a book of maps showing all the streets in a particular city or area. **A to Z** is a trademark. **2** An **A to Z** of a particular subject is a book or programme which gives information on all aspects of it, arranged in alphabetical order.
N-COUNT
N-SING

atrium /'eɪtriəm/ **atriums.** An **atrium** is part of a building such as a hotel or shopping centre, which extends up through several storeys of the building and often has a glass roof.
N-COUNT

atro·cious /ə'trəʊʃəs/. **1** If you describe something as **atrocious**, you are emphasizing that it is extremely bad or unpleasant. *The food here is atrocious.* ...*atrocious weather: snow in the mountains, torrential rain elsewhere.* **2** If you describe someone's behaviour or their actions as **atrocious**, you mean that they are extremely violent, cruel, or shocking. *The judge said he had committed atrocious crimes against women.*
◆◇◇◇ ADJ-GRADED PRAGMATICS

ADJ-GRADED

atroc·ity /ə'trɒsɪti/ **atrocities.** An **atrocity** is a very cruel, shocking action, usually involving violence or killing. *Those who committed this atrocity should be tried and punished.*
◆◆◇◇ N-VAR

at·ro·phy /'ætrəfi/ **atrophies, atrophying, atrophied. 1** If a muscle or other part of the body **atrophies**, it decreases in size or strength, often as a result of an illness. ► Also a noun. ...*exercises to avoid jelling and atrophy of cartilage.* **2** If something **atrophies**, its size, degree, or effectiveness decreases because it is not used or protected. *If you allow your mind to stagnate, this particular talent will atrophy.* ► Also a noun. *After 1904 the industry sank into stagnation and atrophy.*
VERB: V FORMAL
N-UNCOUNT
VERB V
N-UNCOUNT

at·tach /ə'tætʃ/ **attaches, attaching, attached. 1** If you **attach** something to an object, you join it or fasten it to the object. *We attach labels to things before we file them away... The astronauts will attach a motor that will boost the satellite into its proper orbit.* **2** If someone **attaches** himself or herself to you, they join you and stay with you, often without being invited to do so. *Natasha attached herself to the film crew filming at her orphanage.* **3** If people **attach** a quality to someone or something, they consider that the person or thing has that quality. *The Chinese authorities have attached much significance to Mr Maude's visit.* **4** If you **attach** conditions to something such as an agreement, you state that specific things must be done before the agreement is valid. *President Lee has attached impossible conditions to his offer.* **5** See also **attached. ● no strings attached:** see **string.**
◆◆◆◇◇ VERB
V n ton
V n
VERB
V pron-refl to n
V-ERG
V n toto n
VERB
V n ton
Also V n

at·ta·ché /æ'tæʃeɪ, AM ˌætæ'ʃeɪ/ **attachés.** An **attaché** is a member of staff in an embassy, usually with a special responsibility for something. *He was working as a cultural attache in Warsaw.*
N-COUNT

at·taché case, attaché cases. An **attaché case** is a flat, hinged, briefcase.
N-COUNT

at·tached /ə'tætʃt/. **1** If you are **attached to** someone or something, you are very fond of them. *She is very attached to her family and friends.* **2** If someone is **attached to** an organization or group of people, they are working with them, often only for a short time. *Ford was attached to the battalion's first line of transport.* **3** If one organization or institution
◆◆◇◇ ADJ-GRADED: v-link ADJ to n
ADJ: v-link ADJ to n
ADJ:

is **attached to** a larger organization, it is part of that organization and is controlled and administered by it. *The schools were mainly attached to the church.*
v-link ADJ to n

at·tach·ment /ə'tætʃmənt/ **attachments. 1** If you have an **attachment** to someone or something, you are fond of them or loyal to them. *Mother and child form a close attachment.* ...*a feeling of attachment to the land where their ancestors have lived.* **2** An **attachment** is a device that can be fixed onto a machine in order to enable it to do different jobs. *Some models come with attachments for dusting.* **3** If someone is on **attachment** to another company, department, or place, they are working there temporarily. *During her course she worked on attachment for six months at Kew Gardens.*
◆◇◇◇ N-VAR
N-COUNT
N-VAR BRITISH

at·tack /ə'tæk/ **attacks, attacking, attacked. 1** To **attack** a person or place means to try to hurt or damage them using physical violence. *He bundled the old lady into her hallway and brutally attacked her.* ...*attacking forces.* ► Also a noun. *Refugees had come under attack from federal troops.* **2** If something such as a disease, chemical, or insect **attacks** something, it harms or spoils it. *Several key crops failed when they were attacked by pests.* ► Also a noun. ...*leaving the body wide open to attack from other infections.* **3** An **attack** of an illness is a short period in which you suffer badly from it. ...*an attack of asthma.* ● See also **heart attack. 4** If you **attack** a person, their ideas, or their actions, you criticize them strongly. *He publicly attacked people who've been calling for secret ballot nominations... A newspaper ran an editorial attacking him for being a showman.* ► Also a noun. *The role of the state as a prime mover in planning social change has been under attack.* **5** If you **attack** a job or a problem, you start to deal with it in an energetic way. *Any attempt to attack the budget problem is going to have to in some way deal with these issues.* **6** In games such as football, when one team **attacks**, they try to score a goal. *Now the US is controlling the ball and attacking the opponent's goal.* ► Also a noun. ...*some incisive attacks in the second half.* ♦ **at·tack·ing** ...*a more attacking style of football.* **7** See also **counter-attack.**
◆◆◆◆◆ VERB
V n
V-ing
Also V
N-VAR
VERB: V n be V-ed
N-UNCOUNT: also N in pl
N-COUNT: with supp
VERB
V n
V n for-ing
Also V n as n/ adj
N-VAR
VERB
V n
VERB: V
V n
N-COUNT
ADJ-GRADED: ADJ n

at·tack·er /ə'tækə/ **attackers.** You can refer to a person who attacks someone as their **attacker.** *She struggled with her attacker.*
◆◆◇◇ N-COUNT

at·tain /ə'teɪn/ **attains, attaining, attained.** If you **attain** something, you gain or achieve it, often after a lot of effort or difficulty. *Jim is halfway to attaining his pilot's licence.* ...*attaining a state of calmness and confidence.*
◆◇◇◇ VERB
V n
FORMAL

at·tain·able /ə'teɪnəbəl/. Something that is **attainable** can be achieved. *It is unrealistic to believe perfection is an attainable goal.*
ADJ-GRADED

at·tain·ment /ə'teɪnmənt/ **attainments. 1** The **attainment** of an aim is the achieving of it. ...*the attainment of independence.* **2** An **attainment** is a skill you have learnt or something you have achieved. ...*their educational attainments.*
◆◇◇◇ N-UNCOUNT FORMAL
N-COUNT FORMAL

at·tempt /ə'tempt/ **attempts, attempting, attempted. 1** If you **attempt** to do something, especially something difficult, you try to do it, often without success. *They are accused of attempting to murder British soldiers... Before I could attempt a reply he added over his shoulder: 'Wait there.'* ► Also a noun. ...*a deliberate attempt to mislead people.* **2** An **attempt** on someone's life is an attempt to kill them. ...*an attempt on the life of the former Iranian Prime Minister.* **3** If a sportsman or sportswoman makes an **attempt** on a record, they try to beat it.
◆◆◆◆◆ VERB
V to-inf
V n
N-COUNT
N-COUNT: N on n
N-COUNT: N on n

at·tempt·ed /ə'temptɪd/. An **attempted** crime or unlawful action is an unsuccessful effort to commit the crime or action. ...*a case of attempted murder.*
◆◆◇◇ ADJ: ADJ n

at·tend /ə'tend/ **attends, attending, attended. 1** If you **attend** a meeting or other event, you are present at it. *Thousands of people attended the funeral.* **2** If you **attend** an institution such as a school, college, or church, you go there regularly. *They attended college together at the University of*
◆◆◆◆◇ VERB
V n
Also V
VERB
V n
Also V

Pennsylvania. ♦ **at·tend·er, attenders** *He was a* N-COUNT
regular attender at the opera. **3** If you **attend** to VERB
something, you deal with it. If you **attend** to some- V *to n*
one who is hurt or injured, you care for them. *The
staff will helpfully attend to your needs.*

at·tend·ance /əˈtendəns/ **attendances.** ♦♦◇◇◇
1 Someone's **attendance** at an event or an institu- N-UNCOUNT
tion is the fact that they are present at the event or
go regularly to the institution. *Her attendance at
school was sporadic.* **2** The **attendance** at an event N-VAR
is the number of people who are present at it. *Average weekly cinema attendance in February was 2.41
million.* **3** If someone is **in attendance** at a place or PHRASE
an event, they are there. *Police with riot gear and
several fire engines are in attendance.* **4** If someone PHRASE
is **in attendance** on an important person, they are FORMAL
accompanying that person as a servant or assistant.
*He lived in considerable style, travelling widely,
usually with a cook, valet, butler and chauffeur in
attendance.*

at·tend·ant /əˈtendənt/ **attendants. 1** An attend- ♦♦◇◇◇
ant is someone whose job is to serve or help people N-COUNT
in a place such as a petrol station, a car park, or a
cloakroom. *...a car-park attendant.* **2** You use **at-** ADJ
tendant to describe something that results from a
thing already mentioned or that is connected with
it. *Mr Branson's victory, and all the attendant publicity, were well deserved. ...the risks attendant on the
exploration of the unknown.*

at·tend·ee /əˌtenˈdiː/ **attendees.** The attendees at N-COUNT
something such as a conference are the people who AMERICAN
are attending it.

at·ten·tion /əˈtenʃən/ **attentions. 1** If you give ♦♦♦♦
something your **attention**, you look at it, listen to it, N-UNCOUNT:
or think about it carefully. *You have my undivided* also N in pl
*attention... Later he turned his attention to the des-
perate state of housing in the province.* **2** Attention N-UNCOUNT
is great interest that is shown in someone or something, particularly by the general public. *Volume
Two, sub-titled 'The Lawyers', will also attract considerable attention.* **3** If someone or something is N-UNCOUNT
getting **attention**, they are being dealt with or cared
for. *Each year more than two million household injuries need medical attention.* **4** You can refer to N-PLURAL
someone's efforts to help you, or the interest they PRAGMATICS
show in you, as their **attentions**; often used showing disapproval. *The only way to escape the unwanted attentions of the local men was not to go out.*
5 If you bring something to someone's **attention** or N-UNCOUNT
draw their **attention** to it, you tell them about it or
make them notice it. *If we don't keep bringing this to
the attention of the people, nothing will be done.* **6** If PHRASE
someone or something **attracts** your **attention** or
catches your **attention**, you suddenly notice them. *A
faint aroma of coffee attracted his attention.* **7** If you PHRASE
pay attention to someone or something, you watch
them, listen to them, or take notice of them. *More
than ever before, the food industry is paying attention
to young consumers... Both Alistair and Rose were far
too busy to pay any attention to her.*
8 When people such as soldiers **stand to attention** or PHRASE
stand at attention, they stand straight with their feet
together and their arms at their sides.

at·ten·tive /əˈtentɪv/ **1** If you are **attentive**, you ♦◇◇◇◇
are paying close attention to what is being said or ADJ-GRADED
done. ♦ **at·ten·tive·ly** *He questioned Chrissie, and* ADV-GRADED
listened *attentively to what she told him.* **2** Someone ADJ-GRADED
who is **attentive** is helpful and polite. *At society parties he is attentive to his wife. ...courteous and attentive service to each and every guest.* ♦ **at·ten·tive-** N-UNCOUNT
·ness *Anne was both flattered and surprised by
Danny's attentiveness to her.*

at·tenu·ate /əˈtenjueɪt/ **attenuates, attenuat-** VERB
ing, attenuated. To **attenuate** something means V n
to reduce it or weaken it. *You could never eliminate FORMAL
risk, but preparation and training could attenuate it.*

at·test /əˈtest/ **attests, attesting, attested.** To ♦◇◇◇◇
attest something or **attest** to something means to VERB
show or prove that it is true. *Police records attest to* V *to n*
V *that*

his long history of violence... I can personally attest Also V n
that the cold and flu season is here. FORMAL

at·tic /ˈætɪk/ **attics.** An **attic** is a room at the top of ♦◇◇◇◇
a house just below the roof. N-COUNT

at·tire /əˈtaɪə/. Your **attire** is the clothes you are N-UNCOUNT
wearing. *...seven women dressed in their finest attire.* FORMAL

at·tired /əˈtaɪəd/. If you describe how someone is ADJ:
attired, you are describing how they are dressed. *He* v-link ADJ *in*
was faultlessly attired in black coat and striped n,
trousers. adv ADJ

at·ti·tude /ˈætɪtjuːd, AM -tuːd/ **attitudes. 1** Your ♦♦♦♦
attitude to something is the way that you think and N-VAR
feel about it, especially when this shows in the way
you behave. *...the general change in attitude towards
handicapped people. ...negative attitudes to work.
...a critical attitude of mind.* **2** If you refer to a per- N-UNCOUNT
son with **attitude**, you mean someone who has a JOURNALISM
very individual or aggressive style of behaviour.
...women with attitude.

at·ti·tu·di·nal /ˌætɪˈtjuːdɪnəl, AM -ˈtuːd-/. **Attitudi-** ADJ
nal means related to people's attitudes and the way FORMAL
they look at their life. *...an attitudinal change.*

at·tor·ney /əˈtɜːni/ **attorneys.** In the United ♦♦♦◇◇
States, an **attorney** is a lawyer. *...a prosecuting at-* N-COUNT
torney. ● See also **District Attorney.**

At·torney 'General, Attorneys General. A ♦♦◇◇◇
country's **Attorney General** is its chief law officer N-COUNT
who advises its king, queen, or government.

at·tract /əˈtrækt/ **attracts, attracting, attract-** ♦♦♦♦
ed. 1 If something **attracts** people or animals, it VERB
has features that cause them to come to it. *The Car-* V n
diff Bay project is attracting many visitors... Warm V n adv/prep
weather has attracted the flat fish close to shore. **2** If VERB
something **attracts** support, publicity, or money, it V n
receives support, publicity, or money. *His country
would also like to attract investment from private
companies.* **3** If one object **attracts** another, it VERB
causes the second object to move towards it. *Any-* V n *to n*
thing with strong gravity attracts other things to it. Also V n
4 If someone or something **attracts** you, they have VERB
particular qualities which cause you to like or admire V n
them. If a particular quality **attracts** you to a person or V n *to n*
thing, it is the reason why you like them. *The theory
attracted him by its logic... What first attracted me to
her was her incredible experience of life.* **5** If someone VERB
attracts you, you are interested in them sexually. *I* V n
was married to a man who had ceased to attract me. Also be V-ed
♦ **at·tract·ed** *He was nice looking, but I wasn't deeply* to n
attracted to him. ♦ **at·trac·tion** *...our level of attrac-* ADJ-GRADED
tion to the opposite sex. N-UNCOUNT
6 ● to **attract someone's attention**: see **attention.**

at·trac·tion /əˈtrækʃən/ **attractions. 1** An attrac- ♦♦◇◇◇
tion is a feature which makes something interesting N-COUNT
or desirable. *...the attractions of living on the waterfront.* **2** An **attraction** is something that people can N-COUNT
go to for interest or enjoyment, for example a fa-
mous building. *The walled city is an important tourist attraction.* **3** See also **attract.**

at·trac·tive /əˈtræktɪv/. **1** If you find someone at- ♦♦♦◇◇
tractive, especially someone of the opposite sex, ADJ-GRADED
you think that they are pleasant to look at or sexually desirable. *He was immensely attractive to women.*
♦ **at·trac·tive·ness** *...physical attractiveness.* N-UNCOUNT
2 Something that is **attractive** has a pleasant ap- ADJ-GRADED
pearance or sound. *The flat was small but attractive.*
♦ **at·trac·tive·ly** *...an attractively illustrated, de-* ADV-GRADED
tailed guide. ♦ **at·trac·tive·ness** *The forest will* N-UNCOUNT
enhance the attractiveness of the region.* **3** You can ADJ-GRADED
describe something as **attractive** when it seems
worth having or doing. *Smoking is still attractive to
many young people who see it as glamorous.* ♦ **at-**
·trac·tive·ly *The services are attractively priced.* ADV-GRADED
♦ **at·trac·tive·ness** *The attractiveness of the* N-UNCOUNT
schemes depends almost entirely on tax relief.*

at·trib·ut·able /əˈtrɪbjʊtəbəl/. If something **is at-** ♦◇◇◇◇
tributable to something or someone, it is likely that ADJ:
it was caused by them. *10,000 deaths a year from* v-link ADJ *to n*
chronic lung disease are attributable to smoking.*

at·trib·ute, attributes, attributing, attribut- ♦♦◇◇◇
ed. The verb is pronounced /əˈtrɪbjuːt/. The noun

is pronounced /'ætrɪbjuːt/. **1** If you **attribute** one thing to another, you think that it was caused by that other thing. *Women tend to attribute their success to external causes such as luck.* **2** If you **attribute** a particular quality or feature to someone or something, you think that they have got it. *People were beginning to attribute superhuman qualities to him.* ♦ **at·tri·bu·tion** /ˌætrɪ'bjuːʃən/ ...*attribution of evil intent to those who have different views.* **3** If a piece of writing, a work of art, or a remark **is attributed** to someone, people say that they wrote it, created it, or said it. *This, and the remaining frescoes, are not attributed to Giotto.* **4** An **attribute** is a quality or feature that someone or something has. *Cruelty is a normal attribute of human behaviour.*

VERB
V n to n

VERB
V n to n

N-UNCOUNT

VB: usu passive
be V-ed to n

N-COUNT

at·tri·tion /ə'trɪʃən/ **1** Attrition is a process in which you steadily reduce the strength of an enemy by continually attacking them. *The rebels have declared a cease-fire in their war of attrition against the government.* **2** At a university or place of work, **attrition** is the decrease in the number of students or employees caused by people leaving and not being replaced. *The company plans to cut a quarter of its workforce over six years through natural attrition.*

♦◇◇◇
N-UNCOUNT
FORMAL

N-UNCOUNT
AMERICAN

at·tuned /ə'tjuːnd, AM ə'tuːnd/. **1** If you **are attuned to** something, you can understand and appreciate it. *He seemed unusually attuned to people's feelings.* **2** If your ears **are attuned to** a sound, they can hear it and recognize it quickly. *Their ears were still attuned to the sounds of the London suburb.*

ADJ:
v-link ADJ to n

ADJ-GRADED:
v-link ADJ to n

atyp·i·cal /ˌeɪ'tɪpɪkəl/. Someone or something that is **atypical** is not typical of their kind. *He was an atypical English schoolboy.*

ADJ-GRADED

auber·gine /'əʊbəʒiːn/ **aubergines.** An **aubergine** is a vegetable with a smooth, dark purple skin. The usual American word is **eggplant.**

♦◇◇◇
N-VAR
BRITISH

auburn /'ɔːbən/. **Auburn** hair is reddish brown.

COLOUR

auc·tion /'ɔːkʃən/ **auctions, auctioning, auctioned.** **1** An **auction** is a public sale where goods are sold to the person who offers the highest price. *Lord Salisbury bought the picture at auction. ...Britain's two main auction houses, Sotheby's and Christie's.* **2** If something **is auctioned**, it is sold in an auction. *Eight drawings by French artist Jean Cocteau will be auctioned next week.* ▶ **Auction off** means the same as **auction.** *Any fool could auction off a factory full of engineering machinery.*

♦♦◇◇
N-VAR

VERB
be V-ed
be V-ed to n

PHRASAL VB
V P noun

auc·tion·eer /ˌɔːkʃə'nɪə/ **auctioneers.** An **auctioneer** is a person who is in charge of an auction and who calls out the amounts people offer to pay for the goods being sold.

♦◇◇◇
N-COUNT

auda·cious /ɔː'deɪʃəs/. Something or someone that is **audacious** takes risks in order to achieve something. *...an audacious plan to win the presidency.* ♦ **audac·ity** /ɔː'dæsɪti/ *I was shocked at the audacity and brazenness of the gangsters.*

♦◇◇◇
ADJ-GRADED

N-UNCOUNT

audible /'ɔːdɪbəl/. A sound that is **audible** is loud enough to be heard. *The Colonel's voice was barely audible.* ♦ **audibly** /'ɔːdɪbli/ *Hugh sighed audibly.*

♦◇◇◇
ADJ-GRADED

ADV-GRADED

audi·ence /'ɔːdiəns/ **audiences.** **1** The **audience** at a play, concert, film, or public meeting is the group of people watching or listening to it. *The entire audience broke into loud applause... He was speaking to an audience of students.* **2** The **audience** for a television or radio programme consists of all the people who watch or listen to it. *...a worldwide television audience estimated at one thousand million.* ● See also **studio audience.**
3 If you have an **audience** with someone important, you have a formal meeting with them. *The Prime Minister will seek an audience with the Queen later this morning.*

♦♦♦◇
N-COLL-
COUNT

N-COLL-
COUNT

N-COUNT

audio /'ɔːdiəʊ/. **Audio** equipment is used for recording and reproducing sound. *...audio tapes of books for blind people.*

♦♦◇◇
ADJ: ADJ n

audio-visual; also spelled **audiovisual. Audio-visual** equipment and materials involve recorded sound and things such as TV, pictures, charts, or models.

ADJ: ADJ n

audit /'ɔːdɪt/ **audits, auditing, audited.** When an accountant **audits** an organization's accounts, he or she examines the accounts officially in order to make sure that they have been done correctly. ▶ Also a noun. *The bank first learned of the problem when it carried out an internal audit.*

♦◇◇◇
VERB: V n

N-COUNT

audi·tion /ɔː'dɪʃən/ **auditions, auditioning, auditioned.** **1** If an actor, dancer, or musician does an **audition**, they give a short performance so that a director or conductor can decide if they are good enough to be in a play, film, or orchestra. **2** If you **audition** or if someone **auditions** you, you do an audition. *They're auditioning for new members of the cast for 'Miss Saigon' today.*

♦◇◇◇
N-COUNT

V-ERG
V for n
Also V,
V n,
V n for n

audi·tor /'ɔːdɪtə/ **auditors.** An **auditor** is an accountant who officially examines the accounts of organizations.

♦◇◇◇
N-COUNT

audi·to·rium /ˌɔːdɪ'tɔːriəm/ **auditoriums** or **auditoria** /ˌɔːdɪ'tɔːriə/. **1** An **auditorium** is the part of a theatre or concert hall where the audience sits. **2** An **auditorium** is a large room, hall, or building which is used for events such as meetings and concerts.

♦◇◇◇
N-COUNT

N-COUNT
AMERICAN

audi·tory /'ɔːdɪtri, AM -tɔːri/. **Auditory** means related to hearing. *...music, which is organized auditory information.*

ADJ
TECHNICAL

au fait /ˌəʊ 'feɪ/. If you are **au fait with** something, you are familiar with it and know about it. *I am au fait with fashion.*

ADJ-GRADED:
v-link ADJ
with n

Aug. Aug. is a written abbreviation for **August.**

♦♦◇◇

aug·ment /ɔːg'ment/ **augments, augmenting, augmented.** To **augment** something means to make it larger, stronger, or more effective by adding something to it. *...searching for a way to augment the family income.*

♦◇◇◇
VERB
V n
FORMAL

augur /'ɔːgə/ **augurs, auguring, augured.** If something **augurs** well or badly for a person or a future situation or event, it is a sign that things will go well or badly. *The renewed violence this week in Azerbaijan hardly augurs well for smooth or peaceful change.*

VERB
V adv for n
Also V adv
FORMAL

augu·ry /'ɔːgjʊri/ **auguries.** An **augury** is a sign of what will happen in the future. *The auguries of death are fast gathering round his head.*

N-COUNT
LITERARY

august /ɔː'gʌst/. Someone or something that is **august** is dignified and impressive. *The magazine held its party in the august surroundings of the Liberal Club.*

ADJ-GRADED
FORMAL

August /'ɔːgəst/ **Augusts. August** is the eighth month of the year in the Western calendar. See Appendix headed **Dates.**

♦♦♦◇
N-VAR

auk /ɔːk/ **auks. Auks** are a group of birds with heavy bodies and short tails that dive into the sea for their food. Puffins are a type of auk.

N-COUNT

aunt /ɑːnt, ænt/ **aunts.** Someone's **aunt** is the sister of their mother or father, or the wife of their uncle. *...Aunt Vera.* ● See also **agony aunt.**

♦♦♦♦
N-FAMILY;
N-TITLE

auntie /'ɑːnti, 'ænti/ **aunties;** also spelled **aunty.** Someone's **auntie** is their aunt. *...my Auntie Elsie.*

N-FAMILY;
N-TITLE
INFORMAL

au pair /ˌəʊ 'peə, AM ˌɔː -/ **au pairs.** An **au pair** is a young person from a foreign country, usually a woman, who lives with a family in order to learn the language. An au pair usually helps with the children and housework in return for a small wage.

♦◇◇◇
N-COUNT

aura /'ɔːrə/ **auras.** An **aura** is a quality or feeling that seems to surround a person or place or to come from them. *She had an aura of authority.*

♦◇◇◇
N-COUNT

aural /'ɔːrəl, 'aʊrəl/. **Aural** means related to the sense of hearing. Compare **oral.** *...astonishing visual and aural effects.*

♦◇◇◇
ADJ

aus·pi·ces /'ɔːspɪsɪz/. If something is done **under the auspices of** a particular person or organization, it is done with their support and approval. *...a walk in support of Forests of the World, under the auspices of the World Wildlife Fund.*

♦◇◇◇
PHRASE
FORMAL

aus·pi·cious /ɔː'spɪʃəs/. Something that is **auspicious** indicates that success is likely. *His career as a playwright had an auspicious start.*

ADJ-GRADED
FORMAL

A

Aus·sie /ˈɒz/ **Aussies.** Aussie means Australian. ◆◇◇◇◇ ADJ INFORMAL N-COUNT
...*Aussie comedy actor Paul Hogan.* ▶ An **Aussie** is a
person from Australia.

aus·tere /ɔːˈstɪə/ **1** If you describe something as ADJ-GRADED
austere, you approve of its plain and simple ap- PRAGMATICS
pearance. ...*a cream linen suit and austere black
blouse.* ◆ **aus·ter·ity** /ɔːˈsterɪti/ ...*many abandoned* N-UNCOUNT
*buildings, some of which have a compact classical
austerity and dignity.* **2** If you describe someone as ADJ-GRADED
austere, you disapprove of them because they are PRAGMATICS
strict and serious. *I found her a rather austere, distant, somewhat cold person.* **3** An **austere** way of life ADJ-GRADED
is simple and without luxuries. *The life of the troops
was still comparatively austere.* **4** An **austere** eco- ADJ-GRADED
nomic policy reduces people's living standards
sharply. ...*a set of very austere economic measures to
control inflation.* ◆ **austerity** ...*the years of auster-* N-UNCOUNT
ity which followed the war.

authen·tic /ɔːˈθentɪk/ **1** If something is **authentic**, ◆◆◇◇◇ ADJ
it is genuine rather than an imitation or a forgery.
...*authentic Italian food.* ◆ **au·then·tic·ity** N-UNCOUNT
/ˌɔːθenˈtɪsɪti/ *There are factors that have cast doubt
on the statue's authenticity.* ◆ **authen·ti·cal·ly** ADV-GRADED
/ɔːˈθentɪkli/ *Highland Park is not some grisly tourist
trap but something authentically Scottish.* **2** You ADJ-GRADED
can describe something as **authentic** when it is PRAGMATICS
such a good imitation that it is practically the same
as the original; used showing approval. ...*patterns
for making authentic frontier-style clothing.*
◆ **authentically** *The team decided to try and repli-* ADV-GRADED
cate the missing curtains as authentically as possible.
3 An **authentic** account or piece of information is ADJ
reliable and accurate. ◆ **authentically** *The book* ADV-GRADED
*authentically and intimately describes the small de-
tails of her daily life.*

authen·ti·cate /ɔːˈθentɪkeɪt/ **authenticates,
authenticating, authenticated. 1** If you VERB
authenticate something such as a painting, you Vn
state officially that it is genuine after examining it. Also Vn as n
*All the antiques have been authenticated and record-
ed.* ◆ **authen·ti·ca·tion** /ɔːˌθentɪˈkeɪʃən/ *He had* N-UNCOUNT
*purchased a painting in reliance upon the authenti-
cation of a well-regarded expert.* **2** If you **authenti-** VERB: Vn
cate something such as a report, you prove or con- V-ed
firm that it is true. ...*well authenticated reports that
the use of this drug is very occasionally responsible
for heart attacks.*

author /ˈɔːθə/ **authors, authoring, authored.** ◆◆◆◇
1 The **author** of a piece of writing is the person who N-COUNT
wrote it. ...*Jill Phillips, author of the book 'Give Your
Child Music'.* **2** An **author** is a person whose occu- N-COUNT
pation is writing books. *Haruki Murakami is Japan's
best-selling author.* **3** The **author of** a plan or pro- N-COUNT:
posal is the person who thinks of it and works out N of n
the details. **4** To **author** something means to be the VERB
author of it. *Then he opened a restaurant, authored* Vn
a book, and landed his own radio show. ...a UN V-ed
peace plan authored by Cyrus Vance and Lord Owen.

autho·rial /ɔːˈθɔːriəl/. **Authorial** means relating to ADJ: ADJ n
the author of something such as a book or play. *The
book suffers from excessive authorial control.*

author·ise /ˈɔːθəraɪz/. See **authorize**.

authori·tar·ian /ɔːˌθɒrɪˈteəriən, AM -ˈtɔːr-/ ◆◇◇◇◇
authoritarians. If you describe a person or an or- ADJ-GRADED
ganization as **authoritarian**, you are criticizing PRAGMATICS
them for controlling everything rather than letting
people decide things for themselves. ◆ **authori-**
·tari·an·ism /ɔːˌθɒrɪˈteəriənɪzəm, AM -ˈθɔːr-/ ...*the* N-UNCOUNT
long revolt against authoritarianism.

authori·ta·tive /ɔːˈθɒrɪtətɪv, AM əˈθɔːrɪteɪtɪv/ ◆◇◇◇◇
1 An **authoritative** person gives an impression of ADJ-GRADED
power and importance and is likely to be obeyed.
*He has a commanding presence and deep, authorita-
tive voice.* ◆ **authori·ta·tive·ly** *The man pushed his* ADV-GRADED
way authoritatively through the crowd. **2** **Authorita-** ADJ-GRADED
tive means showing a lot of knowledge of a subject.
*The first authoritative study of polio was published
in 1840.* ◆ **authoritatively** *My own life is the only* ADV-GRADED:
thing I can speak authoritatively about. ADV with v

author·ity /ɔːˈθɒrɪti, AM -ˈtɔːr-/ **authorities.** ◆◆◆◆◆
1 The **authorities** are the people or organizations N-PLURAL
who have the power to make decisions, especially
the government. *This provided a pretext for the
authorities to cancel the elections.* **2** An **authority** is
an official organization or government department
that has the power to make decisions. ...*the Health
Education Authority.* ● See also **local authority**.
3 **Authority** is the right to command and control N-UNCOUNT
other people. *The judge had no authority to order a
second trial.* **4** **Authority** is official permission to do N-UNCOUNT
something. *The prison governor has refused to let
him go, saying he must first be given authority from
his own superiors.*
5 If someone has **authority**, they have a quality which N-UNCOUNT
makes other people take notice of what they say. *He
had no natural authority and no capacity for imposing
his will on others.*
6 Someone who is an **authority on** a subject knows a N-COUNT:
lot about it. *He's universally recognized as an author- N on n
ity on Russian affairs.*

author·ize /ˈɔːθəraɪz/ **authorizes, authorizing,** ◆◆◇◇◇
authorized; also spelled **authorise** in British Eng- VERB
lish. If someone in a position of authority **author-** Vn
izes something, they give their official permission Also Vn to-inf
for it to happen. *It would certainly be within his
power to authorize a police raid.* ◆ **authori·za·tion** N-VAR
/ˌɔːθəraɪˈzeɪʃən/ **authorizations** *The United Nations will approve his request for authorization to
use military force to deliver aid.*

author·ship /ˈɔːθəʃɪp/. The **authorship** of a piece N-UNCOUNT
of writing is the identity of the person who wrote it.
Its authorship has been disputed.

autism /ˈɔːtɪzəm/. **Autism** is a severe mental disor- N-UNCOUNT
der that begins in early childhood. People who suf-
fer from autism are unable to respond to other people. ◆ **autis·tic** /ɔːˈtɪstɪk/ ...*autistic children.* ADJ

auto /ˈɔːtəʊ/ **autos.** An **auto** is a car. ...*the auto*
industry. N-COUNT AMERICAN

auto·bio·graphi·cal /ˌɔːtəbaɪəˈɡræfɪkəl/. An ADJ-GRADED
autobiographical piece of writing relates to events
in the life of the person who has written it. ...*a highly autobiographical novel.*

auto·bi·og·ra·phy /ˌɔːtəbaɪˈɒɡrəfi/ **autobiogra-** ◆◆◇◇◇
phies. Your **autobiography** is an account of your N-COUNT
life, which you write yourself.

autoc·ra·cy /ɔːˈtɒkrəsi/ **autocracies. 1** Autocra- N-UNCOUNT
cy is government or management by one person
who has complete power. **2** An **autocracy** is a coun- N-COUNT
try or organization that is ruled by one person who
has complete power.

auto·crat /ˈɔːtəkræt/ **autocrats.** An **autocrat** is a N-COUNT
person in authority who has complete power.

auto·crat·ic /ˌɔːtəˈkrætɪk/. An **autocratic** person ◆◇◇◇◇
or organization has complete power and makes de- ADJ-GRADED
cisions without asking anyone else's advice.

auto·cue /ˈɔːtəʊkjuː/ **autocues.** An **autocue** is a N-COUNT
device used by people speaking on television or at a BRITISH
public event, which displays words for them to
read.

auto·graph /ˈɔːtəɡrɑːf, -ɡræf/ **autographs, auto-** ◆◇◇◇◇
graphing, autographed. 1 An **autograph** of a fa- N-COUNT
mous person is their signature, which they have
specially written for a fan to keep. *He went backstage and asked for her autograph.* ...*autograph
hunters.* **2** If someone famous **autographs** some- VERB: Vn
thing, they put their signature on it. ...*an auto-* V-ed
graphed photo of Clark Gable.

auto-im·mune; also spelled **autoimmune. Auto-** ADJ
immune describes medical conditions in which
normal cells are attacked by the body's immune
system.

auto·mate /ˈɔːtəmeɪt/ **automates, automating,** ◆◇◇◇◇
automated. To **automate** a factory, office, or in- VERB:
dustrial process means to install machines which V-ed
can do the work instead of people. ...*our new automated factory.* ◆ **auto·ma·tion** /ˌɔːtəˈmeɪʃən/ *Auto-* N-UNCOUNT
mation has reduced the work force here by half.

auto·mat·ic /ˌɔːtəˈmætɪk/ **automatics. 1** An ◆◆◆◇◇
automatic machine or device has controls that en- ADJ

A

able it to perform a task without needing to be constantly operated by a person. **Automatic** methods and processes involve the use of such machines. *Modern trains have automatic doors.* **2** An **automatic** is a gun that keeps firing shots until you stop pulling the trigger. *He drew his automatic... The gunmen opened fire with automatic weapons.* **3** An **automatic** is a car in which the gears change automatically as the car's speed increases or decreases. **4** An **automatic** action is one that you do without thinking about it. *All of the automatic body functions, even breathing, are affected.* ♦ **auto·mati·cal·ly** /ˌɔːtəˈmætɪkli/ *You will automatically wake up after this length of time.* **5** If something such as an action or a punishment is **automatic**, it is carried out without people needing to think about it, because it is the result of a fixed rule or method. *Those drivers should face an automatic charge of manslaughter.* ♦ **automatically** *Anyone giving in excess of £100 automatically becomes a member of the Trust.*

N-COUNT N-COUNT ADJ ADV-GRADED ADJ ADV

,**automatic 'pilot**; the form **autopilot** is also used. **1** If you are **on automatic pilot** or **on autopilot**, you are acting without thinking about what you are doing, usually because you have done it many times before. **2** An **automatic pilot** or an **autopilot** is a device in an aircraft that automatically keeps it on a particular course.

PHRASE N-SING

,**automatic trans'mission.** A car that is fitted with **automatic transmission** has a gear system in which the gears change automatically.

N-UNCOUNT

automa·ton /ɔːˈtɒmətən/ **automatons** or **automata** /ɔːˈtɒmətə/. You say that someone is an **automaton** when they behave as if they are so tired or bored that they do things without thinking; used showing disapproval. *I get sick of being thought of as a political automaton.*

N-COUNT PRAGMATICS

auto·mo·bile /ˈɔːtəməbiːl, AM -məʊˈbiːl/ **automobiles.** An automobile is a car.

♦♦◇◇◇ N-COUNT AMERICAN

auto·mo·tive /ˌɔːtəˈməʊtɪv/. Automotive is used to refer to things relating to cars. *...a chain of stores selling automotive parts.*

♦◇◇◇◇ ADJ: ADJ n

autono·mous /ɔːˈtɒnəməs/. An **autonomous** country, organization, or group governs or controls itself rather than being controlled by anyone else. ♦ **autono·mous·ly** *...a highly decentralised company, with each of its subsidiaries operating autonomously.* ♦ **autono·my** /ɔːˈtɒnəmi/ *Activists stepped up their demands for local autonomy.*

♦◇◇◇ ADJ-GRADED ADV N-UNCOUNT

auto·pi·lot /ˈɔːtəʊpaɪlət/. See **automatic pilot.**

autop·sy /ˈɔːtɒpsi/ **autopsies.** An **autopsy** is an examination of a dead body by a doctor who cuts it open in order to try to discover the cause of death.

♦◇◇◇◇ N-COUNT

autumn /ˈɔːtəm/ **autumns.** Autumn is the season between summer and winter when the weather becomes cooler and the leaves fall off the trees. The usual American word is **fall.**

♦♦◇◇ N-VAR

autum·nal /ɔːˈtʌmnəl/. **Autumnal** means relating to autumn or characteristic of autumn. *...the autumnal equinox. ...the autumnal colours of the trees.*

ADJ

aux·ilia·ry /ɔːgˈzɪljəri, AM -ləri/ **auxiliaries. 1** An **auxiliary** is a person who is employed to assist other people in their work. Auxiliaries are often medical workers or members of the armed forces. *...nursing auxiliaries.* **2 Auxiliary** staff and troops assist other staff and troops. **3 Auxiliary** equipment is extra equipment that is available for use when necessary. *...auxiliary fuel tanks.* **4** In grammar, an **auxiliary** or **auxiliary verb** is a verb which is used with a main verb, for example to form different tenses or to make the verb passive. In English, the basic auxiliary verbs are 'be', 'have', and 'do'. Modal verbs such as 'can' and 'will' are also sometimes called auxiliaries.

♦◇◇◇◇ N-COUNT ADJ: ADJ n ADJ: ADJ n N-COUNT

avail /əˈveɪl/ **avails, availing, availed. 1** If you do something **to no avail** or **to little avail**, what you do fails to achieve what you want. *His efforts were to no avail.* **2** If you **avail** yourself of an offer or opportunity, you

♦◇◇◇◇ PHRASE VERB

accept it or make use of it. *Guests should feel at liberty to avail themselves of your facilities.*

V pron-refl of n FORMAL

avail·able /əˈveɪləbəl/. **1** If something you want or need is **available**, you can obtain it. *Since 1978, the amount of money available to buy books has fallen by 17%... There are three small boats available for hire... According to the best available information, the facts are these.* ♦ **avail·abil·ity** /əˌveɪləˈbɪlɪti/ *...the easy availability of guns.* **2** Someone who is **available** is not busy and is therefore free to talk to you or to do a particular task. *Mr Leach is on holiday and is not available for comment.*

♦♦♦♦ ADJ N-UNCOUNT ADJ: v-link ADJ

ava·lanche /ˈævəlɑːntʃ, -læntʃ/ **avalanches. 1** An **avalanche** is a large mass of snow that falls down the side of a mountain. **2** You can refer to a very large quantity of things that all arrive somewhere or happen at the same time as an **avalanche** of them. *The newcomer was greeted with an avalanche of publicity.*

♦◇◇◇◇ N-COUNT N-SING

avant-garde /ˌævɒŋ ˈgɑːd/. **1 Avant-garde** art, music, and literature is very modern and experimental. **2** You can refer to the artists, writers, and musicians who introduce new and very modern ideas as the **avant-garde.** *In Paris he made friends among the avant-garde.*

♦◇◇◇◇ ADJ-GRADED N-SING: the N

ava·ri·cious /ˌævəˈrɪʃəs/. An **avaricious** person is very greedy for money or possessions. ♦ **ava·rice** /ˈævərɪs/. *He paid a month's rent in advance, just enough to satisfy the landlord's avarice.*

ADJ-GRADED LITERARY N-UNCOUNT

Ave. Ave. is a written abbreviation for **avenue** in the names of some streets. *...90 Dayton Ave.*

avenge /əˈvendʒ/ **avenges, avenging, avenged.** If you **avenge** a wrong or harmful act, you hurt or punish the person who is responsible for it. *He has devoted the past five years to avenging his daughter's death... She had decided to avenge herself and all the other women he had abused.* ♦ **aveng·er, avengers.**

♦◇◇◇◇ VERB V n N-COUNT

av·enue /ˈævɪnjuː, AM -nuː/ **avenues. 1** Avenue is used in the names of some streets. *...the most expensive stores on Park Avenue.* **2** An **avenue** is a wide straight road, often with trees on either side. **3** An **avenue** is a way of getting something done. *Talbot was presented with 80 potential avenues of investigation... There is another avenue to pursue – it involves further negotiations.*

♦♦◇◇◇ N-COUNT N-COUNT N-COUNT: with supp

aver /əˈvɜː/ **avers, averring, averred.** If you **aver** that something is the case, you say very firmly that it is the case. *Her girlfriends aver that men find her fascinating and alluring... 'Entertaining is something that everyone in the country can enjoy,' she averred.*

VERB V that V with quote FORMAL

av·er·age /ˈævərɪdʒ/ **averages, averaging, averaged. 1** An **average** is the result that you get when you add two or more numbers together and divide the total by the number of numbers you added together. ▶ Also an adjective. *The average price of goods rose by just 2.2%.* **2** You say **on average** or **on an average** to indicate that a number is the average of several numbers. *Every tonne of coal contains, on average, 30 kilograms of nitrogen.* **3** To **average** a particular amount means to do, get, or produce that amount as an average over a period of time. *We averaged 42 miles per hour.* **4** You use **average** to refer to a number or size that varies but is always approximately the same. *It takes an average of ten weeks for a house sale to be completed.* **5** An amount or quality that is **the average** is the normal amount or quality for a particular group of things or people. *35% of staff time was being spent on repeating work, about the average for a service industry.* ▶ Also an adjective. *£1.50 for a beer is average. ...a woman of average height.* **6** An **average** person or thing is typical or normal. *Packaging is about a third of what is found in an average British dustbin.* **7** If something is **average**, it is neither very good nor very bad. *I was only average academically.* ♦ **av·er·age·ly** *Most children are not geniuses or stars. They just do averagely well.* **8** ● **law of averages:** see **law.**

♦♦♦♦ N-COUNT ADJ: ADJ n PHRASE VERB V n N-SING: a N of amount N-SING: the N ADJ ADJ: ADJ n ADJ-GRADED ADV

average out. If a set of numbers **average out** to a

PHRASAL VB

particular figure or if you **average** them **out** to that figure, their average is calculated to be that figure. *There are six glasses of wine in one bottle, which averages out to 50p a glass... Averaging it out between us there's less than £10 a month each to live on.*

ERG
V P to/atn
V n P
Also V P noun

averse /ə'vɜːs/. If you say that you are not **averse** to something, you mean that you quite like it or quite want to do it. *He's not averse to publicity.*

◆◇◇◇◇
ADJ-GRADED
FORMAL

aver·sion /ə'vɜːʃən, AM -ʒən/ **aversions.** If you have an **aversion** to someone or something, you dislike them very much. *Many people have a natural and emotional aversion to insects.*

◆◇◇◇◇
N-VAR
FORMAL

avert /ə'vɜːt/ **averts, averting, averted. 1** If you **avert** something unpleasant, you prevent it from happening. *Talks with the teachers' union have averted a strike... A fresh tragedy was narrowly averted yesterday.* **2** If you **avert** your eyes or gaze from someone or something, you look away from them. *He avoids any eye contact, quickly averting his gaze when anyone approaches.*

◆◆◇◇◇
VERB
V n

VERB
V n
Also V n from
n

aviary /'eɪvjəri/ **aviaries.** An **aviary** is a large cage or covered area in which birds are kept.

◆◇◇◇◇
N-COUNT

avia·tion /ˌeɪvi'eɪʃən/. **Aviation** is the operation and production of aircraft.

◆◆◇◇◇
N-UNCOUNT

avia·tor /'eɪvieɪtə/ **aviators.** An **aviator** is a pilot of a plane, especially in the early times of aviation.

N-COUNT
DATED

avid /'ævɪd/. You use **avid** to describe someone who is very enthusiastic about something that they do. *...an avid collector of art.* ◆ **av·id·ly** *...a most entertaining magazine, which I read avidly each month.* **2** If someone is **avid** for something, they are very eager to get it. *He was intensely eager, indeed avid, for wealth.* ◆ **avidly** *Western suppliers too are competing avidly for business abroad.*

◆◇◇◇◇
ADJ-GRADED

ADV-GRADED:
ADV with v

ADJ-GRADED:
v-link ADJ

ADV-GRADED:
ADV with v

avi·on·ics /ˌeɪvi'ɒnɪks/. **Avionics** is the science of electronics used in aviation.

N-UNCOUNT
TECHNICAL

avo·ca·do /ˌævə'kɑːdəʊ/ **avocados. Avocados** or **avocado pears** are green pear-shaped tropical fruit. They have hard skins and contain large stones.

◆◇◇◇◇
N-VAR

avoid /ə'vɔɪd/ **avoids, avoiding, avoided. 1** If you **avoid** something unpleasant that might happen, you take action in order to prevent it from happening. *The pilots had to take emergency action to avoid a disaster... Women have to dress modestly, to avoid being harassed by the locals.* **2** If you **avoid** something you do not want or like, you behave in such a way that you do not have to do it or get involved with it. *By borrowing from dozens of banks, he managed to avoid giving any of them an overall picture of what he was up to... The officials said North Korea was trying to avoid dialogue with the South.* **3** If you **avoid** someone, you try to not to see them, speak to them, or have any contact with them. **4** If a person or vehicle **avoids** someone or something, they change the direction they are moving in, so that they do not hit them. **5 ● avoid** someone or something **like the plague**: see **plague**.

◆◆◆◇◇
VERB
V n
V-ing

VERB
V-ing
V n

VERB: V n

VERB

avoid·able /ə'vɔɪdəbəl/. Something that is **avoidable** can be prevented from happening. *The tragedy was entirely avoidable.*

ADJ-GRADED

avoid·ance /ə'vɔɪdəns/. **Avoidance** of someone or something is the act of avoiding them. *Anyone can improve his or her own health by the avoidance of stress.*

◆◇◇◇◇
N-UNCOUNT

avow /ə'vaʊ/ **avows, avowing, avowed.** If you **avow** something, you admit it or declare it. *...a public statement avowing neutrality... The Prime Minister avowed that he saw no need to change his country's policies.*

VERB
V n
Also V with
quote
FORMAL

avowed /ə'vaʊd/. **1** If you are an **avowed** supporter or opponent of something, you have declared that you support it or oppose it. *She is an avowed vegetarian.* ◆ **avow·ed·ly** /ə'vaʊɪdli/ *He remained for some years avowedly radical in his political outlook.* **2** An **avowed** belief or aim is one that you have declared formally or publicly. *...the council's avowed intention to stamp on racism.*

◆◇◇◇◇
ADJ: ADJ n
FORMAL

ADV

ADJ: ADJ n
FORMAL

avun·cu·lar /ə'vʌŋkjʊlə/. An **avuncular** man is friendly and helpful to younger people.

ADJ-GRADED
FORMAL

await /ə'weɪt/ **awaits, awaiting, awaited. 1** If you **await** someone or something, you wait for them. *...as we awaited the arrival of the chairman.* **2** Something that **awaits** you is going to happen or come to you in the future. *A nasty surprise awaited them in Rosemary Lane.*

◆◆◇◇◇
VERB
V n
FORMAL
VERB
V n
FORMAL

awake /ə'weɪk/ **awakes, awaking, awoke, awoken. 1** Someone who is **awake** is not sleeping. *...a large dog, which kept neighbours awake by howling every night.* **2** Someone who is **wide awake** is fully awake. **3** When you **awake** or when something **awakes** you, you wake up. *The sound of many voices awoke her with a start.*

◆◆◇◇◇

v-link ADJ,
ADJ after v
PHRASE
V-ERG: V
V n
V n V prep
LITERARY

awak·en /ə'weɪkən/ **awakens, awakening, awakened. 1** To **awaken** a feeling in a person means to cause them to start having that feeling. *The aim of the cruise was to awaken an interest in and an understanding of foreign cultures.* ◆ **awakening, awakenings.** *...the awakening of national consciousness in people. ...a young woman's sexual awakening.* **2** When you **awaken** to a fact or when someone **awakens** you to it, you become aware of it. *The British never awaken to peril until it is almost too late.* **3** When you **awaken**, or when something or someone **awakens** you, you wake up.

◆◇◇◇◇
VERB
V n
LITERARY

N-COUNT

V-ERG
V to n
V n to n
LITERARY
V-ERG: V
LITERARY

awak·en·ing /ə'weɪkənɪŋ/ **awakenings.** If you have a **rude awakening**, you are suddenly made aware of an unpleasant fact. ● See also **awaken**.

PHRASE

award /ə'wɔːd/ **awards, awarding, awarded. 1** An **award** is a prize or certificate that a person is given for doing something well. *...the Booker Prize, Britain's top award for fiction.* **2** If someone **is awarded** something such as a prize or an examination mark, it is given to them. *She was awarded the prize for both films... The Mayor awarded him a medal of merit.* **3** In law, an **award** is a sum of money that a court decides should be given to someone. *...workmen's compensation awards.* **4** If someone such as a judge or referee **awards** something to someone, they decide that it will be given to that person. *A High Court judge had awarded him £6 million damages.* **5** A pay **award** is an increase in pay for a group of workers. *...this year's average pay award for teachers of just under 8%.*

◆◆◆◇
N-COUNT

VERB
be V-ed n
V n n
Also V n to n

N-COUNT

VERB
V n n
Also V n

N-COUNT
BRITISH

aware /ə'weə/. **1** If you are **aware** of something, you know about it. *Smokers are well aware of the dangers to their own health... He must have been aware that my parents' marriage was breaking up.* ◆ **aware·ness** *The 1980s brought a growing awareness of green issues.* **2** If you are **aware** of something, you realize that it is present or is happening because you hear it, see it, smell it, or feel it. *She was acutely aware of the noise of the city.* **3** Someone who is **aware** notices events that are happening around them, or events that are happening generally in the world. *They are politically very aware.*

◆◆◆◇
ADJ-GRADED:
v-link ADJ

N-UNCOUNT
ADJ-GRADED:
v-link ADJ,
ADJ of n,
ADJ that
ADJ-GRADED:
v-link ADJ

awash /ə'wɒʃ/. **1** If the ground or a floor is **awash**, there is a lot of water on it. **2** If a place is **awash** with something, it contains a large amount of it. *...a company which is awash with cash.*

◆◇◇◇◇
v-link ADJ
v-link ADJ
ADJ:
v-link ADJ

away /ə'weɪ/. **Away** is often used with verbs of movement, such as 'go' and 'drive', and also in phrasal verbs such as 'do away with' and 'fade away'.

◆◆◆◆◇

1 If someone or something moves or is moved **away** from a place, they move or are moved so that they are no longer there. If you are **away** from a place, you are not in the place where people expect you to be. *He walked away from his car... The waitress whipped the plate away... Jason was away on a business trip.* **2** If you put or tidy something **away**, you put it in its proper place. If you hide someone or something **away**, you put them in a place where nobody can see them or find them. *All her letters were carefully filed away in folders... I have $100m hidden away where no one will ever find it.* **3** If something is **away from** a person or place, it is at a distance from that person or place. *The two women were sitting as far away from each other as possible... I was anxious to get him here, away from*

ADV:
ADV after v,
be ADV

ADV:
ADV after v

PHR-PREP

family and friends. **4** When a sports team plays **away**, ADV: ADV after v
it plays on its opponents' ground. ▶ Also an adjective. ADJ: ADJ n
Carlton are about to play an important away match.
5 If you look or turn **away** from something, you move ADV: ADV after v
your head so that you are no longer looking at it.
6 You can use **away** to say that something slowly dis- ADV: ADV after v
appears or becomes less significant. *So much snow
has already melted away... The Liberal Democrats'
support fell away at the last minute.* **7** You use **away** to ADV: be amount ADV
talk about future events. For example, if an event is a
week **away**, it will happen after a week. *...the Washington summit, now only just over two weeks away.* **8** You ADV
use **away** to show that there has been a change or development from one state or situation to another.
*There's been a dramatic shift away from traditional
careers towards business and commerce.*
9 You can use **away** after a verb to emphasize a con- ADV: ADV after v
tinuous or repeated action. *He would often be working
away on his word processor late into the night... She
sighed, her heart banging away against her ribs as she
opened the door.*
10 ● right away: see **right. ● far and away:** see **far.**

awe /ɔː/ **awes, awed. 1 Awe** is the feeling of re- ◇◇◇◇ N-UNCOUNT
spect and amazement that you have when you are
faced with something wonderful and often rather
frightening. *She gazed in awe at the great stones...
The higher we climbed, the more awe-inspiring the
scenery became.* **2** If you **are awed** by someone or VB: usu passive, no cont be V-ed V-ed
something, they make you feel respectful and
amazed, and often rather frightened. *I am still awed
by David's courage... The crowd listened in awed silence.* **3** If you are **in awe** of someone, you have a PHRASE
lot of respect for them and are slightly afraid of
them.
awe·some /ˈɔːsəm/. You say something is **awe-** ◇◇◇◇ ADJ-GRADED
some when it is frightening because of its great size,
strength, or importance. *...the awesome power of the
Zulu soldiers. ...the awesome responsibility of sending men into combat.* ♦ **awe·some·ly** *It was quiet* ADV
in the streets, awesomely quiet.
awe·struck /ˈɔːstrʌk/. If someone is **awestruck**, ADJ-GRADED WRITTEN
they are very impressed and amazed by someone or
something. *I stood and gazed at him, awestruck that
anyone could be so beautiful.*
aw·ful /ˈɔːfʊl/. **1** If you say that someone or some- ◆◆◇◇ ADJ-GRADED PRAGMATICS
thing is **awful**, you dislike them or you think that
they are not very good. *I couldn't stand London!
Bloody awful place... The weather's awful.* ♦ **aw·ful-** N-UNCOUNT
·ness *The programme's awfulness has ensured it is
talked about.* **2** If you say that something is **awful**, ADJ-GRADED
you mean that it is extremely unpleasant, shocking,
or bad. *Her injuries were massive. It was awful...
Some of their offences are so awful they would chill
the blood.* **3** If you look or feel **awful**, you look or ADJ-GRADED: v-link ADJ
feel ill. *I hardly slept at all and felt pretty awful.*
4 You can use **awful** with noun groups that refer to an ADJ: ADJ n PRAGMATICS
amount in order to emphasize how large that amount
is. *I've got an awful lot of work to do.* **5** You can use **aw-** ADV: ADV adj PRAGMATICS AMERICAN
ful with adjectives that describe a quality in order to
emphasize that quality. *Gosh, you're awful pretty...
You know, 10 years sounds like an awful long time.*
aw·ful·ly /ˈɔːfʊli/. You use **awfully** with adjectives ◇◇◇◇ ADV: ADV adj/adv
or adverbs that describe a quality in order to em-
phasize that quality. *The caramel looks awfully
good... I'm awfully sorry.*
awhile /əˈwaɪl/. **Awhile** means for a short time. In ◇◇◇◇ N-UNCOUNT AMERICAN
British English, it is usually written 'a while': See
while. *My mother went over to my aunt's house to
stay for awhile.* ▶ Also an adverb. *He worked awhile* ADV
as a pharmacist.
awk·ward /ˈɔːkwəd/. **1** An **awkward** situation is ◆◆◇◇ ADJ-GRADED
embarrassing and difficult to deal with. *...awkward
questions... There was an awkward moment as couples decided whether to stand next to their partners.*
♦ **awk·ward·ly** *There was an awkwardly long si-* ADV
lence. ...an awkwardly timed meeting. **2** Something ADJ-GRADED
that is **awkward** to use or carry is difficult to use or
carry because of its design. A job that is **awkward** is
difficult to do. *Full-size tripods can be awkward,*

especially if you're shooting a low-level subject. ADV ADJ-GRADED
♦ **awkwardly** *The autoexposure button is awkwardly placed under the lens release button.* **3** An
awkward movement or position is uncomfortable ADV-GRADED:
or clumsy. *Amy made an awkward gesture with her
hands.* ♦ **awkwardly** *He fell awkwardly and went* ADV with v ADJ-GRADED
down in agony clutching his right knee. **4** Someone
who feels **awkward** behaves in a shy or embarrassed way. *They feel awkward taking the initiative* ADV-GRADED
in sex. ♦ **awkwardly** *'This is Malcolm,' the girl said* N-UNCOUNT
awkwardly, to fill the silence. ♦ **awk·ward·ness** *He
displayed all the awkwardness of adolescence.*
5 If you say that someone is **awkward**, you are criti- ADJ-GRADED
cizing them because you find them unreasonable and PRAGMATICS BRITISH
difficult to live with or deal with.
awn·ing /ˈɔːnɪŋ/ **awnings.** An **awning** is a piece of N-COUNT
material attached to a caravan or building which
provides shelter from the rain or sun.
awoke /əˈwəʊk/. **Awoke** is the past tense of **awake.**
awok·en /əˈwəʊkən/. **Awoken** is the past participle
of **awake.**
AWOL /ˈeɪwɒl/. **1** If someone in the armed forces ADJ
goes **AWOL**, they leave their post without the permission of a superior officer. **AWOL** is an abbreviation for 'absent without leave'. **2** If you say that ADJ INFORMAL
someone has gone **AWOL**, you mean that they have
disappeared without telling anyone where they
were going. *His real father had gone AWOL about 17
years earlier, and after that his mother had
remarried.*
awry /əˈraɪ/. **1** If something goes **awry**, it does not ADJ-GRADED: v-link ADJ
happen in the way that it was planned. *She was in a
fury over a plan that had gone awry.* **2** If something ADJ-GRADED: v-link ADJ WRITTEN
is **awry**, it is not in its normal or proper position.
His dark hair was all awry.
axe /æks/ **axes, axing, axed;** spelled **ax** in ◆◆◇◇ N-COUNT
American English. **1** An **axe** is a tool for cutting
wood. It consists of a heavy metal blade sharpened
at one edge and attached by its other edge to the
end of a long handle. See picture headed **tools.** **2** If VB: usu passive be V-ed
someone's job or something such as a public ser-
vice or a television programme **is axed**, it is ended
suddenly and without discussion. **3** If a person or N-SING: the N JOURNALISM
institution is facing **the axe**, that person is likely to
lose their job or that institution is likely to be
closed. *St Bartholomew's is one of four London hos-
pitals facing the axe.* **4** If you say that someone has PHRASE PRAGMATICS INFORMAL
an axe to grind, you mean their reason for doing
something in a particular situation is motivated by
selfishness.
axe·man /ˈæksmæn/ **axemen.** Someone who N-COUNT JOURNALISM
makes changes in an organization by sacking peo-
ple can be referred to as an **axeman.**
axes. **1 Axes,** pronounced /ˈæksɪz/, is the plural of
axe. **2 Axes,** pronounced /ˈæksiːz/, is the plural of
axis.
axi·om /ˈæksiəm/ **axioms.** An **axiom** is a statement N-COUNT FORMAL
or idea which people accept as being true. *...the
long-held axiom that education leads to higher
income.*
axio·mat·ic /ˌæksiəˈmætɪk/. If something is **axio-** ADJ FORMAL
matic, it seems to be obviously true. *It is axiomatic
that as people grow older they generally become less
agile.*
axis /ˈæksɪs/ **axes. 1** An **axis** is an imaginary line ◆◇◇◇ N-COUNT
through the middle of something. **2** An **axis** of a N-COUNT
graph is one of the two lines on which the scales of
measurement are marked.
axle /ˈæksəl/ **axles.** An **axle** is a rod connecting a ◆◇◇◇ N-COUNT
pair of wheels on a car or other vehicle.
aya·tol·lah /ˌaɪəˈtɒlə/ **ayatollahs.** An **ayatollah** is N-COUNT; N-TITLE
one of a class of Shiite Muslim religious leaders.
aye /aɪ/ **ayes. 1 Aye** means yes in some dialects of CONVENTION
British English. **2 The ayes** are the people who vote N-PLURAL: the N
in favour of something. *The Ayes to the right, 437.
The Noes to the left, 35. So the Ayes have it.*
az·ure /ˈæʒʊə/. **Azure** is used to describe things that COLOUR LITERARY
are bright blue. *...warm azure seas.*

Bb

B, b /biː/ **B's, b's.** **1** B is the second letter of the English alphabet. **2** In music, **B** is the seventh note in the scale of C major. **3** If you get a **B** as a mark for a piece of work or in an exam, your work is fairly good. **4** B or b is used as an abbreviation for words beginning with b, for example 'born'. N-VAR / N-VAR / N-VAR

BA /ˌbiː 'eɪ/ **BAs.** **1** A BA is a first degree in an arts subject. BA is an abbreviation for 'Bachelor of Arts'. **2** BA is written after someone's name to indicate that they have a BA. ...*Helen Kich, BA (Hons).* ◆◇◇◇◇ N-COUNT

bab·ble /'bæbəl/ **babbles, babbling, babbled.** **1** If someone **babbles**, they talk in a confused or excited way. *Momma babbled on and on about how he was ruining me... They all babbled simultaneously.* **2** You can refer to people's voices as a **babble** of sound when they are excited and confused, preventing you from understanding what they are saying. ...*the high babble of voices.* ◆◇◇◇◇ VERB V on/away V / N-SING

babe /beɪb/ **babes.** **1** Some people use **babe** as an affectionate way of addressing someone with whom they have an intimate relationship. *I'm sorry, babe. I didn't mean it.* **2** Some men refer to an attractive young woman as a **babe**. **3** A **babe** is the same as a baby. ...*as innocent as a newborn babe.* ◆◇◇◇◇ N-VOC PRAGMATICS INFORMAL N-COUNT N-COUNT DATED

ba·boon /bæ'buːn/ **baboons.** A **baboon** is a type of monkey that lives in Africa. N-COUNT

baby /'beɪbi/ **babies.** **1** A **baby** is a very young child, especially one that cannot yet walk or talk. *My wife has just had a baby.* **2** If you **are left holding the baby**, you are put in a situation where you are responsible for something, often in an unfair way because other people fail or refuse to take responsibility for it.
3 A **baby** animal is a very young animal.
4 **Baby** vegetables are vegetables picked when they are very small.
5 Some people use **baby** as an affectionate way of addressing someone or referring to someone. *He was confused, poor baby.* ◆◆◆◇◇ N-COUNT PHRASE INFORMAL N-COUNT ADJ: ADJ n N-VOC; N-COUNT INFORMAL

'baby boom, baby booms. A **baby boom** is a period of time when a lot of babies are born in a particular place or country. N-COUNT INFORMAL

baby boom·er /'beɪbi buːmə/ **baby boomers;** also spelled **baby-boomer.** A **baby boomer** is someone who was born in Great Britain or the United States during the years 1945-1949, when there was a baby boom. ...*a now middle-aged baby boomer.* N-COUNT INFORMAL, JOURNALISM

'baby buggy, baby buggies. **1** A **baby buggy** is a small seat with wheels, which a young child can sit in and which can be pushed around. **2** A **baby buggy** is the same as a **pram**. N-COUNT BRITISH N-COUNT AMERICAN

'baby carriage, baby carriages. A **baby carriage** is the same as a **pram**. N-COUNT AMERICAN

ba·by·hood /'beɪbihʊd/. Your **babyhood** is the period of your life when you were a baby. N-UNCOUNT

ba·by·ish /'beɪbiɪʃ/. **Babyish** actions, feelings, or looks are like a baby's. ...*a fat, babyish face.* ADJ-GRADED

baby·sit /'beɪbisɪt/ **babysits, babysitting, babysat.** If you **babysit** for someone or **babysit** their children, you look after their children while they are out. *I promised to babysit for Mrs Plunkett... You can take it in turns to babysit.* ♦ **baby·sitter,** **babysitters** ...*a good babysitter.* ♦ **baby·sitting** *Would you like me to do any babysitting?* ◆◇◇◇◇ VERB V for n V Also V n N-COUNT N-UNCOUNT

'baby talk is the language used by babies when they are just learning to speak, or the way in which some adults speak when they are talking to babies. N-UNCOUNT

bac·ca·lau·re·ate /ˌbækə'lɔːriət/. The **international baccalaureate** is an internationally recognized course of study which can be taken in certain schools throughout the world. N-SING

bach·elor /'bætʃələ/ **bachelors.** **1** A **bachelor** is a man who has never married. **2** **Bachelor** is used in titles such as 'Bachelor of Arts' or 'Bachelor of Science' to indicate that a person has a first degree in the arts or the sciences. N-COUNT N-COUNT

'bachelor's degree, bachelor's degrees. A **bachelor's degree** is a first degree awarded by universities. ● See also **BA, BSc.** N-COUNT

back 1 adverb uses

back /bæk/. In addition to the uses shown below, **back** is also used in phrasal verbs such as 'date back' and 'fall back on'. ◆◆◆◆◆
1 If you move **back**, you move in the opposite direction to the one in which you are facing. *The photographers drew back... She stepped back from the door... She pushes back her chair and stands.* **2** If someone moves **back and forth**, they repeatedly move in one direction and then in the opposite direction. *He paced back and forth. ...tossing a baseball back and forth.*
3 If someone or something goes **back** somewhere, they return to the place where they were before. *I went back to bed... Smith changed his mind and moved back home... I'll be back as soon as I can.* **4** If someone or something is **back** in a particular state, they were in that state before and are now in it again. *Denise hopes to be back at work by the time her daughter is one.* **5** If you give or put something **back**, you return it to the person who had it or to the place where it was before you took it. If you get or take something **back**, you then have it again after not having it for a while. *She handed the knife back... Put it back in the freezer... You'll get your money back.* **6** You can say that you go or come **back** to a particular point in a conversation to show that you are mentioning it again. *Going back to the school, how many staff are there?* **7** You use **back** in expressions like **back in London** or **back at the house** when you are giving an account, to show that you are going to start talking about what happened or was happening in the place you mention. *Meanwhile, back in New York, Sid was back to his old tricks.* **8** If something is or comes **back**, it is fashionable again after it has been unfashionable for some time. *Consensus politics could easily come back.*
9 If you put a clock or watch **back**, you change the time shown on it so that it shows an earlier time.
10 If you talk about something that happened **back in** the past or several years **back**, you are emphasizing that it happened quite a long time ago. *The story starts back in 1950, when I was five. ...that terrorist attack a few years back.* **11** If you think **back** to something that happened in the past, you remember it or try to remember it. *I thought back to the time in 1975 when my son was desperately ill.* ● **to cast your mind back:** see **mind.**
12 If you write or call **back**, you write to or telephone someone after they have written to or telephoned you. If you look **back** at someone, you look at them after they have started looking at you. *If the phone rings say you'll call back... Lee looked at Theodora. She stared back.*
13 If someone or something is kept or situated **back** from a place, they are at a distance away from it. *Keep back from the edge of the platform.* **14** If something is held or tied **back**, it is held or tied so that it does not ADV PHRASE ADV ADV ADV ADV PRAGMATICS ADV PRAGMATICS ADV ADV: ADV after v ADV in PRAGMATICS ADV ADV ADV: ADV after v

hang loosely over something. *Her hair was tied back.* **15** If you lie or sit **back**, you move your body backwards into a relaxed sloping or flat position. *She leaned back in her chair and smiled.* **16** If you look or shout **back** at someone or something, you turn to look or shout at them when they are behind you. *Nick looked back over his shoulder... He called back to her.* `ADV: ADV after v` `ADV`

back 2 opposite of front; noun and adjective uses

back /bæk/ **backs. 1** A person's or animal's **back** is the part of their body between their head and their legs that is on the opposite side to their chest. See picture headed **human body**. *She turned her back to the audience. ...the victims were shot in the back.* `◆◆◆◆` `N-COUNT`

2 If you say that something was done **behind** someone**'s back**, you disapprove of it because it was done without them knowing about it, in an unfair or dishonest way. *You eat her food, enjoy her hospitality and then criticize her behind her back.* **3** If you tell someone to **get off** your **back**, you are telling them angrily to stop criticizing you or putting pressure on you. **4** If you say that you will be glad **to see the back of** someone, you mean that you want them to leave. **5** If you **turn** your **back on** someone or something, you ignore them, leave them, or reject them. *Stacey Lattisaw has turned her back on her singing career.* **6** If someone or something **puts** your **back up** or **gets** your **back up**, they annoy you. **7** If you **break the back of** a task or problem, you do the most difficult part of what is necessary to complete the task or solve the problem. *We've broken the back of inflation in this country.* `PHRASE` `PRAGMATICS` `PHRASE INFORMAL` `PHRASE INFORMAL` `PHRASE` `PHRASE INFORMAL` `PHRASE`

8 The **back** of something is the side or part of it that is towards the rear or farthest from the front. *...a room at the back of the shop. ...the back of her neck... Her room was on the third floor, at the back.* **9** Back is used to refer to the side or part of something that is towards the rear or farthest from the front. *...the back door. ...the back seat of their car. ...the back garden.* **10** You can use **back** in expressions such as **round the back** and **out the back** to refer generally to the area behind a house or other building. *He had chickens and things round the back.* **11** You use **back** in expressions such as **in the back** and **out back** to refer to the area behind a house or other building. You also use **in back** to refer to the rear part of something, especially a car or building. *He would be out back on the patio cleaning his shoes... I sat in back.* **12** If you are wearing something **back to front**, you are wearing it incorrectly, with the back of it at the front of your body. If you do or write something **back to front**, you do or write it the wrong way around. *He wears his baseball cap back to front... The picture was printed back to front.* `N-COUNT` `ADJ: ADJ n` `N-SING: prep the N SPOKEN, BRITISH` `N-UNCOUNT: prep N AMERICAN` `PHRASE`

13 The **back** of a chair or settee is the part that you lean against when you sit on it. **14** The **back** of a piece of paper or an envelope is the side which is less important. *...the back of a postcard.* **15** The **back** of a book is the part nearest the end. *...the index at the back of the book.* **16** In team games such as football and hockey, a **back** is a player who is concerned mainly with preventing the other team from scoring goals. **17** ● **off the back of a lorry:** see **lorry.** ● **to have your back to the wall:** see **wall.** `N-COUNT` `N-COUNT: the N` `N-COUNT: the N` `N-COUNT`

back 3 verb uses

back /bæk/ **backs, backing, backed. 1** If a building **backs** onto something, the back of it faces in the direction of that thing or touches the edge of that thing. *...a ground floor flat which backs on to a busy street.* **2** When you **back** a car or other vehicle somewhere or when it **backs** somewhere, it moves backwards. *He backed his car out of the drive... The train backed out of Adelaide Yard.* **3** If you **back** a person or a course of action, you support them, for example by voting for them. *...a new witness to back his claim that he is a victim of mistaken identity.* ♦ **-backed** *...government-backed loans to Egypt.* **4** If you **back** someone in a competition, you predict that they will win, and usually you bet money that they will win. *It is upsetting to discover that you* `◆◆◆◆` `VERB V onto n` `V-ERG V n V` `VERB V n` `COMB VERB V n`

have *backed a loser.* **5** If a singer **is backed** by a band or by other singers, they provide the musical accompaniment for the singer. **6** See also **backing.** `VERB: be V-ed`

back away. 1 If you **back away** from a commitment that you made or something that you were involved with in the past, you try to show that you are no longer committed to it or involved with it. *He's backing away from the policies and style of his predecessor.* **2** If you **back away**, you walk backwards away from someone or something, often because you are frightened of them. `PHRASAL VB V P from n Also V P` `V P`

back down. If you **back down**, you withdraw a claim, demand, or commitment that you made earlier, because other people are strongly opposed to it. *The Clinton Administration has backed down on its proposal to provide free vaccines to all children.* `PHRASAL VB V P`

back off. 1 If you **back off**, you move away in order to avoid problems or a fight. *They backed off in horror.* **2** If you **back off** from a claim, demand, or commitment that you made earlier, or if you **back off** it, you withdraw it. *The Conservatives were backing off from green policies.* `PHRASAL VB V P` `V P Also V P n`

back out. If you **back out**, you decide not to do something that you previously agreed to do. *The Hungarians backed out of the project in 1989.* `PHRASAL VB V P V P of n`

back up. 1 If someone or something **backs up** a statement, they supply evidence to suggest that it is true. *Radio signals received from the galaxy's centre back up the black hole theory.* **2** If an idea or intention **is backed up** by action, action is taken to support or confirm it. *The declaration must now be backed up by concrete and effective actions... It is time the Government backed up its advert campaigns.* **3** If you **back** someone **up**, you show your support for them. *His employers, Norfolk social services, backed him up.* **4** If you **back** someone **up**, you help them by confirming that what they are saying is true, even if you know it is not true. *The girl denied being there, and the man backed her up.* **5** If you **back up**, the car or other vehicle that you are driving moves back a short distance. *Back up, Hans... He backed up a few feet and rolled the window down.* **6** If you **back up**, you move backwards a short distance. **7** See also **backup.** `PHRASAL VB V P noun` `be V-ed P V P noun Also V n P` `V n P Also V P noun` `V n P Also V P noun` `V P V P amount` `V P`

back·ache /'bækeɪk/ **backaches. Backache** is a dull pain in your back. `N-VAR`

back·bencher /ˌbæk'bentʃə/ **backbenchers.** A **backbencher** is an MP who is not a minister and who does not hold an official position in any party. `◆◇◇◇ N-COUNT BRITISH`

back·benches /ˌbæk'bentʃɪz/; the form **backbench** is used as a modifier. The **backbenches** are the seats in the House of Commons where backbenchers sit. The Members of Parliament who sit on the backbenches are also referred to as the **backbenches.** *...the Conservative Party's backbench committee on Northern Ireland.* `N-PLURAL BRITISH`

back·bit·ing /'bækbaɪtɪŋ/. If you accuse someone of **backbiting**, you mean that they say unpleasant or unkind things about someone who is not present. `N-UNCOUNT`

back·bone /'bækbəʊn/ **backbones. 1** Your **backbone** is the column of small linked bones down the middle of your back. **2** The **backbone** of an organization is the part of it that gives it its main strength. *The small business people of Britain are the economic backbone of the nation.* **3** If you say that someone has no **backbone**, you think they do not have the courage to do things which need to be done. *You might be taking drastic measures and you've got to have the backbone to do that.* `◆◇◇◇ N-COUNT` `N-SING` `N-UNCOUNT`

'back-breaking. Back-breaking work involves a lot of hard physical effort. `ADJ-GRADED`

'back burner. If you put an issue on the back **burner**, you leave it in order to deal with it later. *She has looked after her three children with her career very much on the back burner.* `N-SING`

'back 'catalogue, back catalogues. A musical performer's **back catalogue** is the music which they recorded and released in the past. `N-COUNT`

back·cloth /'bækklɒθ, AM klɔːθ/ **backcloths.** A backcloth is the same as a **backdrop**. N-COUNT BRITISH

back·comb /,bæk'kəum/ **backcombs, back-combing, backcombed.** If you **backcomb** your hair, you move a comb through your hair towards your scalp instead of away from it, so that your hair looks thicker. VERB: V n

,**back 'copy, back copies.** A back copy of a magazine or newspaper is the same as a **back issue**. N-COUNT

'**back country.** The **back country** is an area that is a long way from any city and has very few people living in it. N-SING: theN AMERICAN

back·date /,bæk'deɪt/ **backdates, backdating, backdated;** also spelled **back-date**. If a document or an arrangement **is backdated**, it is valid from a date before the date when it is completed or signed. *The contract that was signed on Thursday morning was backdated to March 11.* VERB beV-ed to n Also V n

back·door /,bæk'dɔː/; also spelled **back door**. If you say that someone is doing something through or by the **backdoor**, you disapprove of them because they are doing it in a secret, indirect, or dishonest way. ► Also an adjective. ...*talk of greedy MPs voting themselves a backdoor pay rise.* N-SING: theN PRAGMATICS
ADJ: ADJ n

back·drop /'bækdrɒp/ **backdrops. 1** A backdrop is a large piece of cloth, often with scenery painted on it, that is hung at the back of a stage while a play is being performed. **2** The **backdrop** to an event is the general situation in which it happens. *The election will take place against a backdrop of increasing instability.* ◆◇◇◇◇ N-COUNT
N-COUNT

back·er /'bækə/ **backers.** A backer is someone who helps or supports a project, organization, or person, often by giving or lending money. ◆◇◇◇◇ N-COUNT

back·fire /,bæk'faɪə, AM -'faɪr/ **backfires, back-firing, backfired. 1** If a plan or project **backfires**, it has the opposite result to the one that was intended. *The President's tactics could backfire.* **2** When a motor vehicle or its engine **backfires**, it produces an explosion in the exhaust pipe. ◆◆◇◇◇ VERB V
VERB: V

back·gam·mon /'bækgæmən/. **Backgammon** is a game for two people in which the players throw dice and move discs around a board. N-UNCOUNT

back·ground /'bækgraund/ **backgrounds. 1** Your **background** is the kind of family you come from and the kind of education or career you have had. *She came from a working-class Yorkshire background.* **2** The **background** to an event or situation consists of the facts that explain what caused it. ...*a background of continuing political violence.* **3** The **background** is sounds which you can hear but which you are not listening to with your full attention. ...*the sound of applause in the background.* **4** You can use **background** to refer to the things in a picture or scene that are less noticeable or important than the main things or people in it. ...*roses patterned on a blue background.* ● Someone who stays **in the background** avoids being noticed, although the things that they do are important. ◆◆◇◇◇ N-COUNT
N-COUNT
N-SING: theN
N-COUNT
PHRASE

back·hand /'bækhænd/ **backhands.** A backhand is a shot in tennis or squash, which you make with your arm across your body. N-VAR

back·hand·ed /,bæk'hændɪd/. **1** A **backhanded** compliment is a remark which appears to be an insult but could also be interpreted as a compliment. A **backhanded** compliment is also a remark which appears to be a compliment but could also be interpreted as an insult. *Even my good reviews have tended to be back-handed compliments.* **2** If you say that someone is doing something in a **backhanded** way, you disapprove of their action because they are doing it in an indirect way. *In a backhanded way, Milton Friedman raises yet another objection to high taxes.* ADJ: ADJ n
ADJ-GRADED: ADJ n
PRAGMATICS

back·hand·er /'bækhændə/ **backhanders.** A backhander is an amount of money that is secretly paid to someone in order to get them to do something illegal. The American word is **kickback**. N-COUNT BRITISH, INFORMAL

back·ing /'bækɪŋ/ **backings. 1** If someone or something has the **backing** of an organization or an ◆◆◆◇◇ N-UNCOUNT important person, they receive support or money from that organization or person in order to do something. *The president had the full backing of his government to negotiate a deal.* **2** A **backing** is a layer of something such as cloth that is put onto the back of something in order to strengthen it. **3** The **backing** of a popular song is the music which is sung or played to accompany the main tune. *Sharon also sang backing vocals for Barry Manilow.* N-VAR
N-COUNT BRITISH

,**back 'issue, back issues.** A back issue of a magazine or newspaper is an edition of it that was published some time ago. N-COUNT

back·lash /'bæklæʃ/. A backlash against a tendency or recent development in society or politics is a sudden strong reaction against it. ...*the male backlash against feminism.* ◆◇◇◇◇ N-SING

back·less /'bækləs/. A backless dress leaves most of a woman's back uncovered. ADJ

back·log /'bæklɒg/ **backlogs.** A backlog is a number of things which have not yet been done but which need to be done. ...*a backlog of repairs and maintenance in schools.* ◆◇◇◇◇ N-COUNT

,**back 'number, back numbers.** A back number of a magazine or newspaper is the same as a **back issue.** N-COUNT

back·pack /'bækpæk/ **backpacks.** A backpack is a bag with straps that go over your shoulders, so that you can carry things on your back. N-COUNT

back·pack·ing /'bækpækɪŋ/. If you go **backpacking**, you go travelling or hiking with a backpack. N-UNCOUNT
♦ **back·pack·er, backpackers** *I'm an experienced backpacker and I'm familiar with the trail.* N-COUNT

,**back 'passage, back passages.** People sometimes refer to their rectum as their **back passage**. N-COUNT BRITISH

'**back pay.** Back pay is money which an employer owes an employee for work he or she did in the past. N-UNCOUNT

,**back-'pedal, back-pedals, back-pedalling, back-pedalled;** spelled **back-pedaling, back-pedaled** in American English. Also spelled **backpedal. 1** If you **back-pedal**, you express a different or less forceful opinion about something from the one you had previously expressed. *Last week he appeared to back-pedal on that statement.* **2** If you say that someone **back-pedals**, you mean that you disapprove of their behaviour because they are not doing what they promised. *The Federal Republic will backpedal on its earlier commitments.* VERB V
VERB PRAGMATICS V on/from n
♦ **back-pedalling** ...*Britain's back-pedalling on reforms.* N-UNCOUNT

back·rest /'bækrest/ **backrests.** The backrest of a seat is the part which you rest your back on. N-COUNT

'**back road, back roads.** A back road is a small country road with very little traffic. N-COUNT

'**back room, back rooms;** also spelled **back-room** or **backroom. 1** A **back room** is a room that is situated at the back of a building, especially a private room. ...*the backroom of the officers' club.* **2** You can use **back room** to refer to people in an organization who do important work but are not seen or known about by the public. ...*Mr Smith's backroom staff.* **3** If you refer to a deal made by someone such as a politician as a **back room** deal, you disapprove of it because it has been made in a secret dishonest way. *They have been calling the Presidency decision a backroom deal.* ◆◇◇◇◇ N-COUNT
N-COUNT
ADJ: ADJ n PRAGMATICS

back·side /,bæk'saɪd/ **backsides.** Your backside is the part of your body that you sit on. *He fell flat on his backside.* ◆◇◇◇◇ N-COUNT INFORMAL

'**back-slapping;** also spelled **backslapping. Back-slapping** is noisy cheerful behaviour which people, especially men, use in order to show affection or congratulate each other. ...*his hearty back-slapping and hand-shaking.* ► Also an adjective. ...*a clutch of back-slapping admirers.* N-UNCOUNT
ADJ: ADJ n

back·slid·ing /'bækslaɪdɪŋ/. If you accuse someone of **backsliding** on something that they have agreed to do, you disapprove of them because they have failed to do it. ...*the government's backsliding on free market reforms.* N-UNCOUNT PRAGMATICS

back·stage /ˌbækˈsteɪdʒ/. In a theatre, **backstage** ◆◇◇◇◇
refers to the areas behind the stage. *He went back-* ADV:
stage and asked for her autograph. ▶ Also an adjec- ADV after v
tive. *...a backstage pass.* ADJ: ADJ n

'back street, back streets; also spelled **back-**
street or **backstreet**. **1** A **back street** in a town or N-COUNT
city is a small narrow street with very little traffic.
...a narrow back street of Port-au-Prince. *...back-*
street garages. **2** The **back streets** of a town or city N-PLURAL
are the areas of small, old streets rather than the
richer or newer areas. *...the back streets of Berlin.*
3 Back street activities are carried out unofficially, ADJ: ADJ n
secretly, and often illegally. *...back street abortions.*

back·stroke /ˈbækstrəʊk/. **Backstroke** is a swim- N-UNCOUNT:
ming stroke that you do lying on your back. also the N

back·track /ˈbæktræk/ **backtracks, backtrack-**
ing, backtracked; also spelled **back-track**. **1** If VERB
you **backtrack** on a statement or decision you have V on/from n
made, you do or say something that shows that you Also V
no longer agree with it or support it. *The finance*
minister backtracked on his decision. ◆ **back-**
·track·ing *Some backtracking is probably inevi-* N-UNCOUNT
table. **2** If you **backtrack**, you go back along a path VERB: V
or route you have just used. *We had to backtrack to* V prep
the corner and cross the street. **3** If you **backtrack** in VERB
an account or explanation, you talk about things V
which happened before the ones you were previously talking about. *Can we just backtrack a little bit*
and look at your primary and secondary education?

back·up /ˈbækʌp/ **backups;** also spelled **back-up**. ◆◇◇◇◇
1 Backup consists of extra equipment, resources, or N-VAR
people that you can get help or support from if necessary. *Alternative treatments can provide a useful*
back-up to conventional treatment. **2** If you have N-VAR
something as **backup**, you have arranged for it to be
available in case something you are doing does not
work. *Computer users should make regular back-up*
copies of their work.

back·ward /ˈbækwəd/. In American English, **back-** ◆◆◇◇◇
ward is usually used as an adverb instead of **back-**
wards. **Backward** is also sometimes used in this
way in formal British English. See **backwards** for
these uses.
1 A **backward** movement or look is in the direction ADJ: ADJ n
that your back is facing. Some people use **backwards**
for this meaning. *...a backward glance... He did a*
backward flip. **2** If someone takes a **backward** step, ADJ: ADJ n
they do something that does not improve their situa-
tion, but causes them to go back a stage. *Many den-*
tists will no longer treat National Health Service pa-
tients, which is a big backward step. **3** A **backward** ADJ-GRADED
country or society does not have modern industries
and machines. *We need to accelerate the pace of*
change in our backward country. ◆ **back·ward-**
·ness *I was astonished at the backwardness of our* N-UNCOUNT
country. **4** A **backward** child has difficulty in learning. ADJ-GRADED
◆ **backwardness** *...her backwardness in practical* N-UNCOUNT
and physical activities.

'backward-looking. If you describe someone or ADJ-GRADED
something as **backward-looking**, you disapprove of PRAGMATICS
their attitudes, ideas, or actions because they are
based on old-fashioned opinions or methods. *...a*
stagnant, backward-looking culture.

back·wards /ˈbækwədz/; spelled **backward** in ◆◆◇◇◇
American English. **1** If you move or look **back-** ADV:
wards, you move or look in the direction that your ADV after v
back is facing. *The diver flipped over backwards into*
the water... He took two steps backward. ▶ Also an ADJ: ADJ n
adjective. *Without so much as a backwards glance,*
he steered her towards the car. **2** If someone or PHRASE
something moves **backwards and forwards**, they
move repeatedly first in one direction and then in
the opposite direction. *...people travelling back-*
wards and forwards. **3** ● to bend over backwards:
see **bend**.
4 If you do something **backwards**, you do it in the op- ADV:
posite way to the usual way. *He works backwards,* ADV after v
building a house from the top downwards. **5** If you say PHRASE
that someone **knows** something **backwards**, you are PRAGMATICS
emphasizing that they know it very well.

6 You use **backwards** to indicate that something ADV:
changes or develops in a way that is not an improve- ADV after v,
ment, but is a return to old ideas or methods. *...un-* n ADV
shakable traditions that look backward. **7** See also
backward.

back·wash /ˈbækwɒʃ/. The **backwash** of an event N-SING
or situation is an unpleasant situation that exists after it and as a result of it. *...the backwash of the*
events of 1989.

back·water /ˈbækwɔːtə/ **backwaters. 1** A **back-** ◆◇◇◇◇
water is a place that is isolated. *...a quiet rural back-* N-COUNT
water. **2** If you refer to a place or institution as a N-COUNT
backwater, you think it is not developing properly PRAGMATICS
because it is isolated from ideas and events in other
places and institutions; used showing disapproval.
...a political backwater with no serious influence.

back·woods /ˈbækwʊdz/. If you refer to an area as N-PLURAL
the **backwoods**, you mean that it is a long way from
large towns and is isolated from modern life.

back·yard /ˌbækˈjɑːd/ **backyards;** also spelled ◆◇◇◇◇
back yard. **1** A **backyard** is an area of land at the N-COUNT
back of a house. **2** If you refer to a country's own N-COUNT:
backyard, you are referring to its own territory. with poss
Cuba, an area that the United States has long re-
garded as its own backyard.

ba·con /ˈbeɪkən/. **1** Bacon is salted meat which ◆◇◇◇◇
comes from the back or sides of a pig. N-UNCOUNT
2 If someone **saves** your **bacon**, they get PHRASE
you out of a dangerous or difficult situation. INFORMAL

bac·te·ria /bækˈtɪəriə/. **Bacteria** are very small or- ◆◆◇◇◇
ganisms. Some bacteria can cause disease. *Chlorine* N-PLURAL
is added to kill bacteria. ◆ **bac·te·rial** /bækˈtɪəriəl/ ADJ: ADJ n
Cholera is a bacterial infection.

bac·te·ri·ol·ogy /bækˌtɪəriˈɒlədʒi/. **Bacteriology** is N-UNCOUNT
the science and study of bacteria. ◆ **bac·te·rio-**
·logi·cal /bækˌtɪəriəˈlɒdʒɪkəl/ *...the national bacte-* ADJ: ADJ n
riological laboratory.

bac·te·rium /bækˈtɪəriəm/. **Bacterium** is the singular of **bacteria**.

bad /bæd/ **worse, worst. 1** Something that is **bad** ◆◆◆◆◆
is unpleasant, harmful, or of poor quality. *...bad* ADJ-GRADED
weather conditions. ...a bad day at work... The pain
is often so bad she wants to scream... The floods are
described as the worst in nearly fifty years... Jeffrey
Faux says a tax cut is a bad idea... Teachers' pay is so
bad. **2** You can say that something is **not bad** to ADJ-GRADED:
mean that it is quite good or acceptable. *'How much* with neg
is he paying you?'—'Oh, five thousand.'—'Not bad.'...
'How are you, mate?'—'Not bad, mate.'
3 Someone who is **bad** at doing something is not skil- ADJ-GRADED
ful or successful at it. *He was a bad driver.*
4 A **bad** person has morally unacceptable attitudes ADJ-GRADED
and behaviour. *I was selling drugs, but I didn't think I*
was a bad person... You are a bad boy for repeating
what I told you. ◆ **bad·ness** *They only recognise bad-* N-UNCOUNT
ness when they perceive it in others. **5** Bad language is ADJ-GRADED
language that contains offensive words such as swear
words.
6 If you are in a **bad** mood, you are cross and behave ADJ-GRADED
unpleasantly to people. **7** If you feel **bad** about some- ADJ-GRADED:
thing, you feel rather sorry or guilty about it. *I feel bad* feel ADJ
that he's doing most of the work.
8 If you have a **bad** back, heart, leg, or eye, it is injured, ADJ
diseased, or weak. *Alastair has a bad back so we have a*
hard bed.
9 Food that has gone **bad** is not suitable to eat be- ADJ
cause it has started to decay.
10 If you say that it is **too bad** that something is the PHRASE
case, you mean you are sorry or sad that it is the case. PRAGMATICS
It is too bad that Eleanor had to leave. **11** If you say CONVENTION
'too bad', you are indicating that nothing can be done PRAGMATICS
to change the situation, and that you do not feel sorry
or sympathetic about this. *Too bad if you missed the*
bus. **12** If nobody has a **bad word to say about** you, PHRASE
you are liked or admired by everyone.
13 See also **worse, worst.** ● to **make the best of a bad**
job: see **best.** ● **bad blood**: see **blood.** ● **to be in**
someone's bad books: see **book.** ● **bad luck**: see **luck.**
● **in a bad way**: see **way.** ● to **go from bad to worse**:
see **worse.**

,bad 'cheque, bad cheques; spelled **bad check** N-COUNT in American English. A **bad cheque** is a bank cheque that will not be paid because there is a mistake on it, or because there is not enough money in the account of the person who wrote it.

,bad 'debt, bad debts. A **bad debt** is a sum of ◆◇◇◇◇ money that has been lent but is not likely to be re- N-COUNT paid. ...£1.1 billion to cover bad debts from business failures.

bad·dy /'bædi/ **baddies;** also spelled **baddie.** Chil- N-COUNT dren use **baddy** to refer to a person in a story or INFORMAL film who is considered to be evil or wicked.

bade /bæd, beɪd/. **Bade** is a past tense of **bid.**

badge /bædʒ/ **badges. 1** A **badge** is a small piece ◆◇◇◇◇ of metal or cloth which you wear on your clothes to N-COUNT show, for example, that you belong to a particular organisation. **2** Any feature which is regarded as a N-SING sign of a particular quality can be referred to as a **badge**. Being a Communist was a badge of honour for thousands of trade union activists.

badg·er /'bædʒə/ **badgers, badgering, badg-** ◆◇◇◇◇ **ered. 1** A **badger** is a wild animal which has a N-COUNT white head with two wide black stripes on it. Badgers live underground and usually come up to feed at night. **2** If you **badger** someone, you repeatedly tell VERB: V n them to do something or repeatedly ask them ques- V n to-inf tions. They kept phoning and writing, badgering me to go back.

badi·nage /'bædɪnɑːʒ, -'nɑːʒ/. **Badinage** is humor- N-UNCOUNT ous or light-hearted conversation that often in- LITERARY volves teasing someone. Gregory tried to respond to the Bishop's light-hearted badinage.

bad·ly /'bædli/ **worse, worst. 1** If something is ◆◆◇◇◇ done **badly** or goes **badly**, it is not very successful ADV-GRADED: or effective. I was angry because I played so badly... ADV with v The whole project was badly managed. **2** If someone ADV-GRADED or something is **badly** hurt or **badly** affected, they are severely hurt or affected. The bomb destroyed a police station and badly damaged a church. ...badly injured. **3** If a person or their job is **badly** paid, ADV-GRADED they are not paid very much for what they do. **4** If ADV-GRADED: you want or need something **badly**, you want or ADV with v need it very much.

5 If someone behaves **badly** or treats other people ADV-GRADED: **badly**, they act in an unkind, unpleasant, or unaccep- ADV with v table way. **6** If something reflects **badly** on someone ADV-GRADED: or makes others think **badly** of them, it harms their ADV after v reputation. Low exam results will reflect badly on them... Few people think badly of him. ● See also **worse, worst.**

,badly 'off, worse off, worst off. 1 If you are ◆◇◇◇◇ **badly off**, you are in a bad situation. The average ADJ-GRADED working week in Japan is 42.3 hours, compared with 41.6 in the UK, so they are not too badly off. **2** If you ADJ-GRADED are **badly off**, you do not have much money.

bad·min·ton /'bædmɪntən/. **Badminton** is a game ◆◇◇◇◇ played on a rectangular court by two or four play- N-UNCOUNT ers. They hit a feathered object called a shuttlecock across a high net.

bad-mouth /'bædmaʊθ/ **bad-mouths, bad-** VERB: V n **mouthing, bad-mouthed.** If someone **bad-mouths** you, they say unpleasant things about you.

,bad-'tempered. Someone who is **bad-tempered** ADJ-GRADED is not very cheerful and gets angry easily.

baf·fle /'bæfəl/ **baffles, baffling, baffled.** If ◆◇◇◇◇ something **baffles** you, you cannot understand it or VERB explain it. The disappearance of Nicholas Newall V n and his wife Elizabeth has baffled detectives. ● **baf- ·fling** I was constantly ill, with a baffling array of ADJ-GRADED symptoms. ● **baf·fled** Police are baffled by the ADJ-GRADED murder.

baf·fle·ment /'bæfəlmənt/. **Bafflement** is the state N-UNCOUNT of being baffled. The general response was one of understandable bafflement.

bag /bæg/ **bags, bagging, bagged. 1** A **bag** is a ◆◆◆◆◇ container made of paper or plastic to put things in. N-COUNT ▶ A **bag** of things is the amount of things contained in a bag. **2** A **bag** is the same as a **handbag. 3** If you N-COUNT **pack** your **bags**, you leave a place where you have PHRASE been staying or living.

4 If you say there is **bags of** something, you mean that QUANT there is a large amount of it. If you say that there are BRITISH, **bags** of things, you mean that there are a large num- INFORMAL ber of them. ...a hotel with bags of character.

5 If you have **bags** under your eyes, you have folds of N-PLURAL skin there, usually because you have not had enough sleep.

6 If someone calls a woman an old **bag** or a stupid N-COUNT **bag**, they are insulting her. RUDE

7 If you **bag** something that a lot of people want, you VERB get it for yourself before anyone else can get it. The V n smart ones will have already bagged their seats. BRITISH, INFORMAL

8 If you say that something is **in the bag**, you mean PHRASE that you are certain that you will get it or achieve it. INFORMAL 'I'll get the Republican nomination,' he assured me. 'It's in the bag.'

9 ● to **let the cat out of the bag:** see **cat.** See also **bum bag, carrier bag, mixed bag, shoulder-bag, sleeping bag, tea bag.**

bag up. If you **bag up** a quantity of something, you PHRASAL VB put it into bags. V P noun

ba·gel /'beɪgəl/ **bagels.** A **bagel** is a ring-shaped N-COUNT bread roll.

bag·gage /'bægɪdʒ/. **1** Your **baggage** consists of ◆◇◇◇◇ the suitcases and bags that you take with you when N-UNCOUNT you travel. **2** You can use **baggage** to refer to N-UNCOUNT someone's emotional problems, fixed ideas, or prejudices. How much emotional baggage is he bringing with him?

bag·gy /'bægi/ **baggier, baggiest.** If a piece of ◆◇◇◇◇ clothing is **baggy**, it hangs loosely on your body. ADJ-GRADED

'bag lady, bag ladies. A **bag lady** is a homeless N-COUNT woman who carries all her possessions in shopping bags.

bag·pipes /'bægpaɪps/. The form **bagpipe** is used N-COUNT as a modifier, and sometimes as a singular. A **bag- pipe** or **bagpipes** are a musical instrument consist- ing of a leather bag and several pipes.

ba·guette /bæ'get/ **baguettes.** A **baguette** is a N-COUNT long narrow loaf of white bread which is traditional- ly made in France.

bah /bɑː, bæ/. **'Bah'** is used to represent a noise that EXCLAM people make in order to express annoyance or con- DATED, tempt. Bah! Did he imagine I would accept that? WRITTEN

bail /beɪl/ **bails, bailing, bailed;** also spelled **bale** ◆◆◇◇◇ for meaning 5, and for meanings 1 and 3 of the phrasal verb. **1** In Britain, if someone who is await- N-UNCOUNT ing trial in a court of law is released on **bail**, they are set free until they are due to appear in court, provided someone agrees to pay a sum of money if they fail to appear. He was freed on bail... The high court set bail at $8,000. **2** If a prisoner **jumps bail,** PHRASE he or she does not come back for his or her trial af- ter being released on bail. **3** If someone who is VERB: awaiting trial **is bailed,** they are set free until they be V-ed are due to appear in court, provided someone be V-ed to-inf agrees to pay a sum of money if they fail to appear. He was bailed to appear before local magistrates on 5 November.

4 In the sport of cricket, the **bails** are the two small N-COUNT pieces of wood that are laid across the top of the stumps to form the wicket.

5 If you **bail**, you use a container to remove water VERB from a boat or from a place which is flooded. We kept V her afloat for a couple of hours by bailing frantically. Also V n ▶ **Bail out** means the same as **bail**. A crew was sent PHRASAL VB down the shaft to close it off and bail out all the water. V P noun

bail out. 1 If you **bail** someone **out**, you help them PHRASAL VB out of a difficult situation, often by giving them mon- V n P ey. They will discuss how to bail the economy out of its Also V P noun slump. **2** If you **bail** someone **out**, you pay bail on V n P their behalf. **3** If a pilot **bails out** of an aircraft that is V P crashing, he or she jumps from it, using a parachute to land safely. The pilot bailed out safely. **4** See bail 5.

bail·iff /'beɪlɪf/ **bailiffs. 1** A **bailiff** is a law officer ◆◇◇◇◇ who makes sure that the decisions of a court are N-COUNT obeyed. **2** A **bailiff** is a minor official in a court of BRITISH law who carries messages or looks after prisoners. N-COUNT AMERICAN **3** A **bailiff** is a person who is employed to look after N-COUNT land or property for the owner. BRITISH

B

bairn /beən/ **bairns.** A **bairn** is a child; used mainly in Scotland and the north of England. *He's such a lovely bairn.*   N-COUNT

bait /beɪt/ **baits, baiting, baited. 1 Bait** is food ◆◆◇◇◇ which you put on a hook or in a trap in order to N-VAR catch fish or animals. **2** When you **bait** a hook or VERB trap, you put bait on it or in it. *He baited his hook* V n *with pie.* **3** If someone or something is being used N-UNCOUNT: as **bait**, they are being used to tempt or encourage also a N someone to do something. *As a bait, he offered a free holiday in Turkey.* **4** If you **bait** someone, you VERB deliberately try to make them angry by teasing V n them. *He delighted in baiting his mother.* **5** If you PHRASE **take the bait** or **rise to the bait**, you react to something that someone has said or done exactly as they intended you to do. *When she attempts to make you feel guilty, don't take the bait.*

-baiting /-beɪtɪŋ/. **1** You use **-baiting** after nouns to COMB refer to the activity of persecuting a particular group of people or the activity of ridiculing someone's beliefs. *...the witch-hunts and red-baiting of Senator McCarthy's Committee.* **2** Badger-**baiting**, bear- COMB **baiting**, and bull-**baiting** involve letting dogs attack these animals as a sport, while ensuring that they are unable to defend themselves.

baize /beɪz/. **Baize** is a thick woollen material N-UNCOUNT which is used for covering things such as snooker tables and card tables.

bake /beɪk/ **bakes, baking, baked. 1** If you ◆◆◇◇◇ **bake**, you prepare and mix together ingredients to VB: no make cakes, biscuits, or bread. You then put them passive, in the oven to cook. *How did you learn to bake* V n *cakes?.* ♦ **bak·ing** *On a Thursday she used to do all* N-UNCOUNT *the baking.* **2** When a cake or bread **bakes** or when V-ERG: V you **bake** it, it cooks in the oven without any extra V n liquid or fat. *Bake the cake for 35 to 50 minutes.* **3** If places or people become extremely hot, you can VERB say that they **bake**. *If you closed the windows you* V *baked.* ● See also **baking**.

baked 'beans. Baked beans are haricot beans N-PLURAL cooked in tomato sauce and are usually sold in cans.

Ba·ke·lite /ˈbeɪkəlaɪt/. **Bakelite** is a type of hard N-UNCOUNT plastic that was used for making things such as telephones and radios. **Bakelite** is a trademark.

bak·er /ˈbeɪkə/ **bakers. 1** A **baker** is a person ◆◇◇◇◇ whose job is to bake and sell bread, pastries, and N-COUNT cakes. **2** A **baker** or a **baker's** is a shop where bread N-COUNT and cakes are sold.

bak·ery /ˈbeɪkəri/ **bakeries.** A **bakery** is a building ◆◇◇◇◇ where bread, pastries, and cakes are baked, or the N-COUNT shop where they are sold.

bak·ing /ˈbeɪkɪŋ/. You can use **baking** to describe ◆◇◇◇◇ weather or a place that is very hot indeed. *...a bak-* ADJ *ing July day. ...the baking Jordanian desert.* ▶ Also ADV: ADV adj an adverb. *...the baking hot summer of 1969.* ● See also **bake**.

'baking powder, baking powders. Baking N-VAR **powder** is an ingredient used in cake making. It causes cakes to rise when they are in the oven.

'baking soda. Baking soda is **bicarbonate of** N-UNCOUNT **soda.**

bala·cla·va /ˌbæləˈklɑːvə/ **balaclavas.** A **balaclava** N-COUNT is a close-fitting woollen hood that covers every part of your head except your face.

bal·ance /ˈbæləns/ **balances, balancing, bal-** ◆◆◆◆◇ **anced. 1** If something or someone **balances** some- V-ERG where or if you **balance** them there, they remain V prep/adv steady and do not fall over. *I balanced on the ledge...* V n prep/adv *She had balanced a glass on her chest.* **2 Balance** is N-UNCOUNT the ability to remain steady when you are standing up. *The medicines you are currently taking could be affecting your balance.* **3** If you **keep** your **balance**, PHRASE you remain steady and do not fall over. If you **lose** your **balance**, you become unsteady and fall over. **4** If you are **off balance**, you are in an unsteady po- PHRASE sition and about to fall. **5** If you **balance** one thing with something different V-RECIP-ERG: or if one thing **balances** with another, each of the V n with n things has the same strength or importance. *The state* V pl-n pl-n V

has got to find some way to balance these two needs... Also V with n *Supply and demand on the currency market will gen- erally balance.* ♦ **bal·anced** *This book is a well bal-* ADJ *anced biography.* **6** A **balance** is a situation or combi- N-SING: nation of things in which all the different parts are with supp equal or correct in strength or importance. *...the eco- logical balance of the forest.* **7** If you say that the **bal-** N-SING: **ance** tips in your favour, you start winning or suc- the N ceeding, especially in a conflict or contest. **8** If you VERB **balance** one thing against another, you consider its V n against n importance in relation to the other one. *She carefully tried to balance religious sensitivities against demo- cratic freedom.* **9** If someone **balances** their budget or if a govern- VERB: V n ment **balances** the economy of a country, they make sure that the amount of money that is spent is not greater than the amount that is received. **10** If you V-ERG **balance** your books or make them **balance**, you prove V n by calculation that the amount of money you have re- Also V ceived is equal to the amount that you have spent. *...teaching them to balance the books.* **11** The **balance** N-COUNT in your bank account is the amount of money you have in it. **12** The **balance** of an amount of money is N-SING: what remains to be paid for something or what re- the N mains when part of the amount has been spent. *They were due to pay the balance on delivery.* ● See also **bank balance.** **13** If something hangs **in the balance**, it is uncertain PHRASE whether it will happen or continue. **14** If you are PHRASE thrown **off balance** by something, you are surprised or confused by it. **15** You can say **on balance** to indi- PHRASE cate that you are stating an opinion after considering PRAGMATICS all the relevant facts or arguments. *On balance he agreed with Christine.*

balance out. If two or more opposite things **bal-** PHRASAL VB **ance out** or if you **balance** them **out**, they become ERG: equal in amount, value, or effect. *The exercise under-* V P *gone could balance out the increased calories.* Also V n P

bal·anced /ˈbælənst/. **1** A **balanced** piece of writ- ◆◆◇◇◇ ing takes into account all the different opinions on ADJ-GRADED something and presents information in a fair and PRAGMATICS reasonable way; used showing approval. *...a fair, balanced, comprehensive report.* **2** Something that ADJ-GRADED is **balanced** is pleasing or beneficial because its dif- PRAGMATICS ferent parts are in the correct proportions; used showing approval. *...a balanced diet.* **3** Someone ADJ-GRADED who is **balanced** remains calm and thinks clearly, PRAGMATICS even in a difficult situation; used showing approval. *I have to prove myself as a respectable, balanced, person.* **4** See also **balance.**

balance of 'payments, balances of pay- ◆◇◇◇◇ **ments.** A country's **balance of payments** is the dif- N-COUNT ference between the payments it makes to other countries for imports and the payments it receives from other countries for exports.

balance of 'power. 1 The **balance of power** is a ◆◇◇◇◇ situation in which power is distributed between ri- N-SING val groups or countries in such a way that no single group or country can dominate the others. *...the balance of power between the United States and the former Soviet Union.* **2** If a small political party N-SING holds the **balance of power** in a parliament, it is able to give a larger party a majority by supporting this larger party.

balance of 'trade, balances of trade. A N-COUNT country's **balance of trade** is the difference in value between the goods it imports and the goods it exports.

'balance sheet, balance sheets. A **balance** ◆◇◇◇◇ **sheet** is a written statement of the amount of mon- N-COUNT ey and property a company has, including amounts of money that it owes or is owed. You can use **bal- ance sheet** to refer to the general financial state of a company. *Rolls-Royce needed a strong balance sheet.*

'balancing act, balancing acts. If you perform N-COUNT a **balancing act**, you try to please two or more peo- ple or groups who are in opposition to each other.

bal·co·ny /ˈbælkəni/ **balconies. 1** A **balcony** is a ◆◆◇◇◇ platform on the outside of a building, above ground N-COUNT level, with a wall or railing around it. **2** The **balcony** N-SING

in a theatre or cinema is an area of seats upstairs, above the main seating area.

bald /bɔːld/ **balder, baldest. 1** Someone who is ◆◆◇◇◇ bald has little or no hair on the top of their head. ADJ-GRADED ♦ **bald·ness** *He wears a cap to cover a spot of bald-* N-UNCOUNT *ness.* **2** If a tyre is **bald**, its tread has worn down and ADJ-GRADED it is no longer safe to use. **3** A **bald** statement is ADJ: ADJ n made plainly and often bluntly, containing no unnecessary words. *...a bald statement from the official news agency.* ♦ **bald·ly** *'The leaders are outdated,'* ADV-GRADED *he stated baldly.* ADV with v

bald·ing /ˈbɔːldɪŋ/. Someone who is **balding** is be- ♦◇◇◇◇ ginning to lose the hair on the top of their head. ADJ

bale /beɪl/ **bales, baling, baled. 1** A **bale** is a ◆◇◇◇◇ large quantity of something such as hay, cloth, or N-COUNT paper, tied into a tight bundle. *...large round bales of hay.* **2** If something such as hay, cloth, or paper VERB: **is baled**, it is tied together in a tight bundle. **3** See be V-ed also **bail**.

bale·ful /ˈbeɪlfʊl/. **Baleful** means harmful, or ex- ADJ-GRADED pressing harmful intentions. *He had a baleful look.* LITERARY ♦ **bale·ful·ly** *He watched balefully as Cassandra* ADV: *walked towards him.* ADV with v

balk /bɔːlk, AM bɔːk/ **balks, balking, balked;** ◆◇◇◇◇ also spelled **baulk**. If you **balk** at something, you VERB are very reluctant to do it or to let it happen. *Even* V at n biology undergraduates may balk at animal experi- v *ments. ...nervous investors balked.*

Bal·kani·za·tion /ˌbɔːlkənaɪˈzeɪʃən/; also spelled N-UNCOUNT **balkanization**. If you refer to the division of a coun- PRAGMATICS try into separate independent states as the **Balkani-** **zation** of that country, you are expressing your dis- approval of such a division.

ball 1 circular objects

ball /bɔːl/ **balls, balling, balled. 1** A **ball** is a ◆◆◆◇ round object that is used in games such as tennis, N-COUNT cricket, and football. *I bounced a ball against the house. ...a golf ball.* **2** A **ball** is something or an N-COUNT amount of something that has a round shape. *Thomas screwed the letter up into a ball.* **3** When V-ERG you **ball** something or when it **balls**, it becomes V n adv/prep round and takes up less space. *He picked up the* V adv/prep *sheets of paper, and balled them tightly in his fists... His hands balled into fists.* ▶ **Ball up** means the PHRASAL VB same as **ball**. *She balled the handkerchief up and* ERG *threw it at his feet.* V n P

4 The **ball** of your foot or the **ball** of your thumb is the N-COUNT rounded part where your toes join your foot or where your thumb joins your hand.

5 A man's **balls** are his testicles; some people find this N-COUNT use offensive. ● See also **balls**. INFORMAL

6 If you say that **the ball is in** a particular person's PHRASE **court**, you mean that it is his or her responsibility to take the next action or decision in a particular situa- tion. **7** If you **get the ball rolling, set the ball rolling,** PHRASE or **start the ball rolling**, you start something happen- ing. **8** If you **keep** several **balls in the air**, you try to do PHRASE several different things at once. *...unhappy mothers trying to juggle ten balls in the air.* **9** If someone is **on** PHRASE **the ball**, they are very alert and aware of what is hap- pening. **10** If someone refuses to **play ball**, they are PHRASE unwilling to do what someone wants them to do. INFORMAL

ball up. See **ball** 3 PHRASAL VB

ball 2 social event

ball /bɔːl/ **balls. 1** A **ball** is a large formal social N-COUNT event at which people dance. **2** If you **are having a** PHRASE **ball**, you are having a very enjoyable time. *Going by* INFORMAL *the gales of laughter, they were having a ball.*

bal·lad /ˈbæləd/ **ballads. 1** A **ballad** is a long song ◆◇◇◇◇ or poem which tells a story in simple language. *...an* N-COUNT *eighteenth century ballad about some lost children.* **2** A **ballad** is a slow, romantic, popular song. N-COUNT

bal·last /ˈbæləst/. **Ballast** is any substance that is ◆◇◇◇◇ used in ships or hot-air balloons to make them N-UNCOUNT heavier and more stable.

ˌball ˈbearing, ball bearings; also spelled **ball-** N-COUNT **bearing**. **Ball bearings** are small metal balls placed between the moving parts of a machine to make the parts move smoothly.

ˈball boy, ball boys. In a tennis match, the **ball** N-COUNT **boys** are the boys whose job is to pick up any balls that go into the net or off the court and to throw them back to the players.

bal·le·ri·na /ˌbæləˈriːnə/ **ballerinas.** A **ballerina** is ◆◇◇◇◇ a female ballet dancer.

bal·let /ˈbæleɪ, AM bæˈleɪ/ **ballets. 1** Ballet is a ◆◆◇◇◇ type of very skilled and artistic dancing with care- N-UNCOUNT fully planned movements. *I trained as a ballet danc- er... She is also keen on the ballet.* **2** A **ballet** is an ar- N-COUNT tistic work that is performed by ballet dancers.

bal·let·ic /bæˈletɪk/. If you describe someone's ADJ-GRADED movements as **balletic**, you mean that they have some of the graceful qualities of ballet. *The subject seems to dance with balletic grace.*

ˈball game, ball games; also spelled **ballgame.** ◆◇◇◇◇ **1** Ball games are games that are played with a ball N-COUNT such as football and tennis. **2** A **ball game** is a base- N-COUNT ball match. *I'd still like to go to a ball game.* **3** You AMERICAN can use **ball game** to describe any situation or activ- N-SING ity, especially one that involves competition. *Two of his biggest competitors are out of the ball-game.* ● If you say that a situation is a **new ball game**, you PHRASE mean that it is completely different from, or much more difficult than other situations that you have experienced before. *He finds himself faced with a whole new ball game.*

ˈball girl, ball girls. In a tennis match, the **ball** N-COUNT **girls** are the girls whose job is to pick up any balls that go into the net or off the court and to throw them back to the players.

ball·gown /ˈbɔːlgaʊn/ **ballgowns.** A **ballgown** is a N-COUNT long dress that women wear to formal dances.

bal·lis·tic /bəˈlɪstɪk/. **Ballistic** means relating to ◆◇◇◇◇ ballistics. *Ballistic tests have matched the weapons* ADJ: ADJ n *with bullets taken from the bodies of victims.*

bal·lis·tics /bəˈlɪstɪks/. **Ballistics** is the study of the N-UNCOUNT movement of objects that are shot or thrown through the air, such as bullets fired from a gun.

bal·loon /bəˈluːn/ **balloons, ballooning, bal-** ◆◆◇◇◇ **looned. 1** A **balloon** is a small, thin, rubber bag N-COUNT that you blow air into so that it becomes larger and rounder or longer. **2** A **balloon** is a large, strong bag N-COUNT filled with gas or hot air, which can carry passengers in a basket or compartment underneath it. *...the first to circle the Earth non-stop by balloon.* **3** When something **balloons**, it increases rapidly in VERB amount. *In London, the use of the Tube has bal-* V *looned... The budget deficit has ballooned to $25 bil-* V to n *lion.* **4** When something **balloons**, it quickly becomes VERB bigger in size and rounder in shape. *Paula's plaid* V *jacket ballooned in the deep water.*

bal·loon·ing /bəˈluːnɪŋ/. **Ballooning** is the sport or N-UNCOUNT activity of travelling through the air by balloon. *...Jacques Montgolfier, pioneer of ballooning.*

bal·loon·ist /bəˈluːnɪst/ **balloonists.** A **balloonist** N-COUNT is a person who flies a hot-air balloon.

bal·lot /ˈbælət/ **ballots, balloting, balloted. 1** A ◆◆◆◇ **ballot** is a secret vote in which people select a can- N-COUNT didate in an election, or express their opinion about something. *Fifty of its members will be elected by di- rect ballot.* **2** A **ballot** is a piece of paper on which N-COUNT you indicate your choice or opinion in a ballot. BRITISH *Election boards will count the ballots by hand.* **3** If VERB you **ballot** a group of people, you find out what they V n think about a subject by organizing a secret vote. *The union said they will ballot members on whether to strike.* ♦ **bal·lot·ing** *International observers say* N-UNCOUNT *the balloting was fair.*

ˈballot box, ballot boxes. 1 A **ballot box** is the ◆◇◇◇◇ box into which ballot papers are put after people N-COUNT have voted. **2** You can refer to the system of demo- N-SING: cratic elections as the **ballot box**. *Martinez ex-* the N *pressed confidence of victory at the ballot box.*

ˈballot paper, ballot papers. A **ballot paper** is a N-COUNT piece of paper on which you indicate your choice or opinion in a ballot.

ˈballot rigging; also spelled **ballot-rigging**. **Ballot** N-UNCOUNT **rigging** is the act of illegally changing the result of

an election by producing a false record of the number of votes. *...allegations of ballot rigging.*

ball·park /'bɔːlpɑːk/ **ballparks;** also spelled **ball park.** A **ballpark** is a park or stadium where baseball is played. N-COUNT

ball·play·er /'bɔːlpleɪə/ **ballplayers;** also spelled **ball player.** A **ballplayer** is a baseball player. N-COUNT AMERICAN

ball·point /'bɔːlpɔɪnt/ **ballpoints.** A **ballpoint** or a **ballpoint pen** is a pen with a very small metal ball at the end which transfers the ink from the pen onto a surface. N-COUNT

ball·room /'bɔːlruːm/ **ballrooms.** A **ballroom** is a very large room that is used for dancing. ◆◇◇◇◇ N-COUNT

,**ballroom 'dancing. Ballroom dancing** is a type of dancing in which a man and a woman dance together using fixed sequences of movements. N-UNCOUNT

balls /bɔːlz/. **1** If you say that someone has **balls,** you mean that they have courage. Some people find this use offensive. *To work on this show you've got to have balls.* **2** If you say **'balls'** or say that what someone says is **balls** you think that it is stupid, wrong, or nonsense. Some people find this use offensive. *What complete and utter balls!* N-UNCOUNT INFORMAL / EXCLAM; N-UNCOUNT PRAGMATICS INFORMAL, BRITISH

'**balls-up, balls-ups.** If you make a **balls-up** of something, you do it very badly and make a lot of mistakes. Some people find this use offensive. N-COUNT INFORMAL, BRITISH

balm /bɑːm/ **balms. 1** Balm is a sweet-smelling oil that is obtained from some tropical trees and is used to make ointments that heal wounds or lessen pain. **2** You can refer to something as a **balm** when it comforts or soothes someone. *Venice was a balm that made Catherine forget the terrible nightmares and horrors of the past.* ◆◇◇◇◇ N-VAR / N-UNCOUNT also a N PRAGMATICS

balmy /'bɑːmi/. **Balmy** weather is pleasantly warm. *...a balmy summer's evening.* ADJ-GRADED

ba·lo·ney /bə'ləʊni/. If you say that an idea or statement is **baloney**, you disapprove of it and think it is foolish or wrong. N-UNCOUNT PRAGMATICS INFORMAL

bal·sa /'bɔːlsə/. Balsa or **balsa wood** is a very light wood from a South American tree. N-UNCOUNT

bal·sam /'bɔːlsəm/. **Balsam** is a sweet-smelling oil that is obtained from certain trees or bushes and is used to make medicines and perfumes. N-UNCOUNT

bal·sam·ic vin·egar /bɔːl,sæmɪk 'vɪnɪgə/. **Balsamic vinegar** is a sweet-tasting type of vinegar which is made from grape juice. N-UNCOUNT

bal·us·trade /,bælə'streɪd/ **balustrades.** A **balustrade** is a railing or wall on a balcony or staircase. N-COUNT

bam·boo /bæm'buː/ **bamboos. Bamboo** is a tall tropical plant with hard hollow stems. The young shoots of the plant can be eaten, and the stems are used to make furniture. ◆◇◇◇ N-VAR

bam·boo·zle /bæm'buːzəl/ **bamboozles, bamboozling, bamboozled.** To **bamboozle** someone means to confuse them greatly and often trick them. *He bamboozled Mercer into defeat... He was bamboozled by con men.* VERB V n into n be V-ed

ban /bæn/ **bans, banning, banned. 1** To ban something means to state officially that it must not be done, shown, or used. *Canada will ban smoking in all offices later this year.* ♦ **ban·ning, bannings** *No reason was given for the banning of the magazine.* **2** A **ban** is an official ruling that something must not be done, shown, or used. *The General also lifted a ban on political parties.* **3** If you **are banned** from doing something, you are officially prevented from doing it. *He was banned from driving for three years.* ◆◆◆◇ VERB V n / N-VAR / N-COUNT / VERB be V-ed from n Also V n

ba·nal /bə'nɑːl, -'næl/. If you describe something as **banal**, you do not like it because you think that it is so ordinary that it is not at all effective or interesting. *The text is banal... Bland, banal music tinkled discreetly from hidden loudspeakers.* ▶ You can refer to banal things as **the banal.** *The allegations ranged from the banal to the bizarre.* ♦ **ba·nal·ity** /bə'nælɪti/ **banalities** *...the banality of life... Neil's ability to utter banalities never ceased to amaze me.* ◆◇◇◇◇ ADJ-GRADED PRAGMATICS / N-SING: the N / N-VAR

ba·na·na /bə'nɑːnə, -'næn-/ **bananas. 1** Bananas are long curved fruit with yellow skins. See picture headed **fruit.** *...a spoonful of cooked sliced banana.* ◆◇◇◇ N-VAR

2 If someone is behaving in a silly or mad way, you can say that they are going **bananas. 3** If someone becomes extremely angry and shouts a lot, you can say that they go **bananas.** *Adamson's going to go bananas on this one.* ADJ INFORMAL / ADJ INFORMAL

ba,nana re'public, banana republics. Poor, unimportant, politically unstable countries are sometimes referred to as **banana republics**; some people find this expression offensive. N-COUNT

ba'nana skin, banana skins. If an important or famous person slips on a **banana skin**, they say or do something that makes them look stupid. N-COUNT JOURNALISM

band /bænd/ **bands, banding, banded. 1** A **band** is a small group of musicians who play popular music such as jazz, rock, or pop. **2** A **band** is a group of musicians who play brass and percussion instruments and sometimes also woodwind instruments. **3** A **band** of people is a group of people who have joined together because they share an interest or belief. *...bands of government soldiers.* **4** A **band** is a flat narrow strip of cloth which you wear round your head or wrists, or which forms part of a piece of clothing. *Almost all hospitals use a wristband of some kind with your name and details on it.* **5** A **band** is a strip of something such as colour, light, land, or cloth which contrasts with the areas on either side of it. *...bands of natural vegetation between strips of crops.* ● See also **banded. 6** A **band** is a strip or loop of metal or other strong material which strengthens something, or which holds several things together. **7** A **band** is a range of numbers or values within a system of measurement. *...a new tax band of 20p in the pound.* **8** If something such as a tax **is banded**, it is divided into bands according to the value of the thing being taxed. *...banding the tax so higher earners would pay more. ...a banding system based on property values.* **9** See also **armband, brass band, elastic band, hatband, one-man band, rubber band, waistband, waveband, wedding band.** ◆◆◆◇ N-COLL-COUNT / N-COLL-COUNT / N-COLL-COUNT: with supp / N-COUNT / N-COUNT: with supp / N-COUNT / N-COUNT / VERB V n V-ing V-ing BRITISH

band together. If people **band together**, they meet and act as a group in order to try and achieve something. PHRASAL VB

band·age /'bændɪdʒ/ **bandages, bandaging, bandaged. 1** A **bandage** is a long strip of cloth which is wrapped around a wounded part of someone's body to protect or support it. **2** If you **bandage** a wound or part of someone's body, you tie a bandage around it. *...a bandaged hand.* ▶ **Bandage up** means the same as bandage. *I bandaged the leg up and gave her aspirin for the pain.* ◆◇◇◇◇ N-COUNT / VERB: V n V-ed / PHRASAL VB V n P

'**Band-Aid, Band-Aids;** also spelled **band-aid. 1** A **Band-Aid** is a type of sticking plaster that you use to cover small cuts on your body. **Band-Aid** is a trade mark. **2** If you refer to a **Band-Aid** solution to a problem, you disapprove of it because you think that it will only be effective for a short period. N-VAR / ADJ: ADJ n PRAGMATICS

ban·dan·na /bæn'dænə/ **bandannas;** also spelled **bandana.** A **bandanna** is a large, brightly-coloured handkerchief which is worn around a person's neck or head. N-COUNT

B&B /,biː ən 'biː/ **B&Bs;** also spelled **b&b. 1** B&B is the same as **bed and breakfast.** *...three nights b&b.* **2** A **B&B** is the same as a **bed and breakfast.** *There are B&Bs all over the islands.* N-UNCOUNT / N-COUNT

band·ed /'bændɪd/. If something is **banded**, it has one or more bands on it, often of a different colour which contrasts with the main colour. *...banded stripes of dyed wool.* ♦ **-banded** *Tables are set with white china and gold-banded silver cutlery.* ADJ / COMB

ban·dit /'bændɪt/ **bandits.** People sometimes refer to armed robbers as **bandits**, especially if they operate in areas where the rule of law has broken down. ◆◇◇◇ N-COUNT

ban·dit·ry /'bændɪtri/. **Banditry** is acts of robbery and violence by bandits. N-UNCOUNT

band·leader /'bændliːdə/ **bandleaders.** A **bandleader** is a person who conducts a band, especially a dance band or a large jazz band. N-COUNT

bands·man /'bændzmən/ **bandsmen.** A **bandsman** is a musician in a military or brass band. N-COUNT

B

band·stand /'bændstænd/ **bandstands.** A bandstand is a platform with a roof where a band can play in the open air. `N-COUNT`

band·wagon /'bændwægən/ **bandwagons. 1** You can refer to an activity or movement that has suddenly become fashionable or is attracting increasing interest or support as a **bandwagon**. ...*the environmental bandwagon.* **2** If you say that someone, especially a politician, has jumped or climbed on the **bandwagon**, you disapprove of their involvement in an activity because you think they are not sincerely interested in it and are only involved in it because it is likely to give them success. ...*many conservative politicians have jumped on the anti-immigrant bandwagon.* `◆◇◇◇◇` `N-COUNT` `N-COUNT` `PRAGMATICS`

ban·dy /'bændi/ **bandies, bandying, bandied.** If you **bandy** words with someone, you argue with them. *The prosecution and defense were bandying accusations back and forth.* `VERB: V n with n V n adv`

bandy about or **bandy around.** If someone's name or something such as an idea **is bandied about** or **is bandied around**, that person or thing is discussed by many people in a casual way; used showing disapproval. *He whispered my name to newspapermen, knowing that it would be bandied about.* `PHRASAL VB PRAGMATICS be V-ed P`

bane /beɪn/ **banes.** If you say that someone or something is the **bane** of someone's life, you mean that they cause unhappiness or distress to that person. *Spots can be the bane of a teenager's life.* `N-COUNT`

bang /bæŋ/ **bangs, banging, banged. 1** A bang is a sudden loud noise such as the noise of an explosion. ...*slamming the door with a loud bang.* **2** If something **bangs**, it makes a sudden loud noise, once or several times. *The engine spat and banged.* **3** If you **bang** a door or if it **bangs**, it closes suddenly with a loud noise. ...*the sound of doors banging... All up and down the street the windows bang shut.* **4** If you **bang** on something or if you **bang** it, you hit it hard, making a loud noise. *There is no point in shouting or banging the table.* **5** If you **bang** something on something else or if you **bang** it down, you quickly and violently put it on a surface, because you are angry. *He banged down the telephone.* **6** If you **bang** a part of your body, you accidentally knock it against something and hurt yourself. *He hurried into the hall, banging his shin against a chair in the darkness.* ► Also a noun. ...*a nasty bang on the head.* **7** If you **bang** into something or someone, you bump or knock them hard, usually because you are not looking where you are going. `◆◆◇◇◇` `N-COUNT; SOUND VERB V` `V-ERG: V n V adj` `VERB: V n V on n` `VERB: V n prep V n adv n` `VERB V n` `N-COUNT` `VERB: V into n`

8 A person's **bangs** are the part of their hair that comes down over their forehead and that is cut straight across. The usual British word is **fringe**. `N-PLURAL AMERICAN`

9 You can use **bang** to emphasize expressions that indicate an exact position or an exact time. *For once you leave bang on time for work.* `ADV: ADV prep PRAGMATICS`

10 If something begins or ends **with a bang**, it begins or ends very successfully, attracting a lot of attention. *Her career began with a bang in 1986.* **11** See also **big bang theory** ● to **bang** your **head against a brick wall**: see **brick**. ● to **bang two people's heads together**: see **head**. `PHRASE`

bang on about. If someone **bangs on about** something, they keep talking about it in a boring or annoying way. *He has been banging on about education reform for years.* `PHRASAL VB no passive INFORMAL`

bang out. 1 If a company **bangs out** a poor quality product, they produce large quantities of it in order to make money; used showing disapproval. ...*factories that banged out the same product year after year.* **2** If someone **bangs out** a tune on a musical instrument such as a piano, they play it loudly and not very well. `PHRASAL VB PRAGMATICS V P noun V P noun`

bang up. When someone is locked in a prison cell for a period of time, you can say they are **banged up** there. `PHRASAL VB be V-ed P INFORMAL`

bang·er /'bæŋə/ **bangers. Banger** is an informal British word. **1 Bangers** are sausages. **2** You can describe a car as an old **banger** if it is old and in very bad condition. `N-COUNT N-COUNT`

ban·gle /'bæŋgəl/ **bangles.** A **bangle** is a decorated metal or wooden ring that you can wear round your wrist or ankle. `N-COUNT`

,bang-'on; also spelled **bang on.** If someone is **bang-on** with something, they are exactly right in their opinions or actions. *If we are not bang-on with our preparations then we could have problems.* `ADJ: v-link ADJ BRITISH, INFORMAL`

ban·ish /'bænɪʃ/ **banishes, banishing, banished. 1** If someone or something **is banished** from a place or area of activity, they are sent away from it and prevented from entering it. *They tried to banish him from politics.* **♦ ban·ish·ment** /'bænɪʃmənt/. ...*banishment from political and industrial life.* **2** If you **banish** something unpleasant, you get rid of it. ...*diseases like malaria that have been banished for centuries.* **3** If you **banish** the thought of something, you stop thinking about it. *The past few days had been banished from his mind.* `◆◇◇◇◇` `VERB be V-ed V n from/to n` `N-UNCOUNT` `VERB V n` `VERB: V n he V-ed`

ban·is·ter /'bænɪstə/ **banisters;** also spelled **bannister.** A **banister** is a rail supported by posts and fixed along the side of a staircase. The plural **banisters** can be used to refer to one of these rails. *I still remember sliding down the banisters.* `N-COUNT`

ban·jo /'bændʒəʊ/ **banjos.** A banjo is a musical instrument that looks like a guitar with a circular body, a long neck, and four or more strings. See picture headed **musical instruments**. `◆◇◇◇◇ N-VAR`

bank 1 finance and storage

bank /bæŋk/ **banks, banking, banked. 1** A bank is an institution where people or businesses can keep their money. **2** A **bank** is a building where a bank provides its services. **3** If you **bank** with a particular bank, you have an account with that bank. *My husband has banked with the Co-op since before the war.* **4** If you **bank** money, you pay it into a bank. `◆◆◆◆◆` `N-COUNT` `N-COUNT` `VERB V with n` `VERB: V n`

5 If you say that the cost of something will not **break the bank**, you mean that it will not cost a large sum of money. `PHRASE`

6 You use **bank** to refer to a store of something. For example, a blood **bank** is a store of blood that is kept ready for use. `N-COUNT with supp`

bank 2 areas and masses

bank /bæŋk/ **banks. 1** The **banks** of a river, canal, or lake are the raised areas of ground along its edge. **2** A **bank** of ground is a raised area of it with a flat top and one or two sloping sides. ...*a grassy bank.* **3** A **bank** of something is a long high mass of it. ...*a bank of fog.* **4** A **bank** of things, especially machines, switches, or dials, is a row of them, or a series of rows. **5** See also **banked**. `◆◆◇◇◇` `N-COUNT` `N-COUNT` `N-COUNT: N of n` `N-COUNT`

bank 3 other verb uses

bank /bæŋk/ **banks, banking, banked.** When an aircraft **banks**, one of its wings rises higher than the other, usually when it is changing direction. `◆◇◇◇◇ VERB: V`

bank on. If you **bank on** something happening, you expect it to happen and rely on it happening. *The Berlin government is banking on the Olympics to save the city money.* `PHRASAL VB V P n`

bank·able /'bæŋkəbəl/. In the entertainment industry, someone or something that is described as **bankable** is very popular and therefore likely to be very profitable. *Madonna had become the world's most bankable star.* `ADJ-GRADED`

'bank account, bank accounts. A bank account is an arrangement with a bank which allows you to keep your money in the bank and to take some out when you need it. `◆◇◇◇◇ N-COUNT`

'bank balance, bank balances. Your bank balance is the amount of money that you have in your bank account at a particular time. `N-COUNT`

'bank card, bank cards; also spelled **bankcard.** A **bank card** is a rectangular piece of plastic which the bank gives you and which you have to show when you pay for something by cheque. `N-COUNT`

banked /bæŋkt/. **1** A **banked** stretch of road is higher on one side than the other. **2** If a place is **banked** with something, it is piled high with that thing. If something is **banked up**, it is piled high. *The snow was banked up along the roadside.* `ADJ` `ADJ: v-link ADJ`

bank·er /'bæŋkə/ **bankers.** A banker is someone who works in banking at a senior level. ◆◆◆◇◇ N-COUNT

bank 'holiday, bank holidays. A bank holiday is a public holiday. The usual American expression is **national holiday**. ◆◇◇◇◇ N-COUNT BRITISH

bank·ing /'bæŋkɪŋ/. Banking is the business activity of banks and similar institutions. ◆◆◇◇◇ N-UNCOUNT

bank·note /'bæŋknəʊt/ **banknotes**; also spelled **bank note**. Banknotes are pieces of paper money. ◆◇◇◇◇ N-COUNT

'bank rate, bank rates. The bank rate is the rate of interest at which a bank lends money. In Britain, the bank rate is now called the **base rate**. N-COUNT

bank·roll /'bæŋkrəʊl/ **bankrolls, bankrolling, bankrolled.** 1 To bankroll a person, organization, or project means to provide the financial resources that they need. *The company has bankrolled a couple of local movies.* 2 A bankroll is the financial resources used to back a person, project, or institution. *We have a guaranteed minimum bankroll of £1.7m over the five LPs.* VERB V n AMERICAN, INFORMAL N-SING AMERICAN

bank·rupt /'bæŋkrʌpt/ **bankrupts, bankrupting, bankrupted.** 1 People or organizations that go bankrupt do not have enough money to pay their debts. *He was declared bankrupt after failing to pay a £114m loan guarantee.* 2 To bankrupt a person or organization means to make them go bankrupt. *The move to the market nearly bankrupted the firm and its director.* 3 A bankrupt is a person who has been declared bankrupt by a court of law. ◆◆◇◇◇ ADJ VERB V n N-COUNT

4 You use **bankrupt** to say that someone or something is completely without a particular quality. *He thinks that European civilisation is morally bankrupt.* ADJ PRAGMATICS

bank·rupt·cy /'bæŋkrʌptsi/ **bankruptcies.** 1 Bankruptcy is the state of being bankrupt. *Many established firms are facing bankruptcy.* 2 A bankruptcy is an instance of an organization or person going bankrupt. *The number of corporate bankruptcies climbed in August.* ◆◆◇◇◇ N-UNCOUNT N-COUNT

3 If you refer to someone's or something's **bankruptcy**, you are emphasizing that it is completely without a particular quality. *The massacre laid bare the moral bankruptcy of the regime.* N-UNCOUNT PRAGMATICS

'bank statement, bank statements. A bank statement is a printed document showing all the money paid into and taken out of a bank account. N-COUNT

ban·ner /'bænə/ **banners.** 1 A banner is a long strip of cloth with a message or slogan on it. 2 If someone does something **under the banner of** a particular cause, idea, or belief, they do it saying that they support that cause, idea, or belief. *...the first country to forge a new economic system under the banner of Marxism.* ◆◆◇◇◇ N-COUNT PHRASE

,banner 'headline, banner headlines. A banner headline is a large headline in a newspaper that stretches across the front page. N-COUNT

bannister /'bænɪstə/. See **banister**.

ban·quet /'bæŋkwɪt/ **banquets.** A banquet is a grand formal dinner. ◆◇◇◇◇ N-COUNT

ban·quet·ing /'bæŋkwɪtɪŋ/. A banqueting hall or room is a large room where banquets are held. ADJ: ADJ n

ban·quette /bæŋ'ket/ **banquettes.** A banquette is a long low cushioned seat, long enough for more than one person to sit on at a time. N-COUNT

ban·shee /bæn'ʃiː, AM 'bænʃi/ **banshees.** In Irish folklore, a banshee is a female spirit who warns you by her long sad cry that someone in your family is going to die. N-COUNT

ban·tam /'bæntəm/ **bantams.** A bantam is a breed of small chicken. N-COUNT

bantam·weight /'bæntəmweɪt/ **bantamweights.** A bantamweight is a boxer who weighs between 51 and 53.5 kilograms, or a wrestler who weighs between 52 and 57 kilograms. N-COUNT

ban·ter /'bæntə/ **banters, bantering, bantered.** 1 Banter is teasing or joking talk that is amusing and friendly. 2 If you banter with someone, you tease them or joke with them in an amusing friendly way. *He and Cosell shared a cocktail and bantered easily... All this was said in a bantering tone.* ◆◇◇◇◇ N-UNCOUNT V-RECIP: V with n pl-n V V-ing

bap /bæp/ **baps.** In some British dialects, a bap is a soft flat bread roll. N-COUNT

bap·tise /bæp'taɪz/. See **baptize**.

bap·tism /'bæptɪzəm/ **baptisms.** A baptism is a Christian ceremony in which a person is baptized. ◆◇◇◇◇ N-VAR

♦ **bap·tis·mal** /bæp'tɪzməl/ *...a biblical scholar who studied the origins of the baptismal ceremony.* ADJ: ADJ n

,baptism of 'fire, baptisms of fire. If someone who has just begun a new job has a **baptism of fire**, they immediately have to cope with many severe difficulties. N-COUNT

bap·tize /bæp'taɪz/ **baptizes, baptizing, baptized**; also spelled **baptise** in British English. When someone **is baptized**, water is sprinkled on them or they are immersed in water as a sign that their sins are forgiven and that they have become a member of the Christian Church. Compare **christen**. VB: usu passive be V-ed

bar /bɑː/ **bars, barring, barred.** 1 A bar is a place where you can buy and drink alcoholic drinks. 2 A bar is a room in a place such as a pub or a hotel where alcoholic drinks are served. 3 A bar is a counter on which alcoholic drinks are served. *He leaned forward across the bar.* ● See also **coffee bar, public bar, singles bar, snack bar, wine bar**. ◆◆◆◇ N-COUNT BRITISH N-COUNT

4 A bar is a long, straight, rigid piece of metal. *...a brick building with bars across the ground floor windows.* 5 If you say that someone is **behind bars**, you mean that they are in prison. N-COUNT PHRASE

6 If you **bar** a door, you place something in front of it or a piece of wood or metal across it, in order to prevent it from being opened. ♦ **barred** *The windows were closed and shuttered, the door was barred.* 7 If you **bar** someone's way, you prevent them from going somewhere or entering a place, by blocking their path. 8 If someone **is barred** from a place or from doing something, they are officially forbidden to go there or to do it. *Many jobs were barred to them.* 9 If something is a **bar** to doing a particular thing, it prevents someone from doing it. *One of the fundamental bars to communication is the lack of a universally spoken, common language.* ● See also **colour bar**. 10 If you say that there are **no holds barred** when people are fighting or competing for something, you mean that they are no longer following any rules in their efforts to win. VERB: V n ADJ VERB: V n VERB: be V-ed to n VERB PHRASE

11 You can use **bar** when you mean 'except'. For example, all the work **bar** the washing means all the work except the washing. ● See also **barring**. ● You use **bar none** to add emphasis to a statement that someone or something is the best of their kind. *He is simply the best goalscorer we have ever had, bar none.* PREP PHRASE

12 A bar of an electric fire is a piece of metal with wire coiled round it that glows and provides heat when the fire is switched on. 13 A bar of something such as soap or chocolate is a piece of it which is roughly rectangular. 14 The Bar is used to refer to the profession of a barrister in England, or of any kind of lawyer in the United States. *Robert was planning to read for the Bar.* 15 In music, a bar is one of the several parts of the same length into which a piece of music is divided. N-COUNT N-COUNT: with supp N-PROPER: the N N-COUNT

barb /bɑːb/ **barbs.** 1 A barb is a sharp curved point near the end of an arrow or fish-hook which makes the arrow or fish-hook difficult to pull out. 2 A barb is an unkind remark meant as a criticism of someone or something. *The barb stung her exactly the way he hoped it would.* N-COUNT N-COUNT

bar·bar·ian /bɑː'beəriən/ **barbarians.** In former times, barbarians were uncivilized and violent European peoples. ◆◇◇◇◇ N-COUNT

bar·bar·ic /bɑː'bærɪk/. If you describe someone's behaviour as **barbaric**, you strongly disapprove of it because you think that it is extremely cruel or uncivilized. *...this barbaric treatment of animals.* ◆◇◇◇◇ ADJ-GRADED PRAGMATICS

♦ **bar·bar·ity** /bɑː'bærɪti/ **barbarities** *Rebellions were put down with appalling barbarity.* N-VAR

bar·ba·rism /'bɑːbərɪzəm/. If you refer to someone's behaviour as **barbarism**, you strongly disapprove of it because you think that it is extremely cruel or uncivilized. N-UNCOUNT

bar·ba·rous /ˈbɑːbərəs/. **1** If you describe something as **barbarous**, you strongly dislike it because you think that it is rough and uncivilized. *He thought the poetry of Whitman barbarous.* **2** If you describe someone's behaviour as **barbarous**, you strongly disapprove of it because you think that it is extremely cruel. *It was a barbarous attack on a purely civilian train.* ADJ-GRADED PRAGMATICS ADJ-GRADED PRAGMATICS

bar·becue /ˈbɑːbɪkjuː/ **barbecues, barbecuing, barbecued. 1** A **barbecue** is a piece of equipment on which you can cook food such as sausages and burgers. You use barbecues out of doors. **2** If someone has a **barbecue**, they cook food on a barbecue and invite friends to eat it with them. **3** If you **barbecue** food, you cook it on a barbecue. *Tuna can be grilled, fried or barbecued. ...barbecued chicken.* ◆◇◇◇◇ N-COUNT N-COUNT VERB: V n be V-ed V-ed Also V

barbecue 'sauce. Barbecue sauce is a spicy sauce used to flavour food, especially meat cooked on a barbecue. N-UNCOUNT

barbed /bɑːbd/. A **barbed** remark or joke seems polite or humorous, but contains a cleverly hidden criticism. *...barbed comments.* ◆◇◇◇◇ ADJ-GRADED

barbed 'wire. Barbed wire is strong wire with sharp points sticking out of it, which is used to make fences. *...a barbed-wire fence.* ◆◇◇◇◇ N-UNCOUNT

bar·ber /ˈbɑːbə/ **barbers. 1** A **barber** is a man whose job is cutting men's hair. **2** A **barber's** is a shop where a barber works. The American term is **barber shop**. ◆◇◇◇◇ N-COUNT N-SING BRITISH

'barber shop, barber shops; also spelled **barbershop.** A **barber shop** is a shop where a barber works. The British term is **barber's.** N-COUNT AMERICAN

bar·bie /ˈbɑːbi/ **barbies. 1** In Britain and Australia, a **barbie** is a piece of equipment you use out of doors and on which you can cook food such as sausages and burgers. It is an abbreviation for **barbecue. 2** If someone has a **barbie**, they cook food such as sausages and burgers on a barbecue out of doors. **Barbie** is an abbreviation for **barbecue.** N-COUNT INFORMAL N-COUNT INFORMAL

bar·bi·tu·rate /bɑːˈbɪtʃʊrɪt/ **barbiturates.** A **barbiturate** is a drug which people take to make them calm or to help them to sleep. N-COUNT

'bar code, bar codes. A **bar code** is a set of numbers and parallel lines printed on goods sold in shops. It can be electronically scanned at a checkout to register the price of the goods. N-COUNT

bard /bɑːd/ **bards.** A **bard** is a poet. *...a bard of national significance.* N-COUNT LITERARY

Bard. People sometimes refer to William Shakespeare as **the Bard.** N-PROPER: the N

bare /beə/ **barer, barest; bares, baring, bared. 1** If a part of your body is **bare**, it is not covered by any clothing. *Her feet were bare.* **2** A **bare** surface is not covered or decorated with anything. *...bare wooden floors.* **3** If a tree or a branch is **bare**, it has no leaves on it. **4** If a room, cupboard, or shelf is **bare**, it is empty. *His fridge was bare apart from three very withered tomatoes.* **5** An area of ground that is **bare** has no plants growing on it. **6** If someone gives you the **bare** facts or the **barest** details of something, they tell you only the most basic and important things. **7** If you talk about the **bare** minimum or the **bare** essentials, you mean the very least that is necessary. *The army would try to hold the western desert with a bare minimum of forces.* **8** **Bare** is used in front of an amount to emphasize how small it is. *Sales are growing for premium wines, but at a bare 2 percent a year.* **9** If you **bare** something, you uncover it and show it. *He bared his muscular, hairy chest for a women's magazine.* **10** If someone does something **with their bare hands**, they do it without using any weapons or tools. *...using their bare hands to reach the trapped miners.* **11** If you **lay** something **bare**, you uncover it completely so that it can then be seen. *Without the shirt, the man's shoulder wound was laid bare.* **12** If you **lay bare** something or someone, you reveal or expose them. *No one wants to expose themselves, lay their feelings* ◆◆◆◇◇ ADJ ADJ-GRADED ADJ-GRADED ADJ-GRADED ADJ-GRADED ADJ-GRADED: det ADJ ADJ-GRADED: det ADJ ADJ: a ADJ amount PRAGMATICS VERB V n WRITTEN PHRASE PHRASE PHRASE

bare. **13** If you **bare** your **soul**, you tell someone your most secret thoughts and feelings. **14 ● the bare bones:** see **bone.** PHRASE

bare·back /ˈbeəbæk/. If you ride **bareback**, you ride a horse without a saddle. ▶ Also an adjective. *...a bareback rider in a circus.* ADV: ADV after v ADJ: ADJ n

bare-'faced; also spelled **barefaced.** You use **bare-faced** to describe someone's behaviour when you want to emphasize that they do not care that they are behaving wrongly; used showing disapproval. *Mr Perry made a mental note of this bare-faced lie.* ADJ: ADJ n PRAGMATICS

bare·foot /ˈbeəfʊt/. Someone who is **barefoot** or **barefooted** is not wearing anything on their feet. ◆◇◇◇◇ ADJ

bare·headed /ˌbeəˈhedɪd/. Someone who is **bare-headed** is not wearing a hat or any other covering on their head. ADJ

bare·ly /ˈbeəli/. **1** You use **barely** to say that something is only just true or only just the case. *Anastasia could barely remember the ride to the hospital.* **2** If you say that one thing had **barely** happened when something else happened, you mean that the first event was followed immediately by the second. *The water had barely come to a simmer when she cracked four eggs into it.* ◆◆◆◇◇ ADV ADV: ADV before v

barf /bɑːf/ **barfs, barfing, barfed.** If someone **barfs**, they vomit. The usual British word is **puke.** VERB: V INFORMAL AMERICAN

bar·fly /ˈbɑːflaɪ/ **barflies.** A **barfly** is a person who spends a lot of time drinking in bars. *...a barfly who likes nothing more than staying up late playing pool.* N-COUNT INFORMAL

bar·gain /ˈbɑːgɪn/ **bargains, bargaining, bargained. 1** Something that is a **bargain** is good value for money, usually because it has been sold at a lower price than normal. *At this price the wine is a bargain.* **2** A **bargain** is an agreement, especially a formal business agreement, in which two people or groups agree what each of them will do, pay, or receive. *The treaty was based on a bargain between the French and German governments.* **3** When people **bargain** with each other, they discuss what each of them will do, pay, or receive. *Shop in small local markets and don't be afraid to bargain.* ♦ **bar·gain·er, bargainers** *A union bargainer said that those jobs have been saved.* ♦ **bar·gain·ing** *The government has called for sensible pay bargaining.* **4** If people **drive a hard bargain**, they argue with determination in order to achieve a deal which is favourable to themselves. *Ukraine was always going to drive a hard bargain before signing the treaty.* **5** If you **keep your side of the bargain**, you do what you have promised or arranged to do. *Dealing with this dictator wasn't an option. He wouldn't have kept his side of the bargain.* **6** You use **into the bargain** when mentioning an additional quantity, feature, fact, or action, to emphasize the fact that it is also involved. *She is rich. Now you say she is a beauty into the bargain.* ◆◆◆◇◇ N-COUNT N-COUNT VERB: V with n V N-COUNT N-UNCOUNT PHRASE PHRASE PHRASE PRAGMATICS

bargain for. If someone gets something they had not **bargained for** or gets more than they **bargained for**, something happens that they did not expect or something happens to a greater degree than they had expected. *...expenses I hadn't bargained for.* PHRASAL VB V P n

bargain 'basement; also spelled **bargain-basement.** **Bargain basement** is used to describe things that are cheap and not very good quality. *...a bargain-basement rock musical.* ADJ: ADJ n

'bargain hunter, bargain hunters; also spelled **bargain-hunter.** A **bargain hunter** is someone who looks for goods that are value for money, usually because they are on sale at a lower price than normal. N-COUNT

'bargaining chip, bargaining chips. In negotiations with other people, a **bargaining chip** is something that you are prepared to give up in order to obtain what you want. *Rubio suggests that oil be used as a bargaining chip in any trade talks.* N-COUNT

'bargaining counter, bargaining counters. A **bargaining counter** is the same as a **bargaining chip.** N-COUNT BRITISH

barge /bɑːdʒ/ **barges, barging, barged. 1** A barge is a long narrow boat that is used for carrying heavy loads, especially on canals. **2** If you **barge through** a place, you rush into it in a rough and rude way. *Students tried to barge into the secretariat buildings.* **3** If you **barge into** someone or **barge past** them, you bump against them roughly and rudely. *He barged past her and sprang at Gillian.*
N-COUNT; also by N
VERB
V into/through n
INFORMAL
VERB
V into/past n
INFORMAL

barge in. If you **barge in** or **barge in on** someone, you rudely interrupt what they are doing or saying. *I'm sorry to barge in like this, but I have a problem I hope you can solve.*
PHRASAL VB
V P on
V P
INFORMAL

barge pole; also spelled **bargepole**. If you say that you **wouldn't touch** something **with a barge pole**, you mean that you would not want to have anything to do with it, either because you do not trust it, or because you do not like it.
PHRASE
BRITISH, INFORMAL

bari·tone /ˈbærɪtəʊn/ **baritones. 1** In music, a baritone is a man with a fairly deep singing voice that is lower than that of a tenor but higher than that of a bass. **2** If a man has a **baritone** speaking voice, his voice is low and pleasant to listen to.
N-COUNT
N-SING

bar·ium /ˈbeəriəm/. **Barium** is a soft silvery-white metal.
N-UNCOUNT

bark /bɑːk/ **barks, barking, barked. 1** When a dog **barks**, it makes a short loud noise, once or several times. *A small dog barked at a seagull.* ► Also a noun. *The Doberman let out a string of roaring barks.* **2** If you **bark** at someone, you shout at them aggressively in a loud rough voice. *A policeman held his gun in both hands and barked an order.* **3** If you say that someone's **bark is worse than** their **bite**, you mean that they seem much more unpleasant or hostile than they really are. ● **be barking up the wrong tree** see **tree**. **4 Bark** is the tough material that covers the outside of a tree.
VERB: V
V at n
N-COUNT
VERB: V
V at n
PHRASE
INFORMAL
N-UNCOUNT

barking mad. If you say that someone is **barking mad**, you mean that they are insane or are acting very foolishly. *The builder looked at me as though I was barking mad.*
ADJ;
v-link ADJ
PRAGMATICS
BRITISH, INFORMAL

bar·ley /ˈbɑːli/. **Barley** is a crop which has seeds that are used in the production of food, beer, and whisky.
N-UNCOUNT

bar·maid /ˈbɑːmeɪd/ **barmaids.** A barmaid is a woman who serves drinks behind a bar.
N-COUNT

bar·man /ˈbɑːmən/ **barmen.** A barman is a man who serves drinks behind a bar.
N-COUNT

bar mitz·vah /ˌbɑː ˈmɪtsvə/ **bar mitzvahs.** A bar mitzvah is a ceremony and celebration that takes place on or close to the thirteenth birthday of a Jewish boy, after which he has the status, religious duties, and responsibilities of an adult man.
N-COUNT

bar·my /ˈbɑːmi/ **barmier, barmiest.** If you say that someone or something is **barmy**, you mean that they are slightly mad or very foolish. *This policy is absolutely barmy.*
ADJ-GRADED
PRAGMATICS
BRITISH, INFORMAL

barn /bɑːn/ **barns.** A barn is a building on a farm in which crops or animal food can be kept.
N-COUNT

bar·na·cle /ˈbɑːnɪkəl/ **barnacles. Barnacles** are small shellfish that fix themselves tightly to rocks and the bottoms of boats.
N-COUNT

barn dance, barn dances. A barn dance is a social event people go to for country dancing.
N-COUNT

barn·storm /ˈbɑːnstɔːm/ **barnstorms, barnstorming, barnstormed.** When people such as politicians, actors, or sports players **barnstorm**, they travel around rural areas making political speeches, putting on shows, or playing matches. *He would ignore the Senate and barnstorm across the nation, rallying the people to the cause.*
VERB: V
V prep/adv
Also V n
AMERICAN

barn·storm·ing /ˈbɑːnstɔːmɪŋ/. If you describe the performance of an actor, a sports player, or a musician as **barnstorming**, you are emphasizing that it is full of energy and very exciting to watch. *...a fabulous version of the classic play, with a barnstorming performance from Gerard Depardieu.*
ADJ: ADJ n
PRAGMATICS
BRITISH

barn·yard /ˈbɑːnjɑːd/ **barnyards.** On a farm, the barnyard is the area in front of or next to a barn.
N-COUNT

ba·rom·eter /bəˈrɒmɪtə/ **barometers. 1** A barometer is an instrument that measures air pressure and shows when the weather is changing. **2** If you describe something as a **barometer** of a particular situation, you mean that it indicates how things are changing or how things are likely to develop. *In past presidential elections, Missouri has been a barometer of the rest of the country.*
N-COUNT
N-COUNT:
with supp

bar·on /ˈbærən/ **barons. 1** A baron is a man who is a member of the lowest rank of the nobility. **2** You can use **baron** to refer to someone who controls a large amount of a particular industry and who is therefore extremely powerful. *...the drug barons.*
N-COUNT
N-COUNT:
with supp

bar·on·ess /ˈbærənes/ **baronesses.** A baroness is a woman who is a member of the lowest rank of the nobility, or who is the wife or widow of a baron.
N-COUNT;
N-TITLE

bar·on·et /ˈbærənɪt/ **baronets.** In Britain, a baronet is a man who has been given a special title as an honour, or has inherited this title from his father. Baronets rank below barons but above knights.
N-COUNT

ba·ro·nial /bəˈrəʊniəl/. **1** If you describe a house or room as **baronial**, you mean that it is large, impressive, and old-fashioned in appearance, and looks as if it belongs to someone from the upper classes. **2 Baronial** means relating to a baron or barons. *...the baronial feuding of the Middle Ages.*
ADJ-GRADED
ADJ: ADJ n

baro·ny /ˈbærəni/ **baronies.** A barony is the rank or position of a baron.
N-COUNT

ba·roque /bəˈrɒk, AM -ˈrəʊk/. **1 Baroque** architecture and art is an elaborate style of architecture and art that was popular in Europe in the seventeenth and early eighteenth centuries. *...the baroque church of San Leonardo.* ► The baroque style and period in art and architecture are sometimes referred to as **the baroque**. **2 Baroque** music is a style of European music that was written in the 18th century. ► The baroque style and period in music are sometimes referred to as **the baroque**. **3 Baroque** things are complicated and elaborate. *...a baroque figure dressed in theatrical, but elegant, clothes.*
ADJ: ADJ n
N-SING:
the N
ADJ: ADJ n
N-SING:
the N
ADJ-GRADED

bar·rack /ˈbærək/ **barracks, barracking, barracked. 1** A barracks is a building or group of buildings where soldiers or other members of the armed forces live and work. **Barracks** is the singular and plural form. **2** If an audience **barracks** public speakers or performers, they interrupt them, for example by making rude remarks. *Fans gained more enjoyment barracking him than cheering on the team.* ♦ **bar·rack·ing** *...the barracking that he got from the crowd.*
N-COUNT
VERB
V n
BRITISH
N-UNCOUNT

bar·ra·cu·da /ˌbærəˈkjuːdə, AM -ˈkuː-/ **barracudas; barracuda** can also be used as the plural form. A barracuda is a large tropical sea fish with a protruding lower jaw and sharp teeth. *Mosley caught twelve barracuda.*
N-COUNT

bar·rage /ˈbærɑːʒ, AM bəˈrɑːʒ/ **barrages, barraging, barraged.** Pronounced /ˈbærɪdʒ/ for meaning 4 in American English. **1** A barrage is continuous firing on an area with a large number of artillery weapons such as heavy guns and tanks. *...a barrage of anti-aircraft fire.* **2** A barrage of something such as criticism or complaints is a large number of them directed at someone, often in an aggressive way. *He was faced with a barrage of angry questions.* **3** If you **are barraged** by people or things, you have to deal with a great number of people or things you would rather avoid. *Hughes was barraged with phone calls from friends who were furious at the indiscreet disclosures.* **4** A barrage is a construction that is built across a river to control the level of the water. *...a hydro-electric tidal barrage.*
N-COUNT
N-COUNT
VB: usu passive,
be V-ed by n
be V-ed with n
N-COUNT

bar·rel /ˈbærəl/ **barrels, barrelling, barrelled;** spelled **barreling, barreled** in American English. **1** In the oil industry, a **barrel** is a unit of measurement equal to 159 litres. *Kuwait was exporting 1.5 million barrels of oil a day.* **2** A **barrel** is a large round container for liquids or food. *...red wines which habitually spend time ageing in oak barrels.* **3** The **barrel** of a gun is the tube through which the
N-COUNT
N-COUNT
N-COUNT

bullet moves when the gun is fired. ♦ **-barrelled** ...a COMB *short-barreled rifle.* ● See also **double-barrelled**. **4** VERB If a vehicle or person **is barreling** in a particular di- V prep/adv rection, they are moving very quickly in that direc- tion. *The car was barreling down the street.*

5 If you say that someone moves or buys something PHRASE **lock, stock, and barrel**, you are emphasizing that PRAGMATICS they move or buy every part or item of it. *They dug up their New Jersey garden and moved it lock, stock, and barrel back home.* **6** If someone **has** you **over a barrel**, PHRASE they have put you in a difficult situation where you INFORMAL have little choice but to do what they want you to do. **7** If you say that someone is **scraping the barrel**, or PHRASE **scraping the bottom of the barrel**, you disapprove of PRAGMATICS the fact that they are using or doing something of ex- INFORMAL tremely poor quality. **8** See also **pork barrel**.

bar·ren /ˈbærən/. **1 Barren** land has very few ◆◇◇◇◇ plants and no trees, especially because the soil is ADJ-GRADED poor and dry. *...barren desert land.* ♦ **bar·ren·** **·ness 2** If you describe something such as an activ- N-UNCOUNT ity or a period of your life as **barren**, you mean that ADJ-GRADED you achieve no success during it or that it has no WRITTEN useful results. *...an empty exercise barren of utility.* ♦ **barrenness** *...the barrenness of contemporary* N-UNCOUNT *life.* **3** If you describe a room or a place as **barren**, ADJ you do not like it because it has almost no furniture PRAGMATICS or other objects in it. *The room was austere, nearly* WRITTEN *barren of furniture.* **4** A **barren** woman or female ADJ animal is unable to have babies. ♦ **barrenness** *...a* DATED *ceremony designed to cure women of barrenness.* N-UNCOUNT

bar·ri·cade /ˈbærɪkeɪd/ **barricades, barricad-** ◆◆◇◇◇ **ing, barricaded**. **1** A **barricade** is a line of vehi- N-COUNT cles or other objects placed across a road or open space to stop people getting past. *Large areas of the city have been closed off by barricades set up by the demonstrators.* **2** If you **barricade** something such VERB as a road or an entrance, you place a barricade V n across it, usually to stop someone getting in. *The ri- oters barricaded streets with piles of blazing tyres.* **3** If you **barricade** yourself inside a room or build- VERB ing, you place barriers across the door or entrance V pron-refl so that other people cannot get in. *The students* prep/adv *have barricaded themselves into their dormitory building.*

bar·ri·er /ˈbæriə/ **barriers**. **1** A **barrier** is some- ◆◆◆◇◇ thing such as a rule, law, or policy that makes it dif- N-COUNT ficult or impossible for something to happen or be achieved. *Duties and taxes are the most obvious bar- rier to free trade.* **2** A **barrier** is a problem that pre- N-COUNT vents two people or groups from agreeing or com- municating with each other. *There is no reason why love shouldn't cross the age barrier.* **3** A **barrier** is N-COUNT something such as a fence or wall that is put in place to prevent people from moving easily from one area to another. *The demonstrators broke through heavy police barriers.* **4** A **barrier** is an ob- N-COUNT ject or layer that physically prevents something from moving from one place to another. *...a natural barrier between the house and the lake.* **5** You can N-SING refer to a particular number or amount as a **barrier** the N, when you think it is a significant level, because it is with supp not exceeded very often or easily. *Unemployment will soon break the barrier of three million.* **6** See also **crash barrier, sound barrier.**

ˈ**barrier method, barrier methods**. **Barrier** N-COUNT **methods** of contraception involve the use of con- doms, diaphragms, or other devices that physically prevent the sperm from reaching the egg.

bar·ring /ˈbɑːrɪŋ/. You use **barring** to indicate that ◆◇◇◇◇ the person, thing, or event that you are mentioning PREP is an exception to your statement. *Barring accidents, I believe they will succeed.*

bar·rio /ˈbɑːriəʊ/ **barrios**. **1** A **barrio** is a mainly N-COUNT Spanish-speaking neighbourhood in an American city. *...the barrios of Santa Cruz.* **2** A **barrio** is an N-COUNT urban district in a Spanish-speaking country. *...the barrios of Mexico City.*

bar·ris·ter /ˈbærɪstə/ **barristers**. A **barrister** is a ◆◆◇◇◇ lawyer who represents clients in the higher courts N-COUNT of law. Compare **solicitor**. BRITISH

bar·room /ˈbɑːruːm/ **barrooms;** also spelled **bar-** N-COUNT **room**. A **barroom** is a room or building in which al- AMERICAN coholic drinks are served over a counter. *...a bar- room brawl.*

bar·row /ˈbærəʊ/ **barrows**. **1** A **barrow** is the same N-COUNT as a **wheelbarrow**. **2** A **barrow** is a cart from which N-COUNT fruit or other goods are sold in the street. *The stolen* BRITISH *goods were then sold off barrows in street-markets.*

bar·tender /ˈbɑːtendə/ **bartenders**. A **bartender** is N-COUNT a person who serves drinks behind a bar. The Brit- AMERICAN ish word is **barman** or **barmaid**.

bar·ter /ˈbɑːtə/ **barters, bartering, bartered**. If ◆◇◇◇◇ you **barter** goods, you exchange them for other VERB: V n goods, rather than selling them for money. *They* V n for n *have been bartering wheat for cotton and timber.* Also V ▶ Also a noun. *Overall, barter is a very inefficient* N-UNCOUNT *means of organizing transactions.*

ba·sal /ˈbeɪsəl/. **1 Basal** means relating to or form- ADJ: ADJ n ing the base of something. *Side shoots should be cut* TECHNICAL *back to one leaf above the basal cluster.* **2** Your **basal** ADJ: ADJ n metabolic rate is the rate at which your body uses TECHNICAL energy when it is at rest.

bas·alt /ˈbæsɔːlt, AM bəˈsɔːlt/ **basalts**. Basalt is a N-VAR type of black rock that is produced by volcanoes.

base 1 lowest or most basic part of something

base /beɪs/ **bases, basing, based; baser bas-** ◆◆◆◆◆ **est. 1** The **base** of something is its lowest edge or N-COUNT part. *There was a cycle path running along this side of the wall, right at its base. ...the base of the head.* **2** The **base** of an object such as a box or vase is the N-COUNT lower surface of it that touches the surface it rests on. *...plunge the base of the pan into a bowl of very cold water.* **3** The **base** of an object that has several N-COUNT sections and that rests on a surface is the lower sec- tion of it. *...a solid bed base.* **4** A **base** is a layer of N-COUNT something which will have another layer added to it. *Spoon the mixture on to the biscuit base.* **5** A position or thing that is a **base** for something is N-COUNT one from which that thing can be developed or achieved. *The family base was crucial to my develop- ment.* **6** If you **base** one thing on another thing, he VERB first thing develops from the second thing. *He based* V n on/upon n *his conclusions on the evidence given by the captured prisoners.* ♦ **based** *Three of the new products are* ADJ: *based on traditional herbal medicines.* **7** The **base** of a v-link ADJ on n substance such as paint or food is the main ingredient N-COUNT of it, to which other substances can be added. **8** A **base** is a system of counting and expressing num- N-COUNT: bers. The decimal system uses base 10, and the binary also N num system uses base 2. **9 Base** behaviour is behaviour that is immoral or dis- ADJ-GRADED honourable. *...the baser emotions.* LITERARY

base 2 place you do something from

base /beɪs/ **bases**. **1** A military **base** is a place N-COUNT which part of an army, navy, or air force works from. **2** Your **base** is the main place where you N-COUNT work, stay, or live. *Her base was her home in Scot- land.* **3** If a place is a **base** for a certain activity, the N-COUNT activity can be carried out at that place or from that place. *Hong Kong and Taiwan increasingly depend upon mainland China as a base for their exports.* **4** A **base** in rounders or baseball is one of the places N-COUNT at each corner of the square on the pitch.

base·ball /ˈbeɪsbɔːl/ **baseballs**. **1** Baseball is a ◆◆◆◇◇ game played by two teams of nine players. Each N-UNCOUNT player from one team hits a ball with a bat and then tries to run round four bases before the other team can get the ball back. **2** A **baseball** is a small hard N-COUNT ball which is used in the game of baseball.

based /beɪst/. If you are **based** in a particular ◆◆◆◆◆ place, that is the place where you live or do most of ADJ: your work. *Both firms are based in Kent.* ▶ Also after v-link ADJ adjectives and nouns referring to places. COMB *...American-based companies.* ● See also **base**.

-based /-beɪst/. **1 -based** combines with nouns to COMB mean that the thing mentioned is a central part or feature. *...computer-based jobs. ...oil-based sauces.* **2 -based** combines with adverbs to mean having a COMB particular kind of basis. *There are growing signs of more broadly-based popular unrest.*

base·less /'beɪsləs/. If you describe an accusation, ADJ rumour, or report as **baseless**, you mean that it is not true and is not based on facts. *Baseless allegations have been made.*

base·line /'beɪslaɪn/ **baselines;** also spelled ◆◇◇◇◇ **base-line. 1** The **baseline** of a tennis or badminton N-COUNT court is one of the lines at each end of the court that mark the limits of play. **2** A **baseline** is a value N-COUNT or starting point on a scale with which other values can be compared. *...a baseline for measuring progress.*

base·ment /'beɪsmənt/ **basements.** The **base-** ◆◆◇◇◇ **ment** of a building is a floor built partly or wholly N-COUNT below ground level.

,**base 'metal, base metals.** A **base metal** is a N-COUNT metal such as copper, zinc, tin, or lead that is not a precious metal.

'**base rate, base rates.** In Britain, the **base rate** ◆◇◇◇◇ is the rate of interest that banks use as a basis when N-COUNT they are calculating the rates that they charge on loans.

bases. 1 Bases, pronounced /'beɪsɪz/, is the plural of **base. 2 Bases,** pronounced /'beɪsiːz/ is the plural of **basis.**

bash /bæʃ/ **bashes, bashing, bashed. 1** A **bash** ◆◆◇◇◇ is a party or celebration. *...one of the biggest showbiz* N-COUNT *bashes of the year.* INFORMAL
2 If someone **bashes** you, they attack you by hitting or VERB punching you hard. *I bashed him on the head... The* V n prep/adv *chef was bashed over the head with a bottle.* ♦ **-bash-** INFORMAL ·**er, -bashers** *...gay-bashers who go around looking* COMB *for homosexuals to beat up.* ♦ **-bash·ing** *He offered to* COMB *make a public service announcement on television condemning gay-bashing.* **3** If you **bash** something, VERB: V n you hit it hard in a rough or careless way. *Too many* V n prep/adv *golfers try to bash the ball out of sand.* Also V prep/ adv
4 To **bash** someone means to criticize them severely, VERB usually in a public way. *The President could continue* V n *to bash Democrats as being soft on crime.* ♦ **-bashing** JOURNALISM *Tory-bashing or Labour-bashing will not be enough to* COMB *shift bored, suspicious voters.*

bash in. If someone **bashes** a person's or animal's PHRASAL VB head **in,** they hit it very hard and cause severe injuries V n P to it. *The butt of a rifle had been used to bash in his* V P noun *skull.*

bash out. If you say that someone **bashes** some- PHRASAL VB thing **out,** you mean that they produce it quickly or in V n P large quantities, but without much care or thought. V P noun *Up to then, they'd merrily bashed out albums in be-* INFORMAL *tween tours.*

bash·ful /'bæʃfʊl/. Someone who is **bashful** is shy ADJ-GRADED and easily embarrassed. *We tend to be bashful about our talent and skills.* ♦ **bash·ful·ly** /'bæʃfʊli/ *'No,'* ADV-GRADED: *Wang Fu said bashfully.* ♦ **bash·ful·ness** *Suddenly* ADV with v *overcome with bashfulness, he lowered his voice.* N-UNCOUNT

ba·sic /'beɪsɪk/. **1** You use **basic** to describe things, ◆◆◆◆◇ activities, and principles that are very important or ADJ-GRADED necessary, and on which others depend. *...the basic skills of reading, writing and communicating. ...access to justice is a basic right.* **2 Basic** goods and ADJ-GRADED services are very simple ones which every human being needs. You can also refer to people's **basic** needs for such goods and services. *...shortages of even the most basic foodstuffs. ...the basic needs of food and water.* **3** If one thing is **basic** to another, it ADJ-GRADED: is absolutely necessary to it, and the second thing v-link ADJ to n cannot exist, succeed, or be imagined without it. *There are certain ethical principles that are basic to all the great religions.* **4** You can use **basic** to em- ADJ: ADJ n phasize that you are referring to what you consider PRAGMATICS to be the most important aspect of a situation, and that you are not concerned with less important details. *There are three basic types of tea... The basic design changed little.*
5 You can use **basic** to describe something that is very ADJ-GRADED simple in style and has only the most necessary features, without any luxuries. *...basic cooking and camping equipment.* **6 Basic** research into a subject ADJ: ADJ n is concerned with gaining knowledge about the subject itself, rather than with its practical applications. **7** ADJ: ADJ n

Basic is used to describe a price or someone's income when this does not include any additional amounts such as special charges or bonuses. *...the basic pay of a typical coalface worker... The basic price for a 10-minute call is only £2.49.* **8** The **basic** rate of income ADJ: ADJ n tax is the lowest or most common rate, which applies to people who earn average incomes. *...the basic level of taxation. ...a basic-rate taxpayer.*

ba·si·cal·ly /'beɪsɪkli/. **1** You use **basically** for em- ◆◆◆◇◇ phasis when you are stating an opinion, or when ADV: you are making an important statement about ADV with cl/ something. *This gun is designed for one purpose –* group *it's basically to kill people... Basically I think he* PRAGMATICS *would be someone who complemented me.* **2** You ADV use **basically** to show that you are describing a PRAGMATICS situation in a simple general way, and that you are not concerned with less important details. *It's basically a vegan diet... Battery charging systems remain basically the same as those in use half a century ago.*

ba·sics /'beɪsɪks/. **1** The **basics** of something are ◆◇◇◇◇ its simplest most important elements, ideas, or N-PLURAL principles, in contrast to more complicated or detailed ones. *...teaching the basics of reading, writing and arithmetic... A strong community cannot be built until the basics are in place... Let's get down to basics.* **2 Basics** are things such as simple foods, N-PLURAL clothes, or equipment that people need in order to live or to deal with a particular situation. *...basics such as bread and milk. ...items that are the basics of a stylish wardrobe.* **3** If you talk about getting PHRASE **back to basics,** you are suggesting that people have become too concerned with complicated details or new theories, and that they should concentrate on simple important ideas or activities. *...a new 'back-to-basics' drive to raise standards of literacy in Britain's schools.*

bas·il /'bæzəl/. **Basil** is a sweet-scented herb that is ◆◇◇◇◇ used in cooking. N-UNCOUNT

ba·sili·ca /bə'zɪlɪkə/ **basilicas.** A **basilica** is a ◆◇◇◇◇ church which is rectangular in shape and has a N-COUNT rounded end, a central nave, and two or four side aisles.

ba·sin /'beɪsən/ **basins. 1** A **basin** is a large or ◆◆◇◇◇ deep bowl that you use for holding liquids, or for N-COUNT mixing or storing food. ▶ A **basin** of something such N-COUNT: as water is an amount of it that is contained in a ba- N of n sin. **2** A **basin** is the same as a **washbasin. 3** The N-COUNT **basin** of a large river is the area of land around it N-COUNT: from which streams run down into it. *...the Amazon* with supp *basin.* **4** A **basin** is a particular region of the world N-COUNT: where the earth's surface is lower than elsewhere. TECHNICAL *...countries around the Pacific Basin.* **5** A **basin** is a N-COUNT partially enclosed area of deep water where boats or ships are kept. *The sheltered yacht basin is right in the centre of town.*

ba·sis /'beɪsɪs/ **bases** /'beɪsiːz/. **1** If something is ◆◆◆◆◇ done on a particular **basis,** it is done according to N-SING: that method, system, or principle. *We're going to be* with supp *meeting there on a regular basis... I've always worked on the basis that if I don't know anything technical I shan't be any worse off.* **2** If you say that you are act- N-SING: ing **on** the **basis** of something, you are giving that as on N the reason for your action. *McGregor must remain* PRAGMATICS *confined, on the basis of the medical reports we have received.* **3** The **basis** of something is its starting N-COUNT point or an important part of it from which it can be further developed. *...the plan as a basis for settling the conflict.* **4** The **basis** for something is a fact N-COUNT or argument that you can use to prove or justify it. *...a common fallacy which has no basis in fact.*

'**basis point, basis points.** A **basis point** is one ◆◇◇◇◇ hundredth of a per cent (.01%). N-COUNT TECHNICAL

bask /bɑːsk, bæsk/ **basks, basking, basked.** ◆◇◇◇◇ **1** If you **bask** in the sunshine, you lie somewhere VERB: sunny and enjoy the warmth. **2** If you **bask** in V in n someone's approval, favour, or admiration, you VERB thoroughly enjoy it. *He has spent a month basking* V in n *in the adulation of the fans back in Jamaica.*

bas·ket /'bɑːskɪt, 'bæs-/ **baskets. 1** A basket is a ◆◆◇◇◇ container made from strips of wood, wicker, plastic, N-COUNT

or metal woven together. ▶ A **basket** of things is a `N-COUNT: N ofn` number of things contained in a basket. ...*a small basket of fruit and snacks.* **2** If you talk about a **basket** of currencies or goods, you are referring to the `N-COUNT TECHNICAL` average or total value of a number of different currencies or goods. **3** In basketball, the **basket** is a net `N-COUNT` hanging from a ring through which players try to throw the ball in order to score points. **4** See also **hanging basket, wastepaper basket.** • **put all** your **eggs in one basket:** see **egg.**

basket·ball /'bɑːskɪtbɔːl, 'bæs-/ **basketballs.** ◆◆◇◇◇
1 Basketball is a game in which two teams of five `N-UNCOUNT` players each try to score goals by throwing a large ball through a circular net fixed to a metal ring at each end of the court. **2** A **basketball** is the large `N-COUNT` ball which is used in the game of basketball.

'**basket case, basket cases.** **1** If you describe a `N-COUNT INFORMAL` country or organization as a **basket case**, you mean that its economy or finances are in a very bad state. **2** If you describe someone as a **basket case**, you `N-COUNT INFORMAL` mean that they are mad or insane.

bas-relief /,bɑːrɪ'liːf, ,bæs-/ **bas-reliefs.** `N-UNCOUNT`
1 Bas-relief is a technique of sculpture in which shapes are carved so that they stand out from the background. **2** A **bas-relief** is a sculpture carved on `N-COUNT` a surface so that it stands out from the background.

bass, basses. Pronounced /beɪs/ for meanings 1 ◆◆◇◇◇
to 4, and /bæs/ for meaning 5. The plural of the noun in meaning 5 is **bass**. **1** A **bass** is a man with a `N-COUNT` very deep singing voice. **2** A **bass** drum, guitar, or `ADJ: ADJ n` other musical instrument produces a very deep sound. **3** In popular music, a **bass** is a bass guitar or `N-VAR` a **double bass**. ◆ **bass·ist, bassists.** A **bassist** is `N-COUNT` someone who plays the bass guitar or the double bass. **4** On a hi-fi or radio, the **bass** is the extent to `N-UNCOUNT` which the lower musical notes can be heard. The **bass** is also the knob which controls this.
5 Bass are edible fish that are found in rivers and the `N-VAR` sea. ▶ **Bass** is a piece of this fish eaten as food. `N-UNCOUNT`

bas·soon /bə'suːn/ **bassoons.** A bassoon is a large `N-VAR` wooden orchestral instrument that is shaped like a tube. You play it by blowing into a curved metal mouthpiece and pressing the keys with your fingers.

bas·tard /'bɑːstəd, 'bæs-/ **bastards.** **1** If someone ◆◆◇◇◇
calls a person, usually a man, a **bastard**, they are in- `N-COUNT PRAGMATICS RUDE` sulting him, for example because he has behaved very unpleasantly. This is an offensive use which you should avoid using. **2** If someone refers to a `N-COUNT PRAGMATICS INFORMAL` person, usually a man, as, for example, a lucky **bastard** or a poor **bastard**, they are expressing strong feelings about him, such as envy or sympathy. Some people find this use offensive. **3** A **bastard** is a per- `N-COUNT DATED` son whose parents were not married to each other at the time that he or she was born. This is an offensive use which you should avoid using. ...*King Arthur's bastard son, Mordred.* **4** If someone de- `N-COUNT PRAGMATICS INFORMAL` scribes a problem or a situation as a **bastard**, they mean that it is extremely annoying or difficult to deal with. Some people find this use offensive. *Life can be a real bastard at times.*

bas·tard·ized /'bɑːstədaɪzd, 'bæs-/; also spelled `ADJ-GRADED FORMAL` **bastardised.** If you refer to something as a **bastardized** form of something else, you mean that the first thing is similar to or copied from the second thing, but is of much poorer quality.

baste /beɪst/ **bastes, basting, basted.** If you `VERB: V n` **baste** meat, you pour hot fat and the juices from the `V` meat itself over it while it is cooking. *Bake for 15-20 minutes, basting occasionally.*

bas·ti·on /'bæstiən, AM -tʃən/ **bastions.** If a sys- ◆◇◇◇◇
tem or organization is described as a **bastion** of a `N-COUNT: with supp FORMAL` particular way of life, it is seen as being important and effective in defending that way of life. ...*a town which had been a bastion of white prejudice.*

bat /bæt/ **bats, batting, batted.** **1** A **bat** is a spe- ◆◆◆◇◇
cially shaped piece of wood that is used for hitting `N-COUNT` the ball in cricket, baseball, rounders, or table-tennis. ...*a baseball bat.* **2** When you **bat**, you have `VERB` a turn at hitting the ball with a bat in cricket, base- `V` ball, or rounders. *Australia, put in to bat, made a*

cautious start. ◆ **bat·ting** *He's likely to open the bat-* `N-UNCOUNT`
ting. **3** If you **go to bat for** someone or **go in to bat** `PHRASE`
for them, you give them your support. *The old judge doesn't like the thought of no one going in to bat for the accused.*

4 A **bat** is a small flying animal that looks like a mouse `N-COUNT`
with leathery wings. Bats fly at night.
5 If you say that someone **doesn't bat an eyelid** when `PHRASE BRITISH`
something surprising happens or when they do something unpleasant, you are surprised or shocked because they remain calm and unemotional. The usual American expression is **doesn't bat an eye**. *The conspirators would have killed thousands of people without batting an eyelid.* **6** If someone does some- `PHRASE BRITISH` thing **off** their **own bat**, they do it without anyone else suggesting it. **7** See also **old bat.**

batch /bætʃ/ **batches.** A **batch** of things or people ◆◆◇◇◇
is a group of them of the same kind, especially a `N-COUNT` group that is dealt with at the same time or is sent to a particular place at the same time. ...*the current batch of trainee priests.*

bat·ed /'beɪtɪd/. If you wait for something with **bat-** `PHRASE FORMAL`
ed breath, you wait anxiously to find out what will happen.

bath /bɑːθ, bæθ/ **baths, bathing, bathed.** When ◆◆◆◇◇
the form **baths** is the plural of the noun it is pronounced /bɑːðz/ or /bæðz/ in British English, and
/bæðz/ in American English. When it is used in the
present tense of the verb, it is pronounced /bɑːθs/
or /bæθs/. **1** A **bath** is a container, usually a long `N-COUNT` rectangular one, which you fill with water and sit in `BRITISH` while you wash your body. The American word is **bathtub. 2** When you have or take a **bath**, you sit or `N-COUNT` lie in a bath filled with water in order to wash your body. **3** If you **bath** someone, especially a child, you `VERB` wash them in a bath. *Don't feel you have to bath* `V n` *your child every day.* ▶ Also a noun. *The midwife* `N-COUNT` *gave him a warm bath.* **4** When you **bath**, you have `VERB` a bath. *The three children all bath in the same bath* `V prep/adv` *water.* **5** See also **bubble bath.** `BRITISH`
6 A **bath** or a **baths** is a public building containing a `N-COUNT` swimming pool, and sometimes other facilities that people can use to have a wash or a bath. The plural **baths** can be used to refer either to one or to more than one of these places.
7 A **bath** is a container filled with a liquid, such as a `N-COUNT` dye or an acid, in which objects are placed, usually as part of a manufacturing or chemical process. ...*a developing photograph placed in a bath of fixer.*
8 See also **bloodbath, Turkish bath.**

bathe /beɪð/ **bathes, bathing, bathed.** **1** If you ◆◆◇◇◇
bathe in a sea, river, or lake, you swim, play, or `VERB` wash yourself in it. *The police have warned the city's* `V prep/adv` *inhabitants not to bathe in the polluted river.* ▶ Also `FORMAL, BRITISH` a noun. *Fifty soldiers were taking an early morning* `N-SING` *bathe in a nearby lake.* ◆ **bath·ing** ...*Britain's 440* `N-UNCOUNT` *designated bathing beaches.* ◆ **bath·er, bathers** `N-COUNT` *The beach was crowded with weekend bathers.*
2 When you **bathe**, you have a bath. *At least 60% of* `VERB` *us now bathe or shower once a day.* **3** If you **bathe** `VERB` someone, especially a child, you wash them in a `AMERICAN` bath. *Shirley plays with, feeds and bathes the baby.*
4 If you **bathe** a part of your body or a wound, you `VERB` wash it gently or soak it in a liquid. *Bathe the infect-* `V n` *ed area in a salt solution.* **5** If a place **is bathed** in `VERB` warmth or a gentle light, it is covered with it. *I was* `be V-ed in n` *led to a small room bathed in soft red light.* **6** See `Also V n in n,` also **sunbathe.** `V n`

bathed /beɪðd/. **1** If someone is **bathed** in sweat or `ADJ:` perspiration, they are sweating or perspiring a great `v-link ADJ in n` deal. **2** If someone is **bathed** in an emotion such as `ADJ:` love, they feel it constantly in a pleasant way. `v-link ADJ in n` `LITERARY`

bath·ing suit /'beɪðɪŋ suːt/ **bathing suits.** A bath- `N-COUNT` ing suit is a piece of clothing which people wear for `AMERICAN` swimming.

bath·ing trunks /'beɪðɪŋ trʌŋks/. **Bathing trunks** `N-PLURAL` are shorts that a man wears for swimming. `BRITISH`

bath·mat /'bɑːθmæt, 'bæθ-/ **bathmats;** also spelled `N-COUNT` **bath mat.** A **bathmat** is a mat which you stand on while you dry yourself after getting out of the bath.

ba·thos /'beɪθɒs/. Bathos is a sudden change in speech or writing from a serious or important subject to a ridiculous or very ordinary one. N-UNCOUNT TECHNICAL

bath·robe /'bɑːθrəʊb/ **bathrobes.** A bathrobe is a loose piece of clothing made of towelling which you wear before or after you have a bath or as a dressing gown. N-COUNT

bath·room /'bɑːθruːm, 'bæθ-/ **bathrooms. 1** A bathroom is a room in a house that contains a bath or shower, a washbasin, and sometimes a toilet. See picture headed **house and flat. 2** A bathroom is a room in a house or public building that contains a toilet. The usual British word is **toilet. 3** When people say that they **are going to the bathroom,** they mean that they are going to use the toilet. The British expression is **go to the toilet.** ◆◆◆◇◇ N-COUNT / N-SING AMERICAN / PHRASE AMERICAN

'**bath towel, bath towels.** A bath towel is a very large towel used for drying your body after you have had a bath. N-COUNT

bath·tub /'bɑːθtʌb, 'bæθ-/ **bathtubs.** A bathtub is a long, usually rectangular, container which you fill with water and sit in to wash your body. The British word is **bath.** N-COUNT AMERICAN

'**bath water;** also spelled **bathwater.** Your **bath water** is the water in which you sit or lie when you have a bath. N-UNCOUNT

ba·tik /bə'tiːk, 'bætɪk/ **batiks. 1** Batik is a process for printing designs on cloth. Wax is put on those areas of the cloth that you do not want to be coloured by dye. **2** A batik is a cloth which has been printed with a batik design. N-UNCOUNT / N-VAR

bat·man /'bætmæn/ **batmen.** In former times, a British army officer's **batman** was his personal servant. N-COUNT

ba·ton /'bætɒn, AM bə'tɑːn/ **batons. 1** A baton is a short heavy stick which is sometimes used as a weapon by the police. **2** A baton is a light thin stick which a conductor uses to conduct an orchestra or a choir. **3** A baton is a long stick with a knob on one end that is sometimes carried by a person marching in a parade. **4** In athletics, the **baton** is a short stick that is passed from one runner to another in a relay race. **5** If someone **passes the baton** to someone else, they pass responsibility for something to that person. If someone **picks up the baton,** they take over responsibility for something. ◆◇◇◇◇ N-COUNT / N-COUNT / N-COUNT / N-COUNT / PHRASE

'**baton charge, baton charges.** A baton charge is an attacking forward movement made by a large group of policemen carrying batons. N-COUNT BRITISH

bats·man /'bætsmən/ **batsmen.** The batsman in a game of cricket is the player who is batting. ◆◆◇◇◇ N-COUNT

bat·tal·ion /bə'tæljən/ **battalions. 1** A battalion is a large group of soldiers that consists of three or more companies. **2** A battalion of people is a large group of them, especially a well-organized efficient group that has a particular task to do. ...battalions of highly paid publicists. ◆◆◇◇◇ N-COUNT / N-COUNT: N of n

bat·ten /'bætən/ **battens, battening, battened. 1** A batten is a long strip of wood that is fixed to something to strengthen it or to hold it firm. **2** If something **is battened** in place, it is made secure by having battens fixed across it or being closed firmly. The roof was never securely battened down. **3 •** batten down the hatches: see hatch. N-COUNT BRITISH / VB: usu passive be V-ed adv/ prep

bat·ter /'bætə/ **batters, battering, battered. 1** If a child or a woman is **battered,** they are regularly hit and badly hurt by a member of their own family. ...boys who witness fathers battering their mothers. ...battered wives. **♦ bat·ter·ing** Leaving the relationship does not mean that the battering will stop. **♦ bat·ter·er** /'bætərə/ **batterers.** ...treatment programs for batterers. **2** To **batter** someone or something means to hit them many times, using fists or a heavy object. He battered her around the head... He was battered unconscious. **♦ bat·tered** Her battered body was discovered in a field. **3** If a place is **battered** by wind, rain, or storms, it has very bad weather for a period of time. The country has been battered by winds of between fifty and seventy miles an hour. **4** See also **battered, battering.** ◆◆◇◇◇ VERB: be V-ed V n V-ed / N-UNCOUNT / N-COUNT / VERB: V n V n prep/adv be V-ed adj / ADJ-GRADED / VB: usu passive be V-ed

5 Batter is a mixture of flour, eggs, and milk. You use batter to make things such as pancakes. N-VAR

6 In sports such as baseball, a **batter** is a person who hits the ball with a wooden bat. N-COUNT

batter down. If you **batter** a door **down,** you hit it so hard that it falls to pieces. They used lorries to batter down embassy gates. PHRASAL VB V n P V P n

bat·tered /'bætəd/. Something that is **battered** is old and in poor condition because it has been used a lot. ...a battered leather suitcase. ◆◇◇◇◇ ADJ-GRADED

bat·ter·ing /'bætərɪŋ/ **batterings.** If something takes a **battering,** it suffers very badly as a result of a particular event or action. Sterling took a battering yesterday as worries grew about the state of Britain's economy. N-COUNT

'**battering ram, battering rams;** also spelled **battering-ram.** A battering ram is a long heavy piece of wood that is used to knock down the locked doors of buildings. N-COUNT

bat·tery /'bætəri/ **batteries. 1** Batteries are the devices that you put in electrical items to provide the power that make these devices work. **2** A car battery is a rectangular box containing acid that is found in a car engine. It provides the electricity needed to start the car. **3 •** to **recharge** your **batteries:** see **recharge. 4** A battery of equipment such as guns, lights, or computers is a large set of them kept together in one place. ...batteries of spotlights set up on rooftops. **5** A battery of people or things is a very large number of them. ...a battery of journalists and television cameras. **6** Battery hens are large numbers of hens kept on farms in very small cages. The eggs they produce are called **battery eggs.** ◆◆◇◇◇ N-COUNT / N-COUNT / N-COUNT / N-COUNT: N of n / ADJ: ADJ n BRITISH

bat·tle /'bætəl/ **battles, battling, battled. 1** A battle is a violent fight between groups of people, especially one between military forces during a war. ...a gun battle. ...men who die in battle. **2** A battle is a conflict, quarrel, or contest in which different people or groups compete for power or advantage, or try to achieve opposite things. ...a renewed political battle over Britain's attitude to Europe. **3** To battle with an opposing group or person means to take part in a fight or contest against them. In American English, you can also say that one group or person **is battling** another. The sides must battle again for a quarter-final place... They're also battling the government to win compensation. **4** If one person or group **does battle** with another, they take part in a battle or contest against them. A British and an American company will do battle in the High Court over the right to press compact discs. **5** If one group or person **battles it out** with another, they take part in a fight or contest against each other until one of them wins or a definite result is reached. Leeds battled it out with the old enemy, Manchester United. **6** See also **pitched battle, running battle. 7** If you say that someone may have **lost the battle** but **won the war,** you mean that, although they have been defeated in a minor conflict, they have won a larger more important one of which it was a part. If you say that someone has **won the battle** but **lost the war,** you mean that they have won the small conflict but lost the larger one. **8** If you refer to a situation as a **battle of wills,** you mean that it involves people who try to defeat each other by refusing to change their opposing aims or demands and hoping that their opponents will weaken first. **9** If you refer to a situation as a **battle of wits,** you mean that it involves people with opposing aims who compete with each other using their intelligence, rather than force. **10** You can use **battle** to refer to someone's efforts to achieve something in spite of very difficult circumstances. ...his brave battle against cancer. **11** To **battle** means to try hard to be successful in spite of very difficult circumstances. In British English, you **battle** against something or with something. In American English, you **battle** something. Doctors battled throughout the night to save her life. ...a lone yachts- ◆◆◆◆◇ N-VAR / N-COUNT / V-RECIP: V with/ against n pl-n V V n Also pl-n V to-inf / PHRASE / PHRASE / PHRASE / PHRASE / PHRASE / N-COUNT / VERB V to-inf V with/ against/ through n V n

man returning from his months of battling with the elements... Firefighters are still battling the two blazes.
12 If you say that something is **half the battle**, you mean that it is the most important step towards achieving something. **13** If you are **fighting a losing battle**, you are trying to achieve something but are not going to be successful. ▸PHRASE

'battle-axe, battle-axes; also spelled **battleaxe**. ▸N-COUNT **1** If you call a middle-aged or older woman a **battle-axe**, you mean you think she is very difficult and unpleasant because of her fierce and determined attitude. **2** A **battle-axe** is a large axe that was used as a weapon. ▸INFORMAL ▸N-COUNT

'battle cruiser, battle cruisers; also spelled **battlecruiser**. A **battle cruiser** is a large fast warship. ▸N-COUNT

'battle cry, battle cries; also spelled **battle-cry**. ▸N-COUNT **1** A **battle cry** is a phrase that is used to urge people to take part in activities connected with a cause or campaign. *Their battle-cry will be: 'Sign this petition before they sign away your country.'* **2** In the past, a **battle cry** was a shout that soldiers uttered as they went into battle. ▸N-COUNT

battle·field /'bætlfiːld/ **battlefields. 1** A **battle-field** is a place where a battle is fought. *...the battle-fields of World War I.* **2** You can refer to an issue or field of activity over which people disagree or compete as a **battlefield**. *Sexuality remains a battlefield for solo female performers.* ▸◆◇◇◇ ▸N-COUNT ▸N-COUNT

battle·ground /'bætlgraʊnd/ **battlegrounds. 1** A **battleground** is the same as a **battlefield**. *...the bloody battleground of Yugoslavia.* **2** You can refer to an issue or field of activity over which people disagree or compete as a **battleground**. *...the battle-ground of education.* ▸◆◇◇◇ ▸N-COUNT ▸N-COUNT

bat·tle·ments /'bætlmənts/. The **battlements** of a castle consist of a wall built round the top, with gaps through which guns or arrows can be fired. ▸N-PLURAL

battle·ship /'bætlʃɪp/ **battleships**. A **battleship** is a very large heavily armoured warship. ▸◆◇◇◇ ▸N-COUNT

bat·ty /'bæti/ **battier, battiest**. If you say that someone is **batty**, you mean that they are rather eccentric or slightly mad. *...some batty uncle of theirs.* ▸ADJ-GRADED ▸INFORMAL ▸BRITISH

bau·ble /'bɔːbəl/ **baubles**. A **bauble** is a small cheap ornament or piece of jewellery. ▸N-COUNT

baulk /bɔːlk, AM bɔːk/. See **balk**.

baux·ite /'bɔːksaɪt/. **Bauxite** is an ore from which aluminium is obtained. ▸N-UNCOUNT

bawdy /'bɔːdi/ **bawdier, bawdiest**. A **bawdy** story, joke, or song contains humorous references to sex. ▸ADJ-GRADED ▸DATED

bawl /bɔːl/ **bawls, bawling, bawled. 1** If you **bawl**, you shout or sing in a very loud voice, for example because you are angry. *Laura and Peter were shouting and bawling at each other... He tried to direct the video like a fashion show, bawling instructions to the girls.* ▸ **Bawl out** means the same as **bawl**. *Someone in the audience bawled out 'Not him again!'* **2** If you say that a child is **bawling**, you mean it is crying loudly and you find this annoying. *...a bawling baby.* ▸◆◇◇◇ ▸VERB ▸V at n ▸V n ▸Also V with quote ▸PHRASAL VB ▸V P ▸VERB: V ▸PRAGMATICS ▸V-ing

bawl out. If someone **bawls** you **out**, they shout at you angrily because you have done something wrong. *Do you think I'm just going to bawl you out and that'll be an end of it?* ▸ See also **bawl** 1. ▸PHRASAL VB ▸V n P ▸Also V P noun

bay /beɪ/ **bays, baying, bayed. 1** A **bay** is a part of a coastline where the land curves inwards. *...San Francisco Bay.* **2** A **bay** is a partly enclosed area, inside or outside a building, that is used for a particular purpose. *The car reversed into the loading bay.* **3** A **bay** is an area of a room which extends beyond the main walls of a house, especially an area with a large window at the front of a house. **4** On an aircraft or ship, a **bay** is a compartment that is used for carrying cargo or equipment. *...in the cargo bays of aircraft.* **5** See also **sick bay**. **6** A **bay** horse is reddish-brown in colour. **7** If a dog or wolf **bays**, it makes loud long cries, often because it is angry or in pain. **8** If you say that a number of people **are baying** for something, you mean ▸◆◆◇◇ ▸N-COUNT ▸N-COUNT ▸N-COUNT ▸N-COUNT ▸ADJ ▸VERB: V ▸VERB ▸V for n

that they are shouting for something or demanding it angrily, usually that someone should be hurt or punished. *The referee ignored voices baying for a penalty.* **9** If you **keep** something or someone **at bay**, or **hold** them **at bay**, you prevent them from reaching, attacking, or affecting you. *Eating oranges keeps colds at bay.* ▸PHRASE ▸PHRASE

'bay leaf, bay leaves. A **bay leaf** is a leaf of a small evergreen tree that can be dried and used as a herb in cooking. ▸◆◇◇◇ ▸N-COUNT

bayo·net /'beɪənət/ **bayonets, bayoneting, bayoneted. 1** A **bayonet** is a long sharp blade that can be fixed to the end of a rifle and used as a weapon. **2** To **bayonet** someone means to stab them with a bayonet. *The soldiers were ordered to bayonet every man they could find.* ▸◆◇◇◇ ▸N-COUNT ▸VERB ▸V n

bayou /'baɪuː/ **bayous**. A **bayou** is a slow-moving, marshy tributary of a lake or river. ▸N-COUNT

,bay 'window, bay windows. A **bay window** is a window that sticks out from the outside wall of a house. See picture headed **house** and **flat**. ▸N-COUNT

ba·zaar /bə'zɑː/ **bazaars. 1** In areas such as the Middle East and India, a **bazaar** is a place where there are many small shops and stalls. **2** A **bazaar** is a sale to raise money for charity. *...a church bazaar.* ▸◆◇◇◇ ▸N-COUNT ▸N-COUNT

ba·zoo·ka /bə'zuːkə/ **bazookas**. A **bazooka** is a long tube-shaped gun that is held on the shoulder and fires rockets. ▸N-COUNT

BBC /ˌbiː biː 'siː/. **1** The **BBC** is a British organization which broadcasts programmes on radio and television. **BBC** is an abbreviation for 'British Broadcasting Corporation'. **2 BBC** is used to refer to television channels and radio stations that are run by the BBC. *...his new series on BBC 2.* ▸◆◆◇◇ ▸N-PROPER: the N

BC /ˌbiː 'siː/. You use **BC** in dates to indicate a number of years or centuries before the year in which Jesus Christ is believed to have been born. *...the fourth century BC.* ▸◆◇◇◇

be 1 auxiliary verb uses

be /bi, STRONG biː/ **am, are, is, being, was, were, been**. In spoken English forms of **be** are often contracted, for example 'I am' is contracted to 'I'm' and 'was not' is contracted to 'wasn't'. ▸◆◆◆◆

1 You use **be** with a present participle to form the continuous tenses of verbs. *This is happening in every school... He had only been trying to help... He's doing better than I am.* ▸ **be going to**: see **going**. ▸AUX ▸AUX -ing

2 You use **be** with a past participle to form the passive voice. *Forensic experts were called in... The cost of electricity from coal-fired stations is expected to fall... Similar action is being taken by the US government.* ▸AUX ▸AUX -ed

3 You can say that something is **to be** seen, heard, or found in a particular place to mean that people can see, hear, or find it in that place. *Little traffic was to be seen... They are to be found all over the world.* ▸AUX ▸AUX -ed

4 You use **be** with an infinitive to indicate that something is planned to happen, that it will definitely happen, or that it must happen. *The talks are to begin tomorrow... It was to be Johnson's first meeting... You are to answer to Brian.* ▸ **be about to**: see **about**. **5** You use **be** with an infinitive to say or ask what should happen or be done in a particular situation, how it should happen, or who should do it. *What am I to do?... Who is to say which of them had more power?... What is to be done?.* **6** You use **was** and **were** with an infinitive to talk about something that happened later than the time you are discussing, and was not planned or certain at that time. *...something that was to change the face of China... A few hours later he was to prove it.* ▸AUX ▸AUX to-inf ▸AUX ▸AUX to-inf ▸AUX ▸AUX to-inf

be 2 other verb uses

be /bi, STRONG biː/ **am, are, is, being, was, were, been**. In spoken English forms of **be** are often contracted, for example 'I am' is contracted to 'I'm' and 'was not' is contracted to 'wasn't'. ▸◆◆◆◆◆

1 You use **be** to introduce more information about the subject, such as its identity, nature, qualities, or position. *She's my mother... He is a very attractive man... My grandfather was a butcher... The sky was black... Cheney was in Madrid... Their last major film project was in 1964... 'Is it safe?'—'Well of course it is.'...* ▸V-LINK ▸V n ▸V adj ▸V prep/adv ▸V

He's still alive isn't he?... I was home and the children weren't.
2 You use **be**, with 'it' as the subject, in clauses where you are describing something or giving your judgement of a situation. *It was too chilly for swimming... Sometimes it is necessary to say no... It is likely that investors will face losses... It's nice having friends to chat to... It's a good thing I brought lots of handkerchiefs... It's no good just having meetings... It's a good idea to avoid refined food... It's up to us to prove it.* **3** You use **be** with the impersonal pronoun 'there' in expressions like **there is** and **there are** to say that something exists or happens. *Clearly there is a problem here... There are very few cars on this street... There were always things to think about.*
4 You use **be** as a link between a subject and a clause and in certain other clause structures, as exemplified below. *It was me she didn't like... What the media should not do is to exploit people's natural fears... Our greatest problem is convincing them... The question was whether protection could be improved... All she knew was that I'd had a broken marriage... It was as if there had been a nuclear explosion.*
5 You use **be** in expressions like **the thing is** and **the point is** to introduce a clause in which you make a statement or give your opinion. *The fact is, the players gave everything they had... The plan is good; the problem is it doesn't go far enough.* **6** You use **be** in expressions like **to be fair**, **to be frank**, or **to be serious** to introduce an additional statement , and to indicate that you are trying to be fair, frank, or serious. *I like living here and to be honest I'm not looking to move... It enabled students to devote more time to their studies, or to be more accurate, more time to relaxation.*
7 The form **'be'** is used occasionally instead of the normal forms of the present tense, especially after 'whether'. *...the appropriate type of practitioner, whether it be your GP, dentist, or optician.*
8 If something **is**, it exists. *It hurt so badly he wished to cease to be. ...to be or not to be.*
9 To **be yourself** means to behave in the way that is right and natural for you and your personality. *She'd learnt to be herself and to stand up for her convictions.*
10 If someone or something is, for example, **as happy as can be** or **as quiet as could be**, they are extremely happy or extremely quiet. **11** If you talk about what would happen **if it wasn't for** someone or something, you mean that they are the only thing that is preventing it from happening. *If it hadn't been for her your father would be alive today.* **12** You say **'Be that as it may'** when you want to move onto another subject or go further with the discussion, without deciding whether what has just been said is right or wrong. *'Is he still just as fat?'—'I wouldn't know,' continued her mother, ignoring the interruption, 'and be that as it may, he has made a fortune.'* **13** If you say that you **are not yourself**, you mean you are not feeling well. *She is not herself. She came near to a breakdown.*

be- /bɪ-/. **Be-** can be added to a noun followed by an '-ed' suffix to form an adjective that indicates that a person is covered with or wearing the specified thing. *...a bespectacled librarian.*

beach /biːtʃ/ **beaches, beaching, beached.**
1 A **beach** is an area of sand or pebbles beside the sea. **2** If you **beach** something such as a boat, or if it **is beached**, it is pulled or forced out of the water and onto land. *The boat beached on a mud flat.*

'beach ball, beach balls. A **beach ball** is a large light ball filled with air, which people play with, especially at the seaside.

'beach bum, beach bums. If you refer to someone as a **beach bum**, you mean that they spend a lot of time enjoying themselves on the beach or in the sea.

beach·comber /'biːtʃkəʊmə/ **beachcombers.** A **beachcomber** is someone who spends their time wandering along beaches looking for usable things, especially objects of value.

beach·front /'biːtʃfrʌnt/. A **beachfront** house, cafe, shop, or hotel is situated on or by a beach.

beach·head /'biːtʃhed/ **beachheads;** also spelled **beach·head.** A **beachhead** is an area of land next to the sea or a river where an attacking army has taken control and can prepare to advance further inland.

bea·con /'biːkən/ **beacons. 1** A **beacon** is a light or a fire, usually on a hill or tower, which acts as a signal or a warning. **2** If someone or something acts as a **beacon** to other people, they inspire or encourage people because they are better than anyone else in some way. *General Rudnicki was a moral beacon for many exiled Poles.*

bead /biːd/ **beads. 1 Beads** are small pieces of coloured glass, wood, or plastic which are often put together on a piece of string or wire to make necklaces or sewn onto clothes for decoration. **2** A **bead** of liquid or moisture is a small drop of it. *...the beads of sweat on his forehead.*

bead·ed /'biːdɪd/. **1** A **beaded** dress, cushion, or other object is decorated with beads. *Some costumes, like elaborately beaded evening dresses, cost more than $2000 each.* **2** If something is **beaded** with a liquid, it is covered in small drops of that liquid. *Although the night was cool, Curtis noted that his brow was beaded with perspiration.*

bead·ing /'biːdɪŋ/. **1 Beading** is a narrow strip of wood that is used for decorating or edging furniture and doors. **2 Beading** is an arrangement of beads used for decorating clothes.

beady /'biːdi/. **1 Beady** eyes are small, round, and bright. *Meg felt the old woman's beady eyes on her.* **2** If someone keeps a **beady** eye on a person or organization, they watch them carefully and suspiciously. *A woman concierge sat at a desk and kept a beady eye on people's comings and goings.*

bea·gle /'biːgəl/ **beagles.** A **beagle** is a short-haired black and brown dog with long ears and short legs.

beak /biːk/ **beaks.** A bird's **beak** is the hard curved or pointed part of its mouth.

beak·er /'biːkə/ **beakers. 1** A **beaker** is a plastic cup used for drinking, usually one with no handle. **2** A **beaker** is a glass or plastic jar which is used in chemistry.

,be-all and 'end-all. If something is **the be-all and end-all** to you, it is the only important thing in your life, or the only important feature of a particular activity. *For some people, competing is the be-all and end-all of their running.*

beam /biːm/ **beams, beaming, beamed. 1** If you say that someone **is beaming**, you mean that they have a big smile on their face because they are happy, pleased, or proud about something. *Frances beamed at her friend... 'Welcome back,' she beamed.* **2** A **beam** is a line of energy, radiation, or particles sent in a particular direction. *...high-energy laser beams.* **3** If something such as radio signals or television pictures **are beamed** somewhere, or **beam** somewhere, they are sent there by means of electronic equipment. *Soon, CMTV will be beaming into British homes. ...a ship which is due to begin beaming radio broadcasts to China.* **4** A **beam** of light is a line of light that shines from an object such as a torch or the sun. **5** If something such as the sun or a lamp **beams** down, it sends light to a place and shines on it. *A sharp white spot-light beamed down on a small stage.* **6** A **beam** is a long thick bar of wood, metal, or concrete, especially one used to support the roof of a building. **7** The **beam** is a piece of gymnastic apparatus that consists of a horizontal wooden bar on which the gymnasts balance and perform movements. **8** See also **off-beam**.

bean /biːn/ **beans. 1 Beans** such as green **beans**, french **beans**, or broad **beans** are the seeds of a tall climbing plant or the long thin cases which contain those seeds. **2** Beans such as soya **beans** and kidney **beans** are the dried seeds of a bean plant. **3** Beans such as coffee **beans** or cocoa **beans** are the seeds of a plant that is used in the production of coffee and chocolate. **4** Beans are baked beans.

5 If someone hasn't got a **bean**, they have no money at all. *It doesn't cost a bean.* **6** If someone is **full of beans**, they are very lively and have a lot of energy and enthusiasm. **7** If you **spill the beans**, you tell someone something that people have been trying to keep secret.
N-SING
INFORMAL PHRASE
PHRASE

'bean bag, bean bags; also spelled **beanbag.** A **bean bag** is a large round cushion which squashes into a comfortable shape when you sit on it.
N-COUNT

'bean counter, bean counters; also spelled **bean-counter.** If you disapprove of an accountant or business manager because you think they are only interested in how much money a business makes and spends, you can describe them as **bean counters**.
N-COUNT
PRAGMATICS

bean·pole /'biːnpəʊl/ **beanpoles.** If you call someone a **beanpole**, you mean that they are extremely tall and thin.
N-COUNT
PRAGMATICS INFORMAL

'bean sprout, bean sprouts; also spelled **beansprout. Bean sprouts** are small, long, thin shoots grown from beans that are used in Chinese cookery.
N-COUNT

bear 1 verb uses

bear /beə/ **bears, bearing, bore, borne. 1** If you **bear** something somewhere, you carry it there or take it there. *They bore the oblong hardwood box into the kitchen.* ♦ **-bearing** ...*food-bearing lorries.* **2** If you **bear** something such as a weapon, you hold it or carry it with you. ...*the constitutional right to bear arms.* ♦ **-bearing** ...*hundreds of flag-bearing marchers.* **3** If something **bears** the weight of something else, it supports the weight of that thing. *The ice was not thick enough to bear the weight of marching men.* ♦ **-bearing** ...*the load-bearing joints of the body.* **4** If something **bears** a particular mark or characteristic, it has that mark or characteristic. *The houses bear the marks of bullet holes.* **5** If you **bear** an unpleasant experience, you accept it because you are unable to do anything about it. *They will have to bear the misery of living in constant fear.* **6** If you can't **bear** someone or something, you dislike them very much. *I can't bear people who make judgements... He can't bear to talk about it.* **7** If someone **bears** the cost of something, they pay for it. *Patients should not have to bear the costs of their own treatment.* **8** If you **bear** the responsibility for something, you accept responsibility for it. *If a woman makes a decision to have a child alone, she should bear that responsibility alone.* **9** If something **bears** no resemblance or no relationship to something else, they are not at all like the second thing. *Their daily menus bore no resemblance whatsoever to what they were actually fed.* **10** When a plant or tree **bears** flowers, fruit, or leaves, it produces them. ♦ **-bearing** ...*a strong, fruit-bearing apple tree.* **11** If something such as a bank account or an investment **bears** interest, interest is paid on it. *The eight-year bond will bear annual interest of 10.5%.* ♦ **-bearing** ...*interest-bearing current accounts.* **12** When a woman **bears** a child, she gives birth to it. *She bore him a daughter.* **13** If you **bear** someone a feeling such as love or hate, you feel that emotion towards them. *She bore no ill will. If people didn't like her, too bad.* **14** If you **bear** yourself in a particular way, you move or behave in that way. *There was elegance and simple dignity in the way he bore himself.* **15** If you **bear** left or **bear** right when you are driving or walking, you turn and continue left or right. **16** If you **bring** something **to bear** on a situation, you use it to deal with that situation. *British scientists have brought computer science to bear on this problem.* **17** If you **bring** pressure or influence **to bear on** someone, you use it to try and persuade them to do something. **18** ● **bear the brunt of:** see **brunt.** ● **bear comparison:** see **comparison.** ● **bear fruit:** see **fruit.** ● **grin and bear it:** see **grin.** ● **bear in mind:** see **mind.** ● **bear witness:** see **witness.** See also **bore, borne.**
VERB
V n adv/prep LITERARY
COMB
VERB
V n FORMAL
COMB
VERB
V n
COMB
VERB
V n
VERB
V n
VB: with neg
V n/-ing V to-inf
VERB
V n
VERB
V n
VERB
V n
VERB: V n
COMB
VERB
V n
COMB
VERB: V n n
V n n DATED VERB: V n n
V n LITERARY
VERB
V pron-refl adv/prep LITERARY
VERB: V adv
PHRASE
PHRASE

bear down. 1 If someone or something **bears down** on you, they move quickly towards you in a threatening way. *A group of half a dozen men entered the pub and bore down on the bar.* **2** To **bear down** on something means to push or press downwards with steady pressure. *The entire weight was bearing down on Adam's plasterwork.*
PHRASAL VB
V P on n Also V P
V P on n Also V P

bear out. If someone or something **bears** a person **out** or **bears out** what that person is saying, they support what that person is saying. *Recent studies have borne out claims that certain perfumes can bring about profound psychological changes.*
PHRASAL VB
V P noun Also V n P

bear up. If you **bear up** when experiencing problems, you remain cheerful and show courage in spite of them. *She was frightened that she would be unable to bear up under the pain of childbirth.*
PHRASAL VB
V P
V P under n

bear with. If you ask someone to **bear with** you, you are asking them to be patient.
PHRASAL VB
V P n

bear 2 noun uses

bear /beə/ **bears. 1** A **bear** is a large strong wild animal with thick fur and sharp claws. See picture headed **animals.** ● See also **polar bear, teddy bear. 2** On the stock market, **bears** are people who sell shares in expectation of a drop in price, in order to make a profit by buying them back again after a short time. Compare **bull.**
N-COUNT
N-COUNT

bear·able /'beərəbəl/. If something is **bearable**, you feel that you can accept it or deal with it. *A cool breeze made the heat pleasantly bearable.*
ADJ-GRADED

beard /bɪəd/ **beards.** A man's **beard** is the hair that grows on his chin and cheeks. ♦ **beard·ed** ...*a bearded 40-year-old sociology professor.*
N-COUNT
ADJ

bear·er /'beərə/ **bearers. 1** The **bearer** of something such as a message is the person who brings it to you. *I hate to be the bearer of bad news.* **2** A **bearer** of a particular thing is a person who carries it, especially in a ceremony. ...*Britain's flag bearer at the Olympic Games opening ceremony.* **3** The **bearer** of something such as a document, a right, or an official position is the person who possesses it or holds it. *Spanish identity documents state the bearer's profession.* **4** The **bearer** of a tradition, idea, or characteristic is someone or something that is particularly associated with it and passes it on to other people or situations. *The lower classes are considered to be the bearers of tradition.* **5** In former times, especially in India, a **bearer** was a native servant of a European. **6** See also **pallbearer, standard bearer.**
N-COUNT
N-COUNT FORMAL
N-COUNT FORMAL
N-COUNT: N of n FORMAL
N-COUNT

'bear hug, bear hugs. A **bear hug** is a rather rough, tight, affectionate hug.
N-COUNT

bear·ing /'beərɪŋ/ **bearings. 1** If something **has a bearing** on a situation or event, it is relevant to it. *Diet has an important bearing on your general health.* **2** Someone's **bearing** is the way in which they move or stand. *She later wrote warmly of his bearing and behaviour.* **3** If you take a **bearing** with a compass, you use it to work out the direction in which a particular place lies or in which something is moving. **4** If you **get** your **bearings** or **find** your **bearings**, you find out where you are or what you should do next. If you **lose** your **bearings**, you do not know where you are or what you should do next. **5 Bearings** are small metal balls that are placed between moving parts of a machine in order to make them move smoothly and easily over each other. ● See also **ball bearing.**
PHRASE
N-SING LITERARY
N-COUNT
PHRASE
N-COUNT

-bearing /-beərɪŋ/. **-bearing** combines with nouns to form adjectives which describe things that hold the specified substance inside them. ...*malaria-bearing mosquitos.*
COMB

bear·ish /'beərɪʃ/. On the stock market, if there is a **bearish** sentiment, prices are expected to fall. Compare **bullish.** *Dealers said investors remain bearish.*
ADJ-GRADED

'bear market, bear markets. A **bear market** is a situation on the stock market when people are selling a lot of shares because they expect that the shares will decrease in value and that they will be able to make a profit by buying them again after a short time. Compare **bull market.**
N-COUNT

bear·skin /'beəskɪn/ **bearskins. 1** A **bearskin** is a N-COUNT
tall fur hat that is worn by British soldiers on
ceremonial occasions. **2** A **bearskin** is the skin and N-COUNT
fur of a bear, used for example as a rug or a cover.

beast /biːst/ **beasts. 1** You can refer to an animal ◆◆◇◇◇
as a **beast**, especially if it is large, dangerous, or un- N-COUNT
usual. ...*the threats our ancestors faced from wild* LITERARY
beasts.
2 If you refer to a man as a **beast**, you mean that his N-COUNT
behaviour, especially his sexual behaviour, is very JOURNALISM
violent and uncontrolled. ...*a sex beast who subjected
two sisters to a terrifying ordeal.* **3** If you call someone N-COUNT;
a **beast**, you strongly disapprove of them because you N-VOC
think that they are behaving in a selfish, cruel, or un- PRAGMATICS
pleasant way. *Bully! Hooligan! Beast! Let me go, let go!* DATED
4 You can use **beast** to refer to something or someone N-COUNT
in a light-hearted way, and to mention that they have
a particular quality. ...*that rare beast, a sports movie
that isn't boring.*

beast·ly /'biːstli/. **1** If you describe something as ADJ-GRADED
beastly, you mean that it is very unpleasant. *The* DATED
weather was beastly. **2** If you describe someone as ADJ-GRADED
beastly, you mean that they are unkind, mean, and DATED
spiteful. *He must be wondering why everyone is being so beastly to him.*

beat 1 striking something or moving in a regular rhythm

beat /biːt/ **beats, beating, beaten.** The form ◆◆◆◆◆
beat is used in the present tense and is also the past
tense. **1** If you **beat** someone or something, you hit VERB: V n
them very hard. *They were beaten to death with* V n to n
baseball bats. ♦ **beat·ing, beatings** ...*prisoners* N-COUNT
showing signs of severe beatings.
2 If someone or something **beats** against something, VERB:
they hit it hard, usually several times or continuously. V against n
Nina managed to free herself and began beating at the V at n
flames with a pillow... *The rain was beating on the* V on n
windowpanes. ► Also a noun. ...*the rhythmic beat of* Also V n
the surf. ♦ **beating** ...*the beating of the rain.* N-SING
3 When your heart or pulse **beats**, it continually VERB
makes regular rhythmic movements. *I felt my heart* V
beating faster. ► Also a noun. *Most people's pulse rate* N-COUNT
is more than 70 beats per minute. ♦ **beat·ing** *I could* N-SING
hear the beating of my heart.
4 If you **beat** a drum or similar instrument, you hit it V-ERG: V n
in order to make a sound. When a drum **beats**, it V
makes a sound. ...*drums beating and pipes playing.*
► Also a noun. ...*the rhythmical beat of the drum.* N-SING
5 The **beat** of a piece of music is the main rhythm that N-COUNT
it has. ...*the thumping beat of rock music.* **6** In music, N-COUNT
a **beat** is a unit of measurement. The number of beats
in a bar of a piece of music is indicated by two numbers at the beginning of the piece. ● See also **upbeat,
downbeat.**
7 If you **beat** eggs, cream, or butter, you mix them VERB: V n
thoroughly using a fork or whisk.
8 When a bird or insect **beats** its wings or when its V-ERG: V n
wings **beat**, its wings move up and down. *Its wings* V
beat slowly.
9 A police officer's **beat** is the area for which he or she N-COUNT
is responsible. **10** A police officer **on the beat** is on PHRASE
duty, walking around the area for which he or she is
responsible.
11 See also **beaten, beaten-up, beat-up. 12** Beat is
used in a large number of expressions which are explained under other words in this dictionary. For example, the expression **beat** someone **black and blue**
is explained at **black.**

beat 2 defeating

beat /biːt/ **beats, beating, beaten.** The form
beat is used in the present tense and is also the past
tense. **1** If you **beat** someone in a competition or an VERB: V n
election, you defeat them. *She was easily beaten into* V n into n
third place. ♦ **beat·ing** *The candidates the govern-* N-SING:
ment liked took a beating. **2** If someone **beats** a rec- a N
ord or achievement, they do better than it. *He was* VERB
as eager as his Captain to beat the record.* **3** If you VERB
beat something that you are fighting against, for ex- V n
ample an organization, a problem, or a disease, you
defeat it. *The Union was not going to beat the
government.*

4 If an attack **is beaten** off or **is beaten** back, it is VERB:
stopped, often temporarily. *South Africa's ruling Na-* be V-ed adv
tional Party has beaten off a right-wing challenge.* V adv n
5 If you say that one thing **beats** another, you mean VB: no cont
that it is better than it. *Being boss of a software firm* V n
beats selling insurance. **6** If you say you can't **beat** a INFORMAL
particular thing you mean that it is the best thing of its VB: no cont
kind. *You can't beat soap and water for cleansing.* V n
7 To **beat** a time limit or an event means to achieve VERB
something before that time or event. *They were trying* V n
to beat the midnight deadline.
8 You use **beat** in expressions such as 'It beats me' or PHRASE
'What beats me is' to indicate that you cannot under- INFORMAL
stand or explain something. *'What am I doing wrong,
anyway?'—'Beats me, Lewis.'*
9 If you tell someone to **beat it**, you are telling them to PHRASE
go away. INFORMAL
10 See also **beaten, beaten-up, beat-up.**
11 If you intend to do something but someone **beats** PHRASE
you **to it**, they do it before you do. **12** If **you can't beat** PHRASE
them, join them means that, if someone is too strong INFORMAL
for you to defeat, it is better to be on the same side as
them. **13** If you say that something will **take some** PHRASE
beating, you mean that it is very good and it is unlike- INFORMAL
ly that anything better will be done or made. **14** ● to
beat the clock: see **clock.** ● to **beat** someone **at their
own game**: see **game.**

beat 3 phrasal verbs

beat /biːt/ **beats, beating, beaten.**

beat down. 1 When the sun **beats down**, it is very PHRASAL VB
hot and bright. *I left the school with the sun beating* V P
down on my head. **2** When the rain **beats down**, it V P
rains very hard. **3** If you **beat down** a person who is V P n
selling you something, you force them to accept a Also V n P
lower price for it than they wanted to get. *Beat down
the seller to the price that suits you.*
beat out. 1 If you **beat out** sounds on a drum or PHRASAL VB
similar instrument, you make the sounds by hitting V P n
the instrument. *Drums and cymbals beat out a solemn
rhythm.* **2** If you **beat out** a fire, you cause it to go out V P n
by hitting it, usually with an object such as a blanket. Also V n P
His brother beat out the flames with a blanket. **3** If you V P n
beat out someone in a competition, you defeat them. Also V n P
Indianapolis has beat out nearly 100 other cities as the AMERICAN
site for a huge United Airlines maintenance facility.
beat up. If someone **beats** a person **up**, they hit or PHRASAL VB
kick the person many times. *The government support-* V n P
ers are beating up anyone they suspect of favouring the* V P noun
demonstrators. ♦ **beat·ing-up, beatings-up** *There* N-COUNT
had been no violence, no beatings-up until then.
beat up on. If someone **beats up on** a person or PHRASAL VB
beats on them, they hit or kick the person many V P P n
times. *He beat up on my brother's kid one time.* Also V P n
AMERICAN

beat·en /'biːtən/. **1** Beaten earth has been pressed ◆◇◇◇◇
down, often by people's feet, until it is hard. ...*a* ADJ: ADJ n
well-worn path of beaten earth. **2** A place that is **off** PHRASE
the beaten track is in an area where not many people live or go.

beaten-'up. A beaten-up car or other object is ◆◇◇◇◇
old and in bad condition. ...*his old, beaten-up black* ADJ-GRADED:
leather jacket. ADJ n

beat·er /'biːtə/ **beaters. 1** A **beater** is a tool or ◆◇◇◇◇
part of a machine which is used for beating things N-COUNT
like eggs and cream. **2** A **beater** is a person who N-COUNT
helps hunters by driving animals and birds into the
open so that they can be shot. **3** See also **world
beater.**

bea·tif·ic /ˌbiːə'tɪfɪk/. A **beatific** expression shows ADJ-GRADED
or expresses great happiness and calmness. ...*an al-* LITERARY
most beatific smile.

beat·nik /'biːtnɪk/ **beatniks.** Beatniks were young N-COUNT
people in the late 1950's who rejected traditional
ways of living, dressing, and behaving. People
sometimes use the word beatnik to refer to anyone
who lives in an unconventional way.

beat-'up. A beat-up car or other object is old and ◆◇◇◇◇
in bad condition. ...*a beat-up old Fiat 131.* ADJ-GRADED:
ADJ n

beau /bəʊ/ **beaux** or **beaus.** A woman's **beau** is N-COUNT
her boyfriend or admirer. DATED

beaut /bjuːt/ **beauts.** If an Australian or a New N-COUNT
Zealander describes something as a **beaut**, they INFORMAL
mean that they think it is very good.

beau·ti·cian /bjuːˈtɪʃən/ **beauticians.** A beauti- N-COUNT
cian is a person whose job is giving people beauty
treatments.

beau·ti·ful /ˈbjuːtɪfʊl/. **1** A **beautiful** person or ◆◆◆◆◇
place is very attractive to look at. ...*the most beauti-* ADJ-GRADED
ful child on earth... New England is beautiful.
♦ **beau·ti·ful·ly** /ˈbjuːtɪfli/ *The children behaved* ADV-GRADED
beautifully. ...a beautifully clear, sunny day. **2** You ADJ-GRADED
can describe something that someone does as
beautiful when they do it very skilfully. *That's a*
beautiful shot! ♦ **beautifully** *Arsenal played beauti-* ADV-GRADED
fully.

beau·ti·fy /ˈbjuːtɪfaɪ/ **beautifies, beautifying,** VERB
beautified. If you **beautify** something, you make it V n
look more beautiful. *Claire worked to beautify the*
garden.

beau·ty /ˈbjuːti/ **beauties. 1** Beauty is the state or ◆◆◆◇
quality of being beautiful. ...*an area of outstanding* N-UNCOUNT
natural beauty. **2** A beautiful woman is sometimes N-COUNT
described as a **beauty**. **3** You can say that some- N-COUNT
thing is a **beauty** when you think it is very good. INFORMAL
The pass was a real beauty. **4** The **beauties** of some- N-COUNT
thing are its attractive qualities or features. ...*the* LITERARY
beauties of nature. **5** If you say that a particular fea- N-COUNT
ture is the **beauty** of something, you mean that this
feature is what makes the thing so good. *There*
would be no effect on animals – that's the beauty of
such water-based materials.

ˈbeauty contest, beauty contests. A beauty N-COUNT
contest is a competition in which young women parade in front of judges who decide which one is the
most beautiful.

ˈbeauty queen, beauty queens. A beauty queen N-COUNT
is a woman who has won a beauty contest.

ˈbeauty salon, beauty salons. A beauty salon is N-COUNT
a place where women can go to have treatment to
make them look more beautiful.

ˈbeauty sleep. If someone goes to bed early say- N-UNCOUNT
ing that they need their **beauty sleep**, they are joking that they need a lot of sleep to help them stay
looking young and beautiful.

ˈbeauty spot, beauty spots. 1 A beauty spot is a N-COUNT
place in the country that is popular because of its BRITISH
beautiful scenery. **2** A **beauty spot** is a small dark N-COUNT
spot on a woman's skin which is supposed to add to
her beauty.

bea·ver /ˈbiːvə/ **beavers, beavering, bea-** ◆◇◇◇◇
vered. A **beaver** is a furry animal with a big flat N-COUNT
tail. ► **Beaver** is the fur of a beaver, when it is used N-UNCOUNT
for making coats, hats, and other clothes.

beaver away. If you **are beavering away** at some- PHRASAL VB
thing, you are working very hard at it. ...*architects bea-* V P at/on n
vering away at a scheme for the rehabilitation of Also V P
District 6. BRITISH

be·bop /ˈbiːbɒp/. **Bebop** is a form of jazz music N-UNCOUNT
with complex harmonies and rhythms. The abbreviation 'bop' is also used.

be·calmed /bɪˈkɑːmd/. **1** If a sailing ship is be- ADJ
calmed, it is unable to move because there is no
wind. **2** If the economy, a company, or a series of ADJ
talks is **becalmed**, it is not progressing at all.

be·came /bɪˈkeɪm/. **Became** is the past tense of **be-**
come.

be·cause /bɪˈkʌz, bɪˈkɒz, AM bɪˈkɔːz/. **1** You use ◆◆◆◆
because when stating the reason for something. *He* CONJ
is called Mitch, because his name is Mitchell... Be-
cause his carvings are fragile, Dan prefers clients to
pick them up at his studio. **2** You use **because** when CONJ
stating the explanation for a statement you have PRAGMATICS
just made. *Maybe they just didn't want to ask too*
many questions, because they rented us a room with-
out even asking to see our papers. **3** If an event or PHR-PREP
situation occurs **because of** something, that thing is
the reason or cause. *Many families break up because*
of a lack of money. **4** You use **just because** when PHR-CONJ
you want to say that a particular situation should INFORMAL,
not necessarily make you come to a particular con- SPOKEN

clusion. *Just because it has a good tune does not*
mean it is great music.

beck /bek/. If one person is **at** another's **beck and** PHRASE
call, they have to be ready to do whatever they ask,
and this seems unfair or undesirable.

beck·on /ˈbekən/ **beckons, beckoning, beck-** ◆◇◇◇◇
oned. 1 If you **beckon** to someone, you signal to VERB:
them to come to you. *I beckoned her over... Fielding* V to n
beckoned his cousin to join them. **2** If something V n adv/prep
beckons, it is so attractive to someone that they feel VERB: V
they must become involved in it. *The bright lights of* V n
Hollywood beckon many. **3** If something **beckons** VERB
for someone, it is very likely to happen to them. *Old* V
age beckons.

be·come /bɪˈkʌm/ **becomes, becoming, be-** ◆◆◆◆◆
came. The form **become** is used in the present
tense and is the past participle. **1** If someone or V-LINK
something **becomes** a particular thing, they start to V adj
change and develop into that thing, or start to de- V n
velop the characteristics mentioned. *The wind be-*
came stronger... He became a professional footballer. PHRASE
2 If you wonder **what has become of** someone or
something, you wonder where they are and what
has happened to them.

3 If something **becomes** someone, it makes them look VB: no
attractive or it seems right for them. *Don't be crude,* passive,
Bernard, it doesn't become you. no cont
V n

be·com·ing /bɪˈkʌmɪŋ/. **1** If you say a piece of ADJ-GRADED
clothing, a colour, or a hairstyle is **becoming**, you DATED
mean it makes the person who is wearing it look attractive. ♦ **be·com·ing·ly** *Her dress was of blue silk* ADV
and becomingly open at the neck. **2** Behaviour that ADJ-GRADED
is **becoming** is appropriate and proper in the
circumstances.

bed /bed/ **beds, bedding, bedded. 1** A **bed** is a ◆◆◆◇
piece of furniture that you lie on when you sleep. N-COUNT:
We finally went to bed at about 4am... Sam and also prep N
Robina put the children to bed. ♦ **-bedded** ...*a* COMB
four-bedded room. ...twin-bedded cabins. **2** When PHRASE
you **make** the **bed**, you neatly arrange the sheets
and covers of a bed. **3** See also **bedding.**

4 To **go to bed** with someone means to have sex with PHRASE
them. **5** If someone **gets** someone else **into bed**, they PHRASE
persuade them to have sex with them. **6** You can use PHRASE
in bed to refer to sexual activity. For example, if you
say that someone is good **in bed**, you mean that they
are a skilful lover.

7 If you say that someone **has made** their **bed,** and PHRASE
now they must **lie in it** or **on it**, you mean that since
they have chosen to do a particular thing, they must
now accept the unpleasant results of their action.

8 A **bed** in a garden or park is an area that has been N-COUNT
specially prepared so that plants can be grown in it.
...*the flower bed.* **9** A **bed** of shellfish or vegetation is N-COUNT
an area in the sea or in a lake where a particular type
of shellfish or vegetation is found in large quantities.
The whole lake was rimmed with thick beds of reeds.
10 ● bed of roses: see **rose. 11** If something is served N-COUNT
on a **bed** of a food such as rice or vegetables, it is
served on a layer of that food.

12 The sea **bed** or a river **bed** is the ground at the bot- N-COUNT
tom of the sea or of a river. **13** A **bed** of rock is a layer N-COUNT
of rock that is found within a larger area of rock.

bed down. If you **bed down** somewhere, you sleep PHRASAL VB
there for the night, instead of in bed. *They bedded* V P prep/adv
down in the fields.

BEd /ˌbiːˈed/ **BEds.** In Britain, a **BEd** is a degree N-COUNT
which qualifies someone to teach in a state school.
BEd is an abbreviation for 'Bachelor of Education'.
Compare **PGCE.**

ˌbed and ˈbreakfast, bed and breakfasts; ◆◇◇◇◇
also spelled **bed-and-breakfast. 1** Bed and break- N-UNCOUNT
fast is a system of accommodation in a hotel or
guest house in which you pay for a room for the
night and for breakfast the following morning. The
abbreviation **B&B** is also used. **2** A **bed and break-** N-COUNT
fast is a guest house that provides bed and breakfast. The abbreviation **B&B** is also used.

be·daz·zled /bɪˈdæzəld/. If you are **bedazzled**, you are so amazed and impressed by someone or something that you feel confused. ADJ-GRADED

bed·chamber /ˈbedtʃeɪmbə/ **bedchambers**. A **bedchamber** is a bedroom in a palace or large house. N-COUNT FORMAL

bed·clothes /ˈbedkləʊðz/. **Bedclothes** are the sheets and covers which you put over yourself when you get into bed. N-PLURAL

bed·ding /ˈbedɪŋ/. **Bedding** consists of sheets, blankets, and covers that are used on beds. ◆◇◇◇◇ N-UNCOUNT

'bedding plant, bedding plants. A **bedding plant** is an outdoor plant which lasts for one year. N-COUNT

be·deck /bɪˈdek/ **bedecks, bedecking, bedecked**. If flags or other ornaments **bedeck** a place, a lot of them are decorating it. ♦ **be·decked** *The hall was bedecked with Christmas holly.* ♦ **-be·decked** ...*a flower-bedecked stage.* VERB: V n LITERARY / ADJ / COMB

be·dev·il /bɪˈdevəl/ **bedevils, bedevilling, bedevilled**; spelled **bedeviling, bedeviled** in American English. If you **are bedevilled** by something unpleasant, it causes you a lot of problems over a period of time. ...*a problem that has bedevilled service industries for decades.* VERB: be V-ed V n FORMAL

bed·fellow /ˈbedfeləʊ/ **bedfellows**. You refer to two things or people as **bedfellows** when they have become associated or related in some way. *Sex and death are strange bedfellows.* N-COUNT

bed·head /ˈbedhed/ **bedheads**; also spelled **bed·head**. A **bedhead** is a board which is fixed to the end of a bed behind your head. N-COUNT BRITISH

bed·lam /ˈbedləm/. **Bedlam** means a great deal of noise and disorder. *He is causing bedlam at the hotel.* N-UNCOUNT

'bed linen. **Bed linen** consists of sheets and pillowcases. N-UNCOUNT

Bedou·in /ˈbeduɪn/ **Bedouins**. **Bedouin** can also be used as the plural form. The members of some nomadic Arab tribes are called **Bedouins**. ...*Bedouin settlements.* N-COUNT

bed·pan /ˈbedpæn/ **bedpans**. A **bedpan** is a shallow bowl shaped like a toilet seat, which is used instead of a toilet by people who are too ill to get out of bed. N-COUNT

bed·post /ˈbedpəʊst/ **bedposts**. A **bedpost** is one of the four vertical supports at the corners of a bed which has an old-fashioned wooden or iron frame. N-COUNT

be·drag·gled /bɪˈdrægəld/. Someone or something that is **bedraggled** looks untidy because they have got wet or dirty. ADJ-GRADED

bed·rid·den /ˈbedrɪdən/. Someone who is **bedridden** is too ill or disabled to get out of bed. ADJ

bed·rock /ˈbedrɒk/. 1 The **bedrock** of something consists of the principles, ideas, or facts on which it is based. *Mutual trust is the bedrock of a relationship.* 2 **Bedrock** is the solid rock in the ground which supports all the soil above it. ◆◇◇◇◇ N-SING / N-UNCOUNT

bed·room /ˈbedruːm/ **bedrooms**. A **bedroom** is a room to sleep in. See picture headed **house** and **flat**. *She wandered back into her bedroom.* ♦ **-bedroomed** ...*a two-bedroomed flat.* ◆◆◆◇◇ N-COUNT / COMB

bed·side /ˈbedsaɪd/. 1 Your **bedside** is the area beside your bed. ...*the bedside table... He drew a chair up to the bedside and sat down.* 2 If you talk about being at someone's **bedside**, you are talking about being near them when they are ill in bed. *She was called to her brother's bedside.* ◆◇◇◇◇ N-SING / N-SING

,bedside 'manner. A doctor's **bedside manner** is the way in which he or she talks to a patient, and the extent to which this is friendly and reassuring. N-SING

bed·sit /ˈbedsɪt/ **bedsits**. A **bedsit** is a rented room that you use for both living and sleeping in. N-COUNT BRITISH

bed·sitter /ˌbedˈsɪtə/ **bedsitters**; also spelled **bed·sitter**. A **bedsitter** is the same as a **bedsit**. N-COUNT BRITISH

bed·sores /ˈbedsɔːz/. **Bedsores** are sore places on a person's skin, caused by having to lie in bed for a long time without changing position. N-PLURAL

bed·spread /ˈbedspred/ **bedspreads**. A **bedspread** is a decorative cover which is put over a bed, on top of the sheets and blankets. N-COUNT

bed·stead /ˈbedsted/ **bedsteads**. A **bedstead** is the metal or wooden frame of an old-fashioned bed. N-COUNT

bed·time /ˈbedtaɪm/. Your **bedtime** is the time when you usually go to bed. ◆◇◇◇◇ N-UNCOUNT

bed-wet·ting /ˈbedwetɪŋ/; also spelled **bed-wetting**. **Bedwetting** means urinating in bed, usually by small children. N-UNCOUNT

bee /biː/ **bees**. 1 A **bee** is an insect with a yellow-and-black striped body that makes a buzzing noise as it flies. See picture headed **insects**. 2 If you have **a bee in** your **bonnet** about something, you are so enthusiastic or worried about it that you keep mentioning it or thinking about it. ◆◆◇◇◇ N-COUNT / PHRASE

Beeb /biːb/. The **Beeb** is the same as the BBC. *He joined the Beeb at 19.* N-PROPER: the N INFORMAL

beech /biːtʃ/ **beeches**. A **beech** or a **beech tree** is a type of tree with a smooth grey trunk. ▶ **Beech** is the wood of this tree. N-VAR / N-UNCOUNT

beef /biːf/ **beefs, beefing, beefed**. **Beef** is the meat of a cow, bull, or ox. • See also **corned beef**. ◆◆◇◇◇ N-UNCOUNT

beef up. If you **beef** something **up**, you increase, strengthen, or improve it. ...*a campaign to beef up security.* PHRASAL VB V n P V P noun

beef·bur·ger /ˈbiːfbɜːɡə/ **beefburgers**. **Beefburgers** are flat round pieces of minced beef mixed with flour and flavourings that you grill or fry. N-COUNT BRITISH

beef·cake /ˈbiːfkeɪk/ **beefcakes**. Attractive men with large muscles can be referred to as **beefcake**. ...*the sort of beefcake bodies usually associated with male strippers.* N-VAR

Beef·eater /ˈbiːfiːtə/ **Beefeaters**. **Beefeaters** are guards at the Tower of London. They wear a uniform made in the style of the sixteenth century. N-COUNT

beef·steak /ˈbiːfsteɪk/ **beefsteaks**; also spelled **beef steak**. **Beefsteak** is **steak**. N-VAR

beefy /ˈbiːfi/ **beefier, beefiest**. Someone, especially a man, who is **beefy** has a big body and large muscles. ADJ-GRADED

bee·hive /ˈbiːhaɪv/ **beehives**. 1 A **beehive** is a structure in which bees are kept. 2 A **beehive** is a woman's hairstyle in which the hair is piled onto the top of the head into a dome shape. N-COUNT / N-COUNT

bee·keeping /ˈbiːkiːpɪŋ/. **Beekeeping** is the practice of owning and taking care of bees. ♦ **bee·keeper, beekeepers** ...*a commercial beekeeper.* N-UNCOUNT / N-COUNT

bee·line /ˈbiːlaɪn/. If you **make a beeline for** a place, you go to it as quickly and directly as you can. PHRASE INFORMAL

been /bɪn, biːn/. 1 **Been** is the past participle of **be**. 2 If you have **been** to a place, you have gone to it or visited it. *Mr Li has already been to Egypt.* VERB V prep/adv

beep /biːp/ **beeps, beeping, beeped**. If something such as a horn **beeps**, or you **beep** it, it makes a short harsh sound. ▶ Also a noun. *He hailed her with a beep of the horn.* V-ERG / N-COUNT; SOUND

beep·er /ˈbiːpə/ **beepers**. A **beeper** is a portable device that makes a beeping noise, for example to tell you to phone someone. N-COUNT

beer /bɪə/ **beers**. **Beer** is a bitter alcoholic drink made from grain. ▶ A glass of beer can be referred to as a **beer**. *Would you like a beer?* ◆◆◆◇◇ N-VAR / N-COUNT

'beer belly, beer bellies. If a man has a **beer belly**, he has a fat stomach because of drinking too much beer. N-COUNT

beer·mat /ˈbɪəmæt/ **beermats**; also spelled **beer mat**. A **beermat** is a cardboard mat for resting your glass of beer on in a bar or pub. The usual American word is **coaster**. N-COUNT BRITISH

beery /ˈbɪəri/. If you describe a person, especially a man, as **beery**, you mean they have drunk a lot of beer. ...*jolly beery farmers.* ADJ-GRADED

bees·wax /ˈbiːzwæks/. **Beeswax** is wax that is made by bees. It is often used for making candles and furniture polish. N-UNCOUNT

beet /biːt/ **beets**. 1 **Beet** is a crop with a thick round root. It is often used to feed cattle. • See also **sugar beet**. 2 **Beets** are dark purple vegetables that are the roots of a crop. They are often pickled in vinegar. The British word is **beetroot**. ◆◇◇◇◇ N-VAR AMERICAN

bee·tle /ˈbiːtəl/ **beetles.** A beetle is an insect with a hard covering to its body. See picture headed **insects.** ◆◇◇◇◇ N-COUNT

beet·root /ˈbiːtruːt/ **beetroots.** Beetroot is a dark purple vegetable that is the root of a crop. It is often pickled in vinegar. The American word is **beet.** ◆◇◇◇◇ N-VAR BRITISH

be·fall /bɪˈfɔːl/ **befalls, befalling, befell, befallen.** If something bad or unlucky **befalls** you, it happens to you. ...*the disaster that befell the island of Flores.* ◆◇◇◇◇ VERB V n LITERARY

be·fit /bɪˈfɪt/ **befits, befitting, befitted.** If something **befits** a person or thing, it is suitable or appropriate for them. *He writes beautifully, as befits a poet.* ◆◇◇◇◇ VERB V n

be·fore /bɪˈfɔː/. In addition to the uses shown below, **before** is used in the phrasal verbs 'go before' and 'lay before'. ◆◆◆◆◆

1 If something happens **before** a particular date, time, or event, it happens earlier than that date, time, or event. ...*a few weeks before Christmas... Before World War II, women were not recruited as intelligence officers... My husband rarely comes to bed before 2 or 3am.* Stock prices have climbed close to the peak they'd registered before the stock market crashed in 1987. **2** If you do something **before** doing something else, you do it earlier than the other thing. *He spent his early life in Sri Lanka before moving to England.* ▶ Also a conjunction. *He took a cold shower and then towelled off before he put on fresh clothes.* **3** If you do something **before** someone else can do something, you do it when they have not yet done it. *Before he could rise, she kicked him again.* **4** If there is a period of time or if several things are done **before** something happens, it takes that amount of time or effort for this thing to happen. *It was some time before the door opened in response to his ring.* **5** If a particular situation has to happen **before** something else happens, this situation must happen or exist in order for the other thing to happen. *There was additional work to be done before all the troops would be ready.* **6** ● before long: see **long. 7** If something happened, for example, the day **before** or the weekend **before** a particular date or event, it happened during the previous day or during the previous weekend. **8** You use **before** when you are saying how much earlier one event was than another. *The war had ended only a month or so before.* ▶ Also a preposition. *He sent me the book twenty days before the deadline for my book.* ▶ Also a conjunction. *He was at Boeing for more than a decade before he joined the union.* **9** If you have done something **before**, you have done it on a previous occasion. If you have not done something **before**, you are doing it for the first time. **10** If you tell someone that one place is a certain distance **before** another, you mean that they will come to the first place first. *The turn is about two kilometres before the roundabout.* **11** If you are **before** something, you are in front of it. *They stopped before a large white vllla.* **12** If someone or something appears or comes **before** a person or group, they are there to be heard or considered officially by that person or group. *The Governor will appear before the committee next Tuesday.* **13** If something happens **before** a particular person or group, it is seen by or happens while that person or group is present. *He beat their champion on points before a crowd of 50,000.* **14** If you have something such as a journey or a task **before** you, you must do it or go through it in the future. *It was the single hardest task before them.* **15** When you want to say that one person or thing is more important than another, you can say that they come **before** another. *Her husband, her children, and the Church came before her needs.*

PREP / CONJ / PREP / CONJ / CONJ / CONJ / ADV: n ADV / ADV: n ADV / PREP / CONJ / ADV: ADV after v / PREP / PREP / PREP FORMAL PREP / PREP / PREP / PREP

before·hand /bɪˈfɔːhænd/. If you do something **beforehand**, you do it earlier than a particular event. *How could she tell beforehand that I was going to go out?... Saunas can be hazardous if misused. Avoid a big meal beforehand.* ◆◇◇◇◇ ADV

be·friend /bɪˈfrend/ **befriends, befriending, befriended.** If you **befriend** someone, especially someone who is lonely, you make friends with them. ◆◇◇◇◇ VERB: V n

be·fud·dle /bɪˈfʌdəl/ **befuddles, befuddling, befuddled.** If something **befuddles** you, it confuses your mind or thoughts. ◆ **be·fud·dled** ...*his befuddled manner... I was usually befuddled with drink.* VERB: V n / ADJ-GRADED

beg /beg/ **begs, begging, begged. 1** If you **beg** someone to do something, you ask them very anxiously or eagerly to do it. *I begged to be allowed to leave... We are not going to beg for help... They dropped to their knees and begged forgiveness.* **2** If someone who is poor is **begging**, they are asking people to give them food or money. *I was surrounded by people begging for food... She was living alone, begging food from neighbors.* **3** If you say that something **is going begging**, you mean that it is available but no one is using it or accepting it. *There is other housing going begging in town.* **4** If you say that something **begs** a particular **question**, you mean that it makes people want to ask that question. Some people consider that this use is incorrect. *Hopewell's success begs the question: why aren't more companies doing the same?* **5** If you say that something **begs** a particular **question**, you mean that it assumes that the question has already been answered and so does not deal with it. *The research begs a number of questions.* **6** You say 'I **beg to differ**' when you are politely telling someone that you disagree with them. **7** ● I beg your pardon: see **pardon.**

◆◆◇◇◇ VERB: V n to-inf V to-inf passive V forn V n / VERB V forn V n / PHRASE / PHRASE / PHRASE LITERARY / PHRASE PRAGMATICS

be·gan /bɪˈgæn/. **Began** is the past tense of **begin.**

be·get /bɪˈget/ **begets, begetting, begot, begotten. 1** To **beget** something means to cause it to happen or be created. *Violence begets further violence.* **2** When a man **begets** a child, the child is born and he is its father. VERB V n FORMAL VERB: V n DATED

beg·gar /ˈbegə/ **beggars.** A **beggar** is someone who lives by asking people for money or food. *The number of beggars grew almost daily.* ◆◇◇◇◇ N-COUNT

'begging bowl, begging bowls. If a country or organization approaches other countries or organizations with a **begging bowl**, it asks them for money. N-COUNT BRITISH

begging 'letter, begging letters. A **begging letter** is a letter from a person or organization in which they ask you to send some money for a particular purpose; used showing disapproval. N-COUNT PRAGMATICS BRITISH

be·gin /bɪˈgɪn/ **begins, beginning, began, begun. 1** When someone or something **begins** to do something, they start doing it. *He stood up and began to move around the room... Snow began falling again.* **2** When something **begins** or when you **begin** it, it takes place from a particular time onwards. *The problems began last November... He has just begun his fourth year in hiding.* **3** If someone **begins** with something, or **begins** by doing something, this is the first thing they do. If a person **began** their career as something, this was the first job they had. *Could I begin with a few formalities? ...a businessman who began by selling golf shirts... He began his career as a sound editor.* **4** You use **begin** to mention the first thing that someone says. *'Professor Theron,' he began, 'I'm very pleased to see you.'* **5** If something **began as** a particular thing, it first existed as that thing. *What began as a local festival has blossomed into an international event.* **6** If you say that a thing or place **begins** somewhere, you are talking about one of its limits or edges. *The fate line begins close to the wrist.* **7** If a word **begins** with a particular letter, that is the first letter of that word. **8** If you say that you cannot **begin** to imagine, understand, or explain something, you are emphasizing that it is almost impossible to imagine, understand, or explain it. **9** You use the phrase **to begin with** when you are talking about the first stage of a situation, event, or pro-

◆◆◆◆◆ VERB V to-inf V -ing / V-ERG V V n / VERB V with n V by -ing Also V n prep / VB: no cont with quote Also V VB: no cont V asn / VB: no cont V prep/adv / VB: no cont V with n / VB: no cont, with brd-neg, V to-inf PRAGMATICS / PHRASE

cess. *It was great to begin with but now it's difficult.*
10 You use the phrase **to begin with** to introduce the first of several things that you want to say. *'What do scientists you've spoken with think about that?' - 'Well, to begin with, they doubt it's going to work.'* _{PHRASE} _{PRAGMATICS}
11 • charity begins at home: see **charity. • begin life:** see **life.**

be·gin·ner /bɪˈɡɪnə/ **beginners.** A **beginner** is someone who has just started learning to do something and cannot do it very well yet. *The course is suitable for beginners.* ◆◆◇◇◇ N-COUNT

be·gin·ning /bɪˈɡɪnɪŋ/ **beginnings. 1** The **beginning** of an event, process, or period of time is the first part of it. *This was the beginning of her recording career.* **2** The **beginnings** of something are the signs or events which form the first part of it. *The discussions were the beginnings of a dialogue with Moscow.* **3** The **beginning** of a piece of written material is the first words or sentences of it. **4** If you talk about the **beginnings** of a person, company, or group, you are referring to their backgrounds or origins. *His views come from his own humble beginnings.* **5** You use **beginning** to describe someone who is in the early stages of learning to do something. *The people that she had in her classroom were beginning learners.* ◆◆◆◇◇ N-COUNT / N-PLURAL / N-COUNT / N-PLURAL / ADJ: ADJ n

be·got /bɪˈɡɒt/. **Begot** is the past tense of **beget.**

be·got·ten /bɪˈɡɒtən/. **Begotten** is the past participle of **beget.**

be·grudge /bɪˈɡrʌdʒ/ **begrudges, begrudging, begrudged. 1** If you say that you do not **begrudge** someone something, you mean that you do not feel angry or jealous that they have it. *I certainly don't begrudge him the Nobel Prize.* **2** If you do not **begrudge** something such as time or money, you do not mind giving it up. *I do not begrudge the money.* VERB V n n / VERB V n

be·grudg·ing·ly /bɪˈɡrʌdʒɪŋli/. If you do something **begrudgingly**, you do it unwillingly. *He agreed to her suggestion begrudgingly.* ADV: ADV with v

be·guile /bɪˈɡaɪl/ **beguiles, beguiling, beguiled. 1** If something **beguiles** you, you are charmed and attracted by it. **2** If someone or something **beguiles** you into doing something, they try to trick you into doing it. *He used his newspapers to beguile the readers into buying shares.* VERB: V n / VERB V n into -ing

be·guil·ing /bɪˈɡaɪlɪŋ/. Something that is **beguiling** is charming and attractive. *Mombasa is a town with a beguiling Arabic flavour.* **♦ be·guil·ing·ly** *He was beguilingly boyish and attractive.* ADJ-GRADED WRITTEN / ADV-GRADED

be·gun /bɪˈɡʌn/. **Begun** is the past participle of **begin.**

be·half /bɪˈhɑːf, -ˈhæf/. **1** If you do something **on** someone's **behalf**, or **on behalf of** someone, you do it as that person's representative. *She made an emotional public appeal on her son's behalf.* **2** If you feel, for example, embarrassed or angry **on** someone's **behalf**, or **on behalf of** someone, you feel embarrassed or angry for them. *'What do you mean?' I asked, offended on Liddie's behalf.* ◆◆◇◇◇ PHRASE / PHRASE

be·have /bɪˈheɪv/ **behaves, behaving, behaved. 1** The way that you **behave** is the way that you do and say things, and the things that you do and say. *He'd behaved badly.* **♦ -behaved** *The children were extremely well-behaved.* **2** If you **behave**, you act in the way that people think is correct and proper. *They were expected to behave themselves.* **3** In science, the way that something **behaves** is the things that it does. *Under certain conditions, electrons can behave like waves.* ◆◆◆◇◇ VERB V prep/adv / COMB / VERB V pron-refl Also V / VERB V prep/adv

be·hav·iour /bɪˈheɪvjə/ **behaviours;** spelled **behavior** in American English. **1** People's or animals' **behaviour** is the way that they behave. *...human sexual behaviour.* **2** If someone is on their **best behaviour**, they are making a big effort to behave nicely. **3** Psychologists refer to a particular way of behaving as a particular **behaviour**. *Was she merely reverting to a learned behavior from force of habit?* **4** In science, the **behaviour** of something is the way that it behaves. *It will be many years before anyone can predict a hurricane's behavior.* ◆◆◆◇◇ N-UNCOUNT: with supp / PHRASE / N-COUNT: with supp / N-UNCOUNT: also N in pl, with poss

be·hav·iour·al /bɪˈheɪvjərəl/; spelled **behavioral** in American English. **Behavioural** means relating to the behaviour of a person or animal, or to the study of their behaviour. *...behavioral scientists.* ◆◇◇◇◇ ADJ: ADJ n

be·hav·iour·ism /bɪˈheɪvjərɪzəm/; spelled **behaviorism** in American English. **Behaviourism** is the belief held by some psychologists that the only valid method of studying the psychology of people or animals is to observe how they behave. **♦ be·hav·iour·ist, behaviourists** *Even the behaviourists are beginning to question their own theory.* N-UNCOUNT / N-COUNT

be·head /bɪˈhed/ **beheads, beheading, beheaded.** If someone **is beheaded**, someone cuts their head off, usually because they have been found guilty of a crime. *Charles I was beheaded by the Cromwellians.* VB: usu passive be V-ed

be·held /bɪˈheld/. **Beheld** is the past tense of **behold.**

be·he·moth /bɪˈhiːmɒθ, AM -məθ/ **behemoths.** If you call something such as an organization a **behemoth**, you mean that it is extremely large and perhaps unpleasant, inefficient, or difficult to manage. *The city is a sprawling behemoth with no heart.* N-COUNT PRAGMATICS JOURNALISM

be·hest /bɪˈhest/ **behests.** If something is done at someone's **behest**, or **at the behest** of someone, it is done because they have ordered or requested it. PHRASE FORMAL

behind 1 preposition and adverb uses

be·hind /bɪˈhaɪnd/. In addition to the uses shown below, **behind** is also used in a few phrasal verbs, such as 'fall behind' and 'lie behind'. ◆◆◆◆◆
1 If something is **behind** a thing or person, it is on the other side of them from you, or nearer their back rather than their front. *I put one of the cushions behind his head... They were parked behind the truck.* ▶ Also an adverb. *He attacked the Aston Villa supporter from behind.* **2** If you are walking or travelling **behind** someone or something, you are following them. *Keith wandered along behind him.* ▶ Also an adverb. *The troopers followed behind.* **3** If someone is **behind** a desk, counter, or bar, they are on the other side of it from where you are. *The colonel was sitting behind a cheap wooden desk.* **4** When you shut a door or gate **behind** you, you shut it after you have gone through it. *He slammed the gate shut behind him.* **5** The people or events **behind** a situation are the causes of it or the things that are responsible for it. *It is still not clear who was behind the killing.* **6** If something or someone is **behind** you, they support you and help you. *He had the state's judicial power behind him.* **7** If you refer to what is **behind** someone's outside appearance, you are referring to a characteristic which is not immediately obvious, but which you think is there. *What lay behind his anger was really the hurt he felt.* **8** If you are **behind** someone, you are less successful than them, or have advanced less. *Food production has already fallen behind the population growth.* ▶ Also an adverb. *She is now far behind, and will need retraining.* **9** If something is **behind** schedule, it is not as far advanced as people had planned. If someone is **behind** schedule, they are not progressing as quickly at something as they had planned. **10** If an experience is **behind** you, it happened in your past and no longer affects you now. *Maureen put the nightmare behind her.* **11** If you have a particular achievement **behind** you, you have achieved something and other people consider it to be important or valuable. *...a popular actress with half a decade of filmmaking behind her.* **12** If you stay **behind**, you remain in a place after other people have gone. **13** If you leave something or someone **behind**, you do not take them with you when you go.
PREP / ADV / PREP / ADV / ADV after v / PREP / PREP / PREP / PREP / PREP / PREP / ADV-GRADED / PREP / PREP / PREP / ADV: ADV after v / ADV: ADV after v

14 • do something behind someone's back: see **back. • behind bars:** see **bar. • behind the scenes:** see **scene.**

behind 2 noun use

be·hind /bɪˈhaɪnd/ **behinds.** Your **behind** is the part of your body that you sit on. N-COUNT INFORMAL

be·hind-the-'scenes. See scene. ◆◇◇◇◇

be·hold /bɪ'həʊld/ **beholds, beholding, beheld.** ◆◇◇◇◇
1 If you **behold** someone or something, you see
them. *She looked into his eyes and beheld madness.*
2 People used to say or write **'Behold'** to draw peo-
ple's attention to something. *Fear Not. Behold The
Saviour.* ● **lo and behold**: see **lo**.
VERB
V n
LITERARY
CONVENTION
DATED,
LITERARY

be·hold·en /bɪ'həʊldən/. If you are **beholden to**
someone, you feel that you have a duty to them because they have helped you. *He was made beholden
to the Mafia.*
ADJ:
v-link ADJ *to* n

be·hold·er /bɪ'həʊldə/ **beholders. 1** If you say that
something such as beauty or art is **in the eye of the
beholder**, you mean that it is a matter of personal
opinion. **2** The **beholder** of something is the person
who is looking at it.
PHRASE
N-COUNT
DATED

be·hove /bɪ'həʊv/ **behoves, behoving, be-
hoved;** spelled **behoove** in American English. If **it
behoves** you to do something, it is necessary or advantageous for you to do it. *I think it behoves us, sir,
to get out of here.*
VERB
it V n to-inf
FORMAL

beige /beɪʒ/. Something that is **beige** is pale brown
in colour.
◆◇◇◇◇
COLOUR

be·ing /'biːɪŋ/ **beings. 1 Being** is the present participle of **be. 2 Being** is used in non-finite clauses
where you are giving the reason for something. *It
being a Sunday, the old men from the square had
the day off... Being young, I did not worry.* **3** You can
refer to any real or imaginary creature as a **being**.
...beings from outer space. ● See also **human being**.
4 Being is existence. Something that is **in being** or
comes **into being** exists. *The Kingdom of Italy formally came into being on 17 March 1861.* **5** See also
well-being. ● **other things being equal**: see **equal**.
● **for the time being**: see **time**.
◆◆◆◇◇
V-LINK
V adj
Also V prep
N-COUNT
N-UNCOUNT

be·jew·elled /bɪ'dʒuːəld/; spelled **bejeweled** in
American English. A **bejewelled** person or object is
wearing a lot of jewellery or is decorated with jewels. *...a bejewelled golden tiara.*
ADJ

be·lat·ed /bɪ'leɪtɪd/. A **belated** action happens later than it should have done. *...the government's belated attempts to alleviate the plight of the poor.*
♦ **be·lat·ed·ly** *People have belatedly become aware
of how fragile the planet is.*
◆◇◇◇◇
ADJ-GRADED
FORMAL
ADV-GRADED:
ADV with v

belch /beltʃ/ **belches, belching, belched. 1** If
someone **belches**, they make a sudden noise in
their throat because air has risen up from their
stomach. *He belched with satisfaction.* ▶ Also a
noun. *He drank and stifled a belch.* **2** If something
belches something such as smoke, or if smoke
belches from something, large amounts of smoke
come from it. *Clouds of steam started to belch from
the engine.* ● **Belch out** means the same as **belch**.
*The power-generation plant belched out five tonnes
of ash an hour.*
◆◇◇◇◇
VERB
V
N-COUNT
V-ERG: V n
V *from/out of*
n
PHRASAL VB
ERG
V P noun

be·lea·guered /bɪ'liːgəd/. **1** A **beleaguered** person
or organization is experiencing a lot of difficulties or
criticism. *...the beleaguered government of Mrs
Aquino.* **2** A **beleaguered** place or army is sur-
rounded by its enemies. *The rebels continue their
push towards the beleaguered capital.*
ADJ-GRADED
FORMAL
ADJ
FORMAL

bel·fry /'belfri/ **belfries.** The **belfry** of a church is
the top part of its tower or steeple, where the bells
are.
N-COUNT

be·lie /bɪ'laɪ/ **belies, belying, belied. 1** If one
thing **belies** another, it hides the true situation and
so creates a false idea or image. *Her looks belie her
50 years.* **2** If one thing **belies** another, it proves that
the other thing is not true or genuine. *The facts of
the situation belie his testimony.*
◆◇◇◇◇
VERB
V n
VERB
V n

be·lief /bɪ'liːf/ **beliefs. 1 Belief** is a feeling of certainty that something exists, is true, or is good. *...a
belief in personal liberty.* **2** Your religious or political **beliefs** are your views on religious or political
matters. *They may not share the same religious beliefs.* **3** If it is your **belief** that something is the case,
it is your strong opinion that it is the case. *It is my
belief that sterling will fall sharply.* **4** You use **beyond belief** to emphasize that something is true or
happened to a very great degree. *We are devastated,*
◆◆◆◇◇
N-UNCOUNT
N-PLURAL
N-SING
PHRASE
PRAGMATICS

shocked beyond belief. **5** You use the expression
contrary to popular belief to introduce a statement
that is the opposite to what most people think is
true. **6** If you do something **in the belief that** something is true or will happen, you do it because you
think, usually wrongly, that it is true or will happen.
*Civilians had broken into the building, apparently in
the belief that it contained food.*
PHRASE
PRAGMATICS
PHRASE

be·liev·able /bɪ'liːvəbəl/. Something that is **believ-
able** makes you think that it could be true or real.
This book is full of believable, interesting characters.
◆◇◇◇◇
ADJ-GRADED

be·lieve /bɪ'liːv/ **believes, believing, believed.
1** If you **believe** that something is true, you think
that it is true. You can say **'I believe'** to indicate that
you are not completely sure about something or to
make a statement sound more factual and less emotional. *We believe them to have been there... 'You've
never heard of him?'—'I don't believe so.'*
2 If you **believe** someone or if you **believe** what they
say, you accept that they are telling the truth. *He did
not sound as if he believed her.* **3** If you **believe** in
fairies, ghosts, or miracles, you are sure that they exist
or happen. If you **believe** in a god, you are sure of the
existence of that god.
4 If you **believe in** a way of life or an idea, you think it
is good or right. *He believed in marital fidelity.* **5** If you
believe in someone or what they are doing, you have
confidence in them and think that they will be successful. *If you believe in yourself you will succeed.*
6 Believe is used in expressions such as **I can't believe
how** or **it's hard to believe that** in order to express
surprise. *Many officers I spoke to found it hard to believe what was happening.* **7** If you say that you cannot **believe your eyes** or cannot **believe your ears,**
you are emphasizing that you are very surprised
about something you have seen or heard. **8** You can
use **believe it or not** to emphasize that what you have
just said is surprising. *That's normal, believe it or not.*
9 If you say **would you believe it,** you are emphasiz-
ing your surprise about something. *And would you
believe it, he's younger than me!* **10** You can use **be-
lieve you me** to emphasize that what you are saying is
true. *It's absolutely amazing, believe you me.*
◆◆◆◆◇
VERB:
V that
V n so/not
Also V n adj
FORMAL
VERB
V n
VERB:
V in n
VERB
V in n
VERB
V in n
VB: with brd-
neg
PRAGMATICS
V wh
Also V that
PHRASE
PRAGMATICS
PHRASE
PRAGMATICS
PHRASE
PRAGMATICS
PHRASE
PRAGMATICS

be·liev·er /bɪ'liːvə/ **believers. 1** If you are a great
believer in something, you think that it is good,
right, or beneficial. *Mum was a great believer in
herbal medicines.* **2** A **believer** is someone who is
sure that God exists or that their religion is true.
◆◇◇◇◇
N-COUNT:
N *in* n
N-COUNT

be·lit·tle /bɪ'lɪtəl/ **belittles, belittling, belittled.**
If you **belittle** someone or something, you say or
imply that they are unimportant or not very good.
We mustn't belittle her outstanding achievement.
◆◇◇◇◇
VERB
V n

bell /bel/ **bells. 1** A **bell** is a device that makes a
ringing sound and is used to give a signal or to attract people's attention. *I've been ringing the door
bell.* **2** A **bell** is a hollow metal object shaped like a
cup which has a piece hanging inside it that hits the
sides and makes a sound. *The church bells were
ringing.* **3** If you say that something **rings a bell,**
you mean that it reminds you of something else,
but you cannot remember exactly what.
◆◆◆◇◇
N-COUNT
N-COUNT
PHRASE
INFORMAL

'bell-bottoms; the form **bell-bottom** is used as a
modifier. **Bell-bottoms** are trousers that are very
wide at the bottom of the leg.
N-PLURAL

bell·boy /'belbɔɪ/ **bellboys.** A **bellboy** is a man or
boy who works in a hotel, carrying bags or bringing
things to the guests' rooms.
N-COUNT

belle /bel/ **belles.** A **belle** is a beautiful woman, especially the most beautiful woman at a party or in a
group. *She was the belle of her Sunday School class.*
N-COUNT
DATED

bel·li·cose /'belɪkəʊs, -kəʊz/. You use **bellicose** to
refer to aggressive behaviour that is likely to start an
argument or a fight. *The statement is the most bellicose yet from Baghdad.*
ADJ-GRADED
LITERARY

bel·lig·er·ent /bɪ'lɪdʒərənt/ **belligerents. 1** A
belligerent person is hostile and aggressive. *He was
almost back to his belligerent mood of twelve
months ago.* ♦ **bel·lig·er·ent·ly** *'Why not?' he asked
belligerently.* ♦ **bel·lig·er·ence** *He could be accused of passion, but never belligerence.* **2** The **bel-**
◆◇◇◇◇
ADJ-GRADED
ADV-GRADED
N-UNCOUNT
N-COUNT

bellow

ligerents in a war are the countries or groups that are fighting each other. FORMAL

bel·low /'beləʊ/ **bellows, bellowing, bellowed.** ◆◇◇◇◇
1 If someone **bellows**, they shout angrily in a loud VERB deep voice. *'I didn't ask to be born!' she bellowed...* V with quote *She prayed she wouldn't come in and find them* V a tn *there, bellowing at each other... He bellowed infor-* V n prep *mation into the mouthpiece of his portable tele-* Also V *phone.* ► Also a noun. *...a bellow of tearful rage.* N-COUNT **2** When a large animal such as bull or an elephant VERB: V **bellows**, it roars loudly and deeply. **3** A **bellows** is or N-COUNT: **bellows** are a device used for blowing air into a fire also a pair of N in order to make it burn more fiercely.

bell·weth·er /'belweðə/ **bellwethers.** If you de- N-COUNT scribe something as a **bellwether**, you mean that it JOURNALISM is an indication of how a situation is changing. *IBM is considered the bellwether stock on Wall Street.*

bel·ly /'beli/ **bellies. 1** The **belly** of a person or ◆◇◇◇◇ animal is their stomach or abdomen. ● See also N-COUNT: **beer belly, pot belly. ♦ -bellied** /-belid/ *The fat-* COMB *bellied officer stood near the door.* **2** If a company PHRASE *goes belly up*, it does not have enough money to INFORMAL pay its debts. *I can't afford to see this company go belly up.*

belly button, belly buttons. Some people, espe- N-COUNT cially children, use **belly button** to refer to their navel.

belly dancer, belly dancers. A **belly dancer** is a N-COUNT woman who performs a Middle Eastern dance in which she moves her hips and abdomen vigorously.

belly laugh, belly laughs. A **belly laugh** is a very N-COUNT loud deep laugh.

be·long /bɪ'lɒŋ, AM -'lɔːŋ/ **belongs, belonging,** ◆◆◆◇◇ **belonged. 1** If something **belongs to** you, you VB: no cont own it. *At one time the jeep had belonged to the* V to n *army.* **2** You say that something **belongs to** a par- VB: no cont ticular person when you are guessing or explaining V to n that it was produced by or is part of that person. *The handwriting belongs to a male.* **3** If a baby or VB: no cont child **belongs to** a particular adult, that adult is its V to n parent or the person who is looking after it. *He de-* *duced that the two children belonged to the couple.* **4** If you say that something **belongs to** someone, you VB: no cont mean that person has the right to it. *...but the last* V to n *word belonged to Rosanne.* **5** If you say that a time **be-** VB: no cont **longs to** a particular system or way of doing some- V to n thing, you mean that that time is or will be character- ized by it. *The future belongs to democracy.* **6** If someone **belongs to** a particular group, they are a VB: no cont member of that group. *I used to belong to a youth club.* V to n **7** If something or someone **belongs in** or **to** a particu- VB: no cont lar category group, they are of that category or group. V in/to n *The judges could not decide which category it belonged in.* **8** If something **belongs to** a particular time, it VB: no cont comes from that time. *The theater belongs to another* V to n *era.* **9** When lovers say that they **belong** together, they are V-RECIP: expressing their closeness or commitment to each V together, other. *He belongs with me.* **10** If a person or thing **be-** V with n **longs** in a particular place or situation, that is where V adv/prep they should be. *This piece really belongs in the concert hall... They need to feel they belong. ♦ **be·long·ing*** *...a* N-UNCOUNT *man utterly without a sense of belonging.*

be·long·ings /bɪ'lɒŋɪŋz, AM -'lɔːŋ-/. Your belong- ◆◇◇◇◇ ings are the things that you own. *I collected my be-* N-PLURAL *longings and left.*

be·lov·ed /bɪ'lʌvɪd/. When the adjective is not fol- ◆◆◇◇◇ lowed by a noun it is pronounced /bɪ'lʌvd/. **1** A **be-** ADJ-GRADED **loved** person or thing is one that you feel great af- fection for. *He lost his beloved wife last year.* **2** Your N-SING **beloved** is the person that you love. DATED

be·low /bɪ'ləʊ/. **1** If something is **below** something ◆◆◆◆◇ else, it is in a lower position. *...the apartment direct-* PREP *ly below Leonard's... The path runs below a long brick wall.* ► Also an adverb. *Spread out below was* ADV *a great crowd.* **2** If something is **below ground**, it is PHRASE in the ground. *...a system which pumps up water from 70m below ground.* **3** You use **below** in a ADV piece of writing to refer to something that is men- tioned later. *Please write to me at the address below.*

bench

4 If something is **below** a particular amount or level, it PREP is less than it. *Night temperatures can drop below 15 degrees Celsius... Rainfall has been below average.* ► Also an adverb. *...temperatures at zero or below.* **5** If ADV someone is **below** you in an organization, they are PREP lower in rank. *...pay rises awarded to all white-collar staff below chief officer level.* **6** ● **below par:** see **par.**

be,low-the-'belt. See **belt.**

belt /belt/ **belts, belting, belted. 1** A **belt** is a ◆◆◆◇◇ strip of leather or cloth that you fasten round your N-COUNT waist. See picture headed **clothes.** ● See also **safety belt, seat belt. 2** If someone is or has a **belt** of a N-COUNT particular colour in judo or karate, they have reached the standard which that colour represents. *He is a black belt in karate.* **3** A **belt** in a machine is a circular strip of rubber that N-COUNT is used to drive moving parts or to move objects along. ● See also **conveyor belt, fan belt. 4** A **belt** of land or sea is a long narrow area of it that N-COUNT: has some special feature. *...miners in Zambia's north-* with supp *ern copper belt.* ● See also **Bible Belt, commuter belt, green belt. 5** If someone **belts** you, they hit you very hard. ► Also VERB: V n a noun. *Father would give you a belt over the head.* INFORMAL **6** If you **belt** somewhere, you move or travel there N-COUNT very fast. *We belted down Iveagh Parade.* VERB V prep/adv **7** If you do or say something that is **below the belt** or INFORMAL hit someone **below the belt,** you do or say something PHRASE that is rather cruel and unfair. *...this kind of below-the-belt discrimination.* **8** If you have to **tighten** your PHRASE **belt,** you must manage without things because you have less money than you used to have. **9** If you have PHRASE something **under** your **belt,** you have already achieved it or done it. *Colvin already has two albums under her belt.* **10** See also **belted.**

belt out. If you **belt out** a song, you sing or play it PHRASAL VB very loudly. *The band belted out Rock Around The* V P n *Clock.* Also V n P INFORMAL

belt up. If someone tells you to **belt up,** they are tell- PHRASAL VB ing you in a very impolite way to stop talking. *'Belt up!'* V P *he snapped.* INFORMAL, BRITISH

belt·ed /'beltɪd/. If someone's jacket or coat, for ex- ADJ ample, is **belted,** it has a belt fastened round it. *She wore a brown suede jacket, belted at the waist.*

belt·er /'beltə/ **belters.** If you describe someone or N-COUNT something as a **belter,** you are emphasizing that PRAGMATICS they are very good, powerful, or impressive. INFORMAL, *Shirley's a real belter.* BRITISH

belt-tightening. If you need to do some **belt-** N-UNCOUNT **tightening,** you must manage without things be- cause you have less money than you used to have.

be·moan /bɪ'məʊn/ **bemoans, bemoaning, be-** ◆◇◇◇◇ **moaned.** If you **bemoan** something, you express VERB sorrow or dissatisfaction about it. *Universities and* V n *other research establishments bemoan their lack of* FORMAL *funds.*

be·muse /bɪ'mjuːz/ **bemuses, bemusing, be-** VERB **mused.** If something **bemuses** you, it puzzles or V n confuses you. *The depiction puzzled and bemused her.*

be·mused /bɪ'mjuːzd/. If you are **bemused,** you ◆◇◇◇◇ are puzzled or confused. *He was rather bemused by* ADJ-GRADED *children.* **♦ be·mus·ed·ly** *He was staring bemused-* ADV-GRADED: *ly at the picture.* ADV after v

bench /bentʃ/ **benches. 1** A **bench** is a long seat ◆◇◇◇◇ of wood or metal that two or more people can sit N-COUNT on. **2** In parliament, different groups sit on different N-PLURAL **benches.** For example, the government sits on the BRITISH government **benches.** *Mr Shekhar has spent most of his life on the opposition benches.* ● See also **back-bencher, backbenches, front bench. 3** If a player is N-SING on the bench for a particular match, he is a substi- the N tute for that match. JOURNALISM **4** A **bench** is a long, narrow table in a factory or la- N-COUNT boratory. **5** In a court of law, **the bench** consists of the judge or N-COLL-SING: magistrates. *The chairman of the bench adjourned the* the N *case.* **6** If someone serves on **the bench,** they work as a N-SING: judge or magistrate. *Allgood served on the bench for* the N *more than 50 years.*

bench·mark /'bentʃmɑːk/ **benchmarks;** also ◆◇◇◇◇ N-COUNT
spelled **bench mark**. A **benchmark** is something
whose quality, quantity, or capability is known and
which can therefore be used as a standard with
which other things can be compared. *The truck industry is a benchmark for the economy.*

bend /bend/ **bends, bending, bent. 1** When you ◆◆◇◇ VERB: V
bend, you move the top part of your body down- V adv/prep
wards and forwards. Other tall upright things also V-ed
bend. *I bent over and kissed her cheek... She was
bent over the sink.* **2** When you **bend** your head, you VERB
move your head forwards and downwards. *Rick ap-* V n
*peared, bending his head a little to clear the top of
the door.*
3 When you **bend** a part of your body such as your V-ERG: V n
arm or leg, or when it **bends**, you change its position V
so that it is no longer straight. *As you walk faster, you
will find the arms bending naturally.* ◆ **bent** *Keep your* ADJ-GRADED
knees slightly bent. **4** If you **bend** something that is flat VERB: V n
or straight, you use force to make it curved or to put V n prep
an angle in it. *Bend the bar into a horseshoe.* ◆ **bent** ADJ-GRADED
...a length of bent wire. **5** When a road or other long V-ERG: V n
thin thing **bends** or when something **bends** it, it V n
changes direction to form a curve or angle. *Glass
bends light of different colours by different amounts.*
6 A **bend** in a road, pipe, or other long thin object is a N-COUNT
curve or angle in it. *The crash occurred on a sharp
bend.*
7 If someone **bends** to your opinion, or if they **bend** VERB:
their opinions, they believe or do something different, V to n
usually reluctantly. *Do you think she's likely to bend* V
on her attitude to Europe?... He would not bend his V n
principles.
8 If you **bend** rules or laws, you interpret them in a VERB
way that allows you to do something they would not V n
normally allow you to do. *A minority of officers were
prepared to bend the rules.* **9** If you **bend** the truth or VERB: V n
bend the facts, you say something that is not exactly
true.
10 If you say that someone **is bending over back-** PHRASE
wards to be helpful or kind, you are emphasizing that PRAGMATICS
they are trying very hard to be helpful or kind.
11 If you say that someone or something **drives you** PHRASE
round the bend, you mean that they annoy or upset PRAGMATICS
you very much. *Your fidgeting drives me completely* INFORMAL,
round the bend. **12** If you say that someone is **round** BRITISH
the bend, you mean that they do foolish or silly PHRASE
things. **13** See also **bent; hairpin bend.** BRITISH,
INFORMAL

bend·er /'bendə/ **benders.** If someone goes on a N-COUNT
bender, they drink a very large amount of alcohol. INFORMAL

bendy /'bendi/ **bendier, bendiest.** A bendy object ADJ-GRADED
bends easily. *...a bendy toy whose limbs bend in* BRITISH
every direction.

be·neath /bɪ'niːθ/. **1** Something that is **beneath** ◆◆◆◇◇
another thing is under it. *She could see the muscles* PREP
*of his shoulders beneath his T-shirt... She found
pleasure in sitting beneath the trees.* ► Also an ad- ADV
verb. *On a shelf beneath he spotted a photo album.*
2 If you talk about what is **beneath** the surface of PREP
something, you are talking about the aspects of it
which are hidden or not obvious. *Somewhere deep
beneath the surface lay a caring character.* **3** If you PREP
say that someone or something is **beneath** you, you
feel that they are not good enough for you. *They decided she was marrying beneath her.*

ben·edic·tion /ˌbenɪ'dɪkʃən/ **benedictions.** A N-VAR
benediction is a prayer or gesture blessing some- FORMAL
one. *...as the minister pronounced the benediction.*

ben·efac·tor /'benɪfæktə/ **benefactors.** A ben- ◆◇◇◇◇
efactor is a person who helps a person or organiza- N-COUNT
tion by giving them money.

be·nefi·cent /bɪ'nefɪsənt/. A **beneficent** person or ADJ-GRADED
thing helps people or results in something good. *In* FORMAL
*1909 nuns were running more than 1,000 beneficent
institutions.*

ben·efi·cial /ˌbenɪ'fɪʃəl/. Something that is **benefi-** ◆◆◇◇◇
cial helps people or improves their lives. *...vitamins* ADJ-GRADED
which are beneficial to our health.

bene·fi·ciary /ˌbenɪ'fɪʃəri, AM -ʃieri/ **benefi-** ◆◇◇◇◇
ciaries. 1 Someone who is a **beneficiary** of some- N-COUNT
thing is helped by it. *The main beneficiaries of pension equality so far have been men.* **2** The **benefi-** N-COUNT
ciaries of a will legally receive money or property
from someone when they die.

ben·efit /'benɪfɪt/ **benefits, benefiting, benefit-** ◆◆◆◇
ed; also spelled **benefitting, benefitted. 1** The **ben-** N-VAR
efit of something is the help that you get from it or
the advantage that results from it. *I'm a great believer in the benefits of this form of therapy.*
2 If something is to your **benefit** or is of **benefit** to you, N-UNCOUNT
it helps you or improves your life. *I hope what I have
written will be of benefit to someone else.* **3** If you say PHRASE
that someone is doing something **for the benefit of** a
particular person, you mean that they are doing it for
that person. *...people working for the benefit of the
community.* **4** If you **benefit** from something or if it V-ERG:
benefits you, it helps you or improves your life. *...a va-* V from n
riety of government programs benefiting children. **5** If V n
you have the **benefit** of some information or equip- N-UNCOUNT:
ment, you are able to use it so that you can achieve N of n
something. *Steve didn't have the benefit of a formal
college education.* **6** If you give someone **the benefit** PHRASE
of the doubt, you treat them as if they are telling the
truth or as if they have behaved properly, even though
you are not sure that this is the case.
7 Benefit is money that the government gives to peo- N-VAR
ple who are poor, ill, or unemployed. *...the removal of* BRITISH
benefit from school-leavers.
8 A **benefit**, or a **benefit** concert or dinner, is an event N-COUNT
that is held in order to raise money for a particular
charity or person.
9 See also **fringe benefit, supplementary benefit, unemployment benefit.**

be·nevo·lent /bɪ'nevələnt/. **1** If you describe ◆◇◇◇◇
someone as **benevolent**, you mean that they are ADJ-GRADED
kind and tolerant. *...a benevolent dictator.* ◆ **be-** ADV-GRADED:
·nevo·lent·ly *Thorne nodded his understanding,* ADV with v
smiling benevolently. ◆ **be·nevo·lence** *He chuckles* N-UNCOUNT
often and radiates benevolence. **2 Benevolent** is ADJ: ADJ n
used in the names of some organizations that give
money and help to people who need it. *...the Army
Benevolent Fund.*

be·night·ed /bɪ'naɪtɪd/. If you describe people or ADJ-GRADED:
the place where they live as **benighted**, you mean ADJ n
that you consider them to be unfortunate or igno- PRAGMATICS
rant. *Moorish Spain displayed none of the bigotry of* LITERARY
benighted fundamentalism.

be·nign /bɪ'naɪn/. **1** You use **benign** to describe ◆◇◇◇◇
someone who is kind, gentle, and harmless. *Critics* ADJ-GRADED
of the scheme take a less benign view. ◆ **be·nign·ly** ADV-GRADED
just smiled benignly. **2** If you describe someone's PHRASE
approach to a problem as one of **benign neglect**, PRAGMATICS
you disapprove of the fact that they are doing nothing and hoping that the problem will solve itself.
3 A **benign** substance or process does not have any ADJ-GRADED
harmful effects. **4** A **benign** tumour will not cause ADJ
death or serious harm. **5 Benign** conditions are pleas- MEDICAL
ant or make it easy for something to happen. *They en-* ADJ-GRADED
joyed an especially benign climate.

bent /bent/. **1 Bent** is the past tense and past parti- ◆◆◇◇◇
ciple of **bend**. **2** If an object is **bent**, it is damaged ADJ GRADED
and no longer has its correct shape. **3** If a person is ADJ-GRADED
bent, their body has become curved because of old WRITTEN
age or disease. *...a bent, frail, old man.* **4** If some- PHRASE
one is **bent double**, the top part of their body is
leaning forward towards their legs, usually because
they are in great pain or because they are laughing
so much.
5 If someone is **bent on** doing something, especially ADJ-GRADED:
something destructive, they are determined to do it. v-link ADJ
He's bent on suicide. on/upon n/-
ing
6 If you have a **bent** for something, you have a natural N-SING:
ability to do it or a natural interest in it. *His bent for* N with supp
natural history directed him towards his first job. **7** If N-SING:
someone is of a particular **bent**, they hold a particular adj N
set of beliefs. *...economists of a socialist bent.*
8 If you say that someone in a position of responsibil- ADJ-GRADED
ity is **bent**, you mean that they are dishonest or do il- INFORMAL,
legal things. *...bent policemen.* BRITISH

B

9 Gay people are sometimes described as **bent**; an offensive word. _ADJ BRITISH_

ben·zene /ˈbenziːn/. **Benzene** is a clear colourless liquid which is used to make plastics and dyes, and also as an insecticide. Benzene is poisonous and catches fire very easily. _N-UNCOUNT_

be·queath /bɪˈkwiːð/ **bequeaths, bequeathing, bequeathed.** **1** If you **bequeath** someone your money or property, you legally state that they should have it when you die. _He bequeathed all his silver to his children._ **2** If someone **bequeaths** an idea or system, they leave it for other people to use or develop. _He bequeaths his successor an economy that is doing quite well._ ♦◇◇◇◇ _VERB: V n n / V n to n FORMAL_ _V n n / Also V n to n, V n FORMAL_

be·quest /bɪˈkwest/ **bequests.** A bequest is money or property which you legally leave to someone when you die. _N-COUNT_

be·rate /bɪˈreɪt/ **berates, berating, berated.** If you **berate** someone, you scold them angrily. _Marion berated Joe for the noise he made._ ♦◇◇◇◇ _VERB: V n / V n for n FORMAL_

be·reaved /bɪˈriːvd/. A **bereaved** person has a relative or close friend who has recently died. ▶ A group of people who have been bereaved can be called the **bereaved**. _ADJ_ _N-PLURAL_

be·reave·ment /bɪˈriːvmənt/ **bereavements.** Bereavement is the grief you feel or the state you are in when a relative or close friend has just died. ♦◇◇◇◇ _N-VAR_

be·reft /bɪˈreft/. If a person or thing is **bereft** of something, they no longer have it. _The place seemed to be utterly bereft of human life._ ♦◇◇◇◇ _ADJ-GRADED FORMAL_

be·ret /ˈbereɪ, AM bəˈreɪ/ **berets.** A beret is a circular flat hat that is made of soft material and has no brim. See picture headed **clothes**. ♦◇◇◇◇ _N-COUNT_

ber·ry /ˈberi/ **berries.** Berries are small round fruit that grow on a bush or a tree. Some berries are edible, for example blackberries and raspberries. ♦♦◇◇◇ _N-COUNT_

ber·serk /bəˈzɜːk, -ˈsɜːk/. **1** Berserk means crazy and out of control. _...a howl of berserk laughter._ **2** If someone **goes berserk**, they lose control of themselves and become very angry or violent. _ADJ-GRADED_ _PHRASE_

berth /bɜːθ/ **berths, berthing, berthed.** **1** If you **give** someone or something **a wide berth**, you avoid them. _She gives showbiz parties a wide berth._ **2** A **berth** is a bed on a boat, train, or caravan. **3** A **berth** is a space in a harbour where a ship stays for a period of time. **4** When a ship **berths**, it sails into harbour and stops at the quay. ♦ **berthed** _There the Gripsholm was berthed next to another ship._ ♦◇◇◇◇ _PHRASE_ _N-COUNT_ _N-COUNT_ _VERB: V_ _ADJ_

be·seech /bɪˈsiːtʃ/ **beseeches, beseeching, beseeched.** If you **beseech** someone to do something, you ask them very insistently and desperately. _She beseeched him to cut his drinking._ _VERB Also V with to-inf / V with quote LITERARY_

be·seech·ing /bɪˈsiːtʃɪŋ/. A **beseeching** expression or tone of voice suggests that the person who has it or makes it very much wants someone to do something. _She clung to him and looked up into his face with beseeching eyes._ _ADJ-GRADED WRITTEN_

be·set /bɪˈset/ **besets, besetting.** The form **beset** is used in the present tense and the past tense and past participle. If someone or something is **beset** by problems or fears, they have many problems or fears which affect them severely. _...the problems now besetting the country._ ♦◇◇◇◇ _VERB: be V-ed by / with n_ _V n_

be·side /bɪˈsaɪd/. **1** Something that is **beside** something else is at the side of it or next to it. _Beside his plate was a pile of books... I moved from behind my desk to sit beside her._ ● See also **besides**. **2** If you are **beside yourself** with anger or excitement, you are extremely angry or excited. ● **beside the point**: see **point**. ♦♦♦◇◇ _PREP_ _PHRASE_

be·sides /bɪˈsaɪdz/. **1** Besides something or beside something means in addition to it. _I think she has many good qualities besides being very beautiful._ ▶ Also an adverb. _My daughter was in poor health and heartbroken besides._ **2** You say **besides** when you are making an additional point. _Common sense can also limit risk. Besides, if investing is risky, what isn't?_ ♦♦♦◇◇ _PREP_ _ADV_ _cl ADV_ _ADV: ADV with cl, ADV not last in cl_ _PRAGMATICS_

be·siege /bɪˈsiːdʒ/ **besieges, besieging, besieged.** **1** If you **are besieged** by people, many ♦♦◇◇◇ _VB: usu_ people want something from you and continually bother you. _She was besieged by the press._ **2** If soldiers **besiege** a place, they surround it and wait for the people in it to surrender. _The Afghan air force was using helicopters to supply the besieged town._ _passive be V-ed VERB: V n_ _V-ed_

be·smirch /bɪˈsmɜːtʃ/ **besmirches, besmirching, besmirched.** If someone **besmirches** you or your reputation, they say that you are a bad person or that you have done something wrong, usually when this is not true. _Lawyers can besmirch reputations and disrupt social harmony._ _VERB V n LITERARY_

be·sot·ted /bɪˈsɒtɪd/. If you are **besotted** with someone, you are so much in love with them that you behave in a foolish way. _ADJ-GRADED_

be·speak /bɪˈspiːk/ **bespeaks, bespeaking, bespoke, bespoken.** If someone's action or behaviour **bespeaks** a particular quality or feeling, it indicates that they have that quality or feeling. _The tone of his text bespeaks a certain tiredness._ _VERB V n DATED or LITERARY_

be·spec·ta·cled /bɪˈspektəkəld/. A **bespectacled** person is wearing spectacles. _ADJ WRITTEN_

be·spoke /bɪˈspəʊk/. **1** A **bespoke** craftsman such as a tailor makes or sells things that are specially made for the customer who orders them. **2** Bespoke things such as clothes are specially made for the customer who orders them. _ADJ: ADJ n FORMAL, BRITISH_ _ADJ: ADJ n FORMAL, BRITISH_

best /best/. **1** Best is the superlative of **good**. **2** Best is the superlative of **well**. **3** Best is used to form the superlative of compound adjectives beginning with 'good' and 'well'. For example, the superlative of 'well-known' is 'best-known'.

4 If you like something **best** or like it **the best**, you prefer it to other things. _What was the role you loved the best?_ **5** You use **best of all** to indicate that what you are about to mention is the thing that you prefer or that has most advantages out of all the things you are mentioning. _It was comfortable and cheap; best of all, most of the rent was being paid by two American friends._ _ADV-SUPERL_ _PHRASE_ _PRAGMATICS_

6 Someone's **best** is the greatest effort or highest achievement or standard that they are capable of. _Miss Blockey was at her best when she played the piano._ **7** If you **look your best**, you are looking as smart and attractive as you can. **8** If you **do** your **best** or **try** your **best** to do something, you try as hard as you can to do it, or do it as well as you can. _She was trying her best to help._ **9** If someone does something **as best** they **can**, they do it as well as they can, although it is very difficult. **10** ● **to the best of your ability**: see **ability**. _N-SING_ _PHRASE_ _PHRASE_ _PHRASE_

11 The **best** is used to refer to things of the highest quality or standard. _He'll have the best of care._ **12** ● **the best of the bunch**: see **bunch**. **13** See also **second best**, **Sunday best**. _N-SING theN_

14 If two people are **the best of friends**, they are close friends, especially when they have had a disagreement or fight in the past. _PHRASE_

15 If you say that something is **for the best**, you mean it is the most desirable or helpful thing that could have happened or could be done, considering all the circumstances. **16** You use **at best** to indicate that even if you consider something as favourably as possible, it is still not very good. _This policy, they say, is at best confused and at worst non-existent._ **17** If you **make the best of** something or **make the best of a bad job**, you try to manage as well as you can in an unsatisfactory situation. **18** If you say that something is **the best** that can be done or hoped for, you think it is the most successful or beneficial thing that can be done or hoped for. _A draw seems the best they can hope for._ **19** ● **to hope for the best**: see **hope**. _PHRASE_ _PHRASE_ _PHRASE_ _N-SING theN_

20 If you say that a particular person **knows best**, you mean that they have a lot of experience and should therefore be trusted to make decisions for other people. _PHRASE_

21 If you say that someone **had best** do something, you mean they ought to do it. Some people consider this use to be non-standard. _You'd best take a look._ _PHR-MODAL_

22 You use **the best thing** when you are advising someone about the best course of action to take. _If_ _PHRASE_

you want further information, the best thing to do is have a word with the driver.

23 You can say **'All the best'** when you are saying goodbye to someone, or at the end of a letter. *Wish him all the best, and tell him we miss him.* CONVENTION PRAGMATICS

24 • to the best of your knowledge: see **knowledge.** **•** best of luck: see **luck.** **•** the best part: see **part.** **•** at the best of times: see **time.** **•** the best of both worlds: see **world.**

bes·tial /'bestɪəl, AM -stʃəl/. If you describe behaviour or a situation as **bestial**, you mean that it is very unpleasant or disgusting. ...*bestial aggression.* ADJ-GRADED

bes·ti·al·ity /ˌbestɪˈælɪti, AM -tʃˈæl-/. **1 Bestiality** is revolting or disgusting behaviour. **2 Bestiality** is sexual activity in which a person has sex with an animal. N-UNCOUNT FORMAL N-UNCOUNT

best 'man. The **best man** at a wedding is the man who acts as an attendant to the bridegroom. ◆◇◇◇◇ N-SING

be·stow /bɪˈstəʊ/ **bestows, bestowing, bestowed.** To **bestow** something **on** someone means to give or present it to them. *The Queen personally visited his quarters at Windsor to bestow on him his knighthood.* ◆◇◇◇◇ VERB V on/upon n n Also V n on/ upon n FORMAL

best 'seller, best sellers; also spelled **bestseller.** A **best seller** is a book of which a great number of copies has been sold. ◆◇◇◇◇ N-COUNT

best-'selling; also spelled **bestselling. 1** A **best-selling** product is very popular and a large quantity of it has been sold. **2** A **best-selling** author is an author who has sold a very large number of copies of his or her book. ◆◇◇◇◇ ADJ: ADJ n ADJ: ADJ n

bet /bet/ **bets, betting.** The form **bet** is used in the present tense and is the past tense and past participle. **1** If you **bet** on the result of a horse race, football match, or other event, you give someone a sum of money which they give you back with extra money if the result is what you predicted, or which they keep if it is not. *I bet £10 on a horse called Premonition... He bet them 500 pounds they would lose.* ► Also a noun. *Do you always have a bet on the Grand National?* **•** **bet·ting** ...*off-course betting shops.* **2** A **bet** is a sum of money which you give to someone when you bet. *You can put a bet on almost anything these days.* ◆◆◆◇◇ VERB: V on n V n on n V n n that N-COUNT N-UNCOUNT N-COUNT

3 If someone **is betting** that something will happen, they are hoping or expecting that it will happen. ...*people who were betting on a further easing of credit conditions.* **4** If you use a phrase such as **'I bet', 'I'll bet'**, or **'you can bet'**, you mean that you are sure something is true. *I bet you were good at games when you were at school.* **5** If you say that it is **a good bet** or a **safe bet** that something is true or will happen, you are saying that it is extremely likely to be true or to happen. *It is a safe bet that the current owners will not sell.* VERB: V that, only cont V on n PHRASE PRAGMATICS INFORMAL PHRASE

6 You can use **my bet** is or **it's my bet** to give your own personal opinion about something. *It's my bet that he's the guy behind this killing.* **7** If you say **don't bet on** something or **I wouldn't bet on** something, you mean that you do not think that something is true or will happen. *'We'll never get a table in there'—'Don't bet on it.'* PHRASE PRAGMATICS INFORMAL PHRASE PRAGMATICS INFORMAL

8 If you tell someone that something is a **good bet**, you are suggesting that it is the thing or course of action that they should choose. *Your best bet is to choose a guest house.* **9** If you **hedge your bets**, you follow two courses of action, because you cannot decide which one is right. PHRASE PHRASE

10 You use **I bet** or **I'll bet** in reply to a statement to show that you agree with it or that you expected it to be true, usually when you are annoyed or amused by it. *'I'd like to ask you something,' I said. 'I bet you would,' she grinned.* **11** You use **'You bet'** or **'you bet your life'** to say yes in an emphatic way or to emphasize a reply or statement. *'It's settled, then?'—'You bet.'.* **12** If you reply **'Do you want to bet?'** or **'Want a bet?'** to someone, you mean you are certain that what they have said is wrong. *'Money can't buy happiness'—'Want to bet?'* PHRASE PRAGMATICS INFORMAL PHRASE PRAGMATICS INFORMAL CONVENTION PRAGMATICS INFORMAL

beta block·er /ˌbiːtə ˈblɒkə, AM ˌbeɪtə -/ **beta blockers.** A **beta blocker** is a drug which is used N-COUNT

to treat people who have high blood pressure or heart problems.

bete noire /bet ˈnwɑː/. If you refer to someone or something as your **bete noire**, you mean that you have a particular dislike for them or that they annoy you a great deal. N-SING FORMAL

be·tide /bɪˈtaɪd/. If you say **woe betide** anyone who does a particular thing, you mean that something unpleasant will happen to them if they do it. *Woe betide anyone who got in his way.* PHRASE PRAGMATICS

be·to·ken /bɪˈtəʊkən/ **betokens, betokening, betokened.** If something **betokens** something else, it is a sign of that thing. *His demeanour betokened embarrassment at his prosperity.* VERB V n FORMAL

be·tray /bɪˈtreɪ/ **betrays, betraying, betrayed.** **1** If you **betray** someone who loves or trusts you, your actions hurt and disappoint them. *When I tell someone I will not betray his confidence I keep my word.* **•** **be·tray·er, betrayers** *She was her friend and now calls her a betrayer.* **2** If someone **betrays** their country or their comrades, they give information to an enemy, putting their country's security or their comrades' safety at risk. *They betrayed the plan to the Chinese.* **•** **be·tray·er 3** If you **betray** an ideal or your principles, you say or do something which goes against those beliefs. *We betray the ideals of our country when we support capital punishment.* **4** If you **betray** a feeling or quality, you show it without intending to. *Jeremy's voice betrayed little emotion.* ◆◆◇◇◇ VERB V n N-COUNT VERB: V n V n to n N-COUNT VERB VERB V n

be·tray·al /bɪˈtreɪəl/ **betrayals.** A **betrayal** is an action which betrays someone or something, or the fact of being betrayed. *She felt that what she had done was a betrayal of Patrick.* ◆◇◇◇◇ N-VAR

be·troth·al /bɪˈtrəʊðəl/ **betrothals.** A **betrothal** is an engagement to be married. N-VAR DATED

be·trothed /bɪˈtrəʊðd/. If a couple are **betrothed**, they are engaged to be married. ► Your **betrothed** is the person you are betrothed to. ADJ DATED N-SING

bet·ter /'betə/ **betters, bettering, bettered. 1 Better** is the comparative of **good. 2 Better** is the comparative of **well. 3 Better** is used to form the comparative of compound adjectives beginning with 'good' and 'well.' For example, the comparative of 'well-off' is 'better-off.' ◆◆◆◆◆

4 If you like one thing **better** than another, you like it more. *They liked it better when it rained.* **5** If you are **better** after an illness or injury, you have recovered. If you feel **better**, you no longer feel so ill. **6** If something changes **for the better**, it improves. ADV-COMPAR: ADV after v ADJ-GRADED: v-link ADJ PHRASE

7 You can tell someone that they **are better** doing one thing than another or **it is better** doing one thing than another when you are advising them about what they should do. *You are better eating just a small snack than hurrying a main meal.* **8** People sometimes say **better not** when they are advising someone not to do something. *Better not say too much aloud.* **9** You use **had better** when you are advising or warning someone, or expressing an opinion about what should happen. *I think we had better go home.* **10** If you say that someone would **be better off** doing something, you are advising them to do it or expressing the opinion that it would benefit them to do it. *Their stance seems to be that a baby or child is better off in its country of birth.* PHRASE PRAGMATICS CONVENTION SPOKEN PHR-MODAL PRAGMATICS PHRASE PRAGMATICS

11 If you **better** someone's situation, you improve the quality of their life. If you **better** yourself, you improve your social status. *He had dedicated his life to bettering the lot of the oppressed people of South Africa.* **12** If someone **betters** a high achievement, they achieve something of a higher standard. *As an account of adolescence it could hardly be bettered.* **13** If you **go one better**, you do something better than it has been done before, or you obtain something better than you had before or than someone else has. *Now General Electric have gone one better than nature and made a diamond purer than the best quality natural diamonds.* VERB V n Also V pron-refl VERB: V n be V-ed PHRASE

14 If you say that you expect or deserve **better**, you mean that you expect or deserve a higher standard of PRON

behaviour or treatment from people than they have shown you.

15 Your **betters** are people who have a higher status or rank than you. *Be quiet in front of your elders and betters.*   N-PLURAL: poss N / DATED

16 If you **get the better of** someone, you defeat them.   PHRASE

17 If a feeling such as jealousy or curiosity **gets the better of** you, it becomes too strong for you to conceal or control.   PHRASE

18 If you think a statement or belief is wrong, you can say you **know better**. *My sister still claims she cheated on us at cards, but I know better.* **19** If you say someone **knows better** or should **know better** than to do something, you mean they have, or ought to have the experience and maturity to know it is the wrong thing to do. *She knew better than to argue with Adeline.*   PHRASE

20 You can say **'so much the better'** or **'all the better'** to indicate that, if something is true, it improves the thing you are talking about. *If there's good skiing, breathtaking scenery and you don't need to catch a plane, all the better!* **21** You can use expressions like **'The** bigger **the better'** or **'The** sooner **the better'** to mean that it will be more beneficial or satisfactory if something is big or happens soon. *The Irish love a party, the bigger the better.* **22** If you say that something has happened **for better or worse**, you mean that you are not sure whether the consequences will be good or bad, but they will have to be accepted because the action cannot be changed.   PHRASE

23 If someone does something **the better** to do something else, they do the first thing in order to be able to do the second thing more effectively. *She came on every ride herself, the better to instruct her eager pupils.*   PHRASE / LITERARY

24 If you intend to do something and then **think better of it**, you decide not to do it because you realize it would not be sensible.   PHRASE

25 ● **better** the **devil** you **know**: see **devil**. ● **discretion** is the better part of **valour**: see **discretion**. ● **your better half**: see **half**. ● **against your better judgment**: see **judgment**. ● be **better than nothing**: see **nothing**. ● the **better part**: see **part**.

bet·ter·ment /'betəmənt/. The **betterment** of something is the act or process of improving its standard or status. *His research is for the betterment of mankind.*   N-UNCOUNT / FORMAL

'betting shop, betting shops. In Britain, a **betting shop** is a place where people can go to bet on something such as a horse race.   ◆◇◇◇◇ N-COUNT

be·tween /bɪ'twiːn/. In addition to the uses shown below, **between** is used in a few phrasal verbs, such as 'come between'.   ◆◆◆◆◆

1 If something is **between** two things or is **in between** them, it has one of the things on one side of it and the other thing on the other side.   PREP

2 If people or things travel **between** two places, they travel regularly from one place to the other and back again. *I often travel between Britain, France and Germany.*   PREP

3 A relationship, discussion, or difference **between** two people, groups, or things is one that involves them both or relates to them both. *I think the relationship between patients and doctors has got a lot less personal.*   PREP

4 If something stands **between** you and what you want, it prevents you from having it. *His sense of duty often stood between him and the enjoyment of life.*   PREP

5 If something is **between** or in **between** two amounts or ages, it is greater or older than the first one and smaller or younger than the second one. *A third of its population is aged between 18 and 30.* **6** If something happens **between** or in **between** two times or events, it happens after the first event and before the second one. *The canal was built between 1793 and 1797.*   PREP
▶ Also an adverb. *The cravings come in peaks lasting a few minutes, with periods of calm in between.*   ADV: ADV with cl/group

7 If you must choose **between** two or more things, you must choose just one of them. *Students will be able to choose between English, French and Russian.*   PREP

8 If people or places have a particular amount of something **between** them, this is the total amount

that they have. *The three sites employ 12,500 people between them.* **9** When something is divided or shared **between** people, they each have a share of it. *There is only one bathroom shared between eight bedrooms.*   PREP

10 When you introduce a statement by saying **'between you and me'** or **'between ourselves'**, you are indicating that you do not want anyone else to know what you are saying.   PHRASE

bev·elled /'bevəld/; spelled **beveled** in American English. If a piece of wood or glass has **bevelled** edges, its edges are cut sloping.   ADJ

bev·er·age /'bevərɪdʒ/ **beverages.** Beverages are drinks. *Alcoholic beverages are served in the hotel lounge.*   ◆◇◇◇◇ N-COUNT / FORMAL

bevy /'bevi/ **bevies.** A **bevy of** people is a group of them all together in one place. *...a bevy of little girls.*   N-COUNT

be·wail /bɪ'weɪl/ **bewails, bewailing, bewailed.** If you **bewail** something, you express great sorrow about it. *The Report bewailed the declining standards of the press.*   VERB / V n

be·ware /bɪ'weə/. If you tell someone to **beware** of a person or thing, you are warning them that the person or thing may harm them or may be dangerous. *Beware of being too impatient with others.*   ◆◇◇◇◇ VB: only imper and inf / V of n/-ing

be·wil·der /bɪ'wɪldə/ **bewilders, bewildering, bewildered.** If something **bewilders** you, it is so confusing or difficult that you cannot understand it. *The silence from Alex had hurt and bewildered her.*   VERB / V n

be·wil·dered /bɪ'wɪldəd/. If you are **bewildered**, you are very confused and cannot understand something or decide what you should do. *Some shoppers looked bewildered by the sheer variety.*   ◆◇◇◇◇ ADJ-GRADED
♦ **be·wil·der·ing** The choice of excursions was bewildering.   ADJ-GRADED

be·wil·der·ment /bɪ'wɪldəmənt/. **Bewilderment** is the feeling of being bewildered. *He shook his head in bewilderment.*   ◆◇◇◇◇ N-UNCOUNT

be·witch /bɪ'wɪtʃ/ **bewitches, bewitching, bewitched.** If someone or something **bewitches** you, you are so attracted to them that you cannot think about anything else. *The doctor is bewitched by Maya's beauty.* ♦ **be·witch·ing** *...bewitching brown eyes.*   VERB / V n   ADJ-GRADED

be·yond /bɪ'jɒnd/. **1** If something is **beyond** a place or barrier, it is on the other side of it. *They heard footsteps in the main room, beyond a door.*   ◆◆◆◆◇ PREP
▶ Also an adverb. *The house had a fabulous view out to the Strait of Georgia and the Rockies beyond.*   ADV

2 If something extends **beyond** a particular thing, it affects or includes other things. *His interests extended beyond the fine arts to international politics and philosophy.*   PREP

3 If something happens **beyond** a particular time or date, it continues after that time or date has passed. *Few jockeys continue race-riding beyond the age of 40.*   PREP
▶ Also an adverb. *The financing of home ownership will continue through the 1990s and beyond.* **4** If something goes **beyond** a particular point or stage, it progresses or increases so that it passes that point or stage. *It seems to me he's beyond caring about what anybody does.*   ADV: and ADV   PREP

5 If something is, for example, **beyond** understanding or **beyond** belief, it is so extreme in some way that it cannot be understood or believed. *By the year 2000, business computing will have changed beyond recognition.* **6** If you say that something is **beyond** someone, you mean that they are incapable of dealing with it. *Any practical help would almost certainly be beyond him.*   PREP

7 You use **beyond** to introduce an exception to what you are saying. *I knew nothing beyond a few random facts.*   PREP

8 ● **beyond the pale**: see **pale**. ● **beyond someone's means**: see **means**. ● **beyond your wildest dreams**: see **dream**. ● **beyond a joke**: see **joke**.

bi- /baɪ-/. **1 Bi-** is used at the beginning of nouns and adjectives that have 'two' as part of their meaning. *...a bi-cultural society.* **2 Bi-** is used to form adjectives and adverbs indicating that something happens twice in a period of time or that happens   PREFIX   PREFIX

B

once in two consecutive periods of time. ...*a bimonthly magazine*.

bias /ˈbaɪəs/. **biases, biasing, biased. 1** Bias is prejudice against one group and favouritism towards another, which may badly affect someone's judgment. *Bias against women permeates every level of the judicial system.* **2** Bias is a concern with or interest in one thing more than others. *The Department has a strong bias towards neuroscience.* **3** If something or someone **biases** you or your decision or opinion, they influence your decision or opinion in favour of a particular choice. *We mustn't allow it to bias our teaching.*
◆◆◇◇ N-VAR

N-VAR: with supp

VERB V n

biased /ˈbaɪəst/. **1** If you describe someone or something as **biased**, you believe they show prejudice against one group and favouritism towards another, or are influenced so much by something that any judgment they make is likely to be unfair. *She claimed that judges were biased against women victims.* **2** If something is **biased towards** one thing, it is more concerned with it than with other things. *University funding was tremendously biased towards scientists.*
◆◇◇◇ ADJ-GRADED

ADJ-GRADED: v-link ADJ towards n

bib /bɪb/. **bibs.** A bib is a piece of cloth or plastic which is worn by very young children to protect their clothes while they are eating.
N-COUNT

Bi·ble /ˈbaɪbəl/. **Bibles. 1** The Bible is the sacred book of the Christian religion. The first part, the Old Testament, is also a sacred book for Jews. **2** A Bible is a copy of the Bible. **3** If someone describes a book or magazine about their job or interest as their **bible**, they mean that it is the best and most useful book about it. *...the photographer's bible – Amateur Photographer.*
◆◆◇◇ N-PROPER: the N
N-COUNT
N-COUNT: poss N

'Bible Belt; also spelled **bible belt**. Parts of the southern United States are referred to as **the Bible Belt** because Protestants with strong beliefs have a lot of influence there.
N-PROPER: the N

bib·li·cal /ˈbɪblɪkəl/. **Biblical** means contained in or relating to the Bible. *...the biblical story of Noah.*
◆◇◇◇ ADJ

bib·li·og·ra·phy /ˌbɪbliˈɒɡrəfi/. **bibliographies. 1** A bibliography is a list of books on a particular subject. **2** A bibliography is a list of the books and articles that are referred to in a particular book.
◆◇◇◇ N-COUNT
N-COUNT

bi·car·bo·nate of soda /baɪˌkɑːbəneɪt əv ˈsəʊdə/. Bicarbonate of soda is a white powder which is used in baking to make cakes rise, and also as a medicine to relieve indigestion.
N-UNCOUNT

bi·cen·tenary /ˌbaɪsenˈtiːnəri, AM -ˈten-/ **bicentenaries.** A bicentenary is the year in which people celebrate something important that happened exactly two hundred years earlier.
N-COUNT

bi·cen·ten·nial /ˌbaɪsenˈtenɪəl/ **bicentennials.** Bicentennial celebrations are held to celebrate a bicentenary. ▶ Also a noun. *...the American bicentennial in 1976.*
ADJ: ADJ n
N-COUNT

bi·ceps /ˈbaɪseps/; **biceps** is both the singular and the plural form. Your **biceps** are the large muscles at the front of the upper part of your arms. Some people use 'bicep' as the singular form of 'biceps'.
N-COUNT

bick·er /ˈbɪkə/ **bickers, bickering, bickered.** When people **bicker**, they argue or quarrel about unimportant things. *I went into medicine to care for patients, not to waste time bickering over budgets. ...as states bicker over territory... He is still bickering with the control tower over admissible approach routes.* ♦ **bick·er·ing** *The election will end months of political bickering.*
◆◇◇◇ V-RECIP: pl-n V
V over/about
n (non recip)
pl-n V over/ about n
V with n
N-UNCOUNT

bi·cy·cle /ˈbaɪsɪkəl/ **bicycles, bicycling, bicycled. 1** A bicycle is a vehicle with two wheels which you ride by sitting on it and pushing two pedals with your feet. You steer it by turning a bar that is connected to the front wheel. **2** If you **bicycle** somewhere, you cycle there. *I bicycled on towards the sea.*
◆◆◇◇ N-COUNT
VERB
V adv/prep
DATED

bi·cy·clist /ˈbaɪsɪklɪst/ **bicyclists.** A bicyclist is someone who rides a bicycle.
N-COUNT
DATED

bid 1 attempting or offering

bid /bɪd/ **bids, bidding.** The form **bid** is used in the present tense and is the past tense and past par-
◆◆◆◇

ticiple. **1** A **bid** for something or a **bid** to do something is an attempt to obtain it or do it. *...Bill Clinton's successful bid for the US presidency... He may have changed his appearance in a bid to evade capture.* **2** A **bid** is an offer to pay a particular amount of money for something. *Hanson made an agreed takeover bid of £351 million.* **3** If you **bid** for something or **bid** to do something, you try to obtain it or do it. *My company was bidding for work in Somalia.* ♦ **bid·der, bidders.** *...bidders for two licences to develop cellular telephone systems.* **4** If you **bid** for something, you offer to pay a particular amount of money for it. *He certainly wasn't going to bid $18 billion for this company.* ♦ **bid·der** *The sale will be made to the highest bidder.* ♦ **bid·ding** *The bidding starts at £2 million.*
N-COUNT: N for n, N to-inf
JOURNALISM
N-COUNT
VERB V for n Also V to-inf
N-COUNT
VERB: V n for n Also V
N-UNCOUNT

bid 2 saying something

bid /bɪd/ **bids, bidding, bade, bidden.** American English sometimes uses the form **bid** for the past tense. **1** If you **bid** someone farewell, you say goodbye to them. If you **bid** them goodnight, you say goodnight to them. *She bade farewell to her son.* **2** If you **bid** someone do something, you ask or invite them to do it.
VERB: V n n
V n to n
FORMAL
VERB: V n inf
LITERARY

bid·den /ˈbɪdən/. **Bidden** is a past participle of **bid**.

bid·ding /ˈbɪdɪŋ/. **1** If you do something at someone's **bidding**, you do it because they have asked you to. **2** If you say that someone **does** another person's **bidding**, you disapprove of the fact that they do exactly what the other person asks them to do, even when they do not want to. **3** See also **bid**.
PHRASE FORMAL
PHRASE
PRAGMATICS
FORMAL

bid·dy /ˈbɪdi/ **biddies.** If someone calls an elderly woman an old **biddy**, they are saying in an unkind way that they think she is silly or unpleasant.
N-COUNT
PRAGMATICS

bide /baɪd/ **bides, biding, bided.** If you **bide** your **time**, you wait for a good opportunity before doing something.
PHRASE

bi·det /ˈbiːdeɪ, AM biːˈdeɪ/ **bidets.** A bidet is a low basin in a bathroom which you can use to wash your bottom.
N-COUNT

bi·en·nial /baɪˈeniəl/ **biennials. 1** A biennial event happens or is done once every two years. **2** A biennial plant that lives for two years.
ADJ: ADJ n
N-COUNT

biff /bɪf/ **biffs, biffing, biffed.** If you biff someone, you hit them with your fist.
VERB: V n
DATED,
INFORMAL

bi·fo·cals /ˌbaɪˈfəʊkəlz/; the form **bifocal** is used as a modifier. **Bifocals** are glasses with lenses made in two halves. The top part is for looking at things some distance away, and the bottom part is for reading and looking at things nearby. *...thick bifocal lenses.*
N-PLURAL

big /bɪɡ/ **bigger, biggest. 1** A big person or thing is large in physical size. *Australia's a big country... Her husband was a big man.* **2** Children often refer to their older brother or sister as their **big** brother or sister.
◆◆◆◆ ADJ-GRADED
ADJ: ADJ n
PRAGMATICS

3 Something that is **big** consists of many people or things. *...the big backlog of applications.* **4** A big organization employs many people and has many customers. *...one of Taiwan's biggest companies.*
ADJ-GRADED
ADJ-GRADED

5 If you describe something such as a problem or change as a **big** one, you mean it is great in degree, extent, or importance. *Her problem was just too big for her to tackle on her own... There could soon be a big increase in unemployment.*
ADJ-GRADED

6 If you say that someone is **big** in a particular organization or activity, you mean that they have a lot of influence or authority in it. *Their father was very big in the army.* **7** If you **make it big**, you become successful or famous.
ADJ-GRADED
INFORMAL
PHRASE
INFORMAL

8 If you call someone a **big** bully or a **big** coward, you are emphasizing your disapproval of them.
ADJ: ADJ n
PRAGMATICS

9 Big words are long or rare words which have meanings that are difficult to understand.
ADJ-GRADED
INFORMAL

10 If you **think big**, you make plans on a large scale, often using a lot of time, effort, or money. **11** ● **in a big way**: see **way**.
PHRASE

biga·my /ˈbɪɡəmi/. Bigamy is the crime of marrying a person when you are already legally married to someone else. *He'd committed bigamy.* ♦ **biga·mist**
N-UNCOUNT
N-COUNT

/ˈbɪɡəmɪst/ **bigamists.** *He later discovered his father was a bigamist.*

Big 'Apple. People sometimes refer to New York as **the Big Apple.** N-PROPER: theN INFORMAL

big 'bang theory. The big bang theory is a theory that suggests that the universe was created as a result of a massive explosion. N-SING: theN

Big 'Brother. If you refer to a government, ruler, or person in authority as **Big Brother,** you are criticizing them because you think that they have too much control over people's lives. *His talk of 'appropriate access' may sound reasonable, but what he wants is to keep us all regimented on footpaths, where Big Brother can keep an eye on us.* N-PROPER PRAGMATICS

big 'business. 1 **Big business** is business or commerce which involves very large companies and very large sums of money. 2 Something that is **big business** is something which people spend a lot of money on, and which has become an important commercial activity. *Sport has become big business.* ◆◇◇◇ N-UNCOUNT

big cat, big cats. Big cats are lions, tigers, and other large wild animals in the cat family. N-COUNT

big 'city. The big city is used to refer to a large city which seems attractive to someone because they think there are many exciting things to do there, and many opportunities to earn a lot of money. *...a country girl who dreams of the big city.* ◆◇◇◇ N-SING: theN

big 'deal. 1 If you say that something is a **big deal,** you mean that it is important or significant in some way. *Winning was such a big deal for the whole family.* 2 If someone **makes a big deal** out of something, they treat it as if it were very important. *The Joneses make a big deal out of being 'different'.* 3 If you say **'big deal'** to someone, you mean that you are not impressed by something or someone that they consider important or impressive. *'You'll miss The Brady Bunch.' 'Big deal.'* ◆◇◇◇ N-SING INFORMAL; PHRASE INFORMAL; CONVENTION PRAGMATICS INFORMAL

big 'fish; big fish is both the singular and the plural form. If you describe someone as a **big fish,** you believe that they are powerful or important in some way. ◆◇◇◇ N-COUNT INFORMAL

big 'game. Large wild animals such as lions and elephants that are hunted for sport are often referred to as **big game.** N-UNCOUNT

big·gie /ˈbɪɡi/ **biggies.** People sometimes refer to something or someone successful, well-known, or big as a **biggie.** *...the first of this summer's Hollywood box-office biggies.* N-COUNT INFORMAL

big·gish /ˈbɪɡɪʃ/. Something that is **biggish** is fairly big. ADJ INFORMAL

big head, big heads. If you describe someone as a **big head,** you disapprove of them because they think they know everything. ♦ **big-'headed.** *What an arrogant, big-headed man.* N-COUNT PRAGMATICS INFORMAL ADJ-GRADED

big-'hearted. If you describe someone as **big-hearted,** you think they are kind and generous to other people. *...the bluff big-hearted Irishman.* ADJ-GRADED

big 'money. Big money is an amount of money that seems very large to you, especially money which you get easily. *They began to make big money during the war.* ◆◇◇◇ N-UNCOUNT

big mouth, big mouths. If you say that someone is a **big mouth** or has a **big mouth,** you mean that they tell other people things that they should keep secret. N-COUNT INFORMAL

big 'name, big names. A **big name** is a person who is successful and famous because of their work. *...all the big names in rock and pop.* ◆◇◇◇ N-COUNT

big noise, big noises. Someone who is a **big noise** has an important position in a group or organization. N-COUNT INFORMAL, BRITISH

big·ot /ˈbɪɡət/ **bigots.** If you describe someone as a **bigot,** you disapprove of them because they have strong, unreasonable prejudices or opinions and will not change them, even when they are proved to be wrong. ♦ **big·ot·ed** /ˈbɪɡətɪd/. *He was bigoted and racist.* ♦ **big·ot·ry.** Bigotry is the fact of having or expressing bigoted attitudes. *He deplored religious bigotry.* N-COUNT PRAGMATICS ADJ-GRADED N-UNCOUNT

big 'screen. You can use the big screen to refer to films that are made for cinema rather than for television. N-UNCOUNT: theN

big shot, big shots. A **big shot** is an important and powerful person in a group or organization. N-COUNT INFORMAL

big-ticket. If you describe something as a **big-ticket** item, you mean that it costs a lot of money. ADJ: ADJ n AMERICAN

big time; also spelled **big-time.** 1 You can use **big time** to refer to the highest level of an activity or sport, or a person who is successful at that level. *...big-time football.* 2 The **big time** is used to refer to fame or success in a particular area of activity. *He hit the big time with films such as Ghost.* 3 You can use **big time** to emphasize the importance or extent of something that has happened. *They screwed things up big time.* ◆◇◇◇ ADJ INFORMAL; N-SING: theN INFORMAL; ADV: ADV after v AMERICAN, INFORMAL

big top. The large round tent that a circus uses for its performances is called the **big top.** N-SING

big·wig /ˈbɪɡwɪɡ/ **bigwigs.** If you refer to an important person as a **bigwig,** you are being rather disrespectful. *He scandalised most of the local bigwigs.* N-COUNT PRAGMATICS INFORMAL

bi·jou /ˈbiːʒuː/. Small houses are sometimes described as **bijou** in order to make them sound attractive or fashionable. ADJ: ADJ n BRITISH

bike /baɪk/ **bikes, biking, biked.** 1 A **bike** is a bicycle or a motorcycle. 2 To **bike** somewhere means to go there on a bicycle. *I biked home from the beach.* ♦♦◇◇ N-COUNT VERB V adv/prep

bik·er /ˈbaɪkə/ **bikers. Bikers** are people who ride around on motorbikes, usually in groups. ◆◇◇◇ N-COUNT

bi·ki·ni /bɪˈkiːni/ **bikinis.** A **bikini** is a two-piece swimming costume worn by women. ◆◇◇◇ N-COUNT

bi·lat·er·al /ˌbaɪˈlætərəl/. **Bilateral** meetings or agreements involve only the two groups or countries that are directly concerned. *...bilateral talks between Britain and America.* ♦ **bi·lat·er·al·ly** The two countries agreed to solve their disagreements bilaterally. ◆◆◇◇ ADJ: ADJ n FORMAL ADV

bile /baɪl/. 1 **Bile** is a liquid produced by your liver which helps you to digest fat. 2 **Bile** is anger or bitterness towards someone or something. *He aims his bile at religion, drugs, and politics.* ◆◇◇◇ N-UNCOUNT N-UNCOUNT LITERARY

bilge /bɪldʒ/ **bilges.** 1 The **bilge** or the **bilges** are the flat bottom part of a ship or boat. 2 If you say that something written or spoken is **bilge,** you think it is untrue or silly. N-COUNT N-UNCOUNT PRAGMATICS INFORMAL

bi·lin·gual /ˌbaɪˈlɪŋɡwəl/. 1 **Bilingual** means involving or using two languages. *...bilingual education.* 2 Someone who is **bilingual** can speak two languages fluently, usually because they learnt both languages as a child. ♦ **bi·lin·gual·ism.** ◆◇◇◇ ADJ: ADJ n; ADJ: v-link ADJ; N-UNCOUNT

bili·ous /ˈbɪliəs/. 1 If you describe a colour as **bilious,** you dislike it and find it rather disgusting. *...the bilious green overstuffed sofas.* 2 If you feel **bilious,** you feel sick and have a headache. 3 **Bilious** remarks or criticisms are very bad-tempered and unpleasant. *...a bilious, rancorous attack on much of the music.* ADJ-GRADED WRITTEN; ADJ-GRADED LITERARY; ADJ-GRADED WRITTEN

bill /bɪl/ **bills, billing, billed.** 1 A **bill** is a written statement of money that you owe for goods or services. *He paid his bill for the newspapers promptly. ...phone bills.* ● If you have to **foot the bill** for something, you have to pay for it. 2 If you **bill** someone for goods or services you have provided them with, you give or send them a bill stating how much money they owe you. *Are you going to bill me for this?* 3 The **bill** in a restaurant is a piece of paper on which the price of the meal you have just eaten is written and which you are given before you pay. The American word is **check.** 4 A **bill** is a piece of paper money. The British word is **note.** *...a large quantity of US dollar bills.* 5 In parliament, a **bill** is a formal statement of a proposed new law that is discussed and then voted on. *This is the toughest crime bill that Congress has passed in a decade.* ● See also **Private Member's Bill.** 6 The **bill** of a show or concert is a list of the entertainers who will take part in it. 7 If someone **is billed** to appear in a particular show, it has been advertised ◆◆◆◇ N-COUNT; PHRASE; VB: no cont V n for Also V n; N-SING: theN BRITISH; N-COUNT AMERICAN; N-COUNT; N-SING; VB: usu passive beV-ed to-inf

that they are going to be in it. *She was billed to play the Red Queen in Snow White.* ♦ **bill·ing** ...*their quarrels over star billing.* **8** If you **bill** a person or event as having particular qualities, you advertise them in a way that makes people think they have those qualities. *They bill it as Britain's most exciting museum.*
9 A bird's **bill** is its beak. ♦ **-billed** ...*yellow-billed ducks.*
10 If you say that someone or something **fits the bill** or **fills the bill**, you mean that they are suitable for a particular job or purpose. *Almost any farmhouse blue cheese will fit the bill.* **11** If a doctor gives you **a clean bill of health**, they tell you that you are fit and healthy.

bill·board /ˈbɪlbɔːd/ **billboards.** A **billboard** is a very large board on which posters are displayed.

bil·let /ˈbɪlɪt/ **billets, billeting, billeted.** **1** If members of the armed forces **are billeted** in a particular place, that place is provided for them to stay in for a period of time. **2** A **billet** is a house or lodging where a member of the armed forces has been billeted.

bill·fold /ˈbɪlfəʊld/ **billfolds.** A **billfold** is the same as a **wallet**.

bil·liards /ˈbɪliədz/; the form **billiard** is used as a modifier. **Billiards** is a game played on a large table, in which you use a long stick called a cue to hit small heavy balls into pockets around the sides of the table.

bil·lion /ˈbɪljən/ **billions.** The plural form is **billion** after a number, or after a word or expression referring to a number, such as 'several' or 'a few'. **1** A **billion** is a thousand million. See Appendix headed **Numbers.** ...*3 billion dollars.* **2** If you talk about **billions of** people or things, you mean that there is a very large number of them but you do not know or do not want to say exactly how many. *Biological systems have been doing this for billions of years.* ▶ Also a pronoun. *He thought that it must be worth billions.*

bil·lion·aire /ˌbɪljəˈneə/ **billionaires.** A **billionaire** is an extremely rich person who has money or property worth at least a thousand million pounds or dollars.

bil·lionth /ˈbɪljənθ/ **billionths.** **1** The **billionth** item in a series is the one you count as number one billion. See Appendix headed **Numbers.** **2** A **billionth** is one of a billion equal parts of something.

bill of 'fare, bills of fare. The **bill of fare** at a restaurant is the menu.

Bill of 'Rights. A **Bill of Rights** is a written list of citizens' rights which is usually part of the constitution of a country.

bil·low /ˈbɪləʊ/ **billows, billowing, billowed.** **1** When something made of cloth **billows**, it swells out and flaps slowly in the wind. *Her pink dress billowed out around her.* **2** When smoke or cloud **billows**, it moves slowly upwards or across the sky. ...*billowing clouds of cigarette smoke.* ▶ Also a noun. ...*billows of almost solid black smoke.*

bil·ly goat /ˈbɪli gəʊt/ **billy goats.** A **billy goat** is a male goat.

bim·bo /ˈbɪmbəʊ/ **bimbos.** If someone calls a young woman a **bimbo**, they think that although she is pretty she is rather stupid.

bi·month·ly /ˌbaɪˈmʌnθli/ A **bimonthly** event or publication happens or appears either twice a month or every two months. ...*bimonthly newsletters.*

bin /bɪn/ **bins, binning, binned.** **1** A **bin** is a container that you put rubbish in. The usual American word is **can.** *He screwed the paper small and chucked it in the bin.* **2** A **bin** is a container that you keep or store things in. ...*a bread bin.* **3** If you **bin** something, you throw it away or reject it. *He advised others to bin the letters... We had to bin that idea.*

bi·na·ry /ˈbaɪnəri/ **1** The **binary** system expresses numbers using only the two digits 0 and 1. It is used especially in computing. ▶ Also a noun. *The machine does the calculations in binary.* **2** Binary

describes something that has two different parts. ...*a binary star.*

bind /baɪnd/ **binds, binding, bound.** **1** If something **binds** people together, it makes them feel as if they are all part of the same group or have something in common. ...*the social and political ties that bind the USA to Britain.*
2 If you **are bound** by something such as a rule, agreement, or restriction, you are forced or required to act in a certain way. *The authorities will be legally bound to arrest any suspects... The treaty binds them to respect their neighbour's independence.* ♦ **bound** *Few of them feel bound by any enduring loyalties.*
3 If you **bind** something or someone, you tie rope, string, or tape around them so that they are held firmly. *Bind the ends of the cord together with thread.*
4 When a book **is bound**, the pages are joined together and the cover is put on. ♦ **-bound** ...*leather-bound stamp albums.*
5 If one chemical or particle **is bound** to another, it becomes attached to it or reacts with it to form a single particle or substance. *These compounds bind with genetic material in the liver.* **6** In cookery, if you **bind** a mixture of food, you form it into a mass by mixing it with a sticky substance.
7 If you are in a **bind**, you are in a difficult situation, usually because you have to make a decision or a choice and whatever decision or choice you make will have unpleasant consequences.
8 See also **binding, bound.**

bind over. If someone **is bound over** by a court or a judge, they are given an order and are legally obliged to do as the order says for a particular period of time. *Demonstrators were bound over to keep the peace. ...a duty on courts to bind over parents when they have no control over their children.*

bind·er /ˈbaɪndə/ **binders.** A **binder** is a hard cover with metal rings inside, which is used to hold loose pieces of paper.

bind·ing /ˈbaɪndɪŋ/ **bindings.** **1** A **binding** agreement or decision must be obeyed or carried out. ...*proposals for a legally binding commitment.*
2 The **binding** of a book is its cover. *Its books are noted for the quality of their paper and bindings.* **3** **Binding** is a piece of rope, cloth, or other material that you wrap around something so that it can be gripped firmly or held in place. **4** See also **bind.**

binge /bɪndʒ/ **binges, bingeing, binged.** If you **binge**, you do too much of something, such as drinking alcohol, eating, or spending money. *I binged on pizzas.* ▶ Also a noun. *She went on occasional drinking binges.*

bin·go /ˈbɪŋɡəʊ/ **1** Bingo is a game in which players aim to match the numbers that someone calls out with the numbers on a card that they have been given. **2** You can say **'bingo!'** when giving an account of something to indicate that something pleasant happened, especially in an unexpected or sudden way. *I was in a market in Tangier and bingo! I found this.*

'bin liner, bin liners. A **bin liner** is a plastic bag that you put inside a waste bin or dustbin.

bin·ocu·lars /bɪˈnɒkjuləz/ **Binoculars** consist of two small telescopes joined together side by side, which you look through in order to look at things that are a long way away.

bio- /baɪəʊ-, baɪˈɒ-/ **Bio-** is used at the beginning of nouns and adjectives that refer to life or to the study of living things. ...*bio-engineering.*

bio·chemi·cal /ˌbaɪəʊˈkemɪkəl/ **Biochemical** changes, reactions, and mechanisms relate to the chemical processes that happen in living things.

bio·chem·is·try /ˌbaɪəʊˈkemɪstri/ **1** Biochemistry is the study of the chemical processes that happen in living things. ♦ **bio·chem·ist** /ˌbaɪəʊˈkemɪst/ **biochemists.** **2** The **biochemistry** of a living thing or of a process involving living things is the chemical reactions that happen in it. ...*understanding the biochemistry of cell division.*

bio·degrad·able /ˌbaɪəʊdɪ'greɪdəbəl/. Something ADJ-GRADED
that is **biodegradable** breaks down or decomposes
naturally without any special scientific treatment,
and can therefore be thrown away without causing
pollution. ...*biodegradable plastic.*

bio·di·ver·sity /ˌbaɪəʊdaɪ'vɜːsɪti/. **Biodiversity** is ◆◇◇◇◇
the existence of a wide variety of plant and animal N-UNCOUNT
species living in their natural environment.

bi·og·raph·er /baɪ'ɒɡrəfə/ **biographers.** ◆◇◇◇◇
Someone's **biographer** is a person who writes an N-COUNT
account of their life.

bio·graphi·cal /ˌbaɪə'ɡræfɪkəl/. **Biographical** ◆◇◇◇◇
facts, notes, or details are concerned with the ADJ
events in someone's life. ...*a 14-minute biographical
film which emphasised his love of family.*

bi·og·ra·phy /baɪ'ɒɡrəfi/ **biographies. 1** A biog- ◆◆◇◇◇
raphy of someone is an account of their life, written N-COUNT
by someone else. **2 Biography** is the branch of lit- N-UNCOUNT
erature which deals with accounts of people's lives.

biol. Biol. is a written abbreviation for 'biology' or
'biological'.

bio·logi·cal /ˌbaɪə'lɒdʒɪkəl/. **1 Biological** is used ◆◆◇◇◇
to describe processes and states that occur in the ADJ
bodies and cells of living things. ♦ **bio·logi·cal·ly** ADV
/ˌbaɪə'lɒdʒɪkli/ *Much of our behaviour is biologically
determined.* **2 Biological** is used to describe activ- ADJ: ADJ n
ities concerned with the study of living things.
...*biological sciences.*

3 Biological describes military or agricultural pro- ADJ
cesses which involve the use of bacteria or other living
organisms. ...*experts on biological warfare.* ...*biological pest control.* **4** A **biological** washing powder con- ADJ
tains enzymes which dissolve dirt. BRITISH

5 A child's **biological** parents are the man and woman ADJ: ADJ n
who caused him or her to be born, but who may not
be the adults who looked after him or her.

bio,logical 'clock, biological clocks. Your bio- N-COUNT
logical clock is your body's way of registering time.
*Whenever we change sleep cycles, our biological
clock has to adjust to the new schedule.*

bio,logical di'versity. Biological diversity is the N-UNCOUNT
same as biodiversity.

bi·ol·ogy /baɪ'ɒlədʒi/. **1 Biology** is the science ◆◆◇◇◇
which is concerned with the study of living things. N-UNCOUNT
♦ **bi·olo·gist** /baɪ'ɒlədʒɪst/ **biologists. 2** The biol- N-COUNT:
ogy of a living thing is the way in which its body or theN of n,
cells behave. *The biology of these diseases is terribly* suppN
complicated. ...*human biology.* **3** See also **molecular biology.**

bi·on·ic /baɪ'ɒnɪk/. In science fiction, a **bionic** per- ADJ
son is someone who has superhuman powers, be-
cause parts of their body have been replaced by
electronic machinery.

bio·pic /'baɪəʊpɪk/ **biopics.** A **biopic** is a film that N-COUNT
tells the story of someone's life. BRITISH

bi·op·sy /'baɪɒpsi/ **biopsies.** A **biopsy** is the re- N-VAR
moval and examination of fluids or tissue from a
patient's body in order to discover why they are ill.

bio·sphere /'baɪəsfɪə/. The **biosphere** is the part ◆◇◇◇◇
of the earth's surface and atmosphere which is in- N-SING
habited by living things. TECHNICAL

biotech /'baɪəʊtek/. **Biotech** means the same as N-UNCOUNT
biotechnology.

bio·tech·nol·ogy /ˌbaɪəʊtek'nɒlədʒi/. **Biotechnol-** ◆◇◇◇◇
ogy is the use of living parts such as cells or bacteria N-UNCOUNT
in industry and medicine. ♦ **bio·tech·nolo·gist** TECHNICAL
/ˌbaɪəʊtek'nɒlədʒɪst/ **biotechnologists.** N-COUNT

bi·par·ti·san /ˌbaɪpɑːtɪ'zæn, AM baɪ'pɑːrtɪzən/. **Bi-** ◆◇◇◇◇
partisan means concerning or involving two differ- ADJ
ent political parties or groups. ...*a bipartisan approach to educational reform.*

bi·ped /'baɪped/ **bipeds.** A **biped** is a creature with N-COUNT
two feet. TECHNICAL

bi·plane /'baɪpleɪn/ **biplanes.** A **biplane** is an old- N-COUNT
fashioned type of aeroplane with two pairs of wings,
one above the other.

bi·po·lar /baɪ'pəʊlə/. **Bipolar** systems or situations ADJ
are dominated by two strong and opposing el- FORMAL
ements. ...*the bipolar world of the Cold War years.*

birch /bɜːtʃ/ **birches.** A **birch** is a tall tree with ◆◇◇◇◇
thin branches. N-VAR

bird /bɜːd/ **birds. 1** A **bird** is a creature with feath- ◆◆◆◇◇
ers and wings. Female birds lay eggs. Most birds can N-COUNT
fly. ● See also **game bird.**

2 Some men refer to young women as **birds**. Most N-COUNT
women find this offensive. INFORMAL,
BRITISH
3 If someone says that as a child they were told about PHRASE
the birds and the bees, they are referring humorously
to being told about sex and sexual reproduction. **4** If PHRASE
you say that **the early bird catches the worm** or **gets
the worm,** you mean that the person who arrives first
in a place is the one who gets what they want. **5** If you PHRASE
refer to two people as **birds of a feather,** you mean
that they have the same interests or are very similar.

6 If you say that doing something will **kill two birds** PHRASE
with one stone, you mean that it will enable you to
achieve two things at the same time. **7** If someone is PHRASE
an **early bird,** they usually get up early in the morning. **8** If you say that a **little bird** told you about some- PHRASE
thing, you mean that someone has told you about it,
but you do not want to say who it was.

bird·cage /'bɜːdkeɪdʒ/ **birdcages;** also spelled N-COUNT
bird cage. A **birdcage** is a cage in which birds are
kept.

birdie /'bɜːdi/ **birdies, birdying, birdied. 1** In ◆◇◇◇◇
golf, if you get a **birdie,** you get the golf ball into a N-COUNT
hole in one stroke fewer than the number of strokes
which has been set as the standard for a good play-
er. **2** If a golfer **birdies** a hole, he or she gets a birdie VERB: V n
at that hole.

bird·life /'bɜːdlaɪf/; also spelled **bird life.** The N-UNCOUNT
birdlife in a place is all the birds that live there.

bird·like /'bɜːdlaɪk/; also spelled **bird-like.** If some- ADJ
one has a **birdlike** manner, they move or look like a
bird.

,bird of 'paradise, birds of paradise. A **bird of** N-COUNT
paradise is a brightly coloured singing bird which is
found mainly in New Guinea.

,bird of 'prey, birds of prey. A **bird of prey** is a N-COUNT
bird such as an eagle or a hawk that kills and eats
other birds and animals.

,bird's eye 'view, bird's eye views. You say N-COUNT
that you have a **bird's eye view** of a place when you
are looking down at it from a great height, so that
you can see a long way but everything looks very
small.

bird·song /'bɜːdsɒŋ, AM -sɔːŋ/ **birdsongs;** also N-UNCOUNT:
spelled **bird song. Birdsong** is the sound of birds also N in pl
calling in a way which sounds musical.

'bird table, bird tables. A **bird table** is a small N-COUNT
wooden platform which some people put in their BRITISH
garden in order to put food for birds on it.

'bird-watching; also spelled **birdwatching. Bird-** N-UNCOUNT
watching is the activity of watching and studying
wild birds in their natural surroundings. ♦ **bird-**
watcher, bird-watchers. N-COUNT

Biro /'baɪərəʊ/ **Biros.** A **Biro** is a pen with a small N-COUNT
metal ball at its tip which transfers the ink onto the BRITISH
paper. **Biro** is a trademark.

birth /bɜːθ/ **births. 1** When a baby is born, you re- ◆◆◆◇◇
fer to this event as its birth. ...*the birth of his grand-* N-VAR
children. **2** When a woman **gives birth,** she pro- PHRASE
duces a baby from her body. ● See also **date of
birth.**

3 If, for example, you are French **by birth,** you are PHRASE
French because your parents are French, or because
you were born in France. **4** Some people talk about a N-UNCOUNT
person's **birth** when they are referring to the social
position of the person's family. ...*men of low birth.*

5 You can refer to the beginning or origin of some- N-UNCOUNT:
thing as its **birth.** ...*the birth of popular democracy.* with poss
6 If something **gives birth to** an idea, situation, or in- PHRASE
stitution, that idea, situation, or institution develops
as a result of that thing. *Strikes at the Lenin shipyards
gave birth to the Solidarity trade union.*

'birth certificate, birth certificates. Your **birth** N-COUNT
certificate is an official document which gives details of the date and place of your birth, and the
names of your parents.

'birth con·trol. Birth control means planning ◆◇◇◇◇ whether to have children and using methods of N-UNCOUNT contraception to prevent unwanted pregnancy.

birth·date /'bɜːθdeɪt/ **birthdates.** Your **birthdate** N-COUNT is the same as your **date of birth**.

birth·day /'bɜːθdeɪ, -di/ **birthdays.** Your **birthday** ◆◆◇◇ is the anniversary of the date on which you were N-COUNT born.

'birthday suit, birthday suits. If you are in your N-COUNT **birthday suit**, you are not wearing any clothes. INFORMAL

birth·ing /'bɜːθɪŋ/. **Birthing** means relating to or ADJ: ADJ n used during childbirth. *Some hospitals provide special birthing stools.*

birth·mark /'bɜːθmɑːk/ **birthmarks.** A **birthmark** N-COUNT is a mark on someone's skin that has been there since they were born.

birth·place /'bɜːθpleɪs/ **birthplaces.** 1 Your ◆◇◇◇ **birthplace** is the place where you were born. 2 The N-COUNT **birthplace** of something is the place where it began N-COUNT or originated. *...Athens, the birthplace of the ancient Olympics.*

'birth rate, birth rates. The **birth rate** in a place ◆◇◇◇ is the number of babies born there for every 1000 N-COUNT people during a particular period of time.

birth·right /'bɜːθraɪt/ **birthrights.** Something that N-COUNT is your **birthright** is something that you feel you have a basic right to have, simply because you are a human being. *Freedom is the natural birthright of every human.*

bis·cuit /'bɪskɪt/ **biscuits.** 1 A **biscuit** is a small ◆◆◇◇ flat cake that is crisp and usually sweet. The usual N-COUNT American word is **cookie**. 2 A **biscuit** is a small dry BRITISH cake that sometimes has dried fruit in it. It can be AMERICAN eaten with butter and jam.

bi·sect /ˌbaɪ'sekt/ **bisects, bisecting, bisected.** VERB If something long and thin **bisects** an area or line, it V n divides the area or line in half. *The main street bisects the town from end to end.*

bi·sexu·al /ˌbaɪ'sekʃuəl/ **bisexuals.** Someone ◆◇◇◇ who is **bisexual** is sexually attracted to both men ADJ and women. ▶ Also a noun. *He was an active bisexual.* ♦ **bi·sexu·al·ity** /ˌbaɪsekʃu'ælɪti/. N-UNCOUNT

bish·op /'bɪʃəp/ **bishops.** 1 A **bishop** is a clergy- N-COUNT, man of high rank in the Roman Catholic, Anglican, N-TITLE and Orthodox churches. 2 In chess a **bishop** is a piece that can be moved diagonally across the board on squares that are the same colour.

bish·op·ric /'bɪʃəprɪk/ **bishoprics.** A **bishopric** is N-COUNT the area for which a bishop is responsible, or the rank or office of being a bishop.

bi·son /'baɪsən/; **bison** is both the singular and the N-COUNT plural form. A **bison** is a large hairy animal that is a member of the cattle family.

bis·tro /'biːstrəʊ/ **bistros.** A **bistro** is a small, infor- N-COUNT mal restaurant or a bar where food is served.

bit /bɪt/ **bits.** 1 A **bit** of something is a small ◆◆◆◆◆ amount of it. *All it required was a bit of work... I got* QUANT *paid a little bit of money.* 2 You use **a bit** before PHRASE 'more' or 'less' to mean a small amount more or a small amount less. *I still think I have a bit more to offer.* 3 A **bit** means to a small extent or degree. *This* PHRASE *girl was a bit strange... She looks a bit like his cousin* PRAGMATICS *Maureen.* 4 You can use **a bit of** to make a state- PHRASE ment less extreme. For example, the statement 'It's PRAGMATICS a bit of a nuisance' is less extreme than 'It's a nuisance'. *It's all a bit of a mess.*

5 If you say that something is **a bit much**, you are an- PHRASE noyed because you think someone has behaved in an PRAGMATICS unreasonable way. *It's a bit much expecting young* BRITISH, *people to carry the can for lenders' past mistakes.* INFORMAL

6 **Quite a bit** means quite a lot. *They're worth quite a* PHRASE *bit of money... He's quite a bit older than me.*

7 If something happens **bit by bit**, it happens in PHRASE stages. *Bit by bit I began to understand.* 8 If you do PHRASE something **for a bit**, you do it for a short period of BRITISH, time. *That should keep you busy for a bit.* INFORMAL

9 If you **do your bit**, you do something that, to a small PHRASE or limited extent, helps to achieve something.

10 You say that one thing is **every bit as** good, inter- PHRASE esting, or important as another to emphasize that the PRAGMATICS

first thing is just as good, interesting, or important as the second.

11 You use **not a bit** when you want to make a strong PHRASE negative statement. *'Are you disappointed?' 'Not a bit'.* PRAGMATICS 12 You say **not a bit of it** to emphasize that something BRITISH that you might expect to be the case is not the case. PHRASE *Did he give up? Not a bit of it!* BRITISH

13 A **bit** of something is a small piece of it. *...a bit of* N-COUNT *string.* 14 A **bit** of something is a small part of it. N-COUNT: *That's the bit of the meeting that I missed... Now comes* with supp *the really important bit.* 15 You can use **bit** to refer to N-COUNT a particular item or to one of a group or set of things. *Not one single bit of work has been started.*

16 You can use **bits and pieces** to refer to a collection PHRASE of different things. In British English, the expression INFORMAL **bits and bobs** is also used.

17 If something is smashed or blown **to bits** it is bro- PHRASE ken into a number of pieces. If something falls **to bits** it comes apart so that it is in a number of pieces. ● **thrilled to bits:** see **thrilled**.

18 In computing, a **bit** is the smallest unit of informa- N-COUNT tion that is held in a computer's memory.

19 A **bit** is a piece of metal that is held in a horse's N-COUNT mouth by the reins and is used to control the horse when you are riding. 20 If someone **is champing at** PHRASE **the bit** or **is chomping at the bit**, they are very impatient to do something, but circumstances prevent them from starting it. 21 If you **get the bit between** PHRASE **your teeth**, or **take the bit between** your teeth, you become very enthusiastic about a job you have to do.

22 **Bit** is the past tense of **bite**.

bitch /bɪtʃ/ **bitches, bitching, bitched.** 1 If ◆◆◇◇◇ someone calls a woman a **bitch**, they are saying in a N-COUNT very rude way that they think she is unpleasant. PRAGMATICS ● See also **son of a bitch.** 2 If you describe a situa- RUDE tion as a **bitch**, you mean that it is very unpleasant N-SING or difficult to deal with; some people find this use PRAGMATICS offensive. 3 If you say that someone is **bitching** INFORMAL about something or someone, you disapprove of the VERB: V fact that they are complaining or saying nasty PRAGMATICS things about them. 4 A **bitch** is a female dog. INFORMAL

bitchy /'bɪtʃi/ **bitchier, bitchiest.** If you say that ADJ-GRADED someone is being **bitchy**, you disapprove of the fact PRAGMATICS that they are saying nasty things about someone INFORMAL else. ♦ **bitchi·ness.** N-UNCOUNT

bite /baɪt/ **bites, biting, bit, bitten.** 1 If you bite ◆◆◆◆◆ something, you use your teeth to cut into it, for ex- VERB: V ample in order to eat it or break it. If an animal or V into n person **bites** you, they use their teeth to hurt you. V n adv/prep *He bit into his sandwich... He had bitten the ciga-* Also V *rette in two.* 2 If a snake or a small insect **bites** you, VERB: V n it makes a mark or hole in your skin, and often V causes the surrounding area of your skin to become painful or itchy. *Male mosquitoes don't bite.* ▶ A N-COUNT **bite** is an injury or a mark on your body where an animal, snake, or small insect has bitten you. 3 If an VERB object **bites** into a surface, it presses hard against it V prep/adv or cuts into it. *The nylon rope bit into his wrists.* 4 A Also V **bite** of something, especially food, is the action of N-COUNT biting it. *You cannot eat a bun in one bite.* ▶ A **bite** N-COUNT is also the amount of food you take into your mouth when you bite it. 5 If you have a **bite** to eat, you N-SING: have a small meal or a snack. *It was time to go home* a N *for a little rest and a bite to eat.* 6 A **bite** of some- N-COUNT thing is a small part or amount of it. *...bites of conversation.*

7 If you say that a food or drink has **bite**, you like it be- N-UNCOUNT cause it has a strong or sharp taste. 8 If the air or the PRAGMATICS wind has a **bite**, it feels very cold. *There was a bite in* N-SING: *the air.* a N

9 When an action or policy begins to **bite**, it begins to VERB: V have a serious or harmful effect. *The recession started* V prep/adv *biting deeply into British industry.*

10 If a fish **bites** when you are fishing, it takes the VERB: V hook or bait at the end of your fishing line in its mouth. ▶ Also a noun. *...if I don't get a bite in a few* N-COUNT *minutes.*

11 If you **bite the hand that feeds** you, you behave PHRASE badly or ungratefully towards someone who you depend on to give you money or other things that you

need. *She may be cynical about the film industry, but ultimately she has no intention of biting the hand that feeds her.* **12** If you **bite** your **lip** or your **tongue**, you stop yourself from saying something that you want to say, because it would be wrong in the circumstances. **13** See also **nail-biting**. ● **someone's bark is worse than their bite**: see **bark**. ● **bite the bullet**: see **bullet**. ● **bite off more than you can chew**: see **chew**. ● **bite the dust**: see **dust**.   *PHRASE*

bite back. 1 If you **bite back** a feeling or something that you were going to say, you stop yourself from expressing it. *Susan bit back the words she would like to have said.* **2** If a person or a group of people who have been defeated, criticized, or insulted **bite back**, they respond strongly or angrily.   *PHRASAL VB V P noun LITERARY*   *V P JOURNALISM*

'bite-sized; also spelled **bite-size. 1 Bite-sized** pieces of food are small enough to fit easily in your mouth. *Cut the pumpkin into bite-sized pieces.* **2** If you describe something as **bite-sized**, you like it because it is small enough to be considered or dealt with easily. *...bite-size newspaper items.*   *ADJ*   *ADJ PRAGMATICS*

bit·ing /ˈbaɪtɪŋ/. **1 Biting** wind or cold is extremely cold. *...a raw, biting northerly wind.* **2 Biting** criticism or wit is very harsh or unkind. *This was the most biting criticism made against her.*   *ADJ-GRADED ADJ-GRADED*

'bit part, bit parts; also spelled **bit-part.** A **bit part** is a small unimportant role in a film or play.   *N-COUNT*

bit·ten /ˈbɪtən/. **Bitten** is the past participle of **bite**.

bit·ter /ˈbɪtə/ **bitterest; bitters. 1** In a **bitter** argument or conflict, people argue very angrily or fight very fiercely. *...the scene of bitter fighting during the Second World War. ...a bitter attack on the Government.* ◆ **bit·ter·ly** *...a bitterly fought football match.* ◆ **bit·ter·ness** *...the growing bitterness of the dispute.* **2** If someone is **bitter** after a disappointing experience or after being treated unfairly, they continue to feel angry about it. *His long life was marked by bitter personal and political memories.* ◆ **bitterly** *...bureaucrats who bitterly resented their loss of power.* ◆ **bitterness** *She still feels bitterness towards him.* **3** You can use **bitter** to emphasize feelings of disappointment. *The statement was greeted with bitter disappointment.* ◆ **bitterly** *I was bitterly disappointed to have lost.* **4 Bitter** weather, or a **bitter** wind, is extremely cold. ◆ **bit·ter·ly** *It's bitterly cold here in Moscow.* **5** A **bitter** taste is sharp, not sweet, and often slightly unpleasant. **6** In Britain, **bitter** is a kind of beer that is light brown in colour. **7** If you say that you will continue doing something **to the bitter end**, especially something difficult or unpleasant, you are emphasizing that you will continue doing it until it is completely finished. **8** ● **a bitter pill**: see **pill**.   *◆◆◆◇◇ ADJ-GRADED*   *ADV-GRADED*   *N-UNCOUNT*   *ADJ-GRADED*   *ADV-GRADED*   *N-UNCOUNT*   *ADJ-GRADED*   *ADV-GRADED*   *ADJ-GRADED*   *ADV: ADV adj*   *ADJ-GRADED*   *N-VAR*   *PHRASE PRAGMATICS*

,bitter-'sweet. 1 If you describe an experience as **bitter-sweet**, you mean that it has some happy aspects and some sad ones. *He's got bitter-sweet memories of his first appearance for the team.* **2** A **bitter-sweet** taste seems bitter and sweet at the same time. *...wine with a bitter-sweet flavour.*   *ADJ*   *ADJ*

bit·ty /ˈbɪti/. If you say that something is **bitty**, you mean that it was formed from a lot of different parts which you think do not fit together well. *The programme was bitty and absolutely meaningless.*   *ADJ-GRADED INFORMAL, BRITISH*

bi·tu·men /ˈbɪtʃʊmɪn, AM bɪˈtuːmən/. **Bitumen** is a black sticky substance which is obtained from petrol and is used in making roads.   *N-UNCOUNT*

bivou·ac /ˈbɪvʊæk/ **bivouacs, bivouacking, bivouacked. 1** A **bivouac** is a temporary camp made by soldiers or mountaineers. **2** If you **bivouac** somewhere, you stop and stay in a bivouac there.   *N-COUNT*   *VERB: V*

bi·week·ly /ˌbaɪˈwiːkli/. A **biweekly** event or publication happens or appears once every two weeks. The usual British word is **fortnightly**. ► Also an adverb. *The group meets on a regular basis, usually weekly or biweekly.*   *ADJ: ADJ n AMERICAN*   *ADV:*   *ADV with v*

biz /bɪz/. **Biz** is sometimes used by journalists to refer to the entertainment business, especially pop music or films. *...a girl in the music biz.*   *◆◇◇◇◇ N-SING INFORMAL*

---

bi·zarre /bɪˈzɑː/. Something that is **bizarre** is very strange. *...the bizarre behaviour of the team's manager.* ◆ **bi·zarre·ly** *She dressed bizarrely.*   *◆◆◇◇◇ ADJ-GRADED*   *ADV-GRADED*

blab /blæb/ **blabs, blabbing, blabbed.** If someone **blabs** about something secret, they tell people about it. *He's going to blab the whole thing to Sis... No blabbing to your mates!*   *VERB: V about n V n V*   *INFORMAL*

black /blæk/ **blacker, blackest; blacks, blacking, blacked. 1** Something that is **black** is of the darkest colour that there is, the colour of the sky at night when there is no light at all. *He was dressed all in black.*   *◆◆◆◆◆ COLOUR*

2 A **black** person belongs to a race of people with dark skins, especially a race from Africa. ► **Black** people are sometimes referred to as **blacks**; some people find this use offensive.   *ADJ*   *N-COUNT*

3 Black coffee or tea has no milk or cream added to it. *I drink coffee black.* **4** If you describe a situation as **black**, you are emphasizing that it is very bad indeed. *It was, he said later, one of the blackest days of his political career.* **5** If someone is in a **black** mood, they feel very miserable and depressed. *In late 1975, she fell into a black depression.* **6** If someone gives you a **black look**, they look at you in a way that shows that they are very angry about something. **7** You use **black** to describe things that you consider to be very cruel or wicked. *...the blackest laws in the country's history.* **8 Black** humour involves jokes about sad or tragic situations. **9** People who believe in **black** magic believe that it is possible to communicate with evil spirits.   *ADJ: ADJ n ADJ n, v n ADJ ADJ-GRADED PRAGMATICS*   *ADJ-GRADED*   *PHRASE*   *ADJ-GRADED LITERARY*   *ADJ-GRADED*   *ADJ: ADJ n*

10 If a group **blacks** particular goods or people, it refuses to handle the goods or to have dealings with the people. *The Union had blacked containerised goods at the London Docks.*   *VERB V n BRITISH, INFORMAL*

11 If someone **blacks** another person's eye, they punch or hit that person in the eye, causing it to bruise and look black. ● See also **black eye**. **12** If you say that someone is **black and blue**, you mean that they are badly bruised. *Whenever she refused, he'd beat her black and blue.*   *VERB: V n*   *PHRASE*

13 If a person or an organization is **in the black**, they do not owe anybody any money.   *PHRASE*

black out. 1 If you **black out**, you lose consciousness for a short time. **2** If a place **is blacked out**, it is in darkness, usually because it has no electricity supply. *Large parts of the rest of the country were temporarily blacked out.* **3** If a film or a piece of writing **is blacked out**, it is prevented from being broadcast or published, usually because it contains information which is secret or offensive. **4** If you **black out** a piece of writing, you colour over it in black so that it cannot be seen. *Welsh activists have started blacking out English language road signs.* **5** If you **black out** the memory of something, you try not to remember it because it upsets you. *I blacked it out. It was the easiest way of coping.* **6** See also **blackout**.   *PHRASAL VB V P be V-ed P*   *be V-ed P*   *V P noun Also V n P*   *V n P Also V P noun*

,Black 'Africa. Black Africa is the part of Africa to the south of the Sahara Desert.   *N-PROPER*

,black and 'white; also spelled **black-and-white. 1** In a **black and white** photograph or film, everything is shown in black, white, and grey. *The pictures were in black and white.* **2** A **black-and-white** television set shows only black-and-white pictures. **3** A **black-and-white** issue or situation is one which involves issues which seem straightforward and simple and therefore easy to make decisions about. *This isn't a simple black and white affair.* **4** You say that something is **in black and white** when it has been written or printed, and not just said. *He'd seen the proof in black and white.*   *◆◆◇◇◇ COLOUR*   *ADJ*   *ADJ*   *PHRASE*

black·ball /ˈblækbɔːl/ **blackballs, blackballing, blackballed.** If the members of a club **blackball** someone, they vote against that person being allowed to join their club.   *VERB: V n*

,black 'belt, black belts. A **black belt** is worn by someone who has reached a very high standard in judo or karate. You can also refer to a person who has a black belt as a **black belt**.   *N-COUNT*

B

black·berry /'blækbəri, AM -beri/ **blackberries.** A ◆◇◇◇◇ blackberry is a small, soft black or dark purple fruit. N-COUNT

black·bird /'blækbɜ:d/ **blackbirds.** A blackbird is N-COUNT a common European bird. The male has black feathers and a yellow beak, and the female has brown feathers.

black·board /'blækbɔ:d/ **blackboards.** In a class- ◆◇◇◇◇ room, the **blackboard** is a dark-coloured board N-COUNT which teachers write on with chalk.

,**black 'box, black boxes.** A black box is an elec- N-COUNT tronic device in an aircraft which records informa- tion about its flights and is designed not to be destroyed in a crash.

black·cur·rant /,blæk'kʌrənt, AM -'kɜːrənt/ **black-** ◆◇◇◇◇ **currants.** Blackcurrants are a type of very small, N-COUNT dark purple fruit that grows in bunches.

,**black e'conomy.** The black economy of a coun- N-SING try consists of the buying, selling, and producing of goods or services that goes on without the govern- ment knowing and without tax being paid.

black·en /'blækən/ **blackens, blackening,** ◆◇◇◇◇ **blackened.** 1 To **blacken** something means to V-ERG make it black or very dark in colour. *The married* Vn women of Shitamachi maintained the custom of Also V *blackening their teeth.* 2 If someone **blackens** your VERB character, they make other people believe that you Vn are a bad person. ...*knowingly spreading falsehoods in an effort to blacken my character.*

,**black 'eye, black eyes.** If someone has a **black** N-COUNT **eye**, they have a dark-coloured bruise around their eye. *Smith gave him a black eye.*

black·head /'blækhed/ **blackheads.** Blackheads N-COUNT are small, dark spots on someone's skin caused by blocked pores.

,**black 'hole, black holes.** 1 Black holes are ◆◇◇◇◇ areas in space, where gravity is so strong that noth- N-COUNT ing, not even light, can escape from them. 2 If you N-COUNT say that something, especially money, has gone into a black hole, you mean that it has disappeared and cannot be recovered.

black·list /'blæklɪst/ **blacklists, blacklisting,** **blacklisted.** 1 If someone is on a **blacklist**, they N-COUNT are considered by a government or other organiza- tion to be one of a number of people who cannot be trusted or who have done something wrong. ...*a 15-year blacklist effectively barring bankrupts from receiving credit.* 2 If someone is **blacklisted** by a VB: usu government or organization, they are put on a passive blacklist. *He has been blacklisted since being convict-* beV-ed *ed of possessing marijuana in 1969.*

black·mail /'blækmeɪl/ **blackmails, blackmail-** ◆◇◇◇◇ **ing, blackmailed.** 1 Blackmail is the action of N-UNCOUNT threatening to do something unpleasant to some- one, such as to reveal a secret about them or to harm them, unless they do something for you or give you something. *It looks like the pictures were being used for blackmail.* 2 If you describe an action N-UNCOUNT as emotional or moral **blackmail**, you disapprove of PRAGMATICS it because someone is using a person's emotions or moral values to persuade them to do something against their will. *The tactics employed can range from overt bullying to subtle emotional blackmail.* 3 If one person **blackmails** another person, they VERB: Vn use blackmail against them. *He was trying to black-* Vn into -ing/n *mail me into saying whatever he wanted.* ♦ **black- ·mail·er, blackmailers.** N-COUNT

,**black 'mark, black marks.** A black mark N-COUNT against someone is something bad that they have done or a bad quality that they have which affects the way people think about them. *The Commission's verdict was an indelible black mark against me.*

,**black 'market, black markets.** If something is ◆◇◇◇◇ bought or sold on the **black market**, it is bought or N-COUNT sold illegally. *There is a plentiful supply of guns on the black market.* ♦ ,**black marke'teer, black** N-COUNT **marketeers** ...*the black marketeers who are mak- ing a profit out of shortages.*

black·ness /'blæknəs/. Blackness is the state of ◆◇◇◇◇ being very dark. *The twilight had turned to a deep* N-UNCOUNT *blackness.* LITERARY

black·out /'blækaʊt/ **blackouts;** also spelled ◆◇◇◇◇ **black-out.** 1 A blackout is a period of time during a N-COUNT war in which towns and buildings are made dark so that they cannot be seen by enemy planes. *The last show had to be over before the blackout began.* 2 If a N-COUNT **blackout** is imposed on a particular piece of news, journalists are prevented from broadcasting or pub- lishing it. *There was a virtual news blackout about the rally.* 3 If there is a power **blackout**, the electric- N-COUNT ity supply to a place is temporarily cut off. 4 If N-COUNT someone has a **blackout**, they temporarily lose consciousness.

,**black 'pepper.** Black pepper is pepper which ◆◇◇◇◇ has been made from the dried berries of the pepper N-UNCOUNT plant, including their black outer cases.

,**black 'pudding, black puddings.** Black pud- N-VAR **ding** is a thick sausage which has a black skin and is BRITISH made from pork fat and pig's blood. The usual American expression is **blood sausage**.

,**black 'sheep.** If you describe someone as the N-COUNT **black sheep** of their family or of a group, you mean that they are considered bad or worthless by other people in that family or group.

black·smith /'blæksmɪθ/ **blacksmiths.** A black- ◆◇◇◇◇ smith is a person whose job is making things out of N-COUNT metal that has been heated to a high temperature.

'**black spot, black spots;** also spelled **blackspot.** N-COUNT 1 If you describe a place, time, or part of a situation BRITISH as a **black spot**, you mean that it is particularly bad or likely to cause problems. *There are recognised black spots in marriages which can lead to trouble... Gainsborough is known as an unemployment blackspot.* 2 A **black spot** is a place on a road where N-COUNT accidents often happen. BRITISH

,**black 'tie;** also spelled **black-tie.** A **black tie** event ADJ is a formal social event such as a party at which the men wear dinner jackets and bow ties and the women wear evening dresses. *Tonight the college is hosting a black-tie dinner.* ▶ Also a noun. *Everyone* N-UNCOUNT *was dressed in black tie.*

black·top /'blæktɒp/. Blacktop is a hard black sub- N-UNCOUNT stance which is used as a surface for roads. The AMERICAN usual British word is **tarmac**.

blad·der /'blædə/ **bladders.** Your bladder is the ◆◇◇◇◇ part of your body where urine is stored until it N-COUNT leaves your body. See also **gall bladder**.

blade /bleɪd/ **blades.** 1 The blade of a knife, axe, ◆◆◇◇◇ or saw is the edge which is used for cutting. *Many of* N-COUNT *them will have sharp blades.* 2 The **blades** of a pro- N-COUNT peller are the long, flat parts that turn round. 3 The **blade** of an oar is the thin flat part that you put into N-COUNT the water. 4 A **blade** of grass is a single piece of N-COUNT grass. 5 See also **razor blade, shoulder blade**.

blag /blæg/ **blags, blagging, blagged.** If some- VERB one **blags** something, they get it free, usually by Vn persuading someone to give it to them. *She'd* V way prep/ *blagged a tape off a friend of his. ...next time you* adv *find yourself unable to blag your way onto the guest* BRITISH, *list.* INFORMAL

blah /blɑː/. You use blah, blah, blah to refer to ◆◇◇◇◇ something that is said or written without giving the CONVENTION actual words, because you think that they are bor- INFORMAL ing or unimportant. ...*the different challenges of their career, their need to change, to evolve, blah blah blah.*

blame /bleɪm/ **blames, blaming, blamed.** 1 If ◆◆◆◇◇ you **blame** a person or thing for something bad, you VERB believe or say that they are responsible for it or that Vn for n they caused it. *The commission is expected to blame* Vn on n *the army for many of the atrocities... The police* Vn *blamed the explosion on terrorists... If it wasn't Sam's fault, why was I blaming him?* 2 The **blame** N-UNCOUNT for something bad that has happened is the respon- sibility for causing it or letting it happen. *Some of the blame for the miscarriage of justice must be borne by the solicitors... He typically shifted the blame to other parties.* 3 If someone or something is PHRASE **to blame** for something bad that has happened, they are responsible for causing it. *The policy is partly to blame for causing the worst unemployment*

in Europe. **4** If you say that you do not **blame** some- | VERB | V n for -ing | V n
one for doing something, you mean that you
consider it was a reasonable thing to do in the circumstances. *I do not blame them for trying to make
some money... He slammed the door and stormed off.
I could hardly blame him.* **5** If you say that someone | PHRASE | PRAGMATICS
has only themselves to blame or **has no-one but
themselves to blame**, you are emphasizing that
they are responsible for something bad that has
happened to them and showing that you have no
sympathy for them. *My life is ruined and I suppose I
only have myself to blame.*

blame·less /'bleɪmləs/. Someone who is **blameless** ADJ-GRADED
has not done anything wrong. *The US itself, of
course, is not entirely blameless in trading matters.
...a blameless life.*

blanch /blɑːntʃ, blæntʃ/ **blanches, blanching,** ◆◇◇◇
blanched. **1** If you **blanch**, you suddenly become VERB: V
very pale. *She felt herself blanch at the unpleasant* V at n
memories. **2** If you say that someone **blanches** at VERB
something, you mean that they find it unpleasant or V at n
shocking and do not want to be involved with it.
*Ministers are likely to blanch at the cost implications
of some of the plans.*
3 If you **blanch** vegetables, fruit, or nuts, you put VERB: V n
them into boiling water for a short time, usually in order to remove their skins, or to prepare them for
freezing.

blanc·mange /blə'mɒndʒ/ **blancmanges. Blanc-** N-VAR
mange is a cold jelly-like dessert that is made from BRITISH
milk, sugar, cornflour, and flavouring.

bland /blænd/ **blander, blandest.** **1** If you de- ◆◆◇◇
scribe someone or something as **bland**, you mean ADJ-GRADED
that they are dull and unexceptional. ♦ **bland·ness** N-UNCOUNT
...the blandness of television. **2** Food that is **bland** ADJ-GRADED
has very little flavour.

blan·dish·ments /'blændɪʃmənts/. Someone's N-PLURAL
blandishments are pleasant things that they say to FORMAL
someone in order to persuade them to do something. *At first Lewis resisted their blandishments.*

bland·ly /'blændli/. If you do something **blandly**, ADV-GRADED:
you do it in a calm, quiet, and unexcited way. *The* ADV with v
nurse smiled blandly.

blank /blæŋk/ **blanks, blanking, blanked.** ◆◆◇◇
1 Something that is **blank** has nothing on it. *He tore* ADJ
a blank page from his notebook. ...blank cassettes.
2 A **blank** is a space which is left in a piece of writ- N-COUNT
ing or on a printed form for you to fill in particular
information. **3** If you look **blank**, your face shows ADJ-GRADED:
no feeling, understanding, or interest. ♦ **blank·ly** ADV with v
She stared at him blankly. ♦ **blank·ness** *His eyes* N-UNCOUNT
have the blankness of someone half-asleep. **4** If your N-SING:
mind or memory is **a blank**, you cannot think of aN
anything or remember anything. **5** If your mind PHRASE
goes blank, you are suddenly unable to think of
anything appropriate to say, for example in reply to
a question. **6** Blanks are gun cartridges which con- N-COUNT
tain explosive but do not contain a bullet, so that
they cause no harm when the gun is fired. **7** If you PHRASE
draw a blank when you are looking for someone or INFORMAL
something, you do not succeed in finding them.
8 See also **point-blank.**

blank out. If you **blank out** a particular feeling or PHRASAL VB
thought, you do not allow yourself to experience that V P noun
feeling or to have that thought. *I learned to blank* V n P
those feelings out.

,**blank 'cheque, blank cheques;** spelled **blank
check** in American English. **1** If someone is given a N-COUNT
blank cheque, they are given the authority to spend
as much money as they need or want. *We are not
prepared to write a blank cheque for companies that
have run into trouble.* **2** If someone is given a **blank** N-COUNT
cheque, they are given the authority to do what JOURNALISM
they think is best in a particular situation. *He has, in
a sense, been given a blank cheque to negotiate the
new South Africa.*

blan·ket /'blæŋkɪt/ **blankets, blanketing,** ◆◆◇◇
blanketed. **1** A **blanket** is a large square or rectan- N-COUNT
gular piece of thick cloth, especially one which you
put on a bed to keep you warm. **2** A **blanket** of N-COUNT

something such as snow is a continuous layer of it
which hides what is below or beyond it. *...a blanket
of fog.* **3** If something such as snow **blankets** an VERB: V n
area, it covers it. **4** You use **blanket** to describe ADJ-GRADED
something when you want to emphasize that it af-
fects or refers to every person or thing in a group,
without any exceptions. *There's already a blanket
ban on foreign unskilled labour.*
5 See also **electric blanket, security blanket, wet
blanket.**

,**blank 'verse. Blank verse** is poetry that does not N-UNCOUNT
rhyme. In English literature it usually consists of
lines with five stressed syllables.

blare /bleə/ **blares, blaring, blared.** If some- ◆◇◇◇
thing such as a siren or radio **blares**, it makes a V-ERG
loud, unpleasant noise. *Music blared from the flat* V
behind me... I blared my horn. ▶ Also a noun. *...the* V n
blare of a radio through a thin wall. ▶ **Blare out** N-SING: N of n
means the same as **blare.** *In the market, music* PHRASAL VB
blares out of cheap cassette recorders. ...giant loud- ERG
speakers which blare out patriotic music. V P
Also V n P

blar·ney /'blɑːni/. **Blarney** is a lot of flattering and N-UNCOUNT
amusing things that someone says in order to PRAGMATICS
please someone else or to persuade them to do
something.

bla·sé /'blɑːzeɪ, AM blɑː'zeɪ/; also spelled **blase.** If ADJ-GRADED
you describe someone as **blasé**, you mean that they
are not easily impressed or worried by things,
usually because they have seen or experienced
them before. *Once people were shocked every time
there was a killing but they have become blase about
it.*

blas·pheme /blæs'fiːm/ **blasphemes, blas-** VERB: V
pheming, blasphemed. If someone **blasphemes**,
they say rude or disrespectful things about God or
religion, or they use God's name as a swear word.
♦ **blas·phem·er, blasphemers.** N-COUNT

blas·phe·my /'blæsfəmi/ **blasphemies.** You can ◆◇◇◇
describe something that shows disrespect for God N-VAR
or a religion as **blasphemy.** ♦ **blas·phe·mous** ADJ
/'blæsfəməs/. *...works which they describe as blas-
phemous or obscene.*

blast /blɑːst, blæst/ **blasts, blasting, blasted.** ◆◆◇◇
1 A **blast** is a big explosion, especially one caused N-COUNT
by a bomb. *250 people were killed in the blast.* **2** If
something **is blasted** into a particular place or state, VERB:
an explosion causes it to be in that place or state. If beV-ed prep/adv
something such as a hole **is blasted** in something, it V n with adv
is created by an explosion. *They're using dynamite* V n
*to blast away rocks to put a road in. ...blasting rock
with gelignite.* ♦ **blast·ing** *There was a salvo of* N-UNCOUNT
blasting in the quarry. **3** To **blast** someone means VERB: V n
to shoot them with a gun. *Suddenly all the men pull* V away
out pistols and begin blasting away. ▶ Also a noun. JOURNALISM
...the man who killed Nigel Davies with a shotgun N-COUNT
blast. **4** If someone **blasts** their way somewhere, VERB:
they get there by shooting at people or causing an V way prep/
explosion. *One armoured column attempted to blast* adv
a path through a barricade of buses and trucks. V n prep/adv
5 If something **blasts** water or air somewhere, it sends VERB:
out a sudden, powerful stream of it. ▶ Also a noun. V n prep/adv
Blasts of cold air swept down from the mountains. N-COUNT
6 If you **blast** something such as a car horn, it makes a V-ERG
sudden, loud sound. If something **blasts** music, the V n
music is very loud. *Jubilant drivers blasted their car* Also V away
*horns... The sound of western music blasted as she en-
tered.* ▶ **Blast out** means the same as **blast.** *A* PHRASAL VB
lunchtime band was blasting out salsa music... Music ERG
blasted out from loudspeakers around the square. V P noun
▶ Also a noun. *...the loud blast of a horn.* **7** If some- N-COUNT
thing such as a radio or a heater is on **full blast**, or PHRASE
at full blast, it is producing as a lot of sound or power,
perhaps as much as it is able to. *The television is on
full blast 24 hours a day.*
8 To **blast** someone or something means to criticize VERB
them strongly. *He blasted the decision to dismiss* V n
Marsh. JOURNALISM
9 Some people say '**blast**' to show that they are EXCLAM
annoyed at something or someone. *Blast! I can't do* PRAGMATICS
anything with this. BRITISH

10 You can use **a blast from the past** as a light-hearted way of referring to something such as an old record or fashion that you hear or notice again, and which reminds you of an earlier time. PHRASE INFORMAL

blast off. When a space rocket **blasts off**, it leaves the ground at the start of its journey. ● See also blast-off. PHRASAL VB V P

blast·ed /'blɑːstɪd, 'blæstɪd/. Some people use **blasted** to express anger or annoyance at something or someone. *I couldn't get that blasted door open.* ADJ: ADJ n PRAGMATICS INFORMAL

'blast furnace, blast furnaces. A **blast furnace** is a furnace in which pure iron metal is obtained from iron ore. N-COUNT

'blast-off. Blast-off is the moment when a rocket leaves the ground and rises into the air to begin a journey into space. *The original planned launch was called off four minutes before blast-off.* N-UNCOUNT

bla·tant /'bleɪtənt/. You use **blatant** to describe something bad in order to emphasize your shock or surprise at it, usually your shock and surprise that it is done in such an open and obvious way. *Outsiders will continue to suffer the most blatant discrimination.* ♦ **bla·tant·ly** *...a blatantly sexist question... Blatantly false assertions have gone unchallenged.* ADJ-GRADED PRAGMATICS ADV-GRADED

blath·er /'blæðə/ **blathers, blathering, blathered.** If you say that someone **is blathering** on about something, you mean that they are talking for a long time about something that you consider boring or irrelevant. *Stop blathering.* ► Also a noun. *Anyone knows that all this is blather.* VERB: V on Also V about n N-UNCOUNT

blaze /bleɪz/ **blazes, blazing, blazed. 1** When a fire **blazes**, it burns strongly and brightly. *...a blazing fire.* **2** A **blaze** is a large fire which is difficult to control and which destroys a lot of things. *...a blaze which swept through a tower block.* **3** If something **blazes** with light or colour, it is extremely bright. ► Also a noun. *I wanted the front garden to be a blaze of colour.* **4** If someone's eyes **are blazing** with an emotion such as anger, their eyes look very bright because they are feeling that emotion so strongly. *Indignation blazed in her eyes.* **5** A **blaze of** publicity or attention is a great amount of it. *He was arrested in a blaze of publicity.* **6** If guns **blaze**, they fire continuously, making a lot of noise. ● **with guns blazing:** see gun. **7** If someone **blazes a trail**, they discover or explore something new. *These surgeons have blazed the trail in the treatment of bomb victims.* VERB: V-ing N-COUNT JOURNALISM VERB: V with n N-COUNT VERB: V with n V LITERARY N-SING: a N of n VERB: V n PHRASE

blaz·er /'bleɪzə/ **blazers.** A **blazer** is a kind of jacket which is often worn by members of a particular group, especially schoolchildren or members of a sports team. N-COUNT

blaz·ing /'bleɪzɪŋ/. **1** You use **blazing** or **blazing hot** to describe the weather when it is very hot and sunny. **2** When people have a **blazing** row, they quarrel in a very noisy and excited way. ADJ: ADJ n ADJ: ADJ n

bldg, bldgs. Bldg is a written abbreviation for **building** which is used especially in the names of buildings. *...Old National Bank Bldg.*

bleach /bliːtʃ/ **bleaches, bleaching, bleached. 1** If you **bleach** something, you use a chemical to make it white or pale in colour. *...peroxide or ammonia, which bleach the hair.* **2** If the sun **bleaches** something, its natural colour fades until it is almost white. *The tree's roots are stripped and hung to season and bleach.* **3** **Bleach** is a chemical that is used to make cloth white, or to clean things thoroughly and kill germs. VERB V-ERG: V n V N-VAR

bleach·ers /'bliːtʃəz/. The **bleachers** is an area of uncovered seating at an outdoor sports stadium, where it is cheap to sit. N-PLURAL AMERICAN

bleak /bliːk/ **bleaker, bleakest. 1** If a situation is **bleak**, it is bad, and seems unlikely to improve. *The immediate outlook remains bleak.* ♦ **bleak·ness** *...the continued bleakness of the American job market.* **2** If you describe a place as **bleak**, you mean that it looks cold, bare, and unattractive. *...bleak inner-city streets.* **3** When the weather is **bleak**, it is cold, dull, and unpleasant. **4** If someone looks or sounds **bleak**, they look or sound depressed, as if ADJ-GRADED N-UNCOUNT ADJ-GRADED ADJ-GRADED ADJ-GRADED

they have no hope or energy. ♦ **bleak·ly** *'There is nothing left,' she says bleakly.* ADV-GRADED

bleary /'blɪəri/. If your eyes are **bleary**, they look dull or tired, as if you have not had enough sleep or have drunk too much alcohol. *I arrived bleary-eyed and rumpled.* ADJ

bleat /bliːt/ **bleats, bleating, bleated. 1** When a sheep or goat **bleats**, it makes the sound that sheep and goats typically make. ► Also a noun. *...the faint bleat of a distressed animal.* **2** If someone **bleats**, they speak in a weak, high voice. *'I don't want it,' Eric bleated.* ► Also a noun. *She wanted to scream, but all that would come out was this faint bleat.* **3** If you say that someone **bleats** about something, you mean that they complain about it in a way which makes them sound weak and irritating. *Don't come bleating to me every time something goes wrong.* VERB: V N-COUNT VERB V with quote WRITTEN N-COUNT VERB: V about n PRAGMATICS V prep/adv Also V that

bled /bled/. **Bled** is the past tense and past participle of **bleed**.

bleed /bliːd/ **bleeds, bleeding, bled. 1** When you **bleed**, you lose blood from your body as a result of injury or illness. *His head had struck the sink and was bleeding... She's going to bleed to death!* ● See also nosebleed. ♦ **bleed·ing** This results in internal bleeding. **2** If the colour of a substance **bleeds**, it accidentally runs onto another substance. **3** If you say that someone **is being bled dry** or is **being bled white**, you disapprove of the fact that someone or something is gradually taking all of their money or resources away. *The war has bled the once-strong Armenian economy dry.* VERB V V to n N-UNCOUNT VERB: V PHRASE PRAGMATICS

bleed·ing /'bliːdɪŋ/. **Bleeding** is a swear word which some people use to emphasize what they are saying, especially when they are angry. Some people find this offensive. ADJ: ADJ n PRAGMATICS BRITISH

bleeding 'heart, bleeding hearts; also spelled **bleeding-heart.** If you refer to someone as a **bleeding heart**, you are criticizing them for being too sympathetic towards people who claim to be poor or suffering, either because you think the people do not deserve sympathy, or because you think that the person you are criticizing is not sincere. ► Also an adjective. *...a sort of 'soft' option that the bleeding heart liberals will push for.* N-COUNT PRAGMATICS ADJ: ADJ n

bleep /bliːp/ **bleeps, bleeping, bleeped. 1** A **bleep** is a short high-pitched sound that is made by an electrical device. **2** If something electronic **bleeps**, it makes a bleep sound. N-COUNT VERB: V

bleep·er /'bliːpə/ **bleepers.** A **bleeper** is the same as a **beeper**. N-COUNT INFORMAL

blem·ish /'blemɪʃ/ **blemishes, blemishing, blemished. 1** A **blemish** is a small mark on something that spoils its appearance. *If there is the slightest blemish it is rejected.* ♦ **blem·ished** *...oily, blemished complexions.* **2** A **blemish** on something is a small fault in it. *...the one blemish on an otherwise resounding success.* **3** If something **blemishes** someone's reputation, it spoils it or makes it seem less good than it was. *He wasn't about to blemish that pristine record.* N-COUNT ADJ-GRADED N-COUNT VERB V n

blend /blend/ **blends, blending, blended. 1** If you **blend** substances together, you mix them together so that they become one substance. *Blend the butter with the sugar... Put the soap and water in a pan and leave to stand until they have blended.* **2** A **blend** of things is a mixture or combination of them that is useful or pleasant. *The public areas offer a subtle blend of traditional charm with modern amenities.* **3** When colours, sounds, or styles **blend**, they come together or are combined in a pleasing way. *...the picture, furniture and porcelain collections that blend so well with the house itself.* **4** If you **blend** ideas, policies, or styles, you use them together in order to achieve something. *...a band that blended jazz, folk and classical music.* V-RECIP-ERG: V pl-n V n with n pl-n V N-COUNT V-RECIP: pl-n V V with n VERB V n Also V n with n

blend in. 1 If something **blends into** the background or **blends in**, it looks or sounds similar to the background, so it is difficult to see or hear it separately. *The toad had changed its colour to blend in with its new environment. ...a continuous pale neutral grey,* PHRASAL VB V P with n V P n Also V P

almost blending into the sky. **2** If someone **blends into** a particular group or situation, or if they **blend in**, they seem to belong there or are not noticeable, because their appearance or behaviour is similar to that of the other people involved. *She felt she would blend in nicely... He blended in with the crowd at the art sale.* `VP n` `VP` `VP with n`

blend·er /'blendə/ **blenders.** A **blender** is an electrical kitchen appliance used for mixing liquids and soft foods or turning soft foods into liquid. `N-COUNT`

bless /bles/ **blesses, blessing, blessed.** **1** When someone asks a priest **blesses** people or things, he asks for God's favour and protection for them. **2 Bless** is used in expressions such as 'God bless' or 'bless you' to express affection, thanks, or good wishes. **3** You can say **bless you** to someone who has just sneezed. **4** See also **blessed, blessing.** `♦♦◇◇◇` `VERB: V n` `CONVENTION` `PRAGMATICS` `INFORMAL` `CONVENTION`

blessed. Pronounced /blest/ for meaning 1, and /'blesɪd/ for meanings 2 and 3. **1** If someone is **blessed with** a particular good quality or skill, they have it. *Both are blessed with uncommon ability to fix things.* **2** You use **blessed** to describe something that you are thankful for or relieved about. *Rainy weather brings blessed relief to hay fever victims.* **♦ bless·ed·ly** *Most British election campaigns are blessedly brief.* **3** Some people use **blessed** to emphasize that they are annoyed about something. *No-one knows a blessed thing.* **4** See also **bless.** `♦◇◇◇◇` `ADJ-GRADED:` `v-link ADJ` `with n` `ADJ: ADJ n` `PRAGMATICS` `ADV` `ADJ: ADJ n` `INFORMAL`

bless·ing /'blesɪŋ/ **blessings. 1** A **blessing** is something good that you are thankful for. *Rivers are a blessing for an agricultural country. ...the blessings of prosperity.* **2** If you tell someone to **count** their **blessings**, you mean they should think about how lucky they are instead of complaining. **3** If you say that something is **a blessing in disguise**, you mean that it causes problems and difficulties at first but later you realize that it was a good thing that it happened. **4** If you say that a situation is **a mixed blessing**, you mean that it has disadvantages as well as advantages. **5** If something is done with someone's **blessing**, it is done with their approval and support. *Thai and Indonesian leaders gave their formal blessing to the idea.* **6** A **blessing** is a prayer asking God to look kindly upon a group of people or an event. `♦♦◇◇◇` `N-COUNT` `PHRASE` `PHRASE` `PHRASE` `N-COUNT` `N-COUNT`

blew /bluː/. **Blew** is the past tense of **blow.**

blight /blaɪt/ **blights, blighting, blighted. 1** You can refer to something as a **blight** when it causes great difficulties or damage to something. *This discriminatory policy has really been a blight on America. ...urban blight and unacceptable poverty.* **2** If something **blights** something else, it damages or spoils it. *An embarrassing blunder nearly blighted his career. ...a strategy to redevelop blighted inner-city areas.* **3 Blight** is a disease which makes plants wither. `♦◇◇◇◇` `N-VAR` `VERB` `V n` `V-ed` `N-UNCOUNT:` `also N in pl`

blight·er /'blaɪtə/ **blighters.** Some people use **blighter** to refer to another person when they want to emphasize the way they feel about them or to express mild criticism of them. *Lucky blighter, thought King.* `N-COUNT` `INFORMAL, BRITISH`

Blighty /'blaɪti/. **Blighty** is a slightly humorous way of referring to England. *See you back in Blighty!* `N-PROPER` `BRITISH, DATED`

bli·mey /'blaɪmi/. You can say **blimey** when you are surprised by something or feel strongly about it. `EXCLAM` `INFORMAL, BRITISH`

blimp /blɪmp/ **blimps.** A **blimp** is the same as an **airship.** `N-COUNT`

blind /blaɪnd/ **blinds, blinding, blinded. 1** Someone who is **blind** is unable to see because their eyes are damaged. *He went blind... How would you explain colour to a blind person?* ● See also **colour blind.** ► **The blind** are people who are blind. **♦ blind·ness** *Early diagnosis and treatment can usually prevent blindness.* **2** If something **blinds** you, it makes you unable to see, either for a short time or permanently. **3** If you are **blind** with something such as tears or a bright light, you are unable to see for a short time because of the tears or light. **♦ blind·ly** *Lettie groped blindly for the glass.* **4** A **blind** corner is one that you cannot see round. `♦♦♦◇◇` `ADJ` `N-PLURAL: the N` `N-UNCOUNT` `VERB: V n` `ADJ: v-link ADJ` `ADV: ADV with v` `ADJ: ADJ n`

5 If you say that someone is **blind to** a fact or a situation, you are criticizing them because they take no notice of it or are unaware of it. *All the time I was blind to your suffering.* **♦ blind·ness** *...blindness in government policy to the very existence of the unemployed.* **6** If something **blinds** you to the real situation, it prevents you from realizing that it exists or understanding it properly. *He never allowed his love of Australia to blind him to his countrymen's faults.* **7** If you describe someone's beliefs or actions as **blind**, you disapprove of them because you think that they do not question or think about what they are doing. *...her blind faith in the wisdom of the Church.* **♦ blind·ly** *Don't just blindly follow what the banker says.* **8** If you say that someone **is turning a blind eye** to something bad or illegal, you mean that they are pretending not to notice that it is happening so that they will not have to do anything about it. *I can't turn a blind eye when someone is being robbed.* **9** A **blind** is a roll of cloth or paper which you can pull down over a window in order to keep out the light. ● See also **Venetian blind.** `ADJ-GRADED:` `v-link ADJ to n` `PRAGMATICS` `N-UNCOUNT` `VERB` `V n to n` `ADJ-GRADED` `PRAGMATICS` `ADV-GRADED` `PHRASE` `N-COUNT`

,blind 'alley, blind alleys. If you describe a situation as a **blind alley**, you mean that no progress is not possible or that there can be no useful reference. `N-COUNT`

,blind 'date, blind dates. A **blind date** is an arrangement for you to spend a romantic evening with someone you have never met before. `N-COUNT`

blind·er /'blaɪndə/ **blinders. 1** If you say that someone such as a sports player or musician has played a **blinder**, you are emphasizing that they have played very well. **2 Blinders** are the same as **blinkers.** `N-COUNT` `INFORMAL, BRITISH` `N-PLURAL` `AMERICAN`

blind·fold /'blaɪndfəʊld/ **blindfolds, blindfolding, blindfolded. 1** A **blindfold** is a strip of cloth that is tied over someone's eyes so that they can't see. **2** If you **blindfold** someone, you tie a blindfold over their eyes. **3** If someone does something **blindfold**, they do it while wearing a blindfold. **4** If you say that you **can** do something **blindfold**, you are emphasizing that you can do it easily, for example because you have done it many times before. `♦◇◇◇◇` `N-COUNT` `VERB: V n` `ADJ:` `ADJ after v` `PHRASE` `PRAGMATICS`

blind·ing /'blaɪndɪŋ/ **1** A **blinding** light or pain is extremely intense. **2** You use **blinding** to emphasize that something is very obvious. *With blinding clarity, I realized that mundane things are of enormous importance.* **♦ blind·ing·ly** *It is blindingly obvious that there is not enough money.* `♦◇◇◇◇` `ADJ` `ADJ: ADJ n` `ADV-GRADED:` `ADV adj/adv`

'blind spot, blind spots. 1 If you say that someone has a **blind spot** about something, you mean that they seem to be unable to understand it or to see how important it is. *There seems to be a blind spot among financial directors about their bank charges.* **2** A **blind spot** is an area in your range of vision that you cannot see properly. For example, when you are driving a car, the area just behind your shoulders is often a blind spot. `N-COUNT` `N-COUNT`

blink /blɪŋk/ **blinks, blinking, blinked. 1** When you **blink** or when you **blink** your eyes, you shut your eyes and very quickly open them again. *Kathryn blinked and forced a smile... She was blinking her eyes rapidly.* ► Also a noun. *He kept giving quick blinks.* **2** If you say that something happens in **the blink of an eye**, you mean that it happens very quickly. *It was all over in the blink of an eye.* **3** When a light **blinks**, it flashes on and off. *A warning light blinked on.* **4** If a machine goes **on the blink**, it stops working properly. `♦♦◇◇◇` `VERB` `V` `V n` `N-COUNT` `PHRASE` `VERB: V` `V on/out/off` `PHRASE` `INFORMAL`

blink·ered /'blɪŋkəd/. A **blinkered** view, attitude, or approach considers only a narrow point of view and does not take into account other people's opinions; used showing disapproval. *He seems to be so blinkered that he cannot see what is happening around him.* `ADJ-GRADED` `PRAGMATICS` `BRITISH`

blink·ers /'blɪŋkəz/. **1** If you describe someone as wearing **blinkers**, you disapprove of them because you think that they are considering only a narrow point of view and are not taking into account other people's opinions. The usual American word is `N-PLURAL` `PRAGMATICS` `BRITISH`

blinders. *At least you have removed your blinkers and can now see the relationship in its true colours.* **2 Blinkers** are pieces of leather which are placed at the side of a horse's eyes so that it can only see straight ahead; the usual American word is **blinders**. N-PLURAL BRITISH

blip /blɪp/ **blips. 1** A **blip** is a small spot of light, sometimes occurring with a short, high-pitched sound, which flashes on and off regularly on a piece of equipment such as a radar screen. **2** A **blip** in a straight line, such as the line on a graph, is a point at which the line suddenly makes a sharp change of direction before returning to its original direction. **3** A **blip** in a situation is a sudden but temporary change in it. *Interest rates generally have been declining since last spring, despite a few upward blips in recent weeks.* ◆◇◇◇ N-COUNT N-COUNT N-COUNT

bliss /blɪs/. **Bliss** is a state of complete happiness. *It was a scene of such domestic bliss.* ◆◇◇◇ N-UNCOUNT

bliss·ful /ˈblɪsfʊl/. **1** A **blissful** situation or period of time is one in which you are extremely happy. *We spent a blissful week together.* ♦ **bliss·ful·ly** /ˈblɪsfʊli/ *We're blissfully happy... The summer passed blissfully.* **2** If someone is in **blissful** ignorance of something unpleasant or serious, they are totally unaware of it. ♦ **blissfully** *He was blissfully unaware of the conspiracy against him.* ◇◇◇◇ ADJ-GRADED ADV-GRADED ADJ: ADJ n ADV

blis·ter /ˈblɪstə/ **blisters, blistering, blistered. 1** A **blister** is a painful swelling on the surface of your skin which contains a clear liquid. Blisters are usually caused by heat or by something rubbing your skin. **2** When your skin **blisters** or when something **blisters** it, blisters appear on it. *The affected skin turns red and may blister... The sap of this plant blisters the skin.* ◆◇◇◇ N-COUNT V-ERG V V n

blis·ter·ing /ˈblɪstərɪŋ/. **1 Blistering** heat is very great heat. *...a blistering summer day.* **2** A **blistering** remark expresses great anger or sarcasm. *The president responded to this with a blistering attack on his critics.* **3 Blistering** is used to describe actions in sport to emphasize that they are done with great speed or force. *Sharon Wild set a blistering pace to take the lead.* ◆◇◇◇ ADJ ADJ-GRADED ADJ: ADJ n PRAGMATICS JOURNALISM

blithe /blaɪð/. **1** You use **blithe** to indicate that something is done casually, without serious or careful thought; used showing disapproval. *...blithe disregard for best scientific practice.* ♦ **blithe·ly** *Your editorial blithely ignores the hard facts.* **2** Someone who is **blithe** is carefree and cheerful. ◇◇◇◇ ADJ-GRADED PRAGMATICS ADV ADJ-GRADED LITERARY

blitz /blɪts/ **blitzes, blitzing, blitzed. 1** If a city or building **is blitzed** during a war, it is attacked by bombs dropped by enemy aircraft. *They blitzed the capital with tanks.* **2** The heavy bombing of British cities by German aircraft in 1940 and 1941 is referred to as **the Blitz. 3** If you have a **blitz** on something, you make a big effort to deal with it or to improve it. *There is to be a blitz on incorrect grammar.* **4** An advertising or publicity **blitz** is a major effort to publicize something. *On December 8 the media blitz began in earnest.* ◇◇◇◇ VERB: be V-ed V n N-PROPER: the N N-COUNT: with supp INFORMAL N-COUNT: with supp

blitz·krieg /ˈblɪtskriːg/ **blitzkriegs. 1** A **blitzkrieg** is a fast and intensive military attack that takes the enemy by surprise and is intended to achieve a very quick victory. **2** A rapid and powerful attack or campaign in sport, politics, or advertising is sometimes referred to as a **blitzkrieg.** *...a blitzkrieg of media hype.* N-COUNT N-COUNT INFORMAL, JOURNALISM

bliz·zard /ˈblɪzəd/ **blizzards. 1** A **blizzard** is a very bad snowstorm with strong winds. **2** You can refer to a large number of things that you do not like or which you think are a nuisance as a **blizzard** of those things. *...the annual blizzard of bills and amendments.* ◆◇◇◇ N-COUNT N-COUNT PRAGMATICS WRITTEN

bloat·ed /ˈbləʊtɪd/. **1** If a part of someone's body is **bloated**, it is much larger than normal, usually because it has a lot of liquid or gas inside it. ♦ **bloat·ing** *A great deal of gas is formed, causing abdominal bloating.* **2** If you feel **bloated** after eating a large meal, you feel very full and uncomfortable. *Diners do not want to leave the table feeling bloated.* ◆◇◇◇ ADJ-GRADED N-UNCOUNT ADJ-GRADED: v-link ADJ

blob /blɒb/ **blobs. 1** A **blob** of thick or sticky liquid is a small, often round, amount of it. *...a blob of chocolate mousse.* **2** You can use **blob** to refer to something that you cannot see very clearly, for example because it is in the distance. *You could just see vague blobs of faces.* ◆◇◇◇ N-COUNT N-COUNT INFORMAL

bloc /blɒk/ **blocs.** A **bloc** is a group of countries which have similar political aims and interests and that act together over some issues. *...the former Soviet bloc.* ● See also **en bloc.** ◆◆◇◇ N-COUNT

block /blɒk/ **blocks, blocking, blocked. 1** A **block** of flats or offices is a large building containing them. See picture headed **house** and **flat.** *...a white-painted apartment block.* **2** A **block** in a town is an area of land with streets on all its sides. *She walked four blocks down High Street.* **3** A **block** of a substance is a large rectangular piece of it. *...a block of ice.* **4** A **block** of something such as tickets or shares is a large quantity of them, especially when they are all sold at the same time and are in a particular sequence or order. *Those booking a block of seats get them at reduced rates.* **5** To **block** a road, channel, or pipe means to put an object across it or in it so that nothing can pass through it or along it. *Some students today blocked a highway that cuts through the center of the city.* **6** If something **blocks** your view, it prevents you from seeing something because it is between you and that thing. *...a row of spruce trees that blocked his view.* **7** If you **block** someone's way, you prevent them from going somewhere or entering a place by standing in front of them. *Mr Calder tried to leave the shop but the police officer blocked his path.* **8** If you **block** something that is being arranged, you prevent it from being done. *The country has tried to block imports of various cheap foreign products.* **9** If you have a **mental block** or a **block**, you are temporarily unable to do something that you can normally do which involves using, thinking about, or remembering something. **10** If someone **lays** their **head on the block,** or **puts** their **head on the block,** they are risking their reputation or position by taking a particular course of action. **11** See also **breeze-block, building block, roadblock, stumbling block, tower block.** ● a chip off the old block: see chip. ◆◆◆◆ N-COUNT N-COUNT N-COUNT N-COUNT VERB V n VERB V n VERB V n VERB V n N-COUNT PHRASE

block in. If you **are blocked in,** someone has parked their car in such a way that you cannot drive yours away. *Oh, is that your car outside? I may have blocked you in.* PHRASAL VB V n P Also V P noun

block off. When you **block off** a door, window, or passage, you put something across it so that nothing can pass through it. *They had blocked off the fireplaces.* PHRASAL VB V P noun Also V n P

block out. 1 If someone **blocks out** a thought, they try not to think about it. *She accuses me of having blocked out the past... I had to block the thought out of my mind.* **2** Something that **blocks out** light prevents it from reaching a place. *Thick chipboard across the window frames blocked out the daylight.* PHRASAL VB V P noun V n P of n Also V n P

block up. If you **block** something **up** or if it **blocks up,** it is blocked completely so that nothing can get through it. *'Any holes in the kitchen where the mice are getting through?'—'I've blocked them up.'... Powdering a sweaty nose will only block up the pores.* PHRASAL VB ERG V P noun V n P Also V P

block·ade /blɒˈkeɪd/ **blockades, blockading, blockaded. 1** A **blockade** of a place is an action that is taken to prevent goods or people from entering or leaving it. *Striking lorry drivers agreed to lift their blockades of main roads.* **2** If a group of people **blockade** a place, they take action to prevent goods or people from reaching it or using it for access. *Warships are blockading the port.* ◆◆◇◇ N-COUNT VERB V n

block·age /ˈblɒkɪdʒ/ **blockages.** A **blockage** in a pipe, tube, or tunnel is an object which blocks it, or the fact that it is blocked. *...a total blockage in one of the coronary arteries.* ◆◇◇◇ N-COUNT

block·bust·er /ˈblɒkbʌstə/ **blockbusters.** A **blockbuster** is a very popular and successful film or ◆◇◇◇ N-COUNT INFORMAL

book. ♦ **block·bust·ing** ...*the blockbusting sci-fi* ADJ: ADJ n
movie 'Suburban Commando'.

,**block 'capitals. Block capitals** are simple capital N-PLURAL
letters that are not decorated in any way.

,**block 'letters. Block letters** are the same as N-PLURAL
block capitals.

,**block 'vote, block votes.** A **block vote** is a large N-COUNT
number of votes that are all cast in the same way by
one person on behalf of a group of people.

bloke /bləʊk/ **blokes.** A **bloke** is a man. *You don't* ◆◇◇◇
know what the blokes in the betting shop are like... I N-COUNT
met this bloke and just completely fell in love with INFORMAL,
him. BRITISH

blonde /blɒnd/ **blondes; blonder.** The form ◆◆◇◇◇
blonde is usually used to refer to women, and
blond to refer to men. **1** Someone who has **blonde** COLOUR
hair has very light brown or light yellow hair.
2 Someone who is **blonde** has blonde hair. *She was* ADJ-GRADED
tall, blonde, and attractive. **3** A **blonde** is a woman N-COUNT
who has blonde hair.

blood /blʌd/. **1 Blood** is the red liquid that flows ◆◆◆◇
inside your body, which you can see if you cut your- N-UNCOUNT
self. **2** If you say that someone has a person's **blood** PHRASE
on their **hands**, you mean that they are responsible
for that person's death. **3** If you say that doing PHRASE
something such as getting information or persuad- PRAGMATICS
ing someone to talk to you is like **getting blood out
of a stone** or **getting blood from a stone**, you are
emphasizing that it is very difficult and that you do
not think people are being very helpful. **4** If you say PHRASE
that something **makes** your **blood boil**, you are em- PRAGMATICS
phasizing that it makes you very angry. *It makes my
blood boil to think two thugs decided to pick on an
innocent young girl.* **5** If you say that something PHRASE
makes your **blood run cold** or **makes** your **blood
freeze**, you mean that it makes you feel very frightened. *The rage in his eyes made her blood run cold.*
6 If you say that someone **sweats blood** trying to do PHRASE
something, you are emphasizing that they try very PRAGMATICS
hard to do it. **7** If you refer to something as involv- PHRASE
ing **blood, sweat, and tears**, you mean that it is a
very hard thing to do and requires a lot of effort.
*...the blood, sweat, tears and heartache involved in
getting a PhD.*
8 You can use **blood** to refer to the race or social class N-UNCOUNT
of someone's parents or ancestors. *There was Greek
blood in his veins... He was of noble blood.* **9** If you say PHRASE
that someone has **blue blood**, you mean that they are
from a family that has a high social rank. ● See also
blue-blooded. 10 If a quality or talent is **in** your PHRASE
blood, it is part of your nature, and other members of
your family have it too. *Diplomacy was in his blood.*
11 If you say that there is **bad blood** between people, PHRASE
you mean that they have argued about something and
dislike each other.
12 If something violent and cruel is done **in cold** PHRASE
blood, it is done deliberately and in an unemotional
way. ● See also **cold-blooded. 13** You can use the ex- PHRASE
pressions **new blood, fresh blood,** or **young blood** to
refer to people who are brought into an organization
to improve it by thinking of new ideas or new ways of
doing things. *There's been a major reshuffle of the
cabinet to bring in new blood.*
14 ● **flesh and blood**: see **flesh.** ● **own flesh and
blood**: see **flesh.**

'**blood bank, blood banks.** A **blood bank** is a N-COUNT
place where blood taken from blood donors is
stored until it is needed for blood transfusions.

blood·bath /blʌdbɑːθ, -bæθ/ **bloodbaths.** If you N-COUNT
describe an event as a **bloodbath**, you are empha- PRAGMATICS
sizing that a lot of people were killed very violently.
...a bloodbath of tribal killings.

'**blood count, blood counts.** Your **blood count** is N-COUNT
the number of blood cells in your bloodstream. *Her
blood count was normal.*

'**blood-curdling**; also spelled **bloodcurdling.** A ADJ-GRADED
blood-curdling sound or story is very frightening
and horrible. ... *a bloodcurdling battle cry.*

'**blood donor, blood donors.** A **blood donor** is N-COUNT
someone who gives some of their blood so that it
can be used for transfusions or operations.

'**blood group, blood groups.** Someone's **blood** N-COUNT
group is the type of blood that they have in their
body.

blood·hound /'blʌdhaʊnd/ **bloodhounds.** A N-COUNT
bloodhound is a large dog with a very good sense of
smell.

blood·less /'blʌdləs/. **1** A **bloodless** coup or victory ADJ-GRADED
is one in which nobody is killed. ♦ **blood·less·ly** ADV-GRADED:
This war had to be fought fast and relatively blood- ADV with v
lessly. **2** If you describe someone's face or skin as ADJ
bloodless, you mean that it is very pale.

'**blood-letting. 1 Blood-letting** is violence or kill- N-UNCOUNT
ing between groups of people, especially between
rival armies. *There's been ferocious blood-letting in
the township.* **2** Journalists sometimes refer to a bit- N-UNCOUNT
ter quarrel between two groups of people, usually
people from within the same organization, as
blood-letting.

blood·line /'blʌdlaɪn/ **bloodlines.** A person's N-COUNT
bloodline is their ancestors over many generations,
and the characteristics they are believed to have inherited from these ancestors.

'**blood lust;** also spelled **blood-lust.** If you say that N-UNCOUNT:
someone is driven by **blood lust**, you mean that also a N
their emotions are aroused by extreme violence.

'**blood poisoning. Blood poisoning** is a serious N-UNCOUNT
illness resulting from an infection in your blood.

'**blood pressure.** Your **blood pressure** is a meas- ◆◆◇◇◇
ure of the force with which blood is pumped N-UNCOUNT
around your body. *...high blood pressure.*

'**blood-red;** also spelled **blood red.** Something that COLOUR
is **blood-red** is bright red in colour.

,**blood re'lation, blood relations.** A **blood rela-** N-COUNT
tion is someone who is related to you by birth rather than by marriage.

,**blood 'relative, blood relatives.** A **blood rela-** N-COUNT
tive is the same as a **blood relation.**

blood·shed /'blʌdʃed/. **Bloodshed** is violence in ◆◇◇◇◇
which people are killed or wounded. *The govern-* N-UNCOUNT
*ment must increase the pace of reforms to avoid fur-
ther bloodshed.*

blood·shot /'blʌdʃɒt/. If your eyes are **bloodshot**, ADJ-GRADED
the parts that are usually white are red or pink.

'**blood sport, blood sports;** also spelled N-COUNT
bloodsport. Blood sports are sports such as hunting in which animals are killed.

blood·stain /'blʌdsteɪn/ **bloodstains.** A **blood-** N-COUNT
stain is a mark on a surface caused by blood.
♦ **blood-stained** /'blʌdsteɪnd/. *Bloodstained cloth-* ADJ-GRADED
ing had been found.

blood·stock /'blʌdstɒk/. Horses that are bred for N-UNCOUNT
racing are referred to as **bloodstock.**

blood·stream /'blʌdstriːm/ **bloodstreams.** Your ◆◇◇◇◇
bloodstream is the blood that flows around your N-COUNT
body. *The disease releases toxins into the bloodstream.*

blood·sucker /'blʌdsʌkə/ **bloodsuckers. 1** A N-COUNT
bloodsucker is any creature that sucks blood from a
wound that it has made in an animal or person. **2** If N-COUNT
you call someone a **bloodsucker**, you disapprove of PRAGMATICS
them because you think that they do not make any
worthwhile contribution to society but live by other
people's efforts. *He was at last free from the financial bloodsuckers.*

'**blood test, blood tests.** A **blood test** is a medi- ◆◇◇◇◇
cal examination of a sample of your blood.

blood·thirsty /'blʌdθɜːstiː/. **Bloodthirsty** people are ADJ-GRADED
eager to use violence or display a strong interest in
violent things. *...this bloodthirsty war.*

'**blood transfusion, blood transfusions.** A N-VAR
blood transfusion is a process in which blood is injected into the body of a person who is badly injured or ill.

'**blood type, blood types.** Someone's **blood type** N-COUNT
is the same as their **blood group.**

'**blood vessel, blood vessels. Blood vessels** are ◆◇◇◇◇
the narrow tubes through which your blood flows. N-COUNT

bloody /'blʌdi/ **bloodier, bloodiest; bloodies,** ◆◆◆◇
bloodying, bloodied. 1 Bloody is a swear word. ADJ-GRADED
Some people use 'bloody' to emphasize what they PRAGMATICS
are saying, especially when they are angry about BRITISH,
something someone has said or done. RUDE

2 If you describe a situation or event as **bloody**, you ADJ-GRADED
mean that it is very violent and a lot of people are
killed. *Forty-three demonstrators were killed in bloody
clashes.* ♦ **blood·i·ly** *Rebellions in the area were* ADV:
bloodily repressed. **3** You can describe someone or ADV with v
something as **bloody** if they are covered in a lot of ADJ-GRADED
blood. *...a bloody knife.* **4** If you have **bloodied** part of VERB
your body, there is blood on it because you have been V n
injured. *One of our children fell and bloodied his knee.*

Bloody Mary /ˌblʌdi 'meəri/ **Bloody Marys;** also N-COUNT
spelled **bloody mary.** A **Bloody Mary** is a drink
made from vodka and tomato juice.

bloody-'minded. If someone is being **bloody-** ADJ-GRADED
minded, they are being deliberately difficult instead PRAGMATICS
of being helpful; used showing disapproval. *He was* INFORMAL,
just being bloody-minded. He could easily have let BRITISH
the car pass. ♦ **bloody-minded·ness** *The relation-* N-UNCOUNT
ship was one of bloody-mindedness.

bloom /blu:m/ **blooms, blooming, bloomed.** ◆◆◇◇◇
1 A **bloom** is the flower on a plant. *...the sweet fra-* N-COUNT
grance of the white blooms. **2** A plant or tree that is LITERARY
in bloom has flowers on it. **3** When a plant or tree PHRASE
blooms, it produces flowers. When a flower **blooms,** VERB
the flower bud opens. *This plant blooms between* V
May and June. ♦ **-blooming** *...the scent of night-* COMB
blooming flowers.

4 If someone or something **blooms,** they develop VERB: V
good, attractive, or successful qualities. *She bloomed* V into n
into an utterly beautiful creature.

5 If something such as someone's skin has a **bloom,** it N-UNCOUNT:
has a fresh and healthy appearance. also a N

6 See also **blooming.**

bloom·ers /'blu:məz/. **Bloomers** are an old- N-PLURAL
fashioned kind of women's underwear which consists of wide, loose trousers gathered at the knees.

bloom·ing /'blu:mɪŋ/. **1 Blooming** is a mild swear ADJ: ADJ n
word used to emphasize what you are saying, PRAGMATICS
especially when you are annoyed. *It's a blooming* BRITISH
nuisance. ▶ Also an adverb. *She was blooming mar-* ADV: ADV adj
vellous. **2** Someone who is **blooming** looks attrac- ADJ
tively healthy and full of energy.

bloop·er /'blu:pə/ **bloopers.** A **blooper** is a silly N-COUNT
mistake. *...television bloopers.* INFORMAL,
AMERICAN

blos·som /'blɒsəm/ **blossoms, blossoming,** ◆◆◇◇◇
blossomed. 1 Blossom consists of the flowers N-VAR
that appear on trees. **2** When a tree **blossoms,** it VERB: V
produces blossom.

3 If someone or something **blossoms,** they develop VERB: V
good, attractive, or successful qualities. *What began* V into n
*as a local festival has blossomed into an international
event.* ♦ **blos·som·ing** *...the blossoming of British* N-UNCOUNT:
art, pop and fashion. N of n

blot /blɒt/ **blots, blotting, blotted. 1** If some- ◆◇◇◇◇
thing is a **blot on** a person's or thing's reputation, it N-COUNT:
spoils their reputation. *This drugs scandal is another* N on n
blot on the Olympics. **2** If you describe something PHRASE
such as a building as a **blot on the landscape,** you
mean that you think it is very ugly and spoils an
otherwise attractive place.

3 A **blot** is a drop of liquid that has been spilled on a N-COUNT
surface and has dried. *...an ink blot.*

4 If you **blot** a surface, you remove liquid from it by VERB
pressing a piece of soft paper or cloth onto it. *Blot the* V n
face with a tissue. Also V n adj

blot out. 1 If one thing **blots out** another thing, it is PHRASAL VB
in front of the other thing and prevents it from being V P noun
seen. *Clouds blotted out the sun. ... with mist blotting* V n P
everything out. **2** If you try to **blot out** a memory, you V P noun
try to forget it. If one thought or memory **blots out** V n P
other thoughts or memories, it becomes the only one
that you can think about. *She's trying to blot out all
memory of the incident... He is blotting certain things
out.*

blotch /blɒtʃ/ **blotches.** A **blotch** is a small N-COUNT
unpleasant-looking area of colour, for example on
someone's skin. *His face was covered in red blotches.*

blotched /blɒtʃt/. Something that is **blotched** has ADJ
blotches on it. *Her narrow face is blotched.*

blotchy /'blɒtʃi/. Something that is **blotchy** has ADJ-GRADED
blotches on it.

blot·ter /'blɒtə/ **blotters.** A **blotter** is a large sheet N-COUNT
of blotting paper kept in a special holder on a desk.

'blotting paper. Blotting paper is thick soft paper N-UNCOUNT
that you use for soaking up and drying ink on a
piece of paper.

blouse /blaʊz, AM blaʊs/ **blouses.** A **blouse** is a ◆◇◇◇◇
kind of shirt worn by a girl or woman. See picture N-COUNT
headed **clothes.**

blow 1 verb uses

blow /bləʊ/ **blows, blowing, blew, blown.** ◆◆◆◇
1 When a wind or breeze **blows,** the air moves. *A* VERB
chill wind blew at the top of the hill. **2** If the wind V
blows something somewhere or if it **blows** there, V-ERG
the wind moves it there. *The wind blew her hair* V n with adv
back from her forehead... Sand blew in our eyes. V adv/prep
Also V,
V n prep

3 If you **blow,** you send out a stream of air from your VERB
mouth. *Danny rubbed his arms and blew on his fingers* V prep/adv
to warm them. **4** If you **blow** something somewhere, Also V
you move it by sending out a stream of air from your VERB
mouth. *He picked up his mug and blew off the steam.* V n with adv
Also V n prep

5 If you **blow** bubbles or smoke rings, you make them VERB: V n
by blowing air out of your mouth through liquid or
smoke.

6 When a whistle or horn **blows** or someone **blows** it, V-ERG: V
they make a sound by blowing into it. *A guard was* V n
blowing his whistle.

7 When you **blow** your nose, you force air out of it VERB: V n
through your nostrils in order to clear it.

8 If someone or something **blows** something out, off, VERB
or away, they violently remove or destroy it with an V n with adv
explosion. *The can exploded, wrecking the kitchen* V n prep
*and bathroom and blowing out windows... Rival gun-
men blew the city to bits.*

9 If you **blow** a large amount of money, you spend it VERB
quickly on luxuries. *My brother lent me some money* V n
and I went and blew the lot. INFORMAL

10 If you **blow** a chance or attempt to do something, VERB
you make a mistake which wastes the chance or V n
causes the attempt to fail. *He has almost certainly* V it
blown his chance of touring India... Oh you fool! INFORMAL
You've blown it!

11 If a fuse **blows** or if something **blows** it, the fuse V-ERG
melts because too much electricity has been sent V
through it, and the electrical current is cut off. *The* Also V n
fuse blew as he pressed the button.

12 If you **blow** a tyre or if it **blows,** a hole suddenly ap- V-ERG
pears in it and all the air comes out of it. *A lorry blew a* V n
tyre and careered into them. ▶ **Blow out** means the Also V
same as **blow.** *A tyre blew out when the coach was on* PHRASAL VB
its way. VP

13 Blow is used in a large number of expressions
which are explained under other words in this dictionary. For example, the expression **to blow away
the cobwebs** is explained at **cobweb.**

blow out. 1 If you **blow out** a flame or a candle, you PHRASAL VB
blow at it so that it stops burning. *I blew out the can-* V P noun
dle. **2** See also **blow 12, blow-out.** Also V n P

blow over. If something such as trouble or an argu- PHRASAL VB
ment **blows over,** it ends without any serious conse- VP
quences. *Wait, and it'll all blow over.*

blow up. 1 If someone **blows** something **up** or if it PHRASAL VB
blows up, it is destroyed by an explosion. *...trying to* ERG
blow up a plane... Their boat blew up. V P noun
VP

2 If you **blow up** something such as a balloon or a V P noun
tyre, you fill it with air. *Other than blowing up a tyre I* Also V P n
hadn't done any car maintenance.

3 If a wind or a storm **blows up,** the weather becomes VP
very windy or stormy.

4 If you **blow up** at someone, you lose your temper V P at n
and shout at them. *I'm sorry I blew up at you.* Also V P
INFORMAL

5 If someone **blows** an incident **up** or if it **blows up,** it ERG
is made to seem more serious or important than it re-

B

ally is. *Newspapers blew up the story... The media* V P noun
may be blowing it up out of proportion. V n P
6 If a photographic image **is blown up**, a large copy is Also V P made of it. *The image is blown up on a large screen.* beV-ed P Also V P noun, V n P
7 See also **blow-up**.

blow 2 noun uses

blow /bləʊ/ **blows. 1** If someone receives a **blow**, ◆◆◇◇ they are hit with a fist or weapon. *He went off to* N-COUNT *hospital after a blow to the face.* **2** If two people or PHRASE groups **come to blows**, they start fighting.
3 If you say that something that happened was a **blow** N-COUNT to someone or something, you mean that it was very upsetting, disappointing, or damaging to them. *When the marriage finally broke up it was obviously a terrible blow to Soames.*
4 Something that **softens the blow** or **cushions the** PHRASE **blow** makes an unpleasant change or piece of news easier to accept. **5** If you **strike a blow for** a particular PHRASE cause or principle, you do something that supports it or makes it more likely to succeed. *The team struck a blow for women's rights by winning the match.*
blow-by-'blow. A blow-by-blow account of an ADJ event describes every stage of it in great detail. *She* INFORMAL *always demanded a blow-by-blow account of what had happened.*
'blow-dry, blow-dries, blow-drying, blow- VERB **dried.** If you **blow-dry** your hair, you dry it with a V n hairdryer, often to give it a particular style. *Blow-dry it forwards.* ▶ Also a noun. *...a cut and blow dry.* N-SING
blow·lamp /'bləʊlæmp/ **blowlamps;** also spelled N-COUNT **blow lamp.** A **blowlamp** is a device which produces BRITISH a hot flame and is used to heat metal or remove old paint. The American word is **blowtorch**.
blown /bləʊn/. **Blown** is the past participle of **blow**.
'blow-out, blow-outs; also spelled **blow out.** **1** A N-COUNT **blow-out** is a large meal at which people may eat INFORMAL too much. **2** If you have a **blow-out** while you are N-COUNT driving a car, one of the tyres suddenly bursts. *A lorry travelling south had a blow-out and crashed.*
blow·torch /'bləʊtɔːtʃ/ **blowtorches.** A **blow-** N-COUNT **torch** is the same as a **blowlamp**.
'blow-up, blow-ups; also spelled **blowup.** A N-COUNT **blow-up** is an enlargement of a photograph or picture. *...yellowing blow-ups of James Dean.*
blub /blʌb/ **blubs, blubbing, blubbed.** If some- VERB one **blubs**, they cry because they are unhappy or V frightened. *I felt very weak and wanted to blub.* INFORMAL, BRITISH
blub·ber /'blʌbə/ **blubbers, blubbering, blub-** **bered. 1** Blubber is the fat of whales, seals, and N-UNCOUNT similar sea animals. **2** If someone **blubbers**, they VERB cry noisily and in an unattractive way. *Their mother* V *started to blubber like a child.* INFORMAL
bludg·eon /'blʌdʒən/ **bludgeons, bludgeoning,** ◆◇◇◇ **bludgeoned. 1** To bludgeon someone means to VERB: V n hit them several times with a heavy object. **2** If VERB someone **bludgeons** you into doing something, they V n into/-ing make you do it by bullying or threatening you. *Their approach simply bludgeons you into submission.*
blue /bluː/ **bluer, bluest; blues. 1** Something ◆◆◆◆◆ that is **blue** is the colour of the sky on a sunny day. COLOUR *...her pale blue eyes.*
2 The blues is a type of music which was developed N-PLURAL: by black American musicians in the southern United theN States. It is characterized by a slow tempo and a strong rhythm.
3 If you have got **the blues**, you feel sad and de- N-PLURAL pressed. *Interfering in-laws are the prime sources of* INFORMAL *the blues.* **4** If you are feeling **blue**, you are feeling sad ADJ-GRADED or depressed, often for is no particular reason. v-link ADJ INFORMAL
5 Blue films, stories, or jokes are about sex. *...a blue* ADJ: ADJ n *movie.*
6 ● bolt from the blue: see **bolt. ● once in a blue moon:** see **moon. ● to scream blue murder:** see **murder.**
blue·bell /'bluːbel/ **bluebells.** Bluebells are plants ◆◇◇◇ that have blue bell-shaped flowers. N-COUNT
blue·berry /'bluːbəri, AM -beri/ **blueberries.** A N-COUNT **blueberry** is a small dark blue fruit that is found in North America.

blue-'black. Something that is **blue-black** is very COLOUR dark blue in colour.
blue-'blooded. A **blue-blooded** person is from a ADJ royal or noble family. **Blue-blooded** can also describe something that is associated with royalty. *While not blue-blooded herself, the Duchess married into the most aristocratic family in Britain.*
'blue book, blue books; also **Blue Book.** A blue N-COUNT **book** is an official government report or register of statistics. *...the office's 1989 Blue Book.*
blue-bottle /'bluːbɒtəl/ **bluebottles.** A bluebottle N-COUNT is a large fly with a shiny dark-blue body.
blue 'chip, blue chips. Blue chip stocks and ◆◇◇◇ shares are investments which are considered rela- N-COUNT tively safe while also being profitable.
blue-'collar. Blue-collar workers work in indus- ADJ: ADJ n try, doing physical work, rather than in offices.
blue-grass /'bluːgrɑːs, -græs/. **Bluegrass** is a style N-UNCOUNT of folk music that originated in the Southern United States. Bluegrass music is characterized by a rapid tempo and strong harmonies.
blue-ish /'bluːɪʃ/. See **bluish**.
blue-print /'bluːprɪnt/ **blueprints. 1** A blueprint ◆◇◇◇ for something is a plan or set of proposals that N-COUNT shows how it is expected to work. *...his blueprint for the country's future.* **2** A blueprint of an architect's N-COUNT building plans or a designer's pattern is a photographic print consisting of white lines on a blue background. Blueprints contain all of the information that is needed to make something. **3** A N-COUNT genetic **blueprint** is a pattern which is contained within all living cells. This pattern determines the hereditary characteristics of the organism. *...the genetic blueprint of each parent.*
blue rib·and /ˌbluː 'rɪbənd/ **blue ribands.** If some- N-COUNT one or something wins the **blue riband** in a compe- BRITISH tition, they win first prize. The trophy that they win is sometimes the shape of a blue ribbon. The American expression is **blue ribbon**.
blue 'ribbon, blue ribbons. A blue ribbon is the N-COUNT same as a **blue riband**. AMERICAN
blue-stocking /'bluːstɒkɪŋ/ **bluestockings;** also N-COUNT spelled **blue-stocking.** If you refer to a woman as a PRAGMATICS **bluestocking**, you mean that she is more concerned with intellectual ideas than behaving in a traditionally feminine way; often used showing disapproval.
bluesy /'bluːzi/. If you describe a song or the way it ADJ is performed as **bluesy**, you mean that it is performed in a way that is characteristic of the blues. *...bluesy sax-and-strings theme music.*
'blue tit, blue tits. A blue tit is a small blue and N-COUNT yellow European bird.
bluff /blʌf/ **bluffs, bluffing, bluffed. 1** A bluff is ◆◇◇◇ an attempt to make someone believe that you will N-VAR do something when you do not really intend to do it. *The letter was a bluff. ...a game of bluff.* ● See also **double bluff**. **2** If you call someone's **bluff**, you PHRASE tell them to do what they have been threatening to do, because you are sure that they will not really do it. **3** If you **bluff** or if you **bluff** someone, you make VERB them believe that you will do something when you V do not really intend to do it, or that you know V n something when you do not really know it. *Either* V way prep *side, or both, could be bluffing... The hijackers bluffed the crew using fake grenades... He tried to bluff his way through another test.*
4 A bluff is a steep cliff or bank, especially by a river or N-COUNT the sea. *...a high bluff over the Congaree River.*
5 If you describe someone, usually a man, as **bluff**, ADJ-GRADED you mean that they have a very direct way of speaking and behaving. *...a man with a bluff exterior. ...bluff, vivid humour.*
blu·ish /'bluːɪʃ/; also spelled **blueish**. Something COLOUR that is **bluish** is slightly blue in colour. *...bluish-grey eyes.*
blun·der /'blʌndə/ **blunders, blundering, blun-** ◆◇◇◇ **dered. 1** A blunder is a stupid or careless mistake. N-COUNT *He made a blunder by announcing it so far ahead of time.* **2** If you **blunder**, you make a stupid VERB: V or careless mistake. **3** If you **blunder** into a danger- VERB

ous or difficult situation, you get involved in it by V *into* n
mistake. *They had blundered into war.*

4 If you **blunder** somewhere, you move there in a VERB
clumsy and careless way. *He had blundered into the* V prep/adv
table, upsetting the flowers.

blunt /blʌnt/ **blunter, bluntest; blunts, blunt-** ◆◆◇◇◇
ing, blunted. 1 If you are **blunt**, you say exactly ADJ-GRADED
what you think without trying to be polite. *She is*
blunt about her personal life. ♦ **blunt·ly** *'I don't be-* ADV-GRADED
lieve you!' Jeanne said bluntly. ♦ **blunt·ness** *His* N-UNCOUNT
bluntness got him into trouble.

2 A **blunt** object has a rounded or flat end rather than ADJ: ADJ n
a sharp one. **3** A **blunt** knife or blade is no longer ADJ-GRADED
sharp and does not cut well.

4 If something **blunts** an emotion, it weakens it. *The* VERB
constant repetition of violence has blunted the human V n
response to it.

blur /blɜː/ **blurs, blurring, blurred. 1** A **blur** is a ◆◆◇◇◇
shape or area which you cannot see clearly because N-COUNT
it has no distinct outline or because it is moving
very fast. *Her face is a blur.* ♦ **blur·ry** /'blɜːri/. ADJ-GRADED
...blurry pictures of Elton John on the screen.

2 When something **blurs** an image, you cannot see V-ERG: V n
it clearly because its edges are no longer distinct. *If* V
you move your eyes and your head, the picture will
blur. ♦ **blurred** *...blurred black and white photo-* ADJ-GRADED
graphs. **3** If your vision **blurs**, you cannot see V-ERG: V
things clearly. *Sweat ran from his forehead into his* V n
eyes, blurring his vision. ♦ **blurred** *...visual disturb-* ADJ-GRADED
ances like eye-strain and blurred vision.

4 If something **blurs** a distinction between things, it VERB: V n
no longer seems clear. ♦ **blurred** *The line between* ADJ-GRADED
fact and fiction is becoming blurred.

blurb /blɜːb/ **blurbs.** The **blurb** about a new book, N-COUNT
film, or exhibition is information about it that is INFORMAL
written in order to attract people's interest. *...the*
blurb on the cover of the paperback.

blurt /blɜːt/ **blurts, blurting, blurted.** If some- ◆◇◇◇◇
one **blurts** something, they say it suddenly, after VERB
trying hard to keep quiet or to keep it secret. *'I was* V with quote
looking for Sally', he blurted. ▶ **Blurt out** means the Also V that
same as **blurt**. *'You're mad,' the driver blurted out...* PHRASAL VB
Richard blurted out what was on his mind. V P with quote
Also V n P

blush /blʌʃ/ **blushes, blushing, blushed.** ◆◇◇◇◇
1 When you **blush**, your face becomes redder than VERB: V
usual because you are ashamed or embarrassed. *I* V colour
blushed scarlet at my stupidity. ▶ Also a noun. *A* N-COUNT
blush spread over Brenda's cheeks. **2** If you **spare** PHRASE
someone's **blushes** or **save** someone's **blushes**, you BRITISH
avoid doing something that will embarrass them.
We don't want to name the man, to spare his
blushes.

blush·er /'blʌʃə/ **blushers. Blusher** is a coloured N-VAR
substance that women put on their cheeks. BRITISH

blus·ter /'blʌstə/ **blusters, blustering, blus-** ◆◇◇◇◇
tered. If you say that someone is **blustering**, you VERB: V
mean that they are speaking aggressively or proudly V with quote
but without authority. *'That's lunacy,' he blustered.*
▶ Also a noun. *...the bluster of the Conservatives'* N-UNCOUNT
campaign.

blus·tery /'blʌstəri/. **Blustery** weather is rough, ADJ-GRADED
windy, and often rainy.

Blvd. Blvd is a written abbreviation for 'Boulevard'.
It is used in addresses and on maps or signs. *...1515*
Wilson Blvd.

'B-movie, B-movies. A **B-movie** is a film which is N-COUNT
produced quickly and cheaply and is often considered to have little artistic value.

bn. bn is a written abbreviation for **billion.** BRITISH

B.O. /ˌbiː 'əʊ/. **B.O.** is an abbreviation for **body** N-UNCOUNT
odour.

boa /'bəʊə/ **boas. 1** A **boa** is a long soft scarf made N-COUNT
of feathers or of short pieces of very light fabric. **2** A N-COUNT
boa is the same as a **boa constrictor.**

boa con'strictor, boa constrictors. A **boa con-** N-COUNT
strictor is a large snake that kills animals by wrapping itself round their bodies and squeezing them
to death. Boa constrictors are found mainly in
South and Central America and the West Indies.

boar /bɔː/ **boars. 1** A **boar** or a **wild boar** is a wild ◆◇◇◇◇
pig. The plural can be 'boar' or 'boars'. **2** A **boar** is a N-COUNT
male pig. N-COUNT

board /bɔːd/ **boards, boarding, boarded. 1** A ◆◆◆◆◇
board is a flat, thin, rectangular piece of wood or N-COUNT
plastic which is used for a particular purpose. *...a*
chopping board. **2** A **board** is a square piece of N-COUNT
wood or stiff cardboard that you use for playing
games such as chess. **3** You can refer to a black- N-COUNT
board or a noticeboard as a **board.** *He wrote a few*
more notes on the board. ● See also **bulletin board.**

4 Boards are long flat pieces of wood which are N-COUNT
used, for example, to make floors or walls.

5 The **board** of a company or organization is the N-COUNT
group of people who control it. *...the September 12*
board meeting. **6 Board** is used in the names of vari- N-COUNT
ous organizations involved in the promotion or distribution of something. *...the Scottish Tourist Board.*

7 When you **board** a train, ship, or aircraft, you get on VERB
it in order to travel somewhere. *I boarded the plane* V n
bound for England. **8** When you are **on board** a train, Also V
ship, or aircraft, you are on it or in it. PHRASE

9 Board is the food which is provided when you stay N-UNCOUNT
somewhere, for example in a hotel. *Free room and*
board are provided for all hotel staff.

10 An arrangement or deal that is **above board** is legal PHRASE
and is being carried out honestly and openly. **11** If a PHRASE
policy or a situation applies **across the board**, it affects everything or everyone in a particular group. *...to*
increase salaries across the board. **12** If someone PHRASE
sweeps the board in a competition or election, they
win nearly everything that it is possible to win. *Spain*
swept the board in boys' team competitions. **13** If you PHRASE
take on board an idea or a problem, you begin to accept it or understand it.

board up. If you **board up** a door or window, you fix PHRASAL VB
pieces of wood over it so that it is covered up. *Shop-* V P noun
keepers have boarded up their windows... Half the V-ed P
shops are boarded up. Also V n P

,board and 'lodging. If you are provided with N-UNCOUNT
board and lodging, you are provided with food and
a place to sleep.

board·er /'bɔːdə/ **boarders.** A **boarder** is a pupil N-COUNT
who lives at school during the term. BRITISH

'board game, board games. A **board game** is a N-COUNT
game such as chess, which people play by moving
small objects around on a board.

board·ing /'bɔːdɪŋ/. **1 Boarding** is an arrangement N-UNCOUNT
by which children live at school during the school
term. *Annual boarding fees are £10,350.* **2 Boarding** N-UNCOUNT
is long, flat pieces of wood which can be used to
make walls, doors, and fences.

'boarding card, boarding cards. A **boarding** N-COUNT
card is the same as a **boarding pass.** BRITISH

'boarding house, boarding houses; also N-COUNT
spelled **boarding-house.** A **boarding house** is a
house which people pay to stay in for a short time.

'boarding pass, boarding pass. A **boarding** N-COUNT
pass is a card which a passenger must have when
boarding a plane or a boat.

'boarding school, boarding schools. A **board-** ◆◇◇◇◇
ing school is a school which some or all of the pu- N-VAR
pils live in during the school term.

board·room /'bɔːdruːm/ **boardrooms;** also ◆◇◇◇◇
spelled **board room.** The **boardroom** is a room N-COUNT
where the board of a company meets.

board·walk /'bɔːdwɔːk/ **boardwalks.** In the Unit- N-COUNT
ed States, a **boardwalk** is a footpath made of wood-
en boards.

boast /bəʊst/ **boasts, boasting, boasted. 1** If ◆◆◇◇◇
someone **boasts** about something that they have VERB
done or that they own, they talk about it too proud- PRAGMATICS
ly in a way that other people may find irritating or V *about/of*
offensive. *Carol boasted about her costume... Furci* n/-ing
boasted that he took part in killing them. ▶ Also a Also V
noun. *...her boast of being a great lover.* ♦ **boast-** N-COUNT
·ful *I am not afraid of seeming boastful.* **2** If some- ADJ-GRADED
one or something can **boast** a particular achieve- VERB
ment or possession, they have achieved or possess V n
that thing. *The houses will boast the latest energy-*

saving technology. ▸ Also a noun. *It is the charity's* N-COUNT
proud boast that it has never yet turned anyone
away.

boat /bəʊt/ **boats. 1** A boat is something in which ◆◆◆◇
people can travel across water. *The island may be*
reached by boat. **2** You can refer to a passenger ship N-COUNT:
as a **boat. 3** See also **gravy boat, rowing boat.**
4 If you say that someone has **missed the boat**, you PHRASE
mean that they have missed an opportunity and may
not get another. **5** If you **push the boat out**, you spend PHRASE
a lot of money on something, especially in order to BRITISH
celebrate. **6** If you say that someone is **rocking the** PHRASE
boat, you mean that they are upsetting a calm situation and causing trouble. **7** If two or more people are PHRASE
in the same boat, they are in the same unpleasant
situation.

boat·building /ˈbəʊtbɪldɪŋ/; also spelled **boat-** N-UNCOUNT
building. **Boatbuilding** is the craft or industry of
making boats. ♦ **boat·builder, boatbuilders.** N-COUNT

boat·er /ˈbəʊtə/ **boaters.** A **boater** is a hard straw N-COUNT
hat with a flat top and brim which is often worn for
certain social occasions in the summer.

boat·house /ˈbəʊthaʊs/ **boathouses;** also spelled N-COUNT
boat house. A **boathouse** is a building at the edge of
a lake, in which boats are kept.

boat·ing /ˈbəʊtɪŋ/. **Boating** is travelling on a lake ◆◇◇◇◇
or river in a small boat for pleasure. *They were killed* N-UNCOUNT
in a boating accident.

boat·load /ˈbəʊtləʊd/ **boatloads;** also spelled **boat** N-COUNT
load. A **boatload** of people or things is a lot of people or things in a boat. ...*the latest boatload of*
refugees.

boat·man /ˈbəʊtmən/ **boatmen.** A **boatman** is a N-COUNT
man who is paid by people to take them across an
area of water in a small boat, or a man who hires
boats out to them for a short time.

'boat people. Boat people are refugees who left ◆◆◇◇◇
their country in a boat to travel to another country N-PLURAL
in the hope that they will be able to live there.

'boat train, boat trains. A **boat train** is a train N-COUNT
that takes you to or from a port.

boat·yard /ˈbəʊtjɑːd/ **boatyards.** A **boatyard** is a N-COUNT
place where boats are built and repaired or kept.

bob /bɒb/ **bobs, bobbing, bobbed. 1** If some- ◆◆◇◇◇
thing **bobs**, it moves up and down, like something VERB:
does when it is floating on water. *The raft bobbed* Also V
along. **2** If you **bob** somewhere, you move there VERB
quickly so that you disappear from view or come BRITISH
into view. *She handed over a form, then bobbed*
down again behind a typewriter. **3** When you **bob** VERB: V n
your head, you move it quickly up and down once.
▸ Also a noun. *The young man smiled with a bob of* N-COUNT
his head.
4 In Britain, people used to refer to a shilling as a **bob**. N-COUNT
The plural form was also **bob**. INFORMAL
5 A **bob** is a hair style in which a woman's hair, except N-COUNT
for the fringe, is cut to the level of her chin.
6 ● **bits and bobs:** see **bit**.

bob·bin /ˈbɒbɪn/ **bobbins.** A **bobbin** is a small N-COUNT
round object on which thread or wool is wound.

bob·ble /ˈbɒbl/ **bobbles.** A **bobble** is a small ball N-COUNT
of material, usually made of wool, which is used for BRITISH
decorating clothes and soft furnishings. The usual
American word is **tassel**.

bob·by /ˈbɒbi/ **bobbies.** A **bobby** is a British N-COUNT
policeman, usually of the lowest rank. INFORMAL

bob·cat /ˈbɒbkæt/ **bobcats.** A **bobcat** is a North N-COUNT
American animal of the cat family which has
reddish-brown fur with dark spots or stripes and a
short tail.

bob·sled /ˈbɒbsled/ **bobsleds.** A **bobsled** is the N-COUNT
same as a **bobsleigh**. AMERICAN

bob·sleigh /ˈbɒbsleɪ/ **bobsleighs.** A **bobsleigh** is a N-COUNT
vehicle with long thin strips of metal fixed to the BRITISH
bottom, which is used for racing downhill on ice.
The American word is **bobsled**.

bod /bɒd/ **bods. 1** A **bod** is a person. ...*an ex-Army* N-COUNT
colonel, *a weird old bod called Pryce-Sampson.* INFORMAL
2 Someone's **bod** is their body. *They've had free use* N-COUNT
of the gym for three months to develop their bods. INFORMAL

bode /bəʊd/ **bodes, boding, boded.** If some- ◆◇◇◇
thing **bodes** ill, it makes you think that something VERB:
bad will happen in the future. If something **bodes** V adv
well, it makes you think that something good will V adv for n
happen. *She says the way the bill was passed bodes* FORMAL
ill for democracy.

bodge /bɒdʒ/ **bodges, bodging, bodged.** If you VERB: V n
bodge something, you make it or mend it in a way BRITISH,
that is not as good as it should be. INFORMAL

bod·ice /ˈbɒdɪs/ **bodices.** The **bodice** of a dress is N-COUNT
the part above the waist.

bodi·ly /ˈbɒdɪli/. **1** Your **bodily** needs and func- ◆◇◇◇
tions are the needs and functions of your body. ADJ: ADJ n
● See also **grievous bodily harm**. **2** You use **bodily** ADV:
to indicate that an action involves the whole of ADV with v
someone's body. *I was hurled bodily to the deck.*

body /ˈbɒdi/ **bodies. 1** Your **body** is all your physi- ◆◆◆◆
cal parts, including your head, arms, and legs.
2 You can refer to the main part of your body, ex- N-COUNT
cluding your arms, head, and legs, as your **body**.
3 You can refer to a person's dead body as a **body**. N-COUNT
4 If someone mentions a possible event and you PHRASE
say **'over** my **dead body'**, you are emphasizing that PRAGMATICS
you feel very strongly that it should not happen, INFORMAL
and that you will do everything you can to prevent
it. *'We'll have her over for dinner.'—'Over my dead*
body!' **5** You use **body and soul** to mean every part PHRASE
of you, including your mind and your emotions. *He*
dedicated himself body and soul to the education of
young men.
6 A **body** is an organized group of people who deal N-COUNT
with something officially. ...*the policemen's repre-*
sentative body, the Police Federation. **7** A **body** of peo- N-COUNT:
ple is a group of people who are together or who are N of n
connected in some way. ...*that large body of people*
which teaches other people how to teach.
8 The **body** of something such as a building or a docu- N-SING:
ment is the main part of it or the largest part of it. ...*the* the N of n
main body of the church. ...*the body of the material.*
9 The **body** of a car or aeroplane is the main part of it, N-COUNT
not including its engine, wheels, or wings.
10 A **body** of water is a large area of water, such as a N-COUNT
lake or a sea. **11** A large **body** of information is a large N-COUNT
amount of it. ...*an increasing body of evidence.*
12 If you say that an alcoholic drink has **body**, you N-UNCOUNT
mean that it has a full and strong flavour.
13 A **body** is the same as a **bodysuit**. N-COUNT
14 See also **heavenly body**.

'body armour; spelled **body armor** in American N-UNCOUNT
English. **Body armour** is special protective clothing
which people such as soldiers and police officers
sometimes wear when they are in danger of being
attacked with guns or other weapons.

'body blow, body blows; also spelled **body-blow**. N-COUNT
If you describe something as a **body blow**, you
mean that it causes great disappointment and difficulty to someone in what they are trying to achieve.
His resignation will be another body blow to the rul-
ing National Liberation Front.

body·building /ˈbɒdibɪldɪŋ/; also spelled **body** N-UNCOUNT
building. **Bodybuilding** is the activity of doing special exercises regularly in order to make your muscles grow bigger. ♦ **body·builder, bodybuilders.** N-COUNT

'body clock, body clocks. Your **body clock** is N-COUNT
the internal biological mechanism which causes BRITISH
your body to automatically behave in particular
ways at particular times of the day. The American
expression is **biological clock**.

'body double, body doubles. A **body double** is N-COUNT
someone who takes the place of an actor when the
actor does not want to be filmed without any
clothes on. *I use my face and my body as I wish and*
if an actress doesn't want to, she can use a body
double.

body·guard /ˈbɒdigɑːd/ **bodyguards.** A **body-** ◆◆◇◇◇
guard is a person or a group of people employed to N-COUNT
protect someone.

'body language. Your **body language** is the way ◆◇◇◇◇
in which you show your feelings or thoughts by N-UNCOUNT
means of the position or movements of your body.

'body odour; spelled **body odor** in American English. **Body odour** is an unpleasant smell caused by stale sweat on a person's body. N-UNCOUNT

,body 'politic. The **body politic** is all the people of a nation when they are considered as a complete political group. N-SING FORMAL

'body search, body searches, body searching, body searched; also spelled **body-search.** If a person **is body searched,** someone such as a police officer searches them while they remain clothed. Compare **strip-search.** *Foreign journalists were body-searched by airport police.* ▶ Also a noun. *...body searches by security guards.* VERB beV-ed Also V n N-COUNT

'body stocking, body stockings. A **body stocking** is a piece of clothing that covers the whole of someone's body and fits tightly. Body stockings are often worn by dancers. N-COUNT

body·suit /'bɒdisuːt/ **bodysuits.** A **bodysuit** is a piece of clothing that fits tightly over the main part of your body, with holes for your legs. N-COUNT

body·work /'bɒdiwɜːk/. The **bodywork** of a motor vehicle is the outside part of it. N-UNCOUNT

Boer /'bəʊə, bɔː/ **Boers.** The **Boers** are the descendants of the Dutch people who went to live in South Africa. N-COUNT

bof·fin /'bɒfɪn/ **boffins.** A **boffin** is a scientist, especially one who is doing research. N-COUNT BRITISH

bog /bɒg/ **bogs, bogging, bogged. 1** A **bog** is an area of land which is very wet and muddy. *The meadow in Dolores Park had become a bog.* **2** The **bog** is another name for the toilet. ◆◆◇◇◇ N-COUNT / N-COUNT BRITISH, INFORMAL

bog down. If a plan or process **is bogged down,** it is delayed and no progress is made. *The talks have bogged down over the issue of military reform.* ● See also **bogged down.** PHRASAL VB ERG: beV-ed P VP

bo·gey /'bəʊgi/ **bogeys. 1** A **bogey** is something or someone that people are worried about, perhaps without much cause or reason. *The universal bogey is AIDS.* ▶ Also an adjective. *...scare stories about bogey policewomen.* **2** A **bogey** is a piece of dried mucus that comes from inside your nose. The American word is **booger.** ◆◇◇◇ N-COUNT / ADJ: ADJ n / N-COUNT INFORMAL, BRITISH

bogey·man /'bəʊgimæn/ **bogeymen;** also spelled **bogey man. 1** A **bogeyman** is someone whose ideas or actions are disapproved of by some people, and who is described by them as evil or unpleasant in order to make other people afraid. *How could he be the left-wing bogeyman that the capitalist media depict him as?* **2** A **bogeyman** is an imaginary evil spirit. N-COUNT PRAGMATICS / N-COUNT

,bogged 'down. If you get **bogged down** in something, it prevents you from making progress or getting something done. *Why get bogged down in legal details?* ◆◇◇◇ ADJ-GRADED

bog·gle /'bɒgəl/ **boggles, boggling, boggled.** If you say that the mind **boggles** at something, you mean that it is so strange or amazing that it is difficult to imagine or understand. *The management group's decision still boggled his mind.* ● See also **mind-boggling.** ◆◇◇◇ V-ERG: V at n V n Also V

bog·gy /'bɒgi/. **Boggy** land is very wet and muddy. ADJ-GRADED

,bog-'standard. If you describe something as **bog-standard** you mean that is an ordinary example of its kind. ADJ-GRADED BRITISH, INFORMAL

bo·gus /'bəʊgəs/. If you describe something as **bogus,** you mean that it is not genuine. *...their bogus insurance claim.* ◆◇◇◇ ADJ-GRADED

bo·he·mian /bəʊ'hiːmiən/ **bohemians.** You can use **bohemian** to describe artistic people who live in an unconventional way. ▶ A **bohemian** is someone who lives in a bohemian way. ◆◇◇◇ ADJ-GRADED / N-COUNT

boil /bɔɪl/ **boils, boiling, boiled. 1** When a hot liquid **boils,** bubbles appear in it and it starts to change into steam or vapour. *Boil the water in the saucepan and add the sage. ...a saucepan of boiling water.* ▶ **Boil up** means the same as **boil.** *Boil up some coffee... Boil it up in half a pint of weak tea.* **2** When you **bring** a liquid **to the boil,** you heat it until it boils. When it **comes to the boil,** it begins to boil. **3** When you **boil** a kettle, or put it on to **boil,** ◆◆◇◇◇ V-ERG: V V n V-ing / PHRASAL VB V P noun V n P / PHRASE / V-ERG

you heat the water inside it until it boils. *He had nothing to do but boil the kettle and make the tea.* V n Also V

4 When you **boil** food, it is cooked in boiling water. *I'd peel potatoes and put them on to boil.* ▶ **Boil up** means the same as **boil.** *They would boil up the potatoes and they'd boil bacon.* V-ERG: V n V PHRASAL VB V P noun

5 If you **are boiling** with anger, you are very angry. VERB: V with n

6 A **boil** is a red, painful swelling on your skin, which contains a thick yellow liquid called pus. N-COUNT

7 See also **boiling.** ● to **make someone's blood boil:** see **blood.**

boil away. When you **boil away** a liquid, it is boiled until all of it changes into steam or vapour. *Check every 20 minutes that the water has not boiled away.* PHRASAL VB ERG: V P noun VP

boil down. When you **boil down** a liquid or food, it is boiled until there is less of it because some of the water in it has changed into steam or vapour. *This may seem a large quantity of mushrooms, but they do boil down.* PHRASAL VB ERG: V P noun VP

boil down to. If you say that a situation or problem **boils down to** a particular thing, you mean that this is the most important or the most basic aspect of it. *For Malcolm work could always be boiled down to one idea: being good in business.* PHRASAL VB ERG: V P P n beV-ed P P n

boil over. 1 When a liquid that is being heated **boils over,** it rises and flows over the edge of the container. **2** When someone's feelings **boil over,** they lose their temper or become violent. *Frustration and anger can boil over into direct and violent action.* PHRASAL VB VP VP / PHRASAL VB

boil up. See boil 1 and 4.

,boiled 'sweet, boiled sweets. Boiled sweets are hard sweets that are made from boiled sugar. N-COUNT BRITISH

boil·er /'bɔɪlə/ **boilers.** A **boiler** is a device which burns fuel in order to provide hot water. ◆◇◇◇ N-COUNT

'boiler suit, boiler suits. A **boiler suit** consists of a single piece of clothing that combines trousers and a shirt. You wear it over your clothes in order to protect them while you are working. The American word is **overalls.** N-COUNT BRITISH

boil·ing /'bɔɪlɪŋ/. Something that is **boiling** or **boiling hot** is very hot. *It's boiling in here.* ◆◆◇◇◇ ADJ

'boiling point. 1 The **boiling point** of a liquid is the temperature at which it starts to change into steam or vapour. **2** If a situation reaches **boiling point,** the people involved have become so angry that they can no longer remain calm. N-UNCOUNT / N-UNCOUNT

bois·ter·ous /'bɔɪstərəs/. Someone who is **boisterous** is noisy, lively, and full of energy. ♦ **bois·ter·ous·ly** *Her friends laughed boisterously.* ◆◇◇◇ ADJ-GRADED / ADV-GRADED

bold /bəʊld/ **bolder, boldest. 1** Someone who is **bold** is not afraid to do things which involve risk or danger. *Poland was already making bold economic reforms.* ♦ **bold·ly** *You can and must act boldly and confidently.* ♦ **bold·ness** *...the boldness of his economic programme.* **2** Someone who is **bold** is not shy or embarrassed in the company of other people. *He was bold enough to ask her a question.* ♦ **boldly** *'You should do it,' the girl said, boldly.* ◆◆◇◇◇ ADJ-GRADED / ADV-GRADED / N-UNCOUNT / ADJ-GRADED / ADV-GRADED

3 A **bold** colour or pattern is very bright and noticeable. ♦ **bold·ly** *The design is pretty startling and very boldly coloured.* **4** Bold lines or designs are drawn in a clear, strong way. ADJ-GRADED / ADV-GRADED / ADJ-GRADED

5 In printing, **bold** print is thicker and looks blacker than ordinary printed letters. N-UNCOUNT TECHNICAL

bo·lero, boleros. Pronounced /'bɒlərəʊ, AM bə'lerəʊ/ for meaning 1, and /bə'leərəʊ/ for meaning 2. **1** A **bolero** is a very short jacket, sometimes without sleeves. Boleros are worn mainly by women. **2** The **bolero** is a traditional Spanish dance. N-COUNT / N-COUNT

bol·lard /'bɒlɑːd/ **bollards. 1 Bollards** are short thick concrete posts that are used to prevent cars from going on to someone's land or on to part of a road. **2** A **bollard** is a strong wooden or metal post on the side of a river or harbour. Bollards are used for mooring boats. N-COUNT BRITISH / N-COUNT

bol·locks /'bɒləks/. **1 Bollocks** is a swear word which is used to express disagreement or irritation; an offensive use. **2** In very informal British English, a man's **bollocks** are his testicles. EXCLAM PRAGMATICS BRITISH / N-PLURAL

Bol·she·vik /ˈbɒlʃɪvɪk/ **Bolsheviks. 1 Bolshevik** is ADJ used to describe the political system and ideas that Lenin and his supporters introduced in Russia after the Russian Revolution of 1917. **2** A **Bolshevik** was a N-COUNT person who supported Lenin and his political ideas.

Bol·she·vism /ˈbɒlʃɪvɪzəm/. **Bolshevism** is the po- N-UNCOUNT litical system and ideas that Lenin and his support-ers introduced in Russia after the Russian Revolu-tion of 1917.

bol·shy /ˈbɒlʃi/; also spelled **bolshie**. If you say that ADJ-GRADED someone is **bolshy**, you mean that they behave in BRITISH, an argumentative and unhelpful way. INFORMAL

bol·ster /ˈbəʊlstə/ **bolsters, bolstering, bol-** ◆◆◇◇◇ **stered. 1** If you **bolster** something such as VERB someone's confidence or courage, you increase it. Vn *An early cut in interest rates bolstered confidence. ...measures intended to bolster morale.* **2** If some- VERB one tries to **bolster** their position in a situation, Vn they try to strengthen it. *Britain is free to adopt poli-cies to bolster its economy.* ▶ **Bolster up** means the PHRASAL VB same as **bolster**. *...an aid programme to bolster up* Together/on their troubled economy.* **3** A **bolster** is a firm pillow N-COUNT shaped like a long tube which is sometimes put across a bed under the ordinary pillows.
bolster up. See **bolster** 2. PHRASAL VB

bolt /bəʊlt/ **bolts, bolting, bolted. 1** A **bolt** is a ◆◆◇◇◇ long metal object which screws into a nut and is N-COUNT used to fasten things together. See picture headed **tools. 2** When you **bolt** one thing to another, you VERB fasten them firmly together, using a bolt. *The safety* Vn ton belt is easy to fit as there's no need to bolt it to seat* Vn with belt anchorage points... Bolt the components togeth-* together/on er. ...a wooden bench which was bolted to the floor.* V-ed
3 A **bolt** on a door or window is a metal bar that you N-COUNT can slide across in order to fasten the door or window.
4 When you **bolt** a door or window, you slide the bolt VERB across to fasten it. *He would have to lock and bolt the* Vn kitchen door after her. ...bolted doors.* V-ed
5 If a person or animal **bolts**, they suddenly start to VERB run very fast, often because something has frightened V them. *The pig rose squealing and bolted... I made some* V prep/adv excuse and bolted for the exit.* **6** If you **bolt** your food, VERB you eat it so quickly that you hardly chew it or taste it. Vn *Being under stress can cause you to miss meals, eat on the move, or bolt your food.* ▶ **Bolt down** means the PHRASAL VB same as **bolt**. *I like to think back to high school, when I* V P noun could bolt down three or four burgers and a pile of* Also V n P french fries.*
7 A **bolt** of lightning is a flash of lightning that is seen N-COUNT: as a white line in the sky. N ofn
8 A **bolt** of cloth is a long wide piece of it that is wound N-COUNT into a roll bound a piece of cardboard.
9 When vegetables such as lettuces or onions **bolt**, VERB: V they grow too quickly and produce flowers and seeds, and therefore become less good to eat.
10 If a piece of news comes like **a bolt from the blue**, PHRASE it is completely unexpected and very surprising. *The decision came as a bolt from the blue.* **11** If someone is PHRASE sitting or standing **bolt upright**, they are sitting or standing very straight.
12 ● **nuts and bolts**: see **nut**.
bolt down. See **bolt** 6. PHRASAL VB
bolt-hole, bolt-holes; also spelled **bolthole**. If N-COUNT you say that someone has a **bolt-hole** to go to, you BRITISH mean that there is somewhere that they can go when they want to get away from people that they know. *The hotel is less than an hour from town and is an ideal bolt-hole for Londoners.*

bomb /bɒm/ **bombs, bombing, bombed. 1** A ◆◆◆◆◇ **bomb** is a device which explodes and damages or N-COUNT destroys a large area. *Bombs went off at two London train stations.* **2** Nuclear weapons are sometimes re- N-SING: ferred to as **the bomb**. *They are generally thought to* the N have the bomb.* **3** When people **bomb** a place, they VERB attack it with bombs. *Airforce jets bombed the air-* Vn port.* ▶ **bomb·ing, bombings** ...aerial bombing of N-VAR rebel positions.* **4** See also **petrol bomb**.
bomb out. If a building or area **is bombed out**, it is PHRASAL VB destroyed by bombs. If people **are bombed out**, their PASSIVE beV-ed P

houses are destroyed by bombs. *London had been bombed out.* ● See also **bombed-out**.

bom·bard /ˌbɒmˈbɑːd/ **bombards, bombarding,** ◆◇◇◇◇ **bombarded. 1** If you **bombard** someone with VERB: something, you make them face a great deal of it. Vn with n *I've been bombarded by the press and television since* beV-ed by n *Norway.* ◆ **bom·bard·ment,** /ˌbɒmˈbɑːdmənt/ N-VAR **bombardments.** ...the constant bombardment of* images urging that work was important.* **2** When VERB soldiers **bombard** a place, they attack it with con-tinuous heavy gunfire or bombs. ◆ **bom·bard-** N-VAR **·ment** ...heavy artillery bombardments.*

bom·bast /ˈbɒmbæst/. **Bombast** is the use of long, N-UNCOUNT important-sounding words with very little meaning PRAGMATICS in an attempt to impress people; used showing disapproval.

bom·bas·tic /ˌbɒmˈbæstɪk/. If you describe some- ADJ-GRADED one as **bombastic**, you are criticizing them because PRAGMATICS they use long, important-sounding words with little meaning in an attempt to impress other people. *...the bombastic style adopted by his predecessor.*

'bomb disposal. Bomb disposal is the job of N-UNCOUNT dealing with unexploded bombs by taking out the fuse or by blowing them up in a controlled explo-sion. *Bomb disposal experts defused the devices.*

bombed-'out. A **bombed-out** building has been ADJ: ADJ n damaged or destroyed by a bomb.

bomb·er /ˈbɒmə/ **bombers. 1** A **bomber** is a mili- ◆◆◇◇◇ tary aircraft which drops bombs. **2 Bombers** are N-COUNT people who plant bombs in public places. *...Detec-* N-COUNT tives hunting the London bombers.*

'bomber jacket, bomber jackets. A **bomber** N-COUNT **jacket** is a short jacket which is gathered into a band at the waist or hips.

bomb·shell /ˈbɒmʃel/ **bombshells.** A **bombshell** ◆◇◇◇◇ is a sudden piece of bad or unexpected news. *His* N-COUNT resignation after thirteen years is a political bomb-shell.* ● If someone **drops a bombshell**, they give PHRASE you a sudden piece of bad or unexpected news.

'bomb site, bomb sites; also spelled **bombsite**. A N-COUNT **bomb site** is an empty area where a bomb has de-stroyed all the buildings.

bona fide /ˌbəʊnə ˈfaɪdi/. If something or someone ◆◇◇◇◇ is **bona fide**, they are genuine or real. *We are happy* ADJ to donate to bona fide charitable causes.* FORMAL

bona fides /ˌbəʊnə ˈfaɪdiz/. Someone's **bona fides** N-PLURAL are their good or sincere intentions. *...establishing* FORMAL or the bona fides of the persons you are dealing with.* LEGAL

bo·nan·za /bəˈnænzə/ **bonanzas.** You can refer to ◆◇◇◇◇ a sudden great increase in wealth, profitability, suc- N-COUNT cess, or luck as a **bonanza**. *The expected sales bo-nanza hadn't materialised.*

bond /bɒnd/ **bonds, bonding, bonded. 1** A ◆◆◆◆◇ **bond** between people is a strong feeling of friend- N-COUNT ship, love, or shared experiences that unites them. *The experience created a very special bond between us.* **2** When people **bond** with each other, they form V-RECIP-ERG: a relationship based on love or shared experiences. V with n You can also say that people **bond** or that some- pl-n V thing **bonds** them. *They all bonded while writing* Also V-ed, graffiti together... What had bonded them instantly* V n with n and so completely was their similar background.* ◆ **bond·ing** *They expect bonding to occur naturally.* N-UNCOUNT **3** A **bond** between people or groups is a close con- N-COUNT: nection that they have with each other, for example with supp because they have a special agreement. *The republic is successfully breaking its bonds with Moscow.*
4 Bonds are feelings, duties, or customs that force you N-PLURAL to behave in a particular way. *...a way to loosen the* LITERARY bonds of tradition.*
5 A **bond** between two things is the way in which they N-COUNT stick to one another or are joined in some way. *...car-bon atoms arranged in a ring with a triple bond be-tween two of them.* **6** When one thing **bonds** with an- V-RECIP-ERG: other, it sticks to it or becomes joined to it in some V with n way. You can also say that two things **bond** together, pl-n V or that something **bonds** them together. *In graphite* together sheets, carbon atoms bond together in rings... Strips of* beV-ed together wood are bonded together and moulded by machine.* Also V n with n
7 When a government or company issues a **bond**, it N-COUNT

borrows money from investors. The certificate which is issued to investors who lend money is also called a **bond**. *Most of it will be financed by government bonds.* ● See also **junk bond, premium bond**.

bond·age /'bɒndɪdʒ/. **1 Bondage** is the condition of being someone's property and having to work for them. *Masters sometimes allowed slaves to buy their way out of bondage.* **2 Bondage** is the condition of not being free because you are strongly influenced by something or someone. *All people, she said, lived their lives in bondage to hunger.* **3 Bondage** is the practice of being tied up, or of tying someone else up, in order to gain sexual pleasure.
— N-UNCOUNT LITERARY; N-UNCOUNT FORMAL; N-UNCOUNT

bond·holder /'bɒndhəʊldə/ **bondholders;** also spelled **bond holder.** A **bondholder** is a person who owns one or more investment bonds. — N-COUNT

bone /bəʊn/ **bones, boning, boned. 1** Your **bones** are the hard parts inside your body which together form your skeleton. *Stephen fractured a thigh bone... The body is made up primarily of bone, muscle, and fat.* **2 -boned** combines with adjectives such as 'big' and 'fine' to form adjectives which describe a person as having a particular type of bone structure or build. *He was about seven years old, small and fine-boned like his mother.* **3** If you say someone is just **skin and bone**, you mean they have become very thin, as a result of illness or lack of food. **4** If you **bone** a piece of meat or fish, you remove the bones from it before cooking it. *The boned fish is so easy to serve.* **5** A **bone** tool or ornament is made of bone. *...a pocketknife with a bone handle.* **6** If you say that you feel or know something **in your bones**, you mean you are certain about it, although you cannot explain why. **7** The **bare bones** of something are the most basic parts or details. *There are not even the bare bones of a garden here.* **8** If something such as costs are cut **to the bone**, they are reduced to an absolute minimum. **9** If you **make no bones** about your feelings, opinions, or intentions, you talk openly about them, rather than trying to keep them a secret. **10** See also **T-bone steak**.

bone 'china. **Bone china** is very fine porcelain that contains powdered bone. — N-UNCOUNT

bone 'dry; also spelled **bone-dry.** If you say that something is **bone dry**, you mean that it is very dry indeed. — ADJ

'bone marrow. **Bone marrow** is the soft fatty substance inside human or animal bones. — N-UNCOUNT

'bone meal; also spelled **bonemeal. Bone meal** is a substance made from animal bones which is used as a fertilizer. — N-UNCOUNT

bone of con'tention, bones of contention. If a particular matter or issue is a **bone of contention**, it is the subject of a disagreement or argument. — N-COUNT

bon·fire /'bɒnfaɪə/ **bonfires.** A **bonfire** is a fire that is made outdoors, usually to burn rubbish. — N-COUNT

bong /bɒŋ/ **bongs.** A **bong** is a long deep sound such as the sound made by a big bell. — N-COUNT; SOUND

bon·go /'bɒŋɡəʊ/ **bongos.** A **bongo** is a small drum that you play with your hands. — N-COUNT

bon·ho·mie /'bɒnəmi/. **Bonhomie** is happy jolly friendliness. *...his soft-spoken bonhomie.* — N-UNCOUNT FORMAL

bonk /bɒŋk/ **bonks, bonking, bonked.** In informal British English, if two people **bonk**, they have sexual intercourse. *He is bonking most of the female staff.* ♦ **bonk·ing** *Basically, bonking in public is illegal.* — V-RECIP; N-UNCOUNT

bonk·ers /'bɒŋkəz/. If you say that someone is **bonkers**, you mean that they are silly or mad. — ADJ; INFORMAL

bon·net /'bɒnɪt/ **bonnets. 1** The **bonnet** of a car is the metal cover over the engine at the front. The American word is **hood**. See picture headed **car and bicycle**. **2** A **bonnet** is a hat worn by babies that has ribbons that are tied under the chin. **3** ● to **have a bee in** your **bonnet**: see **bee**. — N-COUNT BRITISH; N-COUNT

bon·ny /'bɒni/ **bonnier, bonniest.** Someone or something that is **bonny** is attractive and nice to look at; used in Scotland and parts of Northern England. *Jemima was a bonny Highland lassie of 15.* — ADJ-GRADED

bon·sai /'bɒnsaɪ/; **bonsai** is both the singular and the plural form. **1** A **bonsai** is a tree or shrub that has been kept very small by growing it in a little pot and trimming it in a special way. **2 Bonsai** is the art of growing miniature shrubs and trees. — N-COUNT; N-UNCOUNT

bo·nus /'bəʊnəs/ **bonuses. 1** A **bonus** is an extra amount of money that is added to someone's pay, usually because they have worked very hard. **2** A **bonus** is something good that you get in addition to something else, and which you would not usually expect. *It's made from natural ingredients, but with the added bonus of containing 30 per cent less fat.* — N-COUNT

bon vo·yage /ˌbɒn vɔɪˈɑːʒ/. You say **'bon voyage'** to someone who is going on a journey, as a way of saying goodbye and wishing them good luck. — CONVENTION PRAGMATICS

bony /'bəʊni/. **1** Someone who has a **bony** face or **bony** hands, for example, has an unattractively thin face or thin hands. **2** The **bony** parts of a person's or animal's body are the parts made of bone. *...the bony ridge of the eye socket.* **3** If you describe fish that you are eating as **bony**, you mean that it has a lot of bones in it. — ADJ-GRADED PRAGMATICS; ADJ; ADJ-GRADED

boo /buː/ **boos, booing, booed. 1** If you boo a speaker or performer, you shout 'boo' or make other loud sounds to indicate that you do not like them, their opinions, or their performance. *Demonstrators booed and jeered him... He was booed off the stage.* ► Also a noun. *She was greeted with boos and hisses.* ♦ **boo·ing** *The fans are entitled to their opinion but booing doesn't help anyone.* **2** You say **'Boo!'** loudly and suddenly when you want to surprise someone who does not know that you are there. — VERB: V n; Also V; N-COUNT; N-UNCOUNT; EXCLAM

boob /buːb/ **boobs, boobing, boobed. 1** A woman's **boobs** are her breasts. Some people find this use offensive. **2** If you **boob**, you make a mistake. ► Also a noun. *The government once again has made a big boob.* — N-COUNT INFORMAL; VERB: V INFORMAL, BRITISH; N-COUNT

boo·by prize /'buːbi praɪz/ **booby prizes.** The **booby prize** is a prize given as a joke to the person who comes last in a competition. — N-COUNT

booby-trap /'buːbi træp/ **booby-traps, booby-trapping, booby-trapped;** also spelled **booby trap. 1** A **booby-trap** is something such as a bomb which is hidden or disguised and which causes death or injury when it is touched. **2** If something is **booby-trapped**, a booby-trap is placed in it or on it. *His booby-trapped car exploded.* — N-COUNT; VERB: be V-ed, V-ed

boo·ger /'buːɡə/ **boogers.** A **booger** is a piece of dried mucus that comes from inside your nose. The British word is **bogey**. — N-COUNT INFORMAL, AMERICAN

boo·gie /'buːɡi/ **boogies, boogying** or **boogieing, boogied.** When you **boogie**, you dance to fast pop music. — VERB: V INFORMAL

book /bʊk/ **books, booking, booked. 1** A **book** is a number of pieces of paper, usually with words printed on them, which are fastened together and fixed inside a cover of stronger paper or cardboard. **2** In a very long written work such as the Bible, a **book** is one of the sections into which it is divided. **3** A **book** of something such as stamps, matches, or tickets is a small number of them fastened together between thin cardboard covers. **4** See also **cheque book, phone book**. **5** A company's or organization's **books** are its records of money that has been spent and earned, or of the names of people who belong to it. *12 per cent of the people on our books are in the computing industry.* **6** When you **book** something such as a hotel room or a ticket, you arrange to have it or use it at a particular time. *Laurie revealed she had booked herself a flight home. ...three-star restaurants that are normally booked for months in advance.* **7** If a hotel, restaurant, theatre, or transport service is **fully booked** or **booked solid**, it has no rooms, tables, tickets left for a particular time or date. **8** See also **booking**. **9** When a football referee **books** a player who has seriously broken the rules of the game, he or she officially records the player's name. **10** When a police officer **books** someone, he or she officially records their name and the offence that they may be charged with. — N-COUNT; N-PLURAL; VERB: V n, V n n, V-ed; PHRASE; VERB: V n BRITISH; VERB: V n INFORMAL

bookable

11 If someone **is brought to book**, they are punished PHRASE for an offence or are made to explain their behaviour officially. **12** If someone in authority **throws the book** PHRASE **at** someone else who has committed an offence, they give them the greatest punishment that they are allowed to. **13** If you are **in** someone's **bad books**, they are an- PHRASE noyed with you. If you are **in** their **good books**, they are pleased with you. **14** If you say that someone or PHRASE something is a **closed book** to you, you mean that you do not know anything about them. *Economics was a closed book to him.* **15** **In my book** means 'in my PHRASE opinion' or 'according to my beliefs'. *The greatest manager there has ever been, or ever will be in my book, is retiring.* **16** ● to **take a leaf out of someone's book**: see **leaf**.

book in or **book into**. When you **book into** a hotel PHRASAL VB or when you **book in**, you officially state that you have arrived to stay there, usually by signing your name in a register. The American term is **check in**. *Today Mahoney booked himself into one of the best hotels in Sydney... The three men stayed at two hotels in Nottingham, booking in at one the day before the crime.*

book·able /ˈbʊkəbəl/. **1** If something such as a ADJ theatre seat or plane ticket is **bookable**, it can be BRITISH booked in advance. **2** In sports such as football, a ADJ **bookable** offence is a foul for which a player can be officially warned by the referee.

book·bind·ing /ˈbʊkbaɪndɪŋ/; also spelled **book-** N-UNCOUNT **binding**. **Bookbinding** is the work of fastening books together and putting covers on them. ♦ **book·binder** /ˈbʊkbaɪndə/ **bookbinders** *His fa-* N-COUNT *ther was a bookbinder.*

book·case /ˈbʊkkeɪs/ **bookcases**. A bookcase is ◆◇◇◇ a piece of furniture with shelves for books. N-COUNT

book club, **book clubs**. A **book club** is an or- N-COUNT ganization that offers books at reduced prices to its members.

booked 'up. **1** If a hotel, restaurant, theatre, or ADJ-GRADED: transport service is **booked up**, it has no rooms, ta- v-link ADJ bles, or tickets left for a particular time or date. **2** If BRITISH someone is **booked up**, they have made so many ADJ-GRADED: arrangements that they have no more time free for v-link ADJ any other engagements. BRITISH

book·end /ˈbʊkend/ **bookends**; also spelled N-COUNT **book-end**. **Bookends** are a pair of supports used to hold a row of books in an upright position. You place one bookend at each end of the row.

bookie /ˈbʊki/ **bookies**. A **bookie** is the same as a ◆◇◇◇ **bookmaker**. N-COUNT INFORMAL

book·ing /ˈbʊkɪŋ/ **bookings**. A **booking** is the ar- ◆◆◇◇ rangement that you make when you **book** some- N-COUNT thing such as a hotel room or a table at a restaurant. *There was a mistake over his late booking.*

'booking office, booking offices. A **booking of-** N-COUNT **fice** is a room where tickets are sold and booked, es- BRITISH pecially in a theatre or station. The American expression is **ticket office**.

book·ish /ˈbʊkɪʃ/. If you describe someone as ADJ-GRADED **bookish**, you mean they spend a lot of their time reading serious books.

book·keeping /ˈbʊkki:pɪŋ/; also spelled **book-** N-UNCOUNT **keeping**. **Bookkeeping** is the job or activity of keeping an accurate record of the money that is spent and received by a business or other organization. ♦ **book·keeper** /ˈbʊkki:pə/ **bookkeepers** *His* N-COUNT *wife served as billing clerk and bookkeeper.*

book·let /ˈbʊklət/ **booklets**. A **booklet** is a small ◆◆◇◇ book that has a paper cover and that gives you in- N-COUNT formation about something.

book·maker /ˈbʊkmeɪkə/ **bookmakers**. A book- ◆◇◇◇ maker is a person whose job is to take your money N-COUNT when you bet and to pay you money if you win.

book·making /ˈbʊkmeɪkɪŋ/. **Bookmaking** is the N-UNCOUNT activity of taking people's money when they bet and paying them money if they win.

book·mark /ˈbʊkmɑ:k/ **bookmarks**. A bookmark N-COUNT is a narrow piece of card or leather that you put between the pages of a book so that you can find a particular page easily.

book·sell·er /ˈbʊkselə/ **booksellers**. A ◆◇◇◇ **bookseller** is a person who sells books, or a compa- N-COUNT ny that owns bookshops.

book·shelf /ˈbʊkʃelf/ **bookshelves**. A bookshelf ◆◇◇◇ is a shelf on which you keep books. N-COUNT

book·shop /ˈbʊkʃɒp/ **bookshops**. A bookshop is ◆◇◇◇ a shop where books are sold. The American word is N-COUNT **bookstore**. BRITISH

book·stall /ˈbʊkstɔ:l/ **bookstalls**. **1** A bookstall is N-COUNT a long table from which books and magazines are sold, for example in a street market. **2** A bookstall is N-COUNT a small shop with an open front where books and BRITISH magazines are sold. Bookstalls are usually found in railway stations and airports. The usual American word is **newsstand**.

book·store /ˈbʊkstɔ:/ **bookstores**. A bookstore ◆◇◇◇ is a shop where books are sold. The usual British N-COUNT word is **bookshop**. AMERICAN

book·worm /ˈbʊkwɜ:m/ **bookworms**. If you de- N-COUNT scribe someone as a **bookworm**, you mean they are INFORMAL very fond of reading.

boom /bu:m/ **booms, booming, boomed**. **1** If ◆◆◆◇◇ there is a **boom** in the economy, there is an in- N-COUNT crease in economic activity. **2** A **boom** in something N-COUNT is an increase in its amount, frequency, or success. *The boom in the sport's popularity has meant more calls for stricter safety regulations.* **3** If the economy VERB or a business **is booming**, the amount of things be- V ing bought or sold is increasing. *Sales are booming.* **4** On a boat, the **boom** is the long pole which is at- N-COUNT tached to the bottom of the sail and to the mast and which you move when you want to change direction. **5** A **boom** is a large floating barrier that is used for N-COUNT stopping an oil spillage from spreading. **6** When something such as someone's voice, a can- VERB non, or a big drum **booms**, it makes a loud, deep, V with quote echoing sound. *'Ladies,' boomed Helena, 'we all know* V prep/adv *why we're here tonight.'... Thunder boomed like battle-* Also V *field cannons over Crooked Mountain.* ▶ **Boom out** PHRASAL VB means the same as **boom**. *Music boomed out from* ERG: V P *loudspeakers... He boomed out a greeting.* ▶ Also a V P noun N-COUNT; noun. *The stillness of night was broken by the boom of* SOUND *a cannon.* **7** See also **baby boom**.

boom out. See **boom** 6. PHRASAL VB

boom·er·ang /ˈbu:məræŋ/ **boomerangs, boom-** eranging, boomeranged. **1** A boomerang is a N-COUNT curved piece of wood which comes back to you if you throw it in the correct way. **2** If a plan **boomer-** VERB: V **angs**, its result is not the one that was intended and V on/against n is harmful to the person who made the plan. *He risks defeat in the referendum which he called, but which threatens to boomerang against him.*

'boom town, boom towns; also spelled **boom-** N-COUNT **town**. A **boom town** is a town which has become very rich and full of people, usually because industry or business has developed rapidly there.

boon /bu:n/ **boons**. You can describe something ◆◇◇◇ as a **boon** when it makes life a lot better or easier N-COUNT for someone. *This battery booster is a boon for photographers.*

boor·ish /ˈbʊərɪʃ/. **Boorish** behaviour is rough, un- ADJ-GRADED educated, and rude.

boost /bu:st/ **boosts, boosting, boosted**. **1** If ◆◆◇◇ one thing boosts another, it causes it to increase, VERB improve, or be more successful. *The move is de-* V n *signed to boost sales during the peak booking months.* ▶ Also a noun. *It would get the economy* N-COUNT *going and give us the boost that we need.* **2** If some- VERB: V n thing **boosts** your confidence or morale, it improves it. ▶ Also a noun. *It did give me a boost to win such* N-COUNT *a big event.*

boost·er /ˈbu:stə/ **boosters**. **1** A booster is some- ◆◇◇◇ thing that increases a positive or desirable quality. N-COUNT *Praise is a great confidence booster.* **2** A booster is N-COUNT an extra engine in a machine such as a space rocket, which provides an extra amount of power at certain times. **3** A booster is a small injection of a drug N-COUNT that you have some time after a larger injection, in

order to make sure that the first injection will remain effective.

boot /buːt/ **boots, booting, booted. 1 Boots** are ◆◆◇◇◇ N-COUNT shoes that cover your whole foot and the lower part of your leg. See picture headed **clothes**. ● See also **wellington. 2 Boots** are also strong heavy shoes N-COUNT which cover your ankle and which have thick soles. **3** If you **boot** something such as a ball, you kick it VERB hard. *He booted the ball 40 yards back up field.* V n adv/prep **4** If you **get the boot** or **are given the boot**, you are INFORMAL PHRASE told that you are not wanted any more, either in your INFORMAL job or by someone you are having a relationship with. **5** If someone **puts the boot in**, they attack someone PHRASE by saying something cruel, often when the person is INFORMAL, BRITISH already feeling weak or upset. **6** The **boot** of a car is a covered space at the back or N-COUNT front, in which you carry things such as luggage or BRITISH shopping. The American word is **trunk**. See picture headed **car and bicycle. 7** You can say **to boot** when you are mentioning an PHRASE additional thing. *He is making money and receiving* PRAGMATICS *free advertising to boot!*

boot out. If you are **booted out** of a job, organiza- PHRASAL VB tion, or place, you are forced to leave. *Schools are* V P noun *booting out record numbers of unruly pupils.* INFORMAL

'boot camp, boot camps. In the United States, a N-VAR **boot camp** is a camp where army, navy, or marine recruits are trained.

booth /buːð/ **booths. 1** A **booth** is a small area ◆◇◇◇◇ separated from a larger public area by screens or N-COUNT thin walls where, for example, people can make a telephone call or vote in secret. **2** In some restau- N-COUNT rants, **booths** are small areas that are separated from the rest of the room by low screens so that people can have a meal in private. **3** A **booth** is a N-COUNT small tent or stall, usually at a fair, in which you can buy goods or watch some form of entertainment.

boot·leg /ˈbuːtleg/ **bootlegs, bootlegging,** ◆◇◇◇◇ **bootlegged. 1 Bootleg** is used to describe some- ADJ: ADJ n thing that is made secretly and sold illegally. *...a bootleg recording of the band's 1977 tour of Scandi- navia.* **2** To **bootleg** something such as a recording VERB: V n means to make and sell it illegally. *Avid Bob Dylan* V-ed *fans treasure bootlegged recordings.* ▶ Also a noun. N-COUNT *The record was a bootleg.* ◆ **boot·leg·ger, boot-** N-COUNT **leggers** *Bootleggers sold 75 million dollars-worth of copies.*

boot·straps /ˈbuːtstræps/. If you have **pulled** your- PHRASE self **up by** your **bootstraps**, you have achieved suc- cess by your own efforts, starting from very difficult circumstances and without help from anyone else.

boo·ty /ˈbuːti/. **Booty** is a collection of valuable N-UNCOUNT things stolen from a place, especially by soldiers after a battle.

booze /buːz/ **boozes, boozing, boozed.** ◆◇◇◇◇ **1 Booze** is alcoholic drink. *There was even a black* N-UNCOUNT *market in booze.* **2** If people **booze**, they drink alco- INFORMAL VERB: V hol. *...a load of drunken businessmen who had been* INFORMAL *boozing all afternoon.* ◆ **booz·ing** *...the boozing* N-UNCOUNT *and girl-chasing of her husband.*

booz·er /ˈbuːzə/ **boozers. 1** A **boozer** is a pub. *She* N-COUNT *once caught him in a boozer with another woman.* BRITISH, INFORMAL **2** A **boozer** is a person who drinks a lot of alcohol. N-COUNT *We thought he was a bit of a boozer.* INFORMAL

boozy /ˈbuːzi/. A **boozy** person is someone who ADJ drinks a lot of alcohol. INFORMAL

bop /bɒp/ **bops, bopping, bopped. 1** A **bop** is a N-COUNT dance. *People just want a good tune and a good bop.* INFORMAL **2** If you **bop**, you dance. *He was bopping around,* VERB: V *snapping his fingers.* **3** See also **bebop.** INFORMAL

bop·per /ˈbɒpə/. See **teenybopper.**

bo·rax /ˈbɔːræks/. **Borax** is a white powder used, for N-UNCOUNT example, in the making of glass or as a cleaning chemical.

bor·del·lo /ˌbɔːˈdeləʊ/ **bordellos.** A **bordello** is a N-COUNT **brothel.** LITERARY

bor·der /ˈbɔːdə/ **borders, bordering, bordered.** ◆◆◆◇◇ **1** The **border** between two countries or regions is N-COUNT the dividing line between them. Sometimes **the border** also refers to the land close to this line. *They*

fled across the border. ...the Mexican border town of VERB *Tijuana.* **2** A country that **borders** another country, V n a sea, or a river is next to it. *He spent his time in the countries bordering Iran.* ▶ **Border on** means the PHRASAL VB same as **border**. *Both republics border on the Black* V P n *Sea.* **3** If something **is bordered** by another thing, VERB the other thing is situated along the edge of it. *...the* V-ed *mile of white sand beach bordered by palm trees and* Also V n *tropical flowers.* **4** A **border** is a strip or band around the edge of some- N-COUNT thing. *...pillowcases trimmed with a hand-crocheted border.* **5** In a garden, a **border** is a strip of ground N-COUNT planted with flowers along the edge of a lawn.

border on. If you talk about a characteristic or situa- PHRASAL VB tion **bordering on** something, usually something that V P n you consider bad, you mean that it is almost that thing. *...the self-confidence, bordering on arrogance, of his predecessor.* ● See also **border** 2.

bor·der·land /ˈbɔːdəlænd/ **borderlands. 1** The N-SING **borderland** between two things is an area which contains features from both things so that it is not possible to say that it belongs to one or the other. *...rather like being on the borderland between sleep and waking.* **2** The area of land close to the border N-COUNT between two countries or major areas can be called the **borderlands.** *...Lebanon's southern borderlands.*

bor·der·line /ˈbɔːdəlaɪn/ **borderlines. 1** The ◆◇◇◇◇ **borderline** between two different or opposite things N-COUNT is the division between them. *...exploring the borderline between painting and photography.* **2** Something that is **borderline** is only just accept- ADJ-GRADED able as a member of a class or group. *Some were ob- viously unsuitable and could be ruled out at once. Others were borderline cases.*

bore /bɔː/ **bores, boring, bored. 1** If someone or ◆◆◆◇◇ something **bores** you, you find them dull and unin- VERB: V n teresting. *Dickie bored him all through the meal* V n *with stories of the Navy.* **2** If you say that someone PHRASE or something **bores** you **to tears**, **bores** you **to** PRAGMATICS **death**, or **bores** you **stiff**, you mean that they bore INFORMAL you very much indeed. **3** You describe someone as N-COUNT a **bore** when you think that they talk in a very unin- teresting way. **4** You can describe a situation as **a** N-SING: **bore** when you find it annoying or a nuisance. *It's a* aN *bore to be sick, and the novelty of lying in bed all day wears off quickly.* **5** See also **bored, boring. 6** If you **bore** a hole in something, you make a deep VERB: V n round hole in it using a special tool. **7** If someone's VERB: eyes **bore** into you, they stare intensely at you. *Her* V into n *eyes seemed to bore a hole in mine.* V n in n WRITTEN **8** A **bore** is a very large wave that moves quickly up N-COUNT certain river estuaries from the sea at particular times of the year as a result of unusual tides. **9 Bore** is the past tense of **bear**.

-bore /-bɔː/. **-bore** combines with numbers to form COMB adjectives which indicate the diameter of the barrel of a gun. *...a 12-bore shotgun.*

bored /bɔːd/. If you are **bored**, you feel tired and ◆◆◇◇◇ impatient because you have lost interest in some- ADJ-GRADED thing or because you have nothing to do. *I am get- ting very bored with this entire business.*

bore·dom /ˈbɔːdəm/. **1 Boredom** is the state of be- ◆◇◇◇◇ ing bored. *He had given up attending lectures out of* N-UNCOUNT *sheer boredom.* **2** The **boredom** of a state or situa- N-UNCOUNT tion is the quality that it has which makes it boring. *They often find they begin to chat to relieve the bore- dom of the flight.*

bore·hole /ˈbɔːhəʊl/ **boreholes.** A **borehole** is a N-COUNT deep round hole made by a special tool or machine, especially one that is made in the ground when searching for oil or water.

bor·ing /ˈbɔːrɪŋ/. Someone or something that is ◆◆◇◇◇ **boring** is so dull and uninteresting that they make ADJ-GRADED people tired and impatient. *...boring work. ...boring television programmes.* ◆ **bor·ing·ly** *Italian frascati* ADV-GRADED *can be boringly tasteless.*

born /bɔːn/. **1** When a baby **is born**, it comes out V-PASSIVE of its mother's body at the beginning of its life. *My* be V-ed *mother was 40 when I was born.* **2** If you say that V-PASSIVE be someone **is born** of someone or to someone, you V-ed of/to n FORMAL

mean that person is their parent. *He was born of German parents and lived most of his life abroad.* **3** If someone **is born** with a particular disease, handicap, or characteristic, they have it from the time they are born. *Some people are born brainy... We are all born leaders; we just need the right circumstances in which to flourish.* **4** You can use **be born** in front of a particular name to show that a person was given this name at birth, although they may be better known by another name. *She was born Jenny Harvey on June 11, 1946.* **5** You use **born** to describe someone who has a natural ability to do a particular activity or job. For example, if you are a **born** cook, you have a natural ability to cook well. **6** When an idea or organization **is born**, it comes into existence. If something **is born** of a particular emotion or activity, it exists as a result of that emotion or activity. *The idea for the show was born in his hospital room... Energy conservation as a philosophy was born out of the 1973 oil crisis.* **7** See also **-born**; **first born**, **newborn**. ● to **be born and bred**: see **breed**. ● to **be born with a silver spoon in** your **mouth**: see **spoon**.

`V-PASSIVE: be V-ed with n be V-ed adj`
`V-PASSIVE: no cont be V-ed n be V-ed n FORMAL`
`ADJ: ADJ n`
`V-PASSIVE: be V-ed be V-ed out of/of n FORMAL`

-born /-bɔːn/. **-born** combines with adjectives that relate to countries or with the names of towns and areas to form adjectives that indicate where someone was born. *The German-born photographer was admired by writers such as Oscar Wilde.* `COMB JOURNALISM`

borne /bɔːn/. **Borne** is the past participle of **bear**.

-borne /-bɔːn/. **-borne** combines with nouns to form adjectives that describe the method or means by which something is carried or moved. *...waterborne diseases.* `COMB`

bor·ough /ˈbʌrə, AM ˈbɜːrəʊ/ **boroughs**. A **borough** is a town, or a district within a large town, which has its own council. `◆◆◇◇◇ N-COUNT`

bor·row /ˈbɒrəʊ/ **borrows, borrowing, borrowed**. **1** If you **borrow** something that belongs to someone else, you take it or use it for a period of time, usually with their permission. *Can I borrow a pen please?*. **2** If you **borrow** money from someone or from a bank, they give it to you and you agree to pay it back at some time in the future. *Kuwait borrowed $5.5 billion from foreign banks last year... It's so expensive to borrow from finance companies.* ♦ **bor·row·er**, **borrowers** *...borrowers with fixed-rate mortgages.* ♦ **bor·row·ing** *We have allowed spending and borrowing to rise in this recession.* **3** If you **borrow** a book from a library, you take it away for a fixed period of time. *I couldn't afford to buy any, so I borrowed them from the library.* **4** If you **borrow** something such as a word or an idea from another language or from another person's work, you use it in your own language or work. *I borrowed his words for my book's title.* ♦ **bor·row·ing**, **borrowings**. A **borrowing** is something such as a word or idea which has been borrowed. `◆◆◆◇◇`
`VERB V n`
`VERB V n from n V from n Also V n, V`
`N-COUNT`
`N-UNCOUNT: also N in pl`
`VERB V n from n`
`VERB V n`
`N-COUNT`

5 Someone who is **living on borrowed time** or who is **on borrowed time** has continued to live or to do something for longer than was expected, and is likely to die or to stop doing it soon. `PHRASE`

bor·stal /ˈbɔːstəl/ **borstals**. A **borstal** was a kind of prison for young criminals, who were not old enough to be sent to ordinary prisons. `N-VAR BRITAIN`

bos·om /ˈbʊzəm/ **bosoms**. **1** A woman's breasts are sometimes referred to as her **bosom** or her **bosoms**. `◆◇◇◇◇ N-COUNT DATED` **2** If you are in **the bosom** of your family or of a community, you are among people who love, accept, and protect you. *Joan was delighted to welcome her boyfriend into the bosom of her large, close-knit family.* `N-SING: the N of n LITERARY` **3** A **bosom** friend is a friend who you know very well and like very much indeed. *Sakota was her cousin and bosom pal.* `ADJ: ADJ n` **4** If you take someone or something **to your bosom**, you accept them and treat or regard them with great affection. `PHRASE LITERARY`

boss /bɒs/ **bosses, bossing, bossed**. **1** Your **boss** is the person in charge of the organization or department where you work. *He cannot stand his* `◆◆◆◆◇ N-COUNT`

boss. **2** If you say that someone **bosses** you, you mean that they keep telling you what to do in a way that is irritating. *We cannot boss them into doing more.* ▶ **Boss around**, or in British English **boss about**, means the same as **boss**. *He started bossing people around and I didn't like what was happening.* **3** If you **are** your **own boss**, you work for yourself or make your own decisions and do not have anyone telling you what to do. `VERB: V n V n prep/adv`
`PHRASAL VB V n P Also V P noun`
`PHRASE`

boss around or **boss about**. See **boss** 2. `PHRASAL VB`

bossy /ˈbɒsi/. If you describe someone as **bossy**, you mean that they enjoy telling people what to do; used showing disapproval. *...a rather bossy little girl.* `ADJ-GRADED [PRAGMATICS]`

bo·sun /ˈbəʊsən/ **bosuns**. The **bosun** on a ship is the officer whose job it is to look after the maintenance of the ship and its equipment. `N-COUNT`

bo·tan·ic /bəˈtænɪk/. **Botanic** means the same as **botanical**. `ADJ: ADJ n`

bo·tani·cal /bəˈtænɪkəl/ **botanicals**. **1** Botanical books, research, and activities relate to the scientific study of plants. *The area is of great botanical interest.* **2** Botanicals are drugs which are made from plants. `◆◇◇◇◇ ADJ: ADJ n`
`N-COUNT`

bota·ny /ˈbɒtəni/. **Botany** is the scientific study of plants. *...a professor of botany.* ♦ **bota·nist** /ˈbɒtənɪst/ **botanists**. `◆◇◇◇◇ N-UNCOUNT N-COUNT`

botch /bɒtʃ/ **botches, botching, botched**. **1** If you **botch** something that you are doing, you do it badly or clumsily. *It is a silly idea and he has botched it.* ▶ **Botch up** means the same as **botch**. *I hate having builders botch up repairs on my house.* **2** If you make a **botch** of something that you are doing, you botch it. *I rather made a botch of that whole thing.* `◆◇◇◇◇ VERB V n INFORMAL`
`PHRASAL VB V P noun Also V n P`
`N-COUNT INFORMAL`

botch-up, botch-ups. A **botch-up** is the same as a **botch**. *Tony Ward described the case as a 'sad botch-up'.* `N-COUNT INFORMAL`

both /bəʊθ/. **1** You use **both** when you are referring to two people or things and saying that something is true about each of them. *He gripped her suddenly by both arms... Put both vegetables into a bowl.* ▶ Also a quantifier. *Both of us had tears in our eyes.* ▶ Also a pronoun. *Miss Brown and her friend, both from Stoke, were arrested... Well, I'll leave you both then.* **2** You use the structure **both...and** when you are giving two facts or alternatives and emphasizing that each of them is true or possible. *Now women work both before and after having their children.* `◆◆◆◆◆ DET`
`QUANT`
`PRON`
`CONJ`

both·er /ˈbɒðə/ **bothers, bothering, bothered**. **1** If you do not **bother** to do something or if you do not **bother** with it, you do not do it, consider it, or use it because you think it is unnecessary or because you are too lazy. *Lots of people don't bother to go through a marriage ceremony... Most of the papers didn't even bother reporting it... He does not bother with a helmet.* **2** If you say that you **can't be bothered** to do something, you mean that you are not going to do it because you think it is unnecessary or because you are too lazy. *I just can't be bothered to look after the house.* `◆◆◆◇◇ VB: with brd-neg V to-inf V -ing V with/about n Also V`
`PHRASE INFORMAL`

3 Bother means trouble, complication, or difficulty. You can also use **bother** to refer to an activity which causes this, especially when you would prefer not to do it or get involved with it. *I usually buy sliced bread – it's less bother... We did have a bit of bother with the mortgage people... Going to the police is a bother.* **4** If you say '**it's no bother**' after offering to do something for someone, you are emphasizing that you really want to do it and that it will take very little effort. *I'll drive you back to your hotel later. It's no bother.* **5** If something **bothers** you, or if you **bother** about it, it worries, annoys, or upsets you. *It bothered me that boys weren't interested in me... Never bother about people's opinions.* ♦ **both·ered** *I was bothered about the blister on my hand.* `N-UNCOUNT: also a N`
`CONVENTION [PRAGMATICS]`
`V-ERG: V n it V n that/ when V about n`
`ADJ-GRADED: v-link ADJ`

6 If someone **bothers** you, they talk to you when you want to be left alone or interrupt you when you are busy. *I don't know why he bothers me with this kind of rubbish.* `VERB: V n V n with/ about n`

both·er·some /ˈbɒðəsəm/. Someone or something that is **bothersome** is annoying or irritating. `ADJ-GRADED` `DATED`

bot·tle /ˈbɒtəl/ **bottles, bottling, bottled.** **1** A **bottle** is a glass or plastic container in which drinks and other liquids are kept. Bottles are usually round with straight sides and a narrow top. *...two empty beer bottles. ...a bottle of wine.* ▶ A **bottle** of something is an amount of it contained in a bottle. *He had drunk half a bottle of whisky.* **2** A **bottle** is a drinking container for babies, with a special rubber part at the top through which they can suck their drink. ▶ A **bottle** is also the amount of drink contained in a baby's bottle. **3** To **bottle** a drink or other liquid means to put it into bottles after it has been made. *...equipment to automatically bottle the wine.* ♦ **bot·tler, bottlers** *...the nation's largest Coca-Cola bottler.* `◆◆◆◇` `N-COUNT`

4 Bottle is used to refer to courage or boldness. *Will anyone have the bottle to go through with it?* `N-UNCOUNT` `BRITISH,` `INFORMAL` **5** See also **bottled; hot-water bottle, water bottle.**

bottle out. If you **bottle out**, you lose your courage at the last moment and do not do something you intended to do. *I haven't come all this way to bottle out.* `PHRASAL VB` `V P` `BRITISH,` `INFORMAL`

bottle up. If you **bottle up** strong feelings, you do not express them or show them, especially when this makes you tense or angry; used showing disapproval. *Tension in the home increases if you bottle things up... Be assertive rather than bottle up anger.* `PHRASAL VB` `PRAGMATICS` `V n P` `V P noun`

ˈbottle bank, bottle banks. A **bottle bank** is a large container into which people can put empty bottles so that they can be recycled and used again. `N-COUNT` `BRITISH`

bot·tled /ˈbɒtəld/. **Bottled** gas is kept under pressure in special metal cylinders which can be moved from one place to another. ● See also **bottle.** `ADJ`

ˈbottle-feed, bottle-feeds, bottle-feeding, bottle-fed. If you **bottle-feed** a baby, you give it milk in a bottle rather than the baby sucking milk from its mother's breasts. `VERB: V n`

ˌbottle-ˈgreen; also spelled **bottle green.** Something that is **bottle-green** is dark green. `COLOUR`

bottle·neck /ˈbɒtəlnek/ **bottlenecks. 1** A **bottleneck** is a place where traffic slows down or stops, for example because the road narrows or because there is a junction. **2** A **bottleneck** is a situation that stops something from progressing further. *He pushed everyone full speed ahead until production hit a bottleneck.* `N-COUNT` `N-COUNT`

ˈbottle-opener, bottle-openers. A **bottle-opener** is a metal device for removing the tops from bottles. `N-COUNT`

bot·tom /ˈbɒtəm/ **bottoms, bottoming, bottomed. 1** The **bottom** of something is the lowest or deepest part of it. *He sat at the bottom of the stairs... Answers can be found at the bottom of page 8.* **2** The **bottom** of something such as a sea, lake, valley or ditch is the ground underneath it or at its floor. *...the damp sand of the canyon bottom.* **3** The **bottom** thing or layer in a series of things or layers is the lowest one. *...the bottom drawer of the cupboard.* **4** The **bottom** of a hollow object is the flat surface at its lowest point. You can also refer to the inside or outside of this surface as the **bottom.** *Spread the onion slices on the bottom of the dish. ...the bottom of his right foot.* ♦ **-bottomed** /-ˈbɒtəmd/. *...a loose-bottomed cake tin. ...a glass-bottomed boat.* **5** ● to **scrape the bottom of the barrel:** see **barrel.** `◆◆◆◇` `N-COUNT` `N-COUNT` `ADJ: ADJ n` `N-COUNT` `COMB`

6 If you say that **the bottom** has dropped out of a market, you mean that people have stopped buying a particular product. *The bottom had fallen out of the city's property market.* `N-SING:` `theN` `JOURNALISM`

7 The lower part of a bikini, tracksuit, or pair of pyjamas can be referred to as the **bottoms** or the **bottom.** *...blue tracksuit bottoms.* `N-COUNT`

8 The **bottom** of a street, garden, bed, or table is the end of it that is farthest away from where you usually enter it, or from where you are. *...the Cathedral at the bottom of the street.* `N-SING:` `theN`

9 The **bottom** of an organization or career structure is the lowest level in it, where new employees often start. *He had worked in the theatre for many years,* `N-SING:` `theN`

starting at the bottom. **10** If someone is **bottom** or at **the bottom** in a survey, test, or league, their performance is worse than that of all the other people involved. *He was always bottom of the class.* `N-SING:` `theN,` `also no det`

11 Your **bottom** is the part of your body that you sit on. See picture headed **human body.** `N-COUNT`

12 You use **at bottom** to emphasize that you are stating what you think is the real nature of something or the real truth about a situation. *The two systems are, at bottom, conceptual models.* **13** If something is **at the bottom** of a problem or unpleasant situation, it is the real cause of it. *Anger and resentment are at the bottom of the problem.* **14** If you want to **get to the bottom** of a problem, you want to solve it by finding out its real cause. `PHRASE` `PHRASE` `PHRASE`

15 See also **rock bottom.**

bottom out. If a trend such as a fall in prices **bottoms out**, it stops getting worse or decreasing, and remains at a particular level or amount. *He expects the recession to bottom out.* `PHRASAL VB` `V P` `JOURNALISM`

bot·tom·less /ˈbɒtəmləs/. **1** If you describe a supply of something as **bottomless**, you mean that it seems so large that it will never run out. *Princess Anne does not have a bottomless purse... The problem is we don't have a bottomless pit of resources.* **2** If you describe something as **bottomless**, you mean that it is so deep that it seems to have no bottom. *His eyes were like bottomless brown pools.* `ADJ` `ADJ`

ˌbottom ˈline, bottom lines. 1 The **bottom line** in a decision or situation is the most important factor that you have to consider. *The bottom line is that it's not profitable.* **2** The **bottom line** in a business deal is the least a person is willing to accept. *£95,000 is her bottom line.* **3** The **bottom line** is the total amount that a company has made or lost over a particular period of time. *These small promotions were costly and they did nothing to increase his bottom line.* `◆◇◇◇` `N-COUNT` `N-COUNT` `N-COUNT`

botu·lism /ˈbɒtʃʊlɪzəm/. **Botulism** is a serious form of food poisoning. `N-UNCOUNT` `MEDICAL`

bou·doir /ˈbuːdwɑː/ **boudoirs.** A **boudoir** is a woman's bedroom or private sitting room. `N-COUNT` `DATED`

bouf·fant /ˈbuːfɒn, AM buːˈfɑːnt/ **bouffants.** A **bouffant** is a hairstyle in which your hair is combed backwards and upwards so that it is high and full. `N-COUNT`

bou·gain·vil·laea /ˌbuːɡənˈvɪliə/ **bougainvillaeas;** also spelled **bougainvillea. Bougainvillaea** is a climbing plant that has bright red or purple flowers and grows mainly in hot countries. `N-VAR`

bough /baʊ/ **boughs.** A **bough** is a large branch of a tree. `N-COUNT` `LITERARY`

bought /bɔːt/. **Bought** is the past tense and past participle of **buy.**

boul·der /ˈbəʊldə/ **boulders.** A **boulder** is a large rounded rock. `◆◇◇◇` `N-COUNT`

boules /buːl/. **Boules** is a game in which a small ball is thrown and then the players try to throw balls as close to the first ball as possible. `N-UNCOUNT`

boule·vard /ˈbuːləvɑːd, AM ˈbʊl-/ **boulevards.** A **boulevard** is a wide street in a city, usually with trees along each side. *...Lenton Boulevard.* `◆◇◇◇` `N-COUNT`

bounce /baʊns/ **bounces, bouncing, bounced. 1** When an object such as a ball **bounces**, it moves upwards or away from a surface immediately after hitting it. *I bounced a ball against the house... My father would burst into the kitchen bouncing a football. ...a falling pebble, bouncing down the eroded cliff.* ▶ Also a noun. *...two bounces of the ball.* `◆◆◇◇` `V-ERG` `V n prep` `V n` `V prep/adv` `Also V` `N-COUNT`

2 The **bounce** of a sports pitch is the condition of it, which determines how high a ball will go when it bounces on it. **3** If you **bounce** on a soft surface, you jump up and down on it repeatedly. *She lets us do anything, even bounce on our beds.* **4** If you **bounce** a child on your knee, you lift him or her up and down quickly and repeatedly for fun. **5** If sound or light **bounces** or is **bounced off** a surface, it reaches the surface and is reflected back. *...light bouncing off glass.* `N-SING` `BRITISH` `VERB` `V prep/adv` `Also V` `VERB` `V n prep/adv` `V-ERG` `V off n` `Also V n off n`

6 If something **bounces** or if something **bounces** it, it `V-ERG`

swings or moves up and down. *Her long black hair bounced as she walked.*

7 If someone **bounces** somewhere, they move there in an energetic way, because they are feeling happy. *Moira bounced into the office.*

8 If you **bounce** your ideas off someone, you tell them to that person, in order to find out what they think about them. *It was good to bounce ideas off another mind... Let's bounce a few ideas around.*

9 If a cheque **bounces** or if a bank **bounces** it, the bank refuses to accept it and pay out the money, because the person who wrote it does not have enough money in their account. *Our only complaint would be if the cheque bounced.*

bounce back. If you **bounce back** after a bad experience, you quickly return to your previous level of success, enthusiasm, or activity. *We lost two or three early games in the World Cup, but we bounced back... Undaunted, he continues to bounce back from the brink of bankruptcy.*

bounc·er /ˈbaʊnsə/ **bouncers.** A bouncer is a man who stands at the door of a club, prevents unwanted from coming in, and makes people leave if they cause trouble.

bounc·ing /ˈbaʊnsɪŋ/. If you say that someone is **bouncing** with health, you mean that they are very healthy. You can also refer to a **bouncing** baby. *Derek is now the proud father of a bouncing baby girl.* ◆ See also **bounce.**

bouncy /ˈbaʊnsi/. **1** Someone or something that is **bouncy** is very lively. *...good, bouncy pop songs.* **2** A **bouncy** thing can bounce very well or makes other things bounce well. *...a children's paradise filled with bouncy toys.*

'bouncy castle, bouncy castles. A bouncy castle is a large object filled with air, often in the shape of a castle, which children play on at a funfair or other outdoor event.

bound 1 connected

bound /baʊnd/. **1 Bound** is the past tense and past participle of **bind.** **2** If one person, thing, or situation is **bound to** another, they are closely associated with each other, and it is difficult for them to be separated. *We are as tightly bound to the people we dislike as to the people we love.* **3** If something is **bound up in** a particular form or place, it is fixed in that form or contained in that place. *The manager of a company does not like having a large chunk of his wealth bound up in its shares.* **4** If one thing is **bound up with** or **in** another, they are closely connected with each other, and it is difficult to consider the two things separately. *My fate was bound up with hers.*

5 If you say that something **is bound to** happen, you mean that you are sure it will happen, because it is a natural consequence of something that is already known or exists. *There are bound to be price increases next year.* **6** If you say that something **is bound to** happen or be true, you feel confident and certain of it, although you have no definite knowledge or evidence. *I'll show it to Benjamin. He's bound to know.*

7 If a vehicle or person is **bound for** a particular place, they are travelling towards it. *The ship was bound for Italy.* ▶ Also a combining form. *...a Texas-bound oil freighter.*

bound 2 limits

bound /baʊnd/ **bounds, bounding, bounded.** **1 Bounds** are limits which normally restrict what can happen or what people can do. *Changes in temperature occur slowly and are constrained within relatively tight bounds.* **2** If someone's life or situation **is bounded** by certain things, those are its most important aspects and it is limited or restricted by them. *Our lives are bounded by work, family and television.* **3** If you say that a feeling or quality **knows no bounds,** you are emphasizing that it is very strong or intense. *The passion of Argentinian football fans knows no bounds.* **4** If an area of land **is bounded by** something, that thing is situated around its edge. *Kirgizia is bounded by Uzbekistan,*

Also V adv, Vn

VERB V prep/adv

VERB V n off n V n around

V-ERG V Also V n

PHRASAL VB V P V P prep/adv

◆◇◇◇◇ *N-COUNT*

◆◇◇◇◇ *ADJ: v-link ADJ with n, ADJ n*

◆◇◇◇◇ *ADJ-GRADED ADJ-GRADED*

N-COUNT BRITISH

◆◆◇◇◇ *ADJ-GRADED: v-link ADJ to n*

PHRASE

PHRASE

PHR-MODAL

PHR-MODAL PRAGMATICS SPOKEN

ADJ: v-link ADJ for n COMB

◆◆◆◇◇ *N-PLURAL*

V-PASSIVE be V-ed by n

PHRASE

VERB be V-ed by n Also V n

Kazakhstan *and Tajikistan.* **5** If a place is **out of bounds,** people are not allowed to go there. *The area has been out of bounds to foreign journalists.* **6** If something is **out of bounds,** people are not allowed to do it, use it, see it, or know about it. *What questions are considered out of bounds?*

bound 3 leap

bound /baʊnd/ **bounds, bounding, bounded.** **1** If a person or animal **bounds** in a particular direction, they move quickly with large steps or jumps. *He bounded up the steps.* ▶ A **bound** is a long or high jump. *She leaps in one bound onto her pony's back.* **2** If the quantity or performance of something **bounds** ahead, it increases or improves quickly and suddenly. *The Hong Kong Stock Market bounded ahead.* **3** ● **leaps and bounds:** see **leap.**

-bound /-baʊnd/. **-bound** is used to form adjectives which describe someone or something as being greatly affected by a particular thing, especially a thing which prevents them from moving or progressing freely. *Andrew has been left wheelchair-bound after the accident. ...a 12-car pile up on a fog-bound motorway. ...the somewhat tradition-bound officers of the navy.*

bound·a·ry /ˈbaʊndəri/ **boundaries.** **1** The **boundary** of an area of land is an imaginary line that separates it from other areas. *Drug traffickers operate across national boundaries.* **2** The **boundaries** of something such as a subject or activity are the limits that people think that it has. *...the boundaries between history and storytelling.*

bound·er /ˈbaʊndə/ **bounders.** If you call someone a **bounder,** you mean they behave in an unkind, selfish, or improper way.

bound·less /ˈbaʊndləs/. If you describe something as **boundless,** you mean that there seems to be no end or limit to it. *The work demanded boundless energy.*

boun·ti·ful /ˈbaʊntɪfʊl/. **1** A **bountiful** supply or amount of something pleasant is a large one. *...a bountiful harvest of fruits and vegetables.* **2** A **bountiful** area or period of time produces or provides large amounts of something, especially food. *The land is bountiful and no one starves.*

boun·ty /ˈbaʊnti/ **bounties.** **1** You can refer to something that is provided in large amounts as **bounty.** *...autumn's bounty of fruits, seeds and berries.* **2** A **bounty** is money that is offered as a reward for doing something, especially for finding or killing a particular person.

'bounty hunter, bounty hunters. A **bounty hunter** is someone who tries to find or kill someone in order to get the reward that has been offered.

bou·quet /bəʊˈkeɪ, buː-/ **bouquets.** **1** A **bouquet** is a bunch of flowers which is attractively arranged. *...a bouquet of dried violets.* **2** The **bouquet** of something, especially wine, is the pleasant smell that it has.

bou·quet gar·ni /ˌbəʊkeɪ gɑːˈniː, buː-/. A **bouquet garni** is a bunch of herbs that are tied together and used in cooking to add flavour to the food.

bour·bon /ˈbɜːbən/ **bourbons. Bourbon** is a type of whisky that is made mainly in America. ▶ A **bourbon** is a glass of bourbon.

bour·geois /ˈbʊəʒwɑː/. **1** If you describe people, their lifestyles, or their attitudes as **bourgeois,** you disapprove of them because you consider them typical of conventional middle-class people. *He's accusing them of having a bourgeois and limited vision.* **2** Marxists use **bourgeois** when referring to the capitalist system and to the social class that owns most of the wealth in that system. **3** See also **petit bourgeois.**

bour·geoi·sie /ˌbʊəʒwɑːˈziː/. In Marxist theory, **the bourgeoisie** are the middle-class people who own most of the wealth in a capitalist system.

bout /baʊt/ **bouts. 1** If you have a **bout** of an illness or of an unpleasant feeling, you have it for a short period. *...a severe bout of flu.* **2** A **bout** of something that is unpleasant is a short time during

PHRASE

PHRASE

◆◆◆◇◇ *VERB V prep/adv* *N-COUNT* *VERB V adv*

COMB

◆◆◇◇◇ *N-COUNT* *N-COUNT*

N-COUNT BRITISH, DATED

ADJ

ADJ-GRADED *ADJ-GRADED*

◆◇◇◇◇ *N-VAR: with supp LITERARY* *N-COUNT*

N-COUNT

◆◇◇◇◇ *N-COUNT* *N-VAR*

N-SING: also no det

◆◇◇◇◇ *N-VAR*

◆◇◇◇◇ *ADJ-GRADED* PRAGMATICS

ADJ

◆◇◇◇◇ *N-COLL-SING: the N*

◆◇◇◇◇ *N-COUNT* *N-COUNT*

which it occurs a great deal. *The latest bout of vio- N-COUNT
lence has claimed twenty four lives.* **3** A **bout** is a
boxing or wrestling match.

4 Some writers use **'bout** or **bout** to represent **about**
when the first syllable is not pronounced. *How 'bout
some coffee?*

bou·tique /buːˈtiːk/ **boutiques.** A **boutique** is a ◆◇◇◇◇
small shop that sells fashionable clothes, shoes, or N-COUNT
jewellery.

bo·vine /ˈbəʊvaɪn/. **1** Bovine means relating to cat- ADJ
tle. **2** If you describe someone's behaviour or ap- TECHNICAL
pearance as **bovine**, you think that they are stupid ADJ-GRADED
or slow-moving. *I'm depressed by the bovine enthu- PRAGMATICS
siasm of the crowd's response.*

bow 1 bending or submitting

bow /baʊ/ **bows, bowing, bowed. 1** When you ◆◆◇◇◇
bow to someone, you briefly bend your body to- VERB
wards them as a formal way of greeting them or V to n
showing respect. *They bowed low to Louis and* Also V
hastened out of his way. ▶ Also a noun. *I gave a the- N-COUNT
atrical bow.* **2** If you **bow** your head, you bend it VERB
towards the ground, for example because you want V n
to show respect or because you are thinking deeply.
*The Colonel bowed his head and whispered a prayer
of thanksgiving.*

3 If you **bow to** pressure or to someone's wishes, you VERB
agree to do what they want you to do. *Some shops are* V to n
*bowing to consumer pressure and stocking organically
grown vegetables.*

4 If you **are bowed** by something, you are made un- V-PASSIVE
happy and anxious by it, and lose hope. *George Bush* be V-ed
refused to be bowed by the bad poll news. ▶ To **be** PHRASAL VB
bowed down means the same as to **be bowed**. *I am* PASSIVE
bowed down by my sins. be V-ed P

bow down. 1 If you refuse to **bow down** to another PHRASAL VB
person, you refuse to show them respect or to behave V P to n
in a way which you think would make you seem weaker or less important than them. *We should not have to
bow down to anyone.* **2** See also **bow** 5.

bow out. If you **bow out** of something, you stop tak- PHRASAL VB
ing part in it. *Dr Owen indicated that he would bow* V P of n
out of politics after the next election. Also V P
WRITTEN

bow 2 part of a ship

bow /baʊ/ **bows.** The front part of a ship is called ◆◇◇◇◇
the **bow** or the **bows.** The plural **bows** can be used N-COUNT
to refer either to one or to more than one of these
parts. *...spray from the ship's bows.*

bow 3 objects

bow /bəʊ/ **bows. 1** A **bow** is a knot with two loops ◆◇◇◇◇
and two loose ends that is used in tying shoelaces N-COUNT
and ribbons. *...a length of ribbon tied in a bow.* **2** A N-COUNT
bow is a weapon for shooting arrows which consists
of a long piece of curved wood with a string attached to both its ends. **3** The **bow** of a violin or N-COUNT
other stringed instrument is a long thin piece of
wood with fibres stretched along it, which you move
across the instruments' strings in order to play it.
4 ● another **string** to your **bow**: see **string**.

bowd·ler·ize /ˈbaʊdləraɪz/, AM ˈbəʊd- **bowdler-** VERB: V n
izes, bowdlerizing, bowdlerized; also spelled PRAGMATICS
bowdlerise in British English. To **bowdlerize** a book
or film means to cut parts of it out before publishing it or showing it; used showing disapproval.

bowed. Pronounced /bəʊd/ for meaning 1, and
/baʊd/ for meaning 2. **1** Something that is **bowed** is ADJ-GRADED
curved. *...an old lady with bowed legs.* **2** If a per- ADJ-GRADED
son's body is **bowed**, it is bent forward. *Head
bowed, she was listening or praying.* **3** See also **bow**.

bow·el /ˈbaʊəl/ **bowels. 1** Your **bowels** are the ◆◆◇◇◇
tubes in your body through which digested food N-COUNT
passes from your stomach to your anus. **2** You can N-PLURAL
refer in a polite way to someone defecating by saying that they move, open, or empty their **bowels.**
3 You can refer to the parts deep inside something N-PLURAL:
as **the bowels of** that thing. *...deep in the bowels of* the N of n
the earth.

bow·er /ˈbaʊə/ **bowers.** A **bower** is a shady leafy ◆◇◇◇◇
shelter in a garden or wood. N-COUNT
LITERARY

bowl /bəʊl/ **bowls, bowling, bowled. 1** A **bowl** ◆◆◇◇◇
is a round container with a wide uncovered top, N-COUNT

used for mixing and serving food, and also for eating from. See picture headed **kitchen utensils.**
▶ The contents of a bowl can be referred to as a N-COUNT
bowl of something. *Lili sat beside us eating a bowl
of muesli.* ◆ **bowl·ful, bowlfuls.** *They ate a large* N-COUNT
bowlful of cereal. **2** A washing-up **bowl** is a large N-COUNT
plastic container that you wash dishes in. **3** You can N-COUNT
refer to the hollow rounded part of an object as its
bowl. *...the bowl of his pipe. ...the toilet bowl.*

4 Bowls is a game in which players try to roll large N-UNCOUNT
wooden balls as near as possible to a small wooden
ball. Bowls is usually played outdoors on grass. **5** A set N-COUNT
of **bowls** is a set of round wooden balls that you play
bowls with. **6** If you **bowl**, you play the game of bowls VERB: V
or the game of bowling.

7 In cricket, to **bowl** a ball means to throw it down the VERB: V n
pitch towards a batsman. *He was injured and unable* V
to bowl. ◆ **bow·ler, bowlers** ◆ **bowl·ing** *...excellent* N-COUNT
fielding and bowling from Birmingham. **8** In cricket, N-UNCOUNT
when a batsman **is bowled**, he has to leave the pitch VERB:
because the bowler has hit the wicket with the ball. be V-ed
▶ If a batsman **is bowled out**, he is bowled. *He was* PHRASAL VB
bowled out first ball. Also V n P
9 If you **bowl** along in a car or on a boat, you move VERB
along very quickly, especially when you are enjoying V prep/adv
yourself. *Veronica looked at him, smiling, as they
bowled along.*

10 A large stadium where sports or concerts take N-COUNT
place is sometimes called a **Bowl.** *...the Crystal Palace
Bowl.*
11 A competition in which American football teams N-COUNT
compete can be referred to as a **bowl.**
12 See also **bowling; begging bowl, mixing bowl,
sugar bowl.**

bowl out. In cricket, if a team **is bowled out**, they PHRASAL VB
have to stop batting because all the batsman are out. be V-ed P
Middlesex defeated Derbyshire by bowling out the op- V P n
position. ● See also **bowl** 9. Also V n P

bowl over. 1 To **bowl** someone **over** means to push PHRASAL VB
into them and make them fall to the ground. *Some* be V-ed P
people had to cling to trees as the flash flood bowled V n P
them over. **2** If you **are bowled over** by something, be V-ed P
you are very impressed or surprised by it. *...a man* V n P
who bowled her over with his humour and charm. Also V P noun

bow·ler /ˈbəʊlə/ **bowlers. 1** A **bowler** is the same ◆◆◇◇◇
as a **bowler hat. 2** See also **bowl.** N-COUNT

bowler 'hat, bowler hats. A **bowler hat** is a N-COUNT
round, hard, black hat with a narrow curved brim
which used to be worn by British businessmen.

bowl·ing /ˈbəʊlɪŋ/. **1** Bowling is a game in which ◆◆◇◇◇
you roll a heavy ball down a narrow track towards a N-UNCOUNT
group of wooden objects and try to knock down as
many of them as possible. **2** See also **bowl.**

bowling alley, bowling alleys. A **bowling alley** N-COUNT
is a building which contains several tracks for ten-
pin bowling.

bowling green, bowling greens. A **bowling** N-COUNT
green is an area of very smooth, short grass on
which the game of bowls is played.

bow tie /ˌbəʊ ˈtaɪ/ **bow ties;** also spelled **bow-tie.** N-COUNT
A **bow tie** is a tie in the form of a bow. Bow ties are
worn by men, especially for formal occasions.

box /bɒks/ **boxes, boxing, boxed. 1** A **box** is a ◆◆◆◆◇
square or rectangular container with hard or stiff N-COUNT
sides. *They sat on wooden boxes. ...the box of tissues
on her desk.* ▶ A **box** of something is an amount of N-COUNT
it contained in a box. ◆ **boxed** /bɒkst/. *A boxed set* ADJ: ADJ n
or collection of things is sold in a box. **2** You can N-COUNT
use **box** to refer to something such as a letter-box or
telephone box, when the thing has already been
mentioned. *I begged Tom's telephone number, and
called him from the box down the road.* **3** A **box** is a N-COUNT
square or rectangle marked by lines, that is printed
or drawn on a piece of paper, road, or other surface.
Simply tick the appropriate box. **4** On a soccer N-SING
pitch, the **box** is the same as the **penalty area. 5** In N-COUNT
a theatre or at a sports ground, a **box** is a small area
of seats or room where a small number of people
can sit to watch the performance or game.
6 Television is sometimes referred to as **the box.** N-SING

B

Prince Michael of Kent appeared on the box the other day. **7 Box** is used before a number as a postal address by organizations that receive a lot of mail. *...Country Crafts, Box 111, Landisville.* BRITISH, INFORMAL N-COUNT

8 Box is a small evergreen tree with dark leaves which is often used to form hedges. N-UNCOUNT

9 To **box** means to fight someone according to the rules of boxing. *At school I boxed and played rugby.* ♦ **box·er, boxers.** VERB V Also V n N-COUNT

10 See also **boxing**; **black box**, **chocolate box**, **lunch box**, **phone box**, **post office box**, **post box**, **signal box**.

box in. 1 If you **are boxed in**, you are unable to move from a particular place because you are surrounded by other people or cars. *The black cabs cut in front of them, trying to box them in.* **2** If something **boxes** you **in**, it puts you in a situation where you have very little choice about what you can do. *The Government has appeared to have boxed itself in... President Clinton is boxed in – he must choose among a host of unappetizing choices.* PHRASAL VB be V-ed P Also V P noun V n P V-ed P Also V P noun

box·er /ˈbɒksə/ **boxers. 1** A **boxer** is a dog with short hair and a rather flat face. **2** See also **box**. ♦♦◇◇◇ N-COUNT

boxer shorts. Boxer shorts are loose-fitting men's underpants that are shaped like the shorts worn by boxers. N-PLURAL

box·ing /ˈbɒksɪŋ/. **Boxing** is a sport in which two people wearing large padded gloves fight on a square platform, according to special rules. ♦♦◇◇◇ N-UNCOUNT

Boxing Day. In Britain, **Boxing Day** is the 26th of December, the day after Christmas Day. N-UNCOUNT

boxing ring, boxing rings. A **boxing ring** is a raised square platform with ropes around it in which boxers fight. N-COUNT

box number, box numbers. A **box number** is a number used as an address, especially one given by a newspaper for replies to a private advertisement. N-COUNT

box office, box offices; also spelled **box-office. 1** The **box office** in a theatre, cinema, or concert hall is the place where the tickets are sold. **2** When people talk about the **box office**, they are referring to the success of a film or play in terms of the number of people who go to see it. *It took £20m at the box office... The film was a huge box-office success.* ♦♦◇◇◇ N-COUNT N-SING

box·wood /ˈbɒkswʊd/. **Boxwood** is a type of wood which is obtained from a box tree. N-UNCOUNT

boxy /ˈbɒksi/. If something is **boxy**, it is square in shape, like a box. *Boxy new skyscrapers dominate the skyline.* ADJ-GRADED

boy /bɔɪ/ **boys. 1** A **boy** is a male child. *I knew him when he was a little boy.* **2** You can refer to a young man as a **boy**, especially when talking about relationships between boys and girls. *...the age when girls get interested in boys.* **3** Someone's **boy** is their son. *Eric was my cousin Edward's boy.* **4** You can refer to a man as a **boy**, especially when you are talking about him in an affectionate way. *...the local boy who became President.* **5** If you describe someone as **one of the boys**, you mean they are accepted by a group of male friends who do things that are thought of as typically masculine. **6** The police are sometimes referred to as **the boys in blue**. **7** You can use **boy** when giving instructions to a horse or dog. *Down, boy!* **8** Some people say **boy** or **oh boy** in order to express strong feelings of excitement or admiration. *Oh boy! Just think what I could tell him.* **9** See also **bully boy**, **head boy**, **office boy**, **old boy**, **stable boy**, **teddy boy**. ♦♦♦♦♦ N-COUNT N-COUNT N-COUNT N-COUNT: with supp PRAGMATICS INFORMAL PHRASE PHRASE INFORMAL N-VOC EXCLAM INFORMAL, AMERICAN

boy·cott /ˈbɔɪkɒt/ **boycotts, boycotting, boycotted.** If a country, group, or person **boycotts** a country, organization, or activity, they refuse to be involved with it because they disapprove of it. *The main opposition parties are boycotting the elections.* ▶ Also a noun. *...the lifting of the economic boycott against Israel.* ♦♦◇◇◇ VERB V n N-COUNT

boy·friend /ˈbɔɪfrend/ **boyfriends.** Someone's **boyfriend** is a man or boy with whom they are having a romantic or sexual relationship. *...Brenda and her boyfriend Anthony.* ♦♦◇◇◇ N-COUNT

boy·hood /ˈbɔɪhʊd/. **Boyhood** is the period of a male person's life during which he is a boy. *He has been a Derby County supporter since boyhood.* ♦◇◇◇◇ N-UNCOUNT

boy·ish /ˈbɔɪɪʃ/. **1** If you describe a man as **boyish**, you mean that he is like a boy in his appearance or behaviour, and you find this characteristic quite attractive. ♦ **boy·ish·ly** *John grinned boyishly.* **2** If you describe a girl or woman as **boyish**, you mean that she looks like a boy, for example because she has short hair or small breasts. ♦◇◇◇◇ ADJ-GRADED PRAGMATICS ADV-GRADED ADJ-GRADED

boy racer, boy racers. Young men who drive very fast are sometimes referred to as **boy racers**; used showing disapproval. N-COUNT PRAGMATICS BRITISH

Boy Scout, Boy Scouts; also **boy scout. 1** The **Boy Scouts** is an organization for boys which teaches them to become disciplined, practical, and self-sufficient. **2** A **Boy Scout** is a boy who is a member of the Boy Scouts. N-COLL-PROPER: the N N-COUNT

bozo /ˈbəʊzəʊ/ **bozos.** If you say that someone is a **bozo**, you mean they are stupid. N-COUNT PRAGMATICS INFORMAL

Br. **Br.** is a written abbreviation for **British**.

bra /brɑː/ **bras.** A **bra** is an item of underwear that women wear to support their breasts. See picture headed **clothes**. ♦◇◇◇◇ N-COUNT

brace /breɪs/ **braces, bracing, braced. 1** If you **brace** yourself for something unpleasant or difficult, you prepare yourself for it. *He braced himself for the icy plunge into the black water.* **2** If you **brace** yourself **against** something, you press against it in order to steady your body or to avoid falling. *He braced his back against one wall of the pit.* **3** If you **brace** part of your body, you keep it stiffly in a particular position. **4** To **brace** something such as a roof means to strengthen or support it. **5** A **brace** is a device attached to a part of a person's body in order to strengthen or support it. *...a neck brace.* **6** A **brace** is a metal device that can be fastened to a child's teeth in order to help them grow straight. **7** You can refer to two things of the same kind as a **brace** of that thing. The plural form is also **brace**. *...a few brace of grouse.* **8 Braces** are a pair of straps that pass over your shoulders and fasten to your trousers at the front and back in order to keep them in place. The usual American word is **suspenders**. ♦♦◇◇◇ VERB V pron-refl VERB V n against n VERB: V n VERB: V n N-COUNT N-COUNT N-COUNT N-PLURAL BRITISH

brace·let /ˈbreɪslɪt/ **bracelets.** A **bracelet** is a chain or band, usually made of metal, which you wear around your wrist as jewellery. ♦◇◇◇◇ N-COUNT

brac·ing /ˈbreɪsɪŋ/. If you describe something, especially a place, climate, or activity as **bracing**, you mean that it refreshes you and makes you feel full of energy. *...a bracing walk.* ADJ-GRADED

brack·en /ˈbrækən/. **Bracken** is a plant like a large fern that grows on hills and in woods. N-UNCOUNT

brack·et /ˈbrækɪt/ **brackets, bracketing, bracketed. 1** If you say that someone or something is in a particular **bracket**, you mean that they come within a particular range. *Do you fall outside that age bracket?... They're in a low income bracket.* **2** If two or more people or things **are bracketed** together, they are considered to be similar or related. *Austrian wine styles are often bracketed with those of northern Germany.* **3 Brackets** are pieces of metal, wood, or plastic that are fastened to a wall in order to support something such as a shelf. **4 Brackets** are a pair of written marks such as ( ) that you place round a word, expression, or sentence in order to indicate that you are giving extra information. *The prices in brackets are special rates for the under 18s.* **5 Brackets** are pair of marks that are placed around a series of symbols in a mathematical expression to indicate that those symbols function as one item within the expression. ♦◇◇◇◇ N-COUNT VB: pl-n be V-ed together be V-ed with n N-COUNT N-COUNT N-COUNT

brack·ish /ˈbrækɪʃ/. **Brackish** water is slightly salty and unpleasant. ADJ

brag /bræg/ **brags, bragging, bragged.** If someone **brags**, they talk very proudly about what they have done or what they have; used showing disapproval. *He's always bragging about his prowess as a cricketer... He'll probably go around bragging to his* ♦◇◇◇◇ VERB: V V about n V ton V that

friends... The chairman never tires of bragging that he and Mr. Bush are old friends.

Brah·man /'brɑːmən/ **Brahmans.** A **Brahman** is the same as a **Brahmin.**

Brah·min /'brɑːmɪn/ **Brahmins.** A **Brahmin** is a N-COUNT Hindu of the highest caste.

braid /breɪd/ **braids, braiding, braided. 1** **Braid** ◆◇◇◇◇ is a narrow piece of decorated cloth or twisted N-UNCOUNT threads, used to decorate clothes or curtains. ✦ **braid·ed.** A piece of clothing that is **braided** is ADJ decorated with braid. **2** If you **braid** hair or a group VERB: V n of threads, you twist three or more lengths of them AMERICAN over and under each other to make one thick length. The usual British word is **plait.** ► A **braid** is N-COUNT a length of hair which has been braided. The usual British word is **plait.**

Braille /breɪl/. **Braille** is a system of printing for N-UNCOUNT blind people. The letters are printed as groups of raised dots that you can feel with your fingers.

brain /breɪn/ **brains. 1** Your **brain** is the organ in- ◆◆◆◇ side your head that controls your body's activities and enables you to think and to feel things. **2** Your N-COUNT **brain** is your mind and the way that you think. *Once you stop using your brain you soon go stale.* **3** If you say that someone has **brains** or a good N-COUNT **brain**, you mean they have the ability to learn and understand things quickly, to solve problems, and to make good decisions. **4** If you refer to someone N-COUNT as the **brains** behind an idea or an organization, INFORMAL you mean that he or she conceived that idea or that they make the important decisions about how that organization is managed. *Some investigators regard-ed her as the brains of the gang.* **5** If you **pick** PHRASE someone's **brains**, you ask them to help you with a INFORMAL problem because they know more about the subject than you. **6** To **blow** someone's **brains out** means PHRASE to shoot them in the head, killing them. **7** See also INFORMAL **hare-brained;** ● to **rack** your **brains**: see **rack**.

brain·child /'breɪntʃaɪld/. Someone's **brainchild** is ◆◇◇◇◇ an idea or invention that they have thought up or N-SING: created. *The record was the brainchild of rock star* with poss *Bob Geldof.*

brain 'dead. 1 If someone is declared **brain dead**, ADJ they have suffered brain death. **2** If you say that ADJ-GRADED someone is **brain dead**, you are saying in a cruel PRAGMATICS way that you think they are very stupid.

'brain death. Brain death occurs when someone's N-UNCOUNT brain stops functioning, even though their heart may be kept beating using a machine.

'brain drain. When people talk about a **brain** N-SING **drain**, they are referring to large numbers of scien-tists or academics leaving their own country for other countries where conditions and salaries are better.

brain·less /'breɪnləs/. If you describe someone or ADJ-GRADED something as **brainless**, you think they are stupid. PRAGMATICS

brain·power /'breɪnpaʊə/. A person's **brainpower** N-UNCOUNT is their intelligence. A country's **brainpower** is its JOURNALISM intelligent people, for example its scientists.

brain·storm /'breɪnstɔːm/ **brainstorms, brain-storming, brainstormed. 1** If you have a **brain-** N-COUNT **storm**, you suddenly have a clever idea, often a ra- AMERICAN ther unusual one. The usual British word is **brainwave. 2** If a group of people **brainstorm**, they VERB have a meeting in which they all put forward as V many ideas and suggestions as they can think of. Also V n *The women meet twice a month to brainstorm.* ✦ **brain·storming.** N-UNCOUNT

'brain teaser, brain teasers; also spelled **brain-** N-COUNT **teaser.** A **brain teaser** is a question, problem, or puzzle that is difficult to answer or solve, but is not serious or important.

brain·wash /'breɪnwɒʃ/ **brainwashes, brain-** VERB: V n **washing, brainwashed.** If you **brainwash** V n into-ing someone, you force them to believe something by beV-ed to-inf continually telling them that it is true, and prevent-ing them from thinking about it properly. *They brainwash people into giving up all their money... We were brainwashed to believe we were all equal.*

brain·wave /'breɪnweɪv/ **brainwaves. 1** If you N-COUNT have a **brainwave**, you suddenly have a clever idea, BRITISH often a rather unusual one. The usual American word is **brainstorm. 2 Brainwaves** are electrical sig- N-PLURAL nals produced by the brain which can be recorded and measured.

brainy /'breɪni/ **brainier, brainiest.** Someone who ADJ-GRADED is **brainy** is clever and good at learning. INFORMAL

braise /breɪz/ **braises, braising, braised.** When VERB: V n you **braise** meat or a vegetable, you fry it quickly and then cook it slowly in a covered dish with a small amount of liquid.

brake /breɪk/ **brakes, braking, braked.** ◆◆◇◇◇ **1 Brakes** are devices in a vehicle that make it go N-COUNT slower or stop. See picture headed **car and bicycle.** *The bus crashed when the brakes failed.* **2** When a VERB vehicle or its driver **brakes**, the driver makes it slow V to n down or stop by using the brakes. *She braked sharp-* Also V n *ly to avoid another car... She braked to a halt.* **3** You N-COUNT can use **brake** in a number of expressions to indi-cate that something has slowed down or stopped. *Illness had put a brake on his progress... You can take the financial brakes off in June.*

bram·ble /'bræmbəl/ **brambles. Brambles** are N-COUNT wild, thorny bushes that produce blackberries.

bran /bræn/. The small brown flakes that are left ◆◇◇◇◇ when grain has been used to make white flour are N-UNCOUNT known as **bran.** *...oat bran.*

branch /brɑːntʃ, bræntʃ/ **branches, branching,** ◆◆◆◇◇ **branched. 1** The **branches** of a tree are the parts N-COUNT that grow out from its trunk and have leaves, flow-ers, or fruit growing on them.
2 A **branch** of a business or other organization is one N-COUNT of the offices, shops, or groups which belong to it and which are located in different places. *The local branch of Bank of America is handling the accounts.* **3** A N-COUNT: **branch** of an organization such as the government or with supp the police force is a department which has a particular function. *...the Metropolitan Police Special Branch.* **4** A **branch** of a subject is a part or type of it. **5** A N-COUNT **branch** of your family is a group of its members who N-COUNT are descended from one particular person.

branch off. A road or path that **branches off** from PHRASAL VB another one starts from it and goes in a slightly differ- V P prep/adv ent direction. If you **branch off** somewhere, you Also V P change the direction in which you are going. *After a few miles, a small road branched off to the right.*

branch out. If a person or an organization PHRASAL VB **branches out**, they do something different from their V P normal activities or work. *I continued studying moths,* V P prep/adv *and branched out to other insects.*

'branch line, branch lines. A **branch line** is a N-COUNT railway line that goes to small towns rather than be-tween large cities.

brand /brænd/ **brands, branding, branded. 1** A ◆◆◆◇◇ **brand** of a product is the version of it that is made N-COUNT by one particular manufacturer. *Winston is a brand of cigarette. ...a supermarket's own brand.* **2** A N-COUNT: **brand** of something such as a way of thinking or N of n behaving is a particular kind of it. *The British brand of socialism was more interested in reform than revolution.* **3** If someone **is branded** as something VERB: bad, people think they are that thing. *The company* be V-ed as n *has been branded racist by some of its own staff...* be V-ed adj *The US administration recently branded him a war* V n n *criminal.* **4** When someone **brands** an animal, they VERB: V n put a permanent mark on its skin, usually by burn-ing it, in order to show who it belongs to. ► A **brand** N-COUNT is a permanent mark made like this.

brand·ed /'brændɪd/. A **branded** product is one ADJ: ADJ n which is made by a well-known manufacturer and has the manufacturer's label on it.

bran·dish /'brændɪʃ/ **brandishes, brandishing,** ◆◇◇◇◇ **brandished.** If you **brandish** something such as a VERB weapon, you hold it in a threatening way. *He ap-* V n *peared in the lounge brandishing a knife.*

'brand name, brand names. The **brand name** ◆◇◇◇◇ of a product is the name the manufacturer gives it N-COUNT and under which it is sold. *Drugs can be sold under different brand names.*

,brand-'new. A **brand-new** object is completely new. *He went off to buy himself a brand new car.* ◆◆◇◇◇ ADJ

bran·dy /'brændi/ **brandies.** Brandy is a strong alcoholic drink. It is often drunk after a meal. ▶ A **brandy** is a glass of brandy. ◆◇◇◇ N-VAR N-COUNT

brash /bræʃ/ **brasher, brashest.** If you describe someone as **brash**, you disapprove of them because you think that they are excessively confident and aggressive. ♦ **brash·ly** *I brashly announced to the group that NATO needed to be turned around.* ♦ **brash·ness** *He has shown all the brashness of youth.* ◆◇◇◇ ADJ-GRADED PRAGMATICS ADV N-UNCOUNT

brass /brɑːs, bræs/ **brasses. 1** Brass is a yellow-coloured metal made from copper and zinc, used especially for making ornaments and musical instruments. **2 The brass** or **the brass section** is the part of an orchestra which consists of brass wind instruments such as trumpets and horns. **3 Brasses** are flat pieces of brass with writing or a picture cut into them, which are often found in churches. ● See also **brass rubbing**. ◆◆◇◇◇ N-UNCOUNT N-COUNT N-COUNT

,brass 'band, brass bands. A **brass band** is a band made up of brass and percussion instruments. N-COUNT

bras·se·rie /'bræsəri, AM -'riː/ **brasseries.** A **brasserie** is a small, usually cheap restaurant, or a bar in which food is served as well as drinks. ◆◇◇◇ N-COUNT

bras·si·ca /'bræsɪkə/ **brassicas.** Brassicas are vegetables, such as cabbages and broccoli, which grow above or just under the soil and which carry their seeds in a seed case that has two sections. N-COUNT

bras·siere /'bræziə, AM brə'zɪr/ **brassieres.** A **brassiere** is the same as a **bra**. N-COUNT DATED

'brass rubbing, brass rubbings. A **brass rubbing** is a picture made by placing a piece of paper over a brass plate that has writing or a picture on it, and rubbing it with a wax crayon. N-COUNT

brassy /'brɑːsi, 'bræsi/ **brassier, brassiest. 1** If you describe a person's appearance or their behaviour as **brassy**, you mean they dress or behave in a way that is too bright, daring, and lively, and not at all tasteful. *...Alec and his brassy blonde wife.* **2** Something that is **brassy** has a yellow metallic colour and sometimes looks cheap. *...a woman with big brassy ear-rings.* ADJ-GRADED ADJ-GRADED

brat /bræt/ **brats.** If you call a child a **brat**, you mean that he or she behaves badly or annoys you. *He's a spoilt brat.* ◆◇◇◇ N-COUNT INFORMAL

'brat pack, brat packs. A **brat pack** is a group of young people, especially actors or writers, who are popular or successful at the moment. *...the Hollywood Brat Pack.* N-COUNT JOURNALISM

bra·va·do /brə'vɑːdəu/. **Bravado** is an appearance of courage or confidence that someone shows in order to impress other people. ◆◇◇◇ N-UNCOUNT

brave /breɪv/ **braver, bravest; braves, braving, braved. 1** Someone who is **brave** is willing to do things which are dangerous, and does not show fear in difficult or dangerous situations. *He was not brave enough to report the loss of the documents.* ♦ **brave·ly** *The enemy fought bravely.* **2** If you say that someone **is putting on a brave face** or that they **are putting a brave face on** a difficult situation, you mean they are pretending that they are happy when they are not, or that they can deal with the situation easily when they cannot. **3** If you **brave** unpleasant or dangerous conditions, you deliberately expose yourself to them, usually in order to achieve something. *Thousands have braved icy rain to demonstrate their support.* ◆◆◇◇◇ ADJ-GRADED ADV-GRADED PHRASE VERB V n WRITTEN

brav·ery /'breɪvəri/. **Bravery** is brave behaviour or the quality of being brave. ◆◇◇◇ N-UNCOUNT

bra·vo /,brɑː'vəu/. Some people say **'bravo'** to express appreciation when someone has done something well. EXCLAM

bra·vu·ra /brə'vjuərə, AM -'vurə/. If you say that someone does something with **bravura**, you mean that they do it in an elaborate and confident way that emphasizes their skill or importance. ▶ A **bravura** performance is done with bravura. N-UNCOUNT LITERARY ADJ

brawl /brɔːl/ **brawls, brawling, brawled. 1** A **brawl** is a rough disorganized fight. *He had been in a drunken street brawl.* **2** If people **brawl**, they fight in a rough disorganized way. *He was suspended for a year from University after brawling with police.* ♦ **brawl·ing** *...brawling between the England fans and locals.* ◆◇◇◇ N-COUNT V-RECIP: pl-n V with n N-COUNT

brawn /brɔːn/. **1** If someone has **brawn**, they look physically strong because they have large muscles. *He's got plenty of brains as well as brawn.* ♦ **brawny** /'brɔːni/. *Oscar turned out to be a brawny young man.* **2** In Britain, **brawn** is a kind of food made from pieces of pork and jelly pressed together so that it can be sliced. N-UNCOUNT ADJ N-UNCOUNT

bray /breɪ/ **brays, braying, brayed. 1** When a donkey **brays**, it makes the loud harsh sound that donkeys typically make. **2** If someone **brays**, they make a loud harsh sound or talk in a loud harsh way. *Neil brayed with angry laughter.* ▶ Also a noun. *...a wild bray of laughter.* VERB: V VERB: V V with n WRITTEN N-COUNT

bra·zen /'breɪzən/ **brazens, brazening, brazened.** If you describe a person as **brazen**, you mean that they are very bold and do not care what other people think about them. *They're quite brazen about their bisexuality.* ♦ **bra·zen·ly** *He was brazenly running a $400,000-a-month drug operation.* ◆◇◇◇ ADJ-GRADED ADV-GRADED

brazen out. If you have done something wrong and you **brazen** it **out**, you behave confidently in order not to appear ashamed, even though you may feel ashamed. *Mr Mellor is as determined as ever to brazen out the scandals.* PHRASAL VB V it P V P noun Also V n P

bra·zi·er /'breɪziə, AM -ʒəs/ **braziers.** A **brazier** is a large metal container in which coal or charcoal is burned to keep people warm when they are outside in cold weather, for example because of their work. N-COUNT

breach /briːtʃ/ **breaches, breaching, breached. 1** If you **breach** an agreement, a law, or a promise, you break it. ▶ Also a noun. *His employer sued him for breach of contract.* **2** A **breach** in a relationship is a serious disagreement which often results in the relationship ending. *...a serious breach in relations between the two countries.* **3** If someone or something **breaches** a barrier, they make an opening in it, usually leaving it weakened or destroyed. **4** If someone **breaches** security or defences, they manage to get through and attack an area that is heavily guarded and protected. ▶ Also a noun. *...widespread breaches of security at Ministry of Defence bases.* **5** If you **step into the breach**, you do a job or task which someone else was supposed to do or has done in the past, because they are suddenly unable to do it. ◆◆◇◇◇ VERB: V n N-VAR N-COUNT FORMAL VERB: V n FORMAL VERB: V n N-COUNT PHRASE

,breach of the 'peace, breaches of the peace. A **breach of the peace** is noisy or violent behaviour in a public place which is illegal because it disturbs other people. N-VAR LEGAL

bread /bred/ **breads, breading, breaded. 1** Bread is a very common food made from flour, water, and often yeast, mixed into a soft dough and baked in an oven. *...a loaf of bread.* **2** If you earn your **bread** doing a particular job or activity, you earn your money doing it. **3** If food such as fish or meat **is breaded**, it is covered in breadcrumbs. It can then be fried or grilled. *...a breaded chicken fillet.* ◆◆◇◇◇ N-VAR N-UNCOUNT INFORMAL VERB: be V-ed V-ed

,bread and 'butter; also spelled **bread-and-butter. 1** Something that is the **bread and butter** of a person or organization is the activity or work that provides the main part of their income. *The mobile phone business was actually his bread and butter.* **2 Bread and butter** issues or matters are ones which are important to most people, because they affect them personally. ◆◇◇◇ N-UNCOUNT ADJ: ADJ n

bread·crumb /'bredkrʌm/ **breadcrumbs.** Breadcrumbs are tiny pieces of dry bread. ◆◇◇◇ N-COUNT

bread·line /'bredlaɪn/. Someone who is on the **breadline** is very poor. *We lived on the breadline to get our son through college.* N-SING

breadth /bretθ, AM bredθ/. **1** The **breadth** of something is the distance between its two sides. *The* ◆◇◇◇ N-UNCOUNT

breadth of the whole camp was 400 paces. **2 Breadth** is the quality of including or involving many different things. *Older people have a tremendous breadth of experience.* **3** If you say that something happens throughout or across **the length and breadth of** a place, you are emphasizing that it happens everywhere in that place. ● See also **hair's breadth**.

bread·win·ner /ˈbredwɪnə/ **breadwinners.** The **breadwinner** in a family is the person in it who earns the money that the family needs for essential things.

break /breɪk/ **breaks, breaking, broke, broken.** **1** When an object **breaks**, it suddenly separates into two or more pieces, often because it has been hit or dropped. *He fell through the window, breaking the glass... Break the cauliflower into florets... The plane broke into three pieces.* **2** If you **break** a part of your body such as your leg or your nose, or if a bone **breaks**, you are injured because a bone cracks or splits. *Old bones break easily.* ▶ Also a noun. *It has caused a bad break to Gabriella's leg.* **3** If a surface, cover, or seal **breaks**, a hole or tear is made in it, so that a substance can pass through. *Once you've broken the seal of a bottle there's no way you can put it back together again. ...broken skin.* **4** When a tool or piece of machinery **breaks**, it is damaged and no longer works. *He accused her of breaking the stereo. ...broken washing machines.* **5** If you **break** a rule, promise, or agreement, you do something that you should not do according to it. *We didn't know we were breaking the law. ...broken promises.* **6** If you **break** free or loose, you free yourself from something or escape from it. *She broke free by thrusting her elbow into his chest.* **7** If someone **breaks** something, especially a difficult or unpleasant situation that has existed for some time, they end it or change it. *...to break the vicious circle between disadvantage and crime.* ▶ Also a noun. *...a break in the deadlock.* **8** If someone **breaks** a silence, they make a noise after a long period of silence, or they talk about something that they have not talked about for a long time. *The unearthly silence was broken by a shrill screaming.* **9** If you **break** with a group of people or a traditional way of doing things, or you **break** your connection with them, you stop being involved with that group or stop doing things in that way. *Poland and Czechoslovakia were beginning to break their links with communist ideology.* ▶ Also a noun. *...the need for a break with the past.* **10** If you **break** a habit or if someone **breaks** you of it, you no longer have that habit. *The professor hoped to break the students of the habit of looking for easy answers.* **11** To **break** someone means to destroy their determination and courage, their success, or their career. *He never let his jailers break him.* **12** If there is a **break** in the cloud or weather, it changes and there is a short period of sunshine or fine weather. **13** If the weather **breaks** or a storm **breaks**, it suddenly becomes rainy or stormy after a period of sunshine. *She hoped she'd be able to reach the hotel before the storm broke.* **14** If someone **breaks** for a short period of time, they rest or change from what they are doing for a short period. *They broke for lunch.* **15** A **break** is a short period of time when you have a rest or a change from what you are doing, especially if you are working. *Do you want to have a little break?* ● See also **coffee break, lunch break, tea break.** **16** A **break** is a short holiday. *They are currently taking a short break in Spain.* **17** You can say **'give me a break'** to show that you are annoyed by what someone has said or done. *'I'm a real intellectual-type guy, Tracy,' James joked. 'Oh, give me a break,' Tracy moaned.* **18** To **break** the force of something such as a blow or fall means to weaken its effect, for example by getting in the way of it. *He sustained serious neck injuries after he broke someone's fall.* **19** When a piece of news **breaks**, people hear about it

from the newspapers, television, or radio. *The news broke that the Prime Minister had resigned.* **20** When you **break** a piece of bad news to someone, you tell it to them as kindly as you can. *Then Louise broke the news that she was leaving me.* **21** A **break** is also a lucky opportunity that someone gets to achieve something. *He went into TV and got his first break playing opposite Sid James in the series Citizen James.* **22** If you **break** a record, you beat the previous record for a particular achievement. **23** When day or dawn **breaks**, it starts to grow light after the night has ended. ● See also **daybreak.** **24** The **break of day** or the **break of dawn** is the time when it begins to grow light after the night. **25** When a wave **breaks**, it passes its highest point and turns downwards, for example when it reaches the shore. **26** If you **break** a secret code, you work out how to understand it. **27** If someone's voice **breaks** when they are speaking, it changes its sound or becomes hesitant, for example because they are sad or afraid. *Godfrey's voice broke, and halted.* **28** When an adolescent boy's voice **breaks**, it becomes deeper and sounds more like a man's voice. **29** In tennis, if you **break** your opponent's serve, you win a game in which your opponent is serving. ▶ Also a noun. *A single break of serve settled the first two sets.* **30** If you **make a break** or **make a break for it**, you run to escape from something. *Dan made a break for his car only to find the driver's door locked.* **31** See also **broke, broken; heartbreak, heartbreaking, heartbroken, outbreak.** ● **to break the bank:** see **bank.** ● **to break cover:** see **cover.** ● **to break even:** see **even.** ● **to break new ground:** see **ground.** ● **to break someone's heart:** see **heart.** ● **all hell breaks loose:** see **hell.** ● **to break the ice:** see **ice.** ● **to break ranks:** see **rank.**

break away. 1 If you **break away** from someone who is trying to hold you or catch you, you free yourself and run away. *I broke away from him and rushed out into the hall.* **2** If you **break away** from something or someone that restricts you or controls you, you succeed in freeing yourself from them. *Talabani was once a member of the KDP, but broke away in the 1970s to form his own party.*

break down. 1 If a machine or a vehicle **breaks down**, it stops working. **2** If a discussion, relationship, or system **breaks down**, it fails because of a problem or disagreement. *Talks with business leaders broke down last night.* **3** If someone **breaks down**, they lose control of themselves and start crying. **4** To **break down** something such as an idea or statement means to separate it into smaller parts in order to make it easier to understand or deal with. *These rules tell us how a sentence is broken down into phrases.* **5** When a substance **breaks down**, a biological or chemical process causes it to separate into the substances which make it up. *The oil is attacked by naturally occurring microbes which break it down.* **6** If you **break down** a door or barrier, you hit it so hard that it falls to the ground. *His father failed to break the door down.* **7** To **break down** barriers or prejudices that separate people or restrict their freedom means to change people's attitudes so that the barriers or prejudices no longer exist. *His early experience enabled him to break down barriers between Scottish Catholics and Protestants.* **8** See also **breakdown, broken-down.**

break in. 1 If someone, usually a thief, **breaks in**, they get into a building by force. *Masked robbers broke in and made off with $8,000.* ● See also **break-in. 2** If you **break in** on someone's conversation or activity, you interrupt them. *'She told you to stay here,' Mike broke in.* **3** If you **break** someone in, you get them used to a new job or situation. *The band are breaking in a new backing vocalist.* **4** If you **break in** something new, you gradually use it or wear it more and more until it is ready to be used or worn all the time. *When*

breaking in an engine, you probably should refrain from high speed for the first thousand miles.

break into. 1 If someone **breaks into** a building, they get into it by force. *There was no one nearby who might see him trying to break into the house.* **2** If someone **breaks into** something, they suddenly start doing it. For example if someone **breaks** into a run, they suddenly start running, and if they **break into** song, they suddenly start singing. **3** If you **break into** a profession or area of business, especially one that is difficult to succeed in, you manage to have some success in it. *She finally broke into films after an acclaimed stage career.*   PHRASAL VB   VP n   VP n   VP n

break off. 1 If part of something **breaks off**, it comes off or is removed from something. *Grace broke off a large piece of the clay... They've torn down wooden fences and broken branches off trees.* **2** If you **break off** when you are doing or saying something, you suddenly stop doing it or saying it. *North Korea broke off the talks.* **3** If someone **breaks off** a relationship, they end it. *The two West African states had broken off relations two years ago... He doesn't seem to have the courage to break it off with her... His family broke off with him when he married my mother.*   PHRASAL VB   ERG: VP   VP noun   VnP n   VP   VP noun   V it P with n   VP with n

break out. 1 If something such as war, fighting, or disease **breaks out**, it begins suddenly. *He was 29 when war broke out.* **2** If a prisoner **breaks out** of a prison, they escape from it. *The two men broke out of their cells.* ● See also **breakout**. **3** If you **break out** of a dull situation or routine, you manage to change it or escape from it. *If her marriage becomes too restrictive, she will break out and seek new horizons.* **4** If you **break out** in a rash or a sweat or if it **breaks out** on your body, it appears on your skin. *A person who is allergic to cashews may break out in a rash when he consumes these nuts.*   PHRASAL VB   VP   VP of n   Also V P   VP of n   VP   VP in n   Also V P

break through. 1 If you **break through** a barrier, you succeed in forcing your way through it. *About fifteen inmates broke through onto the roof.* **2** If you **break through**, you achieve success despite difficulties and obstacles. *I broke through the poverty barrier and it was education that did it.* **3** When something that was previously hidden or unseen **breaks through**, it appears. *Elizabeth's human side keeps breaking through.* **4** See also **breakthrough**.   PHRASAL VB   VP n   VP   VP   VP n   Also V P n

break up. 1 When something **breaks up** or when you **break** it **up**, it separates or is divided into several smaller parts. *Break up the chocolate and melt it... He broke the bread up into chunks.* **2** If you **break up** with your boyfriend, girlfriend, husband, or wife or your relationship with them **breaks up**, the relationship ends. *My girlfriend had broken up with me... Fred has given me no good reason for wanting to break up our marriage... She had a child but the marriage broke up.* **3** When a meeting or gathering **breaks up**, it is brought to an end and the people involved in it leave. *Police used tear gas to break up a demonstration.* **4** When a school or the pupils in it **break up**, the school term ends and the pupils start their holidays. *...the last week before they break up.* **5** See also **break-up**.   PHRASAL VB   ERG: VP   VP noun   V n P   RECIP-ERG   VP with n   VP noun   VP   Also pl–n V P   ERG: VP   Also V n P   VP   BRITISH

break·able /ˈbreɪkəbəl/ **breakables. Breakable** objects are easy to break by accident. ▶ **Breakables** are breakable objects. *Keep any breakables out of reach of very young children.*   ADJ-GRADED   N-PLURAL

break·age /ˈbreɪkɪdʒ/ **breakages. 1 Breakage** is the act of breaking something. *Check that your insurance policy covers breakages and damage during removals.* **2** A **breakage** is something that has been broken. *You have to repair breakages.*   N-VAR   N-COUNT

break·away /ˈbreɪkəweɪ/. A **breakaway** group is a group of people who have separated from a larger group, for example because of a disagreement.   ◆◇◇◇   ADJ: ADJ n

break·down /ˈbreɪkdaʊn/ **breakdowns. 1** The **breakdown** of something such as a relationship, plan, or discussion is its failure or ending. *...the breakdown of trade talks between the US and EC officials.* **2** If you have a **breakdown**, you become very depressed, so that you are unable to cope with   ◆◆◇◇   N-COUNT   N-COUNT

your life. *They often seem depressed and close to emotional breakdown.* ● See also **nervous breakdown. 3** If a car or a piece of machinery has a **breakdown**, it stops working. *Her old car was unreliable, so the trip was plagued by breakdowns.* **4** A **breakdown** of something is a list of its separate parts. *The organisers were given a breakdown of the costs.*   N-COUNT   N-COUNT

break·er /ˈbreɪkə/ **breakers. Breakers** are big sea waves, especially at the point when they just reach the shore. ● See also **law-breaker**, **record-breaker**, **strike-breaker**.   ◆◇◇◇   N-COUNT

break·fast /ˈbrekfəst/ **breakfasts, breakfasting, breakfasted. 1 Breakfast** is the first meal of the day. It is usually eaten in the early part of the morning. ● See also **bed and breakfast**, **continental breakfast**, **English breakfast. 2** When you **breakfast**, you have breakfast. *All the ladies breakfasted in their rooms.*   ◆◆◇◇   N-VAR   VERB   V   FORMAL

'breakfast table, breakfast tables. You refer to a table as **the breakfast table** when it is being used for breakfast. *...reading the morning papers at the breakfast table.*   N-COUNT

,breakfast 'television. Breakfast television refers to television programmes which are broadcast in the early morning.   N-UNCOUNT   BRITISH

'breakfast time; also spelled **breakfast-time. Breakfast time** is the period of the morning when most people have their breakfast. *By breakfast-time he was already at his desk.*   N-UNCOUNT

'break-in, break-ins. If there has been a **break-in**, someone has got into a building by force. *The break-in had occurred just before midnight.*   ◆◆◇◇   N-COUNT

'breaking point. If something or someone has reached **breaking point**, they have so many problems or difficulties that they may soon collapse or be unable to continue. *My nerves are almost at breaking point.*   N-UNCOUNT: also a N

break·neck /ˈbreɪknek/. If you say that something happens or travels at **breakneck** speed, you mean that it happens or travels very fast.   ADJ: ADJ n

break·out /ˈbreɪkaʊt/ **breakouts;** also spelled **break-out.** If there has been a **breakout**, someone has escaped from prison. *High Point prison had the highest number of breakouts of any jail in Britain.*   N-COUNT

break·through /ˈbreɪkθruː/ **breakthroughs.** A **breakthrough** is an important development or achievement. *The company looks poised to make a significant breakthrough in China.*   ◆◆◇◇   N-COUNT

'break-up, break-ups. 1 The **break-up** of a marriage, relationship, or association is the act of it finishing or coming to an end. *Since the break-up of his marriage he had not formed any new relationships.* **2** The **break-up** of an organization or a country is the act of it separating or dividing into several parts. *...the break-up of British Rail for privatisation.*   ◆◆◇◇   N-COUNT   N-COUNT

break·water /ˈbreɪkwɔːtə/ **breakwaters.** A **breakwater** is a wooden or stone wall that extends from the shore into the sea and protects a harbour or beach from the force of the waves.   N-COUNT

breast /brest/ **breasts. 1** A woman's **breasts** are the two soft round pieces of flesh on her chest that can produce milk to feed a baby. ♦ **-breasted** *She was slim and muscular and full-breasted.* **2** A person's **breast** is the upper part of his or her chest. *He struck his breast.* **3** If you say that someone **beats** their **breast**, you are emphasizing that they are very angry or upset about something, or that they are pretending to be very angry or upset about it. *The president beat his breast and called that deal a mistake.* **4** The **breast** is often considered to be the part of your body where your emotions are. *The verse rose up to fire his breast with inspiration.* **5** The **breast** of a shirt, jacket, or coat is the part which covers the top part of the chest. *...reaching for something inside the breast of his overcoat.* ● See also **double-breasted**, **single-breasted. 6** A bird's **breast** is the front part of its body. *...a wild robin with a red breast.* ♦ **-breasted** *...flocks of red-breasted*   ◆◆◇◇   N-COUNT   COMB   N-COUNT: poss N   LITERARY   PHRASE   PRAGMATICS   N-COUNT   LITERARY   N-SING: the N   N-COUNT   COMB

parrots. **7** A piece of **breast** is a piece of meat that is cut from the front of a bird or lamb. N-VAR

breast·bone /'brestbəʊn/ **breastbones;** also spelled **breast bone.** Your **breastbone** is the long flat bone which goes from your throat to the bottom of your ribs and to which your ribs are attached. N-COUNT

'**breast-feed, breast-feeds, breast-feeding, breast-fed;** also spelled **breastfeed** or **breast feed.** When a woman **breast-feeds** her baby, she feeds it with milk from her breasts, rather than from a bottle. *...breast-fed babies.* ♦ **breast-feeding** *There are many advantages to breast feeding.* ◆◇◇◇ VERB: V n / V-ed / Also V — N-UNCOUNT

'**breast milk.** Breast milk is the white liquid produced by women to breast-feed their babies. N-UNCOUNT

breast·plate /'brestpleɪt/ **breastplates.** A **breast-plate** is a piece of armour that covers and protects the chest. N-COUNT

,**breast 'pocket, breast pockets.** The breast **pocket** of a man's coat or jacket is a pocket, usually on the inside, next to his chest. N-COUNT: with poss

breast·stroke /'breststrəʊk/. **Breaststroke** is a swimming stroke which you do lying on your front, moving your arms and legs horizontally in a circular motion. N-UNCOUNT

breath /breθ/ **breaths. 1** Your **breath** is the air that you let out through your mouth when you breathe. If someone has bad **breath** their breath smells unpleasant. *I could smell the whisky on his breath.* ◆◆◇◇ N-VAR

2 When you take a **breath,** you breathe in once. *He took a deep breath... He spoke for one and a half hours and barely paused for breath.* **3** If you do not have time to **draw breath,** you do not have time to have a break from what you are doing. **4** If you go outside **for a breath of fresh air** or **for a breath of air,** you go outside because it is stuffy indoors. N-VAR / PHRASE / PHRASE

5 When you **get** your **breath** back after doing something energetic, you start breathing normally again. **6** When you **catch** your **breath** while you are doing something energetic, you stop for a short time so that you can start breathing normally again. **7** If something makes you **catch** your **breath,** it makes you take a short breath of air, usually because it shocks you. *Kenny caught his breath as Nikko nearly dropped the bottle.* **8** If you **hold** your **breath,** you make yourself stop breathing for a few moments, for example because you are under water. **9** If you are **out of breath,** you are breathing very quickly and with difficulty because you have been doing something energetic. **10** If you are **short of breath,** you find it difficult to breathe properly, for example because you are ill. You can also say that someone suffers from **shortness of breath.** PHRASE / BRITISH / PHRASE / PHRASE / PHRASE / PHRASE / PHRASE

11 If you say that there is not a **breath** of wind or air, you are emphasizing that there is no wind and the air is very still. *There's hardly a breath of air even in here with the fans going.* **12** A **breath of** something, is a small amount of it. *It was left to Martina to add a breath of common sense to the proceedings.* **13** If you describe something new or different as **a breath of fresh air,** you mean that it makes a situation or subject more interesting or exciting; used showing approval. *Her brisk treatment of an almost taboo subject was a breath of fresh air.* N-SING / PRAGMATICS / WRITTEN — N-SING: N of n / WRITTEN / PHRASE / PRAGMATICS

14 If you say that someone **is holding** their **breath,** you mean that they are waiting anxiously or excitedly for something to happen. *The whole world holds its breath for this speech.* **15** If you say that you **won't hold** your **breath,** you mean that you do not expect something to happen even though someone has suggested that it might. *'Next thing you know, I'll be dancing at your wedding', he cried. 'Don't hold your breath',* my father replied. **16** If you say that something **takes** your **breath away,** you are emphasizing that it is extremely beautiful or surprising. *I heard this song on the radio and it just took my breath away.* PHRASE / WRITTEN / PHRASE / INFORMAL / PHRASE / PRAGMATICS

17 You can use **in the same breath** or **in the next breath** to indicate that someone says two very different or contradictory things, especially when you are criticizing them. *He hailed this week's arms agreement but in the same breath expressed suspicion about the* PHRASE / PRAGMATICS

motivations of the United States. **18** If you say something **under** your **breath,** you say it in a very quiet voice, often because you do not want other people to hear what you are saying. PHRASE

19 ● **with bated breath:** see **bated.** ● **to fight for breath:** see **fight.**

breath·able /'briːðəbəl/. A **breathable** fabric allows air to pass through it easily, so that it is cool and comfortable to wear. ADJ

breatha·lyze /'breθəlaɪz/ **breathalyzes, breathalyzing, breathalyzed;** also spelled **breathalyse.** If the driver of a car **is breathalyzed** by the police, they ask him or her to breathe into a special device in order to test whether he or she has drunk too much alcohol. ● **breatha·lyz·er** /'breθəlaɪzə/ **breathalyzers.** A breathalyzer is a bag or electronic device that is used to breathalyze someone. VB: usu passive BRITISH — N-COUNT

breathe /briːð/ **breathes, breathing, breathed. 1** When people or animals **breathe,** they take air into their lungs and let it out again. When they **breathe** smoke or a particular kind of air, they take it into their lungs and let it out again as they breathe. *No American should have to drive out of town to breathe clean air... A thirteen year old girl is being treated after breathing in smoke.* ♦ **breathing** *Her breathing became slow and heavy.* **2** If someone **breathes** something, they say it very quietly. *'You don't understand,' he breathed.* **3** If you do not **breathe** a word about something, you say nothing about it, because it is a secret. *He never breathed a word about our conversation.* **4** If someone **breathes** life, confidence, or excitement **into** something, they improve it by adding this quality. *It is the readers who breathe life into a newspaper with their letters.* ◆◆◆◇◇ VERB: V / V n / V n with in/ out — N-UNCOUNT / VERB: V n / V with quote / LITERARY / VB: with brd-neg, no cont / V n — VERB / V n into / WRITTEN

5 If you let wine **breathe,** you open the bottle to allow the air to get in and improve its flavour before you drink it. VERB: V

6 ● **to be breathing down someone's neck:** see **neck.** ● **to breathe a sigh of relief:** see **sigh.**

breathe in. When you **breathe in,** you take some air into your lungs. PHRASAL VB V P

breathe out. When you **breathe out,** you send air out of your lungs through your nose or mouth. PHRASAL VB V P

breath·er /'briːðə/ **breathers.** If you take a **breather,** you stop what you are doing for a short time and have a rest. N-COUNT INFORMAL

'**breathing space, breathing spaces.** A **breathing space** is a short period of time between two activities in which you can recover from the first activity and prepare for the second one. *We hope that it will give us some breathing space.* ♦◇◇◇◇ N-VAR

breath·less /'breθləs/. **1** If you are **breathless,** you have difficulty in breathing properly, for example because you have been running or because you are afraid or excited. ♦ **breath·less·ly** *'I'll go in,' he said breathlessly.* ♦ **breath·less·ness** *Asthma causes wheezing and breathlessness.* **2** You use **breathless** for emphasis when you are describing feelings of excitement or exciting situations. *Technology has advanced at a breathless pace.* ♦ **breath·less·ly** *Nancy waited breathlessly for him to go on.* ◆◇◇◇◇ ADJ-GRADED / ADV-GRADED / N-UNCOUNT / ADJ: ADJ n / PRAGMATICS — ADV

breath·taking /'breθteɪkɪŋ/; also spelled **breath-taking.** If you say that something is **breathtaking,** you are emphasizing that it is extremely beautiful or amazing. *The house has breathtaking views from every room.* ♦ **breath·taking·ly** *...a breathtakingly simple gadget.* ADJ-GRADED / PRAGMATICS — ADV-GRADED

'**breath test, breath tests.** A **breath test** is a test carried out by police in which a motorist blows into a special device to show how much alcohol he or she has drunk. N-COUNT

breathy /'breθi/. If someone has a **breathy** voice, you can hear their breath when they speak or sing. ADJ

bred /bred/. **1 Bred** is the past tense and past participle of **breed. 2** See also **pure-bred, well-bred.**

breeches /'brɪtʃɪz/. **Breeches** are trousers which reach as far as your knees. N-PLURAL DATED

breed /briːd/ **breeds, breeding, bred. 1** A **breed** ◆◆◆◇◇ N-COUNT of a pet or farm animal is a particular type of it. For example, terriers are a breed of dog. **2** You can refer to someone or something as one of a N-COUNT particular **breed** of person or thing when you want to talk about what they are like. *Sue is one of the new breed of British women squash players.* **3** If you **breed** animals or plants, you keep them for VERB: V n the purpose of producing more animals or plants with V n prep particular qualities, in a controlled way. *He used to beV-ed to inf breed dogs for the police... These dogs are bred to fight.* ● See also **cross-breed.** ♦ **breed·er, breeders.** *Her* N-COUNT *father was a racehorse breeder.* ♦ **breed·ing** ...*selec-* N-UNCOUNT *tive breeding for better yields.* **4** When animals **breed,** VERB: V they mate and produce offspring. ♦ **breeding** *Dur-* N-UNCOUNT *ing the breeding season the birds come ashore.* **5** If you say that something **breeds** bad feeling or bad VERB behaviour, you mean that it causes it to develop. *If* V n *they are unemployed it's bound to breed resentment.* **6** If you say that someone **has been bred** for a particu- V-PASSIVE lar lifestyle or **has been bred** to behave in a particular beV-ed to inf way, you mean that they have been prepared for that lifestyle or behaviour ever since childhood. *They have been bred to compete and succeed.* **7** Someone who PHRASE was **born and bred** in a place was born there and spent their childhood there. *I'm a Londoner born and bred.* **8** See also **breeding; pure-bred, well-bred.**

breed·ing /'briːdɪŋ/. If someone says that a person N-UNCOUNT has **breeding,** they mean that they think the person is from a good social background and has good manners. *It's a sign of good breeding to know the names of all your staff.* ● See also **breed.**

'**breeding ground, breeding grounds. 1** If you N-COUNT refer to a situation or place as a **breeding ground** for something bad such as crime, you mean that this thing easily develops there. *Flaws in the system have created a breeding ground for financial scandals.* **2** The **breeding ground** for a particular type of N-COUNT: creature is the place where this creature breeds. with supp *Warm milk is the ideal breeding ground for bacteria.*

breeze /briːz/ **breezes, breezing, breezed. 1** A ◆◆◇◇◇ **breeze** is a gentle wind. **2** If you **breeze** into a place N-COUNT or a position, you enter it in a very casual and care- VERB free way. *He was late, but eventually he breezed in.* V prep/adv **3** If you **breeze through** something such as a game VERB or test, you cope with or win it easily. *Jennifer* V through n *Capriati breezed through her opening match.* **4** If Also V through you say that something is **a breeze,** you mean that it N-SING: is very easy to do or to achieve. *Making the pastry is* a N *a breeze if you have a food processor.* INFORMAL

'**breeze-block, breeze-blocks;** also spelled N-COUNT **breeze block.** A **breeze-block** is a large, grey- BRITISH coloured brick made from ashes and cement.

breezy /'briːzi/. **1** If you describe someone as ◆◇◇◇◇ **breezy,** you mean that they behave in a casual, ADJ-GRADED cheerful, and confident manner. *...his bright and breezy personality.* ♦ **breezi·ly** /'briːzɪli/. *'Oh,* ADV-GRADED *yeah,' he replied as breezily as possible.* **2** If you de- ADJ-GRADED scribe something as **breezy,** you mean that it is JOURNALISM bright, lively, and cheerful. *This album is bright, breezy and playful.* **3** When the weather is **breezy,** ADJ-GRADED there is a fairly strong but pleasant wind.

breth·ren /'breðrɪn/. You can refer to the members ◆◇◇◇◇ of an organization or group, especially a religious N-PLURAL group, as **brethren.** *Sri Lankans share a common* DATED *ancestry with their Indian brethren.*

brev·ity /'breviti/. **1** The **brevity** of something is N-UNCOUNT the fact that it lasts for only a short time. *The bonus* FORMAL *of this homely soup is the brevity of its cooking time.* **2 Brevity** is the use of only a few words to say or N-UNCOUNT write something. FORMAL

brew /bruː/ **brews, brewing, brewed. 1** If you ◆◆◇◇◇ **brew** tea or coffee, you make it by pouring hot wa- VERB: V n ter over tea leaves or ground coffee. **2** A **brew** is a N-COUNT pot of tea or coffee. It can also be a particular kind of tea or coffee. *...a mild herbal brew.* **3** If someone **brews** beer, they make it. *Beer has been* VERB: V n *brewed on this spot for the last 300 years.* ♦ **brew·ing** N-UNCOUNT ...*the brewing of home-made alcohol.* **4** A **brew** is a N-COUNT

particular kind of beer. *...low-alcohol brews.* ● See also **home-brew.** **5** If a storm **is brewing,** large, dark clouds are begin- VERB: V ning to form because there is going to be a storm. **6** If VERB an unpleasant or difficult situation **is brewing,** it is V starting to develop. *A crisis was brewing.* **7** A **brew** of several things is a mixture of them. *...a* N-COUNT *complex brew of pollutants.*

brew up. 1 If someone **brews up** or if they **brew up** PHRASAL VB some tea, they make tea. *Brew up, Curly. We could all* V P *do with a cup of tea.* **2** If someone is **brewing up** an BRITISH, unpleasant situation or if an unpleasant situation is INFORMAL **brewing up,** it is starting to develop. *I realized the ex-* V P noun *tent of the trouble that Mary Morse was brewing up...* V P *There's another security scandal brewing up.*

brew·er /'bruːə/ **brewers.** Brewers are people or ◆◇◇◇◇ companies who make beer. N-COUNT

brew·ery /'bruːəri/ **breweries.** A **brewery** is a ◆◇◇◇◇ place where beer is made. N-COUNT

bri·ar /braɪə/ **briars.** A **briar** is a wild rose with long N-COUNT thorny stems.

bribe /braɪb/ **bribes, bribing, bribed. 1** A **bribe** ◆◆◇◇◇ is a sum of money or something valuable that one N-COUNT person offers or gives to another in order to per- suade him or her to do something. *He was being in- vestigated for receiving bribes.* **2** If someone **bribes** VERB: V n another person, they give him or her a bribe. *The* V n to-inf *government bribed the workers to be quiet.*

brib·ery /'braɪbəri/. **Bribery** is the act of offering ◆◇◇◇◇ someone a bribe. N-UNCOUNT

bric-a-brac /'brɪkəbræk/. **Bric-a-brac** is an assort- N-UNCOUNT ment of small ornamental objects of no great value.

brick /brɪk/ **bricks, bricking, bricked. 1** Bricks ◆◆◇◇◇ are rectangular blocks of baked clay used for build- N-VAR ing walls. **Brick** is the material made up of these blocks. See picture headed **house and flat.** *...high brick walls.* **2** You can use **bricks and mortar** to re- PHRASE fer to houses and other buildings, especially when BRITISH they are considered as an investment. *It's far better to put your money into bricks and mortar.* **3** If someone or something **hits a brick wall** or **comes** PHRASE **up against a brick wall,** they are unable to make pro- INFORMAL gress because something stops them. *The discussions in Brussels hit a brick wall.* **4** If you say that someone PHRASE **is banging their head against a brick wall,** you mean INFORMAL that what they are saying or doing is not having any effect although they keep saying or doing it.

brick up. If you **brick up** a hole, you close it with a PHRASAL VB wall of bricks. *We bricked up our windows.* V P noun

brick·bat /'brɪkbæt/ **brickbats.** Brickbats are very N-COUNT critical or insulting remarks which are made in pub- lic about someone or something. *...endless brickbats from the Scottish media.*

brickie /'brɪki/ **brickies.** A **brickie** is the same as a N-COUNT **bricklayer.** BRITISH, INFORMAL

brick·layer /'brɪkleɪə/ **bricklayers.** A **bricklayer** is N-COUNT a person whose job is to build walls using bricks.

brick·work /'brɪkwɜːk/. You can refer to the bricks N-UNCOUNT in the walls of a building as the **brickwork.**

brid·al /'braɪdəl/. **Bridal** is used to describe some- ◆◇◇◇◇ thing that belongs or relates to a bride, or to both a ADJ: ADJ n bride and her bridegroom. *...a floor length bridal gown.*

bride /braɪd/ **brides.** A **bride** is a woman who is ◆◆◇◇◇ getting married or who has just got married. N-COUNT

bride·groom /'braɪdgruːm/ **bridegrooms.** A N-COUNT **bridegroom** is a man who is getting married.

brides·maid /'braɪdzmeɪd/ **bridesmaids.** A ◆◇◇◇◇ **bridesmaid** is a woman or a girl who helps and ac- N-COUNT companies a bride on her wedding day.

'**bride-to-'be, brides-to-be.** A **bride-to-be** is a N-COUNT woman who is soon going to be married.

bridge /brɪdʒ/ **bridges, bridging, bridged. 1** A ◆◆◆◆◇ **bridge** is a structure that is built over a railway, riv- N-COUNT er, or road so that people or vehicles can cross from one side to the other. **2** See also **suspension bridge.** **3** To **bridge** the gap between two people or things VERB means to make it easier for the differences or dis- PRAGMATICS agreements between them to be reduced or over- V n come. *It is unlikely that the two sides will be able to*

bridge their differences. ▶ Also a noun. *We hope this* N-COUNT
book will act as a bridge between doctor and patient.

4 Something that **bridges** the gap between two very VERB
different things has some of the qualities of each of Vn
these things. *...the singer who bridged the gap between*
pop music and opera.

5 The **bridge** is a structure or cabin on a ship from N-COUNT
which it is steered.

6 The **bridge** of your nose is the thin top part of it, be- N-COUNT
tween your eyes. **7** The **bridge** of a pair of glasses is N-COUNT
the part that rests on your nose. **8** The **bridge** of a vio- N-COUNT
lin, guitar, or other stringed instrument is the small
piece of wood under the strings that holds them up.

9 Bridge is a card game for four players. N-UNCOUNT

10 If you **burn your bridges**, you do something which PHRASE
forces you to continue with a particular course of action, and makes it impossible for you to return to an
earlier situation or relationship. • **water under the**
bridge: see **water**.

bridge·head /'brɪdʒhed/ **bridgeheads.** A **bridge-** N-COUNT
head is a good position which an army has taken in
the enemy's territory and from which it can advance or attack. *A bridgehead was established.*

'bridging loan, bridging loans. A **bridging loan** N-COUNT
is money that a bank or other company lends you .BRITISH
for a short time to cover the period until you get
money from somewhere else, for example so that
you can buy another house before you have sold
the one you already own.

bri·dle /'braɪdəl/ **bridles, bridling, bridled. 1** A ◆◇◇◇◇
bridle is a set of straps that is put around a horse's N-COUNT
head and mouth so that the person riding or driving
the horse can control it. **2** If someone **bridles** at VERB
something, they are angry about it or take offence. V at n
Alex bridled at the shortness of Pamela's tone. Also V
LITERARY

'bridle path, bridle paths; also spelled N-COUNT
bridlepath. A **bridle path** is the same as a
bridleway.

bridle·way /'braɪdəlweɪ/ **bridleways.** A **bridleway** N-COUNT
is a path intended for people riding horses. BRITISH

Brie /briː/; also spelled **brie. Brie** is a type of cheese N-UNCOUNT
that comes from France. It is soft and creamy with a
hard greyish-white skin.

brief /briːf/ **briefer, briefest; briefs, briefing,** ◆◆◆◇
briefed. 1 Something that is **brief** lasts for only a ADJ-GRADED
short time. *...a brief appearance on television.* **2** A ADJ-GRADED
brief speech or piece of writing does not contain
too many words or details. *...a brief statement.* **3** If ADJ-GRADED:
you are **brief**, you say what you want to say in as v-link ADJ
few words as possible. *I hope to be brief and to the*
point. **4** You can describe a period of time as **brief** if ADJ-GRADED
you want to emphasize that it is very short. *For a* PRAGMATICS
few brief minutes we forgot the anxiety.

5 If you refer to something **in brief**, you are referring PHRASE
to a shortened version of it with few details. *...and now*
sport in brief. **6** You can say **in brief** to indicate that PHRASE
you are about to say something in as few words as
possible or to summarize what you have just said. *In*
brief, take no risks.

7 Men's or women's underpants can be referred to as N-PLURAL:
briefs. also a pair of N

8 If someone **briefs** you, especially about a piece of VERB: V n
work or a serious matter, they give you information
that you need before you do it or consider it. ♦ **brief-**
·er /'briːfə/ **briefers.** *...military briefers.* **9** See also N-COUNT
briefing.

10 If someone gives you a **brief**, they officially give N-COUNT
you the responsibility for dealing with a particular FORMAL
thing. *...customs officials with a brief to stop foreign*
porn coming into Britain.

brief·case /'briːfkeɪs/ **briefcases.** A **briefcase** is a ◆◇◇◇◇
case used for carrying documents in. N-COUNT

brief·er /'briːfə/. See **brief**.

brief·ing /'briːfɪŋ/ **briefings.** A **briefing** is a meet- ◆◆◇◇◇
ing at which information or instructions are given N-VAR
to people, especially before they do something.
• See also **brief**.

brief·ly /'briːfli/. **1** Something that happens or is ◆◆◇◇◇
done **briefly** happens or is done for a very short pe- ADV-GRADED:
riod of time. *He smiled briefly... Guerillas captured* ADV with v

and briefly held an important provincial capital. **2** If ADV-GRADED:
you say or write something **briefly**, you use very few ADV with v
words or give very few details. *There are four basic*
alternatives; they are described briefly below. **3** You ADV-GRADED:
can say **briefly** to indicate that you are about to say ADV with cl
something in as few words as possible. *Briefly, no*
less than nine of our agents have passed information
to us.

brig /brɪg/ **brigs.** A **brig** is a type of ship with two N-COUNT
masts and square sails.

Brig. /ˌbrɪgə'dɪə/. **Brig.** is a written abbreviation for
brigadier. *...Brig. Douglas Erskin Crum.*

bri·gade /brɪ'geɪd/ **brigades. 1** A **brigade** is one ◆◆◇◇◇
of the groups which an army is divided into. • See N-COLL-
also **fire brigade. 2** You can use **brigade** humorous- COUNT
ly to refer to a group of people who believe strongly N-SING:
in a particular thing or who share a particular char- n N
acteristic. *...the healthy eating brigade.*

briga·dier /ˌbrɪgə'dɪə/ **brigadiers.** A **brigadier** is a ◆◇◇◇◇
senior officer in the armed forces. N-COUNT;
N-TITLE
,brigadier 'general, brigadier generals; also N-COUNT:
spelled **brigadier-general.** In the United States, a N-TITLE
brigadier general is a senior officer in the armed
forces.

brig·and /'brɪgənd/ **brigands.** A **brigand** is some- N-COUNT
one who attacks people and steals their property, LITERARY
especially in mountainous areas or forests.

bright /braɪt/ **brighter, brightest. 1** A **bright** col- ◆◆◆◇
our is strong and noticeable, and not dark. *...a* ADJ-GRADED
bright red dress. ...the bright uniforms of the guards.
♦ **bright·ly** *...brightly coloured wallpaper trimmed* ADV-GRADED
in pink and blue. ♦ **bright·ness** *...the brightness* N-UNCOUNT
and the beauty of the colors. **2** A **bright** light, object, ADJ-GRADED
or place is shining strongly or is full of light. *...a*
bright October day... She leaned forward, her eyes
bright with excitement. ♦ **bright·ly** *...a warm,* ADV-GRADED
brightly lit room... The sun shone brightly.
♦ **bright·ness** *...the brightness of each star.* N-UNCOUNT

3 If you describe someone as **bright**, you mean that ADJ-GRADED
they are quick at learning things. **4** A **bright** idea is ADJ-GRADED
clever and original.

5 If someone looks or sounds **bright**, they look or ADJ-GRADED
sound cheerful and lively. *'May I help you?' said a*
bright American voice over the telephone. ♦ **bright·ly** ADV-GRADED:
He smiled brightly as Ben approached. **6** If you say the ADV with v
future looks **bright**, you mean it is likely to be pleasant ADJ-GRADED
or successful. **7** If you **look on the bright side**, you try PHRASE
to be cheerful about a bad situation by thinking of
some advantages that could result from it, or thinking
that it is not as bad as it could have been.

bright·en /'braɪtən/ **brightens, brightening,** ◆◇◇◇◇
brightened. 1 If someone **brightens** or their face VERB: V
brightens, they suddenly look happier. ▶ **Brighten** PHRASAL VB
up means the same as **brighten**. *He brightened up a* V P
bit. **2** If your eyes **brighten**, you suddenly look in- VERB: V
terested or excited. *Her tearful eyes brightened with* V with n
interest.

3 If someone or something **brightens** a place, they VERB
make it more colourful and attractive. *Tubs planted* V n
with wallflowers brightened the area outside the door.
▶ **Brighten up** means the same as **brighten**. *David* PHRASAL VB
spotted the pink silk lampshade in a shop and thought V P noun
it would brighten up the room... Why don't you start to V P n
brighten the apartment up? **4** If someone or some- V-ERG: V n
thing **brightens** a situation or the situation **brightens**, V
it becomes more pleasant, enjoyable, or favourable. *It*
is undeniable that the economic picture is brightening.
▶ **Brighten up** means the same as **brighten**. *His* PHRASAL VB
cheerful face brightens up the dullest of days. ERG
V P noun
5 When a light **brightens** a place or when a place V-ERG: V
brightens, it becomes brighter or lighter. *The late* V n
afternoon sun brightened the interior of the church.
6 If the weather **brightens**, it becomes less cloudy or VERB: V
rainy, and the sun starts to shine. ▶ **Brighten up** PHRASAL VB
means the same as **brighten**. *Hopefully it will bright-* it V P
en up.

,bright 'lights. If someone talks about the **bright** N-PLURAL:
lights, they are referring to life in a big city, where the N
you can do a lot of enjoyable and exciting things.
The bright lights of Hollywood.

B

'bright spark, bright sparks. If you say that some **bright spark** had a particular idea or did something, you mean that their idea or action was clever, or that it seemed clever but was silly in some way.   N-COUNT INFORMAL, BRITISH

brill /brɪl/. If you say that something is **brill**, you are very pleased about it or think that it is very good. *What a brill idea!*   ◆◇◇◇ ADJ-GRADED BRITISH, INFORMAL

bril·liant /'brɪliənt/. **1** A **brilliant** person, idea, or performance is extremely clever or skilful. *She had a brilliant mind.* ♦ **bril·liant·ly** *...a very high quality production, brilliantly written and acted.* ♦ **bril·liance** *He was a deeply serious musician who had shown his brilliance very early.* **2** You can say that something is **brilliant** when you are very pleased about it or think that it is very good. *My sister's given me this brilliant book.* **3** You can also say something is **brilliant** when it is very successful. *...his brilliant career.* ♦ **brilliantly** *The strategy worked brilliantly.*   ◆◆◇◇ ADJ-GRADED / ADV-GRADED / N-UNCOUNT / ADJ-GRADED INFORMAL, BRITISH / ADJ-GRADED / ADV-GRADED

4 A **brilliant** colour is extremely bright. *The woman had brilliant green eyes. ...a brilliant white open-necked shirt.* ♦ **bril·liant·ly** *Brilliantly coloured flowers burst from the rich earth.* ♦ **bril·liance** *...an iridescent blue butterfly in all its brilliance.* **5** You describe light, or something that reflects light, as **brilliant** when it shines very brightly. *...brilliant sunshine.* ♦ **bril·liant·ly** *...a brilliantly sunny morning.* ♦ **bril·liance** *...the brilliance of the sun outside.*   ADJ-GRADED ADJ n / ADV-GRADED: ADV adj/-ed N-UNCOUNT ADJ-GRADED / ADV-GRADED / N-UNCOUNT

brim /brɪm/ **brims, brimming, brimmed. 1** The **brim** of a hat is the wide part that sticks outwards round the bottom. ♦ **-brimmed** *...a wide-brimmed straw-hat.*   ◆◇◇◇ N-COUNT / COMB

2 If you say that someone or something **is brimming with** something, especially a particular quality, you mean that they are full of that thing. *England are brimming with confidence after two straight wins in the tournament.* ▶ **Brim over** means the same as **brim**. *I noticed Dorabella was brimming over with excitement.* **3** If your eyes **are brimming with** tears, they are full of fluid because you are upset, although you are not actually crying. ▶ **Brim over** means the same as **brim**. *When she saw me, her eyes brimmed over with tears.* **4** If something **brims** with particular things, it is packed full of them. *The flowerbeds brim with a mixture of lilies and roses.* **5** If something, especially a container, **is filled to the brim** or **full to the brim** with something, it is filled right up to the top.   VERB V with n / PHRASAL VB V P with n V P / VERB: V with n / PHRASAL VB V P with n / VERB V with n / PHRASE

brim·stone /'brɪmstəʊn/. **1** Brimstone is the same as **sulphur**. **2** If someone threatens you with **fire and brimstone**, they are referring to hell and emphasizing how people are punished there after death.   N-UNCOUNT DATED / PHRASE

brine /braɪn/ **brines.** Brine is salty water, especially salty water that is used for preserving food.   N-VAR

bring /brɪŋ/ **brings, bringing, brought. 1** If you **bring** someone or something with you when you come to a place, they come with you or you have them with you. *Remember to bring an apron or an old shirt to protect your clothes... Someone went upstairs and brought down a huge kettle.* **2** If you **bring** something somewhere, you move it there. *Reaching into her pocket, she brought out a cigarette.* **3** If you **bring** something that someone wants or needs, you fetch it for them or carry it to them. *He poured a brandy for Dena and brought it to her... The stewardess kindly brought me a blanket.* **4** To **bring** something or someone to a place or position means to cause them to come to the place or move into that position. *I told you about what brought me here. ...a gas blast which brought her home crashing down.* **5** If you **bring** something new to a place or group of people, you introduce it to that place or to those people. *...a brave reporter who had risked death to bring the story to the world.* **6** To **bring** someone or something into a particular state or condition means to cause them to be in that state or condition. *He brought the car to a stop... They have brought down income taxes.* **7** If something **brings** a particular feeling, situation,   ◆◆◆◆ VERB V n / V n with adv / VERB V n with adv / VERB V n to/for n V n n Also V n / VERB V n prep/adv V n -ing / VERB V n to n / VERB V n prep V n with adv / VERB

or quality, it makes people experience it or have it. *I hope that the election will bring peace to Cambodians... He brought to the job not just considerable experience but passionate enthusiasm... Her three children brought her joy.* **8** If a period of time **brings** a particular thing, it happens during that time. *For Sandra, the new year brought disaster.*   V n to/on/ from n V to n V n n / VERB V n

9 If you **bring** a legal action against someone or **bring** them to trial, you officially accuse them of doing something unlawful. *The ship's captain and crew may be brought to trial.*   VERB be V-ed to n Also V n against n

10 If a television or radio programme **is brought** to you by an organization, they make it, broadcast it, or pay for it to be made or broadcast. *You're listening to Science in Action, brought to you by the BBC World Service.*   VERB be V-ed to n to by Also V n n

11 When you are talking, you can say that something **brings** you to a particular point in order to indicate that you have now reached that point and are going to talk about a new subject. *Which brings me to a delicate matter I should like to raise.*   VERB PRAGMATICS V n to n

12 If you cannot **bring** yourself to do something, you cannot do it because you find it too painful, embarrassing, or disgusting. *I just cannot bring myself to talk about it.*   VB: with brd- neg V pron-refl to-inf

13 • to **bring** something **alive**: see **alive**. • to **bring** something **to bear**: see **bear**. • to **bring the house down**: see **house**. • to **bring up the rear**: see **rear**.

bring about. To **bring** something **about** means to cause it to happen. *The only way to bring about political change is by putting pressure on the country.*   PHRASAL VB V P noun Also V n P

bring along. If you **bring** someone or something **along**, you bring them with you when you come to a place. *They brought along Laura Jane in a pram... Dad brought a notebook along.*   PHRASAL VB V P noun V n P

bring around. See **bring round**.   PHRASAL VB

bring back. 1 If something **brings back** a memory, it makes you think about it. *Your article brought back sad memories for me.* **2** When people **bring back** a practice or fashion that existed at an earlier time, they introduce it again. *...to debate once again whether to bring back the death penalty.*   PHRASAL VB V P noun Also V n P / Also V n P

bring down. 1 When people or events **bring down** a government or ruler, they cause the government or ruler to lose power. *They were threatening to bring down the government.* **2** If someone or something **brings down** a person or aeroplane, they cause them to fall, usually by shooting them. *Military historians may never know what brought down the jet.*   PHRASAL VB V P noun Also V n P / Also V n P

bring forward. 1 If you **bring forward** a meeting or event, you arrange for it to take place at an earlier date or time than had been planned. *He had to bring forward an 11 o'clock meeting so that he could attend the funeral on time.* **2** If you **bring forward** an argument or proposal, you state it so that people can consider it. *The Government will bring forward proposals for legislation.*   PHRASAL VB V P noun Also V n P BRITISH / V P noun Also V n P

bring in. 1 When a government or organization **brings in** a new law or system, they introduce it. *The government brought in a controversial law under which it could take any land it wanted.* **2** Someone or something that **brings in** money makes it or earns it. *I have three part-time jobs, which bring in about £6,000 a year.* **3** If you **bring in** someone from outside a team or organization, you invite them to do a job or participate in an activity or discussion. *The firm decided to bring in a new management team.* **4** When a jury or inquest **brings in** a verdict, the verdict is officially decided. *The jury took 23 hours to bring in its verdict.*   PHRASAL VB V P noun Also V n P / V P noun Also V n P / V P noun Also V n P / V P noun

bring off. If you **bring off** something difficult, you do it successfully. *They were about to bring off an even bigger coup.*   PHRASAL VB V P noun Also V n P

bring on. If something **brings on** an illness, pain, or feeling, especially one that you often suffer from, it causes you to have it. *Severe shock can bring on an attack of acne.*   PHRASAL VB V P noun Also V-ed P, V P noun

bring out. 1 When a person or company **brings out** a new product, especially a new book or record, they produce it and put it on sale. *A journalist all his life, he's now brought out a book.* **2** Something that **brings**   PHRASAL VB V P noun Also V n P / V P noun

out a particular kind of behaviour or feeling in you causes you to show it, especially when it is something you do not normally show. *Sea air seems to bring out the lover in some people.*   Also V n P

bring round or **bring around.** The form **bring round** is mainly used in British English. **1** If you **bring** someone **round** when they are unconscious, you make them conscious again. **2** If you **bring** someone **round**, you cause them to change their opinion about something so that they agree with you. *We will do everything we can to bring parliament round to our point of view.*   PHRASAL VB   V n P   V n P to n   Also V n P

bring to. If you **bring** someone **to** when they are unconscious, you make them conscious again.   PHRASAL VB

bring up. 1 When someone **brings up** a child, they look after it until it is grown up. *She brought up four children... He was brought up in North Yorkshire... I bring my children up to be trusting, honest and helpful.* **2** If you **bring up** a particular subject, you introduce it into a discussion or conversation. *He brought up a subject rarely raised during the course of this campaign.* **3** If someone **brings up** food or wind, food or air is forced up from their stomach through their mouth. *It's hard for the baby to bring up wind.*   PHRASAL VB   V P noun   V n P to-inf   V P noun   Also V n P   V P noun   Also V n P

bring·er /ˈbrɪŋə/ **bringers.** A **bringer** of something is someone who brings or provides it. *He was the bringer of great glad tidings.*   N-COUNT: with supp LITERARY

brink /brɪŋk/. If you are on the **brink** of something important, terrible, or exciting, you are just about to do it or experience it. *...a nation on the brink of war.*   ◆◆◇◇◇ N-SING

brink·man·ship /ˈbrɪŋkmənʃɪp/. **Brinkmanship** is a method of behaviour, especially in politics, in which you deliberately get into dangerous situations which could result in disaster but which could also bring success.   N-UNCOUNT

bri·oche /briˈɒʃ/ **brioches.** Brioche is a kind of sweet bread that is often made into small buns.   N-VAR

brisk /brɪsk/ **brisker, briskest. 1** A **brisk** action is done quickly and in an energetic way. *...a brisk walk.* ♦ **brisk·ly** *Eve walked briskly down the corridor.* ♦ **brisk·ness** *He sat up with surprising briskness.* **2** If trade or business is **brisk**, things are being sold very quickly and a lot of money is being made. *...a brisk trade in souvenirs.* **3** If the weather is **brisk**, it is cold and refreshing. *...a brisk winter's day.* **4** If someone's behaviour is **brisk**, they behave in a busy confident way which shows that they want to get things done quickly. *Her voice was brisk and professional.* ♦ **brisk·ly** *'Anyhow,' she added briskly, 'it's none of my business.'* ♦ **brisk·ness** *...her familiar briskness.*   ◆◆◇◇◇ ADJ-GRADED   ADV-GRADED   N-UNCOUNT   ADJ-GRADED   ADJ-GRADED   ADJ-GRADED   ADV-GRADED: ADV with v   N-UNCOUNT

bris·ket /ˈbrɪskɪt/. Brisket is a cut of beef that comes from the breast of the cow.   N-UNCOUNT

bris·tle /ˈbrɪsəl/ **bristles, bristling, bristled. 1** Bristles are the short hairs that grow on a man's chin after he has shaved. **2** The **bristles** of a brush are the thick hairs or hair-like pieces of plastic which are attached to it. **3** An animal's **bristles** are thick strong hairs on its body that feel hard and rough. **4** If the hair on a person's or animal's body **bristles**, it rises away from their skin because they are cold, frightened, or angry. **5** If you **bristle** at something, you react to it angrily, and show this in your expression or the way you move. *Ellis bristles at accusations that Berkeley's experiment is ill-conceived.* **6** If you say that a place or thing **bristles with** people or with other things, you are emphasizing that it contains a great number of them. *The country bristles with armed groups.*   ◆◇◇◇◇ N-COUNT   N-COUNT   N-COUNT   VERB: V   VERB V at n Also V   VERB: V with n PRAGMATICS

bris·tling /ˈbrɪslɪŋ/. **1 Bristling** means thick, hairy, and rough. It is used to describe things such as moustaches, beards, or eyebrows. *...a bristling white moustache.* **2** If you describe someone's attitude as **bristling**, you are emphasizing that it is full of energy and enthusiasm. *...his bristling determination.*   ADJ: ADJ n   ADJ: ADJ n PRAGMATICS

bris·tly /ˈbrɪsli/. **1 Bristly** hair is rough, coarse, and thick. **2** If a man's chin is **bristly**, it is covered with bristles because he has not shaved recently.   ADJ-GRADED   ADJ-GRADED

Brit /brɪt/ **Brits.** British people are sometimes referred to as **Brits.** *...holiday mad Brits.*   ◆◆◇◇◇ N-COUNT INFORMAL

Brit·ish /ˈbrɪtɪʃ/. **1 British** means belonging or relating to the United Kingdom, or to its people or culture. *...the British government.* **2** The **British** are the people of the United Kingdom.   ◆◆◆◆◇ ADJ   N-PLURAL

British 'Asian, British Asians. A British Asian person is someone of Indian, Pakistani, or Bangladeshi origin who has grown up in Britain. ▸ A **British Asian** is someone who is British Asian.   ADJ   N-COUNT

Brit·on /ˈbrɪtən/ **Britons.** A **Briton** is a British citizen, or a person of British origin. *...seventeen-year-old Briton Jane March.*   ◆◆◇◇◇ N-COUNT JOURNALISM

brit·tle /ˈbrɪtəl/. **1** A **brittle** object or substance is hard but easily broken. **2** If you describe a situation, relationship, or someone's mood as **brittle**, you mean that it is unstable, and may easily change. *The brittle structure of Communist power collapsed quickly in Eastern Europe.* **3** Someone who is **brittle** seems rather sharp and insensitive and says things which are likely to hurt other people's feelings. **4** A **brittle** sound is short, loud, and sharp. *Myrtle gave a brittle laugh.*   ◆◇◇◇◇ ADJ-GRADED   ADJ-GRADED   ADJ-GRADED   ADJ-GRADED

broach /brəʊtʃ/ **broaches, broaching, broached.** When you **broach** a subject, especially a sensitive one, you mention it in order to start a discussion on it.   VERB: V n

broad /brɔːd/ **broader, broadest; broads. 1** Something that is **broad** is wide. *His shoulders were broad. ...the broad river.* **2** A **broad** smile is one in which your mouth is stretched very wide because you are very pleased or amused. ♦ **broad·ly** *Charles grinned broadly.* **3** You use **broad** to describe something that includes a large number of different things or people. *A broad range of issues was discussed.* **4** You use **broad** to describe a word or meaning which covers or refers to a wide range of different things. *The term Wissenschaft has a much broader meaning than the English word 'science'.* ♦ **broadly** *The new EC code defines sexual harassment very broadly.* **5** You use **broad** to describe a feeling or opinion that is shared by many people, or by people of many different kinds. *The agreement won broad support in the US Congress.* ♦ **broadly** *The new law has been broadly welcomed.* **6** A **broad** description or idea is general rather than detailed. *...a broad outline of the Society's development.* ♦ **broadly** *There are, broadly speaking, three ways in which this is done.* **7** A **broad** hint is a very obvious one. *They've been giving broad hints about what to expect.* ♦ **broadly** *He hinted broadly that he would like to come.* **8** A **broad** accent is strong and noticeable. *...a broad Yorkshire accent.* **9** Some men refer to women as **broads**. This is an offensive use. **10** See also **broadly. 11** ● **in broad daylight:** see **daylight.**   ◆◆◆◇ ADJ-GRADED   ADJ-GRADED   ADV-GRADED   ADJ-GRADED   ADJ-GRADED   ADV-GRADED   ADJ-GRADED: ADJ n   ADV-GRADED: ADV with v   ADV-GRADED   ADJ-GRADED: ADJ n ADV   ADJ-GRADED   N-COUNT AMERICAN

broad 'bean, broad beans. Broad beans are flat light green beans that are eaten as a vegetable.   N-COUNT BRITISH

broad-'brush; also spelled **broad brush.** A **broad-brush** approach, strategy, or solution deals with a problem in a general way rather than concentrating on details. *...Perot's broad-brush approach on the economy.*   ADJ

broad·cast /ˈbrɔːdkɑːst, -kæst/ **broadcasts, broadcasting.** The form **broadcast** is used in the present tense and is the past tense and past participle of the verb. **1** A **broadcast** is a programme, performance, or speech on the radio or on television. **2** To **broadcast** a programme means to send it out by radio waves, so that it can be heard on the radio or seen on television. *The concert will be broadcast live on television and radio.*   ◆◆◆◇◇ N-COUNT   VERB be V-ed adv/ prep Also V, V n

broad·cast·er /ˈbrɔːdkɑːstə, -kæst-/ **broadcasters.** A **broadcaster** is someone who gives talks or takes part in interviews and discussions on radio or television programmes.   ◆◆◇◇◇ N-COUNT

broad·cast·ing /'brɔːdkɑːstɪŋ, -kæst-/. Broadcasting is the making and sending out of television and radio programmes. ◆◆◆◇◇ N-UNCOUNT

broad·en /'brɔːdən/ broadens, broadening, broadened. 1 When something broadens, it becomes wider. *The smile broadened to a grin.* 2 If you broaden something such as your experience or popularity or if it broadens, the number of things or people that it includes or affects becomes greater. *We must broaden our appeal... The political spectrum has broadened.* 3 If an experience broadens your mind, it makes you more willing to accept other people's beliefs and customs. ◆◇◇◇ VERB: V into/to n V-ERG V n V PHRASE

broaden out. 1 If something such as a discussion broadens out or if someone broadens it out, the number of things or people that it includes or affects becomes greater. *We'll broaden the discussion out in a minute.* 2 When something such as a river or road broadens out, it becomes wider. PHRASAL VB ERG: V P V n P Also V P noun V P

broad·ly /'brɔːdli/. You can use broadly to indicate that something is generally true. *The idea that software is capable of any task is broadly true in theory.* ● See also broad. ◆◆◇◇ ADV-GRADED ADV with cl

broadly-'based. Something that is broadly-based involves many different kinds of things or people. *...a more broadly-based education.* ADJ-GRADED

broad·minded /,brɔːd'maɪndɪd/. If you describe someone as broadminded, you mean they are willing to accept types of behaviour which other people consider immoral; used showing approval. ADJ-GRADED PRAGMATICS

broad·sheet /'brɔːdʃiːt/ broadsheets. A broadsheet is a newspaper that is printed on large sheets of paper measuring approximately 38 cm by 61 cm. Broadsheets are generally considered to be more serious than other newspapers. Compare tabloid. N-COUNT

broad·side /'brɔːdsaɪd/ broadsides. 1 A broadside is a strong written or spoken attack on a person or institution. 2 If a ship is broadside to something, it has its longest side facing in the direction of that thing. *The ship was moored broadside to the pier.* N-COUNT ADV TECHNICAL

bro·cade /brə'keɪd/ brocades. Brocade is a thick, expensive fabric with a silky pattern woven into it. *...a cream brocade waistcoat.* N-VAR

broc·co·li /'brɒkəli/. Broccoli is a vegetable with green stalks and green or purple flower buds. See picture headed vegetables. ◆◇◇◇ N-UNCOUNT

bro·chure /'brəʊʃə, AM brəʊ'ʃʊr/ brochures. A brochure is a magazine or booklet with pictures that gives you information about a product or service. *...travel brochures.* ◆◆◇◇ N-COUNT

brogue /brəʊg/ brogues. 1 If someone has a brogue, they speak English with a strong accent, especially Irish or Scots. *Gill speaks in a quiet Irish brogue.* 2 Brogues are thick leather shoes which have an elaborate pattern punched into the leather. N-SING N-COUNT

broil /brɔɪl/ broils, broiling, broiled. When you broil food, you grill it. *...broiled chicken.* VERB: V n V-ed AMERICAN

broke /brəʊk/. 1 Broke is the past tense of break. 2 If you are broke, you have no money. *He was all but broke when I married him.* 3 If a company or person goes broke, they lose money and are unable to continue in business or to pay their debts. 4 If you go for broke, you take the most extreme or risky of the possible courses of action in order to try and achieve success. ADJ-GRADED INFORMAL PHRASE INFORMAL PHRASE INFORMAL

bro·ken /'brəʊkən/. 1 Broken is the past participle of break. 2 A broken line is not continuous but has gaps or spaces in it. 3 You can use broken to describe a marriage that has ended in divorce, or a home in which the parents of the family are divorced, when you think this is a sad or bad thing. *...children from broken homes.* 4 If someone talks in broken English, for example, or in broken French, they speak slowly and make a lot of mistakes because they do not know the language very well. ◆◇◇◇ ADJ: ADJ n ADJ: ADJ n PRAGMATICS ADJ: ADJ n

broken-'down. A broken-down vehicle or machine no longer works because it has something wrong with it. ◆◇◇◇ ADJ

broken-'hearted. Someone who is broken-hearted is very sad and upset because they have had a serious disappointment. ADJ

bro·ker /'brəʊkə/ brokers, brokering, brokered. 1 A broker is a person whose job is to buy and sell shares, foreign money, or goods for other people. 2 If a country or government brokers an agreement, they try to negotiate or arrange it. *The United Nations brokered a peace in Mogadishu.* ◆◆◆◇◇ N-COUNT VERB V n

bro·ker·age /'brəʊkərɪdʒ/ brokerages. 1 A brokerage or a brokerage firm is a company of brokers. 2 A brokerage fee or commission is the money charged by a broker for his services. ◆◇◇◇ N-COUNT N-UNCOUNT

brol·ly /'brɒli/ brollies. A brolly is the same as an umbrella. N-COUNT BRITISH, INFORMAL

bro·mide /'brəʊmaɪd/ bromides. Bromide is a drug which used to be given to people to calm their nerves when they were worried or upset. N-VAR

bron·chial /'brɒŋkiəl/. Bronchial means affecting or concerned with the bronchial tubes. *...bronchial asthma.* ADJ: ADJ n MEDICAL

bronchial 'tube, bronchial tubes. Your bronchial tubes are the tubes which connect your windpipe to your lungs. N-COUNT MEDICAL

bron·chi·tis /brɒŋ'kaɪtɪs/. Bronchitis is an illness like a very bad cough, in which your bronchial tubes become sore and infected. N-UNCOUNT

bron·co /'brɒŋkəʊ/ broncos. A bronco is a wild horse that cowboys ride in order to try to tame it. N-COUNT

bronze /brɒnz/ bronzes. 1 Bronze is a yellowish-brown metal which is a mixture of copper and tin. 2 A bronze is a statue or sculpture made of bronze. *...a bronze of Napoleon on horseback.* 3 A bronze is a bronze medal. 4 Something that is bronze is yellowish-brown in colour. *Her hair shone bronze and gold.* ◆◆◇◇ N-UNCOUNT N-COUNT N-COUNT COLOUR

'Bronze Age. The Bronze Age was a period of time in pre-history which began when people started making things from bronze about 4,000 - 6,000 years ago. N-PROPER: the N

bronzed /brɒnzd/. Someone who is bronzed is attractively sun-tanned. ADJ-GRADED

bronze 'medal, bronze medals. If you win a bronze medal, you come third in a competition, especially a sports contest, and are often given a medal made of bronze as a prize. ◆◇◇◇ N-COUNT

bronz·ing /'brɒnzɪŋ/. A bronzing powder or gel is used to give your skin a healthy, bronze, sun-tanned appearance. ADJ: ADJ n

brooch /brəʊtʃ/ brooches. A brooch is a small piece of jewellery which has a pin at the back so it can be fastened on a dress, blouse, or coat. N-COUNT

brood /bruːd/ broods, brooding, brooded. 1 A brood is a group of baby birds that were born at the same time to the same mother. 2 You can refer to someone's young children as their brood when you want to emphasize that there are a lot of them. 3 If someone broods over something, they think about it a lot, seriously and often unhappily. *She constantly broods about her family.* ◆◇◇◇ N-COUNT N-COUNT PRAGMATICS VERB V over/on/ about n Also V

brood·ing /'bruːdɪŋ/. 1 Brooding is used to describe an atmosphere or feeling that causes you to feel disturbed or slightly afraid. *The same heavy, brooding silence descended on them.* 2 If you describe someone's expression or appearance as brooding, you mean that they look as if they are thinking deeply and seriously about something. *...his dark, brooding eyes.* ◆◇◇◇ ADJ-GRADED WRITTEN ADJ-GRADED WRITTEN

broody /'bruːdi/. 1 You say that someone is broody when they are thinking a lot about something in an unhappy way. *He became very withdrawn and broody.* 2 A broody hen is ready to lay or sit on eggs. 3 If you describe a young woman as broody, you mean that she wants to have a baby and she keeps thinking about it. ADJ-GRADED ADJ ADJ-GRADED BRITISH, INFORMAL

brook /brʊk/ brooks, brooked, brooking. 1 A brook is a small stream. 2 If someone in a position of authority is reported as saying that they will brook no interference or opposition, they mean that they will not accept interference ◆◇◇◇ N-COUNT VERB V n

or opposition from others. *The Chinese leadership has said it will brook no interference in China's internal affairs.*

broom /bruːm/ **brooms. 1** A **broom** is a kind of brush with a long handle. You use a broom for sweeping the floor. **2 Broom** is a wild bush with a lot of tiny yellow flowers which grows on waste ground or sandy ground. ◆◇◇◇ N-COUNT / N-UNCOUNT

broom·stick /'bruːmstɪk/ **broomsticks. 1** A **broomstick** is a broom which has a bundle of twigs at the end instead of bristles. **2** A **broomstick** is the handle of a broom. N-COUNT / N-COUNT

Bros. Bros. is an abbreviation for **brothers**. It is usually used as part of the name of a company. *...Lazard Bros of New York.*

broth /brɒθ, AM brɔːθ/ **broths. Broth** is a kind of soup. It usually has vegetables or rice in it. ◆◇◇◇ N-VAR

broth·el /'brɒθəl/ **brothels.** A **brothel** is a building where men pay to have sex with prostitutes. ◆◇◇◇ N-COUNT

broth·er /'brʌðə/ **brothers.** The old-fashioned form **brethren** /'breðrən/ is still sometimes used as the plural for meanings 2 and 3. **1** Your **brother** is a boy or a man who has the same parents as you. *Oh, so you're Peter's younger brother.* ● See also **half-brother, stepbrother. 2** You might describe as your **brother** a man who belongs to the same race, religion, country, profession, or trade union as you, or who has ideas that are similar to yours. *...the Cardinal and his brother bishops.* **3 Brother** is a title given to a man who belongs to a religious community such as a monastery. *...Brother Otto.* ◆◆◆◆ N-COUNT / N-COUNT / N-TITLE; N-COUNT; N-VOC

brother·hood /'brʌðəhʊd/ **brotherhoods. 1 Brotherhood** is the affection and loyalty that you feel for people who you have something in common with. *He believed in socialism and the brotherhood of man.* **2** A **brotherhood** is an organization whose members all have the same political aims and beliefs or the same job or profession. *...the Brotherhood of Locomotive Engineers.* ◆◇◇◇ N-UNCOUNT / N-COUNT

brother-in-law, brothers-in-law. Someone's **brother-in-law** is the brother of their husband or wife, or the man who is married to their sister. ◆◇◇◇ N-COUNT

broth·er·ly /'brʌðəli/. A man's **brotherly** feelings are feelings of love and loyalty which you expect a brother to show. *...family loyalty and brotherly love.* ADJ-GRADED

brought /brɔːt/. **Brought** is the past tense and past participle of **bring**.

brou·ha·ha /'bruːhɑːhɑː/. A **brouhaha** is an excited and critical fuss or reaction to something; used showing disapproval. *...the recent brouhaha over a congressional pay raise.* N-SING: also no det PRAGMATICS JOURNALISM

brow /braʊ/ **brows. 1** Your **brow** is your forehead. *He wiped his brow with the back of his hand.* ● to **knit your brow**: see **knit. 2** Your **brows** are your eyebrows. **3** The **brow** of a hill is the top part of it. ◆◇◇◇ N-COUNT / N-COUNT / N-COUNT

brow·beat /'braʊbiːt/ **browbeats, browbeating, browbeaten.** The form **browbeat** is used in the present tense and is also the past tense. If someone tries to **browbeat** you, they try to bully you and force you to do what they want. *An older kid tried to browbeat me into it.* ♦ **brow·beat·en** *...the browbeaten employees.* VERB: V n / V n into n / ADJ-GRADED

brown /braʊn/ **browner, brownest; browns, browning, browned. 1** Something that is **brown** is the colour of earth or of wood. *...her deep brown eyes.* ◆◆◆◆ COLOUR

2 You can describe a white-skinned person as **brown** when they have been in sitting in the sun until their skin is darker than usual. *I don't want to be really really brown, just have a nice light golden colour.* **3** If someone **browns** in the sun or if the sun **browns** them, they become brown in colour. *...gorgeous females busy browning themselves.* ADJ-GRADED / V-ERG: V V n

4 A **brown** person is someone who belongs to a race of people who have brown-coloured skins. *...a slim brown man with a speckled turban.* ADJ

5 When food **browns** or when you **brown** food, you cook it, usually for a short time on a high flame. *Cook for ten minutes until the sugar browns.* V-ERG V Also V n

brownie /'braʊni/ **brownies;** also spelled **Brownie** for meanings 2, 3, and 4. **1 Brownies** are small flat biscuits or cakes. They are usually chocolate flavoured and have nuts in them. *...chocolate brownies.* **2 The Brownies** is a junior version of the Girl Guides for girls between the ages of seven and ten. Members of the Brownies attend a weekly meeting where they play games, sing songs, and learn practical skills. **3** A **brownie** is a girl who is a member of the Brownies. **4 Brownies** is one of the weekly meetings of the Brownies. *He had to leave at 5pm to pick his daughter up from Brownies.* ◆◇◇◇ N-COUNT / N-COLL-PROPER: theN / N-COUNT / N-UNCOUNT

brownie point, brownie points. If someone does something to score **brownie points**, they do it because they think they will be recognized or congratulated for it; used showing disapproval. *They're just trying to score brownie points with politicians.* N-COUNT PRAGMATICS

brown·ish /'braʊnɪʃ/. Something that is **brownish** is slightly brown in colour. COLOUR

brown 'rice. Brown rice is rice that has not had its outer covering removed. It is cooked and eaten with savoury food. N-UNCOUNT

brown·stone /'braʊnstəʊn/ **brownstones.** In the United States, a **brownstone** is a type of house which was built during the 19th century. Brownstones have a front that is made from a reddish-brown sandstone. N-COUNT

browse /braʊz/ **browses, browsing, browsed. 1** If you **browse** in a shop, you look at things in a fairly casual way, in the hope that you might find something you like. *I stopped in several bookstores to browse... I'm just browsing around.* ▶ Also a noun. *...a browse around the shops.* ♦ **brows·er, browsers** *...a casual browser.* **2** If you **browse** through a book or magazine, you look through it in a fairly casual way. *...sitting on the sofa browsing through the TV pages of the paper.* **3** When animals **browse**, they feed on plants. *...deer stags browsing 50 yards from my lodge.* ◆◇◇◇ VERB / V prep/adv / N-COUNT / N-COUNT / VERB V prep / VERB V Also V n

bruise /bruːz/ **bruises, bruising, bruised. 1** A **bruise** is an injury which appears as a purple mark on your body, although the skin is not broken. *How did you get that bruise?* **2** If you **bruise** a part of your body, a bruise appears on it, for example because something hits you. If you **bruise** easily, bruises appear when something hits you only slightly. *I had only bruised my knee.* ♦ **bruised** *...severely bruised legs.* **3** If you **bruise** a fruit, vegetable, or plant, or if it **bruises**, you damage it by handling it roughly, so that there is a mark on the skin and the taste of the fruit is spoilt. *Be sure to store them carefully as they bruise easily.* ▶ Also a noun. *...bruises on the fruit's skin.* ◆◇◇◇ N-COUNT / V-ERG V n Also V adv/prep / ADJ-GRADED / V-ERG: V n V adv Also V / N-COUNT

4 If you **are bruised** by an unpleasant experience, it makes you feel unhappy or emotionally weakened. *The government will be severely bruised by yesterday's events.* ♦ **bruis·ing** *...the bruising experience of near-bankruptcy.* VB: usu passive be V-ed / ADJ-GRADED

bruis·er /'bruːzə/ **bruisers.** A **bruiser** is someone who is strong and aggressive, and enjoys a fight or an argument; used showing disapproval. *Dad was a docker and a bit of a bruiser in his day.* N-COUNT PRAGMATICS

bruis·ing /'bruːzɪŋ/. **1** If someone has **bruising** on their body, they have bruises on it. *...severe bruising and a cut lip.* **2** In a **bruising** battle or encounter, people fight or compete with each other in a very aggressive or determined way. *...another bruising battle over civil rights.* ◆◇◇◇ N-UNCOUNT FORMAL / ADJ-GRADED JOURNALISM

brunch /brʌntʃ/ **brunches. Brunch** is a meal that is eaten in the late morning. It is a combination of breakfast and lunch. N-VAR

bru·nette /bruː'net/ **brunettes.** A **brunette** is a white-skinned woman or girl with dark brown hair. N-COUNT

brunt /brʌnt/. If someone or something **bears the brunt** or **takes the brunt** of something unpleasant, they suffer the main part or force of it. *Young people are bearing the brunt of unemployment.* ◆◇◇◇ PHRASE

brush /brʌʃ/ **brushes, brushing, brushed. 1** A **brush** is an object which has a large number of bristles fixed to it. You use brushes for painting, for ◆◆◆◇ N-COUNT

cleaning things, and for tidying your hair. *...paint and brushes. ...a hair brush.* **2** If you **brush** something or **brush** something such as dirt off it, you clean it or tidy it using a brush. *Using a small brush, he brushed away the fine sawdust.* ► Also a noun. *I gave it a quick brush with my hairbrush.* **3** If you **brush** something with a liquid, you apply a layer of that liquid using a brush. *Take a sheet of filo pastry and brush it with melted butter.* [VERB: V n] [V n with adv] [Also V n prep] [N-SING: a N] [VERB] [V n with n]

4 If you **brush** something somewhere, you remove it with quick light movements of your hands. *He brushed his hair back with both hands... He brushed the snow off the windshield.* **5** If one thing **brushes** against another or if you **brush** one thing against another, the first thing touches the second thing lightly while passing it. *I felt her dark brown hair brushing the back of my shoulder... She knelt and brushed her lips softly across Michael's cheek.* **6** If you **brush** past someone or **brush** by them, you almost touch them as you go past them. *My father would burst into the kitchen, brushing past my mother.* [VERB] [V n with adv] [V n prep] [V-ERG:] [V prep] [V n] [V n prep] [VERB] [V prep/adv] [WRITTEN]

7 If you have a **brush** with someone, you have an argument or disagreement with them. You use **brush** when you want to make an argument or disagreement sound less serious than it really is. *It is his third brush with the law in less than a year.* **8** If you have a **brush** with a particular situation, usually an unpleasant one, you almost experience it. *The corporation is fighting to survive its second brush with bankruptcy.* [N-COUNT] [PRAGMATICS] [N-COUNT: N with n]

9 Brush is an area of rough open land covered with small bushes and trees. You also use **brush** to refer to the bushes and trees on this land. *...a meadow of low brush and grass.* [N-UNCOUNT]

10 See also **broad-brush.** ● **tarred with the same brush:** see **tar.**

brush aside or **brush away.** If you **brush aside** or **brush away** an idea, remark, or feeling, you refuse to consider it because you think it is not important or useful, even though it may be. *Perhaps you shouldn't brush the idea aside too hastily.* [PHRASAL VB] [V P noun] [V n P]

brush off. If someone **brushes** you **off** when you speak to them, they refuse to talk to you or be nice to you. *When I tried to talk to her about it she just brushed me off.* ► Also a noun *One of his most regretted remarks was the tetchy brush-off he once gave.* [PHRASAL VB] [V n P] [Also V P noun] [N-SING]

brush up or **brush up on.** If you **brush up** something or **brush up on** it, you practise it or improve your knowledge of it. *Eleanor spent much of the summer brushing up on her driving.* [PHRASAL VB] [V P noun] [V P P n]

brush·stroke /ˈbrʌʃstrəʊk/ **brushstrokes.** Brushstrokes are the marks made on a surface by a painter with a paintbrush. [N-COUNT]

brusque /brʌsk/. If you describe a person as **brusque**, you mean that they deal with things, or say things, quickly and abruptly and do not show much consideration for other people. *The doctors are brusque and busy.* ◆ **brusque·ly** *'It's only a sprain,' Paula said brusquely.* [ADJ-GRADED] [ADV-GRADED: ADV with v]

brus·sels sprout /ˌbrʌsəlz ˈspraʊt/ **brussels sprouts;** also spelled **Brussels sprout.** Brussels sprouts are vegetables that look like tiny cabbages. See picture headed **vegetables.** [N-COUNT]

bru·tal /ˈbruːtəl/. **1** A **brutal** act or person is cruel and violent. *...the brutal suppression of anti-government protests.* ◆ **bru·tal·ly** *Her real parents had been brutally murdered.* **2** If someone expresses something unpleasant with **brutal** honesty or frankness, they express it in a clear and accurate way, without attempting to disguise its unpleasantness. *It was refreshing to talk about themselves and their feelings with brutal honesty.* ◆ **brutally** *The talks had been brutally frank.* **3 Brutal** is used to describe things that have an unpleasant effect on people, especially when there is no attempt by anyone to reduce their effect. *...a brutal adjustment from communism to capitalism.* ◆ **brutally** *The Maastricht referendum has brutally exposed the flaws in France's constitution.* [◆◆◇◇◇] [ADJ-GRADED] [ADV-GRADED] [ADJ-GRADED] [ADV-GRADED] [ADJ-GRADED] [ADV-GRADED]

bru·tal·ise /ˈbruːtəlaɪz/. See **brutalize.**

bru·tal·ity /bruːˈtælɪti/ **brutalities.** Brutality is cruel and violent treatment or behaviour. A **brutality** is an instance of cruel and violent treatment or behaviour. *...police brutality. ...the atrocities and brutalities committed by a former regime.* [◆◇◇◇◇] [N-VAR]

bru·tal·ize /ˈbruːtəlaɪz/ **brutalizes, brutalizing, brutalized;** also spelled **brutalise** in British English. **1** If an unpleasant experience **brutalizes** someone, it makes them cruel, violent, or uncaring. *The occupation brutalized many French men and women.* **2** If one person **brutalizes** another, they treat them in a cruel or violent way. *The policemen brutalized him.* [VERB] [V n] [VERB] [V n]

brute /bruːt/ **brutes.** **1** If you call someone, usually a man, a **brute**, you mean that they are rough and insensitive. *Custer was an idiot and a brute and he deserved his fate.* **2** When you refer to **brute** strength or force, you are contrasting it with gentler methods or qualities. *He used brute force to take control.* **3 Brute** emotions or facts are basic, unthinking feelings or responses to a situation, or the basic, fundamental facts of this situation. *...the brute ugliness of nationalism.* [◆◇◇◇◇] [N-COUNT] [ADJ: ADJ n] [ADJ: ADJ n]

brut·ish /ˈbruːtɪʃ/. If you describe a person or their behaviour as **brutish**, you think that they are brutal and uncivilized. *...brutish bullying.* [ADJ-GRADED]

BS /ˌbiː ˈes/. **1 BS** is an abbreviation for 'British Standard', a standard that something sold in Britain must reach in a test to prove that it is satisfactory or safe. Each standard has a number for reference. *Does your electric blanket conform to BS 3456?* **2** A **BS** is the same as a **BSc.** [◆◇◇◇◇] [AMERICAN]

BSc /ˌbiː es ˈsiː/ **BScs.** **1** A **BSc** is a first degree in a science subject. **BSc** is an abbreviation for 'Bachelor of Science'. *He completed his BSc in chemistry in 1934.* **2 BSc** is written after someone's name to indicate that they have a BSc. *...J. Hodgkinson BSc.* [◆◇◇◇◇] [N-COUNT]

BSE /ˌbiː es ˈiː/. **BSE** is a fatal disease which affects the nervous system of cattle. It is an abbreviation for 'bovine spongiform encephalopathy'. [N-UNCOUNT]

'B-side, B-sides. The **B-side** of a pop record has the less important or less popular song on it. [N-COUNT]

bub·ble /ˈbʌbəl/ **bubbles, bubbling, bubbled.** **1 Bubbles** are small balls of air or gas in a liquid. *...a bubble of gas.* **2** A **bubble** is a hollow, delicate ball of soapy liquid that is floating in the air or standing on a surface. *...soap bubbles.* **3** When a liquid **bubbles**, bubbles move in it, for example because it is boiling or moving quickly. *The fermenting wine has bubbled up and over the top.* [◆◆◇◇◇] [N-COUNT] [N-COUNT] [VERB: V] [V adv/prep]

4 In a comic or cartoon, a speech **bubble** is the shape which surrounds the words which a character is thinking or saying. [N-COUNT]

5 If something **bubbles**, it is very active. *The press bubbles with stories of the sale of Russian arms to Serbia.* **6** A feeling, influence, or activity that **is bubbling** away continues to occur. *...political tensions that have been bubbling away for years.* **7** Someone who is **bubbling with** a good feeling is so full of it that they keep expressing the way they feel to everyone around them. *She came to the phone bubbling with excitement.* ► **Bubble over** means the same as **bubble.** *He was quite tireless, bubbling over with vitality.* ► Also a noun. *...a bubble of optimism.* [VERB: V] [WRITTEN] [VERB] [V adv/prep] [VERB] [V with n] [PHRASAL VB] [V P with n] [N-COUNT]

8 If you say that **the bubble has burst**, or that **the bubble has been pricked**, you mean that a situation or idea which seemed wonderful has ended or has stopped seeming wonderful. *It was only a matter of time before this bubble burst.* [PHRASE]

bubble over. See **bubble 7.** [PHRASAL VB]

bubble up. A feeling that **is bubbling up** inside you is growing stronger and stronger. *She could feel the anger growing, bubbling up inside her.* [PHRASAL VB] [V P]

'bubble bath, bubble baths. 1 Bubble bath is a liquid that smells nice and makes a lot of foam when you add it to your bath water. **2** When you have a **bubble bath**, you lie in a bath of water with bubble bath in it. [N-UNCOUNT] [N-COUNT]

'bubble gum; also spelled **bubblegum.** Bubble gum is a sweet substance similar to chewing gum. [N-UNCOUNT]

You can blow it out of your mouth so it makes the shape of a bubble.

bub·bly /'bʌbli/. **1** Someone who is **bubbly** is very lively and cheerful and talks a lot; used showing approval. *...a bubbly girl who loves to laugh.* **2** Champagne is sometimes called **bubbly**. *Guests were presented with glasses of bubbly.* **3** If something is **bubbly**, it has a lot of bubbles in it. *...a nice hot bubbly bath.* ◆◇◇◇◇ ADJ-GRADED PRAGMATICS N-UNCOUNT INFORMAL ADJ-GRADED

bu·bon·ic plague /bjuː,bɒnɪk 'pleɪg, AM buː-/. **Bubonic plague** is an infectious disease spread to people from rats. It causes swellings in the armpit and groin, delirium, and sometimes death. N-UNCOUNT

buc·ca·neer /,bʌkə'nɪə/ **buccaneers. 1** A **buccaneer** was a pirate, especially one who attacked and stole from Spanish ships in the 17th and 18th centuries. **2** If you describe someone as a **buccaneer**, you mean they are clever and successful, especially in business, but you do not completely trust them. N-COUNT N-COUNT

buc·ca·neer·ing /,bʌkə'nɪərɪŋ/. If you describe someone as **buccaneering**, you mean they enjoy being involved in risky or even dishonest activities, especially in order to make money. *...a buccaneering British businessman.* ADJ-GRADED: ADJ n

buck /bʌk/ **bucks, bucking, bucked. 1** A **buck** is a US or Australian dollar. *That would probably cost you about fifty bucks.* **2** When someone makes **a fast buck** or makes **a quick buck**, they earn a lot of money quickly and easily, often by doing something which is considered to be dishonest. **3** If you are trying to **make a buck**, you are trying to earn some money. *The owners don't want to overlook any opportunity to make a buck.* **4** A **buck** is the male of various animals, including the deer and rabbit. **5** A **buck** is a young man. *He'd been a real hell-raiser as a young buck.* **6** If someone has **buck** teeth, their upper front teeth stick forward out of their mouth. **7** If a horse **bucks**, it kicks both of its back legs wildly into the air, or jumps into the air wildly with all four feet off the ground. **8** If someone or something **bucks** against something, they move very suddenly against it. *Fiona bucked against her captor and fought for breath.* **9** If someone or something **bucks** the trend or **bucks** the system, they do something to resist it. *While other newspapers are losing circulation, we are bucking the trend.* **10** If you **pass the buck**, you refuse to accept responsibility for something, and say that someone else is responsible. *David says the responsibility is Mr Smith's and it's no good trying to pass the buck.* **11** If you say **'The buck stops here'** or **'The buck stops with me'**, you mean that you have to take responsibility for something and will not try to pass the responsibility on to someone else. ◆◆◇◇◇ N-COUNT INFORMAL PHRASE INFORMAL PHRASE INFORMAL N-COUNT N-COUNT AMERICAN, INFORMAL ADJ: ADJ n VERB: V VERB V prep/adv Also V AMERICAN VERB V n PHRASE INFORMAL PHRASE INFORMAL

buck up. 1 If you **buck** someone **up** or **buck up** their spirits, you say or do something to make them more cheerful. *The aim, it seemed, was to buck up their spirits in the face of the recession.* **2** If you tell someone to **buck up** or to **buck up** their ideas, you are telling them to start behaving in a more positive and efficient manner. *If we don't buck up we'll be in trouble.* PHRASAL VB V P noun INFORMAL V P Also V P noun INFORMAL

buck·et /'bʌkɪt/ **buckets, bucketing, bucketed. 1** A **bucket** is a round metal or plastic container with a handle attached to its sides. Buckets are often used for holding and carrying water. ▶ A **bucket** of water is the amount of water contained in a bucket. **2** **Buckets** or **bucket-loads** of something means a large amount of it. *They didn't exactly sell bucket-loads of records the first time around.* **3** If someone cries **buckets**, they cry a great deal because they are very upset. If it rains **buckets**, it rains a great deal. *The rain was still coming down in buckets.* ◆◆◇◇◇ N-COUNT N-COUNT QUANT INFORMAL N-PLURAL INFORMAL

buck·et·ful /'bʌkɪtfʊl/ **bucketfuls.** A **bucketful** of something is the amount contained in a bucket. N-COUNT

buck·le /'bʌkəl/ **buckles, buckling, buckled.** **1** A **buckle** is a piece of metal or plastic attached to one end of a belt or strap, which is used to fasten it. ◆◇◇◇◇ N-COUNT

2 When you **buckle** a belt or strap, you fasten it. **3** If an object **buckles** or if something **buckles** it, it becomes bent as a result of very great heat or force. *A freak wave had buckled the deck.* **4** If your legs or knees **buckle**, they bend because they have become very weak or tired. VERB: V n V-ERG: V Vn VERB: V

buckle down. If you **buckle down** to something, you start working seriously at it. *I just buckled down and got on with playing.* PHRASAL VB V P to n V P INFORMAL

buckle under. If you **buckle under** to a person or a situation, you do what they want you to do, even though you do not want to do it. *Protesters accused Wilson of buckling under to right-wing religious groups.* PHRASAL VB V P to n Also V P

buck·led /'bʌkəld/. **Buckled** shoes have buckles on them, either to fasten them or as decoration. ADJ: ADJ n

,Bucks 'Fizz; also spelled **Buck's Fizz. Bucks Fizz** is a drink made by mixing champagne or another sparkling white wine with orange juice. N-UNCOUNT BRITISH

buck·shot /'bʌkʃɒt/. **Buckshot** consists of large pellets of lead shot used for hunting animals. N-UNCOUNT

buck·skin /'bʌkskɪn/. **Buckskin** is soft, strong leather made from the skin of a deer or a goat. N-UNCOUNT

buck·wheat /'bʌkwiːt/. **Buckwheat** is a type of small black grain used for feeding animals and making flour. **Buckwheat** also refers to the flour itself. N-UNCOUNT

bu·col·ic /bjuː'kɒlɪk/. **Bucolic** means relating to the countryside. *...the bucolic surroundings of Chantilly.* ADJ LITERARY

bud /bʌd/ **buds, budding, budded. 1** A **bud** is a small pointed lump that appears on a tree or plant and develops into a leaf or flower. *...early summer, just before the buds open.* **2** When a tree or plant **is budding**, buds are appearing on it or are beginning to open. **3** When a tree or plant is **in bud** or has come **into bud**, it has buds on it. *...trees that should come into bud soon.* **4** Some men use **bud** as a way of addressing other men. *You heard what the boss said, bud.* **5** If you **nip** something such as bad behaviour **in the bud**, you stop it before it can develop very far. *It is important to recognize jealousy and to nip it in the bud before it gets out of hand.* **6** See also **budding**; **cotton bud, taste bud.** ◆◆◇◇◇ N-COUNT VERB: V PHRASE N-VOC AMERICAN, INFORMAL PHRASE INFORMAL

Bud·dha /'bʊdə/ **Buddhas. 1 Buddha** is the title given to Gautama Siddhartha, who was a religious teacher and the founder of Buddhism. **2** A **Buddha** is a statue or picture of the Buddha. ◆◇◇◇◇ N-PROPER N-COUNT

Bud·dhism /'bʊdɪzəm/. **Buddhism** is a religion which teaches that the way to end suffering is by overcoming your desires. ◆◇◇◇◇ N-UNCOUNT

Bud·dhist /'bʊdɪst/ **Buddhists.** A **Buddhist** is a person whose religion is Buddhism. ▶ Also an adjective. *...Buddhist monks. ...Buddhist philosophy.* ◆◇◇◇◇ ▶ N-COUNT ADJ

bud·ding /'bʌdɪŋ/. **1** If you describe someone as, for example, a **budding** businessman or a **budding** artist, you mean that they are starting to succeed or become interested in business or art. *...budding entrepreneurs.* **2** You use **budding** to describe a situation that is just beginning. *...our budding romance.* ◆◇◇◇◇ ADJ: ADJ n ADJ: ADJ n

bud·dy /'bʌdi/ **buddies. 1** A **buddy** is a close friend, usually a male friend of a man. *We became great buddies.* **2** Men sometimes address other men as **buddy**. *Hey, no way, buddy.* ◆◇◇◇◇ N-COUNT INFORMAL N-VOC INFORMAL

budge /bʌdʒ/ **budges, budging, budged. 1** If someone will not **budge** on a matter, or if nothing **budges** them, they refuse to change their mind or to compromise. *The Americans are adamant that they will not budge on this point... No amount of prodding will budge him.* **2** If someone or something will not **budge**, they will not move. If you cannot **budge** them, you cannot make them move. *Her mother refused to budge from London... I got a grip on the boat and pulled but I couldn't budge it.* V-ERG: with brd-neg V n V-ERG: with brd-neg V n

budg·eri·gar /'bʌdʒərigɑː/ **budgerigars.** **Budgerigars** are small, brightly-coloured birds from Australia that people often keep as pets. ◆◇◇◇◇ N-COUNT

budg·et /'bʌdʒɪt/ **budgets, budgeting, budgeted. 1** Your **budget** is the amount of money that you have available to spend. The **budget** for something is the amount of money that a person, organization, ◆◆◆◆◇ N-COUNT: with supp

or country has available to spend on it. *Someone had furnished the place on a tight budget.* **2** The **budget** of an organization or country is its financial situation, considered as the difference between the money it receives and the money it spends. *The hospital obviously needs to balance the budget each year.* **3** In Britain, the **Budget** is the financial plan announced by the government which states how much money they intend to raise through taxation and how they intend to spend it. The **Budget** is also used to refer to the speech in which this plan is announced. **4** If you **budget** certain amounts of money for particular things, you decide that you can afford to spend those amounts on those things. *The movie is only budgeted at $10 million... I'm learning how to budget... The authorities had budgeted for some non-payment.* ♦ **budg·et·ing** ...*our budgeting for the current year.* **5 Budget** is used in advertising to suggest that something is being sold cheaply. *Cheap flights are available from budget travel agents.*

-budget /-bʌdʒɪt/. **-budget** combines with adjectives such as 'low' and 'big' to form adjectives which indicate how much money has been allocated to something, especially the making of a film. ...*a big-budget adventure movie.*

budg·et·ary /'bʌdʒɪtəri, AM -teri/. A **budgetary** matter or policy is concerned with the amount of money that is available to a country or organization, and how it is to be spent. *There are huge budgetary pressures on all governments in Europe to reduce their armed forces.*

budgie /'bʌdʒi/ **budgies.** A budgie is the same as a **budgerigar.**

buff /bʌf/ **buffs, buffing, buffed. 1** Something that is **buff** is pale brown in colour. ...*a largish buff envelope.* **2** You use **buff** to describe someone who knows a lot about a particular subject. ...*an avid film buff.* **3** If you **buff** the surface of something, for example your car or your shoes, you rub it with a piece of soft material in order to make it shine. ♦ **buff·ing** *Regular buffing helps prevent nails from splitting.*

buf·fa·lo /'bʌfələʊ/ **buffaloes.** The plural can be either **buffaloes** or **buffalo. 1** A **buffalo** is a wild animal like a large cow with horns that curve upwards. Buffalo are usually found in southern and eastern Africa. See picture headed **animals. 2** A **buffalo** is the same as a **bison.**

buff·er /'bʌfə/ **buffers, buffering, buffered. 1** A **buffer** is something that prevents something else from being harmed or that prevents two things from harming each other. *Keep savings as a buffer against unexpected cash needs.* **2** If something **is buffered,** it is protected from harm. *The company is buffered by long-term contracts with growers.* **3** The **buffers** on a train or at the end of a railway line are two metal discs on springs that reduce the shock when a train hits them. **4** If you say an elderly man is an old **buffer,** you think he is rather foolish.

'buffer zone, buffer zones. A **buffer zone** is a neutral area created to separate opposing forces or groups.

buf·fet, buffets, buffeting, buffeted. Pronounced /'bʌfeɪ, AM bʊ'feɪ/ for meanings 1 to 3, and /'bʌfɪt/ for meanings 4 and 5. **1** A **buffet** is a meal of cold food that is displayed on a long table at a party or public occasion. Guests usually serve themselves. **2** A **buffet** is a café, usually in a hotel or station. ...*the station buffet.* **3** On a train, the **buffet** or the **buffet car** is the carriage where meals and snacks are sold. **4** If something **is buffeted** by strong winds or by stormy seas, it is repeatedly struck or blown around by them. *Their plane had been severely buffeted by storms.* ♦ **buf·fet·ing, buffetings** ...*the buffetings of the winds.* **5** If an economy or government **is buffeted** by difficult or unpleasant situations, it experiences many of

them. *The whole of Africa had been buffeted by social and political upheavals.*

buf·foon /bʌ'fuːn/ **buffoons.** If you call someone a **buffoon,** you think they are foolish and you do not really respect them.

buf·foon·ery /bʌ'fuːnəri/. **Buffoonery** is foolish behaviour that makes you laugh.

bug /bʌg/ **bugs, bugging, bugged. 1** A **bug** is an insect or similar small creature. See picture headed **insects. 2** A **bug** is an illness which is caused by small organisms such as bacteria. ...*a stomach bug... There was a bug going around.* **3** If there is a **bug** in a computer programme, there is an error in it. **4** A **bug** is a tiny hidden microphone which transmits what people are saying. **5** If someone **bugs** a place, they hide tiny microphones in it which transmit what people are saying. ♦ **bug·ging** ...*an electronic bugging device.* **6** You can say that someone has been bitten by a particular **bug** when they suddenly become very enthusiastic about something. *I've definitely been bitten by the gardening bug.* **7** If someone or something **bugs** you, they worry or annoy you. *I only did it to bug my parents.*

bug·bear /'bʌgbeə/ **bugbears.** Something or someone that is your **bugbear** worries or upsets you. *Money is my biggest bugbear.*

'bug-eyed. A **bug-eyed** person or animal has eyes that bulge out.

bug·gy /'bʌgi/ **buggies. 1** A **buggy** is a lightweight folding pram. **2** A **buggy** is a small lightweight carriage pulled by one horse.

bu·gle /'bjuːgəl/ **bugles.** A **bugle** is a simple brass musical instrument that looks like a small trumpet. See picture headed **musical instruments.**

build /bɪld/ **builds, building, built** /bɪlt/. **1** If you **build** something, you make it by joining things together. *Developers are now proposing to build a hotel on the site... Workers at the plant build the F-16 jet fighter.* ♦ **build·ing** *The building of Kansai airport continues.* ♦ *Even newly built houses can need repairs... It's a product built for safety.* **2** If you **build** something into a wall or object, you make it in such a way that it is in the wall or object, or is part of it. *The TV was built into the ceiling.* **3** If people **build** an organization, a society, or a relationship, they gradually form it. *Their purpose is to build a fair society and a strong economy.* ♦ **building** ...*the building of the great civilisations of the ancient world.* **4** If you **build** an organization, system, or product on something, you base it on it. ...*a firmer foundation of fact on which to build theories.* **5** If you **build** something into a policy, system, or product, you make it part of it. *We have to build computers into the school curriculum.* **6** If someone or something **builds** someone's confidence or trust, that person gradually becomes more confident or trusting. *Usually when we're six months or so into a recovery, confidence begins to build.* ▶ **Build up** means the same as **build.** *The delegations had begun to build up some trust in one another... We will start to see the confidence in the housing market building up again.* **7** If pressure, speed, sound, or excitement **builds,** it gradually becomes greater. *The last chords of the suite build to a crescendo.* ▶ **Build up** means the same as **build.** *We can build up the speed gradually and safely... Economists warn that enormous pressures could build up.* **8** If you **build** on the success of something, you take advantage of this success in order to make further progress. *Build on the qualities you are satisfied with and work to change those you are unhappy with.* **9** Someone's **build** is the shape that their bones and muscles give to their body. *He is of medium build.* **10** See also **building, built.**

build up. 1 If you **build up** something, it gradually becomes bigger, for example because more is added to it. *The regime built up the largest army in Africa...*

Slowly a thick layer of fat builds up on the pan's surface. **2** If you **build** someone **up**, you help them to feel stronger or more confident, especially when they have had a bad experience or have been ill. **3** If you **build** someone or something **up**, you make them seem important or exciting, for example by talking about them a lot. *The media will report on it and the tabloids will build it up... I'd built him up in my head as being the love of my life.* **4** See also **build** 6 and 7, **build-up**, **built-up**.
Also V n P, V P to n, V n P
V n P
V n P, V n P as n/-ing

build up to. If you **build up to** something you want to do or say, you try to prepare people for it by starting to do it or introducing the subject gradually.
PHRASAL VB
V P P n

build·er /'bɪldə/ **builders.** A **builder** is a person whose job it is to build or repair buildings.
◆◆◇◇◇
N-COUNT

build·ing /'bɪldɪŋ/ **buildings.** A **building** is a structure that has a roof and walls, for example a house or a factory. *...the upper floor of the building. ...the Parliament building.*
◆◆◆◆◇
N-COUNT

'**building block, building blocks.** If you describe something as a **building block** of something, you mean it is one of the separate parts that combine to make that thing. *...molecules that are the building blocks of all life on earth.*
◆◇◇◇◇
N-COUNT

'**building site, building sites.** A **building site** is an area of land on which a building or group of buildings is in the process of being built or altered.
◆◇◇◇◇
N-COUNT

'**building society, building societies.** In Britain, a **building society** is a business in which you can invest money and which will lend you money when you want to buy a house.
◆◇◇◇◇
N-COUNT

'**build-up, build-ups;** also spelled **buildup** or **build up**. **1** A **build-up** is a gradual increase in something. *There has been a build-up of troops on both sides of the border.* **2** The **build-up** to an event is the way that journalists, advertisers, or other people talk about it a lot in the period of time immediately before it, and try to make it seem important and exciting. *...the build-up to Christmas.*
◆◆◇◇◇
N-COUNT
N-COUNT

built /bɪlt/. **1** Built is the past tense and past participle of **build**. **2** If you say that someone is **built** in a particular way, you are describing the kind of body they have. *All the Trollope boys were heavily built... He was a huge man, built like an oak tree.* ● See also **well-built**.
◆◇◇◇◇
ADJ:
adv ADJ,
ADJ like n,
ADJ for n/-ing

'**built-'in.** **Built-in** devices or features are included in something as a part of it, rather than being separate. *...modern cameras with built-in flash units. ...built-in cupboards in the bedrooms.*
ADJ: ADJ n

'**built-up.** A **built-up** area is an area such as a town, where there are a lot of buildings.
ADJ-GRADED

bulb /bʌlb/ **bulbs.** **1** A **bulb** is the glass part of an electric lamp, which gives out light when electricity passes through it. **2** A **bulb** is a root shaped like an onion that grows into a flower or plant. *...tulip bulbs.*
◆◆◇◇◇
N-COUNT
N-COUNT

bulb·ous /'bʌlbəs/. Something that is **bulbous** is round and fat in an ugly way. *...his bulbous purple nose.*
ADJ-GRADED

bulge /bʌldʒ/ **bulges, bulging, bulged.** **1** If something such as a person's stomach bulges, it sticks out. *He bulges out of his black T-shirt... His eyes were bulging.* **2 Bulges** are lumps that stick out from a surface which is otherwise flat or smooth. *...those bulges on your hips and thighs.* **3** If you say that something **is bulging** with things, you are emphasizing that it is full of them. *Wolchak was coming out of the office carrying a bulging briefcase.* **4** If there is a **bulge** in something, there is a sudden large increase in it. *...a bulge in aircraft sales.*
◆◇◇◇◇
VERB:
V adv/prep
V
N-COUNT
VERB:
V with n
PRAGMATICS
V-ing
Also V
N-COUNT

bu·limia /bu:'lɪmiə/. Bulimia or bulimia nervosa is a mental illness in which a person eats very large amounts and then makes themselves vomit. ♦ **bu·limic** /bu:'lɪmɪk/. *Nobody knew I was bulimic.* ♦ **bulimics, bulimics** *...a former bulimic.*
◆◇◇◇◇
N-UNCOUNT
ADJ
N-COUNT

bulk /bʌlk/ **bulks, bulking, bulked.** **1** You can refer to the **bulk** of a person or thing when you want to indicate that they are very large and heavy. *Despite his bulk he moved lightly on his feet.* **2** The **bulk** of something is most of it. *The bulk of the text*
◆◆◇◇◇
N-SING
QUANT

is essentially a review. ► Also a pronoun. *They come from all over the world, though the bulk is from the Indian subcontinent.* **3** If you buy or sell something in **bulk**, you buy or sell it in large quantities. *...bulk purchasing.*
PRON
N-UNCOUNT:
in N,
N n

bulk up or **bulk out.** To **bulk up** or **bulk out** something or someone means to make them bigger or heavier. *Use extra vegetables to bulk up the omelette... Holyfield has bulked up to 15st using weights.*
PHRASAL VB
ERG
V P noun
V P
Also V n P

bulk·head /'bʌlkhed/ **bulkheads.** A **bulkhead** is a wall which divides the inside of a ship or aeroplane into separate sections.
◆◇◇◇◇
N-COUNT
TECHNICAL

bulky /'bʌlki/ **bulkier, bulkiest.** Something or someone that is **bulky** is large and heavy. *...bulky items like lawn mowers.*
◆◇◇◇◇
ADJ-GRADED

bull /bʊl/ **bulls.** **1** A **bull** is a male animal of the cow family. Some other male animals, including elephants and whales are also called **bulls**. See picture headed **animals**. **2** If you **take the bull by the horns**, you do something that you feel you ought to do even though it is difficult or dangerous. *Now is the time for the Chancellor to take the bull by the horns and announce a two per cent cut in interest rates.* **3** On the stock market, **bulls** are people who buy shares in expectation of a price rise, in order to make a profit by selling the shares again after a short time. Compare **bear**. **4** If you say that something is **bull**, you mean that it is complete nonsense or absolutely untrue.
5 See also **cock-and-bull story**, **pit bull terrier**.
◆◆◇◇◇
N-COUNT
PHRASE
N-COUNT
N-UNCOUNT
INFORMAL

bull·dog /'bʊldɒɡ, AM -dɔːɡ/ **bulldogs.** A **bulldog** is a fairly small dog with a large square head and powerful jaws.
N-COUNT

bull·doze /'bʊldəʊz/ **bulldozes, bulldozing, bulldozed.** **1** If people **bulldoze** something such as a house or other building, they knock it down using a bulldozer. **2** If people **bulldoze** earth, stone, or other heavy material, they move it using a bulldozer. **3** If you say that someone **bulldozes** something through, you disapprove of them because they get what they want in an unpleasantly forceful way. *The Red Guards planned to bulldoze through a full socialist programme... My parents bulldozed me into going to college.*
VERB: V n
VERB: V n
VERB
PRAGMATICS
V n with
through
V n into n/-ing
Also V n

bull·doz·er /'bʊldəʊzə/ **bulldozers.** A **bulldozer** is a large tractor with a broad metal blade at the front, which is used for knocking down buildings or moving large amounts of earth.
◆◇◇◇◇
N-COUNT

bul·let /'bʊlɪt/ **bullets.** **1** A **bullet** is a small piece of metal, which is fired out of a gun. *...bullet holes in the windscreen.* ● See also **plastic bullet**, **rubber bullet**. **2** If someone **bites the bullet**, they accept that they have to do something unpleasant but necessary. *Tour operators may be forced to bite the bullet and cut prices.*
◆◆◇◇◇
N-COUNT
PHRASE

bul·letin /'bʊlɪtɪn/ **bulletins.** **1** A **bulletin** is a short news report on the radio or television. *...the early morning news bulletin.* **2** A **bulletin** is a short official announcement made publicly to inform people about an important matter. *A bulletin was released announcing that the president was out of immediate danger.* **3** A **bulletin** is a regular newspaper or leaflet that is produced by an organization or group such as a school or church.
◆◆◇◇◇
N-COUNT
N-COUNT
N-COUNT

'**bulletin board, bulletin boards.** **1** A **bulletin board** is a board attached to a wall in order to display notices giving information about something. The usual British word is **noticeboard**. **2** In computing, a **bulletin board** is a system that enables computer users to send and receive messages of general interest.
N-COUNT
AMERICAN
N-COUNT

'**bullet-proof;** also spelled **bulletproof**. Something that is **bullet-proof** is made of a strong material that bullets cannot pass through. *...bullet-proof glass.*
ADJ

bull·fight /'bʊlfaɪt/ **bullfights.** A **bullfight** is a traditional entertainment in Spain, Portugal, and Latin America in which people tease, and usually kill, a fierce bull. ♦ **bull·fighter, bullfighters.** *...a Spanish bullfighter.* ♦ **bull·fighting** *Bullfighting is part of Spain's heritage.*
N-COUNT
N-COUNT
N-UNCOUNT

bull·horn /ˈbʊlhɔːn/ **bullhorns.** A **bullhorn** is a device shaped like a hollow cone for making your voice sound louder in the open air. The usual British word is **loudhailer** or **megaphone**. N-COUNT AMERICAN

bul·lion /ˈbʊliən/. **Bullion** is gold or silver in the form of lumps or bars. N-UNCOUNT

bull·ish /ˈbʊlɪʃ/. **1** On the stock market, if there is a **bullish** sentiment, prices are expected to rise. Compare **bearish**. **2** If someone is **bullish** about something, they are optimistic about it. *Faldo was bullish about his chances of winning.* ◆◇◇◇◇ ADJ-GRADED

'bull market, bull markets. A **bull market** is a situation on the stock market when people are buying a lot of shares because they expect that the shares will increase in value and that they will be able to make a profit by selling them again after a short time. Compare **bear market**. N-COUNT

bull·ock /ˈbʊlək/ **bullocks.** A **bullock** is a young bull that has been castrated. N-COUNT

bull·ring /ˈbʊlrɪŋ/ **bullrings.** A **bullring** is a circular area of ground surrounded by rows of seats where bullfights take place. N-COUNT

'bull's-eye, bull's-eyes. 1 The **bull's-eye** is the small circular area at the centre of a target. *Five of his bullets had hit the bull's-eye.* **2** A **bull's-eye** is a shot or throw of a dart that hits the bull's-eye. **3** If something that you do or say hits the **bull's eye**, it has exactly the effect that you intended it to have. N-COUNT N-COUNT INFORMAL

bull·shit /ˈbʊlʃɪt/ **bullshits, bullshitting, bullshitted. 1** If you say that something is **bullshit**, you are saying that it is nonsense or completely untrue. Some people find this use offensive. **2** If you say that someone **is bullshitting** you or **is bullshitting**, you mean that what they are telling you is nonsense or completely untrue. Some people find this use offensive. N-UNCOUNT; also EXCLAM INFORMAL VERB: Vn, V INFORMAL

bull 'terrier, bull terriers. A **bull terrier** is a breed of strong dog with a short whitish-coloured coat and a thick neck. ● See also **pit bull terrier**. N-COUNT

bul·ly /ˈbʊli/ **bullies, bullying, bullied. 1** If you describe someone as a **bully**, you mean they use their strength or power to hurt or frighten other people. **2** If someone **bullies** you, they use their strength or power to hurt or frighten you. ♦ **bul·ly·ing** *...schoolchildren who were victims of bullying.* **3** If someone **bullies** you into something, they make you do it by using force or threats. *The government says it will not be bullied by the press.* ◆◆◇◇◇ N-COUNT VERB: Vn N-UNCOUNT VERB: Vn into n/-ing be V-ed Also Vn

'bully boy, bully boys; also spelled **bully-boy.** If you describe a man as a **bully boy**, you disapprove of him because he is rough and aggressive. *He accuses me of bully-boy tactics.* PRAGMATICS BRITISH

bul·wark /ˈbʊlwək/ **bulwarks.** Something that is a **bulwark** against something protects you against it. Something that is a **bulwark** of something protects it. *The House of Lords is the only bulwark of democracy in this country.* N-COUNT

bum /bʌm/ **bums, bumming, bummed. 1** A **bum** is a person who has no permanent home or job and who gets money by doing occasional work or by begging. ● See also **beach bum. 2** If you **bum** something off someone, you ask them for it and they give it to you. *Mind if I bum a cigarette?* **3** Someone's **bum** is the part of their body which they sit on. *I almost injured my bum sitting on a cassette.* **4** If you say that the organizers of an event such as a concert want to put **bums on seats**, you disapprove of them because they want a lot of people to attend it but do not care not about the quality of the entertainment. **5** Some people use **bum** to describe a situation that they find unpleasant or annoying. *You're getting a bum deal.* ◆◇◇◇◇ N-COUNT AMERICAN VERB Vn INFORMAL N-COUNT INFORMAL PHRASE PRAGMATICS INFORMAL, BRITISH ADJ: ADJ n INFORMAL

'bum bag, bum bags. A **bum bag** consists of a pouch attached to a belt which you wear round your waist. You use it to carry money and keys. The American expression is **fanny pack**. N-COUNT BRITISH

bumble·bee /ˈbʌmbəlbiː/ **bumblebees;** also spelled **bumble bee**. A **bumblebee** is a large hairy bee. N-COUNT

bum·bling /ˈbʌmblɪŋ/. If you describe a person or their behaviour as **bumbling**, you are critical of them because you think they are confused and disorganized, and make a lot of mistakes. ADJ: ADJ n PRAGMATICS

bumf /bʌmf/; also spelled **bumph**. **Bumf** consists of documents written for your information which you may not need or find interesting. N-UNCOUNT INFORMAL, BRITISH

bum·mer /ˈbʌmə/ **bummers.** If you say that something is a **bummer**, you mean that it is unpleasant or annoying. N-COUNT INFORMAL

bump /bʌmp/ **bumps, bumping, bumped. 1** If you **bump** into something or someone, you accidentally hit them while you are moving. *The boat bumped against something... He bumped his head.* ▶ Also a noun. *Small children often cry after a minor bump.* **2** If you have a **bump** while you are driving a car, you have a minor accident in which you hit something. **3** A **bump** is the action or the dull sound of two heavy objects hitting each other. *The child took five steps, and then sat down with a bump.* **4** You use **with a bump** to emphasize that someone suddenly gets into an unpleasant situation or becomes aware of it. For example, if someone comes down to earth **with a bump**, they suddenly start recognizing unpleasant facts after a period of time when they have not been doing this. **5** A **bump** is a minor swelling that you get if you bump into something or if something hits you. *She fell against our coffee table and got a large bump on her forehead.* ● See also **goose bumps. 6** A **bump** on a road is a raised uneven part. *The truck hit a bump and bounced.* **7** If a vehicle **bumps** over a surface, it travels in a rough bouncing way because the surface is very uneven. *The aircraft bumped along erratically.* ◆◆◇◇◇ VERB V into/against V n N-COUNT N-COUNT INFORMAL, BRITISH N-COUNT PHRASE PRAGMATICS N-COUNT N-COUNT V prep/adv Also V way adv/prep

bump into. If you **bump into** someone you know, you meet them unexpectedly. *I happened to bump into Mervyn Johns in the hallway.* PHRASAL VB V P n INFORMAL

bump off. To **bump** someone **off** means to kill them. *They will probably bump you off anyway. ...the hit man he's hired to bump off his wife.* PHRASAL VB V n P V P noun INFORMAL

bump up. If you **bump up** an amount, you increase it suddenly, usually by a lot. *The extra cost will bump up the price.* PHRASAL VB V P noun Also V n P INFORMAL

bump·er /ˈbʌmpə/ **bumpers. 1 Bumpers** are bars at the front and back of a vehicle which protect it if it bumps into something. See picture headed **car and bicycle**. ● If traffic is **bumper to bumper**, the vehicles are very close to one another and are moving very slowly. **2** A **bumper** crop or harvest is one that is larger than usual. *It's been a bumper year for corn.* **3** If you say that something is **bumper** size, you mean that it is very large. *...bumper profits. ...a bumper pack of matches.* ◆◇◇◇◇ N-COUNT PHRASE ADJ: ADJ n ADJ: ADJ n

'bumper sticker, bumper stickers. A **bumper sticker** is a sticker, usually with a political, religious, or humorous message, that is designed for sticking onto the back of your car. N-COUNT

bumph /bʌmf/. See **bumf**.

bump·kin /ˈbʌmpkɪn/ **bumpkins.** If you refer to someone as a **bumpkin**, you think they are uneducated and stupid because they come from the countryside. *...unsophisticated country bumpkins.* N-COUNT PRAGMATICS

bump·tious /ˈbʌmpʃəs/. If you say that someone is **bumptious**, you disapprove of them because they continually express their own opinions and ideas in a self-important way. ADJ-GRADED PRAGMATICS

bumpy /ˈbʌmpi/ **bumpier, bumpiest. 1** A **bumpy** road or path has a lot of bumps on it. *...a long bumpy track lined with bilberry shrubs.* **2** A **bumpy** journey is uncomfortable and rough. *...a hot and bumpy ride across the desert.* ◆◇◇◇◇ ADJ-GRADED ADJ-GRADED

bun /bʌn/ **buns. 1 Buns** are small bread rolls. They can be sweet and contain currants or spices, or they can be savoury and eaten with hamburgers or hot dogs. **2 Buns** are small sweet cakes. They often have icing on the top. **3** If a woman has her hair in a **bun**, she has fastened it tightly on top of her head or at the back of her head in the shape of a ball. ◆◇◇◇◇ N-COUNT N-COUNT N-COUNT

bunch /bʌntʃ/ **bunches, bunching, bunched.** ◆◆◇◇
1 A **bunch** of people is a group of people who share N-COUNT
one or more characteristics or who are doing some- INFORMAL
thing together. *My neighbours are a bunch of busy-*
bodies... The players were a great bunch. **2** If you say PHRASE
someone or something is **the best of the bunch** or INFORMAL
the pick of the bunch, you mean they are the best
of a group of people or things.
3 A **bunch** of flowers is a number of flowers with their N-COUNT
stalks held or tied together. **4** A **bunch** of bananas or N-COUNT
grapes is a group of them growing on the same stem.
5 A **bunch** of keys is a set of keys kept together on a N-COUNT
metal ring.
6 A **bunch** of things is a number of things, especially a QUANT
large number. *We did a bunch of songs together.* AMERICAN
▶ Also a pronoun. *I'd like to adopt a multi-racial* PRON
child. In fact, I'd love a whole bunch.
7 If a girl has her hair in **bunches**, it is parted down the N-PLURAL
middle and tied on each side of her head with some- BRITISH
thing such as a ribbon.
8 If clothing **bunches** around a part of your body, it VERB
forms a set of creases around it. *She clutches the sides* V around n
of her skirt until it bunches around her waist.
bunch up or **bunch together.** If people or things PHRASAL VB
bunch up or **bunch together**, they move close to each ERG:
other so that they form a small tight group. *They need* V P
to bunch aircraft more closely together to bring in one V n P
that is short of fuel.

bun·dle /ˈbʌndəl/ **bundles, bundling, bundled.** ◆◆◇◇
1 A **bundle** of things is a number of them that are N-COUNT
tied together or wrapped in a cloth or bag so that
they can be carried or stored. *...a bundle of five*
pound notes. ...bundles of clothing. **2** If you de- N-SING:
scribe someone as, for example, a **bundle** of fun, a N of n
you are emphasizing that they are full of fun. *He* PRAGMATICS
confessed to having been a bundle of nerves. **3** If you N-COUNT:
refer to a **bundle** of things, you are emphasizing N of n
that there is a wide range of them. *The profession* PRAGMATICS
offers a bundle of benefits.
4 If someone or something **is bundled** somewhere, VERB
someone pushes them there in a rough and hurried be V-ed
way. *He was bundled into a car.* prep/adv
bundle off. If someone **is bundled off** somewhere, PHRASAL VB
they are sent there or taken there in a hurry. *We want* be V-ed
to bundle them off to bed quickly. V n P to n
Also V n P
bundle up. 1 If you **bundle up** a mass of things, you PHRASAL VB
make them into a bundle by gathering or tying them V P noun
together. *Francis bundled up her clothes again into* Also V n P
their small sack. **2** If you **bundle** someone **up**, you V P noun
dress them in a lot of warm clothes. *Eleanor bundled* Also V n P,
up the baby and carried him to New York. V P

bung /bʌŋ/ **bungs, bunging, bunged. 1** A **bung** N-COUNT
is a round piece of wood, cork, or rubber which you
use to close the hole in a container such as a barrel
or flask. **2** If you **bung** something somewhere, you VERB
put it there in a quick careless way. *Pour a whole lot* V n prep/adv
of cold water over the rice, and bung it in the oven. BRITISH,
3 If something is **bunged up** it is blocked. *The sink's* INFORMAL
bunged up again... My nose is all bunged up. ADJ
BRITISH,
INFORMAL
bun·ga·low /ˈbʌŋɡələʊ/ **bungalows.** A **bungalow** ◆◇◇◇
is a house which has only one storey. See picture N-COUNT
headed **house** and **flat**.
bungee jumping /ˈbʌndʒi dʒʌmpɪŋ/. **Bungee** N-UNCOUNT
jumping is an activity in which someone jumps
from a high place such as a bridge or crane with a
long piece of strong elastic cord tied around their
ankle connecting them to the bridge or crane.
bun·gle /ˈbʌŋɡəl/ **bungles, bungling, bungled.** ◆◇◇◇
If you **bungle** something, you fail to do it properly, VERB
because you make mistakes or are clumsy. *Two* V n
prisoners bungled an escape bid. ▶ Also a noun. *...an*
appalling administrative bungle. ◆ **bun·gling** *...a* ADJ-GRADED
bungling burglar. ◆ **bun·gler, bunglers** *The stu-* N-COUNT
pid bungler!
bun·ion /ˈbʌnjən/ **bunions.** A **bunion** is a large N-COUNT
painful lump on the place where a person's big toe
joins their foot.
bunk /bʌŋk/ **bunks, bunking, bunked. 1** A ◆◇◇◇
bunk is a bed that is fixed to a wall, especially in a N-COUNT
ship or caravan. **2** If you **do a bunk**, you suddenly PHRASE

leave a place without telling anyone. *James's live-in* BRITISH,
lover has done a bunk because he won't marry her. INFORMAL
bunk off. If you **bunk off** from school or work, you PHRASAL VB
leave without permission and do something else. *We* V P n
thought *nothing of bunking off school and travelling* Also V P
100 miles to find this or that record. BRITISH,
INFORMAL
'bunk bed, bunk beds. Bunk beds are two beds, N-COUNT
one above the other, held in a frame.
bun·ker /ˈbʌŋkə/ **bunkers, bunkering, bun-** ◆◆◇◇
kered. 1 A **bunker** is a place, usually underground, N-COUNT
that has been built with strong walls to protect it
against heavy gunfire and bombing. **2** A **bunker** is a N-COUNT
container for coal or other fuel. **3** On a golf course, N-COUNT
a **bunker** is a large hollow filled with sand that golfers must try and avoid. **4** In golf, if you **bunker** a VERB: V n
shot, you hit your ball into the bunker.
bun·kum /ˈbʌŋkəm/. If you say that something that N-UNCOUNT
has been said or written is **bunkum**, you mean that PRAGMATICS
you think it is completely untrue or very stupid. *It's* DATED,
a load of bunkum. INFORMAL
bun·ny /ˈbʌni/ **bunnies.** Children sometimes use ◆◇◇◇
bunny or **bunny rabbit** to refer to a rabbit. N-COUNT
bunt·ing /ˈbʌntɪŋ/. **Bunting** consists of rows of N-UNCOUNT
small coloured flags that are used to decorate
streets and buildings on special occasions.
buoy /bɔɪ, AM ˈbuːi/ **buoys, buoying, buoyed.** ◆◇◇◇
1 A **buoy** is a floating object that is used to show N-COUNT
ships and boats where they can go and to warn
them of danger. **2** If someone in a difficult situation VERB
is buoyed by something, it makes them feel more be V-ed by n
cheerful and optimistic. *Party leaders are buoyed by* Also V n
Clinton's recent rise in the polls. ▶ **Buoy up** means PHRASAL VB
the same as **buoy**. *They are buoyed up by a sense of* be V-ed P
hope. Also V n P
buoy·ant /ˈbɔɪənt/. **1** If you are in a **buoyant** ◆◇◇◇
mood, you feel cheerful and behave in a lively way. ADJ-GRADED
She was in a buoyant mood and they were looking
forward to their new life. ◆ **buoy·an·cy** *...a mood of* N-UNCOUNT
buoyancy and optimism. **2** A **buoyant** economy is a ADJ-GRADED
successful one in which there is a lot of trade and
economic activity. ◆ **buoyancy** *The slump will be* N-UNCOUNT
followed *by a period of buoyancy.* **3** A **buoyant** ob- ADJ-GRADED
ject floats on a liquid. ◆ **buoyancy** *Air can be* N-UNCOUNT
pumped into the diving suit to increase buoyancy.
bur·ble /ˈbɜːbəl/ **burbles, burbling, burbled. 1** If VERB
something **burbles**, it makes a low continuous bub- V
bling sound. *The water burbled over gravel.* **2** If VERB
someone **is burbling**, they are talking in a confused V n
way. *He burbled something incomprehensible.* Also V that,
V on about n
bur·den /ˈbɜːdən/ **burdens, burdening, bur-** ◆◆◇◇
dened. 1 If you describe a problem or a respon- N-COUNT
sibility as a **burden**, you mean that it causes someone a lot of difficulty, worry, or hard work. *Her*
death will be an impossible burden on Paul. **2** If VERB
someone **burdens** you with something that is likely V n with n
to worry you, they tell you about it. *We decided not* Also V n
to burden him with the news. ◆ **bur·dened** *Nicara-* ADJ-GRADED:
gua was burdened with a foreign debt of $11 billion. ADJ with/by n
3 The **burden of proof** is the task of proving that PHRASE
you are correct, for example when you have ac-
cused someone of a crime. *The burden of proof is on*
the prosecution. **4** A **burden** is a heavy load that is N-COUNT
difficult to carry. ◆ **burdened** *Anna and Marie ar-* FORMAL
rived burdened by bags and food baskets. ADJ-GRADED:
ADJ with/by n
bur·den·some /ˈbɜːdənsəm/. If you describe some- ADJ-GRADED
thing as **burdensome**, you mean it is worrying or WRITTEN
hard to deal with. *...a large and burdensome debt.*
bu·reau /ˈbjʊərəʊ/. The usual plural in British ◆◆◇◇
English is **bureaux**. The usual plural in American
English is **bureaus. 1** A **bureau** is an office, organi- N-COUNT
zation, or government department that collects and
distributes information. *...The National Bureau of*
Economic Research. **2** A **bureau** is an office of a N-COUNT
company or organization which has its head-
quarters in another town or country. *...the Wall*
Street Journal's Washington bureau. **3** A **bureau** is a N-COUNT
writing desk with shelves and drawers and a lid that BRITISH
opens to form the writing surface. **4** A **bureau** is the N-COUNT
same as a **chest of drawers**. AMERICAN

bu·reau·cra·cy /bjʊˈrɒkrəsi/ **bureaucracies.** ♦♦◇◇◇
1 A **bureaucracy** is an administrative system N-COUNT
operated by a large number of officials. *State bu-*
reaucracies can tend to stifle enterprise. **2 Bureau-** N-UNCOUNT
cracy refers to all the rules and procedures followed PRAGMATICS
by government departments and similar organiza-
tions. *People usually complain about too much bu-*
reaucracy. ♦ **bu·reau·crat·ic** /ˌbjʊərəˈkrætɪk/. *The* ADJ-GRADED
department has become a bureaucratic nightmare.

bu·reau·crat /ˈbjʊərəkræt/ **bureaucrats. Bureau-** ♦♦◇◇◇
crats are officials who work in a large administrative N-COUNT
system. You can refer to officials as bureaucrats espe- PRAGMATICS
cially if you disapprove of them because they seem to
follow rules and procedures too strictly. *The economy*
is still controlled by bureaucrats.

bu·reaux /ˈbjʊərəʊz/. **Bureaux** is a plural form of
bureau.

bur·geon /ˈbɜːdʒən/ **burgeons, burgeoning,** ♦◇◇◇◇
burgeoned. If something **burgeons**, it grows or V-ing
develops rapidly. *...Japan's burgeoning satellite-TV* LITERARY
industry.

burg·er /ˈbɜːgə/ **burgers.** A **burger** is a flat round ♦◇◇◇◇
mass of minced meat or vegetables, which is fried N-COUNT
and often eaten in a bread roll. *...burger and chips.*

burgh·er /ˈbɜːgə/ **burghers.** The **burghers** of a N-COUNT
town or city are the people who live there, especial- DATED
ly the richer or more respectable people.

bur·glar /ˈbɜːglə/ **burglars.** A **burglar** is a thief ♦◇◇◇◇
who enters a house or other building by force. N-COUNT

'burglar alarm, burglar alarms. A **burglar** N-COUNT
alarm is an electric device that makes a bell ring
loudly if someone tries to enter a building by force.

bur·glar·ize /ˈbɜːgləraɪz/ **burglarizes, burglariz-** VERB:
ing, burglarized. If a building **is burglarized**, a beV-ed
thief enters it by force and steals things. The usual AMERICAN
British word is **burgle.**

bur·gla·ry /ˈbɜːgləri/ **burglaries.** If someone ♦◇◇◇◇
commits a **burglary**, they enter a building by force N-VAR
and steal things. **Burglary** is the act of doing this.
He's been arrested for burglary.

bur·gle /ˈbɜːgl/ **burgles, burgling, burgled.** If a VERB:
building **is burgled**, a thief enters it by force and beV-ed
steals things. The American word is **burglarize.** BRITISH

bur·gun·dy /ˈbɜːgəndi/ **burgundies. 1 Burgundy** ♦◇◇◇◇
is used to describe things that are purplish-red in COLOUR
colour. **2 Burgundy** is a type of wine which comes N-VAR
from the region of France called Burgundy.

bur·ial /ˈberiəl/ **burials.** A **burial** is the act or cer- ♦◇◇◇◇
emony of putting a dead body into a grave in the N-VAR
ground. *The priest prepared the body for burial.*

'burial ground, burial grounds. A **burial ground** N-COUNT
is a place where bodies are buried, especially an ancient site.

bur·lap /ˈbɜːlæp/. **Burlap** is a thick rough fabric that N-UNCOUNT
is used for making sacks. The usual British word is AMERICAN
hessian.

bur·lesque /bɜːˈlesk/ **burlesques.** A **burlesque** is N-VAR
a performance or a piece of writing that makes fun
of something by copying it in an exaggerated way.
You can also use **burlesque** to refer to a real-life
situation that shows this kind of exaggeration.

bur·ly /ˈbɜːli/ **burlier, burliest.** A **burly** man has a ♦◇◇◇◇
broad body and strong muscles. *A burly officer* ADJ-GRADED
stepped forward.

burn /bɜːn/ **burns, burning, burned, burnt.** The ♦♦♦♦◇
past tense and past participle is **burned** in American English, and **burned** or **burnt** in British English.
1 If there is a fire or a flame somewhere, you say VERB
that there is a fire or flame **burning** there. *Fires were*
burning out of control. **2** If something **is burning**, it VERB
is on fire. *When I arrived one of the vehicles was still* V
burning. ♦ **burn·ing** *...a terrible smell of burning.* N-UNCOUNT
3 If you **burn** something, you destroy or damage it VERB
with fire. *Protesters set cars on fire and burned a* V n
building. ♦ **burning** *...burning of a US flag.* N-UNCOUNT
4 If you **burn** a fuel or if it **burns**, it is used to produce V-ERG
heat, light, or energy. *The power stations burn coal* V n
from the Ruhr region. Also V
5 If you **burn** something that you are cooking or if it V-ERG:V

burns, you spoil it by using too great a heat. *I burnt* V n
the toast. ♦ **burnt** *...the smell of burnt toast.* ADJ-GRADED
6 If you **burn** part of your body, **burn** yourself, or are VERB
burnt, you are injured by fire or by something very V n
hot. *Take care not to burn your fingers... If you are bad-* Also V pron-
ly burnt, seek medical attention. ► Also a noun. *She* refl
suffered appalling burns to her back. **7** If you **burn** or V-ERG
get **burned** in the sun, the sun makes your skin be- V
come red and sore. *Build up your tan slowly and don't* Also V n
allow your skin to burn. **8** If a part of your body **burns** V-ERG: V
or if something **burns** it, it has a painful, hot or sting- V n
ing feeling. *...delicious Indian recipes which won't*
burn your throat. **9** If someone **is burnt** or **is burnt** to VERB:
death, they are killed by fire. *At least 80 people were* beV-ed
burnt to death when their bus caught fire. beV-ed to n
10 If a light **is burning**, it is shining. VERB: V
11 If your face **is burning**, it is red because you are VERB
embarrassed or upset.
12 If you **are burning** with an emotion or **are burning** VERB
to do something, you feel that emotion or the desire to V with n
do that thing very strongly. *The young boy was burn-* Also V to-inf
ing with a fierce ambition.
13 If you **are burned** or get **burned**, you lose some- VB: usu
thing as a result of taking a risk, usually in a business passive
deal. *They always took chances and got burned very* be/get V-ed
badly in past years.
14 See also **burning.**
15 ● to **burn the candle at both ends**: see **candle.**
● to **get your fingers burned**: see **finger.** ● to **be**
burnt to the ground: see **ground.** ● to **burn the mid-**
night oil: see **midnight.**

burn down. If a building **burns down** or if someone PHRASAL VB
burns it **down**, it is completely destroyed by fire. *Six* ERG
months after Bud died, the house burned down... An- V P
archists burnt down a restaurant. V P noun
Also V n P

burn off. 1 If someone **burns off** energy, they use it. PHRASAL VB
This will improve your performance and help you V P noun
burn off calories. **2** To **burn off** something unwanted V P noun
means to get rid of it by burning it. *The bushfire actu-* Also V n P
ally helped to burn off a lot of dead undergrowth.

burn out. 1 If a fire **burns** itself out, it stops burning PHRASAL VB
because there is nothing left to burn. *Fire officials let* V pron-refl P
the fire burn itself out. **2** If you **burn** yourself **out**, you V pron-refl P
make yourself exhausted or ill by working too hard.
3 See also **burn-out, burnt-out.**

burn up. 1 If something **burns up** or if a fire **burns** it PHRASAL VB
up, it is completely destroyed by a fire or by strong ERG:
heat. *Fires have burned up 180,000 acres of timber.* **2** If V P
something **burns up** fuel or energy, it uses it. *Brisk* V P noun
walking can burn up more calories than slow jogging. Also V n P

,burned-'out. See **burnt-out.**

burn·er /ˈbɜːnə/ **burners.** A **burner** is a device ♦◇◇◇◇
which produces heat or a flame. ● See also **back** N-COUNT
burner, front burner.

burn·ing /ˈbɜːnɪŋ/. **1** You use **burning** to describe ♦♦◇◇◇
something that is extremely hot. *...the burning des-* ADJ
ert of Central Asia. ● Also an adverb. *He touched* ADV: ADV adj
the boy's forehead. It was burning hot.
2 If you have a **burning** interest in something or a ADJ: ADJ n
burning desire to do something, you are extremely
interested in it or want to do it very much. *I had a*
burning ambition to become a journalist. **3** A **burning** ADJ-GRADED:
issue or question is a very important or urgent one ADJ n
that people feel very strongly about. *The burning*
question in this year's debate over the federal budget is:
whose taxes should be raised?

bur·nish /ˈbɜːnɪʃ/ **burnishes, burnishing, bur-** VERB
nished. To **burnish** the image of someone or V n
something means to improve their image. *The Euro-* JOURNALISM
pean Parliament badly needs a president who can
burnish its image.

bur·nished /ˈbɜːnɪʃt/. You can describe something ADJ
as **burnished** when it is bright or smooth. *The* LITERARY
clouds glowed like burnished gold.

,burn-'out. If someone suffers **burn-out**, they ex- N-UNCOUNT
haust themselves early in their life or career be- INFORMAL
cause they have achieved too much too quickly.

burnt /bɜːnt/. **Burnt** is a past tense and past participle of **burn.**

burnt-'out; also spelled **burned-out.** Burnt-out ◆◇◇◇◇
vehicles or buildings have been very badly damaged ADJ
by fire.

burp /bɜːp/ **burps, burping, burped.** When VERB: V
someone **burps**, they make a noise because air from
their stomach has been forced up through their
throat. ▶ Also a noun. ...*a barely audible burp.* N-COUNT

burr /bɜː/ **burrs;** also spelled **bur** for meaning one. N-COUNT
1 A **burr** is the part of some plants which contains
seeds and which has little hooks on the outside so
that it sticks to clothes or fur. **2** If someone has a N-COUNT
burr, they speak English with a regional accent in
which 'r' sounds are more noticeably pronounced.

bur·row /'bʌrəʊ, AM 'bɜː-/ **burrows, burrowing,** ◆◇◇◇◇
burrowed. 1 A **burrow** is a tunnel or hole in the N-COUNT
ground that is dug by an animal such as a rabbit.
2 If an animal **burrows** into the ground or into a VERB
surface, it moves through it by making a tunnel or V prep/adv
hole. *The larvae burrow into cracks in the floor.*

3 If you **burrow** in a container or pile of things, you VERB
search there for something using your hands. *He bur-* V prep/adv
rowed through old records. **4** If you **burrow** into some- VERB
thing, you move underneath it or press against it, V prep/adv
usually in order to feel warmer or safer. *She turned her
face away from him, burrowing into her heap of
covers.*

bur·sar /'bɜːsə/ **bursars.** The **bursar** of a school or N-COUNT
college is the person who is in charge of its finance
or general administration.

bur·sa·ry /'bɜːsəri/ **bursaries.** A **bursary** is a sum N-COUNT
of money which is given to someone to allow them
to study in a college or university.

burst /bɜːst/ **bursts, bursting.** The form **burst** is ◆◆◆◇◇
used in the present tense and is the past tense and
past participle. **1** When something **bursts** or when V-ERG
you **burst** it, it suddenly breaks open or splits open V
and the air or other substance inside it comes out. *A* V n
tyre burst... It is not a good idea to burst a blister.
2 If a dam **bursts**, or if something **bursts** it, it V-ERG
breaks apart because the force of the river is too V
great. *A dam burst and flooded their villages.* **3** If a Also V n
river **bursts** its banks, the banks break apart and VERB: V n
water overflows. **4** If you say that someone is about VERB
to **burst** with pride, anger, or another emotion, you PRAGMATICS
are emphasizing the intensity of their emotion. *He* V with n
almost burst with pride when his son John began to WRITTEN
excel at football.

5 When a door or lid **bursts** open, it opens very sud- VERB
denly and violently because someone pushes it or V open/apart
there is great pressure behind it. *The door burst open
and an angry young nurse appeared.* **6** If someone or VERB
something **bursts** into or out of a place, they suddenly V prep/adv
enter or leave it with a lot of energy or force. *Gunmen
burst into his home and opened fire.* **7** If you say that VERB
something **bursts** onto the scene, you mean that it V onto/upon n
suddenly starts or becomes active, usually after devel- WRITTEN
oping quietly for some time. *Chinese companies have
burst upon the scene with millions of dollars in their
pockets.*

8 When a firework or bomb **bursts** in the air, it ex- VERB: V
plodes. **9** A **burst** of something is a sudden short peri- N-COUNT
od of it. ...*a burst of machine-gun fire.*

10 ● to **burst** into flames: see **flame**.

burst into. 1 If you **burst into** tears, laughter, or PHRASAL VB
song, you suddenly begin to cry, laugh, or sing. *She* V P n
burst into tears and ran from the kitchen. **2** When V P n
plants **burst into** leaf or flower, their leaves or flowers WRITTEN
suddenly open. ...*rows of wallflowers promising to
burst into bloom.* **3** If you say that something **bursts** V P n
into a particular situation or state, you mean that it
suddenly changes into that situation or state. *This
weekend's fighting is threatening to burst into full-
scale war.*

burst out. 1 If someone **bursts out** laughing, crying, PHRASAL VB
or making another noise, they suddenly start making ERG
that noise. *The class burst out laughing... Everyone* V P -ing
burst out into conversation. **2** If someone **bursts out** V P into/inn
something, they say it suddenly and loudly. '*I want to* Also V P
be just like you', she bursts out. **3** If a situation or prob- WRITTEN
V P prep/adv

lem **bursts out**, it suddenly appears. *Malaria is burst-* Also V P
ing out again all over the world.

burst·ing /'bɜːstɪŋ/. **1** If a place is **bursting** with ◆◇◇◇◇
people or things, it is full of them. *The place appears* ADJ:
to be bursting with women directors. **2** If you say v-link ADJ
that a place is **bursting at the seams** or **full to** PHRASE
bursting, you are emphasizing that it is very full. PRAGMATICS
3 If you say that someone is **bursting with** a feeling or ADJ:
quality, you mean that they have a great deal of it. *I* v-link ADJ
was bursting with curiosity. **4** If you are **bursting** to do with n
something, you are very eager to do it. *She was burst-* ADJ:
ing to tell everyone. v-link ADJ to-
5 See also **burst**. inf
INFORMAL

bury /'beri/ **buries, burying, buried. 1** To **bury** ◆◇◇◇◇
something means to put it into a hole in the ground VERB
and cover it up with earth. ...*squirrels who bury nuts* V n
and seeds.

2 To **bury** a dead person means to put their body into VERB: V n
a grave and then cover it with earth. **3** If you say you VERB: V n
have buried one of your relatives, you mean that one
of your relatives has died and has been buried or
cremated.

4 If you **bury** something under a large quantity of VERB
things, you put it there, often in order to hide it. ...*my* V n prep/adv
*handbag, which was buried under a pile of old news-
papers.* **5** If something **buries** a place or person, it VERB
falls on top of them so that it completely covers them V n
and often harms them in some way. *Mud slides buried
entire villages.*

6 If you **bury** your head or face in something, you VERB
press your head or face against it, often because you V n prep/adv
are unhappy. *She buried her face in the pillows.* **7** If VERB
something **buries** itself somewhere, or if you **bury** it V pron-refl
there, it is pushed very deeply in there. *The missile* Also V n
buried itself deep in the grassy hillside. prep/adv

8 If you **bury** a feeling, you try not to show it. If you VERB: V n
bury a memory, you try to forget it. *When we feel an-* WRITTEN
ger, we bury the emotion and feel guilty instead. **9** If VERB
you **bury** yourself **in** a place or an activity such as V pron-refl in
your work, you spend all your time in that place or do- n
ing that activity, usually because you want to forget
about things. **10** If you **bury** your head in something VERB
such as a book or newspaper, or **bury** yourself in it, V n in/on
you look at it closely and concentrate very hard on it. Also V pron-
My father buried his head in his newspaper. refl in n
11 ● to **bury** the hatchet: see **hatchet**.

bus /bʌs/ **buses, busses, bussing, bussed.** ◆◆◆◇◇
Buses is the plural of the noun. **Busses** is the third
person singular of the verb. American English uses
the spellings **buses, busing, bused** for the verb. **1** A N-COUNT:
bus is a large motor vehicle which carries passen- also by N
gers from one place to another. *They had to travel
everywhere by bus.* **2** When someone is **bussed** to a V-ERG
particular place or when they **bus** there, they travel be V-ed adv/
there on a bus. *On May Day hundreds of thousands* prep
used to be bussed in to parade through East Berlin. Also V adv/
prep

bush /bʊʃ/ **bushes. 1** A **bush** is a large plant ◆◆◇◇◇
which is smaller than a tree and has a lot of N-COUNT
branches. **2** The wild uncultivated parts of some hot N-SING
countries are referred to as the **bush**. ...*the dense
Mozambican bush.* **3** If you tell someone not to PHRASE
beat about the bush, you mean that you want them PRAGMATICS
to tell you something immediately and quickly. *Stop
beating about the bush. What's he done?*

bush·el /'bʊʃəl/ **bushels.** A **bushel** is a unit of vol- ◆◇◇◇◇
ume that is used for measuring agricultural produce N-COUNT
such as corn or beans. A bushel is equivalent in volume to eight gallons.

Bush·man /'bʊʃmæn/ **Bushmen.** A **Bushman** is an N-COUNT
aboriginal person from the southwestern part of Africa, especially the Kalahari desert region.

bushy /'bʊʃi/ **bushier, bushiest. 1** Bushy hair or ◆◇◇◇◇
fur is very thick. ...*bushy eyebrows.* ...*bushy-tailed* ADJ-GRADED
possums. **2** A **bushy** plant has a lot of leaves very ADJ-GRADED
close together.

busi·ly /'bɪzɪli/. If you do something **busily**, you do ◆◇◇◇◇
it in a very active way. *The two saleswomen were* ADV-GRADED:
busily trying to keep up with the demand. ADV with v

busi·ness /'bɪznɪs/ **businesses. 1** Business is ◆◆◆◆◇
work relating to the production, buying, and selling N-UNCOUNT

B

of goods or services. ...*young people seeking a career in business. ...Harvard Business School.* **2 Business** is used when talking about how many products or services a company is able to sell. ...*German companies would lose business... Business is booming.* **3** A **business** is an organization which produces and sells goods or which provides a service. *The majority of small businesses go broke within the first twenty-four months.* **4 Business** is an activity that you do as part of your job and not for pleasure. *I'm here on business. ...business trips.* **5** You can use **business** to refer to a particular area of work or activity in which the aim is to make a profit. *May I ask you what business you're in?* • See also **show business, big business**. N-UNCOUNT N-COUNT N-UNCOUNT N-SING

6 If two people or companies **do business** with each other, one sells goods or services to the other. *I was fascinated by the different people who did business with me.* **7** A company that is **in business** is currently operating and trading. **8** If a shop or company goes **out of business**, it has to stop trading because it is not making enough money. PHRASE PHRASE PHRASE

9 You can use **business** to refer to something that you are doing or concerning yourself with. ...*recording Ben as he goes about his business.* **10** In a difficult situation, if you say it is **business as usual**, you mean that people will continue doing what they normally do. *The Queen was determined to show it was business as usual.* **11** You can use **business** to refer to important matters that you have to deal with. *I've got some unfinished business to attend to.* **12** If you say that something is your **business**, you mean that it concerns you personally and that other people have no right to ask questions about it or disagree with it. *If she doesn't want the police involved, that's her business.* N-SING: with supp PHRASE N-UNCOUNT N-UNCOUNT: with poss

13 If you say that someone **has no business** to be in a place or to do something, you mean that they have no right to be there or to do it. *I had no business to be there at all.* **14** If you say to someone '**mind** your **own business**' or '**it's none of** your **business**', you are rudely telling them not to ask about something that does not concern them. PHRASE PHRASE PRAGMATICS INFORMAL

15 You can use **business** to refer in a general way to an event, situation, or activity. For example, you can say something is 'a wretched business'. *This whole business is very puzzling.* N-SING: supp N

16 If you say you **are in business**, you mean you have everything you need to start something immediately. *All you need is a microphone, and you're in business.* PHRASE SPOKEN

17 If you say that someone **means business**, you mean they are serious and determined about what they are doing. *Now people are starting to realise that he means business.* PHRASE INFORMAL

18 If you **make it your business** to do something, you decide to do it, because you are interested in it or because you want to find out something. **19** If you say that you **are not in the business of** doing something, you mean that you do not do it, usually when you are annoyed or surprised that someone thinks you do. *We are not in the business of subsidising scroungers.* PHRASE PHRASE PRAGMATICS

'business card, business cards. A person's **business card** or their **card** is a small card which they give to other people, and which has their name and details of their job and company printed on it. N-COUNT

'business class. On aeroplanes, **business class** accommodation costs less than first-class but more than economy accommodation. N-UNCOUNT

'business end. The **business end** of a tool or weapon is the end of it which does the work or causes damage rather than the end that you hold. N-SING INFORMAL

'business hours. Business hours are the hours of the day in which a shop or a company is open for business. N-PLURAL

business·like /ˈbɪznəslaɪk/. If you describe someone as **businesslike**, you mean that they deal with things in an efficient way without wasting time. ◆◇◇◇◇ ADJ-GRADED

business·man /ˈbɪznɪsmæn/ **businessmen.** A **businessman** is a man who works in business. ◆◆◆◇◇ N-COUNT

'business person, business people. Business people are people who work in business. N-COUNT

business·woman /ˈbɪznɪswʊmən/ **business-women.** A **businesswoman** is a woman who works in business. ◆◇◇◇◇ N-COUNT

busk /bʌsk/ **busks, busking, busked.** People who **busk** play music or sing for money in the streets or other public places. ♦ **busk·ing** *Passers-by in the area have been treated to some high-quality busking.* ♦ **busk·er** /ˈbʌskə/ **buskers.** VERB: V BRITISH N-UNCOUNT N-COUNT

bus·load /ˈbʌsləʊd/ **busloads.** A **busload** of people is a large number of them who have arrived somewhere in a bus. ...*a busload of 12-year-old schoolgirls.* N-COUNT

'bus-shelter, bus-shelters. A **bus-shelter** is a small covered structure where you can wait for a bus. N-COUNT

'bus stop, bus stops. A **bus stop** is a place on a road where buses stop to let passengers on and off. ◆◇◇◇◇ N-COUNT

bust /bʌst/ **busts, busting, busted.** The form **bust** is used as the present tense of the verb, and can also be used as the past tense and past participle. **1** If you **bust** something, you break it or damage it so badly that it cannot be used. *They will have to bust the door to get him out.* ◆◆◇◇◇ VERB Vn INFORMAL

2 If someone **is busted**, the police arrest them. *They were busted for possession of cannabis.* **3** If police **bust** a place, they raid it in order to arrest people who are doing something illegal. ► Also a noun. ...*6 tons of cocaine seized last week in Panama's biggest drug bust.* VERB: V n VERB: V n INFORMAL N-COUNT

4 If a company **goes bust**, it loses so much money that it is forced to close down. PHRASE INFORMAL

5 A **bust** is a statue of the head and shoulders of a person. ...*a bronze bust of the Queen.* N-COUNT

6 You can refer to a woman's breasts as her **bust**, especially when you are talking about their size. *Good posture also helps your bust look bigger.* N-COUNT

-buster /-bʌstə/ **-busters. 1 -buster** is used to form nouns which refer to someone who breaks a particular law. *The Security Council will consider taking future actions against sanction-busters.* **2 -buster** is used to form nouns which refer to someone or something that stops an undesirable activity or situation. *Hoover was building his reputation as a crime-buster.* COMB COMB

bust·ier /ˈbʌstiə/ **bustiers.** A **bustier** is a type of close-fitting strapless top worn by women. N-COUNT BRITISH

bus·tle /ˈbʌsəl/ **bustles, bustling, bustled. 1** If someone **bustles** somewhere, they move there in a hurried and determined way, often because they are very busy. *My mother bustled around the kitchen.* **2** A place that **is bustling** with people or activity is full of people who are very busy or lively. ...*the bustling market.* **3 Bustle** is busy noisy activity. *There was a good deal of cheerful bustle.* ◆◇◇◇◇ VERB V prep/adv VERB: V with n V-ing N-UNCOUNT

'bust-up, bust-ups. A **bust-up** with someone is a serious quarrel, often resulting in the end of a relationship or partnership. N-COUNT INFORMAL

busty /ˈbʌsti/. If you describe a woman as **busty**, you mean that she has very large breasts. Some people find this word offensive. ADJ-GRADED INFORMAL

busy /ˈbɪzi/ **busier, busiest; busies, busying, busied. 1** If you are **busy**, you are working hard or concentrating on a task, so that you are not free to do anything else. *They are busy preparing for a hectic day's activity... She would be too busy to come.* **2** A **busy** time is a period of time during which you have a lot of things to do. ...*her busy schedule.* **3** If you say that someone is **busy** thinking or worrying about something, you mean that it is taking all their attention, often so that they are unable to think about anything else. *Companies are so busy analysing the financial implications that they overlook the effect on workers.* **4** If you **busy** yourself with something, you occupy yourself by dealing with it. *She busied herself getting towels ready.* ◆◆◆◇◇ ADJ-GRADED ADJ-GRADED ADJ-GRADED: v-link ADJ VERB: V pron-refl with n/-ing

5 A **busy** street or place is full of traffic and people moving about. ADJ-GRADED

6 When a telephone line is **busy**, you cannot make your call because the line is already being used by someone else. ADJ AMERICAN

7 See also **busily**.

busy·body /'bɪzɪbɒdi/ **busybodies.** A busybody is someone who interferes in other people's affairs in a way which you do not approve of. · N-COUNT PRAGMATICS INFORMAL

but /bət, STRONG bʌt/ **buts. 1** You use **but** to introduce something which contrasts with what you have just said, or to introduce something which adds to what you have just said. *'You said you'd stay till tomorrow.'—'I know, Bel, but I think I would rather go back.'. ...until the cider is very hot but not boiling... I still can't figure out why he did what he did – but anyway, he succeeded.* **2** You use **but then** or **but then again** before a remark which slightly contradicts what you have just said. *Perhaps he was wishing they'd divorced, but then again, he did not believe in divorce.* **3** You use **but then** before a remark which suggests that what you have just said should not be regarded as surprising. *Sonia might not speak the English language well, but then who did?* **4** You use **but** when you have made an excuse or apology for what you are just about to say. *I'm sorry, but it's nothing to do with you.* **5** You use **but** to introduce a reply to someone when you want to indicate surprise, disbelief, refusal, or protest. *'I don't think I should stay in this house.'—'But why?'* **6** But is used to mean 'except'. *Europe will be represented in all but two of the seven races... He didn't speak anything but Greek.* **7** You use **but for** to introduce the only factor that causes a particular thing not to happen or not to be completely true. *...the small square below, empty but for a delivery van.* **8** But is used to mean 'only'. *This is but one of the methods used. ...Napoleon and Marie Antoinette, to name but two who had stayed in the great state rooms.* **9** You use **buts** in expressions like **'no buts'** and **'ifs and buts'** to refer to reasons someone gives for not doing something, especially when you do not think that they are good reasons. *There's no ifs or buts. He has to leave Kuwait.* **10** You use **cannot but**, **could not but**, and **cannot help but** when you want to emphasize that you believe something must be true and that there is no possibility of anything else being the case. *The pistol was positioned where I couldn't help but see it.* **11 ● all but:** see **all. ● anything but:** see **anything.**
◆◆◆◆ CONJ / PHRASE / PHRASE / CONJ / CONJ / PREP / PHRASE / ADV; ADV, n; ADV num FORMAL / N-PLURAL / PHRASE FORMAL

bu·tane /'bjuːteɪn/. Butane is a gas that is obtained from petroleum and is used as a fuel. · N-UNCOUNT

butch /butʃ/. **1** If you describe a woman as **butch**, you mean that she behaves or dresses in a masculine way; an offensive use. **2** If you describe a man as **butch**, you mean that he behaves in an exaggeratedly masculine way. ◆◇◇◇◇ ADJ-GRADED / ADJ-GRADED INFORMAL

butch·er /'butʃə/ **butchers, butchering, butchered. 1** A **butcher** is a shopkeeper who sells meat. You can refer to a shop where meat is sold as a **butcher** or a **butcher's. ♦ butch·ery.** Butchery is the work of cutting up meat and preparing it for sale. **2** To **butcher** an animal means to kill it and cut it up for meat. **3** You refer to someone as a **butcher** when they have killed a lot of people in a very cruel way, and you want to express your horror and disgust. **♦ butch·ery** *In her view, war is simply a legalised form of butchery.* **4** You say that someone **has butchered** people when they have killed a lot of them in a very cruel way, and you want to express your horror and disgust. *Guards butchered 1,350 prisoners.* ◆◇◇◇◇ N-COUNT / N-UNCOUNT / VERB: V n / N-COUNT PRAGMATICS / N-UNCOUNT VERB PRAGMATICS V n

but·ler /'bʌtlə/ **butlers.** A **butler** is the most important male servant in a wealthy house. ◆◇◇◇◇ N-COUNT

butt /bʌt/ **butts, butting, butted. 1** Someone's **butt** is their bottom. Some people find this use offensive. **2** The **butt** or the **butt end** of a weapon or tool is the thick end of its handle. **3** The **butt** of a cigarette or cigar is the small part that is left when you have finished smoking it. **4** A **butt** is a large barrel used for collecting or storing liquid. **5** See also **water butt. 6** If someone or something is the **butt** of jokes or criticism, people often make fun of them or criticize them. N-COUNT AMERICAN, INFORMAL / N-COUNT / N-COUNT / N-COUNT / N-SING

7 If a person or animal **butts** you, they hit you with the top of their head. **8** See also **head-butt.** VERB: V n

butt in. If you say that someone **is butting in**, you mean they are joining in a conversation or activity without being asked to, and you find this annoying. *'I should think not,' Sarah butted in.* PHRASAL VB V p PRAGMATICS V P with quote Also V P on n

butt out. If someone tells you to **butt out**, they are telling you rudely to go away or not to interfere with what they are doing. *The time has come for parents to butt out of the adolescent's daily life.* PHRASAL VB V P V P ofn INFORMAL, AMERICAN

but·ter /'bʌtə/ **butters, buttering, buttered. 1** Butter is a soft yellow substance made from cream. You spread it on bread or use it in cooking. **2** When you **butter** bread, you spread butter on it. **3** See also **bread and butter, peanut butter.** ◆◆◇◇ N-VAR / VERB: V n

butter up. If someone **butters** you **up**, they try to please you because they want you to help or support them. *He accused Mr Delors of buttering up farmers to boost his chances of becoming French president.* PHRASAL VB V n P V P noun INFORMAL, BRITISH

'butter bean, butter beans. Butter beans are the yellowish flat round seeds of a kind of bean plant. N-COUNT

butter·cup /'bʌtəkʌp/ **buttercups.** A buttercup is a small plant with bright yellow flowers. N-COUNT

butter·fly /'bʌtəflaɪ/ **butterflies. 1** A butterfly is an insect with large colourful wings and a thin body. See picture headed **insects. 2** Butterfly is a swimming stroke which you do lying on your front, kicking your legs and bringing your arms over your head together. **3** If you have **butterflies in** your **stomach**, you are very nervous or excited about something. ◆◆◇◇ N-COUNT / N-UNCOUNT / PHRASE INFORMAL

butter·milk /'bʌtəmɪlk/. Buttermilk is the liquid that remains when fat has been removed from cream when butter is being made. You can drink it or use it in cooking. N-UNCOUNT

butter·scotch /'bʌtəskɒtʃ/. **1** Butterscotch is a hard yellowish-brown sweet made from butter and sugar boiled together. **2** A butterscotch flavoured or coloured thing has the flavour or colour of butterscotch. *...butterscotch sauce.* N-UNCOUNT / N-UNCOUNT

but·tery /'bʌtəri/. Buttery food contains butter or is covered with butter. *...buttery new potatoes.* ADJ-GRADED

but·tock /'bʌtək/ **buttocks.** Your buttocks are the two rounded fleshy parts of your body you sit on. ◆◇◇◇◇ N-COUNT

but·ton /'bʌtən/ **buttons, buttoning, buttoned. 1** Buttons are small, hard objects sewn on to pieces of clothing, which you use to fasten the clothing. **2** If you **button** a shirt, coat, or other piece of clothing, you fasten it by pushing its buttons through the buttonholes. **▶ Button up** means the same as **button.** *I buttoned up my mink coat.* **3** A **button** is a small object on a machine or electrical device that you press in order to operate the machine or device. *He reached for the remote control and pressed the 'play' button.* **4** If you say that someone **presses the right button** or **pushes the right button,** you mean that they get what they want from a person or situation in a clever way. **5** A **button** is a small piece of metal or plastic which you pin onto your clothes in order to show that you support a particular movement, organization, or person. The British word is **badge.** ◆◆◆◇◇ N-COUNT / VERB: V n / PHRASAL VB V P noun Also V n P / N-COUNT / PHRASE INFORMAL / N-COUNT AMERICAN

button up. See **button** 2. PHRASAL VB

'button-down. A **button-down** shirt or a shirt with a **button-down** collar has a button under each end of the collar which you can fasten. ADJ: ADJ n

buttoned 'up; also spelled **buttoned-up.** If you describe someone as **buttoned up,** you mean they do not talk about their thoughts or feelings. ADJ-GRADED INFORMAL

button·hole /'bʌtənhəʊl/ **buttonholes, buttonholing, buttonholed. 1** A **buttonhole** is a hole that you push a button through in order to fasten a piece of clothing. **2** A **buttonhole** is a flower that you wear on the lapel of your jacket. **3** If you **buttonhole** someone, you stop them and make them listen to you. N-COUNT / N-COUNT BRITISH / VERB: V n

but·tress /'bʌtrəs/ **buttresses, buttressing, buttressed. 1** Buttresses are supports, usually made of stone or brick, that support a wall. **2** To **buttress** an argument, system, or person means to ◆◇◇◇◇ N-COUNT / VERB: V n; V n with n

give them support and strength. *He sought to buttress some of his arguments with quotations from Mein Kampf.*

but·ty /'bʌti/ **butties.** A **butty** is a sandwich. ...*a bacon butty.* N-COUNT BRITISH, INFORMAL

bux·om /'bʌksəm/. If you describe a woman as **buxom**, you mean that she looks healthy and attractive and has a rounded body and big breasts. ADJ-GRADED

buy /baɪ/ **buys, buying, bought. 1** If you **buy** something, you obtain it by paying money for it. *He could not afford to buy a house... Lizzie bought herself a mountain bike... I'd like to buy him lunch.* VERB ♦♦♦♦♦ V n V n n

♦ **buy·er, buyers** *Car buyers are more interested in safety... I was a buyer for the women's clothing department.* N-COUNT **2** If you talk about what an amount of money **buys**, you are referring to the quantity or standard of goods you can buy with that amount. *About £25,000 buys a habitable house... $244 will buy you a return flight to Gerona.* **3** If something is a good **buy**, it is of good quality and is not very expensive. VERB V n V n n N-COUNT: supp N

4 If you say that a person can be **bought**, you mean they can be bribed to give their help or loyalty to someone. VB: usu passive be V-ed

5 If you **buy** something like time, freedom, or victory, you obtain it but only by offering or giving up something in return. *It was a risky operation, but might buy more time.* VERB V n

6 If you **buy** an idea or a theory, you believe it and accept it. *And this talk about police protection. We are not buying it.* ▶ **Buy into** means the same as **buy.** *I bought into the popular myth that when I got the new car or the next house, I'd finally be happy.* VERB V n INFORMAL PHRASAL VB V P n

buy into. If someone **buys into** a company or an organization, they buy part of it, often in order to gain some control of it. ● See also **buy** 6. PHRASAL VB V P n

buy off. If one person **buys off** another person, the first person bribes the second person not to act against them; used showing disapproval. ...*policies designed to buy off the working-class vote.* PHRASAL VB PRAGMATICS V P noun Also V n P

buy out. 1 If you **buy** someone **out,** you buy their share of something such as a company or piece of property that you previously owned together. *The bank had to pay to buy out most of the 200 former partners.* ● See also **buyout. 2** If you **buy** someone **out** of the armed forces or another organization, you pay a sum of money so that they can leave before the end of the period they agreed to stay for. *Carling eventually bought himself out of the army.* PHRASAL VB V P noun Also V n P V n P

buy up. If you **buy up** land, property, or a commodity, you buy large amounts of it, or all that is available. *The mention of price rises sent citizens out to their shops to buy up as much as they could.* PHRASAL VB V P noun Also V n P

buyer's market, buyer's markets. When there is a **buyer's market** for a type of product, there are more products of that type for sale than there are people who want to buy them, so buyers have a lot of choice and can make prices come down. N-COUNT

buy·out /'baɪaʊt/ **buyouts.** A **buyout** is the buying of a company, especially by its managers or employees. ...*a management buyout.* ♦◇◇◇◇ N-COUNT

buzz /bʌz/ **buzzes, buzzing, buzzed. 1** If something **buzzes**, it makes a long continuous sound, like a bee. *Helicopters buzzed across the city.* ▶ Also a noun. ...*the irritating buzz of an insect.* ♦ **buzz·ing** *He switched off the transformer and the buzzing stopped.* **2** You can use **buzz** to refer to a long continuous sound, especially one caused by a lot of people talking at once. ...*the excited buzz of conversation.* **3** If you **buzz** someone, you call them, usually using an internal telephone line or a buzzer. ▶ Also a noun. *We'll give him a buzz when we get to Maybury Street.* **4** If an aircraft **buzzes** a place, it flies low over it. **5** If people **are buzzing** around, they are moving around quickly and busily. *A few tourists were buzzing about.* **6** If a place **is buzzing** with activity or conversation, there is a lot of activity or conversation there, especially because something important or exciting is VERB: V N-COUNT N-UNCOUNT N-SING VERB: V n INFORMAL N-SING: a N VERB: V n VERB V adv/prep WRITTEN VERB: V with n V-ing Also V,

about to happen. ...*Hong Kong's buzzing, pulsating atmosphere.* V prep

7 If something gives you a **buzz,** it makes you feel very happy or excited for a short time. N-SING INFORMAL

8 You can use **buzz** to describe a word, idea, or activity which has recently become extremely popular. *Sex education in schools was the buzz topic.* ADJ: ADJ n

buzz off. If someone **buzzes off,** they go away. People sometimes say **buzz off** as a rude way of telling someone to go away. *He buzzed off downstairs.* PHRASAL VB V P INFORMAL, BRITISH

buz·zard /'bʌzəd/ **buzzards. 1** A **buzzard** is a large bird of prey. **2** Some people refer to a person as a **buzzard** when they think that person is unpleasant or very mean. N-COUNT N-COUNT INFORMAL

buzz·er /'bʌzə/ **buzzers.** A **buzzer** is an electrical device that is used to make a buzzing sound, for example to attract someone's attention. ♦◇◇◇◇ N-COUNT

buzz·word /'bʌzwɜːd/ **buzzwords;** also spelled **buzz word.** A **buzzword** is a word or expression that has become used in a particular field and is being used a lot by the media. *Biodiversity was the buzzword of the Rio Earth Summit.* N-COUNT

by. The preposition is pronounced /baɪ/. The adverb is pronounced /baɪ/. In addition to the uses shown below, **by** is used in phrasal verbs such as 'abide by', 'put by', and 'stand by'. ♦♦♦♦♦

1 If something is done **by** a person or thing, that person or thing does it. *The feast was served by his mother... The town has been under attack by rebel groups.* PREP

2 If you say that something such as a book, a piece of music, or a painting is **by** a particular person, you mean that this person wrote it or created it. ...*a painting by Van Gogh.* PREP

3 If you do something **by** a particular thing, you do it using that thing. ...*if you're travelling by car.* ...*dinners by candlelight.* **4** If you achieve one thing **by** doing another thing, your action enables you to achieve the first thing. *Make the sauce by boiling the cream... By allowing the body to digest food properly, you will get the maximum benefit.* PREP PREP

5 You use **by** in phrases such as 'by chance' or 'by accident' to indicate whether or not an event was planned. *He opened Ingrid's letter by mistake.* PREP

6 If someone is a particular type of person **by** nature, **by** profession, or **by** birth, they are that type of person because of their nature, their profession, or the family they were born into. *Her parents were in fact American by birth.* PREP

7 If something must be done **by** law, the law requires that it should be done. If something is the case **by** particular standards, it is the case according to those standards. ...*evening wear that was discreet by his standards.* PREP

8 If you say what someone means **by** a particular word or expression, you are saying what they intend the word or expression to refer to. *Stella knew what he meant by 'start again'.* PREP

9 If you hold someone or something **by** a particular part of them, you hold that part. *He caught her by the shoulder... He picked up the photocopy by one corner.* PREP

10 Someone or something that is **by** something else is beside it and close to it. ...*a rocking-chair by the window... Felicity Maxwell stood by the bar.* ▶ Also an adverb. *Large numbers of security police stood by.* PREP ADV: ADV after v

11 When a person or vehicle goes **by** you, they move past you without stopping. *A few cars passed close by me.* ▶ Also an adverb. *The bomb went off as a police patrol went by.* PREP ADV: ADV after v

12 If you stop **by** a place, you visit it for a short time. *We had made arrangements to stop by her house.* ▶ Also an adverb. *I'll stop by after dinner and we'll have that talk.* PREP ADV: ADV after v

13 If something happens **by** a particular time, it happens at or before that time. *By eight o'clock he had arrived... We all knew by then that the affair was practically over.* PREP

14 If you do something **by** day, you do it during the day. If you do it **by** night, you do it during the night. PREP

15 In maths, you use **by** before the second number PREP

in a multiplication or division sum. *230cm divided by 22cm is 10.45cm.*

16 You use **by** to talk about measurements of area. PREP For example, if a room is 6 metres **by** 4 metres, it measures 6 metres in one direction and 4 metres in the other direction.

17 You use **by** when you are mentioning the amount PREP of an increase or a decrease. *Violent crime has increased by 10 percent since last year.*

18 Things that are made or sold **by** the million or **by** PREP the dozen are made or sold in those quantities. *Parcels arrived by the dozen from America... House wines are sold by the litre.*

19 You use **by** in expressions such as 'minute by minute' and 'drop by drop' to talk about things that happen gradually, rather than all at once. *His father began to lose his memory bit by bit.*

20 If you are **by yourself**, you are alone. **21** If you do PHRASE something **by yourself**, you succeed in doing it without anyone helping you. *I didn't know if I could raise a child by myself.*

bye /baɪ/. **Bye** and **bye-bye** are informal ways of ◆◆◇◇◇ saying goodbye. CONVENTION

'**bye-law.** See bylaw.

'**by-election, by-elections.** A by-election is an ◆◇◇◇◇ election that is held to choose a new member of N-COUNT parliament when a member has resigned or died.

by·gone /ˈbaɪgɒn, AM -gɔːn/ **bygones. 1** Bygone ◆◇◇◇◇ means happening or existing a very long time ago. ADJ: ADJ n *...memories of a bygone age. ...bygone generations.* **2** If two people **let bygones be bygones**, they decide PHRASE to forget about unpleasant things that have happened between them in the past.

by·law /ˈbaɪlɔː/ **bylaws**; also spelled **bye-law, by-** N-COUNT **law**. A **bylaw** is a law which is made by a local authority and which applies only in their area.

'**by-line, by-lines**; also spelled **byline**. A **by-line** is N-COUNT a line at the top of an article in a newspaper or TECHNICAL magazine giving the author's name.

by·pass /ˈbaɪpɑːs, -pæs/ **bypasses, bypassing,** ◆◆◇◇◇ **bypassed. 1** If you **bypass** someone or something VERB: V n that you would normally have to get involved with, you ignore them or do not get involved with them, often because you want to achieve something more quickly. *Regulators worry that controls could easily*

be bypassed.

2 A **bypass** is a surgical operation performed on or N-COUNT near the heart, in which the flow of blood is redirected so that it does not flow through a part of the heart which is diseased or blocked. *...heart bypass surgery.*

3 A **bypass** is a main road which takes traffic around N-COUNT the edge of a town rather than through its centre. *...the Hereford bypass.* **4** If a person or route **bypasses** a VERB: V n place, they go around it rather than through it.

'**by-product, by-products. 1** A **by-product** is ◆◇◇◇◇ something which is produced during the manufac- N-COUNT ture or processing of another product. *The raw material for the tyre is a by-product of petrol refining.* **2** Something that is a **by-product** of an event or N-COUNT situation happens as a result of it, although it is usually not expected or planned. *A by-product of their meeting was the release of these fourteen men.*

byre /baɪə/ **byres**. A cowshed is sometimes called a N-COUNT **byre**. BRITISH

by·stander /ˈbaɪstændə/ **bystanders**. A **by-** ◆◇◇◇◇ **stander** is a person who is present when something N-COUNT happens but does not take part in it.

byte /baɪt/ **bytes**. In computing, a **byte** is a unit of N-COUNT storage approximately equivalent to one printed character.

by·way /ˈbaɪweɪ/ **byways. 1** A **byway** is a small N-COUNT road which is not used by many cars or people. **2** The **byways** of a subject are the less important or N-COUNT less well known areas of it. *...the byways of children's literature.*

by·word /ˈbaɪwɜːd/ **bywords. 1** Someone or some- N-COUNT: thing that is a **byword** for a particular quality is well N for n known for having that quality. *...a region that had become a byword for violence. ...the Rolls-Royce brand name, a byword for quality.* **2** A **byword** is a N-COUNT word or phrase which people often use. *Loyalty, support, and secrecy became the bywords of the day.*

byz·an·tine /bɪˈzæntaɪn, AM ˈbɪzəntiːn/; also spelled **Byzantine. 1** Byzantine means related to or con- ADJ: ADJ n nected with the Byzantine Empire.

2 If you describe a system or process as **byzantine**, ADJ-GRADED you disapprove of it because it is complicated or se- PRAGMATICS cretive. *...a byzantine system of rules and trading arrangements.*

C c

C, c /siː/ **C's, c's. 1** C is the third letter of the Eng- N-VAR lish alphabet. **2** In music, **C** is the first note in the N-VAR scale of C major. **3** If you get a **C** as a mark for a N-VAR piece of work or in an exam, your work is average.

4 c. is written in front of a date or number to indicate that it is approximate. **c.** is an abbreviation for **circa**. *...the museum's recreation of a New York dining-room (c. 1825-35).* **5** C or c is used as an abbreviation for words beginning with c, such as 'copyright' or 'Celsius'. *Heat the oven to 180°C.*

6 See also **C-in-C, c/o.**

cab /kæb/ **cabs. 1** A cab is a taxi. *...the red London* ◆◆◇◇◇ *buses and black cabs moving along Piccadilly.* N-COUNT **2** The **cab** of a lorry is the front part in which the N-COUNT driver sits.

ca·bal /kəˈbæl/ **cabals**. If you refer to a group of N-COUNT politicians or other people as a **cabal**, you disap- PRAGMATICS prove of them because they meet and decide things secretly. *Harding had been chosen by a cabal of fellow senators.*

caba·ret /ˈkæbəreɪ, AM -ˈreɪ/ **cabarets**. Cabaret is ◆◇◇◇◇ live entertainment consisting of dancing, singing, or N-VAR comedy acts that are performed in the evening in

restaurants or nightclubs. *Peter and I also did a cabaret at the Corn Exchange.*

cab·bage /ˈkæbɪdʒ/ **cabbages**. A cabbage is a ◆◆◇◇◇ round vegetable with green leaves that you usually N-VAR chop up and boil in water before eating. See picture headed **vegetables**.

cab·ble /ˈkæbi/ **cabbies**. A **cabbie** is a person who ◆◇◇◇◇ drives a taxi. *On the way to the airport, the cabbie* N-COUNT *asked us why we were going.* INFORMAL

ca·ber /ˈkeɪbə/ **cabers**. In traditional Scottish N-COUNT sports, a **caber** is a long, heavy, wooden pole that is tossed into the air as a test of strength.

cab·in /ˈkæbɪn/ **cabins. 1** A cabin is a small room ◆◆◇◇◇ in a ship or boat. **2** A cabin is one of the areas in- N-COUNT side a plane. *...the First Class cabin.* **3** A cabin is a N-COUNT small wooden house, especially one in an area of N-COUNT forests or mountains. *...a log cabin.*

'**cabin crew, cabin crews**. The cabin crew on an N-COLL- aircraft are the people whose job it is to look after the COUNT passengers.

'**cabin cruiser, cabin cruisers**. A cabin cruiser N-COUNT is a motor boat which has a cabin for people to live or sleep in.

cabi·net /'kæbɪnɪt/ **cabinets. 1** A **cabinet** is a cupboard used for storing things such as medicine or alcoholic drinks or for displaying decorative things in. ● See also **filling cabinet**. **2** The **Cabinet** is a group of the most senior ministers in a government, who meet regularly to discuss policies. *...a three-hour Cabinet meeting in Downing Street.* N-COUNT

'cabinet maker, cabinet makers; also spelled **cabinetmaker.** A **cabinet maker** is a person who makes high-quality wooden furniture. N-COUNT

ca·ble /'keɪbəl/ **cables, cabling, cabled. 1** Cable is used to refer to television systems in which the signals are sent along underground wires rather than by radio waves. *In addition to being broadcast on cable television, the movie also is being distributed on video-cassettes... They ran commercials on cable systems across the country.* **2** If a country, a city, or someone's home **is cabled**, cables and other equipment are put in place so that the people there can receive cable television. N-UNCOUNT; VB: usu passive be V-ed

3 A **cable** is a thick wire, or a bundle of wires inside a rubber or plastic covering, which is used to carry electricity or electronic signals. *...overhead power cables.* ◆ **ca·bling.** Cabling is used to refer to electrical or electronic cables. *...offices equipped with computer cabling.* **4** A **cable** is a kind of very strong, thick rope, made of wires twisted together. N-VAR; N-UNCOUNT; N-VAR

5 A **cable** is a message that is sent by means of electricity along a wire over a long distance. *She sent a cable to her mother.* **6** If you **cable** someone, you send them a message in the form of a cable. *'Don't do it again,' Franklin cabled her when he got her letter... She had to decide whether or not to cable the news to Louis.* N-COUNT; VERB: V n, V n with quote, V n prep/adv, Also V n n, V

'cable car, cable cars. A **cable car** is a vehicle for taking people up mountains or steep hills. It is pulled by a moving cable. N-COUNT

cache /kæʃ/ **caches.** A **cache** is a quantity of things such as weapons that have been hidden. *A huge arms cache was discovered by police.* N-COUNT: with supp

ca·chet /'kæʃeɪ, AM kæ'ʃeɪ/. If someone or something has a certain **cachet**, they have a quality which makes people admire them or approve of them. *A Mercedes carries a certain cachet.* N-SING WRITTEN

cack·le /'kækəl/ **cackles, cackling, cackled.** If someone **cackles**, they laugh in a loud unpleasant way, often at someone else's misfortune. *Newington threw his head back and cackled with laughter.* ▶ Also a noun. *He let out a brief cackle.* VERB: V, Also V with quote; N-COUNT

ca·copho·ny /kə'kɒfəni/ **cacophonies.** You can describe a loud, unpleasant mixture of sounds as a **cacophony**. *All around was bubbling a cacophony of voices.* ◆ **ca·copho·nous** /kə'kɒfənəs/ *...'60s-sounding guitars and cacophonous vocals.* N-COUNT; ADJ-GRADED

cac·tus /'kæktəs/ **cactuses** or **cacti** /'kæktaɪ/. A **cactus** is a thick fleshy plant that grows in deserts. Cacti have no leaves and many of them are covered in spikes. N-COUNT

cad /kæd/ **cads.** If you call a man a **cad**, you mean that he treats other people badly or unfairly. *He's a scoundrel! A cad!* N-COUNT DATED

ca·dav·er /kə'dævə/ **cadavers.** A **cadaver** is a dead body. N-COUNT FORMAL

ca·dav·er·ous /kə'dævərəs/. If you describe someone as **cadaverous**, you mean they are extremely thin and pale. ADJ-GRADED WRITTEN

cad·die /'kædi/ **caddies, caddying, caddied;** also spelled **caddy. 1** In golf, a **caddie** is a person who carries golf clubs and other equipment for a player. **2** If you **caddie** for a golfer, you act as their caddie. *Lil caddied for her son.* N-COUNT; VERB V for n

ca·dence /'keɪdəns/ **cadences. 1** The **cadence** of someone's voice is the way their voice gets higher and lower as they speak. *He recognized the Polish cadences in her voice.* **2** A **cadence** is a series of chords that ends a section of music or a complete piece of music. N-COUNT FORMAL; N-COUNT

ca·den·za /kə'denzə/ **cadenzas.** In classical music, a **cadenza** is a long and technically difficult solo passage in a piece for soloist and orchestra. N-COUNT

ca·det /kə'det/ **cadets.** A **cadet** is a young person who is being trained in the armed forces or the police. N-COUNT

cadge /kædʒ/ **cadges, cadging, cadged.** If someone **cadges** food, money, or help from you, they ask you for it and succeed in getting it. *Can I cadge a cigarette?* VERB V n INFORMAL, BRITISH

cad·mium /'kædmiəm/. **Cadmium** is a soft white metal used in industry and electronics. N-UNCOUNT

ca·dre /'kɑːdə, AM -dreɪ/ **cadres. 1** A **cadre** is a small group of people who have been specially chosen and trained for a particular purpose. *...an elite cadre of Euro-managers.* **2** In some political parties, a **cadre** is a party worker or official. N-COUNT; N-COUNT

Cae·sar·ean /sɪ'zeəriən/ **Caesareans.** A **Caesarean** or a **Caesarean section** is an operation in which a baby is lifted out of a woman's womb through an opening cut in her abdomen. N-COUNT: also by N

café /'kæfeɪ, AM kæ'feɪ/ **cafés. 1** A **café** is a place where you can buy drinks, simple meals, and snacks. In Britain cafés do not serve alcoholic drinks. **2** A street **café** or a pavement **café** is a café which has tables and chairs on the pavement outside it where people can eat and drink. These cafes are common in European cities. *...an Italian street café.* N-COUNT; N-COUNT: n N

caf·eteria /,kæfɪ'tɪəriə/ **cafeterias.** A **cafeteria** is a restaurant where you choose your food from a counter and carry it to your table yourself after paying for it. Cafeterias are usually found in hospitals, colleges, and hotels. N-COUNT

caff /kæf/ **caffs.** A **caff** is a cafe which serves simple British food such as fried eggs, bacon, and sausages. *...a transport caff.* N-COUNT INFORMAL, BRITISH

caf·feine /'kæfiːn, AM kæ'fiːn/. **Caffeine** is a chemical substance found in coffee, tea, and cocoa, which makes your brain and body more active. N-UNCOUNT

caf·tan /'kæftæn/ **caftans;** also spelled **kaftan.** A **caftan** is a long loose garment with long sleeves. N-COUNT

cage /keɪdʒ/ **cages.** A **cage** is a structure of wire or metal bars in which birds or animals are kept. ● See also **rib cage**. N-COUNT

caged /keɪdʒd/. A **caged** bird or animal is inside a cage. ADJ

cag·ey /'keɪdʒi/. If you say that someone is being **cagey** about something, you think that they are deliberately not giving you much information about it. *He is cagey about what he was paid.* ADJ-GRADED PRAGMATICS

ca·hoots /kə'huːts/. If you say that one person is **in cahoots** with another, you do not trust the first person because you think that they are planning something secretly with the other; used showing disapproval. *They were all in cahoots with the other.* PHRASE PRAGMATICS

cairn /keən/ **cairns.** A **cairn** is a pile of stones which marks a boundary, a route across rough ground, or the top of a mountain. A cairn is sometimes also built in memory of someone. N-COUNT

ca·jole /kə'dʒəʊl/ **cajoles, cajoling, cajoled.** If you **cajole** someone, you get them to do something after persuading them for some time. *It was he who had cajoled Garland into doing the film... He cajoled Mr Izetbegovic to accept the peace plan.* VERB: V n, V n into -ing, V n to-inf, Also V n, V

cake /keɪk/ **cakes. 1** A **cake** is a sweet food made by baking a mixture of flour, eggs, sugar, and fat in an oven. *...a piece of cake.* **2** Food that is formed into flat round shapes before it is cooked can be referred to as **cakes**. *...fish cakes.* **3** A **cake** of soap is a small block of it. N-VAR; N-COUNT; N-COUNT

4 If you think that someone wants the benefits of doing two things when it is only reasonable to expect the benefits of doing one, you can say that they want to **have their cake and eat it**; used showing disapproval. **5** If things are **selling like hot cakes**, a lot of people are buying them. **6** If you think something is very easy to do, you can say it is **a piece of cake**. *Getting rid of him will be a piece of cake.* **7** ● the **icing on the cake**: see **icing**. PHRASE PRAGMATICS; PHRASE INFORMAL; PHRASE INFORMAL

caked /keɪkt/. If something is **caked** with mud, blood, or dirt, it is covered with a thick dry layer of ADJ

it. *Her shoes were caked with mud.* ▶ Also a combining form. *...blood-caked bandages.* COMB

'**cake mix, cake mixes.** Cake mix is a powder-like substance that you mix with eggs and water or milk, to make a cake. N-VAR

'**cake tin, cake tins. 1** A **cake tin** is a metal container with a lid, which you put a cake into in order to keep it fresh. **2** A **cake tin** is a metal container which you bake a cake in. N-COUNT BRITISH / N-COUNT BRITISH

cal /kæl/ **cals.** Cals are units of measurement for the energy value of food. **Cal** is an abbreviation for **calorie.** *...325 cals per serving.* N-COUNT

ca·lam·ity /kə'læmɪti/ **calamities.** A calamity is an event that causes a great deal of damage, destruction, or personal distress. *...the calamity of war.* ♦ **ca·lami·tous** /kə'læmɪtəs/ *...a calamitous air crash.* ◆◇◇◇ N-VAR FORMAL / ADJ-GRADED

cal·cium /'kælsiəm/. **Calcium** is a soft white element which is found in bones and teeth, and also in limestone, chalk, and marble. ◆◆◇◇◇ N-UNCOUNT

cal·cu·late /'kælkjʊleɪt/ **calculates, calculating, calculated. 1** If you **calculate** a number or amount, you discover it from information that you already have, by using arithmetic, mathematics, or a special machine. *From this you can calculate the total mass in the Galaxy... We calculate that the average size farm in Lancaster County is 65 acres.* ♦ **cal·cu·la·tion** /,kælkjʊ'leɪʃən/ **calculations** *Leonard made a rapid calculation: he'd never make it in time.* **2** If you **calculate** the effects of something, especially a possible course of action, you think about them in order to form an opinion or decide what to do. *I believe I am capable of calculating the political consequences accurately.* ♦ **calculation** *Mr Mitterrand has two years of power left and he is deep in his calculations.* ◆◆◇◇◇ VERB / V n / V that / Also V, V wh / N-VAR / VERB / V n / Also V that / N-VAR

cal·cu·lat·ed /'kælkjʊleɪtɪd/. **1** If something is **calculated** to have a particular effect, it is specially done or arranged in order to have that effect. *Their movements through the region were calculated to terrify landowners into abandoning their holdings.* **2** You can describe a clever or dishonest action as **calculated** if it is very carefully planned or arranged. *...a calculated attempt to cover up her crime.* **3** If you take a **calculated** risk, you do something which you think might be successful, although you have fully considered the possible bad consequences of your action. ◆◆◆◇◇ ADJ: v-link ADJ to-inf / ADJ-GRADED / ADJ: ADJ n

cal·cu·lat·ing /'kælkjʊleɪtɪŋ/. If you describe someone as **calculating**, you disapprove of the fact that they deliberately plan to get what they want, often by hurting or harming other people. *...a cool, calculating and clever criminal.* ♦ **calculation** *...cold, unspeakably cruel calculation.* ◆◇◇◇ ADJ-GRADED / N-UNCOUNT

calculation. See **calculate, calculating.**

cal·cu·la·tor /'kælkjʊleɪtə/ **calculators.** A calculator is a small electronic device that you use for making mathematical calculations. ◆◇◇◇ N-COUNT

cal·cu·lus /'kælkjʊləs/. **Calculus** is an advanced branch of mathematics which deals with variable quantities. N-UNCOUNT

cal·en·dar /'kælɪndə/ **calendars. 1** A calendar is a chart or device which displays the date and the day of the week, and often the whole of a particular year divided up into months, weeks, and days. **2** A **calendar** is a particular system for dividing time into periods such as years, months, and weeks, often starting from a particular point in history. *...the Julian calendar of the Romans.* **3** You can use **calendar** to refer to a series or list of events and activities which take place on particular dates, and which are important for a particular organization, community, or person. *...the British sporting calendar's most prestigious events.* ◆◆◇◇◇ N-COUNT / N-COUNT / N-COUNT

,**calendar 'month, calendar months.** A calendar month is a period of approximately 30 days that is known by a particular name, such as January, May, or September. N-COUNT

,**calendar 'year, calendar years.** A calendar year is a period of 365 or 366 days that begins on January 1st and ends on December 31st. N-COUNT

calf /kɑːf, AM kæf/ **calves** /kɑːvz, AM kævz/. **1** A calf is a young cow. **2** Some other young animals, including elephants and whales, are called **calves. 3** Your **calf** is the thick part at the back of your leg, between your ankle and your knee. See picture headed **human body.** ◆◇◇◇ N-COUNT / N-COUNT / N-COUNT

cali·brate /'kælɪbreɪt/ **calibrates, calibrating, calibrated.** If you **calibrate** an instrument or tool, you mark or adjust it so that you can use it to measure something accurately. *...instructions on how to calibrate a thermometer.* ♦ **cali·bra·tion, calibrations** *The main instruments are backlit, with calibrations etched on the glass.* VERB / V n / TECHNICAL / N-VAR

cali·bre /'kælɪbə/ **calibres;** spelled **caliber** in American English. **1** If you talk about the **calibre** of someone or something, you are referring to their qualities, abilities, or high standards; often used showing approval. *I was impressed by the high calibre of the researchers... The calibre of teaching was very high.* **2** The **calibre** of a gun is the width of the inside of its barrel. ◆◇◇◇ N-UNCOUNT: with supp / N-COUNT TECHNICAL

cali·co /'kælɪkəʊ/ **calicoes. Calico** is plain white fabric made from cotton. N-VAR

cali·per /'kælɪpə/ **calipers. 1** Calipers are an instrument consisting of long, thin pieces of metal joined together, which is used to measure the size of things. **2** Calipers are devices consisting of metal rods held together by straps, which are used to support a person's legs when they are unable to walk properly. N-PLURAL / N-COUNT

ca·liph /'keɪlɪf/ **caliphs;** also spelled **calif.** A Caliph was a Muslim ruler. N-COUNT

cal·is·then·ics /,kælɪs'θenɪks/. **Calisthenics** are simple exercises that you can do to keep fit and healthy. N-PLURAL

call /kɔːl/ **calls, calling, called. 1** If you **call** someone or something by a particular name or title, you give them that name or title. *I always wanted to call the dog Mufty... Everybody called each other by their surnames.* ♦ **called** *There are two Labour politicians called Jim Callaghan.* ● See also **so-called. 2** If you **call** someone or something a particular thing, you suggest they are that thing or describe them as that thing. *The speech was interrupted by members of the Conservative Party, who called him a traitor... She calls me lazy... He called it particularly cynical to begin the releases on Christmas Day.* **3** If you **call** something, you say it in a loud voice, because you are trying to attract someone's attention. *He could hear the others downstairs in different parts of the house calling his name.* ▶ **Call out** means the same as **call.** *The butcher's son called out a greeting... The train stopped and a porter called out, 'Middlesbrough!'* **4** If you **call** someone, you ask them to come to you by shouting to them. *She called her young son: 'Here, Stephen, come and look at this!'* **5** If you **call** someone, you telephone them. *'May I speak with Mr Coyne, please?'—'May I ask who's calling?'* **6** If you **call** someone such as a doctor or the police, you ask them to come to you by telephoning them. *He screamed for his wife to call an ambulance.* **7** When you make a telephone **call,** you telephone someone. *I made a phone call to the United States.* **8** If you **call in sick,** you telephone your workplace to tell them you will not be coming to work because you are ill. **9** If someone in authority **calls** something such as a meeting, rehearsal, or election, they arrange for it to take place at a particular time. *The Committee decided to call a meeting of the All India Congress.* **10** If someone **is called** before a court or committee, they are ordered to appear there, usually to give evidence. *The child waited two hours before she was called to give evidence.* **11** If you **call** somewhere, you make a short visit there. *A market researcher called at the house where he* ◆◆◆◆◆ VERB / V n n / V n by n / ADJ: v-link ADJ / VERB / V n n / V n adj / V it adj to-inf / VERB / V n / Also V with quote / PHRASAL VB / V P noun / V P with quote / VERB / V n / VERB: V n / V / VERB / V n / N-COUNT / PHRASE / VERB / V n / VB: usu passive / be V-ed to-inf / Also be V-ed / VERB / V prep/adv / Also V

was living. ▶ Also a noun. *He decided to pay a call on* N-COUNT
Tommy Cummings.

12 When a train, bus, or ship **calls** somewhere, it VERB
stops there for a short time to allow people to get on or V prep/adv
off. *The steamer calls at several palm-fringed ports
along the way.*

13 If there is a **call** for something, someone demands N-COUNT
that it should happen. *There have been calls for a new
kind of security arrangement.* **14** If there is little or no N-UNCOUNT:
call for something, very few people want it to be done with brd-neg,
or provided. *'Have you got just plain chocolate?'—'No,* N for n
I'm afraid there's not much call for that.'* **15** If you say PHRASE
that **there is no call for** someone to behave in a par- PRAGMATICS
ticular way, you mean that you disapprove of their behaviour, usually because you think it is rude.

16 The **call** of something such as a place is the strong N-SING:
attraction or fascination that it has for you. *You must* with poss
be feeling exhilarated by the call of the new.

17 The **call** of a particular bird or animal is the char- N-COUNT
acteristic sound that it makes.

18 If someone has **first call on** something, they will be PHRASE
asked before anyone else whether they want to buy it
or use it. *Why should they get first call on the best
property?*

19 If someone is **on call**, they are ready to go to work PHRASE
at any time if they are needed, especially when there is
an emergency. *...a doctor on call.*

20 Call is used in a large number of expressions
which are explained under other words in this dictionary. For example, the expression **to call
someone's bluff** is explained at **bluff**.

call back. If you **call** someone **back**, you telephone PHRASAL VB
them again or in return for a telephone call that they V n P
have made to you. *If we're not around she'll take a* Also V P
message and we'll call you back.

call for. **1** If you **call for** someone, you go to the PHRASAL VB
building where they are to meet them, so that you can V P n
go somewhere else together. *I shall be calling for you
at seven o'clock.* **2** If you **call for** something, you de- V P n
mand that it should happen. *They angrily called for
Robinson's resignation.* **3** If something **calls for** a par- V P n
ticular action or quality, it needs it or requires it. *...a
situation that calls for a blend of delicacy and force.*

call in. **1** If you **call** someone **in**, you ask them to PHRASAL VB
come and help you or do something for you. *Call in* V P noun
an architect or surveyor to oversee the work. **2** If you Also V n P
call in somewhere, you make a short visit there. *He* V P
just calls in occasionally.

call off. If you **call** something **off** an event that has been PHRASAL VB
planned, you cancel it. *He has called off the trip...* V P noun
There was no explanation given to me when the deal Also V P
was called off.

call on or **call upon. 1** If you **call on** someone to do PHRASAL VB
something, you say publicly that you want them to do V P n to-inf
it. *One of Kenya's leading churchmen has called on the
government to resign.* **2** If you **call on** someone, you V P n
pay them a short visit. *Sofia was intending to call on
Miss Kitts.*

call out. If you **call** someone **out**, you order or re- PHRASAL VB
quest that they come to help, especially in an emer- V P noun
gency. *Colombia has called out the army and imposed* Also V n P
emergency measures. ● See also **call 3**.

call up. 1 If you **call** someone **up**, you telephone PHRASAL VB
them. *When I'm in Pittsburgh, I call him up... I called* V n P
up the Ackroyd house and was told that the lady was V P noun
having her hair done in town. **2** If someone **is called** V P noun
up, they are ordered to join the army, navy, or air be-V-ed P
force, or chosen to play in a sports team. *The United* Also V n P
*States has called up some 150,000 military reservists...
Steve Cutler has been called up for the Australian
squad at the World Cup in October.* ● See also **call-up**.

call upon. See **call on**. PHRASAL VB

'**call box, call boxes;** also spelled **call-box.** A **call** N-COUNT
box is a telephone box.

call·er /'kɔːlə/ **callers. 1** A **caller** is a person who ◆◆◇◇◇
is making a telephone call. *An anonymous caller* N-COUNT
told police what had happened. **2** A **caller** is a per- N-COUNT
son who comes to see you for a short visit.

cal·lig·ra·pher /kə'lɪgrəfə/ **calligraphers.** A **cal-** N-COUNT
ligrapher is a person who is skilled in the art of calligraphy.

cal·lig·ra·phy /kə'lɪgrəfi/. **Calligraphy** is the art of N-UNCOUNT
producing beautiful handwriting using a brush or a
special pen.

call·ing /'kɔːlɪŋ/ **callings.** A **calling** is a profession ◆◇◇◇◇
or career which someone is strongly attracted to, N-COUNT
especially one which involves helping other people.
*He was a consultant physician, a serious man dedi-
cated to his calling.*

'**calling card, calling cards.** A **calling card** is a N-COUNT
small card with personal information about you on
it, such as your name and address, which you can
give to people when you go to visit them.

cal·lous /'kæləs/. A **callous** person or action is very ◆◇◇◇◇
cruel and shows no concern for other people or ADJ-GRADED
their feelings. *...his callous disregard for human life.*
♦ **cal·lous·ness** *...the callousness of Raymond's* N-UNCOUNT
murder. ♦ **cal·lous·ly** *...callously ill-treating his* ADV-GRADED
wife.

cal·loused /'kæləst/; also spelled **callused.** A foot or ADJ-GRADED
hand that is **calloused** is covered in calluses.

cal·low /'kæləʊ/. A **callow** young person has very ADJ-GRADED
little experience or knowledge of the way they
should behave as an adult.

'**call sign, call signs.** A **call sign** is the letters and N-COUNT
numbers which identify a person, vehicle, or organization that is broadcasting on the radio or
sending messages by radio.

'**call-up, call-ups. 1** A **call-up** is an occasion on ◆◇◇◇◇
which people are ordered to report for service in the N-COUNT
armed forces. *The Ministry of Defence served call-up* BRITISH
papers on 390 army reservists. **2** If someone receives N-COUNT
a **call-up** to a sports team, such as the national JOURNALISM
football team, they are chosen to play for that team.

cal·lus /'kæləs/ **calluses.** A **callus** is an area of un- N-COUNT
wanted, unnaturally thick skin, usually on the palms
of your hands or the soles of your feet, which has
been caused by rubbing.

calm /kɑːm/ **calmer, calmest; calms, calm-** ◆◆◆◇◇
ing, calmed. 1 A **calm** person does not show or ADJ-GRADED
feel any worry, anger, or excitement. *She is usually a
calm and diplomatic woman... Try to keep calm and
just tell me what happened. ...a soft, calm voice.*
▶ Also a noun. *He felt a sudden sense of calm.* N-UNCOUNT:
♦ **calm·ly** *Alan looked at him and said calmly, 'I* also a N
don't believe you.' ♦ **calm·ness** *...a feeling of secu-* ADV-GRADED
rity and calmness. **2** If you **calm** someone, you do N-UNCOUNT
something to make them feel less angry, worried, or V n
excited. *She was breathing quickly and tried to calm
herself.* ♦ **calm·ing** *...a very calming effect on the* ADJ-GRADED
mind.

3 Calm is used to refer to a quiet, still, or peaceful at- N-UNCOUNT
mosphere in a place. *...the rural calm of Grand Rap-
ids, Michigan.* **4** If a place is **calm**, it is free from fight- ADJ-GRADED
ing or public disorder, when trouble has recently oc- JOURNALISM
curred there or had been expected. ▶ Also a noun. N-UNCOUNT:
Community and church leaders have appealed for also a N
calm. **5** If someone or something **calms** a situation, VERB
they reduce the amount of trouble, violence, or panic V n
there is somewhere. *Officials hoped admitting fewer
foreigners would calm the situation.*

6 If the sea or a lake is **calm**, the water is not moving ADJ-GRADED
very much and there are no big waves. **7 Calm** weath- ADJ-GRADED
er is pleasant weather with little or no wind. **8** In sail- N-COUNT
ing, a flat **calm** or a dead **calm** is a condition of the sea TECHNICAL
or the weather in which there is very little wind or
movement of the water. **9** When the sea **calms**, it be- VERB: V
comes still because the wind stops blowing strongly.
When the wind **calms**, it stops blowing strongly.

calm down. 1 If you **calm down** or if someone PHRASAL VB
calms you **down**, you become less angry, upset, or ex- ERG:
cited. *I'll try a herbal remedy to calm him down.* **2** If V P
things **calm down**, or someone or something **calms** V n P
things **down**, the amount of activity, trouble, or panic ERG:
somewhere is reduced. *Neil Howorth, director of the* V P
academy, tried to calm things down. V n P

calm·ly /'kɑːmli/. You can use **calmly** to empha- ◆◇◇◇◇
size that someone is behaving in a very controlled ADV:
ADV before v

or ordinary way in a frightening or unusual situation. *She walked up to her lover's wife and calmly shot her in the head.* ● See also **calm**. [PRAGMATICS]

ca·lor·ic /kə'lɒrɪk/. **Caloric** means the same as **calorific**. *...a daily caloric intake of from 400 to 1200 calories.* ADJ: ADJ n

ca·lo·rie /'kæləri/ **calories**. Calories are units of measurement for the energy value of food. People who are on diets try to eat food that does not contain many calories. *A glass of wine does have quite a lot of calories.* ► Also a combining form. *...low-calorie margarine.* ◆◇◇◇ N-COUNT ... COMB

ca·lo·rif·ic /ˌkælə'rɪfɪk/. The **calorific** value of something, or its **calorific** content, is the number of calories it contains. *...food with a high calorific value.* ADJ-GRADED BRITISH

ca·lum·ny /'kæləmni/ **calumnies**. **Calumny** or a **calumny** is an untrue statement made about someone in order to reduce other people's respect and admiration for him. *He was the victim of calumny.* N-VAR FORMAL

calve /kɑːv, AM kæv/ **calves, calving, calved.** 1 When a cow **calves**, it gives birth to a calf. 2 **Calves** is the plural of **calf**. VERB: V

ca·lyp·so /kə'lɪpsəʊ/ **calypsos**. A **calypso** is a song about something topical or interesting, sung in a style which comes from the West Indies. N-COUNT

ca·ma·ra·de·rie /ˌkæmə'rɑːdəri, AM ˌkɑːm-/. **Camaraderie** is a feeling of trust and friendship among a group of people who have usually known each other for a long time or gone through some kind of experience together. *...the cohesiveness and camaraderie of the wartime Army.* N-UNCOUNT

cam·ber /'kæmbə/ **cambers**. A camber is a gradual downward slope from the centre of a road to each side of it. N-COUNT

cam·cord·er /'kæmkɔːdə/ **camcorders**. A camcorder is a portable video camera. ◆◇◇◇ N-COUNT

came /keɪm/. Came is the past tense of **come**.

cam·el /'kæməl/ **camels**. A camel is a desert animal with a long neck and one or two humps on its back. See picture headed **animals**. ◆◇◇◇ N-COUNT

Cam·em·bert /'kæmɒmbeə/ **Camemberts**. Camembert is a soft, creamy, French cheese with a hard greyish-white skin. N-VAR

cameo /'kæmiəʊ/ **cameos**. 1 A cameo is a short description or piece of acting which expresses cleverly and neatly the nature of a situation, event, or person's character. *...a succession of memorable cameos of Scottish history.* 2 A cameo is a piece of jewellery, usually oval, consisting of a raised design fixed onto a flat stone of another colour. ◆◇◇◇ N-COUNT ... N-COUNT

cam·era /'kæmrə/ **cameras**. 1 A camera is a piece of equipment that is used for taking photographs, making films, or producing television pictures. *Her gran lent her a camera for a school trip to Venice and Egypt. ...a video camera.* 2 If someone or something is **on camera**, they are being filmed. *Fay was so impressive on camera that a special part was written in for her.* 3 If a trial is held **in camera**, the public and the press are not allowed to attend. *This morning's appeal was held in camera.* ◆◆◆◇ N-COUNT ... PHRASE ... PHRASE

camera·man /'kæmrəmæn/ **cameramen**. A cameraman is a person who operates a camera for television or film making. ◆◇◇◇ N-COUNT

camera·work /'kæmrəwɜːk/. The **camerawork** in a film is the technique or distinctive style used in filming it. *The director employs sensuous, atmospheric camerawork.* N-UNCOUNT

cami·sole /'kæmɪsəʊl/ **camisoles**. A camisole is a piece of underwear like a vest, which women wear under a shirt or blouse. *...silk camisoles.* N-COUNT

camo·mile /'kæməmaɪl/; also spelled **chamomile**. Camomile is a scented plant with daisy-like flowers. It is often used to make herbal tea. ◆◇◇◇ N-UNCOUNT

camou·flage /'kæməflɑːʒ/ **camouflages, camouflaging, camouflaged.** 1 Camouflage consists of things such as leaves, branches, or brown and green paint, which are used to make it difficult for an enemy to find military forces and equipment. *...a camouflage jacket.* 2 If military buildings or vehicles **are camouflaged**, things such ◆◇◇◇ N-UNCOUNT: also a N ... VB: usu passive beV-ed

as leaves, branches, or brown and green paint are used to make it difficult for an enemy to see them. *You won't see them from the air. They'd be very well camouflaged.* 3 If you **camouflage** something such as a feeling or a situation, you hide it or make it appear to be something different. *He has never camouflaged his desire to better himself.* ► Also a noun. *The frenzied merry-making of her later years was a desperate camouflage for her grief.* 4 Camouflage is the way in which some animals are coloured and shaped to blend in with their natural surroundings. *This gives the animal's fur a greenish tinge, which acts as a camouflage among the leaves.* VERB V n ... N-UNCOUNT: also a N ... N-UNCOUNT: also a N

camp /kæmp/ **camps, camping, camped.** 1 A camp is a collection of huts and other buildings that is provided for a particular group of people, such as refugees, prisoners, or soldiers, as a place to live or stay. *...refugee camps.* 2 A camp is an outdoor area with buildings, tents, or caravans where people stay on holiday. *They have a 200- or 300-acre summer camp nearby.* 3 A camp is a collection of tents or caravans where people are living or staying, usually temporarily while they are travelling. *We'll make camp on that hill ahead.* 4 If you **camp** somewhere, you stay or live there for a short time in a tent or caravan, or in the open air. *We camped near the beach.* ► **Camp out** means the same as **camp**. *For six months they camped out in a caravan in a meadow at the back of the house.* ♦ **camp·er, campers** *There were at least 100 tents for campers.* ♦ **camp·ing** *They went camping in the wilds.* 5 You can refer to a group of people who all support a particular person, policy, or idea as a particular **camp**. *The press release provoked furious protests from the Clinton camp.* 6 If you describe someone's behaviour, performance, or style of dress as **camp**, you mean that it is exaggerated and often amusing in a sexually suggestive way. **Camp** behaviour is sometimes associated with gay people. *James Barron turns in a delightfully camp performance as the lovely Lisa's wicked husband.* ► Also a noun. *The days of platform-soled high camp are long over.* 7 See also **concentration camp, holiday camp, labour camp, prison camp, training camp**. ◆◆◆◆ N-COUNT ... N-VAR ... N-VAR ... VERB V ... PHRASAL VB V P ... N-COUNT ... N-UNCOUNT ... N-COUNT ... ADJ-GRADED INFORMAL ... N-UNCOUNT

camp out. If people **camp out** somewhere in the open air, they stay there for a long time, because they are waiting for something to happen. *...reporters who had camped out in anticipation of her arrival.* ● See also **camp** 4. PHRASAL VB V P

cam·paign /ˌkæm'peɪn/ **campaigns, campaigning, campaigned.** 1 A campaign is a planned set of activities that people carry out over a period of time in order to achieve something such as social or political change. *During his election campaign Clinton promised to put the economy back on its feet.* 2 If someone **campaigns** for something, they carry out a planned set of activities over a period of time in order to achieve their aim. *They have been campaigning to improve the legal status of women.* ♦ **cam·paign·er, campaigners** *...campaigners for multi-party democracy.* 3 In a war, a campaign is a series of planned movements carried out by armed forces. *...a bombing campaign.* ◆◆◆◆ N-COUNT ... VERB: V for/against V to-inf Also V ... N-COUNT ... N-COUNT

'camp bed, camp beds. A camp bed is a small bed that you can fold up. N-COUNT BRITISH

camped /kæmpt/. If people are **camped** or **camped out** somewhere in the open air, they are living, staying, or waiting there, often in tents. *You will wake to find film crews camped in your backyard.* ● See also **camp**. ◆◇◇◇ ADJ: v-link ADJ

camp·er /'kæmpə/ **campers**. A camper is a van which is equipped with beds and cooking equipment so that you can live, cook, and sleep in it. ● See also **camp**. ◆◇◇◇ N-COUNT

ˌcamp 'fire, camp fires. A camp fire is a fire that you light out of doors when you are camping. N-COUNT

camp·ground /'kæmpɡraʊnd/ **campgrounds.** A campground is the same as a **campsite**. N-COUNT AMERICAN

cam·phor /'kæmfə/. **Camphor** is a strong-smelling N-UNCOUNT white substance used in various medicines, in mothballs and in making plastics.

camp·site /'kæmpsaɪt/ **campsites.** A **campsite** or N-COUNT a **camping site** is a place where people who are on BRITISH holiday can stay in tents.

cam·pus /'kæmpəs/ **campuses.** A **campus** is the ◆◆◇◇◇ area of land that contains the main buildings of a N-COUNT: university. *Automobiles are not allowed on* also prep N *campus.*

cam·shaft /'kæmʃɑːft, -ʃæft/ **camshafts.** A **cam-** N-COUNT **shaft** is a rod in an engine which works to change TECHNICAL circular motion into motion up and down or side to side.

can /kən, STRONG kæn/. **Can** is a modal verb. It is ◆◆◆◆◆ used with the base form of a verb. The form **cannot** is used in negative statements. The usual spoken form of **cannot** is **can't**, pronounced /kɑːnt/.

1 You use **can** when you are mentioning a quality or MODAL fact about something which people may make use of if they want to. *Iron can be reworked and mistakes don't have to be thrown away... A central reservation number operated by the resort can direct you to accommodations that best suit your needs. ...the statue which can still be seen in the British Museum.* **2** You use **can** MODAL to indicate that someone has the ability or opportunity to do something. *Don't worry yourself about me, I can take care of myself... I can't give you details... How can I ever thank you for being so kind?... See if you can find Karlov... The United States will do whatever it can to help Greece... I cannot describe it, I can't find the words... You can't be with your baby all the time.* **3** You MODAL use **cannot** to indicate that someone is not able to do something because circumstances make it impossible for them to do it. *...people who can't afford to go to the theatre... We cannot buy food, clothes and pay for rent and utilities on $20 a week... She cannot sleep.* **4** You use **can** to indicate that someone is allowed to MODAL do something. You use **cannot** or **can't** to indicate that someone is not allowed to do something. *You must buy the credit life insurance before you can buy the disability insurance... Can I really have your jeans when you go?... I can't tell you what he said.* **5** You use MODAL **cannot** or **can't** to emphasize that you think that it is PRAGMATICS very important or necessary that something should not happen or that someone should not do something. *It is an intolerable situation and it can't be allowed to go on.* **6** You use **can** to indicate that something is true MODAL sometimes or is true in some circumstances. *...long-* PRAGMATICS *term therapy that can last five years or more... A vacant lot or a bombsite can, to the amateur naturalist, produce an extraordinary variety of flora and fauna... Exercising alone can be boring.* **7** You use **cannot** and **can't** to state that you are cer- MODAL tain that something is not true or will not happen. *She* PRAGMATICS *feels sure that that person can't have been Douglas... You can't be serious, Mrs Lorimer?* **8** You use **can** in MODAL questions with 'how' to indicate that you feel strongly PRAGMATICS about something. *How can millions of dollars go* SPOKEN *astray?... How can you say such a thing?... How can he put up with that awful woman?* **9** You use **can**, usually in questions, in order to make MODAL suggestions or to offer to do something. *What can I do* PRAGMATICS *around here?... Can I help you?'... You can always try the beer.* **10** You use **can** in questions in order to make MODAL polite requests. You use **can't** in questions in order to PRAGMATICS request strongly that somebody does something. *Can I have a look at that?... Can you please help?... Why can't you leave me alone?* **11** You use **can** as a polite MODAL way of interrupting someone or of introducing what PRAGMATICS you are going to say next. *Can I just ask something...* FORMAL, *But if I can interrupt, Joe, I don't think anybody here is* SPOKEN *personally blaming you.* **12** You use **can** with verbs MODAL such as 'imagine', 'think', and 'believe' in order to PRAGMATICS emphasize how you feel about a particular situation. INFORMAL *You can imagine he was terribly upset... You can't think how glad I was to see them all go... I can't understand why folks complain about false teeth.*

can /kæn/ **cans, canning, canned.** **1** A **can** is a ◆◆◇◇◇ metal container in which something such as food, N-COUNT drink, or paint is put. The container is usually sealed to keep the contents fresh. *...empty beer cans.* **2** When food or drink **is canned**, it is put into a VB: usu metal container and sealed so that it will remain passive fresh. *...fruits and vegetables that will be canned,* be V-ed *skinned, diced or otherwise processed.* ● See also **canned.** **3** If you have to **carry the can**, you have to PHRASE take all the blame for something. *We are a luxury* INFORMAL, *restaurant and if people have a bad experience, we* BRITISH *have to carry the can.* **4** If you say that something PHRASE such as a job that you are doing is **in the can**, you INFORMAL mean that it is completely finished.

ca·nal /kə'næl/ **canals.** **1** A **canal** is a long narrow ◆◆◇◇◇ stretch of water that has been made for boats to N-COUNT travel along. **2** A **canal** is a narrow tube inside your N-COUNT body for carrying food, air, or other substances.

ca'nal boat, canal boats. A **canal boat** is a long N-COUNT narrow boat used for travelling on canals.

cana·pé /'kænəpeɪ/ **canapés.** **Canapés** are small N-COUNT pieces of biscuit or toast with food such as meat, cheese, or paté on top. They are often served with drinks at parties.

ca·nard /'kænɑːd, AM kə'nɑːrd/ **canards.** A **canard** N-COUNT is an idea or piece of information that is false, although it is believed by many people. *The charge that Harding was a political stooge may be a canard.*

ca·nary /kə'neəri/ **canaries.** Canaries are small ◆◇◇◇◇ yellow singing birds which are often kept as pets. N-COUNT

'can-can, can-cans. The **can-can** is a dance in N-COUNT which women kick their legs in the air to fast music. *...the can-can girls in Paris's Moulin Rouge cabaret.*

can·cel /'kænsəl/ **cancels, cancelling, can-** ◆◆◆◇◇ **celled;** spelled **canceling, canceled** in American English. **1** If you **cancel** something that has been ar- VERB: V n ranged, you stop it from happening. If you **cancel** V an order for goods or services, you tell the person or organization supplying them that you no longer wish to receive them. *There is normally no refund should a client choose to cancel.* ◆ **can·cel·la·tion** N-VAR /ˌkænsə'leɪʃən/ **cancellations** *Outbursts of violence forced the cancellation of Haiti's first free elections in 1987.* **2** If someone in authority **cancels** a docu- VERB ment, an insurance policy, or a debt, they officially V n declare that it is no longer valid or no longer legally exists. *...a government order cancelling his passport.* ◆ **cancellation** *...a march by groups calling for* N-UNCOUNT: *cancellation of Third World debt.* **3** To **cancel** a with supp stamp or a cheque means to mark it to show that it VERB has already been used and cannot be used again. V n *The new device can also cancel the check after the transaction is complete.*

cancel out. If one thing **cancels out** another thing, PHRASAL VB the two things have opposite effects, so that when V n P they are combined no real effect is produced. *He won-* Also V P noun *ders if the different influences might not cancel each other out... The goal was cancelled out just before half-time by Craig McLurg.*

can·cer /'kænsə/ **cancers.** Cancer is a serious dis- ◆◆◆◇ ease in which cells in a person's body increase rap- N-VAR idly in an uncontrolled way, producing abnormal growths. *Ninety per cent of lung cancers are caused by smoking.*

can·cer·ous /'kænsərəs/. **Cancerous** cells or ◆◇◇◇◇ growths are cells or growths that are the result of ADJ cancer. *Nine out of ten lumps are not cancerous.*

can·de·la·bra /ˌkændə'lɑːbrə/ **candelabras.** A N-COUNT **candelabra** is an ornamental holder for two or more candles.

can·did /'kændɪd/. **1** If you are **candid** about ◆◇◇◇◇ something or with someone, you speak honestly. *I* ADJ-GRADED *haven't been completely candid with him. ...a candid interview.* ◆ **can·did·ly** *He has stopped taking* ADV-GRADED *heroin now, but admits candidly that he will always be a drug addict.* **2** A **candid** photograph of some- ADJ: ADJ n one is one that was taken when the person did not know they were being photographed.

can·di·da·cy /ˈkændɪdəsi/ **candidacies.** ◆◇◇◇◇
Someone's **candidacy** is their position of being a N-VAR
candidate in an election. *Today he is formally an-*
nouncing his candidacy for President.

can·di·date /ˈkændɪdeɪt/ **candidates.** 1 A candi- ◆◆◆◇
date is someone who is being considered for a posi- N-COUNT
tion, for example someone standing in an election
or applying for a job. *...the Democratic candidate...*
He is a candidate for the office of Governor. 2 A can- N-COUNT
didate is someone who is taking an examination.
The papers were taken by more than 150,000 candi-
dates this summer. 3 A candidate is a person or N-COUNT
thing that is regarded as being suitable for a particular purpose or as being likely to do or be a particular thing. *Those who are overweight or indulge in*
high-salt diets are candidates for hypertension.

can·di·da·ture /ˈkændɪtətʃə/ **candidatures.** N-VAR
Someone's **candidature** is their candidacy. *There* BRITISH,
have been calls for him to withdraw his candidature FORMAL
for the presidency.

can·died /ˈkændid/. **Candied** fruit has been covered ADJ
with sugar or has been cooked in sugar syrup.

can·dle /ˈkændəl/ **candles.** 1 A candle is a stick of ◆◆◇◇
hard wax with a piece of string called a wick N-COUNT
through the middle which you light so the candle
produces light. 2 If one person or thing **can't hold a** PHRASE
candle to another, the first person or thing is not
nearly as good as the second. *Girls today can't hold*
a candle to the beauties of the Fifties. 3 If you **burn** PHRASE
the candle at both ends, you try to do too many
things in too short a period of time so that you have
to stay up very late at night and get up very early in
the morning to get them done.

candle·light /ˈkændəllaɪt/. **Candlelight** is the light N-UNCOUNT
that a candle produces. *They dined by candlelight.*

candle·lit /ˈkændəllɪt/. A **candlelit** room or table is ADJ
lit by the light of candles. *...a candlelit dinner.*

candle·stick /ˈkændəlstɪk/ **candlesticks.** A ◆◇◇◇
candlestick is a narrow object with a hole at the top N-COUNT
which holds a candle.

can-'do. If you say that someone has a **can-do** at- ADJ: ADJ n
titude, you approve of them because they are confi- PRAGMATICS
dent and willing to deal with problems or new tasks.
America is once again being seen as a strong, can-do
nation.

can·dour /ˈkændə/; spelled **candor** in American N-UNCOUNT
English. **Candour** is the quality of speaking honestly
and openly about things. *...a brash, forceful man,*
noted both for his candour and his quick temper.

can·dy /ˈkændi/ **candies.** Sweet foods such as tof- ◆◇◇◇
fees, chocolates, and mints are referred to as **candy.** N-VAR
The British word is **sweets.** AMERICAN

candy·floss /ˈkændiflɒs, AM -flɔːs/. 1 **Candyfloss** is N-UNCOUNT
a large pink or white mass of sugar threads that is BRITISH
eaten from a stick. The American term is **cotton**
candy. 2 If you think something such as a record or N-UNCOUNT
film has no real value, you can say that it is **candy-** PRAGMATICS
floss. *She took to writing candyfloss romances.* BRITISH

cane /keɪn/ **canes, caning, caned.** 1 Cane is ◆◇◇◇
used to refer to the long, hollow, hard stems of N-VAR
plants such as bamboo. Strips of cane are often
used to make furniture, and some types of cane can
be crushed and processed to make sugar. *Bamboo*
produces an annual crop of cane. ...cane furniture.
● See also **sugar cane.**

2 A **cane** is a specially-shaped stick which you can N-COUNT
carry to support yourself when you are walking, or
which some people used to carry as a fashion. *He wore*
a grey suit and leaned heavily on his cane.

3 In Britain, a **cane** is a long, thin, flexible stick which N-COUNT
is sometimes used to hit schoolchildren as a punish-
ment. ▶ **The cane** is used to refer to the punishment N-SING:
of being hit with a cane. *In school, you knew if you* theN
misbehaved you would get the cane. 4 If a child is VERB
caned, he or she is hit with a cane as a punishment. be/getV-ed
Boys were caned for speaking Welsh in the play- for-ing/n
ground... I have caned my son when necessary. Vn

5 A **cane** is a tall, narrow stick, usually made of bam- N-COUNT
boo, which is used for supporting plants in gardens. BRITISH

ca·nine /ˈkeɪnaɪn/ **canines.** 1 Canine means relat- ADJ: ADJ n
ing to dogs. *...research into canine diseases.* 2 Ca- N-COUNT
nine **teeth** or canines are pointed teeth near the
front of the mouth of humans and some animals.

can·is·ter /ˈkænɪstə/ **canisters.** 1 A canister is a ◆◇◇◇
strong metal container used to hold gases or chemi- N-COUNT
cal substances. *Riot police hurled tear gas canisters*
and smoke bombs into the crowd. 2 A canister is a N-COUNT
metal, plastic, or china container with a lid. It is
used for storing food such as sugar and flour. 3 A N-COUNT
canister is a flat round container. It is usually made
of metal and is used to store photographic film.

can·ker /ˈkæŋkə/ **cankers.** 1 A canker is some- N-COUNT
thing evil that spreads and affects things or people. FORMAL
The canker of anti-Semitism is growing again in
America. 2 Canker is a disease which affects the N-VAR
wood of shrubs and trees.

can·na·bis /ˈkænəbɪs/. **Cannabis** is the leaves and ◆◇◇◇
flowers of the hemp plant when they are used as a N-UNCOUNT
drug. Cannabis is illegal in many countries.

canned /kænd/. **Canned** music, laughter, or ap- ADJ
plause on the television or radio has been recorded
beforehand and is added to the programme to make
it sound as if there is a live audience. ● See also
can.

can·nery /ˈkænəri/ **canneries.** A cannery is a fac- N-COUNT
tory where food is canned.

can·ni·bal /ˈkænɪbəl/ **cannibals.** Cannibals are ◆◇◇◇
people who eat the flesh of other human beings.
♦ **can·ni·bal·ism** /ˈkænɪbəlɪzəm/ *They were forced* N-UNCOUNT
to practise cannibalism in order to survive. ♦ **can-**
·ni·bal·is·tic /ˌkænɪbəˈlɪstɪk/ *...lurid cannibalistic* ADJ
feasts.

can·ni·bal·ize /ˈkænɪbəlaɪz/ **cannibalizes, can-**
nibalizing, cannibalized; also spelled **cannibal-**
ise in British English. 1 If you **cannibalize** some- VERB
thing, you take it to pieces and use it to make some- Vn
thing else. *They cannibalized damaged planes for*
the parts. 2 If one of a company's products canni- VERB
balizes the company's sales, people buy it instead Vn
of any of the company's other products. *Coke then*
believed that selling a diet soda under the Coke label
would cannibalize Coke's sales.

can·non /ˈkænən/ **cannons, cannoning,** ◆◆◇◇
cannoned. 1 A cannon is a large gun, usually on N-COUNT
wheels, which was formerly used in battles. 2 A N-COUNT
cannon is a heavy automatic gun, especially one
that is fired from an aircraft. 3 If one person or VERB
thing **cannons** into another, they bump into them V prep
with great force. *The ball cannoned off the back of a* BRITISH
Spartak defender and into the net. 4 If you say that PHRASE
someone is a **loose cannon,** you mean that they behave in an independent headstrong way and nobody can predict what they are going to do. ● See
also **water cannon.**

ˈcannon-ball, cannon balls. A **cannon-ball** is a N-COUNT
heavy metal ball that is fired from a cannon.

ˈcannon fodder. If someone in authority regards N-UNCOUNT
people they are in charge of as **cannon fodder,** they
do not care if these people are harmed or lost in the
course of their work. *Many cynical managers see*
employees as cannon fodder.

can·not /ˈkænɒt, kəˈnɒt/. **Cannot** is the negative
form of **can.**

can·ny /ˈkæni/ **cannier, canniest.** A canny per- ◆◇◇◇
son is clever and able to think quickly. *...a canny po-* ADJ-GRADED
litical manoeuvre. ♦ **can·ni·ly** /ˈkænɪli/ *She built up* ADV-GRADED
her fortune by cannily playing the stock market.

ca·noe /kəˈnuː/ **canoes.** A canoe is a small, nar- ◆◇◇◇
row boat that you row using a paddle. N-COUNT

ca·noe·ing /kəˈnuːɪŋ/. **Canoeing** is the sport of N-UNCOUNT
paddling and racing a canoe. ♦ **ca·noe·ist** N-COUNT
/kəˈnuːɪst/ **canoeists.** A canoeist is a person who
goes canoeing.

can·on /ˈkænən/ **canons.** 1 A canon is a member ◆◇◇◇
of the clergy who is on the staff of a cathedral. 2 A N-COUNT
canon is a general rule or principle. *The very first* N-COUNT
canon of nursing is to keep the air inside as fresh as FORMAL
the air outside.

ca·noni·cal /kəˈnɒnɪkəl/. If something has **canoni·cal** status, it is accepted as having all the qualities that a thing of its kind should have. *Without these experts, the words 'Sotheby's' and 'Christie's' could never have assumed the canonical quality they hold in the minds of the public.* ADJ: ADJ n

can·on·ize /ˈkænənaɪz/ **canonizes, canonizing, canonized;** also spelled **canonise** in British English. In the Catholic church, if a dead person **is canonized**, it is officially announced that that person is a saint. *Joan of Arc was finally canonized by Pope Benedict XV in 1920.* **♦ can·oni·za·tion** /ˌkænənaɪˈzeɪʃən, AM -nɪ-/. *...a celebration of the saint's canonization.* VB: usu passive beV-ed | N-UNCOUNT

,canon 'law. Canon law is a set of rules for running the affairs of a Christian church, for example the Roman Catholic Church or the Anglican Church. N-UNCOUNT

ca·noo·dle /kəˈnuːdəl/ **canoodles, canoodling, canoodled.** If two people **are canoodling**, they are kissing and cuddling each other a lot. *Inside, freckled girls are canoodling with their boyfriends in dark corners.* V-RECIP: pl-n V / V with n BRITISH, INFORMAL

'can opener, can openers. A **can opener** is the same as a **tin opener**. N-COUNT

cano·pied /ˈkænəpid/. A **canopied** building or piece of furniture has a roof or cover supported by poles. *...a canopied Elizabethan bed.* ADJ

cano·py /ˈkænəpi/ **canopies. 1** A **canopy** is a decorated cover, often made of cloth, which is placed above something such as a bed or a throne. **2** A **canopy** is a layer of something that spreads out and covers an area, for example the branches and leaves that spread out at the top of trees in a forest. *The trees formed such a dense canopy that all beneath was a deep carpet of pine-needles.* ♦◇◇◇ N-COUNT | N-COUNT

cant /kænt/. If you refer to moral or religious statements as **cant**, you disapprove of them because you think the person making them does not really believe what they are saying. *...politicians holding forth with their usual hypocritical cant.* N-UNCOUNT PRAGMATICS

can't /kɑːnt, AM kænt/. **Can't** is the usual spoken form of **cannot**.

can·tan·ker·ous /kænˈtæŋkərəs/. A **cantankerous** person is always finding things to argue or complain about. ADJ-GRADED

can·ta·ta /kænˈtɑːtə/ **cantatas.** A **cantata** is a fairly short musical work for singers and instruments. N-COUNT

can·teen /kænˈtiːn/ **canteens. 1** A **canteen** is a place in a factory, shop, or college where meals are served to the people who work or study there. **2** A **canteen** is a small plastic bottle for carrying water and other drinks. Canteens are used by soldiers. **3** A **canteen** of cutlery is a set of knives, forks, and spoons in a specially designed box. ♦◇◇◇ N-COUNT | N-COUNT | N-COUNT

cant·er /ˈkæntə/ **canters, cantering, cantered.** When a horse **canters**, it moves at a speed that is slower than a gallop but faster than a trot. *The competitors cantered into the arena.* ▶ Also a noun. *Carnac set off at a canter.* ♦◇◇◇ VERB V prep/adv Also V | N-COUNT

can·ti·lever /ˈkæntɪliːvə/ **cantilevers.** A **cantilever** is a long piece of metal or wood used in a structure such as a bridge. One end is fastened to something and the other end is used to support part of the structure. *...the old steel cantilever bridge.* **♦ can·ti·levered** /ˈkæntɪliːvəd/. A **cantilevered** structure is constructed using cantilevers. N-COUNT | ADJ

can·ton /ˈkænton/ **cantons.** A **canton** is a political or administrative region in some countries, for example Switzerland. ♦◇◇◇ N-COUNT

can·ton·ment /kænˈtuːnmənt, AM -ˈtəun-/ **cantonments.** A **cantonment** is a group of buildings or a camp where soldiers live. N-COUNT

can·vas /ˈkænvəs/ **canvases. 1** Canvas is a strong heavy cloth, usually made of cotton or linen, that is used for making things such as tents, sails, and bags. **2** If you are living and sleeping **under canvas**, you are living in a tent. *...thousands decided to spend the holiday under canvas.* **3** A **canvas** is a piece of canvas or similar material on ♦♦◇◇ N-UNCOUNT | PHRASE | N-VAR

which an oil painting can be done. **4** A **canvas** is a painting that has been done on canvas. *...canvases by masters like Carpaccio, Canaletto and Guardi.* N-COUNT

can·vass /ˈkænvəs/ **canvasses, canvassing, canvassed. 1** If you **canvass** for a particular person, political party, or project, you go round an area trying to persuade people to vote for them or support them. *She works her way around the room canvassing support for the project.* **♦ can·vass·er, canvassers** *...a Conservative canvasser.* **2** If you **canvass** public opinion, you find out how people feel about a particular subject. *The poll canvassed the views of almost eighty economists.* ♦◇◇◇ VERB: V forn / V n | N-COUNT | VERB V n

can·yon /ˈkænjən/ **canyons.** A **canyon** is a long narrow valley with very steep sides. *...the Grand Canyon.* ♦◇◇◇ N-COUNT

cap /kæp/ **caps, capping, capped. 1** A **cap** is a soft flat hat with a curved part at the front which is called a peak. *...a dark blue baseball cap.* **2** If you go **cap in hand** to someone, you go to them very humbly, because you are asking them to give you something. The usual American expression is **hat in hand.** ♦♦♦◇ N-COUNT | PHRASE BRITISH

3 If a sports player represents their country in a team game such as football or cricket, you can say that they have won a **cap**. *Mark Davis will win his first cap for Wales in Sunday's Test match.* **4** If a sports player is **capped**, they are chosen to represent their country in a team game such as football or cricket. *...Underwood, England's most capped rugby union player.* N-COUNT BRITISH | VERB: beV-ed V-ed BRITISH

5 The **cap** of a bottle is its lid. **6** If you **cap** one thing with another, you put the second thing on top. *...homemade scones capped with cream.* ● See also **snow-capped. 7** If someone's teeth **are capped**, coverings are fixed over them so that they look better. *I had my teeth capped.* N-COUNT | VERB: V n with n V-ed | VERB: beV-ed haven V-ed

8 If the government **caps** a local authority or council, it limits the amount of money that the authority is allowed to spend. **♦ cap·ping** *80 councils face significant spending cuts or capping.* VERB: V n | N-UNCOUNT

9 You can say that the last event in a series of good or bad events **caps** the others. *The unrest capped a weekend of right-wing attacks on foreigners.* VERB V n

10 A **cap** is a round rubber device that a woman can use as a contraceptive. N-COUNT BRITISH

11 A **cap** is a small amount of explosive that is wrapped in paper. Caps are often used in toy guns. N-COUNT

12 See also **ice cap.**

ca·pa·bil·ity /ˌkeɪpəˈbɪlɪti/ **capabilities.** A country's military **capability** is its ability to fight in a war. ● See also **capable.** ♦♦◇◇ N-VAR

ca·pable /ˈkeɪpəbəl/. **1** If a person or thing is **capable** of doing something, they have the ability, capacity, or potential to do it. *He appeared hardly capable of conducting a coherent conversation... I realised he was capable of murder.* **♦ capability** /ˌkeɪpəˈbɪlɪti/ **capabilities** *The standards set four years ago will be far below the athletes' capabilities now.* **2** A **capable** person is competent, efficient, or practical. *She's a very capable speaker.* **♦ ca·pably** /ˈkeɪpəbli/. *It was all dealt with very capably by the police.* ♦♦♦◇ ADJ-GRADED: v-link ADJ of -ing/n | N-VAR | ADJ-GRADED | ADV-GRADED: ADV with v

ca·pa·cious /kəˈpeɪʃəs/. Something that is **capacious** has a lot of space to put things in. *...her capacious handbag.* ADJ-GRADED FORMAL

ca·paci·tor /kəˈpæsɪtə/ **capacitors.** A **capacitor** is a device for accumulating electric charge. N-COUNT

ca·pac·ity /kəˈpæsɪti/ **capacities. 1** Your **capacity** for something is your ability to do it, or the amount of it that you are able to do. *Our capacity for giving care, love and attention is limited.* ♦♦♦◇ N-VAR

2 The **capacity** of something such as a factory, industry, or region is the quantity of things that it can produce or deliver. *Bread factories are working at full capacity... Britain must still keep the nuclear and conventional capacity to deal with all conceivable threats.* N-UNCOUNT

3 The **capacity** of a piece of equipment is its size, power, or volume, often measured in particular units. *...an aircraft with a bomb-carrying capacity of 454 kg. ...a feature which gave the vehicles a much greater fuel* N-COUNT

capacity. **4** The **capacity** of a building, place, or vehicle is the number of people or things that it can hold. If a place is filled **to capacity**, it is as full as it can possibly be. *Each stadium had a seating capacity of about 50,000.* ▶ A **capacity** crowd or audience completely fills a place. **5** If you do something in a particular **capacity**, you do it as part of a particular job or duty, or because you are representing a particular organization or person. *Mr Haughey is touring European capitals in his capacity as President of the European Community... Since 1928, Major Thomas has served the club in many capacities.*

cape /keɪp/ **capes.** **1** A **cape** is a large piece of land that sticks out into the sea from the coast. **2** A **cape** is a short cloak. *...a woollen cape.*

ca·per /ˈkeɪpə/ **capers, capering, capered.** **1 Capers** are the small green buds of caper plants. They are usually sold pickled in vinegar. **2** If you **caper** about, you run and jump around because you are happy or excited. **3** A dishonest or illegal activity can be referred to as a **caper**. *She served six months in prison for the helicopter caper.* **4** Books, films, or activities that are not at all serious can be referred to as **capers**. *...his latest film, a light-hearted caper through the canals of Venice.*

ca·pil·lary /kəˈpɪləri, AM ˈkæpəleri/ **capillaries.** **Capillaries** are tiny blood vessels in your body.

cap·i·tal /ˈkæpɪtl/ **capitals.** **1 Capital** is a large sum of money which you use to start or expand a business, or which you invest in order to make more money. *Companies are having difficulty in raising capital.* **2** You can use **capital** to refer to buildings or machinery which are necessary to produce goods or to make companies more efficient, but which do not make money directly. **3** See also **working capital**. **4 Capital** is the part of an amount of money borrowed or invested which does not include interest. **5** The **capital** of a country is the city or town where its government or parliament meets. *...Kathmandu, the capital of Nepal.* **6** If you say that a place is the **capital** of a particular industry or activity, you mean that it is famous for it, because it happens in that place more than anywhere else. *...New York, the fashion capital of the world.* **7 Capitals** or **capital letters** are written or printed letters in the form which is used at the beginning of sentences or names. 'T', 'B', and 'F' are capitals. *The name and address are written in capitals.* **8** You can use phrases such as 'Life **with a capital** L', to emphasize that a word has a particular significance in the situation you are talking about. *She's not feminist with a capital F but she's fairly controversial.* **9** A **capital** offence can be punished by death. *...Americans wrongly convicted of capital crimes.* **10** If you say that someone **is making capital out of** an unfortunate situation, you are criticizing them for gaining an advantage from it.

capital 'gains. **Capital gains** are the profits that you make when you buy something and then sell it at a higher price.

'capital goods. **Capital goods** are used to make other products. Compare **consumer goods**.

capi·tal·ise /ˈkæpɪtəlaɪz/. See **capitalize**.

capi·tal·ism /ˈkæpɪtəlɪzəm/. **Capitalism** is an economic and political system in which property, business, and industry are owned by private individuals and not by the state.

capi·tal·ist /ˈkæpɪtəlɪst/ **capitalists.** **1** A **capitalist** country or system supports or is based on the principles of capitalism. ♦ **capi·tal·ist·ic** /ˌkæpɪtəlˈɪstɪk/ *...capitalistic economic growth.* **2** A **capitalist** is someone such as a politician or businessman who supports or applies the principles of capitalism.

capi·tal·ize /ˈkæpɪtəlaɪz/ **capitalizes, capitalizing, capitalized;** also spelled **capitalise** in British English. **1** If you **capitalize** on a situation, you use it to gain some advantage for yourself. *The rebels seem to be trying to capitalize on the public's discontent*

with the government. **2** To **capitalize** something such as a business means to provide money for it. ♦ **capi·tali·za·tion** /ˌkæpɪtəlaɪˈzeɪʃən/ *...a massive capitalization programme.* **3** If you **capitalize** something that belongs to you, you sell it in order to make money.

,capital 'letter, capital letters. Capital letters are the same as **capitals**.

,capital 'punishment. Capital punishment is the legal killing of a criminal.

ca·pitu·late /kəˈpɪtʃʊleɪt/ **capitulates, capitulating, capitulated.** If you **capitulate**, you stop resisting and do what someone else wants you to do. *Cohen capitulated to virtually every demand.* ♦ **ca·pitu·la·tion** /kəˌpɪtʃʊˈleɪʃən/ *They criticised the government decision as a capitulation to terrorist organisations.*

ca·pon /ˈkeɪpən/ **capons.** A **capon** is a male chicken that has had its sex organs removed and has been specially fattened up to be eaten.

cap·puc·ci·no /ˌkæpʊˈtʃiːnəʊ/ **cappuccinos.** Cappuccino is coffee which has hot frothy milk and sometimes powdered chocolate on top.

ca·price /kæˈpriːs/ **caprices.** A **caprice** is an unexpected action or decision which has no strong reason or purpose.

ca·pri·cious /kæˈprɪʃəs/. **1** Someone who is **capricious** often changes their mind unexpectedly and for no good reason. **2** Something that is **capricious** often changes unexpectedly. ♦ **ca·pri·cious·ness** *...the capriciousness and inhospitality of the English weather.*

cap·si·cum /ˈkæpsɪkəm/ **capsicums.** A **capsicum** is a mild-tasting, hollow vegetable with seeds. It can be red, yellow, or green. The usual American expression is **bell pepper** or **sweet pepper**.

cap·size /kæpˈsaɪz, AM ˈkæpsaɪz/ **capsizes, capsizing, capsized.** If a boat **capsizes**, it turns upside down in the water. *I didn't count on his capsizing the raft.*

cap·stan /ˈkæpstən/ **capstans.** A **capstan** is a machine consisting of a drum that turns round and pulls in a heavy rope or something attached to a rope, for example an anchor.

cap·sule /ˈkæpsjuːl, AM ˈkæpsəl/ **capsules.** **1** A **capsule** is a very small tube containing powdered or liquid medicine, which you swallow. *...cod liver oil capsules.* **2** In some plants, a **capsule** is a part which forms a case or container for seeds, fruit, or spores. **3** A space **capsule** is the part of a spacecraft in which people travel, and which often separates from the main rocket.

Capt. **Capt.** is a written abbreviation for 'captain'.

cap·tain /ˈkæptɪn/ **captains, captaining, captained.** **1** A **captain** is a military officer of middle rank. **2** In the United States and some other countries, a **captain** is a police officer of fairly senior rank. **3** The **captain** of a sports team is the player in charge of it. **4** The **captain** of a ship or aeroplane is the sailor or pilot in charge of it. **5** The **captain** of an aeroplane is the pilot in charge of it. **6** If you **captain** a team or a ship, you are the captain of it.

cap·tain·cy /ˈkæptɪnsi/. The **captaincy** of a team is the position of being captain. *His captaincy of the team was ended by mild eye trouble.*

,captain of 'industry, captains of industry. You can refer to the owners or senior managers of industrial companies as **captains of industry**.

cap·tion /ˈkæpʃən/ **captions, captioning, captioned.** **1** A **caption** is the words printed underneath a picture or cartoon which explain what it is about. **2** When someone **captions** a picture or cartoon, they put a caption under it. *The Sun had captioned a picture of Princess Diana 'Princess of Veils'.*

cap·ti·vate /ˈkæptɪveɪt/ **captivates, captivating, captivated.** If you **are captivated** by someone or something, you find them fascinating and attractive. *For 40 years she has captivated the world*

with her radiant looks. ♦ **cap·ti·vat·ing** ...her captivating smile. `ADJ-GRADED`

cap·tive /'kæptɪv/ **captives. 1** A **captive** animal or person is being kept in a particular place and is not allowed to escape. **2** If someone **takes** or **holds** you **captive**, they take or keep you as a prisoner. **3** A **captive** is someone who is being held captive. **4** You can refer to a group of people as a **captive** audience or market when they have no choice but to watch or listen to someone, or to buy a particular product from someone. *We all performed action songs, sketches and dances before a captive audience of parents.* `♦♦◇◇◇ ADJ` `PHRASE` `N-COUNT` `ADJ: ADJ n`

cap·tiv·ity /kæp'tɪvɪti/. **Captivity** is the state of being kept imprisoned or enclosed. *The great majority of barn owls are reared in captivity.* `♦◇◇◇◇ N-UNCOUNT`

cap·tor /'kæptə/ **captors.** You can refer to the person who has captured someone as their **captor**. `♦◇◇◇◇ N-COUNT`

cap·ture /'kæptʃə/ **captures, capturing, captured. 1** If you **capture** someone or something, you catch them or take possession of them, especially in a war, or after a struggle or chase. *The guerrillas shot down one aeroplane and captured the pilot. ...the murders of fifteen thousand captured Polish soldiers.* ► Also a noun. *...the final battles which led to the army's capture of the town... The man was trying to evade capture by the security forces.* **2** If you **capture** something that you are trying to obtain in competition with other people, you succeed in obtaining it. *In 1987, McDonald's captured 19 per cent of all fast-food sales.* **3** If something **captures** your attention or imagination, you begin to be interested in or excited by it. If someone or something **captures** your heart, you begin to love them or like them very much. **4** If something or someone **captures** a particular quality, feeling, or atmosphere, they represent or express it successfully. *Their mood was captured by one who said, 'Students don't know or care about campus issues.'* **5** If an event **is captured** in a photograph or on film, it is photographed or filmed. *The images were captured by TV crews filming outside the base. ...photographers who captured the traumatic scene.* `♦♦♦◇◇ VERB V n V-ed` `VERB Vn` `VERB: Vn` `VERB: Vn` `VERB: be V-ed on/in n be V-ed V n`

car /kɑː/ **cars. 1** A **car** is a motor vehicle with room for a small number of passengers. *They arrived by car.* **2** In America, the separate sections of a passenger train or a freight train are called **cars**. **3** In Britain, railway carriages can be called **cars** when they are used for a particular purpose. *...the dining car.* **4** See also **cable car**. `♦♦♦♦ N-COUNT: also by N` `N-COUNT` `N-COUNT`

ca·rafe /kə'ræf/ **carafes.** A **carafe** is a glass container in which you serve water or wine. ► A **carafe** of water or wine is the amount of it contained in a carafe. `N-COUNT` `N-COUNT`

cara·mel /'kærəml/ **caramels. 1** A **caramel** is a chewy sweet made from sugar, butter, and milk. **2 Caramel** is burnt sugar used for colouring and flavouring food. `♦◇◇◇◇ N-VAR` `N-UNCOUNT`

cara·mel·ize /'kærəməlaɪz/ **caramelizes, caramelizing, caramelized;** also spelled **caramelise** in British English. **1** If sugar **caramelizes**, it turns to caramel. **2** If you **caramelize** something such as fruit, you cook it with sugar so that it is coated with caramel. *...caramelised apples and pears.* `VERB: V` `VERB: V n V-ed`

cara·pace /'kærəpeɪs/ **carapaces. 1** A **carapace** is the protective shell on the back of some animals such as tortoises or crabs. **2** You can refer to an attitude that someone has in order to protect themselves as their **carapace**. *This arrogance became his protective carapace.* `N-COUNT TECHNICAL` `N-COUNT LITERARY`

car·at /'kærət/ **carats. 1** A **carat** is a unit for measuring the weight of diamonds and other precious stones. It is equal to 0.2 grams. *...a huge eight-carat diamond.* **2 Carat** is used after a number to indicate the purity of gold. The purest gold is 24-carat gold. *...a 14-carat gold fountain pen.* `♦◇◇◇◇ N-COUNT` `COMB`

cara·van /'kærəvæn/ **caravans. 1** A **caravan** is a vehicle with beds and other equipment inside, in which people live or spend their holidays. Caravans `♦◇◇◇◇ N-COUNT`

are usually pulled by a car. The usual American word is **trailer**. ♦ **cara·van·ning** /'kærəvænɪŋ/. *He was on a caravanning holiday.* **2** A **caravan** is a group of people and animals or vehicles who travel together for safety in places like the desert. `N-UNCOUNT` `N-COUNT`

cara·way /'kærəweɪ/. **Caraway** is a plant with strong-tasting seeds that are often used to flavour bread and cakes. `N-UNCOUNT`

car·bine /'kɑːbaɪn, AM -biːn/ **carbines.** A **carbine** is a lightweight automatic rifle. `N-COUNT`

car·bo·hy·drate /ˌkɑːbəʊ'haɪdreɪt/ **carbohydrates. Carbohydrates** are substances, found in certain kinds of food, that provide you with energy. The foods that contain these substances, for example bread and potatoes, can also be referred to as **carbohydrates**. `♦♦◇◇◇ N-VAR`

car·bol·ic acid /kɑːˌbɒlɪk 'æsɪd/. **Carbolic acid** or **carbolic** is a liquid that is used as a disinfectant or antiseptic. `N-UNCOUNT`

car·bon /'kɑːbən/ **carbons. 1 Carbon** is the common chemical element that diamonds and coal are made up of. **2** A **carbon** is a sheet of carbon paper. `♦♦♦◇◇ N-UNCOUNT` `N-COUNT`

car·bon·ate /'kɑːbəneɪt/ **carbonates. Carbonate** is used in the names of some compounds that are formed with carbon dioxide and water. `N-VAR TECHNICAL`

car·bon·at·ed /'kɑːbəneɪtɪd/. **Carbonated** drinks contain small bubbles of carbon dioxide. `ADJ`

'carbon copy, carbon copies. 1 If you say that one person or thing is a **carbon copy** of another, you mean that they look or behave exactly like them. **2** A **carbon copy** is a copy of a piece of writing that is made using carbon paper. `N-COUNT` `N-COUNT`

carbon di'oxide. Carbon dioxide is a gas produced by animals and people breathing out, and by chemical reactions. `♦♦◇◇◇ N-UNCOUNT`

carbon mon'oxide. Carbon monoxide is a poisonous gas that is produced especially by the engines of vehicles. `♦◇◇◇◇ N-UNCOUNT`

'carbon paper. Carbon paper is thin paper with a dark substance on one side which you use to make copies of documents. `N-UNCOUNT`

car 'boot sale, car boot sales. A **car boot sale** is a sale where people sell things they own and do not want from a little stall or from the back of their car. The American expression is **yard sale**. `N-COUNT BRITISH`

car·bun·cle /'kɑːbʌŋkəl/ **carbuncles.** A **carbuncle** is a large swelling under the skin. `N-COUNT`

car·bu·ret·tor /ˌkɑːbə'retə, AM 'kɑːbəreɪtə/ **carburettors;** spelled **carburetor** in American English. A **carburettor** is the part of an engine in which air and petrol are mixed together. `N-COUNT`

car·cass /'kɑːkəs/ **carcasses;** also spelled **carcase. 1** A **carcass** is the body of a dead animal. *...a mound of sheep carcasses.* **2** The **carcass** of a vehicle or building is its remains after most of it has decayed or been destroyed. *...the carcass of a rusted tractor.* `♦◇◇◇◇ N-COUNT` `N-COUNT`

car·cino·gen /kɑː'sɪnədʒən, 'kɑːsɪnədʒen/ **carcinogens.** A **carcinogen** is a substance which can cause cancer. ♦ **car·cino·gen·ic** *We were worried the dye could be carcinogenic.* `N-COUNT MEDICAL` `ADJ-GRADED`

car·ci·no·ma /ˌkɑːsɪ'nəʊmə/ **carcinomas. 1 Carcinoma** is the same as cancer. **2** A **carcinoma** is a malignant tumour. `N-UNCOUNT MEDICAL` `N-COUNT`

card /kɑːd/ **cards. 1** A **card** is a piece of stiff paper or thin cardboard on which something is written or printed. **2 Card** is strong stiff paper or thin cardboard. **3** A **card** is a folded piece of stiff paper with a picture and sometimes a message printed on it, which you send to someone on a special occasion. *She sends me a card on my birthday.* **4** A **card** is the same as a **postcard**. **5** A **card** is a piece of cardboard or plastic, or a small document, which shows information about you and which you carry, for example to prove your identity. *...her membership card.* **6** A **card** is a piece of thin cardboard which business people give to other people, usually showing their name, business address and telephone number. **7** A **card** is a rectangular piece of plastic, issued by a bank, company, or shop, `♦♦♦♦ N-COUNT` `N-UNCOUNT` `N-COUNT` `N-COUNT` `N-COUNT` `N-COUNT` `N-COUNT`

which you can use to buy things or obtain money. *...an American Express card.*

8 Cards are thin pieces of cardboard with numbers or pictures printed on them which are used to play various games. *...a pack of cards.* **9** If you are playing **cards**, you are playing a game using cards. N-COUNT N-UNCOUNT

10 You can use **card** to refer to something that gives you an advantage in a particular situation. If you play a particular **card**, you use that advantage. *This permitted Western manufacturers to play their strong cards: capital and technology.* **11** If you say that someone will achieve success if they **play** their **cards right**, you mean that they will achieve success if they act skilfully and use the advantages that they have. **12** If you **put** or **lay your cards on the table**, you deal with a situation by speaking openly about your feelings, ideas, or plans. **13** If something is **on the cards**, it is likely to happen. The American expression is **in the cards**. *A New Year marriage was on the cards.* N-COUNT PHRASE PHRASE PHRASE BRITISH

14 See also **bank card**, **business card**, **calling card**, **cash card**, **cheque card**, **Christmas card**, **identity card**, **index card**, **playing card**, **report card**, **smart card**, **wild card**.

car·da·mom /ˈkɑːdəməm/ **cardamoms;** also spelled **cardamon**. **Cardamom** is a spice. It comes from the seeds of a plant grown in Asia. N-VAR

card·board /ˈkɑːdbɔːd/. **Cardboard** is thick stiff paper that is used, for example, to make boxes and models. ◆◇◇◇ N-UNCOUNT

'card-carrying. A **card-carrying** member of an organization, especially a political party, is an official, fully committed member. ADJ

'card game, card games. A **card game** is a game that is played using a set of playing cards. N-COUNT

card·holder /ˈkɑːdhəʊldə/ **cardholders.** A **cardholder** is someone who has a bank card or credit card. N-COUNT

car·di·ac /ˈkɑːdiæk/. **Cardiac** means relating to the heart. ◆◇◇◇ ADJ: ADJ n MEDICAL

,cardiac ar'rest, cardiac arrests. A **cardiac arrest** is a heart attack. N-VAR MEDICAL

cardie /ˈkɑːdi/ **cardies.** In Britain, a **cardie** is the same as a **cardigan**. N-COUNT INFORMAL

car·di·gan /ˈkɑːdɪgən/ **cardigans.** A **cardigan** is a knitted woollen jumper that fastens at the front with buttons or a zip. See picture headed **clothes**. ◆◇◇◇ N-COUNT

car·di·nal /ˈkɑːdɪnəl/ **cardinals. 1** A **cardinal** is a high-ranking priest in the Catholic church. ◆◇◇◇ N-TITLE

2 A **cardinal** rule or quality is the one that is considered to be especially important. *Your cardinal rule is to bend over backwards to satisfy a customer.* ADJ: ADJ n FORMAL

,cardinal 'number, cardinal numbers. A **cardinal number** is a number such as 1, 3, or 10, that tells you how many things there are in a group but not the order that they are in. Compare **ordinal number**. N-COUNT

,cardinal 'sin, cardinal sins. If you describe an action as a **cardinal sin**, you are indicating in a humorous way that some people strongly disapprove of it. *I committed the physician's cardinal sin: I got involved with my patients.* N-COUNT

'card index, card indexes. A **card index** is a number of cards with information written on them which are arranged, usually in alphabetical order, so that you can find the information you want easily. N-COUNT

car·di·ol·ogy /ˌkɑːdiˈɒlədʒi/. **Cardiology** is the study of the heart and its diseases. ♦ **car·di·olo·gist, cardiologists.** N-UNCOUNT N-COUNT

car·dio·vas·cu·lar /ˌkɑːdiəʊˈvæskjʊə/. **Cardiovascular** means relating to the heart and blood vessels. *...cardiovascular fitness.* ◆◇◇◇ ADJ: ADJ n MEDICAL

'card table, card tables; also spelled **card-table**. A **card table** is a light folding table which is sometimes used for playing games of cards on. N-COUNT

care /keə/ **cares, caring, cared. 1** If you **care** about something, you feel that it is important and are concerned about it. *...a company that cares about the environment. ...young men who did not care whether they lived or died... Does anybody* ◆◆◆◆◆ VB: no cont V about n V wh

know we're here, does anybody care? **2** If you **care** for someone, you feel a lot of affection for them. *He still cared for me. ...people who are your friends, who care about you.* ♦ **car·ing** *...the 'feminine' traits of caring and compassion.* **3** If you say that you do not **care** for something or someone, you mean that you do not like them. *She had met both sons and did not care for either.* **4** If you say that you **couldn't care less** about someone or something, you are emphasizing that you are not interested in them or not worried about them. *I couldn't care less about the bloody woman.* **5** You can say **for all** I **care** to emphasize that it does not matter at all to you what someone does. *You can go right now for all I care.* **6** You can say **'Who cares?'** to emphasize that something does not matter to you at all. *Who cares about some stupid vacation... 'But we might ruin the stove.'—'Who cares?'* **7** If someone asks you if you would **care** for something, or if you would **care** to do something, they are asking you politely if you would like to have it or do it. *Would you care for some orange juice?... He said he was off to the beach and would we care to join him.* **8** If you say that someone does something when they **care** to do it, you mean that they do it, although they should do it more willingly or more often. *Experts reveal only as much as they care to.* VB: no cont V for/about n Also V N-UNCOUNT VB: no cont with brd-neg V for n DATED PHRASE PRAGMATICS PHRASE PRAGMATICS PHRASE PRAGMATICS PHRASE PRAGMATICS VB: no cont PRAGMATICS V for n V to-inf VB: no cont V to-inf

9 If you **care** for someone or something, you look after them and keep them in a good state or condition. *They hired a nurse to care for her. ...well-cared-for homes.* ► Also a noun. *Most of the staff specialise in the care of children. ...sensitive teeth which need special care.* **10** Children who are in **care** are looked after by the state because their parents are dead or unable to look after them properly. *She was taken into care as a baby.* **11** If you **take care of** someone or something, you look after them and prevent them from being harmed or damaged. *There was no one else to take care of their children... You have to learn to take care of your possessions.* **12** If you **take care of** a problem, task, or situation, you deal with it. *They leave it to the system to try and take care of the problem... 'Do you need clean sheets?' 'No. Mrs. May took care of that.'* **13** See also **caring**; **after-care**, **day care**, **intensive care**. **14** If you do something with **care**, you do it in a detailed or attentive way because you do not want to make any mistakes or cause any damage. *Condoms are an effective method of birth control if used with care... We'd taken enormous care in choosing the location.* **15** If you **take care** to do something, you make sure that you do it. *Take care to keep the baby warm.* **16** You can say **'Take care'** when saying goodbye to someone. **17** Your **cares** are your worries, anxieties, or fears. *Lean back in a hot bath and forget all the cares of the day... Johnson seemed without a care in the world.* **18** If someone sends you a letter or parcel **care of** a particular person or place, they send it to that person or place, and it is then passed on to you. *Please write to me care of the publishers.* VERB V for n V-ed N-UNCOUNT N-UNCOUNT BRITISH PHRASE PHRASE N-UNCOUNT PHRASE CONVENTION PRAGMATICS N-COUNT PHRASE

ca·reen /kəˈriːn/ **careens, careening, careened.** If someone or something **careens** somewhere, they rush forward in an uncontrollable way. *He stood to one side as they careened past him.* VERB V prep/adv

ca·reer /kəˈrɪə/ **careers, careering, careered. 1** A **career** is the job or profession that someone does for a long period of their life. *She is now concentrating on a career as a fashion designer. ...a career in journalism. ...a political career.* **2** Your **career** is the part of your life that you spend working. *During his career, he wrote more than fifty plays.* **3 Careers** advice or guidance consists of information about different jobs and help with deciding what kind of job you want to do. **4** If a person or vehicle **careers** somewhere, they move fast and in an uncontrolled way. *His car careered into a river.* ◆◆◆◇ N-COUNT N-COUNT ADJ: ADJ n BRITISH VERB V prep/adv

ca·reer·ist /kəˈrɪərɪst/ **careerists.** **Careerist** people are ambitious and think that their career is ADJ

more important than anything else. *...careerist poli-* N-COUNT
ticians. ► Also a noun. *...a singleminded careerist
with few friends.*

ca·reer woman, career women. A career wom- N-COUNT
an is a woman who is interested in working and
progressing in her career, rather than staying at
home doing housework and looking after children.

care·free /ˈkeəfriː/. A carefree person or period of ◆◇◇◇◇
time doesn't have or involve any problems or re- ADJ-GRADED
sponsibilities. *...carefree past summers at the beach.*

care·ful /ˈkeəfʊl/. **1** If you are **careful**, you give se- ◆◆◆◆◇
rious attention to what you are doing, in order to ADJ-GRADED
avoid damage or mistakes. If you are **careful** to do
something, you make sure that you do it. *Be very
careful with this stuff, it can be dangerous... We had
to be very careful not to be seen.* ◆ **care·ful·ly** *Drive* ADV-GRADED:
carefully... He had chosen his words carefully. **2** If ADV with v
you tell someone to be **careful about** doing some- v-link ADJ
thing, you mean that they should think seriously about -ing
before they do it, because you think it is probably PRAGMATICS
wrong. *I think you should be careful about talking of
the rebels as heroes.* **3** You can say **'You can't be too** PHRASE
careful' as a way of advising someone to take pre- PRAGMATICS
cautions, even when these may seem unnecessary. SPOKEN
*You can't be too careful when a young child is near
water.*
4 Careful work, thought, or examination is thorough ADJ-GRADED
and shows a concern for details. *What we now know
about the disease was learned by careful study of dis-
eased organs.* ◆ **carefully** *...carefully planned thefts.* ADV-GRADED:
5 If you are **careful** with something such as money or ADV with v
resources, you use or spend only what is necessary. *It* ADJ-GRADED
*would force industries to be more careful with natural
resources.*

'care giver, care givers; also spelled **caregiver.** A N-COUNT
care giver is someone who is responsible for looking after another person, for example, a person who
is ill, or very young. *She is the primary care giver of
the family.*

care·less /ˈkeələs/. **1** If you are **careless**, you do ◆◇◇◇◇
not pay enough attention to what you are doing, ADJ-GRADED
and so you make mistakes, or cause damage. *I'm
sorry. How careless of me... Some parents are accused
of being careless with their children's health. ...care-
less driving.* ◆ **care·less·ly** *a carelessly discarded* ADV-GRADED
cigarette. ◆ **care·less·ness** *This is simple careless-* N-UNCOUNT
ness. **2** If someone is **careless** about something such
as their health or appearance, they do not seem to
be concerned about it. *He had shown himself careless of personal safety.*
3 If you describe someone's movements as **careless**, ADJ-GRADED
you mean that they are relaxed or confident, and do LITERARY
not seem to require much effort or thought. *With a
careless flip of his wrists, he sent the ball quickly on its
way.*

care·less·ly /ˈkeələsli/. If someone does something ADV-GRADED:
carelessly, they do it without much thought or ef- ADV with v
fort. *Houston carelessly tossed the notebooks on the* WRITTEN
bed. ● See also **careless**.

car·er /ˈkeərə/ **carers.** A **carer** is someone who ◆◇◇◇◇
looks after another person, especially a child or an N-COUNT
old or disabled person. The American word is **care-** BRITISH
taker. *We are looking for foster carers who can care
for a child for a few days.*

ca·ress /kəˈres/ **caresses, caressing, ca-** ◆◇◇◇◇
ressed. If you **caress** someone, you stroke them VERB
gently and affectionately. *He was gently caressing* V n
her golden hair. ► Also a noun. *Margaret took me to* N-COUNT
one side, holding my arm in a gentle caress.

care·taker /ˈkeəteɪkə/ **caretakers. 1** A **caretaker** ◆◇◇◇◇
is a person whose job is to look after a large build- N-COUNT
ing such as a school and deal with small repairs. BRITISH
The American word is **janitor**. **2** A **caretaker** gov- ADJ: ADJ n
ernment or leader is in charge temporarily until a
new one is appointed. **3** A **caretaker** is someone N-COUNT
who is responsible for looking after another person, AMERICAN
for example, a disabled person or a child.

'care worker, care workers. A **care worker** is a N-COUNT
person whose work involves looking after people

who cannot look after themselves, for example in an
old people's home.

care·worn /ˈkeəwɔːn/. A person who looks **care-** ADJ-GRADED
worn looks worried, tired, and unhappy.

car·go /ˈkɑːɡəʊ/ **cargoes.** The **cargo** of a ship or ◆◆◇◇◇
plane is the goods that it is carrying. *...a cargo of ba-* N-VAR
nanas. ...cargo planes.

Car·ib·bean /ˌkærəˈbiːən, AM kəˈrɪbiən/ ◆◆◇◇◇
Caribbeans. 1 The **Caribbean** is the sea which is N-PROPER:
between the West Indies, Central America and the theN
north coast of South America. **2 Caribbean** means ADJ
belonging or relating to the Caribbean Sea and its
islands, or to its people. *...the Caribbean island of St
Thomas.* ► A **Caribbean** is a person from a Carib- N-COUNT
bean island. ● See also **Afro-Caribbean**.

cari·bou /ˈkærɪbuː/; **caribou** is both the singular N-COUNT
and the plural form. A **caribou** is a large north
American deer.

cari·ca·ture /ˈkærɪkətʃʊə, AM -tʃər/ **caricatures,** ◆◇◇◇◇
caricaturing, caricatured. 1 A **caricature** of N-COUNT
someone is a drawing or description of them that
exaggerates their appearance or behaviour in a humorous or satirical way. *...a caricature of Hitler with
a devil's horns.* **2** If you **caricature** someone, you VERB: V n
draw or describe them in an exaggerated way in or- be V-ed as n
der to be humorous or satirical. *He was caricatured* Also V n as n
as a turnip. **3** If you refer to something as a **carica-** N-COUNT
ture of an event or situation, you mean that it is a
very exaggerated account of it. *Hall is angry at what
he sees as a caricature of the training offered to social workers.*

car·ies /ˈkeəriz/. **Caries** is decay in teeth. *Fluoride* N-UNCOUNT
appears to prevent dental caries. TECHNICAL

car·ing /ˈkeərɪŋ/ **1** If someone is **caring**, they are ◆◆◇◇◇
affectionate, helpful, and sympathetic. *...a loving,* ADJ-GRADED
caring husband. **2** The **caring** professions are those ADJ: ADJ n
such as nursing and social work that are involved
with looking after people who are ill or need help.

car·jacking /ˈkɑːdʒækɪŋ/ **carjackings.** A N-VAR
carjacking is an attack on a person in their own car JOURNALISM
during which they may be robbed or harmed physi-
cally. *...a bill to combat carjacking.*

car·load /ˈkɑːləʊd/ **carloads.** A **carload** of people N-COUNT
or things is as many people or things as a car can
carry. *...a carload of soldiers.*

car·mine /ˈkɑːmaɪn, -mɪn/. **Carmine** is a deep COLOUR
bright red colour. *...a tulip with carmine petals.* LITERARY

car·nage /ˈkɑːnɪdʒ/. **Carnage** is the violent killing ◆◇◇◇◇
of large numbers of people, especially in a war. *...his* N-UNCOUNT
strategy for stopping the carnage in Bosnia. LITERARY

car·nal /ˈkɑːnəl/. **Carnal** desires and feelings are ADJ
purely sexual and physical. *...carnal love.* FORMAL

car·na·tion /kɑːˈneɪʃən/ **carnations.** A **carnation** ◆◇◇◇◇
is a plant with white, pink, or red flowers. N-COUNT

car·ni·val /ˈkɑːnɪvəl/ **carnivals.** A **carnival** is a ◆◆◇◇◇
public festival during which people play music and N-COUNT
dance in the streets.

car·ni·vore /ˈkɑːnɪvɔː/ **carnivores. 1** A **carnivore** ◆◇◇◇◇
is an animal that eats meat. ◆ **car·nivo·rous** N-COUNT
/kɑːˈnɪvərəs/. *Snakes are carnivorous, mainly eating* ADJ
small animals such as rats and frogs. **2** If you say N-COUNT
someone is a **carnivore**, you mean that they are not
a vegetarian. *This is a vegetarian dish that carnivores love.* ◆ **carnivorous** *Meat is also served for* ADJ
carnivorous guests.

car·ob /ˈkærəb/. **Carob** is a fairly sweet food that is N-UNCOUNT
sometimes substituted for chocolate.

car·ol /ˈkærəl/ **carols.** Carols are Christian reli- ◆◇◇◇◇
gious songs that are sung at Christmas. N-COUNT

ca·rouse /kəˈraʊz/ **carouses, carousing, ca-** VERB: V
roused. If people **are carousing**, they are enjoying
themselves noisily and drinking a lot of alcohol.
◆ **ca·rous·ing** *The singing and carousing did not* N-UNCOUNT
end until after midnight.

carou·sel /ˌkærəˈsel/ **carousels. 1** A **carousel** at a N-COUNT
funfair is a large round mechanical device with
seats, often in the shape of animals or cars, on
which children sit and go round and round. The
British word is **merry-go-round** or **roundabout**.

2 At an airport, a **carousel** is a moving belt from which passengers can collect their luggage. `N-COUNT`

carp /kɑːp/ **carps, carping, carped. Carp** can also be used as the plural form for meaning 1. **1** A **carp** is a kind of freshwater fish. ◆◆◇◇◇ `N-VAR`

2 If you **carp**, you keep criticizing or complaining about someone or something. *She's constantly carping at him.* ♦ **carp·ing** *She was in no mood to put up with Blanche's carping.* `VERB` `V at/about n` `Also V` `N-UNCOUNT`

'car park, car parks; also spelled **carpark.** A **car park** is an area or building where people can leave their cars. The usual American term is **parking lot.** ◆◆◇◇◇ `N-COUNT` `BRITISH`

car·pen·ter /ˈkɑːpɪntə/ **carpenters.** A **carpenter** is a person whose job is making and repairing wooden things. ◆◇◇◇◇ `N-COUNT`

car·pen·try /ˈkɑːpɪntri/. **Carpentry** is the activity of making and repairing wooden things. `N-UNCOUNT`

car·pet /ˈkɑːpɪt/ **carpets, carpeting, carpeted. 1** A **carpet** is a thick covering of soft material which is laid over a floor or a staircase. *They put down wooden boards, and laid new carpets on top.* **2** If a floor or room **is carpeted,** a carpet is laid on the floor. *The main gaming room was thickly carpeted.* **3** If the ground **is carpeted** with something such as leaves or plants, it is completely covered by them. *The ground was thickly carpeted with pine needles.* ▶ Also a noun. *...the carpet of leaves in my yard.* **4** See also **carpeting; red carpet.** • to **sweep** something **under the carpet:** see **sweep.** ◆◆◇◇◇ `N-VAR` `VB: usu passive V-ed` `be V-ed with n LITERARY N-COUNT`

carpet·bag·ger /ˈkɑːpɪtbægə/ **carpetbaggers.** If you call someone a **carpetbagger,** you disapprove of them because they are trying to become a politician in an area which is not their home, because they think they are more likely to succeed there. `N-COUNT` `PRAGMATICS AMERICAN`

'carpet bombing. Carpet bombing is heavy bombing from aircraft, with the intention of hitting as many places as possible in a particular area. `N-UNCOUNT`

car·pet·ing /ˈkɑːpɪtɪŋ/. You use **carpeting** to refer to a carpet, or to the type of material that is used to make carpets. *...wall-to-wall carpeting.* `N-UNCOUNT`

'car pool, car pools. A **car pool** is a number of cars that are owned by an organization for the use of its employees. `N-COUNT`

'car port, car ports; also spelled **carport.** A **car port** is a shelter for one or two cars next to a house. It consists of a flat roof supported on pillars. `N-COUNT`

car·riage /ˈkærɪdʒ/ **carriages. 1** A **carriage** is an old-fashioned vehicle which is pulled by horses. *He kept a carriage and horses.* **2** A **carriage** is one of the separate sections of a train that carries passengers. The usual American word is **car. 3** A **carriage** is the same as a **baby carriage. 4 Carriage** is the cost or action of transporting or delivering goods. *It costs £10.86 for one litre including carriage.* ◆◆◇◇◇ `N-COUNT` `N-COUNT BRITISH` `N-COUNT AMERICAN` `N-UNCOUNT FORMAL`

carriage·way /ˈkærɪdʒweɪ/ **carriageways.** A **carriageway** is one of the two sides of a motorway or major road. Each carriageway may have two or more lanes. *Following a serious accident both carriageways are blocked.* ◆◇◇◇◇ `N-COUNT BRITISH`

car·ri·er /ˈkæriə/ **carriers. 1** A **carrier** is a vehicle that is used for carrying people, especially soldiers, or things. *...armoured personnel carriers and tanks.* • See also **aircraft carrier. 2** A **carrier** is a passenger airline. *...Switzerland's national carrier, Swissair.* ◆◆◇◇◇ `N-COUNT` `N-COUNT`

'carrier bag, carrier bags. A **carrier bag** is a paper or plastic bag which you carry shopping in. `N-COUNT BRITISH`

car·ri·on /ˈkæriən/. **Carrion** is the decaying flesh of dead animals. *Crows circled, looking for carrion.* `N-UNCOUNT`

car·rot /ˈkærət/ **carrots. 1 Carrots** are long, thin, orange-coloured vegetables that grow mainly underground. See picture headed **vegetables. 2** Something that is offered to people in order to persuade them to do something can be referred to as a **carrot.** *They will be set targets, with a carrot of extra cash and pay if they achieve them.* ◆◆◇◇◇ `N-VAR` `N-COUNT`

,carrot and 'stick. If an organization has a **carrot and stick** approach or policy, it offers people things in order to persuade them to do something and punishes them if they refuse to do it. `ADJ: ADJ n`

car·ry /ˈkæri/ **carries, carrying, carried. 1** If you **carry** something, you take it with you, holding it so that it does not touch the ground. *He was carrying a briefcase... She carried her son to the car.* **2** If you **carry** something, you have it with you wherever you go. *You have to carry a bleeper.* ◆◆◆◆◇ `VERB` `V n` `V n prep/adv` `VERB` `V n`

3 To **carry** someone or something means to transport them or take them somewhere. *The delegation was carrying a message of thanks to President Mubarak... The ship could carry seventy passengers.* `VERB` `V n adv/prep` `V n`

4 If a person or animal **is carrying** a disease, they are infected with it and can pass it on to other people or animals. *...people carrying the AIDS virus.* ♦ **car·ri·er, carriers** *...an typhoid carrier.* `VERB` `V n` `N-COUNT`

5 If an action or situation has a particular quality or consequence, you can say that it **carries** it. *Check that any medication you're taking carries no risk for your developing baby.* **6** If a crime **carries** a particular punishment, a person who is found guilty of that crime will receive that punishment. *Treason carries the death sentence in Kenya.* `VB: no passive, no cont` `VB: no cont V n`

7 If a quality or advantage **carries** someone into a particular position or through a difficult situation, it helps them to achieve that position or deal with that situation. *The warmth and strength of their relationship carried them through difficult times.* `VERB` `V n prep/adv`

8 If you **carry** an idea or method further, you develop it, use it more, or apply it in new circumstances. *It's not such a new idea, but I carried it to extremes.* `VERB` `V n prep/adv`

9 If a newspaper or poster **carries** a picture or a piece of writing, it publishes or displays it. `VERB: V n`

10 In a debate, if a proposal or motion **is carried,** a majority of people vote in favour of it. *A motion backing its economic policy was carried by 322 votes to 296.* `VB: usu passive beV-ed`

11 If a candidate or party **carries** a state or area, they win the election there. The usual British word is **take.** *George Bush carried the state with 56 percent of the vote.* `VB: no passive V n AMERICAN`

12 If a sound **carries,** it can be heard a long way away. *Leaphorn doubted if the sound would carry far.* `V adv` `Also V`

13 If you **carry** yourself in a particular way, you walk and move in that way. *They carried themselves with great pride.* `VERB` `V pron-refl prep/adv`

14 If you **get carried away,** you are so eager or excited about something that you do something hasty or foolish. *I got completely carried away and almost cried.* `PHRASE`

15 • to **carry the can:** see **can.** • to **carry conviction:** see **conviction.** • to **carry the day:** see **day.** • to **carry weight:** see **weight.**

carry off. 1 If you **carry** something **off,** you do it successfully. *He's got the experience and the authority to carry it off.* **2** If you **carry off** a prize, you win it. *It carried off the Evening Standard drama award for best play.* `PHRASAL VB` `V n P` `V P n` `Also V n P`

carry on. 1 If you **carry on** doing something, you continue to do it. *The assistant carried on talking... Her bravery has given him the will to carry on with his life.* **2** If you **carry on** an activity, you do it or take part in it for a period of time. *The consulate will carry on a political dialogue with the Soviet Union.* `PHRASAL VB` `V P -ing` `Also V P n` `V P noun`

3 If you say that someone **is carrying on,** you are irritated with them because they are talking very excitedly and saying a lot of silly things. *He was carrying on about some stupid television series.* `V P` `PRAGMATICS` `V P about n` `INFORMAL`

4 If a person **is carrying on** with someone they are not married to, they are having a sexual relationship; used showing disapproval. *If his wife found him carrying on with anybody else she would leave him.* `PRAGMATICS` `V P with n` `Also V P n` `INFORMAL`

carry out. If you **carry out** a threat or instruction, you do it or act according to it. *Commitments have been made with very little intention of carrying them out.* `PHRASAL VB` `V P noun` `Also V n P`

carry over. If something **carries over** or **is carried over** from one situation to another, it continues to exist or apply in the new situation. *Priestley's rational outlook in science carried over to religion. ...a custom which was carried over into Christian times.* `PHRASAL VB` `ERG` `V P into/to n` `beV-ed P` `into/to n`

carry through. If you **carry** something **through,** you do it or complete it, often in spite of difficulties. `PHRASAL VB` `V n P` `Also V P noun`

The state announced a clear-cut policy and set out to carry it through.

car·ry·cot /'kærɪkɒt/ **carrycots.** A **carrycot** is a cot designed for small babies which has handles so it can be carried. N-COUNT BRITISH

cart /kɑːt/ **carts, carting, carted. 1** A **cart** is an old-fashioned wooden vehicle used for transporting goods or people. Some carts are pulled by animals. *...horse-drawn carts.* **2** A **cart** is a small motor vehicle. *Transportation is by electric cart or by horse and buggy.* **3** A **cart** or a **shopping cart** is a large metal basket on wheels which is provided by supermarkets for customers to use while they are in the shop. **4** If you **cart** things or people somewhere, you carry them or transport them there, often with some difficulty. *He carted off the entire contents of the house... Removal men had begun carting boxes from the official residence.* ◆◆◇◇◇ N-COUNT / N-COUNT AMERICAN / N-COUNT AMERICAN / VERB V n with adv V n prep INFORMAL

carte blanche /ˌkɑːt 'blɒnʃ/. If someone gives you **carte blanche**, they give you the authority to do whatever you think is right. *The decorators were given en carte blanche.* N-UNCOUNT

car·tel /kɑː'tel/ **cartels.** A **cartel** is an association of companies or countries involved in the same industry who act together to control competition and prices. *The company runs the world's diamond cartel.* ◆◆◇◇◇ N-COUNT

cart·horse /'kɑːthɔːs/ **carthorses.** A **carthorse** is a large, powerful horse that is used to pull carts or farm machinery. N-COUNT BRITISH

car·ti·lage /'kɑːtɪlɪdʒ/ **cartilages. Cartilage** is a strong, flexible substance in your body, especially around your joints. *He had injured knee ligaments and cartilage in competition.* ◆◇◇◇ N-VAR

car·tog·ra·phy /kɑː'tɒgrəfi/. **Cartography** is the activity or profession of making maps. ♦ **car·tog·ra·pher, cartographers** *...working as a cartographer for the U.S. government.* N-UNCOUNT / N-COUNT

car·ton /'kɑːtən/ **cartons. 1** A **carton** is a plastic or cardboard container in which food or drink is sold. *...a two-pint carton of milk.* **2** A **carton** is a large, strong cardboard box. ◆◇◇◇ N-COUNT / N-COUNT

car·toon /kɑː'tuːn/ **cartoons. 1** A **cartoon** is a humorous drawing or series of drawings in a newspaper or magazine. *...one of Britain's best-loved cartoon characters, Rupert the Bear.* **2** A **cartoon** is a film in which all the characters and scenes are drawn rather than being real people or objects. ◆◆◇◇◇ N-COUNT / N-COUNT

car·toon·ist /kɑː'tuːnɪst/ **cartoonists.** A **cartoonist** is a person whose job is to draw cartoons for newspapers and magazines. ◆◇◇◇ N-COUNT

car·tridge /'kɑːtrɪdʒ/ **cartridges. 1** In a gun, a **cartridge** is a tube containing a bullet and an explosive substance. **2** A **cartridge** is a part of a machine that can be easily removed and replaced when it is worn out or empty. *Change the filter cartridge as often as instructed by the manufacturer.* ◆◇◇◇ N-COUNT / N-COUNT

cart·wheel /'kɑːtwiːl/ **cartwheels, cartwheeling, cartwheeled. 1** If you do a **cartwheel**, you do a fast, circular movement with your body. You fall sideways, put your hands on the ground, swing your legs over, and return to a standing position. **2** If a person or vehicle **cartwheels** down or across something, they turn over and over in an uncontrollable way. *Suddenly I was cartwheeling down the slope.* N-COUNT / VERB V P/adv Also V

carve /kɑːv/ **carves, carving, carved. 1** If you **carve** an object, you make it by cutting it out of a substance such as wood or stone. You **carve** wood or stone in order to make the object. *One of the prisoners has carved a beautiful wooden chess set.* ♦ **carv·er, carvers** *...Charlie Easterfield, the Scottish sculptor and wood carver.* **2** If you **carve** writing or a design on an object, you cut it into the surface of the object. *He carved his name on his desk.* **3** If you **carve** a piece of meat such as chicken or beef, you cut slices from it. **4** If you **carve** a career or a niche for yourself, you succeed in getting the career or the position that you want by your own efforts. *She has carved a niche for* ◆◇◇◇ VERB Also V, V n prep / N-COUNT / VERB V n in/on n / VERB: V n / VB: no passive V n for pronrefl

herself as a comic actor. ▶ **Carve out** means the same as **carve**. *He is hoping to carve out a much greater role for himself... William has not had much luck in carving out a career.* PHRASAL VB: no passive V P n for pron-refl V P n

5 If a road **is carved** through a place, it is built so that it goes through that place. *Two three-lane roads will be carved through countryside.* VB: usu passive be V-ed prep

6 See also **carving**.

carve out See **carve** 4. PHRASAL VB

carve up. 1 If you say that someone **carves** something **up**, you disapprove of the way they have divided it into small parts. *He has set about carving up the company which Hammer created from almost nothing... They have begun carving the country up like a pie.* **2** To **carve** someone **up** means to hurt them badly using a knife. *He wanted to go into the street and carve someone's face up.* PHRASAL VB PRAGMATICS V P noun V n P / V n P Also V P n INFORMAL

carv·ing /'kɑːvɪŋ/ **carvings. 1** A **carving** is an object or design that has been cut out of a material such as stone or wood. *...a wood carving of a human hand.* **2 Carving** is the art of carving objects or designs. ◆◇◇◇ N-COUNT / N-UNCOUNT

'carving knife, carving knives. A **carving knife** is a long sharp knife that is used to cut cooked meat. N-COUNT

cas·cade /kæs'keɪd/ **cascades, cascading, cascaded. 1** If you refer to a **cascade** of something, you mean that there is a large amount of it. *...lustrous cascades of black hair.* **2** When water **cascades** somewhere, it pours or flows downwards very fast and in large quantities. *The freezing, rushing water cascaded past her.* **3** If one thing **cascades** over another, it falls or hangs over it. *Pink geraniums cascade over my balcony.* ◆◇◇◇ N-COUNT LITERARY / VERB V adv/prep Also V / VERB V prep Also V LITERARY

case 1 instances and other abstract meanings

case /keɪs/ **cases. 1** A particular **case** is a particular situation or incident, especially one that you are using as an example of something more general. *Surgical training takes at least nine years, or 11 in the case of obstetrics... Suffering can have beneficial results and certainly I know that was true in my case... In extreme cases, insurance companies can prosecute.* ◆◆◆◆ N-COUNT

2 A **case** is a person or their particular problem that a doctor, social worker, or other professional is dealing with. *Some cases of arthritis respond to a gluten-free diet... Child protection workers were meeting to discuss her case.* N-COUNT

3 If you say that someone is a sad **case** or a hopeless **case**, you mean that they are in a sad or hopeless situation. *I knew I was going to make it – that I wasn't a hopeless case.* ● See also **basket case**. N-COUNT: adj N

4 A **case** is a crime or mystery that the police are investigating. *They haven't discounted her connection with the kidnapping case.* **5** In law, a **case** is a trial or other legal inquiry. *It can be difficult for public figures to win a libel case.* ● See also **test case**. N-COUNT / N-COUNT

6 In an argument or debate, the **case** for or against a plan or idea consists of the facts and reasons used to support it or oppose it. *He sat there while I made the case for his dismissal... These facts strengthen the case against hanging.* N-COUNT

7 You say **in any case** when you are adding something which is more important than what you have just said, but which supports or corrects it. *The concert was booked out, and in any case, most of the people gathered in the square could not afford the price of a ticket.* **8** You say **in any case** after talking about things that you are not sure about, to emphasize that your next statement is the most important thing or the thing that you are sure about. *Either he escaped, or he came to grief. In any case, he was never seen again.* PHRASE PRAGMATICS / PHRASE PRAGMATICS

9 If you do something or have something **in case** or **just in case** a particular thing happens, you do it or have it because that thing might happen. *In case anyone was following me, I made an elaborate detour... Extra boiling water should be kept at hand just in case.* PHR-CONJ

10 If you do something or have something **in case of** a particular thing, you do it or have it because that thing might happen. *Many shops along the route have been* PHR-PREP

boarded up *in case of trouble.* **11** You say **in case** PHRASE
or **in which case** to indicate that what you are going to
say is true if the possible situation that has just been
mentioned actually exists. *Perhaps you've some
doubts about the attack. In that case it may interest
you to know that Miss Woods witnessed it.* **12** You can PHRASE
say that you are doing something **just in case** to refer
vaguely to the possibility that a thing might happen or
be true, without saying exactly what it is. *I guess we've
already talked about this but I'll ask you again just in
case.*
13 You use **in case** in expressions like 'in case you PHRASE
didn't know' or 'in case you've forgotten' in a rather PRAGMATICS
irritated way, when you are telling someone something that you think is either obvious or none of their
business. *'I'm waiting for Mary Ann,' she said, 'in case
you're wondering.'*
14 You say **as the case may be** or **whatever the case** PHRASE
may be to indicate that the statement you are making
applies equally to the two or more alternatives that
you have mentioned. *They know how everything
works – or doesn't work, as the case may be.*
15 If you say that a task or situation is **a case of** a par- PHRASE
ticular thing, you mean that it consists of that thing or
can be described as that thing. *It's a case of relaxing,
then playing.* **16** If you say that something is **a case in** PHRASE
point, you mean that it is a good example of something you have just mentioned. *In many cases religious persecution is at the root of mass flights. A case in
point is colonial India.* **17** If you say that something **is** PHRASE
the case, you mean that it is true or correct. *You'll
probably notice her having difficulty swallowing. If
this is the case, give her plenty of liquids.*

case 2 containers

case /keɪs/ **cases. 1** A case is a container that is ◆◆◇◇◇
specially designed to hold or protect something. *...a* N-COUNT
*black case for his spectacles. ...a 10-foot-long stuffed
alligator in a glass case.* ● See also **attaché case,
bookcase, briefcase, packing case, pillowcase,
showcase, suitcase. 2** A case is the same as a suit- N-COUNT
case. **3** A **case** of wine or other alcoholic drink is a N-COUNT
box containing several bottles, usually twelve.

case 3 grammar term

case /keɪs/ **cases. 1** In the grammar of many lan- N-COUNT
guages, the **case** of a noun, pronoun, or adjective is
the form it has which shows its function in the sentence. See **accusative, nominative. 2** See also **lower
case, upper case.**
case·book /'keɪsbʊk/ **casebooks.** A casebook is a N-COUNT
written record of the cases dealt with by someone
such as a doctor or social worker.
case 'history, case histories. A person's case N-COUNT
history is the record of past events or problems that
have affected them, especially their medical history.
'case law. Case law is law that has been estab- N-UNCOUNT
lished by following decisions made by judges in ear- LEGAL
lier cases.
case·load /'keɪsləʊd/ **caseloads.** The caseload of N-COUNT
someone such as a doctor or lawyer is the number
of cases that they have to deal with. *The court's
caseload has doubled in the last two years.*
case·ment /'keɪsmənt/ **casements.** A casement N-COUNT
or a **casement window** is a window that opens by WRITTEN
means of hinges, usually at the side.
'case study, case studies. A case study is a ◆◇◇◇◇
written account that gives detailed information N-COUNT
about a person, group, or thing and their development over a period of time. *...a large case study of
malaria in West African children.*
case·work /'keɪswɜːk/. **Casework** is social work N-UNCOUNT
that involves actually dealing or working with the
people who need help. ♦ **case·worker, case-** N-COUNT
workers *...a child support caseworker.*
cash /kæʃ/ **cashes, cashing, cashed. 1 Cash** is ◆◆◆◇
money in the form of notes and coins. *...two thou-* N-UNCOUNT
sand pounds in cash. ● See also **hard cash, petty
cash. 2 Cash** means the same as money, especially N-UNCOUNT
money which is immediately available. **3** If you INFORMAL
cash a cheque, you exchange it at a bank for the VERB: V n
amount of money that it is worth.

cash in. 1 If you say that someone **cashes in** on a PHRASAL VB
situation, you mean that they use it to gain an advan- PRAGMATICS
tage, often in an unfair or dishonest way. *Gang leaders* V P on n
had cashed in on the violence to seize valuable land.
2 If you **cash in** something such as an insurance poli- V P noun
cy, you exchange it for money. *Avoid cashing in a poli-* Also V n P
cy early as you could lose out heavily.
cash-and-'carry, cash-and-carries. A cash- N-COUNT
and-carry is a large store where shopkeepers, and BRITISH
sometimes the public, can buy goods very cheaply,
but must pay for them in cash and take them away
themselves.
'cash card, cash cards; also spelled **cashcard.** A N-COUNT
cash card is a card that banks give to their customers so that they can get money out of a cashpoint.
'cash cow, cash cows. In business, a product or N-COUNT
investment can be described as a **cash cow** when it
steadily continues to be profitable.
'cash crop, cash crops. A **cash crop** is a crop N-COUNT
that is grown in order to be sold, rather than to feed
the farmer and his family.
'cash desk, cash desks. A **cash desk** is a place N-COUNT
in a large shop where you pay for the things you BRITISH
want to buy.
'cash dispenser, cash dispensers. A cash dis- N-COUNT
penser is a machine built into the wall of a bank or BRITISH
other building, which allows people to take money
out of their bank account by using a cash card.
cash·ew /'kæʃuː, kæˈʃuː/ **cashews.** A cashew or a N-COUNT
cashew nut is a curved nut that you can eat.
'cash flow; also spelled **cashflow.** The **cash flow** of ◆◇◇◇◇
a business is the amount of money it has available N-UNCOUNT
to pay its expenses so that it can continue to operate. *The company ran into cash-flow problems.*
cash·ier /kæˈʃɪə/ **cashiers, cashiering, cash-** ◆◇◇◇◇
iered. 1 A **cashier** is a person that customers pay N-COUNT
money to or get money from in a shop or a bank.
2 If a person in the armed forces **is cashiered**, he or VERB:
she is forced to leave because they have done some- be V-ed
thing seriously wrong.
cash·mere /ˌkæʃˈmɪə, AM 'kæʒmɪr/. **Cashmere** is a ◆◇◇◇◇
kind of very fine, soft wool.
cash·point /'kæʃpɔɪnt/ **cashpoints.** A cashpoint N-COUNT
is the same as a **cash dispenser.** Cashpoint is a BRITISH
trademark. The usual American word is **ATM.**
'cash register, cash registers. A **cash register** N-COUNT
is a machine in a shop, pub, or restaurant that is
used to add up and record how much money people pay, and in which the money is kept.
'cash-starved. A **cash-starved** company or or- ADJ
ganization does not have enough money to operate JOURNALISM
properly, usually because another organization,
such as the government, is not giving them the
money that they need.
'cash-strapped. If someone describe a person or ADJ
organization as **cash-strapped**, they mean that they BRITISH,
do not have enough money to pay for the things JOURNALISM
they need.
cas·ing /'keɪsɪŋ/ **casings.** A casing is a substance N-COUNT
or object that covers something and protects it.
...the outer casings of missiles.
ca·si·no /kəˈsiːnəʊ/ **casinos.** A casino is a build- ◆◆◇◇◇
ing or room where people play gambling games N-COUNT
such as roulette.
cask /kɑːsk, kæsk/ **casks.** A cask is a wooden bar- N-COUNT
rel that is used for storing things, especially alcoholic drink.
cas·ket /'kɑːskɪt, 'kæsk-/ **caskets. 1** A casket is a N-COUNT
small box in which you keep valuable things. **2** A N-COUNT
casket is a coffin. AMERICAN
cas·sa·va /kəˈsɑːvə/. **Cassava** is a South American N-UNCOUNT
plant with thick roots. It is grown for food. You can
also refer to the substance that comes from the
roots of this plant as **cassava.**
cas·se·role /'kæsərəʊl/ **casseroles, casserol-** ◆◇◇◇◇
ing, casseroled. 1 A casserole is a dish made of N-COUNT
meat and vegetables that have been cooked slowly
in a liquid. **2** If you **casserole** meat and vegetables, VERB: V n
you cook them slowly in a liquid. **3** A **casserole** or a N-COUNT

casserole dish is a large heavy container with a lid used for cooking casseroles.

cas·sette /kə'set/ **cassettes.** A **cassette** is a small, flat, rectangular plastic container with magnetic tape inside which is used for recording and playing back sounds. ◆◇◇◇ N-COUNT also on N

cas'sette player, cassette players. A **cassette player** is a machine that is used for playing cassettes and sometimes also for recording them. N-COUNT

cas'sette recorder, cassette recorders. A **cassette recorder** is a machine that is used for recording and listening to cassettes. N-COUNT

cas·sock /'kæsək/ **cassocks.** A **cassock** is a long robe, often black, that is worn by some members of the clergy. N-COUNT

cast /kɑːst, kæst/ **casts, casting.** The form **cast** is used in the present tense and is the past tense and past participle. **1** The **cast** of a play or film is all the people who act in it. **2** To **cast** an actor in a play or film means to choose them to act a particular role in it. *He was cast as a college professor.* ◆ **cast·ing** *...the casting of the director's daughter in a central role.* **3** To **cast** someone in a particular way or as a particular thing means to describe them in that way or to suggest that they are that thing. *Democrats have been worried about being cast as the party of the poor.* **4** If you **cast** something somewhere, you throw it there. *He cast the stone away in a disparaging fashion.* **5** When someone **casts** a fishing line or **casts,** they throw one end of the fishing line into the water. **6** If you **cast** your eyes or **cast** a look in a particular direction, you look quickly in that direction. *He cast a stern glance at the two men.* **7** If something **casts** a light or shadow somewhere, it causes it to appear there. *The moon cast a bright light over the yard.* **8** If you **cast** doubt on something, you cause people to be unsure about it. *New tests have cast doubt on the cause of the blast.* **9** When you **cast** your vote in an election, you vote. **10** To **cast** an object means to make it by pouring a liquid such as hot metal into a specially shaped container and leaving it there until it becomes hard. *The stair grips, cast in either brass or bronze, resemble exotic sea shells.* ▶ Also a noun. *He suggested that the museum make casts of the skeletons.* **11** A **cast** is the same as a **plaster cast.** **12** See also **casting.** • to **cast aspersions**: see **aspersions.** • **the die is cast:** see **die.** • to **cast your mind back:** see **mind.** ◆◆◆◇ N-COLL VERB: V n V n in/as n N-UNCOUNT VERB V n as/in n VERB LITERARY VERB: V n, V V n prep/adv WRITTEN VERB V n prep WRITTEN VERB V n on n VERB: V n V-ed in n Also V n in n N-COUNT N-COUNT

cast around for. If you **cast around for** something or **cast about for** it, you try to find it or think of it. *She had been casting around for a good excuse.* PHRASAL VB V P P n

cast aside. If you **cast aside** someone or something, you get rid of them because they are no longer necessary or useful to you. *Sweden needs to cast aside outdated policies and thinking.* PHRASAL VB V P noun Also V n P

cast down. If someone **is cast down** by something, they are sad or worried because of it. PHRASAL VB PASSIVE LITERARY

cast off. 1 If you **cast off** something, you get rid of it because it is no longer necessary, or because it is harmful to you. *The essay exhorts women to cast off their servitude to husbands.* • See also **cast-off. 2** If you are on a boat and you **cast off,** you untie the rope that is keeping the boat in a fixed position. PHRASAL VB V P noun Also V n P LITERARY V P

cast out. To **cast out** something or someone means to get rid of them because you do not like or need them. *One of the roles which science plays is that of casting out superstition.* PHRASAL VB V P noun Also V n P LITERARY

cas·ta·nets /ˌkæstə'nets/. **Castanets** are a Spanish musical instrument consisting of two small round pieces of wood or plastic held together by a cord. See picture headed **musical instruments.** N-PLURAL: also a pair of N

cast·away /'kɑːstəweɪ, 'kæst-/ **castaways.** A **castaway** is a person who has managed to swim or float to a lonely island or shore after their boat has been wrecked. N-COUNT

caste /kɑːst, kæst/ **castes. 1** A **caste** is one of the traditional social classes into which people are divided in a Hindu society. **2 Caste** is the system of ◆◆◇◇ N-COUNT N-UNCOUNT

dividing people in a society into different social classes.

cas·tel·lat·ed /'kæstəleɪtɪd/. A **castellated** wall or building has turrets and battlements like a castle. ADJ TECHNICAL

cast·er /'kɑːstə, 'kæstə/. See **castor.**

'caster sugar; also spelled **castor sugar.** In Britain, **caster sugar** is white sugar that has been very finely ground. ◆◇◇◇ N-UNCOUNT

cas·ti·gate /'kæstɪgeɪt/ **castigates, castigating, castigated.** If you **castigate** someone or something, you scold them or criticize them severely. *She castigated him for having no intellectual interests.* ◆ **cas·ti·ga·tion** /ˌkæstɪ'geɪʃən/. *...Helen's merciless castigation of Michelle.* ◆◇◇◇ VERB: V n V n for n/-ing FORMAL N-UNCOUNT

cast·ing /'kɑːstɪŋ, 'kæst-/ **castings.** A **casting** is an object which has been made by pouring a liquid such as hot metal into a container, so that when it hardens it has the required shape. • See also **cast.** ◆◇◇◇ N-COUNT

,casting 'vote, casting votes. When a committee has given an equal number of votes for and against a proposal, the chairperson can give a **casting vote.** This vote decides whether or not the proposal will be passed. N-COUNT

,cast 'iron. 1 Cast iron is iron which contains a small amount of carbon. It is hard and cannot be bent so it has to be made into objects by casting. **2** A **cast-iron** guarantee or alibi is one that is absolutely certain to be effective. *...cast-iron guarantees to invest in long-term projects.* ◆◇◇◇ N-UNCOUNT ADJ

cas·tle /'kɑːsəl, 'kæsəl/ **castles. 1** A **castle** is a large building with thick high walls. Castles were built by important people, such as kings, in former times, often for protection during wars and battles. • See also **sand castle. 2** In chess, a **castle** is a piece that can be moved forwards, backwards, or sideways. ◆◆◆◇ N-COUNT N-COUNT

'cast-off, cast-offs; also spelled **castoff. Cast-off** things, especially clothes, are ones which you give to someone else or throw away because you no longer use them. *...cast-off clothing.* ▶ Also a noun. *...a cousin's cast-offs.* ◆◇◇◇ ADJ: ADJ n N-COUNT

cas·tor /'kɑːstə, 'kæst-/ **castors;** also spelled **caster. Castors** are small wheels fitted to a piece of furniture so that it can be moved more easily. N-COUNT BRITISH

'castor oil. Castor oil is a thick yellow oil that is obtained from the seeds of the castor oil plant. N-UNCOUNT

'castor sugar. See **caster sugar.**

cas·trate /kæ'streɪt, AM 'kæstreɪt/ **castrates, castrating, castrated.** To **castrate** a male animal means to remove its testicles so that it cannot reproduce. ◆ **cas·tra·tion** /kæ'streɪʃən/ **castrations** *...the castration of male farm animals.* ◆◇◇◇ VERB: V n N-VAR

cas·ual /'kæʒʊəl/. **1** If you are **casual,** you are, or you pretend to be, relaxed and not very concerned about what is happening. *...a young man with a casual sort of attitude towards money.* ◆ **casu·al·ly** *'No need to hurry,' Ben said casually.* ◆ **casu·al·ness** *Baydon asked the question with studied casualness.* **2 Casual** is used to describe things which people do by chance or without planning. *A casual remark could be misinterpreted.* **3 Casual** clothes are ones that you normally wear at home or on holiday, and not on formal occasions. ◆ **casu·al·ly** *They were smartly but casually dressed.* **4 Casual** work is for short periods and not on a permanent or regular basis. *...establishments which employ people on a casual basis.* ◆◆◇◇ ADJ-GRADED ADV-GRADED N-UNCOUNT ADJ: ADJ n ADJ-GRADED: ADJ n ADV-GRADED ADJ: ADJ n

casu·al·ty /'kæʒʊəlti/ **casualties. 1** A **casualty** is a person who is injured or killed in a war or in an accident. *The casualties on our side were frightful.* **2** A **casualty** of an event or situation is someone or something that has suffered badly as a result of it. *Fiat has been one of the greatest casualties of the recession.* **3** In Britain, **casualty** is an informal name for the department of a hospital where people are taken for emergency treatment. The usual American expression is **emergency room.** ◆◆◆◇ N-COUNT N-COUNT N-UNCOUNT

casu·ist·ry /'kæzjuɪstri, AM 'kæʒu-/. **Casuistry** is reasoning that is extremely subtle and designed to mislead other people. N-UNCOUNT FORMAL

cat /kæt/ **cats.** **1** A **cat** is a small furry animal with ♦♦♦◇◇ a tail, whiskers, and sharp claws. Cats are often kept N-COUNT as pets. See picture headed **animals**. **2** **Cats** are a N-COUNT group of animals which includes lions, tigers, and domestic cats. **3** In a fight or contest, if the stronger PHRASE person or group plays **cat and mouse** with the other, they choose to defeat their opponent slowly, using skill and deceit, rather than force or violence. *It's a cat-and-mouse game to him, and I'm the bloody mouse.* **4** If you **let the cat out of the bag**, you tell people PHRASE about something that was being kept secret, often by mistake. **5** See also **Cheshire cat**, **fat cat**, **wildcat**.

cat·a·clysm /'kætəklɪzəm/ **cataclysms.** A **cata-** N-COUNT **clysm** is an event that causes great change or harm. FORMAL ♦ **cata·clys·mic** *Few had expected that change to* ADJ-GRADED *be as cataclysmic as it turned out.*

cat·a·comb /'kætəku:m, AM -kəum/ **catacombs.** N-COUNT **Catacombs** are a series of ancient underground passages and rooms, which used to be used for burial.

cata·logue /'kætəlɒg/ **catalogues, catalogu-** ♦♦◇◇◇ **ing, catalogued;** spelled **catalog** in American English. **1** A **catalogue** is a list of things, such as N-COUNT goods you can buy from a particular company or the objects in a museum. **2** To **catalogue** things VERB: V n means to make a list of them. **3** If you **catalogue** a VERB series of similar events or qualities, especially bad V n ones, you list them. *Speaker after speaker lined up to catalogue a series of failures under his leadership.* ▶ Also a noun. *...a catalogue of nuclear disasters.* N-COUNT: N of n

cata·lyse /'kætəlaɪz/ **catalyses, catalysing, catalysed;** spelled **catalyze** in American English. **1** If something **catalyses** a thing or a situation, it VERB makes it active. *Any unexpected circumstance that* V n *arises may catalyze a sudden escalation of violence.* **2** In science, if something **catalyses** a reaction or VERB: V n event, it makes it happen. TECHNICAL

cata·ly·sis /kə'tæləsɪs/. Catalysis is the speeding N-UNCOUNT up of a chemical reaction by adding a catalyst to it. TECHNICAL

cata·lyst /'kætəlɪst/ **catalysts.** **1** You can de- ♦◇◇◇◇ scribe a person or thing as a **catalyst** when they N-COUNT cause a change or event to happen. *He said he saw the bank's role as a catalyst to encourage foreign direct investment.* **2** A **catalyst** is a substance that N-COUNT causes a chemical reaction to take place more quickly.

cata·lyt·ic /,kætə'lɪtɪk/. **1** A **catalytic** substance is ♦◇◇◇◇ one which increases the speed of a chemical reac- ADJ: ADJ n tion. **2** If you describe a person or thing as having a TECHNICAL **catalytic** effect, you mean that they cause things to ADJ-GRADED happen or they increase the speed at which things happen. *Governments do, however, have a vital catalytic role in orchestrating rescue operations.*

catalytic con·vert·er, catalytic converters. A N-COUNT **catalytic converter** is a device which is fitted to a car's exhaust to reduce the amount of pollutants coming from the exhaust.

cata·ma·ran /,kætəmə'ræn/ **catamarans.** A cata- N-COUNT **maran** is a sailing boat with two parallel hulls that are held in place by a single deck.

cata·pult /'kætəpʌlt/ **catapults, catapulting,** ♦◇◇◇◇ **catapulted.** **1** A **catapult** is a device for shooting N-COUNT small stones. It consists of a Y-shaped stick with a BRITISH piece of elastic tied between the two top parts. The usual American word is **slingshot**. **2** A **catapult** is a N-COUNT device that is used to launch aircraft from an aircraft carrier. **3** If someone or something **catapults** V-ERG or **is catapulted** through the air, they move or are V prep thrown very suddenly and violently through it. *The* be V-ed *car catapulted out of the pits... He was catapulted* prep/adv *into the side of the van.* **4** If something **catapults** Also V n you into a new state or situation, you are suddenly prep/adv and unexpectedly caused to be in that state or that VERB situation. *It was 'Psycho' that catapulted him to* V n prep/adv *stardom.*

cata·ract /'kætərækt/ **cataracts.** **1** Cataracts are ♦◇◇◇◇ layers which develop over a person's eyes that pre- N-COUNT vent them from seeing properly. **2** A **cataract** is a N-COUNT large waterfall. LITERARY

ca·tarrh /kə'tɑ:/. **Catarrh** is a medical condition in N-UNCOUNT which a lot of mucus is produced in your nose and throat.

ca·tas·tro·phe /kə'tæstrəfi/ **catastrophes.** A ca- ♦♦◇◇◇ **tastrophe** is an unexpected event that causes great N-COUNT suffering or damage. *From all points of view, war would be a catastrophe.*

cata·stroph·ic /,kætə'strɒfɪk/. **1** Something that ♦◇◇◇◇ is **catastrophic** involves or causes a sudden terrible ADJ-GRADED disaster. *The church suffered catastrophic damage by bombing.* ♦ **cata·stroph·i·cal·ly** /,kætə'strɒfɪkli/. ADV-GRADED *The faulty left-hand engine failed catastrophically.* **2** If you describe something as **catastrophic**, you ADJ-GRADED mean that it is very bad or very unsuccessful. *His mother's untimely death had a catastrophic effect on him.* ♦ **catastrophically** *Prices had fallen* ADV-GRADED *catastrophically.*

cata·ton·ic /,kætə'tɒnɪk/. If you describe someone ADJ-GRADED as being in a **catatonic** state, you mean that they are not moving or responding at all, usually as a result of illness or drug abuse.

cat·call /'kætkɔ:l/ **catcalls.** Catcalls are loud N-COUNT noises that people make to show that they disapprove of something that they are watching or listening to. *My speeches were accompanied by catcalls.*

catch /kætʃ/ **catches, catching, caught.** **1** If ♦♦♦♦◇ you **catch** a person or animal, you capture them af- VERB ter pursuing them, or by using a trap or net. *Police* V n say they are confident of catching the gunman. *...an* V-ed *animal caught in a trap.* **2** When people have been N-COUNT fishing, their **catch** is the total number of fish that they have caught. **3** If you **catch** an object that is moving through the air, VERB: V n you seize it with your hands. ▶ Also a noun. *He missed* N-COUNT *the catch and the match was lost.* **4** If you **catch** a part VERB of someone's body, you take or seize it with your V n hand, often in order to stop them going somewhere. V n prep *Liz caught his arm... Garrido caught her by the wrist.* **5** If the wind or water **catches** something, it carries or VERB: V n pushes it along. **6** If something which is moving **catches** something VERB else, it hits it. *The stinging slap almost caught his* V n *face... He caught her on the side of her head with his* V n on n *other fist.* **7** If something **catches** on or in an object or V-ERG **is caught** on or in it, it accidentally becomes attached V prep to the object or becomes trapped. *Her heel caught on* V n prep *a rusty bedspring... A man caught his foot in the lawnmower.* **8** When you **catch** a bus, train, or plane, you get on it VERB: V n in order to travel somewhere. **9** If you **catch** someone doing something wrong, you VERB see or find them doing it. *He caught a youth breaking* V n -ing *into a car... They caught him with $30,000 cash in a* V n prep *briefcase.* **10** If you **catch** yourself doing something, VERB you suddenly become aware that you are doing it. *I* V pron-refl *caught myself feeling almost sorry for poor Mr* -ing *Laurence.* **11** You can say things such as '**You** PHRASE **wouldn't catch me doing that**' to emphasize that you PRAGMATICS would never do something. **12** If someone **is caught** INFORMAL **with their trousers down** or **caught with their pants** PHRASE **down**, something happens that they are unprepared for and that reveals something embarrassing or shocking about them, for example that they are having an affair. **13** If you **are caught** in a storm or other unpleasant V-PASSIVE situation, it happens when you cannot avoid its ef- be/get V-ed fects. *Visitors to the area were caught between police* prep *and the rioters.* **14** If you **are caught between** two al- V-PASSIVE ternatives or two people, you do not know which one be V-ed to choose or follow. *She was caught between envy and* between pl-n *admiration.* **15** If you **catch** something or **catch** a glimpse of it, you VERB notice it or manage to see it briefly. *He caught a* V n *glimpse of the man's face in a shop window.* **16** If V n something **catches** your attention or your eye, you VERB notice it or become interested in it. *A quick movement* V n. *across the aisle caught his eye.* **17** If you **catch** some- VERB thing that someone says, you manage to hear it. *I do* V n *not believe I caught your name... The men out in the* V wh *corridor were trying to catch what they said.* **18** If you VERB

catch a TV or radio programme or an event, you manage to see it or listen to it. *Bill turns on the radio to catch the local news.* **19** If you **catch** someone, you manage to contact or meet them, especially when they are just about to go somewhere else. *I dialled Elizabeth's number thinking I might catch her before she left for work.*

20 If something or someone **catches** you by surprise or at a bad time, you were not expecting them or do not feel ready or able to deal with them. *She looked as if the photographer had caught her by surprise.*

21 If someone or something **catches** a mood or an atmosphere, they successfully represent it or reflect it. *There's no doubt Mr Yeltsin's speech caught the mood of most deputies.*

22 If you **catch** a cold or a disease, you become ill with it. **23** See also **catching**.

24 To **catch** liquids or small pieces that fall from somewhere means to collect them in a container. *...a specially designed breadboard with a tray to catch the crumbs.*

25 If something **catches** the light or if the light **catches** it, it reflects the light and looks bright or shiny. *They saw the ship's guns, catching the light of the moon.*

26 A **catch** on a window, door, or container is a device that fastens it.

27 A **catch** is a hidden problem or difficulty in a plan or in an offer that seems surprisingly good. *'It's your money. You deserve it.'—'What's the catch?'*

28 If you describe someone as a good **catch**, you mean that they have lots of good qualities and you think their partner or employer is very lucky to have found them. *All my friends said what a good catch he was.*

29 ● to **catch your breath**: see **breath**. ● to **catch fire**: see **fire**. ● to **catch hold of something**: see **hold**. ● to **be caught between a rock and a hard place**: see **rock**. ● to **catch sight of** someone or something: see **sight**.

catch on. 1 When you **catch on** to something, you understand it, or realize that it is happening. *He got what he could out of me before I caught on to the kind of person he'd turned into.* **2** If something **catches on**, it becomes popular. *The idea has been around for ages without catching on.*

catch out. To **catch** someone **out** means to cause them to make a mistake that reveals that they are lying about something. *Detectives followed him for months hoping to catch him out in some deception.*

catch up. 1 If you **catch up** with someone who is in front of you, you reach them by walking faster than they are walking. *I stopped and waited for her to catch up..* **2** To **catch up** with someone means to reach the same standard, stage, or level that they have reached. *During the evenings, the school is used by kids who want to catch up on English and mathematics.* **3** If you **catch up** on an activity that you have not had much time to do, you spend time doing it. *I was catching up on a bit of reading.* **4** If you **catch up** on friends who you have not seen for some time, you talk to them and find out what has happened in their lives since you last talked together. *The ladies spent some time catching up on each other's health and families.*

5 If you are **caught up** in something, you are involved in it, usually unwillingly. *The people themselves weren't part of the conflict; they were just caught up in it.*

catch up with. 1 When people **catch up with** someone who has done something wrong, they succeed in finding them in order to arrest or punish them. *The law caught up with him yesterday.* **2** If something **catches up with** you, you are forced to deal with something unpleasant that happened in the past, which you have been able to avoid until now. *His criminal past caught up with him.*

Catch 22 /ˌkætʃ twentiˈtuː/. If you describe something as a **Catch 22** or a **Catch 22** situation, you mean it is an impossible situation because you cannot do one thing until you do another thing, but you cannot do the second thing until you do the

first thing. *It's a Catch 22 situation here. Nobody wants to support you until you're successful, but without the support how can you ever be successful?*

'catch-all, catch-alls. A **catch-all** is a term or category which includes many different things. *Cancer is a catch-all name for a series of different diseases.*

catch·er /ˈkætʃə/ **catchers. 1** In baseball, the **catcher** is the player who stands behind the batter. The catcher has a special glove for catching the ball. **2** You can refer to someone who catches something as a **catcher**. *...the catcher of the largest fish.*

catch·ing /ˈkætʃɪŋ/. **1** If an illness or a disease is **catching**, it is easily passed on or given to someone else. *There are those who think eczema is catching.* **2** If a feeling or emotion is **catching**, it has a strong influence on other people and spreads quickly. *Enthusiasm is very catching.*

catch·ment /ˈkætʃmənt/ **catchments.** The **catchment** of a river is the area of land from which water flows into the river.

'catchment area, catchment areas. The **catchment area** of a school, hospital, or other service is the area that it serves.

'catch-phrase, catch-phrases; also spelled **catch phrase.** A **catch-phrase** is a sentence or phrase which becomes popular or well-known, often because it is frequently used by a famous person. *Mr Bresslaw, whose catch phrase was 'I only asked', died in hospital last night.*

catchy /ˈkætʃi/ **catchier, catchiest.** If you describe a tune, name, or phrase as **catchy**, you mean that it is attractive and easy to remember. *The songs were both catchy and cutting.*

cat·echism /ˈkætɪkɪzəm/ **catechisms.** In some Christian churches, the **catechism** is a series of questions and answers about religious beliefs, which has to be studied by people before they can become full members of their Church.

cat·egori·cal /ˌkætɪˈɡɒrɪkəl, AM -ˈɡɔːr-/. If you are **categorical** about something, you state your views with certainty and firmness. *...his categorical denial of the charges of sexual harassment.* ♦ **cat·egori·cal·ly** /ˌkætɪˈɡɒrɪkli, AM -ˈɡɔːr-/ *He stated categorically that this would be his last season in Formula One.*

cat·ego·rize /ˈkætɪɡəraɪz/ **categorizes, categorizing, categorized;** also spelled **categorise** in British English. If you **categorize** people or things, you divide them into sets or you say which set they belong to. *Make a list of your child's toys and then categorise them as sociable or antisocial.* ♦ **cat·ego·ri·za·tion** /ˌkætɪɡəraɪˈzeɪʃən/ **categorizations** *Her first novel, defies easy categorisation.*

cat·ego·ry /ˈkætɪɡri, AM -ɡɔːri/ **categories.** If people or things are divided into **categories**, they are divided into groups in such a way that the members of each group are similar to each other in some way. *This book clearly falls into the category of fictionalised autobiography.*

ca·ter /ˈkeɪtə/ **caters, catering, catered. 1** To **cater for** a group of people means to provide all the things that they need or want. In American English, you **cater to** a person or group of people. *We cater to an exclusive clientele.* **2** To **cater for** something means to take it into account. In American English, you **cater to** something. *Exercise classes cater to all levels of fitness.* **3** If a person or company **caters** for an occasion such as a wedding or a party, they provide food and drink for all the people there. *The chef is pleased to cater for vegetarian diets... Does he cater parties too?* ♦ **ca·ter·er** /ˈkeɪtərə/ **caterers** *The caterers were already laying out the tables for lunch.* ♦ **ca·ter·ing** *He recently did the catering for a presidential reception.* ● See also **self-catering**.

cat·er·pil·lar /ˈkætəpɪlə/ **caterpillars.** A **caterpillar** is a small, worm-like creature that feeds on plants and eventually develops into a butterfly or moth.

cat·fish /'kætfɪʃ/; catfish is both the singular and plural form. Catfish are fish with long thin spines that look like whiskers around their mouths. N-VAR

ca·thar·sis /kə'θɑːsɪs/. Catharsis is the getting rid of unhappy memories or strong emotions such as anger or sadness by expressing them in some way. *He wrote out his rage and bewilderment, which gradually became a form of catharsis leading to understanding.* N-UNCOUNT FORMAL

ca·thar·tic /kə'θɑːtɪk/. Something that is cathartic has the effect of catharsis. ...*a cathartic experience.* ADJ-GRADED FORMAL

ca·thedral /kə'θiːdrəl/ cathedrals. A cathedral is a very large and important church which has a bishop in charge of it. ...*St. Paul's Cathedral.* N-COUNT

cath·eter /'kæθɪtə/ catheters. A catheter is a tube which is used in medicine to introduce liquids into a human body or to withdraw liquids from it. N-COUNT

cath·ode /'kæθəʊd/ cathodes. A cathode is the negative electrode in a cell such as a battery. ● See also anode. N-COUNT

'cathode-ray tube, cathode-ray tubes. A cathode-ray tube is a device used in televisions and computer terminals. It sends an image onto the screen. N-COUNT

Catho·lic /'kæθlɪk/ Catholics. 1 The Catholic Church is the branch of the Christian Church that accepts the Pope as its leader and that is based in the Vatican in Rome. ...*Catholic priests.* ...*the Catholic faith.* 2 A Catholic is a member of the Catholic Church. ADJ N-COUNT

3 If you describe a collection of things or people as **catholic**, you are emphasizing that they are very varied. *He was a man of catholic tastes, a lover of grand opera, history and the fine arts.* ADJ-GRADED PRAGMATICS

Ca·tholi·cism /kə'θɒlɪsɪzəm/. Catholicism is the beliefs, traditions, and religious practices of Catholics. ...*her conversion to Catholicism.* N-UNCOUNT

cat·suit /'kætsuːt/ catsuits. A catsuit is a piece of women's clothing that is made in one piece and fits tightly over the body and legs. N-COUNT BRITISH

cat·tery /'kætəri/ catteries. A cattery is a place where you leave your cat when you go on holiday. N-COUNT BRITISH

cat·tle /'kætəl/. Cattle are cows and bulls. ...*the finest herd of beef cattle for two hundred miles.* N-PLURAL

cattle·man /'kætəlmæn/ cattlemen. A cattleman is a man who looks after or owns cattle, especially in North America or Australia. N-COUNT

'cattle market, cattle markets. 1 A cattle market is a market where live cattle are bought and sold. 2 If you refer to an event such as a disco or a beauty contest as a cattle market, you disapprove of the event because it involves women being considered only in terms of their sexual attractiveness or availability. N-COUNT / N-COUNT PRAGMATICS BRITISH

'cattle prod, cattle prods. A cattle prod is an object shaped like a long stick. Farmers make cattle move in a particular direction by pushing the cattle prod against the bodies of the animals. N-COUNT

cat·ty /'kæti/ cattier, cattiest. If you say that someone, especially a woman or girl, is being catty, you mean that they are being unpleasant and spiteful. ...*catty remarks.* ADJ-GRADED INFORMAL

cat·walk /'kætwɔːk/ catwalks. 1 At a fashion show, the catwalk is a narrow platform that models walk along to display clothes. 2 A catwalk is a narrow bridge high in the air between two parts of a tall building or on the outside of a large structure. N-COUNT / N-COUNT

Cau·ca·sian /kɔː'keɪʒən/ Caucasians. 1 A Caucasian person is a white person. ...*a 25-year-old Caucasian male.* ► A Caucasian is someone who is Caucasian. 2 Anthropologists use Caucasian to refer to someone from a racial grouping coming from Europe, North Africa and western Asia. ...*blue eyes and Caucasian features.* ► A Caucasian is someone who is Caucasian. ADJ FORMAL / N-COUNT / ADJ TECHNICAL / N-COUNT

cau·cus /'kɔːkəs/ caucuses. A caucus is a group of people within an organization who share similar aims and interests or who have a lot of influence. ...*the Black Caucus of minority congressmen.* N-COUNT FORMAL

caught /kɔːt/. Caught is the past tense and past participle of catch. N-VAR

caul·dron /'kɔːldrən/ cauldrons; also spelled caldron. 1 A cauldron is a very large, round metal pot used for cooking over a fire. 2 If you describe a situation as a cauldron, you mean that it is unstable or dangerous. *Azerbaijan is a cauldron of ethnic unrest.* N-COUNT LITERARY / N-COUNT JOURNALISM

cau·li·flow·er /'kɒliflaʊə, AM 'kɔː-/ cauliflowers. Cauliflower is a hard roundish white vegetable that is surrounded by green leaves. See picture headed vegetables. N-VAR

caus·al /'kɔːzəl/. If there is a causal relationship between two things, one thing is responsible for causing the other thing. *It is impossible to prove a causal link between the drug and the deaths.* ADJ FORMAL

cau·sal·ity /kɔː'zælɪti/. Causality is the relationship of cause and effect. *An explanation of an earthquake is a description of the chain of causality that produces it.* N-UNCOUNT FORMAL

cau·sa·tion /kɔː'zeɪʃən/. 1 The causation of something, usually something bad, is the factors that have caused it. *Therefore it is clear that the gene is only part of the causation of illness.* 2 Causation is a study of the factors involved in causing something. N-UNCOUNT FORMAL / N-UNCOUNT FORMAL

causa·tive /'kɔːzətɪv/. Causative factors are ones which are responsible for causing something. ...*the prime causative agent of AIDS.* ADJ: ADJ n FORMAL

cause /kɔːz/ causes, causing, caused. 1 The cause of an event is the thing that makes it happen. *Smoking is the biggest preventable cause of death and disease.* 2 To cause something means to make it happen. *This was a genuine mistake, but it did cause me some worry... It attacks other proteins, causing disease to spread. ...the damage to Romanian democracy caused by events of the past few days.* 3 If you have cause for a particular feeling or action, you have good reasons for feeling it or doing it. *Both had much cause to be grateful for the secretiveness of government in Britain.* N-COUNT / VERB: V n, V n n, V n to-inf, V-ed / N-UNCOUNT: N for n, N to-inf

4 A cause is an aim or principle which a group of people supports or is fighting for. *Refusing to have one leader has not helped the cause either.* ● See also lost cause. 5 If one group of people makes common cause with another, they act together in order to achieve a particular aim, even though their aims and beliefs are normally very different. 6 If you say that something is in a good cause or for a good cause, you mean that it is worth doing or contributing to because it will help other people, for example by raising money for charity. N-COUNT / PHRASE / PHRASE

cause cé·lè·bre /,kəʊz seɪ'lebrə/ causes célèbres; also spelled cause celebre. A cause célèbre is a controversial issue, person, or criminal trial that has attracted a lot of public attention. *The Kravchenko trial became a cause celebre.* N-COUNT FORMAL

cause·way /'kɔːzweɪ/ causeways. A causeway is a raised path or road that crosses water or marshes. N-COUNT

caus·tic /'kɔːstɪk/. 1 Caustic chemical substances are very powerful and can dissolve other substances. 2 A caustic remark is extremely critical, cruel, or bitter. *He was often caustic and mocking.* ♦ **caus·ti·cal·ly** /'kɔːstɪkli/ *His new book is caustically about western history and culture.* ADJ-GRADED / ADJ-GRADED / ADV-GRADED

cau·tion /'kɔːʃən/ cautions, cautioning, cautioned. 1 Caution is great care which you take in order to avoid possible danger. *Extreme caution should be exercised when buying part-worn tyres.* ● to err on the side of caution: see err. ● If you throw caution to the wind, you do something without worrying about the risks and dangers involved. 2 If someone cautions you about something, they warn you about problems or danger connected with it. *Tony cautioned against misrepresenting the situation... He cautioned that opposition attacks on the Communist Party would not further political cooperation.* ► Also a noun. *There was a note of caution for the Treasury in the figures.* 3 If someone who has broken the law is cautioned by the police, they are warned that if they break the law again N-UNCOUNT / PHRASE / VERB: V n against/about n/-ing, V against n/-ing, V that, Also V n that / N-COUNT / VERB: be V-ed BRITISH

official action will be taken against them. ▶ Also a N-COUNT
noun. *Paula escaped with a caution.* **4** If someone VERB:
who has been arrested **is cautioned**, the police *be* V-*ed*
warn them that anything that they say may be used
as evidence in a trial.

cau·tion·ary /ˈkɔːʃənri, AM -neri/. A **cautionary** ◆◇◇◇◇
story is one that is intended to give a warning to ADJ-GRADED
people. *...a cautionary tale of the pitfalls of international mergers.*

cau·tious /ˈkɔːʃəs/. **1** Someone who is **cautious** ◆◆◆◇◇
acts very carefully in order to avoid possible danger. ADJ-GRADED
*The scientists are cautious about using enzyme
therapy on humans.* ♦ **cau·tious·ly** *David moved* ADV-GRADED
cautiously forward and looked over the edge. **2** If ADJ-GRADED
you describe someone's attitude or reaction as **cautious**, you mean that it is limited or careful. *...a
more cautious approach to economic reform.*
♦ **cautiously** *Rebel sources have so far reacted cau-* ADV-GRADED
tiously to the threat.

cav·al·cade /ˌkævəlˈkeɪd/ **cavalcades.** A **caval-** N-COUNT
cade is a procession of people on horses or in
vehicles.

cava·lier /ˌkævəˈlɪə/. If you describe a person or ADJ-GRADED
their behaviour as **cavalier**, you disapprove of them PRAGMATICS
because you think that they do not consider other
people's feelings or take account of the seriousness
of a situation. *The Editor takes a cavalier attitude to
the concept of fact checking.*

cav·al·ry /ˈkævəlri/. **1** The **cavalry** is the part of an ◆◆◇◇◇
army that uses fast armoured vehicles for fighting. N-SING
2 In the past, the **cavalry** was the group of soldiers N-SING
in an army who rode horses.

cav·al·ry·man /ˈkævəlrimæn/ **cavalrymen.** In the N-COUNT
past, a **cavalryman** was a soldier who was in the
cavalry and rode a horse.

cave /keɪv/ **caves, caving, caved.** A **cave** is a ◆◆◇◇◇
large hole in the side of a cliff or hill, or one that is N-COUNT
under the ground.

cave in. 1 If something such as a roof or a ceiling PHRASAL VB
caves in, it collapses inwards. *Part of the roof has* VP
caved in. ● See also **cave-in. 2** If you **cave in**, you sud- VP
denly stop arguing or resisting something as a result VP *ton*
of pressure from other people. *The Prime Minister has* VP *on* n
*caved in to backbench pressure... He's caved in on capi-
tal punishment.*

ca·veat /ˈkæviæt, AM ˈkeɪv-/ **caveats.** A **caveat** is a N-COUNT
warning of a specific limitation on something such FORMAL
an agreement. *There was one caveat: he was not to
enter into a merger.*

ca·veat emp·tor /ˌkæviæt ˈemptɔː, AM ˌkeɪv-/. **Ca-** CONVENTION
veat emptor means 'buyer beware', and is a warn- PRAGMATICS
ing for someone buying something that it is their FORMAL
responsibility to identify any faults in it. *If you buy
at auction it is caveat emptor.*

ˈcave-in, cave-ins. A **cave-in** is the sudden col- ◆◇◇◇◇
lapse of the roof of a cave or mine.

cave·man /ˈkeɪvmæn/ **cavemen. Cavemen** were N-COUNT
people in prehistoric times who lived mainly in
caves.

cav·er /ˈkeɪvə/ **cavers.** A **caver** is someone who N-COUNT
explores caves as a pastime.

cav·ern /ˈkævən/ **caverns. 1** A **cavern** is a large ◆◇◇◇◇
deep cave. **2** If you describe the inside of a building N-COUNT
or a room as a **cavern**, you mean that it is very large N-COUNT
and, usually, dark or without much furniture.

cav·ern·ous /ˈkævənəs/. A **cavernous** room or ◆◇◇◇◇
building is so large inside that it reminds you of a ADJ-GRADED
cave.

cavi·ar /ˈkæviɑː/ **caviars;** also spelled **caviare.** ◆◇◇◇◇
Caviar is the salted eggs of a fish called a sturgeon. N-VAR
Caviar is very expensive, luxury food.

cav·il /ˈkævəl/ **cavils, cavilling, cavilled;** spelled VERB:
caviling, caviled in American English. If someone V *atn*
cavils at something, they object to it. *Since the gov-* V
ernment has insisted that cash will be shifted into FORMAL
this area, the opposition can hardly cavil. ▶ Also a N-COUNT
noun. *These cavils aside, most of the essays are very
good indeed.*

cav·ity /ˈkæviti/ **cavities. 1** A **cavity** is a space or ◆◇◇◇◇
hole in something such as a solid object or a per- N-COUNT
FORMAL

son's body. **2** In dentistry, a **cavity** is a hole in a N-COUNT
tooth, caused by decay.

ˌcavity ˈwall, cavity walls. A **cavity wall** is a wall N-COUNT
that consists of two separate walls with a space between them.

ca·vort /kəˈvɔːt/ **cavorts, cavorting, cavorted.** VERB
1 When people **cavort**, they leap about in an excit- V
ed way. *You can enjoy a quick snack while your children cavort in the sand.* **2** When people **cavort**, they VERB
take part in light-hearted sexual activities. *It was* V *with* n
claimed she cavorted with a police sergeant in a JOURNALISM
jacuzzi.*

cay·enne pep·per /kaɪˌen ˈpepə/. **Cayenne pepper** N-UNCOUNT
or **cayenne** is a very hot-tasting red powder made
from dried chillies. It is used to flavour and add colour to food.

CB /ˌsiː ˈbiː/. **CB**, an abbreviation for 'Citizens' N-UNCOUNT
Band', is a range of radio waves which the general
public is allowed to use to transmit messages.

cc /ˌsiː ˈsiː/. **1 cc** is an abbreviation for 'cubic centimetres'. You use 'cc' when referring to the volume
or capacity of something such as the size of a car
engine. *...1,500 cc sports cars.* **2 cc** is used at the
end of a business letter to indicate that a copy is being sent to another person. *...cc J. Chater, S. Cooper.*

CD /ˌsiː ˈdiː/ **CDs. CD** is an abbreviation for 'com- ◆◆◆◇◇
pact disc'. CDs are small shiny discs on which N-COUNT
sound, especially music, is recorded.

ˈCD player, CD players. A **CD player** is a ma- ◆◇◇◇◇
chine on which you can play the music or other N-COUNT
sounds recorded on a CD.

Cdr. Cdr is the written abbreviation for 'Command- N-TITLE
er' when it is used as a title. *...Cdr A.C. Moore.* BRITISH

CD-ROM /ˌsiː diː ˈrɒm/ **CD-ROMs.** A **CD-ROM** is a ◆◇◇◇◇
shiny disc which can be read by a computer, and on N-COUNT
which a very large amount of data, such as text, images, and sound, is stored. CD-ROM is an abbreviation for 'compact disc read-only memory'. *The collected Austen novels on CD-ROM will cost £35.*

CD-ROM drive /ˌsiː diː ˈrɒm draɪv/ **CD-ROM** N-COUNT
drives. A **CD-ROM drive** is the machine, or part of
the machine, that you use with a computer to access CD-ROMs.

cease /siːs/ **ceases, ceasing, ceased. 1** If ◆◆◆◇◇
something **ceases**, it stops happening or existing. *At* VERB: V
one o'clock the rain had ceased.* **2** If someone or FORMAL
something **ceases** to do something, they stop doing VERB:
it. *A small number of firms have ceased trading...* V to-inf
The London Evening News ceased publication. V n
FORMAL

cease·fire /ˈsiːsfaɪə/ **ceasefires;** also spelled ◆◆◇◇◇
cease-fire. A **ceasefire** is an arrangement in which N-COUNT
countries or groups of people that are fighting each
other agree to stop fighting. *The fragile ceasefire appears to be holding.*

cease·less /ˈsiːsləs/. If you describe something, es- ADJ-GRADED
pecially something unpleasant, as **ceaseless**, you FORMAL
mean that it continues for a long time without stopping or changing. *There is a ceaseless struggle from
noon to night.* ♦ **cease·less·ly** *They complain* ADV
ceaselessly about food queues.

ce·dar /ˈsiːdə/ **cedars.** A **cedar** is a large evergreen ◆◇◇◇◇
tree with wide branches and small leaves shaped N-COUNT
like needles. ▶ **Cedar** is the wood of this tree. N-UNCOUNT

cede /siːd/ **cedes, ceding, ceded.** If someone in ◆◇◇◇◇
a position of authority **cedes** land or power to VERB:
someone else, they let them have it, often as a result V n ton
of military or political pressure. *The General had* V n
promised to cede power by January. FORMAL

cei·lidh /ˈkeɪli/ **ceilidhs.** A **ceilidh** is an informal N-COUNT
entertainment, especially in Scotland or Ireland, at
which there is folk music, singing, and dancing.

ceil·ing /ˈsiːlɪŋ/ **ceilings. 1** A **ceiling** is the hori- ◆◆◇◇◇
zontal surface that forms the top part or roof inside N-COUNT
a room. *The study was lined from floor to ceiling
with bookcases.* **2** A **ceiling** on something such as N-COUNT
prices or wages is an official upper limit that cannot
be exceeded. *The agreement sets the ceiling of 22.5
million barrels a day on OPEC production.*

ce·leb /sɪˈleb/ **celebs.** A **celeb** is the same as a **ce-** N-COUNT
lebrity. *In fact, celeb-spotters were rather thicker on* INFORMAL,
the ground than celebs. JOURNALISM

cel·ebrant /ˈselɪbrənt/ **celebrants.** A **celebrant** is N-COUNT
a person who performs or takes part in a religious FORMAL
ceremony.

cel·ebrate /ˈselɪbreɪt/ **celebrates, celebrating,** ◆◆◇◇◇
celebrated. 1 If you **celebrate** something, you do VERB
something enjoyable because of a special occasion V
or to honour someone's success. *I was in a mood to* V n
celebrate... The England football team have been cel-
ebrating their victory. **2** If a person or organization VERB
celebrates a birthday or anniversary, they reach it. V n
Tom celebrated his 24th birthday two days ago... The
Forth Rail Bridge celebrates its centenary today.
3 When priests **celebrate** Holy Communion or VERB: V n
Mass, they officially perform the actions and ceremonies that are involved in it.

cel·ebrat·ed /ˈselɪbreɪtɪd/. A **celebrated** person or ◆◆◇◇◇
thing is famous and much admired. *...Rebel Without* ADJ-GRADED
Cause, his most celebrated film.

cel·ebra·tion /ˌselɪˈbreɪʃən/ **celebrations. 1** A ◆◆◆◇◇
celebration is a special enjoyable event that people N-COUNT
organize because something pleasant has happened
or because it is someone's birthday or anniversary.
...his eightieth birthday celebrations. **2** If you de- N-SING
scribe an event or piece of writing as a **celebration**
of a particular thing, you mean it expresses praise
and appreciation of that thing. *He sees the poem as*
a celebration of human love.

cel·ebra·tory /ˌselɪˈbreɪtəri, AM ˈselɪbrətɔːri/. A ADJ
celebratory meal or other activity takes place to celebrate something such as a victory or birthday. *That*
night she, Nicholson and the crew had a celebratory
dinner.

ce·leb·rity /sɪˈlebrɪti/ **celebrities. 1** A **celebrity** is ◆◆◇◇◇
someone who is famous, especially in areas of en- N-COUNT
tertainment such as films, music, or sport. *At the*
age of 30, Hersey suddenly became a celebrity. **2** Ce- N-UNCOUNT
lebrity means the same as **fame.** *Nobody reading*
this book could fail to identify the reason for her
celebrity.

cel·ery /ˈseləri/. **Celery** is a vegetable with long ◆◇◇◇◇
pale green stalks. It is eaten raw in salads. See pic- N-UNCOUNT
ture headed **vegetables.**

ce·les·tial /sɪˈlestiəl/. **Celestial** is used to describe ◆◇◇◇◇
things relating to heaven or to the sky. *...celestial* ADJ
bodies. LITERARY

celi·bate /ˈselɪbət/ **celibates. 1** Someone who is ADJ
celibate does not marry or have sex, because of
their religious beliefs. ▶ A **celibate** is someone who N-COUNT
is celibate. **♦ celi·ba·cy** /ˈselɪbəsi/. *...a monk who* N-UNCOUNT
took the vow of celibacy. **2** Someone who is **celibate** ADJ
does not have sex during a particular period of their
life. **♦ celibacy** *She went through an extended peri-* N-UNCOUNT
od of celibacy when she was 29.

cell /sel/ **cells. 1** A **cell** is the smallest part of an ◆◆◆◇◇
animal or plant that is able to function indepen- N-COUNT
dently. Every animal and plant is made up of mil-
lions of cells. **2** A **cell** is a small room in which a N-COUNT
prisoner is locked. A **cell** is also a small room in
which a monk or nun lives. **3** A **cell** is a small group N-COUNT
of people specially trained to work together as part
of a larger organization. *...Communist Party cells.*

cel·lar /ˈselə/ **cellars. 1** A **cellar** is a room under- ◆◆◇◇◇
neath a building, which is often used for storing N-COUNT
things. **2** A person's or restaurant's **cellar** is their N-COUNT
collection of different wines.

cel·lo /ˈtʃeləʊ/ **cellos.** A **cello** is a large musical ◆◇◇◇◇
instrument in the violin family. You play it while N-VAR
sitting down and holding the instrument upright
between your legs. See picture headed **musical in-**
struments. ♦ cel·list /ˈtʃelɪst/ **cellists.** A **cellist** is N-COUNT
someone who plays the cello.

cel·lo·phane /ˈseləfeɪn/. **Cellophane** is a thin N-UNCOUNT
transparent material that is used to wrap things
such as cigarette packets or boxes of chocolates.

cell·phone /ˈselfəʊn/ **cellphones;** also spelled N-COUNT
cell-phone. A **cellphone** is the same as a **cellular** INFORMAL
phone.

cel·lu·lar /ˈseljʊlə/. **Cellular** means relating to ani- ◆◇◇◇◇
mal or plant cells. *The residues interfere with cellu-* ADJ
lar activity.

cellular 'phone, cellular phones. A **cellular** N-COUNT
phone or **cellular telephone** is a type of telephone
which does not need wires to connect it to a telephone system.

cel·lu·lite /ˈseljʊlaɪt/. **Cellulite** is lumpy fat which ◆◇◇◇◇
people may get under their skin, especially on their N-UNCOUNT
thighs.

cel·lu·loid /ˈseljʊlɔɪd/. **Celluloid** is sometimes used N-UNCOUNT
to refer to films and the cinema. *King's works seem*
to lack something on celluloid.

cel·lu·lose /ˈseljʊləʊs/. **Cellulose** is a substance N-UNCOUNT
that exists in the cell walls of plants. It is used to
make paper, plastic, and various textiles and fibres.

Celsius /ˈselsiəs/. **Celsius** is a scale for measuring ◆◇◇◇◇
temperature, in which water freezes at 0 degrees ADJ:
and boils at 100 degrees. It is represented by the n/num ADJ
symbol °C. *Highest temperatures 11° Celsius, that's*
52° Fahrenheit. ▶ Also a noun. *The thermometer* N-UNCOUNT
shows the temperature in Celsius.

Celt /kelt, selt/ **Celts.** If you describe someone as a ◆◇◇◇◇
Celt, you mean that they are part of the racial group N-COUNT
which comes from Scotland, Wales, Ireland, and
some other areas such as Brittany. **♦ Celt·ic** /-/ *im-* ADJ
portant figures in Celtic tradition.

ce·ment /sɪˈment/ **cements, cementing, ce-** ◆◆◇◇◇
mented. 1 **Cement** is a grey powder which is N-UNCOUNT
mixed with sand and water in order to make con-
crete. **2** **Cement** is the same as **concrete.** *...the hard* N-UNCOUNT
cold cement floor. **3** Some types of glue are called N-UNCOUNT
cement. *Stick the pieces on with tile cement.* **4** If VERB:
things **are cemented** together, they are stuck or fas- be V-ed
tened together using a type of cement. **5** Something prep/adv
that **cements** a relationship or agreement makes it VERB
stronger. *Nothing cements a friendship between* V n
countries so much as trade. **6** Anything which makes N-UNCOUNT
a relationship or agreement stronger and more
long-lasting can be referred to as a **cement.** *In the*
old days, television was the cement of society.

cem·etery /ˈsemətri, AM -teri/ **cemeteries.** A ◆◆◇◇◇
cemetery is a place where dead people's bodies or N-COUNT
their ashes are buried.

ceno·taph /ˈsenətɑːf, -tæf/ **cenotaphs.** A **ceno-** N-COUNT
taph is a monument that is built in honour of soldiers who died in a war.

cen·sor /ˈsensə/ **censors, censoring, cen-** ◆◇◇◇◇
sored. If someone in authority **censors** letters, the VERB: V n
media, or works of art, they officially examine them
and cut out any information that is regarded as
secret, immoral, or inappropriate. ▶ A **censor** is a N-COUNT
person who has been officially appointed to censor
letters, the media, or works of art. **♦ cen·sor·ship.** N-UNCOUNT
Censorship is the fact or activity of censoring letters, the media, or works of art. *The government to-*
day announced that press censorship was being lift-
ed... I am totally against censorship.

cen·so·ri·ous /senˈsɔːriəs/. If you describe some- ADJ-GRADED
one as **censorious,** you disapprove of them because PRAGMATICS
they are too critical of other people's behaviour. *De-* FORMAL
spite strong principles he was never censorious.

cen·sure /ˈsenʃə/ **censures, censuring, cen-**
sured. If you **censure** someone for something that VERB
they have done, you criticize them strongly. *I would* V n for-ing/n
not presume to censure Osborne for hating his moth- Also V n
er. ▶ Also a noun. *...a controversial policy which has* FORMAL
attracted international censure. N-UNCOUNT

cen·sus /ˈsensəs/ **censuses.** A **census** is an offi- ◆◆◇◇◇
cial survey of the population of a country that is N-COUNT
carried out in order to find out how many people
live there and to obtain details of such things as
people's ages and occupations.

cent /sent/ **cents.** A **cent** is a small unit of money ◆◆◇◇◇
worth one hundredth of the main unit of money in N-COUNT
many countries, for example the dollar in the US
and Australia. ● See also **per cent.**

cen·taur /ˈsentɔː/ **centaurs.** In classical mythol- N-COUNT
ogy, a **centaur** is a creature with the head, arms,

and upper body of a man, and the body and legs of a horse.

cen·te·nary /sen'ti:nəri, AM -'ten-/ **centenaries.** ◆◇◇◇◇ N-COUNT BRITISH
A **centenary** is the 100th anniversary of an event. *Today is the centenary of the death of Lord Tennyson.*

cen·ten·ni·al /sen'teniəl/. A **centennial** is the same ◆◇◇◇◇ N-SING AMERICAN
as a **centenary**.

cen·ter /'sentə/. See **centre**.

cen·ti·grade /'sentɪɡreɪd/. **Centigrade** is the same ADJ
as **Celsius**. ...*daytime temperatures of up to forty degrees centigrade.* ▶ Also a noun. *The number at the* N-UNCOUNT *bottom is the recommended water temperature in Centigrade.*

cen·ti·li·tre /'sentɪliːtə/ **centilitres;** spelled **centi-** N-COUNT **liter** in American English. A **centilitre** is a unit of volume in the metric system equal to ten millilitres or one-hundredth of a litre.

cen·ti·me·tre /'sentɪmiːtə/ **centimetres;** spelled ◆◇◇◇◇ **centimeter** in American English. A **centimetre** is a N-COUNT unit of length in the metric system equal to ten millimetres or one-hundredth of a metre.

cen·ti·pede /'sentɪpiːd/ **centipedes.** A **centipede** N-COUNT is a small, long, thin creature with a lot of legs.

cen·tral /'sentrəl/. **1** A **central** group or organiza- ◆◆◆◆◆ tion makes all the important decisions that are fol- ADJ: ADJ n lowed throughout a larger organization or a country. ...*the central committee of the Cuban communist party.* ♦ **cen·tral·ly** ...*a centrally planned economy.* ADV **2** Something that is **central** is in the middle of a place ADJ or area. ...*a rich woman living in central London.* ♦ **centrally** ...*a full-sized double bed centrally placed.* ADV **3** A place that is **central** is easy to reach because it is in ADJ-GRADED the centre of a city. ...*a central location in the capital.* ♦ **centrally** ...*this centrally located hotel.* **4** The **cen-** ADV-GRADED **tral** people or things in a situation are the most im- ADJ-GRADED portant ones. *Black dance music has been central to mainstream pop since the early '60s.* ♦ **cen·tral·ity** N-UNCOUNT ...*the centrality of the German economy to the welfare of Europe.* ♦ **centrally** *We must be positively and* ADV-GRADED *centrally involved in this debate.*

central 'government, central governments. ◆◆◇◇◇ The **central government** in a country is the govern- N-VAR ment of the whole country, in contrast to smaller authorities which govern local areas.

central 'heating. **Central heating** is a heating ◆◇◇◇◇ system in which air or water is heated and passed N-UNCOUNT round a building through pipes and radiators.

cen·tral·ise /'sentrəlaɪz/. See **centralize**.

cen·tral·ism /'sentrəlɪzəm/. **Centralism** is a way of N-UNCOUNT governing a country, or organizing something such as industry or education, which involves having one central authority giving instructions to regional groups. ♦ **cen·tral·ist** /'sentrəlɪst/ **centralists** ...*a* ADJ *strong centralist state.*

cen·tral·ize /'sentrəlaɪz/ **centralizes, centraliz-** ◆◇◇◇◇ **ing, centralized;** also spelled **centralise** in British VERB English. To **centralize** a country or organization V n means to create a system in which one central authority gives instructions to regional groups. *Multinational firms tended to centralize their opera-* ♦ **cen·trali·za·tion** /,sentrəlaɪ'zeɪʃən/. ...*bu-* N-UNCOUNT *reaucratic centralization.*

centrally 'heated. A **centrally heated** building or ADJ room has central heating.

central 'nervous system, central nervous N-COUNT **systems.** Your **central nervous system** is the part of your nervous system that consists of the brain and spinal cord.

central reser'vation, central reservations. N-COUNT BRITISH The **central reservation** is the strip of ground that separates the two sides of a motorway or dual carriageway.

cen·tre /'sentə/ **centres, centring, centred;** ◆◆◆◆◆ spelled **center** in American English. **1** A **centre** is a N-COUNT building or group of buildings where people go to take part in a particular activity or get help of some kind. *They were taken to the medical centre.* ...*the National Exhibition Centre.*
2 If an area or town is a **centre** for an industry or activ- N-COUNT:

ity, that industry or activity is very important there. with supp *London is also the major international insurance centre.* **3** If an industry or event **is centred** in a place, it V-ERG takes place to the greatest extent there. ...*the silk in-* beV-ed prep *dustry, which was centered in Valencia... The disturb-* V prep *ances have centred round the two main university areas.*
4 The **centre** of something is the middle of it. *A large* N-COUNT *wooden table dominates the centre of the room.*
5 **-centred** can be added to adjectives and nouns to COMB indicate what kind of a centre something has. ...*lemon-centered white chocolates.* **6** If you **centre** VERB something, you move it so that it is at the centre of V n something else. *Centre the design on the cloth.* **7** The N-COUNT **centre** of a town or city is the part where there are the most shops and businesses and where a lot of people come from other areas to work or shop. ...*the city centre.*
8 If something or someone is at the **centre** of a situa- N-COUNT tion or someone's work, they are the most important thing or person involved. ...*the man at the centre of the controversy.* **9** If someone or something is the **centre** N-COUNT of attention or interest, people are giving them a lot of attention. *The centre of attraction was Pierre Auguste Renoir's oil painting.* **10** If something **centres** or **is** V-ERG **centred** on a particular thing or person, that thing or V on/around n person is the main feature or subject of attention. beV-ed on/ ...*talks which centred on the Cambodia problem... All* around n *his concerns were centred around himself rather than Rachel.* ♦ **-centred** ...*a child-centred approach to* COMB *teaching.* ● See also **self-centred**.
11 In politics, the **centre** consists of groups, such as N-SING: liberals and social democrats, that are considered to theN be neither left-wing nor right-wing. ● See also **left-of-centre, right-of-centre.**
12 **Centre** is used in a large number of expressions which are explained under other words in this dictionary. For example, the expression **community centre** is explained at **community**.

centre·fold /'sentəfəʊld/ **centrefolds;** spelled N-COUNT **centerfold** in American English. A **centrefold** is a picture that covers the two central pages of a magazine, especially a photograph of a naked or semi-naked woman in a pornographic magazine.

centre-'forward, centre-forwards. A **centre-** ◆◇◇◇◇ **forward** in a team sport such as football or hockey N-COUNT is the player or position in the middle of the front row of attackers.

centre of 'gravity, centres of gravity. The N-COUNT **centre of gravity** of an object is the point on the object at which it balances perfectly.

centre·piece /'sentəpiːs/ **centrepieces;** spelled ◆◇◇◇◇ **centerpiece** in American English. **1** The **centrepiece** N-COUNT of a number of things is something that is shown as the best one among them or as the biggest attraction. *This year the centrepiece of the Festival will be its presentation of two rarely performed operas.* **2** A N-COUNT **centrepiece** is an ornament which you put in the middle of something, especially a dinner table.

centre 'stage; also spelled **centre-stage**, and ◆◇◇◇◇ spelled **center stage** in American English. If some- N-UNCOUNT thing or someone takes **centre stage**, they become very prominent or noticeable. *Unilateralism is returning to centre-stage in American trade policy.*

cen·tri·fu·gal force /sentrɪ,fjuːɡəl 'fɔːs/. **Centrifu-** N-UNCOUNT **gal force** is the force that makes objects move out- TECHNICAL wards when they are spinning around something or travelling in a curve.

cen·tri·fuge /'sentrɪfjuːdʒ/ **centrifuges.** A **centri-** N-COUNT **fuge** is a machine that spins mixtures of different substances around very quickly so that they separate by centrifugal force.

cen·trist /'sentrɪst/ **centrists. Centrist** policies ◆◇◇◇◇ and parties are moderate rather than extreme. ▶ A ADJ-GRADED N-COUNT **centrist** is someone with centrist views.

cen·tu·ri·on /sen'tjʊəriən, AM -'tʊr-/ **centurions.** N-COUNT A **centurion** was an officer in the Roman army.

cen·tu·ry /'sentʃəri/ **centuries. 1** A **century** is a ◆◆◆◆◆ period of 100 years that is used when stating a date. N-COUNT For example, the 19th century was the period from

1801 to 1900. **2** A **century** is any period of 100 years. `N-COUNT`
The drought there is the worst in a century. **3** In `N-COUNT`
cricket, a **century** is a total of 100 runs scored by a
batsman in one innings.

ce·ram·ic /sɪˈræmɪk/ **ceramics. 1 Ceramic** is clay ◆◇◇◇
that has been heated to a very high temperature so `N-VAR`
that it becomes hard. **2 Ceramics** are ceramic orna- `N-COUNT`
ments or objects. **Ceramics** is also the art of making
ceramic objects.

ce·real /ˈsɪəriəl/ **cereals. 1 Cereal** is a food made ◆◆◇◇
from grain. In Britain, it is mixed with milk and eat- `N-VAR`
en for breakfast. **2 Cereals** are plants such as wheat, `N-COUNT`
maize, or rice that produce grain. *...4 million hectares of cereal crops.*

cere·bral /ˈserɪbrəl/. **1** If you describe someone or ◆◇◇◇
something as **cerebral**, you mean that they are in- `ADJ-GRADED`
tellectual and rational rather than emotional. *Some* `FORMAL`
think him too cerebral to win the support of voters.
2 Cerebral means relating to the brain. *...a cerebral* `ADJ: ADJ n`
haemorrhage. `MEDICAL`

cerebral 'palsy. Cerebral palsy is an illness `N-UNCOUNT`
caused by damage to a baby's brain before it is
born, which makes its limbs and muscles permanently uncontrollable or weak.

cer·e·mo·nial /ˌserɪˈməʊniəl/ **ceremonials.** ◆◇◇◇
1 Something that is **ceremonial** relates to a ceremo- `ADJ: ADJ n`
ny or is used in a ceremony. *He represented the na-
tion on ceremonial occasions.* ♦ **cer·e·mo·ni·al·ly** `ADV:`
Corporal Andrew Satchell ceremonially rolled up the `ADV with v`
flag. **2** A position, function, or event that is **ceremo-** `ADJ`
nial is considered to be representative of an institution, but has very little authority or influence. *Up to
now the post of president has been largely ceremo-
nial.* **3** A **ceremonial** is a formal ceremony. All the `N-VAR`
impressive things that are associated with it can
also be called **ceremonial** or **ceremonials**. *...the
ceremonials leading up to the young Emperor's
wedding.*

cer·e·mo·ni·ous·ly /ˌserɪˈməʊniəsli/. If someone `ADV:`
does something **ceremoniously**, they do it in an ex- `ADV with v`
tremely formal way. *The waiter ceremoniously lifted* `WRITTEN`
rolls from a basket with a pair of silver tongs.

cer·e·mo·ny /ˈserɪməni, AM -məʊni/ **ceremonies.** ◆◆◇◇
1 A **ceremony** is a formal event such as a wedding `N-COUNT`
or a coronation. *Today's award ceremony took place
at the British Embassy.* **2 Ceremony** consists of the `N-UNCOUNT`
special things that are said and done on very formal
occasions. *...the pomp and ceremony of the Pope's
visit.* **3** If you do something **without ceremony**, `N-UNCOUNT:`
you do it quickly and casually. *'Is Hilton here?' she* `withoutN`
asked without ceremony. **4** See also **master of
ceremonies.**

ce·rise /səˈriːs/. Something that is **cerise** is a bright `COLOUR`
pinkish red.

cert /sɜːt/ **certs.** If you say that someone or some- `N-COUNT`
thing is a **cert**, you mean you are certain they will `INFORMAL,`
succeed. *He was a cert for the Premiership.* `BRITISH`

cert., certs. Cert. is a written abbreviation for ◆◇◇◇
certificate.

cer·tain /ˈsɜːtən/. **1** If you are **certain** about some- ◆◆◆◇
thing or if it is **certain**, you firmly believe it is true `ADJ-GRADED`
and have no doubt about it. If you are not **certain**
about something, you do not have definite knowledge or views about it. *She's absolutely certain she's
going to make it... It wasn't a balloon – I'm certain of
that... It is certain that Rodney arrived the previous
day... The scheme is certain to meet opposition... The
Prime Minister is heading for certain defeat.* **2** If you `PHRASE`
know something **for certain**, you have no doubt
about it. *She couldn't know what time he'd go, or
even for certain that he'd go at all.* **3** If you have **cer-** `ADJ-GRADED:`
tain knowledge that something is true, you know `ADJ n`
that it is definitely true. *He had been there four
times to my certain knowledge.* **4** If you **make cer-** `PHRASE`
tain that something is the way you want or expect it
to be, you take action to ensure that it is. *He had
made certain he hadn't shown his face at all at the
party.*

cer·tain /ˈsɜːtən/. **1** You use **certain** to indicate ◆◆◆◇
that you are referring to one particular thing, per- `ADJ:`
son, or group, although you are not saying exactly `det ADJ,`
which it is. *There will be certain people who'll say 'I* `ADJ n`
*told you so!'... You owe a certain person a sum of
money.* **2** When you refer to **certain of** a group of `QUANT`
people or things, you are referring to some particu- `FORMAL`
lar members of that group. *They'll have to give up
completely on certain of their studies.* **3** You can use `ADJ:`
a certain before the name of a person in order to `a ADJ n-`
indicate that you do not know the person or any- `proper`
thing else about them. *She managed to arrange for
them to be hidden in the house of a certain Father
Boduen.* **4** You use **a certain** to indicate that some- `ADJ:`
thing such as a quality or condition exists, and often `a ADJ sing-n/`
to suggest that it is not great in amount or degree. *I* `n-uncount`
received a certain amount of sympathy.

cer·tain·ly /ˈsɜːtənli/. **1** You can use **certainly** to ◆◆◆◆
emphasize what you are saying. *The public is cer-* `ADV-GRADED:`
tainly getting tired of hearing about it... Certainly, `ADV with cl/`
pets can help children develop friendship skills. `PRAGMATICS`
2 You use **certainly** when you are agreeing strongly `ADV`
with what someone has said. *'You keep out of their* `PRAGMATICS`
way don't you?'—'I certainly do.' **3** You say **certain-** `ADV`
ly not when you want to say 'no' in a strong way. `PRAGMATICS`
*'Perhaps it would be better if I withdrew
altogether.'—'Certainly not!'*

cer·tain·ty /ˈsɜːtənti/ **certainties. 1 Certainty** is ◆◆◇◇
the state of having no doubts at all about some- `N-UNCOUNT`
thing. *I have told them with absolute certainty
there'll be no change of policy.* **2 Certainty** is the fact `N-UNCOUNT:`
that something is certain to happen. *A general elec-* `also a N`
tion became a certainty three weeks ago. **3 Certain-** `N-COUNT`
ties are things that nobody has any doubts about. *In
politics there are never any certainties.*

cer·ti·fi·able /ˌsɜːtɪˈfaɪəbəl/. **1** If you describe `ADJ-GRADED`
someone as **certifiable**, you mean their behaviour is `PRAGMATICS`
extremely unreasonable or foolish. *By the time we
left he must have considered that all film crews were
certifiable.* **2** Someone who is **certifiable** is mentally `ADJ`
ill and can be declared insane.

cer·tifi·cate /səˈtɪfɪkət/ **certificates. 1** A **certifi-** ◆◆◇◇
cate is an official document stating that particular `N-COUNT`
things are true. *...birth certificates.* **2** A **certificate** is `N-COUNT:`
an official document that you receive when you `with supp`
have completed a course of study or training. The
qualification that this document represents can also
be called a **certificate**. *...the Post-Graduate Certificate of Education.* ♦ **cer·tifi·cat·ed** /səˈtɪfɪkeɪtɪd/. `ADJ`
...a certificated teacher.

cer·ti·fy /ˈsɜːtɪfaɪ/ **certifies, certifying, certi-** ◆◇◇◇
fied. 1 If someone in an official position **certifies** `VERB`
something, they officially state that it is true or `V that`
genuine. *The president certified that the project* `V n`
would receive at least $650m... The National Election `be V-ed as adj`
*Council is supposed to certify the results... It has
been certified as genuine.* ♦ **cer·ti·fi·ca·tion** `N-VAR`
/ˌsɜːtɪfɪˈkeɪʃən/ **certifications. 1** *...written certification that the relative is really ill.* **2** If someone **is** `VB: usu`
certified as a particular kind of worker, they are giv- `passive`
en a certificate stating that they have successfully `getV-ed as n`
completed a course of training in their profession. `V-ed`
*They wanted to get certified as divers... Mary hopes
to qualify as a certified accountant.* ♦ **certification** `N-UNCOUNT`
...training leading to the certification of their skill.

cer·ti·tude /ˈsɜːtɪtjuːd, AM -tuːd/ **certitudes. Cer-** `N-UNCOUNT:`
titude is the same as **certainty**. *We have this definite* `also N in pl`
certitude that Cicippio will be freed. `FORMAL`

cer·vi·cal /ˈsɜːvɪkəl, səˈvaɪkəl/. **1 Cervical** means ◆◇◇◇
relating to the cervix. *...cervical cancer.* **2 Cervical** `ADJ: ADJ n`
means relating to the neck. *...the cervical spine.* `MEDICAL`
`ADJ: ADJ n`

cer·vix /ˈsɜːvɪks/ **cervixes** or **cervices** ◆◇◇◇
/səˈvaɪsiːz/. The **cervix** is the entrance to the womb. `N-COUNT`
`MEDICAL`

ces·sa·tion /seˈseɪʃən/. The **cessation** of some- `N-UNCOUNT:`
thing is the stopping of it. *He would not agree to a* `also a N`
cessation of hostilities. `FORMAL`

cess·pit /ˈsespɪt/ **cesspits.** A **cesspit** is a hole or `N-COUNT`
tank in the ground into which waste water and sew- `BRITISH`
age flow.

cess·pool /'sespu:l/ **cesspools.** A **cesspool** is the N-COUNT same as a **cesspit**.

ce·ta·cean /sɪ'teɪʃən/ **cetaceans.** Whales, dol- N-COUNT phins, and porpoises belong to the family of crea- tures known as **cetaceans**.

cetera. See **etcetera**.

cf. Cf. is used in writing to introduce something ◆◇◇◇◇ that should be considered in connection with the subject you are discussing. *For the more salient re- marks on the matter, cf. Isis Unveiled, Vol. I.*

CFC /,si: ef 'si:/ **CFCs.** CFCs are chemicals that are ◆◇◇◇◇ used in aerosols, refrigerators, and cooling systems, N-COUNT and in the manufacture of various plastics. **CFC** is an abbreviation for 'chlorofluorocarbon'.

ch., chs. Ch. is a written abbreviation for **chapter**.

cha-cha-cha /,tʃɑ: tʃɑ: 'tʃɑ:/ **cha-cha-chas.** The N-COUNT cha-cha-cha is a Latin American dance with small fast steps.

chafe /tʃeɪf/ **chafes, chafing, chafed. 1** If V-ERG something **chafes** your skin, it rubs against it and V n makes it sore. *The shorts were chafing my thighs...* V against n His wrists began to chafe against the cloth strips Also V binding them. **2** If you **chafe** at a restriction, you VB: no passive feel annoyed about it. *He had chafed at having to* V at/under/ take orders from another.* against n/-ing FORMAL

chaff /tʃɑːf, tʃæf/. **Chaff** is the outer part of grain N-UNCOUNT such as wheat.

chaf·finch /'tʃæfɪntʃ/ **chaffinches.** A chaffinch is N-COUNT a small European songbird. Male chaffinches have reddish-brown fronts and grey heads.

cha·grin /'ʃægrɪn, AM ʃə'grɪn/. **Chagrin** is a feeling N-UNCOUNT of annoyance or disappointment. *To the chagrin of* FORMAL *fans, tournaments are being won by nonentities.*

♦ cha·grined /'ʃægrɪnd, AM ʃə'grɪnd/. *The commit-* ADJ-GRADED *tee did not appear chagrined by the compromises.*

chain /tʃeɪn/ **chains, chaining, chained. 1** A ◆◆◇◇◇ chain consists of metal rings connected together in N-COUNT a line. **2** If a person or thing **is chained** to some- VERB thing, they are fastened to it with a chain. *The dog* be V-ed *was chained to the leg of the garden seat... She* prep/adv *chained her bike to the railings.* ▶ **Chain up** means V n P the same as **chain**. *I'll lock the doors and chain you* V n P *up.* **3** If prisoners are **in chains**, they have chains *in* N-PLURAL: round their wrists or ankles to prevent them from *in* N escaping. **4** If you say that someone **is chained to** a person or a V-PASSIVE situation, you are emphasizing that there are reasons PRAGMATICS why they cannot leave that person or situation, even be V-ed to n though they might like to. *Women used to be chained to unhappy marriages for financial or social reasons.* **5** You can refer to feelings and duties which prevent N-PLURAL you from doing what you want to do as **chains**. *...the* LITERARY *chains of habit that bound him to the present.* **6** A **chain** of things is a group of them existing or ar- N-COUNT: ranged in a line. *...a chain of islands known as the* N of n *Windward Islands.* **7** A **chain** of shops, hotels, or oth- N-COUNT: er businesses is a number of them owned by the same with supp person or company. *...a large supermarket chain.* **8** A N-SING: **chain** of events is a series of them happening one af- N of n ter another. **9** See also **food chain**.

chain up. See **chain** 4. PHRASAL VB

'chain gang, chain gangs. In the United States, N-COUNT a **chain gang** was a group of prisoners who were chained to do work outside their prison.

'chain letter, chain letters. A **chain letter** is a N-COUNT letter, often with a promise of money, that is sent to several people who send copies on to several more people. Chain letters are illegal in some countries.

,chain 'mail. Chain mail is armour made from N-UNCOUNT small metal rings joined together so that they are like a piece of cloth.

,chain re'action, chain reactions. 1 A chain ◆◇◇◇◇ **reaction** is a series of chemical changes, each of N-COUNT which causes the next. **2** A **chain reaction** is a series N-COUNT of events, each of which causes the next. *The pow- der immediately ignited and set off a chain reaction of explosions.*

'chain saw, chain saws; also spelled **chainsaw.** N-COUNT A **chain saw** is a big saw with teeth fixed in a chain that is driven round by a motor.

'chain-smoke, chain-smokes, chain- VERB: V **smoking, chain-smoked.** Someone who **chain- smokes** smokes cigarettes or cigars continuously, one after another. **♦ chain-smoker, chain-** N-COUNT **smokers.**

'chain store, chain stores; also spelled **chain-** N-COUNT **store.** A **chain store** is one of several similar shops that are owned by the same person or company.

chair /tʃeə/ **chairs, chairing, chaired. 1** A chair ◆◆◆◆◇ is a piece of furniture for one person to sit on, with N-COUNT a back and four legs. **2** At British universities, a N-COUNT **chair** is the post of professor. **3** The person in char- N-COUNT ge of a committee or meeting is sometimes called the **chair**. **4** If you **chair** a meeting or a committee, VERB: V n you are the person in charge of it. **5** If you **are in** PHRASE **the chair** or **take the chair** at a meeting, you are the person in charge of it.

'chair lift, chair lifts; also spelled **chairlift.** A N-COUNT **chair lift** is a line of chairs that hang from a moving cable and carry people up and down a mountain or ski slope.

chair·man /'tʃeəmən/ **chairmen. 1** The **chairman** ◆◆◆◆◇ of a committee or organization is the head of it. N-COUNT *Glyn Ford is chairman of the Committee which pro- duced the report.* **♦ chair·man·ship, chairman-** N-VAR **ships.** The **chairmanship** of a committee or or- ganization is the position of being its chairman, or the period when a particular person is chairman. *...a committee under the chairmanship of Professor Roy Goode.* **2** The **chairman** of a meeting or debate N-COUNT is the person in charge, who decides when each person is allowed to speak.

chair·person /'tʃeəpɜ:sən/ **chairpersons.** The N-COUNT **chairperson** of a meeting, committee, or organiza- tion is the person in charge of it.

chair·woman /'tʃeəwʊmən/ **chairwomen.** The N-COUNT **chairwoman** of a meeting, committee, or organiza- tion is the woman in charge of it.

chaise longue /,ʃeɪz 'lɒŋ/ **chaises longues;** the N-COUNT singular and the plural are both pronounced in the same way. A **chaise longue** is a couch with only one arm and usually a back along half its length.

cha·let /'ʃæleɪ, AM ʃæ'leɪ/ **chalets.** A chalet is a ◆◇◇◇◇ small wooden house, especially in a mountain area N-COUNT or a holiday camp.

chal·ice /'tʃælɪs/ **chalices. 1** A chalice is a large N-COUNT gold or silver cup with a stem. Chalices are used to hold wine in the Christian service of Holy Com- munion. **2** If you refer to something that someone PHRASE offers you as a **poisoned chalice**, you mean it seems very attractive, but you believe that accepting it would bring you trouble or failure.

chalk /tʃɔ:k/ **chalks, chalking, chalked.** ◆◇◇◇◇ **1 Chalk** is a type of soft white rock. *...the highest* N-UNCOUNT *chalk cliffs in Britain.* **2 Chalk** is small sticks of N-UNCOUNT: chalk, or a substance similar to chalk, used for writ- also N in pl ing or drawing with. *...drawing a small picture with coloured chalks.* **3** If you **chalk** something, you VERB draw or write it using a piece of chalk. *He chalked* V n *the message on the blackboard.* **4** If you say that two PHRASE people or things are as different as **chalk and** PRAGMATICS **cheese**, you are emphasizing that they are com- BRITISH pletely different.

chalk up. If you **chalk up** a success or a number of PHRASAL VB points in a game, you achieve it. *The team chalked up* V P noun *another victory.* Also V n P

chalk·board /'tʃɔ:kbɔ:d/ **chalkboards.** In a class- N-COUNT room, the **chalkboard** is a board which teachers write on with chalk.

chalky /'tʃɔ:ki/. **1** Something that is **chalky** con- ADJ-GRADED tains chalk or is covered with chalk. *...the chalky soil around Saumur.* **2** Something that is **chalky** is a ADJ-GRADED pale dull colour or has a powdery texture. *Her face became a chalky white.*

chal·lenge /'tʃælɪndʒ/ **challenges, challeng-** ◆◆◆◆◇ **ing, challenged. 1** A challenge is something new N-VAR and difficult which requires great effort and deter- mination. *The new government's first challenge is the economy.* **2** If someone **rises to the challenge,** PHRASE they successfully act in response to a very difficult

situation. *They rose to the challenge of entertaining 80 schoolchildren.*

3 A **challenge** to something is a questioning of its truth or value. A **challenge** to someone is a questioning of their authority. *The demonstrators have now made a direct challenge to the authority of the government.* **4** If you **challenge** an idea, you question its truth or value. *The move was immediately challenged by two of the republics.* **5** If you **challenge** someone to do something, you ask them to defend their actions or to prove their authority. *Rose challenged him to come on stage and explain his opinions... I challenged him on the hypocrisy of his political attitudes.* N-VAR / VERB: V n / VERB V n to-inf V n on/about n Also V with quote

6 If you **challenge** someone, you invite them to fight or compete with you in some way. *Corineus, who was a famous wrestler, challenged him to a bout... He left a note at the scene of the crime, challenging detectives to catch him.* ► Also a noun. *A third presidential candidate emerged to mount a serious challenge.* ♦ **chal·leng·er, challengers** *Mr Portillo is emerging as a right wing challenger to the leadership.* **7** If someone **is challenged** by a guard, they are ordered to stop and say who they are or why they are there. VERB V n V n to-inf Also V n / N-COUNT / N-COUNT / VERB: be V-ed

8 See also **challenged, challenging.**

chal·lenged /'tʃælɪndʒd/. If you say that someone is **challenged** in a particular way, you mean that they have a disability in that area. **Challenged** is often used for humorous effect. *She ran off with an intellectually challenged ski instructor.* ADJ: adv ADJ

chal·leng·ing /'tʃælɪndʒɪŋ/. **1** A **challenging** task or job requires great effort and determination. **2** If you do something in a **challenging** way, you seem to be inviting people to argue with you or compete against you in some way. *Mona gave him a challenging look.* ADJ-GRADED ADJ-GRADED

cham·ber /'tʃeɪmbə/ **chambers. 1** A **chamber** is a large room, especially one that is used for formal meetings. **2** You can refer to a country's parliament or to one section of it as a **chamber**. *More than 80 parties are contesting seats in the two-chamber parliament.* **3** A **chamber** is a room designed and equipped for a particular purpose. *For many, the dentist's surgery remains a torture chamber.* ● See also **gas chamber. 4** The offices used by judges and barristers are referred to as **chambers**. N-COUNT / N-COUNT / N-COUNT: with supp / N-PLURAL

cham·ber·lain /'tʃeɪmbəlɪn/ **chamberlains.** A **chamberlain** is the person in charge of the household affairs of a monarch or high-ranking person. N-COUNT

chamber·maid /'tʃeɪmbəmeɪd/ **chambermaids.** A **chambermaid** is a woman who cleans and tidies the bedrooms in a hotel. N-COUNT

'chamber music. Chamber music is classical music written for a small number of instruments. N-UNCOUNT

,chamber of 'commerce, chambers of commerce. A **chamber of commerce** is a business organization that promotes local commercial interests. N-COUNT

'chamber orchestra, chamber orchestras. A **chamber orchestra** is a small orchestra which plays classical music. N-COUNT

'chamber pot, chamber pots. A **chamber pot** is a round container shaped like a very large cup. Chamber pots used to be kept in bedrooms for people to urinate in. N-COUNT

cha·me·le·on /kə'miːliən/ **chameleons.** A **chameleon** is a lizard whose skin changes colour to match the colour of its surroundings. N-COUNT

cham·ois. Chamois is both the singular and the plural form; it is pronounced /'ʃæmwɑː/ for meaning 1 in British English, and /'ʃæmi/ for both meanings in American English, and for meaning 2 in British English. **1 Chamois** are small goat-like antelope that live in the mountains of Europe and South West Asia. **2** A **chamois** or a **chamois leather** is a soft leather cloth used for cleaning and polishing. N-COUNT / N-COUNT

chamo·mile /'kæməmaɪl/. See **camomile**.

champ /tʃæmp/ **champs.** A **champ** is the same as a champion. *...boxing champ Mike Tyson.* N-COUNT INFORMAL

cham·pagne /,ʃæm'peɪn/ **champagnes. Champagne** is an expensive French sparkling white wine. It is often drunk to celebrate something. N-VAR

champ·ers /'ʃæmpəz/. **Champers** is champagne. *We were slurping champers by the glassful.* N-UNCOUNT INFORMAL, BRITISH

cham·pi·on /'tʃæmpiən/ **champions, championing, championed. 1** A **champion** is someone who has won the first prize in a competition, contest, or fight. *...a former Olympic champion. ...champion boxer Lennox Lewis.* **2** If you are a **champion** of a person, a cause, or a principle, you support or defend them. *He was once known as a champion of social reform.* **3** If you **champion** a person, a cause, or a principle, you support or defend them. *He passionately championed the poor.* N-COUNT / N-COUNT: with supp / VERB V n

cham·pi·on·ship /'tʃæmpiənʃɪp/ **championships. 1** A **championship** is a competition to find the best player or team in a particular sport. *...the world chess championship.* **2** The **championship** refers to the title or status of being a sports champion. *He went on to take the championship.* N-COUNT / N-SING: the N

chance /tʃɑːns, tʃæns/ **chances, chancing, chanced. 1** If there is a **chance** of something happening, it is possible that it will happen. *Tim's chances of survival were still slim... There was really very little chance that Ben would ever have led a normal life.* **2** If you have a **chance** to do something, you have the opportunity to do it. *All eligible people would get a chance to vote... I felt I had to give him a chance.* **3** If you say that someone **stands a chance** of achieving something, you mean that they are likely to achieve it. If you say that they do not **stand a chance**, you mean that they cannot possibly achieve it. N-VAR / N-SING / PHRASE

4 A **chance** meeting or event is one that is not planned or expected. ► Also a noun. *...a victim of chance and circumstance.* **5** If you **chance** to do something or **chance** on something, you do it or find it although you had not planned or tried to. *It was just then that I chanced to look round. ...Christopher Columbus, who chanced upon the Dominican Republic nearly 500 years ago.* **6** Something that happens **by chance** has not been planned by anyone. *He had met Mr Heseltine by chance.* ADJ: ADJ n / N-UNCOUNT / VERB V to-inf V upon/on/ across n FORMAL / PHRASE

7 If you **chance** something, you do it even though there is a risk that you may not succeed or that something bad may happen. *No assassin would chance a shot from amongst that crowd.* **8** When you **take a chance**, you try to do something although there is a large risk of danger or failure. *You take a chance on the weather if you holiday in the UK.* VERB V n / PHRASE

9 You can use **by any chance** when you are asking questions in order to find out whether something that you think might be true is actually true. *Are they by any chance related?* **10** See also **off-chance.** PHRASE PRAGMATICS

chan·cel /'tʃɑːnsəl, 'tʃænsəl/ **chancels.** The **chancel** is the part of a church containing the altar, where the clergy and the choir usually sit. N-COUNT

chan·cel·lery /'tʃɑːnsələri, 'tʃæns-/ **chancelleries. 1** A **chancellery** is the building where a chancellor has his offices. **2** The **chancellery** refers to the officials who work in a chancellor's office. N-COUNT / N-SING

Chan·cel·lor /'tʃɑːnslə, 'tʃæns-/ **Chancellors. 1** **Chancellor** is the title of the head of government in Germany and Austria. **2** In Britain, the **Chancellor** is the Chancellor of the Exchequer. **3** The **Chancellor** of a British university is the official, honorary head of the university. **4** The head of some American universities is called the **Chancellor. 5** See also **vice-chancellor.** N-TITLE / N-COUNT / N-COUNT / N-COUNT

Chancellor of the Ex'chequer, Chancellors of the Exchequer. The **Chancellor of the Exchequer** is the minister in the British government who makes decisions about finance and taxes. N-COUNT

chan·cel·lor·ship /'tʃɑːnsləʃɪp, 'tʃæns-/. The **chancellorship** is the position of chancellor. Someone's **chancellorship** is the period of time when they are chancellor. N-SING

chanc·er /'tʃɑːnsə, 'tʃænsə/ **chancers.** If you refer to someone as a **chancer**, you mean that they N-COUNT PRAGMATICS INFORMAL

exploit situations to their own advantage, often dis- BRITISH
honestly. ...*some silver-tongued chancer trying to
pull a fast one on a gullible British company.*

Chan·cery /'tʃɑːnsəri, 'tʃæns-/. In Britain, the N-SING:
Chancery or **Chancery Division** is the Lord Chan- also in N
cellor's court, which is a division of the High Court.

chancy /'tʃɑːnsi, 'tʃænsi/. Something that is **chancy** ADJ-GRADED
involves a lot of risk or uncertainty. *Investment is* INFORMAL
becoming a chancy business.

chan·de·lier /ˌʃændə'lɪə/ **chandeliers.** A chande- ◆◇◇◇◇
lier is a large decorative frame which holds light N-COUNT
bulbs or candles and hangs from the ceiling.

change /tʃeɪndʒ/ **changes, changing,** ◆◆◆◆◆
changed. 1 If there is a **change** in something, it N-VAR
becomes different. *What is needed is a change of attitude on the part of architects... Political change is
on its way.* ● See also **sea change. 2** If you say that N-SING
something is a **change** or makes a **change**, you PRAGMATICS
mean that it is enjoyable because it is different from
what you are used to. *It is a complex system, but it
certainly makes a change.* **3** When something V-ERG: V
changes, it becomes different. *The mood gradually* V from V to n
changed from resignation to rage... She has now V into n
changed into a happy, self-confident woman... They V n
should change the law to make it illegal to own rep- Also V n into n
lica weapons. **4** If you **change** from one thing to an- VERB
other, you stop doing or using the first thing and V to n
start doing or using the second one. *He would gladly have changed to a different job but it would have
meant a drop in income.* **5** If you say that some- PHRASE
thing is happening **for a change**, you mean that you
are glad that it is happening because usually it does
not. *Now let me ask you a question, for a change.*

6 To **change** something means to replace it with VERB
something new or different. *All they did was change a* V n
fuse. ▶ Also a noun. *A change of leadership alone will* N-COUNT
not be enough. **7** When you **change** your clothes, you VERB: V n
take some or all of them off and put on different ones. V
They had allowed her to shower and change... I V into/out of n
changed into a tracksuit... I've got to get changed first. get V-ed
▶ A **change of** clothes is an extra set of clothes that into/out of n
you take with you somewhere. **8** When you **change** a VERB: V n
baby or **change** its nappy, you take off its dirty nappy
and put on a clean one. **9** When you **change** a bed or VERB: V n
change the sheets, you take off the dirty sheets and
put on clean ones. **10** When you **change** buses, trains, VERB: V n
or planes, you get off one bus, train, or plane and get V
on to another in order to continue your journey. *We
were turned off the train at Hanover, where we had to
change.* **11** When you **change** gear or **change** into an- VERB: V n
other gear, you move the gear lever on a car, bicycle, V prep
or other vehicle in order to use a different gear. In BRITISH
American English, you **shift** gears. *He looked up into
the mirror as he changed through his gears.*

12 Your **change** is the money that you receive when N-UNCOUNT
you pay for something with too much money because
you do not have exactly the right amount. **13** Change N-UNCOUNT
refers to coins, rather than notes. *...a sack of loose
change.* ● See also **small change. 14** If you have N-UNCOUNT
change for a note or a large coin, you have the same
amount of money in smaller notes or coins. **15** When VERB: V n
you **change** money, you exchange it for the same V n into n
amount of money in a different currency, or in smaller coins or notes. *...an agency that will change one foreign currency directly into another.*

16 Change is used in a large number of expressions
which are explained under other words in this dictionary. For example, the expression **to change hands**
is explained at **hand.**

change down. When you **change down**, you move PHRASAL VB
the gear lever in the vehicle you are driving in order to V P
use a lower gear. In American English, you **shift** V P to n
down. *I braked at the second corner and changed* BRITISH
down to third.

change over. If you **change over** from one thing to PHRASAL VB
another, you stop doing one thing and start doing the V P from/to n
other. *We are gradually changing over to a completely* Also V P
metric system. ● See also **changeover.**

change up. When you **change up**, you move the PHRASAL VB

gear lever in the vehicle you are driving in order to use V P
a higher gear. In American English, you **shift up.** BRITISH

change·able /'tʃeɪndʒəbəl/. Someone or some- ADJ-GRADED
thing that is **changeable** is likely to change many
times. *The forecast is for changeable weather.*

change of 'life. The change of life is the same as N-SING:
the menopause. the N

change·over /'tʃeɪndʒəʊvə/ **changeovers.** A N-COUNT
changeover is a change from one activity or system
to another. *He again called for a faster changeover to
a market economy.*

'changing room, changing rooms. A changing N-COUNT
room is a room where you can change your clothes BRITISH
and usually have a shower, for example at a sports
centre. The American expression is **locker room.**

chan·nel /'tʃænəl/ **channels, channelling,** ◆◆◆◆◇
channelled; spelled **channeling, channeled** in
American English. **1** A **channel** is a wavelength or system N-COUNT
which television programmes or radio messages are
broadcast. *...the only serious current affairs programme on either channel.*

2 If you do something through a particular **channel**, N-COUNT
that is the system or organization that you use to
achieve your aims or to communicate. *The government will surely use the diplomatic channels
available.* **3** If you **channel** money or resources into VERB
something, you arrange for them to be used for that V n prep
thing, rather than for a wider range of things. *...a system set up to channel funds to the poor countries.* **4** If VERB
you **channel** your energies or emotions into some- V n into n
thing, you concentrate on or do that one thing, rather Also V n adv
than a range of things. *Stephen is channelling his energies into a novel.*

5 A **channel** is a passage along which water flows. **6** A N-COUNT
channel is a route used by boats. **7** The **Channel** or N-COUNT
the English Channel is the narrow area of water be- N-PROPER:
tween England and France. the N

chant /tʃɑːnt, tʃænt/ **chants, chanting, chant-** ◆◆◇◇◇
ed. 1 A **chant** is a word or group of words that is N-COUNT
repeated over and over again. *He was greeted by the
chant of 'Judas! Judas!'.* **2** If you **chant** something, VERB
you repeat the same words over and over again. *De-* V with quote
monstrators chanted slogans... The crowd chanted V-ing
'We are with you.' ...thousands of chanting demon- Also V
strators. ♦ **chant·ing** *A lot of the chanting was in* N-UNCOUNT
support of the deputy Prime Minister. **3** A **chant** is a N-COUNT
religious song or prayer that is sung on only a few
notes. *...a Gregorian chant.* **4** If you **chant**, you sing VERB
a religious song or prayer. *Muslims chanted and* V
prayed. ♦ **chanting** *The chanting inside the temple* N-UNCOUNT
stopped.

Cha·nu·kah /'hɑːnəkə/. **Chanukah** is the same as N-UNCOUNT
Hanukkah.

cha·os /'keɪɒs/. **Chaos** is a state of complete disor- ◆◆◆◇◇
der and confusion. *The world's first transatlantic* N-UNCOUNT
balloon race ended in chaos.

cha·ot·ic /keɪ'ɒtɪk/. Something that is **chaotic** is in ◆◇◇◇◇
a state of complete disorder and confusion. ♦ **cha-** ADJ-GRADED
·oti·cal·ly *His words poured out chaotically.* ADV

chap /tʃæp/ **chaps. 1** In British English, a **chap** is ◆◇◇◇◇
a man or boy. **2** See also **chapped.** N-COUNT
INFORMAL

chap., chaps. Chap. is a written abbreviation for
chapter.

chap·el /'tʃæpəl/ **chapels. 1** A **chapel** is a part of ◆◆◇◇◇
a church which has its own altar and which is used N-COUNT
for private prayer. **2** A **chapel** is a small church at- N-COUNT
tached to a school, school, or prison. **3** A **chapel** is N-VAR
a building used for worship by members of some
Christian churches. Chapel refers to the religious
services that take place there. *On Sundays, the family went three times to chapel.*

chap·er·one /'ʃæpərəʊn/ **chaperones, chaper-**
oning, chaperoned; also spelled **chaperon. 1** A N-COUNT
chaperone is someone who accompanies another
person somewhere in order to make sure that they
do not come to any harm. **2** If you **are chaperoned** VERB:
by someone, they act as your chaperone. be V-ed

chap·lain /'tʃæplɪn/ **chaplains.** A **chaplain** is a ◆◇◇◇◇
member of the Christian clergy who does religious N-COUNT

work in a place such as a hospital, school, prison, or in the army.

chap·lain·cy /'tʃæplɪnsi/ **chaplaincies. 1** A chaplaincy is the building or office in which a chaplain works. **2** A **chaplaincy** is the position or work of a chaplain. N-COUNT

chapped /tʃæpt/. If your skin is **chapped**, it is dry, cracked, and sore. ADJ-GRADED

chap·py /'tʃæpi/ **chappies.** A **chappy** is the same as a **chap.** N-COUNT INFORMAL, BRITISH

chap·ter /'tʃæptə/ **chapters. 1** A **chapter** is one of the parts that a book is divided into. *Turn to Chapter 1.* **2** A **chapter** in someone's life or in history is a period of time during which a major event or series of related events takes place. *This had been a particularly difficult chapter in Lebanon's recent history.* **3** If you say that someone gives you **chapter and verse** on a particular subject, you are emphasizing that they tell you every detail about it. ◆◆◆◇ N-COUNT N-COUNT: supp N WRITTEN PHRASE PRAGMATICS

4 A **chapter** consists of a group of Christian clergy who work in or who are connected with a cathedral. N-COLL-COUNT **5** A **chapter** is a branch of a society, club, or union. N-COUNT

'chapter house, chapter houses. A **chapter house** is the building or set of rooms in the grounds of a cathedral where the members of the clergy hold their meetings. N-COUNT

char /tʃɑː/ **chars, charring, charred. 1** If food **chars**, it burns slightly and turns black as it is cooking. *Halve the peppers and char the skins under a hot grill.* **2** See also **charred.** ◆◇◇◇ V-ERG: V V n

chara·banc /'ʃærəbæŋ/ **charabancs.** A charabanc is a large old-fashioned coach with several rows of seats. N-COUNT BRITISH

char·ac·ter /'kærɪktə/ **characters. 1** The **character** of a person or place consists of all the qualities they have that make them distinct from other people or places. *There is a negative side to his character... The character of this country has been formed by immigration.* **2** You can use the word **character** to refer to the qualities that people from a particular place are believed to have. *Individuality is a valued and inherent part of the British character.* **3** Someone's **character** is their reputation. If someone is of good **character**, they are believed to be reliable and honest. *He's begun a series of personal attacks on my character.* **4** If you say that someone's actions are **in character**, you mean they are what you would expect them to do, knowing what kind of person they are. If their actions are **out of character**, they are not what you would expect them to do. **5** If something has a particular **character**, it has a particular quality. *Measures of a revolutionary character are necessary.* **6** You use **character** to say what kind of person someone is. For example, if you say that someone is a strange **character**, you mean they are strange. **7** If you say that someone is a **character**, you mean that they are interesting, unusual, or amusing. **8** If you say that someone has **character**, you mean that they have the ability to deal effectively with difficult, unpleasant, or dangerous situations; used showing approval. *I didn't know Ron had that much strength of character.* **9** If you say that a place has **character**, you mean that it has some interesting or unusual quality which makes you notice it and like it; used showing approval. ◆ **char·ac·ter·ful** /'kærɪktəful/. *One of the most characterful places to eat early evening is Mon Plaisir.* ◆ **char·ac·ter·less** /'kærɪktələs/. *...characterless, modern hotels.* ◆◆◆◇ N-COUNT N-SING: supp N N-VAR PHRASE N-SING: also in N N-COUNT N-COUNT INFORMAL N-UNCOUNT PRAGMATICS N-UNCOUNT PRAGMATICS ADJ-GRADED ADJ-GRADED

10 The **characters** in a film, book, or play are the people that it is about. N-COUNT **11** A **character** is a letter, number, or other symbol that is written or printed. N-COUNT

'character actor, character actors. A **character actor** is an actor who specializes in playing unusual or eccentric people. N-COUNT

'character assassination, character assassinations. **Character assassination** is a deliberate attempt to destroy someone's reputation, especially N-VAR by criticizing them unfairly or dishonestly when they are not present.

char·ac·ter·is·tic /ˌkærɪktə'rɪstɪk/ **characteristics. 1** The **characteristics** of a person or thing are the qualities or features that belong to them and make them recognizable. *Genes determine the characteristics of every living thing.* **2** A quality or feature that is **characteristic** of someone or something is one which is often seen in them and which seems typical of them. *Refusal to admit defeat was characteristic of Davis.* ◆ **char·ac·ter·is·ti·cal·ly** /ˌkærɪktə'rɪstɪkli/. *He replied in characteristically robust style.* ◆◆◆◇ N-COUNT ADJ-GRADED ADV-GRADED

char·ac·teri·za·tion /ˌkærɪktəraɪ'zeɪʃən/ **characterizations;** also spelled **characterisation** in British English. **Characterization** is the way an author or an actor portrays a character. ● See also **characterize.** ◆◇◇◇ N-VAR

char·ac·ter·ize /'kærɪktəraɪz/ **characterizes, characterizing, characterized;** also spelled **characterise** in British English. **1** If something **is characterized** by a particular feature or quality, that feature or quality is very evident in it. *This election campaign has been characterized by violence.* **2** If you **characterize** someone or something **as** a particular thing, you describe them as that thing. *Both companies have characterized the relationship as friendly.* ◆ **char·ac·teri·za·tion, characterizations** *I don't fully agree with that characterization of the welfare system.* ◆◆◇◇ VERB be V-ed Also V n FORMAL VERB V n as adj/n FORMAL N-VAR

cha·rade /ʃə'rɑːd, AM -'reɪd/ **charades. 1** If you describe someone's actions as a **charade**, you mean that their actions are very obviously a pretence; used showing disapproval. *I wondered why he had gone through the elaborate charade.* **2 Charades** is a game for teams of players in which one team mimes a word or phrase, syllable by syllable, until other players guess the whole word or phrase. ◆◇◇◇ PRAGMATICS N-UNCOUNT

char·coal /'tʃɑːkəʊl/. **Charcoal** is a black substance obtained by burning wood without much air. It can be burned as a fuel or used for drawing. ◆◇◇◇ N-UNCOUNT

chard /tʃɑːd/. **Chard** is a plant with a round root, large leaves, and a thick stalk. N-UNCOUNT

charge /tʃɑːdʒ/ **charges, charging, charged. 1** If you **charge** someone an amount of money, you ask them to pay that amount for something that you have sold to them or done for them. *Local nurseries charge £100 a week. ...the architect who charged us a fee of seven hundred pounds.* **2** If you **charge** something **to** a person or organization, you tell the people providing it to send the bill to them. If you **charge** something **to** someone's account, you add it to their account so they do not have to pay for it immediately. *Go out and buy a pair of glasses, and charge it to us.* **3** A **charge** is an amount of money that you have to pay for a service. *We can arrange this for a small charge.* **4** If something is **free of charge**, it does not cost anything. **5** A **charge** is a formal accusation that someone has committed a crime. *He may still face criminal charges.* **6** When the police **charge** someone, they formally accuse them of having done something illegal. *Police have charged Mr Bell with murder.* **7** If you **charge** someone **with** doing something wrong or unpleasant, you publicly say that they have done it. *He charged the minister with lying about the economy.* **8** If you take **charge** of someone or something, you make yourself responsible for them and take control over them. If someone or something is in your **charge**, you are responsible for them. *A few years ago Bacryl took charge of the company.* **9** If you are **in charge** in a particular situation, you are the most senior person and have control over something or someone. *...the Swiss governess in charge of the smaller children.* **10** If someone is your **charge**, you have been asked to look after them and you are responsible for them. **11** If you **charge** towards someone or something, you move quickly and aggressively towards them. *He charged through the door to my mother's office.* ▶ Also a noun. *...a bayonet charge.* ◆◆◆◆◆ VERB V n n V n n Also V VERB V n to n N-COUNT PHRASE N-COUNT VERB: V n VERB with n/n VERB V n with-ing/n WRITTEN N-UNCOUNT PHRASE N-COUNT VERB V prep/adv Also V N-COUNT

12 To **charge** a battery means to pass an electrical current through it in order to make it more powerful or to make it last longer. ▶ **Charge up** means the same as **charge**. *You have to drive it every day to charge up the battery.* ♦ **charg·er, chargers** ...*a new battery charger.* **13** An electrical **charge** is an amount of electricity that is held in or carried by something.   VERB: V n / PHRASAL VB / V P noun / Also V n P / N-COUNT / N-COUNT

14 The **charge** in a cartridge or shell is the explosive inside it. You can also refer to the cartridge or shell itself as a **charge**.   N-COUNT

15 See also **charged**; **baton charge**, **cover charge**, **depth charge**, **service charge**.

charge up See **charge** 8.   PHRASAL VB

charge·able /'tʃɑːdʒəbəl/. **1** If something is **chargeable**, you have to pay a sum of money for it. *Carriage is chargeable as an extra cost.* **2** If something is **chargeable**, you have to pay tax on it. ...*the taxpayer's chargeable gain.*   ADJ / BRITISH / ADJ / BRITISH

'charge card, charge cards. **1** A **charge card** is a plastic card that you use to buy goods on credit from a particular store or group of stores. Compare **credit card**. **2** A **charge card** is the same as a **credit card**.   N-COUNT / BRITISH / N-COUNT / AMERICAN

charged /tʃɑːdʒd/. **1** If a situation is **charged**, it is filled with emotion and very tense or exciting. *There was a highly charged atmosphere.* **2 Charged** particles carry an electrical charge. ...*negatively charged ions.*   ADJ-GRADED / ADJ

char·gé d'af·faires /ˌʃɑːʒeɪ dæˈfeə/ **chargés d'affaires.** **1** A **chargé d'affaires** is a person appointed to act as head of a diplomatic mission in a foreign country while the ambassador is away. **2** A **chargé d'affaires** is the head of a minor diplomatic mission in a foreign country.   N-COUNT / N-COUNT

'charge nurse, charge nurses. A **charge nurse** is a male nurse who is in charge of a hospital ward.   N-COUNT / BRITISH

charg·er /'tʃɑːdʒə/ **chargers.** **1** A **charger** was a strong horse that a knight in the Middle Ages used to ride in battle. **2** See also **charge**.   ◆◇◇◇◇ / N-COUNT

'charge sheet, charge sheets; also spelled **charge-sheet.** A **charge sheet** is the official form which is used by the police when they write down legal charges against a person.   N-COUNT / BRITISH

'char-grilled; also spelled **chargrilled. Char-grilled** meat or fish has been cooked so that it burns slightly and turns black.   ADJ

chari·ot /'tʃæriət/ **chariots.** In ancient times, **chariots** were fast-moving vehicles with two wheels that were pulled by horses.   ◆◇◇◇◇ / N-COUNT

chari·ot·eer /ˌtʃæriəˈtɪə/ **charioteers.** In ancient times, a **charioteer** was a chariot driver.   N-COUNT

cha·ris·ma /kəˈrɪzmə/. Someone who has **charisma** can attract and influence people by their personal qualities.   ◆◇◇◇◇ / N-UNCOUNT

char·is·mat·ic /ˌkærɪzˈmætɪk/. **1** A **charismatic** person attracts and influences people by their personal qualities. **2** The **charismatic** church is the part of the Christian Church that believes that people can obtain supernatural gifts from God, for example prophecy and healing.   ◆◇◇◇◇ / ADJ-GRADED / ADJ

chari·table /'tʃærɪtəbəl/. **1** A **charitable** organization or activity helps and supports people who are ill, handicapped, or very poor. **2** If you are **charitable** to someone, you are kind and tolerant, and try to interpret their actions in the best possible way. *The record of most intelligence services is, to be charitable, mixed.* ♦ **chari·tably** /'tʃærɪtəbli/. *Still, he reflected charitably, it was hardly her fault.*   ◆◆◇◇◇ / ADJ: ADJ n / ADJ-GRADED / ADV-GRADED: ADV with v

char·ity /'tʃærɪti/ **charities.** **1** A **charity** is an organization which raises money in order to help people who are ill, handicapped, or very poor. **2** If you give money to **charity**, you give it to one or more charitable organizations. If you do something for **charity**, you do it in order to raise money for one or more charitable organizations. **3** People who live on **charity** live on money or goods which other people give them because they are poor. **4 Charity** is kindness and tolerance towards other people. **5** If you say **charity begins at home**, you mean that people   ◆◆◆◇◇ / N-COUNT / N-UNCOUNT / N-UNCOUNT / N-UNCOUNT / FORMAL / PHRASE

should deal with the needs of people close to them before they think about helping others.

'charity shop, charity shops. A **charity shop** is a shop that sells second-hand goods cheaply and gives its profits to a charity. The usual American expression is **thrift shop**.   N-COUNT / BRITISH

char·la·tan /'ʃɑːlətən/ **charlatans.** If you describe someone as a **charlatan**, you mean that they pretend to have skills or knowledge that they do not really possess.   N-COUNT / FORMAL

charm /tʃɑːm/ **charms, charming, charmed.** **1 Charm** is the quality of being pleasant or attractive. *The 1937 Disney classic has lost none of its original charm.* **2** Someone who has **charm** behaves in a friendly, pleasant way that makes people like them. ...*a man of great charm and distinction.* **3** If you say that someone **turned on the charm**, you mean that they behaved in a way that seemed very friendly but which you think was insincere. **4** If you **charm** someone, you please them using your charm. If you **charm** them into doing something, you persuade them to do it by pleasing them like this. *She can charm you into believing her... He charmed his way out of trouble... He is good at charming money out of companies.*   ◆◆◇◇◇ / N-VAR / N-UNCOUNT / PHRASE / PRAGMATICS / BRITISH / VERB: V n / V n into -ing / V way prep / V n from/out of n

5 A **charm** is a small ornament that is fixed to a bracelet or necklace.   N-COUNT

6 A **charm** is an act, saying, or object that is believed to have magic powers. ...*a good luck charm.* **7** If you say that something **worked like a charm**, you mean that it was very effective or successful.   N-COUNT / PHRASE

charmed /tʃɑːmd/. **1** A **charmed** place, time, or situation is one that is very beautiful or pleasant, and seems slightly separate from the everyday life. ...*the charmed atmosphere of Oxford in the Twenties.*   ◆◇◇◇◇ / ADJ: ADJ n / LITERARY

2 If you say that someone **leads** or **has a charmed life**, you mean that they always seem to be lucky, as if they are protected or helped by magic.   PHRASE / BRITISH

,charmed 'circle. If you refer to a group of people as a **charmed circle**, you disapprove of the fact that they have unfair power or influence and rarely allow anyone else to join their group.   N-SING / PRAGMATICS

charm·er /'tʃɑːmə/ **charmers.** If you refer to someone, especially a man, as a **charmer**, you think that they behave in a very charming but rather insincere way; used showing disapproval. ● See also **snake charmer.**   N-COUNT / PRAGMATICS

charm·ing /'tʃɑːmɪŋ/. **1** If you say that something is **charming**, you mean that it is very pleasant or attractive. ...*a charming little fishing village.* ♦ **charm·ing·ly** *There's something charmingly old-fashioned about his brand of entertainment.* **2** If you describe someone as **charming**, you mean they behave in a friendly, pleasant way that makes people like them. ♦ **charmingly** *Calder smiled charmingly.* **3** You can say **'Charming!'** to indicate your disapproval when someone has just been rude to you or told you about someone's bad behaviour.   ◆◆◇◇◇ / ADJ-GRADED / PRAGMATICS / ADV-GRADED / ADJ-GRADED / ADV-GRADED: ADV after v / CONVENTION / PRAGMATICS

charm·less /'tʃɑːmləs/. If you say that something or someone is **charmless**, you mean that they are unattractive or uninteresting. ...*flat, charmless countryside.*   ADJ-GRADED / WRITTEN

charred /tʃɑːd/. **Charred** plants, buildings, or vehicles are black as a result of being badly burnt. ...*the charred remains of a tank.*   ◆◇◇◇◇ / ADJ-GRADED

chart /tʃɑːt/ **charts, charting, charted.** **1** A **chart** is a diagram, picture, or graph which displays information. *Male unemployment was 14.2%, compared with 5.8% for women (see chart on next page).* ● See also **flow chart, pie chart.** **2** A **chart** is a map of the sea or stars. **3** If you **chart** an area of land, sea, or sky, or a feature in that area, you make a map of the area or show the feature in it. *Portuguese explorers had charted the west coast of Africa.* **4** If you **chart** the development or progress of something, you observe and record it carefully. You can also say that a report or graph **charts** the development or progress of something. *One GP has charted a dramatic rise in local childhood asthma.* **5** If a person or plan **charts** a course of action, they   ◆◆◆◇◇ / N-COUNT / N-COUNT / VERB: V n / VERB: V n / VERB: V n / FORMAL

describe what should be done in order to achieve something. *We've charted a possible way forward.*
6 The **charts** are the official lists that show which pop records have sold the most copies each week. *...Number One in the charts.* **7** If a musical performer or one of their records **charts**, their record sells enough copies to be in the list of best-selling records for a particular week. — N-COUNT / VERB: V / JOURNALISM

char·ter /'tʃɑːtə/ **charters, chartering, chartered. 1** A **charter** is a formal document describing the rights, aims, or principles of an organization or group of people. *...the United Nations Charter... They described the Home Office scheme as a 'charter for cheats'.* **2** A **charter** plane or boat is hired for use by a particular group or company and is not part of a regular service. *...charter flights to Spain.* **3** If a person or organization **charters** a plane, boat, or other vehicle, they hire it for their own use. *He chartered a jet to fly her home.* — ◆◆◇◇ / N-COUNT: with supp / ADJ: ADJ n / VERB V n

char·tered /'tʃɑːtəd/. A **chartered** accountant or **chartered** surveyor has formally qualified in their profession. — ◆◇◇◇ / ADJ: ADJ n / BRITISH

chary /'tʃeəri/. If you are **chary** of doing something, you are fairly cautious about doing it. *She is chary of labelling herself a feminist.* — ADJ-GRADED: v-link ADJ

chase /tʃeɪs/ **chases, chasing, chased. 1** If you **chase** someone, or **chase** after them, you run after them or follow them quickly in order to catch or reach them. *She chased the thief for 100 yards. ...waiting journalists, who chased after him as he left.* ► Also a noun. *He was reluctant to give up the chase.* **2** If you **give chase**, you run after someone or follow them quickly in order to catch them. **3** If someone **chases** you from a place, they force you to leave by using threats or violence. *Many farmers will then chase you off their land... Angry demonstrators chased him away.* **4** If you **chase** somewhere, you run or rush there. *They chased down the stairs into the narrow, dirty street.* **5** If you **are chasing** something you want, such as work or money, you are trying hard to get it. *14 people are chasing every job. ...publishers and booksellers chasing after profits.* ► Also a noun. *They took an invincible lead in the chase for the championship.* **6** If someone **chases** someone that they are attracted to, or **chases** after them, they try hard to persuade them to have a sexual relationship with them. *I was always chasing after men who just couldn't handle intimacy.* ► Also a noun. *The chase is always much more exciting than the conquest.* **7** If you talk about **the thrill of the chase**, you are referring to the excitement that people feel when they are trying very hard to get something. **8** The **chase** is the activity of hunting animals. *...lion hides, and other trophies of the chase.* **9** See also **wild goose chase**. — ◆◆◇◇ / VERB V n / V after n / N-COUNT / PHRASE / VERB V n from/out of/off n / V n away/ off/out / VERB V prep/adv / VERB V n / V after n / N-SING: N for n / VERB / V after n / Also V n / N-SING: the N / PHRASE / N-SING: the N / DATED

chase away. If someone or something **chases away** worries, fears, or other bad feelings, they cause those feelings to change and become happier. *Ellery's return will help to chase away some of the gloom.* — PHRASAL VB V P noun

chase down. If you **chase** someone or something **down**, you manage to catch them or find them. *Ness chased the thief down and held him until police arrived... Bank officials argued that it is not their job to chase down every asset of every bank debtor.* — PHRASAL VB V P noun

chase up. If you **chase up** something or someone that you need to deal with, you try to find them or find out about them, in order to deal with them as soon as possible. *When I didn't hear from the suppliers or receive a refund, I chased the matter up. ...a man who comes to Hollywood to chase up a client.* — PHRASAL VB V n P / V P noun / BRITISH

chas·er /'tʃeɪsə/ **chasers.** A **chaser** is a strong alcoholic drink that you have to accompany a weaker one. — ◆◇◇◇ / N-COUNT

chasm /'kæzəm/ **chasms. 1** A **chasm** is a very deep crack in rock, earth, or ice. **2** If you say that there is a **chasm** between two things or two groups of people, you mean that there is a very big difference between them. *...the chasm that divides the worlds of university and industry.* **3** A **chasm** is a — ◆◇◇◇ / N-COUNT / N-COUNT / N-COUNT

problem or negative emotion that is so large or intense it seems impossible to overcome it. *The two sides are now divided by a chasm of hatred and mistrust.*

chas·sis /'ʃæsi/; **chassis** /'ʃæsiz/ is the plural form. A **chassis** is the framework that a vehicle is built on. — ◆◇◇◇ / N-COUNT

chaste /tʃeɪst/. **1** If you describe a person or their behaviour as **chaste**, you mean that they do not have sex with anyone, or they only have sex with their husband or wife. *Abramov did not live a chaste life.* **2** Something that is **chaste** is very simple in style, without very much decoration. *...chaste clothes.* — ADJ-GRADED / DATED / ADJ: ADJ n

chas·ten /'tʃeɪsən/ **chastens, chastening, chastened.** If you **are chastened** by something, it makes you feel sorry that you have behaved badly or foolishly. *He has clearly not been chastened by his thirteen days in detention.* ♦ **chas·tened** *He now seems a more chastened and less confident politician.* ♦ **chas·ten·ing** *From this chastening experience he learnt some useful lessons.* — VB: usu passive be V-ed by n / FORMAL / ADJ-GRADED / ADJ-GRADED

chas·tise /tʃæs'taɪz/ **chastises, chastising, chastised.** If you **chastise** someone, you scold or punish them for something wrong that they have done. *Thomas Rane chastised Peters for his cruelty.* ♦ **chas·tise·ment** *...unnecessary or cruel chastisement of an animal.* — VERB V n / FORMAL / N-UNCOUNT: also a N

chas·tity /'tʃæstɪti/. **Chastity** is the state of not having sex with anyone, or of only having sex with your husband or wife. *He took a vow of chastity.* — N-UNCOUNT / DATED

chat /tʃæt/ **chats, chatting, chatted.** When people **chat**, they talk to each other in an informal and friendly way. *I was chatting to him the other day... We chatted about old times.* ► Also a noun. *I had a chat with John.* — ◆◆◇◇ / V-RECIP V to/with n / pl-n V about n / Also pl-n V / N-COUNT

chat up. If you **chat** someone **up**, usually someone you do not know very well, you talk to them in a friendly way because you are sexually attracted to them. *He'd spent most of that evening chatting up one of my friends.* — PHRASAL VB V P noun / Also V n P / BRITISH, INFORMAL

châ·teau /'ʃætəʊ/ **châteaux** /'ʃætəʊz/; also spelled **chateau**. A **château** is a large country house or castle in France. — N-COUNT

chat·line /'tʃætlaɪn/ **chatlines.** People phone in to **chatlines** to have conversations with other people who have also phoned in. — N-COUNT / BRITISH

'**chat show, chat shows.** A **chat show** is a television or radio show in which an interviewer and his or her guests talk in a friendly informal way about different topics. The usual American expression is **talk show.** — N-COUNT / BRITISH

chat·tel /'tʃætəl/ **chattels. Chattels** are things that belong to you. *They were slaves, to be bought and sold as chattels.* — N-VAR / DATED

chat·ter /'tʃætə/ **chatters, chattering, chattered. 1** If you **chatter**, you talk quickly and continuously, usually about unimportant things. *Everyone's chattering away in different languages... Erica was friendly and chattered about Andrew's children.* ► Also a noun. *...idle chatter.* **2** If your teeth **chatter**, they click together repeatedly because you are very cold or very nervous. *She was so cold her teeth chattered.* **3** If objects **chatter**, they make repeated rattling sounds. *The telex chattered all day and night.* ► Also a noun. *...the chatter of the chairlift cable over the pulley wheel.* **4** When birds or animals **chatter**, they make high-pitched noises. *Birds were chattering somewhere.* ► Also a noun. *...the chatter of crickets.* — ◆◇◇◇ / VERB: V / V adv/prep / V about n / N-UNCOUNT / VERB V / VERB V / N-UNCOUNT / VERB V / LITERARY / N-UNCOUNT

chatter·box /'tʃætəbɒks/ **chatterboxes.** A **chatterbox** is someone who talks a lot. — N-COUNT / INFORMAL

'**chattering classes.** The **chattering classes** is a term used to describe fashionable or middle-class people who regularly discuss current affairs, and who are thought to have an excessive influence on politics and in the media; used showing disapproval. *Radical feminism is currently the fashionable topic among the chattering classes.* — N-PLURAL / PRAGMATICS / BRITISH

chat·ty /'tʃæti/. **1** Someone who is **chatty** talks a lot in a friendly informal way. **2** A **chatty** style of — ADJ-GRADED / ADJ-GRADED

writing or talking is friendly and informal. *He wrote a chatty letter to his wife.*

'chat-up line, chat-up lines. A chat-up line is a remark that someone makes in order to start a conversation with a person who they do not know but who they find sexually attractive. N-COUNT BRITISH

chauf·feur /'ʃəʊfə, ʃəʊ'fɜ:/ **chauffeurs, chauffeuring, chauffeured. 1** The **chauffeur** of someone rich or important is the person who is employed to look after their car and drive them around in it. **2** If you **chauffeur** someone somewhere, you drive them there in a car, often as part of your job. *It was certainly useful to have her there to chauffeur him around.* ◆◇◇◇◇ N-COUNT VERB V n adv/prep Also V n

chau·vin·ism /'ʃəʊvɪnɪzəm/. **1** If you accuse a man of **chauvinism**, you are criticizing him because he believes that men are naturally better and more important than women. ◆ **chau·vin·ist, chauvinists** *It is ironic that a feminist who values independence should marry a chauvinist.* ◆ **chau·vin·is·tic** *...a chauvinistic culture which emphasized caricatured sexual relations.* **2** Chauvinism is a strong unreasonable belief that your own country is more important and better than other people's. ◆ **chau·vin·ist** *He has been vilified in the media as a demagogue and a chauvinist.* ◆ **chau·vin·is·tic** *...national narrow-mindedness and chauvinistic arrogance.* ◆◇◇◇◇ N-UNCOUNT PRAGMATICS N-COUNT ADJ-GRADED N-UNCOUNT PRAGMATICS N-COUNT ADJ-GRADED

cheap /tʃi:p/ **cheaper, cheapest. 1** Goods or services that are **cheap** cost less money than usual or than you expected. *Smoke detectors are cheap and easy to put up... Running costs are coming down because of cheaper fuel.* ◆ **cheap·ly** *It will produce electricity more cheaply than a nuclear plant.* ◆ **cheap·ness** *...the cheapness and simplicity of the design.* **2** If you describe goods as **cheap**, you mean they cost less money than similar products but their quality is poor. *...some cheap material.* **3** If you describe the cost of someone's work as **cheap**, you disapprove of the way people are taking advantage of a situation to pay someone less than they should for the work that they do. *...unscrupulous employers who treat children as a cheap source of labour.* **4** If you say that someone does or buys something **on the cheap**, you mean they spend less money on it than is required because they are more concerned with what it costs than its quality. **5** If you describe someone's remarks or actions as **cheap**, you mean that they are unkindly or insincerely using a situation to benefit themselves or to harm someone else. *These tests will inevitably be used by politicians to make cheap political points.* **6** If you say that **life is cheap**, you mean that a situation such as a war has made it normal for large numbers of people to die unnecessarily and often violently without anyone caring. ◆◆◆◇ ADJ-GRADED ADV-GRADED: ADV after v N-UNCOUNT ADJ: ADJ n ADJ: ADJ n PRAGMATICS PHRASE INFORMAL, BRITISH ADJ: ADJ n PRAGMATICS PHRASE

cheap·en /'tʃi:pən/ **cheapens, cheapening, cheapened.** If something **cheapens** a person or thing, it lowers their reputation or dignity. *When America boycotted the Moscow Olympics it cheapened the medals won.* VERB V n

cheapo /'tʃi:pəʊ/. **Cheapo** things are very inexpensive and usually of poor quality. *...my cheapo rental car.* ADJ: ADJ n INFORMAL

,cheap 'shot, cheap shots. A cheap shot is a comment which you consider unfair or unkind. N-COUNT PRAGMATICS

cheap·skate /'tʃi:pskeɪt/ **cheapskates.** If you say that someone is a **cheapskate**, you think that they are mean and very reluctant to spend money. *Tell your husband not to be a cheapskate.* N-COUNT PRAGMATICS

cheat /tʃi:t/ **cheats, cheating, cheated. 1** If someone **cheats**, they do not obey a set of rules which they should be obeying, for example in a game or exam. *Students may be tempted to cheat.* ◆ **cheat·ing** *He was accused of cheating.* **2** A **cheat** is someone who does not obey a set of rules which they should be obeying. *Cheats will be disqualified.* **3** If someone **cheats** you out of something, they get it from you by behaving dishonestly. *...a deliberate effort to cheat them out of their pensions... Many brokers* ◆◆◇◇ VERB V N-UNCOUNT N-COUNT VERB V n out of/on V n

were charged with cheating customers. **4** If you **feel cheated**, you feel that you have been let down or treated unfairly. *The storyline is fatally compromised by an ending that leaves you feeling horribly cheated.* **5** If you say that someone **cheats death**, you mean they narrowly avoid being killed. PHRASE PHRASE JOURNALISM

cheat on. 1 If someone **cheats on** their husband, wife, or partner, they have a sexual relationship with another person. **2** If someone **cheats on** something such as an agreement or their taxes, they do not do what they should do under a set of rules. *Their job is to check that none of the signatory countries is cheating on the agreement.* PHRASAL VB V P n INFORMAL V P n AMERICAN

cheat·er /'tʃi:tə/ **cheaters.** A **cheater** is someone who cheats. N-COUNT

check /tʃek/ **checks, checking, checked. 1** If you **check** something such as a piece of information or a document, you make sure that it is correct or satisfactory. *I think there is an age limit, but I'd have to check... She hadn't checked whether she had a clean ironed shirt... I shall need to check with the duty officer.* ● See also **cross-check.** ▶ Also a noun. *...regular checks on his blood pressure.* ◆ **check·er, checkers.** A checker is a person or machine that checks something. *Janie worked as a checker at the A&P... Modern word processors usually have spelling checkers.* ● See also **checker. 2** If you **check** on someone or something, you make sure they are in a safe or satisfactory condition. *Stephen checked on her several times during the night.* **3** To **check** something, usually something bad, means to stop it from spreading or continuing. *Sex education is also expected to help check the spread of AIDS.* **4** If you **check** yourself or if something **checks** you, you suddenly stop what you are doing or saying. *He was about to lose his temper but checked himself in time.* **5** If something or someone **is held** or **kept in check**, they are prevented from becoming too great or powerful. *Life on Earth will become unsustainable unless population growth is held in check.* **6** At an airport, when you **check** your luggage, you give it to an official so that it can be taken aboard the plane you will be travelling on. *You can check your baggage right through to its final destination.* ▶ **Check in** means the same as **check**. *They checked in their luggage and found seats in the departure lounge.* **7** The **check** in a restaurant is a piece of paper on which the cost of your meal is written and which you are given before you pay. **8** A **check** or **check mark** is a written mark like a V with the right side extended. It is used to show that something is correct or has been selected or dealt with. The usual British word is **tick**. *Put a check under the circle.* **9** In a game of chess, you say **check** when you are attacking your opponent's king. **10** A pattern of squares, usually of two colours, can be referred to as **checks** or a **check**. See picture headed **patterns.** ◆ **checked** *He was wearing blue jeans and checked shirt.* **11** See also **cheque, double-check, rain check, spot check.** ◆◆◆◇ VERB: V n V V n/that V with n N-COUNT N-COUNT VERB V on n VERB V n VERB V pron-refl Also V n PHRASE VERB: V n V n prep/adv PHRASAL VB V P noun Also V n P N-COUNT AMERICAN N-COUNT AMERICAN CONVENTION N-COUNT ADJ

check in. 1 When you **check in** or **check into** a hotel or clinic, you arrive and go through the necessary procedures before you stay there. *I'll tell them we'll check in tomorrow... He has checked into an alcohol treatment centre.* **2** When you **check in** at an airport, you arrive and show your ticket before going on a flight. ● See also **check-in, check 6.** PHRASAL VB V P n V P n VP

check off. When you **check** things **off**, you check or count them while referring to a list of them, to make sure you have considered all of them. *...once you've checked off the items you ordered.* PHRASAL VB V P noun Also V n P

check out. 1 When you **check out** of a hotel or clinic where you have been staying, you pay the bill and leave. *They packed and checked out of the hotel... I was disappointed to miss Bryan, who had just checked out.* **2** If you **check out** someone or something, you find out information about them to make sure that everything is correct or satisfactory. *We ought to check him* PHRASAL VB V P of n V P V n P V P n

C

out on the computer... The police had to check out the call. **3** See also **checkout.**

check up on. If you **check up on** something or someone, you find out information about them. *It is certainly worth checking up on your benefit entitlements.* PHRASAL VB / V P P n

check·book /'tʃekbʊk/. See **cheque book**.

check·er /'tʃekə/. **Checkers** is a game for two people, played with 24 round pieces on a board. The British word is **draughts**. ● See also **check.** N-UNCOUNT / AMERICAN

checker·board /'tʃekəbɔːd/ **checkerboards;** also spelled **chequerboard** in British English. **1** A **checkerboard** is a board used to play chess or draughts on. The usual British word is **chessboard.** **2** A **checkerboard** pattern is made up of equal-sized squares of two different colours. N-COUNT / AMERICAN / ADJ: ADJ n

check·ered /'tʃekəd/. See **chequered.**

'**check·in, check·ins.** At an airport, the **check-in** is the counter or desk where you check in. ◆◇◇◇ N-COUNT

'**checking account, checking accounts.** A **checking account** is a personal bank account which you can take money out of at any time using your cheque book or cash card. The usual British expression is **current account.** N-COUNT / AMERICAN

check·list /'tʃeklɪst/ **checklists.** A checklist is a list of all the things that you need to do, information that you want to find out, or things that you need to take somewhere, which you make in order to ensure that you do not forget anything. *...a checklist of the tools and materials you will need.* ◆◇◇◇ N-COUNT

check·mate /'tʃekmeɪt/. In chess, **checkmate** is a situation in which you cannot stop your king being captured and so you lose the game. N-UNCOUNT

check·out /'tʃekaʊt/ **checkouts;** also spelled **check-out.** In a supermarket, a **checkout** is a counter where you pay for things you are buying. ◆◇◇◇ N-COUNT

check·point /'tʃekpɔɪnt/ **checkpoints.** A **checkpoint** is a place where traffic is stopped so that it can be checked. ◆◇◇◇ N-COUNT

'**check-up, check-ups.** A **check-up** is an examination by your doctor or dentist to make sure that there is nothing wrong with your health or teeth. ◆◇◇◇ N-COUNT

ched·dar /'tʃedə/ **cheddars.** Cheddar is a type of hard yellow cheese. ◆◇◇◇ N-VAR

cheek /tʃiːk/ **cheeks. 1** Your **cheeks** are the sides of your face below your eyes. See picture headed **human body.** *She kissed him lightly on both cheeks.* **♦ -cheeked** *...rosy-cheeked children.* **2** If you **turn the other cheek** when someone harms or insults you, you do not harm them in return. **3** ● **cheek by jowl:** see **jowl. 4** You say that someone has a **cheek** when you are annoyed or shocked at something unacceptable they have done. *I'm amazed they had the cheek to ask.* ◆◇◇◇ N-COUNT / COMB / PHRASE / N-SING: also no det INFORMAL, BRITISH

cheek·bone /'tʃiːkbəʊn/ **cheekbones.** Your **cheekbones** are the bones in your face just below your eyes. *She was very beautiful, with high cheekbones.* ◆◇◇◇ N-COUNT

cheeky /'tʃiːki/ **cheekier, cheekiest.** If you describe someone as **cheeky**, you think that they are slightly rude or disrespectful but in a charming or amusing way. *The boy was cheeky and casual. ...a cheeky grin.* **♦ cheeki·ly** /'tʃiːkɪli/. *He strolled cheekily past the commissionaires for a free wash in the gentlemen's cloakroom.* ◆◇◇◇ ADJ-GRADED / ADV-GRADED

cheer /tʃɪə/ **cheers, cheering, cheered. 1** When people **cheer**, they shout loudly to show approval or encouragement of someone, for example at a sports event. *Swiss fans cheered Jakob Hlasek during yesterday's match.* ▶ Also a noun. *The colonel was rewarded with a resounding cheer.* **2** If you **are cheered** by something, it makes you happier or less worried. *The people around him looked cheered by his presence... The thought did nothing to cheer him.* **♦ cheer·ing** *...very cheering news.* **3 Cheer** is a feeling of cheerfulness and well-being. *They were impressed by his steadfast good cheer.* **4** People sometimes say '**Cheers**' to each other just before they drink an alcoholic drink. **5** Some people say '**Cheers**' as an informal way of saying 'thank you'. ◆◆◆◇ VERB: V / V n / N-COUNT / VERB / V-ed / V n / ADJ-GRADED / N-UNCOUNT / CONVENTION / CONVENTION BRITISH

cheer on. When you **cheer** someone **on**, you shout loudly in order to encourage them, for example when they are taking part in a game. *A thousand supporters packed into the stadium to cheer them on.* PHRASAL VB / V n P / Also V P noun

cheer up. When you **cheer up** or when something **cheers** you **up**, you stop feeling depressed and become more cheerful. *I was standing next to his hospital bed singing in a vain effort to cheer him up... Cheer up, better times may be ahead.* PHRASAL VB / ERG / V n P / V P / Also V P noun

cheer·ful /'tʃɪəfʊl/. **1** Someone who is **cheerful** is happy and shows this in their behaviour. *They are both very cheerful in spite of their colds.* **♦ cheer·ful·ly** *'We've come with good news,' Pat said cheerfully.* **♦ cheer·ful·ness** *...his unfailing cheerfulness.* **2** Something that is **cheerful** is pleasant and makes you feel happy. *The nursery is bright and cheerful, with plenty of toys.* **3** If you describe someone's attitude as **cheerful**, you mean they are not worried about something, and you think that they should be. *There is little evidence to support many of Mr Will's cheerful assumptions.* **♦ cheer·ful·ly** *...cheerfully ignoring medical advice.* ◆◇◇◇ ADJ-GRADED / ADV-GRADED: ADV with v / N-UNCOUNT / ADJ-GRADED / ADJ-GRADED / ADV: ADV before v

cheerio /,tʃɪəri'əʊ/. People sometimes say '**Cheerio**' as a way of saying goodbye. *Say cheerio to Shona for me.* CONVENTION BRITISH, INFORMAL

cheer·leader /'tʃɪəliːdə/ **cheerleaders. 1** A **cheerleader** is one of the people who leads the crowd in cheering at a large public event, especially a sports event. **2** If you say that someone is a **cheerleader** for a particular cause or politician, you mean that they are one of the chief supporters of this cause or politician and work hard to raise support for them. *Chancellor Helmut Kohl was the leading cheerleader for German unification.* ◆◇◇◇ N-COUNT / N-COUNT

cheer·less /'tʃɪələs/. A place that is **cheerless** is gloomy and depressing. *The kitchen was dank and cheerless.* ADJ-GRADED

cheery /'tʃɪəri/ **cheerier, cheeriest.** If someone is **cheery**, they are cheerful and happy. *...her father's cheery voice.* **♦ cheeri·ly** *'Come on in,' she said cheerily.* ◆◇◇◇ ADJ-GRADED / ADV-GRADED

cheese /tʃiːz/ **cheeses. 1** Cheese is a solid food made from milk. It is usually white or yellow. **2** See also **cottage cheese, cream cheese, goat cheese.** ● **as different as chalk and cheese:** see **chalk.** ◆◆◇◇ N-VAR

cheese·board /'tʃiːzbɔːd/ **cheeseboards.** A **cheeseboard** is a wooden or plastic board from which a selection of cheeses are served at a meal. N-COUNT

cheese·burg·er /'tʃiːzbɜːgə/ **cheeseburgers.** A **cheeseburger** is a flat piece of cooked meat with a layer of cheese, served in a bread bun. N-COUNT

cheese·cake /'tʃiːzkeɪk/ **cheesecakes.** Cheesecake is a dessert consisting of a base made from crumbled biscuits covered with a soft mixture containing cream cheese. N-VAR

cheese·cloth /'tʃiːzklɒθ, AM -klɔːθ/. **Cheesecloth** is cotton cloth that is very thin and light. N-UNCOUNT

cheesed off /,tʃiːzd 'ɒf/. If you are **cheesed off**, you are annoyed, bored, or disappointed. *Jean was thoroughly cheesed off by the whole affair.* ADJ-GRADED: v-link ADJ BRITISH, INFORMAL

cheesy /'tʃiːzi/. **1 Cheesy** food tastes or smells of cheese. *The sauce was too runny and not cheesy enough.* **2** Something that is **cheesy** is considered to be cheap, unpleasant, or insincere. *...a cheesy Baghdad hotel.* ADJ-GRADED / ADJ-GRADED AMERICAN, INFORMAL

chee·tah /'tʃiːtə/ **cheetahs.** A cheetah is a wild animal like a large cat which can run very fast. See picture headed **animals.** N-COUNT

chef /ʃef/ **chefs.** A chef is a cook in a restaurant or hotel. ◆◆◇◇ N-COUNT

chemi·cal /'kemɪkəl/ **chemicals. 1 Chemical** means involving or resulting from a reaction between two or more substances, or relating to the substances that something consists of. *...chemical reactions. ...the chemical composition of the ocean.* **♦ chemi·cal·ly** /'kemɪkli/. *...chemically treated foods.* **2 Chemicals** are substances that are used in a chemical process or made by a chemical process. *...the over-use of chemicals in agriculture. ...a chemicals company.* ◆◆◆◇ ADJ: ADJ n / ADV / N-COUNT

,**chemical engi'neering.** Chemical engineering N-UNCOUNT is the designing and constructing of machines that are needed for industrial chemical processes.
♦ **chemi·cal en·gi·neer, chemical engineers** N-COUNT

chem·ist /'kemɪst/ **chemists. 1** A chemist or a ♦♦♦◇◇ **chemist's** is a shop where medicines are sold or giv- N-COUNT en out. You can also refer to the specially qualified BRITISH person who prepares and sells the medicines in this shop as a **chemist. 2** A **chemist** is a person who N-COUNT studies chemistry. ...*a research chemist.*

chem·is·try /'kemɪstri/. **1** Chemistry is the ♦♦◇◇◇ scientific study of the characteristics and composi- N-UNCOUNT tion of substances and of the way that they react with other substances. **2** If you talk about the N-UNCOUNT **chemistry** of something, you are referring to the chemical substances that make it up and the chemi- cal reactions that go on inside it. ...*the chemistry of our planet's atmosphere.* **3** If you say that there is N-UNCOUNT **chemistry** between two people, you mean that is obvious they are attracted to each other or like each other very much. ...*the extraordinary chemistry be- tween Ingrid and Bogart.*

chemo·thera·py /ˌkiːməʊ'θerəpi/. **Chemotherapy** ♦◇◇◇ is the treatment of disease using chemicals. It is of- N-UNCOUNT ten used in treating cancer.

che·nille /ʃə'niːl/. **Chenille** is cloth or clothing N-UNCOUNT made from a thick furry yarn.

cheque /tʃek/ **cheques;** spelled **check** in Ameri- ♦♦◇◇◇ can English. A **cheque** is a printed form on which N-COUNT you write an amount of money and who it is to be also by N paid to. Your bank then pays the money to that per- son from your account. *He wrote them a cheque for £10,000... I'd like to pay by cheque.* ● See also **blank cheque, traveller's cheque.**

'**cheque book, cheque books;** also spelled N-COUNT **chequebook.** Spelled **checkbook** in American Eng- lish. A **cheque book** is a book of blank cheques.

'**cheque card, cheque cards.** In Britain, a N-COUNT **cheque card** is a small plastic card which you have to show when you are paying for something by cheque or when you are cashing a cheque.

chequer·board /'tʃekəbɔːd/. See **checkerboard.**

cheq·uered /'tʃekəd/; spelled **checkered** in Ameri- can English. **1** If a person or organization has had a ADJ-GRADED **chequered** career or history, they have had a varied past with both good and bad periods. *He had a chequered political career spanning nearly forty years.* **2** A **chequered** pattern consists of squares of ADJ: ADJ n two or more different colours. ...*red chequered tablecloths.*

cher·ish /'tʃerɪʃ/ **cherishes, cherishing, cher-** ♦◇◇◇◇ **ished. 1** If you **cherish** something such as a hope VERB or a pleasant memory, you keep it in your mind for V n a long period of time. *The president will cherish the memory of this visit to Ohio.* ♦ **cher·ished** ...*the* ADJ-GRADED *cherished dream of a world without wars.* **2** If you VERB: V n **cherish** someone or something, you take good care of them because you love them. ♦ **cherished** ...*his* ADJ-GRADED: *most cherished possession.* **3** If you **cherish** a right, ADJ n a privilege, or a principle, you regard it as important VERB and try hard to keep it. *Chinese people cherish their* V n *independence.* ♦ **cherished** ...*some deeply cher-* ADJ-GRADED: *ished beliefs.* ADJ n

che·root /ʃə'ruːt/ **cheroots.** A **cheroot** is a cigar N-COUNT with both ends cut flat.

cher·ry /'tʃeri/ **cherries. 1** Cherries are small ♦♦◇◇◇ round fruit with red skins. See picture headed **fruit.** N-COUNT **2** A **cherry** or a **cherry tree** is a tree that cherries grow N-COUNT on.

cher·ub /'tʃerəb/ **cherubs.** A **cherub** is an angel N-COUNT that is represented in art as a plump naked child with wings.

che·ru·bic /tʃə'ruːbɪk/. If you say that someone ADJ looks **cherubic**, you mean that they look plump, LITERARY sweet, and innocent like a cherub.

cher·vil /'tʃɜːvɪl/. **Chervil** is a herb that tastes of N-UNCOUNT aniseed.

Chesh·ire cat /ˌtʃeʃə 'kæt/. If you say that some- PHRASE one is grinning **like a Cheshire cat**, you mean that they are smiling very widely.

chess /tʃes/. **Chess** is a game for two people, ♦♦◇◇◇ played on a chessboard. Each player has 16 pieces, N-UNCOUNT including a king. Your aim is to move your pieces so your opponent's king cannot escape being taken.

chess·board /'tʃesbɔːd/ **chessboards.** A **chess-** N-COUNT **board** is a board used to play chess or draughts on. BRITISH The usual American word is **checkerboard.**

chest /tʃest/ **chests. 1** Your **chest** is the top part ♦♦♦◇◇ of the front of your body where your ribs, lungs, N-COUNT and heart are. See picture headed **human body.** *He was shot in the chest... He complained of chest pain.* ♦ **-chested** *He was bare-chested.* **2** If you **get** COMB something **off** your **chest**, you talk about something PHRASE that has been worrying you. **3** A **chest** is a large N-COUNT heavy box used for storing things.

chest·nut /'tʃesnʌt/ **chestnuts. 1** A **chestnut** or ♦◇◇◇◇ **chestnut tree** is a tall tree with broad leaves. ● See N-COUNT also **horse chestnut. 2** Chestnuts are the nuts that N-COUNT grow on chestnut trees. **3** If you refer to a state- PHRASE ment, a story, or a joke as an **old chestnut**, you mean that it has been repeated so often that it is no longer interesting. **4** Something that is **chestnut** is COLOUR dark reddish-brown. ...*a woman with chestnut hair.*

,**chest of 'drawers, chests of drawers.** A **chest** N-COUNT **of drawers** is a low flat piece of furniture with draw- ers in which you keep clothes and other things.

chesty /'tʃesti/. If you have a **chesty** cough, you ADJ: ADJ n have a lot of catarrh in your lungs. BRITISH

chev·ron /'ʃevrɒn/ **chevrons.** A **chevron** is a V ◇◇◇◇ shape, for example one that is worn on the sleeve of N-COUNT someone in the armed forces or police force.

chew /tʃuː/ **chews, chewing, chewed. 1** When ♦♦◇◇◇ you **chew** food, you use your teeth to break it up in VERB: V n your mouth so that it becomes easier to swallow. V at/on n *Daniel leaned back on the sofa, still chewing on his* Also V *apple.* **2** If you **chew** an object, you keep biting it. VERB *He chewed his lower lip nervously... The animal* V n *chewed through electric cables.* **3** A **chew** is a sweet V prep that you have to chew very hard before it becomes N-COUNT soft. BRITISH

4 If you say that someone **has bitten off more than** PHRASE they **can chew**, you mean that they are trying to do something which is too difficult for them. **5** ● to **chew the cud:** see **cud.**

chew over. If you **chew** something **over**, you keep PHRASAL VB thinking about it. *He tends to chew things over too* V n P much in his mind. Also V P noun

chew up. 1 If you **chew** food **up**, you chew it until it PHRASAL VB is completely crushed or softened. *I took one of the* V n P pills and chewed it up. **2** If something **is chewed up**, be V-ed P has been destroyed or badly damaged in some way. V P noun ...*rebels who are now chewing up Croatian territory.* Also V n P INFORMAL

'**chewing gum. Chewing gum** is a kind of sweet N-UNCOUNT that you can chew for a long time.

chewy /'tʃuːi/ **chewier, chewiest.** If food is ADJ-GRADED **chewy**, it needs to be chewed a lot before it be- comes soft enough to swallow.

chic /ʃiːk/. **1** Something or someone that is **chic** is ♦◇◇◇◇ fashionable and sophisticated. ...*very chic bars and* ADJ-GRADED *restaurants.* **2** Chic is used to refer to a particular N-UNCOUNT style or to the quality of being chic. ...*French design- er chic.*

chi·can·ery /ʃɪ'keɪnəri/ **chicaneries. Chicanery** is N-UNCOUNT: trickery and deliberately deceitful behaviour. also N in pl FORMAL

chi·ca·no /tʃɪ'keɪnəʊ/ **chicanos.** A **chicano** is a citi- N-COUNT zen of the United States whose family originally came from Mexico.

chick /tʃɪk/ **chicks. 1** A **chick** is a baby bird. ...*a* ♦♦◇◇◇ *newly-hatched chick.* N-COUNT

2 Some men refer to women as **chicks.** Some women N-COUNT find this use offensive. INFORMAL

chick·en /'tʃɪkɪn/ **chickens, chickening,** ♦♦♦◇◇ **chickened. 1** Chickens are birds which are kept N-COUNT on a farm for their eggs and for their meat. See pic- ture headed **animals.** ▸ Chicken is the flesh of this N-UNCOUNT bird eaten as food.

2 If someone calls you a **chicken**, they mean that you N-COUNT are afraid to do something. ...*accusing him of being a* INFORMAL *chicken.* ▸ Also an adjective. *Why are you so chicken,* ADJ-GRADED *Gregory?*

3 If you describe a situation as a **chicken and egg** situation, you mean that it is impossible to decide which of two things caused the other one. **4** If you say that someone is **running round like a headless chicken**, you mean they are doing unnecessary tasks very quickly when they should be thinking more carefully about what needs to be done. **5** • **chickens come home to roost**: see **roost**. PHRASE

chicken out. If someone **chickens out** of something, they do not do it because they are afraid. *I had never ridden on a motor-cycle before. But it was too late to chicken out.* PHRASAL VB / V P of n / V P / INFORMAL

'chicken feed; also spelled **chickenfeed**. If you refer to an amount of money as **chicken feed**, you mean it is so small it is hardly worth having. N-UNCOUNT

chicken·pox /'tʃɪkɪnpɒks/; also spelled **chicken pox**. Chickenpox is a disease which gives you a high temperature and red spots that itch. N-UNCOUNT

'chicken wire. Chicken wire is a type of thin wire netting. N-UNCOUNT

'chick pea, chick peas; also spelled **chickpea**. Chick peas are hard round seeds that look like pale brown peas. They can be cooked and eaten. N-COUNT

chick·weed /'tʃɪkwiːd/. Chickweed is a plant with small leaves and white flowers which grows close to the ground. N-UNCOUNT

chico·ry /'tʃɪkəri/. Chicory is a plant with crunchy bitter-tasting leaves. It is eaten in salads. N-UNCOUNT

chide /tʃaɪd/ **chides, chiding, chided.** If you **chide** someone, you scold them because they have done something wicked or foolish. *Cross chided himself for worrying.* VERB: V n for/about -ing/n / DATED

chief /tʃiːf/ **chiefs. 1** The **chief** of something such as an organization or department is the person in charge of it or who is its leader. *...the police chief. ...the chief test pilot.* **2** The **chief** cause, part, or member of something is the most important one. *The job went to one of his chief rivals.* N-COUNT: with supp / ADJ: ADJ n

,Chief 'Constable, Chief Constables. A Chief Constable is the officer in charge of the police force in a particular county or area in Britain. N-COUNT; N-TITLE

,Chief 'Justice, Chief Justices. A Chief Justice is the most important judge of a court of law, especially a supreme court. N-COUNT; N-TITLE

chief·ly /'tʃiːfli/. You use **chiefly** to indicate that a particular reason, emotion, method, or feature is the main or most important one. *He joined the consular service in China, chiefly because this was one of the few job vacancies... His response to attacks on his work was chiefly bewilderment.* ADV

,Chief of 'Staff, Chiefs of Staff. The Chiefs of Staff are the highest-ranking officers of each service of the armed forces. N-COUNT

chief·tain /'tʃiːftən/ **chieftains.** A chieftain is the leader of a tribe. N-COUNT

chif·fon /'ʃɪfɒn, AM ʃɪ'fɑːn/ **chiffons.** Chiffon is a kind of very thin silk or nylon cloth. N-VAR

chi·gnon /'ʃiːnjɒn, AM ʃiː'njɑːn/ **chignons.** A chignon is a knot of hair worn at the back of a woman's head. N-COUNT

chi·hua·hua /tʃɪ'wɑːwɑː/ **chihuahuas.** A chihuahua is a very small short-haired dog. N-COUNT

chil·blain /'tʃɪlbleɪn/ **chilblains.** Chilblains are painful red swellings which people sometimes get on their fingers or toes in cold weather. N-COUNT

child /tʃaɪld/ **children** /'tʃɪldrən/. **1** A child is a human being who is not yet an adult. *...when I was a child... It was only suitable for children.* **2** Someone's **children** are their sons and daughters of any age. *His children have left home.* N-COUNT

child·bearing /'tʃaɪldbeərɪŋ/. **1** Childbearing is the process of giving birth to babies. **2** A woman of **childbearing** age is of an age when women are normally able to give birth to children. N-UNCOUNT / ADJ: ADJ n

,child 'benefit. In Britain, **child benefit** is an allowance paid weekly by the state to families for each of their children. N-UNCOUNT

child·birth /'tʃaɪldbɜːθ/. Childbirth is the act of giving birth to a child. *She died in childbirth.* N-UNCOUNT

child·care /'tʃaɪldkeə/. Childcare refers to looking after children, and to the facilities which help parents to do so. *Both partners shared childcare. ...state-run pre-school childcare.* N-UNCOUNT

child·hood /'tʃaɪldhʊd/ **childhoods.** A person's **childhood** is the period of their life when they are a child. *She had a happy childhood. ...a story heard in childhood.* N-VAR

child·ish /'tʃaɪldɪʃ/. **1** Childish means relating to or typical of a child. *...childish enthusiasm.* **2** If you describe someone, especially an adult, as **childish**, you mean their behaviour is silly and more like that of a child than an adult. ♦ **child·ish·ly** *Such remarks were childishly simplistic.* ♦ **child·ish·ness** *...regressing into childishness.* ADJ / ADJ-GRADED / PRAGMATICS / ADV-GRADED / N-UNCOUNT

child·less /'tʃaɪldləs/. Someone who is **childless** has no children. ADJ

child·like /'tʃaɪldlaɪk/. You describe someone as **childlike** when they seem like a child in their character, appearance, or behaviour. ADJ-GRADED

child·minder /'tʃaɪldmaɪndə/ **childminders.** A childminder is someone whose job is to look after children, usually in their own home. ♦ **child·minding** *The extra cash could come in handy to pay for childminding.* N-COUNT BRITISH / N-UNCOUNT

,child 'prodigy, child prodigies. A child prodigy is a child with a very great talent. N-COUNT

child·proof /'tʃaɪldpruːf/; also spelled **child proof.** Something that is **childproof** is designed in a way which ensures that children cannot harm it or be harmed by it. *A medicine chest should be secure and childproof.* ADJ

chil·dren /'tʃɪldrən/. Children is the plural of **child**.

chili /'tʃɪli/. See **chilli**.

chill /tʃɪl/ **chills, chilling, chilled. 1** When you **chill** something, you lower its temperature so that it becomes colder but does not freeze. *Wait for the pastry to chill. ...a glass of chilled champagne.* **2** When something **chills** a person or a place, it makes that person or that place feel very cold. *...his chilled hands. ...the chilling wind.* **3** Chill weather is cold and unpleasant. ► Also a noun. *...the cold chill of the night.* V-ERG: V n / V-ed / V-ing / VERB: V n / V-ed / V-ing / ADJ: ADJ n / N-SING

4 If something that you see, hear, or feel **chills** you, it frightens you. *Some films chill you to the marrow of your bones.* **5** If something sends a **chill** through you, it gives you a sudden feeling of fear or anxiety. **6** A **chill** is a mild illness which can give you a slight fever and headache. *He caught a chill.* V n to n / WRITTEN / N-COUNT / N-COUNT

chill out. If you **chill out**, you relax after doing something tiring or stressful. *After raves, we used to chill out in each others' bedrooms.* PHRASAL VB / V P / INFORMAL

chill·er /'tʃɪlə/ **chillers.** A chiller is a very frightening film or novel. N-COUNT

chil·li /'tʃɪli/ **chillies**; also spelled **chili. 1** Chillies are small red or green seed pods. They have a hot spicy taste and are used in cooking. **2** Chilli or chilli **con carne** is a dish made from minced meat, beans, and powdered or fresh chillies. N-VAR / N-UNCOUNT

chill·ing /'tʃɪlɪŋ/. If you describe something as **chilling**, you mean it frightens and upsets you, because it deals with horrific events. ♦ **chill·ing·ly** *...the murder of a London teenager in chillingly similar circumstances.* ADJ-GRADED / ADV-GRADED

'chilli powder; also spelled **chili powder.** Chilli **powder** is a very strong-tasting spice made from dried chillies. N-UNCOUNT

chil·ly /'tʃɪli/ **chillier, chilliest. 1** Something that is **chilly** is uncomfortably cold. *It was a chilly afternoon.* **2** If you feel **chilly**, you feel rather cold. *I'm a bit chilly. I'm going up to my room to get a cardigan.* **3** You say that relations between people are **chilly** or that a person's response is **chilly** when they are not at all friendly or enthusiastic. ADJ-GRADED / ADJ-GRADED: v-link ADJ / ADJ-GRADED

chime /tʃaɪm/ **chimes, chiming, chimed. 1** When a bell or a clock **chimes**, it makes ringing sounds. *The Guildhall clock chimed three o'clock.* **2** A **chime** is a ringing sound made by a bell, especially when it is part of a clock. *The chimes of midnight struck.* **3** Chimes are a set of small objects VERB: V / V n / N-COUNT / N-PLURAL

which make a ringing sound when they are blown by the wind.

chime in. If someone **chimes in**, they say something just after someone else has spoken. *'Why?' Pete asked impatiently.—'Yes, why?' Bob chimed in.* PHRASAL VB / V P with quote / Also V P

chime in with or **chime with.** If one thing **chimes in with** another thing or **chimes with** it, the two things are similar or consistent with each other. *...a response to each new political development that chimes in with most Germans' instinct.* PHRASAL VB / V P P n / Also V P n / BRITISH

chi·mera /kaɪˈmɪərə/ **chimeras. 1** If you describe an idea as a **chimera**, you mean it is unrealistic. *Religious unity remained as much a chimera as ever.* **2** In Greek mythology, a **chimera** is a monster with a lion's head, a goat's body, and a snake's tail. N-COUNT / FORMAL

chim·ney /ˈtʃɪmni/ **chimneys.** A **chimney** is a pipe through which smoke goes up into the air, usually through the roof of a building. See picture headed **house and flat.** ◆◇◇◇◇ / N-COUNT

'chimney breast, chimney breasts. A **chimney breast** is the part of a wall in a room which is built out round a chimney. N-COUNT / BRITISH

chimney·piece /ˈtʃɪmnɪpiːs/ **chimneypieces.** A **chimneypiece** is the same as a **mantlepiece**. N-COUNT / BRITISH

'chimney pot, chimney pots. A **chimney pot** is a short pipe which is fixed on top of a chimney. N-COUNT

'chimney stack, chimney stacks. A **chimney stack** is the brick or stone part of a chimney that is above the roof of a building. N-COUNT / BRITISH

'chimney sweep, chimney sweeps. A **chimney sweep** is a person whose job is to clean the soot out of chimneys. N-COUNT

chimp /tʃɪmp/ **chimps.** A **chimp** is the same as a **chimpanzee.** N-COUNT / INFORMAL

chim·pan·zee /ˌtʃɪmpænˈziː/ **chimpanzees.** A **chimpanzee** is a kind of small African ape. See picture headed **animals**. ◆◇◇◇◇ / N-COUNT

chin /tʃɪn/ **chins. 1** Your **chin** is the part of your face that is below your mouth and above your neck. See picture headed **human body. 2** If you say that someone **took** something **on the chin**, you mean that they accepted an unpleasant situation bravely and without making a lot of fuss. ◆◆◇◇◇ / N-COUNT / PHRASE / INFORMAL

chi·na /ˈtʃaɪnə/ **1 China** is a kind of very thin clay from which cups, saucers, plates, and ornaments are made. ● See also **bone china. 2** Cups, saucers, plates, and ornaments made of china are referred to as **china**. *Judy collects blue and white china.* ◆◆◇◇◇ / N-UNCOUNT / N-UNCOUNT

,China 'tea. **China tea** is tea made from large dark green or reddish-brown tea leaves. N-UNCOUNT

China·town /ˈtʃaɪnətaʊn/ **Chinatown** is the name given to an area in a city where there are many Chinese shops and restaurants, and which is a social centre for the Chinese community. N-UNCOUNT

chink /tʃɪŋk/ **chinks, chinking, chinked. 1** A **chink** in a surface is a very narrow crack or opening in it. *...a chink in the curtains.* **2** If you say that someone has a **chink in** their **armour**, you mean that they have a small weakness in their character or in their ideas which makes it easy to harm them. **3** A **chink of** light is a small patch of light that shines through a small opening in something. **4** When objects **chink**, they touch each other, making a light ringing sound. *...cutlery chinking in the silence.* N-COUNT / PHRASE / N-COUNT: N of n / VERB: V / BRITISH

chi·nos /ˈtʃiːnəʊz/ **Chinos** are casual loose trousers made from cotton. N-PLURAL

chintz /tʃɪnts/ **chintzes.** **Chintz** is a patterned cotton fabric. N-VAR

chintzy /ˈtʃɪntsi/ Something that is **chintzy** is decorated or covered with chintz. *...chintzy armchairs.* ADJ-GRADED / BRITISH

chip /tʃɪp/ **chips, chipping, chipped. 1 Chips** are long thin pieces of potato fried in oil or fat and eaten hot. The American expression is **French fries. 2** Potato **chips** are very thin slices of potato fried until they are hard and crunchy and eaten cold as a snack. The British word is **crisps. 3** A silicon **chip** is a very small piece of silicon with electronic circuits on it which is part of a computer or other piece of machinery. ◆◆◆◇◇ / N-COUNT / BRITISH / N-COUNT / AMERICAN / N-COUNT

4 If you **chip** something, a small piece is broken off it. *A singer chipped a tooth on his microphone... Steel baths are lighter but chip easily.* ♦ **chipped** *They drank out of chipped mugs.* **5** A **chip** is a small piece of something, especially a piece which has been broken off something. *...chocolate chips. ...wood chips.* **6** A **chip** in a piece of crockery or furniture is a mark where a small piece has been broken off it. **7** If you describe someone as **a chip off the old block**, you mean that they are just like one of their parents in character or behaviour. **8 Chips** are plastic counters used in gambling to represent money. **9** In discussions between people or governments, a **chip** or a **bargaining chip** is something of value which one side holds, which can be exchanged for something they want from the other side. *He was not expected to be released because he was considered a valuable chip in this game.* **10** See also **blue chip. 11** If you say that something happens **when the chips are down**, you mean it happens when a situation gets very difficult. **12** If you say that someone has **a chip on** their **shoulder**, you mean that they behave rudely and aggressively, because they believe they have been treated unfairly. V-ERG: V n / V / ADJ-GRADED / N-COUNT / N-COUNT / PHRASE / N-COUNT / N-COUNT / PHRASE / INFORMAL / PHRASE / PRAGMATICS / INFORMAL

chip away at. If you **chip away at** something such as an idea or amount, you gradually reduce its power or size by repeated efforts. *The rebels want to chip away at her authority.* PHRASAL VB / V P P n

chip in. 1 When a number of people **chip in**, each person gives some money so that they can pay for something together. *The brothers chip in a certain amount of money each month.* **2** If someone **chips in** during a conversation, they interrupt it in order to say something. *'That's true,' chipped in Quaver.* PHRASAL VB / V P / V P noun / INFORMAL / V P / V P with quote / INFORMAL

chip·board /ˈtʃɪpbɔːd/ **Chipboard** is a hard material made out of wood chips, often used for making doors and furniture. N-UNCOUNT

chip·munk /ˈtʃɪpmʌŋk/ **chipmunks.** A **chipmunk** is a small North American animal which looks like a squirrel but which has a striped back. N-COUNT

chip·per /ˈtʃɪpə/ **Chipper** means cheerful and lively. *He looked so chipper and well rested.* ADJ-GRADED / DATED

chip·pings /ˈtʃɪpɪŋz/ Wood or stone **chippings** are small pieces of wood or stone which are used, for example, to cover roads or paths. N-PLURAL

chip·py /ˈtʃɪpi/ **chippies**; also spelled **chippie**. In Britain, a **chippy** is the same as a **chip shop**. N-COUNT / INFORMAL

'chip shop, chip shops. In Britain, a **chip shop** is a shop where fish and chips are cooked and sold for people to take away. N-COUNT

chi·ropo·dy /kɪˈrɒpədi/ **Chiropody** is the professional treatment and care of people's feet. The usual American word is **podiatry**. ♦ **chi·ropo·dist, chiropodists.** A **chiropodist** is a person whose job is chiropody. N-UNCOUNT / BRITISH / N-COUNT

chi·ro·prac·tic /ˈkaɪərəpræktɪk/ **Chiropractic** is the treatment of injuries and other medical conditions by the manipulation of people's joints, especially the backbone. ♦ **chi·ro·prac·tor, chiropractors.** A **chiropractor** is a person who treats diseases by chiropractic. N-UNCOUNT / N-COUNT

chirp /tʃɜːp/ **chirps, chirping, chirped. 1** When a bird or an insect **chirps**, it makes short high-pitched sounds. ► Also a noun. *...the chirps of the small garden birds.* ♦ **chirp·ing** *...the chirping of birds.* **2** You say that a person **chirps** when they say something in a cheerful high-pitched voice. *'See you soon, I hope!' chirped my mother.* VERB: V / N-COUNT / N-UNCOUNT / V with quote / WRITTEN

chirpy /ˈtʃɜːpi/ **chirpier, chirpiest.** If you describe a person or their behaviour as **chirpy**, you mean they are very cheerful and lively. ADJ-GRADED / INFORMAL

chir·rup /ˈtʃɪrəp/, AM /ˈtʃɜːrəp/ **chirrups, chirruping, chirruped.** If a person or bird **chirrups**, they make short high-pitched sounds. *'My gosh,' she chirruped.* VERB: V / V with quote / Also V n

chis·el /ˈtʃɪzəl/ **chisels, chiselling, chiselled;** spelled **chiseling, chiseled** in American English. **1** A **chisel** is a tool that is used for cutting and shaping ◆◇◇◇◇ / N-COUNT

wood and stone. See picture headed **tools**. **2** If you **chisel** wood or stone, you cut and shape it using a chisel. VERB: V n

chis·elled /'tʃɪzəld/; spelled **chiseled** in American ADJ English. If you say that someone, usually a man, has **chiselled** features, you mean that their face has a strong well-defined bone structure.

chit /tʃɪt/ **chits**. A **chit** is a short official note, such N-COUNT as a receipt, which is usually signed by someone in authority.

'chit-chat; also spelled **chitchat**. **Chit-chat** is infor- N-UNCOUNT mal talk about things that are not very important.

chiv·al·ry /'ʃɪvəlri/. **1** Chivalry is polite, kind, and N-UNCOUNT unselfish behaviour, especially by men towards women. ♦ **chiv·al·rous** /'ʃɪvəlrəs/ *I was taught to* ADJ-GRADED *be chivalrous, to pull a chair out for ladies*. **2** In the N-UNCOUNT Middle Ages, **chivalry** was the set of rules and con- ventions which knights had to follow. ♦ **chiv·al·ric** ADJ *...chivalric ideals*.

chives /tʃaɪvz/. **Chives** are long thin leaves of a ◆◇◇◇ herb with a flavour similar to onions. N-PLURAL

chiv·vy /'tʃɪvi/ **chivvies, chivvying, chivvied**. If VERB: V n you **chivvy** someone, you keep urging them to do V n into-ing/n something that they do not want to do. *The health* Also V n to-inf *care authority chivvies doctors into doing more pre-* BRITISH *ventive medicine. ...sending their representatives to the front to chivvy army commanders along*.

chlo·ride /'klɔːraɪd/ **chlorides**. **Chlorides** are ◆◇◇◇ chemical compounds of chlorine and another sub- N-VAR stance. For example, sodium chloride is a com- pound of chlorine and sodium.

chlo·rin·at·ed /'klɔːrɪneɪtɪd/. **Chlorinated** water ADJ has been disinfected by adding chlorine to it.

chlo·rine /'klɔːriːn/. **Chlorine** is a strong-smelling ◆◇◇◇ gas that is used to disinfect water and to make N-UNCOUNT cleaning products.

chloro·fluoro·car·bon /ˌklɔːrəʊˈfluərəʊkɑːbən/ N-COUNT **chlorofluorocarbons**. **Chlorofluorocarbons** are the same as **CFCs**.

chlo·ro·form /'klɒrəfɔːm, AM 'klɔːr-/. **Chloroform** N-UNCOUNT is a colourless liquid with a strong sweet smell, which makes you unconscious if you breathe its vapour.

chlo·ro·phyll /'klɒrəfɪl, AM 'klɔːr-/. **Chlorophyll** is N-UNCOUNT a green substance in plants which enables them to use the energy from sunlight in order to grow.

chock-a-block /ˌtʃɒk ə 'blɒk/. A place that is ADJ **chock-a-block** with people or things is very full of INFORMAL, them. BRITISH

chock-full /ˌtʃɒk 'fʊl/. Something that is **chock-full** ADJ of things is completely full of them. INFORMAL

choco·ho·lic /ˌtʃɒkəˈhɒlɪk, AM ˌtʃɔːkəˈhɔːlɪk/ N-COUNT **chocoholics**. A **chocoholic** is someone who eats a great deal of chocolate.

choco·late /'tʃɒklɪt, AM 'tʃɔːk-/ **chocolates**. ◆◆◇◇ **1** Chocolate is a sweet hard food made from cocoa N-VAR beans. It is usually brown and is eaten as a sweet. *...a bar of chocolate. ...chocolate cake.* ● See also **milk chocolate, plain chocolate**. **2** Chocolate or N-UNCOUNT **hot chocolate** is a hot drink made from a powder containing chocolate. ► A cup of chocolate can be N-COUNT referred to as a **chocolate**. **3** Chocolates are small N-COUNT sweets or nuts covered with a layer of chocolate. *...a box of chocolates*. **4** Chocolate can be used to de- COLOUR scribe things that are dark brown.

'chocolate box. When people talk about ADJ-GRADED **chocolate-box** places, they mean that the places are PRAGMATICS very pretty but in a boring or conventional way; BRITISH used showing disapproval. *...a village of chocolate- box timbered houses*.

choice /tʃɔɪs/ **choices; choicer, choicest**. **1** If ◆◆◆◇ there is a **choice** of things, there are several of them N-COUNT and you can choose the one you want. *It's available in a choice of colours... At lunchtime, there's a choice between the buffet or the set menu*. **2** Your **choice** is N-COUNT someone or something that you choose from a range of things. *His choice of words made Rodney angry*. **3** The thing or person **of** your **choice** is the PHRASE one that you choose. *...tickets to see the football team of your choice*. **4** If you **have no choice** but to PHRASE

do something or **have little choice** but to do it, you cannot avoid doing it.

5 Choice means of very high quality. *...Fortnum and* ADJ-GRADED *Mason's choicest chocolates*. ADJ FORMAL

choir /kwaɪə/ **choirs. 1** A **choir** is a group of peo- N-COUNT ple who sing together, for example in a church or school. **2** In a church building, the **choir** is the area N-COUNT in front of the altar where the choir sits.

choir·boy /'kwaɪəbɔɪ/ **choirboys**. A **choirboy** is a N-COUNT boy who sings in a church choir.

choir·master /'kwaɪəmɑːstə, -mæst-/ **choir- N-COUNT masters**. A **choirmaster** is a person whose job is to train a choir.

choke /tʃəʊk/ **chokes, choking, choked. 1** If ◆◆◇◇ you **choke** on something, it prevents you from V-ERG: breathing properly. *Dense smoke swirled and bil-* V on n *lowed, its rank fumes choking her... The girl choked* V n *to death after breathing in smoke*. **2** To **choke** some- VERB: V n one means to squeeze their neck until they are dead. **3** If a place is **choked** with things or people, it VERB is full of them and they prevent movement in it. *The* be V-ed with n *village's roads are choked with traffic*. Also be V-ed

4 A vehicle's **choke** is a device that reduces the N-COUNT amount of air going into the engine and makes it easi- er to start.

choke back. If you **choke back** tears or a strong PHRASAL VB emotion, you force yourself not to show your V P n emotion.

choke off. If something **chokes off** financial PHRASAL VB growth, it restricts or controls the rate at which a V P noun country's economy can grow. *Raising taxes in the Budget could choke off the recovery*.

choked /tʃəʊkt/. **1** If you say something in a ADJ **choked** voice, your voice does not have its full sound, because you are upset or frightened. **2** If you ADJ-GRADED feel **choked** about something, you are very upset v-link ADJ about it. INFORMAL

chok·er /'tʃəʊkə/ **chokers**. A **choker** is a necklace N-COUNT that fits very closely round a woman's neck.

chol·era /'kɒlərə/. **Cholera** is a serious disease that ◆◇◇◇ affects people's digestive organs. It is caused by N-UNCOUNT drinking infected water or by eating infected food.

chol·er·ic /'kɒlərɪk/. A **choleric** person gets angry ADJ-GRADED very easily. You can also use **choleric** to describe a FORMAL person who is very angry. *...his choleric disposition*.

cho·les·ter·ol /kəˈlestərɒl, AM -rɔːl/. **Cholesterol** ◆◇◇◇ is a substance that exists in the fat, tissues, and N-UNCOUNT blood of all animals. Too much cholesterol in a per- son's blood can cause heart disease.

chomp /tʃɒmp/ **chomps, chomping, chomped**. VERB If a person or animal **chomps** on food, they chew it V prep/adv noisily. *I chomped hungrily through the large steak*. V n ● **to chomp at the bit**: see **bit**. INFORMAL

choose /tʃuːz/ **chooses, choosing, chose**, ◆◆◆◆ **chosen. 1** If you **choose** someone or something V n from several people or things that are available, you V n to-inf decide which person or thing you want to have. Also V, *They will be able to choose their own leaders... He* V from/ *has chosen Clarence Thomas to replace Thurgood* between n *Marshall*. **2** If you **choose** to do something, you do VERB it because you want to or because you feel that it is V to-inf right. *The NRDC chose to inform the public about* Also V *the risks*. **3** If there is **little to choose between** peo- PHRASE ple or things or **nothing to choose between** them, it is difficult to decide which is better or more suit- able. **4** If you refer to a group of people as the **cho-** PHRASE **sen few**, you mean they are a small group who are treated differently from other people or who are more privileged than other people. *Learning should no longer be an elitist pastime for the chosen few*. **5** ● **to pick and choose**: see **pick**.

choosy /'tʃuːzi/. Someone who is **choosy** is diffi- ADJ-GRADED cult to please because they will only accept some- thing if it is exactly what they want. *Skiers should be particularly choosy about the insurance policy they buy*.

chop /tʃɒp/ **chops, chopping, chopped. 1** If ◆◆◆◇ you **chop** something, you cut it into pieces with VERB: V n strong downward movements of a knife or an axe. V n into n *Chop the butter into small pieces*.

2 A **chop** is a small piece of meat cut from the ribs of a sheep or pig. ...*grilled lamb chops.* `N-COUNT`

3 When people **chop and change**, they keep changing their minds about what to do or how to act. `PHRASE` `INFORMAL`

4 If something is **for the chop** or is going to **get the chop**, it is going to be stopped or closed. If someone is **for the chop**, they are going to lose their job or position. *He won't say which programmes are for the chop.* `PHRASE` `INFORMAL, BRITISH`

chop down. If you **chop down** a tree, you cut through its trunk with an axe so that it falls to the ground. *Sometimes they have to chop down a tree for firewood.* `PHRASAL VB` `V P noun` `Also V n P`

chop off. To **chop off** something such as a part of someone's body means to cut it off. *She chopped off her golden, waist-length hair.* `PHRASAL VB` `V P noun` `Also V n P`

chop up. If you **chop** something **up**, you chop it into small pieces. *Chop up three firm tomatoes.* `PHRASAL VB` `V n P`

chop·per /ˈtʃɒpə/ **choppers.** A **chopper** is a helicopter. *Overhead, the chopper roared and the big blades churned the air.* ◆◇◇◇◇ `N-COUNT` `INFORMAL`

'**chopping board, chopping boards.** A **chopping board** is a wooden or plastic board that you chop meat and vegetables on. `N-COUNT`

chop·py /ˈtʃɒpi/ **choppier, choppiest.** When water is **choppy**, there are a lot of small waves on it because there is a wind blowing. `ADJ-GRADED`

chop·stick /ˈtʃɒpstɪk/ **chopsticks. Chopsticks** are a pair of thin sticks which people in China and the Far East use to eat their food with. `N-COUNT`

chop suey /ˌtʃɒp ˈsuːi/. **Chop suey** is a Chinese-style dish that consists of meat and vegetables that have been stewed together. `N-UNCOUNT`

cho·ral /ˈkɔːrəl/. **Choral** music is sung by a choir. ...*choral works by Mozart.* ◆◇◇◇◇ `ADJ`

cho·rale /kɒˈrɑːl, -ˈræl/ **chorales.** A **chorale** is a piece of music sung as part of a church service. `N-COUNT`

chord /kɔːd/ **chords. 1** A **chord** is a number of musical notes played or sung at the same time with a pleasing effect. ...*the opening chords of 'Stairway to Heaven'.* • See also **vocal cords. 2** If something **strikes a chord** with you, it makes you feel sympathy or enthusiasm. *Mr Jenkins' arguments for stability struck a chord with Europe's two most powerful politicians.* ◆◆◇◇◇ `N-COUNT` `PHRASE`

chore /tʃɔː/ **chores. 1** A **chore** is a task that you must do but that you find unpleasant or boring. *Making pasta by hand with a rolling pin can be a real chore.* **2 Chores** are tasks such as cleaning, washing, and ironing that have to be done regularly at home. ◆◇◇◇◇ `N-COUNT` `N-COUNT`

cho·reo·graph /ˈkɒriəgrɑːf, AM ˈkɔːriəgræf/ **choreographs, choreographing, choreographed.** When someone **choreographs** a ballet or other dance, they invent the steps and movements and tell the dancers how to perform them. *Achim had choreographed the dance in Act II himself.* ♦ **cho·reog·ra·pher** /ˌkɒriˈɒgrəfə, AM ˌkɔː-/ **choreographers** ...*dancer and choreographer Rudolph Nureyev.* `VERB` `V n` `Also V` `N-COUNT`

cho·reo·graphed /ˈkɒriəgrɑːft, AM ˈkɔːriəgræft/. You describe an activity involving several people as **choreographed** when it is arranged but is intended to appear natural. *Political conventions are more choreographed and less spontaneous than they used to be.* `ADJ-GRADED`

cho·reog·ra·phy /ˌkɒriˈɒgrəfi, AM ˌkɔː-/. **Choreography** is the inventing of steps and movements for ballets and other dances. ♦ **cho·reo·graph·ic** /ˌkɒriəˈgræfɪk, AM ˌkɔː-/. ...*his choreographic work for The Birmingham Royal Ballet.* ◆◇◇◇◇ `N-UNCOUNT` `ADJ`

chor·is·ter /ˈkɒrɪstə, AM ˈkɔː-/ **choristers.** A **chorister** is a singer in a church choir. `N-COUNT`

chor·tle /ˈtʃɔːtəl/ **chortles, chortling, chortled.** When you **chortle**, you laugh loudly, producing a sound that is halfway between a laugh and a snort. *Larry began chortling like an idiot.* ▶ Also a noun. *He gave a chortle.* `VERB` `V` `Also V with quote` `N-COUNT`

cho·rus /ˈkɔːrəs/ **choruses, chorusing, chorused. 1** A **chorus** is a part of a song which is repeated after each verse. **2** A **chorus** is a piece of ◆◆◇◇◇ `N-COUNT` `N-COUNT`

classical music written to be sung by a large group of people.

3 A **chorus** is a large group of people who sing together. **4** A **chorus** is a group of singers or dancers who perform together in a show, in contrast to the soloists. *Students played the lesser parts and sang in the chorus.* `N-COUNT` `N-COUNT`

5 See also **dawn chorus**.

6 When there is a **chorus** of criticism, disapproval, or praise, that attitude is expressed by a lot of people at the same time. `N-COUNT`

7 When people **chorus** something, they say it or sing it together. *'Hi,' they chorused.* ▶ Also a noun. *He was greeted with a rousing chorus of Happy Birthday.* `VERB` `V with quote` `N-COUNT:` `also in N`

'**chorus girl, chorus girls.** A **chorus girl** is a young woman who sings or dances in the chorus of a show or film. `N-COUNT`

chose /tʃəʊz/. **Chose** is the past tense of **choose**.

cho·sen /ˈtʃəʊzən/. **Chosen** is the past participle of **choose**.

chow /tʃaʊ/ **chows. 1** Food can be referred to as **chow**. *He'd made a point of standing next to me in the chow line.* **2** A **chow** is a kind of dog that has a thick coat and a curled tail. `N-UNCOUNT` `INFORMAL, AMERICAN` `N-COUNT`

chow·der /ˈtʃaʊdə/ **chowders. Chowder** is a thick soup containing pieces of fish. `N-VAR`

chow mein /ˌtʃaʊ ˈmeɪn, - ˈmiːn/. **Chow mein** is a Chinese-style dish that consists of fried noodles, cooked meat, and vegetables. `N-UNCOUNT`

Christ /kraɪst/ **1 Christ** is Jesus, whom Christians believe to be the son of God and whose teachings are the basis of Christianity. **2** Some people say '**Christ!**' when they are surprised, shocked, or annoyed, or in order to emphasize what they are saying. Some people find this use offensive. ◆◆◇◇◇ `N-PROPER` `EXCLAM` `PRAGMATICS` `INFORMAL`

chris·ten /ˈkrɪsən/ **christens, christening, christened. 1** When a baby **is christened**, he or she is given a name during the Christian ceremony of baptism. *She was christened Susan.* ♦ **chris·ten·ing** /ˈkrɪsənɪŋ/ **christenings** ...*my granddaughter's christening.* **2** You say that you **christen** a person, place, or object a particular name if you choose a name for them and start calling them by that name. *The English newspapers christened him 'Le Brat'.* **3** You say that you **christen** something new when you use it for the first time, especially if you do something special to mark the occasion. *To christen the new hall, a number of great orchestras have been invited to play.* ◆◇◇◇◇ `VERB:` `be V-ed` `N-COUNT` `VERB` `V n n` `INFORMAL` `VERB` `V n` `INFORMAL`

Chris·ten·dom /ˈkrɪsəndəm/. All the Christian people and countries in the world can be referred to as **Christendom**. `N-PROPER` `DATED`

Chris·tian /ˈkrɪstʃən/ **Christians.** A **Christian** is someone who follows the teachings of Jesus Christ. ▶ Also an adjective. ...*the Christian Church.* ◆◆◆◆◇ `N-COUNT` `ADJ`

Chris·ti·an·ity /ˌkrɪstiˈænɪti/. **Christianity** is a religion that is based on the teachings of Jesus Christ. ◆◆◇◇◇ `N-UNCOUNT`

'**Christian name, Christian names.** Some people refer to their first names as their **Christian names**. `N-COUNT`

Christ·mas /ˈkrɪsməs/ **Christmases. Christmas** is the period around the 25th of December when Christians celebrate the birth of Jesus Christ. **Christmas** day is the 25th of December. *Merry Christmas... He'll be in the hospital over Christmas.* ◆◆◆◆◇ `N-VAR`

'**Christmas cake, Christmas cakes.** A **Christmas cake** is a rich, dark, heavy cake which is usually eaten at Christmas. `N-VAR`

'**Christmas card, Christmas cards. Christmas cards** are greetings cards which people send to friends and family at Christmas. ◆◇◇◇◇ `N-COUNT`

ˌ**Christmas 'Eve. Christmas Eve** is the 24th of December, the day before Christmas Day. ◆◇◇◇◇ `N-UNCOUNT`

ˌ**Christmas 'pudding, Christmas puddings. Christmas pudding** is a rich, dark, heavy pudding which is eaten at Christmas. `N-VAR`

'**Christmas tree, Christmas trees.** A **Christmas tree** is a fir tree, or an artificial tree, which people put in their houses at Christmas. ◆◇◇◇◇ `N-COUNT`

chrome /krəʊm/. **Chrome** is metal plated with chromium. ...*old-fashioned chrome taps.* ◆◇◇◇◇ `N-UNCOUNT`

chro·mium /ˈkrəʊmiəm/. **Chromium** is a hard ◆◇◇◇◇ shiny metallic element, used to make steel alloys N-UNCOUNT and to coat other metals.

chro·mo·some /ˈkrəʊməsəʊm/ **chromosomes.** ◆◇◇◇◇ A **chromosome** is a part of a cell in an animal or N-COUNT plant. It contains genes which determine what characteristics the animal or plant will have. ♦ **chro·mo·so·mal** /ˌkrəʊməˈsəʊməl/. ...*chromosomal* ADJ: ADJ n *abnormalities.*

chron·ic /ˈkrɒnɪk/. **1** A **chronic** illness or ◆◆◇◇◇ disability lasts for a very long time. Compare **acute.** ADJ ...*chronic back pain.* ♦ **chroni·cal·ly** /ˈkrɒnɪkli/. ADV *Most of them were chronically ill.* **2** You can ADJ: ADJ n describe someone's bad habits or behaviour as **chronic** when they have behaved like that for a long time and do not seem to be able to stop themselves. ...*a chronic worrier.* **3** A **chronic** ADJ situation or problem is a very severe and unpleasant one. *One cause of the artist's suicide seems to have been chronic poverty.* ♦ **chronically** ADV: *Research and technology are said to be chronically* ADV adj/-ed *underfunded.*

chroni·cle /ˈkrɒnɪkəl/ **chronicles, chronicling,** ◆◇◇◇◇ **chronicled. 1** To **chronicle** a series of events VERB: V n means to write about them or show them in broadcasts in the order in which they happened. ♦ **chroni·cler, chroniclers** ...*the chronicler of the* N-COUNT *English civil war.* **2** A **chronicle** is an account or N-COUNT record of a series of events. ...*this vast chronicle of Napoleonic times.* **3** The word **Chronicle** is sometimes used as part of the name of a newspaper. ...*the San Francisco Chronicle.*

chrono·logi·cal /ˌkrɒnəˈlɒdʒɪkəl/. **1** If things are ◆◇◇◇◇ described or shown in **chronological** order, they are ADJ described or shown in the order in which they happened. *I have arranged these stories in chronological order.* ♦ **chrono·logi·cal·ly** *The exhibition is or-* ADV *ganised chronologically.* **2** Someone's **chronological** ADJ: ADJ n age is the number of years that they have lived, in FORMAL contrast to their mental age or the stage they have reached in their physical or emotional development.

chro·nol·ogy /krəˈnɒlədʒi/ **chronologies. 1** The N-UNCOUNT **chronology** of a series of past events is the times at which they happened in the order in which they happened. ...*the chronology of her brief liaison.* **2** A N-COUNT **chronology** is an account or record of the times and the order in which a series of past events took place. *Duffy's book is a detailed chronology of the Reformation.*

chro·nom·eter /krəˈnɒmɪtə/ **chronometers.** A N-COUNT **chronometer** is an extremely accurate clock that is used especially by sailors at sea.

chrysa·lis /ˈkrɪsəlɪs/ **chrysalises. 1** A **chrysalis** is N-COUNT a butterfly or moth in the stage between being a larva and an adult. **2** A **chrysalis** is the hard protective N-COUNT covering that a chrysalis has.

chry·san·themum /krɪˈzænθəməm/ **chrysan-** ◆◇◇◇◇ **themums.** A **chrysanthemum** is a large garden N-COUNT flower with many long thin petals.

chub·by /ˈtʃʌbi/ **chubbier, chubbiest.** A **chubby** ADJ-GRADED person is rather fat. *Do you think I'm too chubby?*

chuck /tʃʌk/ **chucks, chucking, chucked.** ◆◆◇◇◇ **1** When you **chuck** something somewhere, you VERB throw it there in a casual or careless way. *I chucked* V n prep/adv *it in the dustbin... This is as far as she's ever chucked* V n *a javelin.* Also V n n
INFORMAL

2 If you **chuck** your job or some other activity, you VERB stop doing it. *He chucked his 10-year career as a Lon-* V n *don stockbroker.* ▶ **Chuck in** and **chuck up** mean the INFORMAL same as **chuck.** *Almost half the British public think* PHRASAL VB *about chucking in their jobs and doing their own* V P noun *thing.* ● If someone **chucks it all, chucks it all up,** or PHRASE **chucks it all in,** they stop doing their job, and usually move somewhere else, before starting to do something less well-paid or less secure. **3** If your girlfriend VERB: V n or boyfriend **chucks** you, they end the relationship. INFORMAL **4** A **chuck** is a device for holding a tool in a machine N-COUNT such as a drill.

chuck away. If you **chuck** something **away,** you PHRASAL VB

throw it away or waste it. *You cannot chuck money* V n P *away on little luxuries like that.* INFORMAL

chuck in. See **chuck** 2. PHRASAL VB

chuck out. 1 If you **chuck** something **out,** you PHRASAL VB throw it away, because you do not need it or cannot V P noun use it. *Many companies have struggled valiantly to use* Also V n P *less energy and chuck out less rubbish.* **2** If someone **is** beV-ed P **chucked out** of a place, they are forced by other peo- INFORMAL, ple to leave. *Any head teacher who made errors like* BRITISH *this would be chucked out.*

chuck up. See **chuck** 2. PHRASAL VB

chuck·le /ˈtʃʌkəl/ **chuckles, chuckling,** ◆◇◇◇◇ **chuckled.** When you **chuckle,** you laugh quietly. VERB: V *The banker chuckled and said, 'Of course not.'* ▶ Also a noun. *He gave a little chuckle.* N-COUNT

chuffed /tʃʌft/. If you are **chuffed** about some- ADJ-GRADED: thing, you are very pleased about it. *She had just* v-link ADJ *moved into a new house and was pretty chuffed* INFORMAL, *about that.* BRITISH

chug /tʃʌg/ **chugs, chugging, chugged.** When ◆◇◇◇◇ a vehicle **chugs** somewhere, it goes there slowly VERB with its engine making short thudding sounds. *The* V prep/adv *train chugs down the track.* ▶ Also a noun. ...*the* N-SING *chug of farm machinery.*

chum /tʃʌm/ **chums.** Your **chums** are your ◆◇◇◇◇ friends. ...*his old chum Anthony... Her chums were* N-COUNT *all waiting at the station for her.* INFORMAL, BRITISH

chum·my /ˈtʃʌmi/ **chummier, chummiest.** If ADJ-GRADED people or social events are **chummy,** they are pleas- INFORMAL ant and friendly. ...*chummy gatherings in the draw-* *ing room.* ♦ **chum·mi·ness** /ˈtʃʌminəs/. ...*his wife's* N-UNCOUNT *escalating chumminess with the Halcyon-Wilsons.*

chump /tʃʌmp/ **chumps.** If you call someone who N-COUNT you like a **chump,** you are telling them that they PRAGMATICS have done something rather stupid or foolish. INFORMAL

chunk /tʃʌŋk/ **chunks. 1 Chunks** of something ◆◆◇◇◇ are thick solid pieces of it. ...*floating chunks of ice.* N-COUNT **2** A **chunk** of something is a large amount or large INFORMAL part of it. ...*a chunk of farmland near Gatwick Airport.*

chunky /ˈtʃʌŋki/ **chunkier, chunkiest. 1** A ◆◇◇◇◇ **chunky** person is broad and heavy. ...*a chunky girl* ADJ-GRADED *from California.* **2** A **chunky** object is large and ADJ-GRADED thick. ...*a chunky sweater.*

church /tʃɜːtʃ/ **churches. 1** A **church** is a build- ◆◆◆◇ ing in which Christians worship. You usually refer N-VAR to this place as **church** when you are talking about the time that people spend there. *I didn't see you in church on Sunday.* **2** A **Church** is one of the groups N-COUNT of people within the Christian religion that have their own beliefs, clergy, and forms of worship. ...*the Catholic Church.*

3 You can refer to an organization, group, or area of PHRASE activity as a **broad church** when it includes a wide BRITISH range of opinions, beliefs, or styles. *Rock'n'roll was a very broad church indeed.*

church·goer /ˈtʃɜːtʃgəʊə/ **churchgoers;** also N-COUNT spelled **church-goer.** A **churchgoer** is a person who goes to church regularly.

church·man /ˈtʃɜːtʃmən/ **churchmen.** A church- ◆◇◇◇◇ **man** is the same as a clergyman. ...*one of Kenya's* FORMAL *leading churchmen.*

'church school, church schools. A **church** N-COUNT **school** is a school which has a special relationship with a particular branch of the Christian church, and where there is strong emphasis on worship and the teaching of religion.

church·warden /ˌtʃɜːtʃˈwɔːdən/ **church-** N-COUNT **wardens.** In some churches, a **churchwarden** is a person who has been chosen by a congregation to help the vicar of a parish with administration and other duties.

church·yard /ˈtʃɜːtʃjɑːd/ **churchyards.** A ◆◇◇◇◇ **churchyard** is an area of land around a church N-COUNT where dead people are buried.

churl·ish /ˈtʃɜːlɪʃ/. Someone who is **churlish** is un- ADJ-GRADED friendly, bad-tempered, or impolite. *It seemed churlish to argue.*

churn /tʃɜːn/ **churns, churning, churned. 1** A ◆◇◇◇◇ **churn** is a container which is used for making N-COUNT

butter. **2** If something **churns** water, mud, or dust, it moves it about violently. *Ferries churn the waters of Howe Sound.* ▶ **Churn up** means the same as **churn.** *The recent rain had churned up the waterfall into a muddy whirlpool.* **3** If you say that your stomach **is churning,** you mean that you feel sick. You can also say that something **churns** your stomach. *My stomach churned as I stood up.*   VERB Vn / PHRASAL VB VPnoun Also VnP / V-ERG Also Vn / V Also Vn

churn out. To **churn out** something means to produce large quantities of it very quickly. *He began to churn out literary compositions in English.*   PHRASAL VB Also VnP INFORMAL

churn up. See churn 2.   PHRASAL VB

churn·ing /'tʃɜ:nɪŋ/. **Churning** water is moving about violently. *...the brown, churning water below.*   ADJ: ADJn LITERARY

chute /ʃu:t/ **chutes.** **1** A **chute** is a steep narrow slope down which people or things can slide. *...sliding down emergency chutes.* **2** A **chute** is a parachute. *You can release the chute with either hand.*   N-COUNT / N-COUNT INFORMAL

chut·ney /'tʃʌtni/ **chutneys.** Chutney is a cold sauce made from fruit, vinegar, sugar, and spices.   N-VAR

chutz·pah /'hʊtspə/. If you say that someone has **chutzpah,** you mean that you admire the fact that they are not afraid or embarrassed to do or say things that shock, surprise, or annoy other people.   N-UNCOUNT PRAGMATICS INFORMAL

CIA /ˌsi: aɪ 'eɪ/. The CIA is the United States agency that tries to obtain secret information about the political and military activities of other countries. CIA is an abbreviation for 'Central Intelligence Agency'.   N-PROPER: theN

ciabatta /tʃə'bætə/. Ciabatta or ciabatta bread is a type of flattish white bread that is made with olive oil and that has a crisp crust.   N-UNCOUNT

ciao /tʃaʊ/. Some people say **'Ciao'** as a way of saying goodbye to someone who they expect to see again soon.   CONVENTION PRAGMATICS INFORMAL

ci·ca·da /sɪ'kɑ:də, AM -'keɪdə/ **cicadas.** A cicada is a large insect that lives in hot countries and makes a loud high-pitched noise.   N-COUNT

CID /ˌsi: aɪ 'di:/. The CID is the branch of the police force in Britain concerned with finding out who has committed crimes. CID is an abbreviation for 'Criminal Investigation Department'.   N-PROPER

ci·der /'saɪdə/ **ciders.** Cider is a drink made from apples. In Britain, cider is alcoholic. In the United States, cider is usually non-alcoholic. ▶ A glass of cider can be referred to as a **cider.**   N-VAR / N-COUNT

ci·gar /sɪ'gɑ:/ **cigars.** Cigars are rolls of dried tobacco leaves which people smoke.   N-COUNT

ciga·rette /ˌsɪgə'ret/ **cigarettes.** Cigarettes are small tubes of paper containing tobacco which people smoke.   N-COUNT

ciga·rette end, cigarette ends. A cigarette end is the part of a cigarette that you throw away when you have finished smoking.   N-COUNT

ciga·rette holder, cigarette holders. A cigarette holder is a narrow tube that you can put a cigarette into in order to hold it while you smoke it.   N-COUNT

ciga·rette lighter, cigarette lighters. A cigarette lighter is a device which you use to light a cigarette or cigar.   N-COUNT

cig·gy /'sɪgi/ **ciggies;** also spelled **ciggie.** A ciggy is a cigarette. *Nip outside if you want a ciggie.*   N-COUNT INFORMAL

C-in-'C. A C-in-C is the same as a **commander-in-chief.**   N-SING

cinch /sɪntʃ/. If you say that something is **a cinch,** you mean that you think it is very easy to do. *Compared to full-time work it was a cinch.*   N-SING: aN INFORMAL

cin·der block /'sɪndə blɒk/ **cinder blocks.** A cinder block is a large grey-coloured brick made from coal cinders and cement which is used for building. The British word is **breeze-block.**   N-COUNT AMERICAN

cin·ders /'sɪndəz/. Cinders are the pieces of blackened material that are left after something such as wood or coal has burned.   N-PLURAL

cine /'sɪni/. Cine is used to refer to things that are used in or connected with the making or showing of films. *...cine film.*   ADJ: ADJn

cin·ema /'sɪnɪmɑ:/ **cinemas. 1** A cinema is a place where people go to watch films for entertainment. The American term is **movie theater** or **movie house. 2** You can talk about the cinema   N-COUNT BRITISH / N-SING:

when you are talking about seeing a film in a cinema. The American term is the **movies.** *...the last time we went to the cinema.* **3** Cinema is the business and art of making films. ◆ **cin·emat·ic** *...a genuine cinematic masterpiece.*   theN BRITISH / N-UNCOUNT / ADJ

cin·ema·tog·ra·phy /ˌsɪnɪmə'tɒɡrəfi/. Cinematography is the technique of making films for the cinema. ◆ **cin·ema·tog·ra·pher** /ˌsɪnɪmə'tɒɡrəfə/ cinematographers.   N-UNCOUNT / N-COUNT

cin·na·mon /'sɪnəmən/. Cinnamon is a sweet spice used for flavouring food.   N-UNCOUNT

ci·pher /'saɪfə/ **ciphers;** also spelled **cypher. 1** A cipher is a secret system of writing that you use to send messages. *They cracked the cipher.* **2** If you describe someone as a **cipher,** you mean that they have no power and are used by other people to achieve a particular purpose. *...a cipher who faithfully carried out the Fuehrer's commands.*   N-COUNT / N-COUNT

cir·ca /'sɜ:kə/. Circa is used in front of a particular year to say that this is the approximate date when something happened or was made. *...circa 1850.*   PREP FORMAL

cir·cle /'sɜ:kəl/ **circles, circling, circled. 1** A circle is a shape consisting of a curved line completely surrounding an area. Every part of the line is the same distance from the centre of the area. See picture headed **shapes.** *The flag was red, with a large white circle in the center.* **2** A circle of something is a round flat piece or area of it. *Cut out 4 circles of pastry.* **3** A circle of objects or people is a group of them arranged in the shape of a circle. *The monument consists of a circle of gigantic stones.* **4** If something **circles** an object or place, or **circles** around it, it forms a circle around it. *...the long curving driveway that circled around the vast clipped lawn.* **5** If you **circle** something on a piece of paper, you draw a circle around it. **6** If an aircraft or a bird **circles** or **circles** something, it moves round in a circle in the air. *There were two helicopters circling around.* **7** To **circle** around someone or something, or to **circle** them, means to move around them. *Emily kept circling around her mother.* **8** You can refer to a group of people as a **circle** when they meet each other regularly because they are friends or share the same interests. *He has a small circle of friends.* **9** In a theatre or cinema, the circle is an area of seats on the upper floor. **10** See also **Arctic Circle, dress circle, inner circle, vicious circle, virtuous circle. 11** If you say that you **have come full circle** or **have turned full circle,** you mean that after a long series of events or changes the same situation that you started with still exists. **12** If you say that someone **is going round in circles,** you mean that they are not achieving anything because they keep coming back to the same point or problem.   N-COUNT / N-COUNT / N-COUNT / VERB: Vn Varound/ roundn / VERB: Vn / VERB: V Vadv/prep Also Vn / VERB Varound/ roundn Also Vn / N-COUNT: with supp / N-SING: theN / PHRASE / PHRASE BRITISH

cir·cuit /'sɜ:kɪt/ **circuits. 1** An electrical circuit is a complete route which an electric current can flow around. ● See also **closed circuit, short-circuit. 2** A circuit is a series of places that are visited regularly by someone, especially as a part of their job. *He joined the professional circuit.* **3** A racing circuit is a track on which cars, motorbikes, or cycles race. **4** A circuit of a place or area is a journey all the way round it. *She made a slow circuit of the room.*   N-COUNT / N-COUNT / N-COUNT BRITISH / N-COUNT FORMAL

'circuit breaker, circuit breakers. A circuit breaker is a device which can stop the flow of electricity around a circuit by switching itself off if anything goes wrong.   N-COUNT

cir·cui·tous /sə'kju:ɪtəs/. A circuitous route is long and complicated rather than simple and direct. *...a circuitous route, from mainland China through Hong Kong to Europe.*   ADJ-GRADED FORMAL

cir·cuit·ry /'sɜ:kɪtri/. Circuitry is a system of electric circuits.   N-UNCOUNT

'circuit training. Circuit training is a type of fitness training in which you do a series of different exercises, each for a few minutes.   N-UNCOUNT

cir·cu·lar /'sɜ:kjʊlə/ **circulars. 1** Something that is **circular** is shaped like a circle. *...a circular hole*   ADJ

twelve feet wide. ...a circular motion. ● See also **semi-circular. 2** A **circular** journey or route is one in which you go to a place and return by a different route. *...this circular walk.* **3** A **circular** argument or theory is not valid because it uses a statement to prove something which is then used to prove the statement. **4** A **circular** is an official letter or advertisement that is sent to a large number of people at the same time. `ADJ` `ADJ-GRADED` `N-COUNT`

,**circular 'saw, circular saws.** A **circular saw** is a rotating metal disc with a sharp serrated edge. It is powered by an electric motor and is used for cutting wood and other materials. `N-COUNT`

cir·cu·late /'sɜːkjuleɪt/ **circulates, circulating, circulated. 1** If a piece of writing **circulates** or is **circulated**, copies of it are passed round among a group of people. *The document was previously circulated in New York... Public employees, teachers and liberals are circulating a petition for his recall.* ♦ **cir·cu·la·tion** /,sɜːkjʊ'leɪʃən/ *...the circulation of 'unacceptable literature'.* **2** If something such as a rumour **circulates** or is **circulated**, the people in a place tell it to each other. *I deeply resented those sort of rumours being circulated.* **3** When something **circulates**, it moves easily and freely within a closed place or system. *...a virus which circulates via the bloodstream.* ♦ **circulation** *...free circulation of goods.* `◆◆◇◇◇` `V-ERG` `be V-ed` `V n` `Also V` `N-UNCOUNT` `V-ERG: V` `be V-ed` `VERB` `V` `Also V prep` `N-UNCOUNT`

cir·cu·la·tion /,sɜːkjʊ'leɪʃən/ **circulations. 1** The **circulation** of a newspaper or magazine is the number of copies that are sold each time it is produced. *The Daily News once had the highest circulation of any daily in the country.* **2** Your **circulation** is the movement of blood through your body. *...cold spots in the fingers caused by poor circulation.* ♦ **cir·cu·la·tory** /,sɜːkjʊ'leɪtəri, AM 'sɜːkjʊlətɔːri/. *...the human circulatory system.* **3** If something such as money is **in circulation**, it is being used by the public. If something is **out of circulation** or has been **withdrawn from circulation**, it is no longer available for use by the public. *...America, with perhaps 180 million guns in circulation.* **4** If someone is **out of circulation**, they do not appear in public or at social gatherings for a period of time. *Political trials were being used to keep prominent activists out of circulation.* **5** See also **circulate.** `◆◆◇◇◇` `N-COUNT:` `with supp` `N-UNCOUNT` `ADJ: ADJ n` `PHRASE` `PHRASE`

cir·cum·cise /'sɜːkəmsaɪz/ **circumcises, circumcising, circumcised. 1** If a boy or man is **circumcised**, the loose skin at the end of his penis is cut off. ♦ **cir·cum·ci·sion** /,sɜːkəm'sɪʒən/. *Jews and Moslems practise circumcision for religious reasons.* **2** In some cultures, if a girl or woman is **circumcised**, parts of her genitals are slit or cut out. ♦ **circumcision.** `◆◇◇◇◇` `VB: usu` `passive` `N-UNCOUNT:` `also a N` `VB: usu` `passive` `N-UNCOUNT`

cir·cum·fer·ence /sə'kʌmfrəns/. **1** The **circumference** of a circle, place, or round object is the distance around its edge. *The island is 3.5 km in circumference.* **2** The **circumference** of a circle, place, or round object is its edge. *Cut the salmon into long strips and wrap it round the circumference of the bread.* `N-UNCOUNT` `N-UNCOUNT`

cir·cum·flex /'sɜːkəmfleks/ **circumflexes.** A **circumflex** or a **circumflex accent** is a symbol written over a vowel in French and other languages, usually to indicate that it should be pronounced longer than usual. It is used for example in the word 'rôle'. `N-COUNT`

cir·cum·lo·cu·tion /,sɜːkəm'ləʊˈkjuːʃən/ **circumlocutions.** A circumlocution is a way of saying or writing something using more words than are necessary instead of being clear and direct. `N-VAR` `FORMAL`

cir·cum·navi·gate /,sɜːkəm'nævɪgeɪt/ **circumnavigates, circumnavigating, circumnavigated.** If someone **circumnavigates** the world or an island, they sail all the way around it. ♦ **cir·cum·navi·ga·tion** /,sɜːkəmnævɪ'geɪʃən/ **circumnavigations** *...a two-year circumnavigation of the globe in his yacht.* `VERB: V n` `FORMAL` `N-VAR`

cir·cum·scribe /'sɜːkəmskraɪb/ **circumscribes, circumscribing, circumscribed.** If someone's `VERB` `be V-ed` `Also V n`

power or freedom **is circumscribed**, it is limited or restricted. *The army evidently fears that, under him, its activities would be severely circumscribed.* `FORMAL`

cir·cum·spect /'sɜːkəmspekt/. If you are **circumspect**, you are cautious in what you do and say. *The banks should have been more circumspect in their dealings.* ♦ **cir·cum·spec·tion** /,sɜːkəm'spekʃən/. *The angry man would have to be handled with circumspection.* `ADJ-GRADED` `FORMAL` `N-UNCOUNT`

cir·cum·stance /'sɜːkəmstæns/ **circumstances. 1** The **circumstances** of a particular situation are the conditions which affect what happens. *60 per cent favor abortion under certain circumstances... I wish we could have met under happier circumstances.* **2** You can use **in the circumstances** or **under the circumstances** before or after a statement to indicate that you have considered the conditions affecting the situation before making the statement. *In the circumstances, Paisley's plans looked highly appropriate.* **3** You can emphasize that something must not or will not happen by saying that it must not or will not happen **under any circumstances**. *Under no circumstances would she cancel the trip.* **4** The **circumstances** of an event are the way it happened or the causes of it. *...the circumstances of Mary Dean's murder.* **5** Your **circumstances** are the conditions of your life, especially the amount of money that you have. *...help and support for the single mother, whatever her circumstances.* **6** Events and situations which cannot be controlled can be referred to as **circumstance**. *There are those, you know, who, by circumstance, end up homeless.* `◆◆◆◇◇` `N-COUNT` `PHRASE` `PRAGMATICS` `PHRASE` `PRAGMATICS` `N-PLURAL:` `with supp` `N-PLURAL` `N-UNCOUNT`

cir·cum·stan·tial /,sɜːkəm'stænʃəl/. **1** Circumstantial evidence is evidence that makes it seem likely that something happened, but does not prove it. **2** Something that is **circumstantial** is related to a particular circumstance. *The reasons for the project collapsing were circumstantial.* `ADJ` `FORMAL` `ADJ` `FORMAL`

cir·cum·vent /,sɜːkəm'vent/ **circumvents, circumventing, circumvented. 1** If someone **circumvents** a rule or restriction, they avoid having to obey the rule or restriction, in a clever and perhaps dishonest way. *Military planners tried to circumvent the treaty.* ♦ **cir·cum·ven·tion** /,sɜːkəm'venʃən/. *America won't countenance any such circumvention of the sanctions.* **2** If you **circumvent** someone, you cleverly prevent them from achieving something, especially when they are trying to harm you. `◆◇◇◇◇` `VERB` `V n` `FORMAL` `N-UNCOUNT` `VERB: V n` `FORMAL`

cir·cus /'sɜːkəs/ **circuses. 1** A **circus** is a group that consists of clowns, acrobats, and animals which travels around to different places and performs shows. You can also refer to their show as a **circus. 2** If you describe a group of people or an event as a **circus**, you disapprove of them because they attract a lot of attention but do not achieve anything useful. *...the travelling circus of political journalists.* **3** In Britain, **Circus** is sometimes used as part of the name of a street which goes in a circle. *...Piccadilly Circus.* `◆◆◇◇◇` `N-COUNT` `N-SING` `PRAGMATICS`

cir·rho·sis /sɪ'rəʊsɪs/. Cirrhosis or cirrhosis of the liver is a disease which destroys a person's liver and which can kill them. `N-UNCOUNT`

cis·sy /'sɪsi/. See **sissy.**

cis·tern /'sɪstən/ **cisterns.** A **cistern** is a container which holds water, for example to flush a toilet or to store the water supply for a building. `N-COUNT`

cita·del /'sɪtədəl/ **citadels. 1** In the past, a **citadel** was a strongly fortified building in or near a city. **2** If you describe a system or organization as a **citadel** of a particular way of life, usually one you disapprove of, you mean that it is powerful and effective in defending that way of life. *He sees Hollywood as the citadel of a politically correct elite.*   `N-COUNT` `N-COUNT` `PRAGMATICS`

ci·ta·tion /saɪ'teɪʃən/ **citations. 1** A **citation** is an official document or speech which praises a person for something brave or special that they have done. **2** A **citation** from a book or other piece of writing is a passage or phrase from it. **3** A **citation** is an `◆◇◇◇◇` `N-COUNT` `N-COUNT` `N-COUNT`

cite official order to appear in a court of law. The usual British word is **summons**. `AMERICAN`

cite /saɪt/ **cites, citing, cited. 1** If you **cite** something, you quote it or mention it, especially as an example or proof of what you are saying. *She cites a favourite poem by George Herbert... I am merely citing his reaction as typical of British industry.* **2** In a legal case, to **cite** a person means to officially name them. To **cite** a reason or cause means to state it as the official justification for your case. *They cited Alex's refusal to return to the marital home.* `◆◆◇◇` `VERB` `V n` `V n as adj/n` `FORMAL` `VERB` `V n` `LEGAL`

citi·zen /'sɪtɪzən/ **citizens. 1** Someone who is a **citizen** of a particular country is legally accepted as belonging to that country. *...American citizens.* **2** The **citizens** of a town or city are the people who live there. **3** See also **senior citizen**. `◆◆◆◇` `N-COUNT`

citi·zen·ry /'sɪtɪzənri/. The people living in a country, state, or city can be referred to as the **citizenry**. `N-COLL-SING`

citi·zen·ship /'sɪtɪzənʃɪp/. **1** If you have **citizenship** of a country, you are legally accepted as belonging to it. *He has finally decided to apply for American citizenship.* **2 Citizenship** is the fact of belonging to a community, and the duties and responsibilities that this brings. *Their German peers had a more developed sense of citizenship.* `◆◇◇◇` `N-UNCOUNT` `N-UNCOUNT`

cit·ric acid /ˌsɪtrɪk 'æsɪd/. **Citric acid** is a weak acid found in many kinds of fruit, especially citrus fruit such as oranges and lemons. `N-UNCOUNT`

cit·rus /'sɪtrəs/. A **citrus** fruit is a juicy, sharptasting fruit such as an orange, lemon, or grapefruit. `◆◇◇◇` `ADJ: ADJ n`

city /'sɪti/ **cities**. A **city** is a large town. *...a busy city centre.* `◆◆◆◆` `N-COUNT`

City /'sɪti/. **The City** is the part of London where many important financial institutions have their main offices. People often refer to these financial institutions as the **City**. *The City fears that profits could fall.* `◆◆◆◇` `N-PROPER: the N`

city 'fathers; also **City Fathers**. You can refer to the members of a city council as the **city fathers**. `N-PLURAL`

city 'hall, city halls; also **City Hall**. The **city hall** is the building which a city council uses as its main offices. `◆◇◇◇` `N-COUNT; N-PROPER`

city 'slicker, city slickers. If you refer to people as **city slickers**, you mean that they have well-paid jobs in a town or city, and that they appear to be clever and sophisticated, although you do not approve of them. *The city slicker has always considered himself a cut above his country cousin.* `N-COUNT` `PRAGMATICS`

civ·ic /'sɪvɪk/. **1** You use **civic** to describe people or things that have an official status in a town or city. *...the businessmen and civic leaders of Manchester.* **2** You use **civic** to describe the duties or feelings that people have because they belong to a particular community. *...a sense of civic pride.* `◆◆◇◇` `ADJ: ADJ n` `ADJ: ADJ n`

civ·ics /'sɪvɪks/. **Civics** is the study of the rights and duties of the citizens of a society. `N-UNCOUNT`

civ·il /'sɪvəl/. **1** You use **civil** to describe events that happen within a country and that involve the different groups of people in it. *...civil unrest.* **2** You use **civil** to describe people or things in a country that are not connected with its armed forces. *...the US civil aviation industry.* **3** You use **civil** to describe things that are connected with the state rather than with a religion. *They were married on August 9 in a civil ceremony.* **4** You use **civil** to describe the rights that people have within a society. *...a United Nations covenant on civil and political rights.* **5** Someone who is **civil** is polite in a formal way, but not particularly friendly. ♦ **civ·il·ly** *The man nodded civilly to Sharpe.* ♦ **ci·vil·ity** /sɪ'vɪlɪti/ **civilities** *She treats the press with civility.* `◆◆◆◇` `ADJ: ADJ n` `ADJ` `ADJ: ADJ n` `ADJ: ADJ n` `ADJ-GRADED` `FORMAL` `ADV-GRADED` `N-VAR`

civil de'fence; spelled **civil defense** in American English. **Civil defence** is the organization and training of ordinary people in a country so that they can help the armed forces or medical services in a national emergency. `◆◇◇◇` `N-UNCOUNT`

civil diso'bedience. Civil disobedience is the refusal by ordinary people in a country to obey laws or pay taxes, usually as a protest. `N-UNCOUNT`

civil engi'neering. Civil engineering is the planning, design, and construction of roads, bridges, harbours, and public buildings. ♦ **civ·il en·gi·neer, civil engineers**. `N-UNCOUNT` `N-COUNT`

ci·vil·ian /sɪ'vɪliən/ **civilians**. In a military situation, a **civilian** is anyone who is not a member of the armed forces. *...deliberate targeting of the civilian population.* `◆◆◆◇` `N-COUNT`

civi·li·sa·tion /ˌsɪvɪlaɪ'zeɪʃən/. See **civilization**.

civi·lise /'sɪvɪlaɪz/. See **civilize**.

ci·vil·ity /sɪ'vɪlɪti/. See **civil**.

civi·li·za·tion /ˌsɪvɪlaɪ'zeɪʃən/ **civilizations;** also spelled **civilisation** in British English. **1** A **civilization** is a human society with its own social organization and culture. *...the ancient civilizations of Central and Latin America.* **2 Civilization** is the state of having an advanced level of social organization and a comfortable way of life. *...our advanced state of civilisation.* **3** You can refer to a place where you can enjoy the comforts that you consider to be necessary as **civilization**. *I am anxious to return to civilization.* `◆◆◇◇` `N-VAR` `N-UNCOUNT` `N-UNCOUNT`

civi·lize /'sɪvɪlaɪz/ **civilizes, civilizing, civilized;** also spelled **civilise** in British English. To **civilize** a person or society means to educate them and improve their way of life. `◆◇◇◇` `VERB: V n`

civi·lized /'sɪvɪlaɪzd/; also spelled **civilised** in British English. **1** If you describe a society as **civilized**, you mean that it is advanced and has sensible laws and customs. *I believed that in civilized countries, torture had ended long ago.* **2** If you describe a person or their behaviour as **civilized**, you mean that they are polite and reasonable. `◆◇◇◇` `ADJ-GRADED` `ADJ-GRADED`

civil 'law. Civil law consists of laws concerned with the private affairs of citizens, for example marriage and property ownership, rather than with crime. `N-UNCOUNT`

civil 'liberties; the form **civil liberty** is used as a modifier. A person's **civil liberties** are the rights they have to say, think, and do what they want as long as they respect other people's rights. *...civil liberty campaigners.* `◆◇◇◇` `N-PLURAL`

'Civil List. In Britain, **the Civil List** is money paid by the state every year to members of the Royal Family to cover their living expenses. `N-PROPER: the N`

civil 'rights. Civil rights are the rights that people have in a society to equal treatment and equal opportunities, whatever their race, sex, or religion. *...the civil rights movement.* `◆◆◇◇` `N-PLURAL`

civil 'servant, civil servants. A civil servant is a person who works in the Civil Service in Britain and some other countries, or for the local, state, or federal government in the United States. `◆◆◇◇` `N-COUNT`

Civil 'Service. The Civil Service of a country consists of all the government departments and all the people who work in them. `◆◇◇◇` `N-SING`

civil 'war, civil wars. A civil war is a war which is fought between different groups of people who live in the same country. `◆◇◇◇` `N-COUNT`

civ·vies /'sɪviz/. People in the armed forces use **civvies** to refer to ordinary clothes that are not part of a uniform. *They might have been soldiers in civvies.* `N-PLURAL` `INFORMAL`

cl. cl is a written abbreviation for **centilitre**.

clack /klæk/ **clacks, clacking, clacked.** If things **clack**, they make a short loud noise, especially when they hit each other. *He clacked one ski hard against the other.* `V-ERG: V` `V n`

clad /klæd/. **1** If you are **clad** in particular clothes, you are wearing them. *...posters of scantily clad women.* ► Also a combining form. *...the leatherclad biker.* **2** A building, part of a building, or mountain that is **clad** with something is covered by that thing. *The walls and floors are clad with ceramic tiles.* ► Also a combining form. *...the distant shapes of snow-clad mountains.* `◆◇◇◇` `ADJ` `v-link ADJ in` `adv ADJ` `COMB` `ADJ:` `v-link ADJ in/` `with n` `COMB`

clad·ding /'klædɪŋ/. **Cladding** is a covering of tiles, wooden boards, or other material that is fixed to the outside of a building to protect or decorate it. `N-UNCOUNT`

claim /kleɪm/ **claims, claiming, claimed. 1** If someone **claims** that something is true, they say that it is true but they have not proved it and it may be false. *He claimed that it was all a conspiracy against him. ...a man claiming to be a journalist... He claims a 70 to 80 per cent success rate.* ► Also a noun. *He repeated his claim that the people of Trinidad and Tobago backed his action.* **2** If someone **claims** responsibility or credit for something, they say that they are responsible for it, but they have not proved that they are. *An underground organisation has claimed responsibility for the bomb explosion.* **3** If you **claim** something, you try to get it because you think you have a right to it. *Now they are returning to claim what was theirs.* **4** A **claim** is a demand for something that you think you have a right to. *Rival claims to Macedonian territory caused conflict in the Balkans.* **5** If you have a **claim on** someone or their attention, you have the right to demand things from them or to demand their attention. *He was surrounded by people, all with claims on his attention.* **6** If you **lay claim** to something you do not have, you say that it belongs to you. **7** Someone's **claim to fame** is something quite important or interesting that they have done or that is connected with them. *Barbara Follett's greatest claim to fame is that she taught Labour MPs how to look good on television.* **8** If someone **claims** a record, title, or prize, they gain or win it. **9** If you say that a war, disease, or accident **claims** someone's life, you mean that they are killed in it or by it. **10** If you **claim** money from the government, an insurance company, or another organization, you officially apply to them for it, because you think you are entitled to it according to their rules. *25 per cent of the people who are entitled to claim State benefits do not do so.* ► Also a noun. *...the office which has been dealing with their claim for benefit.* **11** If you **claim** money or other benefits from your employers, you demand them because you think you deserve or need them. *The National Union of Teachers claimed a pay rise worth four times the rate of inflation.* ► Also a noun. *They are making substantial claims for improved working conditions.* **12** See also **no claims.** ● to **stake a claim**: see **stake**.

claim·ant /kleɪmənt/ **claimants. 1** A **claimant** is someone who is receiving money from the state because they are unemployed or unable to work because of sickness. **2** A **claimant** is someone who demands something such as compensation or an insurance payment which they think they are entitled to.

clair·voy·ant /ˌkleəˈvɔɪənt/ **clairvoyants.** Someone who is believed to be **clairvoyant** is believed to know about future events or to be able to communicate with dead people. ► Also a noun. *I'm not a clairvoyant, I'm just an expert.* ♦ **clair·voy·ance** *...powers of telepathy and clairvoyance.*

clam /klæm/ **clams, clamming, clammed.** **Clams** are a kind of shellfish which can be eaten.

clam up. If you **clam up**, you stop talking, often because you are shy or to avoid revealing a secret.

clam·ber /ˈklæmbə/ **clambers, clambering, clambered.** If you **clamber** somewhere, you climb there with difficulty, usually using your hands as well as your feet. *They clambered up the stone walls.*

clam·my /ˈklæmi/. Something that is **clammy** is unpleasantly damp or sticky.

clam·or·ous /ˈklæmərəs/. If people or their voices are **clamorous**, they are talking loudly or shouting.

clam·our /ˈklæmə/ **clamours, clamouring, clamoured;** spelled **clamor** in American English. **1** If people **are clamouring** for something, they are demanding it in a desperate, noisy, or angry way. *My two grandsons were clamouring to go swimming.* ► Also a noun. *...the clamour for his resignation.* **2 Clamour** is used to describe the loud noise of a large group of people talking or shouting together. *She could hear a clamour in the road outside.*

clamp /klæmp/ **clamps, clamping, clamped. 1** A **clamp** is a device that holds two things firmly together. **2** When you **clamp** one thing to another, you fasten the two things together with a clamp. **3** To **clamp** something in a particular place means to put it or hold it there firmly and tightly. *Simon finished dialing and clamped the phone to his ear... He clamped his lips together.* **4** A **clamp** is a large metal device which is fitted to the wheel of an illegally parked vehicle in order to prevent it from being driven away. **5** To **clamp** a car means to fit a clamp to one of its wheels so that it cannot be driven away. ♦ **clamp·ing** *...laws to regulate clamping firms.* ♦ **clamp·er, clampers** *Private clampers demanded £57 to release her van.*

clamp down. To **clamp down** on people or activities means to take strong official action to stop or control them. *The authorities are now determined to clamp down on the media.*

clamp·down /ˈklæmpdaʊn/ **clampdowns;** also spelled **clamp-down.** A **clampdown** is a sudden restriction on a particular activity by a government or other authority. *...a clampdown on the employment of illegal immigrants.*

clan /klæn/ **clans. 1** A **clan** is a group which consists of families that are related to each other. **2** You can refer to a group of people with the same interests as a **clan.** *...a powerful clan of industrialists.*

clan·des·tine /klænˈdestɪn/. Something that is **clandestine** is hidden or kept secret, often because it is illegal. ♦ **clan·des·tine·ly** *He left the country clandestinely.*

clang /klæŋ/ **clangs, clanging, clanged.** When a large metal object **clangs,** it makes a loud noise. ► Also a noun. *He pulled the gates to with a clang.* ♦ **clang·ing** *...the clanging of the cell doors.*

clang·er /ˈklæŋə/ **clangers.** You can refer to something stupid or embarrassing that someone does or says as a **clanger.** ● If you say that you have **dropped a clanger,** you mean that you have done or said something stupid or embarrassing.

clank /klæŋk/ **clanks, clanking, clanked.** When metal objects **clank,** they make a noise because they are banging together or banging against something hard. *The train clanked into a tiny station.* ► Also a noun. *I could hear the clank and scrape of bulldozers.*

clans·man /ˈklænzmən/ **clansmen.** Clansmen are people who are members of the same clan.

clap /klæp/ **claps, clapping, clapped. 1** When you **clap,** you hit your hands together to express appreciation or attract attention. *Midge clapped her hands, calling them back to order.* ► Also a noun. *As long as the crowd give them a clap, they're quite happy.* **2** If you **clap** your hand or an object onto something, you put it there quickly and firmly. *I clapped a hand over her mouth.* **3** If you **clap** someone **on** the back or on the shoulder, you hit their back or shoulder with your hand in a friendly way. **4** A **clap of thunder** is a sudden loud noise of thunder. **5** ● to **clap eyes on** someone: see **eye.**

clap·board /ˈklæpbɔːd, ˈklæbəd/. A **clapboard** building has walls which are covered with long narrow pieces of wood, usually painted white.

clapped-out; also spelled **clapped out.** If you describe a person or a machine as **clapped-out,** you mean that they are old and no longer able to work properly.

clapper·board /ˈklæpəbɔːd/ **clapperboards.** A **clapperboard** consists of two pieces of wood that are connected by a hinge and banged together before each scene when making a film.

clap·trap /ˈklæptræp/. If you describe something that someone says as **claptrap,** you mean that it is stupid or meaningless.

clar·et /ˈklærət/ **clarets. 1 Claret** is a type of French red wine. **2** Something that is **claret** is purplish-red in colour.

clari·fy /ˈklærɪfaɪ/ **clarifies, clarifying, clarified. 1** To **clarify** something means to make it

easier to understand, usually by explaining it in more detail. ♦ **clari·fi·ca·tion** /ˌklærɪfɪˈkeɪʃən/ FORMAL N-VAR **clarifications** *The union has written to Zurich asking for clarification of the situation.* **2** To **clarify** a substance means to make it clearer, usually by removing impurities from it. *...clarified butter.* VERB: V n V-ed

clari·net /ˌklærɪ'net/ **clarinets.** A **clarinet** is a musical instrument of the woodwind family in the shape of a pipe with a single reed. See picture headed **musical instruments.** ♦ **clari·net·tist, clarinettists;** also spelled **clarinetist.** *...the brilliant young French clarinettist, Louis Sclavis.* ♦◇◇◇◇ N-VAR N-COUNT

clarion call, clarion calls. A **clarion call** is a strong and emotional appeal to people to do something. *This is a clarion call for our country to face the challenges of the end of the Cold War.* N-COUNT LITERARY

clar·ity /ˈklærɪti/ **1** The **clarity** of something such as a book or argument is its quality of being well explained and easy to understand. *...the ease and clarity with which the author explains difficult technical and scientific subjects.* **2 Clarity** is the ability to think clearly. *...clarity of thought.* **3 Clarity** is the quality of being clear in outline or sound. *This remarkable technology provides far greater clarity than conventional x-rays.* **4** The **clarity** of a liquid, of glass, or of the air is the degree to which it is clear and free from impurities. ♦◇◇◇◇ N-UNCOUNT N-UNCOUNT N-UNCOUNT N-UNCOUNT

clash /klæʃ/ **clashes, clashing, clashed. 1** When people **clash,** they fight, argue, or disagree with each other. *The United States and Israel clashed over demands for a UN investigation into the killings.* ► Also a noun. *...clashes between police in riot gear and demonstrators.* **2** Sports journalists sometimes say that two individuals or teams who compete against each other **clash.** *Lewis has recently recovered his fitness and will clash with Christie in the 4x100m relay.* ► Also a noun. *...Australia's rugby union team for the return clash with New Zealand.* **3** Beliefs, ideas, or qualities that **clash** are very different from each other and therefore are opposed. *Don't make any policy decisions which clash with official company thinking.* ► Also a noun. *...a clash of views.* **4** If one event **clashes** with another, the two events happen at the same time so that you cannot attend both of them. *We'll go to both of them if the times don't clash.* **5** If one colour or style **clashes** with another, the colours or styles look ugly together. *So what if the colours clashed?* **6** When metal objects **clash,** they make a lot of noise by being hit together. *The golden bangles on her arms clashed and jingled.* ♦♦♦◇◇ V-RECIP: pl-n V Also V with n JOURNALISM V-RECIP: pl-n V V with n JOURNALISM N-COUNT V-RECIP: pl-n V V with n N-COUNT: N of n V-RECIP: V with n pl-n V V-RECIP: pl-n V V with n pl-n V VERB LITERARY

clasp /klɑːsp, klæsp/ **clasps, clasping, clasped. 1** If you **clasp** someone or something, you hold them tightly in your hands or arms. *He paced the corridor, hands clasped behind his back.* ► Also a noun. *With one last grasp of his hand, she left him.* **2** A **clasp** is a small device that fastens something. *...the clasp of her handbag.* ♦◇◇◇◇ V-ed N-COUNT N-COUNT

class /klɑːs/ **classes, classing, classed. 1** A **class** is a group of pupils or students who are taught together. **2** A **class** is a course of teaching in a particular subject. *He acquired a law degree by taking classes at night.* **3** If you do something **in class,** you do it during a lesson in school. **4** The students in a school or university who finish their course in a particular year can be referred to as the **class of** that year. *...two members of Yale's Class of '57.* **5** A **class** of things is a group of them with similar characteristics. *...the division of the stars into six classes of brightness.* **6** If someone or something **is classed as** a particular thing, they are regarded as belonging to that group of things. *I class myself as an ordinary working person.* **7** If you say that someone or something is **in a class of** their own, you mean that they have more of a particular skill or quality than anyone else or any similar thing. **8 Class** refers to the division of people in a society into groups according to their social status. *...the British class structure.* ♦♦♦♦◇ N-COUNT N-COUNT N-UNCOUNT: in N N-SING: N of date AMERICAN N-COUNT VERB: be V-ed as n/ adj V n as n/adj PHRASE N-VAR

9 If you say that someone or something has **class,** you mean that they are elegant and sophisticated. **10** If you describe someone or something as a **class** person or thing, you mean that they are very good. *Kite is undoubtedly a class player.* ● A **class act** is someone who is very good at what they do. N-UNCOUNT ADJ: ADJ n INFORMAL PHRASE

11 See also **business class, chattering classes, first-class, middle class, second-class, third-class, top-class, upper class, working class, world-class.**

clas·sic /ˈklæsɪk/ **classics. 1** A **classic** example of a thing or situation has all the features which you expect such a thing or situation to have. *His first two goals were classic cases of being in the right place at the right time.* ► Also a noun. *It was a classic of interrogation: first the bully, then the kind one.* ♦ **clas·si·cal·ly** /ˈklæsɪkli/. *Classically, overweight people underestimate the volume of food that they consume.* **2** A **classic** film, piece of writing, or piece of music is of very high quality and has become a standard against which similar things are judged. *...the classic children's film Huckleberry Finn. ...a classic study of the American penal system.* ► Also a noun. *...a film classic.* **3** A **classic** is a book which is well-known and considered to be of a very high literary standard. **4 Classic** style is simple and traditional and is not affected by changes in fashion. *Wear classic clothes which feel good and look good.* ♦ **classically** *Older women look best in classically elegant styles.* **5 Classics** is the study of the ancient Greek and Roman civilizations, especially their languages, literature, and philosophy. ♦♦♦♦◇ ADJ N-COUNT ADV ADJ: ADJ n N-COUNT N-COUNT ADJ-GRADED ADV: ADJ adj/-ed N-UNCOUNT

clas·si·cal /ˈklæsɪkəl/ **1** You use **classical** to describe something that is traditional in form, style, or content. *...the steps of classical ballet.* ♦ **classi·cal·ly** *...a classically trained musician.* **2 Classical** is used to describe things which relate to or remind people of the ancient Greek or Roman civilizations. *...the healers of ancient Egypt and classical Greece.* ♦ **classically** *...the classically inspired church of S. Francesco.* **3** A **classical** language is a form of a language that was used in ancient times and is now no longer used, or only used in formal writing. *...a line of classical Arabic poetry.* ♦♦♦◇◇ ADJ ADV-ed ADJ ADV: ADJ adj/-ed ADJ: ADJ n

clas·si·cism /ˈklæsɪsɪzəm/. **Classicism** is a style of art practised especially in the 18th century in Europe. It has simple regular forms and the artist does not attempt to express strong emotions. ♦ **clas·si·cist, classicists** *The romantic does not, as does the classicist, regard himself as a craftsman.* N-UNCOUNT N-COUNT

clas·si·cist /ˈklæsɪsɪst/ **classicists. 1** A **classicist** is someone who studies the ancient Greek and Roman civilizations, especially their languages, literature, and philosophy. **2** See also **classicism.** N-COUNT

clas·si·fi·ca·tion /ˌklæsɪfɪˈkeɪʃən/ **classifications.** A **classification** is a division or category in a classifying system. *...engineering companies, a classification that includes the car companies.* ● See also **classify.** ♦◇◇◇◇ N-COUNT

clas·si·fied /ˈklæsɪfaɪd/. **Classified** information or documents are officially secret. *The document was highly classified.* ♦◇◇◇◇ ADJ

classified 'ad, classified ads. Classified ads or **classified advertisements** are small advertisements in a newspaper or magazine which are placed in categories according to their subject. N-COUNT

clas·si·fieds /ˈklæsɪfaɪdz/. The **classifieds** are the same as **classified ads.** N-PLURAL

clas·si·fy /ˈklæsɪfaɪ/ **classifies, classifying, classified.** To **classify** things means to divide them into groups or types so that things with similar characteristics are in the same group. *The coroner immediately classified his death as a suicide.* ♦ **clas·si·fi·ca·tion** /ˌklæsɪfɪˈkeɪʃən/ **classifications** *...the arbitrary classification of knowledge into fields of study.* ♦♦◇◇◇ VERB: V n V n as n N-VAR

class·less /ˈklɑːsləs, ˈklæs-/. When politicians talk about a **classless** society, they mean a society in which people are not affected by differences in social status; used showing approval. ♦ **class·less·ness** *...the myth of classlessness.* ♦◇◇◇◇ ADJ-GRADED PRAGMATICS N-UNCOUNT

class·mate /'klɑːsmeɪt, 'klæs-/ **classmates.** Your
classmates are students who are in the same class
as you at school or college. ◆◇◇◇◇ N-COUNT

class·room /'klɑːsruːm, 'klæs-/ **classrooms.** A
classroom is a room in a school where lessons take
place. ◆◆◇◇◇ N-COUNT

classy /'klɑːsi, 'klæsi/ **classier, classiest.** If you
describe someone or something as **classy**, you
mean they are stylish and sophisticated. *They need
classier brand names to sell upmarket cars.* ◆◇◇◇◇ ADJ-GRADED INFORMAL

clat·ter /'klætə/ **clatters, clattering, clattered.**
1 If you say that people or things **clatter** somewhere, you mean that they move there noisily. *He
turned and clattered down the stairs.* **2** If something
hard **clatters**, it makes repeated short noises as it
hits against another hard thing. *She set her cup
down, and it clattered against the saucer.* ▶ Also a
noun. *...the clatter of a typewriter.* ◆◇◇◇◇ VERB V prep/adv / VERB V prep LITERARY / N-SING

clause /klɔːz/ **clauses. 1** A **clause** is a section of a
legal document. *He has a clause in his contract
which entitles him to a percentage of the profits.* **2** In
grammar, a **clause** is a group of words containing a
verb. Sentences contain one or more clauses. ● See
also **main clause, relative clause, subordinate
clause**. ◆◆◇◇◇ N-COUNT / N-COUNT

claus·tro·pho·bia /ˌklɔːstrəˈfəʊbiə/. **1** Someone
who suffers from **claustrophobia** feels very uncomfortable or anxious when they are in a very small or
enclosed place. ◆ **claus·tro·pho·bic**
/ˌklɔːstrəˈfəʊbɪk/ *The churning, pressing crowds
made her feel claustrophobic.* **2** If you talk about the
claustrophobia of a place or situation, you mean it
makes you feel uncomfortable or unhappy because
you are enclosed or restricted. *Work provided an escape from the inevitable claustrophobia of family
life.* ◆ **claus·tro·pho·bic** *The house felt too
claustrophobic.* N-UNCOUNT / ADJ-GRADED / N-UNCOUNT / ADJ-GRADED

claw /klɔː/ **claws, clawing, clawed. 1** The
claws of a bird or animal are the thin, hard, curved
nails at the end of its feet. **2** The **claws** of a lobster,
crab, or scorpion are the two pointed parts at the
end of its legs which are used for grasping things.
3 If an animal **claws** something, it scratches or
damages it with its claws. *The wolf clawed the tree
and howled.* **4** When people or animals **claw** at
something, they try to get hold of it or damage it by
using their nails or claws. *His fingers clawed at
Blake's wrist.*
5 If you **claw** your **way** somewhere, you move there
with great difficulty, trying desperately to find things
to hold on to. *Some did manage to claw their way up
iron ladders to the safety of the upper deck.* **6** If someone **claws** their **way** to a successful position, they
achieve it with great determination in spite of many
difficulties. *Gino clawed his way out of underworld
obscurity to become a millionaire hotelier.* ◆◇◇◇◇ N-COUNT / N-COUNT / VERB V n / VERB V at n Also V n / VERB V way prep/adv / VERB V way prep/adv

claw back. 1 If someone **claws back** some of the
money or power which they had lost, they get some of
it again. *They will eventually be able to claw back all or
most of the debt.* **2** When a government **claws back**
money, it finds a way of taking money back from peo-
ple that it gave money to in another way. PHRASAL VB V P noun Also V n P BRITISH / V P noun TECHNICAL

clay /kleɪ/ **clays. 1** Clay is a kind of earth that is
soft when it is wet and hard when it is dry. Clay is
shaped and baked to make things such as pots and
bricks. **2** In tennis, matches played on **clay** are
played on courts whose surface is covered with
finely crushed stones or brick. *...Frana, a clay court
specialist.* **3** If you say that a person who is respected or admired has **feet of clay** or has **clay feet**, you
mean that they have serious faults which you or
other people did not know about before. ◆◆◇◇◇ N-VAR / N-UNCOUNT / PHRASE FORMAL

clay 'pigeon, clay pigeons. Clay pigeons are
discs of baked clay which are thrown into the air by
a machine as targets for gun shooting practice.
...clay-pigeon shooting. N-COUNT

clean /kliːn/ **cleaner, cleanest; cleans, cleaning, cleaned. 1** Something that is **clean** is free
from dirt or unwanted marks. *He wore his cleanest
slacks, a clean shirt and a navy blazer... Tiled kitch-* ◆◆◆◆◇ ADJ-GRADED

en floors are easy to keep clean. **2** If you **clean** something or **clean** dirt off it, you make it free from dirt
and unwanted marks, for example by washing or
wiping it. *It took half an hour to clean the orange
powder off the bath... Wood flooring not only cleans
easily, but it's environmentally friendly.* ▶ Also a
noun. *Give the cooker a good clean.* **3** You say that
people or animals are **clean** when they keep themselves or their surroundings clean. **4** A **clean** fuel or
chemical process does not create many harmful or
polluting substances. *Fans of electric cars say they
are clean, quiet and economical.* ◆ **clean·ly** *Manufacturers are working with new fuels to find one that
burns more cleanly than petrol.* **5** If you **clean** a
room or house, you make the inside of it and the
furniture in it free from dirt and dust. *With them
also lived Mary Burinda, who cooked and cleaned.*
◆ **clean·ing** *I do the cleaning myself.*
6 If you describe something such as a book, joke, or
lifestyle as **clean**, you think that they are not sexually
immoral or offensive; used showing approval. *They're
trying to show clean, wholesome, decent movies.* **7** If
someone has a **clean** reputation or record, they have
never done anything illegal or wrong. *...a clean driving licence.* **8** A **clean** game or fight is carried out fairly, according to the rules. *It was a clean match, well
refereed.* ◆ **cleanly** *The game had been cleanly
fought.*
9 If you describe a flavour, smell, or colour as **clean**,
you like it because it is light and fresh. *Soft tones of
blue and grey create a clean, bright look.*
10 A **clean** sheet of paper has no writing or drawing
on it.
11 If you make a **clean** break or start, you end a situation completely and start again in a different way.
*Voters have chosen to make a clean break with the
communist past.* **12** **Clean** is used to emphasize that
something was done completely. *The thief got clean
away with the money.* **13** You can describe an action
as **clean** to indicate that it is carried out simply and
quickly without mistakes. *Paul had arrested countless
men like this one before and was expecting a clean,
quick job.* ◆ **cleanly** *I struck the ball cleanly and my
shot was on target.*
14 A **clean** shape is simple and regular, with definite,
smooth edges. *The drill should be slowly rotated to ensure a clean hole.* ◆ **clean·ly** *Cut horizontally and
cleanly through the stem.*
15 If you **come clean** about something that you have
been keeping secret, you admit it or tell people about
it. *It would be better if you came clean about it and let
her know what kind of man she is seeing.*
16 ● to **clean up** your **act**: see **act**. ● a **clean bill of
health**: see **bill**. ● a **clean slate**: see **slate**. ● to **wipe
the slate clean**: see **slate**. ● a **clean sweep**: see **sweep**.
● **clean as a whistle**: see **whistle**.

V-ERG: V n / V n prep/adv / V adv / N-SING / ADJ-GRADED / ADJ-GRADED / ADV-GRADED: ADV after v / VERB: V n V / N-UNCOUNT / ADJ-GRADED PRAGMATICS / ADJ-GRADED / ADJ-GRADED / ADV / ADJ-GRADED PRAGMATICS / ADJ / ADJ: ADJ n / ADV PRAGMATICS INFORMAL ADJ-GRADED / ADV-GRADED / ADJ-GRADED / ADV-GRADED: ADV with v / PHRASE INFORMAL

clean out. 1 If you **clean out** something such as a
cupboard, room, or container, you take everything
out of it and clean the inside of it thoroughly. *Mr Wall
asked if I would help him clean out the bins.* **2** If someone **cleans** you **out**, they take all the money and valuables you have. If they **clean out** a place, they take
everything of value that is in it. *I'm sure the burglars
waited until my insurance claim was through and
came back to clean me out again.* PHRASAL VB V P noun Also V n P / V n P Also V P noun INFORMAL

clean up. 1 If you **clean up** a mess or **clean up** a
place where there is a mess, you make things tidy and
free of dirt again. *Nina and Mary were in the kitchen,
cleaning up after dinner.* **2** To **clean up** something
such as the environment or an industry means to reduce the pollution that affects it or is caused by it.
Many regional governments cleaned up their beaches.
3 If the police or authorities **clean up** a place or area
of activity, they make it free from crime, corruption,
and other unacceptable forms of behaviour. *After
years of neglect and decline the city was cleaning itself
up.* PHRASAL VB V P noun V P Also V n P / V P noun Also V n P / V P noun V n P

clean up after. If you **clean up after** someone, you
clean or tidy a place after they have made it dirty or
untidy. PHRASAL VB V P P n

,clean-'cut. Someone, especially a boy or man, ADJ-GRADED
who is **clean-cut** has a neat, tidy appearance. *...his
clean-cut good looks.*

clean·er /'kli:nə/ **cleaners. 1** A **cleaner** is some- ◆◇◇◇
one who is employed to clean the rooms and furni- N-COUNT
ture inside a building. **2** A **cleaner** is someone N-COUNT:
whose job is to clean a particular type of thing. *He* nN
was a window cleaner. **3** A **cleaner** is a substance or N-VAR
device used for cleaning things. *...oven cleaner. ...an
air cleaner.* ● See also **pipe cleaner**, **vacuum clean-**
er. 4 A **cleaner** or a **cleaner's** is a shop where things N-COUNT
such as clothes are dry-cleaned.
5 If someone **takes** you **to the cleaners**, they unfairly PHRASE
take a lot of your money, for example in a business INFORMAL
deal or in gambling.

'cleaning lady, cleaning ladies. A **cleaning lady** N-COUNT
is a woman who is employed to clean the rooms
and furniture inside a building.

clean·li·ness /'klenlinəs/. **Cleanliness** is the de- ◆◇◇◇
gree to which people keep themselves and their sur- N-UNCOUNT
roundings clean. *Many of Britain's beaches fail to
meet minimum standards of cleanliness.*

cleanse /klenz/ **cleanses, cleansing,** ◆◆◇◇
cleansed. 1 To **cleanse** a place, person, or organi- VERB
zation of something dirty, unpleasant, or evil means Vn ofn
to make them free from it. *It urged the party to* Also V n
*cleanse its own ranks of those found guilty of human
rights violations.* **2** If you **cleanse** your skin or a VERB: V n
wound, you clean it. ◆ **cleans·er, cleansers** *...a* N-VAR
facial cleanser suitable for dry complexions. **3** If a VERB:
person or their soul **is cleansed**, they are made pure be V-ed
or free from sin. *Confession cleanses the soul.* **4** See V n
also **ethnic cleansing**.

,clean-'shaven. If a man is **clean-shaven**, he does ADJ
not have a beard or a moustache.

'clean-up, clean-ups; spelled **cleanup** in Ameri- ◆◆◇◇
can English. A **clean-up** is the removing of dirt, pol- N-COUNT
lution, crime, or corruption from somewhere. *The
Governor has now called in the National Guard to
assist the clean-up operation.*

clear /klɪə/ **clearer, clearest; clears, clearing,** ◆◆◆◆◆
cleared. 1 Something that is **clear** is easy to ADJ-GRADED
understand, see, or hear. *The book is clear, readable
and adequately illustrated... The space telescope has
taken the clearest pictures ever of Pluto.* ◆ **clear·ly**
*It was important for children to learn to express ADV-GRADED
themselves clearly.* **2** Something that is **clear** is obvi- ADJ-GRADED
ous and impossible to be mistaken about. *It was a
clear case of homicide... It became clear that I hadn't
been able to convince Mike.* ◆ **clearly** *Clearly, the* ADV-GRADED:
police cannot break the law in order to enforce it. ADV with cl/
3 If you **make** something **clear**, you say something group
in a way that makes it impossible for there to be PHRASE
any doubt about your meaning, wishes, or inten-
tions. **4** If you are **clear** about something, you ADJ-GRADED
understand it completely. *It is important to be clear
about what Chomsky is doing here.* **5** You can say 'Is CONVENTION
that clear?' or 'Do I make myself clear?' after you PRAGMATICS
have told someone your wishes or instructions, to
make sure that they have understood you, and to
emphasize your authority. *You're not going to buy
anything. Is that clear?*
6 If your mind or your way of thinking is **clear**, you are ADJ-GRADED
able to think sensibly, reasonably, and logically, and
you are not affected by confusion or by
alcohol. *She needed a clear head to carry out her instructions.* ◆ **clearly** *The only time I can think clearly* ADV-GRADED:
is when I'm alone. **7** To **clear** your mind or your head ADV after v
means to free it from confused thoughts or from the VERB: V n
effects of a drug such as alcohol. *Our therapists will* V n ofn
show you how to clear your mind of worries.
8 A **clear** substance is one which you can see through ADJ
and which has no colour, like clean water. *...a clear
glass panel. ...a clear gel.* **9** A **clear** colour is bright and ADJ-GRADED
strong. *Ladybird pupae vary in colour from brown to
clear orange.* **10** **Clear** eyes look healthy, attractive, ADJ-GRADED
and shining. **11** If your skin is **clear**, it is healthy and ADJ-GRADED
free from spots. **12** If it is a **clear** day or if the sky is ADJ-GRADED
clear, there is no mist, rain, or cloud. **13** When fog or VERB: V
mist **clears**, it gradually disappears.

14 If a surface, place, or view is **clear**, it is free of ob- ADJ
structions or unwanted objects. *The runway is clear –
go ahead and land.* **15** When you **clear** an area or VERB: V n
place or **clear** something from it, you remove things Vn ofn
from it that you do not want to be there. *Workers* Also Vn with
could not clear the tunnels of smoke... Firemen were adv
still clearing rubble from apartments.
16 If something or someone **clears** the way or the VERB:
path **for** something to happen, they make it possible. V n for n to-inf
The Prime Minister resigned today, clearing the way V n for n
for the formation of a new government.
17 If you say that your conscience is **clear**, you mean ADJ
you do not think you have done anything wrong. *I can
look back on things with a clear conscience.*
18 If something or someone is **clear** of something ADJ:
else, it is not touching it or is a safe distance away v-link ADJ of
from it. *He lifted him clear of the deck with one arm.* n, v n ADJ
19 If something or someone is a certain amount **clear** PHR-PREP
of a competitor, they are that amount ahead of them BRITISH
in a competition or race. *He crossed the line three seconds clear of Tom Snape.* **20** If an animal or person VERB
clears an object or **clears** a certain height, they jump V n
over the object, or over something that might be, without touching it. *Sotomayor, the Cuban holder of the
world high jump record, cleared 2.36 metres.*
21 When a bank **clears** a cheque, it agrees to pay the V-ERG: V n
sum of money mentioned on it. *Allow time for the* V
cheque to clear. **22** If a course of action **is cleared**, VERB:
people in authority give permission for it to happen. be V-ed
Within an hour, the helicopter was cleared for take-off. be V-ed for n
23 If someone **is cleared**, they are proved to be not VERB
guilty of a crime or mistake. *She was cleared of murder* be V-ed ofn/
and jailed for just five years for manslaughter. ...a final -ing
effort to clear her name. **24** If someone is **in the clear**, V n
they are free from blame, suspicion, or danger. *The* PHRASE
*Audit Commission said that the ministry was in the
clear.*
25 If you **steer clear** or **stay clear** of someone or PHRASE
something, you avoid them. *The rabbis try to steer
clear of political questions.*
26 See also **clearing**; **crystal clear**. ● **to clear the air**:
see **air**. ● **the coast is clear**: see **coast**. ● **to clear the
decks**: see **deck**. ● **loud and clear**: see **loud**. ● **to clear
your throat**: see **throat**.

clear away. When you **clear** things **away** or **clear** PHRASAL VB
away, you put away the things that you have been V P noun
using, especially for eating or cooking. *The waitress* V P
had cleared away the plates and brought coffee... Also V n P
Tania cooked, served, and cleared away.

clear off. If you tell someone to **clear off**, you are PHRASAL VB
telling them rather rudely to go away. *They looked at* V P
me as if I was nuts and told me to clear off. INFORMAL

clear out. **1** If you tell someone to **clear out** of a PHRASAL VB
place or to **clear out**, you are telling them rather rude- V P ofn
ly to leave the place. *'Clear out!' he bawled. 'Private* V P
property!' **2** If you **clear out** a container, room, or V P noun
house, you tidy it and throw away the things in it that Also V n P
you no longer want. *I took the precaution of clearing
out my desk before I left.* ● See also **clear-out**.

clear up. **1** When you **clear up** or **clear** a place **up**, PHRASAL VB
you tidy things and put them away. *I cleared up my* V P
room. **2** To **clear up** a problem, misunderstanding, or V P noun
mystery means to settle it or find a satisfactory expla- Also V n P
nation for it. *There should be someone to whom you* V P noun
can turn for any advice or to clear up any problems. Also V n P
● See also **clear-up**. **3** To **clear up** a medical problem, ERG:
infection, or disease means to cure it or get rid of it. If V P noun
a medical problem **clears up**, it goes away. *Acne often* V P
clears up after the first three months of pregnancy. Also V n P
4 When the weather **clears up**, it stops raining or be- V P
ing cloudy.

clear·ance /'klɪərəns/ **clearances. 1** Clearance ◆◇◇◇
is the removal of old buildings, trees, or other things N-VAR
that are not wanted from an area. *The UN pledged
to help supervise the clearance of mines.* **2** If you get N-VAR
clearance to do or have something, you get official
approval or permission to do or have it. *Thai Airways said the plane had been given clearance to
land.* **3** The **clearance** of a bridge is the distance be- N-VAR
tween the lowest point of the bridge and the road or

the water under the bridge. *The lowest fixed bridge has 12.8m clearance.*

,clear-'cut. Something that is **clear-cut** is easy to recognize and quite distinct. *This was a clear-cut case of the original land owner being in the right.* ◆◇◇◇ ADJ-GRADED

,clear-'headed. If you describe someone as **clear-headed**, you mean that they are sensible and think clearly, especially in difficult situations. ADJ-GRADED

clear·ing /'klɪərɪŋ/ **clearings.** A **clearing** is a small area in a forest where there are no trees or bushes. *A helicopter landed in a clearing in the dense jungle.* ◆◆◇◇ N-COUNT

'clearing bank, clearing banks. The **clearing banks** are the major banking organizations in Britain. Clearing banks use the central clearing house in London to deal with their transactions. N-COUNT

'clearing house, clearing houses; also spelled **clearing-house. 1** If an organization acts as a **clearing house**, it collects, sorts, and distributes specialized information. *The centre will act as a clearing house for research projects for former nuclear scientists.* **2** A **clearing house** is a central bank which deals with all the transactions between the banks that use its services. N-COUNT

'clear-out, clear-outs. When you have a **clear-out**, you collect together all the things that you do not want and throw them away. N-COUNT BRITISH, INFORMAL

'clear-up. The **clear-up** rate for a crime or in an area is the percentage of criminals caught by the police, compared to the total number of crimes reported. *The Metropolitan Police say clear-up figures were improved.* ◆◇◇◇ ADJ: ADJ n BRITISH

cleat /kliːt/ **cleats.** A **cleat** is a kind of double hook which is used for securing rope, especially on sailing boats. N-COUNT

cleav·age /'kliːvɪdʒ/ **cleavages. 1** A woman's **cleavage** is the space between her breasts, especially the top part which you see if she is wearing a low-cut dress. **2** A **cleavage** between two people or things is a division or disagreement between them. *...the economic cleavages between the two regions.* ◆◇◇◇ N-COUNT / N-COUNT FORMAL

cleave /kliːv/ **cleaves, cleaving.** The past tense can be either **cleaved** or **clove**; the past participle can be **cleaved, cloven,** or **cleft** for meaning 1, and is **cleaved** for meaning 2. **1** When you **cleave** something, you split or divide it into two separate parts, often violently. **2** If someone **cleaves** to something or someone, they have a strong attachment and loyalty to them. *As Morisot and Manet cleaved to each other, previous bonds weakened.* VERB: V n LITERARY / VERB V to n FORMAL

cleav·er /'kliːvə/ **cleavers.** A **cleaver** is a knife with a large square blade, used for chopping meat or vegetables. N-COUNT

cleft /kleft/ **clefts. 1** A **cleft** in a rock or in the ground is a narrow opening in it. **2** If someone has a **cleft** in their chin, their chin has a shallow vertical indentation in the middle. **3** Cleft is a past participle of **cleave.** N-COUNT / N-COUNT

clema·tis /'klemətɪs, klə'meɪtɪs/ **clematises;** the plural form can be **clematis** or **clematises.** A **clematis** is a type of climbing flowering shrub. ◆◇◇◇ N-VAR

clem·en·cy /'klemənsi/. If someone is granted **clemency**, they receive merciful treatment from a person who has the authority to punish them. *Their pleas for clemency were turned down.* N-UNCOUNT FORMAL

clem·ent /'klemənt/. **Clement** weather is pleasantly mild and dry. ADJ-GRADED FORMAL

clench /klentʃ/ **clenches, clenching, clenched. 1** When you **clench** your fist, you curl your fingers up tightly, usually because you are very angry. *He turned on her, fists clenching. ...angry protestors with clenched fists.* **2** When you **clench** your teeth, you squeeze your teeth together firmly, usually because you are angry or upset. *Slowly, he released his breath through clenched teeth.* **3** If you **clench** something in your hand or in your teeth, you hold it tightly with your hand or your teeth. *I clenched the arms of my chair.* ◆◇◇◇ V-ERG: V n / V-ed / VERB: V n / V-ed / Also V / VERB V n

cler·gy /'klɜːdʒi/. The **clergy** are the religious leaders of a particular group of believers. *Stalin deported Catholic clergy to Siberia.* ◆◇◇◇ N-PLURAL

clergy·man /'klɜːdʒimən/ **clergymen.** A **clergyman** is a male member of the clergy. ◆◇◇◇ N-COUNT

cler·ic /'klerɪk/ **clerics.** A **cleric** is a member of the clergy. ◆◇◇◇ N-COUNT

cleri·cal /'klerɪkəl/. **1 Clerical** jobs, skills, and workers are concerned with work that is done in an office. *...a clerical error.* **2 Clerical** means relating to the clergy. *...Iran's clerical leadership.* ◆◇◇◇ ADJ: ADJ n / ADJ: ADJ n

clerk /klɑːk, AM klɜːrk/ **clerks, clerking, clerked. 1** A **clerk** is a person who works in an office, bank, or law court and whose job is to look after the records or accounts. *She was offered a job as an accounts clerk with a travel firm.* **2** A **clerk** is a receptionist. *...a hotel clerk.* **3** To **clerk** means to work as a clerk. *He clerked for the chief justice of the Supreme Court.* ◆◆◇◇ N-COUNT / N-COUNT / VERB: V / V for n

clev·er /'klevə/ **cleverer, cleverest. 1** Someone who is **clever** is intelligent and able to understand things easily or plan things well. *My sister was always a lot cleverer than I was... Her mother was clever at many things.* ◆ **clev·er·ly** *She would cleverly pick up on what I said.* ◆ **clev·er·ness** *Her cleverness seems to get in the way of her emotions.* **2** A **clever** idea, book, or invention is extremely effective and shows the skill of the people involved. *It is a clever and gripping novel. ...this clever new gadget.* ◆ **clev·er·ly** *...a cleverly designed swimsuit.* ◆◆◆◇ ADJ-GRADED / ADV-GRADED / N-UNCOUNT / ADJ-GRADED / ADV-GRADED

cli·ché /'kliːʃeɪ, AM kliː'ʃeɪ/ **clichés;** also spelled **cliche.** A **cliché** is an idea or phrase which has been used so much that it is no longer interesting or effective or no longer has much meaning; used showing disapproval. *It has become a cliche to describe Asia-Pacific as the world's most dynamic economic area.* ◆ **cli·chéd** /'kliːʃeɪd, AM kliː'ʃeɪd/. *It's very easy to fall back on cliched images in travel writing.* ◆◇◇◇ N-COUNT PRAGMATICS / ADJ-GRADED

click /klɪk/ **clicks, clicking, clicked. 1** If something **clicks** or if you **click** it, it makes a short, sharp sound. *He clicked off the radio... Blake clicked his fingers at a passing waiter. ...a click of a button.* **2** When you suddenly understand something, you can say that it **clicks.** *It suddenly clicked that this was fantastic fun.* **3** If you **click** with someone, you like each other and become friends as soon as you meet. *They clicked immediately.* **4** ● to **click** your **heels:** see **heel.** ● to **click** **into place:** see **place.** ◆◆◇◇ V-ERG: V / V n with off/ on / V n / N-COUNT / VERB: V / it V that INFORMAL / V-RECIP: V with n / pl-n V INFORMAL

cli·ent /'klaɪənt/ **clients.** A **client** of a professional person or organization is a person or company that receives a service from them in return for payment. *The company required clients to pay substantial fees in advance.* ◆◆◆◇ N-COUNT

cli·en·tele /ˌkliːɒn'tel, ˌklaɪən-/. The **clientele** of a place or organization are its customers or clients. *This pub had a mixed clientele.* ◆◇◇◇ N-COLL-SING

,client 'state, client states. A **client state** is a country which is controlled or influenced by another larger and more powerful state, or which is dependent on this state for support and protection. N-COUNT

cliff /klɪf/ **cliffs.** A **cliff** is a high area of land with a very steep side, especially one next to the sea. *The car rolled over the edge of a cliff.* ◆◆◇◇ N-COUNT

'cliff-hanger, cliff-hangers. A **cliff-hanger** is a part of a play, film, or situation that is very exciting or frightening because you are left for a long time not knowing what will happen next. *The series always had a cliff-hanger ending.* N-COUNT

cliff·top, clifftops. A **clifftop** is the area of land around the top of a cliff. *I have this beautiful house on a clifftop.* N-COUNT

cli·mac·tic /klaɪ'mæktɪk/. A **climactic** moment in a story or situation is one in which a very exciting or important event occurs. *...the film's climactic scene.* ADJ-GRADED: ADJ n FORMAL

cli·mate /'klaɪmət/ **climates. 1** The **climate** of a place is the general weather conditions that are typical of it. *...the hot and humid climate of Cyprus.* **2** You can use **climate** to refer to the general ◆◇◇◇ N-VAR / N-COUNT

atmosphere or situation somewhere. ...*the existing climate of violence and intimidation.*

cli·mat·ic /klaɪˈmætɪk/. **Climatic** conditions, changes, and effects relate to the general weather conditions of a place. ◆◇◇◇◇ ADJ: ADJ n

cli·ma·tolo·gist /ˌklaɪməˈtɒlədʒɪst/ **climatologists.** A **climatologist** is a person who studies climates. N-COUNT

cli·max /ˈklaɪmæks/ **climaxes, climaxing, climaxed. 1** The **climax** of something is the most exciting or important moment in it, usually near the end. *For Pritchard, reaching an Olympics was the climax of her career.* **2** The event that **climaxes** a sequence of events is an exciting or important event that comes at the end. You can also say that a sequence of events **climaxes** with a particular event. ...*a sell-out UK tour that climaxed with a three-night stint at Brixton Academy.* **3** A **climax** is an orgasm. **4** When someone **climaxes**, they have an orgasm. ◆◆◇◇◇ N-COUNT / V-ERG: V n / V with n / Also V / JOURNALISM / N-VAR / VERB: V

climb /klaɪm/ **climbs, climbing, climbed. 1** If you **climb** something such as a tree, mountain, or ladder, or **climb** up it, you move towards the top of it. If you **climb** down it, you move towards the bottom of it. *Climb up the steps on to the bridge... Children love to climb.* ▶ Also a noun. ...*an hour's leisurely climb through olive groves.* **2** If you **climb** somewhere, you move there carefully, and sometimes awkwardly, for example because you are moving into a small space or trying to avoid falling. *The girls hurried outside, climbed into the car, and drove off.* **3** When something such as an aeroplane **climbs**, it moves upwards to a higher position. When the sun **climbs**, it moves higher in the sky. *The plane climbed to 370 feet.* **4** When something **climbs**, it increases in value or amount. *Prices have climbed by 21%... The FA Cup Final's audience climbed to 12.3 million.* **5** See also **climbing**. ◆◆◆◇◇ VERB: V n / V up/down n / V / Also V up/ down / N-COUNT / VERB / V prep/adv / VERB / V / Also V prep / VERB: V / V by amount / V to/from / amount / Also V amount

climb down. If you **climb down** in an argument or dispute, you admit that you are wrong, or change your intentions or demands. *He has climbed down on pledges to reduce capital gains tax.* ▶ **Climb-down** is also a noun. *However, the government has made its first climb-down.* PHRASAL VB / V P / V P on/overn / BRITISH / N-COUNT

climb·er /ˈklaɪmə/ **climbers. 1** A **climber** is someone who climbs rocks or mountains as a sport or a hobby. ● See also **rock climber**. **2** A **climber** is a plant that grows upwards by attaching itself to other plants or objects. ● See also **social climber**. ◆◇◇◇ N-COUNT / N-COUNT

climb·ing /ˈklaɪmɪŋ/. **Climbing** is the activity of climbing rocks or mountains. ● See also **climb**. ◆◆◇◇◇ N-UNCOUNT

'climbing frame, climbing frames. A **climbing frame** is a structure made of joined metal or wooden bars, for children to climb and play on. N-COUNT / BRITISH

clime /klaɪm/ **climes.** You use **clime** in expressions such as **warmer climes** and **foreign climes** to refer to a place that has a particular kind of climate. *He left Britain for the sunnier climes of Southern France.* N-COUNT

clinch /klɪntʃ/ **clinches, clinching, clinched. 1** If you **clinch** something you are trying to achieve, such as a business deal or victory in a contest, you succeed in obtaining it. *He is about to clinch a deal with an American engine manufacturer.* **2** The thing that **clinches** an uncertain matter settles it or provides a definite answer. *This information clinched the matter.* **3** A **clinch** is a romantic embrace. *They were caught in a clinch when their parents returned home unexpectedly.* ◆◆◇◇◇ VERB: V n / V n with n / VERB / V n / N-COUNT / JOURNALISM

clinch·er /ˈklɪntʃə/ **clinchers.** A **clincher** is something that finally proves something, settles an argument or decision, or helps someone achieve a victory. *DNA fingerprinting has proved the clincher in many criminal and other forensic identifications.* N-COUNT / INFORMAL

cling /klɪŋ/ **clings, clinging, clung. 1** If you **cling** to someone or something, you hold onto them tightly. *Another man was rescued as he clung to the riverbank... We walked along clinging together like lovers.* **2** Something that **is clinging** to something else is stuck on it or just attached to it. *Her glass had bits of orange clinging to the rim.* **3** Clothes that ◆◇◇◇ VERB / V to/onto n / V together / VERB / V to n / VERB:

cling to you stay pressed against your body when you move. ♦ **cling·ing** ...*clinging black garments.* V to n / ADJ-GRADED

4 If someone **clings** to a position or a possession they have, they do everything they can to keep it even though this may be very difficult. *He appears determined to cling to power.* **5** If you **cling** to an idea or way of behaving, you continue to believe in its value or importance, even though it may no longer be valid or useful. *They're clinging to the past.* **6** If someone **clings to** someone they are fond of, they do not allow that person to have enough freedom or independence; used showing disapproval. *I was terrified he would leave me, so I was clinging to him.* ♦ **clinging** *She was anxious not to appear clinging.* VERB / V to/onto n / V on/on / to n / VERB / Also to n / VERB / PRAGMATICS / V to n / ADJ-GRADED

cling·film /ˈklɪŋfɪlm/; also spelled **cling film. Clingfilm** is a thin, clear, stretchy plastic which you use to cover food to keep it fresh. The American term is **plastic wrap**. N-UNCOUNT / BRITISH

clingy /ˈklɪŋi/. **1** If you describe someone as **clingy**, you mean that they become very attached to people and too dependent on them; used showing disapproval. ...*a very clingy child.* **2** Clingy clothes fit tightly round your body. ADJ-GRADED / PRAGMATICS / ADJ-GRADED

clin·ic /ˈklɪnɪk/ **clinics.** A **clinic** is a building where people go to receive medical advice or treatment. ...*a family planning clinic.* ◆◆◆◇◇ N-COUNT

clini·cal /ˈklɪnɪkəl/. **1 Clinical** means involving or relating to the medical treatment or testing of patients. ...*a clinical psychologist.* ♦ **clini·cal·ly** /ˈklɪnɪkli/. ...*clinically depressed.* **2** You use **clinical** to describe thought or behaviour which is very logical and detached and does not involve any emotion; used showing disapproval. *All this questioning is so analytical and clinical.* ◆◆◇◇◇ ADJ: ADJ n / MEDICAL / ADV / ADJ-GRADED / PRAGMATICS

cli·ni·cian /klɪˈnɪʃən/ **clinicians.** A **clinician** is a doctor who specializes in clinical work. ◆◇◇◇ N-COUNT

clink /klɪŋk/ **clinks, clinking, clinked.** When objects made of glass, pottery, or metal **clink**, they touch each other and make a short, light sound. *She clinked her glass against his... They clinked glasses... The fork handle clinked against her plate.* ▶ Also a noun. ...*the clink of a spoon in a cup.* V-RECIP-ERG: / pl-n V / V n against/ / with n / V pl-n / V against n / N-COUNT; / SOUND

clip /klɪp/ **clips, clipping, clipped. 1** A **clip** is a small device, usually made of metal or plastic, that is specially shaped for holding things together. *She took the clip out of her hair.* **2** When you **clip** something to something else, you fasten it to that thing by means of one or more clips. You can also say that something **clips** to something else. *He clipped his safety belt to a fitting on the deck... He clipped his cufflinks neatly in place.* ◆◆◇◇◇ N-COUNT / V-ERG / V n to/onto n / V n prep/adv / Also V to n

3 A **clip** from a film or a radio or television programme is a short piece of it that is broadcast separately. ...*an historical film clip of Lenin speaking.* **4** If you **clip** something, you cut small pieces from it, especially in order to shape it. *I saw an old man out clipping his hedge.* ▶ Also a noun. *Give hedges a last clip.* **5** If you **clip** something out of a newspaper or magazine, you cut it out. **6** If you **clip** a small amount off the time taken to do something, you reduce it by that amount. *Boardman finished in 1hr 43mins, clipping 49 seconds from his own course record.* **7** If something **clips** something else, it hits it accidentally at an angle before moving off in a different direction. *The lorry clipped the rear of a tanker.* **8** If something moves or happens **at a** fast **clip**, it moves or happens quickly. **9** See also **clipping, clipped; paper clip**. ● to **clip** someone's **wings**: see **wing**. N-COUNT / VERB / V n / N-SING / VERB: / V n from/out / of n / VERB / V amount / off/from n / VERB / V n / PHRASE / INFORMAL

clip·board /ˈklɪpbɔːd/ **clipboards.** A **clipboard** is a board with a clip at the top. It is used to hold together pieces of paper that you need to carry around, and provides a firm base for writing. N-COUNT

'clip-on. A **clip-on** object is designed to be fastened to something by means of a clip. ...*a clip-on tie.* ADJ: ADJ n

clipped /klɪpt/. **1 Clipped** means neatly trimmed. ...*a quiet street of clipped hedges.* **2** If you say that someone has a **clipped** way of speaking, you mean ◆◇◇◇ ADJ / ADJ

they speak with quick, short sounds. *...the Chief Constable's clipped tones.*

clip·per /'klɪpə/ **clippers. 1 Clippers** are a tool ◆◇◇◇◇ used for cutting small amounts from something, es- N-PLURAL pecially from someone's hair or nails, or from a hedge. **2** In the past, a **clipper** was a fast sailing N-COUNT ship.

clip·ping /'klɪpɪŋ/ **clippings. 1** A **clipping** is an ◆◇◇◇◇ article, picture, or advertisement that has been cut N-COUNT from a newspaper or magazine. *...bulletin boards crowded with newspaper clippings.* **2 Clippings** are N-COUNT small pieces of something that have been cut from something larger. *...grass clippings.*

clique /kliːk/ **cliques.** If you describe a group of ◆◇◇◇◇ people as a **clique**, you mean that they spend a lot N-COUNT of time together and seem unfriendly towards peo- PRAGMATICS ple who are not in the group; used showing disap- proval. *...the male clique which she believes holds back women in television.* ♦ **cli·quey** /'kliːki/. *...cli-* ADJ-GRADED *quey gossip.*

clito·ral /'klɪtərəl/. **Clitoral** means concerned with ADJ: ADJ n or relating to the clitoris.

clito·ris /'klɪtərɪs/ **clitorises.** A woman's **clitoris** is N-COUNT the small sensitive lump above her vagina.

Cllr. Cllr is a written abbreviation for **Councillor.** *...Cllr Ned Dewitt.*

cloak /kləʊk/ **cloaks, cloaking, cloaked. 1** A ◆◇◇◇◇ **cloak** is a loose, sleeveless piece of clothing which N-COUNT someone wears over their other clothes when they go out. **2** A **cloak** of something such as mist or N-SING: snow completely covers and hides something. *To-* N of n *day most of England will be under a cloak of thick mist.* **3** If you refer to something as a **cloak**, you N-SING: mean that it is intended to hide the truth about N of/for n something. *Preparations for the wedding were made under a cloak of secrecy.* **4** To **cloak** something VERB: V n means to cover it or hide it. *...the decision to cloak* V n in n *major tourist attractions in unsightly hoardings.* WRITTEN

,cloak-and-'dagger; also spelled **cloak and dag-** ADJ **ger.** A **cloak-and-dagger** activity is one which in- volves mystery and secrecy. *She was released from prison in a cloak and dagger operation yesterday.*

cloak·room /'kləʊkruːm/ **cloakrooms. 1** In a N-COUNT public building, the **cloakroom** is the place where people can leave their coats, umbrellas, and so on. **2** A **cloakroom** is a room in a public building con- N-COUNT taining toilets and washbasins, or a downstairs BRITISH room in someone's house containing a toilet.

clob·ber /'klɒbə/ **clobbers, clobbering, clob-** ◆◇◇◇◇ **bered. Clobber** is an informal word.

1 You can refer to someone's belongings, especially N-UNCOUNT their clothes, as their **clobber**. *He nipped down to Mr* BRITISH *Byrite on Oxford Street for some new clobber.* **2** If you VERB **clobber** someone, you hit them. *Hillary clobbered* V n *him with a vase.* **3** If a person or company **is clob-** VERB **bered** by something, they are very badly affected by it. be V-ed *The construction industry was clobbered by recession.* Also V n

cloche /klɒʃ/ **cloches. 1** A **cloche** is a long, low N-COUNT cover made of glass or clear plastic that is put over young plants to protect them from the cold. **2** A N-COUNT **cloche** or a **cloche hat** is a tight-fitting woman's hat shaped like a bell. Cloche hats were popular in the 1920s.

clock /klɒk/ **clocks, clocking, clocked. 1** A ◆◆◇◇◇ **clock** is an instrument, for example in a room or on N-COUNT the outside of a building, that shows what time of day it is. *He also repairs clocks and watches. ...a digi- tal clock.* **2** A time **clock** in a factory or office is a N-COUNT device that is used to record the hours that people work. **3** In a car, the **clock** is an instrument that N-COUNT shows the speed of the car or the distance it has BRITISH travelled. *The car had 160,000 miles on the clock.* **4** To **clock** a particular time or speed in a race means VERB: V n to reach that time or speed. **5** If something or some- VB: usu one **is clocked** at a particular time or speed, their time passive or speed is measured at that level. *He has been clocked* be V-ed at *at 11 seconds for 100 metres.* amount Also be V-ed **6** If you are doing something **against the clock**, you PHRASE are doing it in a great hurry, because there is very little time. *The emergency services were working against the*

clock as the tide began to rise. **7** If someone **beats the** PHRASE **clock**, they finish doing something or succeed in do- ing something before the time allowed for doing it has ended. **8** If something is done **round the clock** or PHRASE **around the clock**, it is done all day and all night with- out stopping. **9** If you want to **turn the clock back** or PHRASE **put the clock back**, you want to return to a situation that used to exist, for example because you would like to have avoided certain things that have happened since then. **10** If you **are watching the clock**, you keep PHRASE looking to see what time it is, usually because you are INFORMAL bored by something and want it to end as soon as possible.

11 See also **alarm clock, biological clock, body clock, cuckoo clock, grandfather clock, o'clock.**

clock in. When you **clock in** at work, you arrive PHRASAL VB there or put a special card into a device to show what V P time you arrived. *I have to clock in by eight.*

clock in at. If something such as a record or film PHRASAL VB **clocks in at** a particular amount of time, it is that V P P amount amount of time long. *There are four more songs, each clocking in at around 12 minutes.*

clock off. When you **clock off** at work, you leave PHRASAL VB work or put a special card into a device to show what V P time you left. BRITISH

clock on. To **clock on** means the same as to **clock** PHRASAL VB **in.** BRITISH

clock out. Clock out means the same as **clock off.** PHRASAL VB

clock up. If you **clock up** a large number or total of PHRASAL VB things, you reach that number or total. *Rude taxi driv-* V P noun *ers clocked up a total of 239 offences in 1990.* BRITISH

'clock tower, clock towers. A **clock tower** is a N-COUNT tall, narrow building with a clock at the top.

clock·wise /'klɒkwaɪz/. When something is mov- ◆◇◇◇◇ ing **clockwise**, it is moving in a circle in the same ADV: direction as the hands on a clock. ► Also an adjec- ADV after v tive. *...a clockwise direction.* ADJ: ADJ n

clock·work /'klɒkwɜːk/. **1** A **clockwork** toy or de- ◆◇◇◇◇ vice has machinery inside it which makes it move or ADJ: ADJ n operate when it is wound up with a key. **2** If you say PHRASE that something happens **like clockwork**, you mean that it happens without any problems or delays, or happens regularly. *The Queen's holiday is arranged to go like clockwork.*

clod /klɒd/ **clods.** A **clod** of earth is a large lump of N-COUNT earth.

clog /klɒg/ **clogs, clogging, clogged. 1** When ◆◇◇◇◇ something **clogs** a hole or place, it blocks it so that VERB nothing can pass through. *The traffic clogged the* V n *Thames bridges.* ♦ **clogged** *The streets were clogged* ADJ-GRADED *with people.* **2 Clogs** are heavy leather or wooden N-COUNT shoes with thick wooden soles.

clog up. When something **clogs up** a hole or a place, PHRASAL VB the hole or place becomes blocked so that nothing ERG can pass through. *...with 22,000 tourists clogging up* V P noun *the pavements... The lungs clog up with a thick mucus.* V P ♦ **clogged up** *The drains are badly clogged up.* ADJ-GRADED

clois·ter /'klɔɪstə/ **cloisters.** A **cloister** is a paved N-COUNT and covered area round a square in a monastery or a cathedral.

clois·tered /'klɔɪstəd/. If you have a **cloistered** way ADJ-GRADED of life, you live quietly and are not involved in the normal busy life of the world around you. *...the cloistered world of royalty.*

clone /kləʊn/ **clones, cloning, cloned. 1** If you ◆◇◇◇◇ say that someone is a **clone** of someone else, you N-COUNT disapprove of them because they try to copy this PRAGMATICS person and have no individuality of their own. *They believe we all want to be supermodel clones.* **2** A N-COUNT **clone** is an animal or plant that has been produced, either naturally or artificially, from the cells of an- other animal or plant. The clone is identical to the original animal or plant. **3** To **clone** an animal or VERB: V n plant means to produce it as a clone. **4** A **clone** of a N-COUNT computer is a cheaper close copy of it.

close 1 shutting or completing

close /kləʊz/ **closes, closing, closed. 1** When ◆◆◆◆◆ you **close** something such as a door or lid, it moves V-ERG so that a hole, gap, or opening is covered. *If you are* V n *cold, close the window... Zacharias heard the door*

close. **2** When you **close** something such as an open book or umbrella, you move the different parts of it together. *Slowly he closed the book.* **3** When you **close** your eyes, your eyelids move downwards, so that you can no longer see. *Bess closed her eyes and fell asleep... Let your eyes close gently.* **4** To **close** a road or border means to block it in order to prevent people from using it. `VERB V n` `V-ERG V n` `V` `VERB: V n`

5 When a shop or other public place **closes** or **is closed**, work or activity stops there for a short period, for example during the night or at lunchtime. *Shops close only on Christmas Day and New Year's Day.* **6** If a place such as a factory, shop, or school **closes**, or if it **is closed**, all work or activity stops there permanently. *If they do close the local college I'll have to go to Worcester.* ► **Close down** means the same as **close**. *Minford closed down the business and went into politics... Many of the smaller stores have closed down... If there is any rowdiness I will not hesitate to close the bars down.* ♦ **clos·ing** *...since the closing of the steelworks.* `V-ERG V Also V` `V-ERG: V V n` `PHRASAL VB ERG V P noun V P V n P` `N-SING`

7 If you **close** a bank account, you take all your money out of it and inform the bank that you will no longer be using the account. `VERB: V n`

8 To **close** a conversation, event, or matter means to bring it to an end or to complete it. *He needs another $30,000 to close the deal. ...the closing ceremony of the National Political Conference.* **9** The **close** of a period of time or an activity is the end of it. To bring or draw something to a **close** means to end it. *By the close of business last night, most of the big firms were hailing yesterday's actions as a success.* `VERB V n V-ing` `N-SING`

10 On the stock market or the currency markets, if a share price or a currency **closes** at a particular value, that is its value at the end of the day's business. *Dawson shares closed at 219p, up 5p.* `VERB V prep/adv`

11 See also **closed**, **closing**. ● to **close the door on** something: see **door**. ● to **close your eyes to** something: see **eye**. ● to **close ranks**: see **rank**.

close down. See **close** 5 `PHRASAL VB`

close off. To **close** something **off** means to separate it from other things or people so that they do not have access to it. *Police closed off about 12 blocks of a major San Francisco thoroughfare.* `PHRASAL VB V P noun Also V n P`

close up. 1 If someone **closes** up a building, they shut it completely and securely, often because they are going away. *Just close up the shop.* **2** If an opening, gap, or something hollow **closes** up, it becomes closed or covered. *Don't use cold water as it shocks the blood vessels into closing up.* `PHRASAL VB V P noun` `ERG V P Also V n P`

close 2 nearness; adjective uses

close /kləʊs/ **closer, closest. 1** If one thing or person is **close** to another, there is only a very small distance between them. *The man moved closer, lowering his voice... The tables were pushed close together.* ♦ **close·ly** *Wherever they went they were closely followed by security men.* `ADJ-GRADED: v-link ADJ, ADJ after v` `ADV-GRADED`

2 You say that people are **close** to each other when they like each other very much and know each other very well. *She and Linda became very close. ...a close friend from school.* ♦ **close·ness** *I asked whether her closeness to her mother ever posed any problems.* `ADJ-GRADED` `N-UNCOUNT`

3 Your **close** relatives are the members of your family who are most directly related to you, for example your parents and your brothers or sisters. **4** A **close** ally or partner of someone knows them well and is very involved in their work. *A senior source close to Mr Major told us: 'Our position has not changed.'* **5** Close contact or co-operation involves seeing or communicating with someone often. *He lived alone, keeping close contact with his three grown-up sons.* ♦ **closely** *We work closely with the careers officers in schools.* `ADJ-GRADED: ADJ n` `ADJ-GRADED ADJ n` `ADJ-GRADED: ADJ n` `ADV-GRADED: ADV after v`

6 If there is a **close** connection or resemblance between two things, they are strongly connected or are very similar. *There is a close connection between pain and tension. ...Clare's close resemblance to his elder sister.* ♦ **closely** *...a pattern closely resembling a cross.* **7** If something is **close** to or comes **close** to something else, it almost is, does, or experiences that thing. *An airliner came close to disaster... Her desire was closer to passion than love.* **8** A **close** competition or elec- `ADJ-GRADED` `ADV-GRADED` `ADJ-GRADED: v-link ADJ`

tion is won or seems likely to be won by only a small amount. *It is still a close contest between two leading opposition parties.* ♦ **closely** *...a closely fought race.* **9** Close inspection or observation of something is careful and thorough. *Let's have a closer look.* ♦ **closely** *...if you look closely at many of the problems in society.* `ADV-GRADED` `ADJ-GRADED: ADJ n` `ADV-GRADED: ADV with v`

10 If you are **close** to something or if it is **close**, it is likely to happen or come soon. If you are **close** to doing something, you are likely to do it soon. *She sounded close to tears... A senior White House official said the agreement is close... He's close to signing a contract.* `ADJ-GRADED: v-link ADJ`

11 If the atmosphere somewhere is **close**, it is uncomfortably warm with not enough air. `ADJ-GRADED`

12 Something that is **close by** or **close at hand** is near to you. *His wife remains behind in Germany, but Jason, his 18-year-old son, is closer at hand.* **13** If you describe an event as a **close shave**, a **close thing**, or a **close call**, you mean that an accident or a disaster very nearly happened. *You had a close shave, but you knew when you accepted this job that there would be risks.* **14** If you **keep a close eye** on someone or something or **keep a close watch** on them, you observe them carefully to make sure they are progressing as you want them to. **15** Close to or **close on** a particular amount or distance means slightly less than that amount or distance. *Sisulu spent close to 30 years in prison.* **16** If you look at something **close up** or **close to**, you look at it when you are very near to it. *They always look smaller close up.* ● See also **close-up**. **17** ● at close quarters: see **quarter**. ● at close range: see **range**. `PHRASE` `PHRASE` `PHRASE` `PHR-PREP` `PHRASE`

close 3 nearness; verb uses

close /kləʊz/ **closes, closing, closed.** If you are **closing** on someone or something that you are following, you are getting nearer and nearer to them. *I was within 15 seconds of the guy in second place and closing on him.* `◆◆◆◇◇ VERB V on n Also V`

close in. 1 If a group of people **close in** on a person or place, they come nearer and nearer to them and gradually surround them. *Soviet forces were closing in on Berlin.* **2** When winter or darkness **closes in**, it arrives. *The dark nights and cold weather are closing in.* `PHRASAL VB V P on n Also V P` `V P`

close 4 used as a road name

Close /kləʊs/. **Close** is used in the names of some streets in Britain. *...116 Dendridge Close.*

close-cropped /ˌkləʊs ˈkrɒpt/. **Close-cropped** hair or grass is cut very short. `ADJ-GRADED`

closed /kləʊzd/. **1** A **closed** group of people does not welcome new people or ideas from outside. *It is a closed society in the sense that they've not been exposed to many things.* **2** See also **close**. ● a **closed book**: see **book**. ● **behind closed doors**: see **door**. `◆◇◇◇ ADJ-GRADED`

closed 'circuit. A **closed circuit** television or video system is one that operates within a limited area such as a building. `ADJ: ADJ n`

closed 'shop, closed shops. If a factory, shop, or other business is a **closed shop**, the employees must be members of a particular trade union. `N-COUNT`

close-fitting /ˌkləʊs ˈfɪtɪŋ/. **Close-fitting** clothes fit tightly and show the shape of your body. `ADJ-GRADED`

close-knit /ˌkləʊs ˈnɪt/. A **close-knit** group of people do a lot of things together, know a lot about each other, and take a strong interest in each other. `ADJ-GRADED`

close-run /ˌkləʊs ˈrʌn/. If you describe something such as a race or contest as a **close-run** thing, you mean that it is only won by a very small margin. `ADJ-GRADED: ADJ n`

close sea·son /ˈkləʊs siːzən/. In football and some other sports, the **close season** is the period of the year when the sport is not played professionally. `◆◇◇◇ N-SING BRITISH`

clos·et /ˈklɒzɪt/ **closets. 1** A **closet** is a piece of furniture with doors at the front and shelves inside, which is used for storing things. The usual British word is **cupboard**. **2** A **closet** is a very small storage room, especially one without windows. **3** Closet is used to describe a person who has beliefs, habits, or feelings which they keep secret, often because they are embarrassed about them. *He is a closet Fascist.* `◆◇◇◇ N-COUNT AMERICAN` `N-COUNT AMERICAN` `ADJ: ADJ n`

4 If someone **comes out of the closet**, they reveal a belief or habit they have which they had previously `PHRASE`

kept secret, often because they were embarrassed about it. You can also say that an issue **comes out of the closet** when it starts to be publicly discussed. **5** See also **closeted**. ● **a skeleton in the closet**: see **skeleton**.

clos·et·ed /ˈklɒzɪtɪd/. If you are **closeted** with someone, you are talking privately to them. *The prime minister has been closeted with his finance ministers for the past 12 hours.*
ADJ:
v-link ADJ

close-up /ˈkləʊs ʌp/ **close-ups.** A **close-up** is a photograph or a picture in a film that shows a lot of detail because it is taken very near to the subject. ● If you see something **in close-up**, you see it in great detail in a photographic or film close-up.
◆◇◇◇◇
N-COUNT

PHRASE

clos·ing /ˈkləʊzɪŋ/. The **closing** part of an activity or period of time is the final part of it. *He entered RAF service in the closing stages of the war. ...closing remarks.* ● See also **close**.
◆◇◇◇◇
ADJ: ADJ n

'closing price, closing prices. On the Stock Exchange, the **closing price** of a share is its price at the end of a day's business.
N-COUNT

'closing time, closing times. Closing time is the time when something such as a shop, library, or pub closes and people have to leave.
N-VAR

clo·sure /ˈkləʊʒə/ **closures. 1** The **closure** of a place such as a business or factory is the permanent ending of the work or activity there. *Almost three in four clinics say they face closure.* **2** The **closure** of a road or border is the blocking of it in order to prevent people from using it.
◆◆◇◇◇
N-VAR

N-COUNT

clot /klɒt/ **clots, clotting, clotted. 1** A **clot** is a sticky lump that forms when blood dries up or thickens. *He needed emergency surgery to remove a blood clot from his brain.* **2** When blood **clots**, it thickens and forms a lump.
◆◇◇◇◇
N-COUNT

VERB: V

cloth /klɒθ, AM klɔːθ/ **cloths. 1** Cloth is fabric which is made by weaving or knitting a substance such as cotton, wool, silk, or nylon. **2** A **cloth** is a piece of cloth which you use for a particular purpose, such as cleaning something or covering something. *Clean the surface with a damp cloth.* **3** The **cloth** is sometimes used to refer to Christian priests and ministers. *...a man of the cloth.*
◆◆◇◇◇
N-VAR

N-COUNT

N-SING:
the N

'cloth 'cap, cloth caps. A **cloth cap** is a soft flat cap, usually worn by a man, with a stiff, curved part at the front called a peak.
N-COUNT

clothe /kləʊð/ **clothes, clothing, clothed.** To **clothe** someone means to provide them with clothes to wear. ● See also **clothed, clothes, clothing.**
VERB: V n

clothed /kləʊðd/. **1** If you are **clothed** in a certain way, you are dressed in that way. *He lay down on the bed fully clothed... She was clothed in a flowered dress.* **2** If a place or thing is **clothed in** something, it is covered in that thing. *The south side of the gorge is now clothed in trees.*
◆◇◇◇◇
ADJ:
adv ADJ,
v-link ADJ in n
ADJ:
v-link ADJ in n
LITERARY

clothes /kləʊðz/. **Clothes** are the things that people wear, such as shirts, coats, trousers, and dresses. *He dressed quickly in casual clothes.* ● **plain-clothes:** see **plain.**
◆◆◆◇
N-PLURAL

'clothes horse, clothes horses. A **clothes horse** is a folding frame used inside someone's house to hang washing on while it dries.
N-COUNT

clothes·line /ˈkləʊðzlaɪn/ **clotheslines;** also spelled **clothes line.** A **clothesline** is a thin rope on which you hang washing so that it can dry.
N-COUNT

'clothes peg, clothes pegs. A **clothes peg** is a small device which you use to fasten clothes to a washing line. The American word is **clothespin.**
N-COUNT
BRITISH

clothes·pin /ˈkləʊðzpɪn/ **clothespins.** A **clothespin** is the same as a **clothes peg.**
N-COUNT
AMERICAN

cloth·ing /ˈkləʊðɪŋ/. **Clothing** is the things that people wear. *...the clothing industry.*
◆◆◆◇
N-UNCOUNT

clotted 'cream. Clotted cream is very thick cream made by heating milk gently and taking the cream off the top.
N-UNCOUNT
BRITISH

cloud /klaʊd/ **clouds, clouding, clouded. 1** A **cloud** is a mass of water vapour that floats in the sky. Clouds are usually white or grey. *The sky was almost entirely obscured by cloud.* **2** A **cloud** of
◆◆◇◇
N-VAR

something such as smoke or dust is a mass of it floating in the air. *...a cloud of dust.* **3** If glass **clouds**, tiny drops of water cover it, making it difficult to see through. *I ran the water very hot, clouding the mirror.*
V-ERG: V
V n

4 If you say that something **clouds** your view of a situation, you mean that it makes you unable to understand the situation or judge it properly. *In his latter years religious mania clouded his mind.* **5** If you say that something **clouds** a situation, you mean that it makes it unpleasant. *Poor job prospects have clouded the outlook for the economy.* **6** If your eyes or face **cloud** or if sadness or anger **clouds** them, your eyes or your face suddenly show sadness or anger. *Trish's face clouded with disappointment.* ▶ **Cloud over** means the same as **cloud.** *I saw Sean's face cloud over at this blatant lie.*
VERB
V n

VERB
V n

V-ERG
V with n
Also V n
LITERARY
PHRASAL VB
V P

7 If you say that someone is **on cloud nine,** you are emphasizing that they are very happy. *When Michael was born I was on cloud nine.* **8** If someone is **under a cloud,** people have a poor opinion of them because of something they have done. *The military are under a cloud for killing civilians while breaking up a demonstration.* **9** ● **every cloud has a silver lining:** see **silver lining.**
PHRASE
PRAGMATICS
INFORMAL
PHRASE

cloud over. If the sky **clouds over,** it becomes covered with clouds. *The sky had clouded over and suddenly rain lashed against the windows.* ● See also **cloud 5.**
PHRASAL VB
V P

cloud·burst /ˈklaʊdbɜːst/ **cloudbursts.** A **cloudburst** is a sudden, very heavy fall of rain.
N-COUNT

,cloud-'cuckoo-land. If you say that someone is living in **cloud-cuckoo-land,** you are criticizing them because they think that things will happen exactly as they want them to without any problems, when this is obviously not the case.
N-UNCOUNT
also a N
PRAGMATICS
INFORMAL

cloud·less /ˈklaʊdləs/. If the sky is **cloudless,** there are no clouds in it.
ADJ

cloudy /ˈklaʊdi/ **cloudier, cloudiest. 1** If it is **cloudy,** there are a lot of clouds in the sky. *...a windy, cloudy day.* **2** A **cloudy** liquid is less clear than it should be. **3** Ideas or opinions that are **cloudy** are confused or uncertain. *...an absurdly cloudy political debate.*
◆◇◇◇◇
ADJ-GRADED
ADJ-GRADED
ADJ-GRADED

clout /klaʊt/ **clouts, clouting, clouted. 1** If you **clout** someone, you hit them. *The officer clouted her on the head.* ▶ Also a noun. *I was half tempted to give one of them a clout.* **2** A person or institution that has **clout** has influence and power. *The two firms wield enormous clout in financial markets.*
◆◇◇◇◇
VERB: V n
V n on n
INFORMAL
N-COUNT
N-UNCOUNT
INFORMAL

clove /kləʊv/ **cloves. 1** Cloves are small dried flower buds which are used as a spice. **2** A **clove** of garlic is one of the sections of a garlic bulb. **3** Clove is a past tense of **cleave.**
◆◇◇◇◇
N-VAR
N-COUNT

clo·ven hoof /ˌkləʊvən ˈhuːf/ **cloven hooves** or **cloven hoofs.** Animals that have **cloven hooves** have feet that are divided into two parts.
N-COUNT

clo·ver /ˈkləʊvə/ **clovers. 1** Clover is a small plant with pink or white ball-shaped flowers. **2** If you say that someone is **in clover,** you mean that they are living a luxurious and comfortable life.
N-VAR
PHRASE

clown /klaʊn/ **clowns, clowning, clowned. 1** A **clown** is a performer in a circus who wears funny clothes and bright make-up, and does silly things in order to make people laugh. **2** If you **clown,** you do silly things in order to make people laugh. ▶ **Clown around** and **clown about** mean the same as **clown.** *Bev made her laugh, the way she was always clowning around.* ♦ **clown·ing** *Behind the clowning there is a terrible sense of anguish.* **3** If you say that someone is a **clown,** you mean that they say or do silly things to amuse people. **4** If you describe someone as a **clown,** you disapprove of them and have no respect for them. *I still think I could do a better job than those clowns.*
◆◇◇◇◇
N-COUNT

VERB: V
PHRASAL VB
V P

N-UNCOUNT
N-COUNT
N-COUNT
PRAGMATICS
INFORMAL

cloy·ing /ˈklɔɪɪŋ/. You use **cloying** to describe something that you find unpleasant because it is excessively sweet and sickly, or too sentimental. *Her cheap, cloying scent enveloped him.* ♦ **cloy·ing·ly** *The film is too cloyingly sentimental.*
ADJ-GRADED

ADV-GRADED:
ADV adj/adv

club /klʌb/ **clubs, clubbing, clubbed. 1** A club ♦♦♦♦ is an organization of people interested in a particu- N-COUNT lar activity or subject who usually meet on a regular basis. ...*the Chorlton Conservative Club*. ...*a youth club*. **2** A **club** is a team which competes in profes- N-COUNT sional or amateur sporting competitions. **3** A **club** is N-COUNT a place where the members of a club meet. **4** A **club** N-COUNT is the same as a **nightclub**. **5** A **club** is a long, thin, metal stick with a piece of N-COUNT wood or metal at one end that you use to hit the ball in golf. **6** A **club** is a thick heavy stick that can be used as a N-COUNT weapon. **7** To **club** a person or animal means to hit VERB: V n them hard with a thick heavy stick or a similar weap- V n to n on. *Riot police clubbed a student to death.* **8 Clubs** is one of the four suits in a pack of playing N-COLL- cards. Each card in a suit is marked with one or UNCOUNT more black symbols: ♣. ...*the ace of clubs*. ▶ A **club** is N-COUNT a playing card of this suit.

club together. If people **club together** to do some- PHRASAL VB thing, they all give money towards the cost of it. *My* V P friends clubbed together and bought me a watch.* BRITISH

club·bing /'klʌbɪŋ/. **Clubbing** is the activity of go- N-UNCOUNT ing to night clubs. ♦ **club·ber, clubbers.** A **club-** N-COUNT **ber** is someone who often goes to night clubs.

club·by /'klʌbi/. If you describe an institution or a ADJ-GRADED group of people as **clubby**, you mean that all the INFORMAL people in it are friendly with each other and do not BRITISH welcome other people in.

,**club 'foot, club feet.** If someone is born with a N-COUNT **club foot**, their foot is twisted and deformed.

club·house /'klʌbhaʊs/ **clubhouses;** also spelled ♦◇◇◇◇ **club house.** A **clubhouse** is the place where the N-COUNT members of a sports club meet.

club·land /'klʌblænd/. A city's **clubland** is the area N-UNCOUNT that contains most of the nightclubs. BRITISH

cluck /klʌk/ **clucks, clucking, clucked. 1** When VERB: V a hen **clucks**, it makes short, abrupt noises. **2** If you VERB say that someone **clucks** over someone or some- PRAGMATICS thing, you are showing your disapproval of the fact V over/around that they behave in a fussy or protective way. *I've n never been one to cluck over babies.* **3** If someone VERB: **clucks** at someone or something, they make disap- V at n proving noises or say things in a disapproving way. V *He clucks in disapproval... Teddy clucked his tongue V n like a disapproving English matron.*

clue /klu/ **clues. 1** A **clue** to a puzzle or mystery is ♦♦◇◇◇ something that helps you to find the answer to it. N-COUNT *How a man shaves may be a telling clue to his age... It's a clue in a crossword Donald is trying to solve.* **2** A **clue** is an object or piece of information that N-COUNT helps the police or a detective to solve a crime. ...*the vital clue to the killer's identity.* **3** If you **haven't a** PHRASE **clue** about something, you do not know anything INFORMAL about it or you have no idea what to do about it. *I haven't a clue what I'll give Carl for his birthday.*

,**clued-'up;** also spelled **clued up.** If you say that ADJ-GRADED someone is **clued-up** on a particular subject, you PRAGMATICS are showing your approval of the fact that they have INFORMAL a great deal of detailed knowledge and information BRITISH about it.

clue·less /'klu:ləs/. If you describe someone as ADJ-GRADED **clueless**, you disapprove of them because they do PRAGMATICS not know anything about a particular subject, or be- INFORMAL cause they are incapable of doing a particular thing properly.

clump /klʌmp/ **clumps, clumping, clumped.** ♦◇◇◇◇ **1** A **clump** of things is a small group of them grow- N-COUNT ing together or collected together in one place. ...*a clump of trees bordering a side road... I was comb- ing my hair and it was just falling out in clumps.* **2** If things **clump together**, they gather together VERB: and form small groups or lumps. **3** If someone V together **clumps** somewhere, they walk there with heavy VERB clumsy footsteps. *They went clumping up the stairs.* V prep/adv

clumpy /'klʌmpi/ **clumpier, clumpiest. Clumpy** ADJ-GRADED means big and clumsy. ...*clumpy shoes.*

clum·sy /'klʌmzi/ **clumsier, clumsiest. 1** A ♦◇◇◇◇ **clumsy** person moves or handles things in a care- ADJ-GRADED less awkward way, often so that things are knocked over or broken. ♦ **clum·si·ly** /'klʌmzili/. *She moved* ADV-GRADED *up the small slope clumsily.* ♦ **clum·si·ness** N-UNCOUNT *clumsiness and ineptitude with the wooden sticks.* **2** A **clumsy** action or statement is not skilful or is ADJ-GRADED tactless and likely to upset people. ...*a clumsy at- tempt to topple the Janata Dal government.* ♦ **clum·si·ly** *If the matter were handled clumsily, it* ADV-GRADED *could cost Miriam her life.* ♦ **clum·si·ness** *I was* N-UNCOUNT *ashamed at my clumsiness and insensitivity.* **3** An ADJ-GRADED object that is **clumsy** is not neat in design or ap- pearance, and is often awkward to use. *The key- board is a large and clumsy instrument.*

clung /klʌŋ/. **Clung** is the past tense and past parti- ciple of **cling.**

clunk /klʌŋk/ **clunks, clunking, clunked. 1** A N-COUNT **clunk** is a sound made by a heavy object hitting something hard. *Something fell to the floor with a clunk.* **2** If a heavy object **clunks** on or against VERB something, it hits it and makes a dull sound. *His feet* V prep *clunked on the wooden steps.*

clunky /'klʌŋki/. If you describe something as ADJ-GRADED **clunky**, you mean that it is solid, heavy, and rather awkward. ...*a clunky piece of architecture.*

clus·ter /'klʌstə/ **clusters, clustering, clus-** ♦♦◇◇◇ **tered. 1** A **cluster** of people or things is a small N-COUNT group of them close together. **2** If people **cluster** to- VERB: gether, they gather together in a small group. *The* V together *children clustered around me... Officials were clus-* V around/ *tered at every open office door.* round n V-ed

'**cluster bomb, cluster bombs.** A **cluster bomb** N-COUNT is a type of bomb which is dropped from an aircraft. It contains a large number of smaller bombs that spread out before they hit the ground.

clutch /klʌtʃ/ **clutches, clutching, clutched.** ♦♦◇◇◇ **1** If you **clutch** something, you hold it tightly, VERB: V n usually because you are afraid or anxious. *I stag-* V at n *gered and had to clutch at a chair for support.* **2** If someone is in another person's **clutches**, that per- N-PLURAL son has captured them or has power over them. **3** ♦ **to clutch at straws**: see **straw**. **4** In a vehicle, the **clutch** is the mechanism which en- N-COUNT ables power from the engine to be disconnected from the drive shaft in order to allow you to change gear. You can also refer to the pedal that you press before you change gear as the **clutch**. See picture headed **car and bicycle. 5** A **clutch** of eggs is a number of eggs laid by a bird at N-COUNT one time. **6** A **clutch** of people or things is a small N-COUNT: group of them. ...*a clutch of young southern liberals.* N of n WRITTEN

clut·ter /'klʌtə/ **clutters, cluttering, cluttered.** ♦◇◇◇◇ **1 Clutter** is a lot of things in an untidy state, espe- N-UNCOUNT cially things that are not useful or necessary. *Caro- line prefers her worktops to be clear of clutter.* **2** If VERB: V n things or people **clutter** a place, they fill it untidily. be V-ed with n *The roads were cluttered with cars.* ▶ **Clutter up** PHRASAL VB means the same as **clutter**. *Vehicles cluttered up the* V P noun *car park.* ♦ **clut·tered** ...*a sad, dirty, cluttered* ADJ-GRADED *room.*

cm. **cm** is the written abbreviation for **centimetre.** ♦♦◇◇◇ *His height had increased by 2.5 cm.*

Cmdr. **Cmdr** is a written abbreviation for **Com- mander.**

c/o. You write **c/o** before an address on an en- ♦◇◇◇◇ velope when the address does not belong to the person you are sending it to, but they are staying or working there temporarily. **c/o** is an abbreviation for 'care of'.

co- /kəʊ-/. **1 co-** is used to form verbs or nouns that PREFIX refer to people sharing things or doing things to- gether. *He co-produced the album with Bowie.* **2 co-** PREFIX is used to form nouns that refer to people who share a job or task with someone else. *His co- workers hated him.*

Co. **1 Co.** is used as an abbreviation for **company** ♦♦♦♦◇ when it is part of the name of an organization. **2 Co.** is used as a written abbreviation for **county** before the names of some counties, especially in Ireland. ...*Co. Waterford.* **3** You can use **and co.** af- PHRASE ter someone's name to mean the group of people INFORMAL

associated with that person. *Wayne Hussey and co. will be playing two live sets each evening.*

C.O. /ˌsiː ˈəʊ/ **C.O.s.** A soldier's **C.O.** is his or her **commanding officer.** N-COUNT

coach /kəʊtʃ/ **coaches, coaching, coached.** ◆◆◆◇
1 When someone **coaches** a person or a team, he or she trains them in a particular sport. *Beckenbauer coached the West Germans to success in the World Cup final.* ▶ A **coach** is someone who trains a person or team like this. *...the former football coach at Columbia University.* **2** If you **coach** someone, you give them special teaching in a particular subject, especially in order to prepare them for an examination. *He gently coached me in French.* ▶ A **coach** is N-COUNT someone who gives people this kind of teaching. *What you need is a drama coach.*
3 A **coach** is a large comfortable bus that carries passengers on long journeys. *I hate travelling by coach.* N-COUNT
4 A **coach** is one of the separate sections of a train that N-COUNT carries passengers. **5** A **coach** is an enclosed four-wheeled vehicle pulled by horses, in which people used to travel. BRITISH N-COUNT

coach·load /ˈkəʊtʃləʊd/ **coachloads.** A N-COUNT **coachload** of people is a group of people who are BRITISH travelling somewhere in a coach. *...coachloads of tourists.*

coach·man /ˈkəʊtʃmən/ **coachmen.** A **coachman** N-COUNT was a man who drove a horse-drawn coach. DATED

'coach station, coach stations. A **coach station** N-COUNT is an area or building which coaches leave from or BRITISH arrive at on regular journeys.

co·agu·late /kəʊˈæɡjʊleɪt/ **coagulates, coagu-** VERB: V **lating, coagulated.** When a liquid **coagulates,** it becomes very thick. ♦ **co·agu·la·tion** N-UNCOUNT /kəʊˌæɡjʊˈleɪʃən/ *Blood becomes stickier to help coagulation in case of a cut.*

coal /kəʊl/ **coals. 1 Coal** is a hard black substance ◆◆◆◇◇ that is extracted from the ground and burned as N-UNCOUNT fuel. **2 Coals** are burning pieces of coal. *It is impor-* N-PLURAL *tant to get the coals white-hot.* **3** If a person in PHRASE authority **hauls** someone **over the coals,** they speak to them severely about something foolish or wrong that they have done.

coa·lesce /ˌkəʊəˈles/ **coalesces, coalescing,** VERB: V **coalesced.** If two or more things **coalesce,** they FORMAL come together and form a larger group or system.

coal·field /ˈkəʊlfiːld/ **coalfields.** A **coalfield** is a N-COUNT region where there is coal under the ground.

coa·li·tion /ˌkəʊəˈlɪʃən/ **coalitions. 1** A **coalition** ◆◆◇◇◇ is a government consisting of people from two or N-COUNT more political parties. *...a coalition government.* **2** A N-COUNT **coalition** is a group consisting of people from different political or social groups who are co-operating to achieve a particular aim.

'coal mine, coal mines. A **coal mine** is a place ◆◇◇◇◇ where coal is dug out of the ground. N-COUNT

'coal miner, coal miners; also spelled N-COUNT **coalminer.** A **coal miner** is a person whose job is mining coal.

'coal tar. **Coal tar** is a thick black liquid made N-UNCOUNT from coal which is used for making drugs and chemical products.

coarse /kɔːs/ **coarser, coarsest. 1 Coarse** ◆◆◇◇◇ things have a rough texture because they consist of ADJ-GRADED thick strands or large pieces. *...a beach of coarse sand.* ♦ **coarse·ly** *...coarsely ground black pepper.* ADV
2 If you describe someone as **coarse,** you mean that ADJ-GRADED they talk or behave in a rude and offensive way.
♦ **coarsely** *The women laughed coarsely at some* ADV-GRADED *vulgar joke.* ♦ **coarse·ness** *...the coarseness of her* N-UNCOUNT *cursing amazed the workmen.*

coars·en /ˈkɔːsən/ **coarsens, coarsening,** V-ERG: V **coarsened.** If something **coarsens,** it becomes Vn thicker or rougher. *He had coarsened his voice.*

coast /kəʊst/ **coasts, coasting, coasted. 1** The ◆◆◆◆◇ **coast** is an area of land that is next to the sea. N-COUNT
♦ **coast·al** /ˈkəʊstəl/ *...local radio stations serving* ADJ: ADJ n *coastal areas.*
2 If a vehicle **coasts,** it moves with the motor switched VERB: V off, or without being pushed or pedalled. *My gearbox* V prep/adv

broke with a crunch and I coasted into the pits to retire.
3 If a person or a team **is coasting,** they are doing VERB something easily and without effort. *Charles was* V *coasting at school... Ivan Lendl coasted to a 6-3, 6-2,* V ton *6-3 victory.* ▶ **Coast along** means the same as **coast.** PHRASAL VB *Matthew had no drive. He coasted along on his good* VP *looks.*
4 If you say that **the coast is clear,** you mean it is safe PHRASE to do something, often something wrong, because there is nobody around to see you.

coast·er /ˈkəʊstə/ **coasters. 1** A **coaster** is a ◆◇◇◇◇ small mat that you put underneath a glass or mug N-COUNT to protect the surface of a table. **2** See also **roller-coaster.**

coast·guard /ˈkəʊstɡɑːd/ **coastguards.** A **coast-** ◆◇◇◇◇ **guard** is an official who watches the sea near a N-COUNT coast in order to get help for sailors when they need it and to prevent smuggling. ▶ **The coastguard** is N-SING: the organization to which coastguards belong. the N

coast·line /ˈkəʊstlaɪn/ **coastlines.** A country's ◆◇◇◇◇ **coastline** is the outline of its coast. N-VAR

coat /kəʊt/ **coats, coating, coated. 1** A **coat** is ◆◆◇◇◇ a long-sleeved garment which you wear over your N-COUNT other clothes when you go outside. See picture headed **clothes.** ♦ **-coated** *...white-coated doctors.* COMB
2 An animal's **coat** is the fur or hair on its body. **3** If VERB: you **coat** something in a substance, you cover it V n with/in n with a thin layer of the substance. *TV pictures* V-ed *showed a dying bird coated with oil.* ♦ **-coated** COMB *...chocolate-coated sweets.* **4** A **coat** of paint or var- N-COUNT nish is a thin layer of it on a surface.

'coat hanger, coat hangers. A **coat hanger** is a N-COUNT curved piece of wood, metal, or plastic that you hang a piece of clothing on.

coat·ing /ˈkəʊtɪŋ/ **coatings.** A **coating** of a sub- ◆◇◇◇◇ stance is a thin layer of it spread over a surface. N-COUNT

,coat of 'arms, coats of arms. The **coat of arms** N-COUNT of a family, town, or organization is a design in the form of a shield that they use as an emblem.

'coat-tails; also spelled **coattails. 1** A man's **coat-** N-PLURAL **tails** are the two long pieces at the back of a formal coat. **2** If someone does something **on the coat-** PHRASE **tails of** someone else, they are able to do it because of the other person's success, and not because of their own efforts.

,co-'author, co-authors, co-authoring, co- ◆◇◇◇◇ **authored. 1** The **co-authors** of a book, play, or re- N-COUNT port are the people who have written it together.
2 If two or more people **co-author** a book, play, or VERB: V n report, they write it together.

coax /kəʊks/ **coaxes, coaxing, coaxed.** If you ◆◇◇◇◇ **coax** someone into doing something, you gently VERB: persuade them to do it. If you **coax** something out V n into-ing of someone, you gently persuade them to give it to V n to-inf you. *The government coaxed them to give up their* V n out of/ *strike. ...her role in trying to coax vital information* from n *from the young victim.*

cob /kɒb/ **cobs. 1** A **cob** is a heavily-built type of ◆◇◇◇◇ horse or pony. **2** See also **corn on the cob.** N-COUNT

co·balt /ˈkəʊbɔːlt/. **1 Cobalt** is a hard silvery-white ◆◇◇◇◇ metal which is used in hardening steel and for pro- N-UNCOUNT ducing a blue dye. **2 Cobalt** or **cobalt blue** is used COLOUR to describe things that are deep blue.

cob·ble /ˈkɒbəl/ **cobbles, cobbling, cobbled.** N-COUNT **Cobbles** are the same as **cobblestones.** ♦ **cob·bled** ADJ /ˈkɒbəld/. A **cobbled** street has a surface made of cobblestones.

cobble together. If you say that someone has **cob-** PHRASAL VB **bled** something **together,** you mean that they have V n P made or produced it roughly or quickly; used showing PRAGMATICS disapproval. *The group had cobbled together a few de-* V P noun *cent songs.*

cob·ler /ˈkɒblə/ **cobblers. 1** A **cobbler** is a per- N-COUNT son whose job is to make or mend shoes. **2** If you DATED describe something that someone has just said as N-UNCOUNT **cobblers,** you mean that you think it is nonsense. BRITISH, INFORMAL

cobble·stone /ˈkɒbəlstəʊn/ **cobblestones.** N-COUNT **Cobblestones** are stones with a rounded upper surface which were once used for making streets. *...narrow, cobblestone streets.*

co·bra /ˈkəʊbrə/ **cobras.** A **cobra** is a kind of poisonous snake. N-COUNT

cob·web /ˈkɒbweb/ **cobwebs.** **1** A **cobweb** is the net which a spider makes for catching insects, especially a dusty one indoors. ♦ **cob·webbed** /ˈkɒbwebd/. A **cobwebbed** surface is covered with cobwebs. **2** If something **blows** or **clears away the cobwebs,** it makes you feel more alert and lively when you had been feeling tired. N-COUNT ADJ PHRASE

co·caine /kəˈkeɪn/. **Cocaine** is a powerful drug which some people take for pleasure, but which they can become addicted to. ◆◆◇◇◇ N-UNCOUNT

coc·cyx /ˈkɒksɪks/ **coccyxes.** The **coccyx** is the small triangular bone at the lower end of the spine in human beings and some apes. N-COUNT

cochi·neal /ˌkɒtʃɪˈniːl/. **Cochineal** is a red substance that is used for colouring food. N-UNCOUNT

coch·lea /ˈkɒkliə/ **cochleae.** The **cochlea** is the spiral shaped part of the inner ear. N-COUNT

cock /kɒk/ **cocks, cocking, cocked. 1** A **cock** is an adult male chicken. The usual American word is **rooster.** **2** You can refer to a male bird, especially a male game bird, as a **cock.** ...*a cock pheasant.* **3** If you **cock** a part of your body in a particular direction, you lift it or point it in that direction. *He paused and cocked his head.* **4** If someone **cocks** their ear, they try very hard to hear something from a particular direction. *He suddenly cocked an ear and listened.* **5** When someone **cocks** a gun, they set a small device in the gun so that it is ready to fire. **6** See also **stopcock.** **7** ● to **cock a snook at** someone: see **snook.** ◆◆◇◇◇ N-COUNT BRITISH N-COUNT VERB V n VERB V n VERB: V n

cock up. If you **cock** something **up,** you ruin it by doing something wrong. *'Seems like I've cocked it up,'* Egan said... *They've cocked up the address.* ● See also **cock-up.** PHRASAL VB V n P V P noun BRITISH, INFORMAL

cock-a-'hoop. If you are **cock-a-hoop,** you are extremely pleased about something. ADJ DATED, BRITISH

cock-and-'bull story, cock-and-bull stories. If you describe something that someone tells you as a **cock-and-bull story,** you mean that you do not believe it is true. N-COUNT INFORMAL

cocka·too /ˌkɒkəˈtuː/ **cockatoos.** A **cockatoo** is a kind of parrot which has a crest on its head. N-COUNT

cocked 'hat, cocked hats. A **cocked hat** is a hat with three corners that used to be worn with some uniforms. N-COUNT

cock·er·el /ˈkɒkərəl/ **cockerels.** A **cockerel** is a young male chicken. N-COUNT

cock·er span·iel /ˌkɒkə ˈspænjəl/ **cocker spaniels.** A **cocker spaniel** is a breed of small dog. N-COUNT

cock·eyed /ˈkɒkaɪd/; also spelled **cock-eyed. 1** If you say that an idea or scheme is **cockeyed,** you mean that you think it is not sensible. **2** If something is **cockeyed,** it is not level or straight. *A life-size portrait hangs cockeyed on the stairs.* ADJ-GRADED ADJ-GRADED

cock·le /ˈkɒkəl/ **cockles.** **Cockles** are small edible shellfish. N-COUNT

cock·ney /ˈkɒkni/ **cockneys. 1** A **cockney** is a person who was born in the East End of London. ...*a Cockney cab driver.* **2 Cockney** is the dialect and accent of the East End of London. ◆◇◇◇◇ N-COUNT N-UNCOUNT

cock·pit /ˈkɒkpɪt/ **cockpits.** In an aeroplane or racing car, the **cockpit** is the part where the pilot sits. ◆◆◇◇◇ N-COUNT

cock·roach /ˈkɒkrəʊtʃ/ **cockroaches.** A **cockroach** is a large brown insect that is sometimes found in warm places or where food is kept. See picture headed **insects.** ◆◇◇◇◇ N-COUNT

cock·sure /ˌkɒkˈʃʊə/. Someone who is **cocksure** is very self-confident and rather cheeky. ADJ-GRADED DATED

cock·tail /ˈkɒkteɪl/ **cocktails. 1** A **cocktail** is an alcoholic drink which contains several ingredients. ...*a champagne cocktail.* ...*a cocktail party.* **2** A **cocktail** is a mixture of a number of different things, especially ones that do not go together well. *Children and guns are a potentially lethal cocktail.* **3** See also **fruit cocktail, prawn cocktail, Molotov cocktail.** ◆◆◇◇◇ N-COUNT N-COUNT

'cocktail dress, cocktail dresses. A **cocktail dress** is a short dress that is suitable for formal social occasions. N-COUNT

'cock-up, cock-ups. If you make a **cock-up** of something, you ruin it by doing something wrong. *This was just an administrative cock-up.* N-COUNT BRITISH, INFORMAL

cocky /ˈkɒki/ **cockier, cockiest.** Someone who is **cocky** is very self-confident and rather cheeky; used showing disapproval. *He had a confident, even cocky, air.* ♦ **cocki·ness** *The pair of them were both blinded by their own cockiness.* ◆◇◇◇◇ ADJ-GRADED PRAGMATICS INFORMAL N-UNCOUNT

co·coa /ˈkəʊkəʊ/. **1 Cocoa** is a brown powder that is used in making chocolate. **2 Cocoa** is a hot drink made from cocoa powder and milk or water. ◆◇◇◇◇ N-UNCOUNT N-UNCOUNT

coco·nut /ˈkəʊkənʌt/ **coconuts. 1** A **coconut** is a very large nut with a hairy shell, which has white flesh and milky juice inside it. **2 Coconut** is the white flesh of a coconut. ◆◇◇◇◇ N-COUNT N-UNCOUNT

'coconut milk. Coconut milk is the milky juice inside coconuts. N-UNCOUNT

'coconut palm, coconut palms. A **coconut palm** is a tall tree on which coconuts grow. N-COUNT

co·coon /kəˈkuːn/ **cocoons, cocooning, cocooned. 1** A **cocoon** is a covering of silky threads that the larvae of moths and other insects make for themselves before they grow into adults. **2** If you are in a **cocoon** of something, you are wrapped up in it or surrounded by it. *One eye was visible through a cocoon of dressings... He stood there in a cocoon of golden light.* **3** If you are living in a **cocoon,** you are in an environment in which you feel protected and safe. ...*her innocent desire to envelop her beloved in a cocoon of love.* **4** If something **cocoons** you from something, it protects you or isolates you from it. *The playwright cocooned himself in a world of pretence.* ♦ **co·cooned** *They have been cocooned from the experience of illness.* N-COUNT N-COUNT N-COUNT VERB: V n from/in n V pron-refl in n ADJ-GRADED

co·cooned /kəˈkuːnd/. If someone is **cocooned** in blankets or clothes, they are completely wrapped in them. *She is comfortably cocooned in pillows.* ADJ

cod /kɒd/. **1 Cod** are a type of large edible fish. The form 'cod' is also used as the plural. ► **Cod** is this fish eaten as food. **2** You use **cod** to describe something which is not genuine and which is intended to deceive or amuse people by looking or sounding like the real thing. *The product is a cod documentary on what animals think of living in a zoo.* ◆◇◇◇◇ N-VAR N-UNCOUNT ADJ: ADJ n INFORMAL, BRITISH

coda /ˈkəʊdə/ **codas. 1** A **coda** is a passage at the end of something such as a book or a speech that finishes it off. **2** In music, a **coda** is the final part of a fairly long piece of music which is added in order to finish it off in a pleasing way. N-COUNT N-COUNT

cod·dle /ˈkɒdəl/ **coddles, coddling, coddled.** If you say that someone **coddles** another person, you are showing your disapproval of the fact that they treat the person too kindly or protect them too much. *She coddled her youngest son madly.* VERB PRAGMATICS V n

code /kəʊd/ **codes. 1** A **code** is a set of rules about how people should behave or about how something must be done. ...*Article 159 of the Turkish penal code.* **2** See also **Highway Code.** **3** A **code** is a system of replacing the words in a message with other words or symbols, so that nobody can understand it unless they know the system. *If you can't remember your number, write it in code in a diary.* **4** A **code** is a group of numbers or letters which is used to identify something such as a postal address or part of a telephone system. *Callers dialing the wrong area code will not get through.* **5** A **code** is any system of signs or symbols that has a meaning. *It will need other chips to reconvert the digital code.* **6** See also **bar code, machine code, morse code, postcode, zip code.** ◆◆◆◇◇ N-COUNT N-COUNT: also in N N-COUNT N-COUNT

cod·ed /ˈkəʊdɪd/. **1 Coded** messages have words or symbols which represent other words, so that the message is secret unless you know the system behind the code. *In a coded telephone warning, Scotland Yard were told four bombs had been planted in the area.* **2** If you say that someone is using **coded** ◆◇◇◇◇ ADJ ADJ

language, you mean that they are expressing their opinion in an indirect or obscure way, usually because that opinion is likely to offend people. *...coded references to homosexuality.* **3 Coded** electronic signals use a binary system of digits which can be decoded by an appropriate machine.

ADJ: ADJ n
TECHNICAL

co·deine /'kəʊdiːn/. **Codeine** is a drug which is used to relieve pain.

N-UNCOUNT

'code name, code names, code naming, code named; also spelled **codename, code-name. 1** A **code name** is a name used for someone or something in order to keep their identity secret. *His Secret Service code name is 'Eagle'.* **2** If a military or police operation **is code-named** something, it is given a name which only the people involved in it know. *The operation was code-named Moonlight Sonata.*

N-COUNT

VB: usu
passive
be V-ed n

,code of 'conduct, codes of conduct. The **code of conduct** for a group or organization is a voluntary agreement on rules of behaviour for its members.

◆◇◇◇◇
N-COUNT

,code of 'practice, codes of practice. A **code of practice** is a set of written rules which explains how people working in a particular profession should behave.

◆◇◇◇◇
N-COUNT

'code word, code words; also spelled **codeword** or **code-word. 1** A **code word** is a word or phrase that has a special meaning, different from its normal meaning, for the people who have agreed to use it in this way. *Their instructions were to volunteer for a special mission when we gave them a code-word.* **2** A **code word** is a word or phrase that someone, especially a public figure, uses in order to avoid saying something else. *'Tired and emotional' is a code word for being drunk.*

N-COUNT

N-COUNT

codg·er /'kɒdʒə/ **codgers.** Old men are sometimes referred to in a disrespectful way as old **codgers.**

N-COUNT
PRAGMATICS

codi·fy /'kəʊdɪfaɪ, AM 'kɑːd-/ **codifies, codifying, codified.** If you **codify** a set of rules, you define them or present them in a clear and ordered way. *The latest draft of the agreement codifies the panel's decision.* ◆ **codi·fi·ca·tion** /,kəʊdɪfɪ'keɪʃən, AM ,kɑːd-/ *The codification of the laws began in the 1840s.*

VERB
V n

N-UNCOUNT

cod·ing /'kəʊdɪŋ/. **Coding** is a method of making types of things distinguishable from each other, for example by marking them in different colours. *This colour coding makes it easily identifiable.*

◆◇◇◇◇
N-UNCOUNT

,cod-liver 'oil; also spelled **cod liver oil. Cod liver oil** is a thick yellow oil which is often given to children, because it is full of vitamins A and D.

N-UNCOUNT

'co-ed, co-eds; also spelled **coed. 1** A **co-ed** school or college is the same as a co-educational school or college. **2** In America, a **co-ed** is a female student at a co-educational college or university.

ADJ

N-COUNT
INFORMAL

,co-edu'cational. A **co-educational** school, college, or university is attended by both boys and girls.

ADJ

co·ef·fi·cient /,kəʊɪ'fɪʃənt/ **coefficients.** A **coefficient** is a number that expresses a measurement of a particular quality of a substance or object under specified conditions. *A coefficient of one means the markets move perfectly in step.*

N-COUNT
TECHNICAL

co·erce /kəʊ'ɜːs/ **coerces, coercing, coerced.** If you **coerce** someone into doing something, you make them do it against their will. *Potter had argued that the government coerced him into pleading guilty.* ◆ **co·er·cion** /kəʊ'ɜːʃən/ *It was vital that the elections should be free of coercion or intimidation.*

◆◇◇◇◇
VERB
V n into-ing/n
Also V n to-inf
FORMAL

N-UNCOUNT

co·er·cive /kəʊ'ɜːsɪv/. **Coercive** measures are intended to force people to do something that they do not want to do. *...increasingly coercive measures on the part of the state.*

◆◇◇◇◇
ADJ-GRADED

co·ex·ist /,kəʊɪg'zɪst/ **coexists, coexisting, co-existed;** also spelled **co-exist.** If one thing **coexists** with another, the two things exist together at the same time or in the same place. You can also say that two things **coexist.** *Bankers and clockmakers have coexisted in the City for hundreds of years.*

V-RECIP:
V n
pl-n V

co·ex·ist·ence /,kəʊɪg'zɪstəns/ *He also believed in coexistence with the West.*

◆◇◇◇◇
N-UNCOUNT

cof·fee /'kɒfi, AM 'kɔːfi/ **coffees. 1 Coffee** is a hot brown drink that you make by pouring boiling water onto ground roasted coffee beans, or onto instant coffee powder. ▶ A **coffee** is a cup of coffee. *I made a coffee.* **2 Coffee** is the roasted seeds or powder from which the drink is made. *...superior quality coffee.*

◆◆◇◇
N-UNCOUNT

N-COUNT

N-VAR

'coffee bar, coffee bars. A **coffee bar** is a small café where non-alcoholic drinks and snacks are sold.

N-COUNT

'coffee bean, coffee beans. Coffee beans are small dark brown beans that are roasted and ground to make coffee. They are the seeds of the coffee plant.

N-COUNT

'coffee break, coffee breaks. A **coffee break** is a short period of time when you stop working and have a cup of coffee.

N-COUNT

'coffee cup, coffee cups; also spelled **coffee-cup.** A **coffee** cup is a cup from which coffee is drunk. Coffee cups are usually smaller than tea cups.

N-COUNT

'coffee house, coffee houses; also spelled **coffee-house.** A **coffee house** is a kind of bar where people sit to drink coffee and talk. Coffee houses were especially popular in the 18th century.

N-COUNT

'coffee morning, coffee mornings. In Britain, a **coffee morning** is a social event that takes place in the morning in someone's house, and is usually intended to raise money for charity.

N-COUNT

'coffee pot, coffee pots; also spelled **coffeepot.** A **coffee pot** is a tall narrow pot with a spout and a lid, in which coffee is made or served.

N-COUNT

'coffee shop, coffee shops; also spelled **coffee-shop.** A **coffee shop** is a kind of restaurant that sells coffee, tea, cakes, and sometimes sandwiches and light meals.

◆◇◇◇◇
N-COUNT

'coffee table, coffee tables; also spelled **coffee-table.** A **coffee table** is a small low table in a living-room.

◆◇◇◇◇
N-COUNT

'coffee-table book, coffee-table books. A **coffee-table book** is a large expensive book with a lot of pictures, which is designed to be looked at rather than to be read properly, and is usually placed where people can see it easily.

N-COUNT

cof·fer /'kɒfə/ **coffers. 1** In the past, a **coffer** was a large strong chest used for storing valuables such as money or gold. **2** The **coffers** of an organization consist of the money that it has to spend. *Other smaller sell-offs are likely to swell the Treasury's coffers.*

◆◇◇◇◇
N-COUNT

N-PLURAL:
with supp

cof·fin /'kɒfɪn, AM 'kɔːfɪn/ **coffins. 1** A **coffin** is a box in which a dead body is buried or cremated. **2** If you say that one thing is **a nail in** the **coffin** of another thing, you mean that it will help bring about its end or failure. *A fine would be the final nail in the coffin of the airline.*

◆◆◇◇
N-COUNT

PHRASE

cog /kɒg/ **cogs. 1** A **cog** is a wheel with square or triangular teeth around the edge, which is used in a machine to turn another wheel or part. **2** If you describe someone as **a cog in a machine** or **wheel,** you mean that they are a small part of a large organization or group. *Mr Lake was an important cog in the Republican campaign machine.*

N-COUNT

PHRASE

co·gent /'kəʊdʒənt/. A **cogent** reason, argument, or example is strong and convincing. *There were perfectly cogent reasons why Julian Cavendish should be told.* ◆ **co·gent·ly** *He tried to convey the information as cogently as he could.*

ADJ-GRADED
FORMAL

ADV-GRADED:
ADV with v

cog·nac /'kɒnjæk, AM 'kɒʊn-/ **cognacs;** also spelled **Cognac. Cognac** is a type of brandy made in the south west of France. *...one of the world's finest cognacs.* ▶ A **cognac** is a glass of cognac.

◆◇◇◇◇
N-VAR

N-COUNT

cog·nate /'kɒgneɪt/. **Cognate** things are related to each other. *...cognate words.*

ADJ
FORMAL

cog·ni·sant /'kɒgnɪzənt/. See **cognizant.**

cog·ni·tion /kɒg'nɪʃən/. **Cognition** is the mental process involved in knowing, learning, and understanding things.

N-UNCOUNT
TECHNICAL

cog·ni·tive /ˈkɒgnɪtɪv/. **Cognitive** means relating to the mental process involved in knowing, learning, and understanding things. *As children grow older, their cognitive processes become sharper.* ◆◇◇◇◇ ADJ: ADJ n TECHNICAL

cog·ni·zant /ˈkɒgnɪzənt/; also spelled **cognisant**. If someone is **cognizant** of something, they are aware of it or understand it. *Walter was cognizant of the limitations of his argument.* ADJ-GRADED v-link ADJ FORMAL

co·gno·scen·ti /ˌkɒnjəˈʃenti/. The people who know a lot about a particular subject are sometimes called the **cognoscenti**. *She has an international reputation among film cognoscenti.* N-PLURAL FORMAL

co·hab·it /kəʊˈhæbɪt/ **cohabits, cohabiting, co-habited.** If two people **are cohabiting**, they are living together and have a sexual relationship, but are not married. *The dentist left his wife of 15 years and openly cohabited with his receptionist... The proportion of single women cohabiting soared.* ◆◇◇◇◇ V-RECIP: pl-n V V with n V (non-recip) FORMAL ♦ **co·habi·ta·tion** /kəʊˌhæbɪˈteɪʃən/ *The decline in marriage has been offset by a rise in cohabitation.* N-UNCOUNT

co·here /kəʊˈhɪə/ **coheres, cohering, cohered.** If the different elements of a piece of writing, a piece of music, or a set of ideas **cohere**, they fit together well so that they form a united whole. *We make sense of particular beliefs only as they cohere with other beliefs... It failed to cohere as a single work.* ♦ **co·her·ence** /kəʊˈhɪərəns/ *The anthology has a surprising sense of coherence.* V-RECIP: pl-n V V with n V (non-recip) N-UNCOUNT

co·her·ent /kəʊˈhɪərənt/. **1** If something is **coherent**, it is well planned, so that it is clear and sensible and all its parts go well with each other. *He has failed to work out a coherent strategy for modernising the service.* ♦ **co·her·ence** *The campaign was widely criticised for making tactical mistakes and for a lack of coherence.* ♦ **co·her·ent·ly** *The government has to convince voters it is proceeding coherently toward its goals.* **2** If someone is **coherent**, they express their thoughts in a clear and calm way, so that other people can understand what they are saying. *He's so calm when he answers questions in interviews. I wish I could be that coherent.* ♦ **co·her·ence** *This was debated eagerly at first, but with diminishing coherence as the champagne took hold.* ♦ **co·her·ent·ly** *He talked coherently.* ◆◇◇◇ ADJ-GRADED N-UNCOUNT ADV ADJ-GRADED: v-link ADJ N-UNCOUNT ADV-GRADED

co·he·sion /kəʊˈhiːʒən/. If there is **cohesion** within a society, organization, or group, the different members fit together well and form a united whole. *By 1990, it was clear that the cohesion of the armed forces was rapidly breaking down.* ◆◇◇◇◇ N-UNCOUNT

co·he·sive /kəʊˈhiːsɪv/. Something that is **cohesive** consists of parts that fit together well and form a united whole. *'Daring Adventures from '86' is a far more cohesive and successful album.* ♦ **co·he·sive·ness** *They had no group cohesiveness. They were in competition with each other all the time.* ◆◇◇◇◇ ADJ-GRADED N-UNCOUNT

co·hort /ˈkəʊhɔːt/ **cohorts. 1** A person's **cohorts** are their companions, supporters, or associates; used showing disapproval. *Drake and his cohorts were not pleased with my appointment.* **2** A **cohort** of people is a group who have something in common. **Cohort** is used especially when a group is being looked at as a whole for statistical purposes. *She speaks for a whole cohort of young Japanese writers.* ◆◇◇◇◇ N-COUNT PRAGMATICS N-COUNT

coiffed /kwɑːft/. If you say someone's hair is neatly **coiffed**, you mean it is very carefully arranged. ADJ FORMAL

coif·fure /kwɑːˈfjʊə/ **coiffures.** A person's **coiffure** is their hairstyle. N-COUNT FORMAL

coil /kɔɪl/ **coils, coiling, coiled. 1** A **coil** of rope or wire is a length of it that has been wound into a series of loops. *He slung the coil of rope over his shoulder.* **2** A **coil** is one loop in a series of loops. *Pythons kill by tightening their coils so that their victim cannot breathe.* **3** If you **coil** something, you wind it into a series of loops or into the shape of a ring. If it **coils** around something, it forms loops or a ring. *Louisa was dancing, spinning by herself, her skirt flying out and coiling around her feet... A huge rattlesnake lay coiled on the blanket.* ▶ **Coil up** means the same as **coil**. *Once we have the wire, we* ◆◇◇◇◇ N-COUNT N-COUNT V-ERG: V n V prep/adv V-ed PHRASAL VB V n P

can coil it up into the shape of a spring... Her hair was coiled up on top of her head. V-ed P Also V P noun

4 A **coil** is a thick spiral of wire through which an electrical current passes. **5** In a vehicle, the **coil** is the part on a petrol engine that sends electricity to the spark plugs. N-COUNT N-COUNT

6 The **coil** is a contraceptive device used by women. It is fitted inside a woman's womb, for up to five years. N-COUNT

coin /kɔɪn/ **coins, coining, coined. 1** A **coin** is a small piece of metal which is used as money. **2** If you say that someone **is coining it** or **is coining** money, you are emphasizing that they are making a lot of money very quickly, often without really earning it. *One wine shop is coining money selling Wembley-label champagne.* ▶ **Coining in** means the same as **coining**. *She's coining it in with a $10 million contract with Revlon.* **3** If you talk about **the other side of the coin**, you are talking about a different, often contrasting, aspect of a situation. *It's short, but the other side of the coin is that it's very light.* **4** If you say that two things are **two sides of the same coin**, you mean that they are different ways of looking at or dealing with the same situation. *The minister reportedly stressed that economic and political reforms were two sides of the same coin.* **5** If you **coin** a word or a phrase, you are the first person to use it. *Jaron Lanier coined the term 'virtual reality'.* **6** You say **'to coin a phrase'** to show that you realize you are making a pun or using a cliché. *Fifty local musicians have, to coin a phrase, banded together to form the Jazz Umbrella.* ◆◇◇◇◇ N-COUNT VERB: V it PRAGMATICS V n INFORMAL, BRITISH PHRASAL VB V it P PHRASE PRAGMATICS PHRASE VERB V n PHRASE PRAGMATICS

coin·age /ˈkɔɪnɪdʒ/. **1 Coinage** is the coins which are used in a country. *The city produced its own coinage from 1325 to 1864.* **2 Coinage** is the system of money used in a country. *It took four years for Britain just to decimalise its own coinage.* N-UNCOUNT N-UNCOUNT

co·in·cide /ˌkəʊɪnˈsaɪd/ **coincides, coinciding, coincided. 1** If one event **coincides** with another, they happen at the same time. *The beginning of the solar and lunar years coincided every 13 years.* **2** If the ideas or interests of two or more people **coincide**, they are the same. *Japan's long-term interests clearly coincide with those of the United States.* ◆◇◇◇◇ V-RECIP: V with n pl-n V V-RECIP: pl-n V V with n

co·in·ci·dence /kəʊˈɪnsɪdəns/ **coincidences.** A **coincidence** is a situation in which two or more similar or related events occur at the same time by chance and without any planning. *It is probably no coincidence that the attacks have come at the start of the electoral campaign. ...inexplicable coincidences that link our lives.* ◆◆◇◇ N-VAR

co·in·ci·dent /kəʊˈɪnsɪdənt/. **1 Coincident** events happen at the same time. *Coincident with her marriage to Ambassador Davies and his posting to Moscow, she began buying Russian art.* **2 Coincident** opinions, ideas, or policies are the same or are very similar to each other. *The purposes and goals of the US are coincident with the purposes and goals of the UN Security Council.* ADJ FORMAL ADJ-GRADED FORMAL

co·in·ci·dent·al /ˌkəʊɪnsɪˈdentəl/. Something that is **coincidental** is the result of a coincidence and has not been deliberately arranged. *Any resemblance to actual persons, places or events is purely coincidental.* ADJ

co·in·ci·dent·al·ly /ˌkəʊɪnsɪˈdentli/. You say **coincidentally** when you want to draw attention to a coincidence. *Coincidentally, I had once found myself in a similar situation.* ◆◇◇◇◇ ADV: also ADV before v

coir /ˈkɔɪə/. **Coir** is a rough material made from coconut shells which is used to make ropes and mats. N-UNCOUNT

coi·tal /ˈkəʊɪtəl/. **Coital** means connected with or relating to sexual intercourse. *...coital techniques.* ADJ: ADJ n TECHNICAL

coi·tus /ˈkəʊɪtəs/. **Coitus** is sexual intercourse. *Coitus became associated with childbirth.* N-UNCOUNT TECHNICAL

coke /kəʊk/. **1 Coke** is a solid black substance that is produced from coal and is burned as a fuel. **2 Coke** is the same as cocaine. ◆◇◇◇◇ N-UNCOUNT N-UNCOUNT INFORMAL

col., cols. col. is a written abbreviation for 'column' or 'colour'.

Col. Col. is a written abbreviation for 'Colonel'. ◆◇◇◇◇ *...Col. Frank Weldon.* N-TITLE

co·la /ˈkəʊlə/ **colas.** Cola is a sweet brown non- ◆◆◇◇◇ alcoholic fizzy drink. N-VAR

col·an·der /ˈkɒləndə, ˈkʌl-/ **colanders.** A colander N-COUNT is a bowl-shaped container with holes in it which you wash or drain food in.

cold /kəʊld/ **colder, coldest; colds. 1** Some- ◆◆◆◇ thing that is **cold** has a very low temperature or a ADJ-GRADED lower temperature than is normal or acceptable. *Rinse the vegetables under cold running water... Your dinner's getting cold.* ◆ **cold·ness** *She com-* N-UNCOUNT *plained about the coldness of his hands.* **2** If it is ADJ-GRADED **cold**, or if a place is **cold**, the temperature of the air is very low. *The house is cold because I can't afford to turn the heat on... This is the coldest winter I can remember.* ◆ **coldness** *The coldness of the night* N-UNCOUNT *had gone.* **3** Cold weather or low temperatures can N-UNCOUNT: be referred to as the **cold**. *He must have come inside* also the N *to get out of the cold.* **4** If you are **cold**, your body is ADJ-GRADED at an unpleasantly low temperature.
5 Cold food, such as salad or meat that has been ADJ cooked and cooled, is not intended to be eaten hot. *...cold meats.*
6 Cold colours or cold light give an impression of ADJ-GRADED coldness. *...the cold blue light from a streetlamp.*
7 If you say that someone is **cold**, you mean that they ADJ-GRADED do not show much emotion, especially affection, and therefore seem unfriendly and unsympathetic. If you say that someone's voice is **cold**, you mean that they speak in an unfriendly unsympathetic way. *What a cold, unfeeling woman she was.* ◆ **cold·ly** *'I'll see you* ADV-GRADED *in the morning,' Hugh said coldly.* ◆ **cold·ness** *His* N-UNCOUNT *coldness angered her.*
8 If you say that someone is **cold** when they are trying ADJ-GRADED: to guess the answer to a question or puzzle, you mean v-link ADJ that they are thinking about it in the wrong way and are going to give a wrong answer.
9 If you have a **cold**, you have a mild, very common ill- N-COUNT ness which makes you sneeze a lot and gives you a sore throat or a cough. **10** See also **common cold.**
11 If you **catch cold**, or **catch a cold**, you become ill PHRASE with a cold.
12 If something **leaves** you **cold**, it fails to excite or in- PHRASE terest you. *Things that you find funny, leave him cold.*
13 If someone is **out cold**, they are unconscious or PHRASE sleeping very heavily.
14 If you say that a person, group, or country has PHRASE been left **out in the cold**, you mean that you think that you think that they have been ignored by others ra- ther than being invited to take part in some activity with them.
15 ● in cold blood: see blood. ● to **get cold feet**: see foot. ● to **pour cold water on** something: see water.

cold-'blooded. 1 Someone who is **cold-blooded** ADJ-GRADED does not show any pity or emotion; used showing PRAGMATICS disapproval. *This was a brutal and cold-blooded killing.* ◆ **cold-bloodedly** *He cold-bloodedly* ADV-GRADED *stalked his victim for 24 hours.* **2** Cold-blooded ani- ADJ mals such as reptiles have a body temperature that TECHNICAL changes according to the surrounding temperature.

cold 'comfort. If you say that a slightly encourag- N-UNCOUNT ing fact or event is **cold comfort** to someone, you mean that it gives them little or no comfort because their situation is so difficult or unpleasant. *These figures may look good on paper but are cold comfort to the islanders themselves.*

cold 'cream. Cold cream is a cream that people N-UNCOUNT use for softening and cleaning their skin, especially skin on their face.

cold 'fish. If you say that someone is a **cold fish**, N-SING you mean that you think that they are unfriendly PRAGMATICS and unemotional.

'cold frame, cold frames. A **cold frame** is a N-COUNT wooden frame with a glass top in which you grow small plants to protect them from cold weather.

cold-'hearted. A **cold-hearted** person does not ADJ-GRADED feel any affection or compassion for other people; PRAGMATICS used showing disapproval. *That Harriet is a cold-hearted bitch.*

cold-'shoulder, cold-shoulders, cold- shouldering, cold-shouldered. 1 If one person N-SING gives another the **cold-shoulder**, they behave to- wards them in an unfriendly way, to show them that they do not care about them. **2** If one person VERB: V n **cold-shoulders** another, they give them the cold- shoulder.

'cold snap, cold snaps. A **cold snap** is a short N-COUNT period of cold and frosty weather.

'cold sore, cold sores. Cold sores are small sore N-COUNT spots that sometimes appear on or near someone's lips and nose when they have a cold.

cold 'storage. If something such as food is put in N-UNCOUNT **cold storage**, it is kept in an artificially cooled place in order to preserve it.

cold 'sweat, cold sweats. If you are in a **cold** N-COUNT **sweat**, you are sweating and feel cold, for example because you are afraid.

cold 'turkey. Cold turkey is the unpleasant N-UNCOUNT physical reaction that people have when they sud- INFORMAL denly stop taking a drug that they are addicted to.

Cold 'War; also spelled **cold war.** When people ◆◆◇◇◇ refer to **the Cold War**, they are referring to the N-PROPER: situation of extreme political hostility and tension the N which existed between the Soviet bloc and the Unit- ed States together with its allies in the period after the Second World War and before Perestroika.

cole·slaw /ˈkəʊlslɔː/. **Coleslaw** is a salad of N-UNCOUNT chopped cabbage, carrots, onions, and other veg- etables, mixed together in mayonnaise.

col·ic /ˈkɒlɪk/. **Colic** is an illness in which you get N-UNCOUNT severe pains in your stomach and bowels. Babies especially suffer from colic.

co·li·tis /kəˈlaɪtɪs/. **Colitis** is an illness in which N-UNCOUNT your colon becomes inflamed.

col·labo·rate /kəˈlæbəreɪt/ **collaborates, col-** ◆◇◇◇◇ **laborating, collaborated. 1** When one person V-RECIP: or group **collaborates** with another, they work to- V with n gether, especially on a book or on some research. V with n on/in *Much later he collaborated with his son Michael on* n/-ing *the English translation... Students collaborate in* pl-n V on/in *group exercises and projects... The two men met and* n/-ing *agreed to collaborate.* ◆ **col·labo·ra·tor, collabo-** pl-n V **rators** *The Irvine group and their collaborators are* N-COUNT *testing whether lasers do the job better.* **2** If someone VERB **collaborates** with an enemy which has occupied PRAGMATICS their country during a war, he or she helps them; V with n used showing disapproval. *He was accused of having* Also V *collaborated with the Communist secret police.* ◆ **col·labo·ra·tor.** N-COUNT

col·labo·ra·tion /kə,læbəˈreɪʃən/ **collaborations.** ◆◆◇◇◇ **1** Collaboration is the act of working together to N-VAR produce a piece of work, especially a book or some research. *Drummond was working on a book in col- laboration with Zodiac Mindwarp.* **2** A collabora- N-COUNT tion is a piece of work that has been produced as the result of people or groups working together. *He is known for his collaborations with the late John Cage.*
3 Collaboration is the act of helping an enemy which N-UNCOUNT has occupied your country; used showing disapprov- PRAGMATICS al. *...rumors of his collaboration with the occupying forces during the war.*

col·labo·ra·tion·ist /kə,læbəˈreɪʃənɪst/. A **collabo-** ADJ **rationist** government or individual is one that helps PRAGMATICS or gives support to an enemy that has occupied their country; used showing disapproval.

col·labo·ra·tive /kəˈlæbərətɪv, AM -reɪt-/. A **col-** ◆◇◇◇◇ **laborative** piece of work is done by two or more ADJ: ADJ n people or groups working together. *...a collaborative* FORMAL *research project.* ◆ **col·labo·ra·tive·ly** *He was not* ADV: *the kind of artist who worked collaboratively.* ADV with v

col·labo·ra·tor /kəˈlæbəreɪtə/ **collaborators.** See ◆◇◇◇◇ **collaborate.**

col·lage /ˈkɒlɑːʒ, AM kəˈlɑːʒ/ **collages. 1** A col- ◆◇◇◇◇ **lage** is a picture that has been made by sticking N-COUNT things such as photographs or pieces of coloured paper or cloth onto paper. *...a vast collage.* **2** Collage N-UNCOUNT is the method of making pictures by sticking things such as photographs or pieces of

coloured paper or cloth onto paper. **3** You can refer N-COUNT to something that has been made by combining a number of very different things as a **collage** of a particular kind. *Rego's work is a rich collage of 20th-century painting styles.*

col·la·gen /'kɒlədʒən/. **Collagen** is a protein that ◆◇◇◇◇ is found in the bodies of people and animals. It is N-UNCOUNT often used in cosmetics or cosmetic surgery, in order to make the skin look younger.

col·lapse /kə'læps/ **collapses, collapsing, col-** ◆◆◆◇ **lapsed. 1** If a building or other structure **collapses**, VERB: V it falls down very suddenly. *Most of the deaths were* V-ing *caused by landslides and collapsing buildings.* ► Also a noun. *Governor Deukmejian called for an* N-UNCOUNT *inquiry into the freeway's collapse.* **2** If something VERB: V with air inside **collapses**, it falls inwards and be- V-ed comes smaller or flatter. *Vicki suffered a collapsed lung.*

3 If something, for example a system or institution, VERB: V **collapses**, it fails or comes to an end completely and V-ing suddenly. *The rural people have been impoverished by a collapsing economy.* ► Also a noun. *Their economy* N-UNCOUNT *is teetering on the brink of collapse.* **4** If you **collapse**, VERB you suddenly faint or fall down because you are very ill or weak. ► Also a noun. *A few days after his collapse* N-UNCOUNT *he was sitting up in bed.*

5 If you **collapse** onto something, you sit or lie down VERB suddenly because you are very tired. *I'd just collapse* V prep *into bed, exhausted.* Also V

col·laps·ible /kə'læpsɪbəl/. A **collapsible** object is ADJ designed to be folded flat when it is not being used. *...a collapsible chair.*

col·lar /'kɒlə/ **collars, collaring, collared.** ◆◆◇◇◇ **1** The **collar** of a shirt or coat is the part which fits N-COUNT round the neck and is usually folded over. ● See also **blue-collar, dog-collar, white-collar. 2** A **collar** N-COUNT is a band of leather or plastic which is put round the neck of a dog or cat.

3 If you **collar** someone who has done something VERB wrong or who is running away, you catch them and V n hold them so that they cannot escape. *As Kerr fled to-* INFORMAL *wards the exit, Boycott collared him at the ticket barri-* er. **4** If you **collar** someone, you stop them and make VERB: V n them listen to you. *Bernard was once collared by an* be V-ed *aggressive stranger in Soho.* INFORMAL

5 If someone **gets hot under the collar** about some- PHRASE thing, they get very annoyed, angry, or excited about INFORMAL it.

'collar bone, collar bones; also spelled **collar-** N-COUNT **bone.** Your **collar bones** are the two long bones which run from the base of your neck to your shoulders. *...Harold had a broken collarbone.*

col·late /kə'leɪt/ **collates, collating, collated.** ◆◇◇◇◇ When you **collate** pieces of information, you bring VERB them all together and examine them. *They have be-* V n *gun to collate their own statistics.* ◆ **col·la·tion** N-UNCOUNT /kə'leɪʃən/ *...laws governing the collation of personal information.*

col·lat·er·al /kə'lætərəl/. **Collateral** is money or ◆◇◇◇◇ property which is used as a guarantee that someone N-UNCOUNT will repay a loan. *Many people use personal assets as* FORMAL *collateral for small business loans.*

col,lateral 'damage. Collateral **damage** is unin- N-UNCOUNT tentional injury to civilians or damage to civilian buildings which occurs during a military operation.

col·league /'kɒliːg/ **colleagues.** Your **colleagues** ◆◆◆◇ are the people you work with, especially in a profes- N-COUNT sional job. *Without consulting his colleagues he flew from Lisbon to Split... A colleague urged him to see a psychiatrist.*

col·lect /kə'lekt/ **collects, collecting, collect-** ◆◆◆◆◇ **ed. 1** If you **collect** a number of things, you bring VERB them together from several places or from several V n people. *Two young girls were collecting firewood... 1.5 million signatures have been collected.*

2 If you **collect** things, such as stamps or books, as a VERB hobby, you get a large number of them over a period V n of time because they interest you. *I used to collect stamps.* ◆ **col·lect·ing** *...hobbies like stamp collect-* N-UNCOUNT:

ing and fishing. ◆ **col·lec·tor, collectors** *...a re-* with supp *spected collector of Indian art.* N-COUNT

3 When you **collect** someone or something, you go VERB and get them from a place where they are waiting for V n from n you or have been left for you. *David always collects* V n *Alistair from school... After collecting the cash, the kid-* *napper made his escape.* ◆ **col·lec·tion** /kə'lekʃən/ N-UNCOUNT *...public services including mail delivery and garbage collection.*

4 If a substance **collects** somewhere, or something V-ERG **collects** it, it keeps arriving over a period of time and is V prep/adv held in that place or thing. *Methane gas does collect in* V n *the mines. ...water tanks which collect rainwater.* Also V

5 If something **collects** light, energy, or heat, it at- VERB tracts it. *Like a telescope it has a curved mirror to col-* V n *lect the sunlight.*

6 If you **collect** for a charity or for a present for some- VERB: one, you ask people to give you money for it. *They col-* V for n *lected donations for a fund to help military families.* V n for n ◆ **col·lec·tion, collections** *Friends held a collec-* N-COUNT *tion for him.*

7 If you **collect** yourself or **collect** your thoughts, you VERB make an effort to calm yourself or prepare yourself V pron-refl mentally. *She paused for a moment to collect herself.* V n *...a chance to relax and collect his thoughts.*

8 If you **call collect** when you make a telephone call, PHRASE the person who you are phoning pays the cost of the AMERICAN call and not you. The usual British term is to **reverse the charges.** *Should you lose your ticket call collect on STA's helpline.*

collect up. If you **collect up** things, you bring them PHRASAL VB all together, usually when you have finished using V P noun them. *Would you go and collect up the dishes?* Also V n P

col·lect·able /kə'lektəbəl/ **collectables;** also ADJ-GRADED spelled **collectible.** A **collectable** object is valued highly by collectors because it is rare or beautiful. *Many of these cushions have survived and are very collectible.* ► Also a noun. *Pollock Antiques deals in* N-COUNT *silver and small collectables.*

col·lect·ed /kə'lektɪd/. **1** An author's **collected** ◆◆◇◇◇ works or letters are all their works or letters pub- ADJ: ADJ n lished in one book or in a set of books. *...the collect-* ed *works of Rudyard Kipling.* **2** If you say that ADJ-GRADED someone is **collected** in a difficult situation, you mean that they are very calm and well-controlled. *She was cool and collected during her interrogation.* **3** See also **collect.**

col·lect·ible /kə'lektɪbəl/ **collectibles.** See **col-** **lectable.**

col·lect·ing /kə'lektɪŋ/. A **collecting** tin or box is ADJ: ADJ n used to collect money for charity. ● See also **collect.**

col·lec·tion /kə'lekʃən/ **collections. 1** A **collec-** ◆◆◆◇ **tion** of things is a group of similar things that you N-COUNT have deliberately acquired, usually over a period of time. *...the world's largest collection of sculptures by Henry Moore.*

2 A **collection** of stories, poems, or articles is a num- N-COUNT ber of them published in one book. *...a collection of es-* *says from foreign affairs experts.* **3** A **collection** of N-COUNT things is a group of things. *Spon Street is a collection of restored buildings.*

4 A fashion designer's new **collection** consists of the N-COUNT new clothes they have designed for the next season.

5 A **collection** is money that is given by people in N-COUNT church during some Christian services.

6 See also **collect.**

col·lec·tive /kə'lektɪv/ **collectives. 1** Collective ◆◆◆◇ actions, situations, or feelings involve or are shared ADJ: ADJ n by every member of a group of people. *It was a collective decision... The country's politicians are already heaving a collective sigh of relief.* ◆ **col·lec-** **·tive·ly** *They collectively decided to recognize the* ADV *changed situation.* **2** A **collective** amount is the total ADJ: ADJ n obtained by adding together the amounts that each person or thing in a group has. ◆ **collectively** *In* ADV: *1968 the states collectively spent $2 billion on it.* ADV with v

3 The **collective** term for two or more types of thing ADJ: ADJ n is a general word or expression referring to all of them. *Social science is a collective name, covering a*

series of individual sciences. ♦ **collectively** ...*other sorts of cells (known collectively as white corpuscles).* ADV: ADV with v

4 A **collective** is a business or farm whose employees share the decision-making and the profits. N-COUNT

col‚lective 'bargaining. When a trade union engages in **collective bargaining**, it has talks with an employer about its members' pay and working conditions. N-UNCOUNT

col‚lective 'noun, collective nouns. A **collective noun** is a noun such as 'family' or 'team' that refers to a group of people or things. When it is used in the singular, the noun can take a singular or plural verb. Many collective nouns are followed by 'of', as in 'a swarm of bees' or 'a flock of sheep'. N-COUNT

col‚lective un'conscious. The **collective unconscious** is the basic ideas and images that some psychologists believe that people share because they have inherited them. N-SING

col·lec·tiv·ism /kəˈlektɪvɪzəm/. **Collectivism** is the political belief that a country's industries and services should be owned and controlled by the state or by all the people in a country. ♦ **col·lec·tiv·ist** /kəˈlektɪvɪst/ ...*collectivist ideals.* N-UNCOUNT ADJ

col·lec·ti·vize /kəˈlektɪvaɪz/ **collectivizes, collectivizing, collectivized;** also spelled **collectivise** in British English. If farms or factories **are collectivized**, they are brought under state ownership and control, usually by combining a number of small farms or factories into one large one. ♦ **col·lec·tivi·za·tion** /kəˌlektɪvaɪˈzeɪʃən/ ...*the forced collectivisation of agriculture.* VERB: V n N-UNCOUNT

col·lec·tor /kəˈlektə/ **collectors.** You can use **collector** to refer to someone whose job is to take something such as money, tickets, or rubbish from people. ...*a tax collector.* ...*a garbage collector.* ● See also **collect**. ◆◇◇◇ N-COUNT: with supp

col'lector's item, collector's items. A **collector's item** is an object which is highly valued by collectors because it is rare or beautiful. N-COUNT

col·lege /ˈkɒlɪdʒ/ **colleges. 1** A **college** is a place where students study after they have left school. *Joanna is doing business studies at a local college.* ...*I was in art college for three years.* ...*Western New England College in Springfield, Massachusetts.* **2** A **college** is one of the institutions into which some British universities are divided into. *He was educated at Balliol College, Oxford.* **3 College** is used in Britain in the names of some secondary schools. ...*Cheltenham Ladies' College.* ◆◆◆◇ N-VAR N-COUNT

4 A **college** of a particular kind is an organized group of people who have special duties and powers. *He is a member of the Royal College of Physicians.* N-COUNT: with supp FORMAL

col·legi·ate /kəˈliːdʒiət/. **Collegiate** means belonging or relating to a college or to college students. ...*the 1933 national collegiate football championship was won by Michigan.* ◆◇◇◇ ADJ: ADJ n

col·lide /kəˈlaɪd/ **collides, colliding, collided. 1** If two or more moving people or objects **collide**, they crash into one another. If a moving person or object **collides** with a stationary person or object, they crash into them. *Two trains collided head-on... Racing up the stairs, he almost collided with Daisy.* **2** If the aims, opinions, or interests of one person or group **collide** with those of another person or group, they are very different from each other and are therefore opposed. *Nasser regularly collided with the different Western powers, who refused to arm him.* ...*what happens when the two interests collide.* ◆◇◇◇ V-RECIP pl-n V V with n Also V with n (non-recip) V-RECIP V with n pl-n V

col·lie /ˈkɒli/ **collies.** A **collie** or a **collie dog** is a dog with long hair and a long, narrow muzzle. N-COUNT

col·liery /ˈkɒljəri/ **collieries.** A **colliery** is a coal mine and all the buildings and equipment connected with it. ◆◇◇◇ N-COUNT BRITISH

col·li·sion /kəˈlɪʒən/ **collisions. 1** A **collision** occurs when a moving object crashes into something. *Their van was involved in a collision with a car.* ...*a head-on collision between two aeroplanes.* **2** A **collision** of cultures or ideas occurs when two or more ◆◆◇◇ N-VAR N-COUNT

very different people or groups meet and conflict. *The play represents the collision of three generations.*

col'lision course. If two or more people or things are on a **collision course**, there is likely to be a sudden and violent disagreement between them. *Britain's universities are set on a collision course with the government.* N-SING

col·lo·cate, collocates, collocating, collocated. The noun is pronounced /ˈkɒləkət/. The verb is pronounced /ˈkɒləkeɪt/. **1** In linguistics, a **collocate** of a particular word is another word which often occurs with it. **2** In linguistics, if one word **collocates** with another, the two words often occur together. *'Detached' collocates with 'house'.* ♦ **col·lo·ca·tion** /ˌkɒləˈkeɪʃən/ **collocations** ...*the basic notion of collocation.* N-COUNT TECHNICAL V-RECIP V with n pl-n V TECHNICAL N-VAR

col·lo·qui·al /kəˈləʊkwiəl/. **Colloquial** words and phrases are informal and are used mainly in conversation. ...*colloquial Russian.* ♦ **col·lo·qui·al·ly** *Bribes are known colloquially as 'key money'.* ADJ-GRADED ADV-GRADED: ADV with v

col·lo·qui·al·ism /kəˈləʊkwiəlɪzəm/ **colloquialisms.** A **colloquialism** is a colloquial word or phrase. N-COUNT

col·lo·quium /kəˈləʊkwiəm/ **colloquiums** or **colloquia** /kəˈləʊkwiə/. A **colloquium** is a large academic seminar. N-COUNT FORMAL

col·lude /kəˈluːd/ **colludes, colluding, colluded.** If one person **colludes** with another, they co-operate secretly or illegally. *Several local officials are in jail on charges of colluding with the Mafia... The store's 'no refunds' policy makes it harder for dishonest cashiers and customers to collude.* V-RECIP V with n pl-n V Also V in n/-ing, pl-n V to-inf

col·lu·sion /kəˈluːʒən/. **Collusion** is secret or illegal co-operation, especially between countries or organizations. ...*collusion between record companies and retailers... Some stockbrokers, in collusion with bank officials, obtained large sums of money for speculation.* ◆◇◇◇ N-UNCOUNT FORMAL

co·logne /kəˈləʊn/ **colognes. Cologne** is a kind of weak perfume or aftershave. ◆◇◇◇ N-VAR

co·lon /ˈkəʊlən/ **colons. 1** A **colon** is a punctuation mark (:), which you can use in several ways. For example, you can put it before a list of things or before reported speech. **2** Your **colon** is the part of your intestine above your rectum. N-COUNT N-COUNT

colo·nel /ˈkɜːnəl/ **colonels.** A **colonel** is a senior military officer. ◆◆◆◇

co·lo·nial /kəˈləʊniəl/ **colonials. 1 Colonial** means relating to countries that are colonies, or to colonialism. ...*independence from British colonial rule.* ...*the colonial civil service.* **2** People who have lived for a long time in a colony but who belong to the colonizing country are sometimes referred to as **colonials.** ...*a group of ex-colonials.* **3 Colonial** buildings or furniture were built or made in a style that was popular in America in the 17th and 18th centuries. ...*white colonial houses.* ◆◆◇◇ ADJ: ADJ n N-COUNT ADJ

co·lo·ni·al·ism /kəˈləʊniəlɪzəm/. **Colonialism** is a political system in which a powerful country directly controls other parts of the world and the people who live there. ...*the bitter oppression of slavery and colonialism.* ◆◇◇◇ N-UNCOUNT

co·lo·ni·al·ist /kəˈləʊniəlɪst/ **colonialists. 1 Colonialist** means relating to colonialism. ...*the British colonialist connection with India.* **2** A **colonialist** is a person who supports colonialism. ADJ N-COUNT

colo·nist /ˈkɒlənɪst/ **colonists. Colonists** are people who start a colony or who are among the first settlers to live in a colony. ...*the early American colonists.* ◆◇◇◇ N-COUNT

colo·nize /ˈkɒlənaɪz/ **colonizes, colonizing, colonized;** also spelled **colonise** in British English. **1** If people **colonize** a foreign country, they go to live there and take control of it. *The first British attempt to colonize Ireland was in the twelfth century.* ♦ **colo·niz·er, colonizers** *To the former Belgian colonizers, Rwanda was a paradise.* ♦ **colo·ni·za·tion** /ˌkɒlənaɪˈzeɪʃən/ ...*the European colonization of America.* **2** When large numbers of animals or plants **colonize** a place, the animals go to live there ◆◇◇◇ VERB V n N-COUNT N-UNCOUNT VERB V n

fast

or the plants start to grow there. *Toads are colonising the whole place... The area was then colonized by scrub.*

col·on·nade /ˌkɒlə'neɪd/ **colonnades.** A colonnade is a row of evenly spaced columns. N-COUNT

col·on·nad·ed /ˌkɒlə'neɪdɪd/. A **colonnaded** building has evenly spaced columns. ADJ: ADJ n

colo·ny /'kɒləni/ **colonies. 1** A **colony** is an area of the world controlled by a more powerful country. *...France's former North African colonies.* **2** You can refer to a place where a particular group of people lives as a particular kind of **colony.** *...an artists' colony in Stone City, Iowa.* **3** A **colony** of birds, insects, or animals is a group of them that live together. *The Shetlands are famed for their colonies of sea birds.* N-COUNT ♦♦◇◇◇

col·or /'kʌlə/. See **colour.**

col·ora·tion /ˌkʌlə'reɪʃən/. The **coloration** of an animal or a plant is the colours and patterns on it. *...plants with yellow or red coloration.* N-UNCOUNT

'color line. If a black person breaks the **color line,** they take part in an activity or go to a place which is usually only for white people. *...the man who broke the color line in baseball.* N-SING AMERICAN

co·los·sal /kə'lɒsəl/. If you describe something as **colossal,** you are emphasizing that it is very large. *There has been a colossal waste of public money... The task they face is colossal.* ADJ-GRADED PRAGMATICS ♦◇◇◇◇

co·los·sus /kə'lɒsəs/ **colossi** /kə'lɒsaɪ/. If you refer to someone or something as a **colossus,** you think that their abilities, influence, or achievements are extremely great. *He became a colossus of the labour movement.* N-COUNT JOURNALISM

co·los·to·my /kə'lɒstəmi/ **colostomies.** A **colostomy** is a surgical operation in which a permanent opening from the colon is made. N-COUNT MEDICAL

col·our /'kʌlə/ **colours, colouring, coloured;** spelled **color** in American English. **1** The **colour** of something is the appearance that it has as a result of the way in which it reflects light. Red, blue, and green are colours. *'What colour is the car?' – 'Red.'... Her silk dress was sky-blue, the colour of her eyes.* **2** A **colour** is a substance you use to give something a particular colour. Dyes and make-up are sometimes referred to as **colours.** *...The Body Shop Herbal Hair Colour... It is better to avoid all food colours.* **3** If you **colour** something, you use dyes, paint, or crayons to change its colour. *Many women begin colouring their hair in their mid-30s... The petals can be cooked with rice to colour it yellow.* **4** Someone's **colour** is the colour of their skin. People often use **colour** in this way to refer to a person's race. *I don't care what colour she is... Mr Taylor's colour and ethnic origins were utterly irrelevant.* **5** People **of colour** are people who belong to a race with dark skins. *Black communities spoke up to defend the rights of all people of color.* **6** A **colour** television, photograph, or picture shows things in all their colours, and not just in black, white, and grey. **7** If a film or television programme is **in colour,** it has been made so that you see the picture in all its colours, and not just in black, white, or grey. **8** **Colour** is a quality that makes something especially interesting or exciting. *She had resumed the travel necessary to add depth and colour to her novels.* ● See also *local colour.* **9** If something **colours** your opinion, it affects the way that you think about something. *The attitude of the parents toward the usefulness of what is learned must colour the way children approach school.* **10** A country's national **colours** are the colours that are particularly associated with it, such as those on its national flag. You can also use **colours** to refer to the flag itself. *...the Hungarian national colours: green, red and white... Kuwaiti troops raised the country's colors in a special ceremony.* **11** A sports team's **colours** are the colours of the clothes they wear when they play. *I was wearing the team's colours.* **12** If you pass a test **with flying colours,** you have done very well in the test. **13** If someone **nails** their **colours to the mast,** they ♦♦♦♦♦ N-COUNT N-VAR VERB Vn Vncolour N-COUNT PHRASE ADJ PHRASE N-UNCOUNT VERB Vn N-PLURAL N-PLURAL PHRASE PHRASE

say what they really think about something. **14** If you **nail your colours to** a particular **mast,** you show that you support that particular person or issue. *Mr Major had at last nailed his colours to the European mast.* PHRASE

15 If you see someone **in** their **true colours** or if they **show** their **true colours,** you realize what they are really like. *The organization has had time to show its true colours, to show its inefficiency and its bungling.* PHRASE

16 See also **coloured, colouring.**

colour in. If you **colour in** a drawing, you give it different colours using crayons or paints. *Someone had coloured in all the black and white pictures.* PHRASAL VB V P noun Also V n P

col·our·ant /'kʌlərənt/ **colourants;** spelled **colorant** in American English. A **colourant** is a substance that is used to give something a particular colour. *...a new range of hair colourants.* N-COUNT

'colour bar. In some societies, a **colour bar** is a law or rule which does not allow black people to take part in the same activities or go to the same places as white people. N-SING

'colour blind; spelled **color-blind** in American English. **1** Someone who is **colour blind** cannot see the difference between colours, especially between red and green. ♦ **col·our-blind·ness 2** A **colour blind** system or organization does not discriminate against people because of their race or nationality. ADJ N-UNCOUNT ADJ

,colour-'coded. Things that are **colour-coded** use colours to represent different features or functions. *The map is colour-coded and easy to follow.* ADJ

col·oured /'kʌləd/ **coloureds;** spelled **colored** in American English. **1** Something that is **coloured** a particular colour is that colour. *...a cluster of five roses coloured apricot orange. ...a cheap gold-coloured bracelet.* **2** Something that is **coloured** is a particular colour or combination of colours, rather than being just white, black, or the colour that it is naturally. *You can often choose between plain white or coloured and patterned scarves. ...brightly coloured silks.* **3** A **coloured** person belongs to a race of people with dark skins; many people find this use offensive. **4** Coloured people are sometimes referred to as **coloureds;** many people find this use offensive. ♦♦♦◇◇ ADJ ADJ ADJ DATED N-COUNT DATED

'colour fast. A **colour fast** fabric has a colour that will not fade when the fabric is washed or worn. ADJ

col·our·ful /'kʌləful/; spelled **colorful** in American English. **1** Something that is **colourful** has bright colours or a lot of different colours. *The flowers were colourful and the scenery magnificent. ...colorful clothes.* ♦ **col·our·ful·ly** *...dozens of colourfully dressed people.* **2** A **colourful** story is full of exciting details. *...the country's colourful and often violent history.* **3** A **colourful** character is a person who behaves in an interesting and amusing way. *Stengel was probably the most colorful character in baseball.* **4** If someone has had a **colourful** past or a **colourful** career, they have been involved in exciting but often slightly shocking things. **5** Colourful language is rude or offensive. *Bryant is alleged to have used colourful language.* ♦♦◇◇◇ ADJ-GRADED ADV-GRADED ADJ-GRADED ADJ-GRADED ADJ-GRADED ADJ-GRADED

col·our·ing /'kʌlərɪŋ/; also spelled **coloring. 1** The **colouring** of something is the colour or colours that it is. *Other countries vary the coloring of their bank notes.* **2** Someone's **colouring** is the colour of their hair, skin, and eyes. *None of them had their father's dark colouring.* **3** Colouring is a substance that is used to give colour to food. **4** See also **colour.** ♦◇◇◇◇ N-UNCOUNT N-UNCOUNT N-UNCOUNT

'colouring book, colouring books. A **colouring book** is a book of simple drawings which children can colour in. N-COUNT

col·our·ist /'kʌlərɪst/ **colourists;** spelled **colorist** in American English. **1** A **colourist** is someone such as an artist or a fashion designer who uses colours in an interesting and original way. **2** A **colourist** is a hairdresser who specializes in colouring people's hair. N-COUNT N-COUNT

col·our·less /'kʌlələs/; spelled **colorless** in American English. **1** A **colourless** substance is clear or invisible. *...a colourless, almost odourless liquid.* **2** If ADJ ADJ

someone's face is **colourless**, it is very pale, often because they are frightened or ill. **3 Colourless** people or places are dull and uninteresting. *We hurried through the colourless little town.* ADJ-GRADED

'colour scheme, colour schemes. The colour ◆◇◇◇ scheme in a room is the combination of colours N-COUNT that have been used to decorate it. *I was so pleased with the yellow colour scheme.*

,colour 'supplement, colour supplements. A N-COUNT **colour supplement** is a colour magazine which is BRITISH one of the sections of a newspaper.

colt /kəʊlt/ **colts.** A **colt** is a young male horse. *...a* ◆◇◇◇ *rangy chestnut colt.* N-COUNT

col·umn /'kɒləm/ **columns. 1** A **column** is a tall, ◆◆◇◇ often decorated cylinder of stone. *...a London land-* N-COUNT *mark, Nelson's Column. ...fluted Corinthian col-umns.* **2** A **column** is something that has a tall nar- N-COUNT row shape. *...a column of smoke.*

3 A **column** is a group of people, animals, or vehicles N-COUNT moving in a long line. *...columns of military vehicles.*

4 On a printed page, in something such as a diction- N-COUNT ary or newspaper, a **column** is one of several vertical sections which are read separately. *In The Dictionary of Quotations, there are no fewer than one and a half columns devoted to 'kiss'.*

5 In a newspaper or magazine, a **column** is a section N-COUNT that is always written by the same person or is always about the same topic. *She also writes a regular column for the Times Educational Supplement.*

6 See also **agony column, gossip column, spinal col-umn, steering column.**

col·umn·ist /'kɒləmɪst/ **columnists.** A columnist ◆◆◇◇ is a journalist who regularly writes a particular kind N-COUNT of article in a newspaper or magazine. *Clarence Page is a columnist for the Chicago Tribune.*

coma /'kəʊmə/ **comas.** Someone who is in a ◆◇◇◇ **coma** is in a state of deep unconsciousness. *She had* N-COUNT slipped into a coma.* MEDICAL

co·ma·tose /'kəʊmətəʊs/. **1** A person who is co- ADJ **matose** is in a coma. *He lived but remained in a co-* MEDICAL *matose state.* **2** A person who is **comatose** is in a ADJ deep sleep, for example because they have drunk INFORMAL too much alcohol. *Grandpa lies comatose on the sofa.*

comb /kəʊm/ **combs, combing, combed. 1** A ◆◇◇◇ **comb** is a flat piece of plastic or metal with narrow N-COUNT pointed teeth along one side, which you use to tidy your hair. **2** When you **comb** your hair, you tidy it VERB: V n using a comb. *Her reddish hair was cut short and* V-ed *neatly combed.*

3 If you **comb** a place, you search everywhere in it in VERB order to find someone or something. *Officers combed* V n for n *the woods for the murder weapon.* **4** If you **comb** VERB through information, you look at it very carefully in V through n order to find something. *It will take months to comb through all the material.*

com·bat, combats, combating or **com-** ◆◆◇◇ **batting, combated** or **combatted.** The noun is pronounced /'kɒmbæt/. The verb is pronounced /kəm'bæt/. **1 Combat** is fighting that takes place in N-UNCOUNT a war. *Over 16 million men had died in combat.* **2** A N-COUNT **combat** is a battle, or a fight between two people. VERB **3** If people in authority **combat** something, they try V n to stop it happening. *...new government measures to combat crime.*

com·bat·ant /'kɒmbətənt/ **combat-** ◆◇◇◇ **ants.** A **combatant** is a person, group, or country N-COUNT that takes part in the fighting in a war. *The two combatants fell upon one another.*

com·bat·ive /'kɒmbətɪv, AM kəm'bætɪv/. A **com-** ◆◇◇◇ **bative** person is aggressive and eager to fight or ADJ-GRADED argue. *He conducted the meeting in his usual combative style.*

com·bi·na·tion /ˌkɒmbɪ'neɪʃən/ **combinations.** ◆◆◆◇ A **combination** of things is a mixture of them. *...a* N-COUNT *fantastic combination of colours. ...the combination of science and art.*

combi'nation lock, combination locks. A N-COUNT **combination lock** is a lock which can be opened

only by turning a dial or a number of dials according to a particular series of letters or numbers.

com·bine, combines, combining, combined. ◆◆◆◇ The verb is pronounced /kəm'baɪn/. The noun is pronounced /'kɒmbaɪn/. **1** If you **combine** two or V-RECIP-ERG more things or if they **combine**, they exist together. V n with n *The Church has something to say on how to combine* pl-n V freedom with responsibility... Disease and starvation V-ed *combine to kill thousands. ...gradual industrial re-* Also V with n, *form combined with fast economic growth.* **2** If you V pl-n **combine** two or more things or if they **combine,** V-RECIP-ERG they join together to make a single thing. *David* V n with n *Jacobs was given the job of combining the data from* pl-n V *these 19 studies... Combine the flour with 3 table-* Also V n with n *spoons water... Carbon, hydrogen and oxygen com-bine chemically to form carbohydrates and fats.*

3 If someone or something **combines** two qualities or VERB features, they have both those qualities or features at V pl-n the same time. *Their system seems to combine the two* V n with n *ideals... He combines legal expertise with social con-cern.* **4** If someone **combines** two activities, they do VERB them both at the same time. *It is possible to combine a* V n with n /- *career with being a mother... He will combine the two* ing *jobs.* V pl-n

5 If two or more groups or organizations **combine** or V-RECIP-ERG if someone **combines** them, they join to form a single V pl-n group or organization. *...a joint venture that would* pl-n V *combine their brick, tile and concrete operations...* V n with n, *Different states or groups can combine to enlarge their* V n with n *markets.* **6** A **combine** is a group of people or organi- N-COUNT zations that are working or acting together. *...Veba, an energy-and-chemicals combine.*

com·bined /kəm'baɪnd/. **1** A **combined** effort or ◆◆◇◇ attack is made by two or more groups of people at ADJ: ADJ n the same time. *...the combined efforts of the host countries.* **2** The **combined** size or quantity of two ADJ: ADJ n or more things is the total of their sizes or quan-tities added together. *The five have combined assets of £9.3 billion.*

,combine 'harvester, combine harvesters. A N-COUNT **combine harvester** is a large machine used on farms to cut, sort, and clean grain.

com'bining form, combining forms. A combin- N-COUNT **ing form** is a word that is used, only when joined to another word. For example, '-legged' as in 'four-legged' and '-fold' as in 'fivefold' are combining forms.

com·bo /'kɒmbəʊ/ **combos.** A **combo** is a small N-COUNT group of musicians who play jazz, dance, or popular INFORMAL music. *...a new-wave rock combo.*

com·bus·tible /kəm'bʌstɪbəl/. **1** A **combustible** ADJ-GRADED material or gas catches fire and burns easily. *...a* FORMAL build-up of combustible vapours.* **2** A **combustible** ADJ-GRADED situation is likely to result in conflict or trouble. *We moved to less combustible talk.*

com·bus·tion /kəm'bʌstʃən/. **Combustion** is the ◆◇◇◇ act of burning something or the process of burning. N-UNCOUNT TECHNICAL

come /kʌm/ **comes, coming, came.** The form ◆◆◆◆◆ **come** is used both in the present tense and as the past participle. **1** If a person or thing **comes** to a VERB particular place, especially to a place where you are, V prep/adv they move there. *Two police officers came into the* V n *hall... We want you to come to lunch... We heard the* V -ing *train coming... Can I come too?... The sea came rush-ing in.* **2** If someone **comes** to do something, they VERB move to the place where you are in order to do it. V to-inf When they do that thing, you can say, especially in V and v British English, that they **come** and do it, or in V inf American English, that they **come** do it. *Eleanor had come to visit her... Come and meet Roger... I want you to come and see me.* **3** If you **come** to a place, you VERB reach it. *He came to a door that led into a passage-* V to n *way.*

4 If something **comes up** or **down** to a particular VERB point, it is tall enough, deep enough, or long enough V up/down to reach that point. *I wore a large shirt of Jamie's* prep *which came down over my hips.*

5 If something **comes apart** or **comes to pieces,** it VERB breaks into pieces. If something **comes off** or **comes** V adv/prep **away**, it becomes detached from something else. *The*

pistol had to be dismantleable. It had to come to pieces, easily and quickly... The door knobs came off in our hands.

6 You use **come** in expressions such as **come to an end** or **come into operation** to indicate that someone or something enters or reaches a particular state or situation. *The Communists came to power in 1944... I came into contact with very bright Harvard and Yale students... Their worst fears may be coming true.* | VERB V to-n V into n V adj

7 If someone **comes** to do something, they do it at the end of a long process or period of time. *She said it so many times that she came to believe it.* | VERB V to-inf

8 You can ask how something **came** to happen when you want to know what caused it to happen or made it possible. *How did you come to meet him?* | VERB V to-inf

9 When a particular event or time **comes**, it arrives or happens. *The announcement came after a meeting at the Home Office... The time has come for us to move on... There will come a time when the crisis will occur.* | VERB V prep/adv there V n

♦ **com·ing** ...*the coming of summer.* | N-SING

10 You can use **come** before a date, time, or event to mean when that date, time, or event arrives. For example, you can say **come the spring** to mean 'when the spring arrives'. *Come the election on the 20th of May, we will have to decide.* | PREP

11 If a thought, idea, or memory **comes to** you, you suddenly think of it or remember it. *He was about to shut the door when an idea came to him.* | VERB V to n

12 If money or property is going to **come to** you, you are going to inherit or receive it. *He did have pension money coming to him when the factory shut down.* | VERB V to n

13 If a case **comes before** a court or tribunal or **comes to** court, it is presented there so that the court or tribunal can examine it. *The membership application came before the Council of Ministers in September.* | VERB V before n Also V to n

14 If something **comes to** a particular number or amount, it adds up to it. *Lunch came to $80.* | VERB V to amount

15 If someone or something **comes from** a particular place or thing, that place or thing are their origin, source, or starting point. *Nearly half the students come from abroad... Chocolate comes from the cacao tree.* | VERB V from n

16 Something that **comes from** something else or **comes of** it is the result of it. *There is a feeling of power that comes from driving fast.* | VERB V from/of n/-ing

17 If someone or something **comes** first, next, or last, they are first, next, or last in a series, list, or competition. *The two countries have been unable to agree which step should come next.* | VERB V ord

18 If a type of thing **comes** in a particular range of colours, forms, styles, or sizes, it can have any of those colours, forms, styles, or sizes. *The wallpaper comes in black and white only.* | VERB V in n

19 You use **come** in expressions such as **it came as a surprise** when indicating a person's reaction to something that happens. *The arrest has come as a terrible shock.* | VERB V as n

20 The next subject in a discussion that you **come to** is the one that you talk about next. *Finally in the programme, we come to the news.* | VERB V to n

21 If you say that someone is, for example, **as** good **as** stupid **as they come**, you are emphasizing that they are extremely good or extremely stupid. *The new finance minister was educated at Oxford and is as financially orthodox as they come.* | PHRASE PRAGMATICS

22 You can use the expression **when it comes down to it** or **when you come down to it** for emphasis, when you are giving a general statement or conclusion. *When you come down to it, however, the basic problems of life have not changed.* | PHRASE PRAGMATICS

23 If you say that someone **has it coming to** them, you mean that they deserve everything bad that is going to happen to them, because they have done something wrong or are a bad person. | PHRASE INFORMAL

24 You use the expression **come to think of it** to indicate that you have suddenly realized something, often something obvious. *He was his distant relative, as was everyone else on the island, come to think of it.* | PHRASE PRAGMATICS

25 When you refer to a time or an event **to come** or one that is still **to come**, you are referring to a future

time or event. *The War will remain a heated topic of debate for some time to come.*

26 You can use the expression **when it comes to** or **when it comes down to** in order to introduce a new topic or a new aspect of a topic that you are talking about. *Knowing such things isn't much help when it comes to shopping and eating.* | PHRASE PRAGMATICS

27 See also **coming**, **comings and goings**.

28 Come is used in a large number of expressions which are explained under other words in this dictionary. For example, the expression **to come to terms with something** is explained at **term**.

come about. When you say how or when something **came about**, you say how or when it happened. *Any possible solution to the Irish question can only come about through dialogue... That came about when we went to Glastonbury last year.* | PHRASAL VB V P through n V P Also it V P that

come across. 1 If you **come across** something or someone, you find them or meet them by chance. *We like to identify and celebrate women's success whenever we come across it.* **2** If someone or what they are saying **comes across** in a particular way, they make that impression on people who meet them or are listening to them. *When sober he can come across as an extremely pleasant and charming young man.* | PHRASAL VB V P n V P as n Also V P adv

come along. 1 If you ask someone to **come along** to a place or event where you are going to be, you are inviting them to come with you or go there. *You're most welcome to come along.* **2** You say 'come along' to someone to encourage them to hurry up, usually when you are rather annoyed with them. *Come along, Osmond. No sense in your standing around.* **3** When something or someone **comes along**, they occur or arrive by chance. *It was lucky you came along.* **4** If something **is coming along**, it is developing or making progress. *Pentagon spokesman Williams says those talks are coming along quite well.* | PHRASAL VB PRAGMATICS V P / CONVENTION PRAGMATICS / V P / V P adv Also V P

come around or **come round. 1** If someone **comes round** to your house, they call there to see you. *Beryl came round this morning to apologize.* **2** If you **come around** to an idea, you eventually change your mind and accept it or agree with it. *It looks like they're coming around to our way of thinking.* **3** When something **comes around**, it happens as a regular or predictable event. *I hope still to be in the side when the World Cup comes around next year.* **4** When someone who is unconscious **comes round**, they recover consciousness. | PHRASAL VB V P / V P to n / V P / V P

come at. If a person or animal **comes at** you, they move towards you in a threatening way and try to attack you. *He was protecting himself from Mr Cox, who came at him with an axe.* | PHRASAL VB V P n with n Also V P n

come back. 1 If something that you had forgotten **comes back** to you, you remember it. *I'll think of his name in a moment when it comes back to me.* **2** When something **comes back**, it becomes fashionable again. *I'm glad hats are coming back.* **3** See also **comeback**. | PHRASAL VB V P to n Also V P

come back to. If you **come back to** a topic or point, you talk about it again later. *'What does that mean please?'—'I'm coming back to that.'* | PHRASAL VB V P P n

come between. If someone or something **comes between** two people, or **comes between** a person and a thing, they make the relationship or connection between them less close or happy. *He's coming between you and your work.* | PHRASAL VB V P pl-n

come by. To **come by** something means to obtain it or find it. *In rural France, English language magazines are rather hard to come by.* | PHRASAL VB V P n

come down. 1 If the cost, level, or amount of something **comes down**, it becomes less than it was before. *If you buy three bottles, the bottle price comes down to £2.42... The price of petrol is coming down by four pence a gallon.* **2** If something **comes down**, it falls to the ground. **3** See also **come-down**. | PHRASAL VB V P / V P to/from n / V P by n / V P

come down on. 1 If you **come down on** one side of an argument, you declare that you support that side. *He clearly and decisively came down on the side of President Rafsanjani.* **2** If you **come down on** someone, you criticize them severely or treat them strictly. | PHRASAL VB V P P n / V P P n

If Douglas came down hard enough on him, Dale would rebel.

come down to. If a problem or decision **comes down to** a particular thing, that thing is the most important factor involved. *Walter Crowley says the problem comes down to money.* PHRASAL VB VPPn

come down with. If you **come down with** an illness, you get it. PHRASAL VB VPPn

come for. If people such as soldiers or police **come for** you, they come to find you, usually in order to harm you or take you away, for example to prison. *Lotte was getting ready to fight if they came for her.* PHRASAL VB VPn

come forward. If someone **comes forward**, they offer to do something or to give some information in response to a request for help. *A vital witness came forward to say that she saw Tanner wearing the boots.* PHRASAL VB VP

come in. 1 If information, a report, or a telephone call **comes in**, it is received. *Reports are now coming in of trouble at yet another jail.* 2 If you have some money **coming in**, you receive it regularly as your income. *She had no money coming in and no funds.* 3 If someone **comes in** on a discussion, arrangement, or task, they join it. *Can I come in here too, on both points?* 4 If you ask where something or someone **comes in**, you are asking what their role is in a particular matter. *Finally, he could do no more, which is where Jacques came in.* 5 When a new idea, fashion, or product **comes in**, it becomes popular or available. 6 When the tide **comes in**, the water in the sea gradually moves so that it covers more of the land. PHRASAL VB VP / VPonn Also VP / VP

come in for. If someone or something **comes in for** criticism or blame, they receive it. *The plans have already come in for fierce criticism.* PHRASAL VB VPPn

come into. 1 If someone **comes into** some money or property, they inherit it. *My father has just come into a fortune in diamonds.* 2 If someone or something **comes into** a situation, they have a role in it. *We don't really know where Hortense comes into all this, Inspector.* PHRASAL VB VPn

come off. 1 If something **comes off**, it is successful or effective. *It was a good try but it didn't quite come off.* 2 If someone **comes off** worst in a contest or conflict, they are in the worst position after it. If they **come off** best, they are in the best position. *Against all odds, they came off worst during the Iran-contra inquiry.* 3 If you **come off** a drug, you stop taking it. *...people trying to come off tranquillizers.* PHRASAL VB VP / VPadv / VPn

come on. 1 You say '**Come on**' to someone to encourage them to do something. *Come on Doreen, let's dance.* 2 You say '**Come on**' to someone to encourage them to hurry up. 3 When something such as a machine or system **comes on**, it starts working or functioning. 4 If you have an illness or a headache **coming on**, you can feel it starting. 5 If a new season or type of weather **is coming on**, it is starting to arrive. *Winter was coming on again.* 6 If you say that something or someone **is coming on** well, you mean that they are developing well or making good progress. *The knee's coming on fine, I'm walking comfortably already.* PHRASAL VB CONVENTION [PRAGMATICS] CONVENTION [PRAGMATICS] VP / VP / VP / VPadv

come on to. When you **come on to** a particular topic, you start discussing it. *We're now looking at a smaller system but I'll come on to that later.* PHRASAL VB VPPn BRITISH

come out. 1 When a new product such as a book or record **comes out**, it becomes available to the public. *Christian Slater has a new movie coming out.* 2 If a fact or the truth **comes out**, it becomes known to people. *The truth is beginning to come out about what happened.* 3 If a gay person **comes out**, they let people know that they are gay. 4 To **come out** in a particular way means to be in the position or state described at the end of a process or event. *In this grim little episode of recent American history, few people come out well... So what makes a good marriage? Faithfulness comes out top of the list.* 5 If you **come out** for or against something, you declare that you support it or that you do not support it. PHRASAL VB VP / VP / VP / VPadv/prep VPadj / VPprep/adv

Helmut Kohl and Francois Mitterrand have come out in favour of direct financial aid. 6 If a group of workers **comes out** on strike, they go on strike. 7 If a photograph does not **come out**, it is blank or unclear when it is developed and printed. 8 When the sun, moon, or stars **come out**, they appear in the sky. VPprep BRITISH / VP / VP

come out in. If you **come out in** spots, you become covered with them. *When I changed to a new soap I came out in a terrible rash.* PHRASAL VB VPPn BRITISH

come out with. If you **come out with** something surprising or funny, you say it. *Everyone who heard it just burst out laughing when he came out with it.* PHRASAL VB VPn

come over. 1 If a feeling or urge **comes over** you, especially a strange or surprising one, it affects you strongly. *As I entered the corridor which led to my room that eerie feeling came over me.* 2 If someone or what they are saying **comes over** in a particular way, they make that impression on people who meet them or are listening to them. *You come over as a capable and amusing companion.* PHRASAL VB VPn / VPasn Also VPadv

come round. See **come around**. PHRASAL VB

come through. 1 To **come through** a dangerous or difficult situation means to survive it and recover from it. *The city had faced racial crisis and come through it.* 2 If a feeling or message **comes through**, it is clearly shown in what is said or done. *I hope my love for the material came through.* 3 If something **comes through**, it arrives, especially after some procedure has been carried out. *The news came through at about five o'clock on election day.* 4 If you **come through** with what is expected or needed from you, you succeed in doing or providing it. *He puts his administration at risk if he doesn't come through on these promises for reform.* PHRASAL VB VPn / VP / VP / VPon/withn Also VPforn

come to. When someone who is unconscious **comes to**, they recover consciousness. PHRASAL VB VP

come under. 1 If you **come under** attack or pressure, for example, people attack you or put pressure on you. *The police came under attack from angry crowds.* 2 If something **comes under** a particular authority, it is managed or controlled by that authority. *They were neglected before because they did not come under the Ministry of Defence.* 3 If something **comes under** a particular heading, it is in the category mentioned. *There was more news about Britain, but it came under the heading of human interest.* PHRASAL VB VPn / VPn / VP

come up. 1 If someone **comes up** or **comes up** to you, they approach you until they are standing close to you. *He came up to me and said: 'Come on, John.'* 2 If something **is coming up**, it is about to happen or take place. *We do have elections coming up.* 3 If something **comes up**, it happens unexpectedly. *I was delayed – something came up at home.* 4 If something **comes up** in a conversation or meeting, it is mentioned or discussed. 5 If a job **comes up** or if something **comes up** for sale, it becomes available. *A research fellowship came up at Girton and I applied for it... The house came up for sale.* 6 In law, when a case **comes up**, it is heard in a court of law. 7 When the sun or moon **comes up**, it rises. PHRASAL VB VP / VPton / VP / VP / VP / VPforn / VP / VP

come up against. If you **come up against** a problem or difficulty, you are faced with it and have to deal with it. *We came up against a great deal of resistance in dealing with the case.* PHRASAL VB VPPn

come up for. If something **comes up** for consideration or action of some kind, the time arrives when it has to be considered or dealt with. *The TV rights contract came up for renegotiation in 1988.* PHRASAL VB VPforn

come upon. 1 If you **come upon** someone or something, you meet them or find them by chance. *I came upon an irresistible item at a yard sale.* 2 If an attitude or feeling **comes upon** you, it begins to affect you. *A sense of impending doom came upon all of us.* PHRASAL VB VPn / VPn LITERARY

come up to. To be **coming up to** a time or state means to be getting near to it. *It's just coming up to ten minutes past eleven now.* PHRASAL VB VPPn

come up with. If you **come up with** something, you are able to produce it or provide it. *Several of the* PHRASAL VB VPPn

members have come up with suggestions of their own...
If Warren can come up with the $15 million, we'll go to
London.

come·back /'kʌmbæk/ **comebacks. 1** If some- ◆◆◇◇◇
one such as an entertainer or sports personality N-COUNT
makes a **comeback**, they return to their profession
or sport after a period of absence. **2** If something N-COUNT
makes a **comeback**, it becomes fashionable again.
Tight fitting T-shirts are making a comeback. **3** If N-UNCOUNT
you have no **comeback** when someone has done with brd-neg
something wrong to you, there is nothing you can
do to have them punished or held responsible, for
example because the law or a rule prevents it.

co·median /kə'miːdiən/ **comedians.** A comedian ◆◆◇◇◇
is an entertainer whose job is to make people laugh, N-COUNT
by telling jokes or funny stories.

co·medic /kə'miːdɪk/. **Comedic** means relating to ADJ
comedy. *She brings an unsuspected comedic touch* FORMAL
to her role.

co·medi·enne /kə,miːdi'en/ **comediennes.** A co- N-COUNT
medienne is a female comedian.

'come·down; also spelled **comedown.** If you say ◆◆◇◇◇
that something is **a come-down**, you think that it is N-SING:
not as good as something else that you have just aN
done or had. *After getting your degree and being on*
a high, it's quite a comedown to experience constant
rejection.

com·edy /'kɒmədi/ **comedies. 1 Comedy** con- ◆◆◆◇◇
sists of types of entertainment, such as plays and N-UNCOUNT
films, or particular scenes in them, that are intended to make people laugh. *...his career in comedy.*
...a TV comedy series. **2** A **comedy** is a play, film, or N-COUNT
television programme that is intended to make
people laugh. **3** The **comedy** of a situation involves N-UNCOUNT
those aspects of it that make you laugh. *Jackie sees*
the comedy in her millionaire husband's thrifty hab-
its. **4** See also **situation comedy.**

come·ly /'kʌmli/ **comelier, comeliest.** A comely ADJ-GRADED
woman is attractive. *...a comely young woman with* DATED
high cheekbones.

'come-on, come-ons. A come-on is a gesture or N-COUNT
remark which someone makes in order to encour- INFORMAL
age another person to make sexual advances to
them.

com·ers /'kʌməz/. If a contest or sporting event is ◆◇◇◇◇
open to **all comers**, anyone is allowed to take part PHRASE
in it or challenge the champion.

com·et /'kɒmɪt/ **comets.** A comet is an object ◆◆◇◇◇
that travels around the sun leaving a bright trail be- N-COUNT
hind it. *Halley's Comet is going to come back in*
2061.

come·up·pance /,kʌm'ʌpəns/. If you say that N-SING
someone has got their **comeuppance**, you approve [PRAGMATICS]
of the fact that they have been punished or have INFORMAL
suffered for something wrong that they have done.
...a bad man who shoots people and gets his
comeuppance.

com·fort /'kʌmfət/ **comforts, comforting,** ◆◆◆◇◇
comforted. 1 If you are doing something in com- N-UNCOUNT
fort, you are physically relaxed and contented, and
are not feeling any pain or other unpleasant sensations. *The shoe has padding around the collar, heel*
and tongue for added comfort.
2 Comfort is a style of life in which you have enough N-UNCOUNT
money to have everything you need. *...ordering our*
busy lives so that we can live in comfort. **3** Comforts N-COUNT
are things which make your life easier and more
pleasant, such as electrical devices you have in your
home. ● See also **creature comforts.**
4 Comfort is a feeling of relief from worries or unhap- N-UNCOUNT
piness. *He found comfort in Eva's blind faith in him.*
● See also **cold comfort. 5** If you refer to a person, N-COUNT
thing, or idea as a **comfort**, you mean that they help
you to stop worrying or they make you feel less unhappy. *It's a comfort talking to you.* **6** If you comfort VERB
someone, you make them feel less worried, unhappy, Vn
or upset, for example by saying kind things to them.
Ned put his arm around her, trying to comfort her.
♦ com·fort·er, comforters *He became Vivien* N-COUNT
Leigh's devoted friend and comforter.

7 If you say that something is, for example, **too close** PHRASE
for comfort, you mean you are worried because it is
closer than you would like it to be. *The bombs fell in*
the sea, many too close for comfort.

com·fort·able /'kʌmftəbəl/. **1** If something such ◆◆◆◇◇
as furniture or clothing is **comfortable**, it makes you ADJ-GRADED
feel physically relaxed when you use it, for example
because it is soft or warm. *...a comfortable fireside*
chair. **♦ comfortably** *...the comfortably furnished* ADV-GRADED
living-room. **2** If you are **comfortable**, you are ADJ-GRADED
physically relaxed and at ease because of the place
or position you are sitting or lying in. *Lie down on*
your bed and make yourself comfortable.
♦ comfortably *Are you sitting comfortably?* ADV-GRADED
3 If you say that someone is **comfortable**, you mean ADJ-GRADED
that they have enough money to be able to live with-
out financial problems. **♦ comfortably** *Cayton de-* ADV-GRADED
scribes himself as comfortably well-off. **4** A comfort- ADJ-GRADED
able life, job, or situation does not cause you any
problems or worries.
5 In a race, competition, or election, if you are in a ADJ-GRADED:
comfortable position, you are likely to win it easily. If ADJ n
you gain a **comfortable** victory, you win it easily.
♦ comfortably *...the Los Angeles Raiders, who com-* ADV-GRADED
fortably beat the Bears earlier in the season.
6 If you feel **comfortable** with a particular situation or ADJ-GRADED:
person, you feel confident and relaxed with them. *I'll* v-link ADJ
talk to them, but I won't feel comfortable about it.
7 If a sick or injured person is said to be **comfortable**, ADJ
they are in a stable physical condition. *He was de-*
scribed as comfortable in hospital last night.

com·fort·ably /'kʌmftəbli/. **1** If someone does ◆◇◇◇◇
something **comfortably**, they do it easily. *Only take* ADV-GRADED:
upon yourself those things that you know you can ADV with v
manage comfortably. **2** If someone is **comfortably** PHRASE
off, they have enough money to be able to live without financial problems. **3** See also **comfortable.**

com·fort·er /'kʌmfətə/ **comforters.** A comforter N-COUNT
is a large cover filled with feathers or similar ma- AMERICAN
terial which you put over yourself in bed instead of
a sheet and blankets. The usual British word is **du-**
vet. ● See also **comfort.**

com·fort·ing /'kʌmfətɪŋ/. If something is **com-** ◆◇◇◇◇
forting, it makes you feel less worried or unhappy. ADJ-GRADED
My mother had just died and I found the book very
comforting. **♦ com·fort·ing·ly** *'Everything's under* ADV-GRADED
control here,' her mother said comfortingly.

com·frey /'kʌmfri/. **Comfrey** is a herb that is used N-UNCOUNT
to make drinks and medicines.

com·fy /'kʌmfi/ **comfier, comfiest. Comfy** ADJ-GRADED
means the same as comfortable. *Loose-fitting shirts* INFORMAL
are comfy. ...a comfy chair.

com·ic /'kɒmɪk/ **comics. 1** If something is **comic**, ◆◆◇◇◇
it makes you laugh, or is intended to make you ADJ-GRADED
laugh. *The novel is comic and tragic.* **2** Comic is ADJ: ADJ n
used to describe comedy as a form of entertain-
ment, and the people who perform it. *Grodin is a*
fine comic actor. **3** A **comic** is an entertainer who N-COUNT
tells jokes in order to make people laugh. **4** A **comic** N-COUNT
is a magazine that contains stories told in pictures. BRITISH
The usual American term is **comic book.**

comi·cal /'kɒmɪkəl/. If something is **comical**, it ◆◇◇◇◇
makes you want to laugh because it seems funny or ADJ-GRADED
silly. *Her expression is almost comical.* **♦ comi·cal·**
·ly /'kɒmɪkli/ *She raised her eyebrows comically.* ADV-GRADED

'comic book, comic books. A comic book is a ◆◇◇◇◇
magazine that contains stories told in pictures. The N-COUNT
usual British word is **comic.** AMERICAN

'comic strip, comic strips. A comic strip is a se- N-COUNT
ries of drawings that tell a story.

com·ing /'kʌmɪŋ/. A **coming** event or time will ◆◆◆◆◆
happen soon. *This obviously depends on the weather* ADJ: ADJ n
in the coming months. ● See also **come.**

,coming of 'age. 1 When something reaches an N-SING:
important stage of development and is accepted by with supp
a large number of people, you can refer to this as its
coming of age. *...postwar Germany's final coming-*
of-age as an independent sovereign state.
2 Someone's **coming of age** is the time when they N-SING:
legally become an adult. with poss

,**comings and 'goings.** The **comings and goings** N-PLURAL:
of people are their arrivals and departures at a par- with poss
ticular place. *Crowds of Somalis gather to watch the
comings and goings of the journalists.*

com·ma /'kɒmə/ **commas.** A comma is the punc- N-COUNT
tuation mark (,) which is used to separate parts of a
sentence or items in a list.

com·mand /kə'mɑːnd, -'mænd/ **commands,** ♦♦♦♦◇◇
commanding, commanded. 1 If someone in VERB:
authority **commands** you to do something, they tell V n to-inf
you to do it. *'Get in your car and follow me,' he com-* V with quote
manded... He commanded that roads be built to link Also V n
castles across the land. ▶ Also a noun. *The tanker* N-VAR
failed to respond to a command to stop. **2** A **com-** N-COUNT
mand is an instruction that you give to a computer.
3 If you **command** something such as respect or VB: no cont
obedience, you obtain it because you are popular, fa- V n
mous, or important. *...an excellent physician who
commanded the respect of all his colleagues.* **4** If N-UNCOUNT
someone has **command** of a situation, they have control of it because they have, or seem to have, power or
authority. *Mr Baker would take command of the cam-*
paign. **5** Your **command** of something such as a for- N-UNCOUNT:
eign language is your knowledge of it and your ability N of n
to use this knowledge. *...a singer with a natural com-*
mand of melody. **6** If you have a particular skill or par- PHRASE
ticular resources **at** your **command,** you have them FORMAL
and can use them fully. *The country should have the
right to defend itself with all legal means at its
command.*
7 If an army or country **commands** a place, they have VERB
total control over it. *Yemen commands the strait at the* V n
southern end of the Red Sea. ▶ Also a noun. *...the* N-UNCOUNT
struggle for command of the air.
8 An officer who **commands** part of an army, navy, or VERB
air force is responsible for controlling and organizing V n
it. *...the French general who commands the UN troops* Also V
in Bosnia. ...Lieutenant Tom Dinsdale, the command-
ing officer at this checkpoint. ▶ Also a noun. *In 1942* N-UNCOUNT
he took command of 108 Squadron. **9** In the armed N-COLL-
forces, a **command** is a part of an army or air force in COUNT
charge of a particular function. *...the Strategic Air
Command.* **10** See also **high command, second-in-**
command.
11 If a place **commands** a view, especially an impres- VB: no cont
sive one, you can see the view clearly from that place. PRAGMATICS
The house commanded some splendid views of Dela- V ii
ware Bay. FORMAL

com·man·dant /'kɒməndænt/ **commandants.** A ♦◇◇◇◇
commandant is an army officer in charge of a par- N-COUNT;
ticular place or group of people. N-TITLE

com,mand e'conomy, command economies. N-COUNT
In a **command economy,** business activities and the
allocation of resources are determined by the government, not by market forces.

com·man·deer /,kɒmən'dɪə/ **commandeers,**
commandeering, commandeered. 1 If the VERB: V n
armed forces **commandeer** a vehicle or building
owned by someone else, they officially take charge
of it so that they can use it. **2** If someone **comman-** VERB
deers something owned by someone else, they take V n
charge of it so that they can use it. *The hijacker
commandeered the plane on a domestic flight.*

com·mand·er /kə'mɑːndə, -'mænd-/ **command-** ♦♦♦◇◇
ers. 1 The **commander** of a military operation or N-COUNT
organization is the officer in charge. **2** A **command-** N-COUNT;
er is an officer in the navy. N-TITLE

com,mander-in-'chief, **commanders-in-** N-COUNT;
chief. A **commander-in-chief** is an officer in char- N-TITLE
ge of all the forces in a particular area.

com·mand·ing /kə'mɑːndɪŋ, -'mænd-/. **1** If you
are in a **commanding** position or situation, you are ADJ-GRADED
in a strong or powerful position or situation. *The
French vessel has a commanding lead.* **2** If you de- ADJ-GRADED
scribe someone as **commanding,** you mean that PRAGMATICS
they are powerful and confident; used showing approval. *The voice at the other end of the line was serious and commanding.* **3** If a building has a **com-** ADJ-GRADED
manding position, it is high up and has good views
of the surrounding area. *What other home offers*

such a commanding view of the capital? **4** See also
command.

com·mand·ment /kə'mɑːndmənt, -'mænd-/ **com-** N-COUNT
mandments. The Ten **Commandments** are the
ten rules of behaviour which, according to the Old
Testament of the Bible, people should obey.

com·man·do /kə'mɑːndəʊ, -'mænd-/ **comman-** ♦◇◇◇◇
dos or **commandoes. 1** A **commando** is soldier N-COUNT
who is a member of a group who have been special-
ly trained to carry out raids. **2** A **commando** is a N-COUNT
group of commandoes. *...a small commando of
marines.*

com'mand post, command posts. A command N-COUNT
post is a place from which a commander in the
army controls and organizes his forces.

com·memo·rate /kə'meməreɪt/ **commemo-** ♦♦◇◇◇
rates, commemorating, commemorated. To VERB: V n
commemorate an important event or person be V-ed
means to remember them by means of a special action or ceremony, or a specially created object. *The
200th anniversary of Mozart's death is being commemorated with concerts featuring his work.*
♦ **com·memo·ra·tion** /kə,memə'reɪʃən/ **com-** N-VAR
memorations *...the 50th Anniversary Commemo-
ration of the Warsaw Ghetto Uprising.*

com·memo·ra·tive /kə'memərətɪv/. A **com-** ♦◇◇◇◇
memorative object or event is intended to make ADJ: ADJ n
people remember an event or person. *...a com-
memorative plaque.*

com·mence /kə'mens/ **commences, com-** ♦◇◇◇◇
mencing, commenced. When something com- V-ERG: V
mences or you **commence** it, it begins. *They com-* V n/-ing
menced a systematic search. FORMAL

com·mence·ment /kə'mensmənt/. **1** The **com-** N-UNCOUNT
mencement of something is its beginning. *All appli-* FORMAL
*cants should be at least 16 years of age at the com-
mencement of this course.* **2** In the United States, N-SING
commencement is a ceremony at a university in
which graduates formally receive their degrees.

com·mend /kə'mend/ **commends, commend-** ♦◇◇◇◇
ing, commended. 1 If you **commend** someone VERB
or something, you praise them formally. *I com-* V n for/on n/
mended her for that action. ♦ **com·men·da·tion** -ing
/,kɒmen'deɪʃən/ **commendations** *The Company* Also V n
received a commendation from the Royal Society of N-COUNT
Arts. **2** If someone **commends** something or some- VERB
one **to** you, they tell you that you will find them V n to n
good or useful. *I can commend it to him as a realistic course of action.* **3** If something **commends** itself VERB
to you, you approve of it. *The Rousseau model com-* V pron-refl to
mended itself to a lot of early socialists.

com·mend·able /kə'mendəbəl/. If you describe ♦◇◇◇◇
someone's behaviour as **commendable,** you ap- ADJ-GRADED
prove of it or are praising it. *Mr Sparrow has acted* PRAGMATICS
with commendable speed. ♦ **com·mend·ably** *Her* FORMAL
manner was commendably restrained. ADV-GRADED

com·men·su·rate /kə'mensərət/. If the level of ADJ
one thing is **commensurate** with another, the first FORMAL
level is in proportion to the second. *Employees are
paid salaries commensurate with those of teachers.*

com·ment /'kɒment/ **comments, commenting,** ♦♦♦♦◇
commented. 1 If you **comment** on something, VERB:
you give your opinion about it or you make a state- V on n/wh
ment about it. *Stuart commented that this was very* V that
true. ▶ Also a noun. *He made his comments at a* Also V,
news conference... Lady Thatcher, who is abroad, V with quote
was not available for comment. **2** People say 'no CONVENTION
comment' as a way of refusing to answer a question, usually when it is asked by a journalist. **3** If N-SING
you say that an event or situation is a **comment** on
something, you mean that it reveals something,
usually something bad, about that thing. *He argues
that family problems are typically a comment on
some unresolved issues in the family.*

com·men·tary /'kɒməntri, AM -teri/ **commen-** ♦♦◇◇◇
taries. 1 A **commentary** is a description of an N-VAR
event while the event is taking place, for example a
description on radio or television. *He gave the listening crowd a running commentary.* **2** A **commen-** N-COUNT
tary is an article, book, or other piece of writing

which explains or discusses something. *Mr Rich will be writing a twice-weekly commentary on American society and culture.*

com·men·tate /ˈkɒmənteɪt/ **commentates, commentating, commentated.** To **commentate** means to give a radio or television commentary on an event. *They are in Sweden to commentate on the European Championships.*
◆◇◇◇◇ VERB V on n Also V

com·men·ta·tor /ˈkɒmənteɪtə/ **commentators.** **1** A **commentator** is a broadcaster who gives a radio or television commentary on an event. **2** A **commentator** is someone who often writes or broadcasts about a particular subject. *...Hugo Young, the political commentator of the Guardian.*
◆◆◆◇◇ N-COUNT
N-COUNT

com·merce /ˈkɒmɜːs/. **Commerce** is the activities and procedures involved in buying and selling things. *They have made their fortunes from industry and commerce.* ● See also **chamber of commerce.**
◆◆◆◇◇ N-UNCOUNT

com·mer·cial /kəˈmɜːʃəl/ **commercials. 1** Commercial means involving or relating to the buying and selling of goods. *...industrial and commercial activity.* **2 Commercial** organizations, activities, and products are concerned with making money or profits, rather than, for example, with scientific research or providing a public service. *British Rail has indeed become more commercial over the last decade. ...the commercial exploitation of forests.* ♦ **com·mer·cial·ly** *Designers are becoming more commercially minded... It was the first commercially available machine to employ artificial intelligence.* **3** A **commercial** vehicle is used for carrying goods or for taking passengers who pay to travel in it. **4 Commercial** television and radio are paid for by the broadcasting of advertisements, rather than by the government. **5** A **commercial** is an advertisement that is broadcast on television or radio. **6** If you use **commercial** to describe something such as a film or a type of music, you mean that it is intended to be popular, and does not have much originality or artistic merit. *There's a feeling among a lot of people that music has become too commercial.*
◆◆◆◆◇ ADJ
ADJ-GRADED
ADV-GRADED
ADJ
ADJ
N-COUNT
ADJ-GRADED

com,mercial 'bank, commercial banks. A **commercial bank** is a large bank with many branches. Commercial banks operate current and deposit accounts and make short-term loans.
◆◇◇◇◇ N-COUNT

com·mer·cial·ism /kəˈmɜːʃəlɪzəm/. **Commercialism** is the practice of making a lot of money from things without caring about their quality; used showing disapproval.
N-UNCOUNT
[PRAGMATICS]

com·mer·cial·ize /kəˈmɜːʃəlaɪz/ **commercializes, commercializing, commercialized;** also spelled **commercialise** in British English. If something **is commercialized,** it is used or changed in such a way that it makes money or profits, often in a way that people disapprove of. *It seems such a pity that a distinguished and honored name should be commercialized in such a manner.* ♦ **com·mer·ciali·za·tion** /kəˌmɜːʃəlaɪˈzeɪʃən/ *...the commercialization of Christmas.* ♦ **com·mer·cial·ized** *Rock'n'roll has become so commercialized and safe since punk.*
VERB be V-ed Also V n
N-UNCOUNT
ADJ-GRADED

com·mie /ˈkɒmi/ **commies.** A **commie** is someone who believes in communism; an offensive word.
N-COUNT AMERICAN

com·mis·er·ate /kəˈmɪzəreɪt/ **commiserates, commiserating, commiserated.** If you **commiserate with** someone, you show them pity or sympathy when something unpleasant has happened to them. *When I lost, he commiserated with me.* ♦ **com·mis·era·tion** /kəˌmɪzəˈreɪʃən/ **commiserations** *Our congratulations go to the winner, and commiserations to all those who came close.*
VERB V with n
N-UNCOUNT: also N in pl

com·mis·sary /ˈkɒmɪsəri, AM -seri/ **commissaries.** A **commissary** is a shop that provides food and equipment in a place such as a military camp or a prison.
N-COUNT AMERICAN

com·mis·sion /kəˈmɪʃən/ **commissions, commissioning, commissioned. 1** If you **commission** something or **commission** someone to do something, you formally arrange for someone to do a piece of work for you, which you usually pay them
◆◆◆◆◇ VERB: V n V n to-inf V-ed

for. *You can commission them to paint something especially for you. ...specially commissioned reports.* ▶ Also a noun. *He approached John Wexley with a commission to write the screenplay of the film.* ♦ **-commissioned** *...Government-commissioned research.*
N-COUNT
COMB

2 Commission is a sum of money paid to a salesperson for every sale that he or she makes. If a salesperson is paid **on commission,** the amount they are paid depends on the amount they sell. **3** If a bank or other company charges **commission,** they charge a fee for providing a service, for example for exchanging money or for issuing an insurance policy.
N-VAR
N-UNCOUNT

4 A **commission** is a group of people who have been appointed to find out about something or to control something. *...the Press Complaints Commission.* **5** See also **High Commission. 6** The **commission** of a crime is the act of committing it. *...an organisation which is actively engaged in the commission of criminal terrorist acts.* **7** If a member of the armed forces receives a **commission,** he or she becomes an officer. **8** If a member of the armed forces **is commissioned,** he or she is made an officer. *He was commissioned as second lieutenant in the Air Force... Only commissioned officers qualify for the Military Cross.* **9** If something such as a ship or machine is **out of commission,** it is broken and cannot be used until it is repaired. *The operator expects the ship to be out of commission until the end of September.*
N-COLL-COUNT
N-UNCOUNT FORMAL
N-COUNT
VB: usu passive beV-ed as n V-ed Also beV-ed
PHRASE

com·mis·sion·er /kəˈmɪʃənə/ **commissioners.** A **commissioner** is an important official in a government department or other organization. *...the European Commissioner for External Affairs.* ● See also **High Commissioner.**
◆◆◆◇◇ N-COUNT

com·mit /kəˈmɪt/ **commits, committing, committed. 1** If someone **commits** a crime or a sin, they do something illegal or bad. *This is a man who has committed murder.* **2** If someone **commits** suicide, they deliberately kill themselves. **3** If you **commit** money or resources to something, you decide to use the money or resources for a particular purpose. *He should not commit American troops without the full consent of Congress.* **4** If you **commit** yourself to a decision or way of life, you accept it fully or definitely decide to act in that way. If you **commit** yourself to a person, you definitely decide that your relationship will be a long-term one. *I'd like a friendship that might lead to something deeper, but I wouldn't want to commit myself too soon.* ♦ **com·mit·ted** *He was a committed socialist.* ♦ **commitment, commitments** *...commitment to the ideals of Bolshevism... They made a commitment to peace.* **5** If you do not want to **commit** yourself on something, you do not want to say what you really think about it or what you are going to do. *She didn't want to commit herself one way or the other.* **6** If you **commit** something **to** paper or to writing, you record it by writing it down. If you **commit** something **to** memory, you memorize it. **7** If someone **is committed** to a hospital, prison, or other institution, they are officially sent there for a period of time. **8** In the British legal system, if someone **is committed for** trial, they are sent by magistrates to stand trial in a crown court. ♦ **com·mit·tal** /kəˈmɪtəl/ **committals** *...committal proceedings.*
◆◆◆◆◇ VERB V n
VERB: V n
VERB: V n to/for n V n
VERB: V pron-refl to -ing/n V pron-refl Also V n, V n to n
ADJ-GRADED
N-VAR
VB: with brd-neg V pron-refl Also V pron-refl on n
VERB: V n to n
VERB: beV-ed to n
VERB: beV-ed for n
N-VAR

com·mit·ment /kəˈmɪtmənt/ **commitments.** A **commitment** is something which regularly takes up some of your time because of an agreement you have made or because of responsibilities you have. *I've got a lot of commitments.* ● See also **commit.**
◆◆◇◇◇ N-COUNT

com·mit·tee /kəˈmɪti/ **committees.** A **committee** is a group of people who meet to make decisions or plans for a larger group or organization that they represent. *...the Committee for Safety in Medicine.*
◆◆◆◆◆ N-COLL-COUNT

com·mode /kəˈməʊd/ **commodes.** A **commode** is a movable piece of furniture shaped like a chair or a stool, which has a large pot below or inside it. It is
N-COUNT

used as a toilet, especially by people who are too ill to be able to walk to the toilet easily.

com·mod·i·ty /kə'mɒdɪti/ **commodities.** Anything which is sold on a large scale can be referred to as a **commodity**. *The government increased prices on several basic commodities like bread and meat.* ◆◆◇◇◇ N-COUNT TECHNICAL

com·mo·dore /'kɒmədɔ:/ **commodores.** A **commodore** is a senior officer in the navy. ◆◇◇◇◇ N-COUNT; N-TITLE

com·mon /'kɒmən/ **commoner commonest; commons. 1** If something is **common**, it is found in large numbers or it happens often. *His name was Hansen, a common name in Norway... Oil pollution is the commonest cause of death for seabirds.* ◆◆◆◆◆ ADJ-GRADED

♦ **com·mon·ly** *Parsley is probably the most commonly used of all herbs.* **2 Common** is used to indicate that someone or something is of the ordinary kind and not special in any way. *...common salt.* ADV-GRADED ADJ: ADJ n

3 When there are more animals or plants of a particular species than there are of related species, then the first species is often called **common**. *...the common house fly.* ADJ: ADJ n

4 If you talk about **common** decency or **common** courtesy, you are referring to the decency or courtesy which most people have. You usually say this when someone has not shown these characteristics in their behaviour. *...if he'd had the common courtesy to ask permission.* ADJ PRAGMATICS

5 If something is **common** to two or more people or groups, it is done, possessed, or used by them all. *Moldavians and Romanians share a common language.* ADJ

6 If two or more things have something **in common**, they have the same characteristic or feature. *In common with most Italian lakes, access to the shores of Orta is restricted.* **7** If two or more people have something **in common**, they share the same interests or experiences. PHRASE

8 You can use the word **common** to describe knowledge, an opinion, or a feeling that is shared by people in general. *It is common knowledge that swimming is one of the best forms of exercise.* ADJ: ADJ n

♦ **commonly** *A little adolescent rebellion is commonly believed to be healthy.* **9** See also **lowest common denominator.** ADV; ADV -ed

10 If you describe someone as **common**, you mean that there is some aspect of them, such as their speech, clothing, or manners, which shows bad qualities that are thought to be characteristic of the lower social classes. Used showing disapproval. ADJ-GRADED PRAGMATICS

11 A **common** is an area of grassy land, usually in or near a village or small town, where the public is allowed to go. N-COUNT

12 The **Commons** is used to refer to the House of Commons or its members. *The Prime Minister is to make a statement in the Commons this afternoon.* N-COLL-PROPER

13 ● to **make common cause with** someone: see **cause.** ● **common ground:** see **ground.**

com·mon·al·ity /kɒmə'nælɪti/ **commonalities.** Commonality is used to refer to a feature or purpose that is shared by two or more people or things. *We don't have the same commonality of interest.* N-VAR FORMAL

common 'cold, common colds. The **common cold** is a mild illness. If you have it, your nose is blocked, you sneeze a lot, and you have a sore throat or a cough. N-COUNT

common 'currency. If an idea or belief has become **common currency**, it is widely used and accepted. *The story that she was trapped in a loveless marriage became common currency.* N-UNCOUNT

common de'nominator, common denominators. 1 A **common denominator** of a group of fractions is a number which all the denominators of the fractions can be divided into. **2** A **common denominator** is a characteristic or attitude that is shared by all members of a group. *Narcissism is the common denominator for our customers.* N-COUNT TECHNICAL N-COUNT

com·mon·er /'kɒmənə/ **commoners.** In countries which have a nobility, **commoners** are the people who are not members of the nobility. ◆◇◇◇◇ N-COUNT

common 'land, common lands. Common land is land which everyone is allowed to go on. N-UNCOUNT: also N in pl

common 'law; also spelled **common-law. 1 Common law** is the system of law which is based on judges' decisions and on custom rather than on written laws. **2** A **common law** relationship is regarded as a marriage because it has lasted a long time, although no official marriage contract has been signed. *...his common law wife.* ◆◇◇◇◇ N-UNCOUNT ADJ: ADJ n

common 'market, common markets. 1 A **common market** is an organization of countries who have agreed to trade freely with each other and make common decisions about industry and agriculture. *...the Central American Common Market.* **2** The **Common Market** is the former name of the European Union. Some people still refer to the European Union as the **Common Market.** ◆◇◇◇◇ N-COUNT N-PROPER: the N

common 'noun, common nouns. A **common noun** is a noun such as 'tree', 'water', or 'beauty' that is not the name of one particular person or thing. Compare **proper noun.** N-COUNT

common-or-'garden. You can use **common-or-garden** to describe something you think is ordinary and not special in any way. *These crumbs were grated on a common-or-garden cheese grater.* ADJ: ADJ n BRITISH

common·place /'kɒmənpleɪs/ **commonplaces. 1** If something is **commonplace**, it happens often or is often found, and is therefore not surprising. *Foreign vacations have become commonplace.* **2** A **commonplace** is something that happens often or is often found. *It's become a commonplace to see people collapsing from hunger in the streets.* **3** A **commonplace** is a remark or opinion that is often expressed and is therefore not original or interesting. *It is a commonplace to say that Northern Ireland is a backwater in the modern Europe.* ◆◇◇◇◇ ADJ-GRADED N-COUNT N-COUNT

'common room, common rooms. A **common room** is a room in a university or school where people can sit, talk, and relax. N-COUNT

common 'sense; also spelled **commonsense.** Your **common sense** is your natural ability to make good judgements and to behave in a practical and sensible way. *Use your common sense. ...a common-sense approach.* ◆◆◇◇◇ N-UNCOUNT

common·wealth /'kɒmənwelθ/. **1** The **Commonwealth** is a voluntary association of independent countries, consisting of the United Kingdom and most of the countries that were formerly under its rule. *...Commonwealth countries.* **2 Commonwealth** is used in the official names of some countries, groups of countries, or parts of countries. *...the Commonwealth of Independent States.* **3** If you refer to a **commonwealth** of nations, you are referring to a group of countries who are friendly towards each other and have something in common. ◆◆◇◇◇ N-PROPER: the N N-SING: the N of n N-SING FORMAL

com·mo·tion /kə'məʊʃən/ **commotions.** A **commotion** is a lot of noise, confusion, and excitement. *Sounds of voices and commotion could be heard downstairs.* ◆◇◇◇◇ N-VAR

com·mu·nal /'kɒmjunəl, AM kə'mju:nəl/. **1** Communal means relating to particular groups in a country or society. *Communal violence broke out in different parts of the country.* **2** You use communal to describe something that is shared by a group of people. *...communal ownership.* ♦ **com·mu·nal·ly** *Meals are taken communally in the dining room.* ◆◆◇◇◇ ADJ: ADJ n ADJ ADV: ADV after v

com·mune, communes, communing, communed. The noun is pronounced /'kɒmju:n/. The verb is pronounced /kə'mju:n/. **1** A **commune** is a group or community of people who live together and share everything. **2** If you say that someone is **communing with** an animal or spirit, or with nature, you mean that they appear to be communicating with it. *He was so happy communing with the dolphin in Dingle Bay.* ◆◇◇◇◇ N-COUNT VERB V with n LITERARY

com·mu·ni·cable /kə'mju:nɪkəbəl/. A **communicable** disease can be passed on from one person to another. ADJ MEDICAL

com·mu·ni·cant /kə'mju:nɪkənt/ **communicants.** A **communicant** is a person in the Christian church who receives communion. N-COUNT FORMAL

com·mu·ni·cate /kə'mju:nɪkeɪt/ **communi-** ◆◆◆◇◇
cates, communicating, communicated. 1 If V-RECIP
you **communicate** with someone, you share or ex- V with n
change information with them, for example by pl-n V
speaking, writing, or using equipment. You can also
say that two people **communicate**. *Officials of the
CIA depend heavily on electronic mail to communicate with each other... They communicated in sign
language.* ♦ **communication** *Lithuania hasn't had* N-UNCOUNT
any direct communication with Moscow. **2** If one V-RECIP:
person **communicates** with another, they success- V with n
fully make each other aware of their feelings and V with n
ideas. You can also say that two people **communi-** Also pl-n V
cate. *Family therapy showed us how to communicate with each other.* ♦ *communi- ...communi-* N-UNCOUNT
nication skills. ♦ **com·mu·ni·ca·tor, communi-** N-COUNT
cators *She's a good communicator.* **3** If you VERB:
communicate information, a feeling, or an idea to V n to n
someone, you let them know about it. *People must* V n
communicate their feelings.

com·mu·ni·ca·tion /kə,mju:nɪ'keɪʃən/ **commu-** ◆◆◆◇◇
nications. 1 Communications are the systems N-PLURAL
and processes that are used to communicate or
broadcast information, especially by means of electricity or radio waves. *...a communications satellite.*
2 A **communication** is a message that is sent to N-COUNT
someone by, for example, making a telephone call, FORMAL
or by sending a letter or a fax. *The ambassador has
brought with him a communication from the
President.*

com·mu·ni·ca·tive /kə'mju:nɪkətɪv/. A **communi-** ADJ-GRADED
cative person talks willingly or easily to other people, for example about his or her feelings. *She has
become a lot more tolerant and communicative.*

com·mun·ion /kə'mju:njən/. **1 Communion** with ◆◇◇◇◇
nature or some other power or spirit, or **commun-** N-UNCOUNT:
ion with a person is the feeling that you are sharing also a N
thoughts or feelings with them.
2 Communion is the Christian ceremony in which N-UNCOUNT
people eat bread and drink wine in memory of
Christ's death. *...the Communion service.*

com·mu·ni·qué /kə'mju:nɪkeɪ, AM -'keɪ/ **commu-** ◆◇◇◇◇
niqués. A **communiqué** is an official statement or N-COUNT
announcement. *Representatives of Jordan, Syria,* FORMAL
*and Lebanon issued a joint communiqué today after
a two-day meeting in Amman.*

com·mun·ist /'kɒmjʊnɪst/ **communists.** A **com-** ◆◆◆◇◇
munist is someone who supports a political system N-COUNT
in which everybody is equal and in which workers
control industry and business. *Some people think
such a system existed in the Soviet Union between
1917 and 1991.* ► *Also an adjective. ...the Commun-* ADJ
ist Party. ♦ **com·mun·ism** /'kɒmjʊnɪzəm/. **Com-** N-UNCOUNT
munism means communist political systems or beliefs. *...the collapse of Communism in Eastern
Europe.*

com·mu·nity /kə'mju:nɪti/ **communities. 1** The ◆◆◆◆◇
community is all the people who live in a particular N-COLL-SING
area or place. *The growth of such vigilante gangs has
worried community leaders.* **2** A particular **commu-** N-COLL-
nity is a group of people who are alike in some way. COUNT
...the business community. **3 Community** is friend- N-UNCOUNT
ship between different people or groups, and a
sense of having something in common. *...a neighbourhood which has no sense of community.*

com'munity centre, community centres. A ◆◇◇◇◇
community centre is a place that is specially pro- N-COUNT
vided for the people, groups, and organizations in a
particular area, where they can go in order to meet
one another and do things.

com,munity po'licing. Community policing is a N-UNCOUNT
system in which police officers work only in one
particular area of the community, so that everyone
knows them.

com,munity 'service. Community service is ◆◇◇◇◇
unpaid work that criminals sometimes do as a pun- N-UNCOUNT
ishment instead of being sent to prison. *He was sentenced to 140 hours community service.*

com·mute /kə'mju:t/ **commutes, commuting,** ◆◆◇◇◇
commuted. 1 If you **commute**, you travel a long VERB: V

distance every day between your home and your V to/from n
place of work. *Mike commutes to London every day...* V between n
McLaren began commuting between Paris and Lon- and n
don. ♦ **com·mut·er, commuters** *The number of* N-COUNT
commuters to London has dropped by 100,000. **2** A N-COUNT
commute is the journey that you make when you AMERICAN
commute. *The average Los Angeles commute is over
60 miles a day.* **3** If a death sentence or prison sentence **is commuted** to a less serious punishment, it VB: usu
is changed to that punishment. *His death sentence* passive
was commuted to life imprisonment. Also be V-ed
com'muter belt, commuter belts. A commuter N-COUNT
belt is the area surrounding a large city, where
many people who work in the city live.

com·pact,   compacts,   compacting, com- ◆◆◇◇◇
pacted. The adjective and verb are pronounced
/kəm'pækt/. The noun is pronounced /'kɒmpækt/.
1 If you describe something as **compact**, you ap- ADJ-GRADED
prove of it because it is small or takes up very little PRAGMATICS
space. *...my compact office in Washington.* ♦ **com-**
·pact·ness *The very compactness of the cottage* N-UNCOUNT
made it all the more snug. **2** A **compact** cassette, ca- ADJ: ADJ n
mera, or car is a small type of cassette, camera, or
car. **3** To **compact** something means to press it so VERB
that it becomes more dense. *The Smith boy was* V n
compacting the trash. ♦ **com·pact·ed** *...a pile of* FORMAL
compacted earth. **4** A **compact** is a small, flat case ADJ-GRADED
that contains face-powder and a mirror. N-COUNT

,**compact 'disc,   compact discs.** Compact ◆◇◇◇◇
discs are small shiny records which are played on N-COUNT:
special machines which use lasers to read their sig- also on N
nals and convert the signals into sound of a very
high quality. The abbreviation 'CD' is also used.

com·pan·ion /kəm'pænjən/ **companions.** A ◆◆◇◇◇
companion is someone who you spend time with or N-COUNT
who you are travelling with. *Fred had been her constant companion for the last six years of her life.*

com·pan·ion·able /kəm'pænjənəbəl/. If you de- ADJ-GRADED
scribe a person as **companionable**, you mean they WRITTEN
are friendly and pleasant to be with.

com·pan·ion·ship /kəm'pænjənʃɪp/. Companion- ◆◇◇◇◇
ship is having someone you know and like with N-UNCOUNT
you, rather than being on your own. *I depended on
his companionship and on his judgement.*

com·pan·ion·way /kəm'pænjənweɪ/ companion- N-COUNT
ways. A **companionway** is a stairway or ladder
that leads from one deck to another on a ship.

com·pa·ny /'kʌmpəni/ **companies. 1** A company ◆◆◆◆◆
is a business organization that makes money by N-COLL-
selling goods or services. *Sheila found some work as* COUNT
a secretary in an insurance company. ● See also
joint-stock company, public company.
2 A **company** is a group of opera singers, dancers, ac- N-COLL-
tors, or other performers who work together. *...the* COUNT
Phoenix Dance Company.
3 A **company** is a group of soldiers that is usually part N-COUNT
of a battalion or regiment, and that is divided into two
or more platoons.
4 Company is the state of having another person or N-UNCOUNT
other people with you, usually when this is pleasant
or stops you feeling lonely. *'I won't stay long.'—'No,
please. I need the company'.* **5** If you **keep** someone PHRASE
company, you spend time with them and stop them
feeling lonely or bored. *Why don't you stay here and
keep Emma company?* **6** When you are **in company**, PHRASE
you are with a person or group of people. *When they
were in company she always seemed to dominate the
conversation.* **7** If you **have company**, you have a visi- PHRASE
tor or friend with you. *He didn't say he had had
company.*
8 You can say **and company** after mentioning a per- PHRASE
son's name, to refer also to the people who are associ- INFORMAL
ated with that person. *Keegan and company
approached the market with understandable caution.*
9 If you say that someone **is in good company**, you PHRASE
mean that they should not be ashamed of a mistake or
opinion, because some important or respected people have made the same mistake or have the same
opinion. *Mr Koo is in good company. The prime minister made a similar slip a couple of years back.*

10 If you feel, believe, or know something **in company with** someone else, you both feel, believe, or know it. *Saudi Arabia, in company with some other Gulf oil states, is concerned to avoid any repetition of the two oil price shocks of the 1970s.* PHR-PREP FORMAL

11 If two or more people **part company**, they go in different directions after going in the same direction together. *The three of them parted company at the bus stop.* **12** If you **part company** with someone, you end your association with them, often because of a disagreement. *Boris Becker has parted company with his Austrian trainer.* PHRASE WRITTEN / PHRASE FORMAL

,company 'car, company cars. A **company car** is a car which is owned or leased by a company but which is given to an employee to use as their own, usually as a benefit of having a particular job. ◆◇◇◇ N-COUNT

,company 'secretary, company secretaries. In Britain, a **company secretary** is a high-ranking official within a company who is responsible for keeping the legal affairs, accounts, and administration in order. N-COUNT

com·pa·rable /'kɒmpərəbəl/. **1** Something that is **comparable** to something else is roughly similar, for example in amount or importance. *Farmers were meant to get an income comparable to that of townspeople.* ◆ **com·pa·rably** /'kɒmpərəbli/ *...comparably qualified students.* **2** If two or more things are **comparable**, they are of the same kind or are in the same situation, and so they can reasonably be compared. *In other comparable countries real wages increased much more rapidly.* ◆ **com·pa·rabil·ity** /ˌkɒmpərə'bɪlɪti/ *...a lack of comparability between the accounts of similar companies. ...a comparability study.* ◆◆◇◇ ADJ / ADV / ADJ / N-UNCOUNT

com·para·tive /kəm'pærətɪv/ **comparatives.** **1** You use **comparative** to indicate that you are judging something against a previous situation, or judging it against something else. For example, **comparative** calm is a situation which is calmer than before or calmer than the situation in other places. *The task was accomplished with comparative ease.* ◆ **com·para·tive·ly** *...a comparatively small nation. ...children who find it comparatively easy to make and keep friends.* **2** A **comparative** study involves the comparison of two or more things of the same kind. **3** In grammar, the **comparative** form of an adjective or adverb is the form that indicates that something has more of a quality than it used to have or than something else has. For example, 'bigger' is the comparative form of 'big'. Compare **superlative.** ▶ Also a noun. *The comparative of 'pretty' is 'prettier'.* ◆◆◇◇ ADJ: ADJ n / ADV: ADV adj/adv / ADJ: ADJ n / ADJ: ADJ n / N-COUNT

com·pare /kəm'peə/ **compares, comparing, compared.** **1** If you **compare** things, you consider them and discover the differences or similarities between them. *Compare the two illustrations in Fig 60... Was it fair to compare independent schools with state schools?* ● to **compare notes**: see **note.** **2** If you **compare** one person or thing to another, you say that they are like the other person or thing. *Some commentators compared his work to that of James Joyce.* **3** If one thing **compares** favourably or unfavourably with another, it is better or worse than the other thing. *Our road safety record compares favourably with that of other European countries.* **4** If you say that something does not **compare with** something else, you mean that it is much worse. *The flowers here do not compare with those at home.* **5** See also **compared.** ◆◆◆◇ VERB V pl-n / V n with n / VERB V n to/with n/-ing / VERB V adv with n Also V adv / VERB V with n

com·pared /kəm'peəd/. You can use **compared with** and **compared to** when you want to contrast two things or situations. For example, if you say that one thing is large **compared with** another or **compared to** another, you mean that it is larger than the other thing. *The room was light and lofty compared with our Tudor ones... Women are smoking two extra cigarettes a week, compared with four years ago.* ◆◆◆◇ PHR-PREP

com·pari·son /kəm'pærɪsən/ **comparisons.** **1** When you make a **comparison**, you consider two ◆◆◆◇ N-VAR

or more things and discover the differences between them. *...a comparison of the British and German economies. ...detailed comparisons between the public and private sectors.* **2** When you make a **comparison**, you say that one thing is like another in some way. *The comparison of her life to a sea voyage simplifies her experience.* **3** If you say, for example, that something is large or small **in comparison with, in comparison to,** or **by comparison with** something else, you mean that it is larger or smaller than the other thing. *Is the human heart weak in comparison with the other organs?* **4** If you say **there is no comparison** between one thing and another, you think that the first thing is much better than the second, or very different from it. *There is no comparison between the knowledge and skill of such a player and the ordinary casual participant.* **5** If you say that someone or something **stands** or **bears comparison with** someone or something else, you mean that they are as good, or almost as good. N-COUNT / PHRASE / PHRASE / PHRASE FORMAL

com·part·ment /kəm'pɑːtmənt/ **compartments.** **1** A **compartment** is one of the separate spaces into which a railway carriage is divided. **2** A **compartment** is one of the separate parts of an object that is used for keeping things in. *I put a bottle of Sainsbury's champagne in the freezer compartment.* ● See also **glove compartment.** ◆◆◇◇ N-COUNT / N-COUNT

com·part·men·tal·ize /ˌkɒmpɑːt'mentəlaɪz/ **compartmentalizes, compartmentalizing, compartmentalized;** also spelled **compartmentalise** in British English. To **compartmentalize** something means to divide it into separate sections. *Traditionally men have compartmentalized their lives, never letting their personal lives encroach upon their professional lives.* ◆ **com·part·men·tal·ized** *...the compartmentalised world of Japanese finance.* VERB V n Also V n into n / ADJ-GRADED

com·pass /'kʌmpəs/ **compasses.** **1** A **compass** is an instrument that you use for finding directions. It has a dial and a magnetic needle that always points to the north. **2** **Compasses** are a hinged V-shaped instrument that you use for drawing circles. **3** Something that is within the **compass** of something or someone is within their limits or their possible range of action or operation. *Within the compass of a normal sized book such a comprehensive survey was not practicable.* ◆◇◇◇ N-COUNT / N-PLURAL: also a pair of N / N-COUNT FORMAL

com·pas·sion /kəm'pæʃən/. **Compassion** is a feeling of pity, sympathy, and understanding for someone who is suffering. *Elderly people need time and compassion from their physicians.* ◆◆◇◇ N-UNCOUNT

com·pas·sion·ate /kəm'pæʃənət/. If you describe someone or something as **compassionate**, you mean that they feel or show pity, sympathy, and understanding for people who are suffering. *My father was a deeply compassionate man.* ◆ **com·pas·sion·ate·ly** *He smiled compassionately at her.* ◆◇◇◇ ADJ-GRADED / ADV-GRADED

com,passionate 'leave. Compassionate leave is time away from your work that your employer allows you for personal reasons, especially when a member of your family dies or is seriously ill. N-UNCOUNT BRITISH

'compass point, compass points. A **compass point** is one of the 32 marks on the dial of a compass that show direction, for example north, south, east, and west. N-COUNT

com·pat·ible /kəm'pætɪbəl/. **1** If things, systems, or ideas are **compatible**, they work well together or can exist together successfully. *Free enterprise, he argued, was compatible with Russian values and traditions.* ◆ **com·pat·ibil·ity** /kəm,pætɪ'bɪlɪti/ *An act of Parliament could be suspended until its compatibility with EC law has been tested.* **2** If you are **compatible** with someone, you have a good relationship with them because you have similar opinions and interests. ◆ **compatibility** *As a result of their compatibility, Haig and Fraser were able to bring about wide-ranging reforms.* **3** If one brand of computer or computer equipment is **compatible** with another, they can be used together and can use the same software.* ◆◆◇◇ ADJ-GRADED / N-UNCOUNT / ADJ-GRADED / N-UNCOUNT / ADJ

com·pat·ri·ot /kəmˈpætriət, AM -ˈpeɪt-/ **compatri-** ◆◇◇◇◇
ots. Your **compatriots** are people from your own N-COUNT
country.

com·pel /kəmˈpel/ **compels, compelling, com-** ◆◆◇◇◇
pelled. If a situation, a rule, or a person **compels** VERB
you to do something, they force you to do it. ...*the* V n to-inf
introduction of legislation to compel cyclists to wear Also V n
a helmet.

com·pel·ling /kəmˈpelɪŋ/. **1** A **compelling** argu- ◆◆◇◇◇
ment or reason convinces you that something is ADJ-GRADED
true or that something should be done. *My second*
and more compelling reason for going to Dearborn
was to see the Henry Ford Museum. **2** If you describe ADJ-GRADED
something such as a film or book as **compelling**,
you mean you want to keep watching it or reading it
because you find it so interesting. ...*a frighteningly*
violent yet compelling film. ♦ **com·pel·ling·ly** *She* ADV-GRADED
wrote compellingly, with great zest.

com·pen·di·um /kəmˈpendiəm/ **compendiums.** A N-COUNT
compendium is a short but detailed collection of
information, usually in a book. *The Roman Catholic*
Church has issued a compendium of its teachings.

com·pen·sate /ˈkɒmpənseɪt/ **compensates,** ◆◆◇◇◇
compensating, compensated. 1 To **compen-** VERB
sate someone for money or things that they have V n for n
lost means to pay them money or give them some- Also V n
thing to replace that money or those things. ...*the*
official promise to compensate people for the price
rise. **2** To **compensate** for something, especially VERB
something harmful or unwanted, means to do V for n
something which balances it or makes it ineffective. Also V
The company agreed to keep up high levels of output
in order to compensate for supplies lost... MPs say it
is crucial that a mechanism is found to compensate
for inflation. **3** If you try to **compensate** for some- VERB
thing that is wrong or missing in your life, you try to V
do something that removes or reduces the harmful Also V for n
effects. *People who sense that they are inferior have*
to compensate.

com·pen·sa·tion /ˌkɒmpənˈseɪʃən/ **compensa-** ◆◆◆◇◇
tions. 1 Compensation is money that some- N-UNCOUNT
one who has undergone loss or suffering claims
from the person or organization responsible, or
from a state fund. *He received one year's salary as*
compensation... The Court ordered Dr Williams to
pay £300 compensation. **2** If something is some N-VAR
compensation for something bad that has happened, it makes you feel better. *Helen gained some*
compensation for her earlier defeat by winning the
final open class.

com·pen·sa·tory /ˌkɒmpənˈseɪtəri, kəmˈpensətɔːri/. ADJ
1 Compensatory payments involve money paid as FORMAL
compensation. *The jury awarded $11.2 million in*
compensatory damages. **2 Compensatory** measures ADJ
are designed to help people who have FORMAL
special problems or disabilities. ...*compensatory*
programmes for deprived pre-school and infant-
school children.

com·pere /ˈkɒmpeə/ **comperes, compering,** N-COUNT
compered. 1 A **compere** is the person who intro- BRITISH
duces the performers or contestants on a radio or
television show or at a live show; the usual American word is **emcee**. **2** The person who **comperes** a VERB
show is the compere of it. *Sarita Sagharwal from TV* V n
Asia compered the programme. Also V
BRITISH

com·pete /kəmˈpiːt/ **competes, competing,** ◆◆◆◇◇
competed. 1 If one person, group, or company V-RECIP
competes with another for something, they try to V with n for n
get that thing for themselves and stop the other get- V with n
ting it. You can also say that two people, groups, or Also V,
companies **compete**. ...*host-country workers, who* pl-n V,
have to compete with foreigners for jobs... The banks pl-n V for n
have long competed with American Express's charge
cards... Schools should not compete with each other
or attempt to poach pupils. **2** If you **compete** in a VERB: V
contest or a game, you take part in it. *Dubbed for-* V prep
eign language films will not be allowed to compete
for best film. **3** See also **competing**.

com·pe·tence /ˈkɒmpɪtəns/. **Competence** is the ◆◇◇◇◇
ability to do something well or effectively. *His com-* N-UNCOUNT

petence as an economist had been reinforced by his
successful fight against inflation.

com·pe·ten·cy /ˈkɒmpɪtənsi/. **Competency** means N-UNCOUNT
the same as **competence**. ...*managerial competency.*

com·pe·tent /ˈkɒmpɪtənt/. Someone who is **com-** ◆◆◇◇◇
petent is efficient and effective. *He was a loyal, dis-* ADJ-GRADED
tinguished and very competent civil servant... Most
adults do not feel competent to deal with a medical
emergency. ♦ **com·pe·tent·ly** *The government per-* ADV-GRADED
formed competently.

com·pet·ing /kəmˈpiːtɪŋ/. **Competing** ideas, re- ◆◆◇◇◇
quirements, or interests cannot all be right or satis- ADJ: ADJ n
fied at the same time. ...*the competing demands of*
work and family. ● See also **compete**.

com·pe·ti·tion /ˌkɒmpɪˈtɪʃən/ **competitions.** ◆◆◆◇◇
1 Competition is a situation in which two or more N-UNCOUNT
people, groups, or companies are trying to get
something which not everyone can have. *There's*
been some fierce competition for the title... Clothing
stores also face heavy competition from factory out-
lets. **2** The **competition** is the person or people you N-SING
are competing with. *I have to change my approach,*
the competition is too good now. **3** A **competition** is N-VAR
an event in which many people take part in order to
find out who is best at a particular activity. ...*a*
surfing competition... He will be banned from inter-
national competition for four years.

com·peti·tive /kəmˈpetɪtɪv/. **1 Competitive** is ◆◆◆◇◇
used to describe situations or activities in which ADJ-GRADED
people or firms compete with each other. *Univer-*
sities are very competitive for the best students.
♦ **com·peti·tive·ly** ...*skiing competitively in events* ADV
for the disabled. **2** A **competitive** person is eager to ADJ-GRADED
be more successful than other people. *He has al-*
ways been ambitious and fiercely competitive.
♦ **competitively** *They worked hard together, com-* ADV-GRADED
petitively and under pressure. ♦ **com·peti·tive-** N-UNCOUNT
·ness *I can't stand the pace, I suppose, and the*
competitiveness. **3** Goods or services that are at a ADJ-GRADED
competitive price or rate are likely to be bought,
because they are less expensive than other goods of
the same kind. ...*a travel company specialising in*
amazingly competitive rates for flights.
♦ **competitively** ...*guitars which were competitive-* ADV-GRADED
ly priced. ♦ **competitiveness** ...*the competitive-* N-UNCOUNT
ness and quality of our goods.

com·peti·tor /kəmˈpetɪtə/ **competitors. 1** A ◆◆◆◇◇
company's **competitors** are other companies who N-COUNT
are trying to sell similar goods or services in the
same market. *The bank isn't performing as well as*
some of its competitors. **2** A **competitor** is a person N-COUNT
who takes part in a competition or contest.

com·pi·la·tion /ˌkɒmpɪˈleɪʃən/ **compilations.** A ◆◇◇◇◇
compilation is a book, record, or broadcast that N-COUNT
contains many different items that have been gathered together, usually ones which have already appeared elsewhere. ...*a compilation of his jazz works*
over the past decade. ● See also **compile**.

com·pile /kəmˈpaɪl/ **compiles, compiling,** ◆◆◇◇◇
compiled. If you **compile** something such as a re- VERB
port, book, or TV programme, you produce it by V n
collecting and putting together many pieces of information. *Councils were required to compile a reg-*
ister of all adults living in their areas.
♦ **compilation** ...*the compilation of data on sus-* N-UNCOUNT
pected terrorists. ♦ **compiler, compilers** ...*an* N-COUNT
18th century dictionary compiler.

com·pil·er /kəmˈpaɪlə/ **compilers.** A **compiler** is a N-COUNT
computer program which converts language that TECHNICAL
people can use into a code that the computer can
understand.

com·pla·cent /kəmˈpleɪsənt/. If you say that ◆◆◇◇◇
someone is **complacent**, you are criticizing them ADJ-GRADED
because they feel that they do not need to worry or PRAGMATICS
do anything about a situation, even though the
situation may be uncertain or dangerous. *We can-*
not afford to be complacent about our health.
♦ **com·pla·cen·cy** /kəmˈpleɪsənsi/ ...*a worrying* N-UNCOUNT
level of complacency about the risks of infection from

AIDS. ♦ **com·pla·cent·ly** *He sat back, smiling* ADV-GRADED
complacently at his own cleverness.

com·plain /kəm'pleɪn/ **complains, complain-** ◆◆◆◇
ing, complained. 1 If you **complain** about a VERB
situation, you say that you are not satisfied with it. V that
Miners have complained bitterly that the govern- V about/of n
ment did not fulfill their promises... The American Also V,
couple complained about the high cost of visiting V with quote
Europe... They are liable to face more mistreatment if
they complain to the police. **2** If you **complain of** VERB
pain or illness, you say that you are feeling pain or V of n
feeling ill. *He complained of a headache.*

com·plain·ant /kəm'pleɪnənt/ **complainants.** A N-COUNT
complainant is a person who makes an official FORMAL
complaint about something.

com·plain·er /kəm'pleɪnə/ **complainers.** If you N-COUNT
call someone a **complainer**, you are criticizing them PRAGMATICS
because they complain a lot.

com·plaint /kəm'pleɪnt/ **complaints. 1** A **com-** ◆◆◆◇
plaint is a statement in which you express your dis- N-VAR
satisfaction with a particular situation. *There's been*
a record number of complaints about the standard
of service on Britain's railways. **2** A **complaint** is a N-COUNT
reason for complaining. *I've got no complaints*
about them. **3** You can refer to an illness as a **com-** N-COUNT
plaint, especially if it is not very serious. *Eczema is a*
common skin complaint.

com·ple·ment, complements, complement- ◆◆◇◇
ing, complemented. The verb is pronounced
/'kɒmplɪment/. The noun is pronounced
/'kɒmplɪmənt/. **1** If one thing **complements** anoth- VERB
er, it goes well with the other thing and makes its V n
good qualities more noticeable. *Nutmeg, parsley*
and cider all complement the flavour of these beans
well. **2** If people or things **complement** each other, VERB
they are different or do something different, which V n
makes them a good combination. *There will be a*
written examination to complement the practical
test. **3** Something that is a **complement** to some- N-COUNT
thing else complements it. *The green wallpaper is*
the perfect complement to the old pine.

4 The **complement** of things or people that some- N-COUNT
thing has is the number of them that it normally has, FORMAL
which enable it to function properly. *Each ship had a*
complement of around a dozen officers and 250 men.

5 In grammar, the **complement** of a link verb is an ad- N-COUNT
jective group or noun group which comes after the
verb and describes or identifies the subject. For example, in the sentence 'They felt very tired', 'very tired' is
the complement.

com·ple·men·tary /ˌkɒmplɪ'mentri/. **1** Comple- ◆◇◇◇
mentary things are different from each other but ADJ
make a good combination. *...two complementary*
strategies are necessary. ♦ **com·ple·men·ta·rity** N-UNCOUNT
/ˌkɒmplɪmen'tærɪti/ *...the complementarity between*
public and private authorities. **2 Complementary** ADJ: ADJ n
medicine consists of treatments which are different BRITISH
from the ones used by most Western doctors. Examples are acupuncture and homoeopathy. *...a*
wide range of complementary therapies.

com·plete /kəm'pliːt/ **completes, completing,** ◆◆◆◆
completed. 1 You use **complete** to emphasize ADJ
that something is as great in extent, degree, or PRAGMATICS
amount as it possibly can be. *...a complete lack of*
understanding by management... The resignation
came as a complete surprise. ♦ **com·plete·ly** *Doz-* ADV
ens of flats had been completely destroyed. **2** You can ADJ: ADJ n
use **complete** to emphasize that you are referring to PRAGMATICS
the whole of something and not just part of it. *A*
complete tenement block was burnt to the ground.

3 If something is **complete**, it contains all the parts ADJ
that it should contain. *No garden is complete without*
a bed of rose bushes. ♦ **com·plete·ness** *...the accu-* N-UNCOUNT
racy and completeness of the information obtained.

4 If something is **complete**, it has been finished. *The* ADJ:
work of restoring the farmhouse is complete. **5** The v-link ADJ
complete works of an author are all their books or ADJ: ADJ n
writings published together in one book or as a set of
books. **6** If one thing comes **complete with** another, it PHR-PREP

has that thing as an extra or additional part. *The diary*
comes complete with a gold-coloured ballpoint pen.

7 To **complete** a set or group means to provide the VB: no cont
last item that is needed to make it a full set or group. V n
Children don't complete their set of 20 baby teeth until
they are two to three years old. **8** If you **complete** VERB: V n
something, you finish doing, making, or producing it. Also get n V-
Peter Mayle has just completed his first novel. ♦ **com-** ed
·ple·tion /kəm'pliːʃən/ **completions** *The project is* N-VAR
nearing completion. **9** If you **complete** something, VB: no cont
you do all of it. *She completed her degree in two years...* V n
We ask candidates to complete a psychometric
questionnaire.

com·plex /'kɒmpleks/ **complexes.** The adjective ◆◆◆◇
is pronounced /kəm'pleks/ in American English.
1 Something that is **complex** has many different ADJ-GRADED
parts, and is therefore often difficult to understand.
...in-depth coverage of today's complex issues. ...a
complex system of voting. ...her complex personality.
...complex machines. **2** In grammar, a **complex** sen- ADJ: ADJ n
tence contains one or more subordinate clauses as
well as a main clause. Compare **compound.**

3 A **complex** is a group of buildings designed for a N-COUNT
particular purpose, or one large building divided into
several smaller areas. *...a new stadium and leisure*
complex. ...a complex of offices and flats. **4** A **complex** N-COUNT
of things is a group or system of things that are con- with supp
nected with each other in a complicated way. *...the*
complex of clans which occupied the land. ...the
military-industrial complex.

5 If someone has a **complex** about something, they N-COUNT
have a mental or emotional problem relating to it, often because of an unpleasant experience in the past. *I*
have never had a complex about my height. ● See also
inferiority complex.

com·plex·ion /kəm'plekʃən/ **complexions. 1** If ◆◇◇◇
you refer to someone's **complexion**, you mean the N-COUNT
natural colour or condition of the skin on their face.
She had short brown hair and a pale complexion.
...oily complexions. **2** The **complexion** of something N-COUNT:
is its general nature or character. *The political com-* with supp
plexion of the government changed... This puts a dif- FORMAL
ferent complexion on things.

com·plex·ity /kəm'pleksɪti/ **complexities.** Com- ◆◆◇◇
plexity is the state of having many different parts N-UNCOUNT:
which are connected or related to each other in a also N in pl
complicated way. *...the increasing complexity of*
modern weapon systems... The issue is surrounded
by legal complexities.

com·pli·ance /kəm'plaɪəns/. **Compliance** with ◆◇◇◇
something, for example a law, treaty, or agreement N-UNCOUNT
means doing what you are required or expected to
do. *Inspectors were sent to visit nuclear sites and*
verify compliance with the treaty. The company
says it is in full compliance with US labor laws.

com·pli·ant /kəm'plaɪənt/. If you say that someone ADJ-GRADED
is **compliant**, you mean they willingly do what they FORMAL
are asked to do. *She was much naughtier than her*
compliant brother.

com·pli·cate /'kɒmplɪkeɪt/ **complicates, com-** ◆◇◇◇
plicating, complicated. To **complicate** some- VERB
thing means to make it more difficult to understand V n
or deal with. *Bad weather continues to complicate*
efforts to deal with oil spilling from the tanker.

com·pli·cat·ed /'kɒmplɪkeɪtɪd/. If something is ◆◆◇◇
complicated, it has so many parts or aspects that it ADJ-GRADED
is difficult to understand or deal with. *...the compli-*
cated voting system.

com·pli·ca·tion /ˌkɒmplɪ'keɪʃən/ **complications.** ◆◆◇◇
1 A **complication** is a problem or difficulty that N-COUNT
makes a situation harder to deal with. *The age dif-*
ference was a complication to the relationship. **2** A N-COUNT
complication is a medical problem that occurs as a
result of another illness or disease. *He died of com-*
plications from a heart attack.

com·plic·it /kəm'plɪsɪt/. If you accuse someone of ADJ
being **complicit** in an illegal activity or plan, you are PRAGMATICS
accusing them of being involved in it with other FORMAL
people. *He is complicit in the death of innocent*
civilians.

C

com·plic·ity /kəm'plɪsɪti/. **Complicity** is involvement with other people in an illegal activity or plan. *Recently a number of policemen were sentenced to death for their complicity in the murder.* ◆◇◇◇◇ N-UNCOUNT FORMAL

com·pli·ment, compliments, complimenting, complimented. The verb is pronounced /'kɒmplɪment/. The noun is pronounced /'kɒmplɪmənt/. **1** If you **compliment** someone, you make a polite remark to show that you like their appearance, appreciate their qualities, or approve of what they have done. *They complimented me on the way I looked.* ▶ Also a noun. *You can do no harm by paying a woman compliments.* **2** If you consider something that a person says or does as a **compliment**, it convinces you of your own good qualities, or that the person appreciates you. *We consider it a compliment to be called 'conservative'.* **3** You can refer to your **compliments** when you want to formally express thanks, good wishes, or respect to someone. *My compliments to the chef.* **4** If you say that someone **returns the compliment**, you mean that they do the same thing to someone else as that person has done to them. *The actors have entertained us so splendidly during this weekend, I think it's time we returned the compliment.* ◆◆◇◇◇ VERB: V n V n on n N-COUNT N-COUNT N-PLURAL PRAGMATICS PHRASE

com·pli·men·tary /ˌkɒmplɪ'mentəri/. **1** If you are **complimentary** about something, you express admiration for it. **2** A **complimentary** seat, ticket, or book is given to you free. ◆◇◇◇◇ ADJ-GRADED ADJ

com·ply /kəm'plaɪ/ **complies, complying, complied.** If you **comply** with an order or set of rules, you do what you are required or expected to do. *There are calls for his resignation, but there is no sign yet that he will comply.* ◆◆◇◇◇ VERB: V with n V

com·po·nent /kəm'pəʊnənt/ **components. 1** The **components** of something are the parts that it is made of. *The management plan has four main components.* **2** The **component** parts of something are the parts that make it up. *Polish workers will now be making component parts for Boeing 757s.* ◆◆◆◇◇ N-COUNT ADJ: ADJ n

com·port /kəm'pɔːt/ **comports, comporting, comported.** If you **comport** yourself in a particular way, you behave in that way. *He comports himself with modesty.* VERB V pron-refl prep/adv FORMAL

com·pose /kəm'pəʊz/ **composes, composing, composed. 1** The things that something **is composed of** are its parts or members. The separate things that **compose** something are the parts or members that form it. *The force would be composed of troops from NATO countries... Protein molecules compose all the complex working parts of living cells.* ◆ **composition** /ˌkɒmpə'zɪʃən/. If you refer to the **composition** of something, you mean the things that compose it. *Forests vary greatly in composition.* **2** If someone **composes** a piece of music, they write it. *Vivaldi composed a large number of very fine concertos.* ◆ **composition, compositions** *Most of his compositions are for one or two cellos... I was studying composition at Boston's Berklee School of Music.* **3** If you **compose** something such as a letter or speech, you write it, often using a lot of concentration or skill. **4** If you **compose** yourself or you **compose** your features, you succeed in becoming calm after you have been angry, excited, or upset. *She quickly composed herself as the car started off.* ◆◆◆◇◇ VERB be V-ed of n V n Also V-ed N-UNCOUNT VERB Also V N-VAR VERB: V n FORMAL VERB V pron-refl Also V n

com·posed /kəm'pəʊzd/. If someone is **composed**, they are calm and able to control their feelings. ADJ-GRADED

com·pos·er /kəm'pəʊzə/ **composers.** A **composer** is a person who writes music, especially classical music. ◆◆◇◇◇ N-COUNT

com·po·site /'kɒmpəzɪt, AM kəm'pɑːzɪt/ **composites.** A **composite** object or item is made up of several different things, parts, or substances. ▶ Also a noun. *Spain is a composite of diverse traditions and people.* ◆◆◇◇◇ ADJ N-COUNT

com·po·si·tion /ˌkɒmpə'zɪʃən/ **compositions. 1** A **composition** is a piece of written work, such as a story or essay, that children do at school. **2** The **composition** of a painting or other work of art is the ◆◇◇◇◇ N-COUNT N-UNCOUNT

way its different parts are arranged, and the skill involved in doing this. **3** See also **compose**.

com·po·si·tion·al /ˌkɒmpə'zɪʃənəl/. **Compositional** refers to the way composers and artists use their skills or techniques in their work. *...a study of Olivier Messiaen's compositional style.* ADJ: ADJ n

com·posi·tor /kəm'pɒzɪtə/ **compositors.** A **compositor** is a person who arranges the text and illustrations of a book, magazine, or newspaper before it is printed. N-COUNT

com·post /'kɒmpɒst, AM -pəʊst/ **composts, composting, composted. 1 Compost** is a mixture of decaying plants and manure, which is added to the soil to help plants grow. *...a small compost heap.* **2 Compost** is a specially treated soil or peat mixed with fertilizer that you buy and use to grow seeds and plants in pots. **3** To **compost** unwanted plants or food means to make them into compost. ◆ **com·post·ing** *Composting is the ideal way of getting rid of vegetable, garden and organic waste.* ◆◆◇◇◇ N-UNCOUNT N-VAR VERB: V n N-UNCOUNT

com·po·sure /kəm'pəʊʒə/. Someone's **composure** is their appearance or feeling of calmness and their control of their feelings, often in a difficult situation. *Stopping only briefly to regain her composure, she described her agonising ordeal.* ◆◇◇◇◇ N-UNCOUNT FORMAL

com·pote /'kɒmpəʊt/ **compotes. Compote** is fruit stewed with sugar or in syrup. N-VAR

com·pound, compounds, compounding, compounded. The noun is pronounced /'kɒmpaʊnd/. The verb is pronounced /kəm'paʊnd/. **1** A **compound** is an enclosed area of land used for a particular purpose. *...a military compound.* **2** In chemistry, a **compound** is a substance that consists of two or more elements. **3** If something is a **compound** of different things, it consists of those things. **4 Compound** is used to indicate that something consists of two or more parts or things. *...a tall shrub with shiny compound leaves.* **5** In grammar, a **compound** noun, adjective, or verb is made up of two or more words, for example 'fire engine', 'bottle-green', and 'force-feed'. **6** In grammar, a **compound** sentence is made up of two or more main clauses. Compare **complex**. **7** To **compound** a problem or mistake means to make it worse by adding to it. *Additional bloodshed and loss of life will only compound the tragedy.* ◆◆◇◇◇ N-COUNT N-COUNT N-COUNT FORMAL ADJ: ADJ n ADJ: ADJ n ADJ: ADJ n VERB V n FORMAL

compound 'interest. Compound interest is interest that is calculated both on an original sum of money and on interest which has previously been added to the sum. N-UNCOUNT

com·pre·hend /ˌkɒmprɪ'hend/ **comprehends, comprehending, comprehended.** If you cannot **comprehend** something, you cannot understand it. *Whenever she failed to comprehend she invariably laughed.* ◆◇◇◇◇ VB: with brd-neg V Also V n FORMAL

com·pre·hen·sible /ˌkɒmprɪ'hensɪbəl/. Something that is **comprehensible** can be understood. *He spoke abruptly, in barely comprehensible Arabic.* ADJ-GRADED FORMAL

com·pre·hen·sion /ˌkɒmprɪ'henʃən/ **comprehensions. 1 Comprehension** is the process of understanding something, or the ability to understand something. *This was utterly beyond her comprehension... They turned to one another with the same expression of dawning comprehension, surprise, and relief.* **2** When pupils do **comprehension**, they do an exercise to find out how well they understand a piece of spoken or written language. ◆◇◇◇◇ N-UNCOUNT FORMAL N-VAR

com·pre·hen·sive /ˌkɒmprɪ'hensɪv/ **comprehensives. 1** Something that is **comprehensive** includes everything that is needed or relevant. *The Rough Guide to Nepal is a comprehensive guide to the region.* **2** In Britain, a **comprehensive** is a state school in which children of all abilities are taught together. ▶ Also an adjective. *He left comprehensive school at the age of 16.* ◆◆◆◇◇ ADJ-GRADED N-COUNT ADJ: ADJ n

com·pre·hen·sive·ly /ˌkɒmprɪ'hensɪvli/. Something that is done **comprehensively** is done very thoroughly. ADV-GRADED

com·press, compresses, compressing, compressed. The verb is pronounced /kəm'pres/.

The noun is pronounced /'kɒmpres/. **1** If you **compress** something or if it **compresses**, it is pressed or squeezed so that it takes up less space. *Poor posture, sitting or walking slouched over, compresses the body's organs. ...vessels filled with compressed air at very high pressure.* ♦ **com·pres·sion** /kəm'preʃən/. *The compression of the wood is easily achieved.* **2** A **compress** is a pad of wet or dry cloth pressed on part of a patient's body to reduce fever.

V-ERG: V
V n
V-ed

N-UNCOUNT

N-COUNT

com·pres·sor /kəm'presə/ **compressors**. A compressor is a machine or part of a machine that squeezes gas or air and makes it take up less space.

N-COUNT

com·prise /kəm'praɪz/ **comprises, comprising, comprised**. **1** If you say that something **comprises** or **is comprised of** a number of things or people, you mean it has them as its parts or members. *The exhibition comprises 50 oils and watercolours.* **2** The things or people that **comprise** something are the parts or members that form it. *...the multitude of ideas, ambitions and regrets that comprises the culture of Russia today.*

♦♦◇◇◇
VERB:
be V-ed of n
V n
FORMAL

VERB
V n
FORMAL

com·pro·mise /'kɒmprəmaɪz/ **compromises, compromising, compromised**. **1** A compromise is a situation in which people accept something slightly different from what they really want, because of circumstances or because they are considering the wishes of other people. *The government's policy of compromise is not universally popular.* **2** If you **compromise** with someone, you reach an agreement with them in which you both give up something that you originally wanted. You can also say that two people or groups **compromise**. *The government has compromised with its critics over monetary policies... 'Nine,' said I. 'Nine thirty,' tried he. We compromised on 9.15... Israel had originally wanted $1 billion in aid, but compromised on the $650 million.* **3** If someone **compromises** themselves or their beliefs, they do something which causes people to doubt their honesty, loyalty, or moral principles. *...members of the government who have compromised themselves by co-operating with the emergency committee.*

♦♦♦◇◇
N-VAR

V-RECIP
V with n over n
V on n
Also pl-n V

VERB: V n
V pron-refl

com·pro·mis·ing /'kɒmprəmaɪzɪŋ/. If you describe information or a situation as **compromising**, you mean that it reveals an embarrassing or guilty secret about someone. *How had this compromising picture come into the possession of the press?*

♦◇◇◇◇
ADJ-GRADED

comp·trol·ler /kən'trəʊlə/ **comptrollers**. A **comptroller** is someone who is in charge of the accounts of a business or a government department.

♦◇◇◇◇
N-COUNT

com·pul·sion /kəm'pʌlʃən/ **compulsions**. **1** A **compulsion** is a strong desire to do something, which you find difficult to control. **2** If someone uses **compulsion** in order to get you to do something, they force you to do it, for example by threatening to punish you if you do not do it.

♦◇◇◇◇
N-COUNT

N-UNCOUNT

com·pul·sive /kəm'pʌlsɪv/. **1** You use **compulsive** to describe people or their behaviour when they cannot stop doing something wrong, harmful, or unnecessary. *...a compulsive liar.* ♦ **com·pul·sive·ly** *John is compulsively neat and clean.* **2** If a book or television programme is **compulsive**, it is so interesting that you do not want to stop reading or watching it. *After a shaky start, the series became compulsive viewing with its fast plots and terrific acting performances.* ♦ **compulsively** *...a series of compulsively readable novels.*

♦◇◇◇◇
ADJ: ADJ n

ADV

ADJ-GRADED
BRITISH

ADV-GRADED

com·pul·so·ry /kəm'pʌlsəri/. If something is compulsory, you must do it or accept it, because it is the law or because someone in a position of authority says you must. ♦ **com·pul·so·ri·ly** /kəm'pʌlsərɪli/ *Senior managers have been made compulsorily redundant.*

♦♦◇◇◇
ADJ

ADV

com·punc·tion /kəm'pʌŋkʃən/. If you say that someone has no **compunction** about doing something, you mean that they do it without feeling ashamed or guilty; used showing disapproval.

N-UNCOUNT
PRAGMATICS

com·pu·ta·tion /ˌkɒmpjʊ'teɪʃən/ **computations**. **Computation** is mathematical calculation. *He took a few notes and made computations.*

N-VAR

com·pu·ta·tion·al /ˌkɒmpjʊ'teɪʃənəl/. **Computational** means using computers or numerical calculations. *...computational linguistics.*

ADJ

com·pute /kəm'pjuːt/ **computes, computing, computed**. To **compute** a quantity or number means to calculate it.

♦◇◇◇◇
VERB: V n

com·put·er /kəm'pjuːtə/ **computers**. A computer is an electronic machine that can quickly make calculations, store, rearrange, and retrieve information, or control another machine. *...a $650,000 computer system..* ♦ See also **personal computer**.

♦♦♦♦◇
N-COUNT:
also by/on N

com'puter game, **computer games**. A computer game is a game that you play on a computer or on a small portable electronic device.

♦◇◇◇◇
N-COUNT

com·put·er·ize /kəm'pjuːtəraɪz/ **computerizes, computerizing, computerized**; also spelled **computerise** in British English. To **computerize** a system or type of work means to introduce computers into it, and so change the way that it is arranged or done. *...computerized records of all companies... Many hospitals simply can't afford to computerize.* ♦ **com·put·eri·za·tion** /kəmˌpjuːtəraɪ'zeɪʃən/ *...the computerization of the company's records.*

♦♦◇◇◇
VERB: V n
V-ed

N-UNCOUNT

com·puter-'literate. If someone is **computerliterate**, they have enough skill and knowledge to be able to use a computer.

ADJ-GRADED

com·put·ing /kəm'pjuːtɪŋ/. **Computing** is the activity of using a computer and writing programs for it. *Courses range from cookery to computing.*

♦♦◇◇◇
N-UNCOUNT

com·rade /'kɒmreɪd, AM -ræd/ **comrades**. **1** Someone's **comrades** are their friends or companions. **2** Socialists or communists sometimes call each other **comrade**, especially in meetings.

♦♦◇◇◇
N-COUNT
LITERARY
N-TITLE;
N-VOC

comrade-in-'arms, **comrades-in-arms**; also **comrade in arms**. A **comrade-in-arms** is someone who works for the same cause or purpose as you and shares the same difficulties and dangers.

N-COUNT

com·rade·ly /'kɒmreɪdli, AM -ræd-/. If you do something in a **comradely** way, you are being pleasant and friendly to other people.

ADJ-GRADED
FORMAL

com·rade·ship /'kɒmreɪdʃɪp, AM -ræd-/. **Comradeship** is friendship between people who are doing the same work or who share the same difficulties.

N-UNCOUNT

con /kɒn/ **cons, conning, conned**. **1** If someone **cons** you, they persuade you to do something or believe something by telling you things that are not true. *The businessman had conned him of £10,000... White conned his way into a job as a warehouseman.* **2** A con is a trick in which someone deceives you by telling you something that is not true. **3** A con is the same as a **convict**. **4** See also **mod cons**. ● **pros and cons**: see **pro**.

♦♦◇◇◇
VERB:
V n of/out
of/into/-ing
V way into n
INFORMAL

N-COUNT
INFORMAL
N-COUNT
INFORMAL

Con. **1** In Britain, **Con**. is the written abbreviation for 'constable'. **2** In Britain, **Con** is the written abbreviation for **Conservative**.

conc. **Conc**. is used to indicate a concessionary fare or price that is charged to pensioners, students, and the unemployed.

BRITISH

con·cave /'kɒnkeɪv, kɒn'keɪv/. A surface that is **concave** curves inwards in the middle.

ADJ-GRADED

con·ceal /kən'siːl/ **conceals, concealing, concealed**. **1** If you **conceal** something, you cover it or hide it carefully. ♦ **con·ceal·ment** *...the concealment of weapons.* **2** If you **conceal** a piece of information or a feeling, you do not let other people know about it. *He was concealing something from her.* ♦ **concealment** *I think there was deliberate concealment of relevant documents.* **3** If something **conceals** something else, it covers it and prevents it from being seen.

♦♦◇◇◇
VERB: V n

N-UNCOUNT
VERB: V n
V n from n

N-UNCOUNT
VERB: V n

con·cede /kən'siːd/ **concedes, conceding, conceded**. **1** If you **concede** something, you admit, often unwillingly, that it is true or correct. *Bess finally conceded that Nancy was right... 'Well,' he conceded, 'I do sometimes mumble a bit.'*
2 If you **concede** something to someone, you allow them to have it as a right or privilege. *Poland's Communist government conceded the right to establish independent trade unions.*
3 If you **concede** something, you give it to the person

♦♦♦◇◇
VERB: V n
V that
V with quote
Also V n n

V n to n
V n
Also V n n

VERB

C

who has been trying to get it from you. *The government conceded some of their demands.*   V n

4 In sport, if you **concede** goals or points, you are unable to prevent your opponent from scoring them. *They conceded four goals to Leeds United.* **5** If you **concede** a game, contest, or argument, you end it by admitting that you can no longer win. *Reiner, 56, has all but conceded the race to his rival.* **6** If you **concede** defeat, you accept that you have lost a struggle.   VERB: V n / Vn to n   VERB Also V n   VERB: V n

con·ceit /kənˈsiːt/ **conceits. 1** Conceit is very great pride in your abilities or achievements that other people feel is undeserved. **2** A **conceit** is a clever or unusual metaphor or comparison.   ◆◇◇◇ N-UNCOUNT: also a N   N-COUNT LITERARY

con·ceit·ed /kənˈsiːtɪd/. If you say that someone is **conceited**, you disapprove of them for being too proud of their abilities or achievements.   ADJ-GRADED PRAGMATICS

con·ceiv·able /kənˈsiːvəbəl/. If something is **conceivable**, you can imagine it or believe it. *It is just conceivable that a single survivor might be found.*   ◆◇◇◇ ADJ

♦ con·ceiv·ably /kənˈsiːvəbli/ *The mission could conceivably be accomplished within a week.*   ADV

con·ceive /kənˈsiːv/ **conceives, conceiving, conceived. 1** If you cannot **conceive** of something, you cannot imagine it or believe it. *He was immensely ambitious but unable to conceive of winning power for himself.* **2** If you **conceive** something as a particular thing, you consider it to be that thing. *We conceive of the family as being in a constant state of change.* **3** If you **conceive** a plan or idea, you think of it and work out how it can be done. *He conceived of the first truly portable computer in 1968.*   ◆◆◇◇ VERB V of n / -ing   VERB: V n asn / -ing V of n asn / -   VERB: V n V of n

4 When a woman **conceives**, she becomes pregnant. *A mother who already has non-identical twins is more likely to conceive another set of twins.*   VERB: V V n

con·cen·trate /ˈkɒnsəntreɪt/ **concentrates, concentrating, concentrated. 1** If you **concentrate** on something, or **concentrate** your mind on it, you give all your attention to it. *At work you need to be able to concentrate... This helps you to be aware of time and concentrates your mind on the immediate task.* **2** If you say that an unpleasant fact or situation **concentrates** someone's **mind**, you mean that it makes them think clearly, because they are aware of the serious consequences if they do not. *A term in prison will concentrate his mind wonderfully.*   ◆◆◆◇ VERB: V on n / -ing V V n on n   PHRASE BRITISH

3 If something **is concentrated** in an area, it is all there rather than being spread around. *Italy's industrial districts are concentrated in its north-central and north-eastern regions.*   VB: usu passive be V-ed prep / adv

4 Concentrate is a liquid or substance from which unnecessary substances such as water have been removed in order to increase its strength or to decrease its bulk. *...orange juice made from concentrate.*   N-VAR

con·cen·trat·ed /ˈkɒnsəntreɪtɪd/. **1** A **concentrated** liquid has been increased in strength by having water removed from it. **2** A **concentrated** activity is directed with great intensity in one place. *...a more concentrated effort to reach out to troubled kids.*   ◆◆◇◇ ADJ-GRADED   ADJ-GRADED

con·cen·tra·tion /ˌkɒnsənˈtreɪʃən/ **concentrations. 1** Concentration on something involves giving all your attention to it. *We lacked concentration and it cost us the goal.* **2** A concentration of something is a large amount of it or large numbers of it in a small area. *...one of the world's greatest concentrations of wildlife.* **3** The **concentration** of a substance is the proportion of essential ingredients or substances in it. *pH is a measure of the concentration of free hydrogen atoms in a solution.*   ◆◆◆◇ N-UNCOUNT   N-VAR   N-VAR: with supp

concen·tration camp, concentration camps. A **concentration camp** is a prison in which large numbers of non-military prisoners are kept in very bad conditions, usually in wartime.   ◆◇◇◇ N-COUNT

con·cen·tric /kənˈsentrɪk/. **Concentric** circles or rings have the same centre point.   ADJ: ADJ n

con·cept /ˈkɒnsept/ **concepts.** A concept is an idea or abstract principle. *The concept of arranged marriages is misunderstood in the west.*   ◆◆◆◇ N-COUNT

con·cep·tion /kənˈsepʃən/ **conceptions. 1** A **conception** of something is an idea that you have of it in your mind. *...someone with not the slightest conception of teamwork.* **2** Conception is the forming of an idea for something in your mind. *The symphony is admirable in conception.* **3** Conception is the process in which the egg in a woman is fertilized and she becomes pregnant.   ◆◇◇◇ N-VAR   N-UNCOUNT   N-VAR

con·cep·tual /kənˈseptʃuəl/. **Conceptual** means related to ideas and concepts formed in the mind. *NATO requires a better international and conceptual framework to guide its thinking.* **♦ con·cep·tu·al·ly** *The method is conceptually simple.*   ◆◇◇◇ ADJ: ADJ n   ADV

con·cep·tu·al·ize /kənˈseptʃuəlaɪz/ **conceptualizes, conceptualizing, conceptualized;** also spelled **conceptualise** in British English. If you **conceptualize** something, you form an idea of it in your mind. *It is nowadays better to conceptualize religion as a cultural resource.* **♦ con·cep·tu·al·i·za·tion** /kənˌseptʃuəlaɪˈzeɪʃən/ **conceptualizations** *...the existing conceptualization of women's liberation.*   VERB: V n V n asn   N-VAR

con·cern /kənˈsɜːn/ **concerns, concerning, concerned. 1** Concern is worry about a situation. *There is no cause for concern.* **2** If something **concerns** you, it worries you. *It concerned her that Bess was developing a crush on Max.* **♦ con·cerned** *I've been concerned about you lately.* **3** A **concern** is a fact or situation that worries you. *Unemployment was the electorate's main concern.* **4** If something is **of concern** to someone, they find it worrying. *The survey's findings are a matter of great concern.*   ◆◆◆◆◆ N-UNCOUNT   VB: no cont, V n it V n that   ADJ-GRADED   N-COUNT   PHRASE

5 Someone's **concern** with something is their feeling that it is important. *...a story that illustrates how dangerous excessive concern with safety can be.* **6** Someone's **concerns** are the things that they consider to be important. *...the concerns of middle-class whites.* **7** If you **concern** yourself with something, you give it attention because you think that it is important. **♦ concerned** *The agency is more concerned with making arty ads than understanding its clients' businesses.* **8** If something is **of concern** to you, it is important to you.   N-VAR   N-COUNT   VERB: V pron-refl with n   ADJ-GRADED v-link ADJ with n   PHRASE

9 Your **concern** for someone is a feeling that you want them to be happy and safe. If you do something out of **concern**, you do it because you want them to be happy and safe. *Without her care and concern, he had no chance at all... He had only gone along out of concern for his two grandsons.*   N-VAR

10 If something such as a book or a piece of information **concerns** a particular subject, it is about that subject. *Chapter 2 concerns itself with the methodological difficulties.* **♦ concerned** *Randolph's work was exclusively concerned with the effects of pollution on health.* **11** You can say **as far as** something is **concerned** to indicate the subject that you are talking about. *As far as starting a family is concerned, the trend is for women having their children later in life.* **12** If a situation, event, or activity **concerns** you, it affects or involves you. **♦ concerned** *It's a very stressful situation for everyone concerned.* **13** If a situation or problem is your **concern**, it is something that you have a duty or responsibility to be involved with. *The technical aspects were the concern of the Army.*   VB: no cont, V n V pron-refl with n   ADJ: v-link ADJ with n   PHRASE PRAGMATICS   VB: no cont, V n ADJ N-SING: with poss

14 You can say **'as far as** I'm **concerned'** to indicate that you are giving your own opinion. *As far as I'm concerned the officials incited the fight.*   PHRASE PRAGMATICS

15 You can refer to a company or business as a **concern**. *If not a large concern, Queensbury Nursery was at least a successful one.* **16** If a company is a **going concern**, it is actually doing business, rather than having stopped trading or not yet having started trading.   N-COUNT FORMAL   PHRASE

concerned /kənˈsɜːnd/. **1** See **concern**. **2** If you are **concerned** to do something, you want to do it because you think it is important. *We were very concerned to keep the staff informed.*   ◆◆◆◇ ADJ-GRADED v-link ADJ to-inf

con·cern·ing /kənˈsɜːnɪŋ/. You use **concerning** to indicate what a question or piece of information is about. *...various questions concerning pollution and the environment.*   ◆◆◇◇ PREP

con·cert /'kɒnsət/ **concerts. 1** A **concert** is a performance of music. ...*a short concert of piano music.* ...*live rock concerts.* **2** If a musician or group of musicians appears **in concert**, they are giving a live performance. **3** If a number of people do something **in concert**, they do it together. *He wants to act in concert with other nations.*
◆◆◆◇◇ N-COUNT
PHRASE
PHRASE FORMAL

con·cert·ed /kən'sɜːtɪd/. **1** A **concerted** action is done by several people or groups working together. **2** If you make a **concerted** effort to do something, you try very hard to do it.
ADJ-GRADED: ADJ n
ADJ-GRADED: ADJ n

con·cer·ti·na /ˌkɒnsə'tiːnə/ **concertinas, concertinaing concertinaed. 1** A **concertina** is a musical instrument consisting of two end-pieces, with stiff paper or cloth that folds up between them. **2** If something **concertinas**, it becomes more compressed. ...*a widescreen film that has been concertinaed for television.*
N-VAR
V-ERG: V beV-ed

con·cer·to /kən'tʃeətəʊ/ **concertos.** A **concerto** is a piece of music written for one or more solo instruments and an orchestra.
◆◇◇◇◇ N-COUNT

con·ces·sion /kən'seʃən/ **concessions. 1** If you make a **concession** to someone, you agree to let them do or have something, especially in order to end an argument or conflict. **2** A **concession** is a special right or privilege that is given to someone. ...*tax concessions for mothers who chose to stay at home with their children.* **3** A **concession** is a special low fare or price for a particular group such as pensioners or students.
◆◆◇◇ N-COUNT
N-COUNT
N-COUNT

con·ces·sion·aire /kən,seʃə'neə/ **concessionaires.** A **concessionaire** is a person or company that has been given particular rights or privileges, for example to sell a particular product or to run a business in a public place.
N-COUNT

con·ces·sion·ary /kən'seʃənri/. A **concessionary** fare or price is a special low one for a particular group such as pensioners or students.
ADJ: ADJ n

conch /kɒntʃ, kɒŋk/ **conches.** A **conch** is a shellfish with a large shell rather like a snail's. A **conch** or a **conch shell** is the shell of this creature.
N-COUNT

con·ci·erge /ˌkɒnsi'eəʒ/ **concierges.** A **concierge** is a person who looks after a block of flats and checks people entering and leaving the building.
N-COUNT

con·cili·ate /kən'sɪlieɪt/ **conciliates, conciliating, conciliated.** If you do something to **conciliate** someone, you do it to try to end a disagreement with them. If you **conciliate**, you try to end a disagreement between other people. *The President has a strong political urge to conciliate.* ♦ **con·cili·ator,** **conciliators** *Douglas Hurd is widely seen as a conciliator.* ♦ **con·cili·ation** /kən,sɪli'eɪʃən/ ...*a mood of conciliation.*
VERB: V n V FORMAL
N-COUNT
N-UNCOUNT

con·cilia·tory /kən'sɪliətri, AM -tɔːri/. When you are **conciliatory** in your actions or behaviour, you show you are willing to end a disagreement with someone. *The next time he spoke he used a more conciliatory tone.* ...*a conciliatory gesture.*
◆◇◇◇◇ ADJ-GRADED

con·cise /kən'saɪs/. **1** Something that is **concise** says everything that is necessary without using any unnecessary words. ♦ **con·cise·ly** *He'd delivered his report clearly and concisely.* **2** A **concise** edition of a book, especially a dictionary, is shorter than the original edition.
◆◇◇◇◇ ADJ-GRADED
ADV-GRADED: ADV with v
ADJ: ADJ n

con·clave /'kɒŋkleɪv/ **conclaves.** A **conclave** is a secret or confidential meeting.
N-COUNT

con·clude /kən'kluːd/ **concludes, concluding, concluded. 1** If you **conclude** that something is true, you decide that it is true using the facts you know. *Larry had concluded that he had no choice but to accept Paul's words...* '*The situation in the inner cities is bad and getting worse,' she concluded.* **2** When you **conclude**, you say the last thing that you are going to say. '*It's a waste of time,' he concluded... I would like to conclude by saying that I do enjoy your magazine.* **3** When someone **concludes** something, they end it. *The evening concluded with dinner and speeches.* **4** If people or groups **conclude** an agreement, such as a treaty or business deal, they arrange it or agree it. *Mexico and the Philip-*
◆◆◆◇◇ VERB V that V with quote
VERB V with quote V
V-ERG: V n V adv/prep FORMAL
V-RECIP: pl-n V n V n with n

pines have both concluded agreements with their commercial bank creditors.

con·clu·sion /kən'kluːʒən/ **conclusions. 1** When you come to a **conclusion** you decide that something is true after you have thought about it carefully. *I've come to the conclusion that she's a very great musician... Other people will no doubt draw their own conclusions.* **2** If you say that someone **jumps to a conclusion**, you are critical of them because they decide too quickly that something is true, when they do not know all the facts. *I didn't want her to jump to the conclusion that the divorce was in any way her fault.* **3** You can refer to something that seems certain to happen as **a foregone conclusion**. *It was a foregone conclusion that I would end up in the same business as him.* **4** The **conclusion** of something is its ending. *At the conclusion of the programme, I asked the children if they had any questions.* **5** You say '**in conclusion**' to introduce the last thing that you want to say. *In conclusion, walking is a cheap, safe, enjoyable and readily available form of exercise.* **6** The **conclusion** of a treaty or a business deal is the act of arranging it or agreeing it.
◆◆◆◇◇ N-COUNT
PHRASE PRAGMATICS
PHRASE
N-SING
PHRASE PRAGMATICS
N-SING

con·clu·sive /kən'kluːsɪv/. **Conclusive** evidence shows with certainty that something is true. *Research on the matter is far from conclusive.* ♦ **con·clu·sive·ly** *A new study proved conclusively that smokers die younger than non-smokers.*
◆◇◇◇◇ ADJ-GRADED
ADV-GRADED: ADV with v

con·coct /kən'kɒkt/ **concocts, concocting, concocted. 1** If you **concoct** an excuse or explanation, you invent one that is not true. **2** If you **concoct** something, especially something unusual, you make it by mixing several things together. *Eugene was concocting Rossini Cocktails.* ♦ **con·coc·tion,** /kən'kɒkʃən/ **concoctions** ...*a concoction of honey, yogurt, oats, and apples.*
◆◇◇◇◇ VERB: V n
VERB V n
N-COUNT

con·comi·tant /kən'kɒmɪtənt/. Something that is **concomitant** with another thing happens at the same time and is connected with it. *New methods had to be learnt, with concomitant delays in successful production.*
ADJ FORMAL

con·cord /'kɒŋkɔːd/. **Concord** is a state of peaceful agreement.
N-UNCOUNT FORMAL

con·cord·ance /kən'kɔːdəns/ **concordances. 1** If there is **concordance** between two things, they are similar to each other or consistent with each other. **2** A **concordance** is a list of the words in a text, with information about where in the text each word occurs and how often it occurs.
N-VAR FORMAL
N-COUNT

con·course /'kɒŋkɔːs/ **concourses.** A **concourse** is a wide hall in a public building, for example a hotel, airport, or station.
N-COUNT

con·crete /'kɒŋkriːt/ **concretes, concreting, concreted. 1** **Concrete** is a substance used for building which is made by mixing cement, sand, small stones, and water. **2** When you **concrete** something such as a path, you cover it with concrete. **3** You use **concrete** to refer to something that is definite and specific. *He had no concrete evidence.* ♦ **con·crete·ly** ...*making their point more concretely.* **4** A **concrete** object is a real, physical object. **5** A **concrete** noun is a noun that refers to a physical object rather than to a quality or idea. **6** If a plan or idea is **set in concrete** or embedded in **concrete**, it is fixed and cannot be changed.
◆◆◆◇◇ N-UNCOUNT
VERB: V n
ADJ-GRADED
ADV-GRADED
ADJ
ADJ: ADJ n
PHRASE

concrete 'jungle, concrete jungles. If you refer to a city or area as a **concrete jungle**, you mean that it has a lot of modern buildings and you think it is ugly or unpleasant to live in.
N-COUNT PRAGMATICS

con·cu·bine /'kɒŋkjʊbaɪn/ **concubines.** In former times, a man's **concubine** was a woman who was not his wife, with whom he had a sexual relationship and whom he supported financially.
N-COUNT

con·cur /kən'kɜː/ **concurs, concurring, concurred.** If two or more people **concur**, they agree. *Local feeling does not necessarily concur with the press.*
◆◇◇◇◇ V-RECIP: pl-n V V with/in n FORMAL

con·cur·rence /kənˈkʌrəns, AM -ˈkɜːr-/ **concurrences. 1** Someone's **concurrence** is their agreement to something. **2** See also **concurrent**.   N-VAR FORMAL

con·cur·rent /kənˈkʌrənt, AM -ˈkɜːr-/. **Concurrent** events or situations happen at the same time. ◆◇◇◇ ADJ ♦ **con·cur·rence** *The concurrence of their disappearances had to be more than coincidental.* ♦ **con·cur·rent·ly** *He was jailed for 33 months to run concurrently with a sentence he is already serving.*   N-UNCOUNT   ADV: ADV with v

con·cussed /kənˈkʌst/. If someone is **concussed**, they are unconscious or are in a sick or confused state, because they have been hit hard on the head.   ADJ-GRADED

con·cus·sion /kənˈkʌʃən/ **concussions.** If you suffer **concussion** after a blow to your head, you lose consciousness or feel sick or confused.   N-VAR

con·demn /kənˈdem/ **condemns, condemning, condemned. 1** If you **condemn** something, you say that it is very bad and unacceptable. *Graham was right to condemn his players for lack of ability.* ♦ **con·dem·na·tion** /ˌkɒndemˈneɪʃən/ **condemnations** *There was widespread condemnation of Saturday's killings.* **2** If someone **is condemned** to a punishment, they are given this punishment. *He was condemned to life imprisonment.* **3** If circumstances **condemn** you to an unpleasant situation, they make it certain that you will suffer in that way. *Mark was condemned to do most of the work.* **4** If authorities **condemn** a building, they officially decide that it is not safe and must be pulled down. **5** See also **condemned**.   ◆◆◆◇◇   VERB: V n, V n for/as n   N-VAR   VB: usu passive be V-ed to n   VERB: V n to n/-ing be V-ed to-inf   VERB: V n

con·demned /kənˈdemd/. A **condemned** man or woman is going to be executed. *...a condemned man's last request.*   ◆◇◇◇◇ ADJ

con·den·sa·tion /ˌkɒndenˈseɪʃən/. **Condensation** consists of small drops of water which form when warm water vapour or steam touches a cold surface such as a window.   N-UNCOUNT

con·dense /kənˈdens/ **condenses, condensing, condensed. 1** If you **condense** something, especially a piece of writing or speech, you make it shorter, usually by including only the most important parts. *We have learnt how to condense serious messages into short, self-contained sentences.* ♦ **con·densed** *...a condensed version of what had already been disclosed.* **2** When a gas or vapour **condenses**, it changes into a liquid. *The compressed gas is cooled and condenses into a liquid.*   ◆◇◇◇◇   VERB: V n, V n into n   ADJ-GRADED   V-ERG: V V into/out of n Also V n

con·densed /kənˈdenst/. **1 Condensed** liquids have been thickened by removing some of the water in them. *...condensed mushroom soup.* **2** See also **condense**.   ADJ-GRADED

con·densed ˈmilk. Condensed milk is very thick sweetened milk.   N-UNCOUNT

con·dens·er /kənˈdensə/ **condensers. 1** A **condenser** is a device that cools gases into liquids. **2** A **condenser** is a device for accumulating electric charge.   N-COUNT   N-COUNT

con·de·scend /ˌkɒndɪˈsend/ **condescends, condescending, condescended. 1** If you say that someone **condescends** to do something, you disapprove of them because they agree to do it in a way which shows that they think they are superior to other people and should not have to do it. **2** If you say that someone **condescends** to other people, you disapprove of them because they behave in a way which shows that they think they are superior to other people. ♦ **con·de·scend·ing** *I'm fed up with your money and your whole condescending attitude.* ♦ **con·de·scend·ing·ly** *James Sinclair smiled condescendingly.* ♦ **con·de·scen·sion** /ˌkɒndɪˈsenʃən/ *There was a tinge of condescension in the way the girl received me.*   VERB: V to-inf [PRAGMATICS]   VERB: V to n [PRAGMATICS]   ADJ-GRADED   ADV-GRADED   N-UNCOUNT

con·di·ment /ˈkɒndɪmənt/ **condiments.** A **condiment** is a flavouring such as salt, pepper, or mustard that you add to food when you eat it.   N-COUNT

con·di·tion /kənˈdɪʃən/ **conditions, conditioning, conditioned. 1** The **condition** of a person or thing is the state that they are in, especially their physical state. *He remains in a critical condition in a California hospital... The two-bedroom chalet is in*   ◆◆◆◆◆   N-SING: also no det, with supp

good condition. **2** The **conditions** under which something is done or happens are all the factors or circumstances which directly affect it. *This change has been timed under laboratory conditions.* **3** The **conditions** in which people live or work are the factors which affect their comfort, safety, or health. *He could not work in these conditions any longer.* **4** The **condition** of a group of people is their situation in life, especially the difficulties or hardship they have. *The government has encouraged its people to better their condition.* **5** To **condition** something such as your hair or skin means to put something on it which will keep it soft and in good condition. ♦ **con·di·tion·er, conditioners** *Massage the conditioner evenly through the hair. ...fabric conditioner.* ♦ See also **air-conditioner**.   N-PLURAL   N-PLURAL   N-SING: with supp FORMAL   VERB: V n   N-COUNT

6 If you say that someone is **in no condition** to do something, you mean that they are too ill, upset, or drunk to do it. **7** If someone is **out of condition**, they are unhealthy and unfit, because they have stopped exercising regularly. **8** ♦ **in mint condition:** see **mint**.   PHRASE   PHRASE

9 A **condition** is something which must happen or be done in order for something else to be possible, especially when this is written into a contract or law. *...terms and conditions of employment.* **10** When you agree to do something **on condition that** something else happens, you mean that you will only do it if this other thing also happens. *He spoke to reporters on condition that he was not identified.*   N-COUNT: with supp   PHR-CONJ

11 If someone has a particular **condition**, they have an illness or other medical problem. *Doctors suspect he may have a heart condition.*   N-COUNT

12 If someone **is conditioned** by their upbringing or environment, they are influenced by it over a period of time so that they do certain things or think in a particular way. *You have been conditioned to believe that it is weak to be scared.* ♦ **con·di·tion·ing** *...social conditioning.*   VERB: be V-ed be V-ed to-inf Also be V-ed into -ing/n   N-UNCOUNT

con·di·tion·al /kənˈdɪʃənəl/. **1** If a situation or agreement is **conditional** on something, it will only happen or continue if this thing happens. *Their support is conditional on his proposals meeting their approval.* ♦ **con·di·tion·al·ly** *Mr Smith has conditionally agreed.* **2** In grammar, a **conditional** clause is a subordinate clause which refers to a situation which may exist or whose possible consequences you are considering. Most conditional clauses begin with 'if' or 'unless'.   ◆◇◇◇◇ ADJ   ADV: ADV with v ADJ: ADJ n

con·ditional ˈdischarge, conditional discharges. In Britain, if someone who is convicted of an offence is given a **conditional discharge** by a court, they are not punished unless they later commit a further offence.   N-COUNT

con·do /ˈkɒndəʊ/ **condos. Condo** is an abbreviation for **condominium**.   N-COUNT

con·do·lence /kənˈdəʊləns/ **condolences. 1** A message of **condolence** is a message in which you express your sympathy for someone because one of their friends or relatives has died recently. **2** When you offer or express your **condolences** to someone, you express your sympathy for them because one of their friends or relatives has died recently.   ◆◇◇◇◇ N-UNCOUNT   N-PLURAL

con·dom /ˈkɒndɒm/ **condoms.** A **condom** is a covering made of rubber which a man can wear on his penis as a contraceptive or as protection against disease during sexual intercourse.   ◆◆◇◇◇ N-COUNT

con·do·min·ium /ˌkɒndəˈmɪniəm/ **condominiums. 1** A **condominium** is a block of flats in which each flat is owned by the person who lives there. **2** A **condominium** is one of the privately owned flats in a condominium.   ◆◇◇◇◇ N-COUNT AMERICAN   N-COUNT AMERICAN

con·done /kənˈdəʊn/ **condones, condoning, condoned.** If someone **condones** behaviour that is wrong, they accept it and allow it to happen. *I have never encouraged nor condoned violence.*   ◆◇◇◇◇ VERB V n

con·dor /ˈkɒndɔː/ **condors.** A **condor** is a large South American bird that eats dead animals.   ◆◇◇◇◇ N-COUNT

con·du·cive /kənˈdjuːsɪv, AM -ˈduːsɪv/. If one thing is **conducive** to another thing, it makes the   ◆◇◇◇◇ ADJ-GRADED

other thing likely to happen. *Make your bedroom as conducive to sleep as possible.*

con·duct, conducts, conducting, conduct- ◆◆◆◆◇
ed. The verb is pronounced /kən'dʌkt/. The noun is pronounced /'kɒndʌkt/. **1** When you **conduct** an activity or task, you organize it and carry it out. *I decided to conduct an experiment.* **2** The **conduct** of a task or activity is the way in which it is organized and carried out. *...the conduct of free and fair elections. ...the conduct of economic policy.* **3** If you **conduct** yourself in a particular way, you behave in that way. *The way he conducts himself reflects on the party... They conduct their private and public lives in accordance with Christian morality.* **4** Someone's **conduct** is the way they behave. *...basic principles of civilised conduct.* **5** When someone **conducts** an orchestra or choir, they stand in front of it and direct its performance. *Solti will continue to conduct here and abroad.* **6** If something **conducts** heat, electricity, or sound, it allows heat, electricity, or sound to pass through it or along it. ♦ **con·duc·tion** /kən'dʌkʃən/. Conduction is the process by which heat, electricity, or sound passes through or along something. **7** If you **conduct** someone to a place, you take them there. ● See also **safe conduct**.

VERB
V n
N-SING:
with supp

VERB
V pron-refl

N-UNCOUNT:
with supp

VERB: V n
V

VERB: V n

N-UNCOUNT

VERB:
V n prep/adv
FORMAL

con,ducted 'tour, conducted tours. A **conducted tour** is a visit to a place during which someone explains everything to you.

N-COUNT
BRITISH

con·duc·tive /kən'dʌktɪv/. A **conductive** substance can conduct things such as heat and electricity. ♦ **con·duc·tiv·ity** /,kɒndʌk'tɪvɪti/ *...a device which monitors the electrical conductivity of the skin.*

ADJ-GRADED
TECHNICAL

N-UNCOUNT

con·duc·tor /kən'dʌktə/ **conductors. 1** A **conductor** is a person who stands in front of an orchestra or choir and directs its performance. **2** On a bus or train, the **conductor** is a person who sells tickets for a journey. **3** A **conductor** is a substance that heat or electricity can pass through or along. ● See also **lightning conductor, semiconductor**.

◆◆◇◇◇
N-COUNT

N-COUNT

N-COUNT

con·duit /'kɒndjʊɪt, AM -duɪt/ **conduits. 1** A **conduit** is a small tunnel or pipe through which water or electrical wires go. **2** A **conduit** is a person or country that carries information or goods between two or more people or countries. *Mr Gorbachev could still act as a conduit for aid from the West.*

◆◇◇◇◇
N-COUNT

N-COUNT

cone /kəʊn/ **cones. 1** A **cone** is a shape with a circular base and smooth curved sides ending in a point at the top. See picture headed **shapes**. *...a twisted cone of paper.* **2** A **cone** is the fruit of a tree such as a pine or fir. It consists of a cluster of woody scales containing seeds. **3** A **cone** is a cone-shaped wafer that is used for holding ice cream. You can also refer to an ice cream that you eat in this way as a **cone**. *...a chocolate cone.* **4** See also **pine cone, traffic cone**.

◆◇◇◇◇
N-COUNT

N-COUNT

N-COUNT

con·fec·tion /kən'fekʃən/ **confections. 1** A **confection** is an elaborately decorated cake or some other sweet food. **2** A **confection** is something that is elaborately made or built. *...an extraordinary architectural confection of old and new.*

N-COUNT
WRITTEN

N-COUNT
WRITTEN

con·fec·tion·er /kən'fekʃənə/ **confectioners.** A **confectioner** is a person whose job is making or selling sweets and chocolates.

N-COUNT

con,fectioners' 'sugar. Confectioners' sugar is very fine white sugar that is used for making icing and sweets. The British term is **icing sugar**.

N-UNCOUNT
AMERICAN

con·fec·tion·ery /kən'fekʃənri, AM -neri/. **Confectionery** is sweets, chocolates, and fancy cakes. *...hand-made confectionery.*

N-UNCOUNT
WRITTEN

con·fed·era·cy /kən'fedərəsi/ **confederacies.** A **confederacy** is a union of states or people who are trying to achieve the same thing.

N-COUNT

con·fed·er·ate /kən'fedərət/ **confederates.** Someone's **confederates** are the people they are working with in a secret activity.

◆◇◇◇◇
N-COUNT

con·fed·era·tion /kən,fedə'reɪʃən/ **confederations.** A **confederation** is an organization or alliance of smaller groups or states, especially one that exists for business or political purposes. *...the Con-*

◆◆◇◇◇
N-COUNT

federation of Indian Industry. ...a confederation of mini-states.*

con·fer /kən'fɜː/ **confers, conferring, conferred. 1** When you **confer** with someone, you discuss something with them in order to make a decision. You can also say that two people **confer**. *He conferred with Hill... His doctors conferred by telephone.* **2** If someone or something **confers** something such as power or an honour on you, they give it to you. *The constitution also confers large powers on Brazil's 25 constituent states... Never imagine that rank confers genuine authority.*

◆◇◇◇◇
V-RECIP
V with n
pl-n V

VERB
V n on n
V n
FORMAL

con·fer·ence /'kɒnfrəns/ **conferences. 1** A **conference** is a meeting, often lasting a few days, which is organized on a particular subject or to bring together people who have a common interest. *...a conference on education. ...the Conservative Party conference.* **2** A **conference** is a meeting at which formal discussions take place. *They sat down at the dinner table, as they always did, before the meal, for a conference... Her employer was in conference with two lawyers.* **3** See also **press conference**.

◆◆◆◆◇
N-COUNT

N-COUNT:
also in N

con·fess /kən'fes/ **confesses, confessing, confessed. 1** If someone **confesses** to doing something wrong or something that they are ashamed of, they admit that they did it. *He had confessed to seventeen murders... I had expected her to confess that she only wrote these books for the money... Most rape victims confess a feeling of help-lessness... He had been forced into confessing.* **2** If someone **confesses** or **confesses** their sins, they tell God or a priest about their sins so that they can be forgiven. *You just go to the church and confess your sins... We have confessed our failures and mistakes to God.* **3** You use expressions like '**I confess**', '**I must confess**', or '**I have to confess**' to apologize for admitting something you are slightly ashamed of or that you think might offend or annoy someone. *I confess it's got me baffled... I must confess I'm not a great enthusiast for long political programmes.*

◆◆◇◇◇
V to n/-ing
V that
V n
V

VERB
V n
V n to n

PHRASE
PRAGMATICS

con·fessed /kən'fest/. You use **confessed** to describe someone who openly admits that they have a particular fault or have done something wrong. *...the confessed killer of Martin Luther King.*

◆◇◇◇◇
ADJ: ADJ n

con·fes·sion /kən'feʃən/ **confessions. 1** A **confession** is a signed statement by someone in which they admit that they have committed a particular crime. *They forced him to sign a confession.* **2** Confession is the act of admitting that you have done something that you are ashamed of or embarrassed about. *The diaries are a mixture of confession and observation... I have a confession to make.* **3** If you make a **confession** of your beliefs or feelings, you publicly tell people that this is what you believe or feel. *...Tatyana's confession of love.* **4** In the Catholic church and in some other churches, if you go to **confession**, you privately tell a priest about your sins and ask for forgiveness.

◆◆◇◇◇
N-COUNT

N-VAR

N-VAR

N-VAR

con·fes·sion·al /kən'feʃənəl/ **confessionals. 1** A **confessional** is the small room in a church where Christians, especially Roman Catholics, go to confess their sins. **2** A **confessional** speech or letter is one in which you confess something. *The convictions rest solely on disputed witness and confessional statements.* **3** A **confessional** is a statement or meeting in which a person or people confess things.

◆◇◇◇◇
N-COUNT

ADJ-GRADED

N-COUNT

con·fes·sor /kən'fesə/ **confessors. 1** A **confessor** is a priest who hears a person's confession. **2** If you describe someone as your **confessor**, you mean that they are the person you can talk to about your secrets or problems. *He had listened in his role of father confessor.*

N-COUNT

N-COUNT

con·fet·ti /kən'feti/. **Confetti** is small pieces of coloured paper that people throw over the bride and groom at a wedding.

N-UNCOUNT

con·fi·dant /'kɒnfɪdænt, -'dænt/ **confidants.** Someone's **confidant** is a man who they are able to discuss their private problems with. *...a close confidant of the president.*

N-COUNT

con·fi·dante /ˈkɒnfɪdænt, -ˈdænt/ **confidantes.** N-COUNT
Someone's **confidante** is a woman who they are able to discuss their private problems with. *You are her closest friend and confidante.*

con·fide /kənˈfaɪd/ **confides, confiding, con-** ◆◇◇◇◇
fided. If you **confide** in someone, you tell them a secret. *She had confided in me a year earlier... He confided to me that he felt like he was being pun-* V inn V on that ◆ **con·fid·ing** *Ford's letters to her are fond* ADJ-GRADED
and confiding.

con·fi·dence /ˈkɒnfɪdəns/ **confidences. 1** If you ◆◆◆◇
have **confidence** in someone, you feel that you can N-UNCOUNT
trust them. *I have every confidence in you. ...the lack of confidence in the police.* **2** If you have **confi-** N-UNCOUNT
dence, you feel sure about your abilities, qualities, or ideas. *The band is on excellent form and brim-* ming with confidence.* **3** If you can say something N-UNCOUNT
with **confidence**, you feel certain it is correct. *I can say with confidence that such rumors were totally groundless.*
4 If you tell someone something in **confidence**, you N-UNCOUNT
tell them a secret. *We told you all these things in confi-* dence.* ● If you **take** someone **into** your **confidence**, PHRASE
you tell them a secret. *If your daughter takes you into her confidence, don't rush off to tell your husband.* **5** A N-COUNT
confidence is a secret that you tell someone. *Gregory shared confidences with Carmen.*
6 See also **vote of no confidence.**

'**confidence trick, confidence tricks.** A confi- N-COUNT
dence trick is a trick in which someone deceives BRITISH
you by telling you something that is not true, often in order to get money from you.

con·fi·dent /ˈkɒnfɪdənt/. **1** If you are **confident** ◆◆◆◇◇
about something, you are certain that it will happen ADJ-GRADED
in the way you want it to. *I am confident that every-* thing will come out right in time... Management is confident about the way business is progressing.*
◆ **con·fi·dent·ly** *I can confidently promise that this* ADV-GRADED:
year is going to be very different.* **2** If a person or ADV with v
their manner is **confident**, they feel sure about their own abilities, qualities, or ideas. *In time he became more confident and relaxed... She is a confident woman.* ◆ **confidently** *She walked confidently* ADV-GRADED
across the hall.* **3** If you are **confident** that some- ADJ-GRADED
thing is true, you are sure that it is true. A **confident** statement is one that the speaker is sure is true. *She is confident that everybody is on her side... 'Bet you I can', comes the confident reply.* ◆ **confidently** *I can* ADV-GRADED:
confidently say that none of them were or are racist.* ADV with v

con·fi·den·tial /ˌkɒnfɪˈdenʃəl/. **1** Information that ◆◆◇◇◇
is **confidential** is meant to be kept secret or private. ADJ-GRADED
...confidential information about her private life.
◆ **con·fi·den·tial·ly** *Any information they give will* ADV-GRADED:
be treated confidentially.* ◆ **con·fi·den·ti·al·ity** ADV with v N-UNCOUNT
/ˌkɒnfɪdenʃɪˈælɪti/ *...the confidentiality of the client-* solicitor relationship.* **2** If you talk to someone in a ADJ-GRADED
confidential way, you talk to them quietly because what you are saying is secret or private. *His face suddenly turned solemn, his voice confidential.*
◆ **con·fi·den·tial·ly** *Nash hadn't raised his voice,* ADV-GRADED:
still spoke rather softly, confidentially.* ADV after v

con·fi·den·tial·ly /ˌkɒnfɪˈdenʃəli/. **Confidentially** is ADV:
used to say that what you are telling someone is a ADV with cl
secret. *Confidentially, I am not sure that it wasn't above their heads.* ● See also **confidential.**

con·figu·ra·tion /kənˌfɪɡʊˈreɪʃən, AM -ˌfɪɡjə-/ **con-** ◆◇◇◇◇
figurations. A **configuration** is an arrangement of N-COUNT
a group of things. *...Stonehenge, in south-western* FORMAL
England, an ancient configuration of giant stones.*

con·fine, confines, confining, confined. The ◆◆◇◇◇
verb is pronounced /kənˈfaɪn/. The noun **confines** is pronounced /ˈkɒnfaɪnz/. **1** To **confine** something VERB:
to a particular place or group means to prevent it V n to n
from spreading beyond that place or group. *The US* V n
will soon be taking steps to confine the conflict.* **2** If VERB
you **confine** yourself or your activities **to** something, V n to n
you do only that thing and nothing else. *Yoko had largely confined her activities to the world of big business.* **3** If someone **is confined to** a mental insti- VB: usu
tution, prison, or other place, they are not allowed passive

to leave it for a period of time. *The army and police* be V-ed to n
had been confined to barracks.*
4 Something that is within the **confines** of an area or N-PLURAL
place is within the boundaries enclosing it. *The movie* FORMAL
is set entirely within the confines of the abandoned fac-* tory.* **5** The **confines** of a situation, system, or activity N-PLURAL
are the limitations or restrictions it involves. *...the confines of the British class system.*

con·fined /kənˈfaɪnd/. **1** If something is **confined** ◆◆◇◇◇
to a particular place, it exists only in that place. If it ADJ:
is **confined** to a particular group, only members of v-link ADJ to n
that group have it. *These dangers are not confined to smokers.* **2** A **confined** space or area is very small. ADJ-GRADED
3 If someone is **confined to** a wheelchair, bed, or ADJ:
house, they have to stay there, because they are dis- v-link ADJ to n
abled or ill.

con·fine·ment /kənˈfaɪnmənt/ **confinements.** ◆◇◇◇◇
1 Confinement is the state of being forced to stay N-UNCOUNT
in a prison or another place which you cannot leave. *She had been held in solitary confinement for four months.* **2** A woman's **confinement** is the peri- N-VAR
od of time just before and during which she gives FORMAL
birth to a child.

con·firm /kənˈfɜːm/ **confirms, confirming, con-** ◆◆◆◇
firmed. 1 If something **confirms** what you believe, VB: no cont
suspect, or fear, it shows that it is definitely true. *X-* V that
rays have confirmed that he has not broken any V n
bones... These new statistics confirm our worst fears.*
◆ **con·fir·ma·tion** /ˌkɒnfəˈmeɪʃən/ *They took her* N-UNCOUNT
resignation from Bendix as confirmation of their sus-* picions.* **2** If you **confirm** something that has been VERB: V n
stated or suggested, you say that it is definitely true. V that
The spokesman confirmed that the area was now in rebel hands. ◆ **confirmation** *She glanced over at* N-UNCOUNT
James for confirmation.*
3 If you **confirm** an arrangement or appointment, VERB
you say that it is definite, usually in a letter or on the V n
telephone. *You make the reservation, and I'll confirm it in writing.* ◆ **confirmation** *Travel arrangements* N-UNCOUNT
are subject to confirmation.*
4 If someone **is confirmed**, they are formally accept- VERB:
ed as a member of a Christian church. ◆ **con·fir·ma-** be V-ed
·tion, confirmations *...when I was being prepared* N-VAR
for Confirmation.*
5 If something **confirms** you **in** your decision, belief, VB: no cont
or opinion, it makes you think that you are definitely V n in n
right. *It has confirmed me in my decision not to be-* come a nun.* **6** If a person or organization **confirms** VERB
their position, role, or power, they do something to V n
make their power, position, or role stronger or more definite. *Edberg confirmed his position as the world's number one tennis player.* **7** If something **con-** VERB
firms you **as** something, it shows that you definitely V n as n
deserve a certain name, role, or position. *His new role could confirm him as one of our leading actors.*

con·firmed /kənˈfɜːmd/. You use **confirmed** to de- ◆◇◇◇◇
scribe someone who has a habit or belief that they ADJ: ADJ n
are unlikely to change. *...a confirmed bachelor.*

con·fis·cate /ˈkɒnfɪskeɪt/ **confiscates, confis-** ◆◇◇◇◇
cating, confiscated. If you **confiscate** something VERB
from someone, you take it away from them, usually V n from n
as a punishment. *There is concern that police use the* Also V n
law to confiscate assets from people who have com-* mitted minor offences.* ◆ **con·fis·ca·tion** N-VAR
/ˌkɒnfɪsˈkeɪʃən/ **confiscations** *...the confiscation of his passport.*

con·fla·gra·tion /ˌkɒnfləˈɡreɪʃən/ **conflagra-** N-COUNT
tions. A **conflagration** is a very large destructive fire.

con·flate /kənˈfleɪt/ **conflates, conflating, con-** V-RECIP-ERG:
flated. If you **conflate** two or more descriptions or V pl-n
ideas, or if they **conflate**, you combine them in or- V n with n
der to produce a single one. *Unfortunately the pub-* pl-n V
lic conflated fiction with reality... The two meanings FORMAL
conflated.* ◆ **con·fla·tion** /kənˈfleɪʃən/ **conflations** N-VAR
The story was a conflation of Greek myths.

con·flict, conflicts, conflicting, conflicted. ◆◆◆◇
The noun is pronounced /ˈkɒnflɪkt/. The verb is pronounced /kənˈflɪkt/. **1 Conflict** is serious dis- N-UNCOUNT
agreement and argument. If two people or groups

are in **conflict**, they have had a serious disagreement and have not yet reached agreement. *Try to keep any conflict between you and your ex-partner to a minimum.* **2 Conflict** is fighting between countries or groups of people. ...*a military conflict.* **3 Conflict** is a state of mind in which you find it impossible to make a decision. ...*the anguish of his own inner conflict.* **4** a **conflict** is a serious difference between two or more beliefs, ideas, or interests. If two beliefs, ideas, or interests are in **conflict**, they are very different. *There is a conflict between what they are doing and what you want.* **5** If ideas, beliefs, or accounts **conflict**, they are very different from each other and it seems impossible for them to exist together. *He held firm opinions which usually conflicted with my own.*
N-VAR

N-UNCOUNT

N-VAR

V-RECIP:
pl-n V
V with n

con·flu·ence /'kɒnfluəns/ **confluences.** **1** The **confluence** of two rivers is the place where they join and become one larger river. **2** If there is a **confluence** of two things, they join or combine. ...*an unusual confluence of events.*
N-SING

N-COUNT
FORMAL

con·form /kən'fɔːm/ **conforms, conforming, conformed.** **1** If something **conforms** to a law or regulation or to someone's wishes, it is of the type or quality that is required or desired. *These activities do not conform with diplomatic rules.* **2** If you **conform**, you behave in the way that you are expected or supposed to behave. *He did not feel obliged to conform to the rules.* **3** If someone or something **conforms** to a pattern or type, they are very similar to it. ...*a young girl who can't make her body conform to the idea of feminine beauty.*
VERB
V to/with n

VERB: V
V to/with n

VERB
V to n

con·form·ist /kən'fɔːmɪst/ **conformists.** Someone who is **conformist** behaves or thinks like everyone else rather than doing things that are original. *Mr Gordon now feels forced into an ever more conformist way of running his practice.* ► A **conformist** is someone who is conformist.
ADJ-GRADED

N-COUNT

con·form·ity /kən'fɔːmɪti/. **1** If something happens in **conformity** with a law or regulation or with someone's wishes, it happens as the law or regulation says it should happen, or as the person wants it to happen. *The prime minister is, in conformity with the constitution, chosen by the president.* **2 Conformity** means behaving in the same way as most other people. *Excessive conformity is usually caused by fear of disapproval.*
N-UNCOUNT

N-UNCOUNT

con·found /kən'faʊnd/ **confounds, confounding, confounded.** If someone or something **confounds** you, they make you feel surprised or confused, often by showing you that your opinion of them was wrong. *He momentarily confounded his critics by his cool handling of the Gulf crisis.*
VERB
V n

con·front /kən'frʌnt/ **confronts, confronting, confronted.** **1** If you **are confronted** with a problem or task, you have to deal with it. *Ministers underestimated the magnitude of the task confronting them.* **2** If you **confront** a difficult situation or issue, you accept the fact that it exists and try to deal with it. *We are learning how to confront death.* **3** If you **are confronted** by something that you find threatening or difficult to deal with, it is in front of you. *I was confronted with an array of knobs, levers, and switches.* **4** If you **confront** someone, you stand or sit in front of them, especially when you are going to fight, argue, or compete with them. *The candidates confronted each other during a televised debate.* **5** If you **confront** someone with something, you present facts or evidence to them in order to accuse them of something. *I could not bring myself to confront him about it.*
VERB:
be V-ed with/
by n
V n
VERB
V n

VB: usu
passive
be V-ed with/
by n
VERB
V n

VERB:
V n with n
V n about n
Also V n

con·fron·ta·tion /ˌkɒnfrʌn'teɪʃən/ **confrontations.** A **confrontation** is a dispute, fight, or battle between two groups of people. ...*confrontation with the enemy.*
N-VAR

con·fron·ta·tion·al /ˌkɒnfrʌn'teɪʃənəl/. If you describe the way that someone behaves as **confrontational**, you disapprove of the fact that they are aggressive and likely to cause a dispute. *Riot police are on hand but have not been confrontational.*
ADJ-GRADED
PRAGMATICS

con·fuse /kən'fjuːz/ **confuses, confusing, confused.** **1** If you **confuse** two things, you get them mixed up, so that you think one of them is the other one. *I can't see how anyone could confuse you with another!* ♦ **con·fu·sion** /kən'fjuːʒən/. *Use different colours of felt pen on your sketch to avoid confusion.* **2** To **confuse** someone means to make it difficult for them to know exactly what is happening or what to do. *German politics surprised and confused him.* **3** To **confuse** a situation means to make it complicated or difficult to understand. *In attempting to present two sides, you managed only to confuse the issue.*
VERB:
V pl-n
V n with n

N-UNCOUNT

VERB
V n

VERB
V n

con·fused /kən'fjuːzd/. **1** If you are **confused**, you do not know exactly what is happening or what to do. *People are confused about what they should eat to stay healthy.* ♦ **con·fus·ed·ly** /kən'fjuːzɪdli/. *He shook his head confusedly.* **2** Something that is **confused** does not have any order or pattern and is difficult to understand. ...*a modern society in which values have become increasingly confused.*
ADJ-GRADED

ADV-GRADED:
ADV with v
ADJ-GRADED

con·fus·ing /kən'fjuːzɪŋ/. Something that is **confusing** makes it difficult for people to know exactly what is happening or what to do. *This situation must be confusing for you.* ♦ **con·fus·ing·ly** *Confusingly, blind people also respond to the light.*
ADJ-GRADED

ADV-GRADED

con·fu·sion /kən'fjuːʒən/ **confusions.** **1** If there is **confusion** about something, it is not clear what the true situation is. *There's still confusion about the number of casualties.* **2 Confusion** is a situation in which everything is in disorder, especially because there are lots of things happening at the same time. *There was confusion when a man fired shots.* **3** If your mind is in a state of **confusion**, you do not know what to believe or what you should do. *We always left his office in a state of confusion.* **4** See also **confuse**.
N-VAR

N-UNCOUNT

N-VAR

con·ga /'kɒŋgə/ **congas.** If people dance a **conga**, they dance in a long winding line, with each person holding on to the back of the person in front.
N-COUNT

con·geal /kən'dʒiːl/ **congeals, congealing, congealed.** When a liquid **congeals**, it becomes very thick and sticky. *The blood had started to congeal.*
VERB
V

con·gen·ial /kən'dʒiːniəl/. A **congenial** person, place, or environment is pleasant. *He is back in more congenial company.*
ADJ-GRADED

con·geni·tal /kən'dʒenɪtəl/. **1** A **congenital** disease or medical condition is one that a person has had from birth. *When John was 17, he died of congenital heart disease.* ♦ **con·geni·tal·ly** ...*congenitally handicapped children.* **2** A **congenital** characteristic or feature in a person is so strong that you cannot imagine it ever changing. *He was a congenital liar.* ♦ **congenitally** *I admit to being congenitally lazy.*
ADJ
MEDICAL

ADV:
ADV adj/-ed
ADJ

ADV

con·ger /'kɒŋgə/ **congers.** A **conger** or a **conger eel** is a large sea eel.
N-VAR

con·gest·ed /kən'dʒestɪd/. **1** A **congested** road or area is extremely crowded and blocked with traffic or people. *Some areas are congested with both cars and people.* **2** If a part of the body is **congested**, it is blocked. *The arteries in his neck had become fatally congested.*
ADJ-GRADED

ADJ-GRADED
FORMAL

con·ges·tion /kən'dʒestʃən/. **1** If there is **congestion** in a place, the place is extremely crowded and blocked with traffic or people. *The problems of traffic congestion will not disappear in a hurry.* **2** If there is **congestion** in a part of the body, it is blocked. ...*nasal congestion.*
N-UNCOUNT

N-UNCOUNT

con·ges·tive /kən'dʒestɪv/. A **congestive** disease is a medical condition where a part of the body becomes blocked. ...*congestive heart failure.*
ADJ: ADJ n
MEDICAL

con·glom·er·ate /kən'glɒmərət/ **conglomerates.** A **conglomerate** is a large business firm consisting of several different companies. *Fiat is Italy's largest industrial conglomerate.*
N-COUNT

con·glom·era·tion /kən,glɒmə'reɪʃən/ **conglomerations.** A **conglomeration** of things is a group of
N-COUNT
FORMAL

many different things, gathered together. ...*a con-glomeration of buildings, all tightly packed together.*

con·gratu·late /kənˈɡrætʃʊleɪt/ **congratulates, congratulating, congratulated. 1** If you **con-gratulate** someone, you say something to show you are pleased that something nice has happened to them. *She congratulated him on the birth of his son.* ♦ **con·gratu·la·tion** /kənˌɡrætʃʊˈleɪʃən/ ...*letters of congratulation.* **2** If you **congratulate** someone, you praise them for something admirable that they have done. *I really must congratulate the organisers for a well run and enjoyable event.* **3** If you **con-gratulate** yourself, you are pleased about something that you have done. *Journalists have been congratu-lating themselves on the role the press has played in the investigations.*

con·gratu·la·tions /kənˌɡrætʃʊˈleɪʃənz/. **1** You say **'Congratulations'** to someone in order to con-gratulate them on something nice that has hap-pened to them or something admirable that they have done. *Congratulations, you have a healthy baby boy.* **2** If you offer someone your **congratula-tions,** you congratulate them.

con·gratu·la·tory /kənˌɡrætʃʊˈleɪtəri/. A **congratu-latory** message expresses congratulations. *He sent Kim a congratulatory letter.*

con·gre·gate /ˈkɒŋɡrɪɡeɪt/ **congregates, con-gregating, congregated.** When people **congre-gate,** they gather together and form a group. *Young-sters love to congregate here in the evenings.*

con·gre·ga·tion /ˌkɒŋɡrɪˈɡeɪʃən/ **congrega-tions.** The people who attend a church service are referred to as the **congregation.**

con·gress /ˈkɒŋɡres/ **congresses.** A **congress** is a large meeting that is held to discuss ideas and policies. *A lot has changed after the party congress.*

Con·gress. Congress is the elected group of poli-ticians that is responsible for making the law in the USA. It consists of two parts: the House of Repre-sentatives and the Senate.

con·gres·sion·al /kənˈɡreʃənəl/. A **congressional** policy, action, or person relates to the US Congress. ...*a congressional report published on September 5th.*

congress·man /ˈkɒŋɡrɪsmən/ **congressmen.** A **congressman** is a male member of the US Congress, especially of the House of Representatives.

congress·woman /ˈkɒŋɡrɪswʊmən/ **congress-women.** A **congresswoman** is a female member of the US Congress, especially of the House of Representatives.

con·gru·ent /ˈkɒŋɡruənt/. If one thing is **congru-ent** with another, there is a similarity between them. *The interests of landowners were by no means congruent with those of industrial capitalists.*

coni·cal /ˈkɒnɪkəl/. A **conical** object is shaped like a cone. ...*conical fur hats.*

co·ni·fer /ˈkɒnɪfə/ **conifers. Conifers** are a type of trees and shrubs that grow in cooler areas of the world. They produce cones and have needle-like leaves which they do not normally lose in winter.

co·nif·er·ous /kəˈnɪfərəs, AM kəʊ-/. A **coniferous** forest or wood is made up of conifers.

con·jec·ture /kənˈdʒektʃə/ **conjectures, con-jecturing, conjectured. 1** A **conjecture** is a guess based on incomplete or doubtful information that you do not know for certain is true. *The atti-tudes of others were matters of conjecture.* **2** When you **conjecture,** you form an opinion or reach a conclusion on the basis of incomplete or doubtful information. *It could be conjectured that Murphy is on track to become the greatest movie comic of all time.*

con·join /kənˈdʒɔɪn/ **conjoins, conjoining, con-joined.** If two or more things **conjoin** or if you **conjoin** them, they are united and joined together. *America's rise in rates was conjoined with higher rates elsewhere.* ...*if we conjoin the two responses.*

con·ju·gal /ˈkɒndʒʊɡəl/. **Conjugal** means relating to marriage and the relationship between a hus-

band and wife, especially their sexual relationship. ...*a man deprived of his conjugal rights.*

con·junc·tion /kənˈdʒʌŋkʃən/ **conjunctions. 1** A **conjunction** of two or more things is the occur-rence of them at the same time or place. ...*a con-junction of religious and social factors.* **2** In gram-mar, a **conjunction** is a word or group of words that joins together words, groups, or clauses. Examples of conjunctions are 'and', 'but', 'although', 'be-cause', and 'when'. **3** If one thing is done or used **in conjunction** with another, the two things are done or used together. *The army should have operated in conjunction with the fleet to raid the enemy's coast.*

con·junc·ti·vi·tis /kənˌdʒʌŋktɪˈvaɪtɪs/. **Conjuncti-vitis** is an eye infection which causes the thin skin that covers the eyeball to become inflamed.

con·jure /ˈkʌndʒə, AM ˈkɑːn-/ **conjures, conjur-ing, conjured.** If you **conjure** something out of nothing, you produce it as if by magic. *They man-aged to conjure a victory.* ▶ **Conjure up** means the same as **conjure.** *Every day a different chef will be conjuring up delicious dishes in the restaurant.*

conjure up. 1 If you **conjure up** a memory, picture, or idea, you create it in your mind. *When he closed his eyes, he could conjure up in exact colour almost every event of his life.* **2** If something such as a word or sound **conjures up** particular images or ideas, it makes you think of them. *Jimmy Buffett's music con-jures up a warm night in the tropics.* **3** See **conjure.**

con·jur·er /ˈkʌndʒərə, AM ˈkɑːn-/ **conjurers;** also spelled **conjuror.** A **conjurer** is a person who enter-tains people by doing magic tricks.

con·jur·or /ˈkʌndʒərə, AM ˈkɑːn-/. See **conjurer.**

conk /kɒŋk/ **conks, conking, conked.**

conk out. If something such as a machine or a vehi-cle **conks out,** it stops working or breaks down. *The dynamo which provided the electricity conked out.*

conk·er /ˈkɒŋkə/ **conkers. 1 Conkers** are round brown nuts which come from horse chestnut trees. **2** In Britain, **conkers** is a children's game in which you tie a conker to a piece of string and try to break your opponent's conker by hitting it as hard as you can with your own.

con man, con men; also spelled **conman.** A **con man** is a man who persuades people to give him their money or property by lying to them.

con·nect /kəˈnekt/ **connects, connecting, connected. 1** If something or someone **connects** one thing to another, or if one thing **connects** to an-other, the two things are joined together. *Connect the wires... Two cables connect to each corner.* **2** If something **connects** two things or places or if they **connect,** they are joined and people or things can pass between them. *The fallopian tubes connect the ovaries with the uterus... His workshop connected with a small building in the garden.* **3** If a piece of equipment or a place **is connected** to a source of power or water, it is joined to that source so that it has power or water. *Ischia was now connected to the mainland water supply.* ▶ **Connect up** means the same as **connect.** *The shower is easy to install – it needs only to be connected up to the hot and cold water supply... They turned the barricade into a po-tential death trap by connecting it up to the mains.* **4** If a telephone operator **connects** you, he or she en-ables you to speak to another person by telephone. *He asked to be connected to the central switchboard.* **5** If one train or plane, for example, **connects** with an-other, it arrives at a time which allows passengers to change to the other one in order to continue their journey. ...*a train connecting with a ferry to Ireland.* **6** If you **connect** a person or thing with something, you realize that there is a link or relationship between them. *I wouldn't have connected the two things.* **7** Something that **connects** a person or thing with something else shows or provides a link or relation-ship between them. *What connects them?* **8** If a per-son or their ideas **connect** with you, you feel a sense of agreement and familiarity with them because you have similar ideas. You can also say that two people

connect. *If you stand on stage and share your view of the world, people will connect with you.*
connect up. See **connect** 3.   PHRASAL VB

con·nect·ed /kə'nektɪd/. If one thing is **connected** ◆◆◇◇◇ with another, there is a link or relationship between ADJ them. *The dispute is not directly connected to the negotiations.* ● See also **connect, well-connected**.

con·nec·tion /kə'nekʃən/ **connections;** also ◆◆◆◇◇ spelled **connexion** in British English. **1** A **connec-** N-VAR **tion** is a relationship between two things, people, or groups. *The police say he had no connection with the security forces.*
2 A **connection** is a joint where two wires or pipes are N-COUNT joined together.
3 If a place has good road, rail, or air **connections,** N-COUNT many places can be directly reached from there by car, train, or plane. *Fukuoka has excellent air and rail connections.* **4** If you get a **connection** at a station or N-COUNT airport, you catch a train, bus, or plane, after getting off another train, bus, or plane, in order to continue your journey. *My flight was late and I missed the connection.*
5 Your **connections** are the people who you know or N-PLURAL are related to, especially when they are in a position to help you. *She used her connections to full advantage.*
6 If you write or talk to someone **in connection with** PHR-PREP something, you write or talk to them about that thing. FORMAL *I am writing in connection with Michael Shower's letter.* **7** You say **in this connection** or **in that connec-** PHRASE **tion** to indicate that what you are talking about is re- PRAGMATICS lated to what you have just mentioned. *It is the 100th* FORMAL *anniversary of his death. We here are having very great celebrations in this connection.*

con,nective 'tissue. Connective tissue is the N-UNCOUNT substance in the bodies of animals and people TECHNICAL which fills in the spaces between organs and connects muscles and bones.

con·nect·or /kə'nektə/ **connectors.** A **connector** N-COUNT is a device that joins two pieces of equipment, wire, or piping together.

con·nex·ion /kə'nekʃən/. See **connection**.

con·niv·ance /kə'naɪvəns/. **Connivance** is a will- N-UNCOUNT ingness to allow or assist something to happen even PRAGMATICS though you know it is wrong; used showing disapproval. *It was stolen by Oliver, with the connivance of Helen.*

con·nive /kə'naɪv/ **connives, conniving, con-** **nived. 1** If you say that one person **connives** with V-RECIP: another to do something, you are critical of them V with n to-inf for secretly trying to achieve something to their PRAGMATICS common advantage. *Senior politicians connived to* pl-n V to-inf *ensure that he was not released.* **2** If you say that Also V with n someone **connives** at something or **connives** in VERB something, you are critical of them because they al- PRAGMATICS low or assist it to happen even though they know V at/in n/-ing that it is wrong. *To buy things cheaply from a poor country is to connive in its poverty.*

con·niv·ing /kə'naɪvɪŋ/. If you describe someone ADJ as **conniving**, you dislike them because they make PRAGMATICS secret plans in order to get things for themselves or harm other people. *...a conniving, greedy woman.*

con·nois·seur /ˌkɒnə'sɜː/ **connoisseurs.** A con- ◆◇◇◇◇ **noisseur** is someone who knows a lot about a par- N-COUNT ticular subject. *...connoisseurs of good food.*

con·no·ta·tion /ˌkɒnə'teɪʃən/ **connotations.** The ◆◇◇◇◇ **connotations** of a word or name are the ideas or N-COUNT qualities it makes you think of. *It's just one of those words that's got so many negative connotations.*

con·note /kə'nəʊt/ **connotes, connoting, con-** VERB **noted.** If a word or name **connotes** something, it V n makes you think of a particular idea or quality. FORMAL *'Shalom' connotes a sense of peace.*

con·quer /'kɒŋkə/ **conquers, conquering, con-** ◆◆◇◇◇ **quered. 1** If one country or group of people **con-** VERB: V n **quers** another, they take complete control of them. be V-ed *In the eleventh century the whole of England was* VERB *again conquered by the Vikings.* **2** If you **conquer** VERB something such as a problem, you succeed in end- V n ing it or dealing with it. *He has never conquered his addiction to smoking.*

con·quer·or /'kɒŋkərə/ **conquerors. 1** The con- ◆◇◇◇◇ **querors** of a country or group of people are the N-COUNT people who have taken complete control of it.
2 The **conqueror** of a person or team is the person N-COUNT or team that beats them in a game or contest.

con·quest /'kɒŋkwest/ **conquests. 1 Conquest** is ◆◇◇◇◇ the act of conquering a country or group of people. N-UNCOUNT: *He had led the conquest of southern Poland in 1939.* also N in pl
2 Conquests are lands that have been conquered in N-COUNT war. *Britain could not have peace unless she returned at least some of her conquests.*
3 If someone makes a **conquest**, they succeed in at- N-COUNT tracting and usually having sex with another person. *...men who boast about their sexual conquests.* **4** You N-COUNT can refer to the person that someone has succeeded in attracting as their **conquest**. *...a womaniser whose conquests included everyone from prostitutes to princesses.*
5 The **conquest** of something such as a problem is N-SING success in ending it or dealing with it. *The conquest of inflation has been the Government's overriding economic priority.*

con·quis·ta·dor /kɒn'kwɪstədɔː/ **conquistadors** N-COUNT or **conquistadores.** The **conquistadors** were the sixteenth century Spanish conquerors of Central and South America.

con·science /'kɒnʃəns/ **consciences. 1** Your ◆◆◇◇◇ **conscience** is the part of your mind that tells you N-COUNT whether what you are doing is right or wrong. *I have battled with my conscience over whether I should actually send this letter. ...a guilty conscience.*
2 Conscience is doing what you believe is right N-UNCOUNT even though it might be unpopular, difficult, or dangerous. *He refused for reasons of conscience to sign a new law legalising abortion.* ● See also **pris-** **oner of conscience**.
3 Conscience is a feeling of guilt because you know N-UNCOUNT you have done something that is wrong. *They have shown a ruthless lack of conscience.* **4** If you have PHRASE something **on** your **conscience**, you feel guilty because you know you have done something wrong. *Now the murderer has two deaths on his conscience.*
5 If you say that you cannot do something **in all con-** PHRASE **science**, you mean that you cannot do it because you think it is wrong. The usual American expression is **in good conscience**.

con·sci·en·tious /ˌkɒnʃi'enʃəs/. Someone who is ◆◇◇◇◇ **conscientious** is very careful to do their work prop- ADJ-GRADED erly. *...a conscientious and dedicated mother.*
♦ **con·sci·en·tious·ly** *He studied conscientiously.* ADV-GRADED
,**conscientious ob'jector, conscientious** N-COUNT **objectors.** A **conscientious objector** is a person who refuses to join the armed forces because they think that it is morally wrong to do so.

con·scious /'kɒnʃəs/. **1** If you are **conscious** of ◆◆◆◇◇ something, you notice it or realize that it is happen- ADJ-GRADED: ing. *He was conscious of the faint, musky aroma of* v-link ADJ *aftershave... He was conscious that he was breathing quickly.* **2 Conscious** memories or thoughts are ADJ: ADJ n ones that you are aware of. *He had no conscious memory of his four-week stay in hospital... I don't think we ever made a conscious decision to have a big family.* ♦ **con·scious·ly** *Sophie was not con-* ADV: *sciously seeking a replacement after her father died...* ADV with v, *Sometimes we are not consciously aware of these* ADV adj *feelings.* **3** If you are **conscious** of something, you ADJ-GRADED: think about it a lot, especially because you are un- v-link ADJ happy about it or because you think it is important. *I'm very conscious of my weight... Children are conscious that high standards are expected of them.*
4 Someone who is **conscious** is awake rather than ADJ asleep or unconscious. *She was fully conscious.*

-conscious /'kɒnʃəs/. **-conscious** combines with COMB words such as 'health', 'fashion', and 'politically' to form adjectives which describe someone who believes that the aspect of life indicated is important. *Environmentally conscious West Germans are worried about the pollution the car produces.*

con·scious·ness /'kɒnʃəsnəs/ **conscious-** ◆◆◆◇◇ **nesses. 1** Your **consciousness** is your mind and N-COUNT

your thoughts. *That idea has been creeping into our consciousness for some time.* ● See also **stream of consciousness**. **2** The **consciousness** of a group of people is their set of attitudes and beliefs. *...a necessary change in the European consciousness.* **3** You use **consciousness** to refer to an interest in and knowledge of a particular subject or idea. *Her political consciousness sprang from her upbringing.*   N-UNCOUNT: with supp / N-UNCOUNT: supp N

4 Consciousness is the state of being awake rather than being asleep or unconscious. If someone **loses consciousness**, they become unconscious. When they **regain consciousness**, they become conscious after being unconscious.   N-UNCOUNT

'consciousness raising. Consciousness raising is the process of developing awareness of an unfair situation, with the aim of making people want to help in changing it. *...consciousness-raising groups.*   N-UNCOUNT

con·script, conscripts, conscripting, conscripted. The noun is pronounced /'kɒnskrɪpt/. The verb is pronounced /kən'skrɪpt/. **1** A **conscript** is a person who has been made to join the armed forces of a country. **2** If someone **is conscripted**, they are officially made to join the armed forces of a country. *He was conscripted into the German army.* ♦ **con·scrip·tion** /kən'skrɪpʃən/. *All adult males will be liable for conscription.*   ♦◇◇◇ / N-COUNT / VB: usu passive beV-ed into n / N-UNCOUNT

con·se·crate /'kɒnsɪkreɪt/ **consecrates, consecrating, consecrated.** When a building, place, or object **is consecrated**, it is officially declared to be holy. When a person **is consecrated**, they are officially appointed to be a bishop. ♦ **con·se·cra·tion** /,kɒnsɪ'kreɪʃən/ *...the consecration of Barbara Harris as a Bishop.*   ♦◇◇◇ / VERB: beV-ed, also V n / N-UNCOUNT

con·secu·tive /kən'sekjʊtɪv/. **Consecutive** periods of time or events happen one after the other without interruption. *It was his second consecutive win... You can do these sessions on consecutive days if you like.* ♦ **con·secu·tive·ly** *...a CD player which plays six CDs consecutively.*   ♦♦◇◇ / ADJ / ADV: ADV after v

con·sen·sual /kən'senʃʊəl/. **1** A **consensual** approach or decision is based on general agreement amongst all the members of a group. *...the consensual character of American leadership.* **2** In **consensual** sexual activity, both partners willingly take part.   ADJ-GRADED / ADJ LEGAL

con·sen·sus /kən'sensəs/. A **consensus** is general agreement amongst a group of people. *...a consensus and broadly shared political consensus... The question of when the troops should leave would be decided by consensus.*   ♦♦◇◇ / N-SING: also no det

con·sent /kən'sent/ **consents, consenting, consented. 1** If you give your **consent** to something, you give someone permission to do it. *Can my child be medically examined without my consent?* **2** If you **consent** to something, you agree to do it or to allow it to be done. *He finally consented to go... He asked Ginny if she would consent to a small celebration after the christening.* **3** See also **age of consent. 4** If something happens **by common consent** or **by mutual consent**, it happens as the result of an agreement between the people involved. *He left the company by mutual consent.* **5** You can use **by common consent** to indicate that most people agree that something is true. *By common consent this election constituted a historic step on the road to democracy.*   ♦♦◇◇ / N-UNCOUNT / VERB V to-inf V to n/-ing Also V / PHRASE / PHRASE

con·sent·ing /kən'sentɪŋ/. A **consenting** adult is a person who is considered old enough to make their own decisions about who they have sex with.   ADJ: ADJ n

con·se·quence /'kɒnsɪkwens/ **consequences. 1** The **consequences** of something are the results or effects of it. *She understood the consequences of her actions and was prepared to go to jail. ...a consequence of cigarette smoking.* **2** If one thing happens and then another thing happens **in consequence**, the second thing happens as a result of the first. *His death was totally unexpected and, in consequence, no plans had been made for his replacement.* **3** If you tell someone that they must **take** or **face the consequences**, you warn them that something un-   ♦♦♦◇ / N-COUNT / PHRASE PRAGMATICS / PHRASE

pleasant will happen to them if they do not stop behaving in a certain way. *These pilots must now face the consequences of their actions and be brought to trial.*

4 Something or someone **of consequence** is important or valuable. If something or someone is **of no consequence**, or **of little consequence**, they are not important or valuable. *...a person of consequence... The religious affiliation of those they choose to marry is of no consequence.*   PHRASE

con·se·quent /'kɒnsɪkwənt/. **Consequent** means happening as a direct result of an event or situation. *...the warming of the Earth and the consequent climatic changes. ...the changes in social work consequent upon reorganization.*   ♦◇◇◇ ADJ

con·se·quen·tial /,kɒnsɪ'kwenʃəl/. **1 Consequential** means the same as **consequent**. *...extra staff and consequential costs.* **2** Something that is **consequential** is important or significant. *A week is usually not a consequential delay.*   ADJ: ADJ n FORMAL / ADJ-GRADED FORMAL

con·se·quent·ly /'kɒnsɪkwentli/. **Consequently** means as a result. *Dingsdale had sustained a broken back while working in the mines. Consequently, he spent the rest of his life in a wheelchair.*   ♦♦◇◇ ADV: ADV with cl PRAGMATICS

con·serv·an·cy /kən'sɜːvənsi/. **Conservancy** is used in the names of organizations that work for the preservation and protection of the environment. *...the Nature Conservancy Council.*   N-UNCOUNT

con·ser·va·tion /,kɒnsə'veɪʃən/. **1 Conservation** is the preservation and protection of wildlife and the environment. *...elephant conservation. ...conservation projects.* **2 Conservation** is the preservation and protection of historical objects or works of art. *...the conservation and rebinding of the Book of Kells.* **3** See also **preservation**.   ♦♦◇◇ / N-UNCOUNT / N-UNCOUNT

con·ser·va·tion·ist /,kɒnsə'veɪʃənɪst/ **conservationists.** A **conservationist** is a someone who works and campaigns for the conservation and protection of wildlife and the environment.   ♦◇◇◇ N-COUNT

con·serva·tism /kən'sɜːvətɪzəm/. **1 Conservatism** is a political philosophy which believes that if changes need to be made to society, they should be made gradually. You can also refer to the political beliefs of a conservative party in a particular country as **Conservatism**. **2 Conservatism** is unwillingness to accept changes and new ideas. *He began his professional life as an accountant, the very model of respectability and conservatism.*   ♦◇◇◇ / N-UNCOUNT / N-UNCOUNT

con·serva·tive /kən'sɜːvətɪv/ **conservatives. 1** A **Conservative** politician or voter is a member of or votes for the Conservative Party. *...Conservative MPs.* ▶ Also a noun. *In 1951 the Conservatives were returned to power.* **2** Someone who is **conservative** has right-wing views. *...counties whose citizens invariably support the most conservative candidate.* ▶ Also a noun. *The new judge is 50-year-old David Suitor who's regarded as a conservative.* **3** Someone who is **conservative** or has **conservative** ideas is unwilling to accept changes and new ideas. *People tend to be more aggressive when they're young and more conservative as they get older.* **4** If someone dresses in a **conservative** way, their clothes are conventional in style. *The girl was well dressed, as usual, though in a more conservative style.* ♦ **con·serva·tive·ly** *She was always very conservatively dressed.* **5** If you make a **conservative** estimate, you are cautious and estimate a low amount which is probably less that the real amount. *A conservative estimate of the bill, so far, is about £22,000.* ♦ **conservatively** *The bequest is conservatively estimated at £30 million.*   ♦♦♦◇ / ADJ / N-COUNT / ADJ-GRADED / N-COUNT / ADJ-GRADED / ADJ-GRADED / ADV-GRADED: ADV with v / ADV-GRADED: ADJ-GRADED / ADV-GRADED: ADV with v

Con'serva·tive Party. The **Conservative Party** is the main right-wing party in the United Kingdom.   ♦◇◇◇ N-PROPER

con·serva·toire /kən'sɜːvətwɑː/ **conservatoires.** A **conservatoire** is an institution where musicians are trained. *...the Paris Conservatoire.*   N-COUNT

con·ser·va·tor /kən'sɜːvətə/ **conservators.** A **conservator** is someone whose job is to maintain and restore historical objects or works of art.   N-COUNT

con·serva·tory /kən'sɜːvətri, AM -tɔːri/ **conservatories. 1** A **conservatory** is a room with   ♦◇◇◇ / N-COUNT

glass walls and a glass roof, which is attached to a house. **2** A **conservatory** is an institution where musicians are trained. *...the New England Conservatory of Music.* N-COUNT

con·serve, conserves, conserving, conserved. The verb is pronounced /kən'sɜːv/. The noun is pronounced /'kɒnsɜːv/. **1** If you **conserve** a supply of something, you use it carefully so that it lasts for a long time. *Factories have closed for the weekend to conserve energy.* ♦ **con·ser·va·tion** *...projects aimed at promoting energy conservation.* **2** To **conserve** something means to protect it from harm, loss, or change. *...aid to help developing countries conserve their forests.* ◆◆◇◇◇ VERB V n; N-UNCOUNT; VERB V n

con·sid·er /kən'sɪdə/ **considers, considering, considered. 1** If you **consider** a person or thing to be something, you think that this is what they are. *We consider them to be our friends... I had always considered myself a strong, competent woman... I consider activities such as jogging and weightlifting as unnatural.* ◆◆◆◆◆ VERB V n to-inf, V n n/adj, V n as adj/n, Also V that

2 If you **consider** something, you think about it carefully. *You do have to consider the feelings of those around you... Consider how much you can afford to pay.* ♦ **con·sid·era·tion** *There should be careful consideration of the future role of the BBC.* **3** You say **all things considered** to indicate that you are making a judgement after taking all the facts into account. *All things considered, I think you have behaved marvellously in coming here.* VERB V n, V wh; N-UNCOUNT; PHRASE PRAGMATICS

4 If you **are considering** doing something, you intend to do it, but have not yet made a final decision whether to do it. *Watersports enthusiasts should consider hiring a wetsuit.* VERB V -ing, Also V n

5 See also **considered, considering.**

con·sid·er·able /kən'sɪdərəbəl/. **Considerable** means great in amount or degree. *Doing it properly makes considerable demands on our time... Vets' fees can be considerable.* ♦ **con·sid·er·ably** *Children vary considerably in the rate at which they learn... Their dinner parties had become considerably less formal.* ◆◆◆◆◇ ADJ-GRADED; ADV-GRADED: ADV with v, ADV compar

con·sid·er·ate /kən'sɪdərət/. Someone who is **considerate** pays attention to the needs, wishes, or feelings of other people. *He's the most charming, most considerate man I've ever known... Try and be considerate of other people.* ♦ **con·sid·er·ate·ly** *He treats everyone equally and considerately.* ♦ **con·sid·era·tion** *Show consideration for other rail travellers.* ◆◇◇◇◇ ADJ-GRADED; ADV-GRADED: ADV with v; N-UNCOUNT

con·sid·era·tion /kənˌsɪdə'reɪʃən/ **considerations. 1** If you **take** something **into consideration**, you think about it because it is relevant to what you are doing. *Safe driving is good driving because it takes into consideration the lives of other people.* ◆◆◇◇◇ PHRASE

2 If something is **under consideration**, it is being discussed. *Several proposals are under consideration.* **3** A **consideration** is something that should be thought about when you are planning or deciding something. *Price has become a more important consideration for shoppers in choosing which store to visit.* **4** See also **consider, considerate.** N-UNCOUNT: under N; N-COUNT

con·sid·ered /kən'sɪdəd/. A **considered** opinion or act is the result of careful thought. *It was Anne's considered opinion that Mavis was a bold-faced liar. ...a considered response to the unions' proposals.* • See also **consider.** ◆◇◇◇◇ ADJ-GRADED: ADJ n

con·sid·er·ing /kən'sɪdərɪŋ/. **1** You use **considering** to indicate that you are thinking about a particular fact when making a judgement or giving an opinion. *The former hostage is in remarkably good shape considering his ordeal.* **2** You use **considering that** to indicate that you are thinking about a particular fact when making a judgement or giving an opinion. *Considering that you are no longer involved with this man, your response is a little extreme.* ◆◆◆◇◇ PREP; CONJ

con·sign /kən'saɪn/ **consigns, consigning, consigned.** To **consign** something or someone **to** a place where they will be forgotten about, or to an unpleasant situation means to put them there. *For decades, many of Malevich's works were consigned to the basements of Soviet museums.* ◆◇◇◇◇ VERB V n to n

con·sign·ment /kən'saɪnmənt/ **consignments.** A **consignment** of goods is a load that is being delivered to a place or person. *The first consignment of food has already left Bologna.* ◆◇◇◇◇ N-COUNT

con·sist /kən'sɪst/ **consists, consisting, consisted. 1** Something that **consists of** particular things or people is formed from them. *My diet consisted almost exclusively of chocolate-covered biscuits and glasses of milk.* **2** Something that **consists in** something else has that thing as its main or only part. *A large proportion of my task consisted in spending long hours watching and waiting.* ◆◆◆◇◇ VERB V of n/-ing; VERB V in n/-ing FORMAL

con·sist·en·cy /kən'sɪstənsi/. The **consistency** of a substance is its degree of thickness or smoothness. *Dilute the paint with water until it is the consistency of milk.* • See also **consistent.** ◆◇◇◇◇ N-UNCOUNT

con·sist·ent /kən'sɪstənt/. **1** Someone who is **consistent** always has the same behaviour or attitudes, or always achieves the same level of success. *Becker has never been the most consistent of players. ...his consistent support of free trade.* ♦ **con·sist·en·cy** *He scores goals with remarkable consistency.* ♦ **con·sist·ent·ly** *It's something I have consistently denied. ...a consistently high standard.* **2** If facts or ideas are **consistent**, they is no contradiction between them or within them. *This result is consistent with the findings... A theory should be internally consistent.* ◆◆◆◇◇ ADJ-GRADED; N-UNCOUNT; ADV-GRADED; ADJ

ˌconsoˈlation prize, consolation prizes. 1 A **consolation prize** is a small prize which is given to a person who fails to win a competition. **2** A **consolation prize** is something that happens or is given to a person to cheer them up when they have failed to achieve something better. *Her appointment was seen as a consolation prize.* N-COUNT; N-COUNT

con·sole, consoles, consoling, consoled. The verb is pronounced /kən'səʊl/. The noun is pronounced /'kɒnsəʊl/. **1** If you **console** someone who is unhappy about something, you try to make them feel more cheerful. *Often they cry, and I have to play the role of a mother, consoling them... He will have to console himself by reading about the success of his compatriots.* ♦ **con·sol·ing** *It is not a consoling thought to Germans to see that Americans have the same kind of problem, too.* ♦ **con·so·la·tion** /ˌkɒnsə'leɪʃən/ **consolations** *He knew then he was right, but it was no consolation.* **2** A **console** is a panel with a number of switches or knobs that is used to operate a machine. ◆◆◇◇◇ VERB V n, V pron-refl; ADJ-GRADED; N-VAR; N-COUNT

con·soli·date /kən'sɒlɪdeɪt/ **consolidates, consolidating, consolidated. 1** If you **consolidate** something such as your power or your success, you strengthen it so that it becomes more effective or more secure. *The question is: will the junta consolidate its power by force?* ♦ **con·soli·da·tion** /kənˌsɒlɪ'deɪʃən/ *...the growth and consolidation of the working class.* **2** To **consolidate** a number of small groups or firms means to make them into one large organization. *Judge Charles Schwartz is giving the state 60 days to disband and consolidate Louisiana's four higher education boards.* ♦ **con·soli·da·tion, consolidations** *Further consolidations in the industry could follow.* ◆◆◇◇◇ VERB V n; N-UNCOUNT; VERB V n; N-VAR

con·som·mé /kɒn'sɒmeɪ, AM ˌkɒnsə'meɪ/ **consommés. Consommé** is thin, clear soup, usually made from meat juices. N-VAR

con·so·nant /'kɒnsənənt/ **consonants. 1** A **consonant** is a sound such as 'p', 'v', or 'n' which you pronounce by stopping the air flowing freely through your mouth. Compare **vowel. 2** Something that is **consonant with** something else fits or agrees with it. *I found their work very much consonant with this way of thinking.* N-COUNT; ADJ-GRADED: v-link ADJ with n FORMAL

con·sort, consorts, consorting, consorted. The verb is pronounced /kən'sɔːt/. The noun is pronounced /'kɒnsɔːt/. **1** If you say that someone **consorts with** a particular person or group, you mean that they spend a lot of time with them, and usually ◆◇◇◇◇ VERB PRAGMATICS V with n FORMAL

C

that you do not think this is a good thing. *He regu-larly consorted with known drug-dealers.* **2** The ruling monarch's wife or husband is called their **consort**. *...her Consort, Prince Albert.* **3** A **consort** of musicians or instruments is a group of them. N-COUNT; N-TITLE / N-COUNT

con·sor·tium /kənˈsɔːtiəm/ **consortia** /kənˈsɔːtiə/ or **consortiums**. A **consortium** is a group of people or firms who have agreed to work in co-operation with each other. *The consortium includes some of the biggest building contractors in Britain.* ◆◇◇◇◇ N-COLL-COUNT

con·spic·u·ous /kənˈspɪkjuəs/. **1** If someone or something is **conspicuous**, people can see or notice them very easily. *...situations where you feel conspicuous.* ♦ **con·spic·u·ous·ly** *...areas where American policies have most conspicuously failed... Johnston's name was conspicuously absent from the list.* **2** If you say that someone or something is **conspicuous by** their **absence**, you are drawing attention to the fact that they are not in a place or situation where you think they should be. ◆◇◇◇◇ ADJ-GRADED / ADV-GRADED: ADV with v, ADV adj / PHRASE

con,spicuous con'sumption. **Conspicuous consumption** means spending your money in a way that shows people how wealthy you are. N-UNCOUNT

con·spira·cy /kənˈspɪrəsi/ **conspiracies**. **1** Conspiracy is the secret planning by a group of people to do something illegal. *He believes there probably was a conspiracy to kill President Kennedy.* **2** A **conspiracy** is an agreement between a group of people which other people think is wrong or is likely to be harmful. *...a conspiracy to dispense with the town centre.* **3** If there is a **conspiracy of silence** about something, people who know about it have agreed that they will not talk publicly about it, although it would be helpful if they did. ◆◆◇◇◇ N-VAR / N-COUNT PRAGMATICS / PHRASE

con'spiracy theory, conspiracy theories. If you say that someone has a **conspiracy theory**, you mean that they think that a group of people are secretly trying to harm someone or achieve something. *Did you ever swallow the conspiracy theory about Kennedy?* N-COUNT

con·spira·tor /kənˈspɪrətə/ **conspirators**. A **conspirator** is a person who joins a conspiracy. ◆◇◇◇◇ N-COUNT

con·spira·to·rial /kənˌspɪrəˈtɔːriəl/. **1** If someone does something such as speak, smile, or wink in a **conspiratorial** way, they do it in a way that suggests they are sharing a secret with someone. *...a conspiratorial whisper.* ♦ **con·spira·to·ri·al·ly** *The officer leaned forward conspiratorially.* **2** Something that is **conspiratorial** is secret and illegal, often with a political purpose. *...a secret and supposedly conspiratorial Communist party meeting.* ADJ-GRADED / ADV-GRADED: ADV after v ADJ

con·spire /kənˈspaɪə/ **conspires, conspiring, conspired.** **1** If two or more people or groups **conspire** to do something illegal or harmful, they make a secret agreement to do it. *Mr Farmer and Mrs Jones both admitted conspiring to murder her husband. ...a defendant convicted of conspiring with his brother to commit robberies... People were conspiring against me.* **2** If events **conspire** to produce a particular result, they seem to work together to cause this result. *History and geography have conspired to bring Greece to a moment of decision.* ◆◇◇◇◇ pl-n V to-inf V with to-inf pl-n V against n / VERB V to-inf Also V against n

con·sta·ble /ˈkʌnstəbəl, ˈkɒn-/ **constables.** In Britain and some other countries, a **constable** is a police officer of the lowest rank. *...Constable Stuart Clark... Thanks for your help, Constable.* ● See also **Chief Constable.** ◆◆◇◇◇ N-COUNT; N-TITLE; N-VOC

con·stabu·lary /kənˈstæbjʊləri, AM -leri/ **constabularies.** In Britain and some other countries, a **constabulary** is the police force of a particular area. *...the Nottinghamshire Constabulary.* ◆◇◇◇◇ N-COUNT

con·stan·cy /ˈkɒnstənsi/. **1 Constancy** is the quality of staying the same even though other things change. *We live in a world without constancy.* **2 Constancy** is faithfulness and loyalty to a particular person or belief even when you are in difficulty or danger. *Even before they were married, she had fretted over his constancy.* N-UNCOUNT / N-UNCOUNT

con·stant /ˈkɒnstənt/ **constants. 1** You use **constant** to describe something that happens all the ◆◆◆◇ ADJ

time or is always there. *Women are under constant pressure to be abnormally thin... He has been her constant companion for four months.* ♦ **con·stant·ly** *The direction of the wind is constantly changing.* **2** If an amount or level is **constant**, it stays the same over a particular period of time. *The temperature remains more or less constant.* **3** A **constant** is a thing or value that always stays the same. *The only constant in my life for all those years was nursing.* ADV-GRADED / ADJ-GRADED / N-COUNT

con·stel·la·tion /ˌkɒnstəˈleɪʃən/ **constellations.** A **constellation** is a group of stars which form a fixed pattern. *...the constellation of Cepheus.* ◆◇◇◇◇ N-COUNT

con·ster·na·tion /ˌkɒnstəˈneɪʃən/. **Consternation** is a feeling of anxiety or fear. *His decision caused consternation in the art photography community.* ◆◇◇◇◇ N-UNCOUNT FORMAL

con·sti·pat·ed /ˈkɒnstɪpeɪtɪd/. Someone who is **constipated** has difficulty in defecating. ADJ-GRADED

con·sti·pa·tion /ˌkɒnstɪˈpeɪʃən/. **Constipation** is a medical condition which causes people to have difficulty defecating. ◆◇◇◇◇ N-UNCOUNT

con·stitu·en·cy /kənˈstɪtjuənsi/ **constituencies. 1** A **constituency** is an area for which someone is elected as the representative in parliament. **2** A particular **constituency** is a section of society that may give political support to a particular party or politician. *In France, farmers are a powerful political constituency.* ◆◆◇◇◇ N-COUNT / N-COUNT

con·stitu·ent /kənˈstɪtjuənt/ **constituents. 1** A **constituent** is someone who lives in a particular constituency. **2** A **constituent** of a mixture, substance, or system is one of the things from which it is formed. *Caffeine is the active constituent of drinks such as tea and coffee.* **3** The **constituent** parts of something are the things from which it is formed. *...a plan to split the company into its constituent parts and sell them separately.* ◆◆◇◇◇ N-COUNT / N-COUNT / ADJ: ADJ n FORMAL

con,stituent as'sembly, constituent assemblies. A **constituent assembly** is a body of representatives elected to create or revise their country's constitution. ◆◇◇◇◇ N-COUNT

con·sti·tute /ˈkɒnstɪtjuːt, AM -tuːt/ **constitutes, constituting, constituted. 1** If something **constitutes** a particular thing, it can be regarded as being that thing. *Testing patients without their consent would constitute a professional and legal offence... The vote hardly constitutes a victory.* **2** If a number of things or people **constitute** something, they are the parts or members that form it. *China's ethnic minorities constitute less than 7 percent of its total population.* **3** When something such as a committee or government **is constituted**, it is formally established and given authority to operate. *On 6 July a People's Revolutionary Government was constituted.* ◆◆◇◇◇ V-LINK: no cont V n / V-LINK: no cont V n / VB: usu passive be V-ed FORMAL

con·sti·tu·tion /ˌkɒnstɪˈtjuːʃən, AM -ˈtuː-/ **constitutions. 1** The **constitution** of a country or organization is the system of laws which formally states people's rights and duties. *The king was forced to adopt a new constitution which reduced his powers. ...the American Constitution.* ♦ **con·sti·tu·tion·al** /ˌkɒnstɪˈtjuːʃənəl, AM -ˈtuː-/ *...efforts to resolve the country's constitutional crisis.* ♦ **con·sti·tu·tion·al·ly** *...constitutionally protected rights.* **2** Your **constitution** is your health. *He must have an extremely strong constitution.* ◆◆◆◇ N-COUNT / ADJ / ADV

con·sti·tu·tion·al·ity /ˌkɒnstɪtjuːʃəˈnælɪti, AM -tuː-/. In a particular political system, the **constitutionality** of a law or action is the fact that it is allowed by the constitution. *They plan to challenge the constitutionality of the law.* N-UNCOUNT FORMAL

con·strain /kənˈstreɪn/ **constrains, constraining, constrained. 1** To **constrain** someone or something means to limit their development or force them to behave in a particular way. *Women are too often constrained by family commitments... Universities are constrained to offer salaries that can only attract mediocre staff.* ♦ **con·strained** *...constrained budgets.* **2** If you **feel constrained** to do something, you feel that you must do it, even though you would prefer not to. *He felt constrained to lower his voice.* ◆◇◇◇◇ VERB: V n be V-ed be V-ed to-inf FORMAL / ADJ-GRADED / PHRASE

con·straint /kən'streɪnt/ **constraints. 1** A con- ◆◆◇◇◇ straint is something that limits or controls what you N-COUNT can do. *...financial constraints... Water shortages in the area will be the main constraint on development.* **2 Constraint** is control over the way you behave N-UNCOUNT which prevents you from doing what you want to do. *The Republics wanted democracy after years of constraint.*

con·strict /kən'strɪkt/ **constricts, constricting,** ◆◇◇◇◇ **constricted. 1** If a part of your body, especially VERB your throat, **is constricted**, something causes it to V n become narrower. *...a drug which constricts the* V-ed *blood vessels... His throat began to feel swollen and constricted.* ◆ **con·stric·tion** /kən'strɪkʃən/ *...con-* N-UNCOUNT *striction of the blood vessels.* **2** If something **con-** VERB **stricts** you, it limits your actions so that you cannot V n do what you want to do. *She objects to the tests the Government's advisers have devised because they constrict her teaching style.* ◆ **con·strict·ed** *Many* ADJ-GRADED *of the women I spoke to left because they felt con-* stricted. ◆ **con·strict·ing** *I find the office environ-* ADJ-GRADED *ment too rigid and constricting.* ◆ **con·stric·tion,** N-VAR **constrictions** *...the constrictions placed upon me as a child.*

con·struct, constructs, constructing, con- ◆◆◆◇◇ **structed.** The verb is pronounced /kən'strʌkt/. The noun is pronounced /'kɒnstrʌkt/. **1** If you **con-** VERB **struct** something, you build it or make it. *The* V n *French constructed a series of fortresses... The boxes* be V-ed *should be constructed from rough-sawn timber.* **2** A from/of/out *construct* is something that is built, made, or creat- ofn ed. *The country was an artificial construct held to-* N-COUNT: *gether by force and intimidation for more than 70* FORMAL *years.* **3** If you **construct** something such as an idea, VERB *piece of writing, or system, you create it by putting* V n *different parts together. Construct a spending plan...* be V-ed *The novel is constructed from a series of on-the-spot* from/out ofn *reports. ...carefully constructed tests.* ◆ **con·struc-** V-ed **·tion** *...the construction of a just system of criminal* N-UNCOUNT: *justice.* **4** A **construct** is a complex idea. *...the* with poss *underlying constructs (beliefs, philosophy, etc.)* N-COUNT *which influence action and behaviour.* FORMAL

con·struc·tion /kən'strʌkʃən/ **constructions.** ◆◆◆◇◇ **1 Construction** is the building of things such as N-UNCOUNT houses, factories, roads, and bridges. *...the only nu- clear power station under construction in Britain. ...the construction industry.* **2** The **construction** of N-UNCOUNT: something is the making of it. *This is the finest wood* with supp *for boat construction.* **3** You can refer to an object N-COUNT *that has been built or made as a* **construction**. *...an impressive steel and glass construction.* **4** You use N-UNCOUNT **construction** to refer to the structure of something and the way it has been built or made. *The chairs were light in construction yet extremely strong.* **5** The **construction** that you put on what someone N-COUNT says or does is your interpretation of what it means. *He put the wrong construction on what he saw.* **6** A grammatical **construction** is a particular arrange- N-COUNT ment of words in a sentence, clause, or phrase. *...com- plex verbal constructions.* **7** See also **construct.**

con·struc·tive /kən'strʌktɪv/. A **constructive** dis- ◆◆◇◇◇ cussion, comment, or approach is useful and help- ADJ-GRADED ful rather than negative and unhelpful. *She wel- comes constructive criticism... At least I'm doing something constructive.* ◆ **con·struc·tive·ly** *We are* ADV-GRADED: *prepared to sit down and talk constructively with* ADV with v *our European partners.*

con·strue /kən'stru:/ **construes, construing,** ◆◇◇◇◇ **construed.** If something **is construed** in a particu- VERB lar way, its nature or meaning is interpreted in that be V-ed as n way. *What may seem helpful behaviour to you can* Also V n *be construed as interference by others.* prep/adv FORMAL

con·sul /'kɒnsəl/ **consuls.** A consul is an official ◆◇◇◇◇ who is sent by their government to live in a foreign N-COUNT city in order to encourage trade with their own country and to help visitors from their own country who are in difficulty. *...the British Consul in Zurich.*

con·su·lar /'kɒnsjʊlə, AM -sə-/. **Consular** means ◆◇◇◇◇ involving or relating to a consul or the work of a ADJ: ADJ n consul. *...British Consular officials.*

con·su·late /'kɒnsjʊlət, AM -sə-/ **consulates.** A ◆◇◇◇◇ consulate is the place where a consul works. *...the* N-COUNT *British consulate in Lyons.*

con·sult /kən'sʌlt/ **consults, consulting, con-** ◆◆◆◇◇ **sulted. 1** If you **consult** an expert or someone sen- VERB ior to you or **consult with** them, you ask them for V n prep wh/ their opinion and advice, or you ask their permis- wh-to-inf sion to do something. *Consult your doctor about* V with n *how much exercise you should attempt... He needed* Also V n *to consult with an attorney.* ◆ **con·sul·ta·tion** N-VAR /ˌkɒnsəl'teɪʃən/ **consultations** *...a consultation with a nutritionist.* **2** If a person or group of people V-RECIP **consults with** other people or **consults** them, they V with n talk and exchange ideas and opinions about what V n *they might decide to do. After consulting with her* Also pl-n V *daughter and manager she decided to take on the part... The two countries will have to consult their allies.* **3** If you **consult** a book or a map, you look in VERB it or at it in order to find some information. *Consult* V n *the chart on page 44 for the correct cooking times.* ◆ **consultation** *...excellent studies available for* N-UNCOUNT *consultation.* **4** See also **consultation.**

con·sul·tan·cy /kən'sʌltənsi/ **consultancies.** ◆◇◇◇◇ **1** A **consultancy** is a company that gives expert N-COUNT advice on a particular subject. *...a management consultancy.* **2 Consultancy** is expert advice on a N-UNCOUNT particular subject which a person or group is paid to provide. *He is acting on a consultancy basis... The project provides both consultancy and training.*

con·sult·ant /kən'sʌltənt/ **consultants. 1** A con- ◆◆◆◇◇ sultant is an experienced doctor who specializes in N-COUNT one area of medicine. *...a consultant heart surgeon.* BRITISH **2** A **consultant** is a person who gives expert advice N-COUNT to a person or organization on a particular subject. *He was a consultant to the Swedish government.*

con·sul·ta·tion /ˌkɒnsəl'teɪʃən/ **consultations.** ◆◇◇◇◇ **1 Consultations** are meetings which are held to dis- N-VAR cuss something. **Consultation** is discussion about something. *Next week he'll be in Florida for consul- tations with President Mitterrand... The plans were drawn up in consultation with the World Health Or- ganisation.* **2** A **consultation** paper or document is ADJ: ADJ n an official document containing ideas for changes in something such as the law or a procedure. It is published or distributed so that people can discuss it and give their opinions. **3** See also **consult.**

con·sul·ta·tive /kən'sʌltətɪv/. A **consultative** ◆◇◇◇◇ committee or document gives advice or makes pro- ADJ posals about a particular problem or subject. *...the consultative committee on local government finance.*

con'sulting room, consulting rooms. A doc- N-COUNT tor's **consulting room** is the room in which they see their patients.

con·sum·able /kən'sju:məbəl, AM -'su:-/. **Consum-** ADJ **able** goods are items which are intended to be FORMAL bought, used, and then replaced.

con·sume /kən'sju:m, AM -'su:m/ **consumes,** ◆◆◇◇◇ **consuming, consumed. 1** If you **consume** VERB something, you eat or drink it. *Martha would con-* V n *sume nearly a pound of cheese per day.* **2** To con- VERB **sume** an amount of fuel, energy, or time means to V n use it. *The most efficient refrigerators consume 70 percent less electricity than traditional models.* ◆ **-consuming** *...oil-consuming countries... It is* COMB *very space-consuming.* **3** If fire **consumes** a building, it totally destroys it. VERB: V n

con·sumed /kən'sju:md, AM -'su:md/. If you are ADJ-GRADED: **consumed** with a feeling or idea, it affects you very v-link ADJ strongly indeed. *They are consumed with envy.* with/by n

con·sum·er /kən'sju:mə, AM -'su:-/ **consumers.** ◆◆◆◆◇ A **consumer** is a person who buys things or uses N-COUNT services. *...claims that tobacco companies failed to warn consumers about the dangers of smoking. ...consumer rights.*

con,sumer 'durable, consumer durables. N-COUNT **Consumer durables** are goods such as refrigerators which are expected to last a long time, and are not often replaced.

con·sumer goods. Consumer goods are items bought by people for their own use, rather than by businesses. ◆◇◇◇◇ N-PLURAL

con·sum·er·ism /kən'sjuːmərɪzəm, AM -'suː-/. **1 Consumerism** is the belief that it is good to buy and use a lot of goods. *They have embraced Western consumerism.* ◆ **con·sum·er·ist** /kən'sjuːmərɪst, AM -'suː-/ *...our consumerist society.* **2 Consumerism** is the protection of the rights and interests of consumers. ◆◇◇◇◇ N-UNCOUNT · ADJ · N-UNCOUNT

con·sum·ing /kən'sjuːmɪŋ, AM -'suː-/. A **consuming** interest is more important to you than anything else. *He has developed a consuming passion for chess.* ● See also **consume**, **time-consuming**. ◆◆◇◇◇ ADJ

con·sum·mate, consummates, consummating, consummated. The adjective is pronounced /'kɒnsjəmət/. The verb is pronounced /'kɒnsəmeɪt/. **1** You use **consummate** to describe someone who is extremely skilful. *...a consummate politician... He acted the part with consummate skill.* **2** If two people **consummate** a marriage or relationship, they make it complete by having sex. ◆ **con·sum·ma·tion** /ˌkɒnsə'meɪʃən/ *...the consummation of their marriage.* **3** To **consummate** an agreement means to complete it. *No one has been able to consummate a deal.* ◆◇◇◇◇ ADJ-GRADED FORMAL · VERB: V n · N-UNCOUNT · VERB V n FORMAL

con·sump·tion /kən'sʌmpʃən/. **1** The **consumption** of fuel or natural resources is the amount of them that is used, or the act of using them. *...a reduction in fuel consumption.* **2** The **consumption** of food or drink is the act of eating or drinking something, or the amount that is eaten or drunk. *The wine was unfit for human consumption... The average daily consumption of fruit and vegetables is around 200 grams.* **3 Consumption** is the act of buying and using things. *They were prepared to put people out of work and reduce consumption by strangling the whole economy. ...the production and consumption of goods and services.* **4** See also **conspicuous consumption**. **5** If you do or say something **for** someone's **consumption**, you intend it to be seen or heard by them. *The hard-line speech appears to be mostly for domestic consumption.* ◆◆◇◇◇ N-UNCOUNT: with supp · N-UNCOUNT FORMAL · N-UNCOUNT TECHNICAL · PHRASE

con·sump·tive /kən'sʌmptɪv/. A **consumptive** person suffers from tuberculosis. ADJ DATED

cont. Cont. is an abbreviation for 'continued'. It is used at the bottom of a page to indicate that a letter or text continues on another page.

con·tact /'kɒntækt/ **contacts, contacting, contacted.** **1 Contact** involves meeting or communicating with someone. *Opposition leaders are denying any contact with the government in Kabul.* **2** If you are **in contact** with someone, you regularly meet them or communicate with them. *He was in direct contact with the kidnappers.* **3** If you come **into contact with** someone or something, you meet that person or thing in the course of your work or other activities. *...doctors I came into contact with... The college has brought me into contact with western ideas.* **4** If you **contact** someone, you telephone them, write to them, or go to see them in order to tell or ask them something. *Contact the Tourist Information Bureau for further details.* **5** Radio **contact** is communication by means of radio. *He lost contact with the control tower.* **6** If you **make contact** with someone, you find out where they are and talk or write to them. **7** If you **lose contact** with someone who you have been friendly with, you no longer see them, speak to them, or write to them. **8** A **contact** is someone you know in an organization who helps you or gives you information. *Their contact in the United States Embassy was called Phil.* **9** If people or things are in **contact**, they are touching each other. *...where the foot and shoe are in contact... The cry occurs when air is brought into contact with the baby's larynx... There was no physical contact.* **10** ● to **make eye contact**: see **eye**. ◆◆◆◇ N-UNCOUNT: also N in pl · PHRASE · N-UNCOUNT: into N with n · VERB V n · N-UNCOUNT · PHRASE · PHRASE · N-COUNT · N-UNCOUNT

'contact lens, contact lenses. Contact lenses are small plastic lenses that you put on the surface of your eyes to help you see better. ◆◇◇◇◇ N-COUNT

con·ta·gion /kən'teɪdʒən/. **1 Contagion** is the spreading of a disease by someone touching another person who already has the disease. *They have been reluctant to admit AIDS patients, because of unfounded fears of contagion.* **2** You can use **contagion** to refer to the spreading of ideas or feelings from one group of people to another; used showing disapproval. *...to continue to insulate his country from the contagion of foreign ideas.* N-UNCOUNT · N-SING PRAGMATICS

con·ta·gious /kən'teɪdʒəs/. **1** A **contagious** disease can be caught by touching people or things that are infected with it. **2** A **contagious** feeling or attitude spreads quickly among a group of people. *Laughing is contagious. ...his contagious enthusiasm.* ◆◇◇◇◇ ADJ-GRADED · ADJ-GRADED

con·tain /kən'teɪn/ **contains, containing, contained.** **1** If something such as a box, bag, room, or place **contains** things, those things are inside it. *The bag contained a Christmas card... The 77,000-acre estate contains five of the highest peaks in Scotland.* **2** If a substance **contains** something, that thing is a part of it. *Greek yogurt contains much less fat than double cream.* **3** If writing, speech, or film **contains** particular information, ideas, or images, it includes them. *This sheet contained a list of problems a patient might like to raise.* **4** If a group or organization **contains** certain people, those people are in it. *The committee contains 11 Democrats and nine Republicans.* **5** If you **contain** something, you control it and prevent it from spreading or increasing. *Firemen are still trying to contain the fire.* ◆ **con·tain·ment.** **Containment** of something is the action of containing it. *...containment of the disease.* **6** If you cannot **contain** a feeling such as excitement or anger, or if you cannot **contain** yourself, you cannot prevent yourself from showing your feelings. *But he was bursting with curiosity, and one day he just couldn't contain himself. 'What are you going to do?' he asked... Evans could barely contain his delight.* **7** See also **self-contained**. ◆◆◆◇ VB: no cont V n · VB: no cont V n · VB: no cont V n · VB: no cont V n · VERB V n · N-UNCOUNT · VERB V pron-refl V n

con·tain·er /kən'teɪnə/ **containers.** **1** A **container** is something such as a box or bottle that is used to hold or store things. *...the plastic containers in which fish are stored and sold.* **2** A **container** is a very large metal or wooden box used for transporting goods so that they can be loaded easily onto ships and lorries. ◆◆◇◇◇ N-COUNT · N-COUNT

con'tainer ship, container ships. A **container ship** is a ship that is designed for carrying goods that are packed in large metal or wooden boxes. N-COUNT

con·tain·ment /kən'teɪnmənt/. **Containment** is the policy of keeping another country's power or area of control within acceptable limits or boundaries. ● See also **contain**. ◆◇◇◇◇ N-UNCOUNT

con·tami·nant /kən'tæmɪnənt/ **contaminants.** A **contaminant** is something that contaminates a substance such as water or food. N-COUNT FORMAL

con·tami·nate /kən'tæmɪneɪt/ **contaminates, contaminating, contaminated.** If something **is contaminated** by dirt, chemicals, or radiation, it becomes polluted by them and is then impure or harmful. *Have any fish been contaminated?* ◆ **con·tami·nat·ed** *...contaminated water.* ◆ **con·tami·na·tion** /kən,tæmɪ'neɪʃən/ *...the contamination of the sea around Capri.* ◆◆◇◇◇ VERB be V-ed Also V n · ADJ-GRADED · N-UNCOUNT

con·tem·plate /'kɒntəmpleɪt/ **contemplates, contemplating, contemplated.** **1** If you **contemplate** an action, you think about whether to do it or not. *He contemplated a career as an army medical doctor... She contemplates leaving for the sake of the kids.* **2** If you **contemplate** an idea or subject, you think about it for a long time. *He cried as he contemplated his future.* ◆ **con·tem·pla·tion** /ˌkɒntəm'pleɪʃən/. *It is a place of quiet contemplation.* **3** If you cannot **contemplate** something, you cannot accept it as a possibility. *That makes it* ◆◆◇◇◇ VERB V n V-ing · VERB V n · N-UNCOUNT · VERB V n

difficult to contemplate the idea that the present policy may not be sustainable.
4 If you **contemplate** something or someone, you look at them for a long time. *He contemplated his hands, still frowning.* ♦ **contemplation** *He was lost in the contemplation of the landscape.*

con·tem·pla·tive /kən'templətɪv/. Someone who is **contemplative** thinks deeply, or is thinking in a serious and calm way. *...a quiet, contemplative sort of chap... I went for long, contemplative walks.*

con·tem·po·ra·neous /kən,tempə'reɪnɪəs/. If two events or situations are **contemporaneous**, they happen or exist during the same period.

con·tem·po·rary /kən'tempərəri, AM -pəreri/ **con·temporaries. 1 Contemporary** things are modern and relate to the present time. *...contemporary music. ...a more contemporary style.* **2 Contemporary** people or things were alive or happened at the same time as something else you are talking about. *...drawing upon official records and the reports of contemporary witnesses.* **3** Someone's **contemporaries** are people who are or were alive at the same time as them. *Like most of my contemporaries, I grew up in a vastly different world. ...Shakespeare and his contemporaries.*

con·tempt /kən'tempt/. **1** If you have **contempt** for someone or something, you have no respect for them, or you think they are unimportant. *He has contempt for those beyond his immediate family circle... I hope voters will treat his advice with the contempt it deserves.* **2 Contempt** means the same as **contempt of court.** *Mr. Kelly was sentenced to six months in prison for contempt.*

con·tempt·ible /kən'temptɪbəl/. If you feel that someone or something is **contemptible**, you feel strong dislike and disrespect for them.

con,tempt of 'court. Contempt of court is the criminal offence of disobeying an instruction from a judge or court of law, or misbehaving in court.

con·temp·tu·ous /kən'temptʃuəs/. If you are **contemptuous** of someone or something, you do not like or respect them at all. *She gave a contemptuous little laugh.* ♦ **con·temp·tu·ous·ly** *'A deal!' she said contemptuously, 'I hate all deals.'*

con·tend /kən'tend/ **contends, contending, contended. 1** If you have to **contend with** a problem or difficulty, you have to deal with it or overcome it. *American businesses could soon have a new kind of lawsuit to contend with.* **2** If you **contend** with someone for something, you compete with them to try to get it. *...the two main groups contending for power. ...with 10 UK construction yards contending with rivals from Norway.*
3 If you **contend** that something is true, you state or argue that it is true. *The government contends that he is fundamentalist.*

con·tend·er /kən'tendə/ **contenders.** A **contender** is someone who takes part in a competition. *...a strong contender for an Olympic gold medal.*

content 1 noun uses
con·tent /'kɒntent/ **contents. 1** The **contents** of a container such as a bottle, box, or room are the things inside it. *Empty the contents of the pan into the sieve. ...Sandon Hall and its contents.* **2** If you refer to the **content** or **contents** of something such as a book, speech, or television programme, you mean the subject that it deals with, the story that it tells, or the ideas that it expresses. *Stricter controls were placed on the content of video films. ...the letter's contents.* **3** The **contents** of a book are its different chapters and sections, usually shown in a list at the beginning of the book. *There is no initial list of contents.* **4** You can use **content** to refer to the amount or proportion of something that a substance contains. *Sunflower margarine has the same fat content as butter.*

content 2 adjective and verb uses
con·tent /kən'tent/ **contents, contenting, contented. 1** If you are **content** to do something or **content with** something, you are willing to do,

have, or accept that thing, rather than wanting something more or better. *I am content to admire the mountains from below... Not content with rescuing one theatre, Sally Green has taken on another.* **2** If you **content** yourself with something, you accept it and do not try to do or have other things. *He wisely contented himself with his family... Most manufacturers content themselves with updating existing models.*
3 If you are **content**, you are happy and satisfied with your way of life. **4 • to your heart's content:** see **heart.**

con·tent·ed /kən'tentɪd/. If you are **contented**, you are satisfied with your life or the situation you are in. *...a soft, contented smile.* ♦ **con·tent·ed·ly** *The landlady sighed contentedly.* ♦ **con·tent·ment** /kən'tentmənt/ *...a feeling of contentment.*

con·ten·tion /kən'tenʃən/ **contentions. 1** Someone's **contention** is the idea or opinion that they are expressing in an argument or discussion. *It is my contention that death and murder always lurk as potentials in violent relationships.*
2 If something is a cause of **contention**, it is a cause of disagreement or argument. *A particular source of contention are plans to privatise state-run companies.*
● See also **bone of contention.**
3 If you are **in contention** in a contest, you have a chance of winning it. *He was in contention for a place in the European championship squad.*

con·ten·tious /kən'tenʃəs/. A **contentious** issue causes a lot of disagreement or arguments. *...a country where land prices are politically contentious.*

con·test, contests, contesting, contested. The noun is pronounced /'kɒntest/. The verb is pronounced /kən'test/. **1** A **contest** is a competition or game in which people try to win. *...a writing contest.* ● See also **beauty contest. 2** If someone **contests** an election or competition, they take part in it and try to win. *He quickly won his party's nomination to contest the elections. ...a closely contested regional flower show.* **3** A **contest** is a struggle to win power or control. *...next year's presidential contest. ...the contest between capitalism and socialism.*
4 If you **contest** a statement or decision, you object to it formally because you think it is wrong or unreasonable. *Your former employer has to reply within 14 days in order to contest the case. ...a hotly contested issue.*

con·test·ant /kən'testənt/ **contestants.** A **contestant** in a competition or quiz is a person who takes part in it.

con·text /'kɒntekst/ **contexts. 1** The **context** of an idea or event is the general situation that relates to it, and which helps it to be understood. *We are doing this work in the context of reforms... It is important that we put Jesus into the context of history.* ♦ **con·tex·tual** /kən'tekstʃuəl/ *...the contextual background of events.* **2** If something is seen **in context**, it is considered together with all the factors that relate to it. *The drugs problem has to be seen in context.*
3 The **context** of a word, sentence, or text consists of the words, sentences, or text before and after it which help to make its meaning clear. **4** If a statement or remark is taken **out of context**, the circumstances in which it was said are not correctly reported, so that it seems to mean something different from the meaning that was intended. *Quotes can be manipulated and used out of context.*

con·tigu·ous /kən'tɪgjuəs/. Things that are **contiguous** are next to each other or touch each other. *Its vineyards are virtually contiguous with those of Ausone.*

con·ti·nent /'kɒntɪnənt/ **continents. 1** A **continent** is a very large area of land, such as Africa or Asia, that consists of several countries. **2** In Britain, the mainland of Europe is sometimes referred to as **the Continent.** *Its shops are among the most stylish on the Continent.*

con·ti·nen·tal /,kɒntɪ'nentəl/ **continentals. 1 Continental** means situated on or belonging to

the mainland of Europe, especially central and southern Europe. *With the completion of the Channel Tunnel, Britain is once again linked to continental Europe.* **2** A **continental** is someone who comes from the mainland of Europe, especially central or southern Europe. N-COUNT BRITISH; INFORMAL

3 **Continental** is used to refer to the main part of a country, rather than its islands or overseas territories. *...the continental United States.* ADJ: ADJ n

,**continental 'breakfast, continental break-fasts.** A **continental breakfast** is breakfast that consists of food such as bread, butter, jam, and a hot drink. N-COUNT

,**continental 'shelf.** The **continental shelf** is the area which forms the edge of a continent, ending in a steep slope to the depths of the ocean. N-SING TECHNICAL

con·tin·gen·cy /kən'tɪndʒənsi/ **contingencies.** **1** A **contingency** is something that might happen in the future. *I need to examine all possible contingencies.* **2** A **contingency** plan or measure is intended to be used if a possible future situation arises. ◆◇◇◇◇ N-VAR / ADJ: ADJ n

con·tin·gent /kən'tɪndʒənt/ **contingents.** **1** A **contingent** of police, soldiers, or military vehicles is a group of them. *...a large contingent of troops.* **2** A **contingent** is a group of people representing a country or organization at a meeting or other event. *...the sole survivor of the five-strong British contingent at the end of the race.* ◆◆◇◇◇ N-COUNT / N-COUNT

3 If something is **contingent** on something else, the first thing depends on the second in order to happen or exist. *Growth is contingent on improved incomes.* ADJ FORMAL

con·tin·ual /kən'tɪnjuəl/. **1** A **continual** process or situation happens or exists without stopping. *The school has been in continual use since 1883. ...continual pain.* ♦ **con·tinu·al·ly** *The large rotating fans whirred continually.* **2** **Continual** events happen again and again. *She suffered continual police harassment.* ♦ **continually** *Malcolm was continually changing his mind.* ◆◆◇◇◇ ADJ: ADJ n / ADV / ADJ: ADJ n / ADV

con·tinu·ance /kən'tɪnjuəns/. The **continuance** of something is its continuation. *...ensuring the continuance of the human species.* N-UNCOUNT FORMAL

con·tinu·ation /kən,tɪnju'eɪʃən/. **1** The **continuation** of something is the fact that it continues, rather than stopping. *It's the coalition forces who are to blame for the continuation of the war.* **2** Something that is a **continuation** of something else is closely connected with it and develops it in some way. *This chapter is a continuation of Chapter 8... What we'll see in the future is, in fact, a continuation of that trend.* ◆◇◇◇◇ N-SING / N-SING

con·tinue /kən'tɪnju:/ **continues, continuing, continued.** **1** If someone or something **continues** to do something, they keep doing it and do not stop. *Interest rates continue to fall... Diana and Roy are determined to continue working when they reach retirement age... There is no reason why you should not continue with any sport or activity you already enjoy... He had hoped to continue as a full-time career officer.* **2** If something **continues** or if you **continue** it, it does not stop happening. *The conflict would continue until conditions were met for a ceasefire... Outside the building people continue their vigil. ...the continued existence of a species.* **3** If you **continue** with something, you start doing it again after a break or interruption. *I went up to my room to continue my packing... She looked up for a moment, then continued drawing.* **4** If something **continues** or if you **continue** it, it starts again after a break or interruption. *The trial continues today... He soon reappeared and continued his activities.* **5** If you **continue**, you begin speaking again after a pause or interruption. *'Anyway, that was what gave us the idea,' she continued after a pause... Please continue.* **6** If you **continue** in a particular direction, you keep walking or travelling in that direction. *He continued rapidly up the path.* **7** If a road or path **continues** somewhere, it goes there after the place you have mentioned. *The main road continues towards Viterbo.* ◆◆◆◆◆ VERB V to-inf / V -ing / V with n / V as n / V-ERG V / V n / V-ed / VERB V with n / V -ing / V-ERG V / V n / VERB V with quote / V / VERB V prep/adv / VERB V prep/adv

con,tinuing edu'cation. Continuing education is education for adults in a variety of subjects, most of which are practical, not academic. N-UNCOUNT

con·ti·nu·ity /,kɒntɪ'nju:ɪti, AM -'nu:-/ **continuities.** **1** You say there is **continuity** when something continues to happen or exist, with no changes or interruptions; used showing approval. *...a tank designed to ensure continuity of fuel supply during aerobatics... He stood for continuity rather than change.* **2** In film-making, **continuity** is the way that things filmed at different times look as if they were filmed at the same time or in the right sequence. ◆◇◇◇◇ N-VAR PRAGMATICS / N-UNCOUNT

con·tinu·ous /kən'tɪnjuəs/. **1** A **continuous** process or event continues for a period of time without stopping. *...all employees who had a record of five years' continuous employment with the firm... There is a continuous stream of phone calls.* ♦ **con·tinu·ous·ly** *The civil war has raged almost continuously since 1976.* **2** A **continuous** line or surface has no gaps or holes in it. *...a continuous line of boats.* **3** In English grammar, **continuous** verb groups are formed using the auxiliary 'be' and the present participle of a verb, as in 'I'm feeling a bit tired' '. Continuous verb groups are used especially when you are focusing on a particular moment. Compare **simple.** ◆◆◇◇◇ ADJ / ADV / ADJ / ADJ

con,tinuous as'sessment. If students undergo **continuous assessment,** they get qualifications because of work they do during the year, rather than because of exam results. N-UNCOUNT

con·tin·uum /kən'tɪnjuəm/. **1** A **continuum** is a set of things on a scale, which have a particular characteristic to different degrees. *These various complaints are part of a continuum of ill-health... It is at one end of the cost continuum.* **2** A **continuum** is a continuous series of closely-connected events. *Development from fertilisation onwards is a continuum.* ◆◇◇◇◇ N-SING FORMAL / N-SING FORMAL

con·tort /kən'tɔ:t/ **contorts, contorting, contorted.** If someone's face or body **contorts** or **is contorted,** it moves into an unnatural and unattractive shape or position. *His face contorts as he screams out the lyrics... Brenner was breathing hard, his face contorted with pain.* ♦ **con·tor·tion, contortions.** Contortions are movements of your body or face into unusual shapes or positions. *...the contortions of the gymnasts.* V-ERG V / V-ed / Also V n / N-COUNT

con·tour /'kɒntʊə/ **contours.** **1** You can refer to the general shape or outline of an object as its **contours.** *...the contours of the body.* **2** A **contour** on a map is a line joining points of equal height and indicating hills, valleys, and the steepness of slopes. *There were three moderate climbs to just below the 450 feet contour.* ◆◇◇◇◇ N-COUNT LITERARY / N-COUNT

con·toured /'kɒntʊəd/. A **contoured** surface has curves and slopes on it, rather than being flat. *...the lush fairways and contoured greens of the course.* ADJ: ADJ n

contra·band /'kɒntrəbænd/. **Contraband** refers to goods that are taken to or from a country illegally. N-UNCOUNT

contra·cep·tion /,kɒntrə'sepʃən/. **Contraception** refers to methods of preventing pregnancy. ◆◇◇◇◇ N-UNCOUNT

contra·cep·tive /,kɒntrə'septɪv/ **contraceptives.** A **contraceptive** is a device or pill used to prevent pregnancy. *...the contraceptive pill.* ◆◇◇◇◇ N-COUNT

con·tract, contracts, contracting, contracted. The noun is pronounced /'kɒntrækt/. The verb is pronounced /kən'trækt/. **1** A **contract** is a legal agreement, usually between two companies or between an employer and employee, which involves doing work for a stated sum of money. *...a prestigious contract for work on Europe's tallest building.* **2** If you are **under contract** to someone, you have signed a contract agreeing to work for them during a fixed period of time. **3** If you **contract** with someone to do something, you legally agree to do it for them or for them to do it for you. *You can contract with us to deliver your cargo.* **4** When something **contracts,** it becomes smaller or shorter. *An excess of meat and salt can contract muscles.* ♦ **con·trac·tion** /kən'trækʃən/ **contractions** *...the contraction and expansion of blood vessels.* ◆◆◆◆◇ N-COUNT / PHRASE / VERB V with n to-inf Also V to-inf FORMAL / V-ERG: V V n / N-VAR

5 If you **contract** a serious illness, you become ill with it.   VERB: V n   FORMAL

contract out. 1 If a company **contracts out** work, they employ other companies to do it. *Firms can contract out work to one another. ...the trend of contracting services out rather than performing them in-house.* **2** If a person or group **contracts out** of a system or scheme, they formally say that they do not want to take part in it. *Employees can contract out of their employer's occupational pension scheme.*   PHRASAL VB   V P noun   V P noun for   V n P   Also V n P ton,   V P   V P ofn   Also V P   BRITISH

con·trac·tion /kənˈtrækʃən/ **contractions.**   ◆◇◇◇◇
1 When a woman who is about to give birth has **contractions**, she experiences a very strong painful tightening of the muscles of her uterus. **2** A **contraction** is a shortened form of a word or words. For example, 'I'm' is a contraction of 'I am'. **3** See also **contract.**   N-COUNT   N-COUNT

con·trac·tor /ˈkɒntræktə, kənˈtræk-/ **contractors.**   ◆◆◇◇◇
A **contractor** is a person or company that does work for other people or organizations.   N-COUNT

con·trac·tual /kənˈtræktʃuəl/. A **contractual** arrangement or relationship involves a legal agreement between people. ♦ **con·trac·tu·al·ly** *Rank was contractually obliged to hand him a cheque for $30 million.*   ◆◇◇◇◇   ADJ   FORMAL   ADV

contra·dict /ˌkɒntrəˈdɪkt/ **contradicts, contradicting, contradicted. 1** If you **contradict** someone, you say that what they have just said is wrong, or suggest that it is wrong by saying something different. *He often talks in circles, frequently contradicting himself.* **2** If one statement or piece of evidence **contradicts** another, the first one makes the second one appear to be wrong. *Her version contradicted the Government's claim.* **3** If one policy or situation **contradicts** another, there appears to be a conflict between them, so that they cannot both exist or be successful. *The cut-backs contradict the Government's commitment to better educational standards.* ♦ **contra·dic·tory** /ˌkɒntrəˈdɪktəri, AM -tɔːri/ *...advice that sometimes is contradictory and confusing.*   ◆◇◇◇◇   VERB: V n   V pron-refl   VERB   V n   VERB   V n   ADJ-GRADED

contra·dic·tion /ˌkɒntrəˈdɪkʃən/ **contradictions. 1** A **contradiction** is an aspect of a situation which appears to conflict with other aspects, so that they cannot all exist or be successful. *...the contradictions between her private life and the public persona... The militants see no contradiction in using violence to bring about a religious state.* **2** If you say that something is a **contradiction in terms**, you mean that it is described as having a quality that it cannot have. *A public service run for profit – a contradiction in terms if there ever was one.*   ◆◆◇◇◇   N-COUNT   PHRASE

contra·flow /ˈkɒntrəfləʊ/ **contraflows.** When there are repairs on a major road, a **contraflow** is a situation in which vehicles travelling in one direction have to use lanes that are normally used by traffic travelling in the opposite direction.   N-COUNT   BRITISH

contra·in·di·ca·tion /ˌkɒntrəˌɪndɪˈkeɪʃən/ **contra·indications;** also spelled **contra-indication. Contraindications** are specific medical reasons for not using a particular treatment for a medical condition in the usual way.   N-COUNT   MEDICAL

con·tral·to /kənˈtræltəʊ/ **contraltos.** In singing, a **contralto** is a woman with a low singing voice.   N-COUNT

con·trap·tion /kənˈtræpʃən/ **contraptions.** You can refer to a device or machine as a **contraption**, especially when it looks strange or you do not know what it is used for.   N-COUNT

con·trar·ian /kənˈtreəriən/ **contrarians.** A **contrarian** is a person who deliberately behaves or thinks in a way that is different from the people around them.   N-COUNT   FORMAL

con·tra·ry /ˈkɒntrəri, AM -treri/. **1** Ideas, attitudes, or reactions that are **contrary** to each other are completely different from each other. *This view is contrary to the aims of critical social research.* **2** If you say that something is true **contrary** to other people's beliefs or opinions, you are emphasizing that it is true and that they are wrong. *Contrary to popular belief, moderate exercise actually decreases*   ◆◆◇◇◇   ADJ   PHR-PREP

your appetite. **3** When a particular idea is being considered, evidence or statements **to the contrary** suggest that this idea is not true or that the opposite is true. **4** You use **on the contrary** or **quite the contrary** when you have just said or implied that something is not true and are going to say that the opposite is true. *It is not an idea around which the Community can unite. On the contrary, I see it as one that will divide us.* **5** You can use **on the contrary** when you are disagreeing emphatically with something that has just been said or implied, or are making a strong negative reply. *'People just don't do things like that.'—'On the contrary, they do them all the time.'*   PHRASE   PHRASE   PRAGMATICS   PHRASE   PRAGMATICS

con·trast, contrasts, contrasting, contrasted. The noun is pronounced /ˈkɒntrɑːst, -træst/. The verb is pronounced /kənˈtrɑːst, -ˈtræst/. **1** A **contrast** is a great difference between two or more things which is clear when you compare them. *...the contrast between town and country.* **2** You say **by contrast** or **in contrast**, or **in contrast to** something, to show that you are mentioning a very different situation from the one you have just mentioned. *The private sector, by contrast, has plenty of money to spend.* **3** If one thing is a **contrast** to another or **in contrast** to it, it is very different from it. *His public statements have always been in marked contrast to those of his son.* **4** If you **contrast** one thing with another, you point out or consider the differences between those things. *In this section we contrast four possible broad approaches.* **5** If one thing **contrasts** with another, it is very different from it. *Paint the wall in a contrasting colour.* **6 Contrast** is the degree of difference between the darker and lighter parts of a photograph or television picture.   ◆◆◇◇   N-VAR   PHRASE   PRAGMATICS   N-VAR   VERB: V n with n   V pl-n   V-RECIP: V with n   V-ing   Also pl-n V   N-UNCOUNT

contra·vene /ˌkɒntrəˈviːn/ **contravenes, contravening, contravened.** To **contravene** a law or rule means to do something that is forbidden by it. ♦ **contra·ven·tion** /ˌkɒntrəˈvenʃən/ **contraventions** *...towns where child labour is exploited in contravention of labour laws.*   ◆◇◇◇◇   VERB: V n   FORMAL   N-VAR

con·tre·temps /ˈkɒntrətɒm/; **contretemps** is both the singular and the plural form. A **contretemps** is a small rather embarrassing disagreement.   N-COUNT   LITERARY

con·trib·ute /kənˈtrɪbjuːt/ **contributes, contributing, contributed. 1** If you **contribute** to something, you say or do things to help to make it successful. *He believes he has something to contribute to a discussion concerning the uprising.* ♦ **con·tri·bu·tion** /ˌkɒntrɪˈbjuːʃən/ **contributions.** If you make a **contribution** to something, you say or do things to help make it successful. *He was awarded a prize for his contribution to world peace.* **2** If a person, organization, or country **contributes** money or resources to something, they give money or resources to help pay for it or achieve it. *The US is contributing $4 billion in loans, credits and grants.* ♦ **con·tribu·tor** /kənˈtrɪbjʊtə/ **contributors** *...the largest net contributors to EC funds.* ♦ **contribution.** A **contribution** is a sum of money that you contribute. *...companies that make charitable contributions.* **3** If you **contribute** to a magazine or book, you write things that are published in it. ♦ **contributor** *...a regular contributor to 'Today' newspaper.* ♦ **contribution.** A **contribution** is a sum of money that you give in order to help pay for something. **4** If something **contributes** to an event or situation, it is one of the causes of it. *Stress, both human and mechanical, may also be a contributing factor.* ♦ **contributor** *Old buses are major contributors to pollution.* ♦ **con·tribu·tory** *Repressing anger is a contributory factor in many physical illnesses.*   ◆◆◇◇   VERB: V to n   V n to n   Also V   N-COUNT   VERB: V n to/   towards n   V n   Also V   N-COUNT   N-COUNT   VERB: V to n   N-COUNT   N-COUNT   VERB: V to n   V-ing   N-COUNT   ADJ

con·trite /kənˈtraɪt, ˈkɒntraɪt/. If you are **contrite**, you are very sorry because you have done something wrong. ♦ **con·tri·tion** /kənˈtrɪʃən/ *He'd be full of contrition, weeping and begging forgiveness.*   ADJ-GRADED   FORMAL   N-UNCOUNT

con·triv·ance /kənˈtraɪvəns/ **contrivances. 1** If you describe something as a **contrivance**, you   N-VAR   PRAGMATICS   FORMAL

disapprove of it because it is unnecessary and artificial. **2** A **contrivance** is an unfair or dishonest scheme to gain an advantage for yourself. *...some contrivance to raise prices.* N-COUNT

con·trive /kən'traɪv/ **contrives, contriving, contrived. 1** If you **contrive** an event or situation, you succeed in making it happen, often by tricking someone. *The oil companies were accused of contriving a shortage of gasoline.* **2** If you **contrive** something such as a device or piece of equipment, you invent and construct it in a clever or unusual way. *We therefore had to contrive a very large black-out curtain.* **3** If you **contrive** to do something difficult, you succeed in doing it. VERB Vn FORMAL / VERB Vn / VERB: V to-inf FORMAL ◇◇◇◇◇

con·trived /kən'traɪvd/ **1** If you say that something someone says or does is **contrived**, you think it is false and deliberate, rather than spontaneous and natural; used showing disapproval. **2** If you say that the plot of a play, film, or novel is **contrived**, you mean that it is unlikely and unconvincing; used showing disapproval. ADJ-GRADED PRAGMATICS / ADJ-GRADED PRAGMATICS ◇◇◇◇◇

con·trol /kən'trəʊl/ **controls, controlling, controlled. 1** If someone has **control** of an organization, place, or system, they have the power to make all the important decisions about the way that it is run. You can also say they are in **control** of it or it is **under** their **control**. *The restructuring involves Mr Ronson giving up control of the company... People feel more in control of their own lives.* **2** The people who **control** an organization or place have the power to take all the important decisions about the way that it is run. *...its controlling interest in both firms.* N-UNCOUNT / VERB: Vn V-ing ◆◆◆◆◆
♦ **-controlled** *AGA Gas is Swedish-controlled.* COMB
♦ **con·trol·ler, controllers** *...the job of controller of BBC 1.* ● See also **air traffic controller.** N-COUNT
3 If you have **control** of something or someone, you are able to make them do what you want them to do. *He lost control of his car... Some teachers have more control over pupils than their parents have.* **4** To **control** a piece of equipment, process, or system means to make it work in the way that you want it to work. *...the controlled production of energy from sugar.* N-UNCOUNT / VERB: Vn V-ed
♦ **-controlled** *...computer-controlled traffic lights.* COMB
5 A **control** is a device such as a switch or lever which you use in order to operate a machine or other piece of equipment. *I practised operating the controls.* ● If someone is at the **controls** of a machine or other piece of equipment, they are operating it. N-COUNT / PHRASE
6 If you show **control**, you prevent yourself behaving in an angry or emotional way. *Sometimes he would completely lose control.* **7** If you **control** yourself, or if you **control** your feelings, voice, or expression, you make yourself behave calmly even though you are feeling angry, excited, or upset. *I couldn't control my temper.* ♦ **con·trolled** *Her manner was quiet and very controlled.* N-UNCOUNT PRAGMATICS / VERB: V pron-refl Vn / ADJ-GRADED
8 When a government **controls** prices, wages, or the activity of a particular group, it uses its power to restrict them. ● Also a noun. *Control of inflation remains the government's absolute priority.* **9 Controls** are the methods that a government uses to restrict something, for example price or wage increases. *They have very strict gun control in Sweden.* **10** To **control** something dangerous means to prevent it from becoming worse or from spreading. *...the need to control environmental pollution.* **11** If something harmful is **out of control**, nobody has any power over it. If it is under control, it is being dealt with successfully. *The fire is burning out of control.* VERB: Vn / N-UNCOUNT: with supp N-VAR / VERB Vn / PHRASE
12 The word **control** is used to refer to a place where your documents or luggage are officially checked when you enter a foreign country. *...border controls.* N-VAR: nN
13 See also **air traffic control, birth control, quality control, remote control, stock control.**

con·trol freak, control freaks. If you say that someone is a **control freak**, you mean that they want to be in control of every situation they find themselves in. N-COUNT INFORMAL

con·trol·lable /kən'trəʊləbəl/. If something is **controllable**, you are able to control or influence it. ADJ-GRADED

con·trol tower, control towers. A **control tower** is a building at an airport from which instructions are given to aircraft when they are taking off or landing. ► You can also refer to the people who work in a control tower as the **control tower.** N-COUNT / N-COLL-COUNT

con·tro·ver·sial /ˌkɒntrə'vɜːʃəl/. If you describe something or someone as **controversial**, you mean that they are the subject of public argument, disagreement, or disapproval. *...the controversial new book.* ♦ **con·tro·ver·sial·ly** *More controversially, he claims that these higher profits cover the cost of finding fresh talent.* ADJ-GRADED / ADV-GRADED ◆◆◆◇◇

con·tro·ver·sy /'kɒntrəvɜːsi, kən'trɒvəsi/ **controversies.** Controversy is a lot of discussion and argument about something, often involving strong feelings of anger or disapproval. *The proposed cuts have caused considerable controversy.* N-VAR ◆◆◆◇◇

con·tu·sion /kən'tjuːʒən, AM -'tuː-/ **contusions.** A contusion is a bruise. N-COUNT MEDICAL

co·nun·drum /kə'nʌndrəm/ **conundrums.** A conundrum is a problem or puzzle which is difficult or impossible to solve. N-COUNT FORMAL ◇◇◇◇◇

con·ur·ba·tion /ˌkɒnə'beɪʃən/ **conurbations.** A conurbation consists of a large city together with the smaller towns around it. N-COUNT BRITISH, FORMAL

con·va·lesce /ˌkɒnvə'les/ **convalesces, convalescing, convalesced.** If you are convalescing, you are resting and regaining your health after an illness or operation. *...many of those convalescing from illness or surgery.* ♦ **con·va·les·cence** /ˌkɒnvə'lesəns/ *I visited him during his convalescence.* ♦ **con·va·les·cent** *...his convalescent wife.* VERB: V V from n FORMAL / N-UNCOUNT / ADJ

con·vec·tion /kən'vekʃən/. Convection is the process by which heat travels through air, water, and other gases and liquids. N-UNCOUNT

con·vene /kən'viːn/ **convenes, convening, convened.** If someone **convenes** a meeting or conference, they arrange for it to take place. *Senior officials convened in October 1991 in London.* VERB: V-ERG: Vn V FORMAL

con·ven·er /kən'viːnə/. See **convenor.**

con·veni·ence /kən'viːniəns/ **conveniences. 1** If something is done for your **convenience**, it is done in a way that is useful or suitable for you. *He was happy to make a detour for her convenience.* ● If something is arranged to happen at your **convenience**, it happens at a time which is suitable for you. *Delivery times are arranged at your convenience.* **2** If you describe something as a **convenience**, you mean that it is useful. **3 Conveniences** are pieces of equipment designed to make your life easier. **4** A public **convenience** is a building containing public toilets. **5** See also **convenient.** N-UNCOUNT: with poss / PHRASE FORMAL / N-COUNT / N-COUNT / N-COUNT BRITISH, FORMAL ◆◇◇◇◇

con·venience 'food. Convenience food is frozen, dried, or tinned food that can be heated and prepared very quickly and easily. N-UNCOUNT

con·venience store, convenience stores. A convenience store is a shop in a residential area which sells mainly groceries and which is usually open until late at night. N-COUNT

con·veni·ent /kən'viːniənt/. **1** If a way of doing something is **convenient**, it is easy, useful or suitable for a particular purpose. *...a flexible and convenient way of paying... It was more convenient to eat in the kitchen.* ♦ **con·veni·ence** *...the convenience of a fast non-stop flight.* ♦ **con·veni·ent·ly** *The body spray slips conveniently into your sports bag.* **2** If you describe a place as **convenient**, you are pleased because it is near to where you are, or because you can reach another place from there quickly and easily. *The town is well placed for easy access of London and convenient for Heathrow Airport.* ♦ **conveniently** *...conveniently close to Los Angeles. ...two conveniently placed push-buttons.* **3** A **convenient** time to do something is a time when you are free to do it or would like to do it. *Would this evening be convenient for you?* **4** If you describe someone's attitudes or actions as **convenient**, you disapprove of them because you think that they are only adopting those attitudes or per- ADJ-GRADED / N-UNCOUNT / ADV-GRADED / ADJ-GRADED PRAGMATICS / ADV-GRADED / ADJ-GRADED / ADJ-GRADED PRAGMATICS ◆◆◇◇◇

forming those actions in order to avoid dealing with a difficult or serious matter. *We cannot make this minority a convenient excuse to turn our backs.*
♦ **conveniently** *They've conveniently forgotten the risk of heart disease.* ADV-GRADED

con·ven·or /kən'viːnə/ **convenors;** also spelled **convener. 1** A **convenor** is a trade union official who organizes the shop stewards at a particular factory. **2** A **convenor** is someone who convenes a meeting. N-COUNT BRITISH / N-COUNT

con·vent /'kɒnvənt/ **convents. 1** A **convent** is a building in which a community of nuns live. **2** A **convent** is the same as a **convent school.** N-COUNT / N-COUNT

con·ven·tion /kən'venʃən/ **conventions. 1** A **convention** is a way of behaving that is considered to be correct or polite by most people in a society. *It's just a social convention that men don't wear skirts.* **2** In art, literature, or the theatre, a **convention** is a traditional method or style. *...the conventions of Western art.* **3** A **convention** is an official agreement between countries or groups of people. *...the UN convention on climate change. ...the Geneva convention.* **4** A **convention** is a large meeting of an organization or political group. *...the annual convention of the Society of Professional Journalists.* N-VAR / N-COUNT / N-COUNT

con·ven·tion·al /kən'venʃənəl/. **1** Someone who is **conventional** has behaviour or opinions that are ordinary and normal. *...a respectable married woman with conventional opinions.* ♦ **con·ven·tion·al·ly** *People still wore their hair short and dressed conventionally.* **2** A **conventional** method or product is one that is usually used or that has been in use for a long time. *...a conventional computer floppy disk.* ♦ **conventionally** *...conventionally grown crops.* **3 Conventional** weapons and wars do not involve nuclear explosives. *...nuclear, chemical and conventional arms.* ADJ-GRADED / ADV-GRADED / ADJ / ADV: ADV with v ADJ

con·ven·tion·eer /kən,venʃə'nɪə/ **conventioneers. Conventioneers** are people who are attending a convention. N-COUNT AMERICAN

'convent school, convent schools. A **convent school** is a school where many of the teachers are nuns. N-COUNT

con·verge /kən'vɜːdʒ/ **converges, converging, converged. 1** If people or vehicles **converge on** a place, they move towards it from different directions. *Competitors from more than a hundred countries have converged on Sheffield for the Games.* **2** If roads or lines **converge**, they meet or join at a particular place. *As they flow south, the five rivers converge.* **3** If different ideas or societies **converge**, they stop being different and become similar to each other. *Their views were converging... The views of the richest householders converged with those of the poorest.* ♦ **con·ver·gence, convergences** *...the need to move towards greater economic convergence.* VERB V on n / VERB pl-n V FORMAL / V-RECIP pl-n V V with n / N-VAR

con·ver·sant /kən'vɜːsənt/. If you are **conversant** with something, you are familiar with it and able to deal with it. *Those in business are not, on the whole, conversant with basic science.* ADJ-GRADED: v-link ADJ FORMAL

con·ver·sa·tion /,kɒnvə'seɪʃən/ **conversations. 1** If you have a **conversation** with someone, you talk with them, usually in an informal situation. *I struck up a conversation with him. ...a telephone conversation.* ♦ **con·ver·sa·tion·al** *...the author's easy, conversational style. ...conversational German.* ♦ **con·ver·sa·tion·al·ly** *Lyrics are written almost conversationally, yet sung with passion.* **2** If you say that people are **in conversation**, you mean that they are talking together. *I found her in conversation with Mrs Williams.* **3** If you **make conversation**, you talk to someone in order to be polite and not because you really want to. N-COUNT / ADJ-GRADED / ADV-GRADED PHRASE / PHRASE

con·ver·sa·tion·al·ist /,kɒnvə'seɪʃənəlɪst/ **conversationalists.** A good **conversationalist** is someone who is able to talk well about interesting things when they have conversations. *Joan is a brilliant conversationalist.* N-COUNT

con·verse, converses, conversing, conversed. The verb is pronounced /kən'vɜːs/. The noun is pronounced /'kɒnvɜːs/. **1** If you **converse** with someone, you talk to them. *Luke sat directly behind the pilot and conversed with him... They were conversing in German.* **2 The converse** of a statement is the opposite or reverse of that statement. *What you do for a living is critical to where you settle and how you live - and the converse is also true.* ♦ **con·verse·ly** *Malaysia and Indonesia rely on open markets for forest and fishery products. Conversely, some Asian countries are highly protectionist.* ◆◇◇◇ V-RECIP V with n pl-n V FORMAL N-SING: the N FORMAL / ADV: ADV with cl

con·ver·sion /kən'vɜːʃən/ **conversions. 1** Conversion is the act or process of changing something into a different form. *...the conversion of disused rail lines into cycle routes. ...a loft conversion.* **2** If someone changes their religion or beliefs, you can refer to their **conversion.** *...his conversion to Christianity.* **3** In rugby, if a player makes or kicks a **conversion**, he scores points by kicking the ball over the crossbar just after a try has been scored. ◆◆◇◇ N-VAR / N-VAR / N-COUNT

con·vert, converts, converting, converted. The verb is pronounced /kən'vɜːt/. The noun is pronounced /'kɒnvɜːt/. **1** If one thing **is converted** or **converts** into another, it is changed into a different form. *The signal will be converted into digital code. ...substances which the body can convert into vitamins. ...a table that converts into an ironing board.* **2** If someone **converts** a room or building, they alter it in order to use it for a different purpose. *By converting the loft, they were able to have two extra bedrooms. ...to convert County Hall into an hotel. ...a converted barn.* **3** If you **convert** a vehicle or piece of equipment, you change it so that it can use a different fuel. *Save money by converting your car to unleaded. ...the programme to convert every gas burner in Britain.* **4** If you **convert** a quantity from one system of measurement to another, you calculate what the quantity is in the second system. *Converting metric measurements to U.S. equivalents is easy.* **5** If someone **converts** you, they persuade you to change your beliefs, especially your religious or political ones. You can also say that someone **converts** to a different set of beliefs. *...converting Godwin to political radicalism... He quickly converted me to the joys of cross-country skiing... He converted to Catholicism in 1917.* **6** A **convert** is someone who has changed their beliefs, especially their religious or political ones. *She, too, was a convert to Roman Catholicism. ...recent converts to vegetarianism.* **7** ● **to preach to the converted: see preach.** ◆◆◇◇ V-ERG be V-ed into/to n V into/to n V into/to n / VERB V n V n into n V-ed / VERB V n to/into n V n / VERB V n prep Also V n / V-ERG V n to n V n V n to n / N-COUNT

con·vert·er /kən'vɜːtə/ **converters.** A **converter** is a device that changes something into a different form. ● See also **catalytic converter.** ◆◇◇◇ N-COUNT

con·vert·ible /kən,vɜːtɪbəl/ **convertibles. 1** A **convertible** is a car with a soft roof that can be folded down or removed. *Her own car is a convertible Golf.* **2 Convertible** investments or money can be easily exchanged for other forms of investments or money. *...the introduction of a convertible currency.* ♦ **con·vert·ibil·ity** /kən,vɜːtɪ'bɪlɪti/ *...the convertibility of the rouble.* ◆◆◇◇ N-COUNT / ADJ TECHNICAL / N-UNCOUNT

con·vex /'kɒnveks/. **Convex** is used to describe something that curves outwards. *...the large convex mirror above the fireplace.* ADJ-GRADED

con·vey /kən'veɪ/ **conveys, conveying, conveyed. 1** To **convey** information or feelings means to cause them to be known or understood by someone. *I tried to convey the wonder of this machine to my husband... In every one of her pictures she conveys a sense of immediacy... The Americans had conveyed their views to the Romanian government.* **2** To **convey** someone or something to a place means to carry or transport them there. *...a branch line to Brightlingsea to convey fish direct to Billingsgate.* ♦ **con·vey·ance** /kən'veɪəns/ *...the conveyance of bicycles on Regional Railways trains.* ◆◆◇◇ VERB V n / VERB V n FORMAL / N-UNCOUNT: with supp

con·vey·anc·ing /kən'veɪənsɪŋ/. **Conveyancing** is the process of transferring the legal ownership of property. N-UNCOUNT LEGAL, BRITISH

con·vey·or belt /kən'veɪə belt/ **conveyor belts.** 1 A conveyor belt or a conveyor is a continuously moving strip of rubber or metal which is used in factories for moving objects along so that they can be dealt with as quickly as possible. 2 If you describe a situation as a conveyor belt, you dislike it because it produces things or people which are all the same or always deals with things or people in the same way. ...conveyor-belt hospital wards.

con·vict, convicts, convicting, convicted. The verb is pronounced /kən'vɪkt/. The noun is pronounced /'kɒnvɪkt/. 1 If someone is convicted of a crime, they are found guilty of it in a law court. There was insufficient evidence to convict him. 2 A convict is someone who is in prison.

con·vic·tion /kən'vɪkʃən/ **convictions.** 1 A conviction is a strong belief or opinion. It is our firm conviction that a step forward has been taken. 2 If you have conviction, you have great confidence in your beliefs or opinions. 'We shall, sir,' said Thorne, with conviction. 3 If something carries conviction, it is likely to be true or likely to be believed. Nor did his denial carry conviction. 4 If someone has a conviction, they have been found guilty of a crime in a court of law. He will appeal against his conviction.

con·vince /kən'vɪns/ **convinces, convincing, convinced.** 1 If someone or something convinces you of something, they make you believe that it is true or that it exists. The waste disposal industry is finding it difficult to convince the public that its operations are safe. ♦ convinced He became convinced of the need for cheap editions of good quality writing. 2 If someone or something convinces you to do something, they persuade you to do it. He convinced her to go ahead and marry Bud.

con·vinc·ing /kən'vɪnsɪŋ/. If you describe someone or something as convincing, you mean that they make you believe that something is true, correct, or genuine. He sounded very convincing. ♦ con·vinc·ing·ly He argued forcefully and convincingly that they were likely to bankrupt the budget.

con·viv·ial /kən'vɪvɪəl/. Convivial people or occasions are pleasant, friendly, and relaxed. The atmosphere was quite convivial.

con·vo·ca·tion /ˌkɒnvə'keɪʃən/ **convocations.** A convocation is a meeting or ceremony attended by a large number of people. ...a convocation of the American Youth Congress.

con·vo·lut·ed /'kɒnvəluːtɪd/. If you describe a sentence, idea, or system as convoluted, you mean that it is complicated and difficult to understand; used showing disapproval. The policy is so convoluted even college presidents are confused.

con·voy /'kɒnvɔɪ/ **convoys, convoying, convoyed.** 1 A convoy is a group of vehicles or ships travelling to a place together. They travel in convoy. 2 To convoy goods or people somewhere means to move them there in a convoy. He ordered the combined fleet to convoy troops to Naples.

con·vulse /kən'vʌls/ **convulses, convulsing, convulsed.** If someone convulses or if they are convulsed by something, their body moves suddenly in an uncontrolled way. He let out a cry that convulsed his bulky frame. ▶ Also an adjective. The opposing team were so convulsed with laughter that they almost forgot to hit the ball. ♦ con·vul·sive Convulsive sobs racked her. ♦ con·vul·sive·ly His arms and legs jerked convulsively.

con·vul·sion /kən'vʌlʃən/ **convulsions.** 1 If someone has convulsions, they suffer uncontrollable movements of their muscles. 2 If there are convulsions in a country, system, or organization, there are major unexpected changes in it. ...the political convulsions that led to de Gaulle's return to power in May 1958.

coo /kuː/ **coos, cooing, cooed.** 1 When doves, pigeons, and certain other birds coo, they make soft sounds. 2 When someone coos, they speak in a very soft quiet voice. She paused to coo at the baby.

cook /kʊk/ **cooks, cooking, cooked.** 1 When you cook a meal, you prepare food for eating and then heat it. Chefs at the St James Court restaurant have cooked for the Queen... We'll cook them a nice Italian meal. ♦ cook·ing Her hobbies include music, dancing, sport and cooking. 2 When you cook food, or when food cooks, it is heated until it is ready to be eaten. Let the vegetables cook gently for about 10 minutes. 3 A cook is a person whose job is to prepare and cook food. They had a butler, a cook, and a maid. 4 If you say that someone is a good cook, you mean that they are good at preparing and cooking food. 5 See also cooking.

cook up. 1 If someone cooks up a dishonest scheme, they plan it. He must have cooked up his scheme on the spur of the moment. 2 If someone cooks up an explanation or a story, they make it up. I know enough about lawyers to know who cooked this up. 3 If you cook up a quantity of food, especially a large quantity, you heat it until it is ready to be eaten. Hot food is available, though the prisoners have to cook it up themselves.

cook·book /'kʊkbʊk/ **cookbooks.** A cookbook is a book that contains recipes for preparing food.

cook·er /'kʊkə/ **cookers.** A cooker is a device, usually consisting of a grill, an oven, and some gas or electric rings, for cooking food. The usual American word is range. ● See also pressure cooker.

cook·ery /'kʊkəri/. Cookery is the activity of preparing and cooking food.

'cookery book, cookery books. A cookery book is the same as a cookbook.

cookie /'kʊki/ **cookies.** A cookie is a sweet biscuit. ...chocolate chip cookies.

cook·ing /'kʊkɪŋ/. 1 Cooking is food which has been cooked. The menu is based on classic French cooking. 2 Cooking ingredients or utensils are ones which are used in cookery. 3 See also cook.

cook·out /'kʊkaʊt/ **cookouts.** A cookout is the same as a barbecue.

cook·ware /'kʊkweə/. Cookware is the range of pans and pots which are used in cooking. ...several lines of popular cookware and utensils.

cool /kuːl/ **cooler, coolest; cools, cooling, cooled.** 1 Something that is cool has a temperature which is low but not very low. The vaccines were kept cool in refrigerators. ♦ cool·ness His knees felt the coolness of the tiled floor. 2 If it is cool, the temperature of the air is low but not very low. Thank goodness it's cool in here... Store grains and cereals in a cool, dry place. ▶ Also a noun. She walked into the cool of the hallway... They could work all night in the cool. ♦ coolness Soon we left the coolness of the olive groves. 3 Clothing that is cool is made of thin material so that you do not become too hot in hot weather. In warm weather, you should wear clothing that is cool and comfortable. 4 Cool colours are light colours which give an impression of coolness. ...a cool colour such as cream. 5 When something cools or when you cool it, it becomes lower in temperature. Huge fans will have to cool the concrete floor. ▶ To cool down means the same as to cool. Avoid putting your car away until the engine has cooled down... The other main way the body cools itself down is by panting. ♦ cool·ing Being immobile in a cold room leads to a cooling of the body temperature. 6 When a feeling or emotion cools, or when you cool it, it becomes less powerful. His weird behaviour had cooled her passion. 7 If you tell someone to cool it, you want them to stop being angry and aggressive. 8 If you say that a person or their behaviour is cool, you mean that they are calm and unemotional, especially in a difficult situation; used showing approval. He was marvelously cool again, smiling as if nothing had happened. ♦ cool·ly Everyone must think this situation through calmly and coolly. ♦ cool·ness Detectives praised him for his coolness. 9 If you keep your cool in a difficult situation, you manage to remain calm. If you lose your cool, you get angry or

upset. **10** If you **play it cool**, you deliberately behave in a calm unemotional way because you do not want people to know you are enthusiastic or angry about something. *PHRASE INFORMAL*

11 If you say that a person or their behaviour is **cool**, you mean that they are unfriendly or unenthusiastic. *I thought he was cool, aloof, and arrogant.* ◆ **cool·ly** *'It's your choice, Nina,' David said coolly.* ◆ **cool·ness** *She seemed quite unaware of the sudden coolness of her friend's manner.* *ADJ-GRADED / ADV-GRADED / N-UNCOUNT*

12 If you say that a person or their behaviour is **cool**, you mean that they are fashionable and attractive. *He was trying to be really cool and trendy.* *ADJ-GRADED PRAGMATICS INFORMAL*

13 If you say that someone is **cool** about something, you mean that they accept it and are not angry or upset about it; used showing approval. *Bev was really cool about it all.* **14** If you say that something is **cool**, you think it is very good. *Kathleen gave me a really cool dress.* *v-link ADJ PRAGMATICS INFORMAL / ADJ-GRADED INFORMAL*

15 You can use **cool** to emphasize that an amount or figure is very large, especially when it has been obtained easily. *Columbia recently re-signed the band for a cool $30 million.* *ADJ-GRADED ADJ n PRAGMATICS INFORMAL*

16 ● **as cool as a cucumber**: see **cucumber**. ● **to cool your heels**: see **heel**.

cool down. 1 See **cool 5. 2** If someone **cools down** or if you **cool** them **down**, they become less angry than they were. *He has had time to cool down and look at what happened more objectively.* *PHRASAL VB ERG: V P Also V P noun*

cool off. If someone or something **cools off**, or if you **cool** them **off**, they become cooler after having been hot. *She made a fanning motion, pretending to cool herself off.* *PHRASAL VB ERG: V P V n P*

cool·ant /'ku:lənt/ **coolants. Coolant** is a liquid used to keep a machine or engine cool. *N-VAR*

cool·er /'ku:lə/ **coolers.** A **cooler** is a container for keeping things cool, especially drinks. ● See also **cool**. *◆◇◇◇ N-COUNT*

cool-'headed. If you describe someone as **cool-headed**, you mean that they stay calm in difficult situations; used showing approval. *...a cool-headed, responsible statesman.* *ADJ-GRADED PRAGMATICS*

coolie /'ku:li/ **coolies.** In former times, unskilled workers in China or other parts of Asia were sometimes referred to as **coolies**. *N-COUNT RUDE*

cooling-'off period, cooling-off periods. A **cooling-off period** is an agreed period of time during which two sides with opposing views try to resolve a dispute before taking any serious action. *...a one-year cooling-off period before couples were granted a divorce.* *N-COUNT*

coop /ku:p/ **coops.** A **coop** is a cage where you keep small animals or birds such as chickens. *N-COUNT*

'co-op, co-ops. A **co-op** is a co-operative. *The co-op sells the art work at exhibitions.* *N-COUNT INFORMAL*

cooped up /ˌku:pt 'ʌp/. If you say that someone is **cooped up**, you mean that they live or are kept in a place which is too small, or which does not allow them much freedom. *He is cooped up in a cramped cell with 10 other inmates.* *ADJ: v-link ADJ*

co-'operate, co-operates, co-operating, co-operated; also spelled **cooperate. 1** If you **co-operate** with someone, you work with them or help them for a particular purpose. *They would co-operate in the raising of their child.* ◆ **co-operation** *...economic co-operation with East Asia.* **2** If you **co-operate**, you do what someone has asked or told you to do. *He agreed to co-operate with the police investigation.* ◆ **co-operation** *...the importance of the public's co-operation in the hunt for the bombers.* *◆◆◇◇ V-RECIP: V with n pl-n V Also V n (non-recip) / N-UNCOUNT VERB: V V with n / N-UNCOUNT*

co-'operative, co-operatives; also spelled **co-operative. 1** A **co-operative** is a business or organization run by the people who work for it, who share its benefits and profits. *The restaurant is run as a co-operative.* **2** A **co-operative** activity is done by people working together. *...a smooth co-operative effort between Egyptian and US authorities.* ◆ **co-operative·ly** *They agreed to work co-operatively.* **3** If you say that someone is **co-operative**, you *◆◇◇◇ N-COUNT / ADJ / ADV-GRADED: ADV after v / ADJ-GRADED*

mean that they do what you ask them to without complaining or arguing. *I made every effort to be co-operative.*

co-'operative so'ciety, co-operative societies. A **co-operative society** is a commercial organization with several shops in a particular district. Customers can join this organization and get a share of its profits. *N-COUNT BRITISH*

co-'opt, co-opts, co-opting, co-opted. 1 If you **co-opt** someone, you persuade them to help or support you. *Sofia co-opted Natasha as her assistant.* **2** If someone **is co-opted** into a group, they are asked by that group to become a member, rather than joining or being elected in the normal way. *He's been authorised to co-opt anyone he wants.* **3** If a group or political party **co-opts** a slogan or policy, they take it, often from another group or political party, and use it themselves. *VERB V n / VERB: be V-ed into/onto n V n / VERB: V n*

co-ordinate, co-ordinates, co-ordinating, co-ordinated; also spelled **coordinate.** The verb is pronounced /kəʊ'ɔ:dɪneɪt/. The noun is pronounced /kəʊ'ɔ:dɪnət/. **1** If you **co-ordinate** an activity, you organize the various people and things involved in it. *...an advisory committee to co-ordinate police work.* ◆ **co-ordinat·ed** *...a rapid and well co-ordinated international rescue operation.* ◆ **co-ordina·tor, co-ordinators** *...the party's campaign co-ordinator.* **2** If you **co-ordinate** clothes or furnishings that are used together, or if they **co-ordinate**, they are similar in some way and look nice together. *...fabric bows that co-ordinate with other furnishings... Colours and looks must fit the themes of the seasons so that the shops co-ordinate well.* **3** **Co-ordinates** are pieces of clothing or soft furnishings which are similar and which are intended to be worn or used together. *...new lingerie co-ordinates.* **4** If you **co-ordinate** the different parts of your body, you make them work together efficiently to perform particular movements. *...treatment which enables them to co-ordinate their limbs better.* **5** The **co-ordinates** of a point on a map or graph are the two sets of numbers or letters that you need in order to find that point. *◆◆◇◇ VERB V n / ADJ-GRADED / N-COUNT / V-RECIP-ERG: V pl-n V with n pl-n V / N-PLURAL / VERB V n / N-COUNT TECHNICAL*

co-'ordinating con'junction, co-ordinating conjunctions. A **co-ordinating conjunction** is a word such as 'and', 'or', or 'but' which joins two or more words, groups, or clauses of equal status, for example two main clauses. Compare **subordinating conjunction**. *N-COUNT*

co-ordi'nation. 1 **Co-ordination** means organizing the activities of two or more groups so that they work together efficiently and know what the others are doing. *...the lack of co-ordination between the civilian and military authorities.* ● If you do something **in co-ordination with** someone else, you both organize your activities so that you work together efficiently. **2** **Co-ordination** is the ability to use the different parts of your body together efficiently. *...clumsiness and lack of co-ordination.* *◆◇◇◇ N-UNCOUNT / PHR-PREP / N-UNCOUNT*

coot /ku:t/ **coots.** A **coot** is a water bird with black feathers and a white patch on its forehead. *N-COUNT*

cop /kɒp/ **cops, copping, copped. 1** A **cop** is a policeman or policewoman. *Frank didn't like having the cops know where to find him.* **2** If you **cop it**, you are punished or scolded by someone for doing something wrong. *Motel owners and restaurant managers copped it for neglecting their clients.* *◆◆◇◇ N-COUNT INFORMAL PHRASE INFORMAL, BRITISH*

cop out. If you say that someone **is copping out**, you mean they are avoiding doing something they should do; used showing disapproval. *'Will you call the board to alert them that I feel I should resign?'—'I'll do it. But I think you're copping out.'* *PHRASAL VB PRAGMATICS V P INFORMAL*

cope /kəʊp/ **copes, coping, coped. 1** If you **cope** with a problem or task, you deal with it successfully. *We managed to cope.* **2** If you have to **cope with** an unpleasant situation, you have to accept it or endure it. *Never before has the industry had to cope with war and recession at the same time.* **3** If a machine or a system can **cope** with some- *◆◆◇◇ VERB: V with n / ing V / VERB V with n / ing / VERB:*

thing, it is large enough or complex enough to deal with it satisfactorily. *The speed of economic change has been so great that the tax-collecting system has been unable to cope.* `V with n` `V`

4 A **cope** is a long cloak worn by some Christian priests on special occasions. `N-COUNT`

copi·er /'kɒpiə/ **copiers.** A **copier** is a machine which makes exact copies of writing or pictures on paper, usually by a photographic process. `N-COUNT`

'co-pilot, co-pilots. The **co-pilot** of an aircraft is a pilot who assists the chief pilot. `N-COUNT`

co·pi·ous /'kəʊpiəs/. A **copious** amount of something is a large amount of it. *I went out for a meal last night and drank copious amounts of red wine.* `♦♦♢♢♢` `ADJ-GRADED`
♦ **co·pi·ous·ly** *The victims were bleeding copiously.* `ADV-GRADED`

'cop-out, cop-outs. If you refer to something as a **cop-out,** you think that it is a way for someone to avoid doing something that they should do; used showing disapproval. *Wallowing in guilt about the past is a cop-out that prevents you from taking responsibility for yourself now.* `N-COUNT` `PRAGMATICS` `INFORMAL`

cop·per /'kɒpə/ **coppers. 1** Copper is reddish brown metal that is used to make things such as coins and electrical wires. **2** Copper is sometimes used to describe things that are reddish-brown in colour. *His hair has reverted back to its original copper hue.* **3** Coppers are brown metal coins of low value. *I gave him a few coppers to spend on himself.* **4** A copper is a policeman or a policewoman. *...your friendly, neighbourhood copper.* `♦♦♢♢♢` `N-UNCOUNT` `ADJ` `LITERARY` `N-COUNT` `BRITISH` `N-COUNT` `BRITISH, INFORMAL`

cop·pery /'kɒpəri/. A **coppery** colour is red-brown like copper. *...pale coppery leaves.* `ADJ`

cop·pice /'kɒpɪs/ **coppices, coppicing, coppiced. 1** A coppice is an area of small trees which are cut very low every few years. The trees then grow shoots which are used to make poles. **2** To coppice trees means to cut them very low, so that they will grow shoots which can be used to make poles. **3** A coppice is the same as a copse. `N-UNCOUNT` `TECHNICAL` `VERB: V n` `TECHNICAL` `N-COUNT`

cops-and-'robbers. A **cops-and-robbers** film, television programme, or book is one whose story involves the police trying to catch criminals. `ADJ: ADJ n`

copse /kɒps/ **copses.** A **copse** is a small group of trees growing very close to each other. `N-COUNT`

cop·ter /'kɒptə/ **copters.** A **copter** is a helicopter. *Sea rescue copter pilot saves crew from death.* `N-COUNT` `INFORMAL`

Cop·tic /'kɒptɪk/. **Coptic** means belonging or relating to a part of the Christian Church which was founded in Egypt. *...the Coptic Church.* `ADJ: ADJ n`

copu·late /'kɒpjʊleɪt/ **copulates, copulating, copulated.** If one animal or person **copulates** with another, they have sex. *Whales take twenty-four hours to copulate.* ♦ **copu·la·tion** /,kɒpjʊ'leɪʃən/ **copulations** *...acts of copulation.* `V-RECIP:` `V with n` `pl-n V` `TECHNICAL` `N-VAR`

copy /'kɒpi/ **copies, copying, copied. 1** If you make a **copy** of something, you produce something that looks like the original thing. *The reporter apparently obtained a copy of Steve's resignation letter.* **2** If you **copy** something, you produce something that looks like the original thing. *He copied the chart from a book by Aesculapius.* **3** If you **copy** a piece of writing, you write it again exactly. *He copied the data into a notebook... We're copying from textbooks.* ▶ **Copy out** means the same as **copy**. *He wrote the title on the blackboard, then copied out the text sentence by sentence.* **4** If you **copy** a person or what they do, you try to do what they do or try to be like them, usually because you admire them. *...the coquettish gestures she had copied from actresses.* ♦ **copy·ing** *Children learn by copying.* **5** A **copy** of a book, newspaper, or record is one of the many identical ones that have been printed or produced. *...a copy of 'USA Today'.* **6** Copy is written material that is ready to be published or used in a broadcast. *...advertising copy.* **7** Copy is news or information that can be used in an article in a newspaper. *...journalists looking for good copy.* **8** See also **back copy, carbon copy, hard copy.** `♦♦♦♢♢` `N-COUNT` `VERB: V n` `V n from n` `VERB: V n` `V n into n` `V n from n` `PHRASAL VB` `V P noun` `Also V n P` `VERB: V n` `V n from n` `N-UNCOUNT` `N-COUNT` `N-UNCOUNT` `N-UNCOUNT` `JOURNALISM`

copy down. If you **copy down** something that `PHRASAL VB`

someone has said or written, you write it down exactly. *I copied it down the way my lawyer read it to me.* `V P n` `V n P`

copy out. See copy 3. `PHRASAL VB`

copy·book /'kɒpibʊk/. A **copybook** action is done perfectly, according to established rules. *Yuri gave a copybook display.* `ADJ` `BRITISH`

copy·cat /'kɒpikæt/ **copycats;** also spelled **copy-cat. 1** A **copycat** crime is committed by someone who is copying someone else. *...a series of copycat attacks.* **2** If you call someone a **copycat,** you are accusing them of copying your behaviour, dress, or ideas; used showing disapproval. `ADJ: ADJ n` `N-COUNT` `PRAGMATICS`

copy·ist /'kɒpiɪst/ **copyists.** A **copyist** copies other people's music or paintings, or makes handwritten copies of documents. *She copies the true artist's signature as part of a painting, as do most copyists.* `N-COUNT`

copy·right /'kɒpirait/ **copyrights.** If someone has **copyright** on a piece of writing or music, it is illegal to reproduce or perform it without their permission. ♦ **copy·right·ed** /'kɒpiraitɪd/. **Copyrighted** material is protected by a copyright. `♦♦♢♢♢` `N-VAR` `ADJ`

copy·writer /'kɒpiraitə/ **copywriters.** A **copywriter** is a person whose job is to write the words for advertisements. `N-COUNT`

co·quette /kɒ'ket, AM kəʊ-/ **coquettes.** A **coquette** is a woman who behaves in a playful way that is intended to make men find her attractive. ♦ **co·quet·tish** /kɒ'ketɪʃ, AM kəʊ-/. *She gave him a coquettish glance.* `N-COUNT` `ADJ-GRADED`

cor /kɔː/. You can say **cor** when you are surprised or impressed. *Cor, look, Annie... Cor, you look just like the Prime Minister.* `EXCLAM` `PRAGMATICS` `INFORMAL, BRITISH`

cor·al /'kɒrəl, AM 'kɔː-/ **corals. 1** Coral is a hard substance formed from the skeletons of very small sea animals. **2** Corals are very small sea animals. **3** Something that is **coral** is dark orangey-pink. `♦♢♢♢♢` `N-VAR` `N-COUNT` `COLOUR`

,coral 'reef, coral reefs. A **coral reef** is a ridge of coral, the top of which is usually just above or just below the surface of the sea. `N-COUNT`

cord /kɔːd/ **cords. 1** Cord is strong thick string. *...a length of nylon cord.* **2** Cord is wire covered in rubber or plastic which connects electrical equipment to an electricity supply. *...electrical cord.* **3** See also **spinal cord, umbilical cord, vocal cords. 4** Cords are trousers made of corduroy. *He had bare feet, a T-shirt and cords on.* **5** Cord means made of corduroy. *...a pair of cord trousers.* `♦♦♢♢♢` `N-VAR` `N-VAR` `N-PLURAL` `ADJ: ADJ n`

cor·dial /'kɔːdiəl, AM -dʒəl/ **cordials. 1** Cordial means friendly. *He had never known him to be so chatty and cordial.* ♦ **cor·di·al·ly** *They all greeted me very cordially.* ♦ **cor·di·al·ity** /,kɔːdi'æliti, AM -dʒæl-/ *...an atmosphere of cordiality.* **2** Cordial is a sweet non-alcoholic drink made from fruit juice. *...fruit cordials.* `♦♢♢♢♢` `ADJ-GRADED` `FORMAL` `ADV-GRADED:` `ADV with v` `N-UNCOUNT` `N-VAR` `BRITISH`

cord·ite /'kɔːdait/. **Cordite** is an explosive substance used in guns and bombs. `N-UNCOUNT`

cord·less /'kɔːdləs/. A **cordless** telephone or piece of electric equipment is operated by a battery fitted inside it and is not connected to the electricity mains. `ADJ`

cor·don /'kɔːdən/ **cordons, cordoning, cordoned.** A **cordon** is a line or ring of police, soldiers, or vehicles preventing people from entering or leaving an area. `♦♢♢♢♢` `N-COUNT`

cordon off. If police or soldiers **cordon off** an area, they prevent people from entering or leaving it, usually by forming a line or ring. *Police cordoned off part of the city centre.* `PHRASAL VB` `V P noun` `Also V n P`

cor·don bleu /,kɔːdɒn 'blɜː/. **Cordon bleu** is used to describe cookery or cooks of the highest standard. *...a cordon bleu cookery course.* `ADJ: ADJ n`

cor·du·roy /'kɔːdərɔi/ **corduroys. 1** Corduroy is thick cotton cloth with parallel raised lines on the outside. **2** Corduroys are trousers made out of corduroy or needle cord. `N-UNCOUNT` `N-PLURAL` `DATED`

core /kɔː/ **cores, coring, cored. 1** The core of a fruit is the central part of it. It contains seeds or pips. *...an apple core.* **2** If you **core** a fruit, you `♦♦♦♢♢` `N-COUNT` `VERB: V n`

remove its core. **3** The **core** of an object, building, N-COUNT or city is the central part of it. *The core of the city is a series of ancient squares.*

4 The **core** of something such as a problem or an issue N-SING: *the*N is the part of it that has to be understood or accepted before the whole thing can be understood or dealt with. *Get straight to the core of a problem.* **5** A **core** N-SING: team or a **core** group is a group of people who do the N n, main part of a job or piece of work. *A core of about six* N *of* n *staff would continue with the project.* **6** In a school or N-SING college, **core** subjects are a group of subjects that have to be studied. *The core subjects are English, mathematics and science.* **7** The **core** businesses or the **core** N-SING activities of an organization are their most important ones. *The core activities of local authorities were reorganised.* **8** See also **hard core**.

9 You can use **to the core** when you are describing PHRASE someone who is a very strong supporter of someone or something and will never change their views. For example, you can say that someone is Republican **to the core**. **10** If someone is shaken **to the core** or PHRASE shocked **to the core**, they are extremely shaken or shocked.

cor·gi /ˈkɔːgi/ **corgis.** A corgi is a type of small dog. N-COUNT

co·ri·an·der /ˌkɒriˈændə, AM ˌkɔː-/. **Coriander** is a ◆◇◇◇ plant with seeds that are used as a spice and leaves N-UNCOUNT that are used as a herb.

cork /kɔːk/ **corks, corking, corked. 1** Cork is a ◆◇◇◇ soft light substance which forms the bark of a type N-UNCOUNT of Mediterranean tree. *...cork floors.* **2** A **cork** is a N-COUNT piece of cork or plastic that is pushed into the opening of a bottle to close it. **3** To **cork** a bottle VERB: V n means to seal it by putting a cork in it.

cork·er /ˈkɔːkə/ **corkers.** If you say that someone N-COUNT or something is a **corker**, you mean that they are DATED, INFORMAL very good. *...an absolute corker of an idea.*

cork·screw /ˈkɔːkskruː/ **corkscrews.** A cork- N-COUNT screw is a device for pulling corks out of bottles. See picture headed **kitchen utensils**.

cor·mo·rant /ˈkɔːmərənt/ **cormorants.** A cormo- N-COUNT rant is a dark-coloured bird which nests near coastal areas.

corn /kɔːn/ **corns. 1** Corn is used to refer to crops ◆◆◇◇ such as wheat and barley. It can also be used to re- N-UNCOUNT fer to the seeds from these plants. The American BRITISH word is **grain**. *...fields of corn.* **2** Corn is the same as N-UNCOUNT maize. *...rows of corn in an Iowa field.* AMERICAN **3** Corns are small painful areas of hard skin which can N-COUNT form on your foot.

corn·bread /ˈkɔːnbred/; also spelled **corn bread.** N-UNCOUNT Cornbread is bread made from ground maize.

'**corn cob, corn cobs.** Corn cobs are the long N-COUNT rounded parts of the maize plant on which small yellow seeds grow.

cor·nea /ˈkɔːniə/ **corneas.** The cornea is the N-COUNT transparent skin covering the outside of your eye. ♦ **cor·neal** /ˈkɔːniəl/ *...corneal scars.* ADJ: ADJ n

corned beef /ˌkɔːnd ˈbiːf/. **Corned beef** is beef N-UNCOUNT which has been cooked and preserved in salt water.

cor·ner /ˈkɔːnə/ **corners, cornering, cornered.** ◆◆◆◇ **1** A corner is a point or an area where two or more N-COUNT edges or sides of something join. *Write 'By Airmail' in the top left hand corner.* **2** The **corner** of a room, N-COUNT box, or other square-shaped space is the area inside it where two or three of its edges or walls meet. *...a card table in the corner of the living room.* **3** The N-COUNT **corner** of your mouth or eye is the side of it. **4** The N-COUNT **corner** of a street is the place where one of its sides ends as it joins another street. *He waited until the man had turned a corner.*

5 In football, hockey, and some other sports, a **corner** N-COUNT is a free kick or shot taken from the corner of the pitch. **6** If you say that something is **around the corner** or PHRASE **round the corner**, you mean that it is very near. *My new place is just around the corner.* **7** If you say that PHRASE something is **around the corner** or **round the corner**, you mean that it will happen very soon. *...economic recovery is just around the corner.*

8 A **corner** is a bend in a road. *We turned a sharp cor-* N-COUNT *ner.* **9** If a car, or the person driving it, **corners** in a VERB

particular way, the car goes round bends in roads in V adv/prep this way. *Peter drove jerkily, cornering too fast.*

10 If you **cut corners**, you do something quickly by PHRASE doing it in a less thorough way than you should; used PRAGMATICS showing disapproval.

11 If you talk about the **corners** of the world, a coun- N-COUNT: try, or some other place, you are referring to places with supp that are far away or difficult to get to. *...a remote corner* WRITTEN *of the Cambodian jungle.* **12** You can use expressions PHRASE such as **the four corners of the world** to refer to WRITTEN places that are a long way from each other. *Young people came from the four corners of the nation.*

13 If you are **in a corner** or **in a tight corner**, you are PHRASE in a situation which is difficult to get out of. *The government is in a corner on interest rates.*

14 If you **corner** a person or animal, you force them VERB: V n into a place they cannot escape from. **15** If you **corner** VERB: V n someone, you force them to speak to you when they have been trying to avoid you. **16** If a company or VERB: V n place **corners** an area of trade, they gain control over it so that no one else can have any success in it.

'**corner shop, corner shops;** also spelled N-COUNT **corner-shop.** A corner shop is a small shop, usually BRITISH on the corner of a street, that sells food and household goods. The American term is **corner store**.

corner·stone /ˈkɔːnəstəʊn/ **cornerstones;** also ◆◇◇◇ spelled **corner-stone.** The **cornerstone** of some- N-COUNT thing is the basic part of it on which its existence, FORMAL success, or truth depends. *Research is the cornerstone of the profession.*

'**corner store, corner stores.** A corner store is a N-COUNT small shop, usually on the corner of a street, that AMERICAN sells food and household goods. The British term is **corner shop**.

cor·net /ˈkɔːnɪt, AM kɔːˈnet/ **cornets. 1** A cornet is N-VAR a musical instrument that looks like a small trumpet. **2** An ice cream **cornet** is a soft thin biscuit N-COUNT shaped like a cone with ice cream in it. BRITISH

'**corn exchange, corn exchanges;** also spelled N-COUNT **Corn Exchange.** A corn exchange is a large building where corn used to be bought and sold.

corn·field /ˈkɔːnfiːld/ **cornfields;** also spelled **corn** N-COUNT **field.** A cornfield is a field in which corn is being grown.

corn·flake /ˈkɔːnfleɪk/ **cornflakes.** Cornflakes are N-COUNT small dry flakes made from maize that are eaten with milk as a breakfast cereal.

corn·flour /ˈkɔːnflaʊə/; also spelled **corn flour.** N-UNCOUNT Cornflour is a fine white powder made from maize BRITISH which is used to thicken sauces and soup. The American word is **cornstarch**.

corn·flower /ˈkɔːnflaʊə/ **cornflowers.** Corn- N-VAR flowers are small plants with bright flowers. The flowers are usually blue.

cor·nice /ˈkɔːnɪs/ **cornices.** A cornice is a strip of N-COUNT plaster, wood, or stone which goes along the top of a wall.

corn·meal /ˈkɔːnmiːl/; also spelled **corn meal.** N-UNCOUNT Cornmeal is a coarse powder made from maize. It is used in cooking.

,**corn on the 'cob, corn on the cobs;** also N-VAR spelled **corn-on-the-cob.** Corn on the cob is the long rounded part of the maize plant on which small yellow seeds grow.

corn·starch /ˈkɔːnstɑːtʃ/; also spelled **corn starch.** N-UNCOUNT Cornstarch is a fine white powder made from AMERICAN maize which is used to thicken sauces, gravy, and soup. The British word is **cornflour**.

cor·nu·co·pia /ˌkɔːnjʊˈkəʊpiə/. A cornucopia of N-SING things is a large number of different things. *...a cor-* WRITTEN *nucopia of career options.*

corny /ˈkɔːni/ **cornier, corniest.** If you describe ADJ-GRADED something as **corny**, you mean that it is obvious or sentimental and not at all original. *I know it sounds corny, but I'm really not motivated by money.*

cor·ol·lary /kəˈrɒləri, AM ˈkɔːrəleri/ **corollaries.** A N-COUNT **corollary** of something is an idea or fact that results FORMAL directly from it. *The number of prisoners increased as a corollary of the government's determination to combat violent crime.*

co·ro·na /kəˈrəʊnə/. The sun's **corona** is its outer atmosphere. `N-SING TECHNICAL`

coro·nary /ˈkɒrənri, AM ˈkɔːrəneri/ **coronaries.** ◆◇◇◇◇ **1** Coronary means belonging or relating to the heart. ...*the coronary arteries.* **2** If someone has a **coronary**, the flow of blood to their heart is blocked by a large blood clot. `ADJ: ADJ n` `MEDICAL` `N-COUNT`

coro·na·tion /ˌkɒrəˈneɪʃən, AM ˌkɔːr-/ **coronations.** A **coronation** is the ceremony at which a king or queen is crowned. ◆◇◇◇◇ `N-COUNT`

coro·ner /ˈkɒrənə, AM ˈkɔːr-/ **coroners.** A **coroner** is an official who is responsible for investigating the deaths of people who have died in a sudden, violent, or unusual way. ◆◇◇◇◇ `N-COUNT`

coro·net /ˈkɒrənət, AM ˌkɔːrəˈnet/ **coronets.** A **coronet** is a small crown. `N-COUNT`

Corp. Corp. is a written abbreviation for 'corporation'. ◆◆◆◇

cor·po·ra /ˈkɔːpərə/. **Corpora** is a plural of **corpus**.

cor·po·ral /ˈkɔːprəl/ **corporals.** A **corporal** is an non-commissioned officer in the army. ◆◇◇◇◇ `N-COUNT; N-TITLE`

corporal 'punishment. Corporal punishment is the punishment of people by beating them. `N-UNCOUNT`

cor·po·rate /ˈkɔːprət/. **Corporate** means relating to business corporations or to a particular business corporation. ...*a corporate lawyer.* ...*a strong corporate image.* ◆◆◆◇◇ `ADJ: ADJ n`

corporate 'raider, corporate raiders. A **corporate raider** is a person or organization that tries to take control of a company by buying a large number of its shares. `N-COUNT`

cor·po·ra·tion /ˌkɔːpəˈreɪʃən/ **corporations.** **1** A **corporation** is a large business or company. ◆◆◆◇◇ `N-COUNT` **2** In some large British cities, the **corporation** is the local authority that is responsible for providing public services. `N-COUNT`

corpo'ration tax. Corporation tax is a tax that companies have to pay on the profits they make. `N-UNCOUNT`

cor·po·rat·ism /ˈkɔːpərətɪzəm/. **Corporatism** is a system in which large groups such as trade unions and employers' associations co-operate closely with the government; often used showing disapproval. `N-UNCOUNT` `PRAGMATICS`

cor·po·rat·ist /ˈkɔːprətɪst/. You use **corporatist** to describe organizations, ideas, or systems which follow the principles of corporatism; used showing disapproval. ... *a corporatist political system.* `ADJ-GRADED` `PRAGMATICS`

cor·po·real /kɔːˈpɔːriəl/. **Corporeal** means involving or relating to the physical world rather than the spiritual world. ...*man's corporeal existence.* `ADJ-GRADED` `FORMAL`

corps /kɔː/; **corps** is both the singular and the plural form. **1** A **corps** is a part of the army which has special duties. ...*the Army Medical Corps.* **2** A **corps** is a small group of people who do a special job. ...*the diplomatic corps.* ◆◆◇◇◇ `N-COUNT:` `supp N`

corpse /kɔːps/ **corpses.** A **corpse** is a dead body, especially the body of a human being. ◆◆◇◇◇ `N-COUNT`

cor·pu·lent /ˈkɔːpjʊlənt/. If you describe someone as **corpulent**, you mean that they are fat. `ADJ-GRADED` `LITERARY`

cor·pus /ˈkɔːpəs/ **corpora** /ˈkɔːpərə/ or **corpuses.** **1** A **corpus** is a large collection of written or spoken texts that is used for language research. ◆◇◇◇◇ `TECHNICAL` **2** See **habeas corpus**.

cor·pus·cle /ˈkɔːpʌsəl, AM -pəsəl/ **corpuscles.** Corpuscles are red or white blood cells. `N-COUNT`

cor·ral /kəˈrɑːl, AM -ˈræl/ **corrals.** In the United States, a **corral** is a space surrounded by a fence where cattle or horses are kept. `N-COUNT`

cor·rect /kəˈrekt/ **corrects, correcting, corrected.** **1** If something is **correct**, it is accurate and has no mistakes. ...*check the label is correct.* ◆ **cor·rect·ly** *Did I pronounce your name correctly?... You have to correctly answer each question.* ◆ **cor·rect·ness** *Ask the investor to check the correctness of what he has written.* **2** If someone is **correct**, what they have said or thought is true. *If Casey is correct, the total cost of the cleanup would come to $110 billion.* **3** The **correct** thing or method is the one that is required, or the one that is most suitable in a particular situation. ...*the correct way to produce a crop* ◆◆◆◆◇ `ADJ` `ADV: ADV with v` `N-UNCOUNT` `ADJ:` `v-link ADJ` `FORMAL` `ADJ: ADJ n`

of tomato plants. ◆ **correctly** *The exercises, correctly performed, will stretch and tone muscles.* `ADV: ADV with v`

4 If you say that someone is **correct** in doing something, you approve of their action. *You are perfectly correct in trying to steer your mother towards increased independence.* ◆ **cor·rect·ly** *When an accident happens, quite correctly questions are asked.* `ADJ` `PRAGMATICS` `ADV: ADV with cl`

5 If you **correct** a problem or fault, you do something which puts it right. ◆ **cor·rec·tion** /kəˈrekʃən/ **corrections** *We will then make the necessary corrections.* **6** When someone **corrects** a piece of writing, they look at it and mark the mistakes in it. **7** If you **correct** someone, you say something which you think is more accurate or appropriate than what they have just said. *I must correct him on a minor point.* **8** You say '**correct me if I'm wrong**' to indicate that you are not entirely sure that what you are about to say is true. *As I recall, but correct me if I am wrong, it was in a car park in Carmarthen.* `VERB: V n` `N-VAR` `VERB: V n` `VERB` `V n` `Also V n with quote` `CONVENTION` `PRAGMATICS`

9 If a person or their behaviour is **correct**, their behaviour is in accordance with social or other rules. *We were rather surprised by their sporting and correct behaviour.* ◆ **cor·rect·ly** *The High Court of Parliament began very correctly with a prayer for the Queen.* ◆ **cor·rect·ness** ...*his stiff-legged gait and formal correctness.* `ADJ-GRADED` `ADV-GRADED: ADV with v` `N-UNCOUNT`

cor·rec·tion /kəˈrekʃən/ **corrections.** **1** Corrections are marks or comments made on a piece of work, especially school work, which indicate where there are mistakes and what are the right answers. **2** See also **correct**. ◆◆◇◇◇ `N-COUNT`

3 Correction is the improvement, usually by punishment, of the behaviour of offenders. ...*the Department of Correction.* `N-UNCOUNT`

cor·rec·tion·al /kəˈrekʃənəl/. **Correctional** institutions, services, or staff are concerned with improving the behaviour of offenders, usually by punishing them. ...*a metropolitan correctional center.* `ADJ: ADJ n`

cor·rec·tive /kəˈrektɪv/ **correctives.** **1** Corrective measures or techniques are intended to put right something that is wrong. ...*corrective surgery.* **2** If something is a **corrective** to a particular view or account, it gives a more accurate or fairer picture than there would have been without it. ...*a useful corrective to the mistaken view that all psychologists are behaviourists.* ◆◇◇◇◇ `ADJ` `N-COUNT` `FORMAL`

cor·re·late /ˈkɒrəleɪt, AM ˈkɔːr-/ **correlates, correlating, correlated.** **1** If one thing **correlates** with another, there is a close similarity or connection between them, often because one thing causes the other. You can also say that two things **correlate** or **are correlated**. *The political opinions of spouses correlate more closely than their heights... The loss of respect for British science is correlated to reduced funding... Earnings and performance aren't always correlated.* **2** If you **correlate** things, you work out the way in which they are connected or the way they influence each other. ...*attempts to correlate specific language functions with particular parts of the brain.* ◆◇◇◇◇ `V-RECIP-ERG:` `V with/to n` `pl-n V` `beV-ed with/ to n` `beV-ed` `FORMAL` `VERB: V n` `V n with n` `FORMAL`

cor·re·la·tion /ˌkɒrəˈleɪʃən, AM ˌkɔːr-/ **correlations.** A **correlation** between things is a connection or link between them. ...*the correlation between smoking and disease.* ◆◇◇◇◇ `N-COUNT` `FORMAL`

cor·re·spond /ˌkɒrɪˈspɒnd, AM ˌkɔːr-/ **corresponds, corresponding, corresponded.** **1** If one thing **corresponds** to another, there is a close similarity or connection between them. You can also say that two things **correspond**. *The two maps of London correspond closely... Her expression is concerned but her body-language does not correspond.* ◆ **cor·re·spond·ing** *March and April sales this year were up 8 per cent on the corresponding period in 1992.* ◆ **cor·re·spond·ing·ly** *As his political stature has shrunk, he has grown correspondingly more dependent on the army.* `V-RECIP:` `V to/with n` `pl-n V` `V (non-recip)` `ADJ: ADJ n` `ADV` ◆◆◇◇◇

2 If you **correspond** with someone, you write letters to them. You can also say that two people **correspond.** *We corresponded regularly.* `V-RECIP:` `V with n` `pl-n V`

cor·re·spond·ence /ˌkɒrɪˈspɒndəns, AM ˌkɔːr-/ ♦♦◇◇◇
correspondences. 1 Correspondence is the act N-UNCOUNT: of writing letters to someone. ...*a long correspond*- also a N *ence with a close college friend.* **2** Someone's **corre-** N-UNCOUNT **spondence** is the letters that they receive or send.
3 If there is a **correspondence** between two things, N-COUNT there is a close similarity or connection between them. ...*correspondences between Eastern religions and Christianity.*

‚corre'spondence course, correspondence N-COUNT **courses.** A **correspondence course** is a course in which you study at home, receiving your work by post and sending it back by post.

cor·re·spond·ent /ˌkɒrɪˈspɒndənt, AM ˌkɔːr-/ **cor-** ♦♦♦◇ **respondents.** A **correspondent** is a newspaper or N-COUNT television reporter, especially one who specializes in a particular type of news. ...*our Diplomatic Correspondent Mark Brayne.*

cor·ri·dor /ˈkɒrɪdɔː, AM ˈkɔːrɪdər/ **corridors. 1** A ♦♦◇◇◇ **corridor** is a long passage in a building or train, N-COUNT with rooms on one or both sides. **2** A **corridor** is a N-COUNT strip of land that connects one country to another or gives it a route to the sea through another country.

cor·robo·rate /kəˈrɒbəreɪt/ **corroborates, cor-** ♦◇◇◇◇ **roborating, corroborated.** To **corroborate** VERB something that has been said or reported means to V n provide evidence or information that supports it. FORMAL ...*a wide range of documents which corroborated the story.* ♦ **cor·robo·ra·tion** /kəˌrɒbəˈreɪʃən/. *He* N-UNCOUNT *could not get a single witness to establish independent corroboration of his version of the accident.*

cor·robo·ra·tive /kəˈrɒbərətɪv, AM -reɪtɪv/. **Cor-** ADJ: ADJ n **roborative** evidence or information supports an FORMAL idea, account, or argument. *The police did not have enough corroborative evidence for a probable conviction.*

cor·rode /kəˈrəʊd/ **corrodes, corroding, cor-** **roded. 1** If metal or stone **corrodes**, it is gradually V-ERG: V destroyed by a chemical or by rust. *The structure* be V-ed *had been corroded by moisture... Acid rain destroys trees and corrodes buildings.* ♦ **cor·rod·ed** *The* ADJ-GRADED *underground pipes were badly corroded.* ♦ **cor·ro-** **·sion** /kəˈrəʊʒən/ *Zinc is used to protect other metals* N-UNCOUNT *from corrosion.* **2** To **corrode** something means to VERB gradually weaken, worsen, or harm it. *He warns that* V n *corruption is corroding Russia.* LITERARY

cor·ro·sive /kəˈrəʊsɪv/. **1** A **corrosive** substance is ADJ-GRADED able to destroy solid materials by a chemical reaction. **2** If you say that something has a **corrosive** ef- ADJ-GRADED fect, you mean that it gradually causes serious FORMAL harm. ...*the corrosive effects of inflation.*

cor·ru·gat·ed /ˈkɒrəgeɪtɪd, AM ˈkɔːr-/. **Corrugated** ♦◇◇◇◇ metal or cardboard has been folded into a series of ADJ small parallel folds to make it stronger.

cor·rupt /kəˈrʌpt/ **corrupts, corrupting, cor-** ♦♦◇◇◇ **rupted. 1** Someone who is **corrupt** behaves in a ADJ-GRADED way that is morally wrong, especially by doing dishonest or illegal things in return for money or power. ♦ **cor·rupt·ly** ...*government officials charged* ADV-GRADED *with acting corruptly.* **2** If someone is **corrupted** by VB: usu something, it causes them to become dishonest and passive unable to be trusted. **3** To **corrupt** someone means VERB to cause them to stop caring about moral standards. V n ...*warning that television will corrupt us all.* **4** If VB: usu something **is corrupted**, it becomes damaged or passive spoiled in some way. ...*corrupted data.* V-ed

cor·rup·tion /kəˈrʌpʃən/ **corruptions. 1** Corrup- ♦♦♦◇◇ **tion** is dishonesty and illegal behaviour by people in N-UNCOUNT positions of authority or power. *The President faces 54 charges of corruption and tax evasion.* **2** A **cor-** N-COUNT **ruption** is a word that is derived from an earlier TECHNICAL word, but which has become changed in some way. '*Morris' is an English corruption of 'Moorish'.*

cor·sage /kɔːˈsɑːʒ/ **corsages.** A **corsage** is a very N-COUNT small bunch of flowers that is fastened to a woman's dress below the shoulder.

cor·set /ˈkɔːsɪt/ **corsets.** A **corset** is a stiff piece of N-COUNT underwear worn by some women. It fits tightly

around their hips and waist and makes them appear slimmer.

cor·tege /kɔːˈteɪʒ, AM -ˈteʒ/ **corteges.** A **cortege** is N-COLL-a procession of people who are walking or riding in COUNT cars to a funeral.

cor·tex /ˈkɔːteks/ **cortices** /ˈkɔːtɪsiːz/. The **cortex** ♦◇◇◇◇ of the brain or of another organ is its outer layer. N-COUNT MEDICAL

cor·ti·sone /ˈkɔːtɪzəʊn/. **Cortisone** is a hormone N-UNCOUNT used in the treatment of arthritis, allergies, and some skin diseases.

co·rus·cat·ing /ˈkɒrəskeɪtɪŋ, AM ˈkɔːr-/. A **corus-** ADJ **cating** speech or performance is lively, intelligent, LITERARY and impressive.

'cos /kəz/; also spelled **cos**. **'Cos** means the same as ♦♦♦♦◇ **because.** CONJ INFORMAL

cosh /kɒʃ/ **coshes, coshing, coshed. 1** A **cosh** N-COUNT is a heavy piece of rubber or metal which is used as BRITISH a weapon. **2** To **cosh** someone means to hit them VERB: V n hard on the head with a cosh or some other blunt BRITISH weapon.

cos·met·ic /kɒzˈmetɪk/ **cosmetics. 1** Cosmetics ♦♦◇◇◇ are substances such as lipstick or powder. N-COUNT ...*beauty-enhancing cosmetics.* **2** If you describe ADJ measures or changes as **cosmetic**, you mean they PRAGMATICS improve the appearance of a situation or thing but do not change its basic nature, and are usually implying that they are inadequate.

cos‚metic 'surgery. Cosmetic surgery is surgery N-UNCOUNT done to make a person look more attractive.

cos·mic /ˈkɒzmɪk/. **1** Cosmic means occurring in, ♦◇◇◇◇ or coming from, the part of space that lies outside ADJ Earth and its atmosphere. ...*cosmic radiation.* **2** Cosmic means belonging or relating to the uni- ADJ verse. ...*the cosmic laws governing our world.*

cosmic 'rays. Cosmic rays are rays that reach N-PLURAL Earth from outer space and consist of atomic nuclei.

cos·mol·ogy /kɒzˈmɒlədʒi/ **cosmologies. 1** A N-VAR **cosmology** is a theory about the origin and nature of the universe. ...*Big Bang cosmology.* **2** Cosmol- N-UNCOUNT **ogy** is the study of the origin and nature of the universe. ♦ **cos·molo·gist, cosmologists** ...*eminent* N-COUNT *cosmologists.* ♦ **cos·mo·logi·cal** /ˌkɒzməˈlɒdʒɪkəl/. ADJ: ADJ n ...*cosmological sciences.*

cos·mo·naut /ˈkɒzmənɔːt/ **cosmonauts.** A **cos-** N-COUNT **monaut** is an astronaut from the former Soviet Union.

cos·mo·poli·tan /ˌkɒzməˈpɒlɪtən/. **1** A **cosmopoli-** ♦◇◇◇◇ **tan** place or society is full of people from many dif- ADJ-GRADED ferent countries and cultures; used showing approv- PRAGMATICS al. **2** Someone who is **cosmopolitan** has had a lot of ADJ-GRADED contact with people and things from many different countries and as a result is very open to different ideas and ways of doing things; used showing approval.

cos·mos /ˈkɒzmɒs, AM -məs/. The **cosmos** is the ♦◇◇◇◇ universe. ...*the natural laws of both this planet and* N-SING: *the cosmos.* the N LITERARY

cos·set /ˈkɒsɪt/ **cossets, cosseting, cosseted;** also spelled **cossetting, cossetted.** If someone **is** VB: usu **cosseted**, everything is done for them and they are passive protected from anything unpleasant. ♦ **cos·set·ed** ADJ-GRADED ...*a cosseted movie queen.*

cost /kɒst, AM kɔːst/ **costs, costing.** The form ♦♦♦♦♦ **cost** is used in the present tense, and is also the past tense and participle, except for meaning 4, where the form **costed** is used. **1** The **cost** of some- N-COUNT thing is the amount of money that is needed in order to buy, do, or make it. *Badges are also available at a cost of £2.50.* **2** If something **costs** a particular VERB: amount of money, you can buy, do, or make it for V amount that amount. *It's going to cost me over $100,000 to* V n amount *buy new trucks.* **3** If you say that something **costs** PHRASE **money**, you mean that it has to be paid for, and perhaps cannot be afforded. **4** When something VB: usu that you plan to do or make **is costed**, the amount passive of money you need is calculated in advance. ...*proj-* V-ed *ects costed at more than $300 million.* BRITISH
5 Your **costs** are the total amount of money that you N-PLURAL must spend on running your home or business. **6** If N-PLURAL

someone is ordered by a court of law to pay **costs**, they have to pay a sum of money towards the expenses of a court case they are involved in.

7 If something is sold at **cost** or at **cost price**, it is sold without any profit, for the same price as it cost the manufacturer to produce it or the seller to buy it. N-UNCOUNT: prep N

8 The **cost** of something is the loss, damage, or injury involved in trying to achieve it. *...factories in the West Country are to be closed at a cost of 150 jobs.* **9** If an event or mistake **costs** you something, you lose that thing as the result of it. *...a six-year-old boy whose life was saved by an operation that cost him his sight.* **10** ● to cost someone **dear**: see **dear**. N-SING / VERB V n n Also V n

11 If someone **counts the cost** of something that has happened or will happen, they consider how the consequences of that action or event affect them. *Several countries in eastern Europe are counting the cost of yesterday's earthquake.* **12** If you know something **to your cost**, you know it because of an unpleasant experience that you have had. *Kathryn knows to her cost the effect of having served a jail sentence.* **13** If you say that something must be avoided **at all costs**, you are emphasizing that it must not be allowed to happen under any circumstances. **14** If you say that something must be done **at any cost**, you are emphasizing that it must be done, even if this requires a lot of effort or money. PHRASE / PHRASE / PHRASE PRAGMATICS / PHRASE PRAGMATICS

'cost accounting. Cost accounting is the recording and analysis of the costs of running a business. N-UNCOUNT

'co-star, co-stars, co-starring, co-starred. **1** An actor's or actress's **co-stars** are the other actors or actresses who also have one of the main parts in a film. **2** If an actor or actress **co-stars** with another actor or actress, the two of them have the main parts in a film. *Wright and Penn met when they co-starred in the movie State Of Grace.* **3** If a film **co-stars** particular actors, they have the main parts in it. N-COUNT / V-RECIP: V with n pl- n V in n Also V in n (non-recip) VERB: V n

,cost-ef'fective. Something that is cost-effective saves or makes a lot of money in comparison with the costs involved. ♦ **cost-effectively** *The management tries to produce the magazine as cost-effectively as possible.* ♦ **cost-effectiveness** *...doubts about the cost-effectiveness of the proposals.* ADJ-GRADED / ADV-GRADED: ADV after v

cost·ing /ˈkɒstɪŋ/ **costings.** A **costing** is an estimation of all the costs involved in something such as a project or a business venture. N-VAR BRITISH

cost·ly /ˈkɒstli, AM ˈkɔːst-/ **costlier, costliest.** **1** If you say that something is **costly**, you mean that it costs a lot of money, often more than you would want to pay. **2** If you describe someone's action or mistake as **costly**, you mean that it results in a serious disadvantage for them. *This sort of scandal in international banking has been politically costly.* ADJ-GRADED / ADJ-GRADED

,cost of 'living. The cost of living is the average amount of money that people in a particular place need in order to be able to afford basic food, housing, and clothing. *Companies are moving jobs to towns with a lower cost of living.* N-SING

,cost 'price. See cost 7.

cos·tume /ˈkɒstjuːm, AM -tuːm/ **costumes.** **1** An actor's or performer's **costume** is the set of clothes they wear while they are performing. **2** The clothes worn by people at a particular time in history, or in a particular country, are referred to as a particular type of **costume**. *...men and women in eighteenth-century costume.* **3** A **costume** play or drama is one which is set in the past and in which the actors wear the type of clothes that were worn in that period. *...a lavish costume drama set in Ireland and the US in the 1890s.* N-VAR / N-UNCOUNT: supp N / ADJ: ADJ n

'costume jewellery. Costume jewellery is jewellery which is not made from precious metals or real jewels. N-UNCOUNT

cosy /ˈkəʊzi/ **cosies; cosier, cosiest;** spelled **cozy** in American English. **1** A **cosy** house or room is comfortable and warm. ♦ **co·si·ly** /ˈkəʊzɪli/ *...the cosily decorated drawing room.* ♦ **co·si·ness** *In the evening a log fire would provide cosiness.* **2** If you are **cosy**, you are comfortable and warm. *I'm cosy in bed.* ♦ **co·si·ly** *He was settled cosily in the corner.* **3** You use **cosy** to describe activities that are pleasant and friendly, and involve people who know each other well. *...a cosy chat between friends.* ♦ **co·si·ness** *...the cosiness and solidity of family life.* **4** A **cosy** is a soft cover which you put over a teapot or a boiled egg to keep it warm. ADJ-GRADED / ADV-GRADED / ADJ-GRADED / N-UNCOUNT / v-link ADJ / ADV-GRADED / ADJ-GRADED / N-UNCOUNT / N-COUNT

cot /kɒt/ **cots. 1** A **cot** is a bed for a baby, with bars or panels round it so that the baby cannot fall out. The American word is **crib**. **2** A **cot** is a narrow bed, usually made of canvas fitted over a frame which can be folded up. The British term is **camp bed**. N-COUNT BRITISH / N-COUNT AMERICAN

'cot death, cot deaths. Cot death is the sudden death of a baby while it is asleep, although the baby had not previously been ill. The usual American term is **crib death**. N-VAR BRITISH

co·terie /ˈkəʊtəri/ **coteries.** A **coterie** of a particular kind is a small group of people who are close friends or have a common interest, and who do not want other people to join them. N-COLL-COUNT FORMAL

cot·tage /ˈkɒtɪdʒ/ **cottages.** A **cottage** is a small house, usually in the country. See picture headed **house and flat**. N-COUNT

,cottage 'cheese. Cottage cheese is a soft, white, lumpy cheese made from sour milk. N-UNCOUNT

,cottage 'industry, cottage industries. A **cottage industry** is a small business that is run from someone's home, especially one that involves a craft such as knitting or pottery. N-COUNT

cot·tag·er /ˈkɒtɪdʒə/ **cottagers.** A **cottager** is a person who lives in a cottage. N-COUNT DATED

cot·tag·ing /ˈkɒtɪdʒɪŋ/. **Cottaging** is homosexual activity between men in public toilets. N-UNCOUNT BRITISH

cot·ton /ˈkɒtən/ **cottons, cottoning, cottoned.** **1** Cotton is a type of cloth made from soft fibres from the cotton plant. *...a cotton shirt.* **2** Cotton is a plant which produces the soft fibres used in making cotton cloth. **3** Cotton is thread that is used for sewing, especially thread that is made from cotton. *...a needle and cotton.* **4** Cotton is soft fluffy cotton, used especially for applying liquids or creams to your skin. The British term is **cotton wool**. N-VAR / N-UNCOUNT / N-VAR BRITISH / N-UNCOUNT AMERICAN

cotton on. If you **cotton on** to something, you understand it or realize it, especially without people telling you about it. *She had already cottoned on to the fact that the nanny was not all she appeared.* PHRASAL VB V P on Also V P BRITISH, INFORMAL

'cotton bud, cotton buds. A **cotton bud** is a small stick with a ball of cotton wool at each end, which people use, for example, for cleaning their ears. The American term is **cotton swab**. N-COUNT BRITISH

,cotton 'candy. Cotton candy is a large pink or white mass of sugar threads that is eaten from a stick. The British word is **candyfloss**. N-UNCOUNT AMERICAN

cotton·wood /ˈkɒtənwʊd/ **cottonwoods.** A **cottonwood** or a **cottonwood tree** is a kind of poplar that grows in North America and has seeds that are covered with cotton-like hairs. N-COUNT

,cotton 'wool. Cotton wool is soft fluffy cotton, used especially for applying liquids or creams to your skin. The American word is **cotton**. N-UNCOUNT BRITISH

couch /kaʊtʃ/ **couches, couching, couched.** **1** A **couch** is a long comfortable seat for two or three people. **2** A **couch** is a bed in a doctor's or psychiatrist's consulting room, which patients lie on while they are being examined or treated. **3** If a statement **is couched** in a particular style of language, it is expressed in that style of language. *His article at the weekend is couched in stronger language... The proposal was couched as an ultimatum.* N-COUNT / N-COUNT / VB: usu passive be V-ed in/as n WRITTEN

'couch potato, couch potatoes. If you describe someone as a **couch potato**, you disapprove of them because they spend most of their time watching television. N-COUNT PRAGMATICS INFORMAL

cou·gar /ˈkuːgə/ **cougars.** A **cougar** is a wild animal that is a member of the cat family. N-COUNT

cough /kɒf, AM kɔːf/ **coughs, coughing, coughed. 1** When you **cough**, you force air out of your throat with a sudden harsh noise. *Graham* VERB V

began to cough violently. ▶ Also a noun. *Coughs and sneezes spread infections.* ◆ **cough·ing** ...*a terrible fit of coughing.* **2** A **cough** is an illness in which you cough often and your chest or throat hurts. ...*a persistent cough.* **3** If you **cough** blood or phlegm, it comes up out of your throat or mouth when you cough. ▶ **Cough up** means the same as **cough.** *Keats became feverish, continually coughing up blood.*

4 If an engine or other machine **coughs**, it makes a sudden harsh noise. *The engine coughed, spluttered and died.*

cough up. If you **cough up** an amount of money, you pay or spend that amount, usually when you would prefer not to. *I'll have to cough up $10,000 a year for tuition... Will this be enough to persuade Congress to cough up?* ● See also **cough** 3.

cough mixture, cough mixtures. Cough mixture is liquid medicine that you take when you have a cough. The American term is **cough syrup.**

could /kəd, STRONG kʊd/. **Could** is a modal verb. It is used with the base form of a verb. **Could** is sometimes considered to be the past form of **can**, but in this dictionary the two words are dealt with separately.

1 You use **could** to indicate that someone had the ability to do something. You use **could not** or **couldn't** to say that someone was unable to do something. *I could see that something was terribly wrong... He could not resist telling her the truth... I couldn't read or write.* **2** You say **'I couldn't'** as a way of refusing an offer of more food or drink. *'More cake?'—'Oh no, I couldn't.'* **3** You use **could** after 'if' when talking about something that you do not have the ability or opportunity to do, but which you are imagining in order to consider what the likely consequences might be. *If I could afford it I'd have four television sets.*

4 You use **could** to indicate that something sometimes happened. *He could be very pleasant when he wanted to.* **5** You use **could have** to indicate that something was a possibility in the past, although it did not actually happen. *He could have made a fortune as a lawyer.* **6** You use **could** to indicate that something is possibly true, or that it may possibly happen. *The disease could have been caused by years of working in smokey clubs.* **7** You use **could not** or **couldn't** to indicate that it is not possible that something is true. *Anne couldn't be expected to understand... He couldn't have been more than fourteen years old.*

8 You use **could not** or **couldn't** with comparatives to emphasize that someone or something has as much as is possible of a particular quality. For example, if you say **I couldn't be happier**, you mean that you are very happy indeed. *The news couldn't have come at a better time.*

9 You use **could** or **couldn't** in questions, when you are making offers and suggestions. *I could call the local doctor... Couldn't you go for walks with your friends?.* **10** You use **could** in questions when you are making a polite request or asking for permission to do something. Speakers sometimes use **couldn't** instead of 'could' to show that they realize that their request may be refused. *Could I stay tonight?... He asked if he could have a cup of coffee... Couldn't I watch you do it?*

11 Speakers sometimes use structures with **if I could** or **could I** as polite ways of interrupting someone or of introducing what they are going to say next. *Well, if I could just interject... Could I begin with an apology for a mistake I made last week?*

12 You use **could** to say emphatically that someone ought to do the thing mentioned, especially when you are annoyed because they have not done it. You use **why couldn't** in questions to express your surprise or annoyance that someone has not done something. *We've come to see you, so you could at least stand and greet us properly... But why couldn't he tell me straight out?*

13 You use **could** when you are expressing strong feelings about something by saying that you feel as if

N-COUNT
N-UNCOUNT
N-COUNT

VERB: V n

PHRASAL VB
V P noun
Also V n P

VERB
V

PHRASAL VB
V P
V P
Also V n P
INFORMAL

N-VAR
BRITISH

◆◆◆◆◆

MODAL

CONVENTION
PRAGMATICS
INFORMAL
MODAL

MODAL

MODAL

MODAL

MODAL

MODAL
PRAGMATICS

MODAL
PRAGMATICS

MODAL
PRAGMATICS

MODAL
PRAGMATICS
FORMAL,
SPOKEN

MODAL
PRAGMATICS

MODAL
PRAGMATICS

you want to do the thing mentioned, although you do not do it. *I could kill you! I swear I could!.* **14** You use **how could** in questions to emphasize that you feel strongly about something bad that has happened. *How could you allow him to do something like that?.* **15** ● **could do with:** see **do.**

couldn't /'kʊdənt/. **Couldn't** is the usual spoken form of **could not.**

could've /'kʊdəv/. **Could've** is the usual spoken form of **could have**, when 'have' is an auxiliary verb.

coun·cil /'kaʊnsəl/ **councils. 1** A **council** is a group of people who are elected to govern a local area such as a city or a county. ...*Cheshire County Council.* **2 Council** houses or flats are owned by the local council, and people pay rent to live in them. **3 Council** is used in the names of some advisory or administrative groups. ...*the National Council for Civil Liberties.* **4** In some organizations, the **council** is the group of people that controls or governs it. ...*the permanent council of the Organization of American States.* **5** A **council** is a specially organized formal meeting that is attended by a particular group of people. *President Najibullah said he would call a grand council of all Afghans.*

coun·cil·lor /'kaʊnsələ/ **councillors;** spelled **councilor** in American English. A **councillor** is a member of a local council.

council·man /'kaʊnsəlmən/ **councilmen.** A **councilman** is a man who is a member of a local council. The British word is **councillor.** ...*a city councilman.*

council of 'war, councils of war. A council of **war** is a meeting that is held in order to decide how a particular threat or emergency should be dealt with.

'council tax. In Britain, the **council tax** is a tax that you pay to your local authority in order to pay for local services such as schools, libraries, and rubbish collection.

coun·cil·woman /'kaʊnsəlwʊmən/ **councilwomen.** A **councilwoman** is a woman who is a member of a local council. The British word is **councillor.** ...*Councilwoman Johnson.*

coun·sel /'kaʊnsəl/ **counsels, counselling, counselled;** spelled **counseling, counseled** in American English. **1 Counsel** is careful advice. *He had always been able to count on her wise counsel.* **2** If you **counsel** someone to take a course of action or if you **counsel** a course of action, you advise that course of action. *My advisers counselled me to do nothing... The prime minister was right to counsel caution about military intervention.* ◆ **coun·sel·ling** /'kaʊnsəlɪŋ/ ...*marriage counseling.* ◆ **coun·sel·lor** /'kaʊnsələ/ **counsellors** ...*a counsellor experienced in bereavement.*

3 If you **counsel** people, you give them advice about their problems. ...*a psychologist who counsels people with eating disorders.* **4** Someone's **counsel** is the lawyer who gives them advice on a legal case and speaks on their behalf in court. **5** If you **keep your own counsel**, you keep quiet about your opinions or intentions.

count /kaʊnt/ **counts, counting, counted. 1** When you **count**, you say all the numbers one after another up to a particular number. *He was counting slowly under his breath... Brian counted to twenty.* **2** You use **count** in expressions such as **a count of three** when you are measuring a length of time by counting slowly up to a certain number. *Hold your breath for a count of five.*

3 If you **count** all the things in a group, you add them up in order to find how many there are. *I counted the money... I counted 34 wild goats grazing.* ▶ **Count up** means the same as **count.** *Couldn't we just count up our ballots and bring them to the courthouse?* ◆ **count·ing** *The counting of the votes was held in a public hall.* **4** A **count** is the action of counting a particular set of things, or the number that you get when you have counted them. *At the last count the police in*

MODAL
PRAGMATICS
SPOKEN

◆◆◆◆◆
N-COLL-
COUNT

ADJ: ADJ n
BRITISH

N-COLL-
COUNT

N-COLL-
COUNT

N-COUNT

◆◆◇◇◇
N-COUNT;
N-TITLE

N-COUNT;
N-TITLE
AMERICAN

N-COUNT
FORMAL

◆◇◇◇◇
N-UNCOUNT:
also the N

N-COUNT;
N-TITLE
AMERICAN

◆◆◆◇◇

N-UNCOUNT
FORMAL

VERB
V n to-inf
V n
Also V with
quote
FORMAL
N-UNCOUNT
N-COUNT

VERB
V n
Also V on n
N-COUNT

PHRASE

◆◆◆◆◇
VERB
V
V to num

N-SING:
N of num

VERB
V n
V num
PHRASAL VB
V P noun
Also V n P
N-UNCOUNT

N-COUNT

the Rimini area had 247 people in custody. **5** If you
keep count of a number of things, you note or keep a
record of how many have occurred. If you **lose count**
of a number of things, you cannot remember how
many have occurred. *She'd lost count of the interviews
she'd been called for.* `PHRASE`

6 You use **count** when referring to the level or amount `N-COUNT:`
of something that someone or something has. *A glass* `nN`
*or two of wine will not significantly add to the calorie
count.* ● See also **blood count, pollen count.**

7 If something or someone **counts** for something or `VERB`
counts, they are important or valuable. *It's as if your* `V`
opinions, your likes and dislikes just don't count... Ex- `V for amount`
perience counts for a lot in poker.

8 If you **count** something when you are making a cal- `VERB`
culation, you include it in that calculation. *Statistics* `Vn`
don't count the people who aren't qualified. `Also V n as n`

9 If something **counts** or **is counted** as a particular `V-ERG`
thing, it is regarded as being that thing, especially in `V as n/-ing/`
particular circumstances or under particular rules. `be V-ed n/adj`
You must remember that a conservatory counts as an `Also V n`
extension... It can be counted a success. `V n as n/-ing/adj`

10 You can use **count** to refer to one or more points `N-COUNT:`
that you are considering. For example, if someone is `on supp N`
wrong **on two counts**, they are wrong in two ways.

11 In law, a **count** is one of a number of charges `N-COUNT`
brought against someone in court. *...two counts of
murder.*

12 If you say that someone should **stand up and be** `PHRASE`
counted, you mean that they should make public
their opinion about something or their involvement
in something, and not hide it or be ashamed of it.

13 ● to **count** your **blessings**: see **blessing.**

count against. If something **counts against** you, it `PHRASAL VB`
may cause you to be rejected or punished, or cause `V P n`
people to have a lower opinion of you. *...his youth
might count against him.*

count in. If you tell someone to **count** you **in**, you `PHRASAL VB`
mean that you want to be included in an activity. `PRAGMATICS`
'Count me in!' said a wiry Scotsman. `V n P`

count on or **count upon. 1** If you **count on** some- `PHRASAL VB`
thing or **count upon** it, you expect it to happen and `V P n/-ing`
include it in your plans. *The Communists thought they
could count on the support of the trades unions.* **2** If `V P n`
you **count on** someone or **count upon** them, you rely `V P n to-inf`
on them to support you or help you. *I can always
count on you to cheer me up.*

count out. 1 If you **count out** a sum of money, you `PHRASAL VB`
count the notes or coins as you put them in a pile one `V P noun`
by one. *Mr. Rohmbauer counted out the money.* **2** If `Also V n P`
you tell someone to **count** you **out**, you mean that you `PRAGMATICS`
do not want to be included in an activity. *If this is the* `V n P`
*standard to which I have to drop to gain membership,
then count me out!*

count towards or **count toward.** If something `PHRASAL VB`
counts towards or **counts toward** an achievement or `V P n`
entitlement, it is included as one of the things that
give you the right to it. *Work from the second year onwards can count towards the final degree.*

count up. See count 2. `PHRASAL VB`

count upon. See count on. `PHRASAL VB`

Count /kaʊnt/ **Counts.** A **Count** is a European `◆◇◇◇`
nobleman with the same rank as a British earl. `N-COUNT;`
...Count Otto Lambsdorff. `N-TITLE; N-VOC`

count·able noun /ˌkaʊntəbəl ˈnaʊn/ **countable** `N-COUNT`
nouns. A **countable noun** is the same as a **count
noun.**

count·down /ˈkaʊntdaʊn/. A **countdown** is the `◆◇◇◇`
counting aloud of numbers in reverse order before `N-SING:`
something happens, especially before a spacecraft is `also no det`
launched. *The countdown has begun for the launch
later today.*

coun·te·nance /ˈkaʊntɪnəns/ **countenances,** `◆◇◇◇`
countenancing, countenanced. 1 If someone `VERB`
will not **countenance** something, they do not agree `V n`
with it and will not allow it to happen. *Jake would* `FORMAL`
*not countenance Janis's marrying while still a stu-
dent.* **2** Someone's **countenance** is their face. *He* `N-COUNT`
met each inquiry with an impassive countenance. `LITERARY`

coun·ter /ˈkaʊntə/ **counters, countering,** `◆◆◆◇◇`
countered. 1 In a place such as a shop or café, a `N-COUNT`
counter is a long narrow table or flat surface at
which customers are served. *...the cosmetics counter.*

2 If a medicine can be bought **over the counter,** `PHRASE`
you do not need a prescription to buy it. **3** If some- `PHRASE`
one buys or sells goods **under the counter,** they
buy or sell them secretly and illegally.

4 If you do something to **counter** a particular action `VERB`
or process, you do something which has an opposite `V n`
effect to it or makes it less effective. *...economic
measures to counter the effects of such a blockade.* **5** `N-SING:`
Something that is **a counter to** something else has an `a N to n`
opposite effect to it or makes it less effective. *...NATO's
traditional role as a counter to the military might of
the Warsaw Pact.* **6** If one thing **runs counter to** an- `PHRASE`
other, or if one thing **is counter to** another, the first `FORMAL`
thing is the opposite of the second thing or conflicts
with it. *Much of the plan runs counter to European
Community agriculture and environmental policy.*

7 If you **counter** something that someone has said, `VERB`
you say something which shows that you disagree `V n`
with them or which proves that they are wrong. *Both* `V with n`
of them had to counter fierce criticism by the Moscow `V by-ing`
intellectuals... The union countered with letters rebut- `Also V that,`
ting the company's claims... The Prime Minister coun- `V with quote`
tered by stating that he had grave misgivings.

8 A **counter** is a device which keeps a count of some- `N-COUNT`
thing and displays the total.

9 A **counter** is a small, flat, round object used in board `N-COUNT`
games.

10 See also **bargaining counter, bean counter,
Geiger counter.**

counter- /ˈkaʊntə-/. **Counter-** is used to form `PREFIX`
words which refer to actions or activities that are intended to prevent other actions or activities or that
respond to them. *...counter-revolutionary activities.*

counter·act /ˈkaʊntərækt/ **counteracts,** `◆◇◇◇`
counteracting, counteracted. To **counteract** `VERB`
something means to reduce its effect by doing `V n`
something that produces an opposite effect. *...pills
to counteract high blood pressure.*

counter-argument, counter-arguments. A `N-COUNT`
counter-argument is an argument that makes an `FORMAL`
opposing point to another argument.

counter-attack, counter-attacks, counter- `◆◇◇◇`
attacking, counter-attacked; also spelled `VERB`
counterattack. If you **counter-attack,** you attack `V`
someone who has attacked you. *The security forces* `Also V n`
counter-attacked the following day. ▶ Also a noun. `N-COUNT`
The army began its counter-attack this morning.

counter·bal·ance /ˈkaʊntəbæləns/ **counterbal-** `VERB`
ances, counterbalancing, counterbalanced; `V n`
also spelled **counter-balance.** To **counterbalance**
something means to balance or correct it with
something that has an equal but opposite effect.
Add honey to counterbalance the acidity. ▶ Also a `N-COUNT`
noun. *...organisations set up as a counterbalance to
groups allied to the ANC.*

counter·clockwise /ˌkaʊntəˈklɒkwaɪz/; also `ADV:`
spelled **counter-clockwise.** If something is moving `ADV after v`
counterclockwise, it is moving in the opposite di- `AMERICAN`
rection to the direction in which the hands of a
clock move. The British word is **anticlockwise.**
▶ Also an adjective. *The dance moves in a counter-* `ADJ: ADJ n`
clockwise direction.

counter-culture, counter-cultures; also `N-VAR`
spelled **counterculture. Counter-culture** is a set of
values, ideas, and ways of behaving that are completely different from those of the rest of society.
...the counterculture of the sixties.

counter-'espionage; also spelled **counter espio-** `N-UNCOUNT`
nage. Counter-espionage consists of the measures
that a country takes in order to find out whether another country is spying on it and to prevent it from
doing so.

counter·feit /ˈkaʊntəfɪt/ **counterfeits, counter-** `◆◇◇◇`
feiting, counterfeited. 1 Counterfeit money, `ADJ`
goods, or documents are not genuine, but have
been made to look exactly like genuine ones in

order to deceive people. ...*counterfeit currency.*
► Also a noun. *Levi Strauss says counterfeits of the* N-COUNT
company's jeans are flooding Europe. **2** If someone VERB: V n
counterfeits something, they make a version of it
that is not genuine but has been made to look
genuine in order to deceive people. ♦ **counter-**
·feit·ing ...*the business of counterfeiting.* N-UNCOUNT
♦ **counter·feit·er, counterfeiters** ...*a gang of* N-COUNT
counterfeiters.

counter·foil /ˈkaʊntəfɔɪl/ **counterfoils.** A N-COUNT
counterfoil is the part of a cheque, ticket, or other BRITISH
document that you keep when you give the other
part to someone else.

counter·mand /ˌkaʊntəˈmɑːnd, -ˈmænd/ **counter-** VERB
mands, countermanding, countermanded. If V n
you **countermand** an order, you cancel it, usually FORMAL
by giving a different order. *I can't countermand an*
order Winger's given.

'counter-measure, counter-measures; also N-COUNT
spelled **countermeasure.** A **counter-measure** is an
action that you take in order to weaken the effect of
another action or a situation, or to make it harmless. *Because the threat never developed, we didn't*
need to take any real countermeasures.

counter·pane /ˈkaʊntəpeɪn/ **counterpanes.** A N-COUNT
counterpane is a decorative cover on a bed. DATED

counter·part /ˈkaʊntəpɑːt/ **counterparts.** ♦♦♦◇◇
Someone's or something's **counterpart** is another N-COUNT:
person or thing that has a similar function in a dif- with supp
ferent place. *The Foreign Secretary telephoned his*
German and Italian counterparts.

counter·point /ˈkaʊntəpɔɪnt/ **counterpoints,**
counterpointing, counterpointed. 1 Some- N-COUNT
thing that is a **counterpoint** to something else con- JOURNALISM
trasts with it in a satisfying way. *Paris is just a short*
train journey away, providing the perfect counter-
point to the peace and quiet of Reims. **2** If one thing VERB
counterpoints another, it contrasts with it in a sat- V n
isfying way. *A good sharp dressing complements* JOURNALISM
the sweetness of the dried fruit. **3** In music, **counter-** N-UNCOUNT
point is a technique in which two or more different
tunes are played together at the same time.

,counter-pro'ductive; also spelled **counterpro-** ♦◇◇◇◇
ductive. Something that is **counter-productive** ADJ-GRADED
achieves the opposite result from the one that you
want. *It is counterproductive to address an inter-*
viewee in patronizing tones.

,counter-revo'lution, counter-revolutions.
1 A **counter-revolution** is a revolution that is in- N-COUNT
tended to reverse the effects of a previous revolution. **2** You can refer to activities that are intended N-UNCOUNT
to reverse the effects of a previous revolution as
counter-revolution. *Such actions would be regarded*
as counter-revolution. ♦ **counter-revolu·tion·ary,** N-COUNT
counter-revolutionaries. A counter-
revolutionary is a person who is trying to reverse
the effects of a previous revolution. ► Also an adjec- ADJ
tive. ...*counter-revolutionary propaganda.*

counter·sign /ˈkaʊntəsaɪn/ **countersigns,** VERB: V n
countersigning, countersigned. If you
countersign a document, you sign it after someone
else has signed it.

counter·ten·or /ˌkaʊntəˈtenə/ **countertenors;** N-COUNT
also spelled **counter-tenor.** A **countertenor** is a
man who sings with a high voice that is similar to a
low female singing voice.

counter·vail·ing /ˌkaʊntəˈveɪlɪŋ/. A **countervailing** ADJ: ADJ n
force or opinion is one which is of equal strength to
another one but is its opposite. *There were two cen-*
tral and countervailing forces in the life of Nikola
Tesla.

counter·weight /ˈkaʊntəweɪt/ **counterweights,**
counterweighting, counterweighted. 1 A N-COUNT
counterweight is an action or proposal that is intended to balance or counter other actions or proposals. *His no-inflation bill serves as a useful*
counterweight to proposals less acceptable to the
Committee. **2** If one action or proposal is intended VERB
to **counterweight** another, it is intended to balance V n

or counter the other action or proposal. *This will be*
used to counterweight the capital gains argument.

Coun·tess /ˈkaʊntɪs/ **Countesses.** A **Countess** is ♦◇◇◇◇
a woman who has the same rank as a count or earl, N-COUNT;
or who is married to a count or earl. N-TITLE;
                                      N-VOC

count·ing /ˈkaʊntɪŋ/. **1** Not counting a particular ♦◇◇◇◇
thing means not including that thing. Counting a PREP
particular thing means including that thing. *That's*
four people, right? Not counting my brother. **2** If you PHRASE
say **and counting** after a number or an amount of
something, you mean that the number or amount is
continuing to increase. ...*sales of 25 million and*
counting.

count·less /ˈkaʊntləs/. **Countless** means very ♦♦◇◇◇
many. *She brought joy to countless people.* ADJ: ADJ n

'count noun, count nouns. A **count noun** is a N-COUNT
noun such as 'bird', 'chair', or 'year' which has a
singular and a plural form and is always used after a
determiner in the singular.

coun·tri·fied /ˈkʌntrɪfaɪd/. **1** You use **countrified** ADJ-GRADED
to describe something that seems or looks like INFORMAL
something in the country, rather than in a town. ...*a*
lovely countrified garden. **2 Countrified** is used to ADJ-GRADED
describe pop music that sounds similar to country JOURNALISM
and western. ...*countrified blues.*

coun·try /ˈkʌntri/ **countries. 1** A **country** is one ♦♦♦♦♦
of the political units which the world is divided into, N-COUNT
covering a particular area of land. *Indonesia is the*
fifth most populous country in the world. **2** The peo- N-SING
ple who live in a particular country can be referred
to as the **country.** *The country had confounded the*
pundits by electing a fourth-term Tory government.
3 If a head of government or a government **goes to** PHRASE
the country, they hold a general election. BRITISH
4 The **country** consists of places such as farms, open N-SING:
fields, and villages which are away from towns and the N
cities. ...*a healthy life in the country.* **5** If you travel PHRASE
across country, you travel through country areas,
avoiding major roads and towns. **6** A particular kind N-UNCOUNT:
of **country** is an area of land which has particular supp N
characteristics or is connected with a well-known
person. ...*mountainous country east of Genoa.* ...*this is*
Elgar country.
7 Country music is the same as country and western N-UNCOUNT
music.

,country and 'western. Country and western is N-UNCOUNT
popular music in the style of white people's folk
music of the southern United States. ...*a successful*
country and western singer.

'country club, country clubs. A **country club** is ♦◇◇◇◇
a club in the country where members can play N-COUNT
sports and attend social events.

,country 'cousin, country cousins. If you refer N-COUNT
to someone who comes from the country as a **coun-** PRAGMATICS
try cousin, you disapprove of them because they
are unsophisticated and are inexperienced in city
ways.

,country 'dancing. Country dancing is tradition- N-UNCOUNT
al dancing in which couples dance in lines or
circles.

,country 'house, country houses. A **country** ♦◇◇◇◇
house is a large attractive house in the country, N-COUNT
usually one that is or was owned by a rich or noble
family.

country·man /ˈkʌntrɪmən/ **countrymen. 1** Your ♦◇◇◇◇
countrymen are people from your own country. *He* N-COUNT
beat his fellow countryman, Andre Agassi. **2** A N-COUNT
countryman is a person who lives in the country rather than in a city or a town.

,country 'seat, country seats. A **country seat** is N-COUNT
a large house and estate in the country which is
owned by someone who also owns a house in a
town. *His family have a country seat in Oxfordshire.*

country·side /ˈkʌntrɪsaɪd/. The **countryside** is ♦♦♦◇◇
land which is away from towns and cities. ...*the* N-UNCOUNT
English countryside.

country·wide /ˌkʌntriˈwaɪd/. Something that hap- ADV
pens or exists **countrywide** happens or exists
throughout the whole of a country. *Armed robbery*
and abduction have been on the increase

countrywide. ► Also an adjective. *...a countrywide* ADJ: ADJ n
network of volunteers.

country·woman /'kʌntriwʊmən/ **country-** N-COUNT
women. 1 A **countrywoman** is a woman who lives
in the country rather than in a city or a town. *She*
had the slow, soft voice of a countrywoman. 2 Your N-COUNT
countrywomen are women from your own country.

coun·ty /'kaʊnti/ **counties.** A **county** is a region ◆◆◆◇
of Britain, Ireland, or the USA which has its own lo- N-COUNT
cal government. *Over 50 events are planned*
throughout the county.

,**county 'council, county councils.** A **county** ◆◇◇◇◇
council is an organization which administers local N-COUNT
government in a county in Britain. *...Devon County*
Council.

,**county 'seat.** See **county town.**

,**county 'town, county towns.** A **county town** is N-COUNT
the most important town in a county, from which BRITISH
the county is administered. The American term is
county seat. *We met in Dorchester, Dorset's bustling*
county town.

coup /kuː/ **coups.** 1 When there is a **coup,** a group ◆◆◇◇◇
of people seize power in a country. *...a military* N-COUNT
coup. 2 A **coup** is an achievement which is thought N-COUNT
to be especially brilliant because it was very difficult. *Regency Opera have scored something of a coup*
by persuading her to undertake the role.

coup de grace /,kuː də 'grɑːs/. To give something N-SING
the **coup de grace** is to finally destroy something, FORMAL
such as an institution, which has been gradually
growing weaker.

coup d'état /,kuː deɪ'tɑː/ **coups d'état.** When ◆◇◇◇◇
there is a **coup d'état,** a group of people seize pow- N-COUNT
er in a country.

cou·pé /'kuːpeɪ, AM 'kuːp/ **coupés.** A **coupé** is a ◆◇◇◇◇
car with a fixed roof, a sloping back, two doors, and N-COUNT
seats for four people.

cou·ple /'kʌpəl/ **couples, coupling, coupled.** ◆◆◆◇
1 If you refer to **a couple of** people or things, you QUANT
mean two or approximately two of them, although INFORMAL
the exact number is not important or you are not
sure of it. *I think the trouble will clear up in a cou-*
ple of days. ► Also a determiner in spoken American DET
English, and before 'more' and 'less'. *...a couple*
weeks before the election... I think I can play maybe
for a couple more years. ► Also a pronoun. *I've got a* PRON
couple that don't look too bad.
2 A **couple** is two people who are married, living to- N-COLL-
gether, or having a sexual relationship. *The couple* COUNT
have no children. 3 A **couple** is two people that you N-COLL-
see together on a particular occasion or that are asso- COUNT
ciated in some way. *The four couples began the open-*
ing dance.
4 If you say that one thing produces a particular effect VERB:
when it **is coupled with** another, you mean that the beV-ed with n
two things combine to produce that effect. *Over-use* V-ed
of those drugs, coupled with poor diet, leads to physical
degeneration. 5 If one piece of equipment **is coupled** VERB:
to another, it is joined to it so that the two pieces of beV-ed ton
equipment work together. *The various elementary de-* beV-ed
tector systems are coupled together in complex arrays. together
♦ **cou·pling** *...the coupling of a particle accelerator* N-SING
and a mass spectrometer. 6 See also **coupling.**

cou·plet /'kʌplɪt/ **couplets.** A **couplet** is two lines N-COUNT
of poetry which come next to each other, especially
two lines that rhyme with each other and are the
same length.

cou·pling /'kʌplɪŋ/ **couplings.** 1 A **coupling** is a ◆◇◇◇◇
device which is used to join two vehicles or pieces N-COUNT
of equipment together. 2 When two different N-COUNT
things, ideas, or activities are combined, or when WRITTEN
two people work together, you can refer to this
combination as a **coupling.** *...the uneasy coupling of*
fascism and conservatism. 3 An act of sexual inter- N-COUNT
course is sometimes referred to as a **coupling.** 4 See FORMAL
also **couple.**

cou·pon /'kuːpɒn/ **coupons.** 1 A **coupon** is a ◆◆◇◇◇
piece of printed paper which is issued by the maker N-COUNT
or supplier of a product and which allows you to
pay less money than usual for it. 2 A **coupon** is a N-COUNT

small form which you send off to ask for information, to order something, or to enter a competition.
3 A **coupon** is a piece of printed paper issued by the N-COUNT
government that gives you the right to buy a product that is rationed.

cour·age /'kʌrɪdʒ, AM 'kɜːr-/. 1 **Courage** is the ◆◆◆◇◇
quality shown by someone who decides to do N-UNCOUNT
something difficult or dangerous, even though they
may be afraid. *They do not have the courage to*
apologise for their actions. ● to **pluck up the cour-**
age: see **pluck.** 2 If you have the **courage of** your PHRASE
convictions, you have the confidence to do what
you believe is right, even though other people may
not agree or approve.

cou·ra·geous /kə'reɪdʒəs/. Someone who is **cou-** ◆◇◇◇◇
rageous shows courage. *It was a courageous deci-* ADJ-GRADED
sion. ♦ **cou·ra·geous·ly** *Smith fought very* ADV-GRADED:
courageously. ADV with v

cour·gette /kʊə'ʒet/ **courgettes.** Courgettes are ◆◇◇◇◇
long thin green vegetables of the marrow family. N-VAR
The American word is **zucchini.** See picture headed BRITISH
vegetables.

cou·ri·er /'kʊriə/ **couriers.** 1 A **courier** is a person ◆◆◇◇◇
who is paid to take letters and parcels direct from N-COUNT
one place to another. 2 A **courier** is a person em- N-COUNT
ployed by a travel company to look after people
who are on holiday.

course /kɔːs/ **courses, coursing, coursed.** ◆◆◆◆◆
1 **Course** is often used in the expression 'of course'.
It is also used instead of 'of course' in informal spoken English. See **of course.**
2 The **course** of a vehicle is the route along which it is N-UNCOUNT:
travelling. *The captain altered course a few degrees to* also a N
the right. 3 If a ship or aircraft is **on course,** it is travel- PHRASE
ling along the correct route. If it is **off course,** it is no
longer travelling along the correct route.
4 A **course** of action is an action or a series of actions N-COUNT
that you can do in a particular situation. *Vietnam is*
trying to decide on its course for the future. 5 If you are PHR-PREP
on course for something, you are likely to achieve it.
England are well on course for a place at the 1998
World Cup Finals. 6 You can refer to the way that N-SING:
events develop as, for example, **the course of history** the N of n
or **the course of events.** *...naval battles which altered*
the course of history. 7 If something happens **in the** PHR-PREP
course of a period of time, it happens during that
time. *We struck up a conversation, in the course of*
which it emerged that he was a sailing man. 8 If some- PHRASE
thing happens or becomes true **in the course of time,**
it happens or becomes true over a long period of time.
9 ● **in due course:** see **due.**
10 A **course** is a series of lessons or lectures on a par- N-COUNT
ticular subject. *...a course in business administration.*
● See also **access course, correspondence course, re-**
fresher course. 11 A **course of** medical treatment is a N-COUNT:
series of treatments that a doctor gives someone. *...a* N of n
course of antibiotics.
12 A **course** is one part of a meal. *...a three-course* N-COUNT
dinner.
13 In sport, a **course** is an area of land where races are N-COUNT
held or golf is played. *...the Tour de France, when 200*
cyclists cover a course of 2,000 miles. 14 If you **stay the** PHRASE
course, you finish something that you have started,
even though it has become very difficult. 15 If some- PHRASE
thing **runs its course** or **takes its course,** it develops
naturally and comes to a natural end. *20,000 cows*
would die before the epidemic had run its course.
16 The **course** of a river is the channel along which it N-COUNT
flows. 17 If a liquid **courses** somewhere, it flows VERB
quickly. *The tears coursed down his cheeks.* V prep/adv
18 If you do something **as a matter of course,** you do LITERARY
it as part of your normal work or way of life. PHRASE

'**course book, course books;** also spelled N-COUNT
coursebook. A **course book** is a textbook that stu- BRITISH
dents and teachers use as part of a course.

'**course work;** also spelled **coursework.** Course N-UNCOUNT
work is work that students do during the year, rather than in exams, especially work that counts towards a student's final grade.

C

cours·ing /'kɔːsɪŋ/. **Coursing** is a sport in which N-UNCOUNT rabbits or hares are hunted with dogs.

court 1 noun uses

court /kɔːt/ **courts. 1** A **court** is a place where le- N-COUNT: gal matters are decided by a judge and jury or by a also *in/at* N magistrate. ...*the divorce courts... He was in court last week.* **2** You can refer to the people in a court, N-COUNT especially the judge, jury, or magistrates, as a **court**. *The court awarded the man one and a half million pounds.* **3** If you **go to court** or **take** someone **to** PHRASE **court**, you take legal action against someone. **4** If a PHRASE legal matter is decided or settled **out of court**, it is decided without legal action being taken in a court of law. ...*an out of court settlement.* **5** See also Crown Court, High Court, kangaroo court.

6 A **court** is an area for playing a game such as tennis, N-COUNT: badminton, or squash. also *on/off* N

7 The **court** of a king or queen is the place where he or N-COUNT she lives and works. Royal people and the people who work closely with them can also be referred to as the **court**. *Their family were certainly well regarded at court.* **8** You can say someone **holds court** when they PHRASE are surrounded by a lot of people who are paying them a lot of attention because they are interesting or famous.

9 In Britain, **Court** is used in the names of large houses and blocks of flats. ...*7 Ivebury Court.*

court 2 verb uses

court /kɔːt/ **courts, courting, courted. 1** If you ◆◆◇◇◇ **are courting** someone of the opposite sex, you are V-RECIP: spending a lot of time with them, because you in- V n tend to get married to them. *She kept the letters he* pl-n V *had written to her when they were courting.* ...*court-* V-ing *ing couples.* **2** To **court** a person or group means to VERB: V n try to please them or improve your relations with JOURNALISM them, often so that they will do something that you want them to do.

3 If you **court** something such as publicity or popular- VERB: V n ity, you try to obtain it for yourself. **4** If you say that VERB someone **is courting** disaster, you think they are act- ing in a way that makes it likely to happen.

cour·teous /'kɜːtɪəs/. Someone who is **courteous** ◆◇◇◇◇ is polite, respectful, and considerate. *He was always* ADJ-GRADED *very courteous.* ♦ **cour·teous·ly** *He nodded cour-* ADV-GRADED *teously to me.*

cour·tesan /ˌkɔːtɪˈzæn/ **courtesans.** In former N-COUNT times, a woman who was looked after by the rich and important men that she had sexual relation- ships with was referred to as a **courtesan.**

cour·tesy /'kɜːtɪsɪ/ **courtesies. 1 Courtesy** is po- ◆◆◇◇◇ liteness, respect, and consideration for others. N-UNCOUNT **2 Courtesies** are polite conventional things that N-COUNT people say in formal situations. *Hugh and John were* FORMAL *exchanging courtesies.* **3** If you refer to the **courtesy** N-SING of doing something, you are referring to a polite ac- FORMAL tion. *By extending the courtesy of a phone call to my clients, I was building a personal relationship with them.* **4 Courtesy** is used to describe services that ADJ: ADJ n are provided free of charge by an organization to its customers. *A courtesy shuttle bus operates between the hotel and the town.*

5 A **courtesy** call or visit is a formal visit that you pay ADJ: ADJ n someone as a way of showing them politeness or re- spect. **6** A **courtesy** title is a title that someone is al- N-UNCOUNT: lowed to use, although it has no legal or official status. N n, by N **7** If you say that something is provided **courtesy of** PHR-PREP someone or **by courtesy of** someone, you are saying PRAGMATICS that they provided it, and often thanking them for it or suggesting that it was provided as a favour. **8** If you PHR-PREP say that one thing happens **courtesy of** another or **by courtesy of** another, you mean that the second thing causes or is responsible for the first thing. *The air was fresh, courtesy of three holes in the roof.*

court·house /'kɔːthaʊs/ **courthouses.** A **court-** ◆◇◇◇◇ **house** is a building in which a court of law meets. N-COUNT The usual British word is **court**. AMERICAN

cour·ti·er /'kɔːtɪə/ **courtiers.** In the past, courti- ◆◇◇◇◇ ers were noblemen and women who spent a lot of N-COUNT time at the court of a king or queen.

court·ly /'kɔːtlɪ/. You use **courtly** to describe some- ADJ-GRADED one whose behaviour is very polite and well- LITERARY mannered, often in a rather old-fashioned way.

court-ˈmartial, court-martials, court- ◆◇◇◇◇ **martialling, court-martialled;** spelled **court- martialing, court-martialed** in American English. **1** A **court-martial** is a trial in a military court of a N-VAR member of the armed forces who is charged with breaking a military law. **2** If a member of the armed VERB: forces **is court-martialled**, he or she is tried in a be V-ed military court.

court of apˈpeal, courts of appeal. A court of ◆◇◇◇◇ **appeal** is a court which deals with appeals against N-COUNT legal judgements.

court of inˈquiry, courts of inquiry. A court of N-COUNT **inquiry** is a group of people who are officially ap- pointed to investigate a serious accident or inci- dent. The investigation is also called a **court of inquiry.**

court of ˈlaw, courts of law. When you refer to N-COUNT a **court of law**, you are referring to a legal court, es- pecially when talking about the evidence that might be given in a trial. *We have a witness who would swear to it in a court of law.*

court·room /'kɔːtruːm/ **courtrooms.** A **court-** ◆◇◇◇◇ **room** is a room in which a legal court meets. N-COUNT

court·ship /'kɔːtʃɪp/ **courtships. 1 Courtship** is ◆◇◇◇◇ the activity of courting, or the time during which a N-VAR man and a woman are courting. ...*a short courtship.* DATED **2** The **courtship** of male and female animals is their N-UNCOUNT behaviour before they mate.

ˈcourt shoe, court shoes. Court shoes are N-COUNT ladies' shoes that are usually made of plain leather BRITISH with no design. The usual American word is **pumps**.

court·yard /'kɔːtjɑːd/ **courtyards.** A **courtyard** is ◆◇◇◇◇ an open area of ground, often paved, which is sur- N-COUNT rounded by buildings or walls.

cous·cous /'kuːskuːs/. **Couscous** is a type of grain N-UNCOUNT that is traditionally eaten in North Africa, or a North African dish consisting of this grain served with a spicy stew.

cous·in /'kʌzən/ **cousins. 1** Your **cousin** is the ◆◆◆◆◇ child of your uncle or aunt. *We are cousins.* ● See N-COUNT also **second cousin**. **2** If you refer to two things or N-COUNT groups of people as **cousins**, you mean that they are equivalents or that there is a connection between them. *The average European kitchen is smaller than its American cousin.* ● See also **country cousin**.

cou·ture /kuːˈtjʊə, AM -ˈtʊr/. **Couture** refers to the ◆◇◇◇◇ designing and making of high-quality fashion N-UNCOUNT clothes, or to the clothes themselves. FORMAL

cou·tu·ri·er /kuːˈtʊərɪeɪ, AM kuːˈtʊriˈeɪ/ **couturiers.** N-COUNT A **couturier** is a person who designs, makes, and sells expensive, high-quality fashion clothes for women.

cove /kəʊv/ **coves.** A **cove** is a small bay on the ◆◇◇◇◇ coast. N-COUNT

cov·en /'kʌvən/ **covens.** A **coven** is a group of N-COLL- witches that meet together. COUNT

cov·enant /'kʌvənənt/ **covenants. 1** A **covenant** ◆◇◇◇◇ is a formal written agreement between two or more N-COUNT people or groups of people which is recognized in law. **2** A **covenant** is a formal written promise to N-COUNT: pay a sum of money each year for a fixed period, es- also by N pecially to a charity.

cov·er /'kʌvə/ **covers, covering, covered. 1** If ◆◆◆◆◇ you **cover** one thing with another, you place the se- VERB: cond thing over it in order to protect it, hide it, or V n with n close it. Something that is over something else like V-ed this **covers** it. ...*the black patch which covered his left eye.* ...*a covered container.* **2** A **cover** is some- N-COUNT thing which is put over an object, usually in order to protect it. ...*a duvet cover.* **3** If you **cover** one VERB: thing with another, you put the second thing all V n with/in n over the surface of the first. Something that is over V n something else like this **covers** it. *Black clouds cov-* V-ed with/ *ered the sky... The desk was covered with papers.* in n ♦ **-covered** ...*chocolate-covered biscuits.* COMB

4 The **covers** on your bed are the sheet, blankets, and N-PLURAL bedspread that you have on top of you. *She slid*

farther under the covers. **5** The **cover** of a book or magazine is the outside part of it. *...the cover of Time magazine... I used to read every issue from cover to cover.* `N-COUNT`

6 If you **cover** a particular distance, you travel that distance. `VERB: V n`

7 To **cover** someone or something means to protect them from attack, by pointing a gun at people who may attack them, and being ready to fire the gun. `VERB: V n`

8 Cover is protection from enemy attack that is provided for troops or ships carrying out an operation. `N-UNCOUNT`

9 Cover is trees, rocks, or other places where you shelter from the weather or from an attack, or hide from someone. *They ran for cover.* ● If you are **under cover**, you are under something that shelters you from the weather or from an attack. **10** If you **take cover**, you shelter from the weather or from an attack. If you **break cover**, you leave the place where you have been sheltering. `N-UNCOUNT` `PHRASE` `PHRASE`

11 Something that is a **cover** for secret or illegal activities seems respectable or normal, and is intended to hide these activities. **12** If you **cover for** someone who is doing something secret or illegal, you give false information in order to protect them. **13** If you do something **under cover of** a particular situation, you do it without being noticed because of that situation. *They move under cover of darkness.* **14** To **blow** someone's **cover** means to cause their true identity or the true nature of their work to be revealed. *...a spy whose cover had been blown.* `N-COUNT` `VERB: V for n` `PHR-PREP` `PHRASE`

15 If you **cover for** someone who is ill or away, you do their work while they are absent. `VERB: V for n`

16 If a sum of money **covers** something, it is enough to pay for it. *...£1.50 to cover postage and administration.* **17** An insurance policy that **covers** a person or thing guarantees that money will be paid in relation to that person or thing. *...travel insurance covering you and your family against theft.* **18** Insurance **cover** is a guarantee from an insurance company that money will be paid by them in relation to particular people or things. **19** If a law **covers** a particular set of people, things, or situations, it applies to them. *Pedigree dogs are covered by the Sale of Goods Act.* `VERB: V n` `VERB: V n` `V n against n` `N-UNCOUNT` `VERB: V n`

20 If you **cover** a particular topic, you discuss it in a lecture, course, or book. *Other subjects covered included nerves and how to overcome them.* **21** If reporters, newspapers, or television companies **cover** an event, they report on it. `VERB: V n` `V-ed` `VERB: V n`

22 To **cover** a song originally performed by someone else means to record a new version of it. **23** A **cover** is the same as a **cover version.** *...a cover of an old Rolling Stones song.* `VERB: V n` `N-COUNT`

24 See also **covered, covering.**

cover up. 1 If you **cover** something or someone **up**, you put something over them in order to protect or hide them. *I covered him up with a duvet.* **2** If you **cover up** something that you do not want people to know about, you conceal the truth about it. *How do we know you're not just covering up for your friend?* ● See also **cover-up.** `PHRASAL VB` `V n P` `Also V P noun` `V P for n` `Also V n P`

cov·er·age /'kʌvərɪdʒ/. The **coverage** of something in the news is the reporting of it. *...TV coverage of college football.* `◆◆◇◇◇` `N-UNCOUNT`

'**cover charge, cover charges.** A **cover charge** is a sum of money that you must pay in some restaurants and nightclubs in addition to the money that you pay for food and drink. `N-COUNT`

cov·ered /'kʌvəd/. A **covered** area is an area that has a roof. *...a covered mall.* `◆◇◇◇◇` `ADJ: ADJ n`

'**cover girl, cover girls.** A **cover girl** is an attractive woman whose photograph appears on the front of a magazine. `N-COUNT`

cov·er·ing /'kʌvərɪŋ/ **coverings.** A **covering** is a layer of something that protects or hides something else. *Sawdust was used as a hygienic floor covering.* `◆◆◇◇◇` `N-COUNT`

,**covering 'letter, covering letters.** A **covering letter** is a letter that you send with a parcel or with another letter in order to give extra information. The American term is **cover letter.** `N-COUNT` `BRITISH`

cov·er·let /'kʌvəlɪt/ **coverlets.** A **coverlet** is the same as a **bedspread.** `N-COUNT` `DATED`

cov·ert /'kʌvət, 'kəʊvɜːt/. **Covert** activities or situations are secret or hidden. *They have been supplying covert military aid to the rebels. ...covert negotiations.* ♦ **cov·ert·ly** *Covertly Isabel watched him go.* `◆◇◇◇◇` `ADJ-GRADED` `FORMAL` `ADV-GRADED`

'**cover-up, cover-ups.** A **cover-up** is an attempt to hide a crime or mistake. *General Schwarzkopf denied there'd been any cover-up.* `◆◇◇◇◇` `N-COUNT`

'**cover version, cover versions.** A **cover version** of a song is a version of it recorded by a singer or band who did not originally perform the song. `◆◇◇◇◇` `N-COUNT`

cov·et /'kʌvɪt/ **covets, coveting, coveted.** If you **covet** something, you strongly want to have it for yourself. *She coveted his job so openly that conversations between them were tense.* `VERB` `V n` `FORMAL`

cov·et·ed /'kʌvɪtɪd/. You use **coveted** to describe something that very many people would like to have. *...one of sport's most coveted trophies.* `◆◇◇◇◇` `ADJ-GRADED`

cov·et·ous /'kʌvɪtəs/. Someone who is **covetous** has a strong desire to possess something, especially something that belongs to another person; used showing disapproval. *A red Lamborghini Diablo sports car attracts covetous stares.* `ADJ-GRADED` `PRAGMATICS` `FORMAL`

cow /kaʊ/ **cows, cowing, cowed. 1** A **cow** is a large female animal that is kept on farms for its milk. People sometimes refer to male and female animals of this species as **cows.** See picture headed **animals.** *...a herd of cows.* ● See also **cattle. 2** Some female animals, including elephants and whales, are called **cows.** *...a cow elephant.* **3** If you say that someone can do something **until the cows come home,** you mean that it will have no effect even if they do it for a very long time. *You can initiate policies until the cows come home, but unless they're monitored at a senior level, you won't get results.* **4** See also **mad cow disease, sacred cow.** `◆◆◇◇◇` `N-COUNT` `N-COUNT` `PHRASE` `PRAGMATICS` `INFORMAL`

5 If someone describes a woman as a **cow,** they dislike her and think that she is unpleasant or stupid; an offensive use. `N-COUNT` `PRAGMATICS`

6 If someone **is cowed,** they are made afraid, or made to behave in a particular way because they have been frightened or oppressed. *The government, far from being cowed by these threats, has vowed to continue its policy. ...cowing them into submission.* ♦ **cowed** *She was so cowed by the beatings that she meekly obeyed.* `VERB` `be V-ed` `V n into n/-ing` `FORMAL` `ADJ-GRADED`

cow·ard /kaʊəd/ **cowards.** If you call someone a **coward,** you disapprove of them because they are easily frightened and avoid dangerous or difficult situations. ♦ **cow·ard·ly** *I was too cowardly to complain. ...a cowardly act of violence.* `◆◇◇◇◇` `N-COUNT` `PRAGMATICS` `ADJ-GRADED`

cow·ard·ice /'kaʊədɪs/. **Cowardice** is cowardly behaviour. `N-UNCOUNT`

cow·bell /'kaʊbel/ **cowbells.** A **cowbell** is a small bell that is hung around a cow's neck so that the ringing sound makes it possible to find the cow. `N-COUNT`

cow·boy /'kaʊbɔɪ/ **cowboys. 1** A **cowboy** is a man employed to look after cattle in the United States, especially in former times. **2** A **cowboy** is a male character in a western. **3** You can refer to someone who runs a business as a **cowboy** if they run it dishonestly or are not experienced, skilful, or careful in their work. `◆◆◇◇◇` `N-COUNT` `N-COUNT` `N-COUNT` `PRAGMATICS` `BRITISH`

cow·er /kaʊə/ **cowers, cowering, cowered.** If you **cower,** you bend forward and downwards because you are very frightened. *The hostages cowered in their seats.* `VERB` `V`

cow·hide /'kaʊhaɪd/. **Cowhide** is leather made from the skin of a cow. *...cowhide boots.* `N-UNCOUNT`

cowl /kaʊl/ **cowls.** A **cowl** is a large loose hood covering a person's head, or their head and shoulders. Cowls are worn especially by monks. `N-COUNT`

cowl·ing /'kaʊlɪŋ/ **cowlings.** A **cowling** is a removable metal covering for an engine, especially on an aircraft. `N-COUNT`

cow·pat /'kaʊpæt/ **cowpats;** also spelled **cow pat.** A **cowpat** is a pile of faeces from a cow. `N-COUNT`

cow·shed /'kaʊʃed/ **cowsheds.** A **cowshed** is a building where cows are kept or milked. `N-COUNT`

cow·slip /'kaʊslɪp/ **cowslips.** A **cowslip** is a small wild plant with yellow, sweet-smelling flowers. `N-COUNT`

cox /kɒks/ **coxes.** In a rowing boat, the cox is the N-COUNT person who tells the rowers which direction to row in.

cox·swain /'kɒksən/ **coxswains.** The coxswain of N-COUNT a lifeboat or other small boat is the person who steers the boat.

coy /kɔɪ/. **1** If you describe someone as coy, you find them irritating because they are shy, or pretend to be shy, about matters of love and sex. *Carol charmed all the men by turning coy.* ♦ **coy·ly** *She smiled coyly at Algie as he took her hand and raised it to his lips.* ♦ **coy·ness** *...her coyness and flirting.* **2** If someone is being coy, they are unwilling to talk about something that they feel guilty or embarrassed about. *The hotel are understandably coy about the incident.* ♦ **coy·ly** *The administration coyly refused to put a firm figure on the war's costs.* ♦ **coy·ness** *...their coyness about financial aid.*

coy·ote /kaɪ'əʊti/ **coyotes.** A coyote is a wild dog N-COUNT which looks like a small wolf. Coyotes live in North America.

cozy /'kəʊzi/. See cosy.

Cpl. Cpl. is the written abbreviation for 'corporal' N-TITLE when it is used as a title.

CPU /,si: pi: 'juː/ **CPUs.** In a computer, the CPU is N-COUNT the part that processes all the data and makes the computer work. CPU is an abbreviation for 'central processing unit'.

crab /kræb/ **crabs.** A crab is a sea creature with a flat round body covered by a shell, and five pairs of legs with large claws on the front pair. ► Crab is the N-UNCOUNT flesh of this creature eaten as food.

'crab apple, crab apples. A crab apple is a tree N-COUNT like an apple tree that produces small sour fruit.

crabbed /'kræbɪd/. **1** Crabbed means the same as crabby. **2** If you describe something, especially handwriting, as crabbed, you mean it does not take up as much room as it should.

crab·by /'kræbi/. Someone who is crabby is bad-tempered and unpleasant to people.

crab·meat /'kræbmiːt/; also spelled crab meat. N-UNCOUNT Crabmeat is the part of a crab that you eat.

crack 1 verb uses

crack /kræk/ **cracks, cracking, cracked. 1** If something hard cracks or if you crack it, it becomes slightly damaged, with lines appearing on its surface. *One of the stones cracked the glass panel in the front door.* ♦ **cracked** *...a cracked mirror.* **2** If something cracks or if you crack it, it makes a sharp sound like the sound of a piece of wood breaking. *He cracked his fingers nervously.* **3** If you crack a hard part of your body, such as your knee or your head, you hurt it by accidentally hitting it hard against something. *He cracked his head on the pavement.* **4** When you crack something such as an egg or a nut, you break its shell in order to reach the inside part. *Crack the eggs into a bowl.* **5** If you crack a problem or a code, you solve it, especially after a lot of thought. *He has finally cracked the system.* **6** If someone cracks, they lose control of their emotions or actions because they are under a lot of pressure. *She's calm and strong, and she is just not going to crack.* **7** If your voice cracks when you are speaking or singing, it changes in pitch because you are feeling a strong emotion. ♦ **cracked** *When he spoke, his voice was hoarse and cracked.* **8** If you crack a joke, you tell it. *He drove a Volkswagen, cracked jokes, and talked about beer and girls.* **9** See also cracked, cracking. **10** If you say that something is not all it's cracked up to be, you mean that it is not as good as other people have said it is.

crack down. If people in authority crack down on a group of people, they become stricter in making the group obey rules or laws. *We are cracking down now. Anyone who gets caught is fired.* ● See also crackdown.

crack up. If someone cracks up, they are under such emotional strain that they become mentally ill. *She would have cracked up if she hadn't allowed herself some fun.*

crack 2 noun and adjective uses

crack /kræk/ **cracks. 1** A crack is a very narrow gap between two things, or between two parts of a thing. *Kathryn had seen him through a crack in the curtains.* **2** If you open something such as a door, window, or curtain a crack, you open it only a small amount. **3** A crack is a line that appears on the surface of something when it is slightly damaged. *The plate had a crack in it.* **4** A crack is a sharp sound, like the sound of a piece of wood breaking. *There was a loud crack and glass flew into the car.* **5** If you have a crack at something, you make an attempt to do or achieve something. *I should love to have a crack at the Olympia title in my last year.* **6** A crack is a slightly rude or cruel joke. *...the crack about the 'famous girl detective'.* **7** You can refer to a situation where people are chatting and having a good time as the crack. *What they most enjoyed about foreign driving was the crack.* **8** Crack is a form of the drug cocaine which has been made into crystals. **9** A crack soldier or sportsman is highly trained and very skilful. *...a crack undercover police officer.* **10** If you say that someone does something at the crack of dawn, you are emphasizing that they do it very early in the morning. **11** If you paper over the cracks, you try to hide all the things that are wrong with something. *The two sides managed only to paper over the cracks on some issues.* **12** If you get a fair crack of the whip, you are allowed a reasonable opportunity to succeed at something. *None of them is expecting any favours, just a fair crack of the whip.*

crack·down /'krækdaʊn/ **crackdowns.** A crackdown is strong official action that is taken to punish people who break laws. *...anti-government unrest that ended with the violent army crackdown.*

cracked /krækt/. If you say that someone is cracked, you think that their behaviour or ideas are very strange.

crack·er /'krækə/ **crackers. 1** A cracker is a thin crisp biscuit which is often eaten with cheese. **2** If you say that someone or something is a cracker, you like and admire them very much. *'Dude' is a cracker of an album.* **3** A cracker is a hollow cardboard tube covered with coloured paper, used mainly at Christmas meals. Crackers make a bang when they are pulled apart and usually contain a small toy, a joke, and a paper hat. **4** If you say that someone is crackers, you think they are mad or are behaving as if they are mad. *They looked at her as though she was crackers.*

'crack house, crack houses. A crack house is a N-COUNT place where crack cocaine is available.

crack·ing /'krækɪŋ/. **1** You use cracking to describe something you think is very good or exciting. *The way Liverpool play, and the way we play, I think it will be a cracking game.* **2** If you tell someone to get cracking, you are telling them to start doing something immediately. *You'd better get cracking, the sooner the better.* **3** If you say that someone or something is moving at a cracking pace, you mean that they are moving very quickly.

crack·le /'krækəl/ **crackles, crackling, crackled.** If something crackles, it makes a rapid series of short, harsh noises. *The fire crackled with dry wood... The radio crackled again.* ► Also a noun. *...the crackle of flames and gunfire.*

crack·ly /'krækəli/. Something that is crackly, especially a recording or broadcast, has or makes a lot of short harsh noises. *...a crackly phone line.*

crack·pot /'krækpɒt/ **crackpots.** If you describe someone or their ideas as crackpot, you disapprove of them because you think that they are strange and crazy. *...crackpot schemes.* ► A crackpot is a crackpot person.

cra·dle /ˈkreɪdəl/ **cradles, cradling, cradled.** ◆◇◇◇◇ N-COUNT
1 A **cradle** is a baby's bed with high sides. Cradles often have curved bases so that they rock. **2** If PHRASE something affects you **from the cradle to the grave**, it affects you throughout your life. **3** A place that is N-COUNT referred to as **the cradle of** something is the place where it began. ...*New York, the cradle of capitalism.* **4** If you **cradle** someone or something in your arms VERB: or hands, you hold them carefully and protectively. V n in n *He was sitting at the big table cradling a large bowl* V n *of milky coffee.* **5** The **cradle** is the part of a tele- N-COUNT phone on which the receiver rests while it is not being used.

craft /krɑːft, kræft/ **crafts, crafting, crafted;** ◆◆◆◇◇ **craft** is both the singular and the plural form for meaning 1. **1** You can refer to a boat, a spacecraft, N-COUNT or an aircraft as a **craft**. *The fisherman manoeuvered his small craft close to the reef.* ● See also **landing craft**.
2 A **craft** is an activity such as weaving, carving, or N-COUNT pottery that involves making things skilfully with your hands. ...*the arts and crafts of the North American Indians.*
3 You can use **craft** to refer to any activity or job that N-COUNT involves doing something skilfully. ...*the craft of writing.* **4** If something **is crafted**, it is made skilfully. VERB: *Many delegates were willing to craft a compromise.* be V-ed / V n

craft·i·ly /ˈkrɑːftɪli, ˈkræft-/. See **crafty**.

crafts·man /ˈkrɑːftsmən, ˈkræft-/ **craftsmen.** A ◆◇◇◇◇ **craftsman** is a man who makes things skilfully with N-COUNT his hands.

crafts·man·ship /ˈkrɑːftsmənʃɪp, ◆◇◇◇◇ ˈkræft-/. N-UNCOUNT
1 Craftsmanship is the skill that someone uses when they make beautiful things with their hands. *It is easy to appreciate the craftsmanship of Armani.*
2 Craftsmanship is the quality that something has N-UNCOUNT when it is beautiful and has been very carefully made. *His canoes are known for their style, fine detail and craftsmanship.*

crafts·people /ˈkrɑːftspiːpəl, ˈkræft-/. **Crafts-** N-PLURAL **people** are people who make things skilfully with their hands.

crafts·woman /ˈkrɑːftswʊmən, ˈkræfts-/ **crafts-** N-COUNT **women.** A **craftswoman** is a woman who makes things skilfully with her hands.

crafty /ˈkrɑːfti, ˈkræfti/ **craftier, craftiest.** If you ◆◇◇◇◇ describe someone as **crafty**, you mean that they ADJ-GRADED achieve what they want in a clever way, often by deceiving people. ...*a crafty, lying character who enjoys plotting against others.* ◆ **crafti·ly** The government ADV-GRADED *has craftily put up all the hidden taxes.*

crag /kræg/ **crags.** A **crag** is a steep rocky cliff or N-COUNT part of a mountain.

crag·gy /ˈkrægi/. **1** A **craggy** cliff or mountain is ADJ-GRADED steep and rocky. ...*tiny villages on craggy cliffs.* **2** A ADJ-GRADED **craggy** face has large features and deep lines. *He's a very small man with a lined, craggy face.*

cram /kræm/ **crams, cramming, crammed.** **1** If ◆◇◇◇◇ you **cram** things or people into a place, you put VERB: them into it, although there is hardly enough room V n prep/adv for them. *I crammed my bag full of swimsuits and* V n full of n *T-shirts... She crammed her mouth with caviar.* **2** If V n with n people **cram** into a place or vehicle or **cram** a place VERB: or vehicle, so many of them enter it at one time that V prep it is completely full. *Friends and admirers crammed* V n *the chapel.* **3** If you **cram** a tightly-fitting hat on, VERB you put it on, especially in a hurry. *I crammed on* V n with on *my cap again. helped the Duke up and tried to dust* Also V n on *him off.* **4** If you **are cramming for** an examination, VERB: you are learning as much as possible in a short time V for n just before you take the examination.

crammed /kræmd/. **1** If a place is **crammed** with ◆◇◇◇◇ things or people, it is full of them, so that there is ADJ hardly room for anything or anyone else. *The house is crammed with priceless furniture and works of art.* **2** If people or things are **crammed** into a place or ADJ: vehicle, it is full of them. *Between two and three* v-link ADJ *thousand refugees were crammed into the church.* prep/adv

cramp /kræmp/ **cramps, cramping, cramped.** ◆◇◇◇◇ **1 Cramp** is a sudden strong pain caused by a mus- N-UNCOUNT: also N in pl cle suddenly contracting. *She started getting stomach cramps.* **2** If someone or something **cramps** PHRASE your **style**, their presence or existence restricts your INFORMAL behaviour in some way. *Like more and more women, she believes wedlock would cramp her style.*

cramped /kræmpt/. A **cramped** room or building ◆◇◇◇◇ is not big enough for the people or things in it. ...*a* ADJ-GRADED *rather cramped little flat in Bristol.*

cran·berry /ˈkrænbəri, AM -beri/ **cranberries.** ◆◇◇◇◇ **Cranberries** are red berries with a sour taste. They N-COUNT are often used to make a sauce or jelly.

crane /kreɪn/ **cranes, craning, craned.** **1** A ◆◆◇◇◇ **crane** is a large machine that moves heavy things by N-COUNT lifting them in the air. **2** A **crane** is a kind of large N-COUNT bird with a long neck and long legs. **3** If you **crane** VERB: V n your neck or head, you stretch your neck in a par- V to-inf ticular direction in order to see or hear something V adv/prep better. *Children craned to get close to him... She craned forward to look at me.*

cra·nium /ˈkreɪniəm/ **craniums** or **crania** N-COUNT /ˈkreɪniə/. Your **cranium** is the round part of your TECHNICAL skull that contains your brain. ◆ **cra·nial** /ˈkreɪniəl/ ADJ: ADJ n ...*cranial distortion.*

crank /kræŋk/ **cranks, cranking, cranked.** **1** If ◆◇◇◇◇ you call someone a **crank**, you think they have pe- N-COUNT culiar ideas or behaviour. *The Labour leader called* PRAGMATICS the Prime Minister 'a crank'. INFORMAL
2 If you **crank** an engine or machine, you make it VERB move or function, especially by turning a handle. *The* V n *chauffeur got out to crank the motor.*

crank up. **1** If you **crank up** a machine or device, PHRASAL VB you make it function harder or at a greater level. V P noun ...*May's warm weather, which caused Americans to* Also V n P *crank up their air conditioners.* **2** If you **crank up** the V P noun volume of something, you turn it up until it is very V n P adj loud. *They're cranking the music up loud again.* **3** To V P noun **crank** something **up** means to increase it or make it Also V n P more intense. *The incident that cranked up the fear was the murder of Brian Smith.*

crank out. If you say that a company or person PHRASAL VB **cranks out** a quantity of similar things, you mean they V P noun produce them quickly, in the same way, and are PRAGMATICS usually implying that the things are unoriginal or of V n P poor quality. *The writer must have cranked it out in* INFORMAL *his lunch-hour.*

crank·shaft /ˈkræŋkʃɑːft, -ʃæft/ **crankshafts.** A N-COUNT **crankshaft** is the main shaft of an internal combustion engine.

cranky /ˈkræŋki/. **1** If you describe ideas or ways of ADJ-GRADED behaving as **cranky**, you disapprove of them be- PRAGMATICS cause you think they are strange. *Vegetarianism has* INFORMAL *shed its cranky image.* **2 Cranky** means bad- ADJ-GRADED tempered. *It was a long trek, and Jack and I both* AMERICAN, *started to get cranky after about ten minutes.* INFORMAL

cran·ny /ˈkræni/ **crannies. Crannies** are very nar- N-COUNT row openings or spaces in something. *They fled like lizards into crannies in the rocks.* ● **every nook and cranny:** see **nook**.

crap /kræp/ **craps, crapping, crapped.** **1** If you ◆◆◇◇◇ describe something as **crap**, you think that it is ADJ-GRADED wrong or of very poor quality; an offensive use. ▶ Also a noun. ...*a tedious, humourless load of crap.* N-UNCOUNT
2 Crap is sometimes used to refer to faeces; an offen- N-UNCOUNT sive use. **3** To **crap** means to get rid of faeces from VERB: V your body; an offensive use.
4 Craps or **crap** is a gambling game, played mainly in N-UNCOUNT the United States, in which you throw two dice and bet on the total score.

crap·py /ˈkræpi/ **crappier, crappiest.** If you de- ADJ-GRADED scribe something as **crappy**, you think it is of very INFORMAL poor quality. Some people find this word offensive. ...*a crappy detective novel.*

crash /kræʃ/ **crashes, crashing, crashed.** **1** A ◆◆◆◆◇ **crash** is an accident in which a moving vehicle hits N-COUNT something and is damaged or destroyed. ...*a car crash.* **2** If a moving vehicle **crashes** or if the driver V-ERG: V **crashes** it, it hits something and is damaged or de- V into n stroyed. *His car crashed into the rear of a van. ...his* V n *death, after crashing his motorcycle on a bridge.* **3** If VERB something **crashes** somewhere, it moves and hits V prep/adv

something else violently, making a loud noise. *The walls above us crashed down.* **4** A **crash** is a sudden, loud noise. *Two people in the flat recalled hearing a loud crash about 1.30 a.m.* N-COUNT

5 If a business or financial system **crashes**, it fails suddenly, often with serious effects. *When the market crashed, they assumed the deal would be cancelled.* ▶ Also a noun. *...a stock market crash.* **6** If a computer or a computer program **crashes**, it fails suddenly. VERB V / N-COUNT VERB: V

crash out. If someone **crashes out** somewhere, they fall asleep where they are because they are very tired or drunk. *I just want to crash out on the sofa.* PHRASAL VB V P INFORMAL

'crash barrier, crash barriers. A **crash barrier** is a strong low fence built along the side of a road at a dangerous corner or between the two halves of a motorway in order to prevent accidents. The usual American word is **guardrail**. N-COUNT BRITISH

,crash 'course, crash courses. A **crash course** in a subject is a short course in which you are taught basic facts or skills, for example before you start a new job. *I did a 15-week crash course in typing.* N-COUNT

'crash helmet, crash helmets. A **crash helmet** is a helmet that motorcyclists wear in order to protect their heads if they have an accident. N-COUNT

,crash-'land, crash-lands, crash-landing, crash-landed; also spelled **crash land**. If a pilot **crash-lands** an aircraft or if it **crash-lands**, the pilot lands the aircraft in an abnormal and dangerous way, for example when it has developed a fault and cannot land normally. *A light aircraft crash-landed on a putting green yesterday.* ♦ **crash-landing, crash-landings** *His plane made a crash-landing during a sandstorm.* V-ERG: V n V / N-COUNT

crass /kræs/ **crasser, crassest.** **Crass** behaviour is stupid and insensitive. *The government has behaved with crass insensitivity.* ♦ **crass·ness** *...the crassness of his conversation.* ♦◇◇◇◇ ADJ-GRADED / N-UNCOUNT

crate /kreɪt/ **crates, crating, crated.** **1** A **crate** is a large box used for transporting or storing things. *...a pile of wooden crates.* **2** If something is **crated**, it is packed in a crate so that it can be transported or stored somewhere safely. *The much repaired plane was crated for the return journey.* **3** A **crate** is a plastic or wire tray divided into sections which is used for carrying bottles. *...a plastic milk crate.* ▶ A **crate** of something is the amount of it that is contained in a crate. *...crates of beer as prizes!* ♦◇◇◇◇ N-COUNT / VB: usu passive be V-ed / N-COUNT / N-COUNT

cra·ter /'kreɪtə/ **craters.** A **crater** is a very large hole in the ground, which has been caused by something hitting it or by an explosion. ♦◇◇◇◇ N-COUNT

cra·vat /krə'væt/ **cravats.** A **cravat** is a piece of cloth which a man wears wrapped around his neck and tucked inside the collar of his shirt. N-COUNT

crave /kreɪv/ **craves, craving, craved.** If you **crave** something, you want to have it very much. *...a vulnerable, unhappy girl who craved affection... You may be craving for some fresh air.* ♦ **crav·ing, cravings** *...a craving for sugar.* ♦◇◇◇◇ VERB V n / Also V to-inf / N-COUNT

cra·ven /'kreɪvən/. If you describe someone as **craven**, you disapprove of them because they are cowardly. *The craven attackers pounced on the boy.* ADJ-GRADED PRAGMATICS WRITTEN

crawl /krɔːl/ **crawls, crawling, crawled.** **1** When you **crawl**, you move forward on your hands and knees. *I began to crawl on my hands and knees towards the door.* **2** When an insect **crawls** somewhere, it moves there quite slowly. *I watched the moth crawl up the outside of the lampshade.* **3** If someone or something **crawls** somewhere, they move or progress slowly or with great difficulty. *Hairpin turns force the car to crawl at 10 miles an hour.* ▶ Also a noun. *The traffic on the approach road slowed to a crawl.* VERB: V / V prep/adv / VERB / V prep / VERB: V prep/adv / N-SING: a N

4 If you say that a place **is crawling with** people or animals, you are emphasizing that it is full of them. *This place is crawling with police.* VB: only cont PRAGMATICS / V with n INFORMAL

5 The crawl is a kind of swimming stroke which you do lying on your front, swinging one arm over your head, and then the other arm. N-SING: the N

6 If something **makes** your **skin crawl** or **makes** your **flesh crawl**, it makes you feel horrified or revolted. PHRASE

7 See also **kerb-crawling, pub crawl**.

cray·fish /'kreɪfɪʃ/ **crayfish** is both the singular and the plural form. A **crayfish** is a small shellfish with five pairs of legs. N-COUNT

cray·on /'kreɪɒn/ **crayons.** A **crayon** is a rod of coloured wax used for drawing. ♦◇◇◇◇ N-COUNT

craze /kreɪz/ **crazes.** If there is a **craze** for something, it is very popular for a short time. *Walking is the latest fitness craze.* ♦◇◇◇◇ N-COUNT

crazed /kreɪzd/. **Crazed** people are wild and uncontrolled, and perhaps insane. *A crazed gunman slaughtered five people last night.* ♦◇◇◇◇ ADJ

-crazed /-kreɪzd/. **-crazed** combines with nouns to form adjectives that describe people whose behaviour is wild and uncontrolled because of the thing the noun refers to. *...a drug-crazed killer.* COMB

cra·zi·ly /'kreɪzili/. If something moves **crazily**, it moves in a way or in a direction that you do not expect. *The ball bounced crazily over his shoulder into the net.* ● See also **crazy**. ADV: ADV after v WRITTEN

cra·zy /'kreɪzi/ **crazier, craziest; crazies.** **1** If you describe someone or something as **crazy**, you think they are very foolish or strange. *People thought they were all crazy to try to make money from manufacturing.* ♦ **cra·zi·ly** *Out in the yard, four tiny figures were dancing around crazily... Our policies are crazily extravagant.* ♦ **cra·zi·ness** *We had to have a sense of humour because of the craziness of it all.* **2** Someone who is **crazy** is insane. *If I sat home and worried about all this stuff, I'd go crazy.* ▶ A **crazy** is someone who is crazy. **3** If something makes you **crazy** or drives you **crazy**, it makes you extremely annoyed or upset. *This sitting around is driving me crazy.* ♦♦♦◇◇ ADJ-GRADED PRAGMATICS INFORMAL / ADV / N-UNCOUNT / ADJ-GRADED INFORMAL / N-COUNT / ADJ-GRADED: v-link ADJ INFORMAL

4 If you are **crazy about** something, you are very enthusiastic about it. If you are not **crazy about** something, you do not like it. *I'm also not crazy about the initial terms of the deal.* ▶ Also a combining form. *...every football-crazy schoolboy in Europe.* **5** If you are **crazy about** someone, you are deeply in love with them. *None of that matters, because we're crazy about each other.* ADJ-GRADED: ADJ about n INFORMAL / COMB / ADJ-GRADED: v-link ADJ about n INFORMAL

6 You use **like crazy** to emphasize that something happens to a great degree. *Some people can diet like crazy and not lose weight.* PHRASE PRAGMATICS INFORMAL

creak /kriːk/ **creaks, creaking, creaked.** If something **creaks**, it makes a short, high-pitched sound when it moves. *The steps creaked beneath his feet.* ▶ Also a noun. *The door was pulled open with a creak.* ♦◇◇◇◇ VERB: V / V prep / N-COUNT

creaky /'kriːki/. **1** A **creaky** object creaks when it moves. *...a creaky door.* **2** If you describe something as **creaky**, you think it is bad in some way because it is old or old-fashioned. *...its creaky and corrupt political system.* ADJ-GRADED / ADJ-GRADED

cream /kriːm/ **creams, creaming, creamed.** **1 Cream** is a thick yellowish-white liquid taken from milk. You can use it in cooking or put it on fruit or puddings. *...strawberries and cream.* ● See also **clotted cream, double cream, single cream, sour cream.** **2 Cream** is used in the names of soups that contain cream or milk. *...cream of mushroom soup.* **3 Cream** is used in expressions such as the **cream of society** to refer to the best people or things of a particular kind. ● You can refer to the best people or things of a particular kind as **the cream of the crop.** ♦♦♦◇◇ N-UNCOUNT / N-UNCOUNT: N of n / N-COLL-SING: the N of n / PHRASE

4 A **cream** is a substance that you rub into your skin, for example to keep it soft or to heal or protect it. *...sun protection creams.* ● See also **face cream**. N-VAR

5 Something that is **cream** is yellowish-white in colour. *...cream silk stockings.* COLOUR

6 See also **ice cream, salad cream, shaving cream**.

cream off. **1** To **cream off** part of a group of people means to take them away and treat them in a special way, because they are better than the others; used showing disapproval. *The private schools cream off many of the best pupils.* **2** If a person or organiza- PHRASAL VB PRAGMATICS V P noun BRITISH / PRAGMATICS

tion **creams off** a large amount of money, they take it and use it for themselves; used showing disapproval. *This means smaller banks can cream off big profits during lending booms.*

V P noun
INFORMAL,
BRITISH

cream 'cheese. Cream cheese is a very rich soft white cheese.

N-UNCOUNT

cream·er /ˈkriːmə/ **creamers. 1** Creamer is a white powder that is used in tea and coffee instead of milk. **2** A creamer is a small jug used for pouring cream or milk. The British term is **milk jug**.

N-VAR

N-COUNT
AMERICAN

cream·ery /ˈkriːməri/ **creameries.** A creamery is a place where milk and cream are made into butter and cheese.

N-COUNT

cream 'tea, cream teas. A cream tea is an afternoon meal that consists of tea to drink and scones with jam and clotted cream to eat.

N-COUNT
BRITISH

creamy /ˈkriːmi/ **creamier, creamiest. 1** Creamy food or drink contains a lot of cream or milk. *...rich, creamy coffee.* **2** Creamy food has a soft smooth texture and appearance. *...creamy mashed potato.*

◆◇◇◇◇
ADJ-GRADED

ADJ-GRADED

crease /kriːs/ **creases, creasing, creased. 1** Creases are lines that are made in cloth or paper when it is crushed or folded. *Papa flattened the creases of the map.* **2** If cloth or paper **creases** or if you **crease** it, lines form in it when it is crushed or folded. *Liz sat down on the bed, lowering herself carefully not to crease her skirt.* ♦ **creased** *His clothes were creased, as if he had slept in them.* **3** If your face **creases** or if an expression **creases** it, lines appear on it because you are frowning or smiling. *His ruddy face still routinely creases with mirth.* **4** Creases in someone's skin are lines which form where their skin folds. *...the tiny creases at the corners of his eyes.* ♦ **creased** *...Jock's creased drunken face.* **5** In cricket, the **crease** is a line on the playing surface near the wicket where the batsman stands.

◆◇◇◇◇
N-COUNT

V-ERG: V
V n

ADJ-GRADED

V
Also V n
WRITTEN

N-COUNT

ADJ-GRADED

N-SING:
the N,
poss N

crease up. If someone or something makes you **crease up** or **creases** you **up**, they make you laugh a lot. *It creases me up every time.*

PHRASAL VB
ERG:
V P
V n P

cre·ate /kriˈeɪt/ **creates, creating, created. 1** To **create** something means to cause it to happen or exist. *She could create a fight out of anything.* ♦ **crea·tion** /kriˈeɪʃən/ *These businesses stimulate the creation of local jobs.* **2** When someone **creates** a new product or process, they invent it or design it. *It is really great for a radio producer to create a show like this.* ♦ **crea·tor, creators** *...Ian Fleming, the creator of James Bond.*

◆◆◆◆◇
VERB
V n

N-UNCOUNT

VERB
V n

N-COUNT

crea·tion /kriˈeɪʃən/ **creations. 1** In many religions, **creation** is the making of the universe, earth, and creatures by God. *For the first time since creation, the survival of the Earth is entirely in our hands.* **2** People sometimes refer to the entire universe as **creation**. *Both gods and goddesses were seen to manifest their energies throughout the whole of creation.* **3** You can refer to something that someone has made as a **creation**, especially if it shows skill, imagination, or artistic ability. *The bathroom is entirely my own creation.* **4** See also **create**.

◆◆◇◇◇
N-UNCOUNT:
also the N

N-UNCOUNT
LITERARY

N-COUNT

crea·tive /kriˈeɪtɪv/ **. 1** A **creative** person has the ability to invent and develop original ideas, especially in the arts. *Like so many creative people he was never satisfied.* ♦ **crea·tiv·ity** /ˌkriːeɪˈtɪvɪti/ *American art reached a peak of creativity in the 50s and 60s.* **2** Creative activities involve the inventing and making of new kinds of things. *...creative writing.* **3** If you use something in a **creative** way, you use it in a new way that produces interesting and unusual results. *...his creative use of words.* ♦ **crea·tive·ly** *Genet teaches you to think creatively.*

◆◆◆◇◇
ADJ-GRADED

N-UNCOUNT

ADJ

ADJ-GRADED

ADV-GRADED

cre·ative ac·counting. If you say that a company or other organization practises **creative accounting**, you are saying in a humorous way that they present or organize their accounts in such a way that they gain money for themselves or give a false impression of their profits.

N-UNCOUNT
PRAGMATICS

crea·tor /kriˈeɪtə/ **.** God is sometimes referred to as **the Creator**. *...the first object placed in the heavens by the Creator.*

◆◆◇◇◇
N-PROPER:
the N

crea·ture /ˈkriːtʃə/ **creatures. 1** You can refer to any living thing that is not a plant as a **creature**, especially when it is of an unknown or unfamiliar kind. *Alaskan Eskimos believe that every living creature possesses a spirit.* **2** If you say that someone is a particular type of **creature**, you are focusing on a particular quality they have. *She's charming, a sweet creature.* **3** If you describe someone as someone else's **creature**, you mean that they are controlled by or depend on that person; used showing disapproval. *We are not creatures of the Conservative government.*

◆◆◇◇◇
N-COUNT

N-COUNT:
with supp
PRAGMATICS

N-COUNT:
with poss
PRAGMATICS

creature 'comforts. Creature comforts are the things that you need to feel comfortable in a place, for example good food and modern equipment. *...all the creature comforts of home.*

N-PLURAL

crèche /kreʃ/ **crèches;** also spelled **creche.** A **crèche** is a place where small children can be left and looked after while their parents are working or doing something else.

◆◇◇◇◇
N-COUNT
BRITISH

cred /kred/ **.** Cred means the same as **street cred**.

BRITISH

cre·dence /ˈkriːdəns/ **. 1** If something lends or gives **credence** to a theory or story, it makes it easier to believe. *Good studies are needed to lend credence to the notion that genuine progress can be made in this important field.* **2** If you give **credence** to a theory or story, you believe it. *You're surely not giving any credence to this story of Hythe's?*

◆◇◇◇◇
N-UNCOUNT
FORMAL

N-UNCOUNT
FORMAL

cre·den·tials /krɪˈdenʃəlz/ **. 1** Someone's **credentials** are their previous achievements, training, and general background, which indicate that they are qualified to do something. *I can testify to the credentials of the clientele.* **2** Someone's **credentials** are a letter or certificate that proves their identity or qualifications. *Britain's new ambassador to Lebanon has presented his credentials to President Hrawi.*

◆◇◇◇◇
N-PLURAL:
with supp

N-PLURAL

credi'bility gap. A **credibility gap** is the difference between what a person says or promises and what they actually think or do. *British economic policy has had a credibility gap since the ERM suspension.*

N-SING

cred·ible /ˈkredɪbəl/ **. 1** Credible means able to be trusted or believed. *Mrs Thatcher's claims seem credible to many.* ♦ **cred·ibil·ity** /ˌkredɪˈbɪlɪti/ *The police have lost their credibility.* ♦ **cred·ibly** /ˈkredɪbli/ *Ministers can equally credibly claim that the opposition is to blame.* **2** A **credible** candidate, policy, or system is one that appears to have a chance of being successful. *Mr Delors would be a credible candidate.* ♦ **credibly** *He was the only figure who could credibly run the country.*

◆◆◇◇◇
ADJ-GRADED

N-UNCOUNT

ADV-GRADED

ADJ-GRADED

ADV-GRADED:
ADV with v

cred·it /ˈkredɪt/ **credits, crediting, credited. 1** If you are allowed **credit**, you are allowed to pay for goods or services several weeks or months after receiving them. *Pay cash or buy on credit.* **2** If someone or their bank account is **in credit**, the bank account has money in it. *I made sure the account stayed in credit.* **3** When a sum of money **is credited** to an account, the bank adds that money to the total in the account. *Midland decided to change the way it credited payments to accounts... Interest is calculated daily and credited once a year.* **4** A **credit** is a sum of money which is added to an account. **5** A **credit** is an entitlement to have a particular amount of money. *...giving families $350 in tax credits per child.* **6** If you get the **credit** for something good, people praise you because you are thought to be responsible for it. *Some of the credit for her relaxed manner must go to Andy.* **7** If people **credit** someone with an achievement or if it **is credited to** them, people say or believe that they were responsible for it. *The staff are crediting him with having saved Hythe's life... The screenplay for 'Gabriel Over the White House' is credited to Carey Wilson.* **8** If you have one or more achievements **to** your **credit**, you have achieved them. *I have countless magazine stories to my credit.* **9** If you **credit** someone **with** a quality, you believe or say that they have it. *Credit him with the same generosity of spirit.* **10** To **give** someone **credit for** a good quality means

◆◆◆◆◇
N-UNCOUNT

N-UNCOUNT:
in N,
N n

VERB:
be V-ed to n
V n to n
be V-ed

N-COUNT
TECHNICAL

N-COUNT
TECHNICAL

N-UNCOUNT

VERB
V n with -ing/
n
be V-ed to n

PHRASE

VERB
V n with n

PHRASE

to believe or say that they have it. *Bruno had more ability than the media gives him credit for.*

11 If you say that someone is, for example, **a credit to their profession**, you are praising them and saying that their qualities or achievements will make people have a better opinion of the group mentioned. **12** If you say that something **does** someone **credit**, you mean that they should be praised or admired because of it. *You're a nice girl, Lettie, and your kind heart does you credit.* **13** If you say that, **to someone's credit**, they did something or do something, you mean that they deserve praise for it. *She had managed to pull herself together and, to her credit, continued to look upon life as a positive experience.*

14 If you cannot **credit** something, you cannot believe that it is true. *He either did not learn of the scandal or refused to credit what he heard.*

15 The list of people who helped to make a film, a record, or a television programme is called the **credits**.

16 A **credit** is the successful completion of a part of a higher education course. At some universities and colleges you need a certain number of credits to be awarded a degree.

cred·it·able /ˈkredɪtəbəl/. A **creditable** performance or achievement is of a reasonably high standard. *They turned out a quite creditable performance.* ♦ **cred·it·ably** /ˈkredɪtəbli/ *British riders performed creditably.*

'credit card, credit cards. A **credit card** is a plastic card that you use to buy goods on credit.

'credit note, credit notes. A **credit note** is a piece of paper that a shop gives you when you return goods that you have bought from them. It states that you are entitled to take goods of the same value without paying for them.

cred·i·tor /ˈkredɪtə/ **creditors.** Your **creditors** are the people who you owe money to.

'credit rating. Your **credit rating** is a judgement of how likely you are to pay money back if you borrow it or buy things on credit.

,credit 'transfer, credit transfers. A **credit transfer** is a direct payment of money from one bank account to another.

credit·worthy /ˈkredɪtwɜːði/; also spelled **credit-worthy**. A **creditworthy** person or organization is one who can safely be lent money or allowed to have goods on credit, for example because in the past they have always paid back what they owe. ♦ **credit·worthi·ness** ...*the creditworthiness of customers.*

cre·do /ˈkriːdəʊ, ˈkreɪ-/ **credos.** A **credo** is a set of beliefs, principles, or opinions that strongly influence the way a person lives or works. *Lord Clarendon's liberal credo was one of the foundations of his political conduct.*

cre·du·lity /krɪˈdjuːlɪti, AM -ˈduː-/. **Credulity** is a willingness to believe that something is real or true. *The plot does stretch credulity.*

credu·lous /ˈkredʒʊləs/. If you describe someone as **credulous**, you have a low opinion of them because they are too ready to believe what people tell them and are easily deceived. *It would be unrealistic for anyone today to consider the female consumer as particularly credulous.*

creed /kriːd/ **creeds. 1** A **creed** is a set of beliefs, principles, or opinions that strongly influence the way people live or work. ...*their devotion to their creed of self-help.* **2** A **creed** is a religion. *The centre is open to all, no matter what race or creed.*

creek /kriːk/ **creeks. 1** A **creek** is a long narrow inlet where the sea comes a long way into the land. **2** A **creek** is a small stream or river. *Follow Austin Creek for a few miles.* **3** If you say that someone is **up the creek** or **up the creek without a paddle**, you mean they are in a bad or difficult situation, or are wrong in some way.

creep /kriːp/ **creeps, creeping, crept. 1** When people or animals **creep** somewhere, they move quietly and slowly. *Back I go to the hotel and creep up to my room.* **2** If something **creeps** somewhere,

it moves very slowly. *Mist had crept in again from the sea.* **3** If a rate or number **creeps** up to a higher level, it gradually reaches that level. *The inflation rate has been creeping up to 9.5 per cent.* **4** If something **creeps** in or **creeps** back, it begins to occur or becomes part of something without people realizing it or wanting it. *An increasing ratio of mistakes, perhaps induced by tiredness, crept into her game.*

5 If you describe someone as a **creep**, you mean that you dislike them, because they are insincere and flatter people. **6** If someone or something **gives** you **the creeps**, they make you feel very uneasy or frightened. *I always hated that statue. It gave me the creeps.* • to **make** someone's **flesh creep**: see **flesh**.

creep up on. 1 If you **creep up on** someone, you move slowly closer to them without being seen by them. *They'll creep up on you while you're asleep.* **2** If a feeling or state **creeps up on** you, you hardly notice that it is beginning to happen to you. *The desire to be a mother may creep up on you unexpectedly.*

creep·er /ˈkriːpə/ **creepers. Creepers** are plants with long stems that wind themselves around objects.

creepy /ˈkriːpi/ **creepier, creepiest.** If you say that something or someone is **creepy**, you mean they make you feel very uneasy or frightened. ...*places that were really creepy at night.*

creepy-crawly /ˌkriːpi ˈkrɔːli/ **creepy-crawlies.** Some children refer to insects as **creepy-crawlies** when they give them a feeling of fear or disgust. See picture headed **insects.**

cre·mate /krɪˈmeɪt, AM ˈkriːmeɪt/ **cremates, cremating, cremated.** When someone **is cremated**, their dead body is burned, usually as part of a funeral service. ♦ **cre·ma·tion** /krɪˈmeɪʃən/ **cremations** ...*the arrangements for her cremation.*

crema·to·rium /ˌkreməˈtɔːriəm/ **crematoria** /ˌkreməˈtɔːriə/ or **crematoriums.** A **crematorium** is a building in which the bodies of dead people are burned.

crème de la crème /ˌkrem də lɑː ˈkrem/. If you refer to someone or something as **the crème de la crème**, you mean they are the very best person or thing of their kind. *Scientists are the crème de la crème of a country's brainpower.*

cren·el·lat·ed /ˈkrenəleɪtɪd/. A **crenellated** wall, for example in a castle, has gaps in the top or openings through which to fire at attackers.

cre·ole /ˈkriːəʊl/ **creoles;** also spelled **Creole. 1** A **creole** is a language that has developed from a mixture of different languages and has become the main language in a particular place. ...*French Creole.* **2** A **Creole** is a person of mixed African and European race, who lives in the West Indies and speaks a creole language. **3** Creole means belonging to or relating to the Creole community. *Coconut Rice Balls is a creole dish.*

creo·sote /ˈkriːəsəʊt/. **Creosote** is a thick dark liquid made from coal tar which is used to prevent wood from rotting.

crepe /kreɪp/ **crepes. 1** Crepe is a thin fabric made of cotton, silk, or wool with an uneven, ridged surface. ...*a crepe bandage.* **2** Crepe is a type of rubber with a rough surface. ...*a pair of crepe-soled ankle-boots.* **3** A **crepe** is a thin pancake. ...*chicken-filled crepes.*

,crepe 'paper. Crepe paper is stretchy paper with an uneven, ridged surface. Coloured crepe paper is often used for making decorations.

crept /krept/. **Crept** is the past tense and past participle of **creep.**

cre·pus·cu·lar /krɪˈpʌskjʊlə/. **Crepuscular** means relating to twilight. *They merged together in the crepuscular light.*

cre·scen·do /krɪˈʃendəʊ/ **crescendos. 1** A **crescendo** is a noise that gets louder and louder. Some people use **crescendo** to refer to the point when a noise is at its loudest. *The applause rose to a crescendo.* **2** People sometimes describe an increase in

the intensity of something, or its most intense point, as a **crescendo**. *There was a crescendo of parliamentary and press criticism.* **3** A **crescendo** is a section of a piece of music in which the music gradually gets louder and louder. `JOURNALISM` `N-COUNT`

cres·cent /'kresənt, 'krez-/ **crescents. 1** A **crescent** is a curved shape like the shape of the moon during its first and last quarters. See picture headed **shapes**. **2** In Britain, **Crescent** is sometimes part of the name of a street or row of houses that is built in a curve. *...44 Colville Crescent.* `N-COUNT`

cress /kres/. **Cress** is a plant with small, strong-tasting green leaves that are used in salads or as a garnish for food. `N-UNCOUNT`

crest /krest/ **crests, cresting, crested. 1** The **crest** of a hill or wave is its top. ● If you say that you are **on the crest of a wave**, you mean that you are feeling very happy and confident because things are going well for you. **2** When someone **crests** a hill, they reach its top. **3** A bird's **crest** is a tuft of feathers on the top of its head. ♦ **crest·ed** *...crested hawks.* **4** A **crest** is a design that is the symbol of a noble family, a town, or an organization. ♦ **crested** *...crested writing paper.* `N-COUNT` `PHRASE` `VERB: V n` `WRITTEN` `N-COUNT` `ADJ: ADJ n` `N-COUNT` `ADJ`

crest·fallen /'krestfɔːlən/. If you look **crestfallen**, you look sad and disappointed about something. `ADJ-GRADED`

cret·in /'kretɪn, AM 'kriːtən/ **cretins**. If you call someone a **cretin**, you think they are very stupid; an offensive word. ♦ **cret·in·ous** /'kretɪnəs, AM 'kriːtənəs/. `N-COUNT` `PRAGMATICS` `RUDE` `ADJ-GRADED`

cre·vasse /krɪ'væs/ **crevasses**. A **crevasse** is a large, deep crack in thick ice or rock. `N-COUNT`

crev·ice /'krevɪs/ **crevices**. A **crevice** is a narrow crack or gap, especially in a rock. `N-COUNT`

crew /kruː/ **crews, crewing, crewed. 1** The **crew** of a ship, an aircraft, or a spacecraft is the people who work on it and operate it. *...the crew of the space shuttle Endeavour... The surviving crew members were ferried ashore.* **2** If you **crew** a boat, you work on it as part of the crew. *There were to be five teams of three crewing the boat.* **3** A **crew** is a group of people with special technical skills who work together on a task or project. *...a two-man film crew.* **4** You can use **crew** to refer to a group of people you disapprove of. *...the motley crew of failed and aspiring actors.* `N-COLL-COUNT` `VERB` `V n` `N-COUNT` `N-COLL-SING` `PRAGMATICS` `INFORMAL`

'crew cut, crew cuts; also spelled **crewcut**. A **crew cut** is a man's hairstyle in which his hair is cut very short. `N-COUNT`

crew·man /'kruːmæn/ **crewmen**. A **crewman** is a member of a crew. `N-COUNT`

'crew neck, crew necks; also spelled **crewneck**. A **crew neck** or a **crew neck** sweater is a sweater with a round neck. `N-COUNT`

crib /krɪb/ **cribs, cribbing, cribbed. 1** A **crib** is a baby's cot. **2** If you **crib**, you copy something that someone else has written and pretend that it is your own work. *You have been cribbing from Bennett... He had been caught cribbing in an exam.* `N-COUNT` `VERB` `V from n` `V` `Also V n from n`

'crib death, crib deaths. Crib death is the sudden death of a baby while it is asleep, although the baby had not previously been ill. The usual British term is **cot death**. `N-VAR` `AMERICAN`

crick /krɪk/ **cricks**. If you have a **crick** in your neck or in your back, you have a pain caused by muscles becoming stiff. `N-COUNT`

crick·et /'krɪkɪt/ **crickets. 1 Cricket** is an outdoor game played between two teams. Players try to score points, called runs, by hitting a ball with a wooden bat. **2** If you say that someone's behaviour is **not cricket**, you mean that they have not behaved in a fair or honourable way. *Their treatment of staff is definitely not cricket.* **3** A **cricket** is a small jumping insect that produces short, loud sounds by rubbing its wings together. See picture headed **insects**. `N-UNCOUNT` `PHRASE` `DATED` `N-COUNT`

crick·et·er /'krɪkɪtə/ **cricketers**. A **cricketer** is a person who plays cricket. `N-COUNT`

crick·et·ing /'krɪkɪtɪŋ/. **Cricketing** means relating to cricket. *...his brief cricketing career.* `ADJ: ADJ n`

cri·er /kraɪə/. See **town crier**.

cri·key /'kraɪki/. Some people say **crikey** in order to express surprise, especially at something they think is not very pleasant. `EXCLAM` `PRAGMATICS` `INFORMAL, BRITISH`

crime /kraɪm/ **crimes. 1** A **crime** is an illegal action or activity for which a person can be punished by law. *...the scene of the crime. ...the growing problem of organised crime.* **2** If you say that doing something is a **crime**, you think it is very wrong or a serious mistake. *It would be a crime to travel all the way to Australia and not stop in Sydney.* `N-VAR` `N-COUNT` `PRAGMATICS`

'crime wave; also spelled **crimewave**. When more crimes than usual are committed in a place, you can say there is a **crime wave** there. `N-SING`

crimi·nal /'krɪmɪnəl/ **criminals. 1** A **criminal** is a person who has committed a crime, or a person who often commits crimes. *A group of gunmen attacked a prison and set free nine criminals.* **2 Criminal** means connected with crime. *He had a criminal record for petty theft. ...criminal assault.* ♦ **crimi·nal·ity** /ˌkrɪmɪ'næləti/ *...a tenfold increase of criminality.* ♦ **crimi·nal·ly** *...a hospital for the criminally insane.* **3** If you describe an action as **criminal**, you think it is very wrong or a serious mistake. *A full-scale dispute involving strikes would be criminal.* ♦ **criminally** *It was, he had said, criminally irresponsible.* `N-COUNT` `ADJ` `N-UNCOUNT` `ADV` `ADJ` `PRAGMATICS` `ADV: ADV adj`

crimi·nal·ize /'krɪmɪnəlaɪz/ **criminalizes, criminalizing, criminalized**; also spelled **criminalise** in British English. If a government **criminalises** an action or person, it officially declares that the action or the person's behaviour is illegal. *...a deliberate campaign to criminalise members of the former Communist leadership.* `VERB` `V n`

crimi·nol·ogy /ˌkrɪmɪ'nɒlədʒi/. **Criminology** is the scientific study of crime and criminals. ♦ **crimi·nolo·gist** /ˌkrɪmɪ'nɒlədʒɪst/ **criminologists** *...a criminologist at the University of Montreal.* `N-UNCOUNT` `N-COUNT`

crimp /krɪmp/ **crimps, crimping, crimped. 1** If you **crimp** something such as fabric or pastry, you make small folds in it. *Crimp the edges to seal them tightly.* **2** To **crimp** something means to restrict or reduce it. *The dollar's recent strength is crimping overseas sales.* `VERB` `V n` `VERB` `V n` `AMERICAN`

Crimp·lene /'krɪmpliːn/. **Crimplene** is an artificial fabric used for making clothes which does not crease easily. **Crimplene** is a trademark. `N-UNCOUNT`

crim·son /'krɪmzən/ **crimsons. 1** Something that is **crimson** is deep red in colour. **2** If a person goes **crimson**, their face becomes red because they are angry or embarrassed. `COLOUR` `ADJ`

cringe /krɪndʒ/ **cringes, cringing, cringed**. If you **cringe** at something, you feel embarrassment or disgusted, and perhaps show this in your expression or by making a slight movement. *Chris had cringed at the thought of using her own family for publicity.* `VERB` `V atn`

crin·kle /'krɪŋkəl/ **crinkles, crinkling, crinkled**. If something **crinkles** or if you **crinkle** it, it becomes slightly creased or folded. *When she laughs, she crinkles her perfectly-formed nose.* ▶ **Crinkles** are small creases or folds. `V-ERG: V` `V n` `N-COUNT`

crin·kly /'krɪŋkli/. A **crinkly** object has many small creases or folds in it. *...her big crinkly face.* `ADJ-GRADED`

crino·line /'krɪnəlɪn/ **crinolines**. A **crinoline** was a frame of hoops worn as an undergarment by women in the 19th century to make their skirts very full. `N-COUNT`

crip·ple /'krɪpəl/ **cripples, crippling, crippled. 1** A person with a physical disability or a serious permanent injury is sometimes referred to as a **cripple**. Some people find this use offensive. *Crutches can help a cripple get around.* **2** If someone is **crippled** by an injury, it is so serious that they can never move their body properly again. *Mr Easton was seriously crippled in an accident.* **3** If you describe someone as an emotional **cripple**, you mean that they have a psychological or emotional problem which prevents them from living a normal life. **4** If something **cripples** a person, it causes them severe psychological or emotional problems. *Howard wanted to be a popular singer, but stage fright* `N-COUNT` `VERB` `beV-ed` `N-COUNT` `VERB` `V n`

crippled him. **5** To **cripple** a machine, organization, or system means to damage it severely or prevent it from working properly. *A total cut-off of supplies would cripple Jordan's economy.* — VERB V n

crip·pling /ˈkrɪplɪŋ/. **1** A **crippling** illness or disability is one that severely damages your health or body. *Arthritis and rheumatism are prominent crippling diseases.* **2** If you say that an action, policy, or situation has a **crippling** effect on something, you mean it has a very harmful effect. *The high cost of capital has a crippling effect on many small American high-tech firms.* ◆ **crip·pling·ly** *...cripplingly high interest rates.* — ◆◇◇◇ ADJ: ADJ n / ADJ / ADV

cri·sis /ˈkraɪsɪs/ **crises** /ˈkraɪsiːz/. A **crisis** is a situation in which something or someone is affected by one or more very serious problems. *Natural disasters have obviously contributed to the continent's economic crisis. ...someone to turn to in moments of crisis.* — ◆◆◆◇ N-VAR

crisp /krɪsp/ **crisper, crispest; crisps, crisping, crisped. 1** **Crisp** food is pleasantly hard and crunchy. *Bake the potatoes for 15 minutes, till they're nice and crisp. ...crisp lettuce.* ◆ **crisp·ness** *The pizza base retains its crispness without becoming brittle.* ◆ **crisp·ly** *...crisply fried onion rings.* **2** If food **crisps** or if you **crisp** it, it becomes pleasantly hard, because you have heated it at a high temperature. *Cook the bacon until it begins to crisp.* **3** **Crisps** are very thin slices of potato that have been fried until they are hard, dry, and crispy. The American word is **chips** or **potato chips. 4** **Crisp** weather is pleasantly fresh, cold, and dry. **5** **Crisp** cloth or paper is clean and has no creases in it. *He wore a panama hat and a crisp white suit.* ◆ **crisply** *...his crisply pressed suit.* **6** Leaves or snow that make a crunching noise when you walk on them can be described as **crisp**. *He crunched through the crisp snow.* **7** If you describe someone's writing or speech as **crisp**, you mean they write or speak very clearly, without mentioning unnecessary details. This may make them seem unfriendly. *'Very well,' I said, adopting a crisp authoritative tone.* ◆ **crisply** *'I'm not a journalist,' said Mary Ann crisply.* — ◆◆◇◇ ADJ-GRADED / N-UNCOUNT / ADV-GRADED: ADV adj/-ed V-ERG V / N-COUNT BRITISH / ADJ-GRADED / ADV-GRADED ADJ-GRADED / ADJ-GRADED / ADV-GRADED

crisp·bread /ˈkrɪspbred/ **crispbreads. Crispbread** is thin dry biscuits made from wheat or rye. It is often eaten instead of bread by people who want to lose weight. — N-VAR BRITISH

crispy /ˈkrɪspi/ **crispier, crispiest. Crispy** food is pleasantly hard and crunchy. *...crispy bread rolls.* — ADJ-GRADED PRAGMATICS

criss-cross /ˈkrɪs krɒs, AM - krɔːs/ **crisscrosses, criss-crossing, criss-crossed;** also spelled **crisscross. 1** If a person or thing **criss-crosses** an area, they travel from one side to the other and back again many times, following different routes. If a number of things **criss-cross** an area, they cross it, and cross over each other. *They criss-crossed the country by bus.* **2** If two sets of lines or things **criss-cross**, they cross over each other. *The roads here are quite a maze, criss-crossing one another in a fashion that at times defies logic.* **3** A **criss-cross** pattern or design consists of lines crossing each other. *Slash the tops of the loaves with a sharp serrated knife in a criss-cross pattern.* — ◆◇◇◇ VERB V n / V-RECIP: pl-n V V pron-recip Also V n / ADJ: ADJ n

cri·teri·on /kraɪˈtɪəriən/ **criteria** /kraɪˈtɪəriə/. A **criterion** is a factor on which you judge or decide something. *The most important criterion for entry is that applicants must design and make their own work.* — ◆◆◇◇ N-COUNT

crit·ic /ˈkrɪtɪk/ **critics. 1** A **critic** is a person who writes reviews and expresses opinions about things such as books, films, music, or art. *Mather was film critic on the Daily Telegraph.* **2** Someone who is a **critic** of a person or system disapproves of them and criticizes them publicly. *Her critics accused her of caring only about success.* — ◆◆◆◇ N-COUNT / N-COUNT

criti·cal /ˈkrɪtɪkəl/. **1** A **critical** time, factor, or situation is extremely important. *The incident happened at a critical point in the campaign... How you finance a business is critical to the success of your venture.* ◆ **criti·cal·ly** /ˈkrɪtɪkli/ *Economic prosper-* — ◆◆◆◇ ADJ-GRADED / ADV-GRADED:

ity depends critically on an open world trading system. **2** A **critical** situation is very serious and dangerous. *The German authorities are considering an airlift if the situation becomes critical.* ◆ **critically** *Moscow is running critically low on food supplies.* **3** If a person is **critical** or in a **critical** condition in hospital, they are seriously ill. ◆ **critically** *She was critically ill.* **4** To be **critical** of someone or something means to criticize them. *...critical remarks.* ◆ **critically** *She spoke critically of Laura.* **5** A **critical** approach to something involves examining and judging it carefully. *...the critical analysis of political ideas.* ◆ **critically** *Wyman watched them critically.* **6** If something or someone receives **critical** acclaim, critics say that it is very good. *The show was also a resounding critical success.* — ADV with v, ADV adj ADJ / ADJ / ADV / ADJ / ADV / ADJ-GRADED ADV-GRADED / ADJ: ADJ n ADV-GRADED / ADV-GRADED ADJ: ADJ n

critical 'mass. 1 The **critical mass** of a substance is the minimum amount of it that is needed for a nuclear chain reaction. **2** A **critical mass** of something is an amount of it that makes it possible for something to happen or continue. *Only in this way can the critical mass of participation be reached.* — N-SING TECHNICAL / N-SING: also no det

criti·cise /ˈkrɪtɪsaɪz/. See **criticize**.

criti·cism /ˈkrɪtɪsɪzəm/ **criticisms. 1 Criticism** is the action of expressing disapproval of something or someone. A **criticism** is a statement that expresses disapproval. *...the criticism that the English do not truly care about their children.* **2 Criticism** is a serious examination and judgement of something such as a book or play. *...literary criticism.* — ◆◆◆◇ N-VAR / N-UNCOUNT

criti·cize /ˈkrɪtɪsaɪz/ **criticizes, criticizing, criticized;** also spelled **criticise** in British English. If you **criticize** someone or something, you express your disapproval of them by saying what you think is wrong with them. *The regime has been harshly criticized for serious human rights violations.* — ◆◆◆◇ VERB V n for/-ing

cri·tique /krɪˈtiːk/ **critiques.** A **critique** is a written examination and judgement of a situation or of a person's work or ideas. *...a feminist critique of Victorian lady novelists.* — N-COUNT FORMAL

crit·ter /ˈkrɪtə/ **critters.** A **critter** is a living creature. *...little furry critters... Look at the poor critter tryin' to get through that door.* — N-COUNT AMERICAN, INFORMAL

croak /krəʊk/ **croaks, croaking, croaked. 1** When a frog or bird **croaks**, it makes a harsh, low sound. **2** If someone **croaks** something, they say it in a hoarse, rough voice. *Tiller moaned and managed to croak, 'Help me.'* ▶ Also a noun. *His voice was just a croak.* — VERB: V / VERB: V n V with quote / N-COUNT

cro·chet /ˈkrəʊʃeɪ, AM krəʊˈʃeɪ/ **crochets, crocheting, crocheted. 1 Crochet** is a way of making cloth out of cotton or wool by using a needle with a small hook at the end. **2** If you **crochet**, you make cloth by using a needle with a small hook at the end. *Ma and I crocheted new quilts.* — N-UNCOUNT / VERB: V n

crock /krɒk/ **crocks. 1** A **crock** is an earthenware pot or jar. *...an earthenware bread crock.* **2** If you describe someone as an old **crock**, you mean that they are old and weak. *But you don't want some old crock like me.* — N-COUNT / N-COUNT DATED / N-COUNT BRITISH, INFORMAL

crock·ery /ˈkrɒkəri/. **Crockery** is the plates, cups, saucers, and dishes that you use at mealtimes. — N-UNCOUNT BRITISH

croco·dile /ˈkrɒkədaɪl/ **crocodiles.** A **crocodile** is a large reptile with a long body and strong jaws. Crocodiles live in rivers and eat meat. — ◆◇◇◇ N-COUNT

crocodile 'tears. If you say that someone is crying **crocodile tears**, you mean that their tears and other expressions of grief are not sincere. — N-PLURAL

cro·cus /ˈkrəʊkəs/ **crocuses. Crocuses** are small white, yellow, or purple flowers that are grown in parks and gardens in the early spring. — N-COUNT

croft /krɒft, AM krɔːft/ **crofts.** In Scotland, a **croft** is a small piece of land which is owned and farmed by one family and which provides them with food. — N-COUNT

croft·er /ˈkrɒftə, AM ˈkrɔːft-/ **crofters.** In Scotland, a **crofter** is the owner or tenant of a croft or small farm. — N-COUNT

croft·ing /ˈkrɒftɪŋ, AM ˈkrɔːft-/. In Scotland, **crofting** is the activity of farming on small pieces of land. — N-UNCOUNT

crois·sant /'kwæsɒn, AM kwɑː'sɑːn/ **croissants.** N-VAR
Croissants are small crescent-shaped pieces of
sweetened bread that are eaten for breakfast.

crone /krəʊn/ **crones. 1** A crone is an old woman. N-COUNT
The shabby old crone took off her shoes. **2** If you re- LITERARY
fer to a woman as a **crone**, you mean that she is old N-COUNT
and ugly; an offensive use. PRAGMATICS

cro·ny /'krəʊni/ **cronies.** Your cronies are the ◆◇◇◇◇
friends who you spend a lot of time with. ...*drinking* N-COUNT
sessions with his business cronies. INFORMAL

cro·ny·ism /'krəʊniɪzəm/. If you accuse someone N-UNCOUNT
in authority of **cronyism**, you mean that they try to PRAGMATICS
use their power or authority to get jobs for their JOURNALISM
friends.

crook /krʊk/ **crooks, crooking, crooked. 1** A ◆◆◇◇◇
crook is a dishonest person or a criminal. *The man* N-COUNT
is a crook and a liar. INFORMAL
2 The crook of your arm or leg is the soft inside part N-COUNT
where you bend your elbow or knee. **3** If you **crook** VERB
your arm or finger, you bend it. *He crooked his finger:* V n
'Come forward,' he said.
4 A crook is a long pole with a large hook at the end. A N-COUNT
crook is carried by a bishop in religious ceremonies,
or by a shepherd.

crooked /'krʊkɪd/. **1** If you describe something as ◆◇◇◇◇
crooked, especially something that is usually ADJ-GRADED
straight, you mean that it is bent or twisted. ...*the*
crooked line of his broken nose. **2** A **crooked** smile ADJ-GRADED
is uneven and bigger on one side than the other.
Polly gave her a crooked grin. ♦ **crook·ed·ly** *Nick* ADV
was smiling crookedly at her. **3** If you describe a ADJ
person or an activity as **crooked**, you mean that INFORMAL
they are dishonest or criminal. ...*crooked business*
deals.

croon /kruːn/ **croons, crooning, crooned. 1** ◆◇◇◇◇
If you **croon**, you sing or hum quietly and VERB: V
gently. *Lewis began to croon another Springsteen* V n
song. **2** If you say someone **croons** something, VERB: V
you mean they say it in a soft gentle voice. *The* V n
man was crooning soft words of encouragement to WRITTEN
his wife.

croon·er /'kruːnə/ **crooners.** A **crooner** was a N-COUNT
male singer who sang sentimental songs, especially
the love songs of the 1930s and 1940s.

crop /krɒp/ **crops, cropping, cropped. 1** Crops ◆◆◆◇◇
are plants such as wheat and potatoes that are N-COUNT
grown in large quantities for food. *Rice farmers here*
still plant and harvest their crops by hand. • See
also **cash crop. 2** The plants or fruits that are col- N-COUNT
lected at harvest time are referred to as a **crop.** *This*
year's corn crop should be about 8 percent more than
last year. **3** When a plant **crops**, it produces fruits or VERB: V
parts which people want. **4** You can refer to a group N-SING:
of people or things that have appeared together as a N of n
crop of people or things. ...*the present crop of books* INFORMAL
and documentaries about Marilyn Monroe. **5** • **the**
cream of the crop: see **cream.**
6 When an animal such as a cow or horse **crops** leaves VERB: V n
or plants, it eats them. **7** To **crop** someone's hair VERB: V n
means to cut it short. ♦ **cropped** *She had cropped* ADJ
grey hair. **8** A **crop** is a short hairstyle. ...*a boyish crop.* N-COUNT
9 If you **crop** a photograph, you cut part of it off, in or- VERB
der to get rid of part of the picture or to be able to V n
frame it. *I decided to crop the picture just above the*
waterline.

crop up. If something **crops up**, it appears or hap- PHRASAL VB
pens, usually unexpectedly. *Problems will crop up* V P
and hit you before you are ready.

cropped /krɒpt/. **Cropped** items of clothing are ◆◇◇◇◇
shorter than normal. *Women athletes wear cropped* ADJ
tops and tight shorts. • See also **crop.**

crop·per /'krɒpə/. If you say that someone **has** PHRASE
come a cropper, you mean that they have had an INFORMAL
unexpected and embarrassing failure. *Several com-*
panies that made use of elastic accounting practices
have since come a cropper.

cro·quet /'krəʊkeɪ, AM krəʊ'keɪ/. Croquet is a game N-UNCOUNT
in which the players use long-handled wooden mallets to hit balls through metal arches stuck in a
lawn.

cross /krɒs, AM krɔːs/ **crosses, crossing,** ◆◆◆◆◇
crossed. 1 If you **cross** something such as a room, VERB
road, or area of land, you move to the other side of V n
it. If you **cross** to a place, you move over a room, V to/into n
road, or area in order to reach that place. *Nine Al-*
banians have crossed the border into Greece... Egan
crossed to the drinks cabinet and poured a Scotch.
2 A road, railway, or bridge that **crosses** an area of VERB
land or water passes over it. *The Defford to* V n
Eckington road crosses the river. **3** When lines or V-RECIP:
roads **cross**, they meet and go across each other. pl-n V
...*where the pilgrimage route crosses the road to* V n
Quimper. **4** If someone or something **crosses** a lim- VERB
it or boundary, for example the limit of acceptable V n
behaviour, they go beyond it. *When prep-school stu-*
dents buy cocaine to sell to their classmates, they
have crossed the line from pranks to delinquency.
5 If an expression **crosses** your face, it appears VERB
there briefly. *A mischievous look crosses his face.* V n
6 A **cross** is a shape or object that consists of a vertical WRITTEN
line or piece with a shorter horizontal line or piece N-COUNT
across it. See picture headed **shapes.** ...*a cross on a sil-*
ver chain. **7** If Christians **cross** themselves, they make VERB:
the sign of a cross by moving their hand across the top V pron-refl
half of their body. **8** If you **cross** your arms, legs, or VERB: V n
fingers, you put one of them on top of the other. *He* V-ed
was sitting there in the living room with his legs
crossed. **9** A **cross** is a written mark in the shape of an N-COUNT
X. You can use it, for example, to indicate that an an-
swer to a question is wrong, to mark the position of
something on a map, or to indicate your vote on a bal-
lot paper. **10** If a cheque **is crossed**, two parallel lines VB: usu
are drawn across it to indicate that it must be paid passive
into a bank account and cannot be cashed. *Postal or-* be V-ed
ders should be crossed and made payable to Newmar- BRITISH
ket Promotions.
11 If you describe something as a **cross** that someone N-COUNT
has to bear, you mean it is a problem or disadvantage
which they have to deal with or endure. *My wife is*
much cleverer than me; it is a cross I have to bear.
12 If you dare to **cross** someone who is likely to get VERB
angry, you dare to oppose them or refuse to do what V n
they want. *If you ever cross him, forget it, you're*
finished.
13 Something that is **a cross between** two things is N-SING:
neither one thing nor the other, but a mixture of both. a N between
'Ha!' It was a cross between a laugh and a bark. pl-n
14 In sports such as football and hockey, a **cross** is the N-COUNT
passing of the ball from the side of the field to a player
in the centre, usually in front of the goal.
15 See also **crossing.** • to **cross** your **fingers:** see **fin-**
ger. • **cross** my **heart:** see **heart.** • to **cross** your
mind: see **mind.** • people's **paths cross:** see **path.**
• to **cross swords:** see **sword.**

cross off. If you **cross off** a word on a list, you draw a PHRASAL VB
line through it, because you have decided that it no V P noun
longer belongs on the list. *They have enough trouble* Also V n P
finding nutritious food without crossing meat off their
shopping lists.

cross out. If you **cross out** words on a page, you PHRASAL VB
draw a line through them, because they are wrong or V P noun
because you want to change them. *He crossed out 'fel-* Also V n P
low subjects', and instead inserted 'fellow citizens'.

cross /krɒs, AM krɔːs/ **crosser, crossest.** Some- ◆◆◇◇◇
one who is **cross** is rather angry or irritated. *I'm ter-* ADJ-GRADED
ribly cross with him. ♦ **cross·ly** *'No, no, no,' Morris* ADV-GRADED:
said crossly. ADV with v

cross·bar /'krɒsbɑː, AM 'krɔːs-/ **crossbars. 1** A N-COUNT
crossbar is a horizontal piece of wood attached to
two upright pieces, for example the top part of the
goal in football. **2** The **crossbar** of a man's or boy's N-COUNT
bicycle is the horizontal metal bar between the
handlebars and the saddle. See picture headed **car**
and bicycle.

cross·bones /'krɒsbəʊnz, AM 'krɔːs-/. See **skull**
and crossbones.

,cross-'border. 1 Cross-border trade occurs be- ◆◇◇◇◇
tween companies in different countries. *More* ADJ: ADJ n

cross-border deals will take place. **2 Cross-border** attacks involve crossing a border and going a short way into another country. *...a cross-border raid.* `ADJ: ADJ n`

cross·bow /ˈkrɒsbəʊ, AM ˈkrɔːs-/ **crossbows.** A **crossbow** is a weapon consisting of a small bow fixed across a piece of wood, which releases an arrow with great power when you press a trigger. `N-COUNT`

'cross-breed, cross-breeds, cross-breeding, cross-bred; also spelled **crossbreed. 1** If one species of animal or plant **is cross-bred** with another or if they **cross-breed**, they reproduce, and new or different animals or plants are produced. *...attempts to cross-breed it with other potatoes... Dr Russel is creating an elite herd by cross-breeding goats from around the globe.* ♦ **cross-breeding** *...centuries of crossbreeding.* **2** A **cross-breed** is an animal that is the result of cross-breeding. `V-RECIP-ERG: V with n / V n with n / V pl-n` `N-UNCOUNT` `N-COUNT`

,cross-'Channel; also **cross-channel. Cross-Channel** travel is travel across the English Channel. *...the cross-channel ferry from Ostend to Dover.* `ADJ: ADJ n`

,cross-'check, cross-checks, cross-checking, cross-checked. If you **cross-check** information, you check that it is correct using a different method or source from the one originally used. *His version will later be cross-checked against that of the university... They want to ensure such claims are justified by cross-checking with other records.* `VERB: V n / be V-ed against n / V with n`

,cross-'country. 1 Cross-country is the sport of running, riding, or skiing across open countryside. *...the world cross-country championships.* **2** A **cross-country** journey involves less important roads or railway lines, or takes you from one side of a country to the other. *...cross-country rail services.* ▶ Also an adverb. *I drove cross-country in his van.* `N-UNCOUNT` `ADJ: ADJ n` `ADV`

,cross-'cultural. Cross-cultural means involving two or more different cultures. *...cross-cultural conflict.* `ADJ: ADJ n`

'cross-current, cross-currents. You can refer to conflicting ideas or traditions as **cross-currents**. *...the cross-currents within the Conservative Party.* `N-COUNT`

,cross-'dress, cross-dresses, cross-dressing, cross-dressed. If someone **cross-dresses**, they wear the clothes of the opposite sex, especially for sexual pleasure. ♦ **cross-dressing** *Myra tolerated Clive's cross-dressing.* `VERB: V` `N-UNCOUNT`

,cross-ex'amine, cross-examines, cross-examining, cross-examined. When a lawyer **cross-examines** someone during a trial or hearing, he or she questions them about the evidence that they have given. *You are liable to be cross-examined mercilessly about the assault.* ♦ **cross-examina·tion** /ˌkrɒs ɪgzæmɪˈneɪʃən/ **cross-examinations** *...the cross-examination of a witness.* `VERB: V n / be V-ed about n` `N-VAR`

'cross-eyed. Someone who is **cross-eyed** has eyes that seem to look towards each other. `ADJ`

cross·fire /ˈkrɒsfaɪə, AM ˈkrɔːs-/; also spelled **cross-fire. 1 Crossfire** is gunfire that comes from two or more different directions and passes through the same area. **2** If you are **caught in the crossfire**, you become involved in an unpleasant situation in which people are arguing with each other. `N-UNCOUNT` `PHRASE`

cross·ing /ˈkrɒsɪŋ, AM ˈkrɔːs-/ **crossings. 1** A **crossing** is a journey by boat or ship to a place on the other side of a sea. *The vessel docked in Swansea after a ten-hour crossing.* **2** A **crossing** is the same as a **pedestrian crossing**. ● See also **pelican crossing, zebra crossing. 3** A **crossing** is the same as a **level crossing**. `N-COUNT` `N-COUNT` `N-COUNT`

,cross-'legged. If someone is sitting **cross-legged**, they are sitting on the floor with their legs bent so that their knees point outwards. `ADV: ADV after v`

cross·over /ˈkrɒsəʊvə, AM ˈkrɔːs-/ **crossovers. 1** A **crossover** of one style and another, especially in music or fashion, is a combination of the two different styles. *...the contemporary crossover of pop, jazz and funk.* **2** A **crossover** is a change from one type of activity to another. *The crossover from actress to singer is easier than singer to actress.* `N-VAR` `N-SING`

,cross-'purposes; also spelled **cross purposes.** If people are **at cross-purposes**, they are talking about or trying to achieve different things without realizing it. `PHRASE`

,cross-qu'estion, cross-questions, cross-questioning, cross-questioned. If you **cross-question** someone, you ask them a lot of questions about something. *The police came back and cross-questioned Des.* `VERB: V n`

,cross-'reference, cross-references, cross-referencing, cross-referenced. 1 A **cross-reference** is a note in a book which tells you that there is relevant or more detailed information in another part of the book. **2** If something such as a book **is cross-referenced**, cross-references are put in it. *Nearly 2,300 plant lists have been checked and cross-referenced.* `N-COUNT` `VB: usu passive be V-ed`

cross·roads /ˈkrɒsrəʊdz, AM ˈkrɔːs-/; **crossroads** is both the singular and the plural form. **1** A **crossroads** is a place where two roads meet and cross each other. **2** If you say that something is at a **crossroads**, you mean that it has reached a very important stage in its development where it could go one way or another. *They had reached a crossroads in their relationship.* `◆◇◇◇` `N-COUNT` `N-SING`

'cross-section, cross-sections. 1 A **cross-section** of things or people is a group of them that you think is typical or representative of them all. *I was surprised at the cross-section of people there.* **2** A **cross-section** of an object is what you would see if you could cut straight through the middle of it. *...a cross-section of an airplane.* `◆◇◇◇` `N-COUNT` `N-COUNT: also in N`

'cross-stitch; also spelled **cross stitch. Cross-stitch** is a type of decorative sewing where one stitch crosses another. `N-UNCOUNT`

cross·wind /ˈkrɒswɪnd, AM ˈkrɔːs-/ **crosswinds;** also spelled **cross-wind.** A **crosswind** is a strong wind that blows across the direction that vehicles, boats, or aircraft are travelling, and makes it difficult for them to keep moving steadily forward. `N-COUNT`

cross·wise /ˈkrɒswaɪz, AM ˈkrɔːs-/. **Crosswise** means diagonally across something. *Rinse and slice the courgettes crosswise.* `ADV: ADV after v`

cross·word /ˈkrɒswɜːd, AM ˈkrɔːs-/ **crosswords.** A **crossword** or **crossword puzzle** is a word game in which you work out the answers to clues, and write the answers in the white squares of a pattern of small black and white squares. `◆◆◇◇` `N-COUNT`

crotch /krɒtʃ/ **crotches. 1** Your **crotch** is the part of your body between the tops of your legs. *Glover kicked him hard in the crotch.* **2** The **crotch** of a pair of trousers or pants is the part that covers the area between the tops of your legs. `N-COUNT` `N-COUNT`

crouch /kraʊtʃ/ **crouches, crouching, crouched. 1** If you **are crouching**, your legs are bent under you so that you are close to the ground and leaning forward slightly. *We were crouching in the bushes... The man was crouched behind the Mercedes.* ▶ Also a noun. *They walked in a crouch.* ▶ **Crouch down** means the same as **crouch**. *He crouched down and reached under the mattress... He crouched down beside him.* **2** If you **crouch over** something, you bend over it so that you are very near to it. *I crouch over a cup of tea in my unheated study.* `◆◆◇◇` `VERB` `V prep/adv V-ed` `N-SING` `PHRASAL VB V P / V P prep/adv` `VERB V prep/adv`

crou·pi·er /ˈkruːpieɪ, AM -iər/ **croupiers.** A **croupier** is the person in charge of a gambling table in a casino. `N-COUNT`

crou·ton /ˈkruːtɒn/ **croutons.** Croutons are small pieces of toasted or fried bread that are added to soup just before you eat it. `N-COUNT`

crow /krəʊ/ **crows, crowing, crowed. 1** A **crow** is a large black bird which makes a loud, harsh noise. **2** When a cock **crows**, it utters a loud sound, often early in the morning. **3** If you say that someone is **crowing** about something they have achieved, you mean that they keep talking about it proudly in a way that annoys you. *We've seen them all crowing that socialism's dead.* **4** If someone **crows**, they make `◆◇◇◇` `N-COUNT` `VERB: V` `VERB: V about/over n` `PRAGMATICS V that` `INFORMAL VERB`

happy sounds or say something happily. *She was crowing with delight... 'I'm not sure I've ever driven a better lap,' crowed a delighted Mansell.* — V with n / V with quote

5 If you say that a place is a particular distance away **as the crow flies**, you mean that it is that distance away measured in a straight line. *I live at Mesa, Washington, about 10 miles as the crow flies from Hanford.* — PHRASE

crow·bar /'krəʊbɑː/ **crowbars.** A **crowbar** is a heavy iron bar which is used as a lever. — N-COUNT

crowd /kraʊd/ **crowds, crowding, crowded.** ◆◆◆◇
1 A **crowd** is a large group of people who have gathered together, for example to watch or listen to something. *Crowds of people were shopping for Mothers' Day.* **2** A particular **crowd** is a group of friends, or a set of people with the same interests or occupation. *All the old crowd have come out for this occasion.* — N-COLL-COUNT / N-COUNT INFORMAL
3 When people **crowd** around someone or something, they gather closely together around them. *Police blocked off the road as hotel staff and guests crowded around.* **4** If people **crowd** into a place or **are crowded** into it, large numbers of them enter it so that it becomes very full. *One group of journalists were crowded into a minibus.* **5** If a group of people **crowd** a place, there are so many of them there that it is full. *Thousands of demonstrators crowded the streets.* **6** If people **crowd** you, they stand very closely around you trying to see or speak to you, so that you start to feel uncomfortable. — VERB: V round / around n / V round / around n / V-ERG: V into n / be V-ed into n / VERB V n / VERB: V n

crowd in. If problems or thoughts **crowd in** on you, you have a lot of them at the same time, so that they occupy all your attention and make you feel unable to escape. *Thoughts crowded in and images flashed into her mind.* — PHRASAL VB V P on n V P

crowd out. If one thing **crowds out** another, it is so successful or widespread that the other thing does not have the opportunity to be successful or exist. *In the 1980s American exports crowded out European films.* — PHRASAL VB V P noun Also V n P

crowd·ed /'kraʊdɪd/ **1** If a place is **crowded**, it is full of people. *The old town square was crowded with people.* **2** A **crowded** area or town has a lot of people living in it. *...a crowded city of 2 million.* **3** If your timetable, life, or mind is **crowded**, it is full of events, activities, or thoughts. *...a long life crowded with incident.* — ADJ-GRADED / ADJ-GRADED / ADJ-GRADED

'crowd-pleaser, crowd-pleasers; also spelled **crowd pleaser.** If you describe a performer, politician, or sports player as a **crowd-pleaser**, you mean they always please their audience. You can also describe an action or event as a **crowd-pleaser**. — N-COUNT

'crowd-puller, crowd-pullers; also spelled **crowd puller.** If you describe a performer or event as a **crowd-puller**, you mean that they attract a large audience. *The exhibition is hardly a crowd-puller.* — N-COUNT BRITISH

crown /kraʊn/ **crowns, crowning, crowned.** ◆◆◆◇
1 A **crown** is a circular ornament, usually made of gold and jewels, which a king or queen wears on their head at official ceremonies. **2** When a king or queen **is crowned**, a crown is placed on their head as part of a ceremony in which they are officially made king or queen. *Juan Carlos was crowned king.* **3** A country's monarchy is referred to as **the Crown** when it is regarded as an institution rather than as an individual person. *The prosecutor in British criminal cases is called the Crown. ...the sovereignty of the Crown.* **4** If one thing **crowns** another, it is on top of it. *Another rugged castle crowns the cliffs and crags.* **5** Your **crown** is the top part of your head, at the back. *He laid his hand gently on the crown of her head.* **6** The **crown** of a hat is the part which covers the top of your head. **7** A **crown** is an artificial top piece fixed over a broken or decayed tooth. **8** An achievement or event that **crowns** something makes it perfect, successful, or complete. *It is an important moment, crowning the efforts of the Cup organisers.* **9** If you **crown** your career with a success or achievement, you have a final success or achievement which is greater than all the others you have had. *He* — N-COUNT / VERB: be V-ed / be V-ed n / N-PROPER: the N / VERB V n LITERARY / N-COUNT / N-COUNT / N-COUNT / VERB V n / VERB V n with n Also V n by -ing

went on to crown a distinguished career in radio and television with his book 'The Price of Victory'. **10** In sport, a **crown** is a title or championship. *...his dream of a fourth Wimbledon crown.* — N-COUNT

,Crown 'Court, Crown Courts. In England and Wales, a **Crown Court** is a court in which criminal cases are tried by a judge and jury rather than by a magistrate. — ◆◆◇◇ N-COUNT

,crown 'jewel, crown jewels. 1 The Crown Jewels consist of the crown, sceptre, and other precious objects which are used on important official occasions by a king or queen. **2** If you describe something as someone's **crown jewel**, you mean it is the most important or valuable thing they have. *The company is also willing to sell 20% of its crown jewel, its credit-card business.* — N-PLURAL: the N / N-COUNT

,Crown 'Prince, Crown Princes. A **Crown Prince** is a prince who will be king of his country when the present king or queen dies. — ◆◇◇◇ N-COUNT

,Crown 'Princess, Crown Princesses. A **Crown Princess** is a princess who is the wife of a Crown Prince, or will be queen of her country when the present king or queen dies. — N-COUNT

'crow's feet. Crow's feet are wrinkles which some older people have at the outside corners of their eyes. — N-PLURAL

cru·cial /'kruːʃəl/. If you describe something as **crucial**, you mean it is extremely important. *Improved consumer confidence is crucial to an economic recovery.* ♦ **cru·cial·ly** *Education is crucially important.* — ◆◆◆◇◇ ADJ-GRADED / ADV-GRADED

cru·ci·ble /'kruːsɪbəl/. A situation in which something is tested or a conflict takes place, and something new is produced as a result, can be referred to as a **crucible**. *The regime served as a crucible for the forging of right-wing ideas and values.* — N-SING LITERARY

cru·ci·fix /'kruːsɪfɪks/ **crucifixes.** A **crucifix** is a cross with a figure of Christ on it. — N-COUNT

Cru·ci·fix·ion /ˌkruːsɪˈfɪkʃən/. The Crucifixion was when Christ was crucified. — ◆◇◇◇◇ N-PROPER: the N

cru·ci·fy /'kruːsɪfaɪ/ **crucifies, crucifying, crucified. 1** If someone **is crucified**, they are killed by being tied or nailed to a cross and left to die. ♦ **cru·ci·fix·ion** /ˌkruːsɪˈfɪkʃən/ **crucifixions** *...the crucifixion of Christians in Rome.* **2** To **crucify** someone means to criticize or punish them severely. *She'll crucify me if she finds you still here.* — ◆◇◇◇◇ VERB: be V-ed / N-VAR / VERB V n INFORMAL

crude /kruːd/ **cruder, crudest; crudes. 1** A **crude** method or measurement is not exact or detailed, but may be useful in a rough, general way. *...an important but crude way of assessing the risk of heart disease.* ♦ **crude·ly** *The donors can be split – a little crudely – into two groups.* **2** If you describe an object that someone has made as **crude**, you mean that it has been made in a very simple way or from very simple parts. *...crude wooden boxes.* ♦ **crudely** *...a crudely carved wooden form.* **3** If you describe someone as **crude**, you disapprove of them because they speak or behave in a rude, offensive, or unsophisticated way. *...crude sexual jokes.* ♦ **crudely** *He hated it when she spoke so crudely.* ♦ **crud·ity** /'kruːdɪti/ *He had not expected such crudity from so sophisticated a minister.* ♦ **crude·ness. 4** Crude substances are in a natural or unrefined state, and have not yet been used in manufacturing processes. *...crude steel.* **5** Crude is the same as crude oil. — ◆◆◇◇ ADJ-GRADED / ADV-GRADED / ADJ-GRADED / ADV-GRADED / ADJ-GRADED PRAGMATICS / ADV-GRADED / N-UNCOUNT / N-UNCOUNT ADJ: ADJ n / N-VAR

,crude 'oil. Crude oil is oil in its natural state before it has been processed or refined. — ◆◇◇◇◇ N-UNCOUNT

crud·ites /'kruːdɪteɪ, AM -'teɪ/. **Crudites** are pieces of raw vegetable, often served before a meal with a dip. — N-PLURAL

cru·el /'kruːəl/ **crueller, cruellest. 1** Someone who is **cruel** deliberately causes pain or distress to people or animals. *Don't you think it's cruel to cage a creature up?* ♦ **cru·el·ly** *Douglas was often cruelly tormented by jealous siblings.* ♦ **cru·el·ty** /'kruːəlti/ **cruelties** *Britain had laws against cruelty to animals but none to protect children.* **2** A situation or event that is **cruel** is very harsh and causes people — ◆◆◇◇ ADJ-GRADED / ADV-GRADED: ADV with v / N-VAR / ADJ-GRADED

distress. *...a cruel world with which they cannot cope.* ♦ **cru·el·ly** *His life has been cruelly shattered by an event not of his own making.* ADV-GRADED

cruise /kruːz/ **cruises, cruising, cruised. 1** A **cruise** is a holiday during which you travel on a ship or boat and visit a number of places. *He and his wife were planning to go on a world cruise.* **2** If you **cruise** a sea, river, or canal, you travel around it or along it on a cruise. *You could cruise to Australia.* ♦ **cruis·ing** *...a 51ft cruising yacht.* **3** If a car, ship, or aircraft **cruises** somewhere, it moves at a constant, comfortable speed. *A black and white police car cruised past.* **4** If a team or sports player **cruises to** victory, they win easily. *She cruised to an easy 6-2, 6-1 victory.* **5** If someone, especially a gay man, **is cruising**, they are looking in public places for a sexual partner. ◆◆◇◇ N-COUNT / VERB: V n, V prep/adv / N-UNCOUNT, VERB V prep/adv / VERB V to n, JOURNALISM VERB: V

cruise 'missile, cruise missiles. A **cruise missile** is a missile which carries a warhead and is guided by a computer. ◆◇◇◇ N-COUNT

cruis·er /ˈkruːzə/ **cruisers. 1** A **cruiser** is a motor boat which has a cabin for people to live or sleep in. *...a large motor cruiser.* **2** A **cruiser** is a large fast warship. ◆◇◇◇ N-COUNT / N-COUNT

cruiser·weight /ˈkruːzəweɪt/ **cruiserweights.** A **cruiserweight** is a professional boxer who weighs between 160 and 175 pounds, or an amateur boxer who weighs between 165 and 179 pounds. N-COUNT

crumb /krʌm/ **crumbs. 1** Crumbs are tiny pieces that fall from bread, biscuits, or cake when you cut or eat them. **2** A **crumb** of something, for example information, is a very small amount of it. *The government were able to draw a few crumbs of comfort from today's unemployment figures.* N-COUNT / N-COUNT

crum·ble /ˈkrʌmbəl/ **crumbles, crumbling, crumbled. 1** If something soft or brittle **crumbles**, it breaks into a lot of small pieces. *Roughly crumble the cheese into a bowl.* **2** If an old building or piece of land **is crumbling**, parts of it keep breaking off. *...a big gray mountain crumbling into the sea.* ► **Crumble away** means the same as **crumble**. *Its apartment blocks, badly in need of restoration, are crumbling away.* **3** If something such as a system, relationship, or hope **crumbles**, it comes to an end. *Their economy crumbled under the weight of United Nations sanctions.* ► **Crumble away** means the same as **crumble**. *Opposition more or less crumbled away.* **4** If someone **crumbles**, they stop resisting or trying to win, or become unable to cope. *Once you stand up to bullies it's amazing how many will crumble.* **5** A **crumble** is a baked pudding made with fruit covered in a crumbly mixture of flour, butter, and sugar. *...apple crumble.* ◆◆◇◇ V-ERG: V, V n / VERB: V, V prep/adv / PHRASAL VB V P / VERB V / PHRASAL VB / VERB V / N VAR BRITISH

crumble away. See **crumble** 2 and 3. PHRASAL VB

crum·bly /ˈkrʌmbli/ **crumblier, crumbliest.** Something that is **crumbly** is easily broken into a lot of little pieces. *...crumbly cheese.* ADJ-GRADED

crum·my /ˈkrʌmi/ **crummier, crummiest.** If you describe something as **crummy**, you mean it is of very poor quality. *Here I am at a crummy hotel.* ADJ-GRADED INFORMAL

crum·pet /ˈkrʌmpɪt/ **crumpets. 1** Crumpets are round flat pieces of a substance similar to bread with small holes in it, which you toast and eat with butter. **2** Some men refer to attractive women as **crumpet**; an offensive use. N-COUNT BRITISH / N-UNCOUNT BRITISH

crum·ple /ˈkrʌmpəl/ **crumples, crumpling, crumpled. 1** If you **crumple** something such as paper or cloth, it is squashed and becomes full of untidy creases and folds. *The front and rear of the car will crumple during a collision.* ► **Crumple up** means the same as **crumple**. *She crumpled up her coffee cup... Nancy looked at the note angrily, then crumpled it up.* ♦ **crum·pled** *His uniform was crumpled.* **2** If someone **crumples**, they collapse in an untidy and helpless way, for example when they have received a shock. *He immediately crumpled to the floor.* **3** If someone's face **crumples**, they suddenly look very disappointed or as if they want to cry. *Then her face crumpled once more.* ◆◇◇◇ V-ERG: V n, V / PHRASAL VB ERG V P noun, V n P / ADJ-GRADED / VERB V / VERB V

crumple up. See **crumple** 1. PHRASAL VB

crunch /krʌntʃ/ **crunches, crunching, crunched. 1** If you **crunch** something hard, you crush it noisily between your teeth. *Richard crunched into the apple.* **2** If something **crunches**, it makes a breaking or crushing noise, for example when you step on it. *He crunched the sheets of paper in his hands.* ► Also a noun. *...the crunch of tires on the gravel driveway.* **3** If you **crunch** across a surface made of very small stones, you move across it causing it to make a crunching noise. *...wheels crunching over a stony surface.* ◆◆◇◇ VERB: V n, V into/on n / V-ERG: V, V n / N-COUNT; SOUND VERB V prep/adv

4 You can refer to a crucial time or event, for example when an important decision has to be made, as the **crunch**. *...a crunch meeting.* ● If you say that something will happen **if** or **when it comes to the crunch**, you mean that it will happen if or when the time comes when something has to be done. *If it comes to the crunch, I'll resign over this.* **5** A situation in which a business or economy has very little money can be referred to as a **crunch**. *The UN is facing a cash crunch.* N-SING / PHRASE / N-COUNT

6 To **crunch** numbers means to do a lot of calculations using a computer or calculator. VERB: V n

crunchy /ˈkrʌntʃi/ **crunchier, crunchiest.** Food that is **crunchy** is pleasantly hard or crisp so that it makes a noise when you eat it. *...a crunchy salad.* ADJ-GRADED PRAGMATICS

cru·sade /kruːˈseɪd/ **crusades, crusading, crusaded. 1** A **crusade** is a long and determined attempt to achieve something for a cause that you feel strongly about. *Footballers launched an unprecedented crusade against racism on the terraces.* **2** If you **crusade** for a particular cause, you make a long and determined effort to achieve something for it. *...a newspaper that has crusaded against the country's cocaine traffickers.* ♦ **cru·sad·er, crusaders** *He has set himself up as a crusader for higher press and broadcasting standards.* **3** The Crusades were the wars that were fought by Christians in Palestine against the Muslims in the eleventh, twelfth, and thirteenth centuries. ♦ **cru·sad·er.** A Crusader was a knight who fought in the Crusades. ◆◇◇◇ N-COUNT / VERB V against/for n / N-COUNT: with supp / N-PROPER-PLURAL: the N / N-COUNT

crush /krʌʃ/ **crushes, crushing, crushed. 1** To **crush** something means to press it very hard so that its shape is destroyed or so that it breaks into pieces. *Andrew crushed his empty can. ...crushed ice.* ♦ **crush·er, crushers.** A **crusher** is a piece of equipment used for crushing things. *...a garlic crusher.* **2** If you **are crushed** against someone or something, you are pushed or pressed against them. *We were at the front, crushed against the stage.* **3** A **crush** is a closely-packed crowd of people, in which it is difficult to move. *His thirteen-year-old son somehow got separated in the crush.* ◆◆◇◇ VERB V n, V-ed / N-COUNT / VB: usu passive beV-ed prep / N-COUNT

4 To **crush** a protest or movement, or a group of opponents, means to defeat it completely, usually by force. *...the first step in a plan to crush the uprising.* ♦ **crush·ing** *...the violent crushing of anti-government demonstrations.* **5** If you **are crushed** by something, it upsets you or affects you very badly. ♦ **crushed** *He felt crushed and desperate.* ♦ **crushing** *...a crushing burden of debt.* VERB V n / N-UNCOUNT beV-ed / ADJ-GRADED / ADJ: ADJ n

6 If you have a **crush** on someone, you feel you are in love with them but you do not have a relationship with them. N-COUNT INFORMAL

crush·ing·ly /ˈkrʌʃɪŋli/. You can use **crushingly** to emphasize the degree of a negative quality. *...a collection of crushingly bad jokes.* ADV-GRADED: ADV adj PRAGMATICS

crust /krʌst/ **crusts. 1** The **crust** on a loaf of bread is the outside part. **2** A pie's **crust** is the cooked pastry on top. **3** A **crust** is a hardened layer of something, especially on top of a softer or wetter substance. *As the water evaporates, a crust of salt is left on the surface.* **4** The earth's **crust** is its outer layer. *Earthquakes leave scars in the earth's crust.* **5** See also **upper crust.** N-COUNT / N-COUNT / N-COUNT / N-COUNT: with supp

crus·ta·cean /krʌˈsteɪʃən/ **crustaceans.** A **crustacean** is an animal with a hard shell and several pairs of legs, which usually lives in water. N-COUNT

crust·ed /ˈkrʌstɪd/. If something is **crusted** with a substance, it is covered with a hard or thick layer of ADJ LITERARY

that substance. ...*flat grey stones crusted with lichen.* ▶ Also a combining form. ...*his mud-crusted boots.* COMB

crusty /'krʌsti/ **crustier, crustiest. 1** Crusty ◆◇◇◇◇ bread has a hard crisp outside. ...*crusty French* ADJ-GRADED *loaves.* **2** If you describe someone, especially an old ADJ-GRADED man, as **crusty**, you mean they are impatient and easily irritated. ...*a crusty old colonel.*

crutch /krʌtʃ/ **crutches. 1** A **crutch** is a stick ◆◇◇◇◇ which someone with an injured foot or leg uses to N-SING support them when walking. **2** If you refer to someone or something as a **crutch**, you mean that they give you help or support. *He gave up the crutch of* N-COUNT *alcohol.* **3** Your **crutch** is the same as your **crotch**. *He kicked him in the crutch.*

crux /krʌks/. **The crux** of a problem or argument is N-SING: the most important or difficult part of it which af- theN fects everything else. *The crux of the matter was economic policy.*

cry /kraɪ/ **cries, crying, cried. 1** When you **cry**, ◆◆◆◇ tears come from your eyes, usually because you are V-ERG: V unhappy or hurt. *He cried with anger and frustra-* V with n *tion.* ▶ Also a noun. *A nurse patted me on the shoul-* N-SING *der and said, 'You have a good cry, dear.'* ♦ **cry·ing** N-UNCOUNT *She had been unable to sleep because of her 13-week-old son's crying.* **2** ● to **cry** your **eyes out**: see **eye**. ● **a shoulder to cry on**: see **shoulder**.

3 If you **cry** something, you shout it or say it loudly. VERB *'Nancy Drew,' she cried, 'you're under arrest!'* ▶ **Cry** V with quote **out** means the same as **cry**. *'You're wrong, quite* PHRASAL VB *wrong!' Henry cried out.* **4** A **cry** is a loud high sound N-COUNT that you make when you feel a strong emotion such as fear, pain, or pleasure. *A cry of horror broke from me.* **5** A bird's or animal's **cry** is the loud high sound that it N-COUNT makes. ...*the cry of a seagull.* **6** A **cry** is a shouted word N-COUNT or phrase, usually intended to attract someone's attention. *Passers-by heard his cries for help.* ● See also **battle cry, rallying cry.**

7 You can refer to a public protest about something or N-COUNT appeal for something as a **cry** of some kind. *There* JOURNALISM *have been cries of outrage about this expenditure.* **8** When people are **in full cry**, they are expressing PHRASE their views very strongly about something. *The main opposition party is already in full cry over this mishandling of security.*

9 If you say something is **a far cry from** something PHRASE else, you mean it is very different from it. *Their lives are a far cry from his own poor childhood.*

10 See also **crying.**

cry off. If you **cry off**, you tell someone that you can- PHRASAL VB not do something that you had agreed or arranged to V P do. The American expression is **beg off**. BRITISH

cry out. If you **cry out**, you call out loudly because PHRASAL VB you are frightened, unhappy, or in pain. *He was crying* V P *out in pain when the ambulance arrived.* ● See also V P in n **cry** 2.

cry out for. If you say that something **cries out for a** PHRASAL VB particular thing or action, you mean it needs that V P P n thing or action very much. *This is a disgraceful state of affairs and cries out for a thorough investigation.*

cry·ing /'kraɪɪŋ/. **1** If you say that there is **a crying** PHRASE **need for** something, you mean that there is a very great need for it. **2** If you say that something is a PHRASE **crying shame**, you are emphasizing what a great PRAGMATICS shame it is, often when you are annoyed about it. **3** See also **cry.**

cryo·gen·ics /ˌkraɪəʊ'dʒenɪks/; the form **cryogenic** N-PLURAL is used as a modifier. Cryogenics is a branch of physics that studies what happens to things at extremely low temperatures.

crypt /krɪpt/ **crypts.** A **crypt** is an underground ◆◇◇◇◇ room beneath a church or cathedral. N-COUNT

cryp·tic /'krɪptɪk/. A **cryptic** remark or message ◆◇◇◇◇ contains a hidden meaning or is difficult to under- ADJ-GRADED stand. ♦ **cryp·ti·cal·ly** *'Not necessarily,' she says* ADV-GRADED *cryptically.* ADV with v

crypto- /'krɪptəʊ-/. **Crypto-** is used to form adjec- COMB tives and nouns which refer to people who have hidden beliefs and principles. *He has been accused of being a crypto-fascist.*

crys·tal /'krɪstəl/ **crystals. 1** A **crystal** is a small ◆◆◆◇◇ piece of a substance that has formed naturally into N-COUNT a regular symmetrical shape. ...*salt crystals.* ● See also **liquid crystal, liquid crystal display. 2** Crystal N-VAR is a transparent rock that is used to make jewellery and ornaments. ...*a strand of crystal beads.* **3** Crys- N-UNCOUNT **tal** is a high quality glass, usually with patterns cut into its surface. ...*crystal glasses.* **4** Glasses and oth- N-UNCOUNT er containers made of crystal are referred to as **crystal**. *Get out your best china and crystal.*

crystal 'ball, crystal balls. If you talk about N-COUNT someone, especially an expert, looking into a **crystal ball**, you mean they are trying to predict the future. Crystal balls are traditionally used by fortune-tellers.

crystal 'clear. 1 Water that is **crystal clear** is ab- ◆◇◇◇◇ solutely clear, like glass. **2** If a message or statement ADJ is **crystal clear**, it is very easy to understand. ADJ

crys·tal·line /'krɪstəlaɪn/. **1** A **crystalline** sub- ADJ stance is in the form of crystals or contains crystals. TECHNICAL **2** Crystalline means clear or bright. ADJ LITERARY

crys·tal·lize /'krɪstəlaɪz/ **crystallizes, crystal-** ◆◇◇◇◇ **lizing, crystallized;** also spelled **crystallise** in British English. **1** If an opinion or idea **crystallizes**, V-ERG: V it becomes fixed and definite. *I hope the above* V n *points have helped to crystallize your thoughts.* ♦ **crys·tal·li·za·tion** /ˌkrɪstəlaɪ'zeɪʃən/ ...*the crys-* N-UNCOUNT *tallization of new values.* **2** If a substance **crystal-** V-ERG **lizes**, it turns into crystals. *Don't stir or the sugar* Also V n *will crystallise.* ♦ **crystallization** ...*the crystallisa-* N-UNCOUNT *tion of glass.*

crys·tal·lized /'krɪstəlaɪzd/. Crystallized fruits and ADJ sweets are covered in sugar which has been melted and then allowed to go hard.

CS 'gas. CS gas is a gas which causes you to cry N-UNCOUNT and makes breathing painful. It is sometimes used to control a crowd which is rioting.

cub /kʌb/ **cubs;** also spelled **Cub** for meanings 2 ◆◇◇◇◇ and 3. **1** A **cub** is a young wild animal such as a lion, wolf, or bear. **2** The Cubs or the Cub Scouts is N-COLL-a junior version of the Scouts for boys between the PROPER: ages of eight and ten. **3** A **cub** or a **cub scout** is a theN N-COUNT boy who is a member of the Cubs.

cubby-hole /'kʌbi həʊl/ **cubby-holes.** A **cubby-** N-COUNT **hole** is a very small room or space for storing things.

cube /kjuːb/ **cubes, cubing, cubed. 1** A **cube** is ◆◆◇◇◇ a solid object with six square surfaces which are all N-COUNT the same size. See picture headed **shapes**. ...*ice cubes.* **2** When you **cube** food, you cut it into VERB: V n cube-shaped pieces. *Serve with cubed bread.* **3** The V-ed **cube** of a number is another number that is pro- N-COUNT duced by multiplying the first number by itself twice. For example, the cube of 2 is 8.

cube 'root, cube roots. The **cube root** of a num- N-COUNT ber is another number that makes the first number when it is multiplied by itself twice. For example, the cube root of 8 is 2.

cu·bic /'kjuːbɪk/. **Cubic** is used in front of units of ◆◇◇◇◇ length to form units of volume, such as **cubic metre** ADJ: ADJ n and **cubic foot**.

cu·bi·cle /'kjuːbɪkəl/ **cubicles.** A **cubicle** is a very ◆◇◇◇◇ small enclosed area, for example one where you can N-COUNT have a shower or change your clothes.

Cub·ism /'kjuːbɪzəm/. **Cubism** is a style of art, be- N-UNCOUNT gun in the early twentieth century, in which objects are represented as if they could be seen from several different positions at the same time, using many lines and geometrical shapes. ♦ **Cub·ist, Cubists.** N-COUNT A **Cubist** is an artist who paints in the style of Cubism. ...*Picasso's first Cubist masterpiece.*

'cub scout. See **cub.**

cuck·old /'kʌkəʊld/ **cuckolds, cuckolding,** **cuckolded. 1** A **cuckold** is a man whose wife is N-COUNT having an affair with another man. **2** If a married LITERARY woman is having an affair, she and her lover are VERB: V n cuckolding her husband. LITERARY

cuckoo /'kʊkuː/ **cuckoos.** A **cuckoo** is a bird that ◆◇◇◇◇ has an easily recognizable call of two quick notes, N-COUNT and that lays its eggs in other birds' nests.

'cuckoo clock, cuckoo clocks. A cuckoo clock N-COUNT
is a clock with a door from which a toy bird comes
out and makes noises like a cuckoo every hour or
half hour.

cu·cum·ber /'kju:kʌmbə/ **cucumbers. 1** A cu- ◆◇◇◇◇
cumber is a long thin vegetable with a hard green N-VAR
skin and wet transparent flesh. It is eaten raw in salads. See picture headed **vegetables. 2** If you say that PHRASE
someone is **as cool as a cucumber**, you are empha- PRAGMATICS
sizing that they are very calm and relaxed, especially when you would not expect them to be.

cud /kʌd/. When animals such as cows or sheep PHRASE
chew the cud, they slowly chew partly digested food
before finally swallowing it.

cud·dle /'kʌdəl/ **cuddles, cuddling, cuddled.** If ◆◇◇◇◇
you **cuddle** someone, you put your arms round V n
them and hold them close as a way of showing your V-RECIP:
affection. *They used to kiss and cuddle in front of* pl-n V
everyone. ▶ Also a noun. *It would have been nice to* N-COUNT
give him a cuddle.

cuddle up. If you **cuddle up** to someone, you sit or PHRASAL VB
lie as near to them as possible. *Then we'd go home and* RECIP:
cuddle up together to watch TV. V P ton
    pl-n V P

cud·dly /'kʌdəli/ **cuddlier, cuddliest. 1** If you ◆◇◇◇◇
describe a person or animal as **cuddly**, you find ADJ-GRADED
them attractive because they are plump or soft and PRAGMATICS
look nice to cuddle. **2 Cuddly** toys are soft stuffed ADJ: ADJ n
toys that look like animals.

cudg·el /'kʌdʒəl/ **cudgels. 1** A **cudgel** is a thick N-COUNT
short stick that is used as a weapon. **2** If you **take** PHRASE
up the cudgels for someone or something, you
speak or fight in support of them.

cue /kju:/ **cues, cueing, cued. 1** A performer's ◆◆◆◇◇
cue is something another performer says or does as N-COUNT
a signal for them to begin speaking, playing, or doing something. *I had never known him miss a cue.*
2 If one performer **cues** another, they say or do VERB: V n
something as a signal for the second performer to
begin speaking, playing, or doing something. **3** If PHRASE
you say that something happened **on cue** or **as if on**
cue, you mean that it happened just when it was expected to happen, or just at the right time. *'It's al-*
most eight o'clock.' As if on cue the bell in the chapel
began to toll. **4** If you say that something that hap- N-COUNT
pens is a **cue** for an action, you mean that people
start doing that action when it happens. *Mr*
Clinton's excitement was the cue for a vigorous lob-
bying campaign. **5** If you **take** your **cue** from some- PHRASE
one or something, you do something similar. *Tak-*
ing his cue from his companion, he apologized.
6 A **cue** is a long thin wooden stick that is used to hit N-COUNT
the ball in games such as snooker and pool.

cuff /kʌf/ **cuffs, cuffing, cuffed. 1** The **cuffs** of a ◆◇◇◇◇
shirt or dress are the parts at the ends of the N-COUNT
sleeves, which are thicker than the rest of the
sleeve. **2** The **cuffs** on a pair of pants or trousers are N-COUNT
the parts at the ends of the legs, which are folded AMERICAN
over. The British term is **turn-up. 3 Cuffs** are the N-PLURAL
same as **handcuffs**. *Get the cuffs off her, she's harm-* INFORMAL
less. **4** If the police **cuff** someone, they put hand- VERB: V n
cuffs on them. INFORMAL
5 If you **cuff** someone, you hit them quickly and light- VERB: V n
ly with your hand, usually on their head or ear. ▶ Also N-COUNT
a noun. *He gave the dog a cuff.*
6 An **off-the-cuff** remark is made without being pre- PHRASE
pared or thought about in advance. *Mr Baker was*
speaking off the cuff when he made those suggestions.

cuff·link /'kʌflɪŋk/ **cufflinks. Cufflinks** are small N-COUNT
decorative objects used for fastening shirt cuffs.

cui·sine /kwɪ'zi:n/ **cuisines. 1** The **cuisine** of a ◆◇◇◇◇
country or district is the style of cooking that is N-VAR
characteristic of that place. **2** The **cuisine** of a res- N-VAR
taurant is the style of food that is served in it. **3** The N-UNCOUNT
skill or profession of cooking unusual or interesting
food can be referred to as **cuisine**.

cul-de-sac /'kʌl dɪ sæk, AM - 'sæk/ **cul-de-sacs.** A N-COUNT
cul-de-sac is a short road which is closed at one
end.

culi·nary /'kʌlɪnəri, AM 'kju:lənəri/. **Culinary** ◆◇◇◇◇
means concerned with cooking. *...culinary skills.* ADJ: ADJ n
    FORMAL

cull /kʌl/ **culls, culling, culled. 1** If items or ◆◇◇◇◇
ideas **are culled from** a particular source or number VERB:
of sources, they are taken and gathered together. be V-ed from n
Laura was passing around photographs she'd culled V n from n
from the albums at home. ...information culled from V-ed
movies he had seen. **2** To **cull** animals means to kill VERB: V n
the weaker ones in a group in order to reduce their
numbers. ▶ Also a noun. *...the annual seal cull off* N-COUNT
the Namibian coast. ♦ **cull·ing** The culling of seal N-UNCOUNT
cubs has led to an outcry.

cul·mi·nate /'kʌlmɪneɪt/ **culminates, culminat-** ◆◇◇◇◇
ing, culminated. If you say that an activity, pro- VERB
cess, or series of events **culminates in** or **with** a V in/with n
particular event, you mean that event happens at
the end of it. *They had an argument, which culmi-*
nated in Tom getting drunk. ♦ **cul·mi·na·tion** N-SING
/ˌkʌlmɪ'neɪʃən/ *Their arrest was the culmination of*
an operation in which 120 other people were
detained.

cul·pable /'kʌlpəbəl/. If someone or their conduct ADJ-GRADED
is **culpable**, they are responsible for something bad FORMAL
that has happened. *...culpable negligence.* ♦ **cul-**
·pabil·ity /ˌkʌlpə'bɪlɪti/ *There was clear culpability* N-UNCOUNT
on the part of the government.

cul·prit /'kʌlprɪt/ **culprits. 1** The person who ◆◇◇◇◇
committed a crime or did something wrong can be N-COUNT
referred to as the **culprit**. *The real culprits in the*
fight have not been identified. **2** The cause of a N-COUNT
problem or bad situation can be referred to as the
culprit. *...carbon dioxide – the main culprit in the*
greenhouse effect.

cult /kʌlt/ **cults. 1** A **cult** is fairly small religious ◆◆◇◇◇
group, especially one which is considered strange. N-COUNT
2 Someone or something that is a **cult** has become N-SING
very popular or fashionable among a group of people. ▶ Also an adjective. *...Monte Hellman, a cult* ADJ
figure among young filmmakers... Fruit beers are de-
veloping a cult following. **3** The **cult** of something is N-COUNT
a situation in which people regard that thing as very PRAGMATICS
important or special; used showing disapproval.
...the cult of youth that recently gripped publishing.

cul·ti·vate /'kʌltɪveɪt/ **cultivates, cultivating,** ◆◆◇◇◇
cultivated. 1 If you **cultivate** land or crops, you VERB: V n
prepare land and grow crops on it. *...the few patches*
of cultivated land. ♦ **cul·ti·va·tion** /ˌkʌltɪ'veɪʃən/ N-UNCOUNT
...the cultivation of fruit and vegetables. ...farmers
with many acres under cultivation. ♦ **cul·ti·va·tor,** N-COUNT
cultivators *...sugar cane cultivators.* **2** If you cul- VERB
tivate an attitude, image, or skill, you try hard to de- V n
velop it and make it stronger or better. *He has culti-*
vated the image of an elder statesman. ♦ **cul·ti·va-**
·tion *...the cultivation of a positive approach to life.* N-UNCOUNT
3 If you **cultivate** someone or **cultivate** a friendship VERB: V n
with them, you try hard to develop a friendship with
them.

cul·ti·vat·ed /'kʌltɪveɪtɪd/. **1** If you describe ◆◇◇◇◇
someone as **cultivated**, you mean they are well- ADJ-GRADED
educated and have good manners. **2 Cultivated** ADJ: ADJ n
plants have been developed for growing on farms or
in gardens.

cul·tur·al /'kʌltʃərəl/. **1 Cultural** means relating to ◆◆◆◇◇
a particular society and its ideas, customs, and art. ADJ
...a deep sense of personal honor which was part of
his cultural heritage. ♦ **cul·tur·al·ly** *Culturally,* ADV
they have much in common with their neighbours
just across the border. **2 Cultural** means involving ADJ: ADJ n
or concerning the arts. *...the sponsorship of sports*
and cultural events by tobacco companies.
♦ **culturally** *...one of our better-governed, culturally* ADV
active regional centres.

cul·ture /'kʌltʃə/ **cultures, culturing, cultured.** ◆◆◆◆◇
1 Culture consists of activities such as the arts and N-UNCOUNT
philosophy, which are considered to be important
for the development of civilization and of people's
minds. *...France's Minister of Culture and Education.*
2 A **culture** is a particular society or civilization, es- N-COUNT
pecially considered in relation to its beliefs, way of
life, or art. *...people from different cultures.* **3** The N-COUNT
culture of a particular organization or group consists of the habits of the people in it and the way

they generally behave. *Social workers say that this has created a culture of dependency.*
4 In science, a **culture** is a group of bacteria or cells N-COUNT which are grown, usually as part of an experiment.
5 In science, to **culture** a group of bacteria or cells VERB: Vn means to grow them, usually as part of an experiment. V-ed
...cultured human blood cells.

cul·tured /ˈkʌltʃəd/. If you describe someone as ◆◇◇◇◇ **cultured**, you mean that they are well educated and ADJ-GRADED know a lot about the arts.

cultured 'pearl, cultured pearls. A **cultured** N-COUNT **pearl** is a pearl that is created by putting sand or grit into an oyster.

'culture shock. Culture shock is a feeling of anxi- N-UNCOUNT: ety and confusion that people sometimes experi- also a N ence when they first arrive in another country.

cul·vert /ˈkʌlvət/ **culverts.** A **culvert** is a water N-COUNT pipe or sewer that crosses under a road or railway.

-cum- /-kʌm-/. **-cum-** is put between two nouns to COMB form a noun referring to something or someone that is partly one thing and partly another. *...a dining-room-cum-study.*

cum·ber·some /ˈkʌmbəsəm/. **1** Something that is ◆◇◇◇◇ **cumbersome** is large, heavy, and difficult to carry, ADJ-GRADED wear, or handle. **2** A **cumbersome** system or pro- ADJ-GRADED cess is complicated and inefficient. *The proposed regulations are ill-defined and cumbersome.*

cum·in /ˈkʌmɪn/. **Cumin** is a sweet-smelling spice N-UNCOUNT used to flavour meat dishes. It is popular in Indian cooking.

cum·mer·bund /ˈkʌməbʌnd/ **cummerbunds.** A N-COUNT **cummerbund** is a wide sash worn round the waist as part of a man's evening dress.

cu·mu·la·tive /ˈkjuːmjʊlətɪv/. If a series of events ◆◇◇◇◇ have a **cumulative** effect, each event makes the ef- ADJ fect greater. ◆ **cu·mu·la·tive·ly** *His administration* ADV *was plagued by one petty scandal after another, cumulatively very damaging.*

cu·mu·lus /ˈkjuːmjʊləs/ **cumuli** /ˈkjuːmjʊlaɪ/. **Cu-** N-VAR **mulus** is a type of thick fluffy white cloud which is formed when hot air rises very quickly.

cun·ni·lin·gus /ˌkʌnɪˈlɪŋɡəs/. **Cunnilingus** is oral N-UNCOUNT sex which involves someone using their mouth to stimulate a woman's genitals.

cun·ning /ˈkʌnɪŋ/. **1** Someone who is **cunning** has ◆◇◇◇◇ the ability to achieve things in a clever way, often by ADJ-GRADED deceiving other people. ◆ **cun·ning·ly** *They were* ADV-GRADED *cunningly disguised in golf clothes.* **2 Cunning** is the N-UNCOUNT ability to achieve things in a clever way, often by deceiving other people.

cup /kʌp/ **cups, cupping, cupped. 1** A cup is a ◆◆◆◆◇ small round container that you drink from. A cup N-COUNT usually has a handle and is made from china or plastic. ▶ A **cup** of something is the amount of it N-COUNT contained in a cup. **2** A **cup** is a large two-handled N-COUNT metal cup on a stem that is given to the person or team that wins a competition. **3 Cup** is used in the N-COUNT names of some sports competitions in which the prize is a cup. *Sri Lanka's cricket team will play India in the final of the Asia Cup.* **4** Things, or parts of N-COUNT things, that are small, round, and hollow can be referred to as **cups**. *...the brass cups of the small chandelier.* **5** If you **cup** your **hands**, you make them VERB: Vn into a curved dish-like shape. *He cupped his hands* Vnprep *around his mouth and called out for Diane... She* V-ed *held it in her cupped hands.* **6** If you **cup** something VERB: Vn in your hands, you make your hands into a curved Vnprep dish-like shape and support it or hold it gently. *He cupped her chin in the palm of his hand.* **7** ● **not** your **cup of tea**: see **tea**.

cup·board /ˈkʌbəd/ **cupboards.** A **cupboard** is a ◆◆◇◇◇ piece of furniture with one or two doors and usually N-COUNT shelves inside, which is used for storage. You also use **cupboard** to refer to a very small storage room. ● **a skeleton in the cupboard**: see **skeleton**.

cup·cake /ˈkʌpkeɪk/ **cupcakes.** A **cupcake** is a N-COUNT small iced cake for one person.

cup·ful /ˈkʌpfʊl/ **cupfuls.** A **cupful** of something is N-COUNT the amount of it a cup can contain. *...a cupful of warm milk.*

cu·pid /ˈkjuːpɪd/ **cupids;** also spelled **Cupid. Cupid** N-PROPER is the Roman god of love. He is usually drawn as a baby boy with wings and a bow and arrow. People, especially journalists, refer to him when talking about people starting a romantic relationship. *...the aristocrat who played Cupid to the Duke and Duchess of York.* ▶ A **cupid** is a representation of Cupid. N-COUNT *I would like my wedding cake decorated with cupids.*

cu·pid·ity /kjuːˈpɪdɪti/. **Cupidity** is a greedy desire N-UNCOUNT for money and possessions. FORMAL

cu·po·la /ˈkjuːpələ/ **cupolas.** A **cupola** is a roof or N-COUNT part of a roof that is shaped like a bowl turned upside-down.

cup·pa /ˈkʌpə/ **cuppas.** A **cuppa** is a cup of tea. N-COUNT *Have you time for a cuppa?* BRITISH, INFORMAL

'cup tie, cup ties; also spelled **cup-tie.** In sport, ◆◇◇◇◇ especially football, a **cup tie** is a match between two N-COUNT teams who are competing in a competition in which BRITISH the prize is a cup.

cur·able /ˈkjʊərəbəl/. If a disease or illness is **cur-** ADJ **able**, it can be cured.

cu·rate, curates, curating, curated. The noun ◆◇◇◇◇ is pronounced /ˈkjʊərət/. The verb is pronounced /kjʊˈreɪt/. **1** A **curate** is a clergyman in the Church N-COUNT of England who helps the vicar or rector of a parish. **2** If an exhibition **is curated** by someone, they organ- VERB: ize it. *He was asked to curate a major exhibition of* beV-ed *landscape photographs.* Vn TECHNICAL

cu·ra·tive /ˈkjʊərətɪv/. Something that has **cura-** ADJ **tive** properties can cure people's illnesses. *...cura-* FORMAL *tive herbs.*

cu·ra·tor /kjʊˈreɪtə/ **curators.** A **curator** is some- ◆◇◇◇◇ one who is in charge of the objects or works of art N-COUNT in a museum or art gallery. ◆ **cu·ra·to·rial** ADJ /ˌkjʊərəˈtɔːriəl/ *...the museum's curatorial team.*

curb /kɜːb/ **curbs, curbing, curbed. 1** If you ◆◆◇◇◇ **curb** something, you control it and keep it within VERB limits. *...advertisements aimed at curbing the spread* Vn *of Aids.* ▶ Also a noun. *He called for much stricter* N-COUNT *curbs on immigration.* **2** If you **curb** an emotion or VERB your behaviour, you keep it under control. *He* Vn *curbed his temper.* **3** See **kerb**.

curd /kɜːd/ **curds.** The thick white substance N-VAR formed when milk turns sour is called **curds**.

cur·dle /ˈkɜːdəl/ **curdles, curdling, curdled.** If V-ERG: V milk or eggs **curdle**, they separate into different Vn bits. *She curdled the mayonnaise.*

cure /kjʊə/ **cures, curing, cured. 1** If a doctor ◆◆◆◇◇ or a medical treatment **cures** someone or **cures** VERB: Vn their illness, they make the person well again. *Now* Vnofn *doctors believe they have cured him of the disease.* **2** A **cure** for an illness is a medicine or other treat- N-COUNT ment that cures the illness. **3** If someone or some- VERB: Vn thing **cures** a problem, they bring it to an end. **4** A N-COUNT **cure** for a problem is something that will bring it to an end. **5** If an action or event **cures** someone of a VERB habit or an attitude, it makes them stop having it. Vnofn *The experience was a detestable ordeal, and it cured* Also Vn *him of any ambitions to direct again.* **6** When food, tobacco, or animal skin **is cured**, it is VERB: dried, smoked, or salted so that it will last for a long beV-ed time. *...sliced cured ham.* V-ed

'cure-all, cure-alls. Something that is believed to N-COUNT be a **cure-all** is believed, usually wrongly, to be able to solve all the problems someone or something has, or to cure a wide range of illnesses.

cur·few /ˈkɜːfjuː/ **curfews.** A **curfew** is a law stat- ◆◆◇◇◇ ing that people must stay inside their houses after a N-VAR particular time at night, for example during a war. *The village was placed under curfew... Crowds of people defied the curfew to celebrate on the streets.*

cu·rio /ˈkjʊəriəʊ/ **curios.** A **curio** is an object such N-COUNT as a small ornament which is unusual or rare.

cu·ri·os·ity /ˌkjʊəriˈɒsɪti/ **curiosities. 1 Curiosity** ◆◆◇◇◇ is a desire to know about something. *Ryle accepted* N-UNCOUNT *more out of curiosity than anything else. ...an enthu- siasm and genuine curiosity about the past... To sat- isfy our own curiosity we traveled to Baltimore.* **2** A N-COUNT **curiosity** is something that is unusual, interesting, and fairly rare. *There is much to see in the way of*

castles, curiosities, and museums... Reed International is seen as a curiosity in the international world of publishing.

cu·ri·ous /'kjʊəriəs/. **1** If you are **curious** about something, you are interested in it and want to know more about it. *Steve was intensely curious about the world I came from. ...a group of curious villagers.* ◆ **cu·ri·ous·ly** *The woman in the shop had looked at them curiously.* **2** If you describe something as **curious**, you mean that it is unusual or difficult to understand. *The pageant promises to be a curious mixture of the ancient and modern... The naval high command's response to these developments is rather curious.* ◆ **curiously** *Harry was curiously silent through all this... Curiously, the struggle to survive has greatly improved her health.*
◆◆◇◇ ADJ-GRADED
ADV-GRADED: ADV after v ADJ-GRADED
ADV-GRADED

curl /kɜːl/ **curls, curling, curled. 1** If you have **curls**, your hair is in the form of tight curves and spirals. *...the little girl with blonde curls. ...a curl of black hair.* **2** If your hair **curls**, it is full of curls. *Maria had curled her hair for the event... Afro hair is short and tightly curled.* **3** A **curl** of something is a piece or quantity of it that is curved or spiral in shape. *A thin curl of smoke rose from a rusty stove. ...curls of lemon peel.* **4** If something **curls** somewhere, it moves there in a spiral or curve. *Smoke was curling up the chimney... He curled the ball into the net.* **5** If your toes, fingers, or other parts of your body **curl**, they form a curved or round shape. *His fingers curled gently round her wrist... Curl the toes and point the foot downwards... She sat with her legs curled under her.* **6** If you **curl** your lip, you raise your upper lip slightly at one side, as a way of showing anger, contempt, or scorn. *He curled his upper lip in a show of scepticism... She had a small, mean mouth that curled disapprovingly.* **7** If a person or animal **curls into** a ball, they move into a position in which their body makes a rounded shape. *He wanted to curl into a tiny ball... The kitten was curled on a cushion on the sofa.* ▶ **Curl up** means the same as **curl**. *In colder weather, your cat will curl up into a tight, heat-conserving ball... He was asleep there, curled up in the fetal position... I just love to curl up with a book.* **8** When a flat object such as a leaf or page **curls**, its edges bend towards the centre. ▶ **Curl up** means the same as **curl**. *The corners of the lino were curling up.*
◆◆◇◇ N-COUNT

V-ERG: V V n V-ed N-COUNT

V-ERG V prep/adv V n prep/adv

V-ERG: V V prep/adv V n V-ed

V-ERG V n V

VERB V into n V-ed

PHRASAL VB V P into n V-ed P V P

VERB: V PHRASAL VB V P

curl up. See **curl** 7 and 8.
PHRASAL VB

curl·er /'kɜːlə/ **curlers. Curlers** are small plastic or metal tubes that women roll their hair round in order to make it curly.
N-COUNT

cur·lew /'kɜːljuː/ **curlews.** A **curlew** is a large brown bird that lives near water, with long legs and a long beak which curves downwards.
N-COUNT

cur·li·cue /'kɜːlɪkjuː/ **curlicues. Curlicues** are decorative twists and curls, usually carved or made with a pen.
N-COUNT LITERARY

curly /'kɜːli/ **curlier, curliest. 1** Curly hair is full of curls. **2 Curly** is used to describe things that are curved or spiral in shape. *...cauliflowers with extra long curly leaves. ...dragons with curly tails.*
◆◇◇◇ ADJ-GRADED ADJ-GRADED

cur·mudg·eon /kə'mʌdʒən/ **curmudgeons.** If you call someone a **curmudgeon**, you do not like them because they are mean or bad-tempered. ◆ **cur·mudg·eon·ly** /kə'mʌdʒənli/ *...the Government's curmudgeonly attitude.*
N-COUNT PRAGMATICS DATED
ADJ-GRADED

cur·rant /'kʌrənt, AM 'kɜːr-/ **currants. 1 Currants** are small dried black grapes, used in baking. **2 Currants** are bushes which produce edible red, black, or white berries. The berries are also called **currants**.
N-COUNT
N-COUNT

cur·ren·cy /'kʌrənsi, AM 'kɜːr-/ **currencies. 1** The money used in a particular country is referred to as its **currency**. *...a single European currency... Tourism is the country's top earner of foreign currency.* **2** If a custom, idea, or word has **currency**, it is used and accepted by a lot of people at a particular time. *His theory of the social contract had wide currency in America... 'Loop' is one of those*
◆◆◆◇ N-VAR

N-UNCOUNT FORMAL

computer words that has gained currency. **3** See also **common currency.**

cur·rent /'kʌrənt, AM 'kɜːr-/ **currents. 1** A **current** is a steady continuous flowing movement in the water of a river, lake, or sea. *The couple were swept away by the strong current.* **2** An air **current** is a steady flowing movement of air. *I felt a current of cool air blowing in my face.* **3** An electric **current** is a flow of electricity through a wire or circuit. ● See also **alternating current, direct current. 4** A **current** is a feeling, idea, or quality that exists within a group of people. *Each party represents a distinct current of thought... A current of terror ran through contemporary fiction.* **5 Current** means happening, being used, or being done at the present time. *The current situation is very different... He plans to repeal a number of current policies.* ◆ **cur·rent·ly** *Twelve potential AIDS vaccines are currently being tested.* **6** Ideas and customs that are **current** are generally accepted and used by most people. *Current thinking suggests that toxins only have a small part to play in the build up of cellulite... This custom was still current in the late 1960s.*
◆◆◆◆◇ N-COUNT

N-COUNT

N-COUNT

N-COUNT: with supp

ADJ

ADV: ADV before v ADJ

current ac'count, current accounts. 1 A **current account** is a personal bank account which you can take money out of at any time using your cheque book or cash card. The American term is **checking account. 2** A country's **current account** is the difference in value between its exports and imports over a period of time.
◆◇◇◇◇ N-COUNT BRITISH

N-COUNT TECHNICAL

current af'fairs. Current affairs are political events and problems in society which are discussed in the media. *I am ill-informed on current affairs. ...the BBC's current affairs programme 'Panorama'.*
◆◇◇◇◇ N-PLURAL

cur·ricu·lum /kə'rɪkjʊləm/ **curriculums** or **curricula** /kə'rɪkjʊlə/. **1** A **curriculum** is all the different courses of study that are taught in a school, college, or university. *Not having Shakespeare in the school curriculum is madness.* ● See also **National Curriculum. 2** A particular **curriculum** is one course of study that is taught in a school, college, or university. *...the history curriculum.*
◆◆◇◇ N-COUNT

N-COUNT

cur·ricu·lum vi·tae /kə,rɪkjʊləm 'viːtaɪ, AM -tiː/. Your **curriculum vitae** is the same as your **CV**. The usual American word is **résumé**.
N-SING BRITISH

cur·ried /'kʌrid, AM 'kɜːrid/. **Curried** meat or vegetables have been flavoured with hot spices.
ADJ: ADJ

cur·ry /'kʌri, AM 'kɜːri/ **curries, currying, curried. 1** Curry is an Indian dish composed of meat or vegetables in a hot spicy sauce. It can be eaten with rice or Indian bread. **2** If one person tries to **curry favour** with another, they do things in order to try to gain their support or co-operation. *...a gesture designed to curry favour with voters.*
◆◇◇◇◇ N-VAR

PHRASE

'curry powder, curry powders. Curry powder is a powder made from a mixture of spices. It is used in cooking, especially when making curry.
N-VAR

curse /kɜːs/ **curses, cursing, cursed. 1** If you **curse**, you use rude or offensive language, usually because you are angry about something. *I cursed and hobbled to my feet.* ▶ Also a noun. *Groans and curses filled the air.* **2** If you **curse** someone or something, you say insulting things to them or complain strongly about them because you are angry. *We set off again, cursing the delay... He cursed himself for not making a note of it.* **3** If you say that there is a **curse** on someone, you mean that there seems to be a supernatural power causing unpleasant things to happen to them. **4** You can refer to something that causes a great deal of trouble or harm as a **curse**. *Apathy is the long-standing curse of British local democracy.*
◆◆◇◇ VERB V WRITTEN N-COUNT
VERB V n V pron-refl

N-COUNT

N-COUNT

cursed /kɜːst/. **1** If you are **cursed with** something, you are very unlucky in having it. *Bulman was cursed with a poor memory.* **2** Someone or something that is **cursed** is suffering as the result of a curse. *The whole family seemed cursed.*
◆◇◇◇◇ ADJ: v-link ADJ with n
ADJ

cur·sor /'kɜːsə/ **cursors.** On a computer screen, the **cursor** is a small, movable shape which indicates where anything typed by the user will appear.
N-COUNT

cur·so·ry /ˈkɜːsəri/. A **cursory** glance or examination is a brief one in which you do not pay much attention to detail. *Burke cast a cursory glance at the menu.* — ADJ-GRADED: ADJ n

curt /kɜːt/. If you describe someone as **curt**, you mean that they speak or reply briefly and rather rudely. *'The matter is closed,' was the curt reply.* ♦ **curt·ly** *'I'm leaving,' she said curtly.* — ◆◇◇◇ ADJ-GRADED / ADV-GRADED

cur·tail /kɜːˈteɪl/ **curtails, curtailing, curtailed.** If you **curtail** something, you reduce or limit it. *The US plans to curtail the number of troops being sent to Somalia... I told Louie that old age would curtail her activities.* ♦ **cur·tail·ment** *...a considerable curtailment of military spending.* — ◆◇◇◇ VERB V n FORMAL / N-SING

cur·tain /ˈkɜːtən/ **curtains. 1 Curtains** are large pieces of material hanging from the top of a window, which can be pulled across it to keep light out or prevent people seeing in. The usual American word is **drapes**. *Her bedroom curtains were drawn.* **2 Curtains** are pieces of very thin material which you hang in front of windows in order to prevent people from seeing in. The usual British word is **net curtains. 3** In a theatre, **the curtain** is the large piece of material that hangs in front of the stage until a performance begins. *The curtain rises toward the end of the Prelude.* **4** You can refer to something as a **curtain** when it is thick and difficult to see through or get past. *...a curtain of cigarette smoke.* ● See also **Iron Curtain. 5** If something **brings the curtain down on** an event or state of affairs, it causes or marks the end of the event or state of affairs. *The night was going to bring the curtain down on Mckenzie's career.* — ◆◆◇◇ N-COUNT BRITISH / N-COUNT AMERICAN / N-SING: the N / N-SING / PHRASE

'curtain call, curtain calls. In a theatre, when actors or performers take a **curtain call**, they come to the front of the stage after a performance in order to receive the applause of the audience. — N-COUNT

cur·tained /ˈkɜːtənd/. A **curtained** window or door has a curtain hanging across it. — ADJ

'curtain-raiser, curtain-raisers. A **curtain-raiser** is an event, especially a sporting event or a performance, that takes place before a more important one, or starts off a series of events. *Yesterday's contest was a curtain raiser to the South African tour.* — N-COUNT JOURNALISM

curt·sy /ˈkɜːtsi/ **curtsies, curtsying, curtsied;** also spelled **curtsey**. If a woman or a girl **curtsies**, she bends her knees briefly, sometimes holding her skirt with both hands, as a way of showing respect for an important person. *We were taught how to curtsy to the Queen.* ▶ Also a noun. *She gave a small curtsy.* — VERB: V / V to n / N-COUNT

cur·va·ceous /kɜːˈveɪʃəs/. If someone describes a woman as **curvaceous**, they think she is attractive because of the curves of her body. Some women find this word offensive. — ADJ-GRADED PRAGMATICS

cur·va·ture /ˈkɜːvətʃə/. The **curvature** of something is its curved shape, especially when this shape is part of the circumference of a circle. *...the curvature of the earth.* — N-UNCOUNT TECHNICAL

curve /kɜːv/ **curves, curving, curved. 1** A **curve** is a smooth, gradually bending line, for example part of the edge of a circle. *...the curve of his lips. ...a curve in the road.* **2** If something **curves**, it has the shape of a curve. *The track curved away below him... A small, unobtrusive smile curved the cook's thin lips.* **3** If something **curves**, it moves in a curve. *The ball curved strangely in the air.* **4** You can refer to a change in something as a particular **curve**, especially when it is represented on a graph. *Each firm will face a downward-sloping demand curve.* ● See also **learning curve.** — ◆◆◇◇ N-COUNT / V-ERG: V / V adv/prep / V n / VERB V / N-COUNT

curved /kɜːvd/. A **curved** object has the shape of a curve or has a smoothly bending surface. *...a small, curved staircase.* — ◆◇◇◇ ADJ-GRADED

curvy /ˈkɜːvi/. If someone describes a woman as **curvy**, they think she is attractive because of the curves of her body. Some women find this word offensive. — ADJ-GRADED PRAGMATICS INFORMAL

cush·ion /ˈkʊʃən/ **cushions, cushioning, cushioned. 1** A **cushion** is a fabric case filled with soft material, which you put on a seat to make it more comfortable. **2** A **cushion** is a soft pad or barrier, especially one that protects something from impact. *...a styrofoam cushion to protect the tablets during shipping.* **3** Something that **cushions** an object when it hits something protects it by reducing the force of the impact. *The suspension is designed to cushion passengers from the effects of riding over rough roads.* **4** To **cushion** the effect of something unpleasant means to reduce it. *The subsidies are designed to cushion farmers against unpredictable weather.* ▶ Also a noun. *Housing benefit provides a cushion against hardship.* — ◆◆◇◇ N-COUNT / N-COUNT / VERB: V n / V n from n / VERB: V n / V n against n / N-SING

cush·ion·ing /ˈkʊʃənɪŋ/. **Cushioning** is something soft that protects an object when it hits something by reducing the force of the impact. *Walkers need cushioning under the ball of the foot.* — N-UNCOUNT

cushy /ˈkʊʃi/. If you describe someone's job or situation as **cushy**, you think it is pleasant because it does not involve much work or effort, and you envy or resent them. *...a cushy job in the civil service.* — ADJ-GRADED PRAGMATICS INFORMAL

cusp /kʌsp/. If you say that someone or something is **on the cusp**, you mean they are between two states, or are about to be in a particular state. *I am sitting on the cusp of middle age.* — PHRASE

cuss /kʌs/ **cusses, cussing, cussed.** If someone **cusses**, they swear at someone or use bad language. *He rails and cusses at those pop stars.* — VERB: V / V at n / Also V n / INFORMAL

cus·tard /ˈkʌstəd/ **custards. Custard** is a sweet yellow sauce made from milk and eggs or from milk and a powder. It is eaten with fruit and puddings. — N-VAR

,custard 'pie, custard pies. Custard pies are creamy fake pies which clowns and comedians sometimes throw at each other. — N-COUNT

cus·to·dial /kʌˈstəʊdiəl/. **1 Custodial** means relating to keeping people in prison. *He will be given a custodial sentence.* **2** If a child's parents are divorced or separated, the **custodial** parent is the parent who has custody of the child. — ADJ: ADJ n FORMAL / ADJ: ADJ n LEGAL

cus·to·dian /kʌˈstəʊdiən/ **custodians.** The **custodian** of an official building, a companies' assets, or something else valuable is the person who is officially in charge of it. *...the custodian of the holy shrines in Mecca and Medina.* — ◆◇◇◇ N-COUNT

cus·to·dy /ˈkʌstədi/. **1 Custody** is the legal right to keep and look after a child, especially the right given to a child's mother or father when they get divorced. *I'm going to go to court to get custody of the children... Child custody is normally granted to the mother.* **2** Someone who is **in custody** or has been taken **into custody** has been arrested, and is being kept in a prison or similar place until they can be tried in a court. — ◆◆◇◇ N-UNCOUNT / PHRASE

cus·tom /ˈkʌstəm/ **customs. 1** A **custom** is an activity, a way of behaving, or an event which is usual or traditional in a particular society or in particular circumstances. *The custom of lighting the Olympic flame goes back centuries... Chung has tried to adapt to local customs.* **2** If it is your **custom** to do something, you usually do it. *It was his custom to approach every problem cautiously.* **3** If a shop has your **custom**, you regularly buy things there. *You have the right to withhold your custom... Providing discounts is not the only way to win custom.* **4** If you use **custom** to describe something such as a vehicle or a piece of clothing, you mean that it has been designed for one particular customer. *...one-of-a-kind custom garments.* ● See also **customs.** — ◆◆◇◇ N-VAR / N-SING / N-UNCOUNT FORMAL, BRITISH / ADJ: ADJ n

cus·tom·ary /ˈkʌstəmri, AM -meri/. **1 Customary** is used to describe things that people usually do in a particular society or in particular circumstances. *It is customary to offer a drink or a snack to guests.* ♦ **cus·tom·ari·ly** /ˈkʌstəməli, AM -ˈeərɪli/ *Marriages in medieval Europe were customarily arranged by the families.* **2 Customary** is used to describe something that a particular person usually does or has. *Yvonne took her customary seat.* — ◆◇◇◇ ADJ-GRADED FORMAL / ADV / ADJ: ADJ n

custom-'built. If something **is custom-built**, it is built according to someone's special requirements. *...a custom-built kitchen.* `V-PASSIVE V-ed`

cus·tom·er /ˈkʌstəmə/ **customers. 1** A **customer** is someone who buys goods or services, especially from a shop. *Our customers have very tight budgets. ...a satisfied customer. ...the quality of customer service.* **2** You can use **customer** in expressions such as **a cool customer** or a **tough customer** to indicate what someone's behaviour or character is like. *...two pretty awkward customers.* `◆◆◆◇ N-COUNT` `N-COUNT: adj N BRITISH, INFORMAL`

cus·tom·ize /ˈkʌstəmaɪz/ **customizes, customizing, customized;** also spelled **customise** in British English. If you **customize** something, you change its appearance or features to suit your tastes or needs. *Kids customised their bikes.* `◆◇◇◇◇ VERB V n`

custom-'made. If something **is custom-made**, it is made according to someone's special requirements. *Furniture can also be custom-made.* `V-PASSIVE be V-ed`

cus·toms /ˈkʌstəmz/ **1 Customs** is the official organization responsible for collecting taxes on goods coming into a country and preventing illegal goods from being brought in. *Spanish customs seized 400lb of marijuana. ...customs officers.* **2 Customs** is the place where people arriving from a foreign country have to declare goods that they bring with them. *He walked through customs.* **3 Customs** duties are taxes that people pay for importing and exporting goods. **4** See also **custom**. `◆◇◇◇◇ N-PROPER` `N-UNCOUNT` `ADJ: ADJ n`

Customs and 'Excise. Customs and Excise is a British government department which is responsible for collecting taxes on imported goods and on some goods produced in Britain. `N-PROPER`

cut /kʌt/ **cuts, cutting.** The form **cut** is used in the present tense and is the past tense and past participle. **1** If you **cut** something, you use a knife or similar tool to divide it into pieces, or to mark it or damage it. If you **cut** a shape or a hole in an object, you make the shape or hole by cutting the object. *Cut the tomatoes in half... The thieves cut a hole in the fence... Mr. Long was now cutting himself a piece of the pink cake.* ▸ Also a noun. *The operation involves making several cuts in the cornea.* ◆ **cut·ter, cutters** *...a pastry cutter. ...wire cutters.* **2** If you **cut** yourself or a part of your body, you accidentally injure yourself on a sharp object so that you bleed. *Johnson cut himself shaving... I started to cry because I cut my finger. ...blood from his cut lip.* ▸ Also a noun. *...a cut on his left eyebrow.* **3** If you **cut** something such as grass, your hair, or your fingernails, you shorten them using scissors or another tool. *The most recent tenants hadn't even cut the grass... You've had your hair cut, it looks great... She had dark red hair, cut short.* ▸ Also a noun. *...£17 for a cut and blow-dry.* ◆ **cutter** *...electric grass cutters.* **4** The way that clothes **are cut** is the way they are designed and made. *It was cut high up the thigh to make her legs look longer.* **5** To **cut through** something means to move or pass through it easily. *...long canoes cutting through the waves.* **6** If you **cut across** or **through** a place, you go through it because it is a short route to another place. *He decided to cut across the heath.* ● See also **short cut**. **7** If you **cut** something, you reduce it. *The first priority is to cut costs. ...an agreement to cut farm subsidies by 30 per cent. ...a deal to cut 50 billion dollars from the federal deficit.* ▸ Also a noun. *The economy needs an immediate 2 per cent cut in interest rates.* ▸ **Cut down** means the same as **cut**. *We'd like politicians to get together and agree ways to cut down atmospheric pollution... We've cut it down to just five years.* ◆ **cutter** *...his credibility as a budget cutter.* **8** If you **cut** a text, broadcast, or performance, you shorten it. If you **cut** a part of a text, broadcast, or performance, you do not publish, broadcast, or perform that part. *We've cut some scenes.* ▸ Also a noun. *It has been found necessary to make some cuts in the text.* **9** To **cut** a supply of something means to stop providing `◆◆◆◆◆` `VERB V n prep/adv V n n` `N-COUNT` `N-COUNT` `VERB V pron-refl V n V-ed` `N-COUNT` `VERB V n have n V-ed` `N-SING` `N-COUNT` `VB: usu passive be V-ed` `VERB V through n` `VERB V across/ through n` `VERB V n V n by amount V amount from/off n N-COUNT PHRASAL VB V P noun V n P to n Also V n P N-COUNT` `VERB V n` `N-COUNT` `VERB V n`

it or stop it being provided. *...cutting food and water supplies.* ▸ Also a noun. *...cuts in electricity and water supplies.* `N-COUNT`

10 If you **cut** a pack of playing cards, you divide it into two. `VERB: V n`

11 When the director of a film says **'cut'**, they want the actors and the camera crew to stop filming. `CONVENTION`

12 When a singer or band **cuts** a record, they make a recording of their music. *She eventually cut her own album.* `VERB V n`

13 When a child **cuts** a tooth, a new tooth starts to grow through the gum. `VERB: V n`

14 If a child **cuts** classes or school, they do not go to school when they are supposed to. `VERB: V n AMERICAN`

15 If you tell someone to **cut** something, you are telling them in an irritated way to stop it. *Let's just cut the pretence.* `VERB PRAGMATICS INFORMAL`

16 A **cut** of meat is a piece or type of meat which is cut in a particular way from the animal, or from a particular part of it. *Use a cheap cut such as spare rib chops.* `N-COUNT: with supp`

17 Someone's **cut** of the profits or winnings from something, especially ones that have been obtained dishonestly, is their share. *The lawyers, of course, take their cut of the little guy's winnings.* `N-SING INFORMAL`

18 If you say that someone or something is **a cut above** other people or things of the same kind, you mean they are better than the others. *Joan Smith's detective stories are a cut above the rest.* **19** If you say that a situation or solution is **cut and dried**, you mean that it is clear and definite. *Things cannot be as cut and dried as many people would like.* **20** If a person or an organization **cuts loose** or **is cut loose**, they become free from the influence or authority of other people. **21** If you say that someone **cuts and runs** in a difficult situation, you disapprove of them because they try to escape from it quickly with the most advantage to themselves, rather than deal with it in a responsible way. **22** If you say that something **cuts both ways**, you mean that it can have two opposite effects, or can have both good and bad effects. *This publicity cuts both ways. It focuses on us as well as on them.* `PHRASE INFORMAL` `PHRASE` `PHRASE` `PHRASE PRAGMATICS INFORMAL` `PHRASE V n`

23 See also **cutting**. ● to **cut** something **to the bone**: see **bone**. ● to **cut corners**: see **corner**. ● to **cut** a particular **figure**: see **figure**. ● to **cut** someone **to the quick**: see **quick**. ● to **cut** someone **down to size**: see **size**. ● to **cut** a long story short: see **story**. ● to **cut your teeth** on something: see **tooth**.

cut across. If an issue or problem **cuts across** the division between two or more groups of people, it affects or matters to people in all the groups. *This health-care issue cuts across all the generations.* `PHRASAL VB V P n`

cut back. If you **cut back on** spending, you reduce it. *They will be concerned to cut back expenditure on unnecessary items... The Government has cut back on defence spending... We have been cutting back a bit.* ● See also **cutback**. `PHRASAL VB V P on n V P on n V P Also V n P`

cut down. 1 If you **cut down** on something, you consume or do less of it. *He cut down on coffee and cigarettes, and ate a balanced diet... Car owners were asked to cut down travel... I was concerned about your drinking and you promised to cut down.* **2** If you **cut down** a tree, you cut through its trunk so that it falls to the ground. *A vandal with a chainsaw cut down a tree.* **3** See **cut** 7. `PHRASAL VB V P on n V P noun V P Also V n P Also V n P`

cut in. If you **cut in** on someone, you interrupt them when they are speaking. *Daniel cut in on Joanne's attempts at reassurance... 'Not true,' the Duchess cut in.* `PHRASAL VB V P on n V P with quote Also V P`

cut off. 1 If you **cut** something **off**, you remove it with a knife or a similar tool. *Mrs Kreutz cut off a generous piece of the meat... He cut me off a slice... He threatened to cut my hair off.* **2** To **cut** someone or something **off** means to separate them from things that they are normally connected with. *One of the goals of the campaign is to cut off the elite Republican Guard from its supplies... The storm has cut us off.* ◆ **cut off** *Without a car we still felt very cut off.* **3** To **cut off** a supply of something means to stop providing it or stop it being provided. *The rebels have cut off electricity from the capital... Our phone's been cut off.* **4** If you get **cut off** when you are on the telephone, the `PHRASAL VB V P noun V n P noun V n P V n P` `V P noun V n P` `ADJ-GRADED V n P Also V n P` `get/be V-ed P V n P Also V P noun`

line is suddenly disconnected and you can no longer speak to the other person. *When you do get through, you've got to say your piece quickly before you get cut off... I'm going to cut you off now because we've got lots of callers waiting.* **5** If you **cut** someone **off** when they are speaking, you interrupt them and stop them from speaking. *'But, sir, I'm under orders to –' Clark cut him off. 'Don't argue with me.'* **6** See also **cut-off**. • to **cut off** your **nose** to spite your **face**: see **nose**.

[V n P; Also V P noun]

cut out. 1 If you **cut** something **out**, you remove or separate it from what surrounds it using scissors or a knife. *Cut out the coupon and send those cheques off today... I cut it out and pinned it to my studio wall.* **2** If you **cut out** a part of a text, you do not print, publish, or broadcast that part, to shorten the text or make it more acceptable. *I listened to the programme and found they'd cut out all the interesting stuff... Her editors wanted her to cut out the poetry from her novel.* **3** To **cut out** something unnecessary means to remove it completely from a situation. For example, if you **cut out** a particular type of food, you stop eating it. *I've simply cut egg yolks out entirely... A guilty plea cuts out the need for a long trial.* **4** If you tell someone to **cut** something **out**, you are telling them in an irritated way to stop it. *Cut it out, Chip... He had better cut out the nonsense.* **5** If you **cut** someone **out** of an activity or inheritance, you do not allow them to be involved in it or to share in it. *Environmentalists say this would cut them out of the debate over what to do with public lands... Cut her out of your will.* **6** If an object **cuts out** the light, it is between you and the light so that you are in the dark. *The curtains were half drawn to cut out the sunlight.* **7** If an engine **cuts out**, it suddenly stops working. **8** See also **cut-out**, **cut out**. • to **have** your **work cut out**: see **work**.

[PHRASAL VB; V P noun; V n P; V P noun; V P noun; from/of n; Also V n P; V n P; V P noun; PRAGMATICS; V it P; V P noun; Also V n P; INFORMAL; V n P of n; V P noun; V P noun; Also V n P; V P]

cut up. 1 If you **cut** something **up**, you cut it into several pieces. *He sits in his apartment cutting up magazines... Halve the tomatoes, then cut them up coarsely.* • See also **cut up**. **2** If one driver **cuts** another **up**, the first driver goes too close in front of the second one, for example after overtaking them. *They were crossing from lane to lane, cutting everyone up.*

[PHRASAL VB; V P noun; V n P; V n P; BRITISH]

,cut and 'dried. See **cut**.

,cut and 'thrust. If you refer to the **cut and thrust** of an activity or situation, you are talking about the argument or fierce competition that takes place in it. *...the cut and thrust of Parliament.*

[N-SING]

cut·away /'kʌtəweɪ/ **cutaways;** also spelled **cut-away**. **1** In a film, a **cutaway** or a **cutaway shot** is a picture that briefly shows something different from the main thing being shown. **2** A **cutaway** or a **cut-away** coat or jacket is one which is cut diagonally from the front to the back, so that the back is longer. The usual British word is **tailcoat**. **3** A **cutaway** picture shows what something such as a machine looks like inside.

[N-COUNT; N-COUNT; AMERICAN; ADJ: ADJ n]

cut·back /'kʌtbæk/ **cutbacks;** also spelled **cut-back**. A **cutback** is a reduction that is made in something. *The jobs are under threat because of cutbacks in defence spending.*

[◆◇◇◇◇; N-COUNT]

cute /kjuːt/ **cuter, cutest. 1** If you describe something or someone as **cute**, you mean that they are very pretty or attractive, or that they are intended to appear pretty or attractive. *Oh, look at that dog! He's so cute. ...a cute little house.* **2** If you describe someone as **cute**, you think they are sexually attractive. *There was this girl, and I thought she was really cute.* **3** If you describe someone as **cute**, you mean that they deal with things cleverly. *That's a cute trick.*

[◆◇◇◇◇; ADJ-GRADED; INFORMAL; ADJ-GRADED; AMERICAN, INFORMAL; ADJ-GRADED; AMERICAN]

cute·sy /'kjuːtsi/. If you describe someone or something as **cutesy**, you dislike them because you think they are too pretty and unpleasantly sentimental. *...cutesy paintings of owls.*

[ADJ-GRADED; PRAGMATICS; INFORMAL]

,cut 'glass; also spelled **cut-glass**. **Cut glass** is glass that has patterns cut into its surface. *...a cut-glass bowl.*

[N-UNCOUNT]

cu·ti·cle /'kjuːtɪkəl/ **cuticles.** Your **cuticles** are the skin at the base of your fingernails and toenails.

[N-COUNT]

cut·lass /'kʌtləs/ **cutlasses.** A **cutlass** is a short sword formerly used by sailors.

[N-COUNT]

cut·lery /'kʌtləri/. The knives, forks, and spoons that you eat with are referred to as **cutlery**. The usual American word is **flatware**.

[◆◇◇◇◇; N-UNCOUNT; BRITISH]

cut·let /'kʌtlət/ **cutlets.** A **cutlet** is a small piece of meat which is usually fried or grilled.

[N-COUNT]

'cut-off, cut-offs; also spelled **cutoff**. **1** A **cut-off** or a **cut-off** point is the level or limit at which you decide that something should stop happening. *The cut-off date for registering is yet to be announced.* **2** The **cut-off** of a supply or service is the complete stopping of it. *A total cut-off of supplies would cripple the country's economy.*

[◆◆◇◇◇; N-COUNT; N-COUNT]

,cut 'out. If you are not **cut out** for a particular type of work, you do not have the right qualities to be able to do it well. *He doesn't feel he is cut out to be a leader.*

[ADJ]

'cut-out, cut-outs. 1 A **cut-out** is a device that turns off a machine automatically in particular circumstances. *Use a kettle with an automatic cut-out.* **2** A cardboard **cut-out** is a shape that has been cut from thick card.

[N-COUNT; N-COUNT]

'cut-price. **Cut-price** goods or services are available at a cheaper price than usual.

[◆◇◇◇◇; ADJ: ADJ n]

'cut-rate. **Cut-rate** means the same as **cut-price**.

[ADJ: ADJ n]

cut·ter /'kʌtə/ **cutters. 1** See **cut**. **2** A **cutter** is a type of boat.

[◆◇◇◇◇; N-COUNT]

'cut-throat. If you describe a situation as **cut-throat**, you mean that the people or companies involved all want success and are willing to harm each other to get it. *...the cut-throat competition in personal computers.*

[ADJ-GRADED]

cut·ting /'kʌtɪŋ/ **cuttings. 1** A **cutting** is an article or photo which has been cut from a newspaper or magazine. The usual American word is **clipping**. *...a stack of old photographs and newspaper cuttings.* **2** A **cutting** from a plant is a part of it that you have cut off so that you can grow a new plant from it. **3** A railway **cutting** is a narrow valley cut through a hill so that a railway line can pass through. **4** A **cutting** remark is unkind and hurtful.

[◆◆◆◇◇; N-COUNT; BRITISH; N-COUNT; N-COUNT; ADJ-GRADED]

,cutting 'edge. 1 If you are at the **cutting edge** of a field of activity, you are involved in its most important or exciting developments. *This shipyard is at the cutting edge of world shipbuilding technology.* **2** If someone or something gives you a **cutting edge**, they give you motivation and energy, and an advantage over your competitors.

[◆◇◇◇◇; N-SING; N-SING]

'cutting room. The **cutting room** in a film production company is the place where the film is edited. *Her scene ended up on the cutting room floor.*

[N-SING]

cuttle·fish /'kʌtəlfɪʃ/ **cuttlefish** is both the singular and the plural form. A **cuttlefish** is a sea animal with a soft body, tentacles, and a hard internal shell.

[N-COUNT]

,cut 'up. If you are **cut up** about something that has happened, you are very upset because of it. *Terry was very cut up about Jim's death.*

[◆◇◇◇◇; ADJ-GRADED; BRITISH, INFORMAL]

CV /ˌsiː 'viː/ **CVs.** Your **CV** is a brief written account of your personal details, your education, and jobs you have had, which you send when you are applying for a job. **CV** is an abbreviation for 'curriculum vitae'. *Send them a copy of your CV.*

[◆◇◇◇◇; N-COUNT]

cya·nide /'saɪənaɪd/. **Cyanide** is a highly poisonous substance. *...a lethal dose of cyanide.*

[◆◇◇◇◇; N-UNCOUNT]

cy·ber·net·ics /ˌsaɪbə'netɪks/. **Cybernetics** is a branch of science which involves studying the way human brains work and developing electronic machines that work similarly.

[N-UNCOUNT]

cy·ber·punk /'saɪbəpʌŋk/. **Cyberpunk** is a type of science fiction. The stories are set in a threatening future society dominated by computer technology.

[N-UNCOUNT]

cy·ber·space /'saɪbəspeɪs/. In computer technology, **cyberspace** refers to data banks and networks, considered as a space.

[N-UNCOUNT]

cy·borg /'saɪbɔːg/ **cyborgs.** In science fiction, a **cyborg** is a being that is part human and part robot, or a robot that looks like a human being.

[N-COUNT]

cyc·la·men /'sɪkləmən/; **cyclamen** is both the singular and the plural form. A **cyclamen** is a plant with white, pink, or red flowers. `N-COUNT`

cy·cle /'saɪkəl/ **cycles, cycling, cycled. 1** If you **cycle**, you ride a bicycle. *He cycled to Ingwold... Over 1000 riders cycled 100 miles around the Vale of York.* ♦ **cy·cling** *Quiet country roads are ideal for cycling.* **2** A **cycle** is a bicycle. `VERB: V n / V prep/adv / N-UNCOUNT / N-COUNT` ♦♦♦◇◇ **3** A **cycle** is a series of events or processes that is continually repeated, always in the same order. *...the life cycle of the plant... They must break out of the cycle of violence.* **4** A **cycle** is a single complete series of movements in an electrical, electronic, or mechanical process. *...10 cycles per second.* **5** A **cycle** is a series of songs or poems that are intended to be performed or read one after the other. `N-COUNT`

cy·cle·way /'saɪkəlweɪ/ **cycleways.** A **cycleway** is a special route or path intended for use by cyclists. `N-COUNT BRITISH`

cy·clic /'sɪklɪk, 'saɪk-/. **Cyclic** means the same as **cyclical**. `ADJ`

cy·cli·cal /'sɪklɪkəl, 'saɪk-/. A **cyclical** process is one in which a series of events happen again and again in the same order. *...the cyclical nature of the airline business.* `♦◇◇◇◇ ADJ`

cy·clist /'saɪklɪst/ **cyclists.** A **cyclist** is someone who rides a bicycle, or is riding a bicycle. `♦◇◇◇◇ N-COUNT`

cy·clone /'saɪkləʊn/ **cyclones.** A **cyclone** is a violent tropical storm. `♦◇◇◇◇ N-COUNT`

cyg·net /'sɪgnɪt/ **cygnets.** A **cygnet** is a young swan. `N-COUNT`

cyl·in·der /'sɪlɪndə/ **cylinders. 1** A **cylinder** is an object with flat round ends and long straight sides. See picture headed **shapes**. *...a cylinder of foam... It was recorded on a wax cylinder.* **2** A gas **cylinder** is a cylinder-shaped container in which gas is kept under pressure. *...oxygen cylinders.* **3** In an engine, `♦♦◇◇◇ N-COUNT / N-COUNT` a **cylinder** is a cylinder-shaped part in which a piston moves.

cy·lin·dri·cal /sɪ'lɪndrɪkəl/. Something that is **cylindrical** is in the shape of a cylinder. `ADJ`

cym·bal /'sɪmbəl/ **cymbals.** A **cymbal** is a flat, round, brass musical instrument. You hit it with a stick or hit two cymbals together. See picture headed **musical instruments**. `N-COUNT`

cyni·cal /'sɪnɪkəl/. If you describe someone as **cynical**, you mean that they have a pessimistic or amoral attitude to life because they believe that people generally act selfishly or dishonourably. *...his cynical view of the world... It has also made me more cynical about relationships.* ♦ **cyn·ic** /'sɪnɪk/ **cynics.** A **cynic** is a cynical person. *Cynics will say that you are just doing this to save your own skin.* ♦ **cyni·cal·ly** /'sɪnɪkli/ *He said cynically, 'He's probably pocketed the difference!'... Fears of disease can be cynically exploited.* ♦ **cyni·cism** /'sɪnɪsɪzəm/ *This talk betrays a certain cynicism about free trade.* `♦♦◇◇◇ ADJ-GRADED / N-COUNT / ADV-GRADED: ADV with v / N-UNCOUNT`

cy·pher /'saɪfə/. See **cipher**.

cy·press /'saɪprəs/ **cypresses.** A **cypress** is a type of conifer. `♦◇◇◇◇ N-COUNT`

cy·ril·lic /sɪ'rɪlɪk/. **1** The **cyrillic** alphabet is the alphabet used to write some Slavonic languages, such as Russian and Bulgarian. **2 Cyrillic** is the cyrillic alphabet. `ADJ: ADJ n / N-UNCOUNT`

cyst /sɪst/ **cysts.** A **cyst** is a growth containing liquid that appears inside your body or under your skin. `♦◇◇◇◇ N-COUNT`

cyst·ic fi·bro·sis /ˌsɪstɪk faɪ'brəʊsɪs/. **Cystic fibrosis** is a serious hereditary disease which affects children from birth and makes breathing difficult. `♦◇◇◇◇ N-UNCOUNT`

cys·ti·tis /sɪ'staɪtɪs/. **Cystitis** is a bladder infection. *...an attack of cystitis.* `N-UNCOUNT MEDICAL`

czar /zɑː/. See **tsar**.

D d

D, d /diː/ **D's, d's. 1** D is the fourth letter of the English alphabet. **2** In music, **D** is the second note in the scale of C major. **3** If you get a **D** as a mark for a piece of work or in an exam, your work is below average or poor. **4 d.** is an abbreviation for **died** when it is written in front of dates, for example on memorials or in reference books. **5 D** or **d** is used as an abbreviation for words beginning with d, such as 'day', 'defeated', or 'district'. `N-VAR / N-VAR / N-VAR`

'd. Pronounced /-d/ after a vowel sound and /-əd/ after a consonant sound. **1 'd** is a short form of **had**, especially when it is an auxiliary verb. *She said she'd met you in England.* **2 'd** is a short form of **would**. *I'd like a word with you.* `SPOKEN / SPOKEN`

d' /d-/. See **d'you**.

D.A. /ˌdiː 'eɪ/ **D.A.s.** In the United States, a **D.A.** is a **District Attorney**. `♦◇◇◇◇ N-COUNT`

dab /dæb/ **dabs, dabbing, dabbed. 1** If you **dab** something, you touch it several times using quick light movements. *She dabbed iodine on the cuts... He dabbed at his lips with the napkin.* **2** A **dab** of something is a small amount of it that is put onto a surface. *...a dab of glue.* `♦◇◇◇◇ VERB: V n / V prep/adv / V at n / N-COUNT: N of n INFORMAL`

dab·ble /'dæbəl/ **dabbles, dabbling, dabbled.** If you **dabble** in something, you take part in it but not very seriously. *Magicians do not dabble, they work hard.* `♦◇◇◇◇ V in/with/at n v`

dab 'hand, dab hands. If you are a **dab hand** at something, you are very good at doing it. *He's a dab hand in the kitchen.* `N-COUNT BRITISH, INFORMAL`

da·cha /'dætʃə, AM 'dɑːtʃə/ **dachas.** A **dacha** is a country house in Russia. `N-COUNT`

dachs·hund /'dækshʊnd, AM 'dɑːksʊnt/ **dachshunds.** A **dachshund** is a small dog that has very short legs and a long body. `N-COUNT`

dad /dæd/ **dads.** Your **dad** is your father. *I talked to Dad... He's living with his mum and dad.* `♦♦♦◇◇ N-FAMILY INFORMAL`

dad·dy /'dædi/ **daddies.** Children often call their father **daddy**. *Look at me, Daddy!* `♦♦◇◇◇ N-FAMILY INFORMAL`

daf·fo·dil /'dæfədɪl/ **daffodils.** A **daffodil** is a yellow trumpet-shaped spring flower with a long stem. `N-COUNT`

daf·fy /'dæfi/. If you describe a person or thing as **daffy**, you mean that they are strange or foolish, but in a rather attractive way. `ADJ-GRADED PRAGMATICS INFORMAL`

daft /dɑːft, dæft/ **dafter, daftest.** If you describe a person or their behaviour as **daft**, you think that they are stupid, impractical, or rather strange. `♦◇◇◇◇ ADJ-GRADED PRAGMATICS BRITISH`

dag·ger /'dægə/ **daggers.** A **dagger** is a weapon like a knife with two sharp edges. `♦◇◇◇◇ N-COUNT`

dahl·ia /'deɪliə/ **dahlias.** A **dahlia** is a garden flower with a lot of brightly coloured petals. `N-COUNT`

dai·ly /'deɪli/ **dailies. 1** If something happens daily, it happens every day. *The Visitor Centre is open daily.* ▶ Also an adjective. *They held daily press briefings.* **2 Daily** quantities or rates relate to a period of one day. *...a diet containing adequate daily amounts of fresh fruit.* **3** A **daily** is a newspaper that is published every day of the week except Sunday. ▶ Also an adjective. *He studied the daily papers.* **4** Your **daily life** is the things that you do every day as part of your normal life. *All of us in our daily life react favourably to people who take our views seriously.* `♦♦♦◇◇ ADV: ADV after v / ADJ: ADJ n / ADJ: ADJ n / N-COUNT / ADJ: ADJ n / PHRASE`

dain·ty /'deɪnti/ **daintier, daintiest.** If you describe a movement, person, or object as **dainty**, you `♦◇◇◇◇ ADJ-GRADED`

mean that they are small, delicate, and pretty.
♦ **dain·ti·ly** *She walked daintily down the steps.* ADV-GRADED

dai·qui·ri /'daɪkɪri, 'dæk-/ **daiquiris.** A daiquiri is a N-COUNT drink made with rum, lime juice, sugar, and ice.

dairy /'deəri/ **dairies.** 1 A dairy is a shop or com- ◆◆◇◇◇ pany that sells milk and food made from milk, such N-COUNT as butter, cream, and cheese. 2 On a farm, the **dairy** N-COUNT is the building where milk is kept or where cream, butter, and cheese are made. 3 **Dairy** is used to re- ADJ: ADJ n fer to foods such as butter and cheese that are made from milk. *...vitamins found in eggs, meat and dairy products.* 4 **Dairy** is used to refer to the use of ADJ: ADJ n cattle to produce milk rather than meat. *...a small vegetable and dairy farm.*

dais /'deɪɪs/ **daises.** A dais is a raised platform in a N-COUNT hall.

dai·sy /'deɪzi/ **daisies.** A daisy is a small wild ◆◇◇◇◇ flower with a yellow centre and white petals. N-COUNT

dale /deɪl/ **dales.** A dale is a valley. *The county is* N-COUNT *renowned for the beauty of the dales.* BRITISH

dal·li·ance /'dæliəns/ **dalliances.** 1 When two N-VAR people have a brief romantic relationship, you can DATED say that they have a **dalliance** with each other. 2 Someone's **dalliance** with something is a brief in- N-COUNT volvement with it. *...my brief dalliance with higher* DATED *education.*

dal·ly /'dæli/ **dallies, dallying, dallied.** If you VERB: V dally, you act or move very slowly, wasting time. *He* V over n/-ing *did not dally over the choice of a suitable partner.* Also V with n DATED

Dal·ma·tian /dæl'meɪʃən/ **Dalmatians.** A Dalma- N-COUNT tian is a large dog with short, smooth, white hair and black or dark brown spots.

dam /dæm/ **dams, damming, dammed.** 1 A ◆◆◇◇◇ dam is a wall that is built across a river in order to N-COUNT stop the water flowing and to make a lake. 2 To VERB: V n **dam** a river means to build a dam across it.

dam·age /'dæmɪdʒ/ **damages, damaging, dam-** ◆◆◆◆◇ **aged.** 1 To **damage** an object means to break it, VERB: V n spoil it physically, or stop it from working properly. 2 **Damage** is physical harm that is caused to an ob- N-UNCOUNT ject. *Extensive damage was caused by the blast.* 3 To **damage** something means to cause it to become VERB less good, pleasant, or successful. *Jackson doesn't* V n *want to damage his reputation as a political personal-ity.* ♦ **dam·ag·ing** *...the resignation will be very dam-* ADJ-GRADED *aging to the Soviet leader.* 4 **Damage** consists of the N-UNCOUNT unpleasant effects that something has on a person, situation, or type of activity. *The scandal stories are doing lasting damage to the Duchess and to her chil-dren.* 5 If you say **'the damage is done'**, you mean that PHRASE it is too late now to prevent the harmful effects of something that has already happened. 6 If a court of law awards **damages** to someone, it or- N-PLURAL ders money to be paid to them by a person who has damaged their reputation or property, or who has in-jured them.

dam·ask /'dæməsk/ **damasks.** Damask is a type of N-VAR heavy cloth with a pattern woven into it.

dame /deɪm/ **dames.** 1 A dame is a woman. *She* ◆◆◇◇◇ *played the kind of dames only the insane would take* N-COUNT *home to mother.* 2 **Dame** is a title given to a woman AMERICAN as a special honour. *...Dame Joan Sutherland.* N-TITLE BRITISH

dam·mit /'dæmɪt/. See **damn.**

damn /dæm/ **damns, damning, damned.** ◆◆◇◇◇ 1 **Damn**, **damn it**, and **dammit** are swear words EXCLAM which some people use to express anger or frustra-tion. 2 **Damn** is a swear word which some people ADJ: :DJ n use to emphasize what they are saying. *There's not a* PRAGMATICS *damn thing you can do about it now.* ▶ Also an ad- ADV: verb. *As it turned out, I was damn right.* ADV adj/adv 3 If you say that someone **does not give a damn** about PHRASE something, you mean that they do not care about it at all. 4 People use **damn near** to emphasize that what PHRASE they are saying is not actually true, but is very close to PRAGMATICS being true. *I damn near went crazy.* INFORMAL 5 If you say that a person or a news report **damns** VERB: V n something such as a policy or action, you mean that they are very critical of it. 6 See also **damned, damning.**

dam·nable /'dæmnəbəl/. You use damnable to em- ADJ: ADJ n phasize that you dislike or disapprove of something PRAGMATICS a great deal. *What a damnable climate we have!* DATED ♦ **dam·nably** /'dæmnəbli/ *It was damnably unfair* ADV: ADV adj *that he should suffer so much.*

dam·na·tion /,dæm'neɪʃən/. 1 According to some N-UNCOUNT religions, if someone suffers **damnation**, they are condemned to stay in hell for ever after their death because of their sin. 2 Some people say **damnation** EXCLAM as a swear word to express anger or frustration.

damned /dæmd/. 1 **Damned** is a swear word that ◆◆◇◇◇ some people use, especially when they are angry or ADJ: ADJ n frustrated, to emphasize what they are saying. PRAGMATICS *They're a damned nuisance most of the time.* ▶ Also ADV: an adverb. *We are making a damned good profit.* ADV adj/adv 2 According to some religions, **the damned** are N-PLURAL: people who have been condemned to stay in hell theN for ever after they have died. 3 If someone says **'I'm** PHRASE **damned if I'm** going to do it' or **'I'll be damned if** PRAGMATICS I'll do it', they are emphasizing that they do not in- INFORMAL tend to do it and think it is unreasonable for anyone to expect them to do it. 4 Some people say **'I'll be** PHRASE **damned!'** when they are expressing surprise at INFORMAL something.

damned·est /'dæmdɪst/. If you say that you will **do** PHRASE your **damnedest** to achieve something, you mean INFORMAL that you will try as hard as you can to do it.

,**damn 'fool.** Damn fool is a mild swear word ADJ-GRADED: meaning 'very stupid'. *What a damn fool thing to* ADJ n *do!* DATED

damn·ing /'dæmɪŋ/. If you describe evidence or a ◆◇◇◇◇ report as **damning**, you mean that it suggests very ADJ-GRADED strongly that someone is guilty of a crime or error.

Damocles /'dæməkliːz/. If you say that someone PHRASE has the **Sword of Damocles** hanging over their head, you mean that they are in a situation in which something very bad could happen to them at any time.

damp /dæmp/ **damper, dampest; damps,** ◆◆◇◇◇ **damping, damped.** 1 Something that is **damp** is ADJ-GRADED slightly wet. 2 **Damp** is moisture that is found on N-UNCOUNT the inside walls of a house or in the air. 3 If you VERB: V n **damp** something, you make it slightly wet.

damp down. To **damp down** something such as a PHRASAL VB strong emotion, an argument, or a crisis means to V P noun make it calmer or less intense. *Mr Major tried to damp down the row yesterday.*

damp·en /'dæmpən/ **dampens, dampening,** ◆◇◇◇◇ **dampened.** 1 To **dampen** something such as VERB: V n someone's enthusiasm or excitement means to make it less lively or intense. ▶ To **dampen** some- PHRASAL VB: thing **down** means the same as to **dampen** it. *Al-* V n P *though unemployment rose last month, this is un-* V P noun *likely to dampen down wage demands.* 2 If you **dampen** something, you make it slightly wet. VERB: V n

damp·er /'dæmpə/ **dampers.** 1 A **damper** is a N-COUNT small sheet of metal in a fire, boiler, or furnace that can be moved to alter the amount of air that enters. 2 If someone or something **puts a damper on** PHRASE something, they stop it being as enjoyable or as suc- INFORMAL cessful as it should be. *Unseasonably cool weather has put a damper on many plans for the day.*

damp·ness /'dæmpnəs/. 1 **Dampness** is moisture N-UNCOUNT in the air, or on the surface of something. *The tins had to be kept away from dampness, soot and cook-ing fumes.* 2 **Dampness** is the quality of being N-UNCOUNT damp. *The dampness of the forest did not agree with him physically.*

dam·sel /'dæmzəl/ **damsels.** A damsel is a young ◆◇◇◇◇ unmarried woman. N-COUNT LITERARY

dam·son /'dæmzən/ **damsons.** A damson is a N-COUNT small, sour, purple plum.

dance /dɑːns, dæns/ **dances, dancing, danced.** ◆◆◆◆◇ 1 When you **dance**, you move your body and feet in VERB: V a way which follows a rhythm, usually in time to V to n music. *I like to dance to the music on the radio.* ♦ **danc·ing** *Let's go dancing tonight.* 2 A **dance** is a N-UNCOUNT particular series of rhythmic movements of your N-COUNT body and feet, which you usually do in time to mu-sic. *She describes the tango as a very sexy dance.*

3 When you **dance** with someone, the two of you take part in a dance together, as partners. You can also say that two people **dance**. *Shall we dance?... He asked her to dance.* ▶ Also a noun. *Come and have a dance with me.* **4 Dance** is the activity of performing dances, as a public entertainment or an art form. **5** If you **dance** a particular kind of dance, you do it or perform it. *We all danced the Tango and the Charleston.*
  V-RECIP:
  V *with* n
  pl-n V
  V (non-recip)
  N-COUNT
  N-UNCOUNT
  VERB
  V n

6 A **dance** is a social event where people dance with each other.   N-COUNT

7 If you **dance** somewhere, you move there lightly and quickly, for example because you are excited. *He danced off down the road.*   VERB V adv/prep

8 If you say that something **dances**, you mean that it moves about, or seems to move about, lightly and quickly. *Patterns of light, reflected by the river, dance along the base of the cliffs.*   VERB V adv/prep

9 ● to **dance** to someone's **tune**: see **tune**. ● to **make a song and dance about** something: see **song and dance**.

'dance floor,   dance floors; also spelled **dancefloor**. In a restaurant or night club, the **dance floor** is the area where people can dance.   ◆◇◇◇◇ N-COUNT

'dance hall, dance halls. Dance halls were large rooms or buildings where people paid to go and dance, usually in the evening.   N-COUNT DATED

danc·er /'dɑːnsə, 'dæns-/ **dancers.** A **dancer** is a person who earns money by dancing, or a person who is dancing.   ◆◆◇◇◇ N-COUNT

'dance studio, dance studios. A **dance studio** is a place where people pay to learn how to dance.   N-COUNT

dan·de·lion /'dændɪlaɪən/ **dandelions.** A **dandelion** is a wild plant which has yellow flowers with lots of thin petals. When the petals drop off, they leave fluffy balls of seeds.   ◆◇◇◇◇ N-COUNT

dan·druff /'dændrʌf/. **Dandruff** consists of small white pieces of dead skin in someone's hair, or fallen from someone's hair.   N-UNCOUNT

dan·dy /'dændi/ **dandies. 1** A **dandy** is a man who thinks a great deal about his appearance and always dresses in smart clothes. **2** If you say that something is **dandy**, you mean it is good or just right. *There's a zoo round here? That's dandy for my kids.*   ◆◇◇◇◇ N-COUNT ADJ DATED, AMERICAN

dan·ger /'deɪndʒə/ **dangers. 1 Danger** is the possibility that someone may be harmed or killed. *My friends endured tremendous danger in order to help me... Your life is in danger.* **2** A **danger** is something or someone that can hurt or harm you. *...the dangers of smoking.* **3** If there is a **danger** of something unpleasant happening, it is possible that it will happen. **4** If someone who has been seriously ill is **out of danger**, they are still ill, but they are not expected to die.   ◆◆◆◇ N-UNCOUNT N-COUNT N-SING: also no det, N that PHRASE

dan·ger·ous /'deɪndʒərəs/. If something is **dangerous**, it is able or likely to hurt or harm you. *...dangerous drugs.* ♦ **dan·ger·ous·ly** *He rushed downstairs dangerously fast.*   ◆◆◆◇ ADJ-GRADED ADV-GRADED

dan·gle /'dæŋgəl/ **dangles, dangling, dangled. 1** If something **dangles** from somewhere, it hangs or swings loosely. *He and I were sitting out on his jetty dangling our legs in the water.* **2** If you say that someone is **dangling** something attractive before you, you mean they are offering it to you in order to try and persuade you to do something or buy something.   ◆◇◇◇◇ V-ERG: V prep/adv V n prep/adv VERB: V n *before/in front of* n

Danish 'pastry, Danish pastries. Danish pastries are cakes made from sweet pastry.   N-COUNT

dank /dæŋk/. A **dank** place is unpleasantly damp and cold.   ADJ

dap·per /'dæpə/. A man who is **dapper** is small, slim, and neatly dressed.   ADJ-GRADED

dap·pled /'dæpəld/. You use **dappled** to describe something that has dark or light patches on it, or that is made up of patches of light and shade. *...a dappled horse.*   ADJ: ADJ n, v-link ADJ *with/in* n

dare /deə/ **dares, daring, dared. Dare** sometimes behaves like an ordinary verb, for example 'He dared to speak' and 'He doesn't dare to speak'   ◆◆◆◇◇

and sometimes like a modal, for example 'He daren't speak'.

1 If you do not **dare** to do something, you do not have enough courage to do it, or you do not want to do it because you fear the consequences. If you **dare** to do something, you do something which requires a lot of courage. *He has also dared to take unpopular, but principled stands at times. ...problems in our family that I didn't dare tell Uncle.* ▶ Also a modal. *Dare she risk staying where she was?... 'Are you coming with me?'—'I can't, Alice. I daren't.'.* **2** You use **'dare I say it'** when you know that what you are going to say will disappoint or annoy someone. *Politicians usually attract younger women, dare I say it, because of the status they have in society.*   VERB V to-inf V inf MODAL PHRASE

3 If you say to someone **'don't you dare'** do something, you are telling someone not to do it and letting them know that you are angry. *Don't you dare go anywhere else.* **4** You say **'how dare you'** when you are very shocked and angry about something that someone has done. *How dare you insult my singing!.*   PHRASE PHRASE

5 If you **dare** someone to do something, you challenge them to prove that they are not frightened of doing it. ▶ Also a noun. *The children said they'd run away for a dare.*   VERB: V n to-inf N-COUNT

6 You can use **'I dare say'** or **'I daresay'** before or after a statement to indicate that you believe it is probably true. *I dare say that the computer would provide a clear answer to that.*   PHRASE SPOKEN

dare·devil /'deədevəl/ **daredevils. 1 Daredevil** people enjoy doing physically dangerous things. ▶ Also a noun. *He was a daredevil when young.* **2** You use **daredevil** to describe actions that are physically dangerous and require courage. *...daredevil feats by cowboys and Indians.*   ADJ: ADJ n N-COUNT ADJ: ADJ n

daren't /deənt/. 'Dare not' is usually said or written as **daren't**.   INFORMAL

dare·say /,deə'seɪ/. See **dare**.

dar·ing /'deərɪŋ/. **1** People who are **daring** are willing to do or say things which are new or which might shock or anger other people. *...a very daring thing to ask.* ♦ **dar·ing·ly** *...a daringly low-cut dress.* **2** A **daring** person is willing to do things that might be dangerous. **3 Daring** is the courage to do things which might be dangerous or which might shock or anger other people. *His daring may have cost him his life.*   ◆◆◇◇◇ ADJ-GRADED ADV-GRADED ADJ-GRADED N-UNCOUNT

dark /dɑːk/ **darker, darkest. 1** When it is **dark**, there is not enough light to see properly, for example because it is night. *People usually draw the curtains once it gets dark... She made her way back through the dark kitchen.* ♦ **dark·ness** *The light went out, and the room was plunged into darkness.* ♦ **dark·ly** *...a darkly lit, seedy dance hall.* **2** The **dark** is the lack of light in a place. *I've always been afraid of the dark.* **3** See also **pitch-dark**. **4** If you do something **after dark**, you do it when night has begun. **5** If you do something **before dark**, you do it before the sun sets and night begins. *They'll be back well before dark.*   ◆◆◆◇ ADJ-GRADED N-UNCOUNT ADV N-SING: the N PHRASE PHRASE

6 If you describe something as **dark**, you mean that it is black in colour, or a shade that is close to black. *He wore a dark suit.* **7** When you use **dark** to describe a colour, you are referring to a shade of that colour which is close to black, or seems to have some black in it. *...a dark blue dress.* **8** If someone has **dark** hair, eyes, or skin, they have brown or black hair, eyes, or skin. **9** If you describe a white person as **dark**, you mean that they have brown or black hair, and often a brownish skin. ♦ **darkly** *He was a slim, solemn, darkly handsome young man.*   ADJ-GRADED COMB ADJ-GRADED ADJ-GRADED ADV: ADV adj

10 A **dark** period of time is unpleasant or frightening. *This was the darkest period of the war.*   ADJ-GRADED

11 A **dark** place or area is mysterious and not fully known about. *...a dark corner of the solar system.*   ADJ-GRADED: ADJ n

12 Dark thoughts are sad, and show that you are expecting something unpleasant to happen. ♦ **darkly** *Her thoughts circled darkly round Bernard's strange behaviour.*   ADJ-GRADED LITERARY ADV-GRADED

13 Dark looks or remarks make you think that the   ADJ-GRADED

person giving them wants to harm you or that something horrible is going to happen. ♦ **darkly** *They shake their heads and mutter darkly.* ADV-GRADED: ADV with v

14 If you describe something as **dark**, you mean that it is related to things that are serious or unpleasant, rather than light-hearted. *...their dark humor.* ADJ-GRADED

♦ **darkly** *The atmosphere after Wednesday's debut was as darkly comic as the film itself.* ADV-GRADED: ADV adj

15 If you are **in the dark** about something, you do not know anything about it. PHRASE **16** If you describe something someone says or does as **a shot in the dark**, you mean they are guessing that what they say is correct or that what they do will be successful. **17** • **leap in the dark**: see **leap**. PHRASE

'dark age, dark ages; also spelled **Dark Age. 1** If you refer to a period as a **dark age**, you think that it is characterized by ignorance and a lack of progress. *The Education Secretary accuses teachers of wanting to return to a dark age.* **2 The Dark Ages** are the period of European history between about 500 A.D. and about 1000 A.D. N-COUNT PRAGMATICS WRITTEN / N-PROPER: the N

dark·en /'dɑːkən/ **darkens, darkening, darkened. 1** If something **darkens** or if someone or something **darkens** it, it becomes darker. *The sky darkened abruptly... She had put on her make-up and darkened her eyelashes.* **2** If someone's mood **darkens**, they suddenly become rather unhappy. *Nothing was going to darken his mood today.* **3** If someone's face **darkens**, they suddenly look angry. ♦◇◇◇◇ V-ERG V WRITTEN V-ERG: V n WRITTEN VERB: V WRITTEN

dark·ened /'dɑːkənd/. A **darkened** building or room has no lights on inside it. ♦◇◇◇◇ ADJ: ADJ n

,dark 'glasses. Dark glasses are glasses which have dark-coloured lenses to protect your eyes in the sunshine. N-PLURAL: also a pair of N

,dark 'horse, dark horses. If you describe someone as a **dark horse**, you mean that people know very little about them. N-COUNT

dark·room /'dɑːkruːm/ **darkrooms. A darkroom** is a room which has been sealed off from natural daylight and is lit only by red light. It is used for developing photographs. ♦◇◇◇◇ N-COUNT

dar·ling /'dɑːlɪŋ/ **darlings. 1** You call someone **darling** if you love them or like them very much. *Thank you, darling.* **2** Some people call other people **darling** as a sign of friendliness. **3** Some people use **darling** to describe someone or something that they love or like very much. *...a darling baby boy.* **4** If you describe someone as a **darling**, you are fond of them and think that they are nice. **5** The **darling** of a group of people is someone who is especially liked by that group. *Rajneesh was the darling of a prosperous family.* ♦♦◇◇ N-VOC PRAGMATICS / N-VOC PRAGMATICS / ADJ: ADJ n / N-COUNT / N-COUNT: with poss

darn /dɑːn/ **darns, darning, darned. 1** When you **darn** something knitted or made of cloth, you mend a hole in it by sewing stitches across the hole and then weaving stitches in and out of them. ♦ **darn·ing** *...chores such as sewing and darning.* **2** A **darn** is a part of a piece of clothing that has been darned. **3** People sometimes use **darn** or **darned** to emphasize what they are saying, often when they are annoyed. *There's not a darn thing he can do about it.* ▶ Also an adverb. *...the desire to be free to do just as we darn well please.* ♦◇◇◇◇ VERB: V n / N-UNCOUNT N-COUNT / ADJ: ADJ n INFORMAL / ADV: ADV adj/adv

dart /dɑːt/ **darts, darting, darted. 1** If a person or animal **darts** somewhere, they move there suddenly and quickly. *Ingrid darted across the deserted street.* **2** If you **dart** a glance at someone or something, or if your eyes **dart** to them, you look at them very quickly. *The conductor's eyes darted to Wilfred.* **3** A **dart** is a small narrow object with a sharp point which can be thrown or shot. **4 Darts** is a game in which you throw darts at a round board which has numbers on it. ♦◇◇◇◇ VERB V prep/adv WRITTEN / VERB: V n at n V prep/adv WRITTEN / N-COUNT / N-UNCOUNT

dart·board /'dɑːtbɔːd/ **dartboards. A dartboard** is a circular board with numbers on it which is used as the target in a game of darts. N-COUNT

dash /dæʃ/ **dashes, dashing, dashed. 1** If you **dash** somewhere, you run or go there quickly and suddenly. *Suddenly she dashed down to the cellar.* ▶ Also a noun. *...a 160-mile dash to hospital.* **2** If you **make a dash for** a place, you run there very quickly, for example to escape from someone or something. **3** If you say that you have to **dash**, you mean that you are in a hurry and have to leave immediately. *I'm sorry but I have to dash.* **4** A **dash** of something is a small quantity of it which you add when you are preparing food or mixing a drink. **5** A **dash** of a quality is a small amount of it that is found in something and often makes it more interesting or distinctive. *...a story with a dash of mystery thrown in.* **6** If you **dash** something somewhere, you throw or push it violently. *She seized the doll and dashed it against the stone wall with tremendous force.* **7** If an event or person **dashes** someone's hopes or expectations, it destroys them by making it impossible that the thing that is hoped for or expected will ever happen. *Investors had their hopes of making a quick profit dashed.* **8** A **dash** is a short fast race. **9** A **dash** is a straight horizontal line (—) used in writing, for example to separate two main clauses whose meanings are closely connected. **10** The **dash** of a car is its dashboard. **11 Dash** is a mixture of stylishness, enthusiasm, and courage. *The Prince was driving his car with great fire and dash.* **12** If you say that someone **cuts a dash**, you mean that they have an attractively stylish appearance. ♦♦◇◇ VERB V adv/prep / N-SING PHRASE / VB: no cont V INFORMAL / N-COUNT / N-COUNT / VERB V n against n Also V n prep / VERB: V n have n V-ed / N-COUNT / N-COUNT / N-COUNT / N-UNCOUNT DATED / PHRASE DATED

dash off. 1 If you **dash off** to a place, you go there very quickly. **2** If you **dash off** a piece of writing, you write it very quickly, without much thought. PHRASAL VB V P to n / V P noun

dash·board /'dæʃbɔːd/ **dashboards.** The **dashboard** in a car is the panel facing the driver's seat where most of the instruments and switches are. See picture headed **car and bicycle**. ♦◇◇◇◇ N-COUNT

dash·ing /'dæʃɪŋ/. A **dashing** person or thing is very stylish and attractive. ♦◇◇◇◇ ADJ-GRADED DATED

das·tard·ly /'dæstədli/. **1** If you describe an action as **dastardly**, you mean it is wicked and planned to hurt someone. *He described the killing as a dastardly act.* **2** If you describe a person as **dastardly**, you mean they are wicked. *...the heiress who is badly treated by her dastardly uncle.* ADJ-GRADED: ADJ n DATED / ADJ-GRADED: ADJ n DATED

DAT /dæt/. **DAT** is an abbreviation for **digital audio tape.** ♦◇◇◇◇ N-UNCOUNT

data /'deɪtə/. the form **data** can be used as a singular or plural. Some people use the form **datum** for the singular. **Data** is information, usually in the form of facts or statistics that you can analyse. *The study was based on data from 2,100 women.* ▶ In formal and technical English, **data** is sometimes a plural noun. *To cope with these data, hospitals bought large mainframe computers.* ♦♦♦◇ N-UNCOUNT N-PLURAL

'data bank, data banks; also spelled **databank.** A **data bank** is the same as a **database.** N-COUNT

data·base /'deɪtəbeɪs/ **databases;** also spelled **data base.** A **database** is a collection of data that is stored in a computer. *...a database of hotels that cater for businesswomen.* ♦◇◇◇◇ N-COUNT

,data 'processing; also spelled **data-processing. Data processing** is the series of operations that are carried out on data, especially by computers, in order to present, interpret, or obtain information. N-UNCOUNT

date /deɪt/ **dates, dating, dated. 1** A **date** is a specific time that can be named, for example a particular day or a particular year. *What's the date today?... You will need to give the dates you wish to stay.* **2** When you **date** something, you give or discover the date when it began or when it was made. *Archaeologists have dated the fort to the reign of Emperor Antoninus Pius.* **3** When you **date** something such as a letter or a cheque, you write that day's date on it. *Once the decision is reached, he can date and sign the sheet.* **4** If you want to refer to an event without saying exactly when it will happen or when it happened, you can say that it will happen or happened **at some date** in ♦♦♦◇ N-COUNT / VERB: V n V n to n / VERB V n / N-SING: with supp, at N

D

the future or past. *Retain copies of all correspondence, since you may need them at a later date.* **5 To date** means up until the present time. *'Dottie' is by far his best novel to date.* PHRASE

6 If something **dates**, it goes out of fashion and becomes unacceptable to modern tastes. ♦ **dat·ed** ...*people in dated dinner-jackets.* **7** If your ideas, what you say, or the things that you like or can remember **date** you, they show that you are quite old or older than the people you are with. *It's going to date me now. I attended that school in nineteen sixty nine.* VERB: V ADJ-GRADED VERB V n

8 A **date** is an appointment to meet someone or go out with them, especially someone with whom you are having, or may soon have, a romantic relationship. *I have a date with Bob.* **9** When you have a date with someone with whom you are having, or may soon have, a romantic relationship, you can refer to that person as your **date**. *His date was one of the girls in the show.* **10** If you **are dating** someone, you go out with them regularly because you are having, or may soon have, a romantic relationship with them. You can also say that two people **are dating**. *For a year I dated a woman who was a research assistant... They've been dating for three months.* N-COUNT N-COUNT V-RECIP pl-n V

11 A **date** is a small, dark-brown, sticky fruit with a stone inside. N-COUNT

12 See also **blind date**, **out of date**, **up to date**.

date back. If something **dates back** to a particular time, it started or was made at that time. *The treasure dates back to the sixth century BC.* PHRASAL VB V P to n Also V P amount

date from. If something **dates from** a particular time, it started or was made at that time. *All the cupboards and appliances dated from the 1950s.* PHRASAL VB V P n

date of 'birth, dates of birth. Your **date of birth** is the exact date on which you were born, including the year. *The registration form showed his date of birth as August 2, 1979.* N-COUNT

'date palm, date palms. A **date palm** is a palm tree on which dates grow. N-COUNT

date 'rape. **Date rape** is when a man rapes a woman after having spent the evening socially with her. N-UNCOUNT

da·tive /'deɪtɪv/. In the grammar of some languages such as Latin, **the dative**, or the **dative** case, is the case used for a noun when it is the indirect object of a verb, or when it comes after some prepositions. N-SING: the N

da·tum /'deɪtəm, 'dɑːtəm/. See **data**.

daub /dɔːb/ **daubs, daubing, daubed.** When you **daub** a substance such as mud or paint on something, you spread it on that thing in a rough or careless way. *They sent death threats and daubed his home with slogans.* VERB: V n prep/adv V n with n

daugh·ter /'dɔːtə/ **daughters.** Someone's **daughter** is their female child. ...*Flora and her daughter Catherine.* ♦♦♦♦◇ N-COUNT

'daughter-in-law, daughters-in-law. Someone's **daughter-in-law** is the wife of their son. ♦◇◇◇◇ N-COUNT

daunt /dɔːnt/ **daunts, daunting, daunted.** If something **daunts** you, it makes you feel slightly afraid or worried about dealing with it. ...*a gruelling journey that would have daunted a woman half her age.* ♦ **daunt·ed** *It is hard to pick up such a book and not to feel a little daunted.* VERB V n ADJ-GRADED: v-link ADJ

daunt·ing /'dɔːntɪŋ/. Something that is **daunting** makes you feel slightly afraid or worried about dealing with it. ...*the daunting task of restoring the gardens to their former splendour.* ♦ **daunt·ing·ly** *She is dauntingly articulate.* ♦◇◇◇◇ ADJ-GRADED ADV-GRADED

dau·phin /'dɔːfɪn, 'dəʊfæn/; also **Dauphin**. In former times, the king of France's eldest son was called the **dauphin**. N-SING: the N

daw·dle /'dɔːdəl/ **dawdles, dawdling, dawdled.** **1** If you **dawdle**, you spend more time than is necessary going somewhere. *Eleanor will be back any moment, if she doesn't dawdle.* **2** If you **dawdle over** something, you spend more time than is necessary doing something. *He got fed up as bank staff dawdled over cashing him a cheque.* VERB V VERB V over n/-ing

dawn /dɔːn/ **dawns, dawning, dawned.** **1** **Dawn** is the time of day when light first appears ♦♦◇◇◇ N-VAR

in the sky, before the sun rises. *Nancy woke at dawn.* • **at the crack of dawn:** see **crack**. **2** When you say that a particular day **dawned**, you mean it arrived or began, when it became light. *The next day dawned sombre and gloomy.* VERB: V V adj WRITTEN

3 The **dawn** of a period of time or a situation is the beginning of it. ...*the dawn of the radio age.* **4** If something **is dawning**, it is beginning to develop or come into existence. *A new railway age, that of the high-speed train, has dawned.* ♦ **dawn·ing** ...*the dawning of the space age.* N-SING LITERARY VERB V WRITTEN N-SING

dawn on or **dawn upon.** If a fact or idea **dawns on** you, you realize it. *It gradually dawned on me that I still had talent and ought to run again.* PHRASAL VB V P n it V P n that

dawn 'chorus. The **dawn chorus** is the singing of birds at dawn. N-SING BRITISH

day /deɪ/ **days.** **1** A **day** is one of the seven twenty-four hour periods of time in a week. **2 Day** is the time when it is light, or the time when you are awake and doing things. *He arranged for me to go down to London one day a week... The snack bar is open during the day.* ♦♦♦♦♦ N-COUNT N-VAR

3 If something happens **day after day**, it happens every day without stopping. ...*doing the same thing day after day.* **4** If something happens **day and night** or **night and day**, it happens all the time without stopping. *He would have a nurse in constant attendance day and night.* **5** If something happens **from day to day** or **day by day**, it happens each day. *Your needs can differ from day to day.* PHRASE PHRASE PHRASE

6 One day or **some day** or **one of these days** means at some time in the future. *I hope some day you will find the woman who will make you happy.* **7** If you say that something happened **the other day**, you mean that it happened a few days ago. *We had lunch the other day at our favorite restaurant.* **8** If it is a month or a year **to the day** since a particular thing happened, it is exactly a month or a year since it happened. *It was January 19, a year to the day since he had arrived in Singapore.* **9 To this day** means up until and including today. *To this day young Zulu boys practise fighting.* PHRASE PHRASE PHRASE PHRASE

10 You can refer to a particular period in history as a particular **day** or as particular **days**. *He began to talk about the Ukraine of his uncle's day... She is doing just fine these days.* **11 In this day and age** means in modern times. *Even in this day and age the old attitudes persist.* N-COUNT: with supp PHRASE

12 If you say that something **has seen better days**, you mean that it is old and in poor condition. *The tweed jacket she wore had seen better days.* **13** If you say that something **has had** its **day**, you mean that the period during which it was most successful has now passed. *Popular music may finally have had its day.* PHRASE PHRASE

14 If you **call it a day**, you decide to stop what you are doing because you are tired with it or because it is not successful. *Faced with mounting debts, the decision to call it a day was inevitable.* **15** If you **carry the day**, you are the winner in a contest such as a battle, debate, or sporting competition. *Those in favour of the liberalisation measures seem to have carried the day.* **16** If something **makes** your day, it makes you feel very happy. *Mrs Thatcher's resignation had made his day.* **17** If someone or something **saves the day** in a situation which seems likely to fail, they manage to make it successful. ...*this story about how he saved the day at his daughter's birthday party.* **18** If a particular person, group, or thing **wins the day**, they win a battle, struggle, or competition. If they **lose the day**, they are defeated. *Few in Westminster doubt that the government will win the day.* **19** If you say that a task is **all in a day's work** for someone, you mean that they do not mind doing it although it may be difficult, because it is part of their job or because they often do it. PHRASE PHRASE PHRASE INFORMAL PHRASE PHRASE PHRASE

20 • **it's early days:** see **early**. • **at the end of the day:** see **end**. • **late in the day:** see **late**. • **see the light of day:** see **light**. • **someone's days are numbered:** see **number**. • **the good old days:** see **old**. • **pass the time of day:** see **time**.

-day /-deɪ/. You use **-day** with a number to say how long something lasts. ...*a two-day visit to Zambia.* COMB

day·break /'deɪbreɪk/. **Daybreak** is the time in the morning when light first appears. N-UNCOUNT

'day care. **Day care** is care that is provided during the day for people who cannot look after themselves, such as small children, old people, or people who are ill. Day care is provided by paid workers. N-UNCOUNT

day·dream /'deɪdriːm/ **daydreams, daydreaming**; also spelled **day-dream**. When you **daydream**, you think about pleasant things for a period of time, usually about things you would like to happen. *He daydreams of being a famous journalist.* ▶ Also a noun. *Janis emerged from her daydream.* VERB: V of n/-ing Also V about n; N-COUNT

Day-glo /'deɪ ɡləʊ/; also spelled **Dayglo**. **Day-glo** colours are shades of orange, pink, green, and yellow which are so bright that they seem to glow. **Day-glo** is a trademark. N-UNCOUNT

day·light /'deɪlaɪt/. **1 Daylight** is the natural light that there is during the day, before it gets dark. *It was still daylight.* **2 Daylight** is the time of day when it begins to get light. *Quinn returned shortly after daylight.* **3** If you say that a crime is committed **in broad daylight**, you are expressing your surprise that it is done during the day when people can see it, rather than at night. N-UNCOUNT; PHRASE PRAGMATICS

'daylight saving time. **Daylight saving time** is a period of time in the summer during which the clocks are set one hour forward, so that people can have extra daylight in the evening. The British word is **summer time**. N-UNCOUNT AMERICAN

,day 'nursery, day nurseries. A **day nursery** is a place where children who are too young to go to school can be left all day while their parents are at work. N-COUNT

,day 'off, days off. A **day off** is a day when you do not go to work, even though it is usually a working day. *It was Mrs Dearden's day off.* N-COUNT

,day of 'reckoning. If someone talks about the **day of reckoning**, they mean a day or time in the future when people will be forced to deal with an unpleasant situation which they have avoided until now. N-SING

,day re'lease; also spelled **day-release**. In Britain, **day release** is a system in which workers spend one day each week at a college in order to study a subject connected with their work. N-UNCOUNT

,day re'turn, day returns. In Britain, a **day return** is a train or bus ticket which allows you to go somewhere and come back on the same day for a lower price than an ordinary return ticket. N-COUNT

'day room, day rooms. A **day room** is a room in a hospital where patients can sit and relax during the day. N-COUNT

'day school, day schools. A **day school** is a school where the pupils go home every evening and do not live at the school. Compare **boarding school**. N-COUNT

day·time /'deɪtaɪm/. The **daytime** is the part of a day between the time when it gets light and the time when it gets dark. *In the daytime he stayed up in his room.* N-SING: the N, also no det

,day-to-'day. **Day-to-day** things or activities exist or happen every day as part of ordinary life. *...the day-to-day lives of students.* ADJ: ADJ n

'day trip, day trips; also spelled **day-trip**. A **day trip** is a journey for pleasure to a place and back again on the same day. N-COUNT

'day-tripper, day-trippers; also spelled **day tripper**. A **day-tripper** is someone who makes a day trip. N-COUNT

daze /deɪz/. If someone is in a **daze**, they are feeling confused and unable to think clearly, often because they have had a shock or surprise. *For 35 minutes I was walking around in a daze.* N-SING

dazed /deɪzd/. If someone is **dazed**, they are confused and unable to think clearly, often because of shock or a blow to the head. *At the end of the interview I was dazed and exhausted.* ADJ-GRADED

daz·zle /'dæzəl/ **dazzles, dazzling, dazzled. 1** If someone or something **dazzles** you, you are extremely impressed by their skill, qualities, or beauty. VERB: V n; V n with n; Also V *George dazzled her with his knowledge of the world.* **2** The **dazzle** of something is a quality it has, such as beauty or skill, which is impressive and attractive. *The dazzle of stardom and status attracts them.* **3** See also **razzle-dazzle**. N-SING: with poss **4** If a bright light **dazzles** you, it makes you unable to see properly for a short time. **5** The **dazzle** of a light is its brightness, which makes it impossible for you to see properly for a short time. VERB: V n; N-UNCOUNT

daz·zling /'dæzlɪŋ/. **1** Something that is **dazzling** is very impressive or beautiful. *He gave Alberg a dazzling smile.* ♦ **daz·zling·ly** *The view was dazzlingly beautiful.* **2** A **dazzling** light is very bright and makes you unable to see properly for a short time. ♦ **dazzlingly** *The bay seemed dazzlingly bright.* ADJ-GRADED; ADJ; ADV-GRADED

DC /,diː 'siː/. **DC** is used to refer to an electric current that always flows in the same direction. **DC** is an abbreviation for 'direct current'. N-UNCOUNT

'D-day. You can use **D-day** to refer to the day that is chosen for the beginning of an important activity. *D-day for my departure was set for 29th June.* N-UNCOUNT

DDT /,diː diː 'tiː/. **DDT** is a poisonous substance which is used for killing insects. N-UNCOUNT

de- /diː-/. **1 De-** is added to a verb in order to change the meaning of the verb to its opposite. *The jury may have become desensitized to the video.* **2 De-** is added to a noun in order to make it a verb referring to the removal of the thing described by the noun. *I've defrosted the freezer.* PREFIX

dea·con /'diːkən/ **deacons. 1** A **deacon** is a member of the clergy who is lower in rank than a priest. **2** A **deacon** is a person who is not ordained but who assists the minister in some Protestant churches. N-COUNT

de·ac·tiv·ate /diːˈæktɪveɪt/ **deactivates, deactivating, deactivated.** To **deactivate** an explosive device or an alarm means to make it harmless or unable to operate. VERB: V n

dead /ded/. **1** A person, animal, or plant that is **dead** is no longer living. *My husband's been dead a year now. ...old newspapers and dead flowers.* ▶ **The dead** are people who are dead. **2** Land or water that is **dead** contains no living things. *...mountainsides of dead earth and stumps of trees.* **3** If you say that a person or animal **dropped dead** or **dropped down dead**, you mean that they died very suddenly and unexpectedly. **4** If you tell someone to **drop dead**, you are insulting them, rudely disagreeing with them or refusing to do something, or telling them to stop bothering you. ● See also **drop-dead**. **5** If you say that someone is **dead and gone**, you are emphasizing that they are dead, and thinking about what happened or will happen after their death. *Often a genius is recognized only after he is dead and gone.* **6** If you say that you **feel dead** or **are half dead**, you mean that you feel very tired or ill and very weak. ADJ; N-PLURAL; ADJ; PHRASE PRAGMATICS; PHRASE PRAGMATICS; PHRASE PRAGMATICS; PHRASE PRAGMATICS **7** If you describe a place or a period of time as **dead**, you mean that there is very little activity taking place in it. *...some dead little town.* ADJ-GRADED **8** Something that is **dead** is no longer being used or is finished. *The dead cigarette was still between his fingers.* **9** If you say that an idea, plan, or subject is **dead**, you mean that people are no longer interested in it or willing to develop it any further. *This brand of politics is dead.* **10** A **dead** language is no longer spoken or written as a means of communication, although it may still be studied. **11** A telephone or piece of electrical equipment that is **dead** is no longer functioning, for example because it no longer has any electrical power. *Duke answered the phone and the line went dead.* ADJ **12** In sport, when a ball is **dead**, it has gone outside the playing area, or a situation has occurred in which the game has to be temporarily stopped, and none of the players can score points or gain an advantage. ADJ **13** A **dead** sound or colour is dull rather than lively or bright. *'That is correct, Meg,' he answered in his cold, dead voice.* ▶ Also a combining form. *The blood drained from his face, leaving the skin dead white.* ADJ-GRADED; COMB

14 Dead is used to mean complete or absolute, espe- ADJ: ADJ n
cially with the words 'centre', 'silence', and 'stop'. *He
adjusted each chess piece so that it stood dead centre in
its square.* **15 Dead** means precisely or exactly. *Mars* ADV:
was visible, dead in the centre of the telescope... A fish- ADV prep/
ing boat came out of nowhere, dead ahead. **16 Dead** is adv/adj
sometimes used to mean very. *His poems sound dead* ADV:
boring, actually. ADV adj/
adv/prep
INFORMAL
17 If you say that you wouldn't **be seen dead** or **be** PHRASE
caught dead in particular clothes, places, or situa- PRAGMATICS
tions, you are expressing strong dislike or disapproval INFORMAL
for them. *I wouldn't be caught dead in such an old-
fashioned place.*
18 If you say that something such as an idea or situa- PHRASE
tion is **dead and buried**, you are emphasizing that you PRAGMATICS
think that it is completely finished or past, and cannot
happen or exist again in the future. **19** If you say that PHRASE
someone or something is **dead in the water**, you are PRAGMATICS
emphasizing that they have failed, and that there is
little hope of them being successful in the future.
20 If something happens **in the dead of night**, **at** PHRASE
dead of night, or **in the dead of winter**, it happens in LITERARY
the middle part of the night or the winter, when it is
darkest or coldest.
21 When Christians say that Jesus Christ **rose from** PHRASE
the dead or **raised** someone **from the dead**, they
mean that Jesus came back to life after he had died, or
brought a dead person back to life.
22 To **stop dead** means to suddenly stop happening, PHRASE
moving, or doing something. To **stop** someone or
something **dead** means to cause them to suddenly
stop happening, moving, or doing something. *We all
stopped dead and looked at it... Conversation stopped
dead.*
23 • a **dead loss**: see **loss. •** a **dead ringer**: see **ringer**.
• to **stop dead** in your **tracks**: see **track**.
dead·beat /'dedbiːt/ **deadbeats.** If you refer to N-COUNT
someone as a **deadbeat**, you think they are lazy and PRAGMATICS
do not want to be part of ordinary society; used AMERICAN,
showing disapproval. *He and a collection of fellow* INFORMAL
hustlers and deadbeats live in an abandoned hotel.
,**dead 'duck, dead ducks.** If you describe some- N-COUNT
one or something as a **dead duck**, you mean that PRAGMATICS
you think they have absolutely no chance of suc- INFORMAL
ceeding in something. *The government is a dead
duck.*
dead·en /'dedən/ **deadens, deadening, dead-** VERB
ened. If something **deadens** a feeling or a sound, it V n
makes it less strong or loud. *He needs morphine to
deaden the pain in his chest.*
,**dead 'end, dead ends. 1** If a street is a **dead** ◆◇◇◇
end, there is no way out at one end of it. **2** A **dead** N-COUNT
end job or course of action does not lead to further N-COUNT
developments or progression. *Waitressing was a
dead-end job.*
dead·en·ing /'dedənɪŋ/. A **deadening** situation de- ADJ
stroys people's enthusiasm and creativity. *...the
deadening routine of her life.*
,**dead 'hand.** You can refer to something which N-SING
has a discouraging or depressing influence on a
particular situation as a **dead hand**. *...removing the
dead hand of the state from economic life.*
'**dead-head, dead-heads, dead-heading,** VERB: V n
dead-headed; also spelled **dead head.** To **dead-
head** a plant which produces flowers means to remove all the dead flowers from it.
,**dead 'heat, dead heats.** If a race or contest is a N-COUNT
dead heat, two or more competitors are joint winners, or are both winning at a particular moment in
the race or contest. In American English, you can
say that a race or contest is in a **dead heat**.
,**dead 'letter, dead letters.** If you say that a law N-COUNT
or agreement is a **dead letter**, you mean that it still
exists but people ignore it.
dead·line /'dedlaɪn/ **deadlines.** A **deadline** is a ◆◆◆◇
time or date before which a particular task must be N-COUNT
finished or a particular thing must be done. *The
deadline for submissions to the competition will be
Easter 1994.*

dead·lock /'dedlɒk/ **deadlocks.** If a dispute or ◆◇◇◇
series of negotiations reaches **deadlock**, neither side N-VAR
is willing to give in at all and no agreement can be
made. *Peace talks between the two sides ended in
deadlock last month.*
dead·locked /'dedlɒkt/. If a dispute or series of ◆◇◇◇
negotiations is **deadlocked**, no agreement can be ADJ:
reached because neither side will give in at all. You v-link ADJ
can also say that the people involved are **deadlocked**. *Talks have been deadlocked over the issue of
human rights since August.*
dead·ly /'dedli/ **deadlier, deadliest. 1** If some- ◆◆◇◇◇
thing is **deadly**, it is likely or able to cause ADJ-GRADED
someone's death, or has already caused someone's
death. *...assault with a deadly weapon. ...a deadly
disease.*
2 If you describe a person or their behaviour as **dead-** ADJ-GRADED
ly, you mean that they will do or say anything to get
what they want. *His mother's voice was one he knew;
ice cold and deadly.*
3 If you describe someone or something as **deadly**, ADJ
you mean that they are very dull and boring. *She finds* INFORMAL
these parties deadly.
4 You can use **deadly** to emphasize an undesirable ADV: ADV adj
quality. *Broadcast news was accurate and reliable but* PRAGMATICS
deadly dull. **5** A **deadly** situation has unpleasant or ADJ-GRADED
dangerous consequences. *...the deadly combination
of low expectations and low achievement.*
6 Deadly enemies or rivals fight or compete in a very ADJ-GRADED
aggressive way. **7** In sport, **deadly** players and actions ADJ-GRADED
are very skilful and successful. *...the fastest and dead-* JOURNALISM
liest bowlers in world cricket today.
dead·pan /'dedpæn/. **Deadpan** humour is when ADJ-GRADED
you appear to be serious and are hiding the fact
that you are joking or teasing someone. *She put the
letter on the desk in front of me, her face deadpan.*
,**dead 'weight, dead weights. 1** A **dead weight** N-COUNT
is a load which is surprisingly heavy and difficult to
lift. *He hoisted the dead weight over his shoulder.*
2 You can refer to something that makes change or N-COUNT
progress difficult as a **dead weight**. *The Labour party must be free of the dead weight of union power.*
,**dead 'wood.** People or things that have been N-UNCOUNT
used for a very long time and that are no longer PRAGMATICS
useful can be referred to as **dead wood**. *Clear away
the dead wood in your life and start completely
afresh.*
deaf /def/ **deafer, deafest. 1** Someone who is ◆◆◇◇◇
deaf is unable to hear anything or is unable to hear ADJ-GRADED
very well. **▶ The deaf** are people who are deaf. N-PLURAL
♦ deaf·ness *Because of her deafness she was hard* N-UNCOUNT
to make conversation with. **2** If you say that some- ADJ:
one is **deaf** to people's pleas, arguments, or criti- v-link ADJ to n
cisms, you disapprove of them because they refuse PRAGMATICS
to pay attention to them. *She kept her eyes down,
deaf to what was happening around her.* **3 •** to **fall
on deaf ears**: see **ear. •** to **turn a deaf ear**: see **ear**.
deaf·en /'defən/ **deafens, deafening, deaf-** ◆◇◇◇
ened. 1 If a noise **deafens** you, it is so loud that VERB
you cannot hear anything else at the same time. *The* V n
noise of the typewriters deafened her. **2** If you **are** VB: usu
deafened by something, you are made deaf by it, or passive
are unable to hear for some time. *He was deafened* be V-ed
by the noise from the gun. **3** See also **deafening**.
deaf·en·ing /'defənɪŋ/. **1** A **deafening** noise is a ◆◇◇◇
very loud noise. **2** If you say there was a **deafening** ADJ-GRADED
silence, you are emphasizing that there was no re- ADJ
action or response to something that was said or PRAGMATICS
done.
,**deaf-'mute, deaf-mutes.** A **deaf-mute** is some- N-COUNT
one who cannot hear or speak. Some people find
this word offensive.

deal 1 quantifier uses
deal /diːl/. **1A** A **great deal of** or a **good deal of** ◆◆◆◇◇
something is a lot of it. *I am in a position to save* QUANT
you a good deal of time. **▶** Also an adverb. *She had* ADV:
*certainly known a good deal more than she'd admit-
ted.* **▶** Also a pronoun. *He knew a good deal about* PRON
Geoffrey. **2** A **deal of** something is a lot of it. *He had* QUANT
a deal of work to do. DATED

deal 2 verb and noun uses

deal /diːl/ **deals, dealing, dealt. 1** If you make a ◆◆◆◆◆
deal or do a **deal**, you complete an agreement or an N-COUNT
arrangement, especially in business. *Japan will have
to do a deal with America on rice imports. ...shady
business deals.*
2 If a person, company, or shop **deals in** a particular VERB
type of goods, their business involves buying or sell- V in n
ing those goods. *They deal in antiques.*
3 If someone **deals** illegal drugs, they sell them. VERB: V n
◆ **deal·ing** ...*drug dealing.* N-UNCOUNT
4 If someone has had a **bad deal**, they have been un- N-COUNT:
fortunate or have been treated unfairly. *The people of adj N
Liverpool have had a bad deal for many, many years.*
● **a raw deal**: see **raw**.
5 When you **deal** playing cards, you give them out to VERB: V n
the players in a game of cards. *The croupier dealt each V n n
player a card, face down.* ▶ **Deal out** means the same Also V
as **deal**. *Dalton dealt out five cards to each player.* PHRASAL VB
                                                           V P noun
6 If an event **deals a blow** to something or someone, it PHRASE
causes them great difficulties or makes failure more JOURNALISM
likely.
7 See also **dealings; wheel and deal.**

deal out. If someone **deals out** a punishment or PHRASAL VB
harmful action, they punish or harm someone. *It also V P noun
deals out sharp criticism to the Department.* ● See also Also V n P
deal 5.   WRITTEN

deal with. 1 When you **deal with** something or PHRASAL VB
someone that needs attention, you give your atten- V P n
tion to them, and often solve a problem or make a
decision concerning them. *...the way that building
societies deal with complaints.* **2** If you **deal with** an PRAGMATICS
unpleasant emotion or an emotionally difficult situa- V P n
tion, you recognize it, and remain calm and in control
of yourself in spite of it. **3** If a book, speech, or film V P n
deals with a particular thing, it has that thing as its
subject or is concerned with it. *...the parts of his
book which deal with contemporary Paris.* **4** If you V P n
deal with a particular person or organization, you
have business relations with them. *When I worked
in Florida I dealt with British people all the time.*

deal·er /diːlə/ **dealers.** A **dealer** is a person ◆◆◆◇◇
whose business involves buying and selling things. N-COUNT
...an antique dealer. ● **wheeler-dealer**: see **wheel**
and deal.

deal·er·ship /diːləʃɪp/ **dealerships.** A **dealership** ◆◇◇◇◇
is a company that sells cars, usually for one car N-COUNT
company.

deal·ings /diːlɪŋz/. Someone's **dealings** with a ◆◆◇◇◇
person or organization are the relations that they N-PLURAL
have with them or the business that they do with
them. *He has learnt little in his dealings with the international community.*

dealt /delt/. **Dealt** is the past tense and past participle of **deal.**

dean /diːn/ **deans. 1** A **dean** is an important ad- ◆◇◇◇◇
ministrator at a university or college. *...the dean of N-COUNT
undergraduate studies.* **2** A **dean** is a priest who is N-COUNT
the main administrator of a large church. *...Alan
Webster, former Dean of St Paul's.*

dear /dɪə/ **dearer, dearest; dears. 1** You use ◆◆◆◇◇
dear to describe someone or something that you ADJ: ADJ n
feel affection for. *Mrs Cavendish is a dear friend of
mine.* **2** If something is **dear to** you or **dear to** your ADJ-GRADED:
heart, you care deeply about it. *His family life was v-link ADJ to n
very dear to him.* **3** You can call someone **dear** as a N-VOC
sign of affection. *You're a lot like me, dear.* **4** You PRAGMATICS
can call someone a **dear** when you are fond of them N-COUNT
and think that they are nice. *He's such a dear.*
5 You use **dear** in expressions such as '**my dear fel-** ADJ: ADJ n
low', '**dear girl**', or '**my dear Richard**' when you are PRAGMATICS
addressing someone whom you know and are fond of.
You can also use expressions like this in an arrogant
way that indicates that you think you are superior to
the person you are addressing.
6 Dear is written at the beginning of a letter, followed ADJ: ADJ n
by the name or title of the person you are writing to.
'Dear sir,' she began.
7 You can use **dear** in expressions such as '**oh dear**', EXCLAM
'**dear me**', and '**dear, dear**' when you are sad, disap- PRAGMATICS

pointed, or surprised about something. *Outside,
Bruce glanced at his watch: 'Dear me, nearly one
o'clock.'*
8 If you say that something is **dear**, you mean that it ADJ-GRADED
costs a lot of money, usually more than you think it PRAGMATICS
should cost. **9** If something that someone does **costs** PHRASE
them **dear**, they suffer a lot as a result of it.

dear·est /dɪərɪst/. **1** You can call someone **dear-** ◆◇◇◇◇
est when you are very fond of them. *What's wrong, N-VOC
my dearest? You look tired.* **2** When you are writing DATED
to someone you are very fond of, you can use **dear-** ADJ-SUPERL:
est at the beginning of the letter before the person's ADJ n
name or before the word you are using to address
them. *Dearest Maria, Aren't I terrible, not coming
back like I promised?* **3** ● **nearest and dearest**: see
near.

dearie /dɪəri/. Some people use **dearie** as a friend- N-VOC
ly or condescending way of addressing someone. PRAGMATICS
The young lady will be with you in a minute, dearie. INFORMAL,
                                                        BRITISH

dear·ly /dɪəli/. **1** If you would **dearly** like to do or ◆◇◇◇◇
have something, you would very much like to do it ADV-GRADED:
or have it. **2** If you love someone **dearly**, you love ADV before v
them very much.   ADV-GRADED:
                                                        ADV with v
3 If you **pay dearly** for doing something or it **costs** you PHRASE
dearly, you suffer a lot as a result. FORMAL

dearth /dɜːθ/. If there is a **dearth** of something, N-SING
there is not enough of it. *...the dearth of good fiction
by English authors.*

death /deθ/ **deaths. 1 Death** is the permanent ◆◆◆◆◇
end of the life of a person or animal. *1.5 million N-VAR
people are in immediate danger of death from star-
vation. ...the thirtieth anniversary of her death.* **2** A N-COUNT:
particular kind of **death** is a particular way of dying. with supp
He died a horrible death. **3** If you say that someone PHRASE
is **at death's door**, you mean that they are very ill in- INFORMAL
deed. **4** If someone is **put to death**, they are execut- PHRASE
ed. **5** You use **to death** to indicate that a particular PHRASE
action or process results in someone's death. *He
was stabbed to death.*
6 If you say that you will **fight to the death** for some- PHRASE
thing, you mean that you will do anything to achieve PRAGMATICS
or preserve it, even if you suffer as a consequence. **7** If PHRASE
you refer to a fight or contest as **a fight to the death**, PRAGMATICS
you are emphasizing that it will not stop until the
death or total victory of one of the opponents. *He now
faces a fight to the death to reach the quarter-finals.*
8 If you say that something is a matter of **life and** PHRASE
death, you are emphasizing that it is extremely im- PRAGMATICS
portant, often because someone may die if people do
not act immediately. *We're dealing with a life-and-
death situation here.*
9 You use **to death** after an adjective or a verb to em- PHRASE
phasize the action, state, or feeling mentioned. For PRAGMATICS
example, if you are **frightened to death** or **bored to
death**, you are very frightened or bored.
10 The **death** of something is its permanent end. *It N-SING
meant the death of everything he had ever been or ever
hoped to be.*

death·bed /deθbed/ **deathbeds.** If someone is on N-COUNT
their **deathbed**, they are in a bed and about to die.
*...after the man who murdered him nearly 40 years
ago made a deathbed confession.*

'death blow; also spelled **death-blow.** If you say N-SING
that an event or action deals a **death blow** to some- JOURNALISM
thing such as a plan or a hope, you mean that it
puts an end to it. *The deportations would be a death
blow to the peace process.*

'death certificate, death certificates. A **death** N-COUNT
certificate is an official certificate signed by a doctor which states the cause of a person's death.

'death duties. Death duties were a tax which had N-PLURAL
to be paid on the money and property of someone BRITISH
who had died. This tax is now called 'inheritance
tax'. The usual American term is 'death taxes'.

'death knell; also spelled **death-knell.** If you say N-SING
that something sounds the **death knell** for something else, you mean that, because the first thing
happens, the other thing will end soon. *The tax increase sounded the death knell for the business.*

D

death·ly /'deθli/. **1** If you say that someone is **deathly** pale or **deathly** still, you are emphasizing that they are as pale or still as a dead person. *She lay deathly still.* **2** If you say that someone is **deathly** afraid, you are emphasizing that they are very afraid. You can also say that someone or something is **deathly** silent, dull, boring, cold, or tired. **3** If you say there is a **deathly** silence or a **deathly** hush, you are emphasizing that it is very quiet.
ADV: ADV adj WRITTEN
ADV-GRADED: ADV adj *PRAGMATICS*
ADJ: ADJ n *PRAGMATICS* *WRITTEN*

'death penalty. The **death penalty** is the punishment of death used in some countries for people who have committed very serious crimes. *If convicted for murder, both youngsters could face the death penalty.*
◆◇◇◇◇ N-SING

'death rate, death rates. The **death rate** is the number of people per thousand who die in a particular area during a particular period of time. *By the turn of the century, Pittsburgh had the highest death rate in the United States.*
◆◇◇◇◇ N-COUNT

death row /,deθ 'rəʊ/. If someone is on **death row**, they are in the part of a prison which contains the cells for criminals who have been sentenced to death. *...death row inmates.*
◆◇◇◇ N-UNCOUNT AMERICAN

'death sentence, death sentences. A **death sentence** is a punishment of death given by a judge to someone who has been found guilty of a serious crime such as murder.
◆◇◇◇ N-COUNT

'death squad, death squads. Death squads are groups of people who operate illegally and carry out the execution of people such as their political opponents or criminals.
◆◇◇◇ N-COUNT

'death throes; also spelled **death-throes**. **1** The **death throes** of something are its final stages, just before it fails completely or ends. *The dead tycoon's sons will remain in their plush offices overseeing the death throes of the family empire.* **2** If a person or animal is in their **death throes**, they are dying and making violent uncontrolled movements, usually because they are in great pain.
N-PLURAL
N-PLURAL

'death toll, death tolls; also spelled **death-toll**. The **death toll** of an accident, disaster, or war is the number of people who die in it.
◆◇◇◇ N-COUNT

'death trap, death traps; also spelled **death-trap**. If you say that a place or vehicle is a **death trap**, you mean it is in such bad condition that it might cause someone's death. *Badly-built kit cars can be death traps.*
N-COUNT INFORMAL

'death warrant, death warrants; also spelled **death-warrant**. **1** A **death warrant** is an official document which orders that someone is to be executed as a punishment. **2** If you say that someone **is signing their own death warrant**, you mean that they are behaving in a way which will cause their ruin or death.
N-COUNT
PHRASE

'death wish; also spelled **death-wish**. A **death wish** is a conscious or unconscious desire to die or be killed.
N-SING

deb /deb/ **debs**. A **deb** is the same as a **debutante**.
N-COUNT

de·ba·cle /deɪ'bɑːkəl, AM dɪ'b-/ **debacles;** also spelled **débacle**. A **debacle** is an event or attempt that is a complete failure. *It will be hard for the republic to recover from this debacle.*
◆◇◇◇◇ N-COUNT

de·bar /dɪ'bɑː, 'diː-/ **debars, debarring, debarred**. If you **are debarred** from doing something, you are prevented from doing it by a law or regulation. *If found guilty, she could be debarred from politics for seven years.*
VB: usu passive be V-ed from n/-ing FORMAL

de·base /dɪ'beɪs/ **debases, debasing, debased**. To **debase** something means to reduce its value or quality. *The popular debate about environmental issues has debased the meaning of the word ecology.* ♦ **de·based** *Debased versions of this gypsy dance are sometimes performed for tourists.*
VERB V n FORMAL
ADJ-GRADED

de·bat·able /dɪ'beɪtəbəl/. If you say that something is **debatable**, you mean that it is not certain. *Whether the Bank of England would do any better is highly debatable.*
◆◇◇◇◇ ADJ-GRADED *PRAGMATICS*

de·bate /dɪ'beɪt/ **debates, debating, debated**. **1** A **debate** is a discussion about a subject on which people have different views. *There has been a lot of*
◆◆◆◇ N-VAR

debate among scholars about this. **2** If people **debate** a topic, they discuss it fairly formally, putting forward different views. You can also say that one person **debates** a topic with another person. *Scholars have debated whether or not Yagenta became a convert... He is a bulky and belligerent newspaperman who debates issues with his friends.* ♦ **de·bat·ing** *...a school debating society.* **3** A **debate** is a formal discussion, for example in a parliament, in which people express different opinions about a subject and then vote on it. *Mr Hamilton was speaking on the second day of a debate on defence spending.*
V-RECIP: pl-n V n pl-n V wh V n with Also V with n
N-UNCOUNT N-COUNT

4 If you **debate** whether to do something or **debate** what to do, you think or talk about possible courses of action before deciding exactly what you are going to do. *I debated going back inside, but weariness won out and I started the car and drove off.*
VERB: V wh V -ing

5 If you say that a matter is **open to debate**, you mean that people have different opinions about it, or it has not yet been firmly decided. *The Government is committed to enforcing some of the recommendations, but others will be open to debate.*
PHRASE

de·bat·er /dɪ'beɪtə/ **debaters**. A **debater** is someone who takes part in debates.
N-COUNT

de·bauched /dɪ'bɔːtʃt/. If you describe someone as **debauched**, you mean they behave in a way that is socially unacceptable, for example because they are sexually promiscuous.
ADJ-GRADED DATED

de·bauch·ery /dɪ'bɔːtʃəri/. You use **debauchery** to refer to drunkenness or sexual activity when you disapprove of it or regard it as excessive.
N-UNCOUNT *PRAGMATICS*

de·ben·ture /dɪ'bentʃə/ **debentures**. A **debenture** is a type of savings bond which offers a fixed rate of interest over a long period. Debentures are usually issued by a company or a government agency.
N-COUNT

de·bili·tate /dɪ'bɪlɪteɪt/ **debilitates, debilitating, debilitated**. **1** If you **are debilitated** by something such as an illness, it causes your body or mind to become gradually weaker. *Stewart took over yesterday when Russell was debilitated by a stomach virus.* ♦ **de·bili·tat·ing** *...a debilitating illness.* ♦ **de·bili·tat·ed** *Occasionally a patient is so debilitated that he must be fed intravenously.* **2** To **debilitate** an organization, society, or government means to gradually make it weaker. ♦ **de·bili·tat·ing** *...people exhausted by years of debilitating economic crisis.* ♦ **de·bili·tat·ed** *...an engineered takeover, designed to keep a debilitated communist party in power.*
◆◇◇◇ VB: usu passive be V-ed by n FORMAL
ADJ-GRADED
ADJ-GRADED
VERB: V n FORMAL
ADJ-GRADED
ADJ-GRADED

de·bil·ity /dɪ'bɪlɪti/ **debilities**. **Debility** is a weakness of a person's body or mind, especially one caused by an illness. *The symptoms are severe anaemia and debility.*
N-VAR FORMAL

deb·it /'debɪt/ **debits, debiting, debited**. **1** When your bank **debits** your account, money is taken from it and paid to someone else. **2** A **debit** is a record of the money taken from your bank account, for example when you write a cheque. *The total of debits must balance the total of credits.* **3** See also **direct debit**.
◆◇◇◇ VERB: V n
N-COUNT

debo·nair /,debə'neə/. A man who is **debonair** is pleasantly confident, charming, and well-dressed; used showing approval.
ADJ-GRADED *PRAGMATICS*

de·brief /,diː'briːf/ **debriefs, debriefing, debriefed**. When someone such as a soldier, diplomat, or astronaut **is debriefed**, they are asked to give a report on a mission or task that they have just completed. *He went to Rio after the CIA had debriefed him.* ♦ **de·brief·ing, debriefings**. *A debriefing would follow this operation.*
VERB: be V-ed V n
N-VAR

de·bris /'deɪbriː, AM deɪ'briː/. **Debris** is pieces from something that has been destroyed, or pieces of rubbish which are strewn around. *A number of people were killed by flying debris.*
◆◆◇◇ N-UNCOUNT

debt /det/ **debts**. **1** A **debt** is a sum of money that you owe someone. *Three years later, he is still paying off his debts.* ● See also **bad debt**. **2** Debt is the state of owing money. *Stress is a main reason for debt.* ● If you are **in debt** or **get into debt**, you owe
◆◆◇◇ N-VAR
N-UNCOUNT
PHRASE

money. If you are **out of debt** or **get out of debt**, you succeed in paying all the money that you owe.
3 You use **debt** in expressions such as **I owe you a debt** or **I am in your debt** when you are expressing gratitude for something that someone has done for you. N-COUNT PRAGMATICS FORMAL

debt·or /'detə/ **debtors.** A debtor is a country, organization, or person who owes money. ...*important improvements in the situation of debtor countries.* ◆◇◇◇◇ N-COUNT

de·bug /ˌdiː'bʌg/ **debugs, debugging, debugged.** When someone **debugs** a computer program, they look for the faults in it and correct them. VERB: V n

de·bunk /ˌdiː'bʌŋk/ **debunks, debunking, debunked.** If you **debunk** a widely held belief, you show that it is false. If you **debunk** something that is widely admired, you show that it is not as good as people think. *Historian Michael Beschloss debunks a few myths.* VERB V n

de·but /'deɪbjuː, AM deɪ'bjuː/ **debuts.** The debut of a performer or sports player is their first public performance, appearance, or recording. ...*her debut album 'Sugar Time'.* ◆◆◇◇◇ N-COUNT

debu·tante /'debjutɑːnt/ **debutantes.** A debutante is a young woman from the upper classes who has started going to social events with other young people. N-COUNT DATED

Dec. Dec. is a written abbreviation for **December**. ◆◆◇◇◇

dec·ade /'dekeɪd/ **decades.** A decade is a period of ten years, especially one that begins with a year ending in 0, for example 1980 to 1989. ...*the last decade of the nineteenth century.* ◆◆◆◇ N-COUNT

deca·dent /'dekədənt/. If you say that a person or society is **decadent**, you mean that they have low standards, especially low moral standards. ...*the excesses and stresses of their decadent rock 'n' roll lifestyles.* ♦ **deca·dence** *The empire had for years been falling into decadence.* ◆◇◇◇◇ ADJ-GRADED PRAGMATICS N-UNCOUNT

decaf /'diːkæf/ **decafs;** also spelled **decaff**. Decaf is decaffeinated coffee. *He only drinks decaf.* N-VAR INFORMAL

de·caf·fein·at·ed /ˌdiː'kæfɪneɪtɪd/. Decaffeinated coffee has had most of the caffeine removed from it. ADJ

de·camp /dɪ'kæmp/ **decamps, decamping, decamped.** If you **decamp**, you go away from somewhere secretly or suddenly. *Bugsy decided to decamp to Hollywood from New York.* VERB V

de·cant /dɪ'kænt/ **decants, decanting, decanted.** If you **decant** a liquid such as wine, you pour some of it carefully from one container into another, making sure any sediment is left behind. *She always used to decant the milk into a jug... Vintage ports must be decanted to remove natural sediments.* VERB V n into n be V-ed Also V n

de·cant·er /dɪ'kæntə/ **decanters.** A decanter is a glass bottle or jug that is used for serving wine, sherry, or port. N-COUNT

de·capi·tate /dɪ'kæpɪteɪt/ **decapitates, decapitating, decapitated.** If someone is **decapitated**, their head is cut off. ...*freshly decapitated chickens.* ♦ **de·capi·ta·tion** /dɪˌkæpɪ'teɪʃən/ **decapitations** *I saw 700 executions by decapitation.* VERB: be V-ed V-ed Also V n FORMAL N-VAR

de·cath·lon /dɪ'kæθlɒn/ **decathlons.** The decathlon is a competition in which athletes compete in 10 different sporting events. N-COUNT

de·cay /dɪ'keɪ/ **decays, decaying, decayed.** **1** When something such as a body, a dead plant, or a tooth decays, it becomes rotten. *The ground was scattered with decaying leaves.* ▶ Also a noun. When not removed, plaque causes tooth decay. ♦ **de·cayed** *Even young children have teeth so decayed they need to be pulled.* **2** If something such as a society, system, or institution decays, it gradually becomes weaker or its condition gets worse. *Congress has tried dozens of approaches to revitalize decaying urban and rural areas.* ▶ Also a noun. *There are problems of urban decay and gang violence.* ◆◆◇◇◇ VERB: V V-ing N-UNCOUNT ADJ-GRADED VERB: V V-ing N-UNCOUNT

de·ceased /dɪ'siːst/ **deceased** is both the singular and the plural form. **1** The **deceased** is used to refer to a person or a group of people who have recently died. *Do you know the last address of the deceased?* **2** A **deceased** person is one who has recently died. ...*his recently deceased mother.* ◆◇◇◇◇ N-COUNT: theN FORMAL ADJ FORMAL

de·ceit /dɪ'siːt/ **deceits.** Deceit is behaviour that is intended to make people believe something which is not true. ◆◇◇◇◇ N-VAR

de·ceit·ful /dɪ'siːtful/. If you say that someone is **deceitful**, you mean that they behave in a dishonest way by making other people believe something that is not true. *The ambassador called the report deceitful and misleading.* ADJ-GRADED

de·ceive /dɪ'siːv/ **deceives, deceiving, deceived.** **1** If you **deceive** someone, you make them believe something that is not true, usually in order to get some advantage for yourself. *The alleged offences include deceiving the council into giving her son a house.* **2** If you **deceive** yourself, you do not admit to yourself something that you know is true. *Alcoholics are notorious for their ability to deceive themselves.* **3** If something **deceives** you, it gives you a wrong impression and makes you believe something that is not true. *It was later than he thought. The midwinter darkness had deceived him.* ◆◇◇◇◇ VERB: V n V n into -ing VERB V pron-refl VERB V n

de·cel·er·ate /ˌdiː'seləreɪt/ **decelerates, decelerating, decelerated.** **1** When a vehicle or machine decelerates or when the driver of a vehicle decelerates, the speed of the vehicle or machine is reduced. **2** When the rate of something such as inflation or economic growth decelerates, it slows down. VERB: V VERB: V

De·cem·ber /dɪ'sembə/ **Decembers.** December is the twelfth and last month of the year in the Western calendar. See Appendix headed **Dates**. ◆◆◆◇ N-VAR

de·cen·cy /'diːsənsi/. **1** If you talk about the **decency** of someone's behaviour, you mean they behave in a way which follows accepted moral standards. *His sense of decency forced him to resign.* **2** If you say that someone did not **have the decency** to do something, you mean there was something which they did not do and you think they ought to have done it. *No-one had the decency to tell me to my face.* ◆◇◇◇◇ N-UNCOUNT PHRASE PRAGMATICS

de·cent /'diːsənt/. **1** Decent is used to describe something which is considered to be of an acceptable standard or quality. *The lack of a decent education did not defeat Rey.* ♦ **de·cent·ly** *The allies say they will treat their prisoners decently.* **2** Decent is used to describe behaviour which is morally correct or acceptable. *She watched his face, as the coffin was lowered into the ground. As soon as it was decent, he plunged through the crowd towards the cars.* ♦ **decently** *There were at least four hours before he could decently go to the pub.* **3** Decent people are honest and behave in a way that most people approve of. *The jury will see what a decent guy he is.* **4** If you say someone should **do the decent thing**, you mean they should do something which they do not want to do, but which you think they are morally obliged to do. *He should do the decent thing and resign.* ◆◆◇◇◇ ADJ ADV-GRADED ADJ ADV-GRADED ADJ-GRADED PHRASE PRAGMATICS DATED

de·cen·tral·ize /ˌdiː'sentrəlaɪz/ **decentralizes, decentralizing, decentralized;** also spelled **decentralise** in British English. To **decentralize** government or a large organization means to move some departments or branches away from the main administrative area, or to give more power to local departments or branches. ...*the need to decentralize and devolve power to regional governments.* ♦ **de·cen·trali·za·tion** /ˌdiːˌsentrəlaɪ'zeɪʃən/ *He seems set against the idea of increased decentralisation.* ◆◇◇◇◇ VERB: V n V N-UNCOUNT

de·cep·tion /dɪ'sepʃən/ **deceptions.** Deception is the act of deceiving someone. *He admitted conspiring to obtain property by deception.* ◆◇◇◇◇ N-VAR

de·cep·tive /dɪ'septɪv/. If something is **deceptive**, it encourages you to believe something which is not true. *First impressions proved deceptive.* ♦ **de·cep·tive·ly** *The storyline is deceptively simple.* ◆◇◇◇◇ ADJ-GRADED ADV

deci·bel /'desɪbel/ **decibels.** A decibel is a unit of measurement which is used to indicate how loud a sound is. N-COUNT

de·cide /dɪ'saɪd/ **decides, deciding, decided.** **1** If you **decide** to do something, you choose to do it, usually after you have thought about the other possibilities. *He has decided that he doesn't want to* ◆◆◆◆◇ VERB: V to-inf V that V against/in favour of n /-

embarrass the movement and will therefore step down... The house needed totally rebuilding, so we decided against buying it. **2** If a person or group of people **decides** something, they choose what something should be like or how a particular problem should be solved. She was still young, he said, and that would be taken into account when deciding her sentence. **3** If you **decide** that something is true, you form that opinion after considering the facts. For a long time I couldn't decide whether the original settlers were insane or just stupid.
ing
Also V,
V wh
VERB
V n

VERB:
V that
V wh

4 If something **decides** you to do something, it is the reason that causes you to choose to do it. What decided him was a cynical question: 'If I fail, I'll be no worse off than I am now, will I?' **5** If an event or fact **decides** something, it makes it certain that a particular choice will be made or that there will be a particular result. The results will decide if he will win a place at a good university... Luck is certainly not the only deciding factor.
VERB:
V n to-inf
V n
Also V n that
VERB: V n
V wh
V-ing

decide on. If you **decide on** something or **decide upon** something, you choose it from two or more possibilities. After leaving university, Therese decided on a career in publishing.
PHRASAL VB
V P n

de·cid·ed /dɪˈsaɪdɪd/. **Decided** means clear and definite. He's a man of very decided opinions.
ADJ-GRADED:
ADJ n

de·cid·ed·ly /dɪˈsaɪdɪdli/. **Decidedly** means to a great extent and in a way that is very obvious. He admits there will be moments when he's decidedly uncomfortable at what he sees.
◆◇◇◇◇
ADV-GRADED:
ADV group

de·cid·er /dɪˈsaɪdə/ **deciders. 1** In sport, a **decider** is one game in a series of games, which establishes which player or team wins the series. **2** In games like football or hockey, the **decider** is the last goal to be scored in a match that is won by a margin of only one goal.
N-COUNT
BRITISH
N-COUNT
BRITISH

de·cidu·ous /dɪˈsɪdjuəs/. A **deciduous** tree or bush loses its leaves every autumn.
ADJ

deci·mal /ˈdesɪməl/ **decimals. 1** A **decimal** system involves counting in units of ten. ...the decimal system of metric weights and measures. **2** A **decimal** is a fraction that is written in the form of a dot followed by one or more numbers which represent tenths, hundredths, and so on: for example .5, .51, .517.
ADJ: ADJ n
N-COUNT

,decimal 'point, decimal points. A **decimal point** is the dot in front of a decimal fraction.
N-COUNT

deci·mate /ˈdesɪmeɪt/ **decimates, decimating, decimated. 1** To **decimate** something such as a group of people or animals means to destroy a very large number of them. The pollution could decimate the river's thriving population of kingfishers. ♦ **deci·ma·tion** /ˌdesɪˈmeɪʃən/ ...the decimation of the great rain forests. **2** To **decimate** a system or organization means to reduce its size and effectiveness greatly. ...a recession which decimated the nation's manufacturing industry.
◆◇◇◇◇
VERB
V n

N-UNCOUNT
VERB
V n

de·ci·pher /dɪˈsaɪfə/ **deciphers, deciphering, deciphered.** If you **decipher** a piece of writing or a message, you work out what it says, even though it is very difficult to read or understand.
◆◇◇◇◇
VERB: V n

de·ci·sion /dɪˈsɪʒən/ **decisions. 1** When you make a **decision**, you choose what should be done or which is the best of various possible actions. The decision to discipline Marshall was taken by the party chairman. **2** Decision is the act of deciding something. The moment of decision can't be too long delayed. **3** A person of **decision** is someone who has the ability to decide quickly and definitely what to do in any situation. He is very quick-thinking and very much a man of decision and action.
◆◆◆◆◆
N-COUNT

N-UNCOUNT

N-UNCOUNT

de'cision-making. Decision-making is the process of reaching decisions, especially in a large organization or in government. She wants to see more women involved in decision making.
◆◆◇◇◇
N-UNCOUNT

de·ci·sive /dɪˈsaɪsɪv/. **1** If a fact, action, or event is **decisive**, it makes it certain that there will be a particular result. The election campaign has now entered its final, decisive phase. ♦ **de·ci·sive·ly** The
◆◆◇◇◇
ADJ-GRADED

ADV

plan was decisively rejected. **2** If someone wins a **decisive** victory, they win by a large margin.
ADJ-GRADED

3 If someone is **decisive**, they have or show an ability to make quick decisions in a difficult or complicated situation. He should give way to a younger, more decisive leader. ♦ **decisively** 'I'll call for you at half ten,' she said decisively. ♦ **de·ci·sive·ness** His supporters admire his decisiveness.
ADJ-GRADED

ADV-GRADED
N-UNCOUNT

deck /dek/ **decks, decking, decked. 1** A **deck** on a bus, ship, or train is a downstairs or upstairs area on it. ...sitting on the top deck of the number 13 bus. ● See also **flight deck. 2** The **deck** of a ship is the top part that forms a floor in the open air which you can walk on. She stood on the deck and waved. **3** If someone or something is **below decks**, they are inside a ship in the part that is underneath the deck.
◆◆◆◇◇
N-COUNT

N-COUNT:
also on N

PHRASE

4 If you **clear the decks**, you get ready to start something new by finishing any work that has to be done or by getting rid of any problems that are in the way.
PHRASE

5 A tape **deck** or record **deck** is a piece of equipment on which you play tapes or records.
N-COUNT

6 A **deck** of cards is a complete set of playing cards. The usual British word is **pack**.
N-COUNT

7 If something **is decked** with pretty things, it is decorated with them. Villagers decked the streets with bunting... The house was decked with flowers.
VERB
V n with n
V-ed
WRITTEN

deck out. If someone or something **is decked out** with or in something, they are decorated with it or wearing it. She had decked him out from head to foot in expensive clothes.
PHRASAL VB
be V-ed P
V n P
Also V P noun

deck·chair /ˈdektʃeə/ **deckchairs.** A **deckchair** is a simple chair with a folding frame and a piece of canvas forming the seat and back. Deckchairs are often used at the seaside.
N-COUNT

-decker /-ˈdekə/. **-decker** is used after adjectives like 'double' and 'single' to indicate how many levels or layers something has. ...a triple-decker peanut butter and jelly sandwich.
COMB

deck·hand /ˈdekhænd/ **deckhands.** A **deckhand** is a person who does the cleaning and other work on the deck of a ship.
N-COUNT

de·claim /dɪˈkleɪm/ **declaims, declaiming, declaimed.** If you **declaim**, you speak dramatically, as if you were acting in a theatre. He raised his right fist and declaimed: 'Liar and cheat!'... I can remember the way he used to declaim French verse to us.
VERB
V with quote
V n
Also V,
V that
WRITTEN

de·clama·tory /dɪˈklæmətri, AM -tɔːri/. A **declamatory** phrase, statement, or way of speaking is dramatic and confident. Rebels like Katharine Hamnett have made a name for bold, declamatory statements.
ADJ-GRADED
FORMAL

dec·la·ra·tion /ˌdekləˈreɪʃən/ **declarations. 1** A **declaration** is an official announcement or statement. They will sign the declaration tomorrow. **2** A **declaration** is a firm, emphatic statement that shows that you have no doubts about what you are saying. She needed time to adjust to Clive's declaration. **3** A **declaration** is a written statement about something which you have signed and which can be used as evidence in a court of law. She had to sign a declaration never to speak about her work.
◆◆◇◇◇
N-COUNT

N-COUNT

N-COUNT

de·clare /dɪˈkleə/ **declares, declaring, declared. 1** If you **declare** that something is true, you say that it is true in a firm, deliberate way. He declared his intention to become the best golfer in the world... Glasses of Madeira wine were brought to us. We declared it delicious. **2** If you **declare** something, you state officially and formally that it exists or is the case. His lawyers are confident that the judges will declare Mr Ashwell innocent... The U.N. has declared it to be a safe zone. **3** If you **declare** goods that you have bought abroad or money that you have earned, you say how much you have bought or earned so that you can pay tax on it.
◆◆◆◆◇
VERB:
V that
V n
V n adj

VERB: V n
V n adj
V n to-inf
Also V that

VERB: V n

declare for. If you **declare for** something or someone, you say that you are in favour of them. Mr. Stenholm had declared for the tax cut.
PHRASAL VB
V P n

de·clas·si·fy /ˌdiːˈklæsɪfaɪ/ **declassifies, declassifying, declassified.** If secret documents or
VERB:
be V-ed

records **are declassified**, it is officially stated that they are no longer secret.

de·cline /dɪ'klaɪn/ **declines, declining, de-** ◆◆◆◆◇
clined. 1 If something **declines**, it becomes less in VERB: V
quantity, importance, or strength. *The number of* V from/to/by
staff has declined from 217,000 to 114,000. **2** If there amount
is a **decline** in something, it becomes less in quan- N-VAR
tity, importance, or quality. *There wasn't such a big
decline in enrollments after all.* **3** If something is **in** PHRASE
decline or **on the decline**, it is gradually decreasing
in importance, quality, or power. *Thankfully the
smoking of cigarettes is on the decline.* **4** If some- PHRASE
thing goes or falls **into decline**, it begins to gradually decrease in importance, quality, or power.
5 If you **decline** something or **decline** to do some- VERB: V n
thing, you politely refuse to accept it or do it. *The band* V to-inf
declined to comment on the story. Also V
FORMAL

de·code /ˌdiː'kəʊd/ **decodes, decoding, decod-**
ed. 1 If you **decode** a message that has been writ- VERB: V n
ten or spoken in a code, you change it into ordinary
language. **2** If you **decode** something such as a play VERB
or a work of art, or someone's behaviour, you man- V n
age to understand its meaning or implications, although they are not obvious. *The critic had been
unable fully to decode the work under review.* **3** A VERB: V n
device that **decodes** a broadcast signal changes it
into a form that can be displayed on a television
screen. ♦ **de·cod·er decoders.** ...*the latest Delta* N-COUNT
Sigma digital decoder.

de·colo·niza·tion /ˌdiːˌkɒlənaɪ'zeɪʃən/; also spelled N-UNCOUNT
decolonisation. Decolonization means giving a
country that was formerly a colony independence.

de·com·mis·sion /ˌdiːkə'mɪʃən/ **decommis-** VERB
sions, decommissioning, decommissioned. be V-ed
When something such as a nuclear reactor or a Also V n
large machine is **decommissioned**, it is taken to
pieces because it is no longer going to be used.
*HMS Warspite would be decommissioned as part of
the defence cuts.*

de·com·pose /ˌdiːkəm'pəʊz/ **decomposes, de-** ◆◇◇◇◇
composing, decomposed. When things such as V-ERG: V
dead plants or animals **decompose**, or something V into n
decomposes them, they change chemically and be- Also V n
gin to rot. *The debris slowly decomposes into compost.* ♦ **de·com·posed** *Be sure to provide well de-* ADJ-GRADED
composed leafmould. ♦ **de·com·po·si·tion** N-UNCOUNT
/ˌdiːˌkɒmpə'zɪʃən/ ...*the four bodies were all in advanced stages of decomposition.*

de·com·pres·sion /ˌdiːkəm'preʃən/. **1** Decom- N-UNCOUNT
pression is the reduction of the force on something
that is caused by the weight of the air. *Decompres-
sion blew out a window in the plane.* **2** Decompres- N-UNCOUNT
sion is the process of bringing someone back to the
normal pressure of the air after they have been
deep underwater.

de·con·gest·ant /ˌdiːkən'dʒestənt/ **decongest-** N-VAR
ants. A **decongestant** is a medicine which helps
someone who has a cold to breathe more easily.

de·con·struct /ˌdiːkən'strʌkt/ **deconstructs,** ◆◇◇◇◇
deconstructing, deconstructed. To **decon-** VERB
struct an idea or text means to show the contradic- V n
tions in its meaning, and to show how it does not TECHNICAL
fully explain what it claims to explain. ...*a fairly
rigorous intellectual framework to deconstruct
various categories of film.* ♦ **de·con·struc·tion** N-UNCOUNT
/ˌdiːkən'strʌkʃən/ ...*the deconstruction of the macho
psyche.*

de·con·tami·nate /ˌdiːkən'tæmɪneɪt/ **decontami-** VERB: V n
nates, decontaminating, decontaminated.
To **decontaminate** something means to remove all
radioactivity, germs, or dangerous substances from
it. ♦ **de·con·tami·na·tion** /ˌdiːkəntæmɪ'neɪʃən/ *The* N-UNCOUNT
land will require public money for decontamination.

de·con·trol /ˌdiːkən'trəʊl/ **decontrols, decon-** VERB: V n
trolling, decontrolled. When governments **de-**
control an activity, they remove controls from it so
that companies or organizations have more freedom. ▶ Also a noun. ...*continuing decontrol of* N-VAR
banking institutions.

de·cor /'deɪkɔː/. The **decor** of a house or room is ◆◇◇◇◇
its style of furnishing and decoration. *The decor is* N-UNCOUNT
simple – black lacquer panels on white walls.

deco·rate /'dekəreɪt/ **decorates, decorating,** ◆◆◆◇◇
decorated. 1 If you **decorate** something, you VERB
make it more attractive by adding things to it. *He* V n with n
decorated his room with pictures. **2** If you **decorate** VERB
a building or room, you paint it or wallpaper it. V n
...*when they came to decorate the rear bedroom... I* have n V-ed
had the flat decorated. ♦ **deco·rat·ing** *I did a lot of* N-UNCOUNT
the decorating myself. ♦ **deco·ra·tion** *The renova-* N-UNCOUNT
tion process and decoration took four months.
♦ **deco·ra·tor, decorators** *The decorator repaint-* N-COUNT
ed the door in half an hour. ♦ **Interior decorator:**
see **interior decoration. 3** If something **decorates** a VERB
place or an object, it makes it look more attractive. V n
Posters decorate the walls. WRITTEN

4 If someone **is decorated**, they are given a medal or VERB:
other honour as an official reward for something that be V-ed
they have done.

deco·ra·tion /ˌdekə'reɪʃən/ **decorations. 1** The ◆◆◇◇◇
decoration of a room is its furniture, wallpaper, and N-UNCOUNT
ornaments. **2 Decorations** are features that are N-VAR
added to something in order to make it look more
attractive. *The only wall decorations are candles.*
3 Decorations are brightly coloured objects such as N-COUNT
balloons, which you put up in a room on special occasions to make it look more attractive.

4 A **decoration** is an official title or honour which is N-COUNT
given to someone, usually in the form of a medal, as a
reward for military bravery or public service.

deco·ra·tive /'dekərətɪv/. Something that is **deco-** ◆◆◇◇◇
rative is intended to look pretty or attractive. *The* ADJ-GRADED
*curtains are for purely decorative purposes and do
not open or close.*

deco·rous /'dekərəs/. **Decorous** behaviour is very ADJ-GRADED
respectable, calm, and polite. *They go for decorous* FORMAL
walks every day. ♦ **deco·rous·ly** *He sipped his* ADV-GRADED
drink decorously.

de·co·rum /dɪ'kɔːrəm/. **Decorum** is behaviour that N-UNCOUNT
people consider to be correct, polite, and respect- FORMAL
able. *I was treated with decorum and respect.*

de·coy /'diːkɔɪ/ **decoys. 1** If you refer to some- ◆◇◇◇◇
thing or someone as a **decoy**, you mean that they N-COUNT
are intended to attract people's attention and deceive them, for example by leading them into a trap
or away from a particular place. *I decided that I
would go out as a decoy to catch the rapist.* **2** A de- N-COUNT
coy is a model of a bird that is used to attract wild
birds towards it.

de·crease,   decreases, decreasing, de- ◆◆◇◇◇
creased. The verb is pronounced /dɪ'kriːs/. The
noun is pronounced /'diːkriːs/. **1** When something V-ERG
decreases or when you **decrease** it, it becomes less V by amount
in quantity, size, or intensity. *Population growth is* V from/to
decreasing by 1.4% each year... The number of inde- V amount
pendent firms decreased from 198 to 96... Raw-steel Also V n
*production by the nation's mills decreased 2.1% last
week.* **2** A **decrease** is a reduction in the quantity, N-COUNT
size, or intensity of something. ...*a decrease in the
number of young people out of work.*

de·cree /dɪ'kriː/ **decrees, decreeing, decreed.** ◆◆◇◇◇
1 A **decree** is an official order or decision, especially N-COUNT:
one made by the ruler of a country. ...*reform by* also by N
presidential decree. **2** If someone in authority **de-** VERB
crees that something must happen, they decide or V that
state this officially. *The government decreed that all* Also V n
*who wanted to live and work in Kenya must hold
Kenyan passports.* **3** A **decree** is a judgement made N-COUNT
by a law court. *Men do not always get their own
way, as court decrees on custody show.*

de·cree 'absolute, decrees absolute. A **decree** N-COUNT
absolute is the final order made by a court in a divorce case which ends a marriage completely.

de·cree nisi /dɪˌkriː 'naɪsaɪ/ **decrees nisi.** A de- N-COUNT
cree nisi is an order made by a court which states
that a divorce must take place at a certain time in
the future unless a good reason is produced to prevent this.

D

de·crep·it /dɪˈkrepɪt/. Something that is **decrepit** is old and in bad condition. Someone who is **decrepit** is old and weak. *...a decrepit old police station. ...a decrepit old man.* ♦ **de·crep·i·tude** /dɪˈkrepɪtjuːd, AM -tuːd/ *There was a general air of decrepitude and neglect.*   ADJ-GRADED   N-UNCOUNT

de·crimi·nal·ize /ˌdiːˈkrɪmɪnəlaɪz/ **decriminalizes, decriminalizing, decriminalized;** also spelled **decriminalise** in British English. When a criminal offence **is decriminalized**, the law changes so that it is no longer a criminal offence. *...whether prostitution should be decriminalized.* ♦ **de·crimi·nali·za·tion** /ˌdiːˌkrɪmɪnəlaɪˈzeɪʃən/ *...the decriminalisation of homosexuality.*   VERB be V-ed Also V n   N-UNCOUNT

de·cry /dɪˈkraɪ/ **decries, decrying, decried.** If someone **decries** an idea or action, they criticize it strongly; used showing disapproval. *He is impatient with those who decry the scheme... Governments also decry the migrants as law-breakers.*   VERB PRAGMATICS V n   V n as n   FORMAL

dedi·cate /ˈdedɪkeɪt/ **dedicates, dedicating, dedicated. 1** If you say that someone **has dedicated** themselves to something, you approve of the fact that they have decided to give a lot of time and effort to it because they think that it is important. *He dedicated himself to politics... Bessie has dedicated her life to caring for others.* ♦ **dedi·cat·ed** *He's quite dedicated to his students.* ♦ **dedi·ca·tion** /ˌdedɪˈkeɪʃən/ *...her courage, compassion and dedication to the cause of humanity.* **2** If someone **dedicates** something such as a book, play, or piece of music to you, they mention your name, for example in the front of a book or when a piece of music is performed, as a way of showing affection or respect for you. *She dedicated her first album to Woody Allen.* ♦ **dedication, dedications.** A **dedication** is a message which is written at the beginning of a book, or a short announcement which is sometimes made before a play or piece of music is performed, as a sign of affection or respect for someone. **3** If a monument, building, or church **is dedicated** to someone, a formal ceremony is held to show that the building will always be associated with them. *A window was dedicated to the memory of the Revd. Michael Scott.* ♦ **dedication** *...the dedication of the Holocaust Museum.*   ♦♦◇◇◇ VERB PRAGMATICS V pron-refl to n/-ing V n to n/-ing   ADJ-GRADED   N-UNCOUNT   VERB V n to n   N-COUNT   VB: usu passive be V-ed to n   N-UNCOUNT

dedi·cat·ed /ˈdedɪkeɪtɪd/. **1** You use **dedicated** to describe someone who enjoys a particular activity very much and spends a lot of time doing it. *...dedicated followers of classical music.* **2** You use **dedicated** to describe something that is made, built, or designed for one particular purpose or thing. *...the world's first museum dedicated to ecology.*   ♦♦◇◇◇ ADJ-GRADED   ADJ

de·duce /dɪˈdjuːs, AM -ˈduːs/ **deduces, deducing, deduced.** If you **deduce** something, you reach that conclusion because of other things that you know to be true. *Alison had got to work and cleverly deduced that I was the author... The date of the document can be deduced from references to the Civil War.*   ♦◇◇◇◇ VERB: V n V that be V-ed from n Also V n from n, V with quote

de·duct /dɪˈdʌkt/ **deducts, deducting, deducted.** When you **deduct** an amount from a total, you subtract it from the total. *The company deducted this payment from his compensation.* ♦ **de·duc·tion** *The profit figure was struck after the deduction of £56,000.*   ♦♦◇◇◇ VERB V n from n Also V n   N-UNCOUNT

de·duc·tion /dɪˈdʌkʃən/ **deductions. 1** A **deduction** is a conclusion that you have reached about something because of other things that you know to be true. *...her own shrewd deductions about what was going on.* **2 Deduction** is the process of reaching a conclusion about something because of other things that you know to be true. *'You are clever to guess. I'm sure I don't know how you did it.'—'Deduction,' James said.* **3** A **deduction** is an amount that has been subtracted from a total. *...tax and National Insurance deductions.*   ♦♦◇◇◇ N-COUNT   N-UNCOUNT   N-COUNT

de·duc·tive /dɪˈdʌktɪv/. **Deductive** reasoning involves deducing conclusions logically from other things that are already known.   ADJ FORMAL

deed /diːd/ **deeds. 1** A **deed** is something that is done, especially something that is very good or very bad. *...the warm feeling one gets from doing a good deed.* **2** A **deed** is a document containing the terms of an agreement, especially an agreement concerning the ownership of land or a building.   ◆◇◇◇◇ N-COUNT LITERARY   N-COUNT LEGAL

'deed poll. In Britain, if you change your name **by deed poll**, you change it officially and legally.   PHRASE

deem /diːm/ **deems, deeming, deemed.** If something **is deemed** to have a particular quality or to do a particular thing, it is considered to have that quality or do that thing. *French and German were deemed essential... He says he would support the use of force if the UN deemed it necessary.*   ♦♦◇◇◇ VERB be V-ed adj/n Also V n to-inf FORMAL

deep /diːp/ **deeper, deepest. 1** If something is **deep**, it extends a long way down from the ground or from the top surface of something. *The water is very deep. ...the deep cut on his left hand.* ► Also an adverb. *Gingerly, she put her hand in deeper.* ♦ **deep·ly** *There isn't time to dig deeply and put in manure or compost.* **2** A **deep** container, such as a wardrobe or cupboard, extends or measures a long distance from front to back. **3** You use **deep** to talk or ask about how much something measures from the surface to the bottom, or from front to back. *I found myself in water only three feet deep... How deep did the snow get?* ► Also a combining form. *...an inch-deep stab wound.* **4** If you say that things or people are two, three, or four **deep**, you mean that there are two, three, or four rows or layers of them there. *...cardboard boxes piled right to the ceiling, ten deep.* **5 The deep** means the sea. *...whales and creatures of the deep.* **6 Deep** in an area means a long way inside it. *Oil and gas were trapped deep inside the earth when it was formed.* **7** In sports such as football and tennis, a **deep** shot is one that sends the ball a long way towards the end of the pitch or court. **8** You use **deep** to emphasize the seriousness, strength, importance, or degree of something. *...a period of deep personal crisis. ...his deep sympathy to the family.* ♦ **deeply** *Our meetings and conversations left me deeply depressed.* **9** If you experience or feel something **deep** inside you or **deep** down, you feel it very strongly although you do not necessarily show it. *Deep in my heart I knew we had no hope.* **10** If you say that something **goes deep** or **runs deep**, you mean that it is very serious or strong and is hard to change. *His anger and anguish clearly went deep.* **11** If you are in a **deep** sleep, you are sleeping peacefully and it is difficult to wake you. ♦ **deeply** *She slept deeply but woke early.* **12** If you are **deep in** thought or **deep in** conversation, you are concentrating very hard on what you are thinking or saying and are not aware of the things that are happening around you. **13** A **deep** gaze or look seems to see right into your mind. *Peter gave him a long deep look.* ► Also an adverb. *He paused, staring deep into Mary's eyes.* ♦ **deeply** *He turned to me, looked deeply into my eyes and said, 'Something's happening.'* **14** A **deep** breath or sigh uses or fills the whole of your lungs. *Caz took a long, deep breath.* ♦ **deeply** *She sighed deeply.* **15** If you say that you **took a deep breath** before doing something dangerous or frightening, you mean that you tried to make yourself feel strong and confident. *I took a deep breath and went in.* **16** You use **deep** to describe colours that are strong and fairly dark. *The sky was peach-colored in the east, deep blue and starry in the west.* ► Also an adjective. *...cushions in traditional deep colours.* **17** A **deep** sound is low in pitch. *His voice was deep and mellow.* **18** If you describe someone as **deep**, you mean that they are reserved in a way that makes you think that they have good qualities such as intelligence or determination. *James is a very deep individual.* **19** If you describe something such as a problem or a piece of writing as **deep**, you mean that it is important, serious, or complicated. *They're written as adventure stories. They're not intended to be deep.*   ♦♦♦♦◇ ADJ-GRADED   ADV-GRADED   ADV-GRADED   ADJ-GRADED   ADJ-GRADED   COMB   ADV: num ADV   N-SING: the N LITERARY   ADV-GRADED   ADJ-GRADED   ADJ-GRADED PRAGMATICS   ADV-GRADED   ADV-GRADED   PHRASE   ADJ-GRADED   ADV-GRADED   v-link ADJ in n   ADJ   ADV-GRADED   ADV-GRADED   ADJ-GRADED   ADV-GRADED   PHRASE   COMB   ADJ-GRADED   ADJ-GRADED   ADJ-GRADED   ADJ-GRADED

20 If you are **deep** in debt, you have a lot of debts. *I* ADV-GRADED: *paid my bills, knowing each cheque got me deeper into* ADV in/into *debt.* ♦ **deeply** *She is now penniless and deeply in* ADV-GRADED: *debt.* ADV in/into

21 ● to go off at the **deep end**: see **end**. ● to be thrown in at the **deep end**: see **end**. ● in **deep water**: see **water**.

deep·en /'di:pən/ **deepens, deepening, deep-** ♦♦◇◇◇
ened. 1 If a situation or emotion **deepens** or if V-ERG: V
something **deepens** it, it becomes stronger and Vn
more intense. *My marriage was rough, but it deepened my emotions.* **2** If you **deepen** your knowledge VERB
or understanding of a subject, you learn more about Vn
it and become more interested in it. *...an exciting
opportunity for anyone wishing to deepen their
understanding of themselves.*
3 When light or a colour **deepens** or **is deepened**, it V-ERG
becomes darker. *Dusk was deepening as they drove* V
back. **4** When a sound **deepens** or **is deepened**, it be- Also Vn
comes lower in tone. *Her voice has deepened and* V-ERG
coarsened with the years. V
5 When your breathing **deepens**, or you **deepen** it, V-ERG
you take more air into your lungs when you breathe. V
He heard her breathing deepen. **6** If people **deepen** VERB
something, they increase its depth by digging out its Vn
lower surface. *A major project has now begun to deep-
en the main approach channel.* **7** Something such as a VERB: V
river or a sea **deepens** where the bottom begins to
slope downwards.

,**deep 'freeze, deep freezes.** A **deep freeze** is the N-COUNT
same as a **freezer**.

,**deep-'fry, deep-fries, deep-frying, deep-** VERB
fried. If you **deep-fry** food, you fry it in a large Vn
amount of fat or oil. *Heat the oil and deep-fry the
fish.*

,**deep-'rooted.** **Deep-rooted** means the same as ADJ-GRADED
deep-seated. *...long-term solutions to a deep-rooted
problem.*

'**deep-sea.** **Deep-sea** activities take place in the ADJ: ADJ n
areas of the sea that are a long way from the coast.
...deep-sea diving.

,**deep-'seated.** A **deep-seated** problem, feeling, ♦◇◇◇◇
or belief is difficult to change because its causes ADJ-GRADED
have been there for a long time. *...deep-seated economic problems.*

'**deep-set.** **Deep-set** eyes have deep sockets. *He* ADJ
had black hair and deep-set brown eyes.

deer /dɪə/; **deer** is both the singular and the plural ♦♦◇◇◇
form. A **deer** is a large wild animal that eats grass N-COUNT
and leaves. A male deer usually has large branching
horns.

de·face /dɪ'feɪs/ **defaces, defacing, defaced.** If VERB: Vn
someone **defaces** something such as a wall or a notice, they spoil it by writing or drawing things on it.

de fac·to /,deɪ 'fæktəʊ/. **De facto** is used to indi- ◇◇◇◇◇
cate that something is a particular thing, although it ADJ: ADJ n
was not specifically planned or intended to be that FORMAL
thing. *This might be interpreted as a de facto recognition of the republic's independence.* ▶ Also an ad- ADV:
verb. *German unity has now de facto replaced the* ADV with cl
signing of such a treaty.

de·fama·tory /dɪ'fæmətri, AM -tɔ:ri/. Speech or ADJ-GRADED
writing that is **defamatory** is likely to damage FORMAL
someone's good reputation by saying something
bad and untrue about them. *The article was highly
defamatory.*

de·fame /dɪ'feɪm/ **defames, defaming, de-** VERB
famed. If you **defame** someone or something, you Vn
say something bad and untrue about them. *Sgt* FORMAL
Norwood complained that the article defamed him.
♦ **defa·ma·tion** /,defə'meɪʃən/ *He was considering* N-UNCOUNT
suing for defamation.

de·fault /dɪ'fɔ:lt/ **defaults, defaulting, default-** ♦♦◇◇◇
ed. Pronounced /'di:fɔ:lt/ for meaning 2. **1** If a per- VERB
son, company, or country **defaults** on something Vn on n
that they have legally agreed to do, such as paying LEGAL
some money before a particular time, they fail to do
it. *More borrowers are defaulting on loans.* ▶ Also a N-UNCOUNT
noun. *The corporation may be charged with default*
on its contract with the government. ♦ **de·fault·er,** N-COUNT
defaulters *...fine defaulters.*
2 A **default** situation is what exists or happens unless ADJ: ADJ n
someone or something changes it. *...default pass-
words being installed on commercial machines.* **3** If PHRASE
something happens **by default**, it happens only be- FORMAL
cause something else which might have prevented it
or changed it has not happened. **4** If something hap- PHR-PREP
pens **in default of** something else, it happens because FORMAL
that other thing does not happen or proves to be
impossible.

de·feat /dɪ'fi:t/ **defeats, defeating, defeated.** ♦♦♦♦◇
1 If you **defeat** someone, you win a victory over VERB
them in a battle, game, or contest. *...the Montreal* Vn
*Canadiens, who defeated the Boston Bruins four
games to one.* **2** If a proposal or motion in a debate VERB:
is defeated, more people vote against it than for it. be V-ed
3 To **defeat** an action or plan means to cause it to VERB: Vn
fail. **4** Defeat is the experience of being beaten in a N-VAR
battle, game, or contest, or of failing to achieve
what you wanted to. *The most important thing is
not to admit defeat.* **5** If a task or a problem **defeats** VERB
you, it is so difficult that you cannot do it or solve it. Vn
*The structural challenges of constructing such a huge
novel almost defeated her.*

de·feat·ist /dɪ'fi:tɪst/ **defeatists.** A **defeatist** is N-COUNT
someone who thinks or talks in a way that suggests
that they expect to be unsuccessful. ▶ Also an ad- ADJ-GRADED
jective. *...a defeatist attitude.* ♦ **de·feat·ism** *Loss of* N-UNCOUNT
confidence can lead to cynicism and defeatism.

def·ecate /'defəkeɪt/ **defecates, defecating,** VERB: V
defecated. When people and animals **defecate**, FORMAL
they get rid of waste matter from their body through
their anus. ♦ **def·eca·tion** /,defə'keɪʃən/ N-UNCOUNT

de·fect, defects, defecting, defected. The ♦♦◇◇◇
noun is pronounced /'di:fekt/. The verb is pro-
nounced /dɪ'fekt/. **1** A **defect** is a fault or imperfec- N-COUNT
tion in a person or thing. *He was born with a hear-
ing defect. ...a defect in the aircraft caused the crash.*
2 If you **defect**, you leave your country, political VERB: V
party, or other group, and join an opposing country, V to/from n
party, or group. *He tried to defect to the West last
year.* ♦ **de·fec·tion** /dɪ'fekʃən/ **defections** *...the* N-VAR
defection of at least sixteen Parliamentary deputies.
♦ **de·fec·tor** /dɪ'fektə/ **defectors.** N-COUNT

de·fec·tive /dɪ'fektɪv/. If something is **defective**, ◇◇◇◇◇
there is something wrong with it and it does not ADJ-GRADED
work properly. *Her sight was becoming defective.*

de·fence /dɪ'fens/ **defences;** spelled **defense** in ♦♦♦♦◇
American English. Pronounced /'di:fens/ for mean-
ing 8 in American English. **1** Defence is action that N-UNCOUNT
is taken to protect someone or something against
attack. *The land was flat, giving no scope for defence.
...wielding a knife in defence.* **2** Defence is the or- N-UNCOUNT
ganization of a country's armies and weapons, and
their use to protect the country or its interests.
*Twenty eight percent of the federal budget is spent on
defense.* **3** The **defences** of a country or region are N-PLURAL
all its armed forces and weapons.
4 A **defence** is something that people or animals can N-COUNT
use or do to protect themselves. *The immune system is
our main defence against disease.* **5** If you come to PHRASE
someone's **defence**, you help them by doing or saying
something to protect them. *Tony sprang to the defence
of the 21-year-old, saying he was not to blame.* **6** A de- N-COUNT:
fence is something that you say or write which sup- also in N
ports ideas or actions that have been criticized or
questioned. *Peking yesterday published a 37,000-
word defence of its rule of Tibet.*
7 In a court of law, an accused person's **defence** is the N-COUNT
process of presenting evidence in their favour. *He has
insisted on conducting his own defence.* **8** The **defence** N-SING
is the case that is presented by a lawyer in a trial for
the person who has been accused of a crime. You can
also refer to this person's lawyers as the **defence.** *The
defence was that the records of the interviews were fabricated by the police... The defence pleaded insanity.*
9 In games such as football or hockey, the **defence** is N-COLL-SING:
the group of players in a team who try to stop the op- also in N
posing players scoring a goal or a point.

de·fence·less /dɪˈfensləs/; spelled **defenseless** in ADJ-GRADED
American English. If someone or something is **defenceless**, they are weak and unable to defend
themselves properly. *...a savage attack on a defenceless young girl.*

de'fence mechanism, defence mechanisms. N-COUNT
A **defence mechanism** is a way of behaving or
thinking which is not conscious or deliberate and is
an automatic reaction to unpleasant experiences or
feelings such as anxiety or fear.

de·fend /dɪˈfend/ **defends, defending, defend-** ◆◆◆◇
ed. **1** If you **defend** someone or something, you VERB: V n
take action in order to protect them. *In 1991 he and* V pron-refl
his friends defended themselves against some white against n
racist thugs. **2** If you **defend** someone or something VERB
when they have been criticized, you argue in sup- V n
port of them. *Clarence's move was unpopular, but* V pron-refl
Matt had to defend it... The author defends herself against n
against charges of racism. **3** When a lawyer **defends** VERB
a person who has been accused of something, the V n
lawyer argues on their behalf in a court of law that Also V
the charges are not true. *...a lawyer who defended*
dissidents in the former Communist state. **4** When a VERB: V n
sports player plays in the tournament which they
won the previous time it was held, you can say that
they **are defending** their title.

de·fend·ant /dɪˈfendənt/ **defendants.** A **defend-** ◆◆◇◇
ant is a person who has been accused of breaking N-COUNT
the law and is being tried in court.

de·fend·er /dɪˈfendə/ **defenders.** **1** If someone is ◆◆◇◇
a **defender** of a particular thing or person that has N-COUNT
been criticized or attacked, they argue or act in support of that thing or person. *...a strong defender of*
human rights or religious freedom. ▶ A **defender** in N-COUNT
a game such as football or hockey is a player whose
main task is to try and stop the other side scoring.

de·fense /dɪˈfens/. See **defence**.

de·fen·sible /dɪˈfensɪbəl/. An opinion, system, or ADJ-GRADED
action that is **defensible** is one that people can argue is right or good. *Her reasons for acting are morally defensible.*

de·fen·sive /dɪˈfensɪv/. **1** You use **defensive** to de- ◆◆◇◇
scribe things that are intended to protect someone ADJ
or something. *The Government hastily organized defensive measures... The union leaders were pushed
into a more defensive position.* **2** Someone who is ADJ-GRADED
defensive is behaving in a way that shows they feel
unsure or threatened. *She heard the blustering, defensive note in his voice.* ♦ **de·fen·sive·ly** *'Oh, I* ADV-GRADED
know, I know,' said Kate, defensively. ♦ **de·fen-** N-UNCOUNT
·sive·ness. **3** If someone is **on the defensive**, they PHRASE
are trying to protect themselves or their interests
because they feel unsure or threatened. *He smiled,
not wanting to put the man on the defensive.* **4** In ADJ-GRADED
sport, **defensive** play is play that is intended to prevent your opponent from scoring goals or points
against you. ♦ **de·fen·sive·ly** *...playing defensively.* ADV-GRADED

de·fer /dɪˈfɜː/ **defers, deferring, deferred.** **1** If ◇◇◇◇
you **defer** an event or action, you arrange for it to VERB
happen at a later date, rather than immediately or V n/-ing
at the previously planned time. *Customers often defer payment for as long as possible.* ♦ **de·fer·ment** N-VAR
/dɪˈfɜːmənt/, **deferments.** *...the deferment of national service for lycée students.* ♦ **de·fer·ral** N-VAR
/dɪˈfɜːrəl/, **deferrals.** *They were granted a deferral
of payments for nine weeks.* **2** If you **defer to** some- VERB
one, you accept their opinion or do what they want V to n
you to do, even when you do not agree with it yourself, because you respect them or their authority.
Doctors are encouraged to defer to experts.

def·er·ence /ˈdefərəns/. **Deference** is a polite and ◇◇◇◇
respectful attitude towards someone, especially be- N-UNCOUNT
cause they have an important position. ♦ **def·er-** ADJ-GRADED
·en·tial /ˌdefəˈrenʃəl/. *All his adult life he had been
surrounded by deferential courtiers.* ♦ **def·er·en-** ADV
·tial·ly *She liked Gertrude, whom she deferentially
called Miss Stein.*

de·fi·ance /dɪˈfaɪəns/. **1** **Defiance** is behaviour or ◆◆◇◇
an attitude which shows that you are not willing to N-UNCOUNT
obey someone. *...his courageous defiance of the gov-*

ernment. **2** If you do something **in defiance of** a PHRASE
person, rule, or law, you do it even though you
know that you are not allowed to do it. *People have
taken to the streets in defiance of the curfew.*

de·fi·ant /dɪˈfaɪənt/. If someone is **defiant**, they ◆◆◇◇
show that they are not willing to obey someone, or ADJ-GRADED
are not worried about someone's disapproval. *The
players are in defiant mood as they prepare for tomorrow's game.* ♦ **de·fi·ant·ly** *They defiantly reject-* ADV-GRADED
ed any talk of a compromise.

de·fi·cien·cy /dɪˈfɪʃənsi/ **deficiencies.** **1** Defi- ◆◆◇◇
ciency in something, especially something that your N-VAR:
body needs, is a lack or shortage of it. *They did* with supp
blood tests on him for signs of vitamin deficiency. FORMAL
2 A **deficiency** is a weakness or imperfection in N-VAR:
someone or something. with supp
FORMAL

de·fi·cient /dɪˈfɪʃənt/. **1** If someone or something ◇◇◇◇
is **deficient** in a particular thing, they do not have ADJ
the full amount of it that they need in order to func- FORMAL
tion normally or work properly. ▶ Also a combining COMB
form. *Vegetarians too can become iron-deficient.*
2 Someone or something that is **deficient** is not ADJ-GRADED
good enough for a particular purpose. *...deficient* FORMAL
landing systems.

defi·cit /ˈdefəsɪt/ **deficits.** A **deficit** is the amount ◆◆◆◇
by which something is less than what is required or N-COUNT
expected, especially the amount by which the total
money received is less than the total money spent.
...the federal budget deficit. ● If an account or or- PHRASE
ganization is **in deficit**, more money has been spent
than has been received.

de·file /dɪˈfaɪl/ **defiles, defiling, defiled.** If some- VERB: V n
one **defiles** something that people think is impor- LITERARY
tant or holy, they do something to it or say something about it which is offensive.

de·fin·able /dɪˈfaɪnəbəl/. Something that is **defin-** ADJ-GRADED
able can be described or identified in a particular
way. *...groups broadly definable as conservative.*

de·fine /dɪˈfaɪn/ **defines, defining, defined.** **1** If ◆◆◆◇
you **define** something, you show, describe, or state VERB: V n
clearly what it is and what its limits are, or what it is V wh
like. *The Supreme Court decision could define how
far Congress can go.* ♦ **de·fined** *...a party with a* ADJ-GRADED
clearly defined programme. **2** If you **define** a word VERB: V n
or expression, you explain its meaning, for example V n as n
in a dictionary. *Collins English Dictionary defines a
workaholic as 'a person obsessively addicted to
work'.*

de·fined /dɪˈfaɪnd/. If something is clearly **defined** ◇◇◇◇
or strongly **defined**, its outline is clear or strong. *A* ADJ-GRADED
clearly defined track leads down to the valley.

defi·nite /ˈdefɪnɪt/. **1** If something such as a deci- ◆◆◇◇
sion or an arrangement is **definite**, it is firm and ADJ-GRADED
clear, and unlikely to be changed. *It's too soon to
give a definite answer.* **2** **Definite** evidence or infor- ADJ
mation is true, rather than being someone's opinion
or guess. *The police had nothing definite against
her.* **3** You use **definite** to emphasize the strength of ADJ-GRADED:
your opinion or belief. *That's a very definite possibil-* ADJ n
ity. **4** Someone who is **definite** behaves or talks in a PRAGMATICS
firm confident way. *Mary is very definite about this.* ADJ-GRADED
5 A **definite** shape or colour is clear and noticeable. ADJ-GRADED

,definite 'article, definite articles. The word N-COUNT
'the' is sometimes called the **definite article.** TECHNICAL

defi·nite·ly /ˈdefɪnɪtli/. **1** You use **definitely** to em- ◆◆◇◇
phasize that something is the case, or to emphasize ADV-GRADED
the strength of your intention or opinion. *I'm defi-* PRAGMATICS
nitely going to get in touch with these people. **2** If ADV:
something has been **definitely** decided, the decision ADV before v
will not be changed. *He told them that no venue had
yet been definitely decided.*

defi·ni·tion /ˌdefɪˈnɪʃən/ **definitions.** **1** A **defini-** ◆◆◇◇
tion is a statement giving the meaning of a word or N-COUNT
expression, for example in a dictionary. *There is no
general agreement on a standard definition of intelligence.* ● If you say that something has a particular PHRASE
quality **by definition**, you mean that it always has PRAGMATICS
this quality, simply because of what it is. *Human
perception is highly imperfect and by definition*

subjective. **2 Definition** is the quality of being clear and distinct. *Their foreign policy lacks definition.* N-UNCOUNT

de·fin·i·tive /dɪˈfɪnɪtɪv/. **1** Something that is **definitive** provides a conclusion that cannot be questioned. *No one has come up with a definitive answer as to why this should be so.* ♦ **de·fin·i·tive·ly** *The Constitution did not definitively rule out divorce.* **2** A **definitive** book or performance is thought to be the best of its kind that has ever been done. ◆◆◇◇◇ ADJ-GRADED ADV ADJ-GRADED

de·flate /dɪˈfleɪt/ **deflates, deflating, deflated. 1** To **deflate** someone or **deflate** their confidence means to cause them to lose confidence. ♦ **de·flat·ed** *When she refused I felt deflated.* **2** When something such as a tyre or balloon **deflates**, all the air comes out of it. *...a deflated balloon.* ◆◇◇◇◇ VERB: V n ADJ-GRADED V-ERG: V V-ed Also V n

de·fla·tion /ˌdiːˈfleɪʃən, dɪf-/. **Deflation** is a reduction in economic activity that leads to lower levels of industrial output, employment, investment, trade, profits, and prices. ♦ **de·fla·tion·ary** /ˌdiːˈfleɪʃənri, AM -neri/. A **deflationary** economic policy or measure is intended to or likely to cause deflation. N-UNCOUNT ADJ

de·flect /dɪˈflekt/ **deflects, deflecting, deflected. 1** If you **deflect** something such as criticism or attention, you act in a way that prevents it from being directed towards you or affecting you. *It's a maneuver just to deflect the attention of the people from what is really happening.* **2** If something or someone **deflects** you from a course of action you have started or decided on, they make you decide not to do it or continue with it. *Never let a little problem deflect you.* **3** If you **deflect** something that is moving, you make it go in a slightly different direction, for example by hitting it or blocking it. *He stuck out his boot and deflected the shot over the bar.* ♦ **de·flec·tion** /dɪˈflekʃən/ **deflections** *...the deflection of light as it passes through the slits in the grating.* ◆◇◇◇◇ VERB: V n V n from n VERB: V n from n/-ing V n VERB: V n V n prep N-VAR

de·flow·er /ˌdiːˈflaʊə/ **deflowers, deflowering, deflowered.** When a woman is **deflowered**, she has sexual intercourse with a man for the first time. VERB: V n LITERARY

de·for·est /ˌdiːˈfɒrɪst, AM -ˈfɔːr-/ **deforests, deforesting, deforested.** If an area is **deforested**, all the trees are cut down or destroyed. ♦ **de·for·esta·tion** /ˌdiːˌfɒrɪsˈteɪʃən, AM -ˈfɔːr-/ *...the disastrous consequences of uncontrolled deforestation.* ◆◇◇◇◇ VERB: be V-ed N-UNCOUNT

de·form /dɪˈfɔːm/ **deforms, deforming, deformed.** If something **deforms** something, usually a person's body, it causes it to have an unnatural shape. *Bad rheumatoid arthritis deforms limbs.* ♦ **de·formed** *He was born with a deformed right leg.* ♦ **de·for·ma·tion** /ˌdiːfɔːˈmeɪʃən/ **deformations** *Changing stresses bring about more cracking and rock deformation.* ◆◇◇◇◇ VERB V n Also V ADJ-GRADED N-VAR

de·form·ity /dɪˈfɔːmɪti/ **deformities. 1** A **deformity** is a part of someone's body which is not the normal shape because of injury or illness, or because they were born this way. **2** Deformity is the condition of having a deformity. *The bones begin to grind against each other, leading to pain and deformity.* N-COUNT N-UNCOUNT

de·fraud /dɪˈfrɔːd/ **defrauds, defrauding, defrauded.** If someone **defrauds** you, they take something away from you or stop you from getting something that belongs to you by means of tricks and lies. *They conspired to defraud the federal government of millions of dollars in income taxes.* ◆◇◇◇◇ VERB: V n V n of/out of n

de·fray /dɪˈfreɪ/ **defrays, defraying, defrayed.** If you **defray** someone's costs or expenses, you give them money which represents the amount that they have spent, for example while they have been doing something for you or acting on your behalf. VERB: V n FORMAL

de·frost /ˌdiːˈfrɒst, AM -ˈfrɔːst/ **defrosts, defrosting, defrosted.** When you **defrost** frozen food or a fridge or freezer, you cause it to become unfrozen. *Once the turkey has defrosted, remove the giblets... Defrost the fridge regularly.* V-ERG: V n V V n

deft /deft/ **defter, deftest.** A **deft** action is skilful and often quick. ♦ **deft·ly** *One of the waiting servants deftly caught him as he fell.* ♦ **deft·ness** *...Dr Holly's surgical deftness and experience.* ◆◇◇◇◇ ADJ-GRADED WRITTEN ADV-GRADED N-UNCOUNT

de·funct /dɪˈfʌŋkt/. If something is **defunct**, it no longer exists, or it has stopped functioning or operating. *...the now defunct Social Democratic Party.* ♦◇◇◇◇ ADJ

de·fuse /ˌdiːˈfjuːz/ **defuses, defusing, defused. 1** If you **defuse** a dangerous or tense situation, you calm it. **2** If someone **defuses** a bomb, they remove the fuse from it so that it cannot explode. ♦◇◇◇◇ VERB: V n VERB: V n

defy /dɪˈfaɪ/ **defies, defying, defied. 1** If you **defy** someone who is trying to stop you doing something, you disobey them and do it. *Nearly eleven-thousand people have been arrested for defying the ban on street trading.* **2** If you **defy** someone to do something, you challenge them to do it when you think that they will be unable to do it or are too frightened to do it. *He looked at me as if he was defying me to argue.* **3** If something **defies** description or understanding, it is so strange, extreme, or surprising that it is almost impossible to understand or explain it. *It's a devastating and barbaric act that defies all comprehension.* ◆◆◇◇◇ VERB V n VERB V n to-inf VB: no passive, no cont V n

de·gen·er·ate, degenerates, degenerating, degenerated. The verb is pronounced /dɪˈdʒenəreɪt/. The adjective and noun are pronounced /dɪˈdʒenərət/. **1** If someone or something **degenerates**, they become worse in some way, for example weaker or poorer in quality. *...a very serious humanitarian crisis which could degenerate into a catastrophe.* ♦ **de·gen·era·tion** /dɪˌdʒenəˈreɪʃən/. *...the degeneration of our political system.* **2** You refer to someone as a **degenerate** when you disapprove of them and are shocked by them because you think they have low standards of morality. ▶ Also an adjective. *...the degenerate attitudes he found among some of his fellow officers.* ♦ **de·gen·era·cy** /dɪˈdʒenərəsi/. *...the moral degeneracy of society.* ♦◇◇◇◇ VERB: V V into n N-UNCOUNT N-COUNT PRAGMATICS ADJ-GRADED N-UNCOUNT

de·gen·era·tive /dɪˈdʒenərətɪv/. A **degenerative** disease or condition gets worse as time progresses. ADJ

de·grade /dɪˈgreɪd/ **degrades, degrading, degraded. 1** Something that **degrades** someone humiliates them and makes them feel they are not respected. *...the notion that pornography degrades women.* ♦ **de·grad·ing** *Mr Porter was subjected to a degrading strip-search.* ♦ **deg·ra·da·tion** /ˌdegrəˈdeɪʃən/, **degradations.** *They were sickened by the scenes of misery and degradation they found.* **2** To **degrade** something means to damage it so that it becomes worse, weaker, or poorer. ♦ **degradation** *...the degradation of democracy.* *...the accelerating degradation of our planet's natural environment.* **3** If a substance **degrades**, it changes chemically and decays or separates into different substances. *...the ability of these enzymes to degrade cellulose.* ♦ **degradation** *...the degradation of salicylic acid in plants.* ♦◇◇◇◇ VERB V n ADJ-GRADED N-VAR VERB: V n FORMAL N-UNCOUNT V-ERG: V Vn TECHNICAL N-UNCOUNT

de·gree /dɪˈgriː/ **degrees. 1** You use **degree** to indicate the extent to which something happens or is the case. *These barriers will ensure a very high degree of protection.* ● If something has a **degree** of a particular quality, it has a small but significant amount of that quality. *Their wages do, however, allow them a degree of independence.* **2** You use **degree** in expressions such as **a matter of degree** and **different in degree** to indicate that you are talking about the comparative quantity, scale, or extent of things, rather than their fundamental nature. *It may be worse for you, but it is a matter of degree.* **3** You use expressions such as **to some degree, to a large degree,** or **to the degree that** in order to indicate the extent to which something is true. **4** A **degree** is a unit of measurement that is used to measure temperatures. It is often written as '°', for example 100°. **5** A **degree** is a unit of measurement that is used to measure angles, and also longitude and latitude. It is often written as '°', for example 45°. **6** If something happens **by degrees**, it happens slowly and gradually. **7** ● **to the nth degree:** see **nth;** see also **third-degree. 8** A **degree** at a university or college is a course of study that you take there, or the qualification that you ◆◆◆◆◇ N-COUNT: with supp PRAGMATICS PHRASE PRAGMATICS N-UNCOUNT: of/in N PRAGMATICS PHRASE PRAGMATICS N-COUNT N-COUNT PHRASE N-COUNT

D

get when you have passed the course. *He returned to take a master's degree in economics at Yale.*

de·hu·man·ize /ˌdiːˈhjuːmənaɪz/ **dehumanizes,** VERB: V n
dehumanizing, dehumanized; also spelled **de-humanise** in British English. If you say that something **dehumanizes** people, you mean it causes them to lose good human qualities such as kindness and individuality. ♦ **de·hu·man·iz·ing** ...*the brutal,* ADJ-GRADED
dehumanising experience of slavery.

de·hy·drate /ˌdiːhaɪˈdreɪt, -ˈhaɪdreɪt/ **dehydrates,** ◆◇◇◇◇
dehydrating, dehydrated. 1 When food **is de-** VB: usu
hydrated, all the water is removed from it, often in passive
order to preserve it. **2** If you **dehydrate,** you lose V-ERG: V
too much water from your body so that you feel V n
weak or ill. *Alcohol quickly dehydrates your body.*
♦ **de·hy·drat·ed** *You should drink lots of water to* ADJ-GRADED
avoid becoming dehydrated. ♦ **de·hy·dra·tion** N-UNCOUNT
/ˌdiːhaɪˈdreɪʃən/ ...*a child who is suffering from
dehydration.*

dei·fy /ˈdeɪfaɪ, AM ˈdiː-/ **deifies, deifying, dei-** VB: usu
fied. If someone or something **is deified,** they are passive
considered to be a god or are respected almost as FORMAL
highly as if they were a god. ♦ **dei·fi·ca·tion** N-UNCOUNT
/ˌdeɪfɪˈkeɪʃən, AM ˌdiː-/. ...*the deification of science
in the 1940s.*

deign /deɪn/ **deigns, deigning, deigned.** If you VERB
say that someone **deigned** to do something, you PRAGMATICS
mean they did it reluctantly, because they thought V to-inf
they were too important to do it; used showing dis- FORMAL
approval. *Weatherby didn't deign to reply.*

de·ity /ˈdeɪɪti, AM ˈdiː-/ **deities.** A **deity** is a god or ◆◇◇◇◇
goddess. N-COUNT
FORMAL

déjà vu /ˌdeɪʒɑː ˈvuː/. **Déjà vu** is the feeling that N-UNCOUNT
you have already experienced the things that are
happening to you now.

de·ject·ed /dɪˈdʒektɪd/. If you are **dejected,** you ADJ-GRADED
feel miserable or unhappy, usually because you
have just been disappointed by something. ♦ **de-** ADV-GRADED:
·ject·ed·ly *Passengers queued dejectedly for the in-* ADV with v
creasingly dirty toilets. ♦ **de·jec·tion** /dɪˈdʒekʃən/. N-UNCOUNT
There was a slight air of dejection about her.

de jure /ˌdeɪ ˈdʒʊəreɪ, AM ˌdiː ˈdʒʊri/. **De jure** is ADJ: ADJ n
used to indicate that something legally exists or is LEGAL
legally a particular thing. ▶ Also an adverb. *Finland* ADV:
had recognised Soviet annexation de facto, but not ADV with cl
de jure.

de·lay /dɪˈleɪ/ **delays, delaying, delayed. 1** If ◆◆◆◇
you **delay** doing something, you do not do it im- VERB
mediately or at the planned or expected time, but V n /-ing
you leave it until later. *I wanted to delay my depar-* V
*ture until June 1980... So don't delay, write in now
for your chance of a free gift.* **2** If there is a **delay,** N-VAR
someone fails to do something or something fails to
happen until later than required, planned, or expected. *We'll send you a quote without delay... Although the tests have caused some delay, flights
should be back to normal this morning.* **3** To **delay** VERB
someone or something means to make them late or V n
to slow them down. *Various set-backs and problems
delayed production.*

de·lec·table /dɪˈlektəbəl/. **1** If you describe some- ADJ-GRADED
thing, especially food or drink, as **delectable,** you
mean it is very pleasant. **2** If you describe someone ADJ-GRADED
as **delectable,** you mean they are very attractive. LITERARY

de·lec·ta·tion /ˌdiːlekˈteɪʃən/. If you do something PHRASE
for someone's **delectation,** you do it to give them FORMAL
enjoyment or pleasure.

del·egate, delegates, delegating, delegated. ◆◆◆◇
The noun is pronounced /ˈdelɪgət/. The verb is pronounced /ˈdelɪgeɪt/. **1** A **delegate** is a person who is N-COUNT
chosen to vote or make decisions on behalf of a
group of other people, especially at a conference or
a meeting. **2** If you **delegate** duties, responsibilities, VERB
or power to someone, you give them those duties or V n to n
responsibilities or that power, so that they can act Also V,
on your behalf. *He talks of delegating more author-* V n
*ity to his deputies... Officials have now been delegat-
ed to start work on a draft settlement.* ♦ **del·ega-
·tion** /ˌdelɪˈgeɪʃən/. ...*the complete delegation of* N-UNCOUNT
responsibility.

del·ega·tion /ˌdelɪˈgeɪʃən/ **delegations.** A **del-** ◆◆◆◇
egation is a group of people who have been sent N-COUNT
somewhere to have talks with other people on behalf of a larger group of people. ...*the Soviet trade
delegation.* • See also **delegate.**

de·lete /dɪˈliːt/ **deletes, deleting, deleted.** If ◆◇◇◇◇
you **delete** something that has been written down VERB: V n
or stored in a computer, you cross it out or remove
it. ♦ **de·letion** /dɪˈliːʃən/ **deletions** ...*the deletion* N-VAR
of a great deal of irrelevant material.

del·eteri·ous /ˌdelɪˈtɪəriəs/. Something that has a ADJ-GRADED
deleterious effect on something has a harmful ef- FORMAL
fect on it. *The fear of crime is having a deleterious
effect on community life.*

de·lib·er·ate, deliberates, deliberating, de- ◆◆◆◇
liberated. The adjective is pronounced /dɪˈlɪbərət/.
The verb is pronounced /dɪˈlɪbəreɪt/. **1** A **deliberate** ADJ-GRADED
action was planned or decided beforehand, and so
it happens intentionally rather than by chance. *It
has a deliberate policy to introduce world war to Britain... Witnesses say the firing was deliberate.* ♦ **de-** ADV-GRADED
·lib·er·ate·ly *It looks as if the blaze was started deliberately.* **2** If a movement or action is **deliberate,** it ADJ-GRADED
is done slowly and carefully. ...*stepping with deliber-
ate slowness up the steep paths.* ♦ **deliberately** ADV-GRADED:
The Japanese have acted calmly and deliberately. ADV after v
3 If you **deliberate,** you think about something care- VERB: V
fully, especially before making a very important deci- V prep
sion. *She deliberated over the decision for a good few* V n
*years before she finally made up her mind... The Court
of Criminal Appeals has been deliberating his case for
almost two weeks.*

de·lib·era·tion /dɪˌlɪbəˈreɪʃən/ **deliberations.** ◆◇◇◇◇
1 Deliberation is careful and often lengthy consid- N-UNCOUNT
eration of a subject. *After deliberation, they rejected
the prosecution's arguments and found Heidi not
guilty.* **2 Deliberations** are formal discussions N-PLURAL
where an issue is considered carefully. **3** If you say N-UNCOUNT
or do something with **deliberation,** you do it slowly
and carefully. *Fred spoke with deliberation.*

deli·ca·cy /ˈdelɪkəsi/ **delicacies.** A **delicacy** is a ◆◇◇◇◇
rare or expensive food that is considered especially N-COUNT
nice to eat. ...*mouthwatering local delicacies.* • See
also **delicate.**

deli·cate /ˈdelɪkət/. **1** Something that is **delicate** is ◆◆◇◇◇
small and beautifully shaped. *He had delicate* ADJ-GRADED
*hands. ...an evergreen tree with large flame-coloured
leaves and delicate blossom.* ♦ **deli·cate·ly** *She was* ADV-GRADED:
a shy, delicately pretty girl with enormous blue eyes. ADV adj/-ed
♦ **deli·ca·cy** ...*the delicacy of a rose. ...a country* N-UNCOUNT
*where the feminine ideal is delicacy, slimness and
grace.* **2** Something that is **delicate** has a colour, ADJ-GRADED
taste, or smell which is pleasant and not strong or
intense. *Young haricot beans have a delicate, subtle
flavour.* ♦ **delicately** ...*a soup delicately flavoured* ADV-GRADED
with nutmeg. **3** If something is **delicate,** it is easy to ADJ-GRADED
harm, damage, or break, and needs to be handled
or treated carefully. ...*a washing machine catering
for every fabric -- even the most delicate.* **4** Some- ADJ-GRADED
one who is **delicate** is not healthy and strong, and
becomes ill easily.
5 You use **delicate** to describe a situation, problem, ADJ-GRADED
matter, or discussion that needs to be dealt with carefully and tactfully in order to avoid upsetting things or
offending people. ...*the delicate issue of adoption.*
♦ **deli·cate·ly** *The president has tried to reject the So-* ADV-GRADED:
viet proposal as delicately as possible. ...his delicately ADV with v
worded assessment of the course. ♦ **deli·ca·cy** *There* N-UNCOUNT
*was a matter of some delicacy... Both countries are be-
having with rare delicacy.* **6** A **delicate** task, move- ADJ-GRADED
ment, action, or product needs or shows great skill
and attention to detail. ...*a long and delicate operation
carried out at a hospital in Florence.* ♦ **deli·cate·ly** ADV-GRADED:
She picked her way delicately over the rocks. ...the deli- ADV with v
cately embroidered sheets. **7** See also **delicacy.**

deli·ca·tes·sen /ˌdelɪkəˈtesən/ **delicatessens.** A N-COUNT
delicatessen is a shop that sells foods such as
cheeses and cold meats that have been imported
from other countries.

de·li·cious /dɪˈlɪʃəs/. **1** Food that is **delicious** has a very pleasant taste. ...*delicious meals*... *Pecan nuts are delicious both raw and cooked.* ♦ **de·li·cious·ly** ADV *This yoghurt has a deliciously creamy flavour.* **2** If you describe something as **delicious**, you mean that it is very pleasant. ...*that delicious feeling of surprise.* ♦ **deliciously** ADV: ADV adj/-ed *It leaves your hair smelling deliciously fresh and fragrant.*

◆◆◇◇ ADJ-GRADED / ADV / ADJ-GRADED

de·light /dɪˈlaɪt/ **delights, delighting, delighted.** **1** Delight is a feeling of very great pleasure. *The views are a constant source of delight... Andrew roared with delight... To my great delight, it worked.* **2** If something **delights** you, it gives you a lot of pleasure. ...*a style of music that has delighted audiences all over the world.* **3** If you **delight** in something, you get a lot of pleasure from it. *Generations of adults and children have delighted in the story.* **4** If someone **takes delight** or **takes a delight** in something, they get a lot of pleasure from it. *Haig took obvious delight in proving his critics wrong.* **5** You can refer to someone or something that gives you great pleasure or enjoyment as a **delight**. *Isn't she a delight?... The aircraft was a delight to fly.*

◆◆◆◇ N-UNCOUNT / VERB Vn / VERB Vinn/-ing / PHRASE / N-COUNT PRAGMATICS

de·light·ed /dɪˈlaɪtɪd/. **1** If you are **delighted**, you are extremely pleased and excited about something. *I know Frank will be delighted to see you... He said that he was delighted with the public response.* ♦ **de·light·ed·ly** ADV *'There!' Jackson exclaimed delightedly.* **2** If someone invites or asks you to do something, you can say that you would be **delighted** to do it, as a way of showing that you are very willing to do it. *'You must come to Tinsley's graduation party.'—'I'd be delighted.'*

◆◆◆◇ ADJ-GRADED / ADV: ADV with v ADJ: v-link ADJ PRAGMATICS

de·light·ful /dɪˈlaɪtfʊl/. If you describe something or someone as **delightful**, you mean they are very pleasant. *It was the most delightful garden I had ever seen.* ♦ **de·light·ful·ly** ...*this delightfully refreshing cologne. ...delightfully packaged foie gras.*

◆◆◇◇ ADJ-GRADED / ADV-GRADED: ADV adj/-ed

de·lim·it /dɪˈlɪmɪt/ **delimits, delimiting, delimited.** If you **delimit** something, you fix or establish its limits. *This is not meant to delimit what approaches social researchers can adopt.*

VERB Vn FORMAL

de·lin·eate /dɪˈlɪnieɪt/ **delineates, delineating, delineated.** **1** If you **delineate** something such as an idea or situation, you describe it or define it, often in a lot of detail. *The relationship between Church and State was delineated in a formal agreement.* ♦ **de·lin·ea·tion** /dɪˌlɪniˈeɪʃən/ ...*his razor-sharp delineation of ordinary life.* **2** To **delineate** a border means to say exactly where it is going to be. *We needed a peace settlement in order to determine and delineate the border.* ♦ **delineation** ...*the delineation of the provincial borders.*

VERB Vn FORMAL / N-UNCOUNT / VERB Vn FORMAL / N-UNCOUNT

de·lin·quent /dɪˈlɪŋkwənt/ **delinquents.** **1** You describe someone, especially a young person as **delinquent** when they repeatedly commit minor crimes. ...*remand homes for delinquent children.* ▶ Also a noun. ...*a nine-year-old delinquent.* ● See also **juvenile delinquent.** ♦ **de·lin·quen·cy, de·linquencies.** Delinquency is criminal behaviour, especially by young people. *He had no history of delinquency. ...a whole range of crimes and delinquencies.* ● See also **juvenile delinquency.** **2** A **delinquent** debtor or taxpayer is someone who has failed to pay their debts or taxes. ♦ **de·lin·quen·cy** ...*increases in mortgage delinquency rates.*

◆◇◇◇ ADJ / N-COUNT / N-UNCOUNT: also N in pl / ADJ: ADJ n AMERICAN, TECHNICAL / N-UNCOUNT: also N in pl

de·liri·ous /dɪˈlɪəriəs/. **1** Someone who is **delirious** is unable to think or speak in a rational way, usually because they are very ill and have a fever. ♦ **de·lir·ium** /dɪˈlɪəriəm/. If someone is suffering from **delirium**, they are delirious. **2** Someone who is **delirious** is extremely excited and happy. *I was delirious with joy.* ♦ **de·liri·ous·ly** *Dora returned from her honeymoon deliriously happy.*

◆◇◇◇ ADJ / N-UNCOUNT / ADJ-GRADED / ADV

de·liv·er /dɪˈlɪvə/ **delivers, delivering, delivered.** **1** If you **deliver** something somewhere, you take it there. *The Canadians plan to deliver more food to southern Somalia... We were told the pizza would be delivered in 20 minutes.* **2** When you **deliver** something that you have promised to do or

◆◆◆◆ VERB Vn to n Also V / VERB V

make, you do it or make it. *They have yet to show that they can really deliver new technologies... His track record so far as prime minister shows that he can't deliver.* **3** ● **deliver the goods**: see **goods.** **4** If someone or something is **delivered** into your care, you are given responsibility for them. *David delivered Holly gratefully into the woman's outstretched arms... He was led in in handcuffs and delivered over to me.* **5** If someone **delivers** you from something, they rescue or save you from it. *I have given thanks to God for delivering me from that pain.* ♦ **de·liv·er·ance** *The opening scene shows them celebrating their sudden deliverance from war... She prayed to God for deliverance.* **6** If you **deliver** a lecture or speech, you give it. **7** When someone **delivers** a baby, they help the woman who is giving birth to the baby. **8** If someone **delivers** a blow to someone else, they hit them. *Those blows to the head could well have been delivered by a woman.*

VERB Vn into/to n beV-ed over FORMAL / VERB Vn from n DATED / N-UNCOUNT / VERB: Vn / VERB: Vn / VERB Vn WRITTEN

de·liv·ery /dɪˈlɪvəri/ **deliveries.** **1** Delivery or a **delivery** is the bringing of letters, parcels, or other goods to a place. *Please allow 28 days for delivery... It is available at £108, including VAT and delivery.* **2** A **delivery** of something is the goods that are delivered. *I got a delivery of fresh eggs this morning.* **3** You talk about someone's **delivery** when you are describing the way in which they give a speech or lecture. *His speeches were magnificently written but his delivery was hopeless.* **4** Delivery is the process of giving birth to a baby. *In the end, it was an easy delivery: a fine baby boy.*

◆◆◆◇ N-VAR / N-COUNT / N-UNCOUNT / N-VAR

dell /del/ **dells.** A **dell** is a small valley with trees growing in it. *The land dipped down into a dell.*

N-COUNT LITERARY

del·phin·ium /delˈfɪniəm/ **delphiniums.** A **delphinium** is a garden plant which has a tall stem with blue flowers growing up it.

N-COUNT

del·ta /ˈdeltə/ **deltas.** A **delta** is an area of low flat land shaped like a triangle, where a river splits and spreads out into several branches before entering the sea. ...*the Mississippi delta.*

◆◇◇◇ N-COUNT

de·lude /dɪˈluːd/ **deludes, deluding, deluded.** **1** If you **delude** yourself, you let yourself believe that something is true, even though it is not true. *The President was deluding himself if he thought he was safe from such action... We delude ourselves that we are in control.* ♦ **de·lud·ed** ...*one man's mad dream and a deluded nation following him.* **2** If something or someone **deludes** you into thinking something, they make you believe something that is not true. *Television deludes you into thinking you have experienced reality, when you haven't.*

VERB V pron-refl V pron-refl that Also V pron-refl into-ing / ADJ-GRADED / VERB Vn into-ing Also Vn

del·uge /ˈdeljuːdʒ/ **deluges, deluging, deluged.** **1** A **deluge** of things is a large number of them which arrive or happen at the same time. *A deluge of manuscripts began to arrive in the post. ...a deluge of criticism.* **2** If a place or person is **deluged** with things, a large number of them arrive or happen at the same time. *Papen's office was deluged with complaints.* **3** A **deluge** is a very heavy fall of rain. ...*Pavarotti rehearsing for his open-air concert in Hyde Park under a deluge of rain.* **4** If rain **deluges** a place, it falls very heavily there, sometimes causing floods. *Two days of torrential rain deluged the capital.*

◆◇◇◇ N-COUNT / VB: usu passive beV-ed with/ by n / N-COUNT / VERB Vn WRITTEN

de·lu·sion /dɪˈluːʒən/ **delusions.** **1** A **delusion** is a false idea. ...*under the delusion that he intended to marry me.* **2** Delusion is the state of believing things that are not true. ...*her capacity for delusion.*

◆◇◇◇ N-COUNT / N-UNCOUNT

deluxe /dɪˈlʌks/; also spelled **de luxe** in British English. **Deluxe** goods or services are better and more expensive than ordinary ones. ...*deluxe wine.*

ADJ: ADJ n

delve /delv/ **delves, delving, delved.** **1** If you **delve** into something, you try to discover new information about it. *Jenny delved into her mother's past.* **2** If you **delve** inside something such as a cupboard or a bag, you search inside it. *She delved into her rucksack and pulled out a folder.*

◇◇◇◇ VERB V into n Also V adv / VERB V prep/adv

dema·gogue /ˈdeməɡɒɡ, AM -ɡɔːɡ/ **demagogues.** A **demagogue** is a political leader who

◆◇◇◇ N-COUNT PRAGMATICS

tries to win support by appealing to people's emotions rather than by rational arguments; used showing disapproval. ♦ **dema·gog·ic** /ˌdeməˈgɒdʒɪk/ ...*a demagogic populist.* ♦ **dema·gogy** /ˈdeməgɒdʒi/. Demagogy refers to the speech or actions of a demagogue.   ADJ-GRADED
N-UNCOUNT

de·mand /dɪˈmɑːnd, -ˈmænd/ **demands, demanding, demanded. 1** If you **demand** something such as information or action, you ask for it in a very forceful way. *The Labour Party has demanded an explanation from the government... Russia demanded that Unita send a delegation to the peace talks... The hijackers are demanding to speak to representatives of both governments.* **2** A **demand** is a firm request for something. *They consistently rejected the demand to remove US troops.* **3** If something is available or happens **on demand**, you can have it or it happens whenever you want it or ask for it. *...providing treatment on demand for drug abusers.*
4 If one thing **demands** another, the first needs the second in order to happen or be dealt with successfully. *The task of reconstruction would demand much patience... He could also turn on the style when the occasion demanded.* **5** The **demands** of something or someone, or their **demands** on you, are the things which they need or which you have to do for them. *...the demands and challenges of a new job... I had no right to make demands on his time.* **6** If you refer to **demand**, or to the **demand** for something, you are referring to how many people want to have it, do it, or buy it. *Demand for coal is down.*
7 If someone or something is **in demand** or **in great demand**, they are very popular and a lot of people want them. *He was much in demand as a lecturer.*
♦♦♦♦♦
VERB
V n from n
V that
V to-inf
Also V with quote

N-COUNT

PHRASE

VERB
V n
V

N-PLURAL

N-UNCOUNT

PHRASE

de·mand·ing /dɪˈmɑːndɪŋ, -ˈmænd-/. **1** A demanding job requires a lot of your time, energy, or attention. **2** People who are **demanding** are not easily satisfied or pleased. *...a very demanding child.*
♦♦◇◇◇
ADJ-GRADED
ADJ-GRADED

de·mar·cate /ˈdiːmɑːkeɪt, AM dɪˈmɑːrk-/ **demarcates, demarcating, demarcated.** If you demarcate something, you establish its boundaries or limits. *A second special UN commission was formed to demarcate the border.* ♦ **de·mar·ca·tion** /ˌdiːmɑːˈkeɪʃən/ ...*the demarcation line between Indian and Pakistani Kashmir.*
VERB
V n
FORMAL

N-UNCOUNT

de·mean /dɪˈmiːn/ **demeans, demeaning, demeaned.** To **demean** someone or something means to make people have less respect for them. *Pornography demeans women and incites rape... I wasn't going to demean myself by acting like a suspicious wife.* ♦ **de·mean·ing** Aid, however it is obtained, is demeaning to the recipients.
VERB
V n
V pron-refl

ADJ-GRADED

de·mean·our /dɪˈmiːnə/ spelled **demeanor** in American English. Your **demeanour** is the way you behave, which gives people an impression of your character and feelings. *From his general demeanour I didn't get the impression he was being ironical.*
♦◇◇◇◇
N-UNCOUNT
FORMAL

de·ment·ed /dɪˈmentɪd/. **1** Someone who is **demented** has a severe mental illness, especially Alzheimer's disease. **2** If you describe someone as **demented**, you think that their actions are strange, foolish, or uncontrolled. *He had been granted his own TV show by some demented executive.*
♦◇◇◇◇
ADJ-GRADED
DATED
ADJ-GRADED
PRAGMATICS
INFORMAL

de·men·tia /dɪˈmenʃə/ **dementias.** Dementia is a serious illness of the mind. *...senile dementia.*
♦◇◇◇◇
N-VAR
MEDICAL

de·merge /ˌdiːˈmɜːdʒ/ **demerges, demerging, demerged.** If a large company **is demerged** or **demerges**, it is broken down into several smaller companies. *Zeneca was at last demerged from its parent firm, ICI... His ultimate aim is to demerge the group. ...why so many companies merge and so few demerge.* ♦ **de·merg·er, demergers.** A demerger is the separation of a large company into smaller companies.
VERB
V-ERG
be V-ed from n
V n
V
Also V n from n
BRITISH

N-COUNT

de·mer·it /ˌdiːˈmerɪt/ **demerits.** The demerits of something or someone are their disadvantages. *...the merits and demerits of the three candidates.*
N-COUNT
FORMAL

demi-god /ˈdemigɒd/ **demi-gods.** If you describe a famous or important person such as a politician or
N-COUNT

writer as a **demigod**, you mean that they are admired or treated by people as if they were divine.

de·mili·ta·rize /ˌdiːˈmɪlɪtəraɪz/ **demilitarizes, demilitarizing, demilitarized;** also spelled de**militarise** in British English. To **demilitarize** an area means to ensure that all military forces are removed from it. *He said the UN had made remarkable progress in demilitarizing the region.* ♦ **de·mili·ta·ri·za·tion** /ˌdiːˌmɪlɪtəraɪˈzeɪʃən/.
♦◇◇◇◇
VERB
V n

N-UNCOUNT

de·mise /dɪˈmaɪz/. The **demise** of something or someone is their end or death. *...the demise of communism in Eastern Europe.*
♦◇◇◇◇
N-SING
FORMAL

demo /ˈdeməʊ/ **demos. 1** A demo is a demonstration by a group of people to show their opposition to something or their support for something. *...an anti-racist demo.* **2** A **demo** is a record or tape with a sample of someone's music recorded on it. *He listened to one of my demo tapes.*
♦◇◇◇◇
N-COUNT
BRITISH
INFORMAL
N-COUNT
INFORMAL

de·mob /diːˈmɒb/. Someone's **demob** is their release from the armed forces. *I didn't get back to Brussels until after my demob.* ♦ **de·mobbed** ...*retraining demobbed soldiers.*
N-UNCOUNT
BRITISH
INFORMAL
ADJ

de·mo·bi·lize /ˌdiːˈməʊbɪlaɪz/ **demobilizes, demobilizing, demobilized;** also spelled demobi**lise** in British English. If a country or armed force **demobilizes** its troops, or if its troops **demobilize**, its troops are released from service and go home. *It is highly unlikely that the rebels will agree to give up their weapons and demobilise.* ♦ **de·mo·bi·li·za·tion** /ˌdiːˌməʊbɪlaɪˈzeɪʃən/ ...*the demobilisation of its 100,000 strong army.*
♦◇◇◇◇
V-ERG
V n
Also V n

N-UNCOUNT

de·moc·ra·cy /dɪˈmɒkrəsi/ **democracies. 1** Democracy is a system of government in which people choose their rulers by voting for them in elections. *...the spread of democracy in Eastern Europe.* **2** A **democracy** is a country in which the people choose their government by voting for it. *The new democracies face tough challenges.* **3** Democracy is a system of running organizations, businesses, and groups in which each member is entitled to vote or participate in decisions. *...the union's emphasis on industrial democracy.*
♦♦♦♦◇
N-UNCOUNT

N-COUNT

N-UNCOUNT

demo·crat /ˈdeməkræt/ **democrats. 1** A Democrat is a member or supporter of a particular political party which has the word 'democrat' or 'democratic' in its title, for example the Democratic Party in the United States. *...a senior Christian Democrat.* **2** A **democrat** is a person who believes in the ideals of democracy, personal freedom, and equality. *This is the time for democrats and not dictators.*
♦♦♦♦◇
N-COUNT

N-COUNT

demo·crat·ic /ˌdeməˈkrætɪk/. **1** A **democratic** country, government, or political system is governed by representatives who are elected by the people. *Bolivia returned to democratic rule in 1982.* ♦ **demo·crati·cal·ly** /ˌdeməˈkrætɪkli/ ...*Russia's first democratically elected President.* **2** Something that is **democratic** is based on the idea that everyone should have equal rights and should be involved in making important decisions. *Education is the basis of a democratic society.* ♦ **democratically** This committee will enable decisions to be made democratically. **3** Democratic is used in the titles of some political parties. *...the Social Democratic Party.*
♦♦♦♦◇
ADJ

ADV

ADJ-GRADED

ADV-GRADED

ADJ: ADJ n

de·moc·ra·tize /dɪˈmɒkrətaɪz/ **democratizes, democratizing, democratized;** also spelled de**mocratise** in British English. If a country or a system **is democratized**, it is made democratic. *He feels there is a further need to democratize the life of society as a whole.* ♦ **de·moc·ra·ti·za·tion** /dɪˌmɒkrətaɪˈzeɪʃən/ ...*the democratisation of Eastern Europe.*
VERB
V n

N-UNCOUNT

de·mog·ra·phy /dɪˈmɒgrəfi/. Demography is the study of such things as the numbers of births, deaths, marriages, and cases of disease in a community over a period of time. ♦ **de·mo·graph·ic** /ˌdeməˈgræfɪk/ ...*demographic trends.*
N-UNCOUNT

ADJ: ADJ n

de·mol·ish /dɪˈmɒlɪʃ/ **demolishes, demolishing, demolished. 1** To **demolish** a building means to destroy it completely. *A storm moved directly over the island, demolishing buildings.*
♦◇◇◇◇
VERB
V n

D

✦ **demo·li·tion** /ˌdeməˈlɪʃən/ **demolitions** The N-VAR
project required the total demolition of the old
bridge. **2** If you **demolish** someone's ideas, you VERB
prove that they are wrong or invalid. Our intention Vn
was quite the opposite – to demolish rumours. **3** If a VERB
person or team **demolishes** their opponents, they Vn
JOURNALISM
defeat them heavily or easily. Millwall demolished
Notts County 6-0 on Saturday. ✦ **demolition** N-UNCOUNT
...Lazio's impressive 3-1 demolition of Inter Milan.

de·mon /ˈdiːmən/ **demons. 1** A demon is an evil ◆◇◇◇◇
spirit. ...a ceremony to rid her of two demons it was N-COUNT
believed possessed her. ✦ **de·mon·ic** /dɪˈmɒnɪk/. ADJ
...demonic forces. **2** Sources of worry or conflict N-COUNT
which torment a person or group of people are
sometimes referred to as **demons**. His private demons drove him to drink excessively. **3** If you ap- N-COUNT
prove of someone because they are very skilled at PRAGMATICS
what they do or because they do it energetically,
you can say that they do it like a **demon**. He played
like a demon. ...a demon organizer. ✦ **demonic** ...a ADJ: ADJ n
demonic drive to succeed.

de·mon·ize /ˈdiːmənaɪz/ **demonizes, demoniz-** VERB
ing, demonized; also spelled **demonise** in British Vn
English. If people **demonize** someone, they convince themselves that that person is evil. Each side
began to demonize the other.

de·mon·ol·o·gy /ˌdiːməˈnɒlədʒi/. **Demonology** is a N-UNCOUNT
set of beliefs which says that a particular situation
or group of people is evil or unacceptable.

de·mon·stra·ble /dɪˈmɒnstrəbəl/. A **demonstrable** ADJ
fact or quality can be shown to be true or to exist. FORMAL
An additive is permitted in food only where there is a
genuine demonstrable need. ✦ **de·mon·stra·bly** ADV
/dɪˈmɒnstrəbli/. ...demonstrably false statements.

dem·on·strate /ˈdemənstreɪt/ **demonstrates,** ◆◆◇◇
demonstrating, demonstrated. 1 To demon- VERB
strate a fact means to make it clear to people. The Vn
study also demonstrated a direct link between obesity V that
and mortality... You have to demonstrate that you V on that
are reliable... They are anxious to demonstrate to the Also V wh
voters that they have practical policies. **2** If you VERB
demonstrate a particular skill, quality, or feeling, Vn
you show by your actions that you have it. The government's going to great lengths to demonstrate its
military might. **3** When people **demonstrate**, they VERB: V
march or gather somewhere to show their opposi- V against/for
tion to something or their support for something. n
Angry farmers arrived in Brussels yesterday to demonstrate against possible cuts in subsidies. ✦ **de·**
·mon·stra·tor, demonstrators ...a crowd of de- N-COUNT
monstrators. **4** If you **demonstrate** something, you VERB
show people how it works or how to do it. The BBC Vn
has just successfully demonstrated a new digital ra- Also V how
dio transmission system. ✦ **de·mon·stra·tor.** N-COUNT

dem·on·stra·tion /ˌdemənˈstreɪʃən/ **demonstra-** ◆◆◆◇◇
tions. 1 A **demonstration** is a march or gathering N-COUNT
which people take part in to show their opposition
to something or their support for something. Riot
police used tear gas and truncheons this afternoon to
break up a demonstration. **2** A **demonstration** of N-COUNT
something is a talk by someone who shows you how
to do it or how it works. ...a cookery demonstration.
3 A **demonstration** of a fact or situation is a clear N-COUNT
proof of it. We want a clear demonstration of
commitment.

de·mon·stra·tive /dɪˈmɒnstrətɪv/ **demonstra-**
tives. 1 Someone who is **demonstrative** shows af- ADJ-GRADED
fection freely and openly. Richard was not normally
demonstrative. ✦ **de·mon·stra·tive·ly** Some chil- ADV-GRADED
dren respond more demonstratively than others.
2 The words 'this', 'that', 'these', and 'those' are N-COUNT
sometimes called **demonstratives**. TECHNICAL

de·mor·al·ize /dɪˈmɒrəlaɪz, AM -ˈmɔːr-/ **demoral-**
izes, demoralizing, demoralized; also spelled VERB: V n
demoralise in British English. If something **demor-**
alizes someone, it makes them lose so much confidence in what they are doing that they want to give
up. ✦ **de·mor·al·ized** ...a demoralized police force. ADJ-GRADED
✦ **de·mor·ali·za·tion** ...the lingering demoraliza- N-UNCOUNT
tion that followed defeat in World War I. ✦ **de·mor-**

·**al·iz·ing** Persistent disapproval or criticism can be ADJ-GRADED
highly demoralizing.

de·mote /dɪˈməʊt/ **demotes, demoting, de-** ◆◇◇◇◇
moted. 1 If someone **demotes** you, they give you a VERB
lower rank or a less important position than you al- Vn
ready have, often as a punishment. It's very difficult
to demote somebody who has been standing in dur-
ing maternity leave. ✦ **de·mo·tion** /dɪˈməʊʃən/ **de-** N-VAR
motions ...an unfair demotion. **2** If a team in a VB: usu
sports league **is demoted**, that team is ordered by passive,
the sport's ruling body to play in a lower division. be V-ed
✦ **demotion** The demotion was imposed as a pun- N-VAR
ishment for infringing the rules.

de·mot·ic /dɪˈmɒtɪk/. **1 Demotic** language is the ADJ
type of informal language used by ordinary people. FORMAL
...television's demotic style of language. **2 Demotic** ADJ
is used to describe someone or something that is FORMAL
typical of ordinary people. He is by instinct a populist, a demotic politician.

de·mur /dɪˈmɜː/ **demurs, demurring, de-** VERB
murred. If you **demur**, you say that you do not V
agree with something or will not do something that FORMAL
you have been asked to do. At first I demurred.

de·mure /dɪˈmjʊə/. **1** If you describe someone, ADJ-GRADED
usually a young woman, as **demure**, you mean they
are quiet and rather shy, and behave very correctly.
✦ **de·mure·ly** Chantal was sitting demurely with ADV-GRADED
her parents. **2 Demure** clothes do not reveal your ADJ-GRADED
body and they give the impression that you are shy WRITTEN
and behave correctly. ...a demure high-necked white
blouse. ✦ **demurely** ...demurely dressed in a black ADV-GRADED
woollen suit.

de·mys·ti·fy /ˌdiːˈmɪstɪfaɪ/ **demystifies, demys-** VERB
tifying, demystified. If you **demystify** some- Vn
thing, you make it easier to understand by giving a
clear explanation of it. To enter the consumer market, it was necessary to demystify the computer.

den /den/ **dens. 1** A **den** is the home of certain ◆◇◇◇◇
types of wild animals such as lions or foxes. **2** Your N-COUNT
den is a quiet room in your house where you can go N-COUNT
to study, work, or carry on a hobby without being AMERICAN
disturbed. **3** A **den** is a secret place where people N-COUNT
meet, usually for a dishonest purpose. ...illegal
drinking dens. ...the crack dens of urban America.
4 If you describe a place as a **den** of a particular N-COUNT:
vice, you mean that a lot of that vice goes on there. N ofn
...the one-bedroomed flat that was to become his den
of savage debauchery. ...a den of greed.

de·na·tion·al·ize /ˌdiːˈnæʃənəlaɪz/ **denational-** VERB: V n
izes, denationalizing, denationalized; also DATED
spelled **denationalise** in British English. To **dena-**
tionalize an industry or business means to transfer
it into private ownership from state ownership.
✦ **de·na·tion·ali·za·tion** /ˌdiːˌnæʃənəlaɪˈzeɪʃən/ N-UNCOUNT
...the denationalisation of industry.

de·ni·al /dɪˈnaɪəl/ **denials. 1** A **denial** of some- ◆◆◇◇◇
thing is a statement that it is not true, does not N-VAR
exist, or did not happen. Despite official denials, differences of opinion lay behind the Ambassador's
decision to quit. ...denial of the Russian Mafia's existence. **2** The **denial** of something to someone is N-UNCOUNT
the act of refusing to let them have it. ...the denial of FORMAL
visas to international relief workers.

den·ier /ˈdeniə/. **Denier** is used when indicating the N-UNCOUNT:
thickness of stockings and tights. ...fifteen-denier num N
stockings.

deni·grate /ˈdenɪgreɪt/ **denigrates, denigrat-** ◆◇◇◇◇
ing, denigrated. If you **denigrate** someone or VERB
something, you criticize them unfairly or insult Vn
them. ...pornographic images which 'denigrate wom-
en'. ✦ **deni·gra·tion** /ˌdenɪˈgreɪʃən/ ...the denigra- N-UNCOUNT
tion of minorities in this country.

den·im /ˈdenɪm/. **Denim** is a thick cotton cloth, ◆◇◇◇◇
usually blue, which is used to make clothes. Jeans N-UNCOUNT
are made from denim. ...a light blue denim jacket...
Dennis was dressed in denim.

den·ims /ˈdenɪmz/. **Denims** are casual trousers N-PLURAL
made of denim. She was dressed in blue denims.

deni·zen /ˈdenɪzən/ **denizens.** A **denizen** of a par- N-COUNT
ticular place is a person, animal, or plant that lives FORMAL

or grows in this place. *Gannets are denizens of the open ocean.*

de·nomi·na·tion /dɪˌnɒmɪˈneɪʃən/ **denominations.** 1 A particular **denomination** is a particular religious group which has slightly different beliefs from other groups within the same faith. *He recommended another church of a similar denomination.* ◆ **de·nomi·na·tion·al** /dɪˌnɒmɪˈneɪʃənəl/ *...Christians from different denominational backgrounds.* 2 The **denomination** of a banknote or coin is its official value. *...a pile of banknotes, mostly in small denominations.*

de·nomi·na·tor /dɪˈnɒmɪneɪtə/ **denominators.** In a fraction, the **denominator** is the number which appears under the line. ● See also **common denominator, lowest common denominator**.

de·note /dɪˈnəʊt/ **denotes, denoting, denoted.** 1 If one thing **denotes** another, it is a sign or indication of it. *Red eyes denote strain and fatigue. ...an amber sash denoting that he was a member of the Home Guard.* 2 What a symbol **denotes** is what it represents. *'Dt' denotes quantity demanded in the current period and 'St' denotes quantity supplied.* 3 What a word or name **denotes** is what it means or refers to. *In the Middle Ages the term 'drab' denoted a very simple type of woollen cloth.*

de·noue·ment /deɪˈnuːmɒn/ **denouements;** also spelled **dénouement.** In a book, play, or series of events, the **denouement** is the sequence of events at the end, when things come to a conclusion.

de·nounce /dɪˈnaʊns/ **denounces, denouncing, denounced.** 1 If you **denounce** a person or an action, you criticize them severely and publicly because you feel strongly that they are wrong or evil. *German leaders all took the opportunity to denounce the attacks... Some 25,000 demonstrators denounced him as a traitor.* ◆ **de·nun·cia·tion** /dɪˌnʌnsɪˈeɪʃən/ **denunciations** *...his denunciation of corrupt and incompetent politicians.* 2 If you **denounce** someone who has broken a rule or law, you report them to the authorities. *...informers who might at any moment denounce them.* ◆ **denunciation** *...the denunciation of French Jews to the Nazis during the Second World War.*

dense /dens/ **denser, densest.** 1 Something that is **dense** contains a lot of things or people in a small area. *...a large, dense forest... Its fur is short, dense and silky. ...the dense crowd.* ◆ **dense·ly** *...a densely populated island.* 2 **Dense** fog or smoke is difficult to see through because it is very heavy and dark. 3 A **dense** substance is very heavy in relation to its volume. *...a small dense star.* 4 If you describe writing or a film as **dense**, you mean that it is difficult to understand because it contains a lot of information and ideas. *His prose is vigorous and dense, occasionally to the point of obscurity.* 5 If you say that someone is **dense**, you mean that they are stupid and that they take a long time to understand simple things. *He's not a bad man, just a bit dense.*

den·sity /ˈdensɪti/ **densities.** 1 **Density** is the extent to which something is filled or covered with people or things. *...the law which restricts the density of housing... Taiwan has a very high population density.* 2 The **density** of a substance or object is the relation of its mass or weight to its volume. *...Jupiter's moon Io, whose density is 3.5 grams per cubic centimetre.*

dent /dent/ **dents, denting, dented.** 1 If you **dent** the surface of something, you make a hollow dip in it by hitting or pressing it. *Its brass feet dented the carpet's thick pile.* 2 A **dent** is a hollow in the surface of something which has been caused by hitting or pressing it. *There was a dent in the bonnet.* 3 If something **dents** your ideas or your pride, it makes you realize that your ideas are wrong, or that you are not as good or successful as you thought. *That sort of thing dents your confidence.* 4 If one thing makes a **dent** in another, it reduces it consid-erably. *I hated to put any dents in his enthusiasm, but I was trying to be realistic.*

den·tal /ˈdentəl/. **Dental** is used to describe things that relate to teeth or to the care and treatment of teeth. *...free prescriptions and dental treatment. ...the dental profession.*

den·tist /ˈdentɪst/ **dentists.** A **dentist** is a person who is qualified to examine and treat people's teeth. *Visit your dentist twice a year for a check-up.* ▶ The **dentist** or the **dentist's** is used to refer to the surgery or clinic where a dentist works.

den·tis·try /ˈdentɪstri/. **Dentistry** is the work done by a dentist.

den·tures /ˈdentʃəz/; the form **denture** is used as a modifier. **Dentures** are artificial teeth worn by people who no longer have all their own teeth.

de·nude /dɪˈnjuːd, AM -ˈnuːd/ **denudes, denuding, denuded.** 1 To **denude** an area means to destroy the plants in it. *Many hillsides had been denuded of trees.* 2 To **denude** something or someone of something means to take that thing away from them. *Mrs Thatcher had claimed that a single European currency would denude Parliament of economic powers.*

de·nun·cia·tion /dɪˌnʌnsɪˈeɪʃən/. See **denounce**.

deny /dɪˈnaɪ/ **denies, denying, denied.** 1 If you **deny** something, you state that it is not true. *She denied both accusations... The government has denied that the authorities have uncovered a plot to assassinate the president.* 2 If you **deny** someone or something, you say that they have no connection with you or do not belong to you. *I denied my father because I wanted to become someone else.* 3 If you **deny** someone something that they need or want, you refuse to let them have it. *His ex-partner denies him access to his children... You will deny yourself the important nutrients that your body requires.*

de·odor·ant /diˈəʊdərənt/ **deodorants.** Deodor-ant is a substance that you can use to hide or prevent the smell of perspiration on your body.

de·part /dɪˈpɑːt/ **departs, departing, departed.** 1 When something or someone **departs** from a place, they leave it and start a journey to another place. *Our tour departs from Heathrow Airport... Mr. Bush departed for Camp David... The coach departs Potsdam in the morning.* ◆ **de·par·ture** /dɪˈpɑːtʃə/ **departures** *...the President's departure for Helsinki... The airline has more than 90 scheduled departures from here every day.* 2 If you **depart** from a traditional or agreed way of doing something, you do it in a different or unexpected way. *...a press conference which departed from the agreed text.* ◆ **departure** *Now she's written a novel which is not a mystery and is a considerable departure from her previous work.* 3 If someone **departs** from a job, they resign from it or leave it. In American English, you can say that someone **departs** a job. *Prime Minister Margaret Thatcher departed from office... A number of staff departed during his reign as rector... He had the good fortune to depart baseball in the '60s.* ◆ **departure** *This would inevitably involve his departure from the post of Prime Minister.* 4 When somebody **departs** this life, or **departs** this earth, they die.

de·part·ed /dɪˈpɑːtɪd/. **Departed** friends or relatives are people who have died. ▶ The **departed** are people who have died.

de·part·ment /dɪˈpɑːtmənt/ **departments.** 1 A **department** is one of the sections in an organization such as a government, business, or university. A department is also one of the sections in a large shop. *...the U.S. Department of Health, Education and Welfare. ...the geography department of Moscow University. ...the jewelry department.* ◆ **de·part·men·tal** /dɪˌpɑːtˈmentəl/ *...a bigger departmental budget.* 2 If you say that a task or area of knowledge **is not** your **department**, you mean that you are not responsible for it or do not know much about it.

de'partment store, department stores. A department store is a large shop which sells many different kinds of goods.   ◆◇◇◇ N-COUNT

de·par·ture /dɪˈpɑːtʃə/. See **depart**.

de·pend /dɪˈpend/ **depends, depending, depended. 1** If you say that one thing **depends** on another, you mean that the first thing will be affected or determined by the second. *The cooking time needed depends on the size of the potato.* ◆ **de·pend·ent** /dɪˈpendənt/ *The results you get from weight training are largely dependent upon how you use those weights.* ◆ **de·pend·ence** *...the dependence of circulation on production.* **2** You use **depend** in expressions such as **it depends** to indicate that you cannot give a clear answer to a question because the answer will be affected or determined by other factors. *'But how long can you stay in the house?'—'I don't know. It depends.'... It all depends on your definition of punk.* **3** You use **depending on** when you are saying that something varies according to the circumstances mentioned. *I tend to have a different answer, depending on the family.* **4** If you **depend** on someone or something, you need them in order to be able to survive physically, financially, or emotionally. *Their survival depends on him.* ◆ **de·pend·ent** *Britain became increasingly dependent upon American technology... In his own way, he was dependent on her.* **5** If you can **depend** on a person, organization, or law, you know that they will support you or help you when you need them. *You can depend on me.*
◆◆◆◆
VERB
V on/upon n
Also V on/
upon wh

ADJ:
v-link ADJ
on/upon n
N-UNCOUNT

VERB
it/that V
it V on n/wh

PHR-PREP

VERB
V on/upon n
-ing

ADJ-GRADED

VERB
V on/upon n

de·pend·able /dɪˈpendəbəl/. If you say that someone or something is **dependable**, you mean you can be sure that they will always act consistently or sensibly, or do what you need or expect them to do; used showing approval. *He was a good friend, a dependable companion.*   ◆◇◇◇ ADJ-GRADED PRAGMATICS

de·pend·ant /dɪˈpendənt/ **dependants;** also spelled **dependent**. Your **dependants** are the people you support financially, such as your children. *...a single man with no dependants.*   ◆◇◇◇ N-COUNT FORMAL

de·pend·ence /dɪˈpendəns/. **1** Your **dependence** on something or someone is your need for them in order to succeed or be able to survive. *...Vietnam's past dependence on the Soviet Union for economic aid.* ◆ **de·pend·en·cy** /dɪˈpendənsi/ *Ukraine is handicapped by its near-total dependency on Russian oil.* **2** If you talk about drug **dependence** or alcohol **dependence**, you are referring to a situation where someone is addicted to drugs or alcohol. ◆ **de·pend·en·cy, dependencies** *He began to show signs of alcohol and drug dependency.*   ◆◇◇◇ N-UNCOUNT

N-UNCOUNT

N-UNCOUNT

N-VAR

de·pend·en·cy /dɪˈpendənsi/ **dependencies.** A **dependency** is a country which is controlled by another country. *...the tiny British dependency of Montserrat.*   ◆◇◇◇ N-COUNT

de·per·son·al·ize /ˌdiːˈpɜːsənəlaɪz/ **depersonalizes, depersonalizing, depersonalized;** also spelled **depersonalise** in British English. **1** To **depersonalize** a system or a situation means to treat it as if it did not really involve people, or to treat it as if the people involved were not really important. *Modern weaponry depersonalised war.* **2** To **depersonalize** someone means to treat them as if they do not matter because their individual feelings and thoughts are not important. *She does not feel that the book depersonalises women.*
VERB
V n

VERB
V n

de·pict /dɪˈpɪkt/ **depicts, depicting, depicted.** To **depict** someone or something means to show or represent them in drawing, painting, or writing. *...pictures depicting Nelson's most famous battles.* ◆ **de·pic·tion** /dɪˈpɪkʃən/ **depictions.** A **depiction** of something is a picture or a written description of it. *The lecture will trace the depiction of horses from earliest times to the present day.*   ◆◆◇◇ VERB Also V n as n

N-VAR

de·pila·tory /dɪˈpɪlətəri, AM -tɔːri/ **depilatories. 1 Depilatory** substances and processes remove unwanted hair from your body. *...a depilatory cream.* **2** A **depilatory** is a depilatory substance.   ADJ: ADJ n

N-COUNT

de·plete /dɪˈpliːt/ **depletes, depleting, depleted.** To **deplete** a stock or amount of something means to reduce it. *...substances that deplete the ozone layer.* ◆ **de·plet·ed** *...Robert E. Lee's worn and depleted army.* ◆ **de·ple·tion** /dɪˈpliːʃən/ *...the depletion of underground water supplies.*   ◆◆◇◇ VERB V n FORMAL ADJ-GRADED N-UNCOUNT

de·plor·able /dɪˈplɔːrəbəl/. If you say that something is **deplorable**, you mean it is very bad and unacceptable, and you disapprove of it. *The Chief Constable said that sexual harassment was deplorable.* ◆ **de·plor·ably** *Reporters travelling with the President behaved deplorably.*   ADJ-GRADED PRAGMATICS FORMAL

ADV-GRADED

de·plore /dɪˈplɔː/ **deplores, deploring, deplored.** If you say that you **deplore** something, you mean that you think it is wrong or immoral. *He deplores violence.*   ◇◇◇◇ VERB PRAGMATICS V n FORMAL

de·ploy /dɪˈplɔɪ/ **deploys, deploying, deployed.** To **deploy** troops or military resources means to organize or position them so that they are ready to be used. *He had no intention of deploying ground troops.* ◆ **de·ploy·ment** /dɪˈplɔɪmənt/ **deployments** *...the deployment of troops.*   ◆◆◇◇ VERB V n

N-VAR

de·popu·late /ˌdiːˈpɒpjuleɪt/ **depopulates, depopulating, depopulated.** To **depopulate** an area means to greatly reduce the number of people living there. *...a war that would depopulate the earth.* ◆ **de·popu·lat·ed** *...a small depopulated part of the south-west.* ◆ **de·popu·la·tion** /ˌdiːˌpɒpjuˈleɪʃən/ *...rural depopulation.*   VERB V n

ADJ-GRADED
N-UNCOUNT

de·port /dɪˈpɔːt/ **deports, deporting, deported.** If a government **deports** someone, usually someone who is not a citizen of that country, it sends them out of the country. *...a government decision earlier this month to deport all illegal immigrants... More than 240 England football fans are being deported from Italy.* ◆ **de·por·ta·tion** /ˌdiːpɔːˈteɪʃən/ **deportations** *...migrants facing deportation.* ◆ **de·por·tee** /ˌdiːpɔːˈtiː/ **deportees.** A **deportee** is someone who is being deported.   ◆◆◇◇ VERB V n beV-ed from/to n Also V n from/to n

N-VAR

N-COUNT

de·port·ment /dɪˈpɔːtmənt/. Your **deportment** is the way you behave, especially the way you walk and move. *Deportment and poise were as important as good marks for young ladies.*   N-UNCOUNT FORMAL

de·pose /dɪˈpəʊz/ **deposes, deposing, deposed.** If a ruler or political leader **is deposed**, they are forced to give up their position. ◆ **de·po·si·tion** /ˌdepəˈzɪʃən/ *It was this issue which led to the deposition of the king.*   ◆◇◇◇ VB: usu passive N-UNCOUNT

de·pos·it /dɪˈpɒzɪt/ **deposits, depositing, deposited. 1** A **deposit** is a sum of money which is part of the full price of something, and which you pay when you agree to buy it. *A £50 deposit is required when ordering.* **2** A **deposit** is a sum of money which you pay when you start renting something. The money is returned to you if you do not damage what you have rented. *...the equivalent of a month's rent as a deposit.* **3** A **deposit** is a sum of money which you have to pay if you want to be a candidate in a parliamentary or European election. The money is returned to you if you receive more than a certain percentage of the votes. **4** A **deposit** is a sum of money which is in a bank account or other savings account. **5** When you **deposit** a sum of money, you pay it into a bank account or other savings account. *The customer has to deposit a minimum of £100 monthly.* ◆ **de·posi·tor** /dɪˈpɒzɪtə/ **depositors.** A bank's **depositors** are the people who have accounts with that bank. **6** A **deposit** is an amount of a substance that has been left somewhere as a result of a chemical or geological process. *...underground deposits of gold and diamonds.* **7** If a substance **is deposited** somewhere, it is left there as a result of a chemical or geological process. *The phosphate was deposited by the decay of marine microorganisms.* ◆ **depo·si·tion** *...continued deposition of silt along the coast... This leads to calcium deposition in the blood-vessels.* **8** To **deposit** someone or something somewhere means to put them or leave them there. *Someone was seen running from the scene after apparently*
◆◆◇◇ N-COUNT

N-COUNT

N-COUNT
BRITAIN

N-COUNT
VERB
V n

N-COUNT

N-COUNT

VB: usu
passive
beV-ed

N-UNCOUNT

VERB
V n
V n prep/adv

depositing the packet... The bus driver deposited the crews in front of their planes. **9** When you **deposit** something somewhere, you put it where it will be safe until it is needed again. *You are advised to deposit valuables in the safe.* VERB V n prep/adv

de'posit account, deposit accounts. A **deposit account** is a type of bank account in which the money earns interest. N-COUNT

depo·si·tion /ˌdepəˈzɪʃən/ **depositions.** A **deposition** is a formal written statement which can be used in a court if the witness cannot be present. ◆◇◇◇◇ N-COUNT

de·posi·tory /dɪˈpɒzɪtəri/ **depositories.** A **depository** is a place where objects can be stored. *They have 2,500 tons of paper stored in their depository.* N-COUNT

de·pot /ˈdepəʊ, AM ˈdiː-/ **depots. 1** A **depot** is a place where large amounts of raw materials, equipment, or other supplies are kept. *...a government arms depot.* **2** A **depot** is a large building or yard where buses or railway engines are kept when they are not being used. **3** A **depot** is a bus station or railway station. *...the bus depot of Ozark, Alabama.* ◆◇◇◇◇ N-COUNT / N-COUNT / N-COUNT

de·prave /dɪˈpreɪv/ **depraves, depraving, depraved.** Something that **depraves** someone makes them morally bad or evil. *...material likely to deprave or corrupt those who see, hear or read it.* VERB V n FORMAL

de·praved /dɪˈpreɪvd/. **Depraved** actions, things, or people are morally bad or evil. *...the most disturbing and depraved film of its kind.* ADJ-GRADED

de·prav·ity /dɪˈprævɪti/. **Depravity** is moral corruption. *...the absolute depravity that can exist in times of war.* N-UNCOUNT FORMAL

dep·re·cate /ˈdeprɪkeɪt/ **deprecates, deprecating, deprecated.** If you **deprecate** something, you speak critically about it. *He also deprecated the low quality of entrants to the profession.* VERB V n FORMAL

dep·re·cat·ing /ˈdeprɪkeɪtɪŋ/. A **deprecating** attitude, gesture, or remark shows that you think that something is not very good, especially something associated with yourself. *...a little deprecating shrug.* ◆ **dep·re·cat·ing·ly** *He speaks deprecatingly of his father.* ADJ-GRADED WRITTEN / ADV: ADV after v

de·pre·ci·ate /dɪˈpriːʃieɪt/ **depreciates, depreciating, depreciated.** If something such as a currency **depreciates** or if something **depreciates** it, it loses some of its original value. *The yuan is depreciating... The demand for foreign currency depreciates the real value of local currencies... The pound depreciated by a quarter.* ◆ **de·pre·cia·tion** /dɪˌpriːʃiˈeɪʃən/ **depreciations** *...miscellaneous costs, including machinery depreciation and wages.* ◆◇◇◇◇ V-ERG / V / V n / V by amount Also V against n / N-VAR

dep·re·da·tion /ˌdeprɪˈdeɪʃən/ **depredations.** The **depredations** of a person, animal, or force are their harmful actions, which usually involve taking or damaging something. *Crops can be all too easily decimated by unchecked depredations by deer.* N-VAR FORMAL

de·press /dɪˈpres/ **depresses, depressing, depressed. 1** If someone or something **depresses** you, they make you feel sad and disappointed. *The state of the country depresses me.* **2** If something **depresses** prices, wages, or figures, it causes them to become less. *The stronger U.S. dollar depressed sales.* ◆◇◇◇◇ VERB V n / VERB V n

de·pressed /dɪˈprest/. **1** If you are **depressed**, you are sad and feel that you cannot enjoy anything, because your situation is so difficult and unpleasant. *He seemed somewhat depressed.* **2** A **depressed** place or industry does not have enough business or employment to be prosperous. *...investment in depressed areas... The construction industry is no longer as depressed as it was.* **3** A **depressed** point on a surface is lower than the parts around it. *Acupressure is manual pressure applied to a specific slightly depressed point on the body.* ◆◆◇◇◇ ADJ-GRADED / ADJ-GRADED / ADJ-GRADED

de·press·ing /dɪˈpresɪŋ/. Something that is **depressing** makes you feel sad and disappointed. *Yesterday's unemployment figures were as depressing as those of the previous 22 months.* ◆ **de·press·ing·ly** *It all sounded depressingly familiar.* ◆◆◇◇◇ ADJ-GRADED / ADV-GRADED

de·pres·sion /dɪˈpreʃən/ **depressions. 1** Depression is a mental state in which you are sad and feel ◆◆◆◇◇ N-VAR

that you cannot enjoy anything, because your situation is so difficult and unpleasant. *Mr Thomas was suffering from depression... I slid into a depression.* **2** A **depression** is a time when there is very little economic activity, which causes a lot of unemployment and poverty. *...the Great Depression of the 1930s.* **3** A **depression** in a surface is an area which is lower than the parts surrounding it. *...an area pockmarked by rainfilled depressions.* **4** A **depression** is a mass of air that has a low pressure and that often causes rain. N-COUNT / N-COUNT / N-COUNT TECHNICAL

de·pres·sive /dɪˈpresɪv/ **depressives. 1** Depressive means relating to depression. *...a severe depressive disorder.* **2** A **depressive** is someone who suffers from depression. *...depressives who feel they can no longer cope.* ● See also **manic-depressive.** ADJ / N-COUNT

de·prive /dɪˈpraɪv/ **deprives, depriving, deprived.** If you **deprive** someone of something that they want or need, you take it away from them, or you prevent them from having it. *The disintegration of the Soviet Union deprived western intelligence agencies of their main enemies.* ◆ **de·prived** *...a deprived inner city area.* ◆ **dep·ri·va·tion** /ˌdeprɪˈveɪʃən/ **deprivations** *...long-term patients who face a life of deprivation.* ◆◆◇◇◇ VERB V n of n / ADJ-GRADED / N-VAR

dept, depts. Dept is used as a written abbreviation for 'department', usually in the name of a department. ◆◇◇◇◇

depth /depθ/ **depths. 1** The **depth** of something such as a river or hole is the distance downwards from its top surface, or between its upper and lower surfaces. *The smaller lake ranges from five to fourteen feet in depth... Pour the vegetable oil into a frying pan to a depth of about 1cm.* **2** If you are **out of your depth**, you are in water that is deeper than you are tall, with the result that you cannot stand up with your head above water. **3** The **depth** of something such as a cupboard or drawer is the distance between its front surface and its back. **4** The **depths** are places that are a long way below the surface of the sea or earth. *Leaves, brown with long immersion, rose to the surface and vanished back into the depths.* **5** If you talk about the **depths** of an area, you mean the parts of it which are very remote. *...somewhere in the depths of the pine forest.* **6** If you say that someone is **out of** their **depth**, you mean that they are in a situation that is much too difficult for them to be able to cope with it. **7** If an emotion is very strongly or intensely felt, you can talk about its **depth**. *I am well aware of the depth of feeling that exists in Londonderry.* **8** The **depth** of a situation is its extent and seriousness. *The country's leadership had underestimated the depth of the crisis.* **9** The **depth** of someone's knowledge is the great amount that they know. **10** If you deal with a subject **in depth**, you deal with it very thoroughly and consider all the aspects of it. *We will discuss these three areas in depth... He demanded an in-depth investigation from the authorities.* **11** If you say that someone or something has **depth**, you mean that they have serious and interesting qualities which are not immediately obvious and which you have to think about carefully before you can fully understand them. *His music lacks depth.* **12** If you are in **the depths of** an unpleasant emotion, you feel that emotion very strongly. *I was in the depths of despair.* **13** If something happens in **the depths of** a difficult or unpleasant period of time, it happens in the middle and most severe or intense part of it. *The country is in the depths of a recession. ...the depths of winter.* **14** The **depth** of a colour is its quality of richness and strength. *White wines tend to gain depth of colour with age.* **15** In photography and art, you say that a picture has **depth** or **depth of field** when you mean that it appears three-dimensional rather than flat. **16** ● to **plumb new depths**: see **plumb.** ● to **plumb the depths**: see **plumb.** ◆◆◆◇◇ N-VAR / PHRASE / N-VAR / N-PLURAL: the N LITERARY / N-PLURAL: the N of n / PHRASE / N-VAR / N-UNCOUNT / N-UNCOUNT / PHRASE / N-UNCOUNT: also N in pl / N-PLURAL: the N of n / N-PLURAL: the N of n / N-UNCOUNT / N-UNCOUNT TECHNICAL

'depth charge, depth charges. A **depth charge** is a type of bomb which explodes under water. N-COUNT

depu·ta·tion /ˌdepjʊˈteɪʃən/ **deputations.** A N-COUNT
deputation is a small group of people who have
been asked to speak to someone on behalf of a larger group of people. *A deputation of elders from the
village arrived headed by its chief.*

de·pute /dɪˈpjuːt/ **deputes, deputing, deputed.** VB: usu
If you **are deputed** to do something, someone in- passive
structs or authorizes you to do it on their behalf. beV-ed to-inf
The Dalai Lama was deputed to lead the Tibetan FORMAL
delegation.

depu·tize /ˈdepjʊtaɪz/ **deputizes, deputizing,** VERB
deputized; also spelled **deputise** in British Eng- V forn
lish. If you **deputize** for someone, you do something V
on their behalf, for example attend a meeting. *I became skilful enough to deputise for him in the kitch-
en... He cannot be here to welcome you and he has
asked me to deputize.*

depu·ty /ˈdepjʊti/ **deputies. 1** A deputy is the se- ◆◆◆◆◇
cond most important person in an organization. N-COUNT
Someone's deputy often acts on their behalf when
they are absent. *...the academy's deputy director.*
2 In some parliaments, the elected members are N-COUNT
called **deputies.**

de·rail /ˌdiːˈreɪl/ **derails, derailing, derailed.** ◆◇◇◇◇
1 If someone or something **derails** a plan or a series VERB
of negotiations, they prevent it from continuing as V n
planned. *...people trying to derail peace talks.* **2** If a V-ERG
train **is derailed** or if it **derails**, it comes off the beV-ed
track on which it is running. *A train was derailed in* V
an isolated mountain region... No-one knows why Also V n
the train derailed. ◆ **de·rail·ment** /ˌdiːˈreɪlmənt/ N-VAR
derailments.

de·ranged /dɪˈreɪndʒd/. Someone who is **deranged** ◆◇◇◇◇
behaves in a wild and uncontrolled way, often as a ADJ-GRADED
result of mental illness. *A deranged man shot and
killed 14 people.*

de·range·ment /dɪˈreɪndʒmənt/. Derangement is N-UNCOUNT
the state of being mentally ill and unable to think or DATED
act in a controlled way. *...mental derangement.*

der·by /ˈdɑːbi, AM ˈdɜːrbi/ **derbies.** A derby is a ◆◇◇◇◇
sporting event between teams from the same area N-COUNT
or city. *...a North London derby between Arsenal and
Tottenham.*

de·regu·late /ˌdiːˈreɡjʊleɪt/ **deregulates, de-** ◆◇◇◇◇
regulating, deregulated. To deregulate some- VERB
thing means to remove government controls and V n
regulations from it. *They all saw the need to deregulate the US airline industry.* ◆ **de·regu·la·tion** N-UNCOUNT
/ˌdiːˌreɡjʊˈleɪʃən/ *Since deregulation, banks are permitted to set their own interest rates.*

der·elict /ˈderɪlɪkt/ **derelicts. 1** A derelict place is ◆◇◇◇◇
empty and in a bad state of repair because it has ADJ-GRADED
not been used or lived in for a long time. *...a derelict
warehouse.* ◆ **der·elic·tion** *The previous owners* N-UNCOUNT
had rescued the building from dereliction. **2** A der- N-COUNT
elict is a person who has no home or job and who FORMAL
has to live on the streets.

dereliction of duty. Dereliction of duty is de- N-UNCOUNT
liberate or accidental failure to do what you should FORMAL
do as part of your job. *Sergeant Slater pleaded guilty
to wilful dereliction of duty.*

de·ride /dɪˈraɪd/ **derides, deriding, derided.** If ◆◇◇◇◇
you **deride** someone or something, you say that VERB
they are stupid or have no value. *Opposition MPs* V n
derided the Government's response to the crisis. FORMAL
◆ **de·ri·sion** /dɪˈrɪʒən/. *He tried to calm them, but* N-UNCOUNT
was greeted with shouts of derision.

de ri·gueur /də rɪˈɡɜː/. If you say that a possession ADJ:
or habit is **de rigueur**, you mean that it is fashion- v-link ADJ
able and therefore necessary for anyone who wants
to avoid being considered old-fashioned or unusual.
*T-shirts now seem almost de rigueur in the West
End.*

de·ri·sive /dɪˈraɪsɪv/. A derisive noise, expression, ADJ-GRADED
or remark expresses contempt. *There was a short,
derisive laugh.* ◆ **de·ri·sive·ly** *Phil's tormentor* ADV-GRADED:
snorted derisively. ADV with v

de·ri·sory /dɪˈraɪsəri/. **1** If you describe something ADJ-GRADED
such as an amount of money as **derisory**, you are PRAGMATICS
emphasizing that it is so small or inadequate that it

seems silly or not worth considering. *She was being
paid what I considered a derisory amount of money.*
2 Derisory means the same as **derisive**. *...derisory* ADJ-GRADED
remarks about the police.

deri·va·tion /ˌderɪˈveɪʃən/ **derivations.** The deri- N-VAR
vation of something is its origin or source. *The deri-
vation of its name is obscure.*

de·riva·tive /dɪˈrɪvətɪv/ **derivatives. 1** A deriva- ◆◇◇◇◇
tive is something which has been developed or ob- N-COUNT
tained from something else. *...a poppy-seed deriva-
tive similar to heroin.* **2** If you say that something is ADJ-GRADED
derivative, you are criticizing it because it is not PRAGMATICS
new or original but has been developed from some-
thing else. *...their dull, derivative debut album.*

de·rive /dɪˈraɪv/ **derives, deriving, derived. 1** If ◆◆◇◇◇
you **derive** something such as pleasure or benefit VERB
from someone or something, you get it from them. V n from n /-
...one of those happy people who derive pleasure FORMAL ing
from helping others. **2** If you say that something V-ERG
such as a word or feeling **derives** or **is derived from** beV-ed from n
something else, you mean that it comes from that V from n
thing. *The name Anastasia is derived from a Greek
word meaning 'of the resurrection'. ...defensive behaviour patterns which derive from our subconscious fears.*

der·ma·ti·tis /ˌdɜːməˈtaɪtɪs/. Dermatitis is a condi- N-UNCOUNT
tion which makes your skin red and painful.

der·ma·tolo·gist /ˌdɜːməˈtɒlədʒɪst/ **dermatolo-** ◆◇◇◇◇
gists. A dermatologist is a doctor who specializes N-COUNT
in the treatment of skin diseases.

de·roga·tory /dɪˈrɒɡətri, AM -tɔːri/. If you make a ADJ-GRADED
derogatory remark or comment, you express your
low opinion of someone or something. *He refused to
withdraw derogatory remarks made about his boss.*

der·rick /ˈderɪk/ **derricks. 1** A derrick is a simple N-COUNT
crane that is used to move cargo on a ship. **2** A der- N-COUNT
rick is a tower built over an oil well which is used to
raise and lower the drill.

derring-do /ˌderɪŋ ˈduː/. Derring-do is the quality N-UNCOUNT
of being bold and daring, often in a rather showy or DATED
foolish way.

der·vish /ˈdɜːvɪʃ/ **dervishes.** If you say that some- N-COUNT
one is like a **dervish**, you mean that they are turning round and round, waving their arms about, or
working very quickly. *...whirling like a dervish.*

de·sali·na·tion /ˌdiːsælɪˈneɪʃən/. Desalination is N-UNCOUNT
the process of removing salt from sea water.

des·cant /ˈdeskænt/ **descants.** A descant is a tune N-COUNT
which is played or sung above the main tune in a
piece of music.

de·scend /dɪˈsend/ **descends, descending, de-** ◆◆◇◇◇
scended. 1 If you **descend** or if you **descend** a VERB
staircase, you move downwards from a higher to a V prep
lower level. *...as we descend to the cellar... She* V n
walked over to the carpeted stairs at the end of the Also V
corridor and descended one flight. FORMAL
2 When a mood or atmosphere **descends**, it affects a VERB: V
place or the people there by spreading among them. on/upon/
An uneasy calm descended on the area. **3** When night, over n
dusk, or darkness **descends**, it starts to get dark. *Dark-* VERB
ness has now descended. **4** If a large group of people V
arrive to see you, especially unexpectedly, you can say V on/upon n
that they **have descended** on you. *Reporters from
around the globe are descending upon the peaceful
villages.*
5 If you say that someone **descends to** something VERB
which you consider unacceptable or unworthy of PRAGMATICS
them, you are expressing your disapproval of the fact V to n/-ing
that they do it. *We're not going to descend to such
methods.* **6** When you want to emphasize that the VERB
situation that someone is entering is very bad, you PRAGMATICS
can say that they **are descending into** that situation. V into n
The country descended into chaos.

de·scend·ant /dɪˈsendənt/ **descendants.** ◆◇◇◇◇
1 Someone's **descendants** are the people in later N-COUNT
generations who are related to them. *...Lord
Cochrane and his descendants.* **2** Something mod- N-COUNT
ern which evolved or developed from an older thing
can be called a **descendant** of it. *His design was a
descendant of a 1956 device.*

de·scend·ed /dɪˈsendɪd/. **1** A person who is **de-** ◆◇◇◇◇
scended from someone who lived a long time ago is ADJ:
directly related to them. *She was descended from* v-link ADJ
some Scottish Lord. **2** An animal that is **descended** ADJ:
from another sort of animal has developed from the v-link ADJ
original sort. *Domestic chickens are descended from from n*
jungle fowl of Southeast Asia.

de·scend·ing /dɪˈsendɪŋ/. When a group of things ADJ: ADJ n
is listed or arranged in **descending** order, each thing
is smaller or less important than the thing before it.

de·scent /dɪˈsent/ **descents.** **1** A **descent** is a ◆◇◇◇◇
movement from a higher to a lower level or posi- N-VAR
tion. *...the crash of an Airbus A300 on its descent into*
Kathmandu airport. **2** A **descent** is a surface that N-COUNT
slopes downwards, for example the side of a steep
hill. *...the castle overlooks a steep descent to the river.*
3 When you want to emphasize that a situation be- N-SING
comes very bad, you can talk about someone's or PRAGMATICS
something's **descent** into that situation. *...his swift*
descent from respected academic to struggling small
businessman.
4 You use **descent** to talk about a person's family N-UNCOUNT
background, for example their nationality or social FORMAL
status. *All the contributors were of African descent.*

de·scribe /dɪˈskraɪb/ **describes, describing,** ◆◆◆◆◇
described. **1** If you **describe** someone or some- VERB
thing, you say what they are like. *We asked her to* V wh
describe what kind of things she did in her spare V n
time. ...a poem by Carver which describes their life
together. **2** If you **describe** someone or something VERB
as a particular thing, you say that they are like that PRAGMATICS
thing. *He described it as an extraordinarily tangled* V n as n
and complicated tale... Even his closest allies describe V n as adj
him as forceful, aggressive and determined. -ing
3 If something **describes** a particular shape, it forms VB: no passive
that shape or makes a movement that follows the line V n
of that shape. *His pass described a perfect arc through* FORMAL
the leaden sky.

de·scrip·tion /dɪˈskrɪpʃən/ **descriptions.** **1** A de- ◆◆◆◇◇
scription of someone or something is an account N-VAR
which explains what they are or what they look like.
Police have issued a description of the man. ...a de-
tailed description of the movements and battle plans
of Italy's fleet. **2** If something is **of** a particular de- N-SING:
scription, it belongs to the general class of items of N
that are mentioned. *Events of this description oc-*
curred daily. **3** You say that something is beyond N-UNCOUNT
description, or that it defies **description** to empha- PRAGMATICS
size that it is very unusual, impressive, dreadful, or
extreme. *His face is weary beyond description.*

de·scrip·tive /dɪˈskrɪptɪv/. **Descriptive** language ◆◇◇◇◇
indicates what something is like. *...the simpler, more* ADJ-GRADED
descriptive title of Angina Support Group.

des·e·crate /ˈdesɪkreɪt/ **desecrates, desecrat-** ◆◇◇◇◇
ing, desecrated. If someone **desecrates** some- VERB
thing which is considered to be sacred or very spe- V n
cial, they deliberately damage or insult it. *She*
shouldn't have desecrated the picture of a religious
leader. **♦ des·e·cra·tion** /ˌdesɪˈkreɪʃən/ *...the des-* N-UNCOUNT
ecration of the cemetery.

de·seed /ˌdiːˈsiːd/ **deseeds, deseeding,** VERB: V n
deseeded; also spelled **de-seed.** To **deseed** a fruit BRITISH
or vegetable means to remove all the seeds from it.

de·seg·re·gate /ˌdiːˈsegrɪgeɪt/ **desegregates,** VERB
desegregating, desegregated. To **desegregate** V n
something such as a place, institution, or service
means to officially stop keeping the people who use
it in separate groups, especially groups defined by
race. *...efforts to desegregate sport.* **♦ de·seg·re·ga-** N-UNCOUNT
·tion /ˌdiːˌsegrəˈgeɪʃən/.

de·sen·si·tize /ˌdiːˈsensɪtaɪz/ **desensitizes, de-** N-UNCOUNT
sensitizing, desensitized; also spelled **desensi-** VERB: V n
tise in British English. To **desensitize** someone V n to n
means to cause them to react less strongly to things
such as pain, anxiety, or other people's suffering.
...the language that is used to desensitize us to the
terrible reality of war.

de·sert, deserts, deserting, deserted. The ◆◆◆◇◇
noun is pronounced /ˈdezət/. The pronunciation
/dɪˈzɜːt/ is used for the verb and for meaning 8. **1** A N-VAR

desert is a large area of land, usually in a hot region,
where there is almost no water, rain, trees, or
plants. **2** If you refer to a place or situation as a **des-** N-COUNT:
ert, you think it is bad for people because it is not with supp
interesting, exciting, or useful in any way. *...a desert* PRAGMATICS
of concrete... Pubs are a cultural desert.
3 If people or animals **desert** a place, they leave it and VERB: V n
it becomes empty. **♦ de·sert·ed** *...a deserted* ADJ-GRADED
sidestreet. **4** If someone **deserts** you, they leave you, VERB: V n
and no longer help or support you. **♦ de·ser·tion** N-VAR
/dɪˈzɜːʃən/, **desertions.** *...her father's desertion.* **5** If VERB: V n
you **desert** something, you stop supporting it, using V
it, or being involved with it. *The paper's new price rise* V n for n
will encourage readers to desert in even greater droves.
...German investors deserting Spain for Eastern
Europe. **♦ desertion** *...possible further desertions* N-VAR
from the party at its conference. **6** If a quality or skill VERB
that you normally have **deserts** you, you suddenly V n
find that you do not have it when you need it or want
it. *A dry sense of humour never deserted him.* **7** If VERB: V
someone **deserts**, they leave a job without permis- V from n
sion, especially a job in the armed forces. *He deserted* Also V n
from army intelligence last month. **♦ de·sert·er, de-** N-COUNT
serters. *...a campaign to hunt down draft dodgers*
and army deserters. **♦ de·ser·tion** *...a growing num-* N-VAR
ber of desertions from the federal army.
8 If you say that someone has got their **just deserts**, PHRASE
you mean that they deserve the unpleasant things
that have happened to them, because they did something bad.

des·er·ti·fi·ca·tion /dɪˌzɜːtɪfɪˈkeɪʃən/. **Desertifica-** N-UNCOUNT
tion is the process by which an area of land be-
comes dry and unsuitable for growing trees or crops
on.

de·sert is·land /ˌdezət ˈaɪlənd/ **desert islands.** A ◆◇◇◇◇
desert island is a small tropical island, where no- N-COUNT
body lives.

de·serve /dɪˈzɜːv/ **deserves, deserving, de-** ◆◆◆◇◇
served. **1** If you say that someone or something VERB: V n
deserves something, you mean that they should V to-inf
have it or receive it because of their qualities or ac- V compar
tions. *His children's books are classics that deserve to*
be much better known... I felt I deserved better than
that. **2** If you say that someone **got what they de-** PHRASE
served, you mean that they deserved the bad thing PRAGMATICS
that happened to them, and you have no sympathy
for them.

de·serv·ed·ly /dɪˈzɜːvɪdli/. You use **deservedly** to ADV
indicate that someone deserved what happened to
them, especially when it was something good. *He*
deservedly won the Player of the Year award... Book
well in advance for this deservedly popular hotel.

de·serv·ing /dɪˈzɜːvɪŋ/. **1** If you describe a person, ◆◇◇◇◇
organization, or cause as **deserving**, you think they ADJ-GRADED
should be helped. **2** If someone is **deserving of** FORMAL
something, they have qualities or have done some- ADJ-GRADED:
thing which makes it right that they should receive v-link ADJ of n
it. *...artists deserving of public subsidy.*

des·ic·cat·ed /ˈdesɪkeɪtɪd/. **1** Desiccated things ADJ
have lost all the moisture that was in them. *...desic-* FORMAL
cated flowers and leaves. **2** Desiccated food has ADJ: ADJ n
been dried in order to preserve it. *...desiccated coco-*
nut is used by confectioners.

de·sign /dɪˈzaɪn/ **designs, designing, de-** ◆◆◆◆◆
signed. **1** When someone **designs** a garment, VERB: V n
building, machine, or other object, they plan it and
make a detailed drawing of it from which it can be
built or made. **♦ de·sign·er, designers.** *Carolyne* N-COUNT
is a fashion designer. **2** When someone **designs** a VERB: V n
survey, policy, or system, they plan and prepare it,
and decide on all the details of it. **3** Design is the N-UNCOUNT
process and art of planning and making detailed
drawings of something. *He was a born mechanic*
with a flair for design. **4** The **design** of something is N-UNCOUNT
the way in which it has been planned and made. *...a*
new design of clock. **5** A **design** is a drawing which N-COUNT
someone produces to show how they would like
something to be built or made.
6 A **design** is a pattern of lines, flowers, or shapes N-COUNT

which is used to decorate something. *Their range of tableware is decorated with a blackberry design.*

7 A **design** is an overall plan or intention that someone has in their mind when they are doing something. *...a grand design to assassinate the War Minister.* **8** If something **is designed** for a purpose, it is intended for that purpose. *This project is designed to help landless people.* **9** If something happens or is done **by design**, someone does it deliberately, rather than by accident. *The pair met often – at first by chance but later by design.* **10** If someone **has designs on** someone or something, they want them and are planning to get them, often in a dishonest way. *His colonel had designs on his wife.* N-COUNT · V-PASSIVE: be V-ed for n / be V-ed to-inf · PHRASE · PHRASE

des·ig·nate, designates, designating, designated. The verb is pronounced /'dezɪgneɪt/. The adjective is pronounced /'dezɪgnət/. **1** When you **designate** someone or something as a particular thing, you formally give them a particular description or name. *...to designate the bridge a historic landmark.* ✦ **des·ig·na·tion** /,dezɪg'neɪʃən/ **des·ig·nations.** *...the Party of Democratic Kampuchea (the formal designation for the Khmer Rouge). ...the designation of Madrid as European City of Culture 1992.* **2** If something **is designated** for a particular purpose, it is set aside for that purpose. *Smoking is allowed in designated areas.* **3** When you **designate** someone as something, you formally choose them to do that particular job. *Designate someone as the spokesperson.* **4 Designate** is used to describe someone who has been formally chosen to do a particular job, but has not yet started doing it. *...Japan's Prime Minister-designate.* ◆◆◇◇◇ · VERB: V n as n / V n n · N-VAR · VERB: be V-ed as/for n, V-ed · VERB V n as n · ADJ: n ADJ

de·sign·er /dɪ'zaɪnə/. **1 Designer** clothes or designer labels are expensive, fashionable clothes created by a famous designer. **2** You can use **designer** to describe things that are worn or bought because they are fashionable. *...designer beers and trendy wines.* **3** See also **design**. ◆◆◇◇◇ · ADJ: ADJ n · ADJ: ADJ n INFORMAL

de·sir·able /dɪ'zaɪərəbəl/. **1** Something that is **desirable** is worth having or doing because it is useful, necessary, or popular. *Prolonged negotiation was not desirable.* ✦ **de·sir·abil·ity** /dɪ,zaɪərə'bɪlɪti/ *...the debate on the desirability of banning the ivory trade.* **2** Someone who is **desirable** is considered to be sexually attractive. ✦ **desirability** *He had not at all overrated Veronica's desirability.* ◆◆◇◇◇ · ADJ-GRADED · N-UNCOUNT · ADJ-GRADED · N-UNCOUNT

de·sire /dɪ'zaɪə/ **desires, desiring, desired. 1** A **desire** is a strong wish to do or have something. *I had a strong desire to help and care for people.* **2** If you **desire** something, you want it. *Fred was bored and desired to go home.* ✦ **de·sired** *His warnings have provoked the desired response.* **3** If you say that someone or something is your **heart's desire**, you mean that you want that person or thing very much.

4 Desire for someone is a strong feeling of wanting to have sex with them. **5** If you **desire** someone, you want to have sex with them. **6 If desired** is used in instructions to indicate that the course of action mentioned is optional. *Transfer this sauce to a saucepan, if desired.* **7** If you say that something **leaves** a lot **to be desired**, you mean that it is not as good as it should be. ◆◆◆◇ · N-COUNT · VERB: V to-inf FORMAL · ADJ-GRADED PHRASE · N-UNCOUNT · VERB: V n · PHRASE WRITTEN · PHRASE

de·sir·ous /dɪ'zaɪərəs/. If you are **desirous of** something, you want it very much. ADJ-GRADED: v-link ADJ

de·sist /dɪ'zɪst/ **desists, desisting, desisted.** If you **desist** from doing something, you stop doing it. *She rubbed her arms, but they hurt and she desisted.* VERB: V from n/n V FORMAL

desk /desk/ **desks. 1** A **desk** is a table, often with drawers, which you sit at to write or work. **2** The place in a hotel, hospital, airport, or other building where you check in or obtain information is referred to as a particular **desk**. *I told the girl on the reception desk that I was terribly sorry.* **3** A particular department of a broadcasting company, or a newspaper or magazine company, can be referred to as a particular **desk**. *Over now to Simon Ingram at the sports desk.* ◆◆◆◇ · N-COUNT · N-SING · N-SING; supp N

'desk clerk, desk clerks. A **desk clerk** is a receptionist in a hotel. N-COUNT AMERICAN

desk·top /'desktɒp/ **desktops;** also spelled **desk-top. 1 Desktop** computers are a convenient size for using on a desk or table, but are not designed to be portable. **2** A **desktop** is a desktop computer. ADJ: ADJ n · N-COUNT

desktop 'publishing; also spelled **desk-top publishing. Desktop publishing** is the production of printed materials such as newspapers and magazines using a desktop computer and a laser printer, rather than using conventional printing methods. N-UNCOUNT

deso·late /'desələt/. **1** A **desolate** place is empty and lacking in comfort. ✦ **deso·la·tion** /,desə'leɪʃən/. *We looked out upon a scene of desolation and ruin.* **2** If someone is **desolate**, they feel very sad, lonely, and without hope. ✦ **desolation** *He felt an overwhelming sense of loneliness and desolation.* ◆◇◇◇◇ · ADJ-GRADED · N-UNCOUNT · ADJ-GRADED · N-UNCOUNT

des·pair /dɪ'speə/ **despairs, despairing, despaired. 1** If you **despair**, you feel that everything is wrong and that nothing will improve. *I despair at the attitude with which their work is received.* ▶ **Despair** is this feeling. *I looked at my wife in despair.* **2** If you **despair of** something, you feel that there is no hope that it will happen or improve. If you **despair of** someone, you feel that there is no hope that they will improve. *He wished to earn a living through writing but despaired of doing so.* ◆◆◇◇◇ · VERB: V V at n · N-UNCOUNT · VERB V of-ing/n

des·patch /dɪ'spætʃ/. See **dispatch**.

des·pe·ra·do /,despə'rɑːdəʊ/ **desperadoes** or **desperados.** A **desperado** is someone who does illegal, violent things without worrying about the danger. N-COUNT DATED

des·per·ate /'despərət/. **1** If you are **desperate**, you are in such a bad situation that you are willing to try anything to change it. *...a desperate attempt to hijack a plane.* ✦ **des·per·ate·ly** *Thousands are desperately trying to leave their battered homes and villages.* **2** If you are **desperate** for something or **desperate** to do something, you want or need it very much indeed. *People are desperate for him to do something.* ✦ **desperately** *He was a boy who desperately needed affection.* **3** A **desperate** situation is very difficult, serious, or dangerous. *People are in desperate need.* ◆◆◇◇◇ · ADJ-GRADED · ADV-GRADED: ADV with v · ADJ-GRADED: v-link ADJ · ADV-GRADED: ADV with v ADJ-GRADED

des·pe·ra·tion /,despə'reɪʃən/. **Desperation** is the feeling that you have when you are in such a bad situation that you will try anything to change it. ◆◇◇◇◇ N-UNCOUNT

des·pic·able /dɪ'spɪkəbəl, AM 'despɪk-/. If you say that a person or action is **despicable**, you are emphasizing that they are extremely nasty or cruel. ADJ-GRADED PRAGMATICS

des·pise /dɪ'spaɪz/ **despises, despising, despised.** If you **despise** something or someone, you dislike them and have a very low opinion of them. *How I despised myself for my cowardice!* ◆◇◇◇◇ · VERB: V n V n for n/-ing

de·spite /dɪ'spaɪt/. **1** You use **despite** to introduce a fact which makes the other part of the sentence surprising. *Despite a thorough investigation, no trace of Dr Southwell has been found.* **2** If you do something **despite** yourself, you do it although you did not really intend or want to. *Despite myself, Harry's remarks had caused me to reflect.* ◆◆◆◇ · PREP · PREP

de·spoil /dɪ'spɔɪl/ **despoils, despoiling, despoiled.** To **despoil** a place means to make it less attractive, valuable, or important by taking things away from it or by destroying it. VERB: V n FORMAL

de·spond·ent /dɪ'spɒndənt/. If you are **despondent**, you are very unhappy because you have been experiencing difficulties that you think you will not be able to overcome. ✦ **de·spond·ent·ly** *I went back and told Bill the news.* ✦ **de·spond·en·cy** /dɪ'spɒndənsi/. *There's a mood of gloom and despondency in the country.* ADJ-GRADED · ADV-GRADED: ADV with v · N-UNCOUNT

des·pot /'despɒt, AM -pət/ **despots.** A **despot** is a ruler or other person who has a lot of power and who uses it unfairly or cruelly. ✦ **des·pot·ic** /dɪ'spɒtɪk/. *...a despotic tyrant.* ✦ **des·pot·ism** /'despətɪzəm/. *...tyranny and despotism.* N-COUNT · ADJ-GRADED · N-UNCOUNT

D

des·sert /dɪˈzɜːt/ **desserts. Dessert** is something ◆◆◇◇◇ N-VAR
sweet, such as fruit or a pudding, that you eat at the
end of a meal.

dessert·spoon /dɪˈzɜːtspuːn/ **dessertspoons;** N-COUNT
also spelled **dessert spoon.** A **dessertspoon** is a
spoon which is midway between the size of a teaspoon and a tablespoon. ▶ A **dessertspoon** of a N-COUNT
food or liquid is the amount of it that a dessertspoon will hold.

des·sert 'wine, dessert wines. A **dessert wine** is N-VAR
a sweet wine, usually a white wine, that is served
with dessert.

de·sta·bi·lize /diːˈsteɪbəlaɪz/ **destabilizes, de-** ◆◇◇◇◇
stabilizing, destabilized; also spelled **destabi-** VERB
lise in British English. To **destabilize** something V n
such as a country or government means to create a
situation which reduces its power or influence.
Their sole aim is to destabilize the Indian govern-
ment. ♦ **de·sta·bi·li·za·tion** /diːˌsteɪbəlaɪˈzeɪʃən/ N-UNCOUNT
...the destabilization of the country.

des·ti·na·tion /ˌdestɪˈneɪʃən/ **destinations.** The ◆◆◇◇◇
destination of someone or something is the place N-COUNT
to which they are going or being sent. *Spain is still*
our most popular holiday destination.

des·tined /ˈdestɪnd/ **1** If something is **destined** to ◆◇◇◇◇
happen or if someone is **destined** to do something, ADJ:
that thing is planned or will definitely happen. *He* v-link ADJ,
feels that he was **destined** to become a musician... ADJ for n
Muriel was destined for great things. **2** If people or ADJ:
goods are **destined for** a particular place, they are v-link ADJ for
travelling towards that place or will be sent to that n
place. *...products destined for Saudi Arabia.*

des·ti·ny /ˈdestɪni/ **destinies. 1** A person's **desti-** ◆◆◇◇◇
ny is everything that happens to them during their N-COUNT
life, including what will happen in the future, especially when it is considered to be controlled by
someone or something else. *We are masters of our*
own destiny. **2 Destiny** is the force which some peo- N-UNCOUNT
ple believe controls the things that happen to you in
your life.

des·ti·tute /ˈdestɪtjuːt, AM -tuːt/. Someone who is ◆◇◇◇◇
destitute has no money or possessions. *...destitute* ADJ-GRADED
children who live on the streets.

des·ti·tu·tion /ˌdestɪˈtjuːʃən, AM -ˈtuː-/. **Destitu-** N-UNCOUNT
tion is the state of having no money or possessions.

de·stroy /dɪˈstrɔɪ/ **destroys, destroying, de-** ◆◆◆◆◇
stroyed. 1 To **destroy** something means to cause VERB
so much damage to it that it is completely ruined or V n
does not exist any more. *...destroying the economy*
and creating chaos... The building was completely
destroyed. ♦ **de·struc·tion** /dɪˈstrʌkʃən/ *...the de-* N-UNCOUNT
struction of the ozone layer. ...weapons of mass de-
struction. **2** To **destroy** someone means to ruin VERB
their life or to make their situation unbearable. *The* V n
criticism would have destroyed me. **3** If an animal **is** VB: usu
destroyed, it is killed, either because it is ill or be- passive,
cause it is dangerous. **4** See also **soul-destroying.** be V-ed

de·stroy·er /dɪˈstrɔɪə/ **destroyers. 1** A destroyer ◆◇◇◇◇
is a small, heavily armed warship. **2** Someone or N-COUNT
something that is described as a **destroyer** destroys N-COUNT:
things or people. *The company is the world's largest* with poss
destroyer of tropical forests.

de·struc·tive /dɪˈstrʌktɪv/. Something that is **de-** ◆◆◇◇◇
structive causes or is capable of causing great ADJ-GRADED
damage, harm, or injury. *...the awesome destructive*
power of nuclear weapons... Guilt can be very de-
structive. ♦ **de·struc·tive·ness** *the destructive-* N-UNCOUNT
ness of their weapons. ♦ **de·struc·tive·ly** *Power* ADV-GRADED
can be used creatively or destructively.

des·ul·tory /ˈdesəltri, AM -tɔːri/. Something that is ADJ-GRADED
desultory is done in an unplanned and disorgan- FORMAL
ized way, and without enthusiasm. *The constables*
made a desultory attempt to keep them away from
the barn.

de·tach /dɪˈtætʃ/ **detaches, detaching, de-** ◆◇◇◇◇
tached. 1 If you **detach** one thing from another V-ERG
that it is fixed to, you remove it. If one thing **de-** V n from n
taches from another, it becomes separated from it. Also V,
Detach the white part of the application form and V from n
keep it for reference... Detach the currants from the

stems. **2** If you **detach** yourself from something, you VERB
become less involved in it or less concerned about V pron-refl
it than you used to. *It helps them detach themselves* from n
from their problems and become more objective. **3** If
you **detach** yourself from a person or place, you VERB
leave them. *Alexis saw his father detach himself* V pron-refl
from the group and walk away. from n

de·tach·able /dɪˈtætʃəbəl/. If a part of an object is ADJ
detachable, it can be removed. *...a cake tin with a*
detachable base.

de·tached /dɪˈtætʃt/. **1** Someone who is **detached** ◆◇◇◇◇
is not personally involved in something or has no ADJ-GRADED
emotional interest in it. *He tries to remain emotion-*
ally detached from the prisoners, but fails. **2** A **de-** ADJ
tached house is one that is not joined to any other
house. See picture headed **house and flat.** ● See
also **semi-detached.**

de·tach·ment /dɪˈtætʃmənt/ **detachments.** ◆◇◇◇◇
1 Detachment is a feeling of not being personally N-UNCOUNT
involved in something or of having no emotional interest in it. *She did not care for the idea of socialis-*
ing with her clients. It would detract from her profes-
sional detachment. **2** A **detachment** is a group of N-COUNT
soldiers who are sent away from the main group to
do a special job. *...a detachment of marines.*

de·tail /ˈdiːteɪl/ **details, detailing, detailed.** The ◆◆◆◆◇
pronunciation /dɪˈteɪl/ is also used in American English. **1** The **details** of something are its individual N-COUNT
features or elements. *...the details of a peace agree-*
ment... No details of the discussions have been giv-
en... I recall every detail of the party. **2 Details** about N-PLURAL
someone or something are facts or pieces of infor-
mation about them. *See the bottom of this page for*
details of how to apply... Full details will be an-
nounced soon. **3** If you **detail** things, you list them VERB
or give information about them. *The report detailed* V n
the human rights abuses committed during the war. Also V how

4 If someone does not **go into details** about a subject, PHRASE
or does not **go into the detail,** they mention it without
explaining it fully or thoroughly. *He said he had been*
in various parts of Britain but did not go into details.
5 If you examine or discuss something **in detail,** you PHRASE
do it thoroughly and carefully.
6 A **detail** is a minor point or aspect of something. N-COUNT
Only minor details now remain to be settled. **7** You can N-UNCOUNT
refer to the small features of something which are often not noticed as **detail.** *We like his attention to de-*
tail. **8** A **detail** of a picture is a small part of it that is N-COUNT
printed separately and enlarged, so that the smaller
features can be clearly seen.
9 If someone **is detailed** to do a task or job, they are VERB
officially ordered to do it. *He detailed a constable to* V n to-inf
take it to the Incident Room. Also V n to n

de·tailed /ˈdiːteɪld, AM dɪˈteɪld/. A **detailed** report ◆◆◆◇◇
or plan contains a lot of details. *...a detailed account* ADJ-GRADED
of the decisions.

de·tain /dɪˈteɪn/ **detains, detaining, detained.** ◆◆◇◇◇
1 When people such as the police **detain** someone, V n
they keep them in a place under their control. *The* FORMAL
act allows police to detain a suspect for up to 48
hours. **2** To **detain** someone means to delay them. VERB
Thank you. We won't detain you any further. V n
FORMAL

de·tainee /ˌdiːteɪˈniː/ **detainees.** A **detainee** is ◇◇◇◇◇
someone who is being held prisoner by a govern- N-COUNT
ment or being held by the police.

de·tect /dɪˈtekt/ **detects, detecting, detected.** ◆◆◇◇◇
1 To **detect** something means to find it or discover V n
that it is present somewhere by using equipment or V n
making an investigation. *...equipment used to detect* V wh
radiation... There is no way of detecting what exact-
ly is happening. **2** If you **detect** something, you no- VERB
tice it or sense it, even though it is not very obvious. V n
Arnold could detect a certain sadness in the old
man's face.

de·tect·able /dɪˈtektəbəl/. Something that is **de-** ADJ-GRADED
tectable can be noticed or discovered. *The disease is*
probably inherited but not detectable at birth.

de·tec·tion /dɪˈtekʃən/. **1 Detection** is the act of ◆◇◇◇◇
noticing or sensing something. *...the early detection* N-UNCOUNT
of breast cancer. **2 Detection** is the discovery of N-UNCOUNT

something which is supposed to be hidden. *They are cheating but are sophisticated enough to avoid detection.* **3 Detection** is the work of investigating a crime in order to find out what has happened and who committed it. N-UNCOUNT

de·tec·tive /dɪˈtektɪv/ **detectives.** A detective is someone whose job is to discover what has happened in a crime or other situation and to find the people involved. Some detectives work in the police force and others work privately. *Detectives are appealing for witnesses who may have seen anything suspicious. ...Detective Inspector Ian Mosley.* ▶ Also a title in American English. *...Detective Nardosa.* ◆◆◆◇◇ N-COUNT / N-TITLE; N-VOC

de·tec·tor /dɪˈtektə/ **detectors.** A detector is an instrument which is used to discover if something is present somewhere, or to measure how much of something there is. *...smoke detectors.* N-COUNT

de·tente /deɪˈtɒnt/; also spelled **détente.** Detente is a state of friendly relations between two countries when previously there had been problems between them. *...their desire to pursue a policy of detente.* ◆◇◇◇◇ N-UNCOUNT: also a N FORMAL

de·ten·tion /dɪˈtenʃən/ **detentions. 1 Detention** is the arrest or imprisonment of someone, especially for political reasons. *...the detention without trial of government critics... The detentions are necessary on national security grounds.* **2 Detention** is a punishment for naughty schoolchildren, who are made to stay at school after the other children have gone home. *The teacher kept the boys in detention after school.* ◆◆◇◇◇ N-UNCOUNT: also N in pl / N-VAR

de·ten·tion centre, detention centres; spelled **detention center** in American English. A **detention centre** is a sort of prison, for example a place where illegal immigrants are kept whilst a decision is made about what to do with them. N-COUNT

de·ter /dɪˈtɜː/ **deters, deterring, deterred.** To **deter** someone from doing something means to make them not want to do it or continue doing it. *Supporters of the death penalty argue that it would deter criminals from carrying guns... Jail sentences have done nothing to deter the protesters.* ◆◆◇◇◇ VERB V n from -ing V n

de·ter·gent /dɪˈtɜːdʒənt/ **detergents.** Detergent is a chemical substance, usually in the form of a powder or liquid, which is used for washing things such as clothes or dishes. ◆◇◇◇◇ N-VAR

de·terio·rate /dɪˈtɪəriəreɪt/ **deteriorates, deteriorating, deteriorated.** If something deteriorates, it becomes worse. *The weather conditions are deteriorating... Grant's health steadily deteriorated.* ♦ **de·terio·ra·tion** /dɪˌtɪəriəˈreɪʃən/ *...the rapid deterioration in relations between the two countries.* ◆◆◇◇◇ VERB V / N-UNCOUNT

de·ter·mi·nant /dɪˈtɜːmɪnənt/ **determinants.** A **determinant** of something causes it to be of a particular kind or to happen in a particular way. *The windows and the views beyond them are major determinants of a room's character.* ◆◇◇◇◇ N-COUNT FORMAL

de·ter·mi·nate /dɪˈtɜːmɪnət/ **Determinate** means fixed and definite. *...the exclusive possession of land for some determinate period.* ADJ

de·ter·mi·na·tion /dɪˌtɜːmɪˈneɪʃən/ **Determination** is the quality that you show when you have decided to do something and you will not let anything stop you. *Everyone concerned acted with great courage and determination... He reaffirmed their determination to tackle inflation.* ◆◆◇◇◇ N-UNCOUNT

de·ter·mine /dɪˈtɜːmɪn/ **determines, determining, determined. 1** If a particular factor determines the nature of a thing or event, it causes it to be of a particular kind. *The size of the chicken pieces will determine the cooking time... What determines whether you are a career success or a failure?* ♦ **de·ter·mi·na·tion** *...the gene which is responsible for male sex determination.* ◆◆◆◆◇ VERB V n V wh / N-UNCOUNT: with supp

2 To **determine** a fact means to discover it as a result of investigation. *The investigation will determine what really happened... Testing needs to be done on each contaminant to determine the long-term effects.* VERB V wh V n Also V that

3 If you **determine** something, you decide it or settle it. *The Baltic people have a right to determine their own future... My aim was first of all to determine what* VERB V n V wh

to do next. ♦ **de·ter·mi·na·tion, determinations** *We must take into our own hands the determination of our future.* **4** If you **determine** to do something, you make a firm decision to do it. *He determined to rescue his two countrymen.* N-COUNT / VERB V to-inf Also V that FORMAL

de·ter·mined /dɪˈtɜːmɪnd/. If you are **determined** to do something, you have made a firm decision to do it and will not let anything stop you. *His enemies are determined to ruin him... He made determined efforts to overcome the scandal.* ♦ **de·ter·mined·ly** *She shook her head, determinedly.* ◆◆◆◇◇ ADJ-GRADED / ADV-GRADED

de·ter·min·er /dɪˈtɜːmɪnə/ **determiners.** A **determiner** is a word which is used at the beginning of a noun group to indicate, for example, which thing you are referring to or whether you are referring to one thing or several. Common English determiners are 'a', 'the', 'some', 'this', and 'each'. N-COUNT

de·ter·min·ism /dɪˈtɜːmɪnɪzəm/ **Determinism** is the belief that all actions and events result from other actions, events, or situations, so people cannot in fact choose what to do. N-UNCOUNT FORMAL

de·ter·min·ist /dɪˈtɜːmɪnɪst/ **determinists. 1** A **determinist** is someone who believes in determinism. **2 Determinist** ideas are based on determinism. *...reactionary and determinist doctrines.* N-COUNT FORMAL / ADJ FORMAL

de·ter·min·is·tic /dɪˌtɜːmɪˈnɪstɪk/. **1 Deterministic** ideas or explanations are based on determinism. **2 Deterministic** forces and factors cause things to happen in a way that cannot be changed. *The rise or decline of the United States is not a function of deterministic forces.* ADJ-GRADED FORMAL / ADJ FORMAL

de·ter·rence /dɪˈterəns, AM -ˈtɜːr-/. **Deterrence** is the prevention of something, especially war or crime, by having something such as weapons or punishment to use as a threat. *...nuclear deterrence.* ◆◇◇◇◇ N-UNCOUNT

de·ter·rent /dɪˈterənt, AM -ˈtɜːr-/ **deterrents. 1** A **deterrent** is something that prevents people from doing something by making them afraid of what will happen to them if they do. *They seriously believe that capital punishment is a deterrent.* **2** A **deterrent** is a weapon or set of weapons designed to prevent potential enemies from attacking by making them afraid to do so. **3** If something has a **deterrent** effect, it discourages people from doing certain things. *Hopefully, that will have a deterrent effect on drug syndicates in the future.* ◆◇◇◇◇ N-COUNT / N-COUNT / ADJ: ADJ n

de·test /dɪˈtest/ **detests, detesting, detested.** If you **detest** someone or something, you dislike them very much. *Jean detested being photographed.* ◆◇◇◇◇ VERB V n/-ing

de·test·able /dɪˈtestəbəl/. If you say that someone or something is **detestable**, you mean you dislike them very much. *I find their views detestable.* ADJ-GRADED FORMAL

de·throne /ˌdiːˈθrəun/ **dethrones, dethroning, dethroned.** If a king, queen, or other powerful person **is dethroned**, they are removed from their position of power. VERB: be V-ed

deto·nate /ˈdetəneɪt/ **detonates, detonating, detonated.** If someone **detonates** a device such as a bomb, or if it **detonates**, it explodes. *...the terrorists who planted and detonated the bomb.* ♦ **deto·na·tion** /ˌdetəˈneɪʃən/ **detonations** *...accidental detonation of nuclear weapons.* ◆◇◇◇◇ V-ERG V n Also V / N-VAR

deto·na·tor /ˈdetəneɪtə/ **detonators.** A **detonator** is a small amount of explosive or a piece of electrical or electronic equipment which is used to explode a bomb or other explosive device. N-COUNT

de·tour /ˈdiːtuə/ **detours, detouring, detoured. 1** If you make a **detour** on a journey, you go by a route which is not the shortest way. **2** If you **detour**, you make a detour. ◆◇◇◇◇ N-COUNT / VERB: V

detox /ˈdiːtɒks/. **Detox** is the same as **detoxification**. *Each patient sees a detox therapist.* ◆◇◇◇◇ N-UNCOUNT

de·toxi·fi·ca·tion /diːˌtɒksɪfɪˈkeɪʃən/. **Detoxification** is treatment given to people who are addicted to drugs or alcohol in order to stop them being addicted. N-UNCOUNT

de·toxi·fy /diːˈtɒksɪfaɪ/ **detoxifies, detoxifying, detoxified. 1** To **detoxify** something means to remove all the poisonous or harmful substances from it. *Seaweed baths can help to detoxify the body.* **2** To VERB V n / VERB: V n

detoxify a poisonous substance means to change it chemically so that it is no longer poisonous.

de·tract /dɪ'trækt/ **detracts, detracting, detracted.** If one thing **detracts** from another, it makes it seem less good or less impressive. *They feared that the publicity surrounding him would detract from their own election campaigns.*
◆◇◇◇◇ VERB V from n Also V n from n

de·trac·tor /dɪ'træktə/ **detractors.** The **detractors** of a person or thing are people who criticize them. *The news will have delighted detractors of the scheme.*
◆◇◇◇◇ N-COUNT

det·ri·ment /'detrɪmənt/. **1** If something happens **to the detriment of** something or to someone's **detriment**, it causes them harm or damage. *These tests will give too much importance to written exams to the detriment of other skills.* **2** If something happens **without detriment** to someone or something, it does not harm them. *These difficulties have been overcome without detriment to performance.*
◆◇◇◇◇ PHRASE

PHRASE

det·ri·men·tal /,detrɪ'mentəl/. Something that is **detrimental** to something else has a harmful or damaging effect on it. *Many foods are suspected of being detrimental to health because of the chemicals and additives they contain.*
◆◇◇◇◇ ADJ-GRADED

de·tri·tus /dɪ'traɪtəs/. **Detritus** is the small pieces of rubbish that remain after an event has finished or when something has been used. *...burnt-out buildings, littered with the detritus of war.*
N-UNCOUNT: with supp FORMAL

deuce /djuːs, AM duːs/ **deuces. Deuce** is the score in a game of tennis when each player has a score of forty.
N-UNCOUNT: also N in pl

de·value /,diː'væljuː/ **devalues, devaluing, devalued. 1** To **devalue** something means to cause it to be thought less impressive or less worthy of respect. *They spread tales about her in an attempt to devalue her work.* ◆ **de·valued** *Selling tickets for a devalued championship is becoming increasingly difficult.* **2** To **devalue** the currency of a country means to reduce its value in relation to other currencies. *India has devalued the Rupee by about eleven per cent.* ◆ **de·valua·tion** /,diː,væljuˈeɪʃən/ **de·valuations** *...the devaluation of the dollar.*
◆◆◇◇◇ VERB V n

ADJ-GRADED

VERB V n by amount

N-VAR

dev·as·tate /'devəsteɪt/ **devastates, devastating, devastated.** If something **devastates** an area or a place, it damages it badly or destroys it totally. *A fire had devastated large parts of Windsor Castle.*
◆◇◇◇◇ VERB V n

dev·as·tat·ed /'devəsteɪtɪd/. If you are **devastated** by something, you are very shocked and upset by it. *He was devastated by news of the Cardinal's death.*
◆◇◇◇◇ ADJ-GRADED: v-link ADJ

dev·as·tat·ing /'devəsteɪtɪŋ/. **1** You describe something as **devastating** when it is very destructive or damaging. *Affairs can have a devastating effect on marriages.* **2** You can use **devastating** to say that something is very shocking, upsetting, or terrible. *The diagnosis was devastating. She had cancer.* **3** You can use **devastating** to emphasize that something or someone is very impressive. *...a devastating display of galloping and jumping.* ◆ **dev·as·tat·ing·ly** *Its advertising is devastatingly successful.*
ADJ-GRADED

ADJ-GRADED

ADJ PRAGMATICS

ADV-GRADED

dev·as·ta·tion /,devəˈsteɪʃən/. **Devastation** is severe and widespread destruction or damage. *A huge bomb blast brought chaos and devastation.*
◆◇◇◇◇ N-UNCOUNT

de·vel·op /dɪ'veləp/ **develops, developing, developed. 1** When someone or something **develops**, they grow or change over a period of time and usually become more advanced or complete. *As children develop, some of the most important things they learn have to do with their sense of self... Most of these settlements developed from agricultural centres... These clashes could develop into open warfare.* ◆ **de·vel·oped** *Their bodies were well-developed.* **2** When a country **develops**, it changes from being a poor agricultural country to a rich industrial country. *All countries, it was predicted, would develop.* ◆ **developed** *The developed nations have to recognize the growing gap between rich and poor around the world.* **3** If someone **develops** a business or industry, or if it **develops**, it becomes bigger and more successful. *...her dreams of developing her own business.*
◆◆◆◆◆ VERB V V from n V into n

ADJ-GRADED VERB V

ADJ-GRADED

V-ERG V n Also V

◆ **developed** *Housing finance is less developed and less competitive in continental Europe.* **4** If a person or company **develops** land or property, they make it more useful or profitable, by building houses or factories or by improving existing buildings. *...the cost of acquiring or developing property.* ◆ **developed** *...developed land.* **5** If someone **develops** a new product, they design it and produce it. *He claims that several countries have developed nuclear weapons secretly.*
ADJ-GRADED VERB V n Also V

ADJ-GRADED VERB V n Also V n from n

6 If you **develop** an idea, theory, story, or theme, or if it **develops**, it gradually becomes more detailed, advanced, or complex. *This point is developed further at the end of this chapter.*
V-ERG V n Also V

7 If you **develop** a habit, reputation, or belief, you start to have it and it then becomes stronger or more noticeable. *She later developed a taste for expensive nightclubs.* **8** If you **develop** a skill, quality, or relationship, or if it **develops**, it becomes better or stronger. *We must develop closer ties with Germany... Their friendship developed.* ◆ **developed** *...a highly developed instinct for self-preservation.* **9** If you **develop** an illness, or if it **develops**, you become affected by it. *Smokers are most prone to develop lung cancer.*
VERB V n

V-ERG V n V

ADJ-GRADED

V-ERG V n Also V

10 If a problem or difficulty **develops**, it begins to occur. **11** If a piece of equipment **develops** a fault, it starts to have it.
VERB: V

VERB: V n

12 To **develop** photographs means to make negatives or prints from a photographic film.
VERB: V n

de·vel·op·er /dɪ'veləpə/ **developers. 1** A **developer** is a person or company that buys land and builds houses, offices, shops, or factories on it, or buys existing buildings and modernizes them. *...common land which would have a high commercial value if sold to developers.* **2** A **developer** of something such as an idea, a design, or a product is someone who develops it. *...a software developer.* **3 Developer** is a chemical used for developing photographs or films.
◆◆◇◇◇ N-COUNT

N-COUNT: with supp

N-UNCOUNT

de·vel·op·ing /dɪ'veləpɪŋ/. If you talk about **developing** countries or the **developing** world, you mean the countries or the parts of the world that are poor and have few industries. *In the developing world cigarette consumption is increasing.*
◆◆◇◇◇ ADJ: ADJ n TECHNICAL

de·vel·op·ment /dɪ'veləpmənt/ **developments. 1 Development** is the gradual growth or formation of something. *...studying the development of the embryo.* **2 Development** is the growth or expansion of something such as a firm or an industry. *...plans for the development of your company.* **3 Development** is the process or result of making a basic design gradually better and more advanced. *...the development of new and innovative telephone services.* **4 Development** is the process of making an area of land or water more useful or profitable. *...the fostering of development in the rural areas.* **5** A **development** is an area of houses or buildings which have been built by property developers. **6** A **development** is an event which has recently happened and is likely to have an effect on the present situation. *...the latest developments in Moscow.*
◆◆◆◆◆ N-UNCOUNT: with supp

N-UNCOUNT: with supp

N-VAR

N-UNCOUNT: with supp

N-COUNT

N-COUNT

de·vel·op·men·tal /dɪ,veləp'mentəl/. **Developmental** means relating to the development of someone or something. *...the emotional, educational, and developmental needs of the child.*
◆◇◇◇◇ ADJ FORMAL

de·vi·ant /'diːviənt/ **deviants. 1 Deviant** behaviour or thinking is different from what people normally consider to be acceptable. *Not all alcoholics and drug abusers produce deviant offspring.* ◆ **de·vi·ance** /'diːviəns/ *...sexual deviance.* **2** A **deviant** is someone whose behaviour or beliefs are different from what people normally consider to be acceptable.
◆◇◇◇◇ ADJ-GRADED

N-UNCOUNT N-COUNT

de·vi·ate /'diːvieɪt/ **deviates, deviating, deviated.** To **deviate** from something means to start doing something different or something that was not planned. *He planned his schedule far in advance, and he didn't deviate from it.* ◆ **de·via·tion** /,diːviˈeɪʃən/ **deviations** *Deviation from the norm is not tolerated.*
◆◇◇◇◇ VERB V from n Also V

N-VAR

de·vi·a·tion /ˌdiːviˈeɪʃən/ **deviations. Deviation** is N-VAR the difference between the value of one number in TECHNICAL a series of numbers and the average value of all the numbers in the series.

de·vice /dɪˈvaɪs/ **devices. 1** A **device** is an object ◆◆◆◇◇ that has been invented for a particular purpose, for N-COUNT example for measuring something. *We believe that an explosive device had been left inside a container.* **2** A **device** is a method of achieving something. *They* N-COUNT *claim that military spending is used as a device for managing the economy.* **3** If you **leave** someone **to** their **own devices**, you PHRASE leave them alone to do as they wish.

dev·il /ˈdevəl/ **devils. 1** In Judaism, Christianity, ◆◇◇◇◇ and Islam, **the Devil** is the most powerful and im- N-PROPER: portant evil spirit. **2** A **devil** is an evil spirit. theN N-COUNT **3** You can use **devil** when you are showing how you N-COUNT feel about someone. For example, if you call someone PRAGMATICS a poor **devil**, you are saying that you feel sorry for INFORMAL them. You can call someone you are fond of an old **devil** or a little **devil**. *Manfred, you're a suspicious old devil.* **4 Devil** can be used to say emphatically what PHRASE you think about someone or something. For example, PRAGMATICS if you say someone is **a devil of a** nuisance, you mean they are very annoying. If you say something is **a devil of a** problem, you mean it is a very difficult problem. **5** If you say that someone does something **like the** PHRASE **devil**, you are emphasizing that they put a lot of effort PRAGMATICS into it. If you say that someone goes or drives **like the devil**, you are emphasizing that they go or drive very fast. *He drives himself on, working like the devil from seven in the morning until midnight.* **6** When you want to emphasize how annoyed or sur- PHRASE prised you are, you can use an expression such as PRAGMATICS **what the devil, how the devil,** or **why the devil.** *'What* INFORMAL *the devil's the matter?'... Tim wondered how the devil they had managed it.* **7** If you say **better the devil you know** or **better the** PHRASE **devil you know than the devil you don't know,** you PRAGMATICS mean that you would prefer to have contact with or do business with a person you already know, even though you don't like them, than with a person you don't know.

dev·il·ish /ˈdevəlɪʃ/. **1** You can use **devilish** to em- ADJ-GRADED phasize how cruel or unpleasant something is. *The* PRAGMATICS *Gulf war showed the devilish destructiveness of mod-ern conventional weapons.* **2** You can use **devilish** ADJ-GRADED to emphasize how extreme or difficult something is. PRAGMATICS *...a devilish puzzle.* ► Also an adverb. *I'd been devil-* ADV *ish lucky.* ♦ **dev·il·ish·ly** *It is devilishly painful.* ADV-GRADED

devil-may-'care. If you say that someone has a ADJ **devil-may-care** attitude, you mean they seem re-laxed and unconcerned about the consequences of their actions.

devil's 'advocate. If you say that you are playing N-UNCOUNT **devil's advocate** in a discussion or debate, you also with det mean you are expressing an opinion which you do not agree with in order to make the argument more interesting.

de·vi·ous /ˈdiːviəs/. **1** You say that someone is **de-** ◆◇◇◇◇ **vious** when they achieve something in a clever, ADJ-GRADED complicated, and dishonest way. *By devious means she tracked down the other woman.* ♦ **de·vi·ous-** N-UNCOUNT **·ness** *...the deviousness of drug traffickers.* **2** A **devi-** ADJ-GRADED **ous** route or path to a place involves many changes in direction, rather than being as straight and direct as possible.

de·vise /dɪˈvaɪz/ **devises, devising, devised.** If ◆◆◇◇◇ you **devise** something, you have the idea for it and VERB design it. *We devised a scheme to help him.* V n

de·void /dɪˈvɔɪd/. If you say that someone or ◆◇◇◇◇ something is **devoid of** a quality or thing, you are ADJ-GRADED: emphasizing that they have none of it. *...a face that* v-link ADJ ofn *was so devoid of feeling.* PRAGMATICS

de·vo·lu·tion /ˌdiːvəˈluːʃən, ˌdev-/. **Devolution** is N-UNCOUNT the transfer of some authority or power from a cen-tral organization or government to smaller organi-zations or government departments. *...the devolu-tion of power to the regions.*

de·volve /dɪˈvɒlv/ **devolves, devolving, de-** ◆◇◇◇◇ **volved.** If you **devolve** power, authority, or respon- V-ERG sibility to a less important or powerful person or V n ton group, or if it **devolves** upon them, it is transferred V n to them. *...the need to decentralize and devolve pow-* Also V upon/ *er to regional governments... The best companies are* onn *those that devolve responsibility.*

de·vote /dɪˈvəʊt/ **devotes, devoting, devoted.** ◆◆◇◇◇ **1** If you **devote** yourself, your time, or your energy VERB to something, you spend all or most of your time or V n ton/-ing energy on it. *He decided to devote the rest of his life to scientific investigation.* **2** If you **devote** part of a VERB piece of writing or a speech to a subject, you deal V n ton with the subject in that part of the writing or speech. *He devoted a major section of his massive report to an analysis of US aircraft design.*

de·vot·ed /dɪˈvəʊtɪd/. **1** Someone who is **devoted** ◆◆◇◇◇ to a person loves that person very much. *...a loving* ADJ-GRADED *and devoted husband.* **2** If you are **devoted** to ADJ-GRADED: something, you care about it a lot and are very en- v-link ADJ to thusiastic about it. *I have personally been devoted to* n, *this cause for many years... Horace is so devoted to* ADJ n *his garden.* **3** Something that is **devoted to** a particular thing ADJ: deals only with that thing or contains only that thing. v-link ADJ ton *...a major touring exhibition devoted to the work of disabled artists.*

de·vo·tee /ˌdevəˈtiː/ **devotees. 1** Someone who is ◆◇◇◇◇ a **devotee** of a subject or activity is very enthusiastic N-COUNT: about it. *...a devotee of Britten's music.* **2** A **devotee** with supp of a religious group is a member of it. *...devotees of* N-COUNT *the Hare Krishna movement.*

de·vo·tion /dɪˈvəʊʃən/. **1 Devotion** is great love, ◆◇◇◇◇ affection, or admiration for someone. *At first she* N-UNCOUNT *was flattered by his devotion.* **2 Devotion** to some- N-UNCOUNT thing you do or believe in is commitment to it. *I don't mean to keep criticising his devotion to his job.* **3 Devotion** is religious worship or strong religious N-UNCOUNT feeling. *He was kneeling by his bed in an attitude of devotion.*

de·vo·tion·al /dɪˈvəʊʃənəl/. **Devotional** activities, ADJ: ADJ n writings, or objects relate to religious worship. *...de-votional pictures and sacred objects.*

de·vo·tions /dɪˈvəʊʃənz/. Someone's **devotions** are N-PLURAL the prayers that they say.

de·vour /dɪˈvaʊə/ **devours, devouring, de-** ◆◇◇◇◇ **voured. 1** If a person or animal **devours** some- VERB thing, they eat it quickly and eagerly. *A medium-* V n *sized dog will devour at least one can of food plus biscuits per day.* **2** If you **devour** a book or maga- VERB zine, for example, you read it quickly and eagerly. V n *She began buying and devouring newspapers when she was only 12.*

de·vout /dɪˈvaʊt/. **1** A **devout** person has deep reli- ◆◇◇◇◇ gious beliefs. *She was a devout Christian.* ► **The de-** ADJ-GRADED **vout** are people who are devout. **2** If you describe N-PLURAL someone as a **devout** supporter or a **devout** oppo- ADJ-GRADED: nent of something, you mean that they support it ADJ n enthusiastically or oppose it strongly. *Devout Marx-ists believed that fascism was the 'last stand of the bourgeoisie'.*

de·vout·ly /dɪˈvaʊtli/. **1 Devoutly** is used to em- ADV-GRADED: phasize how sincerely or deeply you hope for some- ADV with v thing or believe in something. *He devoutly hoped it* PRAGMATICS *was true.* **2 Devoutly** is used to emphasize how FORMAL deep someone's religious beliefs are, or to indicate ADV: that something is done in a devout way. *...in this de-* ADV adj, *voutly Buddhist country.* ADV with v PRAGMATICS

dew /djuː, AM duː/. **Dew** is small drops of water that N-UNCOUNT form on the ground and other surfaces outdoors during the night.

dewy /ˈdjuːi, AM ˈduːi/. **1** Something that is **dewy** is ADJ-GRADED wet with dew. *The satin slippers tread daintily* LITERARY *through the dewy grass.* **2** If your skin looks **dewy**, it ADJ-GRADED looks soft and glows healthily.

dewy-'eyed. If you say that someone is **dewy-** ADJ-GRADED **eyed,** you mean that they are unrealistic and think PRAGMATICS events and situations are better than they really are; used showing disapproval. *...why people become dewy-eyed and sentimental about the past.*

dex·ter·ity /deks'terɪti/. **Dexterity** is skill in using N-UNCOUNT
your hands, or sometimes your mind. *...Reid's dex-*
terity on the guitar.

dex·ter·ous /'dekstrəs/; also spelled **dextrous**. ADJ-GRADED
Someone who is **dexterous** is very skilful and clever
with their hands. *As people grow older they generally*
become less dexterous.

dex·trose /'dekstrəuz, AM -rəus/. **Dextrose** is a N-UNCOUNT
natural form of sugar that is found in fruits, honey,
and in the blood of animals.

dia·be·tes /,daɪə'biːtiːz, AM -tɪs/. **Diabetes** is a ◆◆◇◇◇
medical condition in which someone has too much N-UNCOUNT
sugar in their blood.

dia·bet·ic /,daɪə'betɪk/ **diabetics. 1** A diabetic is ◆◇◇◇◇
a person who suffers from diabetes. ▶ Also an ad- N-COUNT
jective. *...diabetic patients.* **2 Diabetic** means relat- ADJ
ing to diabetes. *He found her in a diabetic coma.* ADJ: ADJ n
3 Diabetic foods are suitable for diabetics. ADJ: ADJ n

dia·bol·ic /,daɪə'bɒlɪk/. **Diabolic** is used to describe ADJ: ADJ n
things that people think are caused by or belong to FORMAL
the Devil. *...the diabolic forces which lurk in all*
violence.

dia·bol·i·cal /,daɪə'bɒlɪkəl/. **1** If you describe some- ADJ-GRADED
thing as **diabolical**, you are emphasizing that it is PRAGMATICS
very bad, extreme, or unpleasant. *The pain was dia-* INFORMAL
bolical. ♦ **dia·bol·i·cal·ly** /,daɪə'bɒlɪkli/ *...diabolical-* ADV
ly difficult clues. **2 Diabolical** is used to emphasize ADJ
how evil something is. *One speaker called the plan* PRAGMATICS
diabolical and sinister.

di·ag·nose /'daɪəgnəuz, AM -nəus/ **diagnoses, di-** ◆◆◇◇◇
agnosing, diagnosed. If someone or something VERB
is diagnosed as having a particular illness or prob- be V-ed as n/
lem, their illness or problem is identified. If an ill- -ing/adj
ness or problem **is diagnosed**, it is identified. *The* V n
soldiers were diagnosed as having flu... He could di- Also be V-ed
agnose an engine problem simply by listening. adj

di·ag·no·sis /,daɪəg'nəusɪs/ **diagnoses. Diagno-** ◆◆◇◇◇
sis is the discovery and identification of what is N-VAR
wrong with someone who is ill or with something
that is not working properly. *Symptoms may not ap-*
pear for some weeks, so diagnosis can be difficult.

di·ag·nos·tic /,daɪəg'nɒstɪk/. **Diagnostic** equip- ◆◇◇◇◇
ment, methods, or systems are used for discovering ADJ: ADJ n
what is wrong with sick people or with things that
do not work properly. *...X-rays and other diagnostic*
tools.

di·ago·nal /daɪ'ægənəl/ **diagonals. 1** A diagonal ◆◇◇◇◇
line or movement goes in a slanting direction. ADJ
♦ **di·ago·nal·ly** *He headed diagonally across the* ADV:
paddock. **2** A **diagonal** is a line that goes in a slant- ADV with v
ing direction. *...checks, stripes, diagonals and trian-* N-COUNT
gles. **3** A **diagonal** is a straight line that joins two N-COUNT
opposite corners in a flat four-sided shape such as a
square.

dia·gram /'daɪəgræm/ **diagrams.** A **diagram** is a ◆◇◇◇◇
simple drawing consisting mainly of lines, that is N-COUNT
used, for example, to explain how a machine works.
...a circuit diagram.

dia·gram·mat·ic /,daɪəgrə'mætɪk/. Something that ADJ
is in **diagrammatic** form is arranged or drawn as a
diagram. *This is the virus in very crude simple dia-*
grammatic form.

dial /daɪəl/ **dials, dialling, dialled;** also spelled ◆◆◇◇◇
dialing, dialed in American English. **1** A **dial** is an N-COUNT
indicator on a clock, meter, or other instrument
which shows you the time or a measurement that
has been recorded. *The luminous dial on the clock*
showed five minutes to seven. **2** A **dial** is a control N-COUNT
on a device or piece of equipment, which you move
in order to adjust the setting, for example to change
the frequency on a radio.
3 A **dial** on some models of telephone is a circular disc N-COUNT
that you rotate according to the number that you
want to call. **4** If you **dial** or if you **dial** a number, you VERB: V
turn the dial or press the buttons on a telephone in or- V n
der to phone someone. *He lifted the phone and dialled*
her number.

dia·lect /'daɪəlekt/ **dialects.** A **dialect** is a form of ◆◇◇◇◇
a language that is spoken in a particular area. *Azer-* N-COUNT:
baijan is a predominantly Islamic country and the also in N

majority of its people speak a dialect of Turkish...
They began to speak rapidly in dialect.

dia·lec·tic /,daɪə'lektɪk/ **dialectics. 1** When peo- N-COUNT:
ple talk about the **dialectic** or **dialectics** of a situa- with supp
tion, they mean the way in which two very different FORMAL
forces or factors interact with each other, and the
way in which their differences are resolved. *...the*
dialectics of class struggle. **2** In philosophy, **dialec-** N-UNCOUNT
tics is a method of reasoning and reaching conclu-
sions by considering theories and ideas together
with ones that contradict them.

dia·lec·ti·cal /,daɪə'lektɪkəl/. **Dialectical** is used to ADJ
describe situations, theories, and methods which
depend on resolving opposing factors. *The essence*
of dialectical thought is division.

'dialling code, dialling codes; spelled **dialing** N-COUNT
code in American English. A **dialling code** is a telephone number which you dial before someone's
personal number in order to be connected to the
right area, town, or village.

'dialling tone, dialling tones. The **dialling tone** N-COUNT
is the noise you hear when you pick up a telephone BRITISH
receiver, which means that you can dial a number.
The usual American term is **dial tone.**

dia·logue /'daɪəlɒg, AM -lɔːg/ **dialogues;** also ◆◆◇◇◇
spelled **dialog** in American English. **1 Dialogue** is N-VAR
communication or discussion between people or
groups such as governments or political parties.
People of all social standings should be given equal
opportunities for dialogue. **2** The **dialogue** in a N-VAR
book, film, or play is the things the characters in it
say to each other. *Although the dialogue is sharp,*
the actors move rather too awkwardly.

'dial tone, dial tones. The **dial tone** is the noise N-COUNT
you hear when you pick up a telephone receiver AMERICAN
and which means that you can dial the number you
want. The usual British term is **dialling tone.**

di·aly·sis /daɪ'ælɪsɪs/. **Dialysis** or **kidney dialysis** is N-UNCOUNT
a method of treating kidney failure by using a ma-
chine to remove waste material from the blood.

dia·man·te /,daɪə'mænti, AM ,diːəmɑː'nteɪ/. **Dia-** N-UNCOUNT
mante jewellery is made from small pieces of cut
glass which look like diamonds.

di·am·eter /daɪ'æmɪtə/ **diameters.** The **diameter** ◆◆◇◇◇
of a circle, sphere, or tube is its width measured by N-COUNT:
a straight line passing through its centre. *...a tiny* also in N
capsule, between 1 and 3 millimetres in diameter.

dia·met·ri·cal·ly /,daɪə'metrɪkli/. If you say that ADV: ADV adj
two things are **diametrically** opposed, you are PRAGMATICS
emphasizing that they are exactly opposite to each
other. *The economic crisis was interpreted in dia-*
metrically opposing ways.

dia·mond /'daɪəmənd/ **diamonds. 1** A **diamond** is ◆◆◇◇◇
a hard, bright, precious stone which is clear and N-VAR
colourless. Diamonds are used in jewellery and for
cutting very hard substances. *...a pair of diamond*
earrings. **2 Diamonds** are jewellery such as neck- N-PLURAL
laces and bracelets which have diamonds set into
them. *Nicole loves wearing her diamonds.*
3 A **diamond** is a shape with four straight sides of N-COUNT
equal length. See picture headed **shapes.** *...forming*
his hands into the shape of a diamond. **4 Diamonds** is N-COLL-
one of the four suits of cards in a pack of playing UNCOUNT
cards. Each card in the suit is marked with one or
more red symbols: ♦. ▶ A **diamond** is a playing card of N-COUNT
this suit.

,diamond 'jubilee, diamond jubilees. A **dia-** N-COUNT
mond jubilee is the sixtieth anniversary of an important event.

dia·per /'daɪəpə/ **diapers.** A **diaper** is a piece of ◆◇◇◇◇
soft towel or absorbent paper, which you put round N-COUNT
a baby's bottom in order to soak up its urine and AMERICAN
faeces. The British word is **nappy.**

di·apha·nous /daɪ'æfənəs/. **Diaphanous** cloth is ADJ
very thin and almost transparent. *...a diaphanous* LITERARY
dress of pale gold.

dia·phragm /'daɪəfræm/ **diaphragms. 1** Your ◆◇◇◇◇
diaphragm is a muscle between your lungs and N-COUNT
your stomach. It is used especially when you
breathe deeply. **2** A **diaphragm** is a circular N-COUNT

D

di·a·rist /'daɪərɪst/ **diarists.** A **diarist** records things in a diary, which is later published. N-COUNT

di·ar·rhoea /ˌdaɪə'riːə/; spelled **diarrhea** in American English. If someone has **diarrhoea**, a lot of liquid faeces comes out of their body at frequent intervals, because they are ill. ◆◇◇◇◇ N-UNCOUNT

di·a·ry /'daɪəri/ **diaries.** A **diary** is a book which has a separate space for each day of the year. You write in it things that you plan to do, or you record in it what happens in your life each day. ◆◆◆◇◇ N-COUNT

di·as·po·ra /daɪ'æspərə/. People who come from a particular nation, or whose ancestors came from it, but who now live in different parts of the world are sometimes referred to as the **diaspora.** ...*the history of peoples from the African diaspora.* N-SING FORMAL

di·a·tribe /'daɪətraɪb/ **diatribes.** A **diatribe** is an angry speech or article which is very critical of someone's ideas or activities. *The last chapter of this book is an extended diatribe against the academic left.* N-COUNT

dice /daɪs/ **dices, dicing, diced. 1** A **dice** is a small cube which has one to six spots or numbers on its sides, and which is used in games to provide random numbers. In old-fashioned English, 'dice' was used only as a plural form, and the singular was **die**, but now 'dice' is used as both the singular and the plural form. **2 Dice** is a game which is played using dice. **3** When you **dice** food, you cut it into small cubes. *Dice the onion.* ◆◇◇◇◇ N-COUNT / N-UNCOUNT / VERB V n

dicey /'daɪsi/ **dicier, diciest.** Something that is **dicey** is slightly dangerous or uncertain. *There was a dicey moment as one of our party made a risky climb up the cliff wall.* ADJ-GRADED INFORMAL, BRITISH

di·choto·my /daɪ'kɒtəmi/ **dichotomies.** If there is a **dichotomy** between two things, there is a very great difference or opposition between them. *There is a dichotomy between the academic world and the industrial world.* N-COUNT FORMAL

dic·tate, dictates, dictating, dictated. The verb is pronounced /dɪk'teɪt, AM 'dɪkteɪt/. The noun is pronounced /'dɪkteɪt/. **1** If you **dictate** something, you say or read it aloud for someone else to write down. *Sheldon writes every day of the week, dictating his novels in the morning.* **2** If someone **dictates** to someone else, they tell them what they should do or can do. *What right has one country to dictate the environmental standards of another?... He cannot be allowed to dictate what can and cannot be inspected... What gives them the right to dictate to us what we should eat?* **3** A **dictate** is an order which you have to obey. *Ensure that the dictates of the Party are followed.* **4 Dictates** are principles or rules which you consider to be extremely important. *We have followed the dictates of our consciences.* **5** If one thing **dictates** another, the first thing causes or influences the second thing. *Of course, a number of factors will dictate how long an apple tree can survive.* ◆◆◇◇◇ / VERB V n Also V / VERB: V ton V n V wh V ton wh / N-COUNT / N-COUNT / VERB: V n V wh Also V that

dic·ta·tion /dɪk'teɪʃən/. **1 Dictation** is the speaking or reading aloud of words for someone else to write down. **2 Dictation** is the giving of orders in a forceful and commanding way. *The Europeans, while keen for partnership with the US, would not accept dictation.* N-UNCOUNT / N-UNCOUNT

dic·ta·tor /dɪk'teɪtə, AM 'dɪkteɪt-/ **dictators.** A **dictator** is a ruler who has complete power in a country, especially power which was obtained by force; used showing disapproval. ◆◆◇◇◇ N-COUNT PRAGMATICS

dic·ta·tor·ial /ˌdɪktə'tɔːriəl/. **1 Dictatorial** means controlled or used by a dictator. *He suspended the constitution and assumed dictatorial powers.* **2** If you describe someone's behaviour as **dictatorial**, you mean that they tell people what to do in a forceful and unfair way; used showing disapproval. *...his dictatorial management style.* ◆◇◇◇◇ ADJ-GRADED / ADJ-GRADED PRAGMATICS

dic·ta·tor·ship /dɪk'teɪtəʃɪp/ **dictatorships. 1 Dictatorship** is government by a dictator. *...military dictatorship.* **2** A **dictatorship** is a country ◆◆◇◇◇ N-VAR / N-COUNT

which is ruled by a dictator or by a very authoritarian government. *...a communist dictatorship.*

dic·tion /'dɪkʃən/. Someone's **diction** is how clearly they speak or sing. *His diction wasn't very good.* N-UNCOUNT

dic·tion·ary /'dɪkʃənri, AM -neri/ **dictionaries. 1** A **dictionary** is a book in which the words and phrases of a language are listed alphabetically, together with their meanings or their translations in another language. *...a Welsh-English dictionary.* **2** A **dictionary** is an alphabetically ordered reference book on one particular subject or limited group of subjects. *The Dictionary of National Biography.* ◆◆◇◇◇ N-COUNT / N-COUNT: with supp

dic·tum /'dɪktəm/ **dictums** or **dicta. 1** A **dictum** is a saying that describes an aspect of life in an interesting or wise way. *...the dictum that it is preferable to be roughly right than precisely wrong.* **2** A **dictum** is a formal statement made by someone in authority. *Disraeli's dictum that the first priority of the government must be the health of the people.* N-COUNT / N-COUNT

did /dɪd/. **Did** is the past tense of **do.**

di·dac·tic /daɪ'dæktɪk/. **1** Something that is **didactic** is intended to teach people something, especially a moral lesson. *In totalitarian societies, art exists for didactic purposes.* **2** Someone who is **didactic** tells people things rather than letting them find things out or discussing things. *He is much more didactic in his approach.* ADJ-GRADED FORMAL / ADJ-GRADED FORMAL

didn't /'dɪdənt/. **Didn't** is the usual spoken form of **did not.** ◆◆◆◆◆

die /daɪ/ **dies, dying, died. 1** When people, animals, and plants **die**, they stop living. *My mother died of cancer... I would die a very happy person if I could stay in music my whole life. ...friends who died young.* **2** If a person, animal, or plant **is dying**, they are so ill or so badly injured that they will not live very much longer. *...people who are dying from lung diseases.* **3** If someone **dies** a violent, unnatural, or painful death, they die in a violent, unnatural, or painful way. *His mother died an agonizing death.* **4** When a machine or device **dies**, it stops completely, especially after a period of functioning more and more slowly or ineffectively. *Then suddenly, the engine coughed, spluttered and died.* **5** When a fire or light **dies**, it stops burning or shining. **6** When an emotion or facial expression **dies**, it disappears completely, usually after a period of gradually becoming weaker and less noticeable. *My love for you will never die.* **7** You say that you **are dying of** thirst, hunger, boredom, or curiosity to emphasize that you are very thirsty, hungry, bored, or curious. **8** You say that you **are dying for** something or **are dying** to do something to emphasize that you very much want to have it or do it. *She was dying to talk to Frank.* **9** You use **die** in expressions such as **I almost died** or **I'd die if anything happened** where you are emphasizing your feelings about a situation, for example to say that it is very shocking, upsetting, embarrassing, or amusing. *I nearly died when I learned where I was ending up... I nearly died of shame.* **10** A **die** is a specially shaped or patterned block of metal which is used to press or cut other metal into a particular shape. **11** See also **dying. 12** You say that **the die is cast** to draw attention to the importance of an event or decision which will affect your future and cannot be changed or avoided. **13** If you say that habits or attitudes **die hard**, you mean that they take a very long time to disappear or change, so that it may not be possible to get rid of them completely. ◆◆◆◆◆ VERB: V, no passive V of/from n V n V adj VERB: V, only cont V of/from n / VB: no passive V n / VERB V / VERB: V / VERB V / VB: only cont PRAGMATICS INFORMAL / VERB: V for n, only cont PRAGMATICS V to-inf / VERB PRAGMATICS V for n INFORMAL / N-COUNT / PHRASE / PHRASE

die away. If a sound **dies away**, it gradually becomes weaker or fainter and finally disappears. PHRASAL VB V P

die back. When a plant **dies back**, its leaves die but its roots remain alive. PHRASAL VB V P

die down. If something **dies down**, it becomes very much quieter or less intense. *The rain remained steady though the wind had died down.* PHRASAL VB V P

die out. If something **dies out**, it becomes less and PHRASAL VB

less common and eventually disappears completely. V P
How did the dinosaurs die out?

die·hard /'daɪhɑːd/ **diehards;** also spelled **die-** N-COUNT
hard. A **diehard** is someone who is very strongly
opposed to change and new ideas, or who is a very
strong supporter of someone or something. *Not
even their diehard supporters can pretend that this
was a great game.*

die·sel /'diːzəl/ **diesels. 1** Diesel or diesel oil is ◆◆◇◇◇
the heavy oil used in a diesel engine. **2** A **diesel** is a N-VAR N-COUNT
vehicle which has a diesel engine.

'diesel engine, diesel engines. A **diesel engine** N-COUNT
is an internal combustion engine in which oil is
burnt by very hot air. Diesel engines are used in
buses and lorries, and in some trains and cars.

diet /'daɪət/ **diets, dieting, dieted. 1** Your **diet** is ◆◆◆◆◇
the type and range of food that you regularly eat. *It's* N-VAR
never too late to improve your diet. ...a healthy diet.
2 If a doctor puts someone on a **diet**, he or she N-COUNT
makes them eat a special type or range of foods in
order to improve their health. *He was put on a diet
of milky food.* **3** If you are on a **diet**, you eat special N-VAR
kinds of food or you eat less food than usual be-
cause you are trying to lose weight. *Diet and exer-
cise will alter your shape.* **4** If you are **dieting**, you VERB: V
eat special kinds of food or you eat less food than
usual because you are trying to lose weight. ♦ **diet-**
·ing *She has already lost around two stone through* N-UNCOUNT
dieting. **5** Diet drinks or foods have been specially ADJ: ADJ n
produced so that they do not contain many calories.
...sugar-free diet drinks.
6 If someone is fed on a **diet** of something, especially N-COUNT
something unpleasant or of poor quality, they receive [PRAGMATICS]
or experience a very large amount of it. *The radio had
fed him a diet of pop songs.*

di·etary /'daɪətri, AM -teri/. **1** You can use the ◆◇◇◇◇
word **dietary** to describe anything that concerns a ADJ
person's diet. *As with all dietary changes, reducing
salt should be done gradually.* **2** You can use the ADJ: ADJ n
word **dietary** to describe substances such as fibre
and fat that are found in food. *Wheat bran is the
commonest source of dietary fibre.*

di·et·er /'daɪətə/ **dieters.** A **dieter** is someone who ◆◇◇◇◇
is on a diet or who regularly goes on diets. N-COUNT

di·etet·ic /ˌdaɪə'tetɪk/. **Dietetic** food or drink is ADJ: ADJ n
food or drink that has been specially produced so AMERICAN,
that it does not contain many calories. FORMAL

di·eti·cian /ˌdaɪə'tɪʃən/ **dieticians;** also spelled N-COUNT
dietitian. A **dietician** is a person whose job is to
give people advice about the kind of food they
should eat. Dieticians often work in hospitals.

dif·fer /'dɪfə/ **differs, differing, differed. 1** If ◆◆◇◇◇
two or more things **differ**, they are unlike each oth- V-RECIP:
er in some way. *The story he told police differed* pl–n V
from the one he told his mother. **2** If people **differ** V from n
about something, they do not agree with each other V-RECIP:
about it. *The two leaders had differed on the issue of* pl–n V
sanctions. **3** ● **'I beg to differ'**: see **beg.** ● **agree to** Also V with n
differ: see **agree.**

dif·fer·ence /'dɪfrəns/ **differences. 1** The **differ-** ◆◆◆◆◇
ence between two things is the way in which they N-COUNT
are unlike each other. *...the vast difference in size...
I'm afraid the difference is that I expect so much of
her, but not of him.*
2 If people have their **differences** about something, N-COUNT
they disagree about it. *The two communities are
learning how to resolve their differences.* **3** If there is a PHRASE
difference of opinion between two or more people or
groups, they disagree about something.
4 A **difference** between two quantities is the amount N-SING
by which one quantity is less than the other. **5** If you PHRASE
split the difference with someone, you agree on an
amount or price which is halfway between two suggested amounts or prices.
6 If something **makes a difference** or **makes** a lot of PHRASE
difference, it affects you and helps in what you are
doing. If something **makes no difference**, it does
not have any effect on what you are doing. *Where you
live can make such a difference to the way you feel.*
7 If you describe a job or holiday, for example, as a job PHRASE

with a difference or a holiday **with a difference**, you INFORMAL
mean that the job or holiday is very interesting and
unusual.

dif·fer·ent /'dɪfrənt/. **1** If two people or things are ◆◆◆◆◆
different, they are not like each other in one or ADJ-GRADED
more ways. *If he'd attended music school, how
might things have been different?... We have totally
different views.* ► In British English, people some- ADJ-GRADED:
times say that one thing is **different to** another. v-link ADJ to n
Some people consider this use to be incorrect. *My
approach is totally different to his.* ► People some- ADJ-GRADED:
times say that one thing is **different than** another. v-link ADJ
This use is often considered incorrect in British than n/cl
English, but it is acceptable in American English. *...a
style of advertising that's different than the rest of the
country.* ♦ **dif·fer·ent·ly** *Every individual learns* ADV-GRADED
differently. ...differently shaped bones. **2** You use ADJ: ADJ n
different to indicate that you are talking about two
or more separate and distinct things of the same
kind. *The number of calories in different brands of
drinks varies enormously.* **3** You can describe some- ADJ-GRADED:
thing as **different** when it is unusual and not like v-link ADJ
others of the same kind. *The result is interesting and
different.*

dif·fer·en·tial /ˌdɪfə'renʃəl/ **differentials. 1** A **dif-** ◆◇◇◇◇
ferential is a difference between two values in a N-COUNT
scale. *Germany and France pledged to maintain the* TECHNICAL
differential between their two currencies. **2** A **differ-** N-COUNT
ential is a difference between rates of pay for differ- BRITISH
ent types of work, especially work done by people in
the same industry or company. *...industrial wage
differentials.* **3** Differential means relating to or ADJ: ADJ n
using a difference between groups or things. *...dif-* FORMAL
ferential voting rights.

dif·fer·en·ti·ate /ˌdɪfə'renʃieɪt/ **differentiates,** ◆◆◇◇◇
differentiating, differentiated. 1 If you **differ-** VERB
entiate between things or you **differentiate** one V between pl–
thing from another, you recognize or show the dif- n
ference between them. *A child may not differentiate* Also V n from
between his imagination and the real world. **2** A VERB
quality or feature that **differentiates** one thing from V n from n
another makes the two things different. *...distinctive
policies that differentiate them from the other parties.* ♦ **dif·fer·en·tia·tion** /ˌdɪfərenʃi'eɪʃən/. N-UNCOUNT

dif·fi·cult /'dɪfɪkəlt/. **1** Something that is **difficult** ◆◆◆◆◇
is not easy to do, understand, or deal with. *Hobart* ADJ-GRADED
*found it difficult to get her first book published...
We're living in difficult times.* **2** Someone who is **dif-** ADJ-GRADED
ficult behaves in an unreasonable and unhelpful
way. *I had a feeling you were going to be difficult
about this.*

dif·fi·cul·ty /'dɪfɪkəlti/ **difficulties. 1** A **difficulty** ◆◆◆◇◇
is a problem. *The country is facing great economic* N-COUNT
difficulties. **2** If you have **difficulty** doing some- N-UNCOUNT
thing, you are not able to do it easily. *Do you have
difficulty getting up?* **3** If you are **in difficulty** or **in** PHRASE
difficulties, you are having a lot of problems. *Rumours spread about banks being in difficulty.*

dif·fi·dent /'dɪfɪdənt/. Someone who is **diffident** is ◆◇◇◇◇
rather shy and does not enjoy talking about them- ADJ-GRADED
selves or being noticed by other people. *Helen was
diffident and reserved.* ♦ **dif·fi·dence** /'dɪfɪdəns/ *He* N-UNCOUNT
*tapped on the door, opened it and entered with a
certain diffidence.* ♦ **dif·fi·dent·ly** *'Would you,' he* ADV-GRADED:
asked diffidently, 'like to talk to me about it?' ADV with v

dif·fuse, diffuses, diffusing, diffused. The ◆◇◇◇◇
verb is pronounced /dɪ'fjuːz/. The adjective is pronounced /dɪ'fjuːs/. **1** If something such as knowl- V-ERG:
edge or information **is diffused**, or if it **diffuses** be V-ed
somewhere, it is made known or becomes available V n
over a wide area or to a lot of people. *...to diffuse* V prep
*new ideas obtained from elsewhere. ...the ideas of
agriculture that diffused across Europe.* ♦ **dif·fu-**
·sion /dɪ'fjuːʒən/ *...the development and diffusion of* N-UNCOUNT:
ideas. with supp
2 To **diffuse** a feeling, especially an undesirable one, VERB
means to cause it to weaken and lose its power to af- V n
fect people. *The arrival of letters from the Pope did
nothing to diffuse the tension.*
3 When something **diffuses** light, it causes the light to VERB

spread faintly and in a lot of directions. *Diffusing a* V n TECHNICAL
light also reduces its power.

4 To **diffuse** or be **diffused** through something means V-ERG
to move and spread through it. *It allows nicotine to* V prep
diffuse slowly and steadily into the bloodstream... The V n prep
moisture present in all foods absorbs the flavour of the Also V,
smoke and eventually diffuses that flavour into its in- V n
terior. ♦ **diffusion** *...rates of diffusion of molecules.* N-UNCOUNT

5 Something that is **diffuse** is not directed towards ADJ-GRADED
one place or concentrated in one place but spread out
over a large area. *A cold, diffuse light filtered in*
through the skylight.

6 If you describe something as **diffuse**, you mean that ADJ-GRADED
it is vague and difficult to understand or explain. *His*
writing is so diffuse, obscure, and overwrought.

dig /dɪg/ **digs, digging, dug. 1** When people or ♦♦♦◊◊
animals **dig**, they make a hole in the ground or in a VERB: V
pile of earth, stones, or debris. *Dig a largish hole* V n
and bang the stake in first... Rescue workers were dig- V through n
ging through the rubble. Also V for n

2 If you **dig** into something such as a deep container, VERB
you put your hand in it to search for something. *He* V into/in n
dug into his coat pocket for his keys. **3** If you **dig** one V-ERG
thing into another or if one thing **digs** into another, V n into n
the first thing is pushed hard into the second, or V into n
presses hard into it. *He could feel the beads digging*
into his palm.

4 If you **dig into** a subject or a store of information, VERB
you study it very carefully in order to discover or V into n
check facts. *He has been digging into the archives.* **5** If PHRASE
you **dig deep**, you do a very thorough investigation
into something.

6 If you say that you **dig** something, you mean that VERB
you like it and understand it. *'They play classic* V n
rock'n'roll,' states her boyfriend. *'My dad digs them* DATED,
too.' INFORMAL

7 A **dig** is an organized activity in which people dig N-COUNT
into the ground in order to discover ancient historical INFORMAL
objects.

8 If you have a **dig** at someone or something, you say N-COUNT
something which is intended to make fun of them or INFORMAL
upset them.

9 If you give someone a **dig** in a part of their body, you N-COUNT
poke them with your finger or your elbow, usually as a
warning or as a joke, or to remind them about a secret
that you both know.

10 If you live in **digs**, you live in a room in someone N-PLURAL
else's house and pay them rent. BRITISH,
INFORMAL

11 If someone **digs into** their **pocket** or **digs into** their PHRASE
purse, they manage after some difficulty to find the
money to pay for something.

12 • to **dig one's heels in**: see **heel**.

dig around. 1 If you **dig around** in a place or con- PHRASAL VB
tainer, you search for something in every part of it. *I* V P in n
went home to dig around in my closets for some old Also V P
tapes. **2** If you **dig around**, you try to find information V P
about someone or something. *They said, after digging*
around, the photo was a phoney.

dig in. 1 If you **dig** a substance **in**, or **dig** it **into** the PHRASAL VB
soil, you mix it into the soil by digging. *I usually dig in* V P noun
a small barrow load of compost in late summer. Also V n P

2 When soldiers **dig in** or **dig** themselves **in**, they dig V pron-refl P
trenches and prepare themselves for an attack by the Also V P
enemy. *The enemy must be digging themselves in now.* V P

3 If you say that someone **is digging in**, you mean that
they are not changing their mind or weakening their
efforts, although they are losing a contest or facing
difficult problems. **4** If someone **digs in**, or **digs into** V P n
some food, they start eating eagerly. If you tell some- Also V P
one to **dig in**, you are inviting them to start eating. INFORMAL
'Listen,' said Daisy, digging into her oatmeal.

dig out. 1 If you **dig** someone or something **out** of a PHRASAL VB
place, you get them out by digging or by forcing them V P of n
from the things surrounding them. *...trying to dig out* V P noun
a trombone from under four saxophones. **2** If you **dig** Also V n P
something **out**, you find it after it has been stored,
hidden, or forgotten for a long time. *Recently, I dug*
out Barstow's novel and read it again.

dig over. If you **dig over** an area of soil, you dig it PHRASAL VB

thoroughly, so that the soil becomes looser and free V P noun
from lumps. *Dig over any ground that is clear of crops.*

dig up. 1 If you **dig up** something, you remove it PHRASAL VB
from the ground where it has been buried or planted. V P noun
You would have to dig up the plant yourself. **2** If you Also V n P
dig up an area of land, you dig holes in it. *Yesterday* V P noun
they continued the search, digging up the back yard of Also V n P
a police station. **3** If you **dig up** information or facts, V P noun
you discover something that has not previously been Also V n P
widely known. *Managers are too expensive and im-*
portant to spend time digging up market information.

di·gest, digests, digesting, digested. The verb ♦♦◊◊◊
is pronounced /daɪˈdʒest/. The noun is pronounced
/ˈdaɪdʒest/. **1** When food **digests** or when you **di-** V-ERG: V
gest it, it passes through your body to your stom- V n
ach. Your stomach removes the substances that
your body needs and gets rid of the rest. *She*
couldn't digest food properly.

2 If you **digest** information, you think about it careful- VERB
ly so that you understand it. *She read everything, di-* V n
gesting every fragment of news. **3** If you **digest** some VERB
unpleasant news, you think about it until you are able V n
to accept it and know how to deal with it. *All this has*
upset me. I need time to digest it all.

4 A **digest** is a collection of pieces of writing. They are N-COUNT
published in a shorter form than they were originally
published. *...the Middle East Economic Digest.*

di·gest·ible /daɪˈdʒestɪbəl/. **1** Digestible food is ADJ-GRADED
food that is easy to digest. *Bananas are easily digest-*
ible and make a satisfying and filling snack. **2** If a ADJ-GRADED
theory or idea is **digestible**, it is very easy to understand. *...the hope of making economic theory more*
digestible.

di·ges·tion /daɪˈdʒestʃən/ **digestions. 1** Diges- ♦◊◊◊◊
tion is the process of digesting food. *...the digestion* N-UNCOUNT
of fats. **2** Your **digestion** is the system in your body N-COUNT
which digests your food.

di·ges·tive /daɪˈdʒestɪv/ **digestives. 1** You can ♦◊◊◊◊
describe things that are related to the digestion of ADJ: ADJ n
food as **digestive**. *...digestive disorders.* **2** In Britain, N-COUNT
a **digestive** or a **digestive biscuit** is a type of biscuit
that is made with wholemeal flour. **Digestive** is a
trademark.

di'gestive system, digestive systems. Your N-COUNT
digestive system is the set of organs in your body
that digest the food you eat.

dig·ger /ˈdɪgə/ **diggers.** A **digger** is a machine that ♦◊◊◊◊
is used for digging. *...a mechanical digger.* N-COUNT

dig·it /ˈdɪdʒɪt/ **digits. 1** A **digit** is a written symbol ♦◊◊◊◊
for any of the ten numbers from 0 to 9. *Her tele-* N-COUNT
phone number differs from mine by one digit. **2** A N-COUNT
digit is a finger, thumb, or toe. *Many animals have* FORMAL
five digits.

digi·tal /ˈdɪdʒɪtəl/. **1** Digital systems record or ♦♦◊◊◊
transmit information in the form of thousands of ADJ
very small signals. Compare **analogue**. *...the new*
digital technology. ♦ **digi·tal·ly** *...digitally recorded* ADV
sound. **2** Digital devices such as watches or clocks ADJ: ADJ n
give information by displaying numbers rather than
by having a pointer which moves round a dial.
Compare **analogue**.

digital 'audio tape. Digital audio tape is a type N-UNCOUNT
of magnetic tape used to make very high quality recordings of sound by recording it in digital form.

digital rec'ording, digital recordings. 1 Digi- N-UNCOUNT
tal **recording** is the process of converting sound or
images into numbers. **2** A **digital recording** is a rec- N-COUNT
ording made by converting sound or images into
numbers.

dig·it·ize /ˈdɪdʒɪtaɪz/ **digitizes, digitizing, digit-** VERB: V n
ized; also spelled **digitise** in British English. To **dig-**
itize information means to turn it into a form that
can be read easily by a computer.

dig·ni·fied /ˈdɪgnɪfaɪd/. If you say that someone or ♦◊◊◊◊
something is **dignified**, you mean they are calmly ADJ-GRADED
impressive and worthy of respect. *He seemed a very*
dignified and charming man.

dig·ni·fy /ˈdɪgnɪfaɪ/ **dignifies, dignifying, digni-**
fied. 1 To **dignify** something means to make it im- VERB
pressive. *It is the function of tragic literature to dig-* V n
LITERARY

nify sorrow and disaster. **2** If you say that a particular reaction or description **dignifies** something you have a low opinion of, you mean that it makes it appear acceptable. *We see no point in dignifying this kind of speculation with a comment.* **VERB / PRAGMATICS / V n**

dig·ni·tary /'dɪgnɪtri, AM -teri/ **dignitaries. Dignitaries** are people who are considered to be important because they have a high rank in government or in the Church. ◆◇◇◇◇ **N-COUNT**

dig·nity /'dɪgnɪti/. **1** If someone behaves or moves with **dignity**, they are calm, controlled, and admirable. *...her extraordinary dignity and composure.* **2** If you talk about the **dignity** of people or their lives or activities, you mean that they are worthy of respect. *...the integrity and the dignity of our lives and feelings.* **3** Your **dignity** is your sense of your own importance and value, and other people's respect for you. *If you were wrong, admit it. You won't lose dignity, but will gain respect.* ◆◆◇◇◇ **N-UNCOUNT** **N-UNCOUNT** **N-UNCOUNT**

di·gress /daɪ'gres/ **digresses, digressing, digressed.** If you **digress**, you move away from the subject you are talking or writing about and talk or write about something different for a while. *She digressed from her prepared speech to pay tribute to the President.* ◆ **di·gres·sion** /daɪ'greʃən/ **digressions** *The text is dotted with digressions.* **VERB: V / V from n** **N-VAR**

dike /daɪk/. See **dyke**.

dik·tat /'dɪktæt, AM dɪk'tɑːt/ **diktats.** You use **diktat** to refer to something such as a law or government which is imposed upon people without their consent; used showing disapproval. **N-VAR / PRAGMATICS**

di·lapi·dat·ed /dɪ'læpɪdeɪtɪd/. A building that is **dilapidated** is old and in a generally bad condition. ◆◇◇◇◇ **ADJ-GRADED**

di·late /daɪ'leɪt/ **dilates, dilating, dilated.** When things such as blood vessels or the pupils of your eyes **dilate** or when something **dilates** them, they become wider or bigger. *Exercise dilates blood vessels.* ◆ **di·lat·ed** *His eyes seemed slightly dilated.* ◆◇◇◇◇ **V-ERG: V / V n** **ADJ-GRADED**

dil·do /'dɪldəʊ/. **dildos.** A dildo is an object which is used as a substitute for an erect penis. **N-COUNT**

di·lem·ma /daɪ'lemə, AM dɪl-/ **dilemmas.** A **dilemma** is a difficult situation in which you have to choose between two or more alternatives. *...the dilemma of whether or not to return to his country.* ◆◆◇◇◇ **N-COUNT**

dil·et·tan·te /ˌdɪlə'tænti, AM -'tɑːnt/ **dilettante** or **dilettanti.** A **dilettante** is someone who seems interested in a subject, especially in art, but who does not really know very much about it; used showing disapproval. **N-COUNT / PRAGMATICS / FORMAL**

dili·gent /'dɪlɪdʒənt/. Someone who is **diligent** works hard in a careful and conscientious way. *Meyers is a diligent and prolific worker.* ◆ **dili·gence** /'dɪlɪdʒəns/ *The police are pursuing their inquiries with great diligence.* ◆ **dili·gent·ly** *...working diligently to resolve their differences.* ◆◇◇◇◇ **ADJ-GRADED** **N-UNCOUNT** **ADV-GRADED: ADV with v**

dill /dɪl/. **Dill** is a herb with yellow flowers and a strong sweet smell. ◆◇◇◇◇ **N-UNCOUNT**

di·lute /daɪ'luːt/ **dilutes, diluting, diluted. 1** If a liquid **is diluted** or **dilutes**, it is added to or mixes with water or another liquid, and becomes weaker. *Dilute it well with cooled, boiled water... The poisons seeping from Hanford's contaminated land quickly dilute in the water.* ◆ **di·lu·tion** *...sewage dilution.* **2** A **dilute** liquid is very thin and weak, usually because it has had water added to it. **3** If someone or something **dilutes** a belief, quality, or value, they make it weaker and less effective. *Serious attention is being given to diluting the value of personal tax allowances.* ◆ **dilution** *...a potentially devastating dilution of earnings per share.* ◆◇◇◇◇ **V-ERG / V n prep / V / Also V n** **N-UNCOUNT / ADJ-GRADED** **VERB: V n** **N-UNCOUNT**

di·lu·tion /daɪ'luːʃən/ **dilutions.** A **dilution** is a liquid that has been diluted with water or another liquid, so that it becomes weaker. **N-COUNT**

dim /dɪm/ **dimmer, dimmest; dims, dimming, dimmed. 1 Dim** light is not bright. *Below decks, the lights were dim.* ◆ **dim·ly** *He followed her into a dimly lit kitchen.* ◆ **dim·ness** *...the dimness of an early September evening.* **2** If you **dim** a light or if it **dims**, it becomes less bright. *Dim the lighting – it is unpleasant to lie with a bright light shining in your* ◆◆◇◇◇ **ADJ-GRADED** **ADV-GRADED** **N-UNCOUNT** **V-ERG / V n / Also V**

eyes. **3** A **dim** place is rather dark because there is not much light in it. *The room was dim and cool.* ◆ **dimness** *...squinting to adjust my eyes to the dimness.* **4** A **dim** figure or object is not very easy to see, either because it is in shadow or darkness, or because it is far away. *Pete's torch picked out the dim figures of Bob and Chang.* ◆ **dimly** *The shoreline could be dimly seen.* **ADJ-GRADED** **N-UNCOUNT** **ADJ-GRADED** **ADV-GRADED**

5 If you have a **dim** memory or awareness of something, it is difficult to remember or unclear in your mind. *It seems that the '60s era of social activism is all but a dim memory.* ◆ **dim·ly** *I was dimly aware that dozens of curious people were looking at us.* **6** If your memories **dim** or if something **dims** them, they become less clear in your mind. *Their memory of what happened has dimmed.* **7** If the prospects for something are **dim**, you have no reason to feel hopeful or optimistic about them. *The prospects for a peaceful solution are dim.* **8** If your prospects, hopes, or emotions **dim** or if something **dims** them, they become less good or less strong. *Forty eight years of marriage have not dimmed the passion between Bill and Helen.* **9** If your eyes **dim** or **are dimmed** by something, they become weaker or unable to see clearly. *Her eyes dimmed with sorrow.* **10** If you describe someone as **dim**, you think that they are stupid. **11** ● **take a dim view**: see **view**. **ADJ-GRADED** **ADV-GRADED** **V-ERG / Also V n** **ADJ-GRADED** **V-ERG / Also V** **V-ERG / V** **ADJ-GRADED / INFORMAL**

dime /daɪm/ **dimes.** A **dime** is an American coin worth ten cents. ◆◇◇◇◇

di·men·sion /daɪ'menʃən, dɪm-/ **dimensions. 1** A particular **dimension** of something is a particular aspect of it. *There is a political dimension to the accusations.* **2** If you talk about the **dimensions** of a situation or problem, you are talking about its extent and size. *He considers the dimensions of the problem.* **3** A **dimension** is a measurement such as length, width, or height. If you talk about the **dimensions** of an object or place, you are referring to its size and proportions. *Drilling will continue on the site to assess the dimensions of the new oilfield.* **4** In mathematics and science, **dimension** is used in describing spatial concepts such as points, lines, and solids. **5** See also **fourth dimension**. ◆◆◇◇◇ **N-COUNT** **N-PLURAL** **N-COUNT** **N-COUNT**

di·men·sion·al /daɪ'menʃənəl, AM dɪm-/. See **two-dimensional, three-dimensional.**

di·min·ish /dɪ'mɪnɪʃ/ **diminishes, diminishing, diminished. 1** When something **diminishes**, it reduces in size, importance, or intensity. *Federalism is intended to diminish the power of the central state. ...diminishing resources.* **2** If you **diminish** someone or something, you talk about them or treat them in a way that makes them appear less important than they really are. ◆◆◇◇◇ **V-ERG: V / V n / V-ing** **VERB: V n**

dimi·nu·tion /ˌdɪmɪ'njuːʃən, AM -'nuː-/. A **diminution** of something is a reduction in its size, importance, or intensity. **N-UNCOUNT / FORMAL**

di·minu·tive /dɪ'mɪnjʊtɪv/ **diminutives. 1** A **diminutive** person or object is very small indeed. **2** A **diminutive** is an informal form of a name. For example, 'Jim' and 'Jimmy' are diminutives of 'James'. **3** A **diminutive** is a suffix which is added to a word to show affection or to indicate that something is small. For example, '-ie' and '-ette' are diminutives, as in 'doggie' and 'statuette'. ◆◇◇◇◇ **ADJ-GRADED** **N-COUNT** **N-COUNT**

dim·mer /'dɪmə/ **dimmers.** A **dimmer** or a **dimmer switch** is a switch that allows you to gradually change the brightness of an electric light. **N-COUNT**

dim·ple /'dɪmpəl/ **dimples.** A **dimple** is a small hollow in someone's cheek or chin, often one that you can see when they smile. ◆ **dim·pled** /'dɪmpəld/. *...a dimpled chin.* **N-COUNT** **ADJ**

dim-'witted. If you describe someone as **dim-witted**, you are saying in quite an unkind way that you do not think they are very clever. **ADJ-GRADED / INFORMAL**

din /dɪn/. A **din** is a very loud and unpleasant noise that lasts for some time. *They tried to make themselves heard over the din of the crowd.* ◆◇◇◇◇ **N-SING**

dine /daɪn/ **dines, dining, dined.** When you **dine**, you have dinner. *That night the two men dined at Wilson's club.* ◆◆◇◇◇ VERB: V V adv/prep

dine on. If you **dine on** a particular sort of food, you have it for dinner. PHRASAL VB V P n

dine out. If you **dine out**, you have dinner away from your home, usually at a restaurant. PHRASAL VB V P

din·er /'daɪnə/ **diners. 1** In American English, a **diner** is a small cheap restaurant that is open all day. **2** The people who are having dinner in a restaurant can be referred to as **diners**. ◆◇◇◇◇ N-COUNT N-COUNT

din·ghy /'dɪŋgi/ **dinghies.** A **dinghy** is a small open boat that you sail or row. ◆◇◇◇◇ N-COUNT

din·go /'dɪŋgəʊ/ **dingoes.** A **dingo** is an Australian wild dog. N-COUNT

din·gy /'dɪndʒi/ **dingier, dingiest.** A **dingy** building or place is rather dark and depressing. ADJ-GRADED

'dining car, dining cars. A **dining car** is a carriage on a train where passengers can have a meal. N-COUNT

'dining room, dining rooms; also spelled **dining-room.** The **dining room** is the room in a house where people have their meals, or a room in a hotel where meals are served. ◆◆◇◇◇ N-COUNT

'dining table, dining tables. A **dining table** is a table that is used for having meals on. ◆◇◇◇◇ N-COUNT

dinky /'dɪŋki/. If you describe something as **dinky**, you mean that it is small and appealing. ADJ-GRADED BRITISH, INFORMAL

din·ner /'dɪnə/ **dinners. 1 Dinner** is the main meal of the day, usually served in the evening. *She invited us to her house for dinner... Would you like to stay and have dinner?* ● See also **TV dinner. 2** Any meal you eat in the middle of the day can be referred to as **dinner. 3** A **dinner** is a formal social event in the evening at which a meal is served. ◆◆◆◇ N-VAR N-VAR BRITISH N-COUNT

'dinner dance, dinner dances. A **dinner dance** is a social event where a large number of people come to have dinner and to dance. N-COUNT BRITISH

'dinner jacket, dinner jackets. A **dinner jacket** is a jacket, usually black, worn by men for formal social events. The usual American word is **tuxedo.** N-COUNT

'dinner party, dinner parties. A **dinner party** is a social event where a small group of people are invited to have dinner and spend the evening at someone's house. ◆◇◇◇◇ N-COUNT

'dinner service, dinner services. A **dinner service** is a set of plates and dishes from which meals are eaten and served. It may also include cups and saucers. N-COUNT

'dinner table, dinner tables. You refer to a table as the **dinner table** when it is being used for dinner. *Sam was left at the dinner table with Peg.* ◆◇◇◇◇ N-COUNT BRITISH

din·ner·time /'dɪnətaɪm/; also spelled **dinner time.** **Dinnertime** is the period of the day when most people have their dinner. N-UNCOUNT

di·no·saur /'daɪnəsɔː/ **dinosaurs. Dinosaurs** were large reptiles which lived in prehistoric times. ◆◆◇◇◇ N-COUNT

dint /dɪnt/. If you achieve a result **by dint of** something, you achieve it by means of that thing. *He succeeds by dint of sheer hard work.* PHR-PREP WRITTEN

dio·cese /'daɪəsɪs/ **dioceses.** A **diocese** is the area over which a bishop has control. ♦ **di·oc·esan** /daɪˈɒsɪsən/. *...diocesan funds.* ◆◇◇◇◇ N-COUNT ADJ

di·ox·ide /daɪˈɒksaɪd/. See **carbon dioxide.**

di·ox·in /daɪˈɒksɪn/ **dioxins. Dioxins** are poisonous chemicals which are a by-product of the manufacture of some weedkillers and disinfectants. N-VAR

dip /dɪp/ **dips, dipping, dipped. 1** If you **dip** something into a liquid, you put it into the liquid for a short time, so that only part of it is covered, and take it out again. *They dip the food into the sauce.* ► Also a noun. *...one dip into the bottle.* ◆◆◇◇◇ VERB V n into/in n N-COUNT

2 A **dip** is a thick sauce into which you dip pieces of raw vegetable or biscuits and then eat them. N-VAR

3 If you **dip** your hand into a container, you put your hand into it in order to take something out of it. *Snoot dipped into a pouch of tobacco.* VERB: V n into n V into n

4 If something **dips**, it makes a downward movement, usually quite quickly. *The sun dipped below the horizon.* ► Also a noun. *...a dip of the head.* **5** If an area of land, a road, or a path **dips**, it goes down to a lower VERB: V V prep N-COUNT VERB: V

level. *...a path which suddenly dips down into a tunnel.* ► Also a noun. *...the road makes a dip.* V adv/prep N-COUNT

6 When farmers **dip** sheep or other farm animals, they put them into a container of liquid with chemicals in it, in order to kill insects which live on the animals' bodies. ♦ **dip·ping** *...sheep dipping.* **7 Dip** is a liquid with chemicals in it which animals or objects can be dipped in to disinfect or clean them. *...sheep dip.* VERB: V n N-UNCOUNT N-UNCOUNT

8 If the amount or level of something **dips**, it becomes smaller or lower, usually only for a short period of time. *Unemployment dipped to 6.9 per cent last month.* ► Also a noun. *...the current dip in farm spending.* VERB: V V prep/adv N-COUNT

9 If you have or take a **dip**, you go for a quick swim in the sea, a river, or a swimming pool. N-COUNT

10 If you are driving a car and **dip** your headlights, you operate a switch that makes them shine downwards, so that they do not shine directly into the eyes of other drivers. VERB: V n BRITISH

11 If you **dip into** a book, you have a brief look at it without reading or studying it closely or seriously. VERB: V into n

12 If you **dip into** your savings, you use some of the money that you had intended to save. VERB: V into n

Dip. Dip. is a written abbreviation for **diploma.**

diph·theria /dɪfˈθɪəriə, dɪp-/. **Diphtheria** is a dangerous infectious disease which causes fever and difficulty in breathing and swallowing. N-UNCOUNT

diph·thong /'dɪfθɒŋ, 'dɪp-/ **diphthongs.** A **diphthong** is a vowel in which the speaker's tongue changes position while it is being pronounced, so that the vowel sounds like a combination of two other vowels. The vowel sound in 'tail' is a diphthong. N-COUNT

di·plo·ma /dɪˈpləʊmə/ **diplomas.** A **diploma** is a qualification which a student may be awarded by a university or college. *...a diploma in social work.* ◆◇◇◇◇ N-COUNT

di·plo·ma·cy /dɪˈpləʊməsi/. **1 Diplomacy** is the activity or profession of managing relations between the governments of different countries. *Today's Security Council resolution will be a significant success for American diplomacy.* ● See also **shuttle diplomacy. 2 Diplomacy** is the skill of being tactful and saying or doing things without offending people. ◆◆◇◇◇ N-UNCOUNT N-UNCOUNT

dip·lo·mat /'dɪpləmæt/ **diplomats.** A **diplomat** is a senior official who negotiates with another country on behalf of his or her own country, usually working as a member of an embassy. ◆◆◆◇◇ N-COUNT

dip·lo·mat·ic /ˌdɪpləˈmætɪk/. **1 Diplomatic** means relating to diplomacy and diplomats. *...before the two countries resume full diplomatic relations.* ♦ **dip·lo·mati·cal·ly** /ˌdɪpləˈmætɪkli/ *The conflict can be resolved diplomatically.* **2** Someone who is **diplomatic** is able to be tactful and say or do things without offending people. ♦ **diplomatically.** ◆◆◇◇◇ ADJ ADV ADJ-GRADED ADV-GRADED

'diplomatic corps; diplomatic corps is both the singular and the plural form. The **diplomatic corps** is the group of all the diplomats who work in one city or country. N-COLL-COUNT

diplomatic im'munity. Diplomatic immunity is the freedom from legal action and from paying taxes that a diplomat has in the country in which he or she is working. N-UNCOUNT

'diplomatic service. The diplomatic service is the government department that employs diplomats to work in foreign countries. N-PROPER: the N

dip·py /'dɪpi/. If you describe someone as **dippy**, you mean that they are slightly odd, but in a way that you find likeable. ADJ-GRADED INFORMAL

dip·stick /'dɪpstɪk/ **dipsticks.** A **dipstick** is a metal rod which is used to measure the amount of liquid in a container, especially the amount of oil in a car engine. N-COUNT

dire /daɪə/. **1 Dire** is used to emphasize how serious or terrible a situation or event is. *He was in dire need of hospital treatment. ...dire poverty.* **2** If you describe something as **dire**, you are emphasizing that it is of very low quality. ◆◇◇◇◇ ADJ-GRADED PRAGMATICS ADJ-GRADED PRAGMATICS

di·rect /daɪˈrekt, dɪ-/ **directs, directing, directed. 1 Direct** means moving towards a place or ob- ◆◆◆◆◇ ADJ-GRADED

ject, without changing direction and without stopping, for example in a journey. *They'd come on a direct flight from the Soviet Union.* ▶ Also an adverb. *You can fly direct to Amsterdam from most British airports.* ♦ **di·rect·ly** *The jumbo jet is due to fly the hostages directly back to London.* **2** If something is in **direct** heat or light, there is nothing between it and the source of heat or light. **3** You use **direct** to describe an experience, activity, or system which only involves the people, actions, or things that are necessary to make it happen. *He seemed to be in direct contact with the Boss.* ▶ Also an adverb. *I can deal direct with your Inspector Kimble.* ♦ **directly** *We cannot measure pain directly. It can only be estimated.* **4** You use **direct** to emphasize the closeness of a connection between two things. *The unfortunate lady had died as a direct result of his injection.* **5** If you describe a person or their behaviour as **direct**, you mean that they are honest and say exactly what they mean. *He avoided giving a direct answer.* ♦ **directly** *Explain simply and directly what you hope to achieve.* ♦ **di·rect·ness** *'I like Rupert enormously,' she said, with a directness which made Pat flush.* **6** If you **direct** something at a particular thing, you aim or point it at that thing. *I reached the cockpit and directed the extinguisher at the fire.* **7** If your attention, emotions, or actions **are directed** at a particular person or thing, you are focusing them on that person or thing. *Do not be surprised if, initially, she directs her anger at you.* **8** If a remark or look **is directed** at you, it concerns you or is addressed to you. *The question was directed towards her.* **9** If you **direct** someone somewhere, you tell them how to get there. *Could you direct them to Dr Lamont's office, please.* **10** When someone **directs** a project or a group of people, they are responsible for organizing the people and activities that are involved. ♦ **di·rec·tion** /daɪ'rekʃən, dɪr-/ *The house was built under the direction of John's partner.* ♦ **di·rec·tor, directors.** *...the director of the intensive care unit at Guy's Hospital.* **11** When someone **directs** a film, play, or television programme, they are responsible for the way in which it is performed and for telling the actors and assistants what to do. *...Miss Birkin's long-held ambition to direct as well as act.* ♦ **di·rec·tion** *...the difference between theatre and film direction.* ♦ **di·rec·tor** *...the film director Franco Zeffirelli.* ♦ **di·rec·to·rial** /daɪrek'tɔ:riəl, dɪr-/. *...his directorial career.* **12** If you **are directed** to do something, someone in authority tells you to do it. *They have been directed to give special attention to the problem of poverty.* **13** If you are a **direct** descendant of someone, you are related to them through your parents and their parents and so on. **14** See also **direction, directly.**

di,rect 'action. Direct action involves doing N-UNCOUNT something such as going on strike or demonstrating in order to put pressure on an employer or government to do what you want.

di,rect 'current, direct currents. A direct cur- N-VAR rent is an electric current that always flows in the same direction. The abbreviation 'DC' is also used.

,direct 'debit, direct debits. If you pay your bills N-VAR to a company by direct debit, you arrange for the bills to be paid directly by your bank, rather than writing a cheque for them each time yourself.

di,rect 'hit, direct hits. If a place suffers a direct N-COUNT hit, a bomb, bullet, or other missile that has been aimed at it lands exactly in that place, rather than some distance away.

di·rec·tion /daɪ'rekʃən/ directions. 1 A direction ◆◆◆◆◇ is the general line that someone or something is N-VAR moving or pointing in. *St Andrews was ten miles in the opposite direction... Civilians were fleeing in all directions.* 2 A direction is the general way in which N-VAR something develops or progresses. *They threatened to lead a mass walk-out if the party did not sharply change direction.* 3 Directions are instructions that N-PLURAL: tell you what to do, how to do something, or how to with supp

get somewhere. *He proceeded to give Dan directions to the computer room.* **4** See also **direct**.

di·rec·tion·al /daɪ'rekʃənəl, dɪr-/. **1** If something ADJ-GRADED such as a radio aerial, microphone, or loudspeaker TECHNICAL is **directional**, it works most effectively in one direction, rather than equally in all directions. **2** Direc- ADJ tional means relating to the direction in which TECHNICAL something is pointing or going.

di·rec·tion·less /daɪ'rekʃənləs, dɪr-/. If you de- ADJ-GRADED scribe an activity or an organization as directionless, you mean that it does not seem to have any point or purpose. If you describe a person as directionless, you mean that they do not seem to have any plans or ideas.

di·rec·tive /daɪ'rektɪv, dɪr-/ directives. A direc- ◆◆◇◇◇ tive is an official instruction that is given by some- N-COUNT one in authority. *...a new EC directive.*

di·rect·ly /daɪ'rektli, dɪr-/. **1** If something is direct- ◆◇◇◇◇ ly above something, below something, or in front of ADV: something, it is in exactly that position. *There, di- ADV prep/adv rectly below me, was a guy... The naked bulb was directly over his head.* **2** If you do one action directly ADV: after another, you do the second action as soon as ADV prep/adv the first one is finished. *Directly after lunch we were packed and ready to go.* **3** If something happens di- ADV: rectly, it happens without any delay. *She'll bring the ADV after v tea directly.* **4** See also direct.

di,rect 'mail; also spelled direct-mail. Direct mail N-UNCOUNT is a method of marketing which involves companies sending advertising material directly to people who they think may be interested in their products.

di,rect 'marketing. Direct marketing is the same N-UNCOUNT as direct mail.

di,rect 'object, direct objects. The direct object N-COUNT of a transitive verb is the noun group which is used to refer to someone or something directly affected by or involved in the action performed by the subject. For example, in 'I saw him yesterday', 'him' is the direct object. Compare indirect object.

di·rec·tor /daɪ'rektə, dɪr-/ directors. **1** The direc- ◆◆◆◆◇ tors of a company are its most senior managers, N-COUNT who meet regularly to make decisions about how it will be run. *...the board of directors.* **2** See also direct.

di·rec·to·rate /daɪ'rektərət, dɪr-/ directorates. ◆◇◇◇◇ **1** A directorate is a board of directors in a company N-COUNT or organization. **2** A directorate is a part of a gov- N-COUNT: ernment department which is responsible for one with supp particular thing. *...the Health and Safety Directorate of the EC.*

di,rector 'general, directors general; also ◆◆◇◇◇ spelled director-general. The director general of a N-COUNT large organization such as the BBC is the person who is in charge of it.

di·rec·tor·ship /daɪ'rektəʃɪp, dɪr-/ directorships. N-COUNT A directorship is the job or position of a company director.

di·rec·tory /daɪ'rektəri, dɪr-/ directories. A direc- ◆◆◇◇◇ tory is a book which gives lists of facts, for example N-COUNT people's names, addresses, and telephone numbers, or the names and addresses of business companies, usually arranged in alphabetical order.

di,rectory en'quiries. In Britain, directory en- N-UNCOUNT quiries is a service which you can telephone to find out someone's telephone number. The usual term in American English is information or directory assistance.

di,rect 'rule. Direct rule is a system in which a N-UNCOUNT central government takes charge of the affairs of a province which had previously had its own parliament or law-making organization.

'direct speech. In grammar, direct speech is N-UNCOUNT speech which is reported by using the exact words that the speaker used.

di,rect 'tax, direct taxes. A direct tax is a tax N-COUNT which a person or organization pays directly to the government, for example income tax.

di,rect tax'ation. Direct taxation is a system in N-UNCOUNT which a government raises money by direct taxes.

dirge /dɜːdʒ/ **dirges.** A **dirge** is a slow, sad song or N-COUNT piece of music. **Dirges** are sometimes performed at funerals.

dirt /dɜːt/. **1** If there is **dirt** on something, there is ◆◆◇◇◇ dust, mud, or a stain on it. *I started to scrub off the* N-UNCOUNT *dirt.* **2** You can refer to the earth on the ground as N-UNCOUNT **dirt**, especially when it is muddy or dusty. **3** A **dirt** ADJ: ADJ n road or track is made from earth, without any gravel or tarmac laid on it.
4 If you say that you have **dirt** on someone, you mean N-SING that you have information that could harm their repu- INFORMAL tation or career. *Both parties use computers to dig up dirt on their opponents.* **5** If you say that someone PHRASE **dishes the dirt** on someone else, you disapprove of PRAGMATICS them because they tell people things about that per- BRITISH, INFORMAL son without worrying if they will hurt that person's feelings. **6** If you say that someone **treats** you **like** PHRASE **dirt**, you are angry with them because you think that they treat you unfairly and with no respect.

,**dirt-'cheap.** If you say that something is **dirt-** ADJ **cheap**, you are emphasizing that it is very cheap PRAGMATICS indeed. INFORMAL

dirty /ˈdɜːti/ **dirtier, dirtiest; dirties, dirtying,** ◆◆◆◇◇ **dirtied. 1** If something is **dirty**, it is marked or cov- ADJ-GRADED ered with stains, spots, or mud, and needs to be cleaned. *...dirty fingernails.* **2** To **dirty** something VERB: V n means to cause it to become dirty.
3 If you describe an action as **dirty**, you disapprove of ADJ-GRADED it and consider it unfair, immoral, or dishonest. *The* PRAGMATICS *gunman had been hired by a rival Mafia family to do the dirty deed.* ▶ Also an adverb. *Jim Browne is the* ADV: *kind of fellow who can fight dirty.* ADV after v
4 If you describe something such as a joke, a book, or ADJ-GRADED someone's language as **dirty**, you mean that it refers PRAGMATICS to sex in a way that some people find offensive. *He laughed at their dirty jokes.* ▶ Also an adverb. *I'm of-* ADV: *ten asked whether the men talk dirty to me.* ADV after v
5 Dirty is sometimes used informally before words of ADJ: ADJ n criticism to emphasize that you do not approve of PRAGMATICS someone or something. *You dirty liar, don't try to be funny with me.*
6 If you say that someone **washes** their **dirty linen in** PHRASE **public**, you disapprove of them discussing or arguing PRAGMATICS about unpleasant or private things in front of other BRITISH people. The usual American expression is **wash** your **dirty laundry in public.**
7 If someone gives you a **dirty look**, they look at you in PHRASE a way which shows that they are angry with you. INFORMAL *Michael gave him a dirty look and walked out.*
8 Dirty old man is an expression some people use to PHRASE describe an older man who they think shows an un- PRAGMATICS natural interest in sex; used showing disapproval.
9 To **do** someone's **dirty work** means to do a task for PHRASE them that is dishonest or unpleasant and which they do not want to do themselves. *The army would send us out to do their dirty work for them.*
10 A **dirty weekend** is a weekend during which two PHRASE people go away together in order to have sex. INFORMAL
11 If you say that an expression is **a dirty word** in a PHRASE group of people, you mean it refers to an idea that they strongly dislike or disagree with. *Marketing became a dirty word at the company.*

,**dirty 'trick, dirty tricks.** You describe the ac- ◆◇◇◇◇ tions of an organization or political group as **dirty** N-COUNT **tricks** when you think they are using illegal meth- ods to harm the effectiveness of their rivals. *He claimed he was the victim of a dirty tricks campaign.*

dis- /dɪs-/. **Dis-** is added to some words that de- PREFIX scribe processes, qualities, or states, in order to form words describing the opposite processes, qual- ities, or states.

dis·abil·ity /ˌdɪsəˈbɪlɪti/ **disabilities. 1** A **disabil-** ◆◆◇◇◇ **ity** is a permanent injury, illness, or physical or N-COUNT mental condition that tends to restrict the way that someone can live their life. *...athletes who have overcome a physical disability to reach the top of their sport.* **2 Disability** is the state of being N-UNCOUNT disabled.

dis·able /dɪˈseɪbəl/ **disables, disabling, dis-** ◆◇◇◇◇ **abled. 1** If an injury or illness **disables** someone, it VERB

affects them so badly that it restricts the way that V n they can live their life. *She did all this tendon dam- age and it really disabled her.* ◆ **dis·abling** *...skin* ADJ-GRADED *ulcers which, although not life-threatening, are dis- figuring and sometimes disabling.* **2** If someone or VERB something **disables** a system or mechanism, they V n stop it working, usually temporarily. *...if you need to disable a car alarm.*

dis·abled /dɪˈseɪbəld/. Someone who is **disabled** ◆◆◇◇◇ has an illness, injury, or condition that tends to re- ADJ-GRADED strict the way that they can live their life, especially by making it difficult for them to move about. *...the practical problems encountered by disabled people.* ▶ People who are disabled are sometimes referred N-PLURAL: to as **the disabled.** the N

dis·able·ment /dɪˈseɪbəlmənt/. **Disablement** is the N-UNCOUNT state of being disabled or the experience of becom- FORMAL ing disabled. *...permanent total disablement result- ing in inability to work.*

dis·abuse /ˌdɪsəˈbjuːz/ **disabuses, disabusing,** VERB **disabused.** If you **disabuse** someone of some- V n of n thing, you tell them or persuade them that what Also V n they believe is in fact untrue. *Their view of country* FORMAL *people was that they like to please strangers. I did not disabuse them of this notion.*

dis·ad·van·tage /ˌdɪsədˈvɑːntɪdʒ, -ˈvæn-/ **disad-** ◆◆◇◇◇ **vantages. 1** A **disadvantage** is a factor which N-COUNT makes something or someone less useful or accept- able than other people or things, or less likely to be successful. *...the advantages and disadvantages of allowing their soldiers to marry.* **2** If you are **at a** PHRASE **disadvantage**, you have a problem or difficulty that many other people do not have, which makes it harder for you to be successful. *The children from poor families were at a distinct disadvantage.* **3** If PHRASE something is **to** your **disadvantage** or works **to** your **disadvantage**, it creates difficulties for you. *Depres- sion is the third thing that works to my patients' dis- advantage.*

dis·ad·van·taged /ˌdɪsədˈvɑːntɪdʒd, -ˈvæn-/. Peo- ◆◇◇◇◇ ple who are **disadvantaged** or live in **disadvantaged** ADJ-GRADED areas live in bad conditions and tend not to get a good education or have a reasonable standard of living. *...the educational problems of disadvantaged children. ...disadvantaged areas of Europe.* ▶ The N-PLURAL: **disadvantaged** are people who are disadvantaged. the N

dis·ad·van·ta·geous /ˌdɪˌsædvənˈteɪdʒəs/. Some- ADJ-GRADED thing that is **disadvantageous** to you puts you in a worse position than other people. *The Second World War started in the most disadvantageous possible way for the western powers.*

dis·af·fect·ed /ˌdɪsəˈfektɪd/. **Disaffected** people ◆◇◇◇◇ no longer fully support something such as an or- ADJ-GRADED ganization or political ideal which they previously supported. *...people disaffected with the government.*

dis·af·fec·tion /ˌdɪsəˈfekʃən/. **Disaffection** is the N-UNCOUNT attitude that people have when they stop support- ing something such as an organization or political ideal. *...the Cuban people's disaffection with their country.*

dis·agree /ˌdɪsəˈɡriː/ **disagrees, disagreeing,** ◆◆◇◇◇ **disagreed. 1** If you **disagree** with someone, you V-RECIP do not accept that what they say is true or correct. V with n You can also say that two people **disagree**. *You* V *must continue to see them no matter how much you* pl-n V prep *may disagree with them... They can communicate even when they strongly disagree... 'I think it is inap- propriate to put up a statue.''Well, I disagree.'...* The two men had disagreed about reincarnation. ● to **agree to disagree**: see **agree**. **2** If you **disagree** with VERB an action or proposal, you disapprove of it and be- V with n lieve that it is wrong. *I respect the president but I* BRITISH *disagree with his decision.* **3** If a food or drink dis- VERB **agrees** with you, it makes you feel unwell. *Orange* V with n *juice seems to disagree with some babies.* BRITISH, INFORMAL

dis·agree·able /ˌdɪsəˈɡriːəbəl/. **1** Something that is ADJ-GRADED **disagreeable** is rather unpleasant. *...a disagreeable odour. ...to make flying an altogether less disagree- able experience.* ◆ **dis·agree·ably** /ˌdɪsəˈɡriːəbli/ ADV *The taste is bitter and disagreeably pungent.*

2 Someone who is **disagreeable** is unfriendly or un- ADJ-GRADED
helpful. *He's a shallow, disagreeable man.*

dis·agree·ment /ˌdɪsəˈɡriːmənt/ **disagree-** ◆◆◇◇◇
ments. 1 Disagreement means objecting to some- N-UNCOUNT
thing such as a proposal. *Britain and France have
expressed some disagreement with the proposal.*
2 When there is **disagreement** about something, N-VAR
people disagree or argue about what should be
done. *A peace conference failed due to disagreement
on who should be allowed to attend... My instructor
and I had a brief disagreement.*

dis·al·low /ˌdɪsəˈlaʊ/ **disallows, disallowing,** ◆◇◇◇◇
disallowed. If something **is disallowed**, it is not VERB
allowed or accepted officially, because it has not be V-ed
been done correctly. *England scored again, but the Also V n
whistle had gone and the goal was disallowed.*

dis·ap·pear /ˌdɪsəˈpɪə/ **disappears, disappear-** ◆◆◆◇◇
ing, disappeared. 1 If you say that someone or VERB: V
something **disappears**, you mean that you can no V prep
longer see them, usually because you or they have
changed position. *The airliner disappeared off their
radar.* **2** If someone or something **disappears**, they VERB
go away or are taken away somewhere where no- V
body can find them. *...a Japanese woman who
disappeared thirteen years ago.* **3** If something **dis-** VERB
appears, it stops existing or happening. *The im-* V
mediate threat of the past has disappeared.

dis·ap·pear·ance /ˌdɪsəˈpɪərəns/ **disappear-** ◆◇◇◇◇
ances. 1 If you refer to someone's **disappearance**, N-VAR
you are referring to the fact that nobody knows
where they have gone. *...thousands of killings and
disappearances over the past few years.* **2** If you refer to the **disappearance** of an object, you are refer- N-COUNT
ring to the fact that it has been lost or stolen. *...the
disappearance from council offices of confidential
files.* **3** The **disappearance** of a type of thing, per- N-UNCOUNT
son, or animal is a process in which it becomes less
common and finally no longer exists. *...the virtual
disappearance of common dolphins from the western Mediterranean.*

dis·ap·point /ˌdɪsəˈpɔɪnt/ **disappoints, disap-** ◆◇◇◇◇
pointing, disappointed. If things or people **dis-** VERB
appoint you, they are not as good as you had V n
hoped, or do not do what you hoped they would do.
She knew that she was fated to disappoint him.

dis·ap·point·ed /ˌdɪsəˈpɔɪntɪd/. **1** If you are **disap-** ◆◆◆◇◇
pointed, you are rather sad because something has ADJ-GRADED
not happened or because something is not as good
as you had hoped. *I was disappointed that Kluge
was not there.* **2** If you are **disappointed in** some- ADJ-GRADED:
one, you are rather sad because they have not be- v-link ADJ in n
haved as well as you expected them to. *You should
have accepted that. I'm disappointed in you.*

dis·ap·point·ing /ˌdɪsəˈpɔɪntɪŋ/. Something that is ◆◆◇◇◇
disappointing is not as good or as large as you ADJ-GRADED
hoped it would be. *The meat was overdone and the
vegetables disappointing.* ♦ **dis·ap·point·ing·ly** ADV
Progress is disappointingly slow.

dis·ap·point·ment /ˌdɪsəˈpɔɪntmənt/ **disappoint-** ◆◆◇◇◇
ments. 1 Disappointment is the state of feeling N-UNCOUNT
disappointed. *Book early to avoid disappointment.*
2 Something or someone that is a **disappointment** N-COUNT
is not as good as you had hoped. *He was such a disappointment to his family.*

dis·ap·prov·al /ˌdɪsəˈpruːvəl/. If you feel or show ◆◇◇◇◇
disapproval of something or someone, you feel or N-UNCOUNT
show that you do not approve of them. *His action
had been greeted with almost universal disapproval.*

dis·ap·prove /ˌdɪsəˈpruːv/ **disapproves, disap-** ◆◇◇◇◇
proving, disapproved. If you **disapprove** of VERB
something or someone, you feel or show that you V of n/-ing
do not like them or do not approve of them. *Her Also V
mother disapproved of her working in a pub.*

dis·ap·prov·ing /ˌdɪsəˈpruːvɪŋ/. A **disapproving** ac- ADJ-GRADED
tion or expression shows that you do not approve of
something or someone. *Janet gave him a disapprov-
ing look.* ♦ **dis·ap·prov·ing·ly** *Antonio looked at* ADV-GRADED:
him disapprovingly. ADV after v

dis·arm /dɪsˈɑːm/ **disarms, disarming, dis-** ◆◇◇◇◇
armed. 1 To **disarm** a person or group means to VERB

take away all their weapons. *We will agree to dis-* V n
arming troops. **2** If a country or group **disarms**, it VERB: V
gives up the use of weapons, especially nuclear V pron-refl
weapons. *We're not ready to disarm ourselves.* **3** If a VERB
person or their behaviour **disarms** you, they cause V n
you to feel less angry, hostile, or critical towards
them. *She did her best to disarm her critics.*

dis·arma·ment /dɪsˈɑːməmənt/. **Disarmament** is ◆◇◇◇◇
the act of reducing the number of weapons, espe- N-UNCOUNT
cially nuclear weapons, that a country has. *...the
pace of nuclear disarmament.*

dis·arm·ing /dɪsˈɑːmɪŋ/. If someone or something ADJ-GRADED
is **disarming**, they make you feel less angry or hostile. *...a disarming smile.* ♦ **dis·arm·ing·ly** *He is, as* ADV
ever, business-like, and disarmingly honest.

dis·ar·ray /ˌdɪsəˈreɪ/. **1** If people or things are in ◆◇◇◇◇
disarray, they are disorganized and confused. *The* N-UNCOUNT
nation is in disarray following rioting. **2** If things or N-UNCOUNT
places are in **disarray**, they are in a very untidy
state. *Her clothes were in disarray.*

dis·as·sem·ble /ˌdɪsəˈsembəl/ **disassembles,** VERB
disassembling, disassembled. To **disassemble** V n
something means to take it to pieces. *Dennet disas-* FORMAL
sembled the cabin and packed it away.

dis·as·so·ci·ate /ˌdɪsəˈsəʊʃieɪt/ **disassociates,**
disassociating, disassociated. 1 If you **disas-** VERB
sociate yourself from something or someone, you V pron-refl
say or show that you are not connected with them. *I* from n
*wish to disassociate myself from this very sad deci-
sion.* **2** If you **disassociate** one group or thing from VERB
another, you separate them. *...an attempt by the* V n from n
president to disassociate the military from politics.

dis·as·ter /dɪˈzɑːstə, -ˈzæs-/ **disasters. 1** A disas- ◆◆◇◇
ter is a very bad accident such as an earthquake or N-COUNT
a plane crash. *It was the second air disaster in the
region in less than two months.* **2** If you refer to N-COUNT
something as a **disaster**, you are emphasizing that PRAGMATICS
you think it is extremely bad or unacceptable. *It
would be a disaster for them not to reach the semi-
finals.* **3 Disaster** is something which has very bad N-UNCOUNT
consequences for you. *For some, the best way of
coping with disaster is not to confront it directly.* **4** If PHRASE
you say that something is **a recipe for disaster**, you
mean that it is very likely to have unpleasant consequences.

dis·aster area, disaster areas. 1 A **disaster** N-COUNT
area is a part of a country or the world which has
been very seriously affected by a disaster such as an
earthquake or flood. **2** If you describe a place, per- N-COUNT
son, or situation as a **disaster area**, you mean that INFORMAL
they are in a state of great disorder or failure. *He's a
disaster area as a politician.*

dis·as·trous /dɪˈzɑːstrəs, -ˈzæs-/. **1** A **disastrous** ◆◆◇◇
event has extremely bad consequences and effects. ADJ-GRADED
*...the recent, disastrous earthquake... The effect on
coffee prices has been disastrous.* ♦ **dis·as·trous·ly** ADV-GRADED
Their scheme went disastrously wrong. **2** If you de- ADJ-GRADED
scribe something as **disastrous**, you mean that it
was very unsuccessful. *England's cricketers have had
another disastrous day.* ♦ **disastrously** *...the* ADV-GRADED
*company's disastrously timed venture into property
development.*

dis·avow /ˌdɪsəˈvaʊ/ **disavows, disavowing,** VERB
disavowed. If you **disavow** something, you say V n
that you are not connected with it or responsible for FORMAL
it. *Dr. Samuels immediately disavowed the newspaper story.*

dis·band /dɪsˈbænd/ **disbands, disbanding,** ◆◇◇◇◇
disbanded. If someone **disbands** a group of peo- V-ERG
ple, or if the group **disbands**, it stops operating as a be V-ed
single unit. *All the armed groups will be disbanded...* Also V n
The rebels were to have fully disbanded by June.

dis·be·lief /ˌdɪsbɪˈliːf/. **Disbelief** is not believing ◆◇◇◇◇
that something is true or real. *She looked at him in* N-UNCOUNT
complete disbelief.

dis·be·lieve /ˌdɪsbɪˈliːv/ **disbelieves, disbeliev-**
ing, disbelieved. 1 If you **disbelieve** someone or VERB
disbelieve something that they say, you do not be- V n
lieve that what they say is true. *There is no reason to* Also V that
disbelieve him. **2** If you **disbelieve in** something, VERB

you do not believe that it exists or that it works. V inn
Frank disbelieved in astrology.

dis·burse /dɪsˈbɜːs/ **disburses, disbursing, dis-** VERB
bursed. To **disburse** an amount of money means V n
to pay it out, usually from a fund which has been FORMAL
collected for a particular purpose. *The bank has dis-*
bursed \$350m for the project.

dis·burse·ment /dɪsˈbɜːsmənt/ **disbursements.** N-UNCOUNT
1 Disbursement is the paying out of a sum of mon- FORMAL
ey, especially from a fund. **2** A **disbursement** is a N-COUNT
sum of money that is paid out. FORMAL

disc /dɪsk/ **discs;** spelled **disk** in American Eng- ◆◆◇◇◇
lish. **1** A **disc** is a flat, circular shape or object. *...a* N-COUNT
revolving disc fitted with replaceable blades. **2** A N-COUNT
disc is one of the thin, circular pieces of cartilage
which separates the bones in your back. **3** A **disc** is N-COUNT
a gramophone record. *This disc includes the piano* DATED
sonata in C minor. **4** See also **disk, compact disc,**
slipped disc.

dis·card /dɪsˈkɑːd/ **discards, discarding, dis-** ◆◆◇◇◇
carded. If you **discard** something, you get rid of it VERB
because you no longer want it or need it. *Read the* V n
manufacturer's guidelines before discarding the box.

dis·cern /dɪˈsɜːn/ **discerns, discerning, dis-** ◆◇◇◇◇
cerned. 1 If you can **discern** something, you are VERB: V n
aware of it and know what it is. *It was hard to dis-* V wh
cern why this was happening. **2** If you can **discern** FORMAL
something, you can just see it, but not clearly. *We* VERB
could just discern a narrow, weedy ditch. V n
FORMAL

dis·cern·ible /dɪˈsɜːnəbəl/. If something is **dis-** ◆◇◇◇◇
cernible, you can see it or recognize that it exists. ADJ-GRADED
Far away the outline of the island is just discernible.

dis·cern·ing /dɪˈsɜːnɪŋ/. If you describe someone ◆◇◇◇◇
as **discerning,** you mean that they are able to judge ADJ-GRADED
which things of a particular kind are good and PRAGMATICS
which are bad; used showing approval. *...holidays to*
suit the more discerning traveller.

dis·cern·ment /dɪˈsɜːnmənt/. **Discernment** is the N-UNCOUNT
ability to judge which things of a particular kind are
good and which are bad.

dis·charge, discharges, discharging, dis- ◆◆◇◇◇
charged. The verb is pronounced /dɪsˈtʃɑːdʒ/. The
noun is pronounced /ˈdɪstʃɑːdʒ/. **1** When someone VERB
is discharged from hospital, prison, or one of the beV-ed
armed services, they are officially allowed to leave, Also V n
or told that they must leave. *He has a broken nose*
but may be discharged today. ► Also a noun. *He was* N-VAR
given a conditional discharge.
2 If someone **discharges** their duties or responsibil- VERB
ities, they do everything that needs to be done in or- V n
der to complete them. If they **discharge** a debt, they FORMAL
pay all the money that needs to be paid. *...the quiet*
competence with which he discharged his many col-
lege duties.
3 If something **is discharged** from inside a place, it VERB
comes out. *The resulting salty water will be discharged* beV-ed prep
at sea. ...discharging blood from the nostrils. **4** When V n prep
there is a **discharge** of a substance, the substance N-VAR
comes out from inside somewhere. *They develop a fe-*
ver and a watery discharge from their eyes.
5 If someone **discharges** a gun, they fire it. *...unlaw-* VERB
fully and dangerously discharging a weapon. V n
DATED

dis·ci·ple /dɪˈsaɪpəl/ **disciples.** If you are ◆◇◇◇◇
someone's **disciple,** you are influenced by their N-COUNT
teachings and try to follow their example. *...a major*
intellectual figure with disciples throughout Europe.

dis·ci·pli·nar·ian /ˌdɪsɪplɪˈneəriən/ **disciplinar-** N-COUNT
ians. If you describe someone as a **disciplinarian,**
you mean that they believe in imposing strict rules
of behaviour and in punishing severely anyone who
disobeys the rules.

dis·ci·pli·nary /ˈdɪsɪplɪnəri, AM -neri/. **Disciplinary** ◆◆◇◇◇
bodies or actions are concerned with making sure ADJ: ADJ n
that people obey rules or regulations and that they
are suitably punished if they do not. *He was unhap-*
py that no disciplinary action was being taken.

dis·ci·pline /ˈdɪsɪplɪn/ **disciplines, disciplining,** ◆◆◆◇◇
disciplined. 1 Discipline is the practice of making N-UNCOUNT
people obey rules or standards of behaviour, and
punishing them when they do not. *...discipline*

problems in the classroom. **2** If someone **is disci-** VERB
plined for something that they have done wrong, beV-ed
they are punished for it. *The workman was disci-* Also V n
plined by his company but not dismissed.
3 Discipline is the quality of being able to behave and N-UNCOUNT
work in a controlled way which involves obeying rules
or standards. *...calm, control and discipline.* **4** If you N-VAR
refer to an activity or situation as a **discipline,** you PRAGMATICS
mean that, in order to be successful in it, you need to
behave in a strictly controlled way and obey rules or
standards. *...the discipline of studying music.* **5** If you VERB:
discipline yourself to do something, you train your- V pron-refl
self to behave and work in a strictly controlled and to-inf
regular way. *I'm very good at disciplining myself.* **6** See V pron-refl
also **self-discipline.**
7 A **discipline** is an area of study, especially a subject of N-COUNT
study in a college or university. *We're looking for peo-* FORMAL
ple from a wide range of disciplines.

dis·ci·plined /ˈdɪsɪplɪnd/. Someone who is **disci-** ◆◇◇◇◇
plined behaves or works in a controlled way. *...be-* ADJ-GRADED
ing very disciplined about how I run my life.

'disc jockey, disc jockeys. A **disc jockey** is N-COUNT
someone who plays and introduces pop records on
the radio or at a disco.

dis·claim /dɪsˈkleɪm/ **disclaims, disclaiming,** VERB
disclaimed. If you **disclaim** knowledge of some- V n
thing or **disclaim** responsibility for something, you FORMAL
say that you did not know about it or are not responsible for it. *Mrs Lee disclaims any knowledge of*
her husband's business concerns.

dis·claim·er /dɪsˈkleɪmə/ **disclaimers.** A **dis-** N-COUNT
claimer is a statement in which someone says that FORMAL
they did not know about something or that they are
not responsible for something.

dis·close /dɪsˈkləʊz/ **discloses, disclosing,** ◆◆◆◇◇
disclosed. If you **disclose** new or secret informa- VERB: V n
tion, you tell people about it. *The company disclosed* V that
that its chairman will step down in May. ♦ **dis·clo-** Also V wh
·sure /dɪsˈkləʊʒə/ **disclosures** *...unauthorised* N-VAR
newspaper disclosures.

dis·co /ˈdɪskəʊ/ **discos.** A **disco** is a place or event ◆◆◇◇◇
at which people dance to pop music. N-COUNT

dis·cog·ra·phy /dɪsˈkɒɡrəfi/ **discographies.** A N-COUNT
discography is a list of all the recordings made by a
particular artist or group.

dis·col·our /dɪsˈkʌlə/ **discolours, discolouring,** V-ERG
discoloured; spelled **discolor** in American Eng- V
lish. If something **discolours** or if it **is discoloured** Also V n
by something else, its original colour changes, so
that it looks unattractive. *A tooth which has been hit*
hard may discolour. ♦ **dis·col·oured** *Some of the* ADJ-GRADED
prints were discoloured. ♦ **dis·col·ora·tion** N-UNCOUNT
/ˌdɪsˌkʌləˈreɪʃən/ *...the discoloration of the soil from*
acid spills.

dis·com·fit /dɪsˈkʌmfɪt/ **discomfits, discomfit-** VERB
ing, discomfited. If you **are discomfited** by beV-ed
something, it causes you to feel slightly embar- Also V n
rassed or confused. *He will be particularly discom-* WRITTEN
fited by the minister's dismissal of his plan.

dis·com·fi·ture /dɪsˈkʌmfɪtʃə/. **Discomfiture** is a N-UNCOUNT
feeling of slight embarrassment or confusion. WRITTEN

dis·com·fort /dɪsˈkʌmfət/ **discomforts. 1** Dis- ◆◆◇◇◇
comfort is a painful feeling in part of your body N-UNCOUNT
when you have been hurt slightly or when you have
been uncomfortable for a long time. *Steve had some*
discomfort, but no real pain. **2** Discomfort is a feel- N-UNCOUNT
ing of worry caused by shame or embarrassment.
He sniffed, fidgeting in discomfort. **3** Discomforts N-COUNT:
are conditions which cause you to feel physically with supp
uncomfortable. *...the discomforts of camping.*

dis·con·cert /ˌdɪskənˈsɜːt/ **disconcerts, discon-** VERB
certing, disconcerted. If something **disconcerts** V n
you, it makes you feel uneasy, confused, or embarrassed. *Antony's smile disconcerted Sutcliffe.* ♦ **dis-**
·con·cert·ed *He was disconcerted to find his fellow* ADJ-GRADED
diners already seated.

dis·con·cert·ing /ˌdɪskənˈsɜːtɪŋ/. If you say that ◆◇◇◇◇
something is **disconcerting,** you mean that it makes ADJ-GRADED
you feel uneasy, confused, or embarrassed. *The re-*
ception desk is not at street level, which is a little

disconcerting. ♦ **dis·con·cert·ing·ly** *She could be* ADV-GRADED
almost disconcertingly absent-minded.

dis·con·nect /ˌdɪskə'nekt/ **disconnects, dis-** ◆◇◇◇◇
connecting, disconnected. 1 If you **disconnect** VERB
a piece of equipment, you detach it from its source V n
of power. *The device automatically disconnects the*
ignition when the engine is switched off. **2** If you **are** VB: usu
disconnected by a gas, electricity, water, or tele- passive
phone company, they turn off the connection to be V-ed
your house. *All their telephone lines were discon-*
nected. ♦ **dis·con·nec·tion** /ˌdɪskə'nekʃən/ **dis-** N-VAR
connections *...the disconnection of his phone.*
3 If you **disconnect** something from something VERB
else, you separate the two things. *He disconnected* V n from n
the IV bottle from the overhead hook.
♦ **disconnection** *...a gradual disconnection from* N-UNCOUNT
the federation.

dis·con·nect·ed /ˌdɪskə'nektɪd/. **Disconnected** ADJ-GRADED
things are not linked in any way. *...sequences of*
utterly disconnected events.

dis·con·so·late /dɪs'kɒnsələt/. Someone who is ADJ-GRADED
disconsolate is very unhappy and depressed. *He did* WRITTEN
not have much success, but tried to keep from getting
too disconsolate. ♦ **dis·con·so·late·ly** *Disconso-* ADV-GRADED:
lately, he walked back down the course. ADV with v

dis·con·tent /ˌdɪskən'tent/ **discontents.** Discon- N-UNCOUNT:
tent is the feeling that you have when you are not also N in pl
satisfied with your situation. *...reports of widespread*
discontent in the capital.

dis·con·tent·ed /ˌdɪskən'tentɪd/. If you are **discon-** ADJ-GRADED
tented, you are not satisfied with your situation.
...farmers discontented with low prices.

dis·con·tin·ue /ˌdɪskən'tɪnjuː/ **discontinues, dis-** ◆◇◇◇◇
continuing, discontinued. 1 If you **discontinue** VERB
something that you have been doing regularly, you V n
stop doing it. *Do not discontinue the treatment* FORMAL
without consulting your doctor. **2** If a product **is dis-** VERB:
continued, the manufacturer stops making it. *The* be V-ed
Leica M2 was discontinued in 1967.

dis·con·ti·nu·ity /ˌdɪs'kɒntɪ'njuːɪti, AM -'nuː-/ **dis-** N-VAR
continuities. Discontinuity in a process is a lack FORMAL
of smooth or continuous development. *The text is*
good in parts, but suffers from discontinuity.

dis·con·tin·u·ous /ˌdɪskən'tɪnjuəs/. A process that ADJ
is **discontinuous** happens in stages with intervals
between them, rather than continuously.

dis·cord /'dɪskɔːd/. **Discord** is disagreement and ◆◇◇◇◇
argument between people. *...arranging schedules so* N-UNCOUNT
as to prevent discord. LITERARY

dis·cord·ant /dɪs'kɔːdənt/. **1** Something that is **dis-** ADJ-GRADED
cordant is strange or unpleasant because it does
not fit in with other things. *His agenda is discordant*
and out of time with ours. **2** A **discordant** sound or ADJ-GRADED
musical effect is unpleasant to hear.

dis·co·theque /'dɪskətek/ **discotheques.** A **dis-** N-COUNT
cotheque is the same as a **disco.**

dis·count, discounts, discounting, discount- ◆◆◇◇◇
ed. Pronounced /'dɪskaʊnt/ for meanings 1 and 2,
and /dɪs'kaʊnt/ for meaning 3. **1** A **discount** is a re- N-COUNT
duction in the usual price of something. *All full-*
time staff get a 20 per cent discount. **2** If a shop or VERB
company **discounts** an amount or percentage from V n
something that they are selling, they deduct the
amount or percentage from the usual price. *This*
has forced airlines to discount fares heavily.
3 If you **discount** an idea, fact, or theory, you consider VERB
that it is not true, not important, or not relevant. *Trad-* V n
ers tended to discount the rumor.

dis·count·er /'dɪskaʊntə/ **discounters.** A **dis-** N-COUNT
counter is a shop or organization which specializes
in selling large quantities of things very cheaply.

dis·cour·age /dɪs'kʌrɪdʒ, AM -'kɜːr-/ **discour-** ◆◆◇◇◇
ages, discouraging, discouraged. 1 If some- VERB
one or something **discourages** you, they cause you
to lose your enthusiasm about doing something. *It*
may be difficult to do at first. Don't let this discour-
age you. ♦ **dis·cour·aged** *She was determined not* ADJ-GRADED
to be too discouraged. ♦ **dis·cour·ag·ing** *Today's* ADJ-GRADED
report is more discouraging for the economy. **2** To VERB
discourage an action or to **discourage** someone V n from -ing

from doing that action means to make them not
want to do it. *...a campaign to discourage children*
from smoking.

dis·cour·age·ment /dɪs'kʌrɪdʒmənt, AM -'kɜːr-/
discouragements. 1 Discouragement is the act N-UNCOUNT
of trying to make someone not want to do something. *He persevered in the face of active discourage-*
ment from those around him. **2** A **discouragement** N-COUNT
is something that makes you unwilling to do something because you are afraid of the consequences.
Uncertainty is one of the many discouragements to
investment.

dis·course, **discourses, discoursing, dis-** ◆◇◇◇◇
coursed. The noun is pronounced /'dɪskɔːs/. The
verb is pronounced /dɪs'kɔːs/. **1 Discourse** is spo- N-UNCOUNT
ken or written communication between people, especially serious discussion of a subject. *...a tradition*
of political discourse. **2** A **discourse** is a serious talk N-COUNT
or piece of writing which is intended to teach or ex- FORMAL
plain something. **3** If someone **discourses** on some- V prep
thing, they talk for a long time about it in an Also V
authoritative way. *He discoursed for several hours on* FORMAL
French and English prose. **4** In linguistics, **discourse** N-UNCOUNT
is natural spoken or written language in context.
...discourse analysis.

dis·cour·teous /dɪs'kɜːtiəs/. If you say that some- ADJ-GRADED
one is **discourteous**, you mean that they are rude FORMAL
and have no consideration for the feelings of other
people. *Staff are often discourteous and sometimes*
downright rude.

dis·cov·er /dɪs'kʌvə/ **discovers, discovering,** ◆◆◆◇
discovered. 1 If you **discover** something that you VERB: V n
did not know about before, you become aware of it V that
or learn of it. *She discovered that they'd escaped... It* V wh
was difficult for the inspectors to discover which
documents were important. **2** If someone or some- VERB
thing **is discovered**, someone finds them, either by be V-ed
accident or because they have been looking for Also V n
them. *A few days later his badly beaten body was*
discovered. **3** When someone **discovers** a new place, VERB: V n
substance, scientific fact, or scientific technique, V wh
they are the first person to find it or become aware Also V that
of it. *They discovered how to form the image in a*
thin layer on the surface. ♦ **dis·cov·er·er, discov-** N-COUNT
erers *...the German discoverer of X-rays.*
4 If you say that someone **has discovered** an activity VERB
or subject, you mean that they have tried doing it or V n
studying it for the first time. *I wish I'd discovered pho-*
tography when I was younger.
5 When a actor, musician, or other performer who is VERB:
not well-known **is discovered**, someone recognizes be V-ed
that they have talent and helps them in their career.

dis·cov·ery /dɪs'kʌvəri/ **discoveries. 1** If some- ◆◆◆◇◇
one makes a **discovery**, they become aware of N-VAR
something or learn of something that they did not
know about before. *I felt I'd made an incredible dis-*
covery. **2** If someone makes a **discovery**, they are N-VAR
the first person to find or become aware of a place,
substance, or scientific fact that no one knew about
before. *...the discovery of the ozone hole over the*
South Pole. **3** If someone makes a **discovery**, they N-VAR
recognize that an actor, musician, or other performer who is not well-known has talent. **4** When the N-VAR
discovery of people or objects happens, someone
finds them, either by accident or as a result of looking for them. *...the discovery and destruction by sol-*
diers of millions of marijuana plants.

dis·cred·it /dɪs'kredɪt/ **discredits, discrediting,** ◆◆◇◇◇
discredited. 1 To **discredit** someone or some- VERB
thing means to cause them to lose people's respect PRAGMATICS
or trust. *...trying to discredit government foreign-aid* V n
policies. ♦ **dis·cred·it·ed** *...the old, discredited re-* ADJ-GRADED
gimes. **2** If someone or something **discredits** an VERB
idea or evidence, they make the idea or evidence V n
appear false or doubtful. *There would be difficulties*
in discrediting the evidence.

dis·cred·it·able /dɪs'kredɪtəbəl/. **Discreditable** be- ADJ-GRADED
haviour is not acceptable because people consider FORMAL
it to be shameful and wrong.

dis·creet /dɪsˈkriːt/. **1** If you are **discreet**, you are polite and careful in what you do or say, because you want to avoid embarrassing or offending someone. *He followed at a discreet distance.* ♦ **dis·creet·ly** *I took the phone, and she went discreetly into the living room.* **2** If you are **discreet** about something you are doing, you do not tell other people about it, in order to avoid being embarrassed or to gain an advantage. *...discreet inquiries.* ♦ **discreetly.** **3** If you describe something as **discreet**, you approve of it because it is small in size or degree, or not easily noticed. *...discreet jewellery.* ♦ **discreetly** *The two rooms were relatively small and discreetly lit.*
◆◆◇◇◇ ADJ-GRADED
ADV-GRADED
ADJ-GRADED
ADV-GRADED
ADJ-GRADED
PRAGMATICS
ADV-GRADED:
ADV -ed/adj

dis·crep·an·cy /dɪsˈkrepənsi/ **discrepancies.** If there is a **discrepancy** between two things that ought to be the same, there is a noticeable difference between them. *...the discrepancy between press and radio reports.*
N-VAR

dis·crete /dɪsˈkriːt/. **Discrete** ideas or things are separate and distinct from each other. *...instruction manuals that break down jobs into discrete steps.*
ADJ
FORMAL

dis·cre·tion /dɪsˈkreʃən/. **1 Discretion** is the quality of behaving in a quiet and controlled way without drawing attention to yourself or giving away private information. *Larsson sometimes joined in the fun, but with more discretion.* **2** If someone in a position of authority has the **discretion** to do something in a situation, they have the freedom and authority to decide what to do. *School governors have the discretion to allow parents to withdraw pupils.* **3** If something happens **at** someone's **discretion**, it can happen only if they decide to do it or give their permission. **4** If you say **discretion is the better part of valour**, you mean that avoiding a dangerous or unpleasant situation is sometimes the most sensible thing to do.
◆◆◇◇◇
N-UNCOUNT
FORMAL
N-UNCOUNT
FORMAL
PHRASE
FORMAL
PHRASE

dis·cre·tion·ary /dɪsˈkreʃənri, AM -neri/. **Discretionary** things are not fixed by rules but are decided on by people in authority, who consider each individual case. *You are entitled to a discretionary grant for your course.*
◆◇◇◇◇
ADJ

dis·crimi·nate /dɪsˈkrɪmɪneɪt/ **discriminates, discriminating, discriminated. 1** If you can **discriminate** between two things, you can recognize that they are different. *He is incapable of discriminating between a good idea and a terrible one.* **2** To **discriminate** against a group of people or in favour of a group of people means to unfairly treat them worse or better than other groups. *...legislation which would discriminate in favour of racial minorities.*
◆◇◇◇◇
VERB
V between pl-n
VERB:
V against n
V in favour of n
Also V

dis·crimi·nat·ing /dɪsˈkrɪmɪneɪtɪŋ/. Someone who is **discriminating** has the ability to recognize things that are of good quality; used showing approval.
ADJ-GRADED
PRAGMATICS

dis·crimi·na·tion /dɪsˌkrɪmɪˈneɪʃən/. **1 Discrimination** is the practice of treating one person or group of people less fairly or less well than other people or groups. *...discrimination against immigrants.* **2 Discrimination** is awareness of what is good or of high quality. *They cooked without skill and ate without discrimination.* **3 Discrimination** is the ability to recognize and understand the differences between two things. *...how colour discrimination and visual acuity develop.*
◆◆◇◇◇
N-UNCOUNT
N-UNCOUNT
N-UNCOUNT

dis·crimi·na·tory /dɪsˈkrɪmɪnətri, AM -tɔːri/. **Discriminatory** laws or practices are unfair because they treat one group of people worse than other groups. *...racially discriminatory laws.*
◆◇◇◇◇
ADJ

dis·cur·sive /dɪsˈkɜːsɪv/. If a style of writing is **discursive**, it includes a lot of facts or opinions that are not necessarily relevant.
ADJ-GRADED
FORMAL

dis·cus /ˈdɪskəs/ **discuses.** A **discus** is a heavy circular object which athletes try to throw as far as they can as a sport.
N-COUNT

dis·cuss /dɪsˈkʌs/ **discusses, discussing, discussed. 1** If people **discuss** something, they talk about it, often in order to reach a decision. *The Cabinet met today to discuss how to respond to the ultimatum.* **2** If you **discuss** something, you write or
◆◆◆◆◇
VERB: V n
V wh-to-inf
Also V wh
VERB

talk about it in detail. *I will discuss the role of diet in cancer prevention in Chapter 7.*
V n

dis·cus·sion /dɪsˈkʌʃən/ **discussions. 1** If there is **discussion** about something, people talk about it, often in order to reach a decision. *The whole question of school curriculum is up for discussion.* ● If something is **under discussion**, it is still being talked about and a final decision has not yet been reached. **2** A **discussion** of a subject is a piece of writing or a lecture in which someone talks about it in detail. *For a discussion of biology and sexual politics, see chapter 4.*
◆◆◆◇
N-VAR
PHRASE
N-COUNT

dis·dain /dɪsˈdeɪn/ **disdains, disdaining, disdained. 1** If you feel **disdain** for someone or something, you dislike them because you think that they are inferior or unimportant. *Janet looked at him with disdain.* **2** If you **disdain** someone or something, you regard them with disdain. *Jackie disdained the servants that her millions could buy.* **3** If you **disdain** to do something, you do not do it, because you feel that you are too superior to do it. *Franklin told Sara that he had himself disdained to take the job.*
◆◇◇◇◇
N-UNCOUNT
VERB
V n
VERB
V to-inf

dis·dain·ful /dɪsˈdeɪnfʊl/. If someone is **disdainful**, they dislike something or someone because they think that thing or person is inferior or unimportant. *He is highly disdainful of anything to do with the literary establishment.* ♦ **dis·dain·ful·ly.**
ADJ-GRADED
ADV-GRADED

dis·ease /dɪˈziːz/ **diseases. 1** A **disease** is an illness which affects people, animals, or plants. *...the rapid spread of disease in the area. ...illnesses such as heart disease.* ♦ **dis·eased** /dɪˈziːzd/ *Clear away dead or diseased plants.* **2** You can refer to a bad attitude or habit, usually one that a group of people have, as a **disease**. *...the wretched disease of racism.*
◆◆◆◇
N-VAR
ADJ
N-COUNT:
with supp
LITERARY

dis·eased /dɪˈziːzd/. If you say that someone's mind is **diseased**, you are emphasizing that you think it is not normal or balanced. *Gardner describes the book as 'the product of a diseased and evil mind'.*
◆◇◇◇◇
ADJ
PRAGMATICS

dis·em·bark /ˌdɪsɪmˈbɑːk/ **disembarks, disembarking, disembarked.** When passengers disembark from a ship, aeroplane, or bus, they leave it at the end of their journey. *Six passengers had disembarked.*
VERB
V
Also V from n
FORMAL

dis·em·bod·ied /ˌdɪsɪmˈbɒdid/. **1 Disembodied** means seeming not to be attached to or to come from anyone. *A disembodied voice sounded from the back of the cabin.* **2 Disembodied** means separated from or existing without a body. *...a disembodied head.*
ADJ
ADJ

dis·em·bow·el /ˌdɪsɪmˈbaʊəl/ **disembowels, disembowelling, disembowelled;** spelled **disemboweling, disemboweled** in American English. **1** To **disembowel** a person or animal means to remove their internal organs. *...a psychopath who hangs and disembowels his prey.* **2** To **disembowel** something means to take out the inside of it. *She disembowelled a melon with a quiet fury.*
VERB
V n
VERB
V n
LITERARY

dis·en·chant·ed /ˌdɪsɪnˈtʃɑːntɪd, -ˈtʃænt-/. If you are **disenchanted** with something, you are disappointed with it and no longer believe that it is good. *I'm disenchanted with the state of British theatre.* ♦ **dis·en·chant·ment** /ˌdɪsɪnˈtʃɑːntmənt, -ˈtʃænt-/ *There's been growing disenchantment with the Government.*
◆◇◇◇◇
ADJ-GRADED
N-UNCOUNT

dis·en·fran·chise /ˌdɪsɪnˈfræntʃaɪz/ **disenfranchises, disenfranchising, disenfranchised.** To **disenfranchise** a group of people means to take away their right to vote for what they want.
VERB: V n

dis·en·gage /ˌdɪsɪnˈgeɪdʒ/ **disengages, disengaging, disengaged. 1** If you **disengage** something, you separate it from something which it has become attached to. If something **disengages**, it separates from something which it is attached to. *John gently disengaged himself from his sister's tearful embrace... His front brake cable disengaged.* **2** If an army **disengages** from an area, it withdraws from that area. *More vigorous action is needed to force the federal army to disengage.*
V-ERG: V n
V pron-refl
from n
Also V n from n
VERB:
V from n
V

dis·en·gaged /ˌdɪsɪnˈɡeɪdʒd/. If someone is **disengaged** from something, they are not as involved with it as you would expect. *The film has the feel of a man curiously disengaged from his material.* ADJ-GRADED

dis·en·gage·ment /ˌdɪsɪnˈɡeɪdʒmənt/. **Disengagement** is a process by which people gradually stop being involved in a conflict, activity, or organization. *...this policy of disengagement from the European war.* N-UNCOUNT

dis·en·tan·gle /ˌdɪsɪnˈtæŋɡəl/ **disentangles, disentangling, disentangled. 1** If you **disentangle** a complicated or confused situation, you make it easier to understand or manage to understand it, by clearly recognizing each separate element. *In this book, Harrison brilliantly disentangles complex debates.* **2** If you **disentangle** someone from an undesirable thing or situation, you separate them from that thing or remove them from that situation. *They are looking at ways to disentangle him from this major policy decision.* **3** If you **disentangle** something, you separate it from things that are twisted around it, or things that it is twisted or knotted around. *She clawed at the bushes to disentangle herself.* VERB / V n / Also V n from n / VERB / V n from n / VERB / V n / Also V n from n

dis·equi·lib·rium /ˌdɪsiːkwɪˈlɪbriəm/. **Disequilibrium** is a state in which things are not stable or certain, but are likely to change suddenly. N-UNCOUNT: also a N / FORMAL

dis·es·tab·lish /ˌdɪsɪsˈtæblɪʃ/ **disestablishes, disestablishing, disestablished.** To **disestablish** a church or religion means to take away the official status that it had. **♦ dis·es·tab·lish·ment** /ˌdɪsɪsˈtæblɪʃmənt/ *...a victim of Welsh Anglican disestablishment.* VERB: V n / FORMAL / N-UNCOUNT

dis·fa·vour /dɪsˈfeɪvə/; spelled **disfavor** in American English. **1** If someone or something is in **disfavour**, people dislike or disapprove of them. *His boss was in disfavour with the communist party.* **2** If you look at someone or something with **disfavour**, the expression on your face shows that you dislike and disapprove of them. *She eyed his unruly collar-length hair with disfavour.* N-UNCOUNT / FORMAL / N-UNCOUNT / FORMAL

dis·fig·ure /dɪsˈfɪɡə, AM -ɡjər/ **disfigures, disfiguring, disfigured. 1** If someone is **disfigured**, their appearance is spoiled. *Many of the wounded had been badly disfigured.* **♦ dis·fig·ured** *...the scarred, disfigured face.* **2** To **disfigure** an object or a place means to spoil its appearance. *Wind turbines are noisy and they disfigure the landscape.* ◆◇◇◇◇ / VERB / be V-ed / ADJ-GRADED / VERB / V n

dis·fig·ure·ment /dɪsˈfɪɡəmənt, AM -ɡjər-/ **disfigurements.** A **disfigurement** is something, for example a scar, that spoils a person's appearance. N-VAR

dis·gorge /dɪsˈɡɔːdʒ/ **disgorges, disgorging, disgorged. 1** If something **disgorges** its contents, it empties them out. *The ground had opened to disgorge a boiling stream of molten lava.* **2** If an animal **disgorges** something it has swallowed, it produces it again from its mouth. VERB / V n / WRITTEN / VERB: V n

dis·grace /dɪsˈɡreɪs/ **disgraces, disgracing, disgraced. 1** If you say that someone is in **disgrace**, you are emphasizing that other people disapprove of them and do not respect them because of something that they have done. *His vice president also had to resign in disgrace.* **2** If you say that something is **a disgrace**, you are emphasizing that it is very bad or wrong. *The way the sales were handled was a complete disgrace.* **3** You say that someone is **a disgrace** to someone else when you want to emphasize that their behaviour causes the other person to feel ashamed. *What went on was a scandal. It was a disgrace to Britain.* **4** If you say that someone **disgraces** someone else, you are emphasizing that their behaviour causes the other person to feel ashamed. *I have disgraced my family's name... I've disgraced myself by the actions I've taken.* ◆◇◇◇◇ / N-UNCOUNT / PRAGMATICS / N-SING: a N / PRAGMATICS / N-SING: a N / PRAGMATICS / VERB / PRAGMATICS / V n / V pron-refl

dis·graced /dɪsˈɡreɪst/. You use **disgraced** to describe someone whose bad behaviour has caused them to lose the approval and respect of the public or of people in authority. *...the disgraced leader of the coup.* ◆◇◇◇◇ / ADJ-GRADED

dis·grace·ful /dɪsˈɡreɪsfʊl/. If you say that something is **disgraceful**, you disapprove of it strongly, and feel that the person responsible should be ashamed of it. *It's disgraceful that they have detained for him so long. ...his disgraceful behaviour.* **♦ dis·grace·ful·ly** *He felt that his brother had behaved disgracefully.* ◆◇◇◇◇ / ADJ-GRADED / ADV-GRADED

dis·grun·tled /dɪsˈɡrʌntəld/. If you are **disgruntled**, you are cross and dissatisfied because things have not happened the way that you wanted them to happen. *Party members are disgruntled at the way the campaign is being handled.* ◆◇◇◇◇ / ADJ-GRADED

dis·guise /dɪsˈɡaɪz/ **disguises, disguising, disguised. 1** If you are in **disguise**, you have altered your appearance so that people will not recognize you. *You'll have to travel in disguise... He was wearing that ridiculous disguise.* **2** If you **disguise** yourself, you alter your appearance so that people will not recognize you. *She disguised herself as a man.* **♦ dis·guised** *The extremists entered the building disguised as medical workers.* **3** To **disguise** something means to hide it or make it appear different so that people will not know about it or will not recognize it. *He made no attempt to disguise his agitation.* **♦ disguised** *...a thinly disguised effort to revive the price controls of the 1970s.* **4 ● a blessing in disguise**: see **blessing**. ◆◆◇◇◇ / N-VAR / VERB: V pron-refl n / ADJ-GRADED / VERB / V n / ADJ-GRADED

dis·gust /dɪsˈɡʌst/ **disgusts, disgusting, disgusted. 1 Disgust** is a feeling of very strong dislike or disapproval. *He spoke of his disgust at the incident... I threw the book aside in disgust.* **2** To **disgust** someone means to make them feel a strong sense of dislike and disapproval. *He disgusted many with his boorish behaviour.* ◆◆◇◇◇ / N-UNCOUNT / VERB / V n

dis·gust·ed /dɪsˈɡʌstɪd/. If you are **disgusted**, you feel a strong sense of dislike and disapproval at something. *I'm disgusted with the way that he was treated... He was disgusted that a British minister could behave so disgracefully.* **♦ dis·gust·ed·ly** *'It's a little late for that,' Ritter said disgustedly.* ◆◇◇◇◇ / ADJ-GRADED / ADV: ADV with v

dis·gust·ing /dɪsˈɡʌstɪŋ/. **1** If you say that something is **disgusting**, you are criticizing it because it is extremely unpleasant. *It tasted disgusting. ...a disgusting habit.* **2** If you say that something is **disgusting**, you mean that you find it completely unacceptable. *It's disgusting that the taxpayer is subsidising this project.* ◆◇◇◇◇ / ADJ-GRADED / ADJ-GRADED

dish /dɪʃ/ **dishes, dishing, dished. 1** A **dish** is a shallow container with a wide uncovered top. You eat and serve food from dishes and cook food in them. *...plastic bowls and dishes. ...a warm serving dish.* **2** The contents of a dish can be referred to as a **dish** of something. *...a dish of spaghetti.* **3** Food that is prepared in a particular style or combination can be referred to as a **dish**. *There are plenty of vegetarian dishes to choose from.* **4** All the objects that have been used to cook, serve, and eat a meal can be referred to as the **dishes**. *He'd cooked dinner and washed the dishes.* **5** You can use the word **dish** to refer to anything that is round and hollow in shape with a wide uncovered top. *...a dish used to receive satellite broadcasts.* **6** See also **satellite dish, side dish. ● to dish the dirt**: see **dirt**. ◆◆◆◇◇ / N-COUNT / N-COUNT / N-COUNT / N-PLURAL / N-COUNT

dish out. 1 If you **dish out** something, you distribute it among a number of people. *Doctors, not pharmacists, are responsible for dishing out drugs.* **2** If someone **dishes out** criticism or punishment, they give it to someone. *Do you usually dish out criticism to someone who's doing you a favour?.* **3** If you **dish out** food, you serve it to people at the beginning of each course of a meal. PHRASAL VB / V P noun / INFORMAL / V P noun / Also V n P / V P n

dish up. If you **dish up** food, you serve it to people at the beginning of each course of a meal. *They dished up a superb meal... I'll dish up and you can grate the Parmesan.* PHRASAL VB / V P noun / V P / Also V n P

dis·har·mo·ny /dɪsˈhɑːməni/. When there is **disharmony**, people disagree about important things and this causes an unpleasant atmosphere. *...the root causes of racial disharmony.* N-UNCOUNT / FORMAL

dish·cloth /ˈdɪʃklɒθ, AM -klɔːθ/ **dishcloths. 1** A N-COUNT **dishcloth** is a cloth used to dry dishes after they have been washed. **2** A **dishcloth** is a cloth used for N-COUNT washing dishes, pans, and cutlery.

dis·heart·ened /dɪsˈhɑːtənd/. If you are **disheart-** ADJ-GRADED **ened**, you feel disappointed about something and have less confidence about it than you did before. *He was disheartened by their hostile reaction.*

dis·heart·en·ing /dɪsˈhɑːtənɪŋ/. Something that is ADJ-GRADED **disheartening** makes you feel disheartened.

di·shev·elled /dɪˈʃevəld/; spelled **disheveled** in ADJ-GRADED American English. If you describe someone's appearance as **dishevelled**, you mean that it is very untidy. *She arrived flushed and dishevelled.*

dis·hon·est /dɪsˈɒnɪst/. If you say that someone is ◆◇◇◇◇ **dishonest**, you mean that they are not honest, and ADJ-GRADED that you cannot trust them. *You have been dishonest with me... It would be dishonest to mislead people.* ♦ **dis·hon·est·ly** *They acted dishonestly.* ADV-GRADED

dis·hon·es·ty /dɪsˈɒnɪsti/. **Dishonesty** is dishonest ◆◇◇◇◇ behaviour. N-UNCOUNT

dis·hon·our /dɪsˈɒnə/ **dishonours, dishonour-ing, dishonoured;** spelled **dishonor** in American English. **1** If you **dishonour** someone, you behave VERB in a way that damages their good reputation. *It* V n *would dishonour my family if I didn't wear the veil.* FORMAL **2 Dishonour** is a state in which people disapprove N-UNCOUNT of you and lose their respect for you. *She refuses to* FORMAL *see her beloved boy die in such dishonor.* **3** If someone **dishonours** an agreement or transaction, they VERB refuse to act according to its conditions. *The bank* V n *had dishonoured some of our cheques.*

dis·hon·our·able /dɪsˈɒnərəbl/; spelled **dishonor-** ADJ-GRADED **able** in American English. Someone who is **dishon-ourable** is not honest and does things which you consider to be morally unacceptable. *Mark had done nothing dishonourable.*

'**dish towel, dish towels.** A **dish towel** is a cloth N-COUNT used to dry dishes after they have been washed. The AMERICAN British word is **tea towel.**

dish·wash·er /ˈdɪʃwɒʃə/ **dishwashers.** A **dish-** ◆◇◇◇◇ **washer** is a machine that washes and dries kitchen N-COUNT and eating utensils.

dish·water /ˈdɪʃwɔːtə/. **Dishwater** is water that N-UNCOUNT dishes, pans, and cutlery have been washed in.

dishy /ˈdɪʃi/. If a woman describes a man as **dishy**, ADJ-GRADED she thinks that he is very good looking. BRITISH, INFORMAL

dis·il·lu·sion /ˌdɪsɪˈluːʒən/ **disillusions, disillu-** ◆◇◇◇◇ **sioning, disillusioned. 1** If something or some- VERB: one **disillusions** you, they make you realize that be V-ed something is not as good as you thought. *He said he had been bitterly disillusioned by his country's fail-ure to change.* ♦ **dis·il·lu·sioned** /ˌdɪsɪˈluːʒənd/ *I've* ADJ-GRADED *become very disillusioned with politics.* ♦ **dis·il·lu-** ·**sion·ment** /ˌdɪsɪˈluːʒənmənt/ *...a general sense of* N-UNCOUNT *disillusionment with the government.* **2 Disillusion** N-UNCOUNT: is the same as **disillusionment.** *There is disillusion* also N in pl *with established political parties.*

dis·in·cen·tive /ˌdɪsɪnˈsentɪv/ **disincentives.** A N-VAR **disincentive** is something which discourages people FORMAL from acting in a particular way. *High tax rates may act as a disincentive to working longer hours.*

dis·in·cli·na·tion /ˌdɪsɪnklɪˈneɪʃən/. A **disinclina-** N-SING **tion** to do something is a feeling that you do not FORMAL want to do it. *They are showing a marked disinclina-tion to pursue these opportunities.*

dis·in·clined /ˌdɪsɪnˈklaɪnd/. If you are **disinclined** ADJ: to do something, you do not want to do it. *He was* v-link ADJ *disinclined to talk about himself.* FORMAL

dis·in·fect /ˌdɪsɪnˈfekt/ **disinfects, disinfecting,** VERB **disinfected.** If you **disinfect** something, you clean V n it using a substance that kills germs. *Chlorine is used to disinfect water.*

dis·in·fect·ant /ˌdɪsɪnˈfektənt/ **disinfectants.** N-VAR **Disinfectant** is a substance that kills germs. *The tank is dosed with disinfectant to kill any harmful organisms.*

dis·in·fla·tion /ˌdɪsɪnˈfleɪʃən/. **Disinflation** is a re- N-UNCOUNT duction in the rate of inflation.

dis·in·for·ma·tion /ˌdɪsɪnfəˈmeɪʃən/. If you accuse N-UNCOUNT someone of spreading **disinformation**, you are ac-cusing them of spreading false information in order to deceive people. *They spread scandal and disinfor-mation in order to discredit certain politicians.*

dis·in·genu·ous /ˌdɪsɪnˈdʒenjuəs/. Someone who ADJ-GRADED is **disingenuous** is slightly dishonest and insincere FORMAL in what they say. *It would be disingenuous to claim that this is a work of beauty.* ♦ **dis·in·genu·ous·ly** ADV-GRADED *He disingenuously remarked that 'he did not under-stand about strategy'.*

dis·in·her·it /ˌdɪsɪnˈherɪt/ **disinherits, disinherit-** VERB: V n **ing, disinherited.** If you **disinherit** someone such as your son or daughter, you arrange that they will not become the owner of your money and property after your death.

dis·in·te·grate /dɪsˈɪntɪɡreɪt/ **disintegrates, dis-** ◆◆◇◇◇ **integrating, disintegrated. 1** If something **dis-** VERB **integrates**, it becomes seriously weakened, and is V divided or destroyed. *During October 1918 the Austro-Hungarian Empire began to disintegrate.* ♦ **dis·in·te·gra·tion** /ˌdɪs,ɪntɪˈɡreɪʃən/ *...the disinte-* N-UNCOUNT *gration of an ordinary marriage.* **2** If an object or V substance **disintegrates**, it breaks into many small pieces or parts and is destroyed. *At 420 mph the windscreen disintegrated.* ♦ **disintegration** *...the* N-UNCOUNT *catastrophic disintegration of the aircraft.*

dis·in·ter /ˌdɪsɪnˈtɜː/ **disinters, disinterring, dis-interred. 1** If you **disinter** something, you start VERB using it again after it has not been used for a long V n time. *...disinterring sixties soul classics for TV com-mercials.* **2** When a dead body **is disinterred**, it is VERB: dug up from out of the ground. be V-ed

dis·in·ter·est /dɪsˈɪntrəst/. If there is **disinterest** in N-UNCOUNT something, people are not interested in it. *At the time I found his disinterest startling.*

dis·in·ter·est·ed /dɪsˈɪntrəstɪd/. **1** Someone who is ADJ-GRADED **disinterested** is not involved in a situation or not likely to benefit from it and is therefore able to act in a fair and unselfish way. *Scientists, of course, can be expected to be impartial and disinterested.* **2** If ADJ-GRADED you are **disinterested** in something, you are not in-terested in it. Some users of English believe that it is not correct to use **disinterested** with this meaning. *Doran was disinterested in food.*

dis·joint·ed /dɪsˈdʒɔɪntɪd/. **1** **Disjointed** words, ADJ-GRADED thoughts, or ideas are not presented in a smooth or logical way. *...disjointed, drunken ramblings.* **2 Dis-** ADJ-GRADED **jointed** societies, systems, and activities are ones in which the different parts are not as closely connect-ed as they should be. *...our increasingly fragmented and disjointed society.*

disk /dɪsk/ **disks.** In a computer, the **disk** is the ◆◇◇◇◇ part where information is stored. *The program takes* N-COUNT *up 2.5 megabytes of disk space.* ● See also **disc, disk drive, floppy disk, hard disk.**

'**disk drive, disk drives;** also spelled **disc drive** in N-COUNT British English. The **disk drive** on a computer is the part that contains the disk or into which a disk can be inserted.

disk·ette /ˌdɪsˈket/ **diskettes.** A **diskette** is the N-COUNT same as a **floppy disk.**

dis·like /ˌdɪsˈlaɪk/ **dislikes, disliking, disliked.** ◆◆◇◇◇ **1** If you **dislike** someone or something, you consid- V-ed er them to be unpleasant and do not like them. *Da-* V n *vid began to dislike all his television heroes who smoked.* **2 Dislike** is the feeling that you do not like N-UNCOUNT someone or something. *...his famous dislike of mod-ern architecture... Kate said nothing and looked at him with dislike.* **3** Your **dislikes** are the things that N-COUNT you do not like. *Consider what your likes and dis-likes are about your job.* **4** If you **take a dislike** to PHRASE someone or something, you decide that you do not like them.

dis·lo·cate /ˈdɪsləkeɪt/ **dislocates, dislocating,** ◆◇◇◇◇ **dislocated. 1** If you **dislocate** a bone or joint in VERB your body, it moves out of its proper position in re- V n lation to other bones. *Harrison dislocated a finger.* V-ed *...a dislocated shoulder.* **2** To **dislocate** something VERB such as a system, process, or way of life means to V n V-ed

D

disturb it greatly or prevent it from continuing as normal. *The strike at the financial nerve centre was designed to dislocate the economy. ...dislocated lives.* ♦ **dis·lo·ca·tion** /ˌdɪslə'keɪʃən/ **dislocations** *Millions of refugees have suffered a total dislocation of their lives.*   N-VAR

dis·lodge /ˌdɪs'lɒdʒ/ **dislodges, dislodging, dislodged.** To **dislodge** something or someone from a place or position means to cause them to leave that place or position, although they were fixed, held, or established there. *Rainfall from a tropical storm dislodged the debris from the slopes of the volcano... He may challenge the Prime Minister even if he decides he cannot dislodge her this time.*   ♦◇◇◇◇   V n from n   V n

dis·loy·al /ˌdɪs'lɔɪəl/. Someone who is **disloyal** to their friends, family, colleagues, or country does not support them or does things that could harm them. *She was so disloyal to her deputy she made his position untenable.* ♦ **dis·loy·al·ty** /ˌdɪs'lɔɪəlti/ *...a feeling of disloyalty to his father.*   ADJ-GRADED   N-UNCOUNT

dis·mal /'dɪzməl/. **1** Something that is **dismal** is depressingly bad. *...Israel's dismal record in the Olympics... My prospects of returning to a suitable job are dismal.* ♦ **dis·mal·ly** *He failed dismally.* **2** Something that is **dismal** is bleak, sad, and depressing. *The main hospital is pretty dismal. ...a dark dismal day.*   ♦◇◇◇◇ ADJ-GRADED   ADV   ADJ-GRADED

dis·man·tle /ˌdɪs'mæntəl/ **dismantles, dismantling, dismantled. 1** If you **dismantle** a machine or structure, you carefully separate it into its different parts. *Tommy sent a telegram instructing Fred to dismantle the machine.* **2** To **dismantle** an organization or system means to cause it to stop functioning by gradually reducing its power or purpose. *...the president's policy of dismantling apartheid.*   ♦♦◇◇◇   VERB   V n   VERB   V n

dis·may /ˌdɪs'meɪ/ **dismays, dismaying, dismayed. 1 Dismay** is a strong feeling of fear, worry, or sadness that is caused by something unpleasant and unexpected. *Lucy discovered to her dismay that she was pregnant... The ministers expressed dismay at the continued practice of ethnic cleansing.* **2** If you **are dismayed** by something, it makes you feel afraid, worried, or sad. *McKee suddenly realized she was crying and the thought dismayed him.* ♦ **dis·mayed** *He was dismayed to find that his hands were shaking.*   ♦♦◇◇◇   N-UNCOUNT   FORMAL   VERB: be V-ed   FORMAL   ADJ-GRADED

dis·mem·ber /ˌdɪs'membə/ **dismembers, dismembering, dismembered. 1** To **dismember** the body of a dead person means to cut or pull it into pieces. *He then dismembered her, hiding parts of her body in the cellar.* ♦ **dis·mem·ber·ment** /ˌdɪs'membəmənt/ *...bodies in various states of decay and dismemberment.* **2** To **dismember** a country or organization means to break it up into smaller parts. *...Hitler's plans to occupy and dismember Czechoslovakia.* ♦ **dismemberment** *...the dismemberment of Pakistan.*   ♦◇◇◇◇   VERB   V n   N-UNCOUNT   VERB   V n   N-UNCOUNT

dis·miss /ˌdɪs'mɪs/ **dismisses, dismissing, dismissed. 1** If you **dismiss** something, you decide or say that it is not important enough for you to think about or consider. *Mr Wakeham dismissed the reports as speculation... I would certainly dismiss any allegations of impropriety by the Labour Party.* ♦ **dis·mis·sal** /ˌdɪs'mɪsəl/ *...high-handed dismissal of public opinion.* **2** If you **dismiss** something from your mind, you stop thinking about it. *'It's been a lovely day,' she said, dismissing the episode.* **3** When an employer **dismisses** an employee, the employer tells the employee that they are no longer needed to do the job that they have been doing. *...the power to dismiss civil servants.* ♦ **dis·mis·sal, dismissals** *...Mr Low's dismissal from his post at the head of the commission.* **4** If you **are dismissed** by someone in authority, they tell you that you can go away from them. *Two more witnesses were called, heard and dismissed.* **5** When a judge **dismisses** a case in court, he or she formally stops the trial, for example when new evidence proves that the defendant is innocent. *A federal*   ♦♦♦♦◇   VERB   V n as n   V n   N-UNCOUNT   VERB: V n from n   V n   VERB   V n   N-VAR   VERB   be V-ed   Also V n   VERB   have V-ed

judge dismissed the charges against the doctor yesterday. ...their attempt to have the case against them dismissed.

dis·mis·sive /ˌdɪs'mɪsɪv/. If you are **dismissive** of someone or something, you say or show that you think they are not important or have no value. *Mr Jones was dismissive of the report. ...the dismissive attitude scientists often take.* ♦ **dis·mis·sive·ly** *He describes Sally dismissively as 'that woman'.*   ♦◇◇◇◇ ADJ-GRADED   ADV-GRADED

dis·mount /ˌdɪs'maʊnt/ **dismounts, dismounting, dismounted.** If you **dismount** from a horse or a bicycle, you get down from it.   VERB: V   FORMAL

dis·obe·di·ent /ˌdɪsə'biːdiənt/. If you are **disobedient**, you deliberately do not do what someone in authority tells you to do. *...a parent ordering a disobedient child to behave itself.* ♦ **dis·obe·di·ence** /ˌdɪsə'biːdiəns/ *The penalty for disobedience was death.*   ADJ-GRADED   N-UNCOUNT

dis·obey /ˌdɪsə'beɪ/ **disobeys, disobeying, disobeyed.** When someone **disobeys** a person or an order, they deliberately do not do what they have been told to do. *...a naughty boy who often disobeyed his mother and father.*   VERB   V n   Also V

dis·or·der /ˌdɪs'ɔːdə/ **disorders. 1** A **disorder** is a problem or illness which affects someone's mind or body. *...a rare nerve disorder that can cause paralysis of the arms. ...a severe mental disorder.* **2 Disorder** is a state of being untidy, badly prepared, or badly organized. *The emergency room was in disorder... Inside all was disorder.* **3 Disorder** is violence or rioting in public. *There are other forms of civil disorder – most notably, football hooliganism.*   ♦♦◇◇◇   N-VAR   N-UNCOUNT   N-VAR

dis·or·dered /ˌdɪs'ɔːdəd/. **1** If you describe something as **disordered**, you mean it is untidy and is not neatly arranged. *Moretti ran a hand through his disordered red hair.* **2** Someone who is mentally **disordered** or who has a **disordered** mind is mentally ill. *...mentally disordered offenders.*   ADJ-GRADED   ADJ-GRADED

dis·or·der·ly /ˌdɪs'ɔːdəli/. **1** If you describe something as **disorderly**, you mean that it is untidy, irregular, or disorganized. *...the large and disorderly room.* **2** If you describe someone as **disorderly**, you mean that they are behaving in a noisy, rude, or violent way in public. *He pleaded guilty to being disorderly on licensed premises... Football matches are disorderly events.* **3** If someone is charged with being **drunk and disorderly**, they are accused of being drunk and behaving in a noisy, offensive, or violent way in public.   ADJ-GRADED   FORMAL   ADJ-GRADED   FORMAL   PHRASE   LEGAL

dis·or·gani·za·tion /ˌdɪsˌɔːɡənaɪ'zeɪʃən/; also spelled **disorganisation** in British English. If something is in a state of **disorganization**, it is disorganized.   N-UNCOUNT

dis·or·gan·ized /ˌdɪs'ɔːɡənaɪzd/; also spelled **disorganised** in British English. **1** Something that is **disorganized** is in a confused state or is badly planned or managed. *He described the police action as confused and disorganised. ...a disorganised, demoralised rabble.* **2** Someone who is **disorganized** is very bad at organizing things in their life. *My boss is completely disorganised.*   ♦◇◇◇◇ ADJ-GRADED   ADJ-GRADED

dis·ori·ent /ˌdɪs'ɔːrient/ **disorients, disorienting, disoriented.** British English also uses the form **disorientate**. If something **disorients** you, you lose your sense of direction, or you generally feel lost and uncertain. *An overnight stay at a friend's house disorients me.* ♦ **dis·ori·ent·ed** *I feel dizzy and disoriented.* ♦ **dis·ori·ent·ing** *An abrupt change of location can be disorienting.* ♦ **dis·ori·en·ta·tion** /ˌdɪsˌɔːriən'teɪʃən/ *He experienced a moment of total disorientation.*   ♦◇◇◇◇   VERB   V n   ADJ-GRADED   ADJ-GRADED   N-UNCOUNT

dis·ori·en·tate /ˌdɪs'ɔːriənteɪt/. See **disorient**.

dis·own /ˌdɪs'əʊn/ **disowns, disowning, disowned.** If you **disown** someone or something, you say or show that you no longer want to have any connection with them. *The man who murdered the girl is no son of mine. I disown him.*   VERB   V n

dis·par·age /ˌdɪs'pærɪdʒ/ **disparages, disparaging, disparaged.** If you **disparage** someone or something, you speak about them in a way which   VERB   V n   FORMAL

D

shows that you do not have a good opinion of them. *...Larkin's tendency to disparage literature.* ♦ **dis·par·age·ment** /dɪsˈpærɪdʒmənt/ *Reviewers have been almost unanimous in their disparagement of this book.* ♦ **dis·par·ag·ing** /dɪsˈpærɪdʒɪŋ/ *The Minister was alleged to have made disparaging remarks about the rest of the Cabinet.* ♦ **dis·par·ag·ing·ly** *Do not talk disparagingly about your company or colleagues in public.* N-UNCOUNT | ADJ-GRADED | ADV-GRADED: ADV with v

dis·par·ate /ˈdɪspərət/. **1** Disparate things are clearly different from each other in quality or type. *Scientists are trying to pull together disparate ideas in astronomy.* **2** A disparate thing is made up of very different elements. *...a very disparate nation.* ◆◇◇◇ ADJ-GRADED FORMAL | ADJ-GRADED FORMAL

dis·par·ity /dɪsˈpærɪti/ **disparities.** If there is a disparity between two or more things, there is a noticeable difference between them. *...the economic disparities between East and West Berlin.* ◆◇◇◇ N-VAR FORMAL

dis·pas·sion·ate /dɪsˈpæʃənət/. Someone who is dispassionate is calm and reasonable, and not affected by emotions. *...the flat, dispassionate tone of a lecturer.* ♦ **dis·pas·sion·ate·ly** *He sets out the facts coolly and dispassionately.* ADJ-GRADED | ADV-GRADED: ADV with v

dis·patch /dɪsˈpætʃ/ **dispatches, dispatching, dispatched;** also spelled **despatch** in British English. **1** If you dispatch someone to a place, you send them there. *The Italian government was preparing to dispatch 4,000 soldiers to search the island.* ▶ Also a noun. *...the despatch of the task force.* **2** If you dispatch a message, letter, or parcel, you send it to a person or place. *The victory inspired him to dispatch a gleeful telegram to Roosevelt.* ▶ Also a noun. *We have 125 cases ready for dispatch.* **3** A dispatch is a special report that is sent to a newspaper or broadcasting organization by a journalist who is in a different town or country. *...this despatch from our West Africa correspondent.* **4** A dispatch is a message or report that is sent, for example, by government officials to their headquarters. *I was carrying dispatches from the ambassador.* ● If a soldier is **mentioned in dispatches,** he or she is considered to have been extremely brave in a battle, and is recommended for a medal. ◆◆◇◇ VERB: V n adv/prep, V n to-inf | N-UNCOUNT | VERB: V n prep/adv FORMAL | N-COUNT | N-COUNT | PHRASE

dis·pel /dɪsˈpel/ **dispels, dispelling, dispelled.** To dispel an idea or feeling means to stop people having it. *The President is attempting to dispel the notion that he has neglected the economy.* ◆◇◇◇ VERB V n

dis·pen·sable /dɪsˈpensəbəl/. If someone or something is dispensable they are not really needed. *All those people in the middle are dispensable.* ADJ-GRADED

dis·pen·sa·ry /dɪsˈpensəri/ **dispensaries.** A dispensary is a place where medicines are prepared and given out. N-COUNT

dis·pen·sa·tion /ˌdɪspenˈseɪʃən/ **dispensations.** **1** A dispensation is special permission to do something that is normally not allowed. *A special dispensation may be obtained from the domestic union.* **2** A dispensation is a religious or political system that has authority at a particular time. N-VAR | N-COUNT

dis·pense /dɪsˈpens/ **dispenses, dispensing, dispensed.** **1** If someone dispenses something that they possess or control, they give, provide, or administer it to a number of people. *I thought of myself as a patriarch, dispensing words of wisdom to all my children.* ♦ **dis·pen·sa·tion** /ˌdɪspenˈseɪʃən/ *...consistent standards in the dispensation of justice.* **2** If you obtain a product by getting it out of a machine, you can say that the machine dispenses the product. ♦ **dis·pens·er** /dɪsˈpensə/ **dispensers.** A dispenser is a machine or container designed to dispense things. **3** When a chemist dispenses medicine, he or she prepares it, and gives or sells it to the patient. ◆◇◇◇ VERB: V n FORMAL | N-UNCOUNT N of n | VERB: V n | N-COUNT | VERB: V n

dispense with. If you dispense with something, you stop using it or get rid of it altogether. *Many households have dispensed with their old-fashioned vinyl turntable.* PHRASAL VB V P n

dis·perse /dɪsˈpɜːs/ **disperses, dispersing, dispersed.** **1** When a group of people disperses or when someone disperses them, the group splits up ◆◆◇◇ V-ERG Also V n

and the people leave in different directions. *The crowd dispersed peacefully.* ♦ **dis·per·sal** /dɪsˈpɜːsəl/ *The police ordered the dispersal of the crowds.* **2** When things disperse or when you disperse them, they spread over a wide area. *The leaflets were dispersed throughout the country by the rebels.* ♦ **dispersal** *Plants have different mechanisms of dispersal for their spores.* **3** When a harmful substance disperses or when you disperse it, it spreads over a wide area and so becomes less concentrated. *The intense currents disperse the sewage.* ♦ **dispersal** *...the dispersal of the oil by rough seas.* N-UNCOUNT | V-ERG Also V | N-UNCOUNT | V-ERG Vn Also V | N-UNCOUNT

dis·persed /dɪsˈpɜːst/. Things that are dispersed are situated in many different places, a long way apart from each other. *They live high in the Andes, in small and dispersed groups.* ◆◇◇◇ ADJ-GRADED

dis·per·sion /dɪsˈpɜːʃən/. **Dispersion** is the spreading of people or things over a wide area. *The threat complicates military planning, forcing greater dispersion of their forces.* N-UNCOUNT FORMAL

dis·pir·it·ed /dɪsˈpɪrɪtɪd/. If you are dispirited, you have lost your enthusiasm and excitement. *I left eventually at six o'clock feeling utterly dispirited.* ADJ-GRADED

dis·pir·it·ing /dɪsˈpɪrɪtɪŋ/. Something that is dispiriting causes you to lose your enthusiasm and excitement. *It's very dispiriting for anyone to be out of a job.* ADJ-GRADED

dis·place /dɪsˈpleɪs/ **displaces, displacing, displaced.** **1** If one thing displaces another, it forces the other thing out of its place, position, or role, and then occupies that place, position, or role itself. *These factories have displaced tourism as the country's largest source of foreign exchange.* ♦ **dis·place·ment** *...the displacement of your reason by your emotions.* **2** If a person or group of people is displaced, they are forced to move away from the area where they live. *...resettling refugees and displaced persons.* ♦ **displacement** *...the gradual displacement of the American Indian.* ◆◆◇◇ VERB Vn | N-UNCOUNT | beV-ed V-ed | N-UNCOUNT

dis·play /dɪsˈpleɪ/ **displays, displaying, displayed.** **1** If you display something, you put it in a place, so that people can see it easily. *...war veterans proudly displaying their medals.* ▶ Also a noun. *...the other artists whose work is on display.* **2** If you display something, you show it to people. *She displayed her wound to the twelve gentlemen of the jury.* **3** A display is an arrangement of things that have been put in a place, so that people can see them easily. *...a display of your work.* **4** A display is a public performance or other event which is intended to entertain people. *...the firework display. ...gymnastic displays.* **5** If you display a characteristic, quality, or emotion, you behave in a way which shows that you have it. *It was unlike Gordon to display his feelings.* ▶ Also a noun. *...an outward display of affection.* **6** When a computer displays information, it shows it on a screen. **7** The display on a computer screen is the information that is shown there. The screen itself can also be referred to as the display. ● See also **liquid crystal display.** ◆◆◆◇ VERB Vn | N-UNCOUNT | VERB: V n ton | N-COUNT | N-COUNT: with supp | VERB Vn | N-VAR | VERB: Vn | N-COUNT

dis·please /dɪsˈpliːz/ **displeases, displeasing, displeased.** If something or someone displeases you, they make you annoyed or rather angry. *Not wishing to displease her, he avoided answering the question.* ♦ **dis·pleased** *Businessmen are displeased with erratic economic policy-making... He was not displeased at the way he had handled the meeting.* VERB Vn | ADJ-GRADED: v-link ADJ

dis·pleas·ure /dɪsˈpleʒə/. Someone's displeasure is a feeling of annoyance that they have about something that has happened. *The population has already begun to show its displeasure at the slow pace of change.* ◆◇◇◇ N-UNCOUNT

dis·pos·able /dɪsˈpəʊzəbəl/ **disposables. 1** A disposable product is designed to be thrown away after it has been used. *...disposable nappies.* ▶ Disposable products can be referred to as **disposables.** **2** Your disposable income is the amount of income ◆◇◇◇ ADJ | N-COUNT | ADJ: ADJ n

you have left after you have paid income tax and social security contributions.

dis·pos·al /dɪsˈpəʊzəl/. If you have something **at** ◆◆◇◇◇
your **disposal**, you are able to use it whenever you PHRASE
want. If you say that you are **at** someone else's **disposal**, you mean that you are willing to help them
in any way you can. *Do you have this information at
your disposal?... If I can be of service, I am at your
disposal.*

dis·pose /dɪsˈpəʊz/ **disposes, disposing, dis-** ◆◆◇◇◇
posed.

dispose of. 1 If you **dispose of** something that you PHRASAL VB
no longer want or need, you throw it away. *Just fold up* VPn
the nappy and dispose of it in the normal manner.
♦ **dis·pos·al** /dɪsˈpəʊzəl/ *...the permanent disposal of* N-UNCOUNT
radioactive wastes. **2** If you **dispose of** a problem, VPn
task, or question, you deal with it. *...the manner in
which you disposed of that problem.* **3** To **dispose of** a VPn
person or an animal means to kill them. *They had* FORMAL
hired an assassin to dispose of him.

dis·posed /dɪsˈpəʊzd/. **1** If you are **disposed** to do ◆◇◇◇◇
something, you are willing or eager to do it. *We* ADJ-GRADED
passed one or two dwellings, but were not disposed FORMAL
to stop. **2** You can use **disposed** when you are talk- ADJ-GRADED
ing about someone's general attitude or opinion FORMAL
about someone or something. *Every government is
ill-disposed to the press, all or some of the time.*
3 If things are **disposed** in a particular way, they are ADJ:
arranged in that way. *...the way colour was disposed* v-link ADJ
within a room. FORMAL

dis·po·si·tion /ˌdɪspəˈzɪʃən/ **dispositions.** ◆◇◇◇◇
1 Someone's **disposition** is the way that they tend N-COUNT
to behave or feel. *...people of a nervous disposition.*
2 A **disposition** to do something is a willingness to N-SING
do it. *They show no disposition to improvise.* FORMAL
3 If you refer to **the disposition of** a number of ob- N-SING:
jects, you mean the way in which they are arranged. theN ofn
...to understand the buildings from the disposition of FORMAL
walls and entrances.
4 The **disposition of** money or property is the act of N-COUNT:
giving or distributing it to a number of people. *...Judge* N ofn
John Stacks, appointed to oversee the disposition of LEGAL
funds.

dis·pos·sess /ˌdɪspəˈzes/ **dispossesses, dispos-** VERB:
sessing, dispossessed. If you **are dispossessed** beV-ed ofn
of something that you own, it is taken away from Vn
you. *They settled the land, dispossessing many of its* Also Vn of/
original inhabitants. ▶ **The dispossessed** are people fromn
who are dispossessed. N-PLURAL:
theN

dis·pro·por·tion /ˌdɪsprəˈpɔːʃən/ **disproportions.** N-VAR
A **disproportion** is a state in which two things are FORMAL
unequal. *...a striking disproportion in the legal resources available to the two sides.*

dis·pro·por·tion·ate /ˌdɪsprəˈpɔːʃənət/. Some- ◆◇◇◇◇
thing that is **disproportionate** is surprising or un- ADJ-GRADED
reasonable in amount or size, compared with something else. *A disproportionate amount of time was
devoted to one topic.* ♦ **dis·pro·por·tion·ate·ly** ADV
*There is a disproportionately high suicide rate
among prisoners facing very long sentences.*

dis·prove /ˌdɪsˈpruːv/ **disproves, disproving,** ◆◇◇◇◇
disproved, disproven. To **disprove** an idea, be- VERB
lief, or theory means to show that it is not true. Vn
...the statistics to prove or disprove his hypothesis.

dis·pute /dɪsˈpjuːt/ **disputes, disputing, dis-** ◆◆◆◇◇
puted. 1 A **dispute** is an argument or disagree- N-VAR
ment between people or groups. *...pay disputes with
the government.* **2** If you **dispute** a fact, statement, VERB: Vn
or theory, you say that it is incorrect or untrue. *No-* V that
body disputed that Davey was clever. **3** When people Also Vwh
dispute something, they fight for control or owner- V-RECIP:
ship of it. *Fishermen from Bristol disputed fishing* Also Vn (non-
rights with the Danes. **4** If two or more people or recip)
groups are **in dispute**, they are arguing or disagree- PHRASE
ing about something. *The two countries are in dispute over the boundaries of their coastal waters... It
is currently in dispute with the government over
price fixing.* **5** If something is **in dispute**, people are PHRASE
questioning it or arguing about it. *All those matters
are in dispute.*

dis·quali·fy /dɪsˈkwɒlɪfaɪ/ **disqualifies, dis-** ◆◇◇◇◇
qualifying, disqualified. When someone **is dis-** VERB:
qualified from an event, an activity, or a competi- beV-ed fromn
tion, they are officially stopped from taking part in Also Vn from
it. *The stewards conferred, and then they eventually
decided to disqualify us.* ♦ **dis·quali·fi·ca·tion** N-VAR
/ˌdɪsˌkwɒlɪfɪˈkeɪʃən/ **disqualifications** *...a four-
year disqualification from athletics.*

dis·qui·et /dɪsˈkwaɪət/ **disquiets, disquieting,** ◆◇◇◇◇
disquieted. 1 Disquiet is a feeling of worry or N-UNCOUNT
anxiety. *There is growing disquiet about the cost of* FORMAL
such policing. **2** If something **disquiets** you, it VERB
makes you feel anxious. *She had been favored with* Vn
some inside information and this disquieted him. FORMAL
♦ **dis·qui·et·ing** *He found her letter disquieting.* ADJ-GRADED

dis·re·gard /ˌdɪsrɪˈɡɑːd/ **disregards, disregard-** ◆◇◇◇◇
ing, disregarded. If you **disregard** something, Vn
you ignore it or do not take account of it. *He disregarded the advice of his executives.* ▶ Also a noun. N-UNCOUNT
...a total disregard for the safety of the public.

dis·re·pair /ˌdɪsrɪˈpeə/. If something is **in disrepair** PHRASE
or is **in a state of disrepair**, it is broken or in bad
condition. *The house was unoccupied and in a bad
state of disrepair.*

dis·repu·table /ˌdɪsˈrepjʊtəbəl/. If you say that ADJ-GRADED
someone or something is **disreputable**, you are PRAGMATICS
critical of them because they are not respectable or
trustworthy. *...enjoying the company of disreputable
women.*

dis·re·pute /ˌdɪsrɪˈpjuːt/. If something is brought ◆◇◇◇◇
into disrepute or falls **into disrepute**, it loses its PHRASE
good reputation, because it is connected with activities that people do not approve of. *It is a disgrace
that such people should bring our profession into
disrepute.*

dis·re·spect /ˌdɪsrɪˈspekt/. **1** If someone shows N-UNCOUNT:
disrespect, they speak or behave in a way that also aN
shows lack of respect for a person, law, or custom.
*...young people with complete disrespect for author-
ity.* **2** You can say '**no disrespect** to someone or PHRASE
something' when you are just about to criticize PRAGMATICS
them, in order to indicate that you are not hostile n
towards them or admire them for other things. *No
disrespect to John Beck, but the club has been happier since he left.*

dis·re·spect·ful /ˌdɪsrɪˈspektfʊl/. If you are **disre-** ADJ-GRADED
spectful, you show no respect in the way that you
speak or behave to someone. *...accusations that he
had been disrespectful to the Queen.* ♦ **dis·re-** ADV-GRADED:
·spect·ful·ly *They get angry if they think they are* ADV with v
being treated disrespectfully.

dis·robe /dɪsˈrəʊb/ **disrobes, disrobing, dis-** VERB: V
robed. When someone **disrobes**, they remove their FORMAL
clothes.

dis·rupt /dɪsˈrʌpt/ **disrupts, disrupting, dis-** ◆◆◇◇◇
rupted. If someone or something **disrupts** an VERB
event, system, or process, they cause difficulties Vn
that prevent it from continuing or operating in a
normal way. *Anti-war protesters disrupted the debate.* ♦ **dis·rup·tion** /dɪsˈrʌpʃən/ **disruptions** *The* N-VAR
*strike is expected to cause delays and disruption to
flights.* ♦ **dis·rup·tive** /dɪsˈrʌptɪv/. *...violent, dis-* ADJ-GRADED
ruptive behavior.

dis·sat·is·fied /ˌdɪsˈsætɪsfaɪd/. If you are **dissatis-** ◆◇◇◇◇
fied with something, you are not contented or ADJ-GRADED
pleased with it. *82% of voters are dissatisfied with
the way their country is being governed.* ♦ **dis·sat-
·is·fac·tion** /ˌdɪsˌsætɪsˈfækʃən/. If you feel **dissatis-** N-UNCOUNT
faction with something, you are not contented or
pleased with it. *...job dissatisfaction among teachers.*

dis·sect /daɪˈsekt, dɪ-/ **dissects, dissecting,** ◆◇◇◇◇
dissected. 1 If someone **dissects** the body of a VERB
dead person or animal, they carefully cut it up in Vn
order to examine it scientifically. *We dissected a frog
in biology class.* ♦ **dis·sec·tion** /daɪˈsekʃən, dɪ-/ N-VAR
dissections *Researchers need a growing supply of
corpses for dissection.* **2** If someone **dissects** some- VERB
thing such as a theory, situation, or piece of writing, Vn
they consider and talk about each detail of it. *People
want to dissect his work and question his motives.*

♦ **dissection** ...*her calm, condescending dissection of my proposals.* N-VAR

dis·sem·ble /dɪˈsembəl/ **dissembles, dissembling, dissembled.** When people **dissemble**, they hide their real motives or emotions. *Henry was not slow to dissemble when it served his purposes.* VERB / Also V / LITERARY

dis·sem·i·nate /dɪˈsemɪneɪt/ **disseminates, disseminating, disseminated.** To **disseminate** information or knowledge means to distribute it so that it reaches many people. *It took years to disseminate information about Aids.* ♦ **dis·sem·i·na·tion** /dɪˌsemɪˈneɪʃən/ ...*the dissemination of scientific ideas.* ◆◇◇◇◇ VERB V n / N-UNCOUNT

dis·sen·sion /dɪˈsenʃən/ **dissensions. Dissension** is disagreement and argument. *The tax cut issue has caused dissension among administration officials.* N-UNCOUNT: also N in pl / FORMAL

dis·sent /dɪˈsent/ **dissents, dissenting, dissented.** If you **dissent**, you express disagreement with a decision or opinion, especially one that is supported by most people or by people in authority. *No one dissents from the decision to unify.* ▸ **Dissent** is strong disagreement or dissatisfaction with a decision or opinion. *He is the toughest military ruler yet and has responded harshly to any dissent.* ♦ **dis·sent·er** /dɪˈsentə/ **dissenters** *The Party does not tolerate dissenters in its ranks.* ◆◇◇◇◇ VERB: V / V from n / FORMAL / N-UNCOUNT / N-COUNT

dis·ser·ta·tion /ˌdɪsəˈteɪʃən/ **dissertations.** A **dissertation** is a long formal piece of writing on a subject, especially for a university degree. ◆◇◇◇◇ N-COUNT

dis·ser·vice /ˌdɪsˈsɜːvɪs/. If you do someone or something a **disservice**, you do something that harms them. *He said the protesters were doing a disservice to the nation.* N-SING / FORMAL

dis·si·dent /ˈdɪsɪdənt/ **dissidents. Dissidents** are people who disagree with and criticize their government, which is totalitarian or repressive. ...*a dissident Chinese novelist.* ◆◆◇◇◇ N-COUNT

dis·simi·lar /ˌdɪsˈsɪmɪlə/. If one thing is **dissimilar** to another, or if two things are **dissimilar**, they are very different from each other. *His methods were not dissimilar to those used by Freud... It would be difficult to find two men who were more dissimilar.* ADJ-GRADED

♦ **dis·simi·lar·ity** /ˌdɪsɪmɪˈlærɪti/ **dissimilarities** ...*the dissimilarity between parents and children.* N-VAR

dis·si·pate /ˈdɪsɪpeɪt/ **dissipates, dissipating, dissipated.** 1 When something **dissipates** or when you **dissipate** it, it becomes less or becomes less strong until it goes away completely. *The tension in the room had dissipated.* ♦ **dis·si·pa·tion** ...*heat dissipation.* 2 When someone **dissipates** money, time, or effort, they waste it in a foolish way. *Her father had dissipated her inheritance.* ♦ **dissipation** ...*the dissipation of my wealth.* ◆◇◇◇◇ V-ERG / V / Also V n / FORMAL / N-UNCOUNT / VERB / V n / FORMAL / N-UNCOUNT

dis·si·pat·ed /ˈdɪsɪpeɪtɪd/. If you describe someone as **dissipated**, you disapprove of them because they spend a lot of time drinking alcohol and enjoying other physical pleasures, and are probably unhealthy because of this. *Flynn was a charming fellow, still handsome though dissipated.* ADJ-GRADED PRAGMATICS / LITERARY

dis·so·ci·ate /dɪˈsəʊsieɪt/ **dissociates, dissociating, dissociated.** 1 If you **dissociate** yourself from something or someone, you say or show that you are not connected with them, usually in order to avoid trouble or blame. *It seems harder and harder for the president to dissociate himself from the scandals.* 2 If you **dissociate** one thing from another, you consider the two things as separate from each other, or you separate them. ...*how to dissociate emotion from reason.* ♦ **dis·so·cia·tion** /dɪˌsəʊsiˈeɪʃən/ *There is a war between the sexes but this should not result in their complete dissociation from one another.* VERB / V pron-refl from n / VERB / V n from n / FORMAL / N-UNCOUNT

dis·so·lute /ˈdɪsəluːt/. Someone who is **dissolute** lives in a way that is considered to be wicked and immoral; used showing disapproval. ADJ-GRADED PRAGMATICS

dis·solve /dɪˈzɒlv/ **dissolves, dissolving, dissolved.** 1 If a substance **dissolves** in liquid or if you **dissolve** it, it becomes mixed with the liquid and disappears. *Heat gently until the sugar dissolves.* 2 If something such as a problem or feeling **dissolves** ◆◆◇◇◇ V-ERG / Also V n / V-ERG

or **is dissolved**, it becomes weaker and disappears. *His new-found optimism dissolved.* ♦ **dis·so·lu·tion** /ˌdɪsəˈluːʃən/ ...*the dissolution of traditional family life.* Also V n / N-UNCOUNT: also a N

3 When an organization, institution, or parliament **is dissolved**, it is officially ended or broken up. *The King agreed to dissolve the present commission.* ♦ **dissolution** *Politicians say it could lead to a dissolution of parliament.* 4 When a marriage or business arrangement **is dissolved**, it is officially ended. ♦ **dissolution** ...*the statutory requirement for granting dissolution of a marriage.* VERB V n / N-UNCOUNT: also a N / VERB: be V-ed / N-UNCOUNT: also a N

dissolve into. If you **dissolve into** or **dissolve in** tears or laughter, you begin to cry or laugh, because you cannot control yourself. *She dissolved into tears at the mention of Munya's name.* PHRASAL VB V P noun

dis·so·nance /ˈdɪsənəns/. **Dissonance** is a lack of agreement or harmony between things. N-UNCOUNT FORMAL

dis·suade /dɪˈsweɪd/ **dissuades, dissuading, dissuaded.** If you **dissuade** someone from doing or believing something, you persuade them not to do or believe it. *He considered emigrating, but his family managed to dissuade him.* ◆◇◇◇◇ VERB V n from / -ing/n / V n / FORMAL

dis·tance /ˈdɪstəns/ **distances, distancing, distanced.** 1 The **distance** between two points or places is the amount of space between them. ...*the distance between the island and the nearby shore.* ...*within walking distance.* ◆◆◆◆◇ N-VAR: with supp

2 When two things are very far apart, you talk about the **distance** between them. *The distance wouldn't be a problem.* 3 If you can see something **in the distance**, you can see it, far away from you. *We suddenly saw her in the distance.* 4 If you **keep** your **distance** from someone or something, you do not get physically close to them. N-UNCOUNT / N-SING: in/into the N / PHRASE

5 When you want to emphasize that two people or things do not have a close relationship or are not the same, you can refer to the **distance** between them. *There was a vast distance between psychological clues and concrete proof.* N-UNCOUNT PRAGMATICS

6 **Distance** is detachment and remoteness in the way that someone behaves so that they do not seem friendly. *There were periods of sulking, of pronounced distance, of coldness.* N-UNCOUNT FORMAL

7 If you **distance** yourself from someone or something or if something **distances** you from them, you feel less friendly or positive towards them, or become less involved with them. *The author distanced himself from some of the comments in his book.* ♦ **dis·tanced** *He'd become too distanced from his fans.* 8 If you **keep** your **distance** from someone or something or **keep** them **at a distance**, you do not become involved with them. *Jay had always tended to keep his girlfriends at a distance.* VERB V pron-refl from n / Also V n from / ADJ-GRADED v-link ADJ / PHRASE

9 If you are **at a distance** from something or if you see it or remember it **from a distance**, you are a long way away from it in space or time. ...*now that I can look back on the whole tragedy from a distance of nearly forty years.* PHRASE

10 If you **go the distance** in a race or sports competition, you continue running or playing until the end of the race or match. *More riders than ever are now determined to go the distance.* PHRASE INFORMAL

dis·tant /ˈdɪstənt/. 1 **Distant** means very far away. *The mountains rolled away to a distant horizon.* ♦ **dis·tant·ly** *They were too distantly seated for any conversation.* ◆◆◇◇◇ ADJ-GRADED WRITTEN / ADV-GRADED

2 You use **distant** to describe a time or event that is very far away in the future or in the past. *Things will improve in the not too distant future.* ADJ-GRADED

3 A **distant** relative is one who you are not closely related to. ♦ **distantly** *His father's distantly related to the Royal family.* ADJ-GRADED / ADV-GRADED

4 If you describe someone as **distant**, you mean that you find them emotionally detached and unfriendly. *He found her cold, ice-like and distant.* ADJ-GRADED: v-link ADJ

5 If you describe someone as **distant**, you mean that they are not concentrating on what they are doing because they are thinking about other things. *There was* ADJ-GRADED

a distant look in her eyes. ♦ **distantly** *'He's in the interview room,' she said distantly.*   ADV-GRADED: ADV after v

dis·tant·ly /ˈdɪstəntli/. **1** If you are **distantly** aware of something or if you **distantly** remember it, you are aware of it or remember it, but not very strongly. *She became distantly aware that the light had grown strangely brighter.* **2** See also **distant**.   ADV-GRADED

dis·taste /dɪsˈteɪst/. If you feel **distaste** for someone or something, you dislike them and consider them to be unpleasant, disgusting, or immoral. *Roger looked at her with distaste.* ♦ **dis·taste·ful** /dɪsˈteɪstfʊl/. If something is **distasteful** to you, you think it is unpleasant, disgusting, or immoral. *The film itself is actually distasteful to him.*   ◆◇◇◇◇ N-UNCOUNT   ADJ-GRADED

dis·tem·per /dɪsˈtempə/. **1 Distemper** is a dangerous and infectious disease that can be caught by animals.   N-UNCOUNT

2 Distemper is a kind of paint sometimes used for painting walls.   N-UNCOUNT

dis·tend /dɪsˈtend/ **distends, distending, distended.** If a part of your body **is distended** or if it **distends**, it becomes swollen and unnaturally large. *The abdominal cavity is distended with carbon dioxide gas... The colon, or large intestine, distends and fills with gas.* ♦ **dis·tend·ed** *...an infant with a distended belly.* ♦ **dis·ten·sion** /dɪsˈtenʃən/.   V-ERG beV-ed V   Also V n MEDICAL   ADJ-GRADED   N-UNCOUNT

dis·til /dɪsˈtɪl/ **distils, distilling, distilled;** spelled **distill** in American English. **1** If a liquid such as whisky **is distilled**, it is heated until it evaporates and then cooled until it becomes liquid again. ♦ **dis·til·la·tion** /ˌdɪstɪˈleɪʃən/ *Any faults in the original cider stood out sharply after distillation.* ♦ **dis·till·er, distillers.** A **distiller** is a person or a company that makes whisky or a similar strong alcoholic drink by a process of distilling. **2** If an oil or liquid **is distilled** from a plant, it is produced by a process which extracts the main part or essence of the plant. To **distil** a plant means to produce an oil or liquid from it by this process. *The oil is distilled from the berries of this small tree. ...the art of distilling rose petals.* ♦ **distillation** *The distillation of rose petals to produce rosewater.* **3** If a thought or idea **is distilled** from previous thoughts, ideas, or experiences, it is derived from them. *Eventually passion was distilled into the natural beauty of a balmy night... Roy distills these messages into something powerful.* ♦ **dis·til·la·tion** *The material below is a distillation of his work.*   ◆◇◇◇◇ VERB: beV-ed   N-UNCOUNT   N-COUNT   VERB beV-ed from n V n Also V n from n   N-UNCOUNT   VERB beV-ed into/ from n V n into n   N-SING

dis·till·ery /dɪsˈtɪləri/ **distilleries.** A **distillery** is a place where whisky or a similar strong alcoholic drink is made by a process of distilling.   ◆◇◇◇◇ N-COUNT

dis·tinct /dɪsˈtɪŋkt/. **1** If something is **distinct** from something else of the same type, it is recognizably different or separate from it. *Engineering and technology are disciplines distinct from one another. ...oily fish, as distinct from fatty meat.* ♦ **dis·tinct·ly** *...a banking industry with two distinctly different sectors.*   ◆◆◇◇◇ ADJ-GRADED   ADV-GRADED: ADV adj

2 If something is **distinct**, you can hear, see, or taste it clearly. *...to impart a distinct flavor with a minimum of cooking fat.* ♦ **distinctly** *I distinctly heard the loudspeaker.* **3** If an idea, thought, or intention is **distinct**, it is clear and definite. *There was a distinct change in her attitude... I have distinct memories of him.* ♦ **distinctly** *I distinctly remember wishing I had not got involved.*   ADJ-GRADED   ADV-GRADED   ADV-GRADED: ADV with v

4 You can use **distinct** to emphasize that something is great enough in amount or degree to be noticeable or important. *Being 6ft 3in tall has some distinct disadvantages!* ♦ **distinctly** *His government is looking distinctly shaky.*   ADJ-GRADED: ADJ n PRAGMATICS   ADV-GRADED: ADV adj/-ed

dis·tinc·tion /dɪsˈtɪŋkʃən/ **distinctions. 1** A **distinction** is a difference between similar things. *...obvious distinctions between the two wine-making areas.* ● If you **draw a distinction** or **make a distinction**, you say that two things are different. *He draws a distinction between art and culture.*   N-COUNT   PHRASE

2 Distinction is the quality of excellence, superiority, and merit. *...pieces of furniture of distinction.* **3** A **distinction** is a special award or honour that is given to   N-UNCOUNT   N-COUNT

someone as a recognition of their very high level of achievement. *I did an M.A. at Liverpool University in Latin American Studies and got a distinction.* **4** If you say that someone or something has the **distinction** of being something, you are drawing attention to the fact that they have the special or unique quality of being that thing. *The book had the distinction of being published in the former Soviet Union.*   N-SING PRAGMATICS

dis·tinc·tive /dɪsˈtɪŋktɪv/. Something that is **distinctive** has a special quality or feature which makes it easily recognizable and different from other things of the same type. *...the distinctive odour of chlorine... His voice was very distinctive.* ♦ **dis·tinc·tive·ly** *...the distinctively fragrant taste of elderflowers.* ♦ **dis·tinc·tive·ness** *His own distinctiveness was always evident at school.*   ◆◆◇◇◇ ADJ-GRADED   ADV-GRADED: ADV adj/-ed N-UNCOUNT

dis·tin·guish /dɪsˈtɪŋgwɪʃ/ **distinguishes, distinguishing, distinguished. 1** If you can distinguish one thing from another, you can see or understand the difference between them. *Could he distinguish right from wrong? ...distinguishing between areas of light and dark.* **2** A feature or quality that **distinguishes** one thing from another causes the two things to be regarded as different. *There is something about music that distinguishes it from all other art forms.* **3** If you can **distinguish** something, you can see, hear, or taste it although it is very difficult to detect. *He could distinguish voices.* **4** If you **distinguish** yourself, you do something that makes you famous or important. *He distinguished himself as a leading constitutional scholar.*   ◆◆◇◇◇ VERB V n from n V between pl-n Also V pl-n   VERB V n from n   VERB V n FORMAL   VERB: V pron-refl V pron-refl as n

dis·tin·guish·able /dɪsˈtɪŋgwɪʃəbəl/. **1** If something is **distinguishable** from other things, it has a quality or feature which makes it possible for you to recognize it and see that it is different. *...features that make their products distinguishable from those of their rivals.* **2** If something is **distinguishable**, you can see or hear it in conditions when it is difficult to see or hear anything. *It would be getting light soon now. Already shapes were more distinguishable.*   ADJ-GRADED   ADJ-GRADED: v-link ADJ

dis·tin·guished /dɪsˈtɪŋgwɪʃt/. **1** If you describe a person or their work as **distinguished**, you mean they have been very successful in their career and have a good reputation. *...a distinguished academic family.* **2** If you describe someone as **distinguished**, you mean that they look very noble and dignified. *...a distinguished gentleman.*   ◆◆◇◇◇ ADJ-GRADED

dis·tort /dɪsˈtɔːt/ **distorts, distorting, distorted. 1** If you **distort** a statement, fact, or idea, you report or represent it in an untrue way. *The media distorts reality.* ♦ **dis·tort·ed** *These figures give a distorted view.* ♦ **dis·tor·tion** /dɪsˈtɔːʃən/ **distortions** *He later accused reporters of wilful distortion and bias.* **2** If something you can see or hear **is distorted** or **distorts**, its appearance or sound is changed so that it seems strange. *A painter may exaggerate or distort shapes and forms... His face was beginning to distort.* ♦ **dis·tort·ed** *Sound was becoming more and more distorted through the use of hearing aids.* ♦ **dis·tor·tion** *Audio signals could be transmitted along cables without distortion.*   ◆◆◇◇◇ VERB V n   ADJ-GRADED   N-VAR   V-ERG V n V   ADJ-GRADED   N-VAR

dis·tract /dɪsˈtrækt/ **distracts, distracting, distracted.** If something **distracts** you or your attention from something, it takes your attention away from it. *Playing video games sometimes distracts him from his homework... Don't let yourself be distracted by fashionable theories.*   ◆◇◇◇◇ VERB: V n V n from n beV-ed

dis·tract·ed /dɪsˈtræktɪd/. If you are **distracted**, you are not concentrating on something because you are worried or are thinking about something else. *She had seemed curiously distracted.* ♦ **dis·tract·ed·ly** *He looked up distractedly. 'Be with you in a second.'*   ◆◇◇◇◇ ADJ-GRADED   ADV: ADV with v

dis·tract·ing /dɪsˈtræktɪŋ/. If you say that something is **distracting**, you mean that it makes it difficult for you to concentrate properly on what you are doing. *I find it slightly distracting to have someone watching me while I work.*   ADJ-GRADED

dis·trac·tion /dɪsˈtrækʃən/ **distractions. 1** A **distraction** is something that turns your attention   ◆◇◇◇◇ N-VAR

away from something you want to concentrate on. *This is getting to be a distraction from what I really want to do.* 2 A **distraction** is an activity which is N-COUNT intended to entertain and amuse you. *Their national distraction is going to the disco.*

dis·traught /dɪ'strɔːt/. If someone is **distraught**, ◇◇◇◇◇ they are so upset and worried that they cannot ADJ-GRADED think clearly. *Mr Barker's distraught parents were last night being comforted by relatives.*

dis·tress /dɪ'stres/ **distresses, distressing,** ◆◆◇◇◇ **distressed. 1 Distress** is a state of extreme sor- N-UNCOUNT row, suffering, or pain. *Jealousy causes distress and painful emotions... Her mouth grew stiff with pain and distress.* 2 **Distress** is the state of being in ex- N-UNCOUNT treme danger and needing urgent help. *He expressed concern that the ship might be in distress.* 3 If some- VERB one or something **distresses** you, they cause you to V n be upset or worried. *The idea of Toni being in danger distresses him enormously.* ♦ **dis·tress·ing** ADJ-GRADED /dɪ'stresɪŋ/ ...*distressing news... I know this must be distressing for you.* ♦ **dis·tress·ing·ly** *Her face had* ADV-GRADED *grown distressingly old.*

dis·trib·ute /dɪ'strɪbjuːt/ **distributes, distribut-** ◆◆◇◇◇ **ing, distributed. 1** If you **distribute** things, you VERB hand them or deliver them to a number of people. V n *Soldiers are working to distribute food and blan-* beV-ed *kets... The furniture was left to the neighbours or* among n *distributed among friends.* 2 When a company VERB: V n **distributes** goods, it supplies them to the shops or businesses that sell them. 3 If you **distribute** things VERB among the members of a group, you share them V n among n among those members. *He began to distribute ma-* Also V n *jor offices among his friends and supporters.* 4 To VERB **distribute** a substance **over** something means to V n over n *scatter it over it. Distribute the topping evenly over* FORMAL *the fruit.*

dis·trib·ut·ed /dɪ'strɪbjuːtɪd/. If things are **distrib-** ◆◆◇◇◇ **uted** throughout an area, object, or group, they exist ADJ throughout it. *These cells are widely distributed throughout the body... Distant galaxies are not as evenly distributed in space as theory predicts.*

dis·tri·bu·tion /ˌdɪstrɪ'bjuːʃən/ **distributions.** ◆◆◆◇◇ **1** The **distribution** of things involves giving or de- N-UNCOUNT livering them to a number of people or places. ...*the distribution of foreign aid. ...distribution problems. ...emergency food distribution.* 2 The **distribution** N-VAR of something is how much of it there is in each place or at each time. ...*a more equitable distribution of wealth.*

dis·tri·bu·tion·al /ˌdɪstrɪ'bjuːʃənəl/. 1 **Distribu-** ADJ **tional** means relating to the distribution of goods. 2 **Distributional** effects and policies relate to the ADJ: ADJ n share of a country's wealth. ...*the distributional ef-* FORMAL *fects of free markets.*

dis·tribu·tive /dɪ'strɪbjuːtɪv/. **Distributive** means ADJ: ADJ n relating to the distribution of goods. ...*the distributive side of this industry.*

dis·tribu·tor /dɪ'strɪbjutə/ **distributors. 1** A **dis-** ◆◆◇◇◇ **tributor** is a company that supplies goods to shops N-COUNT or other businesses. ...*Spain's largest distributor of petroleum products. ...film distributors.* 2 The **dis-** N-COUNT **tributor** in a car or other motor vehicle is a device that sends electric current to the spark plugs in the engine.

dis·trict /'dɪstrɪkt/ **districts. 1** A **district** is an ◆◆◆◇◇ area of a town or country. *I drove around the busi-* N-COUNT *ness district. ...Nashville's shopping district. ...the Lake District.* 2 A **district** is an area of a town or N-COUNT: country which has been given official boundaries with supp for the purpose of administration. ...*Glasgow District Council. ...the district health authority.*

,**District At'torney, District Attorneys.** In the ◇◇◇◇◇ United States, a **District Attorney** is a lawyer who N-COUNT works as the State prosecutor in a district. The abbreviation **D.A.** is also used.

,**district 'nurse, district nurses.** In Britain, a N-COUNT **district nurse** is a nurse who goes to people's houses to give them medical treatment and advice.

dis·trust /ˌdɪs'trʌst/ **distrusts, distrusting, dis-** ◇◇◇◇◇ **trusted. 1** If you **distrust** someone or something, VERB

you think they are not honest, reliable, or safe. *I* V n *don't have any particular reason to distrust them.* 2 **Distrust** is the feeling of suspicion that you have N-UNCOUNT: towards someone or something you distrust. ...*a* also a N *profound distrust of all political authority.*

dis·trust·ful /ˌdɪs'trʌstful/. If you are **distrustful** of ADJ-GRADED someone or something, you think that they are not honest, reliable, or safe. *The older you get the more distrustful you become.*

dis·turb /dɪ'stɜːb/ **disturbs, disturbing, dis-** ◆◆◇◇◇ **turbed. 1** If you **disturb** someone, you interrupt VERB what they are doing and cause them inconvenience. V n *Did you sleep well? I didn't want to disturb you.* 2 If something **disturbs** you, it makes you feel upset VERB or worried. ...*dreams so vivid that they disturb me for* V n *days.* ♦ **dis·turb·ing** /dɪ'stɜːbɪŋ/ *There was some-* ADJ-GRADED *thing about him she found disturbing.* ♦ **dis·turb·** **·ing·ly** ...*the disturbingly high frequency of racial* ADV-GRADED *attacks.* 3 If something **is disturbed**, its position or shape is VERB changed. *He'd placed his notes in the brown envelope.* be V-ed *They hadn't been disturbed.* Also V n 4 If something **disturbs** a situation or atmosphere, it VERB spoils or unsettles it. *Neither Baker nor Levy seemed* V n *eager to disturb the cordial atmosphere.* 5 If someone is accused of **disturbing the peace**, they PHRASE are accused of behaving in a noisy and offensive way LEGAL in public.

dis·turb·ance /dɪ'stɜːbəns/ **disturbances. 1** A ◆◆◇◇◇ **disturbance** is an incident in which people behave N-COUNT violently in public. *During the disturbance which followed, three Englishmen were hurt.* 2 **Disturb-** N-UNCOUNT **ance** means upsetting or disrupting something which was previously in a calm and well-ordered state. *The old people's home would cause less disturbance to local residents than a school.* 3 You can N-VAR: use **disturbance** to refer to a medical or psychologi- with supp cal problem. ...*emotional disturbance. ...heart rhythm disturbances.*

dis·turbed /dɪ'stɜːbd/. 1 A **disturbed** person is ◆◆◇◇◇ very upset emotionally, and often needs special care ADJ-GRADED or treatment. ...*working with severely emotionally disturbed children.* 2 You can say that someone is ADJ-GRADED **disturbed** when they are very worried or anxious. *I was disturbed to hear that the selection committee originally decided not to send a British team.* 3 If ADJ-GRADED you describe a situation or period of time as **disturbed**, you mean that it is unhappy and full of problems. ...*women from disturbed backgrounds.*

dis·turb·ing /dɪ'stɜːbɪŋ/. See **disturb.**

dis·unit·ed /ˌdɪsju'naɪtɪd/. If a group of people are ADJ-GRADED **disunited**, there is disagreement and division among them.

dis·unity /ˌdɪs'juːnɪti/. **Disunity** is lack of agree- N-UNCOUNT ment among people which prevents them from working together effectively.

dis·use /ˌdɪs'juːs/. If something falls into **disuse**, N-UNCOUNT people stop using it. ...*a church which has fallen into disuse. ...years of disuse.*

dis·used /ˌdɪs'juːzd/. A **disused** place or building ◆◇◇◇◇ is empty and no longer used. ...*a disused airfield.* ADJ

ditch /dɪtʃ/ **ditches, ditching, ditched. 1** A ◆◆◇◇◇ **ditch** is a long narrow channel cut into the ground N-COUNT at the side of a road or field. 2 If you **ditch** something that you have or are respon- VERB sible for, you get rid of it, because you no longer want V n it. *I decided to ditch the sofa bed... Unpopular policies* INFORMAL *such as unilateral disarmament were ditched.* 3 If VERB someone **ditches** someone, they end a relationship V n with that person. *I can't bring myself to ditch him and* INFORMAL *start again.* 4 If a pilot **ditches** an aircraft or if it V-ERG **ditches**, the pilot makes an emergency landing. *One* V n *American pilot was forced to ditch his jet.* Also V 5 See also **last-ditch.**

dith·er /'dɪðə/ **dithers, dithering, dithered.** ◆◇◇◇◇ When someone **dithers**, they hesitate because they VERB are unable to make a quick decision about some- V overwh/n thing. *We're still dithering over whether to marry.* V about-ing/ ...*if you have been dithering about buying shares.* wh/n Also V

D

dit·to /ˈdɪtəʊ/. You can use **ditto** to represent a word or phrase that you have just used in order to avoid repeating it. In written lists, **ditto** can be represented by ditto marks (the symbol ʺ) underneath the word that you want to repeat. [PRAGMATICS] [INFORMAL]

dit·ty /ˈdɪti/ **ditties.** A **ditty** is a short or light-hearted song or poem. [N-COUNT] [WRITTEN]

di·uret·ic /ˌdaɪəˈretɪk/ **diuretics.** A **diuretic** is a substance which makes your body increase its production of waste fluids, with the result that you need to urinate more often than usual. *Like caffeine, alcohol acts as a diuretic.* ► Also an adjective. *Certain vitamins have a diuretic effect.* [◆◇◇◇◇] [N-COUNT] [TECHNICAL] [ADJ]

di·ur·nal /daɪˈɜːnəl/. **Diurnal** means happening or active during the daytime. *Kangaroos are diurnal animals.* [ADJ] [FORMAL]

diva /ˈdiːvə/ **divas.** You can refer to a successful and famous female opera singer as a **diva**. [◆◇◇◇◇] [N-COUNT]

Di·va·li /dɪˈvɑːli/. See **Diwali**.

di·van /dɪˈvæn/ **divans.** 1 A **divan** or **divan bed** is a bed that has a thick base under the mattress. 2 A **divan** is a long soft seat that has no back or arms. [N-COUNT] [BRITISH] [N-COUNT]

dive /daɪv/ **dives, diving, dived;** American English sometimes uses the form **dove** for the past tense. 1 If you **dive** into some water, you jump in head-first with your arms held straight above your head. *She was standing by a pool, about to dive in... Joanne had just learnt to dive.* ► Also a noun. *...a dive of 80 feet from the Chasm Bridge.* 2 If you **dive**, you go under the surface of the sea or a lake, using special breathing equipment. ► Also a noun. *...my dive to a sunken wreck off Sardinia.* ♦ **div·er, divers** *Police divers have recovered the body of a sixteen year old boy.* 3 When birds and animals **dive**, they go quickly downwards, head-first, through the air or through water. *The shark dived down and swam under the boat.* 4 If an aeroplane **dives**, it flies or drops down quickly and suddenly. *He was killed when his monoplane stalled and dived into the ground.* ► Also a noun. *The plane failed to pull out of a dive and smashed down in a field.* [◆◆◇◇◇] [VERB: V into n, V in, V] [N-COUNT] [VERB: V] [N-COUNT] [N-COUNT] [VERB: V, V adv/prep] [VERB: V] [VERB: V prep/adv] [N-COUNT]

5 If you **dive** in a particular direction or into a particular place, you jump or move there quickly. *They dived into a taxi... The cashier dived for cover when a gunman opened fire.* ► Also a noun. *He made a sudden dive for Uncle Jim's legs.* 6 If you **dive** into a bag or container, you put your hands into it quickly in order to get something out. [VERB] [V prep/adv] [N-COUNT] [VERB: V into n]

7 If shares, profits, or figures **dive**, their value falls suddenly and dramatically. *Profits have dived from £7.7m to £7.1m... The shares dived 22p to 338p.* ► Also a noun. *Stock prices took a dive.* [VERB: V, V from/to/by, V amount] [N-COUNT]

8 If you describe a bar or club as a **dive**, you mean it is dirty and dark, and not very respectable. [N-COUNT] [PRAGMATICS] [INFORMAL]

ˈ**dive-bomb,** **dive-bombs,** **dive-bombing,** **dive-bombed.** If a plane **dive-bombs** an area, it suddenly flies down low over it to drop bombs onto it. *The Russians had to dive-bomb the cities to regain control.* ♦ **d'ive-bomber, dive bombers.** *...dive-bombers armed with torpedoes.* [VERB] [V n] [Also V] [N-COUNT]

di·verge /daɪˈvɜːdʒ, AM dɪ-/ **diverges, diverging, diverged.** 1 If one thing **diverges** from another similar thing, the first thing is different from the second or develops differently from it. *His interests increasingly diverged from those of his colleagues... Their opinions diverge very little.* ♦ **di·ver·gence** /daɪˈvɜːdʒəns, AM dɪ-/, **divergences** *There's a substantial divergence of opinion within the party.* ♦ **di·ver·gent** *Similar customs were known in widely divergent cultures.* 2 If one road, path, or route **diverges** from another, they lead in different directions after starting from the same place. *...a course that diverged from the Calvert Island coastline... At Orte, the railway lines for Florence and Ancona diverge.* [◆◇◇◇◇] [V-RECIP] [V from n] [pl-n V] [N-VAR] [ADJ-GRADED] [V-RECIP] [V from n] [Also pl-n V]

di·verse /daɪˈvɜːs, AM dɪ-/. If a group or range is **diverse**, it is made up of a wide variety of people or things. *...a much more diverse and perhaps younger audience. ...shops selling a diverse range of gifts.* [◆◆◇◇◇] [ADJ-GRADED]

di·ver·si·fy /daɪˈvɜːsɪfaɪ, AM dɪ-/ **diversifies, diversifying, diversified.** When an organization or person **diversifies** into other things, or **diversifies** their activities, they increase the variety of things that they do or make. *Manufacturers have been encouraged to diversify. ...the need to diversify their markets.* ♦ **di·ver·si·fi·ca·tion** /daɪˌvɜːsɪfɪˈkeɪʃən, AM dɪ-/, **diversifications.** *...diversification of agriculture.* [◆◆◇◇◇] [VERB: V into n/-ing] [V n] [N-VAR]

di·ver·sion /daɪˈvɜːʃən, AM dɪˈvɜːrʒən/ **diversions.** 1 A **diversion** is an action or event that attracts your attention away from what you are doing or concentrating on. *...armed robbers who escaped after throwing smoke bombs to create a diversion.* ♦ **di·ver·sion·ary** /daɪˈvɜːʃənri, AM dɪˈvɜːrʒəneri/. *It's thought the fires were started by the prisoners as a diversionary tactic.* 2 A **diversion** is an activity that you do for pleasure. *Finger painting is very messy but an excellent diversion.* 3 A **diversion** is a special route arranged for traffic to follow when the normal route cannot be used. 4 **The diversion of** something involves changing its course or destination. *...the illegal diversion of profits from secret arms sales.* [◆◇◇◇◇] [N-COUNT] [ADJ] [N-COUNT] [FORMAL] [N-COUNT] [BRITISH] [N-UNCOUNT: the N of n]

di·ver·sity /daɪˈvɜːsɪti, AM dɪ-/ **diversities.** 1 The **diversity** of something is the fact that it contains many very different elements. *...the cultural diversity of British society. ...to introduce more choice and diversity into the education system.* 2 A **diversity of** things is a range of things which are very different from each other. *...how to grow a diversity of vegetables in fall and winter.* [◆◆◇◇◇] [N-VAR] [N-SING] [N of n]

di·vert /daɪˈvɜːt, AM dɪ-/ **diverts, diverting, diverted.** 1 To **divert** vehicles or travellers means to make them follow a different route or go to a different destination than they originally intended. *A new bypass will divert traffic from the A13... We diverted a plane to rescue 100 passengers... She insists on diverting to a village close to the airport.* 2 To **divert** money or resources means to cause them to be used for a different purpose. *The government is trying to divert more public funds from west to east.* 3 To **divert** a phone call means to send it to a different number or place from the one that was dialled by the person making the call. *He instructed switchboard staff to divert all Laura's calls to him.* 4 If you say that someone **diverts** your attention from something important or serious, you disapprove of them doing something which stops you thinking about it. *They want to divert the attention of the people from the real issues.* [◆◆◇◇◇] [V-ERG] [V n from/to n] [V n] [V from/to n] [VERB: V n] [V n prep/adv] [VERB: V n] [V n prep/adv] [VERB] [PRAGMATICS] [V n prep/adv] [Also V n]

di·vert·ing /daɪˈvɜːtɪŋ, AM dɪ-/. If you describe something as **diverting**, you mean that it is amusing or entertaining. [◆◇◇◇◇] [ADJ-GRADED] [DATED]

di·vest /daɪˈvest, AM dɪ-/ **divests, divesting, divested.** 1 If you **divest** yourself of something that you own or are responsible for, you get rid of it or stop being responsible for it. *The company divested itself of its oil interests.* 2 If something or someone **is divested** of a particular quality, they lose that quality or it is taken away from them. *They have divested rituals of their original meaning.* 3 If you **divest** someone of something that they are wearing or carrying, you take it off them or away from them. *...the formalities of divesting her of her coat.* [VERB] [V pron-refl of n] [FORMAL] [VERB: be V-ed of n] [FORMAL] [VERB] [V n of n] [Also V n] [DATED]

di·vide /dɪˈvaɪd/ **divides, dividing, divided.** 1 When people or things **are divided** into smaller groups or parts, they become separated into smaller parts. *It will be easiest if we divide them into groups... Divide the pastry in half and roll out each piece... The egg has divided into clusters of cells... Bacteria reproduce by dividing.* 2 If you **divide** something among people or things, you separate it into several parts or portions which you distribute to the people or things. *Paul divides most of his spare time between the study and his bedroom... Divide the sauce among 4 bowls.* 3 If you **divide** a larger number by a smaller number or **divide** a smaller number into a larger number, you calculate how many times the smaller number can fit [◆◆◆◇] [V-ERG: be V-ed into n, V n into pl-n, V n in fraction, V into pl-n] [VERB] [V n between/among pl-n, Also V n] [VERB] [V n by/into num]

exactly into the larger number. *Measure the floor area of the greenhouse and divide it by six.*

4 If a border or line **divides** two areas, it keeps them separate from each other. *...remote border areas dividing Tamil and Muslim settlements. ...the long frontier dividing Mexico from the United States... Residents have approved a plan that would divide the region in two.* VERB V n V n from n V n in/into n

5 If something **divides** people, it causes strong disagreement between them. *She has done more to divide the Conservatives than anyone else.* ♦ **di·vid·ed** *The democrats are divided over whether to admit him into their group.* **6** A **divide** is a significant distinction between two groups, often one that causes conflict. *...a Hindu-Muslim divide in India. ...the great divide between formality and truth.* VERB V n ADJ-GRADED N-COUNT

7 A **divide** is a line of high ground between areas that are drained by different rivers. The usual British word is **watershed**. N-COUNT AMERICAN

8 You use **divide and rule** to refer to a policy which is intended to keep someone in a position of power by causing disagreements between people who might otherwise unite against them. PHRASE

divide off. If something **divides** an area **off**, it forms a barrier that keeps it separate from another area. *...a bamboo partition dividing off another room.* PHRASAL VB V n P V P noun

divide up. 1 If you **divide** something **up**, you separate it into smaller or more useful groups. *The idea is to divide up the country into four sectors.* **2** If you **divide** something **up**, you share it out among a number of people or groups in approximately equal parts. *The aim was to divide up state property.* PHRASAL VB V n P V P noun V n P V P noun

di·vid·ed 'highway, divided highways. A divided highway is a road which has two lanes of traffic travelling in each direction with a strip of grass or concrete down the middle. The British expression is **dual carriageway**. N-COUNT AMERICAN

div·i·dend /'dɪvɪdend/ **dividends. 1** A dividend is the part of a company's profits which is paid to people who have shares in the company. **2** If something **pays dividends**, it brings advantages at a later date. *Steps taken now to maximise your health will pay dividends later on.* **3** See also **peace dividend**. ♦♦♦◇◇ N-COUNT PHRASE

di·vid·er /dɪ'vaɪdə/ **dividers. 1** A divider is something which forms a barrier between two areas or sets of things. *A curtain acted as a divider between this class and another. ...room dividers.* **2** Dividers are an instrument consisting of two pointed arms jointed by a hinge, used for measuring lines and for marking points along them. N-COUNT N-PLURAL

di'viding line, dividing lines. 1 A dividing line is a distinction which marks the difference between two types of thing or two groups. *There's a very thin dividing line between joviality and hysteria.* **2** The dividing line between two areas is the boundary between them. *...the dividing line between Israel and the occupied territories.* N-COUNT N-SING

divi·na·tion /ˌdɪvɪ'neɪʃən/. Divination is the art or practice of discovering what will happen in the future using supernatural means. N-UNCOUNT FORMAL

di·vine /dɪ'vaɪn/ **divines, divining, divined. 1** You use **divine** to describe something that is provided by or relates to a god or goddess. *...a divine punishment. ...divine inspiration.* ♦ **di·vine·ly** *The law was divinely ordained.* **2** A **divine** is a priest who specializes in the study of theology. **3** People use **divine** to express their pleasure or enjoyment of something. *Darling, how lovely to see you, you look simply divine.* ♦ **divinely** *...divinely glamorous singer Jeffrey McDonald.* ♦♦◇◇ ADJ ADV N-COUNT DATED ADJ-GRADED PRAGMATICS DATED ADV-GRADED

4 If you **divine** something, you discover or learn it by guessing. *We may divine that kings did not sleep any better than peasants.* **5** If you **divine**, you try to find underground supplies of water or minerals, using a special rod or pair of rods. *I was divining for water.* VERB: V n V that LITERARY VERB: V V for n

div·ing /'daɪvɪŋ/. **1** Diving is the activity of working or exploring underwater, using special breathing equipment. **2** Diving is the sport or activity in which you jump into water head first with your ♦♦◇◇ N-UNCOUNT N-UNCOUNT

arms held straight above your head, usually from a diving board.

'diving bell, diving bells. A diving bell is a container shaped like a bell, in which people can breathe air while they work under water. N-COUNT

'diving board, diving boards. A diving board is a board high above a swimming pool from which people can dive into the water. N-COUNT

di·vin·ity /dɪ'vɪnɪti/ **divinities. 1** Divinity is the study of religion. **2** Divinity is the quality of being divine. *...the divinity of Christ's word.* **3** A divinity is a god or goddess. *...Roman divinities.* ♦◇◇◇◇ N-UNCOUNT N-UNCOUNT N-COUNT

di·vis·ible /dɪ'vɪzɪbəl/. If one number is **divisible** by another number, the second number can be divided into the first exactly, with no remainder. ADJ: v-link ADJ by num

di·vi·sion /dɪ'vɪʒən/ **divisions. 1** The division of a large unit into two or more parts is the act of separating it into these parts. *...the unification of Germany, after its division into two states.* **2** The division of something among people or things is its separation into parts which are distributed among them. *...the current division of labor between workers and management.* **3** A **division** is a significant distinction or difference of opinion between two groups, which causes them to be considered as very different and separate. *The division between the prosperous west and the impoverished east remains.* **4** Division is the arithmetical process of dividing one number into another number. **5** In a large organization, a **division** is a group of departments that are located in the same area or concerned with similar tasks. *...the bank's Latin American division.* ♦ **di·vi·sion·al** *...the divisional headquarters.* **6** A **division** is a group of military units which fight as a single unit. *...armoured divisions.* **7** In football and some other sports, a **division** is one of the groups of teams which make up a league. **8** In the British Parliament, a **division** is a vote where the MPs go into separate rooms in order to record their vote. ♦♦♦♦◇ N-UNCOUNT N-UNCOUNT N-VAR N-UNCOUNT N-COUNT ADJ: ADJ n N-COUNT N-COUNT N-COUNT

di·vi·sive /dɪ'vaɪsɪv/. Something that is **divisive** causes hostility and argument between people. *Abortion has always been a divisive issue.* ♦ **di·vi·sive·ness** *...the divisiveness that has separated Miami's black and Latino communities.* ♦◇◇◇◇ ADJ-GRADED N-UNCOUNT

di·vorce /dɪ'vɔːs/ **divorces, divorcing, divorced. 1** A divorce is the formal ending of a marriage by law. *Numerous marriages now end in divorce.* **2** If a man and woman **divorce** or if one of them **divorces** the other, their marriage is legally ended. *He and Lillian had got divorced... Mr Gold is divorcing for the second time.* ♦ **di·vorced** *Princess Margaret is divorced from Lord Snowdon.* **3** A **divorce** between two things is a separation between them. *...this divorce of Christian culture from the roots of faith.* **4** If one thing **is divorced from** another, they become separate from each other. *We have been able to divorce sex from reproduction.* ♦ **divorced** *...speculative theories divorced from political reality... I feel society has got so divorced from natural things.* ♦♦♦◇◇ N-VAR V-RECIP: pl-n V pl-n get V-ed ADJ N-SING VERB: be V-ed from n V n from n v-link ADJ-GRADED: from n

di·vor·cee /dɪvɔː'siː/ **divorcees.** A divorcee is a person who is divorced. N-COUNT

div·ot /'dɪvət/ **divots.** A divot is a small piece of grass and earth which is dug out accidentally, for example by a golf club. N-COUNT

di·vulge /daɪ'vʌldʒ, AM dɪ-/ **divulges, divulging, divulged.** If you divulge secret or private information, you tell it to someone. *Officials refuse to divulge details of the negotiations... I do not want to divulge where the village is.* ♦◇◇◇◇ VERB V n V wh Also V that FORMAL

div·vy /'dɪvi/ **divvies.** If you call someone a **divvy**, you are saying in a humorous way that you think they are rather foolish. *Don't be a divvy!* N-COUNT PRAGMATICS BRITISH, INFORMAL

Di·wa·li /dɪ'wɑːliː/; also spelled **Divali**. Diwali is a Hindu festival celebrated in October or November. N-UNCOUNT

DIY /ˌdiː aɪ 'waɪ/. DIY is the activity of making or repairing things yourself, especially in your home. DIY is an abbreviation for 'do-it-yourself'. *He's useless at DIY.* ♦◇◇◇◇ N-UNCOUNT BRITISH

diz·zy /'dɪzi/ **dizzier, dizziest; dizzies, dizzy-** ◆◆◇◇◇
ing, dizzied. 1 If you feel **dizzy**, you feel that you ADJ-GRADED
are losing your balance and are about to fall. *She
felt slightly dizzy and disoriented.* ♦ **diz·zi·ly** /'dɪzɪli/ ADV-GRADED
Her head spins dizzily as soon as she sits up. ♦ **diz-**
·zi·ness *His complaint causes dizziness and nau-* N-UNCOUNT
sea. **2** If something **dizzies** you, it causes you to feel VERB
unsteady or confused. *The sudden height dizzied* V n
her. ♦ **diz·zy·ing** *We're descending now at dizzying* ADJ-GRADED
speed. **3** You can use **dizzy** to describe a woman ADJ-GRADED
who is careless and forgetful, but likeable. *She is*
famed for playing dizzy blondes. **4** If you say that PHRASE
someone has reached the **dizzy heights** of some- PRAGMATICS
thing, you are emphasizing that they have reached a
very high level by achieving it. *Annie Lennox took
the group to dizzy heights of rock success.*

DJ /ˌdiː'dʒeɪ/ **DJs;** also spelled **dj. 1** A **DJ** is the ◆◆◇◇◇
same as a **disc jockey. 2** A **DJ** is the same as a **din-** N-COUNT
ner jacket. N-COUNT

DNA /ˌdiː en 'eɪ/. **DNA** is an acid that is contained ◆◆◇◇◇
in the cells of living things. It determines the par- N-UNCOUNT
ticular structure and functions of every cell. **DNA** is
an abbreviation for 'deoxyribonucleic acid'.

,DNA 'fingerprinting. DNA fingerprinting is the N-UNCOUNT
same as **genetic fingerprinting.**

do 1 auxiliary verb uses

do /də, STRONG duː/ **does, doing, did, done. Do** ◆◆◆◆◆
is used as an auxiliary with the simple present
tense. **Did** is used as an auxiliary with the simple
past tense. In spoken English negative forms of **do**
are often contracted, for example **do not** is contracted to **don't** and **did not** is contracted to **didn't.**

1 Do is used to form the negative of main verbs, by AUX
putting 'not' after 'do' and before the main verb in its AUX neg inf
infinitive form (without 'to'). *They don't want to
work... I did not know Jamie had a knife.* **2 Do** is used AUX
to form questions, by putting the subject after 'do' AUX n v
and before the main verb in its infinitive form (without 'to'). *Do you like music?... What did he say?* **3 Do** is AUX
used in question tags. *You know about Andy, don't* cl AUX n
*you?... They had some of the same questions last year
didn't they?* **4** You use **do** when you are confirming or AUX
contradicting a statement containing 'do', or giving a AUX
negative or positive answer to a question. *'Did he
think there was anything suspicious going on?'—'Yes,
he did.'... They say they don't care, but they do.* **5 Do** is AUX:
used with a negative to tell someone not to behave in only imper
a certain way. *Don't be silly... Don't touch that!* AUX neg inf

6 Do is used to give emphasis to the main verb when AUX
there is no other auxiliary. *Veronica, I do understand.* AUX inf
7 Do is used as a polite way of inviting or trying to per- AUX:
suade someone to do something. *Do help yourself to* only imper
another drink. PRAGMATICS
AUX inf
8 Do can be used to refer back to another verbal VERB
group when you are comparing or contrasting two V
things. *I make more money than he does... Alcohol in-* as V n
hibits sleep, as do coffee, chocolate and tea... More than than V n
twice as many men kill themselves than do women.
9 You use **do** after 'so' and 'nor' to say that the same VERB
statement is true for two people or groups. *You know* PRAGMATICS
that's true, and so do I. V n

do 2 other verb uses

do /duː/ **does, doing, did, done. 1** When you **do** ◆◆◆◆◆
something, you take some action or perform an ac- VERB
tivity or task. **Do** is often used instead of a more PRAGMATICS
specific verb, to talk about a common action involving a particular thing. For example, you can say 'do
your teeth' instead of 'brush your teeth'. *I was trying to do some work... I did the washing up... Dad
does the garden.* **2 Do** can be used to stand for any VERB
verbal group, or to refer back to another verbal PRAGMATICS
group, including one that was in a previous sen- V n
tence. *What are you doing?... Think twice before doing anything... A lot of people got arrested for looting
so they will think before they do it again... The first
thing is to get some more food. When we've done
that we ought to start again.* **3** You can use **do** at the VERB
beginning of a sentence after words like 'what' and PRAGMATICS
'all', to give special emphasis to the information V n

that comes at the end of the sentence. *All she does is
complain... What I should do is go and see her.*
4 If you **do** a particular thing with something, you use VERB
it in that particular way. *I was allowed to do whatever I* V n with n
wanted with my life... The technology was good, but V amount with
you couldn't do much with it. **5** You can ask someone n
what they **did with** something as another way of ask- PHRASE
ing them where they put it. *What did you do with that
notebook?*
6 If you **do** something about a problem, you take ac- VERB
tion to try to solve it. *They refuse to do anything about* V n about n
the real cause of crime: poverty... Though he didn't like V amount
it there wasn't much he could do about it. **7** If an action about n
or event **does** a particular thing, such as harm or VERB
good, it has that result or effect. *A few bombs can do a* V n
lot of damage... The publicity did her career no harm. V n n
8 You can use **do** to talk about the degree to which a VERB
person, action, or event affects or improves a particu- V amount to-
lar situation. *The current reforms will do much to cre-* inf
ate these conditions... Such incidents do nothing for V amount for n
live music's reputation. **9** You can talk about what Also V n for n
someone or something **does** to someone to mean that V to n
they have a very harmful effect on them. *I saw what
the liquor was doing to her.*
10 If you ask someone what they **do**, you want to VERB: V n
know what their job or profession is.
11 If you **are doing** something, you are busy or active VERB
in some way, or have planned an activity for some V n
time in the future. *Are you doing anything tomorrow
night?*
12 If you say that someone or something **does** well or VERB
badly, you are talking about how successful or unsuc- V adv
cessful they are. *Connie did well at school.*
13 If a person or organization **does** a particular ser- VERB
vice or product, they provide that service or sell that V n
product. *They provide design services and do printing
and packaging.*
14 You can use **do** when referring to the speed or rate VERB
that something or someone achieves or is able to V amount
achieve. *They were doing 70 miles an hour.*
15 If you **do** a subject, author, or book, you study VERB
them at school or college. *I'd like to do maths at uni-* V n
versity... In the first year we did "Julius Caesar".' SPOKEN
16 If you **do** a particular person, accent, or role, you VERB
mimic that person or accent or act that role. *Gina does* V n
accents extremely well.
17 If you say that something will **do** or will **do** you, V
you mean that it is sufficient in quantity or quality to V n
meet your requirements. *Give them a prize. Anything
will do... I just want to get better and then that'll do me.*
18 If you say that you **could do with** something, you PHRASE
mean that you need it or would benefit from it. *I could
do with a cup of tea.* **19** If you ask **what** someone or PHRASE
something **is doing** in a particular place, you are asking why they are there. *What was he doing in Hyde
Park at that time of the morning?* **20** If you say **that** CONVENTION
will do to a child, you are telling them to stop behav- PRAGMATICS
ing in the way that they are. **21** If you say that one PHRASE
thing **has** something **to do with** or **is** something **to do
with** another thing, you mean that the two things are
connected or that the first thing is about the second
thing. *Mr Forlani denies having anything to do with
the episode... They were shouting at each other. It was
something to do with money.* **22 do** is used in a large
number of expressions which are explained under
other words in the dictionary. For example, the expression **easier said than done** is explained at **easy.**

do away with. To **do away with** something means PHRASAL VB
to remove it completely or abolish it. *The long-range* V P P n
goal must be to do away with nuclear weapons.

do down. If someone **does** you **down**, they try to you PHRASAL VB
make other people think that you are unpleasant or V n P
unsuccessful by criticizing you. *Glover thinks that* Also V P noun
Smith did him down, perhaps out of envy. BRITISH, INFORMAL

do for. If you say that you **are done for**, you mean PHRASAL VB
that you are in a disastrous and hopeless situation. *If I* usu passive
can't bring my questions to you, I'm done for. be V-ed P
INFORMAL

do in. To **do** someone **in** means to kill them. *Whoever* PHRASAL VB
did him in removed a man who was brave as well as V n P
ruthless. Also V P noun
INFORMAL

do out. If a room or building is **done out** in a particular way, it is decorated and furnished in that way. ...*a room newly done out in country-house style.* — PHRASAL VB, usu passive, be V-ed P, BRITISH

do out of. If you **do** someone **out of** something, you unfairly cause them not to have or get something that they were expecting to have. *The others have done him out of his share.* — PHRASAL VB, V n P P n, INFORMAL

do over. Do over is an informal expression. — PHRASAL VB

1 If you **do** a task **over**, you perform it again from the beginning. *If she had the chance to do it over, she would have hired a press secretary.* **2** If someone **does** a place **over**, they rob it or search it and leave it very untidy. *The door was open. They had done the place over.* **3** To **do** someone **over** means to hurt them badly, for example by hitting or kicking them. *We could get someone to do him over, couldn't we?* — V n P / AMERICAN / V n P / BRITISH / V n P / Also V P noun / BRITISH

do up. 1 If you **do** something **up**, you fasten it. *Mari did up the buttons... Do your coat up.* **2** If you **do up** an old building, you decorate and repair it so that it is in a better condition. *Nicholas has bought a barn in Provence and is spending August doing it up.* **3** If you say that a person or room **is done up** in a particular way, you mean they are dressed or decorated in that way, often a way that is rather ridiculous or extreme. *...Beatrice, usually done up like the fairy on the Christmas tree... She's had her blond hair done up exactly like Jackie's.* — PHRASAL VB, V n P, V P noun, V n P, Also V P noun, usu passive, be V-ed, prep/adv, have n V-ed P

do without. 1 If you **do without** something you need, want, or usually have, you are able to survive, continue, or succeed although you do not have it. *We can't do without the help of your organisation.* **2** If you say that you could **do without** something, you mean that you would prefer not to have it or it is of no benefit to you. *He could do without her rhetorical questions at five o'clock in the morning.* — PHRASAL VB, V P n, Also V P, V P n, INFORMAL

do 3 noun uses

do /duː/ **dos. 1** A **do** is a party, dinner party, or other social event. *A friend of his is having a do in Stoke... They always have all-night dos there.* **2** If someone tells you the **dos and don'ts** of a situation, they advise you what you should and should not do in that situation. *...the dos and don'ts of carpet care.* — N-COUNT, BRITISH, INFORMAL / PHRASE

do. do. is a written abbreviation for **ditto.** — DATED

d.o.b. d.o.b. is used as a written abbreviation for 'date of birth', especially on official forms.

do·ber·man /ˈdəʊbəmən/ **dobermans.** A **doberman** is a type of large dog with short dark fur. — N-COUNT

doc /dɒk/ **docs.** Some people call a doctor **doc.** *I think I've got a stomach ulcer but the doc says no.* — N-COUNT, INFORMAL

doc·ile /ˈdəʊsaɪl, AM ˈdɑːsəl/. A person or animal that is **docile** is quiet, not aggressive, and easily controlled. *...docile, obedient children.* ♦ **do·cil·i·ty** /dɒˈsɪlɪti/ *Her docility had surprised him.* ♦ **do·cile·ly** *She stands, hands behind her, as if docilely awaiting my decision.* — ◇◇◇◇, ADJ-GRADED / N-UNCOUNT / ADV-GRADED: ADV with v

dock /dɒk/ **docks, docking, docked. 1** A **dock** is an enclosed area in a harbour where ships go to be loaded, unloaded, or repaired. *What other ships are in dock here?* ● See also **dry dock. 2** When a ship **docks** or **is docked**, it is brought into a dock. *The vessel docked at Liverpool... Russian commanders docked a huge aircraft carrier in a Russian port.* **3** A **dock** is a small structure at the edge of water where boats can tie up, especially one that is privately owned. **4** A **dock** is a platform for loading vehicles or trains. *The truck left the loading dock.* **5** When one spacecraft **docks** or **is docked** with another, the two crafts join together in space. *The space shuttle Atlantis is scheduled to dock with Russia's Mir space station.* **6** In a law court, the **dock** is the place where the person accused of a crime stands or sits. *Their father has stood in the dock for attempted murder.* **7** If you **dock** something such as someone's salary, you take some of it away as a punishment. *Soccer's governing body has recommended docking two points from the league champions.* **8** A **dock** is a plant with large leaves which grows wild in Britain and some other northern countries. — ♦♦◇◇◇, N-COUNT: also in/into N / V-ERG, V, V n / N-COUNT, AMERICAN / N-COUNT, AMERICAN / V-ERG-RECIP, V with n, Also V n prep / N-SING, BRITISH / VERB, V n, Also V n n, BRITISH / N-VAR

dock·er /ˈdɒkə/ **dockers.** A **docker** is a person who works in the docks, loading and unloading ships. The usual American word is **longshoreman.** — N-COUNT, BRITISH

dock·et /ˈdɒkɪt/ **dockets. 1** A **docket** is a certificate or ticket which shows the contents of something such as a parcel or cargo, and proves who the goods belong to. **2** A **docket** is a list of cases awaiting trial in a law court. *The Court has about 1,400 appeals on its docket.* — N-COUNT, BRITISH / N-COUNT, AMERICAN

dock·land /ˈdɒklænd/ **docklands.** The **dockland** or **docklands** of a town or city is the area around the docks. — ◇◇◇◇◇, N-VAR, BRITISH

dock·yard /ˈdɒkjɑːd/ **dockyards.** A **dockyard** is a place where ships are built, maintained, and repaired. — N-COUNT

doc·tor /ˈdɒktə/ **doctors, doctoring, doctored. 1** A **doctor** is someone who is qualified in medicine and treats people who are ill. *Don't hesitate to call the doctor if you are at all uneasy... Doctor, you've got to help me.* **2** The **doctor's** is used to refer to the surgery or clinic where a doctor works. *I have an appointment at the doctor's.* **3** A **doctor** is someone who has been awarded the highest academic or honorary degree by a university. *He is a doctor of philosophy.* **4** If someone **doctors** something, they change it in order to deceive people. *They doctored the prints, deepening the lines to make her look as awful as possible.* ♦ **doc·tor·ing** *...the doctoring of the document.* **5** If someone **doctors** food or drink, they add a poison or drug to it. — ♦♦♦♦◇, N-COUNT, N-TITLE; N-VOC / N-COUNT / N-COUNT; N-TITLE / VERB, V n / N-UNCOUNT / VERB: V n

doc·tor·al /ˈdɒktərəl/. A **doctoral** thesis or piece of research is written or done in order to obtain a doctor's degree. — ADJ: ADJ n

doc·tor·ate /ˈdɒktərət/ **doctorates.** A **doctorate** is the highest degree awarded by a university. — ◇◇◇◇◇, N-COUNT

doc·tri·naire /ˌdɒktrɪˈneə/. If you say that someone is **doctrinaire**, you disapprove of them because they have fixed principles which they try to impose on other people. *He is firm but not doctrinaire.* — ADJ-GRADED, PRAGMATICS, FORMAL

doc·trine /ˈdɒktrɪn/ **doctrines. 1** A **doctrine** is a set of principles or beliefs, especially religious ones. *...the Marxist doctrine of perpetual revolution.* ♦ **doc·tri·nal** /dɒkˈtraɪnəl, AM ˈdɑːktrɪnəl/. *Doctrinal differences were vigorously debated.* **2** A **doctrine** is a statement of official government policy, especially foreign policy. — ♦♦◇◇◇, N-VAR / ADJ / N-COUNT, AMERICAN

docu·dra·ma /ˈdɒkjʊdrɑːmə/ **docudramas;** also spelled **docu-drama.** A **docudrama** is a television film based on events that really happened. — N-VAR

docu·ment, documents, documenting, documented. The noun is pronounced /ˈdɒkjəmənt/. The verb is pronounced /ˈdɒkjəment/. **1** A **document** is one or more official pieces of paper with writing on them. *The foreign ministers of the two countries signed the documents today.* **2** If you **document** something, you make a detailed record of it in writing or on film or tape. *...a book documenting his prison experiences.* — ♦♦♦♦◇, N-COUNT / VERB, V n

docu·men·tary /ˌdɒkjəˈmentri/ **documentaries. 1** A **documentary** is a television or radio programme, or a film, which shows real events or provides factual information about a particular subject. **2 Documentary** evidence consists of things that are written down. — ♦♦◇◇◇, N-COUNT / ADJ: ADJ n

docu·men·ta·tion /ˌdɒkjəmenˈteɪʃən/. **Documentation** consists of documents which provide proof or evidence of something, or are a record of something. *Passengers must carry proper documentation.* — ◇◇◇◇◇, N-UNCOUNT

dod·der·ing /ˈdɒdərɪŋ/. If you refer to someone as a **doddering** old man or woman, you are saying in a disrespectful way that they are old and weak. — ADJ, PRAGMATICS

dod·dery /ˈdɒdəri/. Someone who is **doddery** walks in an unsteady and shaky way, especially because of old age. — ADJ-GRADED

dod·dle /ˈdɒdəl/. If you say that something is a **doddle**, you mean that it is very easy to do. *This summer's schedule should be a doddle for him.* — N-SING, a N, BRITISH, INFORMAL

dodge /dɒdʒ/ **dodges, dodging, dodged. 1** If you **dodge** somewhere, you move suddenly, often to avoid being hit, caught, or seen. *He dodged amongst* — ♦♦◇◇◇, VERB, V prep/adv

the seething crowds of men. **2** If you **dodge** something, you avoid it by quickly moving to one side so that it cannot hit or reach you. *He desperately dodged a speeding car trying to run him down.*
3 If you **dodge** something, usually something you ought to do, you deliberately avoid doing it or dealing with it. *He boasts of dodging military service by feigning illness.* ▶ Also a noun. *This was not just a tax dodge.* ♦ **dodgers, dodgers** ...*a crackdown on fare dodgers.* ● See also **draft dodger**.
VERB V n

VERB V n

N-COUNT
N-COUNT

dodg·em /'dɒdʒəm/ **dodgems.** The **dodgems** or **dodgem cars** at a fairground are small electric cars which are driven around a special enclosure and crashed into each other for fun. **Dodgem** is a trademark.
N-COUNT
BRITISH

dodgy /'dɒdʒi/ **dodgier, dodgiest. Dodgy** is an informal word used in British English.
◆◇◇◇◇

1 If you describe someone or something as **dodgy**, you disapprove of them because they seem rather dishonest and unreliable. *He was a bit of a dodgy character.* **2** If you say that something is **dodgy**, you mean that it seems rather risky or unreliable. *Predicting voting trends from economic forecasts is a dodgy business.*
ADJ-GRADED
PRAGMATICS

ADJ-GRADED

3 If you say that someone has a **dodgy** heart or knee, for example, you mean that that part of their body is not very strong or healthy. *My heart's a bit dodgy.*
ADJ-GRADED

dodo /'dəudəu/ **dodos** or **dodoes.** A **dodo** was a very large bird that was unable to fly.
N-COUNT

doe /dəu/ **does.** A **doe** is an adult female rabbit, hare, or deer.
N-COUNT

doer /'du:ə/ **doers.** If you refer to someone as a **doer**, you mean that they act promptly and efficiently, without spending a lot of time thinking about it. *Robertson was a doer, not a thinker.*
N-COUNT

does /dəz, STRONG dʌz/. **Does** is the third person singular in the present tense of **do**.

doesn't /'dʌzənt/. **Doesn't** is the usual spoken form of **does not**.
◆◆◆◆◆

doff /dɒf, AM dɔːf/ **doffs, doffing, doffed.** If you **doff** your hat or coat, you take it off.
VERB: V n
DATED

dog /dɒg, AM dɔːg/ **dogs, dogging, dogged. 1** A **dog** is a very common four-legged animal that is often kept by people as a pet or to guard or hunt. See picture headed **animals. 2** People refer to a sports meeting where dogs, especially greyhounds, race and people bet on which dog will win as **the dogs.** ...*a night out at the dogs.* **3** You use **dog** to refer to a male dog, or to the male of some related species such as wolves or foxes. *Is this a dog or a bitch?* **4** If problems or injuries **dog** you, they are with you all the time. ...*the problems that have dogged him all year.* **5** You use **dog eat dog** to express your disapproval of a situation where everyone wants to succeed and is willing to harm other people in order to do so. *It is very much dog eat dog out there.* **6** If you say that something **is going to the dogs**, you mean that it is becoming weaker and worse in quality.
◆◆◆◇
N-COUNT

N-PLURAL:
the N
BRITISH,
INFORMAL
N-COUNT

VERB
V n

PHRASE
PRAGMATICS

PHRASE
PRAGMATICS

7 See also **dogged; guide dog, prairie dog, sniffer dog.**

dog-collar, dog-collars; also spelled **dog collar. 1** A **dog-collar** is a stiff, round, white collar that is worn by Christian priests and ministers. **2** A **dog-collar** is a collar worn by a dog.
N-COUNT

N-COUNT

dog-eared. A book or piece of paper that is **dog-eared** has been used so much that the corners of the pages are turned down or torn. ...*dog-eared copies of ancient history books.*
ADJ-GRADED

dog·fight /'dɒgfaɪt, AM 'dɔːg-/ **dogfights;** also spelled **dog fight. 1** A **dogfight** is a fight between fighter planes, in which they fly close to one another and manoeuvre very fast. **2** If you say that organizations or people are involved in a **dogfight**, you mean they are struggling very hard against each other. *The airline emerged from its dogfight with recession.*
N-COUNT

N-COUNT

dog·fish /'dɒgfɪʃ, AM 'dɔːg-/; **dogfish** is both the singular and the plural form. A **dogfish** is a small shark.
◆◇◇◇◇
N-COUNT

dogged /'dɒgɪd, AM 'dɔː-/. If you describe someone's actions as **dogged**, you mean that they
◆◇◇◇◇
ADJ-GRADED:
ADJ n

are determined to continue with something, however difficult it becomes. *They have, through sheer dogged determination, slowly gained respect.* ♦ **dog·ged·ly** *She would fight doggedly for her rights.* ♦ **dog·ged·ness** *Most of my accomplishments came as the result of sheer doggedness.*
ADV-GRADED
N-UNCOUNT

dog·ger·el /'dɒgərəl, AM 'dɔː-/. If you refer to a poem as **doggerel**, you think it is very bad.
N-UNCOUNT
PRAGMATICS

dog·gie /'dɒgi, AM 'dɔː-/ **doggies. Doggie** is a child's word for a dog.
N-COUNT

dog·gy /'dɒgi, AM 'dɔː-/ **doggies.** See **doggie**.

dog·house /'dɒghaus, AM 'dɔːg-/ **doghouses;** also spelled **dog-house. 1** If you are **in the doghouse**, people are annoyed with you. *Her husband was in the doghouse for leaving her to cope on her own.* **2** A **doghouse** is a small building made especially for a dog to sleep in. The usual British word is **kennel**.
PHRASE
INFORMAL

N-COUNT
AMERICAN

dog·ma /'dɒgmə, AM 'dɔːg-/ **dogmas.** If you refer to a belief or a system of beliefs as a **dogma**, you are criticizing it for expecting people to accept that it is true, without questioning it. *Their political dogma has blinded them to the real needs of the country.*
◆◇◇◇◇
N-VAR
PRAGMATICS

dog·mat·ic /dɒg'mætɪk, AM dɔːg-/. If you say that someone is **dogmatic**, you are criticizing them for following rules or principles rigidly, without paying any attention to circumstances or to other people's views. *Many writers at this time held rigidly dogmatic views.* ♦ **dog·mati·cal·ly** /dɒg'mætɪkli, AM dɔːg-/. *He would not dogmatically oppose government intervention.* ♦ **dog·ma·tism** /'dɒgmətɪzəm, AM 'dɔːg-/. *We cannot allow dogmatism to stand in the way of progress.*
◆◇◇◇◇
ADJ-GRADED
PRAGMATICS

ADV-GRADED:
ADV with v

N-UNCOUNT

do-'gooder, do-gooders. If you describe someone as a **do-gooder**, you mean that they do things which they think will help other people, although you think that they are interfering.
N-COUNT
PRAGMATICS

dogs·body /'dɒgzbɒdi, AM 'dɔːgz-/ **dogsbodies.** A **dogsbody** is a person who has to do all the boring jobs that nobody else wants to do.
N-COUNT
BRITISH,
INFORMAL

'dog tag, dog tags. Dog tags are metal identification tags that are worn on a chain around the neck by members of the United States armed forces.
N-COUNT

doi·ly /'dɔɪli/ **doilies.** A **doily** is a small round piece of paper or cloth that is put on plates under cakes and sandwiches.
N-COUNT

do·ings /'du:ɪŋz/. Someone's **doings** are their activities at a particular time. ...*the everyday doings of a group of London schoolchildren.*
N-PLURAL

do-it-your'self. Do-it-yourself is the same as **DIY**.
N-UNCOUNT

Dol·by /'dɒlbi/. **Dolby** is a system which reduces the background noise on electronic cassette players. **Dolby** is a trademark.
N-UNCOUNT

dol·drums /'dɒldrəmz/. If an activity or situation is **in the doldrums**, it is very quiet and nothing new or exciting is happening.
◆◇◇◇◇
PHRASE

dole /dəul/ **doles, doling, doled.** The **dole** is money that is given regularly by the government to people who are unemployed. The usual American word is **welfare**. ● Someone who is **on the dole** is registered as unemployed and receives the dole. The usual American expression is **on welfare**.
◆◆◇◇◇
N-UNCOUNT
BRITISH

PHRASE

dole out. If you **dole** something **out**, you give a certain amount of it to each member of a group. *I got out my wallet and began to dole out the money.*
PHRASAL VB
V P noun
Also V n P

dole·ful /'dəulful/. A **doleful** expression, manner, or voice is depressing and miserable. ♦ **dole·ful·ly** *'I don't know why they left,' he said dolefully.*
ADJ-GRADED

ADV-GRADED:
ADV with v

'dole queue, dole queues. When people talk about the **dole queue**, they are talking about the state of being unemployed, especially when saying how many people are unemployed. The usual American expression is **unemployment line**.
N-COUNT
BRITISH

doll /dɒl/ **dolls, dolling, dolled.** A **doll** is a child's toy which looks like a small person or baby.
◆◆◇◇◇
N-COUNT

doll up. If a woman **dolls** herself **up**, she puts on smart or fashionable clothes in order to try and look attractive. *We used to doll ourselves up and go into town.* ♦ **dolled up** *She was dolled up for the occasion.*
PHRASAL VB
V pron-refl P
INFORMAL

ADJ-GRADED

dol·lar /'dɒlə/ **dollars.** The **dollar** is the unit of money used in the USA, Canada, and some other countries. It is represented by the symbol $. ▶ The **dollar** is also used to refer to the American currency system. *The dollar fell sharply against the yen.* ◆◆◆◆◆ N-COUNT N-SING the N

dol·lop /'dɒləp/ **dollops.** A **dollop** of soft or sticky food is a large scoop of it served in a casual way. *...a dollop of cream.* N-COUNT INFORMAL

'doll's house, doll's houses; the form **dollhouse** is used in American English. A **doll's house** is a toy in the form of a small house. N-COUNT

dol·ly /'dɒli/ **dollies.** A **dolly** is a child's word for a doll. ◆◇◇◇◇ N-COUNT

dol·phin /'dɒlfɪn/ **dolphins.** A **dolphin** is a mammal which lives in the sea and looks like a large fish with a pointed mouth. ◆◆◇◇◇ N-COUNT

dolt /dəʊlt/ **dolts.** If you call someone a **dolt**, you think they are stupid. N-COUNT INFORMAL

do·main /dəʊ'meɪn/ **domains. 1** A **domain** is a particular field of thought, activity, or interest. *...the great experimenters in the domain of art.* **2** Someone's **domain** is the area they own or have control over. *The kitchen is by no means his wife's domain.* ● See also **public domain**. ◆◇◇◇◇ N-COUNT FORMAL N-COUNT LITERARY

dome /dəʊm/ **domes. 1** A **dome** is a round roof. *...the dome of St Paul's cathedral.* **2** A **dome** is any object that has a similar shape to a dome. *...the dome of the hill.* **♦ domed** *...the great hall with its domed ceiling.* ◆◆◇◇◇ N-COUNT N-COUNT ADJ

do·mes·tic /də'mestɪk/ **domestics. 1** Domestic political activities, events, and situations happen or exist within one particular country. *...sales in the domestic market... He did not want to intervene in Israel's domestic affairs. ...over 100 domestic flights a day to 15 UK destinations.* ● See also **gross domestic product. ♦ do·mes·ti·cal·ly** /də'mestɪkli/ *Opportunities will improve as the company expands domestically and internationally.* **2** Domestic situations and activities are concerned with the running of a home and family. *...domestic chores. ...a domestic dispute.* **3** Domestic items and services are intended to be used in people's homes rather than in factories or offices. *...domestic appliances.* **4** A **domestic**, a **domestic help**, or a **domestic worker** is a person who is paid to come to help with housework. **5** A **domestic** animal is not wild and is kept as a pet or to produce food. ◆◆◆◇ ADJ ADV ADJ: ADJ n ADJ: ADJ n N-COUNT ADJ

do·mes·ti·cate /də'mestɪkeɪt/ **domesticates, domesticating, domesticated.** When people **domesticate** wild animals, they bring them under control and use them to produce food or as pets. *We domesticated the dog to help us with our hunting.* **♦ do·mes·ti·ca·tion** /də,mestɪ'keɪʃən/ *Sheep are particularly well suited for domestication.* ◆◇◇◇◇ VERB V n N-UNCOUNT

do·mes·ti·cat·ed /də'mestɪkeɪtɪd/. Someone who is **domesticated** willingly does household tasks such as cleaning. ADJ-GRADED

do·mes·ti·city /,dəʊmes'tɪsɪti/. **Domesticity** is the state of being at home with your family. *...cosy domesticity.* N-UNCOUNT

do,mestic 'science. In British schools, **domestic science** was the name used to refer to the subject which involved the teaching of cookery, needlework, and other household skills. The subject is now referred to as **home economics**, which is also the usual American term. N-UNCOUNT

domi·cile /'dɒmɪsaɪl/ **domiciles.** Your **domicile** is the place where you live. **♦ domi·ciled.** If you are **domiciled** in a particular place, you live there. *Frank is currently domiciled in Berlin.* N-COUNT FORMAL ADJ

domi·nant /'dɒmɪnənt/. Someone or something that is **dominant** is more powerful, influential, or noticeable than other people or things. *She was a dominant figure in the French film industry.* **♦ domi·nance** /'dɒmɪnəns/ *...an attempt by each group to establish dominance over the other... Legislation is the only route to ending the car's dominance as a form of transport.* ◆◆◇◇◇ ADJ-GRADED N-UNCOUNT

domi·nate /'dɒmɪneɪt/ **dominates, dominating, dominated. 1** To **dominate** a situation means to ◆◆◆◇ VERB

be the most powerful or important person or thing in it. *The book is expected to dominate the best-seller lists. ...countries where life is dominated by war.* **♦ domi·na·tion** /,dɒmɪ'neɪʃən/ *...the domination of the market by a small number of organizations.* **2** If one person **dominates** another, they have power over them. *Women are no longer dominated by the men in their relationships.* **♦ domi·nat·ing** *He had a very dominating personality.* **♦ domi·na·tion** *They had five centuries of domination by the Romans.* **3** If a building or object **dominates** an area, it is the most noticeable thing there because it is so large or impressive. *...its skyline dominated by the central mosque.* V n Also V N-UNCOUNT VERB: V n Also V ADJ-GRADED N-UNCOUNT VERB: V n V-ed

domi·neer·ing /,dɒmɪ'nɪərɪŋ/. If you say that someone is **domineering**, you disapprove of them because you feel that they try to control other people without considering their feelings or opinions. ADJ-GRADED PRAGMATICS

do·min·ion /də'mɪnjən/ **dominions. 1** Dominion is control or authority. *They truly believe they have dominion over us.* **2** A **dominion** is an area of land that is controlled by a ruler. *The Republic is a dominion of the Brazilian people.* ◆◇◇◇◇ N-UNCOUNT FORMAL N-COUNT

domi·no /'dɒmɪnəʊ/ **dominoes. 1** Dominoes are small rectangular blocks marked with spots on one side, and used for playing games. **2** Dominoes is a game using dominoes. *...some old men playing dominoes.* ◆◇◇◇◇ N-COUNT N-UNCOUNT

'domino effect. If one event causes another similar event, which in turn causes another event, and so on, you can refer to this as a **domino effect.** *...the domino effect that a huge manufacturer such as Boeing can have on other parts of the economy.* N-SING

don /dɒn/ **dons, donning, donned. 1** If you **don** clothing, you put it on. *The crowd threw petrol bombs at the police, who responded by donning riot gear.* **2** A **don** is a lecturer at a university, especially at Oxford or Cambridge University in England. VERB V n WRITTEN N-COUNT

do·nate /dəʊ'neɪt/ **donates, donating, donated. 1** If you **donate** something to a charity or other organization, you give it to them. *Others donated second-hand clothes.* **♦ do·na·tion** /dəʊ'neɪʃən/ **do·nations** *Employees make regular donations to charity.* **2** If you **donate** your blood or a part of your body, you allow doctors to use it to help somebody who is ill. *...people who are willing to donate their organs for use after death.* **♦ donation** *...organ donation.* ◆◆◇◇◇ VERB: V n to n V n N-VAR VERB V n N-UNCOUNT

done /dʌn/. **1** Done is the past participle of **do. 2** A task or activity that is **done** has been completed successfully. *When her deal is done, the client emerges with her purchase.* **3** When something that you are cooking is **done**, it has been cooked long enough and is ready. *As soon as the cake is done, remove it from the oven.* **4** If something is **over and done with**, it is completely finished and you do not have to think about it any more. *Once this is all over and done with she's to go into the clinic for a complete rest.* ◆◆◆◇◇ ADJ: v-link ADJ ADJ: v-link ADJ PHRASE SPOKEN

don·key /'dɒŋki/ **donkeys. 1** A **donkey** is an animal like a horse, but smaller and with longer ears. See picture headed **animals. 2** If you say that something has been happening for **donkey's years**, you are emphasizing that it has been happening for a very long time. ◆◇◇◇◇ N-COUNT PHRASE PRAGMATICS BRITISH, INFORMAL

'donkey jacket, donkey jackets. A **donkey jacket** is a thick, warm jacket worn by workmen. N-COUNT BRITISH

'donkey work. If you do the **donkey work**, you do the hard work or the less interesting part of the work that needs to be done. N-SING BRITISH, INFORMAL

do·nor /'dəʊnə/ **donors. 1** A **donor** is someone who gives a part of their body or some of their blood to be used by doctors to help a person who is ill. **2** Donor organs or parts of the body are available to doctors to use to help sick people. *...the shortage of suitable donor organs.* **3** A **donor** is a person or organization who gives something, especially money, to an organization or country that needs it. ◆◆◇◇◇ N-COUNT ADJ: ADJ n N-COUNT

'donor card, donor cards. A **donor card** is a card N-COUNT which people carry in order to make sure that, when they die, their organs are used by doctors to help sick people.

don't /dəunt/. **Don't** is the usual spoken form of do ♦♦♦♦♦ not.

do·nut /'dəunʌt/ **donuts.** See doughnut.

doo·dle /'duːdəl/ **doodles, doodling, doodled.** **1** A **doodle** is a pattern or picture that you draw N-COUNT when you are bored or thinking about something else. **2** When someone **doodles**, they draw doodles. VERB: V *He began to doodle pictures on a notepad.* V n

doom /duːm/ **dooms, dooming, doomed.** ♦◇◇◇◇ **1 Doom** is a terrible future state or event which you N-UNCOUNT cannot prevent. *...his warnings of impending doom... I awoke with a terrible sense of doom and fear.* **2** If something **dooms** someone to an unpleas- VERB ant fate or they **are doomed** to that fate, they are V n to n certain to suffer it. *That argument was the turning* be V -ed to-inf *point for their marriage, and the one which doomed* Also V n to-inf *it to failure... If he lived, he would be doomed to spend the war as a prisoner.* ♦ **doomed.** Someone ADJ or something that is **doomed** is certain to fail. *...a doomed attempt to rescue the children.*

dooms·day /'duːmzdeɪ/. **1 Doomsday** is a day or N-UNCOUNT time when you expect that something terrible will happen. **2** In the Christian religion, **Doomsday** is N-PROPER the last day of the world, on which God will judge everyone.

door /dɔː/ **doors. 1** A **door** is a piece of wood, ♦♦♦♦♦ glass, or metal fixed to a wall along one side, which N-COUNT is used to open and close the entrance to a building, room, cupboard, or vehicle. *I was knocking at the front door; there was no answer.* **2** A **door** is the N-COUNT space in a wall when a door is open. *She looked through the door.* **3** The **door** is the entrance to a N-COUNT large building such as a shop, hotel, or theatre. *He entered Harrod's by the main door.* **4** You use **doors** N-PLURAL: in expressions such as **a few doors down** or **three** amount N **doors up** when you are referring to a place that is a down/up particular number of buildings away from where INFORMAL you are.

5 When you **answer the door**, you go and open the PHRASE door because a visitor has knocked on it or rung the bell. **6** If you **see** someone **to the** door, you go to the PHRASE door with a visitor when they leave. **7** If someone PHRASE **shows** you **the door**, they ask you to leave because they are angry with you. **8** If someone **shuts** or **slams** PHRASE **the door in** your **face**, they angrily shut the door when you are standing just outside it, because they do not want to see you or talk to you. **9** If someone goes **from** PHRASE **door to door** or goes **door to door**, they go along a street calling at each house in turn, for example sell- ing something. *They are going from door to door col- lecting money from civilians. ...a door-to-door sales- man.* **10** If you talk about a distance or journey **from** PHRASE **door to door** or **door to door**, you are talking about the distance from the place where the journey starts to the place where it finishes. *It took seven hours door-to-door.* **11** When you are **out of doors**, you are PHRASE not inside a building, but in the open air. *The weather was fine enough for working out of doors.*

12 If you say that someone gets something or does PHRASE something **by** or **through the back door**, you are criti- PRAGMATICS cizing them for doing it secretly or unofficially. *They claim the Government is privatising dentistry through the back door.* **13** If people have discussions **behind** PHRASE **closed doors**, they have them in private because they want them to be kept secret. **14** If someone **closes the** PHRASE **door on** something, they stop thinking about it or dealing with it. *We never close the door on a successful series.* **15** If someone or something **opens the door to** PHRASE a new idea or situation, they introduce it or make it possible. *This book opens the door to some of the most exciting findings in solid-state physics.* **16** If you say PHRASE that something helps someone to get their **foot in the door** or their **toe in the door**, you mean that it gives them an opportunity to start doing something new, usually in an area that is difficult to succeed in. *The Philips deal also gives Sparc a foot in the door of a new*

market. **17** If you **lay** something **at** someone's **door**, PHRASE you blame them for something unpleasant that has happened. *The blame is generally laid at the door of the government.*

18 • at death's door: see death. See also next door.

door·bell /'dɔːbel/ **doorbells.** A **doorbell** is a bell ♦◇◇◇◇ on the outside of a house you ring so that the peo- N-COUNT ple inside know that you want to see them. See pic- ture headed house and flat.

door·keep·er /'dɔːkiːpə/ **doorkeepers.** A **door-** N-COUNT **keeper** is a person whose job is to stand at the door of a hotel or public building and help people who are going in or out.

door·knob /'dɔːnɒb/ **doorknobs.** A **doorknob** is a N-COUNT round handle on a door.

door·man /'dɔːmən/ **doormen.** A **doorman** is a N-COUNT person whose job is to stay by the main entrance of a large building, and to help people visiting the building.

door·mat /'dɔːmæt/ **doormats. 1** A **doormat** is a N-COUNT mat by a door which people can wipe their shoes on when they enter a building. **2** If you say that some- N-COUNT one is a **doormat**, you are criticizing them because PRAGMATICS they let other people treat them badly without com- INFORMAL plaining or defending themselves.

door·step /'dɔːstep/ **doorsteps. 1** A **doorstep** is a ♦◇◇◇◇ step in front of a door on the outside of a building. N-COUNT See picture headed house and flat. **2** If something PHRASE is **on** your **doorstep**, it is very near to where you live. *They have to put up with a giant oil refinery right on their doorstep.*

door·stop /'dɔːstɒp/ **doorstops.** A **doorstop** is a N-COUNT heavy object that you use to keep a door open.

,door to 'door. See door.

door·way /'dɔːweɪ/ **doorways. 1** A **doorway** is a ♦♦◇◇◇ space in a wall where a door opens and closes. *He* N-COUNT *stood in the doorway, smiling.* **2** A **doorway** is a cov- N-COUNT ered space just outside the door of a building. *...homeless people sleeping in shop doorways.*

dope /dəup/ **dopes, doping, doped. 1 Dope** is a ♦◇◇◇◇ drug, usually an illegal drug such as cannabis or co- N-UNCOUNT caine. *He has failed a dope test for cocaine. ...dope* INFORMAL *dealers.* **2** If someone **dopes** a person or animal, VERB: V n they force them or trick them into taking drugs. *I'd* be V -ed with n *been doped with Somnolin... They drugged the* V -ed *building's guard dog with doped meatballs.* **3** If N-COUNT someone calls a person a **dope**, they think that the PRAGMATICS person is stupid. *I'm more comfortable with them. I* INFORMAL *don't feel I'm such a dope.*

dopey /'dəupi/. **1** Someone who is **dopey** is sleepy, ADJ-GRADED as though they have been drugged. **2** If you de- ADJ-GRADED scribe someone as **dopey**, you mean that they are INFORMAL rather stupid.

dork /dɔːk/ **dorks.** If you call someone a **dork**, you N-COUNT think they dress badly in old-fashioned clothes, and AMERICAN, behave awkwardly in social situations. INFORMAL

dorm /dɔːm/ **dorms.** A **dorm** is the same as a N-COUNT **dormitory**. INFORMAL

dor·mant /'dɔːmənt/. Something that is **dormant** ♦◇◇◇◇ is not active, growing, or being used at the present ADJ time but is capable of becoming active later on. *...the long dormant volcano... The virus remains dormant in nerve tissue until activated.*

dor·mer /'dɔːmə/ **dormers.** A **dormer** or **dormer** N-COUNT **window** is a window that is built upright in a slop- ing roof.

dor·mi·tory /'dɔːmɪtri, AM -tɔːri/ **dormitories.** ♦◇◇◇◇ **1** A **dormitory** is a large bedroom where several N-COUNT people sleep, for example in a boarding school. **2** A N-COUNT **dormitory** is a building in a college or university AMERICAN where students live. The usual British term is **hall of residence**. **3** A **dormitory** suburb or town is one in ADJ: ADJ n which most of the residents travel to work in a larg- BRITISH er town nearby.

dor·mouse /'dɔːmaus/ **dormice** /'dɔːmaɪs/. A **dor-** N-COUNT **mouse** is a small rodent that looks like a mouse.

dor·sal /'dɔːsəl/. **Dorsal** means relating to the back ADJ: ADJ n of a fish or animal. *...a dolphin's dorsal fin.* TECHNICAL

dos·age /'dəʊsɪdʒ/ **dosages.** A **dosage** is the amount of a medicine that someone takes or should take. *He was put on a high dosage of vitamin C.* ◆◇◇◇◇ N-COUNT

dose /dəʊs/ **doses, dosing, dosed. 1** A **dose** of medicine or a drug is a measured amount of it which is intended to be taken at one time. *One dose of penicillin can wipe out the infection.* **2** You can refer to an amount of something as a **dose** of that thing, especially when you want to emphasize that there is a great deal of it. *She was born with a healthy dose of self-confidence.* **3** If you **dose** a person or animal with medicinal drug, you give them an amount of it. *I dosed myself with quinine.* ▶ **Dose up** means the same as **dose**. *I dosed him up with Valium.* ◆◆◇◇◇ N-COUNT / N-COUNT PRAGMATICS / VERB Vn with n / PHRASAL VB VnP with n

doss /dɒs/ **dosses, dossing, dossed.** If someone doss somewhere, they sleep in a place which is uncomfortable, for example because they have nowhere to live. *...young people dossing in the streets of our great cities.* ▶ **Doss down** means the same as **doss**. *We dossed down in the lounge.* VERB V prep/adv BRITISH, INFORMAL / PHRASAL VB VP prep/adv

dos·ser /'dɒsə/ **dossers.** A **dosser** is someone who does not have a permanent home and sleeps in the streets or in hostels; some people find this word offensive. N-COUNT BRITISH, INFORMAL

'doss-house, doss-houses; also spelled **doss house**. A **doss-house** is a kind of cheap hotel in a city for people who have no home and very little money. N-COUNT BRITISH, INFORMAL

dos·si·er /'dɒsieɪ, -iə/ **dossiers.** A **dossier** is a collection of papers containing information on a particular event or person. *The government kept dossiers on thousands of its citizens.* ◆◇◇◇◇ N-COUNT

dost /dʌst/. **Dost** is an old-fashioned way of saying or writing the second person singular form of the verb 'do'.

dot /dɒt/ **dots, dotting, dotted. 1** A **dot** is a very small round mark, like the one that is used as the top part of the letter 'i'. **2** If you say that someone **dots** the **i's** and **crosses** the **t's**, you mean that they pay great attention to every small detail in a task. **3** You can refer to something that you can see in the distance and that looks like a small round mark as a **dot**. *Soon they were only dots above the hard line of the horizon.* **4** When things **dot** a place or an area, they are scattered or spread all over it. *Small coastal towns dot the landscape.* **5** See also **dotted, polka dots**. **6** If you arrive somewhere or do something **on the dot**, you arrive there or do it at exactly the time that you were supposed to. *Be there at seven on the dot.* **7** The **year dot** is used to mean a very long time ago. *You've wanted to be a barrister since the year dot.* ◆◆◇◇◇ N-COUNT / PHRASE / N-COUNT / VERB Vn / PHRASE / PHRASE INFORMAL

dot·age /'dəʊtɪdʒ/. If someone is in their **dotage**, they are very old and becoming weak. *...spending his dotage in a riverside cottage.* N-UNCOUNT

dote /dəʊt/ **dotes, doting, doted.** If you say that someone **dotes** on a person or a thing, you mean that they love or care about them very much and ignore any faults they may have. *He dotes on his nine-year-old son.* ♦ **dot·ing** *His doting parents bought him his first racing bike at 13.* VERB V on/upon n / ADJ-GRADED

doth /dʌθ/. **Doth** is an old-fashioned way of saying or writing the third person singular form of the verb 'do'.

,dot 'matrix printer, dot matrix printers. A **dot matrix printer** is a computer printer using a device with a series of dots or pins stamped onto it to produce words and numbers. N-COUNT

dot·ted /'dɒtɪd/. **1** A **dotted** line is made of a row of dots. *Cut along the dotted line.* ● If you **sign on the dotted line**, you formally agree to something by signing an official document. **2** You use **dotted** to describe something that is covered with large dots. *...a dotted bow tie.* **3** If a place or object is **dotted with** things, it has many of those things scattered over its surface. *The maps were dotted with the names of small towns.* **4** If things are **dotted** around a place, they can be found in many different parts ◆◇◇◇◇ ADJ PHRASE / ADJ / ADJ: v-link ADJ with n / ADJ: v-link ADJ prep

of that place. *Many pieces of sculpture are dotted around the house.*

dot·ty /'dɒti/ **dottier, dottiest.** If you say that someone is **dotty**, you mean that they are slightly mad or likely to do strange things. *She was obviously going dotty.* ADJ-GRADED PRAGMATICS BRITISH, INFORMAL

dou·ble /'dʌbəl/ **doubles, doubling, doubled. 1** You use **double** to indicate that something includes or is made of two things of the same kind. *...a pair of double doors. ...a lone skier gliding along smooth double tracks.* **2** You use **double** before a singular noun to refer to two things of the same type that occur together, or that are connected in some way. *...an extremely nasty double murder... It was to have been a double wedding.* **3** If something is **double** the amount or size of another thing, it is twice as large. *The offer was to start a new research laboratory at double the salary he was then getting. ...tropical Queensland, more than double the size of Texas.* ▶ Also a pronoun. *On average doctors write just over seven prescriptions each year per patient; in Germany it is double.* **4** You use **double** to describe something which is twice the normal size or twice the normal capacity. *...a large double garage... Allow the loaves to rise until just about double in size.* **5** You use **double** to describe a drink that is the normal measure. *...a double whisky.* ▶ Also a noun. *'Give me a whisky,' Debilly said to Francis. 'Make it a double.'* **6** When something **doubles** or when you **double** it, it becomes twice as great in number, amount, or size. *The program will double the amount of money available to help pay for child care.* **7** A **double** room is a room intended for two people, usually a couple. ▶ Also a noun. *The Great Western Hotel is ideal, costing around £40 a night for a double.* **8** A **double** bed is a bed that is wide enough for two people to sleep in. **9** **Double** is used when you are spelling a word or telling someone a number to show that a letter or digit is repeated. *Ring four two double two double two if you'd like to speak to our financial adviser.* ● **in double figures:** see **figure**. **10** If you refer to someone as a person's **double**, you mean that they look exactly like them. **11** If a person or thing **doubles** as someone or something else, they have a second job or purpose as well as their main one. *...drug dealers who double as police informers.* ▶ **Double up** means the same as **double**. *The lids of the casserole dishes are designed to double up as baking dishes.* **12** In tennis or badminton, when people play **doubles**, they play a match with two people on each team. **13** If you do something **at the double** or **on the double**, you do it very quickly or immediately. *Come to my office, please, at the double.* **14** If you **are seeing double**, there is something wrong with your eyes, and you can see two images instead of one. *I was dizzy, seeing double.* **15** ● **bent double:** see **bent**. ◆◆◆◆◇ ADJ: ADJ n / ADJ: ADJ n / PREDET / PRON / ADJ / ADJ: ADJ n N-COUNT / V-ERG: V Vn / ADJ N-COUNT / ADJ: ADJ n / ADJ: ADJ n / N-COUNT: poss N VERB V as n / PHRASAL VB VP as n / N-UNCOUNT / PHRASE INFORMAL / PHRASE

double back. If you **double back**, you go back in the direction that you came from. PHRASAL VB VP

double up or **double over.** If you **double up** or **double over**, you bend your body quickly or violently, for example because you are laughing a lot or because you are feeling a lot of pain. *She doubled up with laughter... I was doubled over in agony. ...a savage blow in the crutch which doubled him up.* PHRASAL VB ERG V P with/in n be V-ed P with/in n V n P Also V P

'double act, double acts; also spelled **double-act**. Two comedians or entertainers who perform together are referred to as a **double act**. Their performance can also be called a **double act**. *He suggested that we do a double act.* N-COUNT

,double 'agent, double agents. A **double agent** is someone who works as a spy for a particular country or organization, but who also works for its enemies. N-COUNT

'double-barrelled; spelled **double-barreled** in American English. **1** A **double-barrelled** gun has two barrels. **2** A **double-barrelled** surname has two ADJ: ADJ n / ADJ: ADJ n

parts which are joined by a hyphen, for example 'Miss J. Heydon-Smith'.   *BRITISH*

dou·ble bass /ˌdʌbəl ˈbeɪs/ **double basses.** A **double bass** is the largest instrument in the violin family. You play it standing up. See picture headed **musical instruments.**   N-VAR

,**double 'bill, double bills;** also spelled **double-bill.** A **double bill** is a theatre or cinema performance in which there are two shows on the programme.   N-COUNT

,**double 'bluff, double bluffs.** A **double bluff** is an attempt to deceive someone by telling the truth when you know that they will assume you are lying.   N-VAR

,**double-'breasted.** A **double-breasted** jacket or suit has two very wide sections at the front of the jacket which overlap when you button them up.   ADJ

,**double-'check, double-checks, double-checking, double-checked.** If you **double-check** something, you examine or test it a second time to make sure that it is completely correct or safe. *Double-check that the ladder is secure... Don't believe what you are told; double-check with an independent source.*   VERB: V n / V that / Also V

,**double 'chin, double chins.** If someone has a **double chin**, they have a fold of fat under their chin.   N-COUNT

,**double 'cream.**   **Double cream** is very thick cream. The usual American expression is **heavy cream.**   ◆◇◇◇◇ N-UNCOUNT BRITISH

,**double-'cross, double-crosses, double-crossing, double-crossed.** If someone you trust **double-crosses** you, they do something which harms you instead of doing something they had promised to do. ▶ Also a noun. *...a novel about double-crosses, blackmail and intrigue.*   VERB: V n INFORMAL / N-COUNT

,**double-'dealing.** **Double-dealing** is deceitful and dishonest behaviour.   N-UNCOUNT

,**double-'decker, double-deckers. 1** A **double-decker** or a **double-decker bus** is a bus that has two levels, so passengers can sit upstairs or downstairs. **2 Double-decker** items or structures have two layers or levels. *...a double-decker sandwich.*   N-COUNT / ADJ: ADJ n

,**double-'edged. 1** If you say that a comment is **double-edged**, you mean that it has two meanings, so that you are not sure whether the person who said it is being critical or is giving praise. *Even his praise is double-edged.* **2** If you say that something is **double-edged**, you mean that its positive effects are balanced or outweighed by its negative effects. *Tourism is double-edged, for although it's boosting the country's economy, the Reef could be damaged.* • **a double-edged sword:** see **sword.**   ADJ / ADJ-GRADED

dou·ble en·ten·dre /ˌduːbəl ɒnˈtɒndrə/ **double entendres.** A **double entendre** is a word or phrase that has two meanings, one of which is rude and often sexual. *He has a fondness for outrageous double entendre.*   N-VAR

,**double-'glaze, double-glazes, double-glazing, double-glazed.** If someone **double-glazes** a house or its windows, they fit the windows with a second layer of glass which keeps the inside of the house warmer and quieter. *We recently had our house double-glazed. ...double-glazed windows.*   VERB: V n / have V-ed / V-ed
♦ ,**double-'glazing.** *Doreen had double glazing put into their bungalow.*   N-UNCOUNT

,**double-'header, double-headers;** also spelled **doubleheader** in American English. A **double-header** is a sporting contest between two teams that involves two separate games being played.   N-COUNT

,**double 'life, double lives.** If you say that someone is living a **double life**, you mean that they lead two separate and very different lives, and they appear to be a different person in each. *She threatened to publicly expose his double life if he left her.*   N-COUNT

,**double-'park, double-parks, double-parking, double-parked.** If someone **double-parks** their car or their car **double parks**, they park in a road by the side of another parked car. *The car pulled in and double-parked in front of the town hall.*   V-ERG: V n / V

,**double-'quick.** If you say that something does something in **double-quick time**, you are emphasizing that they do it very quickly. *I was over the fence in double-quick time.*   PHRASE PRAGMATICS INFORMAL

double-'speak /ˈdʌbəlspiːk/. If you refer to what someone says as **doublespeak**, you are criticizing them for presenting things in a way that is intended to mislead people and hide the truth. *...the doublespeak so fluently used by governments and their press offices.*   ◆◇◇◇◇ N-UNCOUNT PRAGMATICS

,**double 'standard, double standards.** If you accuse a person or institution of applying **double standards** in their treatment of different groups of people, you mean that they unfairly allow more freedom of behaviour to one group than to another. *A woman now has sexual options, just like a man. This means the death of the double standard.*   ◆◇◇◇◇ N-COUNT PRAGMATICS

dou·blet /ˈdʌblɪt/ **doublets.** A **doublet** was a short, tight-fitting jacket that was worn by men in the fifteenth, sixteenth, and early seventeenth centuries.   N-COUNT

,**double-'take, double-takes.** If you do a **double-take** when you see or hear something strange or surprising, you hesitate for a moment before reacting to it because you wonder if you really saw or heard it.   N-COUNT

'**double-talk;** also spelled **double talk.** If you refer to something someone says as **double-talk**, you mean that it can deceive people or is difficult to understand because it has two possible meanings.   N-UNCOUNT

,**double 'vision.** If someone is suffering from **double vision**, they see a single object as two objects, for example because they are ill or drunk.   N-UNCOUNT

dou·bly /ˈdʌbli/. **1** You use **doubly** to indicate that there are two aspects or features that are having an influence on a particular situation. *She now felt doubly guilty; she had embarrassed Franklin and she had cost her partner money.* **2** You use **doubly** to emphasize that something exists or happens to a greater degree than usual. *Mr. Bush's task is made doubly difficult by his election pledge of 'no new taxes'.*   ◆◇◇◇◇ ADV / ADV: ADV adj/adv

doubt /daʊt/ **doubts, doubting, doubted. 1** If you feel **doubt** or **doubts** about something, you feel uncertain about it and do not know whether it is true or possible. If you have no **doubt** about it, you are certain it is true. *This raises doubts about the point of advertising... They were troubled and full of doubt... There can be little doubt that you can try too hard.* **2** If you are **in doubt** about something, you feel unsure or uncertain about it. *He is in no doubt as to what is needed.*   ◆◆◆◆◇ N-VAR / PHRASE

3 If you say that something is **in doubt**, you mean that nobody knows what it will be like. *The outcome was still in doubt.* **4** You say that something is **beyond doubt** or **beyond reasonable doubt** when you are certain that it is true and it cannot be contradicted or disproved. *A referendum showed beyond doubt that voters wanted independence.* **5** If you say that something is true **without doubt** or **without a doubt**, you are emphasizing that it is definitely true.   PHRASE / PHRASE PRAGMATICS / PHRASE PRAGMATICS

6 If you **doubt** whether something is true or possible, you believe that it is probably not true or possible. *He doubted if he would learn anything new from Marie... She doubted that the accident could have been avoided.* **7** You say **I doubt it** as a response to a question or statement about something that you think is untrue or unlikely. *'Somebody would have seen her.'—'I doubt it, not on Monday.'* **8** If you **doubt** something, you believe that it might not be true or genuine. *No one doubted his ability.* **9** If you **doubt** someone or **doubt** their word, you think that they may not be telling the truth. *Don't think I'm doubting you.*   VERB: V whether / V if / V that / CONVENTION PRAGMATICS / VERB: V n / VERB: V n

10 You use **no doubt** to emphasize that something seems very likely to you. *No doubt many will regard these as harsh words.*   PHRASE PRAGMATICS

11 • **the benefit of the doubt:** see **benefit.** • **a shadow of a doubt:** see **shadow.**

doubt·er /ˈdaʊtə/ **doubters.** If you refer to people as **doubters**, you mean that they have doubts about   N-COUNT

something, especially their religious or political system.

doubt·ful /'daʊtfʊl/. **1** If it is **doubtful** that something will happen, it seems unlikely to happen or you are uncertain whether it will happen. *It is doubtful whether he will appear again this summer.* ◆◆◇◇◇ ADJ-GRADED PRAGMATICS **2** If you are **doubtful** about something, you feel uncertain about it. *I was still very doubtful about the chances for success.* ADJ-GRADED ♦ **doubt·ful·ly** *Keeton shook his head doubtfully.* ADV-GRADED: ADV after v **3** If you say that something is of **doubtful** quality or value, you mean that it is of low quality or value. ADJ-GRADED PRAGMATICS **4** If a sports player is **doubtful** for a match or event, he or she seems unlikely to play, usually because of injury. ADJ-GRADED JOURNALISM

doubt·less /'daʊtləs/. If you say that something is **doubtless** the case, you mean that you think it is probably and almost certainly the case. *He will doubtless try and persuade his colleagues to change their minds.* ◆◇◇◇◇ ADV: ADV with cl/ group PRAGMATICS

douche /duːʃ/ **douches**. A **douche** is a method of washing the vagina with a jet of water, using a device also called a **douche**. N-COUNT

dough /dəʊ/ **dough**. **1 Dough** is a fairly firm mixture of flour, water, and sometimes also fat and sugar. It can be cooked to make bread, pastry, and biscuits. ◆◇◇◇◇ N-VAR N-UNCOUNT **2** You can refer to money as **dough**. INFORMAL

dough·nut /'dəʊnʌt/ **doughnuts**; also spelled **donut**. A **doughnut** is a bread-like cake made from sweet dough that has been cooked in hot fat. ◆◇◇◇◇ N-COUNT

dough·ty /'daʊti/. If you describe someone as a **doughty** fighter or campaigner, you mean they are brave, determined, and not easily defeated. ADJ-GRADED: ADJ n PRAGMATICS DATED

dour /dʊə, daʊə/. If you describe someone as **dour**, you mean that they have a rather severe and unfriendly manner. ♦ **dour·ly** *'They criticized it for being jingoistic,' he says dourly.* ◆◇◇◇◇ ADJ-GRADED ADV-GRADED

douse /daʊs/ **douses, dousing, doused**; also spelled **dowse**. **1** If you **douse** a fire, you stop it burning by pouring a lot of water over it. **2** If you **douse** someone or something with a liquid, you throw a lot of that liquid over them. ◆◇◇◇◇ VERB: V n VERB: V n with/in n

dove, doves; pronounced /dʌv/ for meanings 1 and 2, and /dəʊv/ for meaning 3. **1** A **dove** is a bird that looks like pigeon but is smaller and lighter in colour. **2** People who support the use of peaceful methods to solve difficult situations can be referred to as **doves**. Compare **hawk**. ♦ **dov·ish** *...the most dovish government Israel has had since the 1970s.* ◆◇◇◇◇ N-COUNT N-COUNT JOURNALISM ADJ-GRADED **3 Dove** is sometimes used as the past tense of **dive**. AMERICAN

dove·cote /'dʌvkɒt, -kəʊt/ **dovecotes**. A **dovecote** is a small building or a container for pigeons or doves to live in. N-COUNT

dove·tail /'dʌvteɪl/ **dovetails, dovetailing, dovetailed**. **1** If two ideas or things **dovetail**, they fit together neatly or have some common characteristics. *...areas where U.S. interests can dovetail with Japanese concerns... It is important that we dovetail our respective interests.* **2** A **dovetail** or a **dovetail joint** is a wedge-shaped joint used in carpentry. V-RECIP-ERG: V n with n V with n V pl-n Also V n with n N-COUNT

dowa·ger /'daʊədʒə/ **dowagers**. **1** You use **dowager** to refer to the widow of a duke, emperor, or other high-ranking man. *...the Dowager Countess Spencer.* ▶ Also a noun. **2** If you describe a woman as a **dowager**, you mean that she is old and rich or grand-looking. ADJ: ADJ n, n ADJ N-COUNT N-COUNT LITERARY

dow·dy /'daʊdi/ **dowdier, dowdiest**. If you describe someone or their clothes as **dowdy**, you mean their clothes are dull and unfashionable; used showing disapproval. ADJ-GRADED PRAGMATICS

dow·el /'daʊəl/ **dowels**. A **dowel** is a short thin piece of wood or metal which is used for joining larger pieces of wood or metal together. N-COUNT

down 1 preposition and adverb uses

down /daʊn/. **Down** is often used with verbs of movement, such as 'fall' and 'pull', and also in phrasal verbs such as 'bring down' and 'calm down'. ◆◆◆◆◆

1 If someone or something goes **down** something such as a slope or a pipe, they go towards the ground PREP

or to a lower level. *We're going down a mountain... A man came down the stairs... The tears began flooding down her cheeks.* ▶ Also an adverb. *She went down to the kitchen... Any unauthorized war planes flying in the area are to be shot down.* ADV: ADV after v PREP **2** If you are a particular distance **down** something, you are that distance below the top or surface of it. *...a ledge 40ft down the rock face.* ▶ Also an adverb. *I buried it three inches down.* ADV: amount ADV **3** You use **down** to say that you are looking or facing in a direction that is towards the ground or towards a lower level. *She was still looking down at her papers... She put her head down, her hands over her face.* ADV: ADV after v **4** If you put something **down**, you put it onto a surface. *Danny put down his glass... After two rings I put down the phone.* ADV: ADV after v

5 If you go or look **down** something such as a road or river, you go or look along it. If you are **down** a road or river, you are somewhere along it. *They set off at a jog up one street and down another. ...a few miles down the road at Burnham.* PREP **6** If you are travelling to a particular place, you can say that you are going **down** to that place, especially if you are going towards the south or to a lower level of land. **Down** can also suggest that your journey is casual or unhurried. *I went down to L.A. all the way from Seattle... I have seen him walking down to the shops... I'll take you down to the valley.* ADV: ADV after v SPOKEN **7** If you are **down** a place, you are at that place. If you go **down** a place, you go to that place. Some people believe this use is incorrect. *People are down the pub, getting drunk... We got in the car and went down the supermarket.* PREP INFORMAL **8** If an amount of something goes **down**, it decreases. If an amount of something is **down**, it has decreased and is at a lower level. *Interest rates came down today... My weight went down to seventy pounds... My department had a healthy interest in keeping expenses down.* ADV **9** If you are **down to** a certain amount of something, you have only that amount left. *The poor man's down to his last £3.* PHR-PREP

10 If you say that there are a number of things **down** and a number **to go**, you are saying how many of the things have already been dealt with and how many remain to be dealt with. *Two weeks down, three to go.* PHRASE **11 Down to** a particular detail means including everything, even that detail. **Down to** a particular person means including everyone, even that person. *I was a soldier down to my shoelaces. ...from the chairman right down to the tea ladies.* PHR-PREP **12** If a situation is **down to** a particular person or thing, it has been caused by that person or thing. *Any mistakes are entirely down to us.* PHR-PREP **13** If someone or something is **down for** something, it has been arranged that they will do it or it will happen to them. *Mark had told me that he was down for an interview.* PHR-PREP **14** If you are **down with** an illness, you have that illness. ● See also **come down with**. PHR-PREP INFORMAL **15** If people shout '**down with**' something or someone, they are saying that they dislike them and want to get rid of them. *Demonstrators chanted 'down with communism'.* PHRASE PRAGMATICS

16 ● **up and down**: see **up**. ● **ups and downs**: see **up**. ● **down in the dumps**: see **dump**.

down 2 adjective uses

down /daʊn/. **1** If you are feeling **down**, you are feeling unhappy or depressed. **2** If something is **down** on paper, it has been written on the paper. *That date wasn't down on our news sheet.* **3** If a piece of equipment, especially a computer system, is **down**, it is temporarily not working because of a fault. ADJ-GRADED: v-link ADJ ADJ: v-link ADJ ADJ: v-link ADJ

down 3 verb uses

down /daʊn/ **downs, downing, downed**. **1** If you say that someone **downs** food or a drink, you mean that they eat or drink it. **2** If something or someone **is downed**, they fall to the ground because they have been hurt or damaged in some way. *A bank guard shot him in the leg and downed him.* ◆◆◇◇◇ VERB: V n VERB: be V-ed V n JOURNALISM ♦ **down·ing** *...the downing of an airliner, which killed 107 people.* **3** ● **to down tools**: see **tool**. N-UNCOUNT

down 4 noun uses

down /daʊn/. **1 Down** consists of the small soft N-UNCOUNT
feathers on young birds. **2 Down** is very fine hair. N-UNCOUNT
The whole plant is covered with fine down. ● See
also **downs**.

down-and-'out, down-and-outs; also spelled ADJ-GRADED
down and out. If someone is **down-and-out**, they
have no job and nowhere to live, and they have no
real hope of improving their situation. ▶ Also a N-COUNT
noun in British English. *...some poor down-and-out
in need of a meal.*

down-at-'heel. Something that is **down-at-heel** is ADJ-GRADED
in a in bad condition because it has been used too
much or has not been looked after properly. Someone who is **down-at-heel** is wearing old worn
clothes because they have little money.

down·beat /'daʊnbiːt/. If someone is **downbeat**, ADJ-GRADED
they are feeling cautious or pessimistic about something. *...a downbeat assessment of 1992's economic
prospects.*

down·cast /'daʊnkɑːst, -kæst/. **1** If you are **down-** ADJ-GRADED
cast, you are feeling sad and pessimistic. **2** If your ADJ
eyes are **downcast**, you are looking towards the
ground because you are feeling sad or embarrassed.

down·er /'daʊnə/ **downers. 1 Downers** are drugs N-COUNT
that make you feel sleepy or calm. INFORMAL
2 If you describe a situation as a **downer**, you mean N-COUNT
that it is very depressing. INFORMAL

down·fall /'daʊnfɔːl/. **1** The **downfall** of a success- ◆◇◇◇◇
ful or powerful person or institution is their loss of N-UNCOUNT:
success or power. *His lack of experience had led to* also N in pl
his downfall. **2** The thing that was a person's **down-** N-UNCOUNT
fall caused them to fail or lose power. *His honesty
had been his downfall.*

down·grade /ˌdaʊn'grɪd/ **downgrades, down-** ◆◇◇◇◇
grading, downgraded. 1 If something is **down-** VB: usu
graded, it is given less importance than it used to passive
have, or than you think it should have. *The boy's* beV-ed
*condition has been downgraded from critical to seri-
ous.* **2** If someone **is downgraded**, their job or sta- VERB:
tus is changed so that they become less important beV-ed
or receive less money. *His superiors suspended him,* V n
and then downgraded him.

down·hearted /ˌdaʊn'hɑːtɪd/. If you are **down-** ADJ-GRADED
hearted, you are feeling sad and discouraged.

down·hill /ˌdaʊn'hɪl/. **1** If something or someone is ◆◇◇◇◇
moving **downhill**, they are moving down a slope. If ADV
they are **downhill**, they are located towards the bottom of a slope. *He headed downhill towards the river... It was a clearing just downhill from a peak of
eight thousand feet.* ▶ Also an adjective. *...downhill* ADJ: ADJ n
ski runs. **2** If you say that something is going ADV
downhill, you mean that it is becoming worse or
less successful. *Australian rugby has certainly gone
downhill.* **3** If you say that a task or situation is ADJ:
downhill after a particular stage or time, you mean v-link ADJ
that it is easy to deal with after that stage or time. *I
guess it's all downhill from here.*

Down·ing Street /'daʊnɪŋ striːt/. **Downing Street** ◆◆◇◇◇
is the street in London in which the Prime Minister N-PROPER
and the Chancellor of the Exchequer live. You can
also use **Downing Street** to refer to the Prime Minister and his or her officials.

down·load /'daʊnləʊd/ **downloads, download-** VERB: V n
ing, downloaded. To **download** data means to
transfer it to or from a computer along a line such
as a telephone line, a radio link, or a computer
network.

down·market /ˌdaʊn'mɑːkɪt/; also spelled **down-** ADJ-GRADED
market. A **downmarket** product or service is cheap
and not very good quality. ▶ Also an adverb. *Why is* ADV:
the company going downmarket? ADV after v

'down payment, down payments. If you make N-COUNT
a **down** payment on something, you pay a percentage of the total cost when you buy it. You pay the
remaining amount later.

down·play /ˌdaʊn'pleɪ/ **downplays, downplay-** ◆◇◇◇◇
ing, downplayed. If you **downplay** a fact or fea- VERB
ture, you try to make people think that it is less im- V n

portant or serious than it really is. *He attempted to
downplay the significance of Tory divisions.*

down·pour /'daʊnpɔː/ **downpours**. A **downpour** ◆◇◇◇◇
is a sudden and unexpected heavy fall of rain. N-COUNT

down·right /'daʊnraɪt/. You use **downright** to em- ◆◇◇◇◇
phasize unpleasant or bad qualities or behaviour. ADV: ADV adj
...ideas that would have been downright dangerous if PRAGMATICS
put into practice. ▶ Also an adjective. *...suspicion* ADJ: ADJ n
and downright hostility.

down 'river; also spelled **downriver**. Something ADV
that is moving **down river** is moving towards the
mouth of a river, from a point further up the river.
Something that is **down river** is towards the mouth
of a river. *By 09.30 we had cast off and were heading
down river. ...a big tourist hotel a few hundred yards
down river.*

downs /daʊnz/. **Downs** are areas of gentle hills with N-PLURAL
few trees. BRITISH

down·side /'daʊnsaɪd/. The **downside** of a situa- ◆◇◇◇◇
tion is the aspect of it which is less positive, pleas- N-SING
ant, or useful than its other aspects. *The downside
of this approach is a lack of clear leadership.*

down·size /'daʊnsaɪz/ **downsizes, downsizing**, VERB: V n
downsized. To **downsize** something such as a
business or industry means to make it smaller.
♦ **down·siz·ing** *...a trend toward downsizing in the* N-UNCOUNT
personal computer market.

down·spout /'daʊnspaʊt/ **downspouts**. A **down-** N-COUNT
spout is a pipe attached to the side of a building, AMERICAN
through which water flows from the roof into a
drain. The British word is **drainpipe**. See picture
headed **house and flat**.

'Down's syndrome. American English usually N-UNCOUNT
uses the form **Down syndrome**. **Down's syndrome**
is a genetic disorder in which a person is born with
a flat forehead and sloping eyes and lower than average intelligence.

down·stairs /ˌdaʊn'steəz/. **1** If you go **downstairs** ◆◆◇◇◇
in a building, you go down a staircase towards the ADV:
ground floor. **2** If something or someone is **down-** ADV after v
stairs in a building, they are on the ground floor or ADV:
on a lower floor than you. *...the flat downstairs.* beADV,
▶ Also an adjective. *She repainted the downstairs* n ADV
rooms. ▶ The **downstairs** of a building is its lower ADJ: ADJ n
floor or floors. *The downstairs of the two little* N-SING:
houses had been entirely refashioned. theN

down·stream /ˌdaʊn'striːm/. Something that is ◆◇◇◇◇
moving **downstream** is moving towards the mouth ADV
of a river, from a point further up the river. Something that is **downstream** is further towards the
mouth of a river than where you are. *We had drifted
downstream... Communities downstream have been
alerted.* ▶ Also an adjective. *...Baghdad and other* ADJ: ADJ n
downstream cities.

down·swing /'daʊnswɪŋ/ **downswings**. A **down-** N-COUNT
swing is a sudden decline in something such as an
economy, that had previously been improving.

down-to-'earth. If you say that someone is ◆◇◇◇◇
down-to-earth, you approve of the fact that they ADJ-GRADED
concern themselves with practical things and ac- PRAGMATICS
tions, rather than with abstract theories.

down·town /'daʊntaʊn/. **Downtown** places are in ◆◆◇◇◇
or towards the centre of a large town or city, where ADJ: ADJ n
the shops and places of business are. *...an office in
downtown Chicago.* ▶ Also an adverb. *By day he* ADV
*worked downtown... You have to be downtown in a
hurry.*

down·trod·den /ˌdaʊn'trɒdən/. People who are ADJ
downtrodden are treated very badly by people with
power, and do not have the ability or the energy to
rebel. ▶ The **downtrodden** are people who are N-PLURAL:
downtrodden. theN

down·turn /'daʊntɜːn/ **downturns**. If there is a ◆◇◇◇◇
downturn in the economy or in a company or in- N-COUNT
dustry, it becomes worse or less successful than it
had been.

down 'under. You can refer to Australia and New ◆◇◇◇◇
Zealand as **down under**. *For summer skiing down* PHRASE
under, there is no better place than New Zealand. BRITISH,
INFORMAL

down·wards /'daʊnwədz/. In usual British English, **downwards** is an adverb and **downward** is an adjective. In formal British English and in American English, **downward** is both an adjective and an adverb. ◆◆◇◇◇

1 If you move or look **downwards**, you move or look towards the ground or a lower level. *Benedict pointed downwards again with his stick... The child lay face downwards.* ▶ Also an adjective. *...a firm downward movement of the hands.* **2** If an amount or rate moves **downwards**, it decreases. *Inflation is moving firmly downwards.* ▶ Also an adjective. *...the downward trend in home ownership.* **3** If you want to emphasize that a statement applies to everyone in an organization, you can say that it applies from its leader **downwards**. *...from the Prime Minister downwards.* ADV · ADJ: ADJ n · ADV: ADV after v · ADJ: ADJ n · ADV: from n ADV · PRAGMATICS

down·wind /daʊn'wɪnd/. If something moves **downwind**, it moves in the same direction as the wind. If something is **downwind**, the wind is blowing towards it. *...people who are living downwind of Nevada nuclear test sites.* ▶ Also an adjective. *...the downwind end of the field.* ADV · ADJ: ADJ n

downy /'daʊni/ **downier, downiest. 1** Something that is **downy** is filled or covered with small soft feathers. **2** Something that is **downy** is covered with very fine hairs. *...the baby's downy head.* ADJ-GRADED · ADJ-GRADED

dow·ry /'daʊəri/ **dowries.** A woman's **dowry** is the money and goods which, in some cultures, her family gives to the man that she marries. N-COUNT

dowse /daʊs/ **dowses, dowsing, dowsed.** If someone **dowses** for underground water, minerals, or some other substance, they search for it with the aid of a special rod or a pendulum. *Terry Ross dowses oil and ore in South America.* ● See also **douse.** ◆◇◇◇◇ · VERB: V for n · Also V

doy·en /'dɔɪən, dɔɪ'en/ **doyens.** If you refer to a man as the **doyen** of a group or profession, you mean that he is the oldest and most experienced and respected member of it. *Sir Robin Day is widely regarded as the doyen of political interviewers.* N-COUNT · FORMAL

doy·enne /dɔɪ'en/ **doyennes.** If you refer to a woman as the **doyenne** of a group or profession, you mean that she is the oldest and most experienced and respected woman in it. *Jean Muir has often been described as the doyenne of British fashion.* N-COUNT · FORMAL

doze /dəʊz/ **dozes, dozing, dozed.** When you **doze**, you sleep lightly or for a short period. ▶ Also a noun. *After lunch I had a doze.* ◆◇◇◇◇ · VERB: V · N-SING: a N

doze off. If you **doze off** you fall into a light sleep. *Salter dozed off for a few moments.* PHRASAL VB · V P

doz·en /'dʌzən/ **dozens.** The plural form is **dozen** after a number, or after a word or expression referring to a number, such as 'several' or 'a few'. **1** If you have a **dozen** things, you have twelve of them. *The cake must have contained two dozen eggs.* **2** You can refer to a group of approximately twelve things or people as a **dozen** things or people. You can refer to a group of approximately six things or people as **half a dozen** things or people. *I was sitting only a dozen feet away.* **3** If you refer to **dozens of** things or people, you are emphasizing that there are very many of them. *...a storm which destroyed dozens of homes.* ▶ Also a pronoun. *...Mr Johnson's portraits, of which there are dozens.* ◆◆◆◆◇ · NUMBER · NUMBER · QUANT · PRAGMATICS · PRON

dozy /'dəʊzi/ **dozier, doziest. 1** If you are **dozy**, you are feeling sleepy and not very alert. **2** If you describe someone as **dozy**, you mean they are rather stupid and slow to understand things. ADJ-GRADED · ADJ-GRADED · PRAGMATICS · BRITISH

Dr, Drs; this abbreviation is usually followed by a full stop in American English. **Dr** is a written abbreviation for **Doctor**. ◆◆◆◆◇

drab /dræb/ **drabber, drabbest. 1** If something is **drab**, it is dull and boring to look at or experience. ◆◇◇◇◇ · ADJ-GRADED

♦ **drab·ness** *...the dusty drabness of nearby villages.* **2** See also **dribs and drabs.** N-UNCOUNT

dra·co·nian /drə'kəʊniən/. **Draconian** laws or measures are extremely harsh and severe. ◆◇◇◇◇ · ADJ-GRADED · FORMAL

draft /drɑːft, dræft/ **drafts, drafting, drafted. 1** When you **draft** a letter, book, or speech, you write the first version of it. *He drafted a standard* ◆◆◇◇◇ · VERB · V n

letter to the editors. ▶ Also a noun. *I faxed a first draft of this article to him.* N-COUNT **2** If you **are drafted**, you are ordered to serve in the armed forces. *He was drafted into the US Army.* VERB: beV-ed · beV-ed into n **3** **The draft** is the practice of ordering people to serve in the armed forces for a limited period of time. *...his effort to avoid the draft.* N-SING: the N **4** If people **are drafted** into a place, they are moved there to do a particular job. *Extra police officers had to be drafted in.* VERB: beV-ed prep/adv · Also V n **5** A **draft** is a written order for payment of money by a bank, especially from one bank to another. N-COUNT **6** See also **draught.**

'**draft dodger, draft dodgers.** A **draft dodger** is someone who avoids joining the armed forces when normally they would be obliged to join; used showing disapproval. N-COUNT · PRAGMATICS

draftee /drɑː'fiː, dræft-/ **draftees.** A **draftee** is the same as a **conscript.** N-COUNT · AMERICAN

drafts·man /'drɑːftsmən, 'dræfts-/ **draftsmen.** See **draughtsman.**

drafty /'drɑːfti, 'dræfti/. See **draughty.**

drag /dræg/ **drags, dragging, dragged. 1** To **drag** something or someone means to pull them along the ground, often with difficulty. *He got up and dragged his chair towards the table.* **2** If you **drag** your foot or your leg behind you, you walk with great difficulty because you foot or leg is injured in some way. *He drags his leg, and he can hardly lift his arm.* ◆◆◆◇◇ · VERB · V n prep/adv · VERB: V n prep · V n **3** If someone **drags** you somewhere you do not want to go, they make you go there. *...when you can drag him away from his work.* VERB · V n adv/prep **4** If you say that you **drag** yourself somewhere, you are emphasizing that you have to make a very strong effort to go there. *I find it really hard to drag myself out and exercise regularly.* VERB · PRAGMATICS · V pron-refl adv/prep **5** If you **drag** your **feet** or **drag** your **heels**, you delay doing something or do it very slowly because you do not want to do it. PHRASE **6** If the police **drag** a river or lake, they pull nets or hooks across the bottom of it in order to look for something. VERB: V n **7** If a period of time or an event **drags**, it is very boring and seems to last a long time. *The minutes dragged past.* VERB: V · V adv **8** If something is **a drag on** the development or progress of something, it slows it down or makes it more difficult. *Spending cuts will put a drag on growth.* N-SING: a N on n **9** **Drag** is the resistance to the movement that is experienced by something that is moving through air or through a fluid. *The drag of those extra air molecules brought the satellite crashing to Earth.* N-UNCOUNT · TECHNICAL **10** If you say that something is **a drag**, you mean that it is a nuisance or is very dull. N-SING: a N · INFORMAL **11** If you take a **drag** on a cigarette or pipe that you are smoking, you take in air through it. N-COUNT · INFORMAL **12** **Drag** is the wearing of women's clothes by a male entertainer. *...a drag queen imitating Bette Davis.* ● If a man is **in drag**, he is wearing women's clothes. N-UNCOUNT · PHRASE

drag down. 1 To **drag** someone **down** means to reduce them to a lower social status or standard of behaviour. *There were fears he would be dragged down by the scandal.* **2** Something that **drags** you **down** makes you feel weak or depressed. PHRASAL VB · V n P · beV-ed P by n · V n P

drag in. When you are talking, if you **drag in** a subject, you mention something that is not relevant and that other people do not want to discuss. *They disapproved of my dragging in his wealth.* PHRASAL VB · V P noun · Also V n P

drag into. To **drag** something or someone **into** an event or situation means to involve them in it when it is not necessary or not desirable. *Why should Carmela have dragged him into the argument?* PHRASAL VB · V n P n

drag on. You say that an event or process **drags on** when you disapprove of the fact that it lasts for longer than necessary. PHRASAL VB · V P · PRAGMATICS

drag out. 1 If you **drag** something **out**, you make it last for longer than is necessary. *...a company that was willing and able to drag out the proceedings for years.* **2** If you **drag** something **out** of someone, you persuade them to tell you something that they do not want to tell you. *Every piece of information had to be dragged out of the authorities.* PHRASAL VB · V n P · V P noun · V n P of n

drag up. If someone **drags up** an unpleasant event or a story from the past, they mention it when people do not want to be reminded of it. *I don't want to go back there and drag up that anger again.* PHRASAL VB V P noun Also V n P

drag·net /'drægnet/. If a large number of police officers conduct a **dragnet**, they carefully search a specific area for a particular suspected criminal. N-SING

drag·on /'drægən/ **dragons.** 1 In stories and legends, a **dragon** is an animal like a big lizard. It has wings and claws, and breathes out fire. 2 If someone calls a woman a **dragon**, they mean that she is fierce and unpleasant. N-COUNT N-COUNT RUDE

dragon·fly /'drægənflaɪ/ **dragonflies.** A dragonfly is a brightly-coloured insect with a long thin body and two sets of wings. See picture headed **insects**. N-COUNT

dra·goon /drə'guːn/ **dragoons, dragooning, dragooned.** 1 In European armies in the past, a **dragoon** was a soldier. 2 If someone **dragoons** you into doing something that you do not want to do, they forcefully persuade you to do it. N-COUNT VERB: V n into-ing/n

drain /dreɪn/ **drains, draining, drained.** 1 If you **drain** a liquid from a place or object, you remove the liquid by causing it to flow somewhere else. If a liquid **drains** somewhere, it flows there. *Miners built the tunnel to drain water out of the mines. ...springs and rivers that drain into lakes.* 2 A **drain** is a pipe that carries water or sewage away from a place, or an opening in a surface that leads to the pipe. 3 If you **drain** a place or object, you dry it by causing water to flow out of it. *They have mobilised vast numbers of people to drain flooded land... The soil drains freely.* 4 If you **drain** food, you remove the liquid that it has been in, especially after it has been cooked or soaked in water. *Drain the pasta well... Wash the leeks thoroughly and allow them to drain.* 5 If someone **drains** a glass, they empty it by drinking what is in it. 6 If the colour or the blood **drains** from someone's face, or if their face **drains** of colour, they become very pale. *Thacker's face drained of colour... Jock's face had been suddenly drained of all colour.* 7 If a feeling **drains** out of you, it gradually becomes weaker until you no longer feel it. *And then, suddenly, the euphoria began to drain away... The excitement had been drained completely from her voice.* 8 If something **drains** you, it exhausts you physically and emotionally. ♦ **drained** *United stalked off, stunned and drained.* ♦ **drain·ing** *It is physically exhausting and emotionally draining.* 9 If energy **drains** from you, you lose all energy and become very tired. *As his energy drained away, his despair and worry grew.* ► Also an adjective. *He was too drained of energy to fret further.* V-ERG V n adv/prep V prep/adv Also V n N-COUNT V-ERG V n V V-ERG V n V VERB: V n LITERARY V-ERG: V from n V of n beV-ed of n V-ERG V adv/prep beV-ed from n VERB: V n ADJ-GRADED ADJ-GRADED V-ERG V adv/prep Also V n ADJ-GRADED

10 If you say that something is a **drain** on an organization's finances or resources, you mean that it costs the organization a large amount of money, and you do not consider that it is worth it. ● See also **brain drain.** 11 If you say that a country's or a company's resources or finances **are drained**, you mean that they are used or spent completely. *The state's finances have been drained by drought and civil disorder.* N-SING VERB beV-ed Also V n

12 If you say that something is going **down the drain**, you mean that it is being destroyed or wasted. PHRASE INFORMAL

drain·age /'dreɪnɪdʒ/. **Drainage** is the system or process by which water or other liquids are drained from a place. *Line the pots with pebbles to ensure good drainage.* ♦◇◇◇ N-UNCOUNT

'draining board, draining boards. The **draining board** is the place on a sink unit where things such as plates and cutlery are put to drain after they have been washed. N-COUNT

drain·pipe /'dreɪnpaɪp/ **drainpipes.** A drainpipe is a pipe attached to the side of a building, through which rainwater flows from the roof into a drain. The American word is **downspout**. See picture headed **house and flat**. N-COUNT

drake /dreɪk/ **drakes.** A drake is a male duck. N-COUNT

dram /dræm/ **drams.** A dram is a small measure of whisky; used especially in Scottish English. N-COUNT

dra·ma /'drɑːmə/ **dramas.** 1 A **drama** is a serious play for the theatre, television, or radio. *...television dramas.* 2 You use **drama** to refer to plays in general or to work that is connected with plays and the theatre. *He knew nothing of Greek drama. ...drama school.* 3 You can refer a real situation which is exciting or distressing as **drama**. *...the drama and relief of a hostage release.* ♦♦♦◇ N-COUNT N-UNCOUNT N-VAR

dra·mat·ic /drə'mætɪk/. 1 A **dramatic** change or event happens suddenly and is very noticeable and surprising. *A fifth year of drought is expected to have dramatic effects on the California economy.* ♦ **dra·mati·cal·ly** /drə'mætɪkli/ *At speeds above 50mph, serious injuries dramatically increase.* 2 A **dramatic** action, event, or situation is exciting and impressive. 3 You use **dramatic** to describe things connected with or relating to the theatre, drama, or plays. *...a dramatic arts major in college.* ♦♦♦♦ ADJ-GRADED ADV-GRADED ADJ-GRADED ADJ: ADJ n

dra·mat·ics /drə'mætɪks/. 1 You use **dramatics** to refer to activities connected with the theatre and drama, such as acting in plays or producing them. *...an amateur dramatics class.* 2 You talk about **dramatics** to express your disapproval of behaviour which seems to show too much emotion, and which you think is done deliberately. *...another wearisome outbreak of Nancy's dramatics.* N-UNCOUNT N-PLURAL PRAGMATICS

dra·ma·tis per·so·nae /ˌdræmətɪs pə'səʊnaɪ/. The characters in a play are sometimes referred to as **the dramatis personae.** N-PLURAL: the N FORMAL

drama·tist /'dræmətɪst/ **dramatists.** A dramatist is someone who writes plays. ♦◇◇◇ N-COUNT

drama·tize /'dræmətaɪz/ **dramatizes, dramatizing, dramatized;** also spelled **dramatise** in British English. 1 If a book or story **is dramatized**, it is written or presented as a play, film, or television drama. ♦ **drama·ti·za·tion** /ˌdræmətaɪ'zeɪʃən/ **dramatizations** *...a dramatisation of D H Lawrence's novel, 'Lady Chatterley's Lover.'* 2 If you say that someone **dramatizes** a situation or event, you mean that they try to make it seem more serious, more important, or more exciting than it really is; used showing disapproval. *They have a tendency to show off, to dramatize almost every situation.* 3 If an action or event **dramatizes** a situation, it focuses people's attention on the situation in a dramatic way. *The need for change has been dramatized by plummeting bank profits.* ♦◇◇◇ VB: usu passive N-COUNT: with supp VERB PRAGMATICS V n Also V VERB: V n

drank /dræŋk/. **Drank** is the past tense of **drink.**

drape /dreɪp/ **drapes, draping, draped.** 1 If you **drape** a piece of cloth somewhere, you place it there so that it hangs down in a casual and graceful way. *Natasha took the coat and draped it over her shoulders.* 2 If someone or something **is draped** in a piece of cloth, they are loosely covered by it. *He draped himself in the Canadian flag.* 3 If you **drape** a part of your body somewhere, you lay it there in a relaxed and graceful way. *He draped his arm over Daniel's shoulder.* 4 **Drapes** are pieces of heavy fabric you hang across a window that you can close to keep the light out or stop people looking in. The British word is **curtains.** ♦◇◇◇ VERB V n prep VERB V n in/with n VERB V n prep N-COUNT AMERICAN

drap·er /'dreɪpə/ **drapers.** A draper is a shopkeeper who sells cloth. You can also refer to the shop where a draper works as a **draper** or **draper's.** ♦◇◇◇ N-COUNT BRITISH

dra·pery /'dreɪpəri/ **draperies.** 1 You can refer to cloth, curtains, or clothing hanging in folds as **drapery** or **draperies.** 2 **Drapery** is cloth that you buy in a shop. *My mother ran a couple of drapery shops.* N-UNCOUNT: also N in pl N-UNCOUNT BRITISH

dras·tic /'dræstɪk/. 1 If you take **drastic** action in order to solve a problem, you do something extreme, severe, and radical to solve it. *He's not going to do anything drastic about economic policy.* 2 A **drastic** change is a very great change. ♦ **dras·ti·cal·ly** *Services have been drastically reduced.* ♦♦◇◇ ADJ-GRADED ADJ-GRADED ADV: ADV with v

draught /drɑːft, dræft/ **draughts;** spelled **draft** in American English. 1 A **draught** is a current of air that comes into a place in an undesirable way. 2 **Draught** beer is beer which is kept in barrels rather than bottles. 3 **Draughts** is a game for two people, played with 24 ♦♦◇◇ N-COUNT ADJ N-UNCOUNT

round pieces on a board. The usual American word is checkers. ▶ A **draught** is one of the round pieces which are used in the game of draughts. The usual American word is **checker**. *BRITISH* *N-COUNT*

4 A **draught** animal is one which pulls heavy loads, for example on a farm. *ADJ: ADJ n*

5 A **draught** of liquid is a large amount that you swallow. **6** A **draught** is a medicine in the form of a liquid which you drink. ...*a sleeping draught.* *N-COUNT: N-COUNT DATED*

draughts·man /'drɑːftsmən, 'dræfts-/ **draughtsmen;** spelled **draftsman** in American English. **1** A **draughtsman** is someone whose job is to prepare very detailed drawings of machinery, equipment, or buildings. **2** If someone is a good **draughtsman,** they are very skilled at drawing. *N-COUNT* *N-COUNT*

draughty /'drɑːfti, 'dræfti/ **draughtier, draughtiest;** spelled **drafty** in American English. A **draughty** room or building has currents of cold air blowing through it, usually because the windows and doors do not fit very well. *ADJ-GRADED*

draw /drɔː/ **draws, drawing, drew, drawn.** ♦♦♦♦♦
1 When you **draw** or when you **draw** something, you use a pencil, pen, or crayon to produce a picture, pattern, or diagram. *He starts a painting by quickly drawing simplified shapes.* ♦ **draw·ing** I *like dancing, singing and drawing.* *VERB: V V n* *N-UNCOUNT*

2 When a vehicle **draws** somewhere, it moves there smoothly and steadily. *Claire had seen the taxi drawing away.* **3** If you **draw** somewhere, you move there slowly. *She drew away and did not smile... He did not draw close to her.* **4** If you **draw** something or someone in a particular direction, you move them in that direction, usually by pulling them gently. *He drew his chair nearer the fire... He put his arm around Caroline's shoulders and drew her close to him.* *VERB V adv/prep* *VERB V adv/adj WRITTEN* *VERB V n prep V n adj Also V n with adv WRITTEN*

5 When you **draw** a curtain or blind, you pull it across a window, either to cover or to uncover it. *VERB: V n*

6 If someone **draws** a gun, knife, or other weapon, they pull it out of its holder and threaten you with it. *VERB: V n*

7 If an animal or vehicle **draws** something such as a cart, carriage, or trailer, it pulls it along. *VERB: V n*

8 If you **draw** a deep breath, you breathe in deeply once. **9** If you **draw** on a cigarette, you breathe the smoke from it into your mouth or lungs. *She drew smoke into her lungs.* *VERB: V n* *VERB: V on V n into n*

10 To **draw** something such as water or energy **from** a particular source means to take it from that source. *Villagers still have to draw their water from wells.* *VERB V n from n*

11 If something that hits you or presses part of your body **draws** blood, it cuts your skin so that it bleeds. *VERB: V n*

12 If you **draw** money out of a bank, building society, or savings account, you get it from the account so that you can use it. *She was drawing out cash from a cash machine.* **13** If you **draw** a salary or a sum of money, you receive a sum of money regularly. *He is moving ever closer to drawing his pension.* *VERB: V n from n V n with out* *VERB V n*

14 To **draw** something means to choose it or to be given it at random, as part of a competition, game, or lottery. *We delved through a sackful of letters to draw the winning name.* ▶ Also a noun. ...*the draw for the quarter-finals.* **15** A **draw** is a competition where people pay money for numbered or named tickets, then some of those tickets are chosen at random, and the owners are given prizes. *VERB V n* *N-COUNT* *N-COUNT*

16 To **draw** something **from** a particular thing or place means to take or get it from that thing or place. *I draw strength from the millions of women who have faced this challenge successfully.* *VERB V n from n*

17 If you **draw** a particular conclusion, you decide that that conclusion is true. *He draws two conclusions from this.* **18** If you **draw** a comparison, parallel, or distinction, you compare or contrast two different things. *He draws a comparison between what's going on in Yugoslavia now and what happened in Germany.* *VERB: V n V n from n* *V n Also V n with n*

19 If you **draw** someone's attention to something, you make them aware of it or make them think about it. *He was waving his arms to draw their attention.* *VERB: V n to n V n*

20 If someone or something **draws** a particular reaction, people react to it in that way. *Such a policy would* *VERB V n from n Also V n*

inevitably draw fierce resistance from farmers. **21** If something such as a film or an event **draws** a lot of people, it is so interesting or entertaining that a lot of people go to it. **22** If someone or something **draws** you, it attracts you very strongly. *What drew him to the area was its proximity to central London.* **23** If someone will not **be drawn** or refuses to **be drawn,** they will not reply to questions in the way that you want them to, or will not reveal information or their opinion. *The ambassador would not be drawn on questions of a political nature.* *VERB: V n* *VERB: V n V n to n* *VB: with brd-neg, usu passive be V-ed on n Also be V-ed*

24 In a game or competition, if one person or team **draws** with another one, or if two people or teams **draw,** they have the same number of points at the end of the game. *Holland and the Republic of Ireland drew one-one... Egypt drew two of their matches in Italy.* ▶ Also a noun. *We were happy to come away with a draw against Sweden.* *V-RECIP V with/ against n pl-n V num pl-n V (non-recip) Also pl-n V N-COUNT*

25 See also **drawing.**

26 When an event or period of time **draws to a close** or **draws to an end,** it finishes. *The conflict was drawing to a close.* **27** If an event or period of time **is drawing closer** or **is drawing nearer,** it is approaching. *Next spring's elections are drawing closer.* *PHRASE FORMAL* *PHRASE*

28 • to **draw a blank:** see **blank.** • to **draw breath:** see **breath.** • to **draw the line:** see **line.** • to **draw lots:** see **lot.** • **the luck of the draw:** see **luck.**

draw in. 1 If you say that the nights, evenings, or days **are drawing in,** you mean that it is becoming dark at an earlier time in the evening, because autumn or winter is approaching. **2** If you **draw** someone **in** or **draw** them **into** something you are involved with, you cause them to become involved with it. *Don't let him draw you into his strategy.* **3** If you **draw in** your breath, you breathe in deeply. If you **draw in** air, you take it into your lungs as you breathe in. *Rose drew her breath in sharply.* *PHRASAL VB V P BRITISH* *V n P V n P n Also V P noun* *V P noun V n P*

draw into. See **draw in** 2.

draw off. If a quantity of liquid **is drawn off** from a larger quantity, it is taken from it, usually by means of a syringe or pipe. *He allowed the doctors to open a vein of his arm and draw off a pint of blood.* *PHRASAL VB be V-ed P V P noun Also V n P*

draw on. 1 If you **draw on** or **draw upon** something such as your skills or experience, you make use of it in order to do something. *He drew on his experience as a yachtsman to make a documentary programme.* **2** As a period of time **draws on,** it passes and the end of it gets closer. ...*as the afternoon drew on.* *PHRASAL VB V P n* *V P*

draw out. If you **draw** someone **out,** you make them feel less nervous and more willing to talk. *PHRASAL VB V n P*

draw up. 1 If you **draw up** a document, list, or plan, you prepare it and write it out. ...*a working party to draw up a formal agreement.* **2** If you **draw up** a chair, you move it nearer to a person or place, for example so that you can watch something or join in with something. *He drew up a chair and sat down.* **3** If you **draw** yourself **up,** you make your back very straight, rather than stooping. *He drew himself up to his full height.* *PHRASAL VB V P noun Also V n P V P noun Also V n P* *V pron-refl P V pron-refl P to n*

draw upon. See **draw on** 1.

draw·back /'drɔːbæk/ **drawbacks.** A **drawback** is an aspect of something that makes it less acceptable than it would otherwise be. *The apartment's only drawback was that it was too small.* ♦♦♦♦♦ *N-COUNT*

draw·bridge /'drɔːbrɪdʒ/ **drawbridges.** A **drawbridge** is a bridge that can be pulled up, for example to prevent people from getting into a castle or to allow ships to pass underneath it. *N-COUNT*

draw·er /'drɔːə/ **drawers.** A **drawer** is part of a desk, chest, or other piece of furniture that is shaped like a box and is designed for putting things in. You pull it towards you to open it. • See also **chest of drawers.** ♦♦♦♦♦ *N-COUNT*

draw·ing /'drɔːɪŋ/ **drawings.** A **drawing** is a picture made with a pencil, pen, or crayon. *She did a drawing of me.* • See also **draw.** ♦♦♦♦♦ *N-COUNT*

'drawing board, drawing boards. 1 A **drawing board** is a large flat board on which you place your paper when you are drawing or designing something. **2** If you say that you will have to go **back to the drawing board,** you mean that something ♦♦♦♦♦ *N-COUNT* *PHRASE*

D

which you have done has not been successful and
that you will have to start again or try another idea.

'drawing pin, drawing pins. A **drawing pin** is a N-COUNT
short pin with a broad flat top which is used for fas- BRITISH
tening papers or pictures to a board or other surface. The usual American term is **thumbtack**.

'drawing room, drawing rooms. A **drawing** ◆◇◇◇
room is a room, especially a large room in a large N-COUNT
house, where people sit and relax. FORMAL

drawl /drɔːl/ **drawls, drawling, drawled.** If ◆◇◇◇
someone **drawls**, they speak slowly and not very VERB: V
clearly, with long vowel sounds. *'I guess you guys* V with quote
don't mind if I smoke?' he drawled. ▶ Also a noun. N-COUNT
...Jack's southern drawl.

drawn /drɔːn/ **1 Drawn** is the past participle of ◆◇◇◇
draw. 2 If someone or their face looks **drawn**, their ADJ-GRADED
face is thin and they look very tired, ill, worried, or PRAGMATICS
unhappy.

drawn-'out. You describe something as **drawn-** ◆◇◇◇
out when it lasts or takes longer than you would ADJ-GRADED
like it to. *Pulling out of a recession is a lengthy and*
drawn-out process.

draw·string /'drɔːstrɪŋ/ **drawstrings.** A **draw-** N-COUNT
string is a cord that goes through a seam round an
opening, for example at the top of a bag or a pair of
trousers. When the cord is pulled tighter, the opening gets smaller.

dread /dred/ **dreads, dreading, dreaded. 1** If ◆◆◇◇
you **dread** something which may happen, you feel VERB
very anxious and unhappy about it because you V n/-ing
think it will be unpleasant or upsetting. *I dreaded* Also V that
coming back... I'd been dreading that the birth
would take a long time. **2** If you say that you **dread** PHRASE
to think what might happen, you mean that you are
anxious about it because it is likely to be very unpleasant. *I dread to think what will happen in the*
case of a major emergency. **3 Dread** is a feeling of N-UNCOUNT
great anxiety and fear about something that may
happen. **4 Dread** means terrible and greatly feared. ADJ
...a more effective national policy to combat this LITERARY
dread disease. **5** See also **dreaded.**
6 You can use **dread** to describe something that you ADJ: ADJ n
find annoying when you expect others to sympathize PRAGMATICS
with you. *...the dread phrase 'politically correct'.* INFORMAL

dread·ed /'dredɪd/ **1 Dreaded** means terrible and ◆◇◇◇
greatly feared. *No one knew how to treat this dread-* ADJ-GRADED:
ed disease... Then came the dreaded chemotherapy. ADJ n
2 You can use **dreaded** to describe something that ADJ: ADJ n
you find annoying when you expect others to sym- PRAGMATICS
pathize with you. *She's a victim of the dreaded hay* INFORMAL
fever.

dread·ful /'dredfʊl/ **1** If you say that something is ◆◆◇◇
dreadful, you mean that it is very bad or unpleas- ADJ-GRADED
ant, or very poor in quality. *They told us the dread-*
ful news... My financial situation is dreadful.
♦ **dread·fully** *I do realize that I've behaved abso-* ADV-GRADED
lutely dreadfully. **2 Dreadful** is used to emphasize ADJ: ADJ n
the degree or extent of something bad. *We've made* PRAGMATICS
a dreadful mistake. **3** If someone **looks** or **feels** ADJ-GRADED:
dreadful, they look or feel very ill, tired, or upset. feel/look ADJ

dread·fully /'dredfəli/ You use **dreadfully** to em- ADV
phasize the degree or intensity of something, espe- PRAGMATICS
cially something bad or unpleasant. *He looks dread-* INFORMAL
fully ill. ● See also **dreadful.**

dread·locks /'dredlɒks/. If someone has **dread-** N-PLURAL
locks, their hair is divided into a large number of
long thin sections that look like plaits.

dream /driːm/ **dreams, dreaming, dreamed,** ◆◆◆◆
dreamt. 1 A **dream** is an imaginary series of N-COUNT
events that you experience in your mind while you
are asleep. *He had a dream about Claire.* **2** When VERB: V
you **dream,** you experience imaginary events in V that
your mind while you are asleep. *Ivor dreamed that* V about/of n
he was on a bus... She dreamed about her baby.
3 If you often think about something that you would VERB
very much like to happen or have, you can say that V of/-ing
you **dream** of it. *She had dreamed of becoming an ac-* n/-ing
tress... I dream that my son will attend college. ▶ Also a V that
noun. *...his dream of becoming a full pilot.* N-COUNT
4 You can use **dream** to describe something that you ADJ: ADJ n

think is ideal or perfect, especially if it is something
that you thought you would never be able to have or
experience. *...a dream holiday to Jamaica.* **5** If you de- N-SING:
scribe something as a particular person's **dream,** you poss N
think that it would be ideal for that person and that he
or she would like it very much. *Greece is said to be a*
botanist's dream. **6** If you describe someone or some- PHRASE
thing as the person or thing **of** your **dreams,** you
mean that you consider them to be ideal or perfect.
This could be the man of my dreams. **7** If you say that N-SING:
something is **a dream,** you mean that it is wonderful. a N
The village is a dream. INFORMAL
8 If you say that you would not **dream of** doing some- VB: with neg
thing, you are emphasizing that you would never do V of -ing/n
it. *I wouldn't dream of making fun of you.* **9** If you say VB: with brd-
that you never **dreamed** that something would hap- neg,
pen, you are emphasizing that you did not think that V that
it would happen because it seemed very unlikely. PRAGMATICS
Who could ever dream of a disaster like this? V of n
  Also V
10 If you say that someone does something **like a** PHRASE
dream, you think that they do it very well. If you say
that something happens **like a dream,** you mean that
it happens successfully without any problems. *His*
ship had sailed like a dream.
11 If you say that you could not imagine a particular PHRASE
thing in your **wildest dreams,** you are emphasizing PRAGMATICS
that you think it is extremely strange or unlikely. *Nev-*
er in my wildest dreams could I imagine there would be
this kind of money in the game. **12** If you describe PHRASE
something as being **beyond** your **wildest dreams,** you PRAGMATICS
are emphasizing that it is better than you could have
imagined or hoped for. *...success beyond her wildest*
dreams.
13 See also **pipe dream.**

dream up. If you **dream up** a plan or idea, you work PHRASAL VB
it out or create it in your mind. *His son hadn't* V P noun
dreamed it up. V n P

dream·er /'driːmə/ **dreamers.** If you describe ◆◇◇◇
someone as a **dreamer,** you mean that they spend a N-COUNT
lot of time thinking about and planning for things
that they would like to happen but which are improbable or impractical.

dream·i·ly /'driːmɪli/. If you say or do something ADV
dreamily, you say or do it in a way that shows your
mind is occupied with pleasant relaxing thoughts.

dream·land /'driːmlænd/. If you refer to a situation N-UNCOUNT:
as **dreamland,** you mean that it represents what also a N
someone would like to happen, but that it is com- BRITISH
pletely unrealistic. *His book seems set in dreamland.*

dream·less /'driːmləs/. A **dreamless** sleep is very ADJ
deep and peaceful, and without dreams.

dream·like /'driːmlaɪk/. If something is **dreamlike,** ADJ-GRADED
it seems strange and unreal.

dreamt /dremt/. **Dreamt** is a past tense and past
participle of **dream.**

dream 'ticket. When journalists refer to a par- N-SING
ticular person or small group of people as a **dream**
ticket, they mean that they think the people will be
extremely successful in a particular situation.

dreamy /'driːmi/ **dreamier, dreamiest. 1** If you ◆◇◇◇
say that someone has a **dreamy** expression, you ADJ-GRADED
mean that they are not paying attention to things
around them and look as if they are thinking about
something pleasant. **2** If you describe something as ADJ-GRADED
dreamy, you mean that you like it and that it seems PRAGMATICS
gentle and soft, like something in a dream. *...a*
dreamy, delicate song. **3** If you describe a person or ADJ-GRADED
an idea as **dreamy,** you mean that they are not very
practical.

dreary /'drɪəri/ **drearier, dreariest.** If you de- ◆◇◇◇
scribe something as **dreary,** you mean that it is dull ADJ-GRADED
and depressing. ♦ **dreari·ly** *...a drearily familiar* ADV-GRADED
scenario.

dredge /dredʒ/ **dredges, dredging, dredged.** ◆◇◇◇
When people **dredge** a harbour, river, or other area VERB: V n
of water, they remove mud and unwanted material
from the bottom with a special machine. ♦ **dredg-**
·er, dredgers. A **dredger** is a boat which is fitted N-COUNT
with a special machine for removing mud or other

unwanted material from the bottom of a harbour, river, or canal.

dredge up. 1 If someone **dredges up** a piece of information they learnt a long time ago or if they **dredge up** a distant memory, they manage to remember it. *...an American trying to dredge up some French or German learned in high school.* **2** If someone **dredges up** a damaging or upsetting fact about your past, they remind you of it or tell other people about it. *She dredges up a minor misdemeanour: 'You didn't give me money for the school trip.'*   PHRASAL VB / V P noun / Also V n P / V P noun / Also V n P

dregs /dregz/. **1** The **dregs** of a liquid are the last drops left at the bottom of a container, together with any solid bits that have sunk to the bottom. **2** If you talk about the **dregs** of a society or community, you mean the people in it who you consider to be the most worthless and bad; used showing disapproval.   N-PLURAL / N-PLURAL PRAGMATICS

drench /drentʃ/ **drenches, drenching, drenched.** To **drench** something or someone means to make them completely wet. *...getting drenched by icy water... We were completely drenched and cold.* ♦ **-drenched** *...the rain-drenched streets of the capital.*   ♦◇◇◇ VERB: V n / get V-ed / V-ed / COMB

dress /dres/ **dresses, dressing, dressed. 1** A **dress** is a piece of clothing worn by a woman or girl. It covers her body and extends down over her legs. See picture headed **clothes**. **2** You can refer to clothes worn by men or women as **dress**. *He's usually smart in his dress.* ● See also **evening dress, fancy dress, full dress, morning dress. 3** If someone **dresses** in a particular way, they wear clothes of a particular style or colour. *She used to dress in jeans.* ♦ **dressed** *He was dressed in black, with a gold chain at his throat. ...a tall, elegantly dressed man.* ● See also **well-dressed. 4** If someone is **dressed to kill**, they are wearing very smart or glamorous clothes because they want people to notice them and think they are attractive. **5** When you **dress** or **dress** someone, you put clothes on yourself or on someone else. *He told Sarah to wait while he dressed... She bathed her and dressed her in clean clothes.* ♦ **dressed.** If you are **dressed**, you are wearing clothes rather than being naked or wearing your night clothes. If you get **dressed** you put on your clothes. *He was fully dressed, including shoes.* **6** If you **dress** for something, you put on special clothes for it. *We don't dress for dinner here.* **7** When someone **dresses** a wound, they clean it and cover it. **8** If you **dress** a salad, you cover it with a sauce made from oil, vinegar, and herbs or flavourings. **9** To **dress** meat, poultry, or fish means to prepare it for cooking by cleaning it and removing bits that you cannot eat. **10** See also **dressing**.   ♦♦♦♦◇ N-COUNT / N-UNCOUNT / VERB V in n / ADJ / PHRASE INFORMAL / V / V n / ADJ / VERB V for n / VERB: V n / VERB: V n

dress down. 1 If you **dress down**, you wear clothes that are less smart than usual. **2** If you **dress** someone **down**, you speak angrily to them because they have done something bad or foolish. *Campbell dressed them down in public.* ♦ **dressing down.** If someone gives you a **dressing-down**, they speak angrily to you because you have done something bad or foolish.   PHRASAL VB V P / V n P / Also V P noun / N-SING

dress up. 1 If you **dress up** or **dress** someone **up**, you put different clothes on yourself or on someone else to smarten or disguise yourself or the other person. *You do not need to dress up for dinner... Mother loved to dress me up.* ♦ **dressed up** *You don't have to get dressed up for this party.* **2** If you **dress** something **up**, you try to make it seem more attractive, acceptable, or interesting than it really is. *However you dress it up, a bank only exists to lend money.* ♦ **dressed up.** If you say that something is **dressed up** as something else, you mean that someone has tried to make it more attractive, acceptable, or interesting that it really is by making it seem like that other thing. *The trip would be dressed up as a UN mission.* **3 dressing-up.**   PHRASAL VB ERG / V n P / Also V P n/as n / ADJ-GRADED / V n P / Also V P noun / ADJ: v-link ADJ as/in n

dres·sage /ˈdresɑːʒ/. **Dressage** is a competition in which horse riders have to make their horse perform a series of controlled movements.   N-UNCOUNT

dress 'circle. The **dress circle** is the lowest balcony in a theatre.   N-SING

dress·er /ˈdresə/ **dressers. 1** A **dresser** is a chest of drawers, usually with a mirror on the top. **2** A **dresser** is a piece of furniture which is usually used for storing china. **3** A **dresser** is someone who works in a theatre and helps the actors and actresses to dress. **4** You can use **dresser** to refer to the kind of clothes that a person wears. For example, if you say that someone is a **smart dresser**, you mean that they wear smart clothes.   N-COUNT AMERICAN / N-COUNT BRITISH / N-COUNT / N-COUNT: adj N

dress·ing /ˈdresɪŋ/ **dressings. 1** A salad **dressing** is a mixture of oil, vinegar, and herbs or flavourings, which you pour over a salad. **2** A **dressing** is a covering that is put on a wound to protect it.   ♦◇◇◇ N-VAR / N-COUNT

'dressing gown, dressing gowns; also spelled **dressing-gown.** A **dressing gown** is a long loose garment which you wear over pyjamas or a nightdress when you are not in bed.   ♦◇◇◇ N-COUNT

'dressing room, dressing rooms; also spelled **dressing-room.** A **dressing room** is a room in a theatre or sports stadium where performers or players can change their clothes.   ♦◇◇◇ N-COUNT

'dressing table, dressing tables; also spelled **dressing-table.** A **dressing table** is a small table in a bedroom with drawers underneath.   ♦◇◇◇ N-COUNT

,dressing-'up; also spelled **dressing up.** When children play at **dressing-up**, they put on special or different clothes and pretend to be different people.   ♦◇◇◇ N-UNCOUNT

dress·making /ˈdresmeɪkɪŋ/. **Dressmaking** is the activity or job of making clothes for women or girls. ♦ **dress·maker, dressmakers.**   N-UNCOUNT / N-COUNT

,dress re'hearsal, dress rehearsals. 1 The **dress rehearsal** of a play, opera, or show is the final rehearsal before it is performed, in which the performers wear their costumes. **2** You can describe an event as a **dress rehearsal** for a later more important event when it indicates how the later event will be. *These elections, you could almost say, are a dress rehearsal for the real elections.*   N-COUNT / N-COUNT

,dress 'shirt, dress shirts. A **dress shirt** is a shirt which men wear with a dinner jacket and bow tie.   N-COUNT

dressy /ˈdresi/ **dressier, dressiest.** **Dressy** clothes are smart clothes which you wear when you want to look elegant or formal.   ADJ-GRADED

drew /druː/. **Drew** is the past tense of **draw**.

drib·ble /ˈdrɪbəl/ **dribbles, dribbling, dribbled. 1** If a liquid **dribbles** somewhere, or if you **dribble** it, it drips down slowly or flows in a thin stream. *Sweat dribbled down Hart's face.* **2** If a person **dribbles**, saliva trickles from their mouth. *She's dribbling on her collar.* **3 Dribble** is saliva that has trickled from someone's mouth. **4** A **dribble of** a liquid is a very small amount of it. *Apply a dribble of baby shampoo.* **5** When players **dribble** the ball in a game such as football, they give it several quick kicks or taps in order to keep it moving. *He dribbled past four defenders.* **6** If people or things **dribble** somewhere, they move there slowly and in small numbers. *...as the workers dribbled away from city square.*   ♦◇◇◇ V-ERG / V prep/adv / prep/adv / VERB V / N-UNCOUNT / N-COUNT N of n / VERB: V n / V / VERB V prep/adv

dribs and drabs /ˌdrɪbz ən ˈdræbz/. If people or things arrive **in dribs and drabs**, they arrive in small numbers over a period of time.   PHRASE INFORMAL

dried /draɪd/. **Dried** food or milk has had all the water removed from it so that it will last for a long time. ● See also **dry**.   ♦♦◇◇ ADJ: ADJ n

dri·er /ˈdraɪə/. See **dry, dryer**.

drift /drɪft/ **drifts, drifting, drifted. 1** When something **drifts** somewhere, it is carried there by the movement of wind or water. *We proceeded to drift on up the river.* **2** A **drift** of something is an amount of it that has been created by the movement of wind or water. *There was a drift of smoke above the trees.* **3** If snow **drifts**, it builds up into piles as a result of the movement of the wind. **4** A **drift** is a mass of snow that has built up into a pile as a result of the movement of wind. *...a snow drift.* **5** If someone or something **drifts** into a situation, they   ♦♦♦◇◇ VERB V adv/prep / N-COUNT: with supp / VERB: V / N-COUNT / VERB

get into that situation in a way that is not planned or controlled. *...young people drifting into crime... The country and economy alike are drifting.* **6** If you say that someone **drifts** around, you mean that they travel from place to place without a plan or settled way of life; used showing disapproval. *You've been drifting from job to job without any real commitment.* ♦ **drift-er, drifters** *...a drifter who plays the guitar.*

7 To **drift** somewhere means to move there slowly or gradually. *Investment advisers are tending to drift towards Japan.* ▶ Also a noun. *...the drift towards the cities.*

8 If sounds **drift** somewhere, they can be heard but they are not very loud. *Dance sounds are drifting from the stereo.*

9 The **drift of** an argument or speech is the general point that is being made. *Grace was beginning to get his drift... I follow the drift of her conversation.*

drift off. If you **drift off** to sleep, you gradually fall asleep. *...when he finally drifted off to sleep.*

drift·wood /'drɪftwʊd/. **Driftwood** is wood which has been carried by the motion of the sea or a river.

drill /drɪl/ **drills, drilling, drilled.** **1** A **drill** is a tool or machine that you use for making holes. See picture headed **tools.** *...pneumatic drills. ...a dentist's drill.* **2** When you **drill** into something or **drill** a hole in something, you make a hole in it using a drill. *He drilled into the wall of Lili's bedroom.* **3** When people **drill** for oil or water, they search for it by drilling deep holes in the ground or in the bottom of the sea. *There have been proposals to drill for more oil.* ♦ **drill·ing** *Drilling is due to start early next year.*

4 A **drill** is a way that teachers teach their students something by making them repeat it many times. *The teacher runs them through a drill – the days of the week, the weather and some counting.* **5** If you **drill** people, you teach them to do something by making them repeat it many times. *He drills the choir to a high standard.* ♦ **drilling** *...stimulation rather than repetitive drilling.* **6** A **drill** is a procedure which a group of people, especially soldiers, practice so that they can do something quickly and efficiently. *...the military drill used by soldiers to load and fire the big guns.* **7** A **drill** is a routine exercise or activity, in which people practise what they should do in dangerous situations. *...a fire drill.*

8 Drill is thick cotton material which is used for making uniforms and trousers.

dri·ly /'draɪli/. See **dry.**

drink /drɪŋk/ **drinks, drinking, drank, drunk.** **1** When you **drink** a liquid, you take it into your mouth and swallow it. *He drank his cup of tea... He drank thirstily from the pool.* **2** A **drink** is an amount of a liquid which you drink. *I'll get you a drink of water.* **3** To **drink** means to drink alcohol. *He was smoking and drinking too much.* ♦ **drink·ing** *She had left him because of his drinking.* **4 Drink** is alcohol, such as beer, wine, or whisky. *Too much drink is bad for your health.* ▶ A **drink** is an alcoholic drink. *She felt like a drink after a hard day.*

5 If someone **drinks** you **under the table**, they drink more alcohol than you are able to on a particular occasion. **6** People say '**I'll drink to that**' to show that they agree with and approve of something that someone has just said. **7** ♦ to **drink** someone's **health:** see **health.** See also **drinking.**

drink in. If you **drink in** something that you see or hear, you pay a lot of attention to it and enjoy it. *She stood drinking in the glittering view.*

drink to. When people **drink to** someone or something, they refer to them and raise their glasses before drinking, as a way of celebrating something or showing that they want something to happen. *Let's drink to his memory, eh?*.

drink up. When you **drink up** an amount of liquid, you finish it completely. *Drink up your sherry and we'll go... Drink up, there's time for another.*

drink·able /'drɪŋkəbəl/. **1** Water that is **drinkable** is clean and safe for drinking. **2** If you say that a drink is **drinkable**, you mean that it tastes quite pleasant. *The food was good and the wine drinkable.*

drink·er /'drɪŋkə/ **drinkers.** **1** If someone is a tea **drinker** or a beer **drinker**, for example, they regularly drink tea or beer. **2** When someone is a **drinker**, you mean that they drink alcohol, especially in large quantities. *I'm not a heavy drinker.*

drink·ing /'drɪŋkɪŋ/. Someone's **drinking** friends or companions are people they regularly drink alcohol with. ● See also **drink.**

'drinking fountain, drinking fountains. A **drinking fountain** is a device which supplies water for people to drink in places such as streets, parks, or schools.

'drinking water. Drinking water is water which it is safe to drink.

drip /drɪp/ **drips, dripping dripped. 1** When liquid **drips** somewhere, or you **drip** it somewhere, it falls in individual small drops. *Let the blood drip into a tissue. ...parents trying to stop their children from dripping Coke on the carpets.* **2** When something **drips**, drops of liquid fall from it. *A tap in the kitchen was dripping... Lou was dripping with perspiration.* **3** A **drip** is a small individual drop of a liquid. *...drips of water.*

4 A **drip** is a piece of medical equipment by which a liquid is slowly passed through a tube into a patient's bloodstream. *I spent two days in hospital on a drip.*

5 If you say that something **is dripping with** a particular thing, you mean that it contains a lot of that thing. *...window displays dripping with diamonds and furs.*

6 If you call someone a **drip**, you mean that they are rather stupid and lacking in enthusiasm or energy. **7** See also **drip-dry, dripping.**

,drip-'dry. Drip-dry clothes or sheets are made of a fabric that does not crease when it is hung up wet.

drip·ping /'drɪpɪŋ/. **1 Dripping** is the fat which comes out of meat when it is fried or roasted, and which can be used for frying food. **2** If you are **dripping wet**, you are so wet that water is dripping from you. **3** See also **drip.**

drip·py /'drɪpi/. If you describe someone as **drippy**, you mean that they are rather stupid and weak. If you describe something such as a book or a type of music as **drippy**, you mean that you think it is rather stupid, dull, and sentimental.

drive /draɪv/ **drives, driving, drove, driven. 1** When you **drive** somewhere, you operate a car or other vehicle and control its movement and direction. *She never learned to drive... Mrs Glick drove her own car.* ♦ **driv·ing** *...an outrageous piece of dangerous driving.* ♦ **driv·er, drivers** *The driver got out of his van.* **2** If you **drive** someone somewhere, you take them there in a car or other vehicle. *His daughter Carly drove him to the train station.* **3** A **drive** is a journey in a car or other vehicle. *I thought we might go for a drive.*

4 A **drive** is a wide piece of hard ground, or sometimes a private road, that leads from the road to a person's house. **5 Drive** is used in the names of some streets. *...23 Queen's Drive, Malvern, Worcestershire.*

6 If something **drives** a machine, it supplies the power that makes it work. *...electric motors that drive the wheels.* **7 Drive** is the power supplied by the engine to particular wheels in a car or other vehicle to make the vehicle move. *He put the jeep in four-wheel drive.*

8 You use **drive** to refer to the mechanical part of a computer which reads the data on disks and tapes, or writes data onto them. ● See also **disk drive.**

9 If you **drive** one thing into another, you push it in or hammer it in using a lot of effort. *Drive the pegs into the side of the path.* **10** In games such as cricket, golf, or football, if a player **drives** a ball somewhere, they kick or hit it there with a lot of force. **11** If the wind, rain, or snow **drives** in a particular direction, it moves with great force in that direction. *Rain drove against the window.* ♦ **driv·ing** *...rescuers battling through driving snow.* **12** If you **drive** people or animals

somewhere, you make them go to or from that place. `V n prep`
The last offensive drove thousands of people into Thai- `Also V n with`
land. `adv`

13 To **drive** someone into a particular state or situa- `VERB`
tion means to force them into that state or situation. `Also V n into/to n`
Hospital bills drove them into bankruptcy. **14** The de- `VERB:`
sire or feeling that **drives** someone to do something, `V n to-inf`
especially something extreme, is the desire or feeling `V n to n`
that causes them to do it. *Jealousy drives people to* `Also V n`
murder. **15** If you say that someone has **drive**, you `N-UNCOUNT`
mean they have energy and determination. *John will*
be best remembered for his drive and enthusiasm. **16** A `N-COUNT`
drive is a very strong need or desire in human beings
that makes them act in particular ways. ...*compelling,*
dynamic sex drives. **17** A **drive** is a special effort made `N-SING:`
by a group of people for a particular purpose. ...*a* `with supp`
nationwide recruitment drive.

18 If you ask someone **what** they **are driving at**, you `PHRASE`
are asking what they are trying to say or what they are
indirectly saying. *Cohen didn't understand what*
Millard was driving at.

19 See also **driving**. **20 •** to **drive a hard bargain**: see
bargain.

drive away. To **drive** people **away** means to make `PHRASAL VB`
them want to go away or stay away. *Increased crime in* `V n P`
the Fifth Ward is driving away customers. `V P noun`

drive off. If you **drive** someone or something **off**, `PHRASAL VB`
you force them to go away and to stop attacking you `V n P`
or threatening you. *Men drove off the dogs with stones.* `V P noun`

drive out. To **drive out** something means to make it `PHRASAL VB`
disappear or stop operating. *He cut his rates to drive* `V P noun`
out rivals.

'drive-in, drive-ins. A **drive-in** is a restaurant, ci- ♦◇◇◇◇
nema, or other commercial place which is designed `N-COUNT`
so that customers can use the services provided
while staying in their cars. ...*fast food drive-ins.*
▶ Also an adjective. ...*a drive-in movie theater.* `ADJ`

driv·el /ˈdrɪvəl/. If you describe something that is `N-UNCOUNT`
written or said as **drivel**, you are critical of it be- `PRAGMATICS`
cause you think it is very silly. *What absolute drivel!* `INFORMAL`

driv·en /ˈdrɪvən/. **Driven** is the past participle of
drive.

'driver's license, driver's licenses. A **driver's** `N-COUNT`
license is a card showing that you are qualified to `AMERICAN`
drive. The usual British term is **driving licence**.

'driver's seat. 1 In a vehicle, the **driver's seat** is `N-SING`
the seat where the person who is driving sits. **2** If `PHRASE`
you say that someone **is in the driver's seat**, you
mean that they are in control in a situation. *Now he*
knows he's in the driver's seat and can wait for a bet-
ter deal.

drive·way /ˈdraɪvweɪ/ **driveways.** A **driveway** is a ♦◇◇◇◇
piece of hard ground that leads from the road to a `N-COUNT`
person's garage or front door.

driv·ing /ˈdraɪvɪŋ/. The **driving** force, idea, or mo- ♦◇◇◇◇
tive behind something is the thing that has the `ADJ: ADJ n`
strongest effect on it and makes it happen or be
done in a particular way. *Consumer spending was*
the driving force behind the economic growth. **•** See
also **drive**.

'driving licence, driving licences; also spelled ♦◇◇◇◇
driving license in American English. A **driving li-** `N-COUNT`
cence is a card showing that you are qualified to `BRITISH`
drive. The usual American term is **driver's license**.

'driving school, driving schools. A **driving** `N-COUNT`
school is a business that deals with teaching people
to drive cars.

'driving seat. Driving seat means the same as
driver's seat.

driz·zle /ˈdrɪzəl/ **drizzles, drizzling, drizzled.** If ♦◇◇◇◇
it **is drizzling**, it is raining very lightly. *It was start-* `VERB`
ing to drizzle. ▶ **Drizzle** is light rain falling in fine `/t V`
drops. *The drizzle had now stopped.* `N-UNCOUNT:`
`also a N`

driz·zly /ˈdrɪzəli/. When the weather is **drizzly**, the `ADJ-GRADED`
sky is dull and grey and it is raining softly and
steadily.

droll /drəʊl/. Something or someone that is **droll** is `ADJ-GRADED`
amusing or witty, sometimes in an unexpected way. `WRITTEN`
The band have a droll sense of humour.

drone /drəʊn/ **drones, droning, droned. 1** If ♦◇◇◇◇
something **drones**, it makes a low continuous hum- `VERB`
ming noise. *An invisible plane droned through the* `V`
night sky. ▶ Also a noun. ...*the constant drone of the* `N-SING`
motorways. **♦ dron·ing** ...*the droning of a plane.* `N-SING`

2 If you say that someone **drones**, you mean that they `VERB`
keep talking about something in a boring way. *Cham-* `PRAGMATICS`
bers' voice droned, maddening as an insect around his `V`
head. ▶ Also a noun. *The minister's voice was a relent-* `N-SING`
less drone. ▶ **Drone on** means the same as **drone**. `PHRASAL VB`
Daniel just drones on about American policy. `V P`

3 People who do not contribute anything to society or `N-COUNT`
to an organization are sometimes described as `PRAGMATICS`
drones. *A few are dim-witted drones, but most are tal-*
ented, frustrated, wasted people.

4 A **drone** is a male bee. `N-COUNT`

drone on. See **drone** 2. `PHRASAL VB`

drool /druːl/ **drools, drooling, drooled. 1** If you `VERB:`
say that someone **is drooling** over someone or `V over n`
something, you mean that they are looking at them `PRAGMATICS`
with great pleasure; used showing disapproval. *Ad-* `V prep`
vertisers are already drooling at reports that this `Also V`
might bring 20 million dollars. **2** If a person or ani- `VERB: V`
mal **drools**, saliva trickles from their mouth.

droop /druːp/ **droops, drooping, drooped.** If ♦◇◇◇◇
something **droops**, it hangs or leans downwards `VERB: V`
with no strength or firmness. *Pale wilting roses* `V prep`
drooped from a blue vase. ▶ Also a noun. ...*the* `N-SING`
droop of his shoulders.

droopy /ˈdruːpi/ **droopier, droopiest.** If you de- `ADJ-GRADED`
scribe something as **droopy**, you mean that it hangs
down limply with no strength or firmness. ...*a*
droopy moustache.

drop /drɒp/ **drops, dropping, dropped. 1** If a ♦♦♦♦◇
level or amount **drops** or if someone or something `V-ERG`
drops it, it quickly becomes less. *Temperatures can* `V prep/adv`
drop to freezing at night... His blood pressure had `V`
dropped severely... He had dropped the price of his `V n`
London home by £1.25m. ▶ Also a noun. *He was* `N-COUNT`
prepared to take a drop in wages.

2 If you **drop** something, or if it drops, you accidental- `V-ERG`
ly let it fall. *I dropped my glasses and broke them... His* `V n`
toupee dropped off. **3** If you **drop** something some- `V prep/adv`
where or if it **drops** there, you deliberately let it fall `V-ERG`
there. *He dropped his plate into the sink. ...pots that* `V n prep/adv`
simply drop into their own container. **♦ drop·ping** `V prep/adv`
...*the dropping of the first atomic bomb.* **4** You use `Also V`
drop to talk about vertical distances. For example, a `N-UNCOUNT`
thirty-foot **drop** is a distance of thirty feet between the `N-COUNT`
top of a cliff or wall and the bottom of it.

5 If a person or a part of their body **drops** to a lower `V-ERG`
position, or if they **drop** a part of their body to a lower `V`
position, they move to that position, often in a tired `V prep/adv`
way. *Nancy dropped into a nearby chair... She let her* `Also V n`
head drop. **6** To **drop** is used in expressions such as **to** `prep/adv`
be about to drop and **to dance until you drop** to em- `VB: no cont`
phasize that you are exhausted and can no longer `PRAGMATICS`
continue doing something. *She looked about to drop.* `V`

7 If you **drop** to a lower position in a sports competi- `VERB`
tion, you move to that position. *Britain has dropped* `V prep/adv`
from second to third place.

8 If your voice **drops** or if you **drop** your voice, you `V-ERG`
speak more quietly. *Her voice will drop to a dismissive* `V to n`
whisper... He dropped his voice and glanced round at `V n`
the door. `Also V,`
`V n to n`

9 If you **drop** someone or something somewhere, you `VERB`
take them somewhere and leave them there, usually `V n prep/adv`
in a car or other vehicle. *He dropped me outside the*
hotel. ▶ **Drop off** means the same as **drop**. *Just drop* `PHRASAL VB`
me off at the airport... He was dropping off a late birth- `V n P prep/adv`
day present. `V P noun`

10 If you **drop** an idea, course of action, or habit, you `VERB`
decide not to continue with it. *He was told to drop the* `V n`
idea. **♦ dropping** ...*the factors that led to President* `N-UNCOUNT:`
Suharto's dropping of his previous objections. **11** If `N of n`
someone **is dropped** by a sports team or organiza- `VB: usu`
tion, they are no longer included in that team or em- `passive`
ployed by that organization. *The country's captain* `be V-ed`
was dropped from the tour party. **12** If you want `PHRASE`
someone to **drop the subject**, **drop it**, or **let it drop**,

you want them to stop talking about something, often because you are annoyed that they keep talking about it. *Mary Ann wished he would just drop it.*

13 If you **drop** a game or part of a game in a sports competition, you lose it. *Krickstein dropped a set before beating Jason Stoltenberg of Australia.* VERB Vn

14 A **drop** of a liquid is a very small amount of it shaped like a little ball. In informal English, you can also use **drop** when you are referring to a very small amount of something. *...a drop of blue ink... I'll have another drop of that Italian milk.* **15 Drops** are a kind of medicine which you put drop by drop into your ears, eyes, or nose. N-COUNT / N-PLURAL

16 If you **drop a hint**, you give a hint or say something in a casual way. *If I drop a few hints he might give me a cutting.* PHRASE

17 See also **air-drop.** ● to **drop dead**: see **dead.** ● at the **drop of a hat**: see **hat.** ● to **drop** someone **a line**: see **line.** ● **a drop in the ocean**: see **ocean.**

drop away. If land or ground **drops away**, it slopes down so that it is at a lower level to where you are or from a particular point that has been mentioned. *To the south the hills dropped away to farmland.* PHRASAL VB VP / VP prep

drop by. If you **drop by**, you visit someone informally. *Could you drop by at ten?... He tried to drop by the office.* PHRASAL VB VP / VPn

drop in. If you **drop in** on someone, you visit them informally, usually without having arranged it. *Why not drop in for a chat?* PHRASAL VB VP on n / VP

drop off. 1 See **drop 9. 2** If you **drop off** to sleep, you go to sleep. *Just as I was dropping off, a strange thought crossed my mind.* **3** If the level of something **drops off**, it becomes less. *Sales to the British forces are expected to drop off.* PHRASAL VB VP / VP

drop out. 1 If someone **drops out** of college or a race, for example, they leave it without finishing what they started. *She dropped out after 20 kilometres with stomach trouble.* **2** If someone **drops out**, they reject the accepted ways of society and live outside the usual system. *She encourages people to keep their jobs rather than dropping out to live in a commune.* ● See also **drop-out.** PHRASAL VB VP of n / VP / VP

drop-dead. If you describe someone as, for example, **drop-dead** gorgeous, you mean that they are so gorgeous that people cannot fail to notice them. *The effect is soft and pretty rather than drop-dead sexy.* ▶ Also an adjective. *...the drop-dead glamour of the designer decade.* ADV: ADV adj INFORMAL / ADJ: ADJ n

drop-let /ˈdrɒplət/ **droplets.** A droplet is a very small drop of liquid. *...droplets of sweat.* ◆◇◇◇◇

drop-out, drop-outs; also spelled **dropout. 1** If you describe someone as a **drop-out**, you disapprove of the fact that they have rejected the accepted ways of society, for example by not having a regular job. **2** A **drop-out** is someone who has left school or college before they have finished their studies. *...high-school drop-outs.* **3** If you refer to the **drop-out** rate, you are referring to the number of people who leave a school or college early, or leave a course or other activity before they have finished it. ◆◇◇◇◇ / N-COUNT / N-COUNT / ADJ: ADJ n

drop-per /ˈdrɒpə/ **droppers.** A dropper is an instrument which you use for dropping small amounts of liquid. N-COUNT

drop-pings /ˈdrɒpɪŋz/. **Droppings** are the faeces of birds and small animals. *...pigeon droppings.* ◆◇◇◇◇ N-PLURAL

dross /drɒs, AM drɔːs/. If you describe something as **dross**, you mean that it is of very poor quality or has no value. *What I do write is just dross.* N-UNCOUNT

drought /draʊt/ **droughts.** A drought is a long period of time during which no rain falls. *...drought and famines have killed up to two million people.* ◆◆◇◇◇ N-VAR

drove /drəʊv/. **Drove** is the past tense of **drive.**

drov-er /ˈdrəʊvə/ **drovers.** A drover is someone whose job is to make herds of sheep or cattle walk from one place to another. N-COUNT

droves /drəʊvz/. If you say that people are going somewhere or doing something **in droves**, you are emphasizing that there is a very large number of them. *Scientists are leaving the country in droves.* ◆◇◇◇◇ N-PLURAL PRAGMATICS

drown /draʊn/ **drowns, drowning, drowned.** **1** If someone **drowns** or **is drowned**, they die because they have gone or been pushed under water and cannot breathe. *Forty-eight people have drowned after their boat capsized... Last night a boy was drowned in the river... He walked into the sea and drowned himself.* **2** If you say that someone or something **is drowning** in something, you are emphasizing that they have a very large amount of it, or are completely covered in it. *We were drowning in data... The potatoes were drowned in chilli.* **3** If something **drowns** a sound, it is so loud that you cannot hear that sound properly. *Clapping drowned the speaker's words.* ▶ **Drown out** means the same as **drown.** *Their cheers drowned out the protests of demonstrators... Her voice was drowned out by a loud crash.* **4** If you say that someone **is drowning** their **sorrows**, you mean that they are drinking alcohol in order to forget something sad or upsetting. ◆◆◇◇◇ / V-ERG V beV-ed Vpron-refl Also Vn / VERB PRAGMATICS Vinn beV-ed / VERB Vn / PHRASAL VB VP noun Also VnP / PHRASE

drowse /draʊz/ **drowses, drowsing, drowsed.** If you **drowse**, you are almost asleep or just asleep. VERB: V

drow-sy /ˈdraʊzi/ **drowsier, drowsiest.** If you feel **drowsy**, you feel sleepy and cannot think clearly. *He felt pleasantly drowsy.* ♦ **drowsi-ness** *Big meals during the day cause drowsiness.* ♦ **drowsi-ly** /ˈdraʊzɪli/ *'Mm,' she answered drowsily.* ◆◇◇◇◇ ADJ-GRADED / N-UNCOUNT / ADV-GRADED: ADV with v

drudge /drʌdʒ/ **drudges.** If you describe someone as a **drudge**, you mean they have to work hard at a job which is not very important or interesting. N-COUNT

drudg-ery /ˈdrʌdʒəri/. You use **drudgery** to refer to jobs and tasks which are boring or unpleasant but which must be done. *...the drudgery of their everyday lives.* N-UNCOUNT

drug /drʌg/ **drugs, drugging, drugged. 1** A **drug** is a chemical which is given to people in order to treat or prevent an illness or disease. *The drug will be useful to hundreds of thousands of infected people.* **2 Drugs** are substances that some people smoke or inject into their blood because of their stimulating or pleasurable effects. *His mother was on drugs... She was sure Leo was taking drugs. ... drug abuse.* **3** If you **drug** a person or animal, you give them a chemical substance in order to make them sleepy or unconscious. *They drugged the guard dog.* **4** If food or drink **is drugged**, a chemical substance is added to it in order to make someone sleepy or unconscious when they eat or drink it. *Anyone who knew you would drink that wine could have drugged it.* ◆◆◆◆◇ / N-COUNT / N-COUNT / VERB Vn / VERB Vn

drug-gie /ˈdrʌgi/ **druggies;** also spelled **druggy.** If you refer to someone as a **druggie** you mean they are involved with or addicted to illegal drugs. N-COUNT PRAGMATICS INFORMAL

drug-gist /ˈdrʌgɪst/ **druggists.** A **druggist** or a **druggist's** is a shop where medicines are sold or given out. You can also refer to the specially qualified person who prepares and sells the medicines in this shop as a **druggist.** The British word is **chemist.** N-COUNT AMERICAN

drug-store /ˈdrʌgstɔː/ **drugstores.** In America, a **drugstore** is a shop where medicines, cosmetics, and some other goods are sold. ◆◇◇◇◇ N-COUNT

Dru-id /ˈdruːɪd/ **Druids;** also spelled **druid.** A **Druid** is a priest of the Celtic religion. ◆◇◇◇◇ N-COUNT

drum /drʌm/ **drums, drumming, drummed. 1** A **drum** is a musical instrument consisting of a skin stretched tightly over a round frame. See picture headed **musical instruments.** ♦ **drum-mer, drummers.** A **drummer** is a person who plays the drums in a band or group. ♦ **drum-ming.** **Drumming** is the action of playing the drums. **2** A **drum** is a large cylindrical container which is used to store fuel or other substances. *...an oil drum. ...a drum of chemical waste.* **3** A **drum** is a hollow cylindrical structure which is part of a machine, for example a washing machine. **4** If something **drums** on a surface, it hits it regularly, making a continuous beating sound. *He drummed his fingers on the leather top of his desk.* ♦ **drum-ming** *The steady drumming of rain could be heard.* ◆◆◆◇◇ / N-COUNT / N-COUNT / N-UNCOUNT / N-COUNT / N-COUNT / V-ERG: Vonn Vn on/against / N-UNCOUNT: also aN

drum into. If you **drum** something **into** someone, you keep saying it to them until they understand it or PHRASAL VB usu passive have itV-ed P

remember it. *We had it drummed into us that you need a degree to get a job... They drummed it into her that you were not to know she was working for them.* `n that V it P n that` `Also V P n that`

drum out. If someone **is drummed out of** an organization such as the armed forces or a club, they are forced to leave it in disgrace. *Sailors caught in a drugs scandal are to be drummed out of the service.* `PHRASAL VB usu passive be V-ed P P n`

drum up. If you **drum up** support or business, you try to get it. *...a delegation to drum up international support.* `PHRASAL VB V P noun`

drum·beat /'drʌmbiːt/ **drumbeats. 1** A **drumbeat** is the sound of a beat on a drum. **2** People sometimes describe a series of warnings or continuous pressure on someone to do something as a **drumbeat.** *...the steady drumbeat of pressure to force the President into open conflict with Nazi Germany.* `N-COUNT` `N-COUNT AMERICAN, JOURNALISM`

'drum kit, drum kits. A **drum kit** is a set of drums and cymbals. `N-COUNT`

'drum roll, drum rolls. A **drum roll** is a series of drumbeats that follow each other so quickly that they make a continuous sound. `N-COUNT`

drum·stick /'drʌmstɪk/ **drumsticks. 1** A **drumstick** is the lower part of the leg of a bird such as a chicken which is cooked and eaten. **2** Drumsticks are sticks used for beating a drum. `N-COUNT` `N-COUNT`

drunk /drʌŋk/ **drunks. 1** Someone who is **drunk** has drunk so much alcohol that they cannot speak clearly or behave sensibly. *I got drunk. ...drunk driving.* **2** A **drunk** is someone who is drunk or frequently gets drunk. **3** If you are **drunk** with a strong emotion or an experience, you are in a state of great excitement because of it. *I felt drunk with the excitement of life.* **4 Drunk** is the past participle of **drink.** `◆◆◇◇◇ ADJ-GRADED` `N-COUNT` `ADJ-GRADED: v-link ADJ`

drunk·ard /'drʌŋkəd/ **drunkards.** A **drunkard** is someone who frequently gets drunk. `N-COUNT`

drunk·en /'drʌŋkən/. **1 Drunken** is used to describe events and situations that involve people who are drunk. *The pain roused him from his drunken stupor. ...a drunken brawl.* **2** A **drunken** person is drunk or is frequently drunk; used showing disapproval. *...groups of drunken hooligans.* ♦ **drunk·en·ly** *Bob stormed drunkenly into her house and smashed some chairs.* ♦ **drunk·en·ness** *He was arrested for drunkenness.* `◆◇◇◇◇ ADJ-GRADED: ADJ n` `ADJ-GRADED: ADJ n PRAGMATICS` `ADV-GRADED: ADV with v` `N-UNCOUNT`

dry /draɪ/ **drier** or **dryer, driest; dries, drying, dried. 1** If something is **dry,** there is no water or moisture on it or in it. *Clean the metal with a soft dry cloth... Pat it dry with a soft towel... Once the paint is dry, apply a coat of the red ochre.* ♦ **dry·ness** *...the parched dryness of the air.* **2** When something **dries** or when you **dry** it, it becomes dry. *Leave your hair to dry naturally whenever possible... Wash and dry the lettuce... Mrs. Madrigal picked up a towel and began drying dishes.* **3** If the weather or a period of time is **dry,** there is no rain or there is much less rain than average. *...exceptionally dry weather... The spring had been unusually dry.* ▶ Also a noun. *Such cars, however, do grip the road well, even in the dry.* **4** A **dry** place or climate is one that gets very little rainfall. *It was one of the driest and dustiest places in Africa.* ♦ **dryness** *...the warmth and dryness of Italy.* **5** If a river, lake, or well is **dry,** it is empty of water, usually because of hot weather and lack of rain. *...a dry lake in western Arizona... In the end the Volga's waters will run dry.* **6** If an oil well is **dry,** it is no longer producing any oil. **7** If you say that someone is sucking something **dry** or milking it **dry,** you are criticizing them for taking all the good things from it until there is nothing left. *...a shady rip-off industry that sucks its talent dry then discards it.* **8** If you say that your skin or hair is **dry,** you mean that it is less oily or soft than average or than normal. *Dry hair is damaged by washing it too frequently... My skin's been getting a little dry recently.* ♦ **dryness** *...dryness of the skin.* **9** If you are **dry,** you are thirsty and need to drink something. *She was suddenly thirsty and dry.* **10** If your mouth or throat is **dry,** it has little or no saliva in it, and so feels very unpleasant. *His mouth was still* `◆◆◆◇ ADJ-GRADED` `N-UNCOUNT` `N-UNCOUNT V-ERG V V n` `ADJ-GRADED` `N-SING` `ADJ-GRADED` `N-UNCOUNT` `ADJ-GRADED` `ADJ` `ADJ: v n ADJ PRAGMATICS` `ADJ-GRADED` `N-UNCOUNT` `ADJ-GRADED` `ADJ-GRADED`

dry, he would certainly be glad of a drink. ♦ **dryness** *...frequent dryness in the mouth.* **11** A **dry** cough is one that does not produce any phlegm. **12** If someone has **dry** eyes, there are no tears in their eyes. *She didn't wince and her eyes were dry. Talk about brave. She was unbelievable.* `N-UNCOUNT` `ADJ` `ADJ`

13 Dry humour is very amusing, but in a subtle and clever way; used expressing approval. *Mr Brooke is renowned for his dry wit.* ♦ **dri·ly** *As Rossini drily observed, 'Wagner has lovely moments but awful quarters of an hour.'* ♦ **dryness** *It has a wry dryness you won't recognise.* **14** If you describe a voice as **dry,** you mean that it is cold or dull, and does not express any emotions. *He heard the dry voice of Father Laurence.* ♦ **drily** *'Possible,' I said drily, 'but not likely'.* **15** If you describe something such as a book, play, or activity as **dry,** you mean that it is dull and uninteresting. *...the dry, academic phrases.* `ADJ-GRADED PRAGMATICS` `ADV` `N-UNCOUNT` `ADJ-GRADED WRITTEN` `ADV` `ADJ-GRADED`

16 If a country, state, or city is **dry,** it has laws or rules which forbid anyone to drink, sell, or buy alcoholic drink. *Gujarat has been a totally dry state for the past thirty years.* **17** Dry bread or toast is plain and not covered with butter or jam. **18** Dry sherry or wine does not have a sweet taste. `ADJ INFORMAL` `ADJ: ADJ n` `ADJ`

19 ● **high and dry**: see **high.** ● **home and dry**: see **home.**

dry off. If something **dries off** or if you **dry** it **off,** moisture on its surface disappears or is removed. *They are then scrubbed with clean water and left to dry off... I got out, dried myself off, and dressed.* `PHRASAL VB ERG V P V n P` `Also V P noun`

dry out. 1 If something **dries out** or is **dried out,** it loses all the moisture that was in it and becomes hard. *If the soil is allowed to dry out the tree could die... The cold winds dry out your skin very quickly.* **2** If someone **dries out** or is **dried out,** they are cured of alcoholism. *He checked into Cedars Sinai Hospital to dry out.* `PHRASAL VB ERG V P V P noun ERG V P` `Also V-ed P INFORMAL`

dry up. 1 If something **dries up** or if something **dries** it **up,** it loses all its moisture and becomes completely dry and shrivelled or hard. *As the day goes on, the pollen dries up and becomes hard... Warm breezes from the South dried up the streets.* ♦ **dried-up** *...a tuft or two of dried-up grass.* **2** If a river, lake, or well **dries up,** it becomes empty of water, usually because of hot weather and a lack of rain. ♦ **dried-up** *...a dried-up river bed.* **3** If a supply of something **dries up,** it stops. *The main source of income and employment, tourism, is expected to dry up completely this summer.* **4** If you **dry up** when you are speaking, you stop in the middle of what you were saying, because you cannot think what to say next. **5** If you **dry up** or **dry up** the dishes, you wipe the water off them with a cloth after they have been washed. *He got up and stood beside Julie, drying up the dishes while she washed.* ♦ **drying up.** `PHRASAL VB ERG V P V P noun Also V n P` `ADJ` `V P` `ADJ` `V P` `V P` `V P noun Also V P` `N-UNCOUNT: also the N`

dry-'clean, dry-cleans, dry-cleaning, dry-cleaned. When things such as clothes **are dry-cleaned,** they are cleaned with a liquid chemical rather than with water. `VB: usu passive, be V-ed`

dry 'cleaner, dry cleaners. A **dry cleaner** is someone who has a shop where things can be dry-cleaned. You can also refer to the shop as a **dry-cleaner** or a **dry-cleaner's.** `N-COUNT`

dry-'cleaning; also spelled **dry cleaning. 1** Dry-cleaning is the action or work of dry-cleaning things such as clothes. *He owns a dry-cleaning business.* **2** Dry-cleaning is things that have been dry-cleaned, or that are going to be dry-cleaned. `N-UNCOUNT` `N-UNCOUNT`

dry 'dock, dry docks. A **dry dock** is a dock from which water can be removed so that ships, boats, or barges can be repaired or finished. `N-COUNT`

dry·er /draɪə/ **dryers;** also spelled **drier.** A **dryer** is a machine for drying things. There are different kinds of dryer, for examples ones designed for drying clothes, crops, or people's hair or hands. *...electric hand dryers.* ● See also **dry, tumble dryer.** `◆◇◇◇◇ N-COUNT`

dry-'eyed. If you say that someone is **dry-eyed,** you mean that although they are in a very sad situation they are not actually crying. *At the funeral he held her hand, but she was dry-eyed.* `ADJ`

'dry goods. Dry goods are cloth, thread, and other things that are sold at a draper's shop. `N-PLURAL AMERICAN`

,dry 'land. If you talk about **dry land**, you are re- N-UNCOUNT
ferring to land, in contrast to the sea or the air. *We
were glad to be on dry land again.*

,dry 'rot. Dry rot is a serious disease of wood. N-UNCOUNT

,dry-stone 'wall, dry-stone walls. A **dry-stone** N-COUNT
wall is a wall that has been built by fitting stones together without using any mortar. The American
term is **dry wall**.

DT's /,diː 'tiːz/. When alcoholics have **the DT's**, the N-PLURAL:
alcohol causes their bodies to shake uncontrollably, the N
and makes them unable to think clearly.

dual /'djuːəl, AM 'duː-/. **Dual** means having two ◆◆◇◇◇
parts, functions, or aspects. *...his dual role as head* ADJ: ADJ n
of the party and head of state. ...dual nationality.

,dual 'carriageway, dual carriageways. In N-VAR
Britain, a **dual carriageway** is a road which has two
lanes of traffic travelling in each direction with a
strip of grass or concrete down the middle to separate the two lots of traffic. The American expression
is **divided highway**.

dual·ism /'djuːəlɪzəm, AM 'duː-/. **Dualism** is the N-UNCOUNT
state of having two main parts or aspects, or the be- FORMAL
lief that something has two main parts or aspects.
*...a human being as a simple dualism of body and
soul.*

dual·ity /djuː'ælɪti, AM 'duː-/ **dualities.** A **duality** is N-VAR
a situation in which two contradictory ideas or feel- FORMAL
ings exist at the same time. *We live in a world of
duality, day and night, positive and negative, male
and female, etc.*

dub /dʌb/ **dubs, dubbing, dubbed. 1** If someone ◆◆◇◇◇
or something is **dubbed** a particular thing, they are VERB
given that description or nickname. *Orson Welles* V n n
dubbed her 'the most exciting woman in the world'. Also V n *as n*
2 If a film or soundtrack is **dubbed**, a different VB: usu
soundtrack is added with actors speaking a transla- passive,
tion of the dialogue. *It was dubbed into Spanish for* beV-ed
Mexican audiences. beV-ed into n

du·bi·ous /'djuːbiəs, AM 'duː-/. **1** If you describe ◆◆◇◇◇
something as **dubious**, you mean that you do not ADJ-GRADED
consider it to be completely honest, safe, or reliable.
*Soho was still a highly dubious area... Those figures
alone are a dubious basis for such a conclusion.*
◆ **du·bi·ous·ly** *Carter was dubiously convicted of* ADV-GRADED
shooting three white men in a bar. **2** If you are **dubi-** ADJ-GRADED:
ous about something, you are not completely sure v-link ADJ
about it and have not yet made up your mind about
it. *My parents were a bit dubious about it all at first
but we soon convinced them.* ◆ **dubiously** *He eyed* ADV
Coyne dubiously. **3** If you say that someone has the ADJ-GRADED:
dubious honour or the **dubious** pleasure of doing ADJ n
something, you are indicating that what they are PRAGMATICS
doing is not an honour or pleasure at all, but is, in
fact, unpleasant or bad. *El Salvador has earned the
dubious distinction of having the worst soil erosion
in continental America.*

du·cal /'djuːkəl, AM 'duː-/. **Ducal** places or things ADJ
belong to or are connected with a duke. FORMAL

duch·ess /'dʌtʃɪs/ **duchesses.** A **duchess** is a ◆◇◇◇◇
woman who has the same rank as a duke, or who is N-COUNT
a duke's wife or widow. *...the Duchess of York.*

duchy /'dʌtʃi/ **duchies.** A **duchy** is an area of land ◆◇◇◇◇
that is owned or ruled by a duke. *...the Duchy of* N-COUNT
Cornwall.

duck /dʌk/ **ducks, ducking, ducked. 1** A **duck** ◆◆◇◇◇
is a very common water bird with short legs, N-VAR
webbed feet, a short neck, and a large flat beak. See
picture headed **animals**. ▶ **Duck** is the flesh of this N-UNCOUNT
bird when it is eaten as food. *...honey roasted duck.*
● See also **dead duck, lame duck, sitting duck**.
2 Some people call other people **duck** or **ducks** as a N-VOC
sign of affection. *Oh, I am glad to see you, duck.* BRITISH
3 If you **duck** your head or **duck**, you move your head VERB
quickly downwards in order to avoid being seen or hit V
by something. *He ducked in time to save his head from* V adv/prep
*a blow from the cane... I wanted to duck down and
slip past but they saw me.* **4** If you **duck** something VERB
such as a blow, you avoid it by moving your head or V n
body quickly downwards. *Hans deftly ducked their
blows.* **5** If you **duck** into a place, you move there VERB

quickly, often in an attempt to avoid danger or to V prep/adv
avoid being seen. *Matt ducked into his office.*
6 You say that someone **ducks** a duty or responsibility VERB
when you disapprove of the fact that they avoid it. *The* PRAGMATICS
Opposition reckons the Health Secretary has ducked V n
all the difficult decisions.

duck out. If you **duck out** of something that you are PHRASAL VB
supposed to do, you avoid doing it. *George ducked out* V P of n
of his forced marriage to a cousin. Also V P

duck·ling /'dʌklɪŋ/ **ducklings.** A **duckling** is a N-COUNT
young duck. ● See also **ugly duckling**.

duct /dʌkt/ **ducts. 1** A **duct** is a pipe, tube, or ◆◇◇◇◇
channel which carries a liquid or gas. *...a big air* N-COUNT
duct in the ceiling. **2** A **duct** is a tube in your body N-COUNT:
which carries a liquid such as tears. with supp

dud /dʌd/ **duds. Dud** means not working properly ◆◇◇◇◇
or not successful. *He replaced a dud valve.* ▶ Also a ADJ
noun. *The mine was a dud.* INFORMAL
    N-COUNT

dude /djuːd, AM duːd/ **dudes.** A **dude** is a man. *My* ◆◇◇◇◇
doctor is a real cool dude. INFORMAL

'dude ranch, dude ranches. A **dude ranch** is an N-COUNT
American ranch where people can go on holiday
and do activities such as riding or camping.

dudg·eon /'dʌdʒən/. If you say that someone is **in** PHRASE
high dudgeon, you are emphasizing that they are PRAGMATICS
very angry or resentful about something.

due /djuː, AM duː/ **dues. 1** If an event is **due to** ◆◆◆◇
something, it happens or exists as a direct result of PHR-PREP
that thing. *The country's economic problems are
largely due to the weakness of the recovery... A lot of
this will be due to Mr Green's efforts.* **2** You can say PHR-PREP
due to to introduce the reason for something happening. *Jobs could be lost in the defence industry due
to political changes.*
3 If something is **due** at a particular time, it is expect- ADJ
ed to happen or to arrive at that time. *The results are
due at the end of the month... The first price increases
are due to come into force in July... Mr Carter is due in
London on Monday.* **4** If you say that something will PHRASE
happen **in due course**, you mean that it will happen
eventually, when the time is right. *The arrangements
will be published in due course.* **5** Something that is ADJ:
due, or that is **due** to someone, is owed to them. *No* v-link ADJ
*further pension was due... I've got some leave due to
me.* ▶ Also a preposition. *He had accumulated three* PREP
leave due him. **6** If someone is **due for** something, ADJ:
that thing is planned to happen or be given to them v-link ADJ for
now, or very soon. *Although not due for release until* n
*2001, he was let out of his low-security prison to spend
a weekend with his wife.* ▶ Also a preposition. *I reckon* PREP
I'm due one of my travels.
7 Due attention and consideration is the proper, rea- ADJ: ADJ n
sonable, or deserved amount of it under the circumstances. *After due consideration it was decided to send
him away to live with foster parents.*
8 Dues are sums of money that you pay regularly to an N-PLURAL
organization that you belong to.
9 Due is used before the words 'north', 'south', 'east', ADV:
or 'west' to indicate that something is in exactly the ADV adv/adj
direction mentioned. *They headed due north.*
10 You can say **'to give** him his **due'**, or **'giving** him his PHRASE
due' when you are admitting that there are some good PRAGMATICS
things about someone, even though there are things
that you do not like about them. *To give Linda her due,
she had tried to encourage John in his school work.*
11 You can say **'with due respect'** when you are about PHRASE
to disagree politely with someone. *With all due re-* PRAGMATICS
*spect I submit to you that you're asking the wrong
question.*

duel /'djuːəl, AM 'duː-/ **duels, duelling duelled;** ◆◇◇◇◇
spelled **dueling, dueled** in American English. **1** A N-COUNT
duel is a fight between two people in which they
use guns or swords in order to settle a quarrel.
2 You can refer to a conflict between two people or N-COUNT
groups as a **duel**. *The area has been the scene of sporadic artillery duels.* **3** To **duel** means to fight a duel V-RECIP
or be involved in a conflict. *We duelled for two years* pl-n V
and Peterson made the most of it, playing us off Also V with n,
against each other. V (non-recip)

duet /dju:'et, AM du:-/ **duets.** A **duet** is a piece of music sung or played by two people. ◆◇◇◇◇ N-COUNT

duff /dʌf/ If you describe something as **duff**, you mean it is useless, broken, or of poor quality. *Most of us have had to take a duff job sometime in our lives.* ◆◇◇◇◇ ADJ-GRADED BRITISH, INFORMAL

duf·fel /'dʌfəl/ **duffels. 1** A **duffel** is the same as a **duffel coat. 2** A **duffel** is the same as a **duffel bag.** N-COUNT N-COUNT

duf·fel bag /'dʌfəl bæg/ **duffel bags;** also spelled **duffle bag.** A **duffel bag** is a bag shaped like a cylinder and made of strong fabric such as canvas with a drawstring at one end. N-COUNT

duf·fel coat /'dʌfəl kəʊt/ **duffel coats;** also spelled **duffle coat.** A **duffel coat** is a heavy coat with a hood and long buttons that fasten with loops. N-COUNT

duff·er /'dʌfə/ **duffers.** If you describe someone as a **duffer**, you mean that they are very bad at doing something. *Waugh was a duffer at cricket.* N-COUNT DATED, INFORMAL, BRITISH

duf·fle /'dʌfəl/. See **duffel bag, duffel coat.**

dug /dʌg/. **Dug** is the past tense and past participle of **dig.**

dug·out /'dʌgaʊt/ **dugouts. 1** A **dugout** is a canoe that is made by hollowing out a log. **2** A **dugout** is a shelter made by digging a hole in the ground and then covering it or tunnelling so that the shelter has a roof over it. N-COUNT N-COUNT

duke /dju:k, AM du:k/ **dukes.** A **duke** is a nobleman of high rank. *...the Queen and the Duke of Edinburgh.* ◆◇◇◇◇ N-COUNT

duke·dom /'dju:kdəm, AM 'du:k-/ **dukedoms. 1** A **dukedom** is the rank or title of a duke. *...the present heir to the dukedom.* **2** A **dukedom** is the land owned by a duke. N-COUNT N-COUNT

dul·cet /'dʌlsɪt/. **1** A **dulcet** voice is one that is gentle and pleasant to listen to. *Quickly, in her dulcet voice, Tamara told him what had happened.* **2** People often use the expression **dulcet tones** to refer humorously to someone's voice. *You hear his dulcet tones on the radio.* ADJ: ADJ n LITERARY PHRASE

dull /dʌl/ **duller, dullest; dulls, dulling, dulled. 1** If you describe someone or something as **dull**, you mean they are not interesting or exciting. *They are both nice people but can be rather dull... I felt she found me boring and dull.* ♦ **dull·ness** *...the dullness of their routine life.* **2** Someone or something that is **dull** is not very lively or energetic. *We all feel dull and sleepy between 1 and 3pm.* ♦ **dul·ly** *His eyes looked dully ahead.* ♦ **dull·ness** *Did you notice any unusual depression or dullness of mind?* **3** A **dull** colour or light is not bright. *The stamp was a dark, dull blue colour.* ♦ **dully** *The street lamps gleamed dully.* **4** You say the weather is **dull** when it is very cloudy. *It's always dull and raining.* **5** Dull sounds are not very clear or loud. *The coffin closed with a dull thud.* ♦ **dully** *He heard his heart thump dully but more quickly.* **6** Dull feelings are weak and not intense. *...a dull ache.* ♦ **dully** *His arm throbbed dully.* **7** If something **dulls** or if it **is dulled**, it becomes less intense, bright, or lively. *Her eyes dulled and she gazed blankly... It dulled our senses with facts.* ◆◆◇◇◇ ADJ-GRADED PRAGMATICS N-UNCOUNT ADJ-GRADED ADV N-UNCOUNT ADJ-GRADED ADV ADJ-GRADED ADV ADJ-GRADED: ADJ n ADV V-ERG V V n

dull·ard /'dʌləd/ **dullards.** If you say that someone is a **dullard**, you mean that they are unimaginative and slow to understand things. N-COUNT

duly /'dju:li, AM 'du:-/. **1** If something happens that was expected to happen, you can say that it **duly** happened. *Westcott appealed to Waite for an apology, which he duly received.* **2** If something is **duly** done, it is done in the correct way. *He is a duly elected president of the country.* ◆◇◇◇◇ ADV: ADV before v ADV: ADV before v FORMAL

dumb /dʌm/ **dumber, dumbest. 1** Someone who is **dumb** is completely unable to speak. *...a young deaf and dumb man.* **2** If someone is **dumb** on a particular occasion, they cannot speak because they are angry, shocked, or surprised. *We were all struck dumb for a minute.* ♦ **dumb·ly** *I shook my head dumbly, not believing him.* **3** Something that is **dumb** is done or expressed without words. *...an expression of dumb recognition.* ◆◇◇◇◇ ADJ: v-link ADJ LITERARY ADV ADJ: ADJ n LITERARY

4 If you call a person **dumb**, you mean that they are stupid or foolish. *I've met a lot of dumb people. ...a stereotyped dumb blonde.* **5** If you say that something is **dumb**, you think that it is silly and annoying. *I came up with this dumb idea.* ADJ-GRADED INFORMAL ADJ-GRADED INFORMAL, AMERICAN

dumb-bell /'dʌmbel/ **dumb-bells;** also spelled **dumbbell.** A **dumb-bell** is a short bar with weights on either side which people lift for exercise. N-COUNT

dumb·found /,dʌm'faʊnd/ **dumbfounds, dumbfounding, dumbfounded.** If someone or something **dumbfounds** you, they surprise you very much. *This suggestion dumbfounded Joe.* ♦ **dumb·found·ed** *I stood there dumbfounded, scarcely able to believe the evidence of my senses.* VERB V n ADJ-GRADED

dumb·struck /'dʌmstrʌk/. If you are **dumbstruck**, you are so shocked or surprised that you cannot speak. *We were dumbstruck. We just couldn't believe our eyes when she appeared.* ADJ-GRADED PRAGMATICS

dum·my /'dʌmi/ **dummies. 1** A **dummy** is a model of a person, often used to display clothes. *...the bottom half of a shop-window dummy. ...the ventriloquist's dummy.* **2** You can use **dummy** to refer to things that are not real, but have been made to look or behave as if they are real. *Dummy patrol cars will be set up beside motorways to frighten speeding motorists. ...dummy weapons.* **3** A baby's **dummy** is a rubber or plastic object that you give the baby to suck so that it feels comforted. **4** If you call someone a **dummy**, you mean that you think they are stupid. *'You're a dummy, Mack,' she yelled.* ◆◇◇◇◇ N-COUNT N-COUNT N-COUNT BRITISH N-COUNT PRAGMATICS INFORMAL

dummy 'run, dummy runs. A **dummy run** is a trial or test procedure which is carried out in order to see if a plan or process works properly. N-COUNT BRITISH

dump /dʌmp/ **dumps, dumping, dumped. 1** If you **dump** something somewhere, you put it or unload it there quickly and carelessly. *We dumped our bags at the nearby Grand Hotel and hurried towards the market.* **2** If something **is dumped** somewhere, it is put or left there because it is no longer wanted or needed. *The getaway car was dumped near a motorway tunnel... A million tonnes of untreated sewage is dumped into the sea.* ♦ **dump·ing** *...the dumping of hazardous waste.* **3** To **dump** something such as an idea, policy, or practice means to stop supporting or using it. *It was vital to dump the poll tax before the election.* **4** To **dump** computer data or memory means to copy it from one storage system onto another, such as from disk to magnetic tape. ◆◆◇◇◇ VERB V n prep/adv INFORMAL VERB be V-ed Also V n INFORMAL N-UNCOUNT VERB V n INFORMAL VERB: V n into n TECHNICAL

5 A **dump** is a place where rubbish is left, for example on open ground outside a town. **6** A **dump** is a place where an army stores food, weapons, or ammunition temporarily while it is stationed in a particular place. **7** If you say that a place is a **dump**, you think it is ugly and unpleasant to live in or visit. *'What a dump!' Christabel said, standing in the doorway of the youth hostel.* **8** If you are **down in the dumps**, you are feeling very depressed and miserable. *She's feeling a bit down in the dumps and needs cheering up.* **9** If you **dump** someone, you end your relationship with them. *I thought he was going to dump me for another girl.* **10** If you say that a parent **dumps** a child with someone, you are criticizing the parent for leaving the child to be looked after by that person. *I was sometimes dumped with my grandmother or left with highly unsuitable au pairs.* N-COUNT N-COUNT N-COUNT PRAGMATICS INFORMAL PHRASE INFORMAL VERB V n INFORMAL VERB PRAGMATICS be V-ed with n Also V n in n INFORMAL

'dumper truck, dumper trucks. A **dumper truck** is the same as a **dump truck.** N-COUNT BRITISH

'dumping ground, dumping grounds. If you refer to a place as a **dumping ground** for something, you mean that things are left there, usually in large quantities, and you disapprove of this. *Eastern Europe is rapidly becoming a dumping-ground for radioactive residues.* N-COUNT PRAGMATICS

dump·ling /'dʌmplɪŋ/ **dumplings.** Dumplings are small lumps of dough that are cooked and eaten, either with meat and vegetables or as part of a sweet pudding. N-VAR

Dump·ster /'dʌmpstə/ **Dumpsters.** A **Dumpster** is a large metal container for holding rubbish or N-COUNT AMERICAN

things for recycling. **Dumpster** is a trademark. The usual British word is **skip**.

'dump truck, dump trucks. A **dump truck** is a N-COUNT truck whose carrying part can be tipped backwards so that the load falls out.

dumpy /'dʌmpi/. If you describe someone as ADJ-GRADED **dumpy**, you mean they are short and fat. PRAGMATICS

dun /dʌn/. Something that is **dun** is a dull grey- COLOUR brown colour. ...*her dun mare.*

dunce /dʌns/ **dunces.** If you say that someone is a N-COUNT **dunce**, you think they are rather stupid. PRAGMATICS

dune /dju:n, AM du:n/ **dunes.** A **dune** is a hill of ◆◇◇◇◇ sand near the sea or in a desert. N-COUNT

dung /dʌŋ/. **Dung** is faeces from large animals. ◆◇◇◇◇ ...*little piles of cow dung.* N-UNCOUNT

dun·ga·rees /,dʌŋgə'ri:z/. **Dungarees** are a one- N-PLURAL piece garment consisting of trousers, a piece of cloth which covers your chest, and straps which go over your shoulders. In American English, **dungarees** can also refer to jeans. See picture headed **clothes**.

dun·geon /'dʌndʒən/ **dungeons.** A **dungeon** is a N-COUNT dark underground prison in a castle.

dunk /dʌŋk/ **dunks, dunking, dunked.** If you VERB **dunk** something **in** a liquid, you put it in the liquid V n in n for a short time. *Dunk new plants in a bucket of wa-ter for an hour or so before planting.*

dun·no /də'nəʊ/. **Dunno** is sometimes used to rep- ◆◇◇◇◇ resent a way of saying 'don't know'. *'How did she* WRITTEN, *get it?'—'I dunno.'* INFORMAL

duo /'dju:əʊ, AM 'du:-/ **duos. 1** A **duo** consists of ◆◇◇◇◇ two musicians, singers, or other performers who N-COUNT perform together as a pair. ...*a famous dancing and singing duo.* **2** You can refer to two people together N-COUNT as a **duo**, especially when they have something in common. ...*Britain's golden Olympic duo of Linford Christie and Sally Gunnell.*

duo·denum /,dju:əʊ'di:nəm, AM ,du:-/ **duode-** N-COUNT **nums.** Your **duodenum** is the part of your small in- MEDICAL testine that is just below your stomach. ♦ **duo·de-** **·nal** /,dju:əʊ'di:nəl, AM ,du:-/ ...*duodenal ulcers.* ADJ: ADJ n

dupe /dju:p, AM du:p/ **dupes, duping, duped.** ◆◇◇◇◇ **1** If someone **dupes** you, they trick you into doing VERB something, or into believing something which is not V n into-ing true. ...*a plot to dupe stamp collectors into buying* Also V n *fake rarities.* **2** A **dupe** is someone who is tricked by N-COUNT someone else. *He was accused of being a dupe of the communists.*

du·plex /'dju:pleks, AM 'du:-/ **duplexes. 1** In N-COUNT North America, a **duplex** is a house which has been divided into two separate units for two different families or groups of people. **2** In North America, a N-COUNT **duplex** or a **duplex apartment** is a flat which has rooms on two floors.

du·pli·cate, duplicates, duplicating, dupli- ◆◇◇◇◇ **cated.** The verb is pronounced /'dju:plɪkeɪt, AM 'du:-/. The noun and adjective are pronounced /'dju:plɪkət, AM 'du:-/. **1** If you **duplicate** something VERB that has already been done, you repeat or copy it. V n *His task will be to duplicate his success overseas here at home.* ▶ Also a noun. *He was organising a dupli-* N-COUNT *cate of Operation Gladio.* ● See also **duplication**. **2** To **duplicate** something which has been written, VERB drawn, or recorded onto tape means to make exact V n copies of it. ...*a business which duplicates video and cinema tapes.* ▶ Also a noun. *I've lost my card. I've* N-COUNT: *got to get a duplicate... The genuine mileage is rec-* also in N *orded in duplicate.* **3 Duplicate** is used to describe ADJ: ADJ n things that have been made as an exact copy of oth-er things, usually in order to serve the same pur-pose. ...*a duplicate key.*

du·pli·ca·tion /,dju:plɪ'keɪʃən/. If you say N-UNCOUNT that there has been **duplication** of something, you PRAGMATICS mean that someone has done a task unnecessarily because it has already been done before. ...*unneces-sary duplication of resources.*

du·plic·ity /dju:'plɪsɪti, AM du:-/. If you accuse N-UNCOUNT someone of **duplicity**, you mean that they are de- FORMAL ceitful. *Malcolm believed his former mentor was guilty of duplicity.*

du·rable /'djʊərəbəl, AM 'dʊr-/. Something that is ◆◆◇◇◇ **durable** is strong and lasts a long time. *Fine bone* ADJ-GRADED *china is eminently practical, since it is strong and durable.* ♦ **du·rabil·ity** /,djʊərə'bɪlɪti, AM ,dʊr-/ *Air-* N-UNCOUNT *lines recommend hard-sided cases for durability.*

du·ra·tion /dju'reɪʃən, AM dʊr-/. **1** The **duration** of ◆◆◇◇◇ an event or state is the time during which it hap- N-UNCOUNT pens or exists. *Courses are of two years' duration.* **2** If you say that something will happen **for the du-** PHRASE **ration**, you mean that it will happen for as long as a particular situation continues. *His wounds knocked him out of combat for the duration.*

du·ress /dju'res, AM dʊr-/. If someone does some- N-UNCOUNT thing under **duress**, they do it because someone FORMAL forces them to do it or threatens them.

Du·rex /'djʊəreks, AM 'dʊreks/. **Durex** is both the N-COUNT singular and the plural form. In Britain, a **Durex** is a type of contraceptive sheath. **Durex** is a trademark.

dur·ing /'djʊərɪŋ, AM 'dʊrɪŋ/. **1** If something hap- ◆◆◆◆◆ pens **during** a period of time or an event, it hap- PREP pens continuously, or happens several times be-tween the beginning and end of that period or event. *Sandstorms are common during the Saudi Arabian winter.* **2** If something develops **during** a PREP period of time, it develops gradually from the begin-ning to the end of that period. *Wages have fallen by more than twenty percent during the past two months.* **3** An event that happens **during** a period of PREP time happens at some point or moment in that pe-riod. *The attack is believed to have been carried out during the early morning hours.*

dusk /dʌsk/. **1 Dusk** is the time just before night ◆◇◇◇◇ when the daylight has almost gone but when it is N-UNCOUNT not completely dark. **2** The **dusk** is the dim, rather N-UNCOUNT shadowy light there is at dusk. *She turned and dis-* LITERARY *appeared into the dusk.*

dusky /'dʌski/. **1 Dusky** means rather dark. *Heavy* ADJ-GRADED *gold earrings gleamed against her dusky cheeks.* LITERARY **2** A **dusky** colour is soft rather than bright. ...*dusky* COMB *pink carpet.*

dust /dʌst/ **dusts, dusting, dusted. 1 Dust** con- ◆◆◇◇◇ sists of very small dry particles of earth, sand, or N-UNCOUNT dirt. *Tanks raise huge trails of dust when they move... I could see a thick layer of dust on the stairs.* **2 Dust** is a fine powder which consists of very small N-UNCOUNT particles of a substance such as gold, wood, or coal. **3** When you **dust** something such as furniture, you VERB: V n remove dust from it, usually using a cloth. *She dust-* V *ed, she cleaned, and she did the washing-up.* ♦ **dust·ing** *I don't have to do the washing-up or the* N-UNCOUNT *dusting.* **4** If you **dust** something with a fine sub- VERB: stance such as powder or if you **dust** a fine sub- V n prep/adv stance onto something, you cover it lightly with that V adv/prep substance. *Dust between the toes with baby powder.*

5 If you say that something **has bitten the dust**, you PHRASE are emphasizing that it no longer exists or that it has PRAGMATICS failed. *The allegation has caused one lecturer's career* INFORMAL *to bite the dust.* **6** If you say that something will hap- PHRASE pen when **the dust settles**, you mean that a situation INFORMAL will be clearer after it has calmed down. If you let the **dust settle** before doing something, you let a situation calm down before you try to do anything else. **7** If you PHRASE say that something **is gathering dust**, you mean that it has been left somewhere and nobody is using it or do-ing anything with it.

dust down or **dust off. 1** If you say that someone PHRASAL VB **dusts** something **down** or **dusts** it **off**, you mean they V P noun are reusing something such as an idea which is old ra- Also V n P ther than trying something new. *Critics were busy dusting down the same superlatives they had applied to their first three films.* **2** If you say that someone has V pron-refl P **dusted** himself or herself **down** or **dusted** themselves **off**, you mean that they have managed to recover from a severe setback which has affected their lives. *Tina Turner dusted herself down, got rid of Ike and be-came the greatest show on earth.* **3** If someone **dusts** V P noun **down** something or **dusts** dirt **off** something, they re- Also V n P move dirt or dust from it. *He stood and dusted down his suit and folded the letter away.*

dust·bin /'dʌstbɪn/ **dustbins.** A **dustbin** is a large round container with a lid which people put their rubbish in and which is usually kept outside their house. The usual American term is **garbage can**. See picture headed **house and flat**. ◆◇◇◇◇ N-COUNT BRITISH

dust·er /'dʌstə/ **dusters.** A **duster** is a cloth which you use for removing dust from furniture. N-COUNT

'dust jacket, dust jackets. A **dust jacket** is a loose paper cover which is put on a book to protect it. N-COUNT

dust·man /'dʌstmən/ **dustmen.** A **dustman** is a person whose job is to empty the rubbish from people's dustbins and take it away to be disposed of. The usual American term is **garbage man**. N-COUNT BRITISH

dust·pan /'dʌstpæn/ **dustpans.** A **dustpan** is a small flat container made of metal or plastic. You hold it on the floor and sweep dirt and dust into it. N-COUNT

'dust-up, dust-ups. A **dust-up** is a quarrel that often involves some fighting. N-COUNT INFORMAL

dusty /'dʌsti/ **dustier, dustiest.** Something that is **dusty** is covered with dust. ...a dusty old car... The books looked faded, dusty, and unused. ◆◇◇◇◇ ADJ-GRADED

Dutch /dʌtʃ/. If two or more people **go Dutch**, each of them pays their own bill, for example in a restaurant. We went dutch on the cheap Chinese in Shaftesbury Avenue. ◆◆◆◆ PHRASE INFORMAL

du·ti·ful /'djuːtɪfʊl, AM 'duː-/. If you say that someone is **dutiful**, you mean that they do everything that they are expected to do. The days of the dutiful wife, who sacrifices her career for her husband, are over. ◆ **du·ti·ful·ly** The inspector dutifully recorded the date in a large red book. ◆◇◇◇◇ ADJ-GRADED ◆ ADV: ADV with v

duty /'djuːti, AM 'duːti/ **duties. 1 Duty** is work that you have to do for your job. Staff must report for duty at their normal place of work. **2** If someone such as a policeman or a nurse is **off duty**, they are not working. If someone is **on duty**, they are working. Extra staff had been put on duty. **3** Your **duties** are tasks which you have to do because they are part of your job. I carried out my duties conscientiously. **4** If you say that something is your **duty**, you believe that you ought to do it because it is your responsibility. I consider it my duty to write to you and thank you. **5 Duties** are taxes which you pay to the government on goods that you buy. Import duties still average 30%. ◆◆◆◇ N-UNCOUNT PHRASE N-PLURAL N-SING N-VAR

,duty-'bound; also spelled **duty bound**. If you say you are **duty-bound** to do something, you are emphasizing that you feel it is your duty to do it. 'I didn't want to work on it but felt duty bound to help,' Wilson said. ADJ: v-link ADJ to-inf PRAGMATICS FORMAL

,duty-'free. **Duty-free** goods are sold at airports or on planes or ships at a cheaper price than usual because you do not have to pay import tax on them. ◆◇◇◇◇ ADJ

,duty-'free shop, duty-free shops. A **duty-free shop** is a shop, for example at an airport, where you can buy duty-free goods. N-COUNT

du·vet /'duːveɪ, AM duː'veɪ/ **duvets.** A **duvet** is a large cover filled with feathers or similar material which you put over yourself in bed instead of a sheet and blankets. The usual American word is **comforter**. ◆◇◇◇◇ N-COUNT BRITISH

dwarf /dwɔːf/ **dwarves, dwarfs, dwarfing, dwarfed. 1** If one person or thing is **dwarfed** by another, the second is so much bigger than the first that it makes them look very small. The US air travel market dwarfs that of Britain. **2 Dwarf** plants or animals are much smaller than other plants or animals of the same kind. ...dwarf shrubs. **3** In children's stories, a **dwarf** is an imaginary creature that is like a small man. **4** In former times, people who were much smaller than normal were called **dwarfs**; a use which is now considered offensive. ◆◆◇◇◇ VERB: beV-ed V n ADJ: ADJ n N-COUNT N-COUNT DATED

dwell /dwel/ **dwells, dwelling, dwelt** or **dwelled. 1** If you **dwell** on something, especially something unpleasant, you think, speak, or write about it a lot for a long time. 'I'd rather not dwell on the past,' he told me. **2** If you **dwell** somewhere, you live there. They are concerned for the fate ◆◇◇◇◇ VERB V on/upon n VERB V prep/adv FORMAL

of the forest and the Indians who dwell in it. **3** See also **dwelling**.

dwell·er /'dwelə/ **dwellers.** A city **dweller** or slum **dweller**, for example, is a person who lives in the kind of place or house indicated. ◆◇◇◇◇ N-COUNT: supp N

dwell·ing /'dwelɪŋ/ **dwellings.** A **dwelling** or a **dwelling place** is a place where someone lives. Some 3500 new dwellings are planned for the area. ◆◇◇◇◇ N-COUNT FORMAL

dwelt /dwelt/. **Dwelt** is the past tense and past participle of **dwell**.

dwin·dle /'dwɪndəl/ **dwindles, dwindling, dwindled.** If something **dwindles**, it becomes smaller, weaker, or less in number. The factory's workforce has dwindled from over 4,000 to a few hundred. ...his dwindling authority. ◆◇◇◇◇ VERB V V-ing

dye /daɪ/ **dyes, dyeing, dyed. 1** If you **dye** something, you change its colour by soaking it in a special liquid. The women prepared, spun and dyed the wool. **2 Dye** is a substance which is mixed into a liquid and used to change the colour of something. ...bottles of hair dye. ◆◆◇◇◇ VERB V n N-VAR

,dyed-in-the-'wool. **Dyed-in-the-wool** means having very strong opinions about something which you refuse to change. He was a dyed-in-the-wool conservative. ADJ-GRADED: ADJ n

dy·ing /'daɪɪŋ/. **1 Dying** is the present participle of **die**. **2** A **dying** person or animal is very ill and likely to die soon. ...a dying man. ▶ **The dying** are people who are dying. By the time our officers arrived, the dead and the dying were everywhere. **3** You use **dying** to describe something which happens at the time when someone dies, or is connected with that time. ...the dying wishes of her mother. **4** The **dying** days or **dying** minutes of a state of affairs or an activity are its last days or minutes. ...the dying days of the second world war. **5** A **dying** tradition or industry is becoming less important and is likely to finish altogether. Shipbuilding is a dying business. **6** A **dying** fire is no longer hot and bright and will not burn for much longer. ◆◆◇◇◇ ADJ: ADJ n N-PLURAL: the N ADJ: ADJ n ADJ: ADJ n ADJ: ADJ n ADJ: ADJ n

dyke /daɪk/ **dykes;** also spelled **dike. 1** A **dyke** is a thick wall that is built to stop water flooding onto very low-lying land from a river or from the sea. **2** A **dyke** is a lesbian; this use is considered offensive. ◆◇◇◇◇ N-COUNT N-COUNT INFORMAL

dy·nam·ic /daɪ'næmɪk/ **dynamics. 1** If you describe someone as **dynamic**, you approve of them because they are full of energy or full of new and exciting ideas. ...a dynamic and energetic leader. ◆ **dy·nami·cal·ly** /daɪ'næmɪkli/ ...one of the most dynamically imaginative jazz pianists. **2** If you describe something as **dynamic**, you approve of it because it is very active and energetic. ...the most dynamic economic region in the world. **3** A **dynamic** process is one that constantly changes and progresses. Political debate is dynamic. ◆ **dynamically** Germany has a dynamically growing market at home. **4** The **dynamic** of a system or process is the force that causes it to change or progress. The dynamic of the market demands constant change and adjustment. **5** The **dynamics** of a situation or group of people are the opposing forces within it that cause it to change. The interchange of ideas aids an understanding of family dynamics. **6 Dynamics** are forces which produce power or movement. Scientists observe the same dynamics in fluids. **7 Dynamics** is the scientific study of motion, energy, and forces. ◆◇◇◇◇ ADJ-GRADED PRAGMATICS ADV-GRADED PRAGMATICS ADJ-GRADED PRAGMATICS ADJ ADV N-COUNT N-PLURAL N-UNCOUNT TECHNICAL N-UNCOUNT

dy·na·mism /'daɪnəmɪzəm/. **1** If you say that someone or something has **dynamism**, you are expressing approval of the fact that they are full of energy or full of new and exciting ideas. ...a situation that calls for dynamism and new thinking. **2** If you refer to the **dynamism** of a situation or system, you are referring to the fact that it is changing in an exciting and dramatic way. Such changes are also indicators of economic dynamism. ◆◇◇◇◇ N-UNCOUNT PRAGMATICS N-UNCOUNT

dy·na·mite /'daɪnəmaɪt/ **dynamites, dynamiting, dynamited. 1 Dynamite** is a type of explosive that contains nitroglycerin. **2** If someone dyna- ◆◇◇◇◇ N-UNCOUNT VERB: V n

mites something, they blow it up by using dynamite. **3** If you describe a piece of information as **dynamite**, you think that people will react violently to it. *The book is dynamite, and if she publishes it, there will be no hiding place for her.* **4** If you describe someone or something as **dynamite**, you think that they are exciting and stimulating. *The first kiss is dynamite.* [N-UNCOUNT INFORMAL] [N-UNCOUNT PRAGMATICS INFORMAL]

dy·na·mo /'daɪnəməʊ/ **dynamos. 1** A **dynamo** is a device that uses the movement of a machine or vehicle to produce electricity. **2** If you describe someone as a **dynamo**, you mean that they are very energetic and are always busy and active. *Myles is a human dynamo.* [◆◇◇◇◇ N-COUNT] [N-COUNT]

dy·nas·tic /daɪ'næstɪk/. **Dynastic** means typical of or relating to a dynasty. *The country's democratic rulers were trying to revive dynastic rule.* [ADJ]

dyn·as·ty /'dɪnəsti, AM 'daɪn-/ **dynasties. 1** A **dynasty** is a series of rulers of a country who all belong to the same family. *...the Seljuk dynasty of Syria.* **2** A **dynasty** is a period of time during which a country is ruled by members of the same family. *...the Ming dynasty.* **3** A **dynasty** is a family which has members from two or more generations who are important in a particular field of activity, for ex- [◆◇◇◇◇ N-COUNT] [N-COUNT: with supp] [N-COUNT]

ample in business or politics. *This is a family-owned company – the current president is the fourth in this dynasty.*

d'you /djuː, dʒuː/. **d'you** is a short form of **do you** or **did you**, used in writing to represent informal spoken English. *What d'you say?*

dys·en·tery /'dɪsəntri, AM -teri/. **Dysentery** is an infection in a person's intestines that causes severe diarrhoea. [N-UNCOUNT]

dys·func·tion /dɪs'fʌŋkʃən/ **dysfunctions. 1** If you refer to a **dysfunction** in something such as a relationship or someone's behaviour, you mean it is different from what is considered to be normal. *...his severe emotional dysfunction.* ◆ **dys·func·tion·al** *...a dysfunctional family.* **2** If someone has a physical **dysfunction**, part of their body is not working properly. *...liver dysfunction.* [N-COUNT FORMAL] [ADJ-GRADED] [N-VAR MEDICAL]

dys·lexia /dɪs'leksiə/. If someone suffers from **dyslexia**, they have difficulty with reading because of a slight disorder of their brain. ◆ **dys·lex·ic** /dɪs'leksɪk/ *He was diagnosed as severely dyslexic.* [N-UNCOUNT TECHNICAL] [ADJ]

dys·pep·sia /dɪs'pepsiə, AM -ʃə/. **Dyspepsia** is the same as **indigestion**. [N-UNCOUNT MEDICAL]

dys·tro·phy /'dɪstrəfi/. See **muscular dystrophy**.

Ee

E, e /iː/ **E's, e's. 1** E is the fifth letter of the English alphabet. **2** In music, E is the third note in the scale of C major. **3** E or e is an abbreviation for words beginning with e, such as 'English' and 'east'. [N-VAR] [N-VAR]

each /iːtʃ/. **1** If you refer to **each** thing or person in a group, you mean every member of it, considered as individuals. *Each book is beautifully illustrated... Each year, hundreds of animals are killed in this way.* ▶ Also a pronoun. *...two bedrooms, each with three beds.* ▶ Also an emphasizing pronoun. *We each have different needs.* ▶ Also an adverb. *The children were given one each. ...tickets at six pounds each.* ▶ Also a quantifier. *He handed each of them a page of photos. ...the machines, each of which is perhaps five feet in diameter.* [◆◆◆◆◆ DET] [PRON] [PRON] [ADV: amount ADV] [QUANT]

2 If you refer to **each one** of the members of a group, you are referring in a slightly emphatic way to each of them. *He picked up forty of these publications and read each one of them.* [QUANT PRAGMATICS]

3 You can refer to **each and every** member of a group to emphasize that you mean all the members of it. *They can't destroy truth without destroying each and every one of us.* [PHRASE PRAGMATICS]

4 You use **each other** when you are saying that each member of a group does something to the others or has a particular connection with them. *We looked at each other in silence... Both sides are willing to make allowances for each other's political sensitivities.* [PRON]

eager /'iːgə/. **1** If you are **eager** to do or have something, you want to do or have it very much. *Robert was eager to talk... I became eager for another baby... The low prices still pull in crowds of eager buyers.* ◆ **eager·ness** *...an eagerness to learn.* **2** If you look or sound **eager**, you look or sound as if you expect something interesting or enjoyable to happen. *...the crowd of eager faces around him.* ◆ **eager·ly** *'So what do you think will happen?' he asked eagerly.* ◆ **eager·ness** *...the voice of a woman speaking with breathless eagerness.* [◆◆◆◇◇ ADJ-GRADED] [N-UNCOUNT] [ADJ-GRADED] [ADV-GRADED] [N-UNCOUNT]

eagle /'iːgəl/ **eagles.** An **eagle** is a large bird that lives by eating small animals. [◆◆◇◇◇ N-COUNT]

'eagle eye, eagle eyes. If you talk about someone's **eagle eye**, you mean that they are watching someone or something carefully or are [N-COUNT]

very good at noticing things. *He did the work under the eagle eye of his teacher.* ◆ **'eagle-eyed** *...eagle-eyed police officers.* [ADJ]

ear /ɪə/ **ears. 1** Your **ears** are the two parts of your body, one on each side of your head, with which you hear sounds. See picture headed **human body**. **2** If you have an **ear** for music or language, you are able to hear its sounds accurately and to interpret them or reproduce them well. **3** The word **ear** is often used to refer to people's willingness to listen to what someone is saying. *What would cause the masses to give him a far more sympathetic ear? ...shutting their eyes and ears to everything that had been improved in South Africa.* [◆◆◆◇◇ N-COUNT] [N-SING] [N-COUNT]

4 If someone says that they are **all ears**, they mean that they are ready and eager to listen. **5** If a request **falls on deaf ears** or someone **turns a deaf ear** to it, they take no notice of it. **6** If you say that something **goes in one ear and out the other**, you mean that someone pays no attention to it, or forgets about it immediately. [PHRASE] [PHRASE] [PHRASE]

7 If you **play by ear** or **play** a piece of music **by ear**, you play it by relying on your musical instincts or your memory, rather than by reading printed music. **8** If you **play it by ear**, you decide what to say or do in a situation by responding to events rather than by following a plan which you have formed in advance. [PHRASE] [PHRASE]

9 If someone says that you will be **out on your ear**, they mean that you will be thrown out or dismissed suddenly and unpleasantly. *We never objected. We'd have been out on our ears looking for another job if we had.* **10** If you are **up to your ears** in something, it is taking up all of your time, attention, or resources. *I'm up to my ears in reports.* [PHRASE INFORMAL] [PHRASE]

11 The **ears** of a cereal plant such as wheat are the top parts of the stem, which contain the seeds or grains. **12** ● to **make a pig's ear of** something: see **pig**. ● **music** to your **ears**: see **music**. [N-COUNT]

ear·ache /'ɪəreɪk/ **earaches. Earache** is a pain in the inside part of your ear. [N-VAR]

ear·drum /'ɪədrʌm/ **eardrums;** also spelled **ear drum**. Your **eardrums** are the thin pieces of tightly stretched skin inside each ear, which vibrate when sound reaches them. [N-COUNT]

ear·ful /ˈɪəfʊl/. If you say that you got **an earful**, you mean that someone spoke angrily to you for quite an long time. — N-SING: a N; INFORMAL

earl /ɜːl/ **earls.** An **earl** is a British nobleman. — N-COUNT

earl·dom /ˈɜːldəm/ **earldoms.** An **earldom** is the rank or title of an earl. — N-COUNT

ear·li·er /ˈɜːliə/. **Earlier** is used to refer to a point or period in time before the present or before the one you are talking about. *Earlier, it had been hoped to use the indoor track. ...political reforms announced by the President earlier this year.* ▶ Also an adjective. *...earlier reports of gunshots.* — ◆◆◆◇ ADV-COMPAR; ADJ-COMPAR: ADJ n

ear·li·est /ˈɜːliɪst/. **At the earliest** means not before the date or time mentioned. *The first official results are not expected until Tuesday at the earliest.* — ◆◇◇◇ PHRASE

ear·lobe /ˈɪələʊb/ **earlobes;** also spelled **ear lobe.** Your **earlobes** are the soft parts at the bottom of your ears. See picture headed **human body.** — N-COUNT

ear·ly /ˈɜːli/ **earlier, earliest. 1 Early** means before the usual time that something happens. *I had to get up early... Why do we have to go to bed so early?* ▶ Also an adjective. *...early retirement.* — ◆◆◆◆ ADV-GRADED: ADV after v; ADJ-GRADED
2 Early means before the time that was arranged or expected. *She remembered arriving early... The first snow came a month earlier than usual.* ▶ Also an adjective. *I'm always early.* **3** You can use **as early as** to emphasize that a particular time or period is surprisingly early. *Inflation could fall back into single figures as early as this month.* — ADV-GRADED: ADV after v; ADJ-GRADED; PHRASE; PRAGMATICS
4 Early means near the beginning of a particular period of time. *...the early 1980s... She was in her early teens.* ▶ Also an adverb. *We'll hope to see you some time early next week. ...an incident which occurred much earlier in the game.* **5 Early** means near the beginning of an activity or process, when it is often not clear how the situation will develop. *...the early stages of pregnancy... The early indications look encouraging... It's too early to declare his efforts a success.* ● If you say about something that might be true that **it is early days,** you mean that it is too soon for you to be completely sure about it. *It's early days yet, but the headaches do seem to be getting better.* — ADJ-GRADED: ADJ n; ADV-GRADED; ADJ-GRADED: ADJ n; PHRASE

early-'warning. An **early-warning** system is a system which gives an advance warning that something bad is likely to happen. — ◆◇◇◇ ADJ: ADJ n

ear·mark /ˈɪəmɑːk/ **earmarks, earmarking, earmarked. 1** If money or resources **are earmarked** for a particular purpose, they are reserved for that purpose. *China has earmarked more than $20bn for oil exploration... Some of the money has been earmarked to pay for the re-settlement of people from contaminated areas.* **2** If something **has been earmarked** for closure or disposal, for example, people have decided that it will be closed or disposed of. — ◆◇◇◇ VERB: V n for n; be V-ed to-inf; Also V-ed; VERB: be V-ed for n

ear·muffs /ˈɪəmʌfs/; also spelled **ear muffs. Earmuffs** are two thick soft pieces of cloth which you wear over your ears to protect them from the cold or from loud noise. — N-PLURAL: also a pair of N

earn /ɜːn/ **earns, earning, earned. 1** If you **earn** money, you receive money in return for work that you do. *The dancers can earn anything between £50 and £100 for each session.* **2** If something **earns** money, it produces money as profit or interest. *...a current account which earns little or no interest. ...the money earned from oil imports.* **3** If you **earn** something such as praise, you get it because you deserve it. *Companies must earn a reputation for honesty... I think that's earned him very high admiration.* — ◆◆◆◇ VERB: V n; Also V; VERB: V n; V-ed; VERB: V n; V n n

earn·er /ˈɜːnə/ **earners. 1** An **earner** is someone or something that earns money or produces profit. *...a typical wage earner... Sugar is Fiji's second biggest export earner.* **2** If you refer to a job or activity as a **nice little earner,** you mean that you can make money from it easily. — ◆◇◇◇ N-COUNT; PHRASE BRITISH, INFORMAL

ear·nest /ˈɜːnɪst/. **1** If something is done **in earnest,** it is done to a much greater extent and more seriously than before. *Campaigning will begin in earnest tomorrow.* **2 Earnest** people are very serious — ◆◇◇◇ PHRASE; ADJ-GRADED

and sincere in what they say or do. *Despite their earnest efforts, they still struggle to win support.* ◆ **ear·nest·ly** *'Did you?' she asked earnestly.* ◆ **ear·nest·ness** *He was admired by many for his earnestness.* **3** If you are **in earnest,** you are sincere in what you are doing and saying. *...points made in earnest by Catholic writers.* — ADV-GRADED; N-UNCOUNT; PHRASE

ear·nest·ly /ˈɜːnɪstli/. If you **earnestly** hope or wish for something, you hope or wish strongly and sincerely for it. — ADV-GRADED: ADV before v

earn·ings /ˈɜːnɪŋz/. Your **earnings** consist of the money you earn by working. *Average weekly earnings rose by 1.5% in July.* — ◆◆◆◇ N-PLURAL

earnings-re'lated. An **earnings-related** benefit provides higher or lower payments according to the amount a person was earning while working. *...an Earnings-Related Pension Scheme.* — ADJ

ear·phone /ˈɪəfəʊn/ **earphones. Earphones** are a small piece of equipment which you wear over or inside your ears so that you can listen to a radio or cassette recorder without anybody else hearing. — N-COUNT

ear·piece /ˈɪəpiːs/ **earpieces.** The **earpiece** of a telephone receiver, hearing aid, or other device is the part that is held up to or put into your ear. — N-COUNT

ear·plug /ˈɪəplʌg/ **earplugs;** also spelled **ear plug. Earplugs** are small pieces of a soft material which you put in your ears to keep out noise or water. — N-COUNT

ear·ring /ˈɪərɪŋ/ **earrings. Earrings** are pieces of jewellery which you attach to your earlobes. — ◆◇◇◇ N-COUNT

ear·shot /ˈɪəʃɒt/. If you are **within earshot** of someone or something, you are close enough to be able to hear them. If you are **out of earshot,** you are too far away to hear them. — PHRASE

'ear-splitting. An **ear-splitting** noise is very loud. *...ear-splitting screams.* — ADJ

earth /ɜːθ/ **earths. 1 Earth** or **the Earth** is the planet on which we live. *The space shuttle Atlantis returned safely to earth. ...the Earth's crust.* **2 The earth** is the land surface on which we live and move about. *The earth shook and swayed and the walls of neighbouring houses fell around them.* **3 Earth** is the substance on the land surface of the earth in which plants grow. *The road winds for miles through parched earth.* — ◆◆◆◇ N-PROPER; N-SING: the N; N-UNCOUNT
4 On earth is used for emphasis in questions that begin with words such as 'how', 'what', or 'where'. *What on earth had Luke done?... Why on earth would he want to go to such a place?* **5 On earth** is used for emphasis after some negative noun groups, for example 'no reason'. *There is no feeling on earth like winning for the first time.* **6 On earth** is used for emphasis after a noun group that contains a superlative adjective. *He wanted to be the fastest man on earth.* — PHRASE PRAGMATICS; PHRASE PRAGMATICS; PHRASE PRAGMATICS
7 If you come **down** or **back to earth,** you have to face the reality of everyday life after a period of great excitement. *I was shocked, brought down to earth by this revelation.* **8** If you say that something **cost the earth** or that you **paid the earth** for it, you are emphasizing that it was very expensive. — PHRASE; PHRASE PRAGMATICS INFORMAL
9 The **earth** in an electric plug or appliance is a wire through which electricity can pass into the ground, making the equipment safe even if something goes wrong with it. *The earth wire was not connected.* — N-SING
10 See also **down-to-earth;** ● **hell on earth:** see **hell.** ● to **move heaven and earth:** see **heaven.** ● **salt of the earth:** see **salt.**

earth·bound /ˈɜːθbaʊnd/. **1** If something is **earthbound,** it is unable to fly, or is on the ground rather than in the air or in space. *The Hubble telescope is producing images much sharper than those of earthbound telescopes.* **2** If you describe someone or something as **earthbound,** you mean that they do not have very much imagination. — ADJ; ADJ-GRADED

earth·en /ˈɜːðən/. **1 Earthen** containers and objects are made of clay that is baked so that it becomes hard. *...an earthen jar.* **2** An **earthen** floor or mound is made of hardened or pressed earth. — ADJ: ADJ n; ADJ: ADJ n

earth·en·ware /ˈɜːðənweə/. **1 Earthenware** bowls, pots, or other objects are made of hardened, baked — ADJ: ADJ n

clay. **2** Earthenware objects are referred to as N-UNCOUNT **earthenware.** ...*Italian china and earthenware.*

earth·ling /'ɜːθlɪŋ/ **earthlings.** Some science- N-COUNT fiction writers use **earthlings** to refer to human beings who live on the planet Earth.

earth·ly /'ɜːθli/. **1 Earthly** means happening in the ◆◇◇◇ material world of our life on earth and not in any ADJ: ADJ n spiritual life or life after death. ...*the need to confront evil during the earthly life.* **2 Earthly** is used ADJ: ADJ n in phrases such as **there is no earthly reason** and PRAGMATICS **there is no earthly use** to emphasize that there is no reason at all why something should happen. *There's no earthly use saying it isn't true... What earthly reason would they have for lying?*

earth·quake /'ɜːθkweɪk/ **earthquakes.** An earth- ◆◆◇◇ quake is a shaking of the ground caused by move- N-COUNT ment of the earth's crust.

'earth-shattering. Something that is **earth-** ADJ-GRADED **shattering** is very surprising or shocking. ...*earth-shattering news.*

earth·work /'ɜːθwɜːk/ **earthworks. Earthworks** N-COUNT are large mounds of earth that were built for defence, especially in early historical periods.

earth·worm /'ɜːθwɜːm/ **earthworms.** An earth- N-COUNT worm is a kind of worm which lives in the ground.

earthy /'ɜːθi/ **earthier, earthiest. 1** If you de- ◆◇◇◇ scribe someone as **earthy**, you mean that they are ADJ-GRADED open and direct, and talk about subjects which other people avoid or feel ashamed about. ◆ **earthi-** **·ness** ...*her appealing earthiness.* **2** If you describe N-UNCOUNT something as **earthy**, you mean it looks, smells, or ADJ-GRADED feels like earth. ...*the clean earthy smell of wet clay.*

ear·wig /'ɪəwɪg/ **earwigs.** An **earwig** is a small, N-COUNT thin brown insect that has a pair of pincers at the back end of its body. See picture headed **insects.**

ease /iːz/ **eases, easing, eased. 1** If you do ◆◆◇◇ something **with ease**, you do it without difficulty or PHRASE effort. *Anne was intelligent and capable of passing her exams with ease.* **2** If you talk about the **ease of** N-UNCOUNT: a particular activity, you mean that it is easy to do N of n or has been made easier to do. *For ease of reference, only the relevant extracts of the regulations are included.* ...*the camera's ease of use.* **3 Ease** is the N-UNCOUNT state of being very comfortable and able to live as you want, without any worries or problems. *She lived a life of ease.*

4 If something unpleasant **eases** or if you **ease** it, it is V-ERG reduced in degree, speed, or intensity. *Tensions had* V eased... I gave him some brandy to ease the pain. V n ◆ **eas·ing** ...*editorials calling for the easing of sanc-* N-UNCOUNT tions. **5** If you **ease** your way somewhere or **ease** VERB somewhere, you move there slowly, carefully, and V way prep/ gently. If you **ease** something somewhere, you move adv it there slowly, carefully, and gently. *I eased my way* V prep/adv towards the door... She eased back into the chair... He V n prep/adv eased his foot off the accelerator. Also V n with adj

6 If you are **at ease**, you are feeling confident and re- PHRASE laxed, and are able to talk to people without feeling anxious. If you put someone **at their ease**, you make them feel at ease. **7 'At ease'** or **'Stand at ease'** is an or- PHRASE der given to soldiers to stand with their feet apart and PRAGMATICS their hands behind their backs. **8** If you are **ill at ease,** PHRASE you feel rather uncomfortable or anxious.

ease off. If something **eases off**, or someone or PHRASAL VB something **eases** it **off**, it is reduced in speed or inten- ERG sity. *These days, the pressure has eased off... There is* V P *very little braking effect from the engine when you ease* V P noun *off the power.* Also V n P

ease up. 1 If something **eases up**, it is reduced in PHRASAL VB speed or intensity. *The rain had eased up.* **2** If you V P **ease up**, you start to make less effort. *He told support-* V P *ers not to ease up even though he's leading in the presidential race.* **3** If you **ease up** on someone or V P on n something, your behaviour or attitude towards them INFORMAL becomes less severe or strict. *The manager does not intend to ease up on his players.*

easel /'iːzəl/ **easels.** An **easel** is a wooden frame N-COUNT that supports a picture which an artist is painting or drawing.

easi·ly /'iːzɪli/. **1** You use **easily** to emphasize that ◆◆◇◇ something is very likely to happen or be true. *It* ADV-GRADED *could easily be another year before the economy* PRAGMATICS *starts to show some improvement.* ...*an ancient barn that is easily the length of two tennis courts.* **2** You ADV-GRADED: use **easily** to say that something happens more ADV after v quickly or more often than is usual or normal. *He had always cried very easily.* **3** See also **easy.**

east /iːst/; **East** is one of the four points of the ◆◆◆◆◆ compass. See Appendix headed **Compass.**

east·bound /'iːstbaʊnd/. See Appendix headed **Compass.**

East·er /'iːstə/ **Easters. Easter** is a Christian festi- ◆◇◇◇ val and holiday in March or April, when the resur- N-VAR rection of Jesus Christ is celebrated. *They usually have a walking holiday at Easter.* ...*Easter Sunday.*

'Easter egg, Easter eggs. An **Easter egg** is a N-COUNT chocolate egg that is given as a present at Easter.

east·er·ly /'iːstəli/. See Appendix headed **Compass.**

east·ern /'iːstən/. See Appendix headed **Compass.** ◆◆◆◇

east·ern·er /'iːstənə/ **easterners.** See Appendix headed **Compass.**

east·ern·most /'iːstənməʊst/. See Appendix head- ed **Compass.**

east·ward /'iːstwəd/. See Appendix headed **Com- pass.**

easy /'iːzi/ **easier, easiest. 1** If a job or action is ◆◆◆◆◇ **easy**, you can do it without difficulty or effort, be- ADJ-GRADED cause it is not complicated and causes no problems. *The shower is easy to install... This is not an easy task... The home is situated within easy access of shops.* ◆ **easi·ly** *Dress your child in layers of clothes* ADV-GRADED *you can remove easily.* **2** If you say that something is ADJ-GRADED: **easy** or too **easy**, you are criticizing someone be- v-link ADJ cause you think they have done the least difficult PRAGMATICS thing, and have not considered the situation carefully enough. *That's easy for you to say... It was all too easy to believe it.* **3** If you describe someone or ADJ-GRADED: something as **easy prey** or as an **easy target**, you ADJ n mean that they can easily be attacked or criticized. *Tourists have become easy prey... The World Bank, with its poor environmental record, is an easy target for blame.* **4** If you say that something is **easier said** PHRASE **than done**, you mean that although it sounds like a good idea in theory, you think it would be difficult to actually do it. *Avoiding mosquito bites is easier said than done.*

5 If you describe an action or activity as **easy**, you ADJ-GRADED mean that it is done in a confident, relaxed way, with- out any anxiety. If someone is **easy** about something, they feel relaxed and confident about it. ...*making easy conversation with people she has never met be- fore... He was an easy person to talk to..* ◆ **easily** *They* ADV-GRADED: *talked amiably and easily about a range of topics.* **6** If ADV with v you say that someone has an **easy** life, you mean that ADJ-GRADED they live comfortably without any worries. **7** If some- PHRASE one tells you to **take it easy** or **take things easy**, they PRAGMATICS mean that you should relax and not do very much. INFORMAL

8 You use **easy** in expressions such as **easy on the eye** ADJ-GRADED: or **easy on the ear** when you are describing things that v-link ADJ on are pleasant and do not need much effort to be en- the n joyed or done. *The layout should be clear and easy on the eye.* ...*exercise that's easy on the joints.* **9** If you say CONVENTION **'Easy does it'**, you are telling someone to be careful SPOKEN and not to use too much effort, especially when they are moving something large and awkward. **10** If you PHRASE tell someone to **go easy on** something, you are telling INFORMAL them to use only a small amount of it. **11** If you tell PHRASE someone to **go easy on**, or **be easy on**, a particular PRAGMATICS person, you are telling them not to punish or treat INFORMAL that person very severely. *This agency has been far too easy on the timber industry over the years.*

12 See also **easily.**

'easy chair, easy chairs. An **easy chair** is a large, N-COUNT comfortable padded chair.

,easy-'going. If you describe someone as **easy-** ◆◇◇◇ **going**, you mean that they are not easily annoyed, ADJ-GRADED worried, or upset; used showing approval. PRAGMATICS

eat /iːt/ **eats, eating, ate, eaten. 1** When you VERB: V n **eat** something, you put it into your mouth, chew it, beV-ed V

E

and swallow it. *The bananas should be eaten within two days... We took our time and ate slowly.* **2** If you **eat** sensibly or healthily, you eat food that is good for you. **3** When you **eat**, you have a meal. *Let's go out to eat... We ate lunch together a few times.* **4** If something **is eating** you, it is annoying or worrying you. *What the hell's eating you?* **5** If you have someone **eating out of** your **hand**, they are completely under your control. **6** You can use expressions like '**eat your heart out** Mozart' when you are joking that you can do something better than the person named, or suggesting that they would be jealous of you. *One of my driving faults is speeding. Eat your heart out, Nigel Mansell!*

7 • to **be eaten alive**: see **alive**. **•** to **have** your **cake and eat it**: see **cake**. **•** **dog eat dog**: see **dog**. **•** to **eat humble pie**: see **humble**.

eat away. If one thing **eats away** another or **eats away** at another, it gradually destroys or uses it up. *Water pours through the roof, encouraging rot to eat away the interior of the house... The recession is eating away at their revenues.*

eat into. 1 If something **eats into** your time or resources, it uses them, when they should be used for other things. *Wages were rising faster than productivity and this was eating into profits.* **2** If a substance such as acid or rust **eats into** something, it destroys or damages its surface.

eat up. 1 When you **eat up** your food, you eat all of it. *Some seed fell along the footpath, and the birds came and ate it up.* **2** If something **eats up** time or resources, it uses them or consumes them in great quantities. *Health insurance costs are eating up his income.*

eat·en /'iːtən/. **Eaten** is the past participle of **eat**.

ˌeaten 'up. If someone is **eaten up with** jealousy, curiosity, or desire, they feel it very intensely.

eat·er /'iːtə/ **eaters.** You use the word **eater** to refer to someone who eats in a particular way or who eats particular kinds of food. *...meat eaters.*

eat·ery /'iːtəri/ **eateries.** An **eatery** is a place where you can buy and eat food. *...one of the most elegant old eateries in town.*

'eating apple, eating apples. An **eating apple** is an apple that is eaten raw rather than cooked.

eau de co·logne /ˌəʊ də kə'ləʊn/. **Eau de cologne** is a fairly weak, sweet-smelling perfume.

eaves /iːvz/. The **eaves** of a house are the lower edges of its roof. See picture headed **house and flat**.

eaves·drop /'iːvzdrɒp/ **eavesdrops, eavesdropping, eavesdropped.** If you **eavesdrop**, you listen secretly to what someone is saying. *The government illegally eavesdropped on his telephone conversations.* **♦ eaves·drop·per, eavesdroppers.** **♦ eaves·drop·ping.**

ebb /eb/ **ebbs, ebbing, ebbed. 1** When the tide or the sea **ebbs**, its level gradually falls. **2** The **ebb** or the **ebb** tide is one of the regular periods when the sea gradually falls to a lower level. **3** If a feeling or force **ebbs**, it becomes weaker and gradually disappears. *...as a man's physical strength ebbs.* **▶ Ebb away** means the same as **ebb**. *His little girl's life ebbed away.* **4** If someone or something is at **a low ebb** or at their **lowest ebb**, they are not being very successful or profitable. *Everyone is tired and at a low ebb.* **5** You can use **ebb and flow** to describe the way that something repeatedly increases and decreases or rises and falls. *...the ebb and flow of feeling and moods.*

eb·ony /'ebəni/. **1** Ebony is a very hard, heavy, dark-coloured wood. *...a small ebony cabinet.* **2** Ebony is a very deep black colour. *...soft ebony hair.*

ebul·lient /ɪ'bʌliənt, -'bʊl-/. If you describe someone as **ebullient**, you mean that they are lively and full of enthusiasm or excitement about something. *...the ebullient Russian President.* **♦ ebul·lience** /ɪ'bʌliəns, -'bʊl-/ *...his natural ebullience.*

ec·cen·tric /ɪk'sentrɪk/ **eccentrics.** If you say that someone is **eccentric**, you mean that they have habits or opinions that other people find strange.

He is an eccentric character. ...Mr Thomas, a businessman with eccentric views. **▶** An **eccentric** is an eccentric person. **♦ ec·cen·tri·cal·ly** /ɪk'sentrɪkli/ *...painters, eccentrically dressed and already half drunk.* **♦ ec·cen·tri·city** /ˌeksen'trɪsɪti/ **eccentricities** *...a performer noted for his eccentricity... We all have our eccentricities.*

ec·cle·si·as·ti·cal /ɪˌkliːzi'æstɪkəl/. **Ecclesiastical** means belonging to or connected with the Christian Church. *...the ecclesiastical hierarchy.*

ECG, ECGs /ˌiː siː 'dʒiː/. If someone has an **ECG**, doctors use special equipment to measure the electric currents produced by that person's heart in order to see whether it is working normally. **ECG** is an abbreviation for **electrocardiogram**.

eche·lon /'eʃəlɒn/ **echelons. 1** An **echelon** in an organization or society is a level or rank in it. *...the lower echelons of society.* **2** An **echelon** is a military formation in which soldiers, vehicles, ships, or aircraft follow each other but are spaced out sideways so that they can see ahead.

echo /'ekəʊ/ **echoes, echoing, echoed. 1** An **echo** is a sound which is caused by a noise being reflected off a surface such as a wall. *He listened and heard nothing but the echoes of his own voice.* **2** If sounds **echo**, or a place **echoes** with sounds, the sounds are reflected off a surface there and can be heard again. *The bang came suddenly, echoing across the buildings... The corridor echoed with the barking of a dozen dogs. ...the echoing hall.* **3** If you **echo** someone's words, you repeat them or express agreement with them. *Many phrases in the last two chapters echo earlier passages.* **4** An **echo** is an expression of an attitude or feeling which has already been expressed. *Political attacks work only if they find an echo with voters.*

éclair /ɪ'kleə, AM eɪk-/ **éclairs.** An **éclair** is a long thin cake made of light pastry, filled with cream and topped with chocolate.

ec·lec·tic /ɪ'klektɪk/. If you describe a collection of objects, ideas, or beliefs as **eclectic**, you mean that they are wide-ranging and come from many different sources. **♦ ec·lec·ti·cism** /ɪ'klektɪsɪzəm/ *...her cultural eclecticism.*

eclipse /ɪ'klɪps/ **eclipses, eclipsing, eclipsed. 1** When there is an **eclipse** of the sun or **solar eclipse**, the moon is between the earth and the sun, so that part or all of the sun is hidden. When there is an **eclipse** of the moon or **lunar eclipse**, the earth is between the sun and the moon, so that part or all of the moon is hidden. **2** If one thing **is eclipsed** by a second thing that is bigger, newer, or more important, the first thing is no longer noticed because the second thing gets all the attention. *Nothing is going to eclipse winning the Olympic title.*

eco- /'iːkəʊ-/. **Eco-** combines with nouns and adjectives to form other nouns and adjectives which describe something as being related to ecology. *...the eco-friendly image of cycling. ...the eco-horror of the North Sea oil spill.*

eco·logi·cal /ˌiːkə'lɒdʒɪkəl/. **1** Ecological means involved with or concerning ecology. *...Siberia's delicate ecological balance. ...ecological disasters.* **♦ eco·logi·cal·ly** /ˌiːkə'lɒdʒɪkli/ *It is economical to run and ecologically sound.* **2** Ecological groups consist of people who are concerned with the preservation of the environment and natural resources. **♦ ecolo·gist** /ɪ'kɒlədʒɪst/ **ecologists** *...the new Ecologist Party.*

ecol·ogy /ɪ'kɒlədʒi/. **1** Ecology is the study of the relationships between plants, animals, people, and their environment. **♦ ecolo·gist** *...an ecologist who visited Sri Lanka to study endangered animals.* **2** If you talk about the **ecology** of a place, you are referring to relationships between plants, animals, people, and the environment in that place. *...the extinction of the marshes' unique ecology.*

eco·nom·ic /ˌiːkə'nɒmɪk, ˌek-/. **1** Economic means concerned with the organization of the money, industry, and trade of a country, region, or soci-

ety. ...*Poland's radical economic reforms.* ...*economic growth.* ♦ **eco·nomi·cal·ly** /ˌiːkəˈnɒmɪkli, ˌek-/ ADV-GRADED ...*an economically depressed area.* **2** If something is **economic**, it produces a profit. *The new system may be more economic.*

eco·nomi·cal /ˌiːkəˈnɒmɪkəl, ek-/. **1** Something ◆◇◇◇ that is **economical** does not require a lot of money ADJ-GRADED to operate. *It is more economical to wash a full load of clothes.* ♦ **economically** *Services could be oper-* ADV-GRADED: ADV after v *ated more efficiently and economically.* **2** Someone ADJ-GRADED who is **economical** spends money sensibly and tries not to waste it on unnecessary things. **3** Economi- ADJ-GRADED cal means using the minimum amount of time, effort, or language that is necessary. *His gestures were economical.* ♦ **eco·nomi·cal·ly** ...*Burn's novel, viv-* ADV-GRADED: *idly and economically written.* ADV -ed

eco·nom·ics /ˌiːkəˈnɒmɪks, ek-/. **1** Economics is ◆◆◇◇ the study of the way in which money, industry, and N-UNCOUNT trade are organized in a society. ♦ **econo·mist** N-COUNT /ɪˈkɒnəmɪst/ ...*the monetarist econo-* *mist, Professor Alan Walters.* **2** The **economics** of a N-UNCOUNT society or industry is the system of organizing money and trade in it. ...*the economics of the third world.* **3** See also **home economics**.

econo·mize /ɪˈkɒnəmaɪz/ **economizes, econo-** VERB: V **mizing, economized;** also spelled **economise** in V on n British English. If you **economize**, you save money by spending it more carefully. *Hollywood has been talking about economizing on movie budgets.*

econo·my /ɪˈkɒnəmi/ **economies. 1** A country's ◆◆◆◆ **economy** is the way that money, business, industry, N-COUNT and trade are organized there. ...*Africa's most indus-* *trialised economy...* *The Japanese economy grew at an annual rate of more than 10 per cent.*

2 Economy is the use of the minimum amount of N-UNCOUNT: money, time, or other resources needed to achieve with supp something. ...*improvements in the fuel economy of cars...* *I have never known such economy with words.* **3** If you make **economies**, you try to save money by N-COUNT not spending money on unnecessary things. **4** Economy services such as travel are cheap and have ADJ: ADJ n no luxuries or extras. *Travelling economy class costs 200 marks.* **5** Economy can be used to describe large ADJ: ADJ n packages of goods which are cheaper than buying the same goods in normal-sized packages. ...*an economy pack containing 150 assorted screws.* **6** If you describe PHRASE an attempt to save money as a **false economy**, you mean that you have not saved any money as you will have to spend a lot more later. *A cheap bed can be a false economy.*

eco·sys·tem /ˈiːkəʊsɪstəm, AM ˈekə-/ **ecosys-** ◆◇◇◇ **tems.** An **ecosystem** is all the plants and animals N-COUNT that live in a particular area together with the rela- TECHNICAL tionship that exists between them and their environment.

ec·sta·sy /ˈekstəsi/ **ecstasies. 1** Ecstasy is a feel- ◆◇◇◇ ing of very great happiness. ...*a state of almost reli-* N-VAR *gious ecstasy.* ...*the agony and ecstasy of holiday ro-* *mance.* **2** If you are in **ecstasy** about something, PHRASE you are very excited about it. *She went into ecstasies over actors.* **3** Ecstasy is an illegal drug which acts N-UNCOUNT as a stimulant and can cause hallucinations.

ec·stat·ic /ekˈstætɪk/. If you are **ecstatic**, or have ◆◇◇◇ an **ecstatic** reaction to something, you feel very ADJ-GRADED happy, excited, or enthusiastic about something. ...*the cheers of an ecstatic crowd...* *The production received ecstatic reviews.* ♦ **ec·stati·cal·ly** ADV-GRADED /ekˈstætɪkli/ ...*ecstatically happy.*

ecu /ˈeɪkjuː/ **ecus.** The **ecu** is a unit of money used ◆◆◇◇ for accounting purposes by the European Union's N-COUNT financial institutions, although it is not yet used as currency in any country. **Ecu** is an abbreviation for 'European Currency Unit'.

ecu·meni·cal /ˌiːkjuːˈmenɪkəl, ˌek-/. **Ecumenical** ADJ activities, ideas, and movements try to unite differ- FORMAL ent Christian Churches. ...*ecumenical church services.*

ec·ze·ma /ˈeksmə, AM ɪgˈziːmə/. Eczema is an un- ◆◇◇◇ comfortable skin condition which makes your skin N-UNCOUNT itch and become sore and broken.

-ed. Pronounced /-ɪd/ after /t/ or /d/, and /-t/ after one of the following sounds: /p, f, θ, s, tʃ, ʃ, k/. In other cases, it is pronounced /-d/. **1** -ed is added to SUFFIX verbs to form their past tense or their past partici- ple. *I posted the letter... He danced well... 'I quite understand,' he replied.* **2** -ed is added to nouns to SUFFIX form adjectives that describe someone or some- thing as having a particular feature or features. ...*a fat, bearded man.* ...*coloured flags.* **3** -ed is added SUFFIX to nouns or verbs combined with other words, to form compound adjectives. ...*a cone-shaped con- tainer.* ...*green-tinted glasses.*

ed., eds. ed. is a written abbreviation for **editor.** ◆◆◇◇

eddy /ˈedi/ **eddies, eddying, eddied. 1** An eddy N-COUNT is a rapid, circular movement in water or in the air. VERB **2** To **eddy** means to move round and round in vari- V ous directions. *The dust whirled and eddied in the* LITERARY *sunlight.*

edge /edʒ/ **edges, edging, edged. 1** The edge of ◆◆◆◇ something is the place or line where it stops, or the N-COUNT part of it that is furthest from the middle. *We were on a hill, right on the edge of town... She was stand- ing at the water's edge.* ♦ **-edged** ...*shallow-edged* COMB *lakes.* **2** The **edge** of something sharp such as a N-COUNT knife or an axe is its sharp or narrow side. ...*the sharp edge of the sword.* ♦ **-edged** ...*a blunt-edged* COMB *knife.* **3** The **edge** of something, especially some- N-SING thing bad, is the point at which it may start to hap- pen. *They have driven the rhino to the edge of ex- tinction... She was on the edge of tears.*

4 If someone or something **edges** somewhere, they VERB move very slowly in that direction. *He edged closer to* V prep/adv *the telephone.*

5 If someone or something has an **edge**, they have an N-SING advantage that makes them more likely to be success- ful than another thing or person. *The three days France have to prepare could give them the edge over England... Through superior production techniques they were able to gain the competitive edge.* **6** If you say N-SING: that something has **an edge**, you like it because it ex- aN presses an emotion or idea powerfully and unsentimentally. *I like any music with enthusiasm and an edge to it.* ♦ **-edged** ...*sharp-edged satire.* COMB

7 An **edge** to someone's voice is a quality of sharp- N-SING ness, bitterness, or controlled emotion in it. *Under- neath the humour is an edge of bitterness.*

8 If you or your nerves are **on edge**, you are tense, PHRASE nervous, and unable to relax. **9** If you say that some- PHRASE one is **on the edge of** their **seat** or **chair**, you mean that they are very excited by what is happening or what is going to happen. **10** If you say that a person or PHRASE a piece of entertainment has **rough edges**, you mean that they have some small faults, although generally you approve of them. *The show, despite some rough edges, was an instant success.* **11** If something takes PHRASE **the edge off** a situation or feeling, it makes it less pow- erful or intense. *Drink took the edge off my fear.* **12** See also **edged; cutting edge, double-edged, hard-edged, knife-edge, leading edge.** ● to set your **teeth on edge**: see **tooth.**

edge out. If someone **edges out** someone else, they PHRASAL VB just manage to beat them or get in front of them in a V P noun contest. *Germany and France edged out the British* V n P of n *team by less than a second... McGregor's effort was* Also V n P *enough to edge Johnson out of the top spot.*

edged /edʒd/. If something is **edged** with a par- ◆◆◇◇ ticular thing, that thing forms a border around it. ADJ: ...*a large lawn edged with flowers.* ...*blank pages* v-link ADJ *edged in black.* ► Also a combining form. ...*a lace-* COMB *edged handkerchief.* ♦ **edg·ing, edgings.** Edging N-VAR is material that something is edged with. ...*the satin edging on Randall's blanket.*

edge·ways /ˈedʒweɪz/. The form **edgewise,** PHRASE /ˈedʒwaɪz/, is used in American English. If you say PRAGMATICS that you **cannot get a word in edgeways**, you are INFORMAL complaining that you do not have the opportunity to speak because someone else is talking so much.

edgy /ˈedʒi/ **edgier, edgiest.** If someone is **edgy,** ◆◇◇◇ they are nervous and anxious, and seem likely to ADJ-GRADED lose control of themselves. INFORMAL

ed·ible /'edɪbəl/. If something is **edible**, it is safe to eat and not poisonous. ...*edible fungi.* ◆◇◇◇◇ ADJ

edict /'iːdɪkt/ **edicts.** An **edict** is a command or instruction given by someone in authority. *He issued an edict that none of his writings be destroyed.* ◆◇◇◇◇ N-COUNT FORMAL

edi·fi·ca·tion /,edɪfɪ'keɪʃən/. If something is done for your **edification**, it is done to benefit you in some way. N-UNCOUNT FORMAL

edi·fice /'edɪfɪs/ **edifices. 1** An **edifice** is a large and impressive building. ...*a list of historic edifices.* **2** You can describe a system of beliefs or a traditional institution as an **edifice**. ...*an edifice of British constitutional tradition.* ◆◇◇◇◇ N-COUNT FORMAL N-COUNT FORMAL

edi·fy·ing /'edɪfaɪɪŋ/. **1** If you describe something as **edifying**, you mean that it improves your knowledge or wisdom. *Art was seen, along with music and poetry, as something edifying.* **2** You say that something is not very **edifying** when you want to suggest that there is something unpleasant or unacceptable about it. ...*memories of a not very edifying past.* ADJ-GRADED FORMAL ADJ-GRADED: with brd-neg PRAGMATICS

edit /'edɪt/ **edits, editing, edited. 1** If you **edit** a text such as an article or a book, you correct and adapt it, often by cutting parts of it, so that it is suitable for publishing. ...*an edited version of the speech.* ♦ **edit·ing** *Throughout the editing of this book, we have had much support and encouragement.* **2** If you **edit** a book or a series of books, you collect several pieces of writing by different authors and prepare them for publishing. ...*a collection of essays, edited by Toni Morrison.* ♦ **editing** *Despite some artful editing, the anthology is weak.* **3** If you **edit** a film or a television or radio programme, you choose some of what has been filmed or recorded and arrange it in a particular order. *He taught me to edit and splice film... He is editing together excerpts of some of his films.* ♦ **editing** *He sat in on much of the filming and early editing.* **4** Someone who **edits** a newspaper, magazine, or journal is in charge of it. ♦ **editing** *He took over the editing of the magazine.* **5** An **edit** is the process of examining and correcting a text so that it is suitable for publishing. *The purpose of the edit is fairly simple.* ◆◆◆◇◇ VERB: V n V-ed N-UNCOUNT VERB: V n V-ed N-UNCOUNT VERB V n with together VERB: V n N-UNCOUNT N-COUNT TECHNICAL

edit out. If you **edit** something **out** of a book or film, you remove it. *Her voice will be edited out of the final film... She edited that line out.* PHRASAL VB V P noun V n P

edi·tion /ɪ'dɪʃən/ **editions. 1** An **edition** is a particular version of a book, magazine, or newspaper that is printed at one time. *This is the second edition of a popular book.* ...*a paperback edition.* **2** An **edition** is a single television or radio programme that is one of a series about a particular subject. *They appeared on an edition of BBC2's Arena.* ◆◆◆◇ N-COUNT N-COUNT: with supp

edi·tor /'edɪtə/ **editors. 1** An **editor** is the person who is in charge of a newspaper or magazine and who decides what will be published in it. *Tarmu Tammerk is the editor of the Baltic Independent.* **2** An **editor** is a journalist who is responsible for a particular section of a newspaper or magazine, or for a particular aspect of radio or television news. *Our economics editor, Dominic Harrod, reports.* **3** An **editor** is a person who checks and corrects texts before they are published. **4** An **editor** is a person who prepares a film, or a radio or television programme, by selecting some of what has been filmed or recorded and putting it in a particular order. *She had worked at 20th Century Fox as a film editor.* **5** An **editor** is a person who collects pieces of writing by different authors and prepares them for publication in a book or a series of books. *Michael Rosen is the editor of the anthology.* **6** An **editor** is a computer program that enables you to make alterations and corrections to stored data. ◆◆◆◇ N-COUNT N-COUNT: supp N N-COUNT N-COUNT N-COUNT N-COUNT

edi·to·rial /,edɪ'tɔːriəl/ **editorials. 1 Editorial** means involved in preparing a newspaper, magazine, or book for publication. ...*the editorial staff of 'Private Eye'.* ♦ **edi·to·ri·al·ly** *Rosie Boycott was not involved editorially with Virago.* **2 Editorial** means involving the attitudes, opinions, and content of something such as a newspaper, magazine, or television programme. *We are not about to change our editorial policy.* ♦ **editorially** *The state television stations are editorially independent.* **3** An **editorial** is an article in a newspaper which gives the opinion of the editor or publisher on a topic. *In an editorial, The Independent suggests the victory could turn nasty.* ◆◆◆◇◇ ADJ: ADJ n ADV ADJ: ADJ n ADV N-COUNT

edi·to·ri·al·ize /,edɪ'tɔːriəlaɪz/ **editorializes, editorializing, editorialized;** also spelled **editorialise** in British English. If someone, especially a journalist, **editorializes**, they express their opinion about something rather than just stating facts. VERB: V

edi·tor·ship /'edɪtəʃɪp/ **editorships.** The **editorship** of a newspaper or magazine is the position of its editor, or his or her work as its editor. *Under his editorship, the Economist has introduced regular sports coverage.* N-VAR

edu·cate /'edʒukeɪt/ **educates, educating, educated. 1** When someone, especially a child, is **educated**, he or she is taught at a school or college. *He was educated at Haslingden Grammar School.* **2** To **educate** people means to improve their understanding of a particular problem or issue. ...*to educate people about the destructive effects of alcohol abuse.* ◆◆◇◇ VB: usu passive be V-ed VERB V n

edu·cat·ed /'edʒukeɪtɪd/. An **educated** person has a high standard of learning or knowledge. ◆◆◇◇ ADJ-GRADED

-educated /-'edʒukeɪtɪd/. **1 -educated** combines with nouns and adjectives to form adjectives indicating where someone was educated. ...*the Oxford-educated son of a Liverpool merchant.* **2 -educated** combines with adverbs to form adjectives indicating how much education someone has had. *Many of the immigrants are well-educated.* COMB COMB

,educated 'guess, educated guesses. An **educated guess** is a guess which is based on a certain amount of knowledge and is likely to be correct. N-COUNT

edu·ca·tion /,edʒu'keɪʃən/ **educations. 1 Education** means learning and teaching. *They're cutting funds for education... Paul prolonged his education.* ♦ **edu·ca·tion·al** ...*pupils with special educational needs.* ♦ **edu·ca·tion·al·ly** *They're socially and educationally disadvantaged.* **2 Education** of a particular kind involves teaching the public about a particular issue. ...*better health education.* **3** See also **adult education, further education, higher education.** ◆◆◆◆◆ N-VAR ADJ ADV N-UNCOUNT

edu·ca·tion·al /,edʒu'keɪʃənəl/. An **educational** experience teaches you something. ...*an enjoyable and educational day.* ● See also **education.** ◆◇◇◇ ADJ-GRADED

edu·ca·tion·al·ist /,edʒu'keɪʃənəlɪst/ **educationalists.** An **educationalist** is a specialist in the theories and methods of education. The usual American word is **educator.** N-COUNT BRITISH

edu·ca·tion·ist /,edʒu'keɪʃənɪst/ **educationists.** An **educationist** is the same as an **educationalist.** N-COUNT BRITISH

edu·ca·tive /'edʒukətɪv, AM -keɪt-/. Something that has an **educative** role teaches you something. ...*an educative and moving experience.* ADJ-GRADED FORMAL

edu·ca·tor /'edʒukeɪtə/ **educators. 1** An **educator** is a teacher. **2** An **educator** is a specialist in the theories and methods of education. The usual British word is **educationalist.** N-COUNT N-COUNT AMERICAN

Ed·ward·ian /ed'wɔːdiən/. **Edwardian** means connected with or typical of Britain in the first decade of the 20th century, when Edward VII was King. ...*the Edwardian era.* ...*a baggy Edwardian suit.* ◆◇◇◇ ADJ

eel /iːl/ **eels.** An **eel** is a long, thin fish that looks like a snake. ► **Eel** is the flesh of this fish which is eaten as food. ...*smoked eel.* ◆◆◇◇ N-VAR N-UNCOUNT

eerie /'ɪəri/ **eerier, eeriest.** If you describe something as **eerie**, you mean that it seems strange and makes you feel nervous. *I walked down the eerie dark path.* ♦ **eeri·ly** /'ɪərɪli/ *Monrovia after the fighting is eerily quiet.* ◆◇◇◇ ADJ-GRADED ADV-GRADED

ef·face /ɪ'feɪs/ **effaces, effacing, effaced.** If someone or something **effaces** something, they destroy or remove it so that it becomes forgotten. ...*an event that has helped efface the country's traditional image.* ● See also **self-effacing.** VERB V n FORMAL

ef·fect /ɪˈfekt/ **effects, effecting, effected.** ◆◆◆◆◆ N-VAR
1 The **effect** of one thing on another is the change that the first thing causes in the second thing. *Parents worry about the effect of music on their adolescent's behavior... Head injuries can cause long-lasting psychological effects. ...cause and effect.* **2** An N-COUNT **effect** is an impression that a speaker, artist, or designer deliberately creates by their style. *The whole effect is cool, light and airy.* **3** The **effects** in a film N-PLURAL are the specially created sounds and scenery. **4** If PHRASE you say that someone is doing something **for effect**, you mean that they are doing it in order to impress people and to draw attention to themselves. *Jock paused for effect... The Cockney accent was put on for effect.*
5 If you **put** a plan or idea **into effect** or **bring** or **carry** PHRASE it **into effect**, you cause it to happen in practice. *These and other such measures ought to have been put into effect in 1985.* **6** If a law or policy **takes effect** or **comes** PHRASE **into effect** at a particular time, it officially begins to apply or be valid from that time. *...new logging permits which will take effect from July.* **7** You can say PHRASE that something **takes effect** when it starts to produce the results that are intended. *International sanctions were beginning to take effect.* **8** If you say that some- PHRASE thing will happen **with immediate effect** or **with ef-** BRITISH, **fect** from a particular time, you mean that it will begin FORMAL to happen immediately or from the stated time. *The price of the Saturday edition is going up with effect from 3 November.*
9 You use **effect** in expressions such as **to good effect** PHRASE and **to no effect** in order to indicate how successful or impressive an action is. *Mr Charles complained, to no effect.* **10** You add **in effect** to a statement which you PHRASE feel is a reasonable description or summary of some- PRAGMATICS thing. *That deal would create, in effect, the world's biggest airline.*
11 You use **to this effect** or **to that effect** to refer back PHRASE to something that you have already mentioned or ex- PRAGMATICS plained. *A circular to this effect will be issued in the next few weeks.* **12** You use **to the effect that** to indi- PHRASE cate that you are giving a summary of something that PRAGMATICS was said or written, and not the actual words used. *...a Chinese proverb to the effect that you should never wish ill on your neighbour.*
13 A person's **effects** are the things that they have N-PLURAL; with them at a particular time, for example when they with poss die, are admitted to hospital, or are arrested. FORMAL
14 If you **effect** something that you are trying to VERB achieve, you succeed in causing it to happen. *...pros-* V n *pects for effecting real political change.* **15** See also FORMAL **greenhouse effect, placebo effect, side-effect, sound effect, special effect.**

ef·fec·tive /ɪˈfektɪv/. **1** Something that is **effective** ◆◆◆◆◇ works well and produces the results that were in- ADJ-GRADED tended. *We could be more effective in encouraging students to enter teacher training... Simple antibiotics are effective against this organism. ...an effective public transport system.* ♦ **ef·fec·tive·ly** *...the team* ADV-GRADED *roles which you believe to be necessary for the team to function effectively.* ♦ **ef·fec·tive·ness** *...the ef-* N-UNCOUNT *fectiveness of computers as an educational tool.* ADJ: ADJ n **2 Effective** means having a particular role or result in practice, though not officially or in theory. *They have had effective control of the area since. ...in an effective increase on one of their most popular excursion fares.* **3** When something such as a law or an ADJ: agreement becomes **effective**, it begins officially to v-link ADJ apply or be valid.

ef·fec·tive·ly /ɪˈfektɪvli/. You use **effectively** with ◆◇◇◇ a statement which you feel is a reasonable descrip- ADV tion or summary of a particular situation. *This effec-* PRAGMATICS *tively means that the government does not agree... The region was effectively independent.*

ef·fec·tual /ɪˈfektʃuəl/. If an action or plan is **effec-** ADJ-GRADED **tual**, it succeeds in producing the results that were FORMAL intended.

ef·femi·nate /ɪˈfemɪnət/. If you describe a man or ADJ-GRADED boy as **effeminate**, you disapprove of him because PRAGMATICS you think he behaves or looks like a woman or girl.

ef·fer·ves·cent /ˌefəˈvesənt/. **1** An **effervescent** ADJ liquid contains or releases bubbles of gas. **2** If you ADJ-GRADED describe someone as **effervescent**, you mean that they are lively, enthusiastic, and exciting. *...an effer- vescent blonde actress.* ♦ **ef·fer·ves·cence** *...his* N-UNCOUNT *effervescence, magnetism and commitment.*

ef·fete /ɪˈfiːt/. If you describe someone as **effete**, ADJ-GRADED you are criticizing them for being weak and ineffec- PRAGMATICS tive. *...effete Russian gentry of the 1840s.* FORMAL

ef·fi·ca·cious /ˌefɪˈkeɪʃəs/. If something is **effica-** ADJ-GRADED **cious**, it succeeds in producing the results that were FORMAL intended. *The nasal spray was new on the market and highly efficacious.*

ef·fi·ca·cy /ˈefɪkəsi/. The **efficacy** of something is ◆◇◇◇◇ its effectiveness in producing the results that were N-UNCOUNT intended. FORMAL

ef·fi·cien·cy /ɪˈfɪʃənsi/. **1 Efficiency** is the quality ◆◆◇◇◇ of being able to do a task successfully, without N-UNCOUNT wasting time or energy. *They marvelled at her effi- ciency. ...energy efficiency.* **2 Efficiency** is the differ- N-UNCOUNT: ence between the amount of energy a machine also N in pl needs to make it work, and the amount it produces. TECHNICAL

ef·fi·cient /ɪˈfɪʃənt/. If something or someone is ◆◆◆◇◇ **efficient**, they are able to do tasks successfully, ADJ-GRADED without wasting time or energy. *...today's more effi- cient contraception.* ♦ **ef·fi·cient·ly** *I work very ef-* ADV-GRADED *ficiently and am decisive.*

ef·fi·gy /ˈefɪdʒi/ **effigies. 1** An **effigy** is a roughly N-COUNT made figure that represents someone you dislike. **2** An **effigy** is a statue or carving of a famous N-COUNT person. FORMAL

eff·ing /ˈefɪŋ/. Some people use **effing** to empha- ADJ: ADJ n size a word or phrase, especially when they are feel- PRAGMATICS ing angry or annoyed; an offensive word. BRITISH

ef·flu·ent /ˈefluənt/ **effluents. Effluent** is liquid N-VAR waste that comes out of factories or sewage works. FORMAL

ef·fort /ˈefət/ **efforts. 1** If you make an **effort** to ◆◆◆◆◆ do something, you try very hard to do it. *He made* N-VAR *no effort to hide his disappointment... Finding a cure requires considerable time and effort. ...his efforts to reform and revitalise Italian research.* **2** If you PHRASE **make the effort** to do something, you do it, even though you need extra energy to do it or you do not really want to. *I don't get lonely now because I make the effort to see people.*
3 If you say that someone did something with **effort** N-UNCOUNT or with **an effort**, you mean it was difficult for them to WRITTEN do. *She took a deep breath and sat up slowly and with great effort.* **4** If you say that something is **an effort**, N-SING: you mean that an unusual amount of physical or a N mental energy is needed to do it. *Even carrying the camcorder while hiking in the forest was an effort.*
5 An **effort** is a particular series of activities that is or- N-COUNT ganized by a group of people in order to achieve something. *...a famine relief effort in Angola.*

ef·fort·less /ˈefətləs/. If you describe something as ◆◇◇◇◇ **effortless**, you mean that it has been achieved or ADJ-GRADED accomplished easily. *...effortless and elegant Italian cooking.* ♦ **ef·fort·less·ly** *Peter adapted effortlessly* ADV-GRADED *to his new surroundings.*

ef·fron·tery /ɪˈfrʌntəri/. If you accuse someone of N-UNCOUNT **effrontery**, you are accusing them of bold, rude, or PRAGMATICS cheeky behaviour. *One could only gasp at the sheer* FORMAL *effrontery of the man.*

ef·fu·sion /ɪˈfjuːʒən/ **effusions.** If someone ex- N-VAR presses their emotions or ideas with **effusion**, they express them with more enthusiasm and for longer than is usual or expected. *His employer greeted him with an effusion of relief.* ♦ **ef·fu·sive** /ɪˈfjuːsɪv/ *She* ADJ-GRADED *was very gushing and very effusive.* ♦ **ef·fu·sive·ly** ADV-GRADED *She greeted them effusively.*

EFL /ˌiː ef ˈel/. **EFL** is the teaching of English to N-UNCOUNT people whose first language is not English. **EFL** is an abbreviation for 'English as a Foreign Language'. *...an EFL teacher.*

e.g. /ˌiː ˈdʒiː/. **e.g.** is an abbreviation that means ◆◆◇◇◇ 'for example'. It is used before a noun, or to intro- duce another sentence. *Or consider how you can ac- quire these skills, e.g. by taking extra courses.*

egali·tari·an·ism /ɪˌgælɪˈteəriənɪzəm/. **Egalitarianism** is used to refer to the belief that all people are equal and should have the same rights and opportunities. ♦ **egali·tar·ian. Egalitarian** means supporting or following the ideas of egalitarianism. ...*an egalitarian society.* — N-UNCOUNT / ADJ-GRADED

egg /eg/ **eggs, egging, egged.** **1** An **egg** is a small round or oval object produced by a female bird from which a baby bird later emerges. Reptiles, fish, and insects also lay eggs. ...*a baby bird hatching from its egg.* ...*ant eggs.* **2** In Western countries, **eggs** often means hen's eggs, eaten as food. *Break the eggs into a shallow bowl.* **3** An **egg** is a cell that is produced in the bodies of female animals and humans. **4** If someone puts **all** their **eggs in one basket**, they put all their effort or resources into doing one thing so that, if it fails, they have no alternatives left. **5** If someone has **egg on** their **face** or has **egg all over** their **face**, they have been made to look foolish. **6** See also **Easter egg, nest egg.** • **a chicken and egg situation:** see **chicken.** — N-COUNT / N-VAR / N-COUNT / PHRASE / PHRASE

egg on. If you **egg** someone **on**, you encourage them to do something, especially something daring or foolish. *She was laughing and egging him on... They egged each other on to argue and to fight.* — PHRASAL VB V n P / V n P to-inf

'egg cup, egg cups. An **egg cup** is a container in which you put a boiled egg while you eat it. — N-COUNT

egg·head /ˈeghed/ **eggheads.** If you think someone is more interested in ideas and theories than in practical actions you can say they are an **egghead.** — N-COUNT / PRAGMATICS / INFORMAL

egg·plant /ˈegplɑːnt, -plænt/ **eggplants.** An **eggplant** is the same as an **aubergine.** — N-VAR / AMERICAN

egg·shell /ˈegʃel/ **eggshells;** also spelled **egg shell.** An **eggshell** is the hard covering on the outside of an egg. — N-VAR

'egg timer, egg timers; also spelled **egg-timer.** An **egg timer** is a device that measures the time needed to boil an egg. — N-COUNT

'egg whisk, egg whisks. An **egg whisk** is a piece of kitchen equipment used for mixing the different parts of an egg together. — N-COUNT

ego /ˈiːgəʊ, ˈegəʊ/ **egos.** You refer to someone's **ego** when you are referring to their sense of their own self and their own worth. *He had a massive ego, never would he admit he was wrong.* • See also **alter ego, super-ego.** — N-VAR

ego·cen·tric /ˌiːgəʊˈsentrɪk, ˌeg-/. If you describe someone as **egocentric**, you are criticizing them for thinking only of themselves and their own wants. — ADJ-GRADED / PRAGMATICS

ego·ism /ˈiːgəʊɪzəm, ˈeg-/. **Egoism** is the same as **egotism.** — N-UNCOUNT

ego·ist /ˈiːgəʊɪst, ˈeg-/ **egoists.** An **egoist** is the same as an **egotist.** — N-COUNT

ego·is·tic /ˌiːgəʊˈɪstɪk, ˌeg-/. **Egoistic** means the same as **egotistic.** — ADJ-GRADED

ego·ma·nia /ˌiːgəʊˈmeɪniə, ˌeg-/. If you accuse someone of **egomania**, you are criticizing them for thinking only of themselves and not caring if they harm other people in order to get what they want. ♦ **ego·ma·ni·ac, egomaniacs** *Adam is clever enough, but he's also something of an egomaniac.* — N-UNCOUNT / PRAGMATICS / N-COUNT

ego·tism /ˈiːgəʊtɪzəm, ˈeg-/. If you accuse someone of **egotism**, you are criticizing them for behaving selfishly and believing themselves to be more important than other people. *His ambition demonstrated his insular egotism.* ♦ **ego·tist, egotists** *Wolseley is an egotist and a braggart.* — N-UNCOUNT / PRAGMATICS / N-COUNT

ego·tis·tic /ˌiːgəʊˈtɪstɪk, ˌeg-/. The form **egotistical** is also used. If you describe someone as **egotistic** or **egotistical**, you are criticizing them for behaving selfishly and believing themselves to be more important than other people. — ADJ-GRADED / PRAGMATICS

'ego trip, ego trips. If you say that someone is on an **ego trip**, you are criticizing them for doing something on their own satisfaction, often to show that they think they are more important than other people. *He's on one big ego trip.* — N-COUNT / PRAGMATICS

egre·gious /ɪˈɡriːdʒəs/. **Egregious** means very bad indeed. ...*the most egregious abuses of human rights.* — ADJ-GRADED / FORMAL

eh /eɪ/. **Eh** is used in writing to represent a noise that people make as a response in conversation, for example to express agreement or to ask for something to be explained or repeated. *Let's talk all about it outside, eh?* — ♦♦♢♢♢ CONVENTION

eider·down /ˈaɪdədaʊn/ **eiderdowns.** An **eiderdown** is a bed covering filled with small soft feathers or warm material. The usual American word is **comforter.** — N-COUNT

eight /eɪt/ **eights. Eight** is the number 8. See Appendix headed **Numbers.** *So far eight workers have been killed.* — ♦♦♦♦♦ NUMBER

eight·een /ˌeɪˈtiːn/ **eighteens. Eighteen** is the number 18. See Appendix headed **Numbers.** *He was employed by them for eighteen years.* — ♦♦♦♦♦ NUMBER

eight·eenth /ˌeɪˈtiːnθ/. The **eighteenth** item in a series is the one that you count as number eighteen. See Appendix headed **Numbers.** — ♦♦♦♦♢ ORDINAL

eighth /eɪtθ/ **eighths. 1** The **eighth** item in a series is the one that you count as number eight. See Appendix headed **Numbers. 2** An **eighth** is one of eight equal parts of something. — ♦♦♦♦♢ ORDINAL / FRACTION

eighti·eth /ˈeɪtiəθ/. The **eightieth** item in a series is the one that you count as number eighty. See Appendix headed **Numbers.** — ♦♦♦♦♢ ORDINAL

eighty /ˈeɪti/ **eighties. 1 Eighty** is the number 80. See Appendix headed **Numbers.** *Eighty horses trotted up.* **2** When you talk about the **eighties**, you are referring to numbers between 80 and 89. *He was in his late eighties.* **3** The **eighties** is the decade between 1980 and 1989. — ♦♦♦♦♦ NUMBER / N-PLURAL / N-PLURAL: the N

either /ˈaɪðə, ˈiːðə/. **1** You use **either** in front of the first of two or more alternatives, when you are stating the only possibilities or choices that there are. The other alternatives are introduced by 'or'. *Sightseeing is best done either by tour bus or by bicycles... He should be either put on trial or set free... Either she goes or I go.* **2** You use **either** in a negative statement in front of the first of two alternatives to indicate that the negative statement refers to both the alternatives. ...*music that fails to be either funny or funky... There had been no indication of either breathlessness or any loss of mental faculties.* **3** You can use **either** to refer to one of two things, people, or situations, when you want to say that they are both possible and it does not matter which one is chosen or considered. *There were glasses of iced champagne and cigars. Unfortunately not many of either were consumed.* ► Also a quantifier. *They are able to talk openly to one another whenever either of them feels hurt.* ► Also a determiner. ...*the authority to pursue suspects into either country.* **4** You use **either** in a negative statement to refer to each of two things, people, or situations to indicate that the negative statement includes both of them. *She warned me that I'd never marry or have children.—'I don't want either.'* ► Also a quantifier. *There are no simple answers to either of those questions.* ► Also a determiner. *He sometimes couldn't remember either man's name.* **5** You can use **either** to introduce a noun that refers to each of two things when you are talking about both of them. *The basketball nets hung down from the ceiling at either end of the gymnasium.* **6** You use **either** by itself in negative statements to indicate that there is a similarity or connection with a person or thing that you have just mentioned. *He did not even say anything to her, and she did not speak to him either.* — ♦♦♦♦ CONJ / PRAGMATICS / CONJ / PRAGMATICS / PRON / QUANT / DET / PRON / PRAGMATICS / QUANT / DET / DET / ADV: ADV after v, with brd-neg

ejacu·late /ɪˈdʒækjʊleɪt/ **ejaculates, ejaculating, ejaculated.** When a man **ejaculates**, sperm comes out through his penis. ... *a tendency to ejaculate quickly.* ♦ **ejacu·la·tion** /ɪˌdʒækjʊˈleɪʃən/ **ejaculations** *Each male ejaculation will contain up to 300 million sperm.* — ♦♢♢♢♢ VERB V / N-VAR

eject /ɪˈdʒekt/ **ejects, ejecting, ejected. 1** If you **eject** someone from a place, you force them to leave. *Officials used guard dogs to eject the protesters... He was ejected from a restaurant.* ♦ **ejec·tion** /ɪˈdʒekʃən/ **ejections** ...*the ejection and manhandling of hecklers at the meeting.* **2** To **eject** — ♦♢♢♢♢ VERB V n / V n from n / N-VAR / VERB: V n

something means to remove it or push it out forcefully. **3** When pilots **eject** from their aircraft, they leave the aircraft rapidly by means of ejector seats, usually because the plane is about to crash. VERB: V *from* n

e'jector seat, ejector seats. An **ejector seat** is a special seat which can throw the pilot out of a fast military aircraft in an emergency. N-COUNT

eke /iːk/ **ekes, eking, eked.** If you **eke a living**, you manage to survive with very little money. *He ekes out a living with a market stall.* PHRASE

eke out. If you **eke out** something, you make your supply of it last as long as possible. *Workers can eke out their redundancy money for about 10 weeks.* PHRASAL VB / V P noun / Also V n P

elabo·rate, elaborates, elaborating, elaborated. The adjective is pronounced /ɪˈlæbərət/. The verb is pronounced /ɪˈlæbəreɪt/. **1** You use **elaborate** to describe something that is very complex because it has a lot of different parts. *...an elaborate ceremony that lasts for eight days.* **2** **Elaborate** clothing or material is made with a lot of detailed artistic designs. ♦ **elabo·rate·ly** *...elaborately costumed dolls.* **3** If you **elaborate** a plan or theory, you develop it by making it more complicated and more effective. *...to elaborate policies which would make a market economy compatible with a clean environment.* ♦ **elabo·ra·tion** /ɪˌlæbəˈreɪʃən/ *...the elaboration of specific policies.* **4** If you **elaborate** on something, you give more details about it. *He refused to elaborate on his solicitor's comment.* ♦♦◇◇◇ / ADJ-GRADED / ADJ-GRADED / ADV-GRADED / VERB V n / N-UNCOUNT / VERB V on n Also V

élan /eɪˈlɑːn/; also spelled **elan.** If you say that someone does something with **élan**, you mean that they do it in an energetic and confident way. *This part was taken with elan by a promising young tenor.* N-UNCOUNT LITERARY

elapse /ɪˈlæps/ **elapses, elapsing, elapsed.** When time **elapses**, it passes. *Forty-eight hours have elapsed since his arrest.* ♦◇◇◇ VERB V FORMAL

elas·tic /ɪˈlæstɪk/. **1** **Elastic** is a rubber material that stretches when you pull it and returns to its original size and shape when you let it go. *...my plaid Bermuda shorts with the elastic waist.* **2** Something that is **elastic** is able to stretch easily and then return to its original size and shape. *...an elastic rope.* **3** **Elastic** ideas and policies can change in order to suit new circumstances. *...an elastic interpretation of the rules of boxing.* ♦◇◇◇ N-UNCOUNT / ADJ-GRADED / ADJ-GRADED

elas·ti·cat·ed /ɪˈlæstɪkeɪtɪd/. A piece of clothing that is **elasticated** has elastic sewn or woven into it. *...a pink silk jacket with an elasticated waist.* ADJ BRITISH

e,lastic 'band, elastic bands. An **elastic band** is the same as a **rubber band.** N-COUNT

elas·tici·ty /ˌiːlæˈstɪsɪti, ˌlæst-/ **elasticities.** **1** The **elasticity** of a material or substance is its ability to return to its original shape, size, and condition after it has been stretched. *Daily facial exercises help her to retain the skin's elasticity.* **2** The **elasticity** of something is the degree to which it changes in response to changes in circumstances. *...the elasticity of demand for a single newspaper.* ♦◇◇◇ N-UNCOUNT / N-UNCOUNT: also N in pl

elat·ed /ɪˈleɪtɪd/. If you are **elated**, you are extremely happy and excited because of something that has happened. *'That was one of the races of my life,' said an elated Mansell.* ♦ **ela·tion** /ɪˈleɪʃən/ *His supporters have reacted to the news with elation.* ♦◇◇◇ ADJ-GRADED / N-UNCOUNT

el·bow /ˈelbəʊ/ **elbows, elbowing, elbowed.** **1** Your **elbow** is the part of your arm where the upper and lower halves of the arm are joined. See picture headed **human body.** **2** If you **elbow** someone aside or to one side, you push them out of the way, using your elbows. *The security team elbowed aside a steward... We girls elbow one another out of the way... Mr Smith elbowed me in the face.* **3** If you **elbow** your way somewhere, you move there by pushing other people out of the way, using your elbows. ♦♦◇◇ N-COUNT / VERB V n with aside V n out of n V n in n Also V / VERB: V way prep/ adv

'elbow grease. People use the expression **elbow grease** to refer to the strength and energy that you use when doing physical work. *It took a considerable amount of polish and elbow grease before the brass shone like new.* N-UNCOUNT INFORMAL

'elbow room. **Elbow room** is the freedom to do what you want to do or need to do in a particular situation. *His speech won a standing ovation – but it was also designed to give himself more political elbow room.* N-UNCOUNT INFORMAL

el·der /ˈeldə/ **elders. 1** The **elder** of two people is the one who was born first. *...his elder brother. ...the elder of her two daughters.* **2** A person's **elder** is someone who is older than them, especially someone quite a lot older. *The young have no respect for their elders.* **3** In some societies, an **elder** is one of the respected older people who have influence and authority. **4** In some Christian churches, an **elder** is one of the people who hold a position of responsibility. **5** An **elder** is a bush or small tree which has groups of small white flowers and red or black berries. ♦♦◇◇ ADJ-COMPAR / N-COUNT: poss N FORMAL / N-COUNT / N-COUNT / N-COUNT

elder·berry /ˈeldəberi/ **elderberries. 1** Elderberries are the edible red or black berries that grow on an elder bush or tree. **2** An **elderberry** is an elder bush or tree. N-COUNT / N-VAR

eld·er·ly /ˈeldəli/. **1** You use **elderly** as a polite way of saying that someone is old. *There was an elderly couple on the terrace.* ▶ The **elderly** are people who are old. **2** If you describe an object as **elderly**, you mean that it is rather old or old-fashioned. *Some of those artillery pieces look a little elderly.* ♦♦◇◇ ADJ-GRADED / N-PLURAL / ADJ-GRADED

,elder 'statesman, elder statesmen. 1 An elder statesman is an old and respected politician or former politician who still has influence because of his or her experience. **2** An experienced and respected member of an organization or profession is sometimes referred to as an **elder statesman.** N-COUNT / N-COUNT

eld·est /ˈeldɪst/. The **eldest** person in a group is the one who was born before all the others. *The eldest child was a daughter called Fiona... David was the eldest of three boys.* ♦◇◇◇ ADJ-SUPERL

elect /ɪˈlekt/ **elects, electing, elected. 1** When people **elect** someone, they choose that person to represent them, by voting for them. *Manchester College elected him Principal in 1956. ...electing a woman as its new president.* ♦ **elect·ed** *...the country's democratically elected president.* **2** If you **elect** to do something, you choose to do it. *Those choosing to smoke will be seated at the rear.* **3** **Elect** is added after words such as 'president' or 'governor' to indicate that a person has been elected to the post but has not officially started to carry out the duties involved. *...the president-elect.* ♦♦♦♦ VERB: V n V n n V n as n / ADJ: ADJ n / VERB V to-inf FORMAL / ADJ: n ADJ FORMAL

elec·tion /ɪˈlekʃən/ **elections. 1** An **election** is a process in which people vote to choose a person or group of people to hold an official position. *...Poland's first fully free elections for more than fifty years. ...during his election campaign. ...the final election results.* **2** The **election** of a particular person or group of people is their success in winning an election. *...the election of the Labour government in 1964. ...Vaclav Havel's election as president.* ♦♦♦♦♦ N-VAR / N-UNCOUNT

elec·tion·eer·ing /ɪˌlekʃəˈnɪərɪŋ/. **Electioneering** is the activities that politicians and their supporters carry out in order to persuade people to vote for them or their political party in an election. N-UNCOUNT

elec·tive /ɪˈlektɪv/ **electives. 1** An **elective** post or committee is one to which people are appointed as a result of winning an election. *Buchanan has never held elective office.* **2** **Elective** surgery is surgery that you choose to have in advance rather than wait for it to become essential., for example a hip replacement or a hysterectomy. **3** An **elective** is a subject which a student can choose to study as part of his or her course. *Electives are offered in Tai Chi and advanced dance exercise.* ADJ FORMAL / ADJ FORMAL / N-COUNT AMERICAN

elec·tor /ɪˈlektə/ **electors. Electors** are people who have the right to vote in an election. ♦◇◇◇ N-COUNT

elec·tor·al /ɪˈlektərəl/. **Electoral** is used to describe things that are connected with elections. *...Italy's electoral system of proportional representation.* ♦ **elec·tor·al·ly.** ♦♦◇◇ ADJ: ADJ n / ADV

e·lectoral 'register, electoral registers. In Britain, an **electoral register** is an official list of all the people who have the right to vote in an election. N-COUNT

e·lectoral 'roll, electoral rolls. In Britain, an **electoral roll** is the same as an **electoral register.** N-COUNT

elec·tor·ate /ɪˈlektərət/ **electorates.** The **electorate** of a country or area is all the people in it who have the right to vote in an election. *He has the backing of almost a quarter of the electorate.* ◆◆◇◇◇ N-COLL-COUNT

elec·tric /ɪˈlektrɪk/. **1** An **electric** device or machine works by means of electricity, rather than using some other source of power. **2** An **electric** current, voltage, or charge is one that is produced by electricity. **3 Electric** plugs, sockets, or power lines are designed to carry electricity. **4** The **electric** is the supply of electricity to a house or other place. **5** If you describe the atmosphere of a place or event as **electric**, you mean that people are in a state of great excitement. *The mood in the hall was electric.* ◆◆◆◇◇ ADJ; ADJ: ADJ n; ADJ: ADJ n; N-UNCOUNT INFORMAL; ADJ-GRADED

elec·tri·cal /ɪˈlektrɪkəl/. **1 Electrical** goods, equipment, or appliances work by means of electricity. *...shipments of electrical equipment.* ◆ **elec·tri·cal·ly** /ɪˈlektrɪkli/ *...electrically-powered vehicles.* **2 Electrical** systems or components supply or use electricity. **3 Electrical** energy is energy in the form of electricity. ◆ **electrically. 4 Electrical** industries, engineers, or workers are involved in the production and supply of electricity or electrical goods. ◆◇◇◇ ADJ; ADV; ADV-ed; ADJ; ADJ; ADV; ADJ: ADJ n

e·lectrical engi'neering. Electrical engineering is the designing, constructing, and maintenance of electrical and electronic devices. ◆ **e·lectrical engi'neer, electrical engineers.** N-UNCOUNT; N-COUNT

e·lectric 'blanket, electric blankets. An **electric blanket** is a blanket with wires inside it which carry an electric current that keeps the blanket warm. N-COUNT

e·lectric-'blue. Something that is **electric-blue** is very bright blue in colour. COLOUR

e·lectric 'chair, electric chairs. The **electric chair** is a method of execution in which a person is strapped to a special chair and killed by a powerful electric current. N-COUNT

elec·tri·cian /ɪlekˈtrɪʃən, ˌiːlek-/ **electricians.** An **electrician** is a person whose job is to install and repair electrical equipment. ◆◇◇◇ N-COUNT

elec·tric·ity /ɪlekˈtrɪsɪti, ˌiːlek-/. **Electricity** is a form of energy that can be carried by wires and is used for heating and lighting, and to provide power for machines. *The electricity had been cut off.* ◆◆◆◇◇ N-UNCOUNT

elec·trics /ɪˈlektrɪks/. You can refer to a system of electrical wiring as the **electrics.** N-PLURAL BRITISH

e·lectric 'shock, electric shocks. If you get an **electric shock**, you get a sudden painful feeling when you touch something which is connected to a supply of electricity. N-COUNT

elec·tri·fi·ca·tion /ɪˌlektrɪfɪˈkeɪʃən/. The **electrification** of a house, town, or area is the connecting of that place with a supply of electricity. ● See also **electrify.** N-UNCOUNT

elec·tri·fied /ɪˈlektrɪfaɪd/. An **electrified** fence or other barrier has been connected to a supply of electricity, so that a person or animal that touches it will get an electric shock. ADJ: ADJ n

elec·tri·fy /ɪˈlektrɪfaɪ/ **electrifies, electrifying, electrified. 1** If people **are electrified** by an event or experience, it makes them feel very excited and surprised. *The world was electrified by his courage and resistance.* ◆ **elec·tri·fy·ing** *...an electrifying performance.* **2** When a railway system or railway line **is electrified**, electric cables are put over the tracks, or electric rails are put beside them, so that the trains can be powered by electricity. ◆ **elec·tri·fi·ca·tion** *...the electrification of the Oxted to Uckfield line.* ◆◇◇◇ VERB: be V-ed; ADJ-GRADED; VERB: be V-ed; N-UNCOUNT

electro- /ɪˈlektrəʊ-/. **Electro-** is used to form words that refer to electricity or processes involving electricity. *...electro-magnetic energy.* PREFIX

elec·tro·cute /ɪˈlektrəkjuːt/ **electrocutes, electrocuting, electrocuted. 1** If someone **is electrocuted**, they are accidentally killed or badly in- VERB: be V-ed; V pron-refl

jured when they touch something connected to a source of electricity. *He accidentally electrocuted himself.* **2** If a criminal **is electrocuted**, he or she is executed by means of an electrical apparatus. ◆ **elec·tro·cu·tion** /ɪˌlektrəˈkjuːʃən/ **electrocutions** *...death by electrocution.* VERB: be V-ed; N-VAR

elec·trode /ɪˈlektrəʊd/ **electrodes.** An **electrode** is a small piece of metal or other substance that is used to take an electric current to or from a source of power, a piece of equipment, or a living body. ◆◇◇◇ N-COUNT

elec·troly·sis /ɪlekˈtrɒlɪsɪs, ˌiː-/. **Electrolysis** is the process of passing an electric current through a substance in order to produce chemical changes in the substance. N-UNCOUNT TECHNICAL

elec·tro·lyte /ɪˈlektrəlaɪt/ **electrolytes.** An **electrolyte** is a substance, usually a liquid, which electricity can pass through. N-COUNT TECHNICAL

elec·tro·mag·net·ic /ɪˌlektrəʊmægˈnetɪk/. **Electromagnetic** is used to describe the electrical and magnetic forces or effects produced by an electric current. *...electromagnetic fields.* ◆◇◇◇ ADJ

elec·tron /ɪˈlektrɒn/ **electrons.** An **electron** is a tiny particle of matter that is smaller than an atom and has a negative electrical charge. ◆◆◇◇ N-COUNT TECHNICAL

elec·tron·ic /ɪlekˈtrɒnɪk, ˌiː-/. **1** An **electronic** device is one that has transistors or silicon chips which control and change the electric current passing through the device. **2** An **electronic** process or activity involves the use of electronic devices. *...electronic surveillance.* ◆ **elec·troni·cal·ly.** ◆◆◆◇◇ ADJ: ADJ n; ADJ; ADV

e·lectronic 'mail. Electronic mail is the same as **email.** N-SING

elec·tron·ics /ɪlekˈtrɒnɪks/. **1 Electronics** is the technology of using transistors and silicon chips, especially in devices such as radios, televisions, and computers. *...Europe's three main electronics companies.* **2** You can refer to electronic devices, or the part of a piece of equipment that consists of electronic devices, as the **electronics.** ◆◆◇◇ N-UNCOUNT; N-PLURAL

el·egant /ˈelɪgənt/. **1** If you describe a person or thing as **elegant**, you mean that they are pleasing and graceful in appearance or style. *...an elegant restaurant.* ◆ **el·egance** *...Princess Grace's understated elegance.* ◆ **el·egant·ly** *...a tall, elegantly dressed man with a mustache.* **2** If you describe a piece of writing, an idea, or a plan as **elegant**, you mean that it is simple, clear, and clever. ◆ **elegantly** *...an elegantly simple idea.* ◆◆◆◇◇ ADJ-GRADED; N-UNCOUNT; ADV-GRADED; ADJ-GRADED; ADV-GRADED

el·egi·ac /ˌelɪˈdʒaɪək/. Something that is **elegiac** expresses or shows sadness. ADJ-GRADED LITERARY

el·egy /ˈelɪdʒi/ **elegies.** An **elegy** is a sad poem, often about someone who has died. N-COUNT

el·ement /ˈelɪmənt/ **elements. 1** The different **elements** of something are the different parts it contains. *...one of the key elements of the UN's peace plan.* **2** A particular **element** of a situation, activity, or process is an important quality or feature that it has or needs. *Fitness has now become an important element in our lives.* **3** When you talk about **elements** within a society or organization, you are referring to groups of people who have similar aims, beliefs, or habits. *...criminal elements. ...the hooligan element.* **4** If something has an **element** of a particular quality or emotion, it has a certain amount of this quality or emotion. *These reports clearly contain elements of propaganda.* **5** An **element** is a substance such as gold, oxygen, or carbon that consists of only one type of atom. **6** The **element** in an electric fire or water heater is the part which changes the electric current into heat. **7** You can refer to the weather, especially wind and rain, as the **elements.** *...exposed to the elements.* **8** If you say that someone is **in** their **element**, you mean that they are in a situation they enjoy, or are doing something that they enjoy and do well. *My stepmother was in her element, organizing everything.* ◆◆◆◇ N-COUNT; N-COUNT: with supp; N-COUNT: usu pl, supp N; N-COUNT; N-COUNT TECHNICAL; N-COUNT; N-PLURAL: the N; PHRASE

el·ement·al /ˌelɪˈmentəl/. **Elemental** feelings and types of behaviour are simple, basic, and forceful. ◆◇◇◇ ADJ-GRADED LITERARY

...the elemental life they would be living in this new colony.

el·emen·ta·ry /ˌelɪ'mentri/. Something that is **elementary** is very simple, straightforward, and basic. *...elementary computer skills.* ADJ-GRADED

ele'mentary school, elementary schools. In the United States, an **elementary school** is a school where children are taught for the first six or eight years of their education. N-VAR

el·ephant /'elɪfənt/ **elephants.** An **elephant** is a very large animal with a long, flexible nose called a trunk, which it uses to pick up things. See picture headed **animals.** ● See also **white elephant.** N-COUNT

el·ephan·tine /ˌelɪ'fæntaɪn/. If you describe something as **elephantine**, you mean that you think it is large and clumsy; used showing disapproval. *His legs were elephantine and his body obese.* ADJ-GRADED PRAGMATICS

el·evate /'elɪveɪt/ **elevates, elevating, elevated. 1** When someone or something achieves a more important rank or status, you can say that they **are elevated** to it. *He was elevated to the post of prime minister.* ♦ **el·eva·tion** /ˌelɪ'veɪʃən/ *After his elevation to the papacy, he reigned for two years.* **2** If you **elevate** something to a higher status, you consider it to be better or more important than it really is. *Don't elevate your superiors to superstar status.* **3** To **elevate** something means to increase it in amount or intensity. *Emotional stress can elevate blood pressure.* **4** If you **elevate** something, you raise it above a horizontal level. VB: usu passive beV-ed to n FORMAL / N-UNCOUNT / VERB V n to n / VERB V n FORMAL / VERB: V n FORMAL

el·evat·ed /'elɪveɪtɪd/. **1** An **elevated** person, job, or role is very important or of very high rank. *His career has blossomed and that has given him a certain elevated status.* **2 Elevated** thoughts or ideas are on a high moral or intellectual level. *...the magazine's elevated British tone.* **3 Elevated** land or buildings are raised up higher than the surrounding area. ADJ / ADJ-GRADED / ADJ

el·eva·tion /ˌelɪ'veɪʃən/ **elevations. 1** An **elevation** is the front, back, or side of a building, or a drawing of one of these. *...the addition of two-storey wings on the north and south elevations.* **2** The **elevation** of a place is its height above sea level. *...an elevation of about 13,000 feet above sea level.* **3** An **elevation** is a piece of ground that is higher than the area around it. N-COUNT: with supp TECHNICAL / N-COUNT / N-COUNT

el·eva·tor /'elɪveɪtə/ **elevators.** An **elevator** is a device that carries people up and down inside buildings. The usual British word is **lift.** N-COUNT AMERICAN

elev·en /ɪ'levən/ **elevens.** Eleven is the number 11. See Appendix headed **Numbers.** NUMBER

e,leven-'plus; also spelled **eleven plus.** The **eleven plus** is an exam which is taken by children in Britain at about the age of eleven. N-SING

elev·enth /ɪ'levənθ/. The **eleventh** item in a series is the one that you count as number eleven. See Appendix headed **Numbers.** ORDINAL

e,leventh 'hour. If someone does something at **the eleventh hour**, they do it at the last possible moment. *...last night's eleventh hour agreement.* N-SING

elf /elf/ **elves.** In fairy stories, **elves** are small magical beings who play tricks on people. N-COUNT

elf·in /'elfɪn/. If you describe someone as **elfin**, you think that they are attractive because they are small and have delicate features. *...a little boy with an elfin face.* ADJ-GRADED PRAGMATICS

elic·it /ɪ'lɪsɪt/ **elicits, eliciting, elicited. 1** If you **elicit** a response or a reaction, you do or say something which makes other people respond or react. *Yeltsin's firing of Yakovlev elicited a storm of protest.* **2** If you **elicit** a piece of information, you get it by asking the right questions. *Several phone calls elicited no further information.* VERB V n / VERB V n FORMAL

eli·gible /'elɪdʒɪbəl/. **1** Someone who is **eligible** for something is entitled or able to have it. *Almost half the population are eligible to vote in today's election.* ♦ **eli·gibil·ity** /ˌelɪdʒə'bɪlɪti/ *...the rules covering eligibility for benefits.* **2** An **eligible** man or woman is not yet married and is considered to be a suitable partner. ADJ-GRADED / N-UNCOUNT / ADJ-GRADED

elimi·nate /ɪ'lɪmɪneɪt/ **eliminates, eliminating, eliminated. 1** To **eliminate** something that you do not want or need, means to remove it completely. *Academic departments are being eliminated... If you think you may be allergic to a food or drink, eliminate it from your diet.* ♦ **elimi·na·tion** /ɪˌlɪmɪ'neɪʃən/ *...the prohibition and elimination of chemical weapons.* **2** When a person or team **is eliminated** from a competition, they are defeated and so take no further part in the competition. *If you are eliminated in the show-jumping then you are out of the complete competition.* **3** If someone says that they **have eliminated** an enemy, they mean that they have killed them. *He urged right-wingers to eliminate their opponents.* VERB: V n beV-ed V n from n FORMAL / N-UNCOUNT / V-PASSIVE: be V-ed from n beV-ed / VERB PRAGMATICS V n

elimi·na·tor /ɪ'lɪmɪneɪtə/ **eliminators.** In sport, an **eliminator** is a match or competition which decides which team or player is to go through to the next stage of a competition. N-COUNT

elite /ɪ'liːt, eɪ-/ **elites.** You can refer to the most powerful, rich, or talented people within a particular group, place, or society as the **elite.** *...China's intellectual elite.* ► Also an adjective. *...the elite troops of the President's bodyguard.* N-COUNT / ADJ-GRADED: ADJ n

elit·ism /ɪ'liːtɪzəm, eɪ-/. **1 Elitism** is the feeling of superiority someone has when they believe they are part of an elite. *...the arrogance and elitism of gallery owners.* **2 Elitism** is the belief that a society or country should be ruled by a small group of people who are superior to everyone else. N-UNCOUNT / N-UNCOUNT

elit·ist /ɪ'liːtɪst, eɪ-/ **elitists. 1** If you describe systems, practices, or ideas as **elitist**, you believe that they favour only a small group of powerful, rich, or talented people; used showing disapproval. *Labour has criticised government policy on Hong Kong as elitist.* **2** If you describe an activity or profession as **elitist**, you mean that it is practised only by a small group of powerful, rich, or talented people; used showing disapproval. *The legal profession is starting to be less elitist.* **3** An **elitist** is someone who believes that they are part of an elite or believes in elitism; used showing disapproval. *...intellectual elitists.* ADJ-GRADED PRAGMATICS / ADJ-GRADED PRAGMATICS / N-COUNT PRAGMATICS

elix·ir /ɪ'lɪksə/ **elixirs.** An **elixir** is a liquid that is considered to have magical powers. *...the elixir of life.* N-COUNT LITERARY

Eliza·bethan /ɪˌlɪzə'biːθən/. **Elizabethan** means belonging to or connected with England in the second half of the sixteenth century, when Elizabeth the First was Queen. *...the Elizabethan theatre.* ADJ

elk /elk/ **elks; elk** can also be used as the plural form. The **elk** is the largest type of deer. N-VAR

el·lipse /ɪ'lɪps/ **ellipses.** An **ellipse** is an oval shape like a flattened circle. N-COUNT FORMAL

el·lip·sis /ɪ'lɪpsɪs/. **Ellipsis** means leaving out words rather than repeating them unnecessarily; for example, saying 'I want to go but I can't' instead of 'I want to go but I can't go'. N-UNCOUNT TECHNICAL

el·lip·ti·cal /ɪ'lɪptɪkəl/. **1** Something that is **elliptical** is oval, like a flattened circle. *...the moon's elliptical orbit.* **2 Elliptical** references to something are indirect. *...elliptical references to problems best not aired in public.* ADJ-GRADED FORMAL / ADJ-GRADED FORMAL

elm /elm/ **elms.** An **elm** is a tree that has broad leaves which it loses in winter. ► **Elm** is the wood of this tree. N-VAR / N-UNCOUNT

elo·cu·tion /ˌelə'kjuːʃən/. **Elocution** lessons are lessons in which someone is taught to speak clearly and in an accent that is considered to be standard and acceptable. N-UNCOUNT

elon·gate /'iːlɒŋgeɪt, AM ɪ'lɔːŋ-/ **elongates, elongating, elongated.** If you **elongate** something or if it **elongates**, you stretch it so that it becomes longer. *The fibre can elongate up to 4 per cent before breaking.* V-ERG: V n V FORMAL

elon·gat·ed /'iːlɒŋgeɪtɪd, AM ɪ'lɔːŋ-/. If something is **elongated**, it is very long and thin. *The light from my candle threw his elongated shadow on the walls.* ADJ-GRADED

elope /ɪˈləʊp/ **elopes, eloping, eloped.** When V-RECIP: two people **elope** they go away in secret to get married. *In 1912 he eloped with Frieda von Richthofen.*   pl-n V / V with n

elo·quent /ˈeləkwənt/. **1 Eloquent** speech or writing is well expressed and is very effective in persuading people. *I heard him make a very eloquent speech.* ♦ **elo·quence** *...the eloquence of his prose.* ♦ **elo·quent·ly** *Jan speaks eloquently about her art.* **2** A person who is **eloquent** is good at speaking and able to persuade people; used showing approval. *...one particularly eloquent German critic.* ♦ **elo·quence** *I wish I'd had the eloquence of Helmut Schmidt.*   ◇◇◇◇ ADJ-GRADED / N-UNCOUNT / ADV-GRADED / ADJ-GRADED / PRAGMATICS / N-UNCOUNT

else /els/. **1** You use **else** after words such as 'anywhere', 'someone', and 'what', to refer in a vague way to another person, place, or thing. *If I can't make a living at painting, at least I can teach someone else to paint... What else have you had for your birthday?* ▶ Also an adverb. *I never wanted to live anywhere else.* **2** You use **else** after words such as 'everyone', 'everything', and 'everywhere' to refer in a vague way to all the other people, things, or places except the one you are talking about. *Cigarettes are in short supply, like everything else here.* ▶ Also an adverb. *London seems so much dirtier than everywhere else.*   ♦♦♦♦ ADJ / ADV: adv ADV / ADJ / ADV: adv ADV

3 You use **or else** after stating a logical conclusion, to indicate that what you are about to say is evidence for that conclusion. *Evidently no lessons have been learnt or else the government would not have handled the problem so sloppily.* **4** You use **or else** to introduce a statement that indicates the unpleasant results that will occur if someone does or does not do something. *Make sure you are strapped in very well, or else you will fall out.* **5** You use **or else** to introduce the second of two possibilities when you do not know which one is true. *You are either a total genius or else you must be absolutely raving mad.*   PHR-CONJ / PHR-CONJ / PHR-CONJ

6 Above all else is used to emphasize that a particular thing is more important than other things. *Above all else I hate the cold.* **7** You can say **'if nothing else'** to indicate that what you are mentioning is, in your opinion, the only good thing in a particular situation. *If nothing else, you'll really enjoy meeting them.* **8** You say **'or else'** after a command to warn someone that if they do not obey, you will be angry and may harm or punish them. *Behave, or else!*   PHRASE / PRAGMATICS / PHRASE / PHRASE / PRAGMATICS

else·where /ˌelsˈweə/. **Elsewhere** means in other places or to another place. *Almost 80 percent of the state's residents were born elsewhere... They were living rather well, in comparison with people elsewhere in the world.*   ♦♦♦◇◇ ADV

ELT /ˌiː el ˈtiː/. **ELT** is the teaching of English to people whose first language is not English. **ELT** is an abbreviation for 'English Language Teaching'.   N-UNCOUNT

elu·ci·date /ɪˈluːsɪdeɪt/ **elucidates, elucidating, elucidated.** If you **elucidate** something, you make it clear and easy to understand. *There was no need for him to elucidate.*   VERB: V n / V / FORMAL

elude /ɪˈluːd/ **eludes, eluding, eluded. 1** If something that you want **eludes** you, you fail to obtain it. *Sleep eluded her.* **2** If you **elude** someone or something, you avoid them or escape from them. *He eluded the police for 13 years.* **3** If a fact or idea **eludes** you, you do not succeed in understanding it, realizing it, or remembering it. *The appropriate word eluded him.*   ◇◇◇◇ VB: no passive / V n / VERB / V n / VB: no passive / V n

elu·sive /ɪˈluːsɪv/. Something or someone that is **elusive** is difficult to find, describe, remember, or achieve. *In London late-night taxis are elusive.* ♦ **elu·sive·ness** *...the elusiveness of her character.*   ◇◇◇◇ ADJ-GRADED / N-UNCOUNT

elves /elvz/. **Elves** is the plural of **elf.**

em- /ɪm-/. Often pronounced /em-/, particularly in American English. **Em-** is a form of **en-** that is used before b-, m-, and p-. *I want to empower the businessman.*   PREFIX

ema·ci·at·ed /ɪˈmeɪsieɪtɪd, -ˈmeɪʃ-/. An **emaciated** person is extremely thin and weak because of illness or lack of food.   ADJ-GRADED

email /ˈiːmeɪl/; also spelled **E-mail. Email** is a system of sending written messages electronically from one computer to another. **Email** is an abbreviation of 'electronic mail'.   N-UNCOUNT

ema·nate /ˈeməneɪt/ **emanates, emanating, emanated. 1** If a quality or feeling **emanates** from you, or if you **emanate** a quality or feeling, you give people a strong sense that you have that quality or feeling. *He emanates sympathy.* **2** If something **emanates** from somewhere, it comes from there. *...reports emanating from America.*   ♦◇◇◇◇ V-ERG: / V from n / FORMAL / VERB / V from n / Also V / FORMAL

ema·na·tion /ˌeməˈneɪʃən/ **emanations.** An **emanation** is a form of energy or a mass of tiny particles that comes from something.   FORMAL

eman·ci·pate /ɪˈmænsɪpeɪt/ **emancipates, emancipating, emancipated.** If people **are emancipated**, they are freed from unpleasant or degrading social, political, or legal restrictions. *That war preserved the Union and emancipated the slaves.* ♦ **eman·ci·pa·tion** /ɪˌmænsɪˈpeɪʃən/ *...the emancipation of women.*   ♦◇◇◇◇ VERB: / be V-ed / V n / FORMAL / N-UNCOUNT

eman·ci·pat·ed /ɪˈmænsɪpeɪtɪd/. If you describe someone as **emancipated**, you mean that they behave in a less restricted way than is traditional in their society. *She is an emancipated woman.*   ADJ-GRADED

emas·cu·late /ɪˈmæskjʊleɪt/ **emasculates, emasculating, emasculated. 1** If you say that someone or something **is emasculated**, you disapprove of the fact that they have been made weak and ineffective. *The company tried to emasculate the unions.* **2** If you say that a man **is emasculated**, you disapprove of the fact that he loses his male role, identity, or qualities. *He was clearly emasculated by his girlfriend.*   VERB: / be V-ed / PRAGMATICS / V n / VB: usu passive / PRAGMATICS / be V-ed

em·balm /ɪmˈbɑːm/ **embalms, embalming, embalmed.** If a dead person **is embalmed**, their body is preserved using special substances. ♦ **em·balm·ing** *People often look different after embalming.*   VERB: / be V-ed / N-UNCOUNT

em·bank·ment /ɪmˈbæŋkmənt/ **embankments.** An **embankment** is a thick wall or mound of earth that is built to carry a road or railway over an area of low ground, or to prevent a river or the sea from flooding the area. *...Victoria Embankment.*   ♦◇◇◇◇ N-COUNT

em·bar·go /ɪmˈbɑːɡəʊ/ **embargoes, embargoing, embargoed.** If goods of a particular kind **are embargoed**, people are not permitted to import them from a particular country or export them to a particular country. *They embargoed oil shipments to the U.S..* ▶ Also a noun. *He has called on the government to lift its embargo on trade with Vietnam.*   ♦◇◇◇ VERB: / be V-ed / V n / N-COUNT

em·bark /ɪmˈbɑːk/ **embarks, embarking, embarked. 1** If you **embark** on something new, difficult, or exciting, you start doing it. *He's embarking on a new career as a writer.* **2** When someone **barks** on a ship, they go on board before the start of a voyage. *Bob ordered brigade HQ to embark.* ♦ **em·bar·ka·tion** /ˌembɑːˈkeɪʃən/ *Embarkation was scheduled for just after 4 pm.*   ♦♦◇◇◇ VERB / V on/upon n / V on n / N-UNCOUNT

em·bar·rass /ɪmˈbærəs/ **embarrasses, embarrassing, embarrassed. 1** If something or someone **embarrasses** you, they make you feel shy or ashamed. *It embarrassed him that he had no idea of what was going on.* ♦ **em·bar·rass·ing** /ɪmˈbærəsɪŋ/ *That was an embarrassing situation for me.* ♦ **em·bar·rass·ing·ly** *Stephens had beaten him embarrassingly easily.* **2** If something **embarrasses** a politician or political party, it causes problems for them. *The Government has been embarrassed by the affair.* ♦ **em·bar·rass·ing** *He has put the Bonn government in an embarrassing position.*   ♦♦◇◇◇ VERB: / it V n that / ADJ-GRADED / ADV-GRADED / VERB: V n / be V-ed / ADJ-GRADED

em·bar·rassed /ɪmˈbærəst/. A person who is **embarrassed** feels shy, ashamed, or guilty about something. *...an embarrassed silence.*   ♦♦◇◇◇ ADJ-GRADED

em·bar·rass·ment /ɪmˈbærəsmənt/ **embarrassments. 1 Embarrassment** is a feeling of shyness, shame, or guilt. *We apologise for any embarrassment this may have caused.* **2** An **embarrassment** is an action, event, or situation which causes problems for a politician, political party, government, or other public group. *The poverty figures were undoubtedly*   ♦♦◇◇◇ N-VAR / N-COUNT

E

an embarrassment to the president. **3** If you refer to a person as **an embarrassment**, you mean that you disapprove of them but cannot avoid your connection with them. *You have been an embarrassment to us from the day Douglas married you.* `N-SING: aN`

em·bas·sy /'embəsi/ **embassies.** An **embassy** is a group of government officials, headed by an ambassador, who represent their government in a foreign country. The building in which they work is also called an **embassy**. *The American Embassy has already complained.* `◆◆◇◇ N-COUNT`

em·bat·tled /ɪm'bætəld/. **1** If you describe a person, group, or organization as **embattled**, you mean that they are having a lot of problems or difficulties. *The embattled Sulzer begged him for help.* **2** An **embattled** area is one that is involved in the fighting in a war, especially one that is surrounded by enemy forces. `◆◇◇◇ ADJ-GRADED` `ADJ: ADJ n`

em·bed /ɪm'bed/ **embeds, embedding, embedded.** **1** If an object **embeds** itself in a substance or thing, it becomes fixed there firmly and deeply. *One of the bullets passed through Andrea's chest before embedding itself in a wall.* ♦ **em·bedded** *There is glass embedded in the cut.* **2** If something such as an attitude or feeling **is embedded** in a society or system, or in someone's personality, it becomes a permanent and noticeable feature of it. *This agreement will be embedded in a state treaty to be signed soon.* ♦ **embedded** *I think that hatred of the other is deeply embedded in our society.* `◆◇◇◇ VERB Also V n prep` `ADJ-GRADED VB: usu passive beV-ed inn` `ADJ-GRADED`

em·bel·lish /ɪm'belɪʃ/ **embellishes, embellishing, embellished.** **1** If something **is embellished** with decorative features, they are added to make it look more attractive. *Ivy leaves embellish the front of the dresser.* ♦ **em·bel·lish·ment** /ɪm'belɪʃmənt/ **embellishments.** An embellishment is a decoration added to something. **2** If you **embellish** a story, you make it more interesting by adding details which may be untrue. *I launched into the parable, embellishing the story with invented dialogue and extra details.* `◆◇◇◇ VERB: beV-ed withn V n` `N-VAR` `VERB V n`

em·ber /'embə/ **embers.** The **embers** of a fire are small pieces of wood or coal that remain and glow with heat after the fire has finished burning. `N-COUNT`

em·bez·zle /ɪm'bezl/ **embezzles, embezzling, embezzled.** If someone **embezzles** money that has been entrusted to them, they take it and use it illegally for their own purposes. *One former director embezzled $34 million in company funds.* `VERB V n Also V`

em·bez·zle·ment /ɪm'bezlmənt/. **Embezzlement** is the crime or activity of embezzling money. `◆◇◇◇ N-UNCOUNT`

em·bit·tered /ɪm'bɪtəd/. If you describe someone as **embittered**, you mean that they feel angry and resentful because of unpleasant and unfair things that have happened to them. *He had turned into an embittered, hardened adult.* `ADJ-GRADED`

em·bla·zoned /ɪm'bleɪzənd/. If something is **emblazoned** with a design or letters, they are clearly drawn, printed, or sewn on it. *Jackie was sporting a T-shirt with 'Mustique' emblazoned on it.* `ADJ`

em·blem /'embləm/ **emblems.** **1** An **emblem** is a design representing a country or organization. *...the Red Cross emblem.* **2** An **emblem** is something that represents a quality or idea. *The eagle was an emblem of strength and courage.* `◆◇◇◇ N-COUNT` `N-COUNT`

em·blem·at·ic /,emblə'mætɪk/. **1** If something, such as an object in a picture, is **emblematic** of a particular quality or an idea, it symbolically represents the quality or idea. *In some works, flowers take on a powerful emblematic quality.* **2** If you say that something is **emblematic** of a state of affairs, you mean that it is characteristic of it and represents its most typical features. *Montana is emblematic of America's isolationism.* `ADJ` `ADJ`

em·bodi·ment /ɪm'bɒdimənt/. If you say that someone or something is the **embodiment** of a quality or idea, you mean that that is their most noticeable characteristic or the basis of all they do. *A baby is the embodiment of vulnerability.* `◆◇◇◇ N-SING FORMAL`

em·body /ɪm'bɒdi/ **embodies, embodying, embodied.** **1** If someone or something **embodies** an idea or quality, they are a symbol or expression of that idea or quality. *That stability was embodied in the Gandhi family.* **2** If something **is embodied** in a particular thing, the second thing contains or consists of the first. *The constitution would embody the reforms first proposed by President Ramiz Alia.* `◆◇◇◇ VERB: V n beV-ed in/by n` `VERB: beV-ed in/by n V n`

em·bold·en /ɪm'bəʊldən/ **emboldens, emboldening, emboldened.** If you **are emboldened** by something, it makes you feel confident enough to behave in a particular way. *Four days of non-stop demonstrations have emboldened the anti-government protesters.* `VERB: beV-ed V n`

em·bossed /ɪm'bɒst, AM -'bɔːst/. If a surface such as paper or wood is **embossed** with a design, the design stands up slightly from the surface. *The paper on the walls was pale gold, embossed with swirling leaf designs.* `ADJ`

em·brace /ɪm'breɪs/ **embraces, embracing, embraced.** **1** If you **embrace** someone, you put your arms around them and hold them tightly, usually in order to show your love or affection for them. You can also say that two people **embrace** each other or that they **embrace**. *They embraced passionately.* ▶ Also a noun. *...a young couple locked in an embrace.* **2** If you **embrace** a change, political system, or idea, you start supporting it or believing in it wholeheartedly. *The new rules have been embraced by government watchdog organizations.* ▶ Also a noun. *The marriage signalled James's embrace of the Catholic faith.* **3** If something **embraces** a group of people, things, or ideas, it includes them in a larger group or category. *...a theory that would embrace the whole field of human endeavour.* `◆◆◇◇ V-RECIP: V n pl-n V` `N-COUNT` `VERB: V n beV-ed FORMAL` `N-SING` `VERB V n FORMAL`

em·broi·der /ɪm'brɔɪdə/ **embroiders, embroidering, embroidered.** **1** If something such as clothing or cloth **is embroidered** with a design, the design is stitched into it. *Matilda was embroidering an altar cloth... I have a pillow with my name embroidered on it.* **2** If you **embroider** a story or account of something, or if you **embroider** on it, you try to make it more interesting by adding details which may be untrue. *She embroidered on this theme for about ten minutes.* `◆◇◇◇ VERB: beV-ed with/ in n V n Also V-ed VERB: V n V on n`

em·broi·dery /ɪm'brɔɪdəri/ **embroideries.** **1** **Embroidery** consists of designs stitched into cloth. The panel contains an embroidery. **2** **Embroidery** is the activity of stitching designs onto cloth. *She learned sewing, knitting and embroidery.* `◆◇◇◇ N-VAR` `N-UNCOUNT`

em·broil /ɪm'brɔɪl/ **embroils, embroiling, embroiled.** If someone **embroils** you in a fight or an argument, they get you deeply involved in it. *Any hostilities could result in retaliation and further embroil U.N. troops in fighting.* ♦ **em·broiled** *The Government insisted that troops would not become embroiled in battles in Bosnia.* `VERB V n inn Also V n` `ADJ-GRADED`

em·broiled /ɪm'brɔɪld/. If you become **embroiled** with a person, you become involved in a relationship with them that causes you problems. *As Smith became embroiled with his new lover, the marriage was called off.* `ADJ-GRADED`

em·bryo /'embriəʊ/ **embryos.** **1** An **embryo** is an unborn animal or human being in the very early stages of development. **2** An **embryo** idea, system, or organization is in the very early stages of development, but is expected to grow stronger. *They are an embryo party of government.* **3** Something that is **in embryo** is at a very early stage of its development. *These developments were foreseen in embryo.* `◆◆◇◇ N-COUNT` `ADJ: ADJ n` `PHRASE`

em·bry·on·ic /,embri'ɒnɪk/. An **embryonic** process, idea, organization, or organism is one at a very early stage in its development. *...Romania's embryonic democracy. ...embryonic plant cells.* `ADJ-GRADED FORMAL`

em·cee /,em'siː/ **emcees.** An **emcee** is the same as a **master of ceremonies.** `N-COUNT AMERICAN`

em·er·ald /'emərəld/ **emeralds.** **1** An **emerald** is a bright green precious stone. **2** Something that is **emerald** is bright green in colour. *...an emerald wool gown.* `N-COUNT` `N-COUNT COLOUR`

E

emerge /ɪˈmɜːdʒ/ **emerges, emerging, emerged.** 1 To **emerge** means to come out from an enclosed or dark space, or from a position where you could not be seen. *The postman emerged from his van soaked to the skin.* 2 If you **emerge from** a difficult or bad experience, you come to the end of it. *The nation is emerging from the recession slowly.* 3 If a fact or result **emerges** from a period of thought, discussion, or investigation, it becomes known as a result of it. *...the growing corruption that has emerged in the past few years... It later emerged that much of the story was inaccurate.* 4 If someone or something **emerges** as a particular thing, they become recognised as that thing. *New leaders have emerged.* 5 When something such as an organization or an industry **emerges**, it comes into existence. *The new republic that emerged in October 1917.* ♦ **emer·gence** /ɪˈmɜːdʒəns/. *...the emergence of new democracies in East and Central Europe.*
(♦♦♦♦◇; VERB: V from n; VERB: V from n; VERB: V; it V that; VERB: V as n; VERB: V; JOURNALISM; N-UNCOUNT: with supp)

emer·gen·cy /ɪˈmɜːdʒənsi/ **emergencies.** 1 An **emergency** is an unexpected and difficult or dangerous situation, especially an accident, which arises suddenly and which must be dealt with quickly. *The hospital will cater only for emergencies.* 2 An **emergency** action is one that is done or arranged quickly and not in the normal way, because an emergency has occurred. *The Prime Minister has called an emergency meeting of parliament.* 3 **Emergency** equipment or supplies are those intended for use in an emergency. *They escaped through an emergency exit and called the police.*
(♦♦♦◇◇; N-COUNT; ADJ: ADJ n; ADJ: ADJ n)

e'mergency room, emergency rooms. In the United States, the **emergency room** is the part of a hospital where people are taken for emergency treatment. The usual British expression is **casualty**.
(N-COUNT)

e'mergency services. The **emergency services** are the public organizations whose job is to take quick action to deal with emergencies when they occur, especially the fire brigade, the police, and the ambulance service.
(♦◇◇◇◇; N-PLURAL)

emer·gent /ɪˈmɜːdʒənt/. An **emergent** country, political movement, or social group is one that is becoming powerful or coming into existence. *...an emergent nationalist movement.*
(ADJ: ADJ n; WRITTEN)

emeri·tus /ɪˈmerɪtəs/. **Emeritus** is used with a professional title to indicate that the person bearing it has retired but keeps the title as an honour. *...emeritus professor of physics.*
(ADJ: ADJ n, n ADJ)

emet·ic /ɪˈmetɪk/ **emetics.** An **emetic** is something that is given to someone to swallow, in order to make them vomit.
(N-COUNT)

emi·grant /ˈemɪɡrənt/ **emigrants.** An **emigrant** is a person who has left their own country to live in another country. Compare **immigrant**.
(♦◇◇◇◇; N-COUNT)

emi·grate /ˈemɪɡreɪt/ **emigrates, emigrating, emigrated.** If you **emigrate**, you leave your native country to live in another country. *He emigrated to Belgium.* ♦ **emi·gra·tion** /ˌemɪˈɡreɪʃən/ *...the huge emigration of workers to the West.*
(♦♦◇◇◇; V to n; N-UNCOUNT)

émi·gré /ˈemɪɡreɪ/ **émigrés;** also spelled **emigre.** An **émigré** is someone who has left their own country for political reasons. *...a Polish émigré family.*
(♦◇◇◇◇; N-COUNT)

emi·nence /ˈemɪnəns/. 1 **Eminence** is the quality of being very well-known and highly respected. *Beveridge was a man of great eminence.* 2 You use expressions such as **Your Eminence** or **His Eminence** when you are addressing or referring to a Roman Catholic cardinal.
(♦◇◇◇◇; N-UNCOUNT; N-VOC: poss N)

emi·nent /ˈemɪnənt/. An **eminent** person is well-known and respected. *...an eminent scientist.*
(♦◇◇◇◇; ADJ-GRADED)

emi·nent·ly /ˈemɪnəntli/. You use **eminently** in front of an adjective describing a positive quality in order to emphasize the quality expressed by that adjective. *His family was eminently respectable.*
(ADV-GRADED: ADV adj/-ed; PRAGMATICS)

emir /eˈmɪə/ **emirs.** An **emir** is a Muslim ruler. *...the Emir of Kuwait.*
(♦◇◇◇◇; N-COUNT)

emir·ate /ˈemərət, AM ɪˈmɪərət/ **emirates.** An **emirate** is a country that is ruled by an emir.
(N-COUNT)

em·is·sary /ˈemɪsəri, AM -seri/ **emissaries.** An **emissary** is a messenger or representative sent by
(N-COUNT; FORMAL)

one government or leader to another. *...the President's special emissary to Hanoi.*

emis·sion /ɪˈmɪʃən/ **emissions.** An **emission** of something such as gas or radiation is the release of it into the atmosphere. *Sulfur emissions from steel mills become acid rain.*
(♦♦◇◇◇; N-VAR; FORMAL)

emit /ɪˈmɪt/ **emits, emitting, emitted.** 1 If something **emits** heat, light, gas, or a smell, it produces it and sends it out by means of a physical or chemical process. *...the amount of carbon dioxide emitted.* 2 To **emit** a sound or noise means to produce it. *Polly blinked and emitted a long, low whistle.*
(♦◇◇◇◇; VERB: V n, be V-ed; FORMAL; V n; FORMAL)

emol·lient /ɪˈmɒliənt/ **emollients.** 1 An **emollient** is a liquid or cream which you put on your skin to soften it. 2 An **emollient** cream or other substance softens and soothes skin. 3 If you describe someone, especially a politician, as **emollient**, you mean that they try to be tactful to people and to reduce conflict. *...a deceptively emollient senior figure in a Conservative Government.*
(N-VAR; FORMAL; ADJ: ADJ n; FORMAL; ADJ ADJ-GRADED; FORMAL)

emolu·ment /ɪˈmɒljʊmənt/ **emoluments.** Emoluments are money or other forms of payment which a person receives for doing work. *He could earn up to £1m a year in salary and emoluments.*
(N-COUNT; FORMAL)

emo·tion /ɪˈməʊʃən/ **emotions.** 1 An **emotion** is a feeling such as happiness, love, fear, anger, or hatred, which can be caused by the situation that you are in or the people you are with. *Her voice trembled with emotion.* 2 **Emotion** is the part of a person's character that consists of their feelings, as opposed to their thoughts. *...the split between reason and emotion.*
(♦♦♦◇◇; N-VAR; N-UNCOUNT)

emo·tion·al /ɪˈməʊʃənəl/. 1 **Emotional** means concerned with emotions and feelings. *Victims are left with emotional problems that can last for life.* ♦ **emo·tion·al·ly** *He'd learned never to become emotionally involved.* 2 An **emotional** situation or issue is one that causes people to have strong feelings. *...the emotional issue of euthanasia.* ♦ **emotionally** *It was a very emotionally charged moment.* 3 If someone is or becomes **emotional** they show their feelings very openly, especially because they are upset. *I don't get as emotional as I once did.*
(♦♦♦◇◇; ADJ; ADV: ADV adj/-ed ADJ-GRADED; ADV-GRADED ADV adj/-ed ADJ-GRADED)

emo·tion·less /ɪˈməʊʃənləs/. If you describe someone as **emotionless**, you mean that they do not show any feelings or emotions.
(ADJ-GRADED)

emo·tive /ɪˈməʊtɪv/. An **emotive** situation or issue is likely to make people feel strong emotions. *Embryo research is an emotive issue.*
(♦◇◇◇◇; ADJ-GRADED)

em·pa·thet·ic /ˌempəˈθetɪk/. Someone who is **empathetic** has the ability to share another person's feelings or emotions as if they were their own. *...Clinton's skills as an empathetic listener.*
(ADJ-GRADED; FORMAL)

em·pa·thize /ˈempəθaɪz/ **empathizes, empathizing, empathized;** also spelled **empathise** in British English. If you **empathize** with someone, you understand their problems and feelings, because you have been in a similar situation. *Parents must make use of their natural ability to empathize.*
(VERB: V with n V)

em·pa·thy /ˈempəθi/. **Empathy** is the ability to share another person's feelings and emotions as if they were your own. *He had a natural empathy with children.*
(♦◇◇◇◇; N-UNCOUNT)

em·per·or /ˈempərə/ **emperors.** An **emperor** is a man who rules an empire or is the head of state in an empire.
(♦♦◇◇◇; N-COUNT)

em·pha·sis /ˈemfəsɪs/ **emphases** /ˈemfəsiːz/. 1 **Emphasis** is special or extra importance that is given to an activity or to a part or aspect of something. *Too much emphasis is placed on research... Grant puts a special emphasis on weather in his paintings.* 2 **Emphasis** is extra force that you put on a syllable, word, or phrase when you are speaking in order to make it seem more important. *'Of course, Vassios,' Leonidas said with emphasis.*
(♦♦♦◇◇; N-VAR; N-VAR)

em·pha·size /ˈemfəsaɪz/ **emphasizes, emphasizing, emphasized;** also spelled **emphasise** in British English. To **emphasize** something means to
(♦♦♦◇◇; VERB; V n; V that)

indicate that it is particularly important or true, or to draw special attention to it. *Her tight black jeans emphasize her birdlike legs... Mr Menem emphasized that his government will stick to its program... Your letter should emphasize how your skills will benefit the employer.*

em·phat·ic /ɪmˈfætɪk/. **1** An emphatic response or statement is one made in a forceful way, because the speaker feels very strongly about what he or she is saying. *His response was immediate and emphatic.* **2** If you are **emphatic** about something, you use forceful language because you feel very strongly about what you are saying. *The rebels are emphatic that this is not a surrender.* **3** An **emphatic** win or victory is one in which the winner has won by a large amount or distance.

em·phat·ic·al·ly /ɪmˈfætɪkli/. **1** If you say something **emphatically**, you say it in a forceful way because you feel very strongly about what you are saying. *Mr Craxi has emphatically denied the charges.* **2** You use **emphatically** to emphasize the statement you are making. *Politics is most emphatically back on the agenda.*

em·pire /ˈempaɪə/ **empires**. **1** An **empire** is a number of individual nations that are all controlled by the government or ruler of one particular country. *...the Roman Empire.* **2** You can refer to a group of companies controlled by one person as an **empire**. *...the big Mondadori publishing empire.*

em·pir·i·cal /ɪmˈpɪrɪkəl/. **Empirical** evidence or study relies on practical experience rather than theories. ♦ **em·pir·i·cal·ly** *To some extent it can be demonstrated empirically.*

em·pir·i·cism /ɪmˈpɪrɪsɪzəm/. **Empiricism** is the belief that people should rely on practical experience and experiments, rather than on theories, as a basis for knowledge. ♦ **em·piri·cist, empiricists** *He was an unswerving empiricist.*

em·place·ment /ɪmˈpleɪsmənt/ **emplacements**. **Emplacements** are specially prepared positions from which a heavy gun can be fired.

em·ploy /ɪmˈplɔɪ/ **employs, employing, employed**. **1** If a person or company **employs** you, they pay you to work for them. *More than 3,000 local workers are employed in the tourism industry.* **2** If you are **in the employ of** someone or something, you work for them. *Those in his employ were careful never to enrage him.* **3** If you **employ** certain methods, materials, or expressions, you use them. *The tactics the police are now to employ are definitely uncompromising. ...the vocabulary that she employs.* **4** If someone or someone's time **is employed** in doing something, they are using the time to do that thing. *Your time could be usefully employed in attending to professional matters.*

em·ploy·able /ɪmˈplɔɪəbəl/. **Employable** people have skills or abilities that are likely to make someone want to give them a job. *People need basic education if they are to become employable.*

em·ploy·ee /ɪmˈplɔɪiː/ **employees**. An **employee** is a person who is paid to work for a company or organization. *He is an employee of Fuji Bank. ...a government employee.*

em·ploy·er /ɪmˈplɔɪə/ **employers**. Your **employer** is the person or organization that you work for.

em·ploy·ment /ɪmˈplɔɪmənt/. **1 Employment** is the fact of having a paid job. *She was unable to find employment.* **2 Employment** is the fact of employing someone. *...the employment of children under nine.* **3 Employment** is the availability of work in a country or area. *...economic policies designed to secure full employment.*

em'ployment agency, employment agencies. An **employment agency** is a company that helps people to find work and helps employers to find the workers they need.

em·po·rium /ɪmˈpɔːriəm/ **emporiums** or **emporia**. An **emporium** is a shop.

em·pow·er /ɪmˈpaʊə/ **empowers, empowering, empowered**. **1** If someone or something **empow-**

ers you, they give you the means to achieve something, for example to become stronger or more successful. *What I'm trying to do is to empower people, to give them ways to help them get well.* ♦ **em·pow·er·ment** /ɪmˈpaʊəmənt/ *This government believes very strongly in the empowerment of women.* **2** If someone **is empowered** to do something, they have the authority or power to do it. *His position does not empower him to cite our views without consultation.*

em·press /ˈemprɪs/ **empresses**. An **empress** is a woman who rules an empire or who is the wife of an emperor.

emp·ti·ness /ˈemptinəs/. **1** A feeling of emptiness is an unhappy or frightening feeling that nothing is worthwhile. **2** The **emptiness** of a place is the fact that there is nothing in it. *...the emptiness of space.*

emp·ty /ˈempti/ **emptier, emptiest; empties, emptying, emptied**. **1** An **empty** place, vehicle, or container is one that has no people or things in it. *The room was bare and empty... The roads were nearly empty of traffic.* **2** If you **empty** a container, or **empty** something out of it, you remove its contents, especially by tipping it up. *Empty the noodles and liquid into a serving bowl... He emptied the contents out into the palm of his hand.* **3 Empties** are bottles or containers which no longer have anything in them.
4 If someone **empties** a room or place, or if it **empties**, everyone that is in it goes away. *The stadium emptied at the end of the first day of athletics.*
5 An **empty** gesture, threat, or relationship has no real value or meaning. *Nobody should take this decision as an empty threat.* **6** If you describe a person's life or a period of time as **empty**, you mean that nothing interesting or valuable happens in it. *I feel so empty, my life just doesn't seem worth living any more.*

empty-'handed. If you come away from somewhere **empty-handed**, you have failed to get what you wanted. *Shirley returned home empty-handed from her shopping trip.*

empty-'headed. If you describe someone as **empty-headed**, you mean that they are not very intelligent and often do silly things.

emu /ˈiːmjuː/ **emus**; the plural can be **emus** or **emu**. An **emu** is a large Australian bird which cannot fly.

emu·late /ˈemjʊleɪt/ **emulates, emulating, emulated**. If you **emulate** something or someone, you imitate them because you admire them. *Sons are traditionally expected to emulate their fathers.* ♦ **emu·la·tion** /ˌemjʊˈleɪʃən/ *...a role model worthy of emulation.*

emul·si·fier /ɪˈmʌlsɪfaɪə/ **emulsifiers**. An **emulsifier** is a substance used in food manufacturing which helps to combine liquids of different thicknesses.

emul·si·fy /ɪˈmʌlsɪfaɪ/ **emulsifies, emulsifying, emulsified**. When two liquids of different thicknesses **emulsify** or when they **are emulsified**, they combine. *Whisk the cream into the mixture to emulsify it.*

emul·sion /ɪˈmʌlʃən/ **emulsions**. **1 Emulsion** or **emulsion paint** is a water-based paint that is used for painting walls and ceilings. *...a matt emulsion.* **2** An **emulsion** is a liquid or cream which is a mixture of two or more liquids, such as oil and water, which do not naturally mix together. **3** In photography, **emulsion** is a substance that is used to make photographic film sensitive to light.

en- /ɪn-/. Also pronounced /en-/, particularly in American English. **En-** is added to words to form verbs that describe the process of putting someone into a particular state, condition, or place. *People with disabilities are now doing many things to enrich their lives... He is expected to be enthroned early next year.*

en·able /ɪˈneɪbəl/ **enables, enabling, enabled**. **1** If someone or something **enables** you to do a particular thing, they give you the opportunity to do it. *The new test should enable doctors to detect the*

disease early. ♦ **en·abling** *Researchers describe it as* ADJ
an enabling technology. **2** To **enable** something to VERB
happen means to make it possible for it to happen. V n to-inf
The hot sun enables the grapes to reach optimum V n
ripeness... The working class is still too small to en-
able a successful socialist revolution.

en·act /ɪnˈækt/ **enacts, enacting, enacted.** ♦♦◇◇◇
1 When a government or authority **enacts** a propo- VERB
sal, they make it into a law. *The bill would be sub-* V n
mitted for public discussion before being enacted as TECHNICAL
law. ♦ **en·act·ment** /ɪnˈæktmənt/ **enactments** N-VAR
We support the call for the enactment of a Bill of
Rights. **2** If people **enact** a story or play, they per- VERB: V n
form it by acting. ♦ **enactment** *The main building* N-VAR
was also used for the enactment of mystery plays.
3 If a particular event or situation **is enacted**, it VB: usu
happens, especially as a repetition of something passive
that has happened before. *It was a scene which was* be V-ed
enacted month after month for eight years. JOURNALISM

enam·el /ɪˈnæməl/ **enamels. 1** **Enamel** is a sub- ♦◇◇◇◇
stance like glass which can be heated and put onto N-VAR
metal in order to decorate or protect it. *...a white*
enamel saucepan. **2** **Enamel** is a hard, shiny paint N-VAR
that is used especially for painting metal and wood.
3 **Enamel** is the hard white substance that forms N-UNCOUNT
the outer part of a tooth.

enam·elled /ɪˈnæməld/; spelled **enameled** in Ameri- ADJ: ADJ n
can English. An **enamelled** object is decorated or
covered with enamel. *...enamelled plates.*

enam·el·ling /ɪˈnæməlɪŋ/; spelled **enameling** in N-UNCOUNT
American English. **Enamelling** is the decoration of
something such as jewellery with enamel.

en·am·oured /ɪnˈæməd/; spelled **enamored** in ADJ-GRADED
American English. If you say that you are **enam-** [PRAGMATICS]
oured of something or someone, you mean that you FORMAL
like or admire them a lot. If you say that you are not
enamoured of something, you mean that you dislike or disapprove of it.

en bloc /ˌɒn ˈblɒk/. If a group of people do some- ADV
thing **en bloc**, they do it all together and at the
same time. *Now the governors en bloc are demand-*
ing far more consultation.

en·camped /ɪnˈkæmpt/. If soldiers are **encamped** ADJ
somewhere, they have set up camp there. *Railways*
could now bring food to encamped armies. ♦ **en-**
·camp·ment /ɪnˈkæmpmənt/ **encampments** *...an* N-COUNT
encampment of 2,000 legionnaires.

en·cap·su·late /ɪnˈkæpsjʊleɪt/ **encapsulates,** ♦◇◇◇◇
encapsulating, encapsulated. If something VERB: V n
encapsulates facts or ideas, it represents all the be V-ed in n
most important aspects of those facts or ideas in a Also V n in n
very small space or in a single object or event. *His*
ideas were later encapsulated in a book strangely
called Democratic Ideals and Reality. ♦ **en·cap·su-**
·la·tion /ɪnˌkæpsjʊˈleɪʃən/ **encapsulations** *...a* N-COUNT
witty encapsulation of modern America.

en·case /ɪnˈkeɪs/ **encases, encasing, en-** ♦◇◇◇◇
cased. If a person or an object **is encased** in some- VERB:
thing, they are completely covered or surrounded be V-ed in n
by it. *These weapons also had a heavy brass guard* V n
which encased almost the whole hand. Also V n in/
with n

-ence /-əns/ or **-ency** /-ənsi/. **-ence** and **-ency** are SUFFIX
added to adjectives, usually in place of -ent, to form
nouns. These nouns refer to states, qualities, attitudes, or behaviour. For example, 'affluence' is the
state of being affluent, and 'complacency' is the attitude of someone who is complacent. Nouns like
these are often not defined in this dictionary, but
are treated with the related adjective.

en·chant /ɪnˈtʃɑːnt, -ˈtʃænt/ **enchants, enchant-** ♦◇◇◇◇
ing, enchanted. 1 If you **are enchanted** by some- VERB:
one or something, they cause you to have feelings be V-ed
of great delight or pleasure. *She enchanted you as* V n
she has so many others. ♦ **en·chant·ed** *They were* ADJ-GRADED
enchanted with the novelty of it all. **2** In fairy stories VERB: V n
and legends, to **enchant** someone or something V-ed
means to put a magic spell on them. *...Celtic stories*
of cauldrons and enchanted vessels.

en·chant·ing /ɪnˈtʃɑːntɪŋ, -ˈtʃænt-/. If you de- ♦◇◇◇◇
scribe someone or something as **enchanting**, you ADJ-GRADED

mean that they are attractive, delightful, or charming. *She's an absolutely enchanting child.*

en·chant·ment /ɪnˈtʃɑːntmənt, -ˈtʃænt-/. If you say N-UNCOUNT
that something has **enchantment**, you mean that it
makes you feel great delight or pleasure. Your **en-**
chantment with something is the fact of your feeling great delight or pleasure because of it. *The*
campsite had its own peculiar enchantment.

en·cir·cle /ɪnˈsɜːkəl/ **encircles, encircling, en-** ♦◇◇◇◇
circled. To **encircle** something or someone means VERB: V n
to surround or enclose them, or to go round them. be V-ed
By 22nd November the Sixth Army was encircled.

en·clave /ˈeŋkleɪv/ **enclaves.** An **enclave** is an ♦◇◇◇◇
area within a country or a city that is inhabited by N-COUNT
people of a different nationality or culture from the
inhabitants of the surrounding country or city.

en·close /ɪnˈkləʊz/ **encloses, enclosing, en-** ♦◇◇◇◇
closed. 1 If a place or object **is enclosed** by some- VERB
thing, the place or object is inside that thing or be V-ed in/by
completely surrounded by it. *Samples must be en-* n
closed in two watertight containers... Enclose the pot V n in n
in a clear polythene bag. **2** If you **enclose** something VERB: V n
with a letter, you put it in the same envelope as the V-ed
letter. *The enclosed leaflet shows how Service Care*
can ease all your worries.

en·clo·sure /ɪnˈkləʊʒə/ **enclosures.** An **enclo-** ♦◇◇◇◇
sure is an area of land that is surrounded by a wall N-COUNT
or fence and that is used for a particular purpose.

en·code /ɪnˈkəʊd/ **encodes, encoding, encod-** ♦◇◇◇◇
ed. If you **encode** a message or some information, VERB
you put it into a code or express it in a different V n
form or system of language. *The two parties encode*
confidential data in a form that is not directly read-
able by the other party.

en·com·pass /ɪnˈkʌmpəs/ **encompasses, en-** ♦◇◇◇◇
compassing, encompassed. 1 If something VERB
encompasses particular things, it includes them. V n
His repertoire encompassed everything from Bach to
Schoenberg. **2** To **encompass** a place means to VERB
completely surround or cover it. *The map shows the* V n
rest of the western region, encompassing nine states.

en·core /ˈɒŋkɔː, -ˈkɔː/ **encores. 1** An **encore** is a ♦◇◇◇◇
short extra performance at the end of a longer one, N-COUNT
which an entertainer gives because the audience
asks for it. **2** '**Encore**' is the word shouted by classi- CONVENTION
cal concert audiences when they want a performer
to perform an encore.

en·coun·ter /ɪnˈkaʊntə/ **encounters, encoun-** ♦♦◇◇◇
tering, encountered. 1 If you **encounter** prob- VERB
lems or difficulties, you experience them. *Mothers* V n
who were not teachers encountered great stress. **2** If VERB
you **encounter** someone, you meet them unexpect- V n
edly. *Did you encounter anyone in the building?* FORMAL
3 An **encounter** with someone is a meeting with N-COUNT
them, particularly one that is unexpected or significant. **4** An **encounter** is a particular type of experi- N-COUNT
ence. *...a sexual encounter. ...his first serious en-*
counter with alcohol.

en·cour·age /ɪnˈkʌrɪdʒ, AM -ˈkɜːr-/ **encourages,** ♦♦♦♦◇
encouraging, encouraged. 1 If you **encourage** VERB
someone, you give them confidence, for example by V n
letting them know that what they are doing is good
and telling them that they should continue to do it.
When things aren't going well, he encourages
me, telling me not to give up. **2** If someone **is en-** VB: usu
couraged by something, it gives them hope or con- passive
fidence. *Mr Major said he had been encouraged by* be V-ed by n
recent Irish statements about the issue. ♦ **en·cour-**
·aged *He was encouraged that there seemed to be* ADJ-GRADED
some progress. **3** If you **encourage** someone to do VERB
something, you try to persuade them to do it, for V n to-inf
example by trying to make it easier for them to do V n
it. You can also **encourage** an activity. *We want to*
encourage people to go fishing... Their task is to help
encourage private investment in Russia. **4** If some- VERB
thing **encourages** a particular activity or state, it V n
causes it to happen or increase. *...a natural sub-* V n to-inf
stance that encourages cell growth... Slow music en-
courages supermarket-shoppers to browse longer.

en·cour·age·ment /ɪnˈkʌrɪdʒmənt, AM -ˈkɜːr-/ **en-** ◆◆◇◇◇
couragements. Encouragement is the activity of   N-VAR
encouraging someone, or something that is said or
done in order to encourage them. *Thanks for your
advice and encouragement.*

en·cour·ag·ing /ɪnˈkʌrɪdʒɪŋ, AM -ˈkɜːr-/. Some- ◆◆◇◇◇
thing that is **encouraging** gives people hope or con-   ADJ-GRADED
fidence. *There are encouraging signs of an artistic revival... It was encouraging that he recognised the
dangers facing the company.* ♦ **en·cour·ag·ing·ly**   ADV-GRADED
*She smiled encouragingly. ...encouragingly large
audiences.*

en·croach /ɪnˈkrəʊtʃ/ **encroaches, encroach-** ◆◇◇◇◇
ing, encroached. 1 If one thing **encroaches** on   VERB
another, the first thing spreads or becomes strong-   PRAGMATICS
er, and slowly begins to restrict the power, range, or   V on/upon n
effectiveness of the second thing; used showing   V-ing
disapproval. *The Church is resisting government*   Also V on
attempts to encroach upon its authority. ...the en-   FORMAL
croaching competition of television. ♦ **en·croach**
·ment /ɪnˈkrəʊtʃmənt/ **encroachments.** *It's a*   N-VAR
*sign of the encroachment of commercialism in medi-
cine.* **2** If something **encroaches** on a place, it   VERB:
spreads and takes over more and more of that   V on n
place. *I turned into the dirt road and followed it*   V-ing
through encroaching trees and bushes.   FORMAL

en·crust·ed /ɪnˈkrʌstɪd/. If an object is **encrusted**   ADJ-GRADED
with something, its surface is covered with a layer of
that thing. ▶ Also a combining form. *...a jewel-*   COMB
encrusted ring.

en·cum·ber /ɪnˈkʌmbə/ **encumbers, encumber-**
ing, encumbered. 1 If you **are encumbered** by   VERB: V n
something, it prevents you from moving freely or   be V-ed with n
doing what you want. *It is still labouring under the
debt burden that it was encumbered with in the
1980s.* ♦ **en·cum·bered** *The rest of the world is less*   ADJ-GRADED
encumbered with legislation. **2** If a place **is encum-**   VERB
bered with things, it contains so many of them that   be V-ed prep
it is difficult to move freely there. *The narrow quay
was encumbered by hundreds of carts.*

en·cum·brance /ɪnˈkʌmbrəns/ **encumbrances.**   N-COUNT
An **encumbrance** is something or someone that encumbers you. *Magdalena considered the past an irrelevant encumbrance.*

-ency. See **-ence.**

en·cyc·li·cal /ɪnˈsɪklɪkəl/ **encyclicals.** An **encycli-**   N-COUNT
cal is a religious letter which is sent to many
churches, especially one written by the Pope stating
the official Roman Catholic teaching on a particular
subject.

en·cy·clo·pedia /ɪnˌsaɪkləˈpiːdiə/ **encyclo-** ◆◇◇◇◇
pedias; also spelled **encyclopaedia** in British Eng-   N-COUNT
lish. An **encyclopedia** is a book or set of books in
which facts about many different subjects or about
one particular subject are arranged for reference.

en·cy·clo·pedic /ɪnˌsaɪkləˈpiːdɪk/; also spelled **en-**   ADJ-GRADED
cyclopaedic in British English. If you describe
something as **encyclopedic,** you mean that it is very
full and complete in the amount of knowledge or
information that it has. *He had an encyclopaedic
knowledge of drugs.*

end /end/ **ends, ending, ended. 1** The **end** of ◆◆◆◆◇
something such as a period of time, an event, a   N-SING:
book, or a film is the last part of it or the final point   the N
in it. *The £5 banknote was first issued at the end of
the 18th century... The report is expected by the end
of the year... You will have the chance to ask questions at the end.* **2** When a situation, process, or ac-   V-ERG: V
tivity **ends,** or when something or someone **ends** it,   V n
it reaches its final point and stops. *She began to
weep. That ended our discussion.* ♦ **end·ing** *With*   N-SING
*the ending of the cold war the reconciliation is com-
plete.* **3** If a period of time **ends,** it reaches its final   VERB
point. *The college year ends in March.*   V

4 An **end** to something or the **end** of it is the act or re-   N-COUNT
sult of stopping it so that it does not continue any
longer. *I was worried she would walk out or bring the
interview to an end.* **5** If something is **at an end,** it has   PHRASE
finished and will not continue. *The recession is definitely at an end.* **6** If something **comes to an end,** it   PHRASE

stops. **7** To **put an end to** something means to cause it   PHRASE
to stop. **8** If you do something to **the bitter end** or to   PHRASE
the very end, you continue to do it for as long as you
can, although it may be very unpleasant or dangerous. *We will fight to the bitter end.*

9 If you say that someone or something **ends** a period   V-ERG
of time in a particular way, you are indicating what   V n prep/adv
the final situation was like. You can also say that a pe-   V prep
riod of time **ends** in a particular way. *The markets*   Also V n by
ended the week on a quiet note... The evening ended   -ing,
with a dramatic display of fireworks. **10** If something   V n -ing
such as a book, speech, or performance **ends** with a   V with/on n
particular thing or the writer or performer **ends** it with   V n with on n
that thing, its final part consists of the thing men-   Also V with
tioned. *The book ends on a lengthy description of Ha-*   quote
*waii... Dawkins ends his discussion with a call for lib-
eration.* **11** If a situation or event **ends** in a particular   VERB
way, it has that particular result. *The match ended in a*   V in n
draw... Our conversations ended with him saying he   V with n -ing
would try to be more understanding... Shares ended   V adv/adj
1.7 per cent firmer on the Frankfurt exchange.

12 If you **end** by doing something or **end** in a particu-   VERB:
lar state, you do that thing or get into that state even   V by-ing
though you did not originally intend to. *They'll prob-*   V adv/prep
ably end back on the streets. **13** You say **in the end**   PHRASE
when you are saying what is the final result of a series   PRAGMATICS
of events, or what is your final conclusion after considering all the relevant facts. *I toyed with the idea of
calling the police, but in the end I didn't.* **14** You say **at**   PHRASE
the end of the day when you are talking about what   PRAGMATICS
happens after a long series of events or what appears   INFORMAL
to be the case after you have considered the relevant
facts. *At the end of the day it's up to the Germans to
decide.*

15 A journey, road, or river that **ends** at a particular   VERB
place stops there and goes no further. *The road ended*   V prep/adv
at a T-junction. **16** If a process or person has reached   Also V
the end of the road, they are unable to progress any   PHRASE
further. *Is this the end of the road for the hardliners in
Congress?* **17** If you say that something **ends** at a par-   VERB
ticular point, you mean that it applies or exists up to   V adv/prep
that point, and no further. *Helen is also 25 and from
Birmingham, but the similarity ends there.*

18 The two **ends** of something long and narrow are   N-COUNT:
the two points or parts of it that are furthest away   with supp
from each other. *...both ends of the tunnel. ...a tube
with metal electrodes at each end.* **19** The **end** of a   N-COUNT
long, narrow object such as a finger or a pencil is the
tip or smallest edge of it, usually the part that is furthest away from you. *...the end of her cigarette.* **20** If   VERB
an object **ends with** or **in** a particular thing, it has that   V with/in n
thing on its tip or point, or as its last part. *It has three
pairs of legs, each ending in a large claw.* **21** End is   N-COUNT:
used to refer to either of the two extreme points of a   with supp
scale, or of something that you are considering as a
scale. *The agreement has been criticised by extremist
groups on both ends of the political spectrum.* **22** The   N-COUNT:
other **end** is one of two places that are connected be-   supp N
cause people are communicating with each other by
telephone or writing, or are travelling from one place
to the other. *There was silence at the other end of the
line... Make sure to meet them at the other end.*

23 An **end** is the purpose for which something is done   N-COUNT
or towards which you are working. *The police force is
being manipulated for political ends.* **24** If you con-   PHRASE
sider something to be **an end in itself,** you do it because it seems desirable and not because it is likely to
lead to something else. *While he had originally traveled in order to study, traveling had become an end in
itself.*

25 You can refer to someone's death as their **end.** *He*   N-COUNT
had met a violent end. **26** If someone **ends it all,** they   LITERARY
commit suicide.   PHRASE

27 If you describe something as, for example, the deal   PHRASE
to end all deals or the film **to end all** films, you mean
that it is a very important or successful deal or film
and that compared to it all other deals or films would
seem trivial or second-rate. *It was going to be a party
to end all parties.* **28** If you say that something bad is   PHRASE
not the end of the world, you are trying to stop your-   PRAGMATICS

self or someone else being so upset by it, by suggesting that it is not the worst thing that could happen. *Obviously I'd be disappointed if we don't make it, but it wouldn't be the end of the world.* **29** When something happens for hours, days, weeks, or years **on end**, it happens continuously and without stopping for that time that is mentioned. *I spend days on end in this studio.* **30 No end** means a lot. *The problem was causing the poor woman no end of misery.* PHRASE

PHRASE INFORMAL

31 If you say that someone **has gone off the deep end**, you mean that their mind has stopped working in a normal way and their behaviour has become very strange as a result. **32** If you **are thrown in at the deep end**, you are put in a completely new situation or given something difficult to do without any help or preparation. If you **jump in at the deep end**, you go into a completely new situation or begin to do something difficult without any help or preparation. **33** If you refer to a particular **end** of a project or piece of work, you mean a part or aspect of it, for example a part of it that is done by a particular person or in a particular place. *Let's go up to the office and settle the business end of things.* **34** If you find it difficult to **make ends meet**, you can only just manage financially. *I can't make ends meet from temping.* PHRASE INFORMAL

PHRASE BRITISH

N-COUNT SPOKEN

PHRASE

35 • the end of your tether: see tether. **•** to burn the candle at both ends: see candle. **•** to make your hair stand on end: see hair. **•** a means to an end: see mean. **•** to be on the receiving end: see receive. **•** to get the wrong end of the stick: see stick. **•** to come to a sticky end: see sticky. **•** to be at your wits' end: see wit.

end up. 1 If someone or something **ends up** somewhere, they eventually arrive there, usually by accident. *The painting ended up at the Tate Gallery.* **2** If you **end up** doing something or **end up** in a particular state, you do that thing or get into that state even though you did not originally intend to. *You might end up getting something you don't want... Every time they went dancing they ended up in a bad mood... She could have ended up a millionairess.* PHRASAL VB V P prep/adv

V P -ing V P prep/adv V P n

en·dan·ger /ɪnˈdeɪndʒə/ **endangers, endangering, endangered.** To **endanger** something or someone means to put them in a situation where they might be harmed or destroyed completely. *...endangered species such as lynx, wolf and several species of vulture.* ♦♦◇◇◇ VERB: V n V-ed

en·dear /ɪnˈdɪə/ **endears, endearing, endeared.** If something **endears** you **to** someone or if you **endear** yourself **to** them, you become popular with them and well liked by them. *He has endeared himself to the American public.* ♦◇◇◇◇ VERB: V n to n V pron-refl to n

en·dear·ing /ɪnˈdɪərɪŋ/. If you describe someone's behaviour as **endearing**, you mean that it causes you to feel very fond of them. *...an endearing personality.* **♦ en·dear·ing·ly** *She is endearingly free of pretensions.* ♦◇◇◇◇ ADJ-GRADED: v-link ADJ

ADV-GRADED

en·dear·ment /ɪnˈdɪəmənt/ **endearments.** An **endearment** is a loving or affectionate word or phrase that you say to someone you love. *No term of endearment crossed their lips.* N-VAR

en·deav·our /ɪnˈdevə/ **endeavours, endeavouring, endeavoured;** spelled **endeavor** in American English. **1** If you **endeavour** to do something, you try very hard to do it. *I will endeavour to arrange it.* **2** An **endeavour** is an attempt to do something, especially something new or original. *...the benefits of investment in scientific endeavour.* ♦♦◇◇◇

VERB V to-inf FORMAL N-VAR FORMAL

en·dem·ic /enˈdemɪk/. **1** If a disease or illness is **endemic** in a place, it is frequently found among the people who live there. *Polio was then endemic among children my age.* **2** If you say that a condition or problem is **endemic**, you mean that it is very common and strong, and cannot be dealt with easily. *...powerful radicals with an endemic hatred and fear of the West.* ♦◇◇◇◇ ADJ TECHNICAL

ADJ-GRADED WRITTEN

end·ing /ˈendɪŋ/ **endings. 1** You can refer to the last part of a book, play, or film as the **ending**. *The film has a Hollywood happy ending.* **2** The **ending** ♦♦◇◇◇ N-COUNT

N-COUNT:

of a word is the last part of it. *...common word endings, like 'ing' in walking.* **3** See also **nerve ending**. with supp

en·dive /ˈendɪv, AM -daɪv/ **endives. 1 Endive** is a type of plant with crisp curly leaves that is eaten in salads. **2 Endive** is type of a plant with crunchy sharp-tasting leaves that is eaten in salads. The British word is **chicory**. N-VAR

N-VAR AMERICAN

end·less /ˈendləs/. If you say that something is **endless**, you mean that it is very large or lasts for a very long time, and it seems as if it will never stop. *...an endless street... The war was endless.* **♦ end·less·ly** *They talk about it endlessly. ...endlessly long arcades of shops.* ♦♦◇◇◇ ADJ-GRADED

ADV-GRADED

endo·crine /ˈendəkraɪn/. The **endocrine** system is the system of glands that produce hormones which go directly into the bloodstream, such as the pituitary or thyroid glands. ADJ: ADJ n TECHNICAL

E

en·dorse /ɪnˈdɔːs/ **endorses, endorsing, endorsed. 1** If you **endorse** someone or something, you say publicly that you support or approve of them. *I can endorse their opinion wholeheartedly.* **♦ en·dorse·ment, endorsements** *That adds up to an endorsement of the status quo.* **2** If you **endorse** a product or company, you appear in advertisements for it. *The twins endorsed a line of household cleaning products.* **♦ endorsement** *Her income from endorsements is around $7 million a year.* **3** If someone's driving licence **is endorsed**, an official record is made on it that they have been found guilty of a driving offence. *He also had his licence endorsed with eight penalty points.* **♦ en·dorse·ment** *He has endorsements on his licence.* **4** When you **endorse** a cheque, you write your name on the back of it so that it can be paid into someone else's bank account. ♦♦◇◇◇ VERB V n

N-COUNT VERB V n

N-COUNT

V-PASSIVE: be V-ed have n V-ed N-COUNT VERB: V n

en·dow /ɪnˈdaʊ/ **endows, endowing, endowed. 1** If someone **is endowed** with a particular desirable characteristic or possession, they have it. *You are endowed with wealth, good health and a lively intellect.* **♦ en·dow·ment, endowments** *People differ from each other in their natural mental endowments.* **2** If you **endow** something or someone **with** a particular quality, you think they have it. *The onlooker is tempted to endow the computer with human values such as irony.* **3** If someone **endows** an institution, scholarship, or project, they provide a large amount of money which will produce the annual income needed to pay for it. *The ambassador has endowed a $1 million public-service fellowships program.* **♦ en·dow·ment** *The company revived the finances of the Oxford Union with a £1m endowment.* ♦◇◇◇◇ VB: usu passive be V-ed with n FORMAL N-COUNT

VERB V n with n FORMAL

VERB V n

N-COUNT

en·dow·ment /ɪnˈdaʊmənt/ **endowments.** An **endowment** policy or mortgage is an insurance policy or mortgage which you pay towards each year and which then provides you with a large sum of money at the end of a fixed period. ♦♦◇◇◇ N-COUNT BRITISH

,end 'product, end products. The **end product** of something is the thing that is produced or achieved by means of it. *It is the end product of exhaustive research and development.* N-COUNT

,end re'sult, end results. The **end result** of an activity or a process is the final result or outcome that it produces. *The end result of this will be unity.* ♦◇◇◇◇ N-COUNT

en·dur·ance /ɪnˈdjʊərəns, AM -ˈdʊr-/. **Endurance** is the ability to continue with a difficult experience or activity over a long period of time. *...his powers of endurance.* ♦◇◇◇◇ N-UNCOUNT

en·dure /ɪnˈdjʊə, AM -ˈdʊr/ **endures, enduring, endured. 1** If you **endure** a painful or difficult situation, you do not avoid it or give up, usually because you cannot. *The company endured heavy financial losses... unbearable pain, which they had to endure in solitude.* **2** If something **endures**, it continues to exist without any loss in quality or importance. *Somehow the language persists.* **♦ en·dur·ing** *...the start of an enduring friendship.* ♦♦◇◇◇ VERB V n

VERB V

ADJ-GRADED

en·ema /ˈenɪmə/ **enemas.** If someone has an **enema**, a liquid is put into their rectum in order to N-COUNT

empty their bowels, for example before they have
an operation.

en·e·my /'enəmi/ **enemies. 1** If someone is your ◆◆◆◇◇
enemy, they hate you or want to harm you. **2** If N-COUNT
someone is your **enemy**, they are opposed to what N-COUNT
you think or do. *...the Government's political en-
emies.* **3** The **enemy** is a country, army, or other N-COLL-SING:
force that is opposed to you in a war. *He searched* theN,
the skies for enemy bombers. **4** If one thing is the N-COUNT
enemy of another thing, the second thing cannot FORMAL
happen or succeed because of the first thing. *Reform, as we know, is the enemy of revolution.*

en·er·get·ic /ˌenə'dʒetɪk/. **1** If you are **energetic** in ◆◆◇◇◇
what you do, you have a lot of enthusiasm and ADJ-GRADED
determination. *The next government will play an
energetic role in seeking multilateral nuclear disarmament.* ♦ **en·er·get·i·cal·ly** *He had worked en-* ADV-GRADED:
ergetically all day on his new book. **2** An **energetic** ADV with v
person is very active and does not feel at all tired. ADJ-GRADED
An **energetic** activity involves a lot of physical
movement and power. *Ten year-olds are incredibly
energetic.* ♦ **energetically** *Gretchen chewed ener-* ADV-GRADED:
getically on the steak. ADV with v

en·er·gize /'enədʒaɪz/ **energizes, energizing,** ◆◇◇◇◇
energized; also spelled **energise** in British Eng- VERB
lish. To **energize** someone means to give them the V n
enthusiasm and determination to do something. *He
helped energize and mobilize millions of people
around the nation.* ♦ **en·er·giz·ing** *Acupuncture* ADJ-GRADED
has a harmonizing and energizing effect.

en·er·gy /'enədʒi/ **energies. 1** **Energy** is the abil- ◆◆◆◆◇
ity and strength to do active physical things. *He was* N-UNCOUNT
*saving his energy for next week's race in Belgium...
We try to boost our energy by eating.* **2** **Energy** is de- N-UNCOUNT
termination and enthusiasm about doing things; PRAGMATICS
used showing approval. *You have drive and energy
for those things you are interested in.* **3** Your **ener-** N-COUNT
gies are your efforts and attention, which you can
direct towards a particular aim. *We must concen-
trate our energies on treating addiction first.* **4** **Ener-** N-UNCOUNT
gy is the power from sources such as electricity and
coal that makes machines work or provides heat.
*...nuclear energy... Improve the energy efficiency of
your home.*

en·er·vat·ed /'enəveɪtɪd/. If you feel **enervated**, ADJ-GRADED
you feel tired and weak. ♦ **en·er·vat·ing** *...a hot* FORMAL
and enervating climate. ADJ-GRADED

en·fant ter·ri·ble /ˌɒnfɒn te'riːblə/ **enfants** N-COUNT
terribles. If you describe someone as an **enfant
terrible**, you mean that they are talented but unconventional, and often shock other members of
their profession. *He became known as the enfant
terrible of British theater.*

en·fee·bled /ɪn'fiːbəld/. If someone or something ADJ-GRADED
is **enfeebled**, they have become very weak. *He finds* FORMAL
himself politically enfeebled.

en·fold /ɪn'fəʊld/ **enfolds, enfolding, enfolded.** VERB
1 If something **enfolds** an object or person, they V n
surround or are wrapped around them. *Aurora felt* beV-ed in n
the opium haze enfold her... He was now comfort- Also V n in n
ably enfolded in a woolly dressing-gown. **2** If you LITERARY
enfold someone or something, you hold them close VERB: V n
in a gentle, loving way. LITERARY

en·force /ɪn'fɔːs/ **enforces, enforcing, en-** ◆◆◇◇◇
forced. 1 If people in authority **enforce** a law or a VERB
rule, they make sure that it is obeyed, usually by V n
punishing people who do not obey it. *Until now,
the government has only enforced the ban with regard to American ships.* ♦ **en·force·able** *...the* ADJ-GRADED
creation of legally enforceable contracts. ♦ **en-**
·force·ment *The doctors want stricter enforcement* N-UNCOUNT
of existing laws. **2** To **enforce** something means to VERB: V n
force or cause it to be done or to happen. *David is* V-ed
now living in Beirut again after an enforced absence.

en·fran·chise /ɪn'fræntʃaɪz/ **enfranchises, en-** VERB
franchising, enfranchised. To **enfranchise** V n
someone means to give them the right to vote in FORMAL
elections. *The company voted to enfranchise its 120
women members.* ♦ **en·fran·chise·ment** *...the en-* N-UNCOUNT
franchisement of the country's blacks.

en·gage /ɪn'geɪdʒ/ **engages, engaging, en-** ◆◆◆◇◇
gaged. 1 If you **engage in** an activity, you do it or V inn
are actively involved with it. *I have never engaged in* FORMAL
the drug trade. **2** If something **engages** you or your VERB
attention or interest, it keeps you interested in it. V n
*They never learned skills to engage the attention of
the others.* **3** If you **engage** someone in conversa- VERB
tion, you have a conversation with them. *We want* V n inn
to engage recognized leaders in discussion. **4** If you VERB
engage with something or **with** a group of people, V with n
you feel actively involved and closely connected
with it. *She found it hard to engage with office life.*
♦ **en·gage·ment** *Audiences experience real engage-* N-UNCOUNT
ment with the play.
5 If you **engage** someone to do a particular job, you VERB
appoint them to do it. *We engaged the services of a rec-* V n
ognised engineer. **6** When a part of a machine or other V-ERG
mechanism **engages** or when you **engage** it, it moves V n
into a position where it fits into something else. *Press
the lever until you hear the catch engage. ...how to engage the four-wheel drive.* **7** When a military force **en-** VERB: V n
gages the enemy, it attacks them and starts a battle.
8 See also **engaged, engaging.**

en·gaged /ɪn'geɪdʒd/. **1** Someone who is **engaged** ◆◆◇◇◇
in or **engaged on** a particular activity is doing it or ADJ:
involved with it. *The police said they found the three* v-link ADJ in/
engaged in target practice. **2** When two people are onn
engaged, they have agreed to marry each other. *We* FORMAL
got engaged on my eighteenth birthday... He was en- ADJ
gaged to Miss Julia Maria Boardman. **3** If a tele- ADJ:
phone line is **engaged**, it is already being used by v-link ADJ
someone else so that you are unable to speak to the BRITISH
person you are phoning. The usual American word
is **busy**. *We tried to call you back but you were engaged.* **4** If a public toilet is **engaged**, it is already ADJ:
being used by someone else. The usual American v-link ADJ
term is **occupied**. BRITISH

en·gage·ment /ɪn'geɪdʒmənt/ **engagements.** ◆◇◇◇◇
1 An **engagement** is an arrangement that you have N-COUNT
made to do something at a particular time. *He had* FORMAL
*an engagement at a restaurant in Greek Street at
eight.* **2** An **engagement** is an agreement that two N-COUNT
people have made with each other to get married.
You can refer to the period of time during
which they have this agreement as their **engagement**. *I've broken off my engagement to Arthur... I
felt our engagement was quite an unhappy time.* **3** A N-VAR
military **engagement** is an armed conflict between
two enemies. **4** See also **engage.**

en'gagement ring, engagement rings. An en- N-COUNT
gagement **ring** is a ring worn by a woman when she
is engaged to be married.

en·gag·ing /ɪn'geɪdʒɪŋ/. An **engaging** person or ◆◇◇◇◇
thing is pleasant, interesting, and entertaining. ADJ-GRADED

en·gen·der /ɪn'dʒendə/ **engenders, engender-** ◆◇◇◇◇
ing, engendered. If someone or something **en-** VERB
genders a particular feeling or situation, they cause V n
it to occur. *He has what it takes to engender loyalty.* FORMAL

en·gine /'endʒɪn/ **engines. 1** The **engine** of a car ◆◆◆◇
or other vehicle is the part that produces the power N-COUNT
which makes the vehicle move. *He got into the driving seat and started the engine. ...an engine failure.*
♦ **-engined** *...the world's biggest twin-engined air-* COMB
liner. **2** An **engine** is also the large vehicle that N-COUNT
pulls a railway train. *...a steam engine.*

en·gi·neer /ˌendʒɪ'nɪə/ **engineers, engineering,** ◆◆◆◇
engineered. 1 An **engineer** is a person who uses N-COUNT
scientific knowledge to design, construct, and maintain engines and machines or structures such as
roads, railways, and bridges. ● See also **chemical
engineering, civil engineering, electrical engineering, sound engineer. 2** An **engineer** is a person who N-COUNT
repairs mechanical or electrical devices. *They send a
service engineer to fix the disk drive.* **3** An **engineer** N-COUNT
is a person who is responsible for maintaining the
engine of a ship while it is at sea. **4** When a vehicle, VERB:
bridge, or building is **engineered**, it is planned and beV-ed
constructed using scientific methods. *...the car's bet-* V-ed
ter designed and engineered rivals. **5** If you **engi-** VERB
neer an event or situation, you arrange for it to V n

happen, in a clever or indirect way. *He could stand no more and engineered an escape.*

en·gi·neer·ing /ˌendʒɪˈnɪərɪŋ/. Engineering is the work involved in designing and constructing engines and machinery, or structures such as roads and bridges. Engineering is also the subject studied by people who want to do this work. *...graduates with degrees in engineering.* ● See also **chemical engineering, civil engineering, electrical engineering, genetic engineering.** ◆◆◆◇ N-UNCOUNT

Eng·lish /ˈɪŋɡlɪʃ/. **1** English means belonging or relating to England, or to its people or language. It is also sometimes used to mean belonging or relating to Great Britain, although many people object to this. *...the English way of life.* ▶ The English are English people. **2** English is the language spoken by people who live in Great Britain and Ireland, the United States, Canada, Australia, and many other countries. *He uses tapes of this program to teach English.* ◆◆◆◇ ADJ / N-PLURAL: the N / N-UNCOUNT

English 'breakfast, English breakfasts. An English breakfast is a breakfast consisting of cooked food such as bacon, eggs, sausages, and tomatoes, with toast and tea or coffee. N-COUNT

en·gorged /ɪnˈɡɔːdʒd/. Something that is engorged is swollen, usually because it has been filled with fluid. *...the tissues become engorged with blood.* ADJ

en·grave /ɪnˈɡreɪv/ **engraves, engraving, engraved.** If you engrave something with a design or inscription, or if you engrave a design on it, you cut the design into its surface. *Your wedding ring can be engraved with a personal inscription... Harrods will also engrave your child's name on the side... I'm having 'John Law' engraved on the cup.* ♦ **en·grav·er, engravers** *He was a master engraver.* ◇◇◇◇ VERB be V-ed with n / V n on/in n / have n V-ed / prep Also V n / N-COUNT

en·graved /ɪnˈɡreɪvd/. If you say that something is engraved on your mind or memory or on your heart, you are emphasizing that you will never forget it. *Her image is engraved upon my heart.* ADJ: v-link ADJ in/on/upon n PRAGMATICS

en·grav·ing /ɪnˈɡreɪvɪŋ/ **engravings. 1** An engraving is a picture or design that has been cut into a surface. **2** An engraving is a picture that has been printed from a plate on which designs have been cut. N-COUNT / N-COUNT

en·grossed /ɪnˈɡrəʊst/. If you are engrossed in something, it holds your attention completely. *Tony didn't notice because he was too engrossed in his work.* ADJ-GRADED

en·gross·ing /ɪnˈɡrəʊsɪŋ/. Something that is engrossing is very interesting and holds your attention completely. *He is an engrossing subject for a book.* ADJ-GRADED

en·gulf /ɪnˈɡʌlf/ **engulfs, engulfing, engulfed.** If something such as fire or conflict engulfs a place, it spreads quickly and uncontrollably throughout it. *A revolutionary wave now threatens to engulf the country... The building was engulfed in flames.* ◇◇◇◇ VERB V n / be V-ed in n

en·hance /ɪnˈhɑːns, -ˈhæns/ **enhances, enhancing, enhanced.** To enhance something means to improve its value, quality, or attractiveness. *They'll be keen to enhance their reputation abroad.* ♦ **en·hance·ment, enhancements** *He was concerned with the enhancement of the human condition.* ♦ **en·hanc·er, enhancers** *Cinnamon is an excellent flavour enhancer.* ◆◆◇◇ VERB V n / N-VAR / N-COUNT

enig·ma /ɪˈnɪɡmə/ **enigmas.** If you describe something or someone as an enigma, you mean they are mysterious or difficult to understand. *Iran remains an enigma for the outside world.* ◇◇◇◇ N-COUNT

en·ig·mat·ic /ˌenɪɡˈmætɪk/. Someone or something that is enigmatic is mysterious and difficult to understand. *...an enigmatic smile. ...one of Welles's most enigmatic films.* ♦ **en·ig·mati·cal·ly** *'Corbiere didn't deserve this,' she said enigmatically.* ◇◇◇◇ ADJ-GRADED / ADV-GRADED

en·join /ɪnˈdʒɔɪn/ **enjoins, enjoining, enjoined. 1** If you enjoin someone to do something, you order them to do it. If you enjoin an action or attitude, you order people to do it or have it. *She enjoined me strictly not to tell anyone else... Islam enjoins tolerance... The positive neutrality enjoined on the force has now been overtaken by events.* **2** If a VERB V n to-inf / V-ed / FORMAL

judge enjoins someone from doing something, they order them not to do it. If a judge enjoins an action, they order people not to do it. *The judge enjoined Varityper from using the ad in any way. ...a preliminary injunction enjoining the practice.* V n from -ing/n / V n / AMERICAN / FORMAL

en·joy /ɪnˈdʒɔɪ/ **enjoys, enjoying, enjoyed. 1** If you enjoy something, you find pleasure and satisfaction in doing it or experiencing it. *Ross had always enjoyed the company of women... He was a guy who enjoyed life to the full... I enjoyed playing cricket.* **2** If you enjoy yourself, you do something that you like doing or you take pleasure in the situation that you are in. *I am really enjoying myself at the moment.* **3** If you enjoy something such as a right, benefit, or privilege, you have it. *The average German will enjoy 40 days' paid holiday this year.* ◆◆◆◇ VERB V n/-ing / VERB V pron-refl / VERB V n / FORMAL

en·joy·able /ɪnˈdʒɔɪəbəl/. Something that is enjoyable gives you pleasure. *Shopping for clothes should be an enjoyable experience.* ♦ **en·joy·ably** *...an enjoyably nasty thriller. ...the place in which he has enjoyably spent his working life.* ADJ-GRADED / ADV-GRADED

en·joy·ment /ɪnˈdʒɔɪmənt/. Your enjoyment of something is the feeling of pleasure and satisfaction that you have when you do or experience it. *I apologise if your enjoyment of the movie was spoiled.* ◆◇◇◇ N-UNCOUNT

en·large /ɪnˈlɑːdʒ/ **enlarges, enlarging, enlarged. 1** When you enlarge something or when it enlarges, it becomes bigger. *...the plan to enlarge Ewood Park into a 30,000 all-seater stadium... The glands in the neck may enlarge.* ♦ **en·larged** *...an enlarged peacekeeping force.* ♦ **en·large·ment** *There is insufficient space for enlargement of the buildings.* **2** To enlarge a photograph means to develop a bigger print of it. ♦ **en·large·ment, enlargements** *You can have your film processed and enlargements made.* **3** If you enlarge on something that has been mentioned, you give more details about it. *Mr Dienstbier was enlarging on proposals he made last night.* ◆◆◇◇ V-ERG V n / V / ADJ-GRADED / N-UNCOUNT / VERB: V n / N-COUNT / VERB V on/upon n Also V / FORMAL

en·light·en /ɪnˈlaɪtən/ **enlightens, enlightening, enlightened.** To enlighten someone means to give them more knowledge and greater understanding about something. *This book will entertain, enhance and enlighten the reader.* ♦ **en·light·en·ing** *She gave an enlightening talk.* ♦ **en·light·en·ment** *Stella had a moment of enlightenment.* ◆◇◇◇ VB: no cont V n / FORMAL / ADJ-GRADED / N-UNCOUNT

en·light·ened /ɪnˈlaɪtənd/. If you describe someone or their attitudes as enlightened, you mean that they have sensible, modern attitudes; used showing approval. *He had also been an enlightened and humane reformer. ...an enlightened policy.* ◆◇◇◇ ADJ-GRADED PRAGMATICS

en·light·en·ment /ɪnˈlaɪtənmənt/. **1** In Buddhism, enlightenment is a final blessed state in which there is no desire or suffering. *...lessons for attaining enlightenment.* **2** See also **enlighten.** ◆◇◇◇ N-UNCOUNT

en·list /ɪnˈlɪst/ **enlists, enlisting, enlisted. 1** If someone enlists or is enlisted, they join the army, navy, or air force. *He enlisted in the 82nd Airborne 20 years ago... He enlisted as a private in the Mexican War... Three thousand men were enlisted.* ♦ **en·list·ment, enlistments** *...his enlistment in HM Armed Forces.* **2** If you enlist the help of someone, you persuade them to help or support you in doing something. *I've read that you've enlisted some 12-year-olds to help out in your campaign.* ◆◇◇◇ V-ERG: V / V as n / be V-ed / N-UNCOUNT: also N in pl / V n / V n to-inf

en·list·ed /ɪnˈlɪstɪd/. An enlisted man or woman is a member of the American army or navy who is below the rank of an officer. ADJ

en·liv·en /ɪnˈlaɪvən/ **enlivens, enlivening, enlivened.** To enliven events, situations, or people means to make them more lively or cheerful. *Flirtation can enliven the most mundane situation.* ◆◇◇◇ VERB V n

en masse /ˌɒn ˈmæs/. If a group of people do something en masse, they do it all together and at the same time. *...the arrival en masse of the Latin American delegates.* ◆◇◇◇ ADV

en·meshed /ɪnˈmeʃt/. If you are enmeshed in or with something, usually something bad, you are involved in it and you cannot easily escape from it. *The European Community is becoming increasingly* ADJ-GRADED: v-link ADJ PRAGMATICS

enmeshed in the crisis... Her life gets enmeshed with Andrew's.

en·mi·ty /ˈenmɪti/ **enmities.** Enmity is a long-lasting feeling of hatred towards someone. *There is an historic enmity between them.* N-VAR

en·no·ble /ɪˈnəʊbəl/ **ennobles, ennobling, ennobled. 1** Something that **ennobles** someone or something makes them more dignified and morally better. ♦ **en·no·bling** *...lofty rhetoric about the ennobling and civilizing power of education.* **2** If someone **is ennobled**, they are made a member of the nobility. *...the newly ennobled Lord Archer.* VERB: V n LITERARY / ADJ-GRADED / VERB: be V-ed V-ed FORMAL

en·nui /ˈɒnwiː/ **Ennui** is a feeling of tiredness, boredom, and dissatisfaction. N-UNCOUNT LITERARY

enor·mi·ty /ɪˈnɔːmɪti/ The **enormity** of a problem or difficulty is its very great extent, or seriousness. *I was numbed by the enormity of the responsibility.* N-UNCOUNT

enor·mous /ɪˈnɔːməs/ **1** Something that is **enormous** is extremely large in size or amount. *The main bedroom is enormous... There is, of course, an enormous amount to see.* **2** You can use **enormous** to emphasize the great degree or extent of something. *It was an enormous disappointment. ...his enormous capacity for brutality.* ♦ **enor·mous·ly** *This book was enormously influential... The new database will help horse breeders enormously.* ◆◆◇◇ ADJ-GRADED / ADJ PRAGMATICS / ADV

enough /ɪˈnʌf/ **1 Enough** means as much as you need or as much as is necessary. *They had enough cash for a one-way ticket... There aren't enough tents to shelter them.* ▶ Also an adverb. *I was old enough to work and earn money... Do you believe that sentences for criminals are tough enough?... She graduated with high enough marks to apply for university.* ▶ Also a pronoun. *Although the UK says efforts are being made, they are not doing enough.* ▶ Also a quantifier. *All parents worry about whether their child is getting enough of the right foods.* ▶ Also an adjective. *British charities are in trouble. Sunday's figures were proof enough of that.* **2** If you say that something is **enough**, you mean that you do not want it to continue any longer or get any worse. *I met him only the once, and that was enough... I think I have said enough... You've got enough to think about for the moment.* ▶ Also a quantifier. *Ann had heard enough of this... He had messed up enough of these occasions to give rise to some anxieties.* ▶ Also a determiner. *I've had enough problems with the police, I don't need this... Would you shut up, please! I'm having enough trouble with these children!* ▶ Also an adverb. *Things are difficult enough as they are.* **3** You can also use **enough** to say that something is the case to a moderate or fairly large degree. *Winter is a common enough German surname... The rest of the evening passed pleasantly enough.* ◆◆◆◆ DET / ADV: adj/adv ADV, ADV after v / PRON / QUANT / ADJ: n ADJ / PRON / QUANT / DET / ADV: adj ADV / ADV: adj/adv ADV

4 You use **enough** in expressions such as **strangely enough** and **interestingly enough** to indicate that you think a fact is strange or interesting. *Strangely enough, the last thing he thought of was his beloved Tanya. ...an Italian who, interestingly enough, doesn't speak a word of his native language.* **5** If you say **'enough is enough'**, you mean that you want something that is happening to stop. *Stop asking questions! You should know when enough is enough.* **6** You say **'that's enough'** to tell someone to stop behaving badly. **7** If you say that you **have had enough**, you mean that you are unhappy with a situation and you want it to stop. *I had had enough of other people for one night.* **8** If you say **'enough said'**, you mean that what you have just said is sufficient to make a point clear, and that there is no need to say any more. *My husband is a jazz musician. Enough said.* ADV: adv ADV with cl / PHRASE / CONVENTION PRAGMATICS / PHRASE / CONVENTION PRAGMATICS

9 ♦ **fair enough:** see fair. ♦ **sure enough:** see sure.

en·quire /ɪnˈkwaɪə/ See inquire.

en·quir·er /ɪnˈkwaɪərə/ See inquirer.

en·quiry /ɪnˈkwaɪəri/ See inquiry.

en·rage /ɪnˈreɪdʒ/ **enrages, enraging, enraged.** If you **are enraged** by something, it makes you extremely angry. *He enraged the government by* ◆◇◇◇ VERB: be V-ed V n

renouncing the agreement. ♦ **en·raged** *I began getting more and more enraged at my father.* ADJ-GRADED

en·rap·ture /ɪnˈræptʃə/ **enraptures, enrapturing, enraptured.** If something or someone **enraptures** you, you think they are wonderful or fascinating. *The place at once enraptured me... The 20,000-strong audience listened, enraptured.* VERB V n / V-ed LITERARY

en·rich /ɪnˈrɪtʃ/ **enriches, enriching, enriched. 1** To **enrich** something means to improve its quality. *It is important to enrich the soil prior to planting.* ♦ **-enriched** *...nutrient-enriched water.* ♦ **en·rich·ment** *...a student exchange organization dedicated to fostering cultural enrichment.* **2** To **enrich** someone means to increase the amount of money that they have. *They used inside information to enrich themselves at the expense of the bank.* ♦ **enrichment** *He had been doing his job and had not sought any personal enrichment.* **3** To **enrich** a nuclear fuel such as uranium means to increase the number of atoms of a particular kind in it, so that it can be used to produce more energy or a greater explosion. ◆◇◇◇ VERB V n / COMB / N-UNCOUNT / VERB V n / N-UNCOUNT / VERB: V n TECHNICAL

en·rol /ɪnˈrəʊl/ **enrols, enrolling, enrolled;** spelled **enroll** in American English. If you **enrol** or **are enrolled** on a course, you officially join it and pay a fee for it. *Cherny was enrolled at the University in 1945... She enrolled on a local Women Into Management course... I thought I'd enrol you with an art group at the school.* ♦ **en·rol·ment;** spelled **enrollment** in American English. *A fee is charged for each year of study and is payable at enrolment.* ◆◇◇◇ V-ERG be V-ed prep V prep V n prep Also V / N-UNCOUNT

en route /ˌɒn ˈruːt/ See route.

en·sconce /ɪnˈskɒns/ If you are **ensconced** somewhere, you are settled there comfortably and have no intention of moving. *Brian was ensconced behind the bar.* ADJ: v-link ADJ prep/adv

en·sem·ble /ɒnˈsɒmbəl/ **ensembles. 1** An **ensemble** is a group of musicians, actors, or dancers who regularly perform together. **2 Ensemble** acting or playing is the fact or technique of playing or performing well together. *Foote's most recent play, 'Dividing the Estate,' is an ensemble piece.* **3** An **ensemble** of things or people is a group of things or people considered as a whole rather than as separate individuals. *The state is an ensemble of political and social structures.* **4** An **ensemble** is a set of clothes which have been chosen to look nice together. *...navy and white ensembles.* ◆◇◇◇ N-COUNT / ADJ: ADJ n TECHNICAL / N-COUNT FORMAL / N-COUNT FORMAL

en·shrine /ɪnˈʃraɪn/ **enshrines, enshrining, enshrined.** If an idea or a right **is enshrined** in something such as a constitution or law, it is protected by it. *His new relationship with Germany is enshrined in a new non-aggression treaty.* ◆◇◇◇ VB: usu passive be V-ed in n

en·sign /ˈensaɪn, ˈensən/ **ensigns. 1** An **ensign** is a flag flown on a ship to show what country the ship belongs to. **2** An **ensign** is a junior officer in the United States Navy. ◆◇◇◇ N-COUNT

en·slave /ɪnˈsleɪv/ **enslaves, enslaving, enslaved. 1** If someone **is enslaved**, they are forced to become a slave. *Often entire populations were enslaved.* ♦ **en·slave·ment** *...the enslavement of African people.* **2** If you say that someone **is enslaved** by something, you think they are not free because of it; used showing disapproval. *We are enslaved by greed, anger, and ignorance. ...religions that have enslaved human beings for untold years.* ♦ **enslavement** *...the analysis of women's enslavement to appearance.* VB: usu passive be V-ed / N-UNCOUNT / VB: usu passive PRAGMATICS be V-ed V n / N-UNCOUNT

en·snare /ɪnˈsneə/ **ensnares, ensnaring, ensnared. 1** If you **ensnare** someone, you gain power or control over them, using dishonest or deceitful methods. *Feminism is simply another device to ensnare women.* **2** If someone or something **is ensnared**, they are caught in a trap or snare. *Fiona's foot ensnared itself in a trailing root.* VERB V n / VERB: be V-ed on/in n V n on/in n

en·sue /ɪnˈsjuː, AM -ˈsuː/ **ensues, ensuing, ensued.** If something **ensues**, it happens immediately after another event, usually as a result of it. *A brief but embarrassing silence ensued.* ♦ **en·su·ing** *The ensuing argument had been bitter.* ◆◇◇◇ VB: no cont / ADJ

en suite /ˌɒn 'swiːt/. An **en suite** bathroom is next ADJ: ADJ n
to a bedroom and can only be reached by a door in
that bedroom. An **en suite** bedroom has an en suite
bathroom.

en·sure /ɪnˈʃʊə/ **ensures, ensuring, ensured.** ◆◆◆◇
To **ensure** that something happens, means to make VERB
certain that it happens. *Ensure that it is written into* V that
your contract. Also V n
FORMAL

en·tail /ɪnˈteɪl/ **entails, entailing, entailed.** If ◆◇◇◇◇
one thing **entails** another, it involves it or causes it. VERB: V n
To see the whole thing entails walking nearly a V-ing
mile... I'll never accept parole because that entails V n -ing
me accepting guilt. FORMAL

en·tan·gle /ɪnˈtæŋgəl/ **entangles, entangling,** ◆◇◇◇◇
entangled. 1 If something **is entangled** in some- VERB
thing such as a rope or net, it is caught in it very be V-ed with/
firmly. *The tree was entangled in a mass of creepers.* in n
♦ **en·tan·gled** ...*a whale that became entangled in* Also V n
crab nets. **2** If something **entangles** you in prob- VERB:
lems or difficulties, it involves you in problems or V n in/with n
difficulties from which it is hard to escape.
♦ **entangled** *He became entangled in further* ADJ-GRADED
controversy.

en·tan·gle·ment /ɪnˈtæŋgəlmənt/ **entangle-**
ments. 1 An **entanglement** is a complicated or N-COUNT
adulterous sexual relationship; used showing disap- PRAGMATICS
proval. **2** You can refer to a difficult or complicated N-VAR
situation as an **entanglement**. *The legal entangle-*
ments of Noriega do not end in Miami.

en·tente /ˌɒnˈtɒnt/ **ententes.** An **entente** or an **en-** N-VAR
tente cordiale is a friendly agreement between two
or more countries.

en·ter /ˈentə/ **enters, entering, entered.** ◆◆◆◇
1 When you **enter** a place such as a room or build- VERB
ing, you go into it or come into it. *He entered the* V n
room briskly and stood near the door... As soon as I V
entered, they stopped. **2** If you **enter** an organization VERB
or institution, you start to work there or become a V n
member of it. *She entered a convent.* **3** If someone VERB
or something **enters** a particular situation or period V n
of time, they start to be in it or part of it. ...*as the*
war enters its second month... A million young peo-
ple enter the labour market each year.
4 If something **enters** your head or mind, you VERB: V n
suddenly think about it. • If you say **it did not enter** PHRASE
your head or **it never entered your mind** that something was the case, you mean that you never once
thought that it was the case.
5 If you **enter** a competition, race, or examination, VERB: V n
you officially state that you will compete or take part V for n
in it. *As a boy soprano he entered for many competi-* V
tions... To enter, simply complete the coupon. **6** If you VERB
enter someone for a race or competition, you official- V n for n
ly state that they will compete or take part in it. *His* Also V n
wife Marie secretly entered him for the Championship.
7 If you **enter** information in a notebook or financial VERB
account, you write it down. If you **enter** information V n with in/
into a computer, you record it there, for example by into
typing it on a keyboard. *Each week she meticulously* Also V n
entered in her notebooks all sums received.

enter into. 1 If you **enter into** something such as an PHRASAL VB
agreement, discussion, or relationship with someone, V P n with n
you become involved in it. *They've entered into a* pl-n V n
power-sharing agreement... No correspondence will be be V-ed P
entered into. **2** If something **enters into** a situation, it (non-recip)
is a factor in it. *Issues like race or creed do not enter into* V P n
it. FORMAL

en·ter·prise /ˈentəpraɪz/ **enterprises. 1** An **en-** ◆◆◆◇
terprise is a company or business, often a small N-COUNT
one. **2** An **enterprise** is something new, difficult, or N-COUNT
important that you do or try to do. *Horse breeding is*
indeed a risky enterprise. **3 Enterprise** is the activity N-UNCOUNT
of managing businesses and starting new ones. *He*
is still involved in voluntary work promoting local
enterprise. **4 Enterprise** is the ability to think of new N-UNCOUNT
and effective things to do, together with an eager- PRAGMATICS
ness to do them; used showing approval. ...*the spirit*
of enterprise worthy of a free and industrious people.
♦ **en·ter·pris·ing** *Some enterprising members* ADJ-GRADED
found ways of reducing their expenses.

en·ter·tain /ˌentəˈteɪn/ **entertains, entertain-** ◆◆◆◇
ing, entertained. 1 If someone or something **en-** VERB: V n
tertains you, they amuse you, interest you, or give be V-ed
you pleasure. *They were entertained by top singers,* V
dancers and celebrities... Children's television not
only entertains but also teaches. ♦ **en·ter·tain·ing** ADJ-GRADED
To generate new money the sport needs to be more
entertaining. **2** If you **entertain** guests, you give VERB: V n
them food and hospitality. *The Monroes continued*
to entertain extravagantly. ♦ **entertaining** ...*a cosy* N-UNCOUNT
area for entertaining and relaxing. **3** If you **enter-** VERB
tain an idea or suggestion, you allow yourself to V n
consider it as possible. *I wouldn't entertain the idea* FORMAL
of such an unsociable job.

en·ter·tain·er /ˌentəˈteɪnə/ **entertainers.** An **en-** ◆◇◇◇◇
tertainer is a person whose job is to entertain audi- N-COUNT
ences, for example by telling jokes or dancing.

en·ter·tain·ment /ˌentəˈteɪnmənt/ **entertain-** ◆◆◇◇
ments. Entertainment consists of performances of N-VAR
plays and films, and activities such as reading and
watching television, that give people pleasure.

en·thral /ɪnˈθrɔːl/ **enthrals, enthralling, en-** ◆◇◇◇◇
thralled; the spellings **enthrall** and **enthralls** are VERB:
used in American English. If you **are enthralled** by be V-ed
something, you enjoy it and give it your complete V n
attention and interest. *He enthralled audiences in*
Prague, Vienna, and Paris. ♦ **en·thral·ling** ...*an en-* ADJ-GRADED
thralling race.

en·throne /ɪnˈθrəʊn/ **enthrones, enthroning,**
enthroned. 1 When kings, queens, emperors, or VERB:
bishops **are enthroned**, they officially take on their be V-ed
role during a ceremony in which they are placed on FORMAL
a throne. ♦ **en·throne·ment** /ɪnˈθrəʊnmənt/ N-COUNT
enthronements. ...*the enthronement of their new*
emperor. **2** To **enthrone** an idea means to give it a VERB
prominent place in your life or thoughts because V n
you think it is very important. *He was forcing the*
State to enthrone a particular brand of modernism.

en·thuse /ɪnˈθjuːz, AM -ˈθuːz/ **enthuses, enthus-** ◆◇◇◇◇
ing, enthused. 1 If you **enthuse** about something, VERB:
you talk about it in a way that shows how excited V about/over
you are about it. *'I've found the most wonderful* n
house to buy!' she enthused. **2** If you **are enthused** VERB:
by something, it makes you feel excited and enthu- be V-ed
siastic. *Find a hobby or interest which enthuses you.* V n
Also V n

en·thu·si·asm /ɪnˈθjuːziæzəm, AM -ˈθuː-/ **enthusi-** ◆◆◇◇
asms. 1 Enthusiasm is great eagerness to be in- N-VAR
volved in a particular activity which you like and
enjoy or which you think is important. *The lack of*
enthusiasm for unification among most West Ger-
mans fills him with disappointment. **2** An **enthusi-** N-COUNT
asm is an activity or subject that interests you very
much and that you spend a lot of time on. ♦ **en-**
·thu·si·ast /ɪnˈθjuːziæst, AM -ˈθuː-/ **enthusiasts.** N-COUNT
...*keep-fit enthusiasts.*

en·thu·si·as·tic /ɪnˌθjuːziˈæstɪk, AM -ˌθuː-/. If you ◆◆◇◇
are **enthusiastic** about something, you show how ADJ-GRADED
much you like or enjoy it by the way that you behave and talk. ♦ **en·thu·si·as·ti·cal·ly** ADV-GRADED
/ɪnˌθjuːziˈæstɪkli, AM -ˈθuː-/. *The announcement was*
greeted enthusiastically.

en·tice /ɪnˈtaɪs/ **entices, enticing, enticed.** To ◆◇◇◇◇
entice someone to go somewhere or to do some- VERB:
thing means to try to persuade them to go to that V n to-inf
place or to do that thing. *Shops have battled to en-* V n prep
tice hard-pressed customers over the threshold... Two Also V n with adv
youths tried to entice away her two-year-old son.
♦ **en·tice·ment** /ɪnˈtaɪsmənt/ **enticements.** There N-VAR
is a range of enticements to open an account. ♦ **en-** ADJ-GRADED
·tic·ing ...*many enticing illustrations.* ♦ **en·tic-** ADV-GRADED
·ing·ly *Advertising must display the client's product*
as enticingly as possible.

en·tire /ɪnˈtaɪə/. You use **entire** when you want to ◆◆◆◇
emphasize that you are referring to the whole of ADJ: det ADJ
something. *He had spent his entire life in China as a* PRAGMATICS
doctor... The entire family was staring at him.

en·tire·ly /ɪnˈtaɪəli/. **1 Entirely** means completely ◆◆◆◇
and not just partly. ...*an entirely new approach...* ADV
Their price depended almost entirely on their scar-
city. **2 Entirely** is also used to emphasize what you ADV

E

are saying. *I agree entirely... The official Chinese spokesman asserted that the coup was entirely a domestic affair.* **3** People sometimes use the expression **not entirely** to reduce the force of a strong statement, especially a critical one. *They are not entirely happy with his criticism of the president... We shall see that this is not entirely true.* ADV: *not* ADV / PRAGMATICS

en·tirety /ɪnˈtaɪərɪtɪ/. If something is used or affected **in its entirety**, the whole of it is used or affected. ◆◇◇◇ PHRASE

en·ti·tle /ɪnˈtaɪtəl/ **entitles, entitling, entitled.** **1** If you **are entitled** to something, you have the right to have it or do it. *It entitles you to withdraw cash.* ♦ **en·ti·tle·ment** /ɪnˈtaɪtəlmənt/ **entitlements** *They lose their entitlement to benefit when they start work.* **2** If the title of something such as a book, film, or painting is, for example, 'Sunrise', you can say that it **is entitled** 'Sunrise'. *...a performance entitled 'United States'.* ◆◆◇◇ VERB: V n to n V n to-inf N-VAR / VB: usu passive, be V-ed quote V-ed quote

en·tity /ˈentɪtɪ/ **entities.** An **entity** is something that exists separately from other things and has a clear identity of its own. *...the earth as a living entity... North and South will remain separate entities.* ◆◇◇◇ N-COUNT FORMAL

en·tomb /ɪnˈtuːm/ **entombs, entombing, entombed.** **1** If something **is entombed**, it is buried or permanently trapped by something. *The city was entombed in volcanic lava... The Tel, an artificial mountain, entombs Jericho's ancient past.* **2** When a person's dead body **is entombed**, it is buried in a grave or put into a tomb. *Neither of them had any idea how long the body had been entombed.* VERB be V-ed in n V n FORMAL / VB: usu passive be V-ed FORMAL

ento·mol·ogy /ˌentəˈmɒlədʒɪ/. **Entomology** is the study of insects. *...a professor of entomology.* ♦ **ento·molo·gist** /ˌentəˈmɒlədʒɪst/ **entomologists** *...a research entomologist.* N-UNCOUNT / N-COUNT

en·tou·rage /ˌɒntuˈrɑːʒ/ **entourages.** A famous or important person's **entourage** is the group of assistants, servants, or other people who travel with them. *He was accompanied by an entourage of a dozen police officers.* ◆◇◇◇ N-COUNT

en·trails /ˈentreɪlz/. The **entrails** of people or animals are their inside parts, especially their intestines. *He cut out the steaming entrails.* N-PLURAL

entrance 1 noun uses

en·trance /ˈentrəns/ **entrances.** **1** The **entrance** to a place is the way into it, for example a door or gate. *Beside the entrance to the church, turn right... A marble entrance hall leads to a sitting room.* **2** You can refer to someone's arrival in a place as their **entrance**, especially when you think that they are trying to be noticed and admired. *If she had noticed her father's entrance, she gave no indication.* **3** When a performer makes his or her **entrance** on to the stage, he or she comes on to the stage. *He made his entrance into the parade ring.* **4** If you gain **entrance** to a particular place, you manage to get in there. *Hewitt had gained entrance to the Hall by pretending to be a heating engineer.* **5** If you gain **entrance** to a particular profession, society, or institution, you are accepted as a member of it. *Entrance to universities and senior secondary schools was restricted. ...entrance exams for the French civil service.* **6** If you make an **entrance** into a particular activity or system, you succeed in becoming involved in it. *...his entrance into politics in 1993.* ◆◆◇◇ N-COUNT / N-COUNT / N-COUNT / N-UNCOUNT FORMAL / N-UNCOUNT / N-SING

entrance 2 verb use

en·trance /ɪnˈtrɑːns, -ˈtræns/ **entrances, entrancing, entranced.** If something or someone **entrances** you, they cause you to feel delight and wonder. *Last Friday she entranced the audience with her classical Indian singing.* ♦ **en·tranced** *I became entranced with the idea... For the next three hours we sat entranced.* ♦ **en·tranc·ing** *The light reflected off the stone, creating a golden glow he found entrancing.* ◆◇◇◇ VERB V n / ADJ-GRADED / ADJ-GRADED

'entrance fee, entrance fees. An **entrance fee** is a sum of money which you pay before you go into somewhere such as a cinema or museum, or which you have to pay in order to join an organization or institution. *The entrance fee is £9.50.* N-COUNT

'entrance hall, entrance halls. An **entrance hall** is the area behind the main door of a large house, hotel, or other large building. N-COUNT

en·trant /ˈentrənt/ **entrants.** **1** An **entrant** is a person who has recently become a member of an institution such as a university. *...a young school entrant.* **2** An **entrant** is a person who is taking part in a competition. *All items entered for the competition must be the entrant's own work.* ◆◇◇◇ N-COUNT: with supp / N-COUNT

en·trap /ɪnˈtræp/ **entraps, entrapping, entrapped.** If you **entrap** someone or something, you trap them by tricking or deceiving them. *He overturned the conviction, saying the defendant was entrapped... He claimed the government had entrapped him into doing something that he would not have done otherwise.* VERB: V n V n into n/-ing

en·trap·ment /ɪnˈtræpmənt/. **Entrapment** is the practice of arresting someone by using unfair or illegal methods. *Entrapment is contrary to Home Office guidelines.* N-UNCOUNT LEGAL

en·treat /ɪnˈtriːt/ **entreats, entreating, entreated.** If you **entreat** someone to do something, you ask them very humbly and seriously to do it. *'Call me Earl!' he entreated... I earnestly entreat that we don't get caught out again.* VERB: V n to-inf V with quote V that Also V n, V n with quote FORMAL

en·treaty /ɪnˈtriːtɪ/ **entreaties.** An **entreaty** is a humble, serious request. *The FA has resisted all entreaties to pledge its support to the campaign.* N-VAR FORMAL

en·trée /ˈɒntreɪ/ **entrées;** also spelled **entree.** **1** If you have an **entrée** to a social group, you are accepted and made to feel welcome by them. *She had an entree into the city's cultivated society.* **2** At restaurants or formal banquets, the **entrée** can be the main course, or a dish before the main course. *...a hot entrée of chicken, veal, or lamb.* N-COUNT / N-COUNT

en·trench /ɪnˈtrentʃ/ **entrenches, entrenching, entrenched.** If something such as power, a custom, or an idea **is entrenched**, it is firmly established and difficult to change. *...a series of measures designed to entrench democracy and the rule of law... They have sought to entrench themselves in office.* ♦ **en·trenched** *The recession remains deeply entrenched.* ♦ **en·trench·ment** /ɪnˈtrentʃmənt/ *In South Africa, the entrenchment of democratic norms will be that much harder.* ◆◇◇◇ VERB V n V pron-refl / ADJ-GRADED / N-UNCOUNT

en·tre·pre·neur /ˌɒntrəprəˈnɜː/ **entrepreneurs.** An **entrepreneur** is a person who sets up businesses and business deals. ◆◇◇◇ N-COUNT

en·tre·pre·neur·ial /ˌɒntrəprəˈnɜːrɪəl/. **Entrepreneurial** means having the qualities that are needed for people to succeed as entrepreneurs. *...her prodigious entrepreneurial flair.* ◆◇◇◇ ADJ-GRADED

en·tre·pre·neur·ship /ˌɒntrəprəˈnɜːʃɪp/. **Entrepreneurship** is the state of being an entrepreneur, or the activities associated with being an entrepreneur. N-UNCOUNT

en·tro·py /ˈentrəpɪ/. **Entropy** is a state of disorder, confusion, and disorganization. N-UNCOUNT FORMAL

en·trust /ɪnˈtrʌst/ **entrusts, entrusting, entrusted.** If you **entrust** something important to someone or **entrust** them with it, you make them responsible for it. *He was forced to entrust an assistant with the important task of testing and demonstrating aircraft... They can be entrusted to solve major national questions.* VERB: V n to n V n with n be V-ed to-inf Also V n on n

en·try /ˈentrɪ/ **entries.** **1** If you gain **entry** to a particular place, you are able to go in. *Non-residents were refused entry into Lhasa... The point of entry into Zambia would be the Chirundu border post... Entry to the museum is free. ...entry fees to places of scientific interest.* ● The words **No Entry** are used on signs to indicate that you are not allowed to go into a particular area. **2** You can refer to someone's arrival in a place as their **entry**, especially when you think that they are trying to be noticed and admired. *He made his triumphal entry into Mexico City.* **3** Someone's **entry** into a particular society or group is their joining of it. *...Britain's entry into the European Exchange Rate Mechanism.* **4** An **entry** in a diary, computer file, or reference book ◆◆◆◇ N-UNCOUNT / PHRASE / N-COUNT / N-UNCOUNT / N-COUNT

is a short piece of writing in it. *Violet's diary entry for 20 April 1917 records Brigit admitting to the affair.* **5** An **entry** for a competition is a piece of work, for example a story or drawing, which you complete in order to take part in the competition. *The closing date for entries is 31st December.* **6** Journalists sometimes use **entry** to refer to the total number of people taking part in an event or competition. For example, if a competition has an entry of twenty people, twenty people take part in it. *Our competition has attracted a huge entry.* **7 Entry** in a competition is the act of taking part in it. *Entry to this competition is by invitation only. ...an entry form.*

en·twine /ɪnˈtwaɪn/ **entwines, entwining, entwined. 1** If one thing **is entwined** with another thing, or if you **entwine** two things, the two things are twisted around each other. *His dazed eyes stare at the eels, which still writhe and entwine... The giraffes were managing to entwine their necks in the most astonishing manner... He entwined his fingers with hers.* **2** If two things **entwine** or **are entwined**, they closely resemble or are linked to each other, and they are difficult to separate or identify. *The book entwines the personal and the political... Once, years ago, he told me our lives should entwine.* ♦ **en·twined** *Fuji Heavy Industries, which makes Subaru cars, is becoming increasingly entwined with Nissan.*

E num·ber /ˈiː nʌmbə/ **E numbers. E numbers** are artificial substances which are added to some foods and drinks to improve their flavour or colour or to make them last longer.

enu·mer·ate /ɪˈnjuːməreɪt, AM -ˈnuː-/ **enumerates, enumerating, enumerated.** When you **enumerate** a list of things, you name each one in turn. *I enumerate the work that will have to be done.*

enun·ci·ate /ɪˈnʌnsieɪt/ **enunciates, enunciating, enunciated. 1** When you **enunciate** a word or part of a word, you pronounce it clearly. *She enunciates very slowly and carefully.* ♦ **enun·cia·tion** /ɪnʌnsiˈeɪʃən/ *...his grammar always precise, his enunciation always perfect.* **2** When you **enunciate** a thought, idea, or plan, you express it very clearly and precisely. *He was ever ready to enunciate his views to all who would listen.* ♦ **enunciation** *...the enunciation of grand moral principles.*

en·vel·op /ɪnˈveləp/ **envelops, enveloping, enveloped.** If one thing **envelops** another, it covers or surrounds it completely. *That lovely, rich fragrant smell of the forest enveloped us.*

en·ve·lope /ˈenvələʊp, ˈɒn-/ **envelopes.** An **envelope** is the rectangular paper cover in which you send a letter to someone through the post.

en·vi·able /ˈenviəbəl/. An **enviable** quality is one that someone else has and that you wish you had too. *They have enviable reputations as athletes.*

en·vi·ous /ˈenviəs/. If you are **envious** of someone else, you envy them. *I don't think I'm envious of your success. ...envious thoughts.* ♦ **en·vi·ous·ly** *'You haven't changed,' I am often enviously told.*

en·vi·ron·ment /ɪnˈvaɪərənmənt/ **environments. 1** Someone's **environment** is all the circumstances, people, things, and events around them that influence their life. *Pupils in our schools are taught in a safe, secure environment... The twins were separated at birth and brought up in entirely different environments.* **2** Your **environment** consists of the particular natural surroundings in which you live or exist. *If our environment cools, then messages from the skin alert the body's thermostat. ...the maintenance of a safe environment for marine mammals.* **3** The **environment** is the natural world of land, sea, air, plants, and animals. *...persuading people to respect the environment.*

en·vi·ron·men·tal /ɪnˌvaɪərənˈmentəl/. **1 Environmental** means concerned with the protection of the natural world of land, sea, air, plants, and animals. *...economic and environmental legislation... Environmental groups plan to stage public protests during the conference.* ♦ **en·vi·ron·men·tal·ly** *What is needed are chemicals which are more environmen-*

tally friendly. **2 Environmental** means relating to or caused by the surroundings in which someone lives or something exists. *It protects against environmental hazards such as wind and sun.*

en·vi·ron·men·tal·ism /ɪnˌvaɪərənˈmentəlɪzəm/. **Environmentalism** is used to describe actions and policies which show a concern with protecting and preserving the natural environment.

en·vi·ron·men·tal·ist /ɪnˌvaɪərənˈmentəlɪst/ **environmentalists.** An **environmentalist** is a person who is concerned with protecting and preserving the natural environment.

en·vi·rons /ɪnˈvaɪərənz/. The **environs** of a place consist of the area immediately surrounding it. *The town and its environs are inviting.*

en·vis·age /ɪnˈvɪzɪdʒ/ **envisages, envisaging, envisaged.** If you **envisage** something, you imagine that it is true, real, or likely to happen. *He had never envisaged spending the whole of his working life in that particular job... Personally, I envisage them staying together.*

en·vi·sion /ɪnˈvɪʒən/ **envisions, envisioning, envisioned.** If you **envision** something, you envisage it. *Most people do stop at this point, not envisioning that there is anything beyond.*

en·voy /ˈenvɔɪ/ **envoys. 1** An **envoy** is someone who is sent as a messenger, especially from one government or political group to another. **2** An **envoy** is a diplomat in an embassy who is immediately below the ambassador in rank.

envy /ˈenvi/ **envies, envying, envied. 1 Envy** is the feeling you have when you wish you could have the same thing or quality that someone else has. *They gazed in a mixture of envy and admiration at the beauty of the statue.* **2** If you **envy** someone, you wish that you had the same things or qualities that they have. *I have a rich brother and a lot of people envy the fact... He envied Caroline her peace.* **3** If a thing or quality is **the envy of** someone, they wish very much that they could have or achieve it. *...an economic expansion that was the envy of many other states.* **4** ♦ **green with envy:** see **green.**

en·zyme /ˈenzaɪm/ **enzymes.** An **enzyme** is a chemical substance that is found in living creatures which produces changes in other substances without being changed itself.

eon /ˈiːɒn/. See **aeon.**

EP /ˌiː ˈpiː/ **EPs.** An **EP** is a record which is designed to be played at either 33 rpm or 45 rpm and which lasts for about 8 minutes on each side. **EP** is an abbreviation for 'extended play'.

ep·au·lette /ˌepəˈlet/ **epaulettes;** spelled **epaulet** in American English. **Epaulettes** are decorations worn on the shoulders of certain uniforms, especially military ones.

ephem·era /ɪˈfemərə/. **1** You can refer to things which last for only a short time as **ephemera.** **2 Ephemera** is used to refer to things people collect such as old postcards, posters, and bus tickets which were only intended to last a short time when they were produced. *...one of Britain's best known private collections of tickets and other printed ephemera.*

ephem·er·al /ɪˈfemərəl/. If you describe something as **ephemeral,** you mean that it lasts only for a very short time. *These paintings are in some ways a reminder that earthly pleasures are ephemeral.*

epic /ˈepɪk/ **epics. 1** An **epic** is a long book, poem, or film, whose story extends over a long period of time or tells of great events. *...the Middle High German epic, 'Nibelungenlied'... It is an over-long, standard Hollywood epic.* ▸ Also an adjective. *...epic narrative poems.* **2** If you describe something as **epic,** you mean that it is very impressive or ambitious. *...Columbus's epic voyage of discovery.*

epi·cen·tre /ˈepɪsentə/ **epicentres;** spelled **epicenter** in American English. The **epicentre** of an earthquake is the place on the earth's surface directly above the point where it starts, and where it is felt most strongly.

epi·dem·ic /ˌepɪˈdemɪk/ **epidemics. 1** If there is an **epidemic** of a particular disease somewhere, it spreads quickly to a very large number of people there. *A flu epidemic is sweeping through Moscow. ...a killer epidemic of yellow fever.* **2** If an activity that you disapprove of is increasing or spreading rapidly, you can refer to this as an **epidemic** of that activity. *...an epidemic of serial killings.* ◆◇◇◇ N-COUNT / N-COUNT: with supp PRAGMATICS

epi·der·mis /ˌepɪˈdɜːmɪs/. Your **epidermis** is the thin, protective, outer layer of your skin. N-SING

epi·dur·al /ˌepɪˈdjʊərəl, AM -ˈdʊr-/ **epidurals.** An **epidural** is an anaesthetic which is injected into a person's spine so that pain is relieved from the waist downwards. Epidurals are sometimes given to women who are giving birth. N-COUNT

epi·gram /ˈepɪɡræm/ **epigrams.** An **epigram** is a short saying or poem which expresses an idea in a very clever and amusing way. N-COUNT

epi·lep·sy /ˈepɪlepsi/. **Epilepsy** is a brain condition which causes a person to suddenly lose consciousness and sometimes to have fits. ◆◇◇◇ N-UNCOUNT

epi·lep·tic /ˌepɪˈleptɪk/ **epileptics. 1 Epileptic** means suffering from or relating to epilepsy. *...an epileptic fit.* **2** An **epileptic** is a person who suffers from epilepsy. ADJ / N-COUNT

epi·logue /ˈepɪlɒɡ, AM -lɔːɡ/ **epilogues.** An **epilogue** is a passage or speech which is added to the end of a book or play as a conclusion. N-COUNT

epis·co·pal /ɪˈpɪskəpəl/. **1 Episcopal** means relating to a branch of the Anglican Church in Scotland and the USA. *...the Episcopal bishop of New York.* **2 Episcopal** means relating to bishops. *...episcopal conferences. ...a set of red episcopal vestments.* ADJ: ADJ n / ADJ: ADJ n FORMAL

epi·sode /ˈepɪsəʊd/ **episodes. 1** You can refer to an event or a short period of time as an **episode** if you want to suggest that it is important or unusual, or has some particular quality. *It was a rather sordid episode of my life.* **2** An **episode** of something such as a television serial or a story in a magazine is one of the separate parts in which it is broadcast or published. *...an episode of TV's 'Star Trek'.* **3** An **episode** of an illness is short period in which a person who suffers from it is affected by it particularly badly. *The new drug lessens the severity of pneumonia episodes.* ◆◆◇◇ N-COUNT / N-COUNT / N-COUNT MEDICAL

epi·sod·ic /ˌepɪˈsɒdɪk/. **1** Something that is **episodic** occurs at irregular and infrequent intervals. *...episodic attacks of fever.* **2** An **episodic** piece of writing or film consists of a series of events, often events which seem random or unconnected. ADJ-GRADED FORMAL / ADJ-GRADED

epis·tle /ɪˈpɪsəl/ **epistles. 1** An **epistle** is a letter. *I wrote a lengthy epistle describing the family and its lifestyle.* **2** In the Bible, the **Epistles** are a series of books in the New Testament which were originally written as letters. N-COUNT: supp N LITERARY / N-COUNT

epis·to·lary /ɪˈpɪstələri, AM -leri/. An **epistolary** novel or story is written as a series of letters. ADJ: ADJ n FORMAL

epi·taph /ˈepɪtɑːf, -tæf/ **epitaphs.** An **epitaph** is a short description, thought, or message about someone who is dead, often carved on their gravestone. N-COUNT

epi·thet /ˈepɪθet/ **epithets.** An **epithet** is an adjective or short phrase which is used to describe or refer to someone. *...the religious issue which led to the epithet 'bible-basher'.* N-COUNT

epito·me /ɪˈpɪtəmi/. If you say that a person or thing is the **epitome** of something, you are emphasizing that they are the best possible example of a particular type of person or thing. *Maureen was the epitome of sophistication.* ◆◇◇◇ N-SING PRAGMATICS

epito·mize /ɪˈpɪtəmaɪz/ **epitomizes, epitomizing, epitomized;** also spelled **epitomise** in British English. If you say that something or someone **epitomizes** a particular thing, you mean that they are a perfect example of it. *...a warrior mentality epitomized by Gandhi and Martin Luther King.* ◆◇◇◇ VERB: V n / V-ed

epoch /ˈiːpɒk, AM ˈepək/ **epochs. 1** If you refer to a long period of time as an **epoch**, you mean that important events or great changes took place during it. *The birth of Christ was the beginning of a major epoch of world history.* **2** An **epoch** is a very long ◆◇◇◇ N-COUNT / N-COUNT period of time in the earth's development, marked by particular physical characteristics. *Two main glacial epochs affected both areas.* TECHNICAL

'epoch-making. An **epoch-making** change or declaration is considered to be the extremely important because it is likely to have a significant long-term effect. *...the epoch-making changes now taking place in Eastern Europe.* ADJ

epony·mous /ɪˈpɒnɪməs/. An **eponymous** hero or heroine is the character in a play or book whose name is the title of that play or book. ◆◇◇◇ ADJ: ADJ n FORMAL

Ep·som salts /ˌepsəm ˈsɔːlts/. **Epsom salts** is a white powder which you can mix with water and drink as a medicine to help you empty your bowels. N-UNCOUNT

eq·uable /ˈekwəbəl/. If you describe someone as **equable**, you mean that they are calm, cheerful, and fair with other people, even in difficult circumstances. *He was a man of the most equable temper.* ADJ-GRADED

equal /ˈiːkwəl/ **equals, equalling, equalled;** spelled **equaling, equaled** in American English. **1** If two things are **equal** or if one thing is **equal** to another, they are the same in size, number, or value. *Investors can borrow an amount equal to the property's purchase price. ...equal numbers of men and women... Research and teaching are of equal importance.* ◆ **equal·ly** *...a tendency for property to be divided equally between heirs... All these techniques are equally effective.* **2** If something **equals** a particular number or amount, it is the same as that amount or the equivalent of it. *9 percent interest less 7 percent inflation equals 2 percent... The average pay rise equalled 1.41 times inflation.* **3** If you say **'other** or **all things being equal'** when talking about a possible situation, you are assuming that there will be no unexpected changes. ◆◆◆◇ ADJ / ADV / V-LINK V amount / PHRASE PRAGMATICS

4 If people are **equal**, have **equal** rights, or are given **equal** treatment, they all have the same rights and are treated in the same way. *At any gambling game, everyone is equal. ...the commitment to equal opportunities. ...new legislation allowing building societies to compete on equal terms with their competitors.* ◆ **equal·ity** /ɪˈkwɒlɪti/. *...equality of the sexes.* **5** Someone who is your **equal** has the same ability, status, or rights as you have. *She was one of the boys, their equal... You should have married somebody more your equal.* **6** If you say that someone or something **has no equal**, you think that there is nothing that is as good as them. *The film demands attention, and has no equal in cinema history.* **7** To **equal** something or someone means to be as good or as great as them. *The victory equalled Southend's best in history... No amount of money can equal memories like that.* ADJ-GRADED / N-UNCOUNT N-COUNT: poss N / PHRASE PRAGMATICS / VERB V n

8 If someone is **equal to** a particular job or situation, they have the necessary ability, strength, or courage to deal successfully with it. *She was determined that she would be equal to any test the corporation put to them.* ADJ-GRADED: v-link ADJ to n

equal·ize /ˈiːkwəlaɪz/ **equalizes, equalizing, equalized;** also spelled **equalise** in British English. **1** To **equalize** a situation means to give everyone the same rights or opportunities, for example in education, wealth, or social status. *...modern divorce laws that equalize the rights of husbands and wives... Such measures are needed to equalize wage rates between countries.* ◆ **equali·za·tion** /ˌiːkwəlaɪˈzeɪʃən/ *...the equalization of parenting responsibilities between men and women.* **2** In sports such as football, if someone **equalizes**, they score a goal that makes the scores of the two teams equal. *Keegan equalized with only 16 minutes remaining.* ◆ **equal·iz·er.** An **equalizer** is a goal that makes the scores of two teams equal. ◆◆◇◇ VERB V n / N-UNCOUNT: also a N / VERB V Also V n BRITISH / N-SING

equal·ly /ˈiːkwəli/. **Equally** is used to introduce another comment on the same topic, which balances or contrasts with the previous comment. *In that situation, he would lie. Equally, in my situation, I would want to believe he was lying.* ● See also **equal**. ◆◇◇◇ ADV: ADV with cl PRAGMATICS

'equals sign, equals signs. An **equals sign** is the sign =, which is used in arithmetic to indicate that two numbers or quantities are equal.   N-COUNT

equa·nim·ity /ˌekwəˈnɪmɪti, ˌiːk-/. **Equanimity** is a calm state of mind and attitude to life, so that you never lose your temper or become upset. *The defeat was taken with equanimity by the leadership.*   N-UNCOUNT FORMAL

equate /ɪˈkweɪt/ **equates, equating, equated.** If you **equate** one thing with another, or if you say that one thing **equates** with another, you believe that they are strongly connected. *I'm always wary of men wearing suits, as I equate this with power and authority... The author doesn't equate liberalism and conservatism... The principle of hierarchy does not equate to totalitarian terror.* ♦ **equa·tion** *The equation of gangsterism with business in general in Coppola's film was intended to be subversive.*   ◆◇◇◇ V-ERG / V n with n / V pl-n / V to/with n   N-UNCOUNT

equa·tion /ɪˈkweɪʒən/ **equations. 1** An **equation** is a mathematical statement saying that two amounts or values are the same, for example 6×4=12×2. **2** You can refer to a situation as an **equation** when you are considering two or more aspects of it that are closely connected or dependent on each other. *The equation is simple: research breeds new products.*   ◆◆◇◇ N-COUNT   N-COUNT

equa·tor /ɪˈkweɪtə/. **The equator** is an imaginary line around the middle of the earth at an equal distance from the North and South Poles.   ◆◇◇◇ N-SING: the N

equa·to·rial /ˌekwəˈtɔːriəl, AM ˌiː-/. Something that is **equatorial** is near or at the equator. *...equatorial forests.*   ADJ

eq·uer·ry /ɪˈkweri, AM ˈekwəri/ **equerries.** An **equerry** is a personal assistant to a member of the royal family.   N-COUNT

eques·trian /ɪˈkwestriən/. **Equestrian** means connected with the activity of riding horses. *...equestrian skills.*   ◆◇◇◇ ADJ

eques·tri·an·ism /ɪˈkwestriənɪzəm/. **Equestrianism** refers to sports such as show jumping which involve people demonstrating their skill at riding and controlling a horse.   N-UNCOUNT

equi·dis·tant /ˌiːkwɪˈdɪstənt/. A place that is **equidistant** from two other places is the same distance away from each of these places. *Horsey is equidistant from Great Yarmouth and Mundesley.*   ADJ

equi·lat·eral /ˌiːkwɪˈlætərəl/. An **equilateral** triangle has its sides that are all the same length.   ADJ TECHNICAL

equi·lib·rium /ˌiːkwɪˈlɪbriəm/ **equilibria. Equilibrium** is a state of balance or stability in a situation or in someone's mind. *For the economy to be in equilibrium, income must equal expenditure... He had recovered his equilibrium and even his good humour.*   ◆◇◇◇ N-UNCOUNT: also a N   FORMAL

equine /ˈekwaɪn, AM ˈiːk-/. **Equine** means connected with or relating to horses. *...equine influenza.*   ◆◇◇◇ ADJ: ADJ n

equi·nox /ˈiːkwɪnɒks, ˈek-/ **equinoxes.** The **spring equinox** and the **autumn equinox** are the two days in the year when day and night are of equal length.   N-COUNT

equip /ɪˈkwɪp/ **equips, equipping, equipped. 1** If you **equip** a person or thing with something such as tool or machine, you provide them with it. *...trying to equip their vehicles with gadgets to deal with every possible contingency... The country did not possess the modern guns to equip the reserve army properly. ...well-equipped research buildings.* **2** If something **equips** you for a particular task or experience, it gives you the knowledge, skills, and personal qualities you need for it. *Relative poverty, however, did not prevent Martin from equipping himself with an excellent education... A basic two-hour first aid course would equip you to deal with any of these incidents.*   ◆◆◇◇ VERB / V n with n / V n   V-ed / Also V n to-inf   VERB / V n with n / V n to-inf / Also V n for / n/-ing

equip·ment /ɪˈkwɪpmənt/. **Equipment** consists of the things such as tools or machines which are used for a particular purpose. *...electronic equipment.*   ◆◆◆◇ N-UNCOUNT

equi·table /ˈekwɪtəbəl/. Something that is **equitable** is fair and reasonable in a way that gives equal treatment to everyone. *...an equitable compromise.* ♦ **equi·tably** *...a real attempt to allocate scarce resources more equitably.*   ◆◇◇◇ ADJ-GRADED   ADV-GRADED

equi·ty /ˈekwɪti/. **1** Your **equity** is the sum of your assets, for example the value of your house, minus your debts. ● See also **negative equity. 2 Equity** is the quality of being fair and reasonable in a way that gives equal treatment to everyone. *...social justice and equity.*   ◆◆◆◇ N-UNCOUNT TECHNICAL   N-UNCOUNT

equiva·lence /ɪˈkwɪvələns/. If there is **equivalence** between two things, they have the same use, function, size, or value. *...the equivalence of science and rationality.*   N-UNCOUNT

equi·va·lent /ɪˈkwɪvələnt/ **equivalents. 1** If one amount or value is the **equivalent** of another, they are the same. *Even the cheapest car costs the equivalent of 70 years' salary for a government worker.* ► Also an adjective. *A unit is equivalent to a glass of wine or a single measure of spirits... They will react with hostility to the price rises and calls for equivalent wage increases are bound to be heard.* **2** The **equivalent** of someone or something is a person or thing that has the same function in a different place, time, or system. *...the civil administrator of the West Bank and his equivalent in Gaza.* ► Also an adjective. *...a decrease of 10% in property investment compared with the equivalent period in 1991.*   ◆◆◇◇ N-SING   ADJ-GRADED   N-COUNT   ADJ

equivo·cal /ɪˈkwɪvəkəl/. **1** If you are **equivocal**, you are deliberately vague or ambiguous in what you say. *Many were equivocal about the idea. ...his equivocal response.* **2** If something is **equivocal**, it is difficult to interpret it or be certain about it, often because it has aspects that seem to contradict each other. *Research in this area is somewhat equivocal. ...the equivocal nature of his position.*   ADJ-GRADED FORMAL   ADJ-GRADED FORMAL

equivo·cate /ɪˈkwɪvəkeɪt/ **equivocates, equivocating, equivocated.** If someone **equivocates**, they deliberately use vague and ambiguous language in order to deceive people or to avoid telling the truth. *He is equivocating a lot about what is going to happen if and when there are elections.* ♦ **equivo·ca·tion** /ɪˌkwɪvəˈkeɪʃən/ *Why doesn't the President say so without equivocation?*   VERB / V about/over n / Also V   N-UNCOUNT

er /ɜː/. **Er** is used to represent the sound that people make when they hesitate, especially while they decide what to say next.   ◆◆◆◆◆

-er /-ə/. **1** You add **-er** to adjectives, and a few adverbs, that have one or two syllables in order to make their comparative form. For example the comparative of 'hard' is 'harder', and the comparative of 'early' is 'earlier'. **2** You add **-er** to verbs to form nouns which refer to a person, animal, or thing that does the action described by the verb. For example a 'teacher' is someone who teaches and a 'money-saver' is something that saves money.   SUFFIX   SUFFIX

era /ˈɪərə/ **eras.** You can refer to a period of history or a long period of time as an **era** when you want to draw attention to a particular feature or quality that it has. *...the Reagan-Bush era. ...an era of austerity.*   ◆◆◇◇ N-COUNT

eradi·cate /ɪˈrædɪkeɪt/ **eradicates, eradicating, eradicated.** To **eradicate** something means to get rid of it completely. *They are already battling to eradicate illnesses such as malaria and tetanus.* ♦ **eradi·ca·tion** /ɪˌrædɪˈkeɪʃən/ *...the eradication of their country's Communist past.*   ◆◇◇◇ VERB / V n   FORMAL   N-UNCOUNT

erase /ɪˈreɪz, AM ɪˈreɪs/ **erases, erasing, erased. 1** If you **erase** a thought or feeling, you destroy it completely so that you can no longer remember it or feel it. *They are desperate to erase the memory of that last defeat... Love was a word he'd erased from his vocabulary since Susan's going.* **2** If you **erase** sound which has been recorded on a tape or information which has been stored in a computer, you completely remove or destroy it. *The names were accidentally erased from computer disks.* **3** If you **erase** something such as writing or a mark, you remove it. *A carpet burn can be erased by rubbing raw potato into the burned area.*   ◆◇◇◇ VERB / V n / V n from n   VERB: V n / be V-ed from n / Also V n from n   VERB: V n / be V-ed

eras·er /ɪˈreɪzə, AM -ˈreɪs-/ **erasers.** An **eraser** is an object, usually a piece of rubber, which is used for rubbing out writing.   N-COUNT

ere /eə/. **Ere** means the same as 'before'. *Take the water ere the clock strikes twelve.*   CONJ LITERARY

erect /ɪˈrekt/ **erects, erecting, erected. 1** If people **erect** something such as a building or bridge, they build it; a formal use. *The Eiffel Tower was erected for the World Exhibition in 1889.* ♦ **erec·tion** *...the erection of temporary fencing.* **2** If you **erect** a system, theory, or institution, you create it. *He erected a new doctrine of precedent. ...the whole edifice of free trade which has been erected since the Second World War.* **3** People or things that are **erect** are straight and upright. *...the individual who is unable to stand erect due to muscle weakness... Her head was erect and her back was straight.*

erec·tion /ɪˈrekʃən/ **erections.** If a man has an **erection** his penis is stiff and sticking up because he is sexually aroused.

ergo /ˈɜːɡəʊ/. Some people use **ergo** instead of 'therefore' to introduce a clause in which they mention something that is the logical consequence of what they have just said. *Neither side would have an incentive to start a war. Ergo, peace would reign.*

er·go·nom·ics /ˌɜːɡəˈnɒmɪks/. **Ergonomics** is the study of how equipment and furniture can be arranged so that people can do work or other activities more efficiently and comfortably.

er·mine /ˈɜːmɪn/. **Ermine** is expensive white fur that is obtained from stoats.

erode /ɪˈrəʊd/ **erodes, eroding, eroded. 1** If rock or soil **erodes** or **is eroded** by the weather or sea, it cracks and breaks so that it is gradually destroyed. *By 1980, Miami beach had all but totally eroded... Soil is quickly eroded by wind and rain.* ♦ **erod·ed** *...the deeply eroded landscape.* **2** If something strong or something with a high value **erodes** or **is eroded**, it gradually weakens or decreases. *His fumbling of the issue of reform has eroded his authority... The value of the dollar began to erode rapidly.*

erog·enous /ɪˈrɒdʒɪnəs/. An **erogenous** zone is part of your body where sexual pleasure can be felt.

ero·sion /ɪˈrəʊʒən/. **1 Erosion** is the gradual destruction and removal of rock or soil in a particular area by rivers, the sea, or the weather. *...erosion of the river valleys. ...soil erosion.* **2** The **erosion** of something strong or of high value is its gradual weakening or decrease. *...the erosion of moral standards. ...a dramatic erosion of support for the program.*

erot·ic /ɪˈrɒtɪk/. If you describe something as **erotic**, you mean that it involves or arouses sexual desire. *It wasn't an erotic experience at all. ...nude women in erotic poses.* ♦ **eroti·cal·ly** /ɪˈrɒtɪkli/ *The film is shot seductively, erotically... Everything seemed erotically charged and exciting.*

eroti·ca /ɪˈrɒtɪkə/. **Erotica** is works of art that show or describe people engaged in sexual activity, which are intended to arouse sexual feelings in the viewer or reader.

eroti·cism /ɪˈrɒtɪsɪzəm/. **Eroticism** is sexual excitement, or the quality of being able to arouse sexual excitement. *...an aura of eroticism.*

err /ɜː/ **errs, erring, erred. 1** If you **err**, you make a mistake. *It criticises the main contractor for seriously erring in its original estimates.* **2** If you are uncertain what to do, and you **err on the side of** caution, for example, you decide to act in a cautious way. *He probably erred on the conservative rather than the generous side.*

er·rand /ˈerənd/ **errands.** If you go on or run an **errand** for someone, you make a short trip in order to do a job for them, for example buying something from a shop. *She went off on some errand. ...running dodgy errands for a seedy local villain.*

er·rant /ˈerənt/. **Errant** is used to describe someone whose actions are considered unacceptable or wrong. For example, an **errant** husband is unfaithful to his wife. *...the Government's crackdown on errant fathers.*

er·rat·ic /ɪˈrætɪk/. Something that is **erratic** does not follow a regular pattern, but happens at unexpected times or moves in an irregular way. *...Argentina's erratic inflation rate.* ♦ **er·rati·cal·ly** /ɪˈrætɪkli/ *Police stopped him for driving erratically.*

er·ro·neous /ɪˈrəʊniəs/. **Erroneous** beliefs, statements or methods are not correct. *...the erroneous notion that one can contract AIDS by giving blood.* ♦ **er·ro·neous·ly** *It had been widely and erroneously reported that Armstrong had refused.*

er·ror /ˈerə/ **errors. 1** An **error** is something you have done which is incorrect, or which should not have been done. *NASA discovered a mathematical error in its calculations. ...errors of judgment.* **2** If you do something **in error**, you do it because you have made a mistake, especially in your judgement. *The plane was shot down in error.* **3** If someone sees **the error of** their **ways**, they realize or admit that they have made a mistake or behaved badly. *I wanted an opportunity to talk some sense into him and try to make him see the error of his ways.*

er·satz /ˈeəzæts/. **1** If you describe something as **ersatz**, you dislike it because it is not genuine and is a poor imitation of something better. *...an ersatz Victorian shopping precinct... The ersatz spontaneity of 'Sunday Love' sounds especially hollow.* **2** An **ersatz** product is poor-quality and is used as a substitute for something that is not available. *...ersatz coffee and biscuits.*

erst·while /ˈɜːstwaɪl/. You use **erstwhile** to describe someone that used to be the type of person indicated, but no longer is. *Erstwhile workers may have become managers.*

eru·dite /ˈeruːdaɪt, AM ˈerjə-/. If you describe someone as **erudite**, you mean that they have or show great academic knowledge. You can also use **erudite** to describe something such as a book or a style of writing. *...lengthy, erudite, literary fictions.* ♦ **eru·di·tion** /ˌeruːˈdɪʃən, AM ˌerjə-/. **Erudition** is great academic knowledge. *His erudition was apparently endless.*

erupt /ɪˈrʌpt/ **erupts, erupting, erupted. 1** When a volcano **erupts**, it throws out a lot of hot lava, ash, and steam. ♦ **erup·tion** /ɪˈrʌpʃən/ **eruptions** *...the volcanic eruption of Tambora in 1815.* **2** If violence **erupts** in a place, it suddenly begins or intensifies there. You can also say that the place **erupts** or the people there **erupt**. *Heavy fighting erupted there today after a two-day cease-fire... In Los Angeles, the neighborhood known as Watts erupted into riots.* ♦ **eruption** *...this sudden eruption of violence.* **3** You can say that someone **erupts** when they suddenly have a change in mood, usually becoming quite noisy. *Without warning she erupts into laughter... Union leaders erupted in fury last night over the proposed pay restraints.* ♦ **eruption** *...an eruption of despair.* **4** If your skin **erupts**, sores or spots suddenly appear there. *My skin erupted in pimples.* ♦ **eruption** *...eruptions of adolescent acne.*

es·ca·late /ˈeskəleɪt/ **escalates, escalating, escalated.** If a bad or unpleasant situation **escalates** or if someone or something **escalates** it, it becomes more serious or severe. *The dispute could escalate... Protests escalated into five days of rioting... Defeat could cause one side or other to escalate the conflict.* ♦ **es·ca·la·tion** /ˌeskəˈleɪʃən/ *...the threat of nuclear escalation. ...there was a sudden escalation of violence.*

es·ca·la·tor /ˈeskəleɪtə/ **escalators.** An **escalator** is a moving staircase.

es·ca·lope /ˈeskəlɒp/ **escalopes.** An **escalope** is a thin boneless slice of meat or fish.

es·ca·pade /ˈeskəpeɪd/ **escapades.** An **escapade** is an exciting and rather dangerous adventure. *...Robin Hood's escapades.*

es·cape /ɪˈskeɪp/ **escapes, escaping, escaped. 1** If you **escape** from a place, you succeed in getting away from it. *A prisoner has escaped from a jail in northern England... He tried to escape. ...an escaped prisoner.* ▶ Also a noun. *The man made his escape.* **2** When gas, liquid, or heat **escapes**, it leaks

from a pipe, container, or place. **3** See also **fire escape**.

4 You can say that you **escape** when you survive VERB something such as an accident. *The two officers were* Vn *extremely lucky to escape serious injury... The man's* Vadj *girlfriend managed to escape unhurt... He narrowly es-* Vprep *caped with his life.* ► Also a noun. *I hear you had a* N-COUNT *very narrow escape.*

5 If something is an **escape**, it is a way of avoiding N-COUNT difficulties or responsibilities. *For me television is an escape. ...an escape from the depressing realities of wartime.* **6** You can use **escape** to describe things ADJ: ADJ n which allow you to avoid difficulties or problems. For example, an **escape route** is an activity or opportunity that lets you improve your situation. An **escape clause** is part of an agreement that allows you to avoid having to do something that you do not want to do. *We all need the occasional escape route from the boring, routine aspects of our lives.*

7 If something **escapes** you or your attention, you VERB forget it or are unaware of it. *...an actor whose name* Vn *escapes me for the moment... She was too striking to escape their attention.*

es·cap·ee /ɪˌskeɪˈpiː/ **escapees.** An **escapee** is a N-COUNT person who has escaped from somewhere, especially from prison.

es·cap·ism /ɪˈskeɪpɪzəm/. If you describe an activ- N-UNCOUNT ity or type of entertainment as **escapism**, you mean that it makes people think about pleasant things instead of the uninteresting or unpleasant aspects of their life. *Horoscopes are merely harmless escapism from an ever-bleaker world.* ♦ **es·cap·ist** ADJ-GRADED /ɪˈskeɪpɪst/ *...escapist movies.*

es·carp·ment /ɪˈskɑːpmənt/ **escarpments.** An N-COUNT **escarpment** is a wide, steep slope on a ridge or mountain.

es·chew /ɪsˈtʃuː/ **eschews, eschewing,** ◆◇◇◇ **eschewed.** If you **eschew** something, you deliber- VERB ately avoid doing it or becoming involved in it. *He* FORMAL *eschewed publicity and avoided nightclubs.*

es·cort, escorts, escorting, escorted. The ◆◆◇◇ noun is pronounced /ˈeskɔːt/. The verb is pronounced /ɪsˈkɔːt/. **1** An **escort** is a person or group N-COUNT of people travelling with someone in order to protect or guard them. *He arrived with a police escort.* ● If someone is taken somewhere **under escort**, PHRASE they are accompanied by guards, either because they have been arrested or because they need to be protected. *...his arrival in Benin late last week, handcuffed and under military escort.* **2** An **escort** N-COUNT is a person who accompanies someone of the opposite sex to a social event. Sometimes people are paid to be escorts. **3** If you **escort** someone somewhere, VERB you accompany them there, usually in order to Vn prep/adv make sure that they leave a place or get to their destination. *I escorted him to the door... The vessel was escorted to an undisclosed port.*

Es·ki·mo /ˈeskɪˌməʊ/ **Eskimos.** An **Eskimo** is a ◆◇◇◇◇ member of the group of peoples who live in Alaska, N-COUNT Northern Canada, Eastern Siberia, and other parts of the Arctic. These peoples usually call themselves Inuits or Aleuts, and the term Eskimo is sometimes considered offensive.

ESL /ˌiː es ˈel/. ESL is an abbreviation for 'English as a second language'. ESL is taught to people whose native language is not English but who live in a society in which English is a main language.

esoph·a·gus /ɪˈsɒfəgəs/. See **oesophagus**.

eso·ter·ic /ˌiːsəʊˈterɪk, AM ˌesə-/. Something that ◆◇◇◇◇ is **esoteric** is understood by only a small number of ADJ-GRADED people. *...esoteric knowledge.* FORMAL

esp. esp. is a written abbreviation for **especially**.

ESP /ˌiː es ˈpiː/. **1** ESP is the teaching of English to N-UNCOUNT students whose first language is not English but who need it for a particular job or purpose. ESP is an abbreviation for 'English for specific purposes' or 'English for special purposes'. **2** ESP is an abbrevia- N-UNCOUNT tion for **extra-sensory perception**.

es·pe·cial /ɪˈspeʃəl/. **Especial** means exceptional or ADJ: ADJ n special in some way. *The authorities took especial interest in him because of his trade union work.*

es·pe·cial·ly /ɪˈspeʃəli/. **1** You use **especially** to ◆◆◆◇ emphasize that what you are saying applies more to ADV: one person or thing than to any others. *Re-apply* ADV with cl/ *sunscreen every two hours, especially if you have* group *been swimming.* **2** You use **especially** to emphasize PRAGMATICS a characteristic or quality. *The recession made find-* ADV: ADV adj/adv *ing work especially difficult.* PRAGMATICS

Es·pe·ran·to /ˌespəˈræntəʊ/. **Esperanto** is an in- N-UNCOUNT vented language which consists of parts of several European languages.

es·pio·nage /ˈespiənɑːʒ/. **Espionage** is the activity ◆◇◇◇◇ of finding out the political, military, or industrial se- N-UNCOUNT crets of your enemies or rivals by using spies. *The authorities have arrested several people suspected of espionage.* ● See also **counter-espionage**.

es·pla·nade /ˌespləˈneɪd, AM -ˈnɑːd/ **esplanades.** N-COUNT The **esplanade**, usually in a seaside town, is a wide, open road where people walk for pleasure.

es·pous·al /ɪˈspaʊzəl/. Someone's **espousal** of a N-SING particular cause is their strong support of it. *...his* FORMAL *espousal of the free market.*

es·pouse /ɪˈspaʊz/ **espouses, espousing, es-** ◆◇◇◇◇ **poused.** If you **espouse** a particular cause, you VERB give your strong support to it. *She ran away with* Vn *him to Mexico and espoused the revolutionary cause.* FORMAL

es·pres·so /eˈspresəʊ/ **espressos. Espresso** cof- N-UNCOUNT fee is made by forcing steam or boiling water through ground coffee beans. ► An **espresso** is a N-COUNT cup of espresso coffee.

es·prit de corps /eˌspriː də ˈkɔː/. **Esprit de corps** N-UNCOUNT is a feeling of loyalty and pride that is shared by the FORMAL members of a particular group.

espy /ɪˈspaɪ/ **espies, espying, espied.** If you VERB: Vn **espy** something, you see or notice it. LITERARY

Esq. Esq. is used after men's names as a written abbreviation for 'esquire'.

es·quire /ɪˈskwaɪə, AM ˈeskwaɪr/. **Esquire** is a for- N-TITLE mal title that can be written after a man's name if he has no other title.

es·say /ˈeseɪ/ **essays, essaying, essayed.** The ◆◆◇◇ noun is pronounced /ˈeseɪ/. The verb is pro- nounced /eˈseɪ/. **1** An **essay** is a short piece of writ- N-COUNT ing on one particular subject written by a student. *...an essay about his hometown.* **2** An **essay** is a N-COUNT short piece of writing on one particular subject that is written for publication. *...Thomas Malthus's essay on population.* **3** If you **essay** something, you try to VERB do it. *Sinclair essayed a smile.* ► Also a noun. *...his* Vn *first essay in running a company.* FORMAL N-COUNT

es·say·ist /ˈeseɪɪst/ **essayists.** An **essayist** is a N-COUNT writer who writes essays for publication.

es·sence /ˈesəns/ **essences. 1** The **essence** of ◆◆◇◇ something is its basic and most important charac- N-UNCOUNT teristic. *The essence of consultation is to listen... Ireland's very essence is expressed through the lan- guage.* **2** You use **in essence** to indicate that you are PHRASE talking about the basic and most important charac- teristics of something. *Local taxes are in essence simple.* **3** If you say that something **is of the es-** PHRASE **sence**, you mean that it is absolutely necessary in a particular situation. *Time is of the essence.* **4** Es- N-VAR **sence** is a very concentrated liquid that is used for flavouring food or for its smell. *...a few drops of va- nilla essence.*

es·sen·tial /ɪˈsenʃəl/ **essentials. 1** Something ◆◆◆◇ that is **essential** is extremely important or absolute- ADJ-GRADED ly necessary in a particular situation. *It was abso- lutely essential to separate crops from the areas that animals used... Jordan promised to trim the city budget without cutting essential services.* **2** The **es-** N-COUNT **sentials** are the things that are absolutely necessary in a particular situation. *The flat contained the basic essentials.* **3** The **essential** aspects of something are ADJ-GRADED its most basic or important aspects. *Play is an essen- tial part of a child's development.* **4** The **essentials** N-PLURAL are the most basic or important aspects of some-

thing. *This has stripped the contest down to its essentials.*

es·sen·tial·ly /ɪ'senʃəli/. **1** You use **essentially** to emphasize that you are talking about the most basic and important aspects of someone or something. *He was essentially a simple man... There is nothing essentially different about their approach.* **2** You use **essentially** to indicate that what you are saying is basically or generally true, although it may not be accurate in every detail. *Essentially, the West has only two options... He develops his opinions essentially by reading the newspapers.*
◆◆◇◇◇ ADV-GRADED: ADV with cl/ group PRAGMATICS
ADV: ADV with cl/ group, ADV with v PRAGMATICS

-est /-ɪst/. You add **-est** to many short adjectives to form superlatives. For example, the superlative of 'hard' is 'hardest'; the superlative of 'happy' is 'happiest'. You also add it to some adverbs that do not end in -ly. For example, the superlative of 'soon' is 'soonest'.
SUFFIX

es·tab·lish /ɪ'stæblɪʃ/ **establishes, establishing, established. 1** If someone **establishes** something such as an organization or a set of rules, they create it or introduce it in such a way that it is likely to last for a long time. *The UN has established detailed criteria for who should be allowed to vote.* ◆ **es·tab·lish·ment** *...the establishment of the regional government in 1980.* **2** If you **establish** contact or communication with someone, you start to have contact or communication with them. *They finally established contact.* ◆ **establishment** *...discussions to explore the establishment of diplomatic relations.* **3** If you **establish** that something is true, you discover facts that show that it is definitely true. *Medical tests established that she was not their own child... An autopsy was being done to establish the cause of death... It was established that the missile had landed.* ◆ **es·tab·lished** *...an established medical fact.* **4** If you **establish** yourself or your reputation, you achieve a good reputation or a secure position. *This is going to be the show where up-and-coming comedians will establish themselves... He has established himself as a pivotal figure in US politics.*
◆◆◇◇◇ VERB V n
◆ N-SING
V-RECIP: V n with n pl-n V FORMAL N-SING
VERB V wh/that V n it be V-ed that FORMAL
ADJ-GRADED
VERB V n V n as n

es·tab·lished /ɪ'stæblɪʃt/. If you describe an organization or person as **established**, you mean they have a good reputation or a secure position, usually because they have existed for a long time. *Their religious adherence is not to the established church. ...the established names of Paris fashion.*
◆◆◇◇◇ ADJ-GRADED

es·tab·lish·ment /ɪ'stæblɪʃmənt/ **establishments. 1** An **establishment** is a business or organization occupying a particular building or place. *...a scientific research establishment. ...commercial establishments.* **2** You refer to the people who have power and influence in the running of a country or organization as the **establishment**. *...pillars of the Tory establishment. ...prominent British establishment figures.* **3** See also **establish**.
◆◆◇◇◇ N-COUNT FORMAL
N-SING

es·tate /ɪ'steɪt/ **estates. 1** An **estate** is a large area of land in the country which is owned by a person, family, or organization. *...Lord Wyville's estate.* **2** In Britain, people sometimes use **estate** to refer to a housing estate. *He used to live on the estate.* **3** Someone's **estate** is all the money and property that they leave behind them when they die. *His estate was valued at $150,000.* **4** An **estate** is an estate car. The American term is **station wagon**. **5** See also **housing estate, industrial estate, real estate**.
◆◆◆◇◇ N-COUNT
N-COUNT
N-COUNT LEGAL
N-COUNT BRITISH

es'tate agent, estate agents. An estate agent is someone who works for a company that sells houses and land for people. The American word is **realtor**.
◆◆◇◇◇ N-COUNT BRITISH

es'tate car, estate cars. An estate car is a car with a long body, a door at the rear, and space behind the back seats. The American term is **station wagon**.
N-COUNT BRITISH

es·teem /ɪ'stiːm/. **Esteem** is the admiration and respect that you feel towards another person. *He is held in high esteem by colleagues... He retained immense regard and esteem for the prime minister.* ● See also **self-esteem**.
◆◆◇◇◇ N-UNCOUNT FORMAL

es·teemed /ɪ'stiːmd/. You use **esteemed** to describe someone who you greatly admire and respect. *They look to you as an esteemed colleague.*
ADJ-GRADED FORMAL

es·thete /'iːsθiːt, AM 'es-/. See aesthete.

es·thet·ic /iːs'θetɪk, AM es'θ-/. See aesthetic.

es·ti·ma·ble /'estɪməbəl/. If you describe someone or something as **estimable**, you mean that they deserve admiration. *...the estimable Miss Cartwright.*
ADJ-GRADED FORMAL

es·ti·mate, estimates, estimating, estimated. The verb is pronounced /'estɪmeɪt/. The noun is pronounced /'estɪmət/. **1** If you **estimate** a quantity or value, you make an approximate judgement or calculation of it. *It's difficult to estimate how much money is involved... Some analysts estimate its current popularity at around ten per cent.* ◆ **es·ti·mat·ed** *There are an estimated 90,000 gangsters in the country.* **2** An **estimate** is an approximate calculation of a quantity or value. *...the official estimate of the election result... A recent estimate was that factories were undermanned by about 30 per cent.* **3** An **estimate** is a judgement about a person or situation which you make based on the available evidence. *I hadn't been far wrong in my estimate of his grandson's capabilities.* **4** An **estimate** from someone who you employ to do a job for you, such as a builder or a plumber, is a written statement of how much the job is likely to cost.
◆◆◆◆◇ VERB V wh/that V n amount Also V with quote
ADJ: a ADJ amount
N-COUNT
N-COUNT
N-COUNT

es·ti·ma·tion /,estɪ'meɪʃən/ **estimations.** Your **estimation** of a particular person or situation is the opinion or impression that you have of them. *He has gone down considerably in my estimation. ...Lee Dixon, the best player on the pitch in his manager's estimation.*
N-COUNT

es·tranged /ɪ'streɪndʒd/. **1** You refer to someone as **estranged** from their family or friends when they are living separately from them and not communicating with them because they have quarrelled. *...his estranged wife... Joanna, 30, spent most of her twenties virtually estranged from her father.* ◆ **es·trange·ment, estrangements** *They are anxious to end the estrangement between them.* **2** If someone is **estranged** from something such as society or their profession, they no longer seem to be involved in it. *Arran became increasingly estranged from the mainstream of Hollywood.*
◆◇◇◇◇ ADJ: ADJ n, v-link ADJ from n FORMAL
N-VAR
ADJ-GRADED: v-link ADJ FORMAL

es·tro·gen /'iːstrədʒən, AM 'est-/. See oestrogen.

es·tu·ary /'estʃuri, AM 'estʃueri/ **estuaries.** An **estuary** is the wide part of a river where it joins the sea. *...the Clyde estuary.*
◆◇◇◇◇ N-COUNT

et al. /,et 'æl/. **et al.** is used after a name or a list of names to indicate that other people are also involved, especially when referring to books or articles which were written by more than two people.
◆◆◇◇◇

etc. **etc** is used at the end of a list to indicate that you have mentioned only some of the items involved and have not given a full list. **Etc** is a written abbreviation for 'et cetera'. *She knew all about my schoolwork, my hospital work etc.*
◆◆◆◇◇

et·cet·era /et'setrə/; also spelled **et cetera**. See **etc**.

etch /etʃ/ **etches, etching, etched. 1** If a line or pattern **is etched** into a surface, it is cut into the surface by means of acid or a sharp tool. *Crosses were etched into the walls... Windows are etched with the vehicle identification number.* **2** If you say that feelings **are etched** on someone's face, you mean that you can see the feelings clearly in their appearance. *His grief was etched into every line of his face.* **3** If something **is etched** on your memory, you remember it very clearly because it made a strong impression on you. *The ugly scene in the study was still etched in her mind.*
◆◇◇◇◇ VERB be V-ed into/ in/on n be V-ed with n
VB: usu be V-ed into/ on n LITERARY
V-PASSIVE be V-ed into/ in/on n LITERARY

etch·ing /'etʃɪŋ/ **etchings.** An **etching** is a picture printed from a metal plate that has had a design cut into it with acid.
N-COUNT

eter·nal /ɪ'tɜːnəl/. **1** Something that is **eternal** lasts for ever. *...eternal life. ...the quest for eternal youth.* ◆ **eter·nal·ly** *She is eternally grateful to her family for their support.* **2** If you describe something as **eternal**, you mean that it seems to last forever, often because it is boring or annoying. *In the back-*
◆◆◇◇◇ ADJ
ADV
ADJ

ground was that eternal hum. **3 Eternal** truths, ADJ: ADJ n
values, and questions are believed to be always true
and unchanging. ...the notion of hierarchy as an
eternal truth.

eter·nity /ɪ'tɜːnɪti/. **1 Eternity** is time without an ◆◇◇◇◇
end or a state of existence outside time, especially N-UNCOUNT
the state which some people believe they will pass
into after they have died. ...laying him to rest for all
eternity. **2** If you say that a situation lasted for **an** N-SING:
eternity, you mean that it seemed to last an ex- aN
tremely long time, usually because it was boring or
unpleasant.

ether /'iːθə/. **1 Ether** is a colourless liquid that N-UNCOUNT
burns easily. It is used as a solvent, and in the past
was used as an anaesthetic. **2** The air is sometimes N-SING:
referred to as **the ether**. theN
LITERARY

ethe·real /ɪ'θɪəriəl/. If you describe someone or ◆◇◇◇◇
something as **ethereal**, you mean that they have a ADJ-GRADED
delicate beauty that seems almost supernatural. FORMAL
...hauntingly ethereal melodies.

eth·ic /'eθɪk/. **ethics. 1 Ethics** are moral beliefs ◆◆◇◇◇
and rules about right and wrong. Its members are N-PLURAL
bound by a rigid code of ethics. ...my personal ethics.
2 Ethics is the study of questions about what is N-UNCOUNT
morally right and wrong. **3** An **ethic** of a particular N-SING:
kind is moral belief that influences the behaviour with supp
and attitudes of a group of people. The work ethic is
very strong in their household.

eth·i·cal /'eθɪkəl/. **1 Ethical** means relating to be- ◆◆◇◇◇
liefs about right and wrong. ...the ethical issues sur- ADJ
rounding terminally-ill people. ◆ **eth·i·cal·ly** ADV:
/'eθɪkli/ Attorneys are ethically and legally bound to ADV adj/-ed,
absolute confidentiality. **2** If you describe something ADJ-GRADED
as **ethical**, you mean that it is morally right or acceptable. Does the party think it is ethical to link tax
policy with party fund-raising? ◆ **ethically** ADV-GRADED:
want local companies to behave ethically. ADV after v

Ethio·pian /,iːθi'əupiən/ **Ethiopians. Ethiopian** ◆◆◆◇◇
means belonging or relating to Ethiopia, or to its ADJ
people, language, or culture. ▶ An **Ethiopian** is an N-COUNT
Ethiopian citizen, or a person of Ethiopian origin.

eth·nic /'eθnɪk/. **1 Ethnic** means connected with ◆◆◆◇◇
or relating to different racial or cultural groups of ADJ
people. ...ethnic minorities. ...ethnic tensions. ◆ **eth·ni·cal·ly** /'eθnɪkli/ ...a predominantly ADV
young, ethnically mixed audience. **2** You can use ADJ: ADJ n
ethnic to describe people who belong to a particular racial or cultural group. There are still several
million ethnic Germans in Russia. ◆ **ethnically** ...a ADV: ADV adj
large ethnically Albanian population. **3 Ethnic** ADJ-GRADED
clothing, music, or food is characteristic of the traditions of a particular ethnic group, and is different
from what is usually found in modern Western
culture.

,ethnic 'cleansing. Ethnic cleansing is a policy ◆◇◇◇◇
of forcing certain groups of people to leave a par- N-UNCOUNT
ticular area or country by violence.

eth·nic·ity /eθ'nɪsɪti/ **ethnicities. Ethnicity** is the N-VAR
state or fact or belonging to a particular ethnic
group. He said his ethnicity had not been important
to him.

eth·nog·ra·phy /eθ'nɒɡrəfi/. **Ethnography** is the N-UNCOUNT
branch of anthropology in which different cultures
are studied and described. ◆ **eth·no·graph·ic** ADJ
...ethnographic research.

ethos /'iːθɒs/. An **ethos** is the set of ideas and atti- ◆◇◇◇◇
tudes that is associated with a particular group of N-SING
people or a particular type of activity. ...the radical FORMAL
ethos prevailing in the humanities today.

eti·ol·ogy /,iːti'ɒlədʒi/ **etiologies;** also spelled N-VAR
aetiology. The **etiology** of a disease or a problem is TECHNICAL
the study of its causes.

eti·quette /'etɪket/. **Etiquette** is a set of customs ◆◇◇◇◇
and rules for polite behaviour. ...a great breach of N-UNCOUNT
etiquette. ...the rules of diplomatic etiquette.

ety·mol·ogy /,etɪ'mɒlədʒi/ **etymologies. 1** Ety- N-UNCOUNT
mology is the study of the origins and historical development of words. ◆ **ety·mo·logi·cal** 'Gratifica- ADJ
tion' and 'gratitude' have the same etymological root.
2 The **etymology** of a particular word is its history. N-COUNT

EU. The **EU** is an organization of European coun- N-PROPER
tries which have joint policies on matters such as
trade, agriculture, and finance. EU is an abbreviation for 'European Union'.

euca·lyp·tus /,juːkə'lɪptəs/; **eucalyptus** is both the ◆◇◇◇◇
singular and the plural form. A **eucalyptus** is an N-VAR
evergreen tree, originally from Australia, that provides timber, gum, and a strong-smelling oil.

eugen·ics /juː'dʒenɪks/. **Eugenics** is the study of N-UNCOUNT
methods to improve the human race by selecting TECHNICAL
parents who will produce the strongest children.

eulo·gize /'juːlədʒaɪz/ **eulogizes, eulogizing,** VERB
eulogized; also spelled **eulogise** in British English. V n
If you **eulogize** someone or something, you praise
them very highly. Society eulogizes the mother who
gives up everything for her child.

eulogy /'juːlədʒi/ **eulogies.** A **eulogy** is a speech or N-COUNT
piece of writing that praises someone or something
very much, for example a speech given at a funeral.

eunuch /'juːnək/ **eunuchs.** A **eunuch** is a man N-COUNT
who has been castrated.

euphemism /'juːfəmɪzəm/ **euphemisms.** A ◆◇◇◇◇
euphemism is a polite, pleasant, or neutral word or N-COUNT
expression that is used to refer to something which
people may find upsetting or embarrassing to talk
about. The term 'comfort women' is the euphemism
they applied to women put in army brothels.
◆ **euphemis·tic** ...a formal and euphemistic way of ADJ-GRADED
saying that someone has been lying. ◆ **euphemis-**
ti·cal·ly ...political prisons, called euphemistically ADV-GRADED:
're-education camps'. ADV with v

eupho·ria /juː'fɔːriə/. **Euphoria** is a feeling of in- ◆◇◇◇◇
tense happiness and excitement. ◆ **euphor·ic** It N-UNCOUNT
had received euphoric support from the public. ADJ-GRADED

Eura·sian /juə'reɪʒən/ **Eurasians. 1 Eurasian** ADJ
means concerned with or relating to both Europe
and Asia. ...the Eurasian continent. **2** A **Eurasian** is N-COUNT
a person who has one European and one Asian par-
ent or who is of mixed European and Asian ancestry. ▶ Also an adjective. ...a leading Eurasian family ADJ
in Hong Kong.

eureka /ju'riːkə/. Someone might say **'eureka'** EXCLAM
when they suddenly find or realize something, or
when they solve a problem. 'Eureka! I've got it!'

Euro- /'juərəu-/. **Euro-** is used to form words that PREFIX
describe or refer to something which is connected
with Europe or with the EU. ...German Euro-MPs.

Euro·cen·tric /,juərəu'sentrɪk/. If you describe ADJ-GRADED
something as **Eurocentric**, you disapprove of it be- PRAGMATICS
cause it focuses narrowly on Europe and the needs
of European people. ...the insultingly Eurocentric
bias in the education system.

Euro·crat /'juərəukræt/ **Eurocrats.** Journalists use N-COUNT
Eurocrats to refer to the civil servants and administrators who work for the EU.

Europe /'juərəp/. **1 Europe** is the continent which ◆◆◆◇
is joined to Asia in the east, and which is to the N-PROPER
north of Africa and the Mediterranean Sea and to
the east of the Atlantic Ocean. You can also use
Europe to refer to the people who live there.
2 Europe can refer to all of Europe except for the N-PROPER
United Kingdom. More than four out of ten cars pro- BRITISH
duced in the UK are for the export market, mainly to
Europe. **3** People use **Europe** to refer to all the N-PROPER
countries that are members of the EU. Britain
should stay in Europe.

Euro·pean /,juərə'piːən/ **Europeans. 1 European** ◆◆◆◇
means belonging or relating to, or coming from ADJ
Europe. ...European countries. **2** A **European** is a N-COUNT
person who comes from Europe.

eutha·na·sia /,juːθə'neɪziə, AM -ʒə/. **Euthanasia** is ◆◇◇◇◇
the practice of killing someone painlessly in order N-UNCOUNT
to stop their suffering when they are dying or have
an incurable illness.

evacu·ate /ɪ'vækjueɪt/ **evacuates, evacuating,** ◆◆◇◇◇
evacuated. 1 To **evacuate** someone means to VERB: V n
send them to a place of safety, away from a dangerous building, town, or area. 18,000 people have been
evacuated from the area. ◆ **evacu·ation** N-VAR
/ɪ,vækju'eɪʃən/ **evacuations** ...the evacuation of

the sick and wounded. **2** If people **evacuate** a place, VERB: V n / V
they move out of it for a period of time, especially
because it is dangerous. *Officials ordered the resi-* N-VAR
dents to evacuate. ♦ **evacuation** *...the mass evacu-*
ation of the Bosnian town of Srebrenica.

evac·uee /ˌɪvækjuˈiː/ **evacuees.** An **evacuee** is ◆◇◇◇◇
someone who has been sent away from a dangerous N-COUNT
place to somewhere safe.

evade /ɪˈveɪd/ **evades, evading, evaded. 1** If ◆◇◇◇◇
you **evade** something unpleasant or difficult, you VERB
find a way of not dealing with it or avoiding it hap- V n
pening to you. *By his own admission, he evaded*
taxes... He managed to evade capture. **2** If you **evade** VERB
someone or something, you move so that you can V n
avoid them meeting or touching you. *She evaded his*
kisses... I tried to evade Steve's glare. **3** If something VERB
such as success, glory, or love **evades** you, you do V n
not manage to have it. *...those nights when sleep* LITERARY
evaded him.

evalu·ate /ɪˈvæljueɪt/ **evaluates, evaluating,** ◆◆◇◇◇
evaluated. If you **evaluate** something or someone, VERB: V n
you consider them in order to make a judgement
about them, for example about how good or bad
they are. *The market situation is difficult to evalu-*
ate. ♦ **evalu·ation** /ɪˌvæljuˈeɪʃən/ **evaluations** N-VAR
...the opinions and evaluations of college supervisors.

evalu·ative /ɪˈvæljueɪtɪv/. Something that is **evalu-** ADJ-GRADED
ative is based on an assessment of the value and FORMAL
significance of a particular person or thing. *...evalu-*
ative research.

eva·nes·cent /ˌevəˈnesənt/. Something that is **eva-** ADJ-GRADED
nescent gradually disappears from sight or memory. LITERARY

evan·geli·cal /ˌiːvænˈdʒelɪkəl/. **1 Evangelical** ◆◇◇◇◇
Christians emphasize the importance of the Bible ADJ
and the need for personal belief in Christ in order to
obtain salvation. **2** If you describe someone's be- ADJ-GRADED
haviour as **evangelical**, you mean that it is very enthusiastic. *...his evangelical fervour for education.*

evan·gelism /ɪˈvændʒəlɪzəm/. **Evangelism** is the N-UNCOUNT
teaching of Christianity, especially to people who
are not Christians. ♦ **evan·gelist, evangelists** *He* N-COUNT
says a Texan evangelist has led him to God.

evan·gelize /ɪˈvændʒəlaɪz/ **evangelizes, evan-** VERB: V n
gelizing, evangelized; also spelled **evangelise** in V
British English. If someone **evangelizes** a group or
area, they try to convert people to their religion, especially Christianity. *They felt the call to evangelize.*

evapo·rate /ɪˈvæpəreɪt/ **evaporates, evaporat-** ◆◇◇◇◇
ing, evaporated. 1 When a liquid **evaporates**, or V-ERG: V
is evaporated, it changes from a liquid state to a be V-ed
gas, because its temperature has increased. *The wa-* Also V n
ter is evaporated by the sun. ♦ **evapo·ra·tion** N-UNCOUNT
/ɪˌvæpəˈreɪʃən/ *...the evaporation of the sweat on the*
skin. **2** If a feeling or plan **evaporates**, it gradually VERB
becomes weaker and eventually is forgotten. *My an-* V
ger evaporated and I wanted to cry.

eva·sion /ɪˈveɪʒən/ **evasions.** If you accuse some- ◆◇◇◇◇
one of **evasion**, you mean that they are deliberately N-VAR
avoiding dealing with something unpleasant or difficult. *...an evasion of responsibility. ...tax evasion...*
We want straight answers. No evasions.

eva·sive /ɪˈveɪsɪv/. **1** If you describe someone as **eva-** ◆◇◇◇◇
sive, you mean that they deliberately avoid answering ADJ-GRADED
questions. *He was evasive about the circumstances.*
♦ **eva·sive·ly** *'I can't come to any conclusion about* ADV:
that,' Millson said evasively. ♦ **eva·sive·ness. 2** If a ADV with v
driver or pilot **takes evasive action**, they change direc- N-UNCOUNT
tion in order to avoid being met or hit by someone or PHRASE
something. *At least four high-flying warplanes had to*
take evasive action.

eve /iːv/ **eves.** The **eve** of a particular event or oc- ◆◆◇◇◇
casion is the day before it, or the period of time just N-COUNT
before it. *...on the eve of his 27th birthday.* ● See JOURNALISM
also **Christmas Eve.**

even /ˈiːvən/. **1** You use the word **even** to suggest ◆◆◆◆◆
that what comes just after or just before it in the ADV:
sentence is surprising. *He kept calling me for years,* ADV with cl/
even after he got married... Even dark-skinned wom- group,
en should use sunscreens... He didn't even hear what ADV before v
PRAGMATICS

I said. **2** You use **even so** to introduce a surprising PHRASE
fact which relates to what you have just said. *The* PRAGMATICS
bus was only half full. Even so, a young man asked
Nina if the seat next to her was taken. **3** You use PHRASE
even then to say that something is the case in spite PRAGMATICS
of what has just been stated or whatever the circumstances may be. *There was something about the*
way he moved, but even then I didn't guess.
4 You use **even** with comparative adjectives and ad- ADV:
verbs to emphasize a quality that someone or some- ADV compar
thing has. *It was on television that he made an even* PRAGMATICS
stronger impact as an interviewer... Stan was speaking
even more slowly than usual.
5 You use **even if** or **even though** to indicate that a PHR-CONJ
particular fact does not make the rest of your state-
ment untrue. *He accepted the election result, even if it*
meant defeat for his party.
6 If one thing happens **even as** something else hap- PHR-CONJ
pens, they both happen at exactly the same time. *Even* LITERARY
as she said this, she knew it was not quite true.

even /ˈiːvən/. **1** An **even** measurement or rate stays ◆◆◇◇◇
at about the same level. *How important is it to have* ADJ-GRADED
an even temperature? ♦ **even·ly** *He looked at Ellen,* ADV
breathing evenly in her sleep.
2 An **even** surface is smooth and flat. ADJ-GRADED
3 If there is an **even** distribution or division of some- ADJ-GRADED
thing, each person, group, or area involved has an
equal amount. *Divide the dough into 12 even pieces.*
...an even distribution of weight. ♦ **evenly** *The blood* ADV-GRADED
vessels in the skin are not evenly distributed around
the face and neck. **4** An **even** contest or competition is ADJ-GRADED
equally balanced between the two sides who are tak-
ing part. ♦ **evenly** *...two evenly matched candidates.* ADV-GRADED
5 If you are **even** with someone, you do not owe them ADJ:
anything, such as money or a favour. *You don't owe* v-link ADJ
me. I don't owe you. We're even. **6** If you say that you INFORMAL
are going to **get even** with someone, you mean that PHRASE
you are going to cause them the same amount of INFORMAL
harm or annoyance as they have caused you. *I'm go-*
ing to get even with you for this.
7 If your voice is **even**, you are speaking in a very con- ADJ-GRADED
trolled way which makes it difficult for people to tell LITERARY
what your feelings are. ♦ **evenly** *'Is Mary Ann* ADV-GRADED:
O.K?'—'She's fine,' she said evenly. ADV after v
8 An **even** number can be divided exactly by the num- ADJ
ber two.
9 When a company or a person running a business PHRASE
breaks even, they make neither a profit nor a loss.
10 ● **to be on an even keel**: see **keel.**

even /ˈiːvən/ **evens, evening, evened.** ◆◇◇◇◇
even out. If something **evens out**, or if you **even** it PHRASAL VB
out, the differences between the different parts of it ERG
are reduced. *Rates of house price inflation have evened* V P
out... Foundation make-up evens out your skin tone. V P noun
even up. To **even up** a contest or game means to PHRASAL VB
make it more equally balanced than it was. *I would* V P noun
like to see the championship evened up a little. V-ed P

even-'handed. An **even-handed** person is com- ADJ-GRADED
pletely fair when they are judging other people or
dealing with two groups of people. *...an even-*
handed approach to the war on drugs.

even·ing /ˈiːvnɪŋ/ **evenings.** The **evening** is the ◆◆◆◆◇
part of each day between the end of the afternoon N-VAR
and the time when you go to bed. *All he did that*
evening was sit around. ...6.00 in the evening.

'evening class, evening classes. An **evening** N-COUNT
class is a course for adults that is taught in the
evening.

'evening dress, evening dresses. 1 Evening N-UNCOUNT
dress consists of the formal clothes that people
wear to formal occasions in the evening. **2** An **even-** N-COUNT
ing dress is a special dress, usually a long one, that
a woman wears to a formal occasion in the evening.

evens /ˈiːvənz/. In a race or contest, if you bet on a N-UNCOUNT
horse or competitor that is quoted at **evens**, you will BRITISH
win a sum of money equal to your bet if that horse
or competitor wins.

E

even·song /ˈiːvənsɒŋ, AM -sɔːŋ/. **Evensong** is the evening service in the Church of England. N-UNCOUNT

event /ɪˈvent/ **events. 1** An **event** is something that happens. *...the events of Black Wednesday. ...recent events in Europe. ...major sporting events.* **2** An **event** is one of the races or competitions that are part of an organized occasion such as a sports meeting. *The main events start at 1pm.* ◆◆◆◆◆ N-COUNT N-COUNT

3 You use **in the event of**, **in the event that**, and **in that event** when you are talking about a possible future situation, especially when you are planning what to do if it occurs. *...in the unlikely event of an error being made.* **4** You say **in any event** after you have been discussing a situation, in order to indicate that what you are saying is true, in spite of anything that has happened. *In any event, the bowling alley restaurant proved quite acceptable.* **5** You say **in the event** after you have been discussing what could have happened in a particular situation, in order to indicate that you are now describing what actually did happen. *'Don't underestimate us,' Norman Willis warned last year. There was, in the event, little danger of that.* PHRASE PHRASE PRAGMATICS PHRASE PRAGMATICS BRITISH

even-'tempered. An **even-tempered** person is usually calm and does not easily get angry. ADJ-GRADED

event·ful /ɪˈventfʊl/. If you describe an event or a period of time as **eventful**, you mean that a lot of interesting, exciting, or important things have happened during it. *Our next journey was longer and much more eventful.* ADJ-GRADED

even·tual /ɪˈventʃuəl/. You use **eventual** to indicate that something happens or is the case at the end of a process or period of time. *Civil war will be the eventual outcome of the racial tension.* ◆◆◇◇◇ ADJ: ADJ n PRAGMATICS

even·tu·al·i·ty /ɪˌventʃuˈæliti/ **eventualities.** An **eventuality** is a possible future event or result, especially one that is unpleasant or surprising. *Every eventuality is covered, from running out of petrol to needing water.* ◆◇◇◇◇ N-COUNT: with supp FORMAL

even·tu·al·ly /ɪˈventʃuəli/. **1 Eventually** means in the end, especially after a lot of delays, problems, or arguments. *The flight eventually got away six hours late.* **2 Eventually** means at the end of a situation or process or as the final result of it. *She eventually plans to run her own chain of country inns.* ◆◆◆◇ ADV: ADV with cl, ADV before v ADV: ADV with cl, ADV before v

ever /ˈevə/. **Ever** is an adverb which you use to add emphasis in negative sentences, commands, questions, and conditional structures. ◆◆◆◆◆

1 Ever means at any time. It is used in questions and negative statements. *Neither of us had ever skied... Have you ever experienced failure?... You won't hear from Gaston ever again.* **2** You use **ever** in expressions such as **'did you ever'** and **'have you ever'** to express surprise or shock at something you have just seen, heard, or experienced. *Have you ever seen anything like it?* **3** You use **ever** after comparatives and superlatives to emphasize the degree to which something is true or when you are comparing a present situation with the past or the future. *She's got a great voice and is singing better than ever... 'Fear Of Music' remains among the best albums ever.* **4** You can use **ever** for emphasis after 'never'. *I can never, ever, forgive myself... Felix has never, ever confided in me.* **5** You use **ever** to indicate that a person is showing a particular quality that is typical of them. *He was ever careful to check his scripts.* **6** You say **as ever** in order to indicate that something is not unusual. *He was by himself, alone as ever.* **7** You use **ever** to mean increasingly. *They grew ever further apart... It will become ever more complex.* **8** You use **ever** in questions beginning with words such as 'why', 'when', and 'who' when you want to emphasize your surprise or shock. *Why ever didn't you tell me?* **9** If something has been the case **ever since** a particular time, it has been the case all the time from then until now. *He's been there ever since you left!* ► Also an adverb. *I simply gave in to him, and I've regretted it ever since... Ever since, whenever I have been desperate, she has turned up.* **10** You use **ever** in the expressions **ever such** and **ever**
ADV: ADV before v, ADV adv ADV: in questions, ADV before v PRAGMATICS ADV: ADV after compar than, ADV after adj superl PRAGMATICS ADV: ADV before v PRAGMATICS ADV: ADV adj/n WRITTEN PHRASE ADV: ADV adj/v ADV: quest ADV PRAGMATICS PHR-CONJ ADV: ADV after v, ADV with cl

so to emphasize that someone or something has a lot of a particular quality. *He was very lively and ever such a good dancer... This is in ever such good condition... I like him ever so much.* ADV such/so PRAGMATICS INFORMAL, BRITISH

11 You use the expression **all** someone **ever does** when you want to emphasize that they do the same thing all the time, and this annoys you. *All she ever does is whinge and complain.* PHRASE PRAGMATICS

12 You can write **'Yours ever'** or **'Ever yours'** at the end of a letter before you sign your name, as an affectionate way of ending the letter. CONVENTION BRITISH, DATED

13 See also **forever**.

ever- /ˈevə-/. You use **ever-** in adjectives such as **ever-increasing** and **ever-present**, to show that something exists or continues all the time. *...an ever-changing world.* COMB

ever·green /ˈevəɡriːn/ **evergreens.** An evergreen is a tree or bush which has green leaves all the year round. ► Also an adjective. *Plant evergreen shrubs around the end of the month.* ◆◇◇◇◇ N-COUNT ADJ

ever·last·ing /ˌevəˈlɑːstɪŋ, -ˈlæst-/. **1** Something that is **everlasting** never comes to an end. *...a message of peace and everlasting life.* **2** If you describe something as **everlasting**, you mean that it seems never to change or end. *Sometimes the work can feel unrewarding and everlasting.* ADJ ADJ

ever 'more; also spelled **evermore. Ever more** means for all the time in the future. *They will bitterly regret what they have done for ever more.* ◆◇◇◇◇ ADV: ADV with v

every /ˈevri/. **1** You use **every** to indicate that you are referring to all the members of a group or all the parts of something. *Every village has a green, a church, a pub and a manor house. ...fish of every shape and hue. ...recipes for every occasion.* ► Also an adjective. *His every utterance will be scrutinized.* **2** If you say that someone's **every** whim, wish, or desire will be satisfied, you are emphasizing that everything they want will happen or be provided. **3** You use **every** in order to say how often something happens or to indicate that something happens at regular intervals. *We were made to attend meetings every day... A burglary occurs every three minutes in London.* **4** You use **every** in the expressions **every now and then**, **every now and again**, **every once in a while**, and **every so often** in order to indicate that something happens occasionally. **5** If something happens **every other day** or **every second day**, for example, it happens one day, then does not happen the next day, then happens the day after that, and so on. You can also say that something happens **every third week**, **every fourth year**, and so on. **6** You use **every** in front of a number when you are saying what proportion of people or things something happens to or applies to. *Two out of every three Britons already own a video recorder... For every £1 we spend on food, on average we spend 22p on tobacco.* **7** You can use **every** before some nouns, for example 'sign', 'effort', 'reason', and 'intention' in order to emphasize what you are saying. *There is every chance that you will succeed.* **8** ● **every bit as** good **as**: see **bit**. ◆◆◆◆◆ DET ADJ: poss ADJ n ADJ: poss ADJ n PRAGMATICS DET PHRASE PHRASE DET DET PRAGMATICS

every·body /ˈevribɒdi/. **Everybody** means the same as **everyone**. ◆◆◆◆◇

every·day /ˈevrideɪ/. You use **everyday** to describe something which happens or is used every day, or forms a regular and basic part of your life. *...your everyday routine... A paint finish can transform something everyday and mundane into something more elaborate.* ◆◆◇◇◇ ADJ

every·one /ˈevriwʌn/. The form **everybody** is also used. **1** You use **everyone** or **everybody** to refer to all the people in a particular group. *Everyone in the street was shocked... Everyone else goes home around 7 p.m... Not everyone thinks that the government is being particularly generous.* **2** You use **everyone** or **everybody** to refer to all people. *Everyone needs some free time for rest and relaxation.* ◆◆◆◆◇ PRON-INDEF PRON-INDEF

every·thing /ˈevriθɪŋ/. **1** You use **everything** to refer to all the objects, actions, activities, or facts in a particular situation. *Everything else in his life had changed. ...everything that they will need for the* ◆◆◆◆ PRON-INDEF

day's hike... *Everything in the building had gone silent... We can't think of everything.* **2** You use **everything** to refer to a whole situation or to life in general. *Everything is going smoothly... Is everything all right?* **3** If you say that someone or something has **everything**, you mean they have all the things or qualities that most people consider to be desirable. *This man had everything. He had the house, the sailboat and a full life with friends and family.* **4** If you say that someone or something is **everything**, you mean you consider them to be the most important thing that there is. **5** You say **'and everything'** after mentioning a particular thing or list of things to indicate that they are only examples and that other things are also involved. *He had a bed and a fireplace and everything.*

PRON-INDEF

PRON-INDEF

PRON-INDEF

PHRASE
INFORMAL

every·where /'evriweə/. **1** You use **everywhere** to refer to a whole area or to all the places in a particular area. *Working people everywhere object to paying taxes... We went everywhere together... Dust is everywhere.* **2** You use **everywhere** to refer to all the places that someone goes to. *...travelling everywhere in style... Everywhere he went he was introduced as the current United States Open Champion.* **3** You use **everywhere** to emphasize that you are talking about a large number of places, or all possible places. *I saw her picture everywhere... I looked everywhere. I couldn't find him.* **4** If you say that someone or something is **everywhere**, you mean that they are present in a place in very large numbers. *There were cartons of cigarettes everywhere.*

◆◆◆◇◇
ADV

ADV

ADV
PRAGMATICS

ADV

evict /ɪ'vɪkt/ **evicts, evicting, evicted.** If someone **is evicted** from the place where they are living, they are forced to leave it, usually because they have broken a law or contract. *The city police evicted ten families... The landlord threatened that he would evict Anne from her home.* ◆ **evic·tion** /ɪ'vɪkʃən/ **evictions** *He was facing eviction.*

◆◇◇◇◇
VERB:
be V-ed from n
V n
V n from n

N-VAR

evi·dence /'evɪdəns/ **evidences, evidencing, evidenced.** **1** Evidence is anything that you see, experience, read, or are told that causes you to believe that something is true or has really happened. *He'd seen no evidence of widespread fraud. ...evidence that stress is partly responsible for disease... There is no evidence to support this theory.* **2** If a particular feeling, ability, or attitude **is evidenced** by something or someone, it is seen or felt. *She was not calculating and evidenced no specific interest in money.* **3** Evidence is the information which is used in a court of law to try to prove something. Evidence is obtained from documents, objects, or witnesses. *The evidence against him was purely circumstantial.* **4** If you **give evidence** in a court of law or an official enquiry, you officially say what you know about people or events, or describe an occasion at which you were present. *Cabin crew have been giving evidence at the M1 air crash enquiry.* **5** If someone or something **is in evidence**, they are present and can be clearly seen. *Few soldiers were in evidence.*

◆◆◆◆◇
N-UNCOUNT

VERB:
be V-ed by n
V n
FORMAL

N-UNCOUNT

PHRASE

PHRASE

evi·dent /'evɪdənt/. **1** If something is **evident**, you notice it easily and clearly. *His footprints were clearly evident in the heavy dust.* **2** You use **evident** to emphasize your certainty about a situation or fact and your interpretation of it. *It was evident that she had once been a beauty... The cities are bombarded day after day in an evident effort to force their surrender.* **3** See also **self-evident**.

◆◆◇◇◇
ADJ-GRADED

ADJ-GRADED:
oft it v-link
ADJ that/wh
PRAGMATICS

evi·dent·ly /'evɪdəntli/. **1** You use **evidently** to say that something is true, because you have seen evidence of it yourself or because someone has told you it is true. *The two Russians evidently knew each other... From childhood, he was evidently at once rebellious and precocious.* **2** You can use **evidently** to introduce a statement or opinion and to emphasize that you feel that it is true or correct. *Quite evidently, it has nothing to do with social background.*

◆◆◇◇◇
ADV-GRADED:
ADV with cl/
group,
ADV before v

ADV-GRADED:
ADV with cl
PRAGMATICS
FORMAL

evil /'iːvəl/ **evils. 1** Evil is used to refer to all the wicked and bad things that happen in the world.

◆◆◆◇◇
N-UNCOUNT

...those who see television as the root of all evil... There's always a conflict between good and evil in his plays. **2** An **evil** is a very unpleasant or harmful situation or activity. *Apartheid is even a greater evil. ...the evils of alcohol.* **3** If you describe someone as **evil**, you mean that they are very wicked and take pleasure in doing things that harm other people. *...the country's most evil terrorists.* **4** If you describe something as **evil**, you mean that you think it causes a great deal of harm to people and is morally bad. *...condemning slavery as evil.* **5** If you have two choices, but think that they are both bad, you can describe the one which is less bad as **the lesser of two evils**, or **the lesser evil**.

N-COUNT

ADJ-GRADED

ADJ-GRADED

PHRASE

evil 'eye. 1 Some people believe that **the evil eye** is a magical power used to cast a spell on someone or something, so that bad things happen to them. **2** If you say that someone is giving you the **evil eye**, you mean that they are looking at you in a very unpleasant and hostile way.

N-SING:
the N

N-SING

evince /ɪ'vɪns/ **evinces, evincing, evinced.** If someone or something **evinces** a particular feeling or quality, they show it, often indirectly. *The entire production evinces authenticity.*

VERB
V n

evis·cer·ate /ɪ'vɪsəreɪt/ **eviscerates, eviscerating, eviscerated.** If you say that something will **eviscerate** an organization or system, you mean that it will make it much weaker or much less powerful. *The petition will eviscerate state government.*

VERB
V n
FORMAL

evoca·tive /ɪ'vɒkətɪv/. If you describe something as **evocative**, you mean that it produces pleasant memories, ideas, emotions, and responses in people. *Her story is sharply evocative of Italian provincial life.* ◆ **evoca·tive·ly** *...the collection of islands evocatively known as the South Seas.*

◆◇◇◇◇
ADJ-GRADED

ADV-GRADED

evoke /ɪ'vəʊk/ **evokes, evoking, evoked.** To **evoke** a particular memory, idea, emotion, or response means to cause it to occur. *...the scene evoking memories of those old movies.* ◆ **evo·ca·tion** /ˌiːvə'keɪʃən, ˌev-/ **evocations** *...the faithful evocation of those fateful years.*

◆◆◇◇◇
VERB
V n

N-VAR

evo·lu·tion /ˌiːvə'luːʃən, ˌev-/ **evolutions. 1** Evolution is a process of gradual change that takes place over many generations, during which species of animals, plants, or insects slowly change some of their physical characteristics. *...the evolution of plants and animals.* **2** Evolution is a process of gradual and uninterrupted development in a particular situation or thing over a period of time. *...the evolution of modern physics.*

◆◆◇◇◇
N-UNCOUNT

N-VAR
FORMAL

evo·lu·tion·ary /ˌiːvə'luːʃənri, AM -neri/. **Evolutionary** means relating to a process of gradual change and development. *...an evolutionary process. ...a period of evolutionary change.*

◆◇◇◇◇
ADJ

evolve /ɪ'vɒlv/ **evolves, evolving, evolved. 1** When animals or plants **evolve**, they gradually change and develop into different forms. *Maize evolved from a wild grass in Mexico. ...when amphibians evolved into reptiles.* **2** If something **evolves** or you **evolve** it, it gradually develops over a period of time into something different and usually more advanced. *...a tiny airline which eventually evolved into Pakistan International Airlines... As medical knowledge evolves, beliefs change.*

◆◆◇◇◇
VERB: V
V from n
V into n

V-ERG
V into/from n
V
Also V n

ewe /juː/ **ewes.** A ewe is a adult female sheep.

N-COUNT

ex /eks/ **exes.** Someone's **ex** is the person they used to be married to or used to have a romantic or sexual relationship with.

N-COUNT
INFORMAL

ex- /eks-/. **Ex-** is added to nouns to show that someone or something is no longer the thing referred to by that noun. For example, someone's ex-husband is no longer their husband.

PREFIX

ex·ac·er·bate /ɪg'zæsəbeɪt/ **exacerbates, exacerbating, exacerbated.** If something **exacerbates** a bad situation, it makes it worse. *Mr Powell-Taylor says that depopulation exacerbates the problem.* ◆ **ex·ac·er·ba·tion** /ɪg,zæsə'beɪʃən/ *...the exacerbation of global problems.*

◆◇◇◇◇
VERB
V n
FORMAL

N-UNCOUNT

ex·act /ɪg'zækt/ **exacts, exacting, exacted. 1** Exact means correct in every detail. For example,

◆◆◆◇
ADJ-GRADED

an **exact** copy is the same in every detail as the original. *I don't remember the exact words... The exact number of protest calls has not been revealed.* ♦ **ex·act·ly** *Try to locate exactly where the smells are entering the room... The system worked perfectly, exactly as his training and plans had led him to expect.* **2** You use **exact** before a noun to emphasize that you are referring to that particular thing and no other, especially something that has a particular significance. *Do you really think I could get the exact thing I want?... It may be that you will feel the exact opposite of what you expected.* ♦ **exactly** *These are exactly the people who do not vote.* **3** You say **to be exact** to indicate that you are now giving more detailed information or a slight correction that relates to what you have been saying. *A small number – five, to be exact – have been bad.* **4** If you describe someone as **exact**, you mean that they are very careful and detailed in their work, thinking, or methods. **5** When someone **exacts** something, they demand and obtain it from someone else, especially because they are in a superior or more powerful position. *Already he has exacted a written apology from the chairman of the commission.* **6** If someone **exacts** revenge on a person, they have their revenge on them. *She uses the media to help her exact a terrible revenge.* **7** If something **exacts** a high price, it has a bad effect on a person or situation. *The sheer physical effort had exacted a heavy price.* **8** See also **exactly**.

ADJ: ADJ n
PRAGMATICS

ADV:
ADV n/wh
PHRASE
PRAGMATICS

ADJ-GRADED

VERB
V n from/for n
FORMAL

VERB:
V n on n
V n
VERB
V n
Also V n on n

ex·act·ing /ɪgˈzæktɪŋ/. You use **exacting** to describe something or someone that demands hard work and a great deal of care. *...such an exacting task... Privately they seem to have the same exacting standards.*

ADJ-GRADED

ex·ac·ti·tude /ɪgˈzæktɪtjuːd, AM -tuːd/. **Exactitude** is the quality of being very accurate and careful. *...the exactitude he expected to find in all dimensions of daily life.*

N-UNCOUNT
FORMAL

ex·act·ly /ɪgˈzæktli/. **1** You use **exactly** before an amount, number, or position to emphasize that it is no more, no less, or no different from what you are stating. *Agnew's car pulled into the driveway at exactly five o'clock. ...exactly in the middle of the picture.* **2** If you say '**Exactly**', you are agreeing with someone or emphasizing the truth of what they say. If you say '**Not exactly**', you are telling them politely that they are wrong in part of what they are saying. *'We don't know the answer to that.'—'Exactly, so shut up and stop speculating.'... 'And you refused?'—'Well, not exactly. I couldn't say yes.'* **3** You use **not exactly** to indicate that a meaning or situation is slightly different from what people think or expect. *He's not exactly homeless, he just hangs out in this park.* **4** You use **not exactly** to emphasize in an ironic or sarcastic way what is being said. *This is not exactly what the Church needed just at this moment.* **5** You use **exactly** with a question to emphasize your annoyance with what someone is doing or saying. *Exactly what are you looking for?* **6** See also **exact**.

ADV
PRAGMATICS

ADV
PRAGMATICS

ADV:
not ADV
PRAGMATICS

ADV:
not ADV
PRAGMATICS

ADV with
quest
PRAGMATICS

ex,act 'science. If you say that a particular activity is not an **exact science**, you mean that there are no set rules to follow or it does not produce entirely accurate results. *Forecasting floods is not an exact science.*

N-SING

ex·ag·ger·ate /ɪgˈzædʒəreɪt/ **exaggerates, exaggerating, exaggerated.** **1** If you **exaggerate**, you indicate that something is, for example, worse or more important than it really is. *She did sometimes exaggerate the demands of her job.* ♦ **ex·ag·gera·tion** /ɪgˌzædʒəˈreɪʃən/ **exaggerations** *It would be an exaggeration to call the danger urgent.* **2** If something **exaggerates** a situation, quality, or feature, it makes it appear greater, more obvious, or more important than it really is. *These figures exaggerate the loss of competitiveness.*

VERB: V
V n

N-VAR

VERB
V n

ex·ag·ger·at·ed /ɪgˈzædʒəreɪtɪd/. Something that is **exaggerated** is or seems larger, better, worse, or more important than it needs to be. *...exaggerated*

ADJ-GRADED

claims for what such courses can achieve. ♦ **ex·ag·ger·at·ed·ly** *...an exaggeratedly feminine appearance... She laughed exaggeratedly at their jokes.*

ADV-GRADED:
ADV adj/-ed,
ADV after v

ex·alt /ɪgˈzɔːlt/ **exalts, exalting, exalted.** To **exalt** someone or something means to praise them very highly. *This book exalts her as both mother and muse.* ♦ **ex·al·ta·tion** *The poem, which appeared in 1890, is an exaltation of married love.*

◆◇◇◇◇
VERB
V n
FORMAL
N-UNCOUNT:
also a N

ex·al·ta·tion /ˌegzɔːlˈteɪʃən/. **Exaltation** is an intense feeling of great joy and happiness. *The city was swept up in the mood of exaltation.* ● See also **exalt**.

N-UNCOUNT
FORMAL

ex·alt·ed /ɪgˈzɔːltɪd/. **1** Someone or something that is at an **exalted** level is at a very high level, especially with regard to rank or importance. *...the exalted level of Olympic competition.* **2** If you feel **exalted**, you feel full of joy and happiness. *You do get very excited and exalted by the power of these speeches.*

◆◇◇◇◇
ADJ-GRADED
FORMAL

ADJ-GRADED
FORMAL

exam /ɪgˈzæm/ **exams.** An **exam** is a formal test that you take to show your knowledge of a subject, or to obtain a qualification. *He passed his A-level history exam... Kate's exam results were excellent.*

◆◆◇◇◇
N-COUNT

ex·ami·na·tion /ɪgˌzæmɪˈneɪʃən/ **examinations.** An **examination** is the same as an **exam.** ● See also **examine.**

◆◆◆◇◇
N-COUNT
FORMAL

ex·am·ine /ɪgˈzæmɪn/ **examines, examining, examined.** **1** If you **examine** something, you look at it carefully. *He examined her passport.* ♦ **ex·ami·na·tion** /ɪgˌzæmɪˈneɪʃən/ **examinations** *...an examination of the wreck.* **2** If a doctor **examines** you, he or she checks your body in order to find out how healthy you are. *Another doctor examined her and could still find nothing wrong.* ♦ **examination** *Further examination is needed to exclude the chance of disease.* **3** If an idea or plan **is examined**, it is considered very carefully. *The plans will be examined by EC environment ministers.* ♦ **examination** *The government said it was studying the implications, which 'required very careful examination'.* **4** If you **are examined**, you are given a formal test in order to show your knowledge of a subject. *...learning to cope with the pressures of being judged and examined by our teachers.*

◆◆◆◆◇
VERB
V n
N-VAR

VERB
V n

N-VAR

VERB
V n
N-VAR

VB: usu
passive
be V-ed

ex·ami·nee /ɪgˌzæmɪˈniː/ **examinees.** An **examinee** is someone who is taking an exam.

N-COUNT
FORMAL

ex·am·in·er /ɪgˈzæmɪnə/ **examiners.** An **examiner** is a person who sets or marks an examination. ● See also **medical examiner.**

◆◇◇◇◇
N-COUNT

ex·am·ple /ɪgˈzɑːmpəl, -ˈzæmp-/ **examples.** **1** An **example** of something is a situation, object, or person that illustrates a point you are making, or that supports an argument or opinion. *The doctors gave numerous examples of patients being expelled from hospital.* **2** You use **for example** to emphasize something that illustrates a point you are making, or that supports an argument or opinion. *A few simple precautions can be taken, for example ensuring that desks are the right height.* **3** An **example** is something that represents or is typical of a particular class of objects or styles. *Symphonies 103 and 104 stand as perfect examples of early symphonic construction... The plaque illustrated in Figure 1 is an example of his work at this time.* **4** In a dictionary entry, an **example** is a phrase or sentence which shows how a word is used. **5** If you refer to a person as an **example** to other people, you mean that he or she behaves in a good way that other people should copy. *Their example shows us what we are all capable of.* **6** If you **set an example**, you encourage people by your behaviour to behave in a similar way. *An officer's job was to set an example.* **7** If you **follow** someone's **example**, you copy their behaviour, especially because you admire them. *...following the example set by her father.* **8** To **make an example of** someone who has done something wrong means to punish them severely as a warning to other people not to do the same thing.

◆◆◆◆◆
N-COUNT
PRAGMATICS

PHRASE
PRAGMATICS

N-COUNT

N-COUNT

N-COUNT

PHRASE

PHRASE

PHRASE

ex·as·per·ate /ɪgˈzɑːspəreɪt, -ˈzæs-/ **exasperates, exasperating, exasperated.** If someone

◆◇◇◇◇
VERB
V n

E

or something **exasperates** you, they annoy you and make you feel extremely frustrated. *The sheer futility of it all exasperates her.* ♦ **ex·as·pera·tion** /ɪɡ,zɑːspəˈreɪʃən, -,zæs-/ *Mahoney clenched his fist in exasperation.* `N-UNCOUNT`

ex·as·per·at·ed /ɪɡˈzɑːspəreɪtɪd, -ˈzæs-/. If you describe someone as **exasperated**, you mean that they are feeling frustrated or angry because of something that is happening. *Bertha was exasperated at the delay. ...an exasperated sigh.* `ADJ-GRADED` ◆◇◇◇

ex·as·per·at·ing /ɪɡˈzɑːspəreɪtɪŋ, -ˈzæs-/. If you describe someone or something as **exasperating**, you mean that they make you feel angry or frustrated. *She really is the most exasperating woman.* `ADJ-GRADED`

ex·ca·vate /ˈekskəveɪt/ **excavates, excavating, excavated. 1** When archaeologists or other people **excavate** a piece of land, they remove earth from it and look for things which are buried there, in order to find out about the past. *A new Danish expedition is again excavating the site.* ♦ **ex·ca·va·tion** /,ekskəˈveɪʃən/ *...the excavation of a bronze-age boat... These new excavations will require conservation.* **2** To **excavate** means to dig a hole in the ground, for example in order to build there. *A contractor was hired to drain the reservoir and to excavate soil.* ♦ **excavation** *...the excavation of canals.* `VERB Vn` `N-VAR` `VERB Vn` `N-VAR` ◆◇◇◇

ex·ca·va·tor /ˈekskəveɪtə/ **excavators.** An **excavator** is a large machine that is used for digging. `N-COUNT`

ex·ceed /ɪkˈsiːd/ **exceeds, exceeding, exceeded. 1** If something **exceeds** a particular amount or number, it is greater or larger than that amount or number. *Its research budget exceeds $700 million a year... His performance exceeded all expectations.* **2** If you **exceed** a limit or rule, you go beyond it, even though you are not supposed to. *She was exceeding the speed limit... I would be exceeding my powers if I ordered the march to be halted.* `VERB Vn` `VERB Vn` ◆◆◇◇

ex·ceed·ing·ly /ɪkˈsiːdɪŋli/. **Exceedingly** means very or very much. *...an exceedingly good lunch... I have a case that troubles me exceedingly.* `ADV DATED` ◆◇◇◇

ex·cel /ɪkˈsel/ **excels, excelling, excelled.** If someone **excels** in or at something, they are very good at doing it. *Academically he began to excel... Krishnan excelled himself in all departments of his game.* `VERB: Vin/atn v Vpron-refl` ◆◇◇◇

ex·cel·lence /ˈeksələns/. If someone or something has the quality of **excellence**, they are extremely good at something. *...the top US award for excellence in journalism.* ● See also **par excellence**. `N-UNCOUNT` ◆◆◇◇

Ex·cel·len·cy /ˈeksələnsi/ **Excellencies.** You use expressions such as **Your Excellency** or **His Excellency** when you are addressing or referring to officials of very high rank, for example ambassadors or governors. *...His excellency the President.* `N-VOC: possN poss PRON: poss PRON PRAGMATICS` ◆◇◇◇

ex·cel·lent /ˈeksələnt/. **1** Something that is **excellent** is very good indeed. *The recording quality is excellent... Sue is very efficient and does an excellent job as Fred's personal assistant.* ♦ **ex·cel·lent·ly** *They're both playing excellently... The tournament was excellently organised.* **2** Some people say '**Excellent!**' to show that they approve of something. `ADJ` `ADV-GRADED` `EXCLAM` ◆◆◆◇

ex·cept /ɪkˈsept/. **1** You use **except** to introduce the only thing or person that a statement does not apply to, or a fact that prevents a statement from being completely true. *I wouldn't have accepted anything except a job in Europe... I don't take any drugs whatsoever, except aspirin for colds... Booking is not necessary except in the case of larger parties.* ▶ Also a conjunction. *The log cabin stayed empty, except when we came... Nothing more to do now except wait.* **2** You use **except for** to introduce the only thing or person that prevents a statement from being completely true. *Everyone was late, except for Richard.* `PREP` `CONJ` `PHR-PREP` ◆◆◆◇

ex·cept·ed /ɪkˈseptɪd/. You use **excepted** after you have mentioned a person or thing to show that you do not include them in the statement you are making. *Jeremy excepted, the men seemed personable.* `ADV: n ADV FORMAL`

ex·cept·ing /ɪkˈseptɪŋ/. You use **excepting** to introduce the only thing that prevents a statement from being completely true. *The source of meat for much of this region (excepting Japan) has traditionally been the pig.* `PREP FORMAL`

ex·cep·tion /ɪkˈsepʃən/ **exceptions. 1** An **exception** is a particular thing, person, or situation that is not included in a general statement or rule. *There is, however, one major exception to the general shift towards capitalism... The law makes no exceptions.* **2** You use **with the exception of** to introduce a thing or person that is not included in a general statement. *Yesterday was a day off for everybody, with the exception of Lawrence.* **3** When you are referring to an example which contradicts a statement that you are making, you can say that it is **the exception that proves the rule**, in order to avoid spoiling your argument. *Selling arms to a country that sponsors terrorism is clearly wrong, but it's the exception that proves the rule.* **4** If you make a general statement, and then say that something or someone is **no exception**, you are emphasizing that they are included in that statement. *Marketing is applied to everything these days, and books are no exception.* **5** You use **without exception** to emphasize that the statement you are making is true in all cases. *The vehicles are without exception old, rusty and dented... Almost without exception those convicted were our friends and colleagues.* **6** If you **take exception to** something, you feel offended or annoyed by it. *They take exception to any kind of noise whatsoever.* `N-COUNT` `PHR-PREP` `PHRASE PRAGMATICS` `PHRASE PRAGMATICS` `PHRASE PRAGMATICS` `PHRASE` ◆◆◆◇

ex·cep·tion·al /ɪkˈsepʃənəl/. **1** You use **exceptional** to describe someone or something that has a particular quality to an unusually high degree. *...children with exceptional ability.* ♦ **ex·cep·tion·al·ly** *He's an exceptionally talented dancer... The conditions under ground were exceptionally hot.* **2 Exceptional** situations are unusual and only happen very rarely. *...if the courts hold that this case is exceptional.* ♦ **exceptionally** *Exceptionally, in times of emergency, we may send a team of experts.* `ADJ-GRADED PRAGMATICS` `ADV: ADV adj/adv` `ADJ-GRADED FORMAL` `ADV: ADV with cl` ◆◆◇◇

ex·cerpt /ˈeksɜːpt/ **excerpts.** An **excerpt** is a short piece of writing or music which is taken from a larger piece. `N-COUNT` ◆◆◆◇

ex·cess, excesses. The noun is pronounced /ɪkˈses/. The adjective is pronounced /ˈekses/. **1** An **excess** of something is a larger amount than is needed or usual. *Polyunsaturated oils are essential for health. Excess is harmful, however.* ▶ Also an adjective. *The major reason for excess weight is excess eating.* **2** In **excess of** means more than a particular amount. *Avoid deposits in excess of £20,000 in any one account.* **3 Excess** is behaviour that is unacceptable because it is too extreme or immoral. *She was sick of her life of excess. ...the bloody excesses of warfare.* **4** If you do something **to excess**, you do it too much. *Red meat, eaten to excess, is very high in fat and calories.* **5 Excess** is used to refer to additional amounts of money that need to be paid for services and activities that were not originally taken into account. *...an access fare of £20.* **6** The **excess** on an insurance policy is a sum of money which the insured person has to pay towards the cost of a claim. The insurance company then pays the rest. *...a policy with a £250 excess for under-21s.* `N-VAR: with supp` `ADJ: ADJ n` `PHR-PREP FORMAL` `N-UNCOUNT: also N in pl` `PHRASE` `ADJ: ADJ n FORMAL` `N-COUNT BRITISH, TECHNICAL` ◆◆◆◇

ex·ces·sive /ɪkˈsesɪv/. If you describe the amount or level of something as **excessive**, you disapprove of it because it is more or higher than is necessary or reasonable. *...use of excessive force by police.* ♦ **ex·ces·sive·ly** *...excessively high salaries... Mum had started taking pills and drinking excessively.* `ADJ-GRADED PRAGMATICS` `ADV` ◆◆◇◇

ex·change /ɪksˈtʃeɪndʒ/ **exchanges, exchanging, exchanged. 1** If two or more people **exchange** things of a particular kind, they give them to each other at the same time. *We exchanged addresses... He exchanged a quick smile with her.* ▶ Also a noun. *He ruled out any exchange of prisoners with the militants... There was also a brief ex-* `V-RECIP pl-n V Vn withn` `N-COUNT` ◆◆◆◆

change of views. **2** If you **exchange** something or **ex-** VERB: V n
change it for something else, you replace it with V n for n
something else, especially something that is better.
If the car you have leased is clearly unsatisfactory,
you can always exchange it for another. **3** If you do PHRASE
something for someone or give them something **in**
exchange, you do it or give it because they did
something for you or gave you something. *It is il-*
legal for public officials to solicit gifts or money in
exchange for favors... He paid her a huge salary. In
exchange, he was assured of her vote.
4 An **exchange** of fire, for example, is an incident in N-COUNT
which people use guns or missiles against each other.
...the risk of a nuclear exchange. **5** An **exchange** is an N-COUNT
arrangement in which people from two different
countries visit each other's country, to strengthen
links between them. *...educational exchanges for*
young people. **6** An **exchange** is a brief conversation, N-COUNT
usually an angry one. FORMAL
7 **Exchange** is used in the names of some places
where people used to trade and do business with each
other. **8** The **exchange** is the same as the **telephone** N-COUNT
exchange. **9** See also **corn exchange, foreign ex-**
change, stock exchange.

ex'change rate, exchange rates. The **ex-** ◆◆◆◇◇
change rate of a country's unit of currency is the N-COUNT
amount of another country's currency that you get
in exchange for it.

Ex·cheq·uer /ɪksˈtʃekə/. **The Exchequer** is the de- ◆◇◇◇
partment in the British government which is re- N-PROPER:
sponsible for the money belonging to the state. theN

ex·cise, excises, excising, excised. The noun ◆◇◇◇
is pronounced /ˈeksaɪz/. The verb is pronounced
/ɪkˈsaɪz/. **1** **Excise** is a tax that the government of a N-VAR
country puts on goods such as cigarettes, which are
produced for sale in its own country. *...this year's*
rise in excise duties. **2** If someone **excises** some- VERB: V n
thing, they remove it completely. *...the question of* V n from n
permanently excising madness from the world. FORMAL

ex·cit·able /ɪkˈsaɪtəbəl/. If you describe someone ADJ-GRADED
as **excitable,** you mean that they behave in a nervous way and become excited easily. *Mrs. Anderson*
was not an excitable woman.

ex·cite /ɪkˈsaɪt/ **excites, exciting, excited. 1** If ◆◆◇◇
something **excites** you, it makes you feel very happy VERB
or enthusiastic. *We'd not been excited by anything* V
for about three years... The show really excites
is in the display of avant-garde photography. **2** If VERB
something **excites** a particular emotion or reaction V n
in someone, it causes them to experience it.
Daniel's early exposure to motor racing did not ex-
cite his interest... Reports of the plot of this unusual
film tend to excite revulsion. **3** If something or VERB
someone **excites** you, they cause you to feel sexual V n with n
desire. *Don't try exciting your partner with dirty* Also V n
magazines. ♦ **ex·cit·ed** *She makes you feel warm* ADJ-GRADED
and comfortable, and maybe a little excited. ♦ **ex-**
·cit·ing *...a sexually exciting thought.* ADJ-GRADED

ex·cit·ed /ɪkˈsaɪtɪd/. **1** If you are **excited,** you are ◆◆◇◇
so happy that you cannot relax, especially because ADJ-GRADED
you are thinking about something pleasant that is
going to happen to you. *I'm very excited about the*
possibility of playing for England's first team. ...an
excited teenager. ♦ **ex·cit·ed·ly** *'You're coming?' he* ADV-GRADED:
said excitedly. **2** If you are **excited,** you are very ADV with v
worried or angry about something, and so you can- ADJ-GRADED
not relax. *I don't think there's any reason to get ex-*
cited about inflation. ...excited voices.

ex·cite·ment /ɪkˈsaɪtmənt/ **excitements.** You ◆◆◇◇
use **excitement** to refer to the state of being excited, N-VAR
or to something that excites you. *...in a state of great*
excitement... This game had its challenges, excite-
ments and rewards.

ex·cit·ing /ɪkˈsaɪtɪŋ/. If something is **exciting,** it ◆◆◆◇
makes you feel very happy or enthusiastic. *...the* ADJ-GRADED
most exciting adventure of their lives. ♦ **ex·cit·ing-**
·ly *...an excitingly original writer.* ADV-GRADED

ex·claim /ɪksˈkleɪm/ **exclaims, exclaiming, ex-** ◆◇◇◇
claimed. Writers sometimes use **exclaim** to show VERB
that someone is speaking suddenly, loudly, or em- V with quote
Also V that

phatically. *'He went back to the lab,' Iris exclaimed*
impatiently.

ex·cla·ma·tion /ˌekskləˈmeɪʃən/ **exclamations.** N-COUNT
An **exclamation** is something that is spoken sud- FORMAL
denly, loudly, or emphatically and that expresses
excitement, admiration, shock, or anger. *Sue gave*
an exclamation as we got a clear sight of the house.

excla'mation mark, exclamation marks. An N-COUNT
exclamation mark is the sign (!) which is used in BRITISH
writing to show that a word, phrase, or sentence is
an exclamation. The usual American expression is
exclamation point.

ex·clude /ɪksˈkluːd/ **excludes, excluding, ex-** ◆◆◇◇
cluded. 1 If you **exclude** someone from a place or VERB
activity, you prevent them from entering it or taking V n from n
part in it. *The Academy excluded women from its* Also V n
classes... Many of the youngsters feel excluded. **2** If VERB
you **exclude** something that has some connection V n
with what you are doing, you deliberately do not
use it or consider it. *Christmas carols are being*
modified to exclude any reference to Christ. **3** To **ex-** VERB
clude a possibility means to decide or prove that it V n
is wrong and not worth considering. *...the patho-*
logical evidence, which does not exclude suicide.

ex·clud·ing /ɪksˈkluːdɪŋ/. You use **excluding** be- ◆◇◇◇
fore mentioning a person or thing to show that you PREP
are not including them in your statement. *Excluding*
water, half of the body's weight is protein.

ex·clu·sion /ɪksˈkluːʒən/ **exclusions. 1** The **ex-** ◆◆◇◇
clusion of something is the act of deliberately not N-VAR
using, allowing, or considering it. *...the exclusion of*
all commercial lending institutions from the college
loan program... Certain exclusions and limitations
apply. **2 Exclusion** is the act of preventing someone N-UNCOUNT
from entering a place or taking part in an activity.
...women's exclusion from political power. **3** If PHRASE
something happens **to the exclusion of** something
else, the first thing happens to such a great extent
that it prevents the second thing from being considered or being present. *Diane had dedicated her life*
to caring for him to the exclusion of all else.

ex·clu·sion·ary /ɪksˈkluːʒənri/. Something that is ADJ-GRADED
exclusionary excludes a particular person or group FORMAL
of people. *...exclusionary business practices.*

ex·clu·sive /ɪksˈkluːsɪv/ **exclusives. 1** If some- ◆◆◇◇
thing is **exclusive,** it is limited to people who have a ADJ-GRADED
lot of money or who belong to a high social class,
and is therefore not available to everyone.
...Britain's most exclusive club. ♦ **ex·clu·sive·ness** N-UNCOUNT
...the exclusiveness of the traditional elite. ♦ **ex·clu-**
·siv·ity /ˌeksklu:ˈsɪvɪti/ *...residents enjoy the exclu-* N-UNCOUNT
sivity of their homes. **2** Something that is **exclusive** ADJ
is used or owned by only one person or group, and
not shared with anyone else. *Our group will have*
exclusive use of a 60-foot boat... Many of their
cheeses are exclusive to our stores in Britain.
♦ **exclusivity** *Only 250 are to be sold in Europe, so* N-UNCOUNT
exclusivity is guaranteed. **3** If a newspaper, maga- ADJ
zine, or broadcasting organization describes one of
its articles or reports as **exclusive,** they mean that it
does not appear in any other publication or on any
other channel. *...an exclusive interview.* ♦ An **exclu-** N-COUNT
sive is an exclusive article or report. *Some papers*
thought they had an exclusive. **4** If a company states ADJ
that its prices or goods are **exclusive** of something,
that thing is not included in the stated price, although it usually still has to be paid for. *All charges*
for service are exclusive of value added tax. **5** If two PHRASE
things are **mutually exclusive,** they are very different from each other, so that it is impossible for
them to exist or happen together. *Ambition and*
successful fatherhood can be mutually exclusive.

ex·clu·sive·ly /ɪksˈkluːsɪvli/. **Exclusively** is used to ◆◆◇◇
refer to situations or activities that involve only the ADV
thing or things mentioned, and nothing else. *...an*
exclusively male domain... Instruction in these sub-
jects is almost exclusively by lecture.

ex·com·mu·ni·cate /ˌekskəˈmjuːnɪkeɪt/ **excom-** VERB:
municates, excommunicating, excommuni- beV-ed
cated. If a Roman Catholic or member of the V n

E

Orthodox Church is **excommunicated**, it is publicly stated that the person is no longer allowed to be a member of the Church. This is a punishment for some very great wrong that they have done. *In 1766 he excommunicated the village.* ♦ **ex·com·mu·ni·ca·tion** /ˌekskəmjuːnɪˈkeɪʃən/ N-VAR **tions** *...the threat of excommunication.*

ex·co·ri·ate /ɪkˈskɔːrieɪt/ **excoriates, excoriating, excoriated.** To excoriate a person or organization means to criticize them severely or condemn their actions, usually in public. *He proceeded to excoriate me in front of the nurses.* VERB V n FORMAL

ex·cre·ment /ˈekskrɪmənt/. **Excrement** is the solid waste that is passed out of a person or animal's body through their bowels. N-UNCOUNT FORMAL

ex·cre·ta /ɪkˈskriːtə/. **Excreta** is the waste matter, such as urine or faeces, which is passed out of a person or animal's body. N-UNCOUNT FORMAL

ex·crete /ɪkˈskriːt/ **excretes, excreting, excreted.** When a person or animal **excretes** waste matter from their body, they get rid of it, for example in faeces, urine, or sweat. *Your open pores excrete sweat and dirt.* ♦ **ex·cre·tion** /ɪkˈskriːʃən/ **excretions** *...the excretion of this drug from the body.* ♦◇◇◇◇ V n Also V / N-UNCOUNT: also N in pl

ex·cru·ci·at·ing /ɪkˈskruːʃieɪtɪŋ/. **1** If you describe something as **excruciating**, you mean that it is extremely painful, either physically or emotionally. *I was in excruciating pain. ..excruciating misery and loneliness.* ♦ **ex·cru·ci·at·ing·ly** *He found the transition to boarding school excruciatingly painful... The ball hit him excruciatingly in the most sensitive part of his anatomy.* **2** If you describe something as **excruciating**, you mean that it is very unpleasant to experience, for example because it is very boring or embarrassing. *...a moment of excruciating silence.* ♦ **excruciatingly** *The dialogue is excruciatingly embarrassing. ...the children's chorus goes on excruciatingly about 'Grocer Jack'.* ♦◇◇◇◇ ADJ-GRADED PRAGMATICS / ADV-GRADED / ADJ-GRADED / ADV-GRADED

ex·cur·sion /ɪkˈskɜːʃən, AM -ʒən/ **excursions. 1** You can refer to a short journey as an **excursion**, especially if it is made for pleasure. **2** An **excursion** is a visit to a place of interest, especially one that is arranged by a holiday company. *We also recommend a full day optional excursion to the Upper Douro.* **3** If you describe an activity as an **excursion** into something, you mean that it is an attempt by someone to do something new that they have not experienced before. *...Radio 3's latest excursion into ethnic music.* ♦◇◇◇◇ N-COUNT / N-COUNT / N-COUNT

ex·cus·able /ɪkˈskjuːzəbəl/. If you say that someone's wrong words or actions are **excusable**, you mean that they can be understood and forgiven. *I then realised that he had made a simple but excusable historical mistake.* ADJ-GRADED

ex·cuse, excuses, excusing, excused. The noun is pronounced /ɪkˈskjuːs/. The verb is pronounced /ɪkˈskjuːz/. **1** An **excuse** is a reason which you give in order to explain why something has been done or has not been done, or to avoid doing something. *It is easy to find excuses for his indecisiveness... Once I had had a baby I had the perfect excuse to stay at home.* ● If you say that there is **no excuse** for something, you are emphasizing that it should not happen, or expressing disapproval that it has happened. *Solitude was no excuse for sloppiness.* **2** To **excuse** someone or **excuse** their behaviour means to provide reasons for their actions, especially when other people disapprove of these actions. *He excused himself by saying he was 'forced to rob to maintain his wife and cat'... That doesn't excuse my mother's behaviour.* **3** If you **excuse** someone for something wrong that they have done, you forgive them for it. *Many people might have excused them for shirking some of their responsibilities.* **4** If someone **is excused** from a duty or responsibility, they are told that they do not have to carry it out. *Some MPs will have been officially excused attendance.* **5** If you **excuse** yourself, you use a phrase such as 'Excuse me' as a polite way of saying that you are about ♦♦♦◇◇ N-COUNT / PHRASE PRAGMATICS / VERB V n by·-ing V n / VERB Also V n, V n n / VB: usu passive, be V-ed from n/·-ing be V-ed in / VERB V pron-refl

to leave. *He excused himself and went up to his room.* ● You use **excuse me** or a phrase such as **if you'll excuse me** to indicate that you are about to leave, or that you are about to stop talking to someone because you need to do something else. *Now if you'll excuse me, I've got work to do.* **6** You say **'Excuse me'** when you want to politely get someone's attention, especially when you are about to ask them a question. *Excuse me, but are you Mr Honig?* **7** You use **excuse me** to apologize to someone when you have disturbed or interrupted them. *Excuse me interrupting, but there's a thing I feel I've got to say.* **8** You use **excuse me** to apologize when you have done something slightly embarrassing or impolite, such as burping or sneezing. **9** You say **'Excuse me?'** to show that you want someone to repeat what they have just said. The usual British expression is **pardon** or **I beg your pardon.** CONVENTION PRAGMATICS / CONVENTION PRAGMATICS / CONVENTION PRAGMATICS / CONVENTION PRAGMATICS / CONVENTION PRAGMATICS AMERICAN

ex·di·rec·tory. If a person or his or her telephone number is **ex-directory**, the number is not listed in the telephone directory, and the telephone company will refuse to give it to people who ask for it. The usual American word is **unlisted.** ADJ BRITISH

ex·ecra·ble /ˈeksɪkrəbəl/. If you describe something as **execrable**, you mean that it is very bad or unpleasant. ADJ-GRADED FORMAL

ex·ecute /ˈeksɪkjuːt/ **executes, executing, executed. 1** To **execute** someone means to kill them, usually as a punishment for a serious crime. *One group claimed to have executed the American hostage... This boy's father had been executed for conspiring against the throne.* ♦ **ex·ecu·tion** /ˌeksɪˈkjuːʃən/ **executions** *...execution by lethal injection.* ♦ **executioner** /ˌeksɪˈkjuːʃənə/ **executioners. 2** If you **execute** a plan, you carry it out. *We are going to execute our campaign plan to the letter.* ♦ **execution** *US forces are fully prepared for the execution of any action.* **3** If you **execute** a difficult action or movement, you successfully perform it. *The landing was skilfully executed.* **4** When someone **executes** a work of art, they make or produce it, using an idea as a basis. *A well-executed shot of a tall ship is a joy to behold.* ♦ **execution** *The earliest statues tend to be the most raw and immediate in execution and feeling.* ♦♦♦◇ VERB V n be V-ed for n/·-ing / N-VAR / N-COUNT / VERB FORMAL / N-UNCOUNT / VERB / V-ed / N-UNCOUNT

ex·ecu·tive /ɪgˈzekjʊtɪv/ **executives. 1** An **executive** is someone who is employed by a business at a senior level. Executives decide what the business should do, and ensure that it is done. *...an advertising executive.* **2** The **executive** sections and tasks of an organization are concerned with the making of decisions and with ensuring that decisions are carried out. *I don't envisage I will take an executive role.* **3** **Executive** goods are expensive goods designed or intended for people who are executives or who are at a similar social or economic level. *...an executive briefcase.* **4** The **executive** of an organization such as a political party is a committee which has the authority to make decisions and ensures that these decisions are carried out. *...the executive of the National Union of Students... Some executive members have called for his resignation.* **5** The **executive** is the part of the government of a country that is concerned with carrying out decisions or orders, as opposed to the part that makes laws or the part that deals with criminals. *The government, the executive and the judiciary are supposed to be separate. ...the executive branch of government.* ♦♦♦♦◇ N-COUNT / ADJ: ADJ n / ADJ: ADJ n BRITISH / N-SING: the N, N n / N-SING: the N, N n

ex·ecu·tor /ɪgˈzekjʊtə/ **executors.** An **executor** is someone whose name you write in your will when you want them to be responsible for dealing with your affairs after your death. ♦◇◇◇◇ N-COUNT LEGAL

ex·ege·sis /ˌeksɪˈdʒiːsɪs/ **exegeses** /ˌeksɪˈdʒiːsiːz/. An **exegesis** is an explanation and interpretation of a piece of writing, especially a religious piece of writing, after careful study. *...a substantial exegesis of his work.* N-VAR FORMAL

ex·em·plar /ɪgˈzemplə/ **exemplars. 1** An **exemplar** is someone or something that is considered to be so good that they should be imitated. *They* N-COUNT FORMAL

viewed their new building as an exemplar of taste. **2** An **exemplar** is a typical example of a group of things. *One of the wittiest exemplars of the technique was M. C. Escher.* N-COUNT FORMAL

ex·em·pla·ry /ɪgˈzempləri/. **1** If you describe someone or something as **exemplary**, you mean that you consider them to be extremely good. *...an exemplary record of innovation.* **2** An **exemplary** punishment is an unusually harsh one which is intended to discourage other people from committing similar crimes. ADJ-GRADED ◆◇◇◇◇ ADJ

ex·em·pli·fy /ɪgˈzemplɪfaɪ/ **exemplifies, exemplifying, exemplified.** If something or someone **exemplifies** something such as a situation, quality, or class of things, they are a typical example of it. *...the emotional expressiveness of modern dance as exemplified by the work of Martha Graham.* ◆◇◇◇◇ VERB: V n V-ed FORMAL

ex·empt /ɪgˈzempt/ **exempts, exempting, exempted.** **1** If someone or something is **exempt** from a particular rule or duty, they are not affected or bound by it. *Men in college were exempt from military service... Children under two years are exempt.* ► Also a combining form. *The fund was in danger of losing its tax-exempt status.* **2** To **exempt** a person or thing from a particular rule or duty, means to state officially that they are not bound or affected by it. *Companies with fifty-five or fewer employees would be exempted from the requirements.* ◆◆◇◇◇ ADJ COMB VERB V n from n Also V n

♦ **ex·emp·tion** /ɪgˈzempʃən/ **exemptions** *...new exemptions for students and the low-paid.* N-VAR

ex·er·cise /ˈeksəsaɪz/ **exercises, exercising, exercised.** **1** If you **exercise** something such as your authority, your rights, or a good quality, you use it or put it into effect. *They are merely exercising their right to free speech... Britain has warned travellers to exercise prudence.* ► Also a noun. *...the exercise of political and economic power.* **2** When you **exercise**, you move your body energetically in order to get fit and to remain healthy. *She exercises two or three times a week... Exercising the body does a great deal to improve one's health.* ► Also a noun. *Lack of exercise can lead to feelings of depression.* **3** If a movement or activity **exercises** a part of your body, it causes it to work and keeps it strong. *Rowing exercises every major muscle group.* **4 Exercises** are a series of movements or actions which you do in order to get fit or remain healthy. *...stomach exercises... Do some deep-breathing exercises.* **5** Military **exercises** are operations which are not part of a real war, but which are done as practice. *The military truck was taking 14 men on exercise.* **6** An **exercise** is a short activity or piece of work that you do, for example in school, which is designed to help you learn a particular skill. *Try working through the opening exercises in this chapter.* **7** If you describe an activity as an **exercise** in a particular quality or result, you mean that it has that quality or result, especially when it was not intended to have it. *As an exercise in stating the obvious, this could scarcely be faulted.* **8** If something **exercises** you or your mind, you think or talk about it a great deal, especially because you are worried or concerned about it. *...an issue that has long exercised the finest legal minds.* ◆◆◆◆◇ VERB V n FORMAL N-SING VERB V n VERB V n N-COUNT N-COUNT: also on N N-COUNT N-COUNT VERB V n

exercise book, exercise books. An **exercise book** is a small book with blank pages that pupils and students use for writing in. N-COUNT

ex·ert /ɪgˈzɜːt/ **exerts, exerting, exerted.** **1** If someone or something **exerts** influence, authority, or pressure, they use it or cause it in a way that produces a strong effect. *He exerted considerable influence on the thinking of the scientific community... The cyst was causing swelling and exerting pressure on her brain.* **2** If you **exert** yourself, you make a great physical or mental effort, or work hard to do something. *Do not exert yourself unnecessarily.* ◆◆◇◇◇ VERB V n FORMAL VERB V pron-refl

♦ **ex·er·tion, exertions** *He clearly found the physical exertion exhilarating.* N-UNCOUNT: also N in pl

ex gra·tia /ˌeks ˈgreɪʃə/. An **ex gratia** payment is one that is given as a favour or gift and not because it is legally necessary. ADJ BRITISH, FORMAL

ex·hale /eksˈheɪl/ **exhales, exhaling, exhaled.** When you **exhale**, you breathe out the air that is in your lungs. *Wade exhaled a cloud of smoke and coughed.* ♦ **ex·ha·la·tion** /ˌekshəˈleɪʃən/ **exhalations** *Milton let out his breath in a long exhalation.* ◆◇◇◇◇ VERB: V V n FORMAL N-VAR

ex·haust /ɪgˈzɔːst/ **exhausts, exhausting, exhausted.** **1** If something **exhausts** you, it makes you so tired, either physically or mentally, that you have no energy left. *He took to walking long distances in an attempt to physically exhaust himself.* ♦ **ex·haust·ed** *She was too exhausted and distressed to talk.* ♦ **ex·haust·ing** *It was an exhausting schedule.* ♦ **ex·haus·tion** /ɪgˈzɔːstʃən/ *He is suffering from exhaustion.* **2** If you **exhaust** something such as money or food, you use or finish it all. *Food supplies were almost exhausted.* **3** If you **have exhausted** a subject or topic, you have talked about it so much that there is nothing more to say about it. **4** The **exhaust** or the **exhaust pipe** is the pipe which carries the gas or steam out of the engine of a car, lorry, or motorbike. The more usual American word is **tailpipe**. See picture headed **car and bicycle**. **5** Exhaust is the gas or steam that is produced when the engine of a vehicle is running. *...exhaust fumes.* ◆◆◆◇◇ VERB V n ADJ-GRADED ADJ-GRADED N-UNCOUNT VERB: V n V-ed VERB: V n N-COUNT N-UNCOUNT: also N in pl

ex·haus·tive /ɪgˈzɔːstɪv/. If you describe a study, search, or list as **exhaustive**, you mean that it is very thorough and complete. *This is by no means an exhaustive list... The author's treatment of the subject is exhaustive.* ♦ **ex·haus·tive·ly** *...an exhaustively researched, sensitively written account.* ◆◇◇◇◇ ADJ-GRADED ADV-GRADED

ex·hib·it /ɪgˈzɪbɪt/ **exhibits, exhibiting, exhibited.** **1** If someone or something shows a particular quality, feeling, or type of behaviour, you can say that they **exhibit** it. *He has exhibited symptoms of anxiety... Two cats or more in one house will also exhibit territorial behaviour.* **2** When a painting, sculpture, or object of interest is **exhibited**, it is put in a public place such as a museum or art gallery, so that people can come to look at it. *...a massive elephant exhibited by London Zoo.* ♦ **ex·hi·bi·tion** *Five large pieces of the wall are currently on exhibition in London.* **3** When artists **exhibit**, they show their work in public. *By 1936 she was exhibiting at the Royal Academy.* **4** An **exhibit** is a painting, sculpture, or object of interest that is displayed in a museum or art gallery. *Shona showed me round the exhibits.* **5** An **exhibit** is a public display of paintings, sculpture, or objects of interest, for example in a museum or art gallery. The British word is **exhibition**. *...two tickets to an exhibit at the Metropolitan Museum of Art.* **6** An **exhibit** is an object that a lawyer shows in court as evidence in a legal case. ◆◆◇◇◇ VERB V n FORMAL VB: usu passive N-UNCOUNT VERB V N-COUNT N-COUNT AMERICAN N-COUNT

ex·hi·bi·tion /ˌeksɪˈbɪʃən/ **exhibitions.** **1** An **exhibition** is a public event at which pictures, sculptures, or other objects of interest are displayed, for example at a museum or art gallery. *...an exhibition of expressionist art.* **2** An **exhibition** of a particular skilful activity is a display or example of it that people notice or admire. *...treating the fans to an exhibition of power and speed.* **3** See also **exhibit**. ◆◆◆◇◇ N-COUNT N-SING N of n

ex·hi·bi·tion·ism /ˌeksɪˈbɪʃənɪzəm/. If you describe someone's behaviour as **exhibitionism**, you disapprove of it because they are trying to make people notice their talents in a very obvious way. ♦ **ex·hi·bi·tion·ist, exhibitionists** *Every woman in those pictures is an exhibitionist.* N-UNCOUNT PRAGMATICS N-COUNT

ex·hibi·tor /ɪgˈzɪbɪtə/ **exhibitors.** An **exhibitor** is a person whose work is being shown in an exhibition. *Schedules will be send out to all exhibitors.* ◆◇◇◇◇ N-COUNT

ex·hila·rat·ed /ɪgˈzɪləreɪtɪd/. If you are **exhilarated** by something, it makes you feel very happy and excited. *He felt strangely exhilarated by the brisk, blue morning.* ♦ **ex·hila·rat·ing** *It was exhilarating to be on the road again.* ♦ **ex·hila·ra·tion** /ɪgˌzɪləˈreɪʃən/ *I tried to imagine the exhilaration of flying.* ◆◇◇◇◇ ADJ-GRADED FORMAL ADJ-GRADED N-UNCOUNT

ex·hort /ɪgˈzɔːt/ **exhorts, exhorting, exhorted.** If you **exhort** someone to do something, you try hard to persuade or encourage them to do it. *Kennedy exhorted his listeners to turn away from vio-* ◆◇◇◇◇ VERB V n to-inf Also V n with quote FORMAL

lence. ♦ **ex·hor·ta·tion** /ˌegzɔː'teɪʃən/ **exhorta-** N-VAR
tions *Foreign funds alone are clearly not enough,*
nor are exhortations to reform.

ex·hume /eks'hjuːm, AM ɪg'zuːm/ **exhumes,** VERB:
exhuming, exhumed. If a dead person's body is be V-ed
exhumed, it is taken out of the ground where it is FORMAL
buried. ♦ **ex·hu·ma·tion** /ˌegzjuː'meɪʃən/ **exhu-** N-VAR
mations *Detectives ordered the exhumation.*

exi·gen·cy /'eksɪdʒənsi/ **exigencies.** The **exigen-** N-COUNT
cies of a situation or a job are the demands or diffi- FORMAL
culties that you have to deal with as part of it. ...*the*
exigencies of a wartime economy.

ex·ile /'eksaɪl, 'egz-/ **exiles, exiling, exiled. 1** If ♦♦♦◇◇
someone is living in **exile**, they are living in a for- N-UNCOUNT
eign country because they cannot live in their own
country, usually for political reasons. *He returned*
from exile earlier this year. ...six years of exile...
During his exile, he also began writing books. **2** If VERB
someone **is exiled**, they are living in a foreign coun- be V-ed from n
try because they cannot live in their own country, V n
usually for political reasons. *He was exiled from the*
Soviet Union 18 years ago... They threatened to exile
her. **3** An **exile** is someone who has been exiled. N-COUNT

ex·ist /ɪg'zɪst/ **exists, existing, existed. 1** If ♦♦♦♦◇
something **exists**, it is present in the world as a real VB: no cont
thing. *He thought that if he couldn't see something,* V
it didn't exist... Alfred Adler first postulated in 1908 there V n
that there existed an inborn instinct of aggression.
♦ **ex·ist·ence** ...*the existence of other galaxies.* N-UNCOUNT
...*an immediate threat to his nation's very existence.*
2 To **exist** means to live, especially under difficult VERB: V
conditions or with very little food or money. ...*hav-* V on n
ing to exist on unemployment benefit. ♦ **ex·ist-** N-COUNT:
·ence, existences ...*a miserable existence.* with supp

ex·ist·ent /ɪg'zɪstənt/. You can describe something ADJ
as **existent** when it exists. ...*the range of existent* FORMAL
technology. ● See also **non-existent.**

ex·is·ten·tial /ˌegzɪ'stenʃəl/. **Existential** ADJ: ADJ n
questions or fears relate to human existence and experience. FORMAL

ex·is·ten·tial·ism /ˌegzɪ'stenʃəlɪzəm/. **Existential-** N-UNCOUNT
ism is a philosophical belief which stresses the TECHNICAL
importance of human experience, and says that everyone is responsible for the results of their own actions.
♦ **ex·is·ten·tial·ist, existentialists** ...*the existen-* N-COUNT
tialist philosophy of Jean-Paul Sartre.

ex·ist·ing /ɪg'zɪstɪŋ/. **Existing** is used to describe ♦♦♦◇◇
something which is now present or available, espe- ADJ: ADJ n
cially in contrast to something which is planned for
the future. ...*the need to improve existing products*
and develop new lines. ...*both new and existing*
borrowers.

exit /'egzɪt, 'eksɪt/ **exits, exiting, exited. 1** The ♦♦◇◇◇
exit is the doorway through which you can leave a N-COUNT
public building. ...*a fire exit.* **2** An **exit** on a motor- N-COUNT:
way is a place where traffic can leave it. *Take the* with supp
A422 exit at Old Stratford. **3** If you refer to N-COUNT
someone's **exit**, you are referring to the way that
they left a room or building, or the fact that they left
it. *I made a hasty exit.* **4** If you refer to someone's N-COUNT
exit, you are referring to the way that they left a
situation or activity, or the fact that they left it.
...*England's exit from the European Championship.*
5 If you **exit** from a room or building, you leave it. VERB: V
Allen and his lawyer exited the court. V n
FORMAL

'exit visa, exit visas. An **exit visa** is an official N-COUNT
stamp in someone's passport, or an official docu-
ment, which allows them to leave the country that
they are visiting or living in.

exo·dus /'eksədəs/. If there is an **exodus** of people ♦◇◇◇◇
from a place, a lot of people leave that place at the N-SING
same time. *The medical system is facing collapse be-*
cause of an exodus of doctors.

ex·on·er·ate /ɪg'zɒnəreɪt/ **exonerates, exoner-** VERB: V n
ating, exonerated. If a court, report, or person in V n from n
authority **exonerates** someone, they officially say or FORMAL
show that that person is not responsible for something wrong or unpleasant that has happened. *An*
investigation exonerated the school from any blame.
♦ **ex·on·era·tion** /ɪgˌzɒnə'reɪʃən/ *They expected* N-UNCOUNT
complete exoneration for their clients.

ex·or·bi·tant /ɪg'zɔːbɪtənt/. If you describe a price ADJ-GRADED
or fee as **exorbitant**, you are emphasizing that it is PRAGMATICS
much greater than it should be. ♦ **ex·or·bi·tant·ly** ADV
...*exorbitantly high salaries.*

ex·or·cism /'eksɔːsɪzəm/ **exorcisms. Exorcism** is N-VAR
the removing of evil spirits from a person or place
by the use of prayer. ♦ **ex·or·cist, exorcists.** N-COUNT

ex·or·cize /'eksɔːsaɪz/ **exorcizes, exorcizing,**
exorcized; also spelled **exorcise** in British English.
1 If you **exorcize** a painful or unhappy memory, VERB
you succeed in removing it from your mind. *The* V n
birth of my second daughter has finally exorcised
these feelings of guilt. **2** To **exorcize** an evil spirit or VERB: V n
to **exorcize** a place or person means to force the
spirit to leave by means of prayers and religious
ceremonies.

ex·ot·ic /ɪg'zɒtɪk/. Something that is **exotic** is un- ♦♦◇◇◇
usual and interesting, usually because it comes ADJ-GRADED
from or is related to a distant country. ...*brilliantly*
coloured, exotic flowers. ♦ **ex·oti·cal·ly** ...*exotically* ADV-GRADED
beautiful scenery.

ex·oti·ca /ɪg'zɒtɪkə/. You use **exotica** to refer to N-PLURAL
objects which you think are unusual and interest-
ing, usually because they come from or are related
to a distant country.

ex·oti·cism /ɪg'zɒtɪsɪzəm/. If you talk about the **ex-** N-UNCOUNT
oticism of a place, person, or thing, you mean that
they seem unusual and interesting, usually because
they are connected with a distant country.

ex·pand /ɪk'spænd/ **expands, expanding, ex-** ♦♦♦◇◇
panded. If something **expands**, or someone or V-ERG
something **expands** it, it becomes larger. *The money* V n
supply expanded by 14.6 per cent... We have to ex-
pand the size of the image... I owned a bookshop and
desired to expand the business. ♦ **ex·pan·sion** N-VAR
/ɪk'spænʃən/ **expansions** ...*the rapid expansion of*
private health insurance... The company has aban-
doned plans for further expansion.

expand on or **expand upon.** If you **expand on** or PHRASAL VB
expand upon something, you give more information V P n
or details about it when you write or talk about it. *The*
president used today's speech to expand on remarks he
made last month.

ex·panse /ɪk'spæns/ **expanses.** An **expanse** of ♦◇◇◇◇
something, usually sea, sky, or land, is a very large N-COUNT
amount of it.

ex·pan·sion·ary /ɪk'spænʃənri/. **1 Expansionary** ADJ-GRADED
economic policies are intended to expand the
economy of a country. **2 Expansionary** policies or ADJ-GRADED
actions are intended to increase the amount of land PRAGMATICS
that a particular country rules; used showing disapproval. ...*America's concerns about Soviet expansion-*
ary objectives.

ex·pan·sion·ism /ɪk'spænʃənɪzəm/. If you refer to N-UNCOUNT
a country's **expansionism**, you disapprove of its PRAGMATICS
policy of increasing its land or power. ♦ **ex·pan-**
·sion·ist ...*his expansionist foreign policy.* ADJ-GRADED

ex·pan·sive /ɪk'spænsɪv/. **1** If something is **expan-** ♦◇◇◇◇
sive, it covers or includes a large area or many ADJ: ADJ n
things. ...*an expansive grassy play area.* **2** If you are FORMAL
expansive, you talk a lot, or are friendly or gener- ADJ-GRADED
ous, because you are feeling happy and relaxed. *The*
premier was in expansive mood. ♦ **ex·pan·sive·ly** ADV-GRADED
'I'm here to make them feel good,' he says expansive-
ly, 'to show them how attractive they are.'

ex·pat /'ekspæt/ **expats.** An **expat** is an **expatriate.** N-COUNT
...*exclusive country clubs for British expats.* BRITISH,
INFORMAL

ex·pat·ri·ate /ek'spætriət, -'peɪt-/ **expatriates.** N-COUNT
An **expatriate** is someone who is living in a country
which is not their own. ...*children of expatriate*
families.

ex·pect /ɪk'spekt/ **expects, expecting, ex-** ♦♦♦♦♦
pected. 1 If you **expect** something to happen, you VERB
believe that it will happen. *He expects to lose his job* V to-inf
in the next few weeks... They no longer expect corpo- V n to-inf
rate profits to improve... Few expected that he would V that
declare his candidacy... It is expected that the new it be V-ed that
owner will change the yacht's name... They expect a V n
gradual improvement in sales. **2** If you **are expect-** VERB
ing something or someone, you believe that they V n
V n adv

will be delivered to you or come to you soon. *I am expecting several important letters... We were expecting him home again any day now.* **3** If you **expect** something, or **expect** someone to do something, you believe that it is your right to have that thing, or that person's duty to do it for you. *He wasn't expecting our hospitality... I do expect to have some time to myself... I wasn't expecting you to help... Is this a rational thing to expect of your partner?... She realizes now she expected too much of Helen.* **4** If you tell someone not to **expect** something, you mean that that thing is unlikely to happen as they have planned or imagined. *Don't expect an instant cure... You can't expect to like all the people you will work with... Don't expect me to come and visit you there.* **5** If a woman **is expecting** a baby, she is pregnant. *I hear Dawn's expecting again.*
6 You say **'I expect'** to suggest that a statement is probably correct, or a natural consequence of the present situation, although you have no definite knowledge. *I expect you can guess what follows... I expect you're tired... 'Will Joe be here at Christmas?'—'I expect so.'* **7** You can say **'What can you expect?'** or **'What do you expect?'** to emphasize that there is nothing surprising about a situation or a person's behaviour, especially when you disapprove of it. *It tastes artificial, but at that price what can you expect?*

VERB
V n
V to-inf
V n to-inf
V n ofn
V amount ofn

VB: with brd-neg
PRAGMATICS
V n
V to-inf
V n to-inf
SPOKEN

VB: only cont,
V

PHRASE
PRAGMATICS
SPOKEN

PHRASE
PRAGMATICS

ex·pec·tan·cy /ɪk'spektənsi/. **Expectancy** is the feeling that something exciting, interesting, or good is about to happen. *The supporters had a tremendous air of expectancy.* ● See also **life expectancy**.

◆◇◇◇◇
N-UNCOUNT

ex·pec·tant /ɪk'spektənt/. **1** If someone is **expectant**, they are excited because they think something interesting is about to happen. *An expectant crowd gathered.* ♦ **ex·pect·ant·ly** *The others waited, looking at him expectantly.* **2** An **expectant** mother's or father's baby is going to be born soon.

◆◇◇◇◇
ADJ-GRADED

ADV

ADJ: ADJ n

ex·pec·ta·tion /ˌekspek'teɪʃən/ **expectations.**
1 Your **expectations** are your beliefs that a particular thing will happen. *Contrary to general expectation, he announced that all four had given their approval.* **2** A person's **expectations** are beliefs which they have about the way someone should behave or something should happen. *Chase had determined to live up to the expectations of the Company.*

◆◆◇◇◇
N-UNCOUNT:
also N in pl

N-COUNT

ex·pe·di·ent /ɪk'spiːdiənt/ **expedients.** **1** An **expedient** is an action that achieves a particular purpose, but may not be morally right. *Surgical waiting lists were reduced by the simple expedient of striking off all patients awaiting varicose vein operations.* **2** If it is **expedient** to do something, it is useful or convenient to do it, even though it may not be morally right. *Governments frequently ignore human rights abuses in other countries if it is politically expedient to do so.* ♦ **ex·pe·di·en·cy** *Their enthusiasm was partly motivated by political expediency.*

◆◇◇◇◇
N-COUNT
FORMAL

ADJ-GRADED
FORMAL

N-UNCOUNT

ex·pe·dite /'ekspɪdaɪt/ **expedites, expediting, expedited.** If you **expedite** something, you cause it to be done more quickly. *We tried to help you expedite your plans.*

VERB
V n
FORMAL

ex·pe·di·tion /ˌekspɪ'dɪʃən/ **expeditions. 1** An **expedition** is an organized journey that is made for a particular purpose such as exploration. *...Byrd's 1928 expedition to Antarctica... Forty-three members of the expedition were killed.* **2** An **expedition** is a short journey or outing that you make for pleasure. *Caroline joined them on the shopping expeditions.*

◆◆◇◇◇
N-COUNT

N-COUNT

ex·pe·di·tion·ary force /ˌekspɪ'dɪʃənri fɔːs, AM -neri/ **expeditionary forces.** An **expeditionary force** is a group of soldiers who are sent to fight in a foreign country.

N-COUNT

ex·pe·di·tious /ˌekspɪ'dɪʃəs/. **Expeditious** means quick and efficient. ♦ **ex·pe·di·tious·ly** *The whole job will be done as expeditiously as possible.*

ADJ-GRADED
FORMAL
ADV-GRADED:
ADV with v

ex·pel /ɪk'spel/ **expels, expelling, expelled.**
1 If someone **is expelled** from a school or organization, they are officially told to leave because they have behaved badly. *...a 14-year-old boy expelled from school for refusing to take a shower.* ♦ **ex·pul·sion** /ɪk'spʌlʃən/ **expulsions** *...the high number*

◆◆◇◇◇
VERB:
beV-ed
V-ed

N-VAR

of school expulsions... This led to his suspension and, finally, expulsion from the party. **2** If people **are expelled** from a place, they are made to leave it, often by force. *They were told at first that they should simply expel the refugees.* ♦ **expulsion** *...the expulsion of Yemeni workers.* **3** To **expel** something such as a gas means to force it out. *He groaned, expelling the air from his lungs.* ♦ **expulsion** *...the expulsion of waste products.*

VERB:
beV-ed
V n

N-VAR

VERB
V n

N-UNCOUNT

ex·pend /ɪk'spend/ **expends, expending, expended.** To **expend** energy, time, or money means to use it or spend it.

◆◇◇◇◇
VERB: V n
FORMAL

ex·pend·able /ɪk'spendəbəl/. If you regard someone or something as **expendable**, you think it is acceptable to get rid of them or abandon them when they are no longer needed. *During the recession, training budgets were seen as an expendable luxury.*

ADJ-GRADED
FORMAL

ex·pen·di·ture /ɪk'spendɪtʃə/ **expenditures.**
1 Expenditure is the spending of money on something, or the money that is spent on something. *...reduced public expenditure... They should cut their expenditure on defence.* **2 Expenditure** of time, effort, or energy is using it for a particular purpose.

◆◆◇◇◇
N-VAR
FORMAL

N-UNCOUNT:
N ofn
FORMAL

ex·pense /ɪk'spens/ **expenses. 1 Expense** is the money that something costs you or that you need to spend in order to do something. *He's bought a specially big TV at vast expense... The tunnel is an unnecessary expense. ...household expenses.* **2** Your **expenses** are amounts of money that you spend while doing something in the course of your work, which will be paid back to you afterwards. *Can you claim this back on expenses?* **3** If you do something **at** someone's **expense**, they provide the money for it. *Teachers who signed up did so out of personal choice and at their own expense.* **4** If you **go to the expense** of doing something, you do something which costs a lot of money. If you **go to great expense** to do something, you spend a lot of money in order to achieve it.

◆◆◇◇
N-VAR

N-PLURAL

PHRASE

PHRASE
PRAGMATICS

5 If someone laughs or makes a joke **at** your **expense**, they do it to make you seem foolish. *I think he's having fun at our expense.* **6** If you achieve something **at the expense of** someone or something, you do it in a way which might cause them to be harmed or damaged. *Costs may be trimmed at the expense of the patient... They are worth having but not at the expense of better services.* **7** ♦ to **spare no expense**: see **spare**.

PHRASE

PHRASE

ex'pense account, expense accounts. An **expense account** is an arrangement between an employer and an employee which allows the employee to spend the company's money on things relating to their job.

N-COUNT

ex·pen·sive /ɪk'spensɪv/. If something is **expensive**, it costs a lot of money. *Wine's so expensive in this country. ...a lot of expensive equipment.* ♦ **ex·pen·sive·ly** *She was expensively dressed.*

◆◆◆◇
ADJ-GRADED

ADV-GRADED

ex·pe·ri·ence /ɪk'spɪəriəns/ **experiences, experiencing, experienced. 1 Experience** is knowledge or skill in a particular job or activity, which you have gained because you have done that job or activity for a long time. *He has also had managerial experience on every level... I've had experience with children.* ♦ **ex·pe·ri·enced** *...lawyers who are experienced in these matters. ...experienced and mature professionals.* **2 Experience** is used to refer to the past events, knowledge, and feelings that make up someone's life or character. *Experience has taught me caution... 'If you act afraid, they won't let go,' he says, speaking from experience.* **3** An **experience** is something that happens to you or something that you do, especially something important that affects you. *Moving had become a common experience for me. ...his only experience of gardening.* **4** If you **experience** a particular situation or feeling, you are affected by it or it happens to you. *British business is now experiencing a severe recession... Widows seem to experience more distress than do widowers.*

◆◆◆◆◆
N-UNCOUNT

ADJ-GRADED

N-UNCOUNT

N-COUNT

VERB
V n

ex·pe·ri·en·tial /ɪkˌspɪəri'enʃəl/. **Experiential** means relating to or resulting from experience.

ADJ
FORMAL

ex·per·i·ment, /ɪkˈsperɪmənt/ **experiments, ex-** ◆◆◆◇◇
perimenting, experimented. 1 An **experiment** N-VAR
is a scientific test which is done in order to discover
what happens to something in particular conditions. *The astronauts are conducting a series of experiments... This question can be answered only by
experiment.* **2** If you **experiment with** something or VERB
experiment on it, you do a scientific test on it in or- V with/on n
der to discover what happens to it in particular con- Also V
ditions. *In 1857 Mendel started experimenting with
peas.* ♦ **ex·per·i·men·ta·tion** /ɪkˌsperɪmenˈteɪʃən/ N-UNCOUNT
...the ethical aspects of animal experimentation.
♦ **ex·per·i·ment·er, experimenters. 3** An **ex-** N-COUNT
periment is the trying out of a new idea or method N-VAR
in order to see what it is like and what effects it has.
*As an experiment, we bought Ted a watch. ...the
country's five year experiment in democracy.* **4** To VERB: V
experiment means to try out a new idea or method V with n
to see what it is like and what effects it has. *Students
should be encouraged to experiment with bold ideas.*
♦ **experimentation** *...stories about his sexual* N-UNCOUNT
experimentation.

ex·per·i·men·tal /ɪkˌsperɪˈmentəl/. **1** Something ◆◆◇◇◇
that is **experimental** is new or uses new ideas or ADJ-GRADED
methods, and may not be successful. *...an experimental air conditioning system. ...highly experimental pieces of music.* **2 Experimental** means used in ADJ: ADJ n
or resulting from scientific experiments. *...the main
techniques of experimental science. ...the use of experimental animals... We have experimental and
observational evidence.* ♦ **ex·per·i·men·tal·ly** None ADV:
of the calculations have been tested experimentally. ADV with v
3 An **experimental** action is done in order to see ADJ
what it is like, or what effects it has. *...an experimental lifting of the ban.* ♦ **experimentally** *He* ADV:
touched one of the combs experimentally. ADV with v

ex·pert /ˈekspɜːt/ **experts. 1** An **expert** is a per- ◆◆◆◆◇
son who is very skilled at doing something or who N-COUNT
knows a lot about a particular subject. *Our team of
experts will be on hand to offer help and advice. ...an
expert on trade in that area.* **2** Someone who is **ex-** ADJ-GRADED
pert at doing something is very skilled at it. *...Hal's
expert approach.* ♦ **ex·pert·ly** *Shopkeepers expertly* ADV-GRADED:
rolled spices up in bay leaves. **3** If you say that ADV with v
someone has **expert** hands or an **expert** eye, you ADJ-GRADED:
mean that they are very skilful or experienced in ADJ n
using their hands or eyes for a particular purpose.
*The symptoms are very mild and it takes an expert
eye to see them.* **4 Expert** advice or help is given by ADJ: ADJ n
someone who has studied a subject thoroughly or
who is very skilled at a particular job. *We'll need an
expert opinion.*

ex·per·tise /ˌekspɜːˈtiːz/. **Expertise** is special skill ◆◆◇◇◇
or knowledge that is acquired by training, study, or N-UNCOUNT
practice. *Most local authorities lack the expertise to
deal sensibly in this market.*

ex·pi·ate /ˈekspieɪt/ **expiates, expiating,** VERB
expiated. If you **expiate** guilty feelings or bad be- V n
haviour, you do something to indicate that you are Also V for n
sorry for what you have done. *It seemed that Alice* FORMAL
was expiating her father's sins with her charity work.
♦ **ex·pia·tion** /ˌekspiˈeɪʃən/ *...an often painful pro-* N-UNCOUNT
cess of evaluation and expiation.

ex·pi·ra·tion /ˌekspɪˈreɪʃən/. The **expiration** of a N-UNCOUNT
fixed period of time is its ending. *...a few hours be-* FORMAL
fore the expiration of the midnight deadline.

ex·pire /ɪkˈspaɪə/ **expires, expiring, expired.** ◆◆◇◇◇
1 When something such as a contract, deadline, or VERB
visa **expires**, it comes to an end or is no longer val- V
id. *He had lived illegally in the United States for five
years after his visitor's visa expired.* **2** When some- VERB
one **expires**, they die. *He endured excruciating ago-* V
nies before he finally expired. LITERARY

ex·pi·ry /ɪkˈspaɪəri/. The **expiry** of something such N-UNCOUNT
as a contract, deadline, or visa is the time that it
comes to an end or stops being valid. *Make a note
of credit card numbers and check expiry dates.*

ex·plain /ɪkˈspleɪn/ **explains, explaining,** ◆◆◆◆◇
explained. 1 If you **explain** something, you give VERB: V n
details about it or describe it so that it can be V n to n
V wh

understood. *Don't sign anything until your solicitor* V with quote
has explained the contract to you... Professor Also V that,
Griffiths explained how the drug appears to work... V
'He and Mrs Stein have a plan,' she explained. **2** If VERB: V n
you **explain** something that has happened, you give V pron-refl
people reasons for it, especially in an attempt to V why
justify it. *Let me explain, sir... Amy would have to ex-* V that
plain herself... Explain why you didn't telephone... Also V n to n,
The receptionist apologized for the delay, explaining V with quote
that it had been a hectic day.

explain away. If someone **explains away** a mistake PHRASAL VB
or a bad situation they are responsible for, they try to V P noun
indicate that it is unimportant or that it is not really [PRAGMATICS]
their fault. *I had noticed blood on my husband's cloth-* V n P
ing but he explained it away.

ex·pla·na·tion /ˌekspləˈneɪʃən/ **explanations.** ◆◆◆◇◇
1 If you give an **explanation** of something that has N-COUNT:
happened, you give people reasons for it, especially also of/in N
in an attempt to justify it. *There was a hint of
schoolboy shyness in his explanation... 'It's my ulcer,'
he added by way of explanation.* **2** If you say there is N-COUNT
an **explanation** for something, you mean that there
is a reason for it. *There was no apparent explanation
for the crash... It's the only explanation I can think
of.* **3** If you give an **explanation** of something, you N-COUNT
give details about it or describe it so that it can be
understood. *Haig was immediately impressed by
Charteris's expertise and by his lucid explanation of
the work.*

ex·plana·tory /ɪkˈsplænətri, AM -tɔːri/. **Explana-** ◆◇◇◇◇
tory statements or theories are intended to make ADJ-GRADED
people understand something by describing it or FORMAL
giving the reasons for it. *These statements are accompanied by a series of explanatory notes.*

ex·ple·tive /ɪkˈspliːtɪv/ **expletives.** An **expletive** is N-COUNT
a rude word or expression which you say when you FORMAL
are annoyed, excited, or in pain.

ex·pli·ca·ble /ɪkˈsplɪkəbəl, AM ˈeksplɪk-/. If some- ADJ-GRADED
thing is **explicable**, it can be explained and under- FORMAL
stood because it is logical or sensible. *The older I
grow, the stranger and less explicable the world appears to me.*

ex·pli·cate /ˈeksplɪkeɪt/ **explicates, explicat-** VERB
ing, explicated. To **explicate** something means V n
to explain it and make it clear. *We shall have to ex-* FORMAL
*plicate its basic assumptions before we can assess its
implications.*

ex·plic·it /ɪkˈsplɪsɪt/. **1** Something that is **explicit** ◆◆◇◇◇
is expressed or shown clearly and openly, without ADJ-GRADED
any attempt to hide anything. *...sexually explicit
scenes in films. ...explicit references to age in recruitment advertising.* ♦ **ex·plic·it·ly** *...explicitly politi-* ADV-GRADED
cal activities. **2** If you are **explicit** about something, ADJ-GRADED:
you speak about it very openly and clearly. *He was* v-link ADJ
*explicit about his intention to overhaul the party's
internal voting system.* ♦ **explicitly** *She has been* ADV-GRADED:
talking very explicitly about AIDS. ADV with v

ex·plode /ɪkˈspləʊd/ **explodes, exploding, ex-** ◆◆◆◇◇
ploded. 1 If an object such as a bomb **explodes** or V-ERG: V
if someone or something **explodes** it, it bursts loud- V n
ly and with great force, often causing damage or injury. *...gunfire which exploded the fuel tank.* **2** If VERB: V
something **explodes**, it increases suddenly and rap- V to n
idly in number or intensity. *The population explodes
to 40,000 during the tourist season.* **3** If someone **ex-** VERB: V n
plodes a theory or myth, they prove that it is wrong be V-ed
or impossible. *Such rumours have only recently been
exploded.* **4** If someone **explodes**, they express VERB: V
strong feelings suddenly and violently. *Do you fear* V with n
that you'll burst into tears or explode with anger in V with quote
front of her?... 'What happened!' I exploded. **5** If VERB
something **explodes**, it makes a sudden very loud V
noise. *She heard laughter explode, then die.* LITERARY

ex·ploit, exploits, exploiting, exploited. The ◆◆◆◇◇
verb is pronounced /ɪkˈsplɔɪt/. The noun is pronounced /ˈeksplɔɪt/. **1** If you say that someone **is** VERB
exploiting you, you think that they are treating you V n
unfairly by using your work or ideas and giving you
very little in return. *Critics claim he exploited black
musicians.* ♦ **ex·ploi·ta·tion** /ˌeksplɔɪˈteɪʃən/ *...to* N-UNCOUNT

protect the interests of the staff and prevent exploitation. **2** If you say that someone **is exploiting** a
situation, you disapprove of them because they are
using it to gain an advantage for themselves, rather
than trying to help other people or do what is right.
*The government and its opponents compete to ex-
ploit the troubles to their advantage.*
♦ **exploitation** *...the exploitation of the famine by*
local politicians. ♦ **ex·ploit·er** /ɪkˈsplɔɪtə/
exploiters. *They were accused of being exploiters.*
3 If you **exploit** something, you use it well, and
achieve something or gain an advantage from it.
Cary is hoping to exploit new opportunities in
Europe... So you feel that your skills have never been
fully appreciated or exploited? **4** To **exploit** resources or raw materials means to develop them
and use them for industry or commercial activities.
*I think we're being very short sighted in not exploit-
ing our own coal.* ♦ **exploitation** *...the planned exploitation of its potential oil and natural gas reserves.* **5** If you refer to someone's **exploits,** you
mean the brave, interesting, or amusing things that
they have done. *...his wartime exploits.*

ex·ploita·tive /ɪkˈsplɔɪtətɪv/. If you describe something as **exploitative,** you disapprove of it because it
treats people unfairly by using their work or ideas
for its own advantage, and giving them very little in
return. *The expansion of Western capitalism incorporated the Third World into an exploitative world
system.*

ex·plora·tory /ɪkˈsplɒrətri, AM -ˈplɔːrətɔːri/. Exploratory actions are done in order to discover
something or to learn the truth about something.
Exploratory surgery revealed her liver cancer.

ex·plore /ɪkˈsplɔː/ **explores, exploring, explored. 1** If you **explore** a place, you travel around
it to find out what it is like. *After exploring the old*
part of town there is a guided tour of the cathedral...
We've come to this country, let's explore! ♦ **ex·plo-
·ra·tion** /ˌeksplɔˈreɪʃən/ **explorations** We devote
several days to the exploration of the magnificent
Maya sites of Copan. ♦ **ex·plor·er, explorers.** An
explorer is someone who travels to different places
about which very little is known, in order to discover what is there. **2** If you **explore** an idea or suggestion, you think about it or comment on it in detail,
in order to assess it carefully. *The secretary is expected to explore ideas for post-war reconstruction of the
area.* ♦ **exploration** *I looked forward to the exploration of their theories.* **3** If people **explore** for a
substance such as oil or minerals, they study an
area and do tests on the land to see whether they
can find it. *...the areas of inshore coastal waters to be
explored for oil and gas.* ♦ **exploration** *Oryx is a
Dallas-based oil and gas exploration and production
concern.* **4** If you **explore** something with your
hands or fingers, you touch it to find out what it
feels like. *He explored the wound with his finger.*

ex·plo·sion /ɪkˈspləʊʒən/ **explosions. 1** An **explosion** is a sudden violent burst of energy, for example one caused by a bomb. *...a bomb explosion.*
2 Explosion is the act of deliberately causing a
bomb or similar device to explode. *Bomb disposal
experts blew up the bag in a controlled explosion.*
3 An **explosion** is a large rapid increase in the number or amount of something. *...an explosion in the
diet soft-drink market. ...a population explosion.*
4 An **explosion** is a sudden violent expression of
someone's feelings, especially anger. *...an explosion
of anger against the practices of the occupying forces.*
5 An **explosion** is a sudden serious outbreak of political protest or violence. *A referendum might cause
an explosion in the country.* **6** An **explosion** is a
sudden very loud noise. *There was an explosion of
music.*

ex·plo·sive /ɪkˈspləʊsɪv/ **explosives. 1** An **explosive** is a substance or device that can cause an explosion. *...one-hundred-and-fifty pounds of Semtex
explosive.* **2** Something that is **explosive** is capable
of causing an explosion. *The explosive device was*

timed to go off at the rush hour. ♦ **ex·plo·sive·ly**
*Hydrogen is explosively flammable when mixed with
oxygen.* **3** An **explosive** growth is a sudden rapid increase in the size or quantity of something. *...the explosive growth in casinos.* ♦ **explosively** *These
transactions grew explosively in the early 1980s.* **4** An
explosive situation is likely to have difficult, serious,
or dangerous effects. *He appeared to be treating the
potentially explosive situation with some sensitivity.*
♦ **explosively** *A referendum next year would coincide explosively with the election campaign.* **5** If you
describe someone as **explosive,** you mean that they
tend to express sudden violent anger. *She was unpredictable, explosive, impulsive and easily distracted... He's inherited his father's explosive temper.*
♦ **explosively** *'Are you mad?' David asked explosively.* **6** A sudden loud noise can be described as
explosive. *He made a loud, explosive noise of disgust.* ♦ **explosively** *The sound of her own chewing
and swallowing were explosively loud.*

ex·po·nent /ɪkˈspəʊnənt/ **exponents. 1** An **exponent** of an idea, theory, or plan is a person who explains it, and who argues in favour of it. *...a leading
exponent of test-tube baby techniques.* **2** An **exponent** of a particular skill or activity is a person who
is good at it. *...the great exponent of expressionist
dance, Kurt Jooss.*

ex·po·nen·tial /ˌekspəˈnenʃəl/. **Exponential** means
growing or increasing very rapidly. *...the exponential
growth of public expenditure.* ♦ **ex·po·nen·tial·ly**
*The quantity of chemical pollutants has increased
exponentially.*

ex·port, exports, exporting, exported. The
verb is pronounced /ɪkˈspɔːt/. The noun is pronounced /ˈekspɔːt/. **1** To **export** products or raw
materials means to sell them to another country.
*They expect the antibiotic products to be exported to
Southeast Asia... To earn foreign exchange we must
export.* ► Also a noun. *...the production and export
of cheap casual wear. ...the boom in American exports.* ♦ **ex·port·er** /eksˈpɔːtə, ɪkˈspɔːtə/ **exporters.** *France is the world's second-biggest exporter of
agricultural products.* **2 Exports** are goods which
are sold to another country and sent there. *He did
this to promote American exports... Ghana's main
export is cocoa.* **3** To **export** something means to
introduce it into another country or make it happen
there. *The deal would export jobs to Mexico.*

ex·port·able /ɪkˈspɔːtəbəl/. **Exportable** products
are suitable for being exported. *They are reliant on a
very limited number of exportable products.*

ex·pose /ɪkˈspəʊz/ **exposes, exposing, exposed. 1** To **expose** something that is usually hidden means to uncover it so that it can be seen. *For
an instant his whole back was exposed.* **2** A man
who **exposes** himself shows people his genitals in a
public place. **3** To **expose** a person or situation
means to reveal that they are bad or immoral in
some way. *After the scandal was exposed, Dr Bailey
committed suicide... He has simply been exposed as
an adulterer and a fool.* **4** If someone **is exposed to**
something dangerous or unpleasant, they are put in
a situation in which it might affect them. *A wise
mother never exposes her children to the slightest
possibility of danger.* **5** If someone **is exposed to** an
idea or feeling, usually a new one, they are given experience of it, or introduced to it. *These units exposed children to many viewpoints.*

ex·po·sé /ekˈspəʊzeɪ, AM ˌekspəʊˈzeɪ/ **exposés.** An
exposé is a film or piece of writing which reveals
the truth about a situation or person. *The movie is
an exposé of prison conditions in the South.*

ex·posed /ɪkˈspəʊzd/. If a place is **exposed,** it has
no natural protection against bad weather or enemies, for example because it has no trees or is on
very high ground. *...an exposed hillside.*

ex·po·si·tion /ˌekspəˈzɪʃən/ **expositions. 1** An
exposition of an idea or theory is a detailed explanation or account of it. *The fullest exposition of
Coleridge's thought can be found in the Statesman's*

VERB
PRAGMATICS
V n

N-SING

N of n
N-COUNT

VERB
V n

VERB
V n

N-COUNT

ADJ-GRADED
PRAGMATICS
FORMAL

◆◇◇◇
ADJ

◆◆◆◇◇
VERB
V n
V

N-VAR

N-COUNT

VERB
V n

N-VAR

V for n
be V-ed for n
Also V n for n

N-UNCOUNT

VERB
V n

◆◆◆◇◇
N-COUNT

N-VAR

N-COUNT
with supp

N-COUNT
LITERARY

N-COUNT

N-COUNT
LITERARY

◆◆◇◇◇
N-VAR

ADJ-GRADED

ADV

ADJ-GRADED

ADV-GRADED
ADJ-GRADED

ADV-GRADED
ADV after v
ADJ-GRADED

ADV
ADJ-GRADED

ADV

◆◇◇◇
N-COUNT
FORMAL

N-COUNT
with supp

ADJ
FORMAL

ADV

◆◆◆◇
VERB: V n
be V-ed to n
V
Also V n to n

N-UNCOUNT:
also N in pl

N-COUNT

N-COUNT

VERB: V n
V n to n

ADJ

◆◆◆◇◇
VERB: V n

VERB

VERB: V n
be V-ed as n/
adj
Also V n as n/
adj
VERB:
be V-ed to n
V n to n

VERB:
be V-ed to n
V n to n

N-COUNT

◆◇◇◇
ADJ-GRADED

◆◇◇◇
N-COUNT
FORMAL

Manual. **2** An **exposition** is an exhibition in which something such as goods or works of art are shown to the public. ...an art exposition. N-COUNT

ex·pos·tu·late /ɪk'spɒstʃuleɪt/ **expostulates, expostulating, expostulated.** If you **expostulate**, you express strong `disagreement with someone. 'For heaven's sake!' Dot expostulated... His family expostulated with him. VERB: V / V with quote / V with n / FORMAL

ex·po·sure /ɪk'spəʊʒə/ **exposures. 1** Exposure to something dangerous means being in a situation where it might affect you. Exposure to lead is known to damage the brains of young children. **2** Exposure is the harmful effect on your body caused by very cold weather. At least two people died of exposure. **3** The **exposure** of a well-known person is the revealing of the fact that they are bad or immoral in some way. ...the exposure of Anthony Blunt as a former Soviet spy. **4** Exposure is publicity that a person, company, or product receives. All the candidates have been getting an enormous amount of exposure on television. **5** In photography, an **exposure** is a single photograph. **6** In photography, the **exposure** is the amount of light that is allowed to enter a camera when taking a photograph. Against a deep blue sky or dark storm-clouds, you may need to reduce the exposure. ♦♦♦◇◇ N-UNCOUNT / N-UNCOUNT / N-UNCOUNT / N-UNCOUNT / N-COUNT / N-VAR

ex·pound /ɪk'spaʊnd/ **expounds, expounding, expounded.** If you **expound** an idea or opinion, you give a clear and detailed explanation of it. Schmidt continued to expound his views on economics. ▶ **Expound on** means the same as expound. Lawrence expounded on the military aspects of guerrilla warfare. ♦◇◇◇◇ VERB / V n / FORMAL / PHRASAL VB / V P n

ex·press /ɪk'spres/ **expresses, expressing, expressed. 1** When you **express** an idea or feeling, or express yourself, you show what you think or feel by saying or doing something. He expressed grave concern... He expresses himself easily in English... Children may find it easier to express themselves in a letter than in a formal essay. **2** If an idea or feeling **expresses** itself in some way, it can be clearly seen in someone's actions or in its effects on a situation. The anxiety of the separation often expresses itself as anger. **3** If you **express** a quantity or mathematical problem in a particular way, you write it using particular symbols, figures, or equations. It is expressed as a percentage. **4** An **express** command or order is one that is clearly and deliberately stated. The ship was sunk on express orders from the Prime Minister. ♦ **ex·press·ly** The Duke of Windsor recollected that he had expressly forbidden Goddard to go to see Mrs Simpson. **5** If you refer to an **express** intention or purpose, you are emphasizing that it is a deliberate and specific one. I had obtained my first camera for the express purpose of taking railway photographs. ♦ **expressly** ...projects expressly designed to support cattle farmers. **6** Express is used to describe special services in which things are sent or done faster than usual for a higher price. A special express service is available by fax. **7** An **express** is a fast train or coach which stops at very few places. He had boarded an express for Rome. ...express coaches. ♦♦♦♦◇ VERB / V n / V pron-refl / VERB / V pron-refl / prep / VERB: / V n prep / be V-ed prep / TECHNICAL / ADJ: ADJ n / FORMAL / ADV: / ADV before v / ADJ: ADJ n / PRAGMATICS / ADV / ADJ: ADJ n / N-COUNT

ex·pres·sion /ɪk'spreʃən/ **expressions. 1** The **expression** of ideas or feelings is the showing of them through words, actions, or artistic activities. Laughter is one of the most infectious expressions of emotion. ...freedom of expression... Her concern has now found expression in the new environmental protection act. **2** Your **expression** is the way that your face looks at a particular moment. It shows what you are thinking or feeling. Levin sat there, an expression of sadness on his face... The face is entirely devoid of expression. **3** Expression is the showing of feeling when you are acting, singing, or playing a musical instrument. I put more expression into my lyrics than a lot of other singers do. **4** An **expression** is a word or phrase. She spoke in a quiet voice but used remarkably coarse expressions. **5** An **expression** is a symbol or equation which repre- ♦♦♦◇◇ N-VAR / N-VAR / N-UNCOUNT / N-COUNT / N-COUNT

sents a quantity or problem. This forms the basis for our mathematical expression for the electric field. TECHNICAL

ex·pres·sion·ism /ɪk'spreʃənɪzəm/. **Expressionism** is a style of art, literature, and music which uses symbolism and exaggeration in order to represent emotions rather than representing physical reality. ♦ **ex·pres·sion·ist, expressionists** ...expressionist paintings. N-UNCOUNT / N-COUNT

ex·pres·sion·less /ɪk'spreʃənləs/. If you describe someone's face as **expressionless**, you mean that they are not showing their feelings. ADJ-GRADED

ex·pres·sive /ɪk'spresɪv/. **1** If you describe a person or their behaviour as **expressive**, you mean that their behaviour clearly indicates their feelings or intentions. You can train people to be more expressive. ...intuitive, expressive painting. ♦ **ex·pres·sive·ly** He moved his hands expressively. **2** If something is **expressive** of particular ideas or qualities, it has features which indicate or demonstrate them. Perhaps all his poems were really love poems, expressive of love for someone. ♦◇◇◇◇ ADJ-GRADED / PRAGMATICS / ADV-GRADED / v-link ADJ of n / FORMAL

ex·press·way /ɪk'spreswei/ **expressways.** An **expressway** is a wide road that is designed so that a lot of traffic can move along it very quickly. N-COUNT

ex·pro·pri·ate /ek'sprəʊprieɪt/ **expropriates, expropriating, expropriated.** If a government or other authority **expropriates** someone's property, they take it away from them for public use. The Bolsheviks expropriated the property of the landowners. ♦ **ex·pro·pria·tion** /ek,sprəʊpri'eɪʃən/ **expropriations** ...the expropriation of property. VERB / V n / LEGAL / N-VAR

ex·pul·sion /ɪk'spʌlʃən/ **expulsions.** See also **expel.** ♦♦◇◇◇

ex·punge /ɪk'spʌndʒ/ **expunges, expunging, expunged.** If you **expunge** something, you get rid of it completely, because it causes problems or bad feelings. The experience was something he had tried to expunge from his memory. VERB: V n / V n from n / FORMAL

ex·quis·ite /ɪk'skwɪzɪt, 'ekskwɪzɪt/. **1** Something that is **exquisite** is extremely beautiful or pleasant, especially in a delicate or refined way. Mr Zhang's photography is exquisite. ...her exquisite manners. ♦ **ex·quis·ite·ly** ...exquisitely crafted dolls' houses. **2** Exquisite is used to emphasize that a feeling or quality is very great or intense. She peeled it with exquisite care. ♦♦◇◇◇ ADJ-GRADED / ADV-GRADED / ADJ: ADJ n / PRAGMATICS / LITERARY

ex-'servcieman, ex-servicemen. An **ex-serviceman** is a man who used to be in a country's armed forces. The American word is **veteran.** N-COUNT / BRITISH

ext. Ext. is the written abbreviation for **extension** when it is used to refer to a particular telephone number. ♦♦◇◇◇ N-VAR: / N num

ex·tant /ek'stænt, 'ekstənt/. If something is **extant**, it is still in existence, in spite of being very old. The oldest extant document is dated 1492. ADJ / FORMAL

ex·tem·po·rize /ɪk'stempəraɪz/ **extemporizes, extemporizing, extemporized;** also spelled **extemporise** in British English. If you **extemporize**, you speak, act, or perform something immediately, without preparing it beforehand. VERB: V / FORMAL

ex·tend /ɪk'stend/ **extends, extending, extended. 1** If you say that something, usually something large, **extends** for a particular distance or **extends** from one place to another, you are indicating its size or position. The main stem will extend to around 12ft... Our personal space extends about 12 to 18 inches around us... The high-speed train service is planned to extend from Paris to Bordeax. **2** If you **extend** something, you make it longer or bigger. The building was extended in 1500. ...an extended exhaust pipe. **3** If a piece of equipment or furniture **extends**, its length can be increased. The table extends to 220cm. **4** If an object **extends from** a surface or place, it sticks out from it. Billing's legs extended from the bushes. **5** If someone **extends** their hand, they stretch out their arm and hand to shake hands with someone. The man extended his hand: 'I'm Chuck'. **6** If an event or activity **extends** over a period of time, it continues for that time. ...a playing career in first- ♦♦♦♦◇ VERB: / V for amount / V to amount / V amount / V from n to n / Also V over n, / V to n / VERB: V / V-ed / VERB: V / V to amount / VERB / V from n / VERB / V n / WRITTEN / VERB: / V over n / V from n to n

class cricket that extended from 1894 to 1920. **7** If you   VERB
extend something, you make it last longer than before   V n
or end at a later date. *They have extended the deadline
by twenty-four hours.*

8 If something **extends** to a group of people, things, or   VERB
activities, it includes or affects them. *The service also*   V to n/-ing
extends to wrapping and delivering gifts... His influ-   V beyond n
ence extends beyond the TV viewing audience. **9** If you   VERB
extend something **to** other people or things, you   V n to n
make it include or affect more of them. *It might be
possible to extend the technique to other crop plants.*

ex·tend·ed /ɪkˈstendɪd/. If something happens for ◆◇◇◇◇
an **extended** period of time, it happens for a long   ADJ: ADJ n
period of time. *Obviously, any child who receives
dedicated teaching over an extended period is likely
to improve.* ● See also **extend**.

ex‚tended 'family, extended families. An ex- ◆◇◇◇◇
tended **family** is a family group which includes   N-COUNT
relatives such as uncles, aunts, and grandparents, as
well as parents, children, and brothers and sisters.

ex·ten·sion /ɪkˈstenʃən/ **extensions. 1** An exten- ◆◆◇◇◇
sion is a new room or building which is added to an   N-COUNT
existing building or group of buildings. **2** An exten-   N-COUNT
sion is a new section of a road or rail line that is
added to an existing road or line. *...the Jubilee Line
extension.* **3** An **extension** is a part which is con-   N-COUNT
nected to a piece of equipment in order to make it
reach something further away. *...a 30-foot extension
cord.* **4** An **extension** is an extra period of time for   N-COUNT
which something lasts or is valid, usually as a result
of official permission. *Ian Lentern has been granted
a three-year extension.* **5** Something that is an **ex-**   N-COUNT
tension of something else is a development of it
that includes or affects more people, things, or ac-
tivities. *Many Filipinos see the bases as an extension
of American colonial rule.* **6** An **extension** is a tele-   N-COUNT
phone line that is connected to the switchboard of a
company or institution, and that has its own num-
ber. The written abbreviation 'ext.' is also used. *She
can get me on extension 308.*

ex·ten·sive /ɪkˈstensɪv/. **1** Something that is **ex-** ◆◆◆◇◇
tensive covers or includes a large physical area. *The*   ADJ-GRADED
*palace and its grounds were more extensive than the
city itself.* ♦ **ex·ten·sive·ly** *Mark, however, needs to*   ADV-GRADED:
travel extensively with his varied business interests.   ADV after v
2 Something that is **extensive** covers a wide range   ADJ-GRADED
of details, ideas, or items. *Developments in South
Africa receive extensive coverage... The facilities
available are very extensive.* ♦ **extensively** *All*   ADV-GRADED
these issues have been extensively researched. **3** If   ADJ-GRADED
something is **extensive**, it is very great. *The blast
caused extensive damage... The security forces have
extensive powers of search and arrest.*
♦ **extensively** *Hydrogen is used extensively in in-*   ADV-GRADED
dustry for the production of ammonia.

ex·tent /ɪkˈstent/. **1** If you are talking about how ◆◆◆◇◇
great, important, or serious a difficulty or situation   N-SING:
is, you can refer to the **extent** of it. *Growing up with*   with supp
*him soon made me realise the extent of his determi-
nation... The full extent of the losses was disclosed
yesterday.* **2** The **extent** of something is its length,   N-SING:
area, or size. *Climatic alterations reduced the extent*   with supp
of the rain forest.

3 You use expressions such as **to a large extent**, **to**   PHRASE
some extent, or **to a certain extent** in order to indi-   [PRAGMATICS]
cate that something is partly true, but not entirely
true. *It was and, to a large extent, still is a good show...
To a certain extent it's easier for men to get work... This
also endangers American interests in other regions, al-
though to a lesser extent.* **4** You use expressions such   PHRASE
as **to what extent**, **to that extent**, or **to the extent that**   [PRAGMATICS]
when you are discussing how true a statement is, or in
what ways it is true. *It's still not clear to what extent
this criticism is originating from within the political par-
ty... He could only be sorry to the extent that this affect-
ed his grandchildren. ...the extent to which it helped to
promote Britain's broader strategic interests.* **5** You   PHRASE
use expressions such as **to the extent of**, **to the extent**   [PRAGMATICS]
that, or **to such an extent that** in order to emphasize
that a situation has reached a difficult, dangerous, or

surprising stage. *Ford kept his suspicions to himself,
even to the extent of going to jail for a murder he obvi-
ously didn't commit.*

ex·tenu·at·ing /ɪkˈstenjʊeɪtɪŋ/. If you say that   ADJ
there are **extenuating** circumstances for a bad   FORMAL
situation or wrong action, you mean that there are
reasons or factors which partly excuse it. *The de-
fendants decide to admit their guilt, but insist that
there are extenuating circumstances.*

ex·te·ri·or /ɪkˈstɪəriə/ **exteriors. 1** The **exterior** of ◆◇◇◇◇
something is its outside surface. *In one ad the view-*   N-COUNT
er scarcely sees the car's exterior. **2** You can refer to   N-COUNT
someone's usual appearance or behaviour as their
exterior, especially when it is very different from
their real character. *Pat's tough exterior hides a shy
and sensitive soul.* **3** You use **exterior** to refer to the   ADJ: ADJ n
outside parts of something or things that are out-
side something. *The exterior walls were made of
pre-formed concrete.*

ex·ter·mi·nate /ɪkˈstɜːmɪneɪt/ **exterminates,** ◆◇◇◇◇
exterminating, exterminated. To **exterminate**   VERB
a group of people or animals means to kill all of   V n
them. *A huge effort was made to exterminate the
rats.* ♦ **ex·ter·mi·na·tion** /ɪkˌstɜːmɪˈneɪʃən/ *...the*   N-UNCOUNT
*extermination of hundreds of thousands of their
brethren.*

ex·ter·nal /ɪkˈstɜːnəl/. **1 External** is used to indi- ◆◆◇◇◇
cate that something is on the outside of something   ADJ
or someone, or exists, happens, or comes from out-
side something. *...a much reduced heat loss through
external walls.* ♦ **ex·ter·nal·ly** *Vitamins can be ap-*   ADV
plied externally to the skin. **2** If medicine is **for ex-**   PHRASE
ternal use, it is intended to be used only on the
outside of your body, and not to be eaten or drunk.
3 External means involving or intended for foreign   ADJ: ADJ n
countries. *...the commissioner for external affairs.*
♦ **externally** *...protecting the value of the mark both*   ADV
internally and externally. **4 External** means happen-   ADJ: ADJ n
ing or existing in the world in general and affecting
you in some way. *Such events occur only when the ex-
ternal conditions are favorable.* **5 External** examiners,   ADJ: ADJ n
accountants, or evaluators come into an organization   BRITISH
from outside in order to do a job there that must be
done fairly and independently, or to check that a job is
done properly. ♦ **externally** *There must be external-*   ADV:
ly moderated tests.   ADV -ed

ex·tinct /ɪkˈstɪŋkt/. **1** A species of animal or plant ◆◇◇◇◇
that is **extinct** no longer has any living members. *It*   ADJ
*is 250 years since the wolf became extinct in Britain.
...the bones of extinct animals.* ♦ **ex·tinc·tion**   N-UNCOUNT
/ɪkˈstɪŋkʃən/ *Many species have been shot to the
verge of extinction.* **2** If a particular kind of worker,   ADJ
way of life, or type of activity is **extinct**, it no longer
exists, because of changes in society. *Herbalism had
become an all but extinct skill in the Western world.*
♦ **extinction** *The loggers say their jobs are faced*   N-UNCOUNT
with extinction. **3** An **extinct** volcano is one that   ADJ
does not erupt or is not expected to erupt any more.

ex·tin·guish /ɪkˈstɪŋgwɪʃ/ **extinguishes, extin-** ◆◇◇◇◇
guishing, extinguished. 1 If you **extinguish** a   VERB
fire or a light, you stop it burning or shining. *It took*   V n
about 50 minutes to extinguish the fire. **2** If some-   FORMAL
thing **extinguishes** a feeling or idea, it destroys it.   VERB
The message extinguished her hopes.   V n

ex·tin·guish·er /ɪkˈstɪŋgwɪʃə/ **extinguishers.** An   N-COUNT
extinguisher is the same as a **fire extinguisher**.

extn. Extn. means the same as **ext.**   N-VAR

ex·tol /ɪkˈstəʊl/ **extols, extolling, extolled.** If ◆◇◇◇◇
you **extol** something or someone, you praise them   VERB
enthusiastically. *Now experts are extolling the vir-*   V n
tues of the humble potato.

ex·tort /ɪkˈstɔːt/ **extorts, extorting, extorted.** ◆◇◇◇◇
1 If someone **extorts** money from you, they get it   VERB:
from you using force, threats, or other unfair or il-   V n from n
legal means. *Her kidnapper extorted a £175,000 ran-*   V n
som for her release. ♦ **ex·tor·tion** /ɪkˈstɔːʃən/ *He*   N-UNCOUNT
has been charged with extortion. ♦ **ex·tor·tion·ist**   N-COUNT
/ɪkˈstɔːʃənɪst/ **extortionists** *Wealth and fame will
always be the target of extortionists.* **2** If someone   VERB
extorts something from you, they get it from you   V n

E

with difficulty or by using unfair means. *Some mag-istrates have abused their powers of arrest to extort confessions.*

ex·tor·tion·ate /ɪkˈstɔːʃənət/. If you describe something such as a price as **extortionate**, you are emphasizing that it is far too much. ADJ-GRADED PRAGMATICS

ex·tra /ˈekstrə/ **extras. 1** You use **extra** to de-scribe an amount, person, or thing that is added to others of the same kind, or that can be added to others of the same kind. *Police warned motorists to allow extra time to get to work... Extra staff have been taken on.* **2** If something is **extra**, you have to pay more money for it in addition to what you are already paying for something. *For foreign orders postage is extra.* ► Also a pronoun. *Many of the ad-ditional features now cost extra.* ► Also an adverb. *You may be charged 10% extra for this service.* **3** Ex-tras are additional amounts of money that are add-ed to the price that you have to pay for something. *She is disgusted by big hotels adding so many extras to the bill... There are no hidden extras.* **4** Extras are things which are not necessary, but which make something more comfortable, useful, or enjoyable. *Optional extras include cooking tuition at a top res-taurant.* **5** The **extras** in a film are the people who play unimportant parts, for example as members of a crowd. **6** You can use **extra** in front of adjectives and adverbs to emphasize the quality that they are describing. *I'd have to be extra careful... We were all told to try hard to be nice to him.* **7 ●** to **go the extra mile**: see **mile**. ADJ: ADJ n / v-link ADJ / PRON / ADV / N-COUNT / N-COUNT / N-COUNT / ADV: ADV adj/adv PRAGMATICS INFORMAL

extra- /ˈekstrə-/. **extra-** is used to form adjectives indicating that something is outside something or is not part of something. *The move was extra-constitutional. ...a combination of parliamentary and extra-parliamentary methods.* PREFIX FORMAL

ex·tract, extracts, extracting, extracted. The verb is pronounced /ɪkˈstrækt/. The noun is pro-nounced /ˈekstrækt/. **1** To **extract** a substance means to obtain it from something else, for example by using industrial or chemical processes. *Citric acid can be extracted from the juice of oranges.* **♦ ex-·trac·tion** *Petroleum engineers plan and manage the extraction of oil.* **2** An **extract** is a substance that has been obtained from something else, for exam-ple by means of a chemical or industrial process. *...a plant extract which acts as a natural tonic.* **●** See also **yeast extract. 3** If you **extract** something from a place, you take it out or pull it out. *She reached into the wardrobe and extracted another tracksuit.* **4** When a dentist **extracts** a tooth, he or she removes it from the patient's mouth. *She is to go and have a tooth extracted at 3 o'clock today.* **♦ extraction, extractions** *In those days, dentistry was basic. Extractions were carried out without an-aesthetic.*
5 If you say that someone **extracts** something, you disapprove of them because they take it for them-selves to gain an advantage, often by taking it away from someone else. *His development policies have ex-tracted cash from the city centre.* **6** If you **extract** infor-mation or a response **from** someone, you get it from them with difficulty, because they are unwilling to say or do what you want. *...the mistake of trying to extract further information from our director.* **7** If you **extract** a particular piece of information, you obtain it from a larger amount or source of information. *Britain's trade figures can no longer be extracted from export-and-import documentation at ports.* **8** If printed or published text **is extracted** from a book, it comes from that book. *This material has been extracted from 'Col-lins Good Wood Handbook'.* **9** An **extract** from a book or piece of writing is a small part of it that is printed or published separately. *...this extract from an informa-tion booklet.* VERB: V n beV-ed from n Also V n from n / N-UNCOUNT / N-VAR / VERB: V n LITERARY / VERB: V n have n V-ed / N-VAR / VERB PRAGMATICS V n from n / VERB V n from n / VERB: V n beV-ed from n Also V n from n / V-PASSIVE JOURNALISM / N-COUNT

ex·trac·tion /ɪkˈstrækʃən/. If you say, for example, that someone is of French **extraction**, you mean that they or their family originally came from France. N-UNCOUNT: with supp FORMAL

ex·trac·tor /ɪkˈstræktə/ **extractors.** An extractor or extractor fan is a device that draws smells, steam, or hot air out of a room or building. N-COUNT BRITISH

extra·cur·ricu·lar /ˌekstrəkəˈrɪkjʊlə/; also spelled **extra-curricular. 1 Extracurricular** activities for students are not part of their course. *...extra-curricular sport.* **2 Extracurricular** activities are not part of your normal work. *The money he made from these extra-curricular activities enabled him to pur-sue other ventures.* ADJ: ADJ n FORMAL / ADJ: ADJ n INFORMAL

extra·dite /ˈekstrədaɪt/ **extradites, extraditing, extradited.** If someone is **extradited**, they are offi-cially sent back to their own country to be tried for a crime that they have been accused of. *He was extradited to Britain from the Irish Republic.* **♦ extra·di·tion** /ˌekstrəˈdɪʃən/ **extraditions** *...the British government's request for his extradition.* VERB beV-ed to/ from n FORMAL / N-VAR

extra-·marital; also spelled **extramarital.** An **extra-marital** affair is a sexual relationship between a married person and another person who is not their husband or wife. ADJ

extra-·mural. Extra-mural courses at a college or university are taken by part-time students. ADJ

extra·neous /ɪkˈstreɪniəs/. **Extraneous** things are not relevant or essential to the situation you are in-volved in or the subject you are talking about. *We ought not to bring in extraneous matters.* ADJ FORMAL

extraor·di·naire /ekˌstrɔːdɪˈneə/. If you describe someone as being, for example, a **musician extraordinaire**, you are saying in a slightly humor-ous way that you think they are an extremely good musician. ADJ: n ADJ

extraor·di·nary /ɪkˈstrɔːdənri, AM -neri/. **1** An **extraordinary** person or thing has some extremely good or special quality. *We've made extraordinary progress. ...an extraordinary musician.* **♦ extraor-·di·nari·ly** /ɪkˈstrɔːdənrɪli, AM -nerɪli/ *She's extraor-dinarily disciplined.* **2** If you describe something as **extraordinary**, you mean that it is very unusual or surprising. *What an extraordinary thing to happen!* **♦ extraordinarily** *Apart from the hair, he looked extraordinarily unchanged.* **3** An **extraordinary** meeting is arranged specially to deal with a particu-lar situation or problem, rather than happening regularly. *Representatives of the colonies met in an extraordinary congress.* ADJ-GRADED PRAGMATICS / ADV-GRADED: ADV adj / ADJ-GRADED PRAGMATICS / ADV-GRADED / ADJ: ADJ n FORMAL

ex·trapo·late /ɪkˈstræpəleɪt/ **extrapolates, ex-trapolating, extrapolated.** If you **extrapolate from** known facts, you use them as a basis for gen-eral statements about a present or future situation. *Extrapolating from his American findings, he reck-ons about 80% of these deaths might be attributed to smoking.* **♦ ex·trapo·la·tion** /ɪkˌstræpəˈleɪʃən/ **ex-trapolations** *...an extrapolation of the known inci-dence of the virus.* VERB V from n Also V n from n FORMAL / N-VAR

extra-sensory per·ception. Extra-sensory per-ception means knowing things in a supernatural way, rather than as a result of using your ordinary senses. The abbreviation 'ESP' is also used. N-UNCOUNT

extra·ter·res·trial /ˌekstrətɪˈrestriəl/ **extraterres-trials;** also spelled **extra-terrestrial. 1 Extraterres-trial** means happening, existing, or coming from somewhere beyond the planet Earth. *...a 10-year search for extraterrestrial intelligence.* **2 Extrater-restrials** are living creatures that some people think exist or may exist in another part of the universe. ADJ FORMAL / N-COUNT

extra 'time. If a sports match such as a game of football or hockey goes into **extra time**, the game continues for a set period after it would usually have ended because both teams have the same score. The American term is **overtime**. N-UNCOUNT BRITISH

ex·trava·gance /ɪkˈstrævəgəns/ **extravagances.** An **extravagance** is something that you spend mon-ey on but cannot really afford. *Her only extrava-gance was horses.* N-COUNT

ex·trava·gant /ɪkˈstrævəgənt/. **1** Someone who is **extravagant** spends more money than they can af-ford or uses more of something than is reasonable. *We are not extravagant; restaurant meals are a luxu-ry.* **♦ ex·trava·gant·ly** *Jeff had shopped extrava-* ADJ-GRADED / ADV-GRADED:

E

gantly for presents. ...their days of living extrava- ADV with v
gantly. **◆ ex·trav·a·gance** *...gross mismanagement* N-UNCOUNT
and financial extravagance. **2** Something that is **ex-** ADJ-GRADED
travagant costs more money than you can afford or
uses more of something than is reasonable. *Her
Aunt Sallie gave her an uncharacteristically extravagant gift.* **◆ extravagantly** *Labour's plans would* ADV-GRADED
be extravagantly expensive. **3 Extravagant** behav- ADV adj/-ed
iour is extreme behaviour that is often done for a ADJ-GRADED
particular effect. *...extravagant shows of generosity.*
◆ extravagantly *She had on occasions praised him* ADV-GRADED
extravagantly. ...extravagantly bizarre clothes. **4 Ex-** ADJ-GRADED
travagant claims or ideas are unrealistic or imprac- PRAGMATICS
tical; used showing disapproval. *...adorning their
products with ever more extravagant claims.* **5 Ex-** ADJ-GRADED
travagant entertainments or designs are elaborate
and impressive. *...the wildest and most extravagant
London parties.* **◆ extravagantly** *...his extrava-* ADV-GRADED:
gantly elegant Paris home. ADV adj/-ed

ex·trav·a·gan·za /ɪkˌstrævə'gænzə/ **extravagan-** ◆◇◇◇◇
zas. An **extravaganza** is a very elaborate and N-COUNT
expensive show or performance. *...a magnificent
firework extravaganza.*

ex·treme /ɪk'striːm/ **extremes. 1 Extreme** means ◆◆◆◇◇
very great in degree or intensity. *...people living in* ADJ-GRADED
*extreme poverty. ...the author's extreme reluctance
to generalise.* **2** You use **extreme** to describe situa- ADJ-GRADED
tions and behaviour which are much more severe or
unusual than you would expect. *It is hard to imagine Lineker capable of anything so extreme.* **3** You ADJ-GRADED
use **extreme** to describe opinions, beliefs, or politi- PRAGMATICS
cal movements which you disapprove of because
they are very different from those that most people
would accept as reasonable or normal. *This extreme
view hasn't captured popular opinion.* **4** You can N-COUNT
use **extremes** to refer to situations or types of behaviour that have opposite qualities to each other,
especially when each situation or type of behaviour
has such a quality to the greatest degree possible.
*...a 'middle way' between the extremes of success and
failure.* **5** The **extreme** end or edge of something is ADJ-GRADED:
its furthest end or edge. *...winds from the extreme* ADJ n
north.
6 You use **in the extreme** after an adjective in order to PHRASE
emphasize what you are saying, especially when you PRAGMATICS
want to indicate that it is something which is undesir- FORMAL
able or very surprising. *It is proving controversial in
the extreme.* **7** If someone **goes to extremes**, **takes** PHRASE
something **to extremes**, or **carries** something **to extremes**, they do or say something in a way that people
consider to be unacceptable, unreasonable, or
foolish.

ex·treme·ly /ɪk'striːmli/. You use **extremely** in ◆◆◆◆
front of adjectives and adverbs to emphasize that ADV:
the specified quality is present to a very great de- ADV adj/adv
gree. *My mobile phone is extremely useful... Three of* PRAGMATICS
them are working extremely well.

ex·tre·mis /ɪk'striːmɪs/. See **in extremis**.

ex·trem·ist /ɪk'striːmɪst/ **extremists.** If you de- ◆◆◇◇◇
scribe someone as an **extremist**, you disapprove of N-COUNT
them because they try to bring about political PRAGMATICS
change by using violent or extreme methods. *...a
previously unknown extremist group.* **◆ ex·trem-
·ism** *...right-wing extremism.* N-UNCOUNT

ex·trem·ity /ɪk'stremɪti/ **extremities. 1** The **ex-** N-COUNT:
tremity of something is its furthest end or edge. with supp
...the north-western extremity of the Iberian peninsu- FORMAL
la. **2** Your **extremities** are the ends of your body, N-PLURAL
especially your hands and feet.
3 The **extremity** of a situation or of someone's behav- N-UNCOUNT:
iour is the degree to which it is severe, unusual, or un- also N in pl
acceptable. *In spite of the extremity of her seclusion
she was sane. ...the extremities of their climate.*

ex·tri·cate /'ekstrɪkeɪt/ **extricates, extricating,
extricated. 1** If you **extricate** someone **from** a dif- VERB
ficult or serious situation, you free them from it. *...a* V pron-refl
last ditch attempt by the country to extricate itself from n
from its economic crisis. **2** If you **extricate** someone Also V n from
or something from a place where they are trapped VERB
V n

or caught, you succeed in freeing them. *He endeav-* FORMAL
oured to extricate the car, digging with his hands.

ex·trin·sic /ɪk'strɪnzɪk, AM -sɪk/. **Extrinsic** reasons, ADJ: ADJ n
forces, or factors exist outside the person or situa- FORMAL
tion they affect. *Nowadays there are fewer extrinsic
pressures to get married.*

ex·tro·vert /'ekstrəvɜːt/ **extroverts.** Someone ◆◇◇◇◇
who is **extrovert** is very active, lively, and sociable. ADJ-GRADED
The usual American word is **extroverted.** *His
footballing skills and extrovert personality won the
hearts of the public.* ▶ Also a noun. *...an extrovert* N-COUNT
who revelled in controversy.

ex·tro·vert·ed /'ekstrəvɜːtɪd/. Someone who is ADJ-GRADED
extroverted is very active, lively, and sociable. The
usual British word is **extrovert.** *...young people who
were easy-going and extroverted as children.*

ex·trude /ɪk'struːd/ **extrudes, extruding, ex-** VB: usu
truded. If a substance **is extruded**, it is forced or passive
squeezed out through a small opening. **◆ ex·tru-** FORMAL
·sion /ɪk'struːʒən/ **extrusions** *...the extrusion of* N-VAR
plastic tubes.

exu·ber·ant /ɪg'zjuːbərənt, AM -'zuːb-/. **1** If you ◆◇◇◇◇
are **exuberant**, you are full of energy, excitement, ADJ-GRADED
and cheerfulness. *...the exuberant young girl with
dark hair.* **◆ exu·ber·ance** /ɪg'zjuːbərəns, AM N-UNCOUNT
-'zuːb-/ *...her burst of exuberance.* **◆ exu·ber·ant·ly** ADV-GRADED
They both laughed exuberantly. **2** If you describe ADJ-GRADED
something as **exuberant**, you like it because it is PRAGMATICS
lively, exciting, and full of energy and life. *This is
bold and exuberant cooking.* **◆ exuberance** *...the* N-UNCOUNT
sheer exuberance of the sculpture. **◆ exuberantly** ADV-GRADED
...exuberantly decorated.

ex·ude /ɪg'zjuːd, AM -'zuːd/ **exudes, exuding,** ◆◇◇◇◇
exuded. 1 If someone **exudes** a quality or feeling, V-ERG
or if it **exudes**, they show that they have it to a great V n
extent. *The guerrillas exude confidence... A dogged* FORMAL
air of confidence exuded. **2** If something **exudes** a V-ERG
liquid or smell or if a liquid or smell **exudes** from it, V n
the liquid or smell comes out of it slowly and Also V
steadily. *Nearby was a factory which exuded a pun-* FORMAL
gent smell.

ex·ult /ɪg'zʌlt/ **exults, exulting, exulted.** If you VERB
exult in a triumph or success that you have had, V in/at n
you feel and show great happiness and pleasure be- V with quote
cause of it. *He was exulting in a win at the show...* WRITTEN
*'This is what I've longed for during my entire career,'
Kendall exulted.* **◆ ex·ul·ta·tion** /ˌegzʌl'teɪʃən/ *...a* N-UNCOUNT
tremendous sense of relief and exultation.

ex·ult·ant /ɪg'zʌltənt/. If you are **exultant**, you feel ADJ-GRADED
very happy and triumphant. *An exultant party lead-* FORMAL
er said: 'We had a first class candidate'. **◆ ex·ult-
·ant·ly** *He shouted exultantly.* ADV:
ADV with v

eye /aɪ/ **eyes, eyeing or eying, eyed. 1** Your ◆◆◆◆
eyes are the parts of your body with which you see. N-COUNT
I opened my eyes and looked. **◆ -eyed. -eyed** com- COMB
bines with adjectives to form adjectives which indicate the colour, shape, or size of a person's eyes, or
indicate the kind of expression that they have. *...a
blonde-haired, blue-eyed little girl... She watched
open-eyed.* **2** You say **'an eye for an eye'** to refer to PHRASE
the idea that people should be punished according
to the way in which they offended, for example if
they hurt someone, they should be hurt equally
badly in return. *...a very simple punishment code
based on an eye-for-an-eye.* **3** If you say that there PHRASE
is a type of something, especially a type of scenery, PRAGMATICS
as far as the eye can see, you are emphasizing that
it extends to the horizon and is a lot of it.
*Massive dunes stretched in every direction as far as
the eye could see.* **4** If you **cry** your **eyes** out, you cry PHRASE
very hard. *I've been crying my eyes out all day.* **5** If INFORMAL
you say that something happens **before** your **eyes**, PHRASE
in front of your **eyes**, or **under** your **eyes**, you are PRAGMATICS
emphasizing or saying that it happens where you
can see it clearly or while you are watching it, and
often implying that it is surprising or unpleasant.
6 If something **catches** your **eye**, you suddenly notice PHRASE
it. ● See also **eye-catching. 7** If you **catch** someone's PHRASE
eye, you do something to attract their attention, so
that you can speak to them or ask them something.

8 To **clap eyes on** someone or something, or **set** or **lay eyes on** them, means to see them. ...*the most bare, bleak, barren and inhospitable island I've ever had the misfortune to clap my eyes on.* **9** If you **make eye contact** with someone, you look at them at the same time as they look at you, so that you are both aware that you are looking at each other. **10** If something, especially something surprising or impressive, **meets your eyes**, you see it. ...*the first sight that met my eyes on reaching the front door.* [PHRASE INFORMAL] [PHRASE] [PHRASE]

11 If you say that **all eyes are on** something or that the **eyes of the world are on** something, you mean that everyone is paying careful attention to it and what will happen. *The eyes of the world were now on the police.* [PHRASE JOURNALISM]

12 If you **keep your eyes open** or **keep an eye out** for someone or something, you watch for them carefully. *I ask the mounted patrol to keep their eyes open... You and your friends keep an eye out.* **13** If you **keep an eye on** something or someone, you watch them carefully, for example to make sure that they are satisfactory or safe, or not causing trouble. *We must keep a careful eye on all our running costs.* **14** If someone **has** their **eye on** you, they are watching you carefully to see what you do. **15** When you **take** your **eyes off** the thing you have been watching or looking at, you stop looking at it. *Nina couldn't take her eyes off Philip.* [PHRASE INFORMAL] [PHRASE] [PHRASE] [PHRASE]

16 If you **eye** someone or something in a particular way, you look at them carefully in that way. *Sally eyed Claire with interest... Martin eyed the bottle.* **17** If you **cast** your **eye** or **run** your **eye** over something, you look at it or read it quickly. *I would be grateful if he could cast an expert eye over it.* [VERB V n prep/adv V n] [PHRASE]

18 If you **close** your **eyes to** something bad or if you **shut** your **eyes to** it, you ignore it. *Most governments must simply be shutting their eyes to the problem.* **19** If you say that you did something **with** your **eyes open**, you mean that you were fully aware of the problems and difficulties that you were likely to have. *We want all our members to undertake this trip responsibly, with their eyes open.* **20** If something **opens** your **eyes**, it makes you aware that something is different from the way that you thought it was. *Watching your child explore the world about her can open your eyes to delights long forgotten.* **21** You say **'there's more to** this **than meets the eye'** when you think a situation is not as simple as it seems to be. [PHRASE] [PHRASE] [PHRASE] [PHRASE]

22 You use **eye** when you are talking about a person's ability to judge things or about the way in which they are considering or dealing with things. ...*a man of discernment, with an eye for quality... Their chief negotiator turned his critical eye on the United States... He first learnt to fish under the watchful eye of his grandmother.* **23** If you say that someone **has an eye for** something, you mean that they are good at noticing it or making judgements about it. *Susan has a keen eye for detail.* [N-COUNT] [PHRASE]

24 You use expressions such as **in his eyes** or **to her eyes** to indicate that you are reporting someone's opinion and that other people might think differently. *The other serious problem in the eyes of the new government is communalism... The practice of religion in America sometimes seems strange to European eyes.* **25** If you **see eye to eye** with someone, you agree with them and have the same opinions and views. *Yuriko saw eye to eye with Yul on almost every aspect of the production.* **26** If someone sees or considers something **through** your **eyes**, they consider it in the way that you do, from your point of view. *She tried to see things through his eyes.* **27** If you **have** your **eye on** something, you want to have it. ...*a new outfit you've had your eye on.* **28** If you say that you are **up to** your **eyes** in something, you are emphasizing that you have a lot of it to deal with, and often that you are very busy. *I am up to my eyes in work.* [PHRASE PRAGMATICS] [PHRASE] [PHRASE] [PHRASE INFORMAL] [PHRASE PRAGMATICS INFORMAL]

29 The **eye of** a storm, tornado, or hurricane is the centre of it. **30** If you say that someone or something is at **the eye of the storm**, you mean they are the main subject of a disagreement or controversy. ...*the minister in the eye of the storm.* **31** An **eye** is a small metal loop which a hook fits into, as a fastening on a piece of [N-SING: the N of n PHRASE] [N-COUNT]

clothing. **32** The **eye** of a needle is the small hole at one end which the thread passes through. [N-COUNT]

33 See also **black eye**, **private eye**, **shut-eye**. **34** • **apple of** your **eye**: see **apple**. • to **turn a blind eye**: see **blind**. • to **feast** your **eyes**: see **feast**. • to **look** someone **in the eye**: see **look**. • **in** your **mind's eye**: see **mind**. • **the naked eye**: see **naked**. • to **pull the wool over** someone's **eyes**: see **wool**.

eye up. If someone **eyes** you **up**, they look at you in a way that shows they consider you attractive or sexy. ...*a slob called Drew who spends all day eyeing up the women.* [PHRASAL VB V n P V P noun INFORMAL, BRITISH]

eye·ball /'aɪbɔːl/ **eyeballs. 1** Your **eyeballs** are your whole eyes, rather than just the part which can be seen between your eyelids. **2** If you are **eyeball to eyeball** with someone, you are in their presence and involved in a meeting, dispute, or contest with them. You can also talk about having an **eyeball to eyeball** meeting or confrontation. **3** You use **up to the eyeballs** to emphasize that someone is in an undesirable state to a very great degree. *He's up to his eyeballs in debt.* [◆◇◇◇◇ N-COUNT] [PHRASE INFORMAL] [PHRASE PRAGMATICS]

eye·brow /'aɪbraʊ/ **eyebrows. 1** Your **eyebrows** are the lines of hair which grow above your eyes. **2** If something causes you to **raise an eyebrow** or to **raise** your **eyebrows**, it causes you to feel surprised or disapproving. *An intriguing item on the news pages caused me to raise an eyebrow.* [◆◆◇◇◇ N-COUNT] [PHRASE]

'eye-catching. Something that is **eye-catching** is very noticeable. ...*a series of eye-catching ads.* [◆◇◇◇◇ ADJ-GRADED]

eye·ful /'aɪfʊl/ **eyefuls.** If you get an **eyeful** of something, especially something that you would not normally see, you are able to get a good look at it. *Then she gave him an eyeful of her tattoos.* [N-COUNT INFORMAL]

eye·lash /'aɪlæʃ/ **eyelashes.** Your **eyelashes** are the hairs which grow on the edges of your eyelids. [◆◇◇◇◇ N-COUNT]

eye·let /'aɪlɪt/ **eyelets.** An **eyelet** is a small hole with a metal or leather ring round it which is made in cloth. [N-COUNT]

eye·lid /'aɪlɪd/ **eyelids.** Your **eyelids** are the two flaps of skin which cover your eyes when they are closed. • **not bat an eyelid**: see **bat**. [◆◇◇◇◇ N-COUNT]

eye·liner /'aɪlaɪnə/ **eyeliners. Eyeliner** is a pencil which some women use on the edges of their eyelids next to their eyelashes. [N-VAR]

'eye-opener, eye-openers. If you describe something as an **eye-opener**, you mean that it surprises you and that you learn something new from it. *This summer's tour was an eye-opener for her.* [N-COUNT INFORMAL]

'eye patch, eye patches. See **patch**.

eye·piece /'aɪpiːs/ **eyepieces.** The **eyepiece** of a microscope or telescope is the glass where you put your eye in order to look through the instrument. [N-COUNT]

'eye shadow, eye shadows. Eye shadow is a substance which you can paint on your eyelids in order to make them a different colour. [N-VAR]

eye·sight /'aɪsaɪt/. Your **eyesight** is your ability to see. *He suffered from poor eyesight.* [◆◇◇◇◇ N-UNCOUNT]

'eye socket, eye sockets. Your **eye sockets** are the two hollow bony parts on either side of your face, where your eyeballs are. [N-COUNT]

eye·sore /'aɪsɔː/ **eyesores.** You describe a building or place as an **eyesore** when it is extremely ugly and you dislike it or disapprove of it. ...*slums, which are an eyesore and a health hazard.* [N-COUNT]

'eye strain. If you suffer from **eye strain**, you feel pain around your eyes or at the back of your eyes, because you are very tired or should be wearing glasses. [N-UNCOUNT]

eye·witness /'aɪwɪtnəs/ **eyewitnesses.** An **eyewitness** is a person who was present at an event and can therefore describe it, for example in a law court. *Eyewitnesses say the police then opened fire.* [◆◇◇◇◇ N-COUNT]

ey·rie /'ɪəri, AM 'eri/ **eyries;** spelled **aerie** in American English. **1** If you refer to a place such as a house or a castle as an **eyrie**, you mean it is built high up and is difficult to reach. ...*my 48th floor eyrie in the sky.* **2** An **eyrie** is the nest of an eagle, falcon, or other similar bird. [N-COUNT: with supp LITERARY] [N-COUNT]

F, f

face

F f

F, f /ef/ **F's, f's. 1** F is the sixth letter of the English alphabet. **2** In music, F is the fourth note in the scale of C major. **3** F or f is used as an abbreviation for words beginning with f, such as 'female', 'feminine', 'franc', 'false', and 'Fahrenheit'. *Heat the oven to 400 degrees F.* · N-VAR N-VAR

fab /fæb/. If you say that something is **fab**, you are emphasizing that you think it is very good. · ADJ-GRADED INFORMAL

fa·ble /ˈfeɪbəl/ **fables. 1** A **fable** is a story, often about animals, which teaches a moral lesson. *...the fable of the tortoise and the hare.* **2** You can describe a statement or explanation that is untrue but that many people believe as **fable**. *Is reincarnation fact or fable?* · N-VAR N-VAR

fa·bled /ˈfeɪbəld/. You can describe a famous person, place, or thing as **fabled**, especially when they come from a distant place or period in history. *...the fabled city of Troy.* · ADJ: ADJ n

fab·ric /ˈfæbrɪk/ **fabrics. 1 Fabric** is cloth or other material produced by weaving together cotton, nylon, silk, or other threads. *...small squares of red cotton fabric.* **2** The **fabric** of a society or system is its basic structure, with all the customs and beliefs that make it work successfully. *Years of civil war have wrecked the country's infrastructure and destroyed its social fabric.* **3** The **fabric** of a building is its walls, roof, and the materials with which it is built. · N-VAR N-SING: with supp N-SING

fab·ri·cate /ˈfæbrɪkeɪt/ **fabricates, fabricating, fabricated.** If someone **fabricates** information, they invent it in order to deceive people. *All four claim that officers fabricated evidence against them.* ◆ **fab·ri·ca·tion, fabrications** *China calls the report pure fabrication.* · VERB V n · N-VAR

fab·ri·ca·tion /ˌfæbrɪˈkeɪʃən/. The **fabrication** of goods or materials is the making or manufacture of them. *...micro-circuit fabrication.* · N-UNCOUNT FORMAL

fabu·lous /ˈfæbjʊləs/. **1** If you describe something as **fabulous**, you are emphasizing that you like it a lot or think that it is very good. **2** If you talk about, for example, someone's **fabulous** success or wealth, you are emphasizing that they are extremely successful or wealthy. ◆ **fabu·lous·ly** *...their fabulously rich parents.* · ADJ-GRADED PRAGMATICS ADJ-GRADED PRAGMATICS · ADV-GRADED: ADV adj/adv

fa·cade /fəˈsɑːd/ **facades;** also spelled **façade. 1** The **facade** of a building, especially a large one, is its front wall or the wall that faces the street. **2** A **facade** is an outward appearance which is deliberately false and gives you a wrong impression about someone or something. *They hid the troubles plaguing their marriage behind a facade of family togetherness.* · N-SING

face 1 noun uses

face /feɪs/ **faces. 1** Your **face** is the front part of your head, where your mouth, eyes, and nose are. *He was going red in the face... She had a beautiful face. ...a sad face.* ◆ **-faced** *...a slim, thin-faced man... The committee walked out, grim-faced and shocked.* **2** If you have **a long face**, you look very unhappy or serious. **3** If you **make** or **pull a face**, you show a feeling by putting an exaggerated expression on your face, for example by sticking out your tongue. **4** If you manage to keep **a straight face**, you manage to look serious, although you want to laugh. **5** If you say that someone can do something **until** they are **blue in the face**, you are emphasizing that however much they do it, it will not make any difference. *You can criticise him until you're blue in the face, but you'll never change his personality.* **6** If you **put a brave face on** a bad · N-COUNT · COMB · PHRASE · PHRASE · PHRASE · PHRASE PRAGMATICS · PHRASE

situation or **put on a brave face**, you try not to show how disappointed or upset you are about the situation. In American English the expression **'put on a good face'** is also used. **7** If a feeling **is written all over** your **face** or **is written across** your **face**, it is very obvious to other people from your expression. *Relief and gratitude were written all over his face.* · PHRASE

8 If someone **laughs in** your **face**, they are openly disrespectful towards you. *We can't keep juveniles in custody. They just laugh in your face.* **9** You can say that someone **has set** their **face against** something to indicate that they are stubbornly opposed to it. *This Government has set its face against putting up income tax.* · PHRASE · PHRASE BRITISH

10 If you **show** your **face** somewhere, you go there and see people, although you are not welcome, are unwilling to go, or have not been there for some time. *If she shows her face again back in Massachusetts she'll find a warrant for her arrest waiting.* **11** If something that you have planned **blows up in** your **face**, it goes wrong unexpectedly, with the result that you suffer. **12** If an action or belief **flies in the face of** accepted ideas or rules, it seems to completely contradict them. *...scientific principles that seem to fly in the face of common sense.* **13** If you say something **to** someone's **face**, you say it openly in their presence. *Her opponent called her a liar to her face.* **14** If you come **face to face** with someone, you meet them and can talk to them or look at them directly. *...the first face-to-face meeting between the two men.* **15** If you come **face to face with** a problem, you cannot avoid or ignore it. *I was gradually being brought face to face with the fact that I had very little success.* **16** If you take a particular action or attitude **in the face of** a problem or difficulty, you respond to that problem or difficulty in that way. *The Prime Minister has called for national unity in the face of the violent anti-government protests.* · PHRASE · PHRASE · PHRASE · PHRASE · PHRASE · PHR-PREP

17 If you lose **face**, something happens which makes you appear weak and makes people respect or admire you less. *To cancel the airport would mean a loss of face for the present governor.* · N-UNCOUNT

18 If you say that **the face of** an area, institution, or field of activity is changing, you mean its appearance or nature is changing. *...the changing face of the British countryside... This would change the face of Malaysian politics.* **19** If you refer to **the** particular **face of** an activity, belief, or system, you mean one particular aspect of it, in contrast to other aspects. *He has become a symbol of the unacceptable face of Brussels bureaucracy.* **20** You say **on the face of it** when you are describing how something seems when it is first considered, in order to suggest that people's opinion may change when they know or think more about the subject. *On the face of it that seems to make sense. But the figures don't add up.* · N-SING: the N of n · N-SING: the adj N of n · PHRASE

21 The **face** of a cliff, mountain, or building is a vertical surface or side of it. *...the north face of the Eiger.* **22** The **face** of a clock or watch is the surface with the numbers and hands on it, which shows the time. **23** If someone or something is **face down**, their face or front points downwards. If they are **face up**, their face or front points upwards. *Charles laid down his cards face up.* · N-COUNT: with supp · N-COUNT · PHRASE

24 See also **about-face, bare-faced, face value, po-faced, poker-faced, red-faced, shamefaced, straight-faced, two-faced.** ● **to shut the door in** someone's **face**: see **door.** ● **to have egg** on your **face**: see **egg.** ● **to cut off** your **nose to spite** your **face**: see

nose. ● **shut your face**: see **shut**. ● **a slap in the face**: see **slap**.

face 2 verb and phrasal verb uses

face /feɪs/ **faces, facing, faced. 1** If someone or something **faces** a particular thing, person, or direction, they are positioned opposite that thing or person or are looking in that direction. *They stood facing each other... Face the wall... The garden faces south.* ◆◆◆◆◆ V n / V adv/prep

2 If you have to **face** someone, you have to stand or sit in front of them and talk to them, although it may be difficult or unpleasant. *He faced journalists and told them that there was still a lot to do to bring the economy under control.* **3** If you **are faced** with something difficult or unpleasant, or if it **faces** you, it is going to affect you and you have to deal with it. *Williams faces life in prison. ...the immense difficulties facing European businessmen in Russia... We are faced with a serious problem.* **4** If you **face** the truth, a fact, or a problem, you accept that it is true or really exists and respond to it in a suitable way, although you would prefer to ignore it. *He accused the Government of refusing to face facts about the economy.* ▶ **Face up to** means the same as **face**. *I have grown up now and I have to face up to my responsibilities.* **5** If you cannot **face** something, you do not feel able to do it because it seems so difficult or unpleasant. *My children want me with them for Christmas Day, but I can't face it... I couldn't face seeing anyone.* **6** You use the expression **'let's face it'** when you are stating a fact or making a comment which you think your listener may find unpleasant or be unwilling to admit. *She was always attracted to younger men. But, let's face it, who is not?* VERB V n / VERB V n / VERB V n / be V-ed with n / VERB V n / PHRASAL VB V P P n / VB: with neg V n/-ing / PHRASE PRAGMATICS

face down. If you **face down** an opponent, you defeat them by confronting them openly and refusing to change your mind. *He's confronted crowds before and faced them down.* PHRASAL VB V n P / Also V P noun

face up to. See **face** 5. PHRASAL VB

face·cloth /feɪsklɒθ, AM -klɔːθ/ **facecloths;** also spelled **face cloth**. A **facecloth** is the same as a **face flannel** or **washcloth**. N-COUNT

'face cream, face creams. Face cream is a thick substance that you rub into your face in order to keep it soft. N-VAR

'face flannel, face flannels. A **face flannel** is a small cloth which you use for washing yourself. The usual American word is **washcloth**. N-COUNT BRITISH

face·less /feɪsləs/. If you describe someone or something as **faceless**, you dislike them because they have no character or individuality. *...faceless bureaucrats.* ◆◇◇◇◇ ADJ PRAGMATICS

face·lift /feɪslɪft/ **facelifts;** also spelled **face lift**. **1** If you give a place or thing a **facelift**, you do something to make it look better or more attractive. *Nothing gives a room a faster facelift than a coat of paint.* **2** A **facelift** is an operation in which a surgeon tightens the skin on someone's face in order to make them look younger. N-COUNT / N-COUNT

'face pack, face packs. A **face pack** is a thick substance which you spread on your face, allow to dry for a short time, and then remove, in order to clean your skin thoroughly. N-COUNT

'face powder, face powders. Face powder is a very fine soft powder that you can put on your face in order to make it look smoother. N-VAR

'face-saving. A **face-saving** action or occurrence prevents damage to your reputation or prevents the loss of people's respect for you. *...a face-saving compromise.* ◆ **face-saver, face-savers.** A **face-saver** is a face-saving action or occurrence. *The START agreement offers an important political face-saver to the Kremlin.* ADJ: ADJ n / N-COUNT

fac·et /fæsɪt, -set/ **facets. 1** A **facet** of something is a single part or aspect of it. *The government is involved in every facet of people's lives.* **2** The **facets** of a diamond or other precious stone are the flat surfaces that have been cut on its outside. ◆◇◇◇◇ N-COUNT / N-COUNT

fa·cetious /fəˈsiːʃəs/. If you say that someone is being **facetious**, you are criticizing them because ADJ-GRADED PRAGMATICS

they are making funny remarks or saying things they do not mean in a situation where they ought to be serious. ◆ **fa·cetious·ly** *Al facetiously described himself as the Last Angry Man.* ADV-GRADED: ADV with v

face to 'face. See **face**.

face 'value. 1 The **face value** of things such as coins, banknotes, or tickets is their price or value as stated on the object itself. *Tickets were selling at twice their face value.* **2** If you take something **at face value**, you accept or believe it without thinking about it very much. ◆◇◇◇◇ N-SING / PHRASE

fa·cial /feɪʃəl/ **facials. 1** Facial means appearing on or being part of your face. *His facial expression didn't change. ...facial injuries.* **2** A **facial** is a beauty treatment in which someone's face is massaged, and creams and other substances are rubbed into it. ◆◆◇◇◇ ADJ: ADJ n / N-COUNT

facie /feɪʃiː/. See **prima facie**.

fac·ile /fæsaɪl, AM -səl/. If you describe someone's arguments or suggestions as **facile**, you are criticizing them because their ideas are too simple and indicate a lack of intelligent thinking. ADJ-GRADED PRAGMATICS

fa·cili·tate /fəˈsɪlɪteɪt/ **facilitates, facilitating, facilitated.** To **facilitate** an action or process means to make it easier or more likely to happen. *He's there to facilitate.* ◆ **fa·cili·ta·tor, facilitators.** A **facilitator** is a person or organization that helps another person or organization to do or to achieve a particular thing. ◆◇◇◇◇ VERB: V n / N-COUNT

fa·cil·ity /fəˈsɪlɪti/ **facilities. 1** Facilities are buildings, pieces of equipment, or services that are provided for a particular purpose. *...recreational facilities.* **2** A **facility** is an extra service, option, or feature provided by an organization or a machine. *...an overdraft facility... One of the new models has the facility to reproduce speech.* **3** If you have a **facility** for something, for example learning foreign languages, you find it easy to do. ◆◆◆◆◇ N-COUNT / N-COUNT: with supp / N-COUNT

fac·ing /feɪsɪŋ/ **facings.** A **facing** on a wall is a layer of stone, concrete, or other material that is spread over its surface to make it look attractive. N-VAR

fac·simi·le /fækˈsɪmɪli/ **facsimiles. 1** A **facsimile** of something is an copy or imitation of it. *...a facsimile of his writing desk. ...a facsimile edition of Beethoven's musical manuscripts.* **2** A **facsimile** is the same as a **fax**. N-COUNT FORMAL / N-COUNT FORMAL

fact /fækt/ **facts. 1** You use **the fact that** after some verbs and prepositions, for example in expressions such as **despite the fact that** and **apart from the fact that**, to link the verb or preposition with a clause. *Despite the fact that the disease is so prevalent, treatment is still far from satisfactory... My family now accepts the fact that I don't eat sugar or bread.* ◆◆◆◆ PHRASE PRAGMATICS

2 You use **in fact, in actual fact, as a matter of fact,** or **in point of fact** to indicate that you are giving more detailed information about what you have just said. *We've had a pretty bad time while you were away. In fact, we very nearly split up this time... He apologised as soon as he realised what he had done. In actual fact he wrote a nice little note to me.* **3** You use **in fact, in actual fact, as a matter of fact,** or **in point of fact** to introduce or draw attention to a comment that modifies, contradicts, or contrasts with a previous statement. *That sounds rather simple, but in fact it's very difficult... 'I guess you haven't eaten yet'—'As a matter of fact, I have.'* PHRASE PRAGMATICS / PHRASE PRAGMATICS

4 Facts are pieces of information that can be discovered. *His opponent swamped him with facts and figures... I'll also mention an interesting fact abut this type of fishing.* **5** When you refer to something as **fact**, you mean that it is true or correct. *...a statement of verifiable historical fact... How much was fact and how much fancy no one knew.* **6** If you say that you know something **for a fact**, you are emphasizing that you are completely certain that it is true. *I know for a fact that Graham has kept in close touch with Alan.* **7** You use **the fact is** or **the fact of the matter is** to introduce and draw attention to a summary or statement of the most important point about what you have been saying. *The fact is blindness hadn't stopped* N-COUNT / N-UNCOUNT / PHRASE PRAGMATICS / PHRASE PRAGMATICS

the children doing many of the things that sighted children enjoy. **8** You say **the fact remains** that something is the case when you want to emphasize that the situation must be realized and accepted. *His admirers claim that he came to power perfectly legally, but the fact remains that he did so by exploiting an illegal situation.* PHRASE PRAGMATICS

'fact-finding. If an official group goes on a **fact-finding** mission somewhere, they visit that place to get information about a particular situation. ◆◇◇◇◇ ADJ: ADJ n

fac·tion /'fækʃən/ **factions.** A faction is an organized group of people within a larger group, which opposes some of the ideas of the larger group and fights for its own ideas. *...the leaders of the country's warring factions.* ◆ **fac·tion·al** /'fækʃənəl/. Factional arguments or disputes involve two or more factions. ◆ **fac·tion·al·ism** /'fækʃənəlizəm/. *There has been a substantial amount of factionalism within the movement.* ◆◆◇◇ N-COUNT — ADJ — N-UNCOUNT

,fact of 'life, facts of life. 1 You say that something which is not pleasant is a **fact of life** when there is nothing you can do to change it. *Stress is a fact of life from time to time for all of us.* **2** If a parent tells a child **the facts of life**, he or she tells the child about how babies are conceived and born. ◆◇◇◇◇ N-COUNT — N-PLURAL: the N

fac·tor /'fæktə/ **factors, factoring, factored. 1** A **factor** is anything that affects an event, decision, or situation. *Physical activity is an important factor in maintaining fitness.* **2** If an amount increases, for example, by a **factor** of eight, it becomes eight times bigger. **3** You can use **factor** to refer to a particular level on a scale of measurement. *...a sun-cream with a protection factor of 8.* **4** In mathematics, a **factor** of a whole number is a smaller whole number which can be multiplied by another whole number to produce the first whole number. ◆◆◆◇ N-COUNT — N-COUNT — N-SING — N-COUNT

factor in or **factor into.** If you **factor** a particular cost or element **into** a calculation, or if you **factor** it **in**, you include it. *You'd better consider this and factor this into your decision making... How high would oil have to go now, factoring in inflation?* PHRASAL VB V n P n V P noun Also V n P AMERICAN

fac·to·ry /'fæktri/ **factories.** A **factory** is a large building where machines are used to make large quantities of goods. *...furniture factories.* ◆◆◆◇ N-COUNT

,factory 'floor. The **factory floor** means the workers in a factory, as opposed to the managers. It can also mean the area where they work. *He had worked on the factory floor for 16 years.* N-SING: the N

'fact sheet, fact sheets. A **fact sheet** is a short printed document with information about a particular subject. N-COUNT

fac·tual /'fæktʃuəl/. **Factual** means consisting of facts, or concerned with facts rather than, for example, personal opinions or artistic creation. *The editorial contained several factual errors... Any comparison that is not strictly factual runs the risk of being interpreted as subjective.* ◆ **fac·tu·al·ly** *A number of statements in my talk were factually wrong.* ◆◇◇◇◇ ADJ-GRADED — ADV-GRADED

fac·ul·ty /'fækəlti/ **faculties. 1** Your **faculties** are your physical and mental abilities. *He was drunk and not in control of his faculties. ...the faculty of hearing.* **2** In some universities or colleges, a **faculty** is a group of related departments. *...the Faculty of Social and Political Sciences.* ◆◆◇◇ N-COUNT — N-COUNT

fad /fæd/ **fads.** You use **fad** to refer to an activity or topic of interest that is very popular for a short time, but which people become bored with very quickly. *Hamnett does not believe environmental concern is a passing fad.* ◆◇◇◇ N-COUNT

fad·dish /'fædɪʃ/. If you describe something as **faddish**, you mean that it has no real value and that it will not remain popular for very long. *...faddish footwear.* ADJ-GRADED

fade /feɪd/ **fades, fading, faded. 1** When a coloured object **fades** or when the light **fades** it, it gradually becomes paler. *Ultraviolet will fade the colours in organic materials. ...fading portraits of the Queen.* ◆ **fad·ed** *...faded painted signs on the sides of some of the buildings.* **2** When a light or bright ◆◆◆◇ V-ERG: V V n V-ing — ADJ-GRADED VERB: V

object **fades**, it slowly becomes less bright, for example because it is moving further away. When a sound **fades**, it slowly becomes less loud. *They observed the comet for 70 days before it faded from sight... The sound of the last bomber's engines faded into the distance.* ▶ **Fade away** means the same as **fade**. *We watched the harbour and then the coastline fade away into the morning mist.* V from/into n — PHRASAL VB V P into n Also V P

3 If someone or something **fades**, they become hardly noticeable or very unimportant. *The most prominent poets of the Victorian period had all but faded from the scene.* ▶ **Fade away** means the same as **fade**. *Margaret Thatcher will not fade away into quiet retirement.* **4** If memories, feelings, or possibilities **fade**, they slowly become less strong. *Prospects for peace had already started to fade. ...fading memories of better days.* **5** If someone's smile **fades**, they slowly stop smiling. *Jay nodded, his smile fading.* VERB V into/from n — PHRASAL VB V P into n — VERB V-ing — VERB V

fade away. See **fade** 2 and 3. PHRASAL VB

fade out. 1 When something **fades out**, it slowly becomes less noticeable or less important until it disappears completely. *He thought her campaign would probably fade out soon in any case.* **2** When a light, image, or sound **fades out**, it disappears after gradually becoming weaker. PHRASAL VB V P Also V P of n — V P

fae·cal /'fiːkəl/; spelled **fecal** in American English. **Faecal** means referring or relating to faeces. ADJ FORMAL

fae·ces /'fiːsiːz/; spelled **feces** in American English. **Faeces** is the solid waste substance that people and animals get rid of from their body by excreting it through the anus. ◆◇◇◇ N-UNCOUNT FORMAL

fag /fæg/ **fags. 1** A **fag** is a cigarette. *...floors covered in fag ends and scraps of paper.* **2** A **fag** is a homosexual man; an offensive use. N-COUNT BRITISH, INFORMAL — N-COUNT

fag·got /'fægət/ **faggots.** A **faggot** is a homosexual man; an offensive word. N-COUNT

Fahr·en·heit /'færənhaɪt/. **Fahrenheit** is a scale for measuring temperature, in which water freezes at 32 degrees and boils at 212 degrees. It is represented by the symbol °F. *The temperature was already above 100 degrees Fahrenheit.* ▶ Also a noun. *...the boiling point of water in Fahrenheit.* ADJ: n/num ADJ — N-UNCOUNT

fail /feɪl/ **fails, failing, failed. 1** If you **fail** to do something that you were trying to do, or your attempt **fails**, you do not succeed in doing it. *The Workers' Party failed to win a single governorship... He failed in his attempt to take control of the company... We tried to develop plans for them to get along, which all failed miserably. ...a failed military offensive.* **2** You say **if all else fails** to suggest what could be done in a certain situation if all the other things you have tried are unsuccessful. *If all else fails, I could always drive a truck.* ◆◆◆◆◆ VERB V to-inf V in n V V-ed — PHRASE

3 If someone or something **fails** to do a particular thing that they should have done, they do not do it. *He failed to file tax returns for 1982... The bomb failed to explode.* ● You can use **I fail to see** or **I fail to understand** in order to introduce a statement which indicates that you do not agree with what someone has said or done. *That's how it was in my day and I fail to see why it should be different now.* **4** If someone **fails in** their duty or responsibilities, they do not do everything that they were obliged or expected to do. *Lawyers are accused of failing in their duties to advise clients of their rights.* **5** If someone **fails** you, they do not do what you had expected or trusted them to do. *...communities who feel that the political system has failed them.* **6** If a quality or ability that you have **fails** you or if it **fails**, it is not great or good enough in a particular situation to enable you to do what you need or want to do. *For once, the artist's fertile imagination failed him... Their courage failed.* VERB V to-inf FORMAL — PHRASE PRAGMATICS FORMAL — VERB V in n — VERB V n — VERB V n V

7 If something **fails**, it stops working properly, or does not do what it is supposed to do. *The lights mysteriously failed... Many food crops failed because of the drought.* **8** If a business, organization, or system **fails**, it becomes unable to continue in operation or in existence. *So far this year, 104 banks have failed. ...a failed hotel business.* **9** If something such as your health or a physical quality **is failing**, it is becoming VERB V — VERB V V-ed — VERB V-ing

gradually weaker or less effective. *Here in the hills, the light failed more quickly... An apparently failing memory is damaging for a national leader.* **10** If someone **fails** a test or examination, they do not reach the standard that is required.   VERB: V n

11 You use **without fail** to emphasize that something always happens. *He attended every meeting without fail.* **12** You use **without fail** to emphasize an order or a promise. *On the 30th you must without fail hand in some money for Alex.*   PHRASE PRAGMATICS   PHRASE PRAGMATICS

fail·ing /ˈfeɪlɪŋ/ **failings. 1** The **failings** of someone or something are their faults or unsatisfactory features. *He had invented an imaginary son, in order to make up for his real son's failings.* **2** You use **failing that** to introduce an alternative, in case what you have just said is not possible. *Talk things through, or failing that, write down your thoughts.*   ◆◇◇◇◇ N-COUNT   PHRASE

'fail-safe; also spelled **failsafe.** Something that is **fail-safe** is designed or made in such a way that nothing dangerous can happen if a part of it goes wrong. *Most electrically operated windows do have fail-safe devices.*   ADJ

fail·ure /ˈfeɪljə/ **failures. 1** **Failure** is a lack of success in doing or achieving something. *This policy is doomed to failure. ...feelings of failure.* **2** Your **failure** to do a particular thing is the fact that you do not do it, even though you were expected to do it. *...disgraceful failure to support British citizens arrested overseas.* **3** If someone or something is a **failure**, they are not successful. *The marriage was a failure... I just felt I had been a failure in my personal life.* **4** If someone has a **failure of** a particular quality or ability, they do not have it or show it at a time when it is needed. *There is, too, a simple failure of imagination.* **5** If there is a **failure** of something, for example a machine or part of the body, it stops working or developing properly. *...engine failures... He was being treated for kidney failure.* **6** If there is a **failure** of a business or bank, it is no longer able to continue operating. *Business failures rose 16% last month.*   ◆◆◆◇ N-UNCOUNT   N-UNCOUNT: N to-inf   N-COUNT   N-VAR: N ofn   N-VAR: with supp   N-VAR: with supp

faint /feɪnt/ **fainter, faintest; faints, fainting, fainted. 1** A **faint** sound, colour, mark, feeling, or quality has very little strength or intensity. *...the soft, faint sounds of water dripping... He could see faint lines in her face... There was still the faint hope deep within him.* ♦ **faint·ly** *He was already asleep in the bed, which smelled faintly of mildew... She felt faintly ridiculous.* **2** A **faint** attempt at something is cautious or uncertain, and is not very noticeable. *Caroline made a faint attempt at a laugh. ...the first faint warnings of a worldwide epidemic.* ♦ **faintly** *John smiled faintly and shook his head.* **3** If you **faint**, you lose consciousness for a short time, especially because of hunger, pain, heat, or shock. ▶ Also a noun. *She slumped to the ground in a faint.* **4** Someone who is **faint** feels weak and unsteady as if they are about to lose consciousness. *Toni suddenly felt faint.* ♦ **faint·ness** *One patient suffered headaches, nausea, and faintness.*   ◆◆◇◇◇ ADJ-GRADED   ADV-GRADED   ADJ-GRADED: ADJ n   ADV-GRADED: ADV after v   VERB: V   N-COUNT   ADJ-GRADED: v-link ADJ   N-UNCOUNT

faint·est /ˈfeɪntɪst/. You can use **faintest** for emphasis in negative statements. *He said yesterday that there was not 'the faintest possibility' that the government would bring in such a measure.*   ADJ-SUPERL: ADJ n, with neg PRAGMATICS

,faint-'hearted; also spelled **fainthearted. 1** If you describe someone as **faint-hearted**, you mean that they are not very confident and do not take strong action because they are afraid of failing. **2** If you say that something is **not for the faint-hearted**, you mean that it is an extreme example of its kind, and is not suitable for people who like only safe and familiar things. *It's a film about a serial killer and not for the faint-hearted.*   ADJ-GRADED   PHRASE

fair /feə/ **fairer, fairest; fairs. 1** Something or someone that is **fair** is reasonable, right, and just. *It didn't seem fair to leave out her father... Do you feel they're paying their fair share?... They could not get a fair trial in Los Angeles.* ♦ **fair·ly** *...solving their problems quickly and fairly... Water had to be shared fairly between individuals.* ♦ **fair·ness** *He*   ◆◆◆◇ ADJ-GRADED   ADV-GRADED   N-UNCOUNT

says the new document will guarantee fairness for blacks. ...concern about the fairness of the election campaign. **2** You use **fair** in expressions such as **to be fair** and **let's be fair** when you want to add a favourable comment about someone or something that has just been criticized. *To be fair, the team is young and not yet settled... And, let us be fair, some MPs do work hard.*   PHRASE PRAGMATICS

3 You use **fair enough** when you want to say that a statement, decision, or action seems reasonable to a certain extent, but that perhaps someone has gone beyond what is reasonable. *If you don't like it, fair enough, but that's hardly a justification to attack the whole thing.* **4** You say **fair enough** to acknowledge what someone has just said and to indicate that you understand it. *'The message was addressed to me and I don't see why I should show it to you.'—'Fair enough.'* **5** If you say that someone **plays fair**, you mean that they behave or act in a reasonable and honest way. **6** You use **fair** in expressions such as **It would be fair to say** in order to introduce a statement which you believe to be true and reasonable. *I think it's fair to say that it didn't sound quite right.* **7** If you say that someone won a competition **fair and square**, you mean that they won honestly and without cheating. *We were beaten fair and square.*   PHRASE PRAGMATICS   CONVENTION PRAGMATICS   PHRASE   PHRASE PRAGMATICS   PHRASE

8 A **fair** amount, degree, size, or distance is quite large. *I spent a fair bit of time finding directions.* **9** A **fair** guess or idea about something is one that is likely to be correct. *I have a fair idea of how difficult things can be.* **10** If you describe someone or something as **fair**, you mean that they are average in standard or quality. *Reimar had a fair command of English.* **11** Someone who is **fair**, or who has **fair** hair, has light-coloured hair. **12** **Fair** skin is very pale and usually burns easily. **13** When the weather is **fair**, it is quite sunny and not raining.   ADJ: ADJ n   ADJ: ADJ n   ADJ   ADJ-GRADED   ADJ-GRADED   ADJ-GRADED FORMAL

14 A **fair** is an event held in a park or field at which people pay to ride on various machines for amusement or try to win prizes in games. The usual American word is **carnival**. *...all the fun of the fair.* **15** A **fair** is an event at which people display and sell goods, especially goods of a particular type. *He travels to agricultural shows and country fairs. ...an antiques fair.* ● See also **trade fair. 16** ● **a fair crack of the whip**: see **crack**.   N-COUNT BRITISH   N-COUNT

,fair 'game. If you say that someone is **fair game**, you mean that it is acceptable to criticize or attack them. *Politicians were always considered fair game by cartoonists.*   N-UNCOUNT

fair·ground /ˈfeəɡraʊnd/ **fairgrounds.** A **fairground** is an area of land where a funfair is held.   ◆◇◇◇◇ N-COUNT

fair·ly /ˈfeəli/. **1** **Fairly** means to quite a large degree. *We did fairly well.* **2** You use **fairly** instead of 'very' to add emphasis to an adjective or adverb without making it sound too forceful. *Were you always fairly bright at school?... I'll have no income and no home and will need a job fairly badly.* **3** **Fairly** is used for emphasis when you are describing an action in an exaggerated way. *He fairly flew across the room.* **4** See also **fair**.   ◆◆◆◇ ADV: ADV adj/adv   ADV: ADV adj/adv PRAGMATICS   ADV: ADV before v PRAGMATICS

fair·ness /ˈfeənəs/. **1** You use **fairness** in expressions such as **in fairness to** and **in all fairness** when you want to add a favourable comment about someone or something that has just been criticized. *In fairness to Becker, he was suffering with a leg injury.* **2** See also **fair**.   ◆◇◇◇◇ PHRASE PRAGMATICS

,fair 'play. If you refer to someone's attitude or behaviour as **fair play**, you approve of it because it involves treating everyone in the same reasonable way. *He has an enormous sense of fair play.*   ◆◇◇◇◇ N-UNCOUNT PRAGMATICS

,fair 'sex. If a man talks about **the fair sex**, he is referring to women in general.   N-SING DATED

fair·way /ˈfeəweɪ/ **fairways.** The **fairway** on a golf course is the long strip of short grass between each tee and green.   ◆◇◇◇◇ N-COUNT

'fair-weather. If you describe a person as a **fair-weather** friend or supporter of someone, you disapprove of them because they only give their   ADJ: ADJ n PRAGMATICS

friendship or support when it is rewarding to do so, not during times of difficulty.

fairy /ˈfeəri/ **fairies.** **1** A **fairy** is an imaginary ◆◆◇◇◇ creature with magical powers. Fairies are often por- N-COUNT trayed as small people with wings. **2** If someone N-COUNT describes a man as a **fairy**, they disapprove of the PRAGMATICS fact that he is a homosexual; an offensive use.

fairy ˈgodmother. If you call a woman your **fairy** N-SING: **godmother**, you are saying in a humorous way that poss N she has been very helpful in your life.

fairy·land /ˈfeərilænd/ **fairylands.** **1** Fairyland is N-UNCOUNT the imaginary place where fairies live. **2** If you de- N-VAR scribe a place as a **fairyland**, you mean that it is so beautiful it seems magical. *If you came with me to one of my toy shops, you'd think you were stepping into a fairyland.*

ˈfairy lights. Fairy lights are small, coloured, elec- N-PLURAL tric lights that are hung up as decorations. BRITISH

ˈfairy story, fairy stories. A **fairy story** is the N-COUNT same as a **fairy tale**.

ˈfairy tale, fairy tales; also spelled **fairytale**. **1** A ◆◇◇◇◇ **fairy tale** is a story for children involving magical N-COUNT events and imaginary creatures. **2** A **fairy tale** place ADJ: ADJ n or situation is so wonderful that you can hardly be- lieve that it is real. *It was a fairytale romance.*

fait ac·com·pli /ˌfeɪt əˈkɒmpli, AM -ækoːmˈpliː/ N-COUNT **faits accomplis.** If something is a **fait accompli**, FORMAL it has already been done and cannot be changed. *They were being presented with a fait accompli.*

faith /feɪθ/ **faiths.** **1** If you have **faith** in someone ◆◆◆◇◇ or something, you feel confident about their ability N-UNCOUNT or goodness. *She had placed a great deal of faith in Mr Penleigh... People have lost faith in the British Parliament.* **2** A **faith** is a particular religion, for ex- N-COUNT ample Christianity, Buddhism, or Islam. **3** Faith is N-UNCOUNT strong religious belief in a particular God. *...his loss of his own religious faith.* **4** If you do something **in good faith**, you seriously be- PHRASE lieve that what you are doing is right, honest, or legal, even though this may not be the case. *This report was published in good faith but we regret any confusion which may have been caused.* **5** If you **keep faith with** PHRASE someone you have made a promise to or something you believe in, you continue to support them, even when this is difficult. If you **break faith with** them, you stop supporting them. *Mr Field accused the La- bour leader of breaking faith with working people.* **6** See also **article of faith, leap of faith.**

faith·ful /ˈfeɪθfʊl/ **faithfuls.** **1** Someone who is ◆◆◇◇◇ **faithful** to a person, organization, idea, or activity ADJ-GRADED remains firm in their dedication to them or support for them. *She had been faithful to her promise to guard this secret.* ► **The faithful** are people who are N-PLURAL: faithful to someone or something. *...gatherings of theN the Party faithful.* ◆ **faith·ful·ly** *She had served the* ADV-GRADED *police force faithfully for so many years.* **2** Someone ADJ-GRADED who is **faithful** to their husband, wife, or lover does not have a sexual relationship with anyone else. **3** The faithful are the group of people who believe N-PLURAL: in a particular religion. *The faithful revered him theN then as a prophet.* **4** A **faithful** account, version, or ADJ-GRADED copy of something represents or reproduces the original accurately. *Colin Welland's screenplay is faithful to the novel.* ◆ **faithfully** *I translate from* ADV-GRADED *one meaning to another as faithfully as I can.* **5** You PHRASE can refer to something or someone that has been reliable for a long time as an **old faithful.**

faith·ful·ly /ˈfeɪθfʊli/. When you start a formal or ◆◆◇◇◇ business letter with 'Dear Sir' or 'Dear Madam', you CONVENTION write **Yours faithfully** before your signature at the BRITISH end. The usual American expression is **Sincerely yours.** ● See also **faithful.**

ˈfaith healing; also spelled **faith-healing.** Faith N-UNCOUNT **healing** is the treatment of a sick person by some- one who believes that they are able to heal people through prayer or a supernatural power.

faith·less /ˈfeɪθləs/. If you say that someone is ADJ-GRADED **faithless**, you mean that they are disloyal or that they are dishonest.

fake /feɪk/ **fakes, faking, faked.** **1** A **fake** fur or ◆◆◇◇◇ a **fake** painting, for example, is a fur or painting that ADJ has been made to look valuable or genuine, al- though it is not. *The bank manager is said to have issued fake certificates.* ► A **fake** is something that is N-COUNT fake. *It is filled with famous works of art, and every one of them is a fake.* **2** If someone **fakes** some- VERB thing, they try to make it look genuine, although it V ; is not. *It's safer to fake a tan with make-up... He* V-ed *faked his own death. ...faked evidence.* **3** Someone N-COUNT who is a **fake** is not what they claim to be, for exam- ple because they do not have the qualifications that they claim to have. **4** If you **fake** a feeling, emotion, VERB or reaction, you pretend that you are experiencing it V n when you are not. *I leant against the glass partition and faked a yawn.*

fal·con /ˈfɔːlkən, ˈfælk-/. **falcons.** Falcons are birds N-COUNT of prey, some of which can be trained to hunt other birds and animals. Kestrels are a type of falcon.

fal·con·ry /ˈfɔːlkənri/. **Falconry** is the skill of N-UNCOUNT training falcons and hawks to hunt, and the sport of using them to hunt.

fall /fɔːl/ **falls, falling, fell, fallen.** **1** If someone ◆◆◆◆◆ or something **falls**, they move quickly downwards VERB onto or towards the ground. *Her father fell into the* V prep/adv *sea after a massive heart attack... Prince Charles has* V-ing *again fallen from his horse... He held the bag so that everything fell out... Bombs fell in the town... Twenty people were injured by falling masonry.* ► Also a N-COUNT noun. *...a fall from a bicycle.* **2** If a person or struc- VERB ture that is standing somewhere **falls**, they move V ; from their upright position, so that they are then ly- V prep/adv ing on the ground. *The woman gripped the shoul- ders of her man to stop herself from falling... We watched buildings fall on top of people and pets... He lost his balance and fell backwards.* ► Also a N-COUNT noun. *Mrs Briscoe had a bad fall last week.* ► **Fall** PHRASAL VB **down** means the same as **fall.** *I hit him so hard he* V P *fell down... The building fell down around them.* ◆ **fall·en** *A number of roads have been blocked by* ADJ: ADJ n *fallen trees.* **3** If you say that people **are falling over** PHRASE **themselves** to do something, you mean that they PRAGMATICS are very keen to do it, and often you mean that you INFORMAL disapprove of this. *Within days of his death those same people were falling over themselves to de- nounce him.* **4** When rain or snow **falls**, it comes VERB: V down from the sky. ► Also a noun. *One night there* N-COUNT *was a heavy fall of snow.* ● See also **rainfall, snow- fall.** **5** If you **fall** somewhere, you allow yourself to VERB drop there in a hurried or disorganized way. *He tore* V prep *his clothes off and fell into bed.* **6** If something **falls**, it decreases in amount, value, or VERB strength. *Output will fall by 6% in the EC... Her weight* V byn *fell to under seven stones... Oil product prices fell 0.2* V to/from n *per cent... The rate of convictions has fallen. ...falling* V amount *living standards.* ► Also a noun. *...a sharp fall in the* V-ing *value of the pound.* N-COUNT **7** If a powerful or successful person **falls**, they sud- VERB: V denly lose their power or position. *Mrs Thatcher fell* V from n *from power.* ► Also a noun. *...the fall of the military* N-SING *dictator... Her rise has mirrored his fall.* **8** If a place VERB **falls** in a war or election, an enemy army or a different V to n political party takes control of it. *The city of Zvornik has fallen after a three-day attack... Town after town fell to the Tories.* ► Also a noun. *...the fall of Rome.* **9** If N-SING someone **falls** in battle, they are killed. ◆ **fall·en.** The VERB: V **fallen** are people who have been killed in battle. **10** In LITERARY cricket, when a wicket **falls**, the team who are fielding VERB: V get one of the batsmen out. **11** You can use **fall** to show that someone or some- V-LINK thing passes into another state. For example, if some- V in/into/out one **falls ill**, they become ill. *It is almost impossible to* ofn *visit Florida without falling in love with the state... She* V adj *fell asleep... These women fall victim to exploitation.* V n **12** You can use **fall** in expressions like **fall open** and V-LINK **fall to pieces** to say that something accidentally V adv/prep comes open or breaks into pieces. *The book fell open at page 206.* **13** If you say that something or someone **falls into** a VERB particular group or category, you mean that they be- V into n

long in that group or category. *Both women fall into the highest-risk group.* **14** If the responsibility or blame for something **falls on** someone, they have to take the responsibility or the blame for it. *A vastly disproportionate burden falls on women for child care... A lot of suspicion fell on her.* **15** If a celebration or other special event **falls on** a particular day or date, it is on that day or date. VERB V on n WRITTEN / VERB: V on n

16 If silence or a feeling of sadness or tiredness **falls** on a group of people, they become silent, sad, or tired. *Silence fell on the passengers as the police checked identity cards.* **17** When light or shadow **falls** on something, it covers it. *...the shadow that suddenly fell across the doorway.* **18** If someone's hair or a garment **falls** in a certain way, it hangs downwards in that way. *Her hair was dressed in soft waves, falling on her cheek.* **19** If someone's eyes **fall** on something, they suddenly notice it. *As he laid the flowers on the table, his eye fell upon a note.* **20** When night or darkness **falls**, night begins and it becomes dark. VERB V on/over n WRITTEN / VERB V across/over/on n / V prep/adv / VERB V on/upon n WRITTEN / VERB: V

21 You can refer to a waterfall as the **falls**. *...Niagara Falls.* **22 Fall** is the season between summer and winter when the weather becomes cooler. The British word is **autumn**. *...in the fall of 1991... The Supreme Court will not hear the case until next fall.* **23** In the Christian religion, **the Fall** was the occasion when Adam and Eve sinned and God made them leave the Garden of Eden. **24** In some sports such as judo and wrestling, a **fall** is the act of throwing or forcing your opponent to the floor. N-PLURAL / N-VAR AMERICAN / N-PROPER: the N / N-COUNT

25 See also **fallen**. ● to **fall on** your **feet**: see **foot**. ● to **fall foul** of someone: see **foul**. ● to **fall flat**: see **flat**. ● to **fall from grace**: see **grace**. ● to **fall into place**: see **place**. ● to **fall into the trap**: see **trap**. ● to **fall by the wayside**: see **wayside**.

fall about. If you say that people **are falling about**, you mean that they are laughing a lot about something. *The men at the table fell about laughing.* PHRASAL VB VP / VP -ing BRITISH

fall apart. 1 If something **falls apart**, it breaks into pieces because it is old or badly made. *Bit by bit the building fell apart.* **2** If an organization or system **falls apart**, it becomes disorganized or unable to work effectively. *Europe's monetary system is falling apart.* **3** If you say that someone **is falling apart**, you mean that they are becoming emotionally disturbed and are unable to deal with the difficult situation that they are in. PHRASAL VB VP / VP / VP INFORMAL

fall away. 1 If something **falls away** from the thing it is attached to, it breaks off. *Two engines fell away from the plane.* **2** If you say that land **falls away**, you mean it slopes downwards from a particular point. *On either side of the tracks the ground fell away sharply.* **3** If the degree, amount, or size of something **falls away**, it decreases. *Demand began to fall away.* PHRASAL VB VP / VP / VP

fall back. 1 If you **fall back**, you move backwards a short distance away from someone or something. *He fell back in embarrassment... The congregation fell back from them slightly as they entered.* **2** If an army **falls back** during a battle or war, it retreats. VP / VP from n / VP

fall back on. If you **fall back on** something, you do it or use it after other things have failed. *Unable to defeat him by logical discussion, she fell back on her old habit of criticizing his speech.* PHRASAL VB VP P n

fall behind. If a person or project **falls behind**, they do not progress or produce something as fast as other people, or as fast as they should. *He missed school and fell behind... He faces losing his home after falling behind with the payments... Boris is falling behind all the top players... Construction work fell behind schedule.* PHRASAL VB VP / VP P n / VP with n

fall down. 1 See **fall 2**. **2** If an argument, organization, or person **falls down** on a particular point, they are weak or unsatisfactory on that point. *The report falls down on accuracy and balance... That is where his argument falls down.* PHRASAL VB VP on n / VP

fall for. 1 If you **fall for** someone, you are strongly attracted to them and start loving them. *I just fell for him right away.* **2** If you **fall for** a lie or trick, you believe it or are deceived by it. *It was just a line to get you out here, and you fell for it!* PHRASAL VB VP n / VP n

fall in. 1 If a roof or ceiling **falls in**, it collapses and PHRASAL VB

falls to the ground. **2** If you **fall in** behind or beside someone who is walking along, you start walking behind them or beside them. VP prep

fall into. If you **fall into** conversation or a discussion with someone, usually someone you have just met, you start having a conversation or discussion with them. PHRASAL VB VP n

fall in with. 1 If you **fall in with** an idea, plan, or system, you accept it. *Carmen's reluctance to fall in with Driver's plans led to trouble.* **2** If you **fall in with** someone, you become friends with them and start seeing them a lot. *At university, Taylor had fallen in with a small clique of literature students.* PHRASAL VB VP P n / VP P n

fall off. 1 If something **falls off**, it separates from the thing to which it was attached. *When your exhaust falls off, you have to replace it.* **2** If the degree, amount, or size of something **falls off**, it decreases. *Retail buying has fallen off.* PHRASAL VB VP / VP

fall on. If you **fall on** something when it arrives or appears, you eagerly seize it or welcome it. *They fell on the sandwiches with alacrity.* PHRASAL VB VP n

fall out. 1 If something such as a person's hair or a tooth **falls out**, it separates from their body. **2** If you **fall out** with someone, you have an argument and stop being friendly with them. *Mum and I used to fall out a lot.* **3** See also **fallout**. PHRASAL VB VP RECIP: V P with n pl-n V P

fall over. If a person or object that is standing **falls over**, they accidentally move from their upright position so that they are then lying on the ground or on the surface supporting them. *If he drinks more than two glasses of wine he falls over.* PHRASAL VB VP

fall through. If an arrangement, plan, or deal **falls through**, it fails to happen. *My house sale is just on the verge of falling through.* PHRASAL VB VP

fall to. 1 If a responsibility, duty, or opportunity **falls to** someone, it becomes their responsibility, duty, or opportunity. *No chances have fallen to him... It fell to me to get rid of them.* **2** If someone **falls to** doing something, they start doing it. *When she had departed, they fell to fighting among themselves.* PHRASAL VB VP n it V P n to-inf / VP -ing WRITTEN

fal·la·cy /ˈfæləsi/ **fallacies.** A fallacy is an idea which many people believe to be true, but which is false because it is based on incorrect information or faulty reasoning. *It's a fallacy that the affluent give relatively more to charity.* ♦ **fal·la·cious** /fəˈleɪʃəs/. *Their main argument is fallacious.* ◆◇◇◇◇ N-VAR / ADJ-GRADED

fall·back /ˈfɔːlbæk/. Someone's **fallback** position is what they will do if their plans do not succeed, or if something unexpected happens. ADJ: ADJ n JOURNALISM

fall·en /ˈfɔːlən/. **1 Fallen** is the past participle of **fall**. **2 Fallen** is used in religious or old-fashioned language to describe someone who has sinned or lost their virtue. *...Lucifer, the fallen angel. ...the Victorian cult of saving the fallen woman.* **3** See also **fall**. ADJ: ADJ n

'fall guy, fall guys. If someone is the **fall guy**, they are blamed for something which they did not do or which is not their fault. *He was made the fall guy for the affair.* N-COUNT INFORMAL

fal·lible /ˈfælɪbəl/. If you say that someone or something is **fallible**, you mean that they are not perfect and may make mistakes or fail. *They are only human and all too fallible.* ♦ **fal·libil·ity** /ˌfælɪˈbɪlɪti/ *Errors may have been made due to human fallibility.* ADJ-GRADED N-UNCOUNT

fal·lo·pian tube /fəˌləʊpiən ˈtjuːb, AM -ˈtuːb/ **fallopian tubes.** A woman's **fallopian tubes** are the two tubes in her body along which eggs pass from her ovaries to her uterus. ◆◇◇◇◇ N-COUNT

fall·out /ˈfɔːlaʊt/. **1 Fallout** is the radiation that affects a particular place or area after a nuclear explosion has taken place. *They were exposed to radioactive fallout.* **2** If you refer to the **fallout** from something that has happened, you mean the unpleasant consequences that follow it. *Grundy lost his job in the fallout from the incident.* ◆◇◇◇◇ N-UNCOUNT / N-UNCOUNT

fal·low /ˈfæləʊ/. **1 Fallow** land has been dug or ploughed but nothing has been sown or planted in it, usually so that the soil can recover its quality. *The fields lay fallow.* **2** A **fallow** period is a time when very little is being achieved. ADJ / ADJ

false /fɔːls/. **1** If something is **false**, it is incorrect, ◆◆◆◇◇ untrue, or mistaken. *The President was being given* ADJ *false information... He had deliberately given the hospital a false name and address.* ♦ **false·ly** *...a* ADV *man who is falsely accused of a crime.* ♦ **fal·sity** N-UNCOUNT /'fɔːlsɪti/ *There's no way we can tell the truth or falsity of any one story.* **2** You use **false** to describe ob- ADJ jects which are artificial but which are intended to look like the real thing or to be used instead of the real thing. *...the items she'd secreted in the false bottom of her suitcase. ...a set of false teeth.* **3** If you ADJ-GRADED describe a person or their behaviour as **false**, you PRAGMATICS are criticizing them for being insincere or for hiding their real feelings. *She bowed her head and smiled in false modesty... Even to himself the geniality rang false.* ♦ **falsely** *He was falsely jovial.* ADV-GRADED

false a'larm, false alarms. When you think N-COUNT something dangerous is about to happen, but then discover that you were mistaken, you can say that it was a **false alarm**. *...a bomb threat that turned out to be a false alarm.*

false·hood /'fɔːlshʊd/ **falsehoods. 1 Falsehood** is N-UNCOUNT the quality or fact of being untrue or of being a lie. *...a victory of truth over falsehood.* **2** A **falsehood** is N-COUNT a lie. *He accused them of knowingly spreading false-* FORMAL *hoods about him.*

false 'move. You use **one false move** to introduce PHRASE the very serious or disastrous consequences which will result if someone makes a mistake, even a very small one. *One false move and I knew Sarah would be dead.*

false 'start, false starts. 1 A **false start** is an at- ◆◇◇◇◇ tempt to start something, such as a speech, project, N-COUNT or plan, which fails because you were not properly prepared or ready to begin. **2** If there is a **false start** N-COUNT at the beginning of a race, one of the competitors moves before the starter has given the signal.

fal·set·to /fɔːl'setəʊ/ **falsettos.** If a man sings or N-COUNT speaks in a **falsetto**, his voice is high-pitched, and higher than a man's normal voice. *Even though it's high, it's not a falsetto voice.*

fal·si·fy /'fɔːlsɪfaɪ/ **falsifies, falsifying, falsi-** ◆◇◇◇◇ **fied.** If someone **falsifies** something, they change it VERB in a misleading way or add untrue details to it in or- V n der to deceive people. *Wise allegedly falsified bank records.* ♦ **fal·si·fi·ca·tion** /ˌfɔːlsɪfɪ'keɪʃən/ **falsifi-** N-VAR **cations** *...the falsification of evidence in court.*

fal·ter /'fɔːltə/ **falters, faltering, faltered. 1** If ◆◇◇◇◇ something **falters**, it weakens and seems likely to VERB collapse or to stop. *The economy is faltering. ...the* V *faltering peace process.* **2** If you **falter**, you hesitate V-ing or pause, because you are not confident about what VERB you are doing or saying. *As he neared the house his* V *steps faltered... Her voice faltered and she had to stop a moment to control it.* ♦ **fal·ter·ing** *'Now I feel I* ADJ *can do it,' he said in faltering English.*

fame /feɪm/. If you achieve **fame**, you become very ◆◆◇◇◇ well-known. *At the height of his fame, his every word* N-UNCOUNT *was valued... The film earned him international fame. ...her rise to fame and fortune.* ● **claim to fame**: see **claim.** ♦ **famed** *The city is famed for its* ADJ-GRADED *outdoor restaurants. ...the famed Brazilian photographer Sebastiao Salgado.*

fa·mil·ial /fə'mɪliəl/. **Familial** means relating to ADJ families in general, or typical of a family. *Of all the* FORMAL *familial relationships, daughter/father is the least studied.*

fa·mil·iar /fə'mɪliə/. **1** If someone or something is ◆◆◆◇◇ **familiar** to you, you recognize them or know them ADJ-GRADED well. *He talked of other cultures as if they were more familiar to him than his own... They are already familiar faces on our TV screens.* ♦ **fa·mili·ar·ity** N-UNCOUNT /fəmɪli'ærɪti/ *Tony was unnerved by the uncanny familiarity of her face.* **2** If you are **familiar with** ADJ-GRADED: something, you know or understand it well. *He was* v-link ADJ *not very familiar with the area. ...software developers* with n *familiar with the concepts of artificial intelligence.* ♦ **familiarity** *The enemy would always have the ad-* N-UNCOUNT *vantage of familiarity with the rugged terrain.* **3** If ADJ-GRADED someone you do not know well behaves in a **famili-** PRAGMATICS

ar way towards you, they treat you very informally in a way that you might find offensive; used showing disapproval. *John's 'crime' was being too familiar with the manager and calling him Gouldy.* ♦ **familiarity** *...the easy familiarity with which her* N-UNCOUNT host greeted the head waiter.* ♦ **fa·mili·ar·ly** ADV-GRADED *'Gerald, isn't it?' I began familiarly.*

fa·mil·iar·ize /fə'mɪliəraɪz/ **familiarizes, famil-** VERB: **iarizing, familiarized;** also spelled **familiarise** in V pron-refl British English. If you **familiarize** yourself **with** with n something, or if someone **familiarizes** you **with** it, V n with n you learn about it and start to understand it. *The goal of the experiment was to familiarize the people with the new laws.*

fa·mili·ar·ly /fə'mɪliəli/. **1** If you say that something PHRASE or someone is **familiarly known as** or **familiarly called** a particular thing, you are giving the name that people use informally to refer to it. *...Ann Hamilton's father, familiarly known as 'Dink'.* **2** See also **familiar.**

fami·ly /'fæmɪli/ **families. 1** A **family** is a group of ◆◆◆◆◆ people who are related to each other, especially N-COLL- parents and their children. *...a family of five... His* COUNT *family are completely behind him, whatever he decides... To him the family is the core of society... Does he have any family?* **2** When people talk about hav- N-COLL- ing a **family**, they sometimes mean having children. COUNT *They decided to start a family. ...couples with large families.* **3** When people talk about their **family**, N-COLL- they sometimes mean their ancestors. *Her family* COUNT *came to Los Angeles at the turn of the century. ...the history of mental illness in the family.* **4** You can ADJ: ADJ n use **family** to describe things that belong to a particular family. *He returned to the family home... I was working in the family business.* **5** You can use ADJ: ADJ n **family** to describe things that are designed to be used or enjoyed by both parents and children. *It had been designed as a family house... A wedding is a family event.* **6** A **family** of animals or plants is a N-COUNT: group of related species. *...foods in the cabbage* with supp *family, such as Brussels sprouts.*

family 'doctor, family doctors. A family doc- ◆◇◇◇◇ **tor** is a doctor who does not specialize in any par- N-COUNT ticular area of medicine, but who has a medical practice in which he or she treats all types of illness.

'family man, family men. A **family man** is a man N-COUNT who has a wife and children, especially one who enjoys spending time with them.

'family name, family names. Your **family name** N-COUNT is your surname.

family 'planning. Family planning is the prac- ◆◇◇◇◇ tice of using contraception to control the number of N-UNCOUNT children you have. *...a family planning clinic.*

family 'tree, family trees. A **family tree** is a N-COUNT chart that shows all the people in a family over many generations and their relationship to each other.

fam·ine /'fæmɪn/ **famines. Famine** is a serious ◆◆◇◇◇ shortage of food in a country, which may cause N-VAR many deaths. *Thousands of refugees are trapped by war, drought and famine.*

fam·ished /'fæmɪʃt/. If you are **famished**, you are ADJ very hungry. *Isn't dinner ready? I'm famished.* INFORMAL

fa·mous /'feɪməs/. Someone or something that is ◆◆◆◇◇ **famous** is very well-known. *New Orleans is famous* ADJ-GRADED *for its cuisine. ...England's most famous landscape artist.*

fa·mous·ly /'feɪmsli/. **1** You use **famously** to refer ◆◇◇◇◇ to a fact that is well-known, usually because it is re- ADV markable or extreme. *Authors are famously ignorant about the realities of publishing.* **2** If you get on fa- ADV **mously** with someone, you are very friendly with DATED, each other and enjoy meeting and being together. INFORMAL

fan /fæn/ **fans, fanning, fanned. 1** If you are a ◆◆◆◇◇ **fan** of someone or something, you admire them and N-COUNT are very interested in them. *If you're a Billy Crystal fan, you'll love this movie.* **2** A **fan** is a flat object that you hold in your hand and N-COUNT wave in order to move the air and make yourself feel cooler. **3** If you **fan** yourself or your face when you are VERB:

hot, you wave a fan or other flat object in order to make yourself feel cooler. *Mo kept bringing me out refreshments and fanning me as it was that hot.* **4** A **fan** is a piece of electrical or mechanical equipment with revolving blades which keeps a room or machine cool or which gets rid of unpleasant smells. *V pron-refl V n* *N-COUNT*

5 If you **fan** a fire, you wave something flat next to it in order to make it burn more strongly. *Old Maria was fanning the smoldering fire... Hot winds fan the flames.* **6** If someone **fans** an emotion such as fear, hatred, or passion, they deliberately do things to make people feel the emotion more strongly. *Students were fanning social unrest with their violent protests.* *VERB V n* *VERB V n*

7 ● to fan the flames: see **flame**.

fan out. 1 If a group of people or things **fan out**, they move forwards away from a particular point in different directions. *The main body of British, American, and French troops had fanned out to the west.* **2** If something **fans out** or if you **fan** it **out**, it spreads out or opens out into a flat, semi-circular shape. *The dress's full skirt fanned out in a bright circle... Korontzis fanned out the cards one by one.* *PHRASAL VB V P* *ERG V P V P noun Also V n P*

fa·nat·ic /fə'nætɪk/ **fanatics. 1** If you describe someone as a **fanatic**, you disapprove of them because you consider their behaviour or opinions to be very extreme. *The man is not a religious fanatic but I am a Christian.* ♦ **fa·nat·i·cal** /fə'nætɪkəl/ *As a boy he was a fanatical patriot.* ♦ **fa·nat·i·cal·ly** *He's fanatically hostile to trade unions.* **2** If you say that someone is a **fanatic**, you mean that they are very enthusiastic about a particular activity, sport, or way of life. *Both Rod and Phil are football fanatics.* **3** Fanatic means the same as **fanatical**. *◆◇◇◇◇ N-COUNT PRAGMATICS* *ADJ-GRADED* *ADV-GRADED* *INFORMAL* *ADJ-GRADED*

fa·nat·i·cism /fə'nætɪsɪzəm/. **Fanaticism** is extreme behaviour or opinions; used showing disapproval. *...intolerance and religious fanaticism.* *N-UNCOUNT PRAGMATICS*

'fan belt, fan belts. In a car engine, the **fan belt** is the belt that drives the fan which keeps the engine cool. *N-COUNT*

fan·ci·er /'fænsiə/ **fanciers.** An animal or plant **fancier** is a person who breeds animals or plants of a particular type or who is very interested in them. ● See also **fancy**. *◆◇◇◇◇ N-COUNT: supp N*

fan·ci·ful /'fænsɪfʊl/. **1** If you describe an idea as **fanciful**, you disapprove of it because you think it comes from someone's imagination, and is therefore unrealistic or unlikely to be true. *Designing silicon chips to mimic human organs sounds fanciful.* **2** If you describe the appearance of something as **fanciful**, you mean that it is unusual and elaborate rather than plain and simple. *...fanciful architecture.* *◆◇◇◇◇ ADJ-GRADED PRAGMATICS* *ADJ-GRADED*

'fan club, fan clubs. A **fan club** is an organized group of people who all admire the same person or thing, for example a pop singer or pop group. *◆◇◇◇◇ N-COUNT*

fancy 1 wanting, liking, or thinking

fan·cy /'fænsi/ **fancies, fancying, fancied. 1** If you **fancy** something, you want to have it or to do it. *Do you fancy going to see a movie sometime?... I just fancied a drink.* **2** A **fancy** is a liking or desire for someone or something, especially one that does not last long. *His interest was just a passing fancy.* **3** If you **take a fancy** to someone or something, you start liking them, usually for no understandable reason. *Sylvia took quite a fancy to him.* **4** If something **takes** your **fancy** or **tickles** your **fancy**, you like it a lot when you see it or think of it. *...copying any fashion which takes her fancy.* *◆◆◇◇◇ VERB V -ing/n BRITISH N-COUNT* *PHRASE* *PHRASE*

5 If you **fancy** someone, you feel attracted to them, especially in a sexual way. *'I didn't really fancy him anyway,' she said.* **6** If you **fancy** yourself, you think that you are very clever, attractive, or good at something, or think that you would be good at something if you tried it. *She fancies herself a bohemian... So you fancy yourself as the boss someday?* **7** If you **fancy** that something is the case, you think or suppose that it is so. *He fancied that he saw a shadow pass close to the window.* **8** A **fancy** is an idea that is unlikely, untrue, or imaginary. *...a childhood fancy. ...whims and fancies.* ● **flight of fancy:** see **flight**. *VERB: V n INFORMAL* *VERB: V pron-refl V pron-refl n/-ing V pron-refl as n* *VERB V that* *N-VAR LITERARY*

9 You say **'fancy'** or **'fancy that'** when you want to express surprise or disapproval. *Fancy coming to a funeral in brown boots!... 'Fancy that!' smiled Conti.* *EXCLAM PRAGMATICS*

fancy 2 elaborate or expensive

fan·cy /'fænsi/ **fancier, fanciest. 1** If you describe something as **fancy**, you mean that it is special, unusual, or elaborate. *...fancy jewellery.* **2** If you describe something as **fancy**, you mean that it is very expensive or of very high quality, and you often dislike it because of this. *They sent me to a fancy private school.* *◆◇◇◇◇ ADJ-GRADED* *ADJ-GRADED PRAGMATICS INFORMAL*

,fancy 'dress. Fancy dress is clothing that you wear for a party at which everyone tries to look like a famous person or a person from a story, from history, or from a particular profession. *N-UNCOUNT*

fan·dan·go /fæn'dæŋgəʊ/ **fandangos.** A **fandango** is a Spanish dance in which two people dance very close together. *N-COUNT*

fan·fare /'fænfeə/ **fanfares. 1** A **fanfare** is a short, loud tune played on trumpets or other similar instruments to announce a special event. **2** If something happens with a **fanfare**, it happens or is announced with a lot of publicity. *The company was privatised with a fanfare of publicity in 1986.* *◆◇◇◇◇* *N-VAR JOURNALISM*

fang /fæŋ/ **fangs. Fangs** are the two long, sharp, upper teeth that some animals have. *The cobra sank its venomous fangs into his hand.* *◆◇◇◇◇ N-COUNT*

fan·light /'fænlaɪt/ **fanlights.** A **fanlight** is a small window over a door or above another window. *N-COUNT*

fan·ny /'fæni/ **fannies. 1** Someone's **fanny** is their bottom; an informal use which some people find offensive. **2** A woman's **fanny** is her genitals; an informal use which some people find offensive. *N-COUNT AMERICAN* *N-COUNT BRITISH*

'fanny pack, fanny packs. A **fanny pack** consists of a pouch attached to a belt which you wear round your waist. You use it to carry money and keys. The British expression is **bum bag**. *N-COUNT AMERICAN*

fan·ta·sia /fæn'teɪziə, AM -ʒə/ **fantasias.** A **fantasia** is a piece of music that is not written in a traditional or fixed form. *N-COUNT TECHNICAL*

fan·ta·sist /'fæntəzɪst/ **fantasists.** A **fantasist** is someone who constantly tells lies about their life and achievements in order to make them sound more exciting than they really are. *N-COUNT*

fan·ta·size /'fæntəsaɪz/ **fantasizes, fantasizing, fantasized;** also spelled **fantasise** in British English. **1** If you **fantasize** about an event or situation that you would like to happen, you give yourself pleasure by imagining that it is happening, although it is untrue or unlikely to happen. *Her husband died in 1967, although she fantasised that he was still alive.* **2** If someone **fantasizes**, they try to excite themselves sexually by imagining a particular person or situation. *I tried to fantasize about Christine.* *◆◇◇◇◇* *VERB: V about/n/-ing V that Also V -ing* *VERB: V V about/over n*

fan·tas·tic /fæn'tæstɪk/. The form **fantastical** is also used for meaning 3. **1** If you say that something is **fantastic**, you are emphasizing that you think it is very good or that you like it a lot. *I have a fantastic social life.* **2** A **fantastic** amount or quantity is an extremely large one. *...fantastic amounts of money.* ♦ **fan·tas·ti·cal·ly** /fæn'tæstɪkli/ *...a fantastically expensive restaurant.* **3** You describe something as **fantastic** or **fantastical** when it seems strange and wonderful or unlikely. *The book has many fantastical aspects.* *◆◆◇◇◇ ADJ-GRADED PRAGMATICS INFORMAL* *ADJ: ADJ n INFORMAL* *ADV* *ADJ-GRADED*

fan·ta·sy /'fæntəzi/ **fantasies;** also spelled **phantasy. 1** A **fantasy** is a situation or event that you think about and that you want to happen, especially one that is unlikely to happen. *...fantasies of romance and true love.* **2** You can refer to a story or situation that someone creates from their imagination and that is not based on reality as **fantasy**. *The film is more of an ironic fantasy than a horror story.* **3** Fantasy is the activity of imagining things. *...a world of imagination, passion, fantasy, reflection.* *◆◆◆◇◇ N-COUNT* *N-VAR* *N-UNCOUNT*

fan·zine /'fænziːn/ **fanzines.** A **fanzine** is a magazine written by fans of, for example, a particular pop group or football team, for other fans to read. *◆◇◇◇◇ N-COUNT*

far /fɑː/ **farther** or **further, farthest** or **furthest. Far** has two comparatives, **farther** and **fur-** *◆◆◆◆◆*

ther, and two superlatives, **farthest** and **furthest**. **Farther** and **farthest** are used mainly in sense 1, and are dealt with here. **Further** and **furthest** are dealt with in separate entries.

1 If one place, thing, or person is **far** away from an- ADV-GRADED other, there is a great distance between them. *...a nice little Italian restaurant not far from here... Both of my sisters moved even farther away from home. ...the sea stretching out far below... Is it far?* **2** If you ask how **far** ADV-GRADED: a place is, you are asking what distance it is from you how ADV, or from another place. If you ask how **far** someone as/so ADV as went, you are asking what distance they travelled, or what place they reached. *How far is it to Malcy?... How far can you throw?... She followed the tracks as far as the road.* **3** When there are two things of the same ADJ: ADJ n kind in a place, the **far** one is the one that is a greater distance from you. *He had wandered to the far end of the room.* **4** You can use **far** to refer to the part of an ADJ: ADJ n area or object that is the greatest distance from the centre in a particular direction. *I wrote the date at the far left of the blackboard.*

5 A time or event that is **far** away in the future or the ADV-GRADED past is a long time from the present or from a particular point in time. *...hidden conflicts whose roots lie far back in time... I can't see any farther than the next six months... The first day of term seemed so far away.* **6** You can use **far** to talk about the extent or degree to ADV-GRADED which something happens or is true. *How far did the film tell the truth about Barnes Wallis?* **7** You can use ADV-GRADED **far** when talking about the progress that someone or something makes. *Discussions never progressed very far... I don't think Mr Cavanagh would get far with that trick.* **8** You can use **far** when talking about the ADV-GRADED: degree to which someone's behaviour or actions are ADV with v extreme. *It's still not clear how far the Russian parliament will go to implement its own plans... This time he's gone too far.* **9** You can use **far** in expressions like ADV-GRADED: 'I **wouldn't go that far**' and 'I **would go so far**' to indi- ADV after v cate to what extent you agree with something. *'Does it* PRAGMATICS *sound like music?'—'I wouldn't go that far.'... I would go so far as to say it's positively neurotic.* **10** You can ADV-GRADED: use **far** in expressions like '**as far as I know**' and '**so far** as/so ADV as **as I remember**' to indicate that you are not absolutely PRAGMATICS sure of the statement you are making. *It only lasted a couple of years, as far as I know... So far as I am aware, no proper investigation has ever been carried out.*

11 You can use **far** to mean 'very much' when you are ADV comparing two things and emphasizing the differ- PRAGMATICS ence between them. *Women who eat plenty of fresh vegetables are far less likely to suffer anxiety or depression... These trials are simply taking far too long. ...far in excess of one thousand million pounds.* **12** You use PHRASE the expression **far and away** when you are comparing PRAGMATICS something or someone with others of the same kind, in order to emphasize how great the difference is between them. *Rangers are far and away the best team in Scotland.* **13** You use the expression **by far** when you PHRASE are comparing something or someone with others of PRAGMATICS the same kind, in order to emphasize how great the difference is between them. *By far the most important issue for them is unemployment.*

14 You can describe people with extreme left-wing or ADJ: ADJ n right-wing political views as the **far** left or the **far** right.

15 If you say that something is **far from** a particular PHRASE thing or **far from** being the case, you are emphasizing PRAGMATICS that it is not that particular thing or not at all the case. *Much of what they recorded was far from the truth... It is still far from clear exactly what the Thais intend to do.* **16** You can use the expression '**far from it**' to em- PHRASE phasize a negative statement that you have just made. PRAGMATICS *Being dyslexic does not mean that one is unintelligent. Far from it.*

17 You say **far be it from me** to disagree, or **far be it** PHRASE **from me** to criticize, when you are disagreeing or PRAGMATICS criticizing and you want to appear less hostile. *Far be it from me to criticise, but shouldn't their mother take a share of the blame?*

18 If you say that something is good **as far as it goes** PHRASE or true **so far as it goes**, you mean that it is good or

true only to a limited extent. *His plan for tax relief is fine as far as it goes but will not be sufficient to get the economy moving again.*

19 Someone or something that is **far gone** is in such a PHRASE bad state or condition that not much can be done to help or improve them. *Many of the properties are in a desperate state but none is too far gone to save.*

20 Someone or something that is **not far wrong**, **not** PHRASE **far out**, or **not far off** is almost correct or almost accurate. *I hadn't been far wrong in my estimate.*

21 You can use the expression '**as far as I can see**' PHRASE when stating your opinion of a situation, to indicate PRAGMATICS that it is your personal opinion. *As far as I can see there are only two reasons for such an action.*

22 If you say that something only goes **so far** or can PHRASE only go **so far**, you mean that its extent, effect, or influence is limited. *Their loyalty only went so far.*

23 If you tell or ask someone what has happened **so** PHRASE **far**, you are telling or asking them what has happened up until the present point in a situation or story, and often implying that something different might happen later. *It's been quiet so far... So far, they have met with no success.*

24 You can say '**so far so good**' to express satisfaction PHRASE with the way that a situation or activity is progressing, developing, or happening.

25 Thus **far** means up until the present point in a PHRASE situation or story. *Thus far, the two prime ministers* FORMAL *have achieved no concrete results.*

26 If people come from **far and wide**, they come from PHRASE a large number of places, some of them far away. If things spread **far and wide**, they spread over a very large area or distance. *Volunteers came from far and wide... His fame spread far and wide.*

27 ● **as far as** I am **concerned**: see **concern**. ● **a far cry from**: see **cry**. ● **in so far as**: see **insofar as**. ● **near and far**: see **near**.

far·a·way /ˈfɑːrəˈweɪ/; also spelled **far-away**. **1** A ◆◇◇◇◇ **faraway** place is a long distance from you or from a ADJ-GRADED: particular place. *...photographs of a far away coun-* ADJ n *try.* **2** If you describe someone or their thoughts as ADJ-GRADED: **faraway**, you mean that they are thinking about ADJ n something that is very different from the situation around them. *...a faraway look in her eyes.*

farce /fɑːs/ **farces**. **1** A **farce** is a humorous play ◆◇◇◇◇ in which the characters become involved in compli- N-COUNT cated and unlikely situations. **2** Farce is the style of N-UNCOUNT acting and writing that is typical of farces. **3** If you N-SING: describe a situation or event as a **farce**, you mean also no det that it is so disorganized or ridiculous that you can- PRAGMATICS not take it seriously. *The elections have been reduced to a farce.*

far·ci·cal /ˈfɑːsɪkəl/. If you describe a situation or ADJ-GRADED event as **farcical**, you mean that it is so silly or ex- PRAGMATICS treme that you are unable to take it seriously.

fare /feə/ **fares, faring, fared**. **1** A **fare** is the ◆◆◆◇◇ money that you pay for a journey that you make. *He* N-COUNT *could barely afford the railway fare.* **2** The **fare** at a N-UNCOUNT restaurant or café is the type of food that is served WRITTEN there. *Traditional Portuguese fare in a traditional setting.* **3** If you say that someone or something VERB **fares** well or badly, you are referring to the degree V adv of success they achieve in a particular situation or activity. *It is unlikely that the marine industry will fare any better in September.*

Far 'East. The Far East is used to refer to all the ◆◇◇◇◇ countries of Eastern Asia, including China, Japan, N-PROPER: North and South Korea, and Indochina. the N

fare·well /ˌfeəˈwel/ **farewells**. Farewell means ◆◆◇◇◇ goodbye; an old-fashioned or literary word. ▶ Also a CONVENTION noun. *They said their farewells there at the cafe.* N-COUNT

far-'fetched. If you describe a story or idea as ADJ-GRADED **far-fetched**, you are criticizing it because you think PRAGMATICS it is unlikely to be true or practical. *The storyline was too far-fetched.*

far-'flung, farther-flung, farthest-flung. Far- ADJ-GRADED: **flung** places are a very long distance away from ADJ n where you are or from important places. *...the far-flung corners of Scotland.*

farm /fɑːm/ **farms, farming, farmed. 1** A **farm** ◆◆◆◇◇
is an area of land, together with the buildings on it, N-COUNT
that is used for growing crops or raising animals.
*Farms in France are much smaller than those in the
United States or even Britain.* **2** If you **farm** an area VERB: V n
of land, you grow crops or keep animals on it. *He* V
has lived and farmed in the area for 46 years.

farm out. If you say that someone **farms out** work, PHRASAL VB
especially work that you would normally expect them V P noun
to do themselves, you mean that they give it to other V n P
people to do. *...a trend for corporate legal staffs to do* V P noun to n
*more work in-house, instead of farming it out to law
firms... Farm out work to consultants.*

farm·er /ˈfɑːmə/ **farmers.** A **farmer** is a person ◆◆◆◇◇
who owns or manages a farm. N-COUNT

farm·hand /ˈfɑːmhænd/ **farmhands;** also spelled N-COUNT
farm hand. A **farmhand** is a person who is employed to work on a farm.

farm·house /ˈfɑːmhaʊs/ **farmhouses;** also ◆◇◇◇◇
spelled **farm house.** A **farmhouse** is the main house N-COUNT
on a farm, usually where the farmer lives.

farm·ing /ˈfɑːmɪŋ/. **Farming** is the activity of grow- ◆◆◇◇◇
ing crops or keeping animals on a farm. N-UNCOUNT

farm·land /ˈfɑːmlænd/ **farmlands. Farmland** is N-UNCOUNT:
land which is farmed, or is suitable for farming. also N in pl
N-COUNT

farm·yard /ˈfɑːmjɑːd/ **farmyards.** On a farm, the
farmyard is an area of land near the farmhouse
which is enclosed by walls or buildings.

,**far 'off, further off, furthest off. 1** If you de- ◆◇◇◇◇
scribe a moment in time as **far off**, you mean that it ADJ-GRADED
is a long time from the present. *European political
and monetary union is further off than ever.* **2** If you ADJ-GRADED
describe something as **far off**, you mean that it is a
long distance from you or from a particular place.
...stars in far-off galaxies. ▶ Also an adverb. *The* ADV-GRADED:
band was playing far off. ADV after v

,**far 'out;** also spelled **far-out.** If you describe ◆◇◇◇◇
something as **far out**, you mean that it is very ADJ-GRADED
strange or extreme. *We need to do something really* INFORMAL
far out.

far·ra·go /fəˈrɑːɡəʊ/ **farragoes** or **farragos.** If N-COUNT
you describe something as a **farrago**, you are criti- PRAGMATICS
cal of it because you think it is a confused mixture
of different types of things. *...a farrago of wild emotional outbursts and confused arguments.*

,**far-'reaching.** If you describe actions, events, or ◆◆◇◇◇
changes as **far-reaching**, you mean that they have a ADJ-GRADED
very great influence and affect a great number of
things. *...technology with far-reaching effects on human society.*

far·ri·er /ˈfærɪə/ **farriers.** A **farrier** is a person who N-COUNT
fits horseshoes onto horses.

,**far-'sighted. 1** If you describe someone as **far-** ADJ-GRADED
sighted, you admire them because they understand PRAGMATICS
what is likely to happen in the future, and consequently make wise decisions and plans. *Haven't
far-sighted economists been telling us for some time
now that in the future we will work less?*
2 Far-sighted people cannot see things clearly that ADJ-GRADED
are close to them, and therefore need to wear AMERICAN
glasses. The usual British expression is
long-sighted.

fart /fɑːt/ **farts, farting, farted. 1** If someone ◆◇◇◇◇
farts, air is forced out of their body through their VERB: V
anus; a use which some people find offensive. INFORMAL
▶ Also a noun. *...a loud fart.* **2** If someone de- N-COUNT
scribes another person as an old **fart**, they are N-COUNT
showing in a disrespectful way that they think the PRAGMATICS
person is boring; an offensive use. RUDE

far·ther /ˈfɑːðə/. **Farther** is a comparative form of
far.

far·thest /ˈfɑːðɪst/. **Farthest** is a superlative form of
far.

far·thing /ˈfɑːðɪŋ/ **farthings.** In Britain until 1961, N-COUNT
a **farthing** was a coin that was worth a quarter of an
old penny.

fas·cia /ˈfeɪʃə/ **fascias. 1** In a car, the **fascia** is the N-COUNT
part surrounding the instruments and dials. **2** The N-COUNT
fascia on a shop front is the flat surface above the BRITISH

shop window, on which the name of the shop is
written.

fas·ci·nate /ˈfæsɪneɪt/ **fascinates, fascinating,** ◆◇◇◇◇
fascinated. If something or someone **fascinates** VERB
you, you find them very interesting. *Politics fasci-* V n
nated Franklin's father. ◆ **fas·ci·nat·ed** *I sat on the* ADJ-GRADED
stairs and watched, fascinated. ◆ **fas·ci·nat·ing** ADJ-GRADED
*Madagascar is the most fascinating place I have ever
been to.*

fas·ci·na·tion /ˌfæsɪˈneɪʃən/ **fascinations. 1** Fas- ◆◇◇◇◇
cination is the state of being greatly interested in or N-UNCOUNT
delighted by something. *I've had a lifelong fascination with the sea.* **2** A **fascination** is something that N-COUNT
fascinates people. *...the fascinations of the British
Museum.*

fas·cism /ˈfæʃɪzəm/. **Fascism** is a set of right-wing ◆◆◇◇◇
political beliefs that includes strong control of soci- N-UNCOUNT
ety and the economy by the state, a powerful role
for the armed forces, and the prevention of political
opposition.

fas·cist /ˈfæʃɪst/ **fascists. 1** You use **fascist** to de- ◆◆◇◇◇
scribe organizations, ideas, or systems which follow ADJ
the principles of fascism. *...nationalist and fascist
organisations.* ▶ A **fascist** is someone who has fas- N-COUNT
cist views. **2** If you refer to someone as a **fascist**, N-COUNT
you are expressing disapproval of the fact that they PRAGMATICS
have extreme views on something, and do not tolerate alternative views. *...health fascists who would
meddle in their lives.*

fash·ion /ˈfæʃən/ **fashions, fashioning, fash-** ◆◆◆◆◇
ioned. 1 Fashion is the area of activity that in- N-UNCOUNT
volves styles of clothing and appearance. *...fashion
for men. ...the fashion world.* **2** A **fashion** is a style N-COUNT
of clothing or a way of behaving that is popular at a
particular time. *In the early seventies I wore false
eyelashes, as was the fashion.* ● See also **old-**
fashioned. 3 If something is **in fashion**, it is popu- PHRASE
lar and approved of at a particular time. If it is **out**
of fashion, it is not popular or approved of.
4 If you do something in a particular **fashion**, you do N-SING:
it in that way. *There is another drug called DHE that* with supp
works in a similar fashion. **5** If you say that something PHRASE
was done **after a fashion**, you mean that it was done,
but not very well. *She was educated – after a fashion.*
6 If you **fashion** an object or a work of art, you make it. VERB: V n

fash·ion·able /ˈfæʃənəbəl/. Someone or some- ◆◆◇◇◇
thing that is **fashionable** is popular or approved of ADJ-GRADED
at a particular time. *It became fashionable to eat certain kinds of fish. ...fashionable restaurants.* ◆ **fash-**
·ion·ably *...women who are perfectly made up and* ADV-GRADED
fashionably dressed.

fast /fɑːst, fæst/ **faster, fastest; fasts, fasting,** ◆◆◆◆◇
fasted. 1 Fast means happening, moving, or doing ADJ-GRADED
something at great speed. You also use **fast** in questions or statements about speed. *...fast cars with
flashing lights and sirens. ...a faster pace of political
reform... The only question is how fast the process
will be.* ▶ Also an adverb. *They work terrifically* ADV-GRADED:
fast... He is fast running out of time... How fast were ADV with v
you driving? **2** You use **fast** to say that something ADV-GRADED
happens without any delay. *We'd appreciate your* ADV after v
leaving as fast as possible. ▶ Also an adjective. *...an* ADJ-GRADED
astonishingly fast action on the part of Congress.
3 The **fast** lane on a motorway or other road is in- ADJ: ADJ n
tended for the vehicles which are travelling at the
greatest speeds.
4 If a watch or clock is **fast**, it is showing a time that is ADJ-GRADED:
later than the real time. v-link ADJ
5 If you hold something **fast**, you hold it tightly and ADV-GRADED:
firmly. If something is stuck **fast**, it is stuck very firmly ADV after v
and cannot move. *The tanker is stuck fast on the rocks.*
6 If you hold **fast** to a principle or idea, or if you stand ADV-GRADED:
fast, you do not change your mind about it. *Hold fast* ADV after v
to the age-old values of honesty and decency.
7 If colours or dyes are **fast**, they do not come out of ADJ-GRADED
the fabrics they are used on when they get wet.
8 A **fast** way of life is one which involves a lot of enjoy- ADJ: ADJ n
able and expensive or dangerous activities. *He wanted
the fast life of California.*
9 If you **fast**, you eat no food for a period of time, VERB: V

usually for either religious or medical reasons, or as a protest. ▶ Also a noun. *The fast is broken at sunset.* N-COUNT
♦ **fast·ing** ...*the Muslim holy month of fasting.* N-UNCOUNT
10 If you say that someone **has pulled a fast one** on you, you mean that they have cheated or tricked you. PHRASE *No doubt someone had pulled a fast one on her over a* INFORMAL *procedural matter.*
11 ● **fast asleep**: see **asleep**. ● **make a fast buck**: see **buck**.

fas·ten /'fɑːsən, 'fæs-/ **fastens, fastening, fas-** ◆◇◇◇◇ **tened. 1** When you **fasten** something, or when it V-ERG: V n **fastens**, you do it up or close it by means of buttons V prep or a strap, buckle, or other device. ...*the dress, which* Also V n prep *fastens with a long back zip.* **2** If you **fasten** one VERB thing to another, you attach the first thing to the se- V n prep/adv cond. *Fasten the carrying strap to the box.* ● See also **fastening**.
3 If someone or something **fastens** your attention on V-ERG: a particular thing, or if your attention **fastens** on it, V n on n you start to concentrate on it. *More and more her* V on n *memory and all her thoughts fastened on one event.* VERB
4 If someone or something **fastens** on a particular V on/onto n thing, they start to concentrate on it. *It's a gross over-simplification to fasten on to the red deer as a threat to the environment.*
5 If someone **fastens** on you, they keep following, VERB talking to, or staying with you, when you want them to V on/onto n go away. *He's fastening on that poor girl like a leech.*
fas·ten·er /'fɑːsənə, 'fæs-/ **fasteners.** A fastener is N-COUNT a device such as a button, zip, or small hook that fastens something, especially clothing.
fas·ten·ing /'fɑːsənɪŋ, 'fæs-/ **fastenings.** A fasten- N-COUNT ing is something such as a clasp, cord, or latch that you use to fasten something. *He fumbled with the fastenings of the long canvas bag.*

ˌfast ˈfood. Fast food is hot food that you buy, ◆◇◇◇◇ such as hamburgers and chips, which is served N-UNCOUNT quickly after you order it.

ˌfast ˈforward, fast forwards, fast forward- VERB: V n **ing, fast forwarded;** also spelled **fast-forward.** V n prep/adv When you **fast forward** the tape in a video or tape Also V recorder, or when you **fast forward**, you make the tape go forwards. Compare **rewind.** *He fast-forwarded the tape past the explosion.* ▶ To put a N-UNCOUNT tape on **fast forward** means to fast forward it.

fas·tid·i·ous /fæ'stɪdiəs/. **1** If you say that someone ◆◇◇◇◇ is **fastidious**, you mean that they pay great atten- ADJ-GRADED tion to detail because they like everything to be very neat, accurate, and orderly. *He was fastidious about his appearance.* ♦ **fas·tid·i·ous·ly** *He fastidiously* ADV-GRADED *copied every word of his notes onto clean paper.* **2** If ADJ-GRADED you say that someone is **fastidious**, you mean that they are concerned about cleanliness to an extent that many people consider to be too fussy. ♦ **fastidiously** ...*fastidiously clean.* ADV-GRADED

ˈfast track; also spelled **fast-track.** The **fast track** ◆◇◇◇◇ to a particular goal is the quickest route to achiev- N-SING ing it. *Many Croats and Slovenes saw independence as the fast track to democracy.*

fat /fæt/ **fatter, fattest; fats. 1** If you say that a ◆◆◆◇ person or animal is **fat**, you mean that they have a ADJ-GRADED lot of flesh on their body and that they weigh too PRAGMATICS much. You usually use the word **fat** when you think that this is a bad thing. *I could eat what I liked with-out getting fat.* ...*the fat woman in front of me.* ♦ **fat·ness** ...*a child's tendency towards fat-* N-UNCOUNT *ness.* **2** Fat is the extra flesh that animals and hu- N-UNCOUNT mans have under their skin, which is used to store energy and to help keep them warm. *Because you're not burning calories, everything you eat turns to fat.*
3 Fat is a solid or liquid substance obtained from N-VAR animals or vegetables, which is used in cooking. ...*vegetable fats, such as coconut oil and palm oil.*
4 Fat is a substance contained in foods such as N-VAR meat, cheese, and butter which forms an energy store in your body. ...*low-fat yogurts.*
5 A **fat** object, especially a book, is very thick or wide. ADJ-GRADED *He took out his fat wallet and peeled off some notes.* **6** A ADJ-GRADED: **fat** profit or fee is a large one. *They are set to make a big* N INFORMAL *fat profit.* **7** If you say that there is **fat chance** of some- PHRASE

thing happening, you mean that you do not believe INFORMAL that it will happen. *'Would your car be easy to steal?'—'Fat chance. I've got a device that shuts down* PHRASE *the gas and ignition.'* **8** If you say that a person or or- PRAGMATICS ganization **has grown fat** on something, you are criti-cizing the fact that they have become very rich as a re-sult of it. *Liverpool grew fat on the basis of the slave trade.*

fa·tal /'feɪtəl/. **1** A **fatal** action has very undesirable ◆◆◇◇ effects. *It would clearly be fatal for Europe to quarrel* ADJ-GRADED *seriously with America.* ♦ **fa·tal·ly** *Failure now* ADV-GRADED *could fatally damage his chances.* **2** A **fatal** accident ADJ or illness causes someone's death. ...*the fatal stab-bing of a police sergeant.* ♦ **fatally** *He was shot and* ADV *fatally injured.*
fa·tal·ism /'feɪtəlɪzəm/. **Fatalism** is a feeling that N-UNCOUNT you cannot control events or prevent unpleasant things from happening. ♦ **fa·tal·is·tic** *People we* ADJ-GRADED *spoke to today were really rather fatalistic about what's going to happen.*
fa·tal·ity /fə'tælɪti/ **fatalities. 1** A **fatality** is a ◆◇◇◇◇ death caused by an accident or by violence. ...*drunk* N-COUNT *driving fatalities.* **2** Fatality is the feeling or belief FORMAL that human beings cannot influence or control N-UNCOUNT events.

ˈfat cat, fat cats. If you refer to a businessman or N-COUNT politician as a **fat cat**, you are indicating that you PRAGMATICS disapprove of the way they use their wealth and power.

fate /feɪt/ **fates. 1** Fate is a power that some peo- ◆◆◇◇ ple believe controls and decides everything that N-UNCOUNT: happens, in a way that cannot be prevented or also N in pl changed. You can also refer to the **fates.** *I see no use quarrelling with fate.* **2** The **fate** of a person or thing N-COUNT is what happens to them. *The Russian Parliament will hold a special session later this month to decide his fate.* **3** If something **seals** a person's or thing's PHRASE **fate**, it makes it certain that they will fail or that something unpleasant will happen to them. *Two more penalty goals sealed Munster's fate.* ● to **tempt fate**: see **tempt**.

fat·ed /'feɪtɪd/. If you say that someone is **fated** to ◆◇◇◇◇ do something, or that something is **fated**, you mean ADJ that it seems to have been decided by fate before it happens, and nothing can be done to change it. *He was fated not to score.* ● See also **ill-fated.**

fate·ful /'feɪtfʊl/. If an action, or a time when an ◆◇◇◇◇ event occurred, is described as **fateful**, it is consid- ADJ-GRADED ered to have an important, and often disastrous, ef-fect on future events. *It was a fateful decision, one which was to break the Government.*

fa·ther /'fɑːðə/ **fathers, fathering, fathered.** ◆◆◆◆ **1** Your **father** is the man who made your mother N-FAMILY pregnant with you. You can also call someone your **father** if he brings you up as if he was this man. *His father was a painter... He would be a good father to my children.* **2** When a man **fathers** a child, he VERB: V n makes a woman pregnant and their child is born. V n by n *He fathered at least three children by the wives of other men.* **3** The man who invented or started N-COUNT: something is sometimes referred to as the **father of** N of n that thing. ...*Max Dupain, regarded as the father of modern photography.* **4** In some Christian N-VOC; churches, priests are addressed or referred to as **Fa-** N-TITLE **ther.** ...*Father William.* **5** Christians often refer to N-PROPER; God as **our Father** or address him as **Father.** N-VOC

ˌFather ˈChristmas. Father Christmas is an im- N-PROPER aginary old man with a long white beard and a red coat who is supposed to bring presents for children at Christmas.

ˈfather figure, father figures; also spelled N-COUNT **father-figure.** If someone is a **father figure** to you, you think of them as someone you can turn to for guidance, help, and protection, like a father.

father·hood /'fɑːðəhʊd/. **Fatherhood** is the state of N-UNCOUNT being a father. ...*the joys of fatherhood.*

ˈfather-in-law, fathers-in-law. Someone's ◆◇◇◇◇ **father-in-law** is the father of their husband or wife. N-COUNT

father·land /'fɑːðəlænd/ **fatherlands.** If someone ◆◇◇◇◇ is very proud of the country where they or their an- N-COUNT

cestors were born, they sometimes refer to it as the **fatherland**.

fa·ther·less /'fɑːðələs/. You describe children as **fatherless** when their father has died or does not live with them. *They were left fatherless.* ADJ

fa·ther·ly /'fɑːðəli/. **Fatherly** feelings or actions are like those of a kind father. ...*fatherly concern.* ADJ-GRADED

fath·om /'fæðəm/ **fathoms, fathoming, fathomed. 1** A **fathom** is a measurement of 1.8 metres or 6 feet, used when referring to the depth of water. **2** If you cannot **fathom** something, you cannot understand it, although you think carefully about it. *I really couldn't fathom what Steiner was talking about.* ◆◇◇◇◇ N-COUNT VERB: V n V wh

fa·tigue /fə'tiːg/ **fatigues. 1** Fatigue is a feeling of extreme physical or mental tiredness. ◆ **fa·tigued** *Winter weather can leave you feeling fatigued and tired.* ◆ **fa·tigu·ing** *Jet travel is undeniably fatiguing.* **2** You can say that people are suffering from a particular kind of **fatigue** when they have been doing something for a long time and feel that they can no longer continue to do it. ...*the result of four months of battle fatigue.* **3 Fatigues** are clothes that soldiers wear when they are doing routine jobs or when they are on the battlefield. **4 Fatigue** in metal or wood is a weakness in it that is caused by repeated stress, and that can cause the metal or wood to break. ◆◆◇◇◇ N-UNCOUNT ADJ-GRADED ADJ-GRADED N-UNCOUNT: with supp N-PLURAL N-UNCOUNT

fat·ten /'fætən/ **fattens, fattening, fattened. 1** If an animal **is fattened**, it becomes fatter as a result of eating more. *He hopes to fatten and sell the pigs... The snakes fatten and reproduce.* ► **Fatten up** means the same as **fatten**. *They fattened up ducks and geese... The rabbits fattened up nicely.* **2** If you say that someone is **fattening** something such as a business or its profits, you mean that they are increasing the value of the business or its profits, in a way that you disapprove of. ► **Fatten up** means the same as **fatten**. *The Government is making the taxpayer pay to fatten up a public sector business for private sale.* V-ERG: be V-ed V n V PHRASAL VB ERG V P noun V P VERB: V n PRAGMATICS PHRASAL VB V P noun Also V n P

fat·ten·ing /'fætənɪŋ/. Food that is **fattening** is thought to make people fat easily. PHRASAL VB ADJ-GRADED

fat·ty /'fæti/ **fattier, fattiest; fatties. 1** Fatty food contains a lot of fat. **2 Fatty** acids or fatty tissues contain or consist of fat. **3** If you call someone a **fatty**, you are criticizing or insulting them for being fat. ◆◆◇◇◇ ADJ-GRADED ADJ: ADJ n N-COUNT PRAGMATICS INFORMAL

fatu·ous /'fætʃʊəs/. If you describe a person, action, or remark as **fatuous**, you think that they are extremely silly. ADJ-GRADED PRAGMATICS FORMAL

fat·wa /'fætwɑː/ **fatwas;** also spelled **fatwah**. A **fatwa** is a religious decree issued by a Muslim leader. N-COUNT

fau·cet /'fɔːsɪt/ **faucets.** A **faucet** is a device that controls the flow of a liquid or gas from a pipe or container. Sinks and baths have faucets attached to them. The usual British word is **tap**. N-COUNT AMERICAN

fault /fɔːlt/ **faults, faulting, faulted. 1** If a bad or undesirable situation is your **fault**, you caused it or are responsible for it. *There was no escaping the fact: it was all his fault... Individuals had suffered hardship through no fault of their own.* **2** If someone or something is **at fault**, they are to blame or are responsible for a particular situation that has gone wrong. *He could never accept that he had been at fault.* **3** If you cannot **fault** someone, you cannot find any reason for criticizing them. *It is hard to fault the way he runs his own operation... You can't fault them for lack of invention.* **4** If you **find fault** with something or someone, you look for mistakes and complain about them. **5** A **fault** is a mistake in what someone is doing or in what they have done. *It is a big fault to think that you can learn how to manage people in business school.* **6** A **fault** in someone or something is a weakness or imperfection in them. *His manners had always made her blind to his faults. ...a short delay due to a minor technical fault.* ◆ **faulty** *Their interpretation was faulty... His car has faulty brakes.* **7** If you say that someone has a particular good quality **to a fault**, you ◆◆◇◇◇ N-SING: with poss PHRASE VB: with brd- neg V n V n for n/-ing PHRASE N-COUNT N-COUNT ADJ-GRADED PHRASE PRAGMATICS

are emphasizing that they have more of this quality than is usual or necessary. *Jefferson was generous to a fault.*

8 A **fault** is a large crack in the surface of the earth. ...*the San Andreas Fault.* **9** A **fault** in tennis is a service that is wrong according to the rules. N-COUNT N-COUNT

fault·less /'fɔːltləs/. Something that is **faultless** is perfect and has no mistakes at all. *Hans's English was faultless.* ◆ **fault·less·ly** *Howard was faultlessly dressed in a dark blue suit.* ◆◇◇◇◇ ADJ ADV

fau·na /'fɔːnə/ **faunas.** Animals, especially those in a particular area, can be referred to as **fauna**. Compare **flora**. *The Lake's remarkable flora and fauna are uniquely its own.* N-COLL-COUNT TECHNICAL

faux pas /ˌfəʊ 'pɑː/ **faux pas.** A faux pas is a socially embarrassing action or mistake. N-COUNT FORMAL

fa·vour /'feɪvə/ **favours, favouring, favoured;** spelled **favor** in American English. **1** If you regard something or someone with **favour**, you like or support them. *It remains to be seen if the show will still find favour with a 1990s audience... Such covert programmes are losing favour among American politicians.* **2** If you **favour** something, you prefer it to the other choices available. *They favour a transition to democracy.* ◆ **fa·voured** *The favoured candidate will probably emerge after private discussions.* **3** If you **favour** someone, you treat them better or more kindly than you treat other people. ◆ **favoured** *Her younger brother was the favoured child.* **4** If you are **in favour** of something, you support it and think that it is a good thing. *I wouldn't be in favour of income tax cuts... The vote passed with 111 in favour and 25 against.* **5** If someone or something is **in favour**, people like or support them. If they are **out of favour**, people no longer like or support them. **6** If someone makes a judgment **in your favour**, they decide that you are right. **7** If something is **in your favour**, it helps you or gives you an advantage. *The protection that farmers have enjoyed amounts to a bias in favour of the countryside.* **8** If one thing is rejected **in favour of** another, the second thing is done or chosen instead of the first. *He dropped socialism in favour of enterprise and the market economy.* **9** If you do someone a **favour**, you do something for them even though you do not have to. *I've come to ask you to do me a favour.* **10** If you say that one person gives or sells their **favours** to another, you mean that they have sex with the other person. *Actresses were still expected to give sexual favours in return for parts.* ◆◆◆◇ N-UNCOUNT VERB V n/-ing ADJ-GRADED VERB: V n ADJ-GRADED PHRASE PHRASE PHRASE PHRASE PHRASE N-COUNT N-PLURAL FORMAL

fa·vour·able /'feɪvərəbl/; spelled **favorable** in American English. **1** If your opinion or your reaction is **favourable** to something, you agree with it and approve of it. *We've already had a lot of favourable comment from customers... In Switzerland, banks and big companies are favourable to EC membership.* ◆ **fa·vour·ably** /'feɪvərəbli/. *He listened intently, and responded favourably to both my suggestions.* **2** If something makes a **favourable** impression on you or is **favourable** to you, you like it and approve of it. *These terms were favourable to India.* **3 Favourable** conditions make something more likely to succeed or seem more attractive. *It's believed the conditions in which the elections are being held are too favourable to the government. ...favourable weather conditions.* ◆ **favourably** *Japan is thus favourably placed to maintain its lead as the most successful manufacturing nation.* **4** If you make a **favourable** comparison between two things, you say that the first is better than or as good as the second. *The film bears favourable technical comparison with Hollywood productions costing 10 times as much.* ◆ **favourably** *These figures compare favourably with more established methods.* ◆◆◇◇◇ ADJ-GRADED: ADJ n, v-link ADJ to n ADV-GRADED ADJ-GRADED ADJ-GRADED ADV-GRADED ADJ-GRADED ADV-GRADED

fa·vour·ite /'feɪvərɪt/ **favourites;** spelled **favorite** in American English. **1** Your **favourite** thing or person of a particular type is the one you like most. *Her favourite writer is Hans Christian Andersen.* ► Also a noun. *I love all sports but soccer is my favourite.* **2** If one person is another person's **favourite**, the second person likes them a lot and treats them with ◆◆◆◇ ADJ: ADJ n N-COUNT N-COUNT

special kindness. ...*Robert Carr, Earl of Somerset, a favourite of King James I.* **3** The **favourite** in a race or contest is the runner or competitor that is expected to win. *The Belgian Cup has been won by the favourites F.C. Liege.* **4** If you refer to something as an **old favourite**, you mean that it has been in existence for a long time and everybody knows it or likes it. *...Vivaldi and Schubert and other old favourites.* `N-COUNT` `PHRASE`

fa·vour·it·ism /'feɪvərɪtɪzəm/; spelled **favoritism** in American English. If you accuse someone of **favouritism**, you disapprove of them because you think they unfairly help or favour one person or group. *Maria loved both the children. There was never a hint of favouritism.* `N-UNCOUNT` `PRAGMATICS`

fawn /fɔːn/ **fawns, fawning, fawned. 1** Fawn is a pale yellowish-brown colour. **2** A **fawn** is a very young deer. **3** If you say that someone **fawns** over a powerful or rich person, you disapprove of them because they flatter that person. *People fawn over you when you're famous. ...nauseatingly fawning journalism.* `◆◇◇◇◇` `COLOUR` `N-COUNT` `VERB` `PRAGMATICS` `V over/on/ around n` `V-ing`

fax /fæks/ **faxes, faxing, faxed. 1** A **fax** or a **fax machine** is a piece of equipment used to copy documents by sending information electronically along a telephone line, and to receive copies that are sent in this way. *These days, cartoonists send in their work by fax.* **2** If you **fax** a document to someone, you send it from one fax machine to another. *Did you fax him a reply?... Pop it in the post, or get your secretary to fax it.* ▶ Also a noun. *I sent him a long fax.* `◆◆◇◇◇` `N-COUNT: also by N` `VERB: V n to n V n n` `N-COUNT`

faze /feɪz/ **fazes, fazing, fazed.** If something does not **faze** you, it does not surprise or frighten you, and you are able to deal with it well. *Big concert halls do not faze Melanie.* `VB: no cont V n` `INFORMAL`

FBI /ˌef biː 'aɪ/. The **FBI** is a government agency in the United States that investigates crimes in which a national law is broken or in which the country's security is threatened. **FBI** is an abbreviation for 'Federal Bureau of Investigation'. `◆◆◇◇◇` `N-PROPER: the N`

fear /fɪə/ **fears, fearing, feared. 1** Fear is the unpleasant feeling you have when you think that you are in danger. *I was sitting on the floor shivering with fear. ...boyhood memories of sickness and fear of the dark.* **2** If you **fear** someone or something, you are frightened because you think that they will harm you. *It seems to me that if people fear you they respect you.* **3** If you **fear for** someone or something, you are very worried because you think that they might be in danger. *Carla fears for her son.* ▶ Also a noun. *There are fears for the safety of a 15-year-old girl.* **4** If you **fear** to do something, you are afraid to do it or you do not wish to do it. *Old people fear to leave their homes.* **5** If you **fear** something unpleasant or undesirable, you are worried that it might happen or might have happened. *She had feared she was going down with pneumonia... More than two million refugees have fled the area, fearing attack.* ▶ Also a noun. *My fear of failure always held me back in dealing with relationships... At the back of my mind is the fear that I will never see him again.* **6** If you say that there is a **fear** that something unpleasant or undesirable will happen, you mean that you think it is possible or likely. *There was no fear that anything would be misunderstood... Reporters were told that there was a real fear of an incoming attack.* **7** If you are **in fear of** doing or experiencing something unpleasant or undesirable, you are very worried that you might have to do it or experience it. *The elderly live in fear of assault and murder.* **8** You say you **fear** that a situation is the case when the situation is unpleasant or undesirable, and when you want to express sympathy, sorrow, or regret about it. *I fear that a land war now looks very probable... 'Is anything left at all?'— 'I fear not.'* **9** If you take a particular course of action **for fear of** something, you take the action in order to prevent that thing happening. *No one dared shoot for fear of hitting Pete.* **10** You say **'fear not'** or **'never fear'** to someone when you are telling them not to worry or be `◆◆◆◆◇` `N-VAR` `VERB V n` `VERB V for n N-VAR: N for n` `VERB V to-inf` `VERB V that V n` `N-VAR` `PHRASE` `VERB PRAGMATICS V that V so/not FORMAL` `PHRASE` `PHRASE DATED`

frightened. *Fear not, Darlene will protect me... You'll get the right training, never fear.* **11** If someone or something **puts the fear of God into** you, they frighten or worry you, often deliberately. `PHRASE`

fear·ful /'fɪəfʊl/. **1** If you are **fearful** of something, you are afraid of it. *Bankers were fearful of a world banking crisis.* **♦ fear·ful·ly** *'What are you going to do to me?' Alex asked fearfully.* **2** You use **fearful** to emphasize how serious or bad something is. *The region is in a fearful recession... You gave me a fearful shock!* **♦ fearfully** *This is fearfully expensive compared with the last one I bought.* `◆◇◇◇◇` `ADJ-GRADED FORMAL` `ADV` `ADJ-GRADED: ADJ n PRAGMATICS DATED` `ADV: ADV adj`

fear·less /'fɪələs/. If you say that someone is **fearless**, you mean that they are not afraid at all, and you admire them for this. *...his fearless campaigning for racial justice.* **♦ fear·less·ly** *...an honest and fearlessly outspoken politician.* `◆◇◇◇◇` `ADJ-GRADED PRAGMATICS` `ADV`

fear·some /'fɪəsəm/. **Fearsome** is used to describe things that are frightening, for example because of their large size or extreme nature. *...a fearsome array of weapons.* `◆◇◇◇◇` `ADJ-GRADED`

fea·sible /'fiːzəbəl/. If something is **feasible**, it can be done, made, or achieved. *She questioned whether it was feasible to stimulate investment in these regions... That may be fine for the US, but it's not feasible for a mass European market.* **♦ fea·sibil·ity** /ˌfiːzə'bɪlɪti/. *The committee will study the feasibility of setting up a national computer network.* `◆◇◇◇◇` `ADJ-GRADED` `N-UNCOUNT`

feast /fiːst/ **feasts, feasting, feasted. 1** A **feast** is a large and special meal. *...wedding feasts... A feast was given in King John's honour.* **2** If you **feast** on a particular food, you eat a large amount of it with great enjoyment. *We feasted on nuts and candies and cake.* **3** If you **feast**, you take part in a feast. *Their captors feasted in the castle's banqueting hall.* **♦ feast·ing** *The marriage is celebrated with much dancing and feasting.* **4** A **feast** is a day or time of the year when a special religious celebration takes place. *The Jewish feast of Passover began last night... St. Rose's feast day is August 30.* **5** You can refer to a large number of good, interesting, or enjoyable things as a **feast** of things. *This new series promises a feast of special effects and set designs... Chicago provides a feast for the ears of any music lover.* **6** If you **feast** your **eyes on** something, you look at it for a long time with great attention because you find it very attractive. *She stood feasting her eyes on the view.* `◆◆◇◇◇` `N-COUNT` `VERB V on n` `VERB V` `N-UNCOUNT` `N-COUNT` `N-SING: with supp` `PHRASE`

feat /fiːt/ **feats.** If you refer to an action, or the result of an action, as a **feat**, you admire it because it is an impressive and difficult achievement. *A racing car is an extraordinary feat of engineering.* `◆◆◇◇◇` `N-COUNT` `PRAGMATICS`

feath·er /'feðə/ **feathers. 1** A bird's **feathers** are the soft covering on its body. Each **feather** consists of a lot of smooth hairs on each side of a thin stiff centre. *...black ostrich feathers. ...a feather bed.* ● See also **feathered. 2** If you describe something that someone has achieved as a **feather in** their **cap**, you mean that they can be proud of it or that it might bring them some advantage. *Harry's appointment to this important post was a feather in his cap.* **3** ● **birds of a feather:** see **bird.** ● to **feather one's nest:** see **nest.** ● to **ruffle** someone's **feathers:** see **ruffle.** `◆◆◇◇◇` `N-COUNT` `PHRASE`

feather 'boa. See **boa.**

feath·ered /'feðəd/. If you describe something as **feathered**, you mean that it has feathers on it. *...the proud lady in the feathered hat.* `◆◇◇◇◇` `ADJ`

feather·weight /'feðəweɪt/ **featherweights.** A **featherweight** is a professional boxer who weighs between 53.5 and 57 kilograms, which is one of the lowest weight ranges. `◆◇◇◇◇` `N-COUNT`

feath·ery /'feðəri/. **1** If something is **feathery**, it has an edge divided into a lot of thin parts so that it looks soft. *The foliage was soft and feathery.* **2** **Feathery** things are soft and light. *...flurries of small, feathery flakes of snow.* `ADJ-GRADED` `ADJ-GRADED`

fea·ture /'fiːtʃə/ **features, featuring, featured. 1** A **feature** of something is an interesting or important part or characteristic of it. *The spacious gardens are a special feature of this property.* **2** Your **features** `◆◆◆◇` `N-COUNT: with supp` `N-PLURAL`

are your eyes, nose, mouth, and other parts of your face. *Her features were strongly defined.* **3** When something such as a film or exhibition **features** someone or something, they are an important part of it. *This spectacular event, now in its 5th year, features a stunning catwalk show.* **4** If someone or something **features** in something such as a show, exhibition, or magazine, they are an important part of it. *Jon featured in one of the show's most thrilling episodes.* **5** A **feature** is a special article in a newspaper or magazine, or a special programme on radio or television. *...a special feature on the fundraising project.*

VERB
V n

VERB
V in/on n

N-COUNT

'feature film, feature films. A **feature film** is a full-length film about a fictional situation, as opposed to a short film or a documentary.

N-COUNT

fea·ture·less /ˈfiːtʃələs/. If you say that something is **featureless**, you mean that it has no interesting features or characteristics. *Malone looked out at the grey-green featureless landscape.*

ADJ-GRADED

Feb. Feb. is a written abbreviation for **February**.

fe·brile /ˈfiːbraɪl/. **Febrile** behaviour is intensely and nervously active. *The news plunged the nation into a febrile, agitated state.*

ADJ-GRADED
LITERARY

Feb·ru·ary /ˈfebjʊəri, AM -jʊeri/ **Februaries.** **February** is the second month of the year in the Western calendar. See Appendix headed **Dates**.

N-VAR

fe·cal /ˈfiːkəl/. See **faecal**.

fe·ces /ˈfiːsiːz/. See **faeces**.

feck·less /ˈfekləs/. If you describe someone as **feckless**, you mean that they lack determination or strength, and are unable to do anything properly.

ADJ-GRADED
FORMAL

fe·cund /ˈfiːkənd, ˈfek-/. When you are talking about living things or natural processes, **fecund** means the same as **fertile**. ♦ **fe·cun·dity** /fɪˈkʌndɪti/ *...an island famous for the profusion and fecundity of its bird life.*

ADJ-GRADED
FORMAL

N-UNCOUNT

fed /fed/ **feds**. **1** **Fed** is the past tense and past participle of **feed**. See also **fed up**. **2** The **feds** are agents for the American security agency, the FBI.

N-COUNT
INFORMAL

fed·er·al /ˈfedərəl/ **federals**. **1** A **federal** country or system of government is one in which the different states or provinces of the country have important powers to make their own laws and decisions. *Five of the six provinces are to become autonomous regions in a new federal system of government.* **2** Some people use **federal** to describe a system of government which they disapprove of, in which the different states or provinces are controlled by a strong central government. *He does not believe in a federal Europe with centralising powers.* **3** **Federal** means belonging or relating to the national government of a federal country rather than to one of the states within it. *The federal government controls just 6% of the education budget. ...a federal judge.* ♦ **fed·er·al·ly** *...residents of public housing and federally subsidized apartments.* **4** **Federals** are the same as **feds**.

ADJ-GRADED:
ADJ n

ADJ-GRADED:
ADJ n
PRAGMATICS

ADJ: ADJ n

ADV:
ADV -ed
N-COUNT

fed·er·al·ism /ˈfedərəlɪzəm/. **Federalism** is belief in or support for a federal system of government, or this system itself. *They argue that the amendment undermines Canadian federalism.* ♦ **fed·er·al·ist, federalists**. *Many Quebeckers are federalists. ...the federalist idea of Europe.*

N-UNCOUNT

N-COUNT

fed·er·at·ed /ˈfedəreɪtɪd/. **Federated** states or societies are ones that have joined together for a common purpose.

ADJ:
ADJ n,
v-link ADJ to n

fed·era·tion /ˌfedəˈreɪʃən/ **federations**. **1** A **federation** is a federal country. *...the Russian Federation.* **2** A **federation** is a group of societies or other organizations which have joined together, usually because they share a common interest. *...the British Athletic Federation.*

N-COUNT

N-COUNT

fe·do·ra /fɪˈdɔːrə/ **fedoras**. A **fedora** is a soft hat with a brim.

N-COUNT

,fed 'up. If you are **fed up**, you are unhappy or bored with something, especially something that you have been experiencing for a long time. *I am fed up with reading how women should dress to please men.*

ADJ-GRADED:
v-link ADJ
INFORMAL

fee /fiː/ **fees**. **1** A **fee** is a sum of money that you pay to be allowed to do something. *...his television licence fee.* **2** A **fee** is the amount of money that someone is paid for a particular job or service that they provide. *...solicitor's fees.*

N-COUNT

N-COUNT

fee·ble /ˈfiːbəl/ **feebler, feeblest**. **1** If you describe someone or something as **feeble**, you mean that they are weak. *He was old and feeble.* ♦ **fee·bly** *His left hand moved feebly at his side.* **2** If you describe someone as **feeble**, you are criticizing them because they are afraid of taking strong action or seem to make no effort. *The Government had been feeble.* **3** If you describe something that someone says as **feeble**, you mean that it is not very good or convincing. *This is a particularly feeble argument.* ♦ **feebly** *I said 'Sorry', very feebly, feeling rather embarrassed.*

ADJ-GRADED

ADV-GRADED:
ADV with v
ADJ-GRADED
PRAGMATICS

ADJ-GRADED

ADV-GRADED:
ADV with v

feed /fiːd/ **feeds, feeding, fed**. **1** If you **feed** a person or animal, you give them food to eat. *She fed him a cookie... He fed me on barbecue ribs... He spooned the ice cream into a cup and fed it to her... The cow becomes unable to move or to feed itself.* ▶ Also a noun in British English. *She's had a good feed.* ♦ **feed·ing, feedings** *...the feeding of dairy cows.* **2** To **feed** a family or a community means to supply food for them. *Feeding a hungry family can be expensive... Russia can feed itself, because of its rich resources.* **3** ● **to bite the hand that feeds you**: see **bite**. ● **another mouth to feed**: see **mouth**. **4** When an animal **feeds**, it eats or drinks something. *Slugs feed on decaying plant and animal material.* **5** When a baby **feeds**, it drinks breast milk or milk from its bottle. *When a baby is thirsty, it feeds more often.* **6** Animal **feed** is food given to animals, especially farm animals. **7** To **feed** something to a place means to supply it to that place in a steady flow. *...blood vessels that feed blood to the brain.* **8** If you **feed** one thing into another, you put it into it. *She was feeding documents into a paper shredder.* **9** To **feed** information into a computer means to gradually put it into it. **10** If someone **feeds** you false or secret information, they deliberately tell it to you. *One British officer was feeding him with classified information.* **11** If you **feed** someone's dislike or desire for something, you make it stronger. *The divorce was painfully public, feeding her dislike of the press.* **12** If one thing **feeds** on another, it becomes stronger as a result of the other thing's existence. *The drinking and the guilt fed on each other.*

VERB: V n
V n n
V n on/with n
V n to n
V pron-refl

N-VAR

VERB
V n
V pron-refl

VERB: V
V on/on f n
VERB: V

N-VAR

VERB
V n prep

VERB
V n prep

VERB
V n into/to n
VERB: V n n
V n with n
Also V n in n

VERB
V n

VERB
V on n

feed up. If you **feed** someone **up**, you make them eat extra food so that they put on weight. *She is too thin. Feed her up a bit.*

PHRASAL VB
V n P
Also V P noun

feed·back /ˈfiːdbæk/. **1** If you get **feedback** on your work or progress, someone tells you how well or badly you are doing. **2** **Feedback** is the unpleasant whistling sound you get in a piece of electrical equipment when part of its power goes back into it.

N-COUNT

N-UNCOUNT

feed·er /ˈfiːdə/ **feeders**. **1** A **feeder** road, railway, or river is a smaller one that leads to a more important one. **2** A **feeder** is a container that you fill with food for birds or animals. *She went outside to put seed in her bird feeder.*

ADJ: ADJ n

N-COUNT

'feeding ground, feeding grounds. The **feeding ground** of a group of animals or birds is the place where they find food and eat. *The mud is a feeding ground for large numbers of birds.*

N-COUNT

feel /fiːl/ **feels, feeling, felt**. **1** If you **feel** a particular emotion or physical sensation, you experience it. *I am feeling very depressed... I felt a sharp pain in my shoulder... I felt as if all my strength had gone.* **2** If you talk about how an experience or event **feels**, you are describing the emotions and sensations connected with it. *It feels good to have finished a piece of work... The speed at which everything moved felt strange... It felt like I'd had two babies instead of one... Going to the mountains feels like going home.* **3** If you talk about how an object **feels**, you talk about

V-LINK
V adj
V n
V as if/like

V-LINK: no cont
it V adj to-inf/that
V adj
it V as if/like
V like -ing/n

V-LINK

the physical quality that you notice when you touch it. `V adj V like n` *The metal felt smooth and cold. ...when the clay feels like putty.* ▶ Also a noun. *He remembered the feel of* `N-SING` *her skin.* **4** If you **feel** an object, you touch it deliber- `VERB` ately with your hand, so that you learn what it is like, `V n` for example what shape it is or whether it is rough or `V wh` smooth. *The doctor felt his head... Feel how soft the* `V prep/adv` *skin is... She felt inside the tin.* **5** If you can **feel** some- `VB: no cont,` thing, you are aware of it because it is touching you. `V n` *He felt her leg against his.* **6** If you **feel** something hap- `V n prep/adv` pening, you become aware of it because of the effect it `VERB:` has on your body. *He felt something move beside* `V n-ing` *him... She felt herself lifted from her feet.* `V n inf` `V pron-refl -ed`

7 If you talk about how the weather **feels**, you de- `V-LINK` scribe the weather. *It felt wintry cold that day.* `it V adj`

8 If you **feel** yourself doing something or being in a `VERB:` particular state, you are aware that something is hap- `V n-ing` pening to you which you are unable to control. *I felt* `V n inf` *myself blush... I actually felt my heart quicken.* **9** If you `VB: no cont,` **feel** something such as someone's presence, you be- `V n` come aware of it, even though you cannot see or hear `V that` it. *I could feel that a man was watching me... He almost* `V n-ing` *felt her wincing at the other end of the telephone.*

10 If you **feel** that something is the case, you have a `VB: no cont,` strong idea in your mind that it is the case. *I feel cer-* `V that` *tain that it will all turn out well... I never felt myself a* `V adj that` *real child of the sixties... She felt him to be responsible.* `V pron-refl n` `V n to-inf`

11 If you **feel** that you should do something, you `VB: no cont,` think that you should do it. *You need not feel obliged to* `V-ed to-inf` *contribute... They felt under no obligation to maintain* `V under n` *their employees.* **12** If you talk about how you **feel** `VB: no cont,` about something, you talk about your opinion, atti- `V about n` tude, or reaction to it. *She feels guilty about spending* `V adj/adv` *less time lately with her two kids... He feels deep regret* `about n` *about his friend's death.* `V n about n`

13 If you **feel** like doing something or having some- `VERB` thing, you want to do it or have it because you are in `V like-ing/n` the right mood for it or think you would enjoy it. *Nei-* *ther of them felt like going back to sleep.*

14 If you **feel** the effect or result of something, you ex- `VERB` perience it. *The charity is still feeling the effects of rev-* `V n` *elations about its one-time president.*

15 The **feel** of something, for example a place, is the `N-SING:` general impression that it gives you. *The room has a* `with supp` *warm, cosy feel.* ● If you **get the feel of** something, for `PHRASE` example a place or a new activity, you become famili- ar with it. *He wanted to get the feel of the place.*

16 See also **feeling**, **felt**. ● to **feel** something **in your** **bones**: see **bone**. ● **feel free**: see **free**.

feel for. 1 If you **feel for** something, for example in `PHRASAL VB` the dark, you try to find it by moving your hand `V P n` around until you touch it. *I felt for my wallet... I felt* `V adv/prep P n` *around for a roof light.*
2 If you **feel for** someone, you have sympathy for `V P n` them. *I really felt for her.*

feel·er /ˈfiːlə/ **feelers. 1** An insect's **feelers** are the `N-COUNT` two thin stalks on its head with which it touches and senses things. See picture headed **insects**. **2** If `N-PLURAL` you put out **feelers**, you make careful discreet con- tacts with people in order to get information from them, or to find out what their reaction will be to a later suggestion. *When vacancies occur, the office* *puts out feelers to the universities.*

feel·good /ˈfiːlɡʊd/ **1** A **feelgood** film presents `ADJ: ADJ n` people and life in a way that makes you feel happy and optimistic after seeing it. **2** When journalists re- `PHRASE` fer to **the feelgood factor**, they mean that people are feeling hopeful and optimistic about the future.

feel·ing /ˈfiːlɪŋ/ **feelings. 1** A **feeling** is an emo- ◆◆◆◇ tion, such as anger or happiness. *It gave me a feel-* `N-COUNT` *ing of satisfaction. ...strong feelings of pride.* **2 Bad** `PHRASE` **feeling** or **ill feeling** is resentment, bitterness, or an- ger which exists between people, for example after they have had an argument. *There's been some bad* *feeling between the two families.* **3 Hard feelings** are `PHRASE` feelings of anger or bitterness towards someone. If you say **'no hard feelings'**, you are making an agreement with someone not to be angry or bitter about something. *I don't want any hard feelings be-* *tween our companies.* **4** You say **'I know the feeling'** `CONVENTION`

to show that you understand and sympathize with `PRAGMATICS` the problem that someone is telling you about.
5 Feeling is a way of thinking and reacting to things `N-UNCOUNT` which is emotional and spontaneous rather than logi- cal and rational. *...a voice that trembles with feeling.*
6 If you have a **feeling** that something is the case or is `N-SING` going to happen, you think that it is probably the case or is probably going to happen. *I have a feeling that* *everything will come right for us.* **7** If you have a **feel-** `N-SING:` **ing of** being in a particular situation, you feel that you `N of-ing` are in that situation. *I had the terrible feeling of being* *left behind.*
8 Your **feelings** about something are the things that `N-PLURAL:` you think and feel about it, or your attitude towards it. `with supp` *She has strong feelings about the alleged growth in vio-* *lence... This establishment doesn't represent the feel-* *ings of all young people.* **9 Feeling** is used to refer to a `N-UNCOUNT:` general opinion that a group of people has about `with supp` something. *There is still some feeling in the art world* *that the market for such works may be declining.* **10** If `PHRASE` you **have mixed feelings** about something or some- one, you feel uncertain about them because you can see both good and bad points about them.
11 When you refer to someone's **feelings**, you are `N-PLURAL` talking about the things that might embarrass, offend, or upset them. For example, if you hurt someone's **feelings**, you say or do something that upsets them. *He has no respect, no regard for anyone's feelings.*
12 Feeling for someone is love, affection, sympathy, `N-UNCOUNT` or concern for them. *It's incredible that Peter can be-* *have with such stupid lack of feeling.*
13 If you have a **feeling** of hunger, tiredness, or other `N-COUNT` physical sensation, you experience it. *I also had a* *strange feeling in my neck... Focus on the feeling of re-* *laxation.* **14 Feeling** in part of your body is the ability `N-UNCOUNT` to experience the sense of touch in this part of the body. *After the accident he had no feeling in his legs.*
15 If you have a **feeling for** something, you have an `N-SING:` understanding of it. *Try to get a feeling for the people* `a N for n` *who live here.* **16** If something such as a place or book `N-SING:` creates a particular kind of **feeling**, it creates a par- `with supp` ticular kind of atmosphere. *The room's large, high* *windows give it a feeling of air and light.*
17 See also **feel**.

feet /fiːt/. **Feet** is the plural of **foot**.

feign /feɪn/ **feigns, feigning, feigned.** If some- ◆◇◇◇◇ one **feigns** a particular feeling or attitude, they try `VERB` to make other people think that they have it or are `V n` experiencing it, although this is not true. *I didn't* `Also V to-inf` *want to go to school, and decided to feign illness.* `FORMAL`

feint /feɪnt/ **feints, feinting, feinted. 1** In sport `VERB: V` or military conflict, if someone **feints**, they make a `V prep/adv` brief movement in a different direction from the one they intend to follow, as a way of confusing or deceiving their opponent. *I feinted to the left.* ▶ Also `N-COUNT` a noun. *He placed the ball and tried a couple of* *feints.* **2 Feint** is used to refer to paper that has pale `N-UNCOUNT` lines across it for writing on.

feisty /ˈfaɪsti/. If you describe someone as **feisty**, ◆◇◇◇◇ you mean that they are tough and lively, often when `ADJ-GRADED` you would not expect them to be, for example be- cause they are old or ill. *At 66, she was as feisty* *as ever.*

fe·lic·i·tous /fɪˈlɪsɪtəs/. A **felicitous** remark or idea `ADJ-GRADED` seems particularly suitable or well-chosen in the `FORMAL` circumstances. *Her prose style is not always* *felicitous.*

fe·line /ˈfiːlaɪn/ **felines. 1 Feline** means belonging `ADJ: ADJ n` or relating to the cat family. ▶ A **feline** is a feline `N-COUNT` animal. **2 Feline** features or movements are elegant `ADJ-GRADED` or graceful in a way that makes you think of a cat. `LITERARY` *...a woman with large feline eyes.*

fell /fel/ **fells, felling, felled. 1 Fell** is the past ◆◇◇◇◇ tense of **fall**. **2** If trees are **felled**, they are cut down. `VERB:` **3** To **fell** someone means to knock them down, for `be V-ed` example in a fight. **4** ● **in one fell swoop**: see `VERB: V n` **swoop**.

fel·la /ˈfelə/ **fellas;** also spelled **feller**. You can re- ◆◇◇◇◇ fer to a man as a **fella**. *He's an intelligent man and a* `N-COUNT` *nice fella.* `INFORMAL`

fel·la·tio /fəˈleɪʃiəʊ/. **Fellatio** is oral sex which involves someone using their mouth to stimulate their partner's penis. N-UNCOUNT

fel·low /ˈfeləʊ/ **fellows. 1** You use **fellow** to describe people who are in the same situation as you, or people you feel you have something in common with. ...*her fellow guests.* **2** Your **fellows** are the people who you work with, who you do things with, or who are like you in some way. *He stood out in terms of competence from all his fellows.* ◆◆◆◇◇ ADJ: ADJ n / N-PLURAL: poss N FORMAL

3 A **fellow** of a society or academic institution is a member of it. N-COUNT

fellow 'feeling; also spelled **fellow-feeling**. **Fellow feeling** is sympathy and friendship that exists between people who have shared similar experiences or difficulties. N-UNCOUNT

fel·low·ship /ˈfeləʊʃɪp/ **fellowships. 1** A **fellowship** is a group of people who join together for a common purpose or interest. ...*the National Schizophrenia Fellowship.* **2 Fellowship** is a feeling of friendship that people have when they are talking or doing something together and sharing their experiences. ...*a sense of community and fellowship.* **3** A **fellowship** at a university is a post which involves research work. ◆◇◇◇ N-COUNT: with supp / N-UNCOUNT / N-COUNT

fel·on /ˈfelən/ **felons.** A **felon** is a person who is guilty of committing a felony. *He's a convicted felon.* N-COUNT LEGAL

felo·ny /ˈfeləni/ **felonies.** In countries where the legal system distinguishes between very serious crimes and less serious ones, a **felony** is a very serious crime such as armed robbery. ◆◇◇◇ N-COUNT LEGAL

felt /felt/. **1 Felt** is the past tense and past participle of **feel. 2 Felt** is a thick cloth made from wool or other fibres packed tightly together. N-UNCOUNT

felt-'tip, felt-tips. A **felt-tip** or a **felt-tip pen** is a pen which has a nib made from fibres pressed together. N-COUNT

fem. **fem.** is a written abbreviation for **female** or **feminine**.

fe·male /ˈfiːmeɪl/ **females. 1** Someone who is **female** is a woman or a girl. ...*a female singer... Only 13 per cent of consultants are female.* ◆ **fe·male·ness** ...*a woman who hides her femaleness.* **2** Women and girls are sometimes referred to as **females** when they are being considered as a type. *Hay fever affects males more than females.* **3 Female** matters and things relate to, belong to, or affect women rather than men. ...*female infertility.* **4** You can refer to any creature that can lay eggs or produce babies from its body as a **female**. *Each female will lay just one egg in April or May.* ▶ Also an adjective. ...*the scent given off by the female aphid.* **5** A **female** flower or plant contains the part that will become the fruit when it is fertilized. ◆◆◆◇ ADJ / N-UNCOUNT / N-COUNT / ADJ: ADJ n / N-COUNT / ADJ / ADJ TECHNICAL

fem·i·nine /ˈfemɪnɪn/. **1 Feminine** qualities and things relate to or are considered typical of women. ...*worrying about their women abandoning traditional feminine roles.* ◆ **fem·i·nin·ity** /ˌfemɪˈnɪnɪti/ ...*the ideology of motherhood and femininity.* **2** Someone or something that is **feminine** has qualities that are considered typical of women, especially prettiness or gentleness. ...*very feminine women who are not overpowering.* **3** In some languages, a **feminine** noun, pronoun, or adjective has a different form from a masculine or neuter one, or behaves in a different way. ◆◆◇◇ ADJ / N-UNCOUNT / ADJ-GRADED / ADJ

fem·i·nism /ˈfemɪnɪzəm/. **Feminism** is the belief and aim that women should have the same rights, power, and opportunities as men. ◆ **fem·i·nist,** **feminists.** ...*the feminist movement.* ◆◇◇◇ N-UNCOUNT / N-COUNT

fem·i·nize /ˈfemɪnaɪz/ **feminizes, feminizing, feminized;** also spelled **feminise** in British English. To **feminize** something means to make it into something that involves mainly women or is thought suitable for or typical of women. ...*their governments' policies of feminizing low-paid factory work.* VERB V n FORMAL

femme fa·tale /ˌfæm fəˈtɑːl/ **femmes fatales.** If a woman has a reputation as a **femme fatale**, she is N-COUNT

considered to be very attractive sexually, and to cause problems for men who are attracted to her.

fe·mur /ˈfiːmə/ **femurs.** Your **femur** is the large bone in the upper part of your leg. N-COUNT

fen /fen/ **fens. Fens** are areas of low, flat, wet land, especially in the east of England. ...*the flat fen lands near Cambridge.* ◆◇◇◇ N-VAR

fence /fens/ **fences, fencing, fenced. 1** A **fence** is a barrier between two areas of land, made of wood or wire supported by posts. See picture headed **house and flat. 2** If you **fence** an area of land, you surround it with a fence. ▶ **Fence off** means the same as **fence**. *We could fence off the cliff top.* **3** A **fence** in show jumping or horse racing is a frame or artificial hedge that horses have to jump over. **4** If one country tries to **mend fences** with another, it tries to end a disagreement or quarrel with the other country. *Britain and Argentina have been mending fences.* **5** If you **sit on the fence**, you avoid supporting a particular side in a discussion or argument. ◆◆◆◇ N-COUNT / VERB: V n / PHRASAL VB V P noun / N-COUNT / PHRASE / PHRASE

fence in. 1 If you **fence** something **in**, you surround it with a fence. *He plans to fence in about 100 acres of his ranch.* **2** If you **are fenced in** by someone or something, you are restricted by them in what you can do or where you can go. *She was basically fenced in by what the military wanted to do.* PHRASAL VB V P noun Also V n P / usu passive be V-ed P

fence off. See **fence** 2. PHRASAL VB

fenc·ing /ˈfensɪŋ/. **1 Fencing** is a sport in which two competitors fight each other using very thin swords. **2** Materials such as wood or wire that are used to make fences are called **fencing**. ◆◇◇◇ N-UNCOUNT / N-UNCOUNT

fend /fend/ **fends, fending, fended.** If you have to **fend for** yourself, you have to look after yourself without relying on help from anyone else. ◆◇◇◇ VERB: V for pron-refl

fend off. 1 If you **fend off** unwanted questions, problems, or people, you stop them from affecting you or defend yourself from them. *He fended off questions from the world's Press... He had struggled to pay off creditors but couldn't fend them off any longer.* **2** If you **fend off** someone who is attacking you, you use your arms or something such as a stick to defend yourself from their blows. *He raised his hand to fend off the blow.* PHRASAL VB V P noun V n P / V P noun Also V n P

fend·er /ˈfendə/ **fenders. 1** A **fender** is a low metal wall built around a fireplace, which stops any coals that fall out of the fire from rolling onto the carpet. **2** A **fender** is the same as a **fireguard. 3** The **fenders** of a car are the parts of the body over the wheels. The British word is **wing**. ◆◇◇◇ N-COUNT / N-COUNT / N-COUNT AMERICAN

fen·nel /ˈfenəl/. **Fennel** is a plant with a crisp rounded base and feathery leaves. It can be eaten as a vegetable or used as a herb. ◆◇◇◇ N-UNCOUNT

fe·ral /ˈfɛrəl, ˈfɪər-/. **1 Feral** animals are wild animals, especially ones that belong to species which are normally owned and kept by people. ...*feral cats.* **2** If you describe something or someone as **feral**, you mean that they seem wild, fierce, and uncontrolled. ADJ FORMAL / ADJ LITERARY

fer·ment, ferments, fermenting, fermented. The noun is pronounced /ˈfɜːment/. The verb is pronounced /fəˈment/. **1 Ferment** is excitement and trouble caused by change or uncertainty. *The whole country has been in a state of political ferment.* **2** If a food, drink, or other natural substance **ferments**, a chemical change takes place in it so that alcohol is produced. *The dried grapes are allowed to ferment... Manufacturers ferment the yeast to produce a more concentrated product.* ◆ **fer·men·ta·tion** /ˌfɜːmenˈteɪʃən/ ...*the fermentation that produces alcohol.* ◆◇◇◇ N-UNCOUNT / V-ERG V / V n / N-UNCOUNT

fern /fɜːn/ **ferns.** A **fern** is a plant that has long stems with feathery leaves and no flowers. ◆◇◇◇ N-VAR

fe·ro·cious /fəˈrəʊʃəs/. **1** A **ferocious** animal, person, or action is very fierce and violent. ...*some of the most ferocious violence ever seen on the streets of London.* ◆ **fe·ro·cious·ly** She kicked out ferociously. ◆ **fe·roc·ity** /fəˈrɒsɪti/. *The armed forces seem to have been taken by surprise by the ferocity of the attack.* **2** If you describe actions or feelings as **ferocious**, you mean that they are intense and deter- ◆◇◇◇ ADJ-GRADED / ADV-GRADED / N-UNCOUNT / ADJ-GRADED

mined. ...*a ferocious battle to select a new parliamentary candidate.* ◆ **ferociously** *These days he is ferociously competitive.* ◆ **ferocity** *The ferocity of his feelings alarmed me.*
ADV-GRADED
N-UNCOUNT

fer·ret /ˈferɪt/ **ferrets, ferreting, ferreted. 1** A ferret is a small fierce animal similar to a weasel, used for hunting rabbits and rats. **2** If you **ferret** about for something, you look for it in a lot of different places or in a place where it is hidden. *She nonetheless continued to ferret about for possible jobs... She ferreted among some papers.*
◆◇◇◇
N-COUNT
VERB
V about/ around
V prep
INFORMAL, BRITISH

ferret out. If you **ferret out** some information, you discover it by searching for it very thoroughly. *The team is trying to ferret out missing details.*
PHRASAL VB
V P noun
Also V n P
INFORMAL

fer·rous /ˈferəs/. **Ferrous** means containing or relating to iron.
ADJ: ADJ n

fer·ry /ˈferi/ **ferries, ferrying, ferried. 1** A ferry is a boat that transports passengers and sometimes also vehicles, usually across rivers or short stretches of sea. **2** If a vehicle **ferries** people or goods, it transports them, usually by means of regular journeys between the same two places. *A plane arrives to ferry guests to and from Bird Island Lodge... A helicopter ferried in more soldiers.*
◆◆◇◇
N-COUNT:
also by N
VERB: V n
V n prep/adv
V n with adv

ferry·boat /ˈferibəʊt/ **ferryboats.** A ferryboat is a boat used as a ferry.
N-COUNT

fer·tile /ˈfɜːtaɪl, AM -təl/. **1** Land or soil that is **fertile** is able to support the growth of a large number of strong healthy plants. ◆ **fer·til·ity** /fɜːˈtɪlɪti/ ...*the fertility of the soil.* **2** If you say someone has a **fertile** mind or imagination, you mean they think of a lot of imaginative ideas, which are sometimes ridiculous or wrong. *This was simply a product of Flynn's fertile imagination.* **3** A situation or environment that is **fertile** in relation to a particular activity or feeling encourages the activity or feeling. ...*a fertile breeding ground for this kind of violent racism.* **4** A person or animal that is **fertile** is able to reproduce and have babies or young. ◆ **fertility** *Pregnancy is the only sure test for fertility.*
◆◆◇◇
ADJ-GRADED
N-UNCOUNT
ADJ-GRADED
ADJ-GRADED:
ADJ n
ADJ-GRADED
N-UNCOUNT

fer·ti·lize /ˈfɜːtɪlaɪz/ **fertilizes, fertilizing, fertilized;** also spelled **fertilise** in British English. **1** When a woman or female animal or her egg **is fertilized,** a sperm from the male joins with the egg, causing the process of reproduction to begin. A female plant **is fertilized** when its reproductive parts come into contact with pollen from the male plant. *Certain varieties cannot be fertilised with their own pollen. ...the normal sperm levels needed to fertilise the female egg.* ◆ **fer·ti·li·za·tion** /ˌfɜːtɪlaɪˈzeɪʃən/ *The average length of time from fertilization until birth is about 266 days.* **2** To **fertilize** land means to improve its quality in order to make plants grow well on it, by spreading manure or a chemical mixture on it.
◆◇◇◇
VERB
be V-ed
V n
N-UNCOUNT
VERB: V n

fer·ti·liz·er /ˈfɜːtɪlaɪzə/ **fertilizers;** also spelled **fertiliser** in British English. Fertilizer is a substance such as manure or a chemical mixture that you put on soil in order to improve its quality.
◆◆◇◇
N-VAR

fer·vent /ˈfɜːvənt/. A **fervent** person has or shows strong feelings about something, and is very sincere and enthusiastic about it. ...*a fervent admirer of Morisot's work.* ◆ **fer·vent·ly** *Their claims will be fervently denied.*
◆◇◇◇
ADJ-GRADED
ADV-GRADED

fer·vour /ˈfɜːvə/; spelled **fervor** in American English. **Fervour** for something is a very strong enthusiasm for or belief in it. ...*religious fervour.*
◆◇◇◇
N-UNCOUNT
FORMAL

fes·ter /ˈfestə/ **festers, festering, festered.** **1** If you say that a situation, problem, or feeling is **festering,** you disapprove of the fact that it is being allowed to grow worse, because it is not being properly recognized or dealt with. *Resentments are starting to fester.* **2** If a wound **festers,** it becomes infected, making it worse.
VERB
PRAGMATICS
VERB: V

fes·ti·val /ˈfestɪvəl/ **festivals. 1** A festival is an organized series of events such as musical concerts or drama productions. ...*summer festivals of music, theatre, and dance.* **2** A festival is a day or time of the year when people have a holiday from work and celebrate some special event, often a religious
◆◆◆◇
N-COUNT
N-COUNT

event. *Shavuot is a two-day festival for Orthodox Jews.*

fes·tive /ˈfestɪv/. **1** Something that is **festive** is special, colourful, or exciting, especially because of a holiday or celebration. *The town has a festive holiday atmosphere.* **2** Festive means relating to a holiday or celebration, especially Christmas. *24 top films will be screened over the festive period by the BBC.*
◆◇◇◇
ADJ-GRADED
ADJ: ADJ n

'festive season. People sometimes refer to the Christmas period as the **festive season.**
N-SING

fes·tiv·ity /fesˈtɪvɪti/ **festivities. 1** Festivity is the celebration of something in a happy way. *There was a general air of festivity and abandon.* **2** Festivities are events organized in order to celebrate something. *The festivities included a huge display of fireworks.*
◆◇◇◇
N-UNCOUNT
N-COUNT

fes·toon /feˈstuːn/ **festoons, festooning, festooned.** If something **is festooned** with, for example, lights, or flowers, large numbers of them are hung from it or wrapped around it. ...*a lamppost festooned in political stickers.* ▶ Also a noun. ...*festoons of laurel and of magnolia.*
◆◇◇◇
VERB:
be V-ed with/
in n
V-ed
N-COUNT

fe·tal /ˈfiːtəl/. See **foetus.**

fetch /fetʃ/ **fetches, fetching, fetched. 1** If you **fetch** something or someone, you go and get them from the place where they are. *Sylvia fetched a towel from the bathroom... Fetch me a glass of water... The caddie ran over to fetch something for him.* **2** If something **fetches** a particular sum of money, it is sold for that amount. *The painting is expected to fetch between two and three million pounds.* **3** See also **far-fetched, fetching.**
◆◆◇◇
VERB
V n
V n n
V n for n
VERB
V n

fetch up. If you **fetch up** somewhere, you arrive there, especially when you have not planned to go there.
PHRASAL VB
V P prep/adv
INFORMAL

fetch·ing /ˈfetʃɪŋ/. If you describe someone or something as **fetching,** you mean that they look very attractive. ...*a fetching outfit.*
ADJ-GRADED

fete /feɪt/ **fetes, feting, feted;** spelled **fête** in American English. **1** A fete is an event that is usually held outdoors and includes competitions, entertainments, and the selling of second-hand or home-made goods. **2** If someone **is feted,** they are celebrated, welcomed, or admired by the public.
◆◇◇◇
N-COUNT
VERB:
be V-ed

fet·id /ˈfetɪd, ˈfiː-/; also spelled **foetid** in British English. **Fetid** water or air has a very strong unpleasant smell.
ADJ-GRADED
FORMAL

fet·ish /ˈfetɪʃ/ **fetishes. 1** If someone has a **fetish,** they have an unusually strong liking for a particular object or activity, as a way of getting sexual pleasure. ◆ **fet·ish·ist** /ˈfetɪʃɪst/, **fetishists.** You can refer to someone who has a fetish as a **fetishist.** ...*a foot fetishist.* **2** If you say that someone has a **fetish** for doing something, you disapprove of the fact that they do it very often or enjoy it very much. *The Conservatives said Labour had a fetish for increasing taxes.* **3** In some cultures, a **fetish** is an object which is considered to have religious importance or magical powers.
◆◇◇◇
N-COUNT
N-COUNT
N-COUNT
PRAGMATICS
N-COUNT

fet·lock /ˈfetlɒk/ **fetlocks.** A horse's **fetlock** is the back part of its leg, just above the hoof.
N-COUNT

fet·ter /ˈfetə/ **fetters, fettering, fettered. 1** If you **are fettered** by something, it prevents you from behaving or moving freely. *The government has arrested thousands and fettered the media.* **2** You can use **fetters** to refer to things such as rules or responsibilities that you dislike because they prevent you from behaving in the way you want. ...*the fetters of social convention.* **3** Especially in former times, **fetters** were chains for a prisoner's feet.
VERB:
be V-ed
V n
LITERARY
N-PLURAL
PRAGMATICS
LITERARY
N-COUNT
N-COUNT

fet·tle /ˈfetəl/. If you say that someone or something is **in fine fettle,** you are emphasizing that they are in very good health or condition.
PHRASE
PRAGMATICS
INFORMAL

fe·tus /ˈfiːtəs/. See **foetus.**

feud /fjuːd/ **feuds, feuding, feuded.** If one person or group **feuds** with another, they have a quarrel that lasts a long time. *He feuded with his ex-wife... Their families had feuded since their teenage daughters quarrelled two years ago.* ▶ Also a noun.
◆◇◇◇
V-RECIP
V with n
pl-n V
N-COUNT

...a long and bitter feud between the state government and the villagers.

feu·dal /'fjuːdəl/. **Feudal** means relating to the system in which people were given land and protection by people of higher rank, and worked and fought for them in return. *...the emperor and his feudal barons.* ♦ **feu·dal·ism** /'fjuːdəlɪzəm/. **Feudalism** is a feudal system. ◆◇◇◇◇ ADJ: ADJ n · N-UNCOUNT

fe·ver /'fiːvə/ **fevers. 1** If you have a **fever** when you are ill, you have a body temperature that is higher than usual and a quick heartbeat. ● See also **hay fever, scarlet fever.** ♦ **fe·vered** /'fiːvəd/ *Voices whirled in her fevered brain.* **2** A **fever** is extreme excitement or agitation about something. *Angie waited in a fever of excitement.* ♦ **fevered** *...fevered speculation over the leadership.* ◆◆◇◇◇ N-VAR · ADJ-GRADED · N-COUNT · ADJ-GRADED

fe·ver·ish /'fiːvərɪʃ/. **1 Feverish** activity is done extremely quickly, often in a state of agitation because you want to finish it as soon as possible. *...feverish last minute negotiations.* ♦ **fe·ver·ish·ly** *Volunteers are working feverishly to remove the heavy snow.* **2 Feverish** emotion is characterized by extreme agitation or excitement. *...a state of feverish excitement.* **3** If you are **feverish**, you are suffering from a fever. ♦ **feverishly** *He slept feverishly all afternoon.* ◆◇◇◇◇ ADJ-GRADED · ADV-GRADED: ADV with v · ADJ: ADJ n · ADJ-GRADED · ADV-GRADED

'fever pitch. If something is at **fever pitch**, it is in an extremely active or excited state. *Frances kept talking, her mind at fever pitch.* N-UNCOUNT

few /fjuː/ **fewer, fewest. 1** You use **a few** to indicate that you are talking about a small number of people or things. You can also say **a very few**. *I gave a dinner party for a few close friends... Here are a few more ideas to consider.* ▶ Also a pronoun. *A strict diet is appropriate for only a few.* ▶ Also a quantifier. *...a little tea-party I'm giving for a few of the teachers.* **2** You use **few** after adjectives and determiners to indicate that you are talking about a small number of things or people. *The past few weeks of her life had been the most pleasant she could remember... A train would pass through there every few minutes.* **3** You use **few** to emphasize that there are only a small number of people or things. You can use 'so', 'too', and 'very' in front of **few**. *She had few friends... Very few firms collect the tax.* ▶ Also a pronoun. *The trouble is that few want to buy.* ▶ Also a quantifier. *Few of the beach houses still had lights on.* ▶ Also an adjective. *...spending her few waking hours in front of the TV... His memories of his father are few.* **4 The few** means a small set of people considered as separate from the majority, often because they share an opportunity or quality that the others do not have. *...a system built on academic excellence for the few.* **5** Things that are **few and far between** are very rare or uncommon. *Successful women politicians are few and far between.* **6** You use **as few as** before a number to suggest that it is surprisingly small. *The factory may make as few as 1,500 cars this year.* **7** You use **no fewer than** to emphasize that a number is surprisingly large. *No fewer than thirteen foreign ministers attended the session.* **8** You use **a good few** and **not a few** when you are referring to quite a lot of things or people. *I think a good few of the others were like me, a bit confused.* **9** If you say that someone **has had a few too many** or **has had a few**, you mean that they have drunk too much alcohol. ◆◆◆◆◇ DET · PRON · QUANT · ADJ · DET PRAGMATICS · PRON · QUANT · ADJ-GRADED · N-SING: the N · PHRASE · PHRASE · PHRASE PRAGMATICS · PHRASE · PHRASE

fey /feɪ/. If you describe someone as **fey**, you mean that they behave in a shy, childish, or unpredictable way, and you are often suggesting that this is unnatural or insincere. ADJ-GRADED LITERARY

fez /fez/ **fezzes.** A **fez** is a round red hat with no brim, which has a flat top with a tassel hanging from it. N-COUNT

ff. In a book or journal, when **ff.** is written after a particular page or line number, it means 'and the following pages or lines'. *...p. 173 ff.* ◆◇◇◇◇

fi·an·cé /fi'ɒnseɪ, AM ˌfiːɑːn'seɪ/ **fiancés.** A woman's **fiancé** is the man to whom she is engaged to be married. ◆◇◇◇◇ N-COUNT

fi·an·cée /fi'ɒnseɪ, AM ˌfiːɑː'nseɪ/ **fiancées.** A man's **fiancée** is the woman to whom he is engaged to be married. ◆◇◇◇◇ N-COUNT

fi·as·co /fi'æskəʊ/ **fiascos.** If you describe an event or attempt to do something as a **fiasco**, you are emphasizing that it fails completely. *From our point of view the race had been a complete fiasco.* ◆◇◇◇◇ PRAGMATICS

fiat /'fiːæt, 'faɪ-/ **fiats.** If something is done by **fiat**, it is done because of an official order given by someone in authority. also by N FORMAL

fib /fɪb/ **fibs, fibbing, fibbed. 1** A **fib** is a small unimportant lie. *She told innocent fibs like anyone else.* **2** If someone **is fibbing**, they are telling lies. N-COUNT INFORMAL · VERB: V

fi·bre /'faɪbə/ **fibres;** spelled **fiber** in American English. **1** A **fibre** is a thin thread of a natural or artificial substance, especially one that is used to make cloth or rope. **2** A particular **fibre** is a type of cloth or other material that is made from or consists of threads. *The ball is made of rattan – a natural fibre.* **3** A **fibre** is a thin piece of flesh like a thread which connects nerve cells in your body or which muscles are made of. *...the nerve fibres.* **4 Fibre** consists of the parts of plants or seeds that your body cannot digest. ◆◆◇◇◇ N-COUNT · N-VAR · N-COUNT · N-UNCOUNT

fibre·glass /'faɪbəglɑːs, -glæs/; spelled **fiberglass** in American English. **1 Fibreglass** is plastic strengthened with short thin threads of glass. **2 Fibreglass** is a material made from short thin threads of glass which can be used to stop heat escaping. N-UNCOUNT · N-UNCOUNT

fibre 'optics; spelled **fiber optics** in American English. The form **fibre optic** is used as a modifier. **Fibre optics** is the use of long thin threads of glass to carry information in the form of light. *...fibre optic cables.* N-UNCOUNT

fi·broid /'faɪbrɔɪd/ **fibroids. Fibroids** are lumps of fibrous tissue that form in a woman's uterus, often causing pain. N-COUNT

fi·brous /'faɪbrəs/. A **fibrous** object or substance contains a lot of fibres or fibre, or looks as if it does. ADJ-GRADED

fibu·la /'fɪbjʊlə/ **fibulae.** Your **fibula** is the outer of the two bones in the lower part of your leg. N-COUNT MEDICAL

fick·le /'fɪkəl/. **1** If you describe someone as **fickle**, you disapprove of them because they keep changing their mind about what they like or want. ♦ **fick·le·ness** *...the fickleness of businessmen and politicians.* **2** If you say that something is **fickle**, you mean that it often changes and is unreliable. *Orta's weather can be fickle.* ◆◇◇◇◇ ADJ-GRADED PRAGMATICS · N-UNCOUNT · ADJ-GRADED

fic·tion /'fɪkʃən/ **fictions. 1 Fiction** refers to books and stories about imaginary people and events, rather than about real people or events. *Diana is a writer of historical fiction.* ● See also **science fiction.** ♦ **fic·tion·al** /'fɪkʃənəl/ *Ulverton is a fictional village on the Wessex Downs.* **2** Something that is **fiction** is not true. *The truth or fiction of this story has never been truly determined... Total recycling is a fiction.* ◆◆◇◇◇ N-UNCOUNT: also N in pl · ADJ · N-VAR

fic·tion·al·ize /'fɪkʃənəlaɪz/ **fictionalizes, fictionalizing, fictionalized;** also spelled **fictionalise** in British English. To **fictionalize** an account of something that really happened means to tell it as a story, with some details changed or added. *...a fictionalised account of a true and horrific story.* VERB: V n · V-ed

fic·ti·tious /fɪk'tɪʃəs/. **1 Fictitious** is used to describe something that is false or does not exist, although some people claim that it is true or exists. *We're interested in the source of these fictitious rumours.* **2** A **fictitious** character, thing, or event occurs in a story, play, or film but never really existed or happened. ◆◇◇◇◇ ADJ · ADJ

fid·dle /'fɪdəl/ **fiddles, fiddling, fiddled. 1** If you **fiddle with** an object, you keep moving or touching it with your fingers. *Harriet fiddled with a pen on the desk.* **2** If you **fiddle with** something, you change it in minor ways. *She told Whistler that his portrait of her was finished and to stop fiddling with it.* **3** If you **fiddle with** a machine, you adjust it. *Someone fiddled with the engine, so we couldn't start the car.* **4** If someone **fiddles** financial documents, they alter ◆◇◇◇◇ VERB V with n · VERB V with n · VERB V with n · VERB

them dishonestly so that they get money for them-selves. *Stop fiddling your expenses account.* ♦ **fid·dling** *...evidence of fiddling in the firm's Treasury-bond department.* **5** A **fiddle** is a dishon-est action or scheme in which someone gets money for themselves. *...a £1 million car insurance fiddle.* **6** Some people call violins **fiddles**, especially when they are used to play folk music. ♦ **fid·dler, fiddlers.** A **fiddler** is someone who plays the violin, especially one who plays folk music. **7** If you say that someone **is fiddling while Rome burns** or **fiddling while** some-thing **burns**, you mean that they are not dealing with a dangerous situation but instead are doing useless things or pretending that nothing is wrong. *Congress fiddles while the financial system burns.* **8** If you **play second fiddle** to someone, your position is less im-portant than theirs in something that you are doing together.

fiddle about or **fiddle around.** The form **fiddle about** is mainly used in British English. **1** If you **fiddle about** or **fiddle around** with a machine, you do things to it to try and make it work. *Two of them got out to fid-dle around with the engine.* **2** If someone **fiddles about** or **fiddles around**, they waste time doing unim-portant things instead of dealing with important problems. *He wastes time fiddling about with minor matters.* **3** If you say that someone is **fiddling about with** or **fiddling around with** something, you mean that they are changing it in a way that you disapprove of. *They're fiddling around with the budget.*

fid·dly /'fɪdəli/ **fiddlier, fiddliest.** Something that is **fiddly** is difficult to do or use, because it involves small or complicated objects. *Fish can be fiddly to cook.*

fi·del·i·ty /fɪ'delɪti/. **1 Fidelity** is loyalty to a person, organization, or set of beliefs. **2 Fidelity** is being loyal to your husband, wife, or partner by not hav-ing a sexual relationship with anyone else. **3** The **fidelity** of something such as a report or translation is its degree of accuracy.

fidg·et /'fɪdʒɪt/ **fidgets, fidgeting, fidgeted.** If you **fidget**, you keep changing your position slightly or moving or touching something, for example be-cause you are nervous or bored. *Brenda fidgeted in her seat... He fidgeted with his tie.* ♦ **fidg·ety** *Every-one was restless and fidgety.*

fief /fiːf/ **fiefs.** In former times, a **fief** was a piece of land given to someone by their lord, to whom they had to provide services in return.

field /fiːld/ **fields, fielding, fielded. 1** A **field** is an area of grass, for example in a park or on a farm. A **field** is also an area of land on which a crop is grown. *...a field of wheat... They went for walks to-gether in the fields.* **2** A sports **field** is an area of grass where sports are played. *Hastings was helped from the field with ankle injuries.* **3** A **field** is an area of land or sea bed under which large amounts of a mineral have been found. *...an extensive natu-ral gas field.* **4** A magnetic, gravitational, or electric **field** is the area in which that particular force is strong enough to have an effect. **5** See also **coal-field, minefield, playing field, snowfield. 6** You can refer to the area where fighting or other military action in a war takes place as the **field** or the **field of battle. 7** The **field** is a way of referring to all the competitors taking part in a particular race or sports contest. *The two most broadly experienced rid-ers led the field.* **8** Your **field** of vision or your visual **field** is the area that you can see without turning your head. **9** A particular **field** is a particular subject of study or type of activity. *Each of the authors of the tapes is an expert in his field.* **10** If you say that someone **leads the field** in a particular activity, you mean that they are better, more active, or more successful than everyone else who is involved in it. **11** Work or study that is done in the **field** is done in a real, natural envi-ronment rather than in a theoretical way or in con-trolled conditions. *...field trips to observe plants and animals.*

12 In a game of cricket, baseball, or rounders, the team that **is fielding** is trying to get the other team out by catching and throwing the ball. ♦ **field·er, fields-ers.** *The right fielder threw the ball back.* ♦ **field·ing** *Their bowling performance was very good, their field-ing very sharp.* **13** If a team or political party **fields** certain players or candidates, they choose them to take part in a particular game, contest, or election. **14** If you say that someone **fields** a question or en-quiry, you mean that they answer it or deal with it, usually successfully. **15** If someone **is having a field day**, they are very busy doing something that they en-joy, even though it may be hurtful for other people. *In our absence the office gossips are probably having a field day.* **16** If someone **plays the field**, they have a number of different romantic or sexual relationships.

field event, field events. A **field event** is an ath-letics contest such as the high jump or throwing the javelin, rather than a race.

field 'marshal, field marshals; also spelled **field-marshal.** A **field marshal** is an officer in the army who has the highest rank.

field mouse, field mice; also spelled **fieldmouse.** A **field mouse** is a mouse with a long tail that lives in fields and woods.

field sport, field sports. Hunting, shooting birds, and fishing with a rod are referred to as **field sports** when they are done mainly for pleasure.

field-test, field-tests, field-testing, field-tested. If you **field-test** a new piece of equipment, you test it in a real, natural environment. ► Also a noun. *Field tests are to be carried out.*

field·work /'fiːldwɜːk/. **Fieldwork** is the gathering of information in a real, natural environment, rather than in a laboratory or classroom.

fiend /fiːnd/ **fiends.** A **fiend** is someone who is ex-tremely wicked or cruel. *...such a saint to his pa-tients and such a fiend to his children.*

fiend·ish /'fiːndɪʃ/. **1** A **fiendish** plan, action, or de-vice is very clever or imaginative. *...a fiendish plot.* ♦ **fiend·ish·ly** *This figure is reached by a fiendishly clever equation.* **2** A **fiendish** problem or task is very difficult and challenging. *...the fiendish difficulty of the questions.* ♦ **fiendishly** *America's trade laws are fiendishly complex.* **3** A **fiendish** person enjoys being cruel. *This was a fiendish act of wickedness.*

fierce /fɪəs/ **fiercer, fiercest. 1** A **fierce** animal or person is very aggressive or angry. ♦ **fierce·ly** *'I don't know,' she said fiercely.* **2 Fierce** feelings, ac-tions, or conditions are very intense and strong. *A fierce battle has been raging all day. ...a fierce storm which went on for five days.* ♦ **fiercely** *He has al-ways been ambitious and fiercely competitive... A lorry had just been set on fire and was burning fiercely.*

fiery /'faɪəri/. **1** If you describe something as **fiery**, you mean that it is burning strongly or contains fire. *A helicopter crashed in a fiery explosion in Vallejo.* **2** You can use **fiery** for emphasis when you are re-ferring to bright colours such as red or orange. *Overhead the sky is a fiery red.* **3** If you describe food or drink as **fiery**, you mean that it has a strong, hot, or spicy taste. **4** If you describe someone as **fiery**, you mean that they express very strong emo-tions, especially anger. *She had a fiery temper.*

fi·es·ta /fi'estə/ **fiestas.** A **fiesta** is a time of public entertainment and parties, usually on a religious holiday, especially in Spain or Latin America.

fife /faɪf/ **fifes.** A **fife** is a small pipe-shaped musical instrument.

fif·teen /ˌfɪf'tiːn/. **Fifteen** is the number 15. See Appendix headed **Numbers**.

fif·teenth /ˌfɪf'tiːnθ/. The **fifteenth** item in a series is the one that you count as number fifteen. See Ap-pendix headed **Numbers**.

fifth /fɪfθ/ **fifths. 1** The **fifth** item in a series is the one that you count as number five. See Appendix headed **Numbers**. **2** A **fifth** is one of five equal parts of something.

fif·ti·eth /'fɪftiəθ/. The **fiftieth** item in a series is the one that you count as number fifty. See Appendix headed **Numbers**.
◆◆◆◇ ORDINAL

fif·ty /'fɪfti/ **fifties. 1 Fifty** is the number 50. See Appendix headed **Numbers. 2** When you talk about the **fifties**, you are referring to numbers between 50 and 59. If you are **in your fifties**, you are aged between 50 and 59. If the temperature is **in the fifties**, the temperature is between 50 and 59 degrees. **3 The fifties** is the decade between 1950 and 1959. *He began performing in the early fifties.*
◆◆◆◆◆ NUMBER N-PLURAL

N-PLURAL: the N

fifty-fifty. 1 If something such as money or property is divided **fifty-fifty** between two people, each person gets half of it. *The proceeds of the sale are split fifty-fifty.* ▶ Also an adjective. *The firm was owned on a fifty-fifty basis by the two parent companies.* **2** If there is a **fifty-fifty** chance of something happening, it is equally likely to happen as not to happen. *You've got a fifty-fifty chance of being right.*
ADV: ADV after v INFORMAL

ADJ

ADJ INFORMAL

fig /fɪg/ **figs. 1** A **fig** is a soft sweet fruit that grows in hot countries. It is full of tiny seeds. The tree on which figs grow is called a **fig** or a **fig tree. 2** If you say that someone doesn't **care a fig** or doesn't **give a fig** about something, you are emphasizing that they think it is unimportant or that they are not interested in it. *I do not give a fig what society thinks.*
◆◇◇◇◇ N-COUNT

PHRASE PRAGMATICS DATED, INFORMAL

fig. 1 In books and magazines, **fig.** is used as an abbreviation for **figure** in order to tell the reader which illustration or diagram is being referred to. *Draw the basic outlines in black felt-tip pen (see fig 4).* **2** In some dictionaries and language books, **fig.** is used as an abbreviation for **figurative**.
◆◇◇◇◇

fight /faɪt/ **fights, fighting, fought. 1** If you **fight** something unpleasant, you try in a determined way to prevent it or stop it happening. *More units to fight forest fires are planned... I've spent a lifetime fighting against racism and prejudice.* ▶ Also a noun. *...the fight against drug addiction.* **2** If you **fight** for something, you try in a determined way to get it or achieve it. *We had fought to hold on to the company... The team has fought its way to the cup final.* ▶ Also a noun. *...the fight for justice.*
◆◆◆◆◆ VERB V n V against n

N-COUNT

VERB; V for n V to-inf V way prep/ adv

N-COUNT

3 If two armies or groups **fight** a battle, they oppose each other with weapons. *Police fought a gun battle with a gang which used hand grenades against them... The Sioux had always fought other tribes for territorial rights... The rival militias have been fighting for more than two years.* **4** If a person or army **fights** in a battle or a war, they take part in it. *I would sooner go to prison than fight for this country... My father did leave his university to fight the Germans... Rebels fought their way into the capital.* ● See also **dogfight. ♦ fight·ing** *More than nine hundred people have died in the fighting.* **5** If one person **fights** with another, the two people hit or kick each other because they want to hurt each other. *I did fight him, I punched him but it was like hitting a wall... I refuse to act that way when my kids fight... You get a lot of unruly drunks fighting each other.* ▶ Also a noun. *He had had a fight with Smith.* **6** If one person **fights** with another, they have an angry disagreement or quarrel. *Gwendolen started fighting her teachers... Mostly, they fight about paying bills.* ▶ Also a noun. *He had a big fight with his dad.* **7** To **fight** means to take part in a boxing match. *I'd like to fight him because he's undefeated.* ▶ Also a noun. *The referee stopped the fight.* **8** If you **fight** an election, you are a candidate in the election and try to win it. **9** You can use **fight** to refer to a contest such as an election or a sports match. *...the fight for the US Presidency.* **10** If you **fight** a case or a court action, you persevere in suing someone, or put forward a defence when you are sued or charged with something. *Watkins sued the Army and fought his case in various courts for 10 years.* **11 Fight** is the desire or ability to keep fighting. *I thought that we had a lot of fight in us.* **12** If you **fight** your way to a place, you move towards it with great difficulty, for example because there are a lot of people or obstacles in your way. *Peter fought his way through a blizzard to save one of the chickens.* **13** If you **fight** an emotion or desire, you try very hard
V-RECIP: V with n V n with n V n pl-n V

VERB: V for n V n V way prep/ adv

N-UNCOUNT

V-RECIP: V with n V n pl-n V pron- recip

N-COUNT

V-RECIP: V with n V n pl-n V INFORMAL N-COUNT

VERB: V N-COUNT VERB: V n

N-COUNT JOURNALISM

VERB V n

N-UNCOUNT

VERB V way prep/ adv

VERB: V n

not to feel it, show it, or act on it, but do not always succeed. *He fought with the urge to smoke... He fought to be patient with her.* **14** If you **fight for breath**, you try to breathe but find it very difficult. **15** If you have a **fighting chance** of doing or achieving something, it is possible that you will do or achieve it, but only if you make a great effort or are very lucky. **16** If you describe someone as **fighting fit**, you are emphasizing that they are very fit or healthy.
V with n V to-inf

PHRASE PHRASE

PHRASE PRAGMATICS BRITISH

17 ● to **fight a losing battle**: see **battle. ●** to **fight fire with fire**: see **fire. ●** to **fight for** your **life**: see **life. ●** to **fight shy**: see **shy.**

fight back. 1 If you **fight back** against someone or something that is attacking or harming you, you resist them actively or attack them. *The teenage attackers fled when the two men fought back.* **2** If you **fight back** an emotion or a desire, you try very hard not to feel it, show it, or act on it. *She fought back the tears.*
PHRASAL VB V P against n V P

V P noun Also V n P

fight down. If you **fight down** an emotion or a desire, you try very hard not to feel it, show it, or act on it. *Meg fought down the desire to run.*
PHRASAL VB V P noun Also V n P

fight off. 1 If you **fight off** something, for example an illness or an unpleasant feeling, you succeed in getting rid of it and in not letting it overcome you. *All day she had fought off the impulse to telephone Harry.* **2** If you **fight off** someone who has attacked you, you fight with them, and succeed in making them go away or stop attacking you. *The woman fought off the attacker.*
PHRASAL VB V P noun Also V n P

V P noun Also V n P

fight out. If two people or groups **fight** something **out**, they fight or argue until one of them wins. *He gets up and walks away leaving his team-mates to fight it out... Malcolm continued to fight it out with Julien... He urged the president to fight out the issue in the November election.*
PHRASAL VB RECIP pl-n V it P V it P with n pl-n V P noun V P n with n

fight·back /'faɪtbæk/. A **fightback** is an effort made by a person or group of people to get back into a strong position when they seem likely to lose something such as a sports match. *The West Indies have staged a dramatic fightback.*
N-SING BRITISH, JOURNALISM

fight·er /'faɪtə/ **fighters. 1** A **fighter** or a **fighter plane** is a fast military aircraft that is used for destroying other aircraft. **2** If you describe someone as a **fighter**, you approve of them because they continue trying to achieve things in spite of great difficulties or opposition. **3** A **fighter** is a person who physically fights another person. *...a tough little street fighter.* **4** See also **fire fighter, freedom fighter, prize fighter.**
◆◆◆◇◇ N-COUNT

N-COUNT PRAGMATICS

N-COUNT

fig leaf, fig leaves. 1 A **fig leaf** is a large leaf which comes from the fig tree. A fig leaf is sometimes used in painting and sculpture to cover the genitals of a nude body. **2** In journalism, **fig leaf** is sometimes used to refer disapprovingly to something which is intended to conceal an embarrassing and shameful situation. *This deal is little more than a fig leaf for the continued destruction of the landscape.*
N-COUNT

N-COUNT PRAGMATICS

fig·ment /'fɪgmənt/ **figments.** If you say that something is a **figment of** someone's **imagination**, you mean that it does not really exist and that they are just imagining it.
PHRASE

fig·ura·tive /'fɪgərətɪv, AM -gjər-/. **1** If you use a word or expression in a **figurative** sense, you use it with a more abstract or imaginative meaning than its ordinary literal one. **♦ fig·ura·tive·ly** *I saw that she was, both literally and figuratively, up against a wall.* **2 Figurative** art is a style of art which attempts to show people and things realistically, as they actually look.
◆◇◇◇◇ ADJ

ADV

ADJ

fig·ure /'fɪgə, AM -gjər/ **figures, figuring, figured. 1** A **figure** is a particular amount expressed as a number, especially a statistic. *Government figures predict that one in two marriages will end in divorce.* **2** A **figure** is any of the ten written symbols from 0 to 9 that are used to represent a number. **3** An amount or number that is in single **figures** is between nought and nine. An amount or number that is in double **figures** is between ten and ninety-nine. *Inflation ran to three figures.* ▶ Also a combin-
◆◆◆◆◆ N-COUNT

N-COUNT

N-PLURAL: adj/num N

COMB

ing form. ...*collectors' pieces which change hands for five-figure sums.*

4 You refer to someone that you can see as a **figure** when you cannot see them clearly or when you are describing them. *A figure in a blue dress appeared in the doorway.* **5** In art, a **figure** is a person in a drawing or a painting, or a statue of a person. **6** Your **figure** is the shape of your body. *Janet was a natural blonde with a good figure.* **7** Someone who is referred to as a **figure** of a particular kind is a person who is well-known and important in some way. *The movement is supported by key figures in the three main political parties.* **8** If you say that someone is, for example, a mother **figure** or a hero **figure**, you mean that other people regard them as the type of person mentioned. **9** If you say that someone **cuts** a particular **figure**, you mean that they appear to other people in the way described. *Today she cuts a lonely figure.* **10** If you describe someone as a **figure of fun**, you mean that people think they are ridiculous. **11** In books and magazines, the diagrams which help to explain or illustrate information are referred to as **figures**. *If you look at a world map (see Figure 1) you can identify the major wine-producing regions.* **12** In geometry, a **figure** is a shape, especially a regular shape. ...*a pentagon, a regular five-sided figure.* **13** If you **figure** that something is the case, you think or guess that it is the case. *She figured that both she and Ned had learned a lot from the experience.* **14** If you say '**That figures**' or '**It figures**', you mean that the fact referred to is not surprising. **15** If someone or something **figures** in something, they appear or are included in it. *Human rights violations figured prominently in the report.*

figure on. If you **figure on** something, you assume that it will happen when making your plans. *He hadn't figured on a few obstacles.*

figure out. If you **figure out** a solution to a problem or the reason for something, you succeed in solving it or understanding it. *It took them about one month to figure out how to start the equipment... I don't have to be a detective to figure that out.*

figure·head /ˈfɪɡəhed, AM -gjə-/ **figureheads. 1** If someone is the **figurehead** of an organization or movement, they are recognized as being its leader, although they may have little real power. **2** A **figurehead** is a large wooden model of a person that was put just under the pointed front of a sailing ship in former times.

figure of ˈspeech, figures of speech. A **figure of speech** is an expression or word that is used with a figurative rather than a literal meaning.

ˈfigure skating. **Figure skating** is skating in attractive patterns, usually with spins and jumps.

figu·rine /ˌfɪɡəˈriːn, AM -gjə-/ **figurines.** A **figurine** is a small ornamental model of a person.

fila·ment /ˈfɪləmənt/ **filaments.** A **filament** is a very thin piece or thread of something, for example the piece of wire inside a light bulb.

filch /fɪltʃ/ **filches, filching, filched.** If you say that someone **filches** something, you mean they steal it, especially when you do not consider this to be a very serious crime.

file /faɪl/ **files, filing, filed. 1** A **file** is a box or folder in which letters or documents are kept. **2** A **file** is a collection of information about a particular person or thing. *We already have files on people's tax details.* • Information that is **on file** or on someone's **files** is recorded as part of a collection of information. *We'll keep your details on file.* **3** In computing, a **file** is a set of related data that has its own name. **4** If you **file** a document, you put it in the correct file. *They are all filed alphabetically under author.* ▶ **File away** means the same as **file**. *I'd completed all the case notes and filed them away.* **5** When someone **files** a report or a news story, they send or give it to their employer. *Catherine Bond filed that report for the BBC from Nairobi.* **6** If you **file** a formal or legal accusation, complaint, or request, you

make it officially. *I filed for divorce on the grounds of adultery.* **7** When a group of people **files** somewhere, they walk one behind the other in a line. *The group of children filed out of the house.* **8** A group of people who are walking or standing **single file** or **in single file** are in a line, one behind the other.

9 A **file** is a hand tool which is used for rubbing hard objects to make them smooth, to shape them, or to cut through them. **10** If you **file** an object, you smooth it, shape it, or cut it with a file. *Manicurists are skilled at shaping and filing nails.*

11 See also **rank and file**.

fil·ial /ˈfɪliəl/. You can use **filial** to describe the duties, feelings, or relationships which exist between a son or daughter and his or her parents. *His father would accuse him of neglecting his filial duties.*

fili·bus·ter /ˈfɪlibʌstə/ **filibusters, filibustering, filibustered.** If a politician **filibusters**, he or she makes a long slow speech in order to use up time so that a vote cannot be taken and a law cannot be passed. *Republicans say they don't expect to filibuster the plan.* ▶ A **filibuster** is a long slow speech made for this purpose.

fili·gree /ˈfɪlɪgriː/. The word **filigree** is used to refer to delicate ornamental designs made with gold or silver wire.

ˈfiling cabinet, filing cabinets. A **filing cabinet** is a piece of office furniture, usually made of metal, which has drawers in which files are kept.

fill /fɪl/ **fills, filling, filled. 1** If you **fill** a container or area, an amount of something enters it that is enough to make it full. *Fill a saucepan with water... The victims' lungs fill quickly with fluid... While the bath was filling, he padded about in his underpants.* ▶ **Fill up** means the same as **fill**. *Pass me your cup, Amy, and I'll fill it up for you... Warehouses at the frontier between the two countries fill up with sacks of rice and flour.* **2** If something **fills** a space, it is so big, or there are such large quantities of it, that there is very little room left. *The text fills 231 pages.* ▶ **Fill up** means the same as **fill**. ...*the complicated machines that fill up today's laboratories.* ♦ **filled** ...*four museum buildings filled with historical objects.* ♦ **-filled** ...*the flower-filled courtyard of an old Spanish colonial house.* **3** A play, film, or performer that **fills** a theatre, concert hall, or cinema attracts a very large audience.

4 If you **fill** a crack or hole, you put a substance into it in order to make the surface smooth again. ▶ **Fill in** means the same as **fill**. *If any cracks have appeared in the tart case, fill these in with raw pastry.* **5** When a dentist **fills** a tooth, he or she puts a filling in it.

6 If a sound, smell, or light **fills** a place or the air, it is very strong or noticeable. *The sunset filled the room with a strange purple light.* ♦ **-filled** ...*dusty or smoke-filled environments.* **7** If something **fills** you with an emotion, you experience this emotion strongly. *I could see the pride that filled him.* **8** If you **fill** a period of time with a particular activity, you spend the time in this way. *If she wants a routine to fill her day, let her do community work.* ▶ **Fill up** means the same as **fill**. *She went to her yoga class, glad to have something to fill up the evening.*

9 If something **fills** a need or a gap, it makes the need or gap no longer exist. **10** If something **fills** a role or position, that is their role or position. *I was asked to fill the role of escort.* **11** If a company or organization **fills** a job vacancy, they choose someone to do the job. **12** If you **fill** an order or a prescription, you provide the things that are asked for.

13 If you **have had** your **fill of** something, you have had enough of it, and do not want to experience it any more or do it any more. **14** • **to fill the bill**: see **bill**.

fill in. 1 If you **fill in** a form or other document, you write information in the spaces where it is required. *If you want your free copy of the Patients' Charter fill this form in.* **2** If you **fill in** a shape, you cover the area inside the lines with colour so that none of the back-

ground is showing. *With a lip pencil, outline lips and fill them in.* **3** If you **fill** someone **in**, you give them more details about something that you know about. *He filled her in on Wilbur Kantor's visit.* **4** If you **fill in** for someone, you do the work or task that they normally do because they are unable to do it. *Vice-presidents' wives would fill in for first ladies.* **5** See also **fill** 4.
V n P
V n P on n
INFORMAL
V P for n

fill out. 1 To **fill out** a form means the same as to **fill in** a form. *Fill out the application carefully, and keep copies of it.* **2** If a fairly thin person **fills out**, they become fatter. *A girl may fill out before she reaches her full height.*
PHRASAL VB
V P noun

V P

fill up. 1 A type of food that **fills** you **up** makes you feel that you have eaten a lot, even though you have only eaten a small amount. You can also say you **fill up** on a type of food. *Potatoes fill us up without overloading us with calories... Fill up on potatoes, bread and pasta.* **2** See also **fill** 1, 2, 8.
PHRASAL VB
ERG
V n P
V P on/with n

fill·er /ˈfɪlə/ **fillers. 1** Filler is a substance used for filling cracks or holes, especially in walls, car bodies, or wood. **2** You can describe something as a **filler** when it is being used or done because there is a need for something and nothing better is available.
◆◇◇◇
N-VAR

N-COUNT
INFORMAL

fil·let /ˈfɪlɪt, AM fɪˈleɪ/ **fillets, filleting, filleted. 1** Fillet is a strip of tender meat that has no bones in it. *...chicken breast fillets.* **2** A **fillet** of fish is the side of a fish with the bones removed. **3** When you **fillet** fish or meat, you prepare it by taking the bones out.
◆◇◇◇
N-VAR

N-COUNT

VERB: V n

fill·ing /ˈfɪlɪŋ/ **fillings. 1** A **filling** is a small amount of metal or plastic that a dentist puts in a hole in a tooth to prevent further decay. **2** The **filling** in something such as a cake, pie, or sandwich is a substance that is put inside it. *Spread some of the filling over each cold pancake.* **3** The **filling** in a piece of soft furniture, a cushion, or a quilt is the soft substance inside it. **4** Food that is **filling** makes you feel full when you have eaten it.
◆◇◇◇
N-COUNT

N-VAR

N-VAR

ADJ-GRADED

'filling station, filling stations. A **filling station** is a place where you can buy petrol and oil for your car.
N-COUNT

fil·lip /ˈfɪlɪp/ **fillips.** If someone or something gives a **fillip** to an activity or person, they suddenly stimulate or improve them. *The recent hot weather has given a fillip to fizzy drink makers.*
N-COUNT
WRITTEN

fil·ly /ˈfɪli/ **fillies.** A **filly** is a young female horse.
N-COUNT

film /fɪlm/ **films, filming, filmed. 1** A **film** consists of moving pictures that have been recorded so that they can be shown at the cinema or on television. **2** If you **film** something, you use a camera to take moving pictures which can be shown on a screen or on television. *A South African television crew has been filming recently in Budapest.* ♦ **film·ing** *Filming was due to start next month.* **3** Film of something is moving pictures of a real event that are shown on television or on a screen. *China's national television news showed film of serious flooding.* **4** The making of cinema films, considered as a form of art or a business, can be referred to as **film** or **films**. *Film is a business with limited opportunities for actresses.* **5** A **film** is the narrow roll of plastic that is used in a camera to take photographs. **6** Plastic **film** is a very thin sheet of plastic used to wrap and cover things. ● See also **clingfilm. 7** A **film** of powder, liquid, or grease is a very thin layer of it. *The sea is coated with a film of raw sewage.*
◆◆◆◆
N-COUNT

VERB: V n
V

N-UNCOUNT
N-UNCOUNT

N-UNCOUNT

N-UNCOUNT:
also N in pl

N-VAR
N-UNCOUNT

N-COUNT

film·ic /ˈfɪlmɪk/. **Filmic** means related to films. *...a new filmic style.*
ADJ: ADJ n
FORMAL

'film-maker, film-makers; also spelled **filmmaker.** A **film-maker** is someone involved in making films, in particular a director or producer.
◆◇◇◇
N-COUNT

'film star, film stars. A **film star** is a famous actor or actress who appears in films.
◆◇◇◇
N-COUNT

filmy /ˈfɪlmi/ **filmier, filmiest.** A **filmy** fabric or substance is very thin and almost transparent. *...pictures of women wearing filmy nightgowns.*
ADJ-GRADED

Filo·fax /ˈfaɪləfæks/ **Filofaxes.** A **Filofax** is a type of personal filing system in the form of a small book
N-COUNT

with pages that can easily be added or removed. **Filofax** is a trademark.

fil·ter /ˈfɪltə/ **filters, filtering, filtered. 1** To **filter** a substance means to pass it through a device which is designed to remove certain particles. *The best prevention for cholera is to boil or filter water.* ♦ **fil·tra·tion** /fɪlˈtreɪʃən/. *This enzyme would make the filtration of beer easier.* **2** A **filter** is a device through which a substance is passed when it is being filtered. *...a paper coffee filter.* **3** A **filter** is a device through which sound or light is passed and which blocks or reduces particular frequencies. *You might use a yellow filter to improve the clarity of a hazy horizon.* **4** If light or sound **filters** into a place, it comes in faintly or slowly, either through a small or partly covered opening, or from a long distance away. *Light filtered into my kitchen through the soft, green shade of the honey locust tree.* **5** When news or information **filters** through to people, it gradually reaches them. *News of the attack quickly filtered through the college. ...as indications filter in from polling stations.* **6** A traffic **filter** is a traffic signal or lane which controls the movement of traffic wanting to turn left or right.
◆◆◇◇
VERB
V n

N-UNCOUNT
N-COUNT

N-COUNT

VERB
V into/
through n

VERB:
V through to n
V through n
V in/out

N-COUNT
BRITISH

filter out. To **filter out** something from a substance or from light means to remove it by passing the substance or light through a filter. *Plants and trees filter carbon dioxide out of the air and produce oxygen.*
PHRASAL VB
V P noun
V n P of/from
n
Also V n P

filth /fɪlθ/. **1** Filth is a disgusting amount of dirt. *The living-room floor was littered with filth and tin cans.* **2** People refer to words or pictures, usually ones relating to sex, as **filth** when they think they are very disgusting. *The dialogue was all filth and innuendo.*
◆◇◇◇
N-UNCOUNT

N-UNCOUNT
PRAGMATICS

filthy /ˈfɪlθi/ **filthier, filthiest. 1** Something that is **filthy** is very dirty indeed. *...a filthy old jacket.* **2** If you describe something as **filthy**, you mean that you think it is morally very unpleasant and disgusting, sometimes in a sexual way. *Apparently, well known actors were at these filthy parties.* **3** Filthy weather is very cold, wet, and windy. *...a filthy wet night.* **4** ● **filthy rich:** see **rich.**
◆◇◇◇
ADJ-GRADED
ADJ-GRADED
PRAGMATICS

ADJ-GRADED
INFORMAL

fil·tra·tion /fɪlˈtreɪʃən/. See **filter.**

fin /fɪn/ **fins. 1** A fish's **fins** are the flat objects which stick out of its body and help it to swim and keep its balance. **2** A **fin** on something such as an aeroplane, rocket, or bomb is a flat part which sticks out and helps to control its movement.
◆◆◇◇
N-COUNT

N-COUNT

fi·nal /ˈfaɪnəl/ **finals. 1** In a series of events, things, or people, the **final** one is the last one. *Astronauts will make a final attempt today to rescue a communications satellite... I received a final letter from Clive.* **2** Final means happening at the end of an event or series of events. *The Notting Hill Carnival is in its final hours.* **3** You can use **final** to emphasize that a situation has a particular quality to a very great or severe degree. *...the final humiliation of meeting the bailiff at the door.* **4** If a decision or someone's authority is **final**, it cannot be changed or questioned. *The White House has the final say... I'm not going, and that's final.* **5** The **final** is the last game or contest in a series, which decides the overall winner. *...the Scottish Cup Final.* ● See also **quarter-final, semi-final. 6** The **finals** of a sporting tournament consist of a smaller tournament that includes only players or teams that have won earlier games. The finals decide the winner of the whole tournament. ♦ **fi·nal·ist** /ˈfaɪnəlɪst/ **finalists** *The twelve finalists will be listed in the Sunday Times.* **7** A student's **finals** are the last and most important examinations in a university or college course. *Anna sat her finals in the summer.*
◆◆◆◆
ADJ: det ADJ n

ADJ: ADJ n

ADJ: ADJ n
PRAGMATICS
WRITTEN

ADJ

N-COUNT

N-PLURAL

N-COUNT

N-PLURAL

fi·na·le /fɪˈnɑːli, -ˈnæli/ **finales. 1** The **finale** of a show, piece of music, or series of shows is the last part of it or the last one of them, especially when this is exciting or impressive. *...the finale of Shostakovich's Fifth Symphony.* **2** If you say that an event provides a particular kind of **finale** to something, you mean that it provides it with a particular
◆◇◇◇
N-COUNT

N-COUNT

kind of ending. ...*a sad finale to an otherwise spectacular career.*

fi·nal·ity /faɪˈnælɪti/. **Finality** is the quality of being final and irreversible. If you say something with **finality**, you say it in a way that shows that you have made up your mind about something and do not want to discuss it further. *Young Children have difficulty grasping the finality of death.* — N-UNCOUNT FORMAL

fi·nal·ize /ˈfaɪnəlaɪz/ **finalizes, finalizing, finalized;** also spelled **finalise** in British English. If you **finalize** something such as a plan or an agreement, you complete the arrangements for it. *We are saying nothing until all the details have been finalised... They have not yet finalized the deal with the government.* — ◆◇◇◇◇ VERB: V n / be V-ed / V n with n

fi·nal·ly /ˈfaɪnəli/. **1** You use **finally** to suggest that something happens after a long period of time, usually later than you wanted or expected it to happen. *The food finally arrived... Finally, after ten hours of negotiations, the gunman gave himself up.* **2** You use **finally** to indicate that something is last in a series of actions or events. *The action slips from comedy to melodrama and finally to tragedy.* **3** You use **finally** in speech or writing to introduce a final point, question, or topic. *And finally, a word about the winner.* — ◆◆◆◇ ADV: ADV before v, ADV with cl / ADV: ADV with cl / ADV with cl PRAGMATICS

fi·nance /ˈfaɪnæns, fɪˈnæns/ **finances, financing, financed. 1** When someone **finances** something such as a project or an expensive purchase, they provide the money to pay for it. *Government expenditure is financed by taxation and by borrowing.* ▶ Also a noun. *A United States delegation is in Japan seeking finance for a major scientific project.* **2 Finance** is the commercial or government activity of managing money, debt, credit, and investment. *...the world of high finance. ...the Venezuelan Finance Minister, Mr Roberto Pocaterra.* **3** You can refer to the amount of money that you have and how well it is organized as your **finances.** *Be prepared for unexpected news concerning your finances... Finance is usually the biggest problem for students.* — ◆◆◆◇ VERB: V n, be V-ed / N-UNCOUNT / N-UNCOUNT: also N in pl / N-UNCOUNT: also N in pl

fi·nan·cial /faɪˈnænʃəl, fɪ-/. **Financial** means relating to or involving money. *...in financial difficulties. ...financial advisers.* ♦ **fi·nan·cial·ly** *She would like to be more financially independent.* — ◆◆◆◆ ADJ / ADV

fi,nancial 'year, financial years. A financial **year** is a period of twelve months, used by government, business, and other organizations, according to which they plan and assess their budgets, profits, and losses. The usual American term is **fiscal year.** — ◆◇◇◇◇ N-COUNT BRITISH

fi·nan·ci·er /faɪˈnænsiə, fɪ-/ **financiers.** A financier is a person, company, or government that provides money for projects or enterprises. — ◆◇◇◇◇ N-COUNT

finch /fɪntʃ/ **finches.** A **finch** is a small bird with a short strong beak. — ◆◇◇◇◇ N-COUNT

find /faɪnd/ **finds, finding, found. 1** If you find someone or something, you see them or learn where they are. *The police also found a pistol... I wonder if you could find me a deck of cards?* ♦ **find·er** /ˈfaɪndə/ **finders** *The finder of a wallet who takes it home may be guilty of theft.* **2** If you find something that you need or want, you succeed in achieving or obtaining it. *Many people here cannot find work... We have to find him a job... Does this mean that they haven't found a place for him?* **3** If you **find** the time or money to do something, you succeed in making or obtaining enough time or money to do it. *My sister helped me find the money for a private operation.* **4** If something **is found** in a particular place or thing, it exists in that place. *Fibre is found in cereal foods, beans, fruit and vegetables.* **5** If you **find** someone or something in a particular situation or doing a particular thing, they are in that situation or doing that thing when you see them or come into contact with them. *They found her walking alone and depressed on the beach... She returned to her east London home to find her back door forced open.* **6** If you **find** yourself doing something, you are doing it without deciding or intending to do it. *It's not the* — ◆◆◆◆◆ VERB: V n, V n n / Also V n for n N-COUNT / VERB: V n, V n for n / VERB: V n / V-PASSIVE: be V-ed / VERB: V n -ing, V n -ed, prep/adv / VERB: V pron-refl -ing

first time that you've found yourself in this situation... He found himself quite unable to take it in. **7** If a time or event **finds** you in a particular situation or doing a particular thing, you are in that situation or doing that thing at the time mentioned or when the event occurs. *Mid-afternoon found her among the stylish shops of Buchanan Street.* **8** If you **find** that something is the case, you become aware of it or realize that it is the case. *At my age I would find it hard to get another job... We find her evidence to be based on a degree of oversensitivity... I've never found my diet a problem.* **9** When a court or jury decides that a person on trial is guilty or innocent, you say that the person **has been found** guilty or not guilty. *She was found guilty of manslaughter... When they found us guilty, I just went blank.* **10** You can use **find** to express your reaction to someone or something. *We're sure you'll find it exciting!... I find it ludicrous that nothing has been done to protect passengers from fire... But you'd find him a good worker if you showed him what to do.* **11** If you **find** a feeling such as pleasure or comfort in a particular thing or activity, you experience the feeling mentioned as a result of this thing or activity. *How could anyone find pleasure in hunting and killing this beautiful creature?* — V pron-refl prep/adv / V pron-refl adj / VB: no passive, no cont: V n prep / V n -ing WRITTEN / V that, V itadj to-inf, V n to-inf, V n n / be V-ed adj, V n adj / VERB, V n adj, V itadj that, V n n / VERB: V n in n, V n in -ing

12 If you describe someone or something that has been discovered as a **find,** you mean that they are valuable, interesting, good, or useful. *...the botanical find of the century.* **13** See also **finding, found.** — N-COUNT

14 If you **find** your **way** somewhere, you successfully get there by choosing the right way to go. *He was an expert at finding his way, even in strange surroundings.* **15** If something **finds** its **way** somewhere, it comes to that place, especially by chance. *It is one of the very few Michelangelos that have found their way out of Italy.* **16** ● **to find fault with:** see **fault.** ● **to find one's feet:** see **foot.** — PHRASE / PHRASE

find out. 1 If you **find** something **out,** you learn something that you did not already know, especially by making a deliberate effort to do so. *Watch the next episode to find out what's going to happen... I was relieved to find out that my problems were due to a genuine disorder. ...their campaign to find out the truth.* **2** If you **find** someone **out,** you discover that they have been doing something dishonest. *Her face was so grave, I wondered for a moment if she'd found me out.* — PHRASAL VB: V n P, V P wh, V P that, V P noun, Also V P / V n P

fin de siècle /ˌfæn də siˈeklə/; also spelled **fin-de-siècle. Fin de siècle** is used to describe something that relates to the last few years of a century, especially the nineteenth century. *...fin de siècle decadence.* — ADJ: ADJ n WRITTEN

find·ing /ˈfaɪndɪŋ/ **findings. 1** Someone's **findings** are the information they get or the conclusions they come to as the result of an investigation or some research. *One of the main findings of the survey was the confusion about the facilities already in place.* **2** The **findings** of a court are the decision that it reaches after a trial or an inquiry into some matter. *The government hopes the court will announce its findings before the end of the month.* — ◆◆◇◇◇ N-COUNT / N-COUNT

fine 1 adjective uses

fine /faɪn/ **finer, finest. 1** You use **fine** to describe something or someone that you admire for their good qualities. *There is a fine view of the countryside. ...London's finest art deco cinema. ...an excellent journalist and a very fine man.* ♦ **fine·ly** *They are finely engineered boats.* **2** If you say that you are **fine,** you mean that you are in good health or reasonably happy. *Lina is fine and sends you her love.* **3** If you say that something is **fine,** you mean that it is satisfactory or acceptable. *It's fine to ask questions as we go along, but it's better if you wait until we have finished... If you don't want to give it to me, that's fine, I don't mind... 'It'll take me a couple of days.' – 'That's fine with me.'* ▶ Also an adverb. *All the instruments are working fine.* **4 Fine** objects or clothing are of good quality, delicate, and expensive. **5** When the weather is **fine,** it is not raining. **6** Something that is **fine** is very delicate, narrow, or small. *...the fine hairs on her arms. ...on the fine sand.* — ◆◆◆◇ ADJ-GRADED / ADV-GRADED: ADV -ed, ADJ-GRADED: v-link ADJ / ADJ-GRADED / ADV-GRADED / ADJ-GRADED / ADJ-GRADED / ADJ-GRADED

♦ **finely** *Chop the ingredients finely.* **7** A **fine** adjustment, detail, or distinction is very delicate, small, or exact. *The market likes the broad outline but is reserving judgment on the fine detail.* ♦ **finely** *They had to take the finely balanced decision to let the visit proceed.*

fine 2 punishment

fine /faɪn/ **fines, fining, fined. 1** A **fine** is a punishment in which a person is ordered to pay a sum of money because they have broken the law or a rule. **2** If someone **is fined**, they are punished by being ordered to pay a fine. *She was fined £150 and banned from driving for one month... The magistrates could have jailed or fined him for contempt of court.*
♦♦♦◇◇
N-COUNT

VERB
be V-ed
amount
V n
Also V n
amount

,**fine 'art, fine arts. 1** Painting and sculpture can be referred to as **fine art** or as the **fine arts**. *He deals in antiques and fine art. ...the university of Cairo's faculty of fine arts.* **2** If you **have got** something **down to a fine art**, you are able to do it in a very skilful or efficient way because you have had a lot of experience of doing it.

,**fine 'print.** In a contract or agreement, the **fine print** is the same as the **small print**.

fin·ery /ˈfaɪnəri/. If someone is dressed in their **finery**, they are wearing their best clothes and jewellery that they wear on special occasions.

fi·nesse /fɪˈnes/. If you do something with **finesse**, you do it with great skill and flair.

,**fine-'tune, fine-tunes, fine-tuning, fine-tuned.** If you **fine-tune** something, you make very small and precise adjustments to it in order to make it as successful or effective as possible. *Computers allow the plans to be fine-tuned and to be altered quickly.* ♦ **fine-tuning** *There's a lot of fine-tuning to be done yet.*

fin·ger /ˈfɪŋgə/ **fingers, fingering, fingered. 1** Your **fingers** are the four long jointed parts at the end of each hand. See picture headed **human body**. *There was a ring on each of his fingers.* ● See also **light-fingered. 2** If you **finger** something, you touch or feel it with your fingers. *He fingered the few coins in his pocket.* **3** You can use **finger** to refer to something that is long and thin in shape. *...a thin finger of land. ...sponge fingers.* ● See also **fish finger. 4** If you **finger** a person or organization, you tell someone, usually the police, that the person or organization has done something illegal or wrong. **5** If you **point the finger at** someone, you blame them or accuse them of something. You can also, for example, **point an accusing finger at** someone. **6** If you say that someone did not or must not **lay a finger on** a particular person or thing, you are emphasizing that they did not or must not touch or harm that person or thing at all. **7** If you say that someone does not **lift a finger** to help you, you are criticizing them because they do nothing. *She never lifted a finger around the house.* **8** If you say that someone has **a finger in every pie**, you mean they are involved in a lot of things. **9** If you tell someone to **pull their finger out** or to **get their finger out**, you are telling them rudely that you want them to start doing some work or making an effort. **10** If you **put your finger on** something such as a problem or an idea, you see and identify exactly what it is. *He could never quite put his finger on who or what was responsible for all this.* **11** ● **finger on the pulse**: see **pulse. 12** If you **get your fingers burnt** or **burn your fingers**, you suffer because something you did or were involved in was a failure or a mistake. *He has had his fingers burnt by deals that turned out badly.* **13** If you **cross** your fingers, you put one finger on top of another and hope for good luck. If someone **is keeping their fingers crossed**, they are hoping for good luck. **14** If something or someone **slips through your fingers**, you fail to catch them, get them, or keep them. **15** ● to **have green fingers**: see **green.**
♦♦♦◇
N-COUNT

VERB
V n

N-COUNT:
N of n,
n N

VERB: V n
INFORMAL

PHRASE

PHRASE
PRAGMATICS

PHRASE
PRAGMATICS

PHRASE

PHRASE
PRAGMATICS
INFORMAL

PHRASE

PHRASE

PHRASE

fin·ger·ing /ˈfɪŋgərɪŋ/. When you are playing a musical instrument, **fingering** is the method of using the most suitable finger to play each note.

finger·nail /ˈfɪŋgəneɪl/ **fingernails;** also spelled **finger-nail**. Your **fingernails** are the thin hard areas at the end of each of your fingers. See picture headed **human body**.

finger·print /ˈfɪŋgəprɪnt/ **fingerprints, finger-printing, fingerprinted. 1** Your **fingerprints** are the unique marks made by your fingers which show the lines on the skin. ● If the police **take** someone's **fingerprints**, they make that person press their fingers onto a pad covered with ink, and then onto paper, so that they know what that person's fingerprints look like. **2** If someone **is fingerprinted**, the police take his or her fingerprints.

finger·tip /ˈfɪŋgətɪp/ **fingertips;** also spelled **finger-tip**. **1** Your **fingertips** are the ends of your fingers. **2** If something is **at your fingertips**, you can reach or get it easily. *I had the information at my fingertips.*

fin·icky /ˈfɪnɪki/. If you say that someone is **finicky**, you mean that they are fussy and difficult to please; used showing disapproval.

fin·ish /ˈfɪnɪʃ/ **finishes, finishing, finished. 1** When you **finish** doing or dealing with something, you do or deal with the last part of it, so that there is no more for you to do or deal with. *As soon as he'd finished eating, he excused himself... I've practically finished the ironing.* ▶ In American English, **finish up** means the same as **finish**. *We waited a few minutes outside his office while he finished up his meeting.* **2** When you **finish** something that you are making or producing, you reach the end of making or producing it, so that it is complete. *The consultants had been working to finish a report this week.* ▶ **Finish off** and, in American English, **finish up** mean the same as **finish**. *She is busy finishing off a biography of Queen Caroline.* **3** To **finish** means to reach the end of saying something. *He held up a hand. 'Let me finish.'* **4** If you put **the finishing touches** to something, you add or do the last things that are necessary to complete it.
♦♦♦♦◇
VERB
V n/-ing

PHRASAL VB
V P noun

VERB
V n

PHRASAL VB
V P noun

VERB
V

PHRASE

5 When something such as a course, film, or sale **finishes**, it ends. *The teaching day finishes at around 4pm... The play has finished its run... After each game is finished, a message flashes on the screen.* **6** If you say that a period of time, an event, or a person **finished** in a particular way, you are describing what happened at the end of that time, what that person did then, or what the end was like. You can also say that someone or something **finishes** an event in a particular way. *The evening finished with the welcoming of three new members... The two of them finished by kissing each other goodbye... To finish the meal, I ordered a sponge pudding... Mackinnon finished the day in fifth place.*
VERB
V at/on/by n
V n
V-ed
V-ed
V-ERG
V with n
V by -ing
V n
V n adj/adv/
prep

7 If someone **finishes** second, for example, in a race or competition, they are in second place at the end of the race or competition. **8** The **finish** of a race is the end of it. *...a close finish.*

9 The **finish** of something is the end of it or the last part of it. *I intend to continue it and see the job through to the finish.*

10 If the surface of something that has been made has a particular kind of **finish**, it has the appearance or texture mentioned. *The finish and workmanship of the woodwork was excellent.*

11 See also **finished.**

finish off. 1 If you **finish off** something that you have been eating or drinking, you eat or drink the last part of it. *Kelly finished off his coffee.* **2** To **finish off** a person or animal that is already badly injured means to kill or destroy them. *They meant to finish her off, swiftly and without mercy.* **3** See **finish 2.**

finish up. If you **finish up** in a place or situation, you are in that place or situation after doing or experiencing several things. *They had met by chance at university and finished up getting married... He's probably going to finish up in jail.* ● See also **finish 1, 2.**

finish with. If you **finish with** someone or something, you stop dealing with them, being involved with them, or being interested in them. *My boyfriend*

was threatening to finish with me... Once the DA was finished with him I was able to question him.

fin·ished /ˈfɪnɪʃt/. **1** Someone who is **finished with** something is no longer doing it, dealing with it, or interested in it. *One suspects he will be finished with boxing.* **2** Someone or something that is **finished** is no longer important, powerful, or effective. *Her power over me is finished... I thought I was finished.* **3** Something that is **finished** in a particular way has been given a particular appearance or decoration. *The dining room is finished in deep red.*
◆◆◇◇◇ ADJ: v-link ADJ with n ADJ: v-link ADJ ADJ: v-link ADJ prep

'finishing school, finishing schools. A **finishing school** is a private school where wealthy young women are taught manners and other social skills that are considered to be suitable for them.
N-VAR

fi·nite /ˈfaɪnaɪt/. **1** Something that is **finite** has a definite fixed size or extent. *The fossil fuels (coal and oil) are finite resources.* **2** A **finite** clause is a clause based on a verb group which indicates tense, such as 'went', 'is waiting', or 'will be found', rather than on an infinitive or a participle. Compare **non-finite**.
◆◇◇◇◇ ADJ FORMAL ADJ

fir /fɜː/ **firs.** A **fir** or a **fir tree** is a tall evergreen tree that has thin needle-like leaves and produces cones.
◆◇◇◇◇ N-VAR

fire 1 burning, heat, or enthusiasm

fire /faɪə/ **fires, firing, fired.** **1** **Fire** is the hot bright flames produced by things that are burning. *...a great orange ball of fire.* **2** **Fire** or a **fire** is an occurrence of uncontrolled burning which destroys things. *A family of four has died in a fire... Much of historic Rennes was destroyed by fire in 1720.* **3** If an object or substance **catches fire**, it starts burning. *The aircraft caught fire soon after take-off.* **4** If something is **on fire**, it is burning and being damaged or destroyed by an uncontrolled fire. *The ship was on fire.* **5** If you **set fire to** something or if you **set** it **on fire**, you start it burning in order to damage or destroy it.
◆◆◆◆ N-UNCOUNT

N-VAR

PHRASE

PHRASE

PHRASE

6 A **fire** is a burning pile of wood, coal, or other fuel that you make, for example to use for heat, light, or cooking. *I started to clear the grate to light a fire.* **7** A **fire** is a device that uses electricity or gas to give out heat and warm a room. *...a gas fire.*
N-COUNT

N-COUNT

8 When the engine of a motor vehicle **fires**, an electrical spark is produced which causes the fuel to burn and the engine to work. **9** If a machine **is fired with** a particular fuel, it operates by means of that fuel. ♦ *-fired ...oil-fired power stations.* **10** When a pot or clay object **is fired**, it is heated at a high temperature in a special oven, as part of the process of making it. *After the pot is dipped in this mixture, it is fired.*
VERB: V

VERB: be V-ed with n COMB VERB be V-ed Also V n

11 You can use **fire** to refer in an approving way to someone's energy and enthusiasm. *His punishing schedule seemed to dim his fire at times.* **12** If a situation or event **catches fire**, it begins to be exciting and successful. *The play only really catches fire once Aschenbach falls in love.* **13** If you **fire** someone with enthusiasm, you make them feel very enthusiastic. If you **fire** someone's imagination, you make them feel interested and excited. *It was Allen who fired this rivalry with real passion... Both his grandfathers were fired with an enthusiasm for public speaking.*
N-UNCOUNT [PRAGMATICS]

PHRASE

VERB: V n V n with n V-ed

14 If you **fight fire with fire**, you deal with people attacking or threatening you by using similar methods to the ones that they are using. **15** If you say that someone is **playing with fire**, you mean that they are doing something dangerous that may result in great harm for them and cause many problems. **16** ● **like a house on fire:** see **house.** ● **have irons in the fire:** see **iron.** ● **there's no smoke without fire:** see **smoke.**
PHRASE

PHRASE

fire 2 shooting or attacking

fire /faɪə/ **fires, firing, fired.** **1** If someone **fires a** gun or a bullet, a bullet is sent from a gun that they are using. *Soldiers fired rubber bullets to disperse crowds... Seventeen people were killed when security forces fired on demonstrators.* ♦ **fir·ing** *The firing continued even while the protestors were fleeing.*
◆◆◆◇ VERB V n V on n Also V n N-UNCOUNT

2 You can use **fire** to refer to the shots fired from a gun or guns. *...an exchange of fire during a police raid... The soldiers returned fire after being attacked.* **3** If someone **holds** their **fire** or **holds fire**, they stop
N-UNCOUNT

PHRASE

shooting or they wait before they start shooting. **4** If you are in the **line of fire**, or in someone's **line of fire**, you are in a position where someone is aiming a gun at you. **5** If someone with a gun **opens fire** on you, they start shooting at you. *The troops opened fire on the crowd.* **6** If you come **under fire** or are **under fire**, someone starts shooting at you.
PHRASE

PHRASE

PHRASE

7 You can use **fire** to refer to someone's strong criticisms of something. *He concentrates his fire on the defects of the Maastricht treaty.* **8** If you **hang fire** or **hold fire**, you delay making a decision or taking decisive action. *Last week, banks and building societies were hanging fire on interest rates.* **9** If you come **under fire** from someone, they criticize you strongly.
N-UNCOUNT: poss N PHRASE

PHRASE

10 If you **fire** questions at someone, you ask them a lot of questions very quickly, one after another.
VERB: V n

fire away. If someone wants to ask you something, you can say **'fire away'** as a way of showing that you are ready for them to speak. *'May I ask you something?'—'Sure. Fire away.'*
PHRASAL VB only imper V P INFORMAL

fire off. 1 If you **fire off** a shot, you send a bullet or other projectile from a gun. *A gunman fired off a volley of shots into the air.* **2** If you **fire off** a letter, question, or remark, you send or say it very quickly, often as part of a series.
PHRASAL VB V P noun

V P noun

fire 3 dismiss

fire /faɪə/ **fires, firing, fired.** If an employer **fires** you, they dismiss you from your job. *You're fired!* ♦ **fir·ing, firings** *...yet another round of firings.*
◆◆◇◇◇ VERB: V n be V-ed N-COUNT

'fire alarm, fire alarms. A **fire alarm** is a device that makes a loud noise, for example with a bell, to warn people when there is a fire.
N-COUNT

fire·arm /ˈfaɪərɑːm/ **firearms. Firearms** are guns. *...illegal possession of firearms.*
◆◇◇◇◇ N-COUNT FORMAL

fire·ball /ˈfaɪəbɔːl/ **fireballs.** A **fireball** is a ball of fire, for example at the centre of an explosion.
N-COUNT

fire·bomb /ˈfaɪəbɒm/ **firebombs;** also spelled **fire bomb.** A **firebomb** is a bomb that burns after it has exploded.
N-COUNT

fire·brand /ˈfaɪəbrænd/ **firebrands.** If you refer to someone such as a politician as a **firebrand**, you mean that they are full of anger or enthusiasm, and are usually in favour of strong or extreme action. *...his reputation as a young firebrand.*
N-COUNT

fire·break /ˈfaɪəbreɪk/ **firebreaks;** also spelled **fire break.** A **firebreak** is an area of open land in a wood or forest that has been created to stop a fire from spreading.
N-COUNT

'fire brigade, fire brigades. The **fire brigade** is an organization which has the job of putting out fires. *Get everyone out and call the fire brigade.*
◆◇◇◇◇ N-COLL-COUNT

fire·cracker /ˈfaɪəkrækə/ **firecrackers.** A **firecracker** is a firework that makes several loud bangs when it is lit.
N-COUNT

'fire department, fire departments. The **fire department** is an organization which has the job of putting out fires. The British term is **fire service.**
N-COLL-COUNT AMERICAN

'fire-eater, fire-eaters. **Fire-eaters** are performers who put flaming rods into their mouths in order to entertain people.
N-COUNT

'fire engine, fire engines. A **fire engine** is a large vehicle that carries firemen and equipment for putting out fires.
N-COUNT

'fire escape, fire escapes. A **fire escape** is a metal staircase or ladder on the outside of a building, which can be used to escape from the building if there is a fire.
N-COUNT

'fire extinguisher, fire extinguishers. A **fire extinguisher** is a metal cylinder containing water or chemicals at high pressure which can put out fires.
N-COUNT

fire·fight /ˈfaɪəfaɪt/ **firefights.** A **firefight** is a battle in a war which involves the use of guns rather than bombs or any other sort of weapon. *...a fierce firefight that left more than sixty people dead.*
N-COUNT JOURNALISM

'fire fighter, fire fighters; also spelled **fire-fighter. Fire fighters** are people whose job is to put out fires.
N-COUNT

'fire fighting. **Fire fighting** is the work of putting out fires. *There was no fire-fighting equipment.*
N-UNCOUNT

fire·fly /'faɪəflaɪ/ **fireflies.** A firefly is an insect that N-COUNT glows in the dark.

fire·guard /'faɪəgɑːd/ **fireguards;** also spelled N-COUNT **fire-guard.** A fireguard is a screen made of strong wire mesh that you put round a fire so that people cannot accidentally burn themselves.

'**fire hydrant, fire hydrants.** A fire hydrant is a N-COUNT pipe in the street from which fire fighters can obtain water for putting out a fire.

fire·light /'faɪəlaɪt/. Firelight is the light that comes N-UNCOUNT: from a fire. *He stared into the firelight.* also the N

fire·man /'faɪəmən/ **firemen.** A fireman is a per- ◆◇◇◇◇ son, usually a man, whose job is to put out fires. N-COUNT

fire·place /'faɪəpleɪs/ **fireplaces.** In a room, the ◆◇◇◇◇ fireplace is the place where a fire can be lit and the N-COUNT area on the wall and floor surrounding this place.

fire·power /'faɪəpaʊə/. The firepower of an army ◆◇◇◇◇ or military vehicle is the amount of ammunition it N-UNCOUNT can fire. *America has enough firepower in the area to mount sustained air strikes.*

fire·proof /'faɪəpruːf/. Something that is fireproof ADJ cannot be damaged by fire. *...fireproof clothing.*

'**fire sale, fire sales.** If you describe a sale of N-COUNT goods or other assets as a fire sale, you mean that everything is being sold very cheaply. *They're likely to hold big fire sales to liquidate their inventory.*

'**fire service, fire services.** The fire service is an N-COLL- organization which has the job of putting out fires. COUNT The American term is fire department. BRITISH

fire·side /'faɪəsaɪd/ **firesides.** If you sit by the fire- N-COUNT side in a room, you sit near the fire. *...winter eve- nings by the fireside. ...cosy fireside chats.*

'**fire station, fire stations.** A fire station is a N-COUNT building where fire engines are kept, and where fire fighters wait until they are called to put out a fire.

fire·storm /'faɪəstɔːm/ **firestorms;** also spelled **fire storm. 1** A firestorm is a fire that is burning N-COUNT uncontrollably, usually in a place that has been bombed. **2** If you say that there is a firestorm of N-COUNT protest or criticism, you are emphasizing that there PRAGMATICS is a great deal of very fierce protest or criticism. *The* AMERICAN *speech has resulted in a firestorm of controversy.*

'**fire truck, fire trucks.** A fire truck is a large vehi- N-COUNT cle that carries firemen and equipment for putting AMERICAN out fires. The British term is fire engine.

fire·wood /'faɪəwʊd/. Firewood is wood that has ◆◇◇◇◇ been cut up so that it can be burned on a fire. N-UNCOUNT

fire·work /'faɪəwɜːk/ **fireworks. 1** Fireworks are ◆◇◇◇◇ small objects that are lit to entertain people on spe- N-COUNT cial occasions. They burn brightly, attractively, and often noisily. *Berlin people drank champagne, set off fireworks and tooted their car horns. ...a firework display.* **2** An exciting and impressive performance N-PLURAL or piece of writing can be referred to as fireworks. *...a typically thoughtful production with just enough theatrical fireworks.*

'**firing line. 1** If you are in the firing line, you are N-SING: in a position where someone is aiming a gun at you. the N *Any hostages in the firing line would have been sac- rificed.* **2** If you say that someone is in the firing N-SING: line, you mean that they are being criticized or the N blamed for something.

'**firing squad, firing squads.** A firing squad is a N-COUNT: group of soldiers who are ordered to shoot and kill also by N a person who has been found guilty of a crime.

firm /fɜːm/ **firms, firming, firmed; firmer, firm- ◆◆◆◆◆ est. 1** A firm is an organization which sells or pro- N-COUNT duces something or which provides a service which people pay for. *...a firm of heating engineers.*
2 If something is firm, it is fairly hard and does not ADJ-GRADED change much in shape when it is pressed. *Fruit should be firm and in excellent condition... Choose a soft, me- dium or firm mattress to suit your individuals needs.*
♦ **firm·ness** *Vegetables should retain some firmness* N-UNCOUNT *and should not be soggy.* **3** If something is firm, it does ADJ-GRADED not shake or move when you put weight or pressure on it, because it is strongly made or securely fastened. *To climb up, use a firm platform or a sturdy ladder.*
♦ **firm·ly** *All the windows are firmly shut.* **4** If ADV-GRADED someone's grip is firm or if they perform a physical ADJ-GRADED

action in a firm way, they do it with quite a lot of force or pressure but also in a controlled way. *The quick handshake was firm and cool... He managed to grasp the metal, get a firm grip of it and heave his body upwards.* ♦ **firmly** *She held me firmly by the elbow.* ADV-GRADED:
ADV after v
5 If you describe someone as firm, you mean that ADJ-GRADED they are behaving in a fairly strict or determined way, and will not change their mind. *She had to be firm with him. 'I don't want to see you again.' ...the guiding hand of a firm father figure.* ♦ **firmly** *'A good night's* ADV-GRADED *sleep is what you want,' he said firmly.* ♦ **firm·ness** N-UNCOUNT *...a manner that combines friendliness with compas- sion and firmness.* **6** If someone stands firm, they re- PHRASE fuse to surrender or change their mind about some- thing. *The council is standing firm against the barrage of protest.*
7 A firm decision or opinion is definite and unlikely to ADJ-GRADED change. *It is my firm belief that an effective partner- ship approach between police and the public is abso- lutely necessary.* ♦ **firmly** *He is firmly convinced that it* ADV-GRADED *is vital to do this.* **8** Firm evidence or information is ADJ-GRADED based on facts and so is likely to be true. *This man* ADJ n *may have killed others but unfortunately we have no firm evidence.* **9** You use firm when describing a situa- ADJ-GRADED tion in which something is strongly established and unlikely to be ended or removed. *They have firm con- trol of the territory... The company, a household name in the States, has a firm foothold in the British market. ...firm friends.* ♦ **firm·ly** *This tradition is also firmly* ADV-GRADED *rooted in the past... It placed reggae music firmly in the mainstream of world culture.* **10** If a price, value, or ADJ-GRADED currency is firm, it is not decreasing in value or amount. *Cotton prices remain firm and demand is strong... The shares held firm at 280p.*

firm up. 1 If you firm up something or if it firms up, PHRASAL VB it becomes more solid, and less flabby or floppy. ERG *Treatment helps tone the body, firm up muscles and* V P noun tighten the skin... The mixture will seem too wet at this V P stage, but it will firm up when chilled. **2** If you firm ERG something up or if it firms up, it becomes clearer, V P noun stronger, or more definite. *The Conservatives will firm* also V P up their plans for a cleaner, greener, safer Britain... The ground rules have been firmed up. **3** If a financial insti- V P noun tution firms up the price or value of something, they take action to protect and maintain its price or value. *OPEC has agreed to freeze its global oil production slightly in order to firm up crude prices.*

fir·ma·ment /'fɜːməmənt/. **1** The firmament is the N-SING sky or heaven. **2** The firmament in a particular or- LITERARY ganization or field of activity is the top of it. *...a ris-* N-SING: ing star in the political firmament. the N

first /fɜːst/ **firsts. 1** The first thing or person is the ◆◆◆◆◆ one that happens or comes before all the others of ORDINAL the same kind. See Appendix headed **Numbers.** *...the first month of her diet. ...the first few flakes of snow... Johnson came first in the one hundred metres.*
► Also a pronoun. *The second paragraph startled* PRON *me even more than the first.* **2** If you do something ADV first, you do it before anyone else does, or before you do anything else. *I do not remember who spoke first... First, tell me what you think of my products.* PHRASE **3** You say '**first come first served**' to indicate that a group of people or things will be dealt with or given something in the order in which they arrive. *There will be free buses, first come first served.*
4 When something happens or is done for the first ORDINAL time, it has never happened or been done before.
► Also an adverb. *...two years after they had first start-* ADV: ed going out. **5** An event that is described as a first has ADV with v never happened before. *It is a first for New York. An* N-SING: outdoor exhibition of Fernando Botero's sculpture. a N
6 The first you hear of something or the first you PRON know about it is the time when you first become aware of it. *That was the first we heard of it.*
7 You use first when you are talking about what hap- ADV: pens in the early part of an event or experience, in ADV before v contrast to what happens later. *When he first came home he wouldn't say anything about what he'd been doing.* ► Also an ordinal. *Her first reaction was dis-* ORDINAL gust. **8** You use at first when you are talking about PHRASE

what happens in the early stages of something, or just after something else has happened. *At first, he seemed surprised by my questions.* **9 From the first** means PHRASE ever since something started. *You knew about me from the first, didn't you?*

10 In order to emphasize your determination not to do a particular thing, you can say that rather than do it, you would do something else **first**. *Marry that fat son of a fat cattle dealer? She would die first!* ADV: ADV after v PRAGMATICS

11 You use **first** when you are about to give the first in a series of items. *Certain basic guidelines can be given. First, have a heating engineer check the safety of the heating system.* **12** You use **first of all** to introduce the first of a number of things that you want to say. *The cut in the interest rates has not had very much impact in California for two reasons. First of all, banks are still afraid to loan.* **13** You use **first off** to introduce the first of a number of things that you want to say. *First off, huge apologies for last month's confusing report.* ADV: ADV with cl/group PRAGMATICS / PHRASE PRAGMATICS / PHRASE PRAGMATICS INFORMAL

14 The **first** thing, person, or place in a line is the one that is nearest to you or nearest to the front. *In the first row sat the President.* ORDINAL

15 You use **first** to refer to the best or most important thing or person of a particular kind. *The first duty of any government must be to protect the interests of the taxpayers.* **16** If you say that someone or something **comes first** for a particular person, you mean they treat or consider that person or thing as more important than anything else. *There's no time for boyfriends, my career comes first.* **17** If you **put** someone or something **first**, you treat or consider them as more important than anything else. ORDINAL / PHRASE / PHRASE

18 In British universities, a **first** is an honours degree of the highest standard. N-COUNT

19 If you learn or experience something **at first hand**, you experience it yourself or learn it directly rather than being told about it by other people. *He arrived in Natal to see at first hand the effects of the recent heavy fighting.* **20** If you say that you **do not know the first thing about** something, you are emphasizing that you know absolutely nothing about it. **21** You say **'first things first'** when you are talking about something that should be done or dealt with before anything else because it is the most important. **22** ● **first and foremost**: see **foremost**. PHRASE / PHRASE PRAGMATICS / PHRASE

-first /-fɜːst/. **-first** combines with nouns like 'head' and 'feet' to indicate that someone moves with the part of the body that is mentioned pointing in the direction in which they are moving. *He fell head-first.* COMB

,**first 'aid.** **First aid** is simple medical treatment given as soon as possible to a person who is injured or who suddenly becomes ill. ◆◇◇◇ N-UNCOUNT

'**first born.** Someone's **first born** is their first child. N-SING

,**first-'class;** also spelled **first class**. **1** If you describe something or someone as **first-class**, you mean that they are of the highest quality. *The food was first-class.* **2** You use **first-class** to describe something that is in the group that is considered to be of the highest standard. *...his retirement from first-class cricket.* **3 First-class** accommodation on a train, aeroplane, or ship is the best and most expensive. *...two first-class tickets to fly to Dublin.* ► Also an adverb. *She had never flown first class before.* ► **First-class** is the first-class accommodation on a train, aeroplane, or ship. *...a cabin in first class.* **4** In Britain, **first-class** postage is the quicker and more expensive type of postage. In the United States, **first-class** postage is the type of postage that is used for sending letters and postcards. ► Also an adverb. *It took six days to arrive despite being posted first class.* ◆◆◇◇ ADJ / ADJ: ADJ n / ADJ: ADJ n / ADV: ADV after v N-UNCOUNT / ADJ: ADJ n / ADV: ADV after v

,**first 'cousin, first cousins.** Someone's **first cousin** is the same as their **cousin**. Compare **second cousin**. N-COUNT

'**first degree, first degrees.** People who have gained a higher qualification after completing a basic university degree such as a BA or a BSc refer to that basic degree as their **first degree**. N-COUNT

'**first-degree.** **1 First-degree** is used to describe crimes that are considered to be the most serious of ADJ: ADJ n AMERICAN

their kind. *...first-degree murder.* **2** A **first-degree** burn is one of the least severe kind, where only the surface layer of the skin has been burnt. ADJ: ADJ n

,**first 'ever;** also spelled **first-ever**. Something that is the **first ever** one of its kind has never happened before. *It's the first-ever meeting between leaders of the two countries.* ◆◇◇◇ ADJ

,**first 'floor, first floors.** **1** The **first floor** of a building is the floor immediately above the one at ground level. The American expression is **second floor**. **2** The **first floor** of a building is the one at ground level. The British expression is **ground floor**. N-COUNT BRITISH / N-COUNT AMERICAN

,**first 'fruits.** The **first fruits** of a project or activity are the earliest results or profits. *...the first fruits of a liberalization of foreign investment law.* N-PLURAL

,**first 'hand;** also spelled **first-hand** or **firsthand**. **1 First hand** information or experience is gained or learned directly, rather than from other people. *School trips give children firsthand experience not available in the classroom.* ► Also an adverb. *We've been through Germany and seen first-hand what's happening there.* **2** ● **at first hand**: see **first**. ◆◇◇◇ ADJ: ADJ n / ADV: ADV after v

,**First 'Lady, First Ladies.** The **First Lady** in a country or state is the wife of the president or state governor, or a woman who performs the official duties normally performed by the wife. ◆◇◇◇ N-COUNT

,**first 'language, first languages.** Someone's **first language** is the language that they learnt first and speak best. N-COUNT

first·ly /'fɜːstli/. You use **firstly** when you want to give a reason, make a point, or mention an item that will be followed by others connected with it. *Vitamin C has many roles to play in weight control. Firstly, it is needed for hormone production.* ◆◇◇◇ ADV: ADV with cl/group PRAGMATICS

'**first name, first names.** Your **first name** is the first of the names that were given to you when you were born. You can also refer to all of your names except your surname as your **first names**. ● If two people are **on first name terms**, they know each other well enough to call each other by their first names. ◆◇◇◇ N-COUNT / PHRASE

,**first 'night, first nights.** The **first night** of a show or play is the first public performance of it. ◆◇◇◇ N-COUNT

,**first of'fender, first offenders.** A **first offender** is a person who has been found guilty of a crime for the first time. N-COUNT

,**first-past-the-'post.** A **first-past-the-post** electoral system is one in which the candidate who gets most votes wins. ADJ: ADJ n

,**first 'person.** A clause in **the first person** is a clause about yourself, or about yourself and someone else. The subject of a clause like this is 'I' or 'we'. *He tells the story in the first person.* ◆◇◇◇ N-SING: the N

'**first-rate;** also spelled **first rate**. Something or someone that is **first-rate** is of the highest quality. *...a first-rate professional.* ◆◇◇◇ ADJ

,**first school, first schools.** A **first school** is a school for children aged between five and eight or nine. N-COUNT BRITISH

,**first-'timer, first-timers.** A **first-timer** is someone who does something for the first time. *It is a great introduction to ballet for first-timers.* N-COUNT

fis·cal /'fɪskəl/. **Fiscal** is used to describe something that relates to government money or public money, especially taxes. *...fiscal policy.* ◆ **fis·cal·ly** *They are fiscally responsible.* ● See also **procurator fiscal**. ◆◆◇◇ ADJ: ADJ n / ADV

,**fiscal 'year, fiscal years.** The **fiscal year** is the same as the **financial year**. *...the budget for the coming fiscal year.* ◆◇◇◇ N-COUNT

fish /fɪʃ/ **fishes, fishing, fished**. The form **fish** is usually used for the plural, but **fishes** can also be used. **1** A **fish** is a creature that lives in water and has a tail and fins. ► **Fish** is the flesh of a fish eaten as food. *Does dry white wine go best with fish?* **2** If you feel **like a fish out of water**, you do not feel comfortable or relaxed because you are in an unusual or unfamiliar situation. **3** If you **fish**, you try to catch fish, either for food or as ◆◆◆◇ N-COUNT / N-UNCOUNT / PHRASE INFORMAL / VERB: V

a form of recreation. **4** If you **fish** a particular area of water, you try to catch fish in it. **5** See also **fishing**. VERB: V n

6 If you say that someone **is fishing** for information or praise, you disapprove of the fact that they are trying to get it from someone in an indirect way. *'You don't have to talk to him!' Mike shouted. 'He's just fishing.'* VERB: V form PRAGMATICS V

fish out. If you **fish** something **out** from somewhere, you take or pull it out. *Kelly fished out another beer from his cooler.* PHRASAL VB V n P V P noun

fisher·man /ˈfɪʃəmən/ **fishermen.** A **fisherman** is a person who catches fish as a job or for sport. ◆◆◇◇◇ N-COUNT

fish·ery /ˈfɪʃəri/ **fisheries. 1 Fisheries** are areas of the sea where fish are caught in large quantities for commercial purposes. *...the fisheries off Newfoundland.* **2** A **fishery** is a place where fish are bred and reared. N-COUNT N-COUNT

fish 'finger, fish fingers. Fish fingers are small rectangular pieces of fish covered in breadcrumbs. N-COUNT

fish·ing /ˈfɪʃɪŋ/. **Fishing** is the sport, hobby, or business of catching fish. ◆◆◆◇◇ N-UNCOUNT

'fishing rod, fishing rods. A **fishing rod** is a long thin pole which has a line and hook attached to it and which is used for catching fish. N-COUNT

fish·monger /ˈfɪʃmʌŋgə/ **fishmongers.** The **fishmonger** or the **fishmonger's** is a shop where fish is sold. You can also refer to the shopkeeper of this shop as a **fishmonger**. N-COUNT BRITISH

fish·net /ˈfɪʃnet/. **Fishnet** tights or stockings are made from a stretchy fabric which has wide holes between its strands. N-UNCOUNT

fishy /ˈfɪʃi/. **1** A **fishy** taste or smell reminds you of fish. **2** If you describe a situation as **fishy**, you feel that someone is not telling the truth or behaving completely honestly. *There seems to be something fishy going on.* ADJ-GRADED ADJ-GRADED INFORMAL

fis·sion /ˈfɪʃən/. Nuclear **fission** is the splitting of the nuclei in atoms of uranium or plutonium to produce a large amount of energy or cause a large explosion. N-UNCOUNT

fis·sure /ˈfɪʃə/ **fissures.** A **fissure** is a deep crack in something, especially in rock or in the ground. N-COUNT

fist /fɪst/ **fists. 1** Your hand is referred to as your **fist** when you have bent your fingers in towards the palm in order to hit someone, to make an angry gesture, or to hold something. *...angry protestors with clenched fists.* **2** An **iron fist** policy or approach is one which deals with people and situations in a very strict and ruthless way. *...the iron-fist policy towards the fundamentalists.* ◆◆◇◇◇ N-COUNT PHRASE

fist·ful /ˈfɪstfʊl/ **fistfuls.** A **fistful** of things is the number of them that you can hold in your fist. *Mandy handed him a fistful of coins.* N-COUNT

fisti·cuffs /ˈfɪstikʌfs/. **Fisticuffs** is fighting in which people try to hit each other with their fists. N-UNCOUNT DATED

fit 1 being right or going in the right place

fit /fɪt/ **fits, fitting, fitted.** In American English the form **fit** is used in the present tense and sometimes also as the past tense and past participle of the verb. ◆◆◆◆◇

1 If something **fits**, it is the right size and shape to go onto a person's body or onto a particular object. *The sash, kimono, and other garments were made to fit a child. ...trousers that fit at the waist... Her champagne-coloured suit fit snugly across her slim hips.* **2** If something is a good **fit**, it fits well. *The sills and doors were a reasonably good fit.* VERB V n V prep/adv N-SING: adj N

3 If something **are fitted for** a particular piece of clothing, you try it on so that the person who is making it can see where it needs to be altered. VB: usu passive, be V-ed for n

4 If something **fits** somewhere, it can be put there or is designed to be put there. *...a pocket computer which is small enough to fit into your pocket.* **5** If you **fit** something into a particular space or place, you put it there. *...she fitted her key in the lock.* VERB V prep/adv VERB V n prep/adv

6 If you **fit** something somewhere, you attach it there, or put it there carefully and securely. *Fit hinge bolts to give extra support to the door lock... Peter had built the overhead ladders, and the next day he fitted them to the wall.* VERB V n V n prep

7 If something **fits** something else or **fits** into it, it is VERB

compatible with that thing or able to be part of it. *Her daughter doesn't fit the current feminine ideal... Fostering is a full-time job and you should carefully consider how it will fit into your career.* **8** You can say that something **fits** a particular person or thing when it is appropriate or suitable for them or it. *The punishment must always fit the crime.* V n V in/into Also V VERB V n

9 If something is **fit** for a particular purpose, it is suitable for that purpose. *Of the seven bicycles we had, only two were fit for the road... The meat is fit to eat. ...making your home a fit place to work, rest and play.* ADJ

10 If someone is **fit** to do something, they have the appropriate qualities or skills that will allow them to do it. *You're not fit to be a mother!... I'm over 60 now and only fit for gardening and sleeping... He was not a fit companion for their skipper.* ♦ **fit·ness** *...a debate about his fitness for the highest office... You should consult your doctor about your fitness to travel.* **11** If something **fits** someone for a particular task or role, it makes them good enough or suitable for it. *...a man whose past experience fits him for the top job in education... It is not a person's gender that fits them to be a minister.* ADJ N-UNCOUNT: N forn, N to-inf VERB V n forn V n to-inf FORMAL

12 If you say that something or someone is **fit** to produce some extreme result, you are emphasizing the extreme nature of that thing or that person's activity. *The stink was fit to knock you down.* ▶ Also an adverb. *Wally was laughing fit to burst... You're shivering fit to die, Gracie.* ADJ: v-link ADJ to-inf PRAGMATICS ADV: ADV after v, ADV to-inf

13 If you say that someone **sees fit** to do something, you mean that they decide to do it, but that you disapprove of their decision. *He's not a friend, you say, yet you saw fit to lend him money.* PHRASE PRAGMATICS

14 See also **fitted, fitting.** ● **fit the bill**: see **bill.** ● **not in a fit state**: see **state.**

fit in. 1 If you manage to **fit** a person or task **in**, you manage to find time to deal with them. *I find that I just can't fit in regular domestic work.* **2** If you **fit into** a group or you **fit in**, you seem to belong in the group because you are similar to other people in it. *It's hard to see how he would fit into the team... She was great with the children and fitted in beautifully.* **3** If something **fits into** a particular situation or system or if it **fits in**, that situation or system seems to be the right place for it. *Most film locations broadly fit into two categories... This fits in with what you've told me.* PHRASAL VB V n P V P noun V P n V P V P n with n Also V P

fit out or **fit up.** The form **fit up** is mainly used in British English. If you **fit** someone or something **out**, or you **fit** them **up**, you provide them with equipment and other things that they need. *We helped to fit him out for a trip to the Baltic... I suggest we fit you up with an office suite.* PHRASAL VB V n P V n P forn V n P with n

fit 2 healthy

fit /fɪt/ **fitter, fittest.** Someone who is **fit** is healthy and physically strong. ♦ **fit·ness** *...women who regularly engage in sports and fitness activities.* ● **fighting fit**: see **fight.** ◆◆◆◇◇ ADJ-GRADED N-UNCOUNT

fit 3 uncontrollable movements or emotions

fit /fɪt/ **fits. 1** If someone has a **fit**, they suddenly lose consciousness and their body makes uncontrollable movements. *...epileptic fits.* ◆◆◇◇◇ N-COUNT

2 If you have a **fit of** coughing or laughter, you suddenly start to cough or laugh in an uncontrollable way. N-COUNT: with supp, N ofn

3 If you do something in a **fit of** anger or panic, you are very angry or afraid when you do it. *Pattie shot Tom in a fit of jealous rage.* N-COUNT: N ofn

4 If you say that someone will **have a fit** when they hear about something, you mean that they will be very angry or shocked. *He'd have a fit if he knew what we were up to!* **5** Someone who is **in fits** is laughing uncontrollably. *He was a much more entertaining person, who used to have us all in fits.* **6** Something that happens **in fits and starts** or **by fits and starts** keeps happening and then stopping again. *My slimming attempts tend to go in fits and starts.* PHRASE INFORMAL PHRASE PHRASE

fit·ful /ˈfɪtfʊl/. Something that is **fitful** happens for irregular periods or occurs at irregular times, rather than being continuous. *Colin drifted off into a fitful* ADJ

sleep... *The government is making slow and fitful progress.* ♦ **fit·ful·ly** *The sun shone fitfully.* — ADV

fit·ted /'fɪtɪd/. **1** A **fitted** piece of clothing is designed so that it is the same size and shape as your body rather than being loose. *...baggy trousers with fitted jackets.* **2** A **fitted** piece of furniture, for example a cupboard, is designed to fill a particular space and is fixed in place. *...fitted wardrobes.* **3** A **fitted** carpet is cut to the same shape as a room so that it covers the floor completely. **4** A **fitted** sheet has the corners sewn so that it fits over the corners of the mattress and does not have to be folded. **5** If a room is **fitted** with objects, those objects are in the room and are normally fixed in place. *Bedrooms are fitted with alarm pull cords.* — ◆◇◇◇ ADJ / ADJ / ADJ: ADJ n / ADJ: ADJ n / ADJ: v-link ADJ with n, ADJ n

fit·ter /'fɪtə/ **fitters.** A **fitter** is a person whose job is to put together, adjust, or install machinery or equipment. *George was a fitter at the shipyard.* — N-COUNT

fit·ting /'fɪtɪŋ/ **fittings. 1** A **fitting** is one of the small parts on the outside of a piece of equipment or furniture, for example a handle or a tap. *...brass light fittings.* **2** **Fittings** are things, for example cookers or electric fires, that are fixed inside a building, but that can be removed if necessary. **3** Something that is **fitting** is right or suitable. *...a fitting end to a bitter campaign.* ♦ **fit·ting·ly** *...a fittingly eccentric figure... Fittingly, she will spend her year off training her voice.* **4** If someone has a **fitting**, they try on a piece of clothing that is being made for them to see if it fits. — ◆◆◇◇ N-COUNT / N-PLURAL / ADJ-GRADED / ADV-GRADED / N-COUNT

-fitting /-'fɪtɪŋ/. **-fitting** combines with adjectives or adverbs such as 'close', 'loose', or 'tightly' to show that something is the size indicated in relation to the thing it is on, in, or next to. *...loose-fitting night clothes. ...glass bottles with tight-fitting caps.* — COMB

five /faɪv/ **fives. 1** **Five** is the number 5. See Appendix headed **Numbers. 2** See also **high five.** — ◆◆◆◆ NUMBER

fiv·er /'faɪvə/ **fivers.** A **fiver** is a British five pound note. *...blank videos for a fiver each.* — ◆◇◇◇ N-COUNT INFORMAL

fix /fɪks/ **fixes, fixing, fixed. 1** If something is **fixed** somewhere, it is attached there firmly or securely. *It is fixed on the wall... He fixed a bayonet to the end of his rifle.* **2** If you **fix** something, for example a date, price, or policy, you decide and say exactly what it will be. *He's going to fix a time when I can see him.* **3** If you **fix** something for someone, you arrange it or organize it for them. *I've fixed it for you to see Bonnie Lachlan... Their relatives would be able to fix the visas... He vanished after you fixed him with a job... We fixed for the team to visit our headquarters.* **4** If you **fix** something which is damaged or which does not work properly, you repair it. *If something is broken, we get it fixed.* **5** If you **fix** a problem or a bad situation, you deal with it and make it satisfactory. *It's not too late to fix the problem.* **6** You can refer to a solution to a problem as a **fix.** *Many of those changes could just be a temporary fix.* ● See also **quick fix.** **7** If you **fix** your eyes **on** someone or something, or if your eyes **fix on** them, you look at them with complete attention. *She fixes her steel-blue eyes on an unsuspecting local official... Her soft brown eyes fixed on Kelly.* **8** If you **fix** someone with a particular kind of expression, you look at them in that way. *He fixed me with a lopsided grin.* **9** If you **fix** your attention **on** someone or something, you think about them with complete attention. *Fix your attention on the practicalities of financing your schemes.* **10** If someone or something **is fixed in** your mind, you remember them well, for example because they are very important, interesting, or unusual. *Amy watched the child's intent face eagerly, trying to fix it in her mind.* **11** If someone **fixes** a gun, camera, or radar **on** something, they point it at that thing. *The US crew fixed its radar on the Turkish ship.* **12** If you **fix** the position of something, you find out exactly where it is, usually by using radar or electronic equipment. *He had not been able to fix his position.* ► Also a noun. *The army hasn't been able to get a fix on the transmitter.* — ◆◆◇◇ VERB beV-ed prep/adv Vn prep/adv / VERB Vn / VERB V it for n to-inf Vn with n V for n to-inf / VERB: Vn get/have n V-ed VERB Vn / N-COUNT / V-ERG Vn on n Vonn / VB: no passive Vn on n WRITTEN / Vn on n / VERB: beV-ed in n Vn in n / VERB Vn on n / VERB Vn / N-COUNT

13 If you get a **fix on** someone or something, you have a clear idea or understanding of them. *It's been hard to get a steady fix on what's going on.* — N-SING: a N on n INFORMAL

14 If you **fix** some food or a drink for someone, you prepare it for them. *Let me fix you a drink... Scotty stayed behind to fix lunch.* **15** If you **fix** your hair, clothes, or make-up, you arrange or adjust them so you look neat. *'I've got to fix my hair,' I said.* **16** If you have your teeth **fixed**, you have dental treatment to make your teeth even, straight, and white. — VERB: V n n V n / VB: no passive Vn INFORMAL / VB: usu passive INFORMAL

17 If someone **fixes** a race, election, contest, or other event, they make unfair or illegal arrangements or use trickery to affect the result. *They offered opposing players bribes to fix a decisive league match.* ► Also a noun. *It's all a fix, a deal they've made.* **18** If you accuse someone of **fixing** prices, you accuse them of making unfair arrangements to charge a particular price for something, rather than allowing market forces to decide it. *...a suspected cartel that had fixed the price of steel.* — VERB V n / N-COUNT / PRAGMATICS V n

19 An injection of an addictive drug such as heroin can be referred to as a **fix. 20** You can use **fix** to refer to an amount of something which a person gets or wants and which helps them physically or psychologically to survive. *She needs her daily fix of publicity.* — N-COUNT / N-COUNT: with supp INFORMAL

21 If you are in a **fix**, you are in a difficult situation. *The government has really got itself into a fix.* — N-SING: a N INFORMAL

22 To **fix** something such as a dye or photographic image means to treat it, especially with chemicals, so that it does not fade or disappear. *Egg yolk is used to fix the pigment.* **23** See also **fixed, fixings.** — VERB V n

fix on. If you **fix on** a particular thing, you decide that it is the one you want. *The Vietnamese government has fixed on May 19th to celebrate his anniversary.* — PHRASAL VB V P n

fix up. 1 If you **fix** something **up**, you arrange it. *I fixed up an appointment to see her... Accommodation is never fixed up in advance.* **2** If you **fix** something **up**, you do work that is necessary in order to make it more suitable or attractive. *I've fixed up Matthew's old room... The whole block is being fixed up.* **3** If you **fix** someone **up with** something they need, you provide it for them. *We'll fix him up with a tie... He was fixed up with a job.* — PHRASAL VB V P noun Also V n P / VERB V P noun Also V n P / V n P with n Also V n P

fix·at·ed /fɪk'seɪtɪd, 'fɪkseɪtɪd/. If you say that someone is **fixated** on a particular thing, you mean that they think about it to an extreme and excessive degree. *The media seems so fixated on polls rather than issues.* ► Also a combining form. *...a pop-fixated music journalist.* — ADJ-GRADED: v-link ADJ on/with/by n / COMB

fixa·tion /fɪk'seɪʃən/ **fixations.** If you say that someone has a **fixation** on something or someone, you mean they think about a particular subject or person to an extreme and excessive degree. *...the country's fixation on the war.* — N-COUNT

fixed /fɪkst/. **1** You use **fixed** to describe something that stays the same and does not vary. *They issue a fixed number of shares. ...a world without fixed laws.* **2** If you say that someone has **fixed** ideas or opinions, you mean that they rarely change their ideas and opinions, although perhaps they should. **3** If someone has a **fixed** smile on their face, they are smiling even though they do not feel happy or pleased. *I had to go through the rest of the evening with a fixed smile on my face.* **4** See also **fix.** **5** ● of no **fixed abode:** see **abode.** — ◆◆◇◇ ADJ / ADJ-GRADED / ADJ

fix·ed·ly /'fɪksɪdli/. If you stare **fixedly** at something, you look at it steadily and continuously for a period of time. *I stared fixedly at the statue.* — ADV-GRADED: ADV after v

fix·er /'fɪksə/ **fixers.** If journalists refer to someone as a **fixer**, they mean that he or she is the sort of person who solves problems and gets things done. *...a television 'fixer' with a clipboard.* — N-COUNT

fix·ings /'fɪksɪŋz/. **1 Fixings** are extra items that are used to decorate or complete something, especially a meal. *He bought a hot dog and had it covered with all the fixings.* **2 Fixings** are items such as screws, nuts, and bolts which are used to fix things such as furniture together. *Have you got all the screws and fixings you need?* — N-PLURAL AMERICAN / N-PLURAL

fix·ity /ˈfɪksɪti/. If you talk about the **fixity** of something, you talk about the fact that it does not change or weaken. ...*the fixity of the class system.* `N-UNCOUNT WRITTEN`

fix·ture /ˈfɪkstʃə/ **fixtures. 1 Fixtures** are pieces of furniture or equipment, for example baths and sinks, which are permanently fixed inside a house or other building. ...*fixtures and fittings are included in the purchase price.* **2** If you describe someone or something as a **fixture** in a particular place or occasion, you mean that they always seem to be there. *She was a fixture in New York's nightclubs.* **3** A **fixture** is a sports event which takes place on a particular date. *City won this fixture 3-0.* `N-COUNT` `N-COUNT` `N-COUNT BRITISH`

fizz /fɪz/ **fizzes, fizzing, fizzed. 1** If a drink **fizzes**, it produces lots of little bubbles of gas and makes a hissing sound. ...*a tray of glasses that fizzed.* ► Also a noun. *I wonder if there's any fizz left in the lemonade.* **2** If you say that someone puts **fizz** into something, you mean that they make it more interesting or exciting. *A Brazilian public relations firm has brought some fizz into his campaign.* **3** Champagne or sparkling wine is sometimes called **fizz**. `VERB V` `N-UNCOUNT` `N-UNCOUNT` `N-UNCOUNT INFORMAL`

fiz·zle /ˈfɪzəl/ **fizzles, fizzling, fizzled.** If something **fizzles**, it ends in a weak or disappointing way. *Our relationship fizzled into nothing.* ► To **fizzle out** means the same as to **fizzle.** *The railway strike fizzled out on its second day.* `VERB V into/to n Also V PHRASAL VB V P`

fizzy /ˈfɪzi/ **fizzier, fizziest. Fizzy** drinks are full of little bubbles of carbon dioxide. `ADJ-GRADED BRITISH`

fjord /fjɔːd, ˈfiːɔːd/ **fjords.** A **fjord** is a strip of sea that comes into the land between high cliffs, especially in Norway. `N-COUNT`

flab /flæb/. If you say that someone has **flab**, you mean they have loose flesh on their body because they are rather fat. `N-UNCOUNT PRAGMATICS`

flab·ber·gast·ed /ˈflæbəgɑːstɪd, -gæst-/. If you say that you are **flabbergasted** by something, you are emphasizing that you are extremely surprised by it. *Everybody was flabbergasted when I announced I was going to emigrate to Australia.* `ADJ-GRADED PRAGMATICS`

flab·by /ˈflæbi/ **flabbier, flabbiest. Flabby** people are rather fat, with loose flesh over their bodies. ...*my bulging thighs and flabby stomach.* `ADJ-GRADED`

flac·cid /ˈflæsɪd, ˈflæksɪd/. Something that is **flaccid** is soft and loose or limp, rather than firm. *I picked up her wrist. It was limp and flaccid.* `ADJ-GRADED`

flag /flæg/ **flags, flagging, flagged. 1** A **flag** is a piece of coloured cloth used as a sign, signal, or symbol of something, for example a country. ...*the American flag.* **2** Journalists sometimes refer to the **flag** of a particular country or organization as a way of referring to the country or organization itself. *The airport was opened by Canadian troops operating under the flag of the United Nations.* **3** If you **flag**, or if your spirits **flag**, you begin to lose enthusiasm or energy. *By 4,000m he was beginning to flag.* **4** A **flag** is the same as a **flagstone.** ● See also **flagstone. 5** If you **fly the flag**, you show that you are proud of your country, or that you support a particular cause. *Steve Crabb can fly the flag with distinction for Britain in Barcelona.* `N-COUNT` `N-COUNT: with supp` `VERB V` `N-COUNT` `PHRASE`

flag down. If you **flag down** a vehicle, especially a taxi, you wave at it as a signal for the driver to stop. *They flagged a car down.* `PHRASAL VB V P noun V n P`

flag·el·la·tion /ˌflædʒəˈleɪʃən/. **Flagellation** is the act of beating yourself or someone else, usually as a religious punishment. `N-UNCOUNT FORMAL`

flagged /flægd/. A **flagged** path or area of ground is paved with flagstones. `ADJ`

flag·on /ˈflægən/ **flagons. 1** A **flagon** is a wide bottle in which cider or wine is sold. **2** A **flagon** is a jug with a narrow neck in which drinks can be served. `N-COUNT` `N-COUNT`

flag·pole /ˈflægpəʊl/ **flagpoles.** A **flagpole** is a tall pole on which a flag can be displayed. `N-COUNT`

fla·grant /ˈfleɪgrənt/. You can use **flagrant** to describe an action, situation, or behaviour that seems to be bad or shocking in an obvious or deliberate way. ...*a flagrant violation of international law.* ♦ **fla·grant·ly** *Basic human rights are being flagrantly abused.* `ADJ-GRADED: ADJ n` `ADV-GRADED`

flag·ship /ˈflægʃɪp/ **flagships. 1** A flagship is the most important ship in a fleet of ships, especially the one on which the commander of the fleet is sailing. **2** The **flagship** of a group of things that are owned or produced by a particular organization is the most important one. *The hospital has been the government's flagship.* `N-COUNT` `N-COUNT`

flag·stone /ˈflægstəʊn/ **flagstones. Flagstones** are large flat pieces of stone which are used for paving. `N-COUNT`

'flag-waving. You can use **flag-waving** to refer to the expression of patriotic feelings in a loud or exaggerated way, especially when you disapprove of this. *The real costs of the war have been ignored in the flag-waving of recent months.* `N-UNCOUNT PRAGMATICS`

flail /fleɪl/ **flails, flailing, flailed. 1** If your arms or legs **flail**, or if you **flail** them about, they wave about in an energetic but uncontrolled way. *He gave a choked cry, flailed his arms wildly for a moment, and then went over the edge.* ► **Flail around** means the same as **flail.** *He starting flailing around and hitting Vincent in the chest.* **2** A **flail** is a tool which consists of a piece of wood or metal that can swing freely from a handle. `V-ERG: V V n` `PHRASAL VB V P` `N-COUNT`

flail around. See **flail** 1. `PHRASAL VB`

flair /fleə/. **1** If you have a **flair for** a particular thing, you have a natural ability to do it well. ...*a flair for languages.* **2** If you have **flair**, you do things in an interesting and stylish way. *Their work has all the usual punch, panache and flair you'd expect.* `N-SING: N for n` `N-UNCOUNT`

flak /flæk/. If you get a lot of **flak** from someone, they criticize you severely. If you take the **flak**, you get the blame for something. *The President is getting a lot of flak for that.* `N-UNCOUNT INFORMAL`

flake /fleɪk/ **flakes, flaking, flaked. 1** A **flake** is a small thin piece of something, especially one that has broken off a larger piece. ...*flakes of paint.* ...*oat flakes.* **2** If something such as paint **flakes**, small thin pieces of it come off. ► **Flake off** means the same as **flake.** *The paint had flaked off.* **3** If a food such as fish **flakes**, or if you **flake** it, it breaks into small thin pieces. *Skin, bone and flake the fish.* `N-COUNT` `VERB: V` `PHRASAL VB V P` `V-ERG: V V n`

flake off. See **flake** 2. `PHRASAL VB`

flake out. If you **flake out**, you collapse, go to sleep, or totally relax because you are very tired. `PHRASAL VB V P`

'flak jacket, flak jackets. A **flak jacket** is a thick sleeveless jacket that soldiers and policemen sometimes wear to protect themselves against bullets. `N-COUNT`

flaky /ˈfleɪki/. Something that is **flaky** breaks easily into small thin pieces or tends to come off in small thin pieces. ...*a small patch of red, flaky skin.* `ADJ-GRADED`

flam·bé /ˈflɒmbeɪ, AM flɑːmˈbeɪ/ **flambés, flambéeing, flambéed.** Food that is **flambéed** is served in flaming brandy, rum, or some other alcoholic drink. *Quickly flambé with rum and serve with lashings of cream.* `VERB be V-ed with/ in n Also V n with/inn, V n`

flam·boy·ant /flæmˈbɔɪənt/. If you say that someone or something is **flamboyant**, you mean that they are very noticeable, stylish, and exciting. *Freddie Mercury was a flamboyant star... He wears flamboyant clothes.* ♦ **flam·boy·ance** ...*his usual mixture of flamboyance and flair.* ♦ **flam·boy·ant·ly** *She dressed flamboyantly.* `ADJ-GRADED` `N-UNCOUNT` `ADV-GRADED`

flame /fleɪm/ **flames, flaming, flamed. 1** A **flame** is a hot bright stream of burning gas that comes from something that is burning. *The heat from the flames was so intense that roads melted.* **2** If something **bursts into flames** or **bursts into flame**, it suddenly starts burning fiercely. *She managed to scramble out of the vehicle as it burst into flames.* **3** If something **goes up in flames**, it starts to burn fiercely and is destroyed. **4** Something that is **in flames** is on fire. `N-VAR` `PHRASE` `PHRASE` `PHRASE`

5 If someone or something **fans the flames** of a situation or feeling, usually a bad one, they make it more intense or extreme in some way. *He accused the Tories of 'fanning the flames of extremism'.* **6** See also **flaming, old flame.** `PHRASE`

fla·men·co /fləˈmeŋkəʊ/ **flamencos.** Flamenco is ◆◇◇◇◇ a Spanish dance that is danced to a special type of N-VAR guitar music.

flame·proof /ˈfleɪmpruːf/; also spelled **flame-proof.** ADJ Flameproof cooking dishes can withstand direct heat.

'flame-thrower, flame-throwers. A flame- N-COUNT thrower is a gun that can send out a stream of burning liquid.

flam·ing /ˈfleɪmɪŋ/. **1 Flaming** is used to describe ◆◇◇◇◇ something that is burning and producing a lot of ADJ flames. *The plane, which was full of fuel, scattered flaming fragments over a large area.* **2** Something ADJ: ADJ n that is **flaming** red or orange is bright red or orange in colour. *He has flaming red hair.* **3** A **flaming** ADJ: ADJ n row or a **flaming** temper, for example, is a very angry row or a very bad temper.

fla·min·go /fləˈmɪŋɡəʊ/ **flamingos** or **flamin-** N-COUNT **goes.** A flamingo is a bird with pink feathers, long thin legs, a long neck, and a curved beak.

flam·mable /ˈflæməbəl/. **Flammable** chemicals, ADJ-GRADED gases, cloth, or other things catch fire and burn easily.

flan /flæn/ **flans.** A **flan** is a food that has a base N-VAR and sides of pastry or sponge cake. The base is filled with fruit or savoury food.

flange /flændʒ/ **flanges.** A **flange** is a projecting N-COUNT edge on an object. Its purpose is to strengthen the object or to connect it to another object.

flank /flæŋk/ **flanks, flanking, flanked. 1** An ◆◆◇◇◇ animal's **flank** is its side, between the ribs and the N-COUNT hip. *He put his hand on the dog's flank.* **2** A **flank** of N-COUNT an army or naval force is one side of it when it is or- ganized for battle. **3** If something **is flanked** by VERB: things, it has them on both sides of it, or sometimes be V-ed by n on one side of it. *Bookcases flank the bed... He walks* V n *briskly, flanked by heavily armed guards.* V-ed

flan·nel /ˈflænəl/ **flannels. 1 Flannel** is lightweight ◆◇◇◇◇ cloth used for making clothes. *...a faded red flannel* N-UNCOUNT *shirt.* **2 Flannels** are men's trousers made of flan- N-PLURAL nel. *...chaps dressed in flannels and blazers.* **3** A N-COUNT **flannel** is a small cloth that you use for washing BRITISH yourself. The American word is **washcloth**. **4** If you N-UNCOUNT describe what someone has said as **flannel**, you are [PRAGMATICS] critical of them because they have said a lot but they avoided telling you what you wanted to know.

flap /flæp/ **flaps, flapping, flapped. 1** If some- ◆◆◇◇◇ thing such as a piece of cloth or paper **flaps** or if V-ERG: V you **flap** it, it moves quickly up and down or from V n side to side. *They would flap bath towels from their balconies as they chatted.* **2** If a bird or insect **flaps** V-ERG: its wings or if its wings **flap**, the wings move quickly V pl-n up and down. *A pigeon emerges, wings flapping* V *noisily.* **3** If you **flap** your arms, you move them VERB: V n quickly up and down as if they were wings. **4** A **flap** of cloth or skin, for example, is a flat piece of it N-COUNT that can move freely up and down or from side to side because it is held or attached by only one edge. **5** A N-COUNT **flap** on the wing of an aircraft is an area along the edge of the wing that can be raised or lowered to control the movement of the aircraft. **6** Someone who is in a **flap** is in a state of great excite- N-SING: ment, worry, or panic. *Why did people get in a flap* a N *over nuclear energy?* INFORMAL

flap·jack /ˈflæpdʒæk/ **flapjacks. 1 Flapjacks** are N-VAR thick chewy biscuits made from oats, butter, and BRITISH syrup. **2 Flapjacks** are thin, flat, circular pieces of N-COUNT cooked batter. AMERICAN

flare /fleə/ **flares, flaring, flared. 1** A **flare** is a ◆◆◇◇◇ small device that produces a bright flame. Flares are N-COUNT used as signals, for example on ships. *...a distress flare.* **2** If a fire **flares**, the flames suddenly become VERB larger. *Camp fires flared like beacons in the dark.* V ▶ **Flare up** means the same as **flare**. *Don't spill too* PHRASAL VB *much fat on the barbecue as it could flare up.* V P **3** If something such as trouble, violence, or conflict VERB **flares**, it starts or becomes more violent. *Trouble* V *flared in several American cities.* ▶ **Flare up** means PHRASAL VB the same as **flare**. *Dozens of people were injured as* V P *fighting flared up.* **4** If people's tempers **flare**, they get VERB: V

angry. **5** If someone's nostrils **flare**, or if they **flare** V-ERG: V them, their nostrils become wider, often because the V n person is angry or upset. *He stuck out his tongue and flared his nostrils.* **6** If something such as a dress **flares**, it spreads out- VERB: V wards at one end. ● See also **flared**.

flare up. If a disease or injury **flares up**, it suddenly PHRASAL VB returns or becomes painful again. *Students often find* V P *that their acne flares up before and during exams.* ● See also **flare 2, 3, flare-up**.

flared /fleəd/. **Flared** trousers or skirts are wider at ADJ-GRADED the hem or at the bottom of the legs than at the top.

'flare-up, flare-ups. If there is a **flare-up** of vio- ◆◇◇◇◇ lence or of an illness, it suddenly starts or gets N-COUNT worse. *...a flare-up in her arthritis.*

flash /flæʃ/ **flashes, flashing, flashed. 1** A **flash** ◆◆◇◇◇ is a sudden burst of light or of something shiny or N-COUNT bright. *A sudden flash of lightning lit everything up.* *...a flash of blue feathers.* **2** If a light **flashes**, or if V-ERG you **flash** a light, it shines with a sudden bright V light, especially as quick regular flashes of light. n *Lightning flashed among the distant dark clouds... A driver flashed her headlights as he overtook.* **3** If something **flashes** past or by it, moves past you so VERB fast that you cannot see it properly. *Cars flashed by* V prep/adv *every few minutes.* **4** If something **flashes through** or VERB **into** your mind, you suddenly think about it. *A ludi-* V through/ *crous thought flashed through Harry's mind.* **5** If you into n PHRASE say that something happens **in a flash**, you mean that it happens very quickly. *The answer had come to him in a flash.* **6** If you say that someone reacts to some- PHRASE thing **quick as a flash**, you mean that they react to it extremely quickly. **7** If you **flash** something such as an identity card, you VERB: V n show it to people quickly and then put it away again. **8** If a picture or message **flashes** up on a screen, or if V-ERG: you **flash** it onto a screen, it is displayed there briefly V prep or suddenly, and often repeatedly. *Researchers flash* V n prep *two groups of different letters on a computer screen.* Also V n **9** If you **flash** a look or a smile at someone, you sud- VERB: denly look at them or smile at them. *Meg flashed Cissie* V n at n *a grateful smile.* **10** If someone's eyes **flash**, they sud- V n n denly show a strong emotion, especially anger. VERB: V WRITTEN **11** You talk about a **flash of** something when you are N-COUNT: saying that it happens very suddenly and unexpected- with supp, ly. *'What did Moira tell you?' Liz demanded with a* N of n *flash of anger. ...a flash of wit or humor.* **12 Flash** is the use of flashbulbs to give more light N-UNCOUNT when taking a photograph. *He was one of the first peo- ple to use high speed flash.* **13** A **flash** is the same as a N-COUNT **flashlight**. *Stopping to rest, Pete shut off the flash.* AMERICAN **14** If you describe something as **flash**, you mean that ADJ-GRADED it looks expensive, fashionable, and new. *...a flash* INFORMAL *uptown restaurant.* **15** If you describe an achievement or success as a PHRASE **flash in the pan**, you mean that it is unlikely to be re- [PRAGMATICS] peated; used showing disapproval.

flash back. If your mind **flashes back** to something PHRASAL VB in the past, you remember it or think of it briefly or V P to n suddenly. *His mind kept flashing back to the previous* Also V P *night.*

flash·back /ˈflæʃbæk/ **flashbacks. 1** In a film, ◆◇◇◇◇ novel, or play, a **flashback** to the past is a scene that N-COUNT returns to events in the past. **2** If you have a **flash-** N-COUNT **back** to a past experience, you have a sudden and vivid memory of it. *He has recurring flashbacks to the night his friends died.*

flash·bulb /ˈflæʃbʌlb/ **flashbulbs**; also spelled N-COUNT **flash bulb**. A **flashbulb** is a small lightbulb that can be fixed to a camera. It makes a bright flash of light so that you can take photographs indoors.

flash·er /ˈflæʃə/ **flashers.** A **flasher** is a man who N-COUNT deliberately exposes his genitals to people in public INFORMAL places.

'flash 'flood, flash floods. A **flash flood** is a sud- N-COUNT den rush of water over dry land, usually caused by a great deal of rain.

flash·gun /ˈflæʃɡʌn/ **flashguns.** A **flashgun** is a N-COUNT device that you can attach to, or that is part of, a ca-

mera and that causes a flashbulb to work automatically when the shutter opens.

flash·light /'flæʃlaɪt/ **flashlights.** A **flashlight** is a small portable electric light which gets its power from batteries. The usual British word is **torch**. ◆◇◇◇◇ N-COUNT

flash·point /'flæʃpɔɪnt/ **flashpoints.** 1 A **flashpoint** is the moment at which conflict, especially political conflict, reaches a climax and becomes violent. *The immediate flashpoint was Wednesday's big rally in the city centre.* 2 A **flashpoint** is a place which people think is dangerous because political trouble may start there and then spread to other towns or countries. N-VAR / N-COUNT

flashy /'flæʃi/ **flashier, flashiest.** If you describe a person or thing as **flashy**, you mean they are smart and noticeable, but in a rather vulgar way; used showing disapproval. *...a flashy sports car.* ◆◇◇◇◇ ADJ-GRADED PRAGMATICS INFORMAL

flask /flɑːsk, flæsk/ **flasks.** 1 A **flask** is a bottle which you use for carrying drinks around with you. *He took out a metal flask.* ► A **flask of** liquid is the flask and the liquid which it contains. 2 A **flask** is a bottle or other container which is used in science laboratories and industry for holding liquids. 3 See also **vacuum flask**. ◆◇◇◇◇ N-COUNT / N-COUNT / N-COUNT

flat /flæt/ **flats; flatter, flattest.** 1 A **flat** is a set of rooms for living in, that is part of a larger building. The usual American word is **apartment**. *...a flat in central London. ...a block of flats.* ◆◆◆◇ N-COUNT; also N num BRITISH

2 Something that is **flat** is level, smooth, or even, rather than sloping, curved, or bumpy. *His right hand moved across the cloth, smoothing it flat... The sea was calm, perfectly flat.* ADJ-GRADED

3 **Flat** means horizontal and not upright. *Two men near him threw themselves flat.* ADJ

4 A **flat** object is not very tall or deep in relation to its length and width. *...a square flat box.* ADJ-GRADED

5 **Flat** land is level, with no high hills or other raised parts. *The highway stretched out flat and straight ahead.* ♦ **flat·ness** Notice the flatness and the rich, red earth. 6 **On the flat** means on level ground. *He had angina and was unable to walk for more than 200 yards on the flat.* 7 A low flat area of uncultivated land, especially a marsh, can be referred to as **flats** or a **flat**. ADJ-GRADED / N-UNCOUNT / PHRASE / N-COUNT

8 You can refer to one of the broad flat surfaces of an object as **the flat of** that object. *...the flat of a knife.* N-COUNT

9 **Flat** shoes have no heels or very low heels. 10 A **flat** tyre, ball, or balloon does not have enough air in it. 11 A **flat** is a tyre that does not have enough air in it. 12 A drink that is **flat** is no longer fizzy. 13 A **flat** battery has lost some or all of its electrical charge. 14 If you have **flat** feet, the arches of your feet are too low. ADJ-GRADED / ADJ-GRADED / ADJ-GRADED / ADJ-GRADED

15 A **flat** denial, refusal, or rejection is definite and firm, and is unlikely to be changed. *The Foreign Ministry has issued a flat denial of any involvement.* ♦ **flat·ly** He flatly refused to discuss it. ADJ: ADJ n / ADV

16 If you say that something happened, for example, in ten seconds **flat** or ten minutes **flat**, you are emphasizing that it happened surprisingly quickly and only took ten seconds or ten minutes. *I had it all explained to me in two minutes flat.* ADJ: num n ADJ PRAGMATICS

17 A **flat** rate, price, or percentage is one that is fixed and which applies in every situation. *Sometimes there's a flat fee for carrying out a particular task.* ADJ: ADJ n

18 If trade or business is **flat**, it is slow and inactive, rather than busy and improving or increasing. *For the country overall, house prices have remained flat.* ADJ-GRADED

19 If you describe something as **flat**, you mean that it is dull and not exciting or interesting. *The past few days have seemed comparatively flat and empty.* ♦ **flatness** Kenworthy detected a certain flatness in the days that followed. ADJ-GRADED / N-UNCOUNT

20 You use **flat** to describe someone's voice when they are saying something without expressing any emotion. *'Whatever you say,' he said in a deadly flat voice.* ♦ **flatly** 'I know you,' he said flatly. ADJ-GRADED / ADV-GRADED

21 **Flat** is used after a letter representing a musical note to show that the note should be played or sung half a tone lower than the note which otherwise corresponds to that letter. **Flat** is often represented by the symbol♭ after the letter. ADJ: n ADJ

22 If someone sings **flat** or if a musical instrument plays **flat**, their singing or the instrument is slightly lower in pitch than it should be. ► Also an adjective. *He had been fired because his singing was flat.* ADV-GRADED: ADV after v / ADJ-GRADED

23 If an event or attempt **falls flat** or **falls flat on** its **face**, it is unsuccessful. *Liz meant it as a joke but it fell flat.* PHRASE

24 If you say that you are **flat broke**, you mean that you have no money at all. PHRASE INFORMAL

25 If you do something **flat out**, you do it as fast or as hard as you can. *Everyone is working flat out to try to trap those responsible.* 26 You use **flat out** to emphasize that something is completely the case. *That allegation is a flat-out lie... They say the industry is flat out lying about the effects of deregulation.* PHRASE BRITISH / PHRASE PRAGMATICS INFORMAL, AMERICAN

27 ● **in a flat spin**: see **spin**.

flat 'cap, flat caps. A **flat cap** is the same as a cloth cap. N-COUNT

flat·fish /'flætfɪʃ/ **flatfish** is both the singular and the plural form. **Flatfish** are sea fish with flat wide bodies, for example plaice or sole. N-VAR

flat-'footed. 1 If you are **flat-footed**, the arches of your feet are too low. *All babies look flat-footed.* 2 If you describe a person or action as **flat-footed**, you think they are clumsy, awkward, or foolish. *The government could be caught flat-footed.* ADJ-GRADED / ADJ-GRADED

flat·mate /'flætmeɪt/ **flatmates;** also spelled **flat-mate.** Someone's **flatmate** is a person who shares a flat with them. N-COUNT BRITISH

'flat pack, flat packs; also spelled **flat-pack. Flat pack** furniture, for example wardrobes or cupboards, is sold in ready-cut pieces along with screws and instructions about how to put it together. N-COUNT BRITISH

'flat racing. Flat racing is horse racing which does not involve jumping over fences. N-UNCOUNT

flat·ten /'flætən/ **flattens, flattening, flattened.** 1 If you **flatten** something or if it **flattens**, it becomes flat or flatter. *The dog's ears flattened slightly as Cook spoke. ...flattened oil drums.* ► **Flatten out** means the same as **flatten**. *The hills flattened out just south of the mountain.* 2 To **flatten** something such as a building, town, or plant means to destroy it by knocking it down or crushing it. *...bombing raids flattened much of the area.* 3 If you **flatten** yourself against something, you press yourself flat against it, for example to avoid getting in the way or being seen. *He flattened himself against a brick wall as I passed.* 4 If you **flatten** someone in a contest, or argument, you defeat them completely. ◆◇◇◇◇ V-ERG: V n / V / V-ed / PHRASAL VB ERG / V P / VERB V n / VERB: V n

flat·ter /'flætə/ **flatters, flattering, flattered.** 1 If someone **flatters** you, they praise you in an exaggerated way that is not sincere, because they want to please you or to persuade you to do something. *The president flattered and feted him into taking his side.* 2 If you **flatter** yourself that something good is the case, you believe that it is true, although others may disagree. *I flatter myself that this campaign will put an end to the war.* 3 If something **flatters** you, it makes you appear more attractive. *Orange and khaki flatter those with golden skin tones. ...clothes that flatter.* 4 See also **flat, flattered, flattering**. ◆◇◇◇◇ VERB: V n / V n into -ing / VERB V pron-refl that / VERB V n / V

flat·tered /'flætəd/. If you are **flattered** by something that has happened, you are pleased about it because it makes you feel important or special. *I am flattered that they should be so supportive.* ◆◇◇◇◇ ADJ-GRADED: v-link ADJ

flat·ter·ing /'flætərɪŋ/. 1 If something is **flattering**, it makes you appear more attractive. *Some styles are so flattering that they instantly become classics.* ♦ **flat·ter·ing·ly** The bold necklace flatteringly lightens her skin tone. 2 If someone's remarks are **flattering**, they praise you and say nice things about you. *There were pleasant and flattering obituaries about him.* 3 If you describe something as **flattering**, you mean that it pleases you and makes you feel important or special. *It was flattering to be told how indispensable his taste and talent were.* ◆◇◇◇◇ ADJ-GRADED / ADV-GRADED / ADJ-GRADED / ADJ-GRADED

flat·tery /'flætəri/. **Flattery** consists of flattering words or behaviour. *He is ambitious and susceptible to flattery.* N-UNCOUNT

flatu·lence /'flætʃʊləns/. Flatulence is too much gas in a person's intestines, which causes an uncomfortable feeling. `N-UNCOUNT`

flat·ware /'flætweə/. Flatware refers to the knives, forks, and spoons that you eat your food with. The usual British word is **cutlery**. `N-UNCOUNT AMERICAN`

flaunt /flɔːnt/ **flaunts, flaunting, flaunted. 1** If you say that someone **flaunts** their possessions or qualities, you mean that they display them in a very obvious way; used showing disapproval. *They drove around in Rolls-Royces, openly flaunting their wealth.* **2** If you say that someone **is flaunting** themselves, you disapprove of them because they are behaving in an excessively confident and flirtatious way. *...beach-boys flaunting themselves in designer swimwear.* `◆◇◇◇◇ VERB PRAGMATICS V n` / `VERB PRAGMATICS V pron-refl`

flau·tist /'flɔːtɪst/ **flautists.** A **flautist** is someone who plays the flute. `N-COUNT BRITISH`

fla·vour /'fleɪvə/ **flavours, flavouring, flavoured;** spelled **flavor** in American English. **1** The **flavour** of a food or drink is its taste. *This cheese has a crumbly texture with a strong flavour. ...salt and vinegar flavour crisps.* ◆ **-flavoured** *...fruit-flavored sparkling water.* **2** If you **flavour** food or drink, you add something to it to give it a particular taste. *Flavour your favourite dishes with exotic herbs and spices.* ◆ **fla·voured** *...meat flavoured with herbs.* **3** You can refer to a special quality that something has as its **flavour**. For example, if something has an Italian flavour, it reminds you of Italian things. **4** If you think that something or someone is very popular at a particular time, you can say that they are **flavour of the month**. *Hats were very much flavour of the month.* `◆◆◆◇◇ N-VAR` / `COMB` / `VERB: V n, V n with n` / `ADJ-GRADED` / `N-COUNT` / `PHRASE`

fla·vour·ing /'fleɪvərɪŋ/ **flavourings;** spelled **flavoring** in American English. **Flavourings** are substances that are added to food or drink to give it a particular taste. *...lemon flavoring.* `N-VAR`

fla·vour·less /'fleɪvələs/; spelled **flavorless** in American English. **Flavourless** food is uninteresting because it does not taste strongly of anything. `ADJ`

flaw /flɔː/ **flaws. 1** A **flaw** in something such as a theory or argument is a mistake in it. *...crucial flaws in his monetary theory.* ◆ **flawed** *These tests were so seriously flawed as to render the results meaningless.* **2** A **flaw** in someone's character is an undesirable quality that they have. *The only flaw in his character seems to be a short temper.* ◆ **flawed** *...a flawed genius.* **3** A **flaw** in something such as a pattern or material is a fault in it. ◆ **flawed** *...the unique beauty of a flawed object.* `◆◇◇◇◇ N-COUNT` / `ADJ-GRADED` / `N-COUNT` / `ADJ-GRADED` / `N-COUNT` / `ADJ-GRADED`

flaw·less /'flɔːləs/. If you say that something or someone is **flawless**, you mean that they have no faults or imperfections. *...her flawless complexion... Discovery's takeoff this morning from Cape Canaveral was flawless.* ◆ **flaw·less·ly** *Each stage of the battle was carried off flawlessly.* `◆◇◇◇◇ ADJ-GRADED` / `ADV-GRADED`

flax /flæks/. **Flax** is a plant with blue flowers. Its stem is used for making thread, rope, and cloth, and its seeds are used for making linseed oil. `N-UNCOUNT`

flax·en /'flæksən/. **Flaxen** hair is pale yellow. `ADJ: ADJ n`

flay /fleɪ/ **flays, flaying, flayed.** When someone **flays** an animal or person, they remove their skin, usually after they are dead. `VERB: V n`

flea /fliː/ **fleas.** A **flea** is a very small jumping insect that has no wings and feeds on the blood of humans or animals. See picture headed **insects**. `◆◇◇◇◇ N-COUNT`

'flea market, flea markets. A **flea market** is an outdoor market selling cheap second-hand goods and sometimes also antiques. `N-COUNT`

fleck /flek/ **flecks.** **Flecks** are small marks on a surface, or objects that look like small marks. *He went to the men's room to wash flecks of blood from his shirt.* ◆ **flecked** *His hair was increasingly flecked with grey. ...a plain, mud-flecked uniform.* `N-COUNT` / `ADJ`

fled /fled/. **Fled** is the past tense and past participle of **flee**.

fledg·ling /'fledʒlɪŋ/ **fledglings. 1** A **fledgling** is a young bird that has its feathers and is learning to fly. **2** You use **fledgling** to describe a person, or- `◆◇◇◇◇ N-COUNT` / `ADJ: ADJ n`

ganization, or system that is new or inexperienced. *...fledgling writers. ...Russia's fledgling democracy.*

flee /fliː/ **flees, fleeing, fled.** If you **flee** from something or someone, or **flee** them, you escape from them. *He slammed the bedroom door behind him and fled... In 1984 he fled to Costa Rica to avoid military service. ...refugees fleeing persecution... Thousands have been compelled to flee the country.* `◆◆◆◇◇ VB: no passive V, V prep/adv V n WRITTEN`

fleece /fliːs/ **fleeces, fleecing, fleeced. 1** A sheep's **fleece** is its coat of wool. **2** A **fleece** is the wool, in a single piece, that is cut off one sheep during shearing. **3** If you **fleece** someone, you get a lot of money from them by tricking or overcharging them. *He fleeced her out of thousands of pounds.* `◆◇◇◇◇ N-COUNT` / `N-COUNT` / `VERB V n out of n, Also V n INFORMAL`

fleecy /'fliːsi/. Something that is **fleecy** is soft and fluffy, or looks soft and fluffy. *...fleecy walking jackets. ...a few fleecy white clouds.* `ADJ`

fleet /fliːt/ **fleets. 1** A **fleet** is a group of ships organized to do something together, for example to fight battles or to catch fish. *...restaurants supplied by local fishing fleets.* **2** A **fleet** of vehicles is a group of them, especially when they all belong to a particular organization or business, or when they are all going somewhere together. *With its own fleet of trucks, the company delivers most orders overnight.* `◆◆◆◇◇ N-COUNT` / `N-COUNT`

fleet·ing /'fliːtɪŋ/. **Fleeting** is used to describe something which lasts only for a very short time. *The girls caught only a fleeting glimpse of the driver.* ◆ **fleet·ing·ly** *He smiled fleetingly.* `◆◇◇◇◇ ADJ-GRADED` / `ADV`

'Fleet Street. **Fleet Street** is used to refer to British national newspapers and to the journalists who work for them. *He was the highest-paid sub-editor in Fleet Street.* `◆◇◇◇◇ N-PROPER`

Flem·ish /'flemɪʃ/. **1 Flemish** means belonging or relating to the region of Flanders in northern Europe, or to its people, language, or culture. **2 Flemish** is a language spoken in Belgium. `◆◇◇◇◇ ADJ` / `N-UNCOUNT`

flesh /fleʃ/ **fleshes, fleshing, fleshed. 1** Flesh is the soft part of a person's or animal's body between the bones and the skin. *Illness had wasted the flesh from her tall, willowy body. ...the pale pink flesh of trout and salmon.* **2** You can use **flesh** to refer to human skin and the human body, especially when you are considering it in a sexual way. *...the sins of the flesh.* **3** The **flesh** of a fruit or vegetable is the soft part of it. *Cut the flesh from the olives.* **4** You use **flesh and blood** to emphasize that someone has human feelings or weaknesses, often when contrasting them with machines. *I'm only flesh and blood, like anyone else.* **5** If you say that someone is your **own flesh and blood**, you are emphasizing that they are a member of your family. **6** If something **makes** your **flesh creep** or **makes** your **flesh crawl**, it makes you feel horrified or revolted. **7** If you meet or see someone **in the flesh**, you meet or see them in person. **8** If you **put flesh on** something, you add details and more information to it. *The strength of this book is that it puts flesh on the bare bones of this argument.* **9** ● **pound of flesh:** see **pound.** `◆◆◇◇◇ N-UNCOUNT` / `N-UNCOUNT` / `N-UNCOUNT` / `PHRASE PRAGMATICS` / `PHRASE PRAGMATICS` / `PHRASE` / `PHRASE` / `PHRASE`

flesh out. If you **flesh out** something such as a story or plan, you add details and more information to it. *He talked with him for an hour and a half, fleshing out the details of his original five-minute account.* `PHRASAL VB V P noun Also V n P`

'flesh-coloured; spelled **flesh-colored** in American English. Something that is **flesh-coloured** is yellowish pink in colour. `ADJ`

'flesh wound, flesh wounds. A **flesh wound** is a wound that breaks the skin but does not damage any bones or internal organs. `N-COUNT`

fleshy /'fleʃi/. **1** If you describe someone as **fleshy**, you mean that they are slightly too fat. **2 Fleshy** parts of the body or **fleshy** plants are thick and soft. *...the fleshy part of the thigh. ...fleshy fruits like apples, plums, pears, peaches.* `ADJ-GRADED` / `ADJ-GRADED`

flew /fluː/. **Flew** is the past tense of **fly.**

flex /fleks/ **flexes, flexing, flexed. 1** A **flex** is an electric cable containing two or more wires that is connected to an electrical appliance. **2** If you **flex** your muscles or parts of your body, you bend, `◆◇◇◇◇ N-VAR BRITISH` / `VERB: V n`

move, or stretch them for a short time in order to exercise them. **3 ◆** to **flex** your **muscles**: see **muscle**.

flex·ible /'fleksɪbəl/. **1** A **flexible** object or material can be bent easily without breaking. ...*brushes with long, flexible bristles.* ◆ **flex·i·bil·ity** /,fleksɪ'bɪlɪti/ *The flexibility of the lens decreases with age.* **2** Something or someone that is **flexible** is able to change and adapt easily to new conditions and circumstances. *Look for software that's flexible enough for a range of abilities. ...flexible working hours.* ◆ **flex·ibly** /'fleksɪbli/ *Apply standards flexibly rather than rigidly.* ◆ **flexibility** *The flexibility of distance learning would be particularly suited to busy managers.*
ADJ-GRADED · ◆◆◇◇◇
N-UNCOUNT
ADJ-GRADED
ADV-GRADED
N-UNCOUNT

flexi·time /'fleksitaɪm/; also spelled **flexi-time**. **Flexitime** is a system that allows employees to vary the time that they start or finish work, provided that an agreed total number of hours are spent at work. The American word is **flextime**.
N-UNCOUNT · BRITISH

flick /flɪk/ **flicks, flicking, flicked. 1** If something **flicks** in a particular direction, or if someone **flicks** it, it moves with a short sudden movement. *His tongue flicked across his lips... Shirley flicked a speck of fluff from the sleeve of her black suit.* ▶ Also a noun. ...*a flick of a paintbrush.* **2** If you **flick** something such as a whip or a towel, you hold one end of it and move your hand quickly up and then forward, so that the other end moves. *He helped her up before flicking the reins... She sighed and flicked a dishcloth at the counter.* ▶ Also a noun. ...*a flick of the whip.* **3** If you **flick** a switch, you press it quickly. *He flicked a light-switch... Sam was flicking a flashlight on and off... Pearle flicked off the TV.* **4** If you **flick through** a book or magazine, you turn its pages quickly, for example to get a general idea of its contents or to look for a particular item. *She was flicking through some magazines... He switched on the television, flicking through the channels.* ▶ Also a noun. *I had a flick through the handbook.*
◆◆◇◇◇
V-ERG
V prep/adv
V n prep/adv
Also V,
V n
N-COUNT
VERB
V n
V n prep
N-COUNT
VERB: V n
off
VERB
V through n
N-SING: a N

flick·er /'flɪkə/ **flickers, flickering, flickered. 1** If a light or flame **flickers**, it shines unsteadily. *A television flickered in the corner.* ▶ Also a noun. *Looking through the cabin window I saw the flicker of flames.* **2** A **flicker** of feeling is one that is experienced or visible only faintly and for a very short time. *He felt a flicker of regret.* **3** If an expression **flickers** across your face, it appears very briefly. *A smile flickered across Vincent's grey features.* **4** If someone's eyes or eyelids **flicker**, they make slight, quick movements. *Dirk's eyes flickered towards the pistol... Her eyelids flickered, then opened.*
◆◇◇◇◇
VERB
V
N-COUNT
N-COUNT
VERB
V across/over
VERB
V prep/adv
V
WRITTEN

'flick-knife, flick-knives; also spelled **flick knife.** In British English, a **flick-knife** is a knife with a blade in the handle that springs out automatically when a button is pressed. The usual American word is **switchblade.**
N-COUNT

fli·er /flaɪə/. See **flyer.**

flight /flaɪt/ **flights. 1** A **flight** is a journey made by flying, usually in an aeroplane. *The flight will take four hours.* **2** You can refer to an aeroplane carrying passengers on a particular journey as a particular **flight.** *I'll try to get on the flight down to Karachi tonight... BA flight 286 was two hours late.* **3** **Flight** is the action of flying, or the ability to fly. ...*supersonic flight... These hawks are magnificent in flight.* **4** A **flight** of birds is a group of them flying together. **5** **Flight** is the act of running away from something. *Frank was in full flight when he reached them. ...her hurried flight from the palace in a cart.* ● If someone **takes flight,** they run away. **6** A **flight** of steps or stairs is a set of steps or stairs that lead from one level to another without changing direction. *We walked in silence up a flight of stairs.* **7** An idea or statement that is very imaginative but complicated, silly, or impractical can be referred to as a **flight of fancy.**
◆◆◆◇
N-COUNT
N-COUNT: also N num
N-UNCOUNT
N-COUNT: N of n
N-UNCOUNT
PHRASE
N-COUNT
PHRASE

'flight attendant, flight attendants. On an aeroplane, the **flight attendants** are the people whose job is to look after the passengers and serve their meals.
N-COUNT

'flight deck, flight decks. On a large aeroplane, the **flight deck** is the area at the front where the pilot works and where all the controls are.
N-COUNT

flight·less /'flaɪtləs/. A **flightless** bird or insect is unable to fly because it does not have the necessary type of wings.
ADJ: ADJ n

,flight lieu'tenant, flight lieutenants. In the British air force, a **flight lieutenant** is a junior officer.
N-COUNT

'flight recorder, flight recorders. On an aeroplane, the **flight recorder** is the same as the **black box.**
N-COUNT

flighty /'flaɪti/ **flightier, flightiest.** If you say that someone is **flighty,** you are criticial of them because they are not very serious or reliable and often change their ideas or their partner.
ADJ-GRADED · PRAGMATICS

flim·sy /'flɪmzi/ **flimsier, flimsiest. 1** A **flimsy** object is weak because it is made of a weak material, or is badly made. ...*a flimsy wooden door.* **2** **Flimsy** cloth or clothing is thin and does not give much protection. ...*a very flimsy pink chiffon nightgown.* **3** If you describe something such as evidence or an excuse as **flimsy,** you mean that it is not very good or convincing.
◆◇◇◇◇
ADJ-GRADED
ADJ-GRADED
ADJ-GRADED

flinch /flɪntʃ/ **flinches, flinching, flinched. 1** If you **flinch,** you make a small sudden movement, for example when something shocks you. *She flinched as though he'd slapped her.* **2** If you do not **flinch** from something unpleasant, you do not attempt to avoid it. *He has never flinched from harsh financial decisions... The world community should not flinch in the face of this challenge.*
◆◇◇◇◇
VERB
V
VERB
V from n
V

fling /flɪŋ/ **flings, flinging, flung. 1** If you **fling** something somewhere, you throw it or put it there suddenly using a lot of force, often because you are angry. *The woman flung the cup at him... Peter flung his shoes into the corner.* **2** If you **fling** yourself somewhere or **are flung** there, you move there suddenly and with a lot of force. *He flung himself to the floor.* **3** If you **fling** a part of your body in a particular direction, especially your arms or head, you move it there suddenly. *She flung her arms around my neck and kissed me.* **4** If you **fling** yourself into a particular activity, you do it with a lot of enthusiasm and energy. *She flung herself into her career.* **5** If two people have a **fling,** they have a brief sexual relationship. *She had a brief fling with him 30 years ago.* **6** A **fling** is a short period of enjoyment, especially the last one that you will get an opportunity to have. ...*that last fling before you finally give up and take up a job.*
◆◆◇◇◇
VERB
V n prep/adv
VERB
V pron-refl prep/adv
Also V n
VERB
prep/adv
V n prep/adv
VERB
V pron-refl
into n
N-COUNT
INFORMAL
N-SING

flint /flɪnt/ **flints. 1** **Flint** is a very hard greyish-black stone that was used in prehistoric times for making tools. **2** A **flint** is a small piece of flint or other mineral which can be struck with a piece of steel to produce sparks.
N-UNCOUNT
N-COUNT

flinty /'flɪnti/. If you describe someone as **flinty,** you mean they are harsh and show no emotion. ...*her flinty stare.*
ADJ-GRADED

flip /flɪp/ **flips, flipping, flipped. 1** If you **flip** a switch, you press it or turn it quickly. *He didn't flip on the headlights until he was two blocks away... He walked out, flipping the lights off... He flipped the timer switch.* **2** If you **flip through** a book, you quickly turn its pages, for example to look for a particular item. *He was flipping through a magazine in the living room... He flipped the pages of the diary.* **3** If something **flips** over, or if you **flip** it over, it suddenly turns over. *The plane then flipped over and burst into flames... He flipped it neatly on to the plate.* **4** If you decide something by **flipping** a coin, you spin a coin into the air using your thumb and guess which side will face upwards when it lands. ▶ Also a noun. ...*having gambled all on the flip of a coin.* **5** If someone **flips,** they suddenly lose control of themselves and become extremely upset or angry. **6** If you say that someone is being **flip,** you disapprove of them because you think that they are not be-
◆◆◇◇◇
VERB
V n with on/off
V n
VERB
V through n
V n
V-ERG
V adv/prep
V n prep/adv
VERB: V n
N-SING
VERB: V
INFORMAL
ADJ-GRADED
PRAGMATICS

ing serious enough about something. ...*a flip answer*... *The tone of the book is sometimes too flip.*

'flip-flop, flip-flops, flip-flopping, flip-flopped. N-PLURAL **1** Flip-flops are sandals which are held on your foot by a V-shaped strap that goes between your big toe and the toe next to it. They are often called **thongs** in American English. **2** If you say that someone, especially a politician, **flip-flops** on a decision, you are critical of them because they change their decision, so that they do or think the opposite. *He has been criticized for flip-flopping on several key issues.* ▶ Also a noun. *The President's flip-flops on taxes made him appear indecisive.* VERB PRAGMATICS V on n Also V AMERICAN, INFORMAL N-COUNT

flip·pant /'flɪpənt/. If you describe a person or what they say as **flippant**, you are criticizing them because you think they are not taking something as seriously as they should. *He now dismisses that as a flippant comment.* ♦ **flip·pan·cy** *There was some flippancy in his tone.* ♦ **flip·pant·ly** *He answered carelessly and flippantly.* ADJ-GRADED PRAGMATICS N-UNCOUNT ADV-GRADED: ADV with v

flip·per /'flɪpə/ **flippers. 1** Flippers are flat pieces of rubber that you can wear on your feet to help you swim more quickly. **2** The **flippers** of an animal that lives in water, for example a seal or a penguin, are the two or four flat limbs which it uses for swimming. N-COUNT N-COUNT

flip·ping /'flɪpɪŋ/. Some people use **flipping** to emphasize what they are saying, especially when they are annoyed. *This is such a flipping horrible picture.* ▶ Also an adjective. *I even washed the flipping bed sheets yesterday.* ADV: ADV adj PRAGMATICS BRITISH, INFORMAL ADJ: ADJ n

'flip side; also spelled **flipside. 1** The **flip side** of a record is the side that does not have the main song on it. **2** The **flip side** of a situation is the less obvious or less pleasant aspects of it, which may seem contradictory. *The trade deficit is the flip side of a rapidly expanding economy.* N-SING: the N N-SING

flirt /flɜːt/ **flirts, flirting, flirted. 1** If you **flirt** with someone, you behave as if you are sexually attracted to them, in a playful or not very serious way. *He flirts outrageously.* ♦ **flir·ta·tion** /flɜːˈteɪʃən/ **flirtations** *She was aware of his attempts at flirtation.* **2** Someone who is a **flirt** likes to flirt a lot. *He's a dreadful flirt.* ♦ **flirty** *She is amazingly flirty.* **3** If you **flirt** with an idea or belief, you consider it or adopt it briefly, but do not become completely committed to it. *My mother used to flirt with Socialism.* ♦ **flirtation** *...his flirtation with nationalism.* ♦◇◇◇◇ V-RECIP: V with n V (non-recip) N-VAR N-COUNT ADJ-GRADED VERB V with n N-VAR

flir·ta·tious /flɜːˈteɪʃəs/. Someone who is **flirtatious** behaves towards someone else as if they are sexually attracted to them, usually in a playful or not very serious way. ADJ-GRADED

flit /flɪt/ **flits, flitting, flitted. 1** If you **flit** around, you go to lots of places without staying for very long in any of them. *Laura flits about New York. ...flitting between Florence, Rome and Bologna.* **2** If someone **flits** from one thing or situation to another, they move or turn their attention from one to the other very quickly. *He's prone to flit between subjects with amazing ease.* **3** If something such as a bird or a bat **flits** about, it flies quickly from one place to another. *...the parrot that flits from tree to tree.* **4** If an expression **flits** across your face or an idea **flits** through your mind, it is there for a short time and then goes again. ♦◇◇◇◇ VERB V prep/adv VERB V from n to n V prep VERB V prep/adv VERB: V prep

float /fləʊt/ **floats, floating, floated. 1** If something or someone **is floating** in a liquid, they are being supported by the liquid, on or just below the surface. You can also **float** something on a liquid. *They noticed fifty and twenty dollar bills floating in the water... A tree branch was floating down the river.* **2** A **float** is a light object that is used to help someone or something float. **3** A **float** is a small object attached to a fishing line which floats on the water and moves when a fish has been caught. **4** Something that **floats** in the air hangs in it or moves slowly through it. *The white cloud of smoke floated away.* **5** If a sound or smell **floats** somewhere, it can be heard or smelled faintly there. *Voices floated down from a distant balcony.* ♦♦♦◇◇ V-ERG V prep/adv Also V n N-COUNT N-COUNT VERB V prep/adv VERB V prep/adv LITERARY

6 If you **float** an idea, you suggest it for others to think about. *She floated the idea of a cut in capital-gains tax.* **7** To **float** a new company means to make shares in it available for the public to buy. To **float** new shares means to make them available for the public to buy. *He floated his firm on the stock market.* **8** If a government **floats** its country's currency or allows it to **float**, it allows the currency's value to change freely in relation to other currencies. *59 per cent of people believed the pound should be allowed to float freely.* **9** A **float** is a lorry on which displays and people in special costumes are carried in a festival procession. VERB V n VERB V n V-ERG: V n V TECHNICAL N-COUNT

float around. Something that **is floating around** exists and can be heard, seen, or found regularly. *There were a few forged £50 notes floating around.* PHRASAL VB V P

,floating 'voter, floating voters. A floating voter is a person who is not a firm supporter of any political party. N-COUNT BRITISH

flock /flɒk/ **flocks, flocking, flocked. 1** A flock of birds, sheep, or goats is a group of them. *They kept a small flock of sheep.* **2** You can refer to a group of people or things as a **flock of** them to emphasize that there are a lot of them. *These cases all attracted flocks of famous writers.* **3** If people **flock** to a particular place or event, a very large number of them go there. *The criticisms will not stop people flocking to see the film.* **4** A clergyman's **flock** is the group of Christians who come to his church or live in the area that he has responsibility for. ♦♦◇◇◇ N-COLL-COUNT N-COLL-COUNT: N of n PRAGMATICS VERB: V to/into n V to-inf N-COUNT

floe /fləʊ/. See **ice floe.**

flog /flɒg/ **flogs, flogging, flogged. 1** If someone tries to **flog** something, they try to sell it. *He was spotted trying to flog a luxury-home development in Ventura.* **2** If someone **is flogged**, they are hit very hard with a whip or stick as a punishment. *Flog them soundly.* ♦ **flog·ging, floggings** *He urged the restoration of hanging and flogging.* ♦◇◇◇◇ VERB: BRITISH, INFORMAL VERB: be V-ed N-VAR

flood /flʌd/ **floods, flooding, flooded. 1** If there is a **flood**, a large amount of water covers an area which is usually dry, for example when a river overflows. *More than 70 people were killed in the floods.* ● See also **flash flood. 2** If something such as a river or a burst pipe **floods** an area that is usually dry, or if the area **floods**, it becomes covered with water. *The Chicago River flooded the city's underground tunnel system... The kitchen flooded. ...flooded land.* ♦ **flood·ing** *The flooding is thought to be the worst this century.* **3** If a river **floods**, it overflows. *Many streams have flooded their banks.* **4** If a river is in **flood**, it is overflowing because it has more water in it than normal. **5** If you say that someone was in **floods of tears**, you are emphasizing that they were crying with great intensity because they were very upset. ♦♦♦◇◇ N-VAR V-ERG V n V-ed N-UNCOUNT VERB: V V n PHRASE PHRASE

6 If you say that a **flood** of people or things arrive somewhere, you are emphasizing that a very large number of them arrive there. *The administration is trying to stem the flood of refugees... He received a flood of letters.* **7** If you say that people or things **flood** into a place, you are emphasizing that they arrive there in large numbers. *...the refugees flooding out of Bosnia.* **8** If someone **floods** a place with a particular type of thing, the place becomes full of so many of them that it cannot hold or deal with any more. *...a policy aimed at flooding Europe with exports... German cameras at knock-down prices flooded the British market.* **9** If an emotion, feeling, or thought **floods** you, you suddenly feel it very intensely. If feelings or memories **flood back**, you suddenly remember them very clearly. *Mary Ann was flooded with relief ... The trial brought painful memories flooding back.* **10** If light **floods** a place or **floods** into it, it suddenly fills it. *Morning sunshine flooded in through the open curtains.* N-COUNT PRAGMATICS VERB V prep/adv VERB V n with n V n VERB: V n be V-ed with n V adv LITERARY VERB: V n PRAGMATICS V prep/adv

flood out. If people, places, or things **are flooded out**, the water from a flood makes it impossible for people to stay in that place or to use that thing. *Train lines were flooded out... The river flooded them out every few years.* PHRASAL VB be V-ed P V n P

flood·gates /'flʌdgeɪts/. If events **open the floodgates** to something, they make it possible for that PHRASE

thing to happen much more often or much more seriously than before. *A decision against the cigarette companies could open the floodgates to many more lawsuits.*

flood·light /ˈflʌdlaɪt/ **floodlights, floodlighting, floodlit. 1** Floodlights are very powerful lamps that are used outside to light public buildings, sports grounds, and other places at night. **2** If a building or place **is floodlit**, it is lit by floodlights. *A police helicopter hovered above, floodlighting the area. ...a floodlit forecourt.* ◆◇◇◇◇ N-COUNT / VERB: be V-ed / V n / V-ed

floor /flɔː/ **floors, flooring, floored. 1** The **floor** of a room is the part of it that you walk on. *Jack's sitting on the floor watching TV.* ♦ **floored** *The aisle was floored with ancient bricks. ...the large marble-floored hall.* **2** A **floor** of a building is all the rooms that are on a particular level. *It is on the fifth floor of the hospital.* **3** The ocean **floor** is the ground at the bottom of an ocean. *The valley floor is the ground at the bottom of a valley.* **4** The place where official debates and discussions are held, especially in a parliament or council, is referred to as the **floor**. *The issues were debated on the floor of the House.* ● If you **take the floor**, you start speaking in a debate or discussion. If you **are given the floor**, you are allowed to do this. **5** In a debate or discussion, **the floor** refers to the people who are listening to the arguments being put forward but who are not among the main speakers. *The president is taking questions from the floor.* **6** The **floor** of a stock exchange is the large open area where trading is done. **7** If you **are floored** by something, you are unable to respond to it because you are so surprised by it. *He was floored by the announcement.* ♦ **floored** *We were absolutely floored when the lady contacted us.* **8** If someone **is floored**, they are knocked to the ground. *Police Sergeant John Shepherd floored him with a rugby tackle.* **9** See also **flooring; dance floor, factory floor, first floor, ground floor, shop floor.** **10** If you say that prices or sales have fallen **through the floor**, you mean that they have suddenly decreased to a very low level. **11** If you **wipe the floor with** someone, you defeat them completely in a competition or discussion. ◆◆◆◇ N-COUNT / ADJ / N-COUNT / N-COUNT / PHRASE / N-COLL-SING: the N / N-COUNT / VB: usu passive be V-ed / ADJ-GRADED / VERB V n / PHRASE / PHRASE INFORMAL

floor·board /ˈflɔːbɔːd/ **floorboards.** Floorboards are the long pieces of wood that a wooden floor is made up of. ◆◇◇◇◇ N-COUNT

floor·ing /ˈflɔːrɪŋ/ **floorings.** Flooring is a material that is used to make the floor of a room. ◆◇◇◇◇ N-VAR

'floor show, floor shows; also spelled **floorshow.** A **floor show** is a series of performances by dancers, singers, or comedians at a night club. N-COUNT

flop /flɒp/ **flops, flopping, flopped. 1** If someone or something **flops** somewhere, they fall there heavily or untidily. *She flopped, exhausted, on to a sofa... His hair flopped over his left eye.* **2** If something **flops**, it is completely unsuccessful. *The film flopped badly at the box office.* ▶ Also a noun. *The policy is destined to be another embarrassing flop.* ◆◆◇◇◇ VERB V prep/adv / VERB V / N-COUNT

flop·py /ˈflɒpi/. Something that is **floppy** is loose rather than stiff, and tends to hang downwards. *...the girl with the floppy hat and glasses.* ◆◇◇◇◇ ADJ-GRADED

,floppy 'disk, floppy disks; also spelled **floppy disc** in British English. A **floppy disk** is a small magnetic disk that is used for storing computer data and programs. N-COUNT

flo·ra /ˈflɔːrə/. You can refer to plants as **flora**, especially the plants growing in a particular area. *The soil is rich in lime and affects the flora.* ◆◇◇◇◇ N-COLL-UNCOUNT FORMAL

flo·ral /ˈflɔːrəl/. **1** A floral fabric or design has flowers on it. **2** You can use **floral** to describe something that contains flowers or is made of flowers. *...eye-catching floral arrangements.* ◆◇◇◇◇ ADJ / ADJ: ADJ n

flor·id /ˈflɒrɪd, AM ˈflɔːr-/. **1** Florid language is complicated and extravagant rather than plain and simple; used showing disapproval. **2** Someone who is **florid** always has a red face. ADJ-GRADED PRAGMATICS / ADJ-GRADED

flo·rist /ˈflɒrɪst, AM ˈflɔːr-/ **florists. 1** A **florist** is a shopkeeper who arranges and sells flowers and sells N-COUNT

indoor plants. **2** A **florist** or a **florist's** is a shop where flowers and indoor plants are sold. N-COUNT

floss /flɒs, AM flɔːs/. Dental **floss** is thread used for cleaning between your teeth. ● See also **candyfloss.** N-UNCOUNT

flo·ta·tion /fləʊˈteɪʃən/ **flotations. 1** The **flotation** of a company is the selling of shares in it to the public. **2** A **flotation** compartment helps something to float because it is filled with air or gas. ◆◇◇◇◇ N-VAR / ADJ: ADJ n

flo·til·la /fləˈtɪlə/ **flotillas.** A **flotilla** is a group of small ships, usually military ships. N-COUNT

flot·sam /ˈflɒtsəm/. **1** Flotsam is rubbish or wreckage that is floating on the sea or has been left by the sea on the shore. **2** You can use **flotsam and jetsam** to refer to small or unimportant items that are found together, especially ones that have no connection with each other. N-UNCOUNT / PHRASE

flounce /flaʊns/ **flounces, flouncing, flounced. 1** If you **flounce** somewhere, you walk there quickly with exaggerated movements, in a way that shows you are annoyed or upset. *She will flounce and argue when asked to leave the room.* **2** A **flounce** is a deep frill around the edge of something, for example a skirt or curtain. VERB: V adv/prep V / N-COUNT

floun·der /ˈflaʊndə/ **flounders, floundering, floundered. 1** If something **is floundering**, it has many problems and may soon fail completely. *What a pity that his career was left to flounder.* **2** If you say that someone **is floundering**, you are criticizing them for not being decisive or for not knowing what to say or do. *I know that you're floundering around, trying to grasp at any straw.* **3** If you **flounder** in water or mud, you move in an uncontrolled way, trying not to sink. *Three men were floundering about in the water.* ◆◆◇◇◇ VERB / VERB: V PRAGMATICS V around / VERB V adv/prep Also V

flour /flaʊə/ **flours, flouring, floured. 1** Flour is a white or brown powder that is made by grinding grain. It is used to make bread, cakes, and pastry. **2** If you **flour** a cooking utensil or food, you cover it with flour. ◆◆◇◇◇ N-VAR / VERB: V n

flour·ish /ˈflʌrɪʃ, AM ˈflɜːr-/ **flourishes, flourishing, flourished. 1** If something **flourishes**, it is successful, active, or widespread, and developing quickly and strongly. *Business flourished and within six months they were earning 18,000 roubles a day.* ♦ **flour·ish·ing** *London quickly became a flourishing port.* **2** If a plant or animal **flourishes**, it grows well or is healthy. ♦ **flourishing** *...the largest and most flourishing fox population in Europe.* **3** If you **flourish** an object, you wave it about in a way that makes people notice it. *He flourished the glass to emphasize the point.* **4** If you do something with a **flourish**, you do it in a showy way so that people notice it. *She tended to finish dancing with a flourish.* **5** A **flourish** is a curly line or piece of decoration. *He scrawled his name across the bill, underlining it with a showy flourish.* ◆◆◇◇◇ VERB V / ADJ-GRADED / VERB: V / ADJ-GRADED / VERB V n / N-COUNT

flout /flaʊt/ **flouts, flouting, flouted.** If you flout something such as a law, an order, or an accepted way of behaving, you deliberately disobey it or do not follow it. *...illegal campers who persist in flouting the law.* ◆◇◇◇◇ VERB V n

flow /fləʊ/ **flows, flowing, flowed. 1** If a liquid, gas, or electrical current **flows** somewhere, it moves there steadily and continuously. *A stream flowed gently down into the valley. ...compressor stations that keep the gas flowing.* ▶ Also a noun. *It works only in the veins, where the blood flow is slower.* **2** If a number of people or things **flow** from one place to another, they move there steadily in large groups. *Refugees continue to flow from the troubled region.* ▶ Also a noun. *...the frantic flow of cars and buses along the street.* **3** If information or money **flows** somewhere, it moves freely between people or organizations. *A lot of this information flowed through other police departments... An interest rate reduction is needed to get more money flowing.* ▶ Also a noun. *...the opportunity to control the flow of information.* ● See also **cash flow. 4** If an emotion **flows** through someone, they feel it very intensely. *A surge of hatred flowed through my* ◆◆◆◆ VERB V adv/prep V / N-VAR / VERB V prep/adv / N-VAR / VERB V prep/adv V / N-VAR: with supp / VERB V prep LITERARY

F

blood. **5** If a quality or situation **flows** from something, it comes from that thing or results naturally from it. *Undesirable consequences flow from these misconceptions.* — VERB V from n

6 If someone's words **flow**, they are spoken smoothly and continuously without hesitation. — VERB: V

7 If someone's hair or clothing **flows** about them, it hangs freely and loosely. *...a long white dress which flowed over her body.* — VERB V prep LITERARY

8 Someone who is **in full flow** is talking fluently and easily and seems likely to go on talking for some time. — PHRASE

9 If you say that an activity, or the person who is performing the activity, is **in full flow**, you mean that the activity has started and is being carried out with a great deal of energy and enthusiasm. *Lunch at Harry's Bar was in full flow.* **10** If you **go with the flow**, you let things happen or let other people tell you what to do, rather than trying to control what happens yourself. — PHRASE ... PHRASE

'**flow chart, flow charts.** A **flow chart** or a **flow diagram** is a diagram which represents the sequence of actions in a particular process or activity. — N-COUNT

flow·er /ˈflaʊə/ **flowers, flowering, flowered.** ◆◆◆◇
1 A **flower** is the brightly coloured part of a plant which grows at the end of a stem. *...a bunch of flowers. ...a lawned area surrounded by screening plants and flowers.* **2** When a plant is **in flower** or when it has come **into flower**, its flowers have appeared and opened. **3** When a plant or tree **flowers**, its flowers appear and open. *These rhododendrons will flower this year for the first time.* **4** See also **flowered**. — N-COUNT ... PHRASE ... VERB V

5 When something **flowers**, it gets stronger and more successful. *Their relationship flowered.* ♦ **flow·er·ing** *...the flowering of new thinking.* — VERB: V ... N-UNCOUNT

6 Someone or something that is described as **the flower** of something is the best part or example of it. *Those killed have been described as the flower of Polish manhood.* — N-SING: the N of n LITERARY

flower·bed /ˈflaʊəbed/ **flowerbeds;** also spelled **flower bed.** A **flowerbed** is an area of garden which has been specially prepared so that flowers can be grown in it. See picture headed **house and flat.** — N-COUNT

flow·ered /ˈflaʊəd/. **Flowered** paper or cloth has a pattern of flowers on it. *...a pretty flowered cotton dress.* — ADJ: ADJ n

flower·pot /ˈflaʊəpɒt/ **flowerpots;** also spelled **flower pot.** A **flowerpot** is a container that is used for growing plants. — N-COUNT

'**flower power.** **Flower power** relates to hippies and the culture associated with hippies in the late 1960s and early 1970s. — N-UNCOUNT

flow·ery /ˈflaʊəri/. **1** A **flowery** smell is strong and sweet. *...Isabel's flowery perfume.* **2 Flowery** cloth, paper, or china has a lot of flowers printed or painted on it. **3 Flowery** speech or writing contains long or literary words and expressions. — ADJ-GRADED ADJ-GRADED ADJ-GRADED

flown /fləʊn/. **Flown** is the past participle of **fly.**

fl. oz. **fl. oz** is a written abbreviation for **fluid ounce.** ◆◇◇◇◇

flu /fluː/. **Flu** is an illness which is similar to a bad cold but more serious. — N-UNCOUNT: also the N ◆◇◇◇◇

fluc·tu·ate /ˈflʌktʃueɪt/ **fluctuates, fluctuating, fluctuated.** If something **fluctuates**, it changes a lot in an irregular way. *Body temperature can fluctuate if you are ill.* ♦ **fluc·tua·tion** /ˌflʌktʃuˈeɪʃən/ **fluctuations** *Don't worry about tiny fluctuations in your weight.* — VERB ◆◇◇◇◇ ... N-VAR

flue /fluː/ **flues.** A **flue** is a pipe or shaft that acts as a chimney, taking fumes and smoke away from a boiler or a stove. — N-COUNT

flu·ent /ˈfluːənt/. **1** Someone who is **fluent** in a particular language can speak the language easily and correctly. You can also say that someone speaks **fluent** French, Chinese, or other language. ♦ **flu·en·cy** *To work as a translator, you need fluency in at least one foreign language.* ♦ **flu·ent·ly** *He spoke three languages fluently.* **2** If your speech, reading, or writing is **fluent**, you speak, read, or write easily, with no hesitation or mistakes. *He had* — ADJ-GRADED ◆◇◇◇◇ ... N-UNCOUNT ... ADV-GRADED ... ADJ-GRADED

emerged from being a hesitant and unsure candidate into a fluent debater. ♦ **fluency** *...speeches of remarkable fluency.* ♦ **fluently** *Alex didn't read fluently till he was nearly seven.* — N-UNCOUNT ... ADV-GRADED: ADV with v

fluff /flʌf/ **fluffs, fluffing, fluffed. 1** **Fluff** consists of soft threads or fibres in the form of small light balls or lumps. *...some bits of fluff on the sleeve of her sweater.* **2** If you **fluff** things such as cushions or feathers, you get a lot of air into them, for example by shaking or brushing them, in order to make them seem larger and lighter. ▶ **Fluff up** means the same as **fluff.** *Take the pan off the heat and cover for 5 minutes to fluff up the rice.* **3** If you **fluff** something that you are trying to do, you are unsuccessful or you do it badly. *She fluffed her interview at Oxford.* ◆◇◇◇◇ — N-UNCOUNT ... VERB: V n ... PHRASAL VB V P noun Also V n P ... VERB V n INFORMAL

fluffy /ˈflʌfi/. **1** If you describe something such as a towel or a toy animal as **fluffy**, you mean that it is very soft and woolly. *...fluffy white towels.* **2** A cake or other food that is **fluffy** is very light because it has a lot of air in it. ◆◇◇◇◇ — ADJ-GRADED ... ADJ-GRADED

flu·id /ˈfluːɪd/ **fluids. 1** A **fluid** is a liquid. *Make sure that you drink plenty of fluids.* **2 Fluid** movements, lines, or designs are smooth and graceful. *His painting became less illustrational and more fluid.* ♦ **flu·id·ity** /fluːˈɪdɪti/ *...an exquisite fluidity of movement.* **3** A situation that is **fluid** is unstable and is likely to change often. *The situation is extremely fluid and it can be changing from day to day.* ♦ **fluidity** *...the complexity and fluidity of the crisis.* ◆◆◇◇◇ — N-VAR ... FORMAL ADJ-GRADED ... N-UNCOUNT ... ADJ-GRADED ... N-UNCOUNT

,**fluid 'ounce, fluid ounces.** A **fluid ounce** is a measurement of liquid. There are twenty fluid ounces in a British pint, and sixteen in an American pint. — N-COUNT: num N

fluke /fluːk/ **flukes.** If you say that something good is a **fluke**, you mean that it happened accidentally rather than by being planned or arranged. *The discovery was something of a fluke.* ◆◇◇◇◇ — N-COUNT INFORMAL

flum·mox /ˈflʌməks/ **flummoxes, flummoxing, flummoxed.** If someone **is flummoxed** by something, they are confused by it and do not know what to do or say. ♦ **flum·moxed** *No wonder Josef was feeling a bit flummoxed.* — VERB: be V-ed ... ADJ-GRADED

flung /flʌŋ/. **Flung** is the past tense and past participle of **fling.**

flunk /flʌŋk/ **flunks, flunking, flunked.** If you **flunk** an exam or a course, you fail to reach the required standard. *Your son is upset because he flunked a history exam.* — VERB V n INFORMAL

flunk·ey /ˈflʌŋki/ **flunkeys;** also spelled **flunky.** You use **flunkey** to refer to someone who does small unimportant tasks for someone else; used showing disapproval. — N-COUNT PRAGMATICS

fluo·res·cent /fluəˈresənt/. **1** A **fluorescent** surface, substance, or colour has a very bright appearance when light is directed onto it, as if it is actually shining itself. *...a piece of fluorescent tape.* ♦ **fluo·res·cence** *...the green fluorescence it gives off under ultraviolet radiation.* **2** A **fluorescent** light shines with a very hard bright light and is usually in the form of a long strip. ◆◇◇◇◇ — ADJ ... N-UNCOUNT ... ADJ

fluori·da·tion /ˌfluərɪˈdeɪʃən/. **Fluoridation** is the action or process of adding fluoride to a water supply. — N-UNCOUNT

fluo·ride /ˈfluəraɪd/. **Fluoride** is a mixture of chemicals that is sometimes added to drinking water and toothpaste because it is considered to be good for people's teeth. ◆◇◇◇◇ — N-UNCOUNT

flur·ry /ˈflʌri, AM ˈflɜːri/ **flurries. 1** A **flurry** of something such as activity or speculation is a short intense period of it. *...a flurry of diplomatic activity aimed at ending the war.* **2** A **flurry** of something such as snow is a small amount of it that suddenly appears for a short time and moves in a quick swirling way. ◆◇◇◇◇ — N-COUNT ... N-COUNT

flush /flʌʃ/ **flushes, flushing, flushed. 1** If you **flush**, your face goes red, for example because you are hot or embarrassed. *He turned away embarrassed, his face flushing red.* ▶ Also a noun. *There* ◆◆◇◇◇ — VERB: V V colour ... N-COUNT

was a slight flush on his cheeks. ♦ **flushed** *Her face was flushed with anger.* ADJ-GRADED

2 When someone **flushes** a toilet after using it, they fill the toilet bowl with water in order to clean it, usually by pressing a handle or pulling a chain. You can also say that a toilet **flushes**. *She flushed the toilet and went back in the bedroom.* ► Also a noun. *He heard the flush of a toilet.* **3** If you **flush** something down the toilet, you get rid of it by putting it into the toilet bowl and flushing the toilet. *He was found trying to flush banknotes down the toilet.* V-ERG V n Also V N-COUNT VERB V n down n

4 If you **flush** dirt or a harmful substance out of a place, you get rid of it by using a large amount of liquid. *That won't flush out all the sewage, but it should unclog some stinking drains.* **5** If you **flush** a part of your body, you clean it or make it healthier by using a large amount of liquid to get rid of dirt or harmful substances. *Flush the eye with clean cold water.* ► **Flush out** means the same as **flush**. *...an 'alternative' therapy that gently flushes out the colon to remove toxins.* VERB V n with out VERB V n PHRASAL VB V P noun Also V n P

6 If you **flush** people or animals out of a place where they are hiding, you find or capture them by forcing them to come out of that place. *The Guyana Defence Force is engaged in flushing out illegal Brazilian miners operating in the country.* VERB: V n out of n V n with out

7 If one object or surface is **flush** with another, they are at the same height or distance from something else, so that they form a single smooth surface. *Make sure the tile is flush with the surrounding tiles.* ADJ: v-link ADJ

8 If you are **flush** with money, you have a lot of it, usually only for a short time. *If we're feeling flush we'll probably give them champagne.* ADJ-GRADED: v-link ADJ INFORMAL

9 The **flush of** something is an intense feeling of excitement or pleasure that you have when you are experiencing it and for a short time afterwards. *...the first flush of young love.* N-SING: N of n

flush out. See **flush** 5. PHRASAL VB

flushed /flʌʃt/. If you say that someone is **flushed with** success or triumph, you mean that they are very excited by their success or triumph. *Grace was flushed with the success of the venture.* ADJ-GRADED: v-link ADJ with n

flus·ter /'flʌstə/ **flusters, flustering, flustered.** If you **fluster** someone, you make them feel nervous and confused by rushing or interrupting them. *She was a very calm person. Nothing could fluster her.* ♦ **flus·tered** *She was so flustered that she forgot her reply.* VERB V n ADJ-GRADED

flute /fluːt/ **flutes.** A **flute** is a musical instrument which you play by blowing over a hole near one end while holding it sideways to your mouth. See picture headed **musical instruments.** ◆◇◇◇ N-VAR

flut·ed /'fluːtɪd/. Something that is **fluted** has round, shallow grooves cut or shaped into it. *...the fluted wooden post of the porch.* ADJ

flut·ing /'fluːtɪŋ/. If you describe someone's voice as **fluting**, you mean that it goes up and down a lot, and usually that it is high pitched. *...a fluting and melodic Scottish accent.* ADJ

flut·ter /'flʌtə/ **flutters, fluttering, fluttered.** **1** If something thin or light **flutters**, or if you **flutter** it, it moves up and down or from side to side with a lot of quick light movements. *Her chiffon skirt was fluttering in the night breeze. ...a butterfly fluttering its wings.* ► Also a noun. *...a flutter of white cloth.* **2** If something light such as a small bird or a piece of paper **flutters** somewhere, it moves through the air with small quick movements. *The birds were active, whirring and fluttering among the trees.* **3** If you say that someone **flutters** somewhere, you mean that they walk there with quick light movements, often in a silly way or in a way which suggests that they are nervous. *She'd been fluttering about in the kitchen.* **4** If your heart or stomach **flutters**, you experience a strong feeling of excitement or anxiety. **5** If you have a **flutter**, you have a small bet on something such as a horse race. *I had a flutter on five horses.* ◆◇◇◇ V-ERG V V n N-COUNT VERB: V adv/prep V VERB V adv/prep VERB: V N-COUNT INFORMAL, BRITISH

flux /flʌks/ **fluxes.** **1** If something is in a state of **flux**, it is constantly changing. *Education remains in a state of flux.* **2** You can refer to a flowing mass as a **flux**. *...the flux of cosmic rays.* ◆◇◇◇ N-UNCOUNT N-VAR TECHNICAL

fly /flaɪ/ **flies, flying, flew, flown.** **1** A **fly** is a small insect with two wings. See picture headed **insects.** ● See also **tsetse fly.** **2** If you say that someone wouldn't **hurt a fly** or wouldn't **harm a fly,** you are emphasizing that they are very kind and gentle. **3** If you say that you would like to be **a fly on the wall** in a situation that does not involve you, you mean that you would like to see or hear what happens in that situation. ● See also **fly-on-the-wall.** ◆◆◆◆ N-COUNT PHRASE PRAGMATICS PHRASE

4 When something such as a bird, insect, or aircraft **flies**, it moves through the air. *The planes flew through the clouds... The bird flew away.* ♦ **fly·ing** *...species of flying insects.* VERB V prep/adv Also V ADJ: ADJ n

5 If you **fly** somewhere, you travel there in an aircraft. *He flew to Los Angeles.* ♦ **fly·er, flyers** *...regular business flyers.* **6** When someone **flies** an aircraft, they control its movement in the air. *He flew a small plane to Cuba. ...his inspiration to fly.* ♦ **flying** *...a flying instructor.* ♦ **flyer** *Our chief pilot was a highly experienced flyer.* **7** To **fly** someone or something somewhere means to take or send them there in an aircraft. *It may be possible to fly the women and children out on Thursday.* VERB V prep/adv N-COUNT VERB: V n V n prep/adv V N-UNCOUNT N-COUNT VERB V n adv/prep

8 If something such as your hair **is flying** about, it is moving about freely and loosely in the air. *His long, uncovered hair flew back in the wind.* **9** If you **fly** a flag or if it **is flying**, you display it at the top of a pole. *They flew the flag of the African National Congress.* VERB V adv/prep Also V V-ERG V n Also V

10 If you say that someone or something **flies** in a particular direction, you are emphasizing that they move there with a lot of speed or force. *She flew to their bedsides when they were ill.* **11** If you **send** someone or something **flying**, or if they **go flying**, they move through the air and fall down with a lot of force. *The blow sent the young man flying.* VERB PRAGMATICS V prep/adv PHRASE

12 If rumours or allegations **are flying** around a place, they are being discussed a great deal and by a lot of people within a short period of time. *Rumours had been flying around the workrooms all morning.* VERB V adv/prep Also V

13 The front opening on a pair of trousers is referred to as the **fly,** or in British English the **flies.** N-COUNT

14 In fishing, a **fly** is a model of a small winged insect that is used as a bait. N-COUNT

15 If you **let fly,** you attack someone, either physically by hitting them, or with words by insulting them. *A simmering row ended with her letting fly with a stream of obscenities.* PHRASE

16 If someone or something **gets off to a flying start,** or **makes a flying start,** they start something very well, for example a race or a new job. *Hendry made a flying start to the final.* PHRASE

17 ● **as the crow flies**: see **crow.** ● **to fly in the face of**: see **face.** ● **to fly the flag**: see **flag.** ● **to fly off the handle**: see **handle.** ● **a fly in the ointment**: see **ointment.** ● **sparks fly**: see **spark.** ● **time flies**: see **time.**

fly at. If you **fly at** someone, you attack them, either physically by hitting them, or with words by insulting them. *She flew at him for making a very anti-British remark.* PHRASAL VB V P n

fly into. If you **fly into** a rage or a panic, you suddenly become very angry or anxious and show this in your behaviour. *Losing a game would cause him to fly into a rage.* PHRASAL VB V P n

fly·by /'flaɪbaɪ/ **flybys;** also spelled **fly-by.** A **flyby** is a flight made by an aircraft or a spacecraft over a particular place in order to record detailed observations about it. N-COUNT

'fly-by-night. If you describe a business or a businessman as a **fly-by-night** operator, you are criticizing them because they want to make money very quickly, and they do not care about the quality of the service they offer. ADJ: ADJ n PRAGMATICS INFORMAL

fly·er /'flaɪə/ **flyers;** also spelled **flier.** **1** A **flyer** is a small printed notice which is used to advertise a ◆◇◇◇ N-COUNT

particular company, service, or event. **2** See also **fly, high-flyer.**

'fly-fishing; also spelled **fly fishing. Fly-fishing** is a method of fishing in which a silk or nylon model of a small winged insect is used as bait.   N-UNCOUNT

,flying 'doctor, flying doctors. A **flying doctor** is a doctor, especially in Australia, who travels by aircraft to visit patients who live in distant or isolated areas.   N-COUNT

'flying fish, flying fishes. Flying fish can also be used as the plural form. **Flying fish** are a type of fish that have large fins that enable them to move forward in the air when they jump out of the water.   N-VAR

,flying 'saucer, flying saucers. A **flying saucer** is a round flat object which some people say they have seen in the sky and which they believe to be a spacecraft from another planet.   N-COUNT

'Flying Squad. The Flying Squad is a group of police officers who are always ready to travel quickly to the scene of a serious crime.   N-COLL-PROPER: the N BRITISH

,flying 'visit, flying visits. A **flying visit** is a visit that only lasts a very short time.   N-COUNT

,fly-on-the-'wall. A **fly-on-the-wall** documentary shows people as they do the things they normally do, rather than them being interviewed or being asked to talk directly to the camera. ● **a fly on the wall:** see **fly.**   ADJ: ADJ n

fly·over /'flaɪəʊvə/ **flyovers. 1** A **flyover** is a structure which carries one road over the top of another road. The usual American word is **overpass. 2** A **flyover** is a flight by a group of aircraft in a special formation which takes place on a ceremonial occasion or as a display. The usual British word is **flypast.**   N-COUNT BRITISH / N-COUNT AMERICAN

fly·past /'flaɪpɑːst, -pæst/ **flypasts;** also spelled **fly-past.** A **flypast** is a flight by a group of aircraft in a special formation which takes place on a ceremonial occasion or as a display. The usual American word is **flyover.**   N-COUNT BRITISH

fly·wheel /'flaɪwiːl/ **flywheels.** A **flywheel** is a heavy wheel that is part of some engines. It regulates the engine's rotation, making it operate at a steady speed.   N-COUNT

FM /,ef 'em/. **FM** is a method of transmitting radio waves used to broadcast high quality stereo. FM is an abbreviation for 'frequency modulation'.   ◆◆◇◇◇

foal /fəʊl/ **foals, foaling, foaled. 1** A **foal** is a very young horse. **2** When a female horse **foals,** it gives birth.   ◆◇◇◇◇ N-COUNT VERB: V

foam /fəʊm/ **foams, foaming, foamed. 1** Foam consists of a mass of small bubbles that are formed when air and a liquid are mixed together. *The water curved round the rocks in great bursts of foam. ...shaving foam.* **2** If a liquid **foams,** it is full of small bubbles and keeps moving slightly. **3** Foam or **foam rubber** is soft rubber full of small holes which is used, for example, to make mattresses and cushions.   ◆◇◇◇◇ N-UNCOUNT / VERB: V / N-VAR

foamy /'fəʊmi/. A **foamy** liquid consists of a mass of bubbles. *Whisk the egg whites until they are foamy.*   ADJ-GRADED

fob /fɒb/ **fobs, fobbing, fobbed.** A **fob** is a chain which attaches a watch to a man's waistcoat.   N-COUNT

fob off. If someone **fobs** you **off,** they tell you something just to stop you asking questions or asking for something, especially when this is not really what you wanted; used showing disapproval. *Don't be fobbed off with excuses.*   PHRASAL VB V n P PRAGMATICS be V-ed P with n

fo·cal /'fəʊkəl/. **1** Focal is used to describe something that relates to the point where a number of rays or lines meet. *...the focal plane of the telescope.* **2** Focal is used to describe something that is very important. *...the focal centre of the Far East.*   ◆◇◇◇◇ ADJ: ADJ n / ADJ: ADJ n

'focal point, focal points. The **focal point** of something is the thing that people concentrate on or pay most attention to. *Its Neighbourhood Centre is a focal point for health services.*   ◆◇◇◇◇ N-COUNT

fo·cus /'fəʊkəs/ **foci** /'fəʊsaɪ/ **focuses, focusing, focused.** The spellings **focusses, focussing, focussed** are also used. The plural of the noun can be either **foci** or **focuses. 1** If you **focus** on a par-   ◆◆◆◆◇

ticular topic or if your attention **is focused** on it, you concentrate on it and deal with it, rather than dealing with other topics. *He is currently focusing on assessment and development... Today he was able to focus his message exclusively on the economy.* **2** The **focus** of something is the main topic or main thing that it is concerned with. *The new system is the focus of controversy.* **3** Your **focus** on something is the special attention that you pay it. *His sudden focus on foreign policy was not motivated by presidential politics.* **4** If something is **in focus,** it is being discussed or its purpose and nature are clear. *These issues have been brought into sharp focus by the Gulf crisis.*   V onn / V n onn / N-COUNT / N-COUNT / PHRASE

5 If you say that something has a **focus,** you mean that you can see a purpose in it. *Their latest LP has a focus that the others have lacked.*   N-UNCOUNT

6 If you **focus** your eyes, or if your eyes **focus,** your eyes adjust so that you can clearly see the thing that you want to look at. If you **focus** a camera, telescope, or other instrument, you adjust it so that you can see clearly through it. *His eyes slowly began to focus on what looked like a small dark ball... He found the binoculars and focused them on the boat.* **7** You use **focus** to refer to the fact of adjusting your eyes or a camera, telescope, or other instrument, and to the degree to which you can see clearly. *His focus switched to the little white ball... These factors determine the depth of focus.* **8** If an image or a camera, telescope, or other instrument is **in focus,** the edges of what you see are clear and sharp. If it is **out of focus,** the edges of what you see are blurred.   V-ERG: V n / V onn / V n onn / Also V / N-UNCOUNT / PHRASE

9 If you **focus** rays of light on a particular point, you pass them through a lens or reflect them from a mirror so that they meet at that point. **10** The **focus** of a number of rays or lines is the point at which they meet.   VERB: V n prep / N-COUNT TECHNICAL

fo·cused /'fəʊkəst/; also spelled **focussed.** If you describe someone or something as **focused,** you approve of the fact that they have a clear and definite purpose. *I spent the next year just wandering. I wasn't focused.*   ADJ-GRADED PRAGMATICS

fod·der /'fɒdə/. **1** Fodder is food that is given to cows, horses, and other animals. **2** If you say that something is **fodder** for a particular purpose, you mean that it is useful for that purpose and perhaps nothing else; used showing disapproval. *Old movies were the cheapest broadcast fodder.*   ◆◇◇◇◇ N-UNCOUNT / N-UNCOUNT PRAGMATICS

foe /fəʊ/ **foes.** Someone's **foe** is their enemy. *Would the U.S. resort to nuclear weapons if drawn into a battle against a formidable foe?*   ◆◇◇◇◇ N-COUNT WRITTEN

foet·id /'fiːtɪd/. See **fetid.**

foe·tus /'fiːtəs/ **foetuses;** also spelled **fetus.** A **foetus** is an unborn animal or human being in its later stages of development. ♦ **foe·tal** /'fiːtəl/ *...an early stage of foetal development.*   ◆◇◇◇◇ N-COUNT / ADJ: ADJ n

fog /fɒg/ **fogs, fogging, fogged. 1** When there is **fog,** there are tiny drops of water in the air which form a thick cloud and make it difficult to see things. *The crash happened in thick fog.* **2** A **fog** is an unpleasant cloud of something such as smoke inside a building or room. *...a fog of stale cigarette smoke.* **3** You can use **fog** to refer to a situation which stops people from being able to notice things, understand things, or think clearly. *...a fog of mythology and folklore.* **4** If a window, mirror, or other glass surface **fogs,** or **is fogged,** it becomes covered with very small drops of water so that you cannot see things clearly through it or in it. *The windows fogged immediately... Water had fogged his diving mask and he couldn't remember how to clear it.*   ◆◆◇◇◇ N-VAR / N-SING / N-SING / V-ERG: V / V n

fog·bound /'fɒgbaʊnd/; also spelled **fog-bound.** If you are **fogbound** in a place, or if the place is **fogbound,** thick fog makes it dangerous or impossible to go anywhere. *...a fogbound motorway.*   ADJ

fo·gey /'fəʊgi/ **fogies** or **fogeys.** If you describe so...   ◆...

fog·gy /'fɒgi/ **foggier, foggiest. 1** When it is ◆◇◇◇◇ ADJ-GRADED
foggy, there is fog. *Conditions were damp and foggy.*
2 If you say that you **haven't the foggiest** or you PHRASE PRAGMATICS INFORMAL
haven't the foggiest idea, you are emphasizing that
you do not know something.

fog·horn /'fɒghɔːn/ **foghorns.** A foghorn is a loud N-COUNT
siren that is used to warn ships about the position
of land and other ships in fog.

fogy /'fəʊgi/. See **fogey.**

foi·ble /'fɔɪbəl/ **foibles.** A foible is a habit or char- N-COUNT
acteristic that someone has which is considered
rather strange or foolish, but not particularly
important. *...human foibles and weaknesses.*

foil /fɔɪl/ **foils, foiling, foiled. 1** Foil consists of ◆◆◇◇◇ N-UNCOUNT
sheets of metal as thin as paper. It is used to wrap
food in. *...aluminium foil.*
2 If you **foil** someone's plan or attempt to do some- VERB V n
thing, you succeed in stopping them from doing what JOURNALISM
they want. *A brave police chief foiled an armed robbery
on a jeweller's.*
3 If you refer to one thing or person as a **foil** for anoth- N-COUNT PRAGMATICS
er, you approve of the fact that they contrast with
each other and go well together. *A cold beer is the perfect foil for a curry.*
4 A **foil** is a thin light sword used in fencing. N-COUNT

foist /fɔɪst/ **foists, foisting, foisted.**
foist on. If you say that someone **foists** something PHRASAL VB PRAGMATICS
on you, or **foists** it **upon** you, you dislike the way that V n P
they force you to listen to it or experience it. *I don't see
my role as foisting my beliefs on them.*

fold /fəʊld/ **folds, folding, folded. 1** If you **fold** ◆◆◆◇◇ VERB
something such as a piece of paper or cloth, you V n
bend it so that one part covers another part. *He* V n prep/adv
*folded the paper carefully... Fold the omelette in
half... Fold the blanket back.* **2** A **fold** in a piece of N-COUNT
paper or cloth is a bend that you make in it when
you put one part of it over another part and press
the edge. *Make another fold and turn the ends to-
gether.* **3** The **folds** in a piece of cloth are the curved N-COUNT
shapes which are formed when it is not hanging or
lying flat. **4** If a piece of furniture or equipment V-ERG
folds, or if you can **fold** it, you can make it smaller V adv/prep
or flatter by bending or closing parts of it. *The back* V adj
of the bench folds forward to make a table... This V n
portable seat folds flat for easy storage... Check if you V-ing
*can fold the buggy without having to remove the
raincover. ...a folding beach chair.* ▶ **Fold up** means PHRASAL VB
the same as **fold.** *When not in use it folds up out of* ERG
the way... Fold the ironing board up so that it is flat. V P
♦ **'fold-up** *...a fold-up bed.* V n P ADJ: ADJ n
5 If you **fold** your arms or hands, you bring them to- VERB: V n
gether and cross or link them, for example over your
chest or in your lap.
6 If a business or organization **folds**, it is unsuccessful VERB
and has to close. *2,500 small businesses were folding* V
each week.
7 When someone joins an organization or group, you N-SING:
can say that they have come into the **fold.** *The EC* the/poss N
brought Spain, Greece and Portugal into the fold.
fold in or **fold into.** In cooking, if you **fold in** an in- PHRASAL VB
gredient or **fold** it **into** the other ingredients, you mix V P noun
it very gently into the other ingredients. *Fold in the* Also V n P n
flour.
fold up. If you **fold** something **up**, you make it into a PHRASAL VB
smaller, neater shape by folding it, usually several V n P
times. *She folded it up, and tucked it into her purse...* V P noun
...[fol]ded up his paper and put it away. ● See also

...[com]bines with numbers to form SUFFIX
...[suc]h an amount has in-
...[am]ount increases
...[o]riginal-
...ADJ: ADJ n

fo·lio /'fəʊliəʊ/ **folios.** A folio is a book made with N-COUNT
paper of a large size, used especially in the early
centuries of European printing.

folk /fəʊk/ **folks; folk** can also be used as the plu- ◆◆◆◇◇ N-PLURAL
ral form for meaning 1. **1** You can refer to people as
folk or **folks.** *...country folk... These are the folks
from the local TV station.* ▶ Also a noun. *'It's a ques-* N-VOC
tion of money, folks,' I announced. **2** You can refer INFORMAL
to your close family, especially your mother and father, as your **folks.** *I've been avoiding my folks lately.*
3 Folk art and customs are traditional or typical of ADJ: ADJ n
a particular community or nation. *...South American
folk art. ...Irish folk music.* **4** Folk can be used to ADJ: ADJ n
describe something that relates to the beliefs and
opinions of ordinary people. *Jack was a folk hero in
the Greenwich Village bars.*

folk·lore /'fəʊklɔː/. Folklore refers to the tradition- ◆◇◇◇◇ N-UNCOUNT
al stories, customs, and habits of a particular com-
munity or nation. *In Chinese folklore the bat is an
emblem of good fortune.*

'folk song, folk songs; also spelled **folksong.** A N-COUNT
folk song is a traditional song that is typical of a
particular community or nation.

folk·sy /'fəʊksi/. **1** If you describe something as ADJ-GRADED
folksy, you mean that it is simple and has a style
characteristic of folk craft and tradition. *...folksy
country furniture.* **2** If you describe someone as ADJ-GRADED
folksy, you mean that they are friendly and informal AMERICAN
in their behaviour. *...an elderly, folksy postman.*

fol·li·cle /'fɒlɪkəl/ **follicles.** A follicle is one of the ◆◇◇◇◇ N-COUNT
small hollows in the skin which hairs grow from.

fol·low /'fɒləʊ/ **follows, following, followed.** ◆◆◆◆◆
1 If you **follow** someone who is going somewhere, VERB
you move along behind them because you want to V n prep/adv
go to the same place. *We followed him up the steps* V
*into a large hall... Please follow me, madam... They
took him into a small room and I followed.* **2** If you VERB
follow someone who is going somewhere, you move V n
along behind them without their knowledge, for example in order to find out where they are going. *She
realized that the Mercedes was following her.* **3** If VERB
you **follow** someone to a place where they have re- V n to n
cently gone and where they are now, you go to join
them there. *He followed Janice to New York.*
4 An event, activity, or period of time that **follows** a VERB
particular thing happens or comes after that thing, at V n
a later time. *...the days following Daddy's death... He* V
was arrested in the confusion which followed. **5** If you VERB
follow one thing with another, you do or say the sec- V n with n
ond thing after you have done or said the first thing.
*Warm up first, then follow this with a series of simple
stretching exercises.* ▶ **Follow up** means the same as PHRASAL VB
follow. *The book proved such a success that the* V n P noun
authors followed it up with 'The Messianic Legacy'. Also V P noun
6 You use **followed by** to say what comes after some- with n
thing else in a list or ordered set of things. *Potatoes are* PHRASE
still the most popular food, followed by white bread. PRAGMATICS
7 If it **follows** that a particular thing is the case, that VERB
thing is a logical result of something else being true or *it* V that
being the case. *Just because a bird does not breed one
year, it does not follow that it will fail the next... If the
explanation is right, two things follow.*
8 If you refer to the words that **follow** or **followed**, you VERB
are referring to the words that come next or came next PRAGMATICS
in a piece of writing or speech. *What follows is an eye-* V
witness account... There followed a list of places where *there* V n
Hans intended to visit. **9** You use **as follows** in writing PHRASE
or speech to introduce something such as a list, de- PRAGMATICS
scription, or explanation. *The winners are as follows:
E. Walker; R. Foster; R. Gates; A. Mackintosh.*
10 If you **follow** a path, route, or set of signs, you go VERB
somewhere using the path, route, or signs to direct V n
you. *If they followed the road, they would be certain to
reach a village.* **11** If you **follow** something with your VERB
eyes, you watch it as it moves. *Ann's eyes followed a* V n
...[po]lice car as it drove slowly past. **12** Something that VERB
...[a] particular course of development happens V n
...[tha]t way. *His release turned out to fol-
...[low that] of the other six hostages.*
...[instru]ction, or a recipe, VERB

you act or do something in the way that it indicates. Vn *Take care to follow the instructions carefully.* **14** If you **follow** someone, you do something that they have VERB done because you think it is a good thing or because Also V you want to copy them. *He followed his father and became a surgeon... Where East Germany goes, the rest will surely follow.*

15 If you **follow** something such as an explanation or VERB the plot of a film, you understand it. *Do you follow the* Vn *plot so far?* **16** If you **follow** a score or written copy of a VERB: Vn play, you read it as you listen to it being performed.

17 If you **follow** something, you take an interest in it VERB and keep informed about what happens. *Do you fol-* Vn *low the football at all?* **18** If you **follow** a particular re- VERB: Vn ligion or political belief, you have that religion or that belief.

19 See also **following**. ● to **follow in** someone's **footsteps**: see footstep. ● to **follow** your **nose**: see nose. ● to **follow suit**: see suit.

follow through. If you **follow through** an action or PHRASAL VB plan, you continue doing or thinking about it until it is VP noun completed. *I was trained to be an actress but I didn't* VP with n/- *follow it through... He decided to follow through with* Also VP on n *his original plan.*

follow up. If you **follow up** something that has been PHRASAL VB said, suggested, or discovered, you try to find out VP noun more about it or take action about it. *An officer took a* VP n *statement from me, but no one's bothered to follow it up.* ● See also **follow-up 5, follow-up.**

fol·low·er /ˈfɒləʊə/ **followers.** The **followers** of a ◆◆◇◇ person or belief are the people who support the N-COUNT person or accept the belief. *...followers of the Zulu Inkatha movement.*

fol·low·ing /ˈfɒləʊɪŋ/ **followings. 1** Following a ◆◆◆◇ particular event means after that event. *...the centu-* PREP *ries following Christ's death.* **2** The **following** day, ADJ: det ADJ week, or year is the day, week, or year after the one you have just mentioned. *We went to dinner the following Monday evening.* **3** You use **following** to re- ADJ: det ADJ fer to something that you are about to mention. *The* [PRAGMATICS] *method of helping such patients is explained in the following chapters.* ▶ Also a pronoun. *Do you use* PRON *any of the following? Pager, Answering machine, Mobile phone, Car phone.*

4 A person or organization that has a **following** has a N-COUNT: group of people who support or admire their beliefs with supp or actions. *Australian rugby league enjoys a huge following in New Zealand.*

'follow-on. A **follow-on** is something which is ◆◇◇◇ done as a continuation of something done previ- N-SING: ously. *This course for bridge players with some ex-* also no det *perience is intended as a follow-on to the Beginners' course.*

'follow-through, follow-throughs. 1 A **follow-** ◆◇◇◇ **through** is the completion of an action or planned N-UNCOUNT: series of actions. *...a durable solution to the refugee* also a N *problem as a follow-through to the very temporary measures.* **2** A **follow-through** is the completion of N-VAR a movement such as hitting a ball. *Focus on making a short, firm follow-through.*

'follow-up, follow-ups. A **follow-up** is something ◆◆◇◇ that is done as a continuation or second part of N-VAR something done previously. *Patients are asked to return for a one-day follow-up workshop.*

fol·ly /ˈfɒli/ **follies. 1** If you say that a particular ◆◇◇◇ action or way of behaving is **folly** or a **folly**, you N-VAR mean that it is foolish. *...a reminder of the follies of war.* **2** A **folly** is an imitation castle, temple, or oth- N-COUNT er unusual building that is built as a decoration in a large garden or park.

fo·ment /fəʊˈment/ **foments, fomenting, fo-** VERB **mented.** If someone or something **foments** trou- Vn ble, they cause it to develop. *They accused strike* FORMAL *leaders of fomenting violence.*

fond /fɒnd/ **fonder, fondest. 1** If you are **fond of** ◆◆◇◇ someone, you feel affection for them. *I am very fond* ADJ-GRADED: *of Michael.* ◆ **fond·ness** *...a great fondness for chil-* v-link ADJ of n *dren.* **2** You use **fond** to describe people or their ADJ-GRADED: behaviour when they show affection. *He gave him a* ADJ n *fond smile.* ◆ **fond·ly** *Their eyes meet fondly across* ADV-GRADED

the table. **3** If you are **fond of** something, you like it ADJ-GRADED: very much. *She is fond of collecting rare carpets.* v-link ADJ of ◆ **fond·ness** *I've always had a fondness for jewels.* n/-ing *...his fondness for cooking.* **4** If you have **fond** ADJ-GRADED: memories of someone or something, you remember ADJ n them with pleasure. ◆ **fondly** *I remembered it* ADV-GRADED *fondly.*

5 You use **fond** to describe hopes, wishes, or beliefs ADJ: ADJ n which you think are foolish because they seem un- likely to be fulfilled. *My fond hope is that we will be ready by Christmastime.* ◆ **fondly** *I fondly imagined* ADV: *that surgery meant a few stitches.* ADV with v

fon·dant /ˈfɒndənt/. Fondant is a sweet paste made N-UNCOUNT from sugar and water.

fon·dle /ˈfɒndəl/ **fondles, fondling, fondled.** If VERB: Vn you **fondle** someone or something, you touch them gently with a stroking movement, usually in a sexual way.

fon·due /ˈfɒndjuː, AM -duː/ **fondues.** A fondue is a N-VAR hot sauce into which you dip bread or pieces of meat or vegetables.

font /fɒnt/ **fonts. 1** In printing, a **font** is a set of N-COUNT characters of the same style and size. **2** In a church, N-COUNT a **font** is a bowl which holds the water for baptisms.

food /fuːd/ **foods. 1** Food is what people and ani- ◆◆◆◆◆ mals eat. *Enjoy your food. ...frozen foods.* ● See also N-VAR **convenience food, fast food, health food, junk food, wholefood. 2** If you give someone **food for** PHRASE **thought**, you make them think carefully about something. *Lord Fraser's speech offers much food for thought.*

'food chain, food chains. The **food chain** is a ◆◇◇◇ series of living things which are linked to each other N-COUNT because each thing feeds on the one next to it in the series.

foodie /ˈfuːdi/ **foodies;** also spelled **foody. Foodies** N-COUNT are people who enjoy cooking and eating different INFORMAL kinds of food.

'food mixer, food mixers; also spelled **food-** N-COUNT **mixer.** A **food mixer** is a piece of electrical equip- ment that is used to mix food.

'food poisoning. If you get **food poisoning**, you ◆◇◇◇ become ill because you have eaten food that has N-UNCOUNT gone bad. *...a serious case of food poisoning.*

'food processor, food processors. A **food pro-** ◆◇◇◇ **cessor** is a piece of electrical equipment that is used N-COUNT to mix, chop, whisk, or liquidize food.

'food stamp, food stamps. In the United States, ◆◇◇◇ **food stamps** are vouchers that are given to people N-COUNT with low incomes to exchange for food.

food·stuff /ˈfuːdstʌf/ **foodstuffs. Foodstuffs** are ◆◇◇◇ substances which people eat. *...basic foodstuffs such* N-VAR *as sugar, cooking oil and cheese.*

'food value, food values. The **food value** of a N-VAR particular food is a measure of how good it is for you.

fool /fuːl/ **fools, fooling, fooled. 1** If you call ◆◆◆◇ someone a **fool**, you are indicating that you think N-COUNT they are not at all sensible and show a lack of good judgment. *'You fool!' she shouted... He'd been a fool to get involved with her!* **2** Fool is used to describe a ADJ: ADJ n person or an action that is not sensible and shows a INFORMAL lack of good judgment. *What a damn fool thing to do!* **3** If you **make a fool of** someone, you make PHRASE them seem silly by telling people about something stupid that they have done, or by tricking them. **4** If PHRASE you **make a fool of** yourself, you behave in a way that makes other people think that you are silly or lacking in good judgment. **5** If you **play the fool** or PHRASE **act the fool**, you behave in a playful, childish, and foolish way, usually in order to make other people laugh.

6 If someone **fools** you, they deceive or trick you. *He's* VERB: Vn *fooled a lot of people including the court... They tried to* Vn into -ing *fool you into coming after us.* **7** If you say that some- VERB one **is fooling with** something or someone, you mean V with n that the way they are behaving is likely to cause prob- lems. *He kept telling her that here you did not fool with officials.*

8 ● to **suffer fools gladly**: see suffer.

fool about or **fool around.** If you **fool about** or **fool around**, you behave in a playful, childish, and silly way, often in order to make people laugh. `PHRASAL VB` `VP`

fool around. 1 If you **fool around**, you behave in a silly, dangerous, or irresponsible way. *Have you been fooling around with something you shouldn't?* **2** If someone **fools around** with another person, especially when one of them is married, they have a casual sexual relationship. *Never fool around with the clients' wives.* `PHRASAL VB` `VP` `VP with n` `VP with n` `Also VP`

fool·har·dy /'fu:lhɑ:di/. If you describe behaviour as **foolhardy**, you disapprove of it because it is extremely risky. `ADJ-GRADED` `PRAGMATICS`

fool·ish /'fu:lɪʃ/. **1** If someone's behaviour or action is **foolish**, it is not sensible and shows a lack of good judgment. *It would be foolish to raise hopes unnecessarily.* ◆ **fool·ish·ly** *He admitted that he had acted foolishly.* ◆ **fool·ish·ness** *They don't accept any foolishness.* **2** If you look or feel **foolish**, you look or feel so silly that people are likely to laugh at you. *I just stood there feeling foolish.* ◆ **foolishly** *He saw me standing there, grinning foolishly at him.* `◆◆◇◇` `ADJ-GRADED` `ADV` `N-UNCOUNT` `ADJ-GRADED` `ADV-GRADED:` `ADV after v`

fool·proof /'fu:lpru:f/. Something such as a plan or a machine that is **foolproof** is so well designed, easy to understand, or easy to use that it cannot go wrong or be used wrongly. *I spent the day working out a foolproof plan to save him.* `ADJ-GRADED`

fools·cap /'fu:lzkæp/. In Britain, **foolscap** is paper which is about 34 centimetres by 43 centimetres in size. `N-UNCOUNT`

fool's 'gold. 1 Fool's gold is a substance that is found in rock and that looks very like gold. **2** If you say that a plan for getting money is **fool's gold**, you mean that it is foolish and you are sure that it will fail. `N-UNCOUNT` `N-UNCOUNT` `PRAGMATICS`

foot /fʊt/ **feet. 1** Your **feet** are the parts of your body that are at the ends of your legs, and that you stand on. *...a foot injury. ...his aching arms and sore feet.* ◆ **-footed** *She was bare-footed.* **2** The **foot** of something is the part that is farthest from its top. *David called to the children from the foot of the stairs. ...the foot of Highgate Hill.* **3** A **foot** is a unit of length equalling 12 inches or 30.48 centimetres. The plural can be either 'foot' or 'feet'. *...a shopping and leisure complex of one million square feet. ...a cell 10 foot long, 6 foot wide and 10 foot high.* **4** See also **footing**. `◆◆◆◆` `N-COUNT` `COMB` `N-SING` `N-COUNT`

5 If you are **on** your **feet**, you are standing up. *Everyone was on their feet applauding wildly.* **6** If you get or rise to your **feet**, you stand up. **7** If you **put** your **feet up**, you relax or have a rest, especially by sitting or lying with your feet supported off the ground. `PHRASE` `PHRASE` `PHRASE`

8 If you go somewhere **on foot**, you walk, rather than using any form of transport. **9** To **set foot** in a place means to go there. *A little later I left that place and never set foot in Texas again.* `PHRASE` `PHRASE`

10 If you say that someone or something is **on** their **feet** again after an illness or difficult period, you mean that they have recovered and are back to normal. *You need someone to take the pressure off and help you get back on your feet.* `PHRASE`

11 If you get **cold feet** about something, you become nervous or frightened about it because you think it will fail. *The Government is getting cold feet about the reforms.* **12** If you say that someone is **finding** their **feet** in a new situation, you mean that they are starting to feel confident and to deal with things successfully. *I don't know anyone in England but I am sure I will manage when I find my feet.* **13** If you say that someone has their **feet on the ground**, you approve of the fact that they have a sensible and practical attitude towards life, and do not have unrealistic ideas. **14** If someone has to **stand on** their **own two feet**, they have to be independent and manage their lives without help from other people. **15** If you say that someone always **falls** or **lands on** their **feet**, you mean that they are always successful or lucky, although they do not seem to achieve this by their own efforts. **16** If someone **puts** their **foot in it**, they make a mistake which embarrasses or offends `PHRASE` `PHRASE` `PHRASE` `PRAGMATICS` `PHRASE` `PHRASE` `PHRASE` `INFORMAL`

people. **17** If you never **put a foot wrong**, you never make any mistakes. **18** If you **put** your **best foot forward**, you act in a cheerful, determined way. `PHRASE` `PHRASE` `DATED`

19 If you say that **the boot is on the other foot** or **the shoe is on the other foot**, you mean that a situation has been reversed completely, so that the person who was in the better position before is now in the worse one. `PHRASE`

20 If someone **puts** their **foot down**, they use their authority in order to stop something happening. *He had planned to go skiing on his own in March but his wife had decided to put her foot down.* **21** If someone **puts** their **foot down** when they are driving, they drive as fast as they can. `PHRASE` `PHRASE`

22 If you say that someone is **under** your **feet**, you are annoyed because they are with you or near you, and being a nuisance to you. *The children were running about under everybody's feet.* `PHRASE`

23 ● **foot the bill**: see **bill**. ● **feet of clay**: see **clay**. ● **foot in the door**: see **door**. ● **drag** your **feet**: see **drag**. ● **shoot** yourself **in the foot**: see **shoot**. ● **sweep** someone **off their feet**: see **sweep**. ● **vote with** your **feet**: see **vote**. ● **hand and foot**: see **hand**.

foot·age /'fʊtɪdʒ/. **Footage** of a particular event is a film of it or the part of a film which shows this event. *...exclusive footage from this summer's festivals.* `◆◆◇◇◇` `N-UNCOUNT`

foot-and-'mouth disease. Foot-and-mouth disease is a serious and highly infectious disease that affects cattle, sheep, pigs, and goats. `N-UNCOUNT` `N-UNCOUNT`

foot·ball /'fʊtbɔ:l/ **footballs. 1** Football is a game played by two teams of eleven players using a round ball. Players kick the ball to each other and try to score goals by kicking the ball into a large net. The American word is **soccer**. *Several boys were still playing football. ...Arsenal Football Club.* **2** Football is a game played by two teams of eleven players using an oval ball. Players carry the ball in their hands or throw it to each other as they try to score goals that are called touchdowns. The British term is **American football**. **3** A **football** is a ball that is used for playing football. `◆◆◆◆◇` `N-UNCOUNT` `BRITISH` `N-UNCOUNT` `AMERICAN` `N-COUNT`

foot·ball·er /'fʊtbɔ:lə/ **footballers.** A **footballer** is a person who plays football, especially as a profession. The American term is 'soccer player'. `◆◆◇◇◇` `N-COUNT` `BRITISH`

foot·balling /'fʊtbɔ:lɪŋ/. **Footballing** means relating to the playing of the game that British people call football. *...the best of my footballing life.* `◆◇◇◇◇` `ADJ: ADJ n` `BRITISH`

'football pools. If you do **the football pools**, you take part in a gambling competition in which people try to win money by guessing the results of football matches. `N-PLURAL:` `the N` `BRITISH`

foot·bridge /'fʊtbrɪdʒ/ **footbridges.** A **footbridge** is a narrow bridge for people travelling on foot. `N-COUNT`

'foot-dragging. When journalists talk about a particular person's **foot-dragging**, they are suggesting that the person is deliberately slowing down a plan or process; used showing disapproval. *He accused the company of 'shameful foot-dragging'.* `N-UNCOUNT` `PRAGMATICS`

-footed /-'fʊtɪd/. **-footed** combines with words such as 'heavy', 'light', or 'leaden' to form adjectives which indicate how someone moves. *...a slim, light-footed little man.* ● See also **foot, flat-footed, sure-footed.** `COMB`

foot·fall /'fʊtfɔ:l/ **footfalls.** A **footfall** is the sound that is made by someone walking each time they take a step. *She heard the priest's familiar, flat footfall on the staircase.* `N-COUNT` `LITERARY`

foot·hills /'fʊthɪlz/. The **foothills** of a mountain or a range of mountains are the lower hills or mountains around its base. `◆◇◇◇◇` `N-PLURAL`

foot·hold /'fʊthəʊld/ **footholds. 1** A **foothold** is a strong or favourable position from which further advances or progress may be made. *Companies must establish a firm foothold in Europe.* **2** A **foothold** is a place such as a ledge, crevice, or hollow where you can safely put your foot when climbing. `◆◇◇◇◇` `N-COUNT` `N-COUNT`

foot·ing /'fʊtɪŋ/. **1** You use **footing** to describe the basis on which something is done or exists. *The new law will put official corruption on the same legal* `◆◇◇◇◇` `N-UNCOUNT:` `with supp`

footing as treason... They decided to put their relationship on a more formal footing. **2** If a country or armed force is **on a war footing**, it is ready to fight a war.   PHRASE

3 You use **footing** to refer to your position and how securely your feet are placed on the ground. *He lost his footing and slid into the water.*   N-UNCOUNT: poss N

foot·lights /ˈfʊtlaɪts/. In a theatre, the **footlights** are the row of lights along the front of the stage.   N-PLURAL

foot·loose /ˈfuːtluːs/. If you describe someone as **footloose**, you mean that they have no responsibilities or commitments, and are therefore free to do what they want and go where they want. *People that are single tend to be more footloose.*   ADJ-GRADED

foot·man /ˈfʊtmən/ **footmen**. A **footman** is a male servant who typically does jobs such as opening doors or serving food, and who often wears a special uniform.   N-COUNT

foot·note /ˈfʊtnəʊt/ **footnotes**. **1** A **footnote** is a note at the bottom of a page in a book which provides more detailed information about something that is mentioned on that page. **2** If you refer to what you are saying as a **footnote** to what has just been said, you mean that you are adding a comment which gives some extra information about it. *As a footnote, I should add that there was one point on which his bravado was more than justified.* **3** If you describe an event as a **footnote**, you mean that it is relatively unimportant although it will probably be remembered. *I'm afraid that Marx will now become a footnote in history.*   N-COUNT / N-COUNT PRAGMATICS / N-COUNT

foot·path /ˈfʊtpɑːθ, -pæθ/ **footpaths**. A **footpath** is a path for people to walk on.   N-COUNT

foot·plate /ˈfʊtpleɪt/ **footplates**. On a steam train, the **footplate** is the platform on the engine where the driver stands.   N-COUNT BRITISH

foot·print /ˈfʊtprɪnt/ **footprints**. A **footprint** is a mark in the shape of a foot that a person or animal makes in or on a surface when they walk on it.   N-COUNT

'**foot soldier, foot soldiers**. The **foot soldiers** of a particular organization are people who seem unimportant and who do not have a high position but who do a large amount of very important and often very boring work.   N-COUNT

foot·sore /ˈfʊtsɔː/. If you are **footsore**, you have sore or tired feet after walking a long way.   ADJ-GRADED

foot·step /ˈfʊtstep/ **footsteps**. **1** A **footstep** is the sound or mark that is made by someone walking each time their foot touches the ground. **2** If you **follow in** someone's **footsteps**, you do the same things as they did earlier. *He followed in the footsteps of his father, a former professional boxer.*   N-COUNT / PHRASE

foot·stool /ˈfʊtstuːl/ **footstools**. A **footstool** is a low stool that you can rest your feet on when you are sitting in a chair.   N-COUNT

foot·wear /ˈfʊtweə/. **Footwear** refers to things that people wear on their feet, for example shoes, boots, and sandals. *...the sports footwear industry.*   N-UNCOUNT

foot·work /ˈfʊtwɜːk/. **1 Footwork** is the way in which you move your feet, especially in sports such as boxing, football, or tennis, or in dancing. **2** If you refer to someone's **footwork** in a difficult situation, you mean the clever way they deal with it. *In the end, his brilliant legal footwork paid off.*   N-UNCOUNT / N-UNCOUNT: supp N

fop·pish /ˈfɒpɪʃ/. If you describe a man as **foppish**, you disapprove of the fact that he is vain and dresses in fancy, extravagant clothes.   ADJ-GRADED PRAGMATICS DATED

for /fə, STRONG fɔː/. In addition to the uses shown below, **for** is used in phrasal verbs such as 'account for' and 'make up for'.   ◆◆◆◆◆

1 If something is used or done **for** someone, they are intended to have it or benefit from it. *I have some free advice for you. ...a table for two... He wanted all the running of the business for himself... He picked the bracelet up for me.* **2** If you work **for** someone, you are employed by them. *...a buyer for one of the largest chain stores.* **3** If you feel a particular emotion **for** someone, you feel it on their behalf. *I am so happy for you!*   PREP / PREP / PREP

4 If you are **for** something, you agree with it or support it. If you argue **for** it, you argue in support of it. *Are you for or against public transport?... Another union has voted for industrial action... The case for nuclear power is impressive.* ▶ Also an adverb. *833 delegates voted for, and only 432 against.* ● You can say that you are **all for** doing something when you agree that it should be done, especially when you then go on to mention some difficulties that exist. *I was all for it, but Wolfe said no.* **5** If you say that you are **for** something or something is **for** you, you mean that you like it or intend to do it or have it. *Right, who's for a toasted sandwich then?... I'm afraid German beer isn't for me.* **6** If it is **for** you to do something, it is your responsibility or right to do it. *It is not for me to arrange such matters.* **7** You use **for** after words such as 'time', 'space', 'money', or 'energy' when you say how much there is or whether there is enough of it in order to be able to do or use a particular thing. *Many new trains have space for wheelchair users... It would take three to six hours for a round trip. ...the high level of concentration required for sixth form study.* **8** You use **for** when you state or explain the purpose of an object, action, or activity. *...drug users who use unsterile equipment for injections of drugs. ...a room for rent. ...a comfortable chair, suitable for use in the living room.* **9** You use **for** after nouns expressing reason or cause. *...a speech in parliament explaining his reasons for going... He has now been formally given the grounds for his arrest.* **10** You can use **for** to introduce a clause which gives the reason why you made the statement in the main clause. *She was half glad to see him, for she did not like the dark.* **11 For** is used in conditional sentences, in expressions such as '**if not for**' and '**if it wasn't for**', to introduce the only thing which prevents the main part of the sentence from being true. *She might have forgotten her completely had it not been for recurrent nightmares.* **12** A word or term **for** something is a way of referring to it. *The technical term for sunburn is erythema... Cancer is derived from the Greek word for crab, karkinos.* **13** You use **for** to say how long something lasts or continues. *For a few minutes she sat on her bed... They talked for a bit.* **14** You use expressions such as for **the first time** and **for the last time** when you are talking about how often something has happened. *Mr Lukman is visiting the United States for the second time this year.* **15** You use **for** to say how far something extends. *We drove on for a few miles.* **16** You use **for** with 'every' when you are stating a ratio, to introduce the second part of the ratio. *There had been one divorce for every 100 marriages before the war.* **17** You can use **for** in expressions such as **pound for pound** or **mile for mile** when you are making comparisons between the values or qualities of different things. *He insists any tax cut be matched dollar-for-dollar with cuts in spending.* **18** If something is bought, sold, or done **for** a particular price or amount, that price or amount is the cost of buying, selling, or doing it. *We got the bus back to Tange for 30 cents... The Martins sold their house for about 1.4 million pounds.* **19 For** is the preposition that you use after many nouns, adjectives, or verbs in order to introduce more information. *Reduced-calorie cheese is a great substitute for cream cheese... It might be possible for a single woman to be accepted as a foster parent... Make sure you have ample time to prepare for the new day ahead.* **20** If you feel a particular emotion **for** someone or something, they are the object of that emotion, and you feel it when you think about them. *I'm sorry for Steve, but I think you've made the right decision.* **21** You use **for** when you make a statement about something in order to say how it affects or relates to someone, or what their attitude to it is. *For her, books were as necessary to life as bread... It would be excellent experience for him to travel a little.* **22** You use **for** when you say that an aspect of something or someone is surprising in relation to other aspects of them. *He was tall for an eight-year-old... He had too much money for a young man.*   ADV: ADV after v PHRASE / PREP / PREP / PREP / PREP / PREP / PREP / CONJ LITERARY / PREP / PREP / PREP / PHRASE / PREP / PREP PRAGMATICS / PREP / PREP / PREP / PREP / PREP / PREP

23 If something is planned **for** a particular date or time, it is planned to happen then. *The party was scheduled for 7:00.* **24** If you do something **for** a particular occasion, you do it on that occasion or to celebrate that occasion. *He asked his daughter what she would like for her birthday... I'll be home for Christmas.* **25** If you leave **for** a particular place, or if you take a bus, train, plane, or boat **for** a place, you are going there. *They would be leaving for Rio early the next morning.* **26 ● as for**: see **as**. **● but for**: see **but**. **● for all**: see **all**.   PREP / PREP / PREP

for·age /ˈfɒrɪdʒ, AM ˈfɔːr-/ **forages, foraging, foraged. 1** To **forage** for something such as food means to search for it. *The cat forages for food... We disturbed a wild boar that had been foraging by the roadside.* **2 Forage** is crops that are grown as food for cattle and horses.   ◆◇◇◇ VERB / V for n / N-UNCOUNT

for·ay /ˈfɒreɪ, AM ˈfɔːreɪ/ **forays. 1** If you make a **foray** into a new or unfamiliar type of activity, you start to become involved in it. *...her first forays into politics.* **2** You can refer to a short journey as a **foray**, especially if it is to an unfamiliar place. *Most guests make at least one foray into the town.* **3** If soldiers make a **foray** into enemy territory, they make a quick attack there, then return to their own territory.   ◆◇◇◇ N-COUNT / N-COUNT / N-COUNT

for·bade /fəˈbæd, -ˈbeɪd/. **Forbade** is the past tense of **forbid**.

for·bear /fɔːˈbeə/ **forbears, forbearing, forbore, forborne.** If you **forbear** to do something, you do not do it although you have the opportunity or the right to do it. *Protesters largely forbore from stone-throwing and vandalism.*   VERB: V to-inf / V from -ing/n / FORMAL

for·bear·ance /fɔːˈbeərəns/. If you say that someone has shown **forbearance**, you admire them for showing self-control and patience when something happens that would give them the right to be very upset or angry.   N-UNCOUNT / PRAGMATICS / FORMAL

for·bid /fəˈbɪd/ **forbids, forbidding, forbade, forbidden. 1** If you **forbid** someone to do something, or if you **forbid** an activity, you order that it must not be done. *They'll forbid you to marry... Brazil's constitution forbids the military use of nuclear energy.* **● for·bid·den.** If something is **forbidden**, you are not allowed to do it or have it. *Smoking was forbidden... It is forbidden to drive faster than 20mph.* **2** If something **forbids** a particular course of action or state of affairs, it makes it impossible. *His own pride forbids him to ask Arthur's help.* **3 ● God forbid**: see **God**. **● heaven forbid**: see **heaven**.   ◆◆◇◇ VERB / V n to-inf / V n / ADJ / VERB: V n / V n to-inf

for·bid·den /fəˈbɪdən/. **1 Forbidden** is used to describe things that people strongly disapprove of or feel guilty about, so that they are very rarely mentioned or talked about. *The war was a forbidden subject... Divorce? It was such a forbidden word.* **2** See also **forbid**.   ◆◆◇◇ ADJ-GRADED

for·bid·ding /fəˈbɪdɪŋ/. If you describe a person or place as **forbidding**, you mean they have a severe, unfriendly, or threatening appearance. *...a huge, forbidding building.*   ADJ-GRADED

force /fɔːs/ **forces, forcing, forced. 1** If someone **forces** you to do something, they make you do it even though you do not want to, for example by threatening you. *They forced me to tell them... I cannot force you in this. You must decide... He tried to force her into a car.* **● forced** *...a system of forced labour.* **2** If a situation or event **forces** you to do something, it makes it necessary for you to do something that you would not otherwise have done. *A back injury forced her to withdraw from Wimbledon... Finances forced him back to Australia.* **● forced** *He made a forced landing on a highway.* **3** If someone **forces** something **on** or **upon** you, they make you accept or use it when you would prefer not to. *To force this agreement on the nation is wrong.* **4** If you **force** something into a particular position, you use your strength to move it there. *He forced the key clumsily into the ignition.* **5** If someone **forces** a lock, a door, or a window, they break it   ◆◆◆◆ VERB / V n to-inf / V n / V n prep/adv / ADJ: ADJ n / VERB / V n to-inf / V n prep/adv / ADJ: ADJ n / VERB / V n on/upon n / VERB / V n prep/adv / VERB / V n

violently in order to get into a building without using a key. *Police forced the door of the flat and arrested Mr Roberts.* **6** If someone uses **force** to do something, they take strong and violent physical action in order to achieve it. *...the guerrillas' efforts to seize power by force.* **7 Force** is the power or strength which something has. *The force of the explosion shattered the windows.*   N-UNCOUNT / N-UNCOUNT / N-UNCOUNT

8 If you refer to someone or something as a **force** in a particular type of activity, you mean that they have a strong influence on it. *The FLN is still a big political force in the country... One of the driving forces behind this recent expansion is the growth of services.* **9** The **force** of something is the powerful effect that it has. *He changed our world through the force of his ideas.* **10** You can use **forces** to refer to processes and events that do not appear to be caused by human beings, and are therefore difficult to understand or control. *...the forces of nature: epidemics, predators, floods. ...the principle of market forces.* **11** In physics, a **force** is the pulling, attracting, or pushing effect that something has on something else. *...the earth's gravitational force. ...magnetic forces.* **12** The word **force** is used before a number to indicate a wind of a particular speed or strength, especially a very strong wind. *The airlift was conducted in force ten winds.*   N-COUNT with supp / N-UNCOUNT / N-COUNT / N-VAR / N-UNCOUNT: N num

13 If you **force** a smile or a laugh, you manage to smile or laugh, but with an effort because you are unhappy. *...a forced smile.* **● forced** *She called him darling. It sounded so forced.*   VERB: V n / V-ed / ADJ-GRADED

14 Forces are groups of soldiers or military vehicles that are organized for a particular purpose. *...the deployment of American forces in the region.* **15** The **forces** means the army, the navy, or the air force, or all three. **16** The **force** is sometimes used to mean the police force.   N-COUNT / N-PLURAL / N-SING: det N

17 See also **air force, armed forces, labour force, task force, tour de force, workforce.**

18 By force of is used in expressions to mean 'due to' or 'by means of'. For example, if something happens **by force of** circumstance, it happens due to the circumstances that exist. *They say no group should be allowed to seize or retain power by force of arms.* **19** A law, rule, or system that is **in force** exists or is being used. *Martial law is already in force... The new tax is already in force.* **20** When people do something **in force**, they do it in large numbers. *Voters turned out in force.* **21** If you **join forces** with someone, you work together in order to achieve a common purpose. *African nations last week joined forces to combat cholera.* **22** If you **force** your **way** somewhere, you have to push or break things that are in your way in order to get there. *He forced his way into a house shouting for help.* **23 ●** to **force** someone's **hand**: see **hand**.   PHRASE / PHRASE / PHRASE / PHRASE / PHRASE / PHRASE

force back. If you **force back** an emotion or desire, you manage, with effort, not to be affected by it. *Nancy forced back tears.*   PHRASAL VB / V P noun

force-'feed, force-feeds, force-feeding, force-fed. If you **force-feed** a person or animal, you make them eat or drink by pushing food or drink down their throat.   VERB: V n

force·ful /ˈfɔːsfʊl/. **1** If you describe someone as **forceful**, you approve of them because they express their opinions and wishes in a strong, emphatic, and confident way. **● force·ful·ly** *Steve argued forcefully in favor of the approach.* **● force·ful·ness** *She had inherited her father's forcefulness.* **2** Something that is **forceful** has a very powerful effect and causes you to think or feel something very strongly. *For most people a heart attack is a forceful reminder that they are mortal.* **● forcefully** *Let's get over the hygiene message forcefully but sympathetically.*   ◆◇◇◇ ADJ-GRADED / PRAGMATICS / ADV-GRADED: ADV with v / N-UNCOUNT / ADJ-GRADED / ADV-GRADED: ADV with v

for·ceps /ˈfɔːseps/. **Forceps** are an instrument consisting of two long narrow arms. Forceps are used by a doctor to hold things.   N-PLURAL: also a pair of N

for·ci·ble /ˈfɔːsɪbəl/. **Forcible** action involves physical force or violence. *...the forcible resettlement of villagers from the countryside into towns.*   ◆◇◇◇ ADJ

♦ **for·cibly** *Two student leaders were forcibly re-* ADV:
moved from the university president's office. ADV with v

ford /fɔːd/ **fords, fording, forded.** **1** A **ford** is a ◆◇◇◇◇
shallow place in a river or stream where it is pos- N-COUNT
sible to cross safely without using a boat. **2** If you VERB: V n
ford a river or stream, you cross it without using a
boat, usually at a shallow point.

fore /fɔː/. **1** If someone or something comes **to the** ◆◇◇◇◇
fore in a particular situation or group, they become PHRASE
important or popular. *A number of low-budget inde-*
pendent films brought new directors and actors to
the fore. **2 Fore** is used to refer to parts at the front ADJ: ADJ n
of an animal, ship, or aircraft. *...the fore part of the*
ship. ▶ Also an adverb. *Our yacht was well* ADV:
equipped with two double cabins fore and aft. n ADV,
ADV after v

fore·arm /ˈfɔːrɑːm/ **forearms.** Your **forearm** is ◆◇◇◇◇
the part of your arm between your elbow and your N-COUNT
wrist.

fore·bear /ˈfɔːbeə/ **forebears.** Your **forebears** are N-COUNT
your ancestors. LITERARY

fore·bod·ing /fɔːˈbəʊdɪŋ/ **forebodings. Forebod-** N-VAR
ing is a strong feeling that something terrible is going to happen. *His triumph was overshadowed by an*
uneasy sense of foreboding.

fore·cast /ˈfɔːkɑːst, -kæst/ **forecasts, forecast-** ◆◆◆◇◇
ing, forecasted. The forms **forecast** and **forecast-**
ed can both be used for the past tense and past participle. **1** A **forecast** is a prediction or statement of N-COUNT
what is expected to happen in the future. *...a fore-*
cast of a 2.25 per cent growth in the economy... He
delivered his election forecast. ● See also **weather**
forecast. ♦ **fore·cast·er, forecasters** *...the na-* N-COUNT
tion's top economic forecasters. **2** If you **forecast** fu- VERB
ture events, you say what you think is going to hap- V n
pen in the future. *They forecast a humiliating defeat* V that
for the Prime Minister... He forecasts that average
salary increases will remain around 4 per cent.

fore·close /fɔːˈkləʊz/ **forecloses, foreclosing,** VERB
foreclosed. If the person or organization that lent V on n
someone money **forecloses**, they take possession of TECHNICAL
a property that was bought with the borrowed mon-
ey, for example because regular repayments have
not been made. *The bank foreclosed on the mort-*
gage for his previous home. ♦ **fore·clo·sure, fore-** N-VAR
closures *If they can't keep up the payments, they*
face foreclosure.

fore·court /ˈfɔːkɔːt/ **forecourts.** The **forecourt** of N-COUNT
a large building or petrol station is the open area at BRITISH
the front of it.

fore·father /ˈfɔːfɑːðə/ **forefathers.** Your **fore-** N-COUNT
fathers are your ancestors, especially your male LITERARY
ancestors.

fore·finger /ˈfɔːfɪŋgə/ **forefingers.** Your **fore-** ◆◇◇◇◇
finger is the finger next to your thumb. See picture N-COUNT
headed **human body.**

fore·front /ˈfɔːfrʌnt/. **1** If you are at **the forefront** ◆◇◇◇◇
of a campaign or other activity, you have a leading N-SING
and influential position in it. **2** If something is at N-SING
the forefront of people's minds or attention, they
think about it a lot.

fore·go /fɔːˈgəʊ/ **foregoes, foregoing, fore-** VERB: V n
went, foregone; also spelled **forgo.** If you **forgo** FORMAL
something, you decide not to have it or do it, although you would like to.

fore·go·ing /fɔːˈgəʊɪŋ, ˈfɔːgəʊ-/. You can refer to PRON
what has just been stated or mentioned as **the fore-** FORMAL
going. *You might think from the foregoing that the*
French want to phase accents out. Not at all. ▶ Also ADJ: ADJ n
an adjective. *The foregoing paragraphs were written*
in 1985.

fore·gone /ˈfɔːgɒn/. **1 Foregone** is the past partici- PHRASE
ple of **forego. 2** If you say that a particular result is
a foregone conclusion, you mean you are certain
that it will happen. *It's almost a foregone conclusion*
that you'll get what you want.

fore·ground /ˈfɔːgraʊnd/ **foregrounds,** ◆◇◇◇◇
foregrounding, foregrounded. **1** The **fore-** N-VAR
ground of a picture or scene you are looking at is
the part or area of it that appears nearest to you. *He*
is the bowler-hatted figure in the foreground. **2** If N-SING

something or someone is in the **foreground**, they
receive a lot of attention. *This is another worry that*
has come to the foreground in recent years. **3** To VERB: V n
foreground certain features of a situation means to FORMAL
make them the most important part of a description
or account.

fore·hand /ˈfɔːhænd/ **forehands.** A **forehand** is a N-COUNT
shot in tennis or squash in which the palm of your
hand faces the direction in which you are hitting
the ball.

fore·head /ˈfɒrɪd, ˈfɔːhed/ **foreheads.** Your **fore-** ◆◆◇◇◇
head is the area at the front of your head between N-COUNT
your eyebrows and your hair. See picture headed
human body.

for·eign /ˈfɒrɪn, AM ˈfɔːr-/. **1** Something or some- ◆◆◆◆◇
one that is **foreign** comes from or relates to a coun- ADJ
try that is not your own. *She was on her first foreign*
holiday without her parents. ...a foreign language.
2 In politics and journalism, **foreign** is used to de- ADJ: ADJ n
scribe people and activities relating to countries
that are not the country of the person or government concerned. *...the German foreign minister.*
...the effects of US foreign policy. **3** A **foreign** body ADJ
or object is something that has got into something FORMAL
else, usually by accident, and should not be there.
...a foreign body in the eye. **4** Something that is **for-** ADJ-GRADED
eign to a particular person or thing is not typical of
them or is unknown to them. *The very notion of*
price competition is foreign to many schools.

for·eign·er /ˈfɒrɪnə, AM ˈfɔːr-/ **foreigners.** A **for-** ◆◆◆◇◇
eigner is someone who belongs to a country that is N-COUNT
not your own.

,**foreign ex'change, foreign exchanges.** ◆◆◇◇◇
1 Foreign exchanges are the institutions or systems N-PLURAL
involved with changing one currency into another.
On the foreign exchanges, the US dollar is up point
forty-five. **2 Foreign exchange** is used to refer to N-UNCOUNT
foreign currency that is obtained through the foreign exchange system. *...an important source of for-*
eign exchange.

'**Foreign Office, Foreign Offices.** The **Foreign** ◆◆◇◇◇
Office is the British government department which N-COUNT:
has responsibility for the government's dealings and the N
relations with foreign governments.

fore·knowl·edge /fɔːˈnɒlɪdʒ/. If you have **fore-** N-UNCOUNT
knowledge of an event or situation, you have some
knowledge of it before it actually happens.

fore·leg /ˈfɔːleg/ **forelegs.** A four-legged animal's N-COUNT
forelegs are its two front legs.

fore·lock /ˈfɔːlɒk/ **forelocks. 1** A **forelock** is a N-COUNT
piece of hair that falls over your forehead. **2** If you PHRASE
say that a person **tugs** their **forelock** to another per- PRAGMATICS
son, you are criticizing them for showing too much BRITISH
respect to the second person or being unnecessarily
worried about their opinions.

fore·man /ˈfɔːmən/ **foremen. 1** A **foreman** is a ◆◇◇◇◇
person, especially a man, in charge of a group of N-COUNT
workers. **2** The **foreman** of a jury is the person who N-COUNT
is chosen as their leader.

fore·most /ˈfɔːməʊst/. **1** The **foremost** thing or ◆◇◇◇◇
person in a group is the most important or best. *He* ADJ
was one of the world's foremost scholars of ancient
Indian culture. **2** You use **first and foremost** to em- PHRASE
phasize the most important quality of something or PRAGMATICS
someone. *It is first and foremost a trade agreement.*

fore·name /ˈfɔːneɪm/ **forenames.** Your **forename** N-COUNT
is your first name, as opposed to your surname. FORMAL
Your **forenames** are all of your names other than
your surname.

fo·ren·sic /fəˈrensɪk/. **1 Forensic** is used to de- ◆◇◇◇◇
scribe the physical evidence and the procedures ADJ: ADJ n
that pathologists, laboratory technicians, and other
scientists work with when they help the police to
solve crimes. *They were convicted on forensic evi-*
dence alone... Forensic experts searched the area for
clues. **2 Forensic** means relating to the legal profes- ADJ: ADJ n
sion. *...his forensic skills in cross-examining minis-*
ters. ...a forensic psychiatrist.

fore·play /'fɔːpleɪ/. **Foreplay** is activity such as N-UNCOUNT
kissing and stroking when it takes place before sex-
ual intercourse.

fore·run·ner /'fɔːrʌnə/ **forerunners.** If you de- ◆◇◇◇◇
scribe something or someone as the **forerunner** of N-COUNT
something or someone similar, you mean they existed before them and either influenced their development or were a sign of what was going to happen. ...*a machine which, in some respects, was the
forerunner of the modern helicopter.*

fore·see /fɔː'siː/ **foresees, foreseeing, fore-** ◆◆◇◇◇
saw, foreseen. If you **foresee** something, you ex- VERB
pect and believe that it will happen. *He did not fore-* V n
see any problems... He could never have foreseen that V that
one day his books would sell in millions.

fore·see·able /fɔː'siːəbəl/. **1** If a future event is ◆◇◇◇◇
foreseeable, you know that it will happen or that it ADJ-GRADED
can happen, because it is a natural or obvious consequence of something else that you know. *It seems
to me that this crime was foreseeable and this death
preventable.* **2 The foreseeable future** is the maxi- PHRASE
mum length of time in the future that you feel able
to make predictions about. *Growth looks like being
above average for the foreseeable future... Australia
faces no threats in the foreseeable future.*

fore·shad·ow /fɔː'ʃædəʊ/ **foreshadows, fore-** VERB: V n
shadowing, foreshadowed. If something **fore-**
shadows a change or unpleasant event, it suggests
that it will happen.

fore·shore /'fɔːʃɔː/ **foreshores.** The **foreshore** is N-COUNT
the part of the seashore, or the part of the shore of a
lake or wide river, which is between the highest and
lowest points reached by the water.

fore·short·en /fɔː'ʃɔːtən/ **foreshortens, fore-** VERB:
shortening, foreshortened. If something be V-ed
foreshortened, it is made shorter than it would nor- V n
mally be. *She felt that her husband's unexpected* V-ed
promotion foreshortened his life. ...designs based on FORMAL
exaggeratedly foreshortened perspectives.

fore·sight /'fɔːsaɪt/. Someone's **foresight** is their ◆◇◇◇◇
ability to see what is likely to happen in the future N-UNCOUNT
and to take appropriate action; used showing ap- PRAGMATICS
proval. *They had the foresight to invest in new technology... He was later criticised for his lack of
foresight.*

fore·skin /'fɔːskɪn/ **foreskins.** A man's **foreskin** is N-VAR
the skin that covers the end of his penis if he has
not been circumcised.

for·est /'fɒrɪst, AM 'fɔːr-/ **forests. 1** A **forest** is a ◆◆◆◇◇
large area where trees grow close together. *...25 mil-* N-VAR
lion hectares of forest. **2** A **forest** of tall or narrow N-COUNT:
objects is a group of them standing or sticking with supp
upright. *...a forest of microphones.* LITERARY

fore·stall /fɔː'stɔːl/ **forestalls, forestalling,** ◆◇◇◇◇
forestalled. If you **forestall** someone, you realize VERB
what they are likely to do and prevent them from V n
doing it. *Large numbers of police were in the square
to forestall any demonstrations.*

for·est·ed /'fɒrɪstɪd, AM 'fɔːr-/. A **forested** area is ADJ-GRADED
an area covered in trees growing closely together.

for·est·er /'fɒrɪstə, AM 'fɔːr-/ **foresters.** A **forester** N-COUNT
is a person whose job is to look after the trees in a
forest and to plant new ones. **♦ for·est·ry** *She de-* N-UNCOUNT
cided to try forestry, and was accepted on a course.

fore·taste /'fɔːteɪst/ **foretastes.** If you describe N-COUNT
an event as a **foretaste** of a future situation, you
mean that it suggests to you what that future situation will be like. *This is but a foretaste of what the
emerging technologies will enable us to do.*

fore·tell /fɔː'tel/ **foretells, foretelling, foretold.** VERB
If you **foretell** a future event, you predict that it will V n
happen. *...prophets who have foretold the end of the
world.*

fore·thought /'fɔːθɔːt/. If you act with **fore-** N-UNCOUNT
thought, before you act you think carefully about
what will be needed, or about what the consequences will be. *With a little forethought many accidents could be avoided.*

fore·told /fɔː'təʊld/. **Foretold** is the past tense and
past participle of **foretell.**

for·ev·er /fə'revə/; also spelled **for ever** for mean- ◆◆◇◇◇
ings 1, 2, and 3. **1** If you say that something will ADV:
happen or continue **forever,** you mean that it will ADV with v
always happen or continue. *It was great fun but we
knew it wouldn't go on for ever... I will forever be
grateful for his considerable input.* **2** If something ADV:
has gone or changed **forever,** it has gone or ADV after v
changed completely and permanently. *The old social order was gone forever.* **3** If you say that some- ADV:
thing takes **forever** or lasts **forever,** you are empha- ADV after v
sizing that it takes or lasts a very long time, or that it PRAGMATICS
seems to. INFORMAL

4 If you say that someone is **forever** doing a particular ADV:
thing, you are emphasizing that they do it very often. ADV before v
He was forever attempting to arrange deals. cont

5 You use **forever** to emphasize that someone always ADV: ADV adj
has or shows the quality mentioned. *The young child* PRAGMATICS
is forever watchful.

fore·warn /fɔː'wɔːn/ **forewarns, forewarning,** VERB: V n
forewarned. If you **forewarn** someone, you warn V n of/about n
them that something is going to happen. *The
Macmillan Guide had forewarned me of what to
expect.*

fore·word /'fɔːwɜːd/ **forewords.** The **foreword** to N-COUNT
a book is the introduction.

for·feit /'fɔːfɪt/ **forfeits, forfeiting, forfeited.** ◆◇◇◇◇
1 If you **forfeit** something, you lose it or are forced VERB
to give it up because you have done something V n
wrong. *He was ordered to forfeit more than £1.5m in
profits.* **2** A **forfeit** is something that you have to N-COUNT
give up because you have done something wrong.
That is the forfeit he must pay. **3** If you **forfeit** some- VERB
thing, you give it up voluntarily, so that you can V n
achieve something else. *He has forfeited a lucrative
fee but feels his well-being is more important.*

for·fei·ture /'fɔːfɪtʃə/ **forfeitures.** **Forfeiture** is N-VAR
the action of forfeiting something because the law LEGAL
says you must.

for·gave /fə'geɪv/. **Forgave** is the past tense of
forgive.

forge /fɔːdʒ/ **forges, forging, forged. 1** To **forge** ◆◆◇◇◇
something such as an alliance or relationship V-RECIP:
means to create it with a lot of hard work, so that it V n within n
is strong or lasting. *They agreed to forge closer eco-* pl-n V n
nomic ties... The programme aims to forge links be- V n between n
tween higher education and small businesses... The pl-n
project will help inmates forge new careers. V n

2 If someone **forges** something such as a banknote, a VERB
document, or a painting, they copy it in order to de- V n
ceive people. *She alleged that Taylor had forged her
signature.* **♦ forg·er, forgers** *...the most prolific art* N-COUNT
forger in the country.

3 If someone **forges** an object out of metal, they heat VERB: V n
the metal and then hammer and bend it into the re-
quired shape. **4** A **forge** is a place where someone N-COUNT
makes objects by shaping heated metal.

forge ahead. If you **forge ahead** with something, PHRASAL VB
you continue with it and make a lot of progress with it. V P with n
The two companies forged ahead, innovating and V P
expanding.

for·gery /'fɔːdʒəri/ **forgeries. 1 Forgery** is the ◆◇◇◇◇
crime of forging money, documents, or paintings. N-UNCOUNT
2 You can refer to a forged document, banknote, or N-COUNT
painting as a **forgery.** *The letter was a forgery.*

for·get /fə'get/ **forgets, forgetting, forgot, for-** ◆◆◆◆◇
gotten. 1 If you **forget** something or **forget** how to VERB
do something, you cannot think of it or think how V n
to do it, although you knew it or knew how to do it V wh
in the past. *Sometimes I improvise and change the
words because I forget them... She forgot where she
left the car.* **2** If you **forget** something or **forget** to VERB: V n
do it, you fail to think about it or fail to remember V to-inf
to do it, for example because you are thinking about V that
other things. *She forgot to lock her door one day and* V about n
*two men got in... Don't forget that all dogs need a
supply of fresh water to drink... She forgot about
everything but the sun and the wind.* **3** If you **forget** VERB
something that you had intended to bring with you, V n
you do not bring it because you did not think about
it at the right time. *Once when we were going to Par-*

is, I forgot my passport. **4** If you **forget** something or someone, you deliberately put them out of your mind and do not think about them any more. *I can't forget what happened... I found it very easy to forget about Sumner... She tried to forget that sometimes she heard them quarrelling.* VERB: V n, V wh, V about n, V that

5 If you **forget** yourself, you behave in an unrestrained or unacceptable way which is not the way you usually behave. VERB: V pron-refl **6** You say **'Forget it'** in reply to someone as a way of telling them not to worry or bother about something, or as an emphatic way of saying no to a suggestion. *'Sorry, Liz. I think I was a bit rude to you.'—'Forget it, but don't do it again!'... 'You want more?' roared Claire. 'Forget it, honey.'* CONVENTION PRAGMATICS **7** You say **not forgetting** a particular thing or person when you want to include them in something that you have already mentioned. *Then I add a bit of oregano and maybe a sprinkle of garlic – not forgetting salt and pepper.* PHRASE PRAGMATICS

for·get·ful /fəˈgetful/. Someone who is **forgetful** often forgets things. **✦ for·get·ful·ness** *Her forgetfulness is due to advancing age.* ADJ-GRADED / N-UNCOUNT

for·get-me-not, forget-me-nots. A **forget-me-not** is a small plant with tiny blue flowers. N-COUNT

for·get·table /fəˈgetəbəl/. If you describe something or someone as **forgettable**, you are criticizing them because they do not have any qualities that make them special or interesting. *He has acted in three forgettable action films.* ADJ-GRADED PRAGMATICS

for·giv·able /fəˈgɪvəbəl/. If you say that something bad is **forgivable**, you mean that you can understand and forgive it in the circumstances. *This was a blunder by Mr Baker, but it was a forgivable one.* ADJ-GRADED

for·give /fəˈgɪv/ **forgives, forgiving, forgave, forgiven**. **1** If you **forgive** someone who has done something wrong, or **forgive** what they have done, you stop being angry with them and no longer want to punish them. *She'd find a way to forgive him for the theft of the money... For those flashes of genius, you can forgive him anything.* **✦ for·give·ness** *...a spirit of forgiveness and national reconciliation.* **✦ for·giv·ing** *I don't think people are in a very forgiving mood.* **2** If you say that someone could **be forgiven for** doing something, you mean that they would be wrong or mistaken to do it, but that many people would do the same thing in those circumstances. *Looking at the figures, you could be forgiven for thinking the recession is already over.* **3 Forgive** is used in polite expressions and apologies like **'forgive me'** and **'forgive my ignorance'** when you are saying or doing something that might seem rude or silly. *Forgive me, I don't mean to insult you.* **4** If an organization such as a bank **forgives** a debt, they agree not to ask for that money to be repaid. VERB: V n, V n for n/-ing, V n n / N-UNCOUNT / ADJ-GRADED / V-PASSIVE be V-ed for -ing/n / VERB PRAGMATICS V n / VERB: V n

for·go /fɔːˈgəʊ/. See **forego**.

for·got /fəˈgɒt/. Forgot is the past tense of **forget**.

for·got·ten /fəˈgɒtən/. Forgotten is the past participle of **forget**.

fork /fɔːk/ **forks, forking, forked**. **1** A **fork** is an implement for eating food with. It consists of three or four long thin prongs on the end of a handle. See picture headed **kitchen utensils**. **2** If you **fork** food into your mouth or onto a plate, you put it there using a fork. N-COUNT / VERB: V n into/onto n **3** A garden **fork** is a large tool that you use to break up soil when you are gardening. It consists of three or four long prongs attached to a long handle. See picture headed **tools**. **4** If you **fork** soil, manure, or hay somewhere, you move it from one place to another using a garden fork. **5** See also **tuning fork**. N-COUNT / VERB: V n prep/adv **6** A **fork** in a road, path, or river is a point at which it divides into two parts and forms a 'Y' shape. *Just there is a fork in the road and you take the right-hand track.* N-COUNT **7** If a road, path, or river **forks**, it forms a fork. *The path dipped down to a sort of cove, and then it forked in two directions.* **✦ forked** *Jaegers are swift black birds with long forked tails.* VERB: V prep/adv / ADJ

fork out. If you **fork out** for something, you spend a lot of money on it. *You don't ask people to fork out* PHRASAL VB V P for/on n / V P

every time they drive up the motorways... Britons fork out more than a billion pounds a year on toys. V P n for/on n INFORMAL

'fork-lift truck, fork-lift trucks. A **fork-lift truck** or a **fork-lift** is a small vehicle with two movable parts on the front that are used to lift heavy loads. N-COUNT

for·lorn /fɔːˈlɔːn/. **1** If someone is **forlorn**, they are lonely and unhappy. *A Dutch newspaper photographed the president waiting forlornly in the rain.* **✦ for·lorn·ly 2** If a place is **forlorn**, it is deserted or uncared for, or has little in it. **✦ forlornly** *It is stranded somewhat forlornly in the middle of the plain.* **3** If you describe a hope or attempt as a **forlorn** hope or attempt, you think that it has no chance of success. *Peasants have left the land in the forlorn hope of finding a better life in cities.* ◆◇◇◇ ADJ-GRADED / ADV-GRADED: ADV with v / ADJ-GRADED / ADV-GRADED: ADV with v / ADJ-GRADED

form 1   noun and verb uses to do with shape or type

form /fɔːm/ **forms, forming, formed**. **1** A **form** of something is a type or kind of it. *He contracted a rare form of cancer... I am against hunting in any form.* ◆◆◆◆◆ N-COUNT: with supp **2** When something can exist or happen in several possible ways, you can use **form** to refer to one particular way in which it exists or happens. *Valleys often take the form of deep canyons... In its present form, the law could lead to new injustices.* N-COUNT: with supp **3** The **form** of something is its shape. *...the form of the body.* **4** You can refer to something that you can see as a **form**, especially if you cannot see it clearly. *She thought she'd never been so glad to see his bulky form.* N-COUNT: with supp / N-COUNT **5** When a particular shape **forms** or **is formed**, people or things move or are arranged so that this shape is made. *They formed a circle and sang 'Auld Lang Syne'... The General gave orders for the cadets to form into lines.* V-ERG: V n, V into n **6** If something is arranged or changed so that it has a particular shape or function, you can say that it **forms** something with that shape or function. *All the buildings have names and form a half circle.* VERB V n **7** If something consists of particular things or people, you can say that they **form** that thing. *Cereals form the staple diet of an enormous number of people around the world.* VERB V n **8** When something **takes form**, it develops or begins to be visible. *As plans took form in her mind, she realized the need for an accomplice.* PHRASE **9** If someone **forms** an organization, group, or company, they start it. *They formed themselves into an association.* **✦ for·ma·tion** /fɔːˈmeɪʃən/ *Mr Mugabe will announce the formation of a new government.* **10** When something natural **forms**, it begins to exist and develop. *Huge ice sheets were formed.* **11** If you **form** something such as a relationship, habit, or idea, you begin to have it and develop it. *An idea formed in his mind.* **✦ formation** *...the formation of other important relationships.* **12** If you say that something **forms** a person's character or personality, you mean that it causes them to develop in a particular way. *Anger at injustice formed his character.* **✦ formation** *My profession had an important influence in the formation of my character.* VERB: V n, V pron-refl into n / N-UNCOUNT / V-ERG: V be V-ed / V-ERG: V n / N-UNCOUNT VERB V n / N-UNCOUNT: with supp

form 2   noun uses to do with someone's condition

form /fɔːm/. **1** In sport, **form** refers to the ability or success of a competitor over a period of time. *His form this season has been brilliant.* **2** If you say that someone is **off form**, you mean they are not performing as well as they usually do. If you say that they are **on form**, you mean that they are performing well. **3** If someone or something behaves **true to form**, they do what is expected and is typical of them. *True to form, she kept her guests waiting for more than 90 minutes.* **4** If you say that it is **bad form** to behave in a particular way, you mean that it is rude and impolite. *It was thought bad form to discuss business on social occasions.* **5** If you say that someone is **in good form**, you mean that they seem healthy and cheerful. ◆◆◆◇◇ N-UNCOUNT / PHRASE BRITISH / PHRASE / PHRASE BRITISH / PHRASE BRITISH

form 3   document

form /fɔːm/ **forms**. A **form** is a paper with questions on it and spaces marked where you should write the answers. *You will be asked to fill in a form with details of your birth and occupation.* ◆◆◆◆◇ N-COUNT

for·mal /'fɔːməl/. **1 Formal** speech or behaviour is correct and serious, and is used especially in official situations. *He wrote a very formal letter of apology to Douglas.* ♦ **for·mal·ly** *'Good afternoon, Mr Benjamin,' Schumacher said formally.* ♦ **for·mal·ity** *Lillith's formality and seriousness amused him.* **2** A **formal** action, statement, or request is an official one. *No formal announcement had been made.* ♦ **formally** *They are now formally separated.* **3 Formal** occasions are ones at which people wear smart clothes and behave correctly in accordance with particular conventions. *...a formal dinner.* **4 Formal** clothes are very smart clothes that are suitable for formal occasions. ♦ **formally** *It was really too warm for her to dress so formally.* **5** Something that is done, written, or studied in a **formal** way has a very ordered organized method or style. *This does not encourage the child to analyse the environment in a formal way.* **6 Formal** education or training is given officially, usually in a school, college, or university. *Although his formal education stopped after primary school, he was an avid reader.* **7** A **formal** garden or room is arranged in a very regular and controlled way. **8** See also **formality**.
ADJ-GRADED / ADV-GRADED: ADV with v / N-UNCOUNT: ADJ: ADJ n / ADV / ADJ-GRADED / ADJ-GRADED: ADJ n ADV-GRADED: ADV after v / ADJ-GRADED / ADJ: ADJ n / ADJ

for·mal·de·hyde /fɔː'mældɪhaɪd/. **Formaldehyde** is a strong-smelling gas which is dissolved in water to make a liquid which is used for preserving specimens in biology.
N-UNCOUNT

for·mal·ise /'fɔːməlaɪz/. See **formalize**.

for·mal·ism /'fɔːməlɪzəm/. **Formalism** is a style, especially in art, in which great attention is paid to the outward form or appearance rather than to the inner reality or significance of things. ♦ **for·mal·ist** *...art based on formalist principles.*
N-UNCOUNT / ADJ: ADJ n

for·mal·ity /fɔː'mælɪti/ **formalities. 1** If you say that an action or procedure is just a **formality**, you mean that it is done only because it is normally done, and that it will not have any real effect on the situation. **2 Formalities** are formal actions or procedures that are conventionally carried out as part of an activity or event. *They are whisked through the immigration and customs formalities in a matter of minutes.* **3** See also **formal**.
♦◇◇◇◇ N-COUNT / N-COUNT

for·mal·ize /'fɔːməlaɪz/ **formalizes, formalizing, formalized;** also spelled **formalise** in British English. If you **formalize** a plan, idea, arrangement, or system, you make it formal and official. ♦ **for·mali·za·tion** /,fɔːməlaɪ'zeɪʃən/ **formalizations** *The formalization of co-operation between the republics would produce progress.*
♦◇◇◇◇ VERB: V n / N-VAR

for·mat /'fɔːmæt/ **formats, formatting, formatted. 1** The **format** of something is the way or order in which it is arranged and presented. *I had met with him to explain the format of the programme.* **2** The **format** of a piece of computer software or a musical recording is the type of equipment on which it is designed to be used or played. For example, the formats in which a musical recording is normally available are vinyl, CD, and cassette. **3** To **format** a computer disk means to run a program so that the disk can be written on.
♦♦◇◇◇ N-COUNT / N-COUNT / VERB: V n

for·ma·tion /fɔː'meɪʃən/ **formations. 1** If people or things are in **formation**, they are arranged in a particular pattern as they move. *He was flying in formation with seven other jets.* **2** A rock or cloud **formation** is rock or cloud of a particular shape or structure. **3** See also **form**.
♦♦◇◇◇ N-UNCOUNT: also a N / N-COUNT: n N

forma·tive /'fɔːmətɪv/. A **formative** period of time or experience is one that has an important and lasting influence on a person's character and attitudes. *She was born in Barbados but spent her formative years growing up in east London.*
♦◇◇◇◇ ADJ-GRADED

for·mer /'fɔːmə/. **1 Former** is used to describe what someone or something used to be, but no longer is. *...former President Richard Nixon. ...the former home of Sir Christopher Wren.* **2 Former** is used to describe a situation or period of time which came before the present one. *He would want you to remember him as he was in former years.* **3** When two people, things, or groups have just been men-
♦♦◇◇◇ ADJ: ADJ n / ADJ: ADJ n FORMAL / PRON

tioned, you can refer to the first of them as **the former**. *If the family home and joint pension rights are of equal value, the wife may choose the former and the husband the latter.*

for·mer·ly /'fɔːməli/. If something happened or was true **formerly**, it happened or was true in the past. *He had formerly been in the Navy. ...East Germany's formerly state-controlled companies.*
♦♦◇◇◇ ADV: ADV with cl/ group, ADV before v

For·mi·ca /fɔː'maɪkə/. **Formica** is a hard plastic that is used for covering surfaces such as kitchen tables or worktops. **Formica** is a trademark.
N-UNCOUNT

for·mi·dable /'fɔːmɪdəbəl, fə'mɪd-/. If you describe something or someone as **formidable**, you mean that you feel slightly frightened by them because they are very impressive or considerable. *We have a formidable task ahead of us.* ♦ **for·mi·dably** *Sofia was attractive and formidably intelligent.*
♦♦◇◇◇ ADJ-GRADED / ADV: ADV adj

form·less /'fɔːmləs/. Something that is **formless** does not have a clear or definite structure or shape.
ADJ

for·mu·la /'fɔːmjʊlə/ **formulae** /'fɔːmjʊliː/ or **formulas. 1** A **formula** is a plan that is devised as a way of dealing with a particular problem. *...a formula to unify the divided peninsula.* **2** A **formula** for a particular situation, especially a good one, is a course of action that is likely to result in that situation. *Clever exploitation of the latest technology would be a sure formula for success.* **3** A **formula** is a group of letters, numbers, or other symbols which represents a scientific or mathematical rule. *...a mathematical formula describing the distances of the planets from the Sun.* **4** In science, the **formula** for a substance is a list of the amounts of various substances which make up that substance, or an indication of the atoms that it is composed of. **5 Formula** followed by a number is used to indicate a type of racing car or something relating to that type. *...Formula 1 racing cars.* **6 Formula** is a powder which you mix with water to make artificial milk for babies.
♦♦◇◇◇ N-COUNT / N-SING: N for n / N-COUNT / N-COUNT / N-UNCOUNT: N num / N-UNCOUNT

for·mu·laic /,fɔːmjʊ'leɪɪk/. If you describe something as **formulaic**, you are criticizing it because it is not original, but follows a pattern similar to many other things that have been done in the past. *His paintings are contrived and formulaic.*
ADJ-GRADED / PRAGMATICS

for·mu·late /'fɔːmjʊleɪt/ **formulates, formulating, formulated. 1** If you **formulate** something such as a plan or proposal, you invent it, thinking about the details carefully. ♦ **for·mu·la·tion** /,fɔːmjʊ'leɪʃən/ *...the process of policy formulation.* **2** If you **formulate** a thought, opinion, or idea, you express it using particular words. ♦ **formulation, formulations** *His formulation is far from explicit.*
♦♦◇◇◇ VERB: V n / N-UNCOUNT / VERB: V n / N-VAR

for·mu·la·tion /,fɔːmjʊ'leɪʃən/ **formulations. 1** The **formulation** of something such as a medicine or a beauty product is the way in which different ingredients are combined to make it. You can also refer to the finished product as a **formulation**. *...a formulation containing royal jelly, pollen and vitamin C.* **2** See also **formulate**.
♦◇◇◇◇ N-VAR

for·ni·ca·tion /,fɔːnɪ'keɪʃən/. **Fornication** is having sex with someone who you are not married to; used showing disapproval.
N-UNCOUNT / PRAGMATICS FORMAL

for·sake /fə'seɪk/ **forsakes, forsaking, forsook** /fə'sʊk/ **forsaken. 1** If you **forsake** someone, you leave them when you should have stayed, or stop helping them or looking after them; used showing disapproval. *...children who've been forsaken by individual teachers.* **2** If you **forsake** something, you stop doing it, using it, or having it. *She forsook her notebook for new technology.* **3** If you **forsake** a place, you leave it. *At 53 he has no plans to forsake the hills.*
♦◇◇◇◇ PRAGMATICS LITERARY / VERB: V n V n for n LITERARY / VERB V n LITERARY

for·sak·en /fə'seɪkən/. A **forsaken** place is not lived in, used, or looked after. ● See also **God-forsaken**.
ADJ: ADJ n LITERARY

for·swear /fɔː'sweə/ **forswears, forswearing, forswore, forsworn.** If you **forswear** something, you promise that you will stop doing it, having it, or using it. *The party was offered a share of government if it forswore violence.*
VERB V n FORMAL, LITERARY

for·sythia /fɔːˈsaɪθɪə, AM -ˈsɪθ-/ **forsythias**. For- N-VAR
sythia is a bush that has spiky yellow flowers.

fort /fɔːt/ **forts**. **1** A **fort** is a strong building or a ◆◆◇◇◇
place with a wall or fence around it where soldiers N-COUNT
can stay and be safe from the enemy. **2** If you **hold** PHRASE
the fort for someone, you look after things for them
while they are somewhere else or busy doing something else. *His business partner is holding the fort
while he is away.*

forte /ˈfɔːteɪ/ **fortes**. Pronounced /fɔːt/ in American N-COUNT
English. You can say that a particular activity is your
forte if you are very good at it. *Originality was never
his forte.*

forth /fɔːθ/. In addition to the uses shown below, ◆◆◆◇◇
forth is also used in the phrasal verbs 'put forth'
and 'set forth'.
1 When someone goes **forth** from a place, they leave ADV:
it. *Go forth into the desert.* ADV after v
LITERARY
2 To bring something **forth** means to produce it or ADV:
make it visible. **3** ● **back and forth**: see **back**. ● to ADV after v
hold forth: see **hold**. LITERARY

forth·com·ing /ˌfɔːθˈkʌmɪŋ/. **1** A **forthcoming** ◆◆◇◇◇
event will happen soon. *He will stand again in the* ADJ: ADJ n
forthcoming election. **2** If something that you want, ADJ:
need, or expect is **forthcoming**, it is given to you or v-link ADJ
it happens. *They promised that the money would be* FORMAL
forthcoming. **3** If you say that someone is **forth-** ADJ-GRADED
coming, you mean that they willingly give information when you ask them.

forth·right /ˈfɔːθraɪt/. If you describe someone as ◆◇◇◇◇
forthright, you admire them because they show ADJ-GRADED
clearly and strongly what they think and feel. PRAGMATICS

forth·with /ˌfɔːθˈwɪθ/. **Forthwith** means immedi- ADV:
ately. *I could have you arrested forthwith!* ADV with v
FORMAL

for·ti·eth /ˈfɔːtiəθ/. The **fortieth** item in a series is ◆◆◆◇◇
the one that you count as number forty. See Appen- ORDINAL
dix headed **Numbers**.

for·ti·fi·ca·tion /ˌfɔːtɪfɪˈkeɪʃən/ **fortifications**. N-COUNT
Fortifications are buildings, walls, or ditches that
are built to protect a place against attack. ● See also
fortify.

fortified **wine, fortified wines**. Fortified wine N-VAR
is an alcoholic drink such as sherry or port that is
made by mixing wine with a small amount of brandy or strong alcohol.

for·ti·fy /ˈfɔːtɪfaɪ/ **fortifies, fortifying, fortified**. ◆◇◇◇◇
1 To fortify a place means to make it stronger and VERB
less easy to attack, often by building a wall or ditch V n
round it. *...British soldiers working to fortify an
airbase.* ◆ **for·ti·fied** *He remains barricaded inside* ADJ-GRADED
his heavily-fortified mansion. **2** If food or drink is VB: usu
fortified, another substance is added to it to make it passive
healthier or stronger. *It has also been fortified with* beV-ed with n
vitamin C... All sherry is made from wine fortified V-ed
with brandy. ◆ **for·ti·fi·ca·tion** *In some countries,* N-UNCOUNT
*iron fortification of foods is carried out to reduce
iron deficiency.* **3** If you **are fortified** by something VERB:
such as food, drink, or an idea, it makes you more beV-ed
cheerful, determined, or energetic. *Would you care* ◆ V pron-refl
*for some tea, or even a light meal, to fortify yourself
before your adventure?* **4** To **fortify** something VERB
means to make it more powerful and more likely to V n
succeed. *His declared agenda is to raise standards in* FORMAL
*schools, fortify parent power and decentralise
control.*

for·ti·tude /ˈfɔːtɪtjuːd, AM -tuːd/. If you say that N-UNCOUNT
someone has shown **fortitude**, you admire them for PRAGMATICS
being brave, calm, and uncomplaining when they FORMAL
have experienced something unpleasant or painful.
*He suffered a long series of illnesses with tremendous
dignity and fortitude.*

fort·night /ˈfɔːtnaɪt/ **fortnights**. A **fortnight** is a ◆◆◇◇◇
period of two weeks. *I hope to be back in a fortnight.* N-COUNT
BRITISH

fort·night·ly /ˈfɔːtnaɪtli/. A **fortnightly** event or ADJ: ADJ n
publication happens or appears once a fortnight. BRITISH
The American word is **biweekly**. *They are now holding their fortnightly meetings at The New Invention
Victory Club.* ► Also an adverb. *They recently put my* ADV:
rent up and I pay it fortnightly. ADV after v

for·tress /ˈfɔːtrɪs/ **fortresses**. A fortress is a cas- ◆◇◇◇◇
tle or other large strong building, or a well- N-COUNT
protected place, which is intended to be difficult for
enemies to enter.

for·tui·tous /fɔːˈtjuːɪtəs, AM -ˈtuː-/. You say some- ADJ-GRADED
thing is **fortuitous** when, by chance, it makes something very successful or pleasant. *Their success is the
result of a fortuitous combination of circumstances.*

for·tu·nate /ˈfɔːtʃunɪt/. If someone or something ◆◆◇◇◇
is **fortunate**, they are lucky. *He was extremely fortu-* ADJ-GRADED
*nate to survive... Central London is fortunate in hav-
ing so many large parks and open spaces... It was
fortunate that the water was shallow.*

for·tu·nate·ly /ˈfɔːtʃunɪtli/. **Fortunately** is used ◆◆◇◇◇
when describing a situation that is lucky for some- ADV-GRADED:
one. *Fortunately, the weather that winter was rea-* ADV with cl
*sonably mild... Fortunately for me, my friend saw
that something was seriously wrong.*

for·tune /ˈfɔːtʃuːn/ **fortunes**. **1** You can empha- ◆◆◆◇◇
size how large a sum of money is by referring to it PRAGMATICS
as a **fortune** or a **small fortune**. *He made a small
fortune in the London property boom.* **2** Someone N-COUNT
who has a **fortune** has a very large amount of money. *He made his fortune in car sales.*
3 Fortune or good **fortune** is good luck. Ill **fortune** is N-UNCOUNT
bad luck. *Government ministers are starting to wonder
how long their good fortune can last.* **4** If you talk N-PLURAL:
about someone's or something's **fortunes**, you are with poss
talking about the extent to which they are doing well
or being successful. *The electoral fortunes of the Liberal Democratic party may decline... She kept up with
the fortunes of the Reeves family.* **5** If you talk about N-UNCOUNT
the way someone is treated by **fortune**, you are referring to the good or bad luck that they have. *He is certainly being smiled on by fortune.* **6** When someone PHRASE
tells your **fortune**, they tell you what will happen to
you in the future, which they say is shown, for example, by the lines on your hand.

fortune-teller, fortune-tellers. A fortune-teller N-COUNT
is a person who tells you what will happen to you in
the future, after looking at something such as the
lines on your hand.

for·ty /ˈfɔːti/ **forties**. **1 Forty** is the number 40. See ◆◆◆◆◆
Appendix headed **Numbers**. **2** When you talk about NUMBER
the **forties**, you are referring to numbers between N-PLURAL
40 and 49. For example, if you are **in your forties**,
you are aged between 40 and 49. If the temperature
is **in the forties**, the temperature is between 40 and
49 degrees. **3 The forties** is the decade between N-PLURAL:
1940 and 1949. the N

fo·rum /ˈfɔːrəm/ **forums**. A forum is a place, situa- ◆◆◇◇◇
tion, or group in which people exchange ideas and N-COUNT:
discuss issues that are important to them. *Members* with supp
*of the council agreed that it still had an important
role as a forum for discussion.*

for·ward /ˈfɔːwəd/ **forwards, forwarding, for-** ◆◆◆◆◇
warded. In addition to the uses shown below, **for-**
ward is also used in phrasal verbs such as 'bring
forward' and 'look forward to'. In British English,
forwards is often used as an adverb instead of **for-**
ward in senses 1 and 6.
1 If you move or look **forward** or **forwards**, you move ADV:
or look in a direction that is in front of you. *He came* ADV after v
*forward... She fell forwards on to her face... He con-
tinued to walk, didn't look at the car, kept his face forward.* **2 Forward** means in a position near the front of ADV-GRADED:
something such as a building or vehicle. *The best seats* beADV,
are in the aisle and as far forward as possible. ► Also ADV after v
an adjective. *Reinforcements were needed to allow* ADV-GRADED:
more troops to move to forward positions. **3** If one PHR-PREP
thing is **forward of** another, especially on a ship or
aircraft, the first thing is in front of the second thing or
further ahead. **4** ● **backwards and forwards**: see
backwards.
5 If something or someone is put **forward**, or comes ADV:
forward, they are suggested or offered as suitable for a ADV after v
particular purpose. *Next month the Commission is to
bring forward its first proposals... No witnesses have
come forward.* **6 Forward** and **forwards** are used in ADV
expressions such as **move forward**, **look forward**,

and **the way forward** to indicate that someone is making progress or thinking about how to make progress. *They just couldn't see any way forward... Space scientists and astronomers have taken another step forwards.* ▶ Also an adjective. *The university system requires more forward planning.* **7** If you put a clock or watch **forward**, you change the time shown on it so that it shows a later time, for example when the time changes to summer time.

ADJ: ADJ n
ADV:
ADV after v

8 If a letter or message **is forwarded** to someone, it is sent to the place where they are, after having been sent to a different place earlier. *A hospital appointment letter for Jane was forwarded from the clinic.*

VERB
be V-ed to/
from n

9 If you describe someone as **forward**, you mean they speak very confidently and frankly, sometimes offending people or not showing them enough respect. **♦ for·ward·ness** *He shocked me with his forwardness.*

ADJ-GRADED

N-UNCOUNT

10 In football or hockey, a **forward** is a player whose usual position is in the opponents' half of the field, and whose usual job is to attack or score goals. ● See also **centre-forward**.

N-COUNT

forwarding ad'dress, forwarding addresses. A **forwarding address** is a new or temporary address that you give someone when you leave your home, so they can send your mail to you.

N-COUNT

'forward-looking. If you describe a person or organization as **forward-looking**, you approve of the fact that they think about the future or have modern ideas.

ADJ-GRADED
PRAGMATICS

for·wards /ˈfɔːwədz/. See **forward**.

fos·sil /ˈfɒsəl/ **fossils.** A **fossil** is the hardened remains of a prehistoric animal or plant that are found inside a rock.

♦♦◇◇◇
N-COUNT

fossil 'fuel, fossil fuels; also spelled **fossil-fuel.** **Fossil fuel** is fuel such as coal or oil that is formed from the decayed remains of plants or animals.

♦◇◇◇◇
N-VAR

fos·sil·ize /ˈfɒsɪlaɪz/ **fossilizes, fossilizing, fossilized;** also spelled **fossilise** in British English. **1** If the remains of an animal or plant **fossilize**, they become hard and form a fossil. *...fossilized dinosaur bones.* **2** If you say that ideas, attitudes, or ways of behaving **have fossilized**, you are criticizing the fact that they are fixed and unlikely to change. *Efforts have been made to breathe some new life into these fossilized organisations.*

V-ERG: V
V-ed

V-ERG: V
PRAGMATICS
V-ed

fos·ter /ˈfɒstə, AM ˈfɔːst-/ **fosters, fostering, fostered.** **1** **Foster** parents are people who officially take a child into their family for a period of time, without becoming the child's legal parents. The child is referred to as their **foster** child. **2** If you **foster** a child, you take him or her into your family as your **foster** child. **3** To **foster** something such as an activity or idea means to help it to develop. *Developed countries had a responsibility to foster global economic growth.*

♦♦◇◇◇
ADJ: ADJ n

VERB: V n

VERB
V n

fought /fɔːt/. **Fought** is the past tense and past participle of **fight**.

foul /faʊl/ **fouler, foulest; fouls, fouling, fouled.** **1** If you describe something as **foul**, you mean it is dirty and smells or tastes unpleasant. *...foul polluted water.* **2** If a place **is fouled** by someone or something, they make it dirty. *Two oil-related accidents near Los Angeles have fouled the ocean.* **3** If an animal **fouls** a place, it drops faeces there. **4** **Foul** language is offensive and contains swear words or rude words. **5** If someone is in a **foul** temper or mood, they are very angry. **6** **Foul** weather is unpleasant, windy, and stormy.

♦♦◇◇◇
ADJ-GRADED

VERB:
be V-ed
V n

VERB: V n
ADJ-GRADED
ADJ-GRADED
ADJ-GRADED

7 In sports such as football, a **foul** is an action that is not allowed by the rules. ▶ Also an adjective. *Players were warned twice for foul play.* **8** In sports such as football, if one player **fouls** another, the first player touches or obstructs the second in a way which is not allowed by the rules. **9** If you **cry foul**, you claim that someone, especially an opponent or rival, has acted illegally or unfairly. *Deprived of the crushing victory it was confidently expecting, the party cried foul.*

N-COUNT

ADJ: ADJ n
VERB: V n

PHRASE

10 If you **fall foul of** someone, you do something

PHRASE

which gets you into trouble with them. *He had fallen foul of the FBI.*

BRITISH

foul up. If you **foul up** something such as a plan, you spoil it by doing something wrong or stupid. *There are serious risks that laboratories may foul up these tests.*

PHRASAL VB
V P noun

,foul-'mouthed. If you describe someone as **foul-mouthed**, you disapprove of them because they use a lot of offensive language such as swear words.

ADJ-GRADED
PRAGMATICS

,foul 'play. **Foul play** is criminal violence or activity that results in a person's death. *The report says it suspects foul play was involved in the deaths.*

N-UNCOUNT

found /faʊnd/ **founds, founding, founded.** **1** **Found** is the past tense and past participle of **find**. **2** When an organization, company, or city **is founded** by someone, they start it or create it. *He founded the Centre for Journalism Studies at University College Cardiff.* **♦ foun·da·tion** *...the 150th anniversary of the foundation of Kew Gardens.* **♦ found·er, founders** *He was one of the founders of the university's medical faculty.* **♦ found·ing** I *have been a member of The Sunday Times Wine Club since its founding in 1973.* **3** See also **founded**.

♦♦♦♦◇
VERB:
be V-ed
V n
N-SING:
with poss
N-COUNT
N-SING

foun·da·tion /faʊnˈdeɪʃən/ **foundations.** **1** The **foundation** of something such as a belief or way of life is the things on which it is based. *The issue strikes at the very foundation of our community... This laid the foundations for later modern economic growth.* ● If an event **shakes the foundations** of a society or a system of beliefs, it causes great uncertainty and makes people question their most deeply held beliefs. **2** The **foundations** of a building or other structure are the layer of bricks or concrete below the ground that it is built on. **3** A **foundation** is an organization which provides money for a special purpose such as research or charity. *...the National Foundation for Educational Research.* **4** If a story has no **foundation**, there are no facts to prove that it is true. *The allegations were without foundation.* **5** **Foundation** is a skin-coloured cream that is put on the face before other make-up. **6** See also **found**.

♦♦♦◇◇
N-COUNT

PHRASE

N-PLURAL

N-COUNT

N-UNCOUNT:
with brd-neg

N-VAR

foun'dation course, foundation courses. In Britain, a **foundation course** is a course that you do at some colleges and universities in order to prepare yourself for a longer or more advanced course.

N-COUNT

foun'dation stone, foundation stones. **1** A **foundation stone** is a block of stone built into a public building close to the ground. It is usually unveiled at a ceremony when the building is complete, and has words cut into it which record the occasion. **2** The **foundation stone** for something is the basic, fundamental part which its existence or success depends on. *...these foundation stones of the future: education, training, research, development.*

N-COUNT

N-COUNT

found·ed /ˈfaʊndɪd/. If something is **founded on** a particular thing, it is based on it. *The criticisms are founded on facts as well as on convictions.* ● See also **well-founded**.

♦◇◇◇◇
ADJ:
v-link ADJ on
n

found·er /ˈfaʊndə/ **founders, foundering, foundered.** **1** If something such as a plan or project **founders**, it fails because of a particular problem. **2** If a ship **founders**, it fills with water and sinks. **3** See also **found**.

♦◇◇◇◇
VERB: V
VERB: V

,founder 'member, founder members. A **founder member** of a club or organization is one of its first members, often one who was involved in setting it up.

♦◇◇◇◇
N-COUNT

,founding 'father, founding fathers. **1** The **founding father** of an organization or idea is the person who set it up or first developed it. **2** The **Founding Fathers** of the United States were the members of the American Constitutional Convention of 1787.

♦◇◇◇◇
N-COUNT
LITERARY
N-PROPER-
PLURAL

found·ry /ˈfaʊndri/ **foundries.** A **foundry** is a place where metal is melted and formed into particular objects.

N-COUNT

fount /faʊnt/ **founts.** If you describe a person or thing as the **fount of** something, you are saying that they are an important source or supply of it. *To the young boy his father was the fount of all knowledge.*

N-COUNT
LITERARY

foun·tain /ˈfaʊntɪn/ **fountains. 1** A **fountain** is an ornamental feature in a pool or lake which consists of a jet of water that is forced up into the air by a pump. **2** A **fountain** of a liquid is an amount of it which is sent up into the air and falls back. *The volcano spewed a fountain of molten rock 650 feet in the air.* **3** If you describe a person or thing as a **fountain** of something, you mean they are an important source of it and supply a lot of it. *You are a fountain of ideas.*
◆◆◇◇◇ N-COUNT
N-COUNT LITERARY
N-COUNT: N ofn LITERARY

fountain pen, fountain pens. A **fountain pen** is a pen with a nib that is supplied with ink from a container inside the pen.
N-COUNT

four /fɔː/ **fours. 1 Four** is the number 4. See Appendix headed **Numbers**. **2** If you are **on all fours**, your knees, feet, and hands are on the ground. *She crawled on all fours over to the window.*
◆◆◆◆◆ NUMBER PHRASE

four-letter ʹword, four-letter words. A **four-letter word** is a short word that people consider to be rude or offensive, usually because it refers to sex or other bodily functions.
N-COUNT

four-poster ʹbed, four-poster beds. A **four-poster bed** or a **four-poster** is a large old-fashioned bed with posts at each corner and curtains that can be drawn around it.
N-COUNT

four·some /ˈfɔːsəm/ **foursomes.** A **foursome** is a group of four people or things. *The London-based foursome are set to release their fourth single this month.*
◆◇◇◇◇ N-COLL-COUNT

four-ʹsquare; also spelled **foursquare. 1** If someone **stands four-square behind** someone or **stands four-square with** them, they are firm in their support for them. **2** A **four-square** building or structure is square in shape and looks solid and well-built.
PHRASE
ADJ

four·teen /ˌfɔːˈtiːn/. **Fourteen** is the number 14. See Appendix headed **Numbers**. *I'm fourteen years old.*
◆◆◆◆◆ NUMBER

four·teenth /ˌfɔːˈtiːnθ/. The **fourteenth** item in a series is the one that you count as number fourteen. See Appendix headed **Numbers**.
◆◆◆◇◇ ORDINAL

fourth /fɔːθ/ **fourths. 1** The **fourth** item in a series is the one that you count as number four. See Appendix headed **Numbers**. **2** A **fourth** is one of four equal parts of something. The British word is **quarter**.
◆◆◆◇◇ ORDINAL
FRACTION AMERICAN

fourth diʹmension. In physics, the **fourth dimension** is time. The other three dimensions are length, breadth, and height.
N-SING: theN

fourth·ly /ˈfɔːθli/. You say **fourthly** when you want to make a fourth point or give a fourth reason for something. *Fourthly, the natural enthusiasm of the student teachers should be maintained.*
ADV: ADV with cl PRAGMATICS

Fourth of Juʹly. In the United States, the **Fourth of July** is a public holiday when people celebrate the Declaration of Independence in 1776.
N-SING

fowl /faʊl/ **fowls; fowl** can also be used as the plural form. A **fowl** is a bird, especially a duck, goose, or chicken.
◆◇◇◇◇ N-COUNT

fox /fɒks/ **foxes, foxing, foxed. 1** A **fox** is a wild animal which looks like a dog and has reddish-brown fur, a pointed face and ears, and a thick tail. **2** If you **are foxed** by something, you cannot understand it or solve it. *...a question which foxed one of these formidable experts.* **3** If you describe someone as a **fox**, you mean they are clever, cunning, and deceitful.
◆◆◇◇◇ N-COUNT
VERB: beV-ed V n BRITISH N-SING

fox·glove /ˈfɒksɡlʌv/ **foxgloves.** A **foxglove** is a tall plant that has pink or white flowers shaped like bells growing up the stem.
N-VAR

fox·hole /ˈfɒkshəʊl/ **foxholes.** A **foxhole** is a small pit which soldiers dig as a shelter from the enemy and from which they can shoot.
N-COUNT

fox·hound /ˈfɒkshaʊnd/ **foxhounds.** A **foxhound** is a type of dog that is trained to hunt foxes.
N-COUNT

ʹfox-hunting; also spelled **foxhunting. Fox-hunting** is a leisure activity in which people riding horses, usually accompanied by dogs, chase a fox across the countryside.
N-UNCOUNT

foxy /ˈfɒksi/ **foxier, foxiest. 1** If you describe someone as **foxy**, you mean they are deceitful in a
ADJ-GRADED

clever, secretive way. **2** If a man calls a woman **foxy**, he finds her sexy and attractive.
ADJ-GRADED AMERICAN, INFORMAL

foy·er /ˈfɔɪə, ˈfwaɪeɪ/ **foyers.** A **foyer** is the large area where people meet or wait just inside the main doors of a theatre, cinema, or hotel. *I went and waited in the foyer.*
◆◇◇◇◇ N-COUNT

Fr 1 Fr is a written abbreviation for **French** or **franc**. **2 Fr** is a written abbreviation for **Father** before the name of a Catholic priest.
◆◇◇◇◇

fra·cas /ˈfrækɑː, AM ˈfreɪkəs/. A **fracas** is a rough, noisy quarrel or fight.
N-SING

frac·tal /ˈfræktəl/ **fractals.** In geometry, a **fractal** is an irregular shape made up of a large number of smaller shapes that are all identical to each other.
N-COUNT

frac·tion /ˈfrækʃən/ **fractions. 1** A **fraction** is a tiny amount or proportion of something. *Here's how to eat like the stars, at a fraction of the cost... I opened my eyes just a fraction.* ♦ **frac·tion·al** /ˈfrækʃənəl/. *...a fractional hesitation.* ♦ **frac·tion·al·ly** *Murphy, Sinclair's young team-mate, was fractionally behind him.* **2** A **fraction** is a number that can be expressed as a ratio of two whole numbers. For example, $\frac{1}{2}$ and $\frac{1}{3}$ are fractions.
◆◆◇◇◇ N-COUNT
ADJ-GRADED
ADV
N-COUNT

frac·tious /ˈfrækʃəs/. If you describe someone as **fractious**, you disapprove of them because they get angry or start quarrelling very easily.
ADJ-GRADED PRAGMATICS

frac·ture /ˈfræktʃə/ **fractures, fracturing, fractured. 1** If something such as a bone **is fractured** or **fractures**, it becomes cracked or broken. *You've fractured a rib... One strut had fractured... He suffered a fractured skull.* ▶ Also a noun. *At least one-third of all women over ninety have sustained a hip fracture.* **2** If something such as an organization or society **is fractured** or **fractures**, it splits so that it is in several parts or ceases to exist. *His policy risks fracturing the coalition. ...a society that could fracture along class lines. ...in a world of fractured cultures and global interdependence.*
◆◆◇◇◇ V-ERG V n V-ed N-COUNT
V-ERG V n V-ed FORMAL

frag·ile /ˈfrædʒaɪl, AM -dʒəl/. **1** If you describe a situation as **fragile**, you mean that it is weak or uncertain, and unlikely to be able to resist strong pressure or attack. *...the fragile economies of several southern African nations.* ♦ **fra·gil·ity** /frəˈdʒɪlɪti/ *...the extreme fragility of the Right-wing coalition.* **2** Something that is **fragile** is easily broken or damaged. *He leaned back in his fragile chair.* ♦ **fragility** *...the fragility of their bones.* **3** Something that is **fragile** is very delicate or fine in appearance. *...her fragile beauty.*
◆◆◇◇◇ ADJ-GRADED JOURNALISM
N-UNCOUNT
ADJ-GRADED
N-UNCOUNT
ADJ-GRADED

frag·ment, fragments, fragmenting, fragmented. The noun is pronounced /ˈfræɡmənt/. The verb is pronounced /fræɡˈment/. **1** A **fragment** of something is a small piece or part of it. *...glass fragments... She read everything, digesting every fragment of news.* **2** If something **fragments**, it breaks or separates into small pieces or parts. *Fierce rivalries have traditionally fragmented the region... Buddhism was in danger of fragmenting into small sects.* ♦ **frag·men·ta·tion** /ˌfræɡmenˈteɪʃən/ *...the extraordinary fragmentation of styles on the music scene.* ♦ **frag·ment·ed** *Europe had become infinitely more unstable and fragmented.*
◆◆◇◇◇
N-COUNT
V-ERG: V V into n
N-UNCOUNT
ADJ-GRADED

frag·men·tary /ˈfræɡməntəri, AM -teri/. Something that is **fragmentary** is made up of small or unconnected pieces. *...fragmentary evidence.*
ADJ-GRADED

fra·grance /ˈfreɪɡrəns/ **fragrances. 1** A **fragrance** is a pleasant or sweet smell. *...a shrubby plant with a strong characteristic fragrance.* **2** In advertising, a perfume is sometimes referred to as a **fragrance**.
◆◆◇◇◇ N-VAR
N-VAR

fra·grant /ˈfreɪɡrənt/. Something that is **fragrant** has a pleasant, sweet smell. *The air was fragrant with the smell of orange blossoms.*
◆◇◇◇◇ ADJ-GRADED

frail /freɪl/ **frailer, frailest. 1** Someone who is **frail** is not very strong or healthy. **2** Something that is **frail** is easily broken or damaged. *The frail craft rocked as he clambered in.*
◆◇◇◇◇ ADJ-GRADED ADJ-GRADED

frail·ty /ˈfreɪlti/ **frailties. 1** If you refer to the **frailties** or **frailty** of people, you are referring to their moral weaknesses. *...a triumph of will over human*
N-VAR

frailty. **2 Frailty** is the condition of being weak in health. N-UNCOUNT

frame /freɪm/ **frames, framing, framed. 1** The **frame** of a picture or mirror is the wooden, metal, plastic, or glass part around its edges. *...picture frames. ...a photograph of her mother in a silver frame.* **2** If a picture or photograph **is framed**, it is put in a frame. *...a large framed photograph.* **3** If an object **is framed** by a particular thing, it is surrounded by that thing in a way that makes the object more striking or attractive to look at. *The swimming pool is framed by tropical gardens.* **4** A **frame** of cinema film is one of the many separate photographs that it consists of. *Standard 8mm projects at 16 frames per second.* ◆◆◇◇ N-COUNT; VERB: be V-ed / VERB be V-ed prep; N-COUNT

5 The **frame** of an object such as a building, chair, or window consists of the wooden, metal, or plastic bars between which other material is fitted, and which give the object its strength and shape. *We painted our table to match the window frame.* **6** The **frames** of a pair of glasses are all the metal or plastic parts of it, but not the lenses. *...spectacles with gold wire frames.* **7** You can refer to someone's body as their **frame**, especially when you are describing its general shape. *...their bony frames.* **8** See also **cold frame**. N-COUNT; N-COUNT; N-COUNT

9 If someone **frames** something such as a set of rules, a plan, or a system, they create and develop it. *A convention was set up to frame a constitution.* **10** If someone **frames** something in a particular style or kind of language, they express it in that way. *The story is framed in a format that is part thriller, part love story... Let me frame the question a little differently.* VERB V n WRITTEN / VERB be V-ed prep/adv V n prep/adv

11 If someone **frames** an innocent person, they make other people think that person is guilty of a crime, by lying or inventing evidence. *He claimed that he had been framed by the police.* VERB: V n be V-ed

,frame of 'mind, frames of mind. Your frame **of mind** is your general mood or attitude at a particular time. *Lewis was not in the right frame of mind to continue.* ◆◇◇◇ N-COUNT

,frame of 'reference, frames of reference. A **frame of reference** is a particular set of beliefs, ideas, or observations on which you base your judgment of things. *We know we're dealing with someone with a different frame of reference.* N-COUNT

frame·work /ˈfreɪmwɜːk/ **frameworks. 1** A **framework** is a set of rules or ideas which you use in order to deal with problems or to decide what to do. *...within the framework of federal regulations.* **2** A **framework** is a structure that forms a support or frame for something. *...wooden shelves on a steel framework.* ◆◆◇◇ N-COUNT; N-COUNT

franc /fræŋk/ **francs.** The **franc** is the unit of currency in France, Switzerland, Belgium, and some other countries where French is spoken. *The price of grapes has shot up to 32 francs a kilo.* ► The **franc** is also the currency system of one of these countries. *The French franc has begun rising against the mark.* ◆◆◇◇ N-COUNT: num N / N-SING: the N

fran·chise /ˈfræntʃaɪz/ **franchises, franchising, franchised. 1** If a large company or organization grants a **franchise** to a smaller company, the smaller company is allowed to sell the products of the larger company or participate in an activity controlled by the organization. *...the franchise to build and operate the tunnel... Talk to other franchise holders and ask them what they think.* **2** If a company **franchises** its business, it sells franchises to other companies, allowing them to sell its products. *...the franchised pizza business.* ◆ **fran·chis·er, franchisers.** A **franchiser** is an organization which sells franchises. ◆ **fran·chis·ing** One of the most important aspects of franchising is the reduced risk of business failure it offers to franchisees. **3** In politics, the **franchise** is the right to vote. *The 1867 Reform Act extended the franchise to much of the male working class. ...the introduction of universal franchise.* ◆◆◇◇ N-COUNT; VERB: V n V-ed; N-COUNT; N-UNCOUNT; N-UNCOUNT: also the N

fran·chi·see /ˌfræntʃaɪˈziː/ **franchisees.** A **franchisee** is a person or company that buys a franchise. ◆◇◇◇ N-COUNT

frank /fræŋk/ **franker, frankest; franks, franking, franked. 1** If someone is **frank**, they state or express things openly and honestly. *...a frank discussion... My client has been less than frank with me.* ◆ **frank·ly** You can talk frankly to me... He now frankly admits that much of his former playboy lifestyle was superficial. ◆ **frank·ness** The reaction to his frankness was hostile. **2** You use **frank** in the expressions **'to be frank'** and **'to be frank with you'** when expressing your honest opinion, especially when the person you are talking to might not agree with you. *To be frank, he could also be a bit of a bore.* ◆ **frankly** 'You don't give a damn about my feelings, do you.'—'Quite frankly, I don't.'... Frankly, Thomas, this question of your loan is beginning to worry me.* **3** When a letter or parcel is **franked**, it is marked with a symbol that shows that the proper charge has been paid or that no stamp is needed. *The letter was franked in London on August 6.* ◆◆◇◇ ADJ-GRADED; ADV-GRADED: ADV with v; N-UNCOUNT; v-link ADJ [PRAGMATICS]; ADV-GRADED; VB: usu passive be V-ed

frank·fur·ter /ˈfræŋkfɜːtə/ **frankfurters.** A **frankfurter** is a type of smoked sausage. N-COUNT

frank·in·cense /ˈfræŋkɪnsens/. **Frankincense** is a substance obtained from a tree. It is burned as incense. N-UNCOUNT

fran·tic /ˈfræntɪk/. If someone is **frantic**, they are behaving in a desperate, wild, or disorganized way because they are frightened, worried, or in a hurry. *A bird had been locked in and was by now quite frantic... A busy night in the restaurant can be frantic in the kitchen.* ◆ **fran·ti·cal·ly** /ˈfræntɪkli/ *She clutched frantically at Emily's arm... We have been frantically trying to save her life.* ◆◆◇◇ ADJ-GRADED; ADV-GRADED: ADV with v

fra·ter·nal /frəˈtɜːnəl/. **Fraternal** actions show strong links of friendship between two people or groups. *...the fraternal assistance of our colleagues and comrades.* ADJ-GRADED FORMAL

fra·ter·nity /frəˈtɜːnɪti/ **fraternities. 1** Fraternity is friendship and mutual support between people who feel they are closely linked to each other. *Bob needs the fraternity of others who share his mission.* **2** You can refer to people who have the same profession or interests as a particular **fraternity**. *...the criminal fraternity. ...the sailing fraternity.* **3** In the United States, a **fraternity** is a society of male students at a university or college. ◆◇◇◇ N-UNCOUNT FORMAL; N-COLL-COUNT; N-COUNT

frat·er·nize /ˈfrætənaɪz/ **fraternizes, fraternizing, fraternized;** also spelled **fraternise** in British English. If you **fraternize** with someone, you associate with them in a friendly way. *Executives fraternized with the key personnel of other banks... Groups fraternise in an atmosphere of mutual support.* V-RECIP V with n pl-n V

frat·ri·cid·al /ˌfrætrɪˈsaɪdəl/. In a **fratricidal** war or conflict, people kill members of their own society or social group. ADJ: ADJ n

fraud /frɔːd/ **frauds. 1** Fraud is the crime of gaining money or financial benefits by deceit or trickery. *He was jailed for two years for fraud... Tax frauds are dealt with by the Inland Revenue.* **2** A **fraud** is something or someone that deceives people in an illegal or dishonest way. *Unfortunately the portraits were frauds... He believes many 'psychics' are frauds.* **3** If you call someone or something a **fraud**, you are criticizing them because you think that they are not genuine, or are less good than they claim or appear to be. *You're a fraud and a spy, Simons... UNITA is denouncing the vote as a fraud.* ◆◆◇◇ N-VAR; N-COUNT; N-COUNT [PRAGMATICS]

fraud·ster /ˈfrɔːdstə/ **fraudsters.** A **fraudster** is someone who commits the crime of fraud. N-COUNT BRITISH, JOURNALISM

fraudu·lent /ˈfrɔːdʒʊlənt/. A **fraudulent** activity is deceitful or dishonest. *...fraudulent claims about being a nurse.* ◆ **fraudu·lent·ly** All 5,000 of the homes were fraudulently obtained. ◆◇◇◇ ADJ; ADV: ADV with v

fraught /frɔːt/. **1** If a situation or action is **fraught with** problems or risks, it is filled with them. *Operations employing this technique were fraught with dangers.* **2** If you say that a situation or action is **fraught**, you mean that it is worrying or stressful. *It has been a most fraught day.* ◆◇◇◇ v-link ADJ with n; ADJ-GRADED

fray /freɪ/ **frays, fraying, frayed. 1** If something such as cloth or rope **frays**, or if something **frays** it, ◆◇◇◇ V-ERG V

its threads or fibres start to come apart from each other. *The fabric is very fine or frays easily... The stitching had begun to fray at the edges.* **2** If you say that something **is fraying at the edges** or **is fraying around the edges**, you mean that it is becoming uncertain or unstable. *There are signs that the alliance is now fraying at the edges.* **3** If people's nerves or people's tempers **fray**, or if something **frays** them, they feel irritable and nervous because of mental strain and anxiety. *Tempers began to fray as the two teams failed to score... This kind of living was beginning to fray her nerves.* ♦ **frayed** *Nerves became severely frayed when air traffic problems delayed the flight.* **4 The fray** is an exciting or challenging activity, situation, or argument that you are involved in. *...a second round of voting when new candidates can enter the fray.*

freak /friːk/ **freaks, freaking, freaked.** **1** A freak event or action is very unusual or extreme. *...a freak accident.* **2** People are sometimes referred to as **freaks** when their behaviour or appearance is very different from that of most people; used showing disapproval. *Not so long ago, transsexuals were regarded as freaks.* **3** If you describe someone as a particular kind of **freak**, you are emphasizing that they are very enthusiastic about something. *...health freaks. ...computer freaks.* ● See also **control freak**. **4** If someone **freaks**, or if something **freaks** them, they suddenly feel extremely surprised, upset, angry, or confused. *I saw five cop cars pull into the driveway. And I literally freaked... I think our music freaks people out sometimes.* ► **Freak out** means the same as **freak**. *The first time I went onstage, I freaked out completely... I think our music freaks people out sometimes.*

freak·ish /ˈfriːkɪʃ/. Something that is **freakish** is remarkable because it is not normal or natural. *...his freakish voice.*

freaky /ˈfriːki/ **freakier, freakiest.** If someone or something is **freaky**, they are very unusual in some way. *This guy bore a really freaky resemblance to Jones.*

freck·le /ˈfrekəl/ **freckles.** If someone has **freckles**, they have small light brown spots on their skin. ♦ **freck·led** /ˈfrekəld/. If a part of someone's body is **freckled**, it has freckles on it.

free /friː/ **freer, freest; frees, freeing, freed.** **1** If something is **free**, you can have it or use it without paying for it. *The seminars are free. ...a free brochure.* ● **free of charge**: see **charge**. **2** If you do something or get something **for free**, you do it without being paid or get it without having to pay for it. *I wasn't expecting you to do it for free.* **3** Someone or something that is **free** is not restricted, controlled, or limited, for example by rules, customs, or other people. *The government will be free to pursue its economic policies... The elections were free and fair.* ♦ **free·ly** *They cast their votes freely and without coercion.* **4** You say '**feel free**' to someone who has asked you if they can do something as an informal way of giving them permission. You say '**feel free to** do something' as an informal way of telling someone that you do not mind them doing it. *Go right ahead. Feel free... If you have any questions at all, please feel free to ask me.* **5** If you **free** someone of something that is unpleasant or restricting, you remove it from them. *It will free us of a whole lot of debt.* **6** If someone or something is **free of** or **free from** an unpleasant or unwanted thing, they do not have it or they are not affected by it. *...a future far more free of fear.* ► Also a combining form. *...a salt-free diet.* **7** If a sum of money or type of goods is **free of** tax or duty, you do not have to pay tax or duty on it. ● See also **duty-free**, **interest-free, tax-free**. **8** Someone who is **free** is no longer a prisoner or a slave. *He walked from the court house a free man... More than ninety prisoners have been set free.* **9** To **free** a prisoner or slave means to release them. **10** If something **frees** someone or something, it makes

them available for a task or function that they were previously unavailable for. *Toolbelts free both hands and lessen the risk of dropping hammers... His deal with Disney will run out shortly, freeing him to pursue his own project.* ► **Free up** means the same as **free**. *It can handle even the most complex graphic jobs, freeing up your computer for other tasks.* **11** If you have a **free** period of time or are **free** at a particular time, you are not working or occupied then. *She spent her free time shopping. ...free periods at school.* **12** If something such as a table or seat is **free**, it is not being used or occupied, or is not reserved for someone to use. **13** If you get something **free**, or if it gets **free**, it is no longer trapped by something or attached to something. *...attempts to pull the vessel free of the rig... He pulled his arm free.* **14** If you **free** someone or something, you remove or loosen them from the place where they have been trapped or become fixed. *It took firemen two hours to cut through the drive belt to free him.* **15** When someone is using only one hand to hold or move something, you can refer to their other hand as their **free** one. *He snatched up the receiver and his free hand groped for the switch on the bedside lamp.* **16** ● **to give** someone **a free hand**: see **hand**. **17** If you say that someone is **free with** something such as advice or money, you mean they give or spend a lot of it; used showing disapproval.

free up. 1 See free 10. **2** To **free up** a market, economy, or system means to make it operate with fewer restrictions and controls. *...policies for freeing up markets and extending competition.*

free 'agent, free agents. 1 If you say that someone is a **free agent**, you are emphasizing that they can do whatever they want to do, because they are not responsible to anyone or for anyone. *We are not free agents; we abide by the decisions of our president.* **2** If a sports player is a **free agent**, he or she is free to sign a contract with any team.

free and 'easy. Someone or something that is **free and easy** is casual, informal, and tolerant. *...the free and easy atmosphere of these cafés.*

free·bie /ˈfriːbi/ **freebies.** A **freebie** is something that you are given, usually by a company, without having to pay for it.

free·dom /ˈfriːdəm/ **freedoms. 1** Freedom is the state of being allowed to do what you want. **Freedoms** are instances of this. *...freedom of speech. ...the need for individual freedoms and human rights.* **2** When prisoners or slaves are set free or escape, they gain their **freedom**. *All hostages and detainees would gain their freedom.* **3 Freedom from** something you do not want means not being affected by it. *...freedom from government control.* **4 The freedom of** a particular city is a special honour which is given to a famous person who is connected with that city, or to someone who has performed some special service for the city. *He was given the Freedom of the City of Dublin by the Lord Mayor.*

'freedom fighter, freedom fighters. If you refer to someone as a **freedom fighter**, you mean that they belong to a group that is trying to overthrow the government of their country using violent methods, and you approve of this.

free 'enterprise. Free enterprise is an economic system in which businesses compete for profit without much government control.

'free fall, free falls; also spelled **free-fall. 1** In economics, if the value or price of something goes into **free fall**, it starts to fall uncontrollably. *Sterling went into free fall.* **2** In parachuting, **free fall** is the part of the jump before the parachute opens.

free-'floating. Free-floating things or people are able to move freely and are not controlled or directed by anything. *...a system of free-floating exchange rates.*

Free·fone /ˈfriːfəʊn/; also spelled **Freephone.** A **Freefone** telephone number is one which you can dial without having to pay for the call. The American word is **toll-free. Freefone** is a trademark.

'free-for-all, free-for-alls. A free-for-all is a dis- N-SING
organized fight, argument, or attempt to get something in which everyone joins in.

'free form; also spelled **free-form.** A free form ADJ: ADJ n
work of art or piece of music has not been created
according to a standard style or convention. *...free-
form jazz.*

free·hand /'friːhænd/. A freehand drawing is drawn ADJ: ADJ n
without using instruments such as a ruler or compasses. ▶ Also an adverb. *Use a template or stencil* ADV:
or simply do it freehand. ADV after v

free·hold /'friːhəʊld/ **freeholds. 1** If you have the N-VAR
freehold of a building or piece of land, it is yours
for life and there are no conditions regarding your
ownership. **♦ free·holder, freeholders.** A free- N-COUNT
holder is someone who owns the freehold to a particular piece of land. **2** If a building or piece of land ADJ
is **freehold**, you can own it for life.

,free 'kick, free kicks. In football, when there is ◆◇◇◇◇
a **free kick**, a member of one side can kick the ball N-COUNT
without opposition because a member of the other
side has broken a rule.

free·lance /'friːlɑːns, -læns/ **freelances, free-** ◆◇◇◇◇
lancing, freelanced. 1 Someone who does ADJ
freelance work or who is, for example, a **freelance**
journalist or photographer is not employed by one
organization, but is paid for each piece of work they
do by the organization they do it for. *She decided to*
go freelance. ▶ Also an adverb. *He is now working* ADV:
freelance. ▶ A **freelance** is someone who does free- ADV after v
lance work. **2** If you **freelance**, you do freelance N-COUNT
work. *She has freelanced as a writer and researcher.* VERB
♦ free·lancer, freelancers *As freelancers we* V as n
weren't pinned down to regular jobs. N-COUNT

free·loader /'friːləʊdə/ **freeloaders.** If you refer N-COUNT
to someone as a **freeloader**, you disapprove of them PRAGMATICS
because they take advantage of other people's gen- INFORMAL
erosity, without giving anything in return.

,free 'love. A belief in **free love** is the belief that it N-UNCOUNT
is acceptable and good to have sexual relationships DATED
without marrying, often several relationships at the
same time.

free·ly /'friːli/. **1** You use **freely** to indicate that ◆◆◇◇◇
something happens or is done many times or in ADV-GRADED:
large quantities, often without restraint. *We have re-* ADV after v,
ferred freely to his ideas... Consumer goods are freely ADV adj
available. **2** If you can talk **freely**, you can talk with- ADV-GRADED:
out needing to be careful about what you say. ADV after v
...someone to whom he could talk freely. **3** If some- ADV-GRADED:
one gives or does something **freely**, they give or do ADV with v
it willingly, without being ordered or forced to do it.
Danny shared his knowledge freely. **4** If something ADV-GRADED:
or someone moves **freely**, they move easily and ADV after v
smoothly, without any obstacles or resistance. *The*
clay court was slippery and he was unable to move
freely. **5** See also **free**.

free·man /'friːmən/ **freemen.** Someone who is a N-COUNT
freeman of a city has been given a special honour
by that city, known as the freedom of the city.

,free-market'eer, free-marketeers. A free- N-COUNT
marketeer is a politician who is in favour of letting
market forces regulate the economy.

Free·mason /'friːmeɪsən/ **Freemasons.** A Free- N-COUNT
mason is a man who is a member of a large secret
society. Freemasons promise to help each other,
and use a system of secret signs in order to recognize each other. **♦ Free·masonry** /'friːmeɪsənri/. N-UNCOUNT
Freemasonry refers to the beliefs and practices of
the Freemasons.

Free·phone /'friːfəʊn/. See **Freefone**.

'free port, free ports. A **free port** is a port or air- N-COUNT
port where goods can be brought in from foreign
countries without payment of duty if they are going
to be exported again.

Free·post /'friːpəʊst/. In Britain, **Freepost** is a N-UNCOUNT
system which allows you to send mail to certain
organizations without paying for the postage.
'Freepost' is written on the envelope as part of the
address.

'free-range. **Free-range** means relating to a sys- ADJ
tem of keeping animals in which they can move and
feed freely on open ground. *...free-range eggs.*

free·sia /'friːʒə/ **freesias.** Freesias are small plants N-VAR
with yellow, pink, white, or purple tubular flowers.

,free 'spirit, free spirits. If you describe someone N-COUNT
as a **free spirit**, you admire them because they live PRAGMATICS
as they want to, rather than in a conventional way.

,free-'standing. A **free-standing** object is not ADJ
fixed to anything or stands on its own away from
other things. *...a free-standing cooker.*

free·style /'friːstaɪl/. **Freestyle** is used to describe ◆◇◇◇◇
sports competitions, especially in swimming, wres- ADJ: ADJ n
tling, and skiing, in which competitors can use any
style or method that they like when they take part.
...the 100m freestyle swimming event. ▶ Also a N-SING
noun. *She won the 800 metres freestyle.*

,free-'thinker, free-thinkers. If you refer to N-COUNT
someone as a **free-thinker**, you admire them be- PRAGMATICS
cause they work out their own ideas rather than accepting generally accepted views.

free·way /'friːweɪ/ **freeways.** A freeway is a ma- ◆◇◇◇◇
jor road that has been specially built for fast travel N-COUNT
over long distances. The usual British word is AMERICAN
motorway.

free·wheel /,friːˈwiːl/ **freewheels, freewheel-** VERB: V
ing, freewheeled; also spelled **free-wheel.** If you V adv/prep
freewheel, you travel, usually downhill, on a bicycle
without using the pedals or in a motor vehicle without using the engine. *He freewheeled back down the*
course.

free·wheel·ing /,friːˈwiːlɪŋ/; also spelled **free-** ADJ
wheeling. If you refer to someone's **freewheeling**
lifestyle or attitudes, you mean that they behave in
a casual, relaxed way without feeling restricted by
rules or accepted ways of doing things.

,free 'will. 1 If you believe in **free will**, you believe ◆◇◇◇◇
that people choose what they do and that their ac- N-UNCOUNT
tions are not decided in advance by God or Fate.
2 If you do something **of** your **own free will**, you do PHRASE
it by choice and not because you are forced to.

freeze /friːz/ **freezes, freezing, froze, frozen.** ◆◆◆◇◇
1 If a liquid **freezes**, or if something **freezes** it, it be- V-ERG
comes solid because of low temperature. *If the* V n
temperature drops below 0°C, water freezes. ...how to
freeze water at higher temperatures. **2** If you **freeze** V-ERG
something such as food, you preserve it by storing it V n
at a temperature below freezing point. You can also V adv
talk about how well food **freezes**. *You can freeze the*
soup at this stage... Most fresh herbs will freeze suc-
cessfully. **3** If something such as a pipe or machine VERB: V
freezes, it becomes blocked or stiff with ice or frozen liquid. **4** If you **freeze**, you feel extremely cold. VERB
Your hands will freeze doing this. V

5 If someone who is moving **freezes**, they suddenly VERB
stop and become completely still. *She froze when the* V
beam of the flashlight struck her.

6 If the government or a company **freeze** things such VERB: V n
as prices or wages, they state officially that they will
not allow them to increase for a fixed period of time.
▶ Also a noun. *...a wage freeze.* **7** If a government N-COUNT
freezes a plan or process, they state officially that they VERB: V n
will not allow it to continue for a period of time.
▶ Also a noun. *...a freeze in nuclear weapons pro-* N-COUNT
grams. **8** If someone in authority **freezes** something VERB: V n
such as a bank account, fund, or property, they obtain
a legal order which states that it cannot be used or
sold for a particular period of time. ▶ Also a noun. *...a* N-COUNT:
freeze on private savings. with supp
9 See also **freezing, frozen.**

freeze out. If you **freeze** someone **out** of an activity PHRASAL VB
or situation, you prevent them from being involved in V n P of n
it by creating difficulties or by being unfriendly. *I* V n P
started by freezing her out and keeping information
from her.

freeze over. If something **freezes over**, it becomes PHRASAL VB
covered with a layer of ice or other frozen substance. V P

freeze up. If something **freezes up**, or if something PHRASAL VB
freezes it **up**, it becomes completely covered or ERG
blocked with ice. *...lavatories that often freeze up in* V P
    V P noun

winter... Ice could freeze up their torpedo release mechanisms.

'**freeze-dried.** Freeze-dried food has been pre- ADJ
served by a process of rapid freezing and drying.

'**freeze-frame, freeze-frames.** A **freeze-frame** N-COUNT
from a film is an individual picture from it, produced by stopping the film or video tape at a particular point.

freez·er /'fri:zə/ **freezers.** A **freezer** is a fridge in ◆◇◇◇◇
which the temperature is kept below freezing point N-COUNT
so that you can store food inside it for long periods.

freez·ing /'fri:zɪŋ/ **1** If you say that something or ◆◇◇◇◇
someone is **freezing** or **freezing cold**, you are emphasizing that you are very cold. *...a freezing Janu-*
ary afternoon... 'You must be freezing,' she said. [PRAGMATICS]
2 **Freezing** means the same as **freezing point**. *It's* N-UNCOUNT
15 degrees below freezing. **3** See also **freeze.**

'**freezing point, freezing points;** also spelled
freezing-point. 1 **Freezing point** is 0° Celsius, the N-COUNT
temperature at which water freezes. *The tempera-*
ture remained below freezing point throughout the
day. **2** The **freezing point** of a substance is the tem- N-COUNT
perature at which it freezes.

freight /freɪt/ **freights, freighting, freighted.** ◆◆◇◇◇
1 **Freight** is the movement of goods by lorries, N-UNCOUNT
trains, ships, or aeroplanes. **2** **Freight** is goods that N-UNCOUNT
are transported by lorries, trains, ships, or aero-
planes. *...26 tons of freight.* **3** When goods are VB: usu
freighted, they are transported in large quantities passive
over a long distance. *The grain is freighted down to* beV-ed adv/
Addis Ababa. prep

freight·er /'freɪtə/ **freighters.** A **freighter** is a ◆◇◇◇◇
large ship or aeroplane that is designed for carrying N-COUNT
freight.

'**freight train, freight trains.** A **freight train** is a N-COUNT
train on which goods are transported.

,**French 'bean, French beans.** French beans are N-COUNT
long very narrow beans that are green in colour and BRITISH
are eaten as a vegetable. The American expression
is **string beans**. See picture headed **vegetables.**

,**French 'door, French doors.** French doors are N-COUNT
the same as **French windows.**

,**French 'dressing.** French dressing is a sauce N-UNCOUNT
which you put on salad.

,**French 'fries.** French fries are long thin pieces of N-PLURAL
potato fried in oil or fat.

,**French 'horn, French horns.** A French horn is N-VAR
a musical instrument which is shaped like a long
metal tube wound round in a circle with a wide funnel at one end. See picture headed **musical**
instruments.

,**French 'window, French windows.** French N-COUNT
windows are a pair of glass doors which you go
through into a garden or onto a balcony.

fre·net·ic /frɪ'netɪk/. **Frenetic** activity is fast and ◆◇◇◇◇
energetic, but rather uncontrolled. *...the frenetic* ADJ-GRADED
pace of life in New York. ◆ **fre·neti·cal·ly** ADV
/frɪ'netɪkli/ *Steve and I worked frenetically.*

fren·zy /'frenzi/ **frenzies.** Frenzy or a frenzy is ◆◇◇◇◇
great excitement or wild behaviour that often re- N-VAR
sults from losing control of your feelings. *'Get out!'*
she ordered in a frenzy. ◆ **fren·zied.** Fren- ADJ-GRADED
zied activities or actions are wild, excited, and uncontrolled. *The man was stabbed to death in a fren-*
zied attack.

fre·quen·cy /'fri:kwənsi/ **frequencies. 1** The fre- ◆◆◇◇◇
quency of an event is the number of times it hap- N-UNCOUNT
pens during a particular period. *The frequency of*
Kara's phone calls increased.
2 The **frequency** of a sound wave or a radio wave is N-VAR
the number of times it vibrates within a specified pe- TECHNICAL
riod of time.

fre·quent, frequents, frequenting, frequent- ◆◆◆◇◇
ed. The adjective is pronounced /'fri:kwənt/. The
verb is pronounced /frɪ'kwent/. **1** If something is ADJ-GRADED
frequent, it happens often. *He is a frequent visitor*
to the house. ◆ **fre·quent·ly** *Iron and folic acid sup-* ADV-GRADED
plements are frequently given to pregnant women.
2 If someone **frequents** a particular place, they regu- VERB: V n
larly go there. FORMAL

fres·co /'freskəʊ/ **frescoes** or **frescos.** A fresco ◆◇◇◇◇
is a picture that is painted on a plastered wall when N-COUNT
the plaster is still wet. ● See also **alfresco.**

fresh /freʃ/ **fresher, freshest. 1** A **fresh** thing or ◆◆◆◇
amount replaces or is added to a previous thing or ADJ: ADJ n
amount. *Make fresh inquiries... I need a new chal-*
lenge and a fresh start. **2** Something that is **fresh** ADJ-GRADED
has been done, made, or experienced recently.
There were no fresh car tracks. ...with the memory of
the bombing fresh in her mind. ▶ Also a combining COMB
form. *...a vase of fresh-cut flowers.* ◆ **fresh·ly** ADV:
...freshly baked bread. ADV -ed

3 **Fresh** food has been picked or produced recently, ADJ-GRADED
and has not been preserved. *...locally caught fresh*
fish. ◆ **fresh·ness** As with all seafood, freshness N-UNCOUNT
equals quality. **4** If you describe something as **fresh,** ADJ-GRADED
you like it because it is new and exciting. *These design-*
ers are full of fresh ideas. ◆ **freshness** There was a N-UNCOUNT
freshness and enthusiasm about the new students. **5** If ADJ-GRADED
you describe something as **fresh,** you mean that it is
pleasant, bright, and clean in appearance. *Gingham*
fabrics always look fresh and pretty. ◆ **freshness** N-UNCOUNT
...the crisp freshness of laundered clothes. **6** If some- ADJ-GRADED
thing smells, tastes, or feels **fresh,** it is clean, cool, or
refreshing. *The air was fresh.* ◆ **freshness** *...the* N-UNCOUNT
freshness of early morning.

7 **Fresh** water is water that is not salty, for example ADJ
the water from rivers, lakes, or reservoirs. **8** If you say ADJ-GRADED
that the weather is **fresh,** you mean that it is fairly cold
and windy. **9** If someone has a **fresh** face or complex- ADJ-GRADED
ion, their skin looks healthy. **10** If you feel **fresh,** you ADJ-GRADED
feel full of energy and enthusiasm. *It's vital we are as*
fresh as possible for those matches. **11** If you **are fresh** ADJ:
from a particular place or experience, you have just v-link ADJ
come from that place or you have just had that experi- from/out of n
ence. You can also say that someone **is fresh out of** a
place. *I returned to the office, fresh from Heathrow.*

,**fresh 'air.** You can describe the air outside as ◆◇◇◇◇
fresh air, especially when you mean that it is good N-UNCOUNT:
for you because it is not polluted. also the N

fresh·en /'freʃən/ **freshens, freshening, fresh-** VERB: V
ened. If the wind **freshens,** it becomes stronger
and colder.

freshen up. 1 If you **freshen** something **up,** you PHRASAL VB
make it clean and pleasant in appearance or smell. *A* V n P
thorough brushing helps to freshen up your mouth. V P noun
2 If you **freshen up,** you wash your hands and face V P
and make yourself look neat and tidy.

fresh·er /'freʃə/ **freshers.** Freshers are students N-COUNT
who are in their first year at university or college. INFORMAL,
The usual American term is **freshmen.** BRITISH

fresh·man /'freʃmən/ **freshmen.** Freshman are ◆◇◇◇◇
students who are in their first year at university or N-COUNT
college. The usual British term is **fresher.** AMERICAN

fresh·water /'freʃwɔːtə/. A **freshwater** lake con- ◆◇◇◇◇
tains water that is not salty, usually in contrast to ADJ: ADJ n
the sea. **Freshwater** creatures live in lakes, ponds,
and rivers which are not salty.

fret /fret/ **frets, fretting, fretted. 1** If you **fret** ◆◇◇◇◇
about something, you worry about it. *Congressional* VERB
staffers fret that the project will eventually cost bil- V that
lions more. ◆ **fret·ful** /'fretfʊl/. If someone is **fret-** ADJ-GRADED
ful, they behave in a way that shows that they are
worried or unhappy about something. *Don't assume*
your baby automatically needs feeding if she's fretful.
2 The **frets** on a stringed instrument such as a guitar N-COUNT
are the metal ridges across its neck.

fret·work /'fretwɜːk/. **Fretwork** is wood or metal N-UNCOUNT
that has been decorated by cutting bits of it out to
make a pattern.

Freud·ian /'frɔɪdiən/. **Freudian** means relating to ADJ
the ideas and methods of the psychiatrist Freud.
...the Freudian theory about daughters falling in love
with their father.

,**Freudian 'slip, Freudian slips.** If someone acci- N-COUNT
dentally says something that reveals their subconscious feelings, this is referred to as a **Freudian slip.**

Fri. Fri. is a written abbreviation for **Friday.** ◆◆◇◇◇

fri·ar /'fraɪə/ **friars.** A **friar** is a member of one of ◆◇◇◇◇
several Catholic religious orders. N-COUNT

fric·tion /ˈfrɪkʃən/ **frictions. 1** Friction between people is disagreement and argument between them. *There had been friction between her children.* **2** Friction is the force that makes it difficult for things to move freely when they are touching each other. **3** Friction is the rubbing of one object against another. *...the friction of his leg against hers.*

Fri·day /ˈfraɪdeɪ, -di/ **Fridays.** Friday is the day after Thursday and before Saturday.

fridge /frɪdʒ/ **fridges.** A fridge is a large metal container which is kept cool, usually by electricity, so that food that is put in it stays fresh. The usual American word is **refrigerator**.

friend /frend/ **friends. 1** A friend is someone who you know well and like, but who is not related to you. *...my best friend.* **2** If you are **friends** with someone, you are their friend and they are yours. **3** If you **make friends** with someone, you begin a friendship with them. You can also say that two people **make friends**. **4** The **friends** of an organization, a country, or a cause are the people and organizations who help and support them. *...The Friends of Birmingham Royal Ballet.* **5** If one country refers to another as a **friend**, they mean that the other country is not an enemy of theirs.

friend·less /ˈfrendləs/. Someone who is **friendless** has no friends.

friend·ly /ˈfrendli/ **friendlier, friendliest; friendlies. 1** If someone is **friendly**, they behave in a pleasant kind way, and like to be with other people. *...a man with a pleasant, friendly face.* **♦ friend·li·ness** *She also loves the friendliness of the people.* **2** If you are **friendly** with someone, you like each other and enjoy spending time together. *I'm friendly with his mother.* **3** You can describe a country or their government as **friendly** when they have good relations with your own country rather than being an enemy. *...a worsening in relations between the two previously friendly countries.* **4** In sport, a **friendly** is a match which is not part of a competition, and is played for entertainment or practice, often without any serious effort to win. **▶** Also an adjective. *...a friendly match.*

-friendly /-ˈfrendli/. **1** **-friendly** combines with nouns to form adjectives which describe things that are not harmful to the specified part of the natural world. *Palm oil is environment-friendly. ...ozone-friendly fridges.* **2** **-friendly** combines with nouns to form adjectives which describe things which are intended for or suitable for the specified person. *...customer-friendly banking facilities.* **●** See also **user-friendly**.

ˈfriendly society, friendly societies. A friendly society is an organization to which people regularly pay small amounts of money and which gives them money when they retire or are ill.

friend·ship /ˈfrendʃɪp/ **friendships. 1** A friendship is a relationship between two or more friends. *...the quickest way to end a good friendship.* **2** You use **friendship** to refer in a general way to the state of being friends, or the feelings that friends have for each other. *...a hobby which led to a whole new world of friendship and adventure.* **3** If you have someone's **friendship**, they are your friend. *He had the friendship of Terry Jones.* **4** Friendship is a relationship between two countries in which they help and support each other. *...targets for the future to promote friendship with East Europe.*

frieze /friːz/ **friezes.** A frieze is a decoration high up on the walls of a room or just under the roof of a building. It consists of a long panel of carving or a long strip of paper with a picture or pattern on it.

frig·ate /ˈfrɪɡət/ **frigates.** A frigate is a fairly small naval ship that can move at fast speeds.

frig·ging /ˈfrɪɡɪŋ/. Some people use **frigging** to emphasize that they are angry or annoyed about something; some people find this word offensive.

fright /fraɪt/ **frights. 1** Fright is a sudden feeling of fear. *Franklin uttered a shriek and jumped with fright... To hide my fright I asked a question.* **2** A

fright is an experience which makes you suddenly afraid. *The last time you had a real fright, you nearly crashed the car.* **3** If a person or animal **takes fright** at something, they are suddenly frightened by it. *An untrained horse had taken fright at the sound of gunfire.* **● the fright of your life**: see **life**.

fright·en /ˈfraɪtən/ **frightens, frightening, frightened. 1** If something or someone **frightens** you, they cause you to suddenly feel afraid, anxious, or nervous. *He knew that Soli was trying to frighten him.* **♦ fright·ened** *She was frightened of flying.* **2** If something **frightens the life out of** you, **frightens the wits out of** you, or **frightens** you **out of** your **wits**, it causes you to feel suddenly afraid or gives you a very unpleasant shock.

frighten away or **frighten off. 1** If you **frighten away** a person or animal, or **frighten** them **off**, you make them afraid so that they run away or stay some distance away from you. *The fishermen said the company's seismic survey was frightening away fish.* **2** To **frighten** someone **away** or **frighten** them **off** means to make them nervous so that they decide not to do something. *Building society repossessions have frightened buyers off.*

frighten into. If you **frighten** someone **into** doing something they would not normally do, you make them do it by making them afraid not to do it.

frighten off. See **frighten away**.

fright·en·ing /ˈfraɪtənɪŋ/. If something is **frightening**, it makes you feel afraid, anxious, or nervous. *It was a very frightening experience and they were very courageous.* **♦ fright·en·ing·ly** *The country is frighteningly close to possessing nuclear weapons.*

fright·ful /ˈfraɪtful/. **1** Frightful means very bad or unpleasant. *My father was unable to talk about the war, it was so frightful.* **2** Frightful is used to emphasize the extent or degree of something. *He got himself into a frightful muddle.* **♦ fright·ful·ly** *I'm most frightfully sorry about this.*

frig·id /ˈfrɪdʒɪd/. **1** Frigid means extremely cold. *The water was too frigid to allow him to remain submerged for long.* **2** If a woman is **frigid**, she finds it difficult to become sexually aroused. *My husband says I am frigid.* **♦ fri·gid·ity** /frɪˈdʒɪdɪti/ *After years of frigidity Angie had her first real orgasm.* **3** If you describe the atmosphere in a place or someone's behaviour as **frigid**, you mean that it is very formal and unfriendly. *'Well, dear,' her hostess would reply with a frigid smile.*

frill /frɪl/ **frills. 1** A frill is a long narrow strip of cloth or paper with many folds in it, which is attached to something as a decoration. **♦ frilled** *...a frilled shirt and floppy cravat.* **2** If you describe something as having no **frills**, you mean that it is simple and has no unnecessary or additional features; used showing approval. *This booklet restricts itself to facts without frills.*

frilly /ˈfrɪli/. Frilly items of clothing or fabric have a lot of frills on them. *...maids in frilly aprons.*

fringe /frɪndʒ/ **fringes. 1** A fringe is hair which is cut so that it hangs over your forehead. The usual American word is **bangs**. **2** A fringe is a decoration attached to clothes, or other objects such as lampshades, consisting of a row of hanging strips or threads. **3** To be **on the fringe** or the **fringes** of a place means to be on the outside edge of it. *...black townships located on the fringes of the city.* **4** The **fringe** or the **fringes** of an activity or organization are its less important, least typical, or most extreme parts, rather than its main and central part. *The Communist Party has always been on the fringe of British politics.*

ˈfringe benefit, fringe benefits. Fringe benefits are extra things that some people get from their job in addition to their salary, for example a car.

fringed /frɪndʒd/. **1** Fringed clothes, curtains, or lampshades are decorated with fringes. **2** If a place or object is **fringed with** something, that thing forms a border around it or is situated along its edges. *...tiny islands fringed with golden sand.*

frip·pery /ˈfrɪpəri/ **fripperies.** If you refer to something as **frippery**, you disapprove of it because it is trivial, extravagant, and only done or worn to impress people. *...all the fripperies with which the Edwardian woman indulged herself.* · N-UNCOUNT: also N in pl · PRAGMATICS · BRITISH

Fris·bee /ˈfrɪzbi/ **Frisbees.** A **Frisbee** is a light plastic disc that one person throws to another as a game. **Frisbee** is a trademark. · N-COUNT

frisk /frɪsk/ **frisks, frisking, frisked.** If someone **frisks** you, they search you in order to see if you are hiding a weapon or drugs in your clothes. · VERB: V n

frisky /ˈfrɪski/ **friskier, friskiest.** A **frisky** animal or person is energetic and playful, and may be difficult to control. · ADJ-GRADED

fris·son /ˈfriːsɒn, AM friːˈsɔun/ **frissons.** A **frisson** is a short, sudden feeling of excitement or fear. *A frisson of apprehension rippled round the theatre.* · N-COUNT

frit·ter /ˈfrɪtə/ **fritters, frittering, frittered.** **Fritters** are round pieces of fruit, vegetables, or meat that are dipped in batter and fried. · N-COUNT

fritter away. If someone **fritters away** time or money, they waste it on unimportant or unnecessary things. *The firm soon started frittering away the cash it was generating.* · PHRASAL VB · V P noun · Also V n P

fri·vol·ity /frɪˈvɒlɪti/ **frivolities.** If you refer to an activity as **frivolity**, you think that it is amusing and rather silly, rather than serious and sensible. *He was one of my most able pupils, but far too easily distracted by frivolities.* · N-VAR

frivo·lous /ˈfrɪvələs/. **1** If you describe someone as **frivolous**, you mean they behave in a silly or light-hearted way, rather than being serious and sensible. *Isabelle was a frivolous little fool.* **2** If you describe an activity as **frivolous**, you disapprove of it because it is not useful and wastes time or money. *...wasting public money on what it believes are frivolous projects.* · ◆◇◇◇◇ · ADJ-GRADED · ADJ-GRADED · PRAGMATICS

frizz /frɪz/. **Frizz** is frizzy hair. · N-UNCOUNT

friz·zy /ˈfrɪzi/ **frizzier, frizziest. Frizzy** hair is very thickly and stiffly curled. · ADJ-GRADED

fro /frəʊ/. ● **to and fro:** see **to**.

frock /frɒk/ **frocks.** A **frock** is a woman's or girl's dress. · N-COUNT · DATED

'frock coat, frock coats; also spelled **frock-coat.** A **frock coat** was a long coat that was worn by men in the 19th century. · N-COUNT

frog /frɒg, AM frɔːg/ **frogs. 1** A **frog** is a small creature with smooth skin, big eyes, and long back legs which it uses for jumping. Frogs usually live near water. **2** Some people refer to French people as **Frogs;** some people find this use offensive. · ◆◇◇◇◇ · N-COUNT · N-COUNT · INFORMAL

frog·man /ˈfrɒgmən, AM ˈfrɔːg-/ **frogmen.** A **frogman** is someone whose job involves diving and working underwater. · N-COUNT

'frog-march, frog-marches, frog-marching, frog-marched; also spelled **frogmarch.** If you are **frog-marched** somewhere, someone takes you there by force, holding you by the arms or another part of your body so that you have to walk along with them. *...arresting the men and frog-marching them to the local police station.* · VERB: · be V-ed · prep/adv · V n prep/adv

frog·spawn /ˈfrɒgspɔːn, AM ˈfrɔːg-/; also spelled **frog spawn. Frogspawn** is a soft jelly-like substance which contains the eggs of a frog. · N-UNCOUNT

'fro·ing. ● See **to-ing and fro-ing.**

frol·ic /ˈfrɒlɪk/ **frolics, frolicking, frolicked.** When people or animals **frolic**, they play or move in a lively, happy, and carefree way. *Tourists sunbathe and frolic in the ocean.* ▸ Also a noun. *Their relationship is never short on fun and frolic.* · ◆◇◇◇◇ · VERB · V · N-VAR

from /frəm, STRONG frɒm, AM frʌm/. In addition to the uses shown below, **from** is used in phrasal verbs such as 'date from' and 'grow away from'. · ◆◆◆◆◆

1 You use **from** to say what the source, origin, or starting point of something is. *...an anniversary present from his wife... The results were taken from six surveys. ...wines from Coteaux d'Aix-en-Provence. ...a representative from the Israeli embassy.* **2** If someone or something moves or is moved **from** a place, they leave it or are removed, so that they are no longer there. *The* · PREP · PREP

guests watched as she fled from the room... Remove the bowl from the ice. **3** If you take something **from** an amount, you reduce the amount by that much. *The £103 is deducted from Mrs Adams' salary every month.* · PREP

4 From is used in expressions such as **away from** or **absent from** to say that someone or something is not present in a place where they are usually found. *Her husband worked away from home a lot.* **5** If you return **from** a place or an activity, you return after being in that place or doing that activity. *My son Colin has just returned from Amsterdam... James Morgan is just back from Germany.* **6** If you see or hear something **from** a particular place, you are in that place when you see it or hear it. *They see the painting from behind a plate glass window.* **7** If something hangs or sticks out **from** an object, it is attached to it or held by it. *Hanging from his right wrist is a heavy gold bracelet. ...large fans hanging from ceilings.* **8** You can use **from** when giving distances. For example, if a place is fifty miles **from** another place, the distance between the two places is fifty miles. *...a small park only a few hundred yards from Zurich's main shopping centre... How far is it from here?* **9** If a road or railway line goes **from** one place to another, you can travel along it between the two places. *...the road from St Petersburg to Tallinn.* · PREP · PREP · PREP · PREP · PREP · PREP

10 From is used, especially in the expression **made from**, to say what substance has been used to make something. *...bread made from white flour.* **11** You can use **from** when you are talking about the beginning of a period of time. *She studied painting from 1926.* **12** You say **from** one thing **to** another when you are stating the range of things that are possible, or when saying that the range of things includes everything in a certain category. *There are 94 countries represented in Barcelona, from Algeria to Zimbabwe. ...everything from finance to fixtures and fittings.* **13** If something changes **from** one thing to another, it stops being the first thing and becomes the second thing. *The expression on his face changed from sympathy to surprise.* · PREP · PREP · PREP · PREP

14 You use **from** after some verbs and nouns when mentioning the cause of something. *The problem simply resulted from a difference of opinion... He is suffering from eye ulcers.* **15** You use **from** when you are giving the reason for an opinion. *She knew from experience that Dave was about to tell her the truth... I guessed from his name that Jose must have been Spanish.* **16 From** is used after verbs with meanings such as 'protect', 'free', 'keep', and 'prevent' to introduce the action that does not happen, or that someone does not want to happen. *Such laws could protect the consumer from harmful or dangerous remedies.* · PREP · PREP · PREP

frond /frɒnd/ **fronds.** A **frond** is a long leaf or piece of seaweed which has an edge divided into lots of thin parts. *...palm fronds.* · N-COUNT

front /frʌnt/ **fronts, fronting, fronted. 1** The **front** of something is the part of it that faces you, or that faces forward, or that you normally see or use. *Stand at the front of the line... Her cotton dress had ripped down the front... Attached to the front of the house, there was a large veranda.* ▸ Also an adjective. *I went out there on the front porch... She was only six and still missing her front teeth.* **2** The **front** page of a newspaper is the outside of the first page, where the main news stories are printed. *The Guardian's front page carries a photograph of the two foreign ministers.* ● See also **front-page.** **3** The **front** is a road next to the sea in a seaside town. *...a stroll on the front.* **4** In warfare, the **front** is the place where two armies are fighting each other. *Her husband is fighting at the front.* ● See also **front line.** **5** If something is happening on a particular **front**, it is happening with regard to a particular situation or activity. *...research across a wide academic front.* **6** If someone puts on a particular kind of **front**, they pretend to have a particular quality. *Michael kept up a brave front.* **7** An organization or activity that is a **front** for another one that is illegal or secret is used to hide it. *...a firm* · ◆◆◆◆◆ · N-COUNT · ADJ: ADJ n · ADJ: ADJ n · N-SING · BRITISH · N-COUNT · N-COUNT · N-COUNT · N-COUNT

later identified by the police as a front for crime syndicates.

8 In weather forecasting, a **front** is the line where a [N-COUNT] mass of cold air meets a mass of warm air.

9 The word **Front** is often used in the titles of political organizations with a particular aim. ...the People's Liberation Front.

10 A building or area of land that **fronts** a particular [VERB: V n] place or **fronts** onto it is next to it and faces it. ...de-[V onto] lightful Victorian houses fronting on to the pavement.

11 The person who **fronts** an organization is the most [VERB: V n] senior person in it. [BRITISH]

12 If a person or thing is **in front**, they are ahead of [PHRASE] others in a moving group. ...motorists who speed or drive too close to the car in front.

13 Someone who is **in front** in a competition or con-[PHRASE] test at a particular point is winning at that point. Some preliminary polls show him out in front in the race.

14 If someone or something is **in front of** a particular [PHR-PREP] thing, they are facing it, ahead of it, or close to the front part of it. She sat down in front of her dressing-table mirror... Something darted out in front of my car.

15 If you do or say something **in front of** someone [PHR-PREP] else, you do or say it when they are present. They never argued in front of their children.

16 On the **home front** or on the **domestic front** [PHRASE] means with regard to your own country rather than [JOURNALISM] foreign countries. Its present economic ills on the home front are largely the result of overspending.

front·age /ˈfrʌntɪdʒ/ **frontages**. A **frontage** of a [N-COUNT: building is a wall which faces a place such as a also no det] street or a river. The restaurant has a river frontage.

front·al /ˈfrʌntəl/. **1 Frontal** means relating to or ◆◇◇◇ involving the front of something, for example the [ADJ] front of an army, a vehicle, or the brain. ...a frontal [FORMAL] assault by the rebels. **2** A **frontal** attack or challenge [ADJ] criticizes or threatens something in a very strong, direct way. ...a frontal attack on working-class organizations. **3** See also **full-frontal**.

,**front 'bench, front benches**. In Britain, the [N-COLL-front bench or people who sit on the **front bench** [COUNT] are members of Parliament who are ministers in the Government or who hold official positions in an opposition party. ◆ **front·bencher, frontbenchers** [N-COUNT] ...a front-bencher from his parliamentary team, Julie Manns.

'**front burner**. If an issue is on the **front burner**, it [N-SING] receives a lot of attention because it is considered to be more urgent or important than other issues. Bosnia continues to be on the front burner.

fron·tier /ˈfrʌntɪə, -ˈtɪə/ **frontiers**. **1** A **frontier** is a ◆◆◇◇ border between two countries. The usual American [N-COUNT] word is **border**. It wasn't difficult then to cross the [BRITISH] frontier. **2** You use **frontier** to refer to the border of [N-COUNT] an area of unclaimed land, or to a region beyond its border. ...a far-flung outpost on the frontier. **3** The [N-COUNT] **frontiers** of something, especially knowledge, are the limits to which it extends. ...pushing back the frontiers of science.

,**front 'line, front lines**; also spelled **front-line**. ◆◆◇◇ **1** The **front line** is the place where two armies are [N-COUNT] fighting each other. **2** A **front line** state shares a [ADJ: ADJ n] border with a country that it is at war with or is in conflict with. ...the front-line states bordering South Africa. **3** Someone who is **in the front line** has to [PHRASE] play a very important part in defending or achieving something. Information officers are in the front line of putting across government policies.

'**front man, front men**. If you say that someone is [N-COUNT] a **front man** for a group or organization, you mean [PRAGMATICS] that their role is to represent and give a good impression of it to the public; used showing disapproval.

,**front-'page**. A **front-page** article or picture ap-◆◆◇◇ pears on the front page of a newspaper because it is [ADJ: ADJ n] very important or interesting.

,**front-'runner, front-runners**. In a competition ◆◇◇◇ or contest, the **front-runner** is the person who [N-COUNT] seems most likely to win it.

frost /frɒst, AM frɔːst/ **frosts**. **1** When there is ◆◇◇◇ **frost** or a **frost**, the temperature outside falls below [N-VAR] freezing point and the ground becomes covered in ice crystals. **2** When someone says that there are a [PHRASE] particular number of **degrees of frost** they mean that the temperature is that number of degrees below freezing point.

frost·bite /ˈfrɒstbaɪt, AM ˈfrɔːst-/. **Frostbite** is a [N-UNCOUNT] condition in which parts of your body, such as your fingers or toes, become seriously damaged as a result of being very cold.

frost·ed /ˈfrɒstɪd, AM ˈfrɔːst-/. **1 Frosted** glass has [ADJ] had its surface roughened so that you cannot see through it clearly. The top half of the door to his office was of frosted glass. **2 Frosted** means covered [ADJ] with frost. ...the frosted trees. **3 Frosted** means cov-[ADJ] ered with something that looks like frost. ...frosted blue eye shadow. **4 Frosted** means covered with ic-[ADJ] ing. The usual British word is **iced**. ...a plate of frost-[AMERICAN] ed cupcakes.

frost·ing /ˈfrɒstɪŋ, AM ˈfrɔːst-/. **Frosting** is a sweet [N-UNCOUNT] substance made from powdered sugar that is used [AMERICAN] to cover and decorate cakes. The usual British word is **icing**.

frosty /ˈfrɒsti, AM ˈfrɔːsti/ **frostier, frostiest**. **1** If ◆◇◇◇ the weather is **frosty**, the temperature is below [ADJ-GRADED] freezing. ...sharp, frosty nights. **2** You describe the [ADJ-GRADED] ground or an object as **frosty** when it is covered with frost. ...the frosty stones. **3** If you describe [ADJ-GRADED] someone's behaviour as **frosty**, you think it is unfriendly. The president may get a frosty reception. ◆ **frost·ily** The Prime Minister smiled again, this [ADV-GRADED: time a trifle frostily. ADV with v]

froth /frɒθ, AM frɔːθ/ **froths, frothing, frothed**. ◆◇◇◇ **1 Froth** is a mass of small bubbles on the surface of [N-UNCOUNT] a liquid. ...the froth of bubbles on the top of a glass of beer. **2** If a liquid **froths**, small bubbles appear on [VERB: V] its surface. The sea froths over my feet. **3** If you say [VERB: V] that someone **is frothing**, or that they **are frothing** [PRAGMATICS] at the mouth, you are emphasizing that they are [V with quote] very angry or excited about something. 'No! No! [Also V prep] Never!' he froths. **4** If you refer to an activity or ob-[N-UNCOUNT] ject as **froth**, you disapprove of it because it appears [PRAGMATICS] exciting or attractive, but has very little real value or importance. Falling in love the first time is all froth and fantasy.

frothy /ˈfrɒθi, AM ˈfrɔːθi/ **frothier, frothiest**. A [ADJ-GRADED] **frothy** liquid has lots of bubbles on its surface.

frown /fraʊn/ **frowns, frowning, frowned**. ◆◆◇◇ When someone **frowns**, their eyebrows become [VERB: V at n] drawn together, because they are annoyed, worried, [V-ing] or puzzled, or because they are concentrating. He frowned at her anxiously. ...a frowning man. ▶ Also [N-COUNT] a noun. There was a deep frown on the boy's face.

frown upon or **frown on**. If something **is frowned** [PHRASAL VB] **upon** or **is frowned on**, people disapprove of it. This [be V-ed P] practice is frowned upon as being wasteful... Many [V P noun] teachers frown on such practices.

froze /frəʊz/. **Froze** is the past tense of **freeze**.

fro·zen /ˈfrəʊzən/. **1 Frozen** is the past participle ◆◆◇◇ of **freeze**. **2** If the ground is **frozen**, it has become very hard be-[ADJ] cause the weather is very cold. It was bitterly cold now and the ground was frozen hard. **3 Frozen** food has [ADJ] been preserved by being kept at a very low temperature. Frozen fish is a very healthy convenience food. **4** If [ADJ] you say that you are **frozen**, or a part of your body is [PRAGMATICS] **frozen**, you are emphasizing that you feel very cold. He put one hand up to his frozen face. ● **Frozen stiff** [PHRASE] means the same as **frozen**. He pulled up his collar and was aware of being frozen stiff.

5 If you describe someone as **frozen**, you mean that [ADJ] their body is fixed in a particular position, for example because they are very worried or afraid. Katherine was frozen in horror.

fru·gal /ˈfruːgəl/. **1** People who are **frugal** or who ◆◇◇◇ live **frugal** lives do not eat much or spend much [ADJ-GRADED] money on themselves. She lives a frugal life. ◆ **fru·gal·ity** We must practise the strictest frugality [N-UNCOUNT] and economy. ◆ **fru·gal·ly** He frugally saved various [ADV-GRADED]

bits of the machine. **2** A **frugal** meal is small and inexpensive. *The diet was frugal: cheese and water, rice and beans.* — ADJ-GRADED

fruit /fruːt/ **fruits, fruiting, fruited.** The plural of the noun can be either **fruit** or **fruits**, but is usually **fruit. 1** Fruit or a **fruit** is something which grows on a tree or bush and which contains seeds or a stone covered by edible flesh. Apples, oranges, and bananas are all fruit. *Fresh fruit and vegetables provide fibre and vitamins. ...bananas and other tropical fruits.* ◆ See also **kiwi fruit, passion fruit.** — ◆◆◆◇ / N-VAR

2 The **fruits** of someone's work or activity are the good things that result from it. *The findings are the fruit of more than three years research.* **3** If the effort that you put into something **bears fruit**, it produces good results. *He was naturally disappointed when the talks failed to bear fruit.* **4** The **first fruits** or the **first fruit** of a project or activity are its earliest results or profits. *This project is one of the first fruits of commercial co-operation between the two countries.* — N-COUNT / PHRASE / PHRASE

fruit·cake /ˈfruːtkeɪk/ **fruitcakes;** also spelled **fruit cake.** A **fruitcake** is a cake that contains raisins, currants, and other dried fruit. — N-VAR

fruit 'cocktail, fruit cocktails. Fruit cocktail is a mixture of pieces of different kinds of fruit eaten as part of a meal. — N-VAR

fruit·ful /ˈfruːtfʊl/. **1** Something that is **fruitful** produces good and useful results. *We had a long, happy, fruitful relationship.* ◆ **fruit·ful·ly** *...taking their skills where they can be applied most fruitfully.* **2** Fruitful land or trees produce a lot of crops. *...a landscape that was fruitful and lush.* — ◆◇◇◇ / ADJ-GRADED / ADV-GRADED: ADV with v / ADJ-GRADED

frui·tion /fruˈɪʃən/. If something comes to **fruition**, it starts to succeed and produce the results that were intended or hoped for. *These plans take time to come to fruition.* — ◆◇◇◇ / N-UNCOUNT / FORMAL

fruit·less /ˈfruːtləs/. **Fruitless** actions, events, or efforts do not achieve anything at all. *It was a fruitless search... Talks have so far have been fruitless.* ◆ **fruit·less·ly** *Negotiation ended fruitlessly.* — ◆◇◇◇ / ADJ-GRADED / ADV

'fruit machine, fruit machines. A **fruit machine** is a machine used for gambling. You put money into it and if a particular combination of symbols, especially fruit, appears, you win money. — N-COUNT / BRITISH

fruit 'salad, fruit salads. Fruit salad is a mixture of pieces of different kinds of fruit, usually eaten as a dessert. — N-VAR

fruity /ˈfruːti/ **fruitier, fruitiest. 1** Something that is **fruity** smells or tastes of fruit. *This shampoo smells fruity and leaves the hair beautifully silky. ...a lovely rich fruity wine.* **2** A **fruity** voice or laugh is pleasantly rich and deep. *...a solid, fruity laugh.* — ◆◇◇◇ / ADJ-GRADED / ADJ-GRADED

frumpy /ˈfrʌmpi/. If you describe a woman or her clothes as **frumpy**, you mean that her clothes are dull and unfashionable. *I looked so frumpy next to these women.* — ADJ-GRADED

frus·trate /frʌˈstreɪt, AM ˈfrʌstreɪt/ **frustrates, frustrating, frustrated. 1** If something **frustrates** you, it upsets or angers you because you are unable to do anything about the problems it creates. *These questions frustrated me... Doesn't it frustrate you that audiences in the theatre are so restricted?* ◆ **frus·trat·ed** *...voters who are frustrated with the council.* ◆ **frus·trat·ing** *It was frustrating to be out of government for the next four years.* ◆ **frus·tra·tion** /frʌˈstreɪʃən/ **frustrations** *The results show the level of frustration among hospital doctors.* **2** If someone or something **frustrates** a plan or attempt to do something, they prevent it from succeeding. *The government has deliberately frustrated his efforts to gain work permits.* — ◆◆◇◇ / VERB / V n / ADJ-GRADED / ADJ-GRADED / N-VAR / VERB / V n

fry /fraɪ/ **fries, frying, fried. 1** When you **fry** food, you cook it in a pan that contains hot fat or oil. *Fry the breadcrumbs until golden brown.* **2** Fry are very small, young fish. **3** Fries are the same as **French fries. 4** See also **small fry.** — ◆◆◇◇ / VERB / V n / N-PLURAL / N-PLURAL

fry up. If you **fry up** food, you fry it, especially in order to make a quick, casual meal. *I fried up the beef... She cuts and fries the mixture up into a potato doughnut.* ◆ See also **fry-up.** — PHRASAL VB / V P noun / V n P / INFORMAL

'frying pan, frying pans. A **frying pan** is a flat metal pan with a long handle, in which you fry food. See picture headed **kitchen utensils.** — ◆◇◇◇◇ / N-COUNT

'fry-up, fry-ups. A **fry-up** is a meal consisting of a mixture of foods such as sausages, bacon, and eggs that have been fried. — N-COUNT / BRITISH / INFORMAL

ft ft is a written abbreviation for **feet** or **foot.** *...flying at 1,000 ft. ...an area of 2,750 sq ft.* — ◆◇◇◇ / N-COUNT: num N

fuch·sia /ˈfjuːʃə/ **fuchsias.** A **fuchsia** is a plant or a small bush which has pink, purple, or white flowers which hang downwards. — N-VAR

fuddy-duddy /ˈfʌdidʌdi/ **fuddy-duddies.** If you describe someone as a **fuddy-duddy**, you are criticizing or making fun of them because they are old-fashioned. ▶ Also an adjective. *Perhaps we did acquire a somewhat fuddy-duddy image.* — N-COUNT / PRAGMATICS / ADJ-GRADED: ADJ n

fudge /fʌdʒ/ **fudges, fudging, fudged. 1** Fudge is a soft brown sweet that is made from butter, cream, and sugar. **2** If you **fudge** something, you avoid making a clear and definite decision, distinction, or statement about it. *Both have fudged their calculations and avoided specifics. ...certain issues that can no longer be fudged.* — ◆◇◇◇◇ / N-UNCOUNT / VERB / V n

fuel /ˈfjuːəl/ **fuels, fuelling, fuelled;** spelled **fueling, fueled** in American English. **1** Fuel is a substance such as coal, oil, or petrol that is burned to provide heat or power. *They ran out of fuel.* **2** A machine or vehicle that **is fuelled** by a particular substance works by burning that substance. *...power stations fuelled by oil, coal and gas.* **3** If something **fuels** something such as speculation, controversy, or inflation, it makes it increase or become more intense. *The economic boom was fueled by easy credit.* **4** If something **adds fuel to** a conflict or debate, or **adds fuel to the fire**, it makes the conflict or debate more intense. — ◆◆◆◇ / N-VAR / VERB: be V-ed / V-ed / VERB: V n / PHRASE

fu·gi·tive /ˈfjuːdʒɪtɪv/ **fugitives.** A **fugitive** is someone who is running away or hiding, usually in order to avoid being caught by the police. *The rebel leader is a fugitive from justice.* — ◆◇◇◇ / N-COUNT

fugue /fjuːg/ **fugues.** A **fugue** is a piece of music that begins with a simple tune which is then repeated by other voices or instrumental parts with small variations. — N-COUNT / TECHNICAL

-ful /-fʊl/ **-fuls.** You use **-ful** to form nouns that refer to the quantity of a substance that an object contains or can contain. *...a spoonful of brown sugar.* — SUFFIX

ful·crum /ˈfʊlkrəm/. If someone or something is the **fulcrum** of a situation, they are the most important part of it and affect all the other parts of it. *The decision is the strategic fulcrum of the Budget.* — N-SING / FORMAL

ful·fil /fʊlˈfɪl/ **fulfils, fulfilling, fulfilled;** also spelled **fulfill** and **fulfills**, especially in American English. **1** If you **fulfil** something such as a promise, dream, or ambition, you do what you said or hoped you would do. *President Kaunda fulfilled his promise of announcing a date for the referendum.* ◆ **ful·fil·ment** *Visiting Angkor was the fulfilment of a childhood dream.* **2** To **fulfil** a task, role, or requirement means to do or be what is required, necessary, or expected. *All the necessary conditions were fulfilled.* **3** If something **fulfils** you, you feel happy and satisfied with what you are doing or with what you have achieved. *Women can fulfil themselves without the assistance of a man.* ◆ **ful·filled** *I feel more fulfilled doing this than I've ever done.* ◆ **ful·filling** *...a fulfilling career.* ◆ **fulfilment** *...a great sense of fulfilment.* — ◆◆◆◇ / VERB / V n / N-UNCOUNT / VERB: V n / VERB: V n / V pron-refl / ADJ-GRADED / ADJ-GRADED / N-UNCOUNT

full /fʊl/ **fuller, fullest. 1** If something is **full**, it contains as much of a substance or as many objects as it can. *Once the container is full, it stays shut. ...a full tank of petrol.* **2** If a place or thing **is full of** things or people, it contains a large number of them. *The streets are still full of debris from two nights of rioting. ...a useful recipe leaflet full of ideas.* **3** If someone or something **is full of** a particular feeling or quality, they have a lot of it. *I feel full of confidence. ...an exquisite mousse, incredibly rich and full of flavour.* **4** You say that a place is **full** — ◆◆◆◆◆ / ADJ-GRADED / ADJ-GRADED: v-link ADJ of n / ADJ-GRADED: v-link ADJ of n / ADJ-GRADED

when there is no space left in it for any more people or things. *The main car park was full when I left... The bus was completely full, and lots of people were standing.* **5** If your hands or arms are **full**, you are carrying or holding as much as you can carry. *Sylvia entered, her arms full of packages... People would go into the store and come out with their arms full.* **6** If you feel **full**, you have eaten so much that you do not want anything else. *No, thanks. I'm full.* ♦ **full·ness** *High fibre diets give the feeling of fullness.* **7** If you say to someone, 'you're **full of** yourself', you disapprove of them because they appear very pleased with themselves, thinking that they are very clever, special, or important.

8 You use **full** before a noun to indicate that you are referring to all the details, things, or people that it can possibly include. *Full details will be sent to you once your application has been accepted... May I have your full name?* **9** You say that something has been done or described **in full** when everything that was necessary has been done or described. *The medical experts have yet to report in full.* **10** **Full** is used to describe a sound, light, or physical force which is being produced with the greatest possible power or intensity. *...the sound of Mahler, playing at full volume... The operation will be carried out in full daylight.* ▶ Also an adverb. *...a two-seater Lotus, parked with its headlamps full on.*

11 You use **full** to emphasize the completeness, intensity, or extent of something. *Television cameras are carrying the full horror of this war into homes around the world... The lane leading to the farm was in full view of the house.* **12** Something that is done or experienced **to the full** is done to as great an extent as is possible. *She probably had a good mind, which should be used to the full.* **13** If you say that someone **knows full well** that something is true, especially something unpleasant, you are emphasizing that they are definitely aware of it, although they may behave as if they are not. *He knew full well he'd be ashamed of himself later.* **14** A **full** statement or report contains a lot of information and detail. *Mr Primakov gave a full account of his meeting with the President.* **15** If you say that someone has or leads a **full** life, you approve of the fact that they are always busy and do a lot of different things. **16** You use **full** to emphasize the force or directness with which someone or something is struck. *The burning liquid hit him full in the right eye... She kissed him full on the mouth.* **17** You use **full** to refer to something which gives you all the rights, status, or importance for a particular position or activity, rather than just some of them. *How did the meeting go, did you get your full membership?*

18 A **full** flavour is strong and rich. *...a dry, grapey wine with a full flavour.* **19** If you describe a part of someone's body as **full**, you mean that it is rounded and rather large. *The Juno Collection specialises in large sizes for ladies with a fuller figure. ...his full lips.* **20** A **full** skirt or sleeve is wide and has been made from a lot of fabric. ♦ **fullness** *The coat has raglan sleeves, and is cut to give fullness at the back.* **21** When there is a **full** moon, the moon appears as a bright, complete circle.

22 • **to be full of beans**: see **bean**. • **full blast**: see **blast**. • **to come full circle**: see **circle**. • **to have your hands full**: see **hand**. • **in full swing**: see **swing**.

'**full-back, full-backs**; also spelled **fullback**. In rugby or football, a **full-back** is a defending player whose position is towards the goal which their team is defending.

,**full-'blooded. Full-blooded** behaviour and actions are carried out with great commitment and enthusiasm. *Full-blooded market reform is the only way to save the economy.*

,**full-'blown. Full-blown** means having all the characteristics of a particular type of thing or person. *Before becoming a full-blown director, he worked as the film editor on Citizen Kane.*

,**full 'board**; also spelled **full-board**. If the price at a hotel includes **full board**, it includes all your meals.

,**full 'dress.** Someone who is in **full dress** is wearing all the clothes needed for a ceremony or formal occasion. *...full dress uniform.*

,**full-'flavoured**; spelled **full-flavored** in American English. **Full-flavoured** food or wine has a pleasant and fairly strong taste.

,**full-'fledged. Full-fledged** means the same as **fully-fledged.**

,**full-'frontal**; also spelled **full frontal**. **1** If there is **full-frontal** nudity in a photograph or film, you can see the whole of the front part of someone's naked body. **2** A **full-frontal** attack on something or approach to something is very firm and direct. *A full-frontal attack on the opposition leader is their best hope.*

,**full-'grown.** An animal or plant that is **full-grown** has reached its full adult size and stopped growing.

,**full 'house, full houses.** If a theatre has a **full house** for a particular performance, it has as large an audience as it can hold. *...playing to a full house.*

,**full-'length. 1** A **full-length** book, record, or film is the normal length, rather than being shorter than normal. **2** A **full-length** coat or skirt is long enough to reach the lower part of a person's leg, almost to the ankles. A **full-length** sleeve reaches a person's wrist. **3 Full-length** curtains or other furnishings reach to the floor. **4** A **full-length** mirror or portrait shows the whole of a person. **5** Someone who is lying **full-length** is lying down flat with their legs extended. *She stretched herself out full-length.*

'**full marks. 1** If you get **full marks** in a test or exam, you get everything right and gain the maximum number of marks. **2** If you say that someone gets **full marks** for something, you are praising them for a particular good quality. *Full marks for honesty, perhaps, but a fail for diplomacy.*

full·ness /'fʊlnəs/. **1** See **full**. **2** If you say that something will happen **in the fullness of time**, you mean that it will eventually happen after a long time or after a long series of events.

,**full-'page.** A **full-page** advertisement, picture, or article in a newspaper or magazine uses a whole page.

,**full-'scale. 1 Full-scale** means as complete, intense, or great in extent as possible. *...the possibility of a full-scale nuclear war.* **2** A **full-scale** drawing or model is the same size as the thing that it represents. *...working, full-scale prototypes.*

,**full-'size** or **full-sized.** A **full-size** or **full-sized** model or picture is the same size as the thing or person that it represents.

,**full 'stop, full stops.** A **full stop** is the punctuation mark (.) which you use at the end of a sentence when it is not a question or exclamation. The American expression is **period**.

full-'strength. See **strength**.

,**full-'throated.** A **full-throated** sound coming from someone's mouth, such as a shout or a laugh, is very loud.

,**full-'time**; also spelled **full time**. **1 Full-time** work or study involves working or studying for the whole of each normal working week rather than for part of it. *...a full-time job. ...full-time staff.* ▶ Also an adverb. *Deirdre works full-time.* **2** If you describe a regular activity or task as a **full-time job**, you mean that it takes up so much of your time it is like doing a paid job. *Mothering was a full-time job.* **3** In games such as football, **full time** is the end of a match. *The score at full-time was Arsenal 1, Sampdoria 1.*

,**full-'timer, full-timers.** A **full-timer** is someone who works full-time.

,**full 'up**; also spelled **full-up. 1** Something that is **full up** has no space left for any more people or things. *The prisons are all full up.* **2** If you are **full up**, you have eaten so much that you do not want to eat anything else.

ful·ly /'fʊli/. **1 Fully** means to the greatest degree or extent possible. *She was fully aware of my thoughts... I don't fully agree with that.* **2** If you de-

scribe, answer, or deal with something **fully**, you leave out nothing that should be mentioned or dealt with. *These debates are discussed more fully later in this book.* **3 Fully** is used to emphasize how great an amount is. *Fully 30% of the poor could not even afford access to illegal shanties.* `ADV with v`

ful·ly-'fledged. Fully-fledged means complete or fully developed. *Hungary is to have a fully-fledged Stock Exchange from today.* `ADV: ADV amount` `PRAGMATICS` `WRITTEN` `◆◇◇◇◇` `ADJ: ADJ n`

ful·mi·nate /'fʊlmɪneɪt, 'fʌl-/ **fulminates, fulminating, fulminated.** If you **fulminate** against someone or something, you criticize them and complain about them angrily. *They all fulminated against the new curriculum.* ♦ **ful·mi·na·tion** /ˌfʊlmɪ'neɪʃən, ˌfʌl-/ ...*fulminations against the government.* `VERB` `V against/about n` `FORMAL` `N-VAR`

ful·some /'fʊlsəm/. If you describe expressions of praise, apology, or gratitude as **fulsome**, you disapprove of them because they are exaggerated and elaborate, so that they sound insincere. *Newspapers have been fulsome in their praise of the former president.* ♦ **ful·some·ly** *She chatted to them about the show and praised them fulsomely.* `ADJ-GRADED` `PRAGMATICS` `ADV-GRADED: ADV with v`

fum·ble /'fʌmbəl/ **fumbles, fumbling, fumbled.** **1** If you **fumble** for something or **fumble** with it, you try and reach for it or hold it in a clumsy way. *She crept from the bed and fumbled for her dressing gown... He fumbled his one-handed attempt to light his cigarette.* **2** When you are trying to say something, if you **fumble** for the right words, you speak in a clumsy and unclear way. *He fumbled his lines, not knowing what he was going to say.* `◆◇◇◇◇` `VERB` `V for/with/in n` `V n` `VERB: V for n` `Also V`

fume /fjuːm/ **fumes, fuming, fumed. 1** Fumes are the unpleasant and often unhealthy smoke and gases that are produced by fires or by things such as chemicals, fuel, or cooking. *...car exhaust fumes.* **2** If you **are fuming** over something, you are very angry about it. *'It's monstrous!' Jackie fumed... Mrs. Vine was still fuming.* `◆◇◇◇◇` `N-PLURAL` `VERB: V over/at/ about n` `V with quote`

fu·mi·gate /'fjuːmɪɡeɪt/ **fumigates, fumigating, fumigated.** If you **fumigate** something, you disinfect it using special chemicals, usually in order to get rid of germs or insects. ♦ **fu·mi·ga·tion** /ˌfjuːmɪ'ɡeɪʃən/ *Methods of control involved poisoning and fumigation.* `VERB: V n` `N-UNCOUNT`

fun /fʌn/. **1** You refer to an activity or situation as **fun** if you think it is pleasant and enjoyable and it causes you to feel happy. *This year promises to be terrifically good fun... We had so much fun doing it... It could be fun to watch them... You still have time to join in the fun.* **2** If you do something **for fun**, you do it in order to enjoy yourself rather than because it is important or necessary. *He had just come for the fun of it.* **3** If you say that someone is **fun**, you mean you enjoy being with them because they say and do interesting or amusing things. *Liz was wonderful fun to be with.* **4** If you describe something as a **fun** thing, you mean that you think it is enjoyable. If you describe someone as a **fun** person, you mean that you enjoy being with them. *It was a fun evening... What a fun person he is!* **5** You can refer to playful or enjoyable activities as **fun and games**, especially if you want to contrast them with something more serious or important. *Family life is not, however, all fun and games.* **6** If you **make fun of** someone or something or **poke fun at** them, you tease them, or make jokes about them in a way that causes them to seem ridiculous. **7** If you do something **in fun**, you do it as a joke or for amusement, without intending to cause any harm. *Don't say such things, even in fun.* **8** ● **figure of fun**: see **figure**. `◆◆◆◇` `N-UNCOUNT` `PHRASE` `N-UNCOUNT` `ADJ-GRADED: ADJ n` `INFORMAL` `PHRASE` `INFORMAL` `PHRASE` `PHRASE`

func·tion /'fʌŋkʃən/ **functions, functioning, functioned. 1** The **function** of something or someone is the useful thing that they do or are intended to do. *The main function of the merchant banks is to raise capital for industry.* **2** If a machine or system **is functioning**, it is working or operating. *Conservation programs cannot function without local support.* **3** If someone or something **functions** `◆◆◆◇` `N-COUNT: with supp` `VERB` `V` `VERB`

as a particular thing, they do the work or fulfil the purpose of that thing. *On weekdays, one third of the room functions as workspace.* **4** A **function** is a series of operations that a computer performs, for example when a single key is pressed. **5** If you say that one thing is a **function** of another, you mean that its amount or nature depends on the other thing. *Investment is a function of the interest rate.* **6** A **function** is a large formal dinner or party. `V as n` `N-COUNT` `TECHNICAL` `N-COUNT` `FORMAL` `N-COUNT`

func·tion·al /'fʌŋkʃənəl/. **1 Functional** things are useful rather than decorative. *...modern, functional furniture.* **2 Functional** equipment works or operates in the way that it is supposed to. *We have fully functional smoke alarms on all staircases.* **3 Functional** means relating to the way in which something works or operates. *Protein increases the functional ability of progesterone.* ♦ **func·tion·al·ly** *...blood cells that are functionally similar.* `◆◇◇◇◇` `ADJ-GRADED` `ADJ` `ADJ: ADJ n` `ADV`

func·tion·ary /'fʌŋkʃənəri, AM -neri/ **functionaries.** A **functionary** is a person whose job is to do administrative work, especially for a government or a political party. `N-COUNT` `FORMAL`

fund /fʌnd/ **funds, funding, funded. 1** Funds are amounts of money that are available to be spent. *The concert will raise funds for research into Aids. ...government funds.* ● See also **fundraiser.** **2** A **fund** is an amount of money that is collected or saved for a particular purpose. *...a pension fund. ...a scholarship fund for undergraduate engineering students.* ● See also **trust fund. 3** When a person or organization **funds** something, they provide money for it. *...a new privately funded scheme.* ♦ **-funded** *...government-funded institutions.* ♦ **fund·ing** They hope for government funding for the scheme... Many colleges have seen their funding cut. **4** If you have a **fund** of something, you have a lot of it. *Hill has a matchless fund of experience.* `◆◆◆◆◆` `N-PLURAL` `N-COUNT` `VERB: V n` `V-ed` `COMB` `N-UNCOUNT` `N-COUNT: N of n`

fun·da·men·tal /ˌfʌndə'mentəl/. **1** You use **fundamental** to describe things, activities, and principles that are very important or essential, and that affect the basic nature of other things. *...the fundamental principles of democracy... Technical skill is a fundamental basis for most, if not all, great art.* ● If one thing **is fundamental to** another, it has a very important or essential role in its existence or basic nature. *Better relations with China are fundamental to the well-being of the area.* **2** You use **fundamental** to describe something which exists at a deep and basic level, and is therefore likely to continue. *On this question, the two leaders have very fundamental differences.* ♦ **fun·da·men·tal·ly** *Environmentalists say the treaty is fundamentally flawed... He can be very charming, but he is fundamentally a bully.* `◆◆◆◇◇` `ADJ-GRADED` `PHRASE` `ADJ-GRADED` `ADV-GRADED`

fun·da·men·tal·ism /ˌfʌndə'mentəlɪzəm/. **Fundamentalism** is the belief in the original form of a religion or theory, without accepting any later ideas. ♦ **fun·da·men·tal·ist, fundamentalists** *...fundamentalist Christians.* `◆◆◇◇◇` `N-UNCOUNT` `N-COUNT`

fun·da·men·tals /ˌfʌndə'mentəlz/. The **fundamentals** of something are its simplest, most important elements, ideas, or principle. *...the fundamentals of road safety.* `◆◆◇◇◇` `N-PLURAL`

fund·raiser /'fʌndreɪzə/ **fundraisers;** also spelled **fund-raiser. 1** A **fundraiser** is an event which is intended to raise money for a particular purpose. *Organize a fundraiser for your church.* **2** A **fundraiser** is someone who works to raise money for a particular purpose. *Sir Anthony was a keen fundraiser for the Liberal Democrats.* ♦ **fund·raising** *Encourage her to get involved in fund-raising for charity.* `N-COUNT` `N-COUNT` `N-UNCOUNT`

fu·ner·al /'fjuːnərəl/ **funerals.** A **funeral** is the ceremony that is held when the body of someone who has died is buried or cremated. *His funeral will be on Thursday at Blackburn Cathedral.* `◆◆◇◇◇` `N-COUNT`

'funeral director, funeral directors. A **funeral director** is a person whose job is to arrange funeral ceremonies. `N-COUNT`

'funeral home, funeral homes. A **funeral home** is a place where a funeral director works and where `N-COUNT` `AMERICAN`

dead people are prepared for burial or cremation. The British expression is **funeral parlour**.

fu·ner·ary /ˈfjuːnərəri, AM -reri/. **Funerary** means relating to funerals, burials, or cremations. ADJ: ADJ n

fu·nereal /fjuːˈnɪəriəl/. A **funereal** tone, atmosphere, or colour is very sad and serious. ADJ-GRADED

fun·fair /ˈfʌnfeə/ **funfairs**. A **funfair** is an event held in a park or field at which people pay to ride on machines for amusement or try to win prizes in games. The usual American word is **carnival**. N-COUNT BRITISH

fun·gal /ˈfʌŋgl/. **Fungal** means caused by, consisting of, or relating to fungus. *Athlete's foot is a fungal infection.* ◆◇◇◇ ADJ

fun·gi /ˈfʌŋgiː, ˈfʌndʒaɪ/. **Fungi** is the plural form of **fungus**.

fun·gi·cide /ˈfʌŋgɪsaɪd, ˈfʌndʒ-/ **fungicides**. A **fungicide** is a chemical that can be used to kill fungus or to prevent it from growing. N-VAR

fun·gus /ˈfʌŋgəs/ **fungi**. A **fungus** is a plant that has no flowers, leaves, or green colouring, such as a mushroom or mould. ◆◇◇◇ N-VAR

funk /fʌŋk/. **Funk** is a style of dance music based on jazz and blues, with a strong, repeated bass part. ◆◇◇◇ N-UNCOUNT

funky /ˈfʌŋki/ **funkier, funkiest**. 1 **Funky** jazz, blues, or pop music has a very strong, repeated bass part. *It's a funky sort of rhythm.* 2 If you describe something or someone as **funky**, you like them because they are unconventional or unusual. *It had a certain funky charm, I guess, but it wasn't much of a place to raise a kid.* ◆◇◇◇ ADJ-GRADED / ADJ-GRADED AMERICAN, INFORMAL

fun·nel /ˈfʌnl/ **funnels, funnelling, funnelled**; spelled **funneling, funneled** in American English. 1 A **funnel** is an object with a wide top and a tube at the bottom, which is used to pour substances into a container. See picture headed **kitchen utensils**. 2 A **funnel** is a metal chimney on a ship or railway engine powered by steam. 3 If something **funnels** somewhere or **is funnelled** there, it is directed through a narrow space. *The winds came from the north, across the plains, funnelling down the valley.* 4 If you **funnel** money, goods, or information from one place to another, you cause it to be sent there as it becomes available. *Its Global Programme on AIDS funnelled money from donors to governments.* ◆◇◇◇ N-COUNT / N-COUNT / V-ERG V adv/prep Also V n adv/prep / VERB V n prep/adv

fun·ni·ly /ˈfʌnɪli/. You use **funnily enough** to indicate that, although something is surprising, it is true or really happened. *I didn't, funnily enough, dislike her.* PHRASE PRAGMATICS

fun·ny /ˈfʌni/ **funnier, funniest**. 1 Something or someone that is **funny** is amusing and likely to make you smile or laugh. *I'll tell you a funny story.* 2 If you describe something as **funny**, you mean that you think it is strange, surprising, or puzzling. *It's funny how love can come and go.* 3 If you feel **funny**, you feel slightly ill. *My head had begun to ache and my stomach felt funny.* 4 **Funny business** is dishonest or unacceptable behaviour. *...an inquiry into funny business in Ireland's biggest export industry.* ◆◆◇◇ ADJ-GRADED / ADJ-GRADED / ADJ-GRADED INFORMAL / PHRASE INFORMAL

fur /fɜː/ **furs**. **Fur** is the thick and usually soft hair that grows on the bodies of many mammals, and is sometimes used to make clothes or rugs. You can also refer to an artificial material that resembles this hair as fur. *This creature's fur is short, dense and silky. ...a black coat with a fur collar.* ▶ A **fur** is a coat made from fur. *...women in furs.* ◆◆◇◇ N-VAR / N-COUNT

fu·ri·ous /ˈfjʊəriəs/. 1 Someone who is **furious** is extremely angry. *He is furious at the way his wife has been treated... I am furious that it has taken so long.* ♦ **fu·ri·ous·ly** *He stormed out of the apartment, slamming the door furiously behind him.* 2 **Furious** is also used to describe something that is done with great energy, effort, speed, or violence. *A furious gunbattle ensued.* ♦ **furiously** *Officials worked furiously to repair the centre court.* ◆◆◇◇ ADJ-GRADED / ADV-GRADED / ADJ / ADV

furl /fɜːl/ **furls, furling, furled**. When you **furl** something such as a sail or flag, you roll or fold it up because it is not going to be used. *An attempt was made to furl the headsail.* VERB V n

fur·long /ˈfɜːlɒŋ, AM -lɔːŋ/ **furlongs**. A **furlong** is an imperial unit of length that is equal to 220 yards or 201.2 metres. ◆◇◇◇ N-COUNT

fur·lough /ˈfɜːləʊ/ **furloughs, furloughing, furloughed**. 1 If workers are given **furlough**, they are told to stay away from work for a certain period because there is not enough for them to do. 2 If people who work for a particular organization are **furloughed**, they are given a furlough. *The factories have begun furloughing hundreds of workers.* 3 When soldiers are given **furlough**, they are given official permission to leave the area where they are fighting for a certain period. N-VAR AMERICAN / VERB: be V-ed V n AMERICAN / N-VAR AMERICAN

fur·nace /ˈfɜːnɪs/ **furnaces**. 1 A **furnace** is a container or enclosed space in which a very hot fire is made, for example to melt metal, burn rubbish, or produce steam. 2 If you say that a place is a **furnace**, you mean that it is very hot there. *How can we walk? It's a furnace out there.* ◆◇◇◇ N-COUNT / N-SING INFORMAL

fur·nish /ˈfɜːnɪʃ/ **furnishes, furnishing, furnished**. 1 If you **furnish** a room or building, you put furniture and furnishings into it. *Many proprietors try to furnish their hotels with antiques.* 2 If you **furnish** someone with something, you provide or supply it. *They'll be able to furnish you with the rest of the details.* ◆◇◇◇ VERB: V n / V n with n / V n with n FORMAL

fur·nished /ˈfɜːnɪʃt/. 1 A **furnished** room or house is available to be rented together with the furniture in it. 2 When you say that a room or house is **furnished** in a particular way, you are describing the kind or amount of furniture that it has in it. *...his sparsely furnished house.* ◆◇◇◇ ADJ / ADJ: adv ADJ

fur·nish·ings /ˈfɜːnɪʃɪŋz/. The **furnishings** of a room or house are the furniture, curtains, carpets, and decorations such as pictures. ◆◇◇◇ N-PLURAL

fur·ni·ture /ˈfɜːnɪtʃə/. **Furniture** consists of large movable objects such as tables, chairs, or beds that are used in a room for sitting on or for putting things on or in. *Each piece of furniture in their home suited the style of the house.* ◆◆◇◇ N-UNCOUNT

fu·ro·re /fjʊˈrɔːri, ˈfjʊərɔː/; spelled **furor** in American English. A **furore** is a very angry or excited reaction by people to something. *The disclosure has already caused a furore among MPs.* ◆◇◇◇ N-SING

fur·ri·er /ˈfʌriə, AM ˈfɜːr-/ **furriers**. A **furrier** is a person who makes or sells clothes made from fur. N-COUNT

fur·row /ˈfʌrəʊ, AM ˈfɜːr-/ **furrows, furrowing, furrowed**. 1 A **furrow** is a long thin line in the earth which a farmer makes in order to plant seeds or to allow water to flow along. 2 If you say that someone **ploughs** a particular **furrow** or **ploughs** their **own furrow**, you mean that their activities or interests are different or isolated from those of other people. *Cale has ploughed a more esoteric furrow as a recording artist.* 3 A **furrow** is a deep fold or line in the skin of someone's face. *...the deep furrows that marked the corners of his mouth.* 4 If someone **furrows** their brow or forehead or if it **furrows**, deep folds appear in it because they are frowning. *My bank manager furrowed his brow.* ◆◇◇◇ N-COUNT / PHRASE BRITISH / N-COUNT / V-ERG V n Also V WRITTEN

fur·ry /ˈfɜːri/. 1 A **furry** animal is covered with thick soft hair. *...a guinea-pig, with a long furry tail.* 2 If you describe something as **furry**, you mean that it has a soft rough texture like fur. *...his herringbone tweed coat with its furry lining.* ◆◇◇◇ ADJ / ADJ

fur·ther /ˈfɜːðə/ **furthers, furthering, furthered**. **Further** is a comparative form of **far**. It is also a verb. ◆◆◆◆◆

1 **Further** means to a greater extent or degree. *Inflation is below 5% and set to fall further.* 2 If someone goes **further** in a discussion, they make a more extreme statement or deal with a point more thoroughly. *To have a better comparison, we need to go further and address such issues as repairs and insurance.* 3 If you go or get **further** with something, or take something **further**, you make some progress. *They lacked the scientific personnel to develop the technical apparatus much further.* 4 If you **further** something, you help it to progress, to be successful, or to be achieved. ADV-COMPAR / ADV-COMPAR: ADV after v / ADV-COMPAR: ADV with v / VERB V n

Education needn't only be about furthering your career. ♦ **fur·ther·ance** /'fɜːðərəns/ ...*the furtherance of research in this country.*
N-UNCOUNT: N of n

5 A **further** thing, number of things, or amount of something is an additional thing, number of things, or amount. *There were likely to be further attacks.*
ADJ: ADJ n

6 Further means a greater distance than before or than something else. *Now we live further away from the city centre... He came to a halt at a crossroads fifty yards further on.*
ADV-COMPAR: ADV adv/prep

7 Further is used in expressions such as **'further back'** and **'further ahead'** to refer to a point in time that is earlier or later than the time you are talking about. *Looking still further ahead, by the end of the next century world population is expected to be about ten billion.*
ADV-COMPAR: ADV adv/prep

8 You use **further** to introduce a statement that relates to the same general topic and that gives additional information or makes an additional point. *Dodd made no appeal of his death sentence and, further, instructed his attorney to sue anyone who succeeds in delaying his execution.*
ADV: ADV with cl
PRAGMATICS
FORMAL

9 Further to is used in letters in expressions such as **'further to your letter'** or **'further to our conversation'**, in order to indicate what you are referring to in the letter. *Further to your letter, I agree that there are some problems.*
PHR-PREP
PRAGMATICS
FORMAL, BRITISH

further edu'cation. Further education is education after leaving school, at a college rather than a university. The usual American term is **continuing education.**
N-UNCOUNT
BRITISH

further·more /ˌfɜːðə'mɔː/. Furthermore is used to introduce a piece of information or opinion that adds to or supports the previous one. *Furthermore, they claim that any such interference is completely ineffective.*
ADV: ADV with cl
PRAGMATICS
FORMAL

further·most /'fɜːðəməʊst/. The furthermost one of a number of similar things is the one that is the greatest distance away from a place. *We walked to the furthermost point.*
ADJ: ADJ n

fur·thest /'fɜːðɪst/. Furthest is a superlative form of **far.**
♦◇◇◇

1 Furthest means to a greater or more extreme extent or degree than ever before or than anything or anyone else. *...the south of England, where prices have fallen furthest.*
ADV-SUPERL: ADV with v

2 Furthest means at a greater distance from a particular point than anyone or anything else, or for a greater distance than anyone or anything else. *...those areas furthest from the coast. ...those who have travelled furthest to take part in the Festival.* ▶ Also an adjective. *...the furthest point from earth.*
ADV-SUPERL
ADJ n

fur·tive /'fɜːtɪv/. If you describe someone's behaviour as **furtive**, you disapprove of them behaving as if they want to keep something secret or hidden. *...a furtive glance over her shoulder.* ♦ **fur·tive·ly** *He walked towards the summerhouse, at first furtively.*
ADJ-GRADED
PRAGMATICS

ADV-GRADED

fury /'fjʊəri/. **1** Fury is violent or very strong anger. *She screamed, her face distorted with fury and pain.* **2** If you are **in a fury**, you are very angry. *I had reacted in a fury of grief... He rose to his feet in a fury.*
♦♦◇◇
PHRASE

fuse /fjuːz/. **1** A fuse is a safety device in an electric plug or circuit which stops the flow of electricity when there is a fault in the plug or circuit. *The fuse blew.* **2** When an electric device **fuses** or when you **fuse** it, it stops working because of a fault. *The light fused.*
♦◇◇◇
N-COUNT

V-ERG
V
Also V n

3 A **fuse** is a device on a bomb or firework which delays the explosion so that people can move a safe distance away.
N-COUNT

4 If someone or something **lights the fuse** of a particular situation or activity, they do something which suddenly gets it started. *Hopes for an early cut in German interest rates lit the market's fuse early on.*
PHRASE

5 When one thing **fuses** with another, they join together physically or chemically, usually to become one thing. *The skull bones fuse between the ages of fifteen and twenty-five... Manufactured glass is made by fusing various types of sand... Their solution was to isolate specific clones of B cells and fuse them with cancer*
V-RECIP-ERG:
V with n
pl-n V
V pl-n
V n with n

cells. **6** If something **fuses** two different qualities, ideas, or things, it causes them to join together. *His music of that period fused the rhythms of jazz with classical forms... Past and present fuse.* ♦ **fu·sion** /'fjuːʒən/ **fusions** *His final reform was the fusion of regular and reserve forces.*
V-RECIP-ERG:
V pl-n
V n with n
pl-n V
Also V with n

N-VAR

7 If you **blow a fuse**, you suddenly become very angry and are unable to stay calm. **8** If you say that someone **has a short fuse** or is **on a short fuse** you mean that they are quick to react angrily when something goes wrong.
PHRASE
PHRASE

'fuse box, fuse boxes. The fuse box is the box that contains the fuses for all the electric circuits in a building.
N-COUNT

fused /fjuːzd/. If an electric plug or circuit is **fused**, it has a fuse in it.
ADJ

fu·selage /'fjuːzɪlɑːʒ/ **fuselages.** The fuselage is the main body of an aeroplane, missile, or rocket.
♦◇◇◇
N-COUNT

fu·sil·lade /ˌfjuːzɪ'leɪd, AM -'lɑːd/. A fusillade of shots or objects is a large number of them fired or thrown at the same time. *...a fusillade of bullets fired at close range.*
N-SING

fu·sion /'fjuːʒən/ **fusions. 1** A fusion is something new that is created by joining together different qualities, ideas, or things. *...fusions of jazz, pop and African melodies.* **2** Fusion is the process in which atomic particles combine and produce a large amount of nuclear energy. *...research into nuclear fusion.* **3** See also **fuse.**
♦◇◇◇
N-COUNT

N-UNCOUNT
TECHNICAL

fuss /fʌs/ **fusses, fussing, fussed. 1** Fuss is anxious or excited behaviour which serves no useful purpose. *I don't know what all the fuss is about.* **2** If you **fuss**, you worry or behave in a nervous, anxious way about unimportant things or rush around doing unnecessary things. *Carol fussed about getting me a drink... My wife was fussing over the food.*
♦♦◇◇
N-SING:
no det
VERB: V
V adv/prep
V over n
Also V n

3 If you **fuss over** someone, you pay them a lot of attention and do things to make them happy or comfortable. *Auntie Hilda and Uncle Jack couldn't fuss over them enough.* **4** If you **make a fuss of** someone, you pay them a lot of attention and do things to make them happy or comfortable.
VERB
V over n

PHRASE
BRITISH

5 If you **make a fuss** or **kick up a fuss** about something, you become angry or excited about it and complain. *I don't know why everybody makes such a fuss about a few mosquitoes.*
PHRASE
INFORMAL

fussed /fʌst/. If you say you **are not fussed** about something, you mean you do not mind about it or do not mind what happens. *I'm not fussed as long as we get where we want to go.*
ADJ-GRADED:
with brd-neg,
v-link ADJ
BRITISH,
INFORMAL

fussy /'fʌsi/ **fussier, fussiest. 1** Someone who is **fussy** is very concerned with unimportant details and is difficult to please. *She is not fussy about her food.*
♦◇◇◇
ADJ-GRADED

2 If you describe things as **fussy**, you are criticizing them because they are too elaborate or detailed. *We are not very keen on floral patterns and fussy designs.*
ADJ-GRADED
PRAGMATICS

fus·ty /'fʌsti/ **fustier, fustiest. 1** If you describe something or someone as **fusty**, you disapprove of them because they are old-fashioned in attitudes or ideas. *The fusty old establishment refused to recognise the demand for popular music.*
ADJ-GRADED
PRAGMATICS

2 A **fusty** place or thing has a stale smell. *...fusty old carpets.*
ADJ-GRADED

fu·tile /'fjuːtaɪl, AM -təl/. If you say that something is **futile**, you mean there is no point in doing it, usually because it has no chance of succeeding. *He brought his arm up in a futile attempt to ward off the blow.* ♦ **fu·til·ity** /fjuː'tɪlɪti/ *...the injustice and futility of terrorism.*
♦◇◇◇
ADJ-GRADED

N-UNCOUNT

fu·ton /'fuːtɒn/ **futons.** A futon consists of a thin mattress on a low wooden frame which can be used as a bed or folded up to make a settee.
N-COUNT

fu·ture /'fjuːtʃə/ **futures. 1** The future is the period of time that will come after the present, or the things that will happen then. *No decision on the proposal was likely in the immediate future. ...plans for the future.* **2 Future** things will happen or exist after the present time. *The domestic debate on Denmark's future role in Europe rages on. ...the*
♦♦♦♦
N-SING:
the N

ADJ: ADJ n

future King and Queen. ● **for future reference**: see PHRASE
reference. 3 If you wonder what the **future holds,**
you wonder what will happen in the future.
4 Someone's **future**, or the **future** of something, is N-COUNT
what will happen to them or what they will do after
the present time. *His future as prime minister depends
on the outcome of the elections.* **5** If you say that PHRASE
someone's **future lies** in a particular place or activity,
you think they will be most successful or happy in that
place or doing that activity.
6 If you say that someone or something has a **future**, N-COUNT
you mean that they are likely to be successful or to
survive. *There's no future in this relationship.*
7 When people trade in **futures**, they buy stocks and N-PLURAL
shares, commodities such as coffee or oil, or foreign
currency at a price that is agreed at the time of purchase for items which are delivered some time in the
future.
8 The **future** tense of a verb is the one used to talk ADJ: ADJ n
about things that are going to happen. The **future
perfect** tense of a verb is used to talk about things that
will have happened at some time in the future.
9 You use **in future** when saying what will happen PHRASE
from now on, which will be different from what has

previously happened. *I asked her to be more careful in
future.*
fu·tur·ist /ˈfjuːtʃərɪst/ **futurists.** A **futurist** is N-COUNT
someone who makes predictions about what is go- AMERICAN
ing to happen, on the basis of facts about what is
happening now.
fu·tur·is·tic /ˌfjuːtʃəˈrɪstɪk/. **1** Something that is ◆◇◇◇◇
futuristic looks or seems very modern and unusual, ADJ-GRADED
like something from the future. *...a futuristic steel
and glass structure.* **2** A **futuristic** film or book tells ADJ: ADJ n
a story that is set in the future.
fuzz /fʌz/. **Fuzz** is a mass of short curly hairs. N-UNCOUNT
fuzzy /ˈfʌzi/ **fuzzier, fuzziest. 1** Fuzzy hair sticks ◆◇◇◇◇
up in a soft curly mass. **2** If something is **fuzzy**, it ADJ-GRADED
has a covering that feels soft and like fur. ADJ-GRADED
3 A **fuzzy** picture, image, or sound is unclear and hard ADJ-GRADED
to see or hear. **4** If you or your thoughts are **fuzzy**, you ADJ-GRADED
are confused and cannot think clearly. *He had little
patience for fuzzy ideas.* **5** You describe something as ADJ-GRADED
fuzzy when it is vague and not clearly defined. *The
border between science fact and science fiction gets a
bit fuzzy.*
6 Fuzzy logic is a type of computer logic that is sup- ADJ: ADJ n
posed to imitate the way that humans think.

G g

G, g /dʒiː/ **G's, g's. 1** G is the seventh letter of the N-VAR
English alphabet. **2** In music, **G** is the fifth note in N-VAR
the scale of C major. **3** G or **g** is used as an abbreviation for words beginning with g, such as 'gram'
and 'gallon'. *Oranges contain only 35 calories per
100g.*
gab /gæb/. If you say that someone has **the gift of** PHRASE
the gab, or in American English **the gift of gab**, you INFORMAL
mean that they have the ability to speak easily, confidently, and in a persuasive way. *...salesmen with
the gift of the gab.*
gab·ar·dine /ˌgæbəˈdiːn/ **gabardines;** also spelled N-UNCOUNT
gaberdine. Gabardine is a fairly thick cloth which is also N in pl
used for making coats and suits.
gab·ble /ˈgæbəl/ **gabbles, gabbling, gabbled.** If VERB: V
you **gabble**, you say things so quickly that it is diffi- V adv
cult for people to understand you. *She gabbles on* V n
about drug dealers... One of the soldiers gabbled Also V with
something and pointed at the front door. quote
INFORMAL
ga·ble /ˈgeɪbəl/ **gables.** A **gable** is the triangular N-COUNT
part at the top of the end wall of a building, be-
tween the two sloping sides of the roof. See picture
headed **house and flat.** ♦ **ga·bled** /ˈgeɪbəld/. *...an* ADJ
attractive gabled house.
gad·fly /ˈgædflaɪ/ **gadflies.** If you refer to someone N-COUNT
as a **gadfly**, you believe that they deliberately annoy
or challenge other people, especially people in
authority.
gadg·et /ˈgædʒɪt/ **gadgets.** A **gadget** is a small ◆◇◇◇◇
machine or device which does something useful. N-COUNT
*...kitchen gadgets including toasters, kettles and
percolators.*
gadg·et·ry /ˈgædʒɪtri/. If you refer to a particular N-UNCOUNT
kind of **gadgetry**, you mean small machines or devices which do something useful. *...the latest electronic gadgetry.*
Gael·ic /ˈgeɪlɪk, ˈgælɪk/. **1** Gaelic is a language spo- ◆◇◇◇◇
ken by people in parts of Scotland and Ireland. N-UNCOUNT
► Also an adjective. *...the Gaelic language.* **2** Gaelic ADJ
means coming from or relating to the parts of Scot- ADJ
land and Ireland where Gaelic is spoken. *...an evening of Gaelic music.*
gaffe /gæf/ **gaffes;** also spelled **gaff.** A **gaffe** is a N-COUNT
stupid or careless mistake, for example when you
say or do something that offends or upsets people.

*...social gaffes committed by high-ranking individ-
uals... He made an embarrassing gaffe.*
gaf·fer /ˈgæfə/ **gaffers.** People use **gaffer** to refer N-COUNT:
to the person in charge of the workers at a factory, N-VOC
building-site, or other place of work. INFORMAL
BRITISH
gag /gæg/ **gags, gagging, gagged. 1** If someone ◆◇◇◇◇
gags you, they tie a piece of cloth around your VERB
mouth in order to stop you from speaking. *I gagged* V n
him with a towel. ► Also a noun. *His captors had
put a gag of thick leather in his mouth.* **2** If a person VERB
is gagged by someone in authority, they are pre- be V-ed
vented from expressing their opinion or from pub- Also V n
lishing certain information; used showing disap-
proval. *Judges must not be gagged.* **3** If you **gag**, you VERB
choke and nearly vomit. *I knelt by the toilet and* V
gagged. INFORMAL
4 A **gag** is a joke, especially one told by a professional N-COUNT
comedian. INFORMAL
gaga /ˈgɑːgɑː/. If you say that someone is **gaga** or ADJ-GRADED:
has gone **gaga**, you mean that they are senile. v-link ADJ
INFORMAL
gag·gle /ˈgægəl/ **gaggles.** You can use **gaggle** to N-COLL-
refer to a group of people, usually when you want to COUNT
express contempt for them. *...a gaggle of journalists.* PRAGMATICS
gai·ety /ˈgeɪɪti/. **Gaiety** is a feeling or atmosphere N-UNCOUNT
of liveliness and fun. *Music rang out adding to the* DATED
gaiety and life of the market.
gai·ly /ˈgeɪli/. **1** If you do something **gaily**, you do it ADV-GRADED:
in a lively happy way. *Magda laughed gaily.* ADV with v
2 Something that is **gaily** coloured or **gaily** decorat- ADV-GRADED:
ed is coloured or decorated in a bright pretty way. ADV -ed
...gaily painted front doors.
gain /geɪn/ **gains, gaining, gained. 1** If a person ◆◆◆◆◇
or place **gains** something such as an ability or qual- VERB
ity, they gradually get more of it. *Students can gain* V n
valuable experience by working on the campus ra- V in n
*dio... While it has lost its tranquility, the area has
gained in liveliness.* **2** To **gain** something such as VERB
weight or speed means to have an increase in that V n
particular thing. *The helicopter gained speed as it* V amount
headed toward the mainland... She gained some 25lb Also V
in weight. ► Also a noun. *News on new home sales is* N-VAR
brighter, showing a gain of nearly 8% in June.
3 If you **gain** something, you obtain it, especially after VERB
a lot of effort. *Passing exams is no longer enough to* V n
gain a place at university. **4** If you **gain** from some- VERB

thing such as an event or situation, you get some advantage or benefit from it. *There is absolutely nothing to be gained by feeling bitter... Many areas of the world would actually gain from global warming.* **5** If you do something **for gain**, you do it in order to get some advantage or profit for yourself; used showing disapproval. *...buying art solely for financial gain.* *(V n from/by n/-ing; V from n; PHRASE FORMAL)*

6 If something such as an idea **gains ground**, it gradually becomes more widely known or more popular. *The Christian right has been steadily gaining ground in state politics.* **7** If you do something in order to **gain time**, you do it in order to give yourself enough time to think of a way out of a difficult situation. *Croatia agreed to the truce in order to gain time to buy desperately needed weapons.* *(PHRASE; PHRASE)*

gain on. If you **gain on** someone or something that is moving in front of you, you gradually get closer to them. *The Mercedes began to gain on the van.* *(PHRASAL VB; V P n)*

gain·er /ˈgeɪnə/ **gainers.** A **gainer** is a person or organization that gains something from a particular situation. *Tuesday's notable gainer was Sony, which reached a high of 9,070 yen.* *(N-COUNT)*

gain·ful /ˈgeɪnfʊl/. If you are in **gainful** employment, you have a job for which you are paid and which is not against the law. *...lack of opportunities for gainful employment.* ♦ **gain·ful·ly** *Both parents were gainfully employed.* *(ADJ: ADJ n FORMAL; ADV: ADV -ed)*

gain·say /ˌgeɪnˈseɪ/ **gainsays, gainsaying, gainsaid.** If you say that nobody can **gainsay** something, you mean that it is true or obvious and that everyone would agree with it, although there may be other things connected with it that are more doubtful. *However much people have criticised her style and some of her policies no one will gainsay her courage.* *(VB: with brd-neg PRAGMATICS V n FORMAL)*

gait /geɪt/ **gaits.** A particular kind of **gait** is a particular way of walking. *...a tubby little man in his fifties, with sparse hair and a rolling gait.* *(♦◇◇◇◇ N-COUNT WRITTEN)*

gal /gæl/ **gals. Gal** is used in written English to represent the word 'girl' as it is pronounced in a particular accent. *...a Southern gal.* *(♦◇◇◇◇ N-COUNT; N-VOC)*

gal. gal or **gal. gal.** is a written abbreviation for 'gallon' or 'gallons'.

gala /ˈgɑːlə, AM ˈgeɪlə/ **galas.** A **gala** is a special public celebration, performance, or festival. *...a gala evening at the Royal Opera House.* *(♦◇◇◇◇ N-COUNT)*

gal·axy /ˈgæləksi/ **galaxies;** also spelled **Galaxy.** **1** A **galaxy** is a huge group of stars and planets that extends over many millions of miles. ♦ **ga·lac·tic** /gəˈlæktɪk/ *...the first galactic formations.* **2** The **Galaxy** is the huge group of stars and planets to which the Earth and the Solar System belong. **3** If you talk about a **galaxy of** people from a particular profession, you mean a group of them who are all famous or important. *He is one of a small galaxy of Dutch stars on German television.* *(♦♦◇◇◇ N-COUNT; ADJ: ADJ n; N-PROPER: the N; N-SING: N of n)*

gale /geɪl/ **gales. 1** A **gale** is a very strong wind. *...the ropes that tethered the tents against the fierce winter gales.* **2** You can refer to the loud noise made by a lot of people all laughing at the same time as a **gale of** laughter or **gales of** laughter. *(♦◇◇◇◇ N-COUNT; N of n)*

'gale-force. A **gale-force** wind is very strong. *(ADJ: ADJ n)*

gall /gɔːl/ **galls, galling, galled. 1** You can use **gall** to refer to someone's behaviour when you disapprove of it because it is bold or risky, or does not show enough respect. *I can't get over the gall of the fellow... She had the gall to suggest that I might supply her with information.* **2** If someone's action **galls** you, it makes you feel angry, often because it is unfair to you and you cannot do anything about it. *It must have galled him that Bardo thwarted each of these measures... It was their serenity, their insouciance which galled her most.* ♦ **gall·ing** *It was especially galling to be criticised by this scoundrel.* *(♦◇◇◇◇ N-UNCOUNT PRAGMATICS; VERB it V n that; Also it V n to-inf; ADJ-GRADED)*

gal·lant /ˈgælənt/. Also pronounced /gəˈlænt/ for meaning 3. **1** If someone is **gallant**, they behave bravely and honourably in a dangerous situation. *...the gallant soldiers.* ♦ **gal·lant·ly** *The town responded gallantly to the War.* **2** A **gallant** effort or fight is one in which someone tried very hard to do *(♦◇◇◇◇ ADJ-GRADED; ADV-GRADED; ADJ-GRADED: ADJ n PRAGMATICS)*

something difficult, although in the end they failed; used showing approval. *He died at the age of 82, after a gallant fight against illness.* ♦ **gallantly** *The Spaniard gallantly fought off 11 set points before Seles won 8-6.* **3** If someone is **gallant**, especially a man towards a woman, they are kind, polite, and considerate towards other people. ♦ **gallantly** *He gallantly kissed Marie's hand as we prepared to leave.* *(WRITTEN; ADV-GRADED: ADV with v; ADJ-GRADED DATED; ADV-GRADED: ADV with v)*

gal·lant·ry /ˈgæləntri/. **1** Gallantry is bravery shown by someone who is in danger. *For his gallantry he was awarded a Victoria Cross.* **2** Gallantry is kind and polite behaviour towards other people, especially women. *It's that time of year again, when thoughts turn to romance and gallantry.* *(N-UNCOUNT DATED, FORMAL; N-UNCOUNT DATED)*

'gall bladder, gall bladders. Your **gall bladder** is the organ in your body which contains bile and is next to your liver. *(N-COUNT)*

gal·leon /ˈgæliən/ **galleons.** In former times, a **galleon** was a sailing ship with three masts. *(N-COUNT)*

gal·lery /ˈgæləri/ **galleries. 1** A **gallery** is a place that has permanent exhibitions of works of art in it. *...an art gallery.* **2** A **gallery** is a building or room where works of art are exhibited and sometimes sold. **3** A **gallery** is a raised area at the back or at the sides of a large room or hall, where people can stand or sit. *A crowd already filled the gallery.* **4** The **gallery** in a theatre or concert hall is a raised area like a large balcony that usually contains the cheapest seats. ● If you **play to the gallery**, you do something in public in a way which you hope will impress people. *(♦♦♦◇◇ N-COUNT; N-COUNT; N-COUNT; N-COUNT; PHRASE)*

gal·ley /ˈgæli/ **galleys. 1** On a ship or aircraft, the **galley** is the kitchen. **2** In former times, a **galley** was a ship with sails and a lot of oars. *(♦◇◇◇◇ N-COUNT; N-COUNT)*

Gal·lic /ˈgælɪk/. You use **Gallic** to describe feelings or actions that you think are very typical of France and French people. *Mme Arlette gave a Gallic shrug.* *(♦◇◇◇◇ ADJ-GRADED)*

gal·lon /ˈgælən/ **gallons.** A **gallon** is a unit of measurement for liquids that is equal to eight pints. In Britain, it is equal to 4.564 litres. In America, it is equal to 3.785 litres. *...80 million gallons of water.* *(♦♦◇◇◇ N-COUNT)*

gal·lop /ˈgæləp/ **gallops, galloping, galloped. 1** When a horse **gallops**, it runs very fast so that all four legs are off the ground at the same time in each stride. *The horses galloped away... Staff officers galloped fine horses down the road.* ► Also a noun. *I was forced to attempt a gallop.* **2** If you **gallop**, you ride a horse that is galloping. *Major Winston galloped into the distance.* **3** If you **gallop**, you run somewhere very quickly. *They are galloping around the garden playing football.* **4** If something such as a process **gallops**, it develops very quickly and is often difficult to control. *China's economy galloped ahead.* *(♦◇◇◇◇ V-ERG V adv/prep V n prep/adv; VERB V prep/adv; VERB: V Also V n INFORMAL; VERB V adv)*

gal·lows /ˈgæləʊz/; **gallows** is both the singular and the plural form. A **gallows** is a wooden frame used to execute criminals by hanging. *(N-COUNT)*

gall·stone /ˈgɔːlstəʊn/ **gallstones.** A **gallstone** is a small painful lump which can develop in your gall bladder. *(N-COUNT)*

ga·lore /gəˈlɔː/. You use **galore** to emphasize that something you like exists in very large quantities. *You'll be able to win prizes galore.* *(♦◇◇◇◇ ADJ: n ADJ PRAGMATICS INFORMAL)*

ga·loshes /gəˈlɒʃɪz/. **Galoshes** are waterproof shoes, usually made of rubber, which you wear over your ordinary shoes to prevent them getting wet. *(N-PLURAL)*

gal·va·nize /ˈgælvənaɪz/ **galvanizes, galvanizing, galvanized;** also spelled **galvanise** in British English. To **galvanize** someone means to cause them to take action, for example by making them feel very excited or angry. *They have been galvanised into collective action.* *(♦◇◇◇◇ VERB: V n beV-ed into n/-ing Also V n into n/-ing)*

gal·va·nized /ˈgælvənaɪzd/; also spelled **galvanised.** **Galvanized** metal has been covered with zinc in order to protect it from rust and other damage. *...corrosion-resistant galvanized steel.* *(ADJ)*

gam·bit /ˈgæmbɪt/ **gambits. 1** A **gambit** is an action which you carry out to try to gain an advantage in a situation or game. *Campaign strategists are* *(N-COUNT)*

calling the plan a clever politic gambit. **2** A **gambit** is a remark which you make to someone in order to start or continue a conversation with them. *His favourite opening gambit is: 'You are so beautiful'.* N-COUNT

gam·ble /'gæmbəl/ **gambles, gambling, gambled.** ◆◆◆◇◇ **1** If you **gamble** on something, you take a risky action or decision in the hope of gaining money, success, or an advantage. *Few firms will be willing to gamble on new products... They are not prepared to gamble their careers on this matter... Who wants to gamble with the life of a friend?* ► Also a noun. *...the French president's risky gamble in calling a referendum.* VERB V on n/-ing V n on n V with n Also V, V n, V that N-COUNT **2** If you **gamble** an amount of money, you bet it in a game such as cards or on the result of a race or competition. *John gambled heavily on the horses. ...the only country in Europe that allows minors to gamble... He gambled away his family estates.* VERB: V n V on n V V n with *away* ♦ **gam·bling** /'gæmblɪŋ/. *But opponents of the plan argue that gambling in Chicago will have the opposite effect.* N-UNCOUNT

gam·bler /'gæmblə/ **gamblers.** ◆◇◇◇◇ **1** A **gambler** is someone who gambles regularly, for example in card games or horse racing. N-COUNT **2** If you describe someone as a **gambler**, you mean that they are ready to take risks in order to gain advantages or success. N-COUNT

gam·bol /'gæmbəl/ **gambols, gambolling, gambolled;** spelled **gamboling**, **gamboled** in American English. If animals or people **gambol**, they run or jump about in a playful way. *...newborn lambs gambolling in the fields.* VERB V prep/adv

game /geɪm/ **games.** ◆◆◆◆◆ **1** A **game** is an activity or sport usually involving skill, knowledge, or chance, in which you follow fixed rules and try to win against an opponent or to solve a puzzle. *...the wonderful game of football. ...a video game.* N-COUNT **2** A **game** is one particular occasion on which a game is played. *We won three games against Australia.* N-COUNT **3** A **game** is a part of a match, for example in tennis or bridge, consisting of a fixed number of points. *...the last three points of the second game.* N-COUNT

4 **Games** are an organized event in which competitions in several sports take place. *...the 1996 Olympic Games.* N-PLURAL **5** **Games** are organized sports activities that children do at school. *He is remembered for being bad at games.* N-PLURAL BRITISH **6** Someone's **game** is the degree of skill or the style that they use when playing a particular game. *Once I was through the first set my game picked up.* N-SING

7 You can use **game** to describe a way of behaving in which a person uses a particular plan, usually in order to gain an advantage for himself or herself. *The Americans have been playing a very delicate political game.* N-COUNT **8** If you beat someone **at** their **own game**, you use the same methods that they have used, but more successfully, so that you gain an advantage over them. *To trap the killer they had to play him at his own game.* PHRASE

9 If you say that someone is **playing games**, you are annoyed with them because they are not treating a situation seriously; used showing disapproval. *'Don't play games with me' he thundered.* PHRASE PRAGMATICS **10** If someone or something **gives the game away**, they reveal a secret or reveal their feelings. *She'd never been to a posh mansion, and was afraid she might give the game away... The faces of the two conspirators gave the game away!* PHRASE **11** If you say '**the game is up**', you mean that someone's secret plans or activities have been revealed and therefore must stop because they cannot succeed. PHRASE

12 If you say that someone is **game** or **game for** something, you mean that they are willing to do something new, unusual, or risky. *He still had new ideas and was game to try them... He said he's game for a similar challenge next year.* ADJ-GRADED: v-link ADJ **13** See also **gamely**.

14 Wild animals or birds that are hunted for sport and sometimes cooked and eaten are referred to as **game**. N-UNCOUNT

'**game bird, game birds.** **Game birds** are birds which are shot for food or for sport. N-COUNT

game·keeper /'geɪmkiːpə/ **gamekeepers.** A **gamekeeper** is a person who takes care of the wild animals or birds that are kept on someone's land for hunting. N-COUNT

game·ly /'geɪmli/. If you do something **gamely**, you do it bravely or with a lot of effort. *He gamely defended his organisation's decision.* ADV-GRADED: ADV with v

'**game plan, game plans.** **1** In sport, a team's **game plan** is the strategy they intend to use during a match in order to win it. N-COUNT **2** Someone's **game plan** is the actions they intend to take and the policies they intend to adopt in order to achieve a particular thing. *...if he has a game plan for winning the deal.* N-COUNT JOURNALISM

games·man·ship /'geɪmzmənʃɪp/. **Gamesmanship** is the art or practice of winning a game by clever tactics which are not against the rules but are very close to cheating. N-UNCOUNT

gam·ine /'gæmiːn/. If you describe a girl or a woman as **gamine**, you mean that she is attractive in a boyish way. *She had a gamine charm.* ADJ-GRADED

gam·ing /'geɪmɪŋ/. **Gaming** means the same as **gambling**, especially at cards, roulette, and other games of chance. *...the most fashionable gaming club in London.* ◆◇◇◇◇ N-UNCOUNT

gam·ma /'gæmə/ **gammas.** **Gamma** is the third letter of the Greek alphabet. ◆◇◇◇◇ N-VAR

'**gamma rays.** **Gamma rays** are a type of electromagnetic radiation that has a shorter wavelength and higher energy than X-rays. N-PLURAL

gam·mon /'gæmən/. **Gammon** is smoked or salted meat from a pig, similar to bacon. N-UNCOUNT BRITISH

gam·ut /'gæmət/. **1** The **gamut** of something is the complete range of things of that kind, or a wide variety of things of that kind. *...the whole gamut of financial services... I experienced the gamut of emotions: shock, anger, sadness, disgust, confusion.* N-SING **2** To **run the gamut** of something means to include, express, or experience all the different things of that kind, or a wide variety of them. *The show runs the gamut of 20th century design... The reviews for 'On a Clear Day' ran the gamut from contempt to qualified rapture.* PHRASE

gan·der /'gændə/ **ganders.** A **gander** is a male goose. N-COUNT

gang /gæŋ/ **gangs, ganging, ganged.** ◆◆◆◇◇ **1** A **gang** is a group of people, especially young people, who go around together and often deliberately cause trouble. *...during the fight with a rival gang.* N-COUNT **2** A **gang** is a group of criminals who work together to commit crimes. *...a gang of masked robbers.* N-COUNT **3** A **gang** is a group of manual workers who work together. *...a gang of labourers.* N-COUNT

gang up. If people **gang up** on someone, they unite against them. *All the other parties ganged up to keep them out of power... All the girls in my class seemed to gang up against me.* PHRASAL VB V P on n V P to-inf V P against n INFORMAL

gang·land /'gæŋlænd/. **Gangland** is used to describe activities or people that are involved in organized crime. *They were gangland killings.* ADJ: ADJ n

gan·gling /'gæŋglɪŋ/. **Gangling** is used to describe a young person, especially a man, who is tall, thin, and clumsy in their movements. *...his gangling, bony frame.* ADJ: ADJ n

gan·gly /'gæŋgli/. If you describe someone as **gangly**, you mean that they are tall and thin and have a slightly awkward or clumsy manner. ADJ-GRADED

gang·plank /'gæŋplæŋk/ **gangplanks.** The **gangplank** is a short bridge or platform that can be placed between the side of a boat and the shore, so that people can get on or off. N-COUNT

gan·grene /'gæŋgriːn/. **Gangrene** is the decay that can occur in a part of a person's body if the blood stops flowing to it. N-UNCOUNT

gang·ster /'gæŋstə/ **gangsters.** A **gangster** is a member of an organized group of violent criminals. ◆◇◇◇◇ N-COUNT

gang·way /'gæŋweɪ/ **gangways.** **1** The **gangway** is the gangplank leading onto a ship. N-COUNT **2** The **gangway** is a passage left between rows of seats, for example in a theatre or aircraft, for people to walk along. N-COUNT BRITISH

gan·try /'gæntri/ **gantries.** A gantry is a high metal N-COUNT structure that supports a crane, a set of road signs, railway signals, or other equipment.

gaol /dʒeɪl/ **gaols, gaoling, gaoled.** See **jail.**

gaol·er /'dʒeɪlə/ **gaolers.** See **jailer.**

gap /gæp/ **gaps. 1** A gap is a space between two ♦♦♦◇◇ things or a hole in the middle of something solid. N-COUNT *He pulled the thick curtains together, leaving just a narrow gap. ...the wind tearing through gaps in the window frames.* **2** A gap is a period of time when N-COUNT you are not busy or when you stop doing something that you normally do. *There followed a gap of four years, during which William joined the Army.* **3** If N-COUNT there is something missing from a situation that prevents it being complete or satisfactory, you can say that there is a gap. *China can't fill the economic gap left by the cut in Soviet support.* **4** A gap be- N-COUNT: tween two groups of people, things, or sets of ideas with supp is a big difference between them. *...the gap between rich and poor... America's trade gap widened.*

gape /geɪp/ **gapes, gaping, gaped. 1** If you ♦◇◇◇◇ gape, you look at someone or something in sur- VERB prise, usually with an open mouth. *His secretary* Also V *stopped taking notes to gape at me.* **2** If you say that VERB something such as a hole or a wound **gapes,** you are PRAGMATICS emphasizing that it is big or wide. *A hole gaped in* V *the roof.* ♦ **gaping** *...a gaping wound in her back.* ADJ

'gap-fill, gap-fills. In language teaching, a **gap-fill** N-COUNT test is an exercise in which words are removed from a text and replaced with spaces. The learner has to fill each space with the missing word.

,gap-'toothed. If you describe a person or their ADJ smile as **gap-toothed,** you mean that some of that WRITTEN person's teeth are missing.

gar·age /'gæra:ʒ, -rɪdʒ, AM gə'ra:ʒ/ **garages. 1** A ♦♦◇◇◇ garage is a building in which you keep a car. See N-COUNT picture headed **house and flat.** *...a double garage.* **2** A garage is a place where you can get your car re- N-COUNT paired, buy a car, or buy petrol. *Nelson Garage has the used car you're after.*

garb /ga:b/. You can refer to the clothes someone is N-UNCOUNT wearing as their **garb** when you want to draw atten- WRITTEN tion to these clothes, for example because they are unusual. *He wore the garb of a scout, not a general.* ♦ **garbed** *She was garbed in a bouffant pink ball gown.* ♦ **-garbed** *...the small blue-garbed woman* COMB *with a brown wrinkled face.*

gar·bage /'ga:bɪdʒ/. **1** Garbage is rubbish, espe- ♦◇◇◇◇ cially waste from a kitchen. *...services such as gar-* N-UNCOUNT *bage collection.* **2** If someone says that an idea or N-UNCOUNT opinion is **garbage,** they are emphasizing that they PRAGMATICS believe it is untrue or unimportant. *Furious govern-* INFORMAL *ment officials branded her story 'garbage'.*

'garbage can, garbage cans. A garbage can is a N-COUNT container that you put rubbish into. The usual Brit- AMERICAN ish word is **dustbin.** See picture headed **house and flat.**

gar·bled /'ga:bəld/. A **garbled** message or report ADJ-GRADED contains confused or wrong details.

gar·den /'ga:dən/ **gardens, gardening, gar-** ♦♦♦♦◇ **dened. 1** A garden is a piece of land next to N-COUNT someone's house where they grow flowers or veg- etables. A garden often includes a lawn. In Ameri- can English, the word **yard** is often used instead of **garden. 2** If you **garden,** you do work in your gar- VERB: V den such as weeding or planting. ♦ **gar·den·ing** *I* N-UNCOUNT *have taken up gardening again.* **3** Gardens are N-PLURAL places like a park that have areas of plants, trees, and grass, and that people can visit and walk around. *The Gardens are open from 10.30am until 5pm.* **4** Gardens is sometimes used as part of the name of a street. *He lives at 9, Acacia Gardens.*

'garden centre, garden centres. A garden ♦◇◇◇◇ centre is a large shop where you can buy things for N-COUNT your garden such as plants and gardening tools.

gar·den·er /'ga:dənə/ **gardeners. 1** A gardener is ♦♦◇◇◇ paid to work in someone else's garden. **2** A garden- N-COUNT er is someone who enjoys working in their own gar- N-COUNT den growing flowers or vegetables.

gar·denia /ga:'di:niə/ **gardenias.** A gardenia is a N-COUNT type of large white or yellow flower with a very pleasant smell. A **gardenia** is also the bush on which these flowers grow.

'garden party, garden parties. A garden party N-COUNT is a formal party that is held out of doors, especially in a large private garden, during the afternoon.

gar·gan·tuan /ga:'gæntʃʊən/. If you say that some- ADJ-GRADED thing is **gargantuan,** you are emphasizing that it is PRAGMATICS very large. *...a gargantuan corruption scandal.* WRITTEN

gar·gle /'ga:gəl/ **gargles, gargling, gargled.** If VERB you **gargle,** you wash your mouth and throat by fill- V ing your mouth with a liquid, making a bubbling noise in your throat, then spitting out the liquid. *Try gargling with salt water as soon as a cough begins.* ▶ A **gargle** is a liquid which is used for gargling. *The* N-COUNT *mixture can be used as a gargle.*

gar·goyle /'ga:gɔɪl/ **gargoyles.** A gargoyle is a N-COUNT decorative stone carving on old buildings. It is usually shaped like the head of a strange and ugly creature, and water drains through it from the roof of the building.

gar·ish /'geərɪʃ/. You describe something as **garish** ♦◇◇◇◇ when you dislike it because it is very bright in an ADJ-GRADED unattractive, showy way. *...garish, illuminated signs.* PRAGMATICS ♦ **gar·ish·ly** *...a garishly patterned three-piece suite.* ADV-GRADED

gar·land /'ga:lənd/ **garlands, garlanding, gar-** ♦◇◇◇◇ **landed. 1** A garland is a circular decoration made N-COUNT from flowers and leaves. People sometimes wear garlands of flowers on their heads or around their necks. **2** If people, places, or objects **are garlanded,** VB: usu people hang garlands or similar decorations around passive them. *Players and officials were garlanded with* be V-ed with n *flowers.*

gar·lic /'ga:lɪk/. Garlic is the small, white, round ♦♦◇◇◇ bulb of a plant related to the onion plant, which is N-UNCOUNT used as a flavouring. *...a clove of garlic.* ♦ **gar·licky** ADJ-GRADED *...a garlicky salad. ...garlicky breath.*

gar·ment /'ga:mənt/ **garments.** You can refer to a ♦♦◇◇◇ piece of clothing as a **garment,** especially when you N-COUNT are talking about the manufacture or sale of clothes. *...the garment industry.*

gar·ner /'ga:nə/ **garners, garnering, garnered.** ♦◇◇◇◇ If someone has collected or gained something VERB useful or valuable, you can say that they have **gar-** V n **nered** it. *Durham had garnered three times as many* FORMAL *votes as Carey.*

gar·net /'ga:nɪt/ **garnets.** A garnet is a hard, shiny, N-COUNT usually red stone that is used in making jewellery.

gar·nish /'ga:nɪʃ/ **garnishes, garnishing, gar-** ♦◇◇◇◇ **nished. 1** A garnish is a small amount of salad, N-VAR herbs, or other food that is used to decorate pre- pared food. **2** If you **garnish** prepared food, you VERB: V n decorate it with a garnish.

gar·ret /'gærɪt/ **garrets.** A garret is a small room at N-COUNT the top of a house, especially one that is rented to a writer, artist, or other lodger.

gar·ri·son /'gærɪsən/ **garrisons, garrisoning,** ♦◇◇◇◇ **garrisoned. 1** A garrison is a group of soldiers N-COLL- whose task is to guard the town or building where COUNT they live. You can also refer to the buildings which the soldiers live in as a garrison. **2** A garrison is N-COUNT buildings which the soldiers live in. **3** To garrison a VERB: V n place means to put soldiers there in order to protect be V-ed adv/ it. *No other soldiers were garrisoned there.* prep

gar·rotte /gə'rɒt/ **garrottes, garrotting, garrot-** **ted. 1** If someone **is garrotted,** they are killed by VB: usu being strangled or having their neck broken, using a passive device such as a piece of wire or a metal collar. *The* be V-ed *two guards had been garrotted.* **2** A garrotte is a N-COUNT piece of wire or a metal collar used to garrotte someone.

gar·ru·lous /'gærələs/. If you describe someone as ADJ-GRADED **garrulous,** you mean that they talk a great deal, es- pecially about unimportant things.

gar·ter /'ga:tə/ **garters.** A garter is a piece of elas- N-COUNT tic worn round the top of a stocking or sock in order to prevent it slipping down.

gas /gæs/ **gases, gasses, gassing, gassed.** ♦♦♦♦◇ The form **gases** is the plural of the noun. The form

gasses is the third person singular of the verb. **1 Gas** is a substance like air that is neither liquid nor solid and burns easily. It is used as a fuel for fires, cookers, and central heating. **2** A **gas** is any substance that is neither liquid nor solid, for example oxygen or hydrogen. ...*gas and dust from the volcanic eruption.* **3 Gas** is a poisonous gas that can be used as a weapon. **4** To **gas** a person or animal means to kill them by making them breathe poisonous gas. **5 Gas** is a gas used for medical purposes, for example to make patients feel less pain or go to sleep during an operation. **6 Gas** is the fuel which is used to drive motor vehicles. The British word is **petrol**. ...*a tank of gas.* ...*gas stations.* • If you **step on the gas** when you are driving a vehicle, you go faster. **7** See also **greenhouse gas, natural gas, tear gas, gas chamber, gas mask.**
N-UNCOUNT / *N-VAR* / *N-VAR* / *VERB: V n* / *N-VAR* / *N-UNCOUNT AMERICAN* / *PHRASE*

'gas chamber, gas chambers. A gas chamber is a room that has been specially built so that it can be filled with poisonous gas in order to kill people. *N-COUNT*

gas·eous /ˈɡæsɪəs, ˈɡeɪʃəs/. You use **gaseous** to describe something which is in the form of a gas, rather than a solid or liquid. *Freon exists both in liquid and gaseous states.* *ADJ*

'gas fire, gas fires. A gas fire is a fire that produces heat by burning gas. *N-COUNT*

'gas guzzler, gas guzzlers. If you say that a car is a **gas guzzler** you mean that it is not economical to run because it uses so much petrol. *N-COUNT INFORMAL AMERICAN*

gash /ɡæʃ/ **gashes, gashing, gashed. 1** A gash is a long deep cut in your skin or in the surface of something. **2** If you **gash** something, you accidentally make a long and deep cut in it. *He gashed his leg while felling trees.* ◆◇◇◇◇ *N-COUNT* / *VERB V n*

gas·ket /ˈɡæskɪt/ **gaskets.** A gasket is a flat piece of soft material that you put between two joined surfaces in a pipe or engine in order to make sure that gas and oil cannot escape. *N-COUNT*

'gas mask, gas masks. A gas mask is a device worn over someone's face in order to protect them from poisonous gases. ◆◇◇◇◇ *N-COUNT*

gaso·line /ˈɡæsəliːn/. Gasoline is the fuel which is used to drive motor vehicles. The British word is **petrol**. ◆◇◇◇ *N-UNCOUNT AMERICAN*

gasp /ɡɑːsp, ɡæsp/ **gasps, gasping, gasped. 1** A gasp is a short quick breath of air that you take in through your mouth, especially when you are surprised, shocked, or in pain. *An audible gasp went round the court...* *She gave a small gasp of pain.* **2** When you **gasp**, you take a short quick breath through your mouth, especially when you are surprised, shocked, or in pain. *She gasped for air...* *'Stop!' he gasped.* **3** If you describe something as the **last gasp**, you are emphasizing that it is the final action of something or that it happens in the last possible moment. *This is probably the last gasp of the low labor-cost policy.* ◆◆◇◇ *N-COUNT* / *VERB: V, V with quote* / *PHRASE* [PRAGMATICS]

'gas station, gas stations. A gas station is a place where gasoline is sold. The British expression is **petrol station**. ◆◇◇◇ *N-COUNT AMERICAN*

gas·sy /ˈɡæsi/ **gassier, gassiest.** Something which is **gassy** contains a lot of bubbles or gas. *ADJ-GRADED*

gas·tric /ˈɡæstrɪk/. You use **gastric** to describe processes, pain, or illnesses that occur in someone's stomach. ...*gastric ulcers.* ◆◇◇◇◇ *ADJ: ADJ n MEDICAL*

gas·tro·en·teri·tis /ˌɡæstrəʊentəˈraɪtɪs/; also spelled **gastro-enteritis**. Gastroenteritis is an illness in which the lining of your stomach and intestines becomes swollen, causing sickness and diarrhoea. *N-UNCOUNT MEDICAL*

gas·tro·nome /ˈɡæstrənəʊm/ **gastronomes.** A gastronome is someone who enjoys preparing and eating good food. *N-COUNT FORMAL*

gas·trono·my /ɡæsˈtrɒnəmi/. Gastronomy is the activity and knowledge involved in preparing and appreciating good food. ♦ **gas·tro·nom·ic** *Paris is the gastronomic capital of the world.* ...*gastronomic delights.* *N-UNCOUNT FORMAL* / *ADJ*

gas·works /ˈɡæswɜːks/ **gasworks;** also spelled **gas works.** A gasworks is a factory where gas is made, usually from coal, to be used as a fuel. *N-COUNT*

gate /ɡeɪt/ **gates. 1** A gate is a structure like a door which is used at the entrance to a field, a garden, or the grounds of a building. See picture headed **house and flat. 2** In an airport, a gate is an exit through which passengers reach their aeroplane. ...*the departure gate.* **3 Gate** is used in the names of streets that stand on the site of an old gate into a city. ...*9 Palace Gate.* **4** The **gate** at a sporting event such as a football match is the total number of people who attend it. ◆◆◆◇◇ *N-COUNT* / *N-COUNT* / *N-COUNT* / *N-COUNT*

ga·teau /ˈɡætəʊ/ **gateaux.** A gateau is a very rich, elaborate cake, especially one with cream in it. *N-VAR BRITISH*

gate·crash /ˈɡeɪtkræʃ/ **gatecrashes, gatecrashing, gatecrashed.** If someone **gatecrashes** a party or other social event, they go to it, even though they have not been invited. *He had gatecrashed but he was with other people we knew.* ♦ **gate·crash·er, gatecrashers.** *VERB: V n* / *V INFORMAL* / *N-COUNT*

gate·house /ˈɡeɪthaʊs/ **gatehouses.** A gatehouse is a small house next to a gate in the boundary of a park or country estate. *N-COUNT*

gate·keeper /ˈɡeɪtkiːpə/ **gatekeepers.** A gatekeeper is a person who is in charge of a gate and who allows people through it. *N-COUNT*

'gate money. Gate money is the total amount of money that is paid by the spectators who attend a sports match or other event. *N-UNCOUNT*

gate·post /ˈɡeɪtpəʊst/ **gateposts.** A gatepost is a post in the ground which a gate is hung from, or which it is fastened to when it is closed. *N-COUNT*

gate·way /ˈɡeɪtweɪ/ **gateways. 1** A gateway is an entrance where there is a gate. *The ruined castle has an attractive gateway.* **2** A gateway to something is a way of reaching, achieving, or discovering it. *New York is the great gateway to America... Science A levels are not a gateway to a successful career.* ◆◇◇◇◇ *N-COUNT* / *N-COUNT*

gath·er /ˈɡæðə/ **gathers, gathering, gathered. 1** If people **gather** somewhere or if someone or something **gathers** them there, they come together in a group. *In the evenings, we gathered around the fireplace and talked... The man signalled for me to gather the children together.* **2** If you **gather** things, you collect them together so that you can use them. *I suggest we gather enough firewood to last the night... She stood up and started gathering her things together.* ► **Gather up** means the same as **gather**. *When Sutcliffe had gathered up his papers, he went out.* ♦ **gath·er·er, gatherers.** ...*brazil nut gatherers.* **3** If you **gather** information or evidence, you gradually collect it. ♦ **gatherer** ...*professional intelligence gatherers.* **4** If something **gathers** speed, momentum, or force, it gradually becomes faster or more powerful. *Demands for his dismissal have gathered momentum in recent weeks.* **5** When you **gather** something such as your strength, courage, or thoughts, you make an effort to prepare yourself to do something. *You must gather your strength for the journey.* ► **Gather up** means the same as **gather**. *She was gathering up her courage to approach him.* **6** You use **gather** in expressions such as '**I gather**' and '**as far as I can gather**' when you are introducing information that you have found out, especially when you have found it out in an indirect way. *I gather his report is highly critical of the trial judge... 'He speaks English,' she said to Graham. 'I gathered that.'* **7** If you **gather** fabric or cloth, you make a row of very small pleats in it by sewing a thread through it and then pulling the thread tight. ► Also a noun. *Try soft gathers at the waist on trousers.* **8** • to **gather dust**: see **dust**. ◆◆◆◆◇ *V-ERG V P noun V n with together Also V* / *VERB V n, V n with together* / *PHRASAL VB V P noun Also V n P* / *N-COUNT* / *VERB: V n* / *N-COUNT* / *VERB V n* / *VERB V n* / *PHRASAL VB V P noun Also V n P* / *VERB V that n* [PRAGMATICS] / *VERB: V n* / *N-PLURAL* / *PHRASAL VB*

gather up. See **gather** 2, 5.

gath·er·ing /ˈɡæðərɪŋ/ **gatherings. 1** A gathering is a group of people meeting together. **2** If you refer to the **gathering** dusk, darkness, or gloom, you mean that the light is gradually decreasing. ◆◆◇◇◇ *N-COUNT* / *ADJ: ADJ n*

gator /ˈɡeɪtə/ **gators;** also spelled **'gator.** A gator is the same as an **alligator**. *N-COUNT AMERICAN, INFORMAL*

gauche /gəʊʃ/. If you describe someone as **gauche**, you mean that they are awkward and uncomfortable in the company of other people. `ADJ-GRADED`

gaudy /'gɔːdi/ **gaudier, gaudiest.** If you describe something as **gaudy**, you mean it is very bright-coloured and showy, and often you are suggesting that it is vulgar. *...her gaudy orange-and-purple floral hat.* ◆◇◇◇◇ `ADJ-GRADED`

gauge /geɪdʒ/ **gauges, gauging, gauged. 1** If you **gauge** the speed or strength of something, or if you gauge an amount, you measure or calculate it. *He gauged the wind at over thirty knots.* **2** A **gauge** is a device that measures the amount or quantity of something and shows the amount measured. *...temperature gauges. ...a pressure gauge.* **3** If you **gauge** people's actions, feelings, or intentions in a particular situation, you consider or find out about them, in order to make a judgment about them. *To gauge consumer reaction, we canvassed shoppers in London's West End.* **4** A **gauge** of a situation is a fact or event that can be used to judge it. *The index is the government's chief gauge of future economic activity.* ◆◆◇◇◇ `VERB` `V n` `N-COUNT` `VERB` `V n` `N-SING`

5 A **gauge** is the distance between the two rails on a railway line. *...a narrow gauge railway.* **6** A **gauge** is the thickness of something, especially metal or wire. `N-COUNT` `N-COUNT`

gaunt /gɔːnt/. If someone looks **gaunt**, they look very thin, usually because they have been very ill. ◆◇◇◇◇ `ADJ-GRADED`

gaunt·let /'gɔːntlɪt/ **gauntlets. 1** Gauntlets are long, thick, protective gloves. **2** If you **run the gauntlet**, you are attacked or criticized by a lot of hostile people, especially because you are obliged to pass through a group of them. *She was forced to run a gauntlet of some 300 jeering demonstrators.* **3** If you **throw down the gauntlet** to someone, you say or do something that challenges them to argue or compete with you. If someone **takes up the gauntlet**, they accept a challenge that has been offered. ◆◇◇◇◇ `N-COUNT` `PHRASE` `PHRASE`

gauze /gɔːz/. **Gauze** is a type of light soft cloth with tiny holes in it. ◆ **gauzy** *...thin, gauzy curtains.* `N-UNCOUNT` `ADJ: ADJ n`

gave /geɪv/. **Gave** is the past tense of **give**.

gav·el /'gævəl/ **gavels.** A **gavel** is a small wooden hammer that a judge, auctioneer, or chairman of a meeting bangs on a table to get people's attention. `N-COUNT`

gawd /gɔːd/. **Gawd** is used in written English to represent the word 'god' pronounced in a particular accent or tone of voice. `EXCLAM` `INFORMAL`

gawk /gɔːk/ **gawks, gawking, gawked.** If someone **gawks** at someone or something, they stare at them in a rude, stupid, or unthinking way. *Tens of thousands came to gawk.* `VERB:` `V at n` `V`

gawky /'gɔːki/. If you describe someone, especially a teenager, as **gawky**, you mean they are awkward and clumsy. `ADJ-GRADED`

gawp /gɔːp/ **gawps, gawping, gawped.** To **gawp** means the same as to **gawk**. *Thorpe could only stand and gawp.* `VERB:` `V at n` `V` `BRITISH`

gay /geɪ/ **gays; gayer, gayest. 1** A **gay** person is homosexual. *...gay men. ...the gay community.* ▶ **Gays** are homosexual people, especially homosexual men. *...lesbians and gays.* ◆ **gay·ness** *...Mike's admission of his gayness.* **2** A **gay** person is fun to be with because they are lively and cheerful. **3** A **gay** object is brightly coloured and pretty to look at. ◆◆◆◇ `ADJ` `N-COUNT` `N-UNCOUNT` `ADJ-GRADED` `DATED` `ADJ-GRADED` `DATED`

gay libe'ration. **Gay liberation** is a political movement, started in the 1970s, to fight prejudice and discrimination against gay people. `N-UNCOUNT`

gaze /geɪz/ **gazes, gazing, gazed. 1** If you **gaze** at someone or something, you look steadily at them for a long time, for example because you find them interesting. *He gazed reflectively at the fire... The girls stood still, gazing around the building.* **2** You can talk about someone's **gaze** as a way of describing how they are looking at something, especially when they are looking steadily at it. *She felt increasingly uncomfortable under the woman's steady gaze.* ◆◆◇◇◇ `VERB` `V at n` `V prep/adv` `N-COUNT`

ga·zebo /gə'ziːbəʊ, AM -'zeɪ-/ **gazebos.** A **gazebo** is a small building with open sides. Gazebos are of- `N-COUNT`

ten put up in gardens so that people can sit in them to enjoy the view.

ga·zelle /gə'zel/ **gazelles.** A **gazelle** is a type of small African or Asian antelope. `N-COUNT`

ga·zette /gə'zet/ **gazettes.** A **gazette** is a newspaper or journal. *His detention has been announced officially in the government gazette. ...the Arkansas Gazette.* ◆◇◇◇◇ `N-COUNT`

ga·zump /gə'zʌmp/ **gazumps, gazumping, gazumped.** If you **are gazumped** by someone, they agree to sell their house to you, but then sell it to someone else who offers to pay a higher price. ◆ **ga·zump·ing** *During the 1980s property boom, gazumping was common.* `VB: usu` `passive` `BRITISH,` `INFORMAL` `N-UNCOUNT`

GB /,dʒiː 'biː/. **GB** is the official abbreviation for **Great Britain**. ◆◆◇◇◇

GBH /,dʒiː biː 'eɪtʃ/. **GBH** is an abbreviation for **grievous bodily harm**. `N-UNCOUNT` `BRITISH`

GCE /,dʒiː siː 'iː/ **GCEs. 1** In Britain, GCE examinations are taken by schoolchildren. GCE O levels used to be taken at age fifteen or sixteen. GCE A levels are taken at age seventeen or eighteen. **GCE** is an abbreviation for 'General Certificate of Education'. **2** GCEs are GCE O levels. *He's got eight GCEs.* `ADJ: ADJ n` `N-VAR`

GCSE /,dʒiː siː es 'iː/ **GCSEs.** In Britain, GCSEs are examinations which schoolchildren take when they are fifteen or sixteen years old. **GCSE** is an abbreviation for 'General Certificate of Secondary Education'. *...as soon as she had taken her GCSEs... I have a GCSE in Religious Studies.* ◆◇◇◇◇ `N-VAR`

GDP /,dʒiː diː 'piː/. **GDP** is an abbreviation for 'gross domestic product', which is the total value of goods and services produced within a country in a year. ◆◆◇◇◇ `N-UNCOUNT` `TECHNICAL`

gear /gɪə/ **gears, gearing, geared. 1** In a machine or vehicle, a **gear** is a device or system which controls the rate at which the energy being used is converted into motion. When a vehicle's engine is operating at a particular rate, you can say it is in a particular **gear**. *The BMW accelerated, changing gears... The car was in fourth gear... He put the truck in gear and drove on.* **2** The **gear** involved in a particular activity is the equipment or special clothing that you use. *...100 officers in riot gear.* **3** If someone or something is **geared to** or **towards** a particular purpose, they are organized or designed in order to achieve that purpose. *Colleges are not always geared to the needs of mature students.* ◆◆◆◇◇ `N-COUNT` `also in N` `N-UNCOUNT` `ADJ-GRADED`

gear up. If someone **is gearing up** for a particular activity, they are preparing to do it. If they **are geared up** to it, they are prepared and able to do it. *All the parties will be gearing up for a general election... The factory was geared up to make 1,100 cars a day.* `PHRASAL VB` `usu passive` `V P for/to n` `be V-ed P to-inf`

gear·box /'gɪəbɒks/ **gearboxes.** A **gearbox** is the system of gears in an engine or vehicle. ◆◇◇◇◇ `N-COUNT`

'gear lever, gear levers. A **gear lever** or a **gear stick** is the lever that you use to change gear in a car or other vehicle. The usual American term is **gearshift**. See picture headed **car and bicycle**. `N-COUNT` `BRITISH`

gear·shift /'gɪəʃɪft/ **gearshifts.** A **gearshift** is the same as a **gear lever**. See picture headed **car and bicycle**. `N-COUNT` `AMERICAN`

gee /dʒiː/. People sometimes say **gee** in order to express a strong reaction to something or to introduce a remark or response. *Gee, it's hot... Gee thanks, Stan.* ◆◇◇◇◇ `EXCLAM` `PRAGMATICS` `AMERICAN,` `INFORMAL`

geek /giːk/ **geeks.** If someone, especially a young person, calls a man or a boy a **geek**, they are insulting them by saying that they are weak and unattractive. *Eric was a total geek.* `N-COUNT` `PRAGMATICS` `INFORMAL`

geese /giːs/. **Geese** is the plural of **goose**.

gee·zer /'giːzə/ **geezers.** Some people use **geezer** to refer to a man. *...an old bald geezer. ...just two ordinary geezers.* ◆◇◇◇◇ `N-COUNT` `BRITISH,` `INFORMAL`

Geiger coun·ter /'gaɪgə kaʊntə/ **Geiger counters.** A **Geiger counter** is a device which detects and measures radioactivity. `N-COUNT`

gei·sha /'geɪʃə/ **geishas.** A **geisha** is a Japanese woman who is specially trained to entertain men with music, dancing, and conversation. `N-COUNT`

gel /dʒel/ **gels, gelling, gelled;** also spelled **jell.** ◆◆◇◇◇
1 If people, things, or ideas **gel**, they or their differ- V-RECIP
ent parts begin to work well together to form a suc- V with n
cessful whole. *They have gelled very well with the* V (non-recip)
rest of the team... Their partnership gelled. ...episodes Also pl-n V
that never quite manage to gel into a plot. **2 Gel** is a N-VAR
thick jelly-like substance, especially one used to
keep your hair in a particular style.

gela·tine /'dʒelətiːn, AM -tən/ **gelatines;** also N-VAR
spelled **gelatin. Gelatine** is a clear tasteless powder
that is used to make liquids become firm, for example when you are making jelly.

ge·lati·nous /dʒɪ'lætɪnəs/. **Gelatinous** substances ADJ
or mixtures are sticky and jelly-like.

geld·ing /'geldɪŋ/ **geldings. A gelding** is a male ◆◇◇◇◇
horse which has been castrated. N-COUNT

gel·ig·nite /'dʒelɪgnaɪt/. **Gelignite** is an explosive N-UNCOUNT
substance that is similar to dynamite.

gem /dʒem/ **gems. 1** A **gem** is a jewel or stone that ◆◇◇◇◇
is used in jewellery. *...a pair of cufflinks studded* N-COUNT
with precious gems. **2** If you describe something or N-COUNT
someone as a **gem**, you mean that they are especially good or helpful. *...a gem of a hotel.*

gem·stone /'dʒemstəʊn/ **gemstones. A gemstone** N-COUNT
is a precious stone before it is cut and polished for
jewellery.

Gen. Gen. is a written abbreviation for **General.**

gen·darme /'ʒɒndɑːm/ **gendarmes. A gendarme** N-COUNT
is a member of the French police force.

gen·der /'dʒendə/ **genders. 1** A person's **gender** ◆◆◇◇◇
is the fact that they are male or female. *Women are* N-VAR
sometimes denied opportunities solely because of
their gender. **2** You can refer to all male people or N-COUNT
all female people as a particular **gender.** *...the differ-*
ent abilities and skills of the two genders. **3** In N-VAR
grammar, the **gender** of a noun, pronoun, or adjective is whether it is masculine, feminine, or neuter.
In English, only personal pronouns such as 'she',
reflexive pronouns such as 'itself', and possessive
determiners such as 'his' have gender.

gene /dʒiːn/ **genes. A gene** is the part of a cell in a ◆◆◇◇◇
living thing which controls its physical characteris- N-COUNT
tics, growth, and development.

ge·neal·ogy /ˌdʒiːni'ælədʒi/ **genealogies. 1** Ge- N-UNCOUNT
nealogy is the study of the history of families,
especially through studying historical documents.
♦ **ge·nea·logi·cal** /ˌdʒiːniə'lɒdʒɪkəl/ *...genealogical* ADJ: ADJ n
research on his family. **2** A **genealogy** is the history N-COUNT
of a family over several generations.

gen·era /'dʒenərə/. **Genera** is the plural of **genus**.

gen·er·al /'dʒenrəl/ **generals. 1** A **general** is a ◆◆◆◆◆
high-ranking officer in the armed forces. N-COUNT,
N-TITLE
2 If you talk about the **general** situation somewhere ADJ-GRADED:
or talk about something in **general** terms, you are de- ADJ n
scribing the situation as a whole rather than considering its details or exceptions. *The figures represent a*
general decline in employment... She recounted in very
general terms some of the events of recent months.
3 You use **general** to describe several items or activ- ADJ: ADJ n
ities when there are too many of them or when they
are not important enough to mention separately.
£2,500 for software is soon swallowed up in general
costs. **4** You use **general** to describe something that ADJ-GRADED:
involves or affects most people, or most people in a ADJ n
particular group. *...general awareness about bullying.*
5 If you describe something as **general**, you mean ADJ: ADJ n
that it is not restricted to any one thing or area. *...a*
general ache radiating from the back of the neck. ...a
general sense of well-being. **6 General** is used to de- ADJ-GRADED:
scribe a person who has an average amount of knowl- ADJ n
edge or interest in a particular subject. *This book is in-*
tended for the general reader.
7 A **general** business offers a variety of services or ADJ: ADJ n
goods rather than just one particular kind. *...the gen-*
eral store. **8 General** is used to describe a person's ADJ: ADJ n
job, usually as part of their title, to indicate that they
have complete responsibility for the administration
of an organization or business. *...General Manager.*
9 General workers do a variety of jobs which re- ADJ: ADJ n

quire no special skill or training. *...a tractor driver*
and two general labourers. **10** See also **generally.**
11 You use **in general** to indicate that you are talking PHRASE
about something as a whole, rather than about part of
it. *We need to improve our educational system in gen-*
eral. **12** You say **in general** to indicate that you are re- PHRASE
ferring to most people or things in a particular group.
People in general will support us. **13** You say **in gener-** PHRASE
al to indicate that a statement is true in most cases. *In*
general, it was the better-educated voters who voted
Yes.

general e'lection, general elections. A gen- ◆◆◆◇◇
eral election is an election at which all the citizens N-COUNT
of a country vote for people to represent them in
the national parliament.

gen·er·al·ise /'dʒenrəlaɪz/. See **generalize.**

gen·er·al·is·si·mo /ˌdʒenrə'lɪsɪməʊ/ **generalissi-** N-COUNT,
mos. In some countries, a **generalissimo** is the su- N-TITLE
preme commander of combined military, naval,
and air forces.

gen·er·al·ity /ˌdʒenə'rælɪti/ **generalities. 1** A gen- N-COUNT
erality is a general statement that covers a range of FORMAL
things, rather than being concerned with specific
instances. **2** The **generality** of a statement or de- N-UNCOUNT
scription is the fact that it is general, rather than
specific or detailed. *That there are problems with*
this kind of definition is hardly surprising, given its
level of generality. **3** If someone refers to the **gener-** QUANT
ality of a group of people, they mean the majority FORMAL
of that group. *...the generality of the electorate.*

gen·er·al·ize /'dʒenrəlaɪz/ **generalizes, gener-** ◆◇◇◇◇
alizing, generalized; also spelled **generalise** in VERB: V
British English. If you **generalize**, you say some- V prep
thing that seems to be true in most situations or for
most people, but that may not be completely true in
all cases. *It's hard to generalize about Cole Porter be-*
cause he wrote so many great songs. ♦ **gen·er·ali-**
·za·tion /ˌdʒenrəlaɪ'zeɪʃən/ **generalizations** *He is* N-VAR
making sweeping generalisations.

gen·er·al·ized /'dʒenrəlaɪzd/; also spelled **general-** ◆◇◇◇◇
ised. Generalized means involving many different ADJ-GRADED
things, rather than one or two specific things. *...a*
generalised discussion about admirable singers.
...generalised feelings of inadequacy.

general 'knowledge. General knowledge is N-UNCOUNT
knowledge about many different things, as opposed
to detailed knowledge about one particular subject.

gen·er·al·ly /'dʒenrəli/. **1** You use **generally** to ◆◆◆◆◇
summarize a situation, activity, or idea without re- ADV-GRADED
ferring to the particular details of it. *University*
teachers generally have admitted a lack of enthusi-
asm. **2** You use **generally** to say that something ADV
happens or is used on most occasions but not on
every occasion. *As women we generally say and feel*
too much... It is generally true that the darker the
fruit the higher its iron content.

general 'practice, general practices. 1 Gen- N-UNCOUNT
eral practice is the work of a doctor who usually BRITISH
treats sick people at a surgery or in their homes, rather than in a hospital. **2** A **general practice** is a N-COUNT
place or organization where the doctors who are in- BRITISH
volved in general practice work.

general prac'titioner, general practitioners. N-COUNT
A **general practitioner** is the same as a **GP.** FORMAL

general 'public. You can refer to the people in a ◆◇◇◇◇
society as the **general public.** *Unemployment is 10* N-COLL-SING:
percent among the general public and about 40 per- the N
cent among North African immigrants.

general 'strike, general strikes. A general ◆◇◇◇◇
strike is a situation where most or all of the workers N-COUNT
in a country are on strike.

gen·er·ate /'dʒenəreɪt/ **generates, generating,** ◆◆◆◇◇
generated. 1 To **generate** something means to VERB
cause it to begin and develop. *The reforms would* V n
generate new jobs. **2** To **generate** a form of energy VERB
or power means to produce it. *...schemes to generate* V n
power from landfill gas. ♦ **gen·era·tion** *...nuclear* N-UNCOUNT
power generation.

gen·era·tion /ˌdʒenə'reɪʃən/ **generations. 1** A ◆◆◆◆
generation consists of all the people in a group or N-COUNT:
with supp

country who are of a similar age. ...*the younger generation of Party members.* ...*the leading American playwright of his generation.* **2** A **generation** is the period of time, usually considered to be about thirty years, that it takes for children to grow up and become adults and have children of their own. *Within a generation, flight has become the method used by many travellers.* **3** You can use **generation** to refer to a stage of development in the design and manufacture of machines or equipment. ...*a new generation of IBM/Apple computers.* **4 Generation** is used to indicate how long members of your family have had a particular nationality. For example, second generation means that you were born in the country you live in, but your parents were not. `N-COUNT` `N-COUNT: N of n` `ADJ: ord ADJ n`

gen·er·a·tion·al /ˌdʒenəˈreɪʃənəl/. **Generational** means relating to a particular generation, or to the relationship between particular generations. ...*generational habits and fashions.* `ADJ`

gene'ration gap, generation gaps. If you refer to the **generation gap**, you are referring to a difference in attitude and behaviour between older people and younger people. `N-COUNT`

gen·era·tive /ˈdʒenərətɪv/. If something is **generative**, it is capable of producing something or causing it to develop. ...*the generative power of the sun.* `ADJ FORMAL`

gen·era·tor /ˈdʒenəreɪtə/ **generators.** **1** A **generator** is a machine which produces electricity. **2** A **generator** of something is a person, organization, product, or situation which produces it or causes it to happen. *The US economy is still an impressive generator of new jobs.* `N-COUNT` `N-COUNT: with supp`

ge·ner·ic /dʒɪˈnerɪk/ **generics.** **1** You use **generic** to describe something that refers or relates to a whole class of similar things. *Parmesan is a generic term used to describe a family of hard Italian cheeses.* ♦ **ge·neri·cal·ly** ...*something generically called 'rock 'n' roll.* **2** A **generic** drug or other product is one that does not have a trademark and that is known by a general name. *They encourage doctors to prescribe cheaper generic drugs instead of more expensive brand names.* ► Also a noun. ...*substituting generics for brand-name drugs.* **3** People sometimes use **generic** to refer to something that is exactly typical of the kind of thing mentioned, and that has no special or unusual characteristics. ...*generic California apartments, the kind that have white walls and white drapes.* `ADJ FORMAL` `ADV` `ADJ TECHNICAL` `N-COUNT` `ADJ: ADJ n INFORMAL`

gen·er·ous /ˈdʒenərəs/. **1** A **generous** person gives more of something, especially money, than is usual or expected. *German banks are more generous in their lending... The gift is generous by any standards.* ♦ **gen·er·ous·ly** ...*the judges who gave so generously of their time.* ♦ **gen·er·os·ity** /ˌdʒenəˈrɒsɪti/ *There are stories about his generosity, the huge amounts of money he gave to charities.* **2** A **generous** person is friendly, helpful, and willing to see the good qualities in someone or something. *He was always generous in sharing his enormous knowledge.* ♦ **generously** ...*the event, at which the stars generously gave their services free.* **3** A **generous** amount of something is much larger than is usual or necessary. ...*a generous six weeks of annual holiday.* ♦ **generously** *Season the steaks generously with salt and pepper.* `ADJ-GRADED` `ADV-GRADED: ADV with v` `N-UNCOUNT` `ADJ-GRADED` `ADV-GRADED: ADV with v` `ADJ-GRADED` `ADV-GRADED`

gen·esis /ˈdʒenɪsɪs/. The **genesis** of something is its beginning, birth, or creation. *The project had its genesis two years earlier.* `N-SING FORMAL`

gene 'therapy. **Gene therapy** is the use of genetic material to treat disease. `N-UNCOUNT`

ge,netic engi'neering. **Genetic engineering** is the science or activity of changing the genetic structure of an organism in order to make it stronger or more suitable for a particular purpose. `N-UNCOUNT`

ge,netic 'fingerprinting. **Genetic fingerprinting** is a method of identifying people using a substance called DNA. `N-UNCOUNT`

ge·neti·cist /dʒɪˈnetɪsɪst/ **geneticists.** A **geneticist** is a person who studies genetics. `N-COUNT`

ge·net·ics /dʒɪˈnetɪks/. The form **genetic** is used as a modifier. **1 Genetics** is the study of heredity and how qualities and characteristics are passed on from one generation to another by means of genes. **2** You use **genetic** to describe something that is concerned with genetics or with genes. ...*the most common fatal genetic disease in the United States.* ♦ **ge·neti·cal·ly** /dʒɪˈnetɪkli/ ...*fetuses that are genetically abnormal.* `N-UNCOUNT` `ADJ` `ADV`

gen·ial /ˈdʒiːniəl/. Someone who is **genial** is kind and friendly. *He was a warm-hearted friend and genial host.* ♦ **gen·ial·ly** *'If you don't mind,' Mrs. Dambar said genially.* ♦ **ge·ni·al·ity** /ˌdʒiːniˈælɪti/ *He soon recovered his habitual geniality.* `ADJ-GRADED` `ADV-GRADED` `N-UNCOUNT`

ge·nie /ˈdʒiːni/ **genies.** In stories from Arabia and Persia, a **genie** is a spirit which appears by magic and obeys the person who controls it. `N-COUNT`

geni·tal /ˈdʒenɪtəl/ **genitals.** **1** Someone's **genitals** are their external sexual organs. **2 Genital** means relating to a person's external sexual organs. *Wear loose clothing in the genital area.* `N-PLURAL` `ADJ: ADJ n`

geni·ta·lia /ˌdʒenɪˈteɪliə/. A person's or animal's **genitalia** are their external sexual organs. `N-PLURAL TECHNICAL`

geni·tive /ˈdʒenɪtɪv/. In the grammar of some languages, the **genitive**, or the **genitive case**, is a noun case which is used primarily to show possession. `N-SING: the N`

ge·ni·us /ˈdʒiːniəs/ **geniuses.** **1 Genius** is very great ability or skill in a particular subject or activity. ...*her real genius as a designer... The man had genius.* **2** A **genius** is a highly talented, creative, or intelligent person. `N-UNCOUNT` `N-COUNT`

geno·cide /ˈdʒenəsaɪd/. **Genocide** is the deliberate murder of a whole community or race. ...*acts of genocide and torture.* ♦ **geno·cid·al** /ˌdʒenəˈsaɪdəl/ ...*genocidal crimes.* `N-UNCOUNT FORMAL` `ADJ`

ge·nome /ˈdʒiːnəʊm/ **genomes.** A **genome** is the particular number and combination of certain chromosomes necessary to form the single nucleus of a living cell. `N-COUNT TECHNICAL`

gen·re /ˈʒɒnrə/ **genres.** A **genre** is a particular type of art form which people consider as a class because it has special characteristics. ...*novels in the horror genre.* `N-COUNT FORMAL`

gent /dʒent/ **gents.** **1 Gent** is an informal word for **gentleman.** *Mr Blake was a gent. He knew how to behave.* **2** People sometimes refer to a public toilet for men as **the gents.** `N-COUNT DATED` `N-COLL-SING BRITISH`

gen·teel /dʒenˈtiːl/. A **genteel** person or place is quiet, respectable, and refined. ...*ladies with genteel manners.* ...*a genteel resort on the south coast.* `ADJ-GRADED DATED`

gen·tian /ˈdʒenʃən/ **gentians.** A **gentian** is a small plant with a blue or purple flower which grows in mountain regions. `N-COUNT`

Gen·tile /ˈdʒentaɪl, AM -təl/ **Gentiles;** also spelled **gentile.** When you are talking about non-Jewish people in contrast to Jewish people, you can use **Gentile** to refer to a person who is not Jewish. ► Also an adjective. ...*Gentile German refugees.* `N-COUNT` `ADJ`

gen·til·ity /dʒenˈtɪlɪti/. **1 Gentility** is used to refer to people of high social status, and their typical way of life. *All the gentility of London was there.* **2 Gentility** is polite, well-mannered, and refined behaviour. *He treated her with scrupulous gentility.* `N-UNCOUNT DATED` `N-UNCOUNT DATED`

gen·tle /ˈdʒentəl/ **gentler, gentlest.** **1** Someone who is **gentle** is kind, mild, and calm. *My son was a quiet and gentle man.* ♦ **gen·tly** *She smiled gently at him.* ♦ **gen·tle·ness** ...*the gentleness with which she treated her pregnant mother.* **2 Gentle** actions or movements are performed in a calm and controlled manner, with little force. ...*a gentle game of tennis.* ♦ **gently** *Patrick took her gently by the arm.* **3** If you describe the weather, especially the wind, as **gentle,** you mean it is pleasant and calm. ...*a gentle breeze.* ♦ **gently** *Light airs blew gently out of the south-east.* **4** A **gentle** slope or curve is not steep or severe. ...*gentle, rolling meadows.* ♦ **gently** *With its gently rolling hills it looks like Tuscany... Green meadows sloped gently up from the road.* **5** A **gentle** heat is a fairly low heat. *Cook for 30 minutes over a* `ADJ-GRADED` `ADV-GRADED` `N-UNCOUNT` `ADJ-GRADED` `ADV-GRADED` `ADJ-GRADED` `ADV-GRADED` `ADJ-GRADED` `ADV-GRADED` `ADJ-GRADED`

gentle heat. ♦ **gently** *Add the onion and cook gently for about 5 minutes.* ADV-GRADED; ADV with v

gentle·man /'dʒentəlmən/ **gentlemen.** 1 A **gentleman** is a man who comes from a family of high social standing. *...English gentleman Joseph Greenway.* 2 If you say that a man is a **gentleman**, you mean he is well-behaved, educated, and refined in his manners. *He was always such a gentleman.* ♦ **gentle·man·ly** /'dʒentəlmənli/ *...his kind and gentlemanly consideration.* 3 You can address men as **gentlemen**, or refer politely to them as **gentlemen**. *This way, please, ladies and gentlemen.* 4 A **gentleman's agreement** or **a gentlemen's agreement** is an informal agreement in which people trust one another to do what they have promised. The agreement is not written down and does not have any legal force. 1 A N-COUNT / N-COUNT / ADJ-GRADED / N-VOC PRAGMATICS / PHRASE

gen·try /'dʒentri/. The **gentry** are people of high social status or high birth. *Most of the country estates were built by the landed gentry during the late 19th century.* ◆◇◇◇◇ N-PLURAL DATED, BRITISH

genu·flect /'dʒenjʊflekt/ **genuflects, genuflecting, genuflected.** 1 If you **genuflect**, you bend one or both knees and bow, especially in church, as a sign of respect. 2 You can say that someone is **genuflecting** to something when they are giving it a great deal of attention and respect, especially if you think it does not deserve it; used showing disapproval. *They refrained from genuflecting to the laws of political economy.* VERB: V FORMAL / VERB PRAGMATICS V to n Also V prep JOURNALISM

genu·ine /'dʒenjʊɪn/. 1 **Genuine** is used to describe people and things that are exactly what they appear to be, and are not fake or an imitation. *...genuine leather... They're convinced the picture is genuine.* 2 **Genuine** refers to things such as emotions that are real and not pretended. *If this offer is genuine I will gladly accept it.* ♦ **genu·ine·ly** *He was genuinely surprised.* ♦ **genu·ine·ness** *He needed at least three days to assess the genuineness of their intentions.* 3 If you describe a person as **genuine**, you approve of them because they are honest, truthful, and sincere. *She is very caring and very genuine.* ♦ **genuineness** *I have no doubt about their genuineness.* ◆◆◇◇ ADJ / ADJ-GRADED / ADV-GRADED / N-UNCOUNT / ADJ-GRADED PRAGMATICS / N-UNCOUNT

ge·nus /'dʒenəs, AM 'dʒiː-/ **genera.** A **genus** is a class of similar things, especially a group of animals or plants that includes several related species. N-COUNT TECHNICAL

ge·og·ra·pher /dʒi'ɒgrəfə/ **geographers.** A **geographer** is a person who studies geography. N-COUNT

geo·graphi·cal /ˌdʒiːə'græfɪkəl/. The form **geographic** /ˌdʒiːə'græfɪk/ is also used. **Geographical** or **geographic** means concerned with or relating to geography. *...a vast geographical area.* ♦ **geo·graphi·cal·ly** /ˌdʒiːə'græfɪkli/ *It is geographically more diverse than any other continent.* ◆◆◇◇ ADJ / ADV

ge·og·ra·phy /dʒi'ɒgrəfi/. 1 **Geography** is the study of the countries of the world and of such things as land formations, seas, and climate. 2 The **geography** of a place is the way that features such as rivers, mountains, and towns are arranged. *...policemen who knew the local geography.* ◆◆◇◇ N-UNCOUNT / N-UNCOUNT

geo·logi·cal /ˌdʒiːə'lɒdʒɪkəl/. **Geological** means relating to geology. *...geological maps, books, and atlases. ...a lengthy geological survey.* ♦ **geo·logi·cal·ly** /ˌdʒiːə'lɒdʒɪkli/ *At least 10,000 of these hectares are geologically unsuitable for housing.* ◆◇◇◇ ADJ / ADV

ge·ol·ogy /dʒi'ɒlədʒi/. 1 **Geology** is the study of the Earth's structure, surface, and origins. *Professor of geology at the University of Jordan.* ♦ **ge·olo·gist, geologists.** 2 The **geology** of an area is the structure of its land, together with the types of rocks and minerals that exist within it. ◆◇◇◇ N-UNCOUNT / N-COUNT / N-UNCOUNT

geo·met·ric /ˌdʒiːə'metrɪk/. The form **geometrical** /ˌdʒiːə'metrɪkəl/ is also used. 1 **Geometric** or **geometrical** patterns or shapes consist of regular shapes or lines. *...geometric designs.* ♦ **geo·met·ri·cal·ly** /ˌdʒiːə'metrɪkli/ *...a few geometrically planted trees.* 2 **Geometric** or **geometrical** means relating to or involving the principles of geometry. ◆◇◇◇ ADJ / ADV / ADJ

ge·om·etry /dʒi'ɒmɪtri/. 1 **Geometry** is the branch of mathematics concerned with the properties and relationships of lines, angles, curves, and shapes. 2 The **geometry** of an object is its shape or the relationship of its parts to each other. *...the geometry of the car's nose.* ◆◇◇◇ N-UNCOUNT / N-UNCOUNT FORMAL

geo·physi·cal /ˌdʒiːəʊ'fɪzɪkəl/. **Geophysical** means relating to geophysics. ADJ

geo·physi·cist /ˌdʒiːəʊ'fɪzɪsɪst/ **geophysicists.** A **geophysicist** is someone who studies geophysics. N-COUNT

geo·phys·ics /ˌdʒiːəʊ'fɪzɪks/. **Geophysics** is the branch of geology that uses physics to examine the earth's structure, climate, and oceans. N-UNCOUNT

geo·poli·tics /ˌdʒiːəʊ'pɒlɪtɪks/. **Geopolitics** is the activity or study of politics on a worldwide scale. *The shape of geopolitics has been decisively altered.* ♦ **geo·po·liti·cal** /ˌdʒiːəʊpə'lɪtɪkəl/ *Hungary and Poland have suffered before because of their unfortunate geopolitical position.* N-UNCOUNT / ADJ

Geor·gian /'dʒɔːdʒən/. **Georgian** is used in Britain to describe eighteenth century architecture and the arts. *...the restoration of his Georgian house.* ◆◆◇◇ ADJ

ge·ra·nium /dʒɪ'reɪniəm/ **geraniums.** A **geranium** is a plant with clusters of small red, pink, or white flowers. N-COUNT

ger·bil /'dʒɜːbɪl/ **gerbils.** A **gerbil** is a small furry rodent that is often kept as a pet. N-COUNT

geri·at·ric /ˌdʒeri'ætrɪk/ **geriatrics.** 1 **Geriatric** is used to describe things relating to the illnesses and medical care of old people. *...the future of geriatric care.* 2 **Geriatrics** is the study of the illnesses that affect old people and the medical care of old people. 3 If you describe someone as a **geriatric**, you are being disrespectful, and implying that they are old and that their mental or physical condition is poor. *...such a boring bunch of geriatrics.* ◆◇◇◇ ADJ: ADJ n MEDICAL / N-UNCOUNT / N-COUNT PRAGMATICS INFORMAL

germ /dʒɜːm/ **germs.** 1 A **germ** is a very small organism that causes disease. *Chlorine is widely used to kill germs.* 2 The **germ of** something such as an idea is something which developed or might develop into that thing. *The germ of an idea took root in Rosemary's mind.* 3 See also **wheatgerm.** ◆◇◇◇ N-COUNT / N-SING: N of n

ger·mane /dʒɜː'meɪn/. Something that is **germane** to a situation or idea is connected with it in an important way. *...documents which were very germane to the case.* ADJ-GRADED FORMAL

Ger·man·ic /dʒɜː'mænɪk/. 1 If you describe someone or something as **Germanic**, you think that their appearance or behaviour is typical of German people or things. 2 **Germanic** is used to describe the ancient culture and language of the peoples of northern Europe. ADJ-GRADED / ADJ

German 'measles. German measles is a disease which causes you to have a cough, a sore throat, and red spots on your skin. N-UNCOUNT

ger·mi·nate /'dʒɜːmɪneɪt/ **germinates, germinating, germinated.** 1 If a seed **germinates** or if it is **germinated**, it starts to grow. *First, the researchers germinated the seeds.* ♦ **ger·mi·na·tion** /ˌdʒɜːmɪ'neɪʃən/ *...the poor germination of your seed.* 2 If an idea, plan, or feeling **germinates**, it comes into existence and begins to develop. *...a 'big book' that was germinating in his mind.* ◆◇◇◇ V-ERG: V n TECHNICAL / N-UNCOUNT / VERB Also V into n FORMAL

germ 'warfare. Germ warfare is the use of germs in a war in order to cause disease in enemy troops, or to destroy crops that they might use as food. N-UNCOUNT

ger·on·tol·ogy /ˌdʒerən'tɒlədʒi/. **Gerontology** is the study of the process by which we get old, how our bodies change, and the problems that old people have. N-UNCOUNT

ger·ry·man·der·ing /ˌdʒeri'mændərɪŋ/. **Gerrymandering** is the act of altering political boundaries in order to give an unfair advantage to one political party or group of people; used showing disapproval. N-UNCOUNT PRAGMATICS

ger·und /'dʒerʌnd/ **gerunds.** A **gerund** is a noun formed from a verb which refers to an action, process, or state. In English, gerunds end in '-ing', for example 'running' and 'thinking'. N-COUNT

ge·stalt /gə'ʃtælt/. A **gestalt** is something that you see or think of that has particular qualities when N-SING FORMAL

you consider it as a whole which are not apparent when you consider only the separate parts of it. *...the visual strength of the gestalt.*

ges·ta·tion /dʒeˈsteɪʃən/. **1 Gestation** is the process in which babies grow inside their mother's body before they are born. *...the seventeenth week of gestation.* **2 Gestation** is the process in which an idea or plan develops. *...the prolonged period of gestation of this design.* [N-UNCOUNT TECHNICAL] [N-UNCOUNT FORMAL]

ges·ticu·late /dʒeˈstɪkjuleɪt/ **gesticulates, gesticulating, gesticulated.** If you **gesticulate**, you make movements with your arms or hands. *The architect was gesticulating at a hole in the ground.* ♦ **ges·ticu·la·tion** /dʒe,stɪkjuˈleɪʃən/ **gesticulations** *...signs, gesticulation and mime.* [VERB: V] [V prep] [N-UNCOUNT: also N in pl]

ges·ture /ˈdʒestʃə/ **gestures, gesturing, gestured.** **1** A **gesture** is a movement that you make with a part of your body, especially your hands, to express emotion or information. *Sarah made a menacing gesture with her fist.* ♦ **ges·tur·al** /ˈdʒestʃərəl/ *There is a frank gestural quality to much of this early work.* **2** A **gesture** is something that you say or do in order to express your attitude or intentions, often something that you know will not have much effect. *As a gesture to security, cars were fitted with special locks.* **3** If you **gesture**, you use movements of your hands or head in order to tell someone something or draw their attention to something. *I gestured towards the boathouse.* [N-COUNT] [ADJ] [N-COUNT] [VERB: V] [V prep]

get 1 changing, causing, moving, or reaching

get /get/ **gets, getting, got** or **gotten.** In most of its uses **get** is a fairly informal word. **Gotten** is an American form of the past tense and past participle. [♦♦♦♦♦]

1 You use **get** with adjectives to mean 'become'. For example, if someone **gets cold** or **gets angry**, they become cold or angry. *The boys were getting bored... From here on, it can only get better... It's getting late.* [V-LINK] [V adj] [it V adj]

2 If someone or something **gets** into a particular state or situation, or another person or thing **gets** them into it, they are in a state or situation that they were not in before, as the result of an action, process, or change. *Half the pleasure of an evening out is getting ready... How did we get into this recession, and what can we do to get out of it?... It got to the point where I was so ill I was waiting to die... I don't know if I can get it clean... Brian will get them out of trouble.* **3** If you say **you can't get away from** something or **there is no getting away from** something, you are emphasizing that it is true, even though people might prefer it not to be true. *There is no getting away from the fact that he is on the left of the party.* **4** You can say, for example, **'How lucky can you get?'** or **'How stupid can you get?'** to emphasize that someone has been very lucky or stupid. [V-ERG] [V adj] [V prep/adv] [it V ton] [V n adj] [V n prep] [PHRASE PRAGMATICS] [PHRASE PRAGMATICS INFORMAL]

5 If you **get** someone to do something, they do it because you asked, persuaded, or told them to do it. *...a long campaign to get US politicians to take the Aids epidemic more seriously.* **6** If you **get** something done, you cause it to be done. *He hadn't done anything about getting the car repaired.* **7 Get** is often used in place of 'be' as an auxiliary verb to form the passive. *Does she ever get asked for her autograph?... A pane of glass got broken.* **8 Get** is used in expressions like **get stuffed** and **get lost** which are offensive ways of expressing contempt for someone, disagreement with someone, or refusal to do something. [VERB V n to-inf] [VERB V n -ed] [AUX AUX -ed] [CONVENTION PRAGMATICS]

9 To **get** somewhere means to move there. *I got off the bed and opened the door... I heard David yelling and telling them to get back.* **10** When you get to a place, you arrive there. *Generally I get to work at 9.30am... It was dark by the time she got home.* **11** If you get something or someone into a particular place or position, you move them there by means of a particular action or effort. *Mack got his wallet out... Go and get your coat on... The UN was supposed to be getting aid to where it was most needed.* [VERB V prep/adv] [VERB V to n V adv] [VERB V n with adv V n prep]

12 If you **get** to do something, you manage to do it or have the opportunity to do it. *Do you get to see him often?... They get to stay in nice hotels... No one could figure out how he got to be so wealthy.* **13** You can use **get** [VERB V to-inf] [VERB]

in expressions like **get moving**, **get going**, and **get working** when you want to tell people to begin moving, going, or working quickly. *We need to get thinking, talking and acting on this before it is too late.* **14** You can use **get** to talk about the progress that you are making. For example, you can say that you are **getting somewhere** to mean that you are making progress, and you can say that something **won't get you anywhere** to mean it will not help you to progress at all. *Radical factions say the talks are getting nowhere... This low-key approach does not get you very far sometimes.* **15** If something that has continued for some time **gets to** you, it starts causing you to suffer. *That's the first time I lost my cool in 20 years in this job. This whole thing's getting to me.* **16** If something **gets** you, it annoys you. *What gets me is the attitude of so many of the people.* [V -ing] [V adv V n adv] [V-ERG V n adv V n adv] [VERB V ton] [VB: no passive V n INFORMAL]

get 2 obtaining, receiving, or catching

get /get/ **gets, getting, got** or **gotten.** **1** If you **get** something that you want or need, you obtain it. *The problem was how to get enough food to sustain life... He can't get a good price for his crops... Young men climbed on buses and fences to get a better view... I asked him to get me some information.* **2** If you **get** someone or something, you go and bring them to a particular place. *Get me a large brandy... Go and get your daddy for me.* [♦♦♦♦♦] [VERB V n V n Also V n for n] [VERB: V n n V n for n]

3 If you **get** something, you receive it or are given it. *He gets a lot of letters from women... They get a salary of $11,000 a year... Riyadh, the Saudi capital, got 25 mm of rain in just 12 hours.* **4** You can use **you get** instead of 'there is' or 'there are' to say that something exists, happens, or can be experienced. *You get a lot of youngsters hanging around the Common.* **5** If you can **get** a particular radio or television channel, you are able to receive broadcasts from it on your radio or television. *I only get Channel 7.* **6** If you **get** an illness or disease, you become ill with it. *When I was five I got measles.* [VERB V n] [VERB V n SPOKEN] [VERB V n] [VERB V n]

7 If you **get** a particular result, you obtain it from some action that you take, or from a calculation or experiment. *You could run that race again and get a different result each time... What do you get if you multiply six by nine?* **8** If you **get** the time or opportunity to do something, you have the time or opportunity to do it. *You get time to think in prison... Whenever I get the chance I go to Maxim's for dinner.* **9** If you **get** an idea, impression, or feeling from something, you have it as a result of doing or experiencing that thing. *Charles got a shock when he saw him... I get the feeling that you're an honest man... Doctors can get the wrong impression from even an accurate description... I would like to take pictures professionally because I get so much out of it.* **10** If you **get** a joke or **get** the point of something that is said, you understand it. *Did you get that joke, Ann?... You don't seem to get the point.* [VERB V n] [VERB V n] [VERB V n from/out ofn] [VERB V n]

11 When you **get** a train, bus, plane, or boat, you travel by that means of transport. *What time are you getting your train?* **12** If you **get** a person or animal, you succeed in catching, killing, or hitting them. *We've got him. He's not going to kill anyone else.* **13** See also **getting, got.** [VERB V n] [VERB V n]

get 3 phrasal verbs

get /get/ **gets, getting, got** or **gotten.** [♦♦♦♦♦]

get about. 1 If you **get about**, you move or travel from place to place. *Rail travel through France is the perfect way to get about.* **2** If news **gets about**, it becomes well known as a result of being told to a lot of people. *The story had soon got about that he had been suspended.* [PHRASAL VB V P] [V P BRITISH]

get across. When an idea **gets across** or when you **get** it **across**, you succeed in making other people understand it. *Officers felt their point of view was not getting across to ministers... Wally got his message across very well.* [PHRASAL VB ERG V P ton V n P]

get ahead. If you want to **get ahead**, you want to be successful in your career. [PHRASAL VB V P]

get along. If you **get along with** someone, you have [PHRASAL VB]

a friendly relationship with them. *It's impossible to get along with him... Although at one point their voices were raised they seemed to be getting along fine.* RECIP V P with n pl-n V P

get around or **get round.** **1** If you **get around** something such as a problem, rule, or law, you succeed in doing what you want in spite of it, often by means of a clever or resourceful action. *Although tobacco ads are prohibited, companies get around the ban by sponsoring music shows.* **2** If news **gets around**, it becomes well known as a result of being told to a lot of people. *Word got around that he was taking drugs.* **3** See also **get round.** PHRASAL VB V P n V P

get around. If you **get around**, you visit a lot of different places as part of your way of life. *He claimed to be a journalist, and he got around.* PHRASAL VB V P

get around to or **get round to.** When you **get around to** doing something that you have delayed or have been too busy to do, you finally do it. *I said I would write to you, but as usual I never got around to it.* PHRASAL VB V P P n/-ing

get at. **1** To **get at** something means to succeed in reaching it. *A goat was standing up against a tree on its hind legs, trying to get at the leaves.* **2** If you **get at** the truth about something, you succeed in discovering it. *We want to get at the truth. Who killed him? And why?* **3** If you **get at** someone, you keep criticizing or teasing them in an unkind way. *They don't like my moustache and my long hair, they get at me whenever they can.* **4** If you ask someone what they **are getting at**, you are asking them to explain what they mean. *What are you getting at now?* PHRASAL VB V P n V P n V P n BRITISH, INFORMAL V P

get away. **1** If you **get away**, you succeed in leaving a place or situation that you do not want to be in. *Dr Dunn was apparently trying to get away when he was shot... We want to get away from the politics of outdated dogmatism.* **2** If you **get away**, you go away for a period of time in order to have a holiday. *He is too busy to get away.* • If you **get away from it all**, you have a holiday in a place that is very different from the place where you normally live and work. PHRASAL VB V P V P from n V P PHRASE

get away with. If you **get away with** doing something wrong or risky, you do not suffer any punishment or other bad consequences because of it. *The criminals know how to play the system and get away with it... This is one of the few jobs you can do and get away with being completely drunk.* PHRASAL VB V P P n/-ing

get back. **1** If someone or something **gets back** to a state they were in before, they are then in that state again. *Life started to get back to normal... I couldn't get back to sleep.* **2** If you **get** something **back** after you have lost it or after it has been taken from you, you have it again. *You can cancel the contract and get your money back.* PHRASAL VB V P to n Also V P into n V n P Also V P noun

get back at. If you **get back at** someone, you do something unpleasant to them in order to have revenge for something unpleasant that they did to you. *My wife has left me and I wanted to get back at the first woman I saw.* PHRASAL VB V P P n

get back to. If you **get back to** a previous activity or subject, you start doing the activity or talking about the subject again. *I think I ought to get back to work... We got back to the subject of Tom Halliday.* PHRASAL VB V P P n

get by. If you can **get by** with the few resources you have, you can manage to live or do things satisfactorily. *Melville managed to get by on a small amount of money.* PHRASAL VB V P V P on n

get down. **1** If something **gets** you **down**, it makes you unhappy. *When my work gets me down, I like to fantasize about being a farmer.* **2** If you **get down**, you lower your body until you are sitting, kneeling, or lying on the ground. *She got down on her hands and knees... 'Get down!' she yelled. 'Somebody's shooting!'* **3** If you **get down** your thoughts or someone's words, you write them down. *The idea has been going around in my head for quite a while and now I am getting it down on paper.* PHRASAL VB V n P V P on n V P V n P Also V P noun

get down to. If you **get down to** a piece of work, you begin doing it. *With the election out of the way, the government can get down to business.* PHRASAL VB V P P n

get in. **1** If a political party or a politician **gets in**, PHRASAL VB

they are elected. *If the Conservatives get in they might decide to change it.* **2** If you **get** something **in**, you manage to do it at a time when you are very busy doing other things. *I plan to get a few lessons in.* **3** When a train, bus, or plane **gets in**, it arrives. *We would have come straight here, except our flight got in too late.* **4** If you **get** something **in**, you eventually manage to say it, usually in a situation where other people are talking a lot. *It was hard to get a word in.* V P V n P V P V n P

get in on. If you **get in on** something that other people are already involved in, you take part in it. *Now baseball is trying to get in on the European market.* PHRASAL VB V P P n INFORMAL

get into. **1** If you **get into** a particular kind of work or activity, you manage to become involved in it. *He was eager to get into politics.* **2** If you **get into** a school or university, you are accepted there as a pupil or student. *I was working hard to get into Cambridge.* **3** If you ask what has **got into** someone, you mean that they are behaving in an unexpected way. *He didn't know what could have got into him, to steal a watch.* PHRASAL VB V P n V P n V P n INFORMAL

get in with. If someone tries to **get in with** you, they try to become friendly with you because they think that you have influence and they can gain some advantage from you; used showing disapproval. *She did everything she could to get in with the people she thought would make her look important.* PHRASAL VB PRAGMATICS V P P n

get off. **1** If someone who has broken a law or rule **gets off**, they are not punished, or only slightly punished. *He is likely to get off with a small fine.* **2** If you **get off**, you leave a place because it is time to leave. *At eight I said 'I'm getting off now.'* **3** If you tell someone to **get off** a piece of land or **get off** the premises, you are telling them to leave, because they have no right to be there and you do not want them there. *Get off the farm.* **4** You can tell someone to **get off** when they are touching you and you do not want them to. *I kept telling him to get off... 'Get off me!' I screamed.* **5** If you **get off**, or **get off to sleep**, you succeed in falling asleep. PHRASAL VB V P with n V P V P n V P V P

get off on. If you **get off on** something, you are very excited by it. *I get off on the entertainment we give.* PHRASAL VB V P P n INFORMAL

get off with. If you **get off with** someone, you have a romantic or sexual encounter with them. PHRASAL VB V P P n BRITISH

get on. **1** If you **get on** with someone, you like them and have a friendly relationship with them. *The host fears the guests won't get on... What are your neighbours like? Do you get on with them?* **2** If you **get on** with something, you continue with something that you have started doing or you start something that you were about to do. *Jane got on with her work... Let's get on.* **3** If you say how someone **is getting on**, you are saying how much success they are having with what they are trying to do. *Livy's getting on very well in Russian. She learns very quickly... When he came back to see me I asked how he had got on.* **4** If you try to **get on**, you try to be successful in your career. *Politics is seen as a man's world. It is very difficult for women to get on.* **5** If someone **is getting on**, they are getting old. *I'm nearly 31 and that's getting on a bit for a footballer.* PHRASAL VB RECIP pl-n V P V P with n V P with n V P V P adv V P BRITISH V P INFORMAL

get on to. **1** If you **get on to** a topic when you are speaking, you start talking about it. *We got on to the subject of relationships.* **2** If you **get on to** someone, you contact them in order to ask or tell them something. *I got on to him and explained some of the things.* PHRASAL VB V P P n V P P n BRITISH

get out. **1** If you **get out** of a place or situation, you leave it because you want to, or because someone makes you leave it. *I wanted to get out of the group, but they wouldn't let me... Getting out of the contract would be no problem... I told him to leave and get out.* **2** If you **get out**, you go to places and meet people, usually in order to have a more enjoyable life. *Get out and enjoy yourself, make new friends.* **3** If news or information **gets out**, it becomes known. *If word got out now, a scandal could be disastrous.* PHRASAL VB V P of n V P V P V P

get out of. If you **get out of** doing something that you do not want to do, you succeed in avoiding doing it. *It's amazing what people will do to get out of paying taxes.* PHRASAL VB V P P -ing/n

get over. **1** If you **get over** an unpleasant experience or an illness, you recover from it. *It took me a very long time to get over the shock of her death.* **2** If you **get over** PHRASAL VB V P n V P n

a problem or difficulty, you overcome it, or succeed in spite of it. **3** If you **get** your message **over** to people, they hear and understand it. *We have got to get the message over to the young that smoking isn't cool.*   VnP Also VPnoun

get over with. If **get** something unpleasant **over with**, you do it or experience it quickly, since you cannot avoid it. *The sooner we start, the sooner we'll get it over with.*   PHRASAL VB VnPP

get round. 1 See **get around**. **2** If you **get round** someone, you persuade them to like you or do what you want, by pleasing or flattering them. *Max could always get round her.*   PHRASAL VB VPn

get round to. See **get around to**.   PHRASAL VB

get through. 1 If you **get through** a task, especially a long or difficult one, you complete it. *I think you can get through the first two chapters.* **2** If you **get through** a difficult or unpleasant period of time, you manage to live through it. *It is hard to see how people will get through the winter... We couldn't get through a day without arguing.* **3** If you **get through** an examination or **get through**, you pass it. *Did you have to get through an entrance examination?* **4** If you **get through** a large amount of something, you use it up. *You'll get through at least ten nappies a day.*   PHRASAL VB VPn / VPn / VPn Also VP / VPn BRITISH

5 If you **get through** to someone, you succeed in making them understand something that you are trying to tell them. *An old friend might well be able to get through to her and help her.* **6** If you **get through** to someone, you succeed in contacting them on the telephone. *I can't get through to this number... I've been trying to ring up all day and I couldn't get through.*   VPton Also VP / VPton VP

7 If a law or proposal **gets through**, it is officially approved by something such as a parliament or committee. *Such a radical proposal would never get through parliament.*   VP / VPn

get together. 1 When people **get together**, they meet in order to discuss something or to spend time together. • See also **get-together**. **2** If you collect or assemble things or people for a particular purpose, you can say that you **get** them **together**. *We'll give you three days to get the money together.*   PHRASAL VB VP / VnP Also VPnoun

get up. 1 When someone who is sitting or lying down **gets up**, they rise to a standing position. **2** When you **get up**, you get out of bed. *They have to get up early in the morning.* **3** See also **get-up**.   PHRASAL VB VP / VP

get up to. If you say that someone **gets up to** something, you mean that they do it and you do not approve of it. *They get up to all sorts behind your back.*   PHRASAL VB PRAGMATICS VPPn BRITISH

get·away /'getəweɪ/ **getaways**; also spelled **get-away. 1** If someone makes a **getaway**, they leave a place in a hurry, especially after committing a crime. *They made their getaway along a pavement on a stolen motorcycle. ...the burglar's getaway car.* **2** A **getaway** is a short holiday somewhere, or a place where you can go for a short holiday.   ◆◇◇◇ N-COUNT / N-COUNT JOURNALISM

get·ting /'getɪŋ/ **1 Getting** is the present participle of **get**. **2 Getting on** for means the same as **nearly**. *It was getting on for two o'clock.*   PHR-PREP BRITISH

'get-together, get-togethers. A **get-together** is an informal meeting or party, usually arranged for a particular purpose.   N-COUNT

'get-up. If you refer to a set of clothes as a **get-up**, you think that they are unusual or ridiculous. *I won't wear this get-up.*   ◆◇◇◇ N-SING PRAGMATICS INFORMAL

gey·ser /'giːzə/ **geysers.** A **geyser** is a hole in the Earth's surface from which hot water and steam are forced out.   N-COUNT

ghast·ly /'gɑːstli, 'gæstli/ **1** If you describe a person, thing, or situation as **ghastly**, you dislike them a great deal or find them very unpleasant. **2** If someone looks **ghastly**, they look very ill or unhappy. **3 Ghastly** is used to emphasize that something bad is extremely severe in its effects. *I was making yet another ghastly mistake.* **4 Ghastly** events, situations, or news involve suffering or death. *...a particularly ghastly murder.*   ◆◇◇◇ ADJ-GRADED INFORMAL / ADJ-GRADED v-link ADJ / ADJ-GRADED / ADJ-GRADED

gher·kin /'gɜːkɪn/ **gherkins. Gherkins** are small pickled cucumbers.   N-COUNT BRITISH

ghet·to /'getəʊ/ **ghettos** or **ghettoes**. A **ghetto** is a part of a town in which many poor people or many people of a particular race, religion, or nationality live. *...the black ghettos of New York.*   ◆◆◇◇ N-COUNT

'ghetto blaster, ghetto blasters; also spelled **ghetto-blaster.** A large stereo cassette player which can be carried around is sometimes called a **ghetto blaster.**   N-COUNT INFORMAL

ghost /gəʊst/ **ghosts, ghosting, ghosted. 1** A **ghost** is the spirit of a dead person that someone believes they can see or feel. *The village is haunted by the ghosts of the dead children.* **2** The **ghost of** something, especially of something bad that has happened, is the memory of it. *He is haunted by the ghost of his past.* **3** A **ghost of** something is a faint trace of it. *He gave the ghost of a smile.* **4** To **ghost** means the same as to **ghost-write.**   ◆◆◇◇ N-COUNT / N-COUNT: Nofn / N-SING Nofn VERB

ghost·ly /'gəʊstli/ **1** Something that is **ghostly** seems unreal or supernatural and may be frightening because of this. *The moon shone, shedding a ghostly light on the fields.* **2** A **ghostly** presence is the ghost or spirit of a dead person.   ◇◇◇◇ ADJ / ADJ: ADJn

'ghost town, ghost towns. A **ghost town** is a town which used to be busy and prosperous but is now poor and deserted.   N-COUNT

'ghost-write, ghost-writes, ghost-writing, ghost-wrote, ghost-written; also spelled **ghost write.** If a book or other piece of writing **is ghost-written**, it is written by a writer for another person, for example a politician or sportsman, who then publishes it as his or her own work. • **ghost-writer, ghost-writers.**   VERB: beV-ed / N-COUNT

ghoul /guːl/ **ghouls. 1** A **ghoul** is an imaginary evil spirit. **Ghouls** are said to steal bodies from graves and eat them. • **ghoul·ish** *...the ghoulish appari-tions at the window.* **2** If you describe someone as a **ghoul**, you disapprove of them because they show an unnatural interest in things such as torture, death, or dead bodies. • **ghoulish** *They are there only to satisfy their ghoulish curiosity.*   N-COUNT / ADJ-GRADED / N-COUNT PRAGMATICS / ADJ-GRADED

GHQ /,dʒiː eɪtʃ 'kjuː/. In Britain, **GHQ** is the place where the people who organize military forces or a military operation work. **GHQ** is an abbreviation for 'General Headquarters'.   N-UNCOUNT

GI /,dʒiː 'aɪ/ **GIs.** A **GI** is a soldier in the United States army.   ◆◇◇◇ N-COUNT

gi·ant /'dʒaɪənt/ **giants. 1** Something that is described as **giant** is much larger or more important than most others of its kind. *...Italy's giant car mak-er, Fiat. ...a giant oak table. ...a giant step towards unification.* **2** A large, successful organization or country can be referred to as a **giant.** *...Japanese electronics giant Sony.* **3** In myths and children's stories, a **giant** is a person who is very big and strong. **4** You can refer to someone as a **giant** if they are very impressive, for example if they are one of the most important or successful people in their field. *He was without question one of the giants of Japanese literature.*   ◆◆◇◇ ADJ: ADJn / N-COUNT JOURNALISM / N-COUNT / N-COUNT

'giant-killing, giant-killings. When a weaker team or competitor beats a much stronger, well-known team or competitor, their success can be referred to as a **giant-killing.** • **gi·ant-kil·ler,** **giant-killers.** *Oldham of the Second Division al-ready have a reputation as giant-killers.*   N-COUNT JOURNALISM / N-COUNT

'giant-sized. An object that is **giant-sized** is much bigger than objects of its kind usually are. *...a giant-sized TV.*   ADJ

gib·ber /'dʒɪbə/ **gibbers, gibbering, gibbered.** If someone **is gibbering**, they are talking very fast and in a confused manner. *I was a gibbering wreck by this stage.*   VERB: V / V-ing INFORMAL

gib·ber·ish /'dʒɪbərɪʃ/. If you say that someone talks **gibberish**, you mean that they do not make any sense.   N-UNCOUNT

gib·bon /'gɪbən/ **gibbons.** A **gibbon** is an ape with very long arms and no tail.   N-COUNT

gibe /dʒaɪb/. See **jibe.**

gid·dy /'gɪdi/ **giddier, giddiest. 1** If you feel **gid-dy**, you feel unsteady and think that you are about   ◆◇◇◇ ADJ-GRADED

to fall over, usually because you are not well. ♦ **gid‑**   N-UNCOUNT
·di·ness *A wave of giddiness swept over her.* **2** If   ADJ-GRADED
you feel **giddy** with delight or excitement, you feel
so happy or excited that you find it hard to think or
act normally. *Being there gave me a giddy pleasure.*
♦ **giddiness** *There's almost a giddiness surround‑*   N-UNCOUNT
ing the talks in Houston.

gift /gɪft/ **gifts. 1** A **gift** is something that you give   ◆◆◆◇
someone as a present. **2** If someone has a **gift** for   N-COUNT
doing something, they have a natural ability for do‑   N-COUNT
ing it. *As a youth he discovered a gift for teaching.*
♦ **gift·ed** /gɪftɪd/ *He's the most gifted player at*   ADJ-GRADED
Highbury. **3** ● **God's gift:** see **God.**

gift·ed /gɪftɪd/. A **gifted child** is more intelligent   ◆◇◇◇
than average.   ADJ-GRADED

ˈgift‑wrapped. A **gift‑wrapped** present is wrapped   ADJ
in pretty paper.

gig /gɪg/ **gigs, gigging, gigged. 1** A **gig** is a live   ◆◇◇◇
performance by a pop or jazz musician, comedian,   N-COUNT
or disc jockey. **2** When musicians or other perform‑   INFORMAL
ers **gig**, they perform live in public. ♦ **gig·ging**   VERB: V
...ten years of gigging in bars and clubs.   INFORMAL / N-UNCOUNT

gi·gan·tic /dʒaɪˈgæntɪk/. If you describe something   ◆◇◇◇
as **gigantic**, you are emphasizing that it is extremely   ADJ-GRADED
large in size, amount, or degree.   PRAGMATICS / INFORMAL

gig·gle /ˈgɪgəl/ **giggles, giggling, giggled. 1** If   ◆◆◇◇
someone **giggles**, they laugh in a childlike, helpless   VERB
way, because they are amused, nervous, or embar‑   V with quote
rassed. *'I beg your pardon?' she giggled. ...a giggling*   V-ing
little girl. ► Also a noun. *She gave a little giggle.*   N-COUNT
♦ **gig·gly** /ˈgɪgəli/. *Ray was very giggly and joking*   ADJ-GRADED
all the time. **2** If you say that someone has **the gig‑**   N-PLURAL:
gles, you mean they cannot stop giggling. *She had a*   theN
fit of the giggles. **3** If you say that something is **a gig‑**   INFORMAL / N-SING:
gle, you mean it is fun or is amusing. *I might buy*   aN
one for a friend's birthday as a giggle.   INFORMAL, BRITISH

gigo·lo /ˈdʒɪgələʊ/ **gigolos.** A **gigolo** is a man who   N-COUNT
is paid to be the lover and companion of a rich and
usually older woman.

gild /gɪld/ **gilds, gilding, gilded.** If you **gild** a   ◆◇◇◇
surface, you cover it in a thin layer of gold or gold   VERB: V n
paint. ♦ **gild·ing** *...carved wooden capitals with*   N-UNCOUNT
their original gilding.

gill /gɪl/ **gills. Gills** are the organs on the sides of   N-COUNT
fish and other water creatures through which they
breathe.

gilt /gɪlt/ **gilts. 1** A **gilt** object is covered with a thin   ◆◆◇◇
layer of gold or gold paint. **2 Gilts** are the same as   ADJ / N-COUNT
gilt‑edged stocks or securities.

ˌgilt‑ˈedged. Gilt‑edged stocks or securities are is‑   ADJ: ADJ n
sued by the government for people to invest in for a   BRITISH
fixed period of time at a fixed rate of interest.

gim·mick /ˈgɪmɪk/ **gimmicks.** A **gimmick** is an   ◆◇◇◇
unusual and unnecessary feature or action whose   N-COUNT
purpose is to attract attention or publicity; used   PRAGMATICS
showing disapproval. ♦ **gim·mick·ry** /ˈgɪmɪkri/.   N-UNCOUNT
That's been mostly public relations gimmickry.
♦ **gim·micky** *The campaign was gimmicky, but it*   ADJ-GRADED
had a serious side.

gin /dʒɪn/ **gins. Gin** is a strong colourless alcoholic   ◆◇◇◇
drink made from grain and juniper berries. ► A **gin**   N-VAR
is a glass of gin. *...another gin and tonic.*   N-COUNT

gin·ger /ˈdʒɪndʒə/. **1 Ginger** is the root of a plant   ◆◇◇◇
that is used to flavour food. It has a sweet spicy fla‑   N-UNCOUNT
vour and is often sold in powdered form. **2 Ginger**   COLOUR
is used to describe something, usually a person's
hair, that is orangey‑brown.

ˌginger ˈale, ginger ales. Ginger ale is a fizzy   N-VAR
non‑alcoholic drink flavoured with ginger. ► A glass   N-COUNT
of ginger ale can be referred to as a **ginger ale.**

ˌginger ˈbeer, ginger beers. Ginger beer is a   N-VAR
drink that is made from syrup and ginger and is
sometimes slightly alcoholic.

ginger·bread /ˈdʒɪndʒəbred/. **Gingerbread** is a   N-UNCOUNT
sweet cake or biscuit that is flavoured with ginger.

gin·ger·ly /ˈdʒɪndʒəli/. If you do something **gin‑**   ◆◇◇◇
gerly, you do it in a careful, hesitant manner,   ADV-GRADED:
usually because you expect it to be dangerous, un‑   ADV with v
pleasant, or painful.   WRITTEN

ging·ham /ˈgɪŋəm/. **Gingham** is cotton cloth which   N-UNCOUNT
has a woven pattern of small squares, usually in
white and one other colour.

gin·seng /ˈdʒɪnseŋ/. **Ginseng** is the root of a plant   N-UNCOUNT
found in China, Korea, and America which some
people believe is good for your health.

gip·sy /ˈdʒɪpsi/. See **gypsy.**

gi·raffe /dʒɪˈrɑːf, -ˈræf/ **giraffes.** A **giraffe** is a large   N-COUNT
African animal with a very long neck, long legs, and
dark patches on its body. See picture headed
animals.

gird /gɜːd/ **girds, girding, girded.** If you **gird**   VERB
yourself **for** a battle or contest, you prepare yourself   V pron-refl for n
for it. *Washington has girded itself for terrorist re‑*   LITERARY
taliation. ● to **gird** your **loins:** see **loin.**

gird·er /ˈgɜːdə/ **girders.** A **girder** is a long, thick   N-COUNT
piece of steel or iron that is used in the framework
of buildings and bridges.

gir·dle /ˈgɜːdəl/ **girdles, girdling, girdled. 1** A   N-COUNT
girdle is a piece of women's underwear that fits
tightly around the stomach and hips. **2** Something   VERB: V n
that **girdles** something else surrounds it. *The old*   LITERARY
town centre is girdled by a boulevard lined with
trees.

girl /gɜːl/ **girls. 1** A **girl** is a female child. *...an elev‑*   ◆◆◆◆
en year old girl... We had a little girl. **2** Young wom‑   N-COUNT
en are often referred to as **girls.** Some people find   N-COUNT
this use offensive. *...a pretty twenty‑year old girl.*
3 Some people refer to a man's girlfriend as his **girl.**   N-COUNT
I've been with my girl for nine years.   INFORMAL

girl·friend /ˈgɜːlfrend/ **girlfriends. 1** Someone's   ◆◆◇◇
girlfriend is a girl or woman with whom they are   N-COUNT
having a romantic or sexual relationship. *He had*
been going out with his girlfriend for seven months.
2 A **girlfriend** is a female friend. *I met a girlfriend*   N-COUNT
for lunch.

ˌGirl ˈGuide, Girl Guides. 1 In Britain, the Guides   N-COLL:
used to be called **the Girl Guides. 2** A **Girl Guide**   PROPER: theN
was a girl who was a member of the Girl Guides.   N-COUNT

girl·hood /ˈgɜːlhʊd/. **Girlhood** is the period of a fe‑   N-UNCOUNT
male person's life during which she is a girl. *Her*
girlhood dream had been to study painting.

girlie /ˈgɜːli/. **Girlie** magazines or calendars show   ADJ: ADJ n
photographs of naked or almost naked women   INFORMAL
which are intended to please men.

girl·ish /ˈgɜːlɪʃ/. If you describe a woman as **girlish,**   ADJ-GRADED
you mean she behaves, looks, or sounds like a
young girl, for example because she is shy, excited,
or lively. *She gave a little girlish giggle.*

ˈGirl Scout, Girl Scouts. 1 In the United States,   N-COLL:
the **Girl Scouts** is an organization similar to the   PROPER: theN
Guides. 2 A **Girl Scout** is a girl who is a member of   N-COUNT
the Girl Scouts.

giro /ˈdʒaɪərəʊ/ **giros;** also spelled **Giro.** In Britain,   N-COUNT
a **giro** or a **giro cheque** is a cheque that is given
regularly by the government to a person who is un‑
employed or ill.

girth /gɜːθ/ **girths. 1** The **girth** of an object is its   N-VAR:
width or thickness, measured around its circumfer‑   with supp
ence. *...his ample girth and greying beard.* **2** A **girth**   FORMAL
is a wide strap which is fastened firmly around the   N-COUNT
middle of a horse to keep the saddle or load in the
right place.

gist /dʒɪst/. The **gist** of a speech, conversation, or   N-SING:
piece of writing is its general meaning. *He related*   theN of n
the gist of his conversation to Naseby.

git /gɪt/ **gits.** If someone refers to another person as   N-COUNT
a **git**, they are expressing their dislike and lack of re‑   PRAGMATICS
spect for that person.   BRITISH, RUDE

give 1 used with nouns describing actions

give /gɪv/ **gives, giving, gave, given. 1** You can   VB: no cont
use **give** with nouns that refer to physical actions.   V n
The whole expression refers to the performing of   V nn
the action. For example, **'She gave a smile'** means
almost the same as 'She smiled'. *She stretched her*
arms out and gave a great yawn... He reached for her
hand and gave it a reassuring squeeze.

2 You use **give** to say that a person provides a service   VERB
or performs an action for someone else. For example,   V nn
if you **give** someone a lift, you take them somewhere   V n

in your car. *He was given mouth-to-mouth resuscitation... Sophie asked her if she would like to come and give art lessons.* **3** You use **give** with nouns that refer to information, opinions, or greetings to indicate that something is communicated. For example, if you **give** someone some news, you tell it to them. *He gave no details... He asked me to give his regards to all of you... He gave the cause of death as haemorrhaging.* **4** If you **give** someone or something a length of time, an amount, or a value, you estimate that they will last that time or have that amount or value. *A BBC poll gave the Labour Party a 2 per cent lead.* **5** If someone or something **gives** you a particular idea, impression, or feeling, it causes you to have or experience it. *They gave me the impression that they were doing exactly what they wanted... It will give great pleasure to the many thousands of children who visit the hospital each year.* **6** If you **give** something thought or attention, you think about it, concentrate on it, or deal with it. *I've been giving it some thought... Priority will be given to those who apply early.* **7** If you **give** a performance or speech, you perform or speak in public. *...Mrs Butler who gave us such an interesting talk last year.* **8** If you **give** a party or other social event, you organize it. *I gave a dinner party for a few close friends.*

VERB: V n n
V n
V n to n
V n as n

VERB
V n n

VERB
V n n
Also V n

VERB
V n n
V n to n/-ing

VERB: V n
V n n

VERB
V n

give 2 transferring

give /gɪv/ **gives, giving, gave. 1** If you **give** someone something that you own or have bought, you provide them with it, so that they have it or can use it. *They gave us T-shirts and stickers... Many leading industrialists gave money to the Conservative Party.* **2** If you **give** someone something that you are holding or that is near you, you pass it to them, so that they are then holding it. *He pulled a handkerchief from his pocket and gave it to him.* **3** To **give** someone or something a particular power or right means to allow them to have it. *...a citizen's charter giving rights to gays... I am very conscious of my money giving me power.*

♦♦♦♦♦
VERB
V n n
V n to n

VERB: V n n
V n to n

VERB
V n to n
V n n

give 3 other uses, phrases, and phrasal verbs

give /gɪv/ **gives, giving, gave, given. 1** If something **gives**, it collapses or breaks under pressure. *My knees gave under me.* **2** You say that you **are given** to understand or believe that something is the case when you do not want to say how you found out about it, or who told you. **3** See also **given. 4** If someone **gives as good as** they **get**, they fight or argue as well as the person they are fighting or arguing with. **5** You use **give** in phrases such as **I'd give anything, I'd give my right arm**, and **what wouldn't I give** to emphasize that you are very keen to do or have something. *I'd give anything to be like you.* **6** People use **give** in expressions such as **I don't give a damn** or **I don't give a hoot** to emphasize that they do not care about something. *I don't give a stuff what you think about me.* **7** You use **give me** to say that you would rather have one thing than another, especially when you have just mentioned the thing that you do not want. *Give me a good roast dinner any day.* **8** If you say that something requires **give and take**, you mean that people must compromise for it to be successful. **9 Give or take** is used to indicate that an amount is approximate. For example, if you say that something is fifty years old, **give or take** a few years, you mean that it is approximately fifty years old. *They grow to a height of 12 ins – give or take a couple of inches.* **10** You say **'I'll give you that'** to indicate that you admit that someone has a particular characteristic or ability. *You're a bright enough kid, I'll give you that.* **11 Give** is used in a large number of expressions which are explained under other words in this dictionary. For example, the expression to **give way** is explained at **way**.

♦♦♦♦♦
V
V-PASSIVE:
be V-ed to-inf
FORMAL

PHRASE

PHRASE

PHRASE
PRAGMATICS

VB: no cont,
no passive,
with brd-neg
V n

INFORMAL
PHRASE

PHRASE

PHRASE

PHRASE
PRAGMATICS

give away. 1 If you **give away** something that you own, you give it to someone, rather than selling it, often because you no longer want it. *He was giving his collection away for nothing... We have six copies of the book to give away.* **2** If someone **gives away** an advantage, they accidentally cause their opponent or en-

PHRASAL VB
V n P
V P noun

V P noun
Also V n P

emy to have that advantage. *We gave away a silly goal.* **3** If you **give away** information that should be kept secret, you reveal it to other people. *She would give nothing away... They felt like they were giving away company secrets.* **4** To **give** someone or something **away** means to show their true nature or identity, which is not obvious. *Although they are pretending hard to be young, grey hair and cellulite give them away... I was never tempted for a moment to give her away.* **5** In a Christian wedding ceremony, if someone, traditionally the bride's father, **gives** the bride **away**, they officially present her to her husband.

V n P
V P noun

V n P
Also V P noun

V n P

give back. If you **give** something **back**, you return it to the person who gave it to you. *I gave the textbook back to him... You gave me back the projector.*

PHRASAL VB
V n P
V P to n
V n P noun

give in. 1 If you **give in**, you admit that you are defeated or that you cannot do something. *All right. I give in. What did you do with the ship?* **2** If you **give in**, you agree to do something that you do not want to do. *They won't give in to the workers' demands.*

PHRASAL VB
V P

V P
V P to n

give off or **give out.** If something **gives off** or **gives out** a gas, heat, or a smell, it produces it and sends it out into the air. *...natural gas, which gives off less carbon dioxide than coal.*

PHRASAL VB
V P noun
Also V n P

give out. 1 If you **give out** a number of things, you distribute them among a group of people. *They were giving out leaflets at the Prime Minister's former school.* **2** If you **give out** information, you make it known to people. *How often do you give your phone number out?* **3** If a piece of equipment or part of the body **gives out**, it stops working. *One of his lungs gives out entirely.* **4** If you **give out** something such as a scream or a sigh, you make that sound. *He gave out a scream of pain.* **5** See **give off.**

PHRASAL VB
V P noun
Also V n P

V n P

V P

V P noun
WRITTEN

give over. If you tell someone to **give over**, you are telling them to stop doing something, usually because they are annoying you. *Tell him to give over... She gave over teasing and grinned at him.*

PHRASAL VB
V P
V P -ing/n
INFORMAL

give over to or **give up to.** If something **is given over to** or **given up to** a particular use, it is used entirely for that purpose. *Much of the garden was given over to vegetables.*

PHRASAL VB
usu passive
be V-ed P P n

give up. 1 If you **give up** something, you stop doing it or having it. *Coastguards had given up all hope of finding the two divers alive. ...smokers who give up.* **2** If you **give up**, you decide that you cannot do something and stop trying to do it. *After a fruitless morning sitting at his desk he had given up.* **3** If you **give up** your job, you resign from it. *He is thinking of giving up teaching.* **4** If you **give up** something that you have or that you are entitled to, you allow someone else to have it. *Georgia refuses to give up any territory... One of the men with him gave up his place on the bench.* **5** If you **give** yourself **up**, you let the police or other people know where you are, after you have been hiding from them. *A 28-year-old man later gave himself up and will appear in court today.*

PHRASAL VB
V P n/-ing
V P
Also V n P
V P

V P n/-ing
Also V n P,
V P
V P noun
Also V n P

V pron-refl P
Also V n P

give up on. If you **give up on** something, you decide that you will never succeed in doing it, understanding it, or changing it, and you stop trying to do it. *He urged them not to give up on peace efforts.*

PHRASAL VB
V P P n

give up to. See **give over to.**

PHRASAL VB

give-and-take. See **give.**

give·away /'gɪvəweɪ/ **giveaways;** also spelled **give-away. 1** A **giveaway** is something that makes you realize the truth about a person or situation. *The only giveaway was the look of amusement in her eyes.* **2** A **giveaway** is something that a company or organization gives to people, usually in order to encourage them to buy a particular product. **3** When you talk about **giveaway** prices, you are emphasizing that they are very low.

♦◇◇◇◇
N-SING

N-COUNT

ADJ: ADJ n
PRAGMATICS

giv·en /'gɪvən/. **1 Given** is the past participle of **give. 2** If you are **given to** doing something, you often do it. *I am not very given to emotional displays.* **3** A **given** situation or a **given** time is any particular situation or time that is possible in certain circumstances. *In chess there are typically about 36 legal moves from any given board position.* **4 Given** is used

♦♦♦◇◇

ADJ-GRADED
FORMAL

ADJ: det ADJ

PREP

when indicating a possible situation in which someone has the opportunity or ability to do something. For example, **given the chance** means 'if I had the chance'. *Given patience, successful breeding of this species can be achieved.* **5** If you say **given that** something is the case, you mean taking that fact into account. *This may seem an odd view to take, given that I am strongly in favour of the Maastricht treaty.* **6** If you say **given** something, you mean taking that thing into account. *Given the uncertainty over Leigh's future I was left with little other choice.*   PHR-CONJ   PREP

'**given name, given names.** A **given name** is a person's first name, which they are given at birth in addition to their surname.   N-COUNT   FORMAL

giv·er /'gɪvə/ **givers.** You can refer to a person or organization that gives or supplies a particular thing as a **giver** of that thing. *Germany is the largest giver of aid... Massage is a beautiful experience, both for the giver and the receiver.* ► Also a combining form. *They are legendary party-givers.*   ◆◇◇◇   N-COUNT   COMB

giz·mo /'gɪzməʊ/ **gizmos.** A **gizmo** is a device or machine which performs a particular task, usually in a new and efficient way. People often use **gizmo** to refer to a device or machine when they do not know what it is really called. *...a plastic gizmo for holding a coffee cup on the dashboard.*   N-COUNT

gla·cé /'glæseɪ, AM -'seɪ/. **Glacé** fruits are fruits that have been preserved in a thick sugary syrup and then dried.   ADJ: ADJ n

gla·cial /'gleɪʃəl/. **1** Glacial means relating to or produced by glaciers or ice. *...a true glacial landscape with U-shaped valleys.* **2** If you say that a person, action, or atmosphere is **glacial**, you are emphasizing that they are very unfriendly or hostile. *The Duchess's glare was glacial.* **3** If you describe someone, usually a woman, as **glacial**, you mean they are very beautiful and elegant, but do not show their feelings. *Her glacial beauty is magnetic.*   ◆◇◇◇   ADJ   TECHNICAL   ADJ-GRADED   PRAGMATICS   ADJ

glaci·er /'glæsɪə, AM 'gleɪʃə/ **glaciers.** A **glacier** is a huge mass of ice which moves very slowly, often down a mountain valley.   ◆◇◇◇   N-COUNT

glad /glæd/. **1** If you are **glad** about something, you are happy and pleased about it. *I'm glad I relented in the end... The people seem genuinely glad to see you.* ♦ **glad·ly** *Mallarme gladly accepted the invitation.* ♦ **glad·ness** *...a night of joy and gladness.* **2** If you say that you will be **glad** to do something, usually for someone else, you mean that you are willing and eager to do it. *I'll be glad to show you everything... We should be glad to answer any questions.* ♦ **gladly** *The counselors will gladly baby-sit during their free time.*   ◆◆◇◇   ADJ-GRADED: v-link ADJ   ADV with v   N-UNCOUNT   ADJ-GRADED: v-link ADJ to-inf   PRAGMATICS   ADV with v

glad·den /'glædən/ **gladdens, gladdening, gladdened.** If something **gladdens** you, it makes you feel happy and pleased. *Charles's visit surprised him and gladdened him. ...a conclusion that should gladden the hearts of all animal-rights activists.*   VERB   V n   LITERARY

glade /gleɪd/ **glades.** A **glade** is a grassy space without trees in a wood or forest. *...a woodland glade.*   N-COUNT   LITERARY

gladia·tor /'glædɪeɪtə/ **gladiators.** In the time of the Roman Empire, a **gladiator** was a man who had to fight against other men or wild animals in order to entertain an audience.   N-COUNT

glam·or /'glæmə/. See **glamour.**

glam·or·ize /'glæməraɪz/ **glamorizes, glamorizing, glamorized;** also spelled **glamorise** in British English. If someone **glamorizes** something, they make it look or seem more attractive than it really is; used showing disapproval. *Filmmakers have often been accused of glamorizing organized crime.*   VERB   PRAGMATICS   V n

glam·or·ous /'glæmərəs/. If you describe someone or something as **glamorous**, you mean that they are more attractive, exciting, or interesting than ordinary people or things. *...some of the world's most beautiful and glamorous women.*   ◆◆◇◇   ADJ-GRADED

glam·our /'glæmə/; spelled **glamor** in American English. **Glamour** is the quality of being more attractive, exciting, or interesting than ordinary people or things. *...the glamour of show biz.*   ◆◆◇◇   N-UNCOUNT

glance /glɑːns, glæns/ **glances, glancing, glanced. 1** If you **glance** at something or someone, you look at them very quickly and then look away again. *He glanced at his watch... I glanced back.* ► Also a noun. *Trevor and I exchanged a glance.* **2** If you **glance through** or **at** a newspaper, report, or book, you spend a short time looking at it without reading it very carefully. *I picked up the phone book and glanced through it.* **3** If you see something **at a glance**, you see or recognize it immediately. *One could tell at a glance that she was a compassionate person.* **4** If you say that something is true or seems to be true **at first glance**, you mean that it seems to be true when you first see it or think about it, but that your first impression may be wrong.   ◆◆◆◇◇   VERB   V prep/adv   N-COUNT   VERB   V through/at n   PHRASE   PHRASE

glance off. If an object **glances off** something, it hits it at an angle and bounces away in another direction. *My fist glanced off his jaw.*   PHRASAL VB   V P n

glanc·ing /'glɑːnsɪŋ, 'glæns-/. A **glancing** blow is one that hits something at an angle rather than from directly in front. *The car struck him a glancing blow.*   ADJ: ADJ n

gland /glænd/ **glands.** A **gland** is a cell or organ in the body which produces chemical substances which the body needs in order to function. *...sweat glands.* ♦ **glan·du·lar** /'glændʒʊlə/. *...glandular tissue.*   ◆◇◇◇   N-COUNT   ADJ

,**glandular 'fever.** Glandular fever is a disease which causes swollen glands, fever, and a sore throat.   N-UNCOUNT

glare /gleə/ **glares, glaring, glared. 1** If you **glare** at someone, you look at them with an angry expression on your face. *Jacob glared and muttered something.* ► Also a noun. *His glasses magnified his irritable glare.* **2** If someone is in **the glare of** publicity or public attention, they are constantly being watched and talked about by the public. *Norma is said to dislike the glare of publicity.* **3** If the sun or a light **glares**, it shines with a very bright light which is difficult to look at. ► Also a noun. *...the glare of a car's headlights.*   ◆◆◇◇   VERB: V at n   V   N-COUNT   N-SING: the N of n   VERB: V   N-SING

glar·ing /'gleərɪŋ/. If you describe something bad as **glaring**, you are emphasizing that it is very noticeable. *...a glaring example of misrepresentation.* ♦ **glar·ing·ly** *It was glaringly obvious.*   ◆◇◇◇   ADJ-GRADED   PRAGMATICS   ADV-GRADED

glas·nost /'glæznɒst/. **Glasnost** is a policy of making a government more open and accountable.   ◆◇◇◇   N-UNCOUNT

glass /glɑːs, glæs/ **glasses. 1** Glass is a hard transparent substance that is used to make things such as windows and bottles. *...a pane of glass. ...a sliding glass door.* **2** A **glass** is a container made from glass, which you can drink from. ► The contents of a glass can be referred to as a **glass** of something. **3** Glass is used to mean objects made of glass. *...a glittering array of glass.* **4** Glasses are two lenses in a frame that some people wear in front of their eyes in order to help them see better. *He took off his glasses.* ● See also **dark glasses, magnifying glass.**   ◆◆◆◇   N-UNCOUNT   N-COUNT   N-COUNT   N-UNCOUNT   N-PLURAL

,**glass 'ceiling, glass ceilings.** When people refer to a **glass ceiling**, they are talking about the attitudes and traditions in a society that prevent women from rising to the top jobs.   N-COUNT

,**glassed-'in.** A **glassed-in** room or building has windows instead of walls.   ADJ

,**glass 'fibre;** spelled **glass fiber** in American English. **Glass fibre** is a cloth made from short thin threads of glass. It is used to keep heat in or to strengthen plastic.   N-UNCOUNT

glass·house /'glɑːshaʊs, 'glæs-/ **glasshouses.** A **glasshouse** is a greenhouse, especially a large one which is used for the commercial production of fruit, flowers, or vegetables.   N-COUNT   BRITISH

glass·ware /'glɑːsweə, 'glæs-/. **Glassware** consists of objects made of glass, such as bowls, drinking containers, and ornaments.   N-UNCOUNT

glassy /'glɑːsi, 'glæsi/. **1** If something is **glassy**, it is very smooth and shiny, like glass. *...glassy green pebbles.* **2** If someone's eyes or expression are   ADJ-GRADED   WRITTEN   ADJ-GRADED

glassy, they are showing no feeling, emotion, or awareness. *Henry gave Paul a glassy-eyed stare.* WRITTEN

glau·co·ma /glɔːˈkəʊmə, AM glau-/. **Glaucoma** is an eye disease which can cause people to go gradually blind. N-UNCOUNT

glaze /gleɪz/ **glazes, glazing, glazed. 1** A **glaze** is a thin layer of liquid which is put on a piece of pottery and becomes hard and shiny when the pottery is heated in a very hot oven. ♦ **glazed** *...glazed bowls and plates.* **2** When you **glaze** food such as bread or pastry, you spread a layer of beaten egg, milk, or other liquid onto it before you cook it in order to make its surface shiny and attractive. ▶ A **glaze** is something that you spread onto food like this. *...a butter and sugar glaze.* ♦◇◇◇◇ N-COUNT / ADJ / VERB: V n / N-COUNT

glaze over. If your eyes **glaze over**, they become dull and lose all expression, usually because you are bored or are thinking about something else. PHRASAL VB V P

glazed /gleɪzd/. **1** If you describe someone's eyes as **glazed**, you mean that their expression is dull or dreamy, usually because they are tired or are having difficulty concentrating. *There was a glazed look in her eyes.* **2** A **glazed** door or wall is made partly or entirely of glass. 3 See also **glaze**. ♦◇◇◇◇ ADJ-GRADED / ADJ

gla·zi·er /ˈgleɪziə, AM -ʒər/ **glaziers.** A **glazier** is someone whose job is fitting glass into windows and doors. N-COUNT

gleam /gliːm/ **gleams, gleaming, gleamed. 1** If an object or a surface **gleams**, it is shiny, often because it is very clean. *...a gleaming red sports car.* ▶ Also a noun. *...the gleam of the dark river.* **2** If a light or the sun or moon **gleams**, it shines but is faint or pale. ▶ Also a noun. *...the gleam of the headlights.* **3** If your eyes **gleam**, they look bright and show that you are excited or happy. ▶ Also a noun. *There was a gleam in her eye when she looked at me.* **4** A **gleam** of something is a faint sign of it. *...a gleam of hope for a peaceful settlement.* ♦◆◇◇◇ VERB: V / V-ing / N-SING / VERB: V / WRITTEN / N-COUNT / VERB: V / WRITTEN / N-SING / N-COUNT: N of n

glean /gliːn/ **gleans, gleaning, gleaned.** If you **glean** information or knowledge, you learn or collect it slowly and patiently, and perhaps indirectly. *We're gleaning information from all sources.* ♦◇◇◇◇ VERB: V n / V n from n

glee /gliː/. **Glee** is a feeling of happiness and excitement, often caused by someone else's misfortune. ♦ **glee·ful** *He took an almost gleeful delight in showing how wrong they can be.* ♦ **glee·ful·ly** *The media gleefully reported the government's panicked response.* ♦◇◇◇◇ N-UNCOUNT / ADJ-GRADED / ADV-GRADED / ADV with v

glen /glen/ **glens.** A **glen** is a deep, narrow valley, especially in the mountains of Scotland or Ireland. N-COUNT

glib /glɪb/. If you describe what someone says as **glib**, you disapprove of it because it suggests that something is simple or easy when this is not the case at all. ♦ **glib·ly** *We talk glibly of equality of opportunity.* ADJ-GRADED / PRAGMATICS / ADV-GRADED

glide /glaɪd/ **glides, gliding, glided. 1** If you **glide** somewhere, you move silently and in a smooth and effortless way. *Waiters glide between tightly packed tables bearing trays of pasta.* **2** When birds or aeroplanes **glide**, they float on air currents. ♦◇◇◇◇ VERB / V prep/adv / VERB: V

glid·er /ˈglaɪdə/ **gliders.** A **glider** is an aircraft without an engine, which flies by floating on air currents. ♦ **glid·ing.** Gliding is the sport or activity of flying in a glider. ♦◇◇◇◇ N-COUNT / N-UNCOUNT

glim·mer /ˈglɪmə/ **glimmers, glimmering, glimmered. 1** If something **glimmers**, it produces or reflects a faint, gentle, often unsteady light. ▶ Also a noun. *In the east there was a glimmer of light.* **2** A **glimmer of** something is a faint sign of it. *He is celebrating his first glimmer of success.* ♦◇◇◇◇ VERB: V / N-COUNT / N-COUNT: N of n

glim·mer·ing /ˈglɪmərɪŋ/ **glimmerings.** A **glimmering of** something is a faint sign of it. *...a glimmering of understanding.* N-COUNT: N of n

glimpse /glɪmps/ **glimpses, glimpsing, glimpsed. 1** If you **glimpse** someone or something, you see them very briefly and not very well. ▶ Also a noun. *The driver caught a glimpse of him in his rear-view mirror.* **2** A **glimpse** of something is a brief experience of it or an idea about it that helps ♦♦◇◇◇ VERB: V n / N-COUNT / N-COUNT

you understand it better. *The trip will give them a glimpse of a world they have barely encountered.*

glint /glɪnt/ **glints, glinting, glinted. 1** If something **glints**, it produces or reflects a quick flash of light. *Sunlight glinted on his spectacles.* ▶ Also a noun. *...a glint of silver.* **2** If someone's eyes **glint**, they shine and express a particular emotion. ▶ Also a noun. *...the glint of triumph in his eye.* ♦◇◇◇◇ VERB: V / V on/off n / WRITTEN / N-COUNT / VERB: V / WRITTEN / N-SING

glis·ten /ˈglɪsən/ **glistens, glistening, glistened. 1** If something **glistens**, it shines or sparkles, usually because it is wet or oily. *Darcy's face was white and glistening with sweat.* **2** If you say that someone's eyes **glisten**, you mean their eyes shine, for example because they are about to cry, or because they are happy or excited. ♦◇◇◇◇ VERB: V / V with n / VERB: V / WRITTEN

glitch /glɪtʃ/ **glitches.** A **glitch** is a problem which stops something from working properly or being successful. *Manufacturing glitches have limited the factory's output.* N-COUNT / INFORMAL

glit·ter /ˈglɪtə/ **glitters, glittering, glittered. 1** If something **glitters**, light comes from or is reflected off different parts of it every moment. ♦ **glit·tery** *...a gold suit and a glittery bow tie.* **2** If someone's eyes **glitter**, they are bright and express a particular emotion, for example excitement or greed. **3** You can use **glitter** to refer to the superficial attractiveness or excitement connected with something. *She was blinded by the glitter and the glamour of her own life.* ♦♦◇◇◇ ADJ-GRADED / VERB: V / WRITTEN / N-UNCOUNT

glit·te·ra·ti /ˌglɪtəˈrɑːti/. The **glitterati** are rich and famous people such as actors and rock stars. N-PLURAL / JOURNALISM

glit·ter·ing /ˈglɪtərɪŋ/. You use **glittering** to indicate that something is very impressive or successful. *...a glittering academic career.* ♦◇◇◇◇ ADJ-GRADED: ADJ n

glitz /glɪts/. You use **glitz** to refer to something that you think is exciting and attractive in a showy and rather superficial way. *...the glitz of Beverly Hills.* ♦ **glitzy** *...the glitziest ski resorts in the world.* N-UNCOUNT / ADJ-GRADED

gloat /gləʊt/ **gloats, gloating, gloated.** If you say that someone **is gloating**, you are criticizing them for showing arrogant and unkind pleasure at their own success, or at other people's failure. *Anti-abortionists are gloating over the court's decision.* VERB: V / PRAGMATICS / V over/about n

glob /glɒb/ **globs.** A **glob** of something soft or liquid is a small round amount of it. N-COUNT / INFORMAL

glob·al /ˈgləʊbəl/. **1** You can use the word **global** to describe something that happens in all parts of the world or affects all parts of the world. *...a global ban on nuclear testing.* ♦ **glob·al·ly** *...a globally familiar trade name.* **2** A **global** view or vision of a situation is one in which all its different aspects are considered. *...a global vision of contemporary societies.* ♦♦♦◇◇ ADJ / ADV / ADJ-GRADED

global 'warming. The problem of the gradual rise in the earth's temperature is referred to as **global warming.** ♦♦◇◇◇ N-UNCOUNT

globe /gləʊb/ **globes. 1** You can refer to the world as the **globe** when you are emphasizing how big it is or that something happens in many different parts of it. *...bottles of beer from every corner of the globe.* **2** A **globe** is a ball-shaped object with a map of the world on it. ♦♦◇◇◇ N-SING / N-COUNT

globe 'artichoke, globe artichokes. Globe artichokes are round green vegetables that have fleshy leaves arranged like the petals of a flower. N-VAR

'globe-trotting; also spelled **globetrotting. Globetrotting** means travelling to different parts of the world. ▶ Also an adjective. *...globe-trotting academic superstars.* ♦ **globetrot·ter, globetrotters.** *...TV globetrotter Alan Whicker.* N-UNCOUNT / INFORMAL / N-COUNT

globu·lar /ˈglɒbjʊlə/. A **globular** object is shaped like a ball. *The globular seed capsule contains numerous small seeds.* ADJ / FORMAL

glob·ule /ˈglɒbjuːl/ **globules. Globules** of a liquid or of a soft substance are tiny round particles of it. *...globules of saliva.* N-COUNT

glock·en·spiel /ˈglɒkənʃpiːl/ **glockenspiels.** A **glockenspiel** is a musical instrument which consists of metal bars of different lengths arranged like a N-COUNT

piano keyboard. You play it by hitting the bars with wooden hammers.

gloom /gluːm/. **1 Gloom** is a state of partial darkness. ...*the gloom of a foggy November morning.* **2 Gloom** is a feeling of unhappiness or despair. ...*the deepening gloom over the economy.*
◆◆◇◇◇ N-SING / N-UNCOUNT: also a N

gloomy /ˈgluːmi/ **gloomier, gloomiest. 1** If a place is **gloomy**, it is almost dark so that you cannot see very well. ...*this huge gloomy church.* **2** If people are **gloomy**, they are unhappy and have no hope. *Miller is gloomy about the fate of the serious playwright in America.* ◆ **gloom·ly** *He tells me gloomily that he has been called up for army service.* **3** If a situation is **gloomy**, it does not give you much hope of success or happiness. ...*a gloomy picture of an economy sliding into recession.*
◆◆◇◇◇ ADJ-GRADED / ADJ-GRADED / ADV-GRADED: ADV with v / ADJ-GRADED

glo·ri·fied /ˈglɔːrɪfaɪd/. You use **glorified** to indicate that something is less impressive than its name suggests. For example, if you describe a lake as a **glorified** pond, you mean that it is not much more than a pond. *I'm just a glorified waitress.*
ADJ: ADJ n

glo·ri·fy /ˈglɔːrɪfaɪ/ **glorifies, glorifying, glorified.** If you say that someone **glorifies** something, you mean that they praise it or make it seem good or special, usually when it is not. ...*the banning of songs glorifying war.* ◆ **glo·ri·fi·ca·tion** /ˌglɔːrɪfɪˈkeɪʃən/ ...*the glorification of violence.*
◆◇◇◇ VERB V n / N-UNCOUNT

glo·ri·ous /ˈglɔːriəs/. **1** If you describe something as **glorious**, you are emphasizing that it is very beautiful or wonderful, and makes you feel very happy. ...*a glorious rainbow.* ◆ **glo·ri·ous·ly** ...*a tree, gloriously lit by autumn.* ...*her gloriously happy love life.* **2** A **glorious** career, victory, or occasion involves great fame or success. *Harrison had a glorious career spanning more than six decades.* ◆ **gloriously** *The mission was successful, gloriously successful.* **3** When you describe the weather as **glorious**, you mean it is hot and sunny. *It was a glorious day.* ◆ **gloriously** *It was a gloriously sunny day.*
◆◆◇◇◇ ADJ-GRADED PRAGMATICS LITERARY / ADV-GRADED / ADJ-GRADED / ADV-GRADED / ADV-GRADED: ADV adj

glo·ry /ˈglɔːri/ **glories, glorying, gloried.** **1 Glory** is the fame and admiration that you gain by doing something impressive. *Walsham had his moment of glory when he won a 20km race.* ● If you go out in **a blaze of glory**, you do something very dramatic at the end of your career or your life which makes you famous. *He wanted his presidency to end in a blaze of glory.* **2** The **glory** of something is its great beauty or quality of being impressive. **3** If you **glory in** a situation or activity, you enjoy it very much. *The workers were glorying in their new-found freedom.*
N-UNCOUNT: also N in pl / PHRASE / N-UNCOUNT: also N in pl / VERB V in n

gloss /glɒs, AM glɔːs/ **glosses, glossing, glossed. 1** A **gloss** is a bright shine on the surface of something. **2 Gloss** is the same as **gloss paint**. **3 Gloss** is a type of shiny make-up. ...*lip glosses.* **4 Gloss** is an appearance of attractiveness or good quality which sometimes hides less attractive features or poor quality. *Television commercials might seem more professional but beware of mistaking the gloss for the content.* **5** If you put **a gloss** on a bad situation, you try to make it seem more attractive or acceptable by giving people a false explanation or interpretation of it. *The whole idea was to give history a happy gloss.* **6** If you **gloss** a difficult word or idea, you provide an explanation of it. *Older editors glossed 'drynke' as 'love-potion'.*
◆◇◇◇ N-SING / N-VAR / N-VAR / N-UNCOUNT / N-SING: a N / VERB V n as n Also V n

gloss over. If you **gloss over** a problem, a mistake, or an embarrassing moment, you try and make it seem unimportant by ignoring it or by dealing with it very quickly. *They gloss over the economic facts.*
PHRASAL VB V P noun

glos·sa·ry /ˈglɒsəri, AM ˈglɔːs-/ **glossaries.** The **glossary** of a book or a subject is an alphabetical list of the special or technical words used in it, with explanations of their meanings.
N-COUNT

glossies /ˈglɒsiz, AM ˈglɔːs-/. The **glossies** are expensive magazines printed on thick, glossy paper.
N-PLURAL BRITISH, INFORMAL

gloss paint. Gloss paint is paint that forms a shiny surface when it dries.
N-UNCOUNT

glossy /ˈglɒsi, AM ˈglɔːsi/. **1 Glossy** means smooth and shiny. ...*glossy black hair.* **2** You can describe something as **glossy** if you think that it has been designed to look attractive but is of little practical value or may have hidden defects. ...*a glossy new office.* **3 Glossy** magazines, brochures, or photographs are produced on expensive, shiny paper.
◆◇◇◇ ADJ-GRADED / ADJ-GRADED / ADJ: ADJ n

glove /glʌv/ **gloves. Gloves** are pieces of clothing which cover your hands and wrists and have individual sections for each finger. See picture headed **clothes**. ...*a pair of white cotton gloves.* ● See also **kid gloves** ● **hand in glove**: see **hand**. ◆ **gloved** /glʌvd/. ...*his gloved hand.*
◆◆◇◇◇ N-COUNT / ADJ

'glove compartment, glove compartments. The **glove compartment** in a car is a small cupboard or shelf below the front windscreen. See picture headed **car and bicycle**.
N-COUNT

glow /gləʊ/ **glows, glowing, glowed. 1** If something **glows**, it produces a dull, steady light. *He blew on the charcoal until it glowed orange.* ▶ Also a noun. *The rising sun casts a golden glow over the fields.* **2** If something **glows**, it looks bright because it is reflecting light. *The fall foliage glowed red and yellow in the morning sunlight.* **3** If someone's skin **glows**, it looks healthy and pink, for example because they are excited or have been exercising. ▶ Also a noun. *The moisturiser gave my face a healthy glow.* **4** If someone **glows** with an emotion such as pride or pleasure, the expression in their face shows they feel it. *The expectant mothers that Amy had encountered positively glowed with pride.* ▶ Also a noun. *Exercise will give you a glow of satisfaction.* **5** See also **glowing**.
◆◆◇◇◇ VERB: V V adj / N-SING / VERB: V V adj / VERB: V / N-SING / VERB V with n Also V / N-SING

glow·er /ˈglaʊə/ **glowers, glowering, glowered.** If you **glower** at someone or something, you look at them angrily. *He glowered and glared.*
VERB: V at n V / WRITTEN

glow·ing /ˈgləʊɪŋ/. A **glowing** description of someone or something praises them highly. *The premieres of his plays brought in glowing reviews.*
◆◇◇◇ ADJ-GRADED

glu·cose /ˈgluːkəʊz, -əʊs/. **Glucose** is a type of sugar.
◆◇◇◇ N-UNCOUNT

glue /gluː/ **glues, glueing** or **gluing, glued. 1 Glue** is a sticky substance used for joining things together, often for repairing broken things. ...*a tube of glue.* **2** If you **glue** one object to another, you stick them together using glue. *Glue the fabric around the window.* **3** If you say that someone is **glued to** something, you mean that they are giving it all their attention. *Football enthusiasts will be glued to their televisions.*
◆◇◇◇ N-VAR / VERB V n prep/adv / V-PASSIVE be V-ed to n

'glue sniffing. Glue sniffing is the practice of inhaling the vapour from glue in order to become intoxicated.
N-UNCOUNT

glum /glʌm/ **glummer, glummest.** Someone who is **glum** is sad and quiet because they are disappointed or unhappy. ◆ **glum·ly** *I was still sitting glumly on the settee.*
◆◇◇◇ ADJ-GRADED / ADV-GRADED: ADV with v

glut /glʌt/ **gluts, glutting, glutted. 1** If there is a **glut** of something, there is so much of it that it cannot all be sold or used. *There's a glut of agricultural products in Western Europe.* **2** If a market **is glutted** with something, there is a glut of that thing. *The region is glutted with hospitals.*
◆◇◇◇ N-COUNT / VERB be V-ed with n Also V n

glu·ten /ˈgluːtən/. **Gluten** is a substance found in cereal grains such as wheat.
N-UNCOUNT

glu·ti·nous /ˈgluːtɪnəs/. Something that is **glutinous** is very sticky. ...*soft and glutinous mud.*
ADJ-GRADED

glut·ton /ˈglʌtən/ **gluttons. 1** If you think that someone eats too much and is greedy, you can say they are a **glutton**. ◆ **glut·tony** *We equate fat women with gluttony.* **2** If you say that someone is a **glutton for** something, you mean that they seem to enjoy or need it very much. *He was a glutton for hard work.*
N-COUNT / N-UNCOUNT / N-COUNT: N for n

glyc·er·ine /ˈglɪsərɪn/; spelled **glycerin** in American English. **Glycerine** is a thick, sweet, colourless liquid that is used especially in making medicine, explosives, and antifreeze for cars.
N-UNCOUNT

gm, gms. The plural can be **gm** or **gms. gm** is a written abbreviation for **gram**.
◆◆◇◇◇

GMT /,dʒiː em 'tiː/. **GMT** is an abbreviation for ◆◆◇◇◇
'Greenwich Mean Time', the standard time in Great
Britain which is used to calculate the time in the
rest of the world.

gnarled /nɑːld/. **1** A **gnarled** tree is twisted and ADJ-GRADED
oddly shaped because it is old. **2** If you describe ADJ-GRADED
someone as **gnarled**, you mean they look very old
because their skin is wrinkled or rough, or their
body is bent or twisted. *...his gnarled hands.*

gnash /næʃ/ **gnashes, gnashing, gnashed.** If PHRASE
you say that someone **is gnashing** their **teeth**, you
mean they are angry or frustrated about something.

gnat /næt/ **gnats.** A **gnat** is a very small flying in- N-COUNT
sect that bites.

gnaw /nɔː/ **gnaws, gnawing, gnawed. 1** If peo- ◆◇◇◇◇
ple or animals **gnaw** something, they bite it repeat- VERB: V n
edly. *Woodlice attack living plants and gnaw at the* V at/on n
stems. **2** If a feeling or thought **gnaws at** you, it VERB
causes you to keep worrying. *Worry and doubt were* V at n
gnawing at his mind. LITERARY

gnome /nəʊm/ **gnomes.** In children's stories, a ◆◇◇◇◇
gnome is an imaginary creature that is like a tiny N-COUNT
old man with a beard and pointed hat.

gno·mic /'nəʊmɪk/. A **gnomic** remark is brief and ADJ-GRADED
seems wise but is difficult to understand. WRITTEN

GNP /,dʒiː en 'piː/ **GNPs.** In economics, a ◆◆◇◇◇
country's **GNP** is the total value of all the goods N-VAR
produced and services provided by that country in
one year. **GNP** is an abbreviation for 'Gross National Product'.

gnu /nuː/ **gnus.** A **gnu** is a large African antelope. N-COUNT

go 1 moving or leaving

go /gəʊ/ **goes, going, went, gone.** In most cases ◆◆◆◆◆
the past participle of **go** is **gone**, but occasionally
you use 'been': see **been**.
1 When you **go** somewhere, you move or travel there. VERB
We went to Rome... I went home at the weekend... It V prep/adv
took us an hour to go three miles. ◆ **-going. -going** is V amount
used to form adjectives which describe something as COMB
moving or travelling in a particular place or direction.
...a strong west-going tide. **2** You use **go** to say that VERB
someone leaves the place where they are and does an V -ing
activity, often a leisure activity. *We went swimming* V for n
very early... He went for a walk. **3** When someone **goes** VERB
to do something, they move somewhere in order to do V to-inf
it, and they do it. In British English, someone can also V and v
go and do something. In American English, someone V inf
can also **go** do something, but you say that someone
went and did something. *Paddy had gone to live in*
Canada... I must go and see this film... Go ask whoever
you want.
4 When you **go**, you leave the place where you are. VERB
Let's go. V
5 If you **go to** school, work, or church, you attend it VERB
regularly as part of your normal life. *His son went to a* V to n
top university. ◆ **-goer, -goers.** *They are regular* COMB
church-goers. ...excited party-goers. ◆ **-going** *...the* COMB
cinema-going public. **6** When you say where a road or VERB
path **goes**, you are saying where it begins or ends, or V prep/adv
what places it is in. *...a mountain road that goes from*
Blairstown to Millbrook Village.
7 You can use **go** in expressions such as **'don't go tell-** VB: with brd-
ing everybody', in order to express disapproval of the neg
kind of behaviour you mention. *You don't have to go* [PRAGMATICS]
running upstairs every time she rings. V -ing
8 You can use **go** to indicate how extreme an action, VERB
idea, or result is, or what level it reaches or passes. For V adv/prep
example, you can say that an action **goes further than**
something else or **goes beyond** it to indicate that it is
more extreme or reaches a higher level. *Some physi-*
cists have gone so far as to suggest that the entire Uni-
verse is a sort of gigantic computer.
9 If you say that a period of time **goes** quickly or slow- VERB:
ly, you mean that it seems to pass quickly or slowly. V adv
10 If you say where money **goes**, you are saying what VERB
it is spent on. *Most of my money goes on bills.* **11** If you V prep/adv
say that something **goes to** someone, you mean that it VERB
is given to them. *A lot of credit must go to the chair-* V to n
man... The job went to Yuri Skokov.

12 If someone **goes on** television or radio, they take VERB:
part in a television or radio programme. V on n
13 If something **goes**, someone gets rid of it. *100,000* VERB
jobs will go. **14** If someone **goes**, they leave their job, V
usually because they are forced to. *He had made a hu-* VERB
miliating tactical error and he had to go. V
15 If something **goes into** something else, it is put in it VERB
as one of the parts or elements that form it. *...the really* V into/in n
interesting ingredients that go into the dishes.
16 If something **goes** in a particular place, it fits in VERB
that place or should be put there because it is the right V
size or shape. *He was trying to push it through the hole* V prep/adv
and it wouldn't go... This knob goes here. **17** If some- VERB
thing **goes** in a particular place, it belongs there or V prep/adv
should be put there, because that is where you normally keep it. *The shoes go on the shoe shelf.*
18 If you say that one number **goes into** another VERB
number a particular number of times, you are divid- V into num
ing the second number by the first. *Six goes into thirty* Also V num
five times.
19 If one of a person's faculties or something such as VERB
a light bulb or part of an engine **is going**, it is no longer V
working properly and may soon stop working altogether. *His eyes are going... The battery was going.*
20 If you say that someone **is going** or **has gone**, you VERB: V
are saying in a gentle, indirect way that they are dying
or are dead.

go 2 link verb uses

go /gəʊ/ **goes, going, went, gone. 1** You can ◆◆◆◆◆
use **go** to say that someone or something changes V-LINK:
to another state or condition. For example, if some- V adj
one **goes crazy**, they become crazy, and if some- V prep
thing **goes green**, it changes colour and becomes
green. *50,000 companies have gone out of business.*
2 You can use **go** when indicating whether or not V-LINK
someone wears or has something. For example, if V adj
someone **goes barefoot**, they do not wear any shoes.
But if you arm the police won't more criminals go
armed?
3 You can use **go** to say that something does not have V-LINK:
a particular thing done to it. For example, if some- V-ed
thing **goes unheard**, nobody hears it, and if it **goes**
unseen, nobody sees it.

go 3 other verb uses, noun uses, and phrases

go /gəʊ/ **goes, going, went, gone. 1** You use **go** ◆◆◆◆◆
to talk about how successful an event or situation is. VERB:
For example, if you say that an event or situation V adv
went well, you mean that it was successful, and if
you ask how something **is going**, you are asking
how much success people are having with it. **2** If a VERB
machine or device **is going**, it is working. *...a car* V
that won't go. **3** If a bell **goes**, it makes a noise, VERB: V
usually as a signal for you to do something.
4 If something **goes with** something else, they look or V-RECIP
taste nice together. *Tarragon or fennel both go well* V with n
with fish dishes... Some colours go together and some pl-n V
don't... Wear something else. This won't go. together
5 You use **go** to introduce something you are quoting. V (non-recip)
For example, you say **the story goes** or **the argument** VERB:
goes just before you quote all or part of it. *The story* V that
goes like this... As the saying goes, 'There's no smoke V prep
without fire.' **6** You use **go** when indicating that V with quote
something makes or produces a sound. For example, VERB:
if you say that something **goes 'bang'**, you mean it V with sound
produces the sound 'bang'. **7** You can use **go** instead VERB
of 'say' when you are quoting what someone has said V with quote
or what you think they will say. *They say 'Tom, shut up'* V ton with
and I go 'No, you shut up'... He goes to me: 'Oh, what do quote
you want?' INFORMAL
8 A **go** is an attempt at doing something. *I always* N-COUNT
wanted to have a go at football. **9** If it is your **go** in a N-COUNT:
game, it is your turn to do something. poss N
10 If you **go all out** to do something or **go all out** for PHRASE
something, you make the greatest possible effort to INFORMAL
do it or get it. *They will go all out to get exactly what*
they want. **11** If you say **'Go for it'** to someone, you are CONVENTION
encouraging them to increase their efforts to achieve [PRAGMATICS]
or win something. **12** If someone asks **'Where do we** INFORMAL
go from here?', they are asking what should be done CONVENTION

G

next, usually because a problem has not been solved very satisfactorily.

13 If you say that someone **has gone and done** something, you are expressing your annoyance at the foolish thing they have done.   PHRASE PRAGMATICS

14 If someone **has a go at** you, they criticize you, often in a way that you feel is unfair.   PHRASE INFORMAL

15 If you say that someone is **making a go of** something such as a business or relationship, you mean that they are having some success with it.   PHRASE

16 If you **have** something **on the go**, you have started it and are busy doing it. *Do you like to have many projects on the go at any one time?*   PHRASE

17 You can say **'My heart goes out to him'** or **'My sympathy goes out to him'** to express the strong sympathy you have for someone in a difficult or unpleasant situation.   PHRASE

18 If you say that there are a particular number of things **to go**, you mean that they still remain to be dealt with. *I still had another five operations to go.*   PHRASE

19 If you say that there is a certain amount of time **to go**, you mean that there is that amount of time left before something happens or ends. *There is a week to go until the first German elections.*   PHRASE

20 If you are in a cafe or restaurant and ask for an item of food **to go**, you mean that you want to take it away with you and not eat it there. *Large fries to go.*   PHRASE AMERICAN

21 See also **going**, **gone**.

go 4 phrasal verbs

go /ɡəʊ/ **goes, going, went, gone.**   ◆◆◆◆◆

go about. 1 The way you **go about** a task or problem is the way you approach it and deal with it. **2** When you **are going about** your normal activities, you are doing them. **3** If you **go about** in a particular way, you behave or dress in that way. *He went about looking ill and unhappy.*   PHRASAL VB / VP n/-ing / VP n / VP prep / VP -ing

go after. If you **go after** something, you try to get it, catch it, or hit it. *We're not going after civilian targets.*   PHRASAL VB / VP n

go against. 1 If a person or their behaviour **goes against** your wishes, beliefs, or expectations, their behaviour is the opposite of what you want, believe in, or expect. **2** If a decision, vote, or result **goes against** you, you do not get the decision, vote, or result that you wanted.   PHRASAL VB / VP n / VP n

go ahead. 1 If someone **goes ahead** with something, they begin to do it or make it, especially after planning, promising, or asking permission to do it. *My wife thought it a good idea too so I went ahead.* **2** If a process or an organized event **goes ahead**, it takes place or is carried out.   PHRASAL VB / VP with n / VP / VP

go along. 1 If you **go along** to a meeting, event, or place, you attend or visit it. *You should go along and have a look.* **2** If you describe how something **is going along**, you describe how it is progressing. *Things were going along fairly well.*   PHRASAL VB / VP to n / VP and inf / VP adv

go along with. 1 If you **go along with** a rule, decision, or policy, you accept it and obey it. **2** If you **go along with** a person or an idea, you agree with them.   PHRASAL VB / VP P n / VP P n

go around or **go round. 1** If you **go around** or **go round** to someone's house, you go to visit them at their house. *Mike went round to see them yesterday.* **2** If you **go around** or **go round** in a particular way, you behave or dress in that way. *If they went around complaining publicly, they might not find it so easy to get another job.* **3** If a piece of news or a joke **is going around** or **going round**, it is being told by many people in the same period of time. **4** If there is enough of something to **go around** or **go round**, there is enough of it to be shared among a group of people, or to do all the things for which it is needed.   PHRASAL VB / VP to n / VP to-inf BRITISH / VP prep / VP -ing / Also V P adj / VP

go around with or **go round with.** If you **go around with** or **go round with** a person or group of people, you regularly meet them and go to different places with them.   PHRASAL VB / VP P n / BRITISH

go at. If you **go at** a task or activity, you start doing it in an energetic, enthusiastic way.   PHRASAL VB / VP n

go away. 1 If you **go away**, you leave a place or a person's company. *I think we need to go away and*   PHRASAL VB / VP

think about this. **2** If you **go away**, you leave a place and spend a period of time somewhere else, especially as a holiday. *When you go away on holiday, you need to take extra security precautions.*   VP

go back. 1 If something **goes back** to a particular time in the past, it was made or started at that time. *The feud with the Catholics goes back to the 11th century.* **2** If someone **goes back** to a time in the past, they begin to discuss or consider events that happened at that time. *If you go back to 1960, you'll find that very few jobs were being created.*   PHRASAL VB / VP to n / Also VP n / VP to n / Also VP n

go back on. If you **go back on** a promise or agreement, you do not do what you promised or agreed to do. *The budget crisis has forced the President to go back on his word.*   PHRASAL VB / VP P n

go back to. 1 If you **go back to** a task or activity, you start doing it again after you have stopped doing it for a period of time. *I now look forward to going back to work.* **2** If you **go back to** a particular point in a lecture, discussion, or book, you start to discuss it. *Let me just go back to the point I was making.*   PHRASAL VB / VP P n/-ing / VP P n

go before. 1 Something that has **gone before** has happened or been discussed at an earlier time. *This is a rejection of most of what has gone before.* **2** When people, problems, or cases **go before** a judge, tribunal, or court of law, they are brought or discussed there as part of an official or legal process.   PHRASAL VB / VP / VP n

go by. 1 If you say that time **goes by**, you mean that it passes. **2** If you **go by** something, you use it as a basis for a judgment or action. *If they prove that I was wrong, then I'll go by what they say.*   PHRASAL VB / VP / VP n

go down. 1 If a price, level, or amount **goes down**, it becomes lower or less than it was. *Crime has gone down 70 percent... Average life expectancy went down from about 70 to 67.7.* **2** If you **go down** on your knees or on all fours, you lower your body until it is supported by your knees, or by your hands and knees. **3** When the sun **goes down**, it goes below the horizon. **4** If a ship **goes down**, it sinks. If a plane **goes down**, it crashes out of the sky. **5** In sport, if a person or team **goes down**, they are defeated in a match or contest. *They went down 2-1 to Australia.* **6** In sport, if a team **goes down**, they move to a lower division in a league. **7** If you say that a remark, idea, or type of behaviour **goes down** in a particular way, you mean that it gets that reaction from a person or group of people. *Solicitors advised their clients that a tidy look went down well with the magistrates.* **8** If a computer **goes down**, it stops functioning temporarily.   PHRASAL VB / VP / VP amount / VP from/to/ / by n / VP on n / VP / VP / VP num / Also VP / BRITISH / VP adv / VP

go down as. If you say that an event or action will **go down as** a particular thing, you mean that it will be regarded, remembered, or recorded as that thing. *It will go down as one of the highlights of my career.*   PHRASAL VB / VP P n

go down with. If you **go down with** an illness or a disease, you catch it. *Three members of the band went down with flu.*   PHRASAL VB / VP P n

go for. 1 If you **go for** a particular thing or way of doing something, you choose it. *People tried to persuade him to go for a more gradual reform programme.* **2** If you **go for** someone or something, you like them very much. *I tend to go for large dark men.* **3** If you **go for** someone, you attack them. *Pantieri went for him, gripping him by the throat.* **4** If you say that a statement you have made about one person or thing also **goes for** another person or thing, you mean that the statement is also true of this other person or thing. *It is illegal to dishonour bookings; that goes for restaurants as well as customers.*   PHRASAL VB / VP n / VP n INFORMAL / VP n / VP n

go in. If the sun **goes in**, a cloud comes in front of it and it can no longer be seen.   PHRASAL VB / VP

go in for. If you **go in for** a particular activity, you decide to do it as a hobby or interest. *They go in for tennis and bowls.*   PHRASAL VB / VP P n

go into. 1 If you **go into** something, you describe or examine it fully or in detail. *I don't want to go into details about what was said.* **2** If you **go into** something, you decide to do it as your job or career. *Mr Pok has now gone into the tourism business.* **3** If an amount of time, effort, or money **goes into** something, it is spent   PHRASAL VB / VP n / VP n / VP n

or used to do it, get it, or make it. *Is there a lot of effort and money going into this sort of research?*

go off. 1 If you **go off** something or someone, you stop liking them. *I started to go off the idea.*   PHRASAL VB   V P n
2 If an explosive device or a gun **goes off**, it explodes or fires.   VP   **3** If an alarm bell **goes off**, it makes a sudden loud noise.   VP
4 If an electrical device **goes off**, it stops operating. *All the lights went off.*   VP
5 If you say how an organized event **went off**, you are saying whether everything happened in the way that was planned or hoped. *The meeting went off all right.*   V P adv/prep
6 Food or drink that has **gone off** has become stale, sour, or rotten.   VP   BRITISH

go off with. 1 If someone **goes off with** another person, they leave their husband, wife, or lover and have a relationship with that person. **2** If someone **goes off with** something that belongs to someone else, they leave a place and take it with them. *He's gone off with my passport.*   PHRASAL VB   V P P n   V P P n

go on. 1 If you **go on** doing something, or **go on with** an activity, you continue to do it. *Unemployment is likely to go on rising this year... I'm all right here. Go on with your work.* **2** If a process or institution **goes on**, it continues to happen or exist. *The population failed to understand the necessity for the war to go on.* **3** If something **is going on**, it is happening. *While this conversation was going on, I was listening.* **4** If you say that a period of time **goes on**, you mean that it passes. *Renewable energy will become progressively more important as time goes on.* **5** If you **go on** to do something, you do it after you have done something else. *She went on to say that she had discussed it with the Canadian foreign minister.* **6** If you **go on** to a place, you go to it from the place that you have reached. *He goes on to Holland tomorrow.* **7** If you **go on**, you continue saying something or talking about something. *Meer cleared his throat several times before he went on... 'Go on,' Chee said. 'I'm interested.'* **8** If you **go on** **about** something, or in British English **go on at** someone, you continue talking about the same thing, often in an annoying way. *Expectations have been raised with the Government going on about choice... She's always going on at me to have a baby.* **9** You say 'Go on' to someone to persuade or encourage them to do something. *Go on, it's fun.* **10** If you talk about the information you have to **go on**, you mean the information you have available to base an opinion or judgment on. **11** If an electrical device **goes on**, it begins operating. *A light went on.*   PHRASAL VB   V P -ing   V P with n   Also V P   VP   VP   VP   V P to-inf   V P prep/adv   VP   V P with quote   V P about n   V P atn to-inf   Also V P at n   INFORMAL   only imper   PRAGMATICS   V P   INFORMAL   V P n   VP

go out. 1 If you **go out**, you leave your home in order to do something enjoyable, for example to go to a party, a bar, or the cinema. **2** If you **go out** with someone, the two of you spend time together socially, and have a romantic or sexual relationship. *They've only been going out for six weeks.* **3** If you **go out** to do something, you make a deliberate effort to do it. *It will be a marvellous occasion and they should go out and enjoy it.* **4** If a light **goes out**, it stops shining. **5** If something that is burning **goes out**, it stops burning. **6** If a message **goes out**, it is announced, published, or sent out to people. **7** When a television or radio programme **goes out**, it is broadcast. **8** If a type of thing **goes out**, it ceases to exist or be used, usually because it is replaced by something else. *The weapons had gone out of use.* **9** When the tide **goes out**, the water in the sea gradually moves back to a lower level.   PHRASAL VB   V P   RECIP: V P with n   pl-n V P   V P to-inf   V P and inf   VP   VP   VP   VP   VP   BRITISH   VP   V P of n   VP

go out of. If a quality or feeling **goes out of** someone or something, they no longer have it. *The fun had gone out of it.*   PHRASAL VB   V P P n

go over. If you **go over** a document, incident, or problem, you examine, discuss, or think about it very carefully and systematically. *An accountant has gone over the books.*   PHRASAL VB   V P n

go over to. 1 If someone or something **goes over to** a different way of doing things, they change to it. **2** If you **go over to** a group or political party, you join them after previously belonging to an opposing group or party. *Only a small number of tanks and paratroops have gone over to his side.*   PHRASAL VB   V P P n   V P P n

go round. Go round means the same as **go around**.   PHRASAL VB

go through. 1 If you **go through** an experience or a period of time, especially an unpleasant or difficult one, you experience it. *He was going through a very difficult time.*   PHRASAL VB   V P n
2 If you **go through** a lot of things such as papers or clothes, you look at them, usually in order to sort them into groups or to search for a particular item. *Someone had gone through my possessions.* **3** If you **go through** a list, story, or plan, you read or check it from beginning to end. **4** When someone **goes through** a routine, procedure, or series of actions, they perform it in the way they usually do. **5** If a law, agreement, or official decision **goes through**, it is approved by a parliament or committee.   V P n   V P n   V P n   VP

go through with. If you **go through with** an action you have decided on, you do it, even though it may be very unpleasant or difficult for you.   PHRASAL VB   V P P n

go towards. If an amount of money **goes towards** something, it is used to pay part of the cost of it.   PHRASAL VB   V P n/-ing

go under. 1 If a business or project **goes under**, it becomes unable to continue to operate or exist. **2** If a boat, ship, or person in a sea or river **goes under**, they sink below the surface of the water.   PHRASAL VB   VP   VP

go up. 1 If a price, amount, or level **goes up**, it becomes higher or greater than it was. *The cost has gone up to $1.95 a minute.* **2** When a building, wall, or other structure **goes up**, it is built or fixed in place. **3** In sport, if a team **goes up**, they move to a higher division in a league. **4** If something **goes up**, it explodes or suddenly starts to burn. *The hotel went up in flames.* **5** If a shout or cheer **goes up**, it is made by a lot of people together.   PHRASAL VB   V P   V P to n   V P   VP   BRITISH   VP   V P in n   VP

go with. 1 If one thing **goes with** another thing, the two things officially belong together, so that if you get one, you also get the other. *...the lucrative £150,000 salary that goes with the job.* **2** If one thing **goes with** another thing, they are usually found or experienced together. *...the stigma that goes with being on the dole.*   PHRASAL VB   V P n   V P n

go without. If you **go without** something that you need or usually have or do, you do not get it or do it. *I have known what it is like to go without food for days... We're used to going without.*   PHRASAL VB   V P n/-ing   V P

goad /gəʊd/ **goads, goading, goaded.** If you **goad** someone, you deliberately make them feel angry or irritated because you want them to react in some way. *The psychiatrist was trying to goad him into some unguarded response.* ▶ Also a noun. *Her presence was just one more goad to Joanna's unravelling nerves.*   ◆◇◇◇◇   VERB: V n   V n into n/-ing   N-COUNT

'go-ahead. 1 If you give someone **the go-ahead**, you give them permission or approval to start doing something. *The Greek government today gave the go-ahead for five major road schemes.* **2** A **go-ahead** person or organization is ambitious and tries hard to succeed. *...one of the oldest and the most go-ahead wine producers in South Africa.*   ◆◆◇◇◇   N-SING: the N   ADJ-GRADED: ADJ n   BRITISH

goal /gəʊl/ **goals. 1** In games such as football or hockey, the **goal** is the space into which the players try to get the ball in order to score a point for their team. **2** In games such as football or hockey, if a player scores a **goal**, they get the ball into the goal and score a point. **3** Your **goal** is something that you want to achieve. *The goal is to raise as much money as possible.*   ◆◆◆◆◇   N-COUNT   N-COUNT   N-COUNT

goalie /'gəʊli/ **goalies.** A **goalie** is the same as a goalkeeper.   N-COUNT   INFORMAL

goal·keeper /'gəʊlkiːpə/ **goalkeepers.** A **goalkeeper** is the player in a sports team whose job is to guard the goal.   ◆◆◇◇◇   N-COUNT

goal·keeping /'gəʊlkiːpɪŋ/. **Goalkeeping** refers to the activity of playing in goal. *...the excellent goalkeeping of John Lukic.*   N-UNCOUNT

goal·less /'gəʊləs/. In games such as soccer and hockey, a **goalless** draw is a match which ends with neither team having scored a goal.   ADJ

'goal line, goal lines; also spelled **goal-line**. In games such as soccer and hockey, a **goal line** is one   N-COUNT

G

of the lines at each end of the pitch on which the goalposts stand.

goal·mouth /'gəʊlmaʊθ/ **goalmouths.** In soccer, the **goalmouth** is the area just in front of the goal.   N-COUNT

goal·post /'gəʊlpəʊst/ **goalposts;** also spelled **goal post. 1** A **goalpost** is one of the two upright wooden posts that are connected by a crossbar and form the goal in games such as football and hockey.   N-COUNT **2** If you accuse someone of **moving the goalposts**, you mean that they have changed the rules in a situation or an activity in order to benefit themselves and make it harder for everyone else.   PHRASE PRAGMATICS

goat /gəʊt/ **goats.** A **goat** is an animal about the size of a sheep which has hairs on its chin which resemble a beard. See picture headed **animals**.   ◆◆◇◇◇ N-COUNT

'goat cheese, goat cheeses; also spelled **goat's cheese. Goat cheese** is cheese made from goat's milk.   N-VAR

goatee /ˌgəʊ'tiː/ **goatees.** A **goatee** is a very short pointed beard that a man wears on his chin.   N-COUNT

gob /gɒb/ **gobs. 1** A person's **gob** is their mouth. *Just keep your gob shut, eh.*   N-COUNT BRITISH, RUDE **2** A **gob** of a thick unpleasant liquid is a small amount of it. *...a gob of spit.*   N-COUNT INFORMAL

gob·ble /'gɒbəl/ **gobbles, gobbling, gobbled.** If you **gobble** food, you eat it quickly and greedily. ▶ **Gobble down** and **gobble up** mean the same as **gobble.** *There were dangerous beasts in the river that might gobble you up.*   ◆◇◇◇◇ VERB: V n ▸ PHRASAL VB V n P

gobble down. See **gobble.**   PHRASAL VB

gobble up. 1 If a group or organization **gobbles up** a smaller group or organization, it takes control of it or destroys it. *Banc One of Ohio has built an empire in the mid-west by gobbling up smaller banks.* **2** If someone or something **gobbles up** something such as money, they use or waste a lot of it. *The firm's expenses gobbled up 44% of revenues.* **3** See also **gobble.**   PHRASAL VB V P noun Also V n P ▸ V P noun Also V n P

gob·ble·dy·gook /'gɒbəldiguːk/; also spelled **gobbledegook.** If you describe a speech or piece of writing as **gobbledygook**, you mean that it seems like nonsense to you because it uses official, technical, or complicated language.   N-UNCOUNT INFORMAL

'go-between, go-betweens. If someone acts as a **go-between**, they take messages between people who are unable or unwilling to meet each other.   ◆◇◇◇◇ N-COUNT

gob·let /'gɒblɪt/ **goblets.** A **goblet** is a cup without handles and usually with a long stem.   N-COUNT

gob·lin /'gɒblɪn/ **goblins.** In fairy stories, a **goblin** is a small ugly creature which enjoys causing trouble.   N-COUNT

gob·smacked /'gɒbsmækt/. If you say that you were **gobsmacked** by something, you are emphasizing how amazed and surprised you were by it. *I was absolutely gobsmacked by the place.*   ADJ-GRADED PRAGMATICS BRITISH, INFORMAL

god /gɒd/ **gods. 1** The name **God** is given to the spirit or being who is worshipped as the creator and ruler of the world, especially by Jews, Christians, and Muslims. *He believes in God... God bless you.* ● See also **act of God. 2** The term **a man of God** is sometimes used to refer to Christian priests or ministers. **3** People sometimes use **God** in exclamations to emphasize something that they are saying, or to express surprise, fear, or excitement. Some people find this offensive. *Oh my God he's shot somebody.* **4** In many religions, a **god** is one of the spirits or beings that are believed to have power over a particular part of the world or nature. *...Pan, the God of nature.* **5** Someone who is admired very much by a person or group of people, and who influences them a lot, can be referred to as a **god.** *To his followers he was a god.* **6** If you say that someone **plays God**, you disapprove of them because they act as if they have unlimited power and make decisions that you think nobody has a right to make. **7** If you say that a person thinks they are **God's gift** to someone or something, you are critical of them because they are arrogant and conceited. *...a revolting, slimy character who reckons he's God's gift to women.* **8** If you say **God willing**, you are saying that something will happen if all goes well. *God will-*   ◆◆◆◇ N-PROPER ● PHRASE ● CONVENTION ● N-COUNT ● N-COUNT ● PHRASE PRAGMATICS ● PHRASE PRAGMATICS ● PHRASE

ing, there will be a breakthrough. **9** If you say **God forbid**, you are expressing your hope that something will not happen. *If, God forbid, something goes wrong, I don't know what I would do.* **10** If you want to say that something unpleasant will happen to someone if they do a particular thing, you can say **God help them.** *God help him if he gets in my way... The boss says you must wear a tie. And God help you if you don't.* **11** If you feel sorry for someone because they are in a difficult or unpleasant situation, especially if you think that nobody can help them, you can say **God help them.** *'God help them,' he said. 'They're beyond help.'* **12** If you say **God help us**, you mean that you have negative feelings about the person or situation you are talking about. *God help us, what a prospect.* **13** If someone uses such expressions as **what in God's name, why in God's name,** or **how in God's name**, they are emphasizing how angry, annoyed, or surprised they are. **14** You say **please God** to emphasize a strong hope, wish, or desire that you have. *Please God, let him telephone me now.* **15** You can use **God** in expressions such as **I hope to God,** or **I wish to God,** or **I swear to God** to emphasize what you are saying. **16** You can say **God knows, God only knows,** or **God alone knows** when you do not know something, in order to emphasize that you feel annoyed, angry, worried, surprised, or disappointed by it. **17** ● to **put the fear of God into** someone: see **fear.** ● **honest to God**: see **honest.** ● **for God's sake**: see **sake.** ● **thank God**: see **thank.**   PHRASE PRAGMATICS ● PHRASE PRAGMATICS ● PHRASE ● PHRASE INFORMAL ● PHRASE INFORMAL ● PHRASE INFORMAL ● PHRASE PRAGMATICS ● PHRASE PRAGMATICS ● PHRASE PRAGMATICS

god·child /'gɒdtʃaɪld/ **godchildren.** In the Christian religion, if a younger person is your **godchild**, you agreed to take responsibility for their religious upbringing when they were baptized.   N-COUNT

god·daughter /'gɒddɔːtə/ **goddaughters;** also spelled **god-daughter.** A **goddaughter** is a female godchild.   N-COUNT

god·dess /'gɒdes/ **goddesses.** In many religions, a **goddess** is a female spirit or being that is believed to have power over a particular part of the world or nature. *...Diana, the goddess of war.*   ◆◆◇◇◇ N-COUNT

god·father /'gɒdfɑːðə/ **godfathers. 1** A **godfather** is a male godparent. **2** A powerful man who is at the head of a criminal organization is sometimes referred to as a **godfather. 3** A man who began or developed a type or music or an activity is sometimes referred to as the **godfather of** that music or activity. *...the godfather of soul, James Brown.*   ◆◇◇◇◇ N-COUNT N-COUNT ● N-COUNT: N of n JOURNALISM

'God-fearing. Someone who is **God-fearing** is religious and behaves according to the moral rules of their religion.   ADJ

'God-forsaken. If you say that somewhere is a **God-forsaken** place, you dislike it because you find it very boring and depressing.   ADJ: ADJ n PRAGMATICS

God·head /'gɒdhed/. The **Godhead** is the divine nature of God.   N-SING

god·less /'gɒdləs/. If you say that a person or society is **godless**, you disapprove of them and think they are amoral because they do not believe in God.   ADJ-GRADED PRAGMATICS

god·like /'gɒdlaɪk/. A **godlike** person is admired or respected very much as if he or she were perfect.   ADJ

god·ly /'gɒdli/. A **godly** person is someone who is deeply religious and shows obedience to the rules of their religion. ♦ **god·li·ness** /'gɒdlinəs/. **Godliness** is the quality of being godly.   ADJ-GRADED ♦ N-UNCOUNT

god·mother /'gɒdmʌðə/ **godmothers.** A **godmother** is a female godparent.   N-COUNT

god·parent /'gɒdpeərənt/ **godparents.** In the Christian religion, if you are someone's **godparent**, you agreed to take responsibility for their religious upbringing when they were baptized.   N-COUNT

god·send /'gɒdsend/. If you describe something as a **godsend**, you are emphasizing that it helps you very much. *Pharmacists are a godsend when you don't feel sick enough to call the doctor.*   N-SING: a N PRAGMATICS

god·son /'gɒdsʌn/ **godsons.** A **godson** is a male godchild.   N-COUNT

go·fer /'gəʊfə/ **gofers.** A **gofer** is a person whose job is to do simple but boring tasks for someone.   N-COUNT

go-'getter, go-getters. If you say that someone N-COUNT is a **go-getter**, you approve of them because they PRAGMATICS are very ambitious and energetic.

gog·gle /'gɒgəl/ **goggles, goggling, goggled.** ◆◇◇◇◇ **1** If you **goggle** at something, you stare at it with VERB: your eyes wide open, usually because you are sur- V atn prised by it. *He goggled in bewilderment.* **2 Goggles** INFORMAL are large glasses that fit closely to your face around N-PLURAL: your eyes to protect them from such things as wa- also a pair of N ter, wind, dust, or sparks.

goggle-'eyed. If you say that someone is **goggle-** ADJ **eyed**, you mean that they are very surprised or in- terested by something. *Johnson stared goggle-eyed at Kravis's sumptuous quarters.*

'go-go. **1** A **go-go** dancer dances to pop music in ◆◇◇◇◇ nightclubs wearing very few clothes. ADJ: ADJ n **2** A **go-go** period of time is a time when people make a ADJ: ADJ n lot of money and businesses are growing. *...the go-go* AMERICAN, *years of the mid to late 1980s.* INFORMAL

going /'gəʊɪŋ/. **1** If you say that something is **going** ◆◆◆◆◇ to happen, you mean that it will happen in the fu- PHR-MODAL ture. *I think it's going to be successful... You're going to enjoy this.* **2** You say that you **are going to** do PHR-MODAL something to express your intention or determina- tion to do it. *I'm going to go to bed... He's going to resign... I was not going to compromise.*
3 If you talk about the **going**, you are talking about N-UNCOUNT: how easy or difficult someone is finding it to do some- the N, thing. You can say that something is, for example, adj N **hard going** or **tough going**. *He has her support to fall back on when the going gets tough.* **4** In horse-racing N-UNCOUNT and horse-riding, when you talk about **the going**, you are talking about the condition of the surface the horses are running on. **5** If you say that someone PHRASE should do something **while the going is good**, you are advising them to do it now while conditions are fa- vourable, because you think it will become much more difficult to do later. **6** If you say that something PHRASE that has been achieved is **good going** or **not bad go-** INFORMAL **ing**, you mean that it is better than usual or than ex- pected. *Nine months from dereliction to habitation is not bad going.*
7 The **going** rate for something is the usual amount of ADJ: ADJ n money that you expect to pay or receive for it.
8 If someone or something **has** a lot **going for** them, PHRASE they have a lot of advantages. *This area has a lot going for it.*
9 When you **get going**, you start doing something or PHRASE start a journey, especially after a delay. **10** If you **keep** PHRASE **going**, you continue doing something. **11** If you can PHRASE **keep going** with the money you have, you can man- age to live on it. *Things were difficult, and we needed her wages to keep going.*
12 If you say that something is enough **to be going on** PHRASE **with**, you mean that it is enough for your needs at the BRITISH moment, although you will need sc mething better at some time in the future.
13 You can use **going on** before a number to say that PHRASE something has almost reached that number. For ex- ample, you can say that someone is **going on 40** to in- dicate that they are nearly 40.
14 See also **go, comings and goings. •** going con- cern: see **concern.**

-going /-gəʊɪŋ/. See **go; easy-going, ongoing, out- going, thoroughgoing.**

going-'over. **1** If you give someone or something N-SING a **going-over**, you examine them in order to make INFORMAL sure that they are all right. *Michael was given a complete going-over and then treated for glandular fever.* **2** A **going-over** is a violent attack on or criti- N-SING cism of someone. *He gets a terrible going-over in* INFORMAL *these pages.*

goings-'on. If you describe events or activities as N-PLURAL **goings-on**, you mean that they are strange, interest- INFORMAL ing, amusing, or rather dishonest. *...the goings-on in the factory.*

goi·tre /'gɔɪtə/. **Goitre** is a disease of the thyroid N-UNCOUNT gland that makes your neck very swollen.

'go-kart, go-karts; also spelled **go-cart.** A **go-kart** N-COUNT is a very small motor vehicle with four wheels, used

for racing. **◆ go-karting** *They share a love of go-* N-UNCOUNT *karting.*

gold /gəʊld/ **golds.** **1 Gold** is a valuable, yellow- ◆◆◆◇ coloured metal that is used for making jewellery N-UNCOUNT and ornaments, and as an international currency. *The price of gold was going up. ...gold coins.* **2 Gold** N-UNCOUNT is jewellery and other things that are made of gold. *We handed over all our gold and money.* **3** Some- COLOUR thing that is **gold** is a bright yellow colour. *...Michel's black and gold shirt.* **4** A **gold** is the same N-VAR as a **gold medal**. *The British star is going for gold in* INFORMAL *the Winter Olympics.* **5** If you say that a child is be- PHRASE ing **as good as gold**, you are emphasizing that they PRAGMATICS are behaving very well. **6** If you say that someone PHRASE has a **heart of gold**, you are emphasizing that they are very good and kind. **7** See also **fool's gold. •** to **strike gold**: see **strike. •** worth one's **weight in gold**: see **weight.**

'gold dust. **1 Gold dust** is gold in the form of a N-UNCOUNT fine powder. **2** If you say that a type of thing is **like** N-UNCOUNT **gold dust** or is **gold dust**, you mean that it is very BRITISH difficult to obtain, usually because everyone wants it. *Tickets were like gold dust.*

gold·en /'gəʊldən/. **1** Something that is **golden** is ◆◆◆◇◇ bright yellow. *...her golden hair. ...an endless golden* ADJ *beach.* **2 Golden** things are made of gold. **3** If you ADJ describe something as **golden**, you mean it is won- ADJ: ADJ n derful because it is likely to be successful, or be- cause it is the best of its kind. *There's a golden op- portunity for peace.*

golden 'age, golden ages. A **golden age** is a ◆◇◇◇◇ period of time during which a very high level of N-COUNT achievement is reached in a particular field of activ- ity. *...the golden age of American children's books.*

golden 'handshake, golden handshakes. A N-COUNT **golden handshake** is a large sum of money that a company gives to an employee when he or she leaves, as a reward for long service or good work.

golden 'jubilee, golden jubilees. A **golden ju-** N-COUNT **bilee** is the 50th anniversary of an important or spe- cial event. *The company is celebrating its golden jubilee.*

golden 'oldie, golden oldies. People sometimes N-COUNT refer to something that is still successful or popular INFORMAL even though it is quite old as a **golden oldie**.

golden 'rule, golden rules. A **golden rule** is an N-COUNT important thing to remember to do in order to be successful at something. *The golden rule is to start with the least difficult problems.*

golden 'syrup. In Britain, **golden syrup** is a type N-UNCOUNT of sweet food in the form of a thick, sticky, yellow liquid.

golden 'wedding, golden weddings. A **golden** N-COUNT **wedding** or a **golden wedding anniversary** is the fiftieth anniversary of a wedding.

gold·fish /'gəʊldfɪʃ/; **goldfish** is both the singular ◆◇◇◇◇ and the plural form. A **goldfish** is a small gold or N-COUNT orange-coloured fish which is often kept as a pet in a bowl or a garden pond.

gold 'medal, gold medals. A **gold medal** is a ◆◆◇◇◇ medal made of gold which is awarded as first prize N-COUNT in a contest or competition.

gold·mine /'gəʊldmaɪn/. If you describe something N-SING such as a business or idea as a **goldmine**, you mean that it produces large profits.

gold·smith /'gəʊldsmɪθ/ **goldsmiths.** A **goldsmith** N-COUNT is a person whose job is making jewellery and other objects using gold.

golf /gɒlf/. **Golf** is a game in which you use long ◆◆◆◇◇ sticks called clubs to hit a small, hard ball into holes N-UNCOUNT spread over a large area of grassy land. **◆ golf·er,** N-COUNT **golfers.** *About 150 golfers had arrived for a match.* **◆ golf·ing** *...a golfing holiday in Spain.* N-UNCOUNT

'golf ball, golf balls. A **golf ball** is a small, hard ◆◇◇◇◇ ball which people use when they are playing golf. N-COUNT

'golf club, golf clubs. **1** A **golf club** is a long, ◆◇◇◇◇ thin, metal stick with a piece of wood or metal at N-COUNT one end that you use to hit the ball in golf. **2** A **golf** N-COUNT **club** is a social organization which provides a golf course and a clubhouse for its members.

'golf course, golf courses. A **golf course** is a large area of grass which is specially designed for people to play golf on. ◆◇◇◇◇ N-COUNT

gol·ly /'gɒli/. Some people use **golly** to express surprise or for emphasis. *'Golly,' he says, 'Isn't it exciting!'... By golly we can do something about it this time.* EXCLAM PRAGMATICS INFORMAL, DATED

gon·do·la /'gɒndələ/ **gondolas.** A **gondola** is a long narrow boat that is steered with a pole and used especially in Venice. N-COUNT

gone /gɒn, AM gɔːn/. **1 Gone** is the past participle of **go. 2** When someone is **gone**, they have left the place where you are and are no longer there. When something is **gone**, it is no longer present or no longer exists. *While he was gone she had tea with the Colonel... By morning the smoke will be all gone.* **3** If you say it is **gone** a particular time, you mean it is later than that time. *It was just gone 7 o'clock this evening when I finished.* ◆◆◆◇ ADJ: v-link ADJ / PREP BRITISH, INFORMAL

gon·er /'gɒnə, AM 'gɔːn-/ **goners.** If you say that someone is a **goner**, you mean that they are about to die, or are in such danger that nobody can save them. N-COUNT INFORMAL

gong /gɒŋ, AM gɑːŋ/ **gongs. 1** A **gong** is a large, flat, circular piece of metal that you hit with a hammer to make a sound like a loud bell. **2** People sometimes refer to a medal or honour as a **gong**. ◆◇◇◇ N-COUNT / N-COUNT BRITISH, INFORMAL

gon·na /'gɒnə, AM 'gɑːnə/. **Gonna** is used in written English to represent the words **going to** when they are pronounced informally. *What am I gonna do?*

gon·or·rhoea /ˌgɒnə'riːə/; spelled **gonorrhea** in American English. **Gonorrhoea** is a sexually transmitted disease. N-UNCOUNT

goo /guː/. You can use **goo** to refer to any thick, sticky substance, for example mud or paste. N-UNCOUNT INFORMAL

good /gʊd/ **better, best. 1 Good** means pleasant or enjoyable. *We had a really good time together... There's nothing better than a cup of hot coffee... It's so good to hear your voice after all this time.* **2 Good** means of a high quality, standard, or level. *Exercise is just as important to health as good food... The train's average speed was no better than that of our bicycles. ...good quality furniture.* **3** If you are **good** at something, you are skilful and successful at doing it. *He was very good at his work... I'm not very good at singing... He is one of the best players in the world.* **4** A **good** idea, reason, method, or decision is a sensible or valid one. *It was a good idea to make some offenders do community service... There is good reason to doubt this... Could you give me some advice on the best way to do this?* **5** A **good** estimate or indication of something is an accurate one. *We have a fairly good idea of what's going on... Laboratory tests are not always a good guide to what happens in the world.* **6** If you get a **good** deal or a **good** price when you buy or sell something, you receive a lot in exchange for what you give. *The merchandise is reasonably priced and offers exceptionally good value.* **7** If someone or something is **no good** or is **not any good**, they are not satisfactory or are of a low standard. *If the weather's no good then I won't take any pictures... I was never any good at maths.* **8** Someone who is in a **good** mood is cheerful and pleasant to be with. *He exudes natural charm and good humour... A relaxation session may put you in a better frame of mind.* **9** If people are **good** friends, they get on well together and are very close. *She's my best friend.* **10** A person's **good** eye, arm, or leg is the one that is healthy and strong, if the other one is injured or weak. **11** You say **'Good'** or **'Very good'** to express pleasure, satisfaction, or agreement with something that has been said or done. *Oh good, Tom's just come in... 'Strike Force Three are here, sir.'—'Good.'* **12** People say **'Good for you'** to express approval of your actions. **13** If you describe a piece of news, an action, or an effect as **good**, you mean that it is likely to result in benefit or success. *President Bush called the report very good news for the US economy... I had the good fortune to be selected... This is not a good example to set.* **14** If ◆◆◆◆ ADJ-GRADED / ADJ-GRADED / ADJ-GRADED / ADJ-GRADED / ADJ-GRADED / ADJ-GRADED / N-UNCOUNT: with brd-neg / ADJ-GRADED / ADJ-GRADED: ADJ n / ADJ: ADJ n / CONVENTION PRAGMATICS / CONVENTION / ADJ-GRADED / ADJ-GRADED

you say that **it is good** that something should happen or **it is good** to do something, you mean it is desirable, acceptable, or right. *I think it's good that some people are going... It is always best to choose organically grown foods.* **15** If you say **'It's a good thing'**, or in British English **'It's a good job'**, that something is the case, you mean that it is fortunate or right. *It's a good thing you aren't married.* **16** If something is **good for** someone or something, it benefits them. *Rain water was once considered to be good for the complexion... Nancy chose the product because it is better for the environment.* **17** If something is done for the **good** of a person or organization, it is done in order to benefit them. *Victims want to see justice done not just for themselves, but for the greater good of society... I'm only telling you this for your own good!* **18** If you say that doing something is **no good** or does **not** do **any good**, you mean that doing it is not of any use or will not bring any success. *It's no good worrying about it now... We gave them water and kept them warm, but it didn't do any good.* **19** If you say that something will **do** someone **good**, you mean that it will benefit them or improve them. *It's probably done you good to get away for a few hours.* **20 Good** is what is considered to be right according to moral standards or religious beliefs. *Good and evil may co-exist within one family.* **21** Someone who is **good** is morally correct in their attitudes and behaviour. *I hope I'm a good person.* **22** Someone, especially a child, who is **good** obeys rules and instructions and behaves in a socially correct way. *I'm going to be a good boy now.* **23** Someone who is **good** is kind and thoughtful. *You are good to me.* **24** You use **good** to emphasize the great extent or degree of something. *We waited a good fifteen minutes... This whole thing's got a good bit more dangerous.* **25** See also **best, better, goods. 26** As good as can be used to mean 'almost.' *His career is as good as over... The vote as good as kills the chance of real reform.* **27** If something changes or disappears for **good**, it never changes back or reappears as it was before. *This drug cleared up the disease for good.* **28** If someone **is good for** something, you can rely on them to provide that thing. *Joe was always good for a colorful quote... He'll end up good for nothing, physically or mentally.* **29** If you **make good** some damage, a loss, or a debt, you try to repair the damage, replace what has been lost, or repay the debt. *It may cost several billion roubles to make good the damage.* **30** If someone **makes good** a threat or promise or **makes good on** it, they do what they have threatened or promised to do. **31** If someone **makes good**, they become successful, famous, or rich. *Both men are poor boys made good.* **32** You use **good old** before the name of a person, place, or thing when you are referring to them in an affectionate way. *Good old Harry. Reliable to the end... There is nothing wrong with good old cauliflower cheese.* **33 Good** is used in a large number of expressions which are explained under other words in this dictionary. For example, the expression to **be in someone's good books** is explained at **book.** ADJ-GRADED / PHRASE / ADJ-GRADED v-link ADJ for n / N-SING: with poss / N-UNCOUNT / PHRASE / N-UNCOUNT / ADJ-GRADED / ADJ-GRADED / ADJ-GRADED / ADJ-GRADED / ADJ: a ADJ n / PHRASE / PHRASE / PHRASE / PHRASE / PHRASE / PHRASE / PHRASE / PHRASE PRAGMATICS

,good after'noon. You say **'Good afternoon'** when you are greeting someone in the afternoon. CONVENTION FORMAL

good·bye /ˌgʊd'baɪ/ **goodbyes;** also spelled **good-bye. 1** You say **'Goodbye'** to someone when you or they are leaving, or at the end of a telephone conversation. **2** When you say **goodbye** to someone or say your **goodbyes**, you say something such as 'goodbye' or 'bye' when you leave. *Perry and I exchanged goodbyes... They came to the front door to wave goodbye.* **3** If you **say goodbye** to something that you have or usually want, or **wave goodbye to** it, you accept that you are not going to get it or have it any more or do something that means you will not have it. *He has probably said goodbye to his last chance of Olympic gold.* **4 ●** to **kiss** something **goodbye:** see **kiss.** ◆◆◇◇◇ CONVENTION / N-VAR / PHRASE

,good 'day. People sometimes say **'Good day'** instead of 'Hello' or 'Goodbye'. CONVENTION FORMAL

,good 'evening. You say 'Good evening' when you are greeting someone in the evening. [CONVENTION FORMAL]

,good-for-'nothing, good-for-nothings. If you describe someone as a **good-for-nothing**, you think that they are lazy or irresponsible. ...*a good-for-nothing fourteen-year-old son.* [N-COUNT]

,Good 'Friday. Good Friday is the Friday before Easter Sunday, when Christians remember the crucifixion of Jesus Christ. [N-UNCOUNT]

,good-'humoured. A **good-humoured** person or atmosphere is pleasant and cheerful. [ADJ-GRADED]

goodie /'gʊdi/. See **goody**.

,good-'looking, better-looking, best-looking. Someone who is **good-looking** has an attractive face. [◆◆◇◇◇ ADJ-GRADED]

good·ly /'gʊdli/. A **goodly** amount or part of something is a fairly large amount or part of it. *There were a goodly number of children.* [ADJ: ADJ n FORMAL]

,good 'morning. You say 'Good morning' when you are greeting someone in the morning. [CONVENTION FORMAL]

,good-'natured. A **good-natured** person or animal is naturally friendly and does not get angry easily. *He was good natured about it, he didn't fuss.* [◆◇◇◇◇ ADJ-GRADED]

good·ness /'gʊdnəs/. **1** People sometimes say **'goodness'** or **'my goodness'** to express surprise or for emphasis. *Goodness, I wonder if he knows... My goodness, he's earned millions in his career.* ● **for goodness sake:** see **sake**. ● **thank goodness:** see **thank**. **2 Goodness** is the quality of being kind, helpful, and honest. *He retains a faith in human goodness.* [◆◆◇◇◇ EXCLAM PRAGMATICS] [N-UNCOUNT]

good·night /ˌgʊd'naɪt/; also spelled **good night**. **1** You say **'Goodnight'** to someone late in the evening before one of you goes home or goes to sleep. **2** If you say **goodnight** to someone or kiss someone **goodnight**, you say something such as 'Goodnight' to them or kiss them before one of you goes home or goes to sleep. *Eleanor went upstairs to say goodnight to the children. ...a goodnight kiss.* [◆◇◇◇◇ CONVENTION] [N-UNCOUNT]

goods /gʊdz/. **1 Goods** are things that are made to be sold. *Money can be exchanged for goods or services. ...a wide range of consumer goods.* **2** If you **deliver the goods** or **come up with the goods**, you do what is expected or required of you. [◆◆◆◆◇ N-PLURAL] [PHRASE INFORMAL]

,good-'tempered. A **good-tempered** person or animal is naturally friendly and does not easily get angry. [ADJ-GRADED]

good·will /ˌgʊd'wɪl/. **Goodwill** is a friendly or helpful attitude towards other people, countries, or organizations. *...a gesture of goodwill... They depend on the goodwill of visitors to pick up rubbish.* [◆◆◇◇◇ N-UNCOUNT]

goody /'gʊdi/ **goodies;** also spelled **goodie**. **1** You can refer to exciting, or attractive things as **goodies.** *...a little bag of goodies.* **2** You can refer to the heroes or the morally good characters in a story or situation as the **goodies**. *There are few goodies and baddies in this industrial dispute.* **3** People, especially children, say **goody** in order to express their pleasure or approval of something. *Oh, goody, I like games.* [◆◇◇◇◇ N-COUNT INFORMAL] [N-COUNT INFORMAL] [EXCLAM PRAGMATICS INFORMAL]

'goody bag, goody bags. A **goody bag** is a bag of gifts or free samples, often given away by manufacturers in order to encourage people to try their products. [N-COUNT INFORMAL]

'goody-goody, goody-goodies. If you call someone a **goody-goody**, you dislike them because they behave extremely well in order to please people in authority. [N-COUNT PRAGMATICS INFORMAL]

goo·ey /'guːi/ **gooier, gooiest. 1** If you describe a food or other substance as **gooey**, you mean that it is very soft and sticky. **2 Gooey** is sometimes used to describe foolish, exaggerated ways of expressing love or affection. *Women went gooey over him.* [ADJ-GRADED INFORMAL] [ADJ-GRADED INFORMAL]

goof /guːf/ **goofs, goofing, goofed.** If someone **goofs**, they make a foolish mistake. ► Also a noun. *But was it, in fact, a hideous goof?* [VERB: V INFORMAL] [N-COUNT]

goof around. If someone **goofs around**, they waste time and behave in a childish and silly way. [PHRASAL VB V P INFORMAL]

goof off. If someone **goofs off**, they spend their time doing nothing, often when they should be working. [PHRASAL VB V P INFORMAL]

goofy /'guːfi/ **goofier, goofiest.** If you describe someone or something as **goofy**, you think they are rather silly or ridiculous. *...a goofy smile.* [ADJ-GRADED INFORMAL, AMERICAN]

goose /guːs/ **geese. 1** A **goose** is a large bird that has a long neck and webbed feet. See picture headed **animals. 2 Goose** is the meat from a goose that has been cooked. *...roast goose.* **3** See also **wild goose chase.** [◆◆◇◇◇ N-COUNT] [N-UNCOUNT]

goose·berry /'gʊzbəri, AM 'guːsberi/ **gooseberries.** A **gooseberry** is a small green fruit that has a sharp taste and is covered with tiny hairs. [N-COUNT]

'goose bumps. If you get **goose bumps**, the hairs on your skin stand up so that it is covered with tiny bumps, because you are cold, frightened, or excited. [N-PLURAL]

'goose pimples. Goose pimples are the same as **goose bumps.** [N-PLURAL]

'goose-step, goose-steps, goose-stepping, goose-stepped. When soldiers **goose-step**, they lift their legs high and do not bend their knees as they march. [VERB: V]

go·pher /'gəʊfə/ **gophers. 1** A **gopher** is a small North American animal similar to a rat, which lives in holes in the ground. **2** In computing, **Gopher** is a program that collects information for you from many databases across the Internet network. [N-COUNT] [N-PROPER; also N-COUNT]

gore /gɔː/ **gores, goring, gored. 1** If someone is **gored** by an animal, they are badly wounded by its horns or tusks. *He was gored to death in front of his family.* **2 Gore** is unpleasant-looking blood from a person or animal, for example after they have been involved in an accident. *There were pools of blood and gore on the pavement.* ♦ **gory** *...the gory details of the assassination. ...the gory death scenes.* [◆◆◇◇◇ VERB: be V-ed beV-ed to n Also V n] [N-UNCOUNT] [ADJ-GRADED]

gorge /gɔːdʒ/ **gorges, gorging, gorged. 1** A **gorge** is a deep, narrow valley with very steep sides, usually where a river passes through mountains or an area of hard rock. **2** If you **gorge on** something, you eat lots of it in a very greedy way. *Three men are gorging themselves on grouse and water melon.* [◆◇◇◇◇ N-COUNT] [VERB: V on n V pron-refl on n]

gor·geous /'gɔːdʒəs/. **1** If you say that something is **gorgeous**, you mean that it gives you a lot of pleasure or is very attractive. *It's a gorgeous day.* ♦ **gor·geous·ly** *She has a gorgeously warm speaking voice.* **2** If you describe someone as **gorgeous**, you are emphasizing that you find them very sexually attractive. *All the girls in my house are mad about Ryan, they think he's gorgeous.* **3** If you describe things such as clothes and colours as **gorgeous**, you mean they are bright, rich, and impressive. ♦ **gorgeously** *...gorgeously embroidered clothing.* [◆◆◇◇◇ ADJ-GRADED INFORMAL] [ADV: ADV adj/-ed ADJ-GRADED INFORMAL] [ADJ-GRADED] [ADV-GRADED: ADV adj/-ed]

go·ril·la /gə'rɪlə/ **gorillas.** A **gorilla** is a very large ape. It has long arms, black fur, and a black face. See picture headed **animals.** [◆◇◇◇◇ N-COUNT]

gorm·less /'gɔːmləs/. If you say that someone is **gormless**, you mean that they look or behave as if they are very stupid. [ADJ-GRADED PRAGMATICS BRITISH, INFORMAL]

gorse /gɔːs/. **Gorse** is a dark green European bush that has small yellow flowers and sharp prickles. [N-UNCOUNT]

gosh /gɒʃ/. Some people say **'Gosh'** to express surprise or for emphasis. *Gosh, there's a lot of noise... By gosh, he was absolutely right.* [◆◇◇◇◇ EXCLAM PRAGMATICS DATED]

gos·ling /'gɒzlɪŋ/ **goslings.** A **gosling** is a baby goose. [N-COUNT]

gos·pel /'gɒspəl/ **gospels. 1** In the New Testament of the Bible, the **Gospels** are the four books which describe the life and teachings of Jesus Christ. **2** In the Christian religion, the **gospel** refers to the message and teachings of Jesus Christ, as explained in the New Testament. *I preached the gospel.* **3** You can use **gospel** to refer to a particular way of thinking that a person or group believes in very strongly and that they urge others to accept. *...the gospel according to my mom.* **4** If you take something as **gospel**, or as **gospel truth**, you believe that it is completely true. *The results were not to be taken as gospel... He wouldn't say this if it weren't the gospel truth.* **5 Gospel** or **gospel music** is a style of religious music that uses strong rhythms and vo- [◆◆◇◇◇ N-COUNT] [N-SING: the N] [N-COUNT] [N-UNCOUNT] [N-UNCOUNT]

cal harmony. It is especially popular among black Christians in the southern United States of America.

gos·sa·mer /ˈgɒsəmə/. You use **gossamer** to indicate that something is very light, thin, delicate, or fragile. *...daring gossamer dresses of sheer black lace.* ADJ: ADJ n LITERARY

gos·sip /ˈgɒsɪp/ **gossips, gossiping, gossiped.** **1 Gossip** is informal conversation, often about other people's private affairs. *There has been much gossip about the possible reasons for his absence... Don't you like a good gossip?* **2 If** you **gossip** with someone, you talk informally, especially about other people or local events. *We spoke, debated, gossiped into the night... Mrs Lilywhite never gossiped.* **3 If** you describe someone as a **gossip**, you disapprove of them because they often talk about other people's private affairs. ◆◆◇◇◇ N-UNCOUNT: also a N / V-RECIP: V with n pl-n V V (non-recip) / N-COUNT PRAGMATICS

gossip column, gossip columns. A **gossip column** is a part of a newspaper or magazine where the activities and private lives of famous people are discussed. N-COUNT

gos·sipy /ˈgɒsɪpi/. **1 If** you describe a book or account as **gossipy**, you mean it is informal and full of interesting but often unimportant news or information about people. **2 If** you describe someone as **gossipy**, you are critical of them because they often talk about other people's private affairs. ADJ-GRADED / ADJ-GRADED PRAGMATICS

got /gɒt/. **1 Got** is the past tense and past participle of **get**. **2 In** spoken English, you use **have got** when you are saying that someone owns, possesses, or is holding a particular thing, or when you are mentioning a quality or characteristic that someone or something has. In informal American English, the 'have' is sometimes omitted. *I've got a coat just like this... She hasn't got a work permit... Have you got any ideas?... After a pause he asked, 'You got any identification?'* **3 In** spoken English, you use **have got to** when you are saying that something is necessary or must happen in the way stated. In informal American English, the 'have' is sometimes omitted. *I'm not happy with the situation, but I've just got to accept it... There has got to be a degree of flexibility... See, you got to work very hard.* **4 In** spoken English, people sometimes use **have got to** in order to emphasize that they are certain that something is true. In informal American English, the 'have' is sometimes omitted. *Bill Clinton's got to be happy with these results.* ◆◆◆◆◆ PHRASE / PHR-MODAL / PHR-MODAL PRAGMATICS

Goth·ic /ˈgɒθɪk/. **1 Gothic** is used to describe a style of architecture or church art, dating from the Middle Ages, that is distinguished by tall pillars, high curved ceilings, and pointed arches. **2 Gothic** is used to describe stories in which strange, mysterious adventures happen in dark and lonely places such as the ruins of a castle. **3 Gothic** is used to describe a style of printing or writing in which the letters are very ornate. German books and signs often used to be written in Gothic script. ◆◇◇◇◇ ADJ / ADJ / ADJ

got·ta /ˈgɒtə/. **Gotta** is used in written English to represent the words 'got to' when they are pronounced informally, with the meaning 'have to' or 'must'. *Prices are high and our kid's gotta eat.*

got·ten /ˈgɒtən/. **Gotten** is the past participle of **get** in American English. ● See also **ill-gotten gains**.

gouge /gaʊdʒ/ **gouges, gouging, gouged. 1 If** you **gouge** something, you make a hole or a long cut in it, usually with a sharp object. *...quarries which have gouged great holes in the hills.* ▶ Also a noun. *...a muddy gouge in the ground.* **2 If** you say that a business **gouges** its customers, you disapprove of it because it forces them to pay an unfairly high price for its goods or services. *Credit-card companies have been accused of gouging their customers.* ◆ **goug·ing** *The airline industry has charged the oil companies with price gouging.* ◆◇◇◇◇ VERB: V n / V n prep/adv / N-COUNT / VERB PRAGMATICS / V n INFORMAL / N-UNCOUNT

gouge out. To **gouge out** a piece or part of something means to cut, dig, or force it from the surrounding surface. *...threatening to gouge his eyes out.* PHRASAL VB / V P noun / V n P

gourd /gʊəd, gɔːd/ **gourds. 1 A gourd** is a large fruit that is similar to a marrow. You can also use the word **gourd** to refer to the plant on which this N-COUNT

fruit grows. **2 A gourd** is a container made from the hard dry skin of a gourd fruit. N-COUNT

gour·met /ˈgʊəmeɪ/ **gourmets. 1 Gourmet** food is more unusual or sophisticated than ordinary food. *Flavored coffee is sold at gourmet food stores.* **2 A gourmet** is someone who enjoys good food, and who knows a lot about food and wine. ◆◇◇◇◇ ADJ: ADJ n / N-COUNT

gout /gaʊt/. **Gout** is a disease which causes people's joints to swell painfully, especially in their toes. N-UNCOUNT

Gov., Govs. Gov. is a written abbreviation for **Governor**. N-TITLE

gov·ern /ˈgʌvən/ **governs, governing, governed. 1 To govern** a place such as a country, or its people, means to be officially in charge of the place, and to have responsibility for making laws, managing the economy, and controlling public services. **2 If** a situation or activity **is governed** by a particular factor or rule, it is controlled by or depends on that factor or rule. *Weight is governed by the gravity of a planet. ...rules governing eligibility for unemployment benefit.* ◆◆◆◇◇ VERB: V n / VERB be V-ed V n

gov·ern·ance /ˈgʌvənəns/. **1 The governance** of a country is the way in which it is governed. **2 The governance** of a company or organization is the way in which it is managed or administered. ◆◇◇◇◇ N-UNCOUNT FORMAL / N-UNCOUNT FORMAL

gov·er·ness /ˈgʌvənes/ **governesses. A governess** is a woman who is employed by a family to live with them and educate their children. ◆◇◇◇◇ N-COUNT

gov·ern·ing /ˈgʌvənɪŋ/. A **governing** body or organization is one which controls or regulates a particular activity. ◆◇◇◇◇ ADJ: ADJ n

gov·ern·ment /ˈgʌvənmənt/ **governments. 1 The government** of a country is the group of people who are responsible for governing it. *The Government are to carry out a review of the Shops Act. ...fighting between government forces and left-wing rebels.* ◆ **gov·ern·men·tal** /ˌgʌvənˈmentəl/ *...a governmental agency for providing financial aid.* **2 Government** consists of the activities, methods, and principles involved in governing a country or other political unit. *...our system of government.* ◆ **governmental** *...participation in the governmental process.* ◆◆◆◆◆ N-COLL-COUNT / ADJ: ADJ n / N-UNCOUNT / ADJ: ADJ n

gov·er·nor /ˈgʌvənə/ **governors. 1 In** some systems of government, a **governor** is a person who is in charge of the political administration of a region or state. ◆ **gov·er·nor·ship, governorships.** *The governorship went to a Democrat... He had worked closely with the President during his governorship.* **2 A governor** is a member of a committee which controls an organization such as a school or a hospital. *...the BBC board of governors.* **3 In** some institutions, the **governor** is the most senior official, who is in charge of the institution. *...the prison governor.* ◆◆◆◇◇ N-COUNT; N-TITLE / N-COUNT / N-COUNT / N-COUNT

Governor-'General, Governors-General. A **Governor-General** is a person who is sent to a former colony as the chief representative of the country which used to control that colony. N-COUNT

govt. Govt. is a written abbreviation for **government**.

gown /gaʊn/ **gowns. 1 A gown** is a dress, usually a long dress, which women wear on formal occasions. *...wedding gowns.* **2 A gown** is a loose black cloak worn on formal occasions by people such as lawyers and academics. ◆◆◇◇◇ N-COUNT / N-COUNT

GP /ˌdʒiː ˈpiː/ **GPs. A GP** is a doctor who does not specialize in any particular area of medicine, but who has a medical practice in which he or she treats all types of illness. **GP** is an abbreviation for 'general practitioner'. ◆◆◇◇◇ N-COUNT

grab /græb/ **grabs, grabbing, grabbed. 1 If** you **grab** something, you take or pick it up suddenly and roughly. *I grabbed him by the neck.* **2 ● grab hold:** see **hold.** See also **smash-and-grab. 3 If** you **grab at** something, you try to grab it. ▶ Also a noun. *I made a grab for the knife.* **4 If** you **grab** someone's attention, you do something in order to make them notice you. **5 If** you **grab** something such as food, drink, or sleep, ◆◆◆◇◇ VERB: V n / V n by/round n / VERB: V at n N-COUNT / VERB: V n / VERB: V n

you manage to get some quickly. *Grab a beer.* **6** If you grab something such as a chance or opportunity, you take advantage of it eagerly. *She grabbed the chance of a job interview.* **7** A **grab for** something such as power or fame is an attempt to gain it. *...a grab for personal power.* **8** If something is **up for grabs**, it is available to anyone who is interested. *The famous Ritz hotel is up for grabs for £100m.*

INFORMAL
V n

N-COUNT

PHRASE
INFORMAL

grace /greɪs/ **graces, gracing, graced. 1** If someone moves with **grace**, they move in a smooth, controlled, and attractive way. ♦ **grace·ful** *...grace-ful ballerinas.* ♦ **grace·ful·ly** *She stepped graceful-ly onto the stage.* ♦ **grace·less** *...his right foot left the ground in a graceless pirouette.* **2** If someone behaves with **grace**, they behave in a pleasant, polite, and dignified way, even when they are upset or being treated unfairly. ♦ **graceful** *Aubrey could think of no graceful way to escape Corbet's company.* ♦ **gracefully** *We managed to de-cline gracefully.* ♦ **graceless** *She couldn't stand his blunt, graceless manner.* **3** The **graces** are the ways of behaving and doing things which are considered po-lite and well-mannered. *Her social graces had made her a very pleasant companion.* **4** If you say that some-one **had the grace** or **had the good grace** to do some-thing, you mean that they showed by their behaviour that they were ashamed of something bad that they had done earlier. *He did not even have the grace to apologise.* **5** If you do something unpleasant **with good grace**, you do it cheerfully and without com-plaining. *He accepted the decision with good grace.* **6** ● **airs and graces:** see **air**. **7** If you say that something **graces** a place, you mean that it makes the place more pleasant or attractive. *The Tartar cities were graced with many gates and temples.* **8** If you say that someone important **will grace** an event, you mean that they have kindly agreed to be present at it. **9** In Christianity and some other religions, **grace** is the kindness that God shows to people because he loves them. *It was only by the grace of God that no one died.* **10** If you are talking about someone who is in an unfortunate situation and you say **'There but for the grace of God go I'**, you mean that it is only by luck or God's goodness that you are not in the same situa-tion, and you sympathize with them. **11** Expressions such as **Your Grace** and **His Grace** are used to address or refer to a duke, duchess, or archbishop. **12** See also **coup de grace, saving grace. 13** If you refer to someone's **fall from grace**, you are talking about the fact that they are suddenly no longer ap-proved of or popular, often because they have done something unacceptable. You can also say that some-one **has fallen from grace. 14** You use **grace** in expressions such as **a day's grace** and **a month's grace** to show that you have been giv-en that amount of time before something happens or before you are expected to do something. *We have only a few hours' grace before the soldiers come.*

♦♦◇◇◇
N-UNCOUNT

ADJ-GRADED
ADV with v
ADJ-GRADED

N-UNCOUNT

ADJ-GRADED

ADV-GRADED
ADJ-GRADED

N-PLURAL
DATED

PHRASE

PHRASE

VERB: V n
be V-ed with/
by n
FORMAL
VERB: V n
FORMAL

N-UNCOUNT

PHRASE

N-VOC;
N-PROPER:
det-poss N

PHRASE

N-UNCOUNT

grace·ful /ˈgreɪsfʊl/. **1** Something that is **graceful** is attractive because it has a pleasing shape or style. *...a graceful medieval cathedral.* **2** See also **grace.**

♦◇◇◇◇
ADJ-GRADED

gra·cious /ˈgreɪʃəs/. **1** If you describe someone or their behaviour as **gracious**, you mean that they are very considerate, polite, and pleasant. *...a gracious speech of thanks.* ♦ **gra·cious·ly** *Hospitality at the Presidential guest house was graciously declined.* **2** You use **gracious** to describe the comfortable way of life of wealthy people. *...the gracious suburbs with the swimming pools and tennis courts.* **3** Some peo-ple say **'Good gracious'** or **'Goodness gracious'** in order to express surprise or annoyance.

♦◇◇◇◇
ADJ-GRADED
FORMAL

ADV-GRADED:
ADV with v

ADJ-GRADED

EXCLAM
PRAGMATICS

gra·da·tion /grəˈdeɪʃən, AM greɪˈd-/ **gradations.** Gradations are small differences or changes in things. *TV images require subtle gradations of light and shade.*

N-COUNT
FORMAL

grade /greɪd/ **grades, grading, graded. 1** If something **is graded**, its quality is judged or classi-fied. *South Point College does not grade the students' work. ...a three-tier grading system.* ► The **grade** of

♦♦◇◇◇
VERB:
be V-ed
V n
V-ing

something is its quality. *...a good grade of plywood. ...a grade II listed building.* ► Also a combining form. *...high-grade oil.* **2** Your **grade** in an examina-tion or piece of written work is the mark you get that indicates your level of achievement. *...GCSE O level, grade B.* **3** Your **grade** in a company or or-ganization is your level of importance or your rank. *Staff turnover is particularly high among junior grades.* **4** If someone **makes the grade**, they suc-ceed, especially by reaching a particular standard. *She had a strong desire to be a dancer but failed to make the grade.* **5** In the United States, a **grade** is a group of classes in which all the children are of a similar age. When you are five years old you go into the first grade and you leave school after the twelfth grade. *Mr White teaches first grade in south Georgia.* **6** A **grade** is a slope. The usual British word is **gradient.**

N-COUNT
COMB

N-COUNT:
with supp

N-COUNT:
with supp

PHRASE
INFORMAL

N-COUNT

N-COUNT
AMERICAN

grad·ed /ˈgreɪdɪd/. In this dictionary, a **graded** ad-jective or adverb is one which is sometimes used with an adverb or phrase indicating degree. 'Clever' is an example of a graded adjective.

ADJ

-grader /-greɪdə/ **-graders. -grader** combines with words such as 'first' and 'second' to form nouns which refer to a child or young person who is in a particular grade in the American education system. *...a sixth-grader.*

COMB

grade school, grade schools. In the United States, a **grade school** is the same as an **elementary school.**

N-VAR

gra·di·ent /ˈgreɪdiənt/ **gradients. 1** A gradient is a slope, or the degree to which the ground slopes. *The courses are long and punishing, with steep gra-dients.* **2** The **gradient** of a graph or series of meas-urements is the rate at which one set of amounts changes in relation to another.

♦◇◇◇◇
N-COUNT

N-COUNT:
with supp

grad·ual /ˈgrædʒuəl/. A **gradual** change or process occurs in small stages over a long period of time, ra-ther than suddenly. *You can expect her progress at school to be gradual rather than brilliant.* ♦ **gradu-al·ly** *Gradually we learned to cope.*

♦♦◇◇◇
ADJ-GRADED

ADV-GRADED:
ADV with v

gradu·ate, graduates, graduating, graduat-ed. The noun is pronounced /ˈgrædʒuət/. The verb is pronounced /ˈgrædʒueɪt/. **1** In Britain, when a student **graduates** from university, they have suc-cessfully completed a first degree course. *She graduated in English and Drama from Manchester University.* ► A **graduate** is someone who has graduated from university. *...graduates in engineer-ing.* **2** In the United States, when a student **gradu-ates**, they have successfully completed their univer-sity, college, or school studies. *...when the boys graduated from high school.* **3** In the United States, a **graduate** is a student who has successfully com-pleted high school. **4** If you **graduate** from one thing to another, you go from a less important job or position to a more important one. *From commer-cials she quickly graduated to television shows.*

♦♦♦◇◇

VERB: V
V prep

N-COUNT

VERB: V
V prep

N-COUNT

VERB
V to/from n

gradu·at·ed /ˈgrædʒueɪtɪd/. **Graduated** means in-creasing by regular amounts or grades. *The US mili-tary wants to avoid the graduated escalation that marked the Vietnam War.*

ADJ: ADJ n

graduate school, graduate schools. In the United States, a **graduate school** is a department in a university or college where postgraduate students are taught.

N-VAR

gradua·tion /ˌgrædʒuˈeɪʃən/ **graduations. 1** Graduation is the successful completion of a course of study at a university, college, or school, for which you receive a degree or diploma. *Upon graduation he joined a small law firm.* **2** A gradua-tion is a special ceremony at university, college, or school, at which degrees and diplomas are given to students who have successfully completed their studies. *...at my brother's high school graduation.*

♦◇◇◇◇
N-UNCOUNT

N-COUNT

graf·fi·ti /grəˈfiːtiː/. Graffiti are words or pictures that are written or drawn in public places, for exam-ple on walls.

♦◇◇◇◇
N-COLL-
UNCOUNT

graft /grɑːft, græft/ **grafts, grafting, grafted. 1** If a piece of healthy skin or bone **is grafted** onto a

♦◇◇◇◇
VB: usu
passive,

damaged part of your body, it is attached to that part of your body by a medical operation. ▶ A **graft** is something which is grafted onto your body. *I am having a skin graft on my arm soon.* **2** If a part of one plant or tree **is grafted** onto another plant or tree, they are joined together so that they will become one plant or tree. **3** If you **graft** one idea or system on to another, you join one to the other. *The Japanese tried to graft their own methods on to this different structure.*
4 Graft means hard work. *His career has been one of hard graft.* **5 Graft** refers to the activity of using power or authority to obtain money dishonestly. *...another politician accused of graft.*

Grail /greɪl/. **1** The **Grail** or the **Holy Grail** is the cup that was used by Jesus Christ at the Last Supper. **2** If you describe something as a **grail** or a **holy grail**, you mean it is something that someone is trying very hard to obtain or achieve. *The discovery is being hailed as The Holy Grail of astronomy.*

grain /greɪn/ **grains**. **1** A **grain** of wheat, rice, or other cereal crop is a seed from it. *...rice grains.* **2 Grain** is a cereal crop, especially wheat or corn, that has been harvested and is used for food or in trade. *...a bag of grain.* **3** A **grain** of something such as sand or salt is a tiny hard piece of it. ♦ **-grained** *...coarse-grained salt.* **4** A **grain** of a quality is a very small amount of it. *There's more than a grain of truth in that.*
5 The **grain** of a piece of wood is the direction of its fibres. You can also refer to the pattern of lines on the surface of the wood as **the grain**. *Brush the paint generously over the wood in the direction of the grain.* ♦ **-grained** *...straight-grained wood.* **6** If you say that an idea or action **goes against the grain**, you mean that it is difficult for you to accept it or do it, because it conflicts with your previous ideas or beliefs.

grainy /greɪni/. **1** A **grainy** photograph looks as if it is made up of lots of spots, which make the lines or shapes in it difficult to see. **2 Grainy** means having a rough surface or texture, or containing small bits of something. *...the grainy tree trunk.*

gram /græm/ **grams**; also spelled **gramme**. A **gram** is a unit of weight. One thousand grams are equal to one kilogram.

gram·mar /græmə/ **grammars**. **1 Grammar** is the ways that words can be put together in order to make sentences. *...the difference between Sanskrit and Tibetan grammar.* **2** Someone's **grammar** is the way in which they obey or do not obey the rules of grammar when they write or speak. *...a deterioration in spelling and grammar among teenagers.* **3** A **grammar** is a book that describes the rules of a language.

gram·mar·ian /grəˈmeəriən/ **grammarians**. A **grammarian** is someone who studies the grammar of a language and teaches or writes books about it.

grammar school, grammar schools. A **grammar school** is a school in Britain for children aged between eleven and eighteen who have a high academic ability.

gram·mat·i·cal /grəˈmætɪkəl/. **1 Grammatical** is used to describe something relating to grammar. ♦ **gram·mati·cal·ly** *...grammatically correct language.* **2** If someone's language is **grammatical**, it is considered correct because it obeys the rules of grammar. *...a new test to determine whether students can write grammatical English.* ♦ **grammatically** *...studies showing that up to one in five undergraduates cannot write grammatically.*

gramme /græm/. See gram.

gramo·phone /græməfəʊn/ **gramophones**. A **gramophone** is an old-fashioned type of record player.

gran /græn/ **grans**. Some people refer to or address their grandmother as **gran**.

grana·ry /grænəri/ **granaries**. **1** A **granary** is a building which is used for storing grain. **2** In Britain, **granary** bread contains whole grains of wheat. **Granary** is a trademark.

grand /grænd/ **grander, grandest; grands**. The form **grand** is used as the plural for meaning 6. **1** If you describe a building or a landscape as **grand**, you mean that it is very splendid or impressive. **Grand** is often used in the names of buildings, especially when they are very large. *The scenery of South Island is on a grand scale... They stayed at The Grand Hotel, Budapest.* **2 Grand** plans or actions are ambitious and intended to achieve important results. *The grand design of Europe's monetary union is already agreed.* **3** If you describe people or things such as their jobs or appearances as **grand**, you disapprove of them because they think they are important or socially superior. **4** If you describe someone or something as **grand**, you mean that you admire or approve of them very much. *He was a grand bloke.*
5 A **grand** total is one that is the final amount or the final result of a calculation. **6** A **grand** is a thousand dollars or a thousand pounds. *They're paying you ten grand.* **7** A **grand** is the same as a **grand piano**. **8** See also **grandly**.

gran·dad /grændæd/ **grandads**; also spelled **granddad**. Your **grandad** is your grandfather.

gran·daddy /grændædi/ **grandaddies**; also spelled **granddaddy**. Some people refer to or address their grandfather as **grandaddy**.

grand·child /græntʃaɪld/ **grandchildren**. Someone's **grandchild** is the child of their son or daughter.

grand·dad /grændæd/. See grandad.

grand·daughter /grændɔːtə/ **granddaughters**. Someone's **granddaughter** is the daughter of their son or daughter.

gran·dee /grænˈdiː/ **grandees**. A **grandee** is a Spanish prince of the highest rank.

gran·deur /grændʒə/. **1 Grandeur** is the quality in something which makes it seem impressive and elegant. *...the grandeur of the country mansion.* **2** Someone's **grandeur** is the great importance and social status that they have, or think they have. *...mansions built by nineteenth-century men with delusions of grandeur.*

grand·father /grænfɑːðə/ **grandfathers**. Your **grandfather** is the father of your father or mother.

grandfather clock, grandfather clocks. A **grandfather clock** is an old-fashioned type of clock in a tall wooden case which stands upright on the floor.

gran·dilo·quent /grænˈdɪləkwənt/. If you describe language or behaviour as **grandiloquent**, you are critical of it because it is very formal or exaggerated, and is used by people who want to seem impressive. *...grandiloquent claims from Tory ministers.*

gran·di·ose /grændiəʊs/. If you describe something as **grandiose**, you mean it is bigger or more elaborate than necessary; used showing disapproval. *Not one of Kim's grandiose plans has even begun.*

grand jury, grand juries. A grand jury is a jury, usually in the United States, which considers a criminal case in order to decide if someone should be tried in a court of law.

grand·ly /grændli/. **1** You use **grandly** to say that the name of something makes it sound much more impressive than it really is. *The grandly named European Cricketer Cup is based at Worksop College.* **2** You say that someone speaks or behaves **grandly** when you disapprove of them because they are trying to impress other people. *This, the EEA grandly declared, would require a diplomatic conference.*

grand·ma /grænmɑː/ **grandmas**. Your grandma is your grandmother.

Grand·master /ˌgrændˈmɑːstə, -ˈmæst-/ **Grandmasters**. In chess, a Grandmaster is a player who has achieved a very high standard in tournaments.

grand·mother /grænmʌðə/ **grandmothers**. Your grandmother is the mother of your father or mother.

grand·pa /grænpɑː/ **grandpas**. Your grandpa is your grandfather.

grand·parent /'grænpeərənt/ **grandparents.** ◆◇◇◇◇ N-COUNT
Your **grandparents** are the parents of your father or mother.

grand pi'ano, grand pianos. A **grand piano** is a N-COUNT
large piano whose strings are set horizontally to the ground. See picture headed **musical instruments**.

Grand Prix /,grɒn 'priː, AM ,grænd -/ **Grands Prix** ◆◆◇◇◇
or **Grand Prix.** A **Grand Prix** is one of a series of N-COUNT
races for very powerful racing cars; also used sometimes in the names of competitions in other sports.

Grand 'Slam, Grand Slams. 1 In sport, a ◆◇◇◇◇
Grand Slam tournament is a major one. ► Also a ADJ: ADJ n
noun. *It's my first Grand Slam and I was hoping to* N-COUNT
make a good impression. **2** If someone wins a N-COUNT
Grand Slam, they win all the major tournaments in a season in a particular sport.

grand·son /'grænsʌn/ **grandsons.** Someone's ◆◇◇◇◇
grandson is the son of their son or daughter. N-COUNT

grand·stand /'grændstænd/ **grandstands.** A ◆◇◇◇◇
grandstand is a covered stand with rows of seats for N-COUNT
spectators at sporting events.

gran·ite /'grænɪt/ **granites.** Granite is a very hard ◆◇◇◇◇
rock used in building. N-VAR

gran·ny /'græni/ **grannies;** also spelled **grannie.** ◆◇◇◇◇
Some people refer to their grandmother as **granny**. N-FAMILY

grant /grɑːnt, grænt/ **grants, granting, granted.** ◆◆◆◇◇
1 A **grant** is an amount of money that a govern- N-COUNT
ment or other institution gives to an individual or to an organization for a particular purpose. *They'd got a special grant to encourage research.* **2** If someone VERB: V n n
in authority **grants** you something, you are allowed be V-ed
to have it. *Permission was granted a few weeks ago.*
3 If you **grant** that something is true, especially VERB
someone else's opinion or an unpleasant fact, you V that
accept and agree that it is true. *The magistrates* FORMAL
granted that the RSPCA was justified in bringing the action.
4 If you say that someone **takes** you **for granted**, you PHRASE
are complaining that they benefit from your help, efforts, or presence without showing that they are grateful. **5** If you **take it for granted** that something is PHRASE
the case, or if you **take** something **for granted**, you believe that it is true or you accept it as normal without thinking about it. *He seemed to take it for granted that he should speak as a representative... All the things I took for granted up north just didn't happen in London.*

grant·ed /'grɑːntɪd, 'græntɪd/. You use **granted** or CONJ
granted that at the beginning of a clause to say that PRAGMATICS
something is true, before you make a comment on it. *Granted that the firm has not broken the law, is the law what it should be?* ► Also an adverb. *Grant-* ADV:
ed, he doesn't look too bad for his age, though there's ADV with cl
nothing about his character that would appeal to me.

grant-main'tained. A **grant-maintained** school ◆◇◇◇◇
is one which receives money directly from the na- ADJ
tional government rather than from a local BRITISH
authority.

granu·lar /'grænjʊlə/. **Granular** substances are ADJ
composed of a lot of granules, or feel or look as if FORMAL
they are composed of a lot of granules.

granu·lat·ed sug·ar /,grænjʊleɪtɪd 'ʃʊgə/. **Granu-** N-UNCOUNT
lated sugar is sugar that is in the form of crystal-like grains.

gran·ule /'grænjuːl/ **granules.** Granules are small N-COUNT
pieces of something. *...coffee granules.*

grape /greɪp/ **grapes. 1** Grapes are small green or ◆◆◇◇◇
dark purple fruit which grow in bunches. See pic- N-COUNT
ture headed **fruit**. **2** If you describe someone's atti- PHRASE
tude as **sour grapes**, you mean that they say something is worthless or undesirable because they want it but cannot have it themselves.

grape·fruit /'greɪpfruːt/ **grapefruits.** The plural ◆◇◇◇◇
can be either **grapefruit** or **grapefruits**. A **grapefruit** N-VAR
is a large, round, yellow fruit, similar to an orange, that has a sharp, slightly bitter taste.

grape·vine /'greɪpvaɪn/ **grapevines. 1** If you ◆◇◇◇◇
hear something on **the grapevine**, you hear it in N-SING
casual conversation with other people. *I had heard*

through the grapevine that he was quite critical of what we were doing. **2** A **grapevine** is a climbing N-COUNT
plant on which grapes grow.

graph /grɑːf, græf/ **graphs.** A **graph** is a math- ◆◇◇◇◇
ematical diagram which shows the relationship N-COUNT
between two or more sets of numbers or measurements.

graph·ic /'græfɪk/ **graphics. 1** If you say that a ◆◆◇◇◇
description or account of something unpleasant is ADJ-GRADED
graphic, you mean that it is clear and detailed.
...graphic scenes of drug taking. ♦ **graphi·cal·ly** ADV-GRADED;
/'græfɪkli/ *Here, graphically displayed, was confirma-* ADV with v
tion of the entire story. **2** Graphics is the activity of N-UNCOUNT
drawing or making pictures, especially in publishing, industry, or computing. **3** Graphics are draw- N-COUNT
ings and pictures that are composed using simple lines. *The Agriculture Department today released a new graphic to replace the old symbol.*

graphi·cal /'græfɪkəl/. A **graphical** representation ADJ: ADJ n
of something uses graphs or similar visual devices to represent statistics or figures.

graphic de'sign. Graphic design is the art of de- N-UNCOUNT
signing advertisements, magazines, and books by combining pictures and words. ♦ **graph·ic de-**
·sign·er, graphic designers. N-COUNT

graph·ite /'græfaɪt/. **Graphite** is a hard black sub- ◆◇◇◇◇
stance that is a form of carbon. N-UNCOUNT

'graph paper. Graph paper is paper that has N-UNCOUNT
small squares printed on it so that you can use it for drawing graphs.

grap·ple /'græpəl/ **grapples, grappling, grap-** ◆◇◇◇◇
pled. 1 If you **grapple** with a problem or difficulty, VERB:
you try hard to solve it. *The young man grappled to* V with n
take in what she was saying. **2** If you **grapple** with V to-inf
someone, you take hold of them and struggle with V-RECIP:
them, as part of a fight. You can also say that two V with n
people **grapple**. *They grappled desperately for con-* pl-n V
trol of the weapon.

grasp /grɑːsp, græsp/ **grasps, grasping,** ◆◆◇◇◇
grasped. 1 If you **grasp** something, you take it in VERB: V n
your hand and hold it very firmly. *She was trying to* V at n
grasp at something. ► Also a noun. *His hand was* N-SING:
taken in a warm, firm grasp. ● see also **grasping**. with supp
2 If something is in someone's **grasp**, they possess N-SING:
or control it. If something slips from your **grasp**, with poss
you lose it or lose control of it. *She allowed victory to slip from her grasp.*
3 If you **grasp** something that is complicated or diffi- VERB: V n
cult to understand, you understand it. *He instantly* V that
grasped that Stephen was talking about his wife. **4** A N-SING:
grasp of something is an understanding of it. *They* with supp
have a good grasp of foreign languages. **5** If you say PHRASE
that something is **within** someone's **grasp**, you mean that it is very likely that they will achieve it.

grasp·ing /'grɑːspɪŋ, 'græsp-/. If you describe ADJ-GRADED
someone as **grasping**, you disapprove of them be- PRAGMATICS
cause they want to get as much money as possible for themselves.

grass /grɑːs, græs/ **grasses, grassing,** ◆◆◆◇◇
grassed. 1 Grass is a very common plant consist- N-VAR
ing of large numbers of thin, spiky, green leaves covering the surface of the ground. *The lawn contained a mixture of grasses... I'm going to cut the grass.* **2** If you say to someone that **the grass is** PHRASE
greener somewhere else, you are reminding them that other people's situations always seem better than your own, but may not really be so. **3** If you PHRASE
say that someone is being **put out to grass**, you INFORMAL
mean they are no longer being employed because they are considered to be too old or no longer useful. **4** Grass is the same as **marijuana**. *I started* N-UNCOUNT
smoking grass when I was about sixteen. INFORMAL

5 If you say that one person **grasses on** another, you VERB:
disapprove of the fact that the first person tells the po- V on n
lice or other authorities about something criminal or V
wrong which the second person has done. *He was re-* PRAGMATICS
peatedly attacked by other inmates, who accused him INFORMAL,
of grassing. ► A person who grasses on someone else BRITISH
is called a **grass**. N-COUNT

grass over. If an area of ground **is grassed over**, grass is planted all over it.   PHRASAL VB / be V-ed P

grass·hopper /'grɑːshɒpə, 'græs-/ **grasshoppers.** A **grasshopper** is an insect with long back legs that jumps high into the air and makes a high, vibrating sound. See picture headed **insects**.   N-COUNT

grass·land /'grɑːslænd, 'græs-/ **grasslands.** **Grassland** is land covered with wild grass.   ◆◇◇◇◇ / N-UNCOUNT: also N in pl

‚grass 'roots; also spelled **grass-roots** or **grassroots.** The **grass roots** of an organization or movement are the ordinary people who form the main part of it, rather than its leaders. *You have to join the party at grass-roots level.*   ◆◇◇◇◇ / N-PLURAL

grassy /'grɑːsi, 'græs-/ **grassier, grassiest.** A **grassy** area of land is covered in grass. *Its buildings are half-hidden behind grassy banks.*   ◆◇◇◇◇ / ADJ-GRADED

grata /'grɑːtə/. See **persona non grata.**

grate /greɪt/ **grates, grating, grated. 1** A **grate** is a framework of metal bars in a fireplace, which holds the coal or wood. **2** If you **grate** food such as cheese or carrots, you rub it over a metal tool called a grater so that the food is shredded into very small pieces. See picture headed **kitchen utensils.** ♦ **grat·er, graters.** *...a cheese grater.* **3** When something **grates**, it rubs against something else making a harsh, unpleasant sound. *The gun barrel grated against the floor.* **4** If something such as someone's behaviour **grates on** you or **grates**, it makes you feel annoyed. *His manner always grated on me.* **5** See also **grating.**   ◆◆◇◇◇ / N-COUNT / VERB: V n / N-COUNT / VERB: V / V against/on n / VERB / V on n / Also V

grate·ful /'greɪtfʊl/. If you are **grateful** for something that someone has given you or done for you, you are pleased and wish to thank them. *She was grateful to him for being so good to her.* ♦ **grate·ful·ly** *'That's kind of you, Sally,' Claire said gratefully.*   ◆◆◇◇◇ / ADJ-GRADED / ADV-GRADED

grati·fy /'grætɪfaɪ/ **gratifies, gratifying, gratified. 1** If you are **gratified** by something, it gives you pleasure or satisfaction. *The figures are likely to gratify ministers anxious to portray the council tax as acceptable.* ♦ **grati·fied** *He was gratified to hear that his idea had been confirmed.* ♦ **grati·fy·ing** *...a gratifying development.* **2** If you **gratify** your own or another person's desire, you do what is necessary to please yourself or them. *We gratified our friend's curiosity.* ♦ **grati·fi·ca·tion** *...sexual gratification.*   ◆◇◇◇◇ / VERB: be V-ed / V n / FORMAL / ADJ-GRADED / ADJ-GRADED / VERB / V n / FORMAL / N-UNCOUNT

grat·ing /'greɪtɪŋ/ **gratings. 1** A **grating** is a flat metal frame with rows of bars across it, which is fastened over a window or over a hole in a wall. **2** A **grating** sound is harsh and unpleasant.   N-COUNT / ADJ-GRADED

gra·tis /'grætɪs, 'grɑːt-/. If something is done or provided **gratis**, it does not have to be paid for. *David gives the first consultation gratis.* ► Also an adjective. *What I did for you was free, gratis.*   ADV: ADV after v / Also ADJ

grati·tude /'grætɪtjuːd, AM -tuːd/. **Gratitude** is the state of feeling grateful. *I wish to express my gratitude to Kathy Davis.*   ◆◇◇◇◇ / N-UNCOUNT

gra·tui·tous /grə'tjuːɪtəs, AM -'tuː-/. If you describe something as **gratuitous**, you mean that it is unnecessary, and often harmful or upsetting. *There's too much crime and gratuitous violence on TV.* ♦ **gra·tui·tous·ly** *...something less gratuitously offensive.*   ◆◇◇◇◇ / ADJ-GRADED / ADV

gra·tu·ity /grə'tjuːɪti, AM -'tuː-/ **gratuities. 1** A **gratuity** is a gift of money to someone who has done something for you. *The porter expects a gratuity.* **2** A **gratuity** is large gift of money given to someone when they leave their employment.   N-COUNT / FORMAL / N-COUNT / BRITISH, FORMAL

grave, graves; graver, gravest. Pronounced /greɪv/, except for meaning 6, when it is pronounced /grɑːv/. **1** A **grave** is a place where a dead person is buried. **2** If you say that someone is **digging their own grave**, you are warning them that they are doing something foolish or dangerous that will cause their own failure. **3** If you say that someone who is dead would **turn in their grave** at something that is happening now, you mean that they would be very shocked or upset by it, if they were alive. ● **from the cradle to the grave:** see **cradle.** **4** A **grave** event or situation is very serious, important,   ◆◆◇◇◇ / N-COUNT / PHRASE / PHRASE / ADJ-GRADED

and worrying. ♦ **grave·ly** *They had gravely impaired the credibility of the government.*   ADV

5 A **grave** person is quiet and serious in their appearance or behaviour. ♦ **gravely** *'I think I've covered that business more than adequately,' he said gravely.*   ADJ-GRADED / ADV-GRADED

6 In some languages such as French, a **grave** accent is a symbol that is placed over a vowel in a word to show how the vowel is pronounced. For example, the word 'mère' has a grave accent over the first 'e'.   ADJ: ADJ n

grave·digger /'greɪvdɪɡə/ **gravediggers.** A **gravedigger** is a person whose job is to dig graves for dead people to be buried in.   N-COUNT

grav·el /'grævəl/. **Gravel** consists of very small stones. *...a gravel path leading to the front door.*   ◆◇◇◇◇ / N-UNCOUNT

grav·elled /'grævəld/; spelled **graveled** in American English. A **gravelled** path, road, or area has a surface made of gravel.   ADJ: ADJ n

grav·el·ly /'grævəli/. **1** A **gravelly** voice is low and rather rough and harsh. **2** An **gravelly** area of land is covered in or full of small stones.   ADJ-GRADED / ADJ-GRADED

grave·side /'greɪvsaɪd/ **gravesides.** You can refer to the area around a grave, especially a new grave, as the **graveside.**   N-COUNT

grave·stone /'greɪvstəʊn/ **gravestones.** A **gravestone** is a large stone with words carved into it, which is placed on a grave.   N-COUNT

grave·yard /'greɪvjɑːd/ **graveyards. 1** A **graveyard** is an area of land, sometimes near a church, where dead people are buried. **2** If you call a place a **graveyard** of particular things, you are expressing disapproval that there are many broken or unwanted things of that kind there. *...a graveyard of rusting cranes.* **3** If you call an event or place the **graveyard** for particular people or their hopes, you mean that those people have often failed in such events or in that place. *Europe has been the graveyard for American golfers recently.*   ◆◇◇◇◇ / N-COUNT / N-COUNT / PRAGMATICS / N-COUNT / WRITTEN

grav·i·tas /'grævɪtæs/. Someone who has **gravitas** is able to talk about important things in a serious, intelligent way.   N-UNCOUNT / FORMAL

gravi·tate /'grævɪteɪt/ **gravitates, gravitating, gravitated.** If you **gravitate** towards a particular place, thing, or activity, you are attracted by it and go to it or get involved in it. *Traditionally young Asians in Britain have gravitated towards medicine, law and engineering.*   VERB / V towards/to n / Also V prep/ adv

gravi·ta·tion /ˌgrævɪ'teɪʃən/. **Gravitation** is the force which causes objects to be attracted towards each other because they have mass. ♦ **gravi·ta·tion·al** /ˌgrævɪ'teɪʃənəl/ *...the earth's gravitational pull.*   ◆◇◇◇◇ / N-UNCOUNT / TECHNICAL / ADJ: ADJ n

grav·ity /'grævɪti/. **1** **Gravity** is the force which causes things to drop to the ground. **2** **Gravity** is the same as gravitation. ● See also **centre of gravity.** **3** The **gravity** of a situation or event is its extreme importance or seriousness. *...the gravity of their crime.* **4** The **gravity** of someone's behaviour or speech is the very serious way in which they behave or speak.   ◆◆◇◇◇ / N-UNCOUNT / N-UNCOUNT / N-UNCOUNT / N-UNCOUNT

gra·vy /'greɪvi/ **gravies.** **Gravy** is a sauce made from the juices that come from meat when it cooks.   ◆◇◇◇◇ / N-VAR

'gravy boat, gravy boats. A **gravy boat** is a long narrow jug that is used to serve gravy.   N-COUNT

'gravy train, gravy trains. If journalists think an organization or person earns too much money for the work that they do, they sometimes say that the organization or person is on the **gravy train.**   N-COUNT

gray /greɪ/. See **grey.**

graze /greɪz/ **grazes, grazing, grazed. 1** When animals **graze** or **are grazed**, they eat the grass or other plants that are growing in a particular place. *He used to graze some sheep up on the high slopes.* **2** If you **graze** a part of your body, you injure your skin by scraping against something. ♦ **grazed** *...grazed arms and legs.* **3** A **graze** is a small wound caused by scraping against something. **4** If something **grazes** another thing, it touches that thing lightly as it passes by. *A bullet had grazed his arm.*   ◆◆◇◇◇ / V-ERG: V / V n / VERB: V n / ADJ / N-COUNT / VERB / V n

graz·ing /'greɪzɪŋ/. **Grazing** or **grazing land** is land on which animals graze.   N-UNCOUNT

grease /griːs/ **greases, greasing, greased.**
1 Grease is a thick, oily substance that is used to oil the moving parts of machines. **2** If you **grease** a part of a car, machine, or device, you put grease on it in order to make it work smoothly. **3** Grease is an oily substance that is produced by your skin. *His hair is thick with grease.* **4** Grease is animal fat that is produced by cooking meat. **5** If you **grease** a baking tray, you smear it with animal fat or vegetable oil in order to prevent food sticking to it. **6** See also **elbow grease.**

◆◇◇◇◇ N-UNCOUNT
VERB: V n
N-UNCOUNT
N-UNCOUNT
VERB: V n

grease·paint /ˈgriːspeɪnt/. Greasepaint is an oily substance used by actors as make-up.

N-UNCOUNT

grease·proof paper /ˌgriːspruːf ˈpeɪpə/. Greaseproof paper does not allow grease to pass through it. It is mainly used in cooking.

N-UNCOUNT
BRITISH

greasy /ˈgriːsi, -zi/ **greasier, greasiest.** Something that is **greasy** has grease on it or in it. *...the problem of greasy hair.*

◆◇◇◇◇ ADJ-GRADED

greasy spoon, greasy spoons. If you think a cafe is small, cheap, and unattractive, you can call it a **greasy spoon.**

N-COUNT
INFORMAL

great /greɪt/ **greater, greatest; greats. 1** You use **great** to describe something that is very large. Great is more formal than **big.** *The room had a great bay window. ...a great hall as long and high as a church.* **2** Great is used to emphasize the large amount or degree of something. *I'll take great care of it.* ◆ **great·ly** *People would benefit greatly from a pollution-free vehicle.* **3** You use **great** to describe something that is important, famous, or exciting. *...the great cultural achievements of the past.* ◆ **great·ness** *A nation must take certain risks to achieve greatness.* **4** The **greats** in a particular subject or field of activity are the people or things that have been most successful in it. *...all the greats of Hollywood. ...cycling's all-time greats.* **5** If you describe someone or something as **great,** you approve of them or admire them. *Arturo has this great place in Cazadero... I think she's great.* **6** If you feel **great,** you feel very healthy, energetic, and enthusiastic. **7** You say '**Great**' in order to emphasize that you are pleased or enthusiastic about something. *Oh great! That'll be good for Fergus.* **8** See also **greater.**

◆◆◆◆◆ ADJ-GRADED: ADJ n
ADJ-GRADED
ADV-GRADED
ADJ-GRADED
N-PLURAL: with supp JOURNALISM
ADJ PRAGMATICS INFORMAL
ADJ: feel ADJ
EXCLAM PRAGMATICS

great- /greɪt-/. Great- is used before some nouns that refer to relatives, in order to say that a relative is one generation removed from you. For example, your great-aunt is the aunt of one of your parents.

PREFIX

Great Brit·ain /ˌgreɪt ˈbrɪtən/. Great Britain is the island consisting of England, Scotland, and Wales, which together with Northern Ireland makes up the United Kingdom.

◆◆◇◇◇ N-PROPER

great·coat /ˈgreɪtkəʊt/ **greatcoats;** also spelled **great coat.** A greatcoat is a long thick overcoat that is worn especially as part of a uniform.

N-COUNT

great·er /ˈgreɪtə/. **1** Greater is the comparative of **great. 2** Greater is used with the name of a large city to refer to the city together with the surrounding urban and suburban area. *...Greater London.*

◆◆◇◇◇ ADJ: ADJ n

Gre·cian /ˈgriːʃən/. Grecian is used to describe something which is in the style of things from ancient Greece. *...elegant Grecian columns.*

ADJ

greed /griːd/. Greed is the desire to have more of something than is necessary or fair. *...an insatiable greed for personal power.* ◆ **greedy, greedier.** *He attacked greedy bosses for awarding themselves big rises.* ◆ **greed·ily** *Livy ate the pasties greedily.*

◆◇◇◇◇ N-UNCOUNT
ADJ-GRADED
ADV-GRADED: ADV with v

green /griːn/ **greens; greener, greenest. 1** Green is the colour of grass or leaves. *...shiny red and green apples.* **2** A place that is **green** is covered with grass, plants, and trees. ◆ **green·ness** *...the lush greenness of the river valleys.* **3** Green issues relate to the protection of the environment. *...the power of the Green movement in Germany.* ▶ Greens are members of green political movements. **4** If you say that someone or something is **green,** you mean they harm the environment as little as possible. *...trying to persuade governments to adopt greener*

◆◆◆◆◆ COLOUR
ADJ-GRADED
N-UNCOUNT
ADJ: ADJ n
N-PLURAL
ADJ-GRADED

policies. ◆ **greenness** *...sending teams round factories to ascertain their greenness.*

N-UNCOUNT

5 A **green** is a smooth, flat area of grass around a hole on a golf course. **6** A **green** is an area of grass in the middle of a town or village.

N-COUNT
N-COUNT

7 You can refer to the cooked green leaves of vegetables such as spinach or cabbage as **greens.**

N-PLURAL

8 If you say that someone is **green,** you mean that they are very inexperienced.

ADJ-GRADED

9 If you say that someone is **green with envy,** you mean that they are very envious indeed. **10** If you say that someone has **green fingers,** you mean that they are very good at gardening and their plants grow well. The American expression is **a green thumb. 11** ● to give someone the **green light:** see **light.**

PHRASE
PHRASE
BRITISH

green·back /ˈgriːnbæk/ **greenbacks.** A greenback is a dollar bill. The dollar can be referred to as **the greenback.**

N-COUNT
AMERICAN, INFORMAL

green 'bean, green beans. Green beans are long narrow beans that are green in colour and are eaten as a vegetable.

N-COUNT

green belt, green belts. A green belt is an area of land with fields or parks around a town or city, where people are forbidden by law to build.

N-COUNT
BRITISH

Green 'Beret, Green Berets. A Green Beret is a British or American commando.

N-COUNT
INFORMAL

green card, green cards. A green card is a document showing that someone who is not a citizen of the United States has temporary permission to live and work there.

N-COUNT

green·ery /ˈgriːnəri/. Plants that make a place look attractive are referred to as **greenery.**

◆◇◇◇◇ N-UNCOUNT

green·fly /ˈgriːnflaɪ/ **greenflies.** The plural can be either **greenfly** or **greenflies.** Greenfly are small green winged insects that damage plants.

N-COUNT

green·gage /ˈgriːngeɪdʒ/ **greengages.** A greengage is a greenish-yellow plum with a sweet taste.

N-COUNT
BRITISH

green·grocer /ˈgriːngrəʊsə/ **greengrocers.** A greengrocer is a shopkeeper who sells fruit and vegetables. A shop where fruit and vegetables are sold is a **greengrocer** or a **greengrocer's.**

N-COUNT
BRITISH

green·house /ˈgriːnhaʊs/ **greenhouses. 1** A greenhouse is a glass building in which you grow plants that need to be protected from bad weather. **2** Greenhouse means relating to or causing the greenhouse effect. *...greenhouse gases.*

◆◆◇◇◇ N-COUNT
ADJ: ADJ n

greenhouse effect. The greenhouse effect is the rise in the earth's temperature caused by a build-up of gases in the air around the earth.

◆◇◇◇◇ N-SING: the N

greenhouse gas, greenhouse gases. Greenhouse gases are the gases which are responsible for causing the greenhouse effect.

◆◇◇◇◇ N-VAR

green·ing /ˈgriːnɪŋ/. Journalists talk about the **greening** of someone when they want to say that they are becoming more aware of environmental issues.

N-SING: also no det

green·ish /ˈgriːnɪʃ/. Greenish means slightly green in colour. *...his cold greenish eyes.* ► Also a combining form. *...greenish-yellow flowers.*

ADJ
COMB

Green 'Paper, Green Papers. In Britain, a Green Paper is a document containing ideas about a particular subject that is published by the Government so that people can discuss them before any decisions are made.

N-COUNT

'Green Party. The Green Party is a political party that is particularly concerned about protecting the environment.

◆◇◇◇◇ N-PROPER: the N

green 'pepper, green peppers. A green pepper is an unripe pepper that is used in cooking or eaten raw in salads.

N-COUNT

green revo'lution; also spelled **Green Revolution.** The green revolution is the increase in agricultural production in developing countries that has been made possible by the use of new types of crops and new farming methods.

N-SING

green·room /ˈgriːnruːm/ **greenrooms;** also spelled **green room.** A greenroom is a room in a theatre or television studio where performers can rest.

N-COUNT

‚green 'salad, green salads. A **green salad** is a N-VAR salad made mainly with green salad vegetables.

Green‧wich Mean Time /ˌgrenɪtʃ 'miːn taɪm/. See GMT.

greet /griːt/ **greets, greeting, greeted. 1** When ◆◆◇◇◇ you **greet** someone, you express friendliness or VERB pleasure when you meet them or when they arrive. V n *She liked to be home to greet Steve when he came in from school.* **2** If something **is greeted** in a particu- VERB: lar way, people react to it in that way. *The European* beV-ed adv *Court's decision has been greeted with dismay by* beV-ed with/ *fishermen.* **3** If you **are greeted** by something, it is byn the first thing you notice in a particular place. *I was* beV-ed byn *greeted by a shocking sight... The savoury smell* Vn *greeted them as they went through the door.* LITERARY

greet‧ing /'griːtɪŋ/ **greetings. 1** A **greeting** is ◆◇◇◇◇ something friendly that you say or do when you N-VAR meet someone. *He raised a hand in greeting.* **2** '**Greetings**' is an old-fashioned greeting. CONVENTION

'greetings card, greeting cards; also spelled N-COUNT **greeting card.** A **greetings card** is a folded card with a picture on the front and a message inside that you give someone, for example on their birthday.

gre‧gari‧ous /grɪ'geəriəs/. **1** Someone who is **gre-** ADJ-GRADED **garious** enjoys being with other people. **2 Gregari-** ADJ-GRADED **ous** animals or birds normally live in large groups.

grem‧lin /'gremlɪn/ **gremlins.** A **gremlin** is a tiny N-COUNT imaginary evil spirit that people say is the cause of a problem which they cannot explain properly or locate.

gre‧nade /grɪ'neɪd/ **grenades.** A **grenade** or a ◆◇◇◇◇ **hand grenade** is a small bomb that can be thrown N-COUNT by hand.

grew /gruː/. **Grew** is the past tense of **grow.**

grey /greɪ/ **greyer, greyest;** spelled **gray** in ◆◆◆◆ American English. **1 Grey** is the colour of ashes or COLOUR of clouds on a rainy day. **2** If someone is going **grey,** ADJ-GRADED their hair is becoming grey. **3** If the weather is **grey,** ADJ-GRADED there are many clouds in the sky and the light is dull. *It was a grey, wet April Sunday.* ♦ **grey‧ness** N-UNCOUNT *...winter's greyness.* **4** If you describe someone or ADJ-GRADED something as **grey,** you think that they are boring PRAGMATICS and unattractive. *...little grey men in suits.* ♦ **greyness** *Journalists are frustrated by his appar-* N-UNCOUNT: *ent greyness.* with supp

'grey area, grey areas; spelled **gray area** in N-COUNT American English. If you refer to something as a **grey area,** you mean that it is unclear, for example because nobody is sure how to deal with it or who is responsible for it, or it falls between two separate categories of things.

grey‧hound /'greɪhaʊnd/ **greyhounds.** A **grey-** ◆◇◇◇◇ **hound** is a dog with a thin body and long thin legs, N-COUNT which can run very fast.

grey‧ish /'greɪɪʃ/; spelled **grayish** in American Eng- ADJ lish. **Greyish** means slightly grey. *The building was of greyish plaster.* ► Also a combining form. *...grey-* COMB *ish green leaves.*

grid /grɪd/ **grids. 1** A **grid** is something which is in ◆◇◇◇◇ a pattern of straight lines that cross over each other, N-COUNT forming squares. *...a grid of ironwork. ...a grid of narrow streets.* **2** A **grid** is a network of wires and N-COUNT cables by which sources of power, such as electric- ity, are distributed throughout a country or area.

grid‧dle /'grɪdəl/ **griddles.** A **griddle** is a round, N-COUNT flat, heavy piece of metal which is placed on a stove or fire and used for cooking.

grid‧iron /'grɪdaɪən/. American football is some- N-UNCOUNT times referred to as **gridiron.**

grid‧lock /'grɪdlɒk/. **1 Gridlock** is the situation ◆◇◇◇◇ that exists when all the roads in a particular place N-UNCOUNT are so full of vehicles that none of them can move. **2** You can use **gridlock** to refer to a situation in an N-UNCOUNT argument or dispute when neither side is prepared to give in, so no agreement can be reached.

grief /griːf/ **griefs. 1 Grief** is a feeling of extreme ◆◆◇◇◇ sadness. *...a huge outpouring of national grief for* N-VAR *the victims of the shootings.* **2** If someone or some- PHRASE thing **comes to grief,** they fail or are harmed. *So many marriages have come to grief over lack of*

money. **3** Some people say '**Good grief**' to express EXCLAM surprise or disbelief. PRAGMATICS

'grief-stricken. If someone is **grief-stricken** about ADJ-GRADED something, they are extremely sad about it. FORMAL

griev‧ance /'griːvəns/ **grievances.** If you have a ◆◇◇◇◇ **grievance** about something that has happened or N-VAR been done, you believe that it was unfair.

grieve /griːv/ **grieves, grieving, grieved. 1** If ◆◇◇◇◇ you **grieve** over something, especially someone's VERB: death, you feel very sad about it. *I didn't have any* V prep *time to grieve. ...Margery's grieving family.* **2** If you V-ing **are grieved** by something, it makes you unhappy or VERB: upset. *I was grieved to hear of the suicide of James...* beV-ed by/at *It grieved me to see the poor man in such distress.* n beV-ed to-inf itV N to-inf

griev‧ous /'griːvəs/. If you describe something as ◆◇◇◇◇ **grievous,** you mean that it is extremely serious or ADJ-GRADED worrying in its effects. *...a very grievous mistake.* ♦ **griev‧ous‧ly** *Birds, sea-life and the coastline all* ADV-GRADED: *suffered grievously.* ADV with v

‚grievous bodily 'harm. If someone is accused N-UNCOUNT of **grievous bodily harm,** they are accused of delib- LEGAL erately causing very serious physical injury to someone.

grif‧fin /'grɪfɪn/ **griffins;** also spelled **griffon.** In N-COUNT mythology, a **griffin** is a winged monster with the body of a lion and the head of an eagle.

grill /grɪl/ **grills, grilling, grilled. 1** A **grill** is a ◆◆◇◇◇ part of a cooker which produces strong heat that N-COUNT cooks food placed underneath it. **2** A **grill** is a flat N-COUNT frame of metal bars on which food can be cooked over a fire. ● See also **grille. 3** A **grill** is a dish which N-COUNT consists of food that has been grilled, especially meat. *...a mixed grill.* **4** When you **grill** food, it is V-ERG: V n cooked using very strong heat directly above or be- V low it. *While the chicken is grilling, cook the rice.* ♦ **grill‧ing** *The breast can be cut into portions for* N-UNCOUNT *grilling.* **5** If you **grill** someone about something, you ask them VERB a lot of questions for a long period of time. *The police* V n *grilled him for hours.* ♦ **grilling, grillings** *They gave* INFORMAL *him a grilling about the implications of a united* N-COUNT *Europe.*

grille /grɪl/ **grilles;** also spelled **grill.** A **grille** is a N-COUNT framework of metal bars or wire which is placed in front of a window or a piece of machinery, in order to protect it or to protect people.

grim /grɪm/ **grimmer, grimmest. 1** A situation or ◆◆◇◇◇ piece of information that is **grim** is unpleasant, de- ADJ-GRADED pressing, and difficult to accept. *There was further grim economic news yesterday.* ♦ **grim‧ness** *...an* N-UNCOUNT *unrelenting grimness of tone.* **2** A place that is **grim** ADJ-GRADED is unattractive and depressing in appearance. *...the tower blocks on the city's grim edges.* **3** If a person ADJ-GRADED or their behaviour is **grim,** they are very serious or LITERARY stern, usually because they are worried about some- thing. ♦ **grim‧ly** *'It's too late now to stop him,' Har-* ADV-GRADED *ris said grimly.*

gri‧mace /grɪ'meɪs, 'grɪməs/ **grimaces, grimac-** ◆◇◇◇◇ **ing, grimaced.** If you **grimace,** you twist your VERB: face in an ugly way because you are displeased, dis- V atn gusted, or in pain. *She grimaced at Cerezzi.* ► Also a N-COUNT noun. *'Awful,' he said with a grimace.*

grime /graɪm/. **Grime** is dirt which has collected on N-UNCOUNT the surface of something.

‚Grim 'Reaper. The Grim Reaper is an imaginary N-SING: character who represents death. the N

grimy /'graɪmi/ **grimier, grimiest.** Something that ADJ-GRADED is **grimy** is very dirty.

grin /grɪn/ **grins, grinning, grinned. 1** When ◆◆◇◇◇ you **grin,** you smile broadly. *He just grinned at her.* VERB: V ► Also a noun. *...a big grin on her face.* **2** If you V atn **grin and bear it,** you accept a difficult or unpleas- N-COUNT ant situation without complaining because you PHRASE know there is nothing you can do to make things better. **3** ● to **wipe the grin off** someone's **face:** see **wipe.**

grind /graɪnd/ **grinds, grinding, ground. 1** If ◆◆◇◇◇ you **grind** a substance such as corn, you crush it be- VERB tween two hard surfaces or with a machine until it V n becomes a fine powder. *Grind the pepper as you* V-ed

need it. ...ground coffee. ▶ **Grind up** means the same as **grind.** *He makes his own paint, grinding up the pigment with a little oil.* ♦ **grind·er, grinders.** *Grind walnuts in an electric coffee grinder.* **2** If you **grind** something into a surface, you press and rub it hard into the surface. *'Well,' I said, grinding my cigarette nervously into the granite step.* **3** To **grind** something such as a tool is to make it smooth or sharp by rubbing it against a hard surface. ♦ **grinder.** A **grinder** is a person or machine that sharpens or polishes tools by grinding them.

4 If you refer to routine tasks or activities that you have to do as the **grind,** you are emphasizing that they are boring and take up a lot of time and effort. *The daily grind of government is done by Her Majesty's Civil Service.* ● See also **grinding.**

5 If a country's economy or something such as a process **grinds to a halt,** it gradually becomes slower or less active until it stops. **6** If a vehicle **grinds to a halt,** it stops slowly and noisily. **7** ● to **have an axe to grind:** see **axe.**

grind down. If you say that someone **grinds** you **down,** you mean that they treat you very harshly and cruelly, reducing your confidence or your will to resist.

grind on. If you say that something **grinds on,** you disapprove of the fact that it continues to happen in the same way for a long time.

grind out. To **grind** something **out** means to produce it in a boring or routine manner. *...grinding out novels to support his family.*

grind up. See **grind** 1.

grind·ing /ˈɡraɪndɪŋ/. If you describe a bad situation as **grinding,** you mean it never gets better, changes, or ends. *...grinding poverty.* ● See also **grind.**

grin·go /ˈɡrɪŋɡəʊ/ **gringos. Gringo** is sometimes used by people from Latin America to refer to foreigners, especially people from the United States and Britain; an offensive word.

grip /ɡrɪp/ **grips, gripping, gripped. 1** If you **grip** something, you take hold of it with your hand and continue to hold it firmly. *She gripped the rope.* ▶ Also a noun. *His strong hand eased the bag from her grip.* **2** If things such as shoes or car tyres have **grip,** they do not slip. **3** Someone's **grip** on someone or something is the power and control they have over them. *The president maintains an iron grip on his country.* **4** If you **get a grip** on yourself, you make an effort to control or improve your behaviour or work. **5** If you **lose your grip,** you lose the control you have over yourself and your situation, and become less able to deal with things. **6** If you **get to grips with** a problem or if you **come to grips with** it, you consider it seriously, and start taking action to deal with it. *The government's first task is to get to grips with the economy.* **7** If something **grips** you, it affects you very strongly. *The entire community has been gripped by fear.* **8** If a person, group, or place is **in the grip of** something, they are being severely affected by it. *Britain is still in the grip of recession.* **9** If you **are gripped** by something such as a story or a series of events, your attention is concentrated on it and held by it. ♦ **grip·ping** *The film turned out to be a gripping thriller.*

gripe /ɡraɪp/ **gripes, griping, griped.** If you say that someone is **griping,** you mean they are complaining about something in an annoying way. *I am sick of hearing motorists griping about the state of the roads.* ▶ A **gripe** is a complaint about something. *That's a minor gripe.* ♦ **grip·ing** *Still, the griping went on.*

grip·ing /ˈɡraɪpɪŋ/. A **griping** pain is a sudden, stabbing pain in your stomach or bowels.

gris·ly /ˈɡrɪzli/ **grislier, grisliest;** also spelled **grizzly.** If you describe something as **grisly,** you mean that it is extremely horrible, and involves death and violence. *...grisly murders.*

gris·tle /ˈɡrɪsəl/. **Gristle** is a tough, rubbery substance found in poor quality meat.

grit /ɡrɪt/ **grits, gritting, gritted. 1 Grit** is very small pieces of stone. It is often put on roads in winter to make them less slippery. **2** If someone has **grit,** they have the determination and courage to continue doing something even though it is very difficult. **3 Grits** are coarsely ground grains of corn which are eaten for breakfast or as part of a meal in the southern United States. **4** If you **grit** your teeth, you press your upper and lower teeth tightly together, usually because you are angry about something. *'I have no comment about this,' she seethed through gritted teeth.* **5** If you **grit** your **teeth,** you make up your mind to carry on even if the situation is very difficult.

grit·ty /ˈɡrɪti/ **grittier, grittiest. 1** Something that is **gritty** contains grit, is covered with grit, or has a texture like that of grit. **2** Someone who is **gritty** is determined and courageous. *...a gritty determination to avoid humiliation.* **3** A **gritty** description or portrayal of a tough or unpleasant situation shows it in a very realistic way. *...a gritty low-budget movie about a women's prison.*

griz·zled /ˈɡrɪzəld/. A **grizzled** person or a person with **grizzled** hair has hair that is grey or streaked with grey. *...a grizzled old age pensioner.*

griz·zly /ˈɡrɪzli/ **grizzlies. 1** A **grizzly** or a **grizzly bear** is a large, fierce, greyish-brown bear found in North America. **2** If children are **grizzly,** they whine or cry a lot, often because they are unwell or tired. **3** See also **grisly.**

groan /ɡrəʊn/ **groans, groaning, groaned. 1** If you **groan,** you make a long, low sound because you are experiencing a strong physical feeling, especially pain, or because you want to indicate your disapproval or unhappiness. *He began to groan with pain... 'My leg – I think it's broken,' Eric groaned.* ▶ Also a noun. *A groan of disappointment went up from the crew.* **2** If you **groan** about something, you complain about it. *There's no point in moaning and groaning.* ▶ Also a noun. *Afterwards there were widespread groans about the soft pitch.* **3** If wood **groans,** it makes a loud creaking sound, because it is being pushed, pressed, or moved. **4** If you say that something such as a table is **groaning** under the weight of something, you are emphasizing that it is very heavily loaded. *...tables groaning with ethnic foodstuffs.*

gro·cer /ˈɡrəʊsə/ **grocers.** A **grocer** is a shopkeeper who sells foods such as flour, sugar, and tinned foods. You can refer to a shop where these goods are sold as a **grocer** or a **grocer's.**

gro·cery /ˈɡrəʊsəri/ **groceries. 1** A **grocery** or a **grocery store** is a grocer's shop. **2 Groceries** are foods you buy at a grocer's or at a supermarket. *...two bags of groceries.*

grog /ɡrɒɡ/. **Grog** is a drink made by diluting a strong spirit, such as rum or whisky, with water.

grog·gy /ˈɡrɒɡi/ **groggier, groggiest.** If you feel **groggy,** you feel weak and rather ill.

groin /ɡrɔɪn/ **groins.** Your **groin** is the part of your body where your legs meet your abdomen.

groom /ɡruːm/ **grooms, grooming, groomed. 1** A **groom** is the same as a **bridegroom.** *...the bride and groom.* **2** A **groom** is someone whose job is to look after the horses in a stable and to keep them clean. **3** If you **groom** an animal, you clean its fur, usually by brushing it. **4** If you **are groomed** for a special job, someone prepares you for it by teaching you the skills you will need. *Marshall was groomed to run the family companies.*

groomed /ɡruːmd/. You use **groomed** in expressions such as **well groomed** and **badly groomed** to say how neat, clean, and smart a person is. *She always appeared perfectly groomed.*

groom·ing /ˈɡruːmɪŋ/. **Grooming** refers to the things that people do to keep themselves clean and make their face, hair, and skin look nice. *...a growing concern for personal grooming.*

groove /ɡruːv/ **grooves. 1** A **groove** is a deep line cut into a surface. ♦ **grooved** *...a grooved surface.*

(Right margin grammar codes:)
PHRASAL VB / V P noun / Also V n P
N-COUNT / VERB / V n prep
VERB: V n
N-COUNT
N-SING / INFORMAL
PHRASE
PHRASE
PHRASAL VB / PRAGMATICS
PHRASAL VB / V P / PRAGMATICS
PHRASAL VB / V n P / V P noun / INFORMAL
PHRASAL VB
ADJ: ADJ n
N-COUNT
VERB / V n
N-COUNT
N-COUNT
N-SING: with supp
PHRASE
PHRASE
PHRASE
VERB: V n
PHRASE
VERB: be V-ed
ADJ-GRADED
VERB: V / V about n / INFORMAL
N-COUNT / N-UNCOUNT
ADJ: ADJ n
ADJ-GRADED

N-UNCOUNT
N-UNCOUNT
N-PLURAL
VERB: V n / V-ed
PHRASE
ADJ-GRADED
ADJ-GRADED
ADJ-GRADED
ADJ
N-COUNT
ADJ-GRADED / INFORMAL
VERB: V / V with n / V with quote
N-COUNT
VERB: V about n / V / INFORMAL
N-COUNT
VERB: V
VERB: V under/with / PRAGMATICS / V-ing
N-COUNT
N-COUNT
N-COUNT / AMERICAN / N-PLURAL
N-UNCOUNT
ADJ-GRADED / INFORMAL
N-COUNT
N-COUNT
N-COUNT
VERB: V n
VERB: be V-ed for n / be V-ed to-inf
ADJ
N-UNCOUNT
N-COUNT / ADJ

2 In popular music, a **groove** is a rhythm. ...*Latin and African grooves.* `N-COUNT INFORMAL`

groovy /ˈgruːvi/ **groovier, grooviest.** If you describe something as **groovy**, you mean that it is attractive, fashionable, or exciting. `◆◇◇◇◇ ADJ-GRADED INFORMAL, DATED`

grope /grəʊp/ **gropes, groping, groped. 1** If you **grope** for something that you cannot see, you try to find it by moving your hands around in order to feel it. *Bunbury groped in his breast pocket for his wallet.* **2** If you **grope** your way to a place, you move there, holding your hands in front of you and feeling the way because you cannot see anything. *I didn't turn on the light, but groped my way across the room.* **3** If you **grope** for something, for example the solution to a problem, you try to think of it, when you have no real idea what it could be. *She groped for a simple word to express a simple idea.* ◆ **grop·ing, gropings** *They continue their groping towards a constitutional settlement.* **4** If one person **gropes** another, they touch or grab their body in a rough, sexual way; used showing disapproval. ▶ Also a noun. *It took a good few gropes for me to realise that he was doing this on purpose.* `◆◇◇◇◇ VERB: V for n V adv/prep` `VERB V way prep/ adv` `VERB V for n Also V towards n` `N-VAR` `VERB: V n PRAGMATICS INFORMAL` `N-COUNT`

gross /grəʊs/ **grosser, grossest; grosses, grossing, grossed. 1** You use **gross** to emphasize the degree to which something is unacceptable or unpleasant. *The company were guilty of gross negligence.* ◆ **gross·ly** *Lexicographers are still grossly underpaid.* **2** If you describe someone's speech or behaviour as **gross**, you mean that it is very rude or unacceptable. **3** If you describe something or someone as **gross**, you think that they are very ugly, tasteless, or repulsive. *He wears really gross holiday outfits.* `◆◆◆◇◇ ADJ: ADJ n PRAGMATICS` `ADV-GRADED` `ADJ-GRADED` `ADJ-GRADED INFORMAL`

4 A **gross** amount is the total amount after all the relevant amounts have been added together, and before any deductions are made. ...*a fixed rate account guaranteeing 10.4% gross interest or 7.8% net.* ▶ Also an adverb. ...*a father earning £20,000 gross a year.* **5** If a person or a business **grosses** a particular amount of money, they earn that amount of money before tax has been deducted. *So far the films have grossed more than £590 million.* **6** The **gross** weight of something is its total weight, including its container or wrapping. `ADJ: ADJ n` `ADV` `VERB V amount` `ADJ: ADJ n`

gross domestic 'product, gross domestic products. A country's **gross domestic product** is the total value of all the goods it has produced and the services it has provided in a particular year. `◆◇◇◇◇ N-VAR`

gro·tesque /grəʊˈtesk/. **1** You say that something is **grotesque** when it is so unnatural, unpleasant, or exaggerated that it upsets or shocks you. ...*the grotesque disparities between the wealthy few and nearly everyone else.* ◆ **gro·tesque·ly** *He says the law is grotesquely unfair.* **2** If someone or something is **grotesque**, they are very ugly. ◆ **grotesquely** ...*grotesquely deformed beggars.* `◆◇◇◇◇ ADJ-GRADED PRAGMATICS` `ADV-GRADED` `ADJ-GRADED` `ADV-GRADED: ADV adj/-ed`

grot·to /ˈgrɒtəʊ/ **grottoes** or **grottos.** A **grotto** is a small cave with interesting rocks. `N-COUNT`

grot·ty /ˈgrɒti/ **grottier, grottiest.** If you describe something as **grotty**, you dislike it and think that it is unpleasant or of poor quality. ...*a grotty little flat in Camden.* `PRAGMATICS BRITISH, INFORMAL`

grouchy /ˈgraʊtʃi/. If someone is **grouchy**, they are very bad-tempered and complain a lot. `ADJ-GRADED INFORMAL`

ground /graʊnd/ **grounds, grounding, grounded. 1** The **ground** is the surface of the earth or the floor of a room. *Women were sitting cross-legged on the ground... We slid down the roof and dropped to the ground.* ● Something that is **below ground** is under the earth's surface or under a building. Something that is **above ground** is on top of the earth's surface. **2** If you say that a town or building **is burnt to the ground** or **is razed to the ground**, you are emphasizing that it has been completely destroyed by fire. **3** If you **go to ground**, you hide somewhere where you cannot easily be found. **4** If you say that something takes place on the **ground**, you mean it takes place on the surface of the earth and not in the air. *All ground forces have not arrived in the Persian Gulf.* **5** The **ground** is the soil and `◆◆◆◆◆ N-SING: theN` `PHRASE` `PHRASE PRAGMATICS` `PHRASE` `N-SING` `N-SING`

rock on the earth's surface. ...*the marshy ground of the river delta.*

6 You can refer to land as **ground**, especially when it has very few buildings or when it is considered to be special in some way. ...*a stretch of waste ground... This memorial stands on sacred ground.* **7** You can use **ground** to refer to an area of land, sea, or air which is used for a particular activity. ...*Indian hunting grounds... The best fishing grounds are around the islands.* **8** A **ground** is an area of land which is specially designed and made for playing sport or for some other activity. ...*the city's football ground. ...a parade ground.* **9** The **grounds** of a large or important building are the garden or area of land which surrounds it. ...*the palace grounds. ...the grounds of the University.* `N-UNCOUNT` `N-COUNT: supp N` `N-COUNT: supp N` `N-PLURAL`

10 You can use **ground** to refer to a place or situation in which particular methods or ideas can develop and be successful. *The company has maintained its reputation as the developing ground for new techniques.* `N-VAR: with supp`

11 If an aircraft or its passengers **are grounded**, they are made to stay on the ground and are not allowed to take off. *A hydrogen leak forced NASA to ground the space shuttle.* **12** If a ship or boat **is grounded**, it touches the bottom of the sea, lake, or river it is on, and is unable to move off. *The boat finally grounded on a soft, underwater bank.* **13** The **ground** in an electric plug or piece of electrical equipment is the wire through which electricity passes into the ground and which makes the equipment safe. The British word is **earth.** `VERB: be V-ed V n` `V-ERG: be V-ed V` `N-COUNT AMERICAN`

14 You can use **ground** in expressions such as **on shaky ground** and **the same ground** to refer to a particular subject, area of experience, or basis for an argument. *It's often necessary to go over the same ground more than once.* **15** If you **shift** your **ground** or **change** your **ground**, you change the basis on which you are arguing. **16** If you **stand** your **ground** or **hold** your **ground**, you continue to support a particular argument or to have a particular opinion when other people are opposing you or trying to make you change your mind. `N-UNCOUNT: supp N` `PHRASE` `PHRASE`

17 If you are **on** your **own ground**, you are in a situation or dealing with a subject which you feel confident about because you are very familiar with it. *On her own ground she knows exactly what she's doing.* **18** The **middle ground** between two groups, ideas, or plans involves things which do not belong to either of these groups, ideas, or plans but have elements of each, often in a less extreme form. *There was no middle ground between faith and doubt in Paul's opinion.* **19** If two people or groups find **common ground**, they agree about something, especially when they do not agree about other things. `PHRASE` `PHRASE` `PHRASE`

20 If you say that something is **a ground for** or **grounds for** a particular feeling or course of action, you mean that it is a reason or justification for it. If you say that you are doing something **on the grounds** of a particular thing, you are giving the reason for your action. *Owen was against it, on the grounds of expense.* **21** If an argument, belief, or opinion **is grounded** in something, that thing is used as a justification for it. *Her argument was grounded in fact.* **22** **Ground** is used in expressions such as **gain ground**, **lose ground**, and **give ground** in order to indicate that someone obtains or loses an advantage which they have in a particular situation. *There are signs that the party is gaining ground in the latest polls.* **23** If you **break new ground**, you do something in a completely different way; used showing approval. **24** If something such as a project gets **off the ground**, it begins or starts functioning. *We help small companies to get off the ground.* **25** If you **prepare the ground** for a future event, course of action, or development, you make it easier for it to happen. ...*a political initiative which would prepare the ground for war.* **26** If you **stand** your **ground** or **hold** your **ground**, you do not run away from a danger or threat, but face it bravely. **27** If you say that something such as a person, job, or piece of clothing **suits** someone **down to the ground**, you are emphasizing that it is completely `N-VAR: N for n, on N with supp` `VERB be V-ed in/on n` `N-UNCOUNT JOURNALISM` `PHRASE PRAGMATICS` `PHRASE` `PHRASE` `PHRASE` `PHRASE PRAGMATICS INFORMAL`

suitable or appropriate for them. **28** If people or things of a particular kind are **thin on the ground**, there are very few of them. *Good managers are often thin on the ground.* `PHRASE BRITISH`

29 Ground is the past tense and past participle of **grind**. See also **grounding; home ground**.

ground·break·ing /'graʊndbreɪkɪŋ/; also spelled **ground-breaking**. You use **groundbreaking** to describe things which you think are significant because they provide new and positive ideas. *...groundbreaking research.* `ADJ`

'**ground crew, ground crews**. At an airport, the people who look after the planes when they are on the ground are called the **ground crew**. `N-COLL-COUNT`

,**ground 'floor, ground floors**. The **ground floor** of a building is the floor that is level or almost level with the ground outside. `N-COUNT` ◆◇◇◇

ground·ing /'graʊndɪŋ/. If you have a **grounding** in a subject, you know the basic facts or principles of that subject. *The degree provides a thorough grounding in both mathematics and statistics.* `N-SING` ◆◇◇◇

ground·less /'graʊndləs/. If you say that a fear or story is **groundless**, you mean that it is not valid because it is not based on evidence. `ADJ`

ground·nut /'graʊndnʌt/ **groundnuts**. A **groundnut** is the same as a **peanut**. `N-COUNT BRITISH`

'**ground rent, ground rents**. **Ground rent** is rent that is paid by the owner of a flat or house to the owner of the land on which it is built. `N-VAR BRITISH`

'**ground rule, ground rules**. The **ground rules** for something are the basic principles on which future action will be based. *She worked to establish legal ground rules for child abuse cases.* `N-COUNT` ◆◇◇◇

grounds·man /'graʊndzmən/ **groundsmen**. A **groundsman** is a person whose job is to look after a park or sports ground. `N-COUNT BRITISH`

'**ground staff**. **1** The people who are paid to maintain a sports ground are called the **ground staff**. **2** At an airport, the **ground staff** are the airline employees who do not fly with the planes, but maintain aircraft and runways and help passengers. `N-COLL-COUNT` `N-COLL-COUNT`

ground·swell /'graʊndswel/. A sudden growth of public feeling or support for something is often called a **groundswell**. *There is undoubtedly a groundswell of support for the idea of a strong central authority.* `N-SING: with supp JOURNALISM`

ground·water /'graʊndwɔːtə/. **Groundwater** is water that is found under the ground. `N-UNCOUNT`

ground·work /'graʊndwɜːk/. The **groundwork** for something is the early work on which forms the basis for further work. *Yesterday's meeting was to lay the groundwork for the task ahead.* `N-SING: the N` ◆◇◇◇

group /gruːp/ **groups, grouping, grouped. 1** A **group** of people or things is a number of people or things which are together in one place at one time. *The trouble involved a small group of football supporters... The students work in groups.* **2** A **group** is a set of people who have the same interests or objectives, and who organize themselves to work or act together. *...the Minority Rights Group. ...members of an environmental group.* **3** A **group** is a set of people, organizations, or things which are considered together because they have something in common. *...the most promising players in her age group... As a group, today's old people are still relatively deprived.* **4** A **group** is a number of separate commercial or industrial firms which all have the same owner. *...a French-based insurance group.* **5** A **group** is a number of musicians who perform together, especially ones who play popular music. *...a pop group called The Urge.* **6** If a number of things or people **are grouped together**, they are together in one place or within one organization or system. *The fact sheets are grouped into seven sections. ...the Arab Maghreb Union, which groups together the five North African states... We want to encourage them to group together.* **7** See also **grouping; blood group; pressure group**. `N-COLL-COUNT ◆◆◆◆` `N-COUNT` `N-COUNT` `N-COUNT` `N-COUNT` `V-ERG be V-ed prep V pl-n with together V together Also V n prep`

groupie /'gruːpi/ **groupies**. A **groupie** is someone who is very keen on a particular pop group, singer, `N-COUNT` or other famous person, and keeps following them around.

group·ing /'gruːpɪŋ/ **groupings**. A **grouping** is a set of people or things that have something in common. *There were two main political groupings pressing for independence.* `◆◇◇◇ N-COUNT`

,**group 'therapy**. **Group therapy** is a form of psychiatric treatment in which a group of people discuss their problems with each other. `◆◇◇◇ N-UNCOUNT`

grouse /graʊs/ **grouses, grousing, groused.** The form **grouse** is used as the plural for meaning 1. **1 Grouse** are small fat birds which are often shot for sport and can be eaten. ▶ **Grouse** is the flesh of this bird eaten as food. *...roast grouse.* **2** If you **grouse**, you complain. *'How come we never know what's going on?' he groused... They groused about the parking regulations.* ▶ A **grouse** is a complaint. `◆◇◇◇` `N-COUNT` `N-UNCOUNT` `VERB: V with quote V about n Also V that` `N-COUNT`

grove /grəʊv/ **groves. 1** A **grove** is a group of trees that are close together. *...an olive grove.* **2** **Grove** is often used as part of the name of a street. *...47 Canada Grove, Bognor Regis.* `◆◆◇◇ N-COUNT`

grov·el /'grɒvəl/ **grovels, grovelling, grovelled**; spelled **groveling, groveled** in American English. **1** If you say that someone **grovels**, you mean they behave very humbly towards another person, for example because they are frightened or because they want something; used showing disapproval. *I don't grovel to anybody... The Senator has been accused of grovelling.* **2** If you **grovel**, you crawl on the ground, for example in order to find something. *We grovelled around the club on our knees.* `VERB` `PRAGMATICS` `V to/before n` `V` `VERB` `V prep/adv Also V`

grow /grəʊ/ **grows, growing, grew, grown. 1** When people, animals, and plants **grow**, they increase in size and change physically over a period of time. **2** If a plant or tree **grows** in a particular place, it is alive there. *The station had roses growing at each end of the platform.* **3** If you **grow** a particular type of plant, you put seeds or young plants in the ground and look after them as they develop. *I always grow a few red onions.* **4** When someone's hair **grows**, it gradually becomes longer. Your nails also **grow**. **5** If someone **grows** their hair, or **grows** a beard or moustache, they stop cutting their hair or shaving so that their hair becomes longer. You can also **grow** your nails. **6** If someone **grows**, they develop and improve in character or attitude. *We really grew as a team.* **7** If an amount, feeling, or problem **grows**, it becomes greater or more intense. *Opposition grew and the government agreed to negotiate. ...a growing number of immigrants.* **8** If the economy or a business **grows**, it increases in wealth, size, or importance. *...a fast growing business.* **9** If something such as an idea or a plan **grows out of** something else, it develops from it. *The idea for this book grew out of conversations with Philippa Brewster.* **10** If one thing **grows into** another, it develops or changes until it becomes that thing. *The boys grew into men... This political row threatens to grow into a full blown crisis.* **11** You use **grow** to say that someone or something gradually changes until they have a new quality, feeling, or attitude. *I grew a little afraid of the guy next door... He's growing old... He grew to love his work.* **12** See also **grown**. `◆◆◆◆ VERB: V` `V` `VERB V n` `VERB: V` `VERB: V n` `VERB V` `VERB V-ing` `VERB: V V-ing` `VERB V out of n` `VERB V into n` `V-LINK V adj V to-inf`

grow apart. If people who have a close relationship **grow apart**, they gradually start to have different interests and opinions from each other, and their relationship starts to fail. *It sounds as if you have grown apart from Tom.* `PHRASAL VB RECIP: pl-n V P V P from n`

grow into. When a child **grows into** an item of clothing, he or she becomes taller or bigger so that it fits him or her properly. `PHRASAL VB V P n`

grow on. If someone or something **grows on** you, you start to like them more and more. *Slowly and strangely, the place began to grow on me.* `PHRASAL VB V P n`

grow out. If you **grow out** a hairstyle or let it **grow out**, you let your hair grow so that the style changes or so that you can cut off the part that you do not want. *I also let my hair go darker and grew out my fringe... The red rinse had grown out completely.* `PHRASAL VB ERG V P noun V P`

grow out of. 1 If you **grow out of** a type of behaviour or an interest, you stop behaving in that way or having that interest, as you develop or change. *Most children who stammer grow out of it.* **2** When a child **grows out of** an item of clothing, he or she becomes so tall or big that it no longer fits him or her properly.   PHRASAL VB / VP P n   VP P n

grow up. 1 When someone **grows up**, they gradually change from being a child into being an adult. *She grew up in Tokyo.* ● See also **grown-up**. **2** If you tell someone to **grow up**, you are telling them to stop behaving in a silly or childish way. *It's time you grew up.* **3** If something **grows up**, it starts to exist and becomes larger or more important. *A variety of heavy industries grew up alongside the port.*   PHRASAL VB / VP / PRAGMATICS / VP / INFORMAL / VP

grow·er /ˈɡrəʊə/ **growers.** A **grower** is a person who grows large quantities of a particular plant or crop in order to sell them. *...apple growers.*   ◆◆◇◇◇ N-COUNT

'growing pains. If a person or organization suffers from **growing pains**, they experience temporary difficulties and problems at the beginning of a particular stage of development. *There's some sympathy for this new country's growing pains.*   N-PLURAL

'growing season, growing seasons. The **growing season** in a particular country or area is the period in each year when the weather and temperature is right for plants and crops to grow.   N-COUNT

growl /ɡraʊl/ **growls, growling, growled. 1** When a dog or other animal **growls**, it makes a low rumbling noise, usually because it is angry. ▶ Also a noun. *...a concerted menacing growl.* **2** If someone **growls** something, they say something in a low, rough voice. *He growled some unintelligible words at Pete... 'I should have killed him,' Sharpe growled.* ▶ Also a noun. *...an angry growl of contempt.* **3** If you say that something **growls**, you mean that it makes a deep rumbling noise. *My stomach growled.* ▶ Also a noun. *...a resonating growl from the gearbox.*   ◆◇◇◇◇ VERB: V / N-COUNT / VERB V n / V with quote WRITTEN / N-COUNT / VERB V / N-COUNT

grown /ɡrəʊn/. A **grown** man or woman is one who is fully developed and mature. *Few women can understand a grown man's love of sport... Dad, I'm a grown woman. I know what I'm doing.* ● See also **full-grown**.   ◆◇◇◇◇ ADJ: ADJ n

,grown-'up, grown-ups; also spelled **grownup**. The syllable **up** is not stressed when it is a noun. **1** A **grown-up** is an adult; used by or to children. *Tell children to tell a grown-up if they're being bullied.* **2** Someone who is **grown-up** is mature and no longer dependent on their parents or another adult. *She was a widow with grown-up children.* **3** If you say that someone is **grown-up**, you mean that they behave in an adult way, often when they are in fact still a child. *She's very grown up.* **4** **Grown-up** things seem suitable for or typical of adults. *Her songs tackle grown-up subjects.*   ◆◇◇◇◇ N-COUNT / ADJ / ADJ-GRADED / ADJ-GRADED INFORMAL

growth /ɡrəʊθ/ **growths. 1** The **growth** of something such as an industry, organization, or idea is its development in size, wealth, or importance. *...the growth of nationalism. ...Japan's enormous economic growth.* **2** The **growth** in something is the increase in it. *The area has seen a rapid population growth.* **3** A **growth** industry, area, or market is one which is increasing in size or activity. **4** Someone's **growth** is the development and progress of their character. *...the child's emotional and intellectual growth.* **5** **Growth** in a person, animal, or plant is the process of increasing in physical size and development. *...hormones which control fertility and body growth.* **6** You can use **growth** to refer to plants which have recently developed or which developed at the same time. *This helps to ripen new growth.* **7** A **growth** is a lump that grows inside or on a person, animal, or plant, and that is caused by a disease or other abnormality. *...cancerous growths.*   ◆◆◆◇ N-UNCOUNT / N-UNCOUNT: also a N / ADJ: ADJ n / N-UNCOUNT / N-UNCOUNT / N-VAR / N-COUNT

grub /ɡrʌb/ **grubs. 1** A **grub** is a young insect which has just come out of an egg and looks like a short fat worm. **2** **Grub** is food.   ◆◇◇◇◇ N-COUNT / N-UNCOUNT INFORMAL

grub·by /ˈɡrʌbi/ **grubbier, grubbiest. 1** A **grubby** person or object is rather dirty. *...kids with grubby faces.* **2** If you call an activity or someone's behaviour **grubby**, you mean that it is not completely honest or respectable and you disapprove of it. *...the grubby business of politics.*   ◆◇◇◇◇ ADJ-GRADED / ADJ-GRADED / PRAGMATICS

grudge /ɡrʌdʒ/ **grudges.** If you bear a **grudge** against someone, you have unfriendly feelings towards them because of something they did in the past. *He appears to have a grudge against certain players.*   ◆◇◇◇◇ N-COUNT

'grudge match, grudge matches. You can call a contest between two people or groups a **grudge match** when they dislike each other.   N-COUNT

grudg·ing /ˈɡrʌdʒɪŋ/. A **grudging** feeling or action is felt or done very unwillingly. *He even earned his opponents' grudging respect.* ♦ **grudg·ing·ly** *The film studio grudgingly agreed.*   ◆◇◇◇◇ ADJ-GRADED / ADV-GRADED ADV with v

gru·el /ˈɡruːəl/. **Gruel** is a simple cheap food made by boiling oats with water or milk.   N-UNCOUNT

gru·el·ling /ˈɡruːəlɪŋ/; spelled **grueling** in American English. A **gruelling** activity is extremely difficult and tiring to do.   ◆◇◇◇◇ ADJ-GRADED

grue·some /ˈɡruːsəm/. Something that is **gruesome** is extremely unpleasant and shocking. *...a series of gruesome murders.* ♦ **grue·some·ly** *He was gruesomely tortured.*   ◆◇◇◇◇ ADJ-GRADED / ADV-GRADED

gruff /ɡrʌf/. **1** A **gruff** voice sounds low and rough. ♦ **gruff·ly** *'Never mind now,' he said gruffly.* **2** If you describe someone as **gruff**, you mean that they seem rather unfriendly or bad-tempered. *His gruff exterior concealed one of the kindest hearts.*   ADJ-GRADED / ADV-GRADED / ADJ-GRADED

grum·ble /ˈɡrʌmbəl/ **grumbles, grumbling, grumbled. 1** If someone **grumbles**, they complain about something in a bad-tempered and discontented way. *A tourist grumbled that the waiter spoke too much Spanish... 'This is inconvenient,' he grumbled.* ▶ Also a noun. *My grumble is with the structure and organisation of the material.* ♦ **grum·bling, grumblings** *...grumblings about the party leader.* **2** If something **grumbles**, it makes a low continuous sound. ▶ Also a noun. *...the grumble of guns.*   ◆◇◇◇◇ VERB: V / V that / V with quote / Also V about- / a†n / N-COUNT / N-VAR / VERB: V / LITERARY N-SING

grumpy /ˈɡrʌmpi/ **grumpier, grumpiest.** A **grumpy** person is bad-tempered and miserable. ♦ **grumpi·ly** *'I know, I know,' said Ken, grumpily.*   ◆◇◇◇◇ ADJ-GRADED / ADV-GRADED

grunt /ɡrʌnt/ **grunts, grunting, grunted. 1** If you **grunt**, you make a low rough noise, especially because you are annoyed or uninterested. *'Rubbish,' I grunted... He grunted his thanks.* ▶ Also a noun. *...grunts of acknowledgement.* **2** When an animal, usually a pig, **grunts**, it makes a low rough noise.   ◆◇◇◇◇ VERB: V / V with quote / V n / N-COUNT / VERB: V

G-string /ˈdʒiː strɪŋ/ **G-strings.** A **G-string** is a narrow band of cloth that is worn between a person's legs to cover their sexual organs, and that is held up by a narrow string round the waist.   N-COUNT

gua·no /ˈɡwɑːnəʊ/. **Guano** is the excrement of sea birds and bats. It is used as a fertilizer.   N-UNCOUNT

guar·an·tee /ˌɡærənˈtiː/ **guarantees, guaranteeing, guaranteed. 1** If one thing **guarantees** another, the first is certain to cause the second thing to happen. *...a man whose fame guarantees that his calls will nearly always be returned.* ♦ **guar·an·teed.** If something is **guaranteed** to happen, it is certain to happen. *Reports of this kind are guaranteed to cause anxiety.* **2** Something that is a **guarantee** of something else makes it certain that it will happen or that it is true. *A famous old name on a firm is not necessarily a guarantee of quality.* **3** If you **guarantee** something, you promise that it is definitely true, or that you will do or provide it for someone. *I guarantee that everyone can make a cake in the microwave... We guarantee to refund your money if you are not delighted.* ▶ Also a noun. *The Editor can give no guarantee that they will fulfil their obligations.* **4** A **guarantee** is a written promise by a company that if a product that they sell or work that they do has any faults within a particular time, it will be repaired, replaced, or redone free of charge. **5** If a company **guarantees** its product or work, they provide a guarantee for it.   ◆◆◆◇ VERB V n / V that / Also V n n / ADJ: v-link ADJ / N-COUNT / VERB: V n / V that / V to-inf / Also V n n / N-COUNT / N-COUNT: also under N / VERB: V n

guarantor · 489 · guide

guar·an·tor /ˌgærən'tɔː/ **guarantors.** A guarantor is a person who gives a guarantee or who is legally bound by one. `N-COUNT LEGAL`

guard /gɑːd/ **guards, guarding, guarded. 1** If you **guard** a place, person, or object, you stand near them in order to watch and protect them. **2** If you **guard** someone, you watch them and keep them in a particular place to stop them from escaping. **3** A **guard** is someone such as a soldier, police officer, or prison officer who is guarding a particular place or person. **4** A **guard** is a specially organized group of people, such as soldiers or policemen, who protect or watch someone or something. *We have a security guard around the whole area.* **5** If you **mount guard** or if you **mount a guard**, you organize people to watch or protect a person or place. **6** If someone is **on guard**, they are on duty and responsible for guarding a particular place or person. **7** If you **stand guard**, you stand near a particular person or place because you are responsible for watching or protecting them. **8** If someone is **under guard**, they are being guarded. **9** A **guard** is a person whose job is to check tickets on a train and ensure that the train travels safely and punctually. **10** If you **guard** some information or advantage that you have, you try to protect it or keep it for yourself. *He closely guarded her identity.* **11** A **guard** is a protective device which covers a part of someone's body or a dangerous part of a piece of equipment. *...the chin guard of my helmet.* **12** You use **guard** to refer to someone's attitude of caution or distrust towards someone or something. For example, if you lower your **guard**, you relax when you should be careful and alert. **13** If someone **catches** you **off guard**, they surprise you by doing something when you are not expecting it. **14** If you are **on** your **guard** or if you are **on guard**, you are being very careful because you think a situation might become difficult or dangerous. *He is constantly on guard against any threat of humiliation.* **15** See also **guarded; bodyguard, coastguard, lifeguard, old guard.** `VERB: V n / VERB: V n / N-COUNT / N-COLL-SING / PHRASE / PHRASE / PHRASE / PHRASE / N-COUNT BRITISH / VERB V n / N-COUNT / N-SING: poss N / PHRASE / PHRASE`

guard against. If you **guard against** something, you are careful to prevent it from happening, or to avoid being affected by it. *The armed forces were on high alert to guard against any retaliation.* `PHRASAL VB V P n`

'guard dog, guard dogs. A **guard dog** is a fierce dog that has been specially trained to protect a particular place. `N-COUNT`

guard·ed /'gɑːdɪd/. A **guarded** person is careful not to show their feelings or to give away information. ♦ **guard·ed·ly** *'I am happy, so far,' he says guardedly.* `ADJ-GRADED / ADV-GRADED`

guard·ian /'gɑːdiən/ **guardians. 1** A **guardian** is someone who has been legally appointed to look after the affairs of another person, for example a child or someone who is mentally ill. ♦ **guardi·an·ship** /'gɑːdiənʃɪp/ *...depriving mothers of the guardianship of their children.* **2** If you consider someone a defender or protector of something, you can call them its **guardian.** `N-COUNT / N-UNCOUNT / N-COUNT`

guardian 'angel, guardian angels. A **guardian angel** is a spirit who is believed to protect and guide a particular person. `N-COUNT`

guard of 'honour, guards of honour; spelled **guard of honor** in American English. A **guard of honour** is an official parade of troops, usually to celebrate or honour a special occasion, such as the visit of a head of state. `N-COUNT`

guard·rail /'gɑːdreɪl/ **guardrails;** also spelled **guard rail.** A **guardrail** is a railing that is placed along the edge of a staircase, path, or boat. `N-COUNT`

guards·man /'gɑːdzmən/ **guardsmen;** also spelled **Guardsman. 1** A **guardsman** is a soldier who is a member of one of the regiments called Guards. **2** A **guardsman** is a soldier who is a member of the National Guard. `N-COUNT BRITISH / N-COUNT AMERICAN`

gua·va /'gwɑːvə/ **guavas.** A **guava** is a round yellow tropical fruit with pink or white flesh. `N-VAR`

gu·ber·na·to·rial /ˌguːbənə'tɔːriəl/. **Gubernatorial** means relating to or connected with the post of governor. *...a former Texas gubernatorial candidate.* `ADJ: ADJ n`

guer·ril·la /gə'rɪlə/ **guerrillas;** also spelled **gueril·la.** A **guerrilla** is someone who fights as part of an unofficial army, usually against an official army or police force. `N-COUNT`

guess /ges/ **guesses, guessing, guessed. 1** If you **guess** something, you give an answer or provide an opinion which may not be true because you do not have definite knowledge about the matter concerned. *Wood guessed that he was a very successful publisher or a banker... You can only guess at what mental suffering they endure... Guess what I did for the whole of the first week.* ► Also a noun. *My guess is that the answer will be negative... He'd taken her pulse and made a guess at his blood pressure.* **2** If someone **keeps** you **guessing**, they do not tell you what you want to know. **3** You say **at a guess** to indicate that what you are saying is only an estimate or what you believe to be true, rather than being a definite fact. *At a guess he's been dead for two days.* **4** If you say that something is **anyone's guess** or **anybody's guess**, you mean that nobody can be certain about what is really true. **5** You say **'I guess'** to indicate slight uncertainty or reluctance about what you are saying. *I guess he's right.* **6** You say **'Guess what'** to draw attention to something exciting, surprising, or interesting that you are about to say. *Guess what, I just got my first part in a movie.* **7** If you **guess** that something is the case, you correctly form the opinion that it is the case, although you do not have definite knowledge about it. *He should have guessed what would happen... Someone might have guessed our secret.* `VERB: V n / V that / V at n/wh / V wh / N-COUNT / PHRASE / PHRASE / PHRASE INFORMAL / PHRASE PRAGMATICS INFORMAL / CONVENTION PRAGMATICS INFORMAL / VERB: V that / V wh / V n`

guess·work /'geswɜːk/. **Guesswork** is the process of trying to guess or estimate something without knowing all the facts or information. *The question of who planted the bomb remains a matter of guesswork.* `N-UNCOUNT`

guest /gest/ **guests, guesting, guested. 1** A **guest** is someone who is visiting you or is at an event because you have invited them. *She was a guest at the wedding.* **2** A **guest** is someone who visits a place or organization or appears on a radio or television show because they have been invited to do so. *...a frequent chat show guest.* **3** If someone **guests for** someone or **guests on** something, they perform or take part in a game or programme on a particular occasion because they have been invited to do so. **4** A **guest** is someone who is staying in a hotel. *I was the only hotel guest.* **5** If you say **be my guest** to someone, you are giving them permission to do something. *If anybody wants to work on this, be my guest.* `N-COUNT / N-COUNT / VERB: V prep / N-COUNT / CONVENTION PRAGMATICS`

'guest house, guest houses; also spelled **guesthouse. 1** A **guest house** is a small hotel. **2** A **guest house** is a small house in the grounds of a large house, where visitors can stay. `N-COUNT / N-COUNT AMERICAN`

,guest of 'honour, guests of honour; spelled **guest of honor** in American English. If you say that someone is the **guest of honour** at a social occasion, you mean that they are the most important guest. `N-COUNT`

guff /gʌf/. If you say that what someone has said or written is **guff**, you think that it is nonsense. *Then there was all the guff about looks not mattering.* `N-UNCOUNT PRAGMATICS INFORMAL`

guf·faw /gʌ'fɔː/ **guffaws, guffawing, guffawed.** To **guffaw** means to laugh loudly and heartily. *'Ha, ha,' everyone guffawed.* ► Also a noun. *He bursts into a loud guffaw.* `VERB: V / V with quote / Also V at n / N-COUNT`

guid·ance /'gaɪdəns/. **Guidance** is help and advice. *...the reports which were produced under his guidance.* `N-UNCOUNT`

'guidance system, guidance systems. The **guidance system** of a missile or rocket is the device which controls its course. `N-COUNT`

guide /gaɪd/ **guides, guiding, guided. 1** A **guide** is a book that gives you information or instructions to help you do or understand something. *...the Pocket Guide to Butterflies.* **2** A **guide** is a book that `N-COUNT / N-COUNT`

gives tourists information about a town, area, or country. ...the Rough Guide to Paris.

3 A **guide** is someone who shows tourists around places such as museums or cities. **4** If you **guide** someone around a city, museum, or building, you show it to them and explain points of interest. **5** A **guide** is someone who shows people the way to a place in a difficult or dangerous region. N-COUNT VERB: V n adv/prep N-COUNT

6 A **guide** is something that can be used to help you plan your actions or to form an opinion about something. As a rough guide, a horse needs 2.5 per cent of its body weight in food every day. N-COUNT

7 If you **guide** someone or something somewhere, you go there with them in order to show them the way. He took the bewildered Elliott by the arm and guided him out. **8** If you **guide** a vehicle somewhere, you control it carefully to make sure that it goes in the right direction. Captain Shelton guided his plane down the runway. **9** If something **guides** you somewhere, it gives you the information you need in order to go in the right direction. ...with only a compass to guide them. VERB V n adv/prep VERB V n adv/prep VERB V n

10 If something or someone **guides** you, they influence your actions or decisions. He should have let his instinct guide him. **11** If you **guide** someone through something that is difficult to understand or to achieve, you help them to understand it or to achieve success in it. ...a free helpline to guide businessmen through the maze of government and EC grants. VERB V n VERB V n adv/prep

Guide, Guides. The **Guides** is an organization for girls which teaches them to become disciplined, practical, and self-sufficient. In the United States, there is a similar organization called the **Girl Scouts.** ▶ A **Guide** is a girl who is a member of the Guides. N-COLL-PROPER: the N BRITISH N-COUNT

guide·book /ˈgaɪdbʊk/ **guidebooks;** also spelled **guide book.** **1** A **guidebook** is a book that gives tourists information about a town, area, or country. **2** A **guidebook** is a book that gives you information or instructions to help you do or understand something. ...a series of guidebooks to American politics. N-COUNT N-COUNT

,guided 'missile, guided missiles. A **guided missile** is a missile whose direction can be controlled while it is in the air. N-COUNT

'guide dog, guide dogs. A **guide dog** is a dog that has been trained to lead a blind person. N-COUNT

guide·line /ˈgaɪdlaɪn/ **guidelines. Guidelines** are pieces of advice that an organization or person issues, intended to help you do something. The effects of the sun can be significantly reduced if we follow certain guidelines. ◆◆◇◇◇ N-COUNT

guild /gɪld/ **guilds.** A **guild** is an organization of people who do the same job or who have the same occupation. ...the Writers' Guild of America. ◆◇◇◇ N-COUNT

guile /gaɪl/. **Guile** is the quality of being very cunning and good at deceiving people. N-UNCOUNT

guile·less /ˈgaɪlləs/. A **guileless** person behaves openly and truthfully. ADJ-GRADED LITERARY

guil·lo·tine /ˈgɪlətiːn/ **guillotines, guillotining, guillotined.** **1** A **guillotine** is a device that was used in former times to execute people by chopping their heads off. ▶ If someone **is guillotined,** they are killed with a guillotine. **2** A **guillotine** is a device used for cutting and trimming paper. N-COUNT: also by N VERB: usu passive N-COUNT

guilt /gɪlt/. **1 Guilt** is an unhappy feeling that you have because you have done something wrong or think that you have done something wrong. Some cancer patients experience strong feelings of guilt. **2 Guilt** is the fact that you have done something wrong or illegal. ...the determination of guilt according to criminal law. ◆◆◇◇◇ N-UNCOUNT N-UNCOUNT

guilty /ˈgɪlti/ **guiltier, guiltiest. 1** If you feel **guilty,** you feel unhappy because you think that you have done something wrong or have failed to do something which you should have done. ♦ **guilti·ly** He glanced guiltily over his shoulder. **2 Guilty** is used of an action or fact that you feel guilty about. ...a guilty secret. **3** If someone is **guilty** of doing something wrong or committing a crime, they have ◆◆◆◇◇ ADJ-GRADED ADV-GRADED ADJ: ADJ n ADJ

done it or committed it. Mr Brooke had been guilty of a 'gross error of judgment'. ...guilty of murder.

guinea /ˈgɪni/ **guineas.** A **guinea** is an old British unit of money that was worth £1.05. ◆◇◇◇◇ N-COUNT

'guinea fowl; guinea fowl is both the singular and the plural. A **guinea fowl** is a large grey African bird. N-COUNT

'guinea pig, guinea pigs. 1 If someone is used as a **guinea pig** in an experiment, something is tested on them that has not been tested on people before. The Doctor used himself as a human guinea pig to perfect a treatment. **2** A **guinea pig** is a small furry animal without a tail. ◆◇◇◇◇ N-COUNT N-COUNT

guise /gaɪz/ **guises.** You use **guise** to refer to the outward appearance or form of someone or something, which is often temporary or different from their real nature. ...the men who committed this murder under the guise of a political act. ◆◇◇◇◇ N-COUNT: with supp

gui·tar /gɪˈtɑː/ **guitars.** A **guitar** is a musical instrument with a long neck and six strings that you pluck or strum. See picture headed **musical instruments.** ♦ **gui·tar·ist** /gɪˈtɑːrɪst/ **guitarists.** A **guitarist** is someone who plays the guitar. ◆◆◇◇◇ N-VAR N-COUNT

gulf /gʌlf/ **gulfs;** spelled **Gulf** in sense 3. **1** A **gulf** is an important or significant difference between two people, things, or groups. There is a growing gulf between rich and poor. **2** A **gulf** is a large area of sea which extends a long way into the surrounding land. ...the Gulf of Mexico. **3** The **Gulf** is used to refer to the Persian Gulf and the countries around it. N-COUNT N-COUNT N-PROPER: the N

gull /gʌl/ **gulls.** A **gull** is a common sea bird. N-COUNT

gul·let /ˈgʌlɪt/ **gullets.** Your **gullet** is the tube which goes from your mouth to your stomach. N-COUNT

gul·lible /ˈgʌlɪbəl/. A **gullible** person is easily tricked because they are too trusting. ♦ **gul·li·bil·ity** /ˌgʌləˈbɪlɪti/ Was she taking part of the blame for her own gullibility? ◆◇◇◇◇ ADJ-GRADED N-UNCOUNT

gul·ly /ˈgʌli/ **gullies;** also spelled **gulley.** A **gully** is a long narrow valley with steep sides. ◆◇◇◇◇ N-COUNT

gulp /gʌlp/ **gulps, gulping, gulped. 1** If you **gulp** something, you eat or drink it very quickly by swallowing large quantities of it at once. She quickly gulped her tea. **2** If you **gulp,** you swallow air, often making a noise in your throat as you do so. I gulped, and then proceeded to tell her the whole story... He slumped back, gulping for air. **3** A **gulp** of air, food, or drink, is a large amount of it that you swallow at once. I took in a large gulp of air. ◆◇◇◇◇ VERB V n VERB V V forn Also V n N-COUNT

gulp down. If you **gulp down** food or drink, you quickly eat or drink it all by swallowing large quantities of it at once. He'd gulped it down in one bite. PHRASAL VB V P n V n P

gum /gʌm/ **gums. 1 Gum** is a substance, often mint-flavoured, which you chew for a long time but do not swallow. ● See also **bubble gum, chewing gum. 2** A **gum** is a chewy sweet which feels like firm rubber and usually tastes of fruit. ...wine gums. **3** Your **gums** are the areas of firm pink flesh inside your mouth, which your teeth grow out of. See picture headed **human body. 4 Gum** is a type of glue that is used to stick two pieces of paper together. ♦ **gummed** ...gummed labels. **5 Gum** is a sticky substance which comes from the eucalyptus tree or from various other trees and shrubs. ◆◆◇◇◇ N-VAR N-COUNT N-COUNT N-VAR BRITISH ADJ N-VAR

gump·tion /ˈgʌmpʃən/. **1** If someone has **gumption,** they are able to think what it would be sensible to do in a particular situation, and they do it. **2** If someone has the **gumption** to do something, they have the courage or the audacity to do it. She admired him for having the gumption to disagree. N-UNCOUNT INFORMAL N-UNCOUNT

gun /gʌn/ **guns, gunning, gunned. 1** A **gun** is a weapon from which bullets or other things are fired. ● See also **airgun, machine gun, shotgun, submachine gun. 2** If you **gun** an engine or a vehicle, you make it start or go faster by pressing on the accelerator pedal. The British word is **rev. 3** If you come out **with guns blazing** or **with all guns blazing,** you put all your effort and energy into trying to achieve something. **4** If you **jump the gun,** you do something before everyone else or before the proper or right time. Some booksellers have jumped the gun and decided to sell it early. **5** If you **stick to your guns,** ◆◆◆◇◇ N-COUNT VERB: V n AMERICAN PHRASE PHRASE INFORMAL PHRASE

you continue to have your own opinion about *some- thing, even though other people disagree or try to make you change your mind.* **INFORMAL**

gun down. If someone **is gunned down**, they are shot and severely injured or killed. **PHRASAL VB usu passive**

gun for. If someone **is gunning for** you, they are trying to find a way to harm you or cause you trouble. **PHRASAL VB V P n INFORMAL**

gun·boat /'gʌnbəʊt/ **gunboats.** A **gunboat** is a small ship which has several large guns fixed on it. **N-COUNT**

gun·fire /'gʌnfaɪə/. **Gunfire** is the repeated shooting of guns. *...the sound of gunfire.* **◆◇◇◇◇ N-UNCOUNT**

gunge /gʌndʒ/. You use **gunge** to refer to a soft sticky substance, especially if it is unpleasant. *...some kind of black gunge.* **N-UNCOUNT INFORMAL, BRITISH**

gun·man /'gʌnmən/ **gunmen.** A **gunman** is a man who uses a gun to commit a crime such as murder or robbery. *Gunmen opened fire on their vehicle.* **◆◆◇◇◇ N-COUNT**

gun·ner /'gʌnə/ **gunners. 1** A **gunner** is an ordinary soldier in an artillery regiment. **2** A **gunner** is a member of the crew of a ship, plane, or helicopter who is responsible for firing a gun from it. **◆◇◇◇◇ N-COUNT N-COUNT**

gun·nery /'gʌnəri/. **Gunnery** is the activity of firing large guns. *The area was used for gunnery practice.* **N-UNCOUNT TECHNICAL**

gun·point /'gʌnpɔɪnt/. If you are held **at gunpoint**, someone is threatening to shoot and kill you if you do not obey them. **◆◇◇◇◇ PHRASE**

gun·powder /'gʌnpaʊdə/. **Gunpowder** is an explosive substance which is used to make fireworks or cause explosions. **N-UNCOUNT**

'gun-running. **Gun-running** is the activity of taking or sending guns into a country secretly and illegally. **♦ gun-runner, gun-runners.** **N-UNCOUNT N-COUNT**

gun·ship /'gʌnʃɪp/ **gunships.** See **helicopter gunship.**

gun·shot /'gʌnʃɒt/ **gunshots. 1 Gunshot** is used to refer to bullets that are fired from a gun. **2** A **gunshot** is the firing of a gun or the sound of a gun being fired. **◆◇◇◇◇ N-UNCOUNT N-COUNT**

gup·py /'gʌpi/ **guppies.** A **guppy** is a small brightly-coloured tropical fish. **N-COUNT**

gur·gle /'gɜːgəl/ **gurgles, gurgling, gurgled. 1** If water **is gurgling**, it is making the sound that it makes when it flows quickly and unevenly through a narrow space. *...the sound of hot water gurgling through the van's engine.* ▶ Also a noun. *...the swish and gurgle of water.* **2** If someone, especially a baby, **is gurgling**, they are making a sound in their throat similar to the gurgling of water. ▶ Also a noun. *There was a gurgle of laughter.* **◆◇◇◇◇ VERB V adv/prep N-COUNT VERB: V N-COUNT**

guru /'guːruː/ **gurus. 1** If you refer to someone as a **guru**, you mean that some people regard them as an expert or leader. *...fashion gurus.* **2** A **guru** is a religious and spiritual leader and teacher, especially in Hinduism. **◆◇◇◇◇ N-COUNT N-COUNT; N-TITLE**

gush /gʌʃ/ **gushes, gushing, gushed. 1** When liquid **gushes** out of something, it flows out very quickly and in large quantities. *Piping-hot water gushed out... A supertanker continues to gush oil off the coast of Spain.* ▶ Also a noun. *I heard a gush of water.* **2** If someone **gushes** about something, they express their admiration or pleasure in an exaggerated way. *'Oh, it was brilliant,' he gushes.* **♦ gush·ing** *...a gushing speech.* **◆◇◇◇◇ V-ERG V adv/prep V n N-SING VERB: V V with quote ADJ-GRADED**

gus·set /'gʌsɪt/ **gussets.** A **gusset** is a small strip of cloth sewn into the crotch of underwear to make it wider, stronger, or more comfortable. **N-COUNT**

gust /gʌst/ **gusts, gusting, gusted. 1** A **gust** is a short, strong, sudden rush of wind. *A gust of wind drove down the valley.* **♦ gusty.** **Gusty** winds are strong and irregular. **2** When the wind **gusts**, it blows with short, strong, sudden rushes. *The wind gusted up to 164 miles an hour.* **◆◇◇◇◇ N-COUNT ADJ-GRADED VERB: V V prep/adv**

gus·to /'gʌstəʊ/. If you do something with **gusto**, you do it with energy and enthusiasm. *Hers was a minor part, but she played it with gusto.* **N-UNCOUNT**

gut /gʌt/ **guts, gutting, gutted. 1** A person's or animal's **guts** are all the organs inside them. **2** When someone **guts** a dead animal or fish, they prepare it for cooking by removing all the organs from inside it. **3** The **gut** is the tube inside the ab-**◆◆◇◇◇ N-PLURAL VERB: V n N-SING:**

domen of a person or animal through which food passes while it is being digested. **the/poss N**

4 The **guts** of something, for example a subject or a machine, are the key elements of it, which make it work. *She has a reputation for getting at the guts of a subject.* **N-PLURAL: N of n INFORMAL**

5 Guts is the will and courage to do something which is difficult or unpleasant, or which might have unpleasant results. *The new Chancellor has the guts to push through unpopular tax increases.* **N-UNCOUNT INFORMAL**

6 A **gut** feeling is based on instinct or emotion rather than reason. **N-SING**

7 To **gut** a building means to destroy the inside of it so that only its outside walls remain. *A factory stands gutted and deserted.* **VERB: V n V-ed**

8 If you **hate** someone's **guts**, you dislike them very much indeed. **PHRASE INFORMAL**

9 If you say that you **are working** your **guts out** or **slogging** your **guts out**, you are emphasizing that you are working as hard as you can. **PHRASE PRAGMATICS INFORMAL**

10 See also **gutted**

gut·less /'gʌtləs/. A **gutless** person has a weak character and lacks courage or determination. **ADJ-GRADED**

gutsy /'gʌtsi/ **gutsier, gutsiest.** If you describe someone as **gutsy**, you mean they show courage or determination; used showing approval. *I've always been drawn to tough, gutsy women.* **ADJ-GRADED PRAGMATICS INFORMAL**

gut·ted /'gʌtɪd/. If you are **gutted**, you feel extremely disappointed or depressed. **ADJ-GRADED: v-link ADJ INFORMAL**

gut·ter /'gʌtə/ **gutters. 1** The **gutter** is the edge of a road next to the pavement, where rain water collects and flows away. **2** A **gutter** is a plastic or metal channel fixed to the lower edge of the roof of a building, which rain water drains into. See picture headed **house and flat. 3** You can use **the gutter** to refer to a condition of life in which someone is poor and has no self-respect. *Instead of ending up in jail or in the gutter he was remarkably successful.* **4** See also **gutter press.** **◆◇◇◇◇ N-COUNT N-COUNT N-SING: the N**

gut·ter·ing /'gʌtərɪŋ/. **Guttering** consists of the plastic or metal channels fixed to the lower edge of the roof of a building, which rain water drains into. **N-UNCOUNT**

,gutter 'press. If you refer to particular newspapers and magazines as **the gutter press**, you disapprove of them because they are full of stories about sex, crime, and people's private affairs. **N-SING: the N PRAGMATICS**

gut·tur·al /'gʌtərəl/. **Guttural** sounds are harsh sounds that are produced at the back of a person's throat. **ADJ-GRADED**

guv /gʌv/. **Guv** is sometimes used to address a man, especially a customer or someone you are doing a service for. *Hey, thanks, guv.* **N-VOC INFORMAL, BRITISH**

guy /gaɪ/ **guys. 1** A **guy** is a man. *I was working with a guy from Manchester.* ● See also **wise guy. 2** Americans sometimes address a group of people, whether they are male or female, as **guys** or **you guys**. *Hi, guys. How are you doing?.* **◆◆◆◆◇ N-COUNT INFORMAL N-VOC; N-PLURAL AMERICAN, INFORMAL**

'guy rope, guy ropes. A **guy rope** is a rope or wire that has one end fastened to a tent or pole and the other end fixed to the ground, so that it keeps the tent or pole in position. **N-COUNT**

guz·zle /'gʌzəl/ **guzzles, guzzling, guzzled. 1** If you **guzzle** something, you drink it or eat it quickly and greedily. *Melissa had chain-smoked all evening and guzzled gin and tonics.* **2** If you say that a vehicle **guzzles** fuel, you mean that it uses a lot of it. **♦ -guz·zling** *...petrol-guzzling cars.* **VERB V n Also V INFORMAL VERB: V n COMB**

gym /dʒɪm/ **gyms. 1** A **gym** is a club, building, or large room, usually containing special equipment, where people go to do physical exercise or get fit. **2 Gym** is the activity of doing physical exercises in a gym, especially at school. **◆◆◇◇◇ N-COUNT N-UNCOUNT INFORMAL**

gym·kha·na /dʒɪm'kɑːnə/ **gymkhanas.** A **gymkhana** is a sporting event in which people ride horses in competition. **N-COUNT**

gym·na·sium /dʒɪm'neɪziəm/ **gymnasiums** or **gymnasia.** A **gymnasium** is the same thing as a **gym**. **◆◇◇◇◇ N-COUNT N-COUNT FORMAL**

gym·nas·tics /dʒɪm'næstɪks/. The form **gymnastic** is used as a modifier. **1 Gymnastics** consists of **◆◇◇◇◇ N-UNCOUNT**

physical exercises that develop your strength, co-ordination, and agility. ...*gymnastic exercises.*

♦ **gym·nast** /'dʒɪmnæst/ **gymnasts.** A **gymnast** is someone who is trained in gymnastics. **2** You can use **gymnastics** to refer to an activity which requires great agility and flexibility. *He did some hasty mental gymnastics to assess how much he'd need.*

N-COUNT

N-UNCOUNT: adj N

gy·nae·col·ogy /ˌgaɪnɪ'kɒlədʒi/; spelled **gynecol-ogy** in American English. **Gynaecology** is the branch of medical science which deals with women's diseases and medical conditions. ♦ **gy·nae·colo·gist**, **gynaecologists.** ♦ **gy·nae·co·logi·cal** /ˌgaɪnɪkə'lɒdʒɪkəl/ ...*a routine gynaecological examination.*

N-UNCOUNT

N-COUNT

ADJ: ADJ n

gyp·sum /'dʒɪpsəm/. **Gypsum** is a soft white substance which looks like chalk and which is used to make plaster of Paris.

N-UNCOUNT

gyp·sy /'dʒɪpsi/ **gypsies;** also spelled **gipsy.** A **gypsy** is a member of a race of people who travel from place to place, usually in caravans, rather than living in one place.

N-COUNT

gy·rate /dʒaɪ'reɪt, AM 'dʒaɪreɪt/ **gyrates, gyrat-ing, gyrated. 1** If you say that a person or their body **is gyrating**, you mean that they are dancing or moving their body in a sexually suggestive way. ...*a room stuffed full of gasping, gyrating bodies.* ♦ **gy-·ra·tion** /dʒaɪ'reɪʃən/ **gyrations** *Prince continued his enthusiastic gyrations on stage.* **2** To **gyrate** means to turn round and round in a circle, usually very fast. *The aeroplane was gyrating about the sky.*

VERB: V

V-ing

N-COUNT

VERB

V prep

Also V

gy·ro·scope /'dʒaɪrəskəʊp/ **gyroscopes.** A **gyro-scope** is a device which contains a disc that always maintains the same position. It is used to help ships and planes navigate, especially in bad weather.

N-COUNT

H h

H, h /eɪtʃ/ **H's, h's** /'eɪtʃɪz/. **1** H is the eighth letter of the English alphabet. **2** H or h is an abbreviation for words beginning with h, such as 'hour', 'height', and 'hospital'.

N-VAR

ha /hɑː/; also spelled **hah. Ha** is used in writing to represent a noise that people make to show they are surprised, annoyed, or pleased about something.
● See also **ha ha.**

EXCLAM

ha. ha. is a written abbreviation for **hectare.**

ha·beas cor·pus /ˌheɪbiəs 'kɔːpəs/. **Habeas corpus** is a law that exists in many countries. It states that a person cannot be kept in prison unless he or she has been brought before a judge or a magistrate.

N-UNCOUNT

hab·er·dash·er /'hæbədæʃər/ **haberdashers. 1** A **haberdasher** or a **haberdasher's** is a shop where small articles for sewing and dressmaking are sold. **2** A **haberdasher** is a shopkeeper who makes and sells men's clothes. The British word is **tailor. 3** A **haberdasher** or a **haberdasher's** is a shop where men's clothes are sold. The British word is **tailor** or **tailor's.**

N-COUNT

BRITISH

N-COUNT

AMERICAN

N-COUNT

AMERICAN

hab·er·dash·ery /'hæbədæʃəri/. **Haberdashery** is small articles for sewing and dressmaking such as buttons, zips, thread, and ribbons.

N-UNCOUNT

BRITISH

hab·it /'hæbɪt/ **habits. 1** A **habit** is something that you do often or regularly. *He has an endearing habit of licking his lips when he's nervous. ...a survey on eating habits in the UK.* **2** If you **are in the habit of** doing something or **make a habit of** doing it, you do it regularly or often. If you **get into the habit of** doing something, you begin to do it regularly or often. *You can phone me at work as long as you don't make a habit of it.*

N-VAR

PHRASE

3 A **habit** is an action which is considered bad, that someone does repeatedly and finds it difficult to stop doing. *After twenty years as a chain smoker Mr Nathe has given up the habit.* **4** A drug **habit** is an addiction to a drug such as heroin or cocaine. **5** A **habit** is a piece of clothing shaped like a long loose dress, which a nun or monk wears.

N-COUNT

N-COUNT: supp N

N-COUNT

hab·it·able /'hæbɪtəbəl/. If a place is **habitable**, it is suitable for people to live in.

ADJ-GRADED

habi·tat /'hæbɪtæt/ **habitats.** The **habitat** of an animal or plant is the natural environment in which it normally lives or grows. *In its natural habitat, the hibiscus will grow up to 25ft.*

N-VAR

habi·ta·tion /ˌhæbɪ'teɪʃən/ **habitations. 1** Habita-tion is the activity of living somewhere. *20 per cent of private-rented dwellings are unfit for human habitation.* **2** A **habitation** is a place where people live.

N-UNCOUNT

FORMAL

N-COUNT

FORMAL

ha·bitu·al /hə'bɪtʃuəl/. **1** A **habitual** action, state, or way of behaving is one that someone usually does or has, especially one that is considered to be typical or characteristic of them. *He soon recovered his habitual geniality.* ♦ **ha·bitu·al·ly** *His mother had a patient who habitually flew into rages.* **2** You use **habitual** to describe someone who usually or often does a particular thing. *Three out of four of them would become habitual criminals if actually sent to jail.*

ADJ

ADV

ADJ: ADJ n

ha·bitué /hə'bɪtʃueɪ/ **habitués.** Someone who is a **habitué** of a particular place often visits that place.

N-COUNT

FORMAL

hack /hæk/ **hacks, hacking, hacked. 1** If you **hack** something or **hack** at it, you cut it with strong, rough strokes using a sharp tool such as an axe or knife. *Some were hacked to death with machetes... Matthew desperately hacked through the leather.*
▶ **Hack away** means the same as **hack.** *He started to hack away at the tree bark.* **2** If you **hack** your way through something such as a jungle or wood, you clear a path through it by cutting and chopping trees, bushes, or anything else that is in your way. *We undertook the task of hacking our way through the jungle.*

VERB: V n

be V-ed

prep/adj

V prep

PHRASAL VB

V P at n

VERB

V way prep/

adv

3 If you refer to a professional writer such as a jour-nalist as a **hack**, you disapprove of them because they write for money without worrying very much about the quality of their writing. **4** If you refer to a politician as a **hack**, you disapprove of them because they have gained power by being loyal and obedient to their party and not because they are particularly talented or popular. *Far too many party hacks from the old days still hold influential jobs.*

N-COUNT

PRAGMATICS

N-COUNT

PRAGMATICS

5 When someone **hacks into** a computer system, they break into the system, especially in order to get secret or confidential information that is stored there. ♦ **hack·er** /'hækə/ **hackers** *Once inside their sys-tems, the hackers could steal information or indulge in sabotage.* ♦ **hack·ing** ...*the common and often illegal art of computer hacking.*

VERB:

V into n

N-COUNT

N-UNCOUNT

6 If you **hack** or **go hacking**, you go for a ride on horseback. *The children could be seen hacking across the hillside on their ponies.* ▶ A **hack** is a ride on horseback. ♦ **hacking** *Hacking is a major activity in the horse world.* **7** A **hack** is a horse which people can hire from a stable to go out riding.

VERB: V

V prep/adv

BRITISH

N-COUNT

N-UNCOUNT

N-COUNT

8 If you say that someone **can't hack it** or **couldn't hack it**, you mean that they do not or did not have the qualities needed to do a task or cope with a situation. *Smith tries to convince them that he can hack it as a police chief.*

PHRASE

INFORMAL

hack away. See hack 1.

PHRASAL VB

hack off. If you **hack** something **off**, you cut it off with strong, rough strokes using a sharp tool such as an axe or knife. *Kim even hacked off her long hair.* PHRASAL VB / V n P / V P noun

hack·les /ˈhækəlz/. If something **raises** your **hackles** or makes your **hackles rise**, it makes you feel angry and hostile. *You could see her hackles rising as she heard him outline his plan.* PHRASE

hack·neyed /ˈhæknid/. If you describe something as **hackneyed**, you disapprove of it because it has been used, seen, or heard many times before. *...hackneyed postcard snaps of lochs and glens.* ADJ-GRADED PRAGMATICS

hack·saw /ˈhæksɔː/ **hacksaws.** A **hacksaw** is a small saw used for cutting metal. N-COUNT

had. The auxiliary verb is pronounced /həd, STRONG hæd/. For the main verb, and for the meanings 2 to 5, the pronunciation is /hæd/. **1 Had** is the past tense and past participle of **have. 2 Had** is sometimes used instead of 'if' to begin a clause which refers to a situation that might have happened but did not. For example, the clause 'had he been elected' means the same as 'if he had been elected'. *Had I known what the problem was, we could have addressed it.* AUX / AUX n -ed

3 If you **have been had**, someone has tricked you, for example by selling you something at too high a price. **4** If you say that someone **has had it**, you mean they are in very serious trouble or have no hope of succeeding. *He wants actors who can speak Welsh. Obviously I've had it.* **5** If you say that you **have had it**, you mean that you are very tired of something or very annoyed about it, and do not want to continue doing it or it to continue happening. *I've had it. Let's call it a day.* PHRASE INFORMAL / PHRASE INFORMAL / PHRASE INFORMAL

had·dock /ˈhædək/. **haddock** is both the singular and the plural form. **Haddock** are a type of edible sea fish that are found in the North Atlantic. ▶ **Haddock** is this fish eaten as food. N-VAR / N-UNCOUNT

Hades /ˈheɪdiːz/. In Greek mythology, **Hades** was a place under the earth where people's souls went after they had died. N-PROPER

hadn't /ˈhædənt/. In informal English, **had not** is usually said or written as **hadn't.**

haemo·glo·bin /ˌhiːməˈɡləʊbɪn/; spelled **hemoglobin** in American English. **Haemoglobin** is the red substance in blood, which combines with oxygen and carries it around the body. N-UNCOUNT TECHNICAL

haemo·philia /ˌhiːməˈfɪliə/; spelled **hemophilia** in American English. **Haemophilia** is a medical condition in which a person's blood does not clot properly, so that they continue to bleed for a long time if they are injured. ♦ **haemo·phili·ac** /ˌhiːməˈfɪliæk/ **haemophiliacs** *He had been diagnosed as a haemophiliac five years before.* N-UNCOUNT / N-COUNT

haem·or·rhage /ˈhemərɪdʒ/ **haemorrhages, haemorrhaging, haemorrhaged;** spelled **hemorrhage** in American English. **1** If someone is **haemorrhaging**, they are bleeding heavily because of broken blood vessels inside their body. *If this is left untreated, one can actually haemorrhage to death.* ▶ Also a noun. *He had a massive brain haemorrhage and died.* ♦ **haem·or·rhag·ing** *A post mortem showed he died from shock and haemorrhaging.* **2** If a group or place **is haemorrhaging** people or resources, it is rapidly losing them and is becoming weak. *The figures showed that cash was haemorrhaging from the conglomerate.* ▶ Also a noun. *The move would stem the haemorrhage of talent and enterprise from the colony.* VERB: V / V to n / N-VAR / N-UNCOUNT / V-ERG: V n / V from n / N-SING: N of n

haem·or·rhoid /ˈhemərɔɪdz/ **haemorrhoids;** spelled **hemorrhoids** in American English. **Haemorrhoids** are painful swellings that can appear in the veins inside the anus. N-COUNT MEDICAL

hag /hæɡ/ **hags.** If someone refers to a woman as a **hag**, they mean she is ugly, old, and unpleasant. N-COUNT RUDE

hag·gard /ˈhæɡəd/. Someone who looks **haggard** has a tired expression and shadows under their eyes, especially because they are ill or have not had enough sleep. *Nick glanced around at the haggard faces watching him.* ADJ-GRADED

hag·gis /ˈhæɡɪs/ **haggises.** A **haggis** is a large Scottish sausage made from minced sheep's meat contained in the skin from a sheep's stomach. N-VAR

hag·gle /ˈhæɡəl/ **haggles, haggling, haggled.** If you **haggle**, you argue about something before reaching an agreement, especially about the cost of something that you are buying. *The clinic couldn't afford to haggle with us... Meanwhile, as the politicians haggle, the violence worsens... Of course he'll still haggle over the price.* ▶ Also a noun. *She laughed again, enjoying the haggle.* ♦ **hag·gling** *After months of haggling, they recovered only three-quarters of what they had lent.* ◆◇◇◇◇ V with n / V (non-recip) / N-COUNT / N-UNCOUNT

hah /hɑː/. See **ha.**

ha 'ha; also spelled **ha ha ha. 1 Ha ha** or **ha ha ha** is used in writing to represent the sound that people make when they laugh. **2** People sometimes say **'ha ha'** sarcastically, when they are not amused by what you have said, or do not believe it. ◆◇◇◇◇ EXCLAM / EXCLAM

hail /heɪl/ **hails, hailing, hailed. 1** If a person, event, or achievement **is hailed** as important or successful, they are praised publicly. *US magazines hailed her as the greatest rock'n'roll singer in the world.* **2 Hail** consists of small balls of ice that fall like rain from the sky. **3** A **hail of** things, usually small objects, is a large number of them that hit you at the same time and with great force. *The riot police were met with a hail of stones.* **4** If someone or something **hails from** a particular place or background, they come from it. *I hail from Brighton.* **5** If you **hail** someone, you call to them. *Jill saw him and hailed him, waving him over.* **6** If you **hail** a taxi or a cab, you wave at it in order to stop it and ask the driver to take you somewhere. **7 Hail** is used as a word of greeting. *Hail to the new champion Bengali D'Albret.* ◆◆◇◇◇ VERB: be V-ed as n / adj / V n as n / Also be V-ed n / N-UNCOUNT / N-SING: N of n / VERB V from n FORMAL / VERB: V n LITERARY VERB / CONVENTION DATED

hail·stone /ˈheɪlstəʊn/ **hailstones.** Hailstones are small balls of ice that fall like rain from the sky. N-COUNT

hail·storm /ˈheɪlstɔːm/ **hailstorms;** also spelled **hail storm.** A **hailstorm** is a storm during which hailstones fall. N-COUNT

hair /heə/ **hairs. 1** Your **hair** is all the fine thread-like material that grows in a mass on your head. See picture headed **human body.** *I wash my hair every night... I get some grey hairs but I pull them out.* ♦ **-haired** /-heəd/. *He was a small, dark-haired man.* **2 Hair** is all the short, fine, thread-like material that grows on different parts of your body. *The majority of men have hair on their chest.* **3 Hair** is the rough, thread-like material that covers the body of an animal such as a dog, or makes up a horse's mane and tail. *...dog hairs on the carpet.* **4 Hairs** are very fine thread-like pieces of material that grow on some insects and plants. ◆◆◆◇ N-VAR / COMB / N-VAR / N-VAR / N-COUNT

5 If you **let** your **hair down**, you relax completely and enjoy yourself. *...the world-famous Oktoberfest, a time when everyone in Munich really lets their hair down.* **6** Something that **makes** your **hair stand on end** shocks or horrifies you. **7** If you say that someone **does not turn a hair**, you mean that they do not show any surprise or shock, especially at something that you would expect to surprise or shock them. *No one seems to turn a hair at the thought of the divorced Princess marrying.* PHRASE / PHRASE / PHRASE

hair·brush /ˈheəbrʌʃ/ **hairbrushes.** A **hairbrush** is a brush that you use to brush your hair. N-COUNT

hair care; also spelled **haircare. Hair care** is all the things people do to keep their hair clean, healthy-looking, and attractive. N-UNCOUNT

hair·cut /ˈheəkʌt/ **haircuts. 1** If you have a **haircut**, someone cuts your hair for you. *I told him to get a haircut.* **2** A **haircut** is the style in which your hair has been cut. *Who's that guy with the funny haircut?* ◆◇◇◇◇ N-COUNT / N-COUNT

hair·do /ˈheəduː/ **hairdos.** A **hairdo** is the style in which your hair has been cut and arranged. *...a teenager with a punk hairdo.* N-COUNT INFORMAL

hair·dresser /'heədresə/ **hairdressers.** A hair-dresser is a person who cuts, colours, and arranges people's hair. You can also refer to the shop where a hairdresser works as a **hairdresser** or a **hair-dresser's.** ♦ **hair·dressing** ...personal services such as hairdressing. N-COUNT N-UNCOUNT

hair·dryer /'heədraɪə/ **hairdryers;** also spelled **hairdrier.** A **hairdryer** is a machine that you use to dry your hair. N-COUNT

hair·grip /'heəgrɪp/ **hairgrips;** also spelled **hair-grip.** A **hairgrip** is a small piece of metal or plastic bent back on itself, which someone uses to hold their hair in position. N-COUNT BRITISH

hair·less /'heələs/. A part of your body that is **hair-less** has no hair on it. ADJ

hair·line /'heəlaɪn/ **hairlines. 1** Your **hairline** is the edge of the area where your hair grows on your head. Joanne had a small dark birthmark near her hairline. **2** A **hairline** crack or fracture is very narrow or fine. N-COUNT ADJ: ADJ n

hair·net /'heənet/ **hairnets.** A **hairnet** is a small net that some women wear over their hair in order to keep it tidy. N-COUNT

hair·piece /'heəpiːs/ **hairpieces.** A **hairpiece** is a piece of false hair that some people wear on their head if they are bald or if they want to make their own hair seem longer or thicker. N-COUNT

hair·pin /'heəpɪn/ **hairpins. 1** A **hairpin** is a small piece of metal or plastic bent back on itself which someone uses to hold their hair in position. **2** A **hairpin** is the same as a **hairpin bend.** N-COUNT N-COUNT

hairpin 'bend, hairpin bends. A **hairpin bend** or a **hairpin** is a very sharp bend in a road, where the road turns back in the opposite direction. N-COUNT

'hair-raising. A **hair-raising** experience, event, or story is very frightening but can also be exciting. ...hair-raising rides at funfairs. ADJ-GRADED

'hair's breadth. A **hair's breadth** is a very small degree or amount. The dollar fell to within a hair's breadth of its all-time low. N-SING: a N

hair 'shirt, hair shirts. If you say that someone is wearing a **hair shirt**, you mean that they are trying to punish themselves to show they are sorry for something they have done. No one is asking you to put on a hair shirt and give up all your luxuries. N-COUNT

hair·spray /'heəspreɪ/ **hairsprays. Hairspray** is a sticky substance that you spray out of a can onto your hair in order to hold it in place. N-VAR

hair·style /'heəstaɪl/ **hairstyles.** Your **hairstyle** is the style in which your hair has been cut or arranged. I think her new short hairstyle looks simply great. ♦◇◇◇◇ N-COUNT

hair·stylist /'heəstaɪlɪst/ **hairstylists;** also spelled **hair stylist.** A **hairstylist** is someone who cuts and arranges people's hair, especially in order to get them ready for a photograph or film. N-COUNT

'hair-trigger. If you describe something as **hair-trigger**, you mean that it is likely to change very violently and suddenly. His hair-trigger temper has often led him into ugly nightclub brawls. ADJ: ADJ n

hairy /'heəri/ **hairier, hairiest. 1** Someone or something that is **hairy** is covered with a lot of hair. **2** If you describe a situation as **hairy**, you mean that it is exciting, worrying, and rather frightening. His driving was a bit hairy. ♦◇◇◇◇ ADJ-GRADED ADJ-GRADED INFORMAL

hake /heɪk/; **hake** is both the singular and the plural form. A **hake** is a big fish similar to a cod. ▸ **Hake** is this fish eaten as food. N-VAR N-UNCOUNT

hal·cy·on /'hælsɪən/. A **halcyon** time is a time in the past that was peaceful or happy. ...those halcyon days in 1990, when he won three tournaments. ♦◇◇◇◇ ADJ: ADJ n LITERARY

hale /heɪl/. If you describe people, especially people who are old, as **hale**, you mean that they are healthy. Victims tend to look hale and hearty in the early days of their disease. ♦◇◇◇◇ ADJ-GRADED DATED

half /hɑːf, AM hæf/ **halves** /hɑːvz, AM hævz/. **1** Half of an amount or object is one of two equal parts that together make up the whole number, amount, or object. More than half of all households report incomes above £35,000... Cut the tomatoes in ♦♦♦♦♦ FRACTION

half vertically... The bridge was re-built in two halves. ▸ Also a predeterminer. They had only received half the money promised... She's half his age. ▸ Also an adjective. ...a half measure of fresh lemon juice... Steve barely said a handful of words during the first half hour. **2** In games such as football and rugby, matches are divided into two equal periods of time which are called **halves**. The only goal was scored by Jakobsen early in the second half. **3** A **half** is half a pint of a drink such as beer or cider. ...a half of lager. PREDET ADJ: ADJ n N-COUNT N-COUNT BRITISH

4 You use **half** to say that something is only partly the case or happens to only a limited extent. His refrigerator frequently looked half empty... She'd half expected him to withdraw from the course. **5** You use **half** to say that someone has parents of different nationalities. For example, if you are **half** German, one of your parents is German. ADV: ADV adj, ADV before v ADV: ADV adj

6 You use **half past** to refer to a time that is thirty minutes after a particular hour. The whistle used to go at half past twelve for lunch... I think I got there about four and left about half past. **7 Half** means the same as **half past**. They are supposed to be here at about half four. PHR-PREP PREP INFORMAL

8 You can use the word **half** before an adjective describing an extreme quality, as a way of emphasizing and exaggerating something. He felt half dead with tiredness. ▸ **Half** can also be used in this way with a noun referring to a long period of time or a large quantity. I thought about you half the night... One phone call and half the city's police force will be around to arrest you. **9 Half** is sometimes used in negative statements, with an affirmative meaning, to emphasize a particular fact or quality. For example, if you say **'he isn't half lucky'**, you mean that he is very lucky. I didn't half get into trouble... 'There'd been a tremendous amount of poverty around and presumably this made some impact then.'—'Oh not half.' ADV: ADV adj PRAGMATICS INFORMAL PREDET ADV: with neg PRAGMATICS INFORMAL, BRITISH

10 You use **not half** to emphasize a negative quality that you think someone has. You're not half the man you think you are. ADV: with neg, ADV n, ADV as/so adj

11 If you talk about your **better half** or your **other half** you mean your husband, your wife, or the person of the opposite sex that you live with. My career, my children and my other half might become too much to cope with. **12** If you increase something **by half**, half of the original amount is added to it. If you decrease it **by half**, half of the original amount is taken away from it. The number of 7 year olds who read poorly has increased by half over the past 5 years. **13** If you say that someone never **does things by halves**, you mean that they always do things very thoroughly. Jimmy never did anything by halves. His cruise was planned like a polar expedition. **14** ● **half the battle**: see battle. PHRASE INFORMAL PHRASE PHRASE

,half-'baked. If you describe an idea, opinion, or plan as **half-baked**, you mean that it has not been properly thought out, and so is stupid or impractical. This is another half-baked scheme that isn't going to work. ADJ-GRADED

half 'board; also spelled **half-board**. If you stay at a hotel and have **half board**, you have your breakfast and evening meal at the hotel, but not your lunch. N-UNCOUNT BRITISH

'half-brother, half-brothers. Someone's **half-brother** is a boy or man who has either the same mother or the same father as they have. ♦◇◇◇◇ N-COUNT

'half-caste, half-castes. Someone who is **half-caste** has parents who come from different races. Some people find this word offensive and use the term 'mixed race' instead. He has two half-caste children. ▸ A **half-caste** is someone who is half-caste. ADJ N-COUNT

,half-'day, half-days; also spelled **half day**. A **half-day** is a day when you work only in the morning or in the afternoon, but not all day. ♦◇◇◇◇ N-COUNT

,half-'hearted. If someone does something in a **half-hearted** way, they do it without any real effort, interest, or enthusiasm. ...a half-hearted apology... In truth, her application was a bit half-hearted. ♦◇◇◇◇ ADJ-GRADED

♦ half-heartedly *I can't do anything half-heartedly. I have to do everything 100 per cent.* `ADV-GRADED: ADV with v`

'half-life, half-lives; also spelled **half life.** The **half-life** of a radioactive substance is the amount of time that it takes to lose half its radioactivity. `N-COUNT`

,half-'mast. If a flag is flying **at half-mast**, it is flying from the middle of the pole, not the top, as a sign of mourning for someone who has died. `PHRASE`

,half 'measure, half measures; also spelled **half-measure.** If someone refers to policies or actions as **half measures**, they are critical of them because they think that they are not forceful enough and are therefore of little value. *They have already declared their intention to fight on rather than settle for half-measures.* `N-COUNT` `PRAGMATICS`

half-'penny /ˈheɪpni/ **halfpennies** or **halfpence** /ˈheɪpəns/. A **halfpenny** was a small British coin which was worth one half of a penny. `N-COUNT`

,half-'price. If something is **half-price**, it costs only half what it usually costs. *Main courses are half price from 12.30pm to 2pm... We can get in half-price.* ► Also a noun. *By yesterday she was selling off stock at half price.* `♦◇◇◇◇ ADJ: v-link ADJ, ADJ after v N-UNCOUNT`

'half-sister, half-sisters. Someone's **half-sister** is a girl or woman who has either the same mother or the same father as they have. `N-COUNT`

,half-'term, half-terms; also spelled **half term.** In Britain, **half-term** is a short holiday in the middle of a school term. *...the half-term holidays.* `N-VAR`

,half-'timbered. Half-timbered is used to describe old buildings that have wooden beams showing in the brick and plaster walls. `ADJ`

,half-'time; also spelled **half time. Half-time** is the short rest period between the two parts of a sporting event such as a football match. `♦♦◇◇◇ N-UNCOUNT`

'half-truth, half-truths; also spelled **half truth.** If you describe statements as **half-truths**, you mean that they are only partly based on fact and are intended or likely to deceive people. *The letter had been full of errors and half truths that he felt slandered him.* `N-COUNT`

half-way /ˌhɑːfˈweɪ, AM ˌhæf-/; also spelled **halfway. 1 Halfway** means in the middle of a place or between two points, at an equal distance from each of them. *Half-way across the car-park, he noticed she was walking with her eyes closed... He was halfway up the ladder.* **2 Halfway** means in the middle of a period of time or of an event. *By then, it was October and we were more than halfway through our tour.* ► Also an adjective. *Welsh international Matthew Postle was third fastest at the halfway point.* **3** If you **meet** someone **halfway**, you accept some of the points they are making so that you can come to an agreement with them. *The Democrats are willing to meet the president halfway.* **4 Halfway** means fairly or reasonably. *You need hard currency to get anything halfway decent.* `♦♦◇◇◇ ADV` `ADV: ADV prep/adv` `ADJ: ADJ n` `PHRASE` `ADV: ADV adj INFORMAL`

,halfway 'house, halfway houses. 1 A **halfway house** is a compromise between two things. *A halfway house between the theatre and cinema is possible. Olivier built one in his imaginative 'Henry V' in 1945.* **2** A **halfway house** is a home for people such as former prisoners, mental patients, or drug addicts who can stay there for a limited period of time to get used to life outside prison or hospital. `N-SING` `N-COUNT`

,half-'witted. If you describe someone as **half-witted**, you think that they are very stupid, silly, or irresponsible. `ADJ-GRADED` `PRAGMATICS` `INFORMAL`

,half-'yearly. 1 Half-yearly means happening in the middle of a calendar year or a financial year. *...the Central Bank's half-yearly report on the state of the economy.* **2** A company's **half-yearly** profits are the profits that it makes in six months. *The company announced a half-yearly profit of just £2 million.* **3 Half-yearly** means happening twice a year, with six months between each event. *The latest half-yearly payment had been due almost two months ago.* `ADJ: ADJ n BRITISH` `ADJ: ADJ n` `ADJ`

hali·but /ˈhælɪbət/; **halibut** is both the singular and the plural form. A **halibut** is a large flat fish. ► **Halibut** is this fish eaten as food. `N-VAR`

hali·to·sis /ˌhælɪˈtəʊsɪs/. If someone has **halitosis**, their breath smells unpleasant. `N-UNCOUNT` `N-UNCOUNT FORMAL`

hall /hɔːl/ **halls. 1** In a house or flat, the **hall** is the area just inside the front door, into which some of the other rooms open. *The lights were on in the hall and in the bedroom.* ● See also **entrance hall. 2** A **hall** is a large room or building which is used for public events such as concerts, exhibitions, and meetings. *Its 300 inhabitants will be celebrating with a dance in the village hall. ...the Royal Albert Hall.* ● See also **city hall, town hall. 3** Students who live in **hall** live in university or college accommodation. **4 Hall** is sometimes used as part of the name of a large house on a country estate. *He died at Holly Hall, his wife's family home.* **5** See also **music hall.** `♦♦♦◇◇ N-COUNT` `N-COUNT` `N-COUNT: also prep N`

hal·le·lu·jah /ˌhælɪˈluːjə/; also spelled **alleluia. 1 Hallelujah** is used in hymns and some other types of religious worship as an exclamation of praise and thanks to God. **2** You can use **hallelujah** as an exclamation of joy when something you have been waiting a long time for finally happens. *Hallelujah! College days are over!* `EXCLAM` `EXCLAM`

hall·mark /ˈhɔːlmɑːk/ **hallmarks. 1** The **hallmark** of something or someone is their most typical quality or feature. *It's a technique that has become the hallmark of Amber Films... The killing had the hallmarks of a professional assassination.* **2** A **hallmark** is an official mark that is put on things made of gold, silver, or platinum that indicates the quality of the metal, where the object was made, and who made it. `♦◇◇◇◇ N-COUNT` `N-COUNT`

hal·lo /hæˈləʊ/. See **hello.**

,hall of 'residence, halls of residence. Halls of residence are blocks of rooms or flats, in which students live during the term. The usual American term is **dormitory.** `N-COUNT BRITISH`

hal·lowed /ˈhæləʊd/. **1 Hallowed** is used to describe something that is respected and admired, usually because it is old, important, or has a good reputation. *The hallowed turf of Twickenham is the venue for the Middlesex Rugby Sevens Finals.* **2 Hallowed** is used to describe something that is considered to be holy. *...hallowed ground.* `ADJ-GRADED: ADJ n` `ADJ-GRADED: ADJ n`

Hal·low·een /ˌhæləʊˈiːn/; also spelled **Hallowe'en. Halloween** is the night of the 31st of October and is traditionally said to be the time when ghosts and witches can be seen. `♦◇◇◇◇ N-UNCOUNT`

hal·lu·ci·nate /həˈluːsɪneɪt/ **hallucinates, hallucinating, hallucinated.** If you **hallucinate**, you see things that are not really there, either because you are ill or because you have taken a drug. *If you stared long enough and hard, you could even begin to hallucinate the appearance of small islands.* ♦ **hal·lu·ci·na·tion** /hə,luːsɪˈneɪʃən/ **hallucinations** *The drug induces hallucinations at high doses.* `VERB: V V n Also V that` `N-VAR`

hal·lu·ci·na·tion /hə,luːsɪˈneɪʃən/ **hallucinations.** A **hallucination** is something that is not real that someone sees because they are ill or have taken a drug. *He thought that perhaps the footprint was a hallucination.* `♦◇◇◇◇ N-COUNT`

hal·lu·ci·na·tory /həˈluːsɪnətri, AM -tɔːri/. **Hallucinatory** is used to describe something that is like a hallucination or is the cause of a hallucination. *It was an unsettling show. There was a hallucinatory feel from the start. ...hallucinatory drugs.* `ADJ`

hal·lu·cino·gen /həˈluːsɪnədʒen/ **hallucinogens.** A **hallucinogen** is a substance such as a drug which makes you hallucinate. ♦ **hal·lu·ci·no·gen·ic** /hə,luːsɪnəˈdʒenɪk/. *...hallucinogenic mushrooms.* `N-COUNT` `ADJ`

hall·way /ˈhɔːlweɪ/ **hallways.** A **hallway** is the entrance hall of a house or other building. `♦◇◇◇◇ N-COUNT`

halo /ˈheɪləʊ/ **haloes** or **halos. 1** A **halo** is a circle of light that is shown in pictures round the head of a holy figure such as a saint. **2** A **halo** is a circle of light round a person or thing, or something that `♦◇◇◇◇ N-COUNT` `N-COUNT`

H

looks like a circle of light. *The sun had a faint halo round it.*

halt /hɔːlt/ **halts, halting, halted. 1** When a vehicle or person **halts** or when something **halts** them, they stop moving along and stand still. *The colonel ordered 'Halt!'... She held her hand out flat, to halt him.* **2** If someone or something comes **to a halt**, they stop moving. *The elevator creaked to a halt at the ground floor.*
◆◆◆◇◇ V-ERG
V n
PHRASE

3 When something such as growth, development, or activity **halts** or when you **halt** it, it stops completely. *He criticised the government for failing to halt economic decline.* **4** If something such as growth, development, or activity comes **to a halt** or is brought **to a halt**, it stops completely. *In the ensuing chaos, agricultural production was brought to a halt.* **5** If someone **calls a halt** to an activity, they decide to end it immediately or not to continue with it. *The Russian government had called a halt to the construction of a new project in the Rostov region.*
V-ERG: V
V n
PHRASE
PHRASE

6 ● **to grind to a halt: see grind.**

hal·ter /ˈhɔːltə/ **halters.** A **halter** is a piece of leather or rope that is fastened round the head of a horse so that it can be led easily.
N-COUNT

halt·ing /ˈhɔːltɪŋ/. If you speak or do something in a **halting** way, you speak or do it slowly and with a lot of hesitation. *The officer replied in halting German... Efforts to attract investment have been halting and confused.* ♦ **halt·ing·ly** *She spoke haltingly of her deep upset and hurt.*
ADJ-GRADED
ADV-GRADED:
ADV with v

halve /hɑːv, AM hæv/ **halves, halving, halved. 1** When you **halve** something or when it **halves**, it is reduced to half its previous size or amount. *The work force has been halved in two years... Meanwhile, sales of vinyl records halved in 1992 to just 6.7m.* **2** If you **halve** something, you divide it into two equal parts. *Halve the pineapple and scoop out the inside.* **3 Halves** is the plural of **half**.
◆◆◇◇◇
V-ERG: V n
be V-ed
V
VERB
V n

ham /hæm/ **hams, hamming, hammed. 1** Ham is meat from the top of the back leg of a pig, usually eaten cold. *...a huge baked ham. ...ham sandwiches.* **2** A **ham** is a person whose hobby is using special radio equipment to communicate with other people with the same hobby. *...a ham radio operator.* **3** A **ham** actor acts badly, exaggerating every emotion and gesture. **4** If actors **ham it up**, they exaggerate every emotion and gesture, often deliberately in order to amuse the audience.
◆◆◇◇◇
N-VAR
N-COUNT
N-COUNT
PHRASE

ham·burg·er /ˈhæmbɜːgə/ **hamburgers.** A **hamburger** is a flat, round piece of cooked minced meat, usually served in a bread roll.
◆◇◇◇◇
N-COUNT

ham-'fisted. If you describe someone as **ham-fisted**, you mean that they are clumsy, especially in the way that they use their hands. *They can all be made in minutes by even the most ham-fisted of cooks.*
ADJ-GRADED

ham·let /ˈhæmlɪt/ **hamlets.** A **hamlet** is a very small village.
◆◇◇◇◇
N-COUNT

ham·mer /ˈhæmə/ **hammers, hammering, hammered. 1** A **hammer** is a tool consisting of a heavy piece of metal at the end of a handle. It is used, for example, to hit nails into a surface, or to break things into pieces. See picture headed **tools.** **2** If you **hammer** an object such as a nail, you hit it with a hammer. *Hammer a wooden peg into the hole... Another bloke would be hammering outside.* ♦ **ham·mer·ing** *...the noise of hammering.* **3** If you say that something goes, comes, or is **under the hammer**, you mean that it is going to be sold at an auction. **4** If you **hammer** on a surface, you hit it several times to make a noise, for example because you are angry or impatient. *He hammered his two clenched fists on the table.* ♦ **hammering** *As he said it, there was a hammering outside.* **5** If you **hammer** something such as an idea into people or you **hammer** at it, you keep repeating it forcefully so that it will have an effect on people. *Recent advertising campaigns from the industry have hammered at these themes.* **6** If you say that someone **hammers** another person,
◆◆◇◇◇
N-COUNT
VERB
V
Also V n
N-UNCOUNT
PHRASE
BRITISH
VERB:
V on n
V n on n
Also V
N-SING
VERB
V n into n
V at n
VERB

you mean that they attack, criticize, or punish the other person severely. *The report hammers the private motorist.* ♦ **hammering** *Parents have taken a terrible hammering.* **7** If you say that businesses **are being hammered**, you mean that they are being unfairly harmed, for example by a change in taxes or by bad economic conditions. *The company has been hammered by the downturn in the construction and motor industries.* **8** In sport, if you say that you **hammered** someone, you mean that you defeated them completely and easily. *He hammered the young left-hander in four straight sets.* ♦ **hammering** *Our cricketers are suffering their ritual hammering at the hands of the Aussies.*
V n
BRITISH
N-SING
V-PASSIVE
be V-ed
BRITISH
VERB
V n
INFORMAL
N-SING

9 In athletics, a **hammer** is a heavy weight on a piece of wire, which the athlete throws as far as possible. ▶ The **hammer** is the sport of throwing the hammer.
N-COUNT
N-SING

hammer in. If you **hammer** something **in**, you hit it into a surface using a hammer. *The workers kneel on the ground and hammer the small stones in.*
PHRASAL VB
V n P
Also V P noun

hammer out. If people **hammer out** an agreement, they succeed in producing it after a long or difficult discussion. *The details of the latest deal were hammered out by the American secretary of state and his Soviet counterpart.*
PHRASAL VB
V P noun
V-ed P
Also V n P

ham·mock /ˈhæmək/ **hammocks.** A **hammock** is a type of bed consisting of a piece of cloth or netting hung between two supports.
N-COUNT

ham·per /ˈhæmpə/ **hampers, hampering, hampered. 1** If someone or something **hampers** you, they make it difficult for you to do what you are trying to do. *I was hampered by a lack of information.* **2** A **hamper** is a large basket with a lid, especially one containing food or used for carrying food. *...a picnic hamper.*
◆◆◇◇◇
VERB: V n
be V-ed
N-COUNT

ham·ster /ˈhæmstə/ **hamsters.** A **hamster** is a small animal similar to a mouse, which is often kept as a pet.
N-COUNT

ham·string /ˈhæmstrɪŋ/ **hamstrings, hamstringing, hamstrung. 1** A **hamstring** is a tendon behind your knee which joins the muscles of your thigh to the bones of your lower leg. *...a hamstring injury.* **2** If you **hamstring** someone, you make it very difficult for them to take any action. *If he becomes the major opposition leader, he could hamstring a conservative-led coalition.*
◆◇◇◇◇
N-COUNT
VERB
V n

hand 1 noun uses and phrases

hand /hænd/ **hands. 1** Your **hands** are the parts of your body at the end of your arms. Each hand has four fingers and a thumb. *I put my hand into my pocket... Sylvia, camera in hand, asked, 'Where do we go first?'* **2** If you do something **by hand**, you do it using your hands rather than a machine. *Each pleat was stitched in place by hand.* **3** If someone is bound **hand and foot**, both their hands and both their feet are tied together. **4** If two people **are hand in hand**, or **are holding hands**, they are holding each other's nearest hand, usually while they are walking or sitting together. People often do this to show their affection for each other. *They held hands during much of the flight.* **5** If you are **on your hands and knees**, you are kneeling down and bending forward so that your knees, feet, and the palms of your hands are all on the ground.
◆◆◆◆◆
N-COUNT
PHRASE
PHRASE
PHRASE
PHRASE

6 If someone **throws up** their **hands**, they express their anger, frustration, or disgust when a situation becomes so bad that they can no longer accept it. *Or are they just going to throw up their hands and say you're asking too much?* **7** If you say that your **hands are tied**, you mean that something is preventing you from acting in the way that you want to do. **8** If you **wash your hands of** someone or something, you refuse to be involved with them any more or to take responsibility for them. **9** If you **have your hands full** with something, you are very busy because of it. *She had her hands full with new arrivals.* **10** If someone lives **from hand to mouth**, they have hardly enough food or money to live on. You can also refer to a **hand-to-mouth** existence. *They accepted what terms they*
PHRASE
PHRASE
PHRASE
PHRASE
PHRASE

could get, and lived from hand to mouth by casual
work.
11 If you ask someone for **a hand** with something, N-SING:
you are asking them to help you in what you are do- aN
ing. *I could see you'd want a hand with the children...
Come and give me a hand in the garden... I'd be glad to
lend a hand.* **12** A **hand** is an employee who does hard N-COUNT
physical work, for example in a factory or on a farm.
He met mill hands, miners and farm labourers. **13** If N-SING:
someone asks an audience to give someone **a hand**, aN
they are asking the audience to clap, usually before or
after that person performs. *Let's give 'em a big hand.*
14 If a man asks for a woman's **hand**, he asks her or N-COUNT
her parents for permission to marry her. *He came to* DATED
ask Usha's father for her hand in marriage. **15** Your N-SING
hand is the style in which you write with a pen or pen- LITERARY
cil. *The manuscripts were written in the composer's
own hand.*
16 If you are playing cards, your **hand** is the set of N-COUNT
cards which are dealt to you, or which you hold at a
particular time during the game. *He carefully inspect-
ed his hand.* **17** If you **show** your **hand**, you show how PHRASE
much power you have and the way you intend to act.
*Events in Russia are now forcing Mr Clinton to show
his hand.* **18** If you **win hands down**, you win very PHRASE
easily.
19 The **hands** of a clock or watch are the thin pieces of N-COUNT
metal or plastic that indicate what time it is.
20 A **hand** is a measurement of four inches, used for N-COUNT
measuring the height of a horse.
21 The **hand** of someone or something is their influ- N-SING:
ence in an event or situation. *He thanked all who had* with poss
*a hand in his release... The study will strengthen the
hand of congressmen who want stricter enforcement of
the 14-year-old Act.* **22** If you **force** someone's **hand**, PHRASE
you force them to act sooner than they want to, or to
act in public when they would prefer to keep their actions secret. **23** If someone gives you **a free hand**, PHRASE
they allow you to do what you want in a particular
situation. **24** If someone such as the ruler of a country PHRASE
treats people with a **heavy hand**, they are very strict
and severe with them. *Henry and Richard both ruled
with a heavy hand.*
25 If you say that something is in a particular person's N-PLURAL
hands, you mean that they own it, control it, or are responsible for it. *The government imposed a blockade
of the island, which is in the hands of secessionist rebels... We're in safe hands.* **26** If someone experiences PHR-PREP
a particular kind of treatment, especially unpleasant
treatment, **at the hands of** a person or organization,
they receive it from them. *Too many East Germans
suffered at the hands of the Stasi.* **27** If you have a PHRASE
problem or responsibility **on** your **hands**, you have to
deal with it. If it is **off** your **hands**, you no longer have
to deal with it. *She would like the worry of dealing with
her affairs taken off her hands.* **28** If you **play into** an PHRASE
enemy's or opponent's **hands**, you do something JOURNALISM
which they will be able to take advantage of. *He is
playing into the hands of racists.*
29 When something **changes hands**, its ownership PHRASE
changes, usually because it is sold to someone else.
30 If you **get** your **hands on** something or **lay** your PHRASE
hands on something, you manage to find it or obtain INFORMAL
it, often after some difficulty. *Patty began reading
everything she could get her hands on.* **31** If you tell PHRASE
someone to **keep** or **take** their **hands off** something or PRAGMATICS
someone, you are telling them in a rather aggressive
way not to touch it or interfere with it. *Keep your
hands off my milk.*
32 If you do something to **keep** your **hand in**, you PHRASE
practise a skill or hobby occasionally in order to re- INFORMAL
main fairly good at it. **33** If you **try** your **hand** at an ac- PHRASE
tivity, you attempt to do it, usually for the first time.
*He tried his hand at a variety of jobs – bricklayer, cine-
ma usher, coal man.* **34** If you **turn** your **hand to** PHRASE
something such as a practical activity, you learn
about it and do it for the first time. *...a person who can
turn his hand to anything.*
35 If you work **hand in glove** with someone, you work PHRASE
very closely with them. **36** If two things go **hand in** PHRASE

hand, they are closely connected and cannot be considered separately from each other. *Hand in hand
with the police inquiries the government has also announced a full investigation.*
37 If a situation is **in hand**, it is under control. *The* PHRASE
Olympic organisers say that matters are well in hand.
38 If you **take** someone **in hand**, you take control or PHRASE
responsibility over them, especially in order to improve them. *If somebody doesn't take her in hand she's
going to make herself sick.* **39** If a person or a situation PHRASE
gets **out of hand**, you are no longer able to control
them. *His drinking had got out of hand.*
40 If something is **at hand**, **near at hand**, or **close at** PHRASE
hand, it is very near in place or time. *Realizing that his
retirement was near at hand, he looked for some additional income.* **41** If you have something **to hand** or PHRASE
near to hand, you have it with you or near you, ready
to use when needed. *You may want to keep this brochure safe, so you have it to hand whenever you may
need it.* **42** If someone or something is **on hand**, they PHRASE
are near and able to be used if they are needed. *The
Bridal Department will have experts on hand to give
you all the help and advice you need.*
43 In a competition, if someone has games **in hand**, PHRASE
they have more games left to play than their opponent BRITISH
and therefore have a chance of scoring more points.
*Wales are three points behind Romania in the group
but have a game in hand.* **44** If you have an amount of PHRASE
something **in hand**, you have more of it than you BRITISH
need. *Even with capital in hand they may not want to
be lenders.* **45** The job or problem **in hand** is the job or PHRASE
problem that you are dealing with at the moment.
46 If you dismiss or reject an idea **out of hand**, you re- PHRASE
ject it fully and immediately without any thought of
changing your mind. **47** You use **on the other hand** to PHRASE
introduce the second of two contrasting points, facts, PRAGMATICS
or ways of looking at something. You can use **on the
one hand** in an earlier sentence to introduce the first
part of the contrast. *On the one hand, if the body
doesn't have enough cholesterol, we would not be able
to survive. On the other hand, if the body has too much
cholesterol, the excess begins to line the arteries.*
48 • with one's **bare hands**: see **bare. •** to **bite the
hand that feeds** you: see **bite. •** to **have** someone eating out of your **hand**: see **eat. •** to **shake** someone's
hand: see **shake. •** to **shake hands**: see **shake**.

hand 2 verb uses

hand /hænd/ **hands, handing, handed. 1** If you ◆◆◆◆◇
hand something to someone, you pass it to them. VERB
He handed me a little rectangle of white paper... He V n n
took a thick envelope from an inside pocket and V n to n
handed it to me. **2** You say things such as **You have** PHRASE
to hand it to her or **You've got to hand it to them** INFORMAL
when you admire someone for their skills or
achievements and you think they deserve a lot of
praise.
hand around. See **hand round**. PHRASAL VB
hand back. If you **hand back** something that you PHRASAL VB
have borrowed or taken from someone, you return it V P noun
to them. *He took a saxophone from the Salvation Army* V n P
but was caught and had to hand it back... He handed V n P noun
the book back to her... He unlocked her door and hand- Also V P n to n
ed her back the key.
hand down. 1 If you **hand down** something such as PHRASAL VB
your knowledge or possessions, you give or leave V P noun
them to people of a younger generation. *...a Ukrain-* V-ed P
ian folk heritage handed down from their parents. Also V n P
2 When a particular decision **is handed down** by be V-ed P
someone in authority, they make the decision and Also V n P
impose it. *Tougher sentences are being handed down...
She is expected soon to hand down a ruling.*
hand in. If you **hand** something **in**, you give it to PHRASAL VB
someone in authority, so that they can inspect, con- V n P
sider, or deal with it. *My advice to anyone who finds* V P noun
*anything on a bus is to hand it in to the police... All
eighty opposition members of parliament have handed in their resignation.*
hand on. If you **hand** something **on**, you give it or PHRASAL VB
leave it to someone else, often someone who replaces V P noun
you. *The government is criticised for not handing on* be V-ed P to n
Also V P n to n

information about missing funds... His chauffeur-driven car and company mobile phone will be handed on to his successor.

hand out. If you **hand** something **out**, you give it to a number of people, usually giving each person a share of it. *One of my jobs was to hand out the prizes... Planning permission is handed out sparingly.* ● See also **handout.**
PHRASAL VB
V P noun
Also V n P

hand over. If you **hand** something **over** to someone, you give or transfer it to them, so that they can consider it, deal with it, or take control of it. *He also handed over a letter of apology from the Prime Minister... They would like to hand over their financial affairs to another body.*
PHRASAL VB
V n P to n
V P noun
V P noun to n
Also V n P

hand over to. If you **hand over to** someone, you give them the responsibility for dealing with a particular situation or problem which was previously your responsibility. *The present leaders have to decide whether to stand down and hand over to a younger generation.*
PHRASAL VB
V P P n

hand round or **hand around.** If you **hand round** something such as food, you pass it from one person to another in a group. *...the free Jamaican cigars that were always handed around at official functions.*
PHRASAL VB
V P noun
V-ed P
Also V n P

hand- /'hænd-/. **Hand-** combines with past participles to indicate that something has been made by someone using their hands or small, simple tools. *...handcrafted jewelry. ...handbuilt cars.*
COMB

hand·bag /'hændbæg/ **handbags.** A **handbag** is a small bag which a woman uses to carry things such as her money and keys when she goes out.
◆◇◇◇◇
N-COUNT

hand·ball /'hændbɔːl/. **1** In Britain and some other countries, **handball** is a team sport in which the players try to score goals by throwing or hitting a large ball with their hand. **2** In the United States and some other countries, **handball** is a sport in which players try to score points by hitting a small ball against a wall with their hand. **3** In football, **handball** is the foul of touching the ball with your hand. *He got sent off for deliberate handball.*
N-UNCOUNT
N-UNCOUNT
N-UNCOUNT:
also a N

hand·bill /'hændbɪl/ **handbills.** A **handbill** is a small printed notice which is used to advertise a company, service, or event.
N-COUNT

hand·book /'hændbʊk/. A **handbook** is a book that gives you advice and instructions about a practical subject.
◆◇◇◇◇
N-COUNT

hand·brake /'hændbreɪk/ **handbrakes.** In a car or similar vehicle, the **handbrake** is a brake in the form of a long lever which the driver operates by hand. See picture headed **car and bicycle.**
N-COUNT

hand·cart /'hændkɑːt/ **handcarts;** also spelled **hand-cart.** A **handcart** is a small two-wheeled cart which is pushed or pulled along and is used for transporting goods.
N-COUNT

hand·cuff /'hændkʌf/ **handcuffs, handcuffing, handcuffed. 1** Handcuffs are two metal rings which are joined together and can be locked round someone's wrists, usually by the police during an arrest. *He was led away to jail in handcuffs.* **2** If the police **handcuff** someone, they put handcuffs around that person's wrists.
◆◇◇◇◇
N-PLURAL:
also a pair of N
VERB: V n

-hander /-'hændə/ **-handers. -hander** combines with words like 'two' or 'three' to form nouns which indicate how many characters are involved in a play. *Williams's play is a tense contemporary three-hander about two murderers and a bank-robber.* ● **left-hander:** see **left-handed;** ● **right-hander:** see **right-handed.**
COMB
BRITISH

hand·ful /'hændfʊl/ **handfuls. 1** A **handful** of people or things is a small number of them. *He surveyed the handful of customers at the bar.* **2** A **handful** of something is the amount of it that you can hold in your hand. *She scooped up a handful of sand.* **3** If you say that someone, especially a child, is a **handful**, you mean that they are difficult to control.
◆◆◇◇◇
QUANT
N-COUNT
N-SING
INFORMAL

'hand grenade, hand grenades. A **hand grenade** is the same as a **grenade.**
◆◇◇◇◇
N-COUNT

hand·gun /'hændgʌn/ **handguns;** also spelled **hand gun.** A **handgun** is a gun that you can hold, carry, and fire with one hand.
◆◇◇◇◇
N-COUNT

'hand-held; also spelled **handheld. Hand-held** equipment is small and light enough to be used while you are holding it. *...a hand-held camera.*
◆◇◇◇◇
ADJ

hand·hold /'hændhəʊld/ **handholds.** If you are climbing something such as a rock or a wall, a **handhold** is a small hole that you can put your hand in.
N-COUNT

handi·cap /'hændikæp/ **handicaps, handicapping, handicapped. 1** A **handicap** is a physical or mental disability. *He lost his leg when he was ten, but learnt to overcome his handicap.* **2** If an event or a situation **handicaps** someone or something, it places them at a disadvantage and makes it harder for them to do something. *Greater levels of stress may seriously handicap some students.* ▶ A **handicap** is an event or situation that handicaps you. *She was away from school for 15 weeks, a handicap she could have done without.* **3** An amateur golfer's **handicap** is the number of free strokes they are allowed during a game. As the golfer improves, their handicap gets lower. **4** In horse racing, a **handicap** is a race in which some competitors are given a disadvantage of extra weight in an attempt to give everyone an equal chance of winning.
◆◆◇◇◇
N-COUNT
VERB
V n
N-COUNT
N-COUNT
N-COUNT

handi·capped /'hændikæpt/. Someone who is **handicapped** has a physical or mental disability that prevents them living a totally normal life. *...handicapped kids... Alex was mentally handicapped.* ▶ You can refer to people who are handicapped as **the handicapped.**
◆◆◇◇◇
ADJ-GRADED
N-PLURAL:
the N

handi·crafts /'hændikrɑːft, -kræft/; the form **handicraft** is used as a modifier. **Handicrafts** are activities such as embroidery and pottery which involve making things with your hands in a skilful way. **Handicrafts** are also the objects that are produced by such activities. *Others carried on some small-trading or worked in handicraft centres.*
N-PLURAL

handi·work /'hændiwɜːk/. You can refer to something that you have done or made yourself as your **handiwork.** *The architect stepped back to admire his handiwork... While the government said the fire was accidental, residents of the town alleged it was the handiwork of the security forces.*
N-UNCOUNT

hand·ker·chief /'hæŋkətʃɪf/ **handkerchiefs.** A **handkerchief** is a small square piece of fabric which you use for blowing your nose.
◆◇◇◇◇
N-COUNT

han·dle /'hændəl/ **handles, handling, handled. 1** A **handle** is a small round object or a lever that is attached to a door and is used for opening and closing it. *I turned the handle and went in.* **2** A **handle** is the part of an object such as a tool, bag, or cup that you hold in order to be able to pick up and use the object. *...the handle of a cricket bat. ...a broom handle.* **3** If you have a **handle** on a subject or problem, you have a way of approaching it that helps you to understand it or deal with it. *When you have got a handle on your anxiety you can begin to control it.* **4** When you **handle** something, you use your hands to hold it, use it, or do something with it. *I had never handled an automatic.* **5** If a vehicle **handles** well, it is easy to drive or control. *His ship had handled like a dream!* **6** If you **handle** a particular area of work, you have responsibility for it. *She handled travel arrangements for the press corps during the presidential campaign.* **7** If you talk about the way that someone **handles** a problem or situation, you mean their ability to deal with it, or the methods they use to achieve a successful result. *I think I would handle a meeting with Mr. Siegel very badly... You must learn how to handle your feelings.* ♦ **han·dling** *The family has criticized the military's handling of Robert's death.*
◆◆◆◇
N-COUNT
N-COUNT
N-SING:
a N on n
INFORMAL
VERB
V n
VERB
V adv/prep
VERB
V n
VERB
V n adv
V n
N-UNCOUNT

handle·bar /'hændəlbɑː/ **handlebars.** The **handlebar** or **handlebars** of a bicycle are the metal bar on the front with handles at each end, which you use to steer the bicycle. See picture headed **car and bicycle.**
N-COUNT

handler

han·dler /ˈhændlə/ **handlers.** A handler is someone whose job is to deal with a particular type of object or animal. ...*baggage handlers at Gatwick airport... Fifty officers, including frogmen and dog handlers, are searching for her.* ◆◇◇◇◇ N-COUNT

'hand luggage. If you travel by air, your **hand luggage** is the luggage you have with you in the plane, rather than the luggage that is carried in the hold. N-UNCOUNT

hand·made /ˌhændˈmeɪd/; also spelled **hand-made.** If something is handmade, it is made by someone using their hands or small, simple tools. *The beads they use are handmade in the Jura mountains. ...handmade chocolates.* ◆◇◇◇◇ V-PASSIVE be V-ed V-ed

hand·maiden /ˈhændmeɪdən/ **handmaidens.** A handmaiden is a female servant. N-COUNT DATED

'hand-me-down, hand-me-downs. Hand-me-downs are clothes which have been used by someone else before you and which have been given to you for your use. ▶ Also an adjective. *Most of the boys wore hand-me-down military shirts from their fathers.* N-COUNT ADJ: ADJ n

hand·out /ˈhændaʊt/ **handouts. 1** A handout is an amount of money, clothing, or food which is given free to someone, for example to poor people. A handout is also the act of giving or distributing such things. *Soldiers oversee the food handouts... Many saw Labour as proposing government handouts for the undeserving.* **2** A handout is a printed document giving information. Copies are given to a group of people or a large number of people. ...*a lecture, complete with colored graphs and handouts.* ◆◇◇◇◇ N-COUNT N-COUNT

hand·over /ˈhændəʊvə/ **handovers.** The handover of something is when possession or control of it is given by one person or group of people to another. ...*a further round of talks in Hong Kong about the handover of the colony to China in 1997.* ◆◇◇◇◇ N-COUNT

hand-'pick, hand-picks, hand-picking, hand-picked; also spelled **handpick.** If someone is hand-picked, they are very carefully chosen by someone in authority for a particular purpose or job. *He was hand-picked for this job by the Admiral. ...his hand-picked successor.* VERB be V-ed V-ed Also V n

hand·rail /ˈhændreɪl/ **handrails.** A handrail is a long piece of metal or wood which is fixed near stairs or places where people could fall. People can hold onto the handrail for support. N-COUNT

hand·set /ˈhændset/ **handsets. 1** The handset of a telephone is the part that you hold next to your face in order to speak and listen. **2** You can refer to a device such as the remote control of a television or stereo as a handset. N-COUNT N-COUNT

hand·shake /ˈhændʃeɪk/ **handshakes.** If you give someone a handshake, you take their right hand with your own right hand and hold it firmly or move it up and down, as a sign of greeting or agreement. *John smiled and gave him a hearty handshake.* ● See also golden handshake. ◆◇◇◇◇ N-COUNT

hand·some /ˈhænsəm/. **1** A handsome man has an attractive face. ...*a tall, dark, handsome sheep farmer.* **2** A handsome woman is rather large, and has an attractive, striking appearance. **3** A handsome building or garden is large and well made with an attractive appearance. ...*the ports of Dubrovnik and Zadar, with their handsome Renaissance buildings.* **4** A handsome sum of money is a large or generous amount. *They will make a handsome profit on the property.* ◆ **hand·some·ly** *He was rewarded handsomely for his efforts.* **5** If someone has a handsome win, they achieve it by a large margin. *The opposition won a handsome victory in the election.* ◆ **handsomely** *The car ran perfectly to the finish, and we won handsomely.* ◆◆◇◇◇ ADJ-GRADED ADJ-GRADED ADJ-GRADED ADJ-GRADED: ADJ n ADV-GRADED ADJ: ADJ n ADV

,hands-'on. Hands-on experience or work involves actually doing a particular thing, rather than just talking about it or getting someone else to do it. *Ninety-nine per cent of primary pupils now have hands-on experience of computers.* ◆◇◇◇◇ ADJ-GRADED

hand·stand /ˈhændstænd/ **handstands.** If you do a handstand, you balance yourself upside down on your hands with your body and legs straight up in the air. N-COUNT

,hand-to-'hand; also spelled **hand to hand.** In hand-to-hand fighting, the people are very close together, using either their hands or weapons such as knives. *There was, reportedly, hand-to-hand combat in the streets.* ADJ: ADJ n

,hand-to-'mouth; also spelled **hand to mouth.** See hand. ADJ

'hand tool, hand tools. Hand tools are fairly simple tools which you use with your hands, and which are usually not powered. N-COUNT

hand·writing /ˈhændraɪtɪŋ/. Your handwriting is your style of writing with a pen or pencil. *The address was in Anna's handwriting.* ◆◇◇◇◇ N-UNCOUNT

hand·written /ˌhændˈrɪtən/. A handwritten piece of writing was written with a pen or pencil, rather than being typed. ◆◇◇◇◇ ADJ

handy /ˈhændi/ **handier, handiest. 1** Something that is handy is useful. *The book gives handy hints on looking after indoor plants.* ● If something comes in handy, it is useful in a particular situation. *The $20 check came in very handy.* **2** A thing or place that is handy is nearby and convenient. *It would be good to have a pencil and paper handy... The hotel is handy for West End stores.* **3** Someone who is handy with a particular tool is skilful at using it. *If you're handy with a needle you could brighten up your sweater with giant daisies.* ◆◆◇◇◇ ADJ-GRADED PHRASE ADJ-GRADED ADJ-GRADED: v-link ADJ with n INFORMAL

handy·man /ˈhændimæn/ **handymen.** A handyman is a man who earns money by doing small jobs for people such as making and repairing things in their homes. You can also use handyman to refer to a man who is good at making or repairing things in his own home. N-COUNT

hang /hæŋ/ **hangs, hanging, hung, hanged.** The form hung is used as the past tense and participle. The form hanged is used as the past tense for meaning 6. **1** If something hangs in a high place or position, or if you hang it there, it is attached there so it does not touch the ground. *Notices painted on sheets hang at every entrance... A young woman came out of the house to hang clothes on a line.* ▶ Hang up means the same as hang. *Some of the prisoners climbed onto the roof and hung up a banner.* **2** If something such as a wall is hung with pictures or other objects, they are attached to it. ...*a line of wall hooks hung with old anoraks.* **3** If a piece of clothing or fabric hangs in a particular way or position, that is how it is worn or arranged. ...*a ragged fur coat that hung down to her calves. ...the shawl hanging loose from her shoulders.* **4** If something hangs loose or hangs open, it is partly fixed in position, even in such a way that it moves freely. *She froze, her mouth hanging open.* **5** If something such as someone's breath or smoke hangs in the air, it remains there without appearing to move or change position. *A haze of expensive perfume hangs around her.* **6** If someone is hanged, they are killed, usually as a punishment, by having a rope tied around their neck and the support taken away from under their feet. *She was hanged last month after being found guilty of spying... He hanged himself two hours after arriving at a mental hospital.* ◆ **hang·ing, hangings** ...*a hanging in New Orleans.* **7** If a possibility hangs over you, it worries you because you think it might happen. *The threat of unemployment hangs over thousands of researchers.* **8** See also hanging, hung. **9** If you get the hang of something such as a skill or activity, you begin to understand or realize how to do it. **10** If you tell someone to hang in there or to hang on in there, you are encouraging them to keep trying to do something and not to give up even though it might be difficult. **11** If you let it all hang out, you relax completely and enjoy yourself without worrying about hiding your emotions or behaving politely. ◆◆◆◇ V-ERG V prep/adv V n prep/adv V PHRASAL VB ERG: V P V P noun VERB: be V-ed with n V-ed VERB V adv/prep V adj VERB V adj VERB V prep/adv V-ERG be V-ed V pron-refl Also V, V n N-VAR VERB V over n PHRASE INFORMAL PHRASE PRAGMATICS INFORMAL PHRASE INFORMAL

12 • to **hang by a thread**: see **thread**. • to **hang on** someone's **every word**: see **word**.

hang around or **hang round;** the form **hang about** is also used in British English. **1** If you **hang around**, **hang about**, or **hang round**, you stay in the same place doing nothing, usually because you are waiting for something or someone. *He got sick of hanging around waiting for me. ...those people hanging round the streets at 6 am with nowhere to go.* **2** If you **hang around**, **hang about**, or **hang round** with someone or in a particular place, you spend a lot of time with that person or in that place. *They usually hung around together most of the time... Helen used to hang round with the boys.*
PHRASAL VB
V P
V P -ing
V P n
INFORMAL

V P together
V P with n
Also V P n
INFORMAL

hang back. 1 If you **hang back**, you move or stay slightly behind a person or group, usually because you are nervous about something. **2** If a person or organization **hangs back**, they do not do something immediately. *Even his closest advisers believe he should hang back no longer.*
PHRASAL VB
V P

V P

hang on. 1 If you ask someone to **hang on**, you ask them to wait or stop what they are doing or saying for a moment. *Hang on a sec. I'll come with you.* **2** If you **hang on**, you manage to survive, achieve success, or avoid failure in spite of great difficulties or opposition. *Manchester United hung on to take the Cup.* **3** If you **hang on** to or **hang onto** something that gives you an advantage, you succeed in keeping it for yourself. *The President has been trying hard to hang onto power.* **4** If you **hang on** to or **hang onto** something, you hold it very tightly. *....a flight stewardess who helped save the life of a pilot by hanging onto his legs.* **5** If you **hang on** to or **hang onto** something, you keep it for a longer time than you would normally expect. *In the present climate, owners are hanging on to old ships.* **6** If one thing **hangs on** another, it depends on it in order to be successful. *The survival of the sport hangs on this race.*
PHRASAL VB
PRAGMATICS
V P
INFORMAL
V P

V P n

V P n
Also V P

V P n
to or
INFORMAL

V P n

hang out. 1 If you **hang out** clothes that you have washed, you hang them on a clothes line to dry. *I was worried I wouldn't be able to hang my washing out.* **2** If you **hang out** in a particular place or area, you go and stay there for no particular reason, or spend a lot of time there. *We can just hang out and have a good time.* • See also **hangout**.
PHRASAL VB
V n P
Also V P noun
V P adv/prep
INFORMAL

hang round. See **hang around**.
PHRASAL VB

hang together. 1 If two people or groups **hang together**, they stay with each other and support each other even though they may disagree on some things. **2** If things such as ideas or the parts of something **hang together**, they are properly organized and fit together reasonably. *Her ideas don't always hang together very well as a plot.*
PHRASAL VB
V P

V P

hang up. 1 See **hang** 1. **2** If you **hang up** or you **hang up** the phone, you end a phone call and put back the receiver. If you **hang up** on someone you are speaking to on the phone, you end the phone call suddenly and unexpectedly by putting back the receiver. *Don't hang up!... He said he'd call again, and hung up on me.* **3** You can use **hang up** to indicate that someone stops doing a particular sport or activity that they have regularly done over a long period. For example, when a footballer **hangs up** his boots, he stops playing football. **4** See also **hang-up, hung up**.
PHRASAL VB
V P noun
V P
V P on n

V P noun

hang·ar /'hæŋə/ **hangars.** A **hangar** is a large building in which aircraft are kept.
◆◇◇◇◇
N-COUNT

hang·dog /'hæŋdɒg, AM -dɔːg/; also spelled **hang-dog.** If you say that someone has a **hangdog** expression on their face, you mean that they look sad, and often guilty or ashamed.
ADJ-GRADED

hang·er /'hæŋə/ **hangers.** A **hanger** is the same as a **coat hanger**.
◆◇◇◇◇
N-COUNT

hanger-'on, hangers-on. If you describe someone as a **hanger-on**, you are critical of them because they are trying to be friendly with a richer or more important person, especially in order to gain an advantage for themselves.
N-COUNT
PRAGMATICS

'hang-glider, hang-gliders; also spelled **hang glider. 1** A **hang-glider** is a glider for one person,
N-COUNT

with which they can fly in the air. It consists of a large piece of cloth over a frame which you hang from in a harness. **2** A **hang glider** is a person who flies using a hang-glider.
N-COUNT

'hang-gliding. **Hang-gliding** is the activity of flying in a hang-glider.
N-UNCOUNT

hang·ing /'hæŋɪŋ/ **hangings. 1** A **hanging** is a large piece of cloth that you put as a decoration on a wall. **2** See also **hang** 6.
N-COUNT

hanging 'basket, hanging baskets. A **hanging basket** is a basket with small ropes or chains attached so that it can be hung from a hook. Hanging baskets are usually used for displaying plants or storing fruit and vegetables.
N-COUNT

hang·man /'hæŋmæn/ **hangmen.** A **hangman** is a man whose job is to execute people by hanging them.
N-COUNT

hang·out /'hæŋaʊt/ **hangouts.** If a place is a **hangout** for a particular group of people, they spend a lot of time there because they can relax and meet other people there.
N-COUNT:
with supp
INFORMAL

hang·over /'hæŋəʊvə/ **hangovers. 1** If someone wakes up with a **hangover**, they feel sick and have a headache because they have drunk a lot of alcohol the night before. **2** Something that is a **hangover** from the past is an idea or way of behaving which people used to have in the past but which people no longer generally have. *As a hangover from rationing, they mixed butter and margarine.*
◆◇◇◇◇
N-COUNT

N-COUNT:
with supp

'hang-up, hang-ups. If you have a **hang-up** about something, you have a feeling of fear or embarrassment about it. *I don't have any hang-ups about my body.*
◆◇◇◇◇
N-COUNT
INFORMAL

hank /hæŋk/ **hanks.** A **hank** of wool, rope, or string is a loosely-wound length of it.
N-COUNT

hank·er /'hæŋkə/ **hankers, hankering, hank-ered.** If you **hanker** after something, you want it very much. *I hankered after a floor-length brown suede coat.* ♦ **hank·er·ing, hankerings** *Have you always had a hankering to be an actress?*
VERB
V after/for n
Also V to-inf

N-COUNT

hanky /'hæŋki/ **hankies;** also spelled **hankie.** A **hanky** is the same as a handkerchief.
N-COUNT
INFORMAL

hanky-panky /ˌhæŋki 'pæŋki/. **1** Hanky-panky is used to refer to improper but not very serious sexual activity between two people. **2** If you describe behaviour as **hanky-panky**, you disapprove of it because it involves mischief, trickery, or dishonesty, and often because it is done in secret. *The government has been offering tax credits, accelerated depreciation, and other economic hanky-panky.*
N-UNCOUNT
BRITISH,
INFORMAL
N-UNCOUNT
PRAGMATICS
AMERICAN

han·som /'hænsəm/ **hansoms.** In former times, a **hansom** or a **hansom cab** was a horse-drawn carriage with two wheels and a fixed hood. *They either took the tram from the bottom of the street, or a hansom cab.*
N-COUNT

Ha·nuk·kah /'hɑːnʊkə/; also spelled **Hanukah**. **Ha-nukkah** is a Jewish festival that commemorates the re-dedication of the Temple in Jerusalem in 165 B.C.
N-UNCOUNT

hap·haz·ard /ˌhæp'hæzəd/. If you describe something as **haphazard**, you are critical of it because it is not at all organized or is not arranged according to a plan. *The investigation does seem haphazard.* ♦ **hap·haz·ard·ly** *...books jammed haphazardly in the shelves.*
◆◇◇◇◇
ADJ-GRADED
PRAGMATICS

ADV-GRADED

hap·less /'hæpləs/. A **hapless** person is unlucky; a formal word. *...his hapless victim.*
◆◇◇◇◇
ADJ: ADJ n

hap·pen /'hæpən/ **happens, happening, hap-pened. 1** Something that **happens** occurs or is done without being planned. *The accident happened close to Martha's Vineyard.* **2** If something **happens**, it occurs as a result of a situation or course of action. *She wondered what would happen if her parents found her.* **3** When something, especially something unpleasant, **happens to** you, it takes place and affects you. *If we had been spotted at that point, I don't know what would have happened to us.* **4** If you **happen** to do something, you do it by chance. If it **happens** that something is the case, it occurs by chance. *I looked in the nearest pa-*
◆◆◆◆◆
VERB
V

VERB
V

VERB
V to n

VERB
V to-inf
Also it V that

per, which happened to be the Daily Mail. **5** You use **as it happens** in order to introduce a statement, especially one that is rather surprising. *She called Amy to see if she had any idea of her son's whereabouts. As it happened, Amy had.* — PHRASE · PRAGMATICS

hap·pen·ing /'hæpənɪŋ/ **happenings. 1 Happenings** are things that happen, often in a way that is unexpected or hard to explain. *They plan to hire freelance reporters to cover the latest happenings.* **2** If you describe something or someone as **happening**, you mean that they are exciting or lively, and involved in the newest trends. *...the most happening place at the moment, the Que Club.* — ◆◇◇◇◇ N-COUNT / ADJ-GRADED INFORMAL

hap·pen·stance /'hæpən'stæns/. If you say that something happened by **happenstance**, you mean that it happened because of certain circumstances, although it was not planned. *I came to live at the farm by happenstance.* — N-UNCOUNT: also a N LITERARY

hap·pi·ly /'hæpɪli/. You can add **happily** to a statement to indicate that you are glad that something happened. *Happily, his neck injuries were not serious.* ● See also **happy**. — ◆◇◇◇◇ ADV-GRADED: ADV with cl

hap·py /'hæpi/ **happier, happiest. 1** Someone who is **happy** has feelings of pleasure, usually because something nice has happened or because they feel satisfied with their life. *Marina was a confident, happy child.* ◆ **hap·pi·ly** *Albert leaned back happily.* ◆ **hap·pi·ness** *She was looking for happiness.* **2** A **happy** time, place, or relationship is full of happy feelings and pleasant experiences, or has an atmosphere in which people feel happy. *She had had a particularly happy childhood.* **3** If you are **happy** about a situation or arrangement, you are satisfied with it, for example because you think that something is being done in the right way. *He was really quite happy to let the department run itself.* **4** If you say you are **happy** to do something, you mean that you are very willing to do it. *That's a task I'm happy to take.* ◆ **hap·pi·ly** *I will happily apologise.* **5 Happy** is used in greetings and other conventional expressions to say that you hope someone will enjoy a special occasion. *Happy Birthday!* ● **many happy returns:** see **return**. — ◆◆◇◇◇ ADJ-GRADED / ADV-GRADED / N-UNCOUNT / ADJ-GRADED / ADJ-GRADED: v-link ADJ / ADJ-GRADED: v-link ADJ / ADV-GRADED / ADJ-GRADED: ADJ n

happy-go-'lucky. Someone who is **happy-go-lucky** enjoys life and does not worry at all about the future. — ADJ-GRADED

'happy hour, happy hours. In a pub, **happy hour** is a period when drinks are sold more cheaply than usual. — N-VAR

ha·rangue /hə'ræŋ/ **harangues, haranguing, harangued.** If someone **harangues** you, they try to persuade you in a forceful way to accept their opinions or ideas. *An argument ensued, with various band members joining in and haranguing Simpson and his girlfriend for over two hours.* ▶ A **harangue** is a speech in which someone harangues you. — VERB: V n Also V / N-COUNT

har·ass /'hærəs, hə'ræs/ **harasses, harassing, harassed.** If someone **harasses** you, they trouble or annoy you, for example by attacking you repeatedly or by causing you as many problems as they can. *We are almost routinely harassed by the police.* ◆ **har·ass·ment** *...sexual harassment.* — ◆◆◇◇◇ VERB: V n / N-UNCOUNT

har·assed /'hærəst, hə'ræst/. If you are **harassed**, you are anxious and tense because you have too much to do or too many problems to cope with. — ◆◇◇◇◇ ADJ-GRADED

har·bin·ger /'hɑːbɪndʒə/ **harbingers.** Something that is a **harbinger** of something else is a sign that it is going to happen. *The November air stung my cheeks, a harbinger of winter.* — N-COUNT LITERARY

har·bour /'hɑːbə/ **harbours, harbouring, harboured;** spelled **harbor** in American English. **1** A **harbour** is an area of the sea at the coast which is partly enclosed by land or walls, so that boats can be left there safely. **2** If you **harbour** an emotion, thought, or secret, you have it in your mind over a long period of time. *Townsend harbours no regrets.* **3** If a person or country **harbours** someone who is wanted by the police, they let them stay in their house or country and offer them protection. — ◆◆◆◇◇ N-COUNT / VERB: V n / VERB: V n

har·bour·master /'hɑːbəmɑːstə, -mæs-/ **harbourmasters;** spelled **harbormaster** in American English. A **harbourmaster** is the official in charge of a harbour. — N-COUNT

hard /hɑːd/ **harder, hardest. 1** Something that is **hard** is very firm and stiff to touch and is not easily bent, cut, or broken. *...the hard wooden floor.* ◆ **hard·ness** *...the hardness of the iron railing.* **2** Something that is **hard** is very difficult to do or deal with. *It's hard to tell what effect this latest move will have.* **3** If you **learn** something **the hard way**, you have to make mistakes or face difficulties before you can improve the way that you do things. **4** If someone is **hard put** or **hard pushed** to do something, they have great difficulty doing it. **5** If you say that something is **hard going**, you mean it is difficult and requires a lot of effort. *The talks had been hard going at the start.* **6** If you have a **hard** life or a **hard** period of time, your life or that period is difficult and unpleasant for you. **7** If you work **hard** doing something, you are very active or work intensely, with a lot of effort. *I'll work hard. I don't want to let him down... Am I trying too hard?* ▶ Also an adjective. *I admired him as a true scientist and hard worker.* **8 Hard** work involves a lot of activity and effort. *Their work is hard and unglamorous.* **9** If you look, listen, or think **hard**, you do it carefully and with a great deal of attention. *People are having to think hard about their holiday plans.* ▶ Also an adjective. *...taking a long hard look at your frustrations and resentments.* **10** If you strike or take hold of something **hard**, you strike or take hold of it with a lot of force. *I kicked a dustbin very hard.* ▶ Also an adjective. *He gave her a hard push.* **11** You can use **hard** to indicate that someone does something or something happens intensely and for quite a long time. *I've never seen Terry laugh so hard... It was snowing hard by then.* **12** If a person or their expression is **hard**, they show no kindness or sympathy. *His father was a hard man.* **13** If you are **hard on** someone, you treat them severely or unkindly. *Don't be so hard on him.* ▶ Also an adverb. *He said the security forces would continue to crack down hard on the protestors.* **14** If you say that something is **hard on** a person or thing, you mean it affects them in a way that is likely to cause them damage or suffering. *The grey light was hard on the eyes.* **15** If you feel **hard done by**, you feel that you have not been treated fairly. **16** To be **hard hit** by something means to be affected very severely by it. *California's been particularly hard hit by the recession.* **17** If you **take** something **hard**, you are very upset or depressed by it. **18** If someone **plays hard to get**, they pretend not to be interested in another person or in what someone is trying to persuade them to do. **19** A **hard** winter or a **hard** frost is very cold and severe. **20 Hard** drugs are strong illegal drugs such as heroin or cocaine. **21 Hard** evidence or facts are definitely true and do not need to be questioned. *Yeltsin has no hard information that any American POWs are still alive.* **22 Hard** water contains a lot of lime so that it leaves a whitish coating on kettles. **23** In phonetics, a **hard** sound is one such as 'c' or 'g' as pronounced in the words 'cat' or 'give', and not as in the words 'cinema' or 'gin'. **24** ● to **drive a hard bargain:** see **bargain**. ● to follow **hard on the heels of:** see **heel**. ● a **hard nut to crack:** see **nut**. ● **between a rock and a hard place:** see **rock**. — ◆◆◆◆◆ ADJ-GRADED / N-UNCOUNT / ADJ-GRADED / PHRASE / PHRASE / PHRASE / ADJ-GRADED / ADV-GRADED: ADV after v / ADJ-GRADED / ADJ-GRADED / ADV-GRADED: ADV after v / ADJ-GRADED / ADV-GRADED: ADV after v / ADJ-GRADED / ADJ-GRADED: ADJ n / ADV-GRADED: ADV after v / ADJ-GRADED: v-link ADJ / ADJ-GRADED / ADJ-GRADED: v-link ADJ / ADV-GRADED: v-link ADJ / ADV-GRADED: ADV after v / ADJ-GRADED: v-link ADJ / PHRASE BRITISH / PHRASE / PHRASE / PHRASE / ADJ-GRADED / ADJ: ADJ n / ADJ: ADJ n / ADJ-GRADED / ADJ

hard and 'fast. If you say that there are no **hard and fast** rules, or that there is no **hard and fast** information about something, you mean that there are no fixed or definite rules or facts. *At the moment there's no hard and fast timetable.* — ADJ

hard·back /'hɑːdbæk/ **hardbacks.** A **hardback** is a book which has a stiff hard cover. Compare **paperback** and **softback**. *'The Secret History' was published in hardback last October.* — ◆◇◇◇◇ N-COUNT: also in N

hard-'bitten. If you describe someone as **hardbitten**, you are critical of them because they do not — ADJ-GRADED · PRAGMATICS

show much emotion or have much sympathy for other people, usually because they have experienced many unpleasant things.

hard·board /'hɑːdbɔːd/. Hardboard is a material **N-UNCOUNT** which is made by pressing very small pieces of wood very closely together to form a thin, slightly flexible sheet.

,hard-'boiled; also spelled hard boiled. **1** A hard- ◆◇◇◇◇ boiled egg has been boiled in its shell until the yolk **ADJ** and the white are hard. **2** You use **hard-boiled** to **ADJ-GRADED** describe someone who is tough and does not show much emotion.

,hard 'cash. Hard cash is money in the form of **N-UNCOUNT** notes and coins as opposed to a cheque or a credit card.

,hard 'copy, hard copies. A hard copy of a docu- **N-VAR** ment is a printed version of it, rather than a version that is stored on a computer. ...eight pages of hard copy.

'hard core; also spelled hardcore. **1** You can refer ◆◇◇◇◇ to the members of a group who are the most com- **N-SING** mitted to its activities or who are the most involved in them as a **hard core** of members or as the **hard-core** members. ...a hard-core group of right-wing senators. **2** Hard-core pornography is pornography **ADJ: ADJ n** that shows sex in a very explicit, violent, or unpleasant way. Compare **soft-core**.

,hard 'currency, hard currencies. A hard cur- ◆◇◇◇◇ rency is one which is unlikely to lose its value and **N-VAR** so is considered to be a good one to have or to invest in.

,hard 'disk, hard disks; also spelled hard disc. A **N-COUNT** computer's **hard disk** is a stiff magnetic disk on which data and programs can be stored.

,hard-'drinking. If you describe someone as a **ADJ-GRADED:** hard-drinking person, you mean that they fre- **ADJ n** quently drink large quantities of alcohol.

,hard-'edged. If you describe something such as a **ADJ-GRADED** style, play, or article as **hard-edged**, you mean you **PRAGMATICS** admire it because it is powerful, critical, or unsentimental. ...his fiery, hard-edged acoustic jazz style.

hard·en /'hɑːdən/ hardens, hardening, hard- ◆◆◇◇◇ ened. **1** When something hardens, it becomes stiff **V-ERG: V** or firm. Give the cardboard two or three coats of var- **V n** nish to harden it. **2** When you harden your ideas or **V-ERG: V n** attitudes, they become fixed and you become more **V** determined than ever that you will not change them. The bitter split which has developed within Solidarity is likely to harden further into separation. **♦ hard·en·ing** ...a hardening of the government's **N-SING** attitude. **3** When events harden people, they be- **V-ERG** come less easily affected emotionally and less sym- **V n** pathetic and gentle than they were before. She was **V against n** hardened by the rigours of the Siberian steppes... All of a sudden my heart hardened against her. **4** If you **VERB: V** say that someone's face or eyes harden, you mean that their face or eyes become sterner and more serious, usually because they have become angry about something.

hard·ened /'hɑːdənd/. If you describe someone as **ADJ-GRADED** hardened, you mean that they have had so much experience of something bad or unpleasant that they are no longer affected by it in the way that other people would be. ...hardened criminals.

'hard hat, hard hats. A hard hat is a hat made **N-COUNT** from a hard material, which people wear to protect their heads, for example on building sites.

,hard-'headed. You use hard-headed to describe **ADJ-GRADED** someone who is practical and determined, and who does not allow emotions to affect their actions. ...a hard-headed and shrewd businesswoman.

,hard-'hearted. You describe someone as hard- **ADJ-GRADED** hearted when you disapprove of the fact that they **PRAGMATICS** have no sympathy for other people.

,hard-'hitting. If journalists describe a report or ◆◇◇◇◇ speech as **hard-hitting**, they approve of it because **ADJ-GRADED** it talks about difficult or controversial matters in a bold and direct way. ...a hard-hitting account of violence in the home.

,hard 'labour; spelled hard labor in American Eng- **N-UNCOUNT** lish. **Hard labour** is hard physical work which people have to do as punishment for a crime.

,hard 'left; also spelled hard-left. You use hard left **N-SING:** to describe those members of a left wing political **the N** group or party who have the most extreme beliefs. **BRITISH** ...the hard-left view that foreign forces should not have been sent.

hard·line /,hɑːd'laɪn/; also spelled hard-line. If you ◆◆◇◇◇ describe someone's policy or attitude as **hardline**, **ADJ-GRADED** you mean that it is strict or extreme, and they refuse to change it. ...a hardline Communist state.

hard·liner /,hɑːd'laɪnə/ hardliners. The hard- ◆◆◇◇◇ liners in a group such as a political party are the **N-COUNT** people who support a strict set of ideas that are often extreme, and who refuse to accept any change in them.

,hard 'luck. If someone says that a bad situation **N-UNCOUNT:** affecting you is just your **hard luck**, they do not **poss N** care about it or think you should be helped, often **INFORMAL** because they think it is your fault. The shop assistants didn't really want to discuss the matter, saying it was just my hard luck.

hard·ly /'hɑːdli/. **1** You use hardly to say that ◆◆◆◇ something is only just true. I hardly know you... He **ADV** was given hardly 24 hours to pack his bags. **2** You **ADV ever/any** use **hardly** in expressions such as **hardly ever, hardly any**, and **hardly anyone** to mean almost never, almost none, or almost nobody. We ate chips every night, but hardly ever had fish... Hardly anyone slept that night. **3** You use hardly before a noun group and a verb, fol- **ADV:** lowed by a negative statement in order to emphasize **ADV n** that something is usually the case. For example, if you **PRAGMATICS** say 'hardly a day goes by when I don't eat fruit', you mean that you eat fruit almost every day. **4** When you **ADV:** say you can **hardly** do something, you are emphasiz- **can/could** ing that it is very difficult for you to do it. My garden **ADV inf** was covered with so many butterflies that I could hard- **PRAGMATICS** ly see the flowers. **5** If you say **hardly** had one thing **ADV:** happened when something else happened, you mean **ADV before v** that the first event was followed immediately by the **PRAGMATICS** second. He had hardly collected the papers on his desk when the door burst open. **6** You use **hardly** to mean 'not' when you want to sug- **ADV** gest that you are expecting your listener or reader to **PRAGMATICS** agree with your comment. It's hardly surprising his ideas didn't catch on. **7** You use **'hardly'** to mean 'no', **CONVENTION** especially when you want to express surprise or an- **PRAGMATICS** noyance at a statement that you disagree with. 'They all thought you were marvellous!'—'Well, hardly.'

,hard-'nosed. You use hard-nosed to describe **ADJ-GRADED** someone who is tough and realistic, and who takes **INFORMAL** decisions on practical grounds. ...a hard-nosed government willing to do unpopular things.

,hard of 'hearing. Someone who is hard of hear- **ADJ-GRADED** ing is not able to hear properly.

,hard 'porn. Hard porn is pornography that shows **N-UNCOUNT** sex in a very explicit, violent, or unpleasant way.

,hard-'pressed; also spelled hard pressed. **1** If ◆◇◇◇◇ someone is **hard-pressed**, they are under a great **ADJ-GRADED** deal of strain and worry, usually because they have **JOURNALISM** not got enough money. The region's hard-pressed consumers are spending less on luxuries. **2** If you **ADJ-GRADED:** will be **hard-pressed** to do something, you will have **v-link ADJ to-** great difficulty doing it. This year the airline will be **inf** hard-pressed to make a profit.

,hard 'right; also spelled hard-right. You use hard **N-SING:** right to describe those members of a right wing po- **the N** litical group or party who have the most extreme **BRITISH** beliefs.

,hard 'sell. A hard sell is a method of selling in **N-SING** which the salesperson puts a lot of pressure on someone to make them buy something.

hard·ship /'hɑːdʃɪp/ hardships. Hardship is a ◆◆◇◇◇ situation in which your life is difficult or unpleas- **N-VAR** ant, often because you do not have enough money. Many people are suffering economic hardship.

,hard 'shoulder, hard shoulders. The hard **N-COUNT** shoulder is the area at the side of a motorway **BRITISH**

where you are allowed to stop if your car breaks down.

hard 'up; also spelled **hard-up**. If you are **hard up**, you have very little money. ADJ-GRADED INFORMAL

hard·ware /ˈhɑːdweə/. **1** In computer systems, **hardware** refers to the machines themselves as opposed to the programs: compare **software**. **2** Military **hardware** is the machinery and equipment that is used by the armed forces, such as tanks and missiles. **3 Hardware** refers to tools and equipment that are used in the home and garden, for example saucepans, screwdrivers, and lawnmowers. N-UNCOUNT

'hardware store, hardware stores. A **hardware store** is a shop where articles for the house and garden are sold. The British word is **ironmonger**. N-COUNT AMERICAN

hard-'wearing; also spelled **hard wearing**. Something that is **hard-wearing** is strong and well made so that it lasts for a long time. ...*hard-wearing cotton shirts*. ADJ BRITISH

hard·wood /ˈhɑːdwʊd/ **hardwoods. Hardwood** is wood such as oak and mahogany, which is very strong and hard. ...*hardwood floors*. N-VAR

hard·work·ing /ˌhɑːdˈwɔːkɪŋ/. If you describe someone as **hardworking**, you mean that they work very hard. ADJ-GRADED

har·dy /ˈhɑːdi/ **hardier, hardiest. 1** Plants that are **hardy** are able to survive frost and cold weather. **♦ har·di·ness** ...*the hardiness of other species that have blue flowers*. **2** People and animals that are **hardy** are strong and able to endure difficult conditions. *Hardy antelope wander in from the desert.* **♦ hardiness** *These Pacific oysters are known for their hardiness.* **3** If you describe a group of people as **hardy**, you mean that they have been very patient or loyal, or have been trying hard to do something in difficult conditions. ...*the ten hardy supporters who had made the trek to Dublin.* ADJ-GRADED / N-UNCOUNT / ADJ-GRADED / N-UNCOUNT / ADJ-GRADED

hare /heə/ **hares.** A **hare** is an animal like a rabbit but larger with long ears, long legs, and a small tail. N-VAR

'hare-brained; also spelled **harebrained**. You use **hare-brained** to describe a scheme or theory which you consider to be foolish or unlikely to succeed. ADJ-GRADED PRAGMATICS

har·em /ˌhɑːˈriːm, AM ˈherəm/ **harems. 1** In some Muslim societies, a **harem** was the part of a rich man's house where the women lived. **2** The women who lived in a harem were often referred to as a **harem**. N-COUNT

hari·cot bean /ˈhærɪkəʊ biːn/ **haricot beans.** **Haricot beans** are small white beans that are eaten as a vegetable. N-COUNT

hark /hɑːk/ **harks, harking, harked. 'Hark!'** means 'Listen!'. *Hark. I hear the returning footsteps of my love.* EXCLAM DATED

hark back to. If someone or something **harks back to** an event or situation in the past, they remember it or remind you of it. ...*pitched roofs, which hark back to the Victorian era.* PHRASAL VB VPPn

har·lequin /ˈhɑːlɪkwɪn/. You use **harlequin** to describe something that has a lot of different colours, often in a diamond pattern. ADJ: ADJ n WRITTEN

har·lot /ˈhɑːlət/ **harlots.** If someone describes a woman as a **harlot**, they disapprove of her because she is a prostitute, or because she looks or behaves like a prostitute. N-COUNT PRAGMATICS DATED

harm /hɑːm/ **harms, harming, harmed. 1** To **harm** a person or animal means to cause them physical injury, usually on purpose. *The hijackers seemed anxious not to harm anyone.* **2** To **harm** a thing, or sometimes a person, means to damage them or make them less effective or successful than they were. ...*a warning that the product may harm the environment... Low-priced imports will harm the industry.* **3 Harm** is physical injury or damage which is caused to someone or something. *To cut taxes would probably do the economy more harm than good.* **4** If you say that someone or something **will come to no harm** or that **no harm will come** to them, you mean that they will not be hurt or damaged in any way. *There is always a lifeguard to ensure that no one* VERB V n / VERB V n / N-UNCOUNT / PHRASE

comes to any harm. **5** If you say **it does no harm** to do something or **there is no harm** in doing something, you mean that it might be worth doing, and you will not be blamed for doing it. *They are not always willing to take on untrained workers, but there's no harm in asking.* **6** If you say that something would **do no harm**, or **do someone no harm**, you are recommending a course of action which you think is worthwhile, helpful, or useful. *It would do her no harm to try.* **7** If someone or something is **out of harm's way**, they are in a safe place away from danger. *Workers scrambled to carry priceless objects out of harm's way.* PHRASE / PHRASE PRAGMATICS / PHRASE

harm·ful /ˈhɑːmfʊl/. Something that is **harmful** has a bad effect on something else, especially on a person's health. ...*the harmful effects of smoking.* ADJ-GRADED

harm·less /ˈhɑːmləs/. **1** Something that is **harmless** does not have any bad effects, especially on people's health. *Industry has been working at developing harmless substitutes for these gases.* **♦ harm·less·ly** *Another missile exploded harmlessly outside the town.* **2** If you describe someone or something as **harmless**, you mean that they are not important and therefore unlikely to annoy other people or cause trouble. *He seemed harmless enough. ...a harmless pleasure.* **♦ harmlessly** *It started harmlessly enough.* ADJ-GRADED / ADV: ADV with v ADJ-GRADED / ADJ-GRADED / ADV

har·mon·ic /hɑːˈmɒnɪk/ **harmonics. 1** Harmonic means composed, played, or sung using two or more notes which sound right and pleasing together. ...*harmonic and rhythmic structures.* **2** Harmonics are the higher or lower tones that are not the main tone of a musical note. ADJ / N-COUNT

har·moni·ca /hɑːˈmɒnɪkə/ **harmonicas.** A **harmonica** is a small musical instrument which you play by moving it across your lips and blowing and sucking air through it. See picture headed **musical instruments**. N-COUNT

har·mo·ni·ous /hɑːˈməʊniəs/. **1** A **harmonious** relationship, agreement, or discussion is friendly and peaceful. *Their harmonious relationship resulted in part from their similar goals.* **♦ har·mo·ni·ous·ly** *It is unfortunate when neighbours cannot live harmoniously.* **2** Something that is **harmonious** has parts which go well together and which are in proportion to each other. ...*a harmonious balance of mind, body, and spirit.* **♦ harmoniously** ...*stone paths that blend harmoniously with the scenery.* **3** Musical notes that are **harmonious** produce a pleasant sound when played together. ADJ-GRADED / ADV-GRADED: ADV after v / ADJ-GRADED / ADV-GRADED / ADJ-GRADED

har·mo·nize /ˈhɑːmənaɪz/ **harmonizes, harmonizing, harmonized;** also spelled **harmonise**. In British English. **1** If two or more things **harmonize** with each other, they fit in well with each other. ...*slabs of pink and beige stone that harmonize with the carpet.* **2** When governments or organizations **harmonize** laws, systems, or regulations, they agree in a friendly way to make them the same or similar. *How far will members have progressed towards harmonising their economies?* **♦ har·mo·ni·za·tion** /ˌhɑːmənaɪˈzeɪʃən/ ...*the European harmonisation of their working hours.* **3** When people **harmonize**, they sing or play notes which are different from the main tune but which sound nice with it. V-RECIP V with n Also pl-n V / VERB V n / N-UNCOUNT / VERB: V

har·mo·ny /ˈhɑːməni/ **harmonies. 1** If people are living in **harmony** with each other, they are in a state of peaceful agreement and co-operation. ...*national unity and harmony.* **2 Harmony** is the pleasant combination of different notes of music played at the same time. **3** The **harmony** of something is the way in which its parts are combined into a pleasant arrangement. ...*the ordered harmony of the universe.* N-UNCOUNT / N-VAR / N-UNCOUNT

har·ness /ˈhɑːnɪs/ **harnesses, harnessing, harnessed. 1** If you **harness** something such as an emotion or natural source of energy, you bring it under your control and use it. *Turkey plans to harness the waters of the Tigris and Euphrates rivers.* **2** A **harness** is a set of straps which fit under a person's arms and fasten round their body in order to keep a piece of equipment in place or to prevent VERB V n / N-COUNT

the person moving from a place. **3** A **harness** is a N-COUNT set of leather straps and metal links which are fastened round a horse's head or body so that the horse can have a carriage or fastened to it. **4** If a VB: usu passive horse or other animal **is harnessed**, a harness is put *beV-ed ton* on it, especially so that it can pull a carriage, cart, or Also *beV-ed* plough. *The horses were harnessed to a heavy wagon.* **5** People or things who work or who are **in harness** work together and co-operate in order to BRITISH achieve their aim. *At Opera North he will be in harness with Paul Daniel, the conductor appointed music director last year.*

harp /hɑːp/ **harps, harping, harped.** A **harp** is a ◆◇◇◇ large musical instrument consisting of a row of N-VAR strings stretched from the top to the bottom of a frame. See picture headed **musical instruments**. ◆ **harp·ist, harpists.** A **harpist** is someone who N-COUNT plays the harp.

harp on. If you say that someone **harps on** a subject, PHRASAL VB you mean that they keep on talking about it in a way VPn that other people find annoying. *She concentrated on* V P about n the good parts of her trip instead of harping on about Also VP the bad.

har·poon /hɑːˈpuːn/ **harpoons, harpooning, harpooned. 1** A **harpoon** is a weapon like a spear N-COUNT with a long rope attached to it, which is fired or thrown by people hunting whales or large sea fish. **2** To **harpoon** a whale or large fish means to hit or VERB: Vn pierce it with a harpoon.

harp·si·chord /ˈhɑːpsɪkɔːd/ **harpsichords.** A N-VAR **harpsichord** is a musical instrument rather like a small piano.

har·py /ˈhɑːpi/ **harpies. 1** In classical mythology, N-COUNT the **harpies** were creatures with birds' bodies and women's faces. **2** If you refer to a woman as a **har-** N-COUNT **py**, you mean that she is very cruel or violent. PRAGMATICS

har·ri·dan /ˈhærɪdən/ **harridans.** If you call a N-COUNT woman a **harridan**, you are saying in a rather cruel PRAGMATICS way that you think she is bossy and unpleasant. FORMAL

har·row /ˈhærəʊ/ **harrows.** A **harrow** is a piece of N-COUNT farm equipment consisting of a row of spikes fixed to a heavy frame.

har·row·ing /ˈhærəʊɪŋ/. A **harrowing** experience is ◆◇◇◇ extremely upsetting or disturbing. *...harrowing pic-* ADJ-GRADED *tures of the children who had been murdered.*

har·ry /ˈhæri/ **harries, harrying, harried.** If ◆◇◇◇ someone **harries** you, they keep asking or telling VERB you to do something, so that you feel anxious or an- Vn noyed. *...harrying the government in late-night de-* *bates.* ◆ **har·ried** *...harried businessmen.* ADJ-GRADED

harsh /hɑːʃ/ **harsher, harshest. 1** A **harsh** con- ◆◆◇◇ dition or way of life is severe and difficult. *The* ADJ-GRADED *weather grew harsh, chilly and unpredictable.* ◆ **harsh·ness** *...the harshness of their living condi-* N-UNCOUNT *tions.* **2 Harsh** actions or speech are unkind and ADJ-GRADED show no understanding or sympathy. *...the cold,* *harsh cruelty of her husband.* ◆ **harsh·ly** *Her hus-* ADV-GRADED: *band is being harshly treated in prison.* ADV with v ◆ **harshness** *She apologizes for the harshness of* N-UNCOUNT *her words.* **3** Something that is **harsh** is so hard, ADJ-GRADED bright, or rough that it seems unpleasant or harm-ful. *...harsher detergents that can leave hair brittle.* ◆ **harshness** *...as the wine ages, losing its bitter* N-UNCOUNT *harshness.* **4 Harsh** voices and sounds are ones that ADJ-GRADED are rough and unpleasant to listen to. *It's a pity she* *has such a loud harsh voice.* ◆ **harshly** *Evidently it* ADV-GRADED: *was a bitter joke, they both laughed harshly.* ADV with v

har·vest /ˈhɑːvɪst/ **harvests, harvesting, har-** ◆◆◇◇ **vested. 1** The **harvest** is the gathering of a crop. N-SING: *...there was about 300 million tons of grain in the* theN *fields at the start of the harvest.* **2** A **harvest** is the N-COUNT crop that is gathered in. *...a bumper potato harvest.* **3** When farmers **harvest** a crop, they gather it in. VERB: Vn ◆ **har·vest·ing** *Tremendous losses occurred during* N-UNCOUNT *harvesting.* **4** If you **harvest** a large number of VERB: Vn things, you collect them, often by making great LITERARY efforts.

har·vest·er /ˈhɑːvɪstə/ **harvesters. 1** A **harvester** N-COUNT is a machine which cuts and often collects ripe crops such as wheat, maize, or vegetables. ● See

also **combine harvester. 2** You can refer to a person N-COUNT who cuts, picks, or gathers crops as a **harvester**.

harvest ˈ**festival, harvest festivals.** A **harvest** N-VAR **festival** is a Christian church service held every year to thank God for the harvest.

has. The auxiliary verb is pronounced /həz, STRONG hæz/. The main verb is usually pronounced /hæz/. **Has** is the third person singular of the present tense of **have**.

ˈ**has-been, has-beens.** If you describe someone N-COUNT as a **has-been**, you are indicating in an unkind way PRAGMATICS that they were important or respected in the past, but they are not now. *...various has-beens who foist* *opinions on us.*

hash /hæʃ/. **1** If you **make a hash of** a job or task, ◆◇◇◇ you do it very badly. *Watson had made a thorough* PHRASE *hash of it.* **2 Hash** is a dish made from meat cut into N-UNCOUNT small lumps and fried with other ingredients such as onions or potato. **3 Hash** is the same as hashish. N-UNCOUNT

hash ˈ**browns; also spelled hashed browns. Hash** N-PLURAL **browns** or **hashed browns** are potatoes that have been chopped into small pieces and cooked on a grill or in a frying pan.

hash·ish /ˈhæʃiːʃ/. **Hashish** is a resin taken from N-UNCOUNT the flowers of the hemp plant and used by some people as a drug. Hashish is also referred to as 'can-nabis resin'. It is illegal in many countries.

hasn't /ˈhæzənt/. In informal English, **has not** is usually said or written as **hasn't**.

hasp /ˈhɑːsp, ˈhæsp/ **hasps.** A **hasp** is a flat piece of N-COUNT metal with a slot in it, fastened to the edge of a door or lid. To close the door or lid, you push the slot over a metal loop fastened to the other section and put a padlock through the loop. *There was a pad-* *lock and hasp securing the double doors from the* *outside.*

has·sle /ˈhæsəl/ **hassles, hassling, hassled.** ◆◇◇◇ **1** A **hassle** is a situation that is difficult and involves N-VAR problems, effort, or arguments with people. *...all the* INFORMAL *usual hassles at airport check-in.* **2** If someone **has-** VERB: Vn **sles** you, they cause problems for you, often by re- INFORMAL peatedly telling you or asking you to do something, in an annoying way.

has·sock /ˈhæsək/ **hassocks.** A **hassock** is a cush- N-COUNT ion for kneeling on in a church. BRITISH

hast /hæst/. **Hast** was a way of saying or writing the DATED present tense of 'have'.

haste /heɪst/. **1 Haste** is the quality of doing some- ◆◇◇◇ thing quickly, sometimes too quickly so that you are N-UNCOUNT careless and make mistakes. *The translations bear* *the signs of inaccuracy and haste.* **2** If someone is PHRASE told to **make haste**, they are told to do something DATED quickly and not waste time. *Simon was under orders* *to make haste.*

has·ten /ˈheɪsən/ **hastens, hastening, has-** ◆◇◇◇ **tened. 1** If you **hasten** an event or process, you VERB make it happen faster or sooner. *But if he does this,* Vn *he may hasten the collapse of his own country.* **2** If VERB you **hasten** to do something, you are quick to do it. V to-inf *She more than anyone had hastened to sign the con-* *tract... 'There's no threat in this, Freddie,' Arnold* *hastened to say.* **3** If you **hasten** somewhere, you VERB hurry there. *He hastened with quicksilver steps to-* V prep/adv *wards me.* LITERARY

has·ty /ˈheɪsti/. **1** A **hasty** movement, action, or ◆◆◇◇ statement is sudden, and often done in reaction to ADJ-GRADED something that has just happened. *...in the event* *they need to make a hasty escape.* ◆ **hasti·ly** ADV-GRADED: /ˈheɪstɪli/ *'No, I'm sure it's not,' said Virginia hastily.* ADV with v **2** A **hasty** event or action is one that is completed ADJ-GRADED more quickly than normal. *After the hasty meal, the* *men had moved forward to take up their positions.* ◆ **hastily** *He said good night hastily.* **3** If you de- ADV-GRADED scribe a person or their behaviour as **hasty**, you ADJ-GRADED mean that they are acting too quickly, without PRAGMATICS thinking carefully; used showing disapproval. *The* *United States' allies had urged him not to take a* *hasty decision.* ◆ **hastily** *I decided that nothing* ADV-GRADED: *should be done hastily.* ADV with v

hat /hæt/ **hats. 1** A **hat** is a head covering, often ◆◆◆◇◇
with a brim round it, which is usually worn out of N-COUNT
doors to give protection from the weather. See picture headed **clothes. 2** If you say that someone is N-COUNT:
wearing a particular **hat**, you mean that they are with supp
performing a particular role at that time. ...*putting
on my nationalistic hat. ...various problems, including too many people wearing too many hats.*

3 If you say that you are ready to do something **at the** PHRASE
drop of a hat, you mean that you are willing to do it
immediately, without hesitating. *India is one part of
the world I would go to at the drop of a hat.* **4** If you say PHRASE
that something or someone is **old hat**, you mean that
they have existed or been known for a long time, and
they have become uninteresting and boring. *Religion
is 'old hat' and science has proved this.* **5** If you say that PHRASE
someone **pulled** something **out of the hat**, you mean
that they did something very unexpected and surprising which helped them to succeed, often when they
appeared to be failing. *Southampton had somehow
managed to pull another Cup victory out of the hat.*
6 If you say that you **take** your **hat off to** someone, PHRASE
you mean that you admire them for something that PRAGMATICS
they have done. *I take my hat off to Mr Clarke for taking this action.* **7** If you go **hat in hand** to someone, PHRASE
you go to them very humbly, because you are asking AMERICAN
them to give you something. The usual British expres-
sion is **cap in hand. 8** If you say '**Hats off** to someone', CONVENTION
you are expressing admiration for them. *Hats off to* PRAGMATICS
them for supporting the homeless.

hat·band /'hætbænd/ **hatbands.** A hatband is a N-COUNT
strip of cloth that is put round a hat above the brim
as a decoration.

hat·box /'hætbɒks/ **hatboxes.** A hatbox is a cylin- N-COUNT
drical box in which a hat can be carried and stored.

hatch /hætʃ/ **hatches, hatching, hatched.** ◆◆◇◇◇
1 When a baby bird or animal or an egg **hatches**, or V-ERG: V
when it **is hatched**, the baby bird or animal comes beV-ed
out of its egg by breaking the shell. *The young dis-* Also V n
appeared soon after they were hatched. ► **Hatch out** PHRASAL VB
means the same as **hatch**. *Seeing the eggs hatch out* V P
for the first time is a moment that I will never forget. Also V n P,
2 If you **hatch** a plot or a scheme, you think of it V P noun
and work it out. *He has accused opposition parties of* VERB
hatching a plot to assassinate the Pope. **3** A **hatch** is V n
an opening in the deck of a ship, which is used by N-COUNT
people for coming on deck or going below deck.
You can also refer to the door of this opening as a
hatch. 4 If someone **battens down the hatches**, PHRASE
they prepare themselves so that they will be able to
withstand a coming difficulty or crisis.

hatch out. See hatch 1. PHRASAL VB

hatch·back /'hætʃbæk/ **hatchbacks.** A hatchback N-COUNT
is a car with an extra door at the back which opens
upwards.

hatch·ery /'hætʃəri/ **hatcheries.** A hatchery is a N-COUNT
place where people control the hatching of eggs, especially fish eggs.

hatch·et /'hætʃɪt/ **hatchets. 1** A hatchet is a ◆◇◇◇◇
small axe that you can hold in one hand. ...*men* N-COUNT
*armed with automatic weapons, hatchets and
knives.* **2** Someone with a **hatchet** face has a long ADJ: ADJ n
narrow face with sharp features. **3** If two people PHRASE
bury the hatchet, they become friendly again after
a quarrel or disagreement.

hatchet job, hatchet jobs. To do a **hatchet job** N-COUNT
on someone or something means to say or write INFORMAL
bad things about them and therefore harm their
reputation.

hatchet man, hatchet men. If you use **hatchet** N-COUNT
man to describe a man employed by a person, com- PRAGMATICS
pany, or organization, you disapprove of him because his job is to destroy things or do unpleasant
tasks.

hatch·way /'hætʃweɪ/ **hatchways.** A hatchway is N-COUNT
the same as a hatch.

hate /heɪt/ **hates, hating, hated. 1** If you **hate** ◆◆◆◇◇
someone or something, you have an extremely VERB
strong feeling of dislike for them. *Most people hate* V n
him, but they don't dare to say so. ► Also a noun. N-UNCOUNT
...*eyes that held a look of chronic hate.* ● to hate
someone's **guts**: see gut. ◆ **hat·ed** *He's probably the* ADJ-GRADED:
most hated man in this county. ...the hated ADJ n
Ceauscescu dictatorship. **2** If you say that you **hate** VB: no cont
something such as a particular activity, you mean V n/-ing
that you find it very unpleasant. *She hated hospi-* V to-inf
tals... He hates to be interrupted during training... I V it wh
hate it when people accuse us of that.

3 You can use **hate** in expressions like **I hate to trou-** VB: no cont
ble you or **I hate to bother you** when you are apolo- PRAGMATICS
gizing to someone for interrupting them or asking V to-inf
them to do something. *I hate to rush you but I have
another appointment later on.* **4** You can use **hate** in VB: no cont
expressions such as **I hate to say it** or **I hate to tell you** PRAGMATICS
when you want to express regret about what you are V to-inf
about to say. *I hate to tell you this, but tomorrow's your
last day.* **5** You can use **hate** in expressions like **I hate** VB: no cont
to see or **I hate to think** when are emphasizing that PRAGMATICS
you find a situation or an idea unpleasant. *I just hate* V to-inf
to see you doing this to yourself. **6** You can use **hate** in VB: no cont
expressions like **I'd hate to think** when you hope that V to-inf
something is not true or that something will not happen. *I'd hate to think my job would not be secure if I left
it temporarily.*

hate campaign, hate campaigns. A hate cam- N-COUNT
paign is a series of actions which are intended to
harm or upset someone, or to make other people
have a low opinion of them.

hate·ful /'heɪtfʊl/. **1** Someone or something that is ADJ-GRADED
hateful is extremely unpleasant. *It was a hateful* DATED
thing to say. **2** Someone who is **hateful** hates some- ADJ-GRADED
one else. ...*a lying, hateful and racist campaign.*

hate mail. If someone receives **hate mail**, they re- N-UNCOUNT
ceive unpleasant or threatening letters.

hater /'heɪtə/ **haters.** If you call someone a **hater** N-COUNT:
of something, you mean that they strongly dislike N of n
that thing. *Braccio was a hater of idleness.* ► Also a COMB
combining form. *He was reputed to be a woman-
hater.*

hath /hæθ/. **Hath** is an old-fashioned way of saying
or writing 'has'.

hat·pin /'hætpɪn/ **hatpins.** A hatpin is a metal pin N-COUNT
which can be pushed through a woman's hat and
through her hair to keep the hat in position.

ha·tred /'heɪtrɪd/. **hatreds.** Hatred is an extreme- ◆◆◇◇◇
ly strong feeling of dislike for someone or some- N-UNCOUNT:
thing. *My hatred for her is so intense it seems to be* also N in pl
destroying me. ...racial hatred.

hat·stand /'hætstænd/ **hatstands.** A hatstand is N-COUNT
an upright pole with hooks at the top on which hats
can be hung.

hat-trick, hat-tricks; also spelled **hat trick.** A ◆◇◇◇◇
hat-trick is a series of three achievements, especial- N-COUNT
ly in a sports match, for example three goals scored
by the same person in a football match.

haugh·ty /'hɔːti/. You use **haughty** to describe ADJ-GRADED
someone's behaviour or appearance when they PRAGMATICS
seem to be very proud and to think that they are
better than other people. *He spoke in a haughty
tone.* ◆ **haugh·ti·ly** /'hɔːtɪli/ *Toni looked at him ra-* ADV-GRADED
ther haughtily.

haul /hɔːl/ **hauls, hauling, hauled. 1** If you **haul** ◆◆◇◇◇
something which is heavy or difficult to move, you VERB
move it using a lot of effort. *A crane had to be used* V n prep/adv
to haul the car out of the stream... She hauled up her V adv n
bedroom window and leaned out. **2** If someone **is** Also V n
hauled before someone in authority, they are made VB: usu
to appear before them because they are accused of passive
having done something wrong. *He was hauled be-* beV-ed before
fore the managing director and fired. ► **Haul up** n
means the same as **haul**. *He was hauled up before* PHRASAL VB:
the Board of Trustees. **3** A **haul** of something illegal usu passive
such as drugs or explosives is an amount of them N-COUNT:
found and seized by police or customs. ...*the biggest* with supp
haul of cannabis ever seized. **4** If you say that a task PHRASE
or a journey is a **long haul**, you mean that it takes a
long time and a lot of effort. *Revitalising the Romanian economy will be a long haul.*

haul·age /'hɔːlɪdʒ/. **Haulage** is the business of N-UNCOUNT
transporting goods by road. BRITISH

haul·er /ˈhɔːlə/ **haulers.** A **hauler** is a company or a person that transports goods by road. The British word is **haulier**. `N-COUNT` `AMERICAN`

haul·ier /ˈhɔːliə/ **hauliers.** A **haulier** is a company or a person that transports goods by road. The American word is **hauler**. *A road haulier's tool of trade is the truck.* `N-COUNT` `BRITISH`

haunch /hɔːntʃ/ **haunches. 1** If you squat **on** your **haunches,** you lower yourself towards the ground so that your legs are bent under you and you are balancing on your feet. **2** The **haunches** of an animal or person consist of the area of the body which includes the hips, buttocks, and tops of the legs. `PHRASE` `N-COUNT`

haunt /hɔːnt/ **haunts, haunting, haunted. 1** If something unpleasant **haunts** you, you keep thinking or worrying about it over a long period of time. *The decision to leave her children now haunts her.* **2** Something that **haunts** a person or organization regularly causes them problems over a long period of time. *The stigma of being a bankrupt is likely to haunt him for the rest of his life.* **3** A place that is the **haunt** of a particular person is one which they often visit because they enjoy going there. **4** A ghost or spirit that **haunts** a place or a person regularly appears in the place, or is seen by the person and frightens them. `◆◆◇◇◇` `VERB` `V n` `VERB` `V n` `N-COUNT:` `with supp` `VERB: V n`

haunt·ed /ˈhɔːntɪd/. **1** A **haunted** building or other place is one where a ghost regularly appears. **2** Someone who has a **haunted** expression looks very worried or troubled. *She looked so haunted, I almost didn't recognize her.* `◆◇◇◇◇` `ADJ` `ADJ-GRADED`

haunt·ing /ˈhɔːntɪŋ/. **Haunting** sounds, images, or words remain in your thoughts because they are very beautiful or sad. *...the haunting calls of wild birds.* ♦ **haunt·ing·ly** *Each one of these ancient towns is hauntingly beautiful.* `◆◇◇◇◇` `ADJ-GRADED` `ADV-GRADED`

haute cou·ture /ˌəʊt kuːˈtjʊə/. **Haute couture** refers to the designing and making of high-quality fashion clothes, or to the clothes themselves. `N-UNCOUNT` `FORMAL`

hau·teur /əʊˈtɜː, AM həʊˈtɜː/. **Hauteur** is proud and arrogant behaviour; used showing disapproval. `N-UNCOUNT` `PRAGMATICS` `FORMAL`

have 1 auxiliary verb uses

have /həv, STRONG hæv/ **has, having, had.** In spoken English forms of **have** are often contracted, for example **I have** is contracted to **I've** and **has not** is contracted to **hasn't**. For explanations of the use of inflected forms and contractions, see the individual entries. `◆◆◆◆◆`

1 You use the forms **have** and **has** with a past participle to form the present perfect tense of verbs. *Alex has already gone... I've just seen a play that I can highly recommend... Frankie hasn't been feeling well for a long time.* **2** You use the form **had** with a past participle to form the past perfect tense of verbs. *She had just returned from a job interview... Miss Windham said she had spoken to them over the weekend.* **3 Have** is used in question tags. *You haven't sent her away, have you?... It's happened, hasn't it?* **4** You use **have** when you are confirming or contradicting a statement containing 'have', 'has', or 'had', or giving a negative or positive answer to a question. *'You'd never seen the Marilyn Monroe film?'—'No I hadn't.'* **5** The form **having** with a past participle can be used to introduce a clause in which you mention an action which had already happened before another action began. *He arrived in San Francisco, having left New Jersey on January 19th.* `AUX` `AUX -ed` `AUX been -ing` `AUX` `AUX -ed` `AUX` `cl AUX n` `AUX` `AUX` `AUX` `AUX -ed`

have 2 used with nouns describing actions

have /hæv/ **has, having, had. Have** is used in combination with a wide range of nouns, where the meaning of the combination is mostly given by the noun. `◆◆◆◆◆`

1 You can use **have** followed by a noun to talk about an action or event, when it would also be possible to use a verb. For example, you can say **'I had a look at the photos'** instead of 'I looked at the photos.' *I went out and had a walk around... She rested for a while, then had a wash and changed her clothes... I'll have a think about that.* **2** In normal spoken or written English, people use **have** with a wide range of nouns `VB: no passive` `V n` `VB: no passive` `V n`

when it is clear from the context what it means, often instead of a more specific verb. For example people are more likely to say **'we had ice-cream'** or **'he's had a shock'** than 'we ate ice-cream', or 'he's suffered a shock'. *Come and have a meal with us tonight... She had an operation on her knee... His visit had a great effect on them.*

have 3 other verb uses and phrases

have /hæv/ **has, having, had.** For meanings 1-4, people often use **have got** instead of **have**, especially in spoken English. In this case, **have** is pronounced as an auxiliary verb. For more information and examples of the use of 'have got', see **got**. `◆◆◆◆◆`

1 You use **have** when you are saying that someone or something owns, possesses, or holds a particular thing, or when you are mentioning one of their qualities or characteristics. *Oscar had a new bicycle... I want to have my own business... You have beautiful eyes... Her house had a balcony... Do you have any brothers and sisters?... I have no doubt at all in my own mind about this... I have my microphone with me.* **2** If you **have** something from someone, they give it to you. *You can have my ticket... Can I have your name please?* **3** If you **have** an illness or disability, you suffer from it. *I had a headache... He has a heart condition.* **4** If a woman **has** a baby, she gives birth to it. If she **is having** a baby, she is pregnant. *Do you want to have your baby in hospital or at home?* **5** If you **have** something to do, you are responsible for doing it or must do it. *He had plenty of work to do... I have some important calls to make.* **6** You can use **have** to say that something exists or happens, where it would also be possible to use an impersonal structure with 'there is'. For example, you can say **'you have no alternative'** instead of 'there is no alternative', or **'he had a good view from his window'** instead of 'there was a good view from his window.' *He had two tenants living with him... We haven't any shops on the island.* **7** If you **have** something such a part of your body in a particular position or state, it is in that position or state. *Mary had her eyes closed... They had the curtains open... He had his shirt buttoned.* **8** If someone **has** you by a part of your body, they are holding you there and they are trying to hurt you or force you to go somewhere. *Larry had him by the ear and was beating his head against the pavement.* **9** If you **have** something done, someone does it for you or you arrange for it to be done. *I had your rooms cleaned and aired... You've had your hair cut, it looks great.* **10** If someone or something **has** something happen to them, usually something unpleasant, it happens to them. *We had our money stolen.* **11** If you **have** someone do something or doing something, you persuade, cause, or order them to do it. *If you happen to talk to him, have him call me... Mr Gower had had us all working so hard.* `VB: no passive` `V n` `V n adv/prep` `VB: no passive` `V n` `VB: no passive` `V n` `VB: no passive, V n` `VB: no passive` `V n to-inf` `VB: no passive` `V n` `VB: no passive` `V n adj/adv/ prep` `V n by n` `VB: no passive` `V n -ed` `VB: no passive` `V n -ed` `VB: no passive` `V n inf` `V n -ing`

12 You can use **have** in expressions like **I won't have it** or **I'm not having that**, to mean that you will not allow or put up with something. *I'm not having any of that nonsense.* **13** You can use **has it** in expressions like **'rumour has it that'** or **'as legend has it'** when you are quoting something that you have heard, but you do not necessarily think it is true. *Rumour has it that tickets were being sold for £300.* **14** If someone **has it in for** you, they do not like you and they want to make life difficult for you. *He's always had it in for the Dawkins family.* **15** If you **have it in** you, you have abilities and skills which you do not usually use and which only show themselves in a difficult situation. *He has it in him to succeed.* **16** To **have it off** with someone or **have it away** with someone means to have sex with them; some people find this expression offensive. `VB: with neg` `PRAGMATICS` `V n` `PHRASE` `PHRASE` `PHRASE` `PHRASE` `BRITISH, INFORMAL`

17 ● **to be had:** see **had.** ● **to have had it:** see **had.**

have 4 modal phrases

have /hæv, həf/ **has, having, had. 1** You use **have to** when you are saying that something is necessary, obligatory, or must happen. If you do not **have to** do something, it is not necessary or obligatory for you to do it. *He had to go to Germany...* `◆◆◆◆◆` `PHR-MODAL`

We'll have to find a taxi... They didn't have to pay tax. **2** You can use **have to** in order to say that you feel certain that something is true or will happen. *That has to be the biggest lie ever told.* PHR-MODAL

ha·ven /ˈheɪvən/ **havens.** A **haven** is a place where people or animals feel safe, secure, and happy. *...Lake Baringo, a freshwater haven for a mixed variety of birds.* • See also **safe haven.** N-COUNT ◆◇◇◇◇

'have-nots. If you refer to two groups of people as **haves and have-nots,** you mean that the first group are very wealthy and the second group are very poor. You can also refer generally to poor people as **have-nots.** PHRASE

haven't /ˈhævənt/. **Have not** is usually spoken or written as **haven't.** INFORMAL

hav·er·sack /ˈhævəsæk/ **haversacks.** A **haversack** is a canvas bag that is usually worn over one shoulder. N-COUNT BRITISH

haves /hævz/. • **haves and have-nots:** see **have-nots.**

hav·oc /ˈhævək/. **1** Havoc is chaos, disorder, and confusion. *Rioters caused havoc in the centre of the town.* **2** If one thing **plays havoc** with another or **wreaks havoc on** it, it prevents it from continuing or functioning as normal, or damages it. *The weather played havoc with airline schedules.* N-UNCOUNT ◆◇◇◇◇ PHRASE

haw /hɔː/ **haws, hawing, hawed.** If you **hum and haw** or **hem and haw,** you take a long time to say something because you cannot think of the right words, or because you are not sure what to say. *Tim hemmed and hawed, but finally told his boss the truth.* PHRASE

hawk /hɔːk/ **hawks, hawking, hawked. 1** A **hawk** is a large bird with a short hooked bill, sharp claws, and very good eyesight. Hawks catch and eat small birds and animals. **2** If you refer to someone as a **hawk,** you mean that they tend to be in favour of war and of forceful solutions to problems, rather than peaceful or diplomatic solutions. • **hawk·ish** *He is one of the most hawkish members of the new cabinet.* **3** If someone **hawks** goods, they sell them by walking through the streets or visiting people's houses. • **hawk·er, hawkers** *It was a visitor and not a hawker or tramp at her door.* **4** If you say that someone **is hawking** something, you disapprove of the fact that they are trying to sell it in an aggressive manner. *Developers will be hawking cut-price flats and houses.* ▶ **Hawk around** means the same as **hawk.** *He is hawking around a 15-minute, £5,000 promotional video.* N-COUNT ◆◆◇◇◇ N-COUNT ADJ-GRADED VERB: V n N-COUNT VERB PRAGMATICS V n PHRASAL VB V P noun Also V n P

haw·thorn /ˈhɔːθɔːn/ **hawthorns.** A **hawthorn** is a small tree which has sharp thorns and produces white or pink flowers. N-VAR ◆◇◇◇◇

hay /heɪ/. **1** Hay is grass which has been cut and dried so that it can be used to feed animals. *...bales of hay.* **2** If you say that someone **is making hay** or **is making hay while the sun shines,** you mean that they are taking advantage of a situation that is favourable to them while they have the chance to. N-UNCOUNT ◆◇◇◇◇ PHRASE

'hay fever. If someone suffers from **hay fever,** they have an allergy to pollen which makes their nose, throat, and eyes become inflamed. N-UNCOUNT ◆◇◇◇◇

hay·stack /ˈheɪstæk/ **haystacks. 1** A **haystack** is a large firmly-built pile of hay, often covered with a straw roof to protect it, which is left in the field until it is needed. **2** If you are trying to find something and say that it is like looking for a **needle in a haystack,** you mean that you are very unlikely indeed to find it. N-COUNT PHRASE

hay·wire /ˈheɪwaɪə/. If something goes **haywire,** it becomes completely disordered or out of control. *Many Americans think their legal system has gone haywire.* ADJ-GRADED: v-link ADJ INFORMAL

haz·ard /ˈhæzəd/ **hazards, hazarding, hazarded. 1** A **hazard** is something which could be dangerous to you, your health or safety, or your plans or reputation. *...fungicides which are a hazard to workers and to the environment.* **2** If you **hazard** someone or something, you put them into a situation which might be dangerous for them, because of N-COUNT ◆◆◇◇◇ VERB V n FORMAL

something you are trying to achieve. *...a principle strong enough to hazard lives for.* **3** If you **hazard a guess,** you make a suggestion about something which you know might be wrong. *'Fifteen or sixteen?' Mrs Dearden hazarded.* VERB: V n V with quote Also V that

haz·ard·ous /ˈhæzədəs/. Something that is **hazardous** is dangerous, especially to people's health or safety. *...hazardous waste... Passive smoking can be hazardous to health.* ADJ-GRADED ◆◇◇◇◇

haze /heɪz/ **hazes. 1** Haze is light mist, caused by particles of water or dust in the air, which prevents you from seeing distant objects clearly. *...the shimmering heat haze.* ◆ **hazy** *The air was thin and crisp, filled with hazy sunshine.* **2** If there is a **haze** of something such as smoke or steam, you cannot see clearly through it. *Dan smiled at him through a haze of smoke.* ◆ **hazy** *Possible side effects include pain and hazy vision.* **3** If someone is in a **haze,** they are not thinking clearly or they feel uncertain and confused about something. *His mind was a haze of fear and confusion.* ◆ **hazy** *I have only a hazy memory of what he was really like.* N-VAR ◆◇◇◇◇ ADJ-GRADED N-SING LITERARY ADJ-GRADED N-SING: with supp ADJ-GRADED

ha·zel /ˈheɪzəl/ **hazels. 1** A **hazel** is a small tree which produces nuts that you can eat. **2** Hazel eyes are greenish-brown in colour. N-VAR ◆◇◇◇◇ COLOUR

hazel·nut /ˈheɪzəlnʌt/ **hazelnuts.** Hazelnuts are nuts from a hazel tree, which can be eaten. N-COUNT

'H-bomb, H-bombs. An **H-bomb** is a bomb in which energy is released from hydrogen atoms. N-COUNT

he /hi, STRONG hiː/. **He** is a third person singular pronoun. **He** is used as the subject of a verb. **1** You use **he** to refer to a man, boy, or male animal. *He lives in Rapid City, South Dakota.* **2** Writers sometimes use **he** to refer to a person without saying whether that person is a man or a woman. Some people dislike this use and prefer to use 'he or she' or 'they'. *The teacher should encourage the child to proceed as far as he can.* **3** In some religions, **He** is used to refer to God. PRON ◆◆◆◆ PRON PRON WRITTEN PRON

H.E. **H.E.** is a written abbreviation for 'His Excellency' or 'Her Excellency' and is used as part of the title of an important official such as an ambassador. *...H.E. the Italian Ambassador.* N-TITLE

head /hed/ **heads, heading, headed. 1** Your **head** is the top part of your body, which has your eyes, mouth, and brain in it. See picture headed **human body.** *She turned her head away from him.* ▶ You can also use **head** as a measure of distance, equal to the length of a person's or animal's head. *The third gorilla was taller by a head.* **2** If you **head** a ball, you hit it with your head in order to make it go in a particular direction. *He headed the ball across the face of the goal.* **3** When you are tossing a coin and it comes down **heads,** you can see the side of the coin which has a head on it, for example the head of the king or president. N-COUNT ◆◆◆◆ N-SING: a N VERB: V n V n prep/adv ADV

4 From **head to foot** means all over your body. *Colin had been put into a bath and been scrubbed from head to foot.* **5** If you **stand on** your **head,** you turn your body upside down and rest all your weight on the top part of your head and your hands with your feet directly above you. **6** If you are **head over heels** or **head over heels in love,** you are very much in love. *I was very attracted to men and fell head over heels many times.* **7** If you **bang** peoples' **heads together** or **knock** their **heads together,** you scold them for doing something wrong. **8** If two or more people **put their heads together,** they talk about a problem they have and try to solve it. **9** If you **keep** your **head above water,** you avoid getting into difficulties, especially in business. *We are keeping our head above water, but our cash flow position is not too good.* **10** If you say that **heads will roll** as a result of something bad that has happened, you mean that people will be punished for it, especially by losing their jobs. PHRASE PHRASE PHRASE PHRASE PHRASE JOURNALISM, BRITISH PHRASE PHRASE PHRASE

11 You can use **head** to refer to your mind and your mental abilities. *I can't get that song out of my head. ...an exceptional analyst who could do complex maths in his head.* **12** If you a have a **head for** something, you can deal with it easily in your mind. For example, N-COUNT PHRASE

if you have a **head for figures**, you can understand and do arithmetic easily, and if you have a **head for heights**, you can climb to a great height without feeling afraid. **13** If you **get** something **into** your **head**, you suddenly decide that it is true and you will not change your mind about it. If you **take it into** your **head** to do something, you suddenly decide to do it and you will not change your mind about it. **14** If you say that someone has **got** something **into** their **head**, you mean that they have finally understood or accepted it, and you are usually criticizing them because it has taken them a long time to do this. *You've got to get it into your head that you're on the brink of catastrophe.* **15** If you **keep** your **head**, you remain calm in a difficult situation. If you **lose** your **head**, you panic or do not remain calm. **16** If you say that someone is **off** their **head**, you think that their ideas or behaviour are very strange or foolish or because they are mentally disturbed or have been taking drugs. **17** The **head** of a line of people or vehicles is the front of it, or the first person or vehicle in the line. **18** If someone or something **heads** a line or procession, they are at the front of it. *The parson, heading the procession, had just turned right.* **19** If something **heads** a list or group, it is at the top of it. *Running a business heads the list of ambitions.* ◆ **head·ed. Headed** paper has the name and address of a person or organization at the top. **20** If a piece of writing is **headed** a particular title, it has that title written at the beginning of it. *One chapter is headed, 'Beating the Test'.* **21** The **head** of something is the highest or top part of it. *Every day a different name was placed at the head of the chart.* **22** If you **stand** an idea or argument **on its head** or **turn** it **on its head**, you think about it or treat it in a completely new and different way. *Theirs was a nonconformist relationship which turned the standard notion of marriage on its head.* **23** The **head** on a glass of beer is the layer of small bubbles that form on the top of the beer. **24** The **head** of something long and thin is the end which is wider than or a different shape from the rest. *There should be no exposed screw heads.* **25** The **head** of a school is the teacher who is in charge of a school. *She became head of a girls' school.* **26** The **head** of a company or organization is the person in charge of it. *Heads of government from more than 100 countries gather in Geneva tomorrow. ...the head waiter.* **27** If you **head** a department, company, or organization, you are the person in charge of it. *...the ruling Socialist Party, headed by Dr Franz Vranitzky.* **28** You can use **head** to describe how many animals of a particular type a farmer has. For example, fifty **head** of cattle is fifty cows. **29** You use **a head** or **per head** after stating a cost or amount in order to indicate that that cost or amount is for each person in a particular group. *This simple chicken dish costs less than £1 a head.* **30** If you **are heading** for a particular place or in a particular direction, you are going towards that place or in that direction. You can also say that you **are headed** for a particular place. *It is not clear how many of them will be heading back to Saudi Arabia. ...a truck headed west.* **31** If something or someone **is heading for** a particular result, the situation they are in is developing in a way that makes that result very likely. You can also say that something or someone **is headed** for a particular result. *The centuries-old ritual seems headed for extinction.* **32** See also **heading**. **33** If you **give** someone their **head**, you allow them to do what they want to do, without trying to advise or stop them. **34** If alcoholic drink **goes to** your **head**, it quickly makes you feel drunk. **35** If you say that something such as praise or success **goes to** someone's **head**, you mean that they become arrogant or conceited as a result of it. **36** If you **knock** something **on the head**, you stop doing it or stop it happening. **37** Phrases such as **laugh** your **head off**, **scream** your **head off**, and **shout** your **head off** can be used to emphasize that you are laughing, screaming,

or shouting very much. **38** If an idea or comment goes **over** someone's **head**, it is too difficult for them to understand. **39** If someone does something **over** your **head**, they do it without consulting you. *He was reprimanded for trying to go over the heads of senior officers.* **40** If you say that something unpleasant or embarrassing rears its **ugly head**, you mean that it has appeared or is present, often after having been absent for some time. *The scourge of racial tyranny should never again be allowed to raise its ugly head.* **41** If you say you cannot **make head or tail of** something, you are emphasizing that you cannot understand it at all. **42** If a problem or disagreement **comes to a head** or if you **bring** it **to a head**, it reaches a state where you have to do something urgently about it. *These problems came to a head in September when five of the station's journalists were sacked.* **43 Head** is used in a large number of expressions which are explained under other words in the dictionary. For example, the expression 'off the top of your head' is explained at 'top'.

head off. 1 If you **head off** a person or vehicle, you move to a place in front of them and make them change the direction they are moving in. *He changed direction swiftly, turned into the hallway and headed her off.* **2** If you **head** something **off**, especially something unpleasant, you take action before it is expected to happen in order to prevent it from happening. *He would ask Congress to intervene and head off a strike.*

head·ache /ˈhedeɪk/ **headaches. 1** If you have a **headache**, you have a pain in your head. *I've got a splitting headache.* **2** If you say that something is a **headache**, you mean that it causes you difficulty or worry. *The airline's biggest headache is the increase in the price of aviation fuel.*

head·band /ˈhedbænd/ **headbands;** also spelled **head band.** A **headband** is a narrow strip of material which you can wear around your head across your forehead.

head·board /ˈhedbɔːd/ **headboards.** A **headboard** is an upright board at the end of a bed against which your pillows go.

head 'boy, head boys. The **head boy** of a school is the boy who is the leader of the prefects and who often represents the school on public occasions.

'head-butt, head-butts, head-butting, head-butted; also spelled **headbutt.** If someone **head-butts** you, they hit you with the top of their head. ▶ Also a noun. *The cut was caused by a head-butt.*

'head count, head counts. If you do a **head count**, you count the number of people present. You can also use **head count** to talk about the number of people that are present at an event, or that an organization employs.

head·dress /ˈheddres/ **headdresses;** also spelled **head-dress.** A **headdress** is something that is worn on a person's head for decoration.

head·er /ˈhedə/ **headers.** In football, a **header** is the act of hitting the ball in a particular direction with your head.

'head-'first; also spelled **headfirst.** If you move **head-first** in a particular direction, your head is the part of your body that is furthest forward as you are moving. *He had apparently fallen head-first down the stairwell.*

head·gear /ˈhedgɪə/; also spelled **head gear.** You use **headgear** to refer to hats or other things worn on the head.

'head 'girl, head girls. The **head girl** of a school is the girl who is the leader of the prefects and who often represents the school on public occasions.

head·hunt /ˈhedhʌnt/ **headhunts, headhunting, headhunted.** If someone who works for a particular company is **headhunted**, they leave that company because another company has approached them and offered them another job with better pay and higher status. *They may headhunt her for the vacant position of Executive Producer.* ◆ **head·hunter, headhunters.** *He was a headhunter, supplying high-powered executive talent.*

head·ing /'hedɪŋ/ **headings.** A heading is the title of a piece of writing, which is written or printed at the top of the page. ...*chapter headings.* ● See also **head.** ◆◇◇◇◇ N-COUNT

head·lamp /'hedlæmp/ **headlamps.** A headlamp is a headlight. N-COUNT BRITISH

head·land /'hedlənd/ **headlands.** A headland is a narrow piece of land which sticks out into the sea. N-COUNT

head·less /'hedləs/. If the body of a person or animal is **headless**, the head has been removed. ADJ

head·light /'hedlaɪt/ **headlights.** A vehicle's **headlights** are the large powerful lights at the front. See picture headed **car and bicycle.** ◆◇◇◇◇ N-COUNT

head·line /'hedlaɪn/ **headlines.** **1** A headline is the title of a newspaper story, printed in large letters at the top of it, especially on the front page. *The cover carried the headline, 'It's War.'* ♦ **head·lined** *The Sunday Times ran an article headlined 'The X Brothers'.* **2** The **headlines** are the main points of the news which are read on radio or television. *I'm Claudia Polley with the news headlines.* **3** Someone or something that **hits the headlines** or **grabs the headlines** gets a lot of publicity from the media. *El Salvador first hit the world headlines at the beginning of the 1980s.* ◆◆◇◇◇ N-COUNT / ADJ: v-link ADJ / N-PLURAL / PHRASE

head·long /'hedlɒŋ, AM -lɔːŋ/. **1** If you move **headlong** in a particular direction, you move there very quickly, usually with your head furthest forward. *He ran headlong for the open door.* ► Also an adjective. *The army was in headlong flight.* **2** If you rush **headlong** into something, you do it quickly without thinking carefully about it. *Do not leap headlong into decisions.* ► Also an adjective. ...*the headlong rush to independence.* ◆◇◇◇◇ ADV: ADV after v / ADV / ADV after v / ADJ: ADJ n

head·man /'hedmən/ **headmen.** The headman is the chief or leader of a tribe in a village. N-COUNT

head·master /ˌhed'mɑːstə, -'mæst-/ **headmasters.** A headmaster is a man who is the head teacher of a school. ◆◇◇◇◇ N-COUNT BRITISH

head·mistress /ˌhed'mɪstrɪs/ **headmistresses.** A **headmistress** is a woman who is the head teacher of a school. ◆◇◇◇◇ N-COUNT BRITISH

head of 'state, heads of state. A head of state is the leader of a country, for example a president, king, or queen. ◆◆◇◇◇ N-COUNT

head-'on. 1 If two vehicles hit each other **head-on,** they hit each other with their fronts pointing towards each other. *The car collided head-on with a van.* ► Also an adjective. *Their car was in a head-on smash with an articulated lorry.* **2** A **head-on** conflict or disagreement is firm and direct, without any compromises. ...*a head-on clash between the president and the assembly.* ► Also an adverb. *I chose to confront the issue head-on.* ◆◆◇◇◇ ADV: ADV after v / ADJ: ADJ n / ADJ: ADJ n / ADV: ADV after v

head·phones /'hedfəʊnz/. **Headphones** are a pair of padded speakers which you wear over your ears in order to listen to a radio, record player, or tape recorder without other people hearing it. ◆◇◇◇◇ N-PLURAL

head·quartered /ˌhed'kwɔːtəd/. If an organization **is headquartered** in a particular place, that is where its main offices are. V-PASSIVE: be V-ed prep/adv

head·quarters /'hedkwɔːtəz/. The **headquarters** of an organization are its main offices. ...*fraud squad officers from London's police headquarters.* ◆◆◇◇ N-COLL-SING

head·rest /'hedrest/ **headrests.** A headrest is the part of the back of a seat, especially in a car, on which you can lean your head. N-COUNT

head·room /'hedruːm/. **Headroom** is the amount of space below a roof or bridge. N-UNCOUNT

head·scarf /'hedskɑːf/ **headscarves.** A headscarf is a scarf which is worn on the head, especially by women. N-COUNT

head·set /'hedset/ **headsets.** A headset is a piece of equipment, attached to a radio or a telephone, that has two earpieces and which you can wear on your head so that your hands are free while you are listening. N-COUNT

head·ship /'hedʃɪp/ **headships.** A headship is the position of being the head of a school, college, or department. N-COUNT

head 'start, head starts; also **head-start.** If you have a **head start** on other people, you have an advantage over them in something such as a competition or race. *A good education gives your child a head start in life.* ◆◇◇◇◇ N-COUNT

head·stone /'hedstəʊn/ **headstones.** A headstone is a large stone which stands at one end of a grave, usually with the name of the dead person carved on it. N-COUNT

head·strong /'hedstrɒŋ, AM -strɔːŋ/. If you refer to someone as **headstrong,** you mean they are stubborn and always determined to do what they want, even when this is not sensible. ADJ-GRADED

head 'teacher, head teachers; also spelled **headteacher.** A **head teacher** is a teacher who is in charge of a school. ◆◇◇◇◇ N-COUNT BRITISH

head·way /'hedweɪ/. If you **make headway,** you progress towards achieving something. *Police were making little headway in the investigation.* ◆◇◇◇◇ PHRASE

head·wind /'hedwɪnd/ **headwinds;** also spelled **head-wind.** A **headwind** is a wind which blows in the opposite direction to the one in which you are moving. N-COUNT

head·word /'hedwɜːd/ **headwords.** A headword is a word which is followed by a phrase or paragraph which explains the word's meaning, especially in a dictionary. N-COUNT

heady /'hedi/ **headier, headiest.** A heady drink, atmosphere, or experience strongly affects your senses, for example by making you feel drunk or excited. ...*the heady days just after their marriage.* ◆◇◇◇◇ ADJ-GRADED

heal /hiːl/ **heals, healing, healed. 1** When a broken bone or other injury **heals,** it becomes healthy and normal again. When someone who is ill **heals,** they recover. *Repeated applications of the mixture will help to heal the wound... Therapies like acupuncture do work and many people have been healed by them.* ♦ **heal·ing** *The healing process will be slow and monotonous.* **2** When emotional or psychological damage **heals,** people recover from it and the situation returns to normal. *The new President will also have to try to heal the wounds caused by a bitter presidential campaign.* ♦ **healing** *The healing of grief only occurs over lengthy periods of time.* ◆◆◆◇◇ V-ERG: V / V n / N-UNCOUNT / V-ERG: V / V n / N-UNCOUNT

heal·er /'hiːlə/ **healers.** A healer is a person who treats sick people, especially one who believes that they are able to heal people through prayer or a supernatural power. ◆◇◇◇◇ N-COUNT

health /helθ/. **1** A person's **health** is the condition of their body and the extent to which it is free from illness or is able to resist illness. *Caffeine is bad for your health.* **2 Health** is a state in which a person is not suffering from any illness and is feeling well. *They nursed me back to health.* **3** The **health** of something such as an organization or a system is its success and the fact that it is working well. ...*the future health of the banking industry.* **4** When you **drink to** someone's **health** or **drink** their **health,** you have a drink as a sign of wishing them health and happiness. *In the village pub, regulars drank the health of John and his father.* ◆◆◆◆◆ N-UNCOUNT / N-UNCOUNT / N-UNCOUNT / PHRASE

'health centre, health centres; spelled **health center** in American English. A **health centre** is a building where a group of doctors and other health workers can be visited by their patients. N-COUNT

'health farm, health farms. A health farm is a sort of hotel with facilities for people who want to get fitter or lose weight. N-COUNT BRITISH

'health food, health foods. Health foods are natural foods which people buy because they consider them to be healthy. ◆◇◇◇◇ N-VAR

health·ful /'helθfʊl/. Something that is **healthful** is good for your health. ADJ-GRADED AMERICAN

'health visitor, health visitors. In Britain, a **health visitor** is a nurse who visits people in their homes and offers advice on matters such as how to look after babies or people with physical disabilities. N-COUNT

healthy /'helθi/ **healthier, healthiest. 1** Someone who is **healthy** is well and is not suffering from ◆◆◆◇◇ ADJ-GRADED

any illness. Something that is **healthy** shows that a person is well. *She had a normal pregnancy and delivered a healthy child. ...the glow of healthy skin.* ◆ **health·ly** /ˈhelθɪli/ *What I really want is to live healthily for as long as possible.* **2** Something that is **healthy** is good for your health. *...a balanced healthy diet.* ◆ **healthily** *I try to eat as healthily as possible.* **3** A **healthy** organization or system is successful. *...an economically healthy socialist state.* **4** A **healthy** amount of something is a large amount that shows success. *He predicts a continuation of healthy profits.* **5** If you have a **healthy** attitude about something, you show good sense. *It's very healthy to be afraid when there's something to be afraid of.*

(ADV-GRADED / ADJ-GRADED / ADV-GRADED / ADJ-GRADED / ADJ-GRADED / ADJ-GRADED)

heap /hiːp/ **heaps, heaping, heaped.** **1** A **heap** of things is a pile of them, especially a pile arranged in a rather untidy way. *...a heap of bricks. ...a compost heap.* **2** If you **heap** things somewhere, you put lots of them there in a pile. *Mrs. Madrigal heaped more carrots onto Michael's plate.* ▶ **Heap up** means the same as **heap**. *The militia was heaping up wood for a bonfire.* **3** If you **heap** praise or criticism **on** someone or something, you give them a lot of praise or criticism. *MPs heaped scorn on his programme for the next two years.* **4** **Heaps of** something or a **heap** of something is a large quantity of it. *You have heaps of time... Mansell managed to get himself in a whole heap of trouble.* **5** Someone who is **at the bottom of the heap** or **at the top of the heap** is low or high in the structure of society or of an organization. **6** If someone collapses **in a heap**, they fall heavily and untidily and do not move.

(N-COUNT / VERB / PHRASAL VB / V P noun / Also V n P / VERB / V n on/upon n / QUANT / INFORMAL / PHRASE / PHRASE)

heaped /hiːpt/. **1** A **heaped** spoonful has the contents of the spoon piled up above the edge. *...a heaped teaspoon of baking powder.* **2** A container or a surface that is **heaped with** things has a lot of them in it or on it in a pile, often so many that it cannot hold any more. *The large desk was heaped with papers.*

(ADJ / ADJ: v-link ADJ with n)

hear /hɪə/ **hears, hearing, heard** /hɜːd/. **1** When you **hear** a sound, you become aware of it through your ears. *The trumpet can be heard all over their house... They heard the protesters shout: 'No more fascism!'... We heard the bells ringing out.* **2** If you **hear** something such as a lecture or a piece of music, you listen to it. *You can hear commentary on the match in about half an hour's time... I don't think you've ever heard Doris talking about her emotional life... She can hear it played by a professional orchestra.* ◆ **hear·er, hearers.** *He knew that his hearers wanted to hear this story.* **3** If you say that you can **hear** something that you heard in the past or might hear in the future, you mean that you are able to imagine hearing it in your mind. *Can't you just hear John Motson now?... I can hear him saying it now: 'Rubbish!'* **4** When a judge or a court of law **hears** a case, or evidence in a case, they listen to it officially in order to make a decision about it. *He had to wait months before his case was heard.* **5** If you **hear** from someone, you receive a letter or telephone call from them. *The police are anxious to hear from anyone who may know her.* **6** In a debate or discussion, if you **hear from** someone, you listen to them giving their opinion or information. **7** If you **hear** some news or information about something or someone, you find out about it by someone telling you, or from the radio or television. *My mother heard of this school through Leslie... He had heard that the trophy had been sold... I had waited to hear the result... Have you heard anything of the other Englishman?* **8** If you **have heard** of something or someone, you know a little about them. *Many people haven't heard of reflexology.* **9** If you say that you **have heard** something **before**, you mean that you are not interested in it, or do not believe it, or are not surprised about it.

(VERB: V n / be V-ed / V n inf / Also V / VERB / V n-ing / V n-ed / Also V n inf / N-COUNT / VB: no cont / V n / V n inf/-ing / VERB: V n / be V-ed / FORMAL / VERB / V from n / VERB: V from n / VERB / V of/about n / V that / V n of/about n / VB: no cont / V of n / PHRASE)

10 If you say **'Do you hear?'** or **'Did you hear me?'** to someone, you are telling them in an angry or forceful way to pay attention to what you are saying. *Leave her alone! Do you hear me?* **11** During political debates

(CONVENTION / PRAGMATICS / CONVENTION)

and public meetings, people sometimes say **'Hear hear!'** to express their agreement with what the speaker is saying. **12** If you say that you **can't hear** yourself **think**, you are complaining and emphasizing that there is a lot of noise, and that it is disturbing you or preventing you from doing something. **13** If you say that you **won't hear of** someone doing something, you mean that you refuse to let them do it.
14 ● **you could have heard a pin drop**: see **pin**.

(PRAGMATICS / FORMAL, BRITISH / PHRASE / PRAGMATICS / INFORMAL / PHRASE / PRAGMATICS)

hear out. If you **hear** someone **out**, you listen to them without interrupting them until they have finished saying everything that they want to say. *Perhaps, when you've heard me out, you'll appreciate the reason for secrecy.*

(PHRASAL VB / V n P / Also V P noun)

hear·ing /ˈhɪərɪŋ/ **hearings.** **1** A person's or animal's **hearing** is the sense which makes it possible for them to be aware of sounds. *His mind still seemed clear and his hearing was excellent.* **2** A **hearing** is an official meeting which is held in order to collect facts about an incident or problem. *The judge adjourned the hearing until next Tuesday.* **3** See also **hard of hearing**. **4** If someone gives you **a fair hearing** or **a hearing**, they listen to you when you give your opinion about something. **5** If someone says something **in** your **hearing** or **within** your **hearing**, you can hear what they say because they are near you.

(◆◆◆◇◇ / N-UNCOUNT / N-COUNT / PHRASE / PHRASE)

'hearing aid, hearing aids. A **hearing aid** is a device which people with hearing difficulties wear in their ear to enable them to hear better.

(N-COUNT)

hear·say /ˈhɪəseɪ/. **Hearsay** is information which you have been told indirectly, but which you do not personally know to be true. *Much of what was reported to them was hearsay.*

(N-UNCOUNT)

hearse /hɜːs/ **hearses.** A **hearse** is a large car that carries the coffin at a funeral.

(N-COUNT)

heart /hɑːt/ **hearts.** **1** Your **heart** is the organ in your chest that pumps the blood around your body. People also use **heart** to refer to the area of their chest that is closest to their heart. *...the beating of his heart... He gave a sudden cry of pain and put his hand to his heart.* **2** You can refer to someone's **heart** when you are talking about their deep feelings and beliefs. *Alik's words filled her heart with pride.* **3** You use the word **heart** when you are talking about someone's character and attitude towards other people, especially when they are kind and generous. *She's got a good heart.* **4** If you refer to things of **the heart**, you mean love and relationships. **5** The **heart** of something is the most central and important part of it. *The heart of the problem is supply and demand.* **6** The **heart** of a place is its centre. *...the heart of London's West End.* **7** A **heart** is a shape that is sometimes used as a symbol of love. See picture headed **shapes**. *...heart-shaped chocolates.* **8** **Hearts** is one of the four suits in a pack of playing cards. Each card in the suit is marked with one or more symbols: ♥. **9** A **heart** is one of the thirteen playing cards in the suit of hearts.
10 You can say **'cross my heart'** when you want someone to believe that you are telling the truth. You can also ask **'cross your heart?'**, when you are asking someone if they are really telling the truth. **11** If you feel or believe something **with all** your **heart**, you feel or believe it very strongly. *My own family I loved with all my heart.* **12** If you say something **from the heart** or **from the bottom of** your **heart**, you sincerely mean what you say. *I don't want to go away without thanking you from the bottom of my heart.* **13** If you believe or know something **in** your **heart of hearts**, that is what you really believe or think, even though it may sometimes seem that you do not. *I know in my heart of hearts that I am the right man for that mission.* **14** If someone **breaks** your **heart**, they make you very sad and unhappy, usually because they end a love affair or close relationship with you. **15** If you say that someone has a **broken heart**, you mean that they are deeply upset and sad, for example because a love affair has ended unhappily. **16** If you **lose** your **heart** to someone, you fall in love with them. **17** If something

(◆◆◆◆◇ / N-COUNT / N-COUNT / LITERARY / N-VAR / PRAGMATICS / N-SING: the N / N-SING: N of n / N-SING / N-COUNT / N-COLL: UNCOUNT / N-COUNT / CONVENTION SPOKEN / PHRASE / PRAGMATICS / PHRASE / PHRASE / PHRASE / PRAGMATICS / LITERARY / PHRASE / LITERARY / PHRASE / LITERARY / PHRASE)

breaks your **heart**, it makes you feel very sad and depressed, especially because people are suffering but you can do nothing to help them. *It really breaks my heart to see them this way.* `PRAGMATICS` `LITERARY`

18 If something such as a subject or project is **close to** your **heart** or **near to** your **heart**, it is very important to you and you are very interested in it and concerned about it. **19** If you **open** your **heart** or **pour out** your **heart** to someone, you tell them your most private thoughts and feelings. **20** If you **wear** your **heart on** your **sleeve**, you openly show your feelings or emotions rather than keeping them hidden. **21** If you say that someone's **heart is in the right place** you mean that they are kind, considerate, and generous, although you may disapprove of other aspects of their character. *He is a bit of a wide boy but his heart is in the right place.* `PHRASE` `PHRASE` `PHRASE` `PHRASE`

22 If something **gives** you **heart**, it makes you feel more confident or happy about something. *It gave me heart to see one thug get what he deserves.* **23** If you **take heart** from something, you are made to feel encouraged and optimistic by it. **24** If you **lose heart**, you become sad and depressed and are no longer interested in something, especially because it is not progressing as you would like. **25** If your **heart is in** your **mouth**, you feel very excited, worried, or frightened. *My heart was in my mouth when I walked into her office.* `PHRASE` `PHRASE` `PHRASE` `PRAGMATICS` `PHRASE`

26 If you say that someone is a particular kind of person **at heart**, you mean that that is what they are really like, even though they may seem very different. **27** If you say that someone has your interests or your welfare **at heart**, you mean that they are concerned about you and that is why they are doing something. **28** If you know something such as a poem **by heart**, you have learnt it so well that you can remember it without having to read it. **29** If someone has a **change of heart**, their attitude towards something changes. `PHRASE` `PHRASE` `PHRASE` `PHRASE`

30 If you can do something to your **heart's content**, you can do it as much as you want. *I was delighted to be able to eat my favorite dishes to my heart's content.* **31** If you want to do something but do **not have the heart** to do it, you do not do it because you know it will make someone unhappy or disappointed. **32** If your **heart isn't in** the thing you are doing, you have very little enthusiasm for it, usually because you are depressed or are thinking about something else. **33** If you have **set** your **heart on** something, you want it very much or want to do it very much. **34** If you put your **heart and soul** into something, you do it with a great deal of enthusiasm, dedication, and pleasure. **35** If you **take** something **to heart**, for example someone's behaviour, you are deeply affected and upset by it. *If someone says something critical I take it to heart.* `PHRASE` `PHRASE` `PHRASE` `PHRASE` `PRAGMATICS` `PHRASE`

heart·ache /'hɑːteɪk/ **heartaches. Heartache** is very great sadness and emotional suffering. *...the heartache of her divorce.* ◆◇◇◇◇ N-VAR JOURNALISM

heart attack, heart attacks. 1 If someone has a **heart attack**, blood fails to reach a part of their heart and they feel severe pain in their chest. Heart attacks can be fatal. *He died of a heart attack.* **2** If you say that someone will have **a heart attack** about something, you are emphasizing that they will be very shocked or angry. *She'll have a heart attack if I tell her.* ◆◆◇◇◇ N-COUNT N-SING a N PRAGMATICS INFORMAL

heart·beat /'hɑːtbiːt/ **heartbeats. 1** Your **heartbeat** is the regular movement of your heart as it pumps blood around your body. *Your baby's heartbeat will be monitored continuously.* **2** A **heartbeat** is one of the movements of your heart. *...irregular heartbeats.* ◆◇◇◇◇ N-SING N-COUNT

heart·break /'hɑːtbreɪk/ **heartbreaks. Heartbreak** is very great sadness and emotional suffering, especially after the end of a love affair or close relationship. *...suffering and heartbreak for those close to the victims.* ◆◇◇◇◇ N-VAR

heart·breaking /'hɑːtbreɪkɪŋ/. Something that is **heartbreaking** makes you feel extremely sad and ADJ-GRADED

upset. *They have taken the heartbreaking decision to have no more children.*

heart·broken /'hɑːtbrəʊkən/. Someone who is **heartbroken** is very sad and emotionally upset. ADJ-GRADED

heart·burn /'hɑːtbɜːn/. **Heartburn** is a painful sensation in your chest, caused by indigestion. N-UNCOUNT

-hearted /-'hɑːtɪd/. **-hearted** combines with adjectives such as 'kind' or 'cold' to form adjectives which indicate that someone has a particular character or personality or is in a particular mood. *...kind-hearted strangers... I tried to be light-hearted.* COMB

heart·en /'hɑːtən/ **heartens, heartening, heartened.** If someone **is heartened** by something, it encourages them and makes them cheerful. *The news heartened everybody.* ♦ **heart·ened** *I feel heartened by her progress... The British government is heartened that Germany shares its enthusiasm.* ♦ **heart·ening** *It has been very heartening to see new writing emerging.* ◆◇◇◇ VERB V n ADJ-GRADED: v-link ADJ ADJ-GRADED

heart failure. Heart failure is a serious medical condition in which someone's heart does not work as well as it should, sometimes stopping completely so that they die. ◆◇◇◇◇ N-UNCOUNT

heart·felt /'hɑːtfelt/. **Heartfelt** is used to describe a deep or sincere feeling or wish. *My heartfelt sympathy goes out to all the relatives.* ◆◇◇◇ ADJ-GRADED

hearth /hɑːθ/ **hearths. 1** The **hearth** is the floor of a fireplace, which sometimes extends into the room. *There was a huge fire roaring in the hearth.* **2** A person's home and family life can be referred to as their **hearth and home**. *...a man who leaves his hearth and home to labour as a miner in the inhospitable north.* ◆◇◇◇ N-COUNT PHRASE LITERARY

heart·land /'hɑːtlænd/ **heartlands. 1** Heartland or **heartlands** is used to refer to the area or region where a particular set of activities or beliefs is most significant. *...the industrial heartland of America.* **2** The most central area of a country or continent can be referred to as its **heartland** or **heartlands**. *We then headed west towards the heartland of Tibet.* ◆◇◇◇ N-COUNT: with supp JOURNALISM N-COUNT: with supp WRITTEN

heart·less /'hɑːtləs/. If you describe someone as **heartless**, you mean that they are cruel and unkind, and have no sympathy for anyone. ADJ-GRADED

heart-rending. You use **heart-rending** to describe something that causes you to feel great sadness and pity. *...heart-rending pictures of refugees.* ADJ-GRADED

heart·strings /'hɑːtstrɪŋz/. If you say that someone tugs at your **heartstrings**, you mean that they cause you to feel strong emotions, usually sadness or pity. *She knows exactly how to tug at readers' heartstrings.* N-PLURAL

heart-throb, heart-throbs. If you describe a man as a **heart-throb**, you mean that he is physically very attractive, so that a lot of women fall in love with him. N-COUNT

heart-to-heart, heart-to-hearts. If two people have a **heart-to-heart**, they have a conversation in which they talk about their feelings and personal problems. N-COUNT

heart-warming. Something that is **heart-warming** causes you to feel happy, usually because something nice has happened to people. *...the heart-warming story of enemies who discover a shared humanity.* ADJ-GRADED

hearty /'hɑːti/ **heartier, heartiest. 1** Hearty people or actions are loud, cheerful, and energetic. *...a hearty, bluff, athletic sort of guy.* ♦ **hearti·ly** *He laughed heartily.* **2** Hearty feelings or opinions are strongly felt. *Arnold was in hearty agreement.* ♦ **heartily** *I heartily agree with her favourable comments on Germany and France. ...most Afghans are heartily sick of war.* **3** A hearty meal is large and very satisfying. *The boys ate a hearty breakfast.* ♦ **heartily** *He ate heartily but would drink only beer.* ◆◇◇◇ ADJ-GRADED ADV-GRADED: ADV after v ADJ-GRADED ADV ADJ-GRADED ADV-GRADED: ADV after v

heat /hiːt/ **heats, heating, heated. 1** When you **heat** something, you raise its temperature, for example by using a flame or a special piece of equipment. *Heat the tomatoes and oil in a pan. ...heated swimming pools.* **2 Heat** is warmth or the quality of ◆◆◆◇ VERB V n V-ed N-UNCOUNT

being hot. ...*the fierce heat of the sun.* **3** The **heat** is very hot weather. *He cannot cope with the heat and humidity.* ● **The heat of the day** is the hottest part of the day, especially when this is very hot. **4** The **heat** of something is the temperature of something that is warm or that is being heated. *Warm the milk to blood heat... Adjust the heat of the barbecue.* **5** You use **heat** to refer to a source of heat, for example a cooking ring or the heating system of a house. *Remove the pan from the heat.* N-UNCOUNT / N-UNCOUNT: with supp / N-SING

6 If you do something in the **heat of the moment**, you do it when you are feeling a strong emotion such as anger or excitement, and often regret it later. **7** The **heat of** a particular activity is the point when there is the greatest activity or excitement. ...*in the heat of the election campaign.* PHRASE / N-SING: the N of n

8 A **heat** is one of a series of races or competitions. The winners of a heat take part in another race or competition, against the winners of other heats. ...*the heats of the men's 100m breaststroke.* ● See also **dead heat**. N-COUNT

9 In British English, when a female animal is **on heat**, she is in a state where she is ready for mating. The American term is **in heat**. PHRASE

heat up. 1 When you **heat** something **up**, especially food which has already been cooked and allowed to go cold, you make it hot. *Freda heated up a pie for me.* **2** When something **heats up**, it gradually becomes hotter. ...*when her mobile home heats up like an oven.* **3** When a situation **heats up**, things start to happen much more quickly and with increased interest and excitement among the people involved. *The movement for democracy began to heat up.* PHRASAL VB V n P / V P noun / VP / VP

heat·ed /ˈhiːtɪd/. If someone gets **heated about** something, they get angry and excited about it. A **heated** discussion or quarrel is where the people involved are angry and excited. ◆ **heat·ed·ly** *The crowd continued to argue heatedly about the best way to tackle the problem.* ADJ-GRADED / ADV-GRADED: ADV with v

heat·er /ˈhiːtə/ **heaters.** A **heater** is a piece of equipment or a machine which is used to raise the temperature of something, especially of the air inside a room or a car. N-COUNT

heath /hiːθ/ **heaths.** A **heath** is an area of open land covered with rough grass or heather and with very few trees or bushes. N-COUNT BRITISH

hea·then /ˈhiːðən/ **heathens.** Some people refer to people who have no religion, or who have a religion that is not Christianity, Judaism, or Islam, as **heathens**; often used showing disapproval. *She called us all heathens and hypocrites.* N-COUNT DATED

heath·er /ˈheðə/. **Heather** is a low spreading plant with small purple, pink, or white flowers that grows wild on hills or moorland. N-UNCOUNT

heat·ing /ˈhiːtɪŋ/. **1** **Heating** is the process of heating a building or room, considered especially from the point of view of how much this costs. ...*cottages for £150 a week, including heating.* **2** **Heating** is the system and equipment that is used to heat a building. *There is no heating in the shed.* ● See also **central heating**. N-UNCOUNT / N-UNCOUNT

'heat stroke; also spelled **heatstroke. Heat stroke** is the same as **sunstroke**. N-UNCOUNT

heat·wave /ˈhiːtweɪv/ **heatwaves.** A **heatwave** is a period of time during which the weather is much hotter than usual. N-COUNT

heave /hiːv/ **heaves heaving heaved. 1** If you **heave** something heavy or difficult to move somewhere, you push, pull, or lift it using a lot of effort. *It took five strong men to heave it up a ramp.* ▶ Also a noun. *It took only one heave to hurl him into the river.* **2** If something **heaves**, it moves up and down with large regular movements. *His chest heaved, and he took a deep breath.* **3** If you **heave**, or if your stomach **heaves**, you vomit or feel sick. *He gasped and heaved and vomited again.* **4** If you **heave** a sigh, you give a big sigh. **5** ● to **heave a sigh of relief**: see **sigh**. VERB V n prep/adv / N-COUNT / VERB V / VERB: V / VERB: V n

heave to. When a boat or ship **heaves to**, it stops moving. PHRASAL VB V P TECHNICAL

heav·en /ˈhevən/ **heavens. 1** In some religions, **heaven** is said to be the place where God lives and where good people go when they die. *I believed that when I died I would go to heaven.* ◆ **heav·en·ly** ...*heavenly beings whose function it is to serve God.* **2** If you **move heaven and earth**, you try as hard as you can to do it. **3** You can use **heaven** to refer to a place or situation that you like very much. *We went touring in Wales and Ireland. It was heaven.* ◆ **heavenly** *The idea of spending two weeks with him may seem heavenly.* **4** See also **seventh heaven**. N-PROPER / ADJ PHRASE / N-UNCOUNT INFORMAL / ADJ-GRADED

5 The **heavens** are the sky. ...*looking up at the heavens.* **6** If **the heavens open**, it suddenly starts raining very heavily. **7** You say **'Heaven forbid!'** to emphasize that you very much hope that something will not happen. *Heaven forbid that he should leave because of me!* **8** You say **'Good heavens!'** to express surprise. In British English, you can also just say **'Heavens!'**. *Good Heavens! That explains a lot!* **9** You say **'Heaven help'** someone when you fear that something bad is going to happen to them, often because you disapprove of what they are doing or the way they are behaving. *Heaven help the man she marries.* **10** You can say **'Heaven knows'** to emphasize that you do not know something, or that you find something very surprising. *Heaven knows what they put in it.* **11** You can say **'Heaven knows'** to emphasize something that you feel or believe very strongly. *Heaven knows they have enough money.* **12** ● **for heaven's sake**: see **sake**. ● **thank heavens**: see **thank**. N-PLURAL: the N DATED / PHRASE / PHRASE PRAGMATICS BRITISH EXCLAM / PHRASE PRAGMATICS INFORMAL / PHRASE PRAGMATICS BRITISH, INFORMAL / PHRASE PRAGMATICS BRITISH, INFORMAL / PHRASE PRAGMATICS BRITISH, INFORMAL

,heavenly 'body, heavenly bodies. A **heavenly body** is a planet, star, moon, or other natural object in space. N-COUNT

,heaven 'sent. You use **heaven-sent** to describe something such as an opportunity which is unexpected, but which is very welcome because it occurs at just the right time. ADJ

heav·en·ward /ˈhevənwəd/; The form **heavenwards** is also used. **Heavenward** means towards the sky or to heaven. *He rolled his eyes heavenward.* ADV: ADV after v WRITTEN

heav·i·ly /ˈhevɪli/. If someone says something **heavily**, they say it in a slow way which shows a feeling such as sadness, tiredness, or annoyance. *'I didn't even think about her,' he said heavily.* ● See also **heavy**. ADV: ADV after v

heavy /ˈhevi/ **heavier, heaviest; heavies. 1** Something that is **heavy** weighs a lot. *These scissors are awfully heavy.* ◆ **heavi·ness** ...*a sensation of warmth and heaviness in the muscles.* **2** You use **heavy** to ask or talk about how much someone or something weighs. *How heavy are you?... Protons are nearly 2000 times as heavy as electrons.* **3** A **heavy** machine or piece of military equipment is very large and very powerful. ...*heavy artillery.* **4** Someone or something that is **heavy** is solid or thick in appearance or structure, or is made of a thick material. ...*heavy old brown furniture... He was short and heavy.* ◆ **heavi·ly** *He was a big man of about forty, wide-shouldered and heavily built.* **5** A **heavy** substance is thick in texture. ...*heavy soil.* **6** **Heavy** means great in amount, degree, or intensity. *Heavy fighting has been going on. ...the heavy responsibility that parents take on.* ◆ **heavily** *It has been raining heavily all day. ...heavily armed members of a special anti-robbery squad.* ◆ **heaviness** ...*the heaviness of the blood loss.* **7** A **heavy** meal is large in amount and often difficult to digest. **8** Something that is **heavy with** things is full of them or loaded with them. *The air is heavy with moisture.* **9** If a person's breathing is **heavy**, it is very loud and deep. *Her breathing became slow and heavy.* ◆ **heavily** *She sank back on the pillow and closed her eyes, breathing heavily.* **10** A **heavy** movement or action is done with a lot of force or pressure. *You sustained a heavy blow on the back of the skull.* ◆ **heavily** *I sat down heavily on the ground.* **11** If you describe a period of time or a schedule as **heavy**, you mean it involves a lot of work. *It's been a* ADJ-GRADED / N-UNCOUNT / ADJ-GRADED: how ADJ, as ADJ as, ADJ-compar than / ADJ: ADJ n / ADJ-GRADED / ADV-GRADED: ADV -ed / ADJ-GRADED / ADJ-GRADED / ADV-GRADED / N-UNCOUNT / ADJ-GRADED LITERARY / ADJ-GRADED / ADV-GRADED: ADV after v / ADJ-GRADED: ADJ n / ADV-GRADED: ADV after v / ADJ-GRADED

heavy day and I'm tired. **12 Heavy** work requires a lot of strength or energy. **13** If someone or something is **heavy on** something, they use a lot of it, which is sometimes a bad thing. *Tanks are heavy on fuel.* [ADJ-GRADED] [ADJ-GRADED: v-link ADJ on] [PRAGMATICS]

14 Air or weather that is **heavy** is unpleasantly still, hot, and damp. **15** If you describe a person's face as **heavy**, you mean that it looks sad, tired, or unfriendly. *Leo regarded him with a stern, heavy face.* **16** If your heart is **heavy**, you are sad about something. **17** A situation that is **heavy** is serious and difficult to cope with. *I don't want any more of that heavy stuff.* **18** A **heavy** is a large strong man who is employed to protect a person or place, often by using violence. *They had employed heavies to evict shop squatters.* **19** • a **heavy hand**: see **hand**. [ADJ-GRADED] [ADJ-GRADED LITERARY] [ADJ-GRADED LITERARY] [ADJ-GRADED INFORMAL] [N-COUNT INFORMAL]

heavy-'duty. A **heavy-duty** piece of equipment is very strong and can be used a lot. *...a heavy duty polythene bag.* ◆◇◇◇◇ [ADJ]

heavy-'handed. **1** If you say that someone's behaviour is **heavy-handed**, you mean that they are unnecessarily forceful, rough, and thoughtless. *...heavy-handed police tactics.* **2** If someone is **heavy-handed** with something, they use too much of it or use it in a clumsy way. *...how heavy-handed you are with the paprika.* ◆◇◇◇◇ [ADJ-GRADED] [ADJ-GRADED]

heavy 'industry, heavy industries. Heavy industry consists of industries such as steel-making and shipbuilding, in which the raw materials, the machinery, and the manufactured goods are all large and heavy. ◆◇◇◇◇ [N-VAR]

heavy 'metal, heavy metals. 1 Heavy metal is a type of very loud rock music with a fast beat. **2** A **heavy metal** is a metallic element with a high relative density. ◆◇◇◇◇ [N-UNCOUNT] [N-COUNT TECHNICAL]

heavy-'set. Someone who is **heavy-set** has a large solid body. [ADJ]

heavy·weight /'heviweɪt/ **heavyweights. 1** A **heavyweight** is a boxer weighing more than 175 pounds and therefore in the heaviest class. **2** If you refer to a person or organization as a **heavyweight**, you mean that they have a lot of influence, experience, and importance in a particular field, subject, or activity. *...a political heavyweight.* ◆◆◇◇◇ [N-COUNT] [N-COUNT]

He·brew /'hiːbruː/ **Hebrews. 1 Hebrew** is a language that was spoken by Jews in former times. A modern form of Hebrew is spoken now in Israel. **2** A **Hebrew** was a person in former times who was Jewish and lived in Israel. *...the exodus of the Hebrews from Egypt.* **3 Hebrew** means belonging to or relating to the Hebrew language or people. *...the respected Hebrew newspaper Haarez.* ◆◇◇◇◇ [N-UNCOUNT] [N-COUNT] [ADJ]

heck /hek/. **1** You say **'heck!'** to express slight irritation or surprise. *Oh, heck. What can I write about?... 'Did you start that fight over me, Darren?'—'Heck no.'* **2** People use **a heck of** to emphasize how big something is or how much of it there is. *They're spending a heck of a lot of money.* **3** You use **the heck** in expressions such as **'what the heck'** and **'how the heck'** in order to emphasize a question, especially when you are puzzled or annoyed. *What the heck's that?.* **4** You say **'what the heck'** to indicate your acceptance of a situation that is unsatisfactory in some way but cannot be avoided or changed. *What the heck, I thought, I'll give it a whirl.* ◆◇◇◇◇ [EXCLAM] [PRAGMATICS] [INFORMAL] [PHRASE] [PRAGMATICS] [INFORMAL] [PHRASE] [PRAGMATICS] [INFORMAL] [PHRASE] [PRAGMATICS] [INFORMAL]

heck·le /'hekəl/ **heckles, heckling, heckled.** If people in an audience **heckle** public speakers or performers, they interrupt them, for example by making rude remarks. *A small group of youths stayed behind to heckle and shout abuse.* ▶ Also a noun. *...a heckle from an audience member.* ◆ **heck·ling** *The ceremony was disrupted by unprecedented heckling and slogan-chanting.* ◆ **heck·ler** /'heklə/ **hecklers** *A heckler called out asking for his opinion on gun control.* ◆◇◇◇◇ [VERB: V n V] [N-COUNT] [N-UNCOUNT] [N-COUNT]

hec·tare /'hektɑː/ **hectares.** A **hectare** is a measurement of an area of land which is equal to 10,000 square metres, or 2.471 acres. ◆◇◇◇◇ [N-COUNT]

hec·tic /'hektɪk/. A **hectic** situation is one that is very busy and involves a lot of rushed activity. *...his hectic work schedule.* ◆◇◇◇◇ [ADJ-GRADED]

hec·tor /'hektə/ **hectors, hectoring, hectored.** If someone **hectors** you, they try to make you do something by bothering you and talking to you aggressively; used showing disapproval. *I suppose you'll hector me until I phone him.* ◆ **hec·tor·ing** *In a loud, hectoring tone, Alan told us that he wasn't going to waste time discussing nonsense.* [VERB] [PRAGMATICS] [V n] [ADJ-GRADED]

he'd /hɪd, hiːd/. **1 He'd** is the usual spoken form of 'he had', especially when 'had' is an auxiliary verb. *He'd never learnt to read.* **2 He'd** is a spoken form of 'he would'. *He'd come into the clubhouse every day.*

hedge /hedʒ/ **hedges, hedging, hedged. 1** A **hedge** is a row of bushes or small trees, usually along the edge of a garden, field, or road. See picture headed **house and flat**. **2** If you **hedge** against something unpleasant or unwanted, especially losing money, you do something which will protect you from it. *Today's clever financial instruments make it possible for firms to hedge their risks.* ▶ Something that is a **hedge against** something unpleasant will protect you from its effects. *Gold is traditionally a hedge against inflation.* **3** If you **hedge**, you avoid answering a question or committing yourself to a particular action or decision. *'I can't give you an answer now,' he hedged.* **4** If you **hedge** your **bets**, you reduce the risk of losing a lot by supporting more than one person or thing in a situation where they are opposed to each other. ◆◆◇◇◇ [N-COUNT] [VERB: V against n V n] [N-COUNT: N against n] [VERB: V V with quote] [PHRASE]

hedge about or **hedge around.** If you say that something such as an offer **is hedged about** or **is hedged around with** rules or conditions, you mean that there are so many rules or conditions that it seems as if the person making the offer is deliberately trying to make it difficult for other people to accept. [PHRASAL VB PASSIVE]

hedge·hog /'hedʒhɒg, AM -hɔːg/ **hedgehogs.** A **hedgehog** is a small brown animal with sharp spikes covering its back. ◆◇◇◇◇ [N-COUNT]

hedge·row /'hedʒrəʊ/ **hedgerows.** A **hedgerow** is a row of bushes, trees, and plants, usually growing along a bank bordering a country lane or between fields. ◆◇◇◇◇ [N-VAR]

he·don·ist /'hiːdənɪst/ **hedonists.** A **hedonist** is someone who believes that having pleasure is the most important thing in life. ◆ **he·don·is·tic** /ˌhiːdəˈnɪstɪk/ *...the hedonistic pleasures of the South.* ◆ **he·don·ism** /'hiːdənɪzəm/. **Hedonism** is the belief that gaining pleasure is the most important thing in life. [N-COUNT FORMAL] [ADJ-GRADED] [N-UNCOUNT]

heed /hiːd/ **heeds, heeding, heeded. 1** If you **heed** someone's advice or warning, you pay attention to it and do what they suggest. *Few at the conference in London last week heeded his warning.* **2** If you **take heed** of what someone says or if you **pay heed** to them, you pay attention to them and consider carefully what they say. ◆◇◇◇◇ [VERB] [V n] [FORMAL] [PHRASE] [FORMAL]

heed·less /'hiːdləs/. If you are **heedless** of someone or something, you do not take any notice of them. *Heedless of time or any other consideration, they began to search.* [ADJ FORMAL]

heel /hiːl/ **heels, heeling, heeled. 1** Your **heel** is the back part of your foot, just below your ankle. See picture headed **human body**. **2** See also **Achilles heel**. **3** If a person or an animal is **at your heels**, they are following close behind you. *She strode off down the restaurant with Cavendish following close at her heels.* **4** The **heel** of a shoe is the raised part on the bottom at the back. **5 Heels** are women's shoes that are raised very high at the back. *...two well-dressed ladies in high heels.* **6** If you **click** your **heels**, you make a sharp sound with the heels of your shoes, especially by knocking them together. **7** The **heel of** your hand is the rounded pad at the bottom of your palm. **8** If you **bring** someone **to heel**, you force them to obey you. *...how the president will use his power to bring the republics to heel.* **9** If you **dig** your **heels in** or ◆◆◇◇◇ [N-COUNT] [PHRASE] [N-COUNT] [N-PLURAL] [PHRASE] [N-COUNT: N of n] [PHRASE] [PHRASE]

dig in your **heels**, you refuse to do something such as change your opinions or plans, especially when someone is trying very hard to make you do so. **10** If you are **cooling** your **heels**, someone is deliberately keeping you waiting, so that you get bored or impatient. [PHRASE] [INFORMAL] **11** If you are **kicking** your **heels**, you are having to wait around with nothing to do, so that you get bored or impatient. *The authorities wouldn't grant us permission to fly all the way down to San Francisco, so I had to kick my heels at Tunis Airport.* [PHRASE] [INFORMAL, BRITISH] **12** If you say that one event follows **hard on the heels** of another, or **hot on the heels** of another, you mean that one happens very quickly or immediately after another. [PHRASE] **13** If you say that someone is **hot on** your **heels**, you are emphasizing that they are chasing you and are not very far behind you. [PHRASE] **14** If you **turn on** your **heel** or **spin on** your **heel**, you suddenly turn round, especially because you are angry or surprised. [PHRASE] **15 ● head over heels**: see **head**. **●** to **drag** your **heels**: see **drag**.

heel over. When something **heels over**, it leans over very far as if it is about to fall over. [PHRASAL VB] [V P]

hefty /ˈhefti/ **heftier, heftiest. 1** Hefty means large in size, weight, or amount. *He faces a hefty fine.* **2** A **hefty** movement is forceful and vigorous. *He gave Luckwell a hefty shove.* [◆◇◇◇◇] [ADJ-GRADED] [INFORMAL] [ADJ-GRADED] [INFORMAL]

he·gemo·ny /hɪˈgeməni, AM -ˈdʒem-/. **Hegemony** is the domination or control by one country, organization, or social group over a group of others, especially if it is a member of that group. [◆◇◇◇◇] [N-UNCOUNT] [FORMAL]

heif·er /ˈhefə/ **heifers.** A **heifer** is a young cow that has not yet had a calf. [N-COUNT]

height /haɪt/ **heights. 1** The **height** of a person or thing is their size or length from the bottom to the top. *Her weight is about normal for her height... I am 5'6" in height... The wave here has a length of 250 feet and a height of 10 feet.* **2** **Height** is the quality of being tall. *Her height is intimidating for some men.* **3** A particular **height** is the distance that something is above the ground or above something else mentioned. *...a 6.3 kilogram weight was dropped on it from a height of 1 metre.* **4** A **height** is a high position or place above the ground. *From a height, it looks like a desert.* **5** When an activity, situation, or organization is **at its height**, it is at its most successful, powerful, or intense. *Emigration from Britain to Brittany was at its height.* **6** If you say that something is **the height of** a particular quality, you are emphasizing that it has that quality to the greatest degree possible. *I think it's the height of bad manners to be dressed badly.* **7** If something reaches great **heights**, it becomes very extreme or intense. *...the mid-1980s, when prices rose to absurd heights.* [◆◆◆◇◇] [N-VAR] [N-UNCOUNT] [N-VAR] [N-COUNT] [N-SING: atN with poss] [N-SING: theN of n] [PRAGMATICS] [N-PLURAL: with supp]

height·en /ˈhaɪtən/ **heightens, heightening, heightened.** If something **heightens** a feeling or if the feeling **heightens**, the feeling increases in degree or intensity. *The move has heightened tension in the state... Cross's interest heightened.* [◆◆◇◇◇] [V-ERG] [V n] [V]

hei·nous /ˈheɪnəs/. If you describe something such as a crime as **heinous**, you mean that it is extremely evil or horrible. [ADJ-GRADED] [FORMAL]

heir /eə/ **heirs.** An **heir** is someone who has the right to inherit a person's money, property, or title when that person dies. *His heir, Lord Doune, cuts a bit of a dash in the city.* [◆◆◇◇◇] [N-COUNT]

heir ap'parent, heirs apparent. The **heir apparent** to a particular job or position is the person who is expected to take it over when the person who currently holds it resigns. *He was seen as Mr Olsen's heir apparent.* [N-COUNT] [JOURNALISM]

heir·ess /ˈeərɪs/ **heiresses.** An **heiress** is a woman or girl who has the right to inherit property or a title, or who has inherited it, especially when this involves great wealth. *She is sole heiress to the family's shipping empire.* [N-COUNT]

heir·loom /ˈeəluːm/ **heirlooms.** An **heirloom** is an ornament or other object that has belonged to a family for a very long time and that has been handed down from one generation to another.

heist /haɪst/ **heists.** A **heist** is a burglary or robbery, especially a very daring one. *It was the biggest art heist in the history of the country.* [N-COUNT]

held /held/. **Held** is the past tense and past participle of **hold**.

heli·cop·ter /ˈhelikɒptə/ **helicopters.** A **helicopter** is an aircraft that is capable of hovering or moving vertically and horizontally, by means of large overhead blades which rotate. [◆◆◆◇◇] [N-COUNT]

,helicopter 'gunship, helicopter gunships. A **helicopter gunship** is a helicopter with large guns attached to it. [N-COUNT]

heli·pad /ˈhelipæd/ **helipads.** A **helipad** is a place where helicopters can land and take off. [N-COUNT]

he·lium /ˈhiːliəm/. **Helium** is a very light gas that is colourless and has no smell. [◆◇◇◇◇] [N-UNCOUNT]

he·lix /ˈhiːlɪks/ **helixes.** A **helix** is a spiral shape or form. [N-COUNT] [TECHNICAL]

hell /hel/ **hells. 1** In some religions, **hell** is the place where the Devil lives, and where wicked people are sent to be punished when they die. **2** **Hell** is a swear word used by some people when they are angry or excited, or when they want to emphasize what they are saying; some people find this use offensive. *'Hell, no!' the doctor snapped.* **3** You can use **as hell** after an adjective or adverb to emphasize the adjective or adverb. *The men might be armed, but they sure as hell aren't trained.* **4** You can use **from hell** after a noun when you are emphasizing that something or someone is extremely unpleasant or evil. *...the holiday from hell.* **5** If you say that a particular situation or place is **hell**, you are emphasizing that it is extremely unpleasant. *Bullies can make your life hell.* **6** If you say that a place or a situation is **hell on earth** or a **living hell**, you are emphasizing that it is extremely unpleasant or that it causes great suffering. **7** If you say that someone **gives** you **hell**, you are emphasizing that they shout at you very angrily because of something you have done wrong. *My father saw this in the newspaper and he gave me absolute hell.* **8** If you say that something **is giving** you **hell**, you are emphasizing that it is causing you a lot of trouble or pain. *My back's giving me hell, let me tell you!* **9** If you **go through hell**, or if someone **puts** you **through hell**, you have a very difficult or unpleasant time. *I put Brian through hell.* **10** If you tell someone to **go to hell**, you are angrily telling them to go away and leave you alone; some people find this use offensive. **11** If you tell someone to **get the hell out** of a place, you are telling them angrily or urgently to leave that place immediately; some people find this use offensive. *Get the hell out of my way.* **12** If you say **'to hell with'** something, you are emphasizing that you do not care about something and that it will not stop you from doing what you want to do; some people find this use offensive. *To hell with this, I'm getting out of here.* **13** If someone does something **for the hell of it**, or **just for the hell of it**, they do it for fun or for no particular reason. **14** If you say that someone is going **hell for leather**, you are emphasizing that they are doing something or moving very quickly, and often recklessly. **15** Some people use **like hell** to emphasize how strong an action or quality is. *It hurts like hell.* **16** If you say that **all hell breaks loose**, you are emphasizing that a lot of arguing or fighting suddenly starts. **17** If you talk about **a hell of a lot of** something, or **one hell of a lot of** something, you mean that there is a large amount of it. *The manager took a hell of a lot of money out of the club.* **18** Some people use **a hell of** or **one hell of** to emphasize that something is very good, very bad, or very big. *Whatever the outcome, it's going to be one hell of a fight.* **19** Some people use **the hell out of** for emphasis after verbs such as 'scare', 'irritate', and 'beat'. *I patted the top of her head in the condescending way I knew irri-* [◆◆◆◇◇] [N-PROPER] [EXCLAM] [PRAGMATICS] [INFORMAL] [PHRASE] [INFORMAL] [PHRASE] [INFORMAL] [N-VAR] [PRAGMATICS] [INFORMAL] [PHRASE] [PHRASE] [INFORMAL] [PHRASE] [PRAGMATICS] [INFORMAL] [PHRASE] [INFORMAL] [PHRASE] [PRAGMATICS] [INFORMAL] [PHRASE] [PRAGMATICS] [INFORMAL] [PHRASE] [PRAGMATICS] [INFORMAL] [PHRASE] [INFORMAL] [PHRASE] [PRAGMATICS] [INFORMAL] [PHRASE] [INFORMAL] [PHRASE] [PRAGMATICS] [INFORMAL] [PHRASE] [INFORMAL] [PHRASE] [PRAGMATICS] [INFORMAL] [PHRASE] [PRAGMATICS] [INFORMAL] [PHRASE] [PRAGMATICS] [INFORMAL]

tated the hell out of her. **20** If you say **there'll be hell to pay**, you are emphasizing that there will be serious trouble. **21** If you say that someone **raises hell**, you are emphasizing that they protest strongly and angrily about a situation in order to persuade other people to correct it or improve it.
22 People sometimes use **the hell** for emphasis in questions, after words such as 'what', 'where', and 'why', often in order to express anger; some people find this use offensive. *Where the hell have you been?... What the hell's going on?* **23** You can say **'what the hell'** when you decide to do something in spite of the doubts that you have about it. *What the hell, I thought, at least it will give the lazy old man some exercise.* **24** Some people say **like hell** to emphasize that they strongly disagree with you or are strongly opposed to what you say. *'I'll go myself.'—'Like hell you will!'*

he'll /hɪl, hiːl/. **He'll** is the usual spoken form of 'he will'. *By the time he's twenty he'll know everyone worth knowing in Washington.*

hell-'bent; also spelled **hellbent**. If you are **hell-bent** on doing something, you are determined to do it, whatever the consequences might be.

Hel·len·ic /heˈlenɪk, -ˈliː-/. **Hellenic** is used to describe the people, language, and culture of Ancient Greece.

hell·hole /ˈhelhəʊl/ **hellholes.** If you call a place a **hellhole**, you mean that it is extremely unpleasant. *...stuck in this hellhole of a jail.*

hell·ish /ˈhelɪʃ/. You describe something as **hellish** to emphasize that it is extremely unpleasant. *The atmosphere in Washington is hellish.*

hel·lo /heˈləʊ/ **hellos;** also spelled **hallo** or **hullo**. **1** You say **'Hello'** to someone when you are greeting them or when you are meeting them for the first time in the course of a day. *Hello, Trish. I won't shake hands, because I'm filthy... Do you want to pop your head in and say hallo to my girlfriend?* ► Also a noun. *The salesperson greeted me with a warm hello.* **2** You say **'Hello'** to someone at the beginning of a telephone conversation, either when you answer the phone or before you give your name or say why you are phoning. *Hallo, may I speak to Frank, please.* **3** Radio or television presenters often say **'Hello'** at the beginning of a programme, as part of the introduction. **4** You can call **'hello'** to attract someone's attention. *Very softly, she called out: 'Hallo? Who's there?'*

hell·uva /ˈheləvə/. Some people say **a helluva** or **one helluva** to emphasize that something is very good, very bad, or very big. *Winning the title would mean a helluva lot.*

helm /helm/ **helms. 1** The **helm** of a boat or ship is its wheel or tiller and the position from which the boat is controlled. *I got into our dinghy while Willis took the helm.* **2** You can say that someone is at the **helm** when they are in a position of leadership or control. *He has been at the helm of Lonrho for 31 years.*

hel·met /ˈhelmɪt/ **helmets.** A **helmet** is a close-fitting hat made of a strong material which you wear to protect your head. ● See also **crash helmet.**

helms·man /ˈhelmzmən/ **helmsmen.** The **helmsman** of a boat is the person who is steering it.

help /help/ **helps, helping, helped. 1** If you **help** someone, you make it easier for them to do something, for example by doing part of the work for them or by giving them advice or money. *He has helped to raise a lot of money... America's priority is to help nations defend themselves... You can of course help by giving them a donation directly... He began to help with the chores.* ► Also a noun. *Some of them have qualified for help with monthly payments.* **2** If you say that something **helps**, you mean that it makes something easier to do or get, or that it improves a situation to some extent. *The right style of swimsuit can help to hide, minimise or emphasise what you want it to... It will do very little indeed to help our environment... Understanding these*

rare molecules will help chemists to find out what is achievable. **3** If you say that someone or something has been **a help** or has been some **help**, you mean that they have helped you to do something that you were having difficulty with. *The books were not much help.* **4** If someone or something **is of help**, they make something easier or make a situation better to some extent. *Can I be of help to you?*
5 If you **help** someone go somewhere or move in some way, you give them support so that they can move more easily. *Come and help me up!... She helped her sit up in bed so she could hold her baby.* **6** If you **help** yourself, you try to get yourself out of a difficult situation rather than accept it and think you can do nothing to change it. *He tries to help people with problems, but firmly believes they should do more to help themselves.* **7 Help** is the assistance that someone gives when they go to rescue a person who is in danger. You shout **'help!'** when you are in danger in order to attract someone's attention so that they can come and rescue you. *He was screaming for help.*
8 If you **help** yourself to something, you serve yourself or you take it for yourself. If someone tells you to **help** yourself, they are telling you politely to serve yourself anything you want or to take anything you want. *There's bread on the table. Help yourself... Just help yourself to leaflets.* **9** If someone **helps** themself to something, they steal it. *Has somebody helped himself to some film star's diamonds?* **10** See also **helping.**
11 If you **can't help** the way you feel or behave, you cannot control it or stop it happening. You can also say that you **can't help** yourself. *'Please don't cry.'—'I can't help it.'... Jerry and Lise know their romance inflicts hurt on others, but they can't help themselves.*
12 If you say you **can't help** thinking something, you are expressing your opinion in an indirect way, often because you think it seems rude. *I can't help feeling that this may just be another of her schemes.*

help out. If you **help** someone **out**, you help them by doing some work for them or by lending them some money. *I help out with the secretarial work... He thought you'd been brought in from Toronto to help out the local police.*

help·er /ˈhelpə/ **helpers.** A **helper** is a person who helps another person or group with a job they are doing.

help·ful /ˈhelpʊl/. **1** If you describe someone as **helpful**, you mean that they help you in some way, such as doing part of your job for you or by giving you information. *The staff in the London office are helpful but only have limited information... Thank you, you've been most helpful.* ♦ **help·ful·ly** *They had helpfully provided us with instructions on how to find the house.* **2** If you describe information or advice as **helpful**, you mean that it is useful for you. *The catalog includes helpful information on the different bike models available.* **3** Something that is **helpful** makes a situation more pleasant or more easy to tolerate. *It is often helpful to have your spouse in the room when major news is expected.*

help·ing /ˈhelpɪŋ/ **helpings. 1** A **helping** of food is the amount of it that you get in a single serving. *She gave them extra helpings of ice-cream.* **2** You can refer to an amount of something, especially a quality, as a **helping** of that thing. *It took a generous helping of entrepreneurial confidence to persevere during this incident.*

help·less /ˈhelpləs/. If you are **helpless**, you do not have the strength or power to do anything useful or to control or protect yourself. *Once aboard we were soon helpless with laughter at the absurdity of it... They are not merely helpless victims.* ♦ **help·less·ly** *Their son watched helplessly as they vanished beneath the waves.* ♦ **help·less·ness** *He was wary of letting strangers observe his helplessness.*

help·line /ˈhelplaɪn/ **helplines.** A **helpline** is a special telephone service that people can call to get advice about a particular subject.

help·mate /ˈhelpmeɪt/ **helpmates.** If you say that one person is another person's **helpmate**, you

mean that they help the other person in their life or work, especially by doing boring but necessary jobs for them such as cooking and cleaning. *She was simply a different kind of companion, a helpmate, necessary to his future.*

helter-skelter /ˌheltə 'skeltə/. You use **helter-skelter** to describe something that is hurried and disorganized, especially when things happen very quickly, one after the other. *He now faces another crisis in his helter-skelter existence.* ▶ Also an adverb. *...a panic-stricken crowd running helter-skelter to get away from the tear gas.* — ADJ: ADJ n / ADV: ADV after v

hem /hem/ **hems, hemming, hemmed.** **1** A **hem** on something such as a sheet, cloth, or piece of clothing is an edge that is folded over and stitched down to make it neat and to prevent it from fraying. The **hem** of a skirt or dress is the hem along its lower edge. **2** If you **hem** something, you form a hem along its edge. *Each dress is hemmed and scrupulously checked for imperfections.* **3** • **hem and haw:** see **haw.** — ◆◇◇◇◇ N-COUNT / VERB V n

hem in. **1** If a place **is hemmed in** by mountains, barriers, or other places, it is surrounded by them. *Manchester is hemmed in by green belt countryside and by housing and industrial areas.* **2** If someone **is hemmed in** or if someone **hems** them **in**, they are prevented from moving or changing, for example because they are surrounded by people or obstacles. *BG's competitors complain that they are hemmed in by rigid, legal contracts... Derek told him to get round to the front of the parade to hem her in.* — PHRASAL VB be V-ed P by n / be V-ed P by n V n P

'he-man, he-men. A **he-man** is a strong and virile man, especially one who likes to show everyone how strong and virile he is. — N-COUNT INFORMAL

hemi·sphere /ˈhemɪsfɪə/ **hemispheres.** **1** A **hemisphere** is one half of the earth. *...the depletion of the ozone layer in the northern hemisphere.* **2** A **hemisphere** is one half of the brain. *In most people, the left hemisphere is bigger than the right.* — ◆◇◇◇◇ N-COUNT / N-COUNT

hem·line /ˈhemlaɪn/ **hemlines.** The **hemline** of a dress or skirt is its lower edge; sometimes used to refer to how long the dress or skirt is. *Mickey favoured tight skirts with a hemline at the knee.* — N-COUNT

hem·lock /ˈhemlɒk/. **Hemlock** is a poisonous plant. — N-UNCOUNT

hemo·glo·bin /ˌhiːməˈgləʊbɪn/. See **haemoglobin.**

hemo·philia /ˌhiːməˈfɪliə/. See **haemophilia.**

hemo·phili·ac /ˌhiːməˈfɪliæk/. See **haemophilia.**

hem·or·rhage /ˈhemərɪdʒ/. See **haemorrhage.**

hem·or·rhoid /ˈhemərɔɪd/. See **haemorrhoid.**

hemp /hemp/. **Hemp** is a plant, originally from Asia. It is used for making rope and in the production of cannabis and marijuana. The plant is also referred to as 'cannabis'. — ◆◇◇◇◇ N-UNCOUNT

hen /hen/ **hens.** **1** A **hen** is a female chicken. People often keep hens in order to eat or sell their eggs. **2** The female of any bird can be referred to as a **hen.** *...ostrich hens.* — ◆◆◇◇◇ N-COUNT / N-COUNT

hence /hens/. **1** You use **hence** to indicate that the statement you are about to make is a consequence of what you have just said. *The Socialist Party was profoundly divided and hence very weak.* **2** You use **hence** in expressions such as **'several years hence'** or **'six months hence'** to refer to a time in the future, especially a long time in the future. *The gases that may be warming the planet will have their main effect many years hence.* — ◆◆◇◇◇ ADV cl/group FORMAL / ADV: amount ADV PRAGMATICS FORMAL

hence·forth /ˌhensˈfɔːθ/. **Henceforth** means from this time onwards. *Henceforth, the pope would be elected solely by cardinals.* — ◆◇◇◇◇ ADV: ADV with cl FORMAL

hence·forward /ˌhensˈfɔːwəd/. **Henceforward** means the same as **henceforth.** — ADV: ADV with cl FORMAL

hench·man /ˈhentʃmən/ **henchmen.** If you refer to someone as another person's **henchman,** you mean that they work for or support the other person, especially by doing unpleasant, violent, or dishonest things on their behalf. — N-COUNT PRAGMATICS

hen·na /ˈhenə/. **Henna** is a reddish-brown dye that is made from the leaves of a shrub. — N-UNCOUNT

'hen party, hen parties. A **hen party** or **hen night** is a party to which only women are invited. A — N-COUNT BRITISH

woman often has a hen party just before she gets married.

'hen-pecked; also spelled **henpecked.** You use **hen-pecked** to describe a man when you disapprove of the fact that a woman is always telling him what to do. — ADJ-GRADED PRAGMATICS INFORMAL

hepa·ti·tis /ˌhepəˈtaɪtɪs/. **Hepatitis** is a serious disease which affects the liver. — ◆◇◇◇◇ N-UNCOUNT

hep·tath·lon /hepˈtæθlɒn/ **heptathlons.** The **heptathlon** is an athletics competition for women in which each athlete competes in seven different events. — N-COUNT

her /hə, STRONG hɜː/. **Her** is a third person singular pronoun. **Her** is used as the object of a verb or a preposition. **Her** is also a possessive determiner. **1** You use **her** to refer to a woman, girl, or female animal. *I went in the room and told her I had something to say to her... I really thought I'd lost her. Everybody kept asking me, 'Have you found your cat?'* ▶ Also a possessive determiner. *Liz travelled round the world for a year with her boyfriend James.* **2** Writers sometimes use **her** to refer to a person without saying whether that person is a man or a woman. Some people dislike this use and prefer to use 'him or her' or 'them'. *Talk to your baby, play games, and show her how much you enjoy her company.* ▶ Also a possessive determiner. *The non-drinking, non smoking model should do nothing to risk her reputation.* **3** **Her** is sometimes used to refer to a country or nation. *He hoped to be able to erect a barrier of fortresses around France to protect her from invasion.* ▶ Also a possessive determiner. *Our reporter looks at reactions to Britain's apparently deep-rooted distrust of her EC partner.* **4** People sometimes use **her** to refer informally to a car, ship, or machine. *Kemp got out of his car. 'Just fill her up, thanks.'* ▶ Also a possessive determiner. *This dramatic photograph was taken from Carpathia's deck by one of her passengers.* — ◆◆◆◆◆ PRON / DET-POSS / PRON WRITTEN / DET-POSS / PRON FORMAL / DET-POSS / PRON / DET-POSS

her·ald /ˈherəld/ **heralds, heralding, heralded.** **1** Something that **heralds** a future event or situation is a sign that it is going to happen or appear. *Their discovery could herald a cure for some forms of impotence.* ▶ Also a noun. *For her, it was the herald of summer.* **2** If an important event or action is **heralded** by people, announcements are made about it so that it is publicly known and expected. *Tonight's clash between Real Madrid and Arsenal is being heralded as the match of the season.* **3** In former times, a **herald** was a person who delivered and announced important messages. — ◆◆◇◇◇ VERB V n FORMAL / N-COUNT / VERB: be V-ed by n be V-ed as n FORMAL / N-COUNT

he·ral·dic /həˈrældɪk/. **Heraldic** means relating to heraldry. *...religious and heraldic symbols.* — ADJ: ADJ n

her·al·dry /ˈherəldri/. **Heraldry** is the study of coats of arms and of the history of the families who are entitled to have them. — N-UNCOUNT

herb /hɜːb, AM ɜːb/ **herbs.** A **herb** is a plant whose leaves are used in cookery to add flavour to food, or as a medicine. — ◆◆◇◇◇ N-COUNT

her·ba·ceous /hɜːˈbeɪʃəs, AM ɜːˈb-/. **Herbaceous** plants are soft and fleshy rather than hard and woody. — ◆◇◇◇◇ ADJ: ADJ n

her·baceous 'border, herbaceous borders. A **herbaceous border** is a flower bed containing a mixture of plants that flower every year. — N-COUNT

herb·al /ˈhɜːbəl, AM ɜːrb-/. **Herbal** means made from or using herbs. *...herbal remedies for colds.* — ◆◇◇◇◇ ADJ: ADJ n

herb·al·ism /ˈhɜːbəlɪzəm, AM ɜːrb-/. **Herbalism** is the practice of using herbs to treat illnesses. — N-UNCOUNT

♦ **herb·al·ist** /ˈhɜːbəlɪst, AM ɜːrb-/ **herbalists.** *You'd be advised to consult a qualified herbalist.* — N-COUNT

herbi·cide /ˈhɜːbɪsaɪd, AM ɜːrb-/ **herbicides.** A **herbicide** is a chemical that is used to destroy plants, especially weeds. — ◆◇◇◇◇ N-VAR

her·bi·vore /ˈhɜːbɪvɔː, AM ɜːrb-/ **herbivores.** A **herbivore** is an animal that only eats plants. — N-COUNT

her·cu·lean /ˌhɜːkjuˈliːən/; also spelled **Herculean.** A **herculean** task or ability is one that requires extremely great strength or effort. *Finding a lawyer may seem like a Herculean task if you live in a big city.* — ADJ-GRADED LITERARY

herd /hɜːd/ **herds, herding, herded. 1** A **herd** is `◆◆◇◇◇` `N-COUNT` a large group of animals of one kind that live together. ...*dairy herds.* **2** If you say that someone has `N-SING:` joined **the herd** or follows **the herd**, you are criticiz- `the N` ing them because you think that they behave just `PRAGMATICS` like everyone else and do not think for themselves. **3** If you **herd** people somewhere, you make them `VERB` move there in a group. *The group was herded into a* `V n prep/adv` *bus.* **4** If you **herd** animals, you make them move `VERB: V n` along as a group. *A boy herded half a dozen camels* `V n prep/adv` *down towards the water trough.*

herds·man /'hɜːdzmən/ **herdsmen.** A **herdsman** `N-COUNT` is a man who looks after a herd of animals such as cattle or goats.

here /hɪə/. **1** You use **here** when you are referring `◆◆◆◆◆` to the place where you are. *I'm here all by myself* `ADV:` *and I know I'm going to get lost... Well, I can't stand* `be ADV,` *here chatting all day... Sheila was in here a minute* `ADV after v,` *ago... I'm not going to stay here. I'm out of here, back* `prep ADV` *down to San Diego.* **2** You use **here** when you are `ADV:` pointing towards a place that is near you, in order `ADV after v,` to draw someone else's attention to it. ...*if you will* `prep ADV,` *just sign here... Come and sit here, Lauren.. 'From* `be ADV` *there, pulling a line to here,' he said, making invis-* *ible drawings in the air.* **3** You use **here** in order to `ADV:` indicate that the person or thing that you are talk- `n ADV,` ing about is near you or is being held by you. *My* `ADV after v` *friend here writes for radio... I have a little book here* *by a lady called Mystic Meg.* **4** You use **here** in order `ADV:` to draw attention to something or someone who `ADV with be,` has just arrived in the place where you are, or to `ADV before v` draw attention to the place you have just arrived at. *'Here's the taxi,' she said politely... Here comes your* *husband.* **5** You use **here** to refer to people in general and their `ADV:` life on Earth. ...*where we have come from, where we* `n ADV,` *are going to, or what our purpose here is, if any... Who* `ADV after v` *are we? What are we doing here?* **6** If you say that you `ADV:` are **here** to do something, that is your role or function. `be ADV to-inf` *I'm here to help you... I'm not here to listen to your* *complaints.* **7** You use **here** to refer to a particular `ADV:` point or stage of a situation or subject that you have `it v-link ADV` come to or that you are dealing with. *Both sides will* `that,` *have to sell the agreement to their people. It's here that* `ADV with v,` *the real test will come... The book goes into recent work* `ADV with cl` *in greater detail than I have attempted here.* **8** You use **here** to refer to a period of time, a situation, `ADV:` or an event that is present or happening now. *Eco-* `ADV before v,` *nomic recovery is here... Here is your opportunity to ac-* `ADV with be` *quire a luxurious one bedroom starter home.* **9** You `ADV:` use **here** at the beginning of a sentence in order to `ADV be n/wh` draw attention to something or to introduce some- thing. *From Nairobi here's our East Africa correspond-* *ent, Colin Blane... Now here's what I want you to do.* **10** You use **here** when you are offering or giving `ADV:` something to someone. *You know you can phone me—* `ADV be n` *here's my mother's number... Here's some letters I want* `PRAGMATICS` *you to sign.* **11** You say **'here we are'** or **'here you are'** when the `PHRASE` statement that you are making about someone's `PRAGMATICS` character or situation is unexpected. *Here you are,* *saying these terrible things... Here we are, pretending* *we're winning.* **12** You say **'here we are'** when you `CONVENTION` have just found something that you have been look- ing for. *I rummaged through the drawers and came up* *with Amanda's folder. 'Here we are.'* **13** You say **'here** `CONVENTION` **goes'** when you are about to do or say something diffi- `PRAGMATICS` cult or unpleasant. *Dr Culver nervously muttered* *'Here goes,' and gave the little girl an injection.* **14** You `PHRASE` use expressions such as **'here we go'**, **'here we go** `PRAGMATICS` **again'**, or **'here I go again'** in order to indicate that `INFORMAL` something is happening again in the way that you ex- pected, especially something unpleasant. *At first, he* *was told he was too young and I thought, 'Oh, boy, here* *we go again.'* **15** You use **here and now** to emphasize that some- `PHRASE` thing is happening at the present time, rather than in `PRAGMATICS` the future or past, or that you would like it to happen at the present time. *Instead of staying in the here and* *now, you bring up similar instances from the past.*

16 If something happens **here and there**, it happens `PHRASE` in several different places. *He could only understand a* *word here and there.* **17** You use expressions such as `CONVENTION` **'here's to us'** and **'here's to your new job'** as a toast in `PRAGMATICS` order to wish success to a venture or happiness to a person.

here·abouts /ˌhɪərə'baʊts/. You use **hereabouts** to `ADV:` indicate that you are talking about something near `ADV after v,` you or in the same area as you. *The mountains* `n ADV` *hereabouts reach heights of over 2000 metres.*

here·after /ˌhɪər'ɑːftə, -'æft-/. **1** **Hereafter** means `ADV:` from this time onwards. *My new plan seems* `ADV with cl` *admirable—hereafter for three years my name will* `FORMAL,` *not appear at all.* **2** **Hereafter** is used to introduce `WRITTEN` information about an abbreviation that will be used `ADV:` in the rest of the text to refer to the person or thing `ADV with cl` just mentioned. *Michel Foucault (1972), The Archae-* `PRAGMATICS` *ology of Knowledge; hereafter this text will be abbre-* `WRITTEN` *viated as AK.* **3** The **hereafter** is sometimes used to `N-SING` refer to the time after you have died, or to the life which some people believe you have after you have died. ▸ Also an adverb. *He had a sense of mission in* `ADV:` *both the temporal world and in the life hereafter.* `n ADV,` `ADV with cl`

here·by /ˌhɪə'baɪ/. **1** You use **hereby** to indicate `ADV:` that what you are saying has official status and will `ADV before v` take effect immediately. *I hereby sentence you for life* `PRAGMATICS` *after all the charges against you have been proven* `FORMAL` *true.* **2** You use **hereby** to draw attention to what `ADV:` you are saying or suggesting, and to emphasize your `ADV before v` sincerity. *I hereby predict this fetish will be the death* `PRAGMATICS` *of economics.* `FORMAL`

he·red·i·tary /hɪ'redɪtri/. **1** A **hereditary** character- `◆◇◇◇◇` istic or illness is passed on to a child from its par- `ADJ` ents before it is born. *Cystic fibrosis is the common-* *est fatal hereditary disease.* **2** A title or position in `ADJ` society that is **hereditary** is one that is passed on as a right from parent to child. *British Prime Ministers* *are traditionally offered hereditary peerages.*

he·red·i·ty /hɪ'redɪti/. **Heredity** is the process by `N-UNCOUNT` which features and characteristics are passed on from parents to their children before the children are born. *Only a minority of cancers are thought to* *be directly linked to heredity.*

here·in /ˌhɪər'ɪn/. **1** **Herein** means in this docu- `ADV` ment, text, or book. *The statements and views ex-* `PRAGMATICS` *pressed herein are those of the author and are not* `FORMAL,` *necessarily those of the Wilson Centre.* **2** You can use `WRITTEN` **herein** to introduce a clause where you state an `ADV:` opinion or analysis that relates to your main topic, `ADV cl` usually when you go on to explain it in more detail. `PRAGMATICS,` *The point is that people grew unaccustomed to* `FORMAL,` *thinking and acting in a responsible and independ-* `WRITTEN` *ent way. Herein lies another big problem.*

her·esy /'herɪsi/ **heresies. 1** **Heresy** is a belief or `◆◇◇◇◇` action that most people think is wrong, because it `N-VAR` disagrees with beliefs that are generally accepted. *It* *might be considered heresy to suggest such a notion.* **2** **Heresy** is a belief or action which seriously dis- `N-VAR` agrees with the principles of a particular religion. *He* *said it was a heresy to suggest that women should not* *conduct services.*

her·etic /'herɪtɪk/ **heretics. 1** A **heretic** is some- `N-COUNT` one whose beliefs or actions are considered wrong by most people, because they disagree with beliefs that are generally accepted. **2** A **heretic** is a person `N-COUNT` who belongs to a particular religion, but whose be- liefs or actions seriously disagree with the principles of that religion.

he·reti·cal /hɪ'retɪkəl/. **1** A belief or action that is `ADJ` **heretical** is one that most people think is wrong be- cause it disagrees with beliefs that are generally ac- cepted. *I made the then heretical suggestion that it* *might be cheaper to design new machines.* **2** A belief `ADJ` or action that is **heretical** is one that seriously dis- agrees with the principles of a particular religion. *The Church regards spirit mediums and people* *claiming to speak to the dead as heretical.*

here·to·fore /ˌhɪətuː'fɔː/. **Heretofore** means before `ADV:` this time. *They reported that clouds are an impor-* `ADV with v,` `also ADV adj,`

tant and heretofore uninvestigated contributor to the climate. ADV with cl FORMAL

here·with /ˌhɪəˈwɪθ/. In written English, **herewith** means 'with this document, text, or book'. You can use **herewith** in a letter to say that you are enclosing something with it. *We demand that by 9 a.m. the regime free the 236 revolutionary prisoners whose names are listed herewith... I return herewith your papers.* ADV PRAGMATICS FORMAL

her·it·age /ˈherɪtɪdʒ/ **heritages.** A country's **heritage** is all the qualities, traditions, or features of life that have been continued over many years and passed on from one generation to another, especially ones that are of historical importance or that have had a strong influence on society. *...the rich heritage of Russian folk music.* ◆◆◇◇◇ N-VAR

her·maph·ro·dite /hɜːˈmæfrədaɪt/ **hermaphrodites.** A **hermaphrodite** is a person, animal, or flower that has both male and female reproductive organs. N-COUNT TECHNICAL

her·met·ic /hɜːˈmetɪk/. **1** If a container has a **hermetic** seal, the seal is very tight so that no air can get in or out. ♦ **her·meti·cal·ly** /hɜːˈmetɪkli/ *The batteries are designed to be leak-proof and hermetically sealed.* **2** You use **hermetic** to describe something which you disapprove of because it seems to be socially, physically, or intellectually separate from other people and things in society. *Its film industry operates in its own curiously hermetic way.* ◆◇◇◇◇ ADJ: ADJ n
ADV
ADJ-GRADED PRAGMATICS WRITTEN

her·mit /ˈhɜːmɪt/ **hermits.** A **hermit** is a person who lives alone, away from people and society. ◆◇◇◇◇ N-COUNT

her·nia /ˈhɜːniə/ **hernias.** A **hernia** is a medical condition in which one of your inner organs sticks through a weak point in the surrounding tissue. ◆◇◇◇◇ N-VAR

hero /ˈhɪərəʊ/ **heroes. 1** The **hero** of a book, play, or film is the main male character, who usually has good qualities. **2** A **hero** is someone, especially a man, who has done something brave, new, or good, and who is therefore greatly admired by a lot of people. *He called Mr Mandela a hero who had inspired millions.* **3** If you describe someone as your **hero** you mean that you admire them a great deal. *My boyhood hero was Bobby Charlton.* ◆◆◇◇◇ N-COUNT
N-COUNT

N-COUNT

he·ro·ic /hɪˈrəʊɪk/ **heroics. 1** If you describe a person or their actions as **heroic**, you admire them because they show extreme bravery. *His heroic deeds were celebrated in every corner of India.* ♦ **he·roi·cal·ly** /hɪˈrəʊɪkli/ *He had acted heroically during the liner's evacuation.* **2** If you describe an action or event as **heroic**, you admire it because it involves great effort or determination to succeed. *He finally faltered in the last game of a heroic match.* ♦ **heroically** *Single parents cope heroically in doing the job of two people.* **3 Heroics** are actions involving bravery, courage, or determination. *England need heroics from the captain now.* **4** If you describe someone's actions or plans as **heroics**, you mean that they are foolish or dangerous because they are too difficult for the situation in which they occur; used showing disapproval. *He said his advice was: 'No heroics, stay within the law'.* ◆◆◇◇◇ ADJ-GRADED
ADV-GRADED
ADJ-GRADED PRAGMATICS
ADV
N-PLURAL
N-PLURAL PRAGMATICS SPOKEN

hero·in /ˈherəʊɪn/. **Heroin** is a powerful and dangerous drug which some people become addicted to. It is illegal in most countries. ◆◆◇◇◇ N-UNCOUNT

hero·ine /ˈherəʊɪn/ **heroines. 1** The **heroine** of a book, play, or film is the main female character, who usually has good qualities. **2** A **heroine** is a woman who has done something brave, new, or good, and who is therefore greatly admired by a lot of people. *The national heroine of the day was Xing Fen, winner of the first Gold medal of the Games.* **3** If you describe a woman as your **heroine**, you mean that you admire her greatly. *My heroine was Elizabeth Taylor.* ◆◆◇◇◇ N-COUNT
N-COUNT

N-COUNT PRAGMATICS

hero·ism /ˈherəʊɪzəm/. **Heroism** is great courage and bravery. *...individual acts of heroism.* ◆◇◇◇◇

her·on /ˈherən/ **herons.** A **heron** is a large bird which has long legs and a long beak, and which eats fish. N-COUNT

hero-worship, hero-worships, hero-worshipping, hero-worshipped; the noun is also spelled **hero worship.** If you **hero-worship** someone, you admire them a great deal and think they are special or perfect. *Younger actors started to hero-worship and copy him.* ▶ Also a noun. *Singer Brett Anderson inspires old-fashioned hero-worship.* VERB
V n
N-UNCOUNT

her·pes /ˈhɜːpiːz/. **Herpes** is the name of several viruses which cause painful red spots to appear on the skin. ◆◇◇◇◇ N-UNCOUNT MEDICAL

her·ring /ˈherɪŋ/ **herrings.** The plural can be either **herring** or **herrings.** A **herring** is a long silver-coloured fish. ▶ **Herring** is this fish eaten as food. ● See also **red herring.** ◆◇◇◇◇ N-VAR
N-UNCOUNT

herring·bone /ˈherɪŋbəʊn/. **Herringbone** is a pattern used in fabrics or brickwork, which appears as parallel rows of zigzag lines. See picture headed **patterns.** N-UNCOUNT

hers /hɜːz/. **Hers** is a third person possessive pronoun.
1 You use **hers** to indicate that something belongs or relates to a woman, girl, or female animal. *His hand as it shook hers was warm and firm. ...a great friend of hers.* **2** Writers sometimes use **hers** to refer to a person without saying whether that person is a man or a woman. Some people dislike this use and prefer to use 'his or hers' or 'theirs'. *...results which more or less agree with hers.* **3 Hers** is sometimes used in written English to refer formally to a country or nation. **4** People sometimes use **hers** to refer to a car or a machine. People also sometimes use **hers** to refer to a ship. ◆◆◇◇◇ PRON-POSS
PRON-POSS WRITTEN
PRON-POSS
PRON-POSS INFORMAL

her·self /hɜːˈself/. **Herself** is a third person singular reflexive pronoun. **Herself** is used when the object of a verb or preposition refers to the same person as the subject of the verb, except in meaning 5.
1 You use **herself** to refer to a woman, girl, or female animal. *She let herself out of the room... Robin didn't feel good about herself.* **2** Writers sometimes use **herself** to refer to a person without saying whether that person is a man or a woman. Some people dislike this use and prefer to use 'himself or herself' or 'themselves'. *How can anyone believe stories for which she feels herself to be in no way responsible?* **3 Herself** is sometimes used to refer to a country or nation. *Britain's dream of herself began to fade.* **4** People sometimes use **herself** to refer to a car or a machine. People also use **herself** to refer to a ship. *The ship adjusted herself to the roll and rhythm of the sea.* **5** You use **herself** to emphasize the person or thing that you are referring to. **Herself** is sometimes used instead of 'her' as the object of a verb or preposition. *She's so beautiful herself... Has anyone thought of consulting Bethan herself?* ◆◆◆◆◆ PRON-REFL
V PRON, prep PRON
PRON-REFL WRITTEN
PRON-REFL FORMAL, WRITTEN
PRON-REFL INFORMAL
PRON-REFL PRAGMATICS

he's /hiz, hiːz/. **He's** is the usual spoken form of 'he is' or 'he has', especially when 'has' is an auxiliary verb. *He's working maybe twenty-five hours a week.*

hesi·tant /ˈhezɪtənt/. If you are **hesitant** about doing something, you do not do it quickly or immediately, usually because you are uncertain, embarrassed, or worried. *His advisers are rightfully hesitant to let the United States be sucked into the conflict.* ♦ **hesi·tan·cy** /ˈhezɪtənsi/ *A trace of hesitancy showed in Dr. Stockton's eyes.* ♦ **hesi·tant·ly** *'Would you do me a favour?' she asked hesitantly.* ◆◇◇◇◇ ADJ-GRADED
N-UNCOUNT
ADV-GRADED: ADV with v

hesi·tate /ˈhezɪteɪt/ **hesitates, hesitating, hesitated. 1** If you **hesitate**, you pause slightly while you are doing or saying something, or just before you do or say it, usually because you are uncertain, embarrassed, or worried about it. ♦ **hesi·ta·tion** /ˌhezɪˈteɪʃən/ **hesitations** *Mr Searle said after some hesitation, 'I'll have to think about that.'* **2** If you **hesitate** to do something, you are unwilling to do it, usually because you are worried or not quite certain whether it is correct or right. If you do not **hesitate** to do something, you do it very willingly or with great certainty. *Many women hesitate to discuss money... I will not hesitate to take unpopular decisions.* **3** You can use **hesitate** in expressions such as **'don't hesitate to call me'**, or **'don't hesitate to contact us'**, when you are telling someone ◆◆◇◇◇ VERB: V
N-VAR
VERB V to-inf
VB: only imper, with neg, V to-inf

that they should do something, and that they should not worry about disturbing other people if they do. `PRAGMATICS`

hesi·ta·tion /ˌhezɪˈteɪʃən/ **hesitations. 1** Hesitation is an unwillingness to do something, or a delay in doing it, because you are uncertain, worried, or embarrassed about it. *He promised there would be no more hesitations in pursuing reforms.* • See also **hesitate. 2** If you say that you **have no hesitation** in doing something, you are emphasizing that you will do it immediately or willingly because you are certain that it is the right thing to do. *The board said it had no hesitation in unanimously rejecting the offer.* **3** If you say that someone does something **without hesitation**, you are emphasizing that they do it immediately and willingly. *The boy followed without hesitation.* ◆◇◇◇◇ N-VAR / PHRASE PRAGMATICS / PHRASE PRAGMATICS

hes·sian /ˈhesiən, AM ˈheʃən/. Hessian is a thick rough fabric that is used for making sacks. N-UNCOUNT BRITISH

hetero·dox /ˈhetərədɒks/. Heterodox beliefs, opinions, or ideas are different from the accepted or official ones. *Supporters of this heterodox theory turn to genetics for further evidence.* ADJ FORMAL

hetero·geneous /ˌhetərəˈdʒiːniəs/. A **heterogeneous** group consists of many different types of things or people. ADJ-GRADED FORMAL

hetero·sex·ual /ˌhetərəʊˈsekʃʊəl/ **heterosexuals. 1** A heterosexual relationship is a sexual relationship between a man and a woman. **2** Someone who is heterosexual is sexually attracted to people of the opposite sex. ► Also a noun. *The code will treat heterosexuals and gays on an equal basis.* ◆◆◇◇◇ ADJ / ADJ / N-COUNT
♦ **hetero·sexu·al·ity** /ˌhetərəʊsekʃʊˈælɪti/ *...a challenge to the assumption that heterosexuality was 'normal'.* N-UNCOUNT

het up /ˌhet ˈʌp/. If you get **het up** about something, you get very excited or anxious about it. ADJ-GRADED INFORMAL

heu·ris·tic /hjuəˈrɪstɪk/. A **heuristic** method of learning involves discovery and problem-solving techniques, using reasoning and past experience. ADJ

hew /hjuː/ **hews, hewing, hewed, hewn.** The past participle can be either **hewed** or **hewn. 1** If you **hew** stone or wood, you cut it, for example with an axe. **2** If something **is hewn** from stone or wood, it is cut or formed from stone or wood. **3** See also **rough-hewn.** VERB: V n DATED / VERB: be V-ed from/out of n DATED

hexa·gon /ˈheksəgən, AM -gɒːn/ **hexagons.** A **hexagon** is a geometric shape that has six straight sides. See picture headed **shapes.** ♦ **hex·ago·nal** *...hexagonal glass jars.* N-COUNT / ADJ

hey /heɪ/. In informal situations, you say or shout **'hey'** to attract someone's attention, or to show surprise, interest, or annoyance. *Hey, can I ask you a question?* ◆◆◇◇◇ CONVENTION PRAGMATICS

hey·day /ˈheɪdeɪ/. Someone's **heyday** is the time when they are most powerful, successful, or popular. *In its heyday, the studio's boast was that it had more stars than there are in heaven.* ◆◇◇◇◇ N-SING: with poss

hi /haɪ/. In informal situations, you say **'hi'** to greet someone. *'Hi, Liz' she said shyly.* ◆◆◆◇◇ CONVENTION

hia·tus /haɪˈeɪtəs/. A **hiatus** is a pause in which nothing happens, or a gap where something is missing. *There was a twenty four hour hiatus before a message came back... There was an hiatus in his acting life.* N-SING FORMAL

hi·ber·nate /ˈhaɪbəneɪt/ **hibernates, hibernating, hibernated.** Animals that **hibernate** spend the winter in a state like a deep sleep. VERB: V

hi·bis·cus /hɪˈbɪskəs, AM haɪ-/; **hibiscus** is both the singular and the plural. A **hibiscus** is a tropical bush with large, brightly-coloured, bell-shaped flowers. N-VAR

hic·cup /ˈhɪkʌp/ **hiccups, hiccuping** or **hiccupping, hiccuped** or **hiccupped;** also spelled **hiccough. 1** You can refer to a small problem or difficulty as a **hiccup**, especially if it does not last very long or is easily put right. *A recent sales hiccup is nothing to panic about.* **2** When you have **hiccups**, you make repeated sharp sounds in your throat, often because you have been eating or drinking too ◆◇◇◇◇ / N-COUNT / N-UNCOUNT: also the N

quickly. **3** When you **hiccup**, you make repeated sharp sounds in your throat. VERB: V

hick /hɪk/ **hicks.** If you refer to someone as a **hick**, you think they are uneducated and stupid because they come from the countryside. *...a crummy little hick hotel.* N-COUNT PRAGMATICS

hid /hɪd/. **Hid** is the past tense of **hide.**

hid·den /ˈhɪdən/. **1 Hidden** is the past participle of **hide. 2 Hidden** facts, feelings, activities, or problems are not easy to notice or discover. *There are hidden dangers, especially for children.* **3** A **hidden** place is difficult to find. *As you descend, suddenly you see at last the hidden waterfall.* ◆◆◇◇◇ / ADJ / ADJ

hidden a'genda, hidden agendas. If you say that someone has a **hidden agenda**, you are criticizing them because you think they are secretly trying to achieve a particular thing, while they appear to be doing something else. N-COUNT PRAGMATICS

hide /haɪd/ **hides, hiding, hid, hidden. 1** If you **hide** something or someone, you put them in a place where they cannot easily be seen or found. *He hid the bicycle in the hawthorn hedge.* **2** If you **hide** or if you **hide** yourself, you go somewhere where you cannot easily be seen or found. *They hid themselves behind a tree.* **3** If you **hide** your face, you press your face against something or cover your face with something, so that people cannot see it. **4** If you **hide** what you feel or know, you keep it a secret, so that no one knows about it. *Lee tried to hide his excitement.* **5** If something **hides** an object, it covers it and prevents it from being seen. *The compound was hidden by trees and shrubs.* **6** A **hide** is a place which is built to look like its surroundings. Hides are used by people who want to watch or photograph animals and birds without being seen by them. **7** A **hide** is the skin of a large animal such as a cow, which can be used for making leather. **8** See also **hidden, hiding.** ◆◆◆◇◇ V n / VERB: V V pron-refl / VERB: V n / VERB V n / VERB V n / N-COUNT BRITISH / N-VAR

hide-and-'seek. Hide-and-seek is a children's game in which one player covers his or her eyes until the other players have hidden themselves, and then he or she tries to find them. N-UNCOUNT

hide·away /ˈhaɪdəweɪ/ **hideaways.** A **hideaway** is a place where you go to hide or to get away from other people. N-COUNT

hide·bound /ˈhaɪdbaʊnd/. If you describe someone or something as **hidebound**, you are criticizing them for keeping to outdated traditions, rather than changing or accepting new ideas. ADJ-GRADED PRAGMATICS

hid·eous /ˈhɪdiəs/. **1** If you say that someone or something is **hideous**, you mean that they are very ugly or unattractive. *...hideous new European architecture.* ♦ **hid·eous·ly** *He has been left hideously disfigured by plastic surgery.* **2** You can describe an event, experience, or action as **hideous** when you mean that it is very unpleasant or painful. *His family was subjected to a hideous attack by the gang.* ♦ **hideously** *...a hideously complex program.* ◆◇◇◇◇ ADJ-GRADED / ADV / ADJ-GRADED / ADV-GRADED

hide·out /ˈhaɪdaʊt/ **hideouts.** A **hideout** is a place where someone goes secretly because they do not want anyone to find them, for example if they are running away from the police. N-COUNT

hid·ing /ˈhaɪdɪŋ/ **hidings. 1** If someone is in **hiding**, they have secretly gone somewhere where they cannot be seen or found. *The duchess is expected to come out of hiding to attend the ceremony.* **2** If someone gives you a **hiding**, they punish you by hitting you many times. **3** If you say that someone who is trying to achieve something is **on a hiding to nothing**, you are emphasizing that they have absolutely no chance of being successful. ◆◆◇◇◇ N-UNCOUNT: prep N / N-COUNT INFORMAL / PHRASE PRAGMATICS INFORMAL, BRITISH

'hiding place, hiding places. A **hiding place** is a place where someone or something can be hidden, or where they are hiding. ◆◇◇◇◇ N-COUNT

hi·er·ar·chi·cal /ˌhaɪəˈrɑːkɪkəl/. A **hierarchical** system or organization is one in which people have different ranks, depending on how important they are. ◆◇◇◇◇ ADJ-GRADED

hi·er·ar·chy /ˈhaɪərɑːki/ **hierarchies. 1** A **hierarchy** is a system of organizing people into different ◆◆◇◇◇ N-VAR

levels of importance, for example in society or in a company. *Even in the desert there was a kind of social hierarchy.* **2** The **hierarchy** of an organization such as the Church is the group of people who manage and control it. **3** A **hierarchy** of ideas and beliefs involves organizing them into a system. *...the notion of 'cultural imperialism', implies a hierarchy of cultures.*

N-COLL-COUNT: with supp
N-COUNT FORMAL

hi·ero·glyph·ics /ˌhaɪərə'ɡlɪfɪks/. **Hieroglyphics** are symbols in the form of pictures which are used in some writing systems, for example those of ancient Egypt.

N-PLURAL

hi-fi /'haɪ faɪ/ **hi-fis.** A **hi-fi** is a set of equipment on which you play records and tapes, and which produces stereo sound of very good quality.

◆◇◇◇◇ N-VAR

higgledy-piggle·dy /ˌhɪɡəldi 'pɪɡəldi/. If you say that things are **higgledy-piggledy**, you mean that they are very untidy or disorganized. *Books are often stacked in higgledy-piggledy piles on the floor.* ▶ Also an adverb. *A whole valley of boulders tossed higgledy-piggledy as though by some giant.*

ADJ-GRADED INFORMAL

ADV-GRADED: ADV after v

high /haɪ/ **higher, highest; highs. 1** Something that is **high** extends a long way from the bottom to the top when it is upright. You do not use the word **high** to describe people, animals, or plants. *...a house, with a high wall all around it. ...the highest mountain in the Adirondacks. ...high-heeled shoes.* ▶ Also an adverb. *...wagons packed high with bureaus, bedding, and cooking pots.* **2** You use **high** to talk or ask about how much something upright measures from the bottom to the top. *...an elegant bronze horse only nine inches high... How high is the door?* **3** If something is **high**, it is a long way above the ground, above sea level, or above a person or thing. *I looked down from the high window... The sun was high in the sky, blazing down on us.* ▶ Also an adverb. *...being able to run faster or jump higher than other people.* ● If something is **high up**, it is a long way above the ground, above sea level, or above a person or thing. *...grapes grown high up on the cliff.* **4** When a river is **high**, it contains much more water than usual. **5** You can use **high** to indicate that something is great in amount, degree, or intensity. *Official reports said casualties were high... High winds have knocked down trees and power lines.* ▶ Also an adverb. *He expects the unemployment figures to rise even higher in coming months.* ● You can use phrases such as '**in the high 80s**' to indicate that a number or level is, for example, more than 85 but not as much as ninety. **6** If a food or other substance is **high in** a particular ingredient, it contains a large amount of that ingredient. *...a superb compost, high in calcium.* **7** If something reaches a **high** of a particular amount or degree, that is the greatest it has ever been. *Sales of Russian vodka have reached an all-time high.* **8** If you aim **high**, you try to obtain or to achieve the best that you can. **9** If you say that something is a **high** priority or is **high** on your list, you mean that you consider it to be one of the most important things you have to do. **10** Someone who is **high** in a particular profession or society, or has a **high** position, has an important position and has great authority and influence. ● Someone who is **high up** in a profession or society has an important position. **11** If someone has a **high** reputation, or people have a **high** opinion of them, people think they are very good in some way, for example at their work. **12** If the quality or standard of something is **high**, it is very good indeed. **13** If someone has **high** principles, they are morally good. **14** A **high** sound or voice is close to the top of a particular range of notes. **15** You can use **high** to describe something that is advanced or complex. *...the rise of Japan's high technology industries.* **16** If you say that something came from **on high**, you mean that it came from a person or place of great authority. *Orders had come from on high that extra care was to be taken during this week.* **17** If you say that you were left **high and dry**, you are emphasizing

◆◆◆◆◆ ADJ-GRADED

ADV-GRADED

ADJ: amount ADJ, n ADJ, how ADJ

ADJ-GRADED

ADV-GRADED PHRASE

ADJ-GRADED

ADJ-GRADED

ADV-GRADED: ADV after v

PHRASE

ADJ-GRADED: v-link ADJ in n

N-COUNT

ADV-GRADED: ADV after v

ADJ-GRADED

ADJ-GRADED: v-link ADJ in n, ADJ n PHRASE

ADJ-GRADED

ADJ-GRADED ADJ-GRADED

ADJ-GRADED

ADJ: ADJ n

PHRASE

PHRASE PRAGMATICS INFORMAL

that you were left in a difficult situation and were unable to do anything about it. **18** If you refer to the **highs and lows** of someone's life or career, you are referring to the successful or happy times, and the unsuccessful or bad times.

PHRASE

19 If your spirits are **high**, you feel happy and excited. **20** If someone is **high** on drink or drugs, they are affected by the alcoholic drink or drugs they have taken. **21** A **high** is a feeling or mood of great excitement, stimulation, and happiness. **22** ● **in high dudgeon**: see **dudgeon**. ● **to be high time**: see **time**.

ADJ-GRADED ADJ INFORMAL

N-COUNT INFORMAL

-high /-haɪ/. **-high** combines with words such as 'knee' or 'shoulder' to indicate that someone or something reaches as high as the point that is mentioned. *The grass was knee-high.* ▶ Also a combining form. *The Tibetans lifted the man with the flag shoulder-high.*

COMB

COMB

high·born /'haɪbɔːʳn/; also spelled **high-born**. If someone is **highborn**, their parents are members of the nobility. *Only the highborn knights were spared, all others being thrown into the sea.*

ADJ-GRADED DATED

high·brow /'haɪbraʊ/. **1** If you say that a book or discussion is **highbrow**, you mean that it is intellectual, and is often difficult to understand. *...highbrow classical music.* **2** If you describe someone as **highbrow**, you mean that they are interested in serious subjects of an intellectual nature; often used showing disapproval.

ADJ-GRADED

ADJ-GRADED PRAGMATICS

high chair, high chairs. A **high chair** is a chair with long legs for a small child to sit in while they are eating.

N-COUNT

high-'class; spelled **high class** in American English. If you describe something as **high-class**, you mean that it is of very good quality or of superior social status. *...a high-class jeweller's.*

◆◇◇◇◇ ADJ-GRADED

high com'mand, high commands. The **high command** is the group that consists of the most senior officers in a nation's armed forces.

◆◇◇◇◇ N-COLL-COUNT

High Com'mission, High Commissions. A **High Commission** is an office which houses a High Commissioner and his or her staff.

◆◇◇◇◇ N-COUNT

High Com'missioner, High Commissioners. 1 A **High Commissioner** is a senior representative who is sent by one Commonwealth country to live in another in order to work as an ambassador. **2** A **High Commissioner** is the head of an international commission. *...the United Nations High Commissioner for Refugees.*

◆◇◇◇◇ N-COUNT

N-COUNT

High 'Court, High Courts. In England and Wales, the **High Court** is a court of law which deals with very important non-criminal cases.

◆◆◇◇◇ N-COUNT

high·er /'haɪəʳ/. A **higher** degree or diploma is a qualification of an advanced standard or level. ● See also **high**.

ADJ: ADJ n

higher edu'cation. Higher education is education at universities and colleges.

◆◆◇◇◇ N-UNCOUNT

high ex'plosive, high explosives. High explosive is an extremely powerful explosive substance.

N-VAR

high 'five, high fives; also spelled **high-five**. If you give someone a **high five**, you jump into the air and slap their outstretched hand, especially after a victory or as a greeting.

N-COUNT

high-'flier. See **high-flyer**.

high-'flown. High-flown language is very grand, formal, or literary; used showing disapproval.

ADJ-GRADED PRAGMATICS

high-'flyer, high-flyers; spelled **high-flier** in American English. A **high-flyer** is someone who is very ambitious and who is likely to be successful in their career. ♦ **high-flying** *...her high-flying newspaper-editor husband.*

◆◇◇◇◇ N-COUNT

ADJ-GRADED

high 'ground. 1 When journalists say that a person or organization has **the high ground** in an argument or dispute, they mean that that person or organization has an advantage. *How do we recapture the intellectual high ground?* **2** If you say that someone has taken the **moral high ground**, you mean that they consider that their policies and actions are morally superior to the policies and actions of their rivals.

◆◇◇◇◇ N-SING: the N

PHRASE

,**high-'handed.** If you say that someone is high- ADJ-GRADED
handed, you disapprove of them because they use PRAGMATICS
their authority in an unnecessarily forceful way
without considering other people's feelings. ...*his allegedly high-handed organisation of government
business in parliament.* ♦ **high-handed·ness** N-UNCOUNT
*They have been accused of secrecy and high-
handedness in their dealings.*

,**high 'heels.** High heels are high-heeled shoes. ◆◇◇◇◇
...*a tall girl in high heels.* N-PLURAL

'**high jinks.** High jinks is lively excited behaviour N-COLL:
in which people do things for fun. *Their annual* UNCOUNT
parties are notorious for high jinks. DATED,
INFORMAL

'**high jump.** The high jump is an athletics event N-SING
which involves jumping over a raised bar.

high·lands /ˈhaɪləndz/. Highlands are mountain- ◆◇◇◇◇
ous areas of land. N-PLURAL

'**high life.** You use the high life to refer to an excit- N-SING:
ing and luxurious way of living that involves a great also no det
deal of entertainment, going to parties, and eating
good food.

high·light /ˈhaɪlaɪt/ highlights, highlighting, ◆◆◆◇◇
highlighted. 1 If someone or something high- VERB
lights a point or problem, they emphasize it or V n
make you think about it. ...*a moving ballad which
highlighted the plight of the homeless.* 2 The high- N-COUNT
lights of an event, activity, or period of time are the
most interesting or exciting parts of it. 3 Highlights N-PLURAL
in a person's hair are thin streaks of lighter colour
that have usually been made by dyeing parts of the
hair.

high·light·er /ˈhaɪlaɪtər/ highlighters. N-VAR
1 Highlighter is pale-coloured make-up that someone puts above their eyes or on their cheeks to emphasize the shape of their face. 2 A highlighter is a N-COUNT
felt-tip pen with brightly coloured ink that is used
to make the important parts of a document stand
out more clearly.

high·ly /ˈhaɪli/. 1 Highly is used before some ad- ◆◆◆◆◇
jectives to mean 'very'. ...*a highly successful sales-* ADV
man... It seems highly unlikely that she ever existed. PRAGMATICS
2 You use highly to indicate that someone has an ADV-GRADED:
important position in an organization or set of peo- ADV -ed
ple. ...*highly ranked soccer teams.* 3 If someone is ADV-GRADED:
highly paid, they receive a large salary. 4 If you ADV -ed
think highly of something or someone, you think ADV-GRADED
they are very good indeed. ...*one of the most highly
regarded chefs.*

,**highly-'strung.** If someone is highly-strung, they ADJ-GRADED
are very nervous and easily upset.

,**high-'minded.** If you say that someone is high- ADJ-GRADED
minded, you think they have very strong moral
principles.

High·ness /ˈhaɪnɪs/ Highnesses. Expressions ◆◇◇◇◇
such 'Your Highness' or 'His Highness' are used to N-VOC;
address or refer to a member of the royal family poss N;
other than a king or queen. ...*Her Royal Highness* PRON:
the Duchess of Kent. poss PRON
PRAGMATICS

,**high 'noon.** 1 High noon means the same as N-UNCOUNT
noon. 2 Journalists sometimes use high noon to re- LITERARY
fer to a crisis or event which is likely to decide final- N-UNCOUNT
ly what is going to happen in a conflict or situation.

,**high-per'formance.** A high-performance car or ADJ-GRADED:
other product goes very fast or does a lot. ...*high-* ADJ n
performance computers.

,**high-'pitched;** also spelled high pitched. A ◆◇◇◇◇
high-pitched sound is high and shrill. *A woman* ADJ-GRADED
squealed in a high-pitched voice.

'**high point, high points.** The high point of an ◆◇◇◇◇
event or period of time is the most exciting or en- N-COUNT
joyable part of it.

,**high-'powered.** 1 A high-powered machine or ◆◇◇◇◇
piece of equipment is very powerful and efficient. ADJ-GRADED
...*high powered lasers.* 2 If you describe a job or ac- ADJ-GRADED
tivity as high-powered, you mean that it carries a
lot of responsibility or status, and needs a high degree of expertise. 3 If you describe someone as ADJ-GRADED
high-powered, you mean that they have a high-
powered job or are involved in a high-powered ac-

tivity. *Her father is a very high-powered solicitor in
London.*

,**high 'priest, high priests.** If you call a man the N-COUNT
high priest of a particular thing, you are saying in a PRAGMATICS
slightly mocking way that he is considered by people to be expert in that thing. ...*the high priest of
cheap periodical fiction.*

,**high 'priestess, high priestesses.** If you call a N-COUNT
woman the high priestess of a particular thing, you PRAGMATICS
are saying in a slightly mocking way that she is considered by people to be expert in that thing.

,**high-'profile.** A high-profile person or a high- ◆◇◇◇◇
profile event attracts a lot of attention or publicity. ADJ-GRADED
...*high-profile singers like Prince and Madonna.*

,**high-'ranking.** A high-ranking person has an ◆◇◇◇◇
important position in a particular organization. ADJ: ADJ n

'**high-rise, high-rises.** High-rise buildings are ◆◇◇◇◇
modern buildings which are very tall and have ADJ: ADJ n
many storeys. ▶ A high-rise is a high-rise building. N-COUNT

'**high road, high roads.** A high road is a main N-COUNT
road. The usual American word is highway. *He saw* BRITISH
*another French officer galloping furiously down the
high road.*

,**high-'roller, high-rollers;** also spelled high roll- N-COUNT
er. When journalists refer to high rollers, they are
referring to people who are very rich and who
spend money in an extravagant or risky way, especially by gambling.

'**high school, high schools.** 1 In Britain, a high ◆◇◇◇◇
school is a school for children aged between eleven N-VAR
and eighteen. 2 In the United States, a high school N-VAR
is a school for children aged between fourteen and
eighteen. ...*an 18-year-old inner-city kid who
dropped out of high school.*

'**high season.** The high season is the time of year N-SING:
when a holiday resort, hotel, or tourist attraction re- also no det
ceives most visitors. BRITISH

,**high-'sounding.** High-sounding language and ADJ-GRADED
ideas seem very grand and important, although of- PRAGMATICS
ten they are not at all important; used showing disapproval. ...*high-sounding decrees designed to impress foreigners and attract foreign capital.*

,**high-'spirited.** Someone who is high-spirited is ADJ-GRADED
very lively and easily excited.

'**high spot, high spots.** The high spot of an event N-COUNT
or activity is the most exciting or enjoyable part of
it. *The high spot of her year came when she beat
Novotna.*

,**high street, high streets.** 1 The high street of a ◆◆◇◇◇
town is the main street where most of the shops N-COUNT
and banks are. *Vegetarian restaurants and health* BRITISH
food shops are springing up in every high street.
2 High street banks and retailers are companies ADJ: ADJ n
which have branches in the main shopping areas of BRITISH
most towns. *The scanners are available from high
street stores.*

,**high 'summer.** High summer is the middle of N-UNCOUNT
summer.

,**high 'tea, high teas.** In Britain, some people N-VAR
have high tea in the late afternoon instead of having dinner or supper later in the evening.

,**high 'tech;** also spelled hi tech. High tech activ- ◆◆◇◇◇
ities or equipment involve or result from the use of ADJ-GRADED
high technology. ...*such high-tech industries as computers or telecommunications.*

,**high tech'nology.** High technology is the prac- ◆◇◇◇◇
tical use of advanced scientific research and N-UNCOUNT
knowledge, especially in relation to electronics and
computers, and the development of new advanced
machines and equipment.

,**high-'tension.** A high-tension electricity cable is ADJ: ADJ n
one which is able to carry a very powerful current.

,**high 'tide.** At the coast, high tide is the time when N-UNCOUNT
the sea is at its highest level because the tide is in.

,**high 'treason.** High treason menas the same as N-UNCOUNT
treason.

,**high-'up, high-ups.** 1 A high-up is an important ◆◇◇◇◇
person who has a lot of authority and influence. N-COUNT
2 ● high up: see high. INFORMAL

high 'water. High water is the time at which the
water in a river or sea is at its highest level as a result of the tide. *Fishing is possible for a couple of
hours either side of high water.* ◆◇◇◇◇ N-UNCOUNT

high-'water mark; also spelled **high water mark.**
The **high-water mark** of a process is its highest or
most successful stage of achievement. *This was almost certainly the high-water mark of her career.* N-SING with supp

high·way /'haɪweɪ/ **highways.** A **highway** is a
main road, especially one that connects towns or
cities. ◆◆◇◇◇ N-COUNT AMERICAN

Highway 'Code. In Britain, **the Highway Code** is
an official booklet published by the Department of
Transport, which contains the rules which tell people how to use public roads safely. N-SING: the N

highway·man /'haɪweɪmən/ **highwaymen.** In former times, **highwaymen** were robbers on horseback
who used to threaten to shoot travellers if they did
not hand over their money and valuables. N-COUNT

high 'wire, high wires; also spelled **high-wire.**
1 A **high wire** is a length of rope or wire stretched
tight high above the ground and used for balancing
acts. N-COUNT

2 Journalists talk about a person being on a **high wire**
or performing a **high-wire** act when he or she is involved in a delicate, tricky situation, and is dealing
with it cleverly. *What could have been a mere intellectual high wire act becomes a wholly unexpected
delight.* N-SING

hi·jack /'haɪdʒæk/ **hijacks, hijacking, hijacked.**
1 If someone **hijacks** a plane or other vehicle, they
illegally take control of it by force while it is travelling from one place to another. ► Also a noun. *Every
minute during the hijack seemed like a week.* ♦ **hi-
·jack·er, hijackers** *There was a scuffle between
the hijackers and the pilots.* ♦ **hi·jack·ing,
hijackings** *There have been at least ten attempted
hijackings in the Soviet Union.* **2** If you say that
someone **has hijacked** something, you disapprove
of the way in which they have taken control of it
when they had no right to do so. *A peaceful demonstration had been hijacked by anarchists intent on
causing trouble.* ◆◇◇◇◇ VERB: V n / N-COUNT / N-COUNT / VERB PRAGMATICS V n

hike /haɪk/ **hikes, hiking, hiked. 1** If you **hike**,
you go for a long walk in the country. *You could
hike through the Fish River Canyon.* ► Also a noun. *I
took long hikes through the nearby fields.* ♦ **hik·er,
hikers** *He guided hunters and hikers through the
millions of acres of Adirondack forest.* ♦ **hik·ing**
*...some harder, more strenuous hiking on cliff path-
ways.* ◆◆◇◇◇ VERB: V / V prep/adv / N-COUNT / N-COUNT / N-UNCOUNT

2 A **hike** is a sudden or large increase in prices, rates,
taxes, or quantities. *...a sudden 1.75 per cent hike in
Italian interest rates.* **3** To **hike** prices, rates, or taxes
means to increase them suddenly or by a large
amount. *The federal government hiked the tax on hard
liquor.* ► **Hike up** means the same as **hike.** *The insur-
ers have started hiking up premiums by huge amounts.* N-COUNT / VERB V n / PHRASAL VB V P noun

hi·lari·ous /hɪ'leəriəs/. If something is **hilarious,** it
is extremely funny and makes you laugh a lot. *He
had a fund of hilarious tales on the subject.* ♦ **hi-
·lari·ous·ly** *She found it hilariously funny.* ◆◇◇◇◇ ADJ-GRADED / ADV-GRADED

hi·lar·ity /hɪ'lærɪti/. **Hilarity** is great amusement
and laughter. *My mistake caused a great deal of
hilarity.* N-UNCOUNT

hill /hɪl/ **hills. 1** A **hill** is an area of land that is
higher than the land that surrounds it. *...the shady
street that led up the hill. ...the Black Hills of Dakota.* **2** If you say that someone is **over the hill,** you
are saying rudely that they are old and no longer capable of doing anything useful. *He doesn't take
kindly to suggestions that he is over the hill.* ◆◆◆◇◇ N-COUNT / PHRASE PRAGMATICS INFORMAL

hill·bil·ly /'hɪlbɪli/ **hillbillies.** If you refer to someone as a **hillbilly,** you think they are uneducated
and stupid because they come from a rural area. N-COUNT PRAGMATICS AMERICAN

hill·ock /'hɪlɒk/ **hillocks.** A **hillock** is a small hill. N-COUNT

hill·side /'hɪlsaɪd/ **hillsides.** A **hillside** is the sloping side of a hill. N-COUNT

hill·top /'hɪltɒp/ **hilltops.** A **hilltop** is the top of a
hill. *...a medieval hilltop village.* ◆◇◇◇◇ N-COUNT

hilly /'hɪli/ **hillier, hilliest.** A **hilly** area has a lot of
hills. ◆◇◇◇◇ ADJ-GRADED

hilt /hɪlt/. **'To the hilt'** means to the maximum extent possible or as fully as possible; used for emphasis. *The men who wield the power are certainly
backing him to the hilt.* PHRASE PRAGMATICS INFORMAL

him /hɪm/. **Him** is a third person singular pronoun.
Him is used as the object of a verb or a preposition.
1 You use **him** to refer to a man, boy, or male animal.
*Elaine met him at the bus station... My brother had a
lovely dog. I looked after him for about a week.* **2** Some
people use **him** to refer to any person when it is not
known or not important whether this person is male
or female. Some people dislike this use and prefer to
use 'him or her' or 'them'. **3** In some religions, **Him** is
used to refer to God. *God will help you if you turn to
Him in humility and trust.* ◆◆◆◆◆ PRON / PRON WRITTEN / PRON

him·self /hɪm'self/. **Himself** is a third person singular reflexive pronoun. **Himself** is used when the
object of a verb or preposition refers to the same
person as the subject of the verb, except in meaning 3.
1 You use **himself** to refer to a man, boy, or male animal. *A driver blew up his car and himself... He poured
himself a whisky... William went away muttering to
himself.* **2** Some people use **himself** to refer to any
person when it is not known or not important whether that person is male or female. Some people dislike
this use and prefer to use 'himself or herself' or 'themselves'. *The child's natural way of expressing himself is
play... The student is invited to test each item for himself by means of specific techniques.* **3** You use **himself**
to emphasize the person or thing that you are referring to. **Himself** is sometimes used instead of 'him' as
the object of a verb or preposition. *...the judgment
pronounced by Pope John Paul II himself... There's no
work and no future for students like himself.* ◆◆◆◆◆ PRON-REFL: v PRON, prep PRON / PRON-REFL: v PRON, prep PRON WRITTEN / PRON-REFL PRAGMATICS

hind /haɪnd/ **hinds. 1** An animal's **hind** legs are at
the back of its body. *The cow kicked up its hind legs.*
2 A **hind** is a female deer. ◆◇◇◇◇ ADJ: ADJ n / N-COUNT

hind·er /'hɪndə/ **hinders, hindering, hindered.**
If something **hinders** you, it makes it more difficult
for you to move, make progress, or do something.
*Does the fact that your players are part-timers help
or hinder you?* ◆◇◇◇◇ VERB V n

hind·quarters /'haɪndkwɔːtəz/. The **hindquarters**
of a four-legged animal are its back part, including
its two back legs. N-PLURAL

hin·drance /'hɪndrəns/ **hindrances.** A **hindrance**
is a person, thing, or action that makes it more difficult for you to do something. *The higher rates have
been a hindrance to economic recovery... You would
be more of a hindrance than a help.* N-COUNT: also without N

hind·sight /'haɪndsaɪt/. **Hindsight** is the ability to
understand and realize something about an event
after it has happened, although you did not understand or realize it at the time. *With hindsight, we'd
all do things differently.* ◆◇◇◇◇ N-UNCOUNT

Hin·du /'hɪnduː, hɪn'duː/ **Hindus.** A **Hindu** is a
person who believes in the Indian religion which
has many gods and teaches that people have another life on earth after they die. ► Also an adjective.
...a Hindu temple. ♦ **Hin·du·ism.** Hinduism is the
religion of Hindus. ◆◆◇◇◇ N-COUNT / ADJ / N-UNCOUNT

hinge /hɪndʒ/ **hinges, hinging, hinged.** A **hinge**
is a piece of metal, wood, or plastic that is used to
join a door to its frame or to join two things together so that one of them can swing freely. *The top
swung open on well-oiled hinges.* ♦ **hinged.** Something that is **hinged** is joined to another thing, or
joined together, by means of a hinge. *The hinged
seat lifts up to reveal a useful storage space.* ◆◇◇◇◇ N-COUNT / ADJ

hinge on. Something that **hinges on** one thing or
event depends entirely on it. *The plan hinges on a deal
being struck with a new company.* PHRASAL VB V P n/-ing/on

hint /hɪnt/ **hints, hinting, hinted. 1** A **hint** is a
suggestion about something that is made in an indirect way. *I'd dropped a hint about having an exhibition of his work up here... The statement gave no
hint as to what the measures would be.* ● If you ◆◆◇◇◇ N-COUNT / PHRASE

take the hint, you understand something that is suggested to you indirectly. *I saw Ron elbow Christabel in an effort to make her shut up. For once she took the hint.* 2 If you **hint** at something, you suggest in an indirect way. *The President hinted he might make some changes in the government.* 3 A **hint** is a helpful piece of advice, usually about how to do something. *Here are some helpful hints to make your journey easier.* 4 A **hint** of something is a very small amount of it. *She added only a hint of vermouth to the gin.*

VERB:
V at n
V that
N-COUNT

N-SING:
N of n

hinter·land /'hɪntəlænd/ **hinterlands.** The **hinterland** of a place such an area of coastline or a large town is the area of land behind it or around it. *...the French Mediterranean coast and its hinterland.*

◆◇◇◇◇
N-COUNT

hip /hɪp/ **hips.** 1 Your **hips** are the two areas or bones at the sides of your body, between the tops of your legs and your waist. See picture headed **human body**. *Tracey put her hands on her hips.* 2 If you say that someone is **hip**, you mean that they are very modern and follow all the latest fashions, for example in clothes and ideas. *...a hip young character with tight-cropped blond hair.*

◆◆◇◇◇
N-COUNT

ADJ-GRADED
INFORMAL

'**hip-hop.** Hip-hop is a form of popular culture which started among young black people in the United States in the 1980s. It includes rap music and graffiti art.

◆◇◇◇◇
N-UNCOUNT

hip·pie /'hɪpi/ **hippies;** also spelled **hippy. Hippies** were young people in the 1960s and 70s who rejected conventional society and tried to live a life based on peace and love.

◆◇◇◇◇
N-COUNT

hip·po /'hɪpəʊ/ **hippos.** A **hippo** is the same as a hippopotamus.

N-COUNT
INFORMAL

hippo·pota·mus /ˌhɪpə'pɒtəməs/ **hippopotamuses.** A **hippopotamus** is a very large African animal which lives near rivers. It has short legs and thick hairless skin. See picture headed **animals**.

N-COUNT

hip·py /'hɪpi/. See **hippie**.

hip·ster /'hɪpstə/ **hipsters.** If you refer to someone as a **hipster**, you mean that they are very fashionable. *...a swaggering hipster with a fondness for Teddy Boy clothes.*

N-COUNT
INFORMAL,
DATED

hire /haɪə/ **hires, hiring, hired.** 1 If you **hire** someone, you employ them or pay them to do a job for you. *He will be in charge of all hiring and firing at PHA.* 2 If you **hire** something, you pay money to the owner so that you can use it for a period of time. *To hire a car you must produce a passport and a current driving licence.* ▶ Also a noun. *They booked our hotel, and organised car hire... Pairs of skis, boots and clothing, are all available.* 3 If something is **for hire**, it is available for you to hire.

◆◆◆◇◇
VERB: V n
V

VERB
V n
BRITISH

N-UNCOUNT

PHRASE
BRITISH

hire out. If you **hire out** something such as a car or a person's services, you allow them to be used in return for payment. *His agency hires out security guards and bodyguards.*

PHRASAL VB
V P noun
Also V n P

hire·ling /'haɪəlɪŋ/ **hirelings.** If you refer to someone as a **hireling**, you disapprove of them because they do not care who they work for and they are willing to do illegal or immoral things for money.

N-COUNT
PRAGMATICS

,**hire 'purchase.** Hire purchase is a way of buying goods over a long period of time, with several small, regular payments. The usual American term is **installment plan.**

N-UNCOUNT
BRITISH

hir·sute /'hɜːsjuːt, AM -suːt/. If a man is **hirsute**, he is hairy.

ADJ-GRADED
FORMAL

his /hɪz/. **His** is a third person singular possessive determiner. **His** is also a possessive pronoun.
1 You use **his** to indicate that something belongs or relates to a man, boy, or male animal. *He spent a large part of his career in Hollywood... The dog let his head thump on the floor again.* ▶ Also a possessive pronoun. *He had taken advice, but the decision was his... She gradually raised her eyes and met his.* 2 Some people use **his** to refer to any person when it is not known or not important whether this person is male or female. Some people dislike this use and prefer to use 'his or her' or 'their'. *...the relations between a teacher and his pupils.* ▶ Also a possessive pronoun. *Tools lying around in there could come in very handy for the*

◆◆◆◆◆

DET-POSS

PRON-POSS

DET-POSS
WRITTEN

PRON-POSS

opportunistic burglar who has forgotten his. 3 In some religions, **His** is used to refer to God. *...humble faith in God, and trust in His Church.*

DET-POSS

His·pan·ic /hɪ'spænɪk/ **Hispanics.** If you describe someone from the United States as **Hispanic**, you mean that they or their family originally came from Latin America. *...a group of Hispanic doctors in Washington.* ▶ A **Hispanic** is someone who is Hispanic.

◆◆◇◇◇
ADJ

N-COUNT

hiss /hɪs/ **hisses, hissing, hissed.** 1 To **hiss** means to make a sound like a long 's'. *The tires of Lenny's bike hissed over the wet pavement.* ▶ Also a noun. *...the hiss of water running into the burnt pan.* ♦ **hiss·ing** *...a silence broken only by a steady hissing from above my head.* 2 If you **hiss** something, you say it in a strong angry whisper. *'Now, quiet,' my mother hissed.* 3 If people **hiss** at someone such as a performer or public speaker, they express their disapproval or dislike of that person by making long loud 's' sounds. *One had to listen hard to catch the words of the President's speech as the delegates booed and hissed.* ▶ Also a noun. *After a moment the barracking began. First came hisses, then shouts.*

◆◇◇◇◇
V prep
N-COUNT

N-UNCOUNT

VERB
V with quote

VERB:
V at n
V
Also V n

N-COUNT

his·to·rian /hɪ'stɔːriən/ **historians.** A **historian** is a person who specializes in the study of history, and who writes books and articles about it.

◆◆◇◇◇
N-COUNT

his·tor·ic /hɪ'stɒrɪk, AM -'tɔːr-/. A **historic** event is important in history, or likely to be considered important at some time in the future. *...the historic changes in the Soviet Union.*

◆◆◇◇◇
ADJ

his·tori·cal /hɪ'stɒrɪkəl, AM -tɔːr-/. 1 **Historical** people, situations, or things existed in the past and are considered to be a part of history. *...an important historical figure. ...historical monuments.* ♦ **his·tori·cal·ly** *Historically, royal marriages have been cold, calculating affairs.* 2 **Historical** books, works of art, or studies are concerned with people, situations, or things that existed in the past. 3 If you consider something in a **historical** context, you are concerned with how it was affected by events in the past, as a way of analysing or explaining it.

◆◆◇◇◇
ADJ: ADJ n

ADV

ADJ: ADJ n

ADJ: ADJ n

his·to·ry /'hɪstəri/ **histories.** 1 You can refer to the events of the past as **history**. You can also refer to the past events which concern a particular topic or place as its **history**. *He later studied history and folklore at Indiana University... The Catholic Church has played a prominent role throughout Polish history.* 2 Someone who **makes history** does something that is considered to be important and significant in the development of the world or of a particular society. *Willy Brandt made history by visiting East Germany in 1970.* 3 If someone or something **goes down in history**, people in the future remember them because of particular actions that they have done or because of particular events that have happened. *...a day that will go down in history.* 4 A **history** is an account of events that have happened in the past in a particular subject. *...his magnificent history of broadcasting.* 5 If a person or place has a **history** of something, it has been very common or has happened frequently in their past. *He had a history of drink problems.* 6 Someone's **history** is the set of facts that are known about their past. *He couldn't get a new job because of his medical history.* 7 If you say that an event, thing, or person is **history**, you mean that they are no longer important. *The Charlottetown agreement is history.* 8 If you are telling someone about an event and say **the rest is history**, you mean that you do not need to tell them what happened next because everyone knows it already. *We met at college, the rest is history.* 9 See also **natural history**.

◆◆◆◆◆
N-UNCOUNT

PHRASE

PHRASE

N-COUNT:
with supp

N-COUNT

N-COUNT:
with poss

N-UNCOUNT
INFORMAL

PHRASE

his·tri·on·ics /ˌhɪstri'ɒnɪks/. If you refer to someone's excited or emotional behaviour as **histrionics**, you disapprove of it because it seems exaggerated or insincere. *When I explained everything to my mum and dad, there were no histrionics.* ♦ **his·tri·on·ic** *Dorothea let out a histrionic groan.*

N-PLURAL
PRAGMATICS

ADJ-GRADED

H

hit /hɪt/ **hits, hitting.** The form **hit** is used in the present tense and is the past and present participle. **1** If you **hit** someone or something, you deliberately touch them with a lot of force, with your hand or an object held in your hand. *Find the exact grip that allows you to hit the ball hard... Both men had been hit in the stomach with baseball bats.* **2** When a moving object **hits** another object, it touches it with a lot of force. *The car had apparently hit a traffic sign before skidding out of control. ...multiple-warhead missiles that could hit many targets at a time.* ► Also a noun. *First a house took a direct hit and then the rocket exploded.*
3 If something **hits** a person, place, or thing, it affects them very badly. *The earthquake which hit northern Peru... It is the lower income groups who are hardest hit by crime.* **4** When a feeling or an idea **hits** you, it suddenly affects you or comes into your mind. *It hit me that I had a choice... Then the answer hit me.* **5** If you **hit** a particular high or low point on a scale, you reach it. *Oil prices hit record levels yesterday... Relations between Kenya and the United States hit an all-time low this weekend.*
6 If a record, film, or play is a **hit**, it is very popular and successful. *The song became a massive hit in 1945. ...the surprise hit video of the year.* **7** If two people **hit it off**, they like each other and become friendly as soon as they meet. *They hit it off straight away, Daddy and Walter... He has never hit it off with Douglas Hurd.*
8 ● to **hit the headlines**: see **headline**. ● to **hit home**: see **home**. ● to **hit the nail on the head**: see **nail**. ● to **hit the road**: see **road**. ● to **hit the roof**: see **roof**. ● to **hit someone for six**: see **six**.

[margin: ◆◆◆◆◆ / VERB / Vn / VERB / Vn / N-COUNT / VERB / Vn / JOURNALISM / VERB / itV n that / Vn / VERB / Vn / JOURNALISM / N-COUNT / PHRASE]

hit back. 1 If you **hit back** when someone hits you, or **hit** them **back**, you hit them in return. *Some violent men beat up their sons, until the boys are strong enough to hit back.* **2** If you **hit back** at someone who has criticized or harmed you, you criticize or harm them in return. *The President has hit back at those who have criticised his economic reforms... British Rail immediately hit back with their own cheap fares scheme.*

[margin: PHRASAL VB / V P / Also V n P / V P at n / V P / JOURNALISM]

hit on or **hit upon.** If you **hit on** an idea or a solution to a problem, you think of it. *After running through the numbers in every possible combination, we finally hit on a solution.*

[margin: PHRASAL VB / V P n]

hit out. 1 If you **hit out** at someone, you try to hit them, although you may miss them. *I used to hit out at my husband and throw things at him... I hit out and gave him a black eye.* **2** If you **hit out** at someone or something, you criticize them strongly because you do not agree with them. *The President took the opportunity to hit out at what he sees as foreign interference.*

[margin: PHRASAL VB / V P at n / V P / BRITISH / V P at/against n / Also V P / JOURNALISM]

hit upon. See **hit on**.

[margin: PHRASAL VB]

hit and 'miss; also spelled **hit-and-miss.** Something that is **hit and miss** or **hit or miss** happens in an unplanned way, so that you cannot predict what the result will be. *Our tester found its efficiency a bit hit-and-miss at first... Farming can thus be very much a hit-and-miss affair.*

[margin: ADJ-GRADED]

hit-and-'run. In a **hit-and-run** accident, the driver of a vehicle hits someone and then drives away without stopping. *...a hit-and-run driver in a stolen car.*

[margin: ADJ: ADJ n]

hitch /hɪtʃ/ **hitches, hitching, hitched. 1** A **hitch** is a slight problem which causes a short delay. *After some technical hitches the show finally got under way... The five-hour operation went without a hitch.* **2** If you **hitch**, **hitch** a lift, or **hitch** a ride, you hitchhike. *There was no garage in sight, so I hitched a lift into town... Jean-Philippe had hitched all over Europe in the 1960s.* **3** If you **hitch** something onto something else, you hook it or fasten it there. *Last night we hitched the horse to the cart and moved here.*

[margin: ◆◇◇◇◇ / N-COUNT / VERB / V / INFORMAL / VERB / V n onto/to n]

hitch up. If you **hitch up** a piece of clothing such as a skirt or pair of trousers, you pull it up into a higher position. *She leapt from the car, hitched up her dress and sprinted down the road after him.*

[margin: PHRASAL VB / V P noun / Also V n P]

hitch·hike /'hɪtʃhaɪk/ **hitchhikes, hitchhiking, hitchhiked;** also spelled **hitch-hike.** If you **hitch-hike**, you travel by getting lifts from passing vehicles without paying. *Neff hitchhiked to New York during his Christmas vacation.* ♦ **hitch-hiker hitchhikers** *On my way to Vancouver one Friday night I picked up a hitchhiker.* ♦ **hitch-hik·ing** *She decided hitchhiking was her best method of escape.*

[margin: VERB / V prep/adv / Also V / N-COUNT / N-UNCOUNT]

hi 'tech. See **high tech**.

hith·er /'hɪðə/. **1 Hither** means to the place where you are. *He has sent hither swarms of officers to harass our people.* **2 Hither and thither** means in many different directions or places, and in a disorganized way. The usual American expression is **hither and yon.** *Refugees run hither and thither in search of safety.*

[margin: ADV: ADV after v / DATED / PHRASE / BRITISH]

hither·to /ˌhɪðə'tuː/. You use **hitherto** to indicate that something was true up until the time you are talking about, although it may no longer be the case. *Hitherto, the main emphasis has been on the need to resist aggression... The helicopter is the first in the world to be designed to serve three hitherto very distinct markets.*

[margin: ◆◇◇◇◇ / ADV: / ADV with cl, / ADV adj/-ed, / ADV after v / PRAGMATICS / FORMAL]

'hit list, hit lists. 1 If someone has a **hit list** of people or things, they are intending to take action concerning those people or things. *Some banks also have a hit list of people whom they threaten to sue for damages.* **2** A **hit list** is a list that terrorists or gangsters make, containing the names of people they intend to have killed.

[margin: ◆◇◇◇◇ / N-COUNT / N-COUNT]

hit·man /'hɪtmæn/ **hitmen;** also spelled **hit man.** A **hitman** is a man who is hired by someone in order to kill people.

[margin: N-COUNT]

,hit or 'miss. See **hit and miss**.

'hit parade. The **hit parade** is the list of pop records which have sold most copies over the previous week or month. *Suede are once again riding high in the hit parade with their new single.*

[margin: N-SING: / the N / DATED]

hit·ter /'hɪtə/ **hitters. 1** In sport, a big **hitter** is someone who is good at hitting the ball hard.
2 If you refer to someone such as a politician or a businessman as a heavy **hitter** or a big **hitter**, you mean that they are powerful and influential.

[margin: ◆◇◇◇◇ / N-COUNT / N-COUNT: / adj N]

HIV /ˌeɪtʃ aɪ 'viː/. **1 HIV** is a virus which reduces people's resistance to illness and can cause AIDS. **HIV** is an abbreviation of 'human immunodeficiency virus'. **2** If someone is **HIV positive**, they are infected with the HIV virus, and may develop AIDS.

[margin: ◆◆◆◇◇ / N-UNCOUNT / PHRASE]

hive /haɪv/ **hives, hiving, hived. 1** A **hive** is the same as a **beehive**. *...honey gathered from more than 400 hives.* **2** If you describe a place as a **hive** of activity, you approve of the fact that there is a lot of activity there or that people are busy working there. *In the morning the house was a hive of activity... Stuart Tannahill's shed is a veritable hive of photographic creativity.*

[margin: ◆◇◇◇◇ / N-COUNT / N-COUNT: / N of n / PRAGMATICS]

hive off. If someone **hives off** part of a business, they transfer or sell it to a new owner. *Klockner plans to hive off its loss-making steel businesses.*

[margin: PHRASAL VB / V P noun / Also N P / BRITISH]

hiya /'haɪjə/. You can say **'hiya'** when you are greeting someone. *Hiya. How are you?*

[margin: CONVENTION / PRAGMATICS / INFORMAL]

HM /ˌeɪtʃ 'em/. **HM** is the written abbreviation for 'Her Majesty's' or 'His Majesty's'; it is used as part of the name of some British government organizations, or as part of a person's title. *...his enlistment in HM Armed Forces. ...HM Chief Inspector of Fire Services.*

[margin: ◆◇◇◇◇]

h'm; also spelled **hm. H'm** is used in writing to represent a noise that people make when they are hesitating or thinking before they speak.

[margin: PRAGMATICS]

HMS /ˌeɪtʃ em 'es/. **HMS** is used before the names of ships in the British navy; it is an abbreviation for 'Her Majesty's Ship' or 'His Majesty's Ship'. *...HMS Warrior.*

[margin: ◆◇◇◇◇]

HNC /ˌeɪtʃ en 'siː/. **HNCs.** An **HNC** is a qualification in a technical or practical subject which you can obtain at a British college. **HNC** is an abbreviation for 'Higher National Certificate'. *...passing his HNC in computer studies.*

[margin: N-VAR]

hoard /hɔːd/ **hoards, hoarding, hoarded. 1** If you **hoard** things such as food or money, you save or store them, often in secret, because they are valuable or important to you. *They've begun to hoard food and gasoline and save their money.* ◆ **hoard·er, hoarders** *Most hoarders have favorite hiding places.* **2** A **hoard** is a store of things that you have hoarded or secretly hidden. *The case involves a hoard of silver and jewels valued at up to $40m.*
◆◇◇◇◇ VERB V n Also V
N-COUNT
N-COUNT

hoard·ing /ˈhɔːdɪŋ/ **hoardings.** A **hoarding** is a very large board at the side of a road or on the side of a building, which is used for displaying advertisements and posters. The usual American word is **billboard.**
N-COUNT BRITISH

hoarse /hɔːs/ **hoarser, hoarsest.** If you or your voice are **hoarse**, your voice sounds rough and unclear, for example because your throat is sore. *'So what do you think?' she said in a hoarse whisper... Nick's voice was hoarse with screaming.* ◆ **hoarse·ly** *'Thank you,' Maria said hoarsely.*
◆◇◇◇◇ ADJ-GRADED
ADV-GRADED

hoary /ˈhɔːri/. If you describe a problem or subject as **hoary**, you mean that it is old and familiar. *...the hoary old myth that women are unpredictable.*
ADJ-GRADED

hoax /həʊks/ **hoaxes.** A **hoax** is a trick in which someone tells people something that is not true, for example that there is a bomb somewhere, or that a forged work of art is genuine. *A series of bomb hoaxes has disrupted Christmas shopping in the city centre... He denied making the hoax call.* ◆ **hoax·er, hoaxers.** A **hoaxer** is someone who carries out a hoax.
◆◇◇◇◇ N-COUNT
N-COUNT

hob /hɒb/ **hobs.** A **hob** is a surface on top of a cooker or set into a worktop, which can be heated in order to cook things.
◆◇◇◇◇ N-COUNT BRITISH

hob·ble /ˈhɒbəl/ **hobbles, hobbling, hobbled. 1** If you **hobble**, you walk in an awkward way with small steps, for example because your foot is injured. *He got up slowly and hobbled over to the coffee table.* **2** To **hobble** something or someone means to make it more difficult for them to be successful or to achieve what they want. *The barriers which have until now hobbled intra-Asian trade are being dismantled.*
◆◇◇◇◇ VERB V adv/prep Also V
VERB V n

hob·by /ˈhɒbi/ **hobbies.** A **hobby** is an activity that you enjoy doing in your spare time. *My hobbies are letter writing, football, music, photography, and tennis.* ◆ **hob·by·ist** /ˈhɒbiɪst/ **hobbyists.** A **hobbyist** is someone who has a particular hobby.
◆◆◇◇◇ N-COUNT
N-COUNT

'hobby-horse, hobby-horses. You describe a subject or idea as your **hobby-horse** if you have strong feelings on it and like talking about it whenever you have the opportunity. *Honesty is a favourite hobby-horse for Courau.*
N-COUNT

hob·nob /ˈhɒbnɒb/ **hobnobs, hobnobbing, hobnobbed.** If you disapprove of the way someone is spending a lot of time with rich, powerful, or glamorous people, you can say that he or she is **hobnobbing** with those people. *She hobnobs with Cabinet Ministers; she lunches with the Queen.*
VERB PRAGMATICS V with n Also V INFORMAL

hobo /ˈhəʊbəʊ/ **hobos** or **hoboes.** A **hobo** is someone without a regular home or place of work, who travels around begging or looking for work.
N-COUNT AMERICAN

hock /hɒk/ **hocks. 1 Hock** is a type of dry white wine from Germany. **2** A horse's **hock** is the joint in its back leg that points backwards. **3** If someone is **in hock**, they are in debt. *Even company directors on £100,000 a year can be deeply in hock to the banks.*
N-VAR BRITISH
N-COUNT
PHRASE

hock·ey /ˈhɒki/. **Hockey** is a sport played between two teams of 11 players who use long curved sticks to hit a small ball and try to score goals. *...the British hockey team.* ● See also **ice hockey.**
◆◆◇◇◇ N-UNCOUNT

hocus-pocus /ˌhəʊkəs ˈpəʊkəs/. If you refer to something as **hocus-pocus**, you disapprove of it because you think it is false and intended to trick or deceive people. *It is unlikely he would have mistaken hocus-pocus for genuine knowledge.*
N-UNCOUNT PRAGMATICS

hod /hɒd/ **hods.** A **hod** is a container used by builders for carrying bricks.
N-COUNT

hodge-podge /ˈhɒdʒpɒdʒ/. A **hodgepodge** is a confused or disorderly mixture of different types of things. The usual British word is **hotch-potch.** *...a hodgepodge of maps, small tools, and notebooks.*
N-SING INFORMAL, AMERICAN

hoe /həʊ/ **hoes, hoeing, hoed. 1** A **hoe** is a gardening tool with a long handle and a small square blade, which you use to remove weeds and break up the surface of the soil. See picture headed **tools.** **2** If you **hoe** a field or crop, you use a hoe on the weeds or soil there. *He was hoeing in the vineyard.*
◆◇◇◇◇ N-COUNT
VERB: V n V

hog /hɒg, AM hɔːg/ **hogs, hogging, hogged. 1** A **hog** is a pig. In British English, **hog** usually refers to a large male pig that has been castrated, but in American English it can refer to any kind of pig. **2** If you **hog** something, you take all of it in a greedy or impolite way. *Have you done hogging the bathroom?* **3** If you **go the whole hog**, you do something bold or extravagant in the most complete way possible. *I've had every other sort of haircut, I'll just go the whole hog.* **4** See also **roadhog.**
◆◇◇◇◇ N-COUNT
VERB V n INFORMAL
PHRASE INFORMAL

hog·wash /ˈhɒgwɒʃ, AM ˈhɔːg-/. If you describe what someone says as **hogwash**, you think it is nonsense.
N-UNCOUNT INFORMAL

,ho 'ho. Ho ho is used in writing to represent the sound that people make when they laugh. *'Ha, ha, ho, ho,' he chortled.*
EXCLAM

ho hum /ˌhəʊ ˈhʌm/. You can use **ho hum** to suggest that you are reacting to something in a bored, unenthusiastic, or calm way. **Ho hum** is sometimes used ironically. *My general reaction to this news might be summed up as 'ho-hum'... Ho hum, another nice job down the drain.*
PHRASE PRAGMATICS

hoi pol·loi /ˌhɔɪ pəˈlɔɪ/. If someone refers to the **hoi polloi**, they are referring scornfully to ordinary people, in contrast to rich, well-educated, or upper-class people. *Monstrously inflated costs are designed to keep the hoi polloi at bay.*
N-PLURAL PRAGMATICS

hoist /hɔɪst/ **hoists, hoisting, hoisted. 1** If you **hoist** something heavy somewhere, you lift it or pull it up there. *Hoisting my suitcase on to my shoulder, I turned and headed toward my hotel... Grabbing the side of the bunk, he hoisted himself to a sitting position.* **2** If something heavy is **hoisted** somewhere, it is lifted there using a machine such as a crane. *A twenty-foot steel pyramid is to be hoisted into position on top of the tower.* **3** A **hoist** is a machine for lifting heavy things. **4** If you **hoist** a flag or a sail, you pull it up to its correct position by using ropes.
◆◇◇◇◇ VERB V n prep/adv V pron-refl prep/adv Also V n
VERB be V-ed prep/adv
N-COUNT
VERB: V n

ho·kum /ˈhəʊkəm/. If you describe something as **hokum**, you think it is nonsense.
N-UNCOUNT INFORMAL

hold 1 *physically touching, supporting, or containing*

hold /həʊld/ **holds, holding, held. 1** When you **hold** something, you carry or support it using your hands or your arms. *Hold the knife at an angle... Hold the baby when I load the car.* ▶ Also a noun. *He released his hold on the camera.* **2 Hold** is used in expressions such as **grab hold of, catch hold of,** and **get hold of,** to indicate that you close your hand tightly around something. *Mother took hold of the barking dogs by their collars.* **3** When you **hold** someone, you put your arms round them, usually because you want to show them how much you like them or because you want to comfort them. *If only he would hold her close to him.*
◆◆◆◇ VERB V n prep/adv V n
N-UNCOUNT: N of n
VERB Also V n

4 If you **hold** someone in a particular position, you use force to keep them in that position and stop them from moving. *He then held the man in an armlock until police arrived... I'd got two nurses holding me down.* **5** A **hold** is a particular way of keeping someone in a position using your own hands, arms, or legs. *...use of an unauthorized hold on a handcuffed suspect.* **6** When you **hold** a part of your body in a particular position, you put it into that position and keep it there. *Hold your hands in front of your face.* **7** If one thing **holds** another in a particular position, it keeps it in that position. *...the wooden wedge which held the heavy door open... They used steel pins to hold everything in place.*
VERB V n prep Also V n with adv
N-COUNT
VERB V n prep/adv Also V n adj
VERB V n with adv V n prep

8 If one thing is used to **hold** another, it is used to sto-
VERB

re it. *Two knife racks hold her favourite knives.*   V n

◆ **hold·er, holders.** *....a toothbrush holder.*   N-COUNT

9 If a place **holds** something, it keeps it available for reference or for future use. *We have reviewed the data that we hold for the area.*   VERB / V n

10 If something **holds** a particular amount of something, it can contain that amount. *The small bottles don't seem to hold much.*   VB: no cont

11 In a ship or aeroplane, a **hold** is a place where cargo or luggage is stored.   N-COUNT

12 If you can **hold** your drink, you are able to drink large quantities of alcohol without becoming ill or getting drunk.   VERB: V n

13 If a vehicle **holds** the road well, it remains in close contact with the road and can be controlled safely and easily. *I thought the car handled and held the road really well.*   VERB / V n adv / Also V n

14 See also **holding**.

hold 2 having or doing

hold /hǝʊld/ **holds, holding, held. Hold** is often used to indicate that someone or something has the particular thing, characteristic, or attitude that is mentioned. Therefore it takes most of its meaning from the word that follows it.   ◆◆◆◆◆

1 Hold is used to indicate that someone has a particular opinion or believes that something is true. *He holds certain expectations about the teacher's role... Current thinking holds that obesity is more a medical than a psychological problem... The public, meanwhile, hold architects in low esteem... It's impossible to hold any individual responsible.*   VB: no cont / V that / V n in n / V n adj

2 Hold is used with words such as 'fear' or 'mystery' to indicate someone's feelings towards something, as if those feelings were a characteristic of the thing itself. *Death doesn't hold any fear for me... It held more mystery than even the darkest jungle... This approach, more than any other, holds promise for true reform.*   VB: no passive / V n for n / V n

3 Hold is used with nouns such as 'office', 'power', and 'responsibility' to indicate that someone has a particular position of power or authority. *She has never held ministerial office.* ◆ **holder** *Bellotti became the state's most popular office holder.*   VERB / V n / N-COUNT

4 Hold is used with nouns such as 'permit', 'degree', or 'ticket' to indicate that someone has a particular document that allows them to do something. *He did not hold a firearm certificate.* ◆ **holder** *This season the club has had 73,500 season-ticket holders.*   VERB / V n / N-COUNT

5 Hold is used with nouns such as 'shares' and 'stock' to indicate that someone owns a particular proportion of a business. *The Fisher family holds 40% of the stock.* ◆ **holder** *...Britain's 11 million holders of shares in privatised companies.*   VERB / V n / N-COUNT

6 Hold is used with nouns such as 'party', 'meeting', and 'talks' to indicate that people are organizing a particular activity. *The German sports federation said it would hold an investigation.* ◆ **hold·ing** *They also called for the holding of multi-party general elections.*   VERB / V n / N-UNCOUNT / N of n

7 Hold is used with nouns such as 'conversation', 'interview', and 'consultation' to indicate that two or more people meet and discuss something. *The Prime Minister, is holding consultations with his colleagues... The engineer and his son held frequent consultations concerning technical problems.*   V-RECIP / V n with n / pl-n V / Also V n (non-recip)

8 Hold is used with words such as 'lead' or 'advantage' to indicate that someone is winning or doing well in a contest. *Mestel holds a slight advantage.*   VERB / V n

9 Hold is used with nouns such as 'attention' or 'interest' to indicate that what you do or say keeps someone interested or listening to you. *It's done in a way that will hold children's attention.*   VERB / V n

10 See also **holding**.

hold 3 controlling or remaining

hold /hǝʊld/ **holds, holding, held. 1** If someone **holds** you in a place, they keep you there as a prisoner and do not allow you to leave. *The inside of a van was as good a place as any to hold a kidnap victim... Somebody is holding your wife hostage.* ◆ **holder** *...the holders of British hostages in Lebanon.*   ◆◆◆◆◇ VERB / V n / V n n / N-COUNT

2 If people such as an army or a violent crowd **hold** a place, they control it by using force. *Demonstrators have been holding the square since Sunday.*   VERB / V n

◆ **-held** *...enemy-held territory. ...the rebel-held town.*   COMB

3 If you have a **hold** over someone, you have   N-SING

power over them, for example because you know something about them you can use to threaten them or because you are in a position of authority. *Because he once loved her, she still has a hold on him.*

4 If you ask someone to **hold** when you are answering a telephone call, you are asking them to wait for a short time, for example so that you can find the person they want to speak to. *Could you hold the line and I'll just get my pen.*   VB: no passive / V n / Also V

5 If you **hold** telephone calls for someone, you do not allow the caller to speak to that person, and you take a message instead.   VERB: V n

6 If something **holds** at a particular value or level, or is **held** there, it stays or is kept at that value or level. *They were expecting the jobless rate to hold steady. ...Government action to hold down petrol prices... With proper maintenance your home will hold its value... Cattle prices held at yesterday's sales.*   V-ERG / V prep/adv/ adj / V n prep/ adv/adj / V n / V

7 If an offer or invitation still **holds**, it is still available for you to accept.   VERB: V

8 If a good situation **holds**, it continues and does not get worse or fail. *Would the weather hold?*   VERB / V

9 If an argument or theory **holds**, it is true or valid, even after close examination. ▶ To **hold up** means the same as to **hold**. *Democrats say arguments against the bill won't hold up.*   VERB: V / PHRASAL VB / V P

10 If you say that you **hold** to a particular opinion or belief, you are stating firmly that you continue to have that opinion or belief. *Would you still hold to that view?*   V to n / FORMAL

11 If you **hold** to a promise or to high standards of behaviour, you keep that promise or continue to behave according to those standards. *Will the President be able to hold to this commitment?*   VERB / V to n / FORMAL

12 If someone or something **holds** you **to** a promise or to high standards of behaviour, they make you keep that promise or those standards.   VERB: V n to n

13 See also **holding**.

hold 4 phrases

hold /hǝʊld/ **holds, holding, held. 1** If you **hold forth** on a subject, you speak confidently and for a long time about it.   ◆◆◆◆◇ PHRASE

2 If you **get hold of** an object or some information, you manage to obtain it. If you **get hold of** someone, you manage to contact them. *It is hard to get hold of guns in this country.*   PHRASE

3 If you say **'Hold it'**, you are telling someone to stop what they are doing and to wait.   CONVENTION

4 If you put something **on hold**, you decide not to do it now, but to leave it till later. *He put his retirement on hold to work 16 hours a day, seven days a week to find a solution.*   PHRASE

5 If you **hold** your **own**, you are able to resist someone who is attacking or opposing you. *Croatia could not hold its own against either the federal air force or the federal artillery.*   PHRASE

6 If you can do something well enough to **hold** your **own**, you do not appear foolish when you are compared with someone who is generally thought to be very good at it. *She can hold her own against almost any player.*   PHRASE

7 If you **hold still**, you do not move.   PHRASE

8 If something **takes hold**, it finally gains complete control or influence over something or someone. *She felt a strange excitement taking hold of her.*   PHRASE

9 If you **hold tight**, you put your hand round or against something in order to prevent yourself from falling over. *He held tight to the rope.*   PHRASE

10 Hold is used in a large number of expressions which are explained under other words in this dictionary. For example, the expression to **hold something at bay** is explained at **bay**.

hold 5 phrasal verbs

hold /hǝʊld/ **holds, holding, held.**   ◆◆◆◆◇

hold against. If you **hold** something **against** someone, you resent or dislike them because of something which they did in the past. *Bernstein lost the case, but never held it against Grundy.*   PHRASAL VB / V n P n

hold back. 1 If you **hold back** or something **holds** you **back**, you hesitate before you do something because you are not sure whether it is the right thing to do. *Melancholy and mistrust of men hold her back.*   PHRASAL VB / ERG: / V P / V n P / Also V P noun

2 To **hold** someone or something **back** means to prevent someone from doing something or to prevent something from happening. *Stagnation in home sales is holding back economic recovery.*   V P noun / V n P / Also V n P

3 If you **hold**   V P noun

something **back**, you keep it in reserve to use later. `Also V n P`
Farmers apparently hold back produce in the hope that prices will rise. **4** If you **hold** something **back**, you `V n P` do not tell someone the full details about something. `Also V P noun` *You seem to be holding something back.* **5** If you **hold** `V P noun` **back** something such as tears or laughter, you make `V P` an effort to stop yourself from showing how you feel. *I* `Also V P` *was close to tears with frustration, but I held back.*

hold down. 1 If you **hold down** a job or a place in a `PHRASAL VB` team, you manage to keep it. *He never could hold* `V P noun` *down a job.* **2** If you **hold** someone **down**, you keep `V P noun` them under control and do not allow them to have `Also V n P` much freedom or power or many rights. *Everyone thinks there is some vast conspiracy wanting to hold down the younger generation.*

hold in. If you **hold in** an emotion or feeling, you do `PHRASAL VB` not allow yourself to express it, often making it more `PRAGMATICS` difficult to deal with. *Depression can be traced to hold-* `Also V n P` *ing in anger.*

hold off. 1 If you **hold off** doing something, you de- `PHRASAL VB` lay doing it or delay making a decision about it. *They* `V P -ing` *have threatened military action but held off until now.* `V P` **2** If you **hold off** a challenge in a race or competition, `V P noun` you do not allow someone to overtake you. *Alesi drove* `Also V n P` *his Tyrrell magnificently, holding off a tremendous challenge from Gerhard Berger.*

hold on or **hold onto. 1** If you **hold on**, or **hold** `PHRASAL VB` **onto** something, you keep your hand on it or around `V P` it, for example to prevent the thing from falling or to `V P ton` support yourself. *His right arm was extended up be-* `Also V P n` *side his head, still holding on to a coffee cup.* **2** If you `V P` **hold on**, you manage to achieve success or avoid fail- ure in spite of great difficulties or opposition. *Juanito scored for the Spaniards with only two minutes left, but the Romanians held on.* **3** If you ask someone to `V P` **hold on**, you are asking them to wait for a short time. `SPOKEN`

hold on to or **hold onto. 1** If you **hold on to** some- `PHRASAL VB` thing that gives you an advantage, you succeed in `V P P n` keeping it for yourself, and prevent it from being tak- `V P n` en away or given to someone else. *...a politician who knew how to hold onto power.* **2** If you **hold on to** `V P P n` something, you keep it for a longer time than would `SPOKEN` normally be expected. *People hold onto letters for years and years.* **3** If you **hold on to** your beliefs, you `V P P n` continue to believe in them and do not change them if `Also V P n` others try to influence you or if circumstances cause you to doubt them. *He was imprisoned for 19 years yet held on to his belief in his people.*

hold out. 1 If you **hold out** your hand or something `PHRASAL VB` you have in your hand, you move your hand away `V P noun` from your body, for example to shake hands with `Also V n P` someone or because someone is giving you some- thing. *'I'm Nancy Drew,' she said, holding out her hand.* **2** If you **hold out** for something, you refuse to `V P for n` accept something else that you consider to be of less `V P` value. **3** If you **hold out** hope of something happen- `V P noun` ing, you hope that in the future it will happen as you want it to. **4** If you **hold out**, you succeed in surviving `V P` a difficult situation.

hold over. If something is **held over**, it does not `PHRASAL VB` happen or it is not dealt with until a future date. *We* `be V-ed P` *would have held the story over until the next day.* `V n P` `Also V P noun`

hold together. When you **hold** people **together** or `PHRASAL VB` when they **hold together**, people who have different `ERG` aims, attitudes or interests manage to live or work to- `PRAGMATICS` gether without arguing or disagreeing. *Her 13-year-* `V n P` *old daughter is holding the family together... He sought* `V P noun` *to hold together the warring factions in his party.* `Also V P`

hold up. 1 If you **hold up** your hand or something `PHRASAL VB` you have in your hand, you move it upwards into a `V P noun` particular position and keep it there. *Hold it up so that* `V n P` *we can see it.* **2** If one thing **holds up** another, it is `V P noun` placed under the other thing in order to support it and `V n P` prevent it from falling. *Her legs wouldn't hold her up.* **3** To **hold up** a person or process means to make `V P noun` them late or delay them. *Why were you holding every-* `V n P` *one up?* **4** If someone **holds up** a place such as a bank, `V P noun` they point a weapon at someone to make them `Also V n P` give them money or valuable goods. *A thief ran off with hundreds of pounds yesterday after holding up a*

petrol station. **5** If you **hold up** something such as `V n P ton` someone's behaviour, you make it known to other `beV-ed P asn` people, so that they can criticize or praise it. *She said* `Also V n P asn` *the picture that had appeared in a Sunday newspaper had held her up to ridicule... He had always been held up as an example to the younger ones.*
6 If something such as a type of business **holds up** in `V P` difficult conditions, it stays in a reasonably good state. *Children's wear is one area that is holding up well in the recession.* **7** If an argument or theory **holds** `V P` **up**, it is true or valid, even after close examination. **8** See also **hold-up.**

hold with. If you do not **hold with** an activity or ac- `PHRASAL VB` tion, you do not approve of it. `with brd-neg:` `V P n`

hold·all /ˈhəʊldɔːl/ **holdalls**; also spelled **hold-all.** `N-COUNT` A **holdall** is a large bag which you use to carry your `BRITISH` clothes and other belongings, for example when you are travelling.

hold·ing /ˈhəʊldɪŋ/ **holdings. 1** If you have a `◆◆◇◇◇` **holding** in a company, you own shares in it. *...hold-* `N-COUNT:` *ings in commercial and merchant banks.* **2** A **hold-** `with supp` **ing** is an area of farm land which is owned or rent- `N-COUNT` ed by the person who cultivates it. **3** The **holdings** `N-PLURAL` of a place such as a library or art gallery are the col- lection of items such as books or paintings which are kept there. **4** A **holding** operation or action is a `ADJ: ADJ n` temporary one that is intended to keep a situation under control and to prevent it from becoming worse.

hold·out /ˈhəʊldaʊt/ **holdouts.** A **holdout** is some- `N-COUNT` one who refuses to agree or act with other people in `AMERICAN` a particular situation and by doing so stops the situation from progressing or being resolved.

'hold-up, hold-ups. 1 A **hold-up** is a situation in `◆◇◇◇◇` which someone is threatened with a weapon in or- `N-COUNT` der to make them hand over money or valuables.
2 A **hold-up** is something which causes a delay, for `N-COUNT` example the stopping or very slow movement of traffic after an accident.

hole /həʊl/ **holes, holing, holed. 1** A **hole** is a `◆◆◆◆◇` hollow space in something solid, with an opening `N-COUNT` on one side. *The builders had cut holes into the soft stone.* **2** A **hole** is the home or hiding place of a `N-COUNT` mouse, rabbit, or other small animal. *...a rabbit hole.* **3** A **hole** is an opening in something that goes `N-COUNT` right through it. *These tiresome creatures eat holes in the leaves.* **4** If something such as a building or ship `VB: usu` **is holed**, holes are made in it by guns or other `passive` weapons. **5** If you say that you **need** something or `PHRASE` someone **like a hole in the head**, you are emphasiz- `PRAGMATICS` ing that you do not want them and that they would `INFORMAL` only add to the problems that you already have.
6 A **hole** in a law, theory, or argument is a fault or `N-COUNT` weakness that it has. **7** If you **pick holes in** an argu- `PHRASE` ment or theory, you find weak points in it and criticize `INFORMAL` it.
8 If you refer to a place as a **hole**, you are emphasizing `N-COUNT` that you think it is very unpleasant. `INFORMAL`
9 A **hole** is one of the places on a golf course that the `N-COUNT` ball must drop into, usually marked by a flag. The nine or eighteen sections of a golf course can also be called **holes.** *I played nine holes with Gary Player to-* `day.* **10** If you **hole** in a game of golf, you hit the ball so `VERB: V` that it goes into the hole. *Frost holed a bunker shot* `V n` *from 50 feet to snatch the title by one stroke.* **11** If you `PHRASE` get **a hole in one** in golf, you get the golf ball into the hole with a single stroke.

hole up. If you **hole up** somewhere, you hide or shut `PHRASAL VB` yourself away there, usually so that people cannot `V P` find you or disturb you. ♦ **holed up** *I wanted to spend* `INFORMAL` *Sundays holed up together in our flat.* `ADJ:` `v-link ADJ`

,hole-in-the-'wall. A **hole-in-the-wall** machine is `N-SING` a machine built into the wall of a bank or other `BRITISH,` building, which allows people to take out money `INFORMAL` from their bank account by using a special card.

holi·day /ˈhɒlɪdeɪ/ **holidays, holidaying, holi-** `◆◆◆◆◇` **dayed. 1** A **holiday** is a period of time during `N-COUNT:` which you relax and enjoy yourself away from `also on/from` home. People sometimes refer to their holiday as `N` their holidays. The American word is **vacation.** *We* `BRITISH`

rang Duncan to ask where he was going on holiday... *We're going to Scotland for our holidays.* **2** If you **are** **holidaying** in a place away from home, you are on holiday there. *Vacant rooms on the campus were being used by holidaying families.* **3** A **holiday** is a day when people do not go to work or school because of a religious or national festival. *Bad weather has caused dozens of flight cancellations over the holiday weekend.* ● See also **bank holiday**. **4** The **holidays** are the time when children do not have to go to school. The American word is **vacation**. **5** If you have a particular number of days' or weeks' **holiday**, you do not have to go to work for that number of days or weeks. The American word is **vacation**.

VERB:
V prep/adv
V-ing
BRITISH

N-COUNT

N-PLURAL
BRITISH

N-UNCOUNT
BRITISH

'holiday camp, holiday camps. A **holiday camp** is a place which provides holiday accommodation and entertainment for large numbers of people.

N-COUNT
BRITISH

holi·day·maker /'hɒlɪdeɪmeɪkə/ **holidaymakers;** also spelled **holiday-maker**. A **holidaymaker** is a person who is away from their home on holiday. The American word is **vacationer**.

◆◇◇◇
N-COUNT
BRITISH

holier-than-'thou. If you describe someone as **holier-than-thou**, you disapprove of them because they seem to believe that they are more religious or have better moral qualities than anyone else.

ADJ-GRADED
PRAGMATICS

ho·li·ness /'həʊlɪnəs/. **1** You say **Your Holiness** or **His Holiness** when you address or refer respectfully to the Pope or to leaders of some other religions. **2** See also **holy**.

N-VOC;
PRON
PRAGMATICS

ho·lis·tic /həʊ'lɪstɪk/. **Holistic** means based on the belief that everything in nature is connected in some way. *...practitioners of holistic medicine.*

◆◇◇◇
ADJ
FORMAL

hol·ler /'hɒlə/ **hollers, hollering, hollered.** If you **holler**, you shout loudly. *'Watch out!' he hollered... Cal hollered for help... In a minute he'll be hollering at me for coming in late... Nick hollered for her to pick up her orders.*

◆◇◇◇
VERB: V
V at/for n
V for n to-inf
INFORMAL,
AMERICAN

hol·low /'hɒləʊ/ **hollows, hollowing, hollowed.** **1** Something that is **hollow** has a space inside it, as opposed to being solid all the way through. *...a hollow tree. ...a hollow cylinder.* **2** A **hollow** is a hole inside a tree.

◆◆◇◇
ADJ

N-COUNT

3 A surface that is **hollow** curves inwards. *He looked young, dark and sharp-featured, with hollow cheeks.* **4** A **hollow** is an area that is lower than the surrounding surface. *Water gathers in a hollow and forms a pond.* **5** If something is **hollowed**, its surface is made to curve inwards or downwards. *The mule's back was hollowed by the weight of its burden. ...her high, elegantly hollowed cheekbones.*

ADJ-GRADED

N-COUNT

VB: usu
passive
be V-ed
V-ed

6 If you describe a statement, situation, or person as **hollow**, you mean they have no real value, worth, or effectiveness. *Any threat to bring in the police is a hollow one.* ♦ **hol·low·ness** *One month before the deadline we see the hollowness of these promises.* **7** If someone gives a **hollow** laugh, they laugh in a way that shows that they do not really find something amusing. **8** A **hollow** sound is dull and echoing. *...the hollow sound of a gunshot.*

ADJ

N-UNCOUNT
ADJ: ADJ n

ADJ: ADJ n

hollow out. If you **hollow** something **out**, you remove the inside part of it. *Someone had hollowed out a large block of stone.*

PHRASAL VB
V P noun
Also V n P

hol·ly /'hɒli/ **hollies. Hollies** are a group of evergreen trees and shrubs which have hard, shiny, prickly leaves, and also have bright red berries in winter.

◆◇◇◇
N-VAR

Hol·ly·wood /'hɒliwʊd/. You use **Hollywood** to refer to the American film industry that is based in Hollywood, California, and also to the lifestyles of the rich and famous people living there. *...a major Hollywood studio. ...Hollywood film stars.*

◆◆◇◇
N-PROPER

holo·caust /'hɒləkɔːst/ **holocausts.** **1** A **holocaust** is an event in which there is large-scale destruction and loss of life, especially in war. *A nuclear holocaust seemed a very real possibility in the '50s.* **2** The **holocaust** is used to refer to the killing by the Nazis of millions of Jews during the Second World War.

◆◇◇◇
N-VAR

N-SING:
theN

holo·gram /'hɒləgræm/ **holograms.** A **hologram** is a three-dimensional photographic image created by laser beams.

N-COUNT

hols /hɒlz/. Some people refer to their holidays as their **hols**.

N-PLURAL
INFORMAL,
BRITISH

hol·ster /'həʊlstə/ **holsters.** A **holster** is a holder for a pistol or revolver, which is worn either on a belt around someone's waist or on a strap around their shoulder.

N-COUNT

holy /'həʊli/ **holier, holiest.** **1** If you describe something as **holy**, you mean that it is considered to be special because it is connected with God or a particular religion. *To them, as to all Tibetans, this is a holy place.* ♦ **ho·li·ness** *...the holiness and supreme majesty of God.* **2** If you describe someone as **holy**, you mean that they lead a pure and good life which is dedicated to God or to a particular religion.

◆◆◆◇◇
ADJ-GRADED

N-UNCOUNT
ADJ-GRADED

3 **Holy** is used in exclamations such as 'Holy cow!' to express an emotion such as surprise or panic. **4** See also **holier-than-thou**.

ADJ: ADJ n
PRAGMATICS

Holy 'Ghost. The **Holy Ghost** is the same as the **Holy Spirit**.

N-PROPER:
theN

holy of holies /,həʊli əv 'həʊliz/. A **holy of holies** is a place that is so sacred that only particular people are allowed to enter; often used in informal English to refer ironically to a place where only a few special people can go. *...the Aldeburgh Festival, the holy of holies in the contemporary British music scene.*

N-SING

holy 'orders; also spelled **Holy Orders.** Someone who is in **holy orders** is a member of the Christian clergy. *He took holy orders in 1935.*

N-PLURAL

Holy 'Spirit. In the Christian religion, **the Holy Spirit** is one of the three aspects of God, together with God the Father and God the Son.

N-PROPER:
theN

hom·age /'hɒmɪdʒ/. **Homage** is respect shown towards someone or something you admire, or to someone who is in authority. *...two marvellous films that pay homage to our literary heritage.*

◆◇◇◇
N-UNCOUNT

home 1 noun, adjective, and adverb uses

home /həʊm/ **homes.** **1** Someone's **home** is the house or flat where they live. *Last night they stayed at home and watched TV. ...the allocation of land for new homes.* **2** **Home** means to or at the place where you live. *His wife wasn't feeling too well and she wanted to go home... Hi, Mom, I'm home!* **3** **Home** means made or done in the place where you live. *...cheap but healthy home cooking.* **4** You can refer to a family unit as a **home**. *Single-parent homes are commonplace... She had, at any rate, provided a peaceful and loving home for Harriet.*

◆◆◆◆
N-COUNT

ADV:
ADV after v,
be ADV

ADJ: ADJ n
N-COUNT

5 You can use **a home from home** to refer to a place in which you feel happy and at ease, just as if you were in your own home. In American English, you say **a home away from home**. **6** If you say to a guest 'Make yourself at home', you are making them feel welcome and inviting them to behave in an informal, relaxed way. **7** If you feel **at home**, you feel comfortable and at ease in the place or situation that you are in.

PHRASE
PRAGMATICS
BRITISH

CONVENTION
PRAGMATICS

PHRASE

8 You can use **home** to refer in a general way to the house, town, or country where someone lives now or where they were born, often to emphasize that they feel they belong in that place. *She gives frequent performances of her work, both at home and abroad... Ms Highsmith has made Switzerland her home... Warwick is home to some 550 international students.* **9** **Home** means relating to your own country as opposed to foreign countries. *...the Guardian's home news pages.*

N-UNCOUNT

ADJ: ADJ n

10 If you say that someone is **home and dry** in a contest or other activity, you mean that they have achieved victory or success, or you are certain that they will achieve it.

PHRASE
BRITISH

11 A **home** is a large house or institution where a number of people live and are looked after, usually because they are too old or ill to look after themselves. *...a home for handicapped children.*

N-COUNT

12 If you refer to the **home** of something, you mean the place where it began or where it is most typically found. *This south-west region of France is the home of*

N-SING:
with supp

claret. **13** If you find a **home** for something, you find a place where it can be kept.   N-COUNT

14 If you press, drive, or hammer something **home**, you explain it to your listeners as firmly as possible. *It is now up to all of us to debate this issue and press home the argument.* **15** To **bring** something **home** to someone means to make them understand how important or serious it is. **16** If a situation or message **hits home** or **strikes home**, people accept that it is real or true, even though it may be painful for them to realize. **17** If something that is thrown or fired **strikes home**, it reaches its target.   ADV; ADV after v / PHRASE / PHRASE / PHRASE WRITTEN

18 When a team plays at **home**, they play a game on their own ground, rather than on the opposing team's ground. ▶ Also an adjective. *All three are Chelsea fans, and attend all home games together.*   N-UNCOUNT / ADJ: ADJ n

home 2 phrasal verb uses

home /ˈhəʊm/ **homes, homing, homed.**   ◆◇◇◇◇

home in. 1 If you **home in** on one particular aspect of something, you give all your attention to it. *The critics immediately homed in on the group's essential members.* **2** If something such as a weapon **homes in** on something else, the weapon is aimed at that thing and moves towards it with great accuracy. *Two rockets homed in on it from behind without a sound.* ● See also **homing**.   PHRASAL VB / V P on n / Also V P / V P on n / Also V P

'home-brew. Home-brew is beer that is made in someone's home, rather than in a brewery.   N-UNCOUNT

home·com·ing /ˈhəʊmkʌmɪŋ/ **homecomings.** Your **homecoming** is your return to your home or your country, usually after a fairly long absence.   ◆◇◇◇◇ / N-VAR

Home 'Counties; also spelled **home counties.** The Home Counties are the counties which surround London.   ◆◇◇◇◇ / N-PROPER-PLURAL: the N

home eco'nomics. Home economics is a school subject dealing with how to cook and run a home efficiently.   N-UNCOUNT

home 'ground, home grounds. 1 A sports team's **home ground** is their own playing field, as opposed to that of other teams. **2** If you say that someone is **on** their **home ground**, you mean that they are in or near where they work or live, and feel confident because of this. *Although he was on home ground, his campaign had been rocked by adultery allegations.*   N-VAR / PHRASE

home-'grown. Home-grown fruit and vegetables have been grown in your garden, rather than on a farm, or in your country rather than abroad.   ◆◇◇◇◇ / ADJ

'home help, home helps. A **home help** is a person who is employed by a local authority to help old or disabled people who are living in their own homes.   N-COUNT BRITISH

home·land /ˈhəʊmlænd/ **homelands. 1** Your **homeland** is your native country. *Many are planning to return to their homeland.* **2** The **homelands** were regions within South Africa in which black South Africans had limited self-government. They are now part of the Republic of South Africa.   ◆◆◇◇◇ / N-COUNT WRITTEN / N-COUNT

home·less /ˈhəʊmləs/. Homeless people have nowhere to live. *Thousands have been made homeless.* ▶ The **homeless** are people who are homeless. *...shelters for the homeless.* ◆ **home·less·ness** *The only way to solve homelessness is to provide more homes.*   ◆◆◆◇◇ / ADJ / N-PLURAL: the N / N-UNCOUNT

home·ly /ˈhəʊmli/. **1** If you describe a room or house as **homely**, you like it because it makes you feel comfortable and at ease, and is as you imagine a home should be. *We try and provide a very homely atmosphere.* **2** If you describe a woman as **homely**, you mean that she has a warm, comforting manner and looks like someone who would enjoy being at home and running a family. **3** If you say that someone is **homely**, you mean that they are not very attractive.   ◆◇◇◇◇ / ADJ-GRADED / ADJ-GRADED BRITISH / ADJ-GRADED AMERICAN

home-'made; also spelled **homemade.** Something that is **home-made** has been made in someone's home, rather than in a shop or factory. *...a home-made bomb.*   ◆◇◇◇◇ / ADJ

home·maker /ˈhəʊmmeɪkə/ **homemakers.** A **homemaker** is a woman who spends a lot of time   N-COUNT

looking after her home and family. If you describe a woman as a **homemaker**, you usually mean that she does not have another job.

'Home Office. The **Home Office** is the department of the British Government which is responsible for domestic affairs, including the police, immigration, and broadcasting.   ◆◆◇◇◇ / N-PROPER

homeopa·thy /ˌhəʊmiˈɒpəθi/. In British English, the spelling **homoeopathy** is also used. Homeopathy is a way of treating an illness in which the patient is given very small amounts of a drug that would produce symptoms of the illness if taken in large quantities. ◆ **homeo·path** /ˈhəʊmiəʊpæθ/ **homeopaths.** A **homeopath** is someone who treats illness by homeopathy. ◆ **homeo·path·ic** /ˌhəʊmiəˈpæθɪk/. *...homeopathic remedies.*   ◆◇◇◇◇ / N-UNCOUNT / N-COUNT / ADJ

'home owner, home owners; also spelled **homeowner.** A **home owner** is a person who owns the house or flat that they live in.   N-COUNT

home 'rule. If a country or region has **home rule**, it has its own independent government and laws.   N-UNCOUNT

Home 'Secretary, Home Secretaries. The Home Secretary is the member of the British government who is in charge of the Home Office.   ◆◆◇◇◇ / N-COUNT

home 'shopping; also spelled **home-shopping.** Home shopping is buying things by ordering them by post or telephone, rather than going to a shop to buy them.   N-UNCOUNT

home·sick /ˈhəʊmsɪk/. If you are **homesick**, you feel unhappy because you are away from home and are missing your family, friends, and home. ◆ **home·sick·ness** *There were inevitable bouts of homesickness.*   ◆◇◇◇◇ / ADJ-GRADED / N-UNCOUNT

home·spun /ˈhəʊmspʌn/. **1** You use **homespun** to describe opinions or ideas that are simple and uncomplicated, especially ones that do not seem to have been thought out well. *The book is simple homespun philosophy.* **2** Homespun clothes are made from cloth that has been made at home, rather than in a factory.   ADJ / N-UNCOUNT

home·stead /ˈhəʊmsted/ **homesteads.** A **homestead** is a farmhouse, together with the land around it.   ◆◇◇◇◇ / N-COUNT

'home straight or **home stretch. 1** The home straight or the home stretch is the last part of a race. **2** You can also refer to the last part of any activity that lasts for a long time as the **home straight** or the **home stretch**, especially if the activity is difficult or boring.   N-SING: the N / N-SING: the N

home·town /ˌhəʊmˈtaʊn/ **hometowns;** also spelled **home town.** Someone's **hometown** is the town where they live or the town that they come from.   ◆◇◇◇◇ / N-COUNT: with poss

home 'truth, home truths. Home truths are unpleasant facts that you learn about yourself, usually from someone else.   N-COUNT

home·ward /ˈhəʊmwəd/; also spelled **homewards.** **1** If you are on a **homeward** journey, you are on a journey towards your home. **2** If you are travelling **homeward** or **homewards**, you are travelling towards your home. 'Homewards' is not often used in American English. *John drove homeward through the lanes.*   ADJ: ADJ n / ADV: ADV after v

homeward 'bound. People or things that are **homeward bound** are on their way home. *...homeward-bound commuters.*   ADJ

home·work /ˈhəʊmwɜːk/. **1** Homework is school work that teachers give to pupils to do at home in the evening or at the weekend. *Have you done your homework, Gemma?* **2** If you do your **homework**, you find out what you need to know in preparation for something.   ◆◇◇◇◇ / N-UNCOUNT / N-UNCOUNT

homey /ˈhəʊmi/. If you describe a place as **homey**, you mean that you feel comfortable and relaxed there.   ADJ-GRADED INFORMAL, AMERICAN

homi·ci·dal /ˌhɒmɪˈsaɪdəl/. Homicidal is used to describe someone who is dangerous because they are likely to kill someone.   ADJ

homi·cide /ˈhɒmɪsaɪd/ **homicides.** Homicide is the deliberate and unlawful killing of a person.   ◆◇◇◇◇ / N-VAR

homi·ly /'hɒmɪli/ **homilies.** A homily is a speech or piece of writing in which someone complains about the state of something or tells people how they ought to behave. ...*his homily on moral values.* `N-COUNT` `FORMAL`

hom·ing /'həʊmɪŋ/. A weapon or piece of equipment that has a **homing** system is able to guide itself to a target or to give out a signal that guides people to it. ...*infra-red homing missiles.* `ADJ: ADJ n`

'**homing pigeon, homing pigeons.** A **homing pigeon** is trained to return to a particular place, especially in races with other pigeons. `N-COUNT`

homeo·path /'həʊmiəʊpæθ/. See **homeopathy.**

homo·geneous /'hɒmə,dʒi:niəs, 'həʊ-/ also spelled **homogenous.** Homogeneous is used to describe a group or thing which has members or parts that are all the same. *The unemployed are not a homogeneous group.* ♦ **homo·genei·ty** /'hɒmədʒə,ni:ɪti, 'həʊ-/. *The government panicked into imposing a kind of cultural homogeneity.* ◆◇◇◇◇ `ADJ-GRADED` `FORMAL` `N-UNCOUNT`

ho·mog·enize /hə'mɒdʒənaɪz/ **homogenizes, homogenizing, homogenized;** also spelled **homogenise** in British English. If you say that something has **been homogenized,** you mean that all its parts have been made to seem the same, and you disapprove of this. *Even Brussels bureaucrats can't homogenize national cultures and tastes.* ♦ **ho·mog·enized** ...*an increasingly homogenised and bland America.* `VERB:` `be V-ed` `PRAGMATICS` `V n` `ADJ-GRADED`

ho·mog·enized /hə'mɒdʒənaɪzd/; also spelled **homogenised** in British English. **Homogenized** milk is milk whose fat has been broken up so that is evenly distributed. `ADJ`

ho·mog·enous /hə'mɒdʒənəs/. **Homogenous** means the same as **homogeneous.** `ADJ-GRADED`

homo·pho·bia /,hɒmə'fəʊbiə/. **Homophobia** is a strong and unreasonable dislike of homosexual people, especially homosexual men. ♦ **homo·pho·bic.** **Homophobic** means involving or related to homophobia. ◆◇◇◇◇ `N-UNCOUNT` `ADJ-GRADED`

homo·phone /'hɒməfəʊn/ **homophones.** Homophones are words with different meanings which are pronounced in the same way but are spelled differently. For example, the words 'write' and 'right' are homophones. `N-COUNT` `TECHNICAL`

homo sa·pi·ens /,həʊməʊ 'sæpienz/. **Homo sapiens** is used to refer to human beings in contrast to other species of ape or animal, or to earlier evolutionary forms of humans. `N-UNCOUNT`

homo·sex·ual /'hɒməʊ,sekʃʊəl, 'həʊ-/ **homosexuals.** 1 A **homosexual** relationship is a sexual relationship between people of the same sex. 2 Someone who is **homosexual** is sexually attracted to people of the same sex. ▶ Also a noun. *The judge said that discrimination against homosexuals is deplorable.* ♦ **homo·sex·ual·ity** /'hɒməʊsekʃʊ,ælɪti, 'həʊ-/ ...*a place where gays could openly discuss homosexuality.* ◆◆◆◇◇ `ADJ` `ADJ` `N-COUNT` `N-UNCOUNT`

Hon. /ɒn/. **Hon.** is an abbreviation for 'honourable' and 'honorary' when they are used as part of a person's title. ◆◇◇◇◇ `N-TITLE`

hone /həʊn/ **hones, honing, honed.** 1 If you **hone** something, for example a skill, technique, idea, or product, you carefully develop it over a long period of time so that it is exactly right for your purpose. *His body is honed and kept in trim with constant exercise.* 2 If you **hone** a blade, weapon, or tool, you sharpen it on a stone or with a special device. ◆◇◇◇◇ `VERB: V n` `VERB: V n` `TECHNICAL`

hon·est /'ɒnɪst/. 1 If you describe someone as **honest,** you mean that they always tell the truth, and do not try to deceive people or break the law. ♦ **hon·est·ly** *She fought honestly for a just cause and for freedom.* 2 If you are **honest** in a particular situation, you tell the complete truth or give your sincere opinion, even if this is not very pleasant. *What do you think of the school, in your honest opinion?* ♦ **honestly** *It came as a shock to hear an old friend speak so honestly about Ted... But did you honestly think we wouldn't notice?* 3 You say '**honest**' before or after a statement to emphasize that ◆◆◆◇◇ `ADJ-GRADED` `ADV-GRADED: ADV after v` `ADJ-GRADED` `ADV-GRADED: ADV with v` `ADV: ADV with cl` `PRAGMATICS`

you are telling the truth and that you want people to believe you. *I'm not sure, honest.* ♦ **honestly** *Honestly, I don't know anything about it.* 4 Some people say '**honest to God**' to emphasize their feelings or to emphasize that something is really true. *I wish we weren't doing this, Lillian, honest to God, I really do.* 5 You can say '**to be honest**' before or after a statement to emphasize that you are telling the truth about your own opinions or feelings, especially if you think these will disappoint the person you are talking to. *To be honest the house is not quite our style.* `INFORMAL` `ADV: ADV with cl` `PHRASE` `PRAGMATICS` `INFORMAL` `PHRASE` `PRAGMATICS`

,**honest 'broker, honest brokers.** If a person or country acts as an **honest broker,** they try to resolve a dispute or arrange a deal by talking to all sides and finding out what they want, without favouring any one side. `N-COUNT`

hon·est·ly /'ɒnɪstli/. 1 You use **honestly** to indicate that you are annoyed or impatient. *Oh, honestly, I don't know what they will think of next.* 2 See also **honest.** ◆◆◇◇◇ `ADV: ADV with cl` `SPOKEN`

hon·es·ty /'ɒnɪsti/. 1 **Honesty** is the quality of being honest. *I can answer you with complete honesty.* 2 You say **in all honesty** when you are stating an opinion or fact that might be disappointing or upsetting, and when you want to soften its effect by emphasizing your sincerity. *But in all honesty, I wish it had never happened.* ◆◆◇◇◇ `N-UNCOUNT` `PHRASE` `PRAGMATICS`

hon·ey /'hʌni/ **honeys.** 1 **Honey** is a sweet, sticky, yellowish substance that is made by bees. 2 You call someone **honey** as a sign of affection. ◆◆◇◇◇ `N-VAR` `N-VOC` `AMERICAN`

honey·bee /'hʌnibi:/ **honeybees.** A honeybee is a bee that makes honey. `N-COUNT`

honey·comb /'hʌnikəʊm/ **honeycombs.** A **honeycomb** is a wax structure consisting of rows of six-sided cells where bees store the honey. `N-VAR`

hon·eyed /'hʌnid/. 1 You can describe someone's voice or words as **honeyed** when they are saying something that is soothing and pleasant to listen to, especially if you want to suggest that they are insincere. *His gentle manner and honeyed tones reassured Andrew.* 2 You can describe something as **honeyed** when it tastes or smells of honey, or is the pale yellowish colour of honey. `ADJ` `ADJ-GRADED` `WRITTEN`

honey·moon /'hʌnimu:n/ **honeymoons, honeymooning, honeymooned.** 1 A **honeymoon** is a holiday taken by a man and a woman who have just got married. 2 When a newly married couple **honeymoon** somewhere, they go there on their honeymoon. 3 You can use **honeymoon** to refer to a period of time when someone has just started in a new job or role and everyone is pleased with them and does not criticize them. *The new Prime Minister will enjoy a honeymoon period.* ◆◇◇◇◇ `N-COUNT` `VERB: V adv/prep` `N-COUNT`

honey·pot /'hʌnipɒt/ **honeypots.** When journalists refer to a place as a **honeypot,** they mean that a lot of people are attracted to it for a particular reason. *Like every other tourist honeypot, Bath is plagued by traffic problems.* `N-COUNT` `BRITISH`

honey·suckle /'hʌnisʌkəl/ **honeysuckles.** **Honeysuckle** is a climbing plant with sweet-smelling flowers. `N-VAR`

honk /hɒŋk/ **honks, honking, honked.** 1 If you **honk** the horn of a vehicle, you make the horn produce a short loud sound. *Horns honk. An angry motorist shouts.* 2 If a bird, person, or musical instrument **honks,** they make a short, loud, harsh noise. *A lone mother Canada goose honked a warning to stay away from her nest.* `V-ERG: V n` `V` `VERB: V` `V n`

honky-tonk /'hɒŋki tɒŋk/ **honky-tonks.** 1 In the United States, a **honky-tonk** is a cheap, shabby bar or nightclub. 2 **Honky-tonk** is a kind of ragtime piano music originally played in honky-tonks. `N-COUNT` `N-UNCOUNT`

hon·or /'ɒnə/. See **honour.**

hon·or·able /'ɒnrəbəl/. See **honourable.**

hono·rar·ium /,ɒnə'reəriəm/ **honoraria** /,ɒnə'reəriə/ or **honorariums.** An **honorarium** is a fee that someone receives for doing something which is not a normal part of their job, for example giving a talk. `N-COUNT`

hon·or·ary /'ɒnərəri, AM -reri/. **1** An honorary title ◆◇◇◇◇ or membership is given to someone without their ADJ: ADJ n needing to have the necessary qualifications, usually because of their public achievements. *...an honorary member of the Golf Club.* **2 Honorary** is ADJ: ADJ n used to describe an official job that is done without payment. *...the honorary secretary of the Cheshire Beekeepers' Association.*

hon·or·if·ic /,ɒnə'rɪfɪk/. An **honorific** title or way of ADJ: ADJ n talking is used to show respect or honour to some- FORMAL one. *All employees will refer to each other by the honorific suffix 'san'.*

hon·our /'ɒnə/ **honours, honouring, hon-** ◆◆◆◇◇ **oured**; spelled **honor** in American English. **1 Hon-** N-UNCOUNT **our** means doing what you believe to be right and being confident that you have done what is right. *I do not believe I can any longer serve with honour as a member of your government.*

2 An **honour** is a special award that is given to some- N-COUNT one, usually because they have done something good or because they are greatly respected. *He was show- ered with honours – among them an Oscar in 1950.* **3** If VERB: someone **is honoured**, they are given public praise or beV-ed an award for something they have done. *Two Ameri-* beV-ed with n *can surgeons were last week honoured with the 1990 Nobel Prize for Medicine and Physiology.* **4** If some- PHRASE thing is arranged or happens in someone's **honour**, it is done specially to show appreciation of them. *...an outdoor concert in his honour.*

5 If you describe doing or experiencing something as N-SING an **honour**, you mean you think it is something spe- PRAGMATICS cial and desirable. People often describe something as an **honour** to indicate in a polite and formal way how pleased they are to be doing it or experiencing it. *Tchaikovsky was given a state funeral – the first com- moner to be granted this honour... It's an honour to finally work with her.* **6** If you say that you would **be** V-PASSIVE **honoured** to do something, you are saying very po- beV-ed to-inf litely and formally that you would be pleased to do it. PRAGMATICS If you say that you **are honoured** by something, you beV-ed are saying that you are grateful for it and pleased about it. *It's a very flattering offer, and I'm honoured by your confidence in me.* **7** To **honour** someone VERB means to treat them or regard them with special at- Vn with n tention and respect. *Her Majesty later honoured the* Also Vn *Headmaster with her presence at lunch.* ◆ **hon·oured** ADJ-GRADED: *Mrs Patrick Campbell was an honoured guest.* ADJ n

8 If something is arranged **in honour of** a particular PHR-PREP event, it is arranged in order to celebrate that event. **9** If someone **does the honours** at a social occasion or PHRASE public event, they act as host or perform some official function. **10** Judges are sometimes called **Your Honour** or re- N-VOC; ferred to as **His Honour** or **Her Honour.** PRON **11** If you **honour** an arrangement or promise, you do VERB what you said you would do. *The two sides agreed to* Vn *honour a new ceasefire.* **12 Honours** is a type of university degree which is of a N-UNCOUNT higher standard than a pass or ordinary degree. *...an honours degree in business studies.* **13** See also **guest of honour, lap of honour, maid of honour.**

hon·our·able /'ɒnərəbəl/; spelled **honorable** in ◆◇◇◇◇ American English. **1** If you describe people or ac- ADJ-GRADED tions as **honourable**, you mean that they are worthy of being respected or admired. *Their intentions are honourable.* ◆ **hon·our·ably** /'ɒnərəbli/ *She had not* ADV-GRADED *behaved honorably in the leadership election.* **2 Honourable** is used as a title before the names of ADJ: some members of the nobility, judges, and some the ADJ n- other officials. *...the Honourable Mr Justice Swinton* proper *Thomas.* **3** In debates in the British parliament, one ADJ: ADJ n member of parliament refers to another as the **hon- ourable** member, the **honourable** gentleman, the **honourable** lady or their **honourable** friend.

honourable 'mention, honourable mentions; N-COUNT spelled **honorable mention** in American English. If something that you do in a competition is given an **honourable mention**, it receives special praise from the judges although it does not actually win a prize.

'honours list, honours lists. In Britain, the **hon-** N-COUNT **ours list** is the list of people who have been selected to receive titles or decorations from the Queen in recognition of their achievements.

Hons /ɒnz/. In Britain, **Hons** is an abbreviation for 'Honours', used after the names of some university degrees, mainly first degrees.

hood /hʊd/ **hoods. 1** A **hood** is a part of a coat ◆◇◇◇◇ which you can pull up to cover your head. *...a warm* N-COUNT *hood.* **2** A **hood** is a bag made of cloth, which is put N-COUNT over someone's head and face so that they cannot be recognized or so that they cannot see. **3** The N-COUNT **hood** of a car is the metal cover over the engine at AMERICAN the front. The British word is **bonnet**. See picture headed **car and bicycle. 4** A **hood** is a covering on a N-COUNT vehicle or a piece of equipment, which is usually BRITISH curved and can be moved. *Why aren't all lenses sup- plied with a lens hood?*

hood·ed /'hʊdɪd/. **1** A **hooded** piece of clothing ◆◇◇◇◇ has a hood. *...a waterproof, hooded black cape.* **2** A ADJ: **hooded** person is wearing a hood or a piece of ADJ: ADJ n clothing pulled down over their face, so they are dif- ficult to recognize. *...a hooded gunman.* **3** If some- ADJ: ADJ n one has **hooded** eyes, their eyelids always look as though they are partly closed.

hood·lum /'huːdləm/ **hoodlums.** A **hoodlum** is a N-COUNT violent criminal, especially one who is part of a INFORMAL gang.

hood·wink /'hʊdwɪŋk/ **hoodwinks, hoodwink-** VERB: Vn **ing, hoodwinked.** If someone **hoodwinks** you, beV-ed they trick or deceive you. *Many people are hood- winked by the so-called beauty industry.*

hoof /huːf/ **hoofs** or **hooves.** The **hooves** of an ◆◇◇◇◇ animal such as a horse are the hard, bony parts of N-COUNT its feet.

hook /hʊk/ **hooks, hooking, hooked. 1** A **hook** ◆◆◇◇◇ is a bent piece of metal or plastic that is used for N-COUNT catching or holding things, or for hanging things up. *...curtain hooks... He felt a fish pull at his hook.* **2** If V-ERG you **hook** one thing to another, you attach it there Vn to/onto n using a hook. If something **hooks** somewhere, it can Vonto n be hooked there. *...one of those can openers that* Vprep *hooked onto the wall.* **3** If you **hook** your arm, leg, VERB or foot round an object, you place it like a hook Vn prep round the object in order to move it or hold it. *I hooked my left arm over the side of the dinghy.* **4** If VERB: Vn you **hook** a fish, you catch it with a hook on the end of a line.

5 If you **are hooked into** something, or **hook into** V-ERG something, you get involved with it. *I'm guessing* be/getV-ed *again now because I'm not hooked into the political* into *circles... Eager to hook into a career but can't find one* Vinto n *right for you?* **6** If someone gets **off the hook** or if AMERICAN someone or something lets them **off the hook**, they PHRASE manage to get out of the awkward or unpleasant situation that they are in. *Government officials ac- cused of bribery and corruption get off the hook with monotonous regularity.*

7 A **hook** is a short sharp blow with your fist that you N-COUNT make with your elbow bent, usually in a boxing match.

8 If you take a phone **off the hook**, you take the re- PHRASE ceiver off the part that it normally rests on, so that the phone will not ring. **9** ● **hook, line, and sinker**: see **sinker**.

hook up. 1 When someone **hooks up** a computer or PHRASAL VB other electronic machine, they connect it to other VPnoun similar machines or to a central power supply. *He* VnP *brought it down, hooked it up, and we got the genera-* beV-edP n *tor going. ...if the machine is hooked up to an apart-* Also VnP to n *ment's central wiring system.* **2** If one person, espe- RECIP: cially a musician, **hooks up** with another, the two VPwithn people start working with each other. *It just seemed* pl-nVP *natural that we should hook up.*

hooked /hʊkt/. **1** If you describe something as ◆◇◇◇◇ **hooked**, you mean that it is shaped like a hook. ADJ-GRADED *...hooked claws.* **2** If you are **hooked** on something, ADJ: you enjoy it so much that it takes up a lot of your v-linkADJ interest and attention. *Open this book and read a* INFORMAL

H

few pages and you will be hooked. **3** If you are hooked on a drug, you are addicted to it.   ADJ: v-link ADJ INFORMAL

hook·er /'hʊkə/ **hookers.** A hooker is a prostitute. *She was once a hooker.*   ◆◇◇◇ N-COUNT INFORMAL

hook-'up, hook-ups. A hook-up is a connection between two locations, systems, or pieces of equipment. *Water and electric hook-ups are available.*   N-COUNT

hooky /'hʊki/; also spelled **hookey.** If a child **plays hooky**, they stay away from school without permission to do so.   PHRASE INFORMAL, AMERICAN

hoo·li·gan /'huːlɪgən/ **hooligans.** If you describe young people as **hooligans**, you are critical of them because they behave in a noisy and violent way in a public place. ◆ **hoo·li·gan·ism** /'huːlɪgənɪzəm/. Hooliganism is the behaviour and actions of hooligans. *...football hooliganism.*   ◆◇◇◇ N-COUNT PRAGMATICS / N-UNCOUNT

hoop /huːp/ **hoops.** **1** A hoop is a large ring made of wood, metal, or plastic. *...a stout iron hoop.* **2** A basketball **hoop** is the ring that players try to throw the ball into in order to get a point for their team. **3** If someone makes you **jump through hoops**, they make you do lots of difficult or boring things in order to please them or achieve something.   ◆◇◇◇ N-COUNT / N-COUNT / PHRASE

hoo·ray /huː'reɪ/. People sometimes shout **'Hooray!'** when they are very happy and excited about something.   EXCLAM

hoot /huːt/ **hoots, hooting, hooted.** **1** If you hoot the horn on a vehicle or if it **hoots**, it makes a loud noise on one note. *I never hoot my horn when I pick a girl up for a date... Somewhere in the distance a siren hooted.* ▶ Also a noun. *Mortlake strode on, ignoring the car, in spite of a further warning hoot.* **2** If you **hoot**, you make a loud high-pitched noise when you are laughing or showing disapproval. *Bev hooted with laughter.* ▶ Also a noun. *His confession was greeted with derisive hoots.* **3** When an owl **hoots**, it makes a sound like a long 'oo'. **4** If you say that someone or something is **a hoot**, you think they are very amusing. *Michael Fish is my favourite. He's a hoot.* **5** If you say that you **don't give a hoot** or **don't care two hoots** about something, you are emphasizing that you don't care at all about it. *Alan doesn't care two hoots about Irish politics... They just don't give a hoot.*   ◆◇◇◇ V-ERG / V n / Also V at n / BRITISH / N-COUNT / VERB: V / V with n / N-COUNT / VERB: V / N-SING: a N INFORMAL / PHRASE PRAGMATICS INFORMAL

hoot·er /'huːtə/ **hooters.** **1** A hooter is a device such as a horn or a siren that makes a hooting noise. **2** You can refer to someone's nose as their **hooter**, especially if it is large.   N-COUNT BRITISH / N-COUNT INFORMAL, BRITISH

hoo·ver /'huːvə/ **hoovers, hoovering, hoovered.** **1** A Hoover is a **vacuum cleaner**. Hoover is a trademark. **2** If you **hoover**, you clean a carpet using a vacuum cleaner. *She hoovered the study and the sitting-room.* ◆ **hoo·ver·ing** *I finished off the hoovering upstairs.*   ◆◇◇◇ N-COUNT BRITISH / VERB: V n BRITISH / N-UNCOUNT: also the N

hooves /huːvz/. Hooves is a plural of **hoof**.

hop /hɒp/ **hops, hopping, hopped.** **1** When you hop, you move along by jumping on one foot. *I hopped down three steps.* ▶ Also a noun. *When he walked it was with the little hops and shuffles of a five-year-old.* **2** When birds and some small animals hop, they move along by jumping on both feet. *A small brown fawn hopped across the trail in front of them.* **3** If you **hop** somewhere, you move there quickly or suddenly. *I hopped out of bed quickly... We hopped on the boat.* **4** A **hop** is a short quick journey, usually by plane. *...a 20-minute hop in a private helicopter.* **5** If you tell someone to **hop it**, you are telling them in a rude way to go away. *'Hop it', I snapped at the bloke. 'She's with me.'* **6** Hops are the flowers of a type of plant. They are dried and used for making beer. **7** Someone who is **hopping mad** is very angry. *The family's hopping mad that she left them nothing.* **8** If you are caught **on the hop**, you are surprised by someone doing something when you were not expecting them to and so you are not prepared for it.   ◆◆◇◇ VERB: V / V prep/adv / N-COUNT / VERB V prep/adv / INFORMAL / N-COUNT INFORMAL / PHRASE PRAGMATICS INFORMAL, BRITISH / N-COUNT / PHRASE INFORMAL / PHRASE INFORMAL, BRITISH

hope /həʊp/ **hopes, hoping, hoped.** **1** If you hope that something is true, or you hope for something, you want it to be true or to happen, and you usually believe that it is possible or likely. *The researchers hope that such a vaccine could be available in about ten years' time... I hope to get a job within the next two weeks. ...as though he had been hoping for conversation... 'We'll speak again.'—'I hope so.'... She had decided she must go on as usual, follow her normal routine, and hope and pray.* ◆ **hoped-for.** Hoped-for is used to describe something that people would like to happen, and which they usually think is likely or possible. *The hoped-for economic recovery in Britain did not arrive.* **2** If you say that you cannot hope for something, or if you talk about the only thing that you can hope to get, you mean that you are in a bad situation, and there is very little chance of improving it. *That's the best you can hope for. ...these mountains, which no one can hope to penetrate.* ▶ Also a noun. *The car was smashed beyond any hope of repair.* **3** If you **hope for the best**, you hope that everything will happen in the way you want, although you know that it may not. *Some companies are cutting costs and hoping for the best.* **4** If you **hope against hope** that something will happen, you hope that it will happen, although it seems impossible. **5** Hope is a feeling of desire and expectation that things will go well in the future. *People once again have hope for genuine changes in the system... Kevin hasn't given up hope of being fit.* **6** If someone wants something to happen, and considers it likely or possible, you can refer to their **hopes** of that thing, or to their **hope** that it will happen. *They have hopes of increasing trade between the two regions... My hope is that, in the future, I will go over there and marry her.* **7** If you tell someone not to **get** their **hopes up**, or not to **build** their **hopes up**, you are warning them that they should not become too confident of progress or success. **8** If you have **high hopes** or **great hopes** that something will happen, you are confident that it will happen. If you have **high hopes** or **great hopes** for someone or something, you are confident that they will be successful. **9** If you do one thing **in the hope** of another thing happening, you do it because you think it might cause or help the other thing to happen, which is what you want. *He was studying in the hope of being admitted to an engineering college.* **10** If you **live in hope** that something will happen, you continue to hope that it will happen, although it seems unlikely. *I just live in hope that one day she'll talk to me.* **11** If you think that the help or success of a particular person or thing will cause you to be successful or to get what you want, you can refer to them as your **hope**. *...England's last hope in the English Open Table Tennis Championships.* **12** You use **'I hope'** in expressions such as **'I hope you don't mind'** and **'I hope I'm not disturbing you'**, when you are being polite and want to make sure that you have not offended someone or disturbed them. **13** You say **'I hope'** when you want to warn someone not to do something foolish, something dangerous, or something that you disapprove of. *You're not trying to see him, I hope?* **14** You add **'I hope'** to what you are saying to make it sound more polite and less rude, abrupt, or definite. *Fraulein Wendel is well, I hope?* **15** If you say that someone has **not got a hope in hell** of doing something, you are emphasizing that they will not be able to do it. **16** If you say **'Some hope'**, or **'Not a hope'**, you think there is no possibility that something will happen, although you may want it to happen. *The industry reckons it will see orders swell by 10% this financial year. Some hope.*   ◆◆◆◆◆ VERB V that / V to-inf / V for n / V so/not / V / ADJ: ADJ n / VB: with brd-neg V for n V to-inf / N-VAR / PHRASE / PHRASE / N-UNCOUNT / N-COUNT: with supp / PHRASE PRAGMATICS / PHRASE / PHRASE / PHRASE / N-COUNT: with supp / PHRASE PRAGMATICS / PHRASE PRAGMATICS / PHRASE PRAGMATICS / PHRASE INFORMAL / CONVENTION PRAGMATICS INFORMAL

hope·ful /'həʊpfʊl/ **hopefuls.** **1** If you are hopeful, you are fairly confident that something that you want to happen will happen. *I am hopeful this misunderstanding will be rectified very quickly.* ◆ **hope·ful·ly** *'Am I welcome?' He smiled hopefully, leaning on the door.* **2** If something such as a sign or event   ◆◆◇◇◇ ADJ-GRADED / ADV-GRADED: ADV with v / ADJ-GRADED

is **hopeful**, it makes you feel that what you want to happen will happen. *The leadership election has not been a hopeful sign for Labour's future.* **3** A **hopeful** ADJ: ADJ n action is one that you do in the hope that you will get what you want to get. *We've chartered the aircraft in the hopeful anticipation that the government will allow them to leave.* **4** If you refer to someone N-COUNT as a **hopeful**, you mean that they have a particular ambition and it is possible that they will achieve it. *...his job as football coach to young hopefuls.*

hope·ful·ly /ˈhəʊpfʊli/. You say **hopefully** when ◆◆◇◇◇ mentioning something that you hope will happen. ADV: Some careful speakers of English think that this use group of **hopefully** is not correct, but it is very frequently used. *Hopefully, you won't have any problems after reading this.*

hope·less /ˈhəʊpləs/. **1** If you feel **hopeless**, you ◆◆◇◇◇ feel desperate because there seems to be no pos- ADJ-GRADED sibility of success. *Even able pupils feel hopeless about job prospects.* ◆ **hope·less·ly** *I looked* ADV-GRADED *around hopelessly. ...a young woman hopelessly in love with a handsome hero.* ◆ **hope·less·ness** *She* N-UNCOUNT *had a feeling of hopelessness about the future.* **2** Someone or something that is **hopeless** is ADJ-GRADED certain to fail or be unsuccessful. *I don't believe your situation is as hopeless as you think.* **3** If someone is ADJ-GRADED **hopeless** at something, they are very bad at it. *I'd be* INFORMAL *hopeless at working for somebody else.* **4** You use ADJ-GRADED **hopeless** to emphasize how bad or inadequate something or someone is. *Argentina's economic policies were a hopeless mess.* ◆ **hope·less·ly** *The* ADV-GRADED *story is hopelessly confusing... They were on the other side of Berlin and Harry was hopelessly lost... He was hopelessly in debt.*

hop·per /ˈhɒpə/ **hoppers.** A **hopper** is a device N-COUNT shaped like a large funnel, into which substances such as grain, coal, or animal food can be put and from which they can be released when required.

hop·scotch /ˈhɒpskɒtʃ/. **Hopscotch** is a children's N-UNCOUNT game which involves jumping between squares which are drawn on the ground.

horde /hɔːd/ **hordes.** If you describe a crowd of ◆◇◇◇◇ people as a **horde**, you mean that the crowd is very N-COUNT large and excited and, often, rather frightening and unpleasant. *...a horde of people was screaming for tickets.*

ho·ri·zon /həˈraɪzən/ **horizons. 1** The **horizon** is ◆◆◇◇◇ the line in the far distance where the sky seems to N-SING meet the land or the sea. *The sun had already sunk below the horizon.* **2** Your **horizons** are the limits of N-COUNT what you want to do or of what you are interested or involved in. *As your horizons expand, these new ideas can give a whole new meaning to life.* **3** If PHRASE something is **on the horizon**, it is almost certainly going to happen or be done quite soon. *There is no obvious breakthrough on the horizon.*

hori·zon·tal /ˌhɒrɪˈzɒntəl, AM ˈhɔːr-/ **horizontals.** ◆◇◇◇◇ **1** Something that is **horizontal** is flat and level with ADJ the ground, rather than at an angle to it. *The board consists of vertical and horizontal lines.* ► Also a N-SING: noun. *Do not raise your left arm above the horizon-* the N *tal.* ◆ **hori·zon·tal·ly** *The wind was cold and drove* ADV *the snow at him almost horizontally. ...a horizontally striped tie.* **2** A **horizontal** is a line or structure N-COUNT that is horizontal. *...the hard horizontals and verticals of the urban scene.*

hor·mone /ˈhɔːməʊn/ **hormones.** A **hormone** is a ◆◆◇◇◇ chemical, usually occurring naturally in your body, N-COUNT that stimulates certain organs of your body. ◆ **hor·mo·nal** /hɔːˈməʊnəl/ *...our individual hormonal* ADJ *balance.*

hormone re'placement. If a woman has **hor-** N-UNCOUNT **mone replacement** therapy, she takes doses of the hormone oestrogen, usually in order to control the symptoms of the menopause.

horn /hɔːn/ **horns. 1** On a vehicle such as a car, ◆◆◇◇◇ the **horn** is the device that makes a loud noise as a N-COUNT signal or warning. See picture headed **car and bicycle.** *A car horn honked from the driveway.*
2 The **horns** of an animal such as a cow or deer are the N-COUNT

hard pointed things that grow from its head. *A mature cow has horns.* ◆ **horned.** Horned animals have ADJ horns. **3 Horn** is the hard substance that the horns of N-UNCOUNT animals are made of. ● See also **horn-rimmed.**

4 A **horn** is a musical instrument of the brass family N-COUNT which is shaped like a long metal tube wound round in a circle with a wide funnel at one end. **5** A **horn** is a N-COUNT simple musical instrument consisting of a metal tube that is wide at one end and narrow at the other. *...a hunting horn.* **6** A **horn** is a hollow curved object that N-COUNT is narrow at one end and wide at the other. *...a wind-up gramophone with a big horn.* **7** See also **shoehorn.**
8 If two people **lock horns**, they argue about some- PHRASE thing. *During his six years in office, Seidman has often locked horns with lawmakers.* **9** ● **take the bull by the horns**: see **bull.**

hor·net /ˈhɔːnɪt/ **hornets. 1 Hornets** are large N-COUNT wasps which have powerful stings. **2** If you say that PHRASE someone has stirred up **a hornet's nest**, you mean PRAGMATICS that they have done something which has caused a INFORMAL lot of controversy or produced a situation which is extremely difficult to deal with.

horn-'rimmed. Horn-rimmed spectacles have ADJ: ADJ n plastic frames that look as though they are made of horn.

horny /ˈhɔːni/ **hornier, horniest. 1** If you de- ◆◇◇◇◇ scribe someone as **horny**, you mean that they are ADJ-GRADED sexually aroused or easily aroused. *...horny adoles-* INFORMAL *cent boys.*
2 If you describe someone as **horny**, you mean that ADJ-GRADED they are sexually attractive. *Let's face it, Keanu Reeves* BRITISH, *is horny.* INFORMAL
3 Something that is **horny** is hard, strong, and made ADJ of horn or of a hard substance like horn. *His fingernails had grown long and horny.*

horo·scope /ˈhɒrəskəʊp, AM ˈhɔːr-/ **horoscopes.** ◆◇◇◇◇ Your **horoscope** is a forecast of events which some N-COUNT people believe will happen to you in the future. Horoscopes are based on the position of the stars when you were born.

hor·ren·dous /həˈrendəs, AM hɔːˈr-/. Something ◆◇◇◇◇ that is **horrendous** is very bad or unpleasant. *...hor-* ADJ-GRADED *rendous traffic jams... The violence used was hor- rendous.* ◆ **hor·ren·dous·ly** *Many outings can now* ADV-GRADED *be horrendously expensive for parents with a young family.*

hor·ri·ble /ˈhɒrɪbəl, AM ˈhɔːr-/. **1** If you describe ◆◆◇◇◇ someone or something as **horrible**, you do not like ADJ-GRADED them at all. *...a horrible small boy.* ◆ **hor·ri·bly** ADV-GRADED /ˈhɒrɪbli, AM ˈhɔːr-/ *When trouble comes they behave selfishly and horribly.* **2** You can call something **hor-** ADJ-GRADED **rible** when it causes you to feel great shock, fear, INFORMAL and disgust. *Still the horrible shrieking came out of his mouth.* ◆ **horribly** *A two-year-old boy was hor-* ADV-GRADED *ribly murdered.* **3 Horrible** is used to emphasize ADJ-GRADED: how awful or unpleasant something is. *Unless you* ADJ n *respect other people's religions, horrible mistakes* PRAGMATICS *and conflict will occur.* ◆ **horribly** *Our plans have* ADV-GRADED *gone horribly wrong... You got horribly drunk.* INFORMAL

hor·rid /ˈhɒrɪd, AM ˈhɔːr-/. **1** If you describe some- ◆◇◇◇◇ thing as **horrid**, you mean that it is very unpleasant ADJ-GRADED indeed. *What a horrid smell!* **2** If you describe INFORMAL someone as **horrid**, you mean that they behave in a ADJ-GRADED very unpleasant way towards other people. *I love both my parents, but they're horrid to each other.*

hor·rif·ic /hɒˈrɪfɪk, AM hɔːˈr-/. **1** If you describe a ◆◇◇◇◇ physical attack, accident, or injury as **horrific**, you ADJ-GRADED mean that it is very bad, so that people are shocked when they see it or think about it. *I have never seen such horrific injuries.* ◆ **hor·rifi·cal·ly** *He had been* ADV-GRADED *horrifically assaulted before he died.* **2** If you de- ADJ-GRADED scribe something as **horrific**, you mean that it is so big that it is extremely unpleasant. *...piling up horrific extra amounts of money on top of your origi- nal debt.* ◆ **horrifically** *Opera productions are hor-* ADV-GRADED: *rifically expensive.* ADV adj

hor·ri·fy /ˈhɒrɪfaɪ, AM ˈhɔːr-/ **horrifies, horrify-** ◆◆◇◇◇ **ing, horrified.** If someone is **horrified**, they feel VERB: shocked, disappointed, or disgusted, usually be- be V-ed V n

cause of something that they have seen or heard.
...a crime trend that will horrify all parents.

hor·ri·fy·ing /ˈhɒrɪfaɪɪŋ/. If you describe some- ◆◇◇◇◇
thing as **horrifying**, you mean that it is shocking, ADJ-GRADED
alarming, or disgusting. *These were horrifying ex-*
periences. ♦ **hor·ri·fy·ing·ly** *...horrifyingly high lev-* ADV-GRADED
els of infant mortality... The two cars cartwheeled
horrifyingly into the sand trap at the first corner.

hor·ror /ˈhɒrə, AM ˈhɔːr-/ **horrors. 1 Horror** is a ◆◆◇◇
feeling of great alarm and dismay caused by some- N-UNCOUNT
thing extremely unpleasant. *I felt numb with hor-*
ror... I watched in horror. **2** The **horror** of some- N-SING
thing, especially something that hurts people, is its
very great unpleasantness, which is often frightening and shocking. *...the horror of this most bloody of*
civil wars. **3** You can refer to extremely unpleasant N-COUNT
or frightening experiences as **horrors**. *...all the hor-*
rors we have undergone since I last wrote you?
4 Horror of horrors is used in a humorous way to PHRASE
refer to something that you consider to be the worst [PRAGMATICS]
part of a situation. *He would horror of horrors, refer* INFORMAL
to the great composers as 'those dead guys'.
5 If you have a **horror** of something, you are afraid of N-SING:
it or dislike it very much. *...his horror of death.* N of n
6 A **horror** film or story is intended to be very fright- ADJ
ening. **7** You can refer to an account of a very unpleas- ADJ
ant experience or event as a **horror** story. *Almost*
everyone has a horror story to tell about 'cowboy'
builders.

horror-stricken /ˈhɒrəstrɪkən/. **Horror-stricken** ADJ
means the same as **horror-struck**.

'horror-struck. If you describe someone as ADJ
horror-struck or **horror-stricken**, you mean that
they feel very great horror or dismay at something
that has happened. *When Nightingale had an-*
nounced her nursing ambitions to her rich parents,
they were horror-struck.

hors d'oeu·vre /ˌɔːˈdɜːv/ **hors d'oeuvres. Hors** N-VAR
d'oeuvres are dishes of cold foods that are served in
small portions before the main course of a meal.

horse /hɔːs/ **horses, horsing, horsed. 1** A ◆◆◆◆◇
horse is a large animal which people can ride. See N-COUNT
picture headed **animals**. *...a small man on a grey*
horse. **2** When you talk about **the horses**, you mean N-PLURAL:
horse races in which people bet money on the the N
horse which they think will win.
3 If you hear something **from the horse's mouth**, you PHRASE
hear it from someone who knows that it is definitely
true.
4 See also **clothes horse, dark horse, rocking horse,**
seahorse.

horse around. If you **horse around**, you play PHRASAL VB
roughly and rather carelessly, so that you could hurt V P
someone or damage something. INFORMAL

horse·back /ˈhɔːsbæk/. **1** If you do something on ◆◇◇◇◇
horseback, you do it while riding a horse. **2 Horse-** N-UNCOUNT
back riding is the activity of riding a horse. *...a* ADJ: ADJ n
horseback ride into the mountains. ▶ Also an ad- ADV
verb. *Many people in this area ride horseback.*

'horse box, horse boxes. A **horse box** is a vehi- N-COUNT
cle which is used to take horses from one place to BRITISH
another.

horse 'chestnut, horse chestnuts. 1 A **horse** N-COUNT
chestnut is a large tree which has leaves with several pointed parts and shiny reddish-brown nuts covered with a spiky case. **2 Horse chestnuts** are the N-COUNT
nuts of a horse chestnut tree. They are more commonly called **conkers**.

'horse-drawn; also spelled **horsedrawn.** A **horse-** ADJ: ADJ n
drawn carriage, cart, or other vehicle is one that is
pulled by one or more horses.

horse·hair /ˈhɔːsheə/. **Horsehair** is hair which is N-UNCOUNT
taken from the tails or manes of horses, and was
formerly used to stuff mattresses and furniture such
as armchairs.

horse·man /ˈhɔːsmən/ **horsemen.** A **horseman** is ◆◇◇◇◇
a man who is riding a horse, or who rides horses N-COUNT
well. ♦ **horse·man·ship** /ˈhɔːsmənʃɪp/. **Horse-** N-UNCOUNT
manship is the ability to ride horses well.

horse·play /ˈhɔːspleɪ/. **Horseplay** is rough play in N-UNCOUNT
which people push and hit each other, or behave in
a silly way.

horse·power /ˈhɔːspaʊə/. **Horsepower** is a unit of N-UNCOUNT
power used for measuring how powerful an engine
is. *...a 300-horsepower engine.*

'horse racing; also spelled **horse-racing** or ◆◇◇◇◇
horseracing. Horse racing is a sport in which N-UNCOUNT
horses ridden by jockeys run in races.

horse·radish /ˈhɔːsrædɪʃ/. **1 Horseradish** is a N-UNCOUNT
white vegetable which is the root of a plant. It has a
very strong sharp taste. **2 Horseradish** or **horse-** N-UNCOUNT
radish sauce is a sauce made from horseradish.

horse·shoe /ˈhɔːsʃuː/ **horseshoes.** A **horseshoe** ◆◇◇◇◇
is a piece of metal shaped like a U, which is fixed N-COUNT
with nails to a horse's hoof in order to protect it.

'horse show, horse shows. A **horse show** is a N-COUNT
sporting event in which people riding horses compete in order to demonstrate their skill and control.

'horse-trading. If you describe discussions or ne- N-UNCOUNT
gotiations as **horse-trading**, you disapprove of the [PRAGMATICS]
way in which people are using secret, unofficial,
and perhaps dishonest methods in order to get
what they want. *...the political horse-trading in-*
volved in forming a government.

horse·whip /ˈhɔːswɪp/ **horsewhips, horsewhip-**
ping, horsewhipped; also spelled **horse-whip.** N-COUNT
1 A **horsewhip** is a long thin piece of leather on the
end of a short stiff handle. It is used to train and
control horses. **2** If someone **horsewhips** an animal VERB: V n
or a person, they hit them several times with a
horsewhip in order to hurt or punish them.

horse·woman /ˈhɔːswʊmən/ **horsewomen.** A N-COUNT
horsewoman is a woman who is riding a horse, or
who rides horses well.

horsey /ˈhɔːsi/; also spelled **horsy. 1** Someone who ADJ-GRADED
is **horsey** likes horses or spends a lot of time with INFORMAL
horses. *He comes from a very horsey family.* **2** If you ADJ-GRADED
describe a woman as **horsey**, you are saying in a ra- [PRAGMATICS]
ther rude way that her face reminds you of a horse,
for example because it is long and thin.

hor·ti·cul·ture /ˈhɔːtɪkʌltʃə/. **Horticulture** is the N-UNCOUNT
study and practice of growing plants. ♦ **hor·ti·cul-**
·tur·al /ˌhɔːtɪˈkʌltʃərəl/ *The horticultural show will*
take place in the old covered Victorian Market.
♦ **hor·ti·cul·tur·al·ist** /ˌhɔːtɪˈkʌltʃərəlɪst/ N-COUNT
horticulturalists. A **horticulturalist** is a person
who studies or grows plants, especially as their job.

hose /həʊz/ **hoses, hosing, hosed. 1** A **hose** is a ◆◇◇◇◇
long flexible pipe made of rubber or plastic. Water N-COUNT
is directed through a hose in order to do things
such as put out fires, clean cars, or water gardens.
See picture headed **tools**. *You've left the garden hose*
on. **2** A **hose** is a pipe made of rubber or plastic, N-COUNT
along which a liquid or gas flows, for example from
one part of an engine to another. *Water in the en-*
gine compartment is sucked away by a hose. **3** If you VERB
hose something, you wash or water it using a hose. V n
We wash our cars and hose our gardens without Also V
even thinking of the water that it uses.
4 See also **pantyhose.**

hose down. When you **hose** something or someone PHRASAL VB
down, you clean them using a hose. *A chauffeur wear-* V n P
ing rubber boots was hosing down a limousine. V P noun

hose·pipe /ˈhəʊzpaɪp/ **hosepipes.** A **hosepipe** is a N-COUNT
hose that people use to water their gardens or for BRITISH
washing their cars.

ho·siery /ˈhəʊziəri, AM -ʒəri/. You use **hosiery** to re- N-UNCOUNT
fer to tights, stockings, and socks, especially when FORMAL
they are on sale in shops.

hos·pice /ˈhɒspɪs/ **hospices.** A **hospice** is a hos- ◆◇◇◇◇
pital for people who are dying. N-COUNT

hos·pi·table /hɒˈspɪtəbəl, ˈhɒspɪt-/. **1** A **hospitable** ◆◆◇◇◇
person is friendly, generous, and welcoming to ADJ-GRADED
guests or strangers. *He was very hospitable to me*
when I came to New York. **2** A **hospitable** place, cli- ADJ-GRADED
mate, or environment is one that allows or encour-
ages the existence or development of particular
people, things, or processes. *...hospitable political*
environments.

hos·pi·tal /'hɒspɪtəl/ **hospitals.** A hospital is a ◆◆◆◆ place where people who are ill are looked after by N-VAR nurses and doctors. *Queen Elizabeth Hospital... My mother went into hospital.*

hos·pi·tal·ity /,hɒspɪ'tælɪti/. **1** Hospitality is ◆◇◇◇◇ friendly welcoming behaviour towards guests or to- N-UNCOUNT wards strangers. *...the kindness, charm and hospital-ity of the people.* **2** Hospitality is the food, drink, N-UNCOUNT and other privileges which some companies provide for their visitors or clients at major sporting or other public events.

hos·pi·tal·ize /'hɒspɪtəlaɪz/ **hospitalizes, hospi-** ◆◇◇◇◇ **talizing, hospitalized;** also spelled **hospitalise** in VB: usu British English. If someone **is hospitalized**, they are passive sent or admitted to hospital. ♦ **hos·pi·tali·za·tion** N-UNCOUNT /,hɒspɪtəlaɪ'zeɪʃən/ *Occasionally hospitalization is required to combat dehydration.*

host /həʊst/ **hosts, hosting, hosted. 1** The host ◆◆◆◆ at a party is the person who has invited the guests N-COUNT and provides the food, drink, or entertainment. **2** If VERB: V n someone **hosts** a party, dinner, or other function, they have invited the guests and provide the food, drink, or entertainment.
3 A country, city, or organization that is the **host** of an N-COUNT event provides the facilities for that event to take place. *Barcelona was chosen to be host of the 1992 Olympic games.* **4** If a country, city, or organization VERB: V n **hosts** an event, they provide the facilities for the event to take place. **5** If a person or country **plays host** to an PHRASE event or an important visitor, they host the event or the visit. *Canada played host to the Commonwealth Conference.*
6 The **host** of a radio or television show is the person N-COUNT who introduces it and talks to the people who appear in it. **7** The person who **hosts** a radio or television VERB: V n show introduces it and talks to the people who appear in it.
8 A **host** of things is a lot of them. *...a whole host of* QUANT *gadgets powered by electricity.*
9 If an area is **host** to living things, those creatures live N-COUNT and feed in that area. *Uganda's beautiful highlands are host to a wide range of wildlife.*
10 The **host** of a parasite is the plant or animal it feeds N-COUNT off. TECHNICAL
11 The **Host** is the bread which is used to represent N-COUNT the body of Christ in Christian church services such as TECHNICAL Holy Communion.

hos·tage /'hɒstɪdʒ/ **hostages. 1** A hostage is ◆◆◆◇ someone who has been captured by a person or or- N-COUNT ganization and who may be killed or injured if peo-ple do not do what that person or organization de-mands. **2** If someone **is taken hostage** or **is held** PHRASE **hostage**, they are captured and kept as a hostage.
3 If you say you are **hostage** to something, you N-VAR: mean that your freedom to take action is restricted N to n by things that you cannot control. *The government will be even more a hostage to the whims of the in-ternational oil price.*

hos·tel /'hɒstəl/ **hostels.** A hostel is a large house ◆◆◇◇ where people can stay cheaply for a short period of N-COUNT time. ● See also **youth hostel.** BRITISH

hos·tel·ry /'hɒstəlri/ **hostelries.** A hostelry is a N-COUNT pub or a hotel. *We found a local hostelry for an ex-* BRITISH, *cellent dinner.* FORMAL

host·ess /'həʊstɪs/ **hostesses. 1** The hostess at a ◆◇◇◇◇ party is the woman who has invited the guests and N-COUNT provides the food, drink, or entertainment. **2** A N-COUNT **hostess** at a night club or dance hall is a woman who is paid by a man to be his companion for the evening.

hos·tile /'hɒstaɪl, AM -təl/. **1** If you are hostile to ◆◆◇◇◇ another person or an idea, you disagree with them ADJ-GRADED or disapprove of them, often showing this in your behaviour. *They would be hostile to the idea of for-eign intervention... The Governor faced hostile crowds.* ♦ **hos·til·ity** /hɒ'stɪlɪti/ *There is hostility* N-UNCOUNT *among traditionalists to this method of teaching his-tory.* **2** Someone who is **hostile** is unfriendly and ag- ADJ-GRADED gressive. *The prisoner eyed him in hostile silence.* ♦ **hostility** *...hostility to Black and ethnic groups.* N-UNCOUNT

3 Hostile situations and conditions make it difficult ADJ-GRADED for you to achieve something. *...some of the most hostile climatic conditions in the world.* **4** In a war, ADJ: ADJ n you use the word **hostile** to describe your enemy's forces, organizations, weapons, land, and activities. *The city is encircled by a hostile army.*

hos·til·ities /hɒ'stɪlɪtiz/. You can refer to fighting ◆◇◇◇◇ between two countries or groups who are at war as N-PLURAL **hostilities**. *The authorities have urged people to* FORMAL *stock up on fuel in case hostilities break out.*

hot /hɒt/ **hotter, hottest; hots, hotting, hot-** ◆◆◆◆◇ **ted. 1** Something that is **hot** has a high tempera- ADJ-GRADED ture. *When the oil is hot, add the sliced onion... What he needed was a hot bath and a good sleep.*
2 If it is **hot**, or if a place is **hot**, the temperature of ADJ-GRADED the air is high. *It was too hot even for a gentle stroll. ...a hot, humid summer day.* **3** If you are **hot**, you ADJ-GRADED feel as if your body is at an unpleasantly high tem-perature. *I was too hot and tired to eat.* **4** You use ADJ-GRADED: **hot** to talk or ask about how high the temperature how ADJ, of something is. *Their colour depends on how hot* as ADJ as *they are.* **5** Hot food is intended to be eaten as soon ADJ: ADJ n as it is cooked, as opposed to food that you eat when it has cooled or that you do not cook at all. *You might not want to cook a hot meal every day.*
6 You can say that food is **hot** when it has a strong, ADJ-GRADED burning taste caused by spices such as chilli or cay-enne pepper. *...hot curries.*
7 You can use **hot** to describe an issue or event that is ADJ-GRADED very important or exciting to people at the present INFORMAL time and is receiving a lot of publicity. *The role of women in war has been a hot topic of debate in Ameri-ca... A friend got me a ticket for the hottest show in town.* **8** You can describe a situation as **hot** when it is ADJ-GRADED difficult to deal with, especially because it involves a INFORMAL lot of conflict or disagreement. *It would require changing the constitution, and that is too hot for any politician to handle.* **9** If a person or team is the **hot** fa- ADJ-GRADED: vourite, people think that they are most the likely to ADJ n win a race or competition. *Labour is now hot favourite to win the election.* **10** Someone who has a **hot** temper ADJ-GRADED gets angry very quickly and easily. ● See also **hot-tempered. 11** ● **in hot pursuit**: see **pursuit.**

hot up. When something **hots up**, a lot of activity PHRASAL VB and excitement starts to happen. *The bars rarely hot* V P *up before 1am... Campaigning is expected to start hot-* BRITISH *ting up today.*

hot 'air. If you say that someone's claims or ◆◇◇◇◇ promises are just **hot air**, you are criticizing them N-UNCOUNT because they are made mainly to impress people PRAGMATICS and have no real value or meaning. *I'd come to the* INFORMAL *conclusion by then that he was all hot air.*

hot-'air balloon, hot-air balloons. A hot-air N-COUNT balloon is a large balloon filled with hot air, with a basket underneath in which people can travel.

hot·bed /'hɒtbed/ **hotbeds.** If you say that some- N-COUNT: where is a **hotbed** of something, usually of a politi- with supp cal activity, you are emphasizing that there is a lot PRAGMATICS of the activity going on there. *...a state now known worldwide as a hotbed of racial intolerance.*

hot-'blooded. If you describe someone as **hot-** ADJ-GRADED **blooded**, you mean that they are very quick to ex-press their emotions, especially anger and love.

hotch-potch /'hɒtʃ pɒtʃ/; also **hotchpotch.** A N-SING hotch-potch is a confused or disorderly mixture of BRITISH, different types of things. The usual American word INFORMAL is **hodgepodge**. *The palace is a complete hotch-potch of architectural styles.*

hot dog, hot dogs. A hot dog is a long bread roll ◆◇◇◇◇ with a hot sausage inside it. N-COUNT

ho·tel /,həʊ'tel/ **hotels.** A hotel is a building where ◆◆◆◆◇ people stay, for example on holiday, paying for their N-COUNT rooms and meals.

ho·tel·ier /,həʊ'teliə, AM ,əʊte'ljeɪ/ **hoteliers.** A ◆◇◇◇◇ hotelier is a person who owns or manages a hotel. N-COUNT

hot 'flash, hot flashes. A hot flash is the same as N-COUNT a **hot flush**. AMERICAN

hot 'flush, hot flushes. A hot flush is a sudden N-COUNT hot feeling in the skin which women often experi-ence at the time of their menopause.

hot-'foot, hot-foots, hot-footing, hot-footed;   VERB
also spelled **hotfoot**. If you **hot-foot** it somewhere,   V it adv/prep
you go there in a hurry. *Richard was hot-footing it*   Also V adv/
back to London.   prep · INFORMAL

hot·head /'hɒthed/ **hotheads.** If you refer to   N-COUNT
someone as a **hothead**, you are criticizing them for   PRAGMATICS
doing things hastily, without thinking of the conse-   INFORMAL
quences. ♦ **hot-headed** /,hɒt'hedɪd/ *All too often*   ADJ-GRADED
people his age act in a hot-headed fashion.

hot·house /'hɒthaʊs/ **hothouses. 1** A **hothouse** is   N-COUNT
a glass building which is kept very warm inside so
that tropical plants can be grown in it. **2** You can   N-COUNT
refer to a situation or place as a **hothouse** when
there is intense activity, especially intellectual or
emotional activity. *...the reputation of the College as*
a hothouse of novel ideas.

hot·line /'hɒtlaɪn/ **hotlines;** also spelled **hot line.**   ◆◇◇◇◇
1 A **hotline** is a telephone line that the public can   N-COUNT
use to contact an organization about a particular
subject. *Two leaflets carry details of a telephone*
hotline for gardeners seeking advice. **2** A **hotline** is a   N-COUNT
special, direct telephone line between the heads of
government in different countries.

hot·ly /'hɒtli/. **1** If someone says something **hotly**,   ◆◇◇◇◇
they speak in a lively or angry way, because they   ADV-GRADED:
feel strongly. *The bank hotly denies any wrongdoing.*   ADV with v
2 If something is being **hotly** pursued or **hotly** con-   ADV-GRADED:
tested, the people involved are very determined to   ADV v-ed
catch it or to win it. *He'd snuck out of America hotly*
pursued by the CIA... This year's final will be as hotly
contested as ever.

hot·plate /'hɒtpleɪt/ **hotplates.** A **hotplate** is a flat   N-COUNT
surface which can be heated, usually on a cooker.

hot·pot /'hɒtpɒt/ **hotpots;** also spelled **hot-pot.** In   N-VAR
Britain, a **hotpot** is a dish made from a mixture of
meat, vegetables, and gravy cooked slowly in the
oven.

hot po'tato, hot potatoes. If you describe a   N-COUNT
problem or issue as a **hot potato**, you mean that it
is very controversial and nobody wants to deal with
it. *Birth-control was a political hot potato.*

'hot seat. If you are in the **hot seat**, you are re-   PHRASE
sponsible for making important and difficult deci-   INFORMAL
sions. *He is to remain in the hot seat as the*
company's chief executive.

hot·shot /'hɒtʃɒt/ **hotshots.** If you refer to some-   N-COUNT
one as a **hotshot**, you mean they are very good at
their job and very ambitious, so they are going to be
very successful. *She's a hotshot broker on Wall*
Street.

'hot spot, hot spots; also spelled **hotspot. 1** You   ◆◇◇◇◇
can refer to an exciting place where there is a lot of   N-COUNT
activity or entertainment as a **hot spot**. *...a fancy*   INFORMAL
Manhattan hot spot. **2** You can refer to an area   N-COUNT
where there is some form of trouble such as fighting   JOURNALISM
or political unrest as a **hot spot**. *...such hot spots as*
Somalia and Bosnia.

'hot 'stuff. If you think that someone or something   N-UNCOUNT
is **hot stuff**, you find them exciting or sexually at-   INFORMAL
tractive. *His love letters were hot stuff.*

hot-'tempered. If someone is **hot-tempered**,   ADJ-GRADED
they get angry very quickly and easily.

'hot tub, hot tubs. A **hot tub** is a very large, round   N-COUNT
bath in which several people can bathe together.

hot-'water bottle, hot-water bottles; also   N-COUNT
spelled **hot water bottle**. A **hot-water bottle** is a
rubber container that you fill with hot water and
put in a bed to make it warm.

'hot wire, hot wires, hot wiring, hot wired. To   VERB
hot wire a car means to start its engine using a   V n
piece of wire rather than the key. Car thieves often
hot wire cars in order to steal them. *A youth was in-*
side the car, attempting to hot wire it.

hou·mous /'hu:məs/; also spelled **humous** or **hum-**   N-UNCOUNT
mus. **Houmous** is a smooth food made from chick
peas.

hound /haʊnd/ **hounds, hounding, hounded.**   ◆◆◇◇◇
1 A **hound** is a type of dog that is often used for   N-COUNT
hunting or racing. **2** If someone **hounds** you, they   VERB
constantly disturb or pester you. *Newcomers are*   V n · be V-ed out

constantly hounding them for advice... He has been   of/from n
hounded out of office by the press.

hounds·tooth /'haʊndztu:θ/. A **houndstooth** pat-   ADJ
tern is one that is similar to check, but that has broken squares in it. See picture headed **patterns**.

hour /aʊə/ **hours. 1** An **hour** is a period of sixty   ◆◆◆◆
minutes. *They waited for about two hours... I only*   N-COUNT
slept about half an hour that night. ...a twenty-four
hour strike. **2** If you say that someone does some-   PHRASE
thing **hour after hour**, you are emphasizing that   PRAGMATICS
they do it continually for a long time. **3** People say   N-PLURAL
that something takes or lasts **hours** to emphasize   PRAGMATICS
that it takes or lasts a very long time, or what seems   INFORMAL
like a very long time.
4 **The hour** is used in expressions like **on the hour** to   N-SING:
refer to times when it is exactly one o'clock, two   the N
o'clock, and so on. *Trains will leave Reading at 36*
minutes past the hour... The clock in the church tower
began to strike the hour. **5** You can refer to a particular   N-SING
time or moment as a particular **hour**. *...the hour of his*   LITERARY
execution. **6** If you say that something is done or hap-   PHRASE
pens **at all hours**, you disapprove of it being done or   PRAGMATICS
happening at the time that it does. *She didn't want her*
fourteen-year-old daughter coming home at all hours
of the morning. **7** If something happens **in the early**   PHRASE
hours or **in the small hours**, it happens in the early
morning after midnight. **8** If you refer, for example, to   N-COUNT:
someone's **hour** of need or **hour** of happiness, you   with supp
are referring to the time in their life when they are or   LITERARY
were experiencing that condition. *...the darkest hour*
of my professional life. **9** You can refer to the period of   N-PLURAL:
time during which something happens or operates   with supp
each day as the **hours** during which it happens or operates. *...the hours of darkness... Phone us on this*
number during office hours. **10** You can use **hours** in   N-PLURAL
expressions such as **after hours** and **out of hours** to
talk about the times when businesses normally operate or when people are normally at work. *...a local res-*
taurant where steel workers unwind after hours...
Teachers refused to run out of hours sports matches.
● See also **after-hours.** **11** If you refer to the **hours** in-   N-PLURAL
volved in a job, you are talking about how long you
spend each week doing it and when you do it. *I*
worked quite irregular hours... The job was easy; the
hours were good.
12 See **eleventh hour, lunch hour, rush hour.**

hour·glass /'aʊəglɑ:s/ **hourglasses;** also spelled   N-COUNT
hour glass. An **hourglass** is a device consisting of
two round glass sections with sand flowing between
them, that was used to measure the passing of an
hour.

hour·ly /'aʊəli/. **1** An **hourly** event happens once   ◆◇◇◇◇
every hour. *He flipped on the radio to get the hourly*   ADJ: ADJ n
news broadcast. ▶ Also an adverb. *The hospital is-*   ADV
sued press releases hourly. **2** Your **hourly** earnings   ADJ: ADJ n
are the earnings that you make in one hour. *They*
have little prospect of finding new jobs with the
same hourly pay.

house, houses, housing, housed. The noun is   ◆◆◆◆◆
pronounced /haʊs/. The verb is pronounced /haʊz/.
The form **houses** is pronounced /'haʊzɪz/. **1** A   N-COUNT
house is a building in which people live, usually the
people belonging to one family. You can also refer
to all the people who live together in a house as the
house. *She has moved to a small house... It would*
wake the whole house. **2** To **house** someone means   VERB
to provide a house or flat for them to live in. *Their*   V n
villas housed army officers now... Regrettably we   V n adv/prep
have to house families in these inadequate flats. **3** A   VB: no cont
building or container that **houses** something is the   V n
place where it is located or from where it operates.
...the office complex that used to house the Central
Committee of the Communist Party. **4** **House** is
sometimes used in the names of office buildings
and large private homes. *I was to go to the very top*
floor of Bush House in Aldwych. **5** A **house** is a fami-   N-COUNT:
ly which has been or will be important for many   with supp
generations, especially the family of a king or
queen. *...the Saudi Royal House. ...the House of*
Windsor.

6 House is used in the names of types of companies N-COUNT: and establishments, for example places where people n N go to eat and drink. *...a steak house... She was fired from her job at a publishing house.* **7** A restaurant's ADJ: ADJ n **house** wine is the cheapest wine it sells, which is not listed by name on the wine list. *...a bottle of house red.* **8** If you are given something in a restaurant or pub **on** PHRASE **the house**, you do not have to pay for it. **9** You can refer to the two main bodies of Britain's and N-COUNT the United States of America's parliament as the **House** or a **House**. *Some members of the House and Senate worked all day yesterday.* **10** The **house** is the N-COUNT part of a theatre or cinema where the audience sits. You can also refer to the audience at a particular performance as the **house**. *They played in front of a packed house.* **11** See also **boarding house, chapter house, clearing house, doll's house, full house, opera house, public house, White House.** **12** If a person or their performance in a play or con- PHRASE cert **brings the house down**, the audience claps and cheers loudly for a long time because they are very pleased with the performance. **13** If two people **get** PHRASE **on like a house on fire**, they quickly become close INFORMAL friends, for example because they have many interests in common; an informal expression. **14** If you **keep house**, you do the cleaning and cook- PHRASE ing for your household, and do not go out to work. *He lives with an aunt who keeps house for him.* **15 Open** PHRASE **house** in someone's home or at an establishment such as a school is a time when visitors are welcome to call without making an appointment. *The International Bookstore and Language School holds an open house on September 13... My wife and I keep open house.* **16** If someone **gets** their **house in order, puts** PHRASE their **house in order,** or **sets** their **house in order,** they arrange their affairs and solve their problems. *The challenge for American leadership is this: Can we put our economic house in order?*

house ar'rest. If someone is under **house arrest,** ◆◇◇◇◇ they are officially ordered not to leave their home, N-UNCOUNT because they are suspected of being involved in an illegal activity.

house·boat /'haʊsbəʊt/ **houseboats.** A **house-** N-COUNT **boat** is a small boat on a river or canal which people live in.

house·bound /'haʊsbaʊnd/. Someone who is ADJ **housebound** is unable to go out of their house, usually because they are ill or cannot walk far.

house·break·er /'haʊsbreɪkə/ **housebreakers.** A N-COUNT **housebreaker** is someone who enters another person's house illegally in order to steal their possessions. ♦ **house·break·ing** *...a huge increase in* N-UNCOUNT *housebreaking and car theft.*

house·coat /'haʊskəʊt/ **housecoats.** A **house-** N-COUNT **coat** is a long loose piece of clothing that some women wear over their underwear or nightclothes when they are at home during the day.

house guest, house guests. A **house guest** is a N-COUNT person who is staying at someone's house for a period of time.

house·hold /'haʊshəʊld/ **households. 1** A **house-** ◆◆◇◇◇ **hold** is all the people in a family or group who live N-COUNT together in a house. *...growing up in a male-only household... Many poor households are experiencing real hardship.* **2** The **household** is your home and N-SING everything that is connected with looking after it. *My husband gave me cash to manage the household. ...household chores.* **3** Someone or something that ADJ: ADJ n is a **household** name is very well known. *Today, fashion designers are household names.*

house·holder /'haʊshəʊldə/ **householders.** A ◆◇◇◇◇ **householder** is the legal owner or tenant of a house. N-COUNT

house·husband /'haʊshʌzbənd/ **house-** N-COUNT **husbands;** also **house husband.** A **househusband** is a married man who does not have a paid job, but instead looks after his home and children.

house·keeper /'haʊskiːpə/ **housekeepers.** A ◆◇◇◇◇ **housekeeper** is a person whose job is to cook, N-COUNT clean, and look after a house for its owner.

house·keeping /'haʊskiːpɪŋ/. **1 Housekeeping** is ◆◇◇◇◇ the work and organization involved in running a N-UNCOUNT home, including the shopping and cleaning. **2** The N-UNCOUNT **housekeeping** is the money that you use to buy BRITISH food, cleaning materials, and other things that you need in your home.

'house lights. In a theatre or cinema, the **house** N-PLURAL: **lights** are the lights where the audience sits, which the N are switched off during the performance.

house·maid /'haʊsmeɪd/ **housemaids.** A **house-** N-COUNT **maid** is a female servant who does cleaning and other work in someone's house.

house·man /'haʊsmən/ **housemen. 1** A **house-** N-COUNT **man** is a doctor who has a junior post in a hospital BRITISH and who usually sleeps at the hospital. The American word is **intern**. **2** A **houseman** is a man who is N-COUNT a servant in a house. The usual British word is AMERICAN **manservant.**

house·master /'haʊsmɑːstə, -mæs-/ **house-** N-COUNT **masters.** A **housemaster** is a male teacher who is BRITISH in charge of one of the dormitories or houses in a boarding school.

house·mate /'haʊsmeɪt/ **housemates.** Your N-COUNT **housemate** is someone who shares a house with you, who is not your boyfriend or girlfriend or a member of your family.

,House of 'Commons. The House of Commons ◆◆◇◇◇ is the more powerful of the two parts of parliament N-PROPER: in Britain or Canada, whose members are elected by the N the population. *The House of Commons has overwhelmingly rejected demands to bring back the death penalty.*

,House of 'Lords. The House of Lords is the less ◆◇◇◇◇ powerful of the two parts of parliament in Britain, N-PROPER: whose members hold office because they belong to the N the nobility or have high positions in the church or judiciary.

,House of Repre'sentatives. The House of ◆◇◇◇◇ Representatives is the less powerful of the two N-PROPER: parts of Congress in the United States, or the equi- the N valent part of the system of government in some other countries. *The House of Representatives approved a new budget plan.*

'house party, house parties. A **house party** is a N-COUNT party held at a big house in the country, usually over a weekend.

'house plant, house plants; also spelled N-COUNT **houseplant.** A **house plant** is a plant which is grown in a pot indoors.

house-proud /'haʊspraʊd/; also spelled ADJ-GRADED **houseproud.** Someone who is **house-proud** spends BRITISH a lot of time cleaning and decorating their house.

house·room /'haʊsruːm/; also **house room.** If you PHRASE say that you wouldn't **give** something **houseroom,** [PRAGMATICS] you are emphasizing that you do not want it or do BRITISH not like it at all.

,Houses of 'Parliament. In Britain, **the Houses** ◆◇◇◇◇ **of Parliament** are the British parliament, which N-COLL- consists of two parts, the House of Commons and PROPER: the House of Lords. the N

,house-to-'house; also spelled **house to house.** A ◆◇◇◇◇ **house-to-house** activity involves going to all the ADJ: ADJ n houses in an area one after another. *...house-to-house searches.*

house·wares /'haʊsweəz/. **Housewares** are objects N-PLURAL on sale for use in your house, especially objects re- AMERICAN lated to cooking and cleaning.

house·warm·ing /'haʊswɔːmɪŋ/ N-COUNT **housewarmings.** A **housewarming** is a party that you give when you have just moved to a new house.

house·wife /'haʊswaɪf/ **housewives.** A **house-** ◆◇◇◇◇ **wife** is a married woman who does not have a paid N-COUNT job, but instead looks after her home and children.

house·work /'haʊswɜːk/. **Housework** is the work ◆◇◇◇◇ such as cleaning, washing, and ironing that you do N-UNCOUNT in your home.

hous·ing /'haʊzɪŋ/ **housings. 1** You refer to the ◆◆◆◇ buildings in which people live as **housing** when you N-UNCOUNT are talking about their standard, price, or availability. *...a shortage of affordable housing. ...poor hous-*

ing. **2 Housing** is the job of providing houses for people to live in. *...courses in housing and public administration... Call the housing department about it.* **3** A **housing** is a case or covering which protects parts of a machine.   N-UNCOUNT / N-COUNT

'housing association, housing associations. ◆◇◇◇◇ In Britain, a **housing association** is an organization which owns houses and helps its members to rent or buy them cheaply.   N-COUNT

'housing benefit, housing benefits. In Britain, **housing benefit** is money that the government gives to people with no income or very low incomes to pay for part or all of their rent. *The majority of the long-term unemployed and their families are dependent upon income support and housing benefit.*   ◆◇◇◇◇ N-UNCOUNT also N in pl

'housing development, housing developments. A **housing development** is the same as a **housing estate.**   N-COUNT

'housing estate, housing estates. A **housing estate** is a large number of houses or flats built close together at the same time.   ◆◇◇◇◇ N-COUNT BRITISH

'housing project, housing projects. A **housing project** is a publicly funded and controlled housing estate for low-income families.   ◆◇◇◇◇ N-COUNT AMERICAN

hove /hoʊv/. **Hove** is the past tense and past participle of **heave** in one of its meanings.

hov·el /'hɒvəl, AM 'hʌv-/ **hovels. 1** A **hovel** is a small hut, especially one which is dirty or needs a lot of repair. **2** You describe a house, room, or flat as a **hovel** to express your disapproval or dislike of it because it is dirty, untidy, and in poor condition. *The room I was given was a hovel.*   N-COUNT / N-COUNT PRAGMATICS

hov·er /'hɒvə, AM 'hʌv-/ **hovers, hovering, hovered. 1** To **hover** means to stay in the same position in the air without moving forwards or backwards. *Beautiful butterflies hovered above the wild flowers... A police helicopter hovered overhead.* **2** If you **hover**, you stay in one place and move slightly in a nervous way, for example because you cannot decide what to do. *Judith was hovering in the doorway... His hand hovered over the doorknob. No, he'd better not.* **3** If you **hover**, you are in an uncertain or unsettled situation or state of mind. *She hovered on the brink of death for three months.* **4** If something such as a price, value, or score **hovers** around a particular level, it stays at approximately that level. *His golf handicap hovered between 10 and 12.*   ◆◆◇◇◇ VERB / V / VERB / V prep/adv / VERB / V prep/adv / VERB / V prep/adv

hover·craft /'hɒvəkrɑːft, AM 'hʌvəkræft/. **hovercraft** is both the singular and the plural. A **hovercraft** is a vehicle that can travel across land and water on a cushion of air.   N-COUNT: also by N

how /haʊ/. **1** You use **how** to ask about the way in which something happens or is done. *How do I make payments into my account?... How do you manage to keep the place so tidy?... How are you going to plan for the future?* ▶ Also a conjunction. *I don't want to know how he died.* **2** You use **how** when you are asking someone whether something happened in a successful or enjoyable way. *How was your trip down to Orlando?... How did your date go?... I wonder how Sam got on with him.* **3** You use **how** when you want to say that it does not matter which way something is done. *It's your life, so live it how you want!* **4** You use **how** in expressions such as **'How can you'** and **'How could you...'** to indicate that you disapprove of what someone has done or that you find it hard to believe. *How can you drink so much beer, Luke?... How could he be so indiscreet?* **5** You ask **'How come?'** or **'How so?'** when you are surprised by something and are asking why it happened or was said. *How come he hasn't been able to be as good as this year?* **6** You use **how** after certain adjectives and verbs to introduce a statement or fact. *It's amazing how people collect so much stuff over the years... I remember how Grandma loved to cook.* **7** You use **how** to ask about someone's health or to find out someone's news. *Hi! How are you doing?... How's the job?... She asked how he had been feeling.* **8** **'How do you do'** is a polite way of greeting someone when you meet them for the first   ◆◆◆◆◆ QUESTION / I CONJ / QUESTION / CONJ INFORMAL / QUESTION PRAGMATICS / PHRASE PRAGMATICS INFORMAL / CONJ / QUESTION / CONVENTION PRAGMATICS

time. **9** You use **how** in expressions such as **'how about...'** or **'how would you like...'** when you are making an offer or a suggestion. *How about a cup of coffee?... How about the end of next week?* **10** If you say **'How's that?'** to someone, you are asking whether something is acceptable or satisfactory. *Suppose we meet somewhere for a drink? I'll pay. How's that?*   QUESTION PRAGMATICS / PHRASE PRAGMATICS

11 You use **how** to ask questions about the quantity or degree of something. *How much money are we talking about?... How many full-time staff have we got?... How long will you be staying?... How old is your son now?... How fast were you driving?* **12** You use **how** to emphasize the degree to which something is true. *I didn't realize how heavy that shopping was going to be... How strange!... How anxiously she awaited my answer.*   QUESTION / ADV: ADV adj/adv PRAGMATICS

13 If you ask someone **'How about you?'** you are asking them what they think or want. *Well, I enjoyed that. How about you two?* **14** If you say **'How about that?'** you are drawing attention to something that has been said or done that you think is surprising. *Turns out I know the guy. How about that?* **15** You use **how about** to introduce a new subject which you think is relevant to the conversation you have been having. *Are your products and services competitive? How about marketing?* **16** If you say **'How do you mean?'** to someone, you are asking them to explain or give more details of what they have just said.   CONVENTION PRAGMATICS / CONVENTION PRAGMATICS / PHRASE PRAGMATICS / PHRASE PRAGMATICS INFORMAL BRITISH

how·dy /'haʊdi/. In American English, **'Howdy'** is an informal way of saying 'Hello'.   CONVENTION

how·ever /haʊ'evə/. **1** You use **however** when you are adding a comment which is surprising or which contrasts with what has just been said. *Some of the food crops failed. However, the cotton did quite well.* **2** You use **however** before an adjective or adverb to emphasize that the degree or extent of something cannot change a situation. *However hard she tried, nothing seemed to work... However much it hurt, he could do it.* **3** You use **however** when you want to say that it makes no difference how something is done. *Wear your hair however you want.* **4** You use **however** in expressions such as **or however long it takes** and **or however many there were** to indicate that the figure you have just mentioned may not be accurate but that the exact figure is not important. *...the 20,000 or however many who come to watch.* **5** You can use **however** to ask in an emphatic way how something has happened which you are very surprised about. Some speakers of English think that this form is incorrect and prefer to use 'how ever'. *However did you find this place?*   ◆◆◆◆◇ ADV: ADV with cl PRAGMATICS / ADV: ADV adj/adv, ADV many/ much PRAGMATICS / CONJ / ADV: ADV many/ much, ADV adv / QUESTION PRAGMATICS

how·itz·er /'haʊɪtsə/ **howitzers.** A **howitzer** is a large gun with a short barrel, which fires shells high up into the air.   N-COUNT

howl /haʊl/ **howls, howling, howled. 1** If an animal such as a wolf or a dog **howls**, it utters a long, loud, crying sound. ▶ Also a noun. *The dog let out a savage howl.* **2** If a person **howls**, they make a long, loud cry expressing pain, anger, or unhappiness. ▶ Also a noun. *A minute later there was a howl of anger.* **3** When the wind **howls**, it blows hard and makes a loud noise. *It sank in a howling gale.* **4** If you **howl** something, you say it in a very loud voice. *'Get away, get away,' he howled... The crowd howled its approval.* **5** If you **howl** with laughter, you laugh very loudly. ▶ Also a noun. *His stories caused howls of laughter.*   ◆◆◇◇◇ VERB: V / N-COUNT / VERB: V / N-COUNT / VERB: V V-ing / VERB V with quote V n / VERB: V with n N-COUNT

howl·er /'haʊlə/ **howlers.** A **howler** is a stupid and embarrassing mistake. *I felt as if I had made an outrageous howler.*   N-COUNT INFORMAL

hp. hp is an abbreviation for 'horsepower'.

HP /ˌeɪtʃ 'piː/. **HP** is an abbreviation for 'hire purchase'.   N-UNCOUNT BRITISH

HQ /ˌeɪtʃ 'kjuː/. **HQs.** HQ is an abbreviation for 'headquarters'.   ◆◇◇◇◇ N-VAR

hr, hrs. hr is a written abbreviations for 'hour'. *...1 hr 15 mins.*   ◆◇◇◇◇

HRH /ˌeɪtʃ ɑːr 'eɪtʃ/. **HRH** is an abbreviation for 'His Royal Highness' or 'Her Royal Highness'. *...HRH the Princess of Wales.*   N-TITLE

HRT /ˌeɪtʃ ɑː ˈtiː/. **HRT** is an abbreviation for 'hormone replacement therapy'. The treatment is given to women, usually in order to control the symptoms of menopause. ◆◇◇◇◇ N-UNCOUNT

hub /hʌb/ **hubs. 1** You can describe a place as a **hub** of an activity when it is a very important centre for that activity. *As a hub of finance and communications, Paris is now almost equal to London.* **2** The **hub** of a wheel is the part at the centre. ◆◇◇◇◇ N-COUNT / N-COUNT

hub·bub /ˈhʌbʌb/ **hubbubs. 1** A **hubbub** is a noise made by a lot of people all talking or shouting at the same time. *There was a hubbub of excited conversation.* **2** You can describe a situation where there is great confusion or excitement as a **hubbub**. *In all the hubbub over the election, one might be excused for missing yesterday's announcement.* N-VAR / N-SING: also no det

hub·by /ˈhʌbi/ **hubbies.** You can refer to a woman's husband as her **hubby**. N-COUNT DATED

hub·cap /ˈhʌbkæp/ **hubcaps;** also **hub cap.** A **hubcap** is a metal or plastic disc that covers and protects the hub of a wheel on a vehicle. N-COUNT

hu·bris /ˈhjuːbrɪs/. If you accuse someone of **hubris**, you are accusing them of arrogant pride. *...a tale of how an honourable man pursuing honourable goals was afflicted with hubris and led his nation towards catastrophe.* N-UNCOUNT FORMAL

huck·ster /ˈhʌkstə⁄/ **hucksters.** If you refer to someone as a **huckster**, you are criticizing them for trying to sell useless or worthless things in a dishonest or aggressive way. *A huckster offered to sell Carnegie the formula for guaranteed success for $20,000.* N-COUNT PRAGMATICS AMERICAN

hud·dle /ˈhʌdəl/ **huddles, huddling, huddled. 1** If you **huddle** somewhere, you sit, stand, or lie there holding your arms and legs close to your body, usually because you are cold or frightened. *She huddled inside the porch as she rang the bell.* **2** If people **huddle** together or **huddle** round something, they stand, sit, or lie close to each other, usually because they all feel cold or frightened. *The survivors spent the night huddled around bonfires.* **3** If people **huddle** in a group, they gather together to discuss something quietly or secretly. *The president has been huddling with his most senior aides.... Mr Perot was huddled with advisers at his house in Dallas.* **4** A **huddle** is a small group of people or things that are very close together. *...the huddle of dark houses on the other side of the reservoir.* ◆◇◇◇◇ VERB / V prep/adv / VERB: V adv/prep V-ed / V-RECIP: pl-n V / V with n / V-ed / N-COUNT

hue /hjuː/ **hues. 1** A **hue** is a colour. *The summer collection includes a selection of tops in natural hues and fibres.* **2** If people raise a **hue and cry** about something, they protest angrily about it. ◆◇◇◇◇ N-COUNT LITERARY / PHRASE

huff /hʌf/ **huffs, huffing, huffed. 1** If you **huff**, you indicate that you are annoyed or offended about something, usually by the way that you say something. *'This', huffed Mr Buthelezi, 'was discrimination.'* **2** If someone is **in a huff**, they are behaving in a bad-tempered way because they are annoyed and offended. **3** If someone **huffs and puffs**, they loudly express their annoyance or dissatisfaction with a decision or situation but do not do anything to change it. ◆◇◇◇◇ VERB / V with quote / PHRASE INFORMAL / PHRASE

huffy /ˈhʌfi/. Someone who is **huffy** is obviously annoyed or offended about something. *I, in my turn, became embarrassed and huffy and told her to take the money back.* ◆ **huffi·ly** /ˈhʌfɪli/ *'I appreciate your concern for my feelings,' Bess said huffily, 'but I'm a big girl now.'* ADJ-GRADED INFORMAL / ADV-GRADED

hug /hʌg/ **hugs, hugging, hugged. 1** When two people **hug**, they put their arms around each other and hold each other tightly. *She had hugged him exuberantly and invited him to dinner the next day.* ► Also a noun. *Syvil leapt out of the back seat, and gave him a hug.* **2** If you **hug** something, you hold it close to your body with your arms tightly round it. *She hugged her legs tight to her chest.* **3** Something that **hugs** the ground or a stretch of land or water stays very close to it. *The road hugs the coast for hundreds of miles.* **4** See also **bear hug**. ◆◆◇◇◇ V-RECIP: pl-n V / V n (non-recip) / N-COUNT / VERB: V n / V n adv/prep / VERB V n WRITTEN

huge /hjuːdʒ/ **huger, hugest. 1** Something or someone that is **huge** is extremely large in size, amount or degree. *Several painters were working on a huge piece of canvas... He is furious they are making huge profits out of the misery of young addicts.* ◆ **huge·ly** *She seemed to be enjoying herself hugely.* **2** Something that is **huge** exists or happens on a very large scale, and involves a lot of different people or things. *Another team is looking at the huge problem of debts between companies... The result was human suffering on a huge scale.* ◆◆◆◇ ADJ-GRADED / ADV-GRADED / ADJ-GRADED

-hugging /-hʌgɪŋ/. **-hugging** combines with nouns to form adjectives which describe an item of clothing that fits very tightly. *...a figure-hugging dress.* COMB

huh /hʌ, hɜː/. **Huh** is used in writing to represent a noise that people make at the end of a question if they want someone to agree with them. **Huh** is also used to show that someone is either surprised or unimpressed by something, or that they did not hear it. *Can we just get on with it, huh?... Huh? What's going on? You want to tell me what I did?* ◆◇◇◇

hulk /hʌlk/ **hulks. 1** The **hulk** of something is the large, ruined remains of it. *I could make out the gutted hulk of the tanker.* **2** You use **hulk** to describe anything which is large and seems threatening to you. *I followed his big hulk into the vestry.* ◆ **hulk·ing** /ˈhʌlkɪŋ/. *When I woke up there was a hulking figure staring down at me.* ◆◇◇◇◇ N-COUNT / N-COUNT / ADJ: ADJ n

hull /hʌl/ **hulls, hulling, hulled. 1** The **hull** of a boat or tank is the main body of it. ◆ **-hulled** *...a steel-hulled narrowboat.* **2** If you **hull** strawberries, you remove the central core and the leaves at the top. *Wash and hull the strawberries.* ◆◆◇◇◇ N-COUNT COMB / V n

hul·la·ba·loo /ˌhʌləbəˈluː/. A **hullabaloo** is a lot of noise or fuss made by people who are angry or excited about something. *I was scared by the hullabaloo over my arrival.* N-SING INFORMAL

hul·lo /hʌˈləʊ/. See **hello**.

hum /hʌm/ **hums, humming, hummed. 1** If something **hums**, it makes a low continuous noise. *The birds sang, the bees hummed.* ► Also a noun. *...the hum of traffic.* **2** When you **hum** a tune, you sing it with your lips closed. *He hummed to himself as he opened the trunk.* ◆ **hum·ming** *The guard stopped his humming and turned his head sharply.* **3** If you say that a place **hums**, you mean that it is full of activity. *On Saturday morning, the town hums with activity and life.* **4** See also **ho hum**. ● **hum and haw**: see **haw**. ◆◆◇◇◇ VERB / N-SING / VERB: V n / V / N-UNCOUNT / VERB: V / V with n

hu·man /ˈhjuːmən/ **humans. 1** Human means relating to or concerning people. *...the human body. ...human history.* **2** You can refer to people as **humans**, especially when you are comparing them with animals or machines. *Its rate of growth was fast - much more like that of an ape than that of a human.* **3** If you call feelings, errors, or people **human**, you mean that they are, or have, weaknesses which are typical of people rather than machines. *...an ever growing risk of human error.* ◆◆◆◆◆ ADJ: ADJ n / N-COUNT / ADJ-GRADED

human 'being, human beings. A **human being** is a man, woman, or child. ◆◆◇◇◇ N-COUNT

hu·mane /hjuːˈmeɪn/. **1 Humane** people act in a kind, sympathetic, and compassionate way towards other people and animals, and try to do them as little harm as possible. *Amnesty calls on all parties to abide by international law on the humane treatment of prisoners.* ◆ **hu·mane·ly** *Our horse had to be humanely destroyed after breaking his right foreleg.* **2** A **humane** activity is one that is thought to have a civilizing and improving effect on people. *...the humane values of socialism.* ◆◇◇◇◇ ADJ-GRADED / ADV-GRADED / ADJ

hu·man·ise /ˈhjuːmənaɪz/. See **humanize**.

hu·man·ism /ˈhjuːmənɪzəm/. **Humanism** is the belief that people can achieve happiness and fulfilment without the need for religion. ◆ **hu·man·ist**, **humanists** *He is a practical humanist, who believes in the dignity of mankind.* ◆◇◇◇◇ N-UNCOUNT / N-COUNT

hu·man·ist·ic /ˌhjuːməˈnɪstɪk/. A **humanistic** idea, condition, or practice relates to humanism. *Reli-* ADJ

gious values can often differ greatly from humanistic morals.

hu·mani·tar·ian /hjuː,mænɪˈteəriən/ **humanitarians.** If a person or society has **humanitarian** ideas or attitudes, or behaves in a **humanitarian** way, they try to avoid making people suffer or they help people who are suffering. *Air bombardment raised criticism on the humanitarian grounds that innocent civilians might suffer. ...humanitarian aid.* ► A **humanitarian** is someone who is humanitarian.

hu·mani·tari·an·ism /hjuː,mænɪˈteəriənɪzəm/. **Humanitarianism** is the concern that humanitarians have for the welfare of the human race.

hu·man·ity /hjuːˈmænɪti/ **humanities.** 1 All the people in the world can be referred to as **humanity**. *...a young lawyer full of illusions and love of humanity.* 2 A person's **humanity** is their state of being a human being, rather than an animal or an object. *He was under discussion and it made him feel deprived of his humanity.* 3 **Humanity** is the quality of being kind, thoughtful, and sympathetic towards others. *Her speech showed great maturity and humanity.* 4 The **humanities** are the subjects such as history, philosophy, and literature which are concerned with human ideas and behaviour.

hu·man·ize /ˈhjuːmənaɪz/ **humanizes, humanizing, humanized;** also spelled **humanise** in British English. If you **humanize** a situation or condition, you improve it by changing it in a way which makes it more suitable and pleasant for people. *Their main aim is to humanise East German education.*

human·kind /ˈhjuːmənkaɪnd/. **Humankind** is the same as **mankind**.

hu·man·ly /ˈhjuːmənli/. 1 **Humanly** means relating to human beings. *A mother is not allowed to be humanly flawed; she has to be perfect.* 2 If something is **humanly possible**, it is possible for people to do it. *They had done everything humanly possible for their son.*

,human 'nature. **Human nature** is the natural qualities and ways of behaving that most people have. *It seems to be human nature to worry.*

,human 'race. All the people in the world can be referred to as **the human race.**

,human re'sources. The department of **human resources** is the department within a company that is responsible for dealing with recruiting, training, and staff welfare.

,human 'rights. **Human rights** are basic rights which many societies believe that all people should have, such as freedom of speech.

hum·ble /ˈhʌmbəl/ **humbler, humblest; humbles, humbling, humbled.** 1 A **humble** person is not proud and does not believe that they are better than other people. *He gave a great performance, but he was very humble. ...a humble apology.* ♦ **humbly** *'I'm a lucky man, undeservedly lucky,' he said humbly.* 2 People with low social status are sometimes described as **humble**. *Spyros Latsis started his career as a humble fisherman in the Aegean.* 3 A **humble** place or thing is ordinary and not special in any way. *Varndell made his own reflector for these shots from a strip of humble kitchen foil.* 4 People use the word **humble** in a phrase such as **in my humble opinion** as a polite way of emphasizing what they think, even though they do not feel humble about it. *It is, in my humble opinion, perhaps the best steak restaurant in Great Britain.* ♦ **humbly** *So may I humbly suggest we all do something next time.* 5 If you **eat humble pie**, you speak or behave in a way which tells people that you admit you were wrong about something. 6 If you **humble** someone who is more important or powerful than you, you defeat them easily and humiliate them by doing so. *Honda won fame in the 1980s as the little car company that humbled the industry giants.* 7 If something or someone **humbles** you, they make you realize that you are not as important, capable, or valuable as you thought you were. *I am sure millions of viewers were humbled by this story.* ♦ **humbled** *I came away very humbled.*

♦ **hum·bling** *Giving up an addiction is a humbling experience.*

hum·bug /ˈhʌmbʌg/ **humbugs.** 1 If you describe someone's language or behaviour as **humbug**, you mean that it is dishonest and intended to deceive people. *There was all the usual humbug and obligatory compliments from ministers.* 2 You can also refer to a person as a **humbug** when you think they are being dishonest or insincere. 3 A **humbug** is a hard, striped sweet that tastes of peppermint.

hum·ding·er /,hʌmˈdɪŋə/ **humdingers.** If you describe someone or something as a **humdinger**, you mean that they are marvellous, impressive, or especially enjoyable. *It should be a humdinger of a match.*

hum·drum /ˈhʌmdrʌm/. If you describe someone or something as **humdrum**, you mean that they are ordinary, dull, or boring. *...her lawyer husband, trapped in a humdrum but well-paid job.*

hu·mid /ˈhjuːmɪd/. You use **humid** to describe an atmosphere or climate that is very damp, and usually very hot. *Visitors can expect hot and humid conditions.*

hu·mid·ity /hjuːˈmɪdɪti/. 1 You say there is **humidity** when the air feels very heavy and damp. *The heat and humidity were insufferable.* 2 **Humidity** is the amount of water in the air. *The humidity is relatively low.*

hu·mili·ate /hjuːˈmɪlieɪt/ **humiliates, humiliating, humiliated.** To **humiliate** someone means to say or do something which makes them feel ashamed or stupid. *She had been beaten and humiliated by her husband.* ♦ **hu·mili·at·ed** *I have never felt so humiliated in my life.* ♦ **hu·mili·at·ing** *The Conservatives have suffered a humiliating defeat.*

hu·milia·tion /hjuː,mɪliˈeɪʃən/ **humiliations.** 1 **Humiliation** is the embarrassment and shame you feel when someone makes you appear stupid, or when you make a mistake in public. *She faced the humiliation of discussing her husband's affair.* 2 A **humiliation** is an occasion or a situation in which you feel embarrassed and humiliated. *The result is a humiliation for the prime minister.*

hu·mil·ity /hjuːˈmɪlɪti/. Someone who has **humility** is not proud and does not believe they are better than other people. *For a long time he still thought like a millionaire but he has humility now.*

humming·bird /ˈhʌmɪŋbɜːd/ **hummingbirds.** A **hummingbird** is a small brightly coloured bird that is found in America. Its wings often make a humming sound as they vibrate.

hum·mock /ˈhʌmək/ **hummocks.** A **hummock** is a mound of earth, like a very small hill.

hum·mus /ˈhʌməs/. See **houmous**.

hu·mor /ˈhjuːmə/. See **humour**.

hu·mor·ist /ˈhjuːmərɪst/ **humorists.** A **humorist** is a writer who specializes in writing amusing things. *...a political humorist.*

hu·mor·ous /ˈhjuːmərəs/. If someone or something is **humorous**, they are amusing, especially in a clever or witty way. *He was quite humorous, and I liked that about him. ...a humorous magazine.* ♦ **hu·mor·ous·ly** *He looked at me humorously as he wrestled with the door.*

hu·mour /ˈhjuːmə/ **humours, humouring, humoured;** spelled **humor** in American English. 1 You can refer to the amusing things that people say as their **humour**. *Her humour and determination were a source of inspiration to others.* ● See also **sense of humour.** 2 **Humour** is a quality in something that makes you laugh, for example in a situation, in someone's words or actions, or in a book or film. *She felt sorry for the man but couldn't ignore the humour of the situation.* 3 If you are in a good **humour**, you feel cheerful and happy, and are pleasant to people. If you are in a bad **humour**, you feel bad-tempered and unhappy, and are unpleasant to people. *Christina was still not clear why he had been in such ill humour.* 4 If you do some-

thing with good **humour**, you do it cheerfully and pleasantly. *Hugo bore his illness with great courage and good humour.*   adj N

5 If you **humour** someone who is behaving strangely, you try to please them or pretend to agree with them, so that they will not become upset. *She disliked Dido but was prepared to tolerate her for a weekend in order to humour her husband.*   VERB / V n

hu·mour·less /ˈhjuːmələs/; spelled **humorless** in American English. If you accuse someone of being **humourless**, you mean that they are very serious about everything and do not find things amusing. *He was a straight-faced, humourless character.*   ADJ-GRADED / PRAGMATICS

hump /hʌmp/ **humps, humping, humped. 1** A **hump** is a small hill or raised area. *The path goes over a large hump.* **2** A camel's **hump** is the large lump on its back. **3** A **hump** is a large lump on a person's back, usually caused by illness or old age.   N-COUNT

4 If you **hump** something heavy, you carry it from one place to another with great difficulty. *Charlie humped his rucksack up the stairs to his flat.*   VERB / V n prep/adv / INFORMAL, BRITISH

hump·back /ˈhʌmpbæk/ **humpbacks.** A **humpback** or a **humpback whale** is a large whale with a hump-shaped back and long flippers.   N-COUNT

hu·mun·gous /hjuːˈmʌŋgəs/; also spelled **humungus.** If you describe something or someone as **humungous**, you are emphasizing that they are very large or important. *...a choppy guitar riff coming from humungous speakers.*   ADJ / PRAGMATICS

hu·mus /ˈhuːməs/. **Humus** is the part of soil which consists of plant and animal remains that have begun to decompose.   N-UNCOUNT

hunch /hʌntʃ/ **hunches, hunching, hunched. 1** If you have a **hunch** about something, you are sure that it is correct or true, even though you do not have any proof. *Then Mr. Kamenar, acting on a hunch, ran a computer check at the Federal Election Commission.* **2** If you **hunch** your shoulders or **hunch** forward, you raise your shoulders, put your head down, and lean forwards, often because you are cold, ill, or unhappy. *He got out his map of Yorkshire and hunched over it to read the small print.*   N-COUNT / INFORMAL / VERB: V n / V adv/prep

♦ **hunched** /hʌntʃt/. *He got a stiff neck and a sore back from sitting hunched up for so long.*   ADJ

hunch·back /ˈhʌntʃbæk/ **hunchbacks.** A **hunchback** is an offensive word for a person who has a large lump on their back because their spine is deformed.   N-COUNT / RUDE

hun·dred /ˈhʌndrəd/ **hundreds.** The plural form is **hundred** after a number, or after a word or expression referring to a number, such as 'several' or 'a few'. **1** A **hundred** or one **hundred** is the number 100. See Appendix headed **Numbers**. **2** If you refer to **hundreds of** things or people, you are emphasizing that there are very many of them. *Hundreds of tree species face extinction.* ▶ Also a pronoun. *Hundreds have been killed in the fighting and thousands made homeless.* **3** You can use **a hundred per cent** or **one hundred per cent** to emphasize that you agree completely with something or that it is completely right or wrong. *Are you a hundred per cent sure it's your neighbour?*   NUMBER / QUANT / PRAGMATICS / PRON / PHRASE / PRAGMATICS / INFORMAL

hun·dredth /ˈhʌndrədθ/ **hundredths. 1** The **hundredth** item in a series is the one that you count as number one hundred. See Appendix headed **Numbers**. *...the hundredth anniversary of his birth.* **2** A **hundredth** of something is one of a hundred equal parts of it. See Appendix headed **Numbers**.   ORDINAL / FRACTION

hundred·weight /ˈhʌndrədweɪt/ **hundredweights.** When it has a number in front of it, the plural form is **hundredweight**. A **hundredweight** is a unit of weight that is equal to 112 pounds in Britain and to 100 pounds in the United States. *...a hundredweight of coal.*   N-COUNT

hung /hʌŋ/. **1 Hung** is the past tense and past participle of most of the senses of **hang**. **2** A **hung** parliament, council, or jury consists of different groups of people who have different opinions, but none forms a majority, and so often no clear decisions can be made.   ADJ

hun·ger /ˈhʌŋgə/ **hungers, hungering, hungered. 1 Hunger** is the feeling of weakness or discomfort that you get when you need something to eat. *Seized by morning hunger pangs, Robert made a beeline for the chocolate vending machine.* **2 Hunger** is a severe lack of food which causes suffering or death. *Three hundred people in this town are dying of hunger every day.* **3** If you say that someone **hungers** for something or **hungers** after it, you are emphasizing that they want it very much. *But Jules was not eager for classroom learning, he hungered for adventure.* ▶ Also a noun. *Geffen has a hunger for success that seems bottomless.*   N-UNCOUNT / N-UNCOUNT / VERB / PRAGMATICS / V for/aftern / Also V to-inf / FORMAL / N-SING

'hunger strike, hunger strikes. If someone goes on **hunger strike** or goes on a **hunger strike**, they refuse to eat as a way of protesting about something.   N-VAR

hung·over /ˌhʌŋˈəʊvə/; also spelled **hung-over.** Someone who is **hungover** is unwell because they drank too much alcohol on the previous day.   ADJ-GRADED

hun·gry /ˈhʌŋgri/ **hungrier, hungriest. 1** When you are **hungry**, you want some food because you have not eaten for some time and have an uncomfortable or painful feeling in your stomach. *She is reduced to stealing to feed her hungry family.* ♦ **hun·gri·ly** /ˈhʌŋgrɪli/ *James ate hungrily.* **2** If people go **hungry**, they suffer from hunger, either for a long period because they are poor or for a short period because they miss a meal. *Leonidas' family had been poor, he went hungry for years.* **3** If you say that someone is **hungry** for something, you are emphasizing that they want it very much. *Susan was certainly hungry for a life different from the one she had made for herself.* ▶ Also a combining form. *...power-hungry politicians.* ♦ **hungrily** *He looked at her hungrily. What eyes! What skin!*   ADJ-GRADED / ADV-GRADED / PHRASE / ADJ-GRADED / LITERARY / COMB / ADJ-GRADED: / ADV with v

hung 'up. If you say that someone is **hung up** about a particular person or thing, you are criticizing them for thinking or worrying too much about that person or thing. *It was a time when people weren't as hung up about health.*   ADJ-GRADED: / v-link ADJ / PRAGMATICS / INFORMAL

hunk /hʌŋk/ **hunks. 1** A **hunk** of something is a large piece of it. *The lamb was tender and the hunk of bread was fresh.* **2** If you refer to a man as a **hunk**, you mean that he is big, strong, and sexually attractive.   N-COUNT / N-COUNT / INFORMAL

hunk·er /ˈhʌŋkə/ **hunkers, hunkering, hunkered.**

hunker down. 1 If you **hunker down**, you bend your knees so that you are in a squatting position. *Betty hunkered down on the floor... He ended up hunkering down beside her.* **2** If you say that someone **hunkers down**, you mean that they are trying to avoid doing things that will make them noticed. *Their strategy for the moment is to hunker down and let the furor die.*   PHRASAL VB / V P on n / V P besiden / AMERICAN / V P / AMERICAN

hunt /hʌnt/ **hunts, hunting, hunted. 1** If you **hunt** for something or someone, you try to find them by searching carefully or thoroughly. *Some new arrivals lose hope even before they start hunting for a job.* ▶ Also a noun. *The couple had helped in the hunt for the toddlers.* **2** If you **hunt** a criminal or an enemy, you search for them in order to catch or harm them. *Detectives have been hunting him for seven months.* ▶ Also a noun. *Despite a nationwide hunt for the kidnap gang, not a trace of them was found.* **3** When people or animals **hunt**, they chase and kill wild animals for food or as a sport. *He got up at four and set out on foot to hunt black grouse.* ▶ Also a noun. *He set off for a nineteen-day moose hunt in Nova Scotia.* **4** In Britain, when people **hunt**, they chase a fox on horseback and try to kill it as a sport. *Dogs called hounds are used to find the fox. She liked to hunt as often as she could.* ▶ Also a noun. *The hunt was held on land owned by the Duke of Marlborough.* **5** In Britain, a **hunt** is a group of people who meet regularly to hunt foxes. **6** See also **hunting, witch-hunt.**   VERB / V for n / Also V / N-COUNT / VERB / V n / Also V for n / N-COUNT / VERB: V / V n / N-COUNT / VERB / Also V n / N-COUNT / N-COUNT

hunt down. If you **hunt down** a criminal or an en-   PHRASAL VB

emy, you find them after searching for them. *It took her four months to hunt him down.* `V P noun / V n P`

hunt out. If you **hunt out** something that is hidden or difficult to find, you search for it and eventually find it. *American consumers are accustomed to hunting out bargains and buying on price.* `PHRASAL VB / V P noun / Also V n P`

hunt·er /'hʌntə/ **hunters. 1** A **hunter** is a person who hunts wild animals for food or as a sport. *...a deer hunter.* **2** People who are searching for things of a particular kind are often referred to as **hunters.** *...job-hunters.* ● See also **bargain hunter, headhunt. 3** A **hunter** is a type of fast strong horse that is used in Britain by people who hunt foxes. `◆◆◆◇◇ / N-COUNT / N-COUNT: n N / N-COUNT`

ˌhunter-ˈgatherer, hunter-gatherers. Hunter-gatherers were people who lived by hunting and gathering food rather than by farming. There are still groups of hunter-gatherers in some parts of the world today. *The Basarwa are descendants of the last of the hunter-gatherers of Southern Africa.* `N-COUNT`

hunt·ing /'hʌntɪŋ/. **1 Hunting** is the chasing and killing of wild animals by people or other animals, for food or as a sport. *...a hunting accident.* **2 Hunting** is the activity of searching for a particular thing. *Job hunting should be approached as a job in itself.* ▸ Also a combining form. *Lee has divided his time between flat-hunting and travelling.* `◆◆◇◇◇ / N-UNCOUNT / N-UNCOUNT: n N / COMB`

ˈhunting ground, hunting grounds. 1 If you say that a place is a good **hunting ground** for something, you mean that people who have a particular interest are likely to find something that they want there. *Other people's weddings are the perfect hunting ground for ideas.* **2** A **hunting ground** is an area where people or animals chase and kill wild animals for food or as a sport. `N-COUNT / N-COUNT`

ˌhunt saboˈteur, hunt saboteurs. A **hunt saboteur** is someone who tries to stop blood sports such as fox hunting by distracting the hounds or covering the scent of the fox for example. `N-COUNT`

hunts·man /'hʌntsmən/ **huntsmen.** A **huntsman** is a person who hunts wild animals, especially one who hunts foxes on horseback using dogs. `◆◇◇◇◇ / N-COUNT`

hur·dle /'hɜːdəl/ **hurdles, hurdling, hurdled. 1** A **hurdle** is a problem or difficulty that you must overcome in order to achieve something. *The first hurdle for many women returning to work is finding nursery places.* **2 Hurdles** is a race in which people run and jump over a number of hurdles. You can use **hurdles** to refer to one or more races. *Davis won the 400m. hurdles in a new Olympic time of 49.3 sec.* **3** If you **hurdle,** you jump over something while you are running. *He crossed the lawn and hurdled the short fence.* **4** If you say that someone or something has fallen **at the first hurdle,** you mean they have failed at the first difficulty that had to be overcome in order to be successful. `◆◆◇◇◇ / N-COUNT / N-COLL-COUNT / VERB: V V n / PHRASE`

hur·dler /'hɜːdlə/ **hurdlers.** A **hurdler** is an athlete whose special event is the hurdles. `◆◇◇◇◇ / N-COUNT`

hurl /hɜːl/ **hurls, hurling, hurled. 1** If you **hurl** something, you throw it violently and with a lot of force. *Groups of angry youths hurled stones at police... Simon caught the grenade and hurled it back.* **2** If you **hurl** abuse or insults, you shout insults at someone aggressively. *...being locked in the back of a cab while the driver hurled abuse at you.* `◆◆◇◇◇ / VERB: V n / V n prep / V n with adv / VERB: V n / V n at n`

hurly-burly /'hɜːli ˈbɜːli/. If you talk about the **hurly-burly** of a situation, you are emphasizing how noisy or busy it is. *No one expects him to get involved in the hurly-burly of campaigning.* `N-SING / PRAGMATICS`

hur·ray /hʊ'reɪ/. See **hooray.**

hur·ri·cane /'hʌrɪkən, AM 'hɜːrɪkeɪn/ **hurricanes.** A **hurricane** is an extremely violent wind or storm. `◆◆◇◇◇ / N-COUNT`

hur·ried /'hʌrɪd, AM 'hɜːr-/. **1** A **hurried** action is done quickly. *There had been a hurried overnight re-drafting of the text.* ♦ **hur·ried·ly** *She blushed and hurriedly left the room.* **2** Someone who is **hurried** does things more quickly than they should because they do not have much time to do them. *Parisians on the street often looked worried, hurried and unfriendly.* `ADJ-GRADED / ADV-GRADED / ADJ-GRADED`

hur·ry /'hʌri, AM 'hɜːri/ **hurries, hurrying, hurried. 1** If you **hurry** somewhere, you go there as quickly as you can. *Bob hurried to join him, and they rode home together.* **2** If you **hurry** to do something, you start doing it as soon as you can, or try to do it quickly. *Mrs Hardie hurried to make up for her tactlessness by asking her guest about his holiday.* **3** To **hurry** something means the same as to **hurry up** something. **4** If you **hurry** someone to a place or into a situation, you try to make them go to that place or get into that situation quickly. *I don't want to hurry you.* **5** If you are in a **hurry** to do something, you need or want to do it quickly. If you do something in a **hurry,** you do it quickly or suddenly. **6** If you say to someone **'There's no hurry'** or **'I'm in no hurry'** you are telling them that there is no need for them to do something immediately. **7** If you are **in no hurry** to do something, you are very unwilling to do it. *I love it at St Mirren so I'm in no hurry to go anywhere.* `◆◆◇◇◇ / VERB / VERB / VERB: V to-inf / Also V / VERB: V n / VERB: V n prep/adv V n / N-SING / PHRASE PRAGMATICS / PHRASE PRAGMATICS`

hurry up. If you tell someone to **hurry up,** you are telling them do something more quickly than they were doing. *Hurry up with that coffee, will you.* `PHRASAL VB / V P / V P with n`

hurry up or **hurry along.** If you **hurry** something **up** or **hurry** it **along,** you make it happen faster or sooner than it would otherwise have done. *Some folks might hurry up the process, but Uncle Jack left his whiskey for an additional eight years.* `PHRASAL VB / V n P / V P noun`

hurt /hɜːt/ **hurts, hurting, hurt. 1** If you **hurt** yourself, you feel pain because you have injured yourself. *He fell and hurt his back on a construction job.* **2** If you **hurt** someone, you cause them to feel pain. *I didn't mean to hurt her... Ouch. That hurt.* **3** If a part of your body **hurts,** you feel pain there. *His collar bone only hurt when he lifted his arm.* **4** If you are **hurt,** you have been injured. *His comrades asked him if he was hurt.* **5** If someone **hurts** you, they upset you by saying or doing something rude or inconsiderate. *He is afraid of hurting Bessy's feelings.* **6** If you are **hurt,** you are emotionally upset because of something that someone has said or done. *He gave me a slightly hurt look.* ♦ **hurt·ful** /'hɜːtful/. If you say that someone's comments or actions are **hurtful,** you mean that they make you feel hurt. **7** If you say that you **are hurting,** you mean that you are experiencing emotional pain. **8** A feeling of **hurt** is a feeling that you have when you think that you have been treated badly or judged unfairly. *...feelings of hurt and anger.* **9** You can say that something **hurts** someone or something when it has a bad effect on them or prevents them from succeeding. *They may fear hurting their husbands' careers.* **10** If you say something such as **'It won't hurt** to do something' or **'It never hurts** to do something', you are recommending something which you think is worth doing or is helpful or useful. *It never hurts to ask.* `◆◆◆◇ / VERB: V pron-refl / V n / VERB V n / V / VERB V / ADJ-GRADED / VERB V n / ADJ-GRADED / ADJ-GRADED / VB: only cont / N-VAR / VERB V n / PHRASE PRAGMATICS INFORMAL`

hurt·le /'hɜːtəl/ **hurtles, hurtling, hurtled.** If you **hurtle** somewhere, you move there very quickly, often in a rough or violent way. *A pretty young girl came hurtling down the stairs.* `◆◇◇◇◇ / VERB V prep`

hus·band /'hʌzbənd/ **husbands, husbanding, husbanded. 1** A woman's **husband** is the man she is married to. **2** If you **husband** something valuable, you use it carefully and do not waste it. *Husbanding precious resources was part of rural life.* `◆◆◆◆ / N-COUNT / VERB V n / LITERARY`

hus·band·ry /'hʌzbəndri/. **Husbandry** is farming, especially when it is done carefully and well. `N-UNCOUNT`

hush /hʌʃ/ **hushes, hushing, hushed. 1** You say **'Hush!'** to someone when you are asking or telling them to be quiet. *Hush, my love, it's all right.* **2** If you **hush** someone or they **hush,** they stop speaking or making a noise. *She tried to hush her noisy father.* **3** You say there is a **hush** in a place when everything is quiet and peaceful, or suddenly becomes quiet. *A hush fell over the crowd.* `◆◇◇◇◇ / CONVENTION PRAGMATICS / V-ERG / Also V / N-SING: also no det`

hush up. 1 If someone **hushes** something **up,** they prevent other people from knowing about it. *The Ministry desperately tried to hush up the whole affair.* **2** If people in authority **hush** someone **up,** they try to `PHRASAL VB / V n P / V P noun / V n P`

stop that person revealing information which they want to keep secret.

hushed /hʌʃt/. **1** A **hushed** place is peaceful and much quieter and calmer than usual. ...*a hushed and dignified atmosphere.* **2** A **hushed** voice or **hushed** conversation is very quiet. ◆◇◇◇◇ ADJ-GRADED ADJ-GRADED

hush-'hush. Something that is **hush-hush** is secret and not to be discussed with other people. ADJ-GRADED INFORMAL

'hush money. If a person is paid **hush money,** someone gives them money so that they do not reveal information that they have which could be damaging or embarrassing. N-UNCOUNT INFORMAL

husk /hʌsk/ **husks.** A **husk** is the outer covering of a grain or a seed. N-COUNT

husky /'hʌski/ **huskies. 1** A **husky** voice is rough or hoarse, often in an attractive way. **2** If you describe a man as **husky,** you think that he is tall, strong, and attractive. ◆◇◇◇◇ ADJ-GRADED ADJ-GRADED INFORMAL

3 A **husky** is a strong furry dog, which is used to pull sledges across snow. N-COUNT

hus·sy /'hʌsi, AM 'hʌzi/ **hussies.** If someone refers to a girl or woman as a **hussy,** they are criticizing her for behaving in a shocking, immoral, or immodest way. N-COUNT PRAGMATICS DATED

hus·tings /'hʌstɪŋz/. The political campaigns and speeches before an election are sometimes referred to as the **hustings.** N-PLURAL BRITISH

hus·tle /'hʌsəl/ **hustles, hustling, hustled. 1** If you **hustle** someone, you try to hurry them into doing something, for example by pulling or pushing them along. *The guards hustled Harry out of the car.* **2** If you **hustle,** you go somewhere or do something hurriedly. *He brought straight up the aircraft steps.* **3** If someone **hustles,** they try to earn money or gain an advantage from a situation, often by using dishonest or illegal means. *I hustled some tickets from a magazine and off we went.* ◆ **hus·tler** /'hʌslə/ **hustlers** ...*an insurance hustler.* ◆◇◇◇◇ VERB V n prep/adv VERB: V V prep VERB: V V n from n N-COUNT

4 Hustle is busy noisy activity. ...*the hustle and bustle of London.* N-UNCOUNT

hus·tler /'hʌslə/ **hustlers.** A **hustler** is a male prostitute. ● See also **hustle.** N-COUNT

hut /hʌt/ **huts.** A **hut** is a small simple building, often made of wood, mud, or grass. ◆◆◇◇◇ N-COUNT

hutch /hʌtʃ/ **hutches.** A **hutch** is a cage, often made of wood, that rabbits or other small pet animals are kept in. N-COUNT

hya·cinth /'haɪəsɪnθ/ **hyacinths.** A **hyacinth** is a plant with a lot of small sweet-smelling flowers that grows from a bulb. N-COUNT

hy·brid /'haɪbrɪd/ **hybrids. 1** A **hybrid** is an animal or plant that has been bred from two different species of animal or plant. **2** You can use **hybrid** to refer to anything that is a mixture of other things. ...*a hybrid of solid and liquid fuel.* ◆◆◇◇◇ N-COUNT TECHNICAL N-COUNT

hy·brid·ize /'haɪbrɪdaɪz/ **hybridizes, hybridizing, hybridized;** also spelled **hybridise** in British English. If one species of plant or animal **hybridizes** with another, the species reproduce together to make a hybrid. *All sorts of colours will result as these flowers hybridise freely... Hybridising the two species will reduce the red to orange.* V-RECIP-ERG: V with n pl-n V pl-n Also V n with n

hy·drant /'haɪdrənt/ **hydrants.** See **fire hydrant.**

hy·drate /'haɪdreɪt/ **hydrates, hydrating, hydrated. 1** A **hydrate** is a chemical compound that contains water. ...*aluminium hydrate.* **2** If a substance **hydrates** your skin, it makes it softer and moister, and prevents it from drying out. N-VAR VERB: V n

hy·drau·lic /haɪ'drɒlɪk, AM -'drɔːl-/. Something that is **hydraulic** involves or is operated by a fluid that is under pressure, such as water or oil. *The boat has no fewer than five hydraulic pumps.* ◆ **hy·drau·li·cal·ly** ...*hydraulically operated pistons for raising and lowering the blade.* ◆◇◇◇◇ ADJ: ADJ n ADV: ADV with v

hy·drau·lics /haɪ'drɒlɪks, AM -'drɔːl-/. **Hydraulics** is the study and use of systems that work using hydraulic pressure. N-UNCOUNT

hydro·car·bon /ˌhaɪdrəʊ'kɑːbən/ **hydrocarbons.** A **hydrocarbon** is a chemical compound that is a mixture of hydrogen and carbon. ◆◇◇◇◇ N-COUNT

hydro·chlo·ric acid /ˌhaɪdrəklɒrɪk 'æsɪd/. **Hydrochloric acid** is a colourless strong acid containing hydrogen and chlorine. N-UNCOUNT

hydro-electricity /ˌhaɪdrəʊ ɪlek'trɪsɪti/. **Hydro-electricity** is electricity made from the energy of running water. ◆ **hydro-electric** /ˌhaɪdrəʊɪ'lektrɪk/ ...*a hydro-electric power station.* N-UNCOUNT ADJ: ADJ n

hydro·foil /'haɪdrəfɔɪl/ **hydrofoils.** A **hydrofoil** is a boat which can travel above the surface of the water on a pair of wing-like fins. You can also to refer to the fins themselves as **hydrofoils.** N-COUNT

hydro·gen /'haɪdrədʒən/. **Hydrogen** is a colourless gas that is the lightest and commonest element in the universe. ◆◆◇◇◇ N-UNCOUNT

'hydrogen bomb, hydrogen bombs. A **hydrogen bomb** is a nuclear bomb in which energy is released from hydrogen atoms. N-COUNT

hydrogen per'oxide. **Hydrogen peroxide** is a chemical that is often used as a bleach for hair and as an antiseptic. N-UNCOUNT

hydro·thera·py /ˌhaɪdrəʊ'θerəpi/. **Hydrotherapy** is a method of treating injuries and diseases by making patients swim or do exercises in water. N-UNCOUNT

hy·ena /haɪ'iːnə/ **hyenas.** A **hyena** is a wild animal that makes a sound which is similar to a human laugh. N-COUNT

hy·giene /'haɪdʒiːn/. **Hygiene** is the practice of keeping yourself and your surroundings clean, especially in order to prevent the spread of diseases. ◆◇◇◇◇ N-UNCOUNT

hy·gien·ic /haɪ'dʒiːnɪk, AM ˌhaɪ'dʒienɪk/. Something that is **hygienic** is clean and unlikely to cause illness. ...*it was a kitchen that was easy to keep clean and hygienic.* ADJ-GRADED

hy·gien·ist /haɪ'dʒiːnɪst/ **hygienists.** A **hygienist** or a **dental hygienist** is a person who is trained to clean people's teeth and to give them advice on how to look after their teeth and gums. N-COUNT

hy·men /'haɪmen/ **hymens.** A **hymen** is a piece of skin that often covers part of a girl's or woman's vagina and breaks, usually when she has sex for the first time. N-COUNT

hymn /hɪm/ **hymns. 1** A **hymn** is a religious song that Christians sing in church. **2** If you describe a film, book, or speech as a **hymn to** something, you mean that it praises or celebrates that thing. ...*a hymn to freedom and rebellion.* ◆◇◇◇◇ N-COUNT N-COUNT: N to n

hype /haɪp/ **hypes, hyping, hyped. 1 Hype** is the intensive use of publicity and advertising in order to make people aware of something such as a product or a politician's ideas; used showing disapproval. *My products aren't based on advertising hype, they sell by word of mouth.* **2** To **hype** a product means to advertise it using intensive methods of publicity; used showing disapproval. ▶ **Hype up** means the same as **hype.** *The media seems obsessed with hyping up individuals or groups.* ◆◆◇◇◇ N-UNCOUNT PRAGMATICS VERB: V n PRAGMATICS PHRASAL VB Also V n P

hype up. To **hype** someone **up** means to deliberately make them very excited about something. *Everyone at school used to hype each other up about men all the time.* ● See also **hype** 2. ◆ **hyped up** *We were both so hyped up about buying the house!* PHRASAL VB V n P Also V P noun ADJ-GRADED

hyper /'haɪpə/. If someone is **hyper,** they are very excited and energetic. *I was incredibly hyper. I couldn't sleep.* ◆◇◇◇◇ ADJ-GRADED INFORMAL

hyper- /'haɪpə-/. **Hyper-** is used to form adjectives that describe someone as having a lot or too much of a particular quality. ...*one of those lean, hyper-fit people.* PREFIX

hyper·ac·tive /ˌhaɪpər'æktɪv/. A **hyperactive** person is unable to relax, and is always in a state of great agitation or activity. ◆ **hyper·ac·tiv·ity** /ˌhaɪpəræk'tɪvɪti/ ...*an extreme case of hyperactivity.* ◆◇◇◇◇ ADJ N-UNCOUNT

hyper·bo·le /haɪ'pɜːbəli/. **Hyperbole** is a style of speech and writing where people exaggerate what they are saying in order to make something sound more impressive than it really is. ...*the hyperbole that portrays him as one of the greatest visionaries in the world.* ◆ **hyper·bol·ic** /ˌhaɪpə'bɒlɪk/ ...*hyperbolic propaganda.* N-UNCOUNT FORMAL ADJ

hyper·in·fla·tion /ˌhaɪpərɪnˈfleɪʃən/; also **hyper in-** N-UNCOUNT
flation. Hyperinflation is very severe inflation.

hyper·mar·ket /ˈhaɪpəmɑːkɪt/ **hypermarkets.** A N-COUNT
hypermarket is a very large supermarket. BRITISH

hyper·sen·si·tive /ˌhaɪpəˈsensɪtɪv/. **1** If you say ADJ
that someone is **hypersensitive**, you mean that they
get annoyed or offended very easily. *Student teach-*
ers were hypersensitive to any criticism of their per-
formance. **2** Someone who is **hypersensitive** is ex- ADJ
tremely sensitive to certain drugs or chemicals. MEDICAL

hyper·ten·sion /ˌhaɪpəˈtenʃən/. **Hypertension** is a ◆◇◇◇◇
medical condition in which a person has very high N-UNCOUNT
blood pressure.

hyper·text /ˈhaɪpətekst/. In computing, **hypertext** N-UNCOUNT
is a way of structuring information in a database, so
that users can find particular information without
having to read from beginning or to end.

hyper·ven·ti·late /ˈhaɪpəventɪleɪt/ **hyperventi-** VERB: V
lates, hyperventilating, hyperventilated. If
someone **hyperventilates**, they begin to breathe
very fast in an uncontrollable way. ♦ **hyper·ven·ti-**
·la·tion /ˌhaɪpəˌventɪˈleɪʃən/ *Several notable re-* N-UNCOUNT
searchers are studying the effects of hyperventilation
and its relation to panic attacks.

hy·phen /ˈhaɪfən/ **hyphens.** A hyphen is the punc- N-COUNT
tuation sign (-) used to join words together to make
a compound. ♦ **hy·phen·at·ed** /ˈhaɪfəneɪtɪd/. A ADJ
word that is **hyphenated** is written with a hyphen
between two or more of its parts.

hyp·no·sis /hɪpˈnəʊsɪs/. **1 Hypnosis** is a state of ◆◇◇◇◇
unconsciousness in which a person seems to be N-UNCOUNT
asleep but can still see, hear, or respond to things
said to them. **2 Hypnosis** is the art or practice of N-UNCOUNT
putting people into this state of unconsciousness.

hyp·no·thera·py /ˌhɪpnəʊˈθerəpi/. **Hypnotherapy** N-UNCOUNT
is the practice of hypnotizing people in order to
help them solve problems, for example to give up
smoking. ♦ **hyp·no·thera·pist** /ˌhɪpnəʊˈθerəpɪst/ N-COUNT
hypnotherapists. A **hypnotherapist** is a person
who treats people by using hypnotherapy.

hyp·not·ic /hɪpˈnɒtɪk/. **1** If someone is in a **hyp-** ◆◇◇◇◇
notic state, they have been hypnotized. **2** Some- ADJ
thing that is **hypnotic** makes you feel as if you have ADJ-GRADED
been hypnotized. *...the TV screen's hypnotic power.*

hyp·no·tize /ˈhɪpnətaɪz/ **hypnotizes, hypnotiz-**
ing, hypnotized; also spelled **hypnotise** in British
English. **1** If someone **hypnotizes** you, they put you VERB: V n
into a state of unconsciousness in which you seem
to be asleep but can see or hear certain things or respond to things said to you. ♦ **hyp·no·tism** N-UNCOUNT
/ˈhɪpnətɪzəm/ *...a psychiatrist who used hypnotism to*
help her deal with her fear. ♦ **hyp·no·tist, hypno-** N-COUNT
tists. A **hypnotist** is someone who hypnotizes people, especially as their job. **2** If you **are hypnotized** VB: usu
by someone or something, you are so fascinated by passive
them that you cannot think of anything else. *He's* be V-ed
hypnotized by that black hair and that white face.

hypo·chon·dria /ˌhaɪpəˈkɒndriə/. If someone suf- N-UNCOUNT
fers from **hypochondria**, they continually worry
about their health and imagine that they are ill, although there is really nothing wrong with them.
♦ **hypo·chon·dri·ac** /ˌhaɪpəˈkɒndriæk/ **hypo-** N-COUNT
chondriacs. A **hypochondriac** is someone who
suffers from hypochondria.

hy·poc·ri·sy /hɪˈpɒkrɪsi/ **hypocrisies.** If you ac- ◆◇◇◇◇
cuse someone of **hypocrisy**, you mean that they N-VAR
pretend to have qualities, beliefs, or feelings that PRAGMATICS
they do not really have; used showing disapproval.

hypo·crite /ˈhɪpəkrɪt/ **hypocrites.** If you accuse N-COUNT
someone of being a **hypocrite**, you mean that they PRAGMATICS
pretend to have qualities, beliefs, or feelings that

they do not really have; used showing disapproval.
♦ **hypo·criti·cal** /ˌhɪpəˈkrɪtɪkəl/ *If someone is being* ADJ-GRADED
hypocritical then it is fair to expose that.

hypo·der·mic /ˌhaɪpəˈdɜːmɪk/ **hypodermics.** A ADJ: ADJ n
hypodermic needle or syringe is a medical instrument which is used to give injections. ► Also a N-COUNT
noun. *He lifted the hypodermic, depressed the plung-*
er and inserted the needle in the vial.

hypotenuse /haɪˈpɒtənjuːz, AM -nuːs/ **hypot-** N-COUNT
enuses. The **hypotenuse** of a right-angled triangle
is the side opposite its right angle. *The square of the*
length of the hypotenuse is equal to the sum of the
squares of the lengths of the other two sides.

hypo·ther·mia /ˌhaɪpəʊˈθɜːmiə/. If someone has N-UNCOUNT
hypothermia, their body temperature has become MEDICAL
dangerously low as a result of being in severe cold
for a long time.

hy·poth·esis /haɪˈpɒθɪsɪs/ **hypotheses.** A hy- ◆◇◇◇◇
pothesis is an idea which is suggested as a possible N-VAR
explanation for a particular situation or condition, FORMAL
but which has not yet been proved to be correct.
Work will now begin to test the hypothesis.

hy·poth·esize /haɪˈpɒθɪsaɪz/ **hypothesizes, hy-** VERB:
pothesizing, hypothesized; also spelled **hy-** V that
pothesise in British English. If you **hypothesize** that V n
something will happen, you say that you think that Also V
thing will happen because of various facts you have FORMAL
considered. *I have long hypothesized a connection*
between these factors.

hypo·theti·cal /ˌhaɪpəˈθetɪkəl/. If something is ◆◇◇◇◇
hypothetical, it is based on possible ideas or situa- ADJ
tions rather than actual ones. *...a purely hypotheti-*
cal question. ♦ **hypo·theti·cal·ly** /ˌhaɪpəˈθetɪkli/ ADV
He was invariably willing to discuss the possibilities
hypothetically.

hys·ter·ec·to·my /ˌhɪstəˈrektəmi/ **hysterecto-** ◆◇◇◇◇
mies. A **hysterectomy** is a surgical operation to re- N-COUNT
move a woman's womb.

hys·te·ria /hɪˈstɪəriə, AM -ˈster-/. **1 Hysteria** ◆◇◇◇◇
among a group of people is a state of uncontrolled N-UNCOUNT
excitement, anger, or panic. *No one could help get-*
ting carried away by the hysteria. **2** A person who is N-UNCOUNT
suffering from **hysteria** is in a state of violent and MEDICAL
disturbed emotion as a result of shock. *She was*
screaming, completely overcome with hysteria.

hys·teri·cal /hɪˈsterɪkəl/. **1** Someone who is **hys-** ◆◇◇◇◇
terical is in a state of uncontrolled excitement, an- ADJ-GRADED
ger, or panic. *The almost hysterical crowds struggled*
to approach him. ♦ **hys·teri·cal·ly** /hɪˈsterɪkli/ *I* ADV-GRADED
don't think we can go round screaming hysterically.
♦ **hys·ter·ics** /hɪˈsterɪks/. If someone is in **hyster-** N-PLURAL
ics or is having **hysterics**, they are in a state of uncontrolled excitement, anger, or panic. **2** Someone ADJ-GRADED
who is **hysterical** is in a state of violent and disturbed emotion that is usually a result of shock. *I*
suffered bouts of really hysterical depression. ♦ **hys-**
·teri·cal·ly *I was curled up on the floor in a corner* ADV-GRADED
sobbing hysterically. ♦ **hys·ter·ics.** If someone is in N-PLURAL
hysterics or is having **hysterics**, they are in a state
of violent and disturbed emotion that is usually a
result of shock.
3 Hysterical laughter is loud and uncontrolled. *I had* ADJ
to rush to the loo to avoid an attack of hysterical gig- INFORMAL
gles. ♦ **hys·teri·cal·ly** *She says she hasn't laughed as* ADV
hysterically since she was 13. ♦ **hys·ter·ics.** You can N-PLURAL
say that someone is in **hysterics** or is having **hysterics**
when they are laughing loudly in an uncontrolled
way. **4** If you describe something or someone as **hys-** ADJ-GRADED
terical, you think that they are very funny and they INFORMAL
make you laugh a lot. ♦ **hys·teri·cal·ly** *It wasn't sup-* ADV-GRADED
posed to be a comedy but I found it hysterically funny.

I i

I, i /aɪ/ **I's, i's. I** is the ninth letter of the English N-VAR
alphabet.

I /aɪ/. A speaker or writer uses **I** to refer to himself ◆◆◆◆
or herself. **I** is a first person singular pronoun. **I** is PRON
used as the subject of a verb. *She liked me, I think...
Jim and I are getting married.*

-ian. See **-an.**

ibid /'ɪbɪd/. **Ibid** is used in books and journals to ◆◆◇◇◇
indicate that a quotation is taken from the same CONVENTION
source as the one previously mentioned.

-ibility, /-ɪ'bɪlɪti/ **-ibilities. -ibility** replaces '-ible' at SUFFIX
the end of adjectives to form nouns referring to the
state or quality described by the adjective. *...your
eligibility for State benefits. ...the possibilities that
emerged.*

ice /aɪs/ **ices, icing, iced. 1** Ice is frozen water, ◆◆◆◆
for example on the surface of a lake in cold weather, N-UNCOUNT
or in small pieces to put in drinks. *Glaciers are moving rivers of ice... Hans ground his skate blade
against the ice. ...a bitter lemon with ice. ...an old
refrigerator that couldn't make reliable ice cubes.*
2 An **ice** is a portion of ice cream. *...a quartet of* N-COUNT
Swiss who had just come in demanding ices. BRITISH
3 If you **break the ice** at a party or meeting, or in a new PHRASE
situation, you say or do something to make people
feel relaxed and comfortable. *I do want to get closer to
them. How can I break the ice?* **4** If you say that some- PHRASE
thing **cuts no ice** with you, you mean that you are not
impressed or influenced by it. *That sort of romantic
attitude cuts no ice with money-men.* **5** If someone PHRASE
puts a plan or project **on ice,** they delay doing it.
*Austria's bid to join the European Community has
been put on ice until 1991.* **6** If you say that someone is PHRASE
on thin ice, you mean that they are doing something
risky which may have serious or unpleasant consequences. *I had skated on thin ice on many assignments and somehow had, so far, got away with it.*
7 If you **ice** cakes or buns, you cover them with a layer VERB: V n
of icing. *We were all given little iced cakes.* **8** See also V-ed
iced, icing.

'Ice Age. The Ice Age was a period of time lasting ◆◇◇◇◇
many thousands of years, during which a lot of the N-PROPER:
earth's surface was covered with ice. theN

ice·berg /'aɪsbɜːg/ **icebergs.** An **iceberg** is a large ◆◇◇◇◇
tall mass of ice floating in the sea. ● **the tip of the** N-COUNT
iceberg: see **tip.**

ice·box /'aɪsbɒks/ **iceboxes.** An **icebox** is the N-COUNT
same as a **refrigerator.** *There's tuna fish in the ice-* AMERICAN,
box if you feel hungry. DATED

'ice bucket, ice buckets. An **ice bucket** is a con- N-COUNT
tainer that holds ice cubes or cold water and ice.
You can use it to provide ice cubes to put in drinks,
or to put bottles of wine in and keep the wine cool.

'ice cap, ice caps; also spelled **ice-cap.** An **ice-** N-COUNT
cap is a thick layer of ice and snow that permanently covers an area of land, especially the areas
around the North and South Poles.

'ice-cold. If you describe something as **ice-cold,** ADJ
you are emphasizing that it is very cold. *...delicious
ice-cold beer... The water was ice cold and my hands
were completely blue.*

ice 'cream, ice creams; also spelled **ice-cream.** ◆◆◇◇◇
1 Ice cream is a very cold, sweet-tasting food made N-VAR
from frozen milk, fats, and sugar. It can also contain
vanilla, chocolate, strawberry, or other flavourings.
...vanilla ice cream. **2** An **ice cream** is a portion of N-COUNT
ice cream. Ice-creams are sold in a container, or in
a cone made of thin biscuit. *They stuffed themselves
with ice creams, chocolate and lollies.*

iced /aɪst/. An **iced** drink has been made very cold, ◆◇◇◇◇
often by putting ice in it. *...iced tea.* ● See also **ice.** ADJ: ADJ n

'ice floe, ice floes. An **ice floe** is a large area of ice N-COUNT
floating in the sea.

'ice hockey; also spelled **ice-hockey.** Ice hockey ◆◇◇◇◇
is a game like hockey played on ice. N-UNCOUNT

ice 'lolly, ice lollies. An **ice lolly** is a piece of fla- N-COUNT
voured ice or ice cream on a stick. BRITISH

'ice pick, ice picks. An **ice pick** is a small pointed N-COUNT
tool that you use for breaking the ice that you put
into drinks.

'ice rink, ice rinks. An **ice rink** is an artificial sur- N-COUNT
face of ice, usually inside a building, made for peo-
ple to skate on.

'ice-skate, ice-skates; also spelled **ice skate.** N-COUNT
Ice-skates are boots with a thin metal bar underneath that people wear to move quickly on ice.

'ice-skating; also spelled **ice skating.** Ice-skating N-UNCOUNT
is a sport or leisure activity which involves people
moving about on ice wearing ice-skates. *...British
ice-skating champion Joanne Conway... They went
ice skating on Riley Pond.*

ici·cle /'aɪsɪkəl/ **icicles.** An **icicle** is a long pointed N-COUNT
piece of ice hanging down from a surface. It forms
when water drips slowly off the surface, freezing as
it falls.

ic·ing /'aɪsɪŋ/. **1** Icing is a sweet substance made ◆◇◇◇◇
from powdered sugar that is used to cover and N-UNCOUNT
decorate cakes. *...a birthday cake with yellow icing.*
2 If you describe something as **the icing on the** PHRASE
cake, you mean that it makes a good thing even
better. *Paul's two goals were the icing on the cake.*

'icing sugar. Icing sugar is a powdery white sug- ◆◇◇◇◇
ar which is used for making icing and sweets. The N-UNCOUNT
usual American term is **confectioners' sugar.** BRITISH

-icity /-'ɪsɪti/ **-icities. -icity** replaces '-ic' at the end SUFFIX
of adjectives to form nouns referring to the state,
quality, or behaviour described by the adjective.
*...the authenticity of the document... He soon exhib-
ited signs of eccentricity.*

icon /'aɪkɒn/ **icons. 1** If you describe something or ◆◇◇◇◇
someone as an **icon,** you mean that they are impor- N-COUNT
tant as a symbol of something. *...Britain's favourite
fashion icon, the Princess of Wales. ...Picasso and
the other icons of modernism.* **2** An **icon** is a picture N-COUNT
of Christ, the Virgin Mary, or a saint painted on a
wooden panel. Icons are regarded as holy by some
Christians. **3** An **icon** is a picture on a computer N-COUNT
screen representing a particular computer function.
If you want to use it, you move the cursor onto the
icon using a mouse.

icon·ic /aɪ'kɒnɪk/. An **iconic** image or thing is im- ADJ
portant or impressive because it seems to symbolize FORMAL
something. *The ads helped Nike to achieve iconic
status.*

icono·clast /aɪ'kɒnəklæst/ **iconoclasts.** If you re- N-COUNT
fer to someone as an **iconoclast,** you mean that FORMAL
they often criticize the ideas and customs that are
generally accepted by society. *Cage was an iconoclast. He refused to be bound by western musical
traditions.* ◆ **icono·clas·tic** /aɪ,kɒnə'klæstɪk/ ADJ-GRADED
*...Foucault's iconoclastic approach to the human
sciences.*

ico·no·gra·phy /aɪkə'nɒgrəfi/. The **iconography** of N-UNCOUNT
something consists of the symbols, pictures, and
objects which typically represent it. *The pictures of
the original moon landings are as much a part of the
iconography of the Sixties as Beatles album covers.
...religious iconography.*

icy /ˈaɪsi/ **icier, iciest. 1** If you describe something as **icy** or **icy cold**, you mean that it is extremely cold. ...*an icy wind... His shoes and clothing were wet through and icy cold.* **2** An **icy** road has ice on it. **3** If you describe a person or their behaviour as **icy**, you mean that they are angry or unfriendly, but showing this in a quiet, controlled way. *His response was icy.* ♦ **ic·ly** *'You have nothing to say in the matter,' he said icily... The prison official is icily polite.*

ID /ˌaɪ ˈdiː/ **IDs.** If you have **ID**, you are carrying a document such as an identity card or driving licence which proves that you are a particular person. *I had no ID on me so the police couldn't establish I was the owner of the car... Registrars checked the ID cards of prospective voters.*

I'd /aɪd/. **1 I'd** is the usual spoken form of 'I had', especially when 'had' is an auxiliary verb. *I'd seen her before.* **2 I'd** is the usual spoken form of 'I would'. *There are some questions I'd like to ask.*

idea /aɪˈdiːə/ **ideas. 1** An **idea** is a plan, suggestion, or possible course of action. *It's a good idea to keep a stock of slimmers' meals for when you're too busy or tired to cook... I really like the idea of helping people... She told me she'd had a brilliant idea.* **2** An **idea** is an opinion or belief about what something is like or should be like. *...his ideas about democracy... There may be some truth in the idea that reading too many books ruins your eyes... My idea of physical perfection is to be very slender.* **3** If you have an **idea** of something, or someone or something gives you an **idea** of it, you have some general understanding or knowledge of it, although you may not know many details about it. *This table will give you some idea of how levels of ability in a foreign language can be measured... Could you give us an idea of the range of complaints you've been receiving?... No one has any real idea how much the company will make next year... I had an idea that he joined the army later, after university, but I may be wrong.* **4** You can use **the idea** to introduce an aim, purpose, or intention. *The idea is to lend money to homeowners who are unable to move because their houses are worth less than their mortgages... He sent for a number of books he admired with the idea of re-reading them.* **5** You can use **idea** in expressions such as **I've no idea** or **I haven't the faintest idea** to emphasize that you don't know something. *We haven't the faintest idea where he is.* **6** If someone **gets the idea**, they understand how to do something or understand what you are telling them. *It isn't too difficult once you get the idea.* **7** You can say **you have no idea** to emphasize how good or bad something is. *You have no idea how depressed it made me.*

ideal /aɪˈdiːəl/ **ideals. 1** An **ideal** is a principle, idea, or standard that seems very good and worth trying to achieve. *...socialist ideals... I tried to live up to my ideal of myself... Throughout his career she remained his feminine ideal.* **2** The **ideal** person or thing for a particular task or purpose is the best possible person or thing for it. *She decided that I was the ideal person to take over the job... The conditions were ideal for racing.* ♦ **ide·al·ly** *The hotel is ideally situated for country walks... They were an extremely happy couple, ideally suited.* **3** An **ideal** society or world is the best possible one that you can imagine. *Their ideal society collapsed around them into the Terror... In an ideal world, there would be no such thing as rubbish.*

ideal·ise /aɪˈdiːəlaɪz/. See **idealize**.

ideal·ism /aɪˈdiːəlɪzəm/. **Idealism** is the beliefs and behaviour of someone who has ideals and who tries to base their behaviour on them. *This experience has tempered their idealism.* ♦ **ideal·ist, idealists** *He is not such an idealist that he cannot see the problems.*

ideal·is·tic /ˌaɪdɪəˈlɪstɪk/. If you describe someone as **idealistic**, you mean that they have ideals, and base their behaviour on them, even though this may be impractical and naive. *Older mothers tend to be too idealistic about the pleasures of motherhood.*

ideal·ize /aɪˈdiːəlaɪz/ **idealizes, idealizing, idealized;** also spelled **idealise** in British English. If you **idealize** something or someone, you think of them, or represent them to other people, as being perfect or much better than they really are. *People idealize the past. ...the idealized men depicted in advertisements.* ♦ **ideali·za·tion** /aɪˌdiːəlaɪˈzeɪʃən/ *...Marie's idealisation of her dead husband.*

ideal·ly /aɪˈdiːəli/. If you say that **ideally** a particular thing should be done, you mean that this is what you would like to be done, but you know that it may not be possible or practical. *People should, ideally, be persuaded to eat a diet with much less fat or oil.* ● See also **ideal**.

iden·ti·cal /aɪˈdentɪkəl/. Things that are **identical** are exactly the same. *Nearly all the houses were identical... The two parties fought the last election on almost identical manifestos.* ♦ **iden·ti·cal·ly** /aɪˈdentɪkli/. *...nine identically dressed female dancers.*

id'entical tw'in, identical twins. Identical twins are twins of the same sex who look exactly the same.

iden·ti·fi·able /aɪˌdentɪˈfaɪəbəl/. Something or someone that is **identifiable** can be recognized. *...four dirty, ragged bundles, just identifiable as human beings. ...Stan Dean, easily identifiable by his oddly-shaped hat... Where the risk is clearly identifiable, the tour operators should give advice to holidaymakers on their arrival.*

iden·ti·fi·ca·tion /aɪˌdentɪfɪˈkeɪʃən/. **1** If someone asks you for some **identification**, they want to see something such as a driving licence, which proves who you are. *In many countries, it is a legal requirement to carry identification at all times.* **2** See also **identify**.

iden·ti·fy /aɪˈdentɪfaɪ/ **identifies, identifying, identified. 1** If you **identify** someone or something, you name them or say who or what they are. *Police have already identified around 10 murder suspects... I tried to identify her perfume. ...the man, who identified himself as John Clark.* ♦ **iden·ti·fi·ca·tion, identifications** *He's made a formal identification of the body... Early identification of a disease can prevent death and illness.* **2** If a particular thing **identifies** someone or something, it makes them easy to recognize, by making them different in some way. *She wore a little nurse's hat on her head to identify her... His boots and purple beret identify him as commanding the Scottish Paratroops.* **3** If you **identify** something, you discover or notice its existence. *Scientists claim to have identified chemicals produced by certain plants which have powerful cancer-combating properties... Having identified the problem, the question arises of how to overcome it.* ♦ **identification** *Their work includes the identification of genes which govern the growth rate and fertility.* **4** If you **identify** one person or thing **with** another, you think that they are closely associated or involved in some way. *Moore really hates to play the sweet, passive women that audiences have identified her with.* ♦ **identification** *Throughout the Balkans, there is a close identification of nationhood with language.* **5** If you **identify with** someone or something, you feel that you understand them or their feelings and ideas. *She would only play a role if she could identify with the character... I could speak their language and identify with their problems.* ♦ **iden·ti·fi·ca·tion** *Marilyn had an intense identification with animals.*

iden·ti·kit /aɪˈdentɪkɪt/ **identikits.** An **Identikit** or an **Identikit picture** is a drawing, made up from a special set of smaller drawings, of the face of someone the police want to question. It is made from descriptions given to them by witnesses to a crime. **Identikit** is a trademark. Compare **photofit**.

iden·tity /aɪˈdentɪti/ **identities. 1** Your **identity** is who you are. *Abu is not his real name, but it's one he uses to disguise his identity.* **2** The **identity** of a person or place is the characteristics they have that

distinguish them from others. *I wanted a sense of my own identity. ...the distinct cultural, religious and national identity of many Tibetans.*

i'dentity card, identity cards. An **identity card** is a card with a person's name, photograph, date of birth, and other information about them on it. ◆◇◇◇◇ N-COUNT

i'dentity parade, identity parades. An **identity parade** is a line of people who have been assembled in a police station. One of the people is a suspected criminal, and victims or witnesses of a crime try to identify that person. The usual American word is **line-up.** N-COUNT BRITISH

ideo·gram /ˈɪdiəʊɡræm/ **ideograms. 1** An **ideo-gram** is a sign or symbol that represents a particular idea or thing rather than a word. The writing systems of Japan and China, for example, use ideograms. **2** In languages such as English which are written using letters and words, an **ideogram** is a sign or symbol that can be used to represent a particular word, for example %, @, or &. N-COUNT N-COUNT

ideo·logi·cal /ˌaɪdiəˈlɒdʒɪkəl/. **Ideological** means relating to ideology. *The ideological divisions between the parties aren't always obvious.* ◆ **ideo·logi·cal·ly** /ˌaɪdiəˈlɒdʒɪkli/. *The army was ideologically opposed to the kind of economic solution proposed.* ◆◆◇◇◇ ADJ ADV

ideo·logue /ˈaɪdiəlɒɡ, AM -lɔːɡ/ **ideologues.** If you refer to someone as an **ideologue**, you disapprove of them because they are too rigid in their support for a particular ideology. *He is not an ideologue. He doesn't have a political agenda.* N-COUNT PRAGMATICS

ideol·ogy /ˌaɪdiˈɒlədʒi/ **ideologies.** An **ideology** is a set of beliefs, especially the political beliefs on which people, parties, or countries base their actions. *...capitalist ideology.* ◆ **ideolo·gist** **ideologists.** An **ideologist** is someone who develops or supports a particular ideology. ◆◆◇◇◇ N-VAR /ˌaɪdiˈɒlədʒɪst/ N-COUNT

id·io·cy /ˈɪdiəsi/ **idiocies.** If you refer to the **idiocy** of something, you think it is very stupid. *...the idiocy of continuing government subsidies for environmentally damaging activities. ...his gentle, ironic analysis of the idiocies of Communist rule.* N-VAR PRAGMATICS

idi·om /ˈɪdiəm/ **idioms. 1** A particular **idiom** is a particular style of something such as music or architecture. *McCartney was also keen to write in a classical idiom, rather than a pop one.* **2** An **idiom** is a group of words which have a different meaning when used together from the one they would have if you took the meaning of each word individually. *...the French idiom 'to be comfortable in one's own skin.'* **3 Idiom** of a particular kind is the kind of language and grammatical structures that people use at a particular time or in a particular place. *Nothing was so irritating as the confident way he used archaic idiom.* ◆◇◇◇◇ N-COUNT FORMAL N-COUNT N-UNCOUNT FORMAL

idio·mat·ic /ˌɪdiəˈmætɪk/. **Idiomatic** language uses words in a way that sounds natural to native speakers of the language. *...idiomatic English.* ADJ-GRADED

idio·syn·cra·sy /ˌɪdiəʊˈsɪŋkrəsi/ **idiosyncrasies.** If you talk about the **idiosyncrasies** of someone or something, you are referring to their rather unusual habits or characteristics. *One of his idiosyncrasies was to wear thick orange gloves... The book is a gem of Victorian idiosyncrasy.* ◆ **idio·syn·crat·ic** /ˌɪdiəʊsɪŋˈkrætɪk/. *...a highly idiosyncratic personality. ...his erratic typing and idiosyncratic spelling.* N-VAR ADJ-GRADED

id·iot /ˈɪdiət/ **idiots. 1** If you call someone an **idiot**, you are insulting them by saying that they are stupid or have done something stupid. *I knew I'd been an idiot to stay there.* ▶ Also an adjective. *...a bunch of idiot journalists waiting to ask me stupid questions.* ◆ **idi·ot·ic** /ˌɪdiˈɒtɪk/. *What an idiotic thing to say!* **2** A person of very low intelligence used to be referred to as an **idiot**; people now find this use offensive. *...the village idiot.* ◆◆◇◇◇ N-COUNT PRAGMATICS ADJ: ADJ n ADJ-GRADED N-COUNT DATED, RUDE

idle /ˈaɪdəl/ **idles, idling, idled. 1** If people who were working are **idle**, they have no jobs or work. *Employees have been idle almost a month because of shortages.* **2** If machines or factories are **idle**, they are not working or being used. *The machine is lying idle.* **3** To **idle** a factory or other place of work ◆◆◇◇◇ ADJ: v-link ADJ ADJ: v-link ADJ VERB

means to close it down because there is no work to do or because the workers are on strike. To **idle** workers means to stop them working. *The strike has idled about 55,000 machinists. ...idled assembly plants.* V n V-ed AMERICAN

4 If you say that someone is **idle**, you disapprove of them because they are not doing anything and you think they should be. *...idle bureaucrats who spent the day reading newspapers... I never met such an idle bunch of workers in all my life!* ◆ **idle·ness** *Idleness is a very bad thing for human nature.* ◆ **idly** *We were not idly sitting around.* **5 Idle** is used to describe something that you do for no particular reason, often because you have nothing better to do. *Why am I making idle chatter when there is so much I want to say?... Your reason for going is merely idle curiosity.* ◆ **idly** *We talked idly about magazines.* **6** If you **idle**, you spend time in a lazy way, doing nothing in particular. *We spent many hours idling in one of the cafes.* ◆ **idler** *The Duke resents being seen as a money-eyed idler.* ADJ PRAGMATICS N-UNCOUNT ADV: ADV with v ADJ: ADJ n ADV VERB V Also V adv/ prep N-COUNT

7 If you say that **it is idle** to do something, you mean that it is not worth doing it, because it will not achieve anything. *It would be idle to pretend the system is perfect.* **8** If you refer to an **idle** threat or boast, you think that it is not serious, not true, or not likely to be carried out. *This is no idle threat.* ADJ: it v-link ADJ to-inf ADJ: ADJ n

9 If an engine or vehicle **is idling**, the engine is running slowly and quietly because it is not in gear, and the vehicle is not moving. VERB: V

idle away. If you **idle away** a period of time, you spend it doing very little. *Residents were mowing their lawns, washing their cars and otherwise idling away a pleasant, sunny day.* PHRASAL VB V P noun Also V n P

idol /ˈaɪdəl/ **idols. 1** If you refer to someone such as a film, pop, or sports star as an **idol**, you mean that they are greatly admired or loved by their fans. *A great cheer went up from the crowd as they caught sight of their idol. ...a teen idol.* **2** An **idol** is a statue or other object that is worshipped by people who believe that it is a god. ◆◇◇◇◇ N-COUNT N-COUNT

 idola·try /aɪˈdɒlətri/. **1** Someone who practises **idolatry** worships idols. **2** If you refer to someone's admiration for a particular person as **idolatry**, you are criticizing it because it is too great and unquestioning. *His real view of Roosevelt stood well short of idolatry.* N-UNCOUNT FORMAL N-UNCOUNT PRAGMATICS FORMAL

 idol·ize /ˈaɪdəlaɪz/ **idolizes, idolizing, idolized;** also spelled **idolise** in British English. If you **idolize** someone, you admire them very much. *Naomi idolised her father.* VERB V n

 id·yll /ˈɪdɪl, AM ˈaɪdəl/ **idylls.** If you describe a situation as an **idyll**, you mean that it is idyllic. *She finds that the sleepy town she moves to isn't the rural idyll she imagined.* N-COUNT

 idyl·lic /ɪˈdɪlɪk, AM aɪd-/. If you describe something as **idyllic**, you mean that it is extremely pleasant, simple, and peaceful without any difficulties or dangers. *...an idyllic setting for a summer romance... Married life was not as idyllic as he had imagined.* ◆◇◇◇◇ ADJ-GRADED

i.e. /ˌaɪ ˈiː/. **i.e.** is used to introduce a word or sentence which makes clearer or makes explicit the meaning of what you have just said. *...strategic points – i.e. airports or military bases.* ◆◆◇◇◇ PRAGMATICS

-ied. See **-ed.**

-ier. See **-er.**

-iest. See **-est.**

 if /ɪf/. **1** You use **if** in conditional sentences to introduce the circumstances in which an event or situation might happen or might have happened. *She gets very upset if I exclude her from anything... If you went into town, you'd notice all the pubs have loud jukeboxes... What I did was right and if I had done anything less it would have been wrong... Mix well and taste; adjust the seasoning if necessary... Are you a student with a knack for coming up with great ideas? If so, we would love to hear from you.* **2** You say **'if I were you'** to someone when you are giving them advice. *If I were you, Mrs Gretchen, I just wouldn't worry about it.* **3** You use **if** to introduce a ◆◆◆◆◆ CONJ PHRASE PRAGMATICS CONJ

subordinate clause in which you admit a fact which you regard as less important than the statement in the main clause. *If there was any disappointment it was probably temporary... So what if sometimes they stayed rather late, it doesn't mean anything.* **4** You use **if** in indirect questions where the answer is either 'yes' or 'no'. *He asked if I had left with you, and I said no... I wasn't really sure if he was a killer.* **5** You can use **if** in fairly polite requests at the beginning of a clause, when you want to do something or are asking someone to do something. *But if I can interrupt, Joe, I don't think anybody here is personally blaming the Germans... I wonder if I might have a word with Mr Abbot?... I wonder if you'd be kind enough to give us some information, please?... If you will just sign here.* **6** You use **if** to suggest that something might be slightly different from what you are stating in the main part of the sentence, for example that there might be slightly more or less of a particular quality. *That standard is quite difficult, if not impossible, to achieve... I will be ready in a couple of weeks, if not sooner... What one quality, if any, do you like the most about your partner?... Meat was available once a week if at all.* ● **if anything**: see **anything**. **7** You use **if not** in front of a word or phrase to indicate that your statement does not apply to that word or phrase, but to something closely related to it that you also mention. *A number of recent advances hold out if not the hope of a cure, then at least the possibility of some drug which could stop the spread of the virus... She understood his meaning, if not his words.* **8** You use **if only** with past tenses to introduce what you think is a fairly good reason for doing something, although you realize it may not be a very good one. *She always writes me once a month, if only to scold me because I haven't answered her last letter yet.* **9** You use **if only** to express a wish or desire, especially one that cannot be fulfilled. *If only you had told me that some time ago... If only it were that simple!... 'Hey, listen to me, all that 1980 nonsense is over.'—'If only, Timothy, if only.'* **10** You use **if ever** with past tenses when you are introducing a description of a person or thing, to emphasize how appropriate it is. *If ever a man needed your love, I need it... I became a distraught, worried mother, a useless role if ever there was one.* **11** You use **as if** when you are making a judgement about something that you see or notice. Your belief or impression might be correct, or it might be wrong. *The whole room looks as if it has been lovingly put together over the years.* **12** You use **as if** to describe something or someone by comparing them with another thing or person. *He points two fingers at his head, as if he were holding a gun.* **13** You use **as if** to emphasize that something is not true. *Getting my work done! My God! As if it mattered.* **14** You use **'It's not as if'** to introduce a statement which, if it were true, might explain something puzzling, although in fact it is not true. *I am surprised by the degree of fuss she's making. It's not as if my personality has changed or vanished.*

if·fy /'ɪfi/. If you say that something is **iffy**, you are not convinced that it is good or successful, and you think that there is something wrong or bad about it. *If your next record's a bit iffy, you're forgotten. ...an iffy neighborhood... His political future has looked iffy for most of this year.* ADJ-GRADED INFORMAL

-ify /-ɪfaɪ/ **-ifies, -ifying, -ified.** -ify is used at the end of verbs that refer to making something or someone different in some way. *More needs to be done to simplify the process... Water can be purified by boiling.* SUFFIX

ig·loo /'ɪgluː/ **igloos.** Igloos are dome-shaped Inuit houses built from blocks of snow. N-COUNT

ig·ne·ous /'ɪgniəs/. **Igneous** rocks are formed by volcanic action. ADJ: ADJ n TECHNICAL

ig·nite /ɪg'naɪt/ **ignites, igniting, ignited.** **1** When you **ignite** something or when it **ignites**, it starts burning or explodes. *The bombs ignited a fire* V-ERG V n V

which destroyed some 60 houses. ...pockets of methane gas that ignited. ◆ **ig·ni·tion** The ignition of methane gas killed eight men. **2** If something or someone **ignites** your passions, they cause you to feel passionate about something. *There was one teacher who really ignited my interest in words... The recent fighting in the area could ignite regional passions.* N-UNCOUNT V n LITERARY

ig·ni·tion /ɪg'nɪʃən/ **ignitions.** In a car, the **ignition** is the mechanism which ignites the fuel and starts the engine, usually operated by turning a key. See picture headed **car and bicycle**. *Uncle Jim put the key in the ignition and turned it.* N-COUNT

ig·no·ble /ɪg'nəʊbəl/. If you describe someone's behaviour or circumstances as **ignoble**, you mean that you consider them dishonourable, shameful, or morally unacceptable. *...ignoble thoughts. ...an ignoble episode from their country's past.* ADJ-GRADED PRAGMATICS FORMAL

ig·no·min·i·ous /ˌɪgnə'mɪniəs/. If you describe someone's behaviour or circumstances as **ignominious**, you mean that they are shameful or very embarrassing. *...their ignominious defeat... Many thought that he was doomed to ignominious failure.* ADJ-GRADED FORMAL ◆ **ig·no·min·i·ous·ly** *Their soldiers had to retreat ignominiously.* ADV-GRADED: ADV with v

ig·no·miny /'ɪgnəmɪni/. **Ignominy** is shame or public disgrace. *The defending champion had to suffer the ignominy of defeat in the first round.* N-UNCOUNT FORMAL

ig·no·ra·mus /ˌɪgnə'reɪməs/ **ignoramuses.** If you describe someone as an **ignoramus**, you are criticizing them because they do not have the knowledge you think they ought to have. N-COUNT PRAGMATICS

ig·no·rant /'ɪgnərənt/. **1** If you describe someone as **ignorant**, you mean that they are not very knowledgeable or well educated. If someone is **ignorant** of a fact, they do not know it. *People don't like to ask questions for fear of appearing ignorant... Many people are worryingly ignorant of the facts about global warming.* ◆ **ig·no·rance** I am beginning to feel embarrassed by my complete ignorance of non-European history... In my ignorance I had never heard country & western music. **2** People are sometimes described as **ignorant** when they behave in an impolite or inconsiderate way. Some people think this use is not correct. ADJ-GRADED N-UNCOUNT ADJ-GRADED

ig·nore /ɪg'nɔː/ **ignores, ignoring, ignored.** **1** If you **ignore** someone or something, you pay no attention to them. *She said her husband ignored her... She ignored legal advice to drop the case.* **2** If an argument or theory **ignores** an important aspect of a situation, it fails to consider that aspect. *Such arguments ignore the question of where ultimate responsibility lay.* VERB V n VERB V n

igua·na /ɪ'gwɑːnə, ˌɪgjʊ'ɑːnə/ **iguanas.** An **iguana** is a type of large lizard found in America. N-COUNT

ikon /'aɪkɒn/. See **icon**.

il- /ɪl-/. **Il-** is added to words that begin with the letter 'l' to form words with the opposite meaning. *...an awful illegible signature. ...a charge of illegally importing weapons.* PREFIX

ilk /ɪlk/. If you talk about people or things of the same **ilk**, you mean people or things of the same type as a person or thing that has been mentioned. *He currently terrorises politicians and their ilk on 'Newsnight'.* N-SING: supp N

ill /ɪl/ **ills.** **1** Someone who is **ill** is suffering from a disease or a health problem. *Payne was seriously ill with pneumonia... I was feeling ill.* ► People who are ill in some way can be referred to as, for example, **the mentally ill**. *She became a nun and cared for the terminally ill.* ● If you **fall ill** or **are taken ill**, you suddenly become ill. *She fell ill with measles.* **2** Difficulties and problems are sometimes referred to as **ills**. *His critics maintain that he's responsible for many of Algeria's ills. ...various potions that would cure all ills.* **3** Ill is evil or harm. *They say they mean you no ill.* ● If you say that something will happen **for good or ill**, you mean that it is going to happen, and nobody can know or control what its effects will be. *For good or ill, the cable industry has been deregulated.* ADJ-GRADED N-PLURAL: the adv N PHRASE N-COUNT FORMAL N-UNCOUNT LITERARY PHRASE

4 Ill can be used in front of some nouns to mean 'bad'. *She had brought ill luck into her family... He says that he bears no ill feelings towards Johnson.* ▶ Ill can be used after some verbs to mean 'badly'. *The company's conservative instincts sit ill with competition.* **5** If you say that someone **can ill afford** to do something, or **can ill afford** something, you mean that it would be harmful or embarrassing to them. *I can ill afford to lose him... We can ill afford another scandal.* **6** If something **bodes ill** or **augurs ill** for someone, it gives you a reason to fear that something harmful might happen to them. *It's an ominous development that may bode ill for the Russian parliament.* **7** ● to **speak ill** of someone: see **speak**.

ADJ: ADJ n FORMAL
ADV-GRADED: ADV with v
PHRASE FORMAL
PHRASE FORMAL

ill- /ɪl-/. Ill- is added to words, especially adjectives and past participles, to add the meaning 'badly' or 'inadequately'. *It was an amazingly ill-disciplined attack.*

COMB

I'll /aɪl/. I'll is the usual spoken form of 'I will' or 'I shall'.

,**ill-ad'vised.** If you describe something that someone does as **ill-advised**, you mean that it is not sensible or wise. *They would be ill-advised to do this.*

ADJ-GRADED

ill at 'ease; also spelled **ill-at-ease**. See **ease**.

,**ill ef'fects;** also spelled **ill-effects**. If something has **ill effects**, it causes problems or damage. *Some people are still suffering ill effects from the contamination of their water.*

N-PLURAL

il·le·gal /ɪ'liːgəl/ **illegals. 1** If something is **illegal**, the law says that it is not allowed. *It is illegal to intercept radio messages... Birth control was illegal there until 1978. ...illegal drugs.* ♦ **il·le·gal·ly** *previous government had acted illegally.* ♦ **il·le·gal·ity** /,ɪlɪ'gælɪti/ **illegalities** *There is no evidence of illegality.* **2** Illegal immigrants or workers have travelled into a country or are working without official permission. ▶ Illegal immigrants or workers are sometimes referred to as **illegals**.

♦♦♦◇◇ ADJ
ADV: ADV with v
N-VAR
ADJ: ADJ n
N-COUNT

il·leg·ible /ɪ'ledʒɪbəl/. Writing that is **illegible** is so unclear that you cannot read it.

ADJ-GRADED

il·le·git·i·mate /,ɪlɪ'dʒɪtɪmət/. **1** A person who is **illegitimate** was born of parents who were not married to each other. ♦ **il·le·git·i·ma·cy** *...a steady rise in divorce and illegitimacy.* **2** Illegitimate is used to describe activities and institutions that are not in accordance with the law or with accepted standards of what is right. *The election would have been dismissed as illegitimate by the international community.*

♦◇◇◇◇ ADJ
N-UNCOUNT
ADJ

,**ill-equ'ipped.** Someone who is **ill-equipped** to do something does not have the ability, the qualities, or the equipment necessary to do it. *They often leave prison ill-equipped for life and work on the outside.*

ADJ-GRADED

,**ill-'fated.** If you describe something as **ill-fated**, you mean that it ended or will end in an unsuccessful or unfortunate way. *England's footballers are back home after their ill-fated trip to Algeria.*

♦◇◇◇◇ ADJ

,**ill-'fitting.** An **ill-fitting** piece of clothing does not fit the person who is wearing it properly.

ADJ: ADJ n

,**ill-'founded.** Something that is **ill-founded** is not based on any proper proof or evidence.

ADJ-GRADED

,**ill-gotten 'gains.** Someone's **ill-gotten gains** are things that they have obtained by means of dishonesty or deceit.

N-PLURAL

,**ill 'health.** Someone who suffers from **ill health** has an illness or is often ill.

♦◇◇◇◇ N-UNCOUNT

il·lib·er·al /ɪ'lɪbərəl/. If you describe someone or something as **illiberal**, you are critical of them because they do not allow or approve of much freedom of action. *His illiberal views are the product of emotional insecurity.*

ADJ-GRADED PRAGMATICS

il·lic·it /ɪ'lɪsɪt/. An **illicit** activity or substance is not allowed by law or the social customs of a country. *Dante clearly condemns illicit love. ...the use of illicit drugs.*

♦◇◇◇◇ ADJ

il·lit·er·ate /ɪ'lɪtərət/ **illiterates. 1** Someone who is **illiterate** does not know how to read or write. *A large percentage of the population is illiterate.* ▶ Also a noun. *...an educational centre for illiterates.*

♦◇◇◇◇ ADJ
N-COUNT

♦ **il·lit·era·cy** /ɪ'lɪtərəsi/. *...the problem of illiteracy in the developing world.* **2** If you describe someone as, for example, musically **illiterate** or technologically **illiterate**, you mean that they do not know much about music or technology.

N-UNCOUNT
ADJ

,**ill-'mannered.** If you describe someone as **ill-mannered**, you are criticizing them for being impolite or rude.

ADJ-GRADED PRAGMATICS FORMAL

ill·ness /'ɪlnəs/ **illnesses. 1** Illness is the fact or experience of being ill. *Mental illness is still a taboo subject.* **2** An **illness** is a particular disease such as measles or pneumonia. *She returned to her family home to recover from an illness.*

♦♦♦◇◇ N-UNCOUNT
N-COUNT

il·logi·cal /ɪ'lɒdʒɪkəl/. If an action, feeling, or belief is **illogical**, it is not rational and does not result from logical and ordered thinking. *It is illogical to have two houses of parliament with the same powers.* ♦ **il·logi·cal·ly** /ɪ'lɒdʒɪkli/. *Illogically, I felt guilty.*

♦◇◇◇◇ ADJ-GRADED
ADV-GRADED

,**ill-pre'pared.** If you are **ill-prepared** for something, you have not made the correct preparations for it, for example because you are not expecting it to happen.

ADJ-GRADED

,**ill-'starred.** If you describe something or someone as **ill-starred**, you mean that they were unlucky or unsuccessful. *...an ill-starred attempt to create jobs in Northern Ireland.*

ADJ JOURNALISM

,**ill-'tempered.** If you describe someone as **ill-tempered**, you mean they are angry or hostile, and you may be implying that this is unreasonable. *It was a day of tense and often ill-tempered debate.*

ADJ-GRADED

,**ill-'timed.** If you describe something as **ill-timed**, you mean that it happens or is done at the wrong time, so that it is damaging. *Congressman Rostenkowski argued that the tax cut was ill-timed.*

ADJ-GRADED

,**ill-'treat, ill-treats, ill-treating, ill-treated.** If someone **ill-treats** you, they treat you badly or cruelly. *They said they had not been ill-treated but that their time in captivity had been miserable.* ♦ **ill-treat·ment** *...allegations of torture and ill-treatment of prisoners.*

VERB: V n
be V-ed
N-UNCOUNT

il·lu·mi·nate /ɪ'luːmɪneɪt/ **illuminates, illuminating, illuminated. 1** To **illuminate** something means to shine light on it and to make it brighter. *No streetlights illuminated the street... The black sky was illuminated by forked lightning.* ♦ **il·lu·mi·nat·ed** *...an illuminated sign.* ♦ **il·lu·mi·na·tion** *The only illumination came from a small window.* **2** If you **illuminate** something that is unclear or difficult to understand, you make it clearer by explaining it or giving information about it. *The instructors use games and drawings to illuminate their subject.* ♦ **il·lu·mi·nat·ing** *This is a most illuminating book.* ♦ **il·lu·mi·na·tion** *...a sense of illumination.*

♦◇◇◇◇ VERB
V n
FORMAL
ADJ
N-UNCOUNT
VERB: V n
V n
FORMAL
ADJ-GRADED
N-UNCOUNT

il·lu·mi·nat·ed /ɪ'luːmɪneɪtɪd/. **1** Illuminated manuscripts have brightly coloured drawings and designs round the writing. **2** See also **illuminate**.

♦◇◇◇◇ ADJ: ADJ n

il·lu·mi·na·tion /ɪ,luːmɪ'neɪʃən/ **illuminations. 1** Illuminations are coloured lights which are put up in towns, especially at Christmas, in order to make them look more attractive at night. **2** See also **illuminate**.

♦◇◇◇◇ N-PLURAL
BRITISH

il·lu·mine /ɪ'luːmɪn/ **illumines, illumining, illumined.** To **illumine** something means the same as to **illuminate** it.

VERB: V n
LITERARY

il·lu·sion /ɪ'luːʒən/ **illusions. 1** An **illusion** is a false idea or belief. *No one really has any illusions about winning the war.* **2** An **illusion** is something that appears to exist or to be a particular thing but in reality does not exist or is something else. *Her upswept hair gave the illusion of above average height.*

♦♦◇◇◇ N-VAR
N-COUNT

il·lu·sion·ist /ɪ'luːʒənɪst/ **illusionists.** An **illusionist** is a performer who performs tricks which create the illusion that something strange or impossible is happening, for example that a person has disappeared or been cut in half.

N-COUNT

il·lu·so·ry /ɪ'luːzəri, -səri/. If you describe something as **illusory**, you mean that although it seems

ADJ-GRADED

true or possible, it is in fact false or impossible. *Universalists argue that freedom is illusory.*

il·lus·trate /'ɪləstreɪt/ **illustrates, illustrating, illustrated. 1** If you say that something **illustrates** a situation that you are drawing attention to, you mean that it shows that the situation exists. *The example of the United States illustrates this point... The incident illustrates how tricky it is to design a safe system... The case also illustrates that some women are now trying to fight back.* ♦ **il·lus·tra·tion** /,ɪlə'streɪʃən/ **illustrations** *An illustration of China's dynamism is that a new company is formed in Shanghai every 11 seconds.* **2** If you use an example, story, or diagram to **illustrate** a point, you use it to show that what you are saying is true or to make your meaning clearer. *Throughout, she illustrates her analysis with excerpts from discussions.* ♦ **illustration** *Here, by way of illustration, are some extracts from our new catalogue.* **3** If you **illustrate** a book, you put pictures, photographs or diagrams into it. *He has illustrated the book with black-and-white photographs.* ♦ **il·lus·trat·ed** *The book is beautifully illustrated throughout.* ♦ **il·lus·tra·tion** *...a princess in a nineteenth-century illustration. ...the world of children's book illustration.*

◆◆◇◇◇ VERB V n V wh V that

N-VAR

VERB: V n V n with n

N-VAR VERB: V n V n with n

ADJ-GRADED N-VAR

il·lus·tra·tive /'ɪləstrətɪv/. If you use something as an **illustrative** example, or for **illustrative** purposes, you use it to show that what you are saying is true or to make your meaning clearer. *The following excerpt is illustrative of her interaction with students.*

ADJ-GRADED FORMAL

il·lus·tra·tor /'ɪləstreɪtə/ **illustrators.** An **illustrator** is an artist who draws pictures and diagrams for books and magazines.

N-COUNT

il·lus·tri·ous /ɪ'lʌstriəs/. An **illustrious** person is extremely well known because they have a high position in society, or because they have done something impressive. *...his long and illustrious career.*

◆◇◇◇◇ ADJ-GRADED

,**ill 'will;** also spelled **ill-will. Ill will** is a feeling of hostility or spite that you have towards someone. *He didn't bear anyone any ill will... All this has created considerable ill-will towards the armed forces.*

N-UNCOUNT

,**ill 'wind.** You can describe an unfortunate event as an **ill wind** if someone benefits from it. The expression occurs in the proverb 'It's an ill wind that blows nobody any good', meaning that however bad something is, it usually has some good aspects.

N-SING

im- /ɪm-/. **Im-** is added to words that begin with 'm', 'p', or 'b' to form words with the opposite meaning. *Don't stare at me – it's impolite!*

PREFIX

I'm /aɪm/. **I'm** is the usual spoken form of 'I am'.

im·age /'ɪmɪdʒ/ **images. 1** If you have an **image** of something or someone, you have a picture or idea of them in your mind. *The words 'Cote d'Azur' conjure up images of sunny days in Mediterranean cafes.* **2** The **image** of a person, group, or organization is the way that they appear to other people. *He has cultivated the image of an elder statesman... The tobacco industry has been trying to improve its image.* **3** An **image** is a picture or reflection of someone or something. *...glamorous images of women on record sleeves... A computer in the machine creates an image on the screen.* **4** An **image** is a description or symbolic representation of something in a poem or other work of art. *...the natural images in the poem.* **5** See also **mirror image.** ● the spitting **image of:** see **spit.**

◆◆◆◇ N-COUNT

N-COUNT

N-COUNT FORMAL

N-COUNT

im·age·ry /'ɪmɪdʒri/. You can refer to the descriptions and symbolic representations in something such as a poem or work of art, and the pictures they create in your mind, as its **imagery.** *...the nature imagery of the ballad.*

◆◇◇◇◇ N-UNCOUNT FORMAL

im·agi·nable /ɪ'mædʒɪnəbəl/. **1** You use **imaginable** after a superlative such as 'best' or 'worst' to emphasize that something is extreme in some way. *...their imprisonment under some of the most horrible circumstances imaginable... He had had the worst imaginable day.* **2** You use **imaginable** after a word like 'every' or 'all' to emphasize that you are talking about all the possible examples of some-

◆◇◇◇◇ ADJ: adj-superl n adj-superl ADJ PRAGMATICS ADJ: ADJ n, n ADJ PRAGMATICS

thing. *Parents encourage every activity imaginable. ...a place of no imaginable strategic value.*

im·agi·nary /ɪ'mædʒɪnəri, AM -neri/. An **imaginary** person, place, or thing exists only in your mind or in a story, and not in real life. *Lots of children have imaginary friends.*

◆◇◇◇◇ ADJ

im·agi·na·tion /ɪ,mædʒɪ'neɪʃən/ **imaginations. 1** Your **imagination** is the ability that you have to form pictures or ideas in your mind of things that are new and exciting, or things that you have not experienced or that do not really exist. *Antonia is a woman with a vivid imagination... Long before I ever went there, Africa was alive in my imagination... The Government approach displays a lack of imagination.* **2** If you say that someone or something **captured** your **imagination,** you mean that you thought they were interesting or exciting when you saw them or heard them for the first time. **3** ● by no stretch of the **imagination:** see **stretch.**

◆◆◇◇ N-VAR

PHRASE

im·agi·na·tive /ɪ'mædʒɪnətɪv/. If you describe someone or their ideas as **imaginative,** you are praising them because they are easily able to think of or create new or exciting things. *...hundreds of cooking ideas and imaginative recipes.* ♦ **im·agi·na·tive·ly** *The hotel is decorated imaginatively and attractively.*

◆◆◇◇◇ ADJ-GRADED PRAGMATICS

ADV-GRADED: ADV with v

im·ag·ine /ɪ'mædʒɪn/ **imagines, imagining, imagined. 1** If you **imagine** something, you think about it and your mind forms a picture or idea of it. *He could not imagine a more peaceful scene... Can you imagine how she must have felt?... Imagine you're lying on a beach... I can't imagine you being unfair to anyone, Leigh.* **2** If you **imagine** that something is the case, you think that it is the case. *We tend to imagine that the Victorians were very prim and proper... 'Was he meeting someone?'—'I imagine so.'* **3** If you **imagine** something, you think that you have seen, heard, or experienced something, although actually you haven't. *I realised that I must have imagined the whole thing.*

◆◆◆◇ VERB V n/-ing V wh V n -ing/prep

VERB V that V so/not

VERB V n Also V that

im·ag·ing /'ɪmɪdʒɪŋ/. **Imaging** is the process of forming or obtaining images by electronically tracing something such as sound waves, temperature, or chemicals, rather than by using light rays or ordinary photography. *...thermal imaging cameras.*

◆◇◇◇◇ N-UNCOUNT

im·ag·in·ings /ɪ'mædʒɪnɪŋz/. Your **imaginings** are pictures or ideas of things which you have formed in your mind, but which have not actually happened. *He succeeded with women beyond his wildest imaginings.*

N-PLURAL LITERARY

imam /ɪ'mɑːm/ **imams.** In Islam, an **imam** is a religious leader, especially the leader of a Muslim community or the person who leads the prayers in a mosque.

◆◇◇◇◇ N-COUNT

im·bal·ance /ɪm'bæləns/ **imbalances.** If there is an **imbalance** in a situation, the things involved are not the same size, or are not the right size in proportion to each other. *...the imbalance between the two sides in this war.* ♦ **im·bal·anced** *...the present imbalanced structure of world trade.*

◆◇◇◇◇ N-VAR

ADJ-GRADED

im·be·cile /'ɪmbɪsiːl, AM -səl/ **imbeciles. 1** If you call someone an **imbecile,** you are insulting them by saying that they are stupid or have done something stupid. *Hubert, you imbecile!* **2** A person of very low intelligence used to be referred to as an **imbecile;** people now find this use offensive.

N-COUNT PRAGMATICS

N-COUNT DATED, RUDE

im·bibe /ɪm'baɪb/ **imbibes, imbibing, imbibed. 1** To **imbibe** alcohol means to drink it. *Since no one had to drive home, we could imbibe freely.* **2** If you **imbibe** ideas, arguments, or ways of behaving, you learn or adopt them because you often hear or experience them. *From her mother and father she had imbibed manners, taste, a certain eloquence.*

VERB: V n V FORMAL VERB: V n V n FORMAL

im·bro·glio /ɪm'brəʊliəʊ/ **imbroglios.** An **imbroglio** is a very confusing or complicated situation.

N-COUNT LITERARY

im·bue /ɪm'bjuː/ **imbues, imbuing, imbued.** If someone or something **is imbued** with an idea, feeling, or quality, they become filled with it. *His presence imbued her with a feeling of completeness and*

◆◇◇◇◇ VERB: be V-ed with n V n with n V-ed FORMAL

security. ...*a Guards officer imbued with a military sense of duty.*

IMF /ˌaɪ em 'ef/. **The IMF** is an international agency which is part of the United Nations. It tries to promote trade and improve economic conditions in the countries which belong to it, sometimes by lending them money. **IMF** is an abbreviation for 'International Monetary Fund'. ◆◇◇◇ N-PROPER: the N

imi·tate /'ɪmɪteɪt/ **imitates, imitating, imitated. 1** If you **imitate** someone, you copy what they do or produce. ...*a genuine German musical which does not try to imitate the American model.* ◆ **imi·ta·tor, imitators** *He's survived and most of his imitators haven't.* **2** If you **imitate** a person or animal, you copy the way they speak or behave, often as a joke. ◆◇◇◇ VERB V n / VERB: V n / N-COUNT

imi·ta·tion /ˌɪmɪ'teɪʃən/ **imitations. 1** An **imitation** of something is a copy of it. ...*the most accurate imitation of Chinese architecture in Europe.* **2** **Imitation** means copying someone else's actions. *Molly learned her golf by imitation.* **3 Imitation** things are not genuine but are made to look as if they are. ...*imitation leather.* **4** If someone does an **imitation** of another person, they copy the way they speak or behave, often as a joke. ◆◇◇◇ N-COUNT / N-UNCOUNT / ADJ: ADJ n / N-COUNT

imi·ta·tive /'ɪmɪtətɪv, AM -teɪt-/. People and animals who are **imitative** copy others' behaviour. ADJ-GRADED

im·macu·late /ɪ'mækjʊlət/. **1** If something is **immaculate**, it is extremely clean, tidy, or neat. *Her front room was kept immaculate.* ◆ **im·macu·late·ly** *As always he was immaculately dressed.* **2** If you say that something is **immaculate**, you are emphasizing that it is perfect, without any mistakes or flaws at all. *The 1979 Chevrolet is in immaculate condition.* ◆ **immaculately** *Her solo was so charmingly, immaculately done.* ◆◇◇◇ ADJ-GRADED / ADV-GRADED ADJ-GRADED PRAGMATICS / ADV-GRADED

im·ma·nent /'ɪmənənt/. If you say that a quality is **immanent** in a particular thing, you mean that the thing has that quality, and cannot exist or be imagined without it. *God is immanent in the world.* ADJ FORMAL

im·ma·teri·al /ˌɪmə'tɪəriəl/. If you say that something is **immaterial**, you mean that it is not important or not relevant. *Whether we like him or not is immaterial.* ◆◇◇◇ ADJ: v-link ADJ

im·ma·ture /ˌɪmə'tjʊə, AM -'tʊr/. **1** Something or someone that is **immature** is not yet completely grown or fully developed. ...*babies with particularly immature respiratory systems.* ◆ **im·ma·tu·rity** /ˌɪmə'tjʊərɪti, AM -'tʊr-/. *In spite of some immaturity in the figure drawing and painting, it showed real imagination.* **2** If you describe someone as **immature**, you are criticizing them because they do not behave in a sensible or responsible way. ...*grossly immature drivers who flout the rules of the road... She's just being childish and immature.* ◆ **immaturity** ...*his immaturity and lack of social skills.* ◆◇◇◇ ADJ / N-UNCOUNT / ADJ-GRADED PRAGMATICS / N-UNCOUNT

im·meas·ur·able /ɪ'meʒərəbəl/. If you describe something as **immeasurable**, you are emphasizing how great it is. *His contribution is immeasurable.* ◆ **im·meas·ur·ably** *They have improved immeasurably since the arrival of their Australian coach.* ADJ PRAGMATICS FORMAL / ADV

im·medi·acy /ɪ'miːdiəsi/. **1** If something has a quality of **immediacy**, it has a strong and exciting impact on you as soon as you see or experience it. ...*the immediacy and excitement of raw rock'n'roll.* **2** See also **immediate**. N-UNCOUNT

im·medi·ate /ɪ'miːdiət/. **1** An **immediate** result, action, or reaction happens or is done without any delay. *These tragic incidents have had an immediate effect... My immediate reaction was just disgust.* ◆ **im·medi·ate·ly** *He immediately flung himself to the floor... Ingrid answered Peter's letter immediately.* **2 Immediate** needs and concerns exist at the present time and must be dealt with quickly. *The immediate problem is not a lack of food, but transportation.* ◆ **im·medi·acy** *It brought home to Americans the immediacy of the crisis.* **3** You use **immediate** to describe something or someone that is very close to something else in time or space, or ◆◆◆◇ ADJ / ADV: ADV with v / ADJ-GRADED / N-UNCOUNT / ADJ: ADJ n

in a sequence. ...*the immediate aftermath of the riots... I was seated at Sauter's immediate left. ...his immediate superior, General Geichenko.* ◆ **im·medi·ate·ly** *They wish to begin immediately after dinner... She always sits immediately behind the driver... The man immediately responsible for this misery is the province's governor.* **4** Your **immediate** family are the members of your family who are most closely related to you, that is your parents, children, brothers, and sisters. ADV: ADV prep/ adj/-ed / ADJ: ADJ n

im·medi·ate·ly /ɪ'miːdiətli/. **1** If something is **immediately** apparent, it can be seen or understood without any delay. *The reasons for this may not be immediately obvious.* **2** If one thing happens **immediately** something else happens, it happens after that event, without any delay. *Immediately he had said it, Leonidas cursed himself... If this happens, see a dentist immediately you land.* **3** See also **immediate**. ◆◆◆◇ ADV: ADV adj / CONJ

im·memo·ri·al /ˌɪmɪ'mɔːriəl/. If you say that something has been happening **since time immemorial** or **from time immemorial**, you are emphasizing that it has been happening for many centuries. PHRASE PRAGMATICS LITERARY

im·mense /ɪ'mens/. If you describe something as **immense**, you mean that it is extremely large or great. *With immense relief I stopped running.* ◆ **im·men·si·ty** /ɪ'mensɪti/. *The immensity of the universe is difficult to grasp.* ◆◆◇◇ ADJ-GRADED / N-UNCOUNT

im·mense·ly /ɪ'mensli/. You use **immensely** to emphasize the degree or extent of a quality, feeling, or process. *Chess is immensely popular in Russia... I enjoyed this movie immensely.* ◆◇◇◇ ADV PRAGMATICS

im·merse /ɪ'mɜːs/ **immerses, immersing, immersed. 1** If you **immerse** yourself in something that you are doing, you become completely involved in it. *I had to immerse myself in the new job.* ◆ **im·mersed** *He's really becoming immersed in his work.* ◆ **im·mer·sion** /ɪ'mɜːʃən/. ...*long-term assignments that allowed them total immersion in their subjects.* **2** If something **is immersed** in a liquid, it is put into the liquid so that it is completely covered. ◆ **immersion** *The wood had become swollen from prolonged immersion.* ◆◇◇◇ VERB V pron-refl in n / ADJ-GRADED: v-link ADJ in n n N-UNCOUNT / VERB: be V-ed in n / N-UNCOUNT

im·mi·grant /'ɪmɪgrənt/ **immigrants.** An **immigrant** is a person who has come to live in a country from another country. *We received waves of immigrants from Europe. ...immigrant visas.* ◆◆◆◇ N-COUNT

im·mi·grate /'ɪmɪgreɪt/ **immigrates, immigrating, immigrated.** If someone **immigrates** to a particular country, they leave their native country and come to live in that country. ...*a Russian-born professor who had immigrated to the United States... He immigrated from Ulster in 1848... 10,000 people are expected to immigrate in the next two years.* VERB V to n V from n V

im·mi·gra·tion /ˌɪmɪ'greɪʃən/. **1 Immigration** is the fact or process of people coming into a country in order to live and work there. *The government has decided to tighten its immigration policy. ...immigration into Europe.* **2 Immigration** or **immigration control** is the place at a port, airport, or international border where officials check the passports of people who wish to come into the country. ◆◆◆◇ N-UNCOUNT / N-UNCOUNT

im·mi·nent /'ɪmɪnənt/. If you say that something is **imminent**, especially something unpleasant, you mean it is almost certain to happen very soon. *There appeared no imminent danger... They warned that an attack is imminent.* ◆ **im·mi·nen·ce** *The imminence of war was on everyone's mind.* ◆◆◇◇ ADJ / N-UNCOUNT

im·mo·bile /ɪ'məʊbaɪl, AM -bəl/. **1** Someone or something that is **immobile** is completely still. *He stood immobile in the darkest shadows.* ◆ **im·mo·bil·ity** /ˌɪməʊ'bɪlɪti/. *She froze into immobility.* **2** Someone or something that is **immobile** cannot easily move around or be moved around. *A riding accident left him immobile. ...a very heavy or immobile object.* ◆ **immobility** *Weeks of immobility had left every muscle stiff and weak.* ◆◇◇◇ ADJ-GRADED / N-UNCOUNT ADJ / N-UNCOUNT

im·mo·bi·lize /ɪ'məʊbɪlaɪz/ **immobilizes, immobilizing, immobilized;** also spelled **immobilise** in British English. To **immobilize** something or VERB V n

someone means to stop them from moving or operating. ...*a car alarm system that not only sounds off, but also immobilises the engine.*

im·mod·er·ate /ɪˈmɒdərət/. If you describe something as **immoderate**, you disapprove of it because it is too extreme. *He denounced him in immoderate terms.* ADJ-GRADED PRAGMATICS FORMAL

im·mod·est /ɪˈmɒdɪst/. **1** If you describe someone's behaviour as **immodest**, you disapprove of it because you find it shocking, embarrassing, or rude. **2** If you say that someone is **immodest**, you disapprove of the way in which they often boast about how good, important, or clever they are. ADJ-GRADED PRAGMATICS / ADJ-GRADED PRAGMATICS

im·mor·al /ɪˈmɒrəl, AM -ˈmɔːr-/. If you describe someone or their behaviour as **immoral**, you believe that their behaviour is morally wrong. ...*those who think that birth control and abortion are immoral.* ◆ **im·mo·ral·ity** /ˌɪməˈrælɪti/. ...*a reflection of our society's immorality.* ♦◇◇◇◇ ADJ-GRADED PRAGMATICS / N-UNCOUNT

im·mor·tal /ɪˈmɔːtəl/ **immortals**. **1** Someone or something that is **immortal** is famous and likely to be remembered for a long time. ...*Wuthering Heights, Emily Bronte's immortal love story.* ► Also a noun. *He called Moore 'one of the immortals of soccer'.* ◆ **im·mor·tal·ity** /ˌɪmɔːˈtælɪti/. *Some people want to achieve immortality through their works.* **2** Someone or something that is **immortal** will live or last for ever and never die or be destroyed. ► An **immortal** is an immortal being. ...*porcelain figurines of the Chinese immortals.* ◆ **immortality** *The Greeks accepted belief in the immortality of the soul.* **3** If you refer to someone's **immortal** words, you mean that what they said is well-known or memorable, and you are usually about to quote it. *Everyone knows Teddy Roosevelt's immortal words, 'Speak softly and carry a big stick.'* ♦◇◇◇◇ ADJ / N-COUNT / N-UNCOUNT / N-COUNT / N-UNCOUNT / ADJ: ADJ n

im·mor·tal·ize /ɪˈmɔːtəlaɪz/ **immortalizes, immortalizing, immortalized**; also spelled **immortalise** in British English. If someone or something is **immortalized** in a story, film, or work of art, they appear in that story, film, or work of art, and so will be remembered or are well-known. *The town of Whitby was immortalised in Bram Stoker's famous Dracula story.* ...*Colditz, the grim fortress immortalised by films and TV.* VERB be V-ed V-ed Also V n WRITTEN

im·mov·able /ɪˈmuːvəbəl/. **1** An **immovable** object is fixed and cannot be moved. **2** If someone is **immovable** in their attitude to something, they will not change their mind. ADJ / ADJ

im·mune /ɪˈmjuːn/. **1** If you are **immune** to a particular disease, you cannot be affected by it. *Most adults are immune to Rubella.* ◆ **im·mun·ity** /ɪˈmjuːnɪti/. *Birds in outside cages develop immunity to airborne bacteria.* **2** An **immune** response or reaction is a reaction by the body's immune system to something harmful that is affecting it. **3** If someone is **immune** to something that happens or is done, they are not affected by it. *He did not become immune to the sight of death.* **4** Someone or something that is **immune** from a particular process or situation is able to escape it. *No one is immune from scandal.* ◆ **immunity** *The police are offering immunity to witnesses who help identify the murderers.* ● See also diplomatic immunity. ♦♦♦◇◇ ADJ: v-link ADJ / N-UNCOUNT / ADJ: ADJ n TECHNICAL / ADJ: v-link ADJ / ADJ: v-link ADJ / N-UNCOUNT

im'mune system, immune systems. Your immune system consists of all the cells and processes in your body which protect you from illness and infection. ♦♦◇◇◇ N-COUNT

im·mun·ize /ˈɪmjʊnaɪz/ **immunizes, immunizing, immunized**; also spelled **immunise** in British English. If you **are immunized**, you are made immune to a particular disease, often by being given an injection. *Every college student is immunized against hepatitis B...* *He proposed a national program to immunize children.* ◆ **im·mun·iza·tion** /ˌɪmjʊnaɪˈzeɪʃən/ **immunizations** ...*universal immunization against childhood diseases.* ♦◇◇◇◇ VERB: be V-ed be V-ed against n V n Also be V-ed / N-VAR

im·mu·table /ɪˈmjuːtəbəl/. Something that is **immutable** will never change or cannot be changed. ADJ FORMAL

...*the eternal and immutable principles of right and wrong.*

imp /ɪmp/ **imps**. In fairy stories, an **imp** is a small magical creature. N-COUNT

im·pact, **impacts, impacting, impacted**. The noun is pronounced /ˈɪmpækt/. The verb is pronounced /ɪmˈpækt/. **1** The **impact** that something has on a situation, process, or person is a sudden and powerful effect that it has on them. *They expect the meeting to have a marked impact on the future of the country.* **2** To **impact** on a situation, process, or person means to affect them. *Such schemes mean little unless they impact on people...* *The airline industry is in a slump and that's impacted us in this region.* ◆ **im·pact·ed** *African-Americans and Latinos are the communities most impacted by the AIDS crisis.* **3** An **impact** is the action of one object hitting another, or the force with which one object hits another. *A running track should be capable of absorbing the impact of a runner's foot landing on it.* **4** If one object **impacts** on another, it hits it with great force. ...*the sharp tinkle of metal impacting on stone.* ...*about eighty million years ago when a meteor impacted the Earth.* ♦♦♦♦ N-COUNT / VERB V on/upon n V n / ADJ-GRADED / N-VAR / VERB V on/upon/ with n V n FORMAL

im·pair /ɪmˈpeə/ **impairs, impairing, impaired**. If something **impairs** something such as an ability or the functioning of something, it damages it or makes it worse. *Consumption of alcohol impairs your ability to drive a car.* ◆ **im·paired** ...*permanently impaired hearing.* ◆ **im·pair·ment** /ɪmˈpeəmənt/ **impairments** *He has a visual impairment in the right eye.* ♦◇◇◇◇ VERB V n FORMAL / N-VAR

-impaired /-ɪmˈpeəd/. Someone who is **hearing-impaired**, for example, has a disability affecting their hearing. ► The **hearing-impaired**, for example, are people who have a disability affecting their hearing. ...*giving a voice to the speech-impaired.* COMB / COMB

im·pale /ɪmˈpeɪl/ **impales, impaling, impaled**. To **impale** something means to cause it to be pierced by a pointed object. *Researchers observed one bird impale a rodent on a cactus.* VERB: V n Vn on n Also V n with n

im·part /ɪmˈpɑːt/ **imparts, imparting, imparted**. **1** If you **impart** information to people, you tell it to them. ...*the ability to impart knowledge.* **2** If someone or something **imparts** a particular quality to something, they give it that quality. *His production of Harold Pinter's play fails to impart a sense of excitement or danger.* ♦◇◇◇◇ VERB V n FORMAL / VERB: V n to n FORMAL

im·par·tial /ɪmˈpɑːʃəl/. Someone who is **impartial** is not directly involved in a particular situation, and is therefore able to give a fair opinion or decision about it. *As an impartial observer my analysis is supposed to be objective.* ◆ **im·par·tial·ity** /ˌɪmpɑːʃiˈælɪti/. ...*a justice system lacking impartiality.* ◆ **im·par·tial·ly** *He has vowed to oversee the elections impartially.* ♦◇◇◇◇ ADJ-GRADED / N-UNCOUNT / ADV: ADV with v

im·pass·able /ɪmˈpɑːsəbəl, -ˈpæs-/. If a road, path, or route is **impassable**, it is impossible to travel over because it is blocked or in bad condition. ADJ

im·passe /ˈæmpæs, ˈɪm-/. An **impasse** is a situation in which it is impossible to make any progress. *The company says it has reached an impasse in negotiations with the union.* ♦◇◇◇◇ N-SING

im·pas·sioned /ɪmˈpæʃənd/. If someone makes an **impassioned** speech or plea, they express their strong feelings about an issue in a forceful way. ♦◇◇◇◇ ADJ-GRADED WRITTEN

im·pas·sive /ɪmˈpæsɪv/. An **impassive** person or face does not show any emotion. *Through all these stories, Mike has to remain impassive.* ◆ **im·pas·sive·ly** *The lawyer looked impassively at him.* ♦◇◇◇◇ ADJ-GRADED WRITTEN / ADV: ADV with v

im·pa·tient /ɪmˈpeɪʃənt/. **1** If you are **impatient**, you are annoyed because you have to wait too long for something. *The big clubs are becoming increasingly impatient at the rate of progress.* ◆ **im·pa·tient·ly** *People have been waiting impatiently for a chance to improve the situation.* ◆ **im·pa·tience** /ɪmˈpeɪʃəns/. *There is considerable impatience with the slow pace of political change.* **2** If you are **impatient**, you are easily irritated by things. *Beware of being too impatient with others.* ◆ **im·pa·tient·ly** ♦◇◇◇◇ ADJ-GRADED: v-link ADJ / ADV: ADV with v N-UNCOUNT / ADJ-GRADED / ADV-GRADED:

'Come on, David,' Harry said impatiently. ADV with v
♦ **impatience** There was a hint of impatience in N-UNCOUNT
his tone. **3** If you are **impatient** to do something or ADJ:
impatient for something to happen, you are eager v-link ADJ,
to do it or for it to happen and do not want to wait. ADJ forn
He was impatient to get home. ♦ **im·pa·tience** She N-UNCOUNT:
showed impatience to continue the climb. N for n

im·peach /ɪmˈpiːtʃ/ **impeaches, impeaching,** ◆◇◇◇◇
impeached. If a court or a group in authority **im-** VERB: V n
peaches a president or other senior official, it charges them with committing a crime which makes
them unfit to hold office. ♦ **im·peach·ment** N-VAR
/ɪmˈpiːtʃmənt/ **impeachments** If his action proves
to be unconstitutional, that would be grounds for
impeachment.

im·pec·cable /ɪmˈpekəbəl/. If you describe some- ◆◇◇◇◇
thing such as someone's behaviour or appearance ADJ-GRADED
as **impeccable**, you are emphasizing that it is excel- PRAGMATICS
lent and has no faults. She had impeccable taste in
clothes. ♦ **im·pec·cably** /ɪmˈpekəbli/. He was ADV-GRADED
charming, considerate and impeccably mannered.

im·pecu·ni·ous /ˌɪmpɪˈkjuːniəs/. Someone who is ADJ-GRADED
impecunious has very little money. FORMAL

im·pede /ɪmˈpiːd/ **impedes, impeding, imped-** ◆◇◇◇◇
ed. If you **impede** someone or something, you VERB
make their movement, development, or progress FORMAL
difficult. Debris and fallen rock are impeding the
progress of the rescue workers.

im·pedi·ment /ɪmˈpedɪmənt/ **impediments. 1** An ◆◇◇◇◇
impediment to something prevents it from happen- N-COUNT
ing, or from progressing or developing easily. The FORMAL
current level of rates was not an impediment to economic recovery... There was no legal impediment to
the marriage. **2** Someone who has a speech **impedi-** N-COUNT
ment has a disability which makes speaking difficult.

im·pel /ɪmˈpel/ **impels, impelling, impelled.** VERB
When something such as an emotion **impels** you to V n to-inf
do something, it affects you so strongly that you feel
forced to do it. ...the courage and competitiveness
which impels him to take risks.

im·pend·ing /ɪmˈpendɪŋ/. An **impending** event is ◆◇◇◇◇
one that is going to happen very soon. I awoke with ADJ: ADJ n
a feeling of impending disaster. FORMAL

im·pen·etrable /ɪmˈpenɪtrəbəl/. **1** If you describe ◆◇◇◇◇
something such as a barrier or a forest as **impen-** ADJ-GRADED
etrable, you mean that it is impossible or very difficult to get through. **2** If you describe something ADJ-GRADED
such as a book or a theory as **impenetrable**, you are PRAGMATICS
emphasizing that it is impossible or very difficult to
understand. ♦ **im·pen·etrably** ...seven impen- ADV-GRADED:
etrably detailed reports on product sales. ADV adj

im·pera·tive /ɪmˈperətɪv/ **imperatives. 1** If it is ◆◇◇◇◇
imperative that something is done, that thing is ex- ADJ-GRADED
tremely important and must be done. It was im- FORMAL
perative that he act as naturally as possible. **2** An N-COUNT
imperative is something that is extremely impor- FORMAL
tant and must be done. The most important
political imperative is to limit the number of US
casualties. **3** In grammar, a clause that is in the **im-** N-SING:
perative contains the base form of a verb and theN
usually has no subject. Examples are 'Go away' and
'Please be careful'. Clauses of this kind are typically
used to tell someone to do something. **4** An **im-** N-COUNT
perative is a verb in the base form that is used,
usually without a subject, in an imperative clause.

im·per·cep·tible /ˌɪmpəˈseptɪbəl/. Something that ADJ
is **imperceptible** is so small or slight that it is not
noticed or cannot be seen. Brian's hesitation was almost imperceptible. ♦ **im·per·cep·tibly** The disease ADV
develops gradually and imperceptibly.

im·per·fect /ɪmˈpɜːfɪkt/. **1** Something that is **im-** ◆◇◇◇◇
perfect has faults and is not exactly as you would ADJ-GRADED
like it to be. We live in an imperfect world. ♦ **im-** FORMAL
·per·fect·ly This effect was imperfectly understood ADV-GRADED
by designers... They both spoke English, though imperfectly. ♦ **im·per·fec·tion** /ˌɪmpəˈfekʃən/ **imper-** N-VAR
fections. An **imperfection** is a small fault in something. I was obsessed by my physical imperfections.
2 In grammar, the **imperfect** or the **imperfect** tense N-SING:

of a verb is used in describing continuous situations theN
or repeated actions in the past. In English, the past
continuous (as in 'I was reading') is sometimes called
the **imperfect**.

im·perial /ɪmˈpɪəriəl/. **1 Imperial** is used to refer ◆◆◇◇◇
to things or people that are or were connected with ADJ: ADJ n
an empire. ...the Imperial Palace in Tokyo. **2** The ADJ: ADJ n
imperial system of measurement uses inches, feet,
and yards to measure length, ounces and pounds to
measure weight, and pints and gallons to measure
volume.

im·peri·al·ism /ɪmˈpɪəriəlɪzəm/. **Imperialism** is a ◆◇◇◇◇
system in which a rich and powerful country con- N-UNCOUNT
trols other countries; used showing disapproval. PRAGMATICS
...the age of imperialism. ♦ **im·peri·al·ist, imperi-** N-COUNT
alists. Imperialists are trying to re-establish colonial rule in the country... The developed nations
have all benefited from their imperialist exploitation.

im·peri·al·is·tic /ɪmˌpɪəriəˈlɪstɪk/. If you describe a ADJ
country as **imperialistic**, you disapprove of it be- PRAGMATICS
cause it wants control over other countries.

im·per·il /ɪmˈperɪl/ **imperils, imperilling, imper-** VERB
illed; spelled **imperiling, imperiled** in American V n
English. Something that **imperils** you puts you in FORMAL
danger. You imperilled the lives of other road users.

im·peri·ous /ɪmˈpɪəriəs/. If you describe someone ADJ-GRADED
as **imperious**, you mean that they have a proud WRITTEN
manner and expect to be obeyed. She gave him a
witheringly imperious look. ♦ **im·peri·ous·ly** Im- ADV-GRADED:
periously she beckoned me out of the room. ADV with v

im·per·ish·able /ɪmˈperɪʃəbəl/. Something that is ADJ
imperishable cannot disappear or be destroyed. My LITERARY
memories are within me, imperishable.

im·per·meable /ɪmˈpɜːmiəbəl/. Something that is ADJ
impermeable will not allow fluid to pass through it. FORMAL
The canoe is made from an impermeable wood.

im·per·son·al /ɪmˈpɜːsənəl/. **1** If you describe a ◆◇◇◇◇
place, organization, or activity as **impersonal**, you ADJ-GRADED
mean that it is not very friendly and makes you feel
unimportant because it involves or is used by a
large number of people. ...large impersonal orphan-
ages. **2** If you describe someone's behaviour as **im-** ADJ-GRADED
personal, you mean that they act towards other
people in a detached way, not caring particularly
who they are. We must be as impersonal as a sur-
geon with his knife. ♦ **im·per·son·al·ly** The doctor ADV-GRADED
treated Ted gently but impersonally. **3** An **imper-** ADJ-GRADED
sonal place, statistic, or label does not give any
information about the character of the person to
which it belongs or relates. The room was neat and
impersonal.

im·per·son·ate /ɪmˈpɜːsəneɪt/ **impersonates,** ◆◇◇◇◇
impersonating, impersonated. If someone **im-** VERB
personates a person, they pretend to be that per- V n
son, either to deceive people or to make people
laugh. He was returned to prison in 1977 for impersonating a police officer. ♦ **im·per·sona·tion** N-COUNT
/ɪmˌpɜːsəˈneɪʃən/, **impersonations** She excelled at
impersonations of her teachers. ♦ **im·per·sona·tor** N-COUNT
/ɪmˈpɜːsəneɪtə/, **impersonators.** An **impersonator**
is a performer who impersonates famous people.

im·per·ti·nent /ɪmˈpɜːtɪnənt/. If someone is **imper-** ADJ-GRADED
tinent, they talk or behave in a rather impolite and FORMAL
disrespectful way. Would it be impertinent to ask
where exactly you were?. ♦ **im·per·ti·nence** N-VAR
/ɪmˈpɜːtɪnəns/, **impertinences** The sheer imperti-
nence of this man is phenomenal!

im·per·turb·able /ˌɪmpəˈtɜːbəbəl/. If you describe ADJ-GRADED
someone as **imperturbable**, you mean that they re- WRITTEN
main calm and untroubled, even in a situation that
is disturbing.

im·per·vi·ous /ɪmˈpɜːviəs/. **1** Someone or some- ADJ-GRADED
thing that is **impervious** to someone's actions is not
affected or influenced by them. She seems almost
impervious to the criticism. **2** Something that is **im-** ADJ
pervious to water, heat, or a particular object is able
to resist it or stop it passing through it.

im·petu·ous /ɪmˈpetʃuəs/. If you describe someone ADJ-GRADED
as **impetuous**, you mean that they are likely to act PRAGMATICS
quickly and suddenly without thinking or being

careful. *He was young and impetuous.* ◆ **im·petu·os·ity** /ɪm,petʃʊˈɒsɪtɪ/. *With characteristic impetuosity, he announced he was leaving school.* `N-UNCOUNT`

im·petus /ˈɪmpɪtəs/. Something that gives a process **impetus** or an **impetus** makes it happen or progress more quickly. *This decision will give renewed impetus to the economic regeneration of east London.* `◆◇◇◇◇ N-UNCOUNT: also a N`

im·pinge /ɪmˈpɪndʒ/ **impinges, impinging, impinged.** Something that **impinges** on you affects you. *...the cuts in defence spending that have impinged on two of the region's largest employers.* `VERB V on/upon n FORMAL`

imp·ish /ˈɪmpɪʃ/. If you describe someone or their behaviour as **impish**, you mean that they are rather cheeky or naughty in a playful way. *...his impish sense of humour.* `ADJ-GRADED`

im·plac·able /ɪmˈplækəbəl/. If you say that someone is **implacable**, you mean that they have very strong feelings, usually feelings of hostility or disapproval, which you are unable to change. *...a ruthless and implacable enemy.* ◆ **im·plac·ably** *His union was implacably opposed to the privatization of the company.* `◆◇◇◇◇ ADJ-GRADED` `ADV-GRADED`

im·plant, implants, implanting, implanted. The verb is pronounced /ɪmˈplɑːnt, -ˈplænt/. The noun is pronounced /ˈɪmplɑːnt, -plænt/. **1** To **implant** something into a person's body means to put it there, usually by means of a medical operation. *Surgeons decided to implant the pump, called Heartmate.* ◆ **im·plan·ta·tion** /,ɪmplɑːnˈteɪʃən, -plæn-/. *The embryos were tested to determine their sex prior to implantation.* **2** An **implant** is something that is implanted into a person's body. *A woman had a right to choose to have a breast implant.* **3** When an egg or embryo **implants** in the womb, it becomes established there and can then develop. *Non-identical twins are the result of two fertilised eggs implanting in the uterus at the same time.* ◆ **implantation** *...the 11 days required to allow for normal implantation of a fertilized egg.* **4** If you **implant** an idea or attitude in people, you make it become accepted or believed. *This would implant the idea that the communists are the legitimate rulers of the country.* `◆◇◇◇◇` `VERB: V n in/into n V n` `N-UNCOUNT` `N-COUNT` `VERB V in n Also V` `N-UNCOUNT` `VERB: V n in/into n V n`

im·plau·sible /ɪmˈplɔːzɪbəl/. If you describe something as **implausible**, you believe that it is unlikely to be true. *It sounded like a convenient and implausible excuse.* ◆ **im·plau·sibly** *They are, rather implausibly, close friends.* `ADJ-GRADED` `ADV-GRADED`

im·ple·ment, implements, implementing, implemented. The verb is pronounced /ˈɪmplɪment/. The noun is pronounced /ˈɪmplɪmənt/. **1** If you **implement** something such as a plan, you ensure that what has been planned is done. *The government promised to implement a new system to control financial loan institutions.* ◆ **im·ple·men·ta·tion** /,ɪmplɪmənˈteɪʃən/. *Very little has been achieved in the implementation of the peace agreement.* **2** An **implement** is a tool or other piece of equipment. *...knives and other useful implements.* `◆◆◇◇◇` `VERB V n` `N-UNCOUNT` `N-COUNT FORMAL`

im·pli·cate /ˈɪmplɪkeɪt/ **implicates, implicating, implicated.** To **implicate** someone or something means to show or claim that they were involved in a crime or responsible for something bad. *Allegations had appeared in the press implicating the army and police in some of the killings.* ◆ **im·pli·cat·ed.** If someone or something is **implicated** in a crime or a bad situation, they are shown to be involved in it or responsible for it. ◆ **im·pli·ca·tion** *Implication in a murder finally brought him to the gallows.* `◆◇◇◇◇` `VERB: V n V n in n` `ADJ: v-link ADJ` `N-UNCOUNT`

im·pli·ca·tion /,ɪmplɪˈkeɪʃən/ **implications.** **1** The **implications** of something are the things that are likely to happen as a result of it. *...the political implications of his decision to prosecute.* **2** The **implication** of a statement, event, or situation is what it implies or suggests. *The implication was obvious: vote for us or it will be very embarrassing for you.* ● If you say that something is the case **by implication**, you mean that a statement, event, or situation `◆◆◇◇◇` `N-COUNT` `N-COUNT` `PHRASE`

implies that it is the case. *Now his authority and, by implication, that of the whole management team are under threat.* **3** See also **implicate**.

im·plic·it /ɪmˈplɪsɪt/. **1** Something that is **implicit** is expressed in an indirect way. *It was his intention to make explicit in the film what was only implicit in the play.* ◆ **im·plic·it·ly** *Mr Patten implicitly accepted that there would not be nationwide tests.* **2** If a quality or element is **implicit** in something, it is involved in it or is shown by it. *Try and learn from the lessons implicit in the failure of your marriage.* **3** If you say that someone has an **implicit** belief or faith in something, you mean that they have complete faith in it and no doubts at all. *He had implicit faith in the noble intentions of the Emperor.* ◆ **implicitly** *I trust him implicitly.* `◆◆◇◇◇` `ADJ-GRADED` `ADV: ADV with v ADJ: v-link ADJ in n FORMAL` `ADJ-GRADED` `ADV-GRADED: ADV after v`

im·plode /ɪmˈpləʊd/ **implodes, imploding, imploded.** **1** If something **implodes**, it collapses into itself in a sudden and violent way. **2** If something such as an organization or a system **implodes**, it suddenly fails or ceases to exist. `VERB: V` `VERB: V`

im·plore /ɪmˈplɔː/ **implores, imploring, implored.** If you **implore** someone to do something, you desperately beg them to do it. *'Tell me what to do!' she implored him... Michael, I implore you. Don't say anything... Frank looked at Jim with imploring eyes.* `VERB: V n to-inf V n with quote V n V-ing Also V with quote`

im·ply /ɪmˈplaɪ/ **implies, implying, implied.** **1** If you **imply** that something is the case, you say something which indirectly indicates that it is the case. *You implied that I was a kind of monster by confronting you... She felt undermined by the implied criticism.* **2** If an event or situation **implies** that something is the case, it makes you think it likely that it is the case. *The meeting in no way implies a resumption of contacts with the terrorists.* `◆◆◆◇◇` `VERB V that V-ed Also V n` `VERB: V that V n`

im·po·lite /,ɪmpəˈlaɪt/. If you say that someone is **impolite**, you mean that they are rather rude and do not have good manners. *It would be most ungracious and impolite to refuse a simple invitation.* `ADJ-GRADED`

im·pon·der·able /ɪmˈpɒndərəbəl/ **imponderables.** An **imponderable** is something unknown, which it is difficult or impossible to estimate or make correct guesses about. *The big imponderable, of course, is what's going to happen to interest rates.* `N-COUNT`

im·port, imports, importing, imported. The verb is pronounced /ɪmˈpɔːt/. The noun is pronounced /ˈɪmpɔːt/. **1** To **import** products means to buy them from another country for use in your own country. *To import from Russia, a Ukrainian firm needs Russian roubles.* ▸ Also a noun. *...restrictions on the import of Polish coal.* ◆ **im·por·ta·tion** /,ɪmpɔːˈteɪʃən/. *...restrictions concerning the importation of birds.* ◆ **im·port·er, importers.** An **importer** is a country, firm, or person that buys goods from another country for use in their own country. **2 Imports** are products bought from another country for use in your own country. *...French farmers protesting about what they say are cheap imports from other European countries.* **3** The **import** of something is its importance. *Such arguments are of little import.* **4** The **import** of something is its meaning, especially when the meaning is not clearly expressed. *I have already spoken about the import of his speech.* `◆◆◆◆◇` `VERB: V n V from n` `N-UNCOUNT: also N in pl` `N-UNCOUNT` `N-COUNT` `N-COUNT` `N-UNCOUNT FORMAL` `N-SING: with poss FORMAL`

im·por·tant /ɪmˈpɔːtənt/. **1** Something that is **important** is very significant, highly valued, or necessary. *Her sons are the most important thing in her life. ...an important economic challenge to the government.* ◆ **im·por·tance** *Safety is of paramount importance.* ◆ **im·por·tant·ly** *I was hungry, and, more importantly, my children were hungry.* **2** Someone who is **important** has influence or power within a society or a particular group. *He was the most important person on the island.* ◆ **im·por·tance** *She lost much of her importance both in the religious and social spheres.* `◆◆◆◆◇` `ADJ-GRADED` `N-UNCOUNT` `ADV-GRADED` `ADJ-GRADED` `N-UNCOUNT`

im·por·tune /,ɪmpɔːˈtjuːn, AM -ˈtuːn/ **importunes, importuning, importuned.** If someone **importunes** someone else, they ask that person for `VERB: V n V n forn Also V n to-inf FORMAL`

something or urge them to do something, in an annoying way. *I would visit the kitchen to importune the cook for a spoonful of black treacle.* ♦ **im·por·tu·nate** /ɪmˈpɔːtʃʊnət/. If you describe someone as **importunate**, you think they are annoying because they keep trying to get something from you. ADJ

im·pose /ɪmˈpəʊz/ **imposes, imposing, imposed.** 1 If you **impose** something on people, you use your authority to force them to accept it. *A third of companies reviewing pay since last August have imposed a pay freeze of up to a year.* ♦ **im·po·si·tion** /ˌɪmpəˈzɪʃən/. *...the imposition of a day-time ban on cycling in the city centre.* 2 If you **impose** your opinions or beliefs on other people, you try and make people accept them as a rule or as a model to copy. *Parents of either sex should beware of imposing their own tastes on their children.* 3 If something **imposes** strain, pressure, or hardship on someone or something, it causes them to experience it. *The filming imposed an additional strain on her.* 4 If someone **imposes** on you, they unreasonably expect you to do something for them, for example allow them to stay with you in your home. *I was afraid you'd simply feel we were imposing on you... I didn't want to impose myself on my married friends.* ♦ **im·po·si·tion, impositions** *I know this is an imposition. But please hear me out.* ◆◆◆◆ VERB: V n on n V n N-UNCOUNT VERB V n on n VERB V on/upon n V pron-refl on n N-COUNT

im·pos·ing /ɪmˈpəʊzɪŋ/. An **imposing** thing or person has an impressive appearance or manner. *...the imposing wrought-iron gates at the entrance to the estate.* ◆◆◇◇ ADJ-GRADED

im·pos·si·ble /ɪmˈpɒsɪbəl/. 1 Something that is **impossible** cannot be done or cannot happen. *It was impossible for anyone to get in because no one knew the password... The tax is impossible to administer... You shouldn't promise what's impossible.* ▶ **The impossible** is something which is impossible. *They were expected to do the impossible.* ♦ **im·pos·si·bly** *Mathematical physics is an almost impossibly difficult subject.* ♦ **im·pos·si·bil·ity, impossibilities** *...the impossibility of knowing absolute truth.* 2 An **impossible** situation or an **impossible** position is one that is very difficult to deal with. *The Government was now in an almost impossible position.* 3 If you describe someone as **impossible**, you are annoyed that their bad behaviour or strong views make them difficult to deal with. *You are an impossible man!* ◆◆◆◇ ADJ-GRADED N-SING: the N ADV: ADV adj N-VAR ADJ: ADJ n ADJ-GRADED PRAGMATICS

im·pos·tor /ɪmˈpɒstə/ **impostors;** also spelled **imposter.** Someone who is an **impostor** is dishonestly pretending to be someone else in order to get something they want. *He was an imposter, who masqueraded as a doctor when he was totally unqualified.* N-COUNT

im·po·tent /ˈɪmpətənt/. 1 If someone feels **impotent**, they feel that they have no power to influence people or events. *The aggression of a bully leaves people feeling hurt, angry and impotent.* ♦ **im·po·tence** *...a sense of impotence in the face of deplorable events.* 2 If a man is **impotent**, he is unable to have sex normally, because his penis fails to get hard or stay hard. ♦ **impotence** *...men who suffer from impotence.* ◆◇◇◇ ADJ-GRADED N-UNCOUNT ADJ N-UNCOUNT

im·pound /ɪmˈpaʊnd/ **impounds, impounding, impounded.** If something is **impounded** by police, customs officers, or other officials, they officially take possession of it because a law or rule has been broken. *The police moved in, arrested him and impounded the cocaine.* ◆◇◇◇ VERB: be V-ed V n

im·pov·er·ish /ɪmˈpɒvərɪʃ/ **impoverishes, impoverishing, impoverished.** 1 Something that **impoverishes** a person or a country makes them poor. *We need to reduce the burden of taxes that impoverish the economy.* ♦ **im·pov·er·ished** *The goal is to lure businesses into impoverished areas.* ♦ **im·pov·er·ish·ment** /ɪmˈpɒvərɪʃmənt/. *The economic reforms are to blame for the wholesale impoverishment of the country.* 2 A person or thing that **impoverishes** something makes it worse in quality. *Cutting down trees impoverishes the soil.* ◆◇◇◇ VERB V n ADJ-GRADED N-UNCOUNT VERB V n

♦ **impoverishment** *...the greed and aesthetic impoverishment that characterised their culture.* N-UNCOUNT

im·prac·ti·cable /ɪmˈpræktɪkəbəl/. If something such as a course of action is **impracticable**, it is impossible to do. *Such measures would be highly impracticable and almost impossible to apply.* ADJ-GRADED

im·prac·ti·cal /ɪmˈpræktɪkəl/. 1 If you describe an object, idea, or course of action as **impractical**, you mean that it is not sensible or realistic, and does not work well in practice. *Once there were regularly scheduled airlines, it became impractical to make a business trip by ocean liner.* 2 If you describe someone as **impractical**, you mean that they do not have the abilities or skills to do practical work such as making, repairing, or organizing things. ◆◇◇◇ ADJ-GRADED ADJ-GRADED

im·pre·ca·tion /ˌɪmprɪˈkeɪʃən/ **imprecations.** An **imprecation** is a curse or insult. N-VAR FORMAL

im·pre·cise /ˌɪmprɪˈsaɪs/. Something that is **imprecise** is not clear, accurate, or precise. *Utilitarianism is a very broad, imprecise concept.* ♦ **im·pre·ci·sion** /ˌɪmprɪˈsɪʒən/. *...the confusion and imprecision in their thinking.* ADJ-GRADED N-UNCOUNT

im·preg·na·ble /ɪmˈpregnəbəl/. 1 If you describe a building or other place as **impregnable**, you mean it is so strong or inaccessible that it cannot be broken into. *In those impregnable mountains, the guerrillas could hold out for years.* 2 If you say that a person or group is **impregnable**, or their position is **impregnable**, you think they cannot be defeated by anyone, for example in political competition or in a sporting contest. *The Bundesbank's seemingly impregnable position has begun to weaken.* ADJ ADJ

im·preg·nate /ˈɪmpregneɪt, AM ɪmˈpreg-/ **impregnates, impregnating, impregnated.** 1 If someone or something **impregnates** a thing with a substance, they make the substance spread through it. *...a block of plastic impregnated with a light-absorbing dye.* ♦ **impreg·nat·ed** *...nicotine-impregnated chewing gum.* 2 When a man or a male animal **impregnates** a female, he makes her pregnant. VERB: V n with n V-ed Also V n COMB VERB: V n FORMAL

im·pre·sa·rio /ˌɪmprɪˈsɑːriəʊ/ **impresarios.** An **impresario** is a person who arranges for plays, concerts, and other entertainments to be performed. N-COUNT

im·press /ɪmˈpres/ **impresses, impressing, impressed.** 1 If something **impresses** you, you feel great admiration for it. *What impressed him most was their speed... Cannon's film impresses on many levels.* ♦ **im·pressed** *I'm very impressed with the new airport... He went away suitably impressed.* 2 If you **impress** something on someone, you make them understand its importance or degree. *I had always impressed upon the children that if they worked hard they would succeed in life... He said he'd be telephoning other Western leaders to impress on them the need to support Soviet reforms.* 3 If someone or something **impresses** you as a particular thing, usually a good one, they gives you the impression of being that thing. *Billy Sullivan had impressed me as a fine man.* ◆◆◇◇ VERB V n V ADJ-GRADED: v-link ADJ VERB V on/upon n that V on/upon n n Also V on/ upon n wh VERB V n as n/-ing

im·pres·sion /ɪmˈpreʃən/ **impressions.** 1 Your **impression** of a person or thing is what you think they are like, usually after having seen or heard them. Your **impression** of a situation is what you think is going on. *What were your first impressions of college?... My impression is that they are totally out of control.* 2 If someone or something gives a particular **impression**, they cause you to believe that something is the case, often when it is not actually the case. *I don't want to give the impression that I'm running away from the charges.* 3 If you are **under the impression** that something is the case, you believe that it is the case, usually when it is not. *He had apparently been under the impression that a military coup was in progress.* 4 If someone or something **makes an impression**, they have a strong effect on people or a situation. *He has told me his plans and he's made a good impression on me.* ◆◆◇◇ N-COUNT N-SING PHRASE PHRASE

5 An **impression** by someone is an amusing imitation N-COUNT

I

of a well-known person. ...*doing impressions of Sean Connery and James Mason.*

6 An **impression** of an object is a mark or outline that it has left after being pressed hard onto a surface. ...*fossil impressions.*   N-COUNT

im·pres·sion·able /ɪm'preʃənəbəl/. Someone who is **impressionable** is not very critical and is therefore easy to influence. *The law is intended to safeguard young and impressionable viewers from exploitation.*   ADJ-GRADED

im·pres·sion·ism /ɪm'preʃənɪzəm/. **Impressionism** is a style of painting developed in France between 1870 and 1900 which concentrated on showing the effects of light on things rather than on clear and exact detail. ♦ **im·pres·sion·ist, Impressionists** *The Impressionists revolutionised art and the way we see the world. ...Paris' magnificent collection of Impressionist paintings.*   N-UNCOUNT   N-COUNT

im·pres·sion·ist /ɪm'preʃənɪst/ **impressionists.** **1** An **impressionist** is an entertainer who does amusing imitations of well-known people. **2** See also **Impressionism**.   ♦◇◇◇◇   N-COUNT

im·pres·sion·is·tic /ɪm,preʃə'nɪstɪk/. An **impressionistic** work of art or piece of writing shows the artist's or writer's impressions of something rather than giving clear details.   ADJ-GRADED

im·pres·sive /ɪm'presɪv/. Something that is **impressive** impresses you. *It is an impressive achievement.* ♦ **im·pres·sive·ly** ...*an impressively bright and energetic American woman... The socialists performed impressively in the legislative elections.*   ♦♦♦◇◇   ADJ-GRADED   ADV-GRADED

im·print, imprints, imprinting, imprinted. The noun is pronounced /'ɪmprɪnt/. The verb is pronounced /ɪm'prɪnt/. **1** If something leaves an **imprint** on a place or on your mind, it has a strong and lasting effect on it. *Few cities in America bear the imprint of Japanese money more than Los Angeles.* **2** When something **is imprinted** on your memory, it is firmly fixed so that you will not forget it. *He repeated the names, as if to imprint them in his mind.* **3** An **imprint** is a mark or outline made by the pressure of one object on another. **4** If a surface **is imprinted** with a mark or design, that mark or design is printed on the surface or pressed into it. ...*a racket with the club's badge imprinted on the strings.*   ♦◇◇◇◇   N-COUNT   VERB: beV-ed on/in n; V n on/in n   N-COUNT   VERB: beV-ed with/on n; V-ed

im·pris·on /ɪm'prɪzən/ **imprisons, imprisoning, imprisoned.** If someone **is imprisoned**, they are locked up or kept somewhere, usually as a punishment for a crime or for political opposition. *Dutch colonial authorities imprisoned him for his part in the independence movement.* ♦ **im·pris·on·ment** *She was sentenced to seven years' imprisonment.*   ♦♦◇◇◇   VERB: beV-ed; V n   N-UNCOUNT

im·prob·able /ɪm'prɒbəbəl/. **1** Something that is **improbable** is unlikely to be true or to happen. *It seems improbable that this year's figure will fall much below last year's 75,000.* ♦ **im·prob·abil·ity** /ɪm,prɒbə'bɪlɪti/ **improbabilities** ...*the improbability of such an outcome.* **2** If you describe something as **improbable**, you mean it is strange or ridiculous. *On the face of it, their marriage seems an improbable alliance.* ♦ **im·prob·ably** *The sea is an improbably pale turquoise.*   ♦◇◇◇◇   ADJ-GRADED   N-VAR   ADJ-GRADED   ADV-GRADED

im·promp·tu /ɪm'prɒmptjuː, AM -tuː/. An **impromptu** action is one that you do without planning it in advance. *The children put on an impromptu concert for the visitors.*   ♦◇◇◇◇   ADJ

im·prop·er /ɪm'prɒpə/. **1** **Improper** activities are illegal or dishonest. *Mr Matthews maintained that he had done nothing improper.* ♦ **im·prop·er·ly** *I acted neither fraudulently nor improperly.* **2** **Improper** conditions or methods of treatment are not suitable or adequate for a particular purpose. *The improper use of medicine could lead to severe adverse reactions.* ♦ **improperly** *Doctors were improperly trained.* **3** If you describe someone's behaviour as **improper**, you mean that it is impolite or shocking. *It would be improper to speculate on Dr Holt's suicide.* ♦ **improperly** *Fundamentalist groups have*   ♦◇◇◇◇   ADJ; FORMAL   ADJ-GRADED: ADV with v; ADJ: ADJ n; FORMAL   ADV: ADV with v; ADJ-GRADED; DATED   ADV-GRADED

attacked women they regarded as improperly dressed.

im·pro·pri·ety /,ɪmprə'praɪɪti/ **improprieties.** **Impropriety** is improper behaviour. *He resigned amid allegations of financial impropriety.*   N-VAR   FORMAL

im·prove /ɪm'pruːv/ **improves, improving, improved.** **1** If something **improves**, it gets better. *The weather is beginning to improve... He improved their house.* **2** If a skill you have **improves**, you get better at it. *The other students were improving slightly... He said he was going to improve his football.* **3** If you **improve** after an illness or an injury, your health gets better or you get stronger. **4** If you **improve on** a previous achievement of your own or of someone else, you achieve a better standard or result. *We need to improve on our performance against France.*   ♦♦♦♦   V-ERG   V n   V-ERG   V   VERB: V   VERB   V on n

im·prove·ment /ɪm'pruːvmənt/ **improvements.** **1** If there is an **improvement** in something, it becomes better. If you make **improvements** to something, you make it better. *There is considerable room for improvement in state facilities for treating the mentally handicapped.* **2** If you say that something is an **improvement** on a previous thing or situation, you mean that it is better than that thing. *The system we introduced in 1980 has been a great improvement.*   ♦♦♦◇◇   N-VAR   N-COUNT

im·provi·dent /ɪm'prɒvɪdənt/. If you describe someone as **improvident**, you disapprove of them because they are wasteful and do not think about the future.   ADJ-GRADED; PRAGMATICS; FORMAL

im·pro·vise /'ɪmprəvaɪz/ **improvises, improvising, improvised.** **1** If you **improvise**, you make or do something using whatever you have or without having planned it in advance. *The vet had improvised a harness. ...tents improvised from sheets of heavy plastic draped over wooden poles.* ♦ **im·provi·sa·tion** /,ɪmprəvaɪ'zeɪʃən, AM -vɪz-/, **improvisations** *Funds were not abundant and clever improvisation was necessary.* **2** When performers **improvise**, they invent the music or words as they play, sing, or speak. When they **improvise** on a tune or story, they invent variations of it. *Uncle Richard intoned a chapter from the Bible and improvised a prayer... I think that the art of a storyteller is to take the story and improvise on it.*   ♦◇◇◇◇   VERB: V; V n; V-ed   N-VAR   VERB: V; V n; V on n

im·pru·dent /ɪm'pruːdənt/. If you describe someone's behaviour as **imprudent**, you think it is not sensible or carefully thought out. ...*an imprudent investment he made many years ago.*   ADJ-GRADED; FORMAL

im·pu·dent /'ɪmpjudənt/. If you describe someone as **impudent**, you mean they behave or speak rudely or disrespectfully, or do something they have no right to do. ♦ **im·pu·dence** *One sister had the impudence to wear the other's clothes.*   ADJ-GRADED; FORMAL   N-UNCOUNT

im·pugn /ɪm'pjuːn/ **impugns, impugning, impugned.** If you **impugn** something such as someone's motives or integrity, you imply that they are not entirely honest or honourable. *They have impugned the honour of the Soviet Army.*   VERB; V n; FORMAL

im·pulse /'ɪmpʌls/ **impulses.** **1** An **impulse** is a sudden desire to do something. *Unable to resist the impulse, he glanced at the sea again.* **2** If you do something **on impulse**, you suddenly decide to do it, without planning it. **3** An **impulse** buy or **impulse** purchase is something that you decide to buy when you see it, although you had not planned to buy it. **4** An **impulse** is a short electrical signal that is sent along a wire or nerve or through the air, usually as one of a series.   ♦♦◇◇◇   N-COUNT   PHRASE   ADJ: ADJ n   N-COUNT

im·pul·sive /ɪm'pʌlsɪv/. If you describe someone as **impulsive**, you mean that they do things suddenly without thinking about them carefully first. *Avoid making an impulsive decision.* ♦ **im·pul·sive·ly** *Impulsively she patted him on the arm.* ♦ **im·pul·sive·ness** ...*Walesa's flamboyant impulsiveness.*   ♦◇◇◇◇   ADJ-GRADED   ADV-GRADED: ADV with v   N-UNCOUNT

im·pu·ni·ty /ɪm'pjuːnɪti/. If you say that someone does something bad **with impunity**, you disapprove of the fact that they are not punished for doing it. *These gangs operate with apparent impunity.*   ♦◇◇◇◇   PHRASE; PRAGMATICS

im·pure /ɪmˈpjʊə/. **1** A substance that is **impure** is ADJ-GRADED not of good quality because it has other substances mixed with it. **2** If you describe thoughts and ac- ADJ-GRADED tions as **impure**, you mean they are concerned with DATED sex and you regard them as sinful.

im·pu·rity /ɪmˈpjʊərɪti/ **impurities**. **Impurities** are N-COUNT substances that are present in small quantities in another substance and make it dirty or of an unacceptable quality. *The air in the factory is filtered to remove impurities.*

im·pute /ɪmˈpjuːt/ **imputes, imputing, imputed.** VERB If you **impute** something such as blame or guilt to V n to n someone, you believe and say that they are to FORMAL blame for something. If you **impute** something such as motives or ideas to someone, you believe and say that they have those motives or ideas. *It is grossly unfair to impute blame to the United Nations.*

in 1 position or movement

in /ɪn/. In addition to the uses shown below, **in** is ◆◆◆◆◆ used after some verbs, nouns, and adjectives in order to introduce extra information. **In** is also used with verbs of movement such as 'walk' and 'push', and in phrasal verbs such as 'give in' and 'dig in'.

1 Someone or something that is **in** something else is PREP enclosed by it or surrounded by it. If you put something in a container, you move it so that it is enclosed by the container. *He was in his car... Put the knives in the kitchen drawer... Mix the sugar and the water in a cup.*
2 If something happens **in** a place, it happens there. PREP *Those rockets landed in the desert.* **3** If you **are in**, you ADV: are present at your home or place of work. *My flat-* be ADV *mate was in at the time... He has had to be in every day.*
4 When someone comes **in**, they enter a room or ADV building. *They shook hands and went in.* **5** If a train, ADV boat, or plane has come **in** or is **in**, it has arrived at a station, port, or airport. *...every plane coming in from Melbourne... Look. The train's in. We'll have to run for it now.* **6** When the sea or tide comes **in**, the sea moves ADV towards the shore rather than away from it. *If the tide was in they went swimming.*
7 Something that is **in** a window, especially a shop PREP window, is just behind the window so that you can see it from outside. *There was a camera for sale in the window.* **8** When you see something **in** a mirror, you see PREP its reflection.
9 If you are dressed **in** a piece of clothing, you are PREP wearing it. *...three women in black... She's usually dressed in blue jeans.* **10** Something that is covered or PREP wrapped **in** something else has that thing over or round its surface. *His legs were covered in mud.* **11** If PREP there is something such as a crack or hole **in** something, there is a crack or hole somewhere on its surface. *...an unsightly hole in the garden.*

in 2 inclusion or involvement

in /ɪn/. **1** If something is **in** a book, film, play, or ◆◆◆◆◆ picture, you can read it or see it there. *...one of the* PREP *funniest scenes in the film.* **2** If you are **in** some- PREP thing such as a play or a race, you are one of the people taking part. *Alf offered her a part in the play he was directing.* **3** Something that is **in** a group or PREP collection is a member of it or part of it. *The New England team are the worst in the league.* **4** You use PREP **in** to specify a general subject or field of activity. *...those working in the defence industry. ...future developments in medicine and surgery.*

in 3 time and numbers

in /ɪn/. **1** If something happens **in** a particular year, ◆◆◆◆◆ month, or other period of time, it happens during PREP that time. *In the evening, the people assemble in the mosques... He believes food prices will go up in the future.* **2** If something happens **in** a particular situa- PREP tion, it happens while that situation is going on. *His father had been badly wounded in the last war. ...issues you struggle with in your daily life.*
3 If you do something **in** a particular period of time, PREP that is how long it takes you to do it. *He walked two hundred and sixty miles in eight days.* **4** If something PREP will happen **in** a particular length of time, it will hap-

pen after that length of time. *They'll be back in a few months.*
5 You use **in** to indicate roughly how old someone is. PREP For example, if someone is **in** their fifties, they are between 50 and 59 years old. **6** You use **in** to indicate PREP roughly how many people or things do something. *The jugs were produced in their millions.* **7** You use **in** PREP to express a ratio, proportion, or probability. *Last year, one in five boys left school without a qualification... He was told that he had a one in 500 chance of survival.*

in 4 states and qualities

in /ɪn/. **1** If something or someone is **in** a particular ◆◆◆◆◆ state or situation, that is their present state or situa- PREP tion. *Dave was in a hurry to get back to work... Their equipment was in poor condition.* **2** You use **in** to PREP indicate the feeling or desire which someone has when they do something, or which causes them to do it. *Simpson looked at them in surprise... Carl pushed ahead in his eagerness to reach the wall.* **3** If PREP a particular quality or ability is **in** you, you naturally have it. *I couldn't find it in me to embrace him.*
4 You use **in** when saying that someone or some- PREP thing has a particular quality. *He had all the qualities I was looking for in a partner... There is artistry in what he does.*
5 You use **in** to indicate how someone is expressing PREP something. *...lessons in languages other than Spanish. ...written in a simple but very expressive style.* **6** You PREP use **in** in expressions such as **in a row** or **in a ball** to describe the arrangement or shape of something. *Her ear, shoulder and hip are in a straight line... He was curled up in a ball.* **7** If something is **in** a particular PREP colour, it has that colour. *He saw something written in black on the gravestones.* **8** You use **in** to specify which PREP feature or aspect of something you are talking about. *The movie is nearly two hours in length. ...a real increase in the standard of living.*

in 5 other uses and phrases

in, /ɪn/. **ins.** **1** If you say that something is **in**, or is ◆◆◆◆◆ the **in** thing, you mean it is fashionable or popular. ADJ *A few years ago jogging was the in thing... It is the* INFORMAL *'in' place to go for a quick drink after work.* **2** You PREP use **in** with a present participle to indicate that when you do something, something else happens as a result. *He shifted uncomfortably on his feet. In doing so he knocked over Steven's briefcase.* **3** If you PHRASE say that someone **is in for** a shock or a surprise, you mean that they are going to experience it. *When you venture outside, you are in for a surprise.*
4 If someone **has it in for** you, they dislike you and try PHRASE to cause problems for you. *Marsie really had it in for* INFORMAL *me.* **5** If you are **in on** something, you are involved in it PHR-PREP or know about it. *I'm going to let you in on a little secret.* **6** You use **in that** to introduce an explanation of a PHR-CONJ statement you have just made. *I'm lucky in that I've got four sisters.* **7** The **ins and outs** of a situation are all PHRASE the detailed points and facts about it. *...the ins and outs of high finance.*

in. **in.** is a written abbreviation for **inch**. The plural ◆◆◇◇◇ can be 'in.' or 'ins'.

in- /ɪn-/. **in-** is added to some adjectives, adverbs, PREFIX and nouns to form other adjectives, adverbs, and nouns that have the opposite meaning. For example, something that is incorrect is not correct. *...incomplete answers. ...women who are insecure about themselves.*

in·abil·ity /ˌɪnəˈbɪlɪti/. If you refer to someone's **in-** ◆◆◇◇◇ **ability** to do something, you are referring to the fact N-UNCOUNT that they are unable to do it. *Her inability to concentrate could cause an accident.*

in·ac·ces·sible /ˌɪnəkˈsesɪbəl/. **1** An **inaccessible** ◆◇◇◇◇ place is very difficult or impossible to reach. *The* ADJ-GRADED *route took us through scenery quite inaccessible to the motorist.* ♦ **in·ac·ces·sibil·ity** /ˌɪnəkses·ɪˈbɪlɪti/ N-UNCOUNT *Poor roads and inaccessibility make food distribution very difficult.* **2** If something is **inaccessible**, ADJ-GRADED you are unable to see, use, or buy it. *Ninety-five per cent of its magnificent collection will remain inaccessible to the public.* ♦ **inaccessibility** *The* N-UNCOUNT

problem of inaccessibility of essential goods, especially of food, is reaching a crisis point. **3** Someone or something that is **inaccessible** is difficult or impossible to understand or appreciate. ...using language that is inaccessible to working people. ♦ **inaccessibility** ...the inaccessibility of his literature. `ADJ-GRADED` `N-UNCOUNT`

in·ac·cu·ra·cy /ɪnˈækjʊrəsi/ **inaccuracies.** The **inaccuracy** of a statement or measurement is the fact that it is not accurate or correct. A reporter tries to guard against inaccuracies by checking with a variety of sources. `N-VAR`

in·ac·cu·rate /ɪnˈækjʊrət/. If a statement or measurement is **inaccurate**, it is not accurate or correct. ♦ **in·ac·cu·rate·ly** He claimed his remarks had been reported inaccurately. `ADJ-GRADED` `ADV-GRADED: ADV with v`

in·ac·tion /ɪnˈækʃən/. If you refer to someone's **inaction**, you disapprove of the fact that they are doing nothing. He is bitter about the inaction of the other political parties. `N-UNCOUNT` `PRAGMATICS`

in·ac·tive /ɪnˈæktɪv/. Someone or something that is **inactive** is not doing anything or is not working. The satellite had been inactive since its launch two years ago. ♦ **in·ac·tiv·ity** /ˌɪnækˈtɪvɪti/. The players have comparatively long periods of inactivity. `ADJ-GRADED` `N-UNCOUNT`

in·ad·equa·cy /ɪnˈædɪkwəsi/ **inadequacies.** **1** The **inadequacy** of something is the fact that there is not enough of it, or that it is not good enough. ...the inadequacy of the water supply... The inadequacies of the current system have already been recognised. **2** If someone has feelings of **inadequacy**, they feel that they do not have the qualities and abilities necessary to do something or to cope with everyday life. ...his deep-seated sense of inadequacy. `N-VAR` `N-UNCOUNT`

in·ad·equate /ɪnˈædɪkwət/. **1** If something is **inadequate**, there is not enough of it or it is not good enough. The problem goes far beyond inadequate staffing. ♦ **in·ad·equate·ly** The projects were inadequately funded. **2** If someone feels **inadequate**, they feel that they do not have the qualities and abilities necessary to do something or to cope with everyday life. `ADJ-GRADED` `ADV-GRADED` `ADJ-GRADED`

in·ad·mis·si·ble /ˌɪnədˈmɪsɪbəl/. **1** Inadmissible evidence cannot be used in a court of law. **2** If you say that something that someone says or does is **inadmissible**, you think that it is totally unacceptable. He said the use of force would be inadmissible. `ADJ` `ADJ-GRADED` `PRAGMATICS`

in·ad·vert·ent /ˌɪnədˈvɜːtənt/. An **inadvertent** action is one that you do without realizing what you are doing. The government has said it was an inadvertent error. ♦ **in·ad·vert·ent·ly** You may have inadvertently pressed the wrong button. `ADJ` `ADV: ADV with v`

in·ad·vis·able /ˌɪnədˈvaɪzəbəl/. A course of action that is **inadvisable** should not be carried out because it is not wise or sensible. For three days, it was inadvisable to leave the harbour. `ADJ-GRADED`

in·al·ien·able /ɪnˈeɪljənəbəl/. If you say that someone has an **inalienable** right to something, you are emphasizing that they have a right to it which cannot be changed or taken away. `ADJ` `FORMAL`

in·ane /ɪnˈeɪn/. If you describe someone's behaviour or actions as **inane**, you think they are very silly or stupid. She started asking me inane questions. ♦ **in·ane·ly** He lurched through the bar, grinning inanely. ♦ **in·an·ity** /ɪnˈænɪti/. ...the ludicrous inanity of much of the conversation. `ADJ-GRADED` `PRAGMATICS` `ADV-GRADED` `N-UNCOUNT`

in·ani·mate /ɪnˈænɪmət/. An **inanimate** object is one that has no life. `ADJ`

in·ap·pli·ca·ble /ˌɪnəˈplɪkəbəl, AM ɪnˈæplɪk-/. Something that is **inapplicable** to what you are talking about is not relevant or appropriate to it. His general theory was virtually inapplicable to underdeveloped economies. `ADJ-GRADED`

in·ap·pro·pri·ate /ˌɪnəˈprəʊpriət/. **1** Something that is **inappropriate** is not useful or suitable for a particular situation or purpose. There is no suggestion that clients have been sold inappropriate policies. ♦ **in·ap·pro·pri·ate·ly** He was dressed inappropriately for the heat in a dark suit. **2** If you say that someone's speech or behaviour in a particular situation is **inappropriate**, you are criticizing it be- `ADJ-GRADED` `ADV-GRADED` `ADJ-GRADED` `PRAGMATICS`

cause you think that it is not suitable for that situation. I feel the remark was inappropriate for such a serious issue... It is inappropriate for a judge to belong to a discriminatory club. ♦ **inappropriately** You have the law on your side if the bank is acting inappropriately. `ADV-GRADED`

in·ar·ticu·late /ˌɪnɑːˈtɪkjʊlət/. If someone is **inarticulate**, they are unable to express themselves easily or well in speech. Kempton made an inarticulate noise at the back of his throat as if he were about to choke. `ADJ-GRADED`

in·as·much as /ˌɪnəzˈmʌtʃ æz/; also spelled **in as much as.** You use **inasmuch as** to introduce a statement which explains something you have just said, and adds to it. We were doubly lucky inasmuch as my friend was living on the island and spoke Greek fluently. `PHR-CONJ` `PRAGMATICS` `FORMAL`

in·at·ten·tion /ˌɪnəˈtenʃən/. A person's **inattention** is their lack of attention; used showing disapproval. Vital evidence had been destroyed as a result of a moment's inattention. `N-UNCOUNT` `PRAGMATICS`

in·at·ten·tive /ˌɪnəˈtentɪv/. Someone who is **inattentive** is not paying complete attention to a person or thing. `ADJ-GRADED`

in·audible /ɪnˈɔːdɪbəl/. If a sound is **inaudible**, you are unable to hear it. `ADJ`

in·augu·ral /ɪnˈɔːgjʊrəl/. An **inaugural** meeting or speech is the first meeting of a new organization or the first speech by its new leader. `ADJ: ADJ n`

in·augu·rate /ɪnˈɔːgjʊreɪt/ **inaugurates, inaugurating, inaugurated. 1** When a new leader **is inaugurated**, they are formally given their new position at an official ceremony. ♦ **in·augu·ra·tion** /ɪnˌɔːgjʊˈreɪʃən/ **inaugurations** ...the inauguration of the new Governor. ...his long inauguration speech. **2** When a new building or institution **is inaugurated**, it is declared open in a formal ceremony. ♦ **inauguration** They later attended the inauguration of the University. **3** If you **inaugurate** a new system or service, you start it. Pan Am inaugurated the first scheduled international flight. `VERB: be V-ed` `N-VAR` `VERB: be V-ed` `N-COUNT` `VERB V n` `FORMAL`

in·aus·pi·cious /ˌɪnɔːˈspɪʃəs/. An **inauspicious** event is one that gives signs that success is unlikely. The meeting got off to an inauspicious start with one of the main participants failing to turn up. `ADJ-GRADED` `FORMAL`

in·board /ˈɪnbɔːd/. An **inboard** motor or engine is inside a boat rather than attached to the outside. `ADJ: ADJ n` `TECHNICAL`

in·born /ˌɪnˈbɔːn/. **Inborn** qualities are natural ones which you are born with. He had an inborn talent for languages. `ADJ`

in·bound /ˈɪnbaʊnd/. An **inbound** flight is one that is arriving from another place. `ADJ`

in·bred /ˌɪnˈbred/. **1 Inbred** means the same as **inborn**. ...behaviour patterns that are inbred. **2** People who are **inbred** have ancestors who are all closely related to each other. `ADJ` `ADJ`

in·breed·ing /ˈɪnbriːdɪŋ/. **Inbreeding** is the repeated breeding of closely related animals or people. `N-UNCOUNT`

in·built /ˌɪnˈbɪlt/; also spelled **in-built.** An **inbuilt** quality is one that someone or something has from the time they were born or produced. ...the only answering machine with inbuilt fax and printer. `ADJ` `BRITISH`

inc. In written advertisements, **inc.** is an abbreviation for 'including'. ...a two-night break for £210 per person, inc. breakfast and dinner.

Inc. In the United States, **Inc.** is an abbreviation for 'Incorporated' when it is used after a company's name. ...BP America Inc.

in·cal·cu·la·ble /ɪnˈkælkjʊləbəl/. Something that is **incalculable** cannot be calculated or estimated because it is so great. This has done incalculable damage to his reputation. `ADJ`

in·can·des·cent /ˌɪnkænˈdesənt/. **1 Incandescent** substances or devices give out a lot of light when heated. ...incandescent light bulbs. **2** If you describe someone or something as **incandescent**, you mean that they are very lively and impressive. Gill had an extraordinary, incandescent personality. ♦ **in·can·des·cence** She burned with an incandescence that had nothing to do with her looks. `ADJ` `TECHNICAL` `ADJ` `LITERARY` `N-UNCOUNT`

in·can·ta·tion /ˌɪnkænˈteɪʃən/ **incantations.** An N-COUNT incantation is a series of words that a person says or sings as a magic spell.

in·ca·pable /ɪnˈkeɪpəbəl/ **1** Someone who is **inca-** ◆◇◇◇◇ **pable of** doing something is unable to do it. *He was* ADJ *a man incapable of violence.* **2** An **incapable** person ADJ is weak or stupid.

in·ca·pac·i·tate /ˌɪnkəˈpæsɪteɪt/ **incapacitates,** VERB **incapacitating, incapacitated.** If something V n incapacitates you, it weakens you in some way, so FORMAL that you cannot do certain things. *A serious fall in-capacitated the 68-year-old congressman.* ♦ **in·ca-** **·paci·tat·ed** *He is incapacitated and can't work.* ADJ-GRADED

in·ca·pac·i·ty /ˌɪnkəˈpæsɪti/. The **incapacity** of a N-UNCOUNT person, society, or system to do something is their FORMAL inability to do it. *Patients with no mental incapacity can refuse treatment.*

in·car·cer·ate /ɪnˈkɑːsəreɪt/ **incarcerates, in-** ◆◇◇◇◇ **carcerating, incarcerated.** If people **are incar-** VERB: **cerated,** they are imprisoned. *It can cost $40,000 to* V n *$50,000 to incarcerate a prisoner for a year.* ♦ **in-** FORMAL **·car·cera·tion** *...her mother's incarceration in a* N-UNCOUNT *psychiatric hospital.*

in·car·nate, incarnates, incarnating, incar- **nated.** The adjective is pronounced /ɪnˈkɑːnɪt/. The verb is pronounced /ˈɪnkɑːneɪt/. **1** If you say ADJ: n ADJ that someone is a quality **incarnate,** you mean that they represent that quality or are typical of it in an extreme form. *She is evil incarnate.* **2** If you say that VERB: a quality **is incarnated** in a person, you mean that beV-ed in n they represent that quality or are typical of it in an V n extreme form. *...a writer who incarnates the chang-ing consciousness of the Americas.* **3** You use **incar-** ADJ: **nate** to say that something, especially a god or spir- v-link ADJ, it, is represented in human form. *The pharaoh is* ADJ n *Osiris, the moon bull incarnate.* **4** If you say that VB: usu someone or something **is incarnated** in a particular passive form, you mean that they appear on earth in that beV-ed prep form. *He was the god Vishnu incarnated on earth as a righteous king.*

in·car·na·tion /ˌɪnkɑːˈneɪʃən/ **incarnations. 1** If ◆◇◇◇◇ you say that someone is the **incarnation of** a par- N-COUNT: ticular quality, you mean that they represent that N of n quality or are typical of it in an extreme form. *She is a perfect incarnation of glamour.* **2** An **incarnation** N-COUNT is an instance of being alive on earth in a particular form. Some religions believe that people have sever-al incarnations in different forms. *His industry and persistence suggest that he was an ant in a previous incarnation.*

in·cen·di·ary /ɪnˈsendiəri, AM -eri/ **incendiaries.** ◆◇◇◇◇ **1 Incendiary** weapons or attacks are ones that ADJ: ADJ n cause large fires. *Five incendiary devices were found in her house.* **2** An **incendiary** is an incendiary N-COUNT bomb.

in·cense, incenses, incensing, incensed. ◆◇◇◇◇ The noun is pronounced /ˈɪnsens/. The verb is pro-nounced /ɪnˈsens/. **1 Incense** is a substance that is N-UNCOUNT burned for its sweet smell, often as part of a reli-gious ceremony. **2** If you say that something **in-** VERB **censes** you, you mean that it makes you extremely V n angry. *This proposal will incense conservation cam-paigners.* ♦ **in·censed** *Mum was incensed at his* ADJ-GRADED *lack of compassion.*

in·cen·tive /ɪnˈsentɪv/ **incentives.** If something is ◆◆◇◇◇ an **incentive** to do something, it encourages you to N-VAR do it. *There is little or no incentive to adopt such measures. ...tax incentives for companies that create jobs.*

in·cep·tion /ɪnˈsepʃən/. The **inception** of an insti- ◆◇◇◇◇ tution or activity is the start of it. *Since its inception* N-UNCOUNT: *the company has produced fifty three different air-* with poss *craft designs.* FORMAL

in·ces·sant /ɪnˈsesənt/. An **incessant** process or ◆◇◇◇◇ activity is one that continues without stopping. *...in-* ADJ-GRADED *cessant rain. ...his incessant demands for affection.* ♦ **in·ces·sant·ly** *Dee talked incessantly.* ADV-GRADED

in·cest /ˈɪnsest/. **Incest** is the crime of two mem- ◆◇◇◇◇ bers of the same family, for example a father and N-UNCOUNT daughter, having sexual intercourse.

in·ces·tu·ous /ɪnˈsestʃuəs/. **1** An **incestuous** rela- ADJ tionship is one involving sexual intercourse be-tween two members of the same family, for exam-ple a father and daughter. **2** If you describe a group ADJ-GRADED of people as **incestuous,** you disapprove of the fact PRAGMATICS that they all know everything about each other but are not interested in ideas or people from outside the group.

inch /ɪntʃ/ **inches, inching, inched. 1** An **inch** ◆◆◆◇◇ is an imperial unit of length, approximately equal to N-COUNT 2.54 centimetres. There are twelve inches in a foot. *...a candy tin 6 inches high.* **2 Inch** is used in the N-SING expressions **every inch** and **inch by inch** to empha- PRAGMATICS size how completely or carefully an area is covered. *Every inch of shelf space was crammed with books... The police were searching the area inch by inch.* **3** If PHRASE you say that someone looks **every inch** a certain PRAGMATICS type of person, you are emphasizing that they look exactly like that kind of person. *He looks every inch the City businessman.* **4** To **inch** somewhere means V-ERG to move there very slowly, carefully, or with difficul- V prep/adv ty. *...a climber inching up a vertical wall of rock...* V n prep/adv *He inched the van forward... An ambulance inched* V way prep/ *its way through the crowd.* adv

in·cho·ate /ɪnˈkəʊɪt/. If something is **inchoate,** it is ADJ recent or new, and rather vague or not yet properly FORMAL developed.

in·ci·dence /ˈɪnsɪdəns/ **incidences.** The **inci-** ◆◇◇◇◇ **dence** of something bad, such as a disease, is the N-VAR frequency with which it occurs, or the occasions when it occurs. *...a report about the high incidence of child mortality.*

in·ci·dent /ˈɪnsɪdənt/ **incidents.** An **incident** is ◆◆◆◇◇ something that happens, often something unpleas- N-COUNT: ant. *26 people have been killed in a dramatic shoot-* also withoutN *ing incident... Jason Brown was arrested without in-* FORMAL *cident in San Francisco.*

in·ci·den·tal /ˌɪnsɪˈdentəl/. If one thing is **inciden-** ◆◇◇◇◇ **tal** to another, it is less important than the other ADJ thing or is not a major part of it. *At the bottom of the bill, you will notice various incidental expenses.*

in·ci·den·tal·ly /ˌɪnsɪˈdentli/. **1** You use **inciden-** ◆◆◇◇◇ **tally** to introduce a point which is not directly rel- ADV: evant to what you are saying, often a question or ADV with cl extra information that you have just thought of. *The* PRAGMATICS tower, incidentally, dates from the twelfth century.* **2** If something occurs only **incidentally,** it is less ADV: important than another thing or is not a major part ADV with v of it. *The letter mentioned my great-aunt and uncle only incidentally.*

'incident room, incident rooms. In Britain, an N-COUNT **incident room** is a room used by the police while they are dealing with a major crime or accident.

in·cin·er·ate /ɪnˈsɪnəreɪt/ **incinerates, inciner-** ◆◇◇◇◇ **ating, incinerated. 1** When authorities **inciner-** VERB: V n **ate** rubbish or waste material, they burn it in a fur-nace. ♦ **in·cin·era·tion** /ɪnˌsɪnəˈreɪʃən/ *...an incin-* N-UNCOUNT *eration plant.* **2** If people **are incinerated,** for ex- VERB: ample in a bomb attack or a fire, they are burnt to beV-ed death.

in·cin·era·tor /ɪnˈsɪnəreɪtə/ **incinerators.** An **in-** ◆◇◇◇◇ **cinerator** is a large furnace for burning rubbish. N-COUNT

in·cipi·ent /ɪnˈsɪpiənt/. An **incipient** situation or ADJ: ADJ n quality is one that is starting to happen or develop. FORMAL *There were signs of incipient panic.*

in·cise /ɪnˈsaɪz/ **incises, incising, incised.** If an VERB: object **is incised** with a design, the design is cut into beV-ed its surface with a sharp instrument. *...a set of chairs* V-ed *incised with Grecian scrolls.* FORMAL

in·ci·sion /ɪnˈsɪʒən/ **incisions.** An **incision** is a N-COUNT sharp cut made in something, for example by a sur-geon who is operating on a patient. *The technique involves making a tiny incision in the skin.*

in·ci·sive /ɪnˈsaɪsɪv/. You use **incisive** to describe a ◆◇◇◇◇ person, their thoughts, or their speech when you ADJ-GRADED approve of their ability to think and express their PRAGMATICS ideas clearly, briefly, and forcefully.

in·ci·sor /ɪnˈsaɪzə/ **incisors.** Your **incisors** are the N-COUNT teeth at the front of your mouth which you use for biting into food.

in·cite /ɪnˈsaɪt/ **incites, inciting, incited.** If ◆◇◇◇◇ someone **incites** people to behave in a violent or VERB unlawful way, they encourage people to behave in V n to-inf that way. *He incited his fellow citizens to take their* V n *revenge... The party agreed not to incite its supporters to violence. ...material likely to incite racial hatred.* ♦ **in·cite·ment, incitements** *British law* N-VAR *forbids incitement to murder.*

incl. **1** In written advertisements, **incl.** is an abbreviation for 'including'. *...only £19.95 (incl. VAT and delivery).* **2** In written advertisements, **incl.** is an abbreviation for 'inclusive'. *Double room: £50 per week incl.*

in·clem·ent /ɪnˈklemənt/. **Inclement** weather is un- ADJ-GRADED pleasantly cold or stormy. FORMAL

in·cli·na·tion /ˌɪnklɪˈneɪʃən/ **inclinations.** An in- ◆◇◇◇◇ clination is a feeling that makes you want to act in N-VAR a particular way. *He had neither the time nor the inclination to think of other things... She showed no inclination to go... He set out to follow his artistic inclinations.*

in·cline, inclines, inclining, inclined. The verb ◆◇◇◇◇ is pronounced /ɪnˈklaɪn/. The noun is pronounced /ˈɪnklaɪn/. **1** If you **incline** to a particular view or ac- V-ERG tion, you want to take that view or action, or often V to/towards take it. *I incline to the view that he is right. ...the fac-* n *tors which incline us towards particular beliefs...* V n to/ *Many end up as team leaders, which inclines them* V n to-inf *to co-operate with the bosses.* ♦ **in·clined** *Nobody* ADJ-GRADED: *felt inclined to argue with Smith... He was inclined* v-link ADJ *to self-pity... If you are so inclined, you can watch TV.* **2** If you **incline** your head, you bend your neck VERB: V n so that your head is leaning forward. **3** An **incline** is WRITTEN land that slopes at an angle. *He came to a halt at the* FORMAL *edge of a steep incline.*

in·clined /ɪnˈklaɪnd/. **1** If you say that you are **in-** ◆◇◇◇◇ **clined** to have a particular opinion, you mean that ADJ-GRADED you hold this opinion but you are not expressing it PRAGMATICS strongly. *I am inclined to agree with Alan.* **2** Some- ADJ: one who is mathematically **inclined** or artistically adv ADJ **inclined**, for example, has a natural talent for mathematics or art. **3** See also **incline**.

in·clude /ɪnˈkluːd/ **includes, including, includ-** ◆◆◆◆◆ **ed.** If something such as a group or amount **in-** VERB **cludes** a particular thing, or if someone **includes** it V n in the group or amount, the group or amount has V n *inn* that thing in it as one of its parts. *The trip has been* V-ed *extended to include a few other events... The list includes many British internationals... The President is expected to include this idea in his education plan... Food is included in the price.* ♦ **in·clud·ed** *All of us,* ADJ: *myself included, had been totally committed to the* n ADJ, *Party.* ♦ **in·clu·sion** /ɪnˈkluːʒən/ **inclusions** *...a* v-link ADJ *confident performance which justified his inclusion* N-VAR *in the team. ...the inclusion of the term 'couplehood' in a Dictionary of New Words.*

in·clud·ing /ɪnˈkluːdɪŋ/. You use **including** to ◆◆◆◆◆ introduce examples of people or things that are part PREP of the group of people or things that you are talking PRAGMATICS about. *A number of international stars, including Joan Collins, are expected to attend... Preparation time (not including chilling): 5 minutes.*

in·clu·sive /ɪnˈkluːsɪv/. **1** If a price is stated to be ◆◇◇◇◇ **inclusive**, it includes all the charges connected with ADJ the goods or services offered. *All prices are inclusive of VAT. ...an inclusive price of £32.90.* ▶ Also an ad- ADV: verb. *...a special introductory offer of £5,995 fully in-* amount ADV *clusive.* ● See also **all-inclusive. 2** After mentioning ADJ: n ADJ the first and last item in a set of things, you can add **inclusive** to make it clear that the items stated are included in the set. *Training will commence on 5 October, running from Tuesday to Saturday inclu-* sive. **3** If you describe a group or organization as **in-** ADJ-GRADED **clusive**, you mean that it allows all sorts of people to belong to it or use its facilities. *The academy is far more inclusive now than it used to be.*

in·cog·ni·to /ˌɪnkɒgˈniːtəʊ/. Someone who is **in-** ADJ: **cognito** is using a false name or wearing a disguise, v-link ADJ, in order not to be recognized or identified. *Hotel in-* ADJ after v *spectors have to travel incognito.*

in·co·her·ent /ˌɪnkəʊˈhɪərənt/. **1** If someone is **in-** ◆◇◇◇◇ **coherent**, they are talking in a confused and un- ADJ-GRADED clear way. *The man was almost incoherent with fear.* ♦ **in·co·her·ence** *This rambling incoherence indi-* N-UNCOUNT *cates her stress.* ♦ **in·co·her·ent·ly** *He collapsed on* ADV *the floor, mumbling incoherently.* **2** If you say that ADJ-GRADED something such as a policy is **incoherent**, you are criticizing the fact that it has no clear and consistent purpose. *...an incoherent set of objectives.* ♦ **in- ·co·her·ence** *...the general incoherence of govern-* N-UNCOUNT *ment policy.*

in·come /ˈɪnkʌm/ **incomes.** A person's or organi- ◆◆◆◆◇ zation's **income** is the money that they earn or re- N-VAR ceive, as opposed to the money that they have to spend or pay out. *...families on low incomes... Over a third of their income comes from comedy videos.*

in·comer /ˈɪnkʌmə/ **incomers.** An **incomer** is N-COUNT someone who has recently come to live in a par- BRITISH ticular place or area.

income sup·port. In Britain, **income support** is ◆◇◇◇◇ money that the government gives regularly to peo- N-UNCOUNT ple with no income or very low incomes. *...people on income support.*

income tax, income taxes. Income tax is a ◆◆◇◇◇ certain percentage of your income that you have to N-VAR pay regularly to the government.

in·com·ing /ˈɪnkʌmɪŋ/. **1** An **incoming** message or ◆◇◇◇◇ phone call is one that you receive. *We keep a tape of* ADJ: ADJ n *incoming calls.* **2** An **incoming** plane or passenger is ADJ: ADJ n one that is arriving at a place. *...a passenger off the incoming flight.* **3** An **incoming** official or govern- ADJ: ADJ n ment is one that has just been appointed or elected. *...a surprise victory for incoming Prime Minister Manuel Esquivel.* **4** An **incoming** tide or wave is ADJ: ADJ n coming towards the shore.

in·com·mu·ni·ca·do /ˌɪnkəˌmjuːnɪˈkɑːdəʊ/. **1** If ADJ someone is being kept **incommunicado**, they are not allowed to talk to anyone outside the place where they are. *He was held incommunicado in prison for ten days.* **2** If someone is **incommunica-** ADJ: **do**, they do not want to be disturbed, or are in a v-link ADJ place where they cannot be contacted. *He is incommunicado in a secluded cottage in Wales.*

in·com·pa·rable /ɪnˈkɒmprəbəl/. If you describe ADJ someone or something as **incomparable**, you mean FORMAL that they are extremely good or impressive. *...a play starring the incomparable Edith Evans. ...an area of incomparable beauty.* ♦ **in·com·pa·rably** *British* ADV *industry is in incomparably better shape than at the beginning of the 1980s.*

in·com·pat·ible /ˌɪnkəmˈpætɪbəl/. **1** If one thing or ◆◇◇◇◇ person is **incompatible** with another, they are very ADJ different in important ways, so that what is good or suitable for one is bad or unsuitable for the other. *His behavior has been incompatible with his role as head of state... Their interests were mutually incom-* patible. ♦ **in·com·pat·ibil·ity** /ˌɪnkəmpætɪˈbɪlɪti/ N-UNCOUNT *Incompatibility between the mother's and the baby's blood groups may cause jaundice.* **2** If one type of ADJ computer or computer system is **incompatible** with another, they cannot use the same programs or be linked up together.

in·com·pe·tent /ɪnˈkɒmpɪtənt/ **incompetents.** If ◆◇◇◇◇ you describe someone as **incompetent**, you are ADJ-GRADED criticizing them because they are unable to do their job or a task properly. *I was incompetent at playing the piano... He wants the power to sack incompetent teachers.* ▶ Also a noun. *I'm surrounded by incom-* N-COUNT *petents!* ♦ **in·com·pe·tence** *The incompetence of* N-UNCOUNT *government officials is appalling. ...his incompetence in failing to conduct full inquiries.*

in·com·plete /ˌɪnkəmˈpliːt/. Something that is **in-** ◆◇◇◇◇ **complete** is not yet finished, or does not have all ADJ-GRADED the parts or details that it needs. *The clearing of rubbish and drains is still incomplete... European political union would be incomplete without a defence element.*

in·com·pre·hen·sible /ˌɪnkɒmprɪˈhensɪbəl/. ◆◇◇◇◇ Something that is **incomprehensible** is impossible ADJ-GRADED

to understand. *Her speech was almost incomprehensible. ...incomprehensible mathematics puzzles.*

in·com·pre·hen·sion /ˌɪnkɒmprɪˈhenʃən/. **Incomprehension** is the state of being unable to understand something or someone. *Rosie had a look of incomprehension on her face.* — N-UNCOUNT

in·con·ceiv·able /ˌɪnkənˈsiːvəbəl/. If you describe something as **inconceivable**, you think it is very unlikely to happen or be true. *It was inconceivable to me that Toby could have been my attacker.* — ◆◇◇◇◇ ADJ-GRADED

in·con·clu·sive /ˌɪnkənˈkluːsɪv/. If something is **inconclusive**, it does not provide any clear answer or result. *Research has so far proved inconclusive... The past two elections were inconclusive.* — ◆◇◇◇◇ ADJ-GRADED

in·con·gru·ous /ɪnˈkɒŋɡruəs/. Someone or something that is **incongruous** seems strange when considered together with other aspects of a situation. *The Indian temple is an incongruous sight in the Welsh border country.* ♦ **in·con·gru·ity**, /ˌɪnkɒŋˈɡruːɪti/ **incongruities.** *...the almost absurd incongruity between her wealth and her lifestyle.* ♦ **in·con·gru·ous·ly** *...Western-style buildings perched incongruously in a high green valley.* — ◆◇◇◇◇ FORMAL / N-VAR / ADV-GRADED

in·con·se·quen·tial /ˌɪnkɒnsɪˈkwenʃəl/. Something that is **inconsequential** is not important. *Seemingly inconsequential details can sometimes contain significant clues.* — ADJ-GRADED

in·con·sid·er·able /ˌɪnkənˈsɪdərəbəl/. If you describe an amount or quality as **not inconsiderable**, you are emphasizing that it is, in fact, large or great. *He was a man of great charm and not inconsiderable wit.* — ADJ: with neg PRAGMATICS

in·con·sid·er·ate /ˌɪnkənˈsɪdərət/. If you describe someone as **inconsiderate**, you are criticizing them because they do not take enough care over how their words or actions will affect other people. — ADJ-GRADED PRAGMATICS

in·con·sist·ent /ˌɪnkənˈsɪstənt/. **1** If you describe someone as **inconsistent**, you are criticizing them for not behaving in the same way every time a similar situation occurs. *...the leadership's hesitant and inconsistent behaviour.* ♦ **in·con·sist·en·cy** *His worst fault was his inconsistency.* **2** Someone or something that is **inconsistent** does not stay the same, but is sometimes good and sometimes bad. *We had a terrific start to the season, but recently we've been inconsistent.* **3** If two statements are **inconsistent**, one cannot possibly be true if the other is true. *The evidence given in court was inconsistent with what he had previously told them.* ♦ **in·con·sist·en·cy, inconsistencies.** *We were asked to investigate the alleged inconsistencies in his evidence.* **4** If something is **inconsistent with** a set of ideas or values, it does not fit in well with them or match them. *This legislation is inconsistent with what they call Free Trade... The outburst was inconsistent with the image he has cultivated.* — ◆◇◇◇◇ ADJ-GRADED / N-UNCOUNT / ADJ-GRADED / ADJ / N-VAR / ADJ-GRADED: v-link ADJ with n

in·con·sol·able /ˌɪnkənˈsəʊləbəl/. If you say that someone is **inconsolable**, you mean that they are very sad and cannot be comforted. — ADJ

in·con·spicu·ous /ˌɪnkənˈspɪkjuəs/. **1** Someone who is **inconspicuous** does not attract attention to themselves. ♦ **in·con·spicu·ous·ly** *I sat inconspicuously in a corner.* **2** Something that is **inconspicuous** is not easily seen or does not attract attention because it is small, ordinary, or hidden away. *The studio is an inconspicuous grey building.* — ADJ-GRADED / ADV-GRADED / ADJ-GRADED

in·con·ti·nent /ɪnˈkɒntɪnənt/. Someone who is **incontinent** is unable to control their bladder or bowels, or both. ♦ **in·con·ti·nence** *Incontinence is not just a condition of old age.* — ADJ / N-UNCOUNT

in·con·tro·vert·ible /ˌɪnkɒntrəˈvɜːtɪbəl/. **Incontrovertible** evidence is absolutely certain and cannot be denied or disproved. ♦ **in·con·tro·vert·ibly** *No solution is incontrovertibly right.* — ADJ / ADV

in·con·ven·ience /ˌɪnkənˈviːniəns/ **inconveniences, inconveniencing, inconvenienced.** **1** If someone or something causes **inconvenience**, they cause problems or difficulties for someone. *We apologize for any inconvenience caused during the repairs.* **2** If someone **inconveniences** you, they — ◆◇◇◇◇ N-VAR / VERB

cause problems or difficulties for you. *He promised to be very quick so as not to inconvenience them any further.* — V n

in·con·ven·ient /ˌɪnkənˈviːniənt/. Something that is **inconvenient** causes problems or difficulties for someone. *I know it's inconvenient for you, but I must see you... It's very inconvenient to have to wait so long... She arrived at an extremely inconvenient moment.* ♦ **in·con·ven·ient·ly** *...a comfortable hotel, but rather inconveniently situated.* — ◆◇◇◇◇ ADJ-GRADED / ADV-GRADED

in·cor·po·rate /ɪnˈkɔːpəreɪt/ **incorporates, incorporating, incorporated.** If something such as a group or device **incorporates** a particular thing, or if someone **incorporates** it in the group or device, the group or device has that thing in it as one of its parts. *The new cars will incorporate a number of major improvements... The party vowed to incorporate environmental considerations into all its policies.* ♦ **in·cor·po·ra·tion** /ɪnˌkɔːpəˈreɪʃən/ *...the incorporation of Piedmont Airlines and PSA into US Air.* — ◆◆◇◇◇ VERB / V n / V n into n / FORMAL / N-UNCOUNT

in·cor·rect /ˌɪnkəˈrekt/. Something that is **incorrect** is untrue, inaccurate, or wrong. *He denied that his evidence about the telephone call was incorrect. ...injuries caused by incorrect posture.* ♦ **in·cor·rect·ly** *The magazine suggested, incorrectly, that he was planning to announce his retirement... The doors had been fitted incorrectly.* — ◆◇◇◇◇ ADJ / ADV: ADV with v

in·cor·ri·gible /ɪnˈkɒrɪdʒəbəl, AM -ˈkɔːr-/. If you tell someone they are **incorrigible**, you are saying, often in a humorous way, that they have faults which will never change. *Gamblers are incorrigible optimists.* — ADJ

in·cor·rupt·ible /ˌɪnkəˈrʌptɪbəl/. If you describe someone as **incorruptible**, you approve of the fact that they cannot be bribed or persuaded to do things that they should not do. — ADJ PRAGMATICS

in·crease, increases, increasing, increased. The verb is pronounced /ɪnˈkriːs/. The noun is pronounced /ˈɪnkriːs/. **1** If something **increases**, it becomes greater in number, level, or amount. *The population continues to increase... Japan's industrial output increased by 2%... The company has increased the price of its cars... The increased investment will help stabilise the economy... We are experiencing an increasing number of problems.* **2** If there is an **increase** in the number, level, or amount of something, it becomes greater. *...a sharp increase in productivity... He called for an increase of 1p on income tax. ...an increase of violence along the border.* ● If something is **on the increase**, it is becoming more frequent or greater in number or intensity. *Crime is on the increase... Divorce rates and births outside marriage are on the increase.* — ◆◆◆◆◆ V-ERG / V / V by/from/to amount / V n / V-ed / V-ing / N-COUNT / PHRASE

in·creas·ing·ly /ɪnˈkriːsɪŋli/. You can use **increasingly** to indicate that a situation or quality is becoming greater in intensity or more common. *He was finding it increasingly difficult to make decisions... The U.S. has increasingly relied on Japanese capital... Increasingly, their goals have become more radical.* — ◆◆◆◆◇ ADV

in·cred·ible /ɪnˈkredɪbəl/. **1** If you describe something or someone as **incredible**, you like them very much or are impressed by them, because they are extremely or unusually good. *You're always an incredible help on these cases.* ♦ **in·cred·ibly** /ɪnˈkredɪbli/. *Their father was incredibly good-looking.* **2** If you say that something is **incredible**, you mean that it is very unusual or surprising, and you cannot believe it is really true, although it may be. *It seemed incredible that people would still want to play football during a war. ...the incredible stories that children may tell us.* ♦ **incredibly** *Incredibly, some people don't like the name.* **3** You use **incredible** to emphasize the degree, amount, or intensity of something. *We import an incredible amount of cheese from the Continent... It's incredible how much Francesca wants her father's approval... His panic was incredible.* ♦ **incredibly** *It was incredibly hard work.* — ◆◆◆◇◇ ADJ-GRADED PRAGMATICS / ADV-GRADED: ADV adj/adv / ADJ-GRADED / ADV / ADJ-GRADED PRAGMATICS / ADV: ADV adj/adv

in·cre·du·li·ty /ˌɪnkrɪˈdjuːlɪti, AM -ˈduːl-/. If some- N-UNCOUNT
one reacts with **incredulity** to something, they are
unable to believe it because it is very surprising or
shocking. *The surprise announcement has been met
with incredulity.*

in·credu·lous /ɪnˈkredʒʊləs/. If someone is **in-** ◆◇◇◇◇
credulous, they are unable to believe something be- ADJ-GRADED
cause it is very surprising or shocking. *There was a
brief, incredulous silence.* ♦ **in·credu·lous·ly** 'You ADV-GRADED:
told Pete?' Rachel said incredulously. ADV with v

in·cre·ment /ˈɪnkrɪmənt/ **increments. 1** An incre- N-COUNT
ment in something or in the value of something is FORMAL
an amount by which it increases. *The average yearly
increment in labour productivity in industry was 4.5
per cent.* **2** An **increment** is an amount by which N-COUNT
your salary automatically increases after a fixed pe- FORMAL
riod of time. *Many teachers qualify for an annual
increment.*

in·cre·men·tal /ˌɪnkrɪˈmentəl/. **Incremental** is ADJ
used to describe something that increases in value FORMAL
or worth, often by a regular amount. *We are seeking
continuous, incremental improvements.*

in·crimi·nate /ɪnˈkrɪmɪneɪt/ **incriminates, in-** ◆◇◇◇◇
criminating, incriminated. If something **in-** VERB: V n
criminates you, it suggests that you are responsible V pron-refl
for something bad, especially a crime. *They are
afraid of incriminating themselves and say no more
than is necessary.* ♦ **in·crimi·nat·ing** *Police had re-* ADJ-GRADED
*portedly searched his flat and found incriminating
evidence.*

in·cu·bate /ˈɪnkjubeɪt/ **incubates, incubating,** ◆◇◇◇◇
incubated. 1 When birds **incubate** their eggs, they VERB: V n
keep the eggs warm until the baby birds hatch. ♦ **in-**
·cu·ba·tion /ˌɪnkjʊˈbeɪʃən/. *Male albatrosses share* N-UNCOUNT
in the incubation of eggs. **2** When a germ in your V-ERG
body **incubates** or is **incubated**, it develops for a V
period of time before it starts making you feel ill. Also V n
*The virus can incubate for up to ten days after the
initial infection.* ♦ **incubation** *The illness has an* N-UNCOUNT
incubation period of up to 11 days.

in·cu·ba·tor /ˈɪnkjʊbeɪtə/ **incubators. 1** An incu- N-COUNT
bator is a piece of hospital equipment which weak
or premature babies are put into until they are
strong enough to survive. **2** An **incubator** is a piece N-COUNT
of equipment used to keep eggs or bacteria at the
correct temperature for them to hatch or develop.

in·cul·cate /ˈɪnkʌlkeɪt, AM ɪnˈkʌl-/ **inculcates, in-** VERB:
culcating, inculcated. If you **inculcate** an idea V n in n
or opinion in someone's mind, you teach it to them V n with n
by repeating it until it is fixed in their mind. *The* FORMAL
aim is to inculcate business people with an appreciation of different cultures... Great care was taken to
inculcate the values of nationhood and family.*

in·cum·bent /ɪnˈkʌmbənt/ **incumbents. 1** An in- ◆◆◇◇◇
cumbent is someone who holds an official post at a N-COUNT
particular time. *...measures to secure the re-election* FORMAL
of incumbent congressmen next month. ▶ Also an ADJ: ADJ n
adjective. *...the only candidate who defeated an incumbent senator.* **2** If it is **incumbent** upon you to ADJ:
do something, it is your duty or responsibility to do it-v-link ADJ
it. *I used to think it was incumbent on a woman to* upon/on n
get married and have children. to-inf
FORMAL

in·cur /ɪnˈkɜː/ **incurs, incurring, incurred.** If ◆◇◇◇◇
you **incur** something unpleasant, it happens to you VERB
because of something you have done. *The govern-* V n
ment had also incurred huge debts. ...the terrible V-ed
damage incurred during the past decade. WRITTEN

in·cur·able /ɪnˈkjʊərəbəl/. **1** If someone has an **in-** ◆◇◇◇◇
curable disease, they cannot be cured of it. ♦ **in-** ADJ
·cur·ably /ɪnˈkjʊərəbli/ *...youngsters who are dis-* ADV: ADV adj
abled, or incurably ill. **2** You can use **incurable** to ADJ: ADJ n
indicate that someone has a particular quality or attitude and will not change. *Poor old William is an
incurable romantic.* ♦ **incurably** *I know you think* ADV: ADV adj
I'm incurably nosey.

in·cur·sion /ɪnˈkɜːʃən, -ʒən/ **incursions.** An **in-** ◆◇◇◇◇
cursion into a country is a small, sudden military N-COUNT
invasion of it. *...armed incursions into border areas
by rebel forces.*

in·debt·ed /ɪnˈdetɪd/. **1** If you say that you are **in-** ◆◇◇◇◇
debted to someone for something, you mean that ADJ-GRADED:
you are very grateful to them for something. *I am* v-link ADJ to n
deeply indebted to him for his help. ♦ **in·debt·ed·** N-UNCOUNT
·ness *...his indebtedness to Sir Geoffrey.* **2 Indebt-** ADJ-GRADED
ed countries, organizations, or people are ones that
owe money to other countries, organizations, or
people. *...the most heavily indebted countries.*
♦ **indebtedness** *The company has reduced its in-* N-UNCOUNT
debtedness to just $15 million.

in·de·cen·cy /ɪnˈdiːsənsi/. **1** In law, an act of **inde-** N-UNCOUNT
cency is a sexual act for which you can be prosecut-
ed. *They were found guilty of acts of gross indecency.*
2 See also **indecent**.

in·de·cent /ɪnˈdiːsənt/. **1** If you describe some- ◆◇◇◇◇
thing as **indecent**, you mean that it is shocking and ADJ-GRADED
offensive, usually because it relates to sex or nakedness. *Mr Sharp had insulted him in what he de-
scribed as indecent language.* ♦ **in·de·cen·cy** *...the* N-UNCOUNT
indecency of their language. ♦ **in·de·cent·ly** *He be-* ADV
haved indecently. ...an indecently short skirt. **2** If ADJ
you describe the speed or amount of something as
indecent, you are indicating that it is much quicker
or larger than is usual or desirable. *The legislation
was drafted with indecent haste.* ♦ **indecently** *...an* ADV
indecently large office.

in,decent as'sault. Indecent assault is the crime N-UNCOUNT
of attacking someone in a way which involves
touching or threatening them sexually, but not forcing them to have sexual intercourse.

in,decent ex'posure. Indecent exposure is a N-UNCOUNT
criminal offence that is committed when someone
exposes their genitals in public.

in·de·ci·pher·able /ˌɪndɪˈsaɪfərəbəl/. If writing or ADJ-GRADED
speech is **indecipherable**, you cannot understand
what the words are.

in·de·ci·sion /ˌɪndɪˈsɪʒən/. If you say that someone ◆◇◇◇◇
suffers from **indecision**, you mean that they find it N-UNCOUNT
very difficult to make decisions. *After months of in-* PRAGMATICS
*decision, the government finally gave the plan the
go-ahead.*

in·de·ci·sive /ˌɪndɪˈsaɪsɪv/. **1** If you say that some- ◆◇◇◇◇
one is **indecisive**, you mean that they find it very ADJ-GRADED
difficult to make decisions. *Michael was indecisive* PRAGMATICS
about how to decorate the room. ♦ **in·de·ci·sive·**
·ness *The mayor was criticized by radical reformers* N-UNCOUNT
for his indecisiveness. **2** An **indecisive** result in a ADJ
contest or election is one which is not clear or definite. *The outcome of the battle was indecisive.*

in·deed /ɪnˈdiːd/. **1** You use **indeed** to confirm or ◆◆◆◆◇
agree with something that has just been said. *The* ADV
payments had indeed been made... 'Did you know PRAGMATICS
*him?'—'I did indeed.'... 'Know what I mean?'—
'Indeed I do.'... 'Isn't it a gorgeous day, Father?'—Yes,
indeed!'.* **2** You use **indeed** to introduce a further ADV:
comment or statement which strengthens the point ADV with cl
you have already made. *We have nothing against di-* PRAGMATICS
versity; indeed, we want more of it. **3** You use **in-** ADV:
deed at the end of a clause to give extra force to the adj ADV
word 'very', or to emphasize a particular word. *The* PRAGMATICS
*wine was very good indeed... It's rare indeed for an
Irish Prime Minister to visit Belfast.* **4** You can use ADV:
indeed as a way of repeating a question in order to quest ADV
emphasize it, especially when you do not know the PRAGMATICS
answer. *'And what do we do here?'—'What, indeed?'* SPOKEN

in·de·fati·ga·ble /ˌɪndɪˈfætɪgəbəl/. You use **inde-** ADJ
fatigable to describe someone who never gets tired FORMAL
of doing something. *His indefatigable spirit helped
him to cope with his illness.*

in·de·fen·sible /ˌɪndɪˈfensɪbəl/. **1** If you say that a ADJ-GRADED
statement, action, or idea is **indefensible**, you mean
that it cannot be justified or supported because it is
completely wrong or unacceptable. *His action was
indefensible.* ▶ **The indefensible** is something N-SING
which is indefensible. *To argue otherwise is trying to
defend the indefensible.*
2 Places or buildings that are **indefensible** cannot be ADJ
defended if they are attacked.

in·de·fin·able /ˌɪndɪˈfaɪnəbəl/. An **indefinable** qual- ADJ WRITTEN
ity or feeling cannot easily be described. *There was*
something indefinable in her eyes.

in·defi·nite /ɪnˈdefɪnɪt/. **1** If you describe a situa- ◆◇◇◇◇ ADJ
tion or period as **indefinite**, you mean that people
have not decided when it will end. *The trial was ad-*
journed for an indefinite period. ♦ **in·defi·nite·ly** ADV:
The visit has now been postponed indefinitely. ADV with v
2 Something that is **indefinite** is not exact or clear. ADJ
...at some indefinite time in the future.

in·definite 'article, indefinite articles. The N-COUNT
words 'a' and 'an' are sometimes called the **indefi-**
nite article.

in·definite 'pronoun, indefinite pronouns. An N-COUNT
indefinite pronoun is a pronoun such as 'someone', 'anything', or 'nobody', which you use to refer
in a general way to a person or thing without saying
who or what they are, or what kind of person or
thing you mean.

in·del·ible /ɪnˈdelɪbəl/. **1** If you say that something ADJ-GRADED
leaves an **indelible** impression, you mean that it is
very unlikely to be forgotten. *My visit to India in*
1986 left an indelible impression on me. ♦ **in·del-**
·ibly *The horrors he experienced are imprinted, per-* ADV:
haps indelibly, in his brain. **2 Indelible** ink or an **in-** ADV with v ADJ
delible stain cannot be removed, erased, or washed
out. *...written in indelible ink... It leaves indelible*
stains on clothes.

in·deli·cate /ɪnˈdelɪkət/. If something or someone ADJ-GRADED FORMAL
is **indelicate**, they are rude or embarrassing. *She re-*
ally could not touch upon such an indelicate subject.

in·dem·ni·fy /ɪnˈdemnɪfaɪ/ **indemnifies, indem-** VERB:
nifying, indemnified. To **indemnify** someone V n against n V n
against something bad happening means to FORMAL
promise to protect them, especially financially, if it
happens. *A third party had agreed to indemnify the*
taxpayer against any loss resulting from this
investment.

in·dem·nity /ɪnˈdemnɪti/ **indemnities. 1** If some- ◆◇◇◇◇
thing provides **indemnity**, it provides insurance or N-UNCOUNT FORMAL
protection against damage or loss, especially in the
form of financial compensation. *Political exiles had*
not been given indemnity from prosecution. **2** An **in-** N-VAR
demnity is an amount of money or goods that are FORMAL
received by someone as compensation for some
damage or loss they have suffered. *The government*
has paid the family an indemnity for the missing
pictures.

in·dent /ɪnˈdent/ **indents, indenting, indented.** VERB: V n
When you **indent** a line, you write or print it further
away from the margin than the other lines.

in·den·ta·tion /ˌɪndenˈteɪʃən/ **indentations. 1** An N-COUNT
indentation is a space at the beginning of a line of
writing, between the margin and the beginning of
the writing. **2** An **indentation** is a dent in a surface N-COUNT
or a notch on the edge of something.

in·dent·ed /ɪnˈdentɪd/. If something is **indented**, its ADJ-GRADED
edge or surface is uneven because parts of it have
been worn away or cut away. *...Chile's indented*
coastline.

in·den·tured /ɪnˈdentʃəd/. In the past, an **inden-** ADJ
tured worker was a worker who was forced to work
for someone for a period of time, because of an
agreement made by people in authority.

Inde'pendence Day. A country's **Independence** N-UNCOUNT
Day is the day on which its people celebrate their
independence from another country that ruled
them in the past.

in·de·pend·ent /ˌɪndɪˈpendənt/ **independents.** ◆◆◆◆◆ ADJ
1 If one thing or person is **independent** of another,
they are separate and not connected, so the first
one is not affected or influenced by the second.
Your questions should be independent of each other.
♦ **in·de·pend·ent·ly** *...people working indepen-* ADV
dently in different areas of the world. ...biological
processes which continue to function independently
of any effort we can make. **2** If someone is **independent**, they are free to live as ADJ-GRADED
they want, because they do not need help and have no
obligations to anyone. *She would like to be financially*

independent. ♦ **independently** *...helping disabled* ADV
students to live and study as independently as possible.
...the independently-minded females of the Nineties.
♦ **in·de·pend·ence** *He was afraid of losing his* N-UNCOUNT
independence.
3 An **independent** school or other organization does ADJ
not receive money from the government.
4 Independent countries and states are not ruled by ADJ-GRADED
other countries but have their own government.
♦ **independence** *In 1816, Argentina declared its in-* N-UNCOUNT
dependence from Spain.
5 An **independent** inquiry or opinion is one that in- ADJ: ADJ n
volves people who are not connected with a situation,
and should therefore be fair and unbiased.
6 An **independent** politician is one who does not rep- ADJ
resent any political party. ▶ An **independent** is an in- N-COUNT
dependent politician.

'in-depth. See depth.

in·de·scrib·able /ˌɪndɪˈskraɪbəbəl/. You use **inde-** ADJ
scribable to emphasize that a quality or condition is PRAGMATICS
very intense or extreme, and therefore cannot be
properly described. *The stench from the sewer is in-*
describable. ♦ **in·de·scrib·ably** /ˌɪndɪˈskraɪbəbli/. ADV: ADV adj
...the treacherous and indescribably filthy conditions.

in·de·struct·ible /ˌɪndɪˈstrʌktɪbəl/. If something is ADJ
indestructible, it is very strong and cannot be destroyed. *Molded plastic is almost indestructible.*

in·de·ter·mi·nate /ˌɪndɪˈtɜːmɪnət/. If something is ADJ-GRADED
indeterminate, you cannot say exactly what it is. *Dr*
Amid was a man of indeterminate age. ♦ **in·de·ter-**
·mi·na·cy *...the indeterminacy of language.* N-UNCOUNT

in·dex /ˈɪndeks/ **indices, indexes, indexing, in-** ◆◆◆◇◇
dexed. Indexes is the usual plural, but the form
indices can be used for meanings 1 and 6. **1** An **in-** N-COUNT:
dex is a system by which changes in the value of with supp
something and the rate at which it changes can be
recorded, measured, or interpreted. *...the UK retail*
price index.
2 An **index** is an alphabetical list that is printed at the N-COUNT
back of a book and tells you on which pages impor-
tant topics are referred to. **3** If you **index** a book or a VERB: V n
collection of information, you make an alphabetical be V-ed
list of the items in it. *A quarter of this vast archive has*
been indexed and made accessible to researchers. **4** See
also **card index**.
5 If a quantity or value **is indexed** to another, a system VB: usu
is arranged so that it increases or decreases whenever passive
the other one increases or decreases. *Minimum pen-* be V-ed to n
sions and wages are to be indexed to inflation.
6 In mathematics, **indices** are the small numbers that N-COUNT
show how many times you must multiply a number TECHNICAL
by itself. For example, in the equation $3^2 = 9$, the number 2 is an index.

'index card, index cards. An **index card** is a N-COUNT
small card on which you can write information.

'index finger, index fingers. Your **index finger** is N-COUNT
the finger that is next to your thumb.

index-'linked. Index-linked pensions, payments, ADJ
or welfare benefits are calculated using the index
which measures inflation or the cost of living, and
therefore change as inflation or the cost of living
changes.

Indian 'summer, Indian summers. You can re- N-COUNT
fer to a period of unusually warm and sunny weather during the autumn as an **Indian summer**.

in·di·cate /ˈɪndɪkeɪt/ **indicates, indicating, in-** ◆◆◆◆◇
dicated. 1 If one thing **indicates** another, the first VERB: V n
thing shows that the second is true or exists. *A sur-* V that
vey of retired people has indicated that most are in- V wh
dependent and enjoying life... High school seniors
must indicate which college they'll attend next year.
♦ **in·di·ca·tion** /ˌɪndɪˈkeɪʃən/ **indications.** An **in-** N-VAR
dication is a sign which shows that something is
true or exists. *All the indications are that we are*
going to receive reasonable support... He gave no
indication that he was ready to compromise. **2** If VERB: V n
you **indicate** an opinion, an intention, or a fact, you V that
mention it in an indirect way. *Mr Rivers has indicat-*
ed that he may resign. **3** If one thing **indicates** VERB

indicative

something else, it is a sign of that thing. *Dreams can help indicate your true feelings.* — V n

4 If you **indicate** something to someone, you show them where it is, especially by pointing to it. *He indicated a chair.* — VERB V n FORMAL

5 If a technical instrument **indicates** something, it shows a measurement or reading. *The temperature gauge indicated that it was boiling.* — VERB: V n V that

6 When drivers **indicate**, they make lights flash on one side of their vehicle to show that they are going to turn in that direction. The usual American word is **signal**. *He can tell us when we should indicate left or right.* — VERB: V V adv BRITISH

in·dica·tive /ɪnˈdɪkətɪv/. **1** If one thing is **indicative** of another, it suggests what the other thing is likely to be. *Often physical appearance is indicative of how a person feels.* **2** In grammar, a clause that is in **the indicative**, or in **the indicative mood**, has a subject followed by a verb group. Examples are 'I'm hungry' and 'She was followed'. — ◆◇◇◇◇ ADJ-GRADED FORMAL / N-SING: the N

in·di·ca·tor /ˈɪndɪkeɪtə/ **indicators. 1** An **indicator** is a measurement or value which gives you an idea of what something is like. *...vital economic indicators, such as inflation, growth and the trade gap.* **2** A car's **indicators** are the flashing lights that tell you that it is going to turn left or right. See picture headed **car and bicycle**. — ◆◇◇◇◇ N-COUNT / N-COUNT BRITISH

in·di·ces /ˈɪndɪsiːz/. **Indices** is one of the plural forms of **index**.

in·dict /ɪnˈdaɪt/ **indicts, indicting, indicted.** If someone **is indicted** for a crime, they are officially charged with it. *Carl was eventually indicted for tampering with public records... He was later indicted on corruption charges.* ♦ **in·dict·ment, indictments** *The government's indictment against the three men alleged unlawful trading.* — ◆◇◇◇◇ VERB: be V-ed be V-ed for -ing/n ing V-ed on n LEGAL, AMERICAN N-COUNT

in·dict·ment /ɪnˈdaɪtmənt/ **indictments.** If you say that one thing is an **indictment** of another thing, you mean that it shows how bad the other thing is. *It's a sad indictment of society that policemen are regarded as easy targets by thugs.* — ◆◇◇◇◇ N-COUNT

in·die /ˈɪndi/ **indies. Indie** music refers to rock or pop music produced by new bands working with small independent record companies. ► An **indie** is an indie band or record company. — ◆◆◇◇◇ ADJ: ADJ n INFORMAL N-COUNT

in·dif·fer·ent /ɪnˈdɪfərənt/. **1** If you accuse someone of being **indifferent** to something, you mean that they have a complete lack of interest in it. *People have become indifferent to the suffering of others.* ♦ **in·dif·fer·ence** *...the prejudice and indifference which surround the Aids epidemic.* ♦ **in·dif·fer·ent·ly** *'Not that it matters,' said Tench indifferently.* **2** If you describe something or someone as **indifferent**, you mean that their standard or quality is not very good, and often quite bad. *She had starred in several very indifferent movies.* ♦ **indifferently** *...an eight-year-old girl who reads tolerably and writes indifferently.* — ◆◇◇◇◇ ADJ-GRADED / N-UNCOUNT / ADV-GRADED ADJ-GRADED / ADV-GRADED: ADV with v

in·dig·enous /ɪnˈdɪdʒɪnəs/. **Indigenous** people or things belong to the country in which they are found, rather than coming there or being brought there from another country. — ◆◇◇◇◇ ADJ FORMAL

in·di·gent /ˈɪndɪdʒənt/. Someone who is **indigent** is very poor. — ADJ-GRADED FORMAL

in·di·gest·ible /ˌɪndɪˈdʒestɪbəl/. **1** Food that is **indigestible** cannot be digested easily. **2** If you describe facts or ideas as **indigestible**, you mean that they are difficult to understand, complicated, and dull. — ADJ-GRADED / ADJ-GRADED

in·di·ges·tion /ˌɪndɪˈdʒestʃən/. If you have **indigestion**, you have pains in your stomach and chest that are caused by difficulties in digesting food. — ◆◇◇◇◇ N-UNCOUNT

in·dig·nant /ɪnˈdɪgnənt/. If you are **indignant**, you are shocked and angry, because you think that something is unjust or unfair. *He is indignant at suggestions that they were secret agents.* ♦ **in·dig·nant·ly** *'That is not true,' Erica said indignantly.* ♦ **in·dig·na·tion** /ˌɪndɪgˈneɪʃən/. *He could hardly contain his indignation.* — ◆◇◇◇◇ ADJ-GRADED / ADV-GRADED / N-UNCOUNT

indistinguishable

in·dig·nity /ɪnˈdɪgnɪti/ **indignities.** If you talk about the **indignity** of doing something, you mean that doing it is humiliating or embarrassing. *He suffered the indignity of having to flee angry protesters.* — ◆◇◇◇◇ N-VAR FORMAL

in·di·go /ˈɪndɪgəʊ/. Something that is **indigo** is dark purplish blue in colour. — ◆◇◇◇◇ COLOUR

in·di·rect /ˌɪndaɪˈrekt, -dɪr-/. **1** An **indirect** result or effect is not caused immediately and obviously by a thing or person, but happens because of something else that they have done. *Millions could die of hunger as an indirect result of the war.* ♦ **in·di·rect·ly** *Drugs are indirectly responsible for the violence... The president is indirectly elected by parliament.* **2** An **indirect** route or journey does not use the shortest or easiest way between two places. **3** **Indirect** remarks and information suggest something or refer to it, without actually mentioning it or stating it clearly. *His remarks amounted to an indirect appeal for economic aid.* ♦ **indirectly** *He referred indirectly to the territorial dispute.* — ◆◇◇◇◇ ADJ / ADV / ADJ-GRADED / ADJ-GRADED / ADV: ADV with v

indirect 'object, indirect objects. An **indirect object** is an object which is used with a transitive verb to indicate who benefits from an action or gets something as a result. For example, in 'She gave him her address', 'him' is the indirect object. Compare **direct object**. — N-COUNT

indirect 'question, indirect questions. An **indirect question** is the same as a **reported question**. — N-COUNT

indirect 'speech. Indirect speech is the same as reported speech. — N-UNCOUNT

indirect 'tax, indirect taxes. An **indirect tax** is a tax on goods and services which is added to their price. Compare **direct tax**. — N-COUNT

indirect ta'xation. Indirect taxation is a system in which a government raises money by means of indirect taxes. — N-UNCOUNT

in·dis·ci·pline /ɪnˈdɪsɪplɪn/. If you refer to **indiscipline** in a group or team, you disapprove of their lack of discipline. *...the team's indiscipline on the pitch.* — N-UNCOUNT PRAGMATICS

in·dis·creet /ˌɪndɪˈskriːt/. If you describe someone as **indiscreet**, you mean that they do or say things in public which they should only do or say secretly or in private. *He is notoriously indiscreet about his private life.* — ADJ-GRADED

in·dis·cre·tion /ˌɪndɪˈskreʃən/ **indiscretions.** If you talk about someone's **indiscretion**, you mean that they have done or said something that is risky, careless, or likely to upset people. *They paid for their indiscretion with their lives. ...his mother's youthful indiscretions.* — N-VAR

in·dis·crimi·nate /ˌɪndɪˈskrɪmɪnət/. If you describe an action as **indiscriminate**, you are critical of it because it does not involve any careful thought or choice. *...the indiscriminate killing of refugees.* ♦ **in·dis·crimi·nate·ly** *The men opened fire indiscriminately... I'm afraid this disease strikes indiscriminately.* — ◆◇◇◇◇ ADJ-GRADED PRAGMATICS / ADV-GRADED

in·dis·pen·sable /ˌɪndɪˈspensəbəl/. If someone or something is **indispensable**, they are absolutely essential and other people or things cannot function without them. *She was becoming indispensable to him.* — ◆◇◇◇◇ ADJ-GRADED

in·dis·posed /ˌɪndɪˈspəʊzd/. If you say that someone is **indisposed**, you mean that they are not available because they are ill, or for a reason that you do not want to reveal. — ADJ FORMAL

in·dis·put·able /ˌɪndɪˈspjuːtəbəl/. If you say that something is **indisputable**, you are emphasizing that it cannot be denied or proved wrong. *It is indisputable that birds in the UK are harbouring this illness.* ♦ **in·dis·put·ably** /ˌɪndɪˈspjuːtəbli/. *She has an indisputably lovely voice.* — ◆◇◇◇◇ ADJ PRAGMATICS / ADV

in·dis·tinct /ˌɪndɪˈstɪŋkt/. Something that is **indistinct** is unclear and difficult to see, hear, or recognize. *The lettering is fuzzy and indistinct.* ♦ **in·dis·tinct·ly** *He speaks so rapidly and indistinctly that many listeners haven't a clue what he is saying.* — ADJ-GRADED / ADV-GRADED: ADV after v

in·dis·tin·guish·able /ˌɪndɪˈstɪŋgwɪʃəbəl/. If one thing is **indistinguishable** from another, the two — ◆◇◇◇◇ ADJ

things are so similar that it is difficult to know which is which.

in·di·vid·u·al /ˌɪndɪ'vɪdʒuəl/ **individuals. 1** Individual means relating to one person or thing, rather than to a large group. ...*waiting for the group to decide rather than making individual decisions... Divide the vegetables among four individual dishes.* ♦ **in·di·vid·u·al·ly** ...*cheeses which come in individually wrapped segments... There are 96 pieces and they are worth, individually and collectively, a lot of money.* **2** An **individual** is a person. ...*anonymous individuals who are doing good things within our community.* **3** If you describe someone or something as **individual**, you mean that you admire them because they are very unusual and do not try to imitate other people or things. ...*her very individual personality.*
♦♦♦♦◇ ADJ: ADJ n
ADV
N-COUNT
ADJ-GRADED
PRAGMATICS

in·di·vid·u·al·ist /ˌɪndɪ'vɪdʒulɪst/ **individualists. 1** If you describe someone as an **individualist**, you mean that they like to think and do things in their own way, rather than imitating other people. *Individualists say that you should be able to wear what you want.* ♦ **in·di·vid·u·al·is·tic** /ˌɪndɪvɪdʒu'lɪstɪk/ *Most artists are very individualistic.* ♦ **in·di·vid·u·al·ism. Individualism** is individualist behaviour. **2 Individualist** means relating to the belief that economics and politics should not be controlled by the state. ...*a party fundamentally committed to individualist and consumerist values.* ▶ An **individualist** is a person with individualist views. *They share with earlier individualists a fear of creeping socialism.* ♦ **individualism. Individualism** is the belief that economics and politics should not be controlled by the state.
N-COUNT
ADJ-GRADED
N-UNCOUNT
ADJ
N-COUNT
N-UNCOUNT

in·di·vid·u·al·ity /ˌɪndɪvɪdʒu'ælɪti/. The **individuality** of a person or thing consists of the qualities that make them different from other people or things. *People who want to express their individuality.*
♦◇◇◇◇ N-UNCOUNT

in·di·vid·u·al·ize /ˌɪndɪ'vɪdʒulaɪz/ **individualizes, individualizing, individualized;** also spelled **individualise** in British English. To **individualize** a thing or person means to make them different from other things or people and to give them a recognizable identity. *Unless a document is highly formal, individualize it by adding comments in the margins.* ♦ **in·di·vid·u·al·ized** *A more individualized approach to patients should now be adopted.*
VERB
V n
FORMAL
ADJ-GRADED

in·di·vis·ible /ˌɪndɪ'vɪzɪbəl/. If something is **indivisible**, it cannot be divided into different parts. *The mind and body form an indivisible whole.*
ADJ

Indo- /'ɪndəu-/. **Indo-** combines with nationality adjectives to form adjectives which describe something connected with both India and another country. ...*Indo-Pakistani talks.*
PREFIX

in·doc·tri·nate /ɪn'dɒktrɪneɪt/ **indoctrinates, indoctrinating, indoctrinated.** If people are **indoctrinated**, they are taught a particular belief with the aim that they will reject other beliefs; used showing disapproval. *I wouldn't say that she was trying to indoctrinate us.* ♦ **in·doc·tri·na·tion** /ɪnˌdɒktrɪ'neɪʃən/ ...*political indoctrination classes.*
VERB: be V-ed
PRAGMATICS
V n
N-UNCOUNT

in·do·lent /'ɪndələnt/. Someone who is **indolent** is lazy. ...*indolent teenagers who won't lift a finger to help.* ♦ **in·do·lence** *There was a great deal of indolence in his nature.*
ADJ-GRADED
FORMAL
N-UNCOUNT

in·domi·table /ɪn'dɒmɪtəbəl/. If you say that someone has an **indomitable** spirit, you admire them because they never give up or admit that they have been defeated.
ADJ-GRADED
PRAGMATICS
FORMAL

in·door /'ɪndɔː/. **Indoor** activities or things are ones that happen or are used inside a building and not outside. ...*an indoor market.*
♦♦◇◇◇ ADJ: ADJ n

in·doors /ˌɪn'dɔːz/. If something happens **indoors**, it happens inside a building. *Since she was indoors, she had not been wearing a coat... I think perhaps we should go indoors.*
♦◇◇◇◇ ADV

in·du·bi·table /ɪn'djuːbɪtəbəl, AM -'duːb-/. You use **indubitable** to describe something when you want to emphasize that it is definite and cannot be doubted. *His brilliance as a director and actor ren-*
ADJ
PRAGMATICS
FORMAL

ders this film an indubitable classic.* ♦ **in·du·bi·tably** *His behaviour was indubitably ill-judged.*
ADV

in·duce /ɪn'djuːs, AM -'duːs-/ **induces, inducing, induced. 1** To **induce** a state or condition means to cause it. *Surgery could induce a heart attack.* ♦ **-induced** ...*stress-induced disorders. ...a drug-induced hallucination.* **2** If you **induce** someone to do something, you persuade or influence them to do it. *I would do anything to induce them to stay.* ♦ **in·duce·ment, inducements.** An **inducement** is something that is offered to someone to persuade or influence them to do something. **3** If a doctor or midwife **induces** labour or birth, they cause a pregnant woman to start giving birth by using drugs or other medical means. ♦ **in·duc·tion** ...*if there are obvious medical reasons for induction.*
♦♦◇◇◇ VERB
V n
COMB
VERB
V n to-inf
N-COUNT
VERB: V n
N-SING

in·duct /ɪn'dʌkt/ **inducts, inducting, inducted. 1** If someone is **inducted** into a particular job, rank, or position, they are given the job, rank, or position in a formal ceremony. ...*how Princess Diana was inducted into her arduous royal work. ...as the Countess inducts Nina into the cult.* **2** If someone **is inducted** into the army, they are officially made to join the army. *In December he was inducted into the army.*
VERB
be V-ed into n
V n into n
Also V n
FORMAL
VB: usu passive,
be V-ed into n
be V-ed into n
AMERICAN

in·duc·tion /ɪn'dʌkʃən/ **inductions. 1** Induction is a procedure or ceremony for introducing someone to a new job or way of life. ...*the induction of the girls into the sport. ...Elvis' induction into the army.* **2 Induction** is a method of reasoning in which you use individual ideas or facts to give you a general rule or conclusion. *Science is founded on the principle of induction.* ♦ **in·duc·tive.** /ɪn'dʌktɪv/. Inductive reasoning is based on the process of induction. **3 Induction** is the process by which electricity or magnetism is passed between two objects or circuits without them touching each other. **4** See also **induce.**
♦◇◇◇◇ N-VAR
N-UNCOUNT
ADJ
N-UNCOUNT
TECHNICAL

in·dulge /ɪn'dʌldʒ/ **indulges, indulging, indulged. 1** If you **indulge** in something, you allow yourself to have or do something that you know you will enjoy. *You can indulge yourself without spending a fortune.* **2** If you **indulge** someone, you let them have or do what they want, even if this is not good for them. *He did not really agree with indulging children.*
♦♦◇◇◇ VERB:
V in n
V pron-refl
Also V n
VERB
V n

in·dul·gent /ɪn'dʌldʒənt/. If you are **indulgent**, you treat a person with special kindness, often in a way that is not good for them. *His indulgent mother was willing to let him do anything he wanted.* ♦ **in·dul·gent·ly** *Ned smiled at him indulgently and said, 'Come on over when you feel like it.'* ♦ **in·dul·gence, indulgences** *The king's indulgence towards his sons angered the business community.*
♦◇◇◇◇ ADJ-GRADED
ADV-GRADED
N-VAR

in·dus·trial /ɪn'dʌstriəl/. **1** You use **industrial** to describe things which relate to or are used in industry. ...*industrial machinery and equipment.* **2** An **industrial** city or country is one in which industry is important or highly developed. ...*western industrial countries.*
♦♦♦♦◇ ADJ
ADJ

in'dustrial 'action. If workers take **industrial action**, they join together and do something to show that they are unhappy with their pay or working conditions, for example refusing to work.
♦◇◇◇◇ N-UNCOUNT
BRITISH

in'dustrial estate, industrial estates. An **industrial estate** is an area which has been specially planned for a lot of factories.
♦◇◇◇◇ N-COUNT
BRITISH

in·dus·tri·al·ise /ɪn'dʌstriəlaɪz/. See **industrialize.**

in·dus·tri·al·ism /ɪn'dʌstriəlɪzəm/. **Industrialism** is the state of having an economy that is based on industry.
N-UNCOUNT

in·dus·tri·al·ist /ɪn'dʌstriəlɪst/ **industrialists.** An **industrialist** is a powerful businessman who owns or controls large industrial companies or factories.
♦◇◇◇◇ N-COUNT

in·dus·tri·al·ize /ɪn'dʌstriəlaɪz/ **industrializes, industrializing, industrialized;** also spelled **industrialise** in British English. When a country **industrializes** or **is industrialized**, it develops a lot of industries. *Energy consumption rises as countries*
♦♦◇◇◇ V-ERG
V
V n

I

industrialise... *Stalin's methods had industrialized the Russian economy.* ◆ **in·dus·tri·ali·za·tion** /ɪnˌdʌstriəlaɪˈzeɪʃən/. *Industrialization began early in Spain.*   N-UNCOUNT

in·dus·tri·al·ized /ɪnˈdʌstriəlaɪzd/; also spelled **in·dustrialised**. An **industrialized** area or place is one which has a lot of industries. *...the industrialized world.*   ◆◆◇◇◇ ADJ-GRADED: ADJ n

in,dustrial re'lations. **Industrial relations** refers to the relationship between employers and employees in industry, and the political decisions and laws that affect it.   ◆◇◇◇◇ N-PLURAL

in·dus·tri·ous /ɪnˈdʌstriəs/. An **industrious** person works very hard. *She was an industrious and willing worker.* ◆ **in·dus·tri·ous·ly** *Maggie paints industriously all through the summer.*   ADJ-GRADED / ADV-GRADED: ADV with v

in·dus·try /ˈɪndəstri/ **industries. 1 Industry** is the work and processes involved in collecting raw materials, and making them into products in factories. *...countries where industry is developing rapidly.* **2** A particular **industry** consists of all the people and activities involved in making a particular product or providing a particular service. *...the motor vehicle and textile industries.* **3** If you refer to a social or political activity as an **industry**, you are criticizing it because you think it involves a lot of people in unnecessary or useless work. *Some Afro-Caribbeans are rejecting the whole race relations industry.* **4** See also **captain of industry, cottage industry, service industry.**   ◆◆◆◆◆ N-UNCOUNT / N-COUNT / N-COUNT PRAGMATICS

5 Industry is the fact of working very hard. *No one doubted his ability, his industry or his integrity.*   N-UNCOUNT FORMAL

in·ebri·at·ed /ɪnˈiːbrieɪtɪd/. Someone who is **inebriated** has drunk too much alcohol.   ADJ-GRADED FORMAL

in·ed·ible /ɪnˈedɪbəl/. If you say that something is **inedible**, you mean you cannot eat it, for example because it tastes bad or is poisonous.   ADJ-GRADED

in·ef·fable /ɪnˈefəbəl/. You use **ineffable** to say that something is so great or extreme that it cannot be described in words. *...the ineffable sadness of many of the portraits.* ◆ **in·ef·fably** /ɪnˈefəbli/. *Walters is ineffably entertaining.*   ADJ FORMAL / ADV

in·ef·fec·tive /ˌɪnɪˈfektɪv/. If you say that something is **ineffective**, you mean that it has no effect on a process or situation. *...an ineffective method of controlling your dog.* ◆ **in·ef·fec·tive·ness** *...the ineffectiveness of some of the police's anti-crime strategies.*   ◆◇◇◇◇ ADJ-GRADED / N-UNCOUNT

in·ef·fec·tual /ˌɪnɪˈfektʃuəl/. If someone or something is **ineffectual**, they fail to do what they are expected to do or are trying to do. *The mayor had become ineffectual in the struggle to clamp down on drugs.* ◆ **in·ef·fec·tu·al·ly** *Few are won and many drag on expensively and ineffectually.*   ◆◇◇◇◇ ADJ-GRADED / ADV-GRADED: ADV with v

in·ef·fi·cient /ˌɪnɪˈfɪʃənt/. **Inefficient** people, organizations, systems, or machines do not use time, energy, or other resources in the best way. *...the closure of outdated and inefficient factories.* ◆ **in·ef·fi·cien·cy, inefficiencies** *...the inefficiency of the distribution system.* ◆ **in·ef·fi·cient·ly** *Energy prices have been kept artificially low, so energy is used inefficiently.*   ◆◆◇◇◇ ADJ-GRADED PRAGMATICS / N-VAR / ADV-GRADED: ADV with v

in·el·egant /ɪnˈelɪgənt/. If you say that something is **inelegant**, you mean that it is not attractive or graceful. *The grand piano has been replaced with a small, inelegant electric model.*   ADJ-GRADED

in·eli·gible /ɪnˈelɪdʒəbəl/. If you are **ineligible** for something, you are not qualified for it or entitled to it. *They were ineligible to remain in the USA because of their criminal records.*   ADJ FORMAL

in·ept /ɪnˈept/. If you say that someone is **inept**, you are criticizing them because they do something with a complete lack of skill. *You are completely inept at writing. ...his inept handling of the army.*   ◆◇◇◇◇ ADJ-GRADED PRAGMATICS

in·epti·tude /ɪnˈeptɪtjuːd, AM -tuːd/. If you refer to someone's **ineptitude**, you are criticizing them because they do something with a complete lack of skill. *...anger which sprayed out in all directions at the ineptitude of the police.*   N-UNCOUNT PRAGMATICS

in·equal·ity /ˌɪnɪˈkwɒlɪti/ **inequalities. Inequality** is the difference in social status, wealth, or opportunity between people or groups. *People are concerned about corruption and social inequality.*   ◆◇◇◇◇ N-VAR

in·equi·table /ɪnˈekwɪtəbəl/. If you say that something is **inequitable**, you are criticizing it because it is unfair or unjust. *The welfare system is grossly inequitable and inefficient.*   ADJ-GRADED PRAGMATICS FORMAL

in·equi·ty /ɪnˈekwɪti/ **inequities.** If you refer to the **inequity** of something, you are criticizing it because it is unfair or unjust. *...the inequities in our health care system.*   N-VAR PRAGMATICS FORMAL

in·eradi·cable /ˌɪnɪˈrædɪkəbəl/. You use **ineradicable** to emphasize that a quality, fact, or situation is permanent and cannot be changed. *Divorce is a permanent, ineradicable fact of modern life.*   ADJ PRAGMATICS FORMAL

in·ert /ɪnˈɜːt/. **1** Something that is **inert** does not move at all and appears to be lifeless. *He covered the inert body with a blanket.* **2** If you describe something as **inert**, you are criticizing it because it is not very lively or interesting. *The novel itself remains oddly inert.* **3** An **inert** substance is one which does not react with other substances.   ◆◇◇◇◇ / ADJ-GRADED PRAGMATICS / ADJ TECHNICAL

in·er·tia /ɪnˈɜːʃə/. **1** If you have a feeling of **inertia**, you feel very lazy and unwilling to move or be active. *He resented her inertia, her lack of energy and self-direction.* **2 Inertia** is the tendency of a physical object to remain still or to continue moving, unless a force is applied to it.   N-UNCOUNT / N-UNCOUNT TECHNICAL

in·es·cap·able /ˌɪnɪˈskeɪpəbəl/. If you describe a fact, situation, or activity as **inescapable**, you mean that it is difficult not to notice it or be affected by it. *...common illnesses that most people regard as nothing more than an inescapable nuisance.* ▶ **in·es·cap·ably** /ˌɪnɪˈskeɪpəbli/. *...when your life becomes inescapably dull.*   ◆◇◇◇◇ ADJ / ADV

in·es·ti·mable /ɪnˈestɪməbəl/. If you describe the value, benefit, or importance of something as **inestimable**, you mean that it is extremely great and cannot be calculated. *This gives the professional an inestimable advantage.*   ADJ FORMAL

in·evi·table /ɪnˈevɪtəbəl/. If something is **inevitable**, it is certain to happen and cannot be prevented or avoided. *If the case succeeds, it is inevitable that other trials will follow.* ▶ **The inevitable** is something which is inevitable. *'It's just delaying the inevitable,' he said.* ◆ **in·evi·tably** /ɪnˈevɪtəbli/. *Technological changes will inevitably lead to unemployment.* ◆ **in·evi·tabil·ity** /ɪnˌevɪtəˈbɪlɪti/ **inevitabilities.** *We are all bound by the inevitability of death.*   ◆◆◆◇◇ ADJ / N-SING: the N / ADV / N-VAR

in·ex·act /ˌɪnɪgˈzækt/. Something that is **inexact** is not precise or accurate. *Economics may be an inexact science, but it is a science nonetheless.*   ADJ-GRADED

in·ex·cus·able /ˌɪnɪkˈskjuːzəbəl/. If you say that something is **inexcusable**, you are emphasizing that it cannot be justified or tolerated because it is extremely bad. *He said the killing of innocent people was inexcusable.* ◆ **in·ex·cus·ably** /ˌɪnɪkˈskjuːzəbli/ *She had been inexcusably careless.*   ADJ-GRADED PRAGMATICS / ADV

in·ex·haust·ible /ˌɪnɪgˈzɔːstəbəl/. If there is an **inexhaustible** supply of something, there is so much of it that it cannot all be used up. *His energy was unbounded and his patience inexhaustible.*   ADJ

in·exo·rable /ɪnˈeksərəbəl/. You use **inexorable** to describe a process which cannot be prevented from continuing or progressing. *...the seemingly inexorable rise in unemployment.* ◆ **in·exo·rably** /ɪnˈeksərəbli/. *The crisis is moving inexorably towards war.*   ◆◇◇◇◇ ADJ-GRADED FORMAL / ADV-GRADED: ADV with v

in·ex·pen·sive /ˌɪnɪkˈspensɪv/. Something that is **inexpensive** does not cost very much. *There is a large variety of good inexpensive restaurants.*   ◆◇◇◇◇ ADJ-GRADED

in·ex·pe·ri·ence /ˌɪnɪkˈspɪəriəns/. If you refer to someone's **inexperience**, you mean that they have little knowledge or experience of a particular situation or activity. *Critics attacked the youth and inexperience of his staff.* ◆ **in·ex·pe·ri·enced** /ˌɪnɪkˈspɪəriənst/. *They are inexperienced when it comes to decorating.*   ◆◇◇◇◇ N-UNCOUNT / ADJ-GRADED

in·ex·pli·cable /ˌɪnɪkˈsplɪkəbəl/. If something is inexplicable, you cannot explain why it happens or why it is true. *For some inexplicable reason, the investors decided to pull out.* ♦ **in·ex·pli·cably** /ˌɪnɪkˈsplɪkəbli/. *She suddenly and inexplicably announced her retirement.* ◆◇◇◇◇ ADJ-GRADED / ADV-GRADED

in·ex·press·ible /ˌɪnɪkˈspresɪbəl/. An inexpressible feeling cannot be expressed in words because it is so strong. *He felt a sudden inexpressible loneliness.* ADJ

in ex·tre·mis /ɪn ɪkˈstriːmɪs/. If someone or something is **in extremis**, they are in a very difficult situation and have to use extreme methods. *The use of antibiotics is permitted only in extremis.* PHRASE FORMAL BRITISH

in·ex·tri·cable /ˌɪnɪkˈstrɪkəbəl, ɪnˈekstrɪk-/. If there is an **inextricable** link between things, they cannot be considered separately. *There's an inextricable link between markets and cost.* ♦ **in·ex·tri·cably** /ˌɪnekˈstrɪkəbəli/. *Our survival is inextricably linked to the survival of the rainforest.* ◆◇◇◇◇ ADJ-GRADED FORMAL / ADV-GRADED: ADV with v

in·fal·lible /ɪnˈfælɪbəl/. If a person or thing is **infallible**, they are never wrong. *She had an infallible eye for style.* ♦ **in·fal·libil·ity** /ɪnˌfælɪˈbɪlɪti/ *...exaggerated views of the infallibility of science.* ◆◇◇◇◇ ADJ / N-UNCOUNT

in·fa·mous /ˈɪnfəməs/. **Infamous** people or things are well-known because of something bad. *...the infamous massacre of Indians at Wounded Knee.* ◆◇◇◇◇ ADJ FORMAL

in·fa·my /ˈɪnfəmi/. **Infamy** is the state of being infamous. *...one of the greatest acts of infamy in history.* N-UNCOUNT FORMAL

in·fan·cy /ˈɪnfənsi/. **1 Infancy** is the period of your life when you are a very young child. *...minute details of Deborah's infancy.* **2** If something is in its **infancy**, it is new and has not developed very much. *Computing science was still in its infancy.* N-UNCOUNT / N-UNCOUNT

in·fant /ˈɪnfənt/ **infants. 1** An **infant** is a baby or very young child. *The family were forced to flee with their infant son. ...the infant mortality rate in Britain.* **2 Infants** are children between the ages of five and seven, who go to an infant school. ♦ You use **the infants** to refer to a school or class for such children. *You've been my best friend ever since we started in the infants.* **3 Infant** means designed especially for very young children. *...an infant carrier in the back of a car.* **4** An **infant** organization or system is new and has not developed very much. *The infant company was based in Germany.* ◆◆◇◇◇ N-COUNT / N-COUNT / BRITISH N-UNCOUNT: the N / ADJ: ADJ n / ADJ: ADJ n

in·fan·ti·cide /ɪnˈfæntɪsaɪd/. **Infanticide** is the crime of killing a baby. N-UNCOUNT

in·fan·tile /ˈɪnfəntaɪl/. **1 Infantile** behaviour or illnesses are typical of very young children. *...infantile aggression. ...children with infantile eczema.* **2** If you accuse someone or something of being **infantile**, you think that they are foolish and childish. *This kind of humour is infantile and boring.* ADJ: ADJ n FORMAL / ADJ-GRADED [PRAGMATICS]

in·fan·try /ˈɪnfəntri/. The **infantry** are soldiers who fight on foot rather than in tanks or on horses. *The enemy infantry was hiding. ...regiments of infantry.* ◆◆◇◇◇ N-COLL-UNCOUNT

in·fantry·man /ˈɪnfəntrimən/ **infantrymen.** An **infantryman** is a soldier in an infantry regiment. N-COUNT

infant school, infant schools. In Britain, an **infant school** is a school for children between the ages of approximately 5 and 7. N-VAR

in·fatu·at·ed /ɪnˈfætʃueɪtɪd/. If you are **infatuated** with a person or thing, you have strong feelings of love or passion for them which make you unable to think clearly or sensibly about that person or thing. *He was utterly infatuated with her.* ♦ **in·fat·ua·tion** /ɪnˌfætʃuˈeɪʃən/ **infatuations.** *...his infatuation with bullfighting... Teenagers have their own infatuations.* ADJ-GRADED [PRAGMATICS] / N-VAR

in·fect /ɪnˈfekt/ **infects, infecting, infected. 1** To **infect** people, animals, or plants means to cause them to have a disease or illness. *...people infected with HIV.* ♦ **in·fec·tion** /ɪnˈfekʃən/ *...plants that are resistant to infection.* **2** To **infect** a substance or area means to cause it to contain harmful germs or bacteria. *The birds infect the milk. ...a virus which is spread mainly by infected blood.* ♦ **in·fect·ed** *In heavily infected areas, half the population will become blind.* **3** When people, places, or things are **infected** by a feeling or influence, it spreads to ◆◆◆◇◇ VERB: V n V-ed Also V n with n / N-UNCOUNT / VERB V n V-ed / ADJ-GRADED / VERB: be V-ed by n V n with n

them. *He thought they might infect others with their bourgeois ideas... His urge for revenge would never infect her.* V n

in·fec·tion /ɪnˈfekʃən/ **infections.** An **infection** is a disease caused by germs or bacteria. *Ear infections are a common complication of a sore throat in pre-school children.* ● See also **infect.** ◆◆◆◇◇ N-COUNT

in·fec·tious /ɪnˈfekʃəs/. **1** A disease that is **infectious** can be caught by being near a person who is infected with it. Compare **contagious.** *...infectious diseases such as measles.* **2** If a feeling is **infectious**, it spreads to other people. *She radiates an infectious enthusiasm for everything she does.* ◆◇◇◇◇ ADJ-GRADED / ADJ-GRADED

in·fec·tive /ɪnˈfektɪv/. **Infective** means related to infection or likely to cause infection. *...a mild and very common infective disease of children.* ADJ-GRADED FORMAL

in·fer /ɪnˈfɜː/ **infers, inferring, inferred. 1** If you **infer** that something is the case, you decide that it is true on the basis of information that you already have. *By measuring the motion of the galaxies in a cluster, astronomers can infer the cluster's mass.* **2** Some people use **infer** to mean 'imply', but many people consider this use to be incorrect. *The police inferred, though they didn't exactly say it, that they found her behaviour rather suspicious.* ◆◇◇◇◇ VERB: V that V n / VERB V that

in·fer·ence /ˈɪnfərəns/ **inferences. 1** An **inference** is a conclusion that you draw about something by using information that you already have about it. *There were two inferences to be drawn from her letter.* **2 Inference** is the act of drawing conclusions about something on the basis of information that you already have. *It had an extremely tiny head and, by inference, a tiny brain.* ◆◇◇◇◇ N-COUNT / N-UNCOUNT

in·fe·ri·or /ɪnˈfɪəriə/ **inferiors. 1** Something that is **inferior** is not as good as something else. *The cassettes were of inferior quality... Comprehensive schools were perceived as inferior to grammar schools.* **2** If one person is regarded as **inferior** to another, they are regarded as less important because they have less status or ability. *...the inferior status of women in pre-revolutionary Russia... Most career women make me feel inferior.* ▶ Also a noun. *It was a gentleman's duty always to be civil, even to his inferiors.* ♦ **in·fe·ri·or·ity** /ɪnˌfɪəriˈɒrɪti, AM -ˈɔːr-/ *I found it very difficult to shake off a sense of inferiority.* ◆◆◇◇◇ ADJ-GRADED / ADJ-GRADED / N-COUNT / N-UNCOUNT

inferi'ority complex, inferiority complexes. Someone who has an **inferiority complex** feels that they are of less worth or importance than other people. N-COUNT

in·fer·nal /ɪnˈfɜːnəl/. **1 Infernal** is used to emphasize that something is very annoying or unpleasant. *They can't work in these infernal conditions.* **2 Infernal** is used to describe things that relate to hell. *...the goddess of the infernal regions.* ADJ: ADJ n [PRAGMATICS] DATED / ADJ: ADJ n

in·fer·no /ɪnˈfɜːnəʊ/ **infernos.** If you refer to a fire as an **inferno**, you mean that it is burning fiercely and causing great destruction. *Rescue workers fought to get to victims inside the inferno.* ◆◇◇◇◇ N-COUNT JOURNALISM

in·fer·tile /ɪnˈfɜːtaɪl, AM -təl/. **1** A person or animal that is **infertile** is unable to produce babies. ♦ **in·fer·til·ity** /ˌɪnfəˈtɪlɪti/. *Male infertility is becoming commonplace.* **2 Infertile** soil is of poor quality and plants cannot grow in it. *The polluted waste is often dumped, making the surrounding land infertile.* ◆◇◇◇◇ ADJ / N-UNCOUNT / ADJ-GRADED

in·fest /ɪnˈfest/ **infests, infesting, infested. 1** When pests such as insects or rats **infest** plants or a place, they spread in large numbers and cause damage. *...pests like aphids which infest cereal crops.* ♦ **in·fest·ed** *The prison is infested with rats.* ♦ **-infested** *...the rat-infested slums where the plague flourished.* ♦ **in·fes·ta·tion** /ˌɪnfeˈsteɪʃən/ **infestations.** *The premises were treated for cockroach infestation.* **2** If you say that people or things you disapprove of or regard as dangerous **are infesting** a place, you mean that there are large numbers of them in that place. *Crime and drugs are infesting the inner cities.* ♦ **in·fest·ed** *The road further south was infested with bandits.* ♦ **-infested** *...the shark-infested waters of the Great Barrier Reef.* ◆◇◇◇◇ VERB V n / ADJ / COMB / N-VAR / VERB [PRAGMATICS] V n / ADJ / COMB

I

in·fi·del /'ɪnfɪdəl/ **infidels.** If one person refers to another as an **infidel**, the first person is hostile towards the second person because that person has a different religion or has no religion. ▶ Also an adjective. *He promised to continue the fight against infidel forces.* N-COUNT PRAGMATICS LITERARY / ADJ: ADJ n

in·fi·del·ity /ˌɪnfɪ'delɪti/ **infidelities.** Infidelity occurs when a person who is married or in a steady relationship has sex with another person. *...frightened always that her fears of her husband's infidelity would be confirmed.* ◆◇◇◇◇ N-VAR

'in-fighting. In-fighting is rivalry or quarrelling between members of the same group or organization. *...after a year of in-fighting between right-wingers and moderates in the party.* N-UNCOUNT

in·fill /'ɪnfɪl/ **infills, infilling, infilled. 1** To **infill** a hollow place or gap means to fill it. *The cave was too polluted to enter and the entrance was infilled by the landowner... It is wise to start infilling with a layer of gravel for drainage.* **2 Infill** is something which fills a hollow place or gap. *There is room for infill between the new outer suburbs of the city.* VERB be V-ed V Also V n BRITISH / N-UNCOUNT

in·fil·trate /'ɪnfɪltreɪt/ **infiltrates, infiltrating, infiltrated. 1** If people **infiltrate** a place or organization, or **infiltrate** into it, they enter it secretly in order to spy on it or influence it. *The street protests had been infiltrated by people bent on violence... A reporter tried to infiltrate into the prison.* ♦ **in·fil·tra·tion** /ˌɪnfɪl'treɪʃən/ **infiltrations** *The security zone was set up to prevent guerrilla infiltrations.* **2** To **infiltrate** people **into** a place or organization means to get them into it secretly in order to spy on it or influence it. *...efforts to infiltrate agents into the former Soviet Union.* ◆◇◇◇◇ VERB: V n be V-ed V into/from n / N-VAR / VERB V n into n

in·fil·tra·tor /'ɪnfɪltreɪtə/ **infiltrators.** An **infiltrator** is a person who has infiltrated a place or organization. *He had close on three hundred infiltrators inside the walls, disguised as local soldiers.* N-COUNT

in·fi·nite /'ɪnfɪnɪt/. **1** If you describe something as **infinite**, you are emphasizing that it is extremely great in amount or degree. *...an infinite variety of landscapes... With infinite care, John shifted position.* ♦ **in·fi·nite·ly** *His design was infinitely better than anything I could have done.* **2** Something that is **infinite** has no limit, end, or edge. *Obviously, no company has infinite resources. ...God's infinite mercy.* ▶ The **infinite** is something which is infinite. *...pondering on the infinite.* ♦ **infinitely** *A centimetre can be infinitely divided into smaller units.* ◆◆◇◇◇ ADJ PRAGMATICS / ADV / N-SING / ADV: ADV with v

in·fini·tesi·mal /ˌɪnfɪnɪ'tesɪməl/. Something that is **infinitesimal** is extremely small. *...mineral substances present in infinitesimal amounts in the soil.* ADJ FORMAL

in·fini·tive /ɪn'fɪnɪtɪv/ **infinitives.** The **infinitive** of a verb is the basic form, for example 'do', 'be', 'take', and 'eat'. The infinitive is often used with 'to' in front of it. N-COUNT

in·fi·ni·tum /ˌɪnfɪ'naɪtəm/. See **ad infinitum.**

in·fin·ity /ɪn'fɪnɪti/. **1 Infinity** is a number that is larger than any other number and can never be given an exact value. *These permutations multiply towards infinity.* **2 Infinity** is a point that is further away than any other point and can never be reached. *...the darkness of a starless night stretching to infinity.* ◆◇◇◇◇ N-UNCOUNT: also a N of n / N-UNCOUNT

in·firm /ɪn'fɜːm/. A person who is **infirm** is weak or ill, and usually old. *She moved with her aging, infirm husband into a retirement center.* ▶ The **infirm** are people who are infirm. ♦ **in·fir·mity** **infirmities.** *Older people often try to ignore their infirmities.* ADJ-GRADED / N-PLURAL / N-VAR

in·fir·ma·ry /ɪn'fɜːməri/ **infirmaries.** Some hospitals are called **infirmaries.** *...the Radcliffe Infirmary in Oxford.* ◆◇◇◇◇ N-COUNT

in·flame /ɪn'fleɪm/ **inflames, inflaming, inflamed.** If something **inflames** a situation or **inflames** people's feelings, it makes them angry or passionate about something. *The shooting has only inflamed passions further.* ◆◇◇◇◇ VERB V n JOURNALISM

in·flamed /ɪn'fleɪmd/. If part of your body is **inflamed**, it is red or swollen, usually as a result of an infection, injury, or illness. *Symptoms include red, itchy and inflamed skin.* ADJ-GRADED FORMAL

in·flam·mable /ɪn'flæməbəl/. An **inflammable** material or chemical catches fire and burns easily. *A highly inflammable liquid escaped into the drilling equipment.* ADJ-GRADED

in·flam·ma·tion /ˌɪnflə'meɪʃən/ **inflammations.** An **inflammation** is a painful redness or swelling of a part of your body that results from an infection, injury, or illness. *The drug can cause inflammation of the liver.* ◆◇◇◇◇ N-VAR FORMAL

in·flam·ma·tory /ɪn'flæmətəri, AM -tɔːri/. **1** If you accuse someone of saying or doing **inflammatory** things, you mean that what they say or do is likely to make people react very angrily. *She described his remarks as irresponsible, inflammatory and outrageous.* **2** An **inflammatory** condition or disease is one in which the patient suffers from inflammation. *...the inflammatory reactions that occur in asthma.* ◆◇◇◇◇ ADJ-GRADED PRAGMATICS / ADJ: ADJ n FORMAL

in·flat·able /ɪn'fleɪtəbəl/ **inflatables.** **1** An **inflatable** object is one that you fill with air when you want to use it. *The children were playing on the inflatable castle.* **2** An **inflatable** is an inflatable object, especially a small boat. ◆◇◇◇◇ ADJ / N-COUNT

in·flate /ɪn'fleɪt/ **inflates, inflating, inflated. 1** If you **inflate** something such as a balloon or tyre, or if it **inflates**, it becomes bigger as it is filled with air or a gas. *Don's lifejacket had failed to inflate.* **2** If you say that someone **inflates** the price of something, or that the price **inflates**, you mean that the price increases. *Clothing prices have not inflated as much as automobiles.* ♦ **in·flat·ed** *They had to buy everything at inflated prices at the ranch store.* **3** If someone **inflates** the amount or effect of something, they say it is bigger, better, or more important than it really is, usually so that they can profit from it. *They inflated their clients' medical injuries and treatment to defraud insurance companies.* ◆◇◇◇◇ V-ERG: V n V / V-ERG: V n V / ADJ-GRADED / VERB V n

in·fla·tion /ɪn'fleɪʃən/. **Inflation** is a general increase in the prices of goods and services in a country. *...an inflation rate of only 2.2%.* ◆◆◆◇ N-UNCOUNT

in·fla·tion·ary /ɪn'fleɪʃənri, AM -neri/. **Inflationary** means connected with inflation or causing inflation. *The bank is worried about mounting inflationary pressures.* ◆◇◇◇◇ ADJ-GRADED

in·flect /ɪn'flekt/ **inflects, inflecting, inflected.** If a word **inflects**, its ending or form changes in order to show its grammatical function. If a language **inflects**, it has words in it that inflect. ♦ **in·flect·ed** *Kings, ministers, and Brahmans spoke Sanskrit, the most esteemed and highly inflected language... In all dictionaries to date we give the headword and all the inflected forms.* ♦ **in·flec·tion** /ɪn'flekʃən/ **inflections.** *At this stage the child has not yet acquired the ability to use inflections.* VERB: V / ADJ-GRADED / N-VAR

in·flec·tion /ɪn'flekʃən/ **inflections.** An **inflection** in someone's voice is a change in their tone or intonation as they are speaking. *The man's voice was devoid of inflection.* N-VAR WRITTEN

in·flex·ible /ɪn'fleksɪbəl/. **1** Something that is **inflexible** cannot be altered in any way, even if the situation changes. *Workers insisted the new system was too inflexible.* ♦ **in·flex·ibil·ity** /ˌɪnˌfleksɪ'bɪlɪti/ *The snag about an endowment mortgage is its inflexibility.* **2** If you say that someone is **inflexible**, you are criticizing them because they refuse to change their mind or alter their way of doing things. *His opponents viewed him as stubborn, dogmatic, and inflexible.* ♦ **inflexibility** *Joyce was irritated by the inflexibility of her colleagues.* ◆◇◇◇◇ ADJ-GRADED / N-UNCOUNT / ADJ-GRADED PRAGMATICS / N-UNCOUNT

in·flict /ɪn'flɪkt/ **inflicts, inflicting, inflicted.** To **inflict** harm or damage on someone or something means to make them suffer it. *...the damage being inflicted on Britain's industries by the recession.* ♦ **in·flic·tion** /ɪn'flɪkʃən/. *...without the unnecessary or cruel infliction of pain.* ◆◆◇◇◇ VERB: V n V n on n / N-UNCOUNT

'in-flight; also spelled **inflight.** **In-flight** services are ones that are provided on board an aeroplane. *The in-flight movie was Casablanca.* ADJ: ADJ n

in·flow /ˈɪnfləʊ/ **inflows.** If there is an **inflow** of money or people into a place, a large amount of money or people move into that place. *The Swiss wanted to discourage an inflow of foreign money. ...the inflow of immigrants from East Germany.* ◆◇◇◇ N-COUNT

in·flu·ence /ˈɪnfluəns/ **influences, influencing, influenced. 1** Influence is the power to make other people agree with your opinions or do what you want. *As Hugh grew older, he had less influence and couldn't control him... The government should continue to use its influence for the release of all hostages.* **2** If you **influence** someone, you use your power to make them agree with you or do what you want. *He is trying to improperly influence a witness... My dad influenced me to do electronics.* **3** If someone or something has an **influence** on people or situations, they affect the way people think or act, or what happens. *The Shropshire landscape was an influence on Owen too... Many other medications have an influence on cholesterol levels.* **4** If someone or something **influences** a person or situation, they have an effect on that person's behaviour or that situation. *What you eat may influence your risk of getting cancer... They still influence what's played on the radio.* **5** Someone or something that is a good or bad **influence** on people has a good or bad effect on them. *TV is a bad influence on people.* **6** If you are **under the influence** of someone or something, you are being affected or controlled by them. *The very earliest sculptures were made under the influence of Greek art... He was arrested on suspicion of driving under the influence of alcohol.* **7** If someone is **under the influence,** their mind is affected by alcohol or drugs. *Police charged the man with driving under the influence.* ◆◆◆◆ N-UNCOUNT / VERB / N-COUNT / VERB / N-COUNT / PHRASE / PHRASE INFORMAL

in·flu·en·tial /ˌɪnfluˈenʃəl/. Someone or something that is **influential** has a lot of influence over people or events. *It helps to have influential friends... He had been influential in shaping economic policy.* ◆◆◇◇ ADJ-GRADED

in·flu·en·za /ˌɪnfluˈenzə/. **Influenza** is the same as **flu.** N-UNCOUNT FORMAL

in·flux /ˈɪnflʌks/ **influxes.** An **influx** of people or things into a place is their arrival there in large numbers. *European countries face the possible influx of millions of Russians and others from eastern Europe.* ◆◇◇◇ N-COUNT

info /ˈɪnfəʊ/. **Info** is information. *For more info phone 414-3935.* ◆◇◇◇ N-UNCOUNT INFORMAL

in·fo·mer·cial /ˌɪnfəʊˈmɜːʃəl/ **infomercials.** An **infomercial** is a television programme in which a famous person gives information about a company's products or services, or a politician gives his or her opinions. The word is formed from 'information' and 'commercial'. N-COUNT

in·form /ɪnˈfɔːm/ **informs, informing, informed. 1** If you **inform** someone of something, you tell them about it. *...efforts to inform people about the dangers of AIDS... My daughter informed me that she was pregnant... 'I just added a little soy sauce,' he informs us.* **2** If someone **informs on** a person, they give information about the person to the police or another authority, which causes the person to be suspected or proved guilty of doing something bad. *Somebody must have informed on us.* **3** If a situation or activity **is informed** by an idea or a quality, that idea or quality is very noticeable in it. *The concept of the Rose continued to inform the poet's work.* ◆◆◇◇ VERB / VERB / VERB:beV-ed by n

in·for·mal /ɪnˈfɔːməl/. **1 Informal** speech or behaviour is relaxed and friendly rather than serious, very correct, or official. *She is refreshingly informal.* ♦ **in·for·mal·ly** *She was always there at half past eight, chatting informally to the children.* ♦ **in·for·mal·ity** /ˌɪnfɔːˈmælɪti/. *He was overwhelmed by their cheerfulness and friendly informality.* **2** An **informal** situation is one which is relaxed and friendly and not very serious or official. *The house has an informal atmosphere.* ♦ **informality** *Eleanor enjoyed the relative informality of island life.* **3** You use **informal** to describe something that is done unofficially ◆◆◇◇ ADJ-GRADED

or casually without planning. *...an informal meeting of EC ministers... We had an informal party at a hotel, and people just flooded in.* ♦ **in·for·mal·ly** *He began informally to handle Ted's tax affairs for him.* ADV

in·form·ant /ɪnˈfɔːmənt/ **informants. 1** An **informant** is someone who gives another person a piece of information. **2** An **informant** is the same as an **informer.** ◆◇◇◇ N-COUNT FORMAL / N-COUNT

in·for·ma·tion /ˌɪnfəˈmeɪʃən/. **Information** about someone or something consists of facts about them. *Pat refused to give her any information about Sarah... Each centre would provide information on technology and training... For further information contact the number below.* ◆◆◆◆ N-UNCOUNT

in·for·ma·tion·al /ˌɪnfəˈmeɪʃənəl/. **Informational** means relating to information. *...the informational needs of school-age children. ...the vocabulary and ideas of informational television.* ADJ: ADJ n JOURNALISM

infor·mation tech·nol·ogy. **Information technology** is the theory and practice of using computers to store and analyse information. *...the information technology industry.* ◆◇◇◇ N-UNCOUNT

in·forma·tive /ɪnˈfɔːmətɪv/. Something that is **informative** gives you useful information. *'Holidays That Don't Cost the Earth' is a lively, informative read.* ◆◇◇◇ ADJ-GRADED

in·formed /ɪnˈfɔːmd/. **1** Someone who is **informed** knows about a subject or what is happening in the world. *Informed people know the company is shaky. ...the importance of keeping the public properly informed.* • See also **well-informed. 2** When journalists talk about **informed** sources, they mean people who are likely to give correct information because of their private or special knowledge. *According to informed sources, those taken into custody include at least one major-general.* **3** An **informed** guess or decision is one that likely to be good, because it is based on definite knowledge or information. *Science is now enabling us to make much more informed choices about how we use common drugs.* **4** See also **inform.** ◆◇◇◇ ADJ-GRADED / ADJ: ADJ n / ADJ-GRADED: ADJ n

in·form·er /ɪnˈfɔːmə/ **informers.** An **informer** is someone who tells the police that another person has done something illegal or is about to do something illegal. *...two men suspected of being police informers were attacked and wounded.* ◆◇◇◇ N-COUNT

info·tain·ment /ˌɪnfəʊˈteɪnmənt/. **Infotainment** is used to refer to radio or television programmes that are intended to be entertaining while providing useful information at the same time. The word is formed from 'information' and 'entertainment'. N-UNCOUNT BRITISH

infra-red /ˌɪnfrə ˈred/. **1 Infra-red** radiation is similar to light but has a longer wavelength, so we cannot see it without special equipment. **2 Infra-red** equipment detects infra-red radiation. *...searching with infra-red scanners for weapons and artillery.* ◆◇◇◇ ADJ: ADJ n / ADJ: ADJ n

infra·struc·ture /ˈɪnfrəstrʌktʃə/ **infrastructures.** The **infrastructure** of a country, society, or organization consists of the basic facilities such as transport, communications, power supplies, and buildings, which enable it to function properly. *The infrastructure, from hotels to transport, is old and decrepit.* ◆◆◇◇ N-VAR

in·fre·quent /ɪnˈfriːkwənt/. If something is **infrequent,** it does not happen often. *John Marvell was paying one of his infrequent visits to London.* ♦ **in·fre·quent·ly** *The bridge is used infrequently. ...schools which, not infrequently, were made up of 80 per cent or more of ethnic minorities.* ◆◇◇◇ ADJ-GRADED / ADV-GRADED

in·fringe /ɪnˈfrɪndʒ/ **infringes, infringing, infringed. 1** If someone **infringes** a law or a rule, they break it or do something which disobeys it. *The film exploited his image and infringed his copyright.* ♦ **in·fringe·ment** /ɪnˈfrɪndʒmənt/ **infringements** *Infringement of the regulation is punishable by a fine.* **2** If something **infringes** people's rights, it interferes with these rights and does not allow people the freedom they are entitled to. *It's starting to infringe on our personal liberties.* ♦ **infringement** ◆◇◇◇ VERB: V n / N-VAR / VERB: V n, V on n / N-VAR

...infringement of privacy... They see it as an infringement on their own freedom of action.

in·furi·ate /ɪn'fjʊəriˌeɪt/ **infuriates, infuriating, infuriated.** If something or someone **infuriates** you, they make you extremely angry. *The champion was infuriated by the decision... It infuriates us to have to deal with this particular mayor.* ◆ **in·furi·at·ed** *He knew me well enough to realize how infuriated such a conversation would make me.* ◆ **in·furi·at·ing** *Steve accelerated with infuriating slowness.* ◆ **in·furi·at·ing·ly** *This book is infuriatingly repetitious.*
◆◇◇◇
VERB: V n
be V-ed
it V n to-inf
Also it V n that
ADJ-GRADED
ADJ-GRADED
ADV-GRADED

in·fuse /ɪn'fjuːz/ **infuses, infusing, infused.** **1** To **infuse** a quality into someone or something, or to **infuse** them with a quality, means to fill them with it. *Many of the girls seemed to be infused with excitement on seeing the snow... He argued that a union would infuse unnecessary conflict into the company's employee relations.* **2** If you **infuse** things such as tea leaves or herbs, you put them in hot water or some other liquid for some time so that the water absorbs their flavour. *Herbalists infuse the flowers in oil... Leave the tea to infuse.*
◇◇◇◇
VERB
be V-ed with n
V n into n
Also V n with n
FORMAL
V-ERG: V n
V n in n
V

in·fu·sion /ɪn'fjuːʒən/ **infusions. 1** If there is an **infusion** of one thing into another, the first thing is added to the other thing and makes it stronger or better. *He brought a tremendous infusion of hope to the people.* **2** An **infusion** is a liquid made by leaving herbs in hot water until the flavour is strong.
◆◇◇◇
N-VAR
FORMAL
N-COUNT

-ing. /-ɪŋ/. **1** -ing is added to verbs to form present participles. Present participles are used with auxiliary verbs to make continuous tenses. They are also used like adjectives, describing a person or thing as doing something. *He was walking along the street... It was worth it to see all those smiling faces.* **2** -ing is added to verbs to form uncount nouns referring to activities. *Gardening is very popular in Britain.*
SUFFIX
SUFFIX

in·gen·ious /ɪn'dʒiːniəs/. Something that is **ingenious** is very clever and involves new ideas or equipment. *...a truly ingenious invention.* ◆ **in·gen·ious·ly** *The roof has been ingeniously designed to provide solar heating.*
◆◇◇◇
ADJ-GRADED
ADV-GRADED

in·ge·nue /ˈænʒeɪˌnjuː/ **ingenues.** An **ingenue** is a young, innocent girl in a play or film, or an actress who plays the part of young, innocent girls. *She's not really interested in any more ingenue roles.*
N-COUNT

in·genu·ity /ˌɪndʒə'njuːɪti, AM -'nuː-/. **Ingenuity** is skill at working out how to achieve things or skill at inventing new things.
◆◇◇◇
N-UNCOUNT

in·genu·ous /ɪn'dʒenjuəs/. If you describe someone as **ingenuous**, you mean that they are innocent, trusting, and incapable of deceiving anyone. *With ingenuous sincerity, he captivated his audience.*
ADJ-GRADED
FORMAL

in·gest /ɪn'dʒest/ **ingests, ingesting, ingested.** When animals or plants **ingest** a substance, they take it into themselves, for example by eating or absorbing it. ◆ **in·ges·tion** /ɪn'dʒestʃən/. *Every ingestion of food can affect our mood.*
◆◇◇◇
VERB: V n
TECHNICAL
N-UNCOUNT

in·glo·ri·ous /ɪn'ɡlɔːriəs/. If you describe something as **inglorious**, you mean that it is rather shameful.
ADJ-GRADED

in·got /'ɪŋɡət/ **ingots.** An **ingot** is a lump of metal, usually shaped like a brick. *...gold ingots.*
N-COUNT

in·grained /ˌɪn'ɡreɪnd/. **Ingrained** habits and beliefs are difficult to change or remove. *Morals tend to be deeply ingrained.*
◆◇◇◇
ADJ-GRADED

in·gra·ti·ate /ɪn'ɡreɪʃieɪt/ **ingratiates, ingratiating, ingratiated.** If someone tries to **ingratiate** themselves with you, they do things to try and make you like them; used showing disapproval. *Many politicians are trying to ingratiate themselves with her.* ◆ **in·gra·ti·at·ing** *He said this with an ingratiating smile at John.*
VERB
PRAGMATICS
V pron-refl with n
Also V pron-refl
ADJ-GRADED

in·grati·tude /ɪn'ɡrætɪˌtjuːd, AM -tuːd/. **Ingratitude** is lack of gratitude for something that has been done for you. *It would be the height of ingratitude after all he's done for me.*
N-UNCOUNT

in·gre·di·ent /ɪn'ɡriːdiənt/ **ingredients. 1** Ingredients are the things that are used to make something, especially all the different foods you use
◆◆◇◇
N-COUNT

when you are cooking a particular dish. **2** An **ingredient** of a situation is one of the essential parts of it. *I think that is one of the major ingredients in his success.*
N-COUNT

in·grown /ˌɪn'ɡrəʊn/ or **ingrowing** /ˌɪn'ɡrəʊɪŋ/. An **ingrown** toenail, or in British English an **ingrowing** toenail, is one which is growing into your toe, often causing you pain.
ADJ

in·hab·it /ɪn'hæbɪt/ **inhabits, inhabiting, inhabited.** If a place or region is **inhabited** by a group of people or a species of animal, those people or animals live there. *...the people who inhabit these beautiful islands.*
◆◆◇◇
VERB:
be V-ed
V n
Also V-ed

in·hab·it·ant /ɪn'hæbɪtənt/ **inhabitants.** The **inhabitants** of a place are the people who live there.
◆◆◇◇
N-COUNT

in·ha·la·tion /ˌɪnhə'leɪʃən/ **inhalations. 1** Inhalation is the process or act of breathing in, taking air and sometimes other substances into your lungs. *Accidental inhalation of the powder can be harmful... Take several deep inhalations.* **2** An **inhalation** is a treatment for colds and other illnesses in which you dissolve substances in hot water and breathe in the vapour.
N-VAR
FORMAL
N-COUNT

in·hale /ɪn'heɪl/ **inhales, inhaling, inhaled.** When you **inhale**, you breathe in. When you inhale something such as smoke, you take it into your lungs when you breathe in. *He was treated for the effects of inhaling smoke.*
◆◇◇◇
VERB: V
V n

in·hal·er /ɪn'heɪlə/ **inhalers.** An **inhaler** is a small device for inhaling a drug in order to help you breathe more easily if you have asthma or a cold.
N-COUNT

in·her·ent /ɪn'herənt, -'hɪər-/. The **inherent** qualities of something are the necessary and natural parts of it. *...the dangers inherent in an outbreak of war.* ◆ **in·her·ent·ly** *Aeroplanes are not inherently dangerous.*
◆◆◇◇
ADJ
ADV

in·her·it /ɪn'herɪt/ **inherits, inheriting, inherited. 1** If you **inherit** money or property, you receive it from someone who has died. *...paintings that he inherited from his father.* **2** If you **inherit** something such as a problem or attitude, you get it from the people who used to have it, for example because you have taken over their job or been influenced by them. *A future Labour government would inherit a difficult economic situation.* **3** If you **inherit** a characteristic or quality, you are born with it, because your parents or ancestors also had it. *Her children have inherited her love of sport... Stammering is probably an inherited defect.*
◆◆◇◇
VERB: V n
V n from n
VERB
V n
Also V n from n
VERB
V-ed
Also V n from

in·her·it·ance /ɪn'herɪtəns/ **inheritances. 1** An **inheritance** is money or property which you receive from someone who has died. *Avoiding inheritance tax is straightforward.* **2** If you get something such as a problem or attitude from someone who used to have it, you can refer to this as an **inheritance**. *...starvation and disease over much of Europe and Asia, which was Truman's inheritance as President.* **3** Your **inheritance** is the particular characteristics or qualities which your family or ancestors had and which you are born with. *Eye colour shows more than your genetic inheritance.*
◆◇◇◇
N-VAR
N-COUNT
N-SING:
also no det,
with supp

in·heri·tor /ɪn'herɪtə/ **inheritors.** The **inheritors** of something such as a tradition are the people who live or arrive after it has been established and are able to benefit from it. *...the proud inheritors of the Prussian military tradition.*
N-COUNT

in·hib·it /ɪn'hɪbɪt/ **inhibits, inhibiting, inhibited. 1** If something **inhibits** an event or process, it prevents it or slows it down. *Wine or sugary drinks inhibit digestion.* **2** To **inhibit** someone from doing something means to prevent them from doing it. *It could end up inhibiting the poor from getting the medical care they need.*
◆◇◇◇
VERB: V n
V n
VERB
V n from n
-ing/n

in·hib·it·ed /ɪn'hɪbɪtɪd/. If you say that someone is **inhibited**, you mean they find it difficult to behave naturally and show their feelings, and that you think this is a bad thing. *Men are more inhibited about touching each other than women.*
◆◇◇◇
ADJ-GRADED
PRAGMATICS

in·hi·bi·tion /ˌɪnɪ'bɪʃən/ **inhibitions.** Inhibitions are feelings of fear or embarrassment that make it
◆◇◇◇
N-VAR

difficult for you to behave naturally. *They behave with a total lack of inhibition.*

in·hos·pi·table /ˌɪnhɒˈspɪtəbəl/. An **inhospitable** place is unpleasant to live in. *...the earth's most inhospitable regions.* ADJ-GRADED

in·hu·man /ˌɪnˈhjuːmən/. **1** If you describe something as **inhuman**, you mean that it is extremely cruel or brutal. *The barbaric slaughter of whales is unnecessary and inhuman.* **2** If you describe someone or something as **inhuman**, you mean that they are strange or bad because they do not seem human in some way. *... inhuman shrieks.* ◆◇◇◇ ADJ-GRADED ADJ-GRADED

in·hu·mane /ˌɪnhjuːˈmeɪn/. If you describe something as **inhumane**, you mean that it is extremely cruel. *He was kept under inhumane conditions.* ADJ-GRADED

in·hu·man·ity /ˌɪnhjuːˈmænɪti/ **inhumanities.** **Inhumanity** is extreme cruelty. *...the inhumanity of war.* N-UNCOUNT also N in pl

in·imi·cal /ɪˈnɪmɪkəl/. Conditions that are **inimical** to something make it difficult for that thing to exist or do well. *...a false morality that is inimical to human happiness.* ADJ-GRADED FORMAL

in·imi·table /ɪˈnɪmɪtəbəl/. You use **inimitable** to describe someone, especially a performer, when you admire them because of their special qualities. *He makes his own point in his own inimitable way.* ADJ PRAGMATICS FORMAL

in·iqui·tous /ɪˈnɪkwɪtəs/. If you describe something as **iniquitous**, you mean that it is very unfair or morally bad. ADJ-GRADED FORMAL

in·iqui·ty /ɪˈnɪkwɪti/ **iniquities. Iniquity** is wickedness or injustice. *...the iniquities of capitalism.* N-VAR FORMAL

in·itial /ɪˈnɪʃəl/ **initials, initialling, initialled;** spelled **initialing, initialed** in American English. **1** You use **initial** to describe something that happens at the beginning of a process. *The initial reaction has been excellent.* **2 Initials** are the capital letters which begin each word of a name. For example, if your full name is Michael Dennis Stocks, your initials will be M.D.S. **3** If someone **initials** an official document, they write their initials on it, for example to show that they have seen it or authorize it. *Would you mind initialing this voucher?* ◆◆◇◇ ADJ: ADJ n N-COUNT VERB V n

in·itial·ly /ɪˈnɪʃəli/. **Initially** means soon after the beginning of a process or situation. *Initially, they were afraid of Simon.* ◆◆◆◇◇ ADV

in·iti·ate, **initiates, initiating, initiated.** The verb is pronounced /ɪˈnɪʃieɪt/. The noun is pronounced /ɪˈnɪʃiət/. **1** If you **initiate** something, you start it or cause it to happen. *They wanted to initiate a discussion on economics.* **2** If you **initiate** someone into something, you introduce them to a particular skill or type of knowledge and teach them about it. *He initiated her into the study of other cultures.* **3** If someone **is initiated** into something such as a religion, secret society, or group, they become a member of it by taking part in ceremonies at which they learn its special knowledge or customs. *...the lengthy ceremony that initiated Golden Dawn members into the Second Order.* **4** An **initiate** is a person who has been accepted as a member by a particular group or club and been taught its secrets and skills. ◆◆◇◇ VERB V n VERB V n into n Also V n VERB: be V-ed into n V n into n Also V n N-COUNT

in·itia·tion /ɪˌnɪʃiˈeɪʃən/ **initiations. 1** The **initiation** of something is the starting of it. *There was a year between initiation and completion.* **2** Someone's **initiation** into a particular group is the act or process by which they officially become a member, often involving special ceremonies. *This was my initiation into the peace movement. ...initiation ceremonies.* ◆◇◇◇ N-UNCOUNT N-VAR

in·itia·tive /ɪˈnɪʃətɪv/ **initiatives. 1** An **initiative** is an important act or statement that is intended to solve a problem. *There's talk of a new peace initiative.* **2** In a fight or contest, if you have the **initiative**, you are in a better position than your opponents to decide what to do next. **3** If you have **initiative**, you have the ability to decide what to do next and to do it, without needing other people to tell you what to do. *She was disappointed by his lack of initiative.* **4** If you **take the initiative** in a situation, ◆◆◆◇◇ N-COUNT N-SING: the N N-UNCOUNT PHRASE

tion, you are the first person to act, and are therefore able to control the situation.

ini·tia·tor /ɪˈnɪʃieɪtə/ **initiators.** The **initiator** of a plan or process is the person who was responsible for thinking of it or starting it. N-COUNT

in·ject /ɪnˈdʒekt/ **injects, injecting, injected. 1** To **inject** someone with a substance such as a medicine, or to **inject** it into them, means to use a needle and a syringe to put it into their body. *His son was injected with strong drugs... He needs to inject himself once a month.* **2** If you **inject** a new, exciting, or interesting quality into a situation, you add it. *She kept trying to inject a little fun into their relationship.* **3** If you **inject** money or resources into a business or organization, you provide more money or resources for it. ◆◆◇◇ VERB: V n into n be V-ed with n V pron-refl Also V n, V n with n VERB V n into n VERB V n into n

in·jec·tion /ɪnˈdʒekʃən/ **injections. 1** If you have an **injection**, a doctor or nurse puts a medicine into your body using a needle and a syringe. *It has to be given by injection, usually twice daily.* **2** An **injection** of money or resources into a business or organization is the act of providing more money or resources for it, to help it become more efficient or profitable. *...a £250 million cash injection from the government.* ◆◆◇◇ N-COUNT: also by N N-COUNT: with supp

in·ju·di·cious /ˌɪndʒuːˈdɪʃəs/. If you describe a person or something that they have done as **injudicious**, you are critical of them because they have shown very poor judgement. *He blamed injudicious comments by bankers for last week's devaluation.* ADJ-GRADED FORMAL

in·junc·tion /ɪnˈdʒʌŋkʃən/ **injunctions. 1** An **injunction** is a court order, usually one telling someone not to do something. *He took out a court injunction against the newspaper demanding the return of the document.* **2** An **injunction** to do something is an order or strong request to do it. *We hear endless injunctions to managers to build commitment and a sense of community among their staff.* ◆◇◇◇ N-COUNT LEGAL N-COUNT: with supp FORMAL

in·jure /ˈɪndʒə/ **injures, injuring, injured.** If you **injure** a person or animal, you damage some part of their body. *...stiff penalties for motorists who kill, maim, and injure.* ◆◇◇◇ VERB: V n V

in·jured /ˈɪndʒəd/. **1** An **injured** person or animal has physical damage to part of their body, usually as a result of an accident or fighting. *Many of them will have died because they were so badly injured.* ▶ The **injured** are people who are injured. **2** If you feel **injured** or if your feelings are **injured**, you feel upset because you believe something unjust or unfair has been done to you. *...a look of injured pride.* ◆◆◇◇ ADJ-GRADED N-PLURAL: the N ADJ-GRADED

injured 'party, injured parties. The **injured party** in a court case or in a dispute over unfair treatment is the person who is or claims to be the victim of the unfair treatment. *The injured party got some compensation.* N-COUNT LEGAL

in·ju·ri·ous /ɪnˈdʒʊəriəs/. Something that is **injurious** to someone or to their health or reputation is harmful to them. *Stress in itself is not necessarily injurious.* ADJ-GRADED FORMAL

in·ju·ry /ˈɪndʒəri/ **injuries. 1** An **injury** is damage done to a person's or an animal's body. *The two other passengers escaped serious injury.* **2** ● to **add insult to injury:** see **insult.** ◆◆◆◇ N-VAR

'injury time. Injury time is the period of time added to the end of a football match because play was interrupted during the match when players were injured. N-UNCOUNT BRITISH

in·jus·tice /ɪnˈdʒʌstɪs/ **injustices. 1 Injustice** is a lack of fairness in a situation. *They resented the injustices of the system.* **2** If you say that someone has done you **an injustice**, you mean that they have been unfair in the way that they have judged you or treated you. ◆◆◇◇ N-VAR PHRASE

ink /ɪŋk/ **inks, inking, inked. 1 Ink** is the coloured liquid used for writing or printing. *The letter was handwritten in black ink.* **2** If you **ink** something, you put ink on it. ◆◆◇◇ N-VAR VERB: V n

ink·ling /ˈɪŋklɪŋ/ **inklings.** If you have an **inkling** of something, you have a vague idea about it. *We had an inkling that something might be happening.* N-COUNT

ink·well /ˈɪŋkwel/ **inkwells.** An **inkwell** is a con- N-COUNT
tainer for ink on a desk.

ink·y /ˈɪŋki/. **1 Inky** means black or very dark blue. ADJ
2 If something is **inky**, it is covered in ink. ADJ

in·laid /ˌɪnˈleɪd/. An object that is **inlaid** has a de- ADJ
sign on it which is made by putting materials such
as wood or metal into the surface of the object. ...*a
box delicately inlaid with little triangles.*

in·land The adverb is pronounced /ɪnˈlænd/. The ◆◆◇◇◇
adjective is pronounced /ˈɪnlænd/. **1** If something is ADV
situated **inland**, it is away from the coast, towards
or near the middle of a country. If you go **inland**,
you go away from the coast, towards the middle of a
country. *The vast majority live further inland.* **2 In-** ADJ: ADJ n
land lakes and places are not on the coast, but in or
near the middle of a country.

Inland 'Revenue. In Britain, the **Inland Rev-** ◆◇◇◇◇
enue is the government authority which collects in- N-PROPER
come tax and some other taxes.

'in-laws. Your **in-laws** are the parents and close ◆◇◇◇◇
relatives of your husband or wife. N-PLURAL

in·lay /ˈɪnleɪ/ **inlays.** An **inlay** is a design or pattern N-VAR
on an object which is made by putting materials
such as wood or metal into its surface. ...*desks with
leather inlay.*

in·let /ˈɪnlet/ **inlets. 1** An **inlet** is a narrow strip of ◆◇◇◇◇
water which goes from a sea or lake into the land. N-COUNT
2 An **inlet** is a part of a machine through which a N-COUNT
flow of liquid enters.

in·mate /ˈɪnmeɪt/ **inmates.** The **inmates** of a pris- ◆◆◇◇◇
on or a psychiatric hospital are the prisoners or pa- N-COUNT
tients who are living there.

in·most /ˈɪnmoʊst/. **Inmost** means the same as ADJ: ADJ n
innermost. *He knew in his inmost heart that he was
behaving badly.*

inn /ɪn/ **inns.** An **inn** is a small hotel or pub, ◆◆◇◇◇
usually an old one. ...*the old Anchor Inn... I stayed* N-COUNT
at a seventeenth-century inn. DATED

in·nards /ˈɪnədz/. **1** The **innards** of a person or ani- N-PLURAL
mal are the organs inside their body. **2** A machine's N-PLURAL
innards are the parts inside it. INFORMAL

in·nate /ɪˈneɪt/. An **innate** quality or ability is one ◆◇◇◇◇
which a person is born with. *Americans have an in-* ADJ
nate sense of fairness. ✦ **in·nate·ly** *I believe every-* ADV: ADV adj
one is innately psychic.

in·ner /ˈɪnə/. **1** The **inner** parts of something are ◆◆◆◇◇
the parts which are contained in or enclosed inside ADJ: ADJ n
the other parts, and which are closest to the centre.
She got up and went into an inner office. **2** Your **in-** ADJ: ADJ n
ner feelings are feelings which you have but do not
show to other people. *Michael needed to express his
inner tensions.*

inner 'circle, inner circles. An **inner circle** is a ◆◇◇◇◇
group of people who have a lot of power or control N-COUNT
in a group or organization, and who work together
in secretive ways. ...*the inner circle of scientists who
produced the atomic bomb.*

inner 'city, inner cities; also spelled **inner-city.** ◆◆◇◇◇
You use **inner city** to refer to the areas in or near N-COUNT
the centre of a large city where people live and
where there are often social and economic problems. ...*helping kids deal with the fear of living in
the inner city.* ...*inner-city areas.*

inner·most /ˈɪnəmoʊst/. **1** Your **innermost** ADJ: ADJ n
thoughts and feelings are your most personal and
secret ones. ...*revealing a company's innermost
secrets.* **2** The **innermost** thing is the one that is ADJ: ADJ n
nearest to the centre. *She put the receipt into the
innermost pocket of her bag.*

'inner tube, inner tubes. An **inner tube** is a rub- N-COUNT
ber tube containing air which is inside a car tyre or
a bicycle tyre.

in·ning /ˈɪnɪŋ/ **innings.** An **inning** is a period in a ◆◆◇◇◇
game of baseball when one of the teams is at bat. N-COUNT

in·nings /ˈɪnɪŋz/; **innings** is both the singular and ◆◆◇◇◇
the plural form. An **innings** is a period in a game of N-COUNT
cricket during which a particular team or player is
batting.

inn·keep·er /ˈɪnkiːpə/ **innkeepers.** An **innkeeper** N-COUNT
is someone who owns or manages an inn. DATED

in·no·cence /ˈɪnəsəns/. **1 Innocence** is the quality ◆◆◇◇◇
of having no experience or knowledge of the more N-UNCOUNT
complex or unpleasant aspects of life. *Youngsters
are losing their childhood innocence too quickly.* **2** If N-UNCOUNT
someone proves their **innocence**, they prove that
they are not guilty of a crime.

in·no·cent /ˈɪnəsənt/ **innocents. 1** If someone is ◆◆◆◇◇
innocent, they did not commit a crime which they ADJ
have been accused of. *He was sure that the man was
innocent of any crime.* **2** If someone is **innocent**, ADJ-GRADED
they have no experience or knowledge of the more
complex or unpleasant aspects of life. *They seemed
so young and innocent.* ► An **innocent** is someone N-COUNT
who is innocent. *She had always regarded Ian as a
hopeless innocent where women were concerned.*
✦ **in·no·cent·ly** *The baby gurgled innocently on the* ADV-GRADED
bed. **3** Innocent people are those who are not in- ADJ
volved in a crime, conflict, or other situation, but
who nevertheless get injured or killed. *All those
wounded were innocent victims.* **4** An **innocent** ADJ-GRADED
question, remark, or comment is not intended to offend or upset people, even if it does so. *It was probably an innocent question, but Michael got flustered,
anyway.*

in·no·cent·ly /ˈɪnəsəntli/. If you say that someone ◆◇◇◇◇
does or says something **innocently**, you mean that ADV-GRADED:
they are pretending to be naive or to know nothing ADV with v
about a situation, although they are really being
quite clever and know more than they say. *I tried to
catch Chrissie's eye to find out what she was playing
at, but she only smiled back at me innocently.* ● See
also **innocent**.

in·noc·u·ous /ɪˈnɒkjʊəs/. Something that is **in-** ◆◇◇◇◇
nocuous is not at all harmful or controversial. *Both* ADJ-GRADED
mushrooms look innocuous but are in fact deadly. FORMAL

in·no·vate /ˈɪnəveɪt/ **innovates, innovating, in-** VERB
novated. To **innovate** means to introduce changes V
and new ideas in the way something is done Also V n
or made. ...*his constant desire to innovate and
experiment.*

in·no·va·tion /ˌɪnəˈveɪʃən/ **innovations. 1** An **in-** ◆◆◇◇◇
novation is a new thing or a new method of doing N-COUNT
something. ...*the technological innovations of the industrial age.* **2 Innovation** is the introduction of N-UNCOUNT
new ideas, methods, or things. *We must promote
originality, inspire creativity and encourage
innovation.*

in·no·va·tive /ˈɪnəveɪtɪv/. **1** Something that is **in-** ◆◆◇◇◇
novative is new and original. **2** An **innovative** per- ADJ-GRADED
son introduces changes and new ideas. ADJ-GRADED

in·no·va·tor /ˈɪnəveɪtə/ **innovators.** An **innovator** ◇◇◇◇◇
is someone who introduces changes and new ideas. N-COUNT

in·no·va·tory /ˈɪnəveɪtəri, AM -tɔːri/. **Innovatory** ADJ-GRADED
means the same as **innovative**. *Only the opening se-* BRITISH
quence could claim to be genuinely innovatory.

in·nu·en·do /ˌɪnjuˈendoʊ/ **innuendoes** or **innu-** ◆◇◇◇◇
endos. Innuendo is indirect reference to some- N-VAR
thing rude or unpleasant. ...*magazines which are
full of sexual innuendo.*

in·nu·mer·able /ɪˈnjuːmərəbəl, AM -ˈnuː-/. **Innu-** ◆◇◇◇◇
merable means very many, or too many to be ADJ
counted. *He has invented innumerable excuses, told
endless lies.*

in·ocu·late /ɪˈnɒkjʊleɪt/ **inoculates, inoculat-** VERB: V n
ing, inoculated. To **inoculate** a person or animal be V-ed
means to inject a weak form of a disease into their against n
body as a way of protecting them against the disease. *His dogs were inoculated against rabies.* ✦ **in-**
·ocu·la·tion /ɪˌnɒkjʊˈleɪʃən/ **inoculations** *This* N-VAR
*may eventually lead to routine inoculation of chil-
dren... Cholera inoculations are recommended.*

in·of·fen·sive /ˌɪnəˈfensɪv/. If you describe some- ADJ-GRADED
one or something as **inoffensive**, you mean that
they are not unpleasant or unacceptable in any way,
but are perhaps rather dull.

in·op·er·able /ɪnˈɒpərəbəl/. An **inoperable** tumour, ADJ
is one that cannot be removed or cured by a surgi- FORMAL
cal operation.

in·op·era·tive /ɪnˈɒpərətɪv/. An **inoperative** rule or ADJ
tax is one that does not work any more or that can- FORMAL
not be made to work.

in·op·por·tune /ɪnˈɒpətjuːn, AM -ˈtuːn/. If you de- ADJ-GRADED
scribe something as **inopportune** or if you say that
it happens at an **inopportune** time, you mean that
it happens at an unfortunate or unsuitable time,
and so causes trouble or embarrassment.

in·or·di·nate /ɪnˈɔːdɪnɪt/. If you describe some- ◆◇◇◇◇
thing as **inordinate**, you are emphasizing that it is ADJ
unusually or excessively great in amount or degree. [PRAGMATICS]
...*their inordinate number of pets.* ♦ **in·or·di·nate-** FORMAL
·ly *He is inordinately proud of his wife's achieve-* ADV
ments.

in·or·gan·ic /ɪnɔːˈgænɪk/. **Inorganic** substances ADJ
are substances such as stone and metal that do not
come from living things.

'in-patient, in-patients. An **in-patient** is someone N-COUNT
who stays in hospital while they receive their treatment.

in·put /ˈɪnpʊt/ **inputs, inputting.** The form **input** ◆◆◇◇◇
is used in the present tense and is the past tense
and past participle. **1 Input** consists of information N-VAR
or resources that a group or project receives. *They
may need some additional inputs and advice on how
to improve the management of their farms.* **2** If you VERB
input information into a computer, you feed it in, beV-ed
for example by typing it on a keyboard. *The computer acts as a word processor where the text of a
speech can be input at any time.* ▶ **Input** is informa- N-UNCOUNT
tion that is put into a computer.

in·quest /ˈɪnkwest/ **inquests. 1** An **inquest** is an ◆◇◇◇◇
official inquiry into the cause of someone's death. N-COUNT
2 You can refer to an investigation by the people in- N-COUNT
volved into the causes of a defeat or failure as an **inquest**. *Party chiefs held an inquest into the election
disaster.*

in·quire /ɪnˈkwaɪə/ **inquires, inquiring, in-** ◆◆◇◇◇
quired; also spelled **enquire. 1** If you **inquire** VERB
about something, you ask for information about it. *I* V about n
rang up to inquire about train times... 'Is something V with quote
wrong?' he enquired... 'Who are you?' he enquired of quote
the first man... He asked for his key and inquired V n
whether there had been any messages for him... He Also V forn,
was so impressed that he inquired the young shep- V
herd's name. **2** If you **inquire into** something, you FORMAL
investigate it carefully. *Inspectors were appointed to* V into n/wh
inquire into the affairs of the company.

inquire after. If you **inquire after** someone, you ask PHRASAL VB
how they are or what they are doing. *Elsie called to in-* V P noun
quire after my health. FORMAL

in·quir·er /ɪnˈkwaɪərə/ **inquirers;** also spelled **en-**
quirer. 1 An **inquirer** is a person who asks for infor- N-COUNT
mation about something or someone. *I send each* FORMAL
inquirer a packet of information. **2 Inquirer** is used
in the names of some newspapers and magazines.
...*the National Enquirer.*

in·quir·ing /ɪnˈkwaɪərɪŋ/; also spelled **enquiring.**
1 If you have an **inquiring** mind, you have a great ADJ-GRADED:
interest in learning new things. ...*an inquiring atti-* ADJ n
tude to learning. **2** If someone has an **inquiring** ex- ADJ: ADJ n
pression on their face, they are showing that they WRITTEN
want to know something. *'That's right, dear,' she
said in reply to his enquiring glance.* ♦ **in·quir·ing-**
·ly *She looked at me inquiringly. 'Well?'* ADV

in·quiry /ɪnˈkwaɪəri/ **inquiries;** also spelled **en-** ◆◆◆◇◇
quiry. Sometimes pronounced /ˈɪŋkwɪri/ in American English. **1** An **inquiry** is a question which you N-COUNT
ask in order to get some information. *He made some
inquiries and discovered she had gone to the Conti-
nent.* **2** An **inquiry** is an official investigation. *He* N-COUNT
*believes a police inquiry may not be completely
independent.* **3 Inquiry** is the process of asking N-UNCOUNT
about or investigating something in order to find
out more about it. *The investigation has suddenly
switched to a new line of inquiry.* **4** If someone **is** PHRASE
helping the police with their inquiries, the police
are questioning them about a crime, but have not
yet charged them with it. **5** See also **court of inquiry.**

in·qui·si·tion /ɪnkwɪˈzɪʃən/ **inquisitions.** An **in-** N-COUNT
quisition is an official investigation, especially one
which is very thorough and uses harsh methods of
questioning.

in·quisi·tive /ɪnˈkwɪzɪtɪv/. An **inquisitive** person ◆◇◇◇◇
likes finding out about things, especially secret ADJ-GRADED
things. *Barrow had an inquisitive nature.*

in·quisi·tor /ɪnˈkwɪzɪtə/ **inquisitors.** An **inquisitor** N-COUNT
is someone who is asking someone else a series of
questions, especially in a rather hostile way.

in·quisi·to·rial /ɪnkwɪzɪˈtɔːriəl/. If you describe ADJ
something as **inquisitorial**, you mean they resemble things in an inquisition. *The next hearings will
be structured differently in order to minimize the inquisitorial atmosphere.*

in·roads /ˈɪnrəʊdz/. If one thing **makes inroads** ◆◇◇◇◇
into another, the first thing starts affecting or de- PHRASE
stroying the second. *In Italy, as elsewhere, television
has made deep inroads into cinema.*

in·sane /ɪnˈseɪn/. **1** Someone who is **insane** has a ◆◆◇◇◇
mind that does not work in a normal way, with the ADJ
result that their behaviour is very strange. *Some
people simply can't take it and they just go insane.*
▶ **The insane** are people who are insane. ...*the state* N-PLURAL:
hospital for the criminally insane. ♦ **in·san·ity** the N
/ɪnˈsænɪti/. *The film is a powerful study of a wom-* N-UNCOUNT
an's descent into insanity. **2** If you describe a deci- ADJ-GRADED
sion or action as **insane**, you think it is very foolish
or excessive. ♦ **in·sane·ly** *I would be insanely jeal-* ADV-GRADED
ous if Bill left me for another woman. ♦ **in·san·ity.** N-UNCOUNT
If you describe a decision or action as **insanity**, you
think it is very foolish. ...*the final financial insanity
of the 1980s.*

in·sani·tary /ɪnˈsænɪtri, AM -teri/. If something ADJ-GRADED
such as a place is **insanitary**, it is so dirty that it is FORMAL
likely to have a bad effect on people's health. ...*the
insanitary conditions of slums.*

in·sa·tiable /ɪnˈseɪʃəbəl/. If someone has an **insa-** ◆◇◇◇◇
tiable desire for something, they want as much of it ADJ
as they can possibly get. *A section of the reading
public has an insatiable appetite for dirty stories
about the famous... They were insatiable collectors.*

in·scribe /ɪnˈskraɪb/ **inscribes, inscribing, in-** ◆◇◇◇◇
scribed. If you **inscribe** words on an object, you VERB
write or carve the words on the object. *Some gal-* V n on/with n
leries commemorate donors by inscribing their V-ed
*names on the walls. ...stone slabs inscribed with
Buddhist texts... The book is inscribed: To John
Arlott from Laurie Lee.*

in·scrip·tion /ɪnˈskrɪpʃən/ **inscriptions.** An **in-** ◆◇◇◇◇
scription is a piece of writing carved into a surface, N-COUNT
or written on something such as a book or photo-
graph. An inscription is usually a special message or
saying. *Above its doors was a Latin inscription... The
silver medal bears the sovereign's head and the inscription 'For distinguished service'.*

in·scru·table /ɪnˈskruːtəbəl/. If a person or their ADJ-GRADED
expression is **inscrutable**, it is very hard to know
what they are really thinking or what they mean. *In
some circumstances, it is important to keep a
straight face and to remain inscrutable.*

in·sect /ˈɪnsekt/ **insects.** An **insect** is a small ani- ◆◆◇◇◇
mal that has six legs. Most insects have wings. Ants, N-COUNT
flies, and beetles are all insects. See picture headed
insects.

in·sec·ti·cide /ɪnˈsektɪsaɪd/ **insecticides.** Insec- ◆◇◇◇◇
ticide is a chemical substance that is used to kill in- N-VAR
sects that are a nuisance, for example because they
eat crops. *Spray the plants with insecticide.*

in·secure /ɪnsɪˈkjʊə/. **1** If you are **insecure**, you ◆◆◇◇◇
feel unsure of yourself because you think that you ADJ-GRADED
are not good enough or are not loved. *Most mothers
are insecure about their performance as mothers.*
♦ **in·secu·rity** /ɪnsɪˈkjʊərɪti/ **insecurities** *She is* N-VAR
*always assailed by self-doubt and emotional insecu-
rity.* **2** Something that is **insecure** is not safe or pro- ADJ-GRADED
tected. ...*low-paid, insecure jobs... Cellular phones
are inherently insecure, as anyone can listen to and
record conversations.* ♦ **insecurity** ...*the increase in* N-UNCOUNT

crime, which has created feelings of insecurity in the population.

in·semi·nate /ɪn'semɪneɪt/ **inseminates, inseminating, inseminated. 1** To **inseminate** a woman or female animal means to put a male's sperm into her in order to make her pregnant. *The gadget is used to artificially inseminate cows.* ♦ **in·semi·na·tion** /ɪn,semɪ'neɪʃən/. *The sperm sample is checked under the microscope before insemination is carried out.* **2** See also **artificial insemination.**
VERB Vn — N-UNCOUNT

in·sen·si·tive /ɪn'sensɪtɪv/. **1** If you describe someone as **insensitive** to particular problems or to someone's feelings, you are criticizing that person for being unaware of those problems or feelings, or not caring about them. *My mother was a thinking woman, not an insensitive one... Women's and Latino organizations that say he is insensitive to civil rights.* ♦ **in·sen·si·tiv·ity** /ɪn,sensɪ'tɪvɪti/ *...insensitivity to the environmental consequences.* **2** Someone who is **insensitive** to a physical sensation is unable to feel it. *He had become insensitive to cold.*
ADJ-GRADED [PRAGMATICS] — N-UNCOUNT — ADJ

in·sepa·rable /ɪn'seprəbəl/. **1** If one thing is **inseparable** from another, the things are so closely connected that they cannot be considered separately. *Liberty is inseparable from social justice... For the ancient Mexicans, life and death were inseparable, two halves of the same whole.* ♦ **in·sepa·rably** *In his mind, religion and politics were inseparably intertwined.* **2** If you say that two people are **inseparable**, you mean that they are very good friends and spend a great deal of time together.
ADJ — ADV — ADJ-GRADED

in·sert, **inserts, inserting, inserted.** The verb is pronounced /ɪn'sɜːt/. The noun is pronounced /'ɪnsɜːt/. **1** If you **insert** an object into something, you put the object inside it. *He took a small key from his pocket and slowly inserted it into the lock... Wait for a couple of minutes with your mouth closed before inserting the thermometer.* ♦ **in·ser·tion** /ɪn'sɜːʃən/ **insertions** *...the first experiment involving the insertion of a new gene into a human being.* **2** If you **insert** a comment into a piece of writing or a speech, you include it. *They joined with the monarchists to insert a clause calling for a popular vote on the issue.* ♦ **insertion** *...an item for insertion in the programme.* **3** An **insert** is something that is inserted somewhere, especially an advertisement on a piece of paper that is placed between the pages of a book or magazine.
VERB Vn into n Vn — N-VAR — VERB Vn Also Vn into/inn — N-VAR — N-COUNT

,in-'service. If people working in a particular profession are given **in-service** training, they attend special courses to improve their skills or to learn about new developments in their field. *...in-service courses for people such as doctors, teachers, and civil servants.*
ADJ: ADJ n

in·set /'ɪnset/ **insets. 1** Something that is **inset** with a decoration or piece of material has the decoration or material set inside it. *...a small gold pendant, shaped as a heart and inset with a diamond.* **2** An **inset** is a small picture, diagram, or map that is inside a larger one.
ADJ — N-COUNT

in·shore. The adverb is pronounced /,ɪn'ʃɔː/. The adjective is pronounced /'ɪnʃɔː/. If something is **inshore**, it is in the sea but quite close to the land. If something moves **inshore**, it moves from the sea towards the land. *A barge was close inshore about a hundred yards away. ...a strong wind blowing inshore.* ► Also an adjective. *...inshore reefs.*
ADV: be ADV, ADV after v — ADJ: ADJ n

in·side /,ɪn'saɪd/ **insides.** The preposition is usually pronounced /ɪn'saɪd/. The form **inside of** can also be used as a preposition. This form is more usual in American English.
♦♦♦♦◇

1 Something or someone that is **inside** a place, container, or object is in it or is surrounded by it. *Inside the box were a dozen or so papers... There is a telephone inside the entrance hall.* ► Also an adverb. *The couple chatted briefly on the doorstep before going inside... He ripped open the envelope and read what was inside... I could hear music coming from inside... Inside, Anastasia could see that the house was very pretty... The potato cakes can be shallow or deep-fried until*
PREP — ADV

crisp outside and meltingly soft inside. ► Also a noun. *...the inside of the house... The doors were locked from the inside.* ► Also an adjective. *...an inside lavatory.* **2** The **inside** pages of a newspaper are all the pages except the front page and the back page. **3** On a wide road, the **inside** lane is the one which is closest to the edge of the road. ► Also a noun. *I overtook Charlie on the inside.* **4** Your **insides** are your internal organs, especially your stomach.
N-COUNT — ADJ: ADJ n — ADJ: ADJ n — N-SING: the N — N-SING: the N N-PLURAL INFORMAL

5 Inside knowledge is obtained from someone who is involved in a situation and therefore knows a lot about it. *Sloane used inside diplomatic information to make himself rich... It's fascinating to get the inside story so many years after this incident.* **6** If you are **inside** an organization, you belong to it. *75 percent of chief executives come from inside the company... He hasn't looked very carefully into what was happening inside the Communist Party.* **7** You can say that someone is **inside** when they are in prison. *He's been inside three times.*
ADJ: ADJ n — PREP — ADV INFORMAL

8 If you have a feeling **inside** you, you feel it, often without expressing it. *He felt a great weight of sorrow inside him.* ► Also an adverb. *There is nothing left inside – no words, no anger, no tears.* ► Also a noun. *On the inside he was in turmoil.* **9** If you do something **inside** a particular time, you do it before the end of that time. *They should have everything working inside an hour... New Zealand were ahead inside five minutes.* **10** If something such as a piece of clothing is **inside out**, the part that is normally inside now faces outwards. **11** If you say that you know something or someone **inside out**, you are emphasizing that you know them extremely well. *He knew the game inside out.* **12** If you say that something **has been turned inside out**, you mean that it is the opposite of what you expect or think it should be. *Edinburgh is an American city turned inside out: the rich in the middle, the poor around the outside.*
PREP — ADV — N-SING: the N — PREP — PHRASE — PHRASE [PRAGMATICS] — PHRASE

in·sid·er /,ɪn'saɪdə/ **insiders.** An **insider** is someone who is involved in a situation and who knows more about it than other people. *...Hollywood insiders... She has valuable insider knowledge about the secret workings of large department stores.*
♦♦◇◇ N-COUNT

,insider 'dealing. Insider dealing is the illegal practice of buying or selling shares in a company, by someone who has special or confidential knowledge of that company because they are involved with it in some way.
N-UNCOUNT

in·sidi·ous /ɪn'sɪdiəs/. Something that is **insidious** is unpleasant or dangerous and develops gradually without being noticed. *They focus on overt discrimination rather than insidious aspects of racism.* ♦ **in·sidi·ous·ly** *Delusions are sometimes insidiously destructive.*
♦◇◇◇◇ ADJ-GRADED — ADV-GRADED

in·sight /'ɪnsaɪt/ **insights. 1** If you gain **insight** or an **insight** into a complex situation or problem, you learn something useful or valuable about it. *I hope that this talk has given you some insight into the kind of work that we've been doing.* **2** If someone has **insight**, they are able to understand complex situations. *He was a man of forceful character, with considerable insight and diplomatic skills.*
♦♦◇◇◇ N-VAR — N-UNCOUNT

in·sight·ful /'ɪnsaɪtful/. If you describe a person or their remarks as **insightful**, you mean that they show a very good understanding of people and situations. *She offered some really interesting, insightful observations.*
ADJ-GRADED [PRAGMATICS]

in·sig·nia /ɪn'sɪgniə/; **insignia** is both the singular and the plural form. An **insignia** is a badge or sign which shows that a person or object belongs to a particular organization, often a military one. *...a scarlet tunic bearing the insignia of a captain in the Irish Guards.*
N-COUNT

in·sig·nifi·cant /,ɪnsɪg'nɪfɪkənt/. Something that is **insignificant** is unimportant, especially because it is very small. *In 1949 Bonn was a small, insignificant city.* ♦ **in·sig·nifi·cance** *The event was regarded as of such insignificance that not one major newspaper carried a report.*
♦◇◇◇◇ ADJ-GRADED — N-UNCOUNT

in·sin·cere /ˌɪnsɪnˈsɪə/. If you say that someone is **insincere**, you are criticizing them for saying things they do not really mean, often polite or flattering things. *This apology has been seen as being too late and insincere.* ♦ **in·sin·cer·ity** /ˌɪnsɪnˈserɪti/ ...*a man who knows how to mingle seduction and insincerity.*   ADJ-GRADED PRAGMATICS   N-UNCOUNT

in·sinu·ate /ɪnˈsɪnjueɪt/ **insinuates, insinuating, insinuated. 1** If you say that someone **insinuates** something unpleasant, you mean that they suggest that it is true without stating it openly; used showing disapproval. *The libel claim followed an article which insinuated that the President was lying... Are you insinuating that I smell?... Marcus kept making insinuating remarks.* ♦ **in·sin·ua·tion** /ɪnˌsɪnjuˈeɪʃən/ **insinuations** *I just don't think it's right to bring a good man down by rumour and insinuation.* **2** If you say that someone **insinuates** themselves into a particular situation, you mean that they manage very cleverly to get into that situation; used showing disapproval. ...*a thriller about a young man who insinuates himself into a millionaire's empire by assuming different identities.*   VERB: V n PRAGMATICS V that V-ing   N-VAR   VERB V pron-refl into n Also V n prep

in·sip·id /ɪnˈsɪpɪd/. **1** If you describe food or drink as **insipid**, you dislike it because it has very little taste. **2** If you describe someone or something as **insipid**, you dislike them because they have no strong or striking qualities. *'A Woman and a Man' is an entirely unoriginal, insipid film.*   ADJ-GRADED   ADJ-GRADED

in·sist /ɪnˈsɪst/ **insists, insisting, insisted. 1** If you **insist** that something should be done, you say very firmly that it must be done. If you **insist** on something, you say very firmly that it must be done or provided. *My family insisted that I should not give in, but stay and fight... She insisted on being present at all the interviews... I didn't want to join in, but Kenneth insisted.* **2** If you **insist** that something is true, you say so very firmly and refuse to be contradicted. *The president insisted that he was acting out of compassion, not political opportunism... 'It's not that difficult,' she insists... Crippen insisted on his innocence.*   ♦♦♦♦◇ VERB V that V on-ing/n V   VERB V that V with quote V on n

in·sist·ence /ɪnˈsɪstəns/. Someone's **insistence** on something is the fact that they insist that it should be done or that it is true. ...*Raeder's insistence that naval uniform be worn... She had attended an interview at her boyfriend's insistence.*   ♦♦◇◇◇ N-UNCOUNT

in·sist·ent /ɪnˈsɪstənt/. **1** Someone who is **insistent** keeps insisting that a particular thing should be done or is the case. *Abramov had been insistent that the matter be resolved quickly... He is most insistent on this point.* ♦ **in·sist·ent·ly** *'What is it?' his wife asked again, gently but insistently.* **2** An **insistent** noise or rhythm keeps going on for a long time and holds your attention. ...*the insistent rhythms of the Caribbean and Latin America.*   ◇◇◇◇ ADJ-GRADED   ADV-GRADED: ADV with v   ADJ-GRADED

in situ /ɪn ˈsɪtjuː, AM -ˈsiːtuː/. If something remains **in situ**, especially while something is done to it, it remains where it is. *Major works of painting, sculpture, mosaic and architecture were examined in situ in Venice.*   ADV: ADV after v FORMAL

in·so·far as /ˌɪnsəˈfɑːr æz/; also spelled **in so far as**. You use **insofar as** to introduce a statement which explains and adds to something you have just said. *We are entering a period of less danger insofar as the danger of nuclear war between the superpowers is less.*   ◇◇◇◇ PHR-CONJ

in·sole /ˈɪnsəʊl/ **insoles.** The **insoles** of a pair of shoes are the soft layer of material inside each one, which the soles of your feet rest on.   N-COUNT

in·so·lent /ˈɪnsələnt/. If you say that someone is being **insolent**, you mean they are being rude to someone they ought to respect. ...*her insolent stare... The officer stamped his boot. 'Don't be insolent with me, mademoiselle.'* ♦ **in·so·lence** The most frequent reasons for excluding a pupil were breaking school rules, insolence, and bad language.   ADJ-GRADED   N-UNCOUNT

in·sol·uble /ɪnˈsɒljubəl/. **1** An **insoluble** problem is so difficult that it is impossible to solve. ...*an insoluble dilemma.* **2** If a substance is **insoluble**, it does   ADJ   ADJ

not dissolve in a liquid. *Carotenes are insoluble in water.*

in·sol·vent /ɪnˈsɒlvənt/. A person or organization that is **insolvent** does not have enough money to pay their debts. *The bank was declared insolvent.* ♦ **in·sol·ven·cy** /ɪnˈsɒlvənsi/ **insolvencies** The economy has entered a sharp downturn, and unemployment and insolvencies can be expected to increase. ...*fighting the threat of insolvency.*   ♦◇◇◇◇ ADJ   N-VAR

in·som·nia /ɪnˈsɒmniə/. Someone who suffers from **insomnia** finds it difficult to sleep.   ♦◇◇◇◇ N-UNCOUNT

in·som·ni·ac /ɪnˈsɒmniæk/ **insomniacs.** An **insomniac** is a person who finds it difficult to sleep.   N-COUNT

in·sou·ci·ant /ɪnˈsuːsiənt/. An **insouciant** action or quality shows someone's lack of concern about something which they might be expected to take more seriously. ...*Andy Warhol, who worked with an insouciant disregard for the distinctions between painting, photography and film.* ♦ **in·sou·ci·ance** /ɪnˈsuːsiəns/ *He replied with characteristic insouciance: 'So what?'*   ADJ-GRADED FORMAL   N-UNCOUNT

Insp. Insp. is the written abbreviation for 'Inspector' when it is used as a title. ...*Insp John Downs.*   N-TITLE

in·spect /ɪnˈspekt/ **inspects, inspecting, inspected. 1** If you **inspect** something, you look at it carefully in order to check it or find out what it is like. *Cut the fruit in half and inspect the pips: if they are turning slightly brown it is ready for harvesting.* ♦ **in·spec·tion** /ɪnˈspekʃən/ *'Excellent work,' he said when he had completed his inspection of the painted doors... A long, low table turns out on closer inspection to be a large mirror set on bricks.* **2** When an official **inspects** a place or a group of people, they visit it and check it carefully, for example in order to find out whether regulations are being obeyed. *Each hotel is inspected and, if it fulfils certain criteria, is recommended.* ♦ **inspection** *Officers making a routine inspection of the vessel found fifty kilograms of the drug.*   ♦♦♦◇◇ VERB V n   N-VAR   VERB: V n be V-ed   N-VAR

in·spec·tor /ɪnˈspektə/ **inspectors. 1** An **inspector** is a person, usually employed by a government agency, whose job is to find out whether people are obeying official regulations. *The mill was finally shut down by state safety inspectors.* **2** In Britain, an **inspector** is a police officer who is higher in rank than a sergeant and lower in rank than a superintendent. *I got on the phone to Inspector Joplin at Scotland Yard.*   ♦♦♦◇◇ N-COUNT   N-COUNT; N-TITLE; N-VOC

in·spec·tor·ate /ɪnˈspektərət/ **inspectorates.** An **inspectorate** is an official organization whose job is to inspect a particular type of place or work. ...*the Nuclear Installations Inspectorate.*   ♦◇◇◇◇ N-COUNT BRITISH

in·spi·ra·tion·al /ˌɪnspɪˈreɪʃənəl/. Something that is **inspirational** provides you with inspiration. *Tolstoy was an inspirational figure in forming Gandhi's ideas about nonviolence.*   ♦◇◇◇◇ ADJ-GRADED

in·spire /ɪnˈspaɪə/ **inspires, inspiring, inspired. 1** If a work of art or an action **is inspired** by something, that thing is the source of the idea or the motivation for it. *The book was inspired by a real person, namely Tamara de Treaux... These herbs will inspire you to try out all sorts of exotic-flavoured dishes!... And what inspired you to change your name?* ♦ **in·spi·ra·tion** /ˌɪnspɪˈreɪʃən/ *My inspiration comes from poets like Baudelaire and Jacques Prévert... The inspiration behind the reforms was a paper written in 1985.* ♦ **-inspired** ...*Mediterranean-inspired ceramics in bright yellow and blue... Jamaica's socialist government is adopting US-inspired free market practices.* **2** If someone or something **inspires** you, they give you new ideas and a strong feeling of enthusiasm. *In the 1960s, the electric guitar virtuosity of Jimi Hendrix inspired a generation.* ♦ **in·spi·ra·tion.** An **inspiration** is someone or something that inspires you. *Powell's unusual journey to high office is an inspiration to millions.* ♦ **in·spir·ing** ...*Edward Kennedy and Mario Cuomo, the party's most inspiring orators... England produced an effective, if not inspiring, performance against the CIS.* **3** Someone or something   ♦♦♦♦◇ VB: usu passive be V-ed by n V n to-inf   N-UNCOUNT   COMB   VERB V n   N-SING: a N   ADJ-GRADED   VERB

that **inspires** a particular emotion or reaction in Vn
people makes them feel this emotion or reaction.
*The car's performance is effortless and its handling is
precise and quickly inspires confidence.*

Inst. Inst. is a written abbreviation for 'Institute'.
...the Liverpool Inst. of Higher Ed.

in·stab·il·ity /ˌɪnstəˈbɪlɪti/ **instabilities.** Instability ◆◆◇◇◇
is a lack of stability in a situation, person, or object. N-UNCOUNT:
...social discontent and political instability. ...mental also N in pl
*instability... The slightest instability will cause bear-
ings to fail and rotors to crash.*

in·stall /ɪnˈstɔːl/ **installs, installing, installed.** ◆◆◇◇◇
1 If you **install** a piece of equipment, you fit it or VERB
put it somewhere so that it is ready to be used. *They* Vn
had installed a new phone line in the apartment.
♦ **in·stal·la·tion** *Hundreds of lives could be saved if* N-UNCOUNT
the installation of alarms was more widespread. 2 If VERB
someone **is installed** in a new job or important po- beV-ed as n
sition, they are officially given the job or position, Vn
often in a special ceremony. *The York Synod is the
first since Dr Carey was installed as Archbishop of
Canterbury... The army has promised to install a
new government within a week.* ♦ **installation** *He* N-UNCOUNT
*sent a letter inviting Naomi to attend his installation
as chief of his tribe.* 3 If you **install** yourself in a par- VERB
ticular place, you settle there and make yourself V pron-refl
comfortable. *She had installed herself in a modern* prep/adv
villa. FORMAL

in·stal·la·tion /ˌɪnstəˈleɪʃən/ **installations.** An in- ◆◆◇◇◇
stallation is a place that contains equipment and N-COUNT
machinery which are being used for a particular
purpose. *The building was turned into a secret military installation. ...a nuclear installation.*

in·stal·ment /ɪnˈstɔːlmənt/ **instalments;** spelled ◆◇◇◇◇
installment in American English. 1 If you pay for N-COUNT
something in **instalments,** you pay small sums of
money at regular intervals over a period of time, rather than paying the whole amount at once. *...his
next instalment on the mortgage.* 2 An **instalment** N-COUNT
of a story is one of its separate parts that are published or broadcast one after the other. *...the latest
instalment in Douglas Adams's 'Hitchhiker' trilogy.*

in·stance /ˈɪnstəns/ **instances.** 1 You use for **in-** ◆◆◆◇
stance to introduce something or someone that is PHRASE
an example of what you are talking about. *At the* PRAGMATICS
high-cost end of the spectrum, for instance, is one
Bank of New York account... Let your child make
some of the small decisions concerning his daily routine. For instance, allow him to choose what clothes
he wears at the weekend.* 2 An **instance** is a particu- N-COUNT
lar example or occurrence of something. *...an investigation into a serious instance of corruption.* 3 You PHRASE
say **in the first instance** to mention the first of a se- PRAGMATICS
ries of actions or possibilities. *In the first instance
your child will be seen by an ear, nose and throat
specialist... The post was for one year in the first instance with possible renewal for a further year.*

in·stant /ˈɪnstənt/ **instants.** 1 An **instant** is an ex- ◆◆◆◇◇
tremely short period of time or point in time. *The* N-COUNT
pain disappeared in an instant... At that instant the
museum was plunged into total darkness.* 2 If you PHR-CONJ
say that someone does something **the instant** PRAGMATICS
something else happens, you are emphasizing that
they do the first thing immediately after the second
thing happens. *I had bolted the door the instant I
had seen the bat.* 3 You use **instant** to describe ADJ
something that happens immediately. *He had taken
an instant dislike to Mortlake.* ♦ **in·stant·ly** *The* ADV
man was killed instantly... The songs are instantly
recognisable.* 4 **Instant** food can be prepared very ADJ: ADJ n
quickly, for example by just adding water. *...instant
coffee.*

in·stan·ta·ne·ous /ˌɪnstənˈteɪniəs/. Something that ◆◇◇◇◇
is **instantaneous** happens immediately and very ADJ-GRADED
quickly. *The coroner said that death was instantaneous.* ♦ **in·stan·ta·neous·ly** *Airbags inflate in-* ADV:
stantaneously on impact. ADV with v

'**instant 'replay, instant replays.** An instant re- N-COUNT
play is a repeated showing, usually in slow motion, AMERICAN

of an event that has just been on television. The
usual British term is **action replay.**

in·stead /ɪnˈsted/. 1 If you do one thing **instead of** ◆◆◆◆◇
another, you do the first thing and not the second PHR-PREP
thing, as the result of a choice or a change of behaviour. *She had to spend nearly four months away
from him that summer, instead of the usual two...
Instead of going to work thinking that it will be totally boring, try to be positive.* 2 If you do not do ADV:
something, but do something else **instead,** you do ADV with cl
the second thing and not the first thing. *Frank and
Joe did not reply. Instead, they began a frantic
search... My husband asked why I couldn't just forget
about dieting all the time and eat normally instead.*

in·step /ˈɪnstep/ **insteps.** Your instep is the middle N-COUNT
part of your foot, where it arches upwards. See picture headed **human body.**

in·sti·gate /ˈɪnstɪgeɪt/ **instigates, instigating,** ◆◇◇◇◇
instigated. Someone who **instigates** an event VERB
causes it to happen. *Jenkinson instigated a refur-* Vn
bishment of the old gallery... The violence over the beV-ed
last forty-eight hours was instigated by ex-members
of the secret police.* ♦ **in·sti·ga·tion** /ˌɪnstɪˈgeɪʃən/ N-UNCOUNT
The talks are taking place at the instigation of Germany.* ♦ **in·sti·ga·tor** /ˈɪnstɪgeɪtə/ **instigators** *He* N-COUNT
was accused of being the main instigator of the coup.*

in·stil /ɪnˈstɪl/ **instils, instilling, instilled;** ◆◇◇◇◇
spelled **instill** in American English. If you **instil** an VERB
idea or feeling into someone, especially over a peri- V n in/into n
od of time, you make them think it or feel it. *They* Vn
hope that their work will instil a sense of responsibility in children. ...young men who could instil fear on
football terraces.*

in·stinct /ˈɪnstɪŋkt/ **instincts.** 1 Instinct is the ◆◆◇◇◇
natural tendency that a person or animal has to be- N-VAR
have in a particular way. *I didn't have as strong a
maternal instinct as some other mothers. ...the dog's
natural instinct to hunt... He always knew what
time it was, as if by instinct.* 2 If you have an **in-** N-COUNT
stinct for something, you are naturally good at it or
able to do it. *Farmers are increasingly losing touch
with their instinct for managing the land... Irene is
so incredibly musical and has a natural instinct to
perform.* 3 An **instinct** is a feeling that you have N-VAR
about a particular situation, rather than an opinion
or idea based on facts. *I should've gone with my first
instinct, which was not to do the interview... He
seems so honest and genuine and my every instinct
says he's not.*

in·stinc·tive /ɪnˈstɪŋktɪv/. An **instinctive** feeling, ◆◆◇◇◇
idea, or action is one that you have or do without ADJ
thinking or reasoning. *It's an absolutely instinctive
reaction – if a child falls you pick it up.* ♦ **in·stinc-**
tive·ly *He knew instinctively that here was more* ADV:
bad news.* ADV with v

in·stinc·tual /ɪnˈstɪŋktʃuəl/. An **instinctual** feeling, ADJ
action, or idea is based on instinct. *The relationship
between a parent and a child is instinctual and
stems from basic human nature.*

in·sti·tute /ˈɪnstɪtjuːt, AM -tuːt/ **institutes, insti-** ◆◆◆◇
tuting, instituted. 1 An **institute** is an organiza- N-COUNT
tion or building where a particular type of work is
done, especially research or teaching. *...the National
Cancer Institute... Directly in front of the institute is
Kelly Ingram Park.* 2 If you **institute** a system, rule, VERB
or plan, you start it. *We will institute a number of* Vn
measures to better safeguard the public.* ♦ **in·sti·tu-** FORMAL
tion *...their demands for the institution of multi-* N-UNCOUNT
party democracy.*

in·sti·tu·tion /ˌɪnstɪˈtjuːʃən, AM -ˈtuː-/ **institu-** ◆◆◆◇
tions. 1 An **institution** is an official organization N-COUNT
which is important in society. Parliament, the
Church, and large banks are all institutions. *The
Hong Kong Bank is Hong Kong's largest financial
institution.* 2 An **institution** is a place such as a N-COUNT
mental hospital, children's home, or prison, where
people are kept and looked after. *...Shoal Creek
Mental Institution. ...penal institutions... Larry has
been in an institution since he was four.* 3 An **insti-** N-COUNT
tution is a custom that is considered an important

or typical feature of society, usually because it has existed for a long time. *I believe in the institution of marriage. ...the institution of the family.*

in·sti·tu·tion·al /ˌɪnstɪˈtjuːʃənəl, AM -ˈtuː-/. **1** Institutional means relating to an important official organization. *NATO remains the United States' chief institutional anchor in Europe... The share price will be determined by bidding from institutional investors.* **2** Institutional means relating to a building where people are looked after or held. *Outside the protected environment of institutional care he could not survive.* ADJ: ADJ n ◆◆◇◇◇

in·sti·tu·tion·al·ize /ˌɪnstɪˈtjuːʃənəlaɪz, AM -ˈtuː-/ **institutionalizes, institutionalizing, institutionalized;** also spelled **institutionalise** in British English. **1** If someone such as a sick or old person is **institutionalized**, they are sent to stay in a special hospital or home, usually for a long period. *She became seriously ill and had to be institutionalized for a lengthy period.* ◆ **in·sti·tu·tion·ali·za·tion** /ˌɪnstɪˈtjuːʃənəlaɪzeɪʃən, AM -ˈtuː-/. *For Arnie, institutionalization was necessary when his wife became both blind and violent.* **2** To **institutionalize** something means to establish it as part of a culture, a social system, or organization. *The goal is to institutionalize family planning into community life. ...institutionalized religion.* ◆ **institutionalization** *...the institutionalization of social change.* VB: usu passive be V-ed ◆◇◇◇◇ VERB V n V-ed N-UNCOUNT N-UNCOUNT

in·struct /ɪnˈstrʌkt/ **instructs, instructing, instructed.** **1** If you **instruct** someone to do something, you formally tell them to do it. *The family has instructed solicitors to sue Thomson for compensation.* ◆ **in·struc·tion, instructions** *Many Labour MPs defied a party instruction to vote against the Bill.* **2** Someone who **instructs** people in a subject or skill teaches it to them. *He instructed family members in nursing techniques.* ◆ **in·struc·tion** *All schoolchildren must now receive some religious instruction.* ◆◆◆◇◇ V n to-inf Also V n with quote, V n that N-COUNT VERB V n in/on n N-UNCOUNT

in·struc·tion /ɪnˈstrʌkʃən/ **instructions.** Instructions are clear and detailed information on how to do something. *This book gives instructions for making a wide range of skin and hand creams. ...an instruction booklet.* ◆◆◇◇◇ N-PLURAL

in·struc·tion·al /ɪnˈstrʌkʃənəl/. Instructional books or films are meant to teach people something or to offer them help with a particular problem. *...instructional material designed to help you with your lifestyle... You may wish to take advantage of our instructional session.* ADJ

in·struc·tive /ɪnˈstrʌktɪv/. Something that is **instructive** gives useful information. *It's instructive to compare his technique with Alan Bennett's. ...an entertaining and instructive documentary.* ◆◇◇◇◇ ADJ-GRADED

in·struc·tor /ɪnˈstrʌktə/ **instructors.** An **instructor** is someone who teaches a skill such as driving or skiing. In American English, an **instructor** is also a schoolteacher or a junior university teacher. *...his karate instructor.* ◆◆◆◇◇ N-COUNT

in·stru·ment /ˈɪnstrəmənt/ **instruments. 1** An **instrument** is a tool or device that is used to do a particular scientific task, for example to measure the speed or altitude of a car or plane. *...navigation instruments. ...instruments for cleaning and polishing teeth.* **2** A musical **instrument** is an object such as a piano, guitar, or flute, which you play in order to produce music. **3** Something that is an **instrument** for achieving a particular aim is used by people to achieve that aim. *The veto has been a traditional instrument of diplomacy for centuries.* **4** See also **stringed instrument, wind instrument.** ◆◆◆◇◇ N-COUNT N-COUNT N-COUNT

in·stru·men·tal /ˌɪnstrəˈmentəl/ **instrumentals. 1** Someone or something that is **instrumental** in a process or event helps to make it happen. *He was instrumental in raising the company's wider profile.* **2** **Instrumental** music is performed by instruments and not by voices. ▶ An **instrumental** is a piece of instrumental music. ◆◇◇◇◇ ADJ-GRADED ADJ N-COUNT

in·stru·men·tal·ist /ˌɪnstrəˈmentəlɪst/ **instrumentalists.** An **instrumentalist** is someone who plays a musical instrument. N-COUNT

in·stru·men·ta·tion /ˌɪnstrəmenˈteɪʃən/. **1** Instrumentation is a group or collection of scientific instruments. *Basic flight instrumentation was similar on both planes.* **2** The **instrumentation** of a piece of music is the way in which it is written for different instruments. *The instrumentation is exquisite.* ◆◇◇◇◇ N-UNCOUNT N-UNCOUNT

in·sub·or·di·nate /ˌɪnsəˈbɔːdɪnət/. If you say that someone is **insubordinate**, you mean that they do not obey people who have authority over them. *In industry, a worker who is grossly insubordinate is threatened with discharge.* ◆ **in·sub·or·di·na·tion** /ˌɪnsəbɔːdɪˈneɪʃən/. *Hansen and his partner were fired for insubordination.* ADJ-GRADED FORMAL N-UNCOUNT

in·sub·stan·tial /ˌɪnsəbˈstænʃəl/. Something that is **insubstantial** is not large, solid, or strong. *The prosecutor had considered the insubstantial nature of the evidence.* ADJ-GRADED

in·suf·fer·able /ɪnˈsʌfrəbəl/. If you say that someone or something is **insufferable**, you are emphasizing that they are very unpleasant or annoying. *The heat and humidity were insufferable.* ◆ **in·suf·fer·ably** /ɪnˈsʌfrəbli/. *His letters are insufferably dull... He found most of them insufferably arrogant.* ADJ PRAGMATICS FORMAL ADV: ADV adj

in·suf·fi·cient /ˌɪnsəˈfɪʃənt/. Something that is **insufficient** is not large enough in amount or degree for a particular purpose. *There was insufficient evidence to justify criminal proceedings.* ◆ **in·suf·fi·cien·cy** /ˌɪnsəˈfɪʃənsi/. *Late miscarriages are usually not due to hormonal insufficiency.* ◆ **in·suf·fi·cient·ly** *Food that is insufficiently cooked can lead to food poisoning.* ◆◆◇◇◇ ADJ FORMAL N-UNCOUNT ADV: ADV adj/-ed

in·su·lar /ˈɪnsjʊlə, AM -sə-/. If you say that someone is **insular**, you disapprove of them because they are unwilling to meet new people or to consider new ideas. ◆ **in·su·lar·ity** /ˌɪnsjʊˈlærɪti, AM -sə-/. *They have started to break out of their old insularity.* ◆◇◇◇◇ ADJ-GRADED PRAGMATICS N-UNCOUNT

in·su·late /ˈɪnsjʊleɪt, AM -sə-/ **insulates, insulating, insulated. 1** If a person or group is **insulated** from the rest of society or from outside influences, they are protected from them. *They wonder if their community is no longer insulated from big city problems... Their wealthy families had further insulated them from reality.* ◆ **in·su·la·tion** /ˌɪnsjʊˈleɪʃən, AM -sə-/. *They lived in happy insulation from brutal facts.* **2** To **insulate** something such as a building means to protect it from cold or noise by covering it or surrounding it in a thick layer. *Is there any way we can insulate our home from the noise?... Are your hot and cold water pipes well insulated? ...a light insulating material.* ◆ **insulation** *High electricity bills point to a poor heating system or bad insulation.* ◆ **in·su·la·tor, insulators.** *Fat is an excellent insulator against the cold.* **3** If a piece of equipment is **insulated**, it is covered with rubber or plastic to prevent electricity passing through it and giving the person using it an electric shock. *...electrical insulating tape.* ◆◇◇◇◇ VERB be V-ed from/against n V n from/ against n VERB: V n V n from or noise/ against n V-ing N-UNCOUNT N-COUNT VERB: be V-ed V-ing

in·su·lin /ˈɪnsjʊlɪn, AM -sə-/. **Insulin** is a substance that most people produce naturally in their body and which controls the level of sugar in their blood. ◆◇◇◇◇ N-UNCOUNT

in·sult, insults, insulting, insulted. The verb is pronounced /ɪnˈsʌlt/. The noun is pronounced /ˈɪnsʌlt/. **1** If someone **insults** you, they say something rude to you or offend you by doing or saying something which shows they have a low opinion of you. *I did not mean to insult you... Buchanan said he was insulted by the judge's remarks.* ◆ **in·sult·ed** *I was a bit insulted that they thought I needed bribing.* ◆ **in·sult·ing** *It's insulting to be seen as some object... One of the apprentices made an insulting remark to a passing officer.* ◆ **in·sult·ing·ly** *I have rarely read anything so insultingly sexist as this article.* **2** An **insult** is a rude remark, or something a person says or does which insults you. *Their behaviour was an insult to the people they represent... They shouted insults at each other.* **3** If an action or ◆◆◇◇◇ VERB V n ADJ-GRADED ADJ-GRADED ADV-GRADED N-COUNT PHRASE

event **adds insult to injury**, it makes an unfair or unacceptable situation even worse.

in·su·per·able /ɪn'suːpərəbəl/. An **insuperable** problem or obstacle is impossible to solve or overcome. ADJ FORMAL

in·sup·port·able /ˌɪnsə'pɔːtəbəl/. If you say that something is **insupportable**, you mean it is unbearable or unacceptable. ADJ FORMAL

in·sur·ance /ɪn'ʃʊərəns/ **insurances. 1** Insurance is an arrangement in which you pay money regularly to a company, and they pay money to you if something unpleasant happens to you, for example if your property is stolen or damaged, or if you get a serious illness. *The insurance company paid out for the stolen jewellery... The individual may take out insurance on the lenses.* **2** If you do something as **insurance** against something unpleasant happening, you do it to protect yourself in case the unpleasant thing happens. *Oil was stored as an insurance against sanctions and oil embargoes.* ◆◆◆◇ N-VAR / N-VAR

in·sure /ɪn'ʃʊə/ **insures, insuring, insured. 1** If you **insure** yourself or your property, you pay money to an insurance company so that, if you become ill or die, or if your property is damaged or stolen, the company will pay you or your family a sum of money. *Many people insure against death... The ABTA scheme insures holidaymakers against a travel firm's collapse.* ◆ **in·sur·er, insurers.** An **insurer** is a company that sells insurance. **2** If you **insure** yourself against something unpleasant that might happen in the future, you do something to protect yourself in case it happens, or to prevent it happening. *He insured himself against failure by treating only those he was fairly certain he could cure.* **3** See also **ensure**. ◆◇◇◇ VERB: V n / V against/for n / V n against/ for n / N-COUNT / VERB V pron-refl against n Also V against n

in·sured /ɪn'ʃʊəd/; **insured** is both the singular and the plural form. **The insured** is the person who is insured by a particular insurance policy. N-COUNT LEGAL

in·sur·gen·cy /ɪn'sɜːdʒənsi/ **insurgencies.** An **insurgency** is an attempt by a group of people to remove the government of their country by force. ◆◇◇◇◇ N-VAR
◆ **in·sur·gent, insurgents.** *The insurgents had taken control of the country's main military air base.* N-COUNT

in·sur·mount·able /ˌɪnsə'maʊntəbəl/. An **insurmountable** problem is so severe or difficult that it cannot be solved. ADJ

in·sur·rec·tion /ˌɪnsə'rekʃən/ **insurrections.** An **insurrection** is an attempt by a group of people to remove the government of their country by force. *They were plotting to stage an armed insurrection.* ◆◇◇◇◇ N-VAR FORMAL

int. **Int.** is an abbreviation for **internal** or for **international**. ◆◇◇◇◇

in·tact /ɪn'tækt/. Something that is **intact** is complete and has not been damaged or changed. *His reputation is still intact... The coup leaders left the telephone system intact.* ◆◆◇◇◇ ADJ

in·take /'ɪnteɪk/ **intakes. 1** Your **intake** of a particular kind of food, drink, or air is the amount that you eat, drink, or breathe in. *Your intake of alcohol should not exceed two units per day... Reduce your salt intake.* **2** The people who are accepted into an organization or place at a particular time are referred to as a particular **intake**. *...one of this year's intake of students.* **3** When there is **an intake of breath**, someone breathes in quickly and audibly, usually because they are shocked at something. ◆◆◇◇◇ N-SING: with supp / N-COUNT / PHRASE

in·tan·gible /ɪn'tændʒɪbəl/ **intangibles.** Something that is **intangible** is abstract or is hard to define or measure. ▶ You can refer to intangible things as **intangibles**. *...intangibles such as pride of workmanship, loyalty and good work habits.* ◆◇◇◇◇ ADJ-GRADED / N-PLURAL

in·te·ger /'ɪntɪdʒə/ **integers.** An **integer** is an exact whole number such as 1, 7, or 24 as opposed to a number with fractions or decimals. N-COUNT TECHNICAL

in·te·gral /'ɪntɪɡrəl/. Something that is an **integral** part of something is an essential part of that thing. *Anxiety is integral to the human condition.* ◆◇◇◇◇ ADJ

in·te·grate /'ɪntɪɡreɪt/ **integrates, integrating, integrated. 1** If someone **integrates** into a social group, or **is integrated** into it, they behave in such a V-ERG way that they become part of the group or are accepted into it. *He didn't integrate successfully into the Italian way of life. ...his attempt to integrate the boy into the family unit.* ◆ **in·te·grat·ed** We believe that pupils of integrated schools will have more tolerant attitudes. ◆ **in·te·gra·tion** /ˌɪntɪ'ɡreɪʃən/ ...the integration of disabled people into mainstream society. **2** If you **integrate** one thing with another, the first thing is combined with the second so that they become closely linked or form part of a whole idea or system. *It believes that by integrating the rail lines with its buses it can make them pay... Ann wanted the conservatory to integrate with the kitchen... Little attempt was made to integrate the parts into a coherent whole.* ◆ **in·te·grat·ed** ...an integrated national transport policy. ◆ **in·te·gra·tion** ...closer European integration. ADJ-GRADED / N-UNCOUNT / V-RECIP-ERG V n within / V with n / V pl-n into n / Also V pl-n, pl-n V / ADJ-GRADED / N-UNCOUNT

in·teg·rity /ɪn'teɡrɪti/. **1** If you have **integrity**, you are honest and firm in your moral principles. *I have always regarded him as a man of integrity.* **2** The **integrity** of something such as a group of people or a text is its state of being a united whole. *Separatist movements are a threat to the integrity of the nation.* ◆◆◇◇◇ N-UNCOUNT / N-UNCOUNT: with poss FORMAL

in·tel·lect /'ɪntɪlekt/ **intellects. 1** Intellect is the ability to understand or deal with ideas and information. *The intellect is not the most important thing in life.* **2** Intellect is the quality of being very intelligent or clever. *Her intellect is famed far and wide.* ◆◇◇◇◇ N-VAR / N-VAR

in·tel·lec·tual /ˌɪntɪ'lektʃuəl/ **intellectuals. 1** Intellectual means involving a person's ability to think and to understand ideas and information. *...the intellectual development of children.* ◆ **in·tel·lec·tual·ly** ...intellectually satisfying work... Intellectually, I was completely prepared for that type of work. **2** An **intellectual** is someone who spends a lot of time studying and thinking about complicated ideas. *...teachers, artists and other intellectuals.* ▶ Also an adjective. *They were very intellectual and witty. ...an intellectual elite.* ◆◆◇◇◇ ADJ: ADJ n / ADV / N-COUNT / ADJ-GRADED

in·tel·li·gence /ɪn'telɪdʒəns/. **1** Intelligence is information that is gathered by the government or the army about their country's enemies and their activities. *...the intelligence services... Why was military intelligence so lacking?* **2** See also **intelligent**. ◆◆◇◇ N-UNCOUNT

in·tel·li·gent /ɪn'telɪdʒənt/. **1** A person or animal that is **intelligent** has the ability to think, understand, and learn things quickly and well. *...lively and intelligent conversation... Horses are more intelligent than cattle.* ◆ **in·tel·li·gence** She's a woman of exceptional intelligence. ◆ **in·tel·li·gent·ly** They are incapable of thinking intelligently about politics. **2** Something that is **intelligent** has the ability to think and understand instead of doing things automatically or by instinct. *It's an intelligent, computer controlled system which can continually sense the road surface. ...the biggest-ever search for intelligent life elsewhere in the universe.* ◆ **in·tel·li·gence** Nerve cells, after all, do not have intelligence of their own. ◆◆◆◇◇ ADJ-GRADED / N-UNCOUNT / ADV-GRADED / ADJ / N-UNCOUNT

in·tel·li·gent·sia /ɪnˌtelɪ'dʒentsiə/. The **intelligentsia** in a country or community are the most educated people there, especially those interested in the arts, philosophy, and politics. ◆◇◇◇◇ N-COLL-SING

in·tel·li·gi·ble /ɪn'telɪdʒɪbəl/. Something that is **intelligible** can be understood. *The language of Darwin was intelligible to experts and non-experts alike.* ADJ-GRADED

in·tem·per·ate /ɪn'tempərət/. If you describe someone's language or behaviour as **intemperate**, you disapprove of it because it is unreasonably strong and uncontrolled. ADJ-GRADED PRAGMATICS FORMAL

in·tend /ɪn'tend/ **intends, intending, intended. 1** If you **intend** to do something, you have decided or planned to do it. *She intends to do A levels and go to university... I didn't intend coming to Germany to work... We had always intended that the new series would be live.* **2** If something **is intended** for a particular use or purpose, people have planned that it should have that use or purpose. *This money is intended for the development of the tourist industry... Columns are usually intended in architecture to add* ◆◆◆◇ VERB V to-inf / V -ing / V that / VB: passive beV-ed for n beV-ed to-inf beV-ed n / V-ed

grandeur and status... Originally, Hatfield had been intended as a leisure complex... The intended target had been a military building. **3** If you **intend** a particular idea or feeling in something that you say or do, you want to express it or want it to be understood. He didn't intend any sarcasm... Burke's response seemed a little patronizing, though he undoubtedly hadn't intended it that way... Those who did use the term did not intend it to be a compliment.

in·tense /ɪnˈtens/. **1 Intense** is used to describe something that is very great or concentrated in strength or degree. He was sweating from the intense heat. ...a deep-seated and intense hatred... The battle for third place was intense. ♦ **in·tense·ly** The fast-food business is intensely competitive. ♦ **in·ten·sity** /ɪnˈtensɪti/ **intensities** The attack was anticipated but its intensity came as a shock. **2** If you describe a person as **intense**, you mean that they appear to concentrate very seriously on everything that they do and feel. He's an intense player, but he does enjoy what he's doing... I felt so self-conscious under Luke's mother's intense gaze. ♦ **in·tense·ly** He stared at David intensely. ♦ **in·ten·sity** His intensity and the ferocity of his feelings alarmed me.

in·ten·si·fy /ɪnˈtensɪfaɪ/ **intensifies, intensifying, intensified.** If you **intensify** something or if it **intensifies**, it becomes greater in strength, amount, or degree. Britain is intensifying its efforts to secure the release of three British hostages... The conflict is almost bound to intensify... Groups of refugees are on the move following intensified fighting in the region. ♦ **in·ten·si·fi·ca·tion** /ɪn,tensɪfɪˈkeɪʃən/ ...the intensification of violent rebel attacks.

in·ten·sive /ɪnˈtensɪv/. **1** An **intensive** activity involves the concentration of energy or people on one particular task in order to try to achieve a great deal in a short time. ...several days and nights of intensive negotiations... Each counsellor undergoes an intensive training programme. ♦ **in·ten·sive·ly** Ruth's parents opted to educate her intensively at home. **2 Intensive** farming involves producing as many crops or animals as possible from your land, usually with the aid of chemicals. ♦ **intensively** Will they farm the rest of their land less intensively?

-intensive /-ɪntensɪv/. **-intensive** combines with nouns to form adjectives which indicate that an industry or activity involves the use of a lot of a particular thing. ...energy-intensive industries.

in,tensive 'care. If someone is in **intensive care**, they are in hospital being cared for very thoroughly and watched very closely because they are seriously ill.

in·tent /ɪnˈtent/ **intents. 1** If you are intent on doing something, you are eager and determined to do it. The rebels are obviously intent on keeping up the pressure. ...a well-known retired actress who was intent on a come-back. **2** If someone is **intent**, they appear to be concentrating very seriously on what they are doing or feeling. She looked from one intent face to another... Rodney had been intent on every word. ♦ **in·tent·ly** He listened intently, then slammed down the phone. **3** A person's **intent** is their intention to do something. ...this strong statement of intent on arms control... He was also accused of possessing a firearm with intent to endanger life. **4** You say to **all intents and purposes** to suggest that a situation is not exactly as you describe it but the effect is the same as if it were. To all intents and purposes he was my father.

in·ten·tion /ɪnˈtenʃən/ **intentions.** An **intention** that you have is an idea or plan of what you are going to do. Beveridge announced his intention of standing for parliament... We have no intention of buying American jets... Unfortunately, his good intentions never seemed to last long.

in·ten·tion·al /ɪnˈtenʃənəl/. Something that is **intentional** is deliberate. ...women who are the victims of intentional discrimination. ♦ **in·ten·tion·al·ly** I've never intentionally hurt anyone.

in·ter /ɪnˈtɜː/ **inters, interring, interred.** When a dead person **is interred**, they are buried. ...the spot where bones were originally interred.

inter- /ˈɪntə-/. **Inter-** combines with adjectives and nouns to form adjectives indicating that something moves, exists, or happens between two or more places, things, or groups of people. For example, inter-governmental relations are relations between governments. ...a policy of encouraging inter-racial marriage.

inter·act /,ɪntəˈrækt/ **interacts, interacting, interacted. 1** When you **interact** with another person, you communicate with each other as you work or spend time together. The other children interacted and played together. ♦ **inter·ac·tion** /,ɪntəˈrækʃən/ **interactions** ...superficial interactions with other people. **2** When computers **interact** with people or other machines, information or instructions are exchanged. ...a true global village in which telephones, computers and televisions interact. ♦ **interaction** ...experts on human-computer interaction. **3** When one thing **interacts** with another, the two things affect each other's behaviour or condition. The oxygen interacts with the wine and brings out the flavours more fully... You have to understand how cells interact. ♦ **interaction** ...the interaction between physical and emotional illness.

inter·ac·tive /,ɪntəˈræktɪv/. **1** An **interactive** computer program or television system is one which allows direct communication between the user and the machine. **2** If you describe a group of people or their activities as **interactive**, you mean that the people communicate with each other. This encouraged flexible, interactive teaching in the classroom.

in·ter alia /,ɪntər ˈeɪliə/. You use **inter alia**, meaning 'among other things', when you want to say that there are other things involved apart from the one you are mentioning.

inter·cede /,ɪntəˈsiːd/ **intercedes, interceding, interceded.** If you **intercede** with someone, usually someone in a position of power, you talk to them in order to try to persuade them not to take action against a particular person. He had occasionally tried to intercede for me... The Supreme Court will not intercede to overturn an election.

inter·cept /,ɪntəˈsept/ **intercepts, intercepting, intercepted.** If you **intercept** someone or something that is travelling from one place to another, you stop them before they get to their destination. His letter was intercepted by the Secret Service. ♦ **inter·cep·tion** /,ɪntəˈsepʃən/ **interceptions** ...the interception of a ship off the west coast of Scotland.

inter·cep·tor /,ɪntəˈseptə/ **interceptors.** An **interceptor** is a fighter aircraft or ground based missile system designed to intercept and attack enemy planes or missiles.

inter·ces·sion /,ɪntəˈseʃən/ **intercessions. Intercession** is an act of interceding to try to end a disagreement or to try to persuade someone powerful to be merciful to a weaker person.

inter·change, interchanges, interchanging, interchanged. The noun is pronounced /ˈɪntətʃeɪndʒ/. The verb is pronounced /,ɪntəˈtʃeɪndʒ/. **1** If there is an **interchange** of ideas or information among a group of people, each person talks about his or her ideas or gives information to the others. **2** If you **interchange** one thing with another, each thing takes the place of the other or is exchanged for the other. Your task is to interchange words so that the sentence makes sense. ...the point where the illusions of the stage and reality begin to interchange. ▶ Also a noun. ...the interchange of matter and energy at atomic or sub-atomic levels. **3** An **interchange** on a motorway is a junction where it meets a main road or another motorway.

inter·change·able /,ɪntəˈtʃeɪndʒəbəl/. Things that are **interchangeable** can be exchanged with each other without it making any difference. His greatest innovation was the use of interchangeable parts.

♦ **inter·change·ably** *These expressions are often* ADV:
used interchangeably, but they do have different ADV after v
meanings.

inter·com /'ɪntəkɒm/ **intercoms.** An **intercom** is a N-COUNT
device like a small box with a microphone which is
connected to a loudspeaker in another room.

inter·con·nect /,ɪntəkə'nekt/ **interconnects,** V-RECIP-ERG:
interconnecting, interconnected. Things that pl-n V
interconnect or **are interconnected** are connected V with n
to or with each other. *Their lives interconnect with* be V-ed
those of celebrated figures of the late eighteenth- V-ing
century... The regions are interconnected by an excel- Also V n with n
lent highway system. ...a huge mesh of interconnect-
ing wires. ♦ **inter·con·nec·tion** /,ɪntəkə'nekʃən/ N-VAR
interconnections *...the thematic interconnection*
between the two.

inter·con·ti·nen·tal /,ɪntəkɒntɪ'nentəl/. **Intercon-** ADJ: ADJ n
tinental is used to describe something that exists or
happens between continents. *...intercontinental*
flights.

inter·course /'ɪntəkɔːs/. 1 **Intercourse** is the act ♦♦◇◇◇
of having sex. *...sexual intercourse... We didn't have* N-UNCOUNT
intercourse. 2 Social **intercourse** is communication N-UNCOUNT
between people as they spend time together. DATED

inter·cut /,ɪntə'kʌt/ **intercuts, intercutting.** The VERB
form **intercut** is used in the present tense and is the be V-ed with n
past tense and past participle. If a film **is intercut** Also V n with n
with particular images, those images appear regu- TECHNICAL
larly throughout the film. *The film is set in a night*
club and intercut with images of gangland London.

inter·de·pend·ent /,ɪntədɪ'pendənt/. People or ADJ-GRADED
things that are **interdependent** all depend on each
other. ♦ **inter·de·pend·ence** *...the interdepend-* N-UNCOUNT
ence of nations. ...economic interdependence.

inter·dict, interdicts, interdicting, interdict-
ed. The verb is pronounced /,ɪntə'dɪkt/. The noun
is pronounced /'ɪntədɪkt/. 1 If an armed force VERB
interdicts something or someone, they stop them V n
and prevent them from moving. If they **interdict** a AMERICAN,
route, they block it or cut it off. *Troops could be fer-* FORMAL
ried in to interdict drug shipments. 2 ...i **interdict** is N-COUNT
an official order to ban, prevent, or restrict some- FORMAL
thing. *The National Trust has placed an interdict on*
jet-skis in Dorset.

inter·dic·tion /,ɪntə'dɪkʃən/. The **interdiction** of N-UNCOUNT
something is the prevention of a supply of it from FORMAL
reaching a place. *...the interdiction of drug traffic.*

inter·dis·ci·pli·nary /,ɪntədɪsɪ'plɪnəri, AM -'plɪneri/. ADJ
Interdisciplinary means involving more than one
academic subject.

in·ter·est /'ɪntrəst, -tərest/ **interests, interest-** ♦♦♦♦♦
ing, interested. 1 If you have an **interest** in N-COUNT:
something, you want to learn or hear more about it. also a N
His parents tried to discourage his interest in music...
She'd liked him at first, but soon lost interest... Food
was of no interest to her at all. 2 Your **interests** are N-COUNT
the things that you enjoy doing. *He developed a*
wide range of sporting interests. 3 If something **in-** VERB
terests you, it attracts your attention so that you V n
want to learn or hear more about it or continue do- it V n to-inf
ing it. *These are the stories that interest me... It may*
interest you to know that Miss Woods, the house-
keeper, witnessed the attack. 4 If you are trying to VERB
persuade someone to buy something from you or V n in n/-ing
do something for you, you can say that you are trying to **interest** them **in** it. *I can't interest you in a*
new car, I suppose?

5 If something is in the **interests** of a particular per- N-COUNT
son or group, it will benefit them in some way. *Did*
those directors act in the best interests of their club?...
She was acting against the boy's interests. 6 If you do PHRASE
something **in the interests of** a particular result or
situation, you do it in order to achieve that result or
maintain that situation. *...a call for all businessmen to*
work together in the interests of national stability.
7 You can use **interests** to refer to groups of people N-COUNT
who you think use their power or money to benefit
themselves. *The government accused unnamed 'for-*
eign interests' of inciting the trouble. 8 A person or or- N-COUNT
ganization that has **interests** in a company owns

shares in this company. *Her other business interests*
include a theme park in Scandinavia... Disney will re-
tain a 51 percent controlling interest in the venture.
9 If a person, country, or organization has an **interest** N-COUNT
in a possible event or situation, they want that event
or situation to happen because they are likely to benefit from it. *The West has an interest in promoting*
democratic forces.

10 **Interest** is extra money that you receive if you N-UNCOUNT
have invested a sum of money, or extra money that
you pay if you have borrowed money. *Does your cur-*
rent account pay interest?

11 See also **interested, interesting; compound inter-**
est, self-interest, vested interest. ● **to have**
someone's interests at heart: see heart.

in·ter·est·ed /'ɪntrestɪd/. 1 If you are **interested** in ♦♦♦♦◇
something, you think it is important and you are ADJ-GRADED
keen to learn more about it or spend time doing it.
The young man is getting interested in gardening... I
would be interested in doing a film based on
Hearst... I'd be interested to meet her. 2 An **interest-** ADJ: ADJ n
ed party or group of people is affected by or in-
volved in a particular event or situation. 3 See also
self-interested.

interest-'free. An **interest-free** loan has no inter- ADJ
est charged on it. *Many stores are offering interest-*
free credit. ▶ Also an adverb. *Customers allowed the* ADV:
banks to use their money interest-free. ADV after v

in·ter·est·ing /'ɪntrestɪŋ/. If you find something ♦♦♦♦◇
interesting, it attracts your attention, for example ADJ-GRADED
because you think it is exciting or unusual. *It was*
interesting to be in a different environment. ...a
strange little place with an interesting history... His
third album is by far his most interesting.

in·ter·est·ing·ly /'ɪntrestɪŋli/. You use **interest-** ♦◇◇◇◇
ingly to introduce a piece of information that you ADV-GRADED:
think is interesting or surprising. *Interestingly* ADV with cl
enough, a few weeks later, Benjamin remarried. PRAGMATICS

inter·face /'ɪntəfeɪs/ **interfaces, interfacing,** ♦◇◇◇◇
interfaced. 1 The **interface** between two subjects N-COUNT
or systems is the area in which they affect each oth- FORMAL
er or have links with each other. *...that interface be-*
tween bureaucracy and the working world. 2 If one V-RECIP-ERG:
thing **interfaces** with another, they have connec- V with n
tions with each other or interact. *Unless divisions* pl-n V
consult with one another, the components they prod- Also V n with n
uce are not likely to interface smoothly. FORMAL

3 The user **interface** of a particular piece of comput- N-COUNT
ing software is its presentation on screen and how TECHNICAL
easy it is to operate.

inter·fere /,ɪntə'fɪə/ **interferes, interfering,** ♦♦◇◇◇
interfered. 1 If someone **interferes** in a situation, VERB:
they get involved in it although it does not concern V in/with n
them and their involvement is not wanted. *I wish* PRAGMATICS
everyone would stop interfering. ...interfering neigh- V-ing
bours. ♦ **inter·fer·ence** *The parliament described* N-UNCOUNT
the decree as interference in the republic's internal
affairs. 2 Something that **interferes with** a situation, VERB
activity, or process has a damaging effect on it. V with n
Drug problems frequently interfered with his work.

inter·fer·ence /,ɪntə'fɪərəns/. When there is **inter-** ♦♦◇◇◇
ference, a radio signal is affected by other radio N-UNCOUNT
waves or electrical activity so that it cannot be received properly.

in·ter·im /'ɪntərɪm/. 1 **Interim** is used to describe ♦♦♦◇◇
something that is intended to be used until some- ADJ: ADJ n
thing permanent is done or established. *She was*
sworn in as head of an interim government in
March. ...an interim report. 2 **In the interim** means PHRASE
until a particular thing happens. *He was to remain* FORMAL
in jail in the interim.

in·te·ri·or /ɪn'tɪəriə/ **interiors.** 1 The **interior** of ♦♦♦◇◇
something is the inside part of it. *...the boat's interi-* N-COUNT
or. ...the interior walls.

2 The **interior** of a country or continent is the central N-SING
area of it. *...a 5-day hike into the interior.*

3 A country's **interior** minister, ministry, or depart- ADJ: ADJ n
ment deals with affairs within that country, such as
law and order. 4 A country's minister or ministry of N-SING

the **interior** deals with affairs within that country, such as law and order.

in·terior deco·ration. Interior decoration is the decoration of the inside of a house, using paints, wallpapers, carpets, and furnishings. ♦ **in·te·ri·or deco·ra·tor, interior decorators.** An interior decorator is someone whose job is interior decoration. N-UNCOUNT / N-COUNT

in·terior de·sign. Interior design is the art or profession of designing how the inside of a house is going to be decorated by choosing paints, wallpapers, carpets, and furnishings. ♦ **in·te·ri·or de·sign·er, interior designers.** An interior designer is someone whose job is interior design. N-UNCOUNT / N-COUNT

inter·ject /ˌɪntəˈdʒekt/ interjects, interjecting, interjected. If you interject something, you say it and interrupt someone else who is speaking. 'Surely there's something we can do?' interjected Palin. ♦ **inter·jec·tion** /ˌɪntəˈdʒekʃən/ interjections. An interjection is something you say which interrupts someone else who is speaking. VERB: V n / V with quote / Also V / FORMAL / N-COUNT

inter·jec·tion /ˌɪntəˈdʒekʃən/ interjections. In grammar, an interjection is a word or expression which you use to express a strong feeling such as surprise, pain, or horror. ● See also interject. N-COUNT

inter·laced /ˌɪntəˈleɪst/. If things are interlaced, parts of one thing go over, under, or between parts of another. He sat with his eyes closed and his fingers interlaced. ADJ / WRITTEN

inter·link /ˌɪntəˈlɪŋk/ interlinks, interlinking, interlinked. Things that are interlinked are linked with each other in some way. The question to be addressed is interlinked with the question of human rights. V-RECIP-ERG: be V-ed / be V-ed with n / Also pl-n V

inter·lock /ˌɪntəˈlɒk/ interlocks, interlocking, interlocked. 1 Things that interlock go between or through each other so that they are linked. Interlock your fingers behind your back. 2 If systems, situations, or plans are interlocked, they are very closely connected. The tragedies begin to interlock. ♦◇◇◇◇ / V-RECIP-ERG: pl-n V / V pl-n / Also V with n / V-RECIP-ERG: be V-ed / pl-n V

inter·locu·tor /ˌɪntəˈlɒkjʊtə/ interlocutors. 1 Your interlocutor is the person with whom you are having a conversation. ...staring motionless at his interlocutor. 2 An interlocutor is a person or organization which has the role of a representative, intermediary, or participant in talks or negotiations. N-COUNT / FORMAL / N-COUNT / FORMAL

inter·lop·er /ˈɪntələʊpə/ interlopers. If you describe someone as an interloper, you mean that they have come into a situation or a place where they are not wanted or do not belong. N-COUNT

inter·lude /ˈɪntəluːd/ interludes. An interlude is a short period of time when an activity or situation stops and something else happens. ...a happy interlude in the Kents' life. ♦◇◇◇◇ / N-COUNT

inter·mar·ry /ˌɪntəˈmæri/ intermarries, intermarrying, intermarried. When people from different social, racial, or religious groups intermarry, they marry each other. Some of the traders settled and intermarried with local women. ♦ **inter·mar·riage** /ˌɪntəˈmærɪdʒ/ intermarriages ...intermarriage between members of the old and new ruling classes. V-RECIP: pl-n V / V with n / N-UNCOUNT: also N in pl

inter·medi·ary /ˌɪntəˈmiːdiəri/ intermediaries. An intermediary is a person who passes messages or proposals between two people or groups. ♦◇◇◇◇ / N-COUNT

inter·medi·ate /ˌɪntəˈmiːdiət/ intermediates. 1 An intermediate stage, level, or position is one that occurs between two other stages, levels, or positions. ...Perugia, Assisi, and intermediate stations. 2 Intermediate learners are no longer beginners, but are not yet advanced. ► An intermediate is an intermediate learner. ...beginners, intermediates, and advanced skiers. ♦♦◇◇◇ / ADJ / ADJ / N-COUNT

in·ter·ment /ɪnˈtɜːmənt/ interments. The interment of a dead person is their burial. N-VAR / FORMAL

in·ter·mi·nable /ɪnˈtɜːmɪnəbəl/. If you describe something as interminable, you are emphasizing that it continues for a very long time and indicating that you wish it was shorter or would stop. ...an in- ♦◇◇◇◇ / ADJ / PRAGMATICS

terminable meeting. ♦ **in·ter·mi·nably** He talked to me interminably about his first wife. ADV

inter·min·gle /ˌɪntəˈmɪŋgəl/ intermingles, intermingling, intermingled. When people or things intermingle, they mix with each other. ...an opportunity for them to intermingle with the citizens of other countries. ♦ **inter·min·gled** The ethnic populations are so intermingled that there's bound to be conflict. V-RECIP: pl-n V / V with n / FORMAL / ADJ-GRADED

inter·mis·sion /ˌɪntəˈmɪʃən/ intermissions. An intermission is a short interval between two parts of a film, play, or show. In American English, you can also say that something happens at, after, or during intermission. N-COUNT: also prep N

inter·mit·tent /ˌɪntəˈmɪtənt/. Something that is intermittent happens occasionally rather than continuously. ...after three hours of intermittent rain. ♦ **inter·mit·tent·ly** The talks went on intermittently for three years. ♦◇◇◇◇ / ADJ-GRADED / ADV-GRADED

in·tern, interns, interning, interned. The verb is pronounced /ɪnˈtɜːn/. The noun is pronounced /ˈɪntɜːn/. 1 If someone is interned, they are put in prison for political reasons. He was interned as an enemy alien at the outbreak of the Second World War. ♦ **in·tern·ment** ...the return of internment without trial for terrorists. ♦ **in·ternee** /ˌɪntɜːˈniː/ internees. An internee is a person who has been imprisoned for political reasons.
2 An intern is an advanced student or a recent graduate who is being given practical training under supervision. ♦◇◇◇◇ / VB: usu passive / be V-ed / N-UNCOUNT / N-COUNT / N-COUNT / AMERICAN

in·ter·nal /ɪnˈtɜːnəl/. 1 Internal is used to describe things that exist or happen inside a country or organization. The country stepped up internal security. ...the internal mail box. ♦ **in·ter·nal·ly** The state is not a unified and internally coherent entity. 2 Internal is used to describe things that exist or happen inside a particular person, object, or place. The internal bleeding had been massive. ♦ **internally** Evening primrose oil is used on the skin as well as taken internally... Internally, however, the two computers are so different that programs cannot be switched. ♦♦♦◇◇ / ADJ: ADJ n / ADV / ADJ: ADJ n / ADV

in·ter·nal·ize /ɪnˈtɜːnəlaɪz/ internalizes, internalizing, internalized; also spelled internalise in British English. If you internalize something such as a belief or a set of values, you make it become part of your attitude or way of thinking. ...internalized feelings of what is right and wrong. VERB: V n / V-ed / FORMAL

inter·na·tion·al /ˌɪntəˈnæʃənəl/ internationals. 1 International means between or involving different countries. ...an international agreement against exporting arms to that country. ♦ **inter·na·tion·al·ly** ...internationally recognised certificates in Teaching English as a Foreign Language. 2 An international is a sports match played between teams representing two different countries. 3 An international is a sportsman or sportswoman who plays in a match played between teams representing two different countries. ♦♦♦♦ / ADJ / ADV / N-COUNT / BRITISH / N-COUNT / BRITISH

inter·na·tion·al·ist /ˌɪntəˈnæʃənəlɪst/ internationalists. If someone has internationalist beliefs or opinions, they believe that countries should co-operate with one another and try to understand one another. ...a more genuinely internationalist view of US participation in peace-keeping. ► An internationalist is someone who has internationalist views. ♦ **inter·na·tion·al·ism.** ADJ / N-COUNT / N-UNCOUNT

inter·na·tion·al·ize /ˌɪntəˈnæʃənəlaɪz/ internationalizes, internationalizing, internationalized; also spelled internationalise in British English. If an issue or a crisis is internationalized, it becomes the concern of many nations. They have been trying to internationalise the Kashmir problem. ♦ **inter·na·tion·ali·za·tion** /ˌɪntənæʃənəlaɪˈzeɪʃən/ ...the internationalization of the crisis in Croatia. VERB: be V-ed / V n / JOURNALISM / N-UNCOUNT

,international re'lations. The political relationships between different countries are referred to as international relations. N-PLURAL

inter·necine /ˌɪntəˈniːsaɪn, AM -siːn/. An internecine conflict, war, or quarrel is one which takes ADJ: ADJ n / FORMAL

I

place between opposing groups within a country or organization.

in·ter·nee. See **intern**.

In·ter·net /'ɪntənet/. **The Internet** is the worldwide network of computer links which allows computer users to connect with computers all over the world, and which carries electronic mail.
N-PROPER: the N

in·tern·ment. See **intern**.

inter·per·son·al /,ɪntə'pɜːsənəl/. **Interpersonal** means relating to relationships between people. ...*problems in interpersonal relationships.*
◆◇◇◇◇ ADJ: ADJ n

inter·play /'ɪntəpleɪ/. The **interplay** between two or more things or people is the way that they have an effect on each other or react to each other. ...*the personal interplay between great entertainers and a live public.*
N-UNCOUNT

in·ter·po·late /ɪn'tɜːpəleɪt/ **interpolates, interpolating, interpolated.** If you **interpolate** a comment into a conversation or some words into a piece of writing, you put it in as an addition. *These odd assertions were interpolated into the manuscript some time after 1400.*
VERB: V n be V-ed into n FORMAL

inter·pose /,ɪntə'pəʊz/ **interposes, interposing, interposed.** 1 If you **interpose** something between two people or things, you place it between them. *Strong police forces had to interpose themselves between the two rival groups... The work interposes a glass plate between two circular mirrors.* 2 If you **interpose**, you interrupt with a comment or question. *'He rang me just now,' she interposed... Jacob was silent so long that Livvy interposed.*
VERB V pron-refl between pl-n V n between pl-n FORMAL VERB: V with quote V Also V n FORMAL

in·ter·pret /ɪn'tɜːprɪt/ **interprets, interpreting, interpreted.** 1 If you **interpret** something in a particular way, you decide that this is its meaning or significance. *The move was interpreted as a defeat for Mr Gorbachev and a victory for Mr Yeltsin... The judge has to interpret the law as it's been passed.* ♦ **in·ter·pre·ta·tion, interpretations** *The opposition Labour Party put a different interpretation on the figures.* 2 If you **interpret** something someone is saying, you translate it immediately into another language. *The chambermaid spoke little English, so her husband came with her to interpret.* ♦ **in·ter·pret·er, interpreters.**
◆◆◇◇◇ VERB: V n adv/prep V n as n V n N-VAR VERB: V n V N-COUNT

in·ter·pre·ta·tion /ɪn,tɜːprɪ'teɪʃən/ **interpretations.** A performer's **interpretation** of something such as a piece of music or a role in a play is the particular way in which they choose to perform it. ...*her full-bodied interpretation of the role of Micaela.* ● See also **interpret**.
◆◆◇◇◇ N-COUNT: with supp

in·ter·pre·ta·tive /ɪn'tɜːprɪtətɪv/. See **interpretive**.

in·ter·pre·tive /ɪn'tɜːprɪtɪv/. The form **interpretative** is also used. You use **interpretive** to describe something that provides an interpretation. *History is an interpretive process.*
ADJ: ADJ n

inter·reg·num /,ɪntə'regnəm/. An **interregnum** is a period between the end of one person's time as ruler or leader and the coming to power of the next ruler or leader.
N-SING FORMAL

inter·re·late /,ɪntərɪ'leɪt/ **interrelates, interrelating, interrelated.** If two or more things **interrelate**, there is a connection between them and they have an effect on each other. *Each of these cells have their specific jobs to do, but they also interrelate with each other.*
V-RECIP: pl-n V pl-n V with pron-recip Also V with n

inter·re·la·tion·ship /,ɪntərɪ'leɪʃənʃɪp/ **interrelationships.** An **interrelationship** is a close relationship between two or more things or people. ...*the interrelationships between unemployment, crime, and imprisonment.*
N-COUNT

in·ter·ro·gate /ɪn'terəgeɪt/ **interrogates, interrogating, interrogated.** If someone **interrogates** someone, they question them thoroughly for a long time in order to get some information from them. ♦ **in·ter·ro·ga·tion** /ɪn,terə'geɪʃən/ **interrogations** ...*the right to silence in police interrogations.* ♦ **in·ter·ro·ga·tor, interrogators** *I was well aware of what my interrogators wanted to hear.*
◆◇◇◇◇ VERB: V n N-VAR N-COUNT

in·ter·roga·tive /,ɪntə'rɒgətɪv/ **interrogatives.**
1 An **interrogative** gesture or tone of voice shows
ADJ-GRADED

that you want to know the answer to a question. *Donovan cocked an interrogative eye at his companion, who nodded in reply.* 2 In grammar, a clause that is in **the interrogative**, or in the **interrogative** mood, has its subject following 'do', 'be', 'have', or a modal verb. Examples are 'When did he get back?' and 'Are you all right?'. Clauses of this kind are typically used to ask questions. 3 In grammar, an **interrogative** is a word such as 'who', 'how', or 'why', which can be used to ask a question.
WRITTEN N-SING: the N N-COUNT

in·ter·rupt /,ɪntə'rʌpt/ **interrupts, interrupting, interrupted.** 1 If you **interrupt** someone who is speaking, you say or do something that causes them to stop. *Turkin tapped him on the shoulder. 'Sorry to interrupt, Colonel.'* ♦ **in·ter·rup·tion** /,ɪntə'rʌpʃən/ **interruptions** *The sudden interruption stopped Beryl in mid-flow.* 2 If someone or something **interrupts** a process or activity, they stop it for a period of time. *He has rightly interrupted his holiday in Spain... Their meal was interrupted by a phone call.* ♦ **interruption** ...*interruptions in the supply of food.* 3 If something **interrupts** a line, surface, or view, it stops it from being continuous or makes it look irregular. *Taller plants interrupt the views from the house.*
◆◆◇◇◇ VERB: V n V N-VAR VERB V n be V-ed by n N-VAR VERB V n

inter·sect /,ɪntə'sekt/ **intersects, intersecting, intersected.** 1 If two or more lines or roads **intersect**, they meet or cross each other. *The orbit of this comet intersects the orbit of the Earth.* ♦ **inter·sec·tion** /,ɪntə'sekʃən/ **intersections.** An **intersection** is a place where roads or other lines meet or cross. ...*a busy highway intersection.* 2 If a place, area, or surface **is intersected** by things such as roads or lines, they cross it. *The centre of the city is intersected by three main waterways.* 3 If one thing **intersects** with another, the two things have a connection at a particular point. *Their histories intersect.*
V-RECIP: pl-n V V n Also V with n N-COUNT VB: usu passive be V-ed by n V-RECIP: V with n pl-n V

inter·sperse /,ɪntə'spɜːs/ **intersperses, interspersing, interspersed.** If you **intersperse** one group of things **with** another, you put or include the second things between or among the first things. ...*skilfully interspersing jokes and gossipy anecdotes among his instructions.*
VERB: V n with n V n among n

inter·spersed /,ɪntə'spɜːst/. If one group of things are **interspersed with** another, the second things occur between or among the first things. ...*a series of bursts of gunfire, interspersed with single shots.*
◆◇◇◇◇ ADJ: v-link ADJ prep

inter·state /'ɪntəsteɪt/ **interstates.** 1 **Interstate** means between states, especially the states of the United States. *The action prohibits interstate movement of certain fruits and vegetables.* ...*interstate highways.* 2 An **interstate** is a major road linking states. *He cruised slowly down Interstate 40.*
◆◇◇◇◇ ADJ: ADJ n N-COUNT: also N num AMERICAN

inter·stel·lar /,ɪntə'stelə/. **Interstellar** means between the stars. *The distances involved in interstellar travel posed immense difficulties.*
ADJ: ADJ n FORMAL

inter·twine /,ɪntə'twaɪn/ **intertwines, intertwining, intertwined.** 1 If two or more things **intertwine**, they are closely connected with each other in many ways. *Their destinies are intertwined... He intertwines personal reminiscences with the story of British television.* 2 If two things **intertwine**, they are twisted together or go over and under each other. ...*their three intertwined initials.*
◆◇◇◇◇ V-RECIP-ERG: pl-n V be V-ed V n with n Also V with n V-RECIP: pl-n V V-ed Also V with n

in·ter·val /'ɪntəvəl/ **intervals.** 1 An **interval** between two events or dates is the period of time between them. *There was a long interval of silence.* 2 An **interval** during a play, concert, or game is a short break between two of the parts. *Our price includes a glass of wine in the interval and a programme.* 3 If something happens **at intervals**, it happens several times with gaps or pauses in between. 4 In music, an **interval** is the difference in pitch between two musical notes. 5 If things are placed **at** particular **intervals**, there are spaces of a particular size between them. *Several red and white barriers marked the road at intervals of about a mile.*
N-COUNT N-COUNT PHRASE N-COUNT TECHNICAL PHRASE

inter·vene /ˌɪntəˈviːn/ **intervenes, intervening, intervened.** 1 If you **intervene** in a situation, you become involved in it and try to change it. *The situation calmed down when police intervened.* ♦ **inter·ven·tion** /ˌɪntəˈvenʃən/ **interventions** *...the United States and its intervention in the internal affairs of many countries.* 2 If you **intervene**, you interrupt a conversation in order to add something to it. *'I've told you he's not here,' Irena intervened.* 3 If an event **intervenes**, it happens suddenly in a way that stops, delays, or prevents something from happening. *I pray that death may not intervene to prevent our meeting.*

◆◆◇◇◇
VERB:
V in n
V

N-VAR

VERB: V
V with quote

VERB: V
V to-inf

inter·ven·ing /ˌɪntəˈviːnɪŋ/. 1 An **intervening** period of time is one that separates two events or points in time. *During those intervening years Bridget had married her husband.* 2 An **intervening** object or area comes between two other objects or areas. *...the intervening miles of moorland.*

◆◇◇◇◇
ADJ: ADJ n

ADJ: ADJ n

inter·ven·tion·ist /ˌɪntəˈvenʃənɪst/ **interventionists.** Interventionist policies show an organization's desire to become involved in a problem or a crisis which does not concern it directly. *The United States and Britain want the UN to develop a more interventionist role.* ▶ An **interventionist** is someone who supports interventionist policies.

◆◇◇◇◇
ADJ-GRADED
JOURNALISM

N-COUNT

inter·view /ˈɪntəvjuː/ **interviews, interviewing, interviewed.** 1 An **interview** is a formal meeting at which someone is asked questions in order to find out if they are suitable for a job or a course of study. 2 If you are **interviewed** for a particular job or course of study, someone asks you questions to find out if you are suitable for it. *He was interviewed for a management job and got it.* 3 An **interview** is a conversation in which a journalist puts questions to someone such as a famous person or politician. 4 When a journalist **interviews** someone such as a famous person, they ask them a series of questions. 5 When the police **interview** someone, they ask them questions about a crime that has been committed.

◆◆◆◆◇
N-VAR

VB: usu
passive
be V-ed

N-COUNT

VERB: V n

VERB: V n

inter·viewee /ˌɪntəvjuˈiː/ **interviewees.** An **interviewee** is a person who is being interviewed.

◆◇◇◇◇
N-COUNT

inter·view·er /ˈɪntəvjuːə/ **interviewers.** An **interviewer** is a person who is asking someone questions at an interview.

◆◇◇◇◇
N-COUNT

inter·weave /ˌɪntəˈwiːv/ **interweaves, interweaving, interwove, interwoven.** If two or more things **interweave**, they are very closely connected or are combined with each other. *He was beginning to realize that her grieving was interwoven with guilt.*

◆◇◇◇◇
V-RECIP-ERG:
pl-n V
be V-ed with n
Also V with n

in·tes·tine /ɪnˈtestɪn/ **intestines.** Your **intestines** are the tubes in your body through which food passes when it has left your stomach. ♦ **in·tes·ti·nal** /ɪnˈtestɪnəl/ *...the intestinal wall.*

◆◇◇◇◇
N-COUNT

ADJ: ADJ n

in·ti·ma·cy /ˈɪntɪməsi/ **intimacies.** 1 Intimacy between two people is a very close personal relationship between them. *...a means of achieving intimacy with another person.* 2 **Intimacies** are things that you say or do to someone you have a very close personal relationship with.

◆◇◇◇◇
N-UNCOUNT

N-COUNT

in·ti·mate, intimates, intimating, intimated. The adjective and noun are pronounced /ˈɪntɪmət/. The verb is pronounced /ˈɪntɪmeɪt/. 1 If you have an **intimate** friendship with someone, you know them very well and like them a lot. ▶ An **intimate** is an intimate friend. *They are to have an autumn wedding, an intimate of the couple confides.* ♦ **in·ti·mate·ly** *He did not feel he had got to know them intimately.* 2 If two people are in an **intimate** relationship, they are involved with each other in a loving or sexual way. *...their intimate moments with their boyfriends.* ♦ **intimately** *You have to be willing to get to know yourself and your partner intimately.* 3 An **intimate** conversation or detail, for example, is very personal and private. ♦ **intimately** *It was the first time they had attempted to talk intimately.* 4 If you use **intimate** to describe an occasion or the atmosphere of a place, you like it

◆◆◇◇◇

ADJ-GRADED

N-COUNT

ADV-GRADED

ADJ-GRADED

ADV-GRADED:
ADV after v

ADJ-GRADED

ADV-GRADED:
ADV after v
ADJ-GRADED
PRAGMATICS

because it is quiet and pleasant, and seems suitable for close conversations between friends. *...an intimate candlelit dinner for two.* 5 An **intimate** connection between ideas or organizations, for example, is a very strong link between them. *...an intimate connection between madness and wisdom.* ♦ **intimately** *Property and equities are intimately connected.* 6 An **intimate** knowledge of something is a deep and detailed knowledge of it. ♦ **intimately** *...a golden age of musicians whose work she knew intimately.* 7 If you **intimate** something, you say it in an indirect way. *He went on to intimate that he was indeed contemplating a shake-up of the company.*

ADJ-GRADED

ADV-GRADED:
ADV after v

ADJ-GRADED
ADV-GRADED

VERB: V n
V that
Also V to n n
FORMAL

in·ti·ma·tion /ˌɪntɪˈmeɪʃən/ **intimations.** An **intimation** is an indirect suggestion or sign that something is likely to happen or be true. *I did not have any intimation that he was going to resign.*

N-COUNT
FORMAL

in·tim·i·date /ɪnˈtɪmɪdeɪt/ **intimidates, intimidating, intimidated.** If you **intimidate** someone, you deliberately make them frightened enough to do what you want them to do. *...attempts to intimidate people into voting for the governing party.* ♦ **in·tim·i·da·tion** /ɪnˌtɪmɪˈdeɪʃən/. *...allegations of intimidation.* ♦ **in·tim·i·dat·ing.** If you describe someone or something as **intimidating**, you mean that they are frightening and make people lose confidence. *A lot of men find buying lingerie intimidating.* ♦ **intimidated** *Women can come in here and not feel intimidated.*

◆◆◇◇◇
VERB: V n
V n into -ing

N-UNCOUNT

ADJ-GRADED

ADJ-GRADED

into /ˈɪntuː/. Also pronounced /ˈɪntʊ/, particularly before pronouns and for meaning 14. In addition to the uses shown below, **into** is used after some verbs and nouns in order to introduce extra information. **Into** is also used with verbs of movement, such as 'walk', and in phrasal verbs such as 'enter into'. 1 If you put one thing **into** another, you put the first thing inside the second. *Put them into a dish... All olives were packed into jars by hand.* 2 If you go **into** a place or vehicle, you move from being outside it to being inside it. *I have no idea how he got into Iraq... She got up and went into an inner office... He got into bed.* 3 If one thing goes **into** another, the first thing moves from the outside to the inside of the second thing, by breaking or damaging the surface of it. *Flavell had accidentally discharged a pistol, firing it into the ceiling... The tiger sank its teeth into his leg.* 4 If one thing gets **into** another, the first thing enters the second and becomes part of it. *Poisonous smoke had got into the water supply.* 5 If you are walking or driving a vehicle and you bump **into** something or crash **into** something, you hit it accidentally. *He slipped on a rotting mango and bumped into the wall.* 6 When you get **into** a piece of clothing, you put it on. *She could change into a different outfit in two minutes.* 7 If someone or something gets **into** a particular state, they start being in that state. *That caused him to get into trouble... I slid into a depression.* 8 If you talk someone **into** doing something, you persuade them to do it. *Gerome tried to talk her into taking an apartment in Paris.* 9 If something changes **into** something else, it then has a new form, shape, or nature. *...to turn a nasty episode into a little bit of a joke. ...learning what she needs to know to grow into a competent adult.* 10 If something is cut or split **into** a number of pieces or sections, it is divided so that it becomes several smaller pieces or sections. *Sixteen teams are taking part, divided into four groups.* 11 An investigation **into** a subject or event is concerned with that subject or event. *...research into Aids.* 12 If you move or go **into** a particular career or business, you start working in it. *There are now more women going into medicine.* 13 If something continues **into** a period of time, it continues until after that period of time has begun. *He had three children, and lived on into his sixties.* 14 If you are very interested in something and like it

◆◆◆◆◆

PREP

PREP

PREP

PREP

PREP

PREP

PREP

PREP

PREP

PREP

PREP

PREP

PREP

PREP

very much, you can say that you are **into** it. *I'm into* INFORMAL
electronics myself.

in·tol·er·able /ɪn'tɒlərəbəl/. If you describe some- ◆◇◇◇◇
thing as **intolerable**, you mean that it is so bad or ADJ-GRADED
extreme that no one can bear it or tolerate it. *They
felt this would put intolerable pressure on them.*
♦ **in·tol·er·ably** /ɪn'tɒlərəbli/ ...*intolerably cramped* ADV-GRADED
conditions.

in·tol·er·ant /ɪn'tɒlərənt/. If you describe someone ◆◇◇◇◇
as **intolerant**, you mean that they do not accept be- ADJ-GRADED
haviour and opinions that are different from their [PRAGMATICS]
own; used showing disapproval. *He was intolerant
of both suggestions and criticisms.* ♦ **in·tol·er·ance** N-UNCOUNT
...*his intolerance of any opinion other than his own.*
...*religious intolerance.*

in·to·na·tion /,ɪntə'neɪʃən/ **intonations.** Your **in-** N-VAR
tonation is the way that your voice rises and falls as
you speak. *The words are English, but the intonation
is distinctly Japanese.*

in·tone /ɪn'təʊn/ **intones, intoning, intoned.** If ◆◇◇◇◇
you **intone** something, you say or recite it in a slow VERB: V n
and serious way, with most of the words at one V with quote
pitch. *'But Jesus is here!' the priest intoned.* WRITTEN

in·toxi·cat·ed /ɪn'tɒksɪkeɪtɪd/. **1** Someone who is ADJ-GRADED
intoxicated is drunk. *He was charged with driving* FORMAL
while intoxicated. **2** If you are **intoxicated by** or ADJ-GRADED:
with something such as a feeling or an event, you v-link ADJ
are so excited by it that you find it hard to think by/with n
clearly and sensibly. *They seem to have become in-* LITERARY
toxicated by their success.

in·toxi·cat·ing /ɪn'tɒksɪkeɪtɪŋ/. **1 Intoxicating** ADJ-GRADED
drink contains alcohol and can make you drunk.
2 If you describe something as **intoxicating**, you ADJ-GRADED
mean that it makes you feel a strong sense of excite- LITERARY
ment or happiness. ...*the intoxicating fragrance of
lilies.*

in·toxi·ca·tion /ɪn,tɒksɪ'keɪʃən/. **1 Intoxication** is N-UNCOUNT
the state of being drunk. *Intoxication interferes with* FORMAL
memory and thinking. **2** You use **intoxication** to re- N-UNCOUNT
fer to a quality that something has that makes you LITERARY
feel very excited. ...*the sheer intoxication of cinema.*

in·trac·table /ɪn'træktəbəl/. **1 Intractable** people ◆◇◇◇◇
are very difficult to control or influence. *He protest-* ADJ-GRADED
ed, but Wright was intractable. **2 Intractable** prob- FORMAL
lems or situations are very difficult to deal with. *A* ADJ-GRADED
final settlement of the intractable Afghan conflict is FORMAL
still far off.

in·tran·si·gent /ɪn'trænsɪdʒənt/. If you describe ◆◇◇◇◇
someone as **intransigent**, you mean that they refuse ADJ-GRADED
to behave differently or to change their attitude to PRAGMATICS
something; used showing disapproval. *They put* FORMAL
pressure on the Government to change its intransi-
gent stance. ♦ **in·tran·si·gence** *He often appeared* N-UNCOUNT
*angry and frustrated by the intransigence of both
sides.*

in·tran·si·tive /ɪn'trænsɪtɪv/. An **intransitive** verb ADJ
does not have an object.

intra·venous /,ɪntrə'viːnəs/. **Intravenous** foods or ◆◇◇◇◇
drugs are given to sick people through their veins, ADJ: ADJ n
rather than through their mouths. ...*an intravenous drip.* TECHNICAL
♦ **intra·venous·ly** *Premature babies have to be fed* ADV:
intravenously. ADV after v

'in tray, in trays; also spelled **in-tray**. An **in tray** is N-COUNT
a shallow basket used in offices to put letters and
documents in when they arrive or when they are
waiting to be dealt with.

in·trep·id /ɪn'trepɪd/. An **intrepid** person acts in a ◆◇◇◇◇
brave way; often used humorously. *Driving a car* ADJ-GRADED
yourself in Buenos Aires is recommended only to the DATED
most intrepid foreigner.

in·tri·ca·cies /'ɪntrɪkəsiz/. The **intricacies** of some- N-PLURAL
thing are its complicated details. *Rose explained the
intricacies of the job.*

in·tri·ca·cy /'ɪntrɪkəsi/. **Intricacy** is the state of N-UNCOUNT
being made up of many small parts or details.
*Garments are priced from $100 to several thousand
dollars, depending on the intricacy of the work.*

in·tri·cate /'ɪntrɪkət/. You use **intricate** to describe ◆◇◇◇◇
something that has many small parts or details. ADJ-GRADED

...*intricate patterns and motifs.* ♦ **in·tri·cate·ly** ADV-GRADED
...*intricately carved sculptures.*

in·trigue, intrigues, intriguing, intrigued. The ◆◆◇◇◇
noun is pronounced /'ɪntriːg/. The verb is pronounced /ɪn'triːg/. **1 Intrigue** is the making of se- N-VAR
cret plans to harm or deceive people. ...*the plots
and intrigues in the novel.* **2** If something **intrigues** VERB
you, it interests you and you are curious about it. V n
She had hesitated, even though the job intrigued her.
♦ **in·trigued** *I would be intrigued to hear others'* ADJ-GRADED
views.

in·tri·guing /ɪn'triːgɪŋ/. If you describe someone ◆◆◇◇◇
or something as **intriguing**, you mean that they in- ADJ-GRADED
terest you and you are curious about them. *This intriguing book is both thoughtful and informative.*
♦ **in·tri·guing·ly** *The results are intriguingly differ-* ADV-GRADED
ent each time.

in·trin·sic /ɪn'trɪnsɪk/. If something has **intrinsic** ◆◇◇◇◇
value or **intrinsic** interest, it is valuable or interest- ADJ: ADJ n
ing because of its basic nature or character, and not FORMAL
because of its connection with other things.
*Diamonds have little intrinsic value and their price
depends almost entirely on their scarcity.* ♦ **in·trin-**
·si·cal·ly /ɪn'trɪnsɪkli/. *Sometimes I wonder if peo-* ADV
ple are intrinsically evil.*

intro·duce /,ɪntrə'djuːs, AM -'duːs/ **introduces,** ◆◆◆◇◇
introducing, introduced. 1 To **introduce** some- VERB: V n
thing means to cause it to enter a place or exist in a V n into/to n
system for the first time. *The word 'Pagoda' was
introduced to Europe by the 17th century Portuguese.*
♦ **intro·duc·tion** ...*the introduction of a privacy bill* N-UNCOUNT
to prevent press intrusions into private lives. **2** If VERB
you **introduce** someone **to** something, you cause V n to n
them to learn about it or experience it for the first
time. *He introduced her to both literature and drugs.*
♦ **introduction** *His introduction to League football* N-SING
*would have been gentler if he had started at a small-
er club.* **3** If you **introduce** one person to another, VERB:
or you **introduce** two people, you tell them each V n to n
other's names, so that they can get to know each V pl-n
other. If you **introduce** yourself to someone, you V pron-refl
tell them your name. *Someone introduced us and I
sat next to him... Let me introduce myself.* ♦ **intro-**
·duc·tion, introductions *With considerable shy-* N-VAR
ness, Elaine performed the introductions.
4 The person who **introduces** a television or radio VERB
programme speaks at the beginning of it, and often be V-ed by n
between the different items in it, in order to explain Also V n
what the programme or the items are about. *'Health
Matters' is introduced by Dick Oliver on BBC World
Service.*

intro·duc·tion /,ɪntrə'dʌkʃən/ **introductions.** ◆◆◇◇◇
1 The **introduction** to a book or talk is the part that N-COUNT
comes at the beginning and tells you what the rest
of it is about. **2** If you refer to a book as an **intro-** N-COUNT
duction to a particular subject, you mean that it explains the basic facts about that subject. **3** You can N-COUNT
refer to a new product as an **introduction** when it
becomes available for the first time. *There are two
among their recent introductions that have greatly
impressed me.* **4** See also **introduce**.

intro·duc·tory /,ɪntrə'dʌktəri/. **1** An **introductory** ◆◇◇◇◇
talk or chapter in a book gives a small amount of ADJ: ADJ n
general information about a particular subject,
often before a more detailed explanation. ...*an
introductory course in religion and theology.* **2** An ADJ: ADJ n
introductory offer or price on a new product is
something such as a free gift or a low price that is
meant to attract new customers. *You will be able to
take advantage of an extremely favourable introductory rate.*

intro·spec·tion /,ɪntrə'spekʃən/. **Introspection** is N-UNCOUNT
the examining of your own thoughts, ideas, and
feelings.

intro·spec·tive /,ɪntrə'spektɪv/. **Introspective** peo- ADJ-GRADED
ple spend a lot of time examining their own
thoughts, ideas, and feelings.

intro·vert /'ɪntrəvɜːt/ **introverts. 1** An **introvert** is N-COUNT
a quiet, shy person who finds it difficult to talk to

people. **2 Introvert** means the same as **introverted**. ADJ-GRADED
The music students here are a very introvert lot.

intro·vert·ed /'ɪntrəvɜːtɪd/. **Introverted** people are ADJ-GRADED
quiet and shy and find it difficult to talk to other
people.

in·trude /ɪn'truːd/ **intrudes, intruding, intrud-** ◆◇◇◇◇
ed. 1 If you say that someone **is intruding** into a VERB:
particular place or situation, you mean that they are V into/on/
not wanted or welcome there. *I hope I'm not intrud-* V upon n
ing. **2** If something **intrudes** on your mood or your V
life, it disturbs it or has an unwanted effect on it. V on/into/
There are times when personal feelings cannot be al- upon n
lowed to intrude. **3** If someone **intrudes** into a VERB
place, they go there even though they are not al- V into/onto n
lowed to be there. *We believe they intruded on to the*
field of play.

in·trud·er /ɪn'truːdə/ **intruders.** An **intruder** is a ◆◇◇◇◇
person who goes into a place where they are not N-COUNT
supposed to be.

in·tru·sion /ɪn'truːʒən/ **intrusions. 1** If someone ◆◇◇◇◇
disturbs you when you are in a private place or hav- N-VAR
ing a private conversation, you can call this event
an **intrusion.** *I hope you don't mind this intrusion,*
Jon. **2** An **intrusion** is something that disturbs your N-VAR
mood or your life in an unwelcome way. *...intrusion*
into private grief.

in·tru·sive /ɪn'truːsɪv/. Something that is **intrusive** ◆◇◇◇◇
disturbs your mood or your life in an unwelcome ADJ-GRADED
way. *Staff are courteous but never intrusive.*

in·tu·it /ɪn'tjuːɪt, AM -'tuː-/ **intuits, intuiting, in-** VERB
tuited. If you **intuit** something, you guess what it is V n
on the basis of your intuition or feelings, rather FORMAL
than on the basis of knowledge. *He was an honest*
man trying to intuit what was the right thing to do.

in·tu·i·tion /,ɪntjʊ'ɪʃən, AM -tʊ-/ **intuitions.** Your ◆◇◇◇◇
intuition or your **intuitions** are unexplained feel- N-VAR
ings you have that something is true even when you
have no evidence or proof of it. *Her intuition was*
telling her that something was wrong.

in·tu·i·tive /ɪn'tjuːɪtɪv, AM -'tuː-/. If you have an ◆◇◇◇◇
intuitive idea or feeling about something, you feel ADJ-GRADED
that it is true although you have no evidence or
proof of it. ◆ **in·tu·i·tive·ly** *He seemed to know in-* ADV-GRADED
tuitively that I must be missing my mother.

Inu·it /'ɪnjuɪt/ **Inuits;** the form **Inuit** can also be N-COUNT
used for the plural. The **Inuit** are a race of people
descended from the original inhabitants of Eastern
Canada and Greenland.

in·un·date /'ɪnʌndeɪt/ **inundates, inundating,** ◆◇◇◇◇
inundated. 1 If you say that you **are inundated** VERB:
with things such as letters, demands, or requests, be V-ed with n
you are emphasizing that you receive so many of PRAGMATICS
them that you cannot deal with them all. *They have* V n with n
inundated me with fan letters. **2** If an area of land is Also V n
inundated, it becomes covered with water. *Almost* VB: usu
four hundred thousand square miles have now been passive
inundated. be V-ed

in·ure /ɪ'njʊə/ **inures, inuring, inured.** If an ex- VERB
perience **inures** you to something unpleasant, it V n to n
makes you accustomed to it so that it no longer af- FORMAL
fects you. *Pictures and accounts of the bombed cities*
had not inured the world to such sights. ◆ **in·ured** ADJ-GRADED:
I'm already inured to the sound of the alarm. v-link ADJ to n

in·vade /ɪn'veɪd/ **invades, invading, invaded.** ◆◆◇◇◇
1 To **invade** a country means to enter it by force VERB
with an army. *In autumn 1944 the allies invaded the* V n
Italian mainland at Anzio and Salerno... When the V-ing
Romans and later the Normans came to Britain they Also V
did so as invading armies. **2** If you say that people VERB
or animals **invade** a place, you mean that they enter V n
it in large numbers, often in a way that is unpleasant or difficult to deal with. *People invaded the*
streets in victory processions almost throughout the
day... Victoria has been invaded by giant American
bullfrogs. **3** ● to **invade** someone's **privacy:** see
privacy.

in·vad·er /ɪn'veɪdə/ **invaders. 1** Invaders are sol- ◆◇◇◇◇
diers who are invading a country. **2** You can refer to N-COUNT
a country or army that has invaded or is about to N-COUNT

invade another country as an **invader.** *...action*
against a foreign invader.

in·va·lid, invalids. The noun is pronounced ◆◇◇◇◇
/'ɪnvəlɪd/. The adjective is pronounced /ɪn'vælɪd/.
1 An **invalid** is someone who needs to be cared for N-COUNT
because they have an illness or disability.
2 If an action, procedure, or document is **invalid,** it ADJ
cannot be accepted, because it breaks the law or some
official rule. *The trial was stopped and the results de-*
clared invalid. ◆ **in·va·lid·ity** *...the invalidity of the* N-UNCOUNT
marriage ceremony. **3** An **invalid** argument or con- ADJ
clusion is wrong because it is based on a mistake.

in·vali·date /ɪn'vælɪdeɪt/ **invalidates, invalidat-**
ing, invalidated. 1 To **invalidate** something such VERB
as an argument, conclusion, or result means to V n
prove that it is wrong or cause it to be wrong. *Any*
form of physical activity will invalidate the results.
2 If something **invalidates** something such as a law, VERB
contract, or election, it causes it to be considered il- V n
legal. *An official decree invalidated the vote in the*
capital.

in·val·id·ity /,ɪnvə'lɪdɪti/. **Invalidity** is the state of N-UNCOUNT
being an invalid. *And this takes no account of*
the human cost— intense pain, invalidity and
dependency.

in·valu·able /ɪn'væljəbəl/. If you describe some- ◆◇◇◇◇
thing as **invaluable,** you mean that it is extremely ADJ
useful. *The research should prove invaluable in the*
study of linguistics.

in·vari·able /ɪn'veəriəbəl/. You use **invariable** to ADJ
describe something that never changes. *It was*
normal to pay interest on money borrowed from
friends and relatives, though the practice was not
invariable.

in·vari·ably /ɪn'veəriəbli/. If something **invariably** ◆◆◇◇◇
happens or is **invariably** true, it always happens or ADV
is always true. *They almost invariably get it wrong.*

in·va·sion /ɪn'veɪʒən/ **invasions. 1** If there is an ◆◆◇◇◇
invasion of a country, a foreign army enters it by N-VAR
force. *...the Roman invasion of Britain.* **2** If you re- N-VAR
fer to the arrival of a large number of people or
things as an **invasion,** you are emphasizing that
they are unpleasant or difficult to deal with. *...this*
year's annual invasion of flies, wasps and ants. **3** If N-VAR
you describe an action as an **invasion,** you disap- PRAGMATICS
prove of it because it affects someone or something
in a way that is not wanted. *Is reading a child's diary*
always a gross invasion of privacy?

in·va·sive /ɪn'veɪsɪv/. **1** You use **invasive** to de- ◆◇◇◇◇
scribe something undesirable which spreads very ADJ-GRADED
quickly and which is very difficult to stop from
spreading. *They found invasive cancer during a rou-*
tine examination. **2** An **invasive** medical procedure ADJ-GRADED
is a procedures such as surgery which involves en-
tering a patient's body, for example by cutting it
open.

in·vec·tive /ɪn'vektɪv/. **Invective** is rude and un- N-UNCOUNT
pleasant things that people shout at people they FORMAL
hate or are angry with. *A woman had hurled racist*
invective at the family.

in·veigh /ɪn'veɪ/ **inveighs, inveighing, in-** VERB
veighed. If you **inveigh against** something, you V against n
criticize it strongly. *A lot of his writings inveigh* FORMAL
against luxury and riches.

in·vei·gle /ɪn'veɪgəl/ **inveigles, inveigling, in-** VERB
veigled. If you **inveigle** someone **into** doing some- V n into n/-ing
thing, you cleverly persuade them to do it when FORMAL
they do not really want to. *He inveigles them into*
planning a robbery.

in·vent /ɪn'vent/ **invents, inventing, invented.** ◆◆◇◇◇
1 If you **invent** something such as a machine or VERB
process, you are the first person to think of it or V n
make it. *He invented the first electric clock.* **2** If you VERB
invent a story or excuse, you try to make other peo- V n
ple believe that it is true when in fact it is not. *I*
must invent something I can tell my mother.

in·ven·tion /ɪn'venʃən/ **inventions. 1** An **inven-** ◆◆◇◇◇
tion is a machine, device, or system that has been N-COUNT
invented by someone. *The spinning wheel was a*
Chinese invention. **2 Invention** is the act of invent- N-UNCOUNT

ing something that has never been made or used before. *...the invention of the telephone.* **3 Invention** is the ability to invent things or to have clever and original ideas. *Perhaps, with such powers of invention and mathematical ability, he will be offered a job in computers.* **4** If you refer to someone's account of something as an **invention**, you think that it is untrue and that they have made it up. — N-UNCOUNT, N-VAR

in·ven·tive /ɪnˈvɛntɪv/. An **inventive** person is good at inventing things or has clever and original ideas. *...Stroman's ceaselessly inventive choreography.* ♦ **in·ven·tive·ness** *He has surprised us before with his inventiveness.* — ◆◇◇◇◇ ADJ-GRADED, N-UNCOUNT

in·ven·tor /ɪnˈvɛntə/ **inventors.** An **inventor** is a person who has invented something, or whose job is to invent things. — ◆◇◇◇◇ N-COUNT

in·ven·tory /ˈɪnvəntri, AM -tɔːri/ **inventories.** **1** An **inventory** is a written list of all the objects in a particular place. **2** An **inventory** is a supply or stock of something. *...one inventory of twelve sails for each yacht.* — ◆◆◇◇◇ N-COUNT, N-VAR AMERICAN

in·verse /ˈɪnvɜːs/. **1** If there is an **inverse** relationship between two things, one of them becomes larger as the other becomes smaller. *The tension grew in inverse proportion to the distance from their final destination.* ♦ **in·verse·ly** *The size of the nebula at this stage is inversely proportional to its mass.* **2** The **inverse** of something is its exact opposite. *There is no sign that you bothered to consider the inverse of your logic.* — ADJ TECHNICAL, ADV, N-SING: the N FORMAL

in·ver·sion /ɪnˈvɜːʃən, -ʒən/ **inversions.** When there is an **inversion** of something, it is changed into its opposite. *...a strange inversion of priorities.* — N-VAR FORMAL

in·vert /ɪnˈvɜːt/ **inverts, inverting, inverted.** **1** If you **invert** something, you turn it upside down or back to front. *Invert the cake onto a cooling rack. ...a black inverted triangle.* **2** If you **invert** something, you change it to its opposite. *They may be hoping to invert the presumption that a defendant is innocent until proved guilty. ...inverted moral values.* — ◆◇◇◇◇ VERB V n V-ed FORMAL VERB V n V-ed FORMAL

in·ver·te·brate /ɪnˈvɜːtɪbrət/ **invertebrates.** An **invertebrate** is a creature that does not have a spine, for example an insect or an octopus. ▶ Also an adjective. *...invertebrate creatures.* — N-COUNT TECHNICAL, ADJ

in,verted ˈcommas are **1** Inverted **commas** are punctuation marks that are used in writing to show where speech or a quotation begins and ends. They are usually written or printed as (') or (" "). Inverted commas are also sometimes used round the titles of books, plays, or songs, or round a word or phrase that is being discussed. **2** If you say **in inverted commas** after a word or phrase, you are indicating that you think the word or phrase is inaccurate or unacceptable in some way, or that you are quoting someone else. *They're asked to make objective, in inverted commas, evaluations of these statements.* — N-PLURAL BRITISH, PHRASE PRAGMATICS BRITISH

in·vest /ɪnˈvɛst/ **invests, investing, invested.** **1** If you **invest** in something, or if you **invest** a sum of money, you use your money in a way that you hope will increase its value, for example by paying it into a bank, or buying shares or property. *They intend to invest directly in shares... He wants advice on how to invest the money... He invested all our profits in gold shares.* **2** When a government or organization **invests** in something, it gives or lends money for a purpose that it considers useful or profitable. *Why does Japan invest, on average, twice as much capital per worker per year than the United States?* **3** If you **invest in** something useful, you buy it, because it will help you to do something more efficiently or more cheaply. *The company has invested a six-figure sum in an electronic order-control system.* **4** If you **invest** time or energy in something, you spend a lot of time or energy on something that you consider to be useful or likely to be successful. **5** If you say that someone or something **is invested with** a particular quality, you mean that they seem to have that quality. *The buildings are invested with a* — ◆◆◇◇◇ VERB V in n V n V in n VERB: V in n V in n Also V n in n V VERB: V in n V in n VERB: V n in n VB: usu passive be V-ed with n FORMAL

nation's history. **6** To **invest** someone **with** rights or responsibilities means to give them those rights or responsibilities legally or officially. *The constitution had invested him with certain powers.* — VERB V n with n FORMAL

in·ves·ti·gate /ɪnˈvɛstɪgeɪt/ **investigates, investigating, investigated.** If someone, especially an official, **investigates** an event or allegation, they try to find out what happened or what is the truth. *The two officers were being investigated by the director of public prosecutions... Police are still investigating how the accident happened.* ♦ **in·ves·ti·ga·tion** /ɪnˌvɛstɪˈgeɪʃən/ **investigations** *He is under investigation for corruption.* — ◆◆◆◇ VERB: V n be V-ed V wh Also V, N-VAR

in·ves·ti·ga·tive /ɪnˈvɛstɪgətɪv, AM -geɪt-/. **Investigative** work, especially journalism, involves investigating things. *...an investigative reporter.* — ◆◇◇◇◇ ADJ

in·ves·ti·ga·tor /ɪnˈvɛstɪgeɪtə/ **investigators.** An **investigator** is someone who carries out investigations, especially as part of their job. — ◆◆◇◇◇ N-COUNT

in·ves·ti·ga·tory /ɪnˈvɛstɪgətri, AM -tɔːri/. **Investigatory** means the same as **investigative**. — ADJ: ADJ n

in·ves·ti·ture /ɪnˈvɛstɪtʃə/ **investitures.** An **investiture** is a ceremony in which someone is given an official title. *...Edward VIII's investiture as Prince of Wales in 1911.* — N-COUNT

in·vest·ment /ɪnˈvɛsmənt/ **investments.** **1** Investment is the activity of investing money. *The government must introduce tax incentives to encourage investment. ...investment bankers.* **2** An **investment** is an amount of money that you invest, or the thing that you invest in it. *You'll be able to earn an average rate of return of 8% on your investments. ...people's desire to buy a house as an investment.* **3** If you describe something you buy as an **investment**, you mean that it will be useful, especially because it will help you to do a task more cheaply or efficiently. *A small-screen portable TV can be a good investment.* **4** Investment of time or effort is the spending of time or effort on something in order to make it a success. — ◆◆◆◆◇ N-UNCOUNT, N-VAR, N-COUNT, N-UNCOUNT

in·ves·tor /ɪnˈvɛstə/ **investors.** An **investor** is a person or organization that buys shares or pays money into a bank in order to receive a profit. — ◆◆◆◆◇ N-COUNT

in·vet·er·ate /ɪnˈvɛtərət/. If you describe someone as, for example, an **inveterate** liar or smoker, you mean that they have lied or smoked for a long time and are not likely to stop doing it. — ADJ: ADJ n

in·vidi·ous /ɪnˈvɪdiəs/. **1** If you describe a task or job as **invidious**, you mean that it is unpleasant because it is likely to make you unpopular. **2** An **invidious** comparison or choice between two things is an unfair one because the two things are not comparable or because there is only one thing that you can choose. *It is invidious to make a selection.* — ADJ-GRADED, ADJ

in·vigi·late /ɪnˈvɪdʒɪleɪt/ **invigilates, invigilating, invigilated.** The person who **invigilates** an examination supervises the people who are taking it. ♦ **in·vigi·la·tor, invigilators** *I acted as the invigilator.* — VERB: V n BRITISH, N-COUNT

in·vig·or·ate /ɪnˈvɪgəreɪt/ **invigorates, invigorating, invigorated.** **1** If something **invigorates** you, it makes you feel refreshed and more awake. *Take a deep breath in to invigorate you.* ♦ **in·vig·or·at·ed** *She seemed invigorated, full of life and energy.* ♦ **in·vig·or·at·ing** *...the bright Finnish sun and invigorating northern air.* **2** To **invigorate** a situation or a process means to make it more efficient or more effective. *The tactic could well help invigorate a struggling campaign.* — ◆◇◇◇◇ VERB V n, ADJ-GRADED, ADJ-GRADED, VERB V n

in·vin·cible /ɪnˈvɪnsɪbəl/. **1** If you describe an army or sports team as **invincible**, you believe that they cannot be defeated. *He knocked out the seemingly invincible Mike Tyson.* ♦ **in·vin·cibil·ity** /ɪnˌvɪnsɪˈbɪlɪti/ *...symbols of the invincibility of the Roman army.* **2** If someone has an **invincible** belief or attitude, it cannot be changed. — ◆◇◇◇◇ ADJ-GRADED, N-UNCOUNT, ADJ

in·vio·lable /ɪnˈvaɪələbəl/. **1** If a law or principle is **inviolable**, you must not break it. *The CIA's security rules were tough, logical, and inviolable.* **2** If a country says its borders are **inviolable**, it means they — ADJ-GRADED FORMAL, ADJ FORMAL

inviolate /ɪn'vaɪələt/. If something is **inviolate**, it has not been or cannot be harmed or affected by anything. *We believed our love was inviolate.* ADJ FORMAL

♦ **in·vi·o·labil·ity** /ɪn,vaɪələ'bɪlɪti/ ...*the inviolability of the country's current border with Poland.* N-UNCOUNT

in·vis·ible /ɪn'vɪzɪbəl/ **invisibles. 1** If you describe something as **invisible**, you mean that it cannot be seen, for example because it is transparent, hidden, or very small. *The belt is invisible even under the thinnest garments.* ♦ **in·vis·ibly** /ɪn'vɪzɪbli/. *A thin coil of smoke rose almost invisibly into the sharp, bright sky.* **2** You can use **invisible** when you are talking about something that cannot be seen but has a definite effect. In this sense, **invisible** is often used before a noun which refers to something that can usually be seen. *All the time you are in doubt about the cause of your illness, you are fighting against an invisible enemy.* **3** If you say that you feel **invisible**, you are complaining that you are being ignored by other people. If you say that a particular problem or situation is **invisible**, you are complaining that it is not being considered or dealt with. *It was strange, how invisible a clerk could feel... The problems of the poor are largely invisible.* ♦ **in·vis·ibil·ity** /ɪn,vɪzɪ'bɪlɪti/. *She takes up the issue of the invisibility of women and women's concerns in society.* **4** In stories, **invisible** people or things have a magic quality which makes people unable to see them. **5 Invisible** earnings are the money that a country makes as a result of services such as banking and tourism, rather than by producing goods. *The invisible trade surplus was £900 million lower than reported.* **6 Invisibles** are services such as banking and tourism, which provide a country's invisible earnings. ADJ-GRADED; ADV: ADV with v; ADJ: ADJ n; ADJ-GRADED; N-UNCOUNT; ADJ; ADJ: ADJ n TECHNICAL; N-PLURAL BRITISH

in·vi·ta·tion /,ɪnvɪ'teɪʃən/ **invitations. 1** An **invitation** is a written or spoken request to come to an event such as a party or a meeting. *The Syrians have not yet accepted an invitation to attend... He's understood to be there at the personal invitation of President Daniel Arap Moi.* **2** An **invitation** is the card or paper on which an invitation is written or printed. **3** If you believe that someone's action is likely to have a particular result, especially a bad one, you can refer to the action as an **invitation** to that result. *...a war that most liberal Democrats regarded as an invitation to disaster.* N-COUNT; N-COUNT; N-SING: N to n

in·vite, **invites**, **inviting**, **invited.** The verb is pronounced /ɪn'vaɪt/. The noun is pronounced /'ɪnvaɪt/. **1** If you **invite** someone to something such as a party or a meal, you ask them to come to it. *I invited her in for a coffee... Barron invited her to accompany him to the races.* **2** If you **are invited** to do something, you are formally asked or given permission to do it. *At a future date, managers will be invited to apply for a management buy-out... If a new leader emerged, it would then be for the Queen to invite him to form a government.* **3** If something you say or do **invites** trouble or criticism, it makes trouble or criticism more likely. *Their refusal to compromise will inevitably invite more criticism from the UN.* **4** An **invite** is an invitation to something such as a party or a meal. VERB V n prep/adv V n to-inf; VERB be V-ed to-inf V n to-inf Also V n; VERB V n; N-COUNT INFORMAL

in·vit·ing /ɪn'vaɪtɪŋ/. If you say that something is **inviting**, you mean that it has good qualities that attract you or make you want to experience it. *The February air was soft, cool, and inviting.* ♦ **in·vit·ing·ly** *The waters of the tropics are invitingly clear.* ● See also **invite**. ADJ-GRADED; ADV-GRADED

in vi·tro /ɪn 'viːtrəʊ/. **In vitro** fertilization is a method of helping a woman to conceive by removing an egg from her and fertilizing it outside her body, then replacing the fertilized egg in her uterus. ADJ: ADJ n

in·vo·ca·tion /,ɪnvə'keɪʃən/ **invocations.** An **invocation** is an appeal to a god for help or forgiveness. *...an invocation for divine guidance.* N-VAR FORMAL

in·voice /'ɪnvɔɪs/ **invoices, invoicing, invoiced. 1** An **invoice** is a document that lists goods and services that you have received, and says how much money you owe for them. **2** If you **invoice** someone, you send them an invoice. N-COUNT; VERB: V n

in·voke /ɪn'vəʊk/ **invokes, invoking, invoked. 1** If you **invoke** a law, you state that you are taking a particular action because that law allows or obliges you to. *The judge invoked an international law that protects refugees.* **2** If you **invoke** something such as a saying or a famous person, you refer to them in order to support your argument. *In political matters George Washington went out of his way to avoid invoking the authority of Christ.* **3** If someone **invokes** a god, they appeal to the god for help or forgiveness. **4** If something such as a piece of music **invokes** a feeling or an image, it causes someone to have the feeling or to see the image. Many people consider this use to be incorrect. VERB V n; VERB V n; VERB: V n LITERARY; VERB: V n

in·vol·un·tary /ɪn'vɒləntri, AM -teri/. **1** If you make an **involuntary** movement or exclamation, you make it suddenly and without intending to. *An other surge of pain in my ankle caused me to give an involuntary shudder.* ♦ **in·vol·un·tari·ly** /'ɪnvələntrəli, AM -'teərɪli/. *His left eyelid twitched involuntarily.* **2** You use **involuntary** to describe an action or situation which is forced on someone. *Involuntary repatriation of Haitians began this week.* ADJ; ADV: ADV with v; ADJ

in·volve /ɪn'vɒlv/ **involves, involving, involved. 1** If a situation or activity **involves** something, that thing is a necessary part or consequence of it. *Nicky's job as a public relations director involves spending quite a lot of time with other people.* **2** If a situation or activity **involves** someone, they are taking part in it. *...a riot involving a hundred inmates.* **3** If you say that someone **involves** themselves in something, you mean that they take part in it, often in a way that is unnecessary or unwanted. *I seem to have involved myself in something I don't understand.* **4** If you **involve** someone else in something, you get them to take part in it. *Before too long he started involving me in the more confidential aspects of the job.* **5** If one thing **involves** you in another thing, especially something unpleasant or inconvenient, the first thing causes you to do or deal with the second. *A late booking may involve you in extra cost.* VERB V n/-ing; VERB V n; VERB V pron-refl in n; VERB V n in n/-ing; VERB V n in n

in·volved /ɪn'vɒlvd/. **1** If you are **involved** in a situation or activity, you are taking part in it or have a strong connection with it. *The Farmers' Club is an organisation for people involved in agriculture.* **2** If you are **involved** in something, you give a lot of time or effort to it. *The family were deeply involved in Jewish culture.* **3** The things **involved** in something such as a job or system are the necessary parts or consequences of it. *Let's take a look at some of the figures involved.* **4** If a situation or activity is **involved**, it is very complicated. **5** If one person is **involved** with another, especially someone they are not married to, they are having a close relationship. *He became romantically involved with a married woman.* ADJ-GRADED v-link ADJ; ADJ-GRADED v-link ADJ; ADJ: v-link ADJ; ADJ-GRADED; ADJ-GRADED

in·volve·ment /ɪn'vɒlvmənt/ **involvements. 1** Your **involvement** in something is the fact that you are taking part in it. *She disliked his involvement with the group.* **2 Involvement** is the enthusiasm that you feel when you care deeply about something. *Ben has always felt a deep involvement with animals.* **3** An **involvement** is a close relationship between two people, especially if they are not married to each other. N-UNCOUNT; N-UNCOUNT; N-VAR

in·vul·ner·able /ɪn'vʌlnərəbəl/. If someone or something is **invulnerable**, they cannot be harmed or damaged. ♦ **in·vul·ner·abil·ity** /ɪn,vʌlnərə'bɪlɪti/ *They have a sense of invulnerability to disease.* ADJ-GRADED; N-UNCOUNT

in·ward /'ɪnwəd/. **1** Your **inward** thoughts or feelings are the ones that you do not express or show to other people. *I sighed with inward relief.* ♦ **in·ward·ly** *He pretended to be mildly affronted, but inwardly he was pleased.* **2** An **inward** movement is one towards the inside or centre of something. *...a sharp, inward breath like a gasp.* **3** See also **inwards.** ADJ: ADJ n; ADV; ADJ: ADJ n

'inward-looking. If you describe a people or society as **inward-looking**, you mean that they are more interested in themselves than in other people or societies; used showing disapproval. ADJ-GRADED PRAGMATICS

in·wards /'ɪnwədz/; the form **inward** is also used. In American English, **inward** is more usual. If something moves or faces **inwards**, it moves or faces towards the inside or centre of something. *She pressed back against the door until it swung inwards.* ◆◇◇◇ ADV: ADV after v

,in-your-'face; also spelled **in-yer-face.** If you say that someone has an **in-your-face** attitude, you mean that they seem determined to behave in a way that is unconventional or slightly shocking. *It's in-your-face feminism, and it's meant to shock.* ADJ-GRADED INFORMAL

iodine /'aɪədiːn, AM -daɪn/. **Iodine** is a dark-coloured substance that is used in medicine and photography. ◆◇◇◇ N-UNCOUNT

ion /aɪən/ **ions.** Ions are electrically charged atoms; a technical term in science. ◆◇◇◇ N-COUNT

-ion. See **-ation.**

ion·iz·er /'aɪənaɪzə/ **ionizers;** also spelled **ioniser** in British English. An **ionizer** is a device which is meant to make the air in a room more healthy by removing positive ions. N-COUNT

iota /aɪ'əʊtə/. **1** If you say that there is not **an iota** or not **one iota** of something, you are emphasizing that there is not even a very small amount of it. *He's never before shown an iota of interest in any kind of social work.* **2** You can use **an iota** or **one iota** to emphasize a negative statement. *Not an iota* or *not one iota* means not even to a small extent or degree. *Our credit standards haven't changed one iota.* QUANT PRAGMATICS / PHRASE PRAGMATICS

IOU /,aɪ əʊ 'juː/ **IOUs.** An **IOU** is a written promise that you will pay back some money that you have borrowed. **IOU** is an abbreviation for 'I owe you'. N-COUNT

IQ /,aɪ 'kjuː/ **IQs.** Your **IQ** is your level of intelligence, as indicated by a special test that you do. **IQ** is an abbreviation for 'intelligence quotient'. *His IQ is above average.* ◆◇◇◇ N-VAR

ir- /ɪr-/. **Ir-** is added to words that begin with the letter 'r' to form words with the opposite meaning. *His behaviour was becoming increasingly irrational. ...its mixture of satirical wit, irreverence and spontaneity.* PREFIX

iras·cible /ɪ'ræsɪbəl/. If you describe someone as **irascible**, you mean that they become angry very easily. ADJ-GRADED WRITTEN

irate /aɪ'reɪt/. If someone is **irate**, they are very angry about something. *She then wrote an extremely irate letter to the New Statesman.* ADJ-GRADED

ire /aɪə/. **Ire** is anger. *The government's decision also drew the ire of local MPs.* N-UNCOUNT WRITTEN

iri·des·cent /,ɪrɪ'desənt/. Something that is **iridescent** has many bright colours that seem to keep changing. *...iridescent bubbles.* ADJ LITERARY

iris /'aɪərɪs/ **irises. 1** The **iris** is the round coloured part of a person's eye. *Each area of the iris is said to correspond to a particular part of the body.* **2** An **iris** is a tall plant which has long leaves and large purple, yellow, or white flowers. ◆◇◇◇ N-COUNT / N-COUNT

irk /ɜːk/ **irks, irking, irked.** If something **irks** you, it irritates or annoys you. *The rehearsal process also irked him increasingly... She was irked by their behavior... It irks me to see this guy get all this free publicity.* ◆ **irked** *Claire had seemed a little irked when he left.* VERB: V n / be V-ed / it V n to-inf/ that FORMAL / v-link ADJ

irk·some /'ɜːksəm/. If something is **irksome**, it irritates or annoys you. ADJ-GRADED FORMAL

iron /aɪən/ **irons, ironing, ironed. 1** Iron is an element which usually takes the form of a hard, dark-grey metal, used to make steel and in manufacturing many things such as vehicles and buildings. *The huge, iron gate was locked... Anaemia is usually the result of a low level of iron in the blood.* ● See also **cast iron. 2** You can use **iron** to describe the character or behaviour of someone who is very firm in their decisions and actions, or who can control their feelings well. *...a man of icy nerve and iron will.* **3** Iron is used in expressions such as **an iron hand** and **iron discipline** to describe strong, harsh, or unfair methods of control which do not allow ◆◆◇◇ N-UNCOUNT / ADJ: ADJ n / ADJ: ADJ n

people much freedom. *...people living permanently in the iron grip of poverty.* **4** If someone **pumps iron**, they exercise by lifting weights using special machines. PHRASE INFORMAL

5 An **iron** is an electrical device with a flat metal base. You heat it until the base is hot, then rub it over clothes to remove creases. **6** If you **iron** clothes, you remove the creases from them using an iron. *There's something nice about a freshly ironed shirt.* ◆ **iron·ing** *I managed to get all the ironing done this morning but not much else.* N-COUNT / VERB: V n / V-ed / N-UNCOUNT

7 If someone has a lot of **irons in the fire**, they are involved in several different activities or have several different plans. *Too many irons in the fire can sap your energy and prevent you from seeing which path to take.* PHRASE

iron out. If you **iron out** difficulties, you resolve them and bring them to an end. *It was in the beginning, when we were still ironing out problems.* PHRASAL VB V P n Also V n P

'Iron Age. The **Iron Age** was a period of time which began when people started making things from iron about three thousand years ago. N-PROPER: the N

iron·clad /'aɪənklæd/; also spelled **iron-clad.** If you describe a guarantee or plan as **ironclad**, you think it is absolutely certain to work or be successful. ADJ-GRADED

,Iron 'Curtain. People referred to the border that separated the Soviet Union and its East European allies from the Western European countries as **the Iron Curtain.** ◆◇◇◇ N-PROPER: the N

iron·ic /aɪ'rɒnɪk/ or **ironical** /aɪ'rɒnɪkəl/. **1** When you make an **ironic** remark, you say something that you do not mean, as a joke. *People used to call me Mr Popularity at high school, but they were being ironic.* ◆ **ironi·cal·ly** *'A very good year for women!' she said ironically.* **2** If you say that it is **ironic** that something should happen, you mean that it is odd or amusing because it involves a contrast. *It is ironic that a feminist who values independence should marry a chauvinist.* ◆ **ironically** *Ironically, for a man who hated war, he would have made a superb war cameraman.* ◆◆◇◇ ADJ-GRADED / ADV-GRADED / ADJ-GRADED / ADV-GRADED: ADV with cl

'ironing board, ironing boards. An **ironing board** is a long narrow board covered with cloth on which you iron clothes. N-COUNT

iron·monger /'aɪənmʌŋgə/ **ironmongers.** An **ironmonger** is a shopkeeper who sells articles for the house and garden such as tools, nails, and pans. You can refer to the shop where an ironmonger works as the **ironmonger** or **ironmonger's.** N-COUNT BRITISH

iron·work /'aɪənwɜːk/. Decorative iron objects or structures are referred to as **ironwork.** N-UNCOUNT

irony /'aɪrəni/ **ironies. 1** Irony is a form of humour which involves saying things that you do not mean. *There seemed to be no hint of irony in his voice.* **2** If you talk about the **irony** of a situation, you mean that it is odd or amusing because it involves a contrast. *The irony is this document may become more available in the US than in Britain where it was commissioned.* ◆◆◇◇ N-UNCOUNT / N-VAR

ir·ra·di·ate /ɪ'reɪdieɪt/ **irradiates, irradiating, irradiated. 1** If someone or something is **irradiated**, they are exposed to a large amount of radiation. *...the Chernobyl disaster, which irradiated large parts of Europe.* ◆ **ir·ra·dia·tion** /ɪ,reɪdi'eɪʃən/. *...the harmful effects of irradiation and pollution.* **2** If food **is irradiated**, it is treated with radiation to kill pests and make it last longer. *...the risks and benefits of irradiated food.* ◆ **irradiation** *...doubts about the safety of food irradiation.* ◆◇◇◇ VERB: be V-ed V n TECHNICAL / N-UNCOUNT / VERB: be V-ed V-ed / N-UNCOUNT

ir·ra·tion·al /ɪ'ræʃənəl/. If you describe someone's feelings and behaviour as **irrational**, you mean they are not based on logical reasons or clear thinking. *...an irrational fear of science.* ◆ **ir·ra·tion·al·ly** *My husband is irrationally jealous over my past loves.* ◆ **ir·ra·tion·al·ity** /ɪ,ræʃə'nælɪti/ *...the irrationality of his behaviour.* ◆◇◇◇ ADJ-GRADED / ADV-GRADED / N-UNCOUNT

ir·rec·on·cil·able /ɪ,rekə'nsaɪləbəl/. **1** If two things such as opinions or proposals are **irreconcilable**, they are so different from each other that it is not possible to believe or have both of them. *These old* ADJ FORMAL

concepts are irreconcilable with modern life. **2** An **ir-** ADJ / FORMAL
reconcilable disagreement or conflict is so serious
that it cannot be settled. *...an irreconcilable clash of
personalities.*

ir·re·deem·able /ˌɪrɪˈdiːməbəl/. If someone or ADJ / FORMAL
something has an **irredeemable** fault, it cannot be
corrected. *He is still an irredeemable misogynist.*
♦ **ir·re·deem·ably** /ˌɪrɪˈdiːməbli/. *The applicant* ADV: ADV adj/-ed
was irredeemably incompetent.

ir·re·duc·ible /ˌɪrɪˈdjuːsɪbəl/. **Irreducible** things ADJ / FORMAL
cannot be made simpler or smaller. *...the irreducible
complexity of human life.*

ir·refu·table /ˌɪrɪˈfjuːtəbəl/. **Irrefutable** evidence, ADJ / FORMAL
statements, or arguments cannot be denied or
shown to be incorrect. *Her logic was irrefutable.*

ir·regu·lar /ɪˈregjʊlə/ **irregulars**. **1** If events or ac- ◆◆◇◇◇ / ADJ-GRADED
tions occur at **irregular** intervals, the periods of
time between them are of different lengths. *She was
taken to hospital suffering from an irregular heart-
beat... He worked irregular hours.* ♦ **ir·regu·lar·ly** ADV-GRADED: ADV with v
Epileptic fits occur irregularly and without warning.
♦ **ir·regu·lar·ity** /ɪˌregjʊˈlærɪti/ **irregularities** *...a* N-VAR
dangerous irregularity in heartbeat. **2** Some- ADJ-GRADED
thing that is **irregular** is not smooth or straight, or
does not form a regular pattern. *The paint was dry-
ing in irregular patches.* ♦ **ir·regu·lar·ly** *...the ir-* ADV-GRADED
regularly shaped lake. ♦ **irregularity** *...treatment* N-VAR
of abnormalities or irregularities of the teeth. **3** Ir- ADJ-GRADED
regular behaviour is dishonest or not in accordance
with the normal rules. *...the minister accused of irregular business practices.* ♦ **ir·regu·lar·ity** *...char-* N-VAR
ges arising from alleged financial irregularities.
4 An **irregular** verb, noun, or adjective does not in- ADJ
flect in the same way as most other verbs, nouns, or
adjectives in the language. For example, 'break' is
an irregular verb because its past form is 'broke',
not 'breaked'. **5 Irregular** troops do not belong to ADJ: ADJ n
an official national army. ▶ **Irregulars** are irregular N-COUNT
troops.

ir·rel·evant /ɪˈrelɪvənt/. If you say that something ◆◆◇◇◇ / ADJ-GRADED
is **irrelevant**, you mean that it is not important to or
not connected with the present situation or discussion. *Their old hard-won skills were irrelevant... The
government decided that their testimony would be
irrelevant to the case.* ♦ **ir·rel·evance** *...the utter ir-* N-SING
*relevance of the debate... Whether the book shocks or
not is an irrelevance.* ♦ **ir·rel·evan·cy, irrelevan-** N-COUNT
cies. *Why was he wasting her time with these irrel-
evancies?* ♦ **ir·rel·evant·ly** *She would have hated* ADV-GRADED
the suit, I thought irrelevantly.

ir·repa·rable /ɪˈrepərəbəl/. **Irreparable** damage or ◆◇◇◇◇
harm is so bad that it cannot be repaired or put ADJ / FORMAL
right. ♦ **ir·repa·rably** /ɪˈrepərəbli/. *His brain was ir-* ADV
reparably damaged.

ir·re·place·able /ˌɪrɪˈpleɪsəbəl/. **Irreplaceable** ADJ
things or people are so special that they cannot be
replaced if they are lost.

ir·re·press·ible /ˌɪrɪˈpresɪbəl/. An **irrepressible** ADJ-GRADED
person is lively and energetic and never seems to be
depressed. ♦ **ir·re·press·ibly** /ˌɪrɪˈpresɪbli/. *Gavin* ADV-GRADED
was irrepressibly rebellious.

ir·re·proach·able /ˌɪrɪˈprəʊtʃəbəl/. If you say that ADJ
someone's character or behaviour is **irreproach-
able**, you mean that they behave so well that they
cannot be criticized.

ir·re·sist·ible /ˌɪrɪˈzɪstɪbəl/. **1** If you describe ◆◆◇◇◇ / ADJ-GRADED
something such as a desire or force as **irresistible**,
you mean that it is so powerful that it makes you
act in a certain way, and there is nothing you can
do to prevent this. *It proved an irresistible temptation to Hall to go back. ...irresistible pressure from
the financial markets.* ♦ **ir·re·sist·ibly** /ˌɪrɪˈzɪstɪbli/ ADV-GRADED: ADV with v
*He can see the drawbacks, but is still irresistibly
drawn to them.* **2** If you describe something or ADJ-GRADED / INFORMAL
someone as **irresistible**, you mean that are so
good or attractive that you cannot stop yourself
from liking them or wanting them. *...irresistible
granary bread.* ♦ **irresistibly** *She had a gamine* ADV-GRADED: ADV adj
charm which men found irresistibly attractive.

ir·reso·lute /ɪˈrezəluːt/. Someone who is **irresolute** ADJ-GRADED / FORMAL
cannot decide what to do.

ir·re·spec·tive /ˌɪrɪˈspektɪv/. If you say that some- ◆◇◇◇◇ / PHR-PREP / FORMAL
thing happens or should happen **irrespective of** a
particular thing, you mean that it is not affected or
should not be affected by that thing. *...equality for
all citizens irrespective of ethnic origin... This service
should be available to everybody, irrespective of
whether they can afford it.*

ir·re·spon·sible /ˌɪrɪˈspɒnsɪbəl/. If you describe ◆◇◇◇◇ / ADJ-GRADED / PRAGMATICS
someone as **irresponsible**, you are criticizing them
because they do things without properly considering their possible consequences. *It was irresponsible
to advocate the legalisation of drugs... It would be
irresponsible of me not to advise my company
to abandon this project... Many people have an
irresponsible attitude towards marriage.* ♦ **ir·re-
·spon·sibly** /ˌɪrɪˈspɒnsɪbli/. *They have behaved ir-* ADV-GRADED
responsibly. ♦ **ir·re·spon·sibil·ity** /ˌɪrɪspɒnsɪˈbɪlɪti/. N-UNCOUNT
*...the irresponsibility of people who advocate such
destruction.*

ir·re·triev·able /ˌɪrɪˈtriːvəbəl/. **Irretrievable** dam- ADJ
age or an **irretrievable** situation is so bad that there
is no possibility of putting it right. *...a country in irretrievable decline.* ♦ **ir·re·triev·ably** /ˌɪrɪˈtriːvəbli/ ADV
Her marriage broke down irretrievably.

ir·rev·er·ent /ɪˈrevərənt/. If you describe someone ◆◇◇◇◇ / ADJ-GRADED / PRAGMATICS
as **irreverent**, you mean that they do not show re-
spect for people or things that are generally respected; usually used showing approval. ♦ **ir·rev·er-
·ence** *His irreverence for authority marks him out* N-UNCOUNT
as a troublemaker. ♦ **ir·rev·er·ent·ly** *'Jobs for the* ADV-GRADED
boys,' said Crosby irreverently.

ir·re·vers·ible /ˌɪrɪˈvɜːsɪbəl/. If a change is **irre-** ◆◇◇◇◇ / ADJ
versible, things cannot be changed back to the way
they were before. *She could suffer irreversible brain
damage.* ♦ **ir·re·vers·ibly** *Television has irrevers-* ADV: ADV with v
ibly changed our perception of the Royal Family.

ir·revo·cable /ɪˈrevəkəbəl/. If a decision, action, ◆◇◇◇◇
or change is **irrevocable**, it cannot be changed or ADJ / FORMAL
reversed. *His mother's death was an irrevocable loss.*
♦ **ir·revo·cably** /ɪˈrevəkəbli/. *My relationships with* ADV
friends have been irrevocably altered.

ir·ri·gate /ˈɪrɪgeɪt/ **irrigates, irrigating, irrigat-** ◆◇◇◇◇
ed. To **irrigate** land means to supply it with water VERB: V n / V-ed
in order to help crops grow. *...strips of cultivated
land irrigated by a maze of interconnected canals.*
♦ **ir·ri·ga·tion** /ˌɪrɪˈgeɪʃən/ *...a sophisticated irriga-* N-UNCOUNT
tion system.

ir·ri·table /ˈɪrɪtəbəl/. If you are **irritable**, you are ◆◇◇◇◇ / ADJ-GRADED
easily annoyed. *He had missed his dinner, and grew
irritable.* ♦ **ir·ri·tably** /ˈɪrɪtəbli/. *'Why are you whis-* ADV-GRADED: ADV with v
pering?' he asked irritably. ♦ **ir·ri·tabil·ity** N-UNCOUNT
/ˌɪrɪtəˈbɪlɪti/. *She showed no sign of irritability.*

ir·ri·tant /ˈɪrɪtənt/ **irritants**. **1** If you describe ◆◇◇◇◇
something as an **irritant**, you mean that it keeps N-COUNT / FORMAL
annoying you. **2** An **irritant** is a substance which N-COUNT / FORMAL
causes a part of your body to become tender, sore,
or itchy.

ir·ri·tate /ˈɪrɪteɪt/ **irritates, irritating, irritated.** ◆◆◇◇◇
1 If something **irritates** you, it keeps annoying you. VERB: V n / be V-ed
Perhaps they were irritated by the sound of crying.
♦ **ir·ri·tat·ed** *Her teacher is getting irritated with* ADJ-GRADED
her. ♦ **ir·ri·tat·ing** *They also have the irritating hab-* ADJ-GRADED
it of interrupting. ♦ **ir·ri·tat·ing·ly** *They can be* ADV-GRADED
irritatingly indecisive at times. **2** If something **irri-** VERB: V n
tates a part of your body, it causes it to itch or become sore. ♦ **ir·ri·tat·ing** *In heavy concentrations,* ADJ-GRADED
ozone is irritating to the eyes.

ir·ri·ta·tion /ˌɪrɪˈteɪʃən/ **irritations. 1 Irritation** is ◆◇◇◇◇
a feeling of annoyance. *For the first time Leonard* N-UNCOUNT
*felt irritation at her methods... He tried not to let his
irritation show.* **2** An **irritation** is something that N-COUNT
keeps annoying you. *He describes the tourists as an
irritation.* **3 Irritation** in your skin or eyes is a feel- N-VAR
ing of soreness or itching there.

is /ɪz/. **Is** is the third person singular of the present
tense of **be**. **Is** is often abbreviated to **'s**.

-ise /-aɪz/. See **-ize**.

-ish /-ɪʃ/. **1** -ish is added to adjectives to form adjectives which indicate that someone or something has a quality to a small extent. For example, if you say that something is largish, you mean it is fairly large. *...a tank of greenish water.* **2** -ish is added to nouns and names to form adjectives which indicate that someone or something is like a particular kind of person or thing. For example, 'childish' means like a child, or typical of a child. *...a man of monkish appearance.* **3** -ish is added to words referring to times, dates, or ages to form words which indicate that the time or age mentioned is approximate. *I'll call you guys tomorrow. Noon-ish... The nurse was fiftyish.* SUFFIX

Is·lam /ˈɪzlɑːm, AM ɪsˈlɑːm/. **1** Islam is the religion of Muslims, which teaches that there is only one God and that Mohammed is His prophet. **2** Some people use Islam to refer to all the countries where Islam is the main religion. *...relations between Islam and the West.* ◆◆◆◇◇ N-UNCOUNT / N-UNCOUNT

Is·lam·ic /ɪzˈlæmɪk/. Islamic means belonging or relating to Islam. *...Islamic law.* ◆◆◆◇◇ ADJ: ADJ n

is·land /ˈaɪlənd/ **islands.** An island is a piece of land that is completely surrounded by water. *...the picturesque island of Gozo... We spent a day on Caldey Island.* ◆◆◆◆◇ N-COUNT

is·land·er /ˈaɪləndə/ **islanders.** Islanders are people who live on an island. ◆◇◇◇◇ N-COUNT

isle /aɪl/ **isles.** An isle is an island. *...the Isle of Man... When the Saxons came to these isles, a number of Britons fled across the Channel.* ◆◆◇◇◇ N-COUNT LITERARY

is·let /ˈaɪlət/ **islets.** An islet is a small island. *The tiny islet has been the subject of dispute for many years.* N-COUNT LITERARY

-ism /-ɪzəm/ **-isms. 1** -ism is used to form uncount nouns that refer to political or religious movements and beliefs. *...a time of growing Slovak nationalism.* **2** -ism is used to form uncount nouns that refer to attitudes and behaviour. *...an act of heroism.* **3** -ism is used to form nouns that refer to unfair or illegal discrimination against particular groups of people. *Ageism is obstructing their career ambitions.* SUFFIX / SUFFIX / SUFFIX

isn't /ˈɪzənt/. In informal English, is not is usually said or written as isn't.

iso·late /ˈaɪsəleɪt/ **isolates, isolating, isolated. 1** To isolate a person or organization means to cause them to lose their friends or supporters. *That will further isolate Britain from the mainstream of the European union.* ◆ iso·lat·ed *They are finding themselves increasingly isolated within the teaching profession.* ◆ iso·la·tion /ˌaɪsəˈleɪʃən/ *...the public isolation of the Prime Minister.* **2** If you isolate yourself, or if something isolates you, you become physically or socially separated from other people. *Tweed's habit was never to isolate himself in his room... His radicalism and refusal to compromise isolated him... Police officers had a siege mentality that isolated them from the people they served.* **3** If you isolate something such as an idea or a problem, you separate it from others that it is connected with, so that you can concentrate on it or consider it on its own. *...attempts to isolate a single factor as the cause of the decline of Britain.* **4** To isolate a substance means to obtain it by separating it from other substances using scientific processes. **5** To isolate a sick person or animal means to keep them apart from other people or animals, so that their illness does not spread. ◆◇◇◇◇ VERB: V n / Vn from n / ADJ-GRADED / N-UNCOUNT / VERB V pron-refl / Vn / Vn from n / VERB Vn / VERB: Vn

iso·lat·ed /ˈaɪsəleɪtɪd/. **1** An isolated place is a long way away from large towns and is difficult to reach. *Aubrey's family's farm is very isolated.* **2** If you feel isolated, you feel lonely and without friends or help. *Some patients may become very isolated and depressed.* **3** An isolated example is an example of something that is not very common. *They said the allegations related to an isolated case of cheating.* ◆◆◇◇◇ ADJ-GRADED / ADJ-GRADED / ADJ: ADJ n

iso·la·tion /ˌaɪsəˈleɪʃən/. **1** Isolation is the state of feeling alone and without friends or help. *Many deaf people have feelings of isolation and loneliness.* ◆◆◇◇◇ N-UNCOUNT

2 If something is considered in isolation from other things that it is connected with, it is considered separately. *Punishment cannot, therefore, be discussed in isolation from social and political theory.* PHRASE

3 If someone does something in isolation, they do it without other people being present or without their help. **4** See also isolate. PHRASE

iso·la·tion·ism /ˌaɪsəˈleɪʃənɪzəm/. Isolationism refers to a country's policy when it avoids becoming involved in relationships or disputes between other countries. ◆ iso·la·tion·ist, isolationists. *Some critics are isolationists, who want a Russia-first policy.* N-UNCOUNT / N-COUNT

iso·met·rics /ˌaɪsəˈmetrɪks/; the form isometric is used as a modifier. Isometrics or isometric exercises are exercises in which you make your muscles work against each other or against something else, for example by pressing your hands together. N-PLURAL

iso·tope /ˈaɪsətəʊp/ **isotopes.** Isotopes are atoms of the same substance which have different physical properties because they do not have the same number of neutrons. *...tritium, a radioactive isotope of hydrogen.* ◆◇◇◇◇ N-COUNT TECHNICAL

is·sue /ˈɪʃuː, ˈɪsjuː/ **issues, issuing, issued. 1** An issue is an important subject that people are arguing about or discussing. *Agents will raise the issue of prize-money... Is it right for the Church to express a view on political issues?* ◆ See also side issue. **2** If something is the issue, it is the thing you consider to be the most important part of a situation or discussion. *I was earning a lot of money, but that was not the issue... She avoided the issue.* **3** The question or point at issue is the question or point that is being argued about or discussed. *The point at issue is not when the reserves were released, but where they were released from.* **4** If you make an issue of something, you try to make other people think about it or discuss it, because you are concerned or annoyed about it. *He decided not to make an issue of it.* **5** If you take issue with someone or something they said, you disagree with them, and start arguing about it. *The filmmaker takes issue with the critics who say his works have been deliberately provocative.* **6** An issue of something such as a magazine or newspaper is the version of it that is published, for example, in a particular month or on a particular day. *...the latest issue of the Lancet... I read Germaine Greer's article in the March issue.* **7** If you issue a statement or a warning, you make it known formally or publicly. *Yesterday his kidnappers issued a second threat to kill him.* **8** If you are issued with something, it is officially given to you. *Staff will be issued with new grey-and-yellow designer uniforms.* ▶ Also a noun. *...a standard army issue rifle.* **9** When something such as a liquid, sound, or smell issues from something, it comes out of that thing. ◆◆◆◆◆ N-COUNT / N-SING the N / PHRASE / PHRASE / PHRASE / N-COUNT / VERB Vn / VB: usu passive be V-ed with n / N-UNCOUNT VERB: V from n FORMAL

-ist /-ɪst/ **-ists. 1** -ist is added to nouns instead of '-ism' in order to form nouns and adjectives relating to particular beliefs. *Later he was to become famous as a pacifist. ...fascist organisations.* **2** -ist is used to form nouns referring to people who do a particular kind of work. *Susi Arnott is a biologist.* **3** -ist is used to form nouns that refer to people who play particular musical instruments. *...Hungarian pianist Christina Kiss.* SUFFIX / SUFFIX / SUFFIX

isth·mus /ˈɪsməs/ **isthmuses.** An isthmus is a narrow piece of land with sea on either side, connecting two very large areas of land. N-COUNT

it /ɪt/. It is a third person singular pronoun. It is used as the subject or object of a verb, or as the object of a preposition. ◆◆◆◆◆

1 You use it to refer to an object, animal, or other thing that has already been mentioned, or to a situation that you have just described. *He saw the grey Land-Rover down the by-pass. It was more than a hundred yards from him... My wife has become crippled by arthritis. She is embarrassed to ask the doctor about it... Antonia will not be jealous, or if she is, she will not show it.* **2** You use it to refer to a child or baby PRON / PRON

whose sex you do not know or whose sex is not relevant to what you are saying. *He threw the baby high in the air and it stopped crying.* **3** You use **it** before certain nouns, adjectives, and verbs to introduce your feelings or point of view about a situation. *It was nice to see Steve again... It's a pity you never got married, Sarah... He found it hard to work with a microphone pointing at him... It seems that you are letting things get you down.* **4** You use **it** in passive clauses which report a situation or event. *It has been said that stress causes cancer... Yesterday it was reported that a number of people had been arrested.* **5** You use **it** with some verbs that need a subject or object, although there is no noun that it refers to. *As it turned out, three-fourths of the people in the group were psychiatrists... I like it here.* **6** You use **it** to say what the time, day, or date is. *It's three o'clock in the morning... It was a Monday, so she was at home.* **7** You use **it** to describe the weather, the light, or the temperature. *It was very wet and windy the day I drove over the hill to Milland... It's getting dark. Let's go inside.* **8** You use **it** when you are telling someone who you are, or asking them who they are, especially at the beginning of a phone call. You also use **it** in statements and questions about the identity of other people. *'Who is it?' he called... Hello Freddy, it's only me, Maxine.* **9** When you are emphasizing or drawing attention to something, you can put that thing immediately after **it** and a form of the verb 'be'. *It was the country's Communist rulers who devised this system... It's my father they're accusing.* **10** You use **it** in expressions such as **it's not that** or **it's not just that** when you are saying that something is not the reason, or not the only reason, for what is happening or being done. *It's not that I didn't want to be with my family.* **11 ● if it wasn't for:** see be.

PRON · PRON · PRON · PRON · PRON · PRON · PRON / PRAGMATICS · PRON / PRAGMATICS · PHRASE / PRAGMATICS

ital·ic /ɪ'tælɪk/ **italics. 1** Italics are letters which slope to the right. They can be used to emphasize particular words. The examples in this dictionary are printed in italics. **2** Italic letters slope to the right. *...her beautiful italic script.* N-PLURAL · ADJ: ADJ n

itch /ɪtʃ/ **itches, itching, itched. 1** When you **itch** or when a part of your body **itches**, you have an unpleasant feeling on your skin that makes you want to scratch. *...dry, itching skin.* ▶ Also a noun. *Scratch my back – I've got an itch.* ● **itch·ing** The *itching is caused by contact with irritant material.* ◆ **itchy** *...itchy, sore eyes... Wigs are itchy and uncomfortable.* **2** If you **are itching** to do something, you are very eager or impatient to do it. *I was itching to get involved... The general was itching for a fight.* ▶ Also a noun. *...an insatiable itch to switch from channel to channel.* ◆◇◇◇◇ · VERB: V / V-ing · N-COUNT · N-UNCOUNT · ADJ-GRADED · VERB / V to-inf / V for n / INFORMAL · N-SING

it'd /ɪtəd/. **1 It'd** is a spoken form of 'it would'. **2 It'd** is a spoken form of 'it had', especially when 'had' is an auxiliary verb. *It'd just started.*

item /'aɪtəm/ **items. 1** An **item** is one of a collection or list of objects. *The most valuable item on show will be a Picasso drawing.* ● See also **collector's item. 2** An **item** is one of a list of things for someone to do, deal with, or talk about. *The other item on the agenda is the tour.* **3** An **item** is a report or article in a newspaper or magazine, or on television or radio. *There was an item in the paper about him.* ◆◆◆◇ · N-COUNT · N-COUNT · N-COUNT

item·ize /'aɪtəmaɪz/ **itemizes, itemizing, itemized;** also spelled **itemise** in British English. If you **itemize** a number of things, you make a list of them. *...a fully itemised bill.* VERB: V n / V-ed

itin·er·ant /aɪ'tɪnərənt/ **itinerants. 1** An **itinerant** worker or preacher travels around a region, working for short periods in different places. *...the author's* ADJ: ADJ n / FORMAL

experiences as an itinerant musician. **2** An **itinerant** is someone whose way of life involves travelling around, usually someone who is poor and homeless. *...education programmes for itinerants.* N-COUNT / FORMAL

itin·er·ary /aɪ'tɪnərəri, AM -eri/ **itineraries.** An **itinerary** is a plan of a journey, including the route and the places that you will visit. *The next place on our itinerary was Silistra.* ◆◇◇◇◇ · N-COUNT

it'll /ɪtəl/. **It'll** is a spoken form of 'it will'.

its /ɪts/. **Its** is a third person singular possessive determiner. You use **its** to indicate that something belongs or relates to a thing, place, or animal that has just been mentioned or whose identity is known. You can use **its** to indicate that something belongs or relates to a child or baby. *The Labour Party concludes its annual conference today.* ◆◆◆◆ · DET-POSS

it's /ɪts/. **1 It's** is the usual spoken form of 'it is'. **2 It's** is the usual spoken form of 'it has', especially when 'has' is an auxiliary verb. *It's been such a long time.*

it·self /ɪt'self/. **1 Itself** is used as the object of a verb or preposition when it refers to something that is the same thing as the subject of the verb. *The body rebuilds itself while we sleep... The back part of the chair bends double and folds into itself.* **2** You use **itself** to emphasize the thing you are referring to. *I think life itself is a learning process... The involvement of the foreign ministers was itself a sign of progress.* **3** If you say that someone is, for example, politeness **itself** or kindness **itself**, you are emphasizing they are extremely polite or extremely kind. *He is rarely satisfied with anything less than perfection itself.* **4 ● an end in itself:** see end. ◆◆◆◆ · PRON-REFL: v PRON, prep PRON · PRON-REFL / PRAGMATICS · PRON-REFL: n PRON / PRAGMATICS

ITV /,aɪ tiː 'viː/. **1 ITV** refers to the group of British commercial television companies that broadcasts programmes on one channel. **ITV** is an abbreviation for 'Independent Television'. **2 ITV** is the television channel that is run by ITV. *The first episode will be shown tomorrow at 10.40pm on ITV.* ◆◆◇◇ · N-COLL-PROPER · N-PROPER

-ity /-ɪti/ **-ities. -ity** is added to some adjectives, sometimes in place of '-ious', to form nouns referring to the state, quality, or behaviour described by the adjective. *...life with all its contradictions and complexities.* SUFFIX

IUD /,aɪ juː 'diː/ **IUDs.** An **IUD** is a piece of plastic or metal which is put inside a woman's womb in order to prevent her from becoming pregnant. **IUD** is an abbreviation for 'intra-uterine device'. N-COUNT

I've /aɪv/. **I've** is the usual spoken form of 'I have', especially when 'have' is an auxiliary verb. *I've been invited.*

ivo·ry /'aɪvəri/. **1 Ivory** is a valuable type of bone, which forms most of the tusks of an elephant. *...intricate ivory carvings.* **2 Ivory** is a creamy-white colour. ◆◆◇◇ · N-UNCOUNT · COLOUR

ivory tower, ivory towers. If you describe someone as living in an **ivory tower**, you disapprove of them because you think they have no knowledge or experience of the practical problems of everyday life. N-COUNT / PRAGMATICS

ivy /'aɪvi/ **ivies.** Ivy is an evergreen plant that grows up walls or along the ground. ◆◇◇◇◇ · N-VAR

Ivy League. The **Ivy League** is a group of eight important universities in the eastern part of the United States. N-PROPER: the N

-ize /-aɪz/ **-izes, -izing, -ized;** also spelled **-ise** in British English. Verbs that can end in either '-ize' or '-ise' are dealt with in this dictionary at the '-ize' spelling. Many verbs ending in **-ize** describe processes by which things or people are brought into a new state. *...a way of trying to regularize and standardize practice.* SUFFIX

J j

J, j /dʒeɪ/ **J's, j's. 1** J is the tenth letter of the English alphabet. **2** J or j is an abbreviation for words beginning with j, such as 'joule' or 'Jack'.   N-VAR

jab /dʒæb/ **jabs, jabbing, jabbed. 1** If you **jab** something, you push it with a quick sudden movement and with a lot of force. *Nick jabbed his finger at the clothes on the bed... A needle was jabbed into the baby's arm... Suddenly he jabbed at me with his forefinger.* **2** A **jab** is a sudden sharp punch. **3** A **jab** is an injection to prevent illness. *...anti malaria jabs.*   VERB: V n / V n prep / be V-ed into n / V at n / N-COUNT / N-COUNT INFORMAL BRITISH

jab·ber /'dʒæbə/ **jabbers, jabbering, jabbered.** If you say that someone **is jabbering**, you mean that they are talking very quickly and excitedly, and you cannot understand them; used showing disapproval. *The girl jabbered incomprehensibly... I left them there jabbering away.*   VERB PRAGMATICS V / V away

jack /dʒæk/ **jacks, jacking, jacked. 1** A **jack** is a device for lifting a heavy object such as a car off the ground. **2** A **Jack** is a playing card whose value is between a ten and a queen. **3** See also **jack-of-all-trades, Union Jack.**   N-COUNT / N-COUNT

jack in. If you **jack** something **in**, you stop doing it. *Four of the cast jacked it in about Christmas... After she jacked in the teaching, Jane got herself a job with a shipping line.*   PHRASAL VB V n P / V P n BRITISH

jack up. 1 If you **jack up** a heavy object such as a car, you raise it off the ground using a jack. *All I had to do was get everyone out of the car, jack it up, and put on the spare.* **2** If you say that someone or something **jacks up** a price or amount, you mean it rises to an unreasonable level. *Inflation has jacked up the rate of unemployment.*   V P noun / V P n PRAGMATICS V P n INFORMAL

jack·al /'dʒækɔ:l/ **jackals.** A **jackal** is a wild animal that looks like a dog. It lives in Africa and Southern Asia.   N-COUNT

jack·boot /'dʒækbu:t/ **jackboots. Jackboots** are soldiers' boots that come up to the knee.   N-COUNT

jack·daw /'dʒækdɔ:/ **jackdaws.** A **jackdaw** is a large black and grey bird that lives in Europe and Asia.   N-COUNT

jack·et /'dʒækɪt/ **jackets. 1** A **jacket** is a short coat with long sleeves. See picture headed **clothes. 2** See also **bomber jacket, dinner jacket, flak jacket, life jacket, sports jacket, straitjacket. 3** The **jacket** of a book is the cover that protects it. **4** A **jacket** is the cover in which a record is kept. The British word is **sleeve**.   N-COUNT / N-COUNT / N-COUNT AMERICAN

jacket po'tato, jacket potatoes. A **jacket potato** is a potato that has been baked without being peeled.   N-COUNT BRITISH

'jack-in-the-box, jack-in-the-boxes. A **jack-in-the-box** is a child's toy that consists of a box with a doll inside it that springs out when the lid is opened.   N-COUNT

'jack-knife, jack-knifes, jack-knifing, jack-knifed. If an articulated truck **jack-knifes**, the trailer swings around at a sharp angle to the cab in an uncontrolled way as the truck is moving.   VERB: V

,jack-of-'all-trades. If you refer to someone as a **jack-of-all-trades**, you mean that they are able to do a variety of different jobs. You are also often suggesting that they are not very good at any of these jobs.   N-SING

jack·pot /'dʒækpɒt/ **jackpots. 1** A **jackpot** is a large sum of money which is the most valuable prize in a game or lottery. *...the biggest ever jackpot of more than £5 million.* **2** If you **hit the jackpot**, you have good luck or a great success.   N-COUNT / PHRASE INFORMAL

Jaco·bean /,dʒækə'bi:ən/. A **Jacobean** building, piece of furniture, or work of art was built or produced in the style of the period between 1603 and 1625.   ADJ

Ja·cuz·zi /dʒə'ku:zi/ **Jacuzzis.** A **Jacuzzi** is a large round bath which is fitted with a device that makes the water bubble. **Jacuzzi** is a trademark.   N-COUNT

jade /dʒeɪd/. **Jade** is a hard green type of stone, used for making jewellery and ornaments.   N-UNCOUNT

jad·ed /'dʒeɪdɪd/. If you are **jaded**, you feel bored, tired, and unenthusiastic, because you have had too much of the same thing. *...his air of jaded cynicism.*   ADJ-GRADED

jagged /'dʒægɪd/. Something that is **jagged** has a rough uneven shape or edge with lots of sharp points. *...a piece of iron with jagged edges.*   ADJ-GRADED

jagu·ar /'dʒægjuə, AM -gwɑ:r/ **jaguars.** A **jaguar** is a large animal of the cat family with dark spots on its back.   N-COUNT

jail /dʒeɪl/ **jails, jailing, jailed;** the form **gaol** is also used in British English. **1** A **jail** is a place where criminals are kept in order to punish them. *He recently served two years in jail for fraud.* **2** If someone **is jailed**, they are put into jail.   N-VAR / VB: usu passive

jail·bird /'dʒeɪlbɜ:d/ **jailbirds.** If you refer to someone as a **jailbird**, you mean that they are in prison, or have been in prison.   N-COUNT DATED, INFORMAL

jail·break /'dʒeɪlbreɪk/ **jailbreaks.** A **jailbreak** is an escape from jail.   N-COUNT

jail·er /'dʒeɪlə/ **jailers.** A **jailer** is a person who is in charge of a jail and the prisoners in it.   N-COUNT DATED

jail·house /'dʒeɪlhaʊs/ **jailhouses.** A **jailhouse** is the same as a **prison**.   N-COUNT INFORMAL, AMERICAN

jam /dʒæm/ **jams, jamming, jammed. 1** Jam is a food that is made by cooking fruit with a large amount of sugar. Usually you spread jam on bread. The usual American word is **jelly**. *...strawberry jam.*   N-VAR BRITISH

2 If you **jam** something somewhere, you push or put it there roughly. *Pete jammed his hands into his pockets.*   VERB V n prep

3 If a mechanism **jams**, or if something **jams** it, the mechanism stops moving freely and no longer works properly. *The second time he fired, his gun jammed... A rope jammed the boat's propeller... The intake valve was jammed open... A tree-root had swollen at the base of the gate, jamming it shut.* **4** To **jam** a radio or electronic signal means to interfere with it and prevent it from being received or heard clearly. ♦ **jam·ming** *The plane is used for electronic jamming and radar detection.* **5** If there is a **jam** on a road, there are so many vehicles that they cannot move. *400 trucks may sit in a jam for ten hours.* ● See also **traffic jam.** ♦ **jammed** *Nearby roads and the dirt track to the beach were jammed with cars.* **6** If a lot of people **jam** a place, or **jam** into a place, they are pressed tightly together so that they can hardly move. *Hundreds of people jammed the boardwalk to watch... They jammed into buses provided by the Red Cross.* ♦ **jammed** *The stadium was jammed and they had to turn away hundreds of disappointed fans.* **7** If you say that callers **are jamming** telephone lines, you are emphasizing that there are a lot of people making calls to the same place at the same time. *Hundreds of callers jammed the BBC switchboard for more than an hour.* **8** If someone **is in a jam**, they are in a very difficult situation. **9** When jazz or rock musicians **are jamming**, they are informally playing music that has not been written down or planned in advance. ▶ Also a noun. *...a jam session.*   VERB V-ERG / V n / V-ed / V n adj / VERB: V n / N-UNCOUNT / N-COUNT / ADJ-GRADED / VERB V n / V into n / ADJ-GRADED / VERB V n / N-SING in N INFORMAL / VERB: V INFORMAL / N-COUNT

jamb /dʒæm/ **jambs.** A **jamb** is a post that forms N-COUNT the side part or upright of a door frame or window frame.

jam·bo·ree /ˌdʒæmbəˈriː/ **jamborees.** A **jamboree** N-COUNT is a party or celebration where there is a large number of people and a lot of excitement.

jam-packed. If somewhere is **jam-packed**, it is ADJ-GRADED so full of people or things that there is no room for INFORMAL any more. *His room was jam-packed with fruit, flowers, gifts etc.*

Jan. Jan. is a written abbreviation for **January**.

jan·gle /ˈdʒæŋgəl/ **jangles, jangling, jangled.** ◆◆◇◇◇ **1** When objects strike against each other and make V-ERG: V an unpleasant ringing noise, you can say that they V n **jangle** or are **jangled**. *Jane took out her keys and* V-ing *jangled them. ...her jangling bracelets.* ► Also a N-SING noun. *...a jangle of bells.* **2** If you say that V-ERG: V someone's nerves **are jangling**, or someone or V n something **jangles** them, you mean that that person is very anxious. *The caffeine in coffee can jangle the nerves.*

jani·tor /ˈdʒænɪtə/ **janitors.** A **janitor** is a person N-COUNT whose job is to look after a building. AMERICAN

Janu·ary /ˈdʒænjəri, AM -jʊeri/ **Januaries.** Janu- ◆◆◆◇◇ ary is the first month of the year in the Western cal- N-VAR endar. See Appendix headed **Dates.** *We always have snow in January.*

jape /dʒeɪp/ **japes.** A **jape** is a silly trick that you N-COUNT play on someone. DATED

jar /dʒɑː/ **jars, jarring, jarred. 1** A **jar** is a glass ◆◆◇◇◇ container with a lid that is used for storing food. N-COUNT **2** You can use **jar** to refer to a jar and its contents, N-COUNT or to the contents only. *...two jars of filter coffee.* **3** If something **jars** on you, you find it unpleasant, dis- VERB turbing, or shocking. *Sometimes a light remark jarred* V on n *on her father. ...televised congressional hearings that* V n *jarred the nation's faith in the presidency. ...self-* V *confidence that in less capable hands would jar horri-* *bly.* ◆ **jar·ring** *Dore's comments strike a jarring note.* ADJ-GRADED **4** If an object **jars**, or if something **jars** it, the object V-ERG moves with a fairly hard shaking movement. *The ship* V *jarred a little... The impact jarred his arm.* V n

jar·gon /ˈdʒɑːgən/. You use **jargon** to refer to ◆◇◇◇◇ words and expressions that are used in special or N-UNCOUNT technical ways by particular groups of people, often making the language difficult to understand. *...600,000 C2 males (marketing jargon for skilled manual workers).*

jas·mine /ˈdʒæzmɪn/ **jasmines.** Jasmine is a ◆◇◇◇◇ climbing plant which has small white or yellow N-VAR flowers with a pleasant smell.

jaun·dice /ˈdʒɔːndɪs/. Jaundice is an illness that N-UNCOUNT makes your skin and eyes become yellow.

jaun·diced /ˈdʒɔːndɪst/. If you describe someone's ADJ-GRADED attitudes or views as **jaundiced**, you mean that they are unenthusiastic, pessimistic, or cynical.

jaunt /dʒɔːnt/ **jaunts.** A **jaunt** is a short journey N-COUNT which you go on for pleasure or excitement.

jaun·ty /ˈdʒɔːnti/ **jauntier, jauntiest.** If you de- ◆◇◇◇◇ scribe someone or something as **jaunty**, you mean ADJ-GRADED that they are full of confidence and energy. *...a jaunty little man... Tremain's novel is altogether jauntier.* ◆ **jaun·ti·ly** *The Arsenal striker remains* ADV-GRADED *jauntily confident.*

jave·lin /ˈdʒævlɪn/ **javelins. 1** A **javelin** is a long ◆◇◇◇◇ spear that is thrown in sports competitions. *I want-* N-COUNT *ed to be a javelin-thrower.* **2** You can refer to the N-SING: competition in which the javelin is thrown as **the** the N **javelin.** *...Steve Backley who won the javelin.*

jaw /dʒɔː/ **jaws. 1** Your **jaw** is the lower part of ◆◆◇◇◇ your face below your mouth. See picture headed N-COUNT **human body.** *He scratched at the stubble on his jaw.* **2** If you say that someone's **jaw drops**, you mean PHRASE that they are very surprised. **3** A person's or ani- N-COUNT mal's **jaws** or **jawbones** are the two bones in their head which their teeth are attached to. **4** If you talk N-PLURAL: about the **jaws** of something unpleasant such as N of n death or hell, you are referring to a dangerous or unpleasant situation. *...caught in the jaws of world recession.*

jaw·line /ˈdʒɔːlaɪn/ **jawlines;** also spelled **jaw line.** N-COUNT Your **jawline** is the part of your lower jaw which forms the outline of the bottom of your face. *...high cheekbones and strong jawline.*

jay /dʒeɪ/ **jays.** A **jay** is a brownish-pink bird with ◆◇◇◇◇ blue and black wings that lives in Europe and Asia. N-COUNT

jay·walk·ing /ˈdʒeɪwɔːkɪŋ/. **Jaywalking** is the act of N-UNCOUNT crossing a road or walking in a road in a careless and dangerous way. *The policemen threatened to ar- rest them for jaywalking.*

jazz /dʒæz/ **jazzes, jazzing, jazzed.** Jazz is a ◆◆◇◇◇ style of music that was invented by black American N-UNCOUNT musicians in the early part of the twentieth century. Jazz music has very strong rhythms and often in- volves improvisation.

jazz up. 1 If you **jazz** something **up**, you make it look PHRASAL VB more interesting, colourful, or exciting. *... jazzing up* V P noun *the chilly modern interiors... They're just jazzing it up* V n P *for the media.* **2** If someone **jazzes up** a piece of mu- INFORMAL sic, they change it in order to make it sound more like V n P popular music or jazz.

jazzy /ˈdʒæzi/ **jazzier, jazziest. 1** If you describe ◆◇◇◇◇ something as **jazzy**, you mean that it is colourful ADJ-GRADED and modern. *...spotted fabrics and jazzy prints.* **2** Jazzy music is music in the style of jazz. ADJ-GRADED

jeal·ous /ˈdʒeləs/. **1** If someone is **jealous**, they ◆◆◇◇◇ feel angry or bitter because they think that another ADJ-GRADED person is trying to take a lover or friend, or a pos- session, away from them. *She got insanely jealous and there was a terrible fight.* ◆ **jeal·ous·ly** *He rare-* ADV-GRADED: *ly appears in public and jealously protects his* ADV with v *family's privacy.* ◆ **jeal·ousy** *We all know the sharp* N-UNCOUNT: *stab of jealousy as an old girlfriend comes back into* also N in pl *view.* **2** If you are **jealous** of another person's pos- ADJ-GRADED sessions or qualities, you feel angry or bitter be- cause you do not have them. *You're jealous because the record company rejected your idea.* ◆ **jealously** ADV-GRADED: *Gloria eyed them jealously.* ◆ **jealousy** *Her beauty* ADV after v *causes envy and jealousy.* N-UNCOUNT

jeans /dʒiːnz/. **Jeans** are casual trousers that are ◆◆◇◇◇ usually made of strong blue denim. N-PLURAL

Jeep /dʒiːp/ **Jeeps.** A **Jeep** is a small four-wheeled ◆◇◇◇◇ vehicle that can travel over rough ground. Jeep is a N-COUNT trademark.

jeer /dʒɪə/ **jeers, jeering, jeered.** If people **jeer** ◆◇◇◇◇ at someone, they show disrespect by saying or VERB: shouting rude and insulting things to them. *His* V at n *motorcade was jeered by angry residents... Demon-* be V-ed *strators have jeered the mayor... I didn't come here* V *today to jeer. ...mobs of jeering bystanders.* ► Also a V-ing noun. *...the heckling and jeers of his audience.* N-COUNT ◆ **jeer·ing** *There was constant jeering and interrup-* N-UNCOUNT *tion from the floor.*

Je·ho·vah /dʒɪˈhəʊvə/. **Jehovah** is the name given N-PROPER to God in the Old Testament.

Je,hovah's 'Witness, Jehovah's Witnesses. A N-COUNT **Jehovah's Witness** is a member of a religious or- ganization which accepts some Christian ideas and believes that the world is going to end very soon.

jell /dʒel/. See **gel.**

jel·lied /ˈdʒelid/. **Jellied** food is prepared and eaten ADJ: ADJ n in a jelly. *...jellied eels.*

Jell-O /ˈdʒeləʊ/. **Jell-O** is a clear food made from N-UNCOUNT gelatine, fruit juice, and sugar. The usual British AMERICAN word is **jelly. Jell-O** is a trademark.

jel·ly /ˈdʒeli/ **jellies. 1** Jelly is a transparent, ◆◇◇◇◇ usually coloured food made from gelatine, fruit N-VAR juice, and sugar. The usual American word is **Jell-O.** BRITISH ► A container of jelly can be referred to as a **jelly.** N-COUNT *Turn out the jellies onto serving plates.* **2** Jelly is the N-VAR same as jam. *...a triple-decker peanut butter and jel-* AMERICAN *ly sandwich.* **3** Jelly is a kind of thin, clear jam, eat- N-VAR en with meat. *Crabapple jelly is a fantastic comple-* BRITISH *ment to both hot and cold meats.* **4** If you refer to a N-VAR substance as a **jelly**, you mean that it is clear and partly liquid, partly solid. *...meat in jelly.* **5** If your N-UNCOUNT legs or arms feel like **jelly**, they feel very weak, usually because you are nervous or afraid. *My legs were like jelly when I realised I had won.* **6** See also **royal jelly.**

'jelly bean, jelly beans. Jelly beans are small coloured sweets with hard shells and jelly inside. N-COUNT

jelly·fish /'dʒelifɪʃ/; **jellyfish** is both the singular and the plural form. A **jellyfish** is a sea creature with a clear soft body and tentacles that can sting you. N-COUNT

jeop·ard·ize /'dʒepədaɪz/ **jeopardizes, jeopardizing, jeopardized;** also spelled **jeopardise** in British English. If someone or something **jeopardizes** a situation or activity, they do something that may destroy it or cause it to fail. *The talks may still be jeopardized by disputes.* ◆◇◇◇◇ VERB: V n be V-ed

jeop·ardy /'dʒepədi/. If someone or something is **in jeopardy**, they are in a dangerous situation where they might fail or be destroyed. *A series of setbacks have put the whole project in jeopardy.* ◆◇◇◇◇ PHRASE

jerk /dʒɜːk/ **jerks, jerking, jerked. 1** If you **jerk** something or someone, or if they **jerk** in a particular direction, they move a short distance very suddenly and quickly. *The car jerked to a halt. ...jerking his head in my direction... Eleanor jerked her wrist free.* ► Also a noun. *He indicated the bedroom with a jerk of his head.* **2** See also **knee-jerk.** ◆◆◇◇◇ V-ERG V adv/prep V n adv/prep V n adj Also V n N-COUNT

3 If you call someone a **jerk,** you are insulting them because you think they are stupid or you do not like them. N-COUNT PRAGMATICS INFORMAL

jer·kin /'dʒɜːkɪn/ **jerkins.** A **jerkin** is a sleeveless jacket worn by men or women. N-COUNT DATED

jerky /'dʒɜːki/ **jerkier, jerkiest.** Jerky movements are very sudden and abrupt and do not flow smoothly. *Mr Griffin made a jerky gesture, dismissing that matter.* ♦ **jerki·ly** ... *he moved jerkily towards the car.* ♦ **jerki·ness** *Avoid jerkiness by breathing easily throughout the exercise.* ◆◇◇◇◇ ADJ-GRADED ADV: ADV with v N-UNCOUNT

jer·sey /'dʒɜːzi/ **jerseys. 1** A **jersey** is a woollen piece of clothing that covers the upper part of your body and your arms. **2 Jersey** is a knitted slightly stretchy fabric used especially to make women's clothing. *... a black jersey top.* ◆◆◇◇ N-COUNT DATED N-VAR

jest /dʒest/ **jests, jesting, jested. 1** A **jest** is something that you say that is intended to be amusing. *It was a jest rather than a reproach.* ● If you say something **in jest,** you do not mean it seriously, but want to be amusing. *It was said in jest.* **2** If you **jest,** you tell jokes or say amusing things. *He enjoyed drinking and jesting with his cronies.* ◆◇◇◇◇ N-COUNT FORMAL PHRASE VERB V FORMAL

jest·er /'dʒestə/ **jesters.** In the courts of kings and queens in medieval Europe, the **jester** was the person whose job was to do silly things in order to make people laugh. N-COUNT

Jesu·it /'dʒezjuɪt, AM 'dʒeʒuɪt/ **Jesuits.** A **Jesuit** is a Catholic priest who belongs to the Society of Jesus. ◆◇◇◇◇ N-COUNT

jet /dʒet/ **jets, jetting, jetted. 1** A **jet** is an aeroplane that is powered by jet engines. *We flew to Paris by private jet.* ● See also **jump jet. 2** If you **jet** somewhere, you travel there in a fast aeroplane. *Val will be jetting off on a two-week holiday.* **3** A **jet** of liquid or gas is a strong, fast, thin stream of it. *A jet of water.* ◆◆◇◇ N-COUNT: also by N VERB V adv/prep N-COUNT

4 Jet is a hard black stone that is used in jewellery. N-UNCOUNT

jet 'aircraft; jet aircraft is both the singular and the plural form. A **jet aircraft** is an aircraft that is powered by one or more jet engines. N-COUNT

jet 'black; also spelled **jet-black.** Something that is **jet black** is a very intense black. *...jet-black hair.* ADJ

jet 'engine, jet engines. A **jet engine** works by pushing hot air and gases out at the back. N-COUNT

'jet lag; also spelled **jetlag.** If you are suffering from **jet lag,** you feel tired and slightly confused after a long journey by aeroplane. ♦ **jet-lagged.** *I'm still a little jet-lagged.* ◆◇◇◇◇ N-UNCOUNT ADJ-GRADED

jet·liner /'dʒetlaɪnə/ **jetliners.** A **jetliner** is a large aeroplane, especially one which carries passengers. N-COUNT AMERICAN

jet·sam /'dʒetsəm/. See **flotsam.**

'jet set; also spelled **jet-set.** You can refer to rich and successful people who live in a luxurious way as the **jet set.** ♦ **jet-setting.** *...enjoying his jet-setting lifestyle.* N-SING ADJ: ADJ n

'jet stream, jet streams. The **jet stream** is a very strong wind that blows high in the earth's atmosphere and has an important influence on the weather. N-COUNT TECHNICAL

jet·ti·son /'dʒetɪsən/ **jettisons, jettisoning, jettisoned. 1** If you **jettison** something, for example an idea or a plan, you deliberately reject it or decide not to use it. *The Government seems to have jettisoned the plan.* **2** If someone **jettisons** something that is not needed, they throw it away or get rid of it. *The crew jettisoned excess fuel.* ◆◇◇◇◇ V n VERB V n

jet·ty /'dʒeti/ **jetties.** A **jetty** is a wide stone wall or wooden platform where boats stop to let people get on or off, or to load or unload goods. ◆◇◇◇◇ N-COUNT

Jew /dʒuː/ **Jews.** A **Jew** is a person who believes in and practises the religion of Judaism. *The Old Testament is a sacred book for Jews.* ♦ **Jew·ish** *...the Jewish festival of the Passover.* ♦ **Jew·ish·ness** /'dʒuːɪʃnəs/. *Its Jewishness was never quite certain.* ◆◆◆◇◇ N-COUNT ADJ N-UNCOUNT

jew·el /'dʒuːəl/ **jewels. 1** A **jewel** is a precious stone used to decorate valuable things such as rings or necklaces. *...precious jewels.* ● See also **crown jewel. 2** If you describe something or someone as a **jewel,** you mean that they are better, more beautiful, or more special than other similar things or people. *Our little jewel of a cathedral... Alan, you're a jewel.* **3** If you refer to an achievement or thing as the **jewel in** someone's **crown,** you mean that it is considered to be their greatest achievement. *This book is the jewel in his crown.* ◆◆◇◇ N-COUNT N-COUNT PHRASE

jew·elled /'dʒuːəld/; spelled **jeweled** in American English. **Jewelled** items and ornaments are decorated with precious stones. ADJ

jew·el·ler /'dʒuːələ/ **jewellers;** spelled **jeweler** in American English. **1** A **jeweller** is a person who makes, sells, and repairs jewellery and watches. **2** A **jeweller** or a **jeweller's** is a shop where jewellery and watches are made, sold, and repaired. ◆◇◇◇◇ N-COUNT N-COUNT

jew·el·lery /'dʒuːəlri/; spelled **jewelry** in American English. **Jewellery** consists of ornaments that people wear, for example rings and bracelets. ◆◆◇◇ N-UNCOUNT

Jew·ry /'dʒuəri, AM 'dʒuːri/. **Jewry** is used to refer to all the people who are Jewish, through religion or ancestry. *...the unity of world Jewry.* N-UNCOUNT FORMAL

jib /dʒɪb/ **jibs, jibbing, jibbed. 1** The **jib** is the small triangular sail that is sometimes used at the front of a sailing boat. N-COUNT

2 If you **jib** at something, you are unwilling to do it or to accept it. VERB: V at n/-ing DATED

jibe /dʒaɪb/ **jibes, jibing, jibed. 1** If someone **jibes,** they say something rude and insulting which is intended to make another person look foolish. *'No doubt he'll give me the chance to fight him again,' he jibed.* ► Also a noun. *...another cheap jibe about his loss of hair.* **2** If numbers, statements, or events **jibe,** they are exactly the same as each other or consistent with each other. *The numbers don't jibe... How did your expectations jibe with the reality?* ◆◇◇◇◇ VERB: V with quote WRITTEN N-COUNT V-RECIP: V n with n INFORMAL, AMERICAN

jif·fy /'dʒɪfi/. If you say that you will do something **in a jiffy,** you mean that you will do it very quickly or very soon. PHRASE INFORMAL

jig /dʒɪg/ **jigs, jigging, jigged. 1** A **jig** is a lively folk dance. *She hopped on the coffee table and danced an Irish jig.* **2** To **jig** means to dance or move energetically, especially bouncing up and down. *You didn't just jig about by yourself, I mean you danced properly.* ◆◇◇◇◇ N-COUNT V adv/prep Also V

jig·gle /'dʒɪgəl/ **jiggles, jiggling, jiggled. 1** If you **jiggle** something, you move it quickly up and down or from side to side. *He jiggled the doorknob noisily.* **2** If someone or something **jiggles,** they move quickly up and down or from side to side. *He tapped his feet, hummed tunes and jiggled about.* VERB V n INFORMAL VERB: V V adv INFORMAL

jig·saw /'dʒɪgsɔː/ **jigsaws. 1** A **jigsaw** or **jigsaw puzzle** is a picture on cardboard or wood that has been cut up into odd shapes and has to be put together correctly. **2** You can describe a very complicated situation as a **jigsaw.** *...the jigsaw of high-level diplomacy.* ◆◇◇◇◇ N-COUNT N-COUNT

ji·had /dʒiˈhæd, AM -ˈhɑːd/. A **jihad** is a holy war ◆◇◇◇ which Islam allows Muslims to fight against those N-SING who reject its teachings.

jilt /dʒɪlt/ **jilts, jilting, jilted.** If someone **is jilted** VERB: by the person who they are having a romantic rela- beV-ed tionship with, that person ends the relationship V n suddenly in a way which is surprising and INFORMAL upsetting. *He murdered the woman who jilted him.*

jin·gle /ˈdʒɪŋɡəl/ **jingles, jingling, jingled.** ◆◆◇◇ **1** When something **jingles**, or when you **jingle** it, it V-ERG makes a gentle ringing noise, like small bells. *Brian* V *put his hands in his pockets and jingled some change... Her bracelets jingled like bells.* ► Also a N-SING noun. *...the jingle of money in a man's pocket.* **2** A N-COUNT **jingle** is a short simple tune, often with words, which is used to advertise a product or programme on radio or television. *...advertising jingles.*

jin·go·ism /ˈdʒɪŋɡəʊɪzəm/. If you refer to people's N-UNCOUNT behaviour as **jingoism**, you disapprove of it because PRAGMATICS it shows a strong and unreasonable belief in the su- periority of their country, especially in a war against another country. ♦ **jin·go·is·tic** /ˌdʒɪŋɡəʊˈɪstɪk/. ADJ *The press continued its jingoistic display.*

jink /dʒɪŋk/ **jinks, jinking, jinked.** If someone or VERB something **jinks** somewhere, they move there V adv/prep quickly in an irregular way, rather than by moving Also V in a straight line. *As they reached the start-finish line* INFORMAL *Prost jinked right and drew abreast.* ● See also **high** BRITISH **jinks.**

jinx /dʒɪŋks/ **jinxes.** You can call something or N-COUNT someone that is considered to be unlucky or to bring bad luck a **jinx**. *He was beginning to think he was a jinx.* ♦ **jinxed** *The couple's children now be-* ADJ-GRADED *lieved their home was jinxed and want to move out as soon as possible.*

jit·ters /ˈdʒɪtəz/. If you have the **jitters**, you feel ex- ◆◇◇◇ tremely nervous, for example because you have to N-PLURAL do something important. *I had a case of the jitters* INFORMAL *during my first two speeches.*

jit·tery /ˈdʒɪtəri/. If you say that someone is **jittery**, ◆◇◇◇ you mean that they feel nervous or are showing ADJ-GRADED signs of nervousness. *International investors have* INFORMAL *become jittery about the country's economy.*

jive /dʒaɪv/ **jives, jiving, jived.** If you **jive**, you VERB dance energetically, especially to jazz music or to V rock and roll. *I learnt to jive there when they got the* INFORMAL *jukebox.*

Jnr. **Jnr** is a written abbreviation for 'Junior' that is ◆◇◇◇ used after a man's name to distinguish him from an BRITISH older member of his family with the same name. In American English, the abbreviation **Jr.** is used.

job /dʒɒb/ **jobs. 1** A **job** is the work that someone ◆◆◆◆ does to earn money. *Once I'm in America I can get a* N-COUNT *job... Thousands have lost their jobs... I felt the pres- sure of being the first woman in the job.* **2** A **job** is a N-COUNT particular task. *He said he hoped that the job of put- ting together a coalition wouldn't take too much time... Save major painting jobs for the spring or summer.* **3** The **job** of a particular person or thing is N-COUNT their duty or function. *Their main job is to preserve health rather than treat illness... Drinking a lot helps the kidneys do their job.* **4** If you say that someone is doing a good **job**, or is N-SING making a good **job** of something, you mean that they are doing it well. *We could do a far better job of man- aging it than they have.* **5** If you say that you have a **job** N-SING doing something, you are emphasizing how difficult it PRAGMATICS is. *With all these different pensions, you're going to have a job to keep track.* **6** See also **jobbing**; **hatchet job, on-the-job. 7** If you refer to work as **jobs for the boys**, you mean PHRASE that the work is unfairly given to someone's friends, PRAGMATICS supporters, or relations, even though they may not be BRITISH the best qualified people to do it. *The Party has been accused of creating a 'jobs for the boys' system of gov- ernment.* **8** If you say that something is **just the job**, PHRASE you mean that it is exactly what you wanted or need- BRITISH, ed. *Not only is it just the job for travelling, but it's* INFORMAL *handy for groceries too.* **9** If someone is **on the job**, PHRASE they are actually doing a particular job or task. *There*

was no formal training; they learned on the job. **10** ● **it's a good job**: see **good.** ● **the job in hand**: see **hand.**

job·bing /ˈdʒɒbɪŋ/. A **jobbing** worker does not work ADJ: ADJ n for someone on a regular basis, but does particular BRITISH jobs when they are asked to. *...a jobbing builder.*

'job centre, job centres; also spelled **jobcentre.** N-COUNT A **job centre** is a place where people who are look- BRITISH ing for work can go to get advice on finding a job, and to look at adverts placed by employers.

job·less /ˈdʒɒbləs/. Someone who is **jobless** does ◆◆◇◇ not have a job, although they would like one. *...the* ADJ *number of jobless people.* ► The **jobless** are people N-PLURAL: who are jobless. *...a new training scheme for the job-* theN *less.* ♦ **job·less·ness** *Concern over the rising level* N-UNCOUNT *of joblessness was a feature of yesterday's debate.*

job 'lot, job lots. A **job lot** is a number of similar N-COUNT things which are sold together cheaply, for example in an auction. *I was lucky to get it as part of a job lot at a sale.*

'job seeker, job seekers. The term **job seeker** is N-COUNT sometimes used by the government and journalists to refer to a jobless person.

'job sharing. **Job sharing** is the arrangement by N-UNCOUNT which two people share the same job by working part-time, for example one person working in the mornings and the other in the afternoons.

jock /dʒɒk/ **jocks. 1** A **jock** is a young man who is N-COUNT very enthusiastic about a particular sport or other INFORMAL activity, and spends a lot of time doing it or in- volved with it. *...an all-American football jock.* **2** A N-COUNT **jock** is the same as a **disc jockey.** *...top Radio 1 jock* INFORMAL *Simon Bates.*

jock·ey /ˈdʒɒki/ **jockeys, jockeying, jockeyed.** ◆◆◇◇ **1** A **jockey** is someone who rides a horse in a race. N-COUNT **2** If you say that someone **is jockeying** for some- VERB thing, you mean that they are using whatever meth- V for n ods they can in order to gain an advantage over V to-inf their rivals. *As the big phone companies jockey for position, the real winners will be the customers... Both sides are jockeying to belittle the other side.*

jock·strap /ˈdʒɒkstræp/ **jockstraps.** A **jockstrap** is N-COUNT a piece of clothing worn by sportsmen under their shorts or trousers to support their genitals.

jocu·lar /ˈdʒɒkjʊlə/. If you say that someone has a ADJ-GRADED **jocular** manner, you mean that they are cheerful FORMAL and often make jokes. *The song was written in a light-hearted jocular way.*

jodh·purs /ˈdʒɒdpəz/. **Jodhpurs** are trousers that N-PLURAL people wear when they ride a horse. Jodhpurs are usually loose from the thigh to the knee and tight below the knee.

jog /dʒɒɡ/ **jogs, jogging, jogged. 1** If you **jog**, ◆◇◇◇ you run slowly, often as a form of exercise. *I got up* VERB early the next morning to jog.* ► Also a noun. *He* V *went for another early morning jog.* ♦ **jog·ging** *It* N-COUNT *isn't the walking and jogging that got his weight* N-UNCOUNT *down.* ♦ **jog·ger, joggers.** *The park was full of* N-COUNT *joggers.* **2** If you **jog** something, you push or bump VERB it slightly so that it moves. *Avoid jogging the camera.* V n **3** If something or someone **jogs** your **memory**, they PHRASE cause you to suddenly remember something that you had forgotten. *Police have planned a recon- struction of the crime tomorrow in the hope this will jog the memory of passers-by.*

joie de vi·vre /ˌʒwɑː də ˈviːvrə/. **Joie de vivre** is a N-UNCOUNT feeling of happiness and enjoyment of life. *He has* LITERARY *plenty of joie de vivre.*

join /dʒɔɪn/ **joins, joining, joined. 1** If one per- ◆◆◆◆ son or vehicle **joins** another, they move or go to the VERB same place, for example so that both of them can V n do something together. *His wife and children moved to join him in their new home.* **2** If you **join** an or- VERB ganization, you become a member of it or start V n work as an employee of it. *He joined the Army five years ago.* **3** If you **join** an activity that other people VERB: V n are doing, you take part in it or become involved V n inn/-ing with it. *The pastor requested the women present to* V in -ing *join him in prayer... Last night the group which rep- resents private contractors joined in condemning the*

J

Government's confused stance. **4** If you **join** a queue, you stand at the end of it. *Make sure you join the queue inside the bank.* `VERB V n`

5 To **join** two things means to fix or fasten them together. *...the conjunctiva, the skin which joins the eye to the lid. ...two springs that are joined together by a string.* ▶ Also a noun. *The joins have been carefully concealed.* **6** If something such as a line or path **joins** two things, it connects them. *The car parks are joined by a footpath. ...a global highway of cables joining all the continents together.* **7** If two roads or rivers **join**, or if one road or river **joins** another, the two meet or come together at a particular point. *Do you know the highway to Tulsa? The airport road joins it.* **8** ● **join forces**: see **force**. ● **join the ranks**: see **rank**. `VERB: V pl-n V n prep/adv` `N-COUNT` `VERB: V pl-n beV-ed V-ing` `V-RECIP: pl-n V V n`

join in. If you **join in** an activity, you take part in it or become involved in it. *The songs the woman will sing will be known by everyone present and all will join in as she sings.* `PHRASAL VB V P n V P`

join up. 1 If someone **joins up**, they become a member of the army, the navy, or the air force. *When hostilities broke out he returned to England and joined up.* **2** If a person or thing **joins up** with another, they move or go to the same place. *Hawkins joined up with Mick in Malaga, and the two went touring around the countryside... They began to join up in communities and to contribute to the livelihood of other communities.* `PHRASAL VB V P BRITISH RECIP V P with n pl-n V P`

join·er /ˈdʒɔɪnə/ **joiners.** A **joiner** is a person who makes wooden window frames, door frames, doors, and cabinets. Compare **carpenter**. `N-COUNT BRITISH`

join·ery /ˈdʒɔɪnəri/. **Joinery** is the skill and work of a joiner. `N-UNCOUNT BRITISH`

joint /dʒɔɪnt/ **joints. 1 Joint** means shared by or belonging to two or more people. *She and Frank had never gotten around to opening a joint account.* ◆ **joint·ly** *The Port Authority is an agency jointly run by New York and New Jersey.* `◆◆◆◇ ADJ: ADJ n` `ADV: ADV with v`

2 A **joint** is a part of your body such as your elbow or knee where two bones meet and are able to move together. *Her joints ache if she exercises.* **3** If something puts someone's **nose out of joint**, it upsets or offends them because it makes them feel less important or less valued. *Her sister-in-law's nose is a little out of joint.* **4** If something is **out of joint**, it is not quite right or appropriate, or does not work quite as it should. *The electoral timetable seems to be out of joint with the need for change.* `N-COUNT` `PHRASE INFORMAL` `PHRASE`

5 A **joint** is the place where two things are fastened or fixed together. ● **dovetail joint**: see **dovetail**. **6** A **joint** is a fairly large piece of meat which is suitable for roasting. The usual American word is **roast**. *He carved the joint of beef.* **7** You can refer to a place where people go for some form of entertainment as a **joint**. *She had always wanted to eat in a hamburger joint in Hollywood.* **8** A **joint** is a cigarette which contains cannabis. `N-COUNT` `N-COUNT BRITISH` `N-COUNT INFORMAL` `N-COUNT INFORMAL`

joint·ed /ˈdʒɔɪntɪd/. Something that is **jointed** has joints that move. *The glass cover for this is cleverly jointed in the middle.* `ADJ`

joint-'stock company, joint-stock companies. A **joint-stock company** is a business whose shares can be bought by members of the public. `N-COUNT TECHNICAL`

joist /dʒɔɪst/ **joists.** Joists are long thick pieces of metal, wood, or concrete that form part of the structure which supports a building. `N-COUNT`

jo·jo·ba /həʊˈhəʊbə/. **Jojoba** or **jojoba oil** is oil which is made from the seeds of the jojoba plant. Jojoba oil is used in many cosmetics. `N-UNCOUNT`

joke /dʒəʊk/ **jokes, joking, joked. 1** If you **joke**, you tell funny stories or say amusing things. *She would joke about her appearance... Lorna was laughing and joking with Trevor... The project was taking so long that Stephen joked that it would never be finished.* ▶ Also a noun. *He made a joke about poisoning his wife.* ◆ **jok·er** /ˈdʒəʊkə/ **jokers.** He is, by nature, a joker, a witty man with a sense of fun. `◆◆◇◇ VERB V about n V with n V that Also V with quote N-COUNT` `N-COUNT`

2 If you **joke**, you tell someone something that is not true in order to amuse yourself. *Don't get defensive, Charlie. I was only joking... 'I wish you made as* `VERB V V with quote`

much fuss of me,' Vera joked, going into the scullery to make some fresh tea. ▶ Also a noun. *It was probably just a joke to them, but it wasn't funny to me.* **3** If you say that something or someone is **a joke**, you think they are ridiculous and not worthy of respect. *The police investigation was a joke. A total cover-up.* `N-COUNT` `N-SING: a N PRAGMATICS INFORMAL`

4 If you say that an annoying or worrying situation is **beyond a joke**, you are emphasizing that you do not think it is fair or reasonable. *I'm not afraid of a fair fight but this is beginning to get beyond a joke.* **5** If you describe a situation as **no joke**, you are emphasizing that it is very difficult or unpleasant. *Two hours on a bus is no joke, is it.* **6** If you **make a joke of** something, you laugh at it even though it is in fact rather serious or sad. *I wish I had your courage, Michael, to make a joke of it like that.* **7** If you say that **the joke is on** a particular person, you mean that they have been made to look very foolish. *'For once,' he said, 'the joke's on me. And it's not very funny.'* **8** You say **you're joking** or **you must be joking** to someone when they have just told you something very surprising or difficult to believe. *One hundred and forty quid for a pair of headphones, you've got to be joking!* `PHRASE PRAGMATICS BRITISH` `PHRASE PRAGMATICS INFORMAL` `PHRASE` `PHRASE` `CONVENTION PRAGMATICS SPOKEN`

jok·er /ˈdʒəʊkə/ **jokers. 1** The **joker** in a pack of playing cards is the card which does not belong to any of the four suits. **2** If you describe someone or something as **the joker in the pack**, you mean that they are different from the other people or things in their group, and can be unpredictable. `◆◇◇◇ N-COUNT` `PHRASE`

jok·ey /ˈdʒəʊki/. If something is done in a **jokey** way, it is intended to be amusing, rather than serious. *He was still his old jokey self.* `ADJ-GRADED INFORMAL, BRITISH`

jok·ing·ly /ˈdʒəʊkɪŋli/. If you say or do something **jokingly**, you do it with the intention of amusing someone, rather than with any serious meaning or intention. *Sarah jokingly called her 'my monster'.* `ADV: ADV with v`

jol·lity /ˈdʒɒlɪti/. **Jollity** is cheerful behaviour. *...the singing and jollity of the celebration.* `N-UNCOUNT DATED`

jol·ly /ˈdʒɒli/ **jollier, jolliest. 1** Someone who is **jolly** is happy and cheerful in their appearance or behaviour. *She was a jolly, kind-hearted woman.* **2** A **jolly** event is lively and enjoyable. *I was looking forward to a jolly party.* `◆◆◇◇ ADJ-GRADED` `ADJ-GRADED`

3 You can use **jolly** to give emphasis to an adjective or adverb. *It was jolly hard work, but I loved it... The captain was a jolly nice chap.* **4** You use **jolly well** to emphasize what you are saying, especially when you are annoyed or angry. *She was jolly well not going to let them get away with it.* `ADV: ADV adj/adv BRITISH PHRASE BRITISH, DATED`

jolt /dʒəʊlt/ **jolts, jolting, jolted. 1** If something **jolts**, or if something **jolts** it, it moves suddenly and quite violently. *The train jolted into motion... They were working frantically in the fear that an aftershock would jolt the house again.* ▶ Also a noun. *We were worried that one tiny jolt could worsen her injuries.* **2** If something **jolts** someone, it gives them an unpleasant surprise or shock. *Henderson was momentarily jolted by the news... It is tragic that it needs deaths to jolt authorities into action... She had drifted into a light sleep when an uproar from the hallway jolted her awake.* ▶ Also a noun. *The campaign came at a time when America needed such a jolt.* `◆◇◇◇ V-ERG: V V prep V n` `N-COUNT` `VERB: V n beV-ed V n prep V n adj` `N-COUNT`

jos·tle /ˈdʒɒsəl/ **jostles, jostling, jostled. 1** If people **jostle** you, they bump against you or push you in a way that annoys you, usually when you are in a crowd. *We spent an hour jostling with the crowds as we did our shopping... She was cheered and clapped by tourists who jostled to see her... Mari elbowed and jostled her way through the crowd.* **2** If people or things **are jostling for** something such as attention or a reward, they are competing with other people or things for it. *...the contenders who have been jostling for the top job.* `◆◇◇◇ VERB: V n V prep/adv V to-inf Also V n prep/adv` `VERB V for n`

jot /dʒɒt/ **jots, jotting, jotted. 1** If you **jot** something short such as an address somewhere, you write it down so that you will remember it. *Could you just jot his name on there.* ▶ **Jot down** means the same as **jot**. *Keep a pad handy to jot down que-* `◆◇◇◇ VERB V n prep/adv` `PHRASAL VB V P noun V n P`

ries as they occur... Listen carefully to the instructions and jot them down. **2** If you say that there is not **a jot** or not **one jot** of something, you are emphasizing that there is not even a very small amount of it. *It makes not one jot of difference.* **3** Not **a jot** or **not one jot** means not even to a small extent or degree. *It doesn't affect my judgement one jot.* QUANT PRAGMATICS DATED / PHRASE PRAGMATICS DATED

jot·ting /'dʒɒtɪŋ/ **jottings. Jottings** are brief informal notes that you write down. N-COUNT

joule /dʒuːl/ **joules.** A **joule** is a unit of energy or work. N-COUNT TECHNICAL

jour·nal /'dʒɜːnəl/ **journals. 1** A **journal** is a magazine, especially one that deals with a specialized subject. *All our results are published in scientific journals.* **2** A **journal** is a daily or weekly newspaper. *He was a newspaperman for The New York Times and some other journals. ...The Wall Street Journal.* **3** A **journal** is an account which you write of your daily activities. *On the plane he wrote in his journal.* N-COUNT / N-COUNT / N-COUNT

jour·nal·ism /'dʒɜːnəlɪzəm/. **Journalism** is the job of collecting news or other information, and writing about it in newspapers or magazines or talking about it on television or radio. *He began a career in journalism, working for the North London Press Group. ...an accomplished piece of investigative journalism.* N-UNCOUNT

jour·nal·ist /'dʒɜːnəlɪst/ **journalists.** A **journalist** is a person whose job is to collect news or other information, and write about it in newspapers or magazines or talk about it on television or radio. ♦ **jour·nal·is·tic** /,dʒɜːnə'lɪstɪk/. *He began his journalistic career in the early eighties in Australia. ...journalistic descriptions of countries they visited.* N-COUNT / ADJ: ADJ n

jour·ney /'dʒɜːni/ **journeys, journeying, journeyed. 1** When you make a **journey**, you travel from one place to another. *There is an express service from Paris which completes the journey to Bordeaux in under 4 hours.* **2** You can refer to a person's experience of changing or developing from one state of mind to another as a **journey**. *My films try to describe a journey of discovery, both for myself and the watcher.* **3** If you **journey** somewhere, you travel there. *In February 1935, Naomi journeyed to the United States for the first time... She has journeyed on horseback through Africa and Turkey.* N-COUNT / N-COUNT: with supp / VERB V to n V prep/adv FORMAL

journey·man /'dʒɜːnimən/ **journeymen. 1** In former times, a **journeyman** was a worker who had finished learning a trade and who was employed by someone else rather than working on his or her own. **2** If you refer to someone, especially a sportsman or woman or an entertainer, as a **journeyman**, you mean that they have the basic skill which their job requires, but that they do not have much talent or originality. *Douglas was a 29-year-old journeyman fighter, erratic in his previous fights.* N-COUNT / N-COUNT JOURNALISM

jour·no /'dʒɜːnəʊ/ **journos.** A **journo** is a journalist. *Hundreds of journos jammed themselves onto the boat.* N-COUNT INFORMAL BRITISH

joust /dʒaʊst/ **jousts, jousting, jousted. 1** When two or more people or organizations **joust**, they compete with each other for superiority. *The image of the white bishop jousting with the oppressive tyranny of bureaucrats, oligarchs and politicians is tempting.* ► Also a noun. *There were notable jousts with the Secretary of Commerce.* **2** In medieval times, when two knights on horseback **jousted**, they fought against each other using lances. *Knights joust and frolic.* ♦ **joust·ing** *...medieval jousting tournaments.* V-RECIP pl-n V V with n LITERARY / N-COUNT / V-RECIP pl-n V Also V with n / N-UNCOUNT

jo·vial /'dʒəʊviəl/. If you describe a person as **jovial**, you mean that they are happy and behave in a cheerful way. *Father Whittaker appeared to be in a jovial mood.* ♦ **jo·vi·al·ly** *'No problem,' he said jovially... Both men hooted jovially, clapping him on the back.* ADJ-GRADED WRITTEN / ADV-GRADED: ADV with v

jowl /dʒaʊl/ **jowls. 1** You can refer to someone's lower cheeks as their **jowls**, especially when they hang down and cover their jawbones. **2** If you say N-COUNT LITERARY / PHRASE

that people or things are **cheek by jowl** with each other, you are indicating that they are very close to each other. *She and her family have to live cheek by jowl with these people.*

joy /dʒɔɪ/ **joys. 1 Joy** is a feeling of great happiness. *Salter shouted with joy... He broke down and wept tears of joy.* **2** A **joy** is something or someone that makes you feel happy or gives you great pleasure. *That is one of the joys of being a chef... It was a joy to see her looking so well.* **3** If you get no **joy**, you do not have success or luck in achieving what you are trying to do. *If you don't get any joy, get in touch with your local councillor.* **4** If you say that someone **is jumping for joy**, you mean that they are very pleased or happy about something. *He jumped for joy on being told the news.* ● one's **pride and joy**: see **pride**. ♦♦♦◇◇ N-UNCOUNT / N-COUNT: with supp / N-UNCOUNT: with brd-neg INFORMAL, BRITISH PHRASE

joy·ful /'dʒɔɪfʊl/. **1** Something that is **joyful** causes happiness and pleasure. *A wedding is a joyful celebration of love.* **2** Someone who is **joyful** is extremely happy. *His staff are well spoken, articulate, joyful people who know what they are talking about.* ♦ **joy·ful·ly** *They greeted him joyfully.* ♦◇◇◇ ADJ-GRADED FORMAL / ADJ-GRADED FORMAL / ADV-GRADED

joy·less /'dʒɔɪləs/. Something that is **joyless** produces no happiness or pleasure. *Eating in East Berlin used to be a hazardous and joyless experience.* ADJ-GRADED FORMAL

joy·ous /'dʒɔɪəs/. **Joyous** means extremely happy. *She had made their childhood so joyous and carefree. ...a joyous celebration of life.* ♦ **joy·ous·ly** *Sarah accepted joyously.* ♦◇◇◇ ADJ-GRADED LITERARY / ADV-GRADED

joy·rid·ing /'dʒɔɪraɪdɪŋ/. **Joyriding** is the crime of stealing a car and driving around in it at high speed. ♦ **joy·ride** /'dʒɔɪraɪd/ **joyrides.** *Thieves took a bus on a 400-mile joyride before dumping it.* ♦ **joy·rider, joyriders** *They have not put off the more determined joyrider.* ♦◇◇◇ N-UNCOUNT / N-COUNT / N-COUNT

joy·stick /'dʒɔɪstɪk/ **joysticks. 1** In some computer games, the **joystick** is the lever which the player uses in order to control the direction of the things on the screen. **2** In an aeroplane, the **joystick** is the lever which the pilot uses in order to control the direction and height of the aeroplane. N-COUNT / N-COUNT INFORMAL

JP /,dʒeɪ 'piː/ **JPs.** In Britain, a **JP** is a Justice of the Peace. N-COUNT

Jr. Jr. is a written abbreviation for **Junior**. It is used after a man's name to distinguish him from an older member of his family with the same name. *...Harry Connick Jr.* ♦♦◇◇◇ AMERICAN

ju·bi·lant /'dʒuːbɪlənt/. If you are **jubilant**, you feel extremely happy because of a success. *...the jubilant crowds of Paris.* ♦◇◇◇ ADJ-GRADED

ju·bi·la·tion /,dʒuːbɪ'leɪʃən/. **Jubilation** is a feeling of great happiness and triumph, because of a success. *His resignation was greeted by jubilation on the streets of Sofia.* N-UNCOUNT FORMAL

ju·bi·lee /'dʒuːbɪliː/ **jubilees.** A **jubilee** is a special anniversary of an event, especially the 25th or 50th anniversary. *...Queen Victoria's jubilee.* ● See also **golden jubilee, silver jubilee.** ♦◇◇◇ N-COUNT

Ju·da·ic /dʒuː'deɪɪk/. **Judaic** means belonging or relating to Judaism. ADJ: ADJ n FORMAL

Ju·da·ism /'dʒuːdeɪɪzəm/. **Judaism** is the religion of the Jewish people. It is based on the Old Testament of the Bible and the Talmud. ♦◇◇◇ N-UNCOUNT

jud·der /'dʒʌdə/ **judders, juddering, juddered.** If something **judders**, it shakes and vibrates rather violently. *The lift started off, juddered, and went out of action.* VERB V

judge /dʒʌdʒ/ **judges, judging, judged. 1** A **judge** is the person in a court of law who decides how the law should be applied, for example how criminals should be punished. *Judge Mr Justice Schiemann jailed him for life.* **2** A **judge** is a person who decides who will be the winner of a competition. *A panel of judges is now selecting the finalists.* **3** If you **judge** something such as a competition, you decide who or what is the winner. *Francine Lawrence will judge the competition... Entrants will be judged in two age categories: 5-10 years and 11-14 years... Len Kelly, who judged with Ron Thumwood,* ♦♦♦◇ N-COUNT; N-TITLE / N-COUNT / VERB V n be V-ed V

said he was surprised at the good condition of the birds. ◆ **judg·ing** *The judging was difficult as always.* N-UNCOUNT

4 If you **judge** something or someone, you form an opinion about them after you have examined the evidence or thought carefully about them. *I am ready to judge any book on its merits... It's for other people to judge how much I have improved... He judged that this was the moment to say what had to be said... The UN withdrew its relief personnel because it judged the situation too dangerous.* **5** If you **judge** something, you guess its amount, size, or value or you guess what it is. *I judged him to be about forty... Though the shoreline could be dimly seen, it was impossible to judge how far away it was.* VERB: V n, V n onn, V wh, V that, V n adj, Also V n to-inf / VERB: V n, V n to-inf, V wh, Also V that

6 If someone is a good **judge** of something, they understand it and can make sensible decisions about it. If someone is a bad **judge** of something, they cannot do this. *It would appear that my sister is a poor judge of masculine charm.* **7** You use **judging by**, **judging from**, or **to judge from** to introduce the reasons why you believe or think something. *Judging by the opinion polls, he seems to be succeeding... To judge from his productivity, Mozart clearly enjoyed robust good health throughout his twenties.* N-COUNT / PHR-PREP PRAGMATICS

judg·ment /ˈdʒʌdʒmənt/ **judgments**; also spelled **judgement** in British English. **1** A **judgment** is an opinion that you have or express after thinking carefully about something. *In your judgment, what has changed over the past few years?... I don't really want to make any judgments on the decisions they made.* **2** **Judgment** is the ability to make sensible guesses about a situation or sensible decisions about what to do. *He said that publication of the information was a serious error in judgment.* **3** A **judgment** is a decision made by a judge or by a court of law. *The industry was awaiting a judgment from the European Court.* ◆◆◆◇◇ N-VAR / N-UNCOUNT / N-VAR

4 If something is **against** your **better judgment**, you believe that it would be more sensible or better not to do it. *Against my better judgement I agreed.* **5** If you **pass judgment** on someone or something, you give your opinion about it, especially if you are making a criticism. *It's not for me to pass judgment, it's a personal matter between the two of you.* **6** If you **reserve judgment** on something, you refuse to give an opinion about it until you know more about it. *Doctors are reserving judgement on his ability to travel until later in the week.* **7** To **sit in judgment** means to decide whether or not someone is guilty of doing something wrong. *He argues very strongly that none of us has the right to sit in judgement.* PHRASE / PHRASE / PHRASE / PHRASE

judg·men·tal /ˌdʒʌdʒˈmentəl/; also spelled **judgemental** in British English. If you say that someone is **judgmental**, you are critical of them because they form opinions on people and situations very quickly, when it would be better for them to wait until they know more about the person or situation. *You should not be judgemental about people and their differing sexualities.* ADJ-GRADED PRAGMATICS

ju·di·cial /dʒuːˈdɪʃəl/. **Judicial** means relating to the legal system and to judgements made in a court of law. *...an independent judicial inquiry... The last judicial hanging in Britain was in 1964.* ◆◆◇◇◇ ADJ: ADJ n ◆ **ju·di·cial·ly** *Even if the amendment is passed it can be defeated judicially.* ADV: ADV with v

ju·di·ci·ary /dʒuːˈdɪʃəri, AM -ʃeri/. The **judiciary** is the branch of authority in a country which is concerned with justice and the legal system. *The judiciary must think very hard before jailing non-violent offenders.* ◆◇◇◇◇ N-SING: the N FORMAL

ju·di·cious /dʒuːˈdɪʃəs/. If you describe an action or decision as **judicious**, you approve of it because you think that it shows good judgment and sense. *The President authorizes the judicious use of military force to protect our citizens.* ◆◇◇◇◇ ADJ-GRADED PRAGMATICS FORMAL ◆ **ju·di·cious·ly** *Modern fertilisers should be used judiciously.* ADV-GRADED: ADV with v

judo /ˈdʒuːdəʊ/. **Judo** is a Japanese sport or martial art in which two people wrestle and try to throw each other to the ground. ◆◇◇◇◇ N-UNCOUNT

jug /dʒʌɡ/ **jugs.** A **jug** is a cylindrical container with a handle and a lip or spout, used for holding and pouring liquids. ▶ A **jug** of liquid is the amount that the jug contains. *...a jug of water.* ◆◇◇◇◇ N-COUNT / N-COUNT

jug·ger·naut /ˈdʒʌɡənɔːt/ **juggernauts.** **1** A **juggernaut** is a very large lorry. *...attempts to curb the number of juggernaut lorries passing through the Alps.* **2** If you describe an organization or group as a **juggernaut**, you are critical of them because they are large and extremely powerful, and you think they are not being controlled properly. N-COUNT BRITISH / N-COUNT PRAGMATICS

jug·gle /ˈdʒʌɡəl/ **juggles, juggling, juggled.** **1** If you say that you **juggle** lots of different things, for example your work and your family, you are indicating that it is difficult to fit them all in so that you have enough time for all of them. *Mike juggled the demands of a family of 11 with a career as a TV reporter.* **2** If you **juggle**, you entertain people by throwing things into the air, catching each one and throwing it up again so that there are several of them in the air at the same time. *Soon she was juggling five eggs.* ◆ **jug·gl·ing** *...mime and juggling.* ◆ **jug·gler, jugglers** *David was a professional juggler and performer.* ◆◇◇◇◇ VERB: V n, V n with n, Also V with n / VERB: V, V n / N-UNCOUNT / N-COUNT

'juggling act, juggling acts. If you say that a situation is a **juggling act**, you mean that someone is trying to do two or more things at once, and finding it difficult to do them properly. *Her life became a juggling act. She had to look after the family and the home, and she had a part-time job as well.* N-COUNT

jugu·lar /ˈdʒʌɡjʊlə/ **jugulars.** **1** A **jugular** or **jugular** vein is one of the three important veins in your neck that carry blood from your head back to your heart. **2** If you say that someone **went for the jugular**, you mean that they ruthlessly attacked another person's weakest points. *Mr Black went for the jugular, asking intimate sexual questions.* N-COUNT / PHRASE INFORMAL

juice /dʒuːs/ **juices.** **1** **Juice** is the liquid that can be obtained from a fruit. *...a glass of fresh orange juice.* **2** The **juices** of a joint of meat are the liquid that comes out of it when you cook it. **3** The **juices** in your stomach are the fluids that help you to digest food. ◆◆◆◇◇ N-VAR / N-PLURAL / N-PLURAL: with supp

juicy /ˈdʒuːsi/ **juicier, juiciest.** **1** If food is **juicy**, it has a lot of juice in it and is very enjoyable to eat. *...a thick, juicy steak.* **2** You can describe information as **juicy** if it is exciting or scandalous. *It provided some juicy gossip for a few days.* ◆◇◇◇◇ ADJ-GRADED / ADJ-GRADED INFORMAL

juke·box /ˈdʒuːkbɒks/ **jukeboxes**; also spelled **juke box.** A **jukebox** is a record player in a place such as a pub or a bar. You put a coin in and choose the record you want to hear. N-COUNT

Jul. **Jul.** is a written abbreviation for **July.** ◆◆◇◇◇

July /dʒuˈlaɪ/ **Julys.** **July** is the seventh month of the year in the Western calendar. See Appendix headed **Dates.** ◆◆◆◇◇ N-VAR

jum·ble /ˈdʒʌmbəl/ **jumbles, jumbling, jumbled.** **1** A **jumble** of things is a lot of different things that are all mixed together in a disorganized or confused way. *...a jumble of huge boulders. ...a meaningless jumble of words.* **2** If you **jumble** things, or if they **jumble**, they become mixed together so that they are untidy or not in the correct order. *They jumble together shampoos, toys, chocolate, clothes, electronic goods and hair slides... Jumble spots and stripes to build a whole spectrum of blues... His thoughts jumbled and raced.* ▶ To **jumble up** means the same as to **jumble**. *They had jumbled it all up into a heap... The watch parts fell apart and jumbled up. ...wires jumbled up, tied together, all painted black.* **3** **Jumble** consists of old or unwanted things that people give away to charity. The American word is **rummage.** ◆◇◇◇◇ N-COUNT / V-ERG V n with together V n, V / PHRASAL VB ERG V n P V P / N-UNCOUNT BRITISH

jum·bled /ˈdʒʌmbəld/. If you describe things or ideas as **jumbled**, you mean that they are mixed up and not in order. ADJ-GRADED

'jumble sale, jumble sales. A **jumble sale** is a sale of cheap second-hand goods, usually held to raise money for charity. The usual American expression is **rummage sale.** N-COUNT BRITISH

jum·bo /'dʒʌmbəʊ/ **jumbos. 1** In advertising and in the names of products, very large products are sometimes described as **jumbo** products. ...*a jumbo box of tissues.* **2** A **jumbo** or a **jumbo jet** is a very large jet aeroplane that can carry several hundred passengers. ◆◇◇◇◇ ADJ: ADJ n / N-COUNT

jump /dʒʌmp/ **jumps, jumping, jumped. 1** If you **jump**, you bend your knees, push against the ground with your feet, and move quickly upwards into the air. *I jumped over the fence... I'd jumped seventeen feet six in the long jump, which was a school record.* ▶ Also a noun. ...*the longest jumps by a man.* **2** If you **jump** from something above the ground, you deliberately push yourself into the air so that you drop towards the ground. *He jumped out of a third-floor window... I jumped the last six feet down to the deck.* **3** If you **jump** something such as a fence, you move quickly up and through the air over or across it. *He jumped the first fence beautifully.* **4** If you **jump** somewhere, you move there quickly and suddenly. *She jumped to her feet and ran downstairs.* **5** If something makes you **jump**, it makes you make a sudden movement because you are frightened or surprised. *The phone shrilled, making her jump.* **6** If an amount or level **jumps**, it suddenly increases or rises by a large amount in a short time. *Sales jumped from $94 million to over $101 million... The number of crimes jumped by ten per cent last year.* ▶ Also a noun. ...*a big jump in energy conservation.* **7** If someone **jumps** a queue, they move to the front of it and are served or dealt with before it is their turn. **8** If someone **jumps** you, or **jumps** on you, they attack you suddenly. *One of them jumped him from behind... A week later, the same guys jumped on me on our own front lawn.* **9** If someone **jumps on** you, they quickly criticize you if you do something that they do not approve of. *A lot of people jumped on me about that.* **10** If you **jump at** an offer or opportunity, you accept it quickly and eagerly. *Members of the public would jump at the chance to become part owners.* **11** If you say that someone is **jumping up and down**, you mean they are very excited, happy, or angry about something. **12** See also **bungee jumping**, **high jump**, **long jump**, **show jumping**, **triple jump**. **13** • to **jump bail**: see **bail**. • to **jump on the bandwagon**: see **bandwagon**. • to **jump to a conclusion**: see **conclusion**. • to **jump the gun**: see **gun**. • to **jump for joy**: see **joy**. ◆◆◆◇
VERB V prep/adv V n Also V / N-COUNT / VERB V prep/adv V n Also V / VERB V n / VERB V prep/adv / VERB V / VERB V to/from amount V by amount Also V amount / N-COUNT / VERB: V n BRITISH / VERB V n V on n INFORMAL / VERB V on n / VB: no cont V at n / PHRASE

jump in. If you **jump in**, you act quickly and decisively, often without thinking much about what you are doing. *The Government had to jump in and purchase millions of dollars worth of supplies.* PHRASAL VB V P

jump out. If you say that something **jumps out** at you, you mean that it is easy to notice it because it is different from other things of its type. *Every so often one letter will jump out at you as being a bit different.* PHRASAL VB V P Also V P

jumped-'up. If you describe someone as **jumped-up**, you disapprove of them because they consider themselves to be more important than they really are. *He's nothing better than a jumped-up bank clerk!* ◆◇◇◇◇ ADJ PRAGMATICS BRITISH, INFORMAL

jump·er /'dʒʌmpə/ **jumpers. 1** A **jumper** is a warm knitted piece of clothing which covers the upper part of your body and your arms. See picture headed **clothes**. ...*a knitted woolly jumper.* **2** A **jumper** is a sleeveless dress that is worn over a blouse or sweater. The usual British word is **pinafore**. See picture headed **clothes**. **3** If you refer to a person or a horse as a particular kind of **jumper**, you are describing how good they are at jumping or the way that they jump. *He is a terrific athlete and a brilliant jumper.* ◆◆◇◇◇ N-COUNT BRITISH / N-COUNT AMERICAN / N-COUNT

jumping-'off point. A **jumping-off point** is a place, situation, or occasion which you use as the starting point for something. ...*a bustling market town and the best jumping-off point for a first visit to Le Gers.* N-SING

jump jet, jump jets. A **jump jet** is a jet aircraft that can take off and land vertically. N-COUNT BRITISH

jump·suit /'dʒʌmpsuːt/ **jumpsuits.** A **jumpsuit** is a piece of clothing in the form of a top and trousers in one continuous piece. N-COUNT

jumpy /'dʒʌmpi/. If you are **jumpy**, you are nervous or worried about something. *When he spoke his voice was jumpy.* ADJ-GRADED INFORMAL

Jun. **Jun.** is a written abbreviation for **June**. ◆◆◇◇◇

junc·tion /'dʒʌŋkʃən/ **junctions.** A **junction** is a place where roads or railway lines join. In American English, the more usual word is **intersection**. *Follow the road to a junction and turn left. ...Clapham Junction.* ◆◆◇◇◇ N-COUNT

junc·ture /'dʒʌŋktʃə/ **junctures.** At a particular **juncture** means at a particular point in time, especially when it is a very important time in a series of events. *What's important at this juncture is the ability of the three republics to work together.* N-COUNT

June /dʒuːn/ **Junes.** **June** is the sixth month of the year in the Western calendar. See Appendix headed **Dates**. *He spent two and a half weeks with us in June 1986.* ◆◆◆◇ N-VAR

jun·gle /'dʒʌŋgəl/ **jungles. 1** A **jungle** is a forest in a tropical country where large numbers of tall trees and plants grow very close together. ...*the mountains and jungles of Papua New Guinea.* **2** If you describe a situation as a **jungle**, you dislike it because it is complicated and difficult to get what you want from it. ...*a jungle of complex rules.* ◆◆◇◇◇ N-VAR / N-SING: with supp PRAGMATICS

jun·ior /'dʒuːniə/ **juniors. 1** A **junior** official or employee holds a low-ranking position in an organization or profession. ...*a junior minister attached to the prime minister's office.* ▶ Also a noun. *The Lord Chancellor has said legal aid work is for juniors.* **2** If you are someone's **junior**, you are younger than they are. *She now lives with actor Denis Lawson, 10 years her junior.* **3** In the United States, a student in the third year of a high school or university course is called a **junior**. ◆◆◇◇◇ ADJ-GRADED / N-COUNT / N-SING: poss N / N-COUNT

junior school, junior schools. In England and Wales, a **junior school** is a school for children between the ages of about seven and eleven. N-VAR

ju·ni·per /'dʒuːnɪpə/ **junipers.** A **juniper** is an evergreen bush with purple berries which can be used in cooking and medicine. ◆◇◇◇◇ N-VAR

junk /dʒʌŋk/ **junks, junking, junked. 1** If you describe a group of objects as **junk**, you think that they are old and useless. *What are you going to do with all that junk, Larry?* **2** You can use **junk** to refer to old and second-hand goods that people buy and collect. *Look out for old illustrated books in junk shops.* **3** If you **junk** something, you get rid of it or stop using it. *Consumers will not have to junk their old cassettes to use the new format.* **4** A **junk** is a Chinese sailing boat that has a flat bottom and square sails. ◆◆◇◇◇ N-UNCOUNT PRAGMATICS INFORMAL / N-UNCOUNT / VERB V n INFORMAL / N-COUNT

junk bond, junk bonds. If a company issues **junk bonds**, it borrows money from investors, usually at a high rate of interest, in order to finance a particular deal. ◆◆◇◇◇ N-COUNT

jun·ket /'dʒʌŋkɪt/ **junkets.** If you describe a trip by an official or businessman as a **junket**, you disapprove of it because it is expensive, unnecessary, and often has been paid for with public money. N-COUNT PRAGMATICS INFORMAL

junk food, junk foods. If you refer to food as **junk food**, you mean that it is quick and easy to prepare but is not good for your health. N-VAR

junkie /'dʒʌŋki/ **junkies. 1** A **junkie** is a drug addict. ...*junkies who leave their syringes all over the place.* **2** You can use **junkie** to refer to someone who is very interested in a particular activity, especially when they spend a lot of time on it. ...*a computer junkie.* ◆◇◇◇◇ N-COUNT INFORMAL N-COUNT: n N INFORMAL

junk mail. **Junk mail** consists of advertisements and publicity materials that you receive through the post which you have not asked for. N-UNCOUNT

junk·yard /'dʒʌŋkjɑːd/ **junkyards.** A **junkyard** is the same as a **scrapyard**. N-COUNT

jun·ta /'dʒʌntə, 'hʊntə/ **juntas.** If you refer to a **junta**, you mean that a military government that has ◆◇◇◇◇ N-COLL COUNT

taken power by force, and not through elections; used showing disapproval. `PRAGMATICS`

ju·ris·dic·tion /ˌdʒʊərɪs'dɪkʃən/ **jurisdictions.** ◆◇◇◇
1 Jurisdiction is the power that a court of law or an N-UNCOUNT FORMAL
official has to carry out legal judgments or to enforce laws. *The British police have no jurisdiction over foreign bank accounts.* **2** A **jurisdiction** is a N-COUNT AMERICAN
state or other area in which a particular court and system of laws has authority.

ju·ris·pru·dence /ˌdʒʊərɪs'pruːdəns/. **Jurisprudence** N-UNCOUNT FORMAL
dence is the study of law and the principles on which laws are based.

ju·rist /'dʒʊərɪst/ **jurists.** A **jurist** is a person who is N-COUNT FORMAL
an expert on law.

ju·ror /'dʒʊərə/ **jurors.** A **juror** is a member of a ◆◇◇◇ N-COUNT
jury.

jury /'dʒʊəri/ **juries. 1** In a court of law, the **jury** is ◆◆◇◇ N-COLL-COUNT
the group of people who have been chosen from the general public to listen to the facts about a crime and to decide whether the person accused is guilty or not. **2** A **jury** is a group of people who choose the N-COLL-COUNT
winner of a competition.

just 1 adverb uses

just /dʒʌst/. **1** You use **just** to say that something ◆◆◆◆◆
happened a very short time ago, or is starting to ADV: ADV before v
happen at the present time. For example, if you say that someone **has just arrived**, you mean that they arrived a very short time ago. *I've just bought a new house... I just had the most awful dream... I'm only just beginning to take it in.* **2** If you say that you are ADV: ADV before v
just doing something, you mean that you are doing it now and will finish it very soon. If you say that you are **just about to** do something, or **just going to** do something, you mean that you will do it very soon. *I'm just making the sauce for the cauliflower... I'm just going to walk down the lane now and post some letters.* **3** You can use **just** to emphasize that ADV: ADV adv/
something is happening at exactly the moment of prep, ADV as/when
speaking or at exactly the moment that you are talk- cl
ing about. *Randall would just now be getting the* `PRAGMATICS`
Sunday paper... Just then the phone rang.
4 You use **just** to indicate that something is no more ADV: ADV group/cl
important, interesting, or difficult, for example, than `PRAGMATICS`
you say it is. *It's just a suggestion... I am sure you can tell just by looking at me that I am all right.* **5** You use ADV: ADV n
just to emphasize that you are talking about a small part or sample, not the whole of an amount. *These are just a few of the many options available.* **6** You use **just** ADV: ADV amount
to draw attention to how small an amount is or how `PRAGMATICS`
short a length of time is. *David redecorated a room in just three days.* **7** You can use **just** in front of a verb to ADV: ADV before v
indicate that the result of something is unfortunate or `PRAGMATICS`
undesirable and is likely to make the situation worse rather than better. *Leaving like I did just made it worse.*
8 You use **just** to indicate that what you are saying is ADV: ADV adj/
the case, but only by a very small degree or amount. adv/prep,
Her hand was just visible by the light from the sitting ADV before v
room... He could just reach the man's head with his right hand. **9** You use **just** with 'might', 'may', and ADV: ADV with v
'could', when you mean that there is a small chance of modal
something happening, despite the fact that it is not very likely. *It's an old trick but it just might work.*
10 You use **just** to emphasize the following word or ADV: ADV before v,
phrase, in order to express feelings such as annoy- ADV adj/n
ance, admiration, or certainty. *She just won't relax... I* `PRAGMATICS`
don't see the point in it really. It's just stupid... Isn't he just the most beautiful thing you ever saw? **11** You use ADV: ADV before v
just with instructions, polite requests, or statements `PRAGMATICS`
of intention, to make your request or statement seem less difficult and problematical than someone might think. *I'm just going to ask you a bit more about your father's business... Just add water, milk and butter.*
12 You use **just** in expressions such as **just a minute,** ADV: ADV n
just a moment, and **just a second** when you are ask- `PRAGMATICS`
ing someone to wait for a short time. *'Let me in, Di.'—* SPOKEN
'Okay. Just a minute.' **13** You can use **just** in expres- ADV: ADV n
sions such as **just a minute, just a moment,** and **just a** `PRAGMATICS`
second when you want to interrupt or stop someone. SPOKEN
Well, now just a second, I don't altogether agree.

14 You can use **just** with negative question tags, for ADV:
example **'isn't he just?'** and **'don't they just!'**, to say `PRAGMATICS` BRITISH,
that you agree completely with what has been said. SPOKEN
'That's crazy,' I said. 'Isn't it just?' he said. **15** If you say ADV: ADV before v
that you can **just** see or hear something, you mean that it is easy for you to imagine seeing or hearing it. *I can just hear her telling her friends, 'Well, I blame his mother!'* **16** You use **just** to mean exactly, when you ADV: ADV cl/prep/
are specifying something precisely or asking for pre- adv
cise information. *There are no statistics about just how many people won't vote... My arm hurts too, just here.*
17 You use **just** to emphasize that a particular thing is ADV: ADV n
exactly what is needed or fits a particular description `PRAGMATICS`
exactly. *Kiwi fruit are just the thing for a healthy snack.* **18** You use **just** in expressions such as **just like,** ADV: ADV like n,
just as...as, and **just the same** when you are empha- ADV as adj/
sizing the similarity between two things or two peo- adv,
ple. *Behind the facade they are just like the rest of us...* ADV n
He worked just as hard as anyone. `PRAGMATICS`

19 You use **just about** to indicate that what you are PHRASE
talking about is so close to being the case that it can be regarded as being the case. *What does she read? Just about everything.* **20** You use **just about** to indicate PHRASE
that what you are talking about is in fact the case, but only by a very small degree or amount. *We've got just about enough time to get there.* **21** If things are **just so,** PHRASE
they are done or arranged exactly as they should be or exactly as someone wants them. *I do her hair, and it has to be just so.* **22** You use the expression **it's just** PHRASE
that when you are making a complaint, suggestion, or `PRAGMATICS`
excuse, so that the person you are talking to will not get annoyed with you. *Your hair is all right; it's just that you need a haircut.* **23** ● **just now:** see **now.**
● **only just:** see **only.** ● **it just goes to show:** see **show.**
● **not just:** see **not.**

just 2 adjective use

just /dʒʌst/. If you describe a situation, action, or ◆◇◇◇ ADJ-GRADED
idea as **just,** you mean that it is right or acceptable FORMAL
according to particular moral principles. *She fought honestly for a just cause and for freedom... Was Pol-lard's life sentence just or was it too severe?* ◆ **just·ly** ADV-GRADED:
They were not treated justly in the past. ● to **get** your ADV with v
just deserts: see **desert.**

jus·tice /'dʒʌstɪs/ **justices. 1 Justice** is fairness in ◆◆◆◇
the way that people are treated. *He only wants free- N-UNCOUNT
dom, justice and equality.* ● See also **miscarriage of justice. 2** The **justice** of a cause, claim, or argument N-UNCOUNT
is its quality of being reasonable, justifiable, or right. *We must win people round to the justice of our cause.* **3 Justice** is the legal system that a country N-UNCOUNT
uses in order to deal with people who break the law. *A lawyer is part of the machinery of justice.* **4** If a PHRASE
criminal is **brought to justice,** he or she is punished for a crime by being arrested and tried in a court of law. *They demanded that those responsible be brought to justice.* **5** A **justice** is a judge. *Thomas* N-COUNT
will be sworn in today as a justice on the Supreme AMERICAN
Court. ...Retired High Court Justices. **6 Justice** is N-TITLE
used before the names of judges. *...Mr Justice Hutchison.*
7 If someone or something **does justice** to a person or PHRASE
thing, they describe or reproduce them in a way that shows truly how good or valuable they are. *The photo-graph I had seen didn't do her justice.* **8** If you **do jus-** PHRASE
tice to someone or something, you deal with them properly and completely. *No one article can ever do justice to the topic of fraud.* **9** If you **do** yourself **jus-** PHRASE
tice, you do something as well as you are capable of doing it. *I don't think he could do himself justice play-ing for England.* **10** If you say that something is **rough** PHRASE
justice for someone, you mean that they have not BRITISH
been treated fairly. *It would have been rough justice had he been deprived of this important third European win.*

Justice of the 'Peace, Justices of the N-COUNT
Peace. In Britain, a **Justice of the Peace** is a per-son who is not a lawyer but who is authorized to act as a judge in a local criminal law court. The abbre-viation **JP** is also used.

jus·ti·fi·able /ˌdʒʌstɪˈfaɪəbəl/. An action, situation, emotion, or idea that is **justifiable** is acceptable or correct because there is a good reason for it. *The violence of the revolutionary years was justifiable on the grounds of political necessity.* ♦ **jus·ti·fi·ably** /ˌdʒʌstɪˈfaɪəbli/ *He was justifiably proud of his achievements.* ◆◇◇◇◇ ADJ-GRADED / ADV-GRADED

jus·ti·fi·ca·tion /ˌdʒʌstɪfɪˈkeɪʃən/ **justifications.** A **justification** for something is an acceptable reason or explanation for it. *To me the only justification for a zoo is educational.* ◆◆◇◇◇ N-VAR

jus·ti·fied /ˈdʒʌstɪfaɪd/. **1** If you describe a decision, action, or idea as **justified**, you think it is reasonable and acceptable. *In my opinion, the decision was wholly justified.* **2** If you think that someone is **justified in** doing something, you think that their reasons for doing it are good and valid. *He's absolutely justified in resigning. He was treated shamefully... The report concluded that police were justified in opening fire.* ◆◆◇◇◇ ADJ-GRADED PRAGMATICS / v-link ADJ *in* -ing PRAGMATICS

jus·ti·fy /ˈdʒʌstɪfaɪ/ **justifies, justifying, justified.** If someone or something **justifies** a particular decision, action, or idea, they show or prove that it is reasonable or necessary. *No argument can justify a war.* ◆◆◆◇◇ VERB V n

just·ly /ˈdʒʌstli/. You use **justly** to show that you approve of someone's attitude towards something, because it seems to be based on truth or reality. *Australians are justly proud of their native wildlife.* ● See also **just.** ADV PRAGMATICS

jut /dʒʌt/ **juts, jutting, jutted. 1** If something **juts** out, it sticks out above or beyond a surface. *The northern end of the island juts out like a long, thin finger into the sea.* **2** If you **jut** a part of your body, especially your chin, or if it **juts**, you push it forward in an aggressive or determined way. *His jaw jutted stubbornly forward... Gwen jutted her chin forward, her nose in the air.* ◆◇◇◇◇ VERB V adv/prep / V-ERG V adv/prep V n adv/prep / Also V, V n

jute /dʒuːt/. **Jute** is a substance that is used to make cloth and rope. It comes from a plant which grows mainly in South-East Asia. N-UNCOUNT

ju·venile /ˈdʒuːvənaɪl/ **juveniles. 1** A **juvenile** is a child or young person who is not yet old enough to be regarded as an adult. *Juvenile crime is increasing at a terrifying rate.* **2** If you describe someone's behaviour as **juvenile**, you are critical of it because you think that it is silly or immature. **3** A **juvenile** is a young animal. ◆◆◇◇◇ N-COUNT FORMAL / ADJ-GRADED PRAGMATICS / N-COUNT

'juvenile court, juvenile courts. A **juvenile court** is a court which deals with crimes committed by young people who are not yet old enough to be considered as adults. N-VAR

'juvenile de'linquency. **Juvenile delinquency** is vandalism and other criminal behaviour that is committed by young people who are not old enough to be legally considered as adults. N-UNCOUNT

'juvenile de'linquent, juvenile delinquents. A **juvenile delinquent** is a young person who is guilty of committing crimes. N-COUNT

jux·ta·pose /ˌdʒʌkstəˈpəʊz/ **juxtaposes, juxtaposing, juxtaposed.** If you **juxtapose** two contrasting objects, images, or ideas, you place them together or describe them together, so that the differences between them are strongly emphasized. *The technique Mr Wilson uses most often is to juxtapose things for dramatic effect. ...the celebration of life juxtaposed with the terror of mortality.* ♦ **jux·ta·po·si·tion** /ˌdʒʌkstəpəˈzɪʃən/ **juxtapositions** *...this juxtaposition of brutal reality and lyrical beauty.* VERB V pl-n / V-ed with n / Also V n with n FORMAL / N-VAR

K k

K, k /keɪ/ **K's, k's. 1** K is the eleventh letter of the English alphabet. **2** K or k is used as an abbreviation for words beginning with k, such as 'kilometre', 'kilobyte', or 'king'. **3** K or k is sometimes used to represent the number 1000, especially when referring to sums of money. *I used to make over 40k.* N-VAR / NUMBER INFORMAL

kaf·tan /ˈkæftæn/ **kaftans.** See **caftan.**

kale /keɪl/. **Kale** is a vegetable that is similar to a cabbage. N-UNCOUNT

ka·lei·do·scope /kəˈlaɪdəskəʊp/ **kaleidoscopes. 1** A **kaleidoscope** is a toy in the shape of a tube. If you look through the tube and turn the other end, you can see a pattern of colours which changes as you turn the tube round. **2** You can describe something that is made up of a lot of different and frequently changing colours or elements as a **kaleidoscope**. *...a kaleidoscope of different alliances, groupings and interests.* ♦ **ka·lei·do·scop·ic** /kəˌlaɪdəˈskɒpɪk/ *...a kaleidoscopic range of fabrics.* N-COUNT / ADJ: ADJ n

ka·mi·ka·ze /ˌkæmɪˈkɑːzi/. **1** If someone such as a soldier or terrorist performs a **kamikaze** act, they attack the enemy knowing that they will be killed doing it. *We have volunteers, including kamikaze pilots, ready to attack.* **2** You can use **kamikaze** to describe an action or attitude which involves doing something which is very dangerous and likely to harm the person who does it. *These are kamikaze jobs, the ones almost guaranteed to end your career.* ADJ: ADJ n / ADJ: ADJ n

kan·ga·roo /ˌkæŋgəˈruː/ **kangaroos.** A **kangaroo** is a large Australian animal which moves by jumping on its back legs. Female kangaroos carry their babies in a pouch on their stomachs. ◆◇◇◇◇ N-COUNT

kanga'roo court, kangaroo courts. If you refer to a court or a meeting as a **kangaroo court**, you disapprove of it because it is unofficial or unfair, and is intended to find someone guilty. *Reichmann claims he is the victim of a kangaroo court.* N-COUNT PRAGMATICS

ka·put /kəˈpʊt/. If you say that something is **kaput**, you mean that it is completely broken, useless, or finished. *'What's happened to your car?' – 'It's kaput.'* ADJ INFORMAL

kara·oke /ˌkæriˈəʊki/. **Karaoke** is a form of entertainment in which a machine plays tapes of the tunes of pop songs, and people take it in turns to use a microphone to sing the words. *...the popularity of pub karaoke nights.* ◆◇◇◇◇ N-UNCOUNT

ka·ra·te /kəˈrɑːti/. **Karate** is a Japanese martial art or sport in which people fight without weapons, using only their hands, elbows, feet, and legs. ◆◇◇◇◇ N-UNCOUNT

kar·ma /ˈkɑːmə/. In religions such as Hinduism and Buddhism that accept the idea of reincarnation, **karma** is the belief that your actions in this life affect all your future lives. *Through good deeds, kindness and compassion people can alter their bad karma.* ◆◇◇◇◇ N-UNCOUNT

kart /kɑːt/ **karts.** A **kart** is the same as a **go-kart.** N-COUNT

kay·ak /ˈkaɪæk/ **kayaks.** A **kayak** is a boat like a canoe, used in the sport of canoeing and by Inuit people. N-COUNT

ke·bab /kəˈbæb, AM -ˈbɑːb/ **kebabs.** A **kebab** is a dish consisting of small pieces of grilled meat, and sometimes vegetables, either inside a pitta bread or on a long metal rod. N-VAR

keel /kiːl/ **keels, keeling, keeled. 1** The **keel** of a boat is the long, specially shaped piece of wood or steel along the bottom of it. **2** If you say that someone or something is **on an even keel**, you mean that they are working or progressing smoothly and ◆◇◇◇◇ N-COUNT / PHRASE

steadily, without any sudden changes. *Jason had helped him out with a series of loans, until he could get back on an even keel.*

keel over. If someone **keels over**, they collapse because they are tired or ill. *She must have had a heart attack and keeled over.* — PHRASAL VB / V P / INFORMAL

keen /kiːn/ **keener, keenest; keens, keening, keened. 1** If you are **keen** on doing something, you very much want to do it. If you are **keen** that something should happen, you very much want it to happen. *Both companies were keen on a merger... She's still keen to keep in touch.* ♦ **keen·ness** ...*the country's keenness for better economic ties with China.* **2** If you are **keen on** something or someone, you like them a lot. *Mick has been very keen on Carla... He's not keen on the idea, but he sees the point.* ♦ **keenness** ...*his keenness for the arts.* **3** If someone is **keen**, they have a lot of enthusiasm for a particular activity or for things in general. *I've interviewed him and he seems very keen... She was a keen amateur photographer.* ♦ **keenness** ...*the keenness of the students.* **4** A **keen** interest or emotion is very intense. ...*his keen sense of loyalty.* ♦ **keen·ly** *This is a keenly awaited project.* **5** If you are a **keen** supporter of a cause or idea, you support it enthusiastically. *He is a keen advocate of closer integration in Europe.* **6** If you say that someone has a **keen** intellect, you mean that they are very clever and aware of what is happening around them. *Mr Walsh has a keen appreciation of the priorities of the electorate.* ♦ **keenly** *They're keenly aware that whatever they decide will set a precedent.* **7** If you have a **keen** eye or ear, you are able to notice things that are difficult to detect. ...*an amateur artist with a keen eye for detail.* ♦ **keenly** *Charles listened keenly.* **8** A **keen** fight or competition is one in which the competitors are all trying very hard to win. *They have buried their keen rivalry to work together on the project.* ♦ **keenly** *The 1994 contest should be very keenly fought.* **9** If someone **keens**, they make a wailing sound, usually as a sign of grief because someone has died. *Someone was making a low, keening noise.* — ◆◆◆◇◇ / ADJ-GRADED; v-link ADJ / N-UNCOUNT / ADJ-GRADED; v-link ADJ on n / N-UNCOUNT ADJ-GRADED / N-UNCOUNT / ADJ-GRADED / ADV-GRADED / ADJ-GRADED; ADJ n / ADJ-GRADED; ADJ n / ADV-GRADED / ADV-GRADED / ADJ-GRADED / ADV-GRADED / VERB: V V-ing LITERARY

keep /kiːp/ **keeps, keeping, kept. 1** If someone **is kept** in a particular state, they remain in it. *The noise kept him awake... To keep warm they burnt wood in a rusty oil barrel.* **2** If you **keep** in a particular position, or place, you remain in it. *Keep away from the doors while the train is moving... He kept his head down, hiding his features... Doctors will keep her in hospital for at least another week.* **3** If you **keep** off something or **keep** away from it, you avoid it. If you **keep** out of something, you avoid getting involved in it. *He's going to be a fantastic player if he keeps away from booze... Their main aim is to help keep youngsters out of trouble.* **4** If someone or something **keeps** you from doing something, they prevent you from doing it. *What can you do to keep it from happening again?* **5** If someone or something **keeps** you, they delay you and make you arrive somewhere later than expected. *'What kept you?'—I went in the wrong direction.* **6** If you try to **keep** from doing something, you try to stop yourself from doing it. *She bit her lip to keep from crying.* **7** If you **keep** doing something, you do it repeatedly or continue to do it. If someone or something **keeps** you doing something, they cause you to do it repeatedly or to continue to do it. *I keep forgetting it's December... I will let you have my answer tomorrow. I won't keep you waiting.* ▶ **Keep on** means the same as **keep**. *Did he give up or keep on trying?* **8 Keep** is used in the phrases **keep at it, keep going**, and **keep it up**, to indicate that someone continues doing something that they have started, even if they are tired and would prefer to stop. *'Keep at it!' Thade encouraged me... She forced herself to keep going... You're doing a great job! Keep it up!* **9** If you **keep** something from someone, you do not tell them about it. *He had to keep the truth from his children.* **10** If you **keep** something **to** yourself, you do — ◆◆◆◆◆ / V-LINK-ERG V n adj/prep V adj/prep / V-ERG V adv/prep V n with adv V n prep / V-ERG V prep/adv V n prep/adv / VERB V n from-ing / VERB V n / VERB V from-ing / V-ERG V-ing V n -ing / PHRASAL VB V P-ing / VERB V at it V-ing V it up / VERB: V n from n / PHRASE

not tell anyone else about it. *I have to tell someone. I can't keep it to myself.* **11** If you **keep yourself to yourself** or **keep to yourself**, you stay on your own most of the time and do not mix with other people. *Since she knows little Italian, she keeps to herself.* — PHRASE

12 Keep is used with some nouns to indicate that someone does something for a period of time or continues to do it. For example, if you **keep a grip** on something, you continue to hold or control it. *One of them would keep a look-out on the road behind to warn us of approaching vehicles.* **13** When you **keep** something such as a promise or an appointment, you do what you said you would do. *He had again failed to keep his word.* **14** If you **keep** a record of a series of events, you write down details of it so that they can be referred to later. *Eleanor began to keep a diary.* **15** If you **keep** something, you continue to have it in your possession and do not throw it away, give it away, or sell it. *'I like this dress,' she said. 'Keep it. You can have it,' said Daphne... Lathan had to choose between marrying her and keeping his job.* **16** If you **keep** something in a particular place, you always have it in that place. *She kept her money under the mattress... To make it easier to contact us, keep this card handy.* **17** Something that is **for keeps** is permanent and will not change. *Ensure that whatever you gain now will be for keeps.* **18** If something is **in keeping** with something else, it is appropriate or suitable in relation to that thing. If something is **out of keeping** with something else, it is not suitable or appropriate in relation to that thing. *In keeping with tradition, the Emperor and Empress did not attend the ceremony.* **19** If you **keep** someone, you support them by earning enough money to provide food, clothing, and other necessary things. *I was working nights in a bar to keep myself... He married an Armenian with a good dowry, who kept him in silk cravats.* **20** Someone's **keep** is the cost of food and other things that they need in their daily life. *Ray will earn his keep on local farms while studying.* **21** If you **keep** animals, you own them and take care of them. *We have kept chickens for many years.* **22** You can say or ask how someone **is keeping** as a way of saying or asking whether they are well. *She hasn't been keeping too well lately.* **23** If food **keeps** for a certain length of time, it stays fresh and suitable to eat for that time. *It will keep for 2-3 weeks.* **24** A **keep** is the main tower of a medieval castle, in which people lived. **25** ● to **keep** someone **company**: see **company**. ● to **keep a straight face**: see **face**. ● to **keep your hand in**: see **hand**. ● to **keep your head**: see **head**. ● to **keep house**: see **house**. ● to **keep pace**: see **pace**. ● to **keep the peace**: see **peace**. ● to **keep a secret**: see **secret**. ● to **keep time**: see **time**. ● to **keep track of**: see **track**. — PHRASE / VERB V n / VERB V n / VERB V n / VERB V n / VERB V n prep/adv V n adj / PHRASE INFORMAL / PHRASE / VERB: V n V pron-refl V n in n / N-SING: poss N / VERB: V n / VB: only cont V adv / VERB V / N-COUNT

keep back. If you **keep** some information **back**, you do not tell all that you know about something. *Neither of them is telling the whole truth. Invariably, they keep something back.* — PHRASAL VB V n P

keep down. 1 If you **keep** the number, size, or amount of something **down**, you do not let it increase. *Administration costs were kept down to just £460.* **2** If someone **keeps** a group of people **down**, they keep them in a state of powerlessness, and prevent them from being completely free. *No matter what a woman tries to do to improve her situation, there is some barrier or attitude to keep her down.* **3** If you **keep** food or drink **down**, you manage to swallow it properly and not vomit, even though you feel sick. *I've been trying to make her drink but she can't keep anything down.* — PHRASAL VB V n P V P noun Also V P noun / V n P

keep on. 1 See **keep 7**. **2** If you **keep** someone **on**, you continue to employ them, for example after they are old enough to retire or after other employees have lost their jobs. *A skeleton staff of 20 is being kept on.* — PHRASAL VB V n P be V-ed P Also V P noun

keep to. 1 If you **keep to** a rule, plan, or agreement, you do exactly what you are expected or supposed to do. *You've got to keep to the speed limit.* **2** If you **keep to** something such as a path or river, you do not move away from it as you go somewhere. *Keep to the right* — PHRASAL VB V P n / V P n

until you reach the end of the track. **3** If you **keep** V n P n
something **to** a particular number or quantity, you
limit it to that number or quantity. *Keep costs to a*
minimum.

keep up. 1 If someone or something **keeps up** with PHRASAL VB
another person or thing, the first one moves, pro- V P with n
gresses, or increases as fast as the second. *She shook* V P
her head and started to walk on. He kept up with her...
Things are changing so fast, it's hard to keep up. **2** If V P with n
you **keep up** with your work or with other people, you V P
manage to do or understand all your work, or to do or
understand it as well as other people. *Life here is*
tough for a parent whose kids aren't keeping up in
school. **3** If you **keep up** with what is happening, you V P with n
make sure that you know about it. *She did not bother* Also V P
to keep up with the news.
4 If you **keep** something **up**, you continue to do it or V n P
provide it. *They risk losing their homes because they* V P noun
can no longer keep up the repayments. **5** If you **keep** V n P
something **up**, you prevent it from growing less in V P noun
amount, level, or degree. *Opposition forces are keep-*
ing up the pressure against the government.

keep·er /ˈkiːpə/ **keepers. 1** In football, the **keeper** ◆◆◇◇◇
is the same as the **goalkeeper.** *...the Chelsea keeper's* N-COUNT
unfortunate performance against Manchester Unit- BRITISH
ed. **2** A **keeper** at a zoo is a person who takes care N-COUNT
of the animals. **3** The **keeper** of a museum or art N-COUNT
gallery is the person who is responsible for the
exhibits.

keep-'fit; also spelled **keep fit. Keep-fit** is the ac- ◆◇◇◇◇
tivity of keeping your body in good condition by do- N-UNCOUNT
ing special exercises. BRITISH

keep·sake /ˈkiːpseɪk/ **keepsakes.** A **keepsake** is a N-COUNT
small present that someone gives you so that you
will not forget them.

keg /keg/ **kegs.** A **keg** is a small barrel used for N-COUNT
storing something such as beer or other alcoholic
drinks. *...empty beer kegs.*

kelp /kelp/. **Kelp** is a type of seaweed. N-UNCOUNT

ken·nel /ˈkenəl/ **kennels. 1** A **kennel** is a small ◆◇◇◇◇
building made especially for a dog to sleep in. N-COUNT
2 Kennels or **a kennels** or **a kennel** is a place where N-COUNT
dogs are bred and trained, or looked after when
their owners are away. *Get friends to take the dog, or*
put him in kennels.

kept /kept/. **Kept** is the past tense and past participle of **keep.**

kerb /kɜːb/ **kerbs;** spelled **curb** in American Eng- ◆◇◇◇◇
lish. The **kerb** is the raised edge of a pavement N-COUNT
which separates it from the road.

'kerb-crawling. Kerb-crawling is the illegal activ- N-UNCOUNT
ity of driving slowly along the side of a road in order BRITISH
to hire a prostitute.

ker·chief /ˈkɜːtʃɪf/ **kerchiefs.** A **kerchief** is a piece N-COUNT
of cloth that you wear on your head or around your DATED
neck.

ker·fuf·fle /kəˈfʌfəl/. A **kerfuffle** is noisy and disor- N-SING
derly behaviour, often resulting from an argument. INFORMAL,
There was a bit of a kerfuffle during the race when a BRITISH
dog impeded the leading runners.

ker·nel /ˈkɜːnəl/ **kernels. 1** The **kernel** of a nut is ◆◇◇◇◇
the part that is inside the shell. **2** The **kernel** of N-COUNT
something is the central and most important part of N-COUNT
it. *The kernel of that message was that peace must*
not be a source of advantage or disadvantage for
anyone. **3** A **kernel** of something is a small element N-COUNT
of it. *There may be a kernel of truth in what he says.*

kero·sene /ˈkerəsiːn/. **Kerosene** is a clear, strong- ◆◇◇◇◇
smelling liquid which is used as a fuel, for example N-UNCOUNT
in heaters and lamps.

kes·trel /ˈkestrəl/ **kestrels.** A **kestrel** is a type of N-COUNT
small falcon.

ketch /ketʃ/ **ketches.** A **ketch** is a type of sailing N-COUNT
ship.

ketch·up /ˈketʃʌp/. **Ketchup** is a thick, cold sauce, N-UNCOUNT
usually made from tomatoes.

ket·tle /ˈketəl/ **kettles. 1** A **kettle** is a covered ◆◇◇◇◇
container that you use for boiling water. It has a N-COUNT
handle and a spout. *I'll put the kettle on and make*
us some tea. ▶ A **kettle** of water is the amount of N-COUNT

water contained in a kettle. *Pour a kettle of boiling*
water over the onions. **2** If you say that something is PHRASE
a different kettle of fish, you mean that it is very INFORMAL
different from another related thing that you are
talking about. *Playing for the reserve team is a total-*
ly different kettle of fish.

kettle·drum /ˈketəldrʌm/ **kettledrums.** A kettle- N-COUNT
drum is a large drum which can be tuned to play a
particular note.

key /kiː/ **keys, keying, keyed. 1** A **key** is a spe- ◆◆◆◇
cially shaped piece of metal that you place in a lock N-COUNT
and turn in order to open or lock something such as
a door, or to start or stop the engine of a vehicle.
She reached for her coat and car keys. ● **under lock**
and key: see **lock.** ● See also **master key. 2** The N-COUNT
keys on a computer keyboard or typewriter are the
buttons that you press in order to operate it. **3** The N-COUNT
keys of a piano or organ are the long narrow pieces
of wood or plastic that you press in order to play it.
4 In music, a **key** is a scale of musical notes that starts N-VAR
on one specific note. *...the key of A minor.* **5** The **key** N-COUNT
on a map or diagram or in a book is a list of symbols or
abbreviations used and their meanings.
6 The **key** person or thing in a group is the most im- ADJ: ADJ n
portant one. *Education is likely to be a key issue in the*
next election. **7** The **key** to a desirable situation or re- N-COUNT
sult is the way in which it can be achieved. *Diet and re-*
laxation are two important keys to good health.

key in. If you **key** something **in,** you put information PHRASAL VB
into a computer or you give the computer a particular V P noun
instruction by typing the information or instruction Also V n P
on the keyboard. *Brian keyed in his personal code.*

key·board /ˈkiːbɔːd/ **keyboards. 1** The **keyboard** ◆◆◇◇◇
of a typewriter or computer is the set of keys that N-COUNT
you press in order to operate it. **2** The **keyboard** of N-COUNT
a piano or organ is the set of black and white keys
that you press in order to play it. **3** People some- N-COUNT
times refer to musical instruments that have a keyboard as **keyboards.** *...a band that featured Paul*
Carrack on keyboards.

keyed 'up. If you are **keyed up,** you are very excit- ADJ-GRADED:
ed or nervous before an important or dangerous v-link ADJ
event.

key·hole /ˈkiːhəʊl/ **keyholes.** A **keyhole** is the hole N-COUNT
in a lock that you put a key in.

keyhole 'surgery. Keyhole surgery is a surgical N-UNCOUNT
technique in which the surgeon inserts the instruments through small cuts in the patient's body.

key·note /ˈkiːnəʊt/ **keynotes.** The **keynote** of a ◆◇◇◇◇
policy or speech is the main theme of it or the part N-COUNT
of it that is emphasized the most. *He would be set-*
ting out his plans for the party in a keynote speech.

'key ring, key rings; also spelled **keyring.** A **key** N-COUNT
ring is a metal ring which you use to keep your keys
together.

key·stone /ˈkiːstəʊn/ **keystones.** A **keystone** of a N-COUNT
policy or system is an important part of it, which is
the basis for later developments. *The government's*
determination to beat inflation has so far been the
keystone of its economic policy.

key 'word, key words. In language teaching, **key** N-COUNT
words are the words in a course book which the
writer suggests are the most important for the student to learn.

kg. Kg is an abbreviation for **kilogram** or ◆◇◇◇◇
kilograms.

kha·ki /ˈkɑːki, AM ˈkæki/. **1 Khaki** is a strong ma- ◆◇◇◇◇
terial of a greenish brown colour, used especially to N-UNCOUNT
make uniforms for soldiers. **2** Something that is COLOUR
khaki is greenish brown.

kib·butz /kɪˈbʊts/ **kibbutzim** /ˌkɪbʊˈtsiːm/. A **kib-** N-COUNT
butz is a place of work in Israel, for example a farm
or factory, where the workers live together and
share all the duties.

kick /kɪk/ **kicks, kicking, kicked. 1** If you **kick** ◆◆◆◇
someone or something, you hit them forcefully with V n
your foot. *He threw me to the ground and started to* V
kick... He escaped by kicking open the window... The V n with adj
fiery actress kicked him in the shins. ▶ Also a noun. V n in n
He suffered a kick to the knee. **2** If you say that N-COUNT
PHRASE

K

someone **kicks** you **when** you **are down**, you think they are behaving unfairly because they are attacking you when you are in a weak position. **3** If you describe a situation as **a kick in the teeth**, you are emphasizing that it is a severe setback or disappointment. *We've been struggling for years and it's a real kick in the teeth to see a new band make it ahead of us.* **4** If you say that you could **kick yourself**, you mean that you are very annoyed with yourself for getting something wrong. *I was still kicking myself for not paying attention... You would kick yourself if you were to miss this.*

5 When you **kick** a ball or other object, you hit it with your foot so that it moves through the air. *He kicked the ball away.* ▶ Also a noun. *Schmeichel swooped to save the first kick from Borisov.* **6** If you **kick**, you move your legs with very quick, small, and forceful movements, once or repeatedly. *They were dragged away struggling and kicking... First he kicked the left leg, then he kicked the right.* ▶ **Kick out** means the same as **kick**. *'Help!' I cried, kicking out.* **7** If you say that someone is dragged **kicking and screaming** into a particular course of action, you are emphasizing that they are very reluctant do something.

8 If you **kick** a bad habit, you stop having that habit. *I've kicked cigarettes.*

9 If something gives you **a kick**, it makes you feel very excited or very happy for a short period of time. *I got a kick out of seeing my name in print.* **10** If someone does something **for kicks**, they do it because they think it will be exciting.

11 ● **alive and kicking**: see **alive**. ● **kick** someone's **ass**: see **ass**. ● **kick up a fuss**: see **fuss**.

kick around. 1 If people **kick** an idea **around**, they discuss it informally. *They started to kick around the idea of an electric scraper.* **2** If someone **kicks** you **around**, they treat you badly and unfairly.

kick down or **kick in.** If someone **kicks** something **down** or if they **kick** it **in**, they hit it violently with their foot so that it falls over or breaks to pieces. *She was forced to kick down the front door.*

kick in. 1 If something **kicks in**, it begins to take effect. *I hoped the tablets would kick in soon.* **2** See also **kick down**.

kick off. 1 In football, when the players **kick off**, they start a match by kicking the ball from the centre of the pitch. **2** If an event, game, series, or discussion **kicks off**, it begins. *The Mayor kicked off the party... We kicked off with a slap-up dinner.* **3** If you **kick off** your shoes, you shake your feet so that your shoes come off.

kick out. 1 To **kick** someone **out** of a place means to force them to leave it. *Her family kicked her out.* **2** See also **kick** 6.

kick·back /'kɪkbæk/ **kickbacks.** A **kickback** is a sum of money that is illegally paid to someone in authority, for example for arranging for a company to be chosen to do an important job.

'kick-off, kick-offs. 1 In football, **kick-off** is the time at which a particular match starts. **2** The **kick-off** of an event or activity is its beginning. *...the kick-off of the parade.*

'kick-start, kick-starts, kick-starting, kick-started; also spelled **kickstart. 1** To **kick-start** a process that has stopped working or progressing is to take a course of action that will quickly start it going again. *The President has chosen to kick-start the economy by slashing interest rates.* ▶ Also a noun. *The housing market needs a kick-start.* **2** If you **kick-start** a motorcycle, you press the lever that starts it with your foot.

kid /kɪd/ **kids, kidding, kidded. 1** You can refer to a child as a **kid**. *They've got three kids.* **2** Young people who are no longer children are sometimes referred to as **kids**. *...gangs of kids on motorbikes.* **3** Your **kid brother** or **kid sister** is your younger brother or sister.

4 If you **are kidding**, you are saying something that is not really true, as a joke. *I'm just kidding... I'm not kidding, Frank. There's a cow out there.* **5** You can say '**No**

kidding' to emphasize that what you are saying is true, or that you mean it. *I'm scared. No kidding, really.* **6** You can say '**No kidding?**' to show you are interested or surprised when someone tells you something. *'We won.'—'No kidding?'* **7** You can say '**you've got to be kidding**' to someone if they have said something you think is ridiculous or completely untrue. *You've got to be kidding! I can't live here!*

8 If you **kid** someone, you tease them. *He used to kid me about being chubby.* **9** If people **kid** themselves, they allow themselves to believe something that is not true because they wish that it was true. *I could kid myself that you did this for me, but it would be a lie.*

10 You can use expressions such as '**who is she kidding?**' or '**who are you trying to kid?**' if you think it is obvious that someone is not being sincere and does not mean what they say. *She played the role of a meek, innocent, shy girl. I don't know who she was trying to kid.*

11 A **kid** is a young goat.

kid·die /'kɪdi/ **kiddies;** also spelled **kiddy.** A **kiddie** is a very young child.

,kid 'gloves. If you treat someone or something with **kid gloves**, you are very careful in the way you deal with them, for example because they are very delicate or easily upset, or because they could be dangerous. *Some artists have to be handled with kid gloves.*

kid·nap /'kɪdnæp/ **kidnaps, kidnapping, kidnapped. 1** To **kidnap** someone is to take them away illegally and by force, and usually to hold them prisoner in order to demand something from their family, employer, or government. *Police in Brazil uncovered a plot to kidnap him.* ◆ **kid·nap·per, kidnappers** *His kidnappers have threatened that they will kill him unless three militants are released from prison.* ◆ **kid·nap·ping, kidnappings** *Two youngsters have been arrested and charged with kidnapping.* **2 Kidnap** or a **kidnap** is the crime of taking someone away by force. *Stewart denies attempted murder and kidnap... He was charged with the kidnap of a 25 year-old woman.*

kid·ney /'kɪdni/ **kidneys. 1** Your **kidneys** are the organs in your body that filter waste matter from your blood and send it out of your body in your urine. **2 Kidneys** are the kidneys of an animal, for example a lamb, calf, or pig, that are eaten as meat. *...steak and kidney pie.*

'kidney bean, kidney beans. Kidney beans are fairly large, dark red beans.

kill /kɪl/ **kills, killing, killed. 1** If a person, animal, or other living thing is **killed**, something or someone causes them to die. *Cattle should be killed cleanly and humanely... The earthquake killed 62 people... Heroin can kill.* ◆ **kill·ing, killings** *There is tension in the region following the killing of seven civilians. ...a brutal killing.* **2** The act of killing an animal after hunting it is referred to as the **kill**. *Venison liver is especially good if eaten within one day of the kill.* **3** If you **move in** or **close in for the kill**, you act very determinedly in taking advantage of a changed situation in order to do something that you have been preparing to do. *She is going for the kill by rallying opposition to the prime minister.*

4 If you say that you will **kill** someone for something they have done, you are emphasizing that you are extremely angry with them. *I'm going to kill him when I get hold of him.* **5** If you say that something **is killing** you, you mean that it is causing you physical or emotional pain. *My feet are killing me.* **6** If you say that you will do something **if it kills** you, you are emphasizing that you are determined to do it even though it is extremely difficult or painful. *I'll make this marriage work if it kills me.* **7** If you say that something will not **kill** you, you mean that it is not really as difficult or unpleasant as it might seem. *Three or four more weeks won't kill me!*

8 If someone or something **kills** a project, activity, or idea, they completely destroy or end it. *His objective was to kill the space station project altogether.*

Margin codes (right column of each entry):

- kick in the teeth — PHRASE, PRAGMATICS, INFORMAL
- kick yourself — PHRASE
- kick a ball — VERB: V n, V n with adv, Also V n prep, N-COUNT
- kick (legs) — VERB, V v, V n
- kick out — PHRASAL VB, V P, PHRASE, PRAGMATICS
- kick a habit — VERB, V n, INFORMAL
- a kick — N-SING, a N, INFORMAL
- for kicks — PHRASE, INFORMAL
- kick around — PHRASAL VB, V n P, V P noun, V n P, INFORMAL
- kick down — PHRASAL VB, V P noun, Also V n P
- kick in — PHRASAL VB, V P
- kick off — PHRASAL VB, V P, ERG: V P, V P noun, V P with n, V P n
- kick out — PHRASAL VB, V n P of n, V n P, Also V P noun
- kickback — ◆◇◇◇◇, N-COUNT
- kick-off — ◆◇◇◇◇, N-VAR, N-SING, INFORMAL
- kick-start — ◆◇◇◇◇, VERB, V n, N-COUNT, VERB: V n
- kid — ◆◆◆◇, N-COUNT, INFORMAL, N-COUNT, INFORMAL, INFORMAL, ADJ: ADJ n, INFORMAL
- kidding (verb) — VERB, V, CONVENTION
- kidding (phrases) — PRAGMATICS, INFORMAL, CONVENTION, PRAGMATICS, INFORMAL, PHRASE, PRAGMATICS, INFORMAL, PHRASE
- kid (tease) — VERB: V n, VERB: V pron-refl, V pron-refl that
- who is she kidding — PHRASE, INFORMAL
- kid (goat) — N-COUNT
- kiddie — N-COUNT, INFORMAL
- kid gloves — N-PLURAL
- kidnap — ◆◇◇◇◇, VERB, V n, Also V, N-COUNT, N-VAR, N-VAR
- kidney — ◆◆◇◇◇, N-COUNT, N-VAR
- kidney bean — N-COUNT
- kill — ◆◆◆◆◇, VERB, be V-ed, V n, V, N-VAR, N-COUNT, PHRASE
- kill (angry) — VERB, PRAGMATICS, V n, INFORMAL
- kill (pain) — VB: only cont, V n, INFORMAL, PHRASE, PRAGMATICS
- kill (not difficult) — VERB, V pron, INFORMAL
- kill (project) — VERB, V n

▶ To **kill off** means the same as to **kill**. *He would soon launch a second offensive, killing off the peace process.* **9** If something **kills** pain, it weakens it or gets rid of it. *He was forced to take opium to kill the pain.* **10** If you **are killing** time, you are doing something because you have some time available, not because you really want to do it. *He walked the streets of Leningrad with no purpose other than to kill time.*

PHRASAL VB
V P noun
Also V n P
VERB
V n
VERB
V n

11 ● to **kill two birds with one stone**: see **bird**. ● **dressed to kill**: see **dress**. ● to **be killed outright**: see **outright**.

kill off. 1 See **kill** 8. **2** If things such as animals or germs **are killed off**, all of them are killed or destroyed. *Their natural predators have been killed off... All blood products are now heat treated to kill off any infection.*

PHRASAL VB
be V-ed P
V P noun
Also V n P

kill·er /ˈkɪlə/ killers. 1 A **killer** is a person who has killed someone. *The police are searching for his killers.* **2** You can refer to something that causes death as a **killer**. *Heart disease is the biggest killer of men in most developed countries.*

◆◆◆◇◇
N-COUNT
N-COUNT

killer 'instinct, killer instincts. If you say that a sports player or politician has the **killer instinct**, you admire them for their toughness and determination to succeed. *He quit the sport when he realised he didn't have the killer instinct.*

N-VAR
PRAGMATICS

killer 'whale, killer whales. A **killer whale** is a type of black and white whale.

N-COUNT

kill·ing /ˈkɪlɪŋ/ killings. 1 If you **make a killing**, you make a large profit very quickly and easily. **2** See also **kill**.

◆◆◆◇◇
PHRASE
INFORMAL

kill·joy /ˈkɪldʒɔɪ/ killjoys. If you call someone a **killjoy**, you are criticizing them because they stop other people from enjoying themselves, often by reminding them of something unpleasant. *Don't be such a killjoy!*

N-COUNT
PRAGMATICS

kiln /kɪln/ kilns. A **kiln** is an oven that is used to bake pottery or bricks so that they become hard.

◆◇◇◇
N-COUNT

kilo /ˈkiːləʊ/ kilos. A **kilo** is the same as a **kilogram**.

◆◇◇◇
N-COUNT

kilo- /ˈkɪləʊ-/. Kilo- is added to some nouns that refer to units of measurement in order to form other nouns referring to units a thousand times bigger. *...100 kilojoules of energy. ...an explosion of around 20 kilotons.*

PREFIX

kilo·byte /ˈkɪləbaɪt/ kilobytes. In computing, a **kilobyte** is one thousand bytes of data.

N-COUNT

kilo·gram /ˈkɪləgræm/ kilograms; also spelled **kilogramme**. A **kilogram** is a metric unit of weight. One kilogram is a thousand grams, and is equal to 2.2 pounds.

◆◇◇◇
N-COUNT

kilo·hertz /ˈkɪləhɜːts/; kilohertz is both the singular and the plural form. A **kilohertz** is a unit of measurement of radio waves. One kilohertz is one thousand hertz.

N-COUNT

kilo·metre /ˈkɪləmiːtə, kɪˈlɒmɪtə/ kilometres; spelled **kilometer** in American English. A **kilometre** is a metric unit of distance or length. One kilometre is a thousand metres, and is equal to 0.62 miles.

◆◆◆◇◇
N-COUNT

kilo·watt /ˈkɪləwɒt/ kilowatts. A **kilowatt** is a unit of power. One kilowatt is a thousand watts.

N-COUNT

'kilowatt-hour, kilowatt-hours. A **kilowatt-hour** is a unit of energy that is equal to the energy provided by a thousand watts in one hour.

N-COUNT

kilt /kɪlt/ kilts. A **kilt** is a kind of skirt that men sometimes wear as part of their country's traditional costume, especially in Scotland. Kilts can also be worn by women and girls.

N-COUNT

ki·mo·no /kɪˈməʊnəʊ, AM -nə/ kimonos. A **kimono** is an item of Japanese clothing. It is long, shaped like a coat, and has wide sleeves.

N-COUNT

kin /kɪn/. Your **kin** are your relatives. *...her husband's kin.* ● See also **kith and kin, next of kin**.

◆◇◇◇
N-PLURAL
DATED

kind 1 noun uses and phrases

kind /kaɪnd/ kinds. 1 A particular **kind** of thing is one of the different types or sorts of that thing. *Had Jamie ever been in any kind of trouble?... I'm not the kind of person to get married... This book prize is the biggest of its kind in the world... Ear pain of any kind must never be ignored.* **2** You can use **all kinds**

◆◆◆◆◇
N-COUNT
PHRASE

of to emphasize that there are a great number and variety of particular things or people. *Donations came from all kinds of people... All kinds of remarkable things began to happen.*

PRAGMATICS

3 If you refer to someone's **kind**, you are referring to all the other people that are like them, especially when you disapprove of them. *I hate Lewis and his kind just as much as you do.* **4** If you refer to someone or something as **one of a kind**, you mean that there is nobody or nothing else like them. *She's a very unusual woman, one of a kind.* **5** If you refer, for example, to **two, three,** or **four of a kind**, you mean two, three, or four similar people or things that seem to go well or belong together. *They were two of a kind, from the same sort of background.*

N-COUNT:
poss N
PRAGMATICS
PHRASE
PHRASE

6 You can use **of a kind** to indicate that something is reasonably good or adequate in the circumstances, but is not ideal. *She finds solace of a kind in alcohol.* **7** You use **kind of** when you want to say that something or someone can be roughly described in a particular way. *She wasn't beautiful. But she was kind of cute... It kind of gives us an idea of what's happening.* **8** If you respond or retaliate **in kind**, you react to something that someone has done to you, by doing the same thing to them. *They hurled defiant taunts at the riot police, who responded in kind.* **9** If you pay a debt **in kind**, you pay it in the form of goods or services, and not money. *Inflation and the shortage of banknotes has forced factories to pay their workers in kind.*

PHRASE
PRAGMATICS
PHRASE
SPOKEN
PHRASE
PHRASE

kind 2 adjective uses

kind /kaɪnd/ kinder, kindest. 1 Someone who is **kind** behaves in a gentle, caring, and helpful way towards other people. *She is warm-hearted and kind to everyone... It was very kind of you to come.* ♦ **kind·ly** *'You seem tired this morning, Jenny,' she said kindly.* ♦ **kind·ness** *We have been treated with such kindness by everybody.* **2** You can use **kind** in expressions such as **please be so kind as to** and **would you be kind enough to** in order to ask someone to do something in a firm but polite way. *Please be so kind as to see to it that all the alterations are made at once!... I wonder if you'd be kind enough to call him.* **3** Something that is **kind** emphasizes the good qualities in something or someone, and perhaps makes them appear better than they really are. *Summer clothes are invariable less kind to fuller figures.* **4** See also **kindly, kindness**.

◆◆◇◇◇
ADJ-GRADED
ADV-GRADED:
ADV after v
N-UNCOUNT
ADJ-GRADED:
v-link ADJ
PRAGMATICS
ADJ-GRADED

kin·der·gar·ten /ˈkɪndəgɑːtən/ kindergartens. A **kindergarten** is the same as a **nursery school**. *She's in kindergarten now.*

◆◇◇◇
N-COUNT:
also in/to/at
N

kind-'hearted. If you describe someone as **kind-hearted**, you mean that they are kind, caring, and generous.

ADJ-GRADED

kin·dle /ˈkɪndəl/ kindles, kindling, kindled. 1 If something **kindles** a particular emotion in someone, it makes them start to feel it. *The second world war kindled his enthusiasm for politics... These poems have helped kindle the imagination of generations of children.* **2** If you **kindle** a fire, you light paper or wood in order to start it.

VERB
V n
VERB: V n

kin·dling /ˈkɪndlɪŋ/. Kindling consists of small pieces of dry wood and other materials that you use to start a fire.

N-UNCOUNT

kind·ly /ˈkaɪndli/. 1 A **kindly** person is kind and caring. *...an extremely kindly man.* ♦ **kind·li·ness** *His kindliness and warmth made him particularly effective with staff welfare.* **2** If someone **kindly** does something for you, they show thoughtfulness and care for you. *He had very kindly asked me to the cocktail party.* **3** If someone asks you to **kindly** do something, they are asking you in a way which shows that they have authority over you, or that they are angry with you. *Will you kindly obey the instructions I am about to give?* **4** If you **look kindly on** someone or something, you support them or approve of what they are doing. *Recent historical work looks kindly on the regime.* **5** If someone **does not take kindly to** something or someone, they do not

◆◆◇◇◇
ADJ-GRADED
N-UNCOUNT
ADV-GRADED:
ADV before v
ADV:
ADV before v
PRAGMATICS
FORMAL
PHRASE
PHRASE

K

like it or them. *She did not take kindly to being offered advice on her social life.* **6** See also **kind**.

kind·ness /'kaɪndnəs/ **kindnesses. 1** A kindness is a helpful or considerate act. *I only want to do you a small kindness.* **2** See also **kind**. ◆◇◇◇◇ N-COUNT

kin·dred spir·it /ˌkɪndrɪd 'spɪrɪt/ **kindred spirits.** A **kindred spirit** is a person who has the same view of life or the same interests as you. *He recognized in Bulman a kindred spirit.* N-COUNT

ki·net·ic /kɪ'netɪk/. **Kinetic** is used to describe something that is concerned with movement. *...the kinetic energy of the meteorite.* ADJ TECHNICAL

king /kɪŋ/ **kings. 1** A **king** is the most important man in the royal family of his country, and usually the Head of State. *...the king and queen of Spain. ...when Prince Charles becomes King. ...King Albert.* **2** If you describe a man as **the king** of something, you mean that he is the most important person doing that thing or he is the best at doing it. *He was the king of the big love song.* **3** A **king** is a playing card with a picture of a king on it. *...the king of diamonds.* **4** In chess, the **king** is the most important piece. When you are in a position to capture your opponent's king, you win the game. **5 ● a king's ransom:** see **ransom**. ◆◆◆◇ N-TITLE; N-COUNT

N-COUNT: *the N of n*

N-COUNT

N-COUNT

king·dom /'kɪŋdəm/ **kingdoms. 1** A **kingdom** is a country ruled by a king or queen. *...the United Kingdom. ...the Kingdom of Denmark.* **2** A **kingdom** is a place or area that is thought to be under the control of a person or organization. *It was infamous as a kingdom of brigands, scoundrels, and slave-traders.* **3** A particular **kingdom** is one of the major groups that all natural and living things are divided into. *...the mineral, plant, animal and human kingdoms.* ◆◆◇◇◇ N-COUNT

N-COUNT

N-COUNT

king·fisher /'kɪŋfɪʃə/ **kingfishers.** A **kingfisher** is a brightly-coloured bird which lives near rivers and lakes and catches fish. ◆◇◇◇◇ N-COUNT

king·ly /'kɪŋli/. **Kingly** means like a king, or related to the duties of a king. *Waving his arms in a kingly manner, he led his company back to the royal dwellings... They thought that he should resume his kingly duties.* ADJ-GRADED LITERARY

king·pin /'kɪŋpɪn/ **kingpins.** If you describe someone as the **kingpin** of an organization, you mean that they are the most important person involved in it. *...one of the alleged kingpins of Colombia's largest drugs ring.* N-COUNT INFORMAL

king·ship /'kɪŋʃɪp/. **Kingship** is the fact or position of being a king. *...the duties of kingship.* N-UNCOUNT

'king-size; also spelled **king-sized.** A **king-size** or **king-sized** version of something is a larger size than the standard version, and may be the largest size available. *...a king-size bed. ...king-size cigarettes.* ADJ

kink /kɪŋk/ **kinks.** A **kink** is a curve or twist in something which is otherwise straight. *...a tiny black kitten with tufted ears and a kink in her tail.* N-COUNT

♦ kinked. If something is **kinked**, it has a kink or kinks in it. *The kinked line in chart 1 represents this pattern.* ADJ

kinky /'kɪŋki/ **kinkier, kinkiest.** If you describe something as **kinky**, you mean that it is associated with strange or unusual sexual practices. *...kinky underwear.* ADJ-GRADED INFORMAL

kin·ship /'kɪnʃɪp/. **1 Kinship** is the relationship between members of the same family. *Her father's family could claim kinship with another hero of that war.* **2** If you feel **kinship** with someone, you feel close to them, because you have a similar background or similar feelings or ideas. *...a sense of kinship. ...the warmth and kinship one farmer feels for another.* N-UNCOUNT FORMAL

N-UNCOUNT LITERARY

kins·man /'kɪnzmən/ **kinsmen.** Someone's **kinsman** is their male relative. N-COUNT LITERARY

kins·woman /'kɪnzwʊmən/ **kinswomen.** Someone's **kinswoman** is their female relative. N-COUNT LITERARY

ki·osk /'ki:ɒsk/ **kiosks. 1** A **kiosk** is a small shop on the street, or in public place such as a station. It sells things such as snacks or newspapers which you buy through an open window. *I was getting cigarettes at the kiosk.* **2** A **kiosk** or a **telephone** ◆◇◇◇◇ N-COUNT

kiosk is a public telephone box. *He phoned me from a kiosk.* BRITISH

kip /kɪp/. **Kip** is sleep. *Mason went home for a couple of hours' kip... I had a kip in a field.* N-UNCOUNT: also a N INFORMAL

kip·per /'kɪpə/ **kippers.** A **kipper** is a herring which has been preserved by being hung in smoke. N-COUNT BRITISH

kirsch /kɪəʃ/. **Kirsch** is a strong, colourless, alcoholic drink made from cherries. N-UNCOUNT

kiss /kɪs/ **kisses, kissing, kissed. 1** If you **kiss** someone, you touch them with your lips to show love or affection, or to greet them or say goodbye. *She leaned up and kissed him on the cheek... Her parents kissed her goodbye... They kissed for almost half-a-minute... We kissed goodbye.* ▶ Also a noun. *I put my arms around her and gave her a kiss.* **2** If you **kiss** someone's hand, you touch it lightly with your lips as a sign of respect. *He bowed, kissed her hand, and led her down to the courtyard.* **3** If you **blow** someone **a kiss,** you touch the palm of your hand lightly with your lips, and then blow on your hand towards the person. **4** If say that you **kiss** something **goodbye** or **kiss goodbye** to something, you accept the fact that you are going to lose it, although you do not want to. *I felt sure I'd have to kiss my dancing career goodbye.* ◆◆◇◇ V-RECIP NON-RECIP: V n

V n n RECIP: pl-n V pl-n V n N-COUNT VERB V n

PHRASE

PHRASE INFORMAL

,kiss and 'tell. If someone who has had a love affair with a famous person tells the story of that affair in public, for example in a newspaper or book, you can refer to this as a **kiss and tell** story. *...the publication of a kiss-and-tell book by a woman who claims to have had an affair with him.* ADJ: ADJ n

,kiss of 'death. If you say that a particular event is the **kiss of death** for someone or something, you mean that it is certain to make them fail or be a disaster. *The government fears these accusations will be the kiss of death for foreign sales of other such goods.* N-SING

,kiss of 'life. If you give someone who has stopped breathing the **kiss of life,** you put your mouth onto their mouth and breathe into their lungs to make them start breathing again. N-SING: the N BRITISH

kit /kɪt/ **kits, kitting, kitted. 1** A **kit** is a group of items that are kept together, often in the same container, because they are all used for similar purposes. *...a first aid kit. ...an emergency car-tool kit.* **2 Kit** is special clothing and equipment that you use when you take part in a particular activity or sport. *I forgot my gym kit.* **3** A **kit** is a set of parts that can be put together in order to make something. *...model aeroplane kits.* ◆◆◇◇◇ N-COUNT

N-UNCOUNT BRITISH N-COUNT

kit out. If someone or something **is kitted out,** they have all the clothing or equipment they need at a particular time. *She was kitted out with winter coat, skirts, jumpers... Kit yourself out in crash helmet and goggles.* PHRASAL VB be V-ed P with/in n V n P with/in n BRITISH, INFORMAL

kit·bag /'kɪtbæg/ **kitbags.** A **kitbag** is a long narrow bag in which soldiers or sailors keep clothing and personal belongings. N-COUNT BRITISH

kitch·en /'kɪtʃɪn/ **kitchens.** A **kitchen** is a room that is used for cooking and for household jobs such as washing dishes. See picture headed **house and flat.** ● See also **soup kitchen.** ◆◆◆◇ N-COUNT

kitch·en·ette /ˌkɪtʃɪ'net/ **kitchenettes.** A **kitchenette** is a small kitchen, or a part of a larger room that is used for cooking. N-COUNT

,kitchen 'garden, kitchen gardens. A **kitchen garden** is a part of the garden of a large country house in which vegetables, herbs, and fruit are grown. N-COUNT

kite /kaɪt/ **kites. 1** A **kite** is a toy which you fly in the air while holding it by a long string. It consists of a light frame covered with paper or cloth. **2** A **kite** is a bird of prey with a long forked tail. ◆◇◇◇◇ N-COUNT

N-COUNT

Kite·mark /'kaɪtmɑːk/. In Britain, the **Kitemark** is a symbol like a small kite which is displayed on products that have met official standards of safety and quality. N-SING

kith and kin /ˌkɪθ ən 'kɪn/. Someone's **kith and kin** are their relatives. N-PLURAL

kitsch /kɪtʃ/. You can refer to a work of art or an object as **kitsch** if it is showy and in bad taste, for example because it has been made to appeal to ◆◇◇◇◇ N-UNCOUNT

people's sentimentality. ...*collectors of Fifties kitsch.*
► Also an adjective. *Blue and green eye shadow has* ADJ-GRADED
long been considered kitsch. ...kitsch pop culture.

kit·ten /ˈkɪtən/ **kittens.** A **kitten** is a very young ◆◇◇◇◇
cat. *I am going to get a kitten.* N-COUNT

kit·ty /ˈkɪti/ **kitties. 1** A **kitty** is an amount of mon- N-COUNT
ey consisting of contributions from several people,
used to buy things that these people will share. *You*
haven't put any money in the kitty for three weeks.
2 A **kitty** is the total amount of money which is bet N-COUNT
in a lottery or card game, and which is taken by the
winner or winners. *The total prize kitty is £13.5 mil-*
lion. **3** **Kitty** is sometimes used as an affectionate N-COUNT
way of referring to a cat. INFORMAL

kiwi /ˈkiːwiː/ **kiwis.** A **kiwi** is a type of bird that ◆◇◇◇◇
lives in New Zealand. Kiwis cannot fly. N-COUNT

'kiwi fruit, kiwi fruits; kiwi fruit can also be used N-VAR
as the plural form. A **kiwi fruit** is a fruit with a
brown hairy skin and green flesh. See picture headed **fruit.**

Kleen·ex /ˈkliːneks/. **Kleenex** is both the singular N-COUNT
and the plural form. A **Kleenex** is a piece of soft tissue paper that is used as a handkerchief. **Kleenex** is
a trademark.

klep·to·ma·ni·ac /ˌkleptəˈmeɪniæk/ **kleptomani-** N-COUNT
acs. A **kleptomaniac** is a person with a mental illness which gives them an uncontrollable desire to
steal things.

km, kms; km can also be used as the plural form. ◆◆◇◇◇
Km is a written abbreviation for **kilometre.**

knack /næk/ **knacks.** If you have the **knack** of do- ◆◇◇◇◇
ing something difficult or skilful, you are able to do N-COUNT
it easily and naturally. *He's got the knack of getting*
people to listen.

knack·ered /ˈnækəd/. **1** If you are **knackered,** you ADJ-GRADED
are extremely tired. *I was absolutely knackered at* BRITISH,
the end of the match. **2** If you say that something is ADJ
knackered, you mean that it is completely broken BRITISH,
or worn out. *My tape player's knackered.* INFORMAL

knap·sack /ˈnæpsæk/ **knapsacks.** A **knapsack** is a N-COUNT
canvas bag that you carry on your back, for example
when you are walking in the countryside.

knead /niːd/ **kneads, kneading, kneaded.** ◆◇◇◇◇
1 When you **knead** dough, you press and squeeze it VERB
with your hands so that it becomes smooth and V n
ready to cook. *Lightly knead the mixture on a*
floured surface. **2** If you **knead** a part of someone's VERB
body, you press or squeeze it with your fingers. *She* V n
felt him knead the aching muscles.

knee /niː/ **knees, kneeing, kneed. 1** Your **knee** ◆◆◆◇◇
is the place where your leg bends. See picture head- N-COUNT
ed **human body.** *The snow was up to his knees. ...a*
knee injury. **2** If you **knee** someone, you hit them VERB: V n
using your knee. **3** The **knee** on a piece of clothing N-COUNT
is the part that covers your knee. *...jeans with holes*
at both knees. **4** If something or someone is on N-COUNT:
your **knee** or on your **knees,** they are resting or sit- poss N
ting on the upper part of your legs when you are sitting down. *I sat in the back of the taxi with my son*
on my knee. **5** If you are on your **knees,** you are in a N-PLURAL:
kneeling position, with the lower part of your legs poss N
bent under you and your knees touching the
ground. *She fell to the ground on her knees and*
prayed... She was on her knees in the kitchen. **6** If a PHRASE
country or organization **is brought to its knees,** it is
almost completely destroyed by someone or something. *Our aim is to bring this government to its*
knees, to force it to the negotiating table.

knee·cap /ˈniːkæp/ **kneecaps;** also spelled **knee-** N-COUNT
cap. Your **kneecaps** are the bones at the front of
your knees.

'knee-capping, knee-cappings. Knee-capping N-VAR
is the act of shooting someone in the knee, which is
carried out by some terrorist organizations as a
form of punishment.

,knee-'deep. 1 Something that is **knee-deep** is as ADJ
high as your knees. *...knee-deep snow.* **2** If a person ADJ
or a place is **knee-deep** in something such as water,
the level of the water comes up to a person's knees.
They spent much of their time knee-deep in mud.

'knee-jerk. If you call someone's response to a ADJ
problem a **knee-jerk** reaction, you mean that they PRAGMATICS
react to it quickly and predictably, without thinking
about it; used showing disapproval. *The knee-jerk*
reaction to this is to call for proper security in all
hospitals.

kneel /niːl/ **kneels, kneeling, kneeled, knelt.** ◆◇◇◇◇
The forms **kneeled** and **knelt** can both be used for VERB
the past tense and past participle. When you **kneel,** V prep/adv
you put your body in a position with your knees on V-ing
the ground and your lower legs stretched out be- Also V
hind them. *She knelt by the bed and prayed. ...a*
kneeling position. ► **Kneel down** means the same PHRASAL VB
as **kneel.** *She kneeled down beside him.* V P

'knees-up, knees-ups. A **knees-up** is a party or N-COUNT
celebration. BRITISH,
INFORMAL

knelt /nelt/. **Knelt** is a past tense and past participle
of **kneel.**

knew /njuː, AM nuː/. **Knew** is the past tense of
know.

knick·ers /ˈnɪkəz/; the form **knicker** is used as a ◆◇◇◇◇
modifier. **Knickers** are a piece of underwear worn N-PLURAL
by women and girls. They have holes for the legs BRITISH
and elastic around the waist. *...six pairs of knickers.*

knick-knacks /ˈnɪknæks/. **Knick-knacks** are small N-PLURAL
objects such as ornaments which people like to
keep or collect. *Her flat is spilling over with*
knick-knacks.

knife /naɪf/ **knives; knifes, knifing, knifed** ◆◆◆◇◇
Knives is the plural form of the noun and **knifes** is
the third person singular of the present tense of the
verb. **1** A **knife** is a tool consisting of a flat sharp- N-COUNT
edged piece of metal on the end of a handle. A knife
is used mainly for cutting things, such as food, but
some knives can be used as weapons. See picture
headed **kitchen utensils.** *...a knife and fork. ...a sur-*
geon's knife. **2** To **knife** someone means to attack VERB: V n
and injure them with a knife. *She was knifed in the* be V-ed prep
back six times. ♦ **knif·ing, knifings.** A **knifing** is Also V n prep
an incident in which someone is knifed. *...a post-* N-COUNT
electoral riot that led to knifings, beatings and 27 ar-
rests. **3** If a lot of people want something unpleas- PHRASE
ant to happen to someone, for example if they want BRITISH
them to lose their job, you can say that **the knives**
are out for that person. *The Party knives are out for*
the leader. **4** If you **twist the knife,** you do or say PHRASE
something unpleasant to someone, when they are
already in an unpleasant situation. *Her daughter*
manages to twist the knife still further by claiming
Nancy never loved her. **5** See also **carving knife,**
flick-knife, paper knife, pocket knife, Stanley
knife.

'knife-edge; also spelled **knife edge.** If a situation N-SING
is **on a knife-edge,** it is exciting or tense because
nobody knows what is going to happen next and
one thing is just as likely to happen as another. *The*
game is poised on a knife-edge. One mistake or one
piece of good luck could decide it... Tonight's knife-
edge vote could be uncomfortably close.

knife·man /ˈnaɪfmən/ **knifemen.** A **knifeman** is N-COUNT
someone who has attacked or killed someone with a BRITISH,
knife. *A crazed knifeman attacked three police-* JOURNALISM
women.

knife·point /ˈnaɪfpɔɪnt/; also spelled **knife-point.** If PHRASE
you are attacked or robbed **at knifepoint,** someone JOURNALISM
threatens you with a knife while they attack or rob
you. *He held her at knifepoint and threatened to kill*
her.

knight /naɪt/ **knights, knighting, knighted.** ◆◆◇◇◇
1 In medieval times, a **knight** was a man of noble N-COUNT
birth, who served his king or lord in battle. **2** If VB: usu
someone **is knighted,** they are given a knighthood. passive
He was knighted in the Queen's birthday honours list be V-ed
in June 1988. **3** In chess, a **knight** is a piece which is N-COUNT
shaped like a horse's head. **4** If you refer to a **knight** PHRASE
in shining armour, you mean someone who is kind
and brave, and likely to rescue you from a difficult
situation.

knight·hood /ˈnaɪthʊd/ **knighthoods.** In Britain, ◆◇◇◇◇
a **knighthood** is a title that the queen or king gives N-COUNT

to a man for his outstanding achievements or service. A man with a knighthood can put 'Sir' in front of his name.

knight·ly /ˈnaɪtli/. Knightly describes something that is characteristic of a knight, such as his bravery or honour. ADJ: ADJ n

knit /nɪt/ knits, knitting, knitted. The past tense can be either knit or knitted for meaning 3. 1 If you knit something, especially a piece of clothing, you make it from wool by using two knitting needles or a machine. *I had endless hours to knit and sew... I have already started knitting baby clothes... She knitted him 10 pairs of socks. ...her grey knitted cardigan.* ▶ Also a combining form. *...hand-knit garments.* 2 If someone or something knits things or people together, they make them fit or work together closely and successfully. *The best thing about sport is that it knits the whole family close together.* ▶ Also a combining form. *...a tightly knit society. ...an exceptionally happy and close-knit family.* 3 If you knit your brows, you frown because you are angry or worried. ◆◆◇◇ VERB / V / V n / V n n / V-ed / COMB / VERB / V n with together / Also V n in / into n / COMB / PHRASE / LITERARY

knit·ting /ˈnɪtɪŋ/. 1 Knitting is something, such as a piece of clothing, that is being knitted. *She had been sitting with her knitting at her fourth-floor window.* 2 Knitting is the activity of making clothes out of wool. *...a relaxing hobby, such as knitting. ...knitting patterns.* ◆◇◇◇ N-UNCOUNT / N-UNCOUNT

'knitting needle, knitting needles. Knitting needles are thin plastic or metal rods which you use when you are knitting. N-COUNT

knit·wear /ˈnɪtweə/. Knitwear is clothing that has been knitted, especially clothing made using machines and sold in shops. N-UNCOUNT

knives /naɪvz/. Knives is the plural of knife.

knob /nɒb/ knobs. 1 A knob is a round handle on a door or drawer which you use in order to open or close it. 2 A knob is a rounded lump or ball on top of a post or stick. *A loose brass knob on the bedstead rattled.* 3 A knob is a round switch on a piece of machinery or equipment. *He twiddled a knob on the dashboard, and a red light came on.* 4 A knob of butter is a small amount of it. *Top the steaming hot potatoes with a knob of butter.* ◆◇◇◇ N-COUNT / N-COUNT / N-COUNT / N-COUNT: N of n BRITISH

knob·bly /ˈnɒbli/; the form knobby /ˈnɒbi/ is also used. Something that is knobbly or knobby has lumps on it which stick out and make the surface uneven. ADJ-GRADED

knock /nɒk/ knocks, knocking, knocked. 1 If you knock on something such as a door or window, you hit it, usually several times, to attract someone's attention. *She went directly to Simon's apartment and knocked on the door... He knocked before going in.* ▶ Also a noun. *They heard a knock at the front door.* ♦ knock·ing *...a loud knocking at the door.* 2 If you knock something, you touch or hit it roughly so that it moves or falls over. *She accidentally knocked the tea tin off the shelf... Buckets of roses had been knocked over.* ▶ Also a noun. *...materials to protect against knocks, rain and dust.* 3 To knock someone into a particular position or condition means to hit them very hard so that they fall over or become unconscious. *The third wave was so strong it knocked me backwards... Someone had knocked him unconscious.* 4 If someone knocks two rooms or buildings into one, or knocks them together, they make them form one room or building by removing a wall. *The spacious kitchen was achieved by knocking together three small rooms.* 5 If something knocks, it makes a repeated sharp banging noise. *The walls squeaked and the pipes knocked.* 6 If something unpleasant knocks a particular quality or characteristic out of someone, it makes them lose it. *The stories of his links with the actress had knocked the fun out of him.* 7 If someone or something receives a knock, they have an unpleasant experience which prevents them from achieving so much. *The art market has suffered some severe knocks during the* ◆◆◆◇ VERB / V on/at n / V / N-COUNT / N-SING / VERB / V n prep / V n with adv / Also V n / N-COUNT / VERB / V n prep/adv / V n adj / VERB / V pl-n into n / V pl-n with together / VERB / V / VB: no cont / V n out of n / Also V n / N-COUNT

past two years. 8 If you knock something or someone, you criticize them. *I'm not knocking them: if they want to do it, it's up to them.* VERB / V n / INFORMAL

9 If you tell someone to knock it off, you are telling them to stop doing something that is annoying you. *Will you just knock it off!* PHRASE / INFORMAL

10 ● to knock people's heads together: see head. ● to knock something on the head: see head. ● to knock someone or something into shape: see shape.

knock about. See knock around. PHRASAL VB

knock around; the form knock about is also used in British English. Knock around and knock about are informal expressions. 1 If someone knocks you around or knocks you about, they hit or kick you several times. *He lied to me constantly and started knocking me around.* 2 If someone knocks around or knocks about somewhere, they spend time there, experiencing different situations or just passing time. *...reporters who knock around in troubled parts of the world... They knock around on weekends in grubby sweaters and pants.* 3 If someone or something is knocking around or knocking about, they are present in a particular place. *His paintings look as if they have been knocking around for centuries.* 4 If you knock around or knock about with someone, you spend your spare time with them. *They were knocking around together for about a year before they started living together.* PHRASAL VB / PHRASAL VB / V n P / BRITISH / V P prep/adv / V P / Also V P n / only cont / V P / RECIP: / V P with n / pl-n V P / together

knock back. 1 If you knock back a drink, you drink it quickly. *He was knocking back his 10th gin and tonic of the day.* 2 If an event, situation, or person knocks you back, they prevent you from progressing or achieving something. *That really knocked back any hope for further peace negotiations.* PHRASAL VB / V P noun / Also V n P / V n P / V P noun / BRITISH

knock down or knock over. 1 If someone is knocked down or is knocked over by a vehicle or its driver, they are hit by the vehicle and are injured or killed. *A drunk driver knocked down and killed two girls.* 2 To knock down a building means to demolish it. *They have since knocked down the shack and built a modern villa.* PHRASAL VB / be V-ed P / V P noun / Also V n P / V P noun / Also V P n

knock off. 1 To knock off an amount from a price, time, or level means to reduce it by that amount. *He has knocked 10 seconds off the world record.* 2 If someone knocks something off, they steal it. *Cars can be stolen almost as easily as knocking off a bike.* 3 When you knock off, you finish work at the end of the day or before a break. *If I get this report finished I'll knock off early.* 4 To knock someone off means to kill them. *He had many motives for wanting to knock off Yvonne.* PHRASAL VB / V P amount / V amount P n / V P noun / BRITISH, INFORMAL / V P / INFORMAL / V P noun / INFORMAL

knock out. 1 To knock someone out means to cause them to become unconscious or to go to sleep. *She hit him with a frying pan! Nearly knocked him out.* 2 If a person or team is knocked out of a competition, they are defeated in a game, so that they take no more part in the competition. *The Irish came so close to knocking England out of the European Championships.* ● See also knockout. 3 If something is knocked out by enemy action or bad weather, it is destroyed or stops functioning because of it. *Our bombers have knocked out the mobile launchers.* PHRASAL VB / V n P / Also V P noun / be V-ed P / V n P of n / Also V P n / V P noun

knock over. See knock down. PHRASAL VB

knock up; the form knock together is also used for meaning 1. 1 If you knock something up or knock it together, you make it or build it very quickly, using whatever materials are available. *Any water-skiing enthusiast can knock up a pair of skis in a few hours... Could you possibly knock me up some scrambled eggs?* 2 If you knock someone up, you knock on their door in the night or in the morning in order to wake them up. *He went to knock Rob up at 4.30am.* PHRASAL VB / V P noun / V n P noun / Also V n P / INFORMAL / V n P / Also V P noun / BRITISH, INFORMAL

knock·about /ˈnɒkəbaʊt/. Knockabout comedy is lively and spontaneous, and often involves people doing funny or foolish things. ADJ-GRADED / BRITISH

knock·down /ˈnɒkdaʊn/ knockdowns; also spelled knock-down. A knockdown price is much lower than it would be normally. *...the chance to buy it now at a knockdown price.* ADJ: ADJ n / INFORMAL

knock·er /ˈnɒkə/ knockers. A knocker is a piece of metal on the front door of a building, which you N-COUNT

use to hit the door in order to attract the attention of the people inside.

'knock-on. A knock-on effect or process is one in which one initial action or event causes several other events to happen one after the other. *The peseta's problems had a knock-on effect on the escudo.* ◆◇◇◇◇ ADJ: ADJ n BRITISH

knock·out /'nɒkaʊt/ **knockouts;** also spelled **knock-out.** 1 In boxing, a **knockout** is a situation in which a boxer wins the fight by making his opponent fall to the ground and be unable to stand up before the referee has counted to ten. 2 A **knockout** blow is an action or event that completely destroys an opponent. *He delivered a knockout blow to all of his rivals.* 3 A **knockout** competition is one in which several competitors or teams take part, and the winner of each match goes on to the next round while the loser leaves the competition, until one competitor or team is the winner. 4 If you describe someone or something as **a knockout,** you think they are extremely attractive or impressive. ◆◇◇◇◇ N-COUNT: also by N ADJ: ADJ n ADJ: ADJ n BRITISH N-SING: a N INFORMAL

knoll /nəʊl/ **knolls.** A **knoll** is a low hill with gentle slopes and a rounded top. N-COUNT LITERARY

knot /nɒt/ **knots, knotting, knotted.** 1 If you tie a **knot** in a piece of string, rope, cloth, or other material, you pass one end or part of it through a loop and pull it tight. *One lace had broken and been tied in a knot.* 2 If you **knot** a piece of string, rope, cloth, or other material, you pass one end or part of it through a loop and pull it tight. *He knotted the laces securely together.* 3 If you say that two people **tie the knot,** you mean that they get married. 4 A **knot** of people is a group standing very close together. *A little knot of men stood clapping.* 5 If your stomach **knots** or if something **knots** it, it feels tight because you are afraid or excited. *I felt my stomach knot with apprehension.* ▶ Also a noun. *There was a knot of tension in his stomach.* 6 If part of your face or your muscles **knot,** they become tense, usually because you are worried or angry. *His forehead knotted in a frown.* 7 A **knot** in a piece of wood is a small hard area where a branch grew. 8 A **knot** is a unit of speed. The speed of ships, aircraft, and winds is measured in knots. *...speeds of up to 30 knots.* ◆◆◇◇◇ N-COUNT VERB: V n V n with together PHRASE INFORMAL N-COUNT WRITTEN V-ERG V Also V n N-COUNT VERB V N-COUNT N-COUNT

knot·ty /'nɒti/ **knottier, knottiest.** 1 A **knotty** problem is complicated and difficult to solve. *The new management team faces some knotty problems.* 2 **Knotty** wood has a lot of small hard areas on it where branches once grew. ADJ-GRADED ADJ

know /nəʊ/ **knows, knowing, knew, known.** 1 If you **know** a fact, a piece of information, or an answer, you have it correctly in your mind. *I don't know the name of the place... I know that you led a rifle platoon during the Second World War... I don't know what happened to her husband.. 'How did he meet your mother?'—'I don't know.'... We all know about his early experiments in flying.* 2 If you **know** about a subject, you have studied it or taken an interest in it, and understand part or all of it. *She didn't know anything about music but she liked to sing.* 3 If you **know** a language, you have learnt it and can understand it. *It helps to know French and Creole if you want to understand some of the lyrics.* 4 If you **know** how to do something, you have the necessary skills and knowledge to do it. *The health authorities now know how to deal with the disease.* 5 If you **know** of something, you have heard about it but you do not necessarily have a lot of information about it. *We know of the incident but have no further details.* 6 If you are **in the know** about something, especially something that is not known about or understood by many people, you have information about it. *He takes crucial decisions without consulting people in the know.* 7 If you **know** someone, you are familiar with them because you have met them and talked to them before. *Gifford was a friend. I'd known him for nine years.* ● If you **get to know** someone, you find out what they are like by spending time with them. 8 If ◆◆◆◆◆ VB: no cont V n V that V wh V V about n/-ing VB: no cont, V about n V amount about n VB: no cont V n VB: no cont V wh-to-inf VB: no cont V of n PHRASE VB: no cont V n PHRASE VB: no cont

you **know** something such as a place, a work of art, or an idea, you are familiar with it. *I don't know whether you know Birmingham well... I don't know the play, I've just come to see it.* 9 If you talk about a thing or system **as we know it,** you are referring to the form in which it exists now and which is familiar to most people. *...those values of our culture that are essential to civilisation as we know it.* 10 If you **know** something or someone, you recognize them when you see them or hear them. *Would she know you if she saw you on the street?* 11 If someone or something **is known** as a particular name, they are called by that name. *The disease is more commonly known as Mad Cow Disease... Everyone knew him as Dizzy.* 12 If you **know** someone or something as a person or thing that has particular qualities, you consider that they have those qualities. *Lots of people know her as a very kind woman... Kemp knew him for a meticulous officer.* 13 If you **know** someone or something as a person or thing with a particular job or function, you are familiar with them in that job or function, rather than in any other. *Most of us know her as the woman who used to present the television news.* V n PHRASE VB: no cont V n VB: no cont V n asn be V-ed as n V n asn Also V n by n VERB V n asn V n for n VERB V n asn

14 See also **knowing, known.**

15 You say **I know** to show that you agree with what has just been said. *'This country is so awful.'—'I know, I know.'* 16 You say **I know** to show that you accept that something is true, but think that it is not very important or relevant. *'There are trains straight from Cambridge.'—'I know, but it's no quicker.'* 17 You use **I know** to express sympathy and understanding towards someone. *I'm sorry, George. I know how you feel... I know you must be feeling sad.* 18 You can use **I don't know** to indicate that you do not completely agree with something or do not really think that it is true. *'He should quite simply resign.'—'I don't know about that.'* 19 You can say **I don't know about you** to indicate that you are going to give your own opinion about something and you want to find out if someone else feels the same. *I don't know about the rest of you, but I'm hungry.* 20 You use **I don't know** in expressions which indicate criticism of someone's behaviour. For example, if you say that you **do not know how** someone can do something, you mean that you cannot understand or accept them doing it. *I don't know what those folk think they are playing at.* CONVENTION PRAGMATICS CONVENTION PRAGMATICS PHRASE PRAGMATICS PHRASE PRAGMATICS PHRASE PRAGMATICS PHRASE PRAGMATICS

21 You can use expressions such as **you know what I mean** and **if you know what I mean** to suggest that the person listening to you understands what you are trying to say, and so you do not have to explain any more. *She was a bit stuck up, know what I mean?* 22 You use **you know** to emphasize or to draw attention to what you are saying. *The conditions in there are awful, you know.* 23 Some people use **you know** when they are uncertain about what they are saying or what they are going to say next. *He's generous and, you know, very nice, very polite.* 24 You use **you know** when you are trying to explain more clearly what you mean, by referring to something that the person you are talking to knows about. *Wear the white dress, you know, the one with all the black embroidery.* CONVENTION PRAGMATICS CONVENTION PRAGMATICS SPOKEN CONVENTION PRAGMATICS SPOKEN CONVENTION PRAGMATICS SPOKEN

25 You say **You never know** or **One never knows** to indicate that it is not definite or certain what will happen in the future, and to suggest that there is some hope that things will turn out well. *There might be an even bigger one – I doubt it, but you never know.* 26 People use expressions such as **goodness knows, Heaven knows,** and **God knows** when they do not know something. Some people consider these expressions to be offensive. *'Who's he?'—'God knows.'* 27 People sometimes say **What do you know!** when they are very surprised about something. *Well, what do you know!* 28 You can say **You don't know** in order to emphasize how strongly you feel about the remark you are going to make next. *You don't know how good it is to speak to somebody from home.* 29 You say **Not that I know of** when you think the answer to a question is 'no' but you cannot be sure be- CONVENTION PRAGMATICS PHRASE INFORMAL EXCLAM PRAGMATICS INFORMAL PHRASE PRAGMATICS SPOKEN CONVENTION PRAGMATICS

K

cause you do not know all the facts. *'Is he married?'—* *'Not that I know of.'*

30 Know is used in a large number of expressions which are explained under other words in this dictionary. For example, the expression **to know** something **backwards** is explained at **backwards**.

'know-all, know-alls. If you say that someone is a **know-all**, you are critical of them because they think that they know a lot more than other people. The American word is **know-it-all**. ◆◇◇◇◇ N-COUNT PRAGMATICS BRITISH, INFORMAL

'know-how; also spelled **knowhow. Know-how** is knowledge of the methods or techniques of doing something. *He hasn't got the know-how to run a farm.* N-UNCOUNT INFORMAL

know·ing /'nəʊɪŋ/. A **knowing** gesture or remark is one that shows that you understand something, even though it has not actually been mentioned directly. *Dan exchanged a knowing look with Harry.* ◆ **know·ing·ly** *He smiled knowingly.* ADJ-GRADED

ADV-GRADED

know·ing·ly /'nəʊɪŋli/. If you **knowingly** do something wrong, you know that it is wrong but you do it anyway. *He had never knowingly taken illegal drugs.* ADV-GRADED: ADV before v

'know-it-all, know-it-alls. If you say that someone is a **know-it-all**, you are critical of them because they think they know a lot more than other people. The British word is **know-all**. N-COUNT PRAGMATICS AMERICAN, INFORMAL

knowl·edge /'nɒlɪdʒ/. **1 Knowledge** is information and understanding about a subject which a person has, or which all people have. *She disclaims any knowledge of her husband's business concerns. ...the quest for scientific knowledge.* **2** If you say that something is true **to** your **knowledge** or **to the best of** your **knowledge**, you mean that you believe it to be true but it is possible that you do not know all the facts. *Alec never carried a gun to my knowledge.* **3** If you do something **safe in the knowledge** that something else is the case, you do the first thing confidently because you are sure of the second thing. *You can ventilate your room, safe in the knowledge that your window is secure.* ◆◆◆◇ N-UNCOUNT

PHRASE

PHRASE WRITTEN

knowl·edge·able /'nɒlɪdʒəbəl/. Someone who is **knowledgeable** has a clear understanding of many different facts about the world or about a particular subject. *Do you think you are more knowledgeable about life than your parents were?* ◆ **knowl·edge·ably** *Kaspar had spoken knowledgeably about the state of agriculture in Europe.* ◆◇◇◇ ADJ-GRADED

ADV-GRADED: ADV after v

known /nəʊn/. **1 Known** is the past participle of **know. 2** You use **known** to describe someone or something that is clearly recognized by or familiar to all people or to a particular group of people. *...He was a known drug dealer... Garcia's more known as a good guitarist.* **3** If you **let it be known** that something is the case, or you **let** something **be known**, you make sure that people know it or can find out about it. *The Prime Minister has let it be known that he is against it.* ADJ-GRADED

PHRASE

knuck·le /'nʌkəl/ **knuckles, knuckling, knuckled.** Your **knuckles** are the rounded pieces of bone that form lumps on your hands where your fingers join your hands. See picture headed **human body**. *Jaggery was clutching the rail so tightly his knuckles* ◆◇◇◇◇ N-COUNT

were white. ● **a rap on the knuckles**: see **rap**.

knuckle down. If someone **knuckles down**, they begin to work or study very hard, especially after a period when they have done very little work. *He managed to knuckle down to his lessons long enough to pass his examination.* PHRASAL VB V P V P to n/-ing INFORMAL

knuckle under. If you **knuckle under**, you do what someone else tells you to do or what a situation forces you to do, because you realize that you have no choice. *The United States, he said, did not knuckle under to demands.* PHRASAL VB V P V P to n INFORMAL

'knuckle-duster, knuckle-dusters; also spelled **knuckleduster.** A **knuckle-duster** is a piece of metal that is designed to be worn on a person's hand as a weapon, so that if they hit someone they will hurt them badly. N-COUNT BRITISH

KO /ˌkeɪ 'əʊ/ **KO's, KO'd. 1 KO** is an abbreviation for **knockout. 2** To **KO** someone means to hit them so hard that they become unconscious. N-COUNT VERB: V n INFORMAL

koa·la /kəʊ'ɑːlə/ **koalas.** A **koala** or a **koala bear** is an Australian animal which looks like a small bear with grey fur and small tufted ears. N-COUNT

kohl·ra·bi /ˌkəʊl'rɑːbi/; **kohlrabi** is both the singular and the plural form. **Kohlrabi** is a green vegetable that has a round ball of leaves like a cabbage. N-VAR

kooky /'kuːki/. Someone who is **kooky** is slightly strange or eccentric, but often in a way which makes you like them. ADJ-GRADED

Ko·ran /kɔː'rɑːn/. The **Koran** is the sacred book on which the religion of Islam is based. ◆ **Ko·ran·ic** /kɔː'rænɪk/ *...Koranic schools.* ◆◇◇◇◇ N-PROPER: the N ADJ: ADJ n

ko·sher /'kəʊʃə/. **1** Something, especially food, that is **kosher** is approved of or permitted by the laws of Judaism. *...a kosher butcher.* **2** Something that is **kosher** is generally approved of or considered to be correct. *I guessed something wasn't quite kosher.* ADJ

ADJ-GRADED INFORMAL

kow·tow /ˌkaʊ'taʊ/ **kowtows, kowtowing, kowtowed;** also spelled **kow-tow.** If you say that someone **kowtows** to someone else, you are critical of them for behaving very humbly towards that other person, because they are afraid of them or hope to get something from them. *See how stupidly they kow-tow to persons higher in the hierarchy.* VERB PRAGMATICS V to n Also V INFORMAL

kph /ˌkeɪ piː 'eɪtʃ/. **kph** is an abbreviation for 'kilometres per hour'. It is used to indicate the speed of something such as a vehicle.

Krem·lin /'kremlɪn/. The **Kremlin** is the building in Moscow where Russian government business takes place. ▶ The **Kremlin** is also used to refer to the central government of Russia and of the former Soviet Union. *The Kremlin is still insisting on a diplomatic solution.* ◆◆◇◇◇ N-PROPER: the N N-PROPER: the N

ku·dos /'kjuːdɒs, AM 'kuːdəʊz/. **Kudos** is fame, glory, or admiration that someone gets as a result of a particular action or achievement. *It meant kudos for whoever won the case.* ◆◇◇◇◇ N-UNCOUNT

kung fu /ˌkʌŋ 'fuː/. **Kung fu** is a Chinese martial art or sport in which people fight using only their bare hands and feet. N-UNCOUNT

KW; also spelled **kW. KW** is a written abbreviation for **kilowatt.**

L l

L, l /el/ **L's, l's. 1 L** is the twelfth letter of the English alphabet. **2 L** is the symbol for 'learner driver'. In Britain, a large red 'L' on a white background is attached to cars, motorbikes, or lorries in which people are learning to drive. **3 L** or **l** is used as an abbreviation for words beginning with l, such as 'litre' and 'lire'. N-VAR

N-VAR

La. La is a written abbreviation for **lane,** and is used especially in addresses and on maps or signs.

lab /læb/ **labs. 1** A **lab** is the same as a **laboratory. 2** In Britain, **Lab** is the written abbreviation for **Labour.** *...Ron Brown MP for Edinburgh Leith (Lab).* ◆◆◇◇◇ N-COUNT

la·bel /'leɪbəl/ **labels, labelling, labelled;** spelled **labeling, labeled** in American English. **1** A ◆◆◆◇◇ N-COUNT

label is a piece of paper or plastic that is attached to an object in order to give information about it. **2** If something **is labelled**, a label is attached to it giving information about it. *The produce was labelled 'Made in China'... All the products are labelled with comprehensive instructions.* **3** If you say that someone or something **is labelled** as a particular thing, you mean that people generally describe them that way and you think that this is unfair. *Too often the press are labelled as bad boys... They are afraid to contact the social services in case they are labelled a problem family.* **4** If you say that someone gets a particular **label**, you mean that people describe them with a particular critical word or phrase. *Her treatment of her husband earned her the label of the most hated woman in America.* **5** You can refer to a company that produces and sells records as a particular **label**.

la·bor /ˈleɪbə/. See **labour**.

la·bora·tory /ləˈbɒrətri, AM ˈlæbrətɔːri/ **labora·tories**. **1** A **laboratory** is a building or a room where scientific experiments, analyses, and research are carried out. **2** A **laboratory** in a school or college is a room containing scientific equipment where students are taught science subjects. **3** See also **language laboratory**.

Labor Day. In the United States, **Labor Day** is a public holiday in honour of working people. It is the first Monday in September.

la·bor·er /ˈleɪbərə/. See **labourer**.

la·bo·ri·ous /ləˈbɔːriəs/. If you describe a task or job as **laborious**, you mean that it takes a lot of time and effort. ♦ **la·bo·ri·ous·ly** *He sat behind a desk laboriously writing.*

labor union, labor unions. A **labor union** is an organization that has been formed by workers in order to represent their rights and interests to their employers. The British term is **trade union**.

la·bour /ˈleɪbə/ **labours, labouring, laboured;** spelled **labor** in American English. **1** **Labour** is very hard work, usually physical work. *...the labour of seeding, planting and harvesting... The chef at the barbecue looked up from his labours.* ● See also **hard labour**. ● If you do something as a **labour of love**, you do it because you really want to and not because of any reward you might get for it, even though it involves hard work. **2** Someone who **labours** works hard using their hands. **3** If you **labour** to do something, you do it with difficulty. *For twenty-five years now he has laboured to build a religious community. ...a young man who's labouring under all kinds of other difficulties.* **4** **Labour** is used to refer to the workers of a country or industry, considered as a group. *Latin America lacked skilled labour. ...the struggle between capital and labour.* **5** The work done by a group of workers or by a particular worker is referred to as their **labour**. *The unemployed cannot withdraw their labour.* **6** In Britain, people use **Labour** to refer to the **Labour Party**. *Labour will now have to try and reassess its position... They all vote Labour.* **7** A **Labour** politician or voter is a member of a Labour Party or votes for a Labour Party. **8** If you **labour under** a delusion or misapprehension, you continue to believe something which is not true. **9** If you **labour** a point or an argument, you keep making the same point or saying the same thing, although it is unnecessary. **10** **Labour** is the last stage of pregnancy, in which the baby is gradually pushed out of the womb by the mother. *She was in labour.*

labour camp, labour camps; spelled **labor camp** in American English. A **labour camp** is a kind of prison, where the prisoners are forced to do hard, physical work, usually outdoors.

la·boured /ˈleɪbəd/. **1** If someone's breathing is **laboured**, it is slow and seems to take a lot of effort. **2** If something such as someone's writing or speech is **laboured**, they have put too much effort into it so it seems awkward and unnatural.

la·bour·er /ˈleɪbərə/ **labourers;** spelled **laborer** in American English. A **labourer** is a person who does a job which involves a lot of hard physical work. *...a farm labourer.*

labour force, labour forces. The **labour force** consists of all the people who are able to work in a country or area, or all the people who work for a particular company.

labour market, labour markets. When you talk about the **labour market**, you are referring to all the people who are able to work and want jobs in a country or area, in relation to the number of jobs there are available in that country or area.

Labour Party; spelled **Labor Party** in American English. In Britain, **the Labour Party** is the main left-of-centre party.

labour-saving. A **labour-saving** device or idea makes it possible for you to do something with less effort than usual.

lab·ra·dor /ˈlæbrədɔː/ **labradors**. A **labrador** is a type of large dog with short dense black or gold hair.

la·bur·num /ləˈbɜːnəm/ **laburnums**. A **laburnum** or a **laburnum tree** is a small tree which has long stems of yellow flowers.

laby·rinth /ˈlæbrɪnθ/ **labyrinths**. **1** If you describe a place as a **labyrinth**, you mean that it is made up of a complicated series of paths or passages, through which it is difficult to find your way. *...the labyrinth of corridors.* ♦ **laby·rin·thine** /ˌlæbɪˈrɪnθaɪn/ *The streets of the Old City are narrow and labyrinthine.* **2** If you describe a situation, process, or area of knowledge as a **labyrinth**, you mean that it is very complicated. *...the labyrinth of human nature.* ♦ **labyrinthine** *...the labyrinthine complexities of the situation.*

lace /leɪs/ **laces, lacing, laced**. **1** **Lace** is a very delicate cloth which is made by twisting together fine threads, with holes left in between. **2** **Laces** are thin pieces of material that are used to fasten some types of clothing, especially shoes. *He'd put on his shoes and tied the laces.* **3** If you **lace** something such as a pair of shoes, you tighten the shoes by pulling the laces through the holes, and usually tying them together. ▶ **Lace up** means the same as **lace**. *He sat on the steps, and laced up his boots... Nancy was lacing her shoe up when the doorbell rang.* **4** To **lace** food or drink with a substance such as alcohol or a drug means to put a small amount of the substance into the food or drink. *...a cup of coffee laced with cyanide.* **5** If you **lace** your speech or writing with a particular quality or type of language, you include a lot of it in what you say or write. *...a speech laced with wry humour.*

lace up. See **lace** 3.

lac·er·ate /ˈlæsəreɪt/ **lacerates, lacerating, lacerated**. If something **lacerates** your skin, it cuts it badly and deeply. ♦ **lac·er·ated** *She was suffering from a badly lacerated hand.*

lac·era·tion /ˌlæsəˈreɪʃən/ **lacerations**. **Lacerations** are deep cuts on your skin.

lace-ups; spelled **lace-up** to is used as a modifier. **Lace-ups** are shoes which are fastened with laces.

lach·ry·mose /ˈlækrɪməʊs, -məʊz/. Someone who is **lachrymose** cries very easily and very often.

lack /læk/ **lacks, lacking, lacked**. **1** If there is a **lack** of something, there is not enough of it or it does not exist at all. *Despite his lack of experience, he got the job... The charges were dropped for lack of evidence.* **2** If you say there is **no lack of** something, you are emphasizing there is a great deal of it. *President Clinton displayed no lack of vigor when he began to speak.* **3** If you say that someone or something **lacks** something, or that that thing **is lacking** in them, you mean they do not have any or enough of that thing. *It lacked the power of the Italian cars... Certain vital information is lacking in the room.* ♦ **lack·ing** *She felt nervous, increasingly lacking in confidence about herself... Why was military intelligence so lacking?*

lacka·dai·si·cal /ˌlækəˈdeɪzɪkəl/. If you say that ADJ-GRADED
someone is **lackadaisical**, you mean that they are
rather lazy and do not show much interest or enthusiasm in what they do.

lack·ey /ˈlæki/ **lackeys.** If you describe someone N-COUNT
as a **lackey**, you are critical of them because they PRAGMATICS
follow someone's orders completely, without ever
questioning them.

lack·lustre /ˈlæklʌstə/; spelled **lackluster** in Ameri- ◆◇◇◇◇
can English. If you describe something or someone ADJ-GRADED
as **lacklustre**, you mean that they are not very impressive or lively. *...his party's lackluster performance during the election campaign.*

la·con·ic /ləˈkɒnɪk/. If you describe someone as ADJ-GRADED
laconic, you mean that they use very few words to
say something, so that they seem casual or un-
friendly. ♦ **la·coni·cal·ly** /ləˈkɒnɪkli/ *He laconically* ADV-GRADED:
announced that Digby had been transferred. ADV with v

lac·quer /ˈlækə/ **lacquers. Lacquer** is a special ◆◇◇◇◇
liquid which is painted on wood or metal in order N-VAR
to protect it and to make it shiny. ♦ **lac·quered**
...17th-century lacquered cabinets. ADJ: ADJ n

la·crosse /ləˈkrɒs, AM -ˈkrɔːs/. **Lacrosse** is an out- N-UNCOUNT
door game in which players use long sticks with
nets at the end to catch and throw a small ball, in
order to try and score goals.

lac·ta·tion /lækˈteɪʃən/. **Lactation** is the produc- N-UNCOUNT
tion of milk by women and female mammals during FORMAL
the period after they give birth.

lac·tic acid /ˌlæktɪk ˈæsɪd/. **Lactic acid** is an acid N-UNCOUNT
which is found in sour milk and is also produced by
your muscles when you have been exercising a lot.

lac·tose /ˈlæktəʊs/. **Lactose** is a sugar which is N-UNCOUNT
found in milk and which is sometimes added to
food.

la·cu·na /ləˈkjuːnə/ **lacunae.** If you say that there N-COUNT
is a **lacuna** in something such as a document or a FORMAL
person's argument, you mean that it does not deal
with an important issue and is therefore not effective or convincing.

lacy /ˈleɪsi/ **lacier, laciest. 1 Lacy** things are ◆◇◇◇◇
made from lace or have pieces of lace attached to ADJ-GRADED
them. *...lacy nightgowns.* **2 Lacy** is used to describe ADJ-GRADED
something that looks like lace, especially because it
is very delicate. *...lacy ferns.*

lad /læd/ **lads. 1 A lad** is a young man or boy. *He's* ◆◆◆◇◇
always been a big lad for his age... Come along, lad. N-COUNT
2 Some men refer to their group of male friends or INFORMAL
colleagues as **the lads.** *...having a drink with the* N-PLURAL:
lads... One look at him and you could see he wasn't theN
one of the lads. BRITISH,
INFORMAL

lad·der /ˈlædə/ **ladders. 1 A ladder** is a piece of ◆◆◇◇◇
equipment used for climbing up something or N-COUNT
down from something. It consists of two long pieces
of wood, metal, or rope with steps fixed between
them. **2** You can use **ladder** to refer to something N-SING:
such as a society, organization, or system which has theN
different levels that people can progress up or drop
down. *They want to climb the ladder of success.* **3 A** N-COUNT
ladder in a woman's stocking or tights is a torn part
where some of the vertical threads have broken,
leaving only the horizontal threads.

lad·die /ˈlædi/ **laddies.** A **laddie** is a young man or N-COUNT;
boy. *Now then, laddie, what's the trouble?* N-VOC
INFORMAL

lad·en /ˈleɪdən/. If someone or something is **lad-** ◇◇◇◇◇
en with a lot of heavy things, they are holding or ADJ
carrying them. *I came home laden with cardboard
boxes... Heavily laden lorries were passing.* **2** If you ADJ-GRADED:
describe a person or thing as **laden with** something, v-link ADJ
particularly something bad, you mean that they with n
have a lot of it or are full of it. *We're so laden with
guilt.* ♦ **-laden** *...a fat-laden meal. ...smoke-laden* COMB
air. ...his debt-laden international empire.

'ladies' man. If you say that a man is a **ladies'** N-SING
man, you mean that he enjoys flirting with women DATED
and that women find him attractive.

'ladies' room. Some people refer to a public toilet N-SING
for women as **the ladies' room.**

la·dle /ˈleɪdəl/ **ladles, ladling, ladled. 1** A **ladle** is N-COUNT
a large, round, deep spoon with a long handle, used

for serving soup, stew, or sauce. See picture headed VERB:
kitchen utensils. 2 If you **ladle** food such as soup or V n prep
stew, you serve it, especially with a ladle. *Barry held* V n with adv
*the bowls while Liz ladled soup into them... I ladled
out fruit punch.*

ladle out. If you **ladle out** something such as mon- PHRASAL VB
ey, information, or advice, you give it freely and in V P noun
large quantities. *She was constantly on the phone, la-* Also V n P
dling out inside details to reporters.

lady /ˈleɪdi/ **ladies. 1** You can use the word **lady** ◆◆◆◇
when you are referring to a woman, especially when N-COUNT
you are showing politeness or respect. *Shall we rejoin the ladies? ...a cream-coloured lady's shoe.*
● See also **old lady. 2** You can say **'ladies'** when you N-VOC
are addressing a group of women in a formal and PRAGMATICS
respectful way. *Your table is ready, ladies.* **3** A **lady** N-COUNT
is a woman from the upper classes, especially in
former times. *...the Empress and ladies of the Imperial Palace.* **4** In Britain, **Lady** is a title used in N-TITLE
front of the names of some female members of the
nobility, or the wives of knights or peers. *...Sir Iain
and Lady Noble.* **5** If you say that a woman is a N-COUNT
lady, you mean that she behaves in a polite, dignified, and graceful way. *His wife was great as well,
beautiful-looking and a real lady.* **6** People some- N-SING
times refer to a public toilet for women as **the** BRITISH,
ladies. *Charlotte rushed into the Ladies.* **7** 'Lady' is N-VOC
sometimes used by men as a form of address when AMERICAN,
they are talking to a woman that they do not know. INFORMAL
What seems to be the trouble, lady? **8** See also
First Lady.

lady·bird /ˈleɪdibɜːd/ **ladybirds.** A **ladybird** is a N-COUNT
small round beetle that is red with black spots. The BRITISH
American word is **ladybug.**

lady·bug /ˈleɪdibʌg/ **ladybugs.** See **ladybird.**

'lady friend, lady friends. A man's **lady friend** is N-COUNT
the woman with whom he is having a romantic or DATED
sexual relationship.

lady-in-'waiting, ladies-in-waiting. A **lady-in-** N-COUNT
waiting is a woman from the aristocracy or upper
classes, who acts as a companion to a queen or
princess.

lady·like /ˈleɪdilaɪk/. If you say that a woman or girl ADJ-GRADED
is **ladylike**, you mean that she behaves in a polite,
dignified, and graceful way.

Lady·ship /ˈleɪdiʃɪp/ **Ladyships.** The expressions N-VOC;
Your Ladyship, Her Ladyship, or **Their Ladyships** N-PROPER:
are used to address or refer to female members of det-poss N
the nobility, or the wives of knights or peers. PRAGMATICS

lag /læg/ **lags, lagging, lagged. 1** If one thing or ◆◆◇◇◇
person **lags** behind another thing or person, their VERB:
progress is slower than that of the other thing or V behind n
person. *Black sportsmen have made it in football,* V behind
but other sports are lagging behind... He now lags 10 V amount
points behind the champion... A poll for the Observer behind n
showed Labour on 39 per cent with the Tories lag- V amount
ging a point behind. **2** A time **lag** or a **lag** of a par- behind
ticular length of time is a period of time between Also V
one event and another related event. *There's a time* N-COUNT:
lag between infection with HIV and developing AIDS. with supp
3 If you **lag** the inside of a roof, a pipe, or a water VERB: V n
tank, you cover it with a special material in order to V-ed
prevent heat escaping from it or to prevent it from BRITISH
freezing. *Water tanks should be well lagged.* ● See
also **lagging.**

la·ger /ˈlɑːgə/ **lagers. Lager** is a type of light beer. ◆◇◇◇◇
...a pint of lager. ► A glass of lager can be referred N-VAR
to as a **lager.** BRITISH
N-COUNT

lag·gard /ˈlægəd/ **laggards.** If you describe a N-COUNT
country, company, or product as a **laggard**, you
mean that it is not performing as well as its
competitors.

lag·ging /ˈlægɪŋ/. **Lagging** is special material which N-UNCOUNT
is used to cover pipes, water tanks, or the inside of a BRITISH
roof so that heat does not escape from them or so
they do not freeze.

la·goon /ləˈguːn/ **lagoons.** A **lagoon** is an area of ◆◇◇◇◇
calm sea water that is separated from the ocean by N-COUNT
reefs or sandbanks.

laid /leɪd/. **Laid** is the past tense and past participle of **lay**.

laid-'back. If you describe someone as **laid-back**, you mean that they behave in a calm relaxed way as if nothing ever worries them. ◆◇◇◇◇ ADJ-GRADED INFORMAL

lain /leɪn/. **Lain** is the past participle of **lie**.

lair /leə/ **lairs**. **1** A **lair** is a place where a wild animal lives, usually a place which is underground or well-hidden. *...a fox's lair.* **2** Someone's **lair** is the particular room or hiding place that they go to, especially when they want to get away from other people. N-COUNT / N-COUNT INFORMAL

laird /leəd/ **lairds**. A **laird** is a landowner in Scotland who owns a large area of land. N-COUNT

laissez-faire /ˌleɪseɪˈfeə, ˌles-/. **Laissez-faire** is the policy which is based on the idea that governments, finance, or the conditions of people's working lives. ▶ Also an adjective. *...the Government's laissez-faire attitude toward the use of motor vehicles.* ◆◇◇◇◇ N-UNCOUNT / ADJ-GRADED

la·ity /ˈleɪɪti/. The **laity** are all the people involved in the work of a church who are not clergy, monks, or nuns. ◆◇◇◇◇ N-COLL-SING: also no det

lake /leɪk/ **lakes**. A **lake** is a large area of fresh water, surrounded by land. *They can go fishing in the lake. ...Lake Victoria.* ◆◆◆◇◇ N-COUNT

lake·side /ˈleɪksaɪd/. The **lakeside** is the area of land around the edge of a lake. N-SING

lama /ˈlɑːmə/ **lamas**. A **lama** is a Buddhist priest or monk in Tibet or Mongolia. N-COUNT; N-TITLE

lamb /læm/ **lambs**. **1** A **lamb** is a young sheep. ▶ **Lamb** is the flesh of a lamb eaten as food. *Laura was basting the leg of lamb.* **2** If you say that people do something or go somewhere **like lambs** or **like lambs to the slaughter**, you mean that they do something or go somewhere quietly and obediently, rather than trying to resist. ◆◆◇◇◇ N-COUNT / N-UNCOUNT / PHRASE

lam·bast /læmˈbæst/ **lambasts, lambasting, lambasted**; also spelled **lambaste** /læmˈbeɪst/. If you **lambast** someone, you criticize them severely, usually in public. VERB: V n FORMAL

lamb·ing /ˈlæmɪŋ/. **Lambing** is the time in the spring when female sheep give birth to lambs. *...the lambing season.* N-UNCOUNT

lame /leɪm/ **lamer, lamest**. **1** If someone is **lame**, they are unable to walk properly and they limp because an injury or illness has damaged one or both of their legs. *She was lame in one leg... His horse went lame.* ▶ The **lame** are people who are lame. ♦ **lame·ness** *Inadequate healing may lead to chronic lameness.* **2** If you describe an excuse, argument, or remark as **lame**, you mean that it is poor or weak. *He mumbled some lame excuse about having gone to sleep.* ♦ **lame·ly** *'Lovely house,' I said lamely.* ◆◇◇◇◇ ADJ-GRADED / N-PLURAL: the N / N-UNCOUNT / ADJ-GRADED / ADV-GRADED: ADV with v

lamé /ˈlɑːmeɪ, AM læˈmeɪ/. **Lamé** is cloth that has threads of gold or silver woven into it, which make it sparkle. N-UNCOUNT

lame 'duck, lame ducks. If you describe someone or something as a **lame duck**, you are critical of them because they are weak or unsuccessful. *It is not proper to use British taxpayers' money to support lame-duck industries.* N-COUNT PRAGMATICS

la·ment /ləˈment/ **laments, lamenting, lamented**. **1** If you **lament** something, you express your sadness, regret, or disappointment about it. *He laments that people in Villa El Salvador are suspicious of the police... 'Prices are down 40 per cent since Christmas,' he lamented.* **2** Someone's **lament** is something that they say that expresses their sadness, regret, or disappointment about something. *...the professional woman's lament that a woman's judgment is questioned more than a man's.* **3** A **lament** is a poem, song, or piece of music which expresses sorrow that someone has died. ◆◇◇◇◇ VERB: V n / V that / V with quote / N-COUNT / N-COUNT

lam·en·table /ˈlæməntəbl, ləˈment-/. If you describe something as **lamentable**, you mean that it is very unfortunate or disappointing. *This lamentable state of affairs lasted until 1947.* ♦ **lam·en·tably** ADJ-GRADED FORMAL / ADV

/ˈlæməntəbli/ *There are still lamentably few women surgeons... They have failed lamentably.*

la·men·ta·tion /ˌlæmenˈteɪʃən/ **lamentations**. A **lamentation** is an expression of grief or great sorrow. N-VAR FORMAL

lami·nate /ˈlæmɪneɪt/ **laminates**. A **laminate** is a tough material that is made by bonding together two or more layers of a particular substance. N-VAR

lami·nat·ed /ˈlæmɪneɪtɪd/. **1** Material such as wood or plastic that is **laminated** consists of several thin sheets or layers that are stuck together. *Modern windscreens are made from laminated glass.* **2** A product that is **laminated** is covered with a thin sheet of something, especially clear or coloured plastic, in order to protect it. *The photographs were mounted on laminated cards.* ADJ / ADJ

lamp /læmp/ **lamps**. **1** A **lamp** is a light that works by using electricity or by burning oil or gas. *She switched on the bedside lamp.* **2** A **lamp** is an electrical device which produces a special type of light or heat, used especially in medical or beauty treatment. *...a sun lamp.* ◆◆◇◇◇ N-COUNT / N-COUNT

lamp·light /ˈlæmplaɪt/. **Lamplight** is the light produced by a lamp. N-UNCOUNT

lam·poon /læmˈpuːn/ **lampoons, lampooning, lampooned**. If you **lampoon** someone or something, you criticize them very strongly, using humorous means. ▶ Also a noun. *...his scathing lampoons of consumer culture.* VERB: V n / N-VAR

'lamp-post, lamp-posts. A **lamp-post** is a tall metal or concrete pole that is fixed beside a road and has a light at the top. The more usual American word is **street lamp**. N-COUNT BRITISH

lamp·shade /ˈlæmpʃeɪd/ **lampshades**. A **lampshade** is a decorative covering that is fitted round or over an electric light bulb. N-COUNT

lance /lɑːns, læns/ **lances, lancing, lanced**. **1** If a boil on someone's body **is lanced**, it is pierced with a sharp instrument in order to let the pus drain out. *It is a painful experience having the boil lanced.* **2** A **lance** is a long spear used in former times, especially by soldiers on horseback. ◆◇◇◇◇ VERB: be V-ed / have n V-ed / Also V n / N-COUNT

land /lænd/ **lands, landing, landed**. **1** Land is an area of ground, especially one that is used for a particular purpose such as farming or building. *...agricultural land.* **2** You can refer to an area of land which someone owns as their **land** or their **lands**. **3** If you talk about **the land**, you mean farming and the way of life in farming areas, as opposed to in the cities. *...living off the land.* **4** Land is the part of the world that is ground, rather than sea or air. *It isn't clear whether the plane went down over land or sea.* **5** If you **land** a fish, you succeed in catching it and getting it out of the water. **6** You can use **land** to refer to a country or region, when you do not mean any particular country, when you are talking about an imaginary or ideal place, or when you are talking about your own country in an emotional or patriotic way. *...2,000 miles away in a strange land. ...blessed lands of sun and sea and olive trees.* **7** When someone or something **lands**, they come down to the ground after moving through the air or falling. *He was sent flying into the air and landed 20ft away.* **8** When someone **lands** a plane, ship, or spacecraft, it arrives somewhere after a journey. *The jet landed after a flight of just under three hours.* ♦ **land·ing, landings** *I had to make a controlled landing into the sea.* **9** To **land** goods somewhere means to successfully unload them there at the end of a journey, especially by ship. *The vessels will have to land their catch at designated ports.* **10** If you **land** in an unpleasant situation or place, something causes you to be in it. *This is not the first time his exploits have landed him in trouble.* **11** If someone or something **lands** you with a difficult situation, they cause you to have to deal with the difficulties involved. *The other options simply complicate the situation and could land him with more expense.* **12** If something **lands** somewhere, it arrives there ◆◆◆◆◇ N-UNCOUNT / N-COUNT: poss N / N-SING: the N / N-UNCOUNT: also the N / VERB: V n / N-COUNT: with supp LITERARY / VERB / V / V-ERG: V n / V / N-VAR / VERB / V n BRITISH / V-ERG: V n in n / V n in n / V n with n INFORMAL, BRITISH / VERB

unexpectedly, often causing problems. *The book had already landed on his desk.*   V prep/adv   INFORMAL

13 If you **land** something that is difficult to get and that many people want, you are successful in getting it. *His flair with hair soon landed him a part-time job at his local barbers.*   VERB: V n   V n n   INFORMAL

14 If someone **lands** a blow or punch, they hit someone. *De Leon landed a punch on the Italian's mouth.*   V-ERG: V n   V n prep   Also V

15 ● to **land on** your **feet**: see **foot**.

land up. If you say that you **land up** in a place or situation, you mean that you arrive in it after a long journey or at the end of a long series of events. *We landed up at the Las Vegas at about 6.30.*   PHRASAL VB   V P prep/adv   INFORMAL

land·ed /ˈlændɪd/. **Landed** means owning a large amount of land, especially land that has belonged to the same family for several generations. *...the landed gentry.*   ADJ: ADJ n

land·fall /ˈlændfɔːl/ **landfalls.** Landfall is the first piece of land which you see or arrive at after a voyage at sea.   N-VAR   LITERARY

land·fill /ˈlændfɪl/ **landfills. 1** Landfill is a method of disposing of very large amounts of rubbish by digging a large deep hole and burying it. **2** A landfill is a large deep hole in which very large quantities of rubbish are disposed of.   ◆◇◇◇◇   N-UNCOUNT   N-COUNT

land·ing /ˈlændɪŋ/ **landings. 1** The landing is the area at the top of a staircase which has rooms leading off it.   ◆◆◇◇◇   N-COUNT
2 A landing is an act of unloading troops in a place as part of a military invasion or other operation. **3** A landing is the same as a landing stage.   N-COUNT   N-COUNT

'landing craft; landing craft is both the singular and the plural form. A landing craft is a boat designed for taking troops and equipment from a larger ship to the shore.   N-COUNT

'landing stage, landing stages. A landing stage or a landing is a platform built over water where boats stop to let people get off, or to load or unload goods.   N-COUNT   BRITISH

'landing strip, landing strips. A landing strip is a long flat piece of land from which aircraft can take off and land.   N-COUNT

land·lady /ˈlændleɪdi/ **landladies. 1** Someone's landlady is the woman who allows them to live or work in a building which she owns, in return for payment of rent. **2** The landlady of a pub is the woman who owns or runs it, or the wife of the man who owns or runs it.   ◆◆◇◇◇   N-COUNT   N-COUNT

land·less /ˈlændləs/. Someone who is landless is prevented from owning the land that they farm, usually by large landowners or by the economic system. *...the yeoman farmers and the landless peasants.*   ADJ

land·locked /ˈlændlɒkt/; also spelled **land-locked**. A landlocked country is surrounded by other countries and does not have its own ports.   ADJ

land·lord /ˈlændlɔːd/ **landlords. 1** Someone's landlord is the man who allows them to live or work in a building which he owns, in return for payment of rent. **2** The landlord of a pub is the man who owns or runs it, or the husband of the woman who owns or runs it.   ◆◆◇◇◇   N-COUNT   N-COUNT

land·lubber /ˈlændlʌbə/ **landlubbers.** A landlubber is a person who is not used to travelling by boat or ship, and is not knowledgeable about the sea.   N-COUNT   DATED

land·mark /ˈlændmɑːk/ **landmarks. 1** A landmark is a building or feature which is easily noticed and can be used to judge your position or the position of other buildings or features. *The Ambassador Hotel is a Los Angeles landmark.* **2** You can refer to an important stage in the development of something as a landmark. *...a landmark arms control treaty.*   ◆◆◇◇◇   N-COUNT   N-COUNT

'land mass, land masses. A land mass is a very large area of land such as a continent.   N-COUNT

land·mine /ˈlændmaɪn/ **landmines;** also spelled **land mine**. A landmine is an explosive device which is placed on or under the ground and explodes when a person or vehicle touches it.   N-COUNT

land·owner /ˈlændəʊnə/ **landowners.** A landowner is a person who owns land, especially a large amount of land.   ◆◇◇◇◇   N-COUNT

land·owning /ˈlændəʊnɪŋ/. Landowning is used to describe people who own a lot of land. *...a wealthy Scottish landowning family.*   ADJ: ADJ n

'land reform, land reforms. Land reform is a change in the system of land ownership, especially when it involves giving land to the people who actually farm it and taking it away from people who own large areas for profit.   N-VAR

'land registry, land registries. A land registry is a government office where records are kept about each area of land in a country or region.   N-COUNT   BRITISH

land·scape /ˈlændskeɪp/ **landscapes, landscaping, landscaped. 1** The landscape is everything you can see when you look across an area of land, including hills, rivers, buildings, trees, and plants. *...Arizona's desert landscape.* **2** A landscape is a drawing or painting which shows a scene in the countryside.   ◆◆◆◇◇   N-VAR   N-COUNT
3 A landscape is all the features that are important in a particular situation, and which give it a unique character. *...Russia's political landscape.*   N-COUNT: with supp
4 If an area of land is landscaped, it is redesigned and then altered to create a pleasing artistic effect. *They had landscaped their property with trees, shrubs, and lawns.* ♦ **land·scap·ing** *The landowner insisted on a high standard of landscaping.*   VERB: be V-ed   V n with n   Also V n   N-UNCOUNT

‚landscape 'architect, landscape architects. A landscape architect is the same as a landscape gardener.   N-COUNT

‚landscape 'gardener, landscape gardeners. A landscape gardener is a person who designs gardens or parks so that they look attractive.   N-COUNT

land·slide /ˈlændslaɪd/ **landslides. 1** A landslide is a victory in an election in which a person or political party gets far more votes or seats than their opponents. *He won last month's presidential election by a landslide. ...a landslide victory.* **2** A landslide is a large amount of earth and rocks falling down a cliff or the side of a mountain.   ◆◇◇◇◇   N-COUNT   N-COUNT

land·slip /ˈlændslɪp/ **landslips.** A landslip is a small movement of soil and rocks down a slope.   N-COUNT   BRITISH

lane /leɪn/ **lanes. 1** A lane is a type of road, especially in the country. *...a quiet country lane. ...The Dorchester Hotel, Park Lane.* **2** A lane is a part of a main road which is marked by the edge of the road and a painted line, or by two painted lines. *...the slow lane.* **3** At a swimming pool or athletic track, a lane is a long narrow section which is marked by lines or ropes. **4** A lane is a route that is frequently used by aircraft or ships. *...the busiest shipping lanes in the world.*   ◆◆◆◇◇   N-COUNT   N-COUNT   N-COUNT   N-COUNT

lan·guage /ˈlæŋgwɪdʒ/ **languages. 1** A language is a system of communication which consists of a set of sounds and written symbols which are used by the people of a particular country or region for talking or writing. *...the English language... Students are expected to master a second language.* **2** You can refer to the words used in connection with a particular subject as the language of that subject. *...the language of business.* **3** You can use language to refer to various means of communication involving recognizable symbols, non-verbal sounds, or actions. *...sign languages. ...the digital language of computers.*   ◆◆◆◆◇   N-COUNT   N-UNCOUNT: the N of n, supp N   N-VAR: supp N, N of n
4 Language is the use of a system of communication which consists of a set of sounds or written symbols. *...how children acquire language.* **5** You can refer to someone's use of rude words or swearing as bad language when you find it offensive.   N-UNCOUNT   N-UNCOUNT: adj N, poss N
6 The language of a piece of writing or speech is the style in which it is written or spoken. *...a booklet summarising it in plain language.*   N-UNCOUNT: with supp

'language laboratory, language laboratories. A language laboratory is a classroom equipped with tape recorders and headphones where people can improve their foreign language skills.   N-COUNT

lan·guid /ˈlæŋgwɪd/. If someone is **languid**, they ◆◇◇◇◇ show little energy or interest and are very slow and ADJ-GRADED casual in their movements. *Thin young models hung* LITERARY *around looking languid.* ♦ **lan·guid·ly** *We sat about* ADV-GRADED *languidly after dinner... A tanned blonde in a bikini swims languidly in the clear swimming pool.*

lan·guish /ˈlæŋgwɪʃ/ **languishes, languishing,** ◆◇◇◇◇ **languished. 1** If someone **languishes** somewhere, VERB they are forced to remain and suffer in an unpleas- V prep/adv ant situation. *Pollard continues to languish in pris-* *on.* **2** If something **languishes**, it is not successful, VERB often because of a lack of effort or because of a lot V of difficulties. *The company gradually languished.*

lan·guor /ˈlæŋgə/. **Languor** is a pleasant feeling of N-UNCOUNT being relaxed and not having any energy or interest LITERARY in anything. ♦ **lan·guor·ous** /ˈlæŋgərəs/ ...*languor-* ADJ-GRADED *ous morning coffees on the terrace.*

lank /læŋk/. **Lank** hair is long and lies or hangs in a ADJ-GRADED dull and unattractive way.

lanky /ˈlæŋki/ **lankier, lankiest.** Someone who is ADJ-GRADED **lanky** is tall and thin and moves rather awkwardly.

lan·tern /ˈlæntən/ **lanterns.** A **lantern** is a lamp in ◆◇◇◇◇ a metal frame with glass sides and with a handle on N-COUNT top so you can carry it.

lap /læp/ **laps, lapping, lapped. 1** Your **lap** is the ◆◆◆◇◇ horizontal flat area formed between your stomach N-COUNT: and your knees when you are sitting down. *She* poss N *waited quietly with her hands in her lap.*
2 In a race, a competitor completes a **lap** when he or N-COUNT she has gone round a course once. ...*that last lap of* *the race.* **3** In a race, if you **lap** another competitor, VERB you go past them while they are still on the previous V n lap. ...*his lack of experience at lapping slower cars.*
4 When water **laps** against something such as the VERB: shore or the side of a boat, it touches it gently and V n makes a soft sound. *The building was right on the river* WRITTEN *and the water lapped the walls.* ♦ **lap·ping** *The only* N-UNCOUNT: *sound was the lapping of the waves.* the N of n
5 When an animal **laps** a drink, it uses short quick movements of its tongue to flick liquid up into its mouth. ► **Lap up** means the same as **lap**. *She poured* PHRASAL VB *some water into a plastic bowl. Faust, her Great Dane,* V n P *lapped it up with relish.*
6 If someone lives **in the lap of luxury**, they live in PHRASE conditions of great comfort and wealth.

lap up. If you say that someone **laps up** something PHRASAL VB such as information or attention, you mean that they V P noun accept it eagerly, and often you think they are being V n P foolish for believing that it is sincere. *They just haven't* *been to school before. They're so eager to learn, they lap* *it up.* ● See also **lap 5**

la·pel /ləˈpel/ **lapels.** The **lapels** of a jacket or coat ◆◇◇◇◇ are the two flaps at the front that are folded back on N-COUNT each side.

lap·is lazu·li /ˌlæpɪs ˈlæzjʊlaɪ, AM -liː/. **Lapis lazuli** N-UNCOUNT is a bright blue semi-precious stone.

'lap of honour, laps of honour. If the winner of N-COUNT a race or game does a **lap of honour**, they run or drive slowly around a race track or sports field in order to receive the applause of the crowd.

lapse /læps/ **lapses, lapsing, lapsed. 1** A lapse ◆◇◇◇◇ is a moment or instance of bad behaviour by some- N-COUNT one who usually behaves well. *He showed neither* *decency nor dignity. It was an uncommon lapse.* **2** A N-COUNT: **lapse** of something such as concentration or judg- N of n, ment is a temporary lack of that thing, which can supp N often cause you to make a mistake.
3 If you **lapse** into a quiet or inactive state, you stop VERB talking or being active. *Doris Brown closed her eyes* V into n *and lapsed into sleep.* **4** If you say that someone **lapses** VERB into a particular way of speaking, a particular lan- V into n guage, or a way of behaving, you mean they start speaking or behaving in that way. *She lapsed into a lit-* *tle girl voice to deliver a nursery rhyme.* ► Also a noun. N-COUNT *Her lapse into German didn't seem peculiar.*
5 A **lapse** of time is a period that is long enough for a N-SING situation to change or for people to have a different opinion about it. ...*the restoration of diplomatic rela-* *tions after a lapse of 24 years.* **6** If a period of time VERB

lapses, it passes. ...*in the days that had lapsed since* V *Grace's death.*
7 If a situation or legal contract **lapses**, it is allowed to VERB: V end or to become invalid rather than being con- tinued, renewed, or extended.
8 If a member of a particular religion **lapses**, he or she VERB: V no longer believes in it or follows its rules and prac- V-ed tices. ...*a lapsed Catholic.*

lap·top /ˈlæptɒp/ **laptops.** A **laptop** or a **laptop** N-COUNT **computer** is a small portable computer.

lap·wing /ˈlæpwɪŋ/ **lapwings.** A **lapwing** is a small N-COUNT bird with dark green feathers, a white breast, and a tuft of feathers on its head.

lar·ceny /ˈlɑːsəni/. **Larceny** is the crime of theft. N-UNCOUNT ...*20 years in prison on grand larceny charges.* LEGAL

larch /lɑːtʃ/ **larches.** A **larch** is a tree with needle- N-VAR shaped leaves.

lard /lɑːd/. **Lard** is soft white fat obtained from pigs. N-UNCOUNT It is used in cooking.

lar·der /ˈlɑːdə/ **larders.** A **larder** is a room or cup- N-COUNT board in a house in which food is kept. BRITISH

large /lɑːdʒ/ **larger, largest. 1** A **large** thing or ◆◆◆◆◆ person is greater in size than usual or average. *The* ADJ-GRADED *pike lives mainly in large rivers and lakes... He was a* *large man with a thick square head.* **2** A **large** ADJ-GRADED amount or number of people or things is more than the average amount or number. *The gang finally* *fled with a large amount of cash... There are a large* *number of centres where you can take full-time* *courses.* **3** A **large** organization or business does a ADJ-GRADED lot of work or commercial activity and employs a lot of people. ...*a large company in Chicago.*
4 Large is used to indicate that a problem or issue ADJ-GRADED which is being discussed is very important or serious. ...*the already large problem of under-age drinking.*
5 You use **at large** to indicate that you are talking in a PHRASE general way about most of the people mentioned. ...*the chances of getting reforms accepted by the com-* *munity at large.*
6 If you say that a dangerous person, thing, or animal PHRASE is **at large**, you mean that they have not been cap- tured or made safe.
7 You use **by and large** to indicate that a statement is PHRASE mostly but not completely true. *By and large, the pa-* *pers greet the government's new policy document with* *a certain amount of scepticism.*
8 ● **to a large extent:** see **extent.** ● **larger than life:** see **life.** ● **to loom large:** see **loom.** ● **in large meas- ure:** see **measure.**

large·ly /ˈlɑːdʒli/. **1** You use **largely** to say that a ◆◆◆◇ statement is not completely true but is mostly true. ADV-GRADED *The fund is largely financed through government* *borrowing... The early studies were done on men,* *largely by male researchers.* **2 Largely** is used to ADV: introduce the main reason for a particular event or ADV prep situation. *The French empire had expanded largely* *through military conquest.*

|large-'scale; also spelled **large scale. 1** A **large-** ◆◆◇◇◇ **scale** action or event happens over a very wide area ADJ-GRADED: or involves a lot of people or things. ...*a large scale* ADJ n *military operation.* **2** A **large-scale** map or diagram ADJ-GRADED: represents a small area of land or a building or ma- ADJ n chine on a scale that is large enough for small de- tails to be shown.

lar·gesse /lɑːˈʒes/; also spelled **largess** in American N-UNCOUNT English. **Largesse** is kindness or generosity, espe- FORMAL cially when this involves giving more money to someone than was expected or asked for.

larg·ish /ˈlɑːdʒɪʃ/. **Largish** means fairly large. ...*a* ADJ *largish modern city.*

lar·go /ˈlɑːgəʊ/ **largos. 1 Largo** written above a ADV-GRADED: piece of music means that it should be played slow- ADV after v ly. **2** A **largo** is a piece of music, especially part of a N-COUNT longer piece, that is played slowly.

lark /lɑːk/ **larks, larking, larked. 1** A **lark** is a ◆◇◇◇◇ small brown bird which makes a pleasant sound. N-COUNT
2 If you say that doing something is a **lark**, you mean N-COUNT it is naughty or daring, but also fun. *The children* BRITISH *thought it was a great lark.*
3 You can use **lark** in expressions such as **this acting** N-COUNT:

lark and **the writing lark** to indicate humorously that *the/this* N you think an activity or job is amusing, foolish, or un- *BRITISH* necessary. *He eventually decided the acting lark wasn't half bad.*

lark around or **lark about.** If you **lark around** or PHRASAL VB **lark about**, you behave in a playful, childish, and silly V P way, often in order to make people laugh. *The other INFORMAL, actors complained about me larking about when they BRITISH were trying to concentrate.*

lar·va /ˈlɑːvə/ **larvae** /ˈlɑːviː/. A **larva** is an insect ◆◇◇◇◇ at the stage of its life after it has developed from an N-COUNT egg and before it changes into its adult form. ♦ **lar·val** ...*the larval stage of a beetle.* ADJ: ADJ n

lar·yn·gi·tis /ˌlærɪnˈdʒaɪtɪs/. **Laryngitis** is an infec- N-UNCOUNT tion of the throat in which your larynx becomes swollen and painful.

lar·ynx /ˈlærɪŋks/ **larynxes.** Your **larynx** is the top N-COUNT part of the passage that leads from your throat to your lungs and contains your vocal cords.

la·sa·gne /ləˈsænjə/ **lasagnes**; also spelled **lasa-** N-VAR **gna.** Lasagne is a food dish that consists of layers of pasta, sauce, and a filling such as meat or cheese.

las·civ·ious /ləˈsɪviəs/. If you describe someone as ADJ-GRADED **lascivious**, you disapprove of them because you PRAGMATICS think show an unnaturally strong interest in sex. ...*their lewd and lascivious talk.*

la·ser /ˈleɪzə/ **lasers. 1** A **laser** is a narrow beam of ◆◆◇◇◇ concentrated light produced by a special machine. N-COUNT ...*new laser technology.* **2** A **laser** is a machine that N-COUNT produces a laser beam.

ˈlaser disc, laser discs. A **laser disc** is a shiny N-COUNT flat disc which can be played on a machine which uses lasers to convert signals on the disc into televi- sion pictures and sound of a very high quality.

ˈlaser printer, laser printers. A **laser printer** is a N-COUNT computer printer that produces clear words and pictures by using laser beams.

lash /læʃ/ **lashes, lashing, lashed. 1** Your ◆◆◇◇◇ **lashes** are the hairs that grow on the edge of your N-COUNT upper and lower eyelids.

2 If you **lash** something somewhere, you tie it firmly VERB to something. *Secure the anchor by lashing it to the* V n to n *rail... The shelter is built by lashing poles together... All* V pl-n with *the equipment is very securely lashed down.* together be V-ed adv

3 If wind, rain, or water **lashes** someone or some- VERB: V n thing, it hits them violently. *Suddenly rain lashed* V prep/adv *against the windows.* WRITTEN

4 If someone **lashes** into you, they speak very angrily VERB: to you, criticizing you or scolding you. ...*while she* V into n summoned up the words to lash him.* ▶ Also a noun. V n *Never before had he felt the full lash of John's temper.* N-SING: det N ♦ **lash·ing, lashings** ...*the lashings he got from the* N-COUNT critics.

5 A **lash** is a thin strip of leather at the end of a whip. N-COUNT **6** If someone **lashes** another person, they hit that per- VERB: V n son with a whip. ▶ Also a noun. *The villagers sen-* N-COUNT tenced one man to five lashes.*

lash out. 1 If you **lash out**, you attempt to hit some- PHRASAL VB one quickly and violently with a weapon or with your V P hands or feet. *Her husband has a terrible temper and* V P at n *lashes out at her for no good reason.* **2** If you **lash out** at V P at/against someone or something, you speak to them very angri- n ly or cruelly, criticizing or scolding them.

lash·ing /ˈlæʃɪŋ/ **lashings. 1** **Lashings of** some- QUANT thing means a large quantity or amount of it. ...*jam* BRITISH *and lashings of clotted cream.*

2 **Lashings** are ropes or cables used to tie one thing to N-COUNT another.

lass /læs/ **lasses.** A **lass** is a young woman or girl. ◆◇◇◇◇ ...*a plain-speaking Yorkshire lass who loves nothing* N-COUNT; *more than to share fish and chips with her child-* N-VOC *hood friends... 'What is it, lass?' Finlay cried.* INFORMAL, BRITISH

las·sie /ˈlæsi/ **lassies.** A **lassie** is a young woman N-COUNT or girl. INFORMAL SCOTTISH

las·si·tude /ˈlæsɪtjuːd, AM -tuːd/. **Lassitude** is a N-UNCOUNT state of tiredness, laziness, or lack of interest. ...*peri-* FORMAL *ods of lassitude and inactivity.*

las·so /ˈlæsuː, AM ˈlæsəʊ/ **lassoes, lassoing, las-** N-COUNT **soed. 1** A **lasso** is a long rope with a loop at one end, used especially by cowboys for catching cattle.

2 If you **lasso** an animal, you catch it by throwing a VERB: V n lasso round its neck and pulling it tight.

last 1 uses before a noun

last /lɑːst, læst/. **1** You use **last** in expressions such ◆◆◆◆◆ as **last Friday**, **last night**, and **last year** to refer, for DET example, to the most recent Friday, night, or year. *I got married last July. ...last year's elections.* **2** The ADJ: det ADJ **last** event, person, thing, or period of time is the most recent one. *Much has changed since my last visit... I split up with my last boyfriend three years ago.* ▶ Also a pronoun. *The next tide would be even* PRON *higher than the last.* **3** The **last** thing, person, event, ORDINAL or period of time is the one that happens or comes after all the others of the same kind. *This is his last chance as prime minister. ...the last three pages of the chapter... They didn't come last in their league.* ▶ Also a pronoun. *The trickiest bits are the last on* PRON *the list.*

4 **Last** is used to refer to the only thing, person, or part ADJ: det ADJ of something that remains. *Jed nodded, finishing off the last piece of pizza. ...the freeing of the last hostage.* ▶ Also a noun. *He finished off the last of the wine.* N-SING: **5** You use **last** before numbers to refer to a position the N of n ADJ: det ADJ that someone has reached in a competition after oth- er competitors have been knocked out. For example, if you reach the last four, you are one of four people remaining in a competition.

6 You can use **last** to indicate for example that you ADJ: det ADJ definitely do not want to do something or that some- one is extremely unlikely to have done something. *The last thing I wanted to do was teach.* ▶ Also a pro- PRON noun. *I would be the last to say that science has ex- plained everything.*

last 2 adverb and pronoun uses

last /lɑːst, læst/. **1** If something **last** happened on a ◆◆◆◆◇ particular occasion, that is the most recent occasion ADV: on which it happened. *When were you there last?...* ADV with v *The house is a little more dilapidated than when I last saw it.* **2** If you do something **last**, you do it af- ADV: ter everyone else does, or after you do everything ADV after v else. *I testified last... I was always picked last for the football team.* **3** If you are the **last** to do or know PRON something, everyone else does or knows it before you. **4** The **last** you see of someone or the **last** you PRON hear of them is the final time that you see them or talk to them.

last 3 phrases

last /lɑːst, læst/. **1** You use expressions such as the ◆◆◇◇◇ **night before last**, **the election before last**, and the PHRASE **leader before last**, to refer to the period of time, event, or person that happened or came immedi- ately before the most recent one in a series. **2** You PHRASE can use expressions such as **the last I heard** and PRAGMATICS **the last she heard** to introduce a piece of informa- tion that is the most recent that you have on a par- ticular subject. *The last I heard, Joe and Irene were still happily married.*

3 You can use phrases such as the **last but one**, the PHRASE **last but two**, or **last but three**, to refer to the thing or person that is, for example, one, two, or three before the final person or thing in a group or series. *It's the last but one day in the athletics programme.* **4** The ex- PHRASE pression **last in, first out** is used to say that the last person who started work in an organization should be the first person to leave it, if fewer people are needed. **5** If you **leave** something or someone **until last**, you PHRASE delay using, choosing, or dealing with them until you have used, chosen, or dealt with all the others. **6** If you PHRASE **see the last of** someone, you do not expect to see them or deal with them again. **7** If you say that something has happened **at last** or **at** PHRASE **long last** you mean it has happened after you have been hoping for it for a long time. *I'm so glad that we've found you at last!* **8** You use **every last** to emphasize that you are talking PHRASE about all the people or things in a group without ex- PRAGMATICS ception, or all the parts of something. *I'd spent all I had, every last penny.* **9** If you say that something goes on happening **to the** PHRASE **last**, you mean that it happens throughout a book,

film, or event. ...*a highly readable political thriller with plenty of twists of plot to keep you guessing to the last.* **10** If you say that someone is a particular kind of person **to the last**, you are emphasizing that they are that kind of person. *Armstrong was tall and handsome to the last.* **11** You use expressions such as **to the last detail** and **to the last man** to indicate that a plan, situation, or activity includes every single person, thing, or part involved. PHRASE PRAGMATICS / PHRASE

12 • to **have the last laugh**: see **laugh**. **• last minute**: see **minute**. **•** someone's **last stand**: see **stand**. **• the last straw**: see **straw**. **• last thing**: see **thing**.

last 4 *verb uses*

last /lɑːst, læst/ **lasts, lasting, lasted. 1** If an event, situation, or problem **lasts** for a particular length of time, it continues to exist or happen for that length of time. *The games lasted only half the normal time... Enjoy it because it won't last.* **2** If something **lasts** for a particular length of time, it continues to be able to be used for that time, for example because there is some of it left or because it is in good enough condition. *The repaired sail lasted less than 24 hours... This battery lasts twice as long as batteries made by other battery makers.* **3** You can use **last** in expressions such as **last the game, last the course**, and **last the week**, to indicate that someone manages to take part in an event or situation right to the end, especially when this is very difficult for them. ▶ To **last out** means the same as to **last**. *It'll be a miracle if the band lasts out the tour.* **4** See also **lasting**. ◆◆◇◇ VERB: V for n / V n / V / VERB: V for n / V n / V adv / Also V / VERB: V n / PHRASAL VB: V P / V P noun

,last-'ditch. A **last-ditch** action is done only because there are no other ways left to achieve something or to prevent something happening. It is often done without much hope that it will succeed. *...a last-ditch attempt to prevent civil war.* ◆◇◇◇ ADJ: ADJ n

last·ing /'lɑːstɪŋ, 'læst-/. You can use **lasting** to describe a situation, result, or agreement that continues to exist or have an effect for a very long time. *We are well on our way to a lasting peace.* ◆◆◇◇ ADJ

last·ly /'lɑːstli, 'læst-/. **1** You use **lastly** when you want to make a final point, ask a final question, or mention a final item that is connected with the other ones you have already asked or mentioned. *Lastly, I would like to ask about your future plans.* **2** You use **lastly** when you are saying what happens after everything else in a series of actions or events. *Spot all the differences between the two pictures opposite, then circle them in red. Lastly, complete the tie-breaker in no more than 25 words.* ◆◇◇◇ ADV: ADV with cl/group PRAGMATICS / ADV: ADV cl

,last-'minute. See **minute**.

,last 'rites. The **last rites** consist of a religious ceremony performed by a Christian priest for a dying person. N-PLURAL: the N

latch /lætʃ/ **latches, latching, latched. 1** A **latch** is a fastening on a door or gate. It consists of a metal bar which slots into place to lock the door and which you lift in order to open the door. **2** If you **latch** a door or gate, you fasten it by means of a latch. *He latched the door, tested it, and turned around to speak to Frank.* **3** A **latch** is a lock on a door which locks automatically when you shut the door. ◆◇◇◇ N-COUNT / VERB V n / N-COUNT

latch onto or **latch on. 1** If someone **latches onto** a person or an idea, or **latches on**, they become very interested in the person or idea, often because they find them useful. *Other trades have been quick to latch on.* **2** If one thing **latches onto** another, or if it **latches on**, it attaches itself to it and becomes part of it. *These are substances which specifically latch onto the protein on the cell membrane.* PHRASAL VB V P n / V P / V P n / Also V P

latch·key /'lætʃkiː/. If you refer to a child as a **latchkey** kid, you disapprove of the fact that they have to let themselves into their home after school because their parents are out at work. ADJ: ADJ n PRAGMATICS

late /leɪt/ **later, latest. 1 Late** means near the end of a day, week, year, or other period of time. *It was late in the afternoon... His autobiography was written late in life... The case is expected to end late next week.* ▶ Also an adjective. *The talks eventually broke* ◆◆◆◆◆ ADV-GRADED / ADJ-GRADED:

down in late spring. ...the late 1960's. **2** If it is **late**, it is near the end of the day or it is past the time that you feel something should have been done. *We've got to go now. It's getting late.* ◆ **late·ness** *A large crowd had gathered despite the lateness of the hour.* **3** See also **later, latest**. ADJ n / ADJ-GRADED: v-link ADJ / N-UNCOUNT

4 Late means after the time that was arranged or expected. *Steve arrived late... The talks began some fifteen minutes late.* ▶ Also an adjective. *His campaign got off to a late start... The train was 40 minutes late.* ◆ **lateness** *He apologised for his lateness.* ADV-GRADED / ADJ-GRADED / N-UNCOUNT

5 Late means after the usual time that a particular event or activity happens. *We went to bed very late... He married late.* ▶ Also an adjective. *They had a late lunch in a cafe.* **6 •** a **late night**: see **night**. ADV-GRADED: ADV after v / ADJ-GRADED: ADJ n

7 You use **late** when you are talking about someone who is dead. *...my late husband. ...the late Mr Parkin.* ADJ: det ADJ

8 Someone who is **late of** a particular place or institution lived or worked there until recently. *...Cousin Zachary, late of Bellevue Avenue.* ADJ: v-link ADJ of n FORMAL

9 If you say **better late than never** when someone has done something, you think they should have done it earlier. *It's been a long time coming but better late than never.* **10** If you say that someone is doing something **late in the day**, you mean that it may fail because they have waited too long before doing it. *I'd left it all too late in the day to get anywhere with these strategies.* **11** You use **of late** to refer to an event or state of affairs that happened or began to exist a short time ago. *The dollar has been stronger of late.* **12** If an action or event is **too late** or happens **too late**, it is useless or ineffective because the right time for it has passed. *We realized too late that we were caught like rats in a trap.* CONVENTION / PHRASE / PHRASE FORMAL / PHRASE

late·comer /'leɪtkʌmə/ **latecomers.** A **latecomer** is someone who arrives after the time that they should have done, or later than others. N-COUNT

late·ly /'leɪtli/. **1** You use **lately** to describe events in the recent past, or situations that started not long ago. *Dad's health hasn't been too good lately... Lord Tomas had lately been appointed Chairman of the Centre for Policy Studies.* **2** You can use **lately** to refer to the job a person has been doing until recently. *I spoke to Sir Robert Mark, lately retired as Commissioner of Metropolitan Police.* ◆◆◇◇ ADV / ADV FORMAL

'late-night. 1 Late-night is used to describe events that happen late at night. *...John Peel's late-night show. ...late-night drinking parties.* **2 Late-night** is used to describe services that are available late at night and do not shut when most commercial activities finish. *Saturday night was a late-night shopping night. ...late-night trains.* ◆◇◇◇ ADJ: ADJ n / ADJ: ADJ n

la·tent /'leɪtənt/. **Latent** is used to describe something which is hidden and not obvious at the moment, but which may develop further in the future. *Advertisements attempt to project a latent meaning behind an overt message.* ◆◇◇◇ ADJ

lat·er /'leɪtə/. **1 Later** is the comparative of **late**. **2** You use **later** to refer to a time or situation that is after the one that you have been talking about or after the present one. *He resigned ten years later... Burke later admitted he had lied.* ▶ Also an adjective. *At a later news conference, he said differences should not be dramatized... The competition should have been re-scheduled for a later date.* ◆ **Later on** means the same as **later**. *Later on I'll be speaking to Patty Davis.* **3** You use **later** to refer to the last part of someone's life or career or of a period of history. *He found happiness in later life. ...the later part of the 20th century.* **4 •** sooner or later: see **sooner**. ◆◆◆◆◆ ADV / ADJ-COMPAR: ADJ n / PHRASE / ADJ-COMPAR: ADJ n

lat·er·al /'lætərəl/. **Lateral** means relating to the sides of something, or moving in a sideways direction. *McKinnon estimated the lateral movement of the bridge to be between four and six inches.* ◆ **lat·er·al·ly** *Shafts were sunk, with tunnels dug laterally... The aircraft became laterally unstable.* ◆◇◇◇ ADJ / ADV

,lateral 'thinking. Lateral thinking is a method of solving problems by using your imagination, rather than by using logic or other conventional ways of thinking. *The holiday romance can last – it just requires a bit of lateral thinking.* N-UNCOUNT BRITISH

L

lat·est /ˈleɪtɪst/. **1 Latest** is the superlative of **late**. **2** You use **latest** to describe something that is the most recent thing of its kind. *...her latest book... The resignations are the latest in a series of blows to Mr Amato's government.* **3** You can use **latest** to describe something that is extremely modern and up-to-date, and is therefore better than the other things of its type. *...the latest laser photocopiers... Computers have always represented the latest in technology.* **4** You use **at the latest** in order to indicate that something must happen at or before a particular time. *She should be back by ten o'clock at the latest.* ◆◆◆◇ ADJ-SUPERL

ADJ-SUPERL: oft v-link ADJ in/ofn

PHRASE PRAGMATICS

la·tex /ˈleɪteks/. Latex is a substance obtained from some kinds of trees, which is used to make products like rubber and glue. N-UNCOUNT

lathe /leɪð/ **lathes.** A **lathe** is a machine which is used for shaping wood or metal. ◆◇◇◇ N-COUNT

lath·er /ˈlɑːðə, ˈlæðə/ **lathers, lathering, lathered.** **1** A **lather** is a white mass of bubbles which is produced by mixing a substance such as soap or washing powder with water. *He wiped off the remains of the lather with a towel.* **2** When a substance such as soap or washing powder **lathers**, it produces a white mass of bubbles because it has been mixed with water. *The shampoo lathers and foams so much it's very hard to rinse it all out.* **3** If you **lather** something, you rub a substance such as soap or washing powder on it until a lather is produced, in order to clean it. *Lather your hair as normal... For super-soft skin, lather on a light body lotion before you bathe.* N-SING / VERB V / VERB V n with adv Also V n prep

Lat·in /ˈlætɪn/ **Latins.** **1 Latin** is the language which the ancient Romans used to speak. **2 Latin** countries are countries where Spanish, or perhaps Portuguese, Italian, or French, is spoken. You can also use **Latin** to refer to things and people that come from these countries. *The enthusiasm for Latin music is worldwide.* ▶ **Latins** are people who come from **Latin** countries. *They are role models for thousands of young Latins.* ◆◆◆◇ N-UNCOUNT ADJ / N-COUNT

La·ti·no /læˈtiːnəʊ/ **Latinos.** A **Latino** is a citizen of the United States who originally came from Latin America, or whose family originally came from Latin America. *...the city's office of Latino Affairs.* ◆◇◇◇ N-COUNT

lat·i·tude /ˈlætɪtjuːd, AM -tuːd/ **latitudes.** **1** The **latitude** of a place is its distance from the equator. Compare **longitude**. *In the middle to high latitudes rainfall has risen steadily over the last 20-30 years.* ▶ Also an adjective. *The army must cease military operations above 36 degrees latitude north.* **2 Latitude** is freedom to choose the way in which you do something. *He would be given every latitude in forming a new government.* ◆◇◇◇ N-VAR / ADJ / N-UNCOUNT FORMAL

la·trine /ləˈtriːn/ **latrines.** A **latrine** is a structure, usually consisting of a hole in the ground, that is used as a toilet for example in a military camp. N-COUNT

lat·ter /ˈlætə/. **1** When two people, things, or groups have just been mentioned, you can refer to the second of them as **the latter**. *He tracked down his cousin and uncle. The latter was sick.* ▶ Also an adjective. *The disease may be congenital or acquired. The latter variety is frequently the consequence of infection.* **2** You use **latter** to describe the later part of a period of time or event. *The latter part of the debate concentrated on abortion.* ◆◆◆◇ PRON / ADJ: ADJ n / ADJ: ADJ n

ˈlatter-day. **Latter-day** is used to describe something or someone that is a modern equivalent of something or someone in the past. *He holds the belief that he is a latter-day prophet.* ◆◇◇◇ ADJ: ADJ n

lat·ter·ly /ˈlætəli/. You can use **latterly** to indicate that a situation or event is the most recent one. *City centres were abandoned first by residents, then by shops, and latterly by businesses.* ADV: ADV with cl/ group

lat·tice /ˈlætɪs/ **lattices.** A **lattice** is a pattern or structure made of strips of wood or another material which cross over each other diagonally leaving holes in between. *We were crawling along the narrow steel lattice of the bridge.* ◆ **lat·ticed** *The surface of the brain is pinky-grey and latticed with tiny blood vessels.* N-COUNT / ADJ

lat·tice·work /ˈlætɪswɜːk/. **Latticework** is any structure that is made in the form of a lattice. *...latticework chairs.* N-UNCOUNT

laud /lɔːd/ **lauds, lauding, lauded.** If people **laud** someone, they praise and admire them. *They lauded the former president as a hero... The company also lauded Mr. Bush for his intention to correct market distortions through an international agreement.* ◆ **laud·ed** *...the most lauded actress in New York.* ◆◇◇◇ VERB: V n asn V n forn JOURNALISM / ADJ-GRADED

laud·able /ˈlɔːdəbəl/. Something that is **laudable** deserves to be praised or admired. *One of Diana's less laudable characteristics is her jealousy.* ADJ-GRADED FORMAL

laugh /lɑːf, læf/ **laughs, laughing, laughed.** **1** When you **laugh**, you make a sound with your throat while smiling and show that you are happy or amused. People also sometimes laugh when they feel nervous or are being unfriendly. *He laughed with pleasure when people said he looked like his dad... The British don't laugh at the same jokes as the French... 'They'll carry me away on a stretcher if I win on Sunday,' laughed Lyle.* ▶ Also a noun. *Lysenko gave a deep rumbling laugh at his own joke.* **2** If people **laugh at** someone or something, they mock them or make jokes about them. *I thought they were laughing at me because I was ugly.* **3** If a person or their comments **get a laugh** or **raise a laugh**, they make the people listening to them laugh. *The joke got a big laugh, which encouraged me to continue.* **4** If you do or say something **for a laugh** or **for laughs**, you do or say it as a joke or for fun rather than for any other reason. *They were persuaded onstage for a laugh by their mates.* **5** If you describe a situation as **a laugh**, **a good laugh**, or **a bit of a laugh**, you think that it is fun and do not take it too seriously. *Working there's great. It's quite a good laugh actually.* **6** If you describe someone as **a laugh** or **a good laugh**, you like them because they are amusing and fun to be with. *Mickey was a good laugh and great to have in the dressing room.* **7** If you **have a good laugh about** something, you find it amusing and realize that it is funny, especially when the situation was at first rather upsetting. *We've both had a good laugh about the accident despite what's happened.* **8** If you say that you **have the last laugh**, you mean that you make your critics or opponents look foolish or wrong, by being successful when you were not expected to be. *Des O'Connor is expecting to have the last laugh on his critics by soaring to the top of the Christmas hit parade.* **9 ●** to **laugh in** someone's face: see **face**. **●** to **laugh** your **head off**: see **head**. **●** no laughing matter: see **matter**. **●** to **laugh all the way to the bank**: see **way**. ◆◆◆◆◇ VERB: V V with n V n asn V atn V with quote / N-COUNT / VERB V atn / PHRASE BRITISH / PHRASE / PHRASE / PHRASE BRITISH / PHRASE / PHRASE / PHRASE

laugh off. If you **laugh off** a difficult or serious situation, you try to suggest that it is amusing and unimportant, for example by making a joke about it. *Whilst I used to laugh it off, I'm now getting irritated by it.* PHRASAL VB V P noun V n P

laugh·able /ˈlɑːfəbəl, ˈlæf-/. If you say that something such as an idea or suggestion is **laughable**, you mean that it is so stupid as to be funny and not worth serious consideration. *The idea that TV shows like 'Dallas' or 'Dynasty' represent typical American life is laughable.* ◆ **laugh·ably** *To an outsider, the issues that we fight about would seem almost laughably petty.* ◆◇◇◇ ADJ-GRADED / ADV

laugh·ing·ly /ˈlɑːfɪŋli, ˈlæf-/. If you **laughingly** refer to something with a particular name or description, the description is not appropriate and you think that this is either amusing or annoying. *I spent much of what I laughingly call 'the holidays' working through 621 pages of typescript.* ADV: ADV with cl

ˈlaughing stock, laughing stocks; also spelled **laughing-stock.** If you say that a person or an institution has become a **laughing stock**, you mean that they have been made to seem ridiculous. *...his policies became the laughing stock of the financial community.* N-COUNT

laugh·ter /ˈlɑːftə, ˈlæf-/. **1 Laughter** is the sound of people laughing, for example because they are ◆◆◆◇◇ N-UNCOUNT

amused or happy. *Their laughter filled the corridor... He delivered the line perfectly, and everybody roared with laughter.* **2 Laughter** is the act of laughing, or the feeling of fun and amusement that you have when you are laughing. *Pantomime is about bringing laughter to thousands.* — N-UNCOUNT

launch /lɔːntʃ/ **launches, launching, launched. 1** To **launch** a rocket, missile, or satellite means to send it into the air or into space. *A Delta II rocket was launched from Cape Canaveral early this morning.* ► Also a noun. *This morning's launch of the space shuttle Columbia has been delayed.* **2** To **launch** a ship or a lifeboat means to put it into water, often for the first time after it has been built. *Coastguards launched three lifeboats off Great Ormes.* ► Also a noun. *The launch of a ship was a big occasion.* **3** To **launch** a large and important activity, for example a military attack, means to start it. *Heavy fighting has been going on after the guerrillas had launched their offensive... Mr Gorbachev was on holiday when the coup was launched.* ► Also a noun. *...the launch of a campaign to restore law and order.* **4** If a company **launches** a new product, it makes it available to the public. *Crabtree & Evelyn has just launched a new jam, Worcesterberry Preserve... Marks & Spencer recently hired top model Linda Evangelista to launch its new range.* ► Also a noun. *British Airways has broken new ground with the launch of a new service to Taipei.* **5** A **launch** is a large motorboat that is used for carrying people on rivers and lakes and in harbours. *We'll make a trip by launch to White Island.* — ◆◆◆◆◇ VERB: V n be V-ed / N-VAR / VERB V n / N-COUNT / VERB V n / N-COUNT / VERB V n / N-COUNT / N-COUNT: also by N

launch into. If you **launch into** something such as a speech, task, or fight, you enthusiastically start it. *Geoff has launched himself into fatherhood with great enthusiasm.* — PHRASAL VB V P n / V pron-refl P n

launching pad, launching pads. A **launching pad** is the same as a **launch pad.** — N-COUNT

launch pad, launch pads. 1 A **launch pad** or **launching pad** is a platform from which rockets, missiles, or satellites are launched. **2** A **launch pad** or **launching pad** is a situation, for example a job, which you can use in order to go forward to something better or more important. *Wimbledon has been a launch pad for so many players.* — N-COUNT / N-COUNT

laun·der /ˈlɔːndə/ **launders, laundering, laundered. 1** When you **launder** clothes, bed linen, and towels, you wash and iron them. *She wore a freshly laundered and starched white shirt.* **2** To **launder** money that has been obtained illegally means to process it through a legitimate business or to send it abroad to a foreign bank, so that nobody knows that it was illegally obtained. *The House voted today to crack down on banks that launder drug money.* ♦ **laun·der·er, launderers** *...a businessman and self-described money launderer.* — ◆◇◇◇◇ VERB: V n V-ed / VERB V n / N-COUNT

laun·der·ette /ˌlɔːnˈdret/ **launderettes;** also spelled **laundrette.** A **launderette** is a shop in which there are washing machines and dryers which people can use to wash and dry their clothes. The American word is **laundromat.** — N-COUNT BRITISH

laun·dro·mat /ˈlɔːndrəmæt/ **laundromats.** A **laundromat** is the same as a **launderette.** — N-COUNT AMERICAN

laun·dry /ˈlɔːndri/ **laundries. 1 Laundry** is used to refer to clothes, sheets, and towels that are about to be washed, are being washed, or have just been washed. *I'll do your laundry... He'd put his dirty laundry in the clothes basket.* **2** A **laundry** is a firm that washes and irons clothes, sheets, and towels for people. *We had to have the washing done at the laundry.* **3** A **laundry** or a **laundry room** is a room in a house, hotel, or institution where clothes, sheets, and towels are washed. **4** ● to **wash** your **dirty laundry in public:** see **dirty.** — ◆◇◇◇◇ N-UNCOUNT / N-COUNT / N-COUNT

laundry list, laundry lists. If you describe something as a **laundry list** of things, you mean that it is a long list of them. *...a laundry list of reasons why shareholders should reject the bid.* — N-COUNT

lau·rel /ˈlɒrəl, AM ˈlɔːr-/ **laurels. 1** A **laurel** or a **laurel tree** is a small evergreen tree with shiny — ◆◇◇◇◇ N-VAR

leaves. **2** If someone is **resting on** their **laurels,** they appear to be satisfied with the things they have achieved and have stopped putting effort into what they are doing; used showing disapproval. *The committee's chairman accused NASA of resting on its laurels after making it to the moon.* — PHRASE PRAGMATICS

lava /ˈlɑːvə/ **lavas.** Lava is the very hot molten rock that comes out of a volcano. — ◆◇◇◇◇ N-VAR

lava·tory /ˈlævətri, AM -tɔːri/ **lavatories.** A **lavatory** is the same as a **toilet.** *...a public lavatory.* — ◆◇◇◇◇ N-COUNT BRITISH

lav·en·der /ˈlævɪndə/ **lavenders. 1 Lavender** is a garden plant with sweet-smelling, bluish-purple flowers. **2 Lavender** is used to describe things that are pale bluish-purple in colour. — ◆◇◇◇◇ N-UNCOUNT: also N in pl COLOUR

lav·ish /ˈlævɪʃ/ **lavishes, lavishing, lavished. 1** If you describe something as **lavish,** you mean that a lot of time, effort, or money has been spent on it to make it as impressive as possible. *...a lavish party to celebrate Bryan's fiftieth birthday... The sets and costumes are lavish.* ♦ **lav·ish·ly** *IBM spent lavishly on their workers' education and training.* **2** If you say that something is **lavish,** you mean it is extravagant and excessively wasteful. *...stealing antique jewellery and paintings to finance a lavish lifestyle.* **3** If you **lavish** something such as money, affection, or time on someone or something, you spend a lot of money on them or give them a lot of affection or attention. *The emperor promoted the general and lavished him with gifts.* — ◆◆◇◇◇ ADJ-GRADED / ADV-GRADED ADJ-GRADED / VERB: V n on/upon n V n with n

law /lɔː/ **laws. 1 The law** is a system of rules that a society or government develops in order to deal with crime, business agreements, and social relationships. You can also use the **law** to refer to the people who work in this system. *Obscene and threatening phone calls are against the law... There must be changes in the law quickly... The book analyses why women kill and how the law treats them.* **2 Law** is used to refer to a particular branch of the law, such as **criminal law** or **company law.** *Important questions of constitutional law were involved.* **3** A **law** is one of the rules in a system of law which deals with a particular type of agreement, relationship, or crime. *...the country's liberal political asylum law.* **4** The **laws** of an organization or activity are its rules, which are used to organize and control it. *...the laws of the Church of England.* **5** A **law** is a rule or set of rules for good behaviour which is considered right and important by the majority of people for moral, religious, or emotional reasons. *...inflexible moral laws.* **6** A **law** is a natural process in which a particular event or thing always leads to a particular result, or a scientific rule that someone has invented to explain such a process. *The laws of nature are absolute. ...the law of gravity.* **7 Law** or **the law** is all the professions which deal with advising people about the law, representing people in court, or giving decisions and punishments. *A career in law is becoming increasingly attractive to young people.* **8 Law** is the study of systems of law and how laws work. *He holds a law degree from Bristol University.* **9** See also **court of law, rule of law. 10** If you accuse someone of thinking they are **above the law,** you criticize them for thinking that they are so clever or important that they do not need to obey the law. *One opposition member of parliament accuses the government of wanting to be above the law.* **11** If you have to do something **by law,** or if you are not allowed to do something **by law,** the law states that you have to do it or that you are not allowed to do it. *Minicabs are prohibited by law from touting passers-by for business.* **12** If someone **takes the law into their own hands,** they punish someone according to their own ideas of justice, often when this involves breaking the law. *The speeding motorist was pinned to the ground by angry locals who took the law into their own hands until police arrived.* **13 The law of averages** is the idea that something is sure to happen at some time, considering the number of times it generally happens or is expected to happen. *On the law of averages we just can't go on losing* — ◆◆◆◆◆ N-SING: the N / N-UNCOUNT / N-COUNT / N-PLURAL: the N of n, supp N / N-COUNT / N-COUNT: with supp / N-UNCOUNT / N-UNCOUNT / PHRASE PRAGMATICS / PHRASE / PHRASE / PHRASE

L

and losing and losing. **14** If you say that someone **lays down the law**, you are critical of them because they give other people orders and they think that they are always right. *...traditional parents, who believed in laying down the law for their offspring.* **15** If you say that someone is **a law unto** himself or herself, you think that they behave in an independent way, ignoring laws, rules, or conventional ways of doing things. *Some of the landowners were a law unto themselves. There was nobody to check their excesses and they exploited the people.* `PHRASE PRAGMATICS`

'**law-abiding.** A **law-abiding** person always obeys the law and is considered to be good and honest because of this. *Gun ownership by law-abiding people was not a problem.* `◆◇◇◇◇ ADJ-GRADED`

,**law and 'order.** When there is **law and order** in a country, the laws are generally accepted and obeyed, so that society there functions normally. *If there were a breakdown of law and order, the army might be tempted to intervene.* `◆◆◇◇◇ N-UNCOUNT`

'**law-breaker, law-breakers;** can also be spelled **lawbreaker.** A **law-breaker** is someone who breaks the law. *The money spent on prisons could be better spent on training first-time law-breakers to earn an honest living.* `N-COUNT`

'**law-breaking;** also spelled **law breaking. Law-breaking** is any kind of illegal activity. *Civil disobedience, violent or non-violent, is intentional law breaking.* `N-UNCOUNT`

'**law court, law courts.** A **law court** is a place where legal matters are decided by a judge and jury or by a magistrate. `N-COUNT`

'**law-enforcement.** **Law-enforcement** agencies or officials are responsible for catching people who break the law. *We need to restore respect for the law and for bodies such as the army and the law-enforcement agencies.* `◆◇◇◇◇ N-UNCOUNT FORMAL, AMERICAN`

law·ful /ˈlɔːfʊl/. If an activity, organization, or product is **lawful**, it is allowed by law. *Hunting is a lawful activity.* ♦ **law·ful·ly** *Amnesty International is trying to establish whether the police acted lawfully in shooting him.* `◆◇◇◇◇ ADJ-GRADED FORMAL ADV: ADV with v`

law·less /ˈlɔːləs/. **1 Lawless** actions break the law, especially in a wild and violent way. *The government recognised there were problems in urban areas but these could never be an excuse for lawless behaviour.* ♦ **law·less·ness** *Lawlessness is a major problem.* **2** A **lawless** place or time is one where people do not respect the law. *...lawless inner-city streets plagued by muggings, thefts, assaults and even murder. ...an increasingly lawless and godless age.* `◆◇◇◇◇ ADJ N-UNCOUNT ADJ-GRADED`

law·mak·er /ˈlɔːmeɪkə/ **lawmakers.** A **lawmaker** is someone such as a politician who is responsible for proposing and passing new laws. `◆◇◇◇◇ N-COUNT AMERICAN`

law·man /ˈlɔːmæn/ **lawmen. Lawmen** are men such as policemen or lawyers whose work involves the law. *...the 61-year-old lawman who headed the enquiry.* `N-COUNT JOURNALISM`

lawn /lɔːn/ **lawns.** A **lawn** is an area of grass that is cut short and is usually part of someone's garden or part of a park. See picture headed **house** and **flat**. `◆◆◇◇◇ N-VAR`

lawn·mow·er /ˈlɔːnməʊə/ **lawnmowers;** also spelled **lawn mower.** A **lawnmower** is a machine for cutting grass on lawns. See picture headed **tools**. `N-COUNT`

,**lawn 'tennis. Lawn tennis** is the official name for tennis. `N-UNCOUNT`

law·suit /ˈlɔːsuːt/ **lawsuits.** A **lawsuit** is a case in a court of law which concerns a dispute between two people or organizations. *The dispute culminated last week in a lawsuit against the government.* `◆◆◇◇◇ N-COUNT FORMAL`

law·yer /ˈlɔɪə/ **lawyers.** A **lawyer** is a person who is qualified to advise people about the law and represent them in court. `◆◆◆◇◇ N-COUNT`

lax /læks/ **laxer, laxest.** If you say that a person's behaviour or a system is **lax**, you mean they are not careful or strict in making or obeying rules or maintaining high standards. *One of the problem areas is lax security... I was lax in my duties.* ♦ **lax·ity** The *laxity of export control authorities has made a significant contribution to the problem.* `◆◇◇◇◇ ADJ-GRADED N-UNCOUNT`

laxa·tive /ˈlæksətɪv/ **laxatives.** A **laxative** is something which you eat or drink that stops you being constipated. *Foods that ferment quickly in the stomach are excellent natural laxatives.* ▶ Also an adjective. *The artificial sweetener sorbitol has a laxative effect.* `◆◇◇◇◇ N-VAR ADJ-GRADED`

lay 1 verb and noun uses

lay /leɪ/ **lays, laying, laid.** In standard English, the form **lay** is also the past tense of the verb **lie** in some meanings. In informal English, people sometimes use the word **lay** instead of **lie** in those meanings. `◆◆◆◆◇`

1 If you **lay** something somewhere, you put it there in a careful or neat way. *Mothers routinely lay babies on their backs to sleep.* **2** If you **lay** the table or **lay** the places at a table, you arrange the knives, forks, and other things that people need on the table before a meal. The usual American expression is **set the table**. **3** If you **lay** something such as carpets, cables, or foundations, you put them into their permanent position. *Public utilities dig up roads to lay pipes.* **4** When someone **lays** a trap, they prepare it to catch someone or something. *They were laying a trap for the kidnapper.* **5** When a female bird **lays** an egg, the egg comes out of its body. *Freezing weather in spring hampered the hens' ability to lay.* `VERB V n prep/adv` `VERB: V n BRITISH` `VERB V n` `VERB V n` `VERB: V n V`

6 Lay is used with some nouns to talk about making official preparations for something. For example, if you **lay the basis** for something, or **lay plans** for it, you prepare it carefully so that you can continue with it, develop it, or benefit from it later. *Diplomats meeting in Chile have laid the groundwork for far-reaching environmental regulations.* **7 Lay** is used with some nouns in expressions about accusing or blaming someone. For example, if you **lay the blame** for a mistake on someone, you say it is their fault, or if the police **lay charges** against someone, they officially accuse that person of a crime. *Police have decided not to lay charges over allegations of a telephone tapping operation.* `VERB V n` `VERB: V n prep V n`

8 If you **lay** yourself **open to** criticism or attack, or if something **lays** you **open to** it, something you do makes it possible or likely that other people will criticize or attack you. *Such a statement could lay her open to ridicule.* `PHRASE`

9 ● to **lay** something **bare**: see **bare**. ● to **lay claim to** something: see **claim**. ● to **lay** something **at** someone's **door**: see **door**. ● to **lay eyes on** something: see **eye**. ● to **lay a finger on** someone: see **finger**. ● to **lay** your **hands on** something: see **hand**. ● to **lay down the law**: see **law**. ● to **lay down** your **life**: see **life**. ● to **lay** something **to rest**: see **rest**. ● to **lay siege** to something: see **siege**. ● to **lay waste**: see **waste**.

lay aside. If you **lay aside** a feeling or belief, you reject it or give it up in order to progress with something. *Perhaps the opposed parties will lay aside their sectional interests and rise to this challenge.* `PHRASAL VB V P noun Also V n P`

lay before. If you **lay** an idea or piece of information **before** someone, you present it to them, usually in order to obtain their approval or advice. *Mr Patten laid regulations before Parliament giving himself wide general powers.* `PHRASAL VB V n P n Also V n P FORMAL`

lay down. 1 If you **lay** something **down**, you put it down, usually because you have finished using it. *She laid down her knife and fork and pushed her plate away.* **2** If rules or people in authority **lay down** what people must do, they officially state what they must do. *The Companies Act lays down a set of minimum requirements.* **3** If someone **lays down** their weapons, they stop fighting a battle or war and make peace. `PHRASAL VB V n P V P noun V P noun V P noun`

lay into. To **lay into** someone or something means to start attacking them with physical violence or severe criticism. *A mob of women laid into him with handbags and pointed shoes.* `PHRASAL VB V P n INFORMAL`

lay off. 1 If workers **are laid off**, they are told by their employers to leave their jobs, usually because there is no more work for them to do. *They did not sell a single car for a month and had to lay off workers.* ● See also **layoff. 2** If you tell someone to **lay off**, you mean that they should leave you or someone else alone. *He went* `PHRASAL VB be V-ed P V P noun Also V n P` `V P INFORMAL`

on attacking her until other passengers arrived and told him to lay off.

lay on. If you **lay on** something such as food, entertainment, or a service, you provide or supply it, especially in a generous or grand way. *They laid on a superb evening.*
PHRASAL VB
V P noun
BRITISH

lay out. 1 If you **lay out** a group of things, you spread them out and arrange them neatly. *She took a deck of cards and began to lay them out.* **2** To **lay out** ideas or plans means to explain or present them clearly, for example in a document or a meeting. *Maxwell listened closely as Johnson laid out his plan.* **3** To **lay out** an area of land or a building means to plan and design how its different parts should be arranged. *When we laid out the car parks, we reckoned on one car per four families.* • See also **layout**. **4** If you **lay out** money on something, you spend a large amount of money on it. *You won't have to lay out a fortune for this dining table.*
PHRASAL VB
V P noun
V P noun
V n P
V P noun
Also V n P
V P noun
Also V n P
V P noun
INFORMAL

lay up. If someone **is laid up** with an illness, the illness makes it necessary for them to stay in bed. *I was laid up in bed with acute rheumatism... I was laid up for two months after the accident.*
PHRASAL VB
usu passive
be V-ed P with
n
be V-ed P
INFORMAL

lay 2 adjective uses

lay /leɪ/. **1** You use **lay** to describe people who are involved with a Christian church but are not members of the clergy or are not monks or nuns. *...a Methodist lay preacher.* **2** You use **lay** to describe people who are not experts or professionals in a particular subject or activity. *It is difficult for a lay person to gain access to medical libraries.*
ADJ: ADJ n
ADJ: ADJ n

lay·about /'leɪəbaʊt/ **layabouts.** If you say that someone is a **layabout**, you disapprove of them because you think they are idle and lazy.
N-COUNT
PRAGMATICS
BRITISH

'lay-by, lay-bys. A **lay-by** is a short strip of road by the side of a main road, where cars can stop for a while.
N-COUNT
BRITISH

lay·er /'leɪə/ **layers, layering, layered. 1** A layer of a material or substance is a quantity or piece of it that covers a surface or that is between two other things. *A fresh layer of snow covered the street... Arrange all the vegetables except the potatoes in layers.* **2** If something such as a system or an idea has many **layers**, it has many different levels or parts. *...an astounding ten layers of staff between the factory worker and the chief executive.* **3** If you **layer** something, you arrange it in layers.
◆◆◆◇◇
N-COUNT
N-COUNT
VERB: V n

lay·ered /'leɪəd/. Something that is **layered** is made of or exists in layers. *...a layered white dress.*
◆◇◇◇◇
ADJ

lay·man /'leɪmən/ **laymen.** A **layman** is a person who is not qualified or experienced in a particular subject or activity. *There are basically two types, called in layman's terms, blue and white asbestos.*
◆◇◇◇◇
N-COUNT

lay·off /'leɪɒf, AM -ɔːf/ **layoffs.** When there are **layoffs** in a company, people are made unemployed because there is no more work for them.
◆◇◇◇◇
N-COUNT

lay·out /'leɪaʊt/ **layouts.** The **layout** of a garden, building, or piece of writing is the way in which the parts of it are arranged.
◆◇◇◇◇
N-COUNT

lay·per·son /'leɪpɜːsən/ **laypersons** or **laypeople.** A **layperson** is a person who is not qualified or experienced in a particular subject or activity.
N-COUNT

laze /leɪz/ **lazes, lazing, lazed.** If you **laze** somewhere for a period of time, you relax and enjoy yourself, not doing anything that requires effort. *Fred lazed in an easy chair.* ▶ **Laze around** or **laze about** means the same as **laze.**
VERB: V
V
Also V prep
PHRASAL VB

lazy /'leɪzi/ **lazier, laziest. 1** If someone is **lazy**, they do not want to work or make any effort to do anything. *I was too lazy to learn how to read music.* ♦ **la·zi·ness** *Current employment laws will be changed to reward effort and punish laziness.* **2** You can use **lazy** to describe an activity in which you are very relaxed and which you do without making much effort. *We would have a lazy lunch and then lie on the beach in the sun.* ♦ **la·zi·ly** *Liz went back into the kitchen, stretching lazily.* **3** If you describe something as **lazy**, you mean that it moves or flows slowly and gently. *...the lazy, loose grace of the born*
◆◆◇◇◇
ADJ-GRADED
N-UNCOUNT
ADJ-GRADED:
ADJ n
ADV-GRADED
ADJ: ADJ n
LITERARY

athlete. ♦ **lazily** *White flakes drifted lazily down from a night sky.*
ADV:
ADV with v

lb. **lb** is a written abbreviation for **pound**, when 'pound' refers to weight. *The baby was born three months early at 3 lb 5oz.*
◆◆◇◇◇

LCD /ˌel siː 'diː/ **LCDs.** An **LCD** is a display of information on a screen, which uses liquid crystals that become visible when electricity is passed through them. LCD is an abbreviation for **liquid crystal display.** *...a solar calculator with LCD display.*
◆◇◇◇◇
N-COUNT

lead 1 being ahead or taking someone somewhere

lead /liːd/ **leads, leading, led. 1** If you **lead** a group of moving people, you walk or ride in front of them. *He walks with a stick but still leads his soldiers into battle... Tom was leading, a rifle slung over his back.* **2** If you **lead** someone to a particular place or thing, you take them there. *He took Dickon by the hand to lead him into the house... Leading the horse, Evandar walked to the door.* **3** If a road or door **leads** to a place or **leads** in a particular direction, you can get to that place or go in that direction by following the road or going through the door. *...a main highway leading north.*
◆◆◆◆◆
V n prep/adv
V
VERB:
V n prep/adv
V n
VERB:
V prep/adv

4 If you **are leading** in a race or competition, you are winning. *So far Fischer leads by five wins to two... Aston Villa last led the League in March 1990.* **5** If you have the **lead** or are in the **lead** in a race or competition, you are winning. *England took the lead after 31 minutes.* **6** Someone's **lead** over a competitor in a race or competition is the distance, amount of time, or number of points by which they are ahead of them. *His goal gave Forest a two-goal lead against Southampton... Sainz now has a lead of 28 points.* **7** If one company or country **leads** others in a particular activity, it is more successful or advanced than they are in that activity. *When it comes to pop music we not only lead Europe, we lead the world.* **8** If you **lead** a group of people, an organization, or an activity, you are in charge of the people or the activity. *He led the country between 1949 and 1984.* **9** If you give a **lead**, you do something that other people consider to be a good example or model to follow. *...the need for the president to give a moral lead... Over the next 150 years, many others followed his lead.* **10** You can use **lead** when you are saying what kind of life someone has. For example, if you **lead** a busy life, your life is busy. **11** If something **leads** to a situation or event, usually an unpleasant one, it begins a process which causes that situation or event to happen. *Ethnic tensions among the republics could lead to civil war.* **12** If something **leads** you to do something, it influences or affects you in such a way that you do it. *What was it ultimately that led you to leave Sarajevo for Zagreb?* **13** If someone or something **leads** you to think or expect something, they cause you to think or expect it, although it is not true or does not happen. *It was not as straightforward as we were led to believe.* **14** If you **lead** a conversation or discussion, you control the way that it develops so that you can introduce a particular subject. *After a while I led the conversation around to her job.* **15** You can say that one point or topic in a discussion **leads** you to another in order to introduce a new point or topic that is linked with the previous one. *Well, I think that leads me to the real point.* **16** A **lead** is a piece of information or an idea which may help people to discover the facts in a situation where many facts are not known, for example in the investigation of a crime. *The inquiry team is also following up possible leads after receiving 400 calls from the public.* **17** The **lead** in a play, film, or show is the most important part in it. The person who plays this part can also be called the **lead.** *Nina Ananiashvili and Alexei Fadeyechev from the Bolshoi Ballet dance the leads.* **18** The **lead** in a newspaper is the most important story in it. **19** A dog's **lead** is a long chain or piece of leather attached to the dog's collar so that you can control the dog. **20** A **lead** is a piece of wire covered in
VERB: V
V by amount
N-SING:
the N
N-SING:
with supp
VERB:
V n in n
V n
VERB
V n
N-COUNT
VERB: V n
VERB
V to n
VERB
V n to-inf
VERB:
V n to-inf
be V-ed
VERB:
V n
V n adv/prep
VERB
PRAGMATICS
V n to n
N-COUNT
N-COUNT
N-SING
N-COUNT
N-COUNT

plastic which supplies electricity to a piece of equipment or carries it from one part of the equipment to another.
21 See also **leading, -led.** ● to **lead** someone **astray**: see **astray.** ● **one thing led to another**: see **thing.** ● to **lead the way**: see **way.**

lead off. 1 If a door or path **leads off** a place or **leads off** from it, you can go directly from that place through that door or along that path. *The treatment rooms lead off from the swimming pool... A corridor led off to the left.* **2** If someone **leads off** in an activity or conversation, they start it. *Whenever there was a dance he and I led off.*
PHRASAL VB
V P n
V P from n
V P prep
VP
Also V P noun

lead on. If someone **leads** you **on**, they encourage you to do something, especially by giving you false information or behaving in a misleading way.
PHRASAL VB
V n P

lead on to. If one event or action **leads on to** another, it causes it or makes it possible. *This discovery led on to studies of the immune system.*
PHRASAL VB
V P P n
BRITISH

lead up to. 1 The events that **led up to** a particular event happened one after the other until that event occurred. *...the events that led up to the deaths.* ● See also **lead-up. 2** The period of time **leading up to** an event is the period of time immediately before it happens. *...the weeks leading up to Christmas.*
PHRASAL VB
V P P n
V P P n

lead 2 substances

lead /led/ **leads. 1** Lead is a soft, grey, heavy metal. **2** The **lead** in a pencil is the centre part of it which makes a mark on paper.
◆◆◇◇◇
N-UNCOUNT
N-COUNT

lead·ed /'ledɪd/. **1** Leaded petrol has had lead added to it. **2** Leaded windows are made of small pieces of glass held together by strips of lead.
ADJ: ADJ n
ADJ: ADJ n

lead·en /'ledən/. **1** A leaden sky is dark grey and has no movement of clouds. **2** If your movements are **leaden**, you move slowly and heavily.
ADJ
LITERARY
ADJ
LITERARY

lead·er /'liːdə/ **leaders. 1** The **leader** of a group of people or an organization is the person who is in charge of it. *The Republican Party's leader, Mr Franz Schoenhuber, has resigned.* **2** The **leader** in a race or competition is the person who is winning. *The leaders came in two minutes clear of the field.* **3** The **leader** among a range of products or companies is the one that is most successful. *Procter & Gamble is the leader in the mass market cosmetics industry.* **4** The **leader** of an orchestra is the most senior violin player, who acts as a deputy to the conductor. **5** The **leader** of a band or orchestra is the person who conducts it. **6** In a newspaper, the **leader** is the main article, usually expressing the editor's opinion on the most important news items of the day.
◆◆◆◆◇
N-COUNT

N-COUNT

N-COUNT

N-COUNT
BRITISH
N-COUNT
AMERICAN

N-COUNT
BRITISH

lead·er·ship /'liːdəʃɪp/ **leaderships. 1** You refer to people who are in control of a group or organization as the **leadership.** *...the Labour leadership of Haringey council.* **2** Someone's **leadership** is their position or state of being in control of a group of people. *He praised her leadership during the crisis.* **3** Leadership refers to the qualities that make someone a good leader, or the methods a leader uses to do his or her job. *What people want to see is determined, decisive action and firm leadership.*
◆◆◆◆◇
N-COUNT

N-UNCOUNT

N-UNCOUNT

lead-free /ˌled'friː/. Something such as petrol or paint which is **lead-free**, is made without lead, or has no lead added to it.
ADJ

lead-in /'liːdɪn/ **lead-ins.** A **lead-in** is something that is said or done as an introduction before the main subject or event, especially for a radio or television programme.
N-COUNT

lead·ing /'liːdɪŋ/. **1** The **leading** person or thing in a particular area is the one which is most important or successful. *Britain's future as a leading industrial nation depends on investment.* **2** The **leading** part or role in a play or film is the main part or role. A **leading** lady or man is an actor who plays this role. **3** The **leading** group, vehicle, or participant in a race or procession is the one that is at the front.
◆◆◆◆◇
ADJ: ADJ n

ADJ: ADJ n

ADJ: ADJ n

leading 'article, leading articles. The **leading article** in a newspaper is the main article in it, usually expressing the editor's opinion on the most important news item of the day.
◆◇◇◇◇
N-COUNT

leading 'edge. The **leading edge** of a particular area of research or development is the area of it that seems most advanced or sophisticated. *...a consumer electronics company at the leading edge of developing components.*
N-SING

leading 'light, leading lights. If you say that someone is a **leading light** in an organization, you mean that they are one of the most important or active people in it.
N-COUNT
BRITISH

leading 'question, leading questions. A **leading question** is expressed in such a way that it suggests what the answer should be.
N-COUNT

lead sing·er /ˌliːd 'sɪŋə/ **lead singers.** The **lead singer** of a pop group is the person who sings most of the songs.
◆◇◇◇◇
N-COUNT

lead-up /'liːdʌp/. The **lead-up** to an event is the things that are connected with that event and that happen before it. *The lead-up to the wedding was extremely interesting.*
N-SING

leaf /liːf/ **leaves; leafs, leafing, leafed. 1** The **leaves** of a tree or plant are the parts that are flat, thin, and usually green. *The Japanese maple that stands across the drive had just come into leaf.* ● See also **-leaved. 2** A **leaf** is one of the pieces of paper of which a book is made. **3** If you **take a leaf from** someone's **book**, you behave in the same way as them because you want to be like that person or as successful as they are. **4** If you say that you are going to **turn over a new leaf**, you mean that you are going to start to behave in a better or more acceptable way.
◆◆◆◇◇
N-COUNT

N-COUNT
PHRASE

PHRASE

leaf through. If you **leaf through** a book or magazine, you turn the pages without reading or looking at them very carefully.
PHRASAL VB
V P n

leaf·less /'liːfləs/. If a tree or plant is **leafless**, it has no leaves.
ADJ

leaf·let /'liːflət/ **leaflets, leafleting, leafleted. 1** A **leaflet** is a little book or a piece of paper containing information about a particular subject. *...a leaflet called 'Sexual Harassment at Work'.* **2** If you **leaflet** a place, you distribute leaflets there, for example by handing them to people, or by putting them through letter boxes. *We've leafleted the university today to try to drum up some support.*
◆◆◇◇◇
N-COUNT

VERB
V n
Also V

leafy /'liːfi/. **1** Leafy trees and plants have lots of leaves on them. *...the splendour of the Tuscan hills and leafy trees.* **2** You say that a place is **leafy** when there are lots of trees and plants there. *...leafy suburban areas.*
◆◇◇◇◇
ADJ-GRADED

ADJ-GRADED

league /liːg/ **leagues. 1** A **league** is a group of people, clubs, or countries that have joined together for a particular purpose, or because they share a common interest. *...the League of Nations.* **2** If you say that someone is **in league** with someone else to do something bad, they are working together to do that thing. *Williams operated the smuggling scheme in league with his brother.* **3** A **league** is a group of clubs which play the same sport or activity in competition with each other. *The club are on the brink of promotion to the Premier League.* **4** You use the word **league** to make comparisons between different people or things, especially in terms of their quality. *Their record sales would put them in the same league as The Rolling Stones.*
◆◆◆◆◇
N-COUNT

PHRASE

N-COUNT

N-COUNT:
with supp

leak /liːk/ **leaks, leaking, leaked. 1** If a container or other object **leaks**, or **leaks** a substance such as a liquid or gas, there is a hole or crack in the container which lets the substance escape. You can also say that a substance such as a liquid or gas **leaks** from a container. *The roof leaked... The gas had apparently leaked from a cylinder... A large diesel tank mysteriously leaked its contents into the river.* ► Also a noun. *It's thought a gas leak may have caused the blast.* **2** A **leak** is a crack, hole, or other fault that a substance such as a liquid or gas can pass through. *Engineers found a leak in a hydrogen fuel line.* **3** If a secret document or piece of information **is leaked**, someone lets the public know about it. *Last year, a civil servant was imprisoned for leaking a document to the press... He revealed who leaked a confiden-*
◆◆◆◇◇
V-ERG
V
V prep/adv
V n into n
Also V n

N-COUNT

N-COUNT

V-ERG
V n to n
V
V-ed

tial police report... We don't know how the transcript leaked. ...a leaked report. ▶ Also a noun. *More serious leaks, possibly involving national security, are likely to be investigated by the police.* ▶ **Leak out** means the same as **leak**. *More details are now beginning to leak out.* `N-COUNT` `PHRASAL VB` `ERG` `V P`

leak·age /'liːkɪdʒ/ **leakages.** A leakage is an amount of liquid or gas that is escaping from a pipe or container by means of a crack or hole. *It should be possible to reduce leakage from pipes.* `N-VAR`

leaky /'liːki/ **leakiest.** Something that is **leaky** has holes, cracks, or other faults which allow liquids and gases to pass through. `ADJ-GRADED`

lean /liːn/ **leans, leaning, leaned, leant; leaner, leanest.** The form **leant** can be used as the past tense and past participle in British English. **1** When you **lean** in a particular direction, you bend your body in that direction. *They stopped to lean over a gate.* **2** If you **lean** on or against someone or something, you rest against them so that they partly support your weight. If you **lean** an object on or against something, you place the object so that it is partly supported by the thing it is resting against. *She was feeling tired and was glad to lean against him... Lean the plants against a wall.* **3** If you describe someone as **lean**, you approve of the fact that they are thin but look strong and healthy. *...Mike, tall and lean with clear blue eyes.* **4** If meat is **lean**, it does not have very much fat. **5** If you describe an organization as **lean**, you mean that it has become stronger and more competitive by getting rid of staff or projects which were unprofitable. **6** If you describe periods of time as **lean**, you mean that people have less of something such as money or are less successful than they used to be. *The taxi trade is going through its leanest patch for 30 years.* `◆◆◆◇◇` `VERB` `V adv/prep` `VERB` `V adv/prep` `V n adv/prep` `ADJ-GRADED` `PRAGMATICS` `ADJ-GRADED` `ADJ-GRADED` `ADJ-GRADED`

lean on or **lean upon. 1** If you **lean on** someone or **lean upon** them, you depend on them for support and encouragement. *She leaned on him to help her to solve her problems.* **2** If you **lean on** someone, you try to influence them, especially by threatening them. *He told us to get stuffed so we leaned on his kid.* `PHRASAL VB` `V P n` `V P n` `INFORMAL`

lean towards. If you **lean towards** or **lean toward** a particular idea, belief, or type of behaviour, you have a tendency to think or act in a particular way. *Politically, I lean towards the right.* `PHRASAL VB` `V P n`

lean·ing /'liːnɪŋ/ **leanings.** Your particular **leanings** are the beliefs, ideas, or aims you hold or a tendency you have towards them. *I always had a leaning towards sport.* `N-COUNT`

leant /lent/. **Leant** is a past tense and past participle of **lean**.

'lean-to, lean-tos. A **lean-to** is a building such as a shed or garage which is attached to one wall of a larger building. `N-COUNT`

leap /liːp/ **leaps, leaping, leaped, leapt.** The form **leapt** is the usual past tense and past participle in British English. **1** If you **leap**, you jump high in the air or jump a long distance. *He had leapt from a window in the building and escaped.* ▶ Also a noun. *Smith took Britain's fifth medal of the championships with a leap of 2.37 metres.* **2** If you **leap** somewhere, you move there suddenly and quickly. *The two men leaped into the jeep and roared off.* **3** If a vehicle **leaps** somewhere, it moves there in a short sudden movement. *The car leapt forward.* **4** If you take a **leap in the dark** or a **leap into the unknown**, you do something without having any previous experience in or knowledge of that activity. **5** A **leap** is a large and important change, increase, or advance. *The result has been a giant leap in productivity... Contemporary art has taken a huge leap forward in the last five or six years.* **6** If you **leap** to a particular place or position, you make a large and important change, increase, or advance. *Warwicks leap to third in the table, 31 points behind leaders Essex.* **7** You can use **in leaps and bounds** or **by leaps and bounds** to emphasize that someone or something is improving or increasing quickly and greatly. *The total number of* `◆◆◆◇◇` `VERB: V` `V prep/adv` `N-COUNT` `VERB` `V prep/adv` `VERB` `V adv/prep` `PHRASE` `N-COUNT` `JOURNALISM` `VERB` `V prep` `PHRASE` `PRAGMATICS`

species on the planet appears to be growing by leaps and bounds. **8** If your heart **leaps**, you experience a sudden, very strong feeling of surprise, fear, or happiness. *My heart leaped at the sight of her.* **9** If you **leap** at a chance or opportunity, you accept it quickly and eagerly. `VERB` `V` `VERB:` `V at n`

leap out at. If something **leaps out at** you, it is very obvious or noticeable. *One of the things that does leap out at us is that every side seems to want the others to acknowledge their suffering... She said she felt the colours were leaping out at her, they were so bright.* `PHRASAL VB` `V P P n`

leap·frog /'liːpfrɒg, AM -frɔːg/ **leapfrogs, leapfrogging, leapfrogged. 1** Leapfrog is a game which children play, in which a child bends over, while others jump over their back. **2** If one group of people **leapfrogs** into a particular position, or **leapfrogs** someone else, they use the achievements of another person or group in order to make advances of their own. *It is already obvious that all four American systems have leapfrogged over the European versions... American researchers have now leapfrogged the Japanese and are going to produce a digital system within a year or two.* `N-UNCOUNT` `VERB` `V prep` `V n`

leap of 'faith, leaps of faith. A **leap of faith** is a deliberate decision to accept or believe something that you initially find difficult to accept or believe. `N-COUNT:` `a N in sing`

leapt /lept/. **Leapt** is a past tense and past participle of **leap**.

'leap year, leap years. A **leap year** is a year which has 366 days. The extra day is the 29th of February. There is a leap year every four years. `N-COUNT`

learn /lɜːn/ **learns, learning, learned, learnt.** In British English, the forms **learned** and **learnt** can both be used for the past tense and past participle. **1** If you **learn** something, you obtain knowledge or a skill through studying or training. *Their children were going to learn English... He is learning to play the piano. ...learning how to use new computer systems... Experienced teachers help you learn quickly.* ◆ **learn·er, learners.** *...a new aid for younger children or slow learners... Learner drivers must be supervised by adults.* ◆ **learn·ing** *...a bilingual approach to the learning of English... Oxford is renowned as a place of learning.* **2** If you **learn of** something, you find out about it. *She learned of his affair with Betty... She wasn't surprised to learn that he was involved.* **3** If people **learn** to behave or react in a particular way, they gradually start to behave in that way. *You have to learn to face your problem... We are learning how to confront death.* ◆ **learned** *Some believe the disorder is a learned reaction to a stressful environment.* **4** If you **learn** from an unpleasant experience, you change the way you behave so that it does not happen again or so that if it happens again, you can deal with it more easily. *I am convinced that he has learned from his mistakes... The company failed to learn any lessons from this experience.* **5** If you **learn** something such as a poem or the script of a play, you study or repeat the words so that you can remember them. **6** See also **learned; seat of learning.** • to **learn** something **the hard way**: see **hard**. • to **learn the ropes**: see **rope**. `◆◆◆◆◆` `VERB` `V n` `V to-inf` `V wh` `Also V about n` `N-COUNT` `N-UNCOUNT` `VERB` `V of n` `V that` `Also V wh` `VERB` `V to-inf` `V wh-to-inf` `ADJ` `VERB` `V from n` `V n from n` `VERB: V n`

learned /'lɜːnɪd/. **1** A **learned** person has gained a lot of knowledge by studying. **Learned** books or papers have been written by someone like this. *I met a learned and charming man called Dr Mortimer Manson.* **2** See also **learn.** `◆◇◇◇◇` `ADJ-GRADED`

'learning curve, learning curves. A **learning curve** is a process where people develop a skill by learning from their mistakes. A steep learning curve involves learning very quickly. `N-COUNT`

learnt /lɜːnt/. **Learnt** is a past tense and past participle of **learn.** `BRITISH`

lease /liːs/ **leases, leasing, leased. 1** A **lease** is a legal agreement by which the owner of a building, a piece of land, or something such as a car allows someone else to use it for a period of time in return for money. *He took up a 10 year lease on the house.* **2** If you **lease** property or something such as a car `◆◆◆◇◇` `N-COUNT` `VERB`

from someone, or if they **lease** it to you, they allow you to use it in return for regular payments of money. *He went to Toronto, where he leased an apartment... She hopes to lease the building to students... La Prade could lease him a few acres.* **3** If you say that someone or something has been given **a new lease of life**, you are emphasizing that they are much more lively or successful than they have been in the past. `V n` `V n to n` `V n n` `PHRASE`

lease·hold /ˈliːshəʊld/ **leaseholds.** If you have the **leasehold** of a building or piece of land, you have the legal right to use it for a period of time as arranged according to a lease. ▶ Also an adjective. *...a leasehold property.* ♦ **lease·holder, lease·holders.** *The leaseholder is responsible for drug use by anyone who lives in the apartment.* `N-COUNT` `BRITISH` `ADJ` `N-COUNT`

leash /liːʃ/ **leashes.** A dog's **leash** is a long thin piece of leather or a chain, which you attach to the dog's collar. *All dogs in public places should be on a leash.* `N-COUNT`

least /liːst/. **Least** is often considered to be the superlative form of **little**. `◆◆◆◆◆`
1 You use **at least** to say that a number or amount is the smallest that is possible or likely and that the actual number or amount may be greater. The forms **at the least** and **at the very least** are also used. *...a dinner menu featuring at least 15 different sorts of fish... He would call me on the phone four or five times a day at the least.* **2** You use **at least** to say that something is the minimum that is the case or should be done, although you think that more than this might be possible in the circumstances. The forms **at the least** and **at the very least** are also used. *She could take a nice holiday at least... Why do we not, at the very least, attack the artillery emplacements?* **3** You use **at least** to indicate an advantage that exists in spite of the disadvantage or bad situation that has just been mentioned. *At least we know he is still alive... If something awful happens to you at least you can write about it.* **4** You use **at least** to indicate that you are correcting or changing something that you have just said. *I can live with almost anything – or at least I thought I could.* **5** You use **the least** to mean a smaller amount than anyone or anything else, or the smallest amount possible. *If you like cheese, go for the ones with the least fat... They neglect their duty at the least hint of fun elsewhere.* ▶ Also a pronoun. *On education funding, Japan performs best but spends the least per student.* ▶ Also an adverb. *Damning the river may end up benefiting those who need it the least.* **6** You use **least** to indicate that someone or something has less of a particular quality than most other things of its kind. *The least experienced athletes had caused a great many false-starts.* **7** You use **least** to indicate that something is true or happens to a smaller degree or extent than anything else or at any other time. *He had a way of throwing her off guard with his charm when she least expected it.* **8** You use **least** in structures where you are emphasizing that a particular situation or event is much less important or serious than other possible or actual ones. *Having to get up at three o'clock every morning was the least of her worries.* **9** You use **the least** in structures where you are stating the minimum that should be done in a situation, and suggesting that more should really be done. *The least his hotel could do is provide a little privacy.* ● You use expressions such as **'that's the least that I can do'** to mean that you are very willing to do something, or to acknowledge someone's thanks. *Why not relax and let me teach you how to windsurf? It's the least I can do.* **10** You can use **in the least** and **the least bit** to emphasize a negative. *I'm not like that at all. Not in the least... Alice wasn't the least bit frightened.* **11** You use **last but not least** to say that the last person or thing to be mentioned is as important as all the others. **12** You can use **least of all** after a negative statement to emphasize that it applies especially to the person or thing mentioned. *No one ever reads these articles, least of all me.* **13** You can use **not least** to emphasize a particularly important example or reason. *Dieting it-* `PHRASE` `PRON` `ADV-SUPERL` `ADV-SUPERL: ADV adj/adv` `ADV-SUPERL: ADV with v` `ADJ-SUPERL: ADJ of n` `PRAGMATICS` `PRON` `PRAGMATICS` `PHRASE` `PRAGMATICS` `PHRASE` `PRAGMATICS` `PHRASE` `PHRASE` `PHRASE` `PRAGMATICS` `PHRASE` `PRAGMATICS`

self can be bad for you, not least because it is a cause of chronic stress. **14** You can use **to say the least** to suggest that a situation is actually much more extreme or serious than you say it is. *Accommodation was basic to say the least.* `PHRASE` `PRAGMATICS`

leath·er /ˈleðə/ **leathers. 1 Leather** is treated animal skin which is used for making shoes, clothes, bags, and furniture. *He wore a leather jacket.* **2 Leathers** are leather clothes such as jackets and trousers, especially those worn by motorcyclists. `◆◆◆◇◇` `N-VAR` `N-PLURAL`

leath·ery /ˈleðəri/. If the texture of something, for example someone's skin, is **leathery**, it is tough and hard, like leather. `ADJ-GRADED`

leave /liːv/ **leaves, leaving, left. 1** If you **leave** a place or person, you go away from that place or person. *I simply couldn't bear to leave my little girl... My flight leaves in less than an hour... The last of the older children had left for school.* **2** If you **leave** an institution, group, or job, you permanently stop attending that institution, being a member of that group, or doing that job. *He left school with no qualifications... I am leaving to concentrate on writing fiction. ...a leaving present.* **3** If you **leave** your husband, wife, or some other person with whom you have had a close relationship, you stop living with them or you end the relationship. *He'll never leave you... Bill left me for another woman.* **4** If you **leave** something or someone in a particular place, you let them remain there when you go away, deliberately or because you forget to take them with you. *I left my bags in the car... Leave your key with a neighbour.* **5** If you **leave** a message or an answer, you write it, record it, or give it to someone so that it can be found or passed on. *You can leave a message on our answering machine... I left my phone number with several people.* **6** If you **leave** someone doing something, they are doing that thing when you go away from them. *Salter drove off, leaving Callendar surveying the scene.* **7** If you **leave** someone to do something, you go away from them so that they do it on their own. *I'd better leave you to get on with it, then... Diana took the hint and left them to it... One of the advantages of a department store is that you are left to yourself to try things on.* **8** If someone or something **leaves** an amount of something, they do not use it and it remains available after the rest has been used or taken away. *He always left a little food for the next day... Double rooms at any of the following hotels should leave you some change from £150.* **9** To **leave** someone with something, especially something that is difficult to deal with or that is unpleasant, means to cause them to have it or be responsible for it. *...a crash which left him with a broken collar-bone... He left me with a child to support.* **10** If an event **leaves** people or things in a particular state, they are in that state when the event has finished. *...violent disturbances which have left at least ten people dead... The documentary left me in a state of shock.* **11** If you **leave** food or drink, you do not eat or drink it, often because you do not like it. **12** If something **leaves** a mark, effect, or sign, it causes that mark, effect, or sign to remain as a result. *A muscle tear will leave a scar after healing... She left a lasting impression on him.* **13** If you **leave** something in a particular state, position, or condition, you let it remain in that state, position, or condition. *He left the album open on the table... I've left the car lights on... I left the engine running.* **14** If you **leave** someone or something **alone**, or if you **leave** them **be**, you do not worry about them or bother them. **15** If someone tells you to **leave well alone**, they are telling you not to interfere in something. **16** If you **leave** a space or gap in something, you deliberately make that space or gap. **17** If you **leave** a job, decision, or choice to someone, you give them the responsibility for dealing with it or making it. *Affix the blue airmail label and leave the rest to us... The judge should not have left it to the jury to decide... For the moment, I leave you to take all decisions... The ceasefire leaves a lot to the goodwill of the forces involved.* **18** If someone or something **leaves** `◆◆◆◆◆` `VERB` `V` `V forn` `VERB` `V n` `V` `V-ing` `VERB` `V n` `V forn` `Also V` `VERB` `V n prep/adv` `V n with n` `VERB: V n` `V n prep/adv` `V n with n` `VERB` `V n -ing` `VERB` `V n to-inf` `V n to it` `be V-ed to` `pron-refl` `Also V n to n` `VERB` `V n forn` `V n n` `VERB` `V n with n` `VERB` `V n adj` `V n prep/adv` `VERB` `V n adj` `VERB` `V n` `VERB` `V n adj` `V n adv/prep` `V n -ing` `PHRASE` `PHRASE` `VERB: V n` `VERB` `V n to n` `V it to n to-inf` `V n to-inf` `V amount to n` `VERB`

you only one particular option, it causes you to have V n n
only that one option. *He would have preferred not to
have a fitted kitchen but the limited space left him no
option.*
19 If you **leave** something until a particular time, you VERB
delay doing it or dealing with it until then. *Don't leave* V n until/ton
it all until the last minute. ● If you **leave** something PHRASE
too late, you delay doing it so that when you eventually do it, it is useless or ineffective. **20** If you **leave** a VERB
particular subject, you stop talking about it and start V n
discussing something else. *I think we'd better leave* V n prep/adv
*the subject of Nationalism... I'm afraid we're going to
have to leave it there.* **21** You use the phrase **leaving** PHR-PREP
aside or **leaving to one side** when mentioning a fact PRAGMATICS
or detail that you want to ignore when making a gen-
eral statement. *Leaving aside the question of privacy,
constant surveillance can be remarkably convenient.*
22 If you **leave** property or money to someone, you VERB:
arrange for it to be given to them after you have died. V n ton
23 If you say that someone **leaves** a wife, husband, or VERB:
a particular number of children, you mean that the V n,
wife, husband, or children remain alive after that per- no cont
son has died. FORMAL
24 Leave is a period of time when you are not working N-UNCOUNT
at your job, because you are on holiday or for some
other reason. If you are **on leave**, you are not working
at your job. *Why don't you take a few days' leave?* **25** If N-UNCOUNT:
you ask for **leave** to do something, you ask for permis- N to-inf
sion to do it. *...an application for leave to appeal* FORMAL
against the judge's order. **26** When you **take** your PHRASE
leave or **take leave of** someone, you say goodbye to FORMAL
them and go.
27 See also **left**. ● **to leave a lot to be desired**: see **desire**. ● **to leave someone to their own devices**: see **device**. ● **take it or leave it**: see **take**.

leave behind. 1 If you **leave** someone or something PHRASAL VB
behind, you go away permanently from them. *We* V n P
hear of women who run away, leaving behind their V P noun
homes and families. **2** If someone or something V n P
leaves behind an object or a situation, it remains after V P noun
they have left or gone. *The sunburn will fade over several days, leaving behind a skin that is tanned.* **3** If a V n P
person, country, or organization **is left behind**, they be/getV-ed P
do not achieve or progress as much as others and so
they are at a disadvantage. *We're going to be left behind by the rest of the world.*

leave off. 1 If someone or something **is left off** a list, PHRASAL VB
they are not included on that list. *She has been deliber-* beV-ed P n
ately left off the guest list... The judge left Walsh's name V n P n
off the list of those he wanted arrested. **2** If someone V P -ing
leaves off doing something, they stop doing it. *We all* V P
left off eating... The film takes up where the original left Also V P noun
off and plots the final demise of Billy the Kid.

leave out. If you **leave** someone or something **out** of PHRASAL VB
an activity, collection, discussion, or group, you do V n P of n
not include them in it. *Some would question the wis-* V P noun
dom of leaving her out of the team... If you prefer mild Also V n P
flavours reduce or leave out the chilli. ● If someone PHRASE
feels left out, they feel sad because they are not included in a group or activity.

-leaved /-liːvd/; also spelled **-leafed**. **-leaved** or COMB
-leafed combines with adjectives to form other adjectives which describe the type of leaves a tree or
plant has. *...broad-leaved trees.*

leav·en /ˈlevən/ **leavens, leavening, leavened.** VERB:
If a situation or activity **is leavened** by something, it beV-ed by/
is made more interesting or cheerful. *He leavened* with n
his pictures with a dry wit. V n with n

leave of ˈabsence, leaves of absence. If you N-VAR
have **leave of absence** you have permission to be
away from work for a certain period.

leaves /liːvz/. **Leaves** is the plural form of **leaf**, and
the third person singular form of **leave**.

lech·er /ˈletʃə/ **lechers.** If you describe a man as a N-COUNT
lecher, you disapprove of him because he behaves PRAGMATICS
as if he is only interested in sex. ♦ **lech·er·ous** ADJ-GRADED
/ˈletʃərəs/. *...lecherous old men.*

lec·tern /ˈlektən/ **lecterns.** A **lectern** is a high N-COUNT
sloping desk on which someone puts their notes
when they are standing up and giving a lecture.

lec·ture /ˈlektʃə/ **lectures, lecturing, lectured.** ◆◆◆◇◇
1 A **lecture** is a talk someone gives in order to teach N-COUNT
people about a particular subject, usually at a university or college. **2** If you **lecture** on a particular VERB
subject, you give a lecture or a series of lectures V on/in n
about it. *She then invited him to Atlanta to lecture* V
*on the history of art... She has danced, choreo-
graphed, lectured and taught all over the world.* **3** If VERB
someone **lectures** you about something, they criti- V n about/on
cize you or tell you how they think you should be- n
have. *He used to lecture me about getting too much* V n
sun... Chuck would lecture me, telling me to get a Also V
haircut. ▶ Also a noun. *Our captain gave us a stern* N-COUNT
lecture on safety.

lec·tur·er /ˈlektʃərə/ **lecturers.** A lecturer is a ◆◆◇◇◇
teacher at a university or college. *...a lecturer in law* N-COUNT
at Southampton University. ♦ **lec·ture·ship, lec-** N-COUNT
tureships. A **lectureship** is the position of a lecturer at a university or college.

led /led/. **Led** is the past tense and past participle of
lead.

-led /-led/. **1 -led** is used to form adjectives which COMB
indicate that something is organized, directed, or
controlled by a particular person or group. *...the
student-led democracy movement.* **2 -led** is used to COMB
form adjectives which indicate that something is
mainly caused or influenced by a particular factor.
...a market-led economy.

ledge /ledʒ/ **ledges. 1** A **ledge** is a piece of rock ◆◇◇◇◇
on the side of a cliff or mountain, which is in the N-COUNT
shape of a narrow shelf. **2** A **ledge** is a narrow shelf N-COUNT
along the bottom edge of a window.

ledg·er /ˈledʒə/ **ledgers.** A **ledger** is a book in N-COUNT
which a company or organization writes down the
amounts of money it spends and receives.

lee /liː/. **1** The **lee** of a place is the shelter that it N-SING:
gives from the wind or bad weather. *...the cathedral,* with poss
which nestles in the lee of a hill. **2** The **lee** side of a ADJ: ADJ n
ship is the one that is away from the wind. TECHNICAL

leech /liːtʃ/ **leeches. 1** A **leech** is a small animal ◆◇◇◇◇
which looks like a worm and lives in water. Leeches N-COUNT
feed by sucking the blood of other animals. **2** If you N-COUNT
describe someone as a **leech**, you disapprove of PRAGMATICS
them because they deliberately depend on other
people, often making money out of them.

leek /liːk/ **leeks.** Leeks are long green and white ◆◇◇◇◇
vegetables which smell similar to onions. See pic- N-VAR
ture headed **vegetables**.

leer /lɪə/ **leers, leering, leered.** If someone **leers** ◆◇◇◇◇
at you, they smile unpleasantly, usually in a sexually PRAGMATICS
suggestive way; used showing disapproval. *...men* V at n
standing around, swilling beer and occasionally leer- Also V
ing at passing females. ▶ Also a noun. *When I asked* N-COUNT
*the clerk for my room key, he gave it to me with a
leer.*

leery /ˈlɪəri/. If you are **leery** of something, you are ADJ-GRADED
cautious and suspicious about it and try to avoid it. INFORMAL

lee·way /ˈliːweɪ/. **Leeway** is the flexibility that ◆◇◇◇◇
someone has to change their plans, for example by N-UNCOUNT
taking more time or spending more money than
they had originally intended to. *The President said
that he wanted to give states more leeway to pursue
their own health-care reforms.*

left 1 remaining

left /left/. **1 Left** is the past tense and past partici- ◆◆◆◇◇
ple of **leave**. **2** If there is a certain amount of some- ADJ:
thing **left**, or if you have a certain amount of it **left**, v-link ADJ,
it remains when the rest has gone or been used. *Is* v n ADJ
*there any gin left?... He's got plenty of money left...
They still have six games left to play.* ● If there is a PHRASE
certain amount of something **left over**, or if you
have it **left over**, it remains when the rest has gone
or been used.

left 2 direction and political groupings

left /left/; also written **Left** for meaning 3. **1** The **left** ◆◆◆◆◆
is one of two opposite directions, sides, or posi- N-SING
tions. If you are facing north and you turn to the
left, you will be facing west. In the word 'to', the 't'
is to the left of the 'o'. *In Britain cars drive on the
left. ...the brick wall to the left of the conservatory...*

Beaufort Castle is on your left. ▶ Also an adverb. ADV *Turn left at the crossroads into Clay Lane.* **2** Your ADJ: ADJ n **left** arm, leg, or ear, for example, is the one which is on the left side of your body. Your **left** shoe or glove is the one which is intended to be worn on your left foot or hand. **3** You can refer to political ideas N-SING: which are closer to socialism than capitalism and *the*N conservatism, or to people who support these ideas, as **the left**. *In 1979, Labour moved sharply to the left... The government's industrial policy has been fiercely attacked by the left.*

left-'field. **Left-field** means slightly odd or un- ADJ-GRADED usual. *...a left-field cabaret act.* INFORMAL

'left-hand. **Left-hand** describes the position of ◆◇◇◇ something when it is on the left side. *The keys are in* ADJ: ADJ n *the back left-hand corner of the drawer.*

,left-hand 'drive. A **left-hand drive** car, van, or ADJ lorry has the steering wheel on the left side, and is designed to be used in countries where people drive on the right-hand side of the road.

,left-'handed. Someone who is **left-handed** finds ◆◇◇◇◇ it easier to use their left hand rather than their right ADJ hand for activities such as writing and throwing a ball. ▶ Also an adverb. *My father thought that I'd be* ADV: *at a disadvantage if I wrote left-handed.* ♦ **l'eft-** ADV after v **h'ander, left-handers.** *Left-handers have trouble* N-COUNT *using can-openers.*

left·ist /'leftɪst/ **leftists.** **1** Socialists and Com- ◆◇◇◇◇ munists are sometimes referred to as **leftists**. N-COUNT *Arguments to provoke leftists still in love with the revolution.* **2** If you describe someone, their ideals ADJ: ADJ n or their activities as **leftist**, you mean that they sup- port the ideas of socialism or communism. *...an al- liance of seven leftist parties.* ♦ **left·ism.** N-UNCOUNT

,left-of-'centre; spelled **left of center** in American ADJ English. **Left-of-centre** people or political parties support moderate political ideas which are closer to socialism than to capitalism.

left·over /'leftəʊvə/ **leftovers;** also spelled **left-** ◆◇◇◇◇ **over. 1** You can refer to food that remains uneaten N-PLURAL after a meal as **leftovers**. **2** You use **leftover** to de- ADJ: ADJ n scribe an amount of something that remains after the rest of it has been used or eaten. *...leftover pieces of wallpaper... Leftover chicken makes a wonderful salad.* **3** A **leftover from** a past period of time is N-COUNT: something that still exists after most other things N *from* n connected to that time have disappeared. *My best clothes were leftovers from college.*

left·ward /'leftwəd/. The form **leftwards** is also ADJ: ADJ n used. **Leftward** or **leftwards** means towards a politi- cal position that is closer to socialism than to capi- talism. *...a leftward shift in politics.* ▶ Also an ad- ADV: verb. *He seemed to move leftwards as he grew older.* ADV after v

,left-'wing; also spelled **left wing. 1 Left-wing** ◆◆◇◇◇ people have political ideas that are based on social- ADJ-GRADED ism. *They said they would not be voting for him because he was too left-wing.* ♦ **l'eft-w'inger, left-wingers.** *We were accused of being militant* N-COUNT *left-wingers.* **2** The **left wing** of a group of people, N-SING especially a political party, consists of the members of it whose beliefs are closer to socialism than are those of its other members.

lefty /'lefti/ **lefties;** also spelled **leftie. 1** If you refer N-COUNT to someone as a **lefty**, you mean that they have so- BRITISH, cialist beliefs and you disapprove of this. *...a 'loony'* INFORMAL *policy of trendy lefty politics.* **2** A **lefty** is someone, N-COUNT especially a sports player, who is left-handed. AMERICAN, INFORMAL

leg /leg/ **legs, legging, legged. 1** A person or ◆◆◆◇ animal's **legs** are the long parts of their body that N-COUNT they use to stand on and walk with. See picture headed **human body.** ♦ **-legged** /-legɪd/ *...Sheila, a* COMB *long-legged blonde. ...a large four-legged animal.* **2** The **legs** of a pair of trousers are the parts that N-COUNT cover your legs. **3** A **leg** of lamb, pork, chicken, or N-COUNT: other meat is a piece of meat that consists of the n N, animal's or bird's leg, especially the thigh. *...a chick- N of* n *en leg. ...a leg of mutton.* **4** The **legs** of a table, N-COUNT chair, or other piece of furniture are the parts that rest on the floor and support the furniture's weight. ♦ **-legged** *...a three-legged stool.* COMB

5 If you **leg it**, you run somewhere very quickly, PHRASE usually in order to escape from someone or some- INFORMAL thing. *He was now to be seen legging it across the field.* PHRASE **6** If you say that something or someone is on their **last** INFORMAL **legs**, you mean that the period of time when they were successful or strong is ending. *By the mid-1980s, the copper industry in the US was on its last legs.* **7** If you PHRASE **are pulling** someone's **leg**, you are teasing them by INFORMAL telling them something shocking or worrying as a joke. **8** A **leg** of a long journey is one part of it, usually be- N-COUNT tween two points where you stop. *The first leg of the journey was by boat to Lake Naivasha.* **9** A **leg** of a N-COUNT sports competition is one of a series of games that are BRITISH played to decide an overall winner. **10** ● **an arm and a leg:** see **arm.**

lega·cy /'legəsi/ **legacies. 1** A **legacy** is money or ◆◆◇◇◇ property which someone leaves to you in their will N-COUNT when they die. **2** A **legacy** of an event or period of N-COUNT: history is something which is a direct result of it with supp and which continues to exist after it is over. *...the legacy of inequality and injustice created by Apartheid.*

le·gal /'liːgəl/. **1 Legal** is used to describe things ◆◆◆◇ that relate to the law. *He vowed to take legal action.* ADJ: ADJ n *...the British legal system.* ♦ **le·gal·ly** *It could be a* ADV *bit problematic, legally speaking.* **2** An action or ADJ situation that is **legal** is allowed or required by law. *...drivers who have more than the legal limit of alco- hol.* ♦ **le·gal·ity** /liˈgæliti/. *The auditor has ques-* N-UNCOUNT *tioned the legality of the contracts.* ♦ **le·gal·ly** *A lor-* ADV *ry driver can legally work eighty-two hours a week.*

,legal 'aid. Legal aid is financial assistance given ◆◇◇◇◇ by the government or another organization to peo- N-UNCOUNT ple who cannot afford to pay for a lawyer.

le·gal·ise /'liːgəlaɪz/. See **legalize.**

le·gal·is·tic /,liːgəˈlɪstɪk/. If you say that someone's ADJ-GRADED language or ideas are **legalistic**, you are criticizing PRAGMATICS them for paying too much attention to legal details.

le·gal·ize /'liːgəlaɪz/ **legalizes, legalizing, le-** ◆◇◇◇◇ **galized;** also spelled **legalise** in British English. If VERB something **is legalized**, a law is passed that makes it be V-ed legal. *Divorce was legalized in 1981.* ♦ **le·gali·za-** Also V n **·tion** /,liːgəlaɪˈzeɪʃən/ *She ruled out the legalisation* N-UNCOUNT *of drugs.*

,legal 'tender. Legal tender is money, especially a N-UNCOUNT particular coin or banknote, which is officially part of a country's currency at a particular time.

le·ga·tion /lɪˈgeɪʃən/ **legations. 1** A **legation** is a N-COUNT group of government officials and diplomats who work in a foreign country and represent their government in that country. *...a member of the US legation.* **2** A **legation** is the building in which a le- N-COUNT gation works.

leg·end /'ledʒənd/ **legends. 1** A **legend** is a very ◆◆◇◇◇ old and popular story that may be true. *...the leg-* N-VAR *ends of ancient Greece. ...Irish legend.* **2** If you refer N-COUNT to someone as a **legend**, you mean that they are very famous and admired by a lot of people. *...blues legends John Lee Hooker and B.B. King.*

leg·end·ary /'ledʒəndri, AM -deri/. **1** If you de- ◆◆◇◇◇ scribe someone or something as **legendary**, you ADJ-GRADED mean that they are very famous and that many sto- ries are told about them. *...the legendary Jazz singer Adelaide Hall.* **2** A **legendary** person, place, or ADJ event is mentioned or described in an old legend. *...the resting place of the legendary King Lud.*

-legged /-legɪd/. See **leg.**

leg·gings /'legɪŋz/. **1 Leggings** are close-fitting ◆◇◇◇◇ trousers, usually made out of a stretchy fabric, that N-PLURAL are worn by women and girls. **2 Leggings** are an N-PLURAL outer covering of leather or other strong material that you wear over your normal trousers in order to protect them.

leg·gy /'legi/. If you describe someone, usually a ADJ-GRADED woman, as **leggy**, you mean that they have very long legs. *The leggy beauty was none other than our own Naomi Campbell.*

leg·ible /'ledʒɪbəl/. **Legible** writing is clear enough ADJ-GRADED to read. *My handwriting isn't very legible.*

le·gion /'liːdʒən/ **legions.** 1 A legion is a large group of soldiers who form one section of an army. N-COUNT 2 A legion of people or things is a great number of N-COUNT them. ...*a legion of stories about noisy neighbours.* WRITTEN 3 If you say that things of a particular kind are le-ADJ: gion, you mean that there are a great number of v-link ADJ them. *Books on the subject of Tarot Cards are legion.* FORMAL

leg·is·late /'ledʒɪsleɪt/ **legislates, legislating,** ◆◇◇◇ **legislated.** When a government or state legislates, VERB: V it passes a new law. *Most member countries have al-* V against/ *ready legislated against excessive overtime... You* for/on n *cannot legislate to change attitudes.* V to-inf FORMAL

leg·is·la·tion /ˌledʒɪ'sleɪʃən/. **Legislation** consists ◆◆◇◇ of a law or laws passed by a government. ...*legisla-* N-UNCOUNT *tion to protect women's rights.* FORMAL

leg·is·la·tive /'ledʒɪslətɪv, AM -leɪ-/. **Legislative** ◆◆◇◇ means involving or relating to the process of mak-ADJ: ADJ n ing and passing laws. ...*the first step in the legislative* FORMAL *process.*

leg·is·la·tor /'ledʒɪsleɪtə/ **legislators.** A legislator ◆◇◇◇ is a person who is involved in making or passing N-COUNT laws. FORMAL

leg·is·la·ture /'ledʒɪslətʃə, AM -leɪ-/ **legislatures.** ◆◆◇◇ The legislature of a particular state or country is the N-COUNT group of people in it who have the power to make FORMAL and pass laws.

le·git /lə'dʒɪt/. If you describe a person or thing as ADJ-GRADED legit, you mean that they are in accordance with the INFORMAL law or with a particular set of rules and regulations. *I checked him out, he's legit.*

le·giti·mate, legitimates, legitimating, legiti- ◆◆◇◇ **mated.** The adjective is pronounced /lɪ'dʒɪtɪmət/. The verb is pronounced /lɪ'dʒɪtɪmeɪt/. 1 Something ADJ-GRADED that is legitimate is acceptable according to the law. ...*the restoration of the legitimate government.* ♦ le-·giti·ma·cy /lɪ'dʒɪtɪmɪsi/ ...*the political legitimacy* N-UNCOUNT *of his government.* ♦ le·giti·mate·ly ...*legitimately* ADV-GRADED *elected by the people.* 2 If you say that something ADJ-GRADED such as a feeling or claim is legitimate, you think that it is reasonable and justified. *That's a perfectly legitimate fear.* ♦ le·giti·ma·cy ...*the legitimacy of* N-UNCOUNT *his challenge for the title.* ♦ le·giti·mate·ly *They* ADV-GRADED: *could quarrel quite legitimately with some of my* ADV with v *choices.* 3 A legitimate child is one whose parents ADJ were married before he or she was born. 4 To legiti-VERB mate something means the same as to legitimize it. V n *We want to legitimate this process by passing a law.* FORMAL ♦ le·giti·ma·tion /lɪˌdʒɪtɪ'meɪʃən/ ...*the legitima-* N-UNCOUNT *tion of state constitutions.*

le·giti·mize /lɪ'dʒɪtɪmaɪz/ **legitimizes, legitimiz-** ◆◇◇◇ **ing, legitimized;** also spelled legitimise in British VERB English. To legitimize something, especially some-V n thing bad, means to officially allow it, approve it, or FORMAL to make it seem acceptable. *They will accept no agreement that legitimizes the ethnic division of the country.*

leg·less /'legləs/. 1 A legless person or animal has ADJ: ADJ n no legs, for example as the result of an accident. ...*Douglas Bader, the legless wartime fighter pilot.* 2 If you say that someone is legless, you mean that ADJ-GRADED they are extremely drunk. *They found the locals get-* BRITISH, *ting legless on tequila.* INFORMAL

'**leg room.** Leg room is the amount of space, espe-N-UNCOUNT cially in a car or other vehicle, that is available in front of your legs.

leg·ume /'legjuːm/ **legumes.** Legumes are a group N-COUNT of plants, including clover, peas, and beans, whose TECHNICAL seeds grow in pods.

lei·sure /'leʒə, AM 'liːʒ-/. 1 Leisure is the time ◆◆◇◇ when you are not working and you can relax and do N-UNCOUNT things that you enjoy. ...*a relaxing way to fill my lei-sure time.* 2 If someone does something at leisure PHRASE or at their leisure, they enjoy themselves by doing it when they want to, without hurrying. *Stroll at lei-sure through the gardens.*

'**leisure centre, leisure centres.** A leisure cen-◆◇◇◇ tre is a large public building containing different fa-N-COUNT cilities for leisure activities, such as a sports hall, a BRITISH swimming pool, and rooms for meetings.

lei·sured /'leʒəd, AM 'liːʒ-/. 1 Leisured people are ADJ: ADJ n people who do not work, usually because they are rich. *The owner belonged to the leisured classes.* ADJ-GRADED 2 Leisured activities are done in a relaxed way or do not involve work. ...*this leisured life of reading and writing.*

lei·sure·ly /'leʒəli, AM 'liːʒ-/. 1 A leisurely action is ◆◇◇◇ done in a relaxed and unhurried way. *Tweed walked* ADJ-GRADED *at a leisurely pace.* ► Also an adverb. *We walked lei-* ADV-GRADED: *surely into the hotel.* ADV with v

lei·sure·wear /'leʒəweə, AM 'liːʒ-/. Leisurewear is N-UNCOUNT informal clothing which you wear when you are not FORMAL working.

leit·mo·tif /'laɪtməʊtiːf/ **leitmotifs;** also spelled N-COUNT leitmotiv. A leitmotif in something such as a book FORMAL or film or in a person's life is an idea or an object which occurs again and again. *The title of one of Dietrich's best-known songs could serve as the leit-motif for her life.*

lem·ming /'lemɪŋ/ **lemmings.** 1 A lemming is an N-COUNT animal that looks like a rat with thick fur. 2 If you N-COUNT say that a large group of people are acting like lem-[PRAGMATICS] mings, you are critical of them because they all fol-low each other into an action without thinking about it. *The French crowds pour like lemmings down the motorway to Paris.*

lem·on /'lemən/ **lemons.** 1 A lemon is a bright ◆◆◇◇ yellow fruit with very sour juice. See picture headed N-VAR fruit. ...*oranges, lemons and other citrus fruits.* 2 Lemon is a drink that tastes of lemons. 3 Lemon N-UNCOUNT is the same as lemon yellow. COLOUR

lem·on·ade /ˌlemə'neɪd/ **lemonades.** Lemonade ◆◇◇◇ is a colourless sweet fizzy drink. A drink that is N-UNCOUNT made from lemons, sugar, and water can also be re-ferred to as lemonade. ► A glass of lemonade can N-COUNT be referred to as a lemonade.

,**lemon 'curd.** Lemon curd is a sweet thick yellow N-UNCOUNT food made from lemons which you spread on bread BRITISH or put in tarts.

lem·on·grass /'leməngrɑːs, -græs/; also spelled N-UNCOUNT lemon grass. Lemongrass is a type of grass that grows in tropical countries. It is used as a flavouring in food.

lem·ony /'leməni/. Something that smells or tastes ADJ-GRADED of lemons can be described as lemony. *The salad dressing was too lemony.*

,**lemon 'yellow;** also spelled lemon-yellow. Lem-COLOUR on yellow or lemon is used to describe things that are pale yellow in colour.

le·mur /'liːmə/ **lemurs.** A lemur is an animal that N-COUNT looks like a small monkey and has a long tail and a face similar to that of a fox.

lend /lend/ **lends, lending, lent.** 1 When people ◆◆◇◇ or organizations such as banks lend you money, VERB they give it to you and you agree to pay it back at a V n future date, often with an extra amount as interest. V n n *The bank is reassessing its criteria for lending mon-* Also V *ey... I had to lend him ten pounds to take his chil-dren to the pictures.* ♦ lend·ing ...*a slump in bank* N-UNCOUNT *lending.* ♦ lend·er, lenders ...*the six leading* N-COUNT *mortgage lenders.* 2 If you lend something that you VERB own, you allow someone to have or to use it for a V n n period of time. *Will you lend me your jacket for a lit-* Also V n to n *tle while?*

3 If you lend your support to someone or something, VERB you help them with something they are doing or with V n to n a problem that they have. *He was approached by the* Also V n *organisers to lend support to a benefit concert.*

4 If something lends itself to a particular activity or VERB result, it is easy for it to be used for that activity or to V pron-refl to achieve that result. *The room lends itself well to sum-* n *mer eating with its light, airy atmosphere.* 5 If some-VERB thing lends a particular quality to something else, it V n to n adds that quality to it. *Enthusiastic applause lent a* Also V n n *sense of occasion to the proceedings.*

6 ● to lend your name to something: see name.

lend·er /'lendə/. See lend.

'**lending library, lending libraries.** A lending li-N-COUNT brary is a public library from which people are al-lowed to borrow books.

'lending rate, lending rates. The **lending rate** is the rate of interest that you have to pay when you are repaying a loan. ◆◇◇◇◇ N-COUNT

length /lɛŋθ/ **lengths. 1** The **length** of something is the amount that it measures from one end to the other along the longest side. *It is about a metre in length. ...the length of the fish. ...a length of 22ft.* **2** The **length** of something is its quality of being long. *I noticed, too, the length of her fingers.* **3** The **length** of something such as a piece of writing is the amount of writing that is contained in it. *...a book of at least 100 pages in length.* **4** The **length** of an event, activity, or situation is the period of time from beginning to end for which something lasts. *The exact length of each period may vary. ...his film, over two hours in length.* **5** A **length** of rope, cloth, wood, or other material is a piece of it that is intended to be used for a particular purpose. *Hang lengths of fabric behind the glass.* **6** If you swim a **length** in a swimming pool, you swim the distance between the ends that are furthest from each other. **7** In boat racing or horse racing, a **length** is the distance from the front to the back of the boat or horse and is used as a unit of measurement. *Harvard won by four lengths.* **8** If something happens or exists along the **length** of something, it happens or exists for the whole way along it. *I looked along the length of the building.* **9** See also **full-length**. **10** If someone does something **at length**, they do it after a long period of time. *At length my father went into the house.* **11** If someone does something **at length**, they do it for a long time or in great detail. *They spoke at length.* **12** If you say that someone **goes to great lengths** to achieve something, you mean that they try very hard and perhaps do extreme things in order to achieve it. *Greta Garbo went to great lengths to hide from reporters and photographers.* **13 •** at **arm's length**: see **arm. •** the **length and breadth of**: see **breadth**.
◆◆◇◇◇ N-VAR / N-UNCOUNT / N-VAR / N-VAR / N-COUNT with supp / N-COUNT / N-COUNT / N-SING theN of n / PHRASE LITERARY / PHRASE / PHRASE / PHRASE

-length /-lɛŋθ/. **-length** combines with nouns to form adjectives that describe something that is of a certain length, or long enough to reach the point indicated by the noun. *...shoulder-length hair. ...knee-length boots. •* See also **full-length**. COMB

length·en /ˈlɛŋθən/ **lengthens, lengthening, lengthened.** When something **lengthens** or when you **lengthen** it, it becomes longer. *Vacations have lengthened and the work week has shortened... She began to walk faster, but he lengthened his stride to keep up with her.* ◆◇◇◇◇ V-ERG V n

length·ways /ˈlɛŋweɪz/ or **lengthwise. Lengthways** or **lengthwise** means in a direction or position along the length of something. *Cut the aubergines in half lengthways.* ADV: ADV after v

length·wise /ˈlɛŋθwaɪz/. **Lengthwise** means the same as **lengthways**. ADV: ADV after v

lengthy /ˈlɛŋθi/ **lengthier, lengthiest. 1** You use **lengthy** to describe an event or process which lasts for a long time. *...the lengthy process of filling out passport application forms.* **2** A **lengthy** report, article, book, or document contains a lot of speech, writing, or other material. *...a lengthy report from the Council of Ministers.* ◆◆◇◇◇ ADJ-GRADED / ADJ-GRADED

le·ni·en·cy /ˈliːniənsi/. **Leniency** is a lenient attitude or lenient behaviour. *He said he would show no leniency towards those who stirred up trouble.* N-UNCOUNT

le·ni·ent /ˈliːniənt/. When someone in authority is **lenient**, they are not as strict or severe as expected. *The government already is lenient with drug traffickers.* **♦ le·ni·ent·ly** *He says that reckless drivers are treated too leniently.* ◆◇◇◇◇ ADJ-GRADED / ADV-GRADED: ADV after v

lens /lɛnz/ **lenses. 1** A **lens** is a thin curved piece of glass or plastic used in things such as cameras, telescopes, and pairs of glasses. You look through a lens in order to make things look larger, smaller, or clearer. *I packed your sunglasses with the green lenses.* **2** In your eye, the **lens** is the part behind the pupil that focuses light and helps you to see clearly. ◆◆◇◇ N-COUNT / N-COUNT

3 See also **contact lens, telephoto lens, wide-angle lens, zoom lens**.

lent /lɛnt/. **Lent** is the past tense and past participle of **lend**.

Lent. Lent is the period of forty days before Easter, during which some Christians give up something that they enjoy. N-UNCOUNT

len·til /ˈlɛntɪl/ **lentils. Lentils** are the seeds of a lentil plant. They can be dried and used to make soups and stews. ◆◇◇◇◇ N-COUNT

leo·nine /ˈliːənaɪn/. **Leonine** means like a lion, and is used especially to describe men with a lot of hair on their head, or with big beards. *...a tall leonine grey-haired man.* ADJ LITERARY

leop·ard /ˈlɛpəd/ **leopards.** A **leopard** is a type of large, wild cat. Leopards have yellow fur and black spots, and live in Africa and Asia. See picture headed **animals**. ◆◇◇◇◇ N-COUNT

leo·tard /ˈliːətɑːd/ **leotards.** A **leotard** is a tight-fitting piece of clothing, covering the body but not the legs, that some people wear when they practise dancing or do exercise. N-COUNT

lep·er /ˈlɛpə/ **lepers. 1** A **leper** is a person who has leprosy. **2** If you refer to someone as a **leper**, you mean that people in their community avoid them because they have done something that has shocked or offended people. *The newspaper article had branded her a social leper not fit to be seen in company.* N-COUNT / N-COUNT

lep·ro·sy /ˈlɛprəsi/. **Leprosy** is an infectious disease that damages people's flesh. N-UNCOUNT

les·bian /ˈlɛzbiən/ **lesbians.** A **lesbian** is a woman who is sexually attracted to women. *...a youth group for lesbians, gays and bisexuals. ▶* Also an adjective. *Many of her best friends were lesbian. ...a long-term lesbian relationship.* ◆◆◇◇◇ N-COUNT / ADJ

les·bi·an·ism /ˈlɛzbiənɪzəm/. **Lesbianism** refers to homosexual relationships between women or the preference that a woman shows for sexual relationships with women. *...today's increased public awareness of lesbianism.* N-UNCOUNT

le·sion /ˈliːʒən/ **lesions.** A **lesion** is an injury or wound to someone's body. *...skin lesions. ...a lesion of the spinal cord.* ◆◇◇◇◇ N-COUNT TECHNICAL

less /lɛs/. **Less** is often considered to be the comparative form of **little**. ◆◆◆◆◆

1 You use **less** to indicate that there is a smaller number of things or a smaller amount of something than before or than average, or than something else. You can use 'a little', 'a lot', 'a bit', 'far', and 'much' in front of **less**. *People should eat less fat. ...a dishwasher that uses less water and electricity. ▶* Also a pronoun. *...spending less and saving more. ▶* Also a quantifier. *Last year less of the money went into high-technology companies.* **2** You use **less than** before a number or amount to say that the actual number or amount is smaller than this. *Motorways actually cover less than 0.1 percent of the countryside.* **3** You use **less** to indicate that something or someone has a smaller amount of a quality than they used to or than is average or usual. *I often think about those less fortunate than me... Poverty is less of a problem now than it used to be.* **4** You use **less and less** to say that something is becoming smaller all the time in degree or amount. *The couple seem to spend less and less time together... She sounded less and less eager to return to Ireland.* **5** You use the expressions **still less, much less,** and **even less** after a negative statement in order to introduce and emphasize a further statement, and to make it negative too. *The boy didn't have a girlfriend, much less a wife.* **6** When you are referring to amounts, you use **less** in front of a number or quantity to indicate that it is to be subtracted from another number or quantity already mentioned. *...Fees: £750, less £400... Drivers will pay between ten and twenty five percent, less tax.* **7** You use **less than** to say that something does not have a particular quality. For example, if you describe something as **less than** perfect, you mean that it is not perfect at all. *Her greeting was less than enthusiastic.*
DET / PRON / QUANT / PHR-PREP / ADV-COMPAR / PHRASE / PHR-CONJ PRAGMATICS FORMAL / PREP / PHRASE PRAGMATICS

8 You can use **no less** as an emphatic way of expressing surprise or admiration at the importance of something or someone. *He had returned to England in an aircraft carrier no less.* **9** You use **no less than** before an amount to indicate that the amount is larger than you expected. *He is lined up for no less than four US television interviews.* PHRASE / PRAGMATICS / PHRASE

10 ● **couldn't care less**: see **care**. ● **more or less**: see **more**. ● **nothing less than**: see **nothing**.

-less /-ləs/. **-less** is added to nouns in order to form adjectives that indicate that someone or something does not have the thing that the noun refers to. *...drink and talk and meaningless laughter.* SUFFIX

les·see /ˌleˈsiː/. A **lessee** is a person who has taken out a lease on something such as a house or a piece of land. N-COUNT / LEGAL

less·en /ˈlesən/ **lessens, lessening, lessened.** If something **lessens** or you **lessen** it, it becomes smaller in size, amount, degree, or importance. *Make sure that your immunisations are up to date to lessen the risk of serious illness.* ♦ **less·en·ing** *...a lessening of tension on the border.* ◆◇◇◇◇ / V-ERG: V / V n / N-UNCOUNT

less·er /ˈlesə/. **1** You use **lesser** in order to indicate that something is smaller in extent, degree, or amount than another thing that has been mentioned. *Obvious potential allies are Ireland, Denmark and, to a lesser degree, the Netherlands.* ► Also an adverb. *...lesser known works by famous artists.* **2** You can use **lesser** to refer to something or someone that is less important than other things or people of the same type. *They pleaded guilty to lesser charges of criminal damage.* **3** ● **the lesser of two evils**: see **evil**. ◆◆◇◇◇ / ADJ-COMPAR: / ADJ n, / the ADJ of n / ADV-COMPAR / ADJ-COMPAR: / ADJ n, / the ADJ of n

les·son /ˈlesən/ **lessons. 1** A **lesson** is a fixed period of time when people are taught about a particular subject or taught how to do something. *Johanna took piano lessons.* **2** If something teaches you a **lesson**, it makes you realize the truth or realize what should be done. *There's still one lesson to be learned from the crisis.* ● If you say that you are going to **teach** someone a **lesson**, you mean that you are going to punish them for something that they have done so that they do not do it again. ◆◆◇◇◇ / N-COUNT / N-COUNT / PHRASE

lest /lest/. If you do something **lest** something unpleasant should happen, you do it to try to prevent the unpleasant thing from happening. *I was afraid to open the door lest he should follow me.* ◆◇◇◇◇ / CONJ / FORMAL

let /let/ **lets, letting;** the form **let** is used in the present tense and is the past tense and past participle. **1** If you **let** something happen, you allow it to happen without doing anything to stop or prevent it. *Thorne let him talk... She let the door slam... Let me say a few more words about economic affairs... I can't let myself be distracted.* **2** If you **let** someone do something, you give them your permission to do it. *I love sweets but Mum doesn't let me have them very often... They won't let you into the country.* **3** If you **let** someone into, out of, or through a place, you allow them to enter, leave, or go through it. *I let myself into the flat... I'd better go and let the dog out.* **4** You use **let me** when you are introducing something you want to say. *Let me tell you what I saw last night... Let me explain why.* **5** You say **let's** or, in more formal English, **let us**, to direct the attention of the people you are talking to towards the subject that you want to consider next. *Let's consider ways of making it easier.* **6** Someone in authority, such as a teacher, can use **let's** or, in more formal English, **let us**, in order to give a polite instruction to another person or group of people. *Let's have some hush, please.* **7** You use **let me** when you are offering politely to do something. *Let me get you something to drink... Please let me help in any way I can.* **8** You say **let's** or, in formal English, **let us** when you are making a suggestion that involves both you and the person you are talking to. *I'm bored. Let's go home.* **9** People often use **let** in expressions like **let me see** or **let me think** when they are hesitating or thinking of what to say next. *Now, let's see. Where did I leave my bag?* ◆◆◆◆◆ / VERB / V inf / V pron-refl inf / VERB / V n inf / V n prep/adv / VERB / V n prep/adv / VB: only imper / PRAGMATICS / V me inf / VB: only imper / PRAGMATICS / V us inf / VB: only imper / PRAGMATICS / V us inf / VB: only imper / PRAGMATICS / V me inf / VB: only imper / PRAGMATICS / V us inf / VERB / PRAGMATICS / V pron inf

10 You can use **let** when you are saying what you think someone should do, usually when they are behaving in a way that you think is unreasonable or wrong. *Let him get his own cup of tea.* VB: only imper / PRAGMATICS / V n inf

11 You can use **let** when you are praying for something to happen or when you want it very much to happen. You can use **let** in this way when you are talking to yourself. *Please God, let him telephone me.* VB: only imper / V n inf

12 If you **let** your house or land to someone, you allow them to use it in exchange for money that they pay you regularly. *The reasons for letting a house, or part of one, are varied.* ► **Let out** means the same as **let**. *I couldn't sell the London flat, so I let it out to pay the mortgage.* VERB: / V n to n / V n / PHRASAL VB / V n P / Also V P noun

13 In tennis or badminton, if you serve a **let**, the ball or shuttlecock touches the net but is in the correct part of the court. You then serve again. N-COUNT

14 Let alone is used after a statement, usually a negative one, to indicate that the statement is even more true of the person, thing, or situation that you are going to mention next. *It is incredible that the 12-year-old managed to even reach the pedals, let alone drive the car.* PHR-CONJ / PRAGMATICS

15 To **let** someone **be** means to leave them alone and not interfere in what they are doing. *If your child is really sick and needs sleep and quiet, let him be.* PHRASE

16 If you **let go** of someone or something, you stop holding them. *She let go of Mona's hand and took a sip of her drink.* **17** If you **let** someone **go**, you allow them to leave or to escape. *They held him for three hours and they let him go.* **18** When someone leaves a job, the employer sometimes says that they are **letting** that person **go**. *Peterson was let go after less than two years.* PHRASE / PHRASE / PHRASE

19 If someone says or does something that you think is annoying or stupid and you **let it go**, you do not react to it or say anything about it. *Let it go, he thought. He didn't feel like arguing.* **20** If you **let** yourself **go**, you relax, lose your inhibitions, and behave much more freely than usual. **21** If someone **lets** themselves **go**, they pay less attention to themselves or their appearance than they used to, so that they look untidy or unattractive. PHRASE / PHRASE / PHRASE

22 If you say that you did not know what you were **letting** yourself **in for** when you decided to do something, you mean you did not realize how difficult, unpleasant, or expensive it was going to be. *He got the impression that Miss Hawes had no idea of what she was letting herself in for.* PHRASE

23 If you **let** someone **know** something, you tell them about it or make sure that they know about it. *If you do want to go, please let me know.* **24** If you **let drop**, **let fall**, or **let slip** information, you reveal it casually or by accident, during a conversation about something else. *He might have let something slip in a moment of weakness.* PHRASE / PHRASE

25 If you say that someone has **been let loose** in a place or situation, you mean that they have been given complete freedom to do what they like in that place or situation. *She has all the glee of a little girl let loose in a sweetie shop.* **26** If someone **lets loose** a sound or remark, they make it, often suddenly. *He let loose a long, deep sigh.* PHRASE / PHRASE

27 ● to **let fly**: see **fly**. ● to **let** your **hair down**: see **hair**. ● to **let** someone **off the hook**: see **hook**. ● to **let it be known**: see **known**. ● to **live and let live**: see **live**. ● to **let the side down**: see **side**. ● to **let off steam**: see **steam**.

let down. 1 If you **let** someone **down** you disappoint them, by not doing something that you have said you will do or that they expected you to do. *Don't worry, Xiao, I won't let you down.* ♦ **let down** *...a large number of workers who feel badly let down.* **2** If something **lets** you **down**, it is the reason you are not as successful as you could have been. *Many believe it was his shyness and insecurity which let him down.* **3** If you **let down** something such as a tyre, hot-air balloon, or rubber dinghy, you allow air to escape from it. *I let the tyres down on his car.* PHRASAL VB / V n P / Also V P noun / ADJ-GRADED / V n P / Also V P noun / V n P / Also V P noun / BRITISH

let in. If an object **lets in** something such as air, light, PHRASAL VB

L

or water, it allows air, light, or water to get into it or pass through it. ...*balconies shaded with lattice-work which lets in air but not light.* V P noun Also V n P

let in on. If you **let** someone **in on** something that is a secret from most people, you allow them to know about it. *I'm going to let you in on a little secret.* PHRASAL VB V n P P n

let into. If you **let** someone **into** a secret, you allow them to know it. *I'll let you into a little showbiz secret.* PHRASAL VB V n P n

let off. 1 If someone in authority **lets** you **off** a task or duty, they give you permission not to do it. *Having a new baby lets you off going to boring dinner-parties.* **2** If you **let** someone **off**, you give them a lighter punishment than they expect or no punishment at all. *Because he was a Christian, the judge let him off.* **3** If you **let off** an explosive or a gun, you explode or fire it. *His neighbourhood had let off fireworks to celebrate the Revolution.* PHRASAL VB V n P n/-ing BRITISH V n P / V P noun Also V n P

let on. If you do not **let on** that something is true, you do not tell anyone that it is true. *She never let on that anything was wrong.* PHRASAL VB V P that/wh Also V P INFORMAL

let out. 1 If something or someone **lets** water, air, or breath **out**, they allow it to flow out or escape. *It lets sunlight in but doesn't let heat out.* **2** If you **let out** a particular sound, you make that sound. *When she saw him, she let out a cry of horror.* **3** See also **let** 12. PHRASAL VB V n P Also V P noun V P noun Also V n P WRITTEN

let up. If an unpleasant, continuous process **lets up**, it stops or its intensity is reduced. *The rain had let up.* ● See also **let-up.** PHRASAL VB V P

'**let-down, let-downs;** also spelled **letdown.** A **let-down** is a disappointment that you suffer, usually because something has not happened in the way in which you expected it to happen. *The flat was really very nice, but compared with what we'd been used to, it was a terrible let-down.* N-VAR

le·thal /'li:θəl/. **1** A substance that is **lethal** can kill people or animals. ...*a lethal dose of sleeping pills.* **2** If you describe something as **lethal**, you mean that it is capable of causing a lot of damage. *High-powered cars are lethal weapons in the hands of inexperienced drivers.* ◆◆◇◇◇ ADJ-GRADED / ADJ-GRADED

le·thar·gic /lɪ'θɑːdʒɪk/. If you are **lethargic**, you do not have much energy or enthusiasm. *He felt too miserable and lethargic to get dressed.* ◆◇◇◇◇ ADJ-GRADED

leth·ar·gy /'leθədʒi/. **Lethargy** is the condition or state of being lethargic. ...*tiredness, paleness, and lethargy.* ◆◇◇◇◇ N-UNCOUNT

let's /lets/. **Let us** is usually said or written as **let's.**

let·ter /'letə/ **letters. 1** If you write a **letter** to someone, you write a message on paper and send it to them, usually by post. *I had received a letter from a very close friend.* ...*a letter of resignation.* **2 Letters** are written symbols which represent one of the sounds in a language. ...*the letter E.* **3** If you say that someone carries out instructions **to the letter**, you mean that they do exactly what they are told to do, paying great attention to every detail. *She obeyed his instructions to the letter.* **4** See also **capital letter, covering letter, dead letter, love letter, newsletter, poison-pen letter.** ◆◆◆◆◇ N-COUNT: also by N / N-COUNT / PHRASE

'**letter bomb, letter bombs.** A **letter bomb** is a small bomb which is disguised as a letter or parcel and sent to someone through the post. N-COUNT

let·ter·box /'letəbɒks/ **letterboxes;** also spelled **letter box.** A **letterbox** is a rectangular hole in a door or a small box at the entrance to a building into which letters and small parcels are delivered. See picture headed **house and flat.** N-COUNT BRITISH

let·tered /'letəd/. Something that is **lettered** is covered or decorated with letters or words. ADJ

let·ter·head /'letəhed/ **letterheads.** A **letterhead** is the name and address of a person, company, or organization which is printed at the top of their writing paper. N-COUNT

let·ter·ing /'letərɪŋ/. **Lettering** is writing, especially when you are describing the type of letters used. ...*a small blue sign with white lettering.* N-UNCOUNT

'**letter opener, letter openers.** A **letter opener** is a tool shaped like a blunt knife, which is used for opening envelopes. N-COUNT

let·tuce /'letɪs/ **lettuces.** A **lettuce** is a plant with large green leaves that you eat in salads. See picture headed **vegetables.** ◆◇◇◇◇ N-VAR

'**let-up.** If there is no **let-up** in something, usually something unpleasant, there is no reduction in the intensity of it. *There was no let-up in the battle on the money markets yesterday.* N-UNCOUNT: also a N

leu·kae·mia /luˈkiːmiə/; spelled **leukemia** in American English. **Leukaemia** is a disease of the blood in which the body produces too many white blood cells. ◆◇◇◇◇ N-UNCOUNT

lev·el /'levəl/ **levels, levelling, levelled;** spelled **leveling, leveled** in American English. **1** A **level** is a point on a scale, for example a scale of amount, quality, or difficulty. ...*the lowest level of inflation for some years... Michael's roommate had been pleasant on a superficial level... The exercises are marked according to their level of difficulty.* ● See also **A level, O level.** **2** The **level** of a river, lake, or ocean or the **level** of liquid in a container is the height of its surface. *The water level of the Mississippi River is already 6.5 feet below normal.* ● See also **sea level.** **3** If something is at a particular **level**, it is at that height. *The water came up to her chin and the bubbles were at eye level.* **4** If one thing is **level** with another thing, it is at the same height. *Amy knelt down so that their eyes were level.* **5** When something is **level**, it is completely flat with no part higher than any other. ...*a plateau of fairly level ground.* **6** If someone or something such as a violent storm **levels** a building or area of land, they flatten or demolish it completely. *Further tremors could level more buildings.* **7** If you draw **level** with someone or something, you get closer to them until you are by their side. *Just before we drew level with the gates, he slipped out of the jeep.* ► Also an adjective. *He waited until they were level with the door.* **8** If you keep your voice **level**, you speak in a deliberately calm and unemotional way. *He forced his voice to remain level.* **9** If an accusation or criticism is **levelled** at someone, they are criticized for something they have done or are accused of doing something wrong. *Allegations of corruption were levelled at him and his family... He levelled bitter criticism against the US.* **10** If you **level** an object at someone or something, you lift it and point it in their direction. *The man wheeled around and levelled his gun at Joe.* **11** If you **level** with someone, you tell them the truth and do not keep anything secret. *I'll level with you. I'm no great detective.* **12** If you say that you will do your **level best** to do something, you are emphasizing that you will try as hard as you can to do it, often when the situation makes it very difficult. *We're going to do our level best to help people.* **13** ● a **level playing field:** see **playing field.** ◆◆◆◆◆ N-COUNT: with supp / ● See also / the N / N-SING / N-SING / ADJ: v-link ADJ / ADJ: v-link ADJ / ADV: ADV after v BRITISH / ADJ: v-link ADJ / ADJ-GRADED / ADJ-GRADED WRITTEN / VERB V n / VERB be V-ed at/ against V n at/against n / VERB V n at n Also V n / VERB V with n INFORMAL / PHRASE PRAGMATICS

level off or **level out. 1** If something that is progressing or developing **levels off** or **levels out**, it stops growing or diminishing at such a fast speed. *Inflation is finally levelling out at around 11% a month.* **2** If an aircraft **levels off** or **levels out**, it travels horizontally after having been travelling in an upwards or downwards direction. PHRASAL VB V P V P prep / V P

level out. See **level off.** PHRASAL VB

'**level 'crossing, level crossings.** A **level crossing** is a place where a railway line crosses a road. The usual American term is **grade crossing** or **railroad crossing.** N-COUNT BRITISH

'**level-'headed.** If you describe a person as **level-headed**, you mean that they are calm and sensible even in difficult situations. *His level-headed approach suggests he will do what is necessary.* ADJ-GRADED

lev·el·ler /'levələ/ **levellers;** spelled **leveler** in American English. If you describe something as a **leveller**, you mean that it makes all people seem the same, regardless of factors such as age, race, and social status. *The computer is a leveller, making information available to everyone.* N-COUNT

level 'pegging; also spelled **level-pegging**. If two ADJ: opponents in a competition or contest are **level** v-link ADJ **pegging**, they are equal with each other. BRITISH

lev·er /'liːvə, AM 'lev-/ **levers, levering, lev-** ◆◇◇◇◇ **ered. 1** A **lever** is a handle or bar that is attached N-COUNT to a piece of machinery which you push or pull in order to operate the machinery. *The taps have a lever to control the mix of hot and cold water.* • See also **gear lever. 2** A **lever** is a long bar, one end of N-COUNT which is placed under a heavy object so that when you press down on the other end you can move the object. **3** If you **lever** something in a particular di- VERB rection, you move it there, especially by using a lot V n with adj of effort. *Neighbours eventually levered open the* V n adv/prep *door with a crowbar... Insert the fork about 6in. from the root and simultaneously lever it backwards.* **4** A N-COUNT **lever** is an idea or action that you can use to make people do what you want them to do. *...using the hostages as a lever to gain concessions from the west.*

lev·er·age /'liːvərɪdʒ, AM 'lev-/ **leverages,** ◆◇◇◇ **leveraging, leveraged. 1 Leverage** is the ability N-UNCOUNT to influence situations or people so that you can control what happens to them. *His function as a Mayor affords him the leverage to get things done.* **2 Leverage** is the force that is applied to an object N-COUNT when something such as a lever is used. *...longer shafts, providing better leverage.* **3** In business, to VERB: V n **leverage** a company or investment means to use borrowed money in order to buy it or pay for it. ✦ **lev·er·aged** *...leveraged buyouts.* ADJ-GRADED

le·via·than /lɪ'vaɪəθən/ **leviathans.** A **leviathan** is N-COUNT something which is extremely large and difficult to LITERARY control, and which you find rather frightening.

Levi's /'liːvaɪz; also spelled **Levis**. **Levi's** are jeans. N-PLURAL **Levi's** is a trademark.

levi·tate /'levɪteɪt/ **levitates, levitating, levi-** ◆◇◇◇◇ **tated.** To **levitate** means to rise and float in the air V without any support from other people or objects. Also V n Some people claim to be able to do this through meditation. *The film shows the shaman levitating into the air and then floating across the room.* ✦ **levi·ta·tion** /ˌlevɪ'teɪʃən/ *...levitation, prophecy,* N-UNCOUNT *and healing.*

lev·ity /'levɪti/. **Levity** is behaviour that shows a N-UNCOUNT tendency to treat serious matters in a way that is LITERARY not serious. *At the time, Arnold had disapproved of such levity.*

levy /'levi/ **levies, levying, levied. 1** A **levy** is a ◆◆◇◇ sum of money that you have to pay, for example as N-COUNT a tax to the government. *...an annual motorway levy on all drivers.* **2** If a government or organization VERB: **levies** a tax or other sum of money, it demands it V n on n from people or organizations. *Taxes should not be* V n *levied without the authority of Parliament.*

lewd /ljuːd, AM luːd/. If you describe someone's be- ADJ-GRADED haviour as **lewd**, you are critical of them because PRAGMATICS you think they are interested in sex in a crude and unpleasant way. *...eyeing up the women and making lewd comments.*

lexi·cal /'leksɪkəl/. **Lexical** means relating to the ADJ words of a language. *...the commonest lexical items in the languages.*

lexi·cog·ra·phy /ˌleksɪ'kɒgrəfi/. **Lexicography** is N-UNCOUNT the activity or profession of writing and editing dictionaries. ✦ **lexi·cog·ra·pher, lexicographers.** N-COUNT

lexi·con /'leksɪkən/ **lexicons. 1** The **lexicon** of a N-SING: particular subject is all the terms associated with it. with supp The **lexicon** of a person or group is all the words they commonly use. *...the lexicon of management.* **2** A **lexicon** is an alphabetical list of words of a lan- N-COUNT guage or of a particular subject. **3** A **lexicon** is a dic- N-COUNT tionary, especially of a very old language such as DATED Greek or Hebrew.

lia·bil·ity /ˌlaɪə'bɪlɪti/ **liabilities. 1** If you say that ◆◆◇◇ someone or something is a **liability**, you mean that N-COUNT they cause a lot of problems or embarrassment. *As the president's prestige continues to fall, they're clearly beginning to consider him a liability.* **2** A N-COUNT company or organization's **liabilities** are the sums TECHNICAL of money which it owes. **3** See also **liable**.

lia·ble /'laɪəbəl/. **1** When something **is liable to** ◆◆◇◇◇ happen, it is very likely to happen. *A small minority* PHR-MODAL *of the mentally ill are liable to harm themselves.* **2** If ADJ-GRADED: people or things are **liable to** something unpleas- v-link ADJ to n ant, they are likely to experience it or do it. *...a woman particularly liable to depression.* **3** If you ADJ: are **liable** for something such as a debt, you are le- v-link ADJ gally responsible for it. *The airline's insurer is liable for damages to the victims' families.* ✦ **lia·bil·ity** N-UNCOUNT /ˌlaɪə'bɪlɪti/ *He is claiming damages from London Underground, which has admitted liability.*

li·aise /li'eɪz/ **liaises, liaising, liaised.** When or- ◆◇◇◇◇ ganizations or people **liaise**, or when one organiza- V-RECIP tion **liaises** with another, they work together and V with n keep each other fully informed about what is hap- pl-n V with pening. *Detectives are liaising with Derbyshire po-* pron-recip *lice... The three groups will all liaise with each other.* BRITISH

liai·son /li'eɪzɒn, AM 'liːeɪz-/ **liaisons. 1 Liaison** is ◆◇◇◇◇ co-operation and the exchange of information be- N-UNCOUNT tween different organizations or between different sections of an organization. *Liaison between police forces and the art world is vital to combat art crime.* **2** If someone acts as **liaison** between two or more N-UNCOUNT: groups, their job is to encourage co-operation and also a N the exchange of information between those groups. *She acts as a liaison between patients and staff.* **3** You can refer to a sexual or romantic relationship N-COUNT between two people as a **liaison**.

liar /'laɪə/ **liars.** If you say that someone is a **liar**, ◆◇◇◇◇ you mean that they tell lies. *He was a liar and a* N-COUNT *cheat.*

lib /lɪb/. **Lib** is an abbreviation for 'liberation'. It is ◆◇◇◇◇ used in the names of some political movements N-UNCOUNT that are concerned with freeing people from gov- ernments or traditional ideas which the members believe to be oppressive. *...Women's Lib.* • See also **ad-lib.**

li·ba·tion /laɪ'beɪʃən/ **libations.** In ancient Greece N-COUNT and Rome, a **libation** was an alcoholic drink that LITERARY was offered to the gods.

Lib Dem /ˌlɪb 'dem/ **Lib Dems.** In Britain, you can ◆◇◇◇◇ refer to the Liberal Democrat Party or its members N-PROPER: as the **Lib Dems**. *...Lib-Dem councillors.* the N, N n

li·bel /'laɪbəl/ **libels, libelling, libelled;** spelled ◆◆◇◇◇ **libeling, libeled** in American English. **1 Libel** is N-VAR something in writing which wrongly accuses some- LEGAL one of something, and which is therefore against the law. Compare **slander**. *Warren sued him for li- bel over the remarks.* **2** To **libel** someone means to VERB: V n write or print something in a book or a newspaper LEGAL which wrongly damages that person's reputation and is therefore against the law.

li·bel·lous /'laɪbələs/; spelled **libelous** in American ADJ-GRADED English. If something in a book, newspaper, or magazine is **libellous**, it wrongly accuses someone of something, and is therefore against the law. *The articles were libellous and damaging to the interests of the team.*

lib·er·al /'lɪbərəl/ **liberals. 1** Someone who has ◆◆◆◇ **liberal** views is tolerant of different behaviour or ADJ-GRADED opinions, and believes people should be free to do or think as they like. *She is known to have liberal views on divorce.* ▶ Also a noun. *...free-thinking lib-* N-COUNT *erals.* **2** A **Liberal** politician or voter is a member of ADJ: ADJ n a Liberal Party or votes for a Liberal Party. ▶ Also a N-COUNT noun. *The Liberals hold twenty-three seats.* **3 Liberal** ADJ-GRADED means giving, using, or taking a lot of something, or existing in large quantities. *As always he is liberal with his jokes.* ✦ **lib·er·al·ly** *Chemical products* ADV-GRADED: *were used liberally.* ADV with v

Liberal 'Democrat, Liberal Democrats. In ◆◆◇◇◇ Britain, a **Liberal Democrat** is a member of the Lib- N-PROPER eral Democrat Party.

Liberal 'Democrat Party. The Liberal Demo- N-PROPER: crat Party is the third largest political party in Brit- the N, ain and the main centre party. N n

lib·er·al·ism /'lɪbərəlɪzəm/. **1 Liberalism** is a belief ◆◇◇◇◇ in gradual social progress by reform and by chang- N-UNCOUNT ing laws, rather than by revolution. **2 Liberalism** is N-UNCOUNT the belief that people should have a lot of political

and individual freedom. ...*growing liberalism in the Church.*

lib·er·al·ize /ˈlɪbrəlaɪz/ **liberalizes, liberalizing, liberalized;** also spelled **liberalise** in British English. When a country or government **liberalizes**, or **liberalizes** its laws or its attitudes, it becomes less strict and allows people more freedom in their actions. ...*the decision to liberalize travel restrictions.* ◆ **lib·er·ali·za·tion** /ˌlɪbrəlaɪˈzeɪʃən/ ...*the liberalization of divorce laws.* VERB: V / Vn N-UNCOUNT

'Liberal Party. In Britain, **the Liberal Party** was the main political party of the centre. **Liberal Party** is also used to refer to similar parties in some other countries. N-PROPER: the N, N n

lib·er·ate /ˈlɪbəreɪt/ **liberates, liberating, liberated. 1** To **liberate** a place or the people in it means to free them from the political or military control of another country, area, or group of people. *They planned to march on and liberate the city.* ◆ **lib·era·tion** /ˌlɪbəˈreɪʃən/ ...*a mass liberation movement.* **2** To **liberate** someone from something means to help them escape from it or overcome it, and lead a better way of life. *He asked how committed the leadership was to liberating its people from poverty.* ◆ **lib·er·at·ing** *It can be a very liberating experience.* ◆ **lib·era·tion** ...*the women's liberation movement.* **3** To **liberate** a prisoner or hostage means to set them free. *The government is devising a plan to liberate prisoners held in detention camps.* VERB Vn / N-UNCOUNT / VERB Vn from n Also Vn / ADJ-GRADED / N-UNCOUNT / VERB Vn

lib·er·at·ed /ˈlɪbəreɪtɪd/. If you describe someone as **liberated**, you mean that they do not accept their society's traditional values or restrictive way of behaving. ...*a liberated businesswoman.* ADJ-GRADED

lib·era·tor /ˈlɪbəreɪtə/ **liberators.** A **liberator** is someone who sets people free from a system, situation, or set of ideas that restricts them in some way. *We were the people's liberators from the Bolsheviks.* N-COUNT FORMAL

lib·er·tar·ian /ˌlɪbəˈteəriən/ **libertarians.** If someone is **libertarian** or has **libertarian** attitudes, they believe in or support the idea that people should be free to think and behave in the way that they want. *The town's political climate was libertarian.* ▶ A **libertarian** is someone with libertarian views. ADJ FORMAL / N-COUNT

lib·er·tine /ˈlɪbətiːn/ **libertines.** If you refer to someone as a **libertine**, you think they are immoral and unscrupulous in their sexual activities and do not care about the effect their behaviour has on other people. N-COUNT LITERARY

lib·er·ty /ˈlɪbəti/ **liberties. 1** Liberty is the freedom to live your life in the way that you want, without interference from other people or the authorities. ...*the rights and liberties of the English people.* ● See also **civil liberties. 2** Liberty is the freedom to go wherever you want, which you lose when you are a prisoner. *There is no formal confirmation so far that he is at liberty.* **3** If someone is **at liberty** to do something, they have been given permission to do it. *You're quite at liberty to dismiss me now as your business manager.* **4** If you say that you have **taken the liberty of** doing something, you are saying that you have done it without asking permission because you do not think that anyone will mind. *I took the liberty of going into Assunta's wardrobe, as it was open.* **5** If you **take liberties** or **take a liberty** with someone or something, you act without caution or without concern for that thing or person. *She knew she was taking a big liberty in developing Mick's photos without his knowledge.* N-VAR / N-UNCOUNT / PHRASE / PHRASE PRAGMATICS / PHRASE

li·bidi·nous /lɪˈbɪdɪnəs/. People who are **libidinous** have strong sexual feelings and express them in their behaviour. ADJ-GRADED LITERARY

li·bi·do /lɪˈbiːdəʊ/ **libidos.** A person's **libido** is all their natural instincts and urges, especially their sexual urges. *Lack of sleep is a major factor in loss of libido.* N-VAR

li·brar·ian /laɪˈbreəriən/ **librarians.** A **librarian** is a person who is in charge of a library or who has been specially trained to work in a library. N-COUNT

li·brary /ˈlaɪbrəri, AM -breri/ **libraries. 1** A public **library** is a building where things such as books, newspapers, videos, and music are kept for people to read, use, or borrow. **2** A private **library** is a collection of things such as books or music, that is normally only used with the permission of the owner. *My thanks go to the British School of Osteopathy, for the use of their library.* **3** In some large houses the **library** is the room where most of the books are kept. N-COUNT / N-COUNT / N-COUNT

li·bret·tist /lɪˈbretɪst/ **librettists.** A **librettist** is a person who writes the words that are used in an opera or musical play. N-COUNT

li·bret·to /lɪˈbretəʊ/ **librettos** or **libretti.** The **libretto** of an opera is the words that are sung in it. ...*the author of one or two opera librettos.* N-COUNT

lice /laɪs/. **Lice** is the plural of **louse.**

li·cence /ˈlaɪsəns/ **licences;** spelled **license** in American English. **1** A **licence** is an official document which gives you permission to do, use, or own something. *Smith, who did not have a licence, admitted driving without due care and attention.* ...*a temporary import licence.* **2** If someone does something **under licence**, they do it by special permission from a government or other authority. **3** If you say that something gives someone **licence** or a **licence** to act in a particular way, you disapprove of the fact that it gives them an excuse to behave in an irresponsible or excessive way. *'Dropping the charges has given racists a licence to kill,' said Jim's aunt.* **4** If you describe a commercial activity as a **licence to print money**, you disapprove of the fact that it allows people to gain a lot of money with little effort or responsibility. *Running a television company may no longer be a licence to print money.* N-COUNT / PHRASE / N-UNCOUNT: also a N, N to-inf PRAGMATICS / PHRASE PRAGMATICS

li·cense /ˈlaɪsəns/ **licenses, licensing, licensed.** If a government or other authority **licenses** a person, organization, or activity, they officially give permission for the person or organization to do something, or for the activity to take place. *Under the agreement, the council can license a U.S. company to produce the drug.* VERB: Vn / Vn to-inf Also Vn to n

li·censed /ˈlaɪsənst/. **1** If you are **licensed** to do something, you have official permission from the government or from the authorities to do it. *There were about 250 people on board, about 100 more than the ferry was licensed to carry.* **2** If something that you own or use is **licensed**, you have official permission to own it or use it. ...*a licensed rifle.* **3** If a place such as a restaurant, hotel, or casino is **licensed**, it has been given a licence to sell alcoholic drinks. ADJ / ADJ / ADJ BRITISH

li·cen·see /ˌlaɪsənˈsiː/ **licensees. 1** A **licensee** is a person or organization that has been given a licence. **2** A **licensee** is someone who has been given a licence to sell alcoholic drinks, for example in a pub. N-COUNT FORMAL / N-COUNT BRITISH

'license number, license numbers. The **license number** of a car or other road vehicle is the series of letters and numbers that are shown at the front and back of it. The British term is **registration number.** N-COUNT AMERICAN

'license plate, license plates. A **license plate** is a sign on the front and back of a vehicle that shows its registration number. The British expression is **number plate.** See picture headed **car and bicycle.** N-COUNT AMERICAN

'licensing laws. In Britain, **licensing laws** are the laws which control the selling of alcoholic drinks. N-PLURAL

li·cen·tious /laɪˈsentʃəs/. If you describe a person as **licentious**, you disapprove of them because you think they are very immoral, especially in their sexual behaviour. *There were alarming stories of licentious behaviour.* ◆ **li·cen·tious·ness** ...*moral licentiousness.* ADJ-GRADED PRAGMATICS FORMAL / N-UNCOUNT

li·chen /ˈlaɪkən/ **lichens.** **Lichen** is a cluster of tiny plants that looks like grey or yellow moss and grows on rocks, trees, and walls. N-VAR

lick /lɪk/ **licks, licking, licked. 1** When people or animals **lick** something, they move their tongue across its surface. *She folded up her letter, licking the envelope flap.* ▶ Also a noun. ...*taking tiny licks at a pistachio ice-cream.* VERB Vn / N-COUNT

2 If you **lick** someone or something, you easily defeat them in a fight or competition. *He might be able to lick us all in a fair fight.* VERB V n INFORMAL

3 When flames **lick** something, they touch it lightly and briefly. *The apex of the flames licked the crimson sky.* VERB V n LITERARY

4 A **lick** of something is a small amount of it. *It could do with a lick of paint to brighten up its premises.* N-COUNT INFORMAL

5 A **lick** is a short piece of music which is part of a song and played on a guitar. *...the screeching licks of heavy metal guitar.* N-COUNT INFORMAL

6 • to **lick** your **lips**: see **lip**. **•** to **lick into shape**: see **shape**.

lick·ing /ˈlɪkɪŋ/ **lickings.** A **licking** is a severe defeat by someone in a fight, battle, or competition. *They gave us a hell of a licking.* N-COUNT

lico·rice /ˈlɪkərɪʃ, -ɪs/. See **liquorice**.

lid /lɪd/ **lids. 1** A **lid** of a container is the top which you open to reach inside. **2** Your **lids** are the pieces of skin which cover your eyes when you close them. ◆◆◇◇◇ N-COUNT N-COUNT

lid·ded /ˈlɪdɪd/. **1 Lidded** is used to describe a container that has a lid. *Place the mussels in a lidded pan and place over a high heat for 4 minutes.* ADJ: ADJ n **2** When someone has **lidded** eyes, their eyelids are partly or fully closed. ADJ LITERARY

lido /ˈliːdəʊ/ **lidos.** A **lido** is an open-air swimming pool, or a part of a beach, which is used by the public for swimming or water sports. N-COUNT BRITISH

lie 1 position or situation

lie /laɪ/ **lies, lying, lay, lain. 1** If you **are lying** somewhere, you are in a horizontal position and are not standing or sitting. *There was a child lying on the ground... He lay awake watching her for a long time.* ◆◆◆◆◇ VERB V prep/adv V adj **2** If an object **lies** in a particular place, it is in a flat position in that place. *...a newspaper lying on a nearby couch... Broken glass lay scattered on the carpet.* VERB V prep/adv V adj **3** If you say that a place **lies** in a particular position or direction, you mean that it is situated there. *The islands lie at the southern end of the Kurile chain.* VERB V prep/adv **4** The **lie** of an object or area is its position or the way that it is arranged. *The actual site of a city is determined by the natural lie of the land.* N-SING: with supp **5 Lie** is used, especially on gravestones and memorials, to say that a dead person is buried in a particular place. *The inscription reads: Here lies Catin, the son of Magarus... My father lies in the small cemetery a few miles up this road.* VERB V prep/adv FORMAL **6** You can use **lie** to say that something is or remains in a particular state or condition. For example, if something **lies forgotten**, it has been and remains forgotten. *His country's economy lies in ruins.* V-LINK: V adj V prep **7** You can use **lie** to say what position a competitor or team is in during a competition. *I was going well and was lying fourth... Blyth Tait is lying in second place.* VERB V ordinal V in n BRITISH **8** You can talk about where something such as a problem, solution, or fault **lies** to say what you think it involves or is caused by. *The problem lay in the large amounts spent on defence... He realised his future lay elsewhere.* VERB V prep/adv **9** You use **lie** in expressions such as **lie ahead**, **lie in store**, and **lie in wait** when you are talking about what someone is going to experience in the future, especially when it is something unpleasant or difficult. *The President's most serious challenges lie ahead.* VERB V prep/adv **10 •** to **lie in state**: see **state**. **•** to **take** something **lying down**: see **take**.

lie around; the form **lie about** is also used in British English. **1** If things are left **lying around** or **lying about**, they are not tidied away but left casually somewhere where they can be seen. *My dad had a couple of Bob Dylan and Beatles song-books lying around the house.* **2** If you **lie around** or **lie about**, you spend your time relaxing and being lazy. *On Sunday Cohen lay around the house all day.* PHRASAL VB V P V P n V P n INFORMAL

lie back. If you **lie back**, you relax and lower yourself from a sitting position so that you are resting on your back. PHRASAL VB V P

lie behind. If you refer to what **lies behind** a situation or event, you are referring to the reason the situa- PHRASAL VB V P n

tion exists or the event happened. *It seems that what lay behind the clashes was disagreement over the list of candidates.*

lie down. When you **lie down**, you move into a horizontal position, usually in order to rest or sleep. PHRASAL VB V P

lie 2 things that are not true

lie /laɪ/ **lies, lying, lied. 1** A **lie** is something that someone says or writes which they know is untrue. *'Who else do you work for?'—'No one.'—'That's a lie.'... All the boys told lies about their adventures.* ◆◆◆◇◇ N-COUNT **•** See also **white lie**. **2** If someone **is lying**, they are saying something which they know is not true. *If asked, he lies about his age... She lied to her husband so she could meet her lover... He reportedly called her 'a lying little twit'.* VERB: V V about n V to n V-ing **♦ ly·ing** Lying is something that I will not tolerate. N-UNCOUNT **3** See also **lying**. **4** If something **gives the lie to** a statement, claim, or theory, it suggests or proves that it is not true. *This survey gives the lie to the idea that Britain is moving towards economic recovery.* PHRASE **5** If you say that someone **is living a lie**, you mean that in every part of their life they are hiding the truth about themselves from other people. PHRASE

'lie detector, lie detectors. A **lie detector** is an electronic machine used mainly by the police to find out whether a suspect is telling the truth. *...a lie detector test.* N-COUNT

'lie-down. If you have a **lie-down**, you have a short rest, usually in bed. ◆◇◇◇◇ N-SING BRITISH

'lie-in, lie-ins. If you have a **lie-in**, you rest by staying in bed later than usual in the morning. *I have a lie-in on Sundays.* ◆◇◇◇◇ N-COUNT INFORMAL, BRITISH

lieu /ljuː, AM luː/. If you do, get, or give one thing **in lieu** of another, you do, get, or give it instead of the other thing, because the two things are considered to be of the same value or importance. *He left what little furniture he owned to his landlord in lieu of rent.* ◆◇◇◇◇ PHR-PREP FORMAL

Lieut. Lieut. is a written abbreviation for **lieutenant** when 'lieutenant' is a person's title.

lieu·ten·ant /lefˈtenənt, AM luː-/ **lieutenants. 1** A **lieutenant** is a junior officer in the army, navy, or air force, or in the American police force. ► Also a combining form. *...Lieutenant Colonel Gale Carter.* ◆◆◇◇◇ COMB **2** If you refer to someone as a person's **lieutenant**, you mean they are that person's main assistant in an organization or activity. N-COUNT

life /laɪf/ **lives** /laɪvz/. **1** Life is the quality which people, animals, and plants have when they are not dead, and which objects and substances do not have. *...a baby's first minutes of life. ...the earth's supply of life-giving oxygen.* ◆◆◆◆◆ N-UNCOUNT **2** You can use **life** to refer to things or groups of things which are alive. *Is there life on Mars?... The book includes some useful facts about animal and plant life.* N-UNCOUNT: with supp **3** If you refer to someone's **life**, you mean their state of being alive, especially when there is a risk or danger of them dying. *Your life is in danger... The intense fighting is reported to have claimed many lives.* N-COUNT **4** Someone's **life** is the period of time during which they are alive. *He spent the last fourteen years of his life in retirement.* N-COUNT: poss N **5** You can use **life** to refer to a period of someone's life when they are in a particular situation or job. *That was the beginning of my life in the television business.* N-COUNT: with supp **6** You can use **life** to refer to particular activities which people regularly do during their lives. *My personal life has had to take second place to my career... Most diabetics have a normal sex life.* N-COUNT: supp N **7** You can use **life** to refer to the events and experiences that happen to people while they are alive. *It's the people with insecurities who make life difficult. ...the sort of life we can only fantasise about living.* N-UNCOUNT **8** If you know a lot about **life**, you have gained many varied experiences, for example by travelling a lot and meeting different kinds of people. *I was 19 and too young to know much about life.* N-UNCOUNT **9** You can use **life** to refer to the things that people do and experience that are characteristic of a particular place, group, or activity. *How did you adjust to college life?... Margaret Thatcher had dominated political life* N-UNCOUNT

L

in Britain for over a decade. **10** A person, place, or something such as a film that is full of **life** gives an impression of excitement, energy, or cheerfulness. *The town itself was full of life and character.* **11** If you refer to someone as **the life and soul of the party**, you mean that they are lively and entertaining on social occasions, and are good at mixing with people. — N-UNCOUNT / PHRASE BRITISH

12 If someone is sentenced to **life**, they are sentenced to stay in prison for the rest of their life or for a very long period of time. *He could get life in prison, if convicted.* **13 For life** means for the rest of a person's life. *He was jailed for life... There can be no jobs for life.* — N-UNCOUNT INFORMAL / PHRASE

14 The **life** of something such as a machine or organization is the period of time that it lasts for. *The repairs did not increase the value or the life of the equipment.* — N-COUNT: with poss

15 If you talk about **life after death**, you are discussing the possibility that people may continue to exist in some form after they die. **16** If you say that someone **is fighting for** their **life**, you mean they are in a very serious condition and may die as a result of an accident or illness. **17** If you say that someone does something **for dear life** or **for** their **life**, you mean that they do it using all their effort because they are in a dangerous or urgent situation. *I made for the life raft and hung on for dear life.* — PHRASE / PHRASE JOURNALISM / PHRASE INFORMAL

18 If someone **lays down** their **life** for another person, they die so that the other person can live. **19** If someone **takes** another person's **life**, they kill them. If someone **takes** their own **life**, they kill themselves. — PHRASE LITERARY / PHRASE FORMAL

20 If you say that someone **lives life to the full**, you mean that they make a deliberate effort to gain a lot from life by being always busy and trying new activities. **21** If you tell someone to **get a life**, you are expressing frustration with them because they do not have any interests or activities which you think would make their life interesting or worthwhile. **22** If you say that you **have a life**, you mean that you have interests and activities, particularly outside your work, which make your life enjoyable and worthwhile. — PHRASE / PHRASE PRAGMATICS / PHRASE

23 If you start **a new life**, you move to another place, or change your career, usually to try and recover from an unpleasant experience. **24** If you **live** your **own life**, you live in the way that you want to and accept responsibility for your actions and decisions, without other people's advice or interference. **25** If you say that **life isn't worth living** without someone or something, or that someone or something **makes life worth living**, you mean that you cannot enjoy life without them. — PHRASE / PHRASE / PHRASE

26 If you **bring** something **to life** or if it **comes to life**, it becomes interesting or exciting. *The cold, hard cruelty of two young men is vividly brought to life in this true story... Poems which had seemed dull and boring suddenly came to life.* **27** If something or someone **comes to life**, they become active. *The volcano came to life a week ago.* **28** You can use expressions such as **to come to life**, **to spring to life**, and **to roar into life** to indicate that a machine or vehicle suddenly starts working or moving. *To his great relief the engine came to life.* — PHRASE / PHRASE / PHRASE LITERARY

29 If you say that you cannot remember something **for the life of** you, you are emphasizing that you cannot remember it, however hard you try. *I can't for the life of me understand why ¸ou didn't think of it.* **30** You can say **'Life goes on'** after mentioning something very sad to indicate that although people are very upset or affected by it, they have to carry on living normally. *I can't spend the rest of my life wishing it hadn't happened. Life goes on.* **31** You can use **in all my life** or **in my life** to emphasize that you have never previously experienced something to such a degree. *I have never been so scared in all my life.* **32** You can use expressions such as **the fright** of your **life** or **the race of** your **life** to emphasize, for example, that something has made you more frightened than you have ever been before or that you have run faster than you have ever run before. **33** People say **'That's life'** after an unlucky, unpleasant, or surprising event to show that they realize such events happen occasionally and must be accepted. — PHRASE PRAGMATICS INFORMAL / CONVENTION PRAGMATICS / PHRASE PRAGMATICS / PHRASE PRAGMATICS / CONVENTION PRAGMATICS

34 If you talk about the man or woman in someone's **life**, you mean the person they are having a relationship with, especially a sexual relationship. *There is a new man in her life.* **35** If you say that someone or something is **larger than life**, you mean that they appear or behave in a way that seems more exaggerated or important than usual. *Nobody takes seriously the improbable storylines and larger than life characters.* **36** If something **starts life** or **begins life** as a particular thing, it is that thing when it first starts to exist. *Herr's book started life as a dramatic screenplay.* **37** In art, **life** refers to the producing of drawings, paintings, or sculptures that represent actual people, objects, or landscapes, rather than images from the artist's imagination. **38** See also **fact of life, kiss of life. • a matter of life and death:** see **death. • a new lease of life:** see **lease. • to risk life and limb:** see **limb. • to have the time of** your **life:** see **time. • true to life:** see **true.** — PHRASE / PHRASE / PHRASE / N-UNCOUNT

life-and-'death. See **death.**

'life assurance. Life assurance is the same as **life insurance.** — ◆◇◇◇◇ N-UNCOUNT BRITISH

life-belt /'laɪfbelt/ **lifebelts.** A lifebelt is a large ring used to keep a person afloat and prevent them from drowning when they fall into the sea or other deep water. — N-COUNT

life-blood /'laɪfblʌd/; also spelled **life-blood.** The lifeblood of an organization, area, or person is the most important thing that they need in order to exist or be successful. *Coal and steel were the region's lifeblood.* — N-SING

life-boat /'laɪfbəʊt/ **lifeboats. 1** A lifeboat is a boat that is sent out from a port or harbour in order to rescue people who are in danger at sea. **2** A lifeboat is a boat that is carried on a ship, which people on the ship use to escape when the ship is in danger of sinking. — ◆◇◇◇◇ N-COUNT / N-COUNT

'life cycle, life cycles. 1 The life cycle of an animal or plant is the series of changes and developments that it passes through from the beginning of its life until its death. **2** The life cycle of something such as an idea or organization is the series of developments that take place in it from its beginning until the end of its usefulness. *Each new product would have a relatively long life cycle.* — ◆◇◇◇◇ N-COUNT / N-COUNT

'life-enhancing. If you describe something as **life-enhancing**, you mean that it makes you feel happier and more content. *...a life-enhancing and exciting trip.* — ADJ-GRADED

,life ex'pectancy, life expectancies. The life expectancy of a person, animal, or plant is the length of time that they are normally likely to live. *Smoking reduces life expectancy.* — ◆◇◇◇◇ N-UNCOUNT: also N in pl

'life form, life forms. A life form is any living thing such as an animal or plant. — N-COUN.: with supp

life-guard /'laɪfgɑːd/ **lifeguards.** A lifeguard is a person who works at a beach or swimming pool and rescues people when they are in danger of drowning. *He worked as a lifeguard at Brighton Beach.* — N-COUNT

,life im'prisonment. If someone is sentenced to **life imprisonment**, they are sentenced to stay in prison for the rest of their life, or for a very long period of time. — ◆◇◇◇◇ N-UNCOUNT

'life insurance. Life insurance is a form of insurance in which a person makes regular payments to an insurance company, in return for a sum of money to be paid to them when they reach a certain age, or to a person they have nominated, usually their wife or husband or children, when they die. — ◆◇◇◇◇ N-UNCOUNT

'life jacket, life jackets; also spelled **lifejacket.** A life jacket is a sleeveless jacket which keeps you afloat in water. The American word is **life preserver.** — N-COUNT BRITISH

life-less /'laɪfləs/. **1** If a person or animal is **lifeless**, they are dead, or are so still that they appear to be dead. **2** A **lifeless** place or area does not have anything living or growing there at all. *Dry stone walls may appear stark and lifeless, but they provide a valuable habitat for plants and animals.* **3** If you describe a person, or something such as an artistic performance or a town as **lifeless**, you mean they — ◆◇◇◇◇ ADJ / ADJ-GRADED / ADJ-GRADED

lack any lively or exciting qualities. *With one exception his novels are shallow and lifeless things.*

life·like /ˈlaɪflaɪk/. Something that is **lifelike** has the appearance of being alive. *...a lifelike doll.*   ADJ-GRADED

life·line /ˈlaɪflaɪn/ **lifelines.** A **lifeline** is something that enables an organization or group to survive or to continue with an activity. *The orders will throw a lifeline to Britain's shipyards.*   ◆◇◇◇◇ N-COUNT

life·long /ˈlaɪflɒŋ, AM -lɔːŋ/. **Lifelong** means existing or happening for the whole of a person's life. *...her lifelong friendship with Naomi.*   ◆◇◇◇◇ ADJ: ADJ n

life 'member, life members. If you are a **life member** of a club or organization, your membership will last for the rest of your life.   N-COUNT

life 'peer, life peers. In Britain, a **life peer** is a person who is given a title such as 'Lord' or 'Lady' which they can use for the rest of their life. Life peers have the right to a seat in the House of Lords in the British parliament.   N-COUNT

'life preserver, life preservers. A **life-preserver** is a sleeveless jacket which keeps you afloat in water. The British term is **life jacket**.   N-COUNT AMERICAN

lif·er /ˈlaɪfə/ **lifers.** A **lifer** is a criminal who has been given a life sentence.   N-COUNT INFORMAL

'life raft, life rafts; also spelled **life-raft.** A **life raft** is a small boat which is carried on aeroplanes, helicopters, and large boats to be used in emergencies.   N-COUNT

life·sav·er /ˈlaɪfseɪvə/ **lifesavers.** If you say that something is a **lifesaver**, you mean that it helps people in a very important way, often in a way that is important to their health. *The cervical smear test is a lifesaver.*   N-COUNT

'life-saving. 1 A **life-saving** drug, operation, or action is one that saves someone's life or is likely to save their life. *She decided her child should go to America for life-saving treatment.* 2 You use **life-saving** to refer to the skills and activities connected with rescuing people, especially people who are drowning. *She teaches swimming, life-saving and water aerobics.*   ◆◇◇◇◇ ADJ / N-UNCOUNT

life 'science, life sciences. The **life sciences** are sciences such as zoology, botany, and anthropology, which are concerned with human beings, animals, and plants.   N-COUNT

life 'sentence, life sentences. If someone receives a **life sentence**, they are sentenced to stay in prison for the rest of their life, or for a very long period of time.   ◆◇◇◇◇ N-COUNT

'life-size. A **life-size** representation of someone or something, for example a painting or sculpture, is the same size as the person or thing that they represent. *...a life-sized statue of an Indian boy.*   ADJ

'life-sized. Life-sized means the same as **life-size**.   ADJ

life·span /ˈlaɪfspæn/ **lifespans;** also spelled **life span.** 1 The **lifespan** of a person, animal, or plant is the period of time for which they live or are normally expected to live. *A 15-year lifespan is not uncommon for a dog.* 2 The **lifespan** of a product, organization, or idea is the period of time for which it is expected to work properly or to last.   N-VAR / N-COUNT

life·style /ˈlaɪfstaɪl/ **lifestyles;** also spelled **life style** or **life-style.** The **lifestyle** of a particular person or group of people is the living conditions, behaviour, and habits that are typical of them or are chosen by them. *...the change of lifestyle occasioned by the baby's arrival.*   ◆◆◇◇◇ N-VAR

life-sup'port machine, life-support machines. A **life-support machine** is the equipment that is used to keep a person alive when they are very ill and incapable of breathing without help.   N-COUNT BRITISH

life-sup'port system, life-support systems. A **life-support system** is the same as a **life-support machine**.   N-COUNT

life's 'work. Someone's **life's work** or **life work** is the main activity that they have been involved in during their life, or their most important achievement. *An exhibition of his life's work is being shown in the garden of his home.*   N-SING

'life-threatening. If someone has a **life-threatening** illness or is in a **life-threatening** situa-   ◆◇◇◇◇ ADJ

tion, there is a strong possibility that the illness or the situation will kill them.

life·time /ˈlaɪftaɪm/ **lifetimes.** 1 A **lifetime** is the length of time that someone is alive. *During my lifetime I haven't got around to much travelling.* 2 The **lifetime** of a particular thing is the period of time that it lasts. *...the lifetime of a parliament.* 3 If you describe something, for example an opportunity, as the opportunity **of a lifetime**, you are emphasizing that it is the most memorable or important opportunity that you are ever likely to have. *This could be not just the trip of a lifetime but the experience of a lifetime.*   ◆◆◇◇◇ N-COUNT / N-SING: with poss / PHRASE [PRAGMATICS]

lift /lɪft/ **lifts, lifting, lifted.** 1 If you **lift** something, you move it to another position, especially upwards. *She lifted the last of her drink to her lips.* ▶ **Lift up** means the same as **lift**. *She put her arms around him and lifted him up... Curious shoppers lifted up their children to take a closer look at the parade.* 2 If you **lift** a part of your body, you move it to a higher position. *Amy lifted her arm to wave.* ▶ **Lift up** means the same as **lift**. *Tom took his seat again and lifted his feet up on to the railing.* 3 If you **lift** your eyes or your head, you look up, for example when you have been reading and someone comes into the room. 4 If a government or organization **lifts** people or goods in or out of a country or area, it transports them there by aeroplane, especially in special circumstances such as a war. *The army lifted people off rooftops where they had climbed to escape the flooding.* 5 If fog, cloud, or mist **lifts**, it reduces, for example by moving upwards or by becoming less thick. 6 A **lift** is a device that carries people or goods up and down inside tall buildings. The American word is **elevator**. 7 If you give someone a **lift** somewhere, you take them there in your car as a favour to them. 8 If people in authority **lift** a law or rule that prevents people from doing something, they end it. *Mr Bush said he'd never been enthusiastic about sanctions in the first place and would lift them.* 9 If something **lifts** your spirits or your mood, you start feeling more cheerful. *He used his incredible sense of humour to lift my spirits... As soon as she heard the telephone ring her spirits lifted.* 10 If something gives you a **lift**, it gives you a feeling of greater confidence, energy, or enthusiasm. *My selection for the team has given me a tremendous lift.* 11 To **lift** something means to increase its amount or to increase the level or the rate at which it happens. *The bank lifted its basic home loans rate to 10.99% from 10.75%... A barrage would halt the flow upstream and lift the water level.* 12 ● to **lift a finger**: see **finger**.   ◆◆◆◇ VERB: V n / V n prep/adv / PHRASAL VB / V n P / V P noun / VERB / V n / PHRASAL VB / V n P / VERB: V n / VERB / V n prep/adv / VERB: V / N-COUNT BRITISH / N-COUNT / VERB / V n / V-ERG / V n / V / N-SING INFORMAL / VERB / V n to/from/ by amount / V n

lift off. When an aircraft or rocket **lifts off**, it leaves the ground and rises into the air.   PHRASAL VB V P

lift up. See lift 1, 2.   PHRASAL VB

'lift-off, lift-offs. Lift-off is the act of launching a rocket into space, when it leaves the ground and rises into the air. *The rocket tumbled out of control shortly after lift-off.*   ◆◇◇◇◇ N-VAR

liga·ment /ˈlɪɡəmənt/ **ligaments.** A **ligament** is a band of strong tissue in a person's body which connects bones.   ◆◇◇◇◇ N-COUNT

light 1 brightness or illumination

light /laɪt/ **lights, lighting, lit, lighted; lighter, lightest.** The form **lit** is the usual past tense and past participle, but the form **lighted** is also used. 1 **Light** is the brightness that lets you see things. Light comes from sources such as the sun, moon, lamps, and fire. *Light and water in embassy buildings were cut off... It was difficult to see in the dim light. ...ultraviolet light.* 2 A **light** is something such as an electric lamp which produces light. *The janitor comes round to turn the lights out. ...street lights.* 3 If a place or object is **lit** by something, it has light shining on it. *A giant moon lit the road so brightly you could see the landscape clearly... The room was lit by only the one light. ...the little lighted space at the bottom of the stairwell.* 4 **First light** is the time in the early morning when light first appears and   ◆◆◆◇ N-UNCOUNT: also the N / N-COUNT / VERB V n / V-ed / Also V n with n / PHRASE LITERARY

before the sun rises. **5** When you talk about **the light at the end of the tunnel**, you are referring to a pleasant situation in the future which gives you hope and optimism, especially because you are in a difficult or unpleasant situation at the moment. PHRASE

6 If it is **light**, there is enough natural daylight left to see by even though it is the evening. *It was still light when we arrived.* **7** If a room or building is **light**, it has a lot of natural light in it, for example because it has large windows. ◆ **light·ness** *The dark green spare bedroom is in total contrast to the lightness of the large main bedroom.* ADJ-GRADED · ADJ-GRADED · N-UNCOUNT

8 You can use **lights** to refer to a set of traffic lights. N-PLURAL

9 If someone in authority gives you the **green light**, they give you permission to do something. *The food industry was given a green light to extend the use of these chemicals.* PHRASE

10 If you **light** something such as a cigarette or fire, or if it **lights**, it starts burning. *If the charcoal does fail to light, use a special liquid spray and light it with a long taper. ...a lighted candle.* **11** If someone asks you for a **light**, they want a match or cigarette lighter so they can start smoking. *Have you got a light anybody?* **12** If you **set light to** something, you make it start burning. The usual American expression is **set fire to**. V-ERG: V n · V · V-ed · N-SING: a N · INFORMAL · PHRASE · BRITISH

13 If you say that an object **sees the light of day** or **sees the light**, you mean that it is taken out of the place where it is stored. *Museum basements are stacked full of objects which never see the light of day.* PHRASE

14 If something **sees the light of day** at a particular time, it comes into existence or is made known to the public at that time. *This extraordinary document first saw the light of day in 1966.* **15** If someone or something **sheds light on**, **throws light on**, or **casts light on** something, it makes it easier to understand, because more information is known about it. *A new approach offers an answer, and may shed light on an even bigger question.* **16** If someone **sees the light**, they finally understand something after having thought about it for some time, or after having misunderstood it. PHRASE · PHRASE · PHRASE

17 See also **lighter, lighting; bright lights, pilot light, red light.**

18 If something is presented in a particular **light**, it is presented so that you think about it in a particular way or so that it appears to be of a particular nature. *He has worked hard in recent months to portray New York in a better light.* **19** You can refer to the type of influence that something has on situations, people, or things as the **light of** that situation, person, or thing. *...the harsh light of reality.* **20** If something **comes to light** or **is brought to light**, it becomes obvious or is made known to a lot of people. *Nothing about this sum has come to light... The truth is unlikely to be brought to light by the promised enquiry.* **21** If something is possible or if you make a decision **in the light of** particular information or knowledge, it is possible or you make the decision because you have this information or knowledge. *In the light of this information it is now possible to identify a number of key issues.* N-COUNT: with supp · N-SING: the N of n · WRITTEN · PHRASE · PHR-PREP

light on or **light upon.** If you **light on** something or **light upon** it, you suddenly notice it or find it. PHRASAL VB · V P n

light up. 1 If you **light** something **up** or if it **lights up**, it becomes bright, usually when you shine light on it. *...a keypad that lights up when you pick up the handset... It isn't possible to heat one half of a bedroom or only to light up one half of a sitting room!* **2** If your face or your eyes **light up**, you suddenly look very surprised or happy. *Sue's face lit up with surprise.* **3** If you **light up**, you make a cigarette, cigar, or pipe start burning and you start smoking it. *He takes his time lighting up a cigarette.* PHRASAL VB · ERG · V P · V P noun · V P · V P with n · V P · V P noun · INFORMAL

light upon. See **light on.** PHRASAL VB

light 2 not great in weight, amount, or intensity

light /laɪt/ **lighter, lightest. 1** Something that is **light** does not weigh very much, or weighs less than you would expect it to. *Try to wear light, loose clothes.* ◆ **light·ness** *It is fashioned completely of steel for lightness and strength.* **2** Something that is **light** is not very great in amount, degree, or intensity. *...the usual light traffic in the city. ...a light* ◆◆◆◇◇ ADJ-GRADED · N-UNCOUNT · ADJ-GRADED

breeze. ◆ **light·ly** *Put the onions in the pan and cook until lightly browned.* **3 Light** equipment and machines are small and easily moved, especially because they are not heavy. *...a convoy of light armoured vehicles.* **4** Something that is **light** is very pale in colour. *He is light haired with gray eyes.* ▶ Also a combining form. *We know he has a light green van.* ADV-GRADED · ADJ: ADJ n · ADJ-GRADED · COMB

5 A **light** sleep is one that is easily disturbed and in which you are often aware of the things around you. If you are a **light** sleeper, you are easily woken when you are asleep. ◆ **lightly** *He was dozing lightly in his chair.* **6** A **light** sound, for example someone's voice, is pleasantly quiet. *The voice was sweet and light.* **7** A **light** meal is small in quantity. *...wine and cheese or other light refreshment.* ◆ **lightly** *She found it impossible to eat lightly.* **8** Food that is **light** has a delicate flavour and is easy to digest. *Berti's clear tomato soup is deliciously light. ...light table wines.* ADJ-GRADED: ADJ n · ADV-GRADED · ADJ-GRADED · ADJ-GRADED · ADV-GRADED · ADJ-GRADED

9 Light work does not involve much physical effort. **10** If you describe the result of an action or a punishment as **light**, you mean that it is less serious or severe than you expected. *She confessed her astonishment at her light sentence when her father visited her at the jail.* ◆ **lightly** *One of the accused got off lightly in exchange for pleading guilty to withholding information from Congress.* **11** Movements and actions that are **light** are graceful or gentle and are done with very little force or effort. *There was a light knock at the door.* ◆ **lightly** *He kissed her lightly on the mouth.* ◆ **light·ness** *She danced with a grace and lightness that were breathtaking.* **12** See also **lighter.** ADJ-GRADED · ADJ-GRADED · ADV-GRADED · ADJ-GRADED · ADV-GRADED · N-UNCOUNT

light 3 unimportant or not serious

light /laɪt/ **lighter, lightest. 1** If you describe things such as books, music, and films as **light**, you mean that they entertain you without making you think very deeply. *...a light entertainment programme.* **2** If you say something in a **light** way, you sound as if you think that it is not important or serious. *Talk to him in a friendly, light way about the relationship. ...to finish on a lighter note.* ◆ **light·ly** *'Once a detective, always a detective,' he said lightly.* ◆ **light·ness** *'I'm not an authority on them,' Jessica said with forced lightness.* **3** If you say that something is not a **light** matter, you mean that it should be treated or considered as being important and serious. *It can be no light matter for the Home Office that so many young prisoners should have wanted to kill or injure themselves.* ◆ **lightly** *His allegations cannot be lightly dismissed.* **4** If you **make light of** something, you treat it as though it is not serious or important, when in fact it is. ● **to make light work of:** see **work.** **5** See also **lighter.** ◆◆◆◇◇ ADJ-GRADED · ADJ-GRADED · ADV-GRADED · N-UNCOUNT · ADJ-GRADED · ADV-GRADED · PHRASE

light 'aircraft. Light aircraft is both the singular and plural form. A **light aircraft** is a small aeroplane that is designed to carry a small number of passengers or a small amount of goods. N-COUNT

'light bulb, light bulbs. A **light bulb** or **bulb** is the round glass part of an electric light or lamp which light shines from. ◆◇◇◇◇ N-COUNT

light·en /ˈlaɪtən/ **lightens, lightening, lightened. 1** When something **lightens**, it becomes less dark in colour. *Leslie lightens her hair and has now had it cut into a short, feathered style.* **2** If your attitude, or mood **lightens**, or if someone or something **lightens** it, they make you feel more cheerful, happy, and relaxed. *The sun was streaming in through the window, yet it did nothing to lighten his mood.* **3** If you **lighten** something, you make it less heavy. *It is a good idea to blend it in a food processor as this lightens the mixture.* **4** If someone or something **lightens** your **burden** or your **load**, they do something to make a bad or difficult situation better for you. *In sharing this secret you lighten your burden... If you are responsible for children, lighten the load by asking others to help.* ◆◇◇◇◇ V-ERG: V · V n · V-ERG: V · V n · VERB · V n · PHRASE

lighten up. If someone tells you to **lighten up**, they think you should be less serious and make an effort to be more relaxed and happy. PHRASAL VB · V P

light·er /'laɪtə/ **lighters.** A **lighter** is a small device that produces a flame which you can use to light cigarettes, cigars, and pipes. ◆◇◇◇◇ N-COUNT

light-'fingered. If you say that someone is **light-fingered**, you mean that they steal things. ADJ-GRADED INFORMAL

light-'headed. If you are **light-headed**, you feel rather dizzy and faint, for example because you are ill or because you have drunk too much alcohol. *I felt awfully dizzy and light-headed.* ADJ-GRADED

light-'hearted. 1 Someone who is **light-hearted** is cheerful and happy. *They were light-hearted and prepared to enjoy life.* **2** Something that is **light-hearted** is intended to be entertaining or amusing, and not at all serious. *There have been many attempts, both light-hearted and serious, to locate the Loch Ness Monster.* ◆◇◇◇◇ ADJ-GRADED ADJ-GRADED

light·house /'laɪthaʊs/ **lighthouses.** A **lighthouse** is a tower containing a powerful flashing lamp that is built on the coast or on a small island in the sea. Lighthouses are used to guide ships or to warn them of danger. ◆◇◇◇◇ N-COUNT

light 'industry, light industries. Light industry is industry in which only small items are made, for example household goods and clothes. N-VAR

light·ing /'laɪtɪŋ/. **1** The **lighting** in a place is the way that it is lit, for example by electric lights, by candles, or by windows, or the quality of the light in it. *The whole room is bathed in soft lighting. ...street lighting.* **2** The **lighting** in a film or play is the use of different electric lights to give a particular effect. ◆◆◇◇◇ N-UNCOUNT N-UNCOUNT

light·ning /'laɪtnɪŋ/. **1 Lightning** is the very bright flashes of light in the sky that happen during thunderstorms. **2 Lightning** describes things that happen very quickly or last for only a short time. *Driving today demands lightning reflexes.* ◆◆◇◇◇ N-UNCOUNT ADJ: ADJ n

'lightning conductor, lightning conductors. A **lightning conductor** is a long thin piece of metal on top of a building that attracts lightning and allows it to reach the ground safely. The American expression is **lightning rod**. N-COUNT BRITISH

'lightning rod, lightning rods. 1 A **lightning rod** is a long thin piece of metal on top of a building that attracts lightning and allows it to reach the ground safely. The British expression is **lightning conductor**. **2** If you say that someone **is a lightning rod for** something, you mean that they attract that thing to themselves. *He became a lightning rod for criticism.* N-COUNT AMERICAN PHRASE AMERICAN

'lightning strike, lightning strikes. A **lightning strike** is a strike in which workers stop work suddenly and without any warning, in order to protest about something. N-COUNT

light·ship /'laɪtʃɪp/ **lightships.** A **lightship** is a small ship that stays in one place and that has a powerful flashing lamp like a lighthouse. It is used to guide ships or to warn them of danger. N-COUNT

light·weight /'laɪtweɪt/ **lightweights;** also spelled **light-weight. 1** Something that is **light-weight** weighs less than most other things of the same type. *The company manufactures a range of innovative light-weight cycles.* **2 Lightweight** is a category in some sports, such as boxing, judo, or rowing, based on the weight of the athlete. *By the age of sixteen he was the junior lightweight champion of Poland.* ▶ A **lightweight** is a person who is in the lightweight category in a particular sport. **3** If you describe someone as a **lightweight**, you are critical of them because you think that they are not very important or skilful in a particular area of activity. ▶ Also an adjective. *Some of the discussion in the book is lightweight and unconvincing.* ◆◆◇◇◇ ADJ-GRADED N-UNCOUNT N-COUNT N-COUNT PRAGMATICS ADJ-GRADED

'light year, light years. 1 A **light year** is the distance that light travels in a year. *...a star system millions of light years away.* **2** You can say that two things are **light years** apart to emphasize a very great difference or a very long distance or period of time between them. *She says the French education system is light years ahead of the English one.* ◆◇◇◇◇ N-COUNT N-COUNT PRAGMATICS INFORMAL

lik·able /'laɪkəbəl/. See **likeable**.

like 1 preposition and conjunction uses

like /laɪk/ **likes. 1** If you say that one person or thing is **like** another, you mean that they have similar characteristics or behave in similar ways. *Kathy is a great mate, we are like sisters... It's a bit like going to the dentist; it's never as bad as you fear. ...a mountain shaped like a reclining woman.* **2** If you ask or talk about what something or someone is **like**, you are asking or talking about their qualities, features, or characteristics. *What was Bulgaria like?... What was it like growing up in Hillsborough?* **3** You can use **like** to introduce an example of the set of things or people that you have just mentioned. *The neglect that large cities like New York have received over the past 12 years is tremendous.* **4** You can use **like** to say that someone or something is in the same situation as another person or thing. *It also moved those who, like me, are too young to have lived through the war.* **5** If you say that someone is behaving or doing something **like** something or someone else, you mean that they are behaving in a way or doing something that is typical of that kind of thing or person. *I was shaking all over, trembling like a leaf... Greenfield was behaving like an irresponsible idiot.* **6** You can use **like** in expressions such as **that's just like her** and **it wasn't like him** to indicate that the person's behaviour is or is not typical of their character. *Why does he want to do a mad thing like that? It's not like him.* **7 Like** is sometimes used in order to say that something appears to be the case when it is not. Some people consider this use to be incorrect. *On the train up to Waterloo, I felt like I was going on an adventure.* **8 Like** is sometimes used in order to indicate that something happens or is done in the same way as something else. Some people consider this use to be incorrect. *He spoke exactly like I did... We really were afraid, not like in the cinema.* **9** You can use the expressions **like anything**, **like crazy**, or **like mad** to emphasize that someone is doing something or something is happening in a very intense or noticeable way. *He's working like mad at the moment.* **10** Some people say **like** when they are thinking about what to say next or because it has become their habit to say it. *I decided that I'd go and, like, take a picture of him.* **11** You can use **like** in expressions such as **like attracts like**, when you are referring to two or more people or things that have the same or similar characteristics. *You have to make sure you're comparing like with like.* **12** You say **'and the like'** to indicate that there are other similar things or people that can be included in what you are saying. *...keeping fit through jogging, aerobics, weight training, and the like.* **13** You can talk about the **likes of** someone or something to refer to people or things of a particular type. *Why would somebody like her want to spend an evening with the likes of me?* **14** If you refer to something **the like of which** or **the likes of which** has never been seen before, you are emphasizing how important, great, or noticeable the thing is. *...technological advances the like of which the world had previously only dreamed of.* **15** You use the expression **more like** when mentioning an amount, name, or description that in your opinion is more accurate than one that has already been mentioned. *It's on company advice – well, orders, more like.* **16** You use the expression **something like** with an amount, number, or description to indicate that it is approximately accurate. *They can get something like £3,000 a year.* **17** You can use **like** in expressions such as **nothing like** to make an emphatic negative statement. *Three hundred million dollars will be nothing like enough.* **18** You say **like this**, **like that**, or **like so** when you are showing someone how something is done. *It opens and closes, like this.* **19** You use **like this** or **like that** when you are drawing attention to something that you are doing or that someone else is doing. *I'm sorry to intrude on you like this.* ◆◆◆◆◆ PREP PREP PREP PREP PREP PREP CONJ CONJ PRAGMATICS PHRASE PRAGMATICS INFORMAL CONVENTION PRAGMATICS INFORMAL, SPOKEN N-UNCOUNT PHRASE PHRASE INFORMAL PHRASE PRAGMATICS PHRASE PHRASE PREP PRAGMATICS PHRASE PHRASE

L

like 2 verb and noun uses

like /laɪk/ **likes, liking, liked. 1** If you **like** something or someone, you think they are interesting, enjoyable, or attractive. *I can't think why Grace doesn't like me... Do you like to go swimming?... I like my whisky neat... That's one of the things I like about you.* **2** Someone's **likes** are the things that they enjoy or find pleasant. *I knew everything about Jemma: her likes and dislikes, her political viewpoints.* **3** If you ask someone how they **like** something, you are asking them for their opinion of it. *How do you like America?... How did you like the trip?* **4** If you **like** something such as a particular course of action or way of behaving, you approve of it. *Opal, his wife, didn't really like him drinking so much... I don't like relying on the judges' decisions.* **5** If you say that you **like** to do something or that you **like** something to be done, you mean that you prefer to do it or prefer it to be done as part of your normal life or routine. *I like to get to airports in good time... I hear Mary's husband likes her to be home no later than six o'clock.* **6** If you say that you would **like** something or would **like** to do something, you are indicating a wish or desire that you have. *I'd like a huge bubble bath to sink into up to my neck... If you don't mind, I think I'd like to go home.* **7** You can say that you **would like** to say something to indicate that you are about to say it. *I'd like to apologize... I would like to take this opportunity of telling you about a new service we are offering.* **8** If you ask someone if they **would like** something, you are politely offering them something or inviting them to do something. *Would you like a magazine while you wait?... Would you like to come back for coffee?* **9** If you say to someone that you **would like** something, or ask them if they **would like** to do something, you are politely telling them what you want or what you want them to do. *I'd like an explanation... Would you like to tell me what happened?* **10** You say '**if you like**' when you are making or agreeing to an offer or suggestion in a casual way. *You can stay here if you like.* **11** You say '**If you like**' when you are expressing something in a different way, or in a way that you think some people might disagree with or find strange. *This is more like a down payment, or a deposit, if you like.* **12** See also **liking**.

VB: no cont
V n/-ing
V to-inf
V n adj/prep
V n about/-ing
N-PLURAL

VB: no cont,
no passive
V n/-ing

VB: no cont,
V n
V -ing
V-ing
Also V to-inf

VB: no cont,
no passive
V to-inf
V n to-inf

VB: no cont,
no passive
PRAGMATICS
V n
V to-inf

VB: no cont,
no passive
PRAGMATICS
V to-inf

VB: no cont,
no passive
PRAGMATICS
V n
V to-inf

VB: no cont,
no passive
PRAGMATICS
V n
V to-inf
Also V n to-inf

PHRASE
PRAGMATICS

PHRASE
PRAGMATICS

-like /-laɪk/. **-like** combines with nouns to form adjectives which describe something as being similar to the thing referred to by the noun. *...beautiful purple-red petunia-like flowers.*

COMB

like·able /'laɪkəbəl/; also spelled **likable.** Someone or something that is **likeable** is pleasant and easy to like. *He was an immensely likeable chap.*

ADJ-GRADED

like·li·hood /'laɪklihʊd/. **1** The **likelihood** of something happening is how likely it is to happen. *The likelihood of infection is minimal... There is every likelihood that sanctions will work.* If something is a **likelihood**, it is likely to happen. *The likelihood is that, if the Republicans lose, Mr Baker will retire.* **3** If you say that something will happen **in all likelihood**, you mean that it will probably happen. *Steven had in all likelihood made his decision.*

N-UNCOUNT

N-SING

PHRASE

like·ly /'laɪkli/ **likelier, likeliest. 1** You use **likely** to indicate that something is probably the case or will probably happen in a particular situation. *If this is your first baby, it's far more likely that you'll get to the hospital too early.* ▶ Also an adverb. *Profit will most likely have risen by about £25 million.* **2** If someone or something is **likely** to do something, they will very probably do it. *Once people have seen that something actually works, they are much more likely to accept change.* **3** A **likely** person, place, or thing is one that will probably be suitable for a particular purpose. *He had seemed a likely candidate to become Prime Minister.*

ADJ-GRADED

ADV-GRADED
ADJ-GRADED:
v-link ADJ to-inf

ADJ-GRADED:
ADJ n

4 You can say '**not likely**' as an emphatic way of saying 'no', especially when someone asks you whether you are going to do something. *'How about having a phone out here?'—'Not likely!'*

CONVENTION
PRAGMATICS
INFORMAL

'like-minded. Like-minded people have similar opinions, ideas, attitudes, or interests. *...the opportunity to mix with hundreds of like-minded people.*

ADJ

lik·en /'laɪkən/ **likens, likening, likened.** If you **liken** one thing or person to another thing or person, you say that they are similar. *She likens marriage to slavery.*

VERB
V n to n/-ing

like·ness /'laɪknəs/ **likenesses. 1** If two things or people have a **likeness** to each other, they are similar to each other. *There might be a likeness between their features, but their eyes were totally dissimilar.* **2** A **likeness** of someone is a picture or sculpture of them. *...wax likenesses of every US president.* **3** If you say that a picture of someone is a good **likeness** of them, you mean that it looks just like them.

N-SING

N-COUNT:
with poss
N-COUNT

like·wise /'laɪkwaɪz/. **1** You use **likewise** when you are comparing two methods, states, or situations and saying that they are similar. *The V2 was not an ordinary weapon: it could only be used against cities. Likewise the atom bomb.* **2** If you do something and someone else does **likewise**, they do the same or a similar thing. *He lent money, made donations and encouraged others to do likewise.*

ADV

ADV:
ADV after v

lik·ing /'laɪkɪŋ/. **1** If you have a **liking** for something or someone, you like them. *She had a liking for good clothes.* **2** If something is, for example, too fast **for** your **liking**, you would prefer it to be slower. *He had become too powerful for their liking.* **3** If something is **to** your **liking**, it suits your interests, tastes, or wishes. *London was more to his liking than Rome.*

N-SING:
with supp
PHRASE

PHRASE

PHRASE

li·lac /'laɪlək/ **lilacs; lilac** can also be used as the plural form. **1** A **lilac** or a **lilac tree** is a small tree which has pleasant-smelling purple, pink, or white flowers in large, cone-shaped clusters. **Lilacs** are the flowers which grow on this tree. **2** Something that is **lilac** is pale pinkish-purple in colour.

N-VAR

COLOUR

lilt /lɪlt/. If someone's voice has a **lilt** in it. the pitch of their voice rises and falls in a pleasant way.

N-SING

lilt·ing /'lɪltɪŋ/. A **lilting** voice or song rises and falls in pitch in a pleasant way. *He had a pleasant, lilting northern accent.*

ADJ

lily /'lɪli/ **lilies.** A **lily** is a plant with large flowers that are often white.

N-VAR

,lily of the 'valley, lilies of the valley; lily of the valley can also be used as the plural. **Lily of the valley** are small plants with large leaves and small, white, bell-shaped flowers.

N-VAR

lima bean /'liːmə biːn/ **lima beans. Lima beans** are flat round beans that are light green in colour and are eaten as a vegetable.

N-COUNT

limb /lɪm/ **limbs. 1** Your **limbs** are your arms and legs. *She would be able to stretch out her cramped limbs and rest for a few hours.* **2** The **limbs** of a tree are its branches. *This entire rickety structure was hanging from the limb of an enormous leafy tree.* **3** If someone goes **out on a limb**, they do something they strongly believe in even though it is risky or extreme, and is likely to fail or be criticized by other people. *They can see themselves going out on a limb, voting for a very controversial energy bill.* **4** If someone **risks life and limb**, they do something very dangerous in order to achieve something, usually in a very brave way. *Viewers will remember the dashing hero, Dirk, risking life and limb to rescue Daphne from the dragons.*

N-COUNT

N-COUNT
LITERARY

PHRASE

PHRASE

-limbed /-lɪmd/. **-limbed** combines with adjectives to form other adjectives which indicate that a person or animal has limbs of a particular type or appearance. *He was long-limbed and dark-eyed.*

COMB

lim·ber /'lɪmbə/ **limbers, limbering, limbered.**
  limber up. If you **limber up**, you prepare for a physical activity such as a sport by exercising your muscles and limbs. *A short walk will limber up the legs.*

PHRASAL VB
V P
V P noun

lim·bo /'lɪmbəʊ/. **1** If you say that someone or something is in **limbo**, you mean that they are in a situation where they seem to be caught between two stages and it is unclear what will happen next. *The negotiations have been in limbo since mid-December.* **2** The **limbo** is a West Indian dance in

N-UNCOUNT

N-SING:

which you have to pass under a low bar while lean-   the N, N n
ing backwards. The bar is moved nearer to the floor
each time you go under it.

lime /laɪm/ **limes. 1** A **lime** is a green fruit that ◆◆◇◇◇
tastes like a lemon. Limes grow on trees in tropical   N-VAR
countries. *...peeled slices of lime.* **2 Lime** is a drink   N-UNCOUNT
that tastes of limes.

3 A **lime** is a large tree with pale green leaves. *...dilapi-*   N-COUNT
dated avenues of limes.

4 Lime is a substance containing calcium. It is found   N-UNCOUNT
in soil and water. ► Also a combining form. *...lime-*   COMB
rich sand.

,lime 'green; also spelled **lime-green**. Something   COLOUR
that is **lime green** is light yellowish-green in colour.
She wore a lime-green trouser suit.

lime·light /'laɪmlaɪt/. If someone is in the **lime-** ◆◇◇◇◇
light, a lot of attention is being paid to them, be-   N-UNCOUNT
cause they are famous or because they have done
something very unusual or exciting. *Tony has now
been thrust into the limelight, with a high-profile
job.*

lim·er·ick /'lɪmərɪk/ **limericks**. A **limerick** is a hu- ◆◇◇◇◇
morous poem which has five lines.   N-COUNT

lime·stone /'laɪmstəʊn/ **limestones**. Limestone ◆◇◇◇◇
is a white rock which is used for building and mak-   N-VAR
ing cement.

lim·ey /'laɪmi/ **limeys**. Some Americans refer to   N-COUNT
British people as **limeys**.   INFORMAL

lim·it /'lɪmɪt/ **limits, limiting, limited. 1** A **limit** ◆◆◆◇
is the greatest amount, extent, or degree of some-   N-COUNT
thing that is possible. *Her love for him was being
tested to its limits... There is no limit to how much
fresh fruit you can eat in a day.* **2** A **limit** of a par-   N-COUNT
ticular kind is the largest or smallest amount of
something such as time or money that is allowed
because of a rule, law, or decision. *The three month
time limit will be up in mid-June.* **3** The **limit** of an   N-COUNT:
area is its boundary or edge. *...the city limits of*   with supp
Baghdad. **4** The **limits** of a situation are the facts   N-PLURAL
involved in it which make only some actions or re-
sults possible. *He outlined the limits of British
power.*

5 If you **limit** something, you prevent it from becom-   VERB
ing greater than a particular amount or degree. *He*   V n
limited payments on the country's foreign debt... This   V n to n
would limit unemployment to around 2.5 million. **6** If   VERB
you **limit** yourself to something, or if someone or   V pron-refl to
something **limits** you, the number of things that you   n/-ing
have or do is reduced. *Men should limit themselves to*   V n to n/-ing
20 units of alcohol a week... We limited them to just a   Also V pron-refl
couple of chances. ♦ **lim·it·ing** The conditions laid   ADJ-GRADED
down to me were not too limiting. **7** If something **is**   VB: usu
limited to a particular place or group of people, it ex-   passive
ists only in that place, or is had or done only by that   be V-ed to n/
group. *Entry to this prize draw is limited to UK resi-*   -ing
dents only.

8 If an area or a place is **off limits**, you are not allowed   PHRASE
to go there. *These establishments are off limits to ordi-*
nary citizens. **9** If someone **is over the limit**, they have   PHRASE
drunk more alcohol than they are legally allowed to   BRITISH
when driving a vehicle. **10** If you say **the sky is the**   PHRASE
limit, you mean that there is nothing to prevent
someone or something from being very successful. *In
terms of both salary and career success, the sky is the
limit.* **11** If you add **within limits** to a statement, you   PHRASE
mean that it is true or applies only when talking about
reasonable or normal situations. *We'll tell you what
we can, within limits, of course.*

12 See also **age limit, limited**.

limi·ta·tion /,lɪmɪ'teɪʃən/ **limitations. 1** The **limi-** ◆◆◇◇◇
tation of something is the act or process of control-   N-UNCOUNT
ling or reducing it. *...the limitation of nuclear
weapons.* **2** A **limitation** on something is a rule or   N-VAR
decision which prevents that thing from growing or
extending beyond certain limits. *...a limitation on
the tax deductions for people who make more than
$100,000 a year.* **3** If you talk about the **limitations**   N-PLURAL
of someone or something, you mean that they can
only do some things and not others, or that they
can only achieve a fairly low degree of success or

excellence. *Parents are too likely to blame schools for
the educational limitations of their children.* **4** A   N-VAR
limitation is a fact or situation that allows only
some actions and makes others impossible. *...an
acute disc collapse in the spine, causing limitation of
movement.*

lim·it·ed /'lɪmɪtɪd/. **1** Something that is **limited** is ◆◆◇◇◇
not very great in amount, range, or degree. *They*   ADJ-GRADED
*may only have a limited amount of time to get their
points across.* **2** A **limited** company is one in which   ADJ:
the shareholders are legally responsible for only a   ADJ n,
part of any money that it may owe if it goes bank-   n ADJ
rupt. *They had plans to turn the club into a limited*   BRITISH
company.

,limited e'dition, **limited editions**. A **limited** ◆◇◇◇◇
edition is something like a book, an engraving, or a   N-COUNT
set of coins which has been produced in very small
numbers, so that each one will be valuable in the
future.

lim·it·less /'lɪmɪtləs/. If you describe something as ◆◇◇◇◇
limitless, you mean that there is or appears to be so   ADJ
much of it that it will never be exhausted. *...a potentially limitless supply of energy.*

lim·ou·sine /,lɪmə'ziːn/ **limousines**. A **limousine** ◆◇◇◇◇
is a large and very comfortable car. Limousines are   N-COUNT
usually driven by a chauffeur and are used by very
rich or important people.

limp /lɪmp/ **limps, limping, limped; limper,** ◆◆◇◇◇
limpest. 1 If someone **limps**, they walk with diffi-   VERB: V
culty or in an uneven way because one of their legs   V adv/prep
or feet is hurt. *He had to limp off with a leg injury.*
► Also a noun. *A stiff knee following surgery forced*   N-COUNT
her to walk with a limp. **2** If you describe some-   ADJ-GRADED
thing as **limp**, you mean that it is soft or weak when
it should be firm or strong. *A residue can build up
on the hair shaft, leaving the hair limp and dull
looking.* ♦ **limp·ly** *Flags and bunting hung limply in*   ADV-GRADED:
the still, warm air. **3** If someone is **limp**, their body   ADV with v
has no strength and is not moving, for example be-   ADJ-GRADED
cause they are asleep or unconscious. *He hit his
head against a rock and went limp.*

lim·pet /'lɪmpɪt/ **limpets**. A **limpet** is a small sea   N-COUNT
animal with a cone-shaped shell which attaches it-
self tightly to rocks.

lim·pid /'lɪmpɪd/. **1** If you say that something is   ADJ-GRADED
limpid, you mean that it is very clear and transpar-   LITERARY
ent. *...limpid blue eyes. ...limpid rock-pools.* **2** If   ADJ-GRADED
you describe speech, writing, or music as **limpid**,   LITERARY
you like it because it is clear, simple, and flowing.
*The New York Times thought the speech a model of
its kind, limpid and unaffected.*

linch·pin /'lɪntʃpɪn/ **linchpins**; also spelled   N-COUNT:
lynchpin. If you refer to a person or thing as the   with supp
linchpin of something, you mean that they are the
most important person or thing involved in it. *He's
the lynchpin of our team and crucial to my long-
term plans.*

lin·den /'lɪndən/ **lindens**. A **linden** or a **linden tree** ◆◇◇◇◇
is a large tree with pale green leaves which is often   N-VAR
planted in parks in towns and cities.

line /laɪn/ **lines, lining, lined. 1** A **line** is a long ◆◆◆◆◆
thin mark which is drawn or painted on a surface.   N-COUNT
Lines are often used to divide one part of a surface
from another. *Draw a line down that page's center.
...a dotted line... The ball had clearly crossed the
line.* **2** The **lines** on someone's skin, especially on   N-COUNT
their face, are long thin marks that appear there as
they grow older. *...a large, generous face with deep
lines.*

3 A **line** of people or things is a number of them ar-   N-COUNT
ranged one behind the other or side by side. *The
sparse line of spectators noticed nothing unusual.* **4** A   N-COUNT:
line of people or vehicles is a number of them that are   also in N
waiting one behind another, for example in order to   AMERICAN
buy something or to go in a particular direction.
*...trucks waiting in line to unload their grain... Thou-
sands stood in line for hours to get a seat in the audience.* **5** If people or things **line** a road, room, or other   VERB
place, they are present in large numbers along its
edges or sides. *Thousands of cheering Albanians lined*

the streets of the capital. ♦ **-lined** *...a long tree-lined* COMB
drive.

6 A **line** of a piece of writing is one of the rows of N-COUNT
words, numbers, or other symbols in it. *The next line*
should read: Five days, 23.5 hours. **7** A **line** of a poem, N-COUNT
song, or play is a group of words that are spoken or
sung together. *Learning lines is very easy. Acting is very*
difficult. **8** A particular type of **line** in a conversation is N-COUNT:
a remark that is intended to have a particular effect. with supp
...chat-up lines like 'You've got beautiful eyes'.

9 You can refer to a long piece of wire, string, or cable N-VAR
as a **line** when it is used for a particular purpose. *She*
put her washing on the line. ...a piece of fishing-line.

10 A **line** is a connection which makes it possible for N-COUNT
two people to speak to each other on the telephone.
The telephone lines went dead... She's on the line from
her home in Boston. **11** You can use **line** to refer to a N-COUNT
telephone number which you can ring in order to get
information or to get advice. *...the 24-hour informa-*
tion line.

12 The **line** in which something or someone moves is N-COUNT
the particular route that they take. *Walk in a straight*
line.

13 A **line** is a particular route, involving the same sta- N-COUNT
tions, roads, or stops along which a train or bus ser-
vice regularly operates. *They've got to ride all the way*
to the end of the line... Stay on the Piccadilly Line. **14** A N-COUNT
railway **line** consists of the pieces of metal and wood
which form the track that the trains travel along. **15** A N-COUNT
shipping, air, or bus **line** is a company which provides
services for transporting people or goods by sea, air,
or bus. *The Foreign Office offered to pay the shipping*
line all the costs.

16 You can use **line** to refer to the edge, outline, or N-COUNT:
shape of an object or a person's body. *...the architec-* with supp
tural lines of the conservatory. LITERARY

17 A state or county **line** is a boundary between two N-COUNT
states or counties. *24-hour-a-day gambling casinos sit* AMERICAN
just over the California state line in Nevada. **18** You N-COUNT
can use **lines** to refer to the set of physical defences or
the soldiers that have been established along the
boundary of an area occupied by an army. *Their unit*
was shelling the German lines. **19** A **line** is a route, es- N-COUNT
pecially a dangerous or secret one, along which peo-
ple move or send messages or supplies. *The American*
continent's geography severely limited the lines of at-
tack. ...the guerrillas' main supply lines.

20 The particular **line** that a person or group has to- N-COUNT
wards a problem or topic is the attitude or policy that
they have towards it. *The government has taken a*
hard line against the continuing influx of Albanian
boat people. **21** You can use **line** to refer to the way in N-COUNT
which someone's thoughts or activities develop, particularly if this is logical or systematic. *What are some*
of the practical benefits likely to be of this line of re-
search? **22** If something is organized on particular N-PLURAL:
lines, or along particular **lines**, it is organized accord- on/along N
ing to that method or principle. *...reorganising old* with supp
factories to work along Japanese lines. **23** Your **line** of N-COUNT
business or work is the kind of work that you do. *So*
what was your father's line of business? **24** If someone N-SING:
says that something is your **line**, or that it is **in your** poss N
line, they mean that it is the sort of thing that you of- INFORMAL
ten do because you enjoy doing it. *Perhaps doing vol-*
untary work is more your line?

25 A **line** is a particular type of product that a compa- N-COUNT
ny makes or sells. *His best selling line is the cheapest*
lager at £1.99.

26 You can use **line** to refer to all the generations of a N-COUNT:
family, especially when you are considering the social with supp
status or the physical characteristics that the various
members inherit. *...the old Welsh royal line descended*
from Arthur and Uther Pendragon. **27** You can use N-COUNT
line when you are referring to a number of people
who are ranked according to status or seniority. *He is*
the man who stands next in line for the presidency.
28 A particular **line** of people or things is a series of N-COUNT
them that has existed over a period of time, when they
have all been similar in some way, or done similar
things. *We were part of a long line of artists.*

29 If you **line** a wall, container, or other object, you VERB: V n
put a layer of something on the inside surface of it in V n with n
order to make it stronger, warmer, or cleaner. *Bears*
tend to line their dens with leaves or grass. ♦ **-lined** *...a* COMB
dark, suede-lined case. **30** If something **lines** a con- VERB
tainer or area, especially an area inside a person, ani- V n
mal, or plant, it forms a layer on the inside surface.
...the muscles that line the intestines.

31 If something happens somewhere **along the line** PHRASE
or somewhere **down the line**, it happens during the
course of a situation or activity, often at a point that
cannot be exactly identified. *Somewhere along the*
line he picked up an engineering degree. **32** If you say PHRASE
that something happens all **down the line**, or right INFORMAL
down the line, you mean that it happens in every
case. *Democrats and Republicans differed right down*
the line on what the proper responses were.

33 If you **draw the line** at a particular activity, you re- PHRASE
fuse to do it, because you disapprove of it or because
it is more extreme than what you normally do. *They*
would draw the line at hitting an old lady. **34** If you PHRASE
draw a line between two things, you make a distinction between them. *It is, however, not possible to draw*
a distinct line between the two categories.

35 If you **drop** someone **a line**, you write to them. *My* PHRASE
phone doesn't work, so drop me a line. INFORMAL

36 If you do something or if it happens to you **in the** PHRASE
line of duty, you do it or it happens as part of your
regular work or as a result of it. *More than 3,000 police*
officers were wounded in the line of duty last year.

37 If you refer to a method as **the first line of**, for ex- PHRASE
ample, defence or treatment, you mean that it is the
first or most important method to be used in dealing
with a problem. *Passport checks will remain the first*
line of defence against terrorists.

38 If you are **in line** for something, it is likely to hap- PHRASE
pen to you or you are likely to obtain it. If something is
in line to happen, it is likely to happen. *He must be in*
line for a place in the Guinness Book of Records. **39** If PHRASE
one object is **in line** with others, or moves **into line**
with others, they are arranged in a line. *The device it-*
self was right under the vehicle, almost in line with the
gear lever. **40** If one thing is **in line** with another, or is PHRASE
brought **into line** with it, the first thing is, or becomes,
similar to the second, especially in a way that has
been agreed, planned, or expected. *The structure of*
our schools is now broadly in line with the major coun-
tries of the world. **41** If you keep someone **in line** or PHRASE
bring them **into line**, you make them obey you, or you
make them behave in the way you want them to. *All*
this was just designed to frighten me and keep me in
line.

42 If you do something **on line**, you do it using a com- PHRASE
puter or a computer network. *They can order their re-*
quirements on line. **43** If something such as your job, PHRASE
career, or reputation is **on the line**, you may lose or INFORMAL
harm it as a result of what you are doing or of the
situation you are in. *He wouldn't put his career on the*
line to help a friend.

44 If someone steps **out of line**, they disobey some- PHRASE
one or behave in an unacceptable way. *Any one of my*
players who steps out of line will be in trouble.

45 If you **read between the lines**, you understand PHRASE
what someone really means, or what is really happening in a situation, even though it is not said openly.
Reading between the lines she sensed a certain lack of
sympathy for the deceased.

46 See also **lined, lining; bottom line, branch line,**
dividing line, front line, party line, picket line, pro-
duction line. ● **to sign on the dotted line:** see **dotted.**
● **to line** your **pockets:** see **pocket.** ● **to toe the line:**
see **toe.**

line up. **1** If people **line up** or if you **line** them **up,** PHRASAL VB
they move so that they stand in a row or form a queue. ERG
The senior leaders lined up behind him in orderly V P
rows... The gym teachers lined us up against the ce- V n P
ment walls. **2** If you **line** things **up,** you move them V P noun
into a straight row. *I would line up my toys on this* Also V n P
windowsill and play. **3** If you **line** one thing **up** with RECIP-ERG
another, or one thing **lines up** with another, the first V n P with n
                                                 V P with n

thing is moved into its correct position in relation to the second. You can also say that two things **line up** or **are lined up**. *You have to line the car up with the ones beside you... I just couldn't get it to line up with the surrounding body panels. ...when the images line up exactly.* **4** If you **line up** an event or activity, you arrange for it to happen. If you **line** someone **up** for an event or activity, you arrange for them to be available for that event or activity. *She lined up executives, politicians and educators to serve on the board of directors... Bob Dylan is lining up a two-week UK tour for the New Year.* **5** If you **line up** with, behind, or alongside a person or group, you support them. *Some surprising names have lined up behind the idea.* **6** See also **line-up**.

line·age /'lɪnɪɪdʒ/ **lineages.** Someone's **lineage** is the series of families from which they are directly descended. *They can trace their lineage directly back to the 18th century.*

lin·ear /'lɪnɪə/. **1** A **linear** process or development is one in which something changes or progresses straight from one stage to another, and has a starting point and an ending point. *Her novel subverts the conventions of linear narrative. It has no neat chronology and no tidy denouement.* **2** A **linear** shape or form consists of straight lines. *...the sharp, linear designs of the Seventies and Eighties.* **3** **Linear** movement or force occurs in a straight line rather than in a curve.

lined /laɪnd/. **1** If someone's face or skin is **lined**, it has wrinkles or lines on it. *His lined face was that of an old man.* **2** **Lined** paper has lines printed across it to help you write neatly. **3** See also **line**.

'line drawing, line drawings. A **line drawing** is a drawing which consists only of lines, in which darker or lighter areas are shown by the spacing and thickness of the lines.

'line manager, line managers. Your **line manager** is the person at work who is in charge of the department, shift, or project you are working on.

lin·en /'lɪnɪn/ **linens.** **1** **Linen** is a kind of cloth that is made from a plant called flax. *...a white linen suit.* **2** **Linen** is tablecloths, napkins, sheets, pillowcases, and similar things made of cloth that are used in the house. *All linens and towels are provided.* • to **wash** your **dirty linen in public**: see **dirty**.

,line of 'sight, lines of sight. Your **line of sight** is an imaginary line that stretches between your eye and the object that you are looking at. *He was trying to keep out of the bird's line of sight.*

lin·er /'laɪnə/ **liners.** A **liner** is a large passenger ship. *...luxury ocean liners.* • See also **bin liner**.

'liner note, liner notes. The **liner notes** on record jackets are short pieces of writing that tell you something about the record or the musicians playing on the record. The British term is **sleeve note**.

lines·man /'laɪnzmən/ **linesmen.** A **linesman** is an official in games such as football and tennis who watches the boundary line of the field or court and indicates when the ball goes outside it.

'line-up, line-ups. **1** A **line-up** is a group of people or a series of things that are assembled to take part in a particular activity or event. *The programme is back for a new series with a great line-up of musicians and comedy acts.* **2** At a police **line-up**, a witness to a crime walks past a line of people in order to see if they recognize the person who committed the crime among the people in the line.

lin·ger /'lɪŋɡə/ **lingers, lingering, lingered.** **1** When something such as an idea, feeling, or illness **lingers**, it continues to exist for a long time, often much longer than expected. *The scent of her perfume lingered on in the room... He would rather be killed in a race than die a lingering death in hospital.* **2** If you **linger** somewhere, you stay there for a longer time than is necessary. *Customers are welcome to linger over coffee until around midnight. ...a dreary little town where few would choose to linger.*

lin·gerie /'lænʒəri, AM -'reɪ/. You can refer to women's underwear and nightclothes as **lingerie**.

lin·go /'lɪŋɡəʊ/ **lingos.** **1** People sometimes refer to a foreign language, especially one that they do not understand, as a **lingo**. *I don't speak the lingo.* **2** A **lingo** is a range of vocabulary or a style of language which is used in a special context or by a small group of people. *In record-business lingo, that means he wanted to buy the rights to the song and market it.*

lin·gua fran·ca /,lɪŋɡwə 'fræŋkə/. A **lingua franca** is a language or way of communicating which is used between people who do not speak one another's native language. *English is rapidly becoming the lingua franca of Asia.*

lin·guist /'lɪŋɡwɪst/ **linguists.** **1** A **linguist** is someone who is good at speaking or learning foreign languages. *Her brother was an accomplished linguist.* **2** A **linguist** is someone who studies or teaches linguistics.

lin·guis·tics /lɪŋ'gwɪstɪks/; the form **linguistic** is used as a modifier. **1** **Linguistics** is the study of the way in which language works. *Modern linguistics emerged as a distinct field in the nineteenth century.* **2** **Linguistic** abilities or ideas relate to language or linguistics. *...linguistic skills. ...linguistic theory.* ♦ **lin·guis·ti·cal·ly** /lɪŋ'gwɪstɪkli/ *Somalia is an ethnically and linguistically homogeneous nation.*

lini·ment /'lɪnɪmənt/ **liniments.** **Liniment** is a liquid that you rub into your skin in order to reduce pain or stiffness.

lin·ing /'laɪnɪŋ/ **linings.** **1** The **lining** of something such as a piece of clothing or a curtain is a layer of cloth attached to the inside of it in order to make it thicker or warmer, or in order to make it hang better. *...a padded satin jacket with quilted lining.* **2** You can use **lining** to refer to a layer of a substance that is attached to the inside of something in order to insulate or protect it. *...brake linings... Moss makes an attractive lining to wire baskets.* **3** The **lining** of your stomach or other organ is a layer of tissue on the inside of it. *...the uterine lining.* **4** See also **line**.

link /lɪŋk/ **links, linking, linked.** **1** If someone or something **links** two things or situations or if they **are linked**, there is a logical relationship between them, for example because one thing causes the other to exist or happen. *The study further strengthens the evidence linking smoking with early death... Liver cancer is linked to the hepatitis B virus.* ▶ Also a noun. *...the link between smoking and lung cancer.* • See also **index-linked**. **2** If two places or objects **are linked** or something **links** them, there is a physical connection between them. *...the Rama Road, which links the capital, Managua, with the Caribbean coast:. ...the Channel Tunnel linking Britain and France.* ▶ Also a noun. *Stalin insisted that the radio link with the German Foreign Ministry should remain open.* **3** A **link** between two people, organizations, or places is a friendly or business connection between them. *Kiev hopes to cement close links with Bonn... A cabinet minister came under investigation for links to the Mafia.* **4** A **link** to another person or organization is something that allows you to communicate with them or have contact with them. *She was my only link with the past... The Red Cross was created to provide a link between soldiers in battle and their families at home.* **5** If you **link** one person or thing to another, you claim that there is a relationship or connection between them. *Criminologist Dr Ann Jones has linked the crime to social circumstances.* **6** A **link** is one of the rings in a chain. *I had to shorten my chain by several links.* **7** If you **link** one thing with another, you join them by putting one thing through the other. *He linked the fingers of his hands together on his gross stomach.* • If two or more people **link arms**, or if one person **links arms** with another, they stand next to each other, and each person puts their arm round the arm of the person next to them. *She*

stayed with them, linking arms with the two girls, joking with the boys. **8** See also **link-up.**

link up. 1 If you **link up** with someone, you join them for a particular purpose. *The Russian and American armies linked up for the first time on the banks of the river Elbe.* **2** If one thing **is linked up to** another, the two things are connected to each other. *The television screens of the next century will be linked up to an emerging world telecommunications grid.*

link·age /'lɪŋkɪdʒ/ **linkages. 1** A **linkage** between two things is a link or connection between them. The **linkage** of two things is the act of linking or connecting them. *No one disputes the direct linkage between the unemployment rate and crime. ...the creation of new research materials by the linkage of previously existing sources.* **2 Linkage** is a process in international diplomacy where one country agrees to do something only if another country agrees to do something in return. *There could be no linkage with other Mideast problems.*

'link-up, link-ups. 1 A **link-up** is a connection between two machines or communication systems. *...a live satellite link-up with Bonn.* **2** A **link-up** is a relationship or partnership between two organizations. *The US airline has just announced a formal link-up with British Airways.*

lino /'laɪnəʊ/. **Lino** is the same as **linoleum.** *...the dirty lino on the floor of the kitchen.*

li·no·leum /lɪ'nəʊliəm/. **Linoleum** is a floor covering which is made of cloth covered with a hard shiny substance. *...a gray linoleum floor.*

lin·seed oil /'lɪnsiːd ɔɪl/. **Linseed oil** is an oil made from flax seeds. It is used to make paints and inks, or to protect wooden surfaces.

lint /lɪnt/. **Lint** consists of small unwanted particles of fluff that collects on clothes.

lin·tel /'lɪntəl/ **lintels.** A **lintel** is a piece of stone or wood over a door or window which supports the bricks above it.

lion /'laɪən/ **lions.** A **lion** is a large wild member of the cat family that is found in Africa. Lions have yellowish fur, and male lions have long hair on their head and neck. See picture headed **animals.**

li·on·ess /'laɪənɪs/ **lionesses.** A **lioness** is a female lion. See picture headed **animals.**

li·on·ize /'laɪənaɪz/ **lionizes, lionizing, lionized;** also spelled **lionise** in British English. If someone **is lionized,** they are treated as if they are very important or special, often when they do not really deserve to be. *The press began to lionize him enthusiastically... In 1936, Max Schmeling had been lionised as boxing's great hope.*

'lion's share. If a person, group, or project gets the **lion's share** of something, they get the largest part of it. *The lion's share of the work will go to American companies.*

lip /lɪp/ **lips. 1** Your **lips** are the two outer parts of the edge of your mouth. See picture headed **human body.** *The tip of Ellen's tongue shows between her lips.* ♦ **-lipped** /-lɪpt/. *A thin-lipped smile spread over the captain's face.* ● See also **tight-lipped. 2** The **lip** of something such as a container or a high area of land is its edge. *...the lip of the jug. ...the lip of Mount Etna's smouldering crater.*

3 If you **bite your lip,** you try very hard not to show your anger or distress. *She bit her lip as she recalled the words he'd thrown at her.* **4** If you **lick your lips,** you move your tongue across your lips as you think about or taste something pleasant. *They licked their lips in anticipation.* **5** If you say that something is **on everyone's lips,** you mean that a lot of people are talking about it. *He is the guy whose name is on everyone's lips at the moment.* **6** If you tell someone that your **lips are sealed,** you are promising them that you will keep a secret that they have told you. *I shall reveal all, but until then my lips are sealed.* **7** If you say that someone is keeping a **stiff upper lip,** you mean that they are not showing any emotion even though it is difficult for them not to.

lipo·suc·tion /'lɪpəʊsʌkʃən/. **Liposuction** is a form of cosmetic surgery where fat is removed from under the skin by dissolving it with chemicals and then sucking it out with a tube.

lip-read, lip-reads, lip-reading. The form **lip-read** is pronounced /'lɪpriːd/ when it is the present tense, and /'lɪpred/ when it is the past tense and past participle. If someone can **lip-read,** they can understand what someone else is saying by looking at the way the other person's lips move as they speak, without actually hearing them. *They are not given hearing aids or taught to lip-read.* ♦ **lip-read·ing** *The teacher should not move around too much as this makes lip reading more difficult.*

'lip service. If you say that someone pays **lip service** to an idea, you are critical of them because they say they are in favour of it, but do nothing to support it. *Unhappily, he had done no more than pay lip service to their views.*

lip·stick /'lɪpstɪk/ **lipsticks. Lipstick** is a coloured substance in the form of a stick which women put on their lips. *She was wearing red lipstick.* ► A **lipstick** is a small tube containing this substance.

liq·ue·fy /'lɪkwɪfaɪ/ **liquefies, liquefying, liquefied.** When a gas or solid substance **liquefies** or is **liquefied,** it changes its form and becomes liquid. *You can liquefy the carbon dioxide to separate it from the other constituents.*

li·queur /lɪ'kjʊə, AM -'kɜːr/ **liqueurs. 1** A **liqueur** is a strong alcoholic drink with a sweet taste. ► A **liqueur** is a glass of liqueur. **2 Liqueurs** are a type of chocolate. They contain a sweet substance that has the flavour of an alcoholic liqueur.

liq·uid /'lɪkwɪd/ **liquids. 1** A **liquid** is a substance which is not solid but which flows and can be poured, for example water. *Boil for 20 minutes until the liquid has reduced by half... Solids turn to liquids at certain temperatures.* **2** A **liquid** substance is in the form of a liquid rather than being solid or a gas. *Wash in warm water with liquid detergent. ...liquid nitrogen.* **3 Liquid** assets are the things that a person or company owns which can be quickly turned into cash if necessary. *The bank had sufficient liquid assets to continue operations.* ♦ **li·quid·ity** /lɪ'kwɪdɪti/. *The company maintains a high degree of liquidity.*

liq·ui·date /'lɪkwɪdeɪt/ **liquidates, liquidating, liquidated. 1** To **liquidate** a company is to close it down and sell all its assets, usually because it is in debt. *A unanimous vote was taken to liquidate the company.* ♦ **liq·ui·da·tion** /,lɪkwɪ'deɪʃən/ **liquidations** *The company went into liquidation.* ♦ **liq·ui·da·tor** /'lɪkwɪdeɪtə/ **liquidators** *The firm has been passed into the hands of liquidators.* **2** If a company **liquidates** its assets, its property is sold in order to get money. *The company closed down operations and began liquidating its assets in January.* **3** If someone powerful **liquidates** people, they get rid of them, usually by killing them. *They have not hesitated in the past to liquidate their rivals.*

'liquid crystal, liquid crystals. A **liquid crystal** is a liquid that has some of the qualities of crystals, for example reflecting light from different directions in different ways.

,liquid crystal dis'play, liquid crystal displays. A **liquid crystal display** is a display of information on a screen, which uses liquid crystals that become visible when electricity is passed through them.

liq·uid·ize /'lɪkwɪdaɪz/ **liquidizes, liquidizing, liquidized;** also spelled **liquidise** in British English. If you **liquidize** food, you process it using an electrical appliance in order to make it into a pulp.

liq·uid·iz·er /'lɪkwɪdaɪzə/ **liquidizers;** also spelled **liquidiser.** A **liquidizer** is an electric machine that you use to liquidize food. The usual American word is **blender.**

liq·uor /'lɪkə/ **liquors.** Alcoholic drink such as whisky, vodka, and gin can be referred to as **liquor.**

The British term is **spirits**. ...*a liquor store. ...intoxicating liquors.*

liquo·rice /ˈlɪkərɪʃ, -ɪs/; also spelled **licorice**. **Liquorice** is a firm black substance with a strong taste. It is used for making sweets. *N-UNCOUNT*

lira /ˈlɪərə/ **lire** /ˈlɪərə/. The **lira** is the unit of money that is used in Italy. Turkey and Syria also have a unit of money called a **lira**. ◆◇◇◇◇ *N-COUNT*

lisp /lɪsp/ **lisps, lisping, lisped. 1** If someone has a **lisp**, they pronounce the sounds 's' and 'z' as if they were 'th'. For example, they say 'thing' instead of 'sing'. **2** If someone **lisps** or if they **lisp** something, they say something with a lisp. *Bochmann lisped his congratulations.* *N-COUNT* / *VERB: V / V n*

list /lɪst/ **lists, listing, listed. 1** A **list** of things such as names or addresses is a set of them which all belong to a particular category, written down one below the other. *There were six names on the list. ...fine wine from the hotel's exhaustive wine list.* **2** A **list** of things such as events or priorities is a set of them that you think of as being in the same category and as being in a particular order. *High on the list of public demands is to end military control of broadcasting... 'First City' joined a long list of failed banks.* **3** To **list** several things such as reasons or names means to write or say them one after another, usually in a particular order. *Ingredients are listed in order of the amount used.* **4** To **list** something in a particular way means to include it in that way in a list or report. *A medical examiner has listed the deaths as homicides... He was not listed under his real name on the residents panel.* **5** See also **listed, listing; civil list, hit list, honours list, laundry list, mailing list, shopping list, waiting list.** **6** If something, especially a ship, **lists**, it leans over to one side. *The ship listed again, and she was thrown back across the bunk.* ◆◆◆◆◆ *N-COUNT / N-COUNT / VERB: V n / be V-ed / VERB / V n prep / VERB / V / TECHNICAL*

list·ed /ˈlɪstɪd/. A **listed** building is protected by law against being demolished or altered because it is historically or architecturally important. *...a Grade II Listed 17th century farmhouse.* *ADJ / BRITISH*

lis·ten /ˈlɪsən/ **listens, listening, listened. 1** If you **listen** to someone who is talking or to a sound, you give your attention to them or it. *Sonia was not listening.* ♦ **lis·ten·er, listeners** One or two listeners had fallen asleep while the President was speaking. **2** If you **listen** for a sound, you keep alert and are ready to hear it if it occurs. *They're both asleep upstairs, but you don't mind listening just in case of trouble, do you?* ▶ **Listen out** means the same as **listen**. *I didn't really listen out for the lyrics... Listen out and we'll see what we can find out.* **3** If you **listen** to someone, you do what they advise you to do, or you believe them. *When I asked him to stop, he would not listen.* **4** You say **listen** when you want someone to pay attention to you because you are going to say something important. *Listen, I finish at one.* ◆◆◆◆◇ *VERB: V / V ton / N-COUNT / VERB: V for n / V / PHRASAL VB / V P for n / V P / VERB: V ton / V / CONVENTION / PRAGMATICS*

listen in. If you **listen in** to a private conversation, you secretly listen to it. *He assigned federal agents to listen in on Martin Luther King's phone calls.* *PHRASAL VB / V P to/on n / Also V P*

lis·ten·er /ˈlɪsnə/ **listeners. 1** A **listener** is a person who listens to the radio or to a particular radio programme. *I'm a regular listener to her show.* **2** If you describe someone as a good **listener**, you mean that they listen carefully and sympathetically to you when you talk. *Dr Brian was a good listener.* **3** See also **listen.** ◆◇◇◇◇ *N-COUNT / N-COUNT: adj N*

list·ing /ˈlɪstɪŋ/ **listings.** A **listing** is a published list, or an item in a published list. *A full listing of the companies will be published quarterly.* ◆◆◇◇◇ *N-COUNT*

list·less /ˈlɪstləs/. Someone who is **listless** has no energy or enthusiasm. *He was listless and pale and wouldn't eat much.* ♦ **list·less·ly** Usually, you would just sit listlessly, too hot to do anything. ◆◇◇◇◇ *ADJ-GRADED / ADV-GRADED: ADV with v*

,list 'price, list prices. The **list price** of an item is the price which the manufacturer suggests that a shopkeeper should charge for it. *N-COUNT*

lit /lɪt/. **Lit** is a past tense and past participle of **light**.

lita·ny /ˈlɪtəni/ **litanies. 1** If you describe what someone says, especially when it is a long list of things, as a **litany**, you mean that you have often heard it repeated, and you think it is boring or insincere. *She remained in the doorway, listening to his litany of complaints against her client.* **2** A **litany** is part of a church service in which the priest says a set group of words and the people reply, also using a set group of words. ◆◇◇◇◇ *N-COUNT / PRAGMATICS / N-COUNT*

li·ter /ˈliːtə/. See **litre**.

lit·era·cy /ˈlɪtərəsi/. **Literacy** is the ability to read and write. *Many adults have some problems with literacy and numeracy.* ◆◇◇◇◇ *N-UNCOUNT*

lit·er·al /ˈlɪtərəl/. **1** The **literal** sense of a word or phrase is its most basic sense. *In many cases, the people there are fighting, in a literal sense, for their homes.* **2** A **literal** translation is one in which you translate each word of the original work rather than giving the meaning of each expression or sentence using words that sound natural. *A literal translation of the name Tapies is 'walls'.* ♦ **lit·er·al·ly 2** *The word 'volk' translates literally as 'folk'.* **3** You use **literal** to describe someone who uses or understands words in a plain and simple way. *Dennis is a very literal person.* ◆◇◇◇◇ *ADJ / ADJ / ADV / ADV-GRADED*

lit·er·al·ly /ˈlɪtərəli/. **1** You can use **literally** to emphasize a word or expression which is being used in a creative way to exaggerate a situation. Some careful speakers of English think that this use is incorrect. *We've got to get the economy under control or it will literally eat us up... The views are literally breath-taking.* **2** You use **literally** to emphasize that what you are saying is true, even though it seems exaggerated or surprising. *I literally crawled to the car.* **3** If you **take** something **literally**, you think that a word or expression is being used with its most simple or basic meaning. *If you tell a person to 'step on it' or 'throw on your coat', they may take you literally, with disastrous consequences.* ◆◆◇◇◇ *ADV / PRAGMATICS / ADV / PRAGMATICS / PHRASE*

lit·er·ary /ˈlɪtərəri, AM -reri/. **1 Literary** means concerned with or connected with the writing, study, or appreciation of literature. *She's the literary editor of the 'Sunday Review'. ...a literary masterpiece.* **2 Literary** words and expressions are often unusual in some way and are used to create a special effect in a piece of writing such as a poem, speech, or novel. ◆◆◆◇◇ *ADJ / ADJ-GRADED*

lit·er·ate /ˈlɪtərət/. **1** Someone who is **literate** is able to read and write. *Over one-quarter of the adult population are not fully literate.* **2** If you describe someone as **literate**, you mean that they are intelligent and well-educated, especially about literature and the arts. *Scientists should be literate and articulate as well as able to handle figures.* **3** If you describe someone as **literate** in a particular subject, you mean that they have a good knowledge and understanding of that subject. *Head teachers need to be financially literate.* ● See also **computer-literate**. ◆◇◇◇◇ *ADJ / ADJ-GRADED / ADJ-GRADED*

lit·era·ti /ˌlɪtəˈrɑːti/. **Literati** are well-educated people who are interested in literature; often used showing disapproval. *That Walter Scott was a fervent Tory is something of an embarrassment to the leftist literati.* *N-PLURAL*

lit·era·ture /ˈlɪtrətʃə, AM -tərətʃʊr/ **literatures. 1** Novels, plays, and poetry are referred to as **literature**, especially when they are considered to have artistic merit. *...a Professor of English Literature... I have spent my life getting to know diverse literatures of different epochs.* **2** The **literature** on a particular subject are the books and articles that have been published about it. *The literature on immigration policy is almost unrelievedly critical of the state.* **3 Literature** is written information produced by people who want to sell you something or give you advice. *Some companies have toned down the claims on their promotional literature.* ◆◆◆◇◇ *N-VAR / N-UNCOUNT / N-UNCOUNT*

lithe /laɪð/. A **lithe** person is able to move and bend their body easily and gracefully. *His walk was lithe and graceful.* *ADJ-GRADED*

lithograph

644

li·tho·graph /'lɪθəɡrɑːf, -ɡræf/ **lithographs.** A **lithograph** is a picture made by printing with a piece of stone or metal which has been specially treated so that inks sticks to some parts of it and not to others. **N-COUNT**

liti·gant /'lɪtɪɡənt/ **litigants.** A **litigant** is a person involved in fighting or defending a civil lawsuit. **N-COUNT LEGAL**

liti·gate /'lɪtɪɡeɪt/ **litigates, litigating, litigated.** To **litigate** means to take legal action. ...*the cost of litigating personal injury claims in the county court.* **VERB: V n LEGAL**
♦ **liti·ga·tion** /ˌlɪtɪ'ɡeɪʃən/. ...*more than four years of litigation on behalf of the residents.* **N-UNCOUNT**

liti·ga·tor /'lɪtɪɡeɪtə/ **litigators.** A **litigator** is a lawyer who helps someone take legal action. **N-COUNT**

li·ti·gious /lɪ'tɪdʒəs/. Someone who is **litigious** often makes formal complaints about people to a civil court of law. *People remained litigious, ready to sue.* **ADJ-GRADED FORMAL**

lit·mus test /'lɪtməs test/ **litmus tests.** If you say that something is a **litmus test** of a particular thing, you mean that it is an effective and conclusive way of proving it or measuring it. *Ending the fighting must be the absolute priority, the litmus test of the agreements' validity.* **N-COUNT**

li·tre /'liːtə/ **litres;** spelled **liter** in American English. A **litre** is a metric unit of volume that is a thousand cubic centimetres. It is equal to 1.76 British pints or 2.11 American pints. ...*15 litres of water. ...a Ford Escort with a 1.9-litre engine.* ♦♦◇◇◇ **N-COUNT**

lit·ter /'lɪtə/ **litters, littering, littered. 1** Litter is rubbish that is left lying around outside. *If you see litter in the corridor, pick it up.* **2** If a number of things **litter** a place, they are scattered around untidily on or in it. *Glass from broken bottles litters the pavement.* ▶ Also a noun. *He pushed aside the litter of books and papers and laid two places at the table.* ♦♦◇◇◇ **N-UNCOUNT** **VERB V n** **N-UNCOUNT**
♦ **lit·tered** *Concrete purpose-built resorts are littered across the mountainsides... Debris was littered over the race track.* **3** If you say that something such as history or someone's speech is **littered with** something, you mean that there are many examples of the second thing in the first. *Charles' speech is littered with lots of marketing buzzwords like 'package' and 'product'.* **4** A **litter** is a group of animals born to the same mother at the same time. ...*a litter of pups.* **ADJ: v-link ADJ** **prep ADJ: v-link ADJ with n** **N-COUNT**

litter bin, litter bins. A **litter bin** is a container, usually in a street, park, or public building, into which people can put rubbish. **N-COUNT BRITISH**

little 1 determiner, quantifier, and adverb uses

lit·tle /'lɪtəl/. **1** You use **little** to indicate that there is only a very small amount of something. You can use 'so', 'too', and 'very' in front of **little**. *I find that I need very little sleep these days... There is little doubt that a diet high in fibre is more satisfying.* ▶ Also a quantifier. *They claim that little of the $16.5 million in aid sent by the US government has reached them.* ▶ Also a pronoun. *Little is known about his childhood.* **2** **Little** means not very often or to only a small extent. *On their way back to Marseille they spoke very little.* **3** A **little** of something is a small amount of it, but not very much. You can also say a **very little**. *A little food would do us all some good... I shall be only a very little time.* ▶ Also a pronoun. *They get paid for it. Not much. Just a little.* ▶ Also a quantifier. *Pour a little of the sauce over the chicken.* **4** A **little** or a **little bit** means to a small extent or degree or for a short period. *He walked a little by himself in the garden... He was a little bit afraid of his father's reaction.* **5** If something happens **little by little**, it happens very gradually. *In the beginning he had felt well, but little by little he was becoming weaker.* ♦♦♦♦♦ **DET** **QUANT** **PRON** **ADV-GRADED: ADV with v** **DET** **PRON** **QUANT** **ADV-GRADED: ADV after v, ADV adj/adv** **PHRASE**

little 2 adjective uses

lit·tle /'lɪtəl/ **littler, littlest.** The comparative **littler** and the superlative **littlest** are sometimes used in spoken English for meanings 1, 3, and 4, but otherwise the comparative and superlative forms of the adjective **little** are not used. ♦♦♦♦♦
1 **Little** things are small in size. **Little** is slightly more informal than **small**. *We sat around a little table, eat-* **ADJ-GRADED**

ing and drinking wine. ...the little group of art students. **2** You use **little** to indicate that someone or something is small, in a pleasant and attractive way. ...*a little old lady... James usually drives a little Citroen hatchback.* **3** A **little** child is young. *When I was little I was very hyper-active.* **4** Your **little** sister or brother is younger than you are. **5** A **little** distance, period of time, or event is short in length. *Just go down the road a little way, turn left, and cross the bridge... Why don't we just wait a little while and see what happens.* **6** A **little** sound or gesture is quick. *He turned with a little nod and I watched him walk away.* **7** You use **little** to indicate that something is not serious or important. *Harry found himself getting angry over little things that had never bothered him before.* **ADJ: ADJ n** **PRAGMATICS** **ADJ-GRADED ADJ: ADJ n** **ADJ-GRADED: ADJ n** **ADJ-GRADED: ADJ n** **ADJ: ADJ n**

little 'finger, little fingers. Your **little finger** is the smallest finger on your hand. ♦◇◇◇◇ **N-COUNT**

lit·to·ral /'lɪtərəl/ **littorals.** The area near a sea coast is sometimes referred to as the **littoral**. ...*the littoral countries of the Persian Gulf.* **N-COUNT TECHNICAL**

li·tur·gi·cal /lɪ'tɜːdʒɪkəl/. **Liturgical** things are used in or relate to church services. ...*Jewish liturgical music.* **ADJ FORMAL**

lit·ur·gy /'lɪtədʒi/ **liturgies.** A **liturgy** is a particular form of religious service, usually one that is set and approved by a branch of the Christian Church. ...*the many similarities in ministry, liturgy and style between the two churches.* **N-VAR**

live 1 verb uses

live /lɪv/ **lives, living, lived. 1** If someone **lives in** a particular place or with a particular person, their home is in that place or with that person. *She has lived here for 10 years... She always said I ought to live alone... He still lives with his parents.* **2** If you say that someone **lives** in particular circumstances or that they **live** a particular kind of life, you mean that they are in those circumstances or that they have that kind of life. *We lived quite grandly... We can start living a normal life again now.* ♦♦♦♦♦ **VERB V adv/prep** **VERB V adv/prep V n**
3 To **live** means to be alive, especially after a particular event or point in time. If you say that someone **lives** to a particular age, or to see a particular event, you mean that they stay alive until they are that age or until that event happens. *He's got a terrible disease and will not live long... He lived to see his first grandson... They both lived to a ripe old age... Ian was her only living relative.* **4** If people **live by** doing a particular activity, they get the money, food, or clothing they need by doing that activity. ...*the last indigenous people to live by hunting. ...professional criminals who lived by crime.* **5** If you say that someone **lives for** a particular thing, you mean that it is the most important thing in their life. *Laura lived for those kids.* **6** If a person or occasion **lives** in someone's mind or in history, they are remembered for ever or for a long time because they are significant or important. *The memory of that will live with me for many years to come... The name of Hawker deserves to live in the history of aviation.* ▶ **Live on** means the same as **live.** *Lenin lives on in the minds and hearts of millions of people.* **7** See also **living.** **VERB V adv V to-inf V ton V-ing** **VB: no cont V by-ing/n** **VERB: V forn** **VB: no cont V with n V in n** **PHRASAL VB V P in n Also V P**
8 If you say that someone **lives and breathes** a particular subject or activity, you are emphasizing that they are extremely enthusiastic about it. *'I live and breathe the business,' he says. 'I'm not here to be second best.'* **9** If you tell someone that they **haven't lived** unless they experience a particular thing, you are telling them that thing is extremely good and should be experienced. *You haven't lived until you've used their new micro system.* **10** You can use expressions such as **to live in fear** and **to live in terror** to indicate that someone is always thinking about an unpleasant or frightening event, because they think that it might happen. *One in 10 Californians is unemployed and thousands more live in fear of losing their jobs.* **11** You say **live and let live** as a way of saying that you should let other people behave in the way that they want to and not criticize them for behaving differently from you. *The Smiths have a liberal live and let live attitude.* **12** If you **live it up**, you have a very enjoyable and **PHRASE PRAGMATICS** **PHRASE** **PHRASE** **CONVENTION PRAGMATICS** **PHRASE**

exciting time, for example by going to lots of parties or spending lots of money. **13 •** to **live hand to mouth**: see **hand**. **•** to **live a lie**: see **lie**. **•** to **live beyond** your **means**: see **means**. **•** to **live in sin**: see **sin**. *INFORMAL*

live by. If you **live by** particular standards or rules, you behave in the way that those standards or rules say that you should. *He expected those around him to live by his own superhuman standards.* PHRASAL VB VP n

live down. If you are unable to **live down** a mistake, failure, or bad reputation, you are unable to make people forget about it. *Labor was also unable to live down its reputation as the party of high taxes... I thought I'd never live it down.* PHRASAL VB VP noun V n P

live off. If you **live off** another person, you rely on them to provide you with money. *...a man who all his life had lived off his father.* PHRASAL VB VP n

live on or **live off. 1** If you **live on** or **live off** a particular amount of money, you have that amount of money to buy things. *Most students are unable to live on £3000 per year.* **2** If you **live on** or **live off** a particular source of income, that is where you get the money that you need. *He's been living off state benefits.* **3** If an animal, plant, or bacterium **lives on** or **lives off** a particular food, this is the kind of food that it eats to stay alive. *...white rot fungus, a common organism that lives on dead wood.* **4** If you say that a person **lives on** or **lives off** a particular kind of food, you mean that it is, or seems to be, the only thing that they eat. *The children live on chips.* PHRASAL VB VP amount VP n VP n

live on. 1 See **live** 6. **2** If someone or something **lives on** after a person has died, they continue to be alive or exist, and to remind people of that person. PHRASAL VB VP

live out. 1 If you **live out** your life in a particular place or in particular circumstances, you stay in that place or in those circumstances until the end of your life or until the end of a particular period of your life. *Gein did not stand trial but lived out his days in a mental asylum.* **2** If you **live out** a dream, fantasy, or idea, you do the things that you have thought about. *He began living out his rock 'n' roll fantasy.* PHRASAL VB VP noun Also V n P VP noun Also V n P

live through. If you **live through** an unpleasant event or change, you experience it and survive. *We are too young to have lived through the war.* PHRASAL VB VP n

live together. If two people are not married but live in the same house and have a sexual relationship, you can say that they **live together**. PHRASAL VB VP

live up to. If someone or something **lives up to** what they were expected or desired to be or do, they are as good as they were expected or desired to be. *Sales have not lived up to expectations this year.* PHRASAL VB VP P n

live 2 adjective uses

live /laɪv/. **1 Live** animals or plants are alive, rather than being dead or artificial. *...a protest against the company's tests on live animals.* **2** You use **real live** to say that someone or something is present or exists, when you want to indicate that you think this is exciting and unusual or unexpected. *He had never met a real live admiral.* ADJ: ADJ n PHRASE INFORMAL

3 A **live** television or radio programme is one in which an event or performance is broadcast at exactly the same time as it happens, rather than being recorded first. ► Also an adverb. *It was broadcast live in 50 countries... We'll be going live to Nottingham later in this bulletin.* **4** A **live** performance is given in front of an audience, rather than being recorded and then broadcast or shown in a film. *A live audience will pose the questions.* ► Also an adverb. *Kat Bjelland has been playing live with her new band... She's much happier performing live than in a recording studio.* **5** A **live** album is an album which has on it a recording of a band playing in a concert, rather than in a recording studio. **6** A **live** wire or piece of electrical equipment is directly connected to a source of electricity. **7 Live** bullets are made of metal, rather than rubber or plastic, and are intended to kill people. *They trained in the jungle using live ammunition.* **8** A **live** bomb or missile is one which has not yet exploded. ADJ ADV: ADV after v ADJ ADV: ADV after v ADJ ADJ ADJ ADJ

live-in /ˌlɪv ˈɪn/. **1** A **live-in** partner is someone who lives in the same house as the person they are having a sexual relationship with, but is not married ◆◆◆◇◇ ADJ: ADJ n

---

to them. **2** A **live-in** nanny or servant sleeps and eats in the house where they work. ADJ: ADJ n

live·li·hood /ˈlaɪvlihʊd/ **livelihoods.** Your livelihood is the job or other source of income which gives you the money to buy the things that you need in your daily life. *...fishermen who depend on the seas for their livelihood.* ◆◇◇◇◇ N-VAR

live·ly /ˈlaɪvli/ **livelier, liveliest. 1** You can describe someone as **lively** when they behave in an enthusiastic and cheerful way. **♦ live·li·ness** *Amy could sense his liveliness even from where she stood.* **2** A **lively** event or a **lively** discussion, for example, has lots of interesting and exciting things happening or being said in it. *It turned out to be a very interesting session with a lively debate.* **♦ liveliness** *Some may enjoy the liveliness of such a restaurant.* **3** Someone who has a **lively** mind is intelligent and interested in a lot of different things. A **lively** feeling or awareness is a strong and enthusiastic one. *The papers also show a lively interest in European developments.* ◆◆◇◇◇ ADJ-GRADED N-UNCOUNT ADJ-GRADED N-UNCOUNT ADJ-GRADED ADJ-GRADED: ADJ n

liv·en /ˈlaɪvən/ **livens, livening, livened.**
liven up. 1 If a place or event **livens up**, or if something **livens** it **up**, it becomes more interesting and exciting. *How could we decorate the room to liven it up?... The arena livens up only on Saturdays and Sundays when a flea market is open there.* **2** If people **liven up**, or if something **livens** them **up**, they become more cheerful and energetic. *Talking about her daughters livens her up... George livens up after midnight, relaxing a little.* PHRASAL VB ERG VnP VP Also V P noun ERG VnP VP

liv·er /ˈlɪvə/ **livers. 1** Your **liver** is a large organ in your body which processes your blood and helps to clean unwanted substances out of it. **2** Liver is the liver of some animals, especially lambs, pigs, and cows, which is cooked and eaten. ◆◆◇◇◇ N-COUNT N-VAR

liv·ery /ˈlɪvəri/ **liveries. 1** A servant's **livery** is the special uniform that he or she wears. *...a butler in pale blue livery.* **♦ liv·eried** *The tea was served to guests by liveried footmen.* **2** The **livery** of a particular company is the special design or set of colours associated with it that is put on its products and possessions. *...buffet cars in the company's bright red and yellow livery.* ◆◇◇◇◇ N-VAR ADJ: ADJ n N-COUNT

lives. 1 Lives, pronounced /laɪvz/, is the plural of **life. 2** Lives, pronounced /lɪvz/, is the third person singular of the present tense of **live**.

live·stock /ˈlaɪvstɒk/. Animals such as cattle and sheep which are kept on a farm are referred to as **livestock**. ◆◇◇◇◇ N-COLL-UNCOUNT

live wire /ˌlaɪv ˈwaɪə/ **live wires.** If you describe someone as a **live wire**, you mean that they are lively and energetic. N-COUNT INFORMAL

liv·id /ˈlɪvɪd/. **1** Someone who is **livid** is extremely angry. *I am absolutely livid about it... She is livid that I have invited Dick.* **2** Something that is **livid** is an unpleasant dark colour. *The scarred side of his face was a livid red.* ADJ-GRADED INFORMAL ADJ-GRADED

liv·ing /ˈlɪvɪŋ/ **livings. 1** The work that you do for a **living** is the work that you do in order to earn the money that you need. *He earns his living doing all kinds of things.* **•** If you say that someone **scrapes a living** or **scratches a living**, you mean that they just manage to earn enough to live on, but it is very difficult. **2** You use **living** when you are talking about the quality of people's daily lives. *Olivia has always been a model of healthy living. ...the stresses of urban living.* **3** The **living** area of a house is the part where people sit and relax. *The spacious living quarters were on the second floor.* **4** The **living** are people who are alive, rather than people who have died. **5 •** living proof: see **proof**. **•** in living memory: see **memory**. ◆◆◆◇◇ N-COUNT PHRASE N-UNCOUNT: with supp ADJ: ADJ n N-PLURAL: the N

'living room, living rooms; also spelled **living-room**. The **living room** in a house is the room where people sit and relax. See picture headed **house and flat**. ◆◆◇◇◇ N-COUNT

'living standard, living standards. Living standards refers to the level of comfort in which people live, which usually depends on how much ◆◇◇◇◇ N-COUNT

money they have. *Cheaper housing would vastly improve the living standards of ordinary people.*

living 'wage. A **living wage** is a wage which is just sufficient to enable you to buy food, clothing, and other necessary things. *Many farmers have to depend on subsidies to make a living wage.* — N-SING

liz·ard /ˈlɪzəd/ **lizards.** A **lizard** is a reptile with short legs and a long tail. — ◆◇◇◇◇ N-COUNT

-'ll /-əl/. **'ll** is the short form of 'will' or 'shall' used in spoken English and informal written English. *I'll tell you what I think.*

lla·ma /ˈlɑːmə/ **llamas.** A **llama** is a South American animal with thick hair, which looks like a small camel without a hump. — N-COUNT

lo /ləʊ/. **Lo and behold** or **lo** is used to emphasize a surprising event that is about to be mentioned, or to emphasize in an ironic way that something is not surprising at all. — ◆◇◇◇◇ CONVENTION PRAGMATICS

load /ləʊd/ **loads, loading, loaded. 1** If you **load** a vehicle or a container, or if you **load** things into or onto it, you put a large quantity of things or heavy things into or onto it. *The three men seemed to have finished loading the truck... Mr. Dambar had loaded his plate with lasagne... They load all their equipment into backpacks... She deposited the loaded tray.* ► **Load up** means the same as **load**. *The giggling couple loaded up their red sports car and drove off... She loaded up his collection of vintage wines into crates.* ♦ **load·ing** *...the loading of baggage onto international flights.* **2** A **load** is something, usually a large quantity or heavy object, which is being carried. *He drove by with a big load of hay.* **3** A **load** is a quantity of clothes or sheets which need washing and which are washed together in a washing machine. **4** You can refer to the amount of work you have to do as a **load**. *She's taking some of the load off the secretaries.* **5** The **load** on something is the amount of weight that is pressing down on it or the amount of strain that it is under. *High blood pressure imposes an extra load on the heart.* **6** The **load** of a system or computer is the extent to which it is being used at a particular time. — ◆◆◇◇◇ VERB: V n, V n into/onto n, V-ed | PHRASAL VB: V n P, V P noun | N-SING | N-COUNT | N-COUNT | N-SING | N-COUNT

7 A **load of** something or **loads of** it is a large amount of it. A **load of** people or things or **loads of** them is a large number of them. *I've got loads of money... I used to read loads of Asterix books.* ● You can use **a load of** to refer to a thing or a group of things or people which you do not like. For example, if you say that something is **a load of rubbish**, you are emphasizing that you think it is no good at all or not true at all. — QUANT INFORMAL | PHRASE PRAGMATICS INFORMAL

8 When someone **loads** a weapon such as a gun, they put a bullet or missile in it so that it is ready to use. *He carried a loaded gun.* **9** When someone **loads** a camera or other piece of equipment or when they **load** film, tape, or data into it, they put film, tape, or data into it so that it is ready to use. *A photographer from the newspaper was loading his camera with film.* **10** See also **loaded**. — VERB: V n, V-ed | VERB: V n, V n with n, Also V n into/onto/on n

load down. If you **load** someone **down** with things, especially heavy things, you give them a large number of them. *They had come up from London loaded down with six suitcases.* — PHRASAL VB V n P with n, V-ed P, Also V P

load up. See load 1. — PHRASAL VB

-load /-ləʊd/ **-loads.** **-load** is used to form nouns that refer to the total amount of something that a particular vehicle or container can hold or carry. *...a lorry-load of sheep.* — COMB

load·ed /ˈləʊdɪd/. **1** A **loaded** question or word has more meaning or purpose than it appears to have, because the person who uses it hopes it will cause people to respond in a particular way. *...the loaded word 'sexist'.* **2** If something is **loaded** with a particular characteristic, it has that characteristic to a very great degree. *The President's visit is loaded with symbolic significance.* **3** If you say that something is **loaded** in favour of someone or something, you mean it works unfairly to their advantage. If you say it is **loaded** against them, you mean it works unfairly to their disadvantage. *The article was heavily loaded against Morrissey.* — ◆◆◇◇◇ ADJ-GRADED | ADJ-GRADED | ADJ-GRADED PRAGMATICS

loaf /ləʊf/ **loaves; loafs, loafing, loafed.** **Loaves** is the plural of the noun. **Loafs** is the third person singular present tense of the verb. **1** A **loaf** of bread is bread which has been shaped and baked in one piece. It is usually large enough for more than one person and can be cut into slices. **2** If you **loaf**, you stand or wait in a place, not doing anything interesting or useful. ► **Loaf around** means the same as **loaf**. *We had been at Cambridge together, she studying medicine and me loafing around.* — ◆◇◇◇◇ N-COUNT | VERB: V | PHRASAL VB V P

loaf·er /ˈləʊfə/ **loafers.** **Loafers** are flat slip-on shoes, usually made of leather. — N-COUNT

loam /ləʊm/. **Loam** is soil that contains a lot of decayed vegetable matter and does not contain too much sand or clay. — N-UNCOUNT

loan /ləʊn/ **loans, loaning, loaned. 1** A **loan** is a sum of money that you borrow. *The president wants to make it easier for small businesses to get bank loans. ...loan repayments.* ● See also **bridging loan**, **soft loan**. **2** If someone gives you a **loan** of something, you borrow it from them. *I am in need of a loan of a bike for a few weeks.* **3** If you **loan** something to someone, you lend it to them. *He had kindly offered to loan us all the plants required for the exhibit.* ► **Loan out** means the same as **loan**. *It is common practice for clubs to loan out players to sides in the lower divisions.* **4** If something is **on loan**, it has been borrowed. *...impressionist paintings on loan from the National Gallery.* **5** If a person is **on loan** from one organization to another, they are temporarily working for the second organization while still employed by the first. *She's on loan to us from the CIA.* — ◆◆◆◇ N-COUNT | N-SING: N of n | VERB: V n to n, V n n, Also V n | PHRASAL VB V P noun, Also V n P | PHRASE | PHRASE

'loan shark, loan sharks. If you describe someone as a **loan shark**, you disapprove of them because they lend money to people and charge them very high rates of interest on the loan. — N-COUNT PRAGMATICS

loath /ləʊθ/; also spelled **loth**. If you are **loath** to do something, you do not want to do it. — ADJ-GRADED: v-link ADJ to-inf

loathe /ləʊð/ **loathes, loathing, loathed.** If you **loathe** something or someone, you dislike them very much. *She loathed being the child of impoverished labourers.* ♦ **loath·ing** *She looked at him with loathing.* ♦ **loath·some** /ˈləʊðsəm/. If you describe something or someone as **loathsome**, you dislike them very much. — ◆◇◇◇◇ VERB: V n, V -ing | N-UNCOUNT | ADJ-GRADED

loaves /ləʊvz/. **Loaves** is the plural of loaf.

lob /lɒb/ **lobs, lobbing, lobbed. 1** If you **lob** something, you throw it or launch it so that it goes quite high in the air. *Enemy forces lobbed a series of artillery shells onto the city.* **2** In sport, if you **lob** the ball, you hit or kick it high into the air so that it lands behind your opponent. *Brown lobbed the ball over the Australian goalkeeper.* ► Also a noun. *...long, high lobs that fell precisely on the baseline.* — ◆◇◇◇◇ VERB: V n, V n prep/adv | VERB: V n prep | N-COUNT

lob·by /ˈlɒbi/ **lobbies, lobbying, lobbied. 1** If you **lobby** someone such as a member of a government or council, you try to persuade them that a particular law should be changed or that a particular thing should be done. *Gun control advocates are lobbying hard for new laws.* ♦ **lob·by·ing.** *The aid was frozen in June after intense lobbying by conservative Republicans.* ♦ **lob·by·ist, lobbyists.** *Victoria is a parliamentary lobbyist for disabled rights group RADAR.* **2** A **lobby** is a group of people who represent a particular organization or campaign, and who try to persuade a government or council to change the laws or take action in favour of that organization or campaign. *Agricultural interests are some of the most powerful lobbies in Washington.* **3** A **lobby** is the area near the entrance to a hotel or other large building that has corridors and staircases leading off it. *I met her in the lobby of the museum.* — ◆◆◆◇ VERB: V n, V for/against n, Also V | N-UNCOUNT | N-COUNT | N-COUNT | N-COUNT

lobe /ləʊb/ **lobes. 1** The **lobe** of your ear is the soft fleshy part at the bottom. **2** A **lobe** is a rounded part of something, for example one of the sections of your brain or lungs, or one of the rounded sections along the edges of some leaves. ♦ **-lobed** *...a plant with large three-lobed leaves.* — ◆◇◇◇◇ N-COUNT | N-COUNT | COMB

lo·boto·my /lə'bɒtəmi/ **lobotomies.** A lobotomy is an operation in which some of the nerves in the brain are cut in order to treat severe mental illness. `N-VAR MEDICAL`

lob·ster /'lɒbstə/ **lobsters.** A lobster is a sea creature that has a hard shell, two large claws, and eight legs. ► **Lobster** is the flesh of a lobster eaten as food. `◆◇◇◇◇` `N-UNCOUNT`

lo·cal /'ləʊkəl/ **locals. 1** Local means existing in or belonging to the area where you live, or to the area that you are talking about. *We'd better check on the match in the local paper... Some local residents joined the students' protest.* ► The **locals** are local people. *That's what the locals call the place.* ♦ **lo-·cal·ly** *...a tree known locally as a toothbrush tree.* **2** Local government is elected by people in one area of a country and controls aspects such as education, housing, and transport within that area. ♦ **locally** *The curriculum was to be decided locally.* **3** Your **local** is a pub which is near where you live and where you often go for a drink. **4** A **local** anaesthetic or condition affects only a small area of your body. `◆◆◆◇◇` `ADJ: ADJ n` `N-COUNT` `ADV-GRADED ADJ` `ADV` `N-COUNT BRITISH, INFORMAL` `ADJ MEDICAL`

local au'thority, local authorities. In Britain, a **local authority** is an organization that is officially responsible for all the public services and facilities in a particular area. `◆◆◇◇◇` `N-COUNT`

local 'colour. Local colour is used to refer to customs, traditions, dress, and other things which give a place or a period of history its own particular character. `N-UNCOUNT`

lo·cale /ləʊ'kɑːl/ **locales.** A locale is a small area, for example the place where something happens or where the action of a book or film is set. `N-COUNT FORMAL`

lo·cal·ity /ləʊ'kælɪti/ **localities.** A locality is a small area of a country or city. *Following the discovery of the explosives the president cancelled his visit to the locality.* `◆◇◇◇◇` `N-COUNT FORMAL`

lo·cal·ize /'ləʊkəlaɪz/ **localizes, localizing, localized;** also spelled **localise** in British English. **1** If you **localize** something, you identify precisely where it is. **2** If something **is localized**, the area that it affects is limited and is prevented from spreading. ♦ **lo·cal·ized** *She had localized breast cancer.* `VERB: V n` `VERB: V n` `ADJ-GRADED`

'local time. Local time is the official time in a particular region or country. *It was around 10.15 pm local time, 3.15 am at home.* `N-UNCOUNT`

lo·cate /ləʊ'keɪt, AM 'ləʊkeɪt/ **locates, locating, located. 1** If you **locate** something or someone, you find out where they are. *We've simply been unable to locate the site.* **2** If you **locate** something in a particular place, you put, build, or set it there. *The board had already decided to locate the headquarters in Perth. ...tax incentives for businesses that locate in the inner city.* ♦ **lo·cat·ed** *The restaurant is located near the cathedral. ...Brisbane's centrally located dance studios.* `◆◆◇◇◇` `VERB FORMAL` `VERB V n prep/adv FORMAL` `V prep/adv FORMAL` `ADJ: v-link ADJ prep, adv ADJ`

lo·ca·tion /ləʊ'keɪʃən/ **locations. 1** A location is the place where something happens or is situated. *Macau's small luxury hotel has a beautiful location.* **2** The **location** of someone or something is their exact position. *Leo looked around him, identifying his location.* **3** A location is a place away from a studio where a film or part of a film is made. *We're shooting on location.* `◆◆◆◇◇` `N-COUNT` `N-COUNT: with poss` `N-VAR`

loch /lɒx, lɒk/ **lochs.** A loch is a large area of water in Scotland that is completely or almost completely surrounded by land. `◆◇◇◇◇` `N-COUNT`

loci /'ləʊsaɪ, 'ləʊkaɪ/. Loci is the plural of **locus.**

lock /lɒk/ **locks, locking, locked. 1** When you **lock** something such as a door, drawer, or case, you fasten it with a key, so that other people cannot open it. *Wolfgang moved along the corridor towards the locked door.* **2** The **lock** on something such as a door or a drawer is the device which is used to keep it shut and prevent other people from opening it. *At that moment he heard Gill's key turning in the lock of the door.* ● If something or someone is kept **under lock and key,** they are in a container or room which has been securely locked. **3** If you **lock** something or someone in a place, room, or container, `◆◆◆◇◇` `VERB: V n V-ed` `N-COUNT` `PHRASE` `VERB V n in/into n`

you put them there and fasten the lock. *They beat them up and locked them in a cell.* **4** When you **lock** something in a particular position or place or when it **locks** there, it is held or fitted firmly in that position or place. *He leaned back in the swivel chair and locked his fingers behind his head... The undercarriage locked into position.* `V-ERG V n prep/adv V prep/adv`

5 On a canal or river, a **lock** is a place where walls have been built with gates at each end so that boats can move to a higher or lower section of the canal or river, by gradually changing the water level inside the gates. `N-COUNT`

6 A **lock** of hair is a small bunch of hairs on your head that grow together and curl or curve in the same direction. **7** Your **locks** are your hair. **8** ● **lock, stock, and barrel:** see **barrel.** `N-COUNT` `N-PLURAL WRITTEN`

lock away. 1 If you **lock** something **away** in a place or container, you put or hide it there and fasten the lock. *He asked them to be sure to lock the letters away... He had even locked away all the videos.* **2** To **lock** someone **away** or to **lock** them **up** means to put them in prison or in a secure psychiatric hospital. *Locking them away is not sufficient, you have to give them treatment.* **3** If you **lock** yourself **away,** you go somewhere where you can be alone, and do not come out or see anyone for some time. `PHRASAL VB` `V n P` `V P noun` `V n P` `Also V P noun` `V pron-refl P`

lock in. If you **lock** someone **in,** you put them in a room and lock the door so that they cannot get out. `PHRASAL VB` `V n P`

lock out. 1 If someone **locks** you **out** of a place, they prevent you entering it by locking the doors. *They had had a row, and she had locked him out of the apartment... My husband's locked me out.* **2** If you **lock** yourself **out** of a place, such as your house, you cannot get in because the door is locked and you do not have your keys. *There had been a knock at the door and when she opened it she locked herself out... She was now locked out.* **3** See also **lock-out.** `PHRASAL VB` `V n P ofn` `V P` `V pron-refl P ofn` `V pron-refl P` `V-ed P`

lock up. 1 If you **lock** something **up** in a place or container, you put or hide it there and fasten the lock. *Lock it up and give the key to the neighbours... Lock up your credit cards and buy on a cash basis.* **2** See **lock away** 2. **3** When you **lock up** a building or car or **lock up,** you make sure that all the doors and windows are locked so that nobody can get in. *Don't forget to lock up... Leave your car here and lock it up.* `PHRASAL VB` `V n P` `V P noun` `V P` `V n P`

locked /lɒkt/. If you say that people are **locked in** conflict or **in** battle, you mean they are arguing or fighting in a fierce or determined way, and neither side seems likely to stop. `◆◆◇◇◇` `ADJ: v-link ADJ in n`

lock·er /'lɒkə/ **lockers.** A locker is a small metal or wooden cupboard with a lock, where you can put your personal belongings temporarily, for example in a school or a sports club. `◆◇◇◇◇` `N-COUNT`

'locker room, locker rooms. A locker room is a room in which there are a lot of lockers, for example in a school, place of work, or a sports club. The British expression is **changing room.** `◆◇◇◇◇` `N-COUNT AMERICAN`

lock·et /'lɒkɪt/ **lockets.** A locket is a piece of jewellery containing something such as a picture, which is worn on a chain around the neck. `N-COUNT`

'lock-out, lock-outs; spelled **lockout** in American English. A **lock-out** is a situation in which employers close a place of work and prevent workers from entering it until the workers accept the employer's new proposals on pay or conditions of work. `N-COUNT`

'lock-up, lock-ups; also spelled **lockup. 1** A **lock-up** is the same as a **jail.** *...the maximum-security lock-up in Lucasville.* **2** A **lock-up** is a garage that is not part of someone's main premises. *...a lock-up garage.* `N-COUNT AMERICAN, INFORMAL` `N-COUNT BRITISH`

lo·co·mo·tion /,ləʊkə'məʊʃən/. Locomotion is the ability to move or the act of moving from one place to another. `N-UNCOUNT FORMAL`

lo·co·mo·tive /,ləʊkə'məʊtɪv/ **locomotives.** A locomotive is a railway engine. `◆◆◇◇◇` `N-COUNT`

lo·cum /'ləʊkəm/ **locums.** A locum is a doctor who does the work of another doctor who is ill or on holiday. `N-COUNT BRITISH`

lo·cus /'ləʊkəs/ **loci.** The **locus** of an activity is the most important place where it happens, or from which it spreads to other places. *Barcelona is the* `N-COUNT FORMAL`

locus of Spanish industry... The military remained the locus of real power.

lo·cust /ˈləʊkəst/ **locusts. Locusts** are large insects which live in hot countries. They fly in large groups and eat crops. See picture headed **insects**. ◆◇◇◇◇ N-COUNT

lodge /lɒdʒ/ **lodges, lodging, lodged. 1** A **lodge** is a house or hut in the country or the mountains where people stay on holiday, for example when they want to hunt animals. *...a Victorian hunting lodge. ...a ski lodge.* **2** A **lodge** is a small house at the entrance to the grounds of a large house. **3** In some organizations, such as the Freemasons, a **lodge** is a local branch or meeting place of the organization. ◆◆◇◇◇ N-COUNT / N-COUNT / N-COUNT

4 If you **lodge** somewhere, such as in someone else's house, or if you **are lodged** there, you live or stay there, usually in return for payment. *...the farming family she lodged with as a young teacher... Rebel and government delegates are lodged in different hotels.* ● See also **lodging. 5** If an object **lodges** somewhere, it becomes stuck there. *The bullet lodged in the sergeant's leg... His car has a bullet lodged in the passenger door.* **6** If you **lodge** a complaint, protest, or claim, you officially make it. *He has four weeks in which to lodge an appeal.* VERB V prep/adv be V-ed prep/adv Also V n prep/adv / VERB V prep/adv V-ed / VERB V n

lodg·er /ˈlɒdʒə/ **lodgers.** A **lodger** is a person who pays money to live in someone else's house. *Jennie took in a lodger to help with the mortgage.* ◆◇◇◇◇ N-COUNT BRITISH

lodg·ing /ˈlɒdʒɪŋ/ **lodgings.** You can use **lodging** or **lodgings** to refer to a place, such as a room in someone else's house, where someone stays for a period of time. **Lodgings** can refer to one or more of these places. *He was given free lodging... Many of the single men found lodgings in the surrounding villages.* ● See also **board and lodging.** ◆◇◇◇◇ N-VAR

loft /lɒft, AM lɔːft/ **lofts, lofting, lofted. 1** A **loft** is the space inside the sloping roof of a house or other building, where things are sometimes stored. *We would like to convert the loft into another bedroom.* **2** When someone such as a cricketer, golfer, or footballer **lofts** a ball, they hit or kick it high into the air. *He lofted the ball 60 yards into the top corner of the net.* ◆◇◇◇◇ N-COUNT / VERB V n

lofty /ˈlɒfti, AM ˈlɔːf-/ **loftier, loftiest. 1** A **lofty** ideal or ambition is noble, important, and admirable. *...the gap between lofty ideals and grubby reality.* **2** A **lofty** building or room is very high. *Victorian houses can seem cold with their lofty ceilings and rambling rooms.* **3** If you say that someone behaves in a **lofty** way, you are criticizing them for behaving in a proud way, as if they think they are very important. *...the lofty disdain he often expresses for his profession.* ◆ **lofti·ly** /ˈlɒftɪli, AM ˈlɔːf-/. *'We supply financial information to selected clients,' Crook said loftily.* ◆◇◇◇◇ ADJ-GRADED / ADJ-GRADED FORMAL / ADJ-GRADED PRAGMATICS / ADV-GRADED

log /lɒg, AM lɔːg/ **logs, logging, logged. 1** A **log** is a thick piece of wood cut from a branch or trunk of a tree. *He dumped the logs on the big stone hearth. ...the original log cabin where Lincoln was born.* **2** A **log** is an official written account of what happens each day, for example on a ship. *The family made an official complaint to a ship's officer, which was recorded in the log.* **3** If you **log** an event or fact, you record it officially in writing or on a computer. *Details of the crime are then logged in the computer.* **4** See also **logging.** ◆◆◇◇◇ N-COUNT / N-COUNT / VERB: V n be V-ed

log in or **log on.** When someone **logs in** or **logs on,** or **logs into** a computer system, they gain access to the system, usually by typing their name and a password. *Customers pay to log on and gossip with other users... They would log into their account and take a look at prices and decide what they'd like to do.* PHRASAL VB V P / V P n

log out or **log off.** When someone who is using a computer system **logs out** or **logs off,** they finish using the system by typing a particular command. PHRASAL VB V P

loga·rithm /ˈlɒgərɪðəm, AM ˈlɔːg-/ **logarithms.** In mathematics, the **logarithm** of a number is a number that it can be represented by in order to make difficult calculations simpler. Mathematics books often contain a list of logarithms. N-COUNT

'log book, log books. A **log book** is a book in which someone records details and events relating to something, especially to their car. N-COUNT

log·ger /ˈlɒgə, AM ˈlɔːg-/ **loggers.** A **logger** is a man whose job is to cut down trees. The usual British word is **lumberjack.** ◆◇◇◇◇ N-COUNT AMERICAN

log·ger·heads /ˈlɒgəhedz, AM ˈlɔːg-/. If two or more people are **at loggerheads,** they disagree very strongly with each other. *For months dentists and the health department have been at loggerheads... The European Community is at loggerheads with the rest of the world over its agricultural subsidies.* PHRASE

log·gia /ˈlɒdʒə/ **loggias.** A **loggia** is a roofed area attached to a house. N-COUNT FORMAL

log·ging /ˈlɒgɪŋ, AM ˈlɔːg-/. **Logging** is the activity of cutting down trees in order to sell the wood. *Logging companies would have to leave a central area of the forest before the end of the year.* ◆◇◇◇◇ N-UNCOUNT

log·ic /ˈlɒdʒɪk/. **1 Logic** is a method of reasoning that involves a series of statements, each of which must be true if the statement before it is true. *...a mind which has a natural understanding of mathematical logic and causality.* **2** The **logic** of a conclusion or an argument is its quality of being correct and reasonable. *I don't follow the logic of your argument... There would be no logic in upsetting the agreements.* **3** A particular kind of **logic** is the way of thinking and reasoning about things that is characteristic of a particular type of person or activity. *The plan was based on sound commercial logic.* ◆◆◇◇◇ N-UNCOUNT / N-UNCOUNT / N-UNCOUNT: with supp

logi·cal /ˈlɒdʒɪkəl/. **1** In a **logical** argument or analysis, each step or point must be true if the step before it is true. *Only when each logical step has been checked by other mathematicians will the proof be accepted.* ◆ **logi·cal·ly** /ˈlɒdʒɪkli/. *My professional training has taught me to look at things logically.* **2** A **logical** conclusion can be reasonably deduced or expected, because of facts or requirements that you know already, or because of the rules of logic. *If the climate gets drier, then the logical conclusion is that even more drought will occur... There was a logical explanation... It is logical to take precautions... Connie suddenly struck her as a logical candidate.* ◆ **logically** *Logically, the Universe cannot be younger than any of the stars it contains.* ◆◆◇◇◇ ADJ / ADV / ADJ-GRADED / ADV

-logical. See **-ological.**

-logist. See **-ologist.**

lo·gis·tic /ləˈdʒɪstɪk/ or **logistical** /ləˈdʒɪstɪkəl/. **Logistic** or **logistical** means relating to the organization of something complicated. *Producing a musical so far from home posed a variety of logistical problems.* ◆ **lo·gis·ti·cal·ly** /ləˈdʒɪstɪkli/. *Organised junior football was either restricted or logistically impossible to operate.* ◆◇◇◇◇ ADJ: ADJ n / ADV

lo·gis·tics /ləˈdʒɪstɪks/. If you refer to the **logistics** of doing something complicated that involves a lot of people or equipment, you are referring to the skilful organization of it so that it can be done successfully and efficiently. *The skills and logistics of getting such a big show on the road pose enormous practical problems.* N-COLL-UNCOUNT

log·jam /ˈlɒgdʒæm/ **logjams.** If someone or something breaks the **logjam,** they succeed in ending a disagreement or difficult situation which had prevented progress from being made. N-COUNT

logo /ˈləʊgəʊ/ **logos.** The **logo** of a company or organization is the special design or way of writing its name that it puts on its products, notepaper, or advertisements. ◆◆◇◇◇ N-COUNT

-logy. See **-ology.**

loin /lɔɪn/ **loins. 1** Someone's **loins** are the front part of their body between their waist and thighs, especially their sexual parts. **2 Loin** is meat which comes from the back or sides of an animal, quite near the tail end. *...roast loin of venison.* **3** If you say that someone has to **gird their loins,** you are saying in a humorous way that they have to prepare themselves for a very difficult task. ◆◇◇◇◇ N-PLURAL LITERARY / N-VAR / PHRASE

loin·cloth /ˈlɔɪnklɒθ, AM -klɔːθ/ **loincloths.** A **loincloth** is the only item of clothing worn by men in N-COUNT

some hot parts of the world. It consists of a piece of cloth covering their sexual parts.

loi·ter /ˈlɔɪtə/ **loiters, loitering, loitered.** If you **loiter** somewhere, you stay there or walk about there without any real purpose. *Unemployed young men loiter at the entrance of the factory.* — VERB V

loll /lɒl/ **lolls, lolling, lolled. 1** If you **loll** somewhere, you sit or lie in a very relaxed position. *He lolled back in his comfortable chair. ...spending afternoons lolling around a swimming pool.* **2** If someone's head or tongue **lolls**, it hangs down loosely. *When he let go the head lolled sideways... Tongue lolling, the dog came lolloping back from the forest.* — VERB V prep/adv — VERB V adv/prep V

lol·li·pop /ˈlɒlɪpɒp/ **lollipops.** A **lollipop** is a sweet consisting of a hard piece of a sugary substance on the end of a stick. — N-COUNT

lol·lop /ˈlɒləp/ **lollops, lolloping, lolloped.** If an animal or person **lollops** along, they run along awkwardly and not very fast. *A herd of elephants lolloped across the plains towards a watering hole.* — VERB V prep/adv

lol·ly /ˈlɒli/ **lollies.** A **lolly** is the same as a **lollipop**. ● See also **ice lolly**. — N-COUNT BRITISH

lone /ləʊn/ **1** If you talk about a **lone** person or thing, you mean that they are alone. *He was shot by a lone gunman.* **2** A **lone** parent looks after her or his child or children without the help of a husband, wife, or partner. *Seven out of ten lone parents live on income support.* — ◆◆◇◇◇ ADJ: ADJ n — ADJ: ADJ n BRITISH

lone·ly /ˈləʊnli/ **lonelier, loneliest. 1** A **lonely** person is unhappy because they are alone, or because they do not have any friends. You can also use **lonely** to describe a situation or period of time in which someone feels lonely. *...lonely people who just want to talk... I desperately needed something to occupy me during those long, lonely nights. ...her lonely childhood.* **♦ lone·li·ness** *...the fear and loneliness working class students can feel when they are plunged into the rarefied atmosphere of university.* **2** A **lonely** place is one where very few people come. *It felt like the loneliest place in the world. ...dark, lonely streets.* — ◆◆◆◇◇ ADJ-GRADED — N-UNCOUNT — ADJ-GRADED

lonely 'hearts. A **lonely hearts** section in a newspaper or a **lonely hearts** club is used by people who are trying to find a lover or friend. — ADJ: ADJ n

lon·er /ˈləʊnə/ **loners.** If you refer to someone as a **loner**, you mean that they prefer to be alone rather than with a group of people. — ◆◇◇◇◇ N-COUNT

lone·some /ˈləʊnsəm/ **1** A **lonesome** person is unhappy because they are alone or do not have any friends. *I've grown so lonesome, thinking of you.* **2** A **lonesome** place is one where very few people come. *...featureless buildings clustered around a series of lonesome quadrangles.* — ADJ-GRADED AMERICAN — ADJ-GRADED AMERICAN

long 1 time

long /lɒŋ, AM lɔːŋ/ **longer** /ˈlɒŋɡə, AM ˈlɔːŋɡər/ **longest** /ˈlɒŋɡɪst, AM ˈlɔːŋɡɪst/. **1 Long** means a great amount of time or for a great amount of time. *Repairs to the cable did not take too long... Have you known her parents long?... I learned long ago to avoid these invitations... The railway had obviously been built long after the house... Chess has long been regarded as a measure of intellect.* **2** You use **long** in expressions such as **'long live the Queen'** and **'long may it continue'** to express your support for someone or something and your hope that they will live or last a long time. **3** The expression **for long** is used to mean 'for a great amount of time'. *'Did you live there?'—'Not for long.'... Developing countries won't put up with the situation for much longer... For too long there was a huge gap in the market.* **4** If something will happen **before long**, it will happen soon or after a short period of time. *German interest rates will come down before long.* **5** If you say that someone **won't be long**, you think that they will arrive or return soon. **6** You use **long** to ask or talk about amounts of time. *How long have you lived around here?... He has been on a diet for as long as any of his friends can remember.* ▶ Also an adjective. *How long is the usual stay in hos-* — ◆◆◆◆◆ ADV-GRADED: ADV with v — PHRASE PRAGMATICS — PHRASE — PHRASE — PHRASE SPOKEN — ADV-GRADED — ADJ-GRADED

pital?... The average commuter journey there is five hours long. ▶ Also a combining form. *...a month-long visit to Egypt.* **7 Long** is used in expressions such as **all day long** and **your whole life long** to emphasize that something happens for the whole of a particular period of time. *We played that record all night long... Snow is sometimes found all summer long upon the highest peaks.* **8** Something that is **no longer** true used to be true but is not true now. You can also say that something is not true **any longer**. *Food shortages are no longer a problem... She could no longer afford to keep him at school... I noticed that he wasn't sitting by the door any longer.* **9** If you say that something is true **as long as** or **so long as** something else is true, you mean that it is true only if the second thing is true. *The interior minister said he would still support them, as long as they didn't break the rules.* **10 Long** is used to describe large periods of time, containing a lot of minutes, hours, days, weeks, or years. *He must have started writing his book a long time ago... She was a TV reporter and worked long hours... He predicts it won't be long before foreign players revolutionise the Premier League.* **11 Long** is used to describe something such as a meeting, journey, book, or list that takes a lot of time to experience or deal with, because of its great size or content. *She is planning a long holiday in Egypt and America... I went for a long walk... He was making quite a long speech... This is a long film, three hours and seven minutes.* **12** If you describe a period of time as **long**, you mean that it seems to last for more time than it actually does, for example because you are very busy or worried during it. *This has been the longest week of my life.* **13** If someone has a **long** memory, they are able to remember things that happened far back in the past. **14 So long** means goodbye. **15 ● at long last:** see **last**. **● in the long run:** see **run**. **● in the long term:** see **term**. **● long in the tooth:** see **tooth**. **● to take the long view:** see **view**. — COMB — ADV: n ADV PRAGMATICS — PHRASE — PHR-CONJ — ADJ-GRADED — ADJ-GRADED — ADJ-GRADED — ADJ-GRADED — CONVENTION — PRAGMATICS INFORMAL

long 2 distance and size

long /lɒŋ, AM lɔːŋ/ **longer** /ˈlɒŋɡə, AM ˈlɔːŋɡər/ **longest** /ˈlɒŋɡɪst, AM ˈlɔːŋɡɪst/. **1** Something that is **long** measures a great distance from one end to the other. *...a long table... Lucy was 27, with long dark hair... His destination was Chobham Common, a long way from his Cotswold home.* **2** A **long** piece of clothing covers the whole of someone's legs or more of their legs than usual. Clothes with **long** sleeves cover the whole of someone's arms. *She is wearing a long black dress. ...a long-sleeved blouse.* **3** You use **long** to talk or ask about the distance something measures from one end to the other. *An eight-week-old embryo is only an inch long... How long is the tunnel? ...centipedes as long as a pencil.* ▶ Also a combining form. *...a three-foot-long gash in the tanker's side.* **4 ● as long as** your **arm:** see **arm**. **● a long face:** see **face**. **● a long shot:** see **shot**. **● to go a long way:** see **way**. — ◆◆◆◆◆ ADJ-GRADED — ADJ: ADJ n — ADJ-GRADED: amount ADJ, how ADJ — COMB

long 3 verb uses

long /lɒŋ, AM lɔːŋ/ **longs, longing, longed.** If you **long** for something, you want it very much. *Steve longed for the good old days... I'm longing to meet her... He longed for the winter to be over.* **♦ longed-for** *...the wet weather that prevents your longed-for picnic.* ● See also **longing**. — ◆◆◇◇◇ VERB V for n V to-inf V for n to-inf — ADJ: ADJ n

long- /lɒŋ, AM lɔːŋ/ **longer-, longest-.** Long- is used with past and present participles to form adjectives which indicate that the action or state indicated by the verb has been continuing for a long time. *...long-established social traditions. ...the long-awaited signing of a peace agreement. ...the long-lasting effects of the infection. ...the world's longest-running radio series, Britain's The Archers'.* — ◆◆◆◇◇ COMB

long-'distance. 1 Long-distance is used to describe travel between places that are far apart. *Trains are reliable, cheap and best for long-distance journeys. ...the first long-distance sea voyages made by Portuguese navigators at the end of the 15th century.* **2 Long-distance** telephone calls are between — ◆◇◇◇◇ ADJ: ADJ n — ADJ

L

people who are not in the same town or local area. ▶ Also an adverb. *I phoned Nicola long distance to suggest it.*
ADV: ADV after v

,**long drawn 'out;** also spelled **long-drawn-out**. A **long drawn out** process or conflict lasts an unnecessarily long time or an unpleasantly long time. *...a long drawn out election campaign.*
ADJ-GRADED

lon·gev·i·ty /lɒn'dʒevɪti/. **Longevity** is long life. *Human longevity runs in families... The main characteristic of the strike has been its longevity.*
◆◇◇◇◇ N-UNCOUNT FORMAL

long·hand /'lɒŋhænd, AM 'lɔːŋ-/. If you write something down in **longhand**, you write it by hand using complete words and normal letters rather than typing it or using shortened forms or special symbols.
N-UNCOUNT

'**long-,haul.** **Long-haul** is used to describe the transporting of passengers or goods over long distances. *...long-haul flights.*
◆◇◇◇◇ ADJ: ADJ n

long·ing /'lɒŋɪŋ, AM 'lɔːŋ-/ **longings.** If you feel a **longing** for something, you have a rather sad feeling because you want it very much. *I was overwhelmed with longing for those innocent days of early childhood... Imelda spoke of her longing to return home.*
◆◇◇◇◇ N-VAR

long·ing·ly /'lɒŋɪŋli, AM 'lɔːŋ-/. If you look or think **longingly**, you look at or think about something you want with a feeling of desire. *Claire looked longingly at the sunlit gardens outside the window.*
ADV-GRADED: ADV with v

lon·gi·tude /'lɒndʒɪtjuːd, AM -tuːd/ **longitudes.** The **longitude** of a place is its distance to the west or east of a line passing through Greenwich. Compare **latitude**. *A similar feature is found at 13 degrees North between 230 degrees and 250 degrees longitude.*
N-VAR

lon·gi·tu·di·nal /,lɒndʒɪ'tjuːdɪnəl, AM -'tuː-/. A **longitudinal** measurement, axis, or cross-section goes from one end of an object to the other rather than across it from side to side. *My nails have longitudinal ridges.*
ADJ: ADJ n

'**long johns.** **Long johns** are warm underpants with long legs.
N-PLURAL

'**long jump.** The **long jump** is an athletics event which involves jumping as far as you can from a mark which you run up to.
N-SING: the N

'**long-life.** **Long-life** milk, fruit juice, or batteries are treated so that they last a longer time than ordinary kinds.
ADJ: ADJ n

'**long-,lost.** You use **long-lost** to describe someone or something that you have not seen for a long time. *A number of Albanian tourists are reported to have come to Turkey to visit long-lost relatives. ...finding a long-lost sixth century manuscript.*
ADJ: ADJ n

'**long-,range.** **1** A **long-range** weapon or vehicle is able to reach a target or destination which is a long way away. *...long-range nuclear missiles. ...the growing use on the North Atlantic routes of long-range twin-engined aircraft.* **2** A **long-range** plan or prediction relates to a period extending a long time into the future. *...a bold, complex, and long-range strategy for improving US education.*
◆◆◇◇◇ ADJ-GRADED

ADJ-GRADED

long·shore·man /'lɒnʃɔːmən, AM 'lɔːŋ-/ **longshoremen.** A **longshoreman** is a person who works in the docks, loading and unloading ships. The British word is **docker**.
N-COUNT AMERICAN

,**long-'sighted.** **Long-sighted** people cannot see things clearly that are close to them, and therefore need to wear glasses. The American word is **far-sighted**.
ADJ-GRADED BRITISH

,**long-'standing.** A **long-standing** situation has existed for a long time. *...their long-standing dispute over money. ...long-standing economic links between Europe and much of Africa.*
◆◆◇◇◇ ADJ-GRADED

,**long-'suffering.** Someone who is **long-suffering** patiently bears continual trouble or bad treatment. *He went back to Yorkshire to join his loyal, long-suffering wife.*
◆◇◇◇◇ ADJ-GRADED

'**long-term,** **longer-term. 1** Something that is **long-term** has continued for a long time or will continue for a long time in the future. *...a new training scheme to help the long-term unemployed... The association believes new technology will provide a long-term solution to credit card fraud.* **2** When
◆◆◆◇◇ ADJ-GRADED

N-SING:

you talk about what happens in **the long term**, you are talking about what happens over a long period of time. *In the long term the company hopes to open in Moscow and other major cities.*
the N

'**long-time.** You use **long-time** to describe something that has existed or been a particular thing for a long time. *...her long-time boyfriend. ...a long-time member of the pro-democracy movement.*
◆◆◇◇◇ ADJ: ADJ n

'**long wave.** **Long wave** is a range of radio waves which are used for broadcasting. *...the BBC's plans to take Radio Four off its long-wave frequency.*
N-UNCOUNT

,**long-'winded.** If you describe something that is written or said as **long-winded**, you are criticizing it because it is longer than necessary. *The manifesto is long-winded, repetitious and often ambiguous or poorly drafted.*
ADJ-GRADED PRAGMATICS

loo /luː/ **loos.** A **loo** is a toilet. *I asked if I could go to the loo... All rooms have private loos.*
◆◇◇◇◇ N-COUNT INFORMAL

loo·fah /'luːfə/ **loofahs.** A **loofah** is a long rough sponge which you use to wash yourself in the bath.
N-COUNT

look 1 using your eyes or your mind

look /lʊk/ **looks, looking, looked. 1** If you **look** in a particular direction, you direct your eyes there, especially so that you can see what is there or see what something is like. *He looks at me and looks away again... I looked down the hallway... Ducks! Look, right there!* ▶ Also a noun. *Lucille took a last look in the mirror... Assisi has a couple of churches that are worth a look if you have time.* **2** A **look** is an expression on someone's face or a movement of their eyes, often showing what they are feeling or thinking. *He gave her a blank look, as if he had no idea who she was... Sally spun round, a feigned look of surprise on her face.* **3** If you **look** someone **in the eye** or **in the face**, you look directly at them in a bold, open way, for example in order to make them realize that you are not afraid of them or that you are telling the truth. *She felt so guilty she could barely look Robert in the eye.* **4** If someone **looks** you **up and down**, they direct their eyes from your head to your feet, in a rude and superior way and often as though they disapprove of you. *The sales assistant looked me up and down and told me not to try the dress on because she didn't think I would get into it.* ● to **look down** your **nose at** someone: see **nose**.
◆◆◆◆◆ VERB V prep/adv V

N-SING

N-COUNT

PHRASE

PHRASE

5 If you say that someone **looks the other way**, you are criticizing them because they pay no attention to something unpleasant that is happening, when they should be dealing with it properly. *Politicians routinely looked the other way while people were tortured or killed by police.*
PHRASE PRAGMATICS

6 If someone, especially an expert, **looks** at something, they examine it, and then deal with it or say how it should be dealt with. *Can you look at my back? I think something's wrong.* ▶ Also a noun. *The car has not been running very well and a mechanic had to come over to have a look at it.* **7** If you **look at** a subject, problem, or situation, you think about it or give your attention to it. *Next term we'll be looking at the Second World War period... He visited Florida a few years ago looking at the potential of the area to stage a big match.* ▶ Also a noun. *They're taking a close look at President Bill Clinton's economic proposal... A quick look at Monday's British newspapers shows that there's plenty of interest in foreign news.* **8** If you **look** at a person, situation, or subject from a particular point of view, you judge them or consider them from that point of view. *Brian had learned to look at her with new respect... It depends how you look at it.*
VERB V at n Also V

N-SING

VERB V at n

N-SING

VERB V at n prep/ adv

9 If you **are looking to** do something, you intend to do it. *Israel is looking to negotiate new trade agreements with the EU.*
VB: only cont V to-inf

10 You can use **look** to draw attention to something or someone, for example because you find them very surprising, significant, or annoying. *I mean, look at how many people watch television and how few read books... Look what a mess you've made of your life.*
VB: only imper PRAGMATICS V at n/wh V wh

11 You say **look** when you want someone to pay attention to you because you are going to say
CONVENTION PRAGMATICS

the N

something important. *Look, I'm sorry. I didn't mean it... Now, look, here is how things stand.* **12** You say **look here** when you are going to say something important to someone, especially when you are angry at something they have done or said. *Now look here, Tim, there really is no need for that kind of reaction.*

CONVENTION
PRAGMATICS

13 If you **look** for something that you have lost, or for something that you want or need, you try to find it. *I'm looking for my friend Brady Coyne. He told me he'd be here tonight... He's looking for a way out from this conflict... I looked everywhere for ideas... Have you looked on the piano?* ▶ Also a noun. *Go and have an-other look.*

VERB
V for n
V prep/adv for n
V prep/adv

N-SING

14 If something such as a building or window **looks** somewhere, it has a view of a particular place. *Each front door looks across a narrow alley to the front door opposite.* ▶ **Look out** means the same as **look**. *Nine windows looked out over the sculpture gardens.*

VERB
V prep

PHRASAL VB
V P prep

look after. 1 If you **look after** someone or something, you do what is necessary to keep them healthy, safe, or in good condition. *I love looking after the chil-dren... People don't look after other people's property in the same way as they look after their own.* **2** If you **look after** something, it is your responsibility to deal with it. *...the farm manager who looks after the day-to-day organization.*

PHRASAL VB
V P n

V P n

look ahead. If you **look ahead**, you think about what is going to happen in the future and perhaps make plans for the future. *Its purpose was to review the pill's safety record and to look ahead to its future development.*

PHRASAL VB
V P

look around. See **look round**.

PHRASAL VB

look back. 1 If you **look back**, you think about things that happened in the past. *Looking back, I am staggered how easily it was all arranged.* **2** If you say that someone did something and then **never looked back**, you mean that they were very successful from that time on. *I went freelance when my son Adam was born, and have never looked back.*

PHRASAL VB
V P

V P

look down on. If you say that someone **looks down on** you, you are criticizing them because they consid-er you to be inferior or unimportant. *I wasn't success-ful, so they looked down on me.*

PHRASAL VB
PRAGMATICS
V P P n

look forward to. 1 If you **look forward to** some-thing that is going to happen, you want it to happen because you think you will enjoy it. *He was looking forward to working with the new Prime Minister.* **2** If you say that someone **is looking forward to** some-thing useful or positive, you mean they expect it to happen. *Motor traders are looking forward to a further increase in vehicle sales.*

PHRASAL VB
V P P -ing/n

V P P n

look in. If you **look in** on a person or place, you visit them for a short time, usually when you are on your way somewhere else. *If we get anywhere near Jersey we'll look in on Mother.*

PHRASAL VB
V P on n
Also V P

look into. If a person or organization **is looking into** something, they are examining the facts relating to it before deciding what to do. *It should also look into the possibilities of wind-generated electricity... He had once looked into buying his own island.*

PHRASAL VB
V P n/-ing

look on. 1 If you **look on** while something happens, you watch it happening without taking part yourself. *About 150 local people looked on in silence as the two coffins were taken into the church.*

PHRASAL VB
V P

look on or **look upon.** If you **look on** someone or something as a particular type of person or thing, or if you **look on** them in a particular way, you think of them in that way. *A lot of people looked on him as a healer... Employers look favourably on applicants who have work experience.*

PHRASAL VB
V P n as n
V adv P n
Also V P n
prep/adv

look out. 1 If you say or shout 'look out!' to some-one, you are warning them that they are in danger. *'Look out!' somebody shouted, as the truck started to roll toward the sea.* **2** See **look** 14.

PHRASAL VB
VERB
PRAGMATICS
V P

look out for. 1 If you **look out for** something, you stay alert so that you will notice it if or when it occurs. *Look out for special deals... What are the symptoms to look out for?* **2** If you **look out for** someone, you make sure that they have all the advantages that they can. *I*

PHRASAL VB
V P P n

felt that I had to look out for myself, because I didn't see that anyone else was going to.

look over. If you **look** something **over**, you examine it quite quickly in order to get a general idea of what it is like. *He could have looked over the papers in less than ten minutes.*

PHRASAL VB
V P noun
Also V P n

look round or **look around.** If you **look round** a building or place, you walk round it and look at the different parts of it. *We went to look round the show homes... I'm going to look around and see what I can find.*

PHRASAL VB
V P n
V P

look through. 1 If you **look through** a book, a magazine, or a group of things, you get an idea of what is in it by examining a lot of the items in it. *He hap-pened to be looking through the medical book 'Gray's Anatomy' at the time... Peter starts looking through the mail as soon as the door shuts.* **2** If you say that some-one **looks through** you, you feel ignored because they look at you without seeming to see or recognize you. *As for doctors, when you go to see them they just look right through you.*

PHRASAL VB
V P n

PRAGMATICS

V P n

look to. If you **look to** someone or something for a particular thing that you want, you expect or hope that they will provide it. *...technically unsophisticated photographers, who look to you for instruction... Looking to the future, though, we asked him what the prospects are for a vaccine.*

PHRASAL VB
V P n

look up. 1 If you **look up** a piece of information, you find it out by looking in a book or list. *I looked your ad-dress up in the personnel file... Many people have to look up the meaning of this word in the dictionary.* **2** If you **look** someone **up**, you visit them after not having seen them for a long time. *She looked up some friends of bygone years.* **3** If a situation **is looking up**, it is im-proving. *Things could be looking up in the computer industry.*

PHRASAL VB
V n P
V P noun

V P noun
Also V n P

V P
INFORMAL

look upon. See **look on**.

PHRASAL VB

look up to. If you **look up to** someone, especially someone older than you, you respect and admire them. *You're a popular girl, Grace, and a lot of the younger ones look up to you.*

PHRASAL VB
V P P n

look 2 appearance

look /lʊk/ **looks, looking, looked. 1** You use **look** when describing the appearance of a person or thing or the impression that they give. *I shall use the money to make my home look lovely... They look like stars to the naked eye... What did my father look like?... He looked as if he was going to smile... He looked to be about fourteen years old.* ▶ Also a noun. *She had the look of someone deserted and betrayed... When he came to decorate the kitchen, Kenneth opt-ed for a friendly rustic look.* ♦ **-looking** *...a very peculiar-looking woman.* **2** When you refer to someone's **looks**, you are referring to how physical-ly attractive they are. *I never chose people just because of their looks. ...a young woman with whole-some good looks.* **3** You use expressions such as **by the look of him** and **by the looks of it** when you want to give an opinion based on the appearance of someone or something. *He was not a well man by the look of him... By the look of things, Mr Stone and company will stay busy.* **4** If you **don't like the look of** something or someone, their appearance sug-gests that they might be the cause of something harmful or unpleasant. *I don't like the look of those clouds... I didn't like the look of him one bit.* **5** You use **look** when indicating what you think will hap-pen in the future or how a situation seems to you. *He had lots of time to think about the future, and it didn't look good... It looks like Warner Brothers' gamble is paying off... The Europeans had hoped to win, and, indeed, had looked like winning.*

♦♦♦♦♦
V-LINK
V adj
V like n
V like/as if
V to-inf

N-SING:
with supp

COMB
N-PLURAL

PHRASE

PHRASE

V-LINK
V adj
it V like/as if
V like-ing/n

'**look-alike, look-alikes.** A **look-alike** is someone who has a very similar appearance to another per-son, especially a famous person. *...a Marilyn Monroe look-alike.*

N-COUNT

look·er /'lʊkə/ **lookers.** You can refer to an attrac-tive man or woman as a **looker** or a **good looker**.

N-COUNT
INFORMAL

'**look-in.** If you do not get a **look-in**, you cannot do something because too many other people are

N-SING
BRITISH,
INFORMAL

L

doing it. *They want to make sure the newcomers don't get a look-in.*

'looking glass, looking glasses; also spelled **looking-glass**. A **looking glass** is a mirror.   N-COUNT DATED

look·out /'lʊkaʊt/ **lookouts. 1** A **lookout** is a place from which you can see clearly in all directions. *Troops tried to set up a lookout post inside a refugee camp.* **2** A **lookout** is someone who is watching for danger in order to warn other people about it. **3** If you **are keeping a lookout** or **are on the lookout**, you are alert and careful because you do not want to miss noticing something interesting or important, or something unpleasant that you want to avoid. *He'd failed to keep a proper lookout that night... Nature lovers will be on the lookout for eagles, cormorants, and the occasional whale.*   ◆◇◇◇◇ N-COUNT / N-COUNT / PHRASE

loom /luːm/ **looms, looming, loomed. 1** If something **looms** over you, it appears as a large or unclear shape, often in a frightening way. *...the bleak mountains that loomed out of the blackness.* **2** If a worrying or threatening situation or event **is looming**, it seems likely to happen soon. *The threat of renewed civil war looms ahead.* **3** If a problem or event **looms large**, it occupies a lot of your thoughts and seems to be a frightening prospect that you cannot avoid. *...the terrible problem of armed crime now looming large in our society.* **4** A **loom** is a device that is used for weaving thread into cloth.   ◆◆◇◇◇ VERB V prep/adv Also V / VERB: V V adv/prep / PHRASE / N-COUNT

loom up. If something **looms up**, it comes into sight as a tall unclear shape, often in a frightening way. *The great house loomed up ahead of them.*   PHRASAL VB V P

loony /'luːni/ **loonies.** If you refer to someone as a **loony**, you mean that they behave in a way that seems mad, strange, or eccentric. *They all thought I was a loony. ...loony feminist nonsense.*   ◆◇◇◇◇ N-COUNT INFORMAL

loop /luːp/ **loops, looping, looped. 1** A **loop** is a curved or circular shape in something long, for example in a piece of string. *...a loop of garden hose... We cling anxiously to the thin loops of rope.* **2** If you **loop** something such as a piece of rope around an object, you tie a length of it in a loop around the object. *He looped the rope over the wood.* **3** If something **loops** somewhere, it goes there in a circular direction that makes the shape of a loop. *The enemy was looping around the south side.*   ◆◆◇◇◇ N-COUNT / VERB V n prep / VERB V prep/adv

loop·hole /'luːphəʊl/ **loopholes.** A **loophole** in the law is a small mistake or omission which allows some people to avoid doing something that the law intended them to do. *...exploiting some loophole in the law to avoid prosecution.*   ◆◇◇◇◇ N-COUNT

loose /luːs/ **looser, loosest; looses, loosing, loosed. 1** Something that is **loose** is not firmly held or fixed in place. *...if a tooth feels very loose... Two wooden beams had come loose from the ceiling. ...a loose thread.* ◆ **loose·ly** *Tim clasped his hands together and held them loosely in front of his belly.* **2** Something that is **loose** is not attached to anything, or held or contained in anything. *...racing motorcycles on the loose gravel. ...a handful of loose change... A page came loose and floated onto the tiles.* **3** If people or animals break **loose** or are set **loose**, they are freed after they have been restrained. *She broke loose from his embrace and crossed to the window.* **4** If a person or an animal is **on the loose**, they are free because they have escaped from a person or place. **5** **Loose** clothes are rather large and do not fit closely. *Clothing should be as loose and as comfortable as possible.* ◆ **loosely** *His shirt hung loosely over his thin shoulders.* **6** If your hair is **loose**, it hangs freely round your shoulders and is not tied back. **7** Something that is **loose** is not compact or dense in texture. *...loose soil.* **8** A **loose** grouping, arrangement, or organization is flexible rather than strictly controlled or organized. *Murray and Alison came to some sort of loose arrangement. ...a loose coalition of leftwing forces.* ◆ **loosely** *...a loosely organised group of criminals.* **9** **Loose** words or expressions are not exact but rather   ◆◆◆◇◇ ADJ-GRADED / ADV-GRADED ADV with v / ADJ / ADJ: ADJ after v, ADJ n, v-link ADJ / PHRASE / ADJ-GRADED / ADV-GRADED ADV with v / ADJ / ADJ / ADJ-GRADED / ADV-GRADED ADV with v / ADJ-GRADED

vague. *...a loose translation.* ◆ **loosely** *...four characters, loosely based on my uncles.*   ADV-GRADED

10 If someone describes a woman or someone's behaviour as **loose**, they disapprove of that person because they think she or he has sexual relationships with too many people. *...a loose woman... He was accused of loose morals.*   ADJ-GRADED PRAGMATICS DATED

11 To **loose** something such as ammunition means to release a large amount of it suddenly. *He trained his gun down and loosed a brief burst.*   VERB V n

12 If you **loose** something, you hold it less tightly or unfasten it slightly. *The guards loosed his arms.*   VERB V n

13 ● a **loose cannon:** see **cannon.** ● to **cut loose:** see **cut.** ● **all hell breaks loose:** see **hell.** ● to **be let loose:** see **let.**

,loose 'end, loose ends. 1 A **loose end** is part of a story, situation, or crime that has not yet been explained. *There are some annoying loose ends in the plot.* **2** If you are **at a loose end**, you are bored because you do not have anything to do.   ◆◇◇◇◇ N-COUNT / PHRASE INFORMAL

,loose 'fitting. **Loose fitting** clothes are rather large and do not fit tightly on your body. *...a pale-pink, loose-fitting silk suit.*   ADJ-GRADED

loos·en /'luːsən/ **loosens, loosening, loosened. 1** If someone **loosens** restrictions or laws, they make them less strict or severe. *Taiwan has progressively loosened restrictions on private travel.* ◆ **loos·en·ing** *Domestic conditions did not justify a loosening of monetary policy.* **2** If someone or something **loosens** the ties between people or groups of people, they become weaker. *The ties that bind them together are loosening.* **3** If a government or organization **loosens** its grip on a group of people or an activity, it begins to have less control over it. *The Soviet Union's grip on Eastern Europe loosened.* **4** If you **loosen** your clothing or something that is tied or fastened, you move it or undo it slightly so that it is less tight or less firmly held in place. *Her hair had loosened and was tangled around her shoulders.* **5** If you **loosen** something that is stretched across something else, you make it less stretched or tight. *Insert a small knife into the top of the chicken breast to loosen the skin.* **6** If you **loosen** your grip on something, you hold it less tightly. *When his grip loosened she eased herself away.* **7** If you say that something **has loosened** someone's **tongue**, you mean that it has made them talk about something, especially when they should have remained silent.   ◆◆◇◇◇ VERB: V n / N-SING V-ERG: V n / V-ERG: V n / V-ERG: V n / VERB V n / V-ERG: V n / PHRASE

loosen up. 1 If a person or situation **loosens up**, they become more relaxed and less tense. *I think people have loosened up their standards.* **2** If you **loosen up** your body, you do simple exercises to get your muscles ready for a difficult physical activity, such as running or playing football. *Relax. Let your body loosen up.*   PHRASAL VB V P / V P n / V P / V P n ERG: V P noun / V P / V P noun Also V n P

loot /luːt/ **loots, looting, looted. 1** If people **loot** shops or houses, they steal things from them during a battle, riot, or other disturbance. *...youths taking advantage of the general confusion to loot and steal.* ◆ **loot·ing** *There has been rioting and looting.* ◆ **loot·er, looters** *He saw looters carrying off items from evacuated apartments.* **2** If someone **loots** money or goods, they steal them during a battle, riot, or other disturbance. *...thugs who have looted food supplies and terrorized the population.* **3** **Loot** is stolen money and goods. *Most criminals steal in order to sell their loot for cash on the black market.*   ◆◆◇◇◇ VERB: V n V / N-UNCOUNT / N-COUNT / VERB V n / N-UNCOUNT INFORMAL

lop /lɒp/ **lops, lopping, lopped.**

lop off. 1 If you **lop** something **off**, you cut it away from what it was attached to, usually with a quick, strong stroke. *...men with axes, lopping off branches.* **2** If you **lop** an amount of money or time **off** something such as a budget or a schedule, you reduce the budget or schedule by that amount. *The Air France plane lopped over four hours off the previous best time.*   PHRASAL VB V n P / V P noun / V n P n / V n P / V n P noun / V n P INFORMAL

lope /ləʊp/ **lopes, loping, loped.** If a person or animal **lopes** somewhere, they run in an easy and relaxed way, taking long steps. *He was loping across*   VERB V prep/adv V-ing Also V

the sand toward Nancy... She turned and walked away with long, loping steps.

lop·sid·ed /ˌlɒpˈsaɪdɪd/; also spelled **lop-sided. 1** Something that is **lopsided** is uneven because one side is lower or heavier than the other. ...a friendly, lopsided grin. **2** If you say that a situation is **lopsided**, you mean that one element is much stronger, bigger, or more important than another element. ...lopsided economic relations. `ADJ-GRADED`

lo·qua·cious /ləˈkweɪʃəs/. If you describe someone as **loquacious**, you mean that they talk a lot. The normally loquacious Mr O'Reilly has said little. `ADJ-GRADED` `FORMAL`

lord /lɔːd/ **lords, lording, lorded. 1** A **lord** is a man who has a high rank in the nobility, for example an earl, a viscount, or a marquess. She married a lord. ...Lord Lloyd. ◆◆◆◇ `N-COUNT; N-TITLE` `BRITISH`

2 Senior judges, bishops, and some male members of the nobility are addressed as **'my Lord'**. My lord, I am instructed by my client to claim that the evidence has been tampered with. `N-VOC; myN` `PRAGMATICS` `BRITISH`

3 Lord is used in the titles of some officials of very high rank. He was Lord Chancellor from 1970 until 1974. `BRITISH`

4 The Lords is the same as **the House of Lords**. It's very likely the bill will be defeated in the Lords. `N-COLL-PROPER: theN` `N-COUNT`

5 In former times, especially in medieval times, a **lord** was a man who owned land or property and who had power and authority over people. **6** If you describe a man as the **lord** of a particular area, industry, or thing, you mean that they have total authority and power over it. A century ago the aristocracy were truly lords of the earth. `N-COUNT` `N-COUNT`

7 If someone **lords it over** you, they act in a way that shows that they think that they are better than you, especially by giving lots of orders; used showing disapproval. In Egypt priests were a privileged class, lording it over common folk. `PHRASE` `PRAGMATICS`

8 In the Christian church, people refer to God and to Jesus Christ as the **Lord**. I know the Lord will look after him. `N-PROPER`

9 Lord is used in exclamations such as **'good Lord!'** and **'oh Lord!'** to express surprise, amusement, shock, frustration, or worry about something. **10** You can say **'Lord knows'** to emphasize something that you feel or believe very strongly. I've got to go home, but Lord knows I dread it. **11** You can say **'Lord knows'** to emphasize that you do not know something. He would turn up at meetings, but Lord knows where he came from. `EXCLAM` `PHRASE` `PRAGMATICS` `PHRASE` `PRAGMATICS`

lord·ly /ˈlɔːdli/. **1** If you say that someone's behaviour is **lordly**, you are critical of them because they treat other people in a proud and arrogant way. ...their usual lordly indifference to patients. **2 Lordly** means magnificent, impressive, and suitable for a lord. ...the site of a lordly mansion. `ADJ-GRADED` `PRAGMATICS` `ADJ: ADJ n`

Lord·ship /ˈlɔːdʃɪp/ **Lordships.** You use the expressions **Your Lordship**, **His Lordship**, or **Their Lordships** when you are addressing or referring to a judge, bishop, or male member of the nobility. My name is Richard Savage, your Lordship. ◆◇◇◇◇ `N-VOC; N-PROPER: det-poss N` `PRAGMATICS`

lore /lɔː/. The **lore** of a particular country or culture is its traditional stories and history. ...ancient Catalan lore. ◆◇◇◇◇ `N-UNCOUNT: with supp`

lor·ry /ˈlɒri, AM ˈlɔːri/ **lorries. 1** A **lorry** is a large vehicle that is used to transport goods by road. The American word is **truck**. ...a long-haul container lorry. **2** If someone says that something has fallen **off the back of a lorry**, they mean that they bought something that they knew was stolen. Pete once bought the boys a bicycle cheap off the back of a lorry. ◆◇◇◇ `N-COUNT` `BRITISH` `PHRASE` `BRITISH, INFORMAL`

lose /luːz/ **loses, losing, lost. 1** If you **lose** a contest, a fight, or an argument, you do not succeed because someone does better than you and defeats you. A C Milan lost the Italian Cup Final... No one likes to be on the losing side. ◆◆◆◆◆ `VERB` `V n` `V-ing` `Also V`

2 If you **lose** something, you do not know where it is, for example because you have forgotten where you put it. I lost my keys. **3** If things **are lost**, they are destroyed in a disaster. ...the famous Nankin pottery that was lost in a shipwreck. `VERB` `V n` `VB: usu passive` `beV-ed`

4 If something **loses** you a contest or **loses** you something that you had, it causes you to fail or to no longer have what you had. My own stupidity lost me the match. `VERB` `V n n`

5 You say that you **lose** something when you no longer have it because it has been taken away from you or destroyed. Mr Chirac subsequently lost his job as prime minister. **6** If someone **loses** a quality, ability, attitude, or belief, they no longer have it. He lost all sense of reason... He had lost the use of his legs. **7** If you say that you **have nothing to lose**, you mean that you will not suffer if you do something unsuccessfully. If you say that you **have much to lose**, you mean that you may suffer if you do something unsuccessfully. `VERB` `V n` `VERB` `V n` `PHRASE`

8 If someone or something **loses** heat, their temperature becomes lower. Babies lose heat much faster than adults. **9** If you **lose** blood or fluid from your body, it leaves your body so that you have less of it. **10** If you **lose** weight, you become less heavy, and usually look thinner. `VERB` `V n` `VERB: V n` `VERB: V n`

11 If you **lose** a part of your body, it is cut off in an operation or in a violent accident. He lost a foot when he was struck by a train. `VERB` `V n`

12 If someone **loses** their life, they die. ...the ferry disaster in 1987, in which 192 people lost their lives. **13** If you **lose** a close relative or friend, they die. My Grandma lost her brother in the war. `VERB` `V n` `VERB` `V n`

14 If you **lose** time, you waste it. Police lost valuable time in the early part of the investigation. **15** If you say that someone **loses no time** in doing something, you are emphasizing that they act quickly in order to benefit from a situation. Francine lost no time in defending herself. `VERB` `V n` `PHRASE` `PRAGMATICS`

16 If you **lose** an opportunity, you do not take advantage of it. They did not lose the opportunity to say what they thought of events. **17** If you say that someone **loses no opportunity** to do or say a particular thing, especially something that they will benefit from or that will harm someone else, you are emphasizing that they do it or say it whenever it is possible. He has lost no opportunity to capitalise on his new position. `VERB: V n` `V n to-inf` `PHRASE` `PRAGMATICS`

18 If you **lose** yourself in something, you give a lot of attention to it and do not think about anything else. He was lost in the contemplation of the landscape. `VERB: V pron-refl in n` `beV-ed in n`

19 If a business **loses** money, it earns less money than it spends, and is therefore in debt. `VERB: V n`

20 ● **lose** your **way**: see **way**. **21** See also **lost**. **22 Lose** is used in a large number of expressions which are explained under other words in this dictionary. For example, the expression **lose** your **balance** is explained at **balance**.

lose out. If you **lose out**, you suffer a loss or disadvantage because you have not succeeded in what you were doing. Laura lost out to Tom... Women have lost out in this new pay flexibility. `PHRASAL VB` `V P` `V P to n` `V P inn` `Also V P on n`

los·er /ˈluːzə/ **losers. 1** The **losers** of a game, contest, or struggle are the people who are defeated or beaten. ...the winners and losers of this year's Super Bowl. ● If you say that someone is a **good loser** you approve of the fact that they accept that they have lost a game or contest without complaining. If you say that someone is a **bad loser**, you are critical of them because they hate losing and complain a lot about it. **2** If you refer to someone as a **loser**, you have a low opinion of them because you think they are always unsuccessful. A born loser, he was unable to keep a job. **3** People who are **losers** as the result of an action or event, are in a worse situation because of it and do not benefit from it. Some of Britain's top business leaders of the 1980s have become the country's greatest losers in the recession. ◆◆◇◇◇ `N-COUNT` `PHRASE` `PRAGMATICS` `N-COUNT` `PRAGMATICS` `INFORMAL` `N-COUNT`

loss /lɒs, AM lɔːs/ **losses. 1 Loss** is the fact of no longer having something or having less of it than before. ...loss of sight... The loss of income for the government is about $250 million a month. **2** A **loss** is the disadvantage you suffer when a valuable and useful person or thing leaves or is taken away. His death was a great loss to herself. **3** If a business ◆◆◆◇ `N-VAR` `N-COUNT` `N-VAR`

L

makes a **loss**, it earns less than it spends. *In 1986 Rover made a loss of nine hundred million pounds.*
4 If a business produces something **at a loss**, they PHRASE sell it at a price which is less than it cost them to produce it or buy it.
5 **Loss** of life occurs when people die. *...a terrible loss* N-VAR *of human life.* **6** The **loss** of a relative or friend is their N-UNCOUNT: death. *...the loss of his mother.* **7** **Loss** is the feeling of with supp sadness you experience when someone or something N-UNCOUNT you like is taken away from you. *...your feelings of loss and grief.*
8 The **loss** of something such as heat, blood, or fluid is N-UNCOUNT: the gradual reduction of it or of its level in a system or with supp in someone's body. *With microsurgery, there is minimal blood loss.*
9 If you say that you are **at a loss**, you mean that you PHRASE do not know what to do in a particular situation.
10 If you **cut** your **losses**, you stop doing what you PHRASE were doing in order to prevent the bad situation that you are in becoming worse.
11 If you say that someone or something is a **dead** PHRASE **loss**, you have a low opinion of them because you PRAGMATICS think they are completely useless or unsuccessful. *I'd* BRITISH, *had no experience of organizing anything of that sort. I* INFORMAL *think I was largely a dead loss.*

'loss leader, loss leaders. A **loss leader** is a N-COUNT product that is sold in a shop at such a low price that it makes a loss. This is done to attract customers, in the hope that they will buy other goods in the same shop.

lost /lɒst, AM lɔːst/. **1** **Lost** is the past tense and ◆◆◆◇ past participle of **lose**.
2 If you are **lost** or if you get **lost**, you do not know ADJ where you are or are unable to find your way. *I realised I was lost.* **3** If something is **lost**, or gets **lost**, you ADJ cannot find it, for example because you have forgotten where you put it. *My paper got lost.*
4 If you feel **lost**, you feel very uncomfortable because ADJ-GRADED you are in an unfamiliar situation. *I feel lost and lonely in a strange town alone.* **5** If you describe a person or ADJ group of people as **lost**, you think that they do not have a clear idea of what they want to do or achieve. *...a lost generation in search of an identity.*
6 If you describe something as **lost**, you mean that ADJ you no longer have it or it no longer exists. *...their lost homeland. ...a lost job or promotion.* **7** You use **lost** to ADJ: ADJ n refer to a period or state of affairs that existed in the past and no longer exists. *...his lost youth.*
8 If something is **lost**, it is not used properly and is ADJ considered wasted. *Fox is not bitter about the lost opportunity to compete in the Games.*
9 If you tell someone to **get lost**, you are telling them PHRASE in a very rude way to go away. **10** If advice or a com- PRAGMATICS ment **is lost on** someone, they do not understand it or PHRASE they pay no attention to it. **11** If you **are lost in** PHRASE thought, you give all your attention to what you are thinking about and do not notice what is going on around you. **12** If you say that you **would be lost** PHRASE **without** someone or something, you mean that you would be unhappy or unable to work properly without them.

,lost 'cause, lost causes. If you refer to some- N-COUNT thing or someone as a **lost cause**, you mean that people's attempts to change or influence them have no chance of succeeding.

,lost 'property. 1 **Lost property** consists of things N-UNCOUNT that people have lost or accidentally left in a public place, for example on a train or in a school. **2** **Lost** N-UNCOUNT **property** is a place where lost property is kept.

,lost 'soul, lost souls. If you call someone a **lost** N-COUNT **soul**, you mean that they seem unhappy, and unable to fit in with any particular group of people in society.

lot /lɒt/ **lots. 1** A **lot of** something or **lots of** it is a ◆◆◆◆◆ large amount of it. *A lot of our land is used to grow* QUANT *crops... 'You'll find that everybody will try and help their colleague.'—'Yeah. There's a lot of that.'... Lots of pubs like to deck themselves out with flowers... He drank lots of milk.* ▶ Also a pronoun. *There's lots go-* PRON *ing on... I learned a lot from him.* **2** A **lot** means to a ADV

great extent or degree. *Matthew's out quite a lot doing his research. ...if I went out and accepted a job at a lot less money.* **3** If you do something **a lot**, you ADV: do it often or for a long time. *They went out a lot.* ADV after v
4 You can use **lot** to refer to a set or group of things or N-COUNT: people. *...two lots of 1,000 shares... We've just sacked* num N *one lot of builders.* **5** You can refer to a specific group N-SING: of people as a particular **lot**. *Future generations are* adj N *going to think that we were a pretty boring lot.* INFORMAL
6 You can use **the lot** to refer to the whole of an N-SING: amount that you have just mentioned. *He went to a* the N *betting shop and lost the lot in half an hour.* INFORMAL
7 Your **lot** is the kind of life you have or the things that N-SING you have or experience. *Young people are usually less contented with their lot.* **8** If you **throw in** your **lot** PHRASE **with** a particular person or group, you decide to work with them and support them from then on, whatever happens.
9 A **lot** is a small area of land that belongs to a person N-COUNT or company. *If oil or gold are discovered under your* AMERICAN *lot, you can sell the mineral rights.* ● See also **parking lot.**
10 A **lot** in an auction is one of the objects or groups of N-COUNT objects that are being sold. *Lot 432 is described as a Baroque pearl and diamond pin.*
11 If people **draw lots** to decide who will do some- PHRASE thing, they each take a piece of paper from a container. One or more pieces of paper are marked, and the people who take marked pieces are chosen.

loth /ləʊθ/. See **loath.**

lo·tion /'ləʊʃən/ **lotions.** A **lotion** is a liquid that ◆◇◇◇◇ you use to clean, improve, or protect your skin or N-VAR hair. *...suntan lotion.*

lot·tery /'lɒtəri/ **lotteries. 1** A **lottery** is a type of ◆◇◇◇◇ gambling game in which people buy numbered N-COUNT tickets. Several numbers are then chosen, and the people who have those numbers on their tickets win a prize. **2** If you describe something as **a lot-** N-SING: **tery**, you mean that what happens depends entirely a N on luck or chance. *Which judges are assigned to a case is always a bit of a lottery.*

louche /luːʃ/. If you describe a person or place as ADJ-GRADED **louche**, you mean that they are unconventional and WRITTEN not respectable, but often in a way that people find rather attractive. *...that section of London society which somehow managed to be louche and fashionable at the same time.*

loud /laʊd/ **louder, loudest. 1** If a noise is **loud**, ◆◆◆◇◇ the level of sound is very high and it can be easily ADJ-GRADED heard. Someone or something that is **loud** produces a lot of noise. *There was a loud bang. ...amazingly loud discos.* ▶ Also an adverb. *He turns the televi-* ADV-GRADED *sion up very loud.* ♦ **loud·ly** *His footsteps echoed* ADV-GRADED *loudly in the tiled hall.* ♦ **loud·ness** *The students* N-UNCOUNT *began to enter the classroom and Anna was startled at their loudness.* **2** If you say or read something **out** PHRASE **loud**, you say it or read it so that it can be heard, rather than just thinking it. *Even Ford, who seldom smiled, laughed out loud a few times.*
3 If you tell someone something **loud and clear**, you PHRASE are very easily understood, either because your voice is very clear or because you express yourself very clearly. *Lisa's voice comes through loud and clear... The message is a powerful one, and I hope it will be heard loud and clear by the tobacco industry.* **4** If ADJ-GRADED someone is **loud** in their support for or criticism of something, they express their opinion very often and in a very strong way. *Mr Jones received loud support from his local community.* ♦ **loud·ly** *Mac talked loud-* ADV-GRADED: *ly in favour of the good works done by the Church.* ADV with v
5 If you describe something, especially a piece of ADJ-GRADED clothing, as **loud**, you dislike it because it has very PRAGMATICS bright colours or very large, bold patterns which look unpleasant. *He liked to shock with his gold chains and loud clothes.*

loud·hail·er /ˌlaʊd'heɪlə/ **loudhailers.** A **loud-** N-COUNT **hailer** is a portable device with a microphone at BRITISH one end and a cone-shaped speaker at the other end. You use it when you want people to be able to

hear you from a long way away, especially outdoors. The usual American word is **bullhorn**.

loud·mouth /ˈlaʊdmaʊθ/ **loudmouths** N-COUNT /ˈlaʊdmaʊðz/; also spelled **loud-mouth**. If you describe someone as a **loudmouth**, you are critical of them because they talk a lot, especially in an unpleasant, offensive, or stupid way. ♦ **loud-mouthed** *a loud-mouthed oaf with very little respect for women.* ADJ-GRADED

loud·speak·er /ˌlaʊdˈspiːkə/ **loudspeakers;** also ♦♢♢♢♢ spelled **loud speaker**. A **loudspeaker** is a piece of N-COUNT equipment, for example part of a radio or hi-fi system, through which sound comes out.

lounge /laʊndʒ/ **lounges, lounging, lounged.** ♦♦♢♢♢ **1** A **lounge** is a room in a house where people sit N-COUNT and relax. *The Holmbergs were sitting before a roaring fire in the lounge.* **2** A **lounge** is a room in a ho- N-COUNT tel or club where people can sit and relax. *...the lounge of a big Johannesburg hotel.* **3** A **lounge** is a N-COUNT very large room in an airport where people can sit and wait for aircraft to arrive or depart. *...the departure lounge.* **4** If you **lounge** somewhere, you lean against some- VERB thing or lie somewhere in a relaxed or lazy way. *They* V prep *ate and drank and lounged in the shade.*

lounge about or **lounge around.** The form PHRASAL VB **lounge about** is mainly used in British English. If you V P **lounge about** or **lounge around**, you spend your time V P n in a relaxed and lazy way, sometimes when you should be doing something useful. *He remembered mowing the lawn, lounging around the swimming pool.*

louse /laʊs/ **lice.** Lice are small insects that live on ♦♢♢♢♢ the bodies of people or animals and bite them in N-COUNT order to drink their blood.

lousy /ˈlaʊzi/ **lousier, lousiest. 1** If you describe ♦♢♢♢♢ something as **lousy**, you mean that it is very bad. *He* ADJ-GRADED *blamed Fiona for a lousy weekend... The food was* INFORMAL *lousy and there was never enough of it.* **2** If someone ADJ-GRADED is **lousy** at something, they are very bad at it. *I was* INFORMAL *a lousy secretary.* **3** If you feel **lousy**, you feel very ill. ADJ-GRADED *I wasn't actually sick but I felt lousy.* INFORMAL

lout /laʊt/ **louts.** If you describe a man or boy as a N-COUNT **lout**, you are critical of them because they behave PRAGMATICS in an impolite or aggressive way. *...a drunken lout.* ♦ **lout·ish** /ˈlaʊtɪʃ/ *I was really embarrassed by the* ADJ-GRADED *loutish behaviour of the English.*

lou·vre /ˈluːvə/ **louvres;** spelled **louver** in Ameri- N-COUNT can English. A **louvre** is a door or window with narrow, flat, sloping pieces of wood or glass across its frame.

lov·able /ˈlʌvəbəl/. If you describe someone as ♦♢♢♢♢ **lovable**, you mean that they have attractive qual- ADJ-GRADED ities, and are easy to like.

love /lʌv/ **loves, loving, loved. 1** If you **love** ♦♦♦♦♦ someone, you feel romantically or sexually attracted VERB to them, and they are very important to you. *Oh,* V n *Amy, I love you.* **2** Love is a very strong feeling of af- N-UNCOUNT fection towards someone who you are romantically or sexually attracted to. *Our love for each other has been increased by what we've been through together. ...an old fashioned love story.* **3** If you **fall in love** PHRASE with someone, you start to be in love with them. *We fell madly in love.* **4** If you **are in love** with some- PHRASE one, you feel romantically or sexually attracted to them, and they are very important to you. **5** When PHRASE two people **make love**, they have sex. *Have you ever made love to a girl before?* **6** Love at first sight is PHRASE the experience of starting to be in love with someone as soon as you see them for the first time. **7** You say that you **love** someone when their happi- VERB ness is very important to you, so that you behave in a V n kind and caring way towards them. *You'll never love anyone the way you love your baby.* **8** Love is the feel- N-UNCOUNT ing that a person's happiness is very important to you, and the way you show this feeling in your behaviour towards them. *My love for all my children is unconditional.* **9** You can use expressions such as **'love'**, **'love from'**, CONVENTION and **'all my love'**, followed by your name, as an infor-

mal way of ending a letter to a friend or relation. *...with love from Grandma and Grandpa.* **10** If you N-UNCOUNT: send someone your **love**, you ask another person, poss N who will soon be speaking or writing to them, to tell them that you are thinking about them with affection. *Please give her my love.* **11** If you say that there is **no love lost** between two PHRASE people or groups or there is **little love lost** between them, you mean that they do not like each other at all. *Garry Kasparov and Anatoly Karpov may be fellow countrymen but there's no love lost between them.* **12** If you cannot or will not do something **for love or** PHRASE **money** or **for love nor money**, you are completely unable to do it or you do not intend to do it. *I'm not coming back up here. Never, for love nor money.* **13** If you **love** something, you like it very much. *I love* VERB: V n *taking photographs. ...one of these people that loves to* V n/-ing *be in the outdoors... I love it when I hear you laugh.* V to-inf **14** You can say that you **love** something when you VERB consider that it is important and want to protect or V n support it. *I love my country as you love yours.* **15** Love N-UNCOUNT is a strong liking for something, or a belief that it is important. *This is no way to encourage a love of literature.* **16** If you say someone **would love** to have or do VERB: something, you mean that they very much want to V to-inf have it or do it. *I would love a hot bath and clean* V n *clothes... His wife would love him to give up his job.* V n to-inf **17** If you **fall in love** with something, you start to like PHRASE it very much. *I fell in love with the cinema.* **18** If you PHRASE are **in love** with something, you like it very much. *He had always been in love with the enchanted landscape of the West.* **19** Your **love** is someone or something that you love. N-COUNT *'She is the love of my life,' he said... Music's one of my great loves.* **20** Some people use **love** as an affectionate way of ad- N-VOC dressing someone. *Well, I'll take your word for it then,* INFORMAL *love.* **21** In tennis, **love** is a score of zero. NUMBER **22** See also **-loved, loving; free love, peace-loving, tug-of-love. 23** ● **labour of love:** see **labour.**

'love affair, love affairs. A **love affair** is a ro- ♦♢♢♢♢ mantic and usually sexual relationship between two N-COUNT people who love each other but who are not married or living together. **2** If you refer to someone's N-SING: **love affair** with something, you mean that they like with supp it a lot and are very enthusiastic about it. *...Tom's love affair with France and most things French.*

love·birds /ˈlʌvbɜːdz/. You can refer in a humorous N-PLURAL way to two people as **lovebirds** when they are obviously very much in love.

'love child, love children. If you refer to some- N-COUNT one as a **love child**, you mean that the person was JOURNALISM born as a result of a love affair between two people who have never been married to each other.

-loved /-lʌvd/. **-loved** combines with adverbs to COMB form adjectives that describe how much someone or something is loved. *...the much-loved father and his son.*

'love-'hate relationship, love-hate relation- N-COUNT **ships.** If you have a **love-hate relationship** with someone or something, your feelings towards them change suddenly and often from love to hate.

love·less /ˈlʌvləs/. A **loveless** relationship or situa- ADJ tion is one where there is no love.

'love letter, love letters. A **love letter** is a letter N-COUNT that you write to someone in order to tell them that you love them.

'love life, love lives. Someone's **love life** is the ♦♢♢♢♢ part of their life that consists of their romantic and N-COUNT sexual relationships.

love·lorn /ˈlʌvlɔːn/. **Lovelorn** means the same as ADJ-GRADED **lovesick.** *He was acting like a lovelorn teenager.*

love·ly /ˈlʌvli/ **lovelier, loveliest.** If you describe ♦♦♦♢♢ someone or something as **lovely**, you like them very ADJ-GRADED much. *You look lovely, Marcia... He had a lovely* BRITISH *voice.* ♦ **love·li·ness** *You are a vision of loveliness.* N-UNCOUNT

'love-making. Love-making refers to sexual activ- N-UNCOUNT ities that take place between two people who love

each other. *Their love-making became less and less frequent.*

love nest, love nests. A **love nest** is a house or flat where two people who are having a love affair live or meet.   N-COUNT JOURNALISM

lov·er /'lʌvə/ **lovers. 1** Someone's **lover** is someone who they are having a sexual relationship with but are not married to. *He and Liz became lovers soon after they first met.* **2** If you are a **lover** of something such as animals or the arts, you enjoy them very much and take great pleasure in them. *She is a great lover of horses.*   ◆◆◆◇◇ N-COUNT / N-COUNT: with supp

love·sick /'lʌvsɪk/. If you describe someone as **lovesick**, you mean that they are so in love with someone, usually someone who does not love them, that they are behaving in a strange and foolish way. *Suddenly John felt like a lovesick teenager again.*   ADJ-GRADED

love story, love stories. A **love story** is something such as a novel or film about a love affair.   ◆◇◇◇ N-COUNT

love triangle, love triangles. A **love triangle** is a situation which involves three people who are each in love with at least one other person in the group.   N-COUNT JOURNALISM

lovey-dovey /ˌlʌvi 'dʌvi/. You can use **lovey-dovey** to describe, in a humorous or slightly disapproving way, lovers who show their affection for each other very openly. *All my friends were either lovey-dovey couples or wild, single girls.*   ADJ-GRADED PRAGMATICS INFORMAL

lov·ing /'lʌvɪŋ/. **1** Someone who is **loving** feels or shows love to other people. *Jim was a most loving husband.* ♦ **lov·ing·ly** *Brian gazed lovingly at Mary Ann.* **2 Loving** actions are done with great enjoyment and care. *The house has been restored with loving care.* ♦ **lovingly** *I lifted the box and ran my fingers lovingly over the top.* **3** See also **peace-loving**.   ◆◆◇◇◇ ADJ-GRADED / ADV-GRADED / ADJ-GRADED / ADV-GRADED

low /ləʊ/ **lower, lowest; lows. 1** Something that is **low** measures only a short distance from the bottom to the top, or from the ground to the top. *She put it down on the low table... The country, with its low, rolling hills, was beautiful.* **2** If something is **low**, it is close to the ground, to sea level, or to the bottom of something. *He bumped his head on the low beams... It was late afternoon and the sun was low in the sky.* **3** When a river is **low**, it contains less water than usual.   ◆◆◆◆◆ ADJ-GRADED / ADJ-GRADED / ADJ-GRADED

4 You can use **low** to indicate that something is small in amount or degree or that it is at the bottom of a particular scale. You can use phrases such as **in the low 80s** to indicate that, for example, a number or level is less than 85 but not as little as 80. *British casualties remained remarkably low... They are still having to live on very low incomes.* **5 Low** is used to describe people who are near the bottom of a particular scale or system. *She refused to promote Colin above the low rank of 'legal adviser'.* **6** If something reaches a **low** of a particular amount or degree, that is the smallest it has ever been. *The dollar fell to a new low.* **7** If you drive or ride in a **low** gear, you select a gear which gives you the most control over your car or bike, usually first or second gear. **8** If the quality or standard of something is **low**, it is very poor. *The inquiry team criticises staff at the psychiatric hospital for the low standard of care. ...low-grade coal.* **9** If you describe someone such as a student or a worker as a **low** achiever, you mean that they are not very good at their work, and do not achieve or produce as much as others. **10** If you have a **low** opinion of someone or something, you disapprove of them or dislike them. **11** You can use **low** to describe negative feelings and attitudes. *We are all very tired and morale is low... People had very low expectations.* **12** If you are **low**, you are depressed. **13** If a food or other substance is **low in** a particular ingredient, it contains only a small amount of that ingredient. *They look for foods that are low in calories.* ▶ Also a combining form. *...low-sodium tomato sauce.* **14** If you are **low** on something or if a supply of   ADJ-GRADED / ADJ-GRADED / N-COUNT / ADJ-GRADED / ADJ-GRADED: ADJ n / ADJ-GRADED / ADJ-GRADED / ADJ-GRADED INFORMAL / ADJ-GRADED: v-link ADJ in n / COMB / ADJ-GRADED:

it is **low**, there is not much of it left. *World stocks of wheat were getting very low.* **15** If a sound or noise is **low**, it is deep. **16** If someone's voice is **low**, it is quiet or soft. **17** A light that is **low** is dim and not bright or strong. **18** If a radio, oven, or light is on **low**, it has been adjusted so that only a small amount of sound, heat, or light is produced. *She turned her little kitchen radio on low... Cook the sauce over a low heat until it boils.* **19** See also **lower**. **20** If a disease or illness **lays** you **low**, it makes you weak or ill. **21** If you **are lying low**, you are hiding or not drawing attention to yourself. *Far from lying low, Kuti became more outspoken than ever.* **22** ● **low profile**: see **profile**. ● **to be running low**: see **run**.   v-link ADJ / ADJ-GRADED / ADJ-GRADED / ADJ-GRADED / ADJ-GRADED / PHRASE / PHRASE INFORMAL

low·brow /'ləʊbraʊ/; also spelled **low-brow**. If you say that something is **lowbrow**, you mean that it is simple and undemanding rather than being intellectual or complicated and is therefore sometimes regarded as being of inferior quality. *...a low-brow French comedy.*   ADJ-GRADED

low-·cut. Low-cut dresses and blouses leave a woman's neck and the top part of her chest bare.   ADJ-GRADED

low-down; also spelled **lowdown. 1** If someone gives you **the low-down** on something or someone, they tell you all the important information about them that they think you want or need to know. *We want you to give us the low-down on your teammates.* **2** You can use **low-down** to emphasize how bad, dishonest, or unfair you consider a person or their behaviour to be. *They will stoop to every low-down trick.*   N-SING: the N INFORMAL / ADJ-GRADED: ADJ n PRAGMATICS INFORMAL

low·er /'ləʊə/ **lowers, lowering, lowered. 1** You can use **lower** to refer to the bottom one of a pair of things. *She bit her lower lip... The upper layer of felt should overlap the lower. ...the lower of the two holes.* **2** You can use **lower** to refer to the bottom part of something. *Use a small cushion to help give support to the lower back. ...fires which started in the lower part of a tower block.* **3** You can use **lower** to refer to people or things that are less important than similar people or things. *The nation's highest court reversed the lower court's decision.* **4** If you **lower** something, you move it slowly downwards. *Two reporters had to help lower the coffin into the grave... Sokolowski lowered himself into the black leather chair.* ♦ **low·er·ing** *...the extinguishing of the Olympic flame and the lowering of the flag.* **5** If someone **lowers** their head, eyes, or gaze, they move their head or eyes so that they look downwards, for example because they are sad or embarrassed. **6** If you **lower** something, you make it less in amount, degree, value, or quality. *The Central Bank has lowered interest rates by 2 percent.* ♦ **lowering** *...a package of social measures which included the lowering of the retirement age.* **7** If you say that you would not **lower** yourself by doing something, you mean that you would not behave in a way that would make you or other people respect you less. *Don't lower yourself, don't be the way they are... I've got no qualms about lowering myself to Lemmer's level to get what I want.* **8** If you **lower** your voice, you speak more quietly. *His voice lowers confidentially.* **9** See also **low**.   ◆◆◆◇◇ ADJ-COMPAR: ADJ n, the ADJ ofn / ADJ-COMPAR: ADJ n / ADJ-COMPAR: ADJ n, the ADJ / VERB: V n V n prep/adv V pron-refl prep/adv / N-UNCOUNT / VERB: V n / VERB V n / N-UNCOUNT / VERB V pron-refl V pron-refl to n / V-ERG: V n V

lower 'case; also spelled **lower-case. Lower-case** letters are small letters, not capital letters.   N-UNCOUNT

lower 'class, lower classes; also spelled **lower-class.** Some people use the **lower class** or the **lower classes** to refer to the division of society that they consider to have the lowest social status. *Education now offers the lower classes access to job opportunities.* ▶ Also an adjective. *Bast is a lower-class young man who works as a clerk in an insurance office.*   N-COLL-COUNT / ADJ

lowest common de'nominator, lowest common denominators. 1 Lowest common denominator is used to refer critically to plans, ideas, opinions, or tastes which appeal to the majority of people or will be understood by the majority of people. *Tabloid newspapers pander to the lowest common*   N-COUNT PRAGMATICS

denominator. **2** In mathematics, the **lowest common denominator** is the smallest number that all the numbers on the bottom of a particular group of fractions can be divided into. N-COUNT TECHNICAL

,low-'flying. Low-flying aircraft or birds are flying very close to the ground, or lower than normal. ADJ: ADJ n

,low-'key. If you say that something is low-key, you mean that it is restrained rather than being as showy or intense as it could be. *The wedding will be a very low-key affair.* ◆◇◇◇◇ ADJ-GRADED

low·lands /'ləʊləndz/; the form lowland is used as a modifier. **Lowlands** are an area of low, flat land. *...the lowlands of the United Kingdom. ...lowland areas.* N-PLURAL

'low life; also spelled **low-life**. People sometimes use **low life** to refer critically to people who they find extremely unpleasant and disturbing, especially people who are involved in crime and violence. *...the sort of low-life characters who populate this film.* N-UNCOUNT PRAGMATICS

low·ly /'ləʊli/ lowlier, lowliest. If you describe someone or something as **lowly**, you mean that they are low in rank or importance. *...lowly bureaucrats pretending to be senators.* ◆◇◇◇◇ ADJ-GRADED

,low-'lying. Low-lying land is at, near, or below sea level. ADJ-GRADED

,low-'paid. If you describe someone or their job as **low-paid**, you mean that their work earns them very little money. ▶ **The low-paid** are people who are low-paid. ◆◇◇◇◇ ADJ-GRADED N-PLURAL: the N

,low-'pitched. **1** A sound that is **low-pitched** is deep. *With a low-pitched rumbling noise, the propeller began to rotate.* **2** A voice that is **low-pitched** is very soft and quiet. *He kept his voice low-pitched in case someone was listening.* ADJ-GRADED ADJ-GRADED

,low-'profile. A **low-profile** person or a **low-profile** event does not attract very much attention or publicity. *He is a low-profile figure who spent nearly 40 years in the company.* ADJ-GRADED

'low season. The low season is the time of year when a holiday resort, hotel, or tourist attraction receives the fewest visitors, and fares and holiday accommodation are often cheaper. The usual American term is **off season**. N-SING: the N BRITISH

,low-'slung. Low-slung chairs or cars are very low, so that you are close to the ground when you are sitting in them. ADJ-GRADED

,low-'tech. Low-tech machines or systems are ones that do not use modern sophisticated technology. *But in Tokyo, the police, with their bicycles and dial phones, are decidedly low-tech.* ADJ-GRADED

,low 'tide, low tides. At the coast, low tide is the time when the sea is at its lowest level because the tide is out. *The causeway to the island is only accessible at low tide.* N-VAR

,low 'water. Low water is the same as **low tide**. N-UNCOUNT

loy·al /'lɔɪəl/. If you describe someone as **loyal**, you mean that they remain firm in their friendship or support for someone or something. *He'd always been such a loyal friend to us all.* ◆ **loy·al·ly** *They have loyally supported their party and class.* ◆◆◇◇◇ ADJ-GRADED ADV-GRADED: ADV with v

loy·al·ist /'lɔɪəlɪst/ loyalists. A **loyalist** is a person who remains firm in their support for a government or ruler. ◆◇◇◇◇ N-COUNT

loy·al·ty /'lɔɪəlti/ loyalties. **1** Loyalty is the quality of staying firm in your friendship or support for someone or something. *I have sworn an oath of loyalty to the monarchy.* **2** Loyalties are feelings of friendship, support, or duty towards someone or something. *She had developed strong loyalties to the Manet family.* ◆◆◇◇◇ N-UNCOUNT N-COUNT

loz·enge /'lɒzɪndʒ/ lozenges. **1** Lozenges are sweets which you can suck to soothe a cough or sore throat. **2** A **lozenge** is a shape with four corners. The two corners that point up and down are further apart than the two pointing sideways. N-COUNT N-COUNT

LP /,el 'pi:/ LPs. An **LP** is a record which usually has about 25 minutes of music or speech on each side; **LP** is an abbreviation for 'long-playing record'. ◆◆◇◇◇ N-COUNT

'L-plate, L-plates. L-plates are signs with a red 'L' on them which you attach to a car to warn other drivers that you are a learner. N-COUNT BRITISH

LSD /,el es 'di:/. LSD is a very powerful illegal drug which causes hallucinations. ◆◇◇◇◇ N-UNCOUNT

Lt. Lt is a written abbreviation for **lieutenant**. ◆◇◇◇◇

Ltd. Ltd is a written abbreviation for **limited**; it is used after the name of a company. Compare **plc**. ◆◆◇◇◇ BRITISH

lub·ri·cant /'lu:brɪkənt/ lubricants. A **lubricant** is a substance which you put on the surfaces or parts of something, especially something mechanical, to make the parts move smoothly. ◆◇◇◇◇ N-VAR

lu·bri·cate /'lu:brɪkeɪt/ lubricates, lubricating, lubricated. If you **lubricate** something such as a part of a machine, you put a substance such as oil on it so that it moves smoothly. *...lubricating oil.* ◆ **lu·bri·ca·tion** /,lu:brɪ'keɪʃən/ *Use a touch of linseed oil for lubrication.* ◆◇◇◇◇ VERB: V n V-ing Also V FORMAL N-UNCOUNT

lu·cerne /lu:'sɜ:n/. Lucerne is a plant that is grown for animals to eat and in order to improve the soil. The usual American word is **alfalfa**. N-UNCOUNT BRITISH

lu·cid /'lu:sɪd/. **1** Lucid writing or speech is clear and easy to understand. *Haig was immediately impressed by his lucid explanation of the work.* ◆ **lu·cid·ly** *Both of them had the ability to present complex matters lucidly.* ◆ **lu·cid·ity** /lu:'sɪdɪti/. *His writings were marked by an extraordinary lucidity and elegance of style.* **2** If someone is **lucid**, they are thinking clearly again after a period of illness or confusion. *He wasn't very lucid, he didn't quite know where he was.* ◆ **lucidity** *The pain had lessened in the night, but so had his lucidity.* ◆◇◇◇◇ ADJ-GRADED ADV-GRADED: ADV with v N-UNCOUNT ADJ-GRADED FORMAL N-UNCOUNT

luck /lʌk/. **1** Luck or good luck is success or good things that happen to you, that do not come from your own abilities or efforts. *The Sri Lankans have been having no luck with the weather... The goal, when it came, owed more to good luck than good planning.* **2** Bad luck is lack of success or bad things that happen to you, that have not been caused by yourself or other people. *I had a lot of bad luck during the first half of this season.* **3** If you say that something **brings bad luck** or **brings** someone **good luck**, you believe that it has an influence on whether good or bad things happen to them. *Jean was extremely superstitious and believed the colour green brought bad luck.* **4** You can add **with luck** or **with any luck** to a statement to indicate that you hope that a particular thing will happen. *With any luck, she thought, the money would turn up somewhere.* **5** If you say 'Good luck' or 'Best of luck' to someone, you are telling them that you hope they will be successful in something they are trying to do. **6** You can say 'Bad luck', 'Hard luck', or 'Tough luck' to someone when you want to express your sympathy to them. **7** If you say that something is the luck of the draw, you mean that it is the result of chance and you cannot do anything about it. **8** See also **hard luck**. ● **take pot luck**: see **pot**. **9** You can say someone is in luck when they are in a situation where they can have what they want or need. *You're in luck. The doctor's still in.* **10** If you say that someone is out of luck, you mean that they cannot have something which they can normally have. *'What do you want, Roy? If it's money, you're out of luck.'* **11** If you describe someone as down on their luck, you mean that they have had bad experiences, often because they have not enough money. **12** You can say 'No such luck' when you want to express your disappointment over something. *He must have been hoping for a relaxed time. No such luck.* **13** If you say that someone is pushing their luck, you think they are taking a bigger risk than is sensible, and may get into trouble. **14** If someone tries their luck at something, they try to succeed at it, often when it is very difficult or there is little chance of success. *She was going to try her luck at the Las Vegas casinos.* ◆◆◆◇◇ N-UNCOUNT N-UNCOUNT PHRASE PHRASE PRAGMATICS INFORMAL CONVENTION PRAGMATICS INFORMAL CONVENTION PRAGMATICS INFORMAL PHRASE PHRASE PHRASE PHRASE CONVENTION INFORMAL PHRASE PHRASE

luck·i·ly /'lʌkɪli/. You add **luckily** to a statement to indicate that it is fortunate that something happened or is the case because otherwise the situation ◆◇◇◇◇ ADV-GRADED: ADV with cl

L

would have been difficult or unpleasant. *Luckily, we both love football.*

luck·less /'lʌkləs/. If you describe someone or something as **luckless**, you mean that they are unsuccessful or unfortunate. ADJ-GRADED LITERARY

lucky /'lʌki/ **luckier, luckiest. 1** You say that someone is **lucky** when they have something that is very desirable and when they are in a very desirable situation. *I am luckier than most. I have a job... He is incredibly lucky to be alive.* **2** Someone who is **lucky** seems to always have good luck. *He had always been lucky at cards.* **3** See also **happy-go-lucky. 4** You can use **lucky** in expressions such as **'Lucky you'** and **'Lucky devil'** when you are slightly jealous of someone else's good fortune or success, or surprised at it. **5** If you **strike lucky** or **strike it lucky**, you have some good luck. *You may strike lucky and find a sympathetic and helpful clerk.* **6** A **lucky** object is something that people believe helps them to be successful. *He did not have on his other lucky charm, a pair of green socks.* **7** If you say that it is **third time lucky** for someone, you mean that they have tried to do a particular thing twice before and that this time they will succeed. **8** If you describe a situation or event as **lucky**, you mean that it was fortunate or successful, and that it happened by chance and not as a result of planning. *He was lucky that it was only a can of beer that knocked him on the head.* **9** If you say that someone **will be lucky** to do or get something, you mean that they are very unlikely to be able to do or get it, and certainly will not do or get any more than that. *You'll be lucky if you get any breakfast... Those remaining in work will be lucky to get the smallest of pay increases.* **10** If you say that someone can **count** themselves **lucky**, you mean that the situation they are in or the thing that has happened to them is better than it might have been. *She counted herself lucky to get a job in one of Edinburgh's department stores.* **11 •** to **thank** one's **lucky stars**: see **star**.

lu·cra·tive /'lu:krətɪv/. A **lucrative** activity, job, or business deal is very profitable. ADJ-GRADED

lu·cre /'lu:kə/. People sometimes refer to money or profit as **lucre**, especially when they think that it has been obtained by dishonest means. *...so they can feel less guilty about their piles of filthy lucre.* N-UNCOUNT PRAGMATICS DATED

Lud·dite /'lʌdaɪt/ **Luddites.** If you refer to someone as a **Luddite**, you are criticizing them for opposing changes in industrial methods, especially the introduction of new machines and modern methods. N-COUNT PRAGMATICS

lu·di·crous /'lu:dɪkrəs/. If you describe something as **ludicrous**, you mean that it is foolish, unreasonable, or unsuitable. *It was ludicrous to suggest that the visit could be kept secret.* **♦ lu·di·crous·ly** *By Western standards the prices are ludicrously low.* ADJ-GRADED PRAGMATICS ADV-GRADED

lug /lʌg/ **lugs, lugging, lugged.** If you **lug** a heavy or awkward object somewhere, you carry it there with difficulty. *Nobody wants to lug around huge suitcases... I hastily packed the hamper and lugged it to the car.* VERB V n with adv V n prep Also V n INFORMAL

lug·gage /'lʌgɪdʒ/. **Luggage** is the suitcases and bags that you take with you when you travel. N-UNCOUNT

lu·gu·bri·ous /lu:'gu:brɪəs/. If you say that someone or something is **lugubrious**, you mean that they are sad and gloomy. ADJ-GRADED LITERARY

luke·warm /,lu:k'wɔ:m/. **1** Something, especially a liquid, that is **lukewarm** is only slightly warm. *Wash your face with lukewarm water and a mild soap.* **2** If you describe a person or their attitude as **lukewarm**, you mean that they are not showing much enthusiasm or interest. *Economists have never been more than lukewarm towards him.* ADJ-GRADED ADJ-GRADED

lull /lʌl/ **lulls, lulling, lulled. 1** A **lull** is a period of quiet or calm in a longer period of activity or excitement. *...a lull in the conversation.* **2** If you are **lulled** into feeling safe, someone or something causes you to feel safe at a time when you are not safe. *It is easy to be lulled into a false sense of security... Lulled by almost uninterrupted economic* N-COUNT VERB be V-ed into n/-ing V-ed Also V n into n/-ing

growth, too many European firms assumed that this would last for ever. **3** If someone or something **lulls** you, they cause you to feel calm or sleepy. *The heat and hum of the forest had lulled him to sleep.* VERB: V n V n into/to n

lulla·by /'lʌləbaɪ/ **lullabies.** A **lullaby** is a quiet song which is sung to babies and young children to help them go to sleep. N-COUNT

lum·ba·go /lʌm'beɪgəʊ/. If someone has **lumbago**, they have pains in the lower part of their back. N-UNCOUNT

lum·bar /'lʌmbə/. **Lumbar** means relating to the lower part of your back. *Lumbar support is very important if you're driving a long way.* ADJ: ADJ n MEDICAL

lum·ber /'lʌmbə/ **lumbers, lumbering, lumbered. 1** Lumber consists of trees and large pieces of wood that have been roughly cut up. *The lumber from different trees of the same species will vary in color and texture.* **2** If someone or something **lumbers** from one place to another, they move there very slowly and clumsily. *He turned and lumbered back to his chair. ...a lumbering lorry.* N-UNCOUNT AMERICAN VERB V adv/prep V-ing

lumber with. If you **are lumbered with** someone or something, you have to deal with them even though you do not want to and this annoys you. *She lost her libel action against Channel 4 and was lumbered with a 300,000 pound bill.* PHRASAL VB usu passive PRAGMATICS be V-ed P n INFORMAL, BRITISH

lumber·jack /'lʌmbədʒæk/ **lumberjacks.** A **lumberjack** is a person whose job is to cut down trees. N-COUNT

lu·mi·nary /'lu:mɪnəri, AM -neri/ **luminaries.** If you refer to someone as a **luminary**, you mean that they are an expert in a particular subject or activity. N-COUNT LITERARY

lu·mi·nes·cence /,lu:mɪ'nesəns/. **Luminescence** is a soft, glowing light. N-UNCOUNT LITERARY

lu·mi·nos·ity /,lu:mɪ'nɒsɪti/. The **luminosity** of a star or sun is how bright it is. N-UNCOUNT TECHNICAL

lu·mi·nous /'lu:mɪnəs/. Something that is **luminous** shines or glows in the dark. *The luminous dial on the clock showed five minutes to seven.* ADJ-GRADED

lump /lʌmp/ **lumps, lumping, lumped. 1** A **lump** of something is a solid piece of it. *The potter shaped and squeezed the lump of clay into a graceful shape.* **2** A **lump** of sugar is a small cube of it. *'No sugar,' I said, and Jim asked for two lumps.* **3** A **lump** on or in someone's body is a small, hard swelling that has been caused by an injury or an illness. **4** If you say that you have a **lump in** your throat, you mean that you have a tight feeling in your throat because of a strong emotion such as sorrow or gratitude. **5** See also **lump sum. 6** If you say that someone **will have to lump it**, you mean that they must accept a situation whether they like it or not. *The crew will be sleeping in the hull and will have to lump it.* N-COUNT N-COUNT N-COUNT PHRASE PHRASE INFORMAL, BRITISH

lump together. If a number of different people or things **are lumped together**, they are considered as a group rather than separately. *Because she was lumped together with alcoholics and hard-drug users, Claire felt out of place.* PHRASAL VB usu passive, be V-ed P be V-ed P with n

lump·en /'lʌmpən/. If you describe people as **lumpen**, you think they are dull and clumsy. ADJ-GRADED BRITISH

lump 'sum, lump sums. A **lump sum** is an amount of money that is paid as a large amount on a single occasion rather than as smaller amounts on several separate occasions. *...a tax-free lump sum of £50,000 at retirement age.* N-COUNT

lumpy /'lʌmpi/ **lumpier, lumpiest.** Something that is **lumpy** contains lumps or is covered with lumps. ADJ-GRADED

lu·na·cy /'lu:nəsi/. **1** If you describe someone's behaviour as **lunacy**, you mean that it seems very strange or foolish. **2** Lunacy is severe mental illness. *Lunacy became the official explanation for Hess's actions.* N-UNCOUNT PRAGMATICS N-UNCOUNT DATED

lu·nar /'lu:nə/. **Lunar** means relating to the moon. *...man's first lunar landing.* ADJ: ADJ n

lu·na·tic /'lu:nətɪk/ **lunatics. 1** If you describe someone as a **lunatic**, you think they behave in a dangerous, stupid, or annoying way. *If Sid wanted to behave like a lunatic, that was his choice.* **2** If you describe someone's behaviour or ideas as **lunatic**, N-COUNT PRAGMATICS INFORMAL ADJ-GRADED PRAGMATICS

you think they are very foolish and possibly dangerous. **3** People who were mentally ill used to be called **lunatics**; some people find this use offensive. N-COUNT DATED

'lunatic asylum, lunatic asylums. A lunatic **asylum** was a place where mentally disturbed people used to be locked up. N-COUNT

,lunatic 'fringe. If you refer to a group of people as the **lunatic fringe**, you mean that they are very extreme in their opinions or behaviour. *Demands for a separate Siberia are confined for now to the lunatic fringe.* N-SING

lunch /lʌntʃ/ **lunches, lunching, lunched. 1** Lunch is the meal that you have in the middle of the day. *He did not enjoy business lunches.* **2** When you **lunch**, you have lunch, especially at a restaurant. *Only the extremely rich could afford to lunch at the Mirabelle.* **3** If you say there's no such thing as a **free lunch**, you are saying that most things that are worth having need to be paid for or worked for, and that you cannot expect to get things for nothing. ◆◆◆◇ N-VAR / VERB: V / V adv/prep FORMAL / PHRASE

'lunch box, lunch boxes; also spelled **lunchbox.** A **lunch box** is a small container with a lid. You put food in it to eat for lunch at work or at school. N-COUNT

'lunch break, lunch breaks; also spelled **lunchbreak.** Your **lunch break** is the period in the middle of the day when you stop work in order to have a meal. N-COUNT

'lunch counter, lunch counters. A lunch counter is an informal café or a counter in a shop where people can buy and eat meals. N-COUNT AMERICAN

lunch·eon /'lʌntʃən/ **luncheons. 1** A luncheon is a formal lunch. People are often invited to luncheons to celebrate an important event or to raise money for charity. **2** Luncheon is the meal that you eat in the middle of the day. ◆◇◇◇ N-COUNT / N-VAR FORMAL

'luncheon meat, luncheon meats. Luncheon **meat** is a type of cooked meat that is often sold in tins. It is a mixture of pork and cereal. ◆◇◇◇ N-VAR BRITISH

'lunch hour, lunch hours. Your **lunch hour** is the period in the middle of the day when you stop working, usually for one hour, in order to have a meal. N-COUNT

lunch·time /'lʌntʃtaɪm/ **lunchtimes;** also spelled **lunch time.** Lunchtime is the period of the day when people have their lunch. ◆◆◇◇ N-VAR

lung /lʌŋ/ **lungs.** Your **lungs** are the two organs inside your chest which fill with air when you breathe in. ◆◆◇◇ N-COUNT

lunge /lʌndʒ/ **lunges, lunging, lunged.** If you **lunge** in a particular direction, you move in that direction suddenly and clumsily. *He lunged at me, grabbing me violently.* ▶ Also a noun. *The attacker knocked on their door and made a lunge for Wendy when she answered.* ◆◇◇◇ VERB / V prep/adv / N-COUNT

lung·ful /'lʌŋfʊl/ **lungfuls.** If someone takes a **lungful** of something such as air or smoke, they breathe in deeply so that their lungs feel as if they are full of that thing. N-COUNT

lurch /lɜːtʃ/ **lurches, lurching, lurched. 1** To **lurch** means to make a sudden, unintentional, jerky movement, especially forwards. *Henry looked, stared, and lurched to his feet.* ▶ Also a noun. *The car took a lurch forward but grounded in a deep rut.* **2** If you say that a person or organization **lurches** from one thing to another, you mean they move suddenly from one course of action or attitude to another in an uncontrolled way. *The first round of multilateral trade talks has lurched between hope and despair.* ▶ Also a noun. *The property sector was another casualty of the lurch towards higher interest rates.* **3** If someone **leaves** you **in the lurch**, they go away or stop helping you at a very difficult time. ◆◇◇◇ VERB / V adv/prep / Also V / N-COUNT // VERB: / V from n to n / V prep/adv / N-COUNT // PHRASE INFORMAL

lure /ljʊə, AM lʊr/ **lures, luring, lured. 1** To **lure** someone means to trick them into a particular place or to trick them into doing something that they should not do. *They did not realise that they were being lured into a trap... The company aims to lure smokers back to cigarettes.* **2** A **lure** is something such as bait which is used to attract prey to a certain place so that they can be caught. **3** A **lure** is ◆◆◇◇ VERB / V n prep/adv / N-COUNT / N-COUNT

an attractive quality that something has, or something that you find attractive. *The lure of rural life is proving as strong as ever.*

lu·rid /'ljʊərɪd, AM 'lʊrɪd/. **1** If you say that something is **lurid**, you are critical of it because it involves a lot of violence, sex, or shocking detail. *...lurid accounts of Claire's sexual exploits.* **2** If you describe something as **lurid**, you do not like it because it is very brightly coloured. *She took care to paint her toe nails a lurid red or orange.* ◆◇◇◇ ADJ-GRADED PRAGMATICS / ADJ-GRADED PRAGMATICS

lurk /lɜːk/ **lurks, lurking, lurked. 1** If someone **lurks** somewhere, they wait there secretly so that they cannot be seen, usually because they intend to do something bad. *Their attack came close to the trees where Harper lurked with his seven-barrelled gun.* **2** If something such as a bad memory, suspicion, or danger **lurks**, it exists, but you are only slightly aware of it. *Hidden dangers lurk in every family saloon car... Around every corner lurked doubt and uncertainty.* ◆◇◇◇ VERB V / VERB V

lus·cious /'lʌʃəs/. **1** If you describe a woman or something about her as **luscious**, you mean that you find her sexually attractive. *What I like most about Gabby is her luscious lips!* **2** Luscious food is juicy and delicious. ◆◇◇◇ ADJ-GRADED / ADJ-GRADED

lush /lʌʃ/ **lusher, lushest. 1** Lush fields or gardens have a lot of very healthy grass or plants. **2** If you describe a place or thing as **lush**, you mean that it is very luxurious. ◆◇◇◇ ADJ-GRADED / ADJ-GRADED: / v-link ADJ

lust /lʌst/ **lusts, lusting, lusted. 1** Lust is a feeling of strong sexual desire for someone. *His lust for her grew until it was overpowering.* **2** A lust for something is a very strong and eager desire to have it. *It was Fred's lust for glitz and glamour that was driving them apart.* ◆◇◇◇ N-UNCOUNT / N-UNCOUNT

lust after or **lust for. 1** If you **lust after** someone or **lust for** them, you feel a very strong sexual desire for them. **2** If you **lust after** or **lust for** something, you have a very strong desire to possess it. *Sheard lusted after the Directorship.* PHRASAL VB / V P n / V P n

lust·ful /'lʌstfʊl/. **Lustful** means feeling or expressing strong sexual desire. *He can't stop himself from having lustful thoughts.* ADJ

lus·tre /'lʌstə/; spelled **luster** in American English. **1** Lustre is gentle shining light that is reflected from a surface, for example from polished metal. *Gold retains its lustre for far longer than other metals.* **2** Lustre is the qualities that something has that make it interesting and exciting. *What do you do if your relationship is beginning to lose its lustre?* N-UNCOUNT / N-UNCOUNT

lus·trous /'lʌstrəs/. Something that is **lustrous** shines brightly and gently, because it has a smooth or shiny surface. ADJ-GRADED

lusty /'lʌsti/ **lustier, lustiest.** If you say that something is **lusty**, you mean that it is healthy and full of strength and energy. *...plants with large, lusty roots.* ◆ **lusti·ly** *Bob ate lustily.* ADJ-GRADED / ADV-GRADED

lute /luːt/ **lutes.** A **lute** is a stringed instrument that looks rather like a guitar. You play the lute by plucking the strings. N-VAR

luv /lʌv/. **Luv** is an informal written form of the word 'love', when it is being used as a way of addressing someone. *You'll have to be quick, luv; we've a plane to catch.* N-VOC PRAGMATICS BRITISH

luv·vie /'lʌvi/ **luvvies.** People sometimes refer to actors and actresses as **luvvies** as a humorous way of criticizing their behaviour and pretentiousness. N-COUNT PRAGMATICS INFORMAL, BRITISH

luxu·ri·ant /lʌg'ʒʊəriənt/. **1** Luxuriant plants, trees, and gardens are healthy and growing well. **2** Luxuriant hair is thick and healthy. ADJ-GRADED / ADJ-GRADED

luxu·ri·ate /lʌg'ʒʊərieɪt/ **luxuriates, luxuriating, luxuriated.** If you **luxuriate in** something, you relax in it and enjoy it very much, especially because you find it comfortable and luxurious. *...Ralph was luxuriating in the first real holiday he'd had in years.* VERB V in n

luxu·ri·ous /lʌg'ʒʊəriəs/. **1** If you describe something as **luxurious**, you mean that it is very comfortable and expensive. *She had come to enjoy Roberto's luxurious life-style.* ◆ **luxu·ri·ous·ly** *The dining-room is luxuriously furnished and carpeted.* ◆◇◇◇ ADJ-GRADED / ADV-GRADED

2 Luxurious means feeling or expressing great pleasure and comfort. *Amy tilted her wine in her glass with a luxurious sigh.* ♦ **luxuriously** *Liz laughed, stretching luxuriously.* ADJ-GRADED / ADV-GRADED: ADV after v

luxu·ry /ˈlʌkʃəri/ **luxuries. 1 Luxury** is very great comfort, especially among beautiful and expensive surroundings. *By all accounts he leads a life of considerable luxury.* **2** A **luxury** is something expensive which is not necessary but which gives you pleasure. *A week by the sea is a luxury they can no longer afford.* ▶ Also an adjective. *He could not afford luxury food on his pay.* **3** A **luxury** is a pleasure which you do not often have the opportunity to enjoy. *Hot baths are my favourite luxury.* ♦♦♦◇◇ N-UNCOUNT / N-COUNT / ADJ: ADJ n / N-SING: with supp

'**luxury goods. Luxury goods** are things which are not necessary, but which give you pleasure or make your life more comfortable. *...increased taxes on luxury goods, such as boats, fur coats and expensive cars.* N-PLURAL

LW. LW is an abbreviation for **long wave.**

-ly /-li/ **-lier, -liest. 1 -ly** is added to adjectives to form adverbs that indicate the manner or nature of something. *I saw Louise walking slowly to the bus stop... Sarah has typically British fair skin.* **2 -ly** is added to nouns to form adjectives that describe someone or something as being like or typical of a particular kind of person or thing. *The staff are very friendly... This was a cowardly thing to do.* **3 -ly** is added to nouns referring to periods of time to form adjectives or adverbs that say how often something happens or is done. *...monthly payments. ...the language that we use daily.* SUFFIX / SUFFIX / SUFFIX

ly·chee /ˈlaɪtʃiː, AM ˈliːtʃiː/ **lychees. Lychees** are Chinese fruit which have white flesh and large stones inside and a pinkish-brown skin. N-VAR

Ly·cra /ˈlaɪkrə/ **Lycra** is a type of stretchy fabric, ♦◇◇◇◇ similar to elastic, which is used to make tight-fitting garments such as tights and swimming costumes. **Lycra** is a trademark. N-UNCOUNT

ly·ing /ˈlaɪɪŋ/. **Lying** is the present participle of **lie.**

lymph gland /ˈlɪmf ɡlænd/ **lymph glands. Lymph glands** are small masses of tissue in various parts of your body. They contain special white blood cells which fight infection. N-COUNT

lynch /lɪntʃ/ **lynches, lynching, lynched.** If an angry crowd of people **lynch** someone, they kill that person by hanging them, without letting them have a trial, because they believe that that person has committed a crime. ♦ **lynch·ing, lynchings** *Some towns found that lynching was the only way to drive away bands of outlaws.* ♦♦◇◇◇ VERB: V n / N-VAR

lynch·pin /ˈlɪntʃpɪn/. See **linchpin.**

lynx /lɪŋks/ **lynxes.** A **lynx** is a wild animal similar to a large cat. N-COUNT

lyre /laɪə/ **lyres.** A **lyre** is a stringed instrument that looks like a small harp. N-COUNT

lyr·ic /ˈlɪrɪk/ **lyrics. 1 Lyric** poetry is written in a simple and direct style, and usually expresses personal emotions such as love. **2** The **lyrics** of a song are its words. ♦♦◇◇◇ ADJ: ADJ n / N-COUNT

lyri·cal /ˈlɪrɪkəl/. Something that is **lyrical** is poetic and romantic. *His paintings became more lyrical.* ♦ **lyri·cal·ly** *I'm trying to show children that it's lyrically beautiful out there, wherever you live.* ● to **wax lyrical:** see **wax.** ♦◇◇◇◇ ADJ-GRADED / ADV-GRADED

lyri·cism /ˈlɪrɪsɪzəm/. **Lyricism** is gentle and romantic emotion, often expressed in writing, poetry, or music. *...a natural lyricism which can be expressed through dance and music.* N-UNCOUNT

lyri·cist /ˈlɪrɪsɪst/ **lyricists.** A **lyricist** is someone who writes the words for modern songs or musicals. N-COUNT

M m

M, m /em/ **M's, m's. 1 M** is the thirteenth letter of the English alphabet. **2 m** is a written abbreviation for 'metres' or 'metre'. *The isthmus is only 200m wide.* **3 m** is a written abbreviation for the number 'million'. *Exports reached $150m.* **4 M** or **m** is used as an abbreviation for words beginning with m, such as 'minutes', 'married', 'masculine', and 'male'. N-VAR

-'m /-m/. In spoken English and in informal written English, **'m** is a short form of 'am'. *I'm not hungry.*

ma /mɑː/ **mas.** Some people refer to or address their mother as **ma.** ♦◇◇◇◇ N-FAMILY INFORMAL

MA /ˌem ˈeɪ/ **MAs. 1** An **MA** is a master's degree in an arts or social science subject. **MA** is an abbreviation for Master of Arts. **2 MA** is written after someone's name to indicate that they have an MA. ♦◇◇◇◇ N-COUNT

ma'am /mæm, mɑːm/. People sometimes say **ma'am** as a formal and polite way of addressing a woman whose name they do not know or a woman of superior rank. ♦◇◇◇◇ N-VOC PRAGMATICS

mac /mæk/ **macs.** A **mac** is a raincoat, especially one made from a particular kind of waterproof cloth. N-COUNT BRITISH

maca·bre /məˈkɑːbrə/. You describe something such as an event or story as **macabre** when it is strange and horrible or upsetting, usually because it involves death or injury. ♦◇◇◇◇ ADJ-GRADED

maca·ro·ni /ˌmækəˈrəʊni/. **Macaroni** is a kind of pasta made in the shape of short hollow tubes. N-UNCOUNT

maca·roon /ˌmækəˈruːn/ **macaroons. Macaroons** are sweet biscuits flavoured with almond. N-COUNT

mace /meɪs/ **maces. 1** A **mace** is an ornamental stick carried by an official or placed somewhere as a symbol of authority. **2 Mace** is a spice, usually in the form of a powder, made from the shell of nutmegs. **3 Mace** is a substance that causes tears and sickness, and that is used in sprays as a defence against rioters or attackers. **Mace** is a trademark. N-COUNT / N-UNCOUNT / N-UNCOUNT

mac·er·ate /ˈmæsəreɪt/ **macerates, macerating, macerated.** If you **macerate** food in a liquid, you soak it for a period of time so that it absorbs the liquid. *Cognac is also used to macerate and flavour ingredients... Leave for four to five days to macerate.* V-ERG: V n in n / V

Mach /mɑːk/. **Mach** is used as a unit of measurement in stating the speed of a moving object in relation to the speed of sound. For example, if an aircraft is travelling at Mach 1, it is travelling at exactly the speed of sound. N-UNCOUNT: N n/num TECHNICAL

ma·chete /məˈʃeti/ **machetes.** A **machete** is a large knife with a broad blade. N-COUNT

Machia·vel·lian /ˌmækiəˈveliən/. If you describe someone as **Machiavellian**, you are critical of them because they use cleverness and trickery to get what they want, and they do not care about morals, conventions, or other people. ADJ-GRADED PRAGMATICS

machi·na·tions /ˌmækɪˈneɪʃənz, ˌmæʃ-/. **Machinations** are someone's secret and complicated plans to gain power; used showing disapproval. *...the political machinations that brought him to power.* N-PLURAL PRAGMATICS

ma·chine /məˈʃiːn/ **machines, machining, machined. 1** A **machine** is a piece of equipment which uses electricity or an engine in order to do a ♦♦♦♦◇ N-COUNT: also by N

particular kind of work. *I put the coin in the machine and pulled the lever. ...a color photograph of the sort taken by machine.* **2** If something **is machined**, it is made or worked on using a machine. *The material is machined in a factory.* ♦ **ma·chin·ing** *...our machining, fabrication and finishing processes.* **3** You can use **machine** to refer to a large and well-controlled system or organization. *...Nazi Germany's military machine.* **4** If you say that someone is a **machine**, you mean that they seem to do their work without thinking or feeling anything. **5** See also **fruit machine**, **sewing machine**, **slot machine**, **vending machine**.

ma'chine code. Machine code is a way of expressing instructions and information in a numerical form which can be understood by a computer or microchip.

ma'chine gun, **machine guns**. also spelled **machine-gun**. A **machine gun** is a gun which fires a lot of bullets one after the other very quickly. *...a burst of machine-gun fire.* ● See also **sub-machine gun**.

ma·chin·ery /məˈʃiːnəri/. **1** You can use **machinery** to refer to machines in general, or machines that are used in a factory or on a farm. *...your local garden machinery specialist.* **2** The **machinery** of a government or organization is the system and all the procedures that it uses to deal with things. *The machinery of democracy could be created quickly.*

ma'chine tool, **machine tools**. A **machine tool** is a machine that cuts, shapes, or finishes metal or other materials.

ma·chin·ist /məˈʃiːnɪst/ **machinists**. A **machinist** is a person whose job is to operate a machine, especially in a factory.

ma·chis·mo /məˈtʃɪzməʊ, AM mɑːˈtʃiːz-/. You use **machismo** to refer to men's behaviour or attitudes when they are very conscious and proud of their masculinity.

macho /ˈmætʃəʊ, AM ˈmɑː-/. You use **macho** to describe men who are very conscious and proud of their masculinity. *...displays of macho bravado.*

mac·in·tosh /ˈmækɪntɒʃ/. See **mackintosh**.

macke·rel /ˈmækərəl/; **mackerel** is both the singular and the plural. A **mackerel** is a sea fish with a greeny-blue skin. ▶ **Mackerel** is this fish eaten as food.

mack·in·tosh /ˈmækɪntɒʃ/ **mackintoshes**. A **mackintosh** is a raincoat, especially one made from a particular kind of waterproof cloth.

macro /ˈmækrəʊ/. You use **macro** to indicate that something relates to something general or large in scope, rather than being detailed or specific, especially when talking about business, finance, and management. *...regulation of the economy both at the macro level and at the micro level.* ♦ **macro-** *...macro-economic policy. ...the macro-relationship between unemployment and imprisonment.*

macro·bi·ot·ic /ˌmækrəʊbaɪˈɒtɪk/. **Macrobiotic** food consists of whole grains and vegetables that are grown without chemicals.

macro·cosm /ˈmækrəʊkɒzəm/. A **macrocosm** is a complex organized system such as the universe or a society, considered as a single unit.

mad /mæd/ **madder**, **maddest**. **1** Someone who is **mad** has a mind that does not work in a normal way, with the result that their behaviour is very strange. *She was afraid of going mad.* ♦ **mad·ness** *He was driven to the brink of madness.* **2** You use **mad** to describe people or things that you think are very foolish. *You must be mad to work with him again.* ♦ **madness** *It is political madness.* **3** If someone is **mad**, they are very angry. *You're just mad at me because I don't want to go.* **4** If you say that someone or something **drives** you **mad**, you mean that you find them extremely annoying. *This itching is driving me mad.* **5** If you are **mad about** or **mad on** something or someone, you like them very much indeed. *He's mad about you... He's mad on trains... She's not as mad*

about sport as I am. ▶ Also a combining form. *...his football-mad son.* **6 Mad** behaviour is wild and uncontrolled. *You only have an hour to complete the game so it's a mad dash... The audience went mad.* ♦ **mad·ly** *Down in the streets people were waving madly.* **7** If you do something **like mad**, you do it very energetically or enthusiastically. *He was weight training like mad.* **8** See also **madly**.

mad·am /ˈmædəm/ **madams**. **1** People sometimes say **Madam** as a very formal and polite way of addressing a woman whose name they do not know or a woman of superior rank. **2** You use the expression **'Dear madam'** at the beginning of a formal letter or a business letter when you are writing to a woman. **3 Madam** is sometimes used in front of words such as 'Chairman' to address the woman who holds the position mentioned. *I have to say this, Madam Chairman.* **4** You can call a little girl a **madam** if you are annoyed because she is being naughty and behaving as if she expects other people to do what she wants.

mad·cap /ˈmædkæp/. A **madcap** plan or scheme is very foolish and not likely to succeed.

mad 'cow disease. **Mad cow disease** is a fatal disease which affects the nervous system of cattle.

mad·den /ˈmædən/ **maddens**, **maddening**, **maddened**. To **madden** a person or animal means to make them very angry.

mad·den·ing /ˈmædənɪŋ/. If you describe something as **maddening**, you mean that it makes you feel angry, irritated, or frustrated. ♦ **mad·den·ing·ly** *The service is maddeningly slow.*

made /meɪd/. **1 Made** is the past tense and past participle of **make**. **2** If something is **made of** or **made out of** a particular substance or material, that substance or material was used to build or construct it. *What is the statue made out of?* **3** If you say that someone **has it made** or **has got it made**, you mean that they are certain to be rich or successful.

-made /-meɪd/. **-made** combines with words such as 'factory' to make adjectives that indicate that something has been made or produced in a particular place or in a particular way. *...a British-made car. ...specially-made footwear.*

made-to-'measure. A **made-to-measure** suit, shirt, or other item of clothing is one that is made by a tailor to fit you exactly, rather than one that you buy already made in a shop.

'made-up; also spelled **made up**. **1** If you are **made-up**, you are wearing make-up such as powder or eye shadow. *She was made-up and ready to go. ...heavily made-up eyes.* **2** A **made-up** word, name, or story is invented, rather than really existing or being true.

mad·house /ˈmædhaʊs/ **madhouses**. **1** If you describe a place or situation as a **madhouse**, you mean that it is full of confusion and noise. **2** A **madhouse** is a mental hospital.

mad·ly /ˈmædli/. **1** If one person is **madly** in love with another, they love that person a great deal. *She has fallen madly in love with him.* **2** You can use **madly** in front of an adjective in order to emphasize a particular quality. *Inside it is madly busy.*

mad·man /ˈmædmən/ **madmen**. A **madman** is a man who is insane.

Ma·don·na /məˈdɒnə/. Catholics and other Christians sometimes call Mary, the mother of Jesus Christ, **the Madonna**.

mad·ras /məˈdræs, -ˈdrɑːs/. A **madras** curry is a rather hot spicy curry.

mad·ri·gal /ˈmædrɪgəl/ **madrigals**. A **madrigal** is a song sung by several singers without any musical instruments.

mad·woman /ˈmædwʊmən/ **madwomen**. A **madwoman** is a woman who is insane.

mael·strom /ˈmeɪlstrɒm/ **maelstroms**. If you describe a situation as a **maelstrom**, you mean that it is very confused, violent, or destructive. *Inside, she was a maelstrom of churning emotions.*

maes·tro /ˈmaɪstrəʊ/ **maestros.** A maestro is a skilled and well-known musician or conductor. `◆◇◇◇◇` `N-COUNT`

ma·fia /ˈmæfiə, AM ˈmɑːf-/ **mafias. 1** The Mafia is a criminal organization that gets money illegally, especially by threatening people, dealing in drugs, and prostitution. **2** You can use mafia to refer to an organized group of people who you disapprove of because they use unfair or illegal means in order to get what they want. ...*the south-based education-reform mafia.* `N-COUNT; N-VOC` `N-COLL-COUNT: theN` `N-COUNT` `PRAGMATICS`

mag /mæg/ **mags.** A mag is the same as a magazine. `◆◇◇◇◇` `N-COUNT` `INFORMAL`

maga·zine /ˌmægəˈziːn, AM -zɪːn/ **magazines. 1** A magazine is a publication with a paper cover which is issued regularly, usually weekly or monthly, and which contains articles, stories, photographs, and advertisements. **2** On radio or television, a magazine or a magazine programme is a programme consisting of several items about different topics, people, and events. ...*a live arts magazine.* **3** In a gun, the magazine is the compartment for the cartridges. **4** A magazine is a building in which ammunition and explosives are kept. `◆◆◆◇` `N-COUNT` `N-COUNT` `N-COUNT` `N-COUNT`

ma·gen·ta /məˈdʒentə/ **magentas.** If something is magenta, it is dark reddish-purple. `COLOUR`

mag·got /ˈmægət/ **maggots.** Maggots are tiny creatures that look like very small worms and turn into flies. `◆◆◇◇◇` `N-COUNT`

mag·ic /ˈmædʒɪk/. **1** Magic is the power to use supernatural forces to make impossible things happen, such as making people disappear or controlling events in nature. *They believe in magic... Legends say that Merlin raised the stones by magic.* **2** You can use magic when you are referring to an event or change that is so wonderful, strange, quick, or unexpected that it seems as if supernatural powers have caused it. *All this was supposed to work magic... The fog disappeared like magic.* **3** You use magic to describe something that does things, or appears to do things, by magic. ...*the magic ingredient that helps to keep skin looking smooth.* **4** Magic is the art and skill of performing mysterious tricks to entertain people, for example by making things appear and disappear. **5** If you refer to the magic of something, you mean that it has a special mysterious quality which makes it seem wonderful and exciting to you and which makes you feel happy. *There can be a magic about love that defies all explanation.* ► Also an adjective. ...*those magic moments in the rose-garden.* **6** If you refer to a person's magic, you mean a special talent or ability that they have, which you admire or consider very impressive. **7** You can use expressions such as the magic number and the magic word to talk about a number or word which is significant or desirable in a particular situation. ...*their quest to gain the magic number of 270 electoral votes.* **8** Magic is used in expressions such as there is no magic formula and there is no magic solution to say that someone will have to make an effort to solve a problem, because it will not solve itself. `◆◆◇◇◇` `N-UNCOUNT` `N-UNCOUNT` `ADJ: ADJ n` `N-UNCOUNT` `N-UNCOUNT` `ADJ-GRADED` `N-UNCOUNT` `ADJ: theADJ n` `ADJ: ADJ n, with neg`

magi·cal /ˈmædʒɪkəl/. **1** Something that is magical seems to use magic or to be able to produce magic. ...*a little boy who has magical powers.* **♦ magi·cal·ly** /ˈmædʒɪkli/. *He is magically transported through the cinema screen.* **2** You can say that a place or object is magical when it has a special mysterious quality that makes it seem wonderful and exciting. `◆◆◇◇◇` `N-UNCOUNT` `ADV: ADV with v` `ADJ-GRADED`

magic 'carpet, magic carpets. In stories, a magic carpet is a special carpet that can carry people through the air. `N-COUNT`

ma·gi·cian /məˈdʒɪʃən/ **magicians. 1** A magician is a person who entertains people by doing magic tricks. **2** In fairy stories, a magician is a person, usually a man, who has magic powers. **3** If you call someone a magician, you admire the skilful and exciting way they do something. *Bevan was a magician with words.* `◆◇◇◇◇` `N-COUNT` `N-COUNT` `N-COUNT` `PRAGMATICS`

magic 'wand, magic wands. 1 A magic wand or a wand is a long thin rod that magicians and `N-COUNT`

fairies wave when they are performing tricks and magic. **2** You use magic wand, especially in the expression there is no magic wand, to indicate that someone is dealing with a difficult problem which cannot be solved quickly and easily. *There is no magic wand to secure a just peace.* `N-COUNT`

mag·is·te·rial /ˌmædʒɪˈstɪəriəl/. If you describe someone's behaviour or work as magisterial, you mean that they show great authority or ability. `ADJ-GRADED` `FORMAL`

mag·is·trate /ˈmædʒɪstreɪt/ **magistrates.** A magistrate is a person who is appointed to act as a judge in law courts which deal with minor crimes or disputes. `◆◆◇◇` `N-COUNT`

mag·nani·mous /mægˈnænɪməs/. If you are magnanimous, you behave well and generously towards other people, especially people who are weaker than you or who have been opposed to you in some way. **♦ mag·na·nim·ity** /ˌmægnəˈnɪmɪti/. *Churchill took his defeat with good humour and magnanimity.* **♦ mag·nani·mous·ly** *'You were right, and we were wrong,' he said magnanimously.* `ADJ-GRADED` `FORMAL` `N-UNCOUNT` `ADV-GRADED`

mag·nate /ˈmægneɪt/ **magnates.** A magnate is someone who has earned a lot of money from a particular business or industry. ...*a multimillionaire shipping magnate.* `◆◇◇◇◇` `N-COUNT`

mag·ne·sium /mægˈniːziəm/. Magnesium is a metallic element which is light and silvery-white, and burns with a bright white flame. `◆◇◇◇◇` `N-UNCOUNT`

mag·net /ˈmægnɪt/ **magnets. 1** A magnet is a piece of iron or other material which attracts iron towards it. **2** If you say that something is a magnet or is like a magnet, you mean that people are very attracted by it and want to go to it or look at it. *Prospect Park, with its vast lake, is a magnet for all health freaks.* `◆◇◇◇◇` `N-COUNT` `N-COUNT`

mag·net·ic /mægˈnetɪk/. **1** If something is magnetic, it has the power of a magnet or functions like a magnet. ...*magnetic particles.* **2** You use magnetic to describe something that is caused by or relates to the force of magnetism. ...*magnetic forces.* **♦ mag·neti·cal·ly** /mægˈnetɪkli/ ...*metal fragments held together magnetically.* **3** You use magnetic to describe tapes, parts of devices, and objects which have a coating of a magnetic substance and which contain coded information which can be read or written on by computers. ...*her magnetic strip ID card.* ...*magnetic recording tape.* **4** If you describe something as magnetic, you mean that it is very attractive to people because it has unusual, powerful, and exciting qualities. ...*the magnetic pull of his looks.* `◆◆◇◇` `ADJ-GRADED` `ADJ` `ADV` `ADJ` `ADJ-GRADED`

,magnetic 'field, magnetic fields. A magnetic field is an area around a magnet, or something functioning as a magnet, in which the magnet's power to attract things is felt. `◆◇◇◇◇` `N-COUNT`

mag·net·ism /ˈmægnɪtɪzəm/. **1** Someone or something that has magnetism has unusual, powerful, and exciting qualities which attract people to them. *There was no doubting the animal magnetism of the man.* **2** Magnetism is the natural power of some objects and substances, especially iron, to attract other objects towards them. `N-UNCOUNT` `N-UNCOUNT`

mag·net·ize /ˈmægnɪtaɪz/ **magnetizes, magnetizing, magnetized;** also spelled **magnetise** in British English. **1** If you magnetize something, you make it magnetic. ...*a small metal chessboard with magnetized playing pieces.* **2** If one thing is magnetized towards another, it is attracted to it by magnetic forces. `VERB: V n` `V-ed` `VERB: beV-ed prep/adv`

mag·ni·fi·ca·tion /ˌmægnɪfɪˈkeɪʃən/ **magnifications. 1** Magnification is the degree to which a lens, mirror, or other device can magnify an object, or the degree to which the object is magnified. ...*electron microscopes, capable of magnification of 1 million times.* **2** See also **magnify.** `N-VAR`

mag·nifi·cent /mægˈnɪfɪsənt/. If you say that something or someone is magnificent, you mean that you think they are extremely good, beautiful, or impressive. ...*a magnificent country house.* **♦ mag·nifi·cence** *I shall never forget the magnificence of* `◆◆◇◇` `ADJ-GRADED` `N-UNCOUNT`

the Swiss mountains. ♦ **mag·ni·fi·cent·ly** The team ADV-GRADED
played magnificently.

mag·ni·fy /ˈmæɡnɪfaɪ/ **magnifies, magnifying,** ♦◇◇◇◇
magnified. 1 To **magnify** an object means to VERB: V n
make it appear larger than it really is, by means of a Vⁿⁿ
special lens or mirror. This version of the Digges V-ing
telescope magnifies images 11 times. ...magnifying
lenses. ♦ **mag·ni·fi·ca·tion** Pores are visible with- N-UNCOUNT
out magnification. **2** To **magnify** something means VERB
to increase its effect, size, loudness, or intensity. V n
Poverty and human folly magnify natural disasters.

ˈ**magnifying glass, magnifying glasses.** A N-COUNT
magnifying glass is a piece of glass which makes
objects appear bigger than they actually are.

mag·ni·tude /ˈmæɡnɪtjuːd, AM -tuːd/ **magni-** ♦◇◇◇◇
tudes. 1 If you talk about the **magnitude** of some- N-UNCOUNT
thing, you are talking about its great size, scale, or
importance. An operation of this magnitude is going
to be difficult... No one seems to realise the magnitude of this problem. **2 Magnitude** is used in stating N-VAR
the size or extent of something such as a star, earth- TECHNICAL
quake, or explosion. ...the 1.2 magnitude star Fo-
malhaut... The San Francisco earthquake of 1906
had a magnitude of 8.3. **3** You can use **order of** PHRASE
magnitude when you are giving an approximate
idea of the amount or importance of something.
America and Russia do not face a problem of the
same order of magnitude as Japan. **4** If one amount PHRASE
is an **order of magnitude** larger than another, it is TECHNICAL
ten times larger than the other. If it is two **orders of
magnitude** larger, it is a hundred times larger.

mag·no·lia /mæɡˈnəʊliə/ **magnolias. 1** A magno- ♦◇◇◇◇
lia is a kind of tree with white, pink, yellow, or pur- N-COUNT
ple flowers. **2** You can use **magnolia** to describe COLOUR
things that are creamish-white.

mag·num /ˈmæɡnəm/ **magnums.** A **magnum** is a N-COUNT
wine bottle holding the equivalent of two normal
bottles, approximately 1.5 litres.

ˌ**magnum** ˈ**opus.** A **magnum opus** is the greatest N-SING
or most important work produced by a writer, artist,
musician, or scholar.

mag·pie /ˈmæɡpaɪ/ **magpies. 1** A **magpie** is a bird ♦◇◇◇◇
with black and white markings and a long tail. **2** If N-COUNT
you describe someone as a **magpie**, you mean that N-COUNT
they like collecting and keeping things, often things
that have little value.

ma·ha·ra·ja /ˌmɑːhəˈrɑːdʒə/ **maharajas;** also N-COUNT
spelled **maharajah.** A **maharaja** is the head of one
of the royal families that used to rule parts of India.

ma·hoga·ny /məˈhɒɡəni/. **Mahogany** is a dark ♦◇◇◇◇
reddish-brown wood that is used to make furniture. N-UNCOUNT

maid /meɪd/ **maids.** A **maid** is a woman who ♦♦◇◇◇
works as a servant in a hotel or private house. ● See N-COUNT
also **old maid.**

maid·en /ˈmeɪdən/ **maidens. 1** A **maiden** is a ♦◇◇◇◇
young girl or woman. ...stories of noble princes and N-COUNT
their brave deeds on behalf of beautiful maidens. LITERARY
2 Maiden is used to describe some activities and ADJ: ADJ n
events when they are the first of that kind that a
particular person or thing has done. For example, a
politician's **maiden speech** is the first speech that
he or she makes in parliament after becoming a
member of it. In 1912, the Titanic sank on her maid-
en voyage.

ˈ**maiden name, maiden names.** A married N-COUNT
woman's **maiden name** is her parents' surname,
which she used before she got married and started
using her husband's surname.

ˌ**maid of** ˈ**honour, maids of honour.** A maid of N-COUNT
honour is the chief bridesmaid at a wedding. AMERICAN

mail /meɪl/ **mails, mailing, mailed. 1** The **mail** ♦♦♦◇◇
is the public service or system by which letters and N-SING:
parcels are collected and delivered. Your check is in the N,
the mail... Ford will contact owners by mail... The also by N
museum's director was contacted through the mail
in early April. **2** You can refer to letters and parcels N-UNCOUNT:
that are delivered to you as **mail**. Nora looked also the N
through the mail. **3** If you **mail** a letter or parcel to VERB:
someone, you send it to them by putting it in a post V n ton
box or by taking it to a post office. He mailed me the V nn
V n with n

contract... The Government has already mailed some V n
18 million households with details of the public offer... She had not mailed the letters. ♦ **mail·ing** The N-UNCOUNT
newsletter was printed towards the end of June in
readiness for mailing. **4** To **mail** someone means to VERB: V n
send a message to them electronically by means of beV-ed prep
a computer network. ...if a report must be electroni- Also V nn
cally mailed to an office by 9 am the next day.
▶ Also a noun. Video mail is electronic mail with N-UNCOUNT
sound and moving pictures. **5** See also **mailing;
chain mail, electronic mail, email, hate mail, junk
mail, surface mail.**

mail out. If someone **mails out** things such as let- PHRASAL VB
ters, leaflets, or bills, they send them to a large num- V P noun
ber of people at the same time. This week, the compa- Also V n P
ny mailed out its annual report.

mail·bag /ˈmeɪlbæɡ/ **mailbags;** also spelled **mail
bag. 1** A **mailbag** is a large bag that is used by post- N-COUNT
al workers for carrying mail. **2** In the United States, N-COUNT
the letters that are received by an important person, JOURNALISM
a newspaper, or a television or radio company can
be referred to as the **mailbag**. The British word is
postbag.

mail·box /ˈmeɪlbɒks/ **mailboxes. 1** In the United ♦◇◇◇◇
States, a **mailbox** is a box outside your house where N-COUNT
letters are delivered. **2** A **mailbox** is a metal box N-COUNT
with a hole in it, which you put letters in to be col- AMERICAN
lected. The British word is **post box.**

mail·ing /ˈmeɪlɪŋ/ **mailings. 1** A **mailing** is some- N-COUNT
thing that is sent to people through the postal ser-
vice. The seniors organizations sent out mailings to
their constituencies. **2** See also **mail.**

ˈ**mailing list, mailing lists.** A **mailing list** is a list N-COUNT
of names and addresses that a company or organi-
zation keeps, so that they can send people information or advertisements.

mail·man /ˈmeɪlmæn/ **mailmen.** A **mailman** is a N-COUNT
man whose job is to collect and deliver letters and AMERICAN
parcels that are sent by post. The usual British word
is **postman.**

ˌ**mail** ˈ**order.** **Mail order** is a system of buying and ♦♦◇◇◇
selling goods. You choose the goods you want from N-UNCOUNT
a company by looking at their catalogue, and the
company sends them to you by post. The toys are
available by mail order.

mail·shot /ˈmeɪlʃɒt/ **mailshots.** A **mailshot** is a N-COUNT
letter sent out to a large number of people in order BRITISH
to advertise something or to appeal for money for a
particular charity.

maim /meɪm/ **maims, maiming, maimed.** To ♦◇◇◇◇
maim someone means to injure them so badly that VERB: V n
part of their body is permanently damaged.

main /meɪn/ **mains. 1** The **main** thing is the most ♦♦♦♦◇
important one of several similar things in a particu- ADJ: det ADJ
lar situation. ...one of the main tourist areas of Amsterdam... My main concern now is to protect the
children. **2** If you say that something is true **in the** PHRASE
main, you mean that it is generally true, although PRAGMATICS
there may be exceptions. **3** The **mains** are the pipes N-COUNT
which supply gas or water to buildings, or which
take sewage away from them. The capital has been
without mains water. **4 The mains** are the wires N-PLURAL
which supply electricity to buildings, or the place BRITISH
where the wires end inside the building. ...amplifi-
ers which plug into the mains.

ˌ**main** ˈ**clause, main clauses.** A **main clause** is a N-COUNT
clause that can stand alone as a complete sentence.
Compare **subordinate clause.**

main·frame /ˈmeɪnfreɪm/ **mainframes.** A main- ♦◇◇◇◇
frame or mainframe computer is a large powerful N-COUNT
computer which can be used by many people at the
same time and which can do very large or complicated tasks.

main·land /ˈmeɪnlænd/. You can refer to the large ♦♦◇◇◇
principal part of a country or continent as the N-SING:
mainland, especially when this is being contrasted the N,
with the islands around it. ...the ferry to the main- N n
land. ...the coast of mainland Britain.

main·line /ˈmeɪnlaɪn/. **1** A **mainline** railway or ADJ: ADJ n
route is the principal railway between two places. A

mainline station is situated on a mainline railway. **2** You can use **mainline** to describe people, ideas, and activities that belong to the most central or conventional part of a tradition, institution, or business. ...*the teachings of mainline churches.* `ADJ: ADJ n`

main·ly /'meɪnli/. **1** You use **mainly** to indicate that your statement is broadly true or that it is a generalization. *I gave up university teaching mainly because I had a child... The birds live mainly on nectar.* **2** You use **mainly** when you are referring to a group and stating something that is true of most of it. *The audience was mainly from Senegal or Mali... The spacious main bedroom is mainly blue.* `◆◆◆◇ ADV; ADV with cl/ group, ADV with v` `ADV: ADV with group`

main 'road, main roads. A **main road** is an important road that leads from one town or city to another. `◆◇◇◇ N-COUNT`

main·spring /'meɪnsprɪŋ/ **mainsprings.** If you say that an idea, emotion, or other factor is the **mainspring** of something, you mean that it is the most important reason or motive for that thing. *The mainspring of his actions was his Christian conviction.* `N-COUNT WRITTEN`

main·stay /'meɪnsteɪ/ **mainstays.** If you describe something as the **mainstay** of a particular thing, you mean that it is the most basic and important part of it. *Fish and rice were the mainstays of the country's diet.* `◆◇◇◇ N-COUNT`

main·stream /'meɪnstriːm/ **mainstreams.** People, activities, or ideas that are part of the **mainstream** are regarded as the most typical, normal, and conventional because they belong to the same group or system as most others of their kind. ...*people outside the economic mainstream... The show wanted to attract a mainstream audience.* `◆◆◇◇ N-COUNT`

main·tain /meɪn'teɪn/ **maintains, maintaining, maintained.** **1** If you **maintain** something, you continue to have it, and do not let it stop or grow weaker. *The Department maintains many close contacts with the chemical industry.* **2** If you **maintain** something at a particular rate or level, you keep it at that rate or level. *The government was right to maintain interest rates at a high level.* **3** If you **maintain** a road, building, vehicle, or machine, you keep it in good condition by regularly checking it and repairing it when necessary. ...*a tough campaign to force authorities to maintain roads properly.* **4** If you **maintain** someone, you provide them with money and other things that they need. ...*the basic costs of maintaining a child.* **5** If you say that someone **maintains** that something is true, you mean that they have stated their opinion strongly but not everyone agrees with them or believes them. *He has maintained that the money was donated for international purposes... He had always maintained his innocence.* `◆◆◆◇ VERB V n` `VERB V n atn` `VERB V n` `VERB V n` `VERB V that V n Also V with quote`

main·te·nance /'meɪntɪnəns/. **1** The **maintenance** of a building, vehicle, road, or machine is the process of keeping it in good condition by regularly checking it and repairing it when necessary. ...*maintenance work on government buildings.* **2 Maintenance** is money that someone gives regularly to another person to pay for the things that the person needs. ...*the government's plan to make absent fathers pay maintenance for their children.* **3** If you ensure the **maintenance** of a state or process, you make sure that it continues. ...*the maintenance of peace and stability in Asia.* `◆◇◇◇ N-UNCOUNT` `N-UNCOUNT` `N-UNCOUNT`

mai·son·ette /,meɪzə'net/ **maisonettes.** In Britain, a **maisonette** is a flat with its own door to the outside, which it does not share with other flats in the same building. Most maisonettes have two storeys. `N-COUNT`

maize /meɪz/. **Maize** is a tall plant which produces large cobs of sweetcorn. It is grown as the basic food crop in many parts of the world. `◆◇◇◇ N-UNCOUNT`

Maj. Maj is a written abbreviation for 'Major' when it is used as a title. ...*Maj D B Lee.* `◆◇◇◇ N-TITLE`

ma·jes·tic /mə'dʒestɪk/. If you describe something or someone as **majestic**, you think they are very beautiful, dignified, and impressive. ...*a majestic* `◆◇◇◇ ADJ-GRADED`

country home. ♦ **ma·jes·ti·cal·ly** /mə'dʒestɪkli/ *She rose majestically to her feet.* `ADV-GRADED`

maj·es·ty /'mædʒɪsti/ **majesties.** **1** You use **majesty** in expressions such as **Your Majesty** or **Her Majesty** when you are addressing or referring to a King or Queen. *I quite agree, Your Majesty... His Majesty requests your presence in the royal chambers.* **2 Majesty** is the quality of being beautiful, dignified, and impressive. ...*the majesty of the mainland mountains.* `◆◆◇◇ N-VOC: poss N; PRON: poss PRON PRAGMATICS` `N-UNCOUNT`

ma·jor /'meɪdʒə/ **majors, majoring, majored.** **1** You use **major** when you want to describe something that is more important, serious, or significant than other things in a group or situation. *The major factor in the decision to stay or to leave was usually professional... Drug abuse has long been a major problem.* **2** A **major** is a middle-ranking officer in the army. **3** In European music, a **major** scale is one in which the third note is two tones higher than the first. ...*Mozart's Symphony No 35 in D Major.* **4** An economics **major** or an English **major**, for example, is a university student whose main subject is economics or English. **5** A student's **major** is the main subject that he or she is studying at university. *He switched his major in college to business.* **6** If someone **majors** in a particular subject, they study it as their main subject at university. `◆◆◆◇ ADJ-GRADED: ADJ n` `ADJ: n ADJ, ADJ n` `N-COUNT supp N AMERICAN` `N-COUNT AMERICAN` `VERB V in n AMERICAN`

ma·jor·ette /,meɪdʒə'ret/ **majorettes.** A **majorette** is one of a group of girls or young women who march at the front of a musical band in a procession. `N-COUNT`

ma·jor·ity /mə'dʒɒrɪti, AM -'dʒɔːr-/ **majorities.** **1** The **majority** of people or things in a group is more than half of them. *The majority of my patients come to me from out of town... The vast majority of our cheeses are made with pasteurised milk.* ● If a group is **in a majority** or **in the majority**, they form more than half of a larger group. ...*the south eastern part of Lithuania where Poles are in a majority.* **2** In an election or vote, a **majority** is the difference between the number of votes or parliamentary seats that the winner gets and the number of votes or seats that the next person or party gets. *Members of parliament approved the move by a majority of ninety-nine... He is set to win a clear majority in the elections.* **3 Majority** is the state of legally being an adult. In Britain, people reach their majority at the age of eighteen. *The age of majority in Romania is eighteen.* **4** See also **absolute majority, moral majority** `◆◆◆◇ N-COLL-SING` `PHRASE` `N-COUNT` `N-UNCOUNT`

make 1 carrying out an action

make /meɪk/ **makes, making, made.** **1** You can use **make** with a wide range of nouns to indicate that someone performs an action or says something. For example, if someone **makes** a suggestion, they suggest something. *I made a few phone calls... I think you're making a serious mistake... She had made us an offer too good to refuse.* **2** You can use **make** with certain nouns to indicate that someone does something well or badly. For example, if you **make** a success of something, you do it successfully. *He made a mess of his audition... Make a better job of it this time.* **3** If you **make** as if to do something or **make** to do something, you behave in a way that makes it seem that you are just about to do it. *Mary made as if to protest, then hesitated... He made to chase Davey.* **4** In cricket, if a player **makes** a particular number of runs, they score that number of runs. In baseball or American football, if a player **makes** a particular score, they achieve that score. **5** If you **make do** with something, you use or have it instead of something else that you do not have, although it is not as good. *Why make do with a copy if you can afford the genuine article?* **6** If you **make like** you are doing something, you act as if you are doing it, and if you **make like** someone, you act as if you are that person. *Bob makes like he's a fish blowing bubbles.* **7 Make** is used in a large number of expressions which are explained under other words in this `◆◆◆◆ VERB V n V n n` `VERB V n ofn` `VERB V as if to-inf V to-inf WRITTEN` `VERB: V amount` `PHRASE` `PHRASE INFORMAL`

dictionary. For example, the expression 'to make sense' is explained at 'sense'.

make 2 causing or changing

make /meɪk/ **makes, making, made. 1** If something **makes** you do something, it causes you to do it. *Grit from the highway made him cough... I was made to feel guilty and irresponsible.* **2** If you **make** someone do something, you force them to do it. *Mama made him clean up the plate... All non-payers of poll tax will be traced and made to pay.* **3** You use **make** to talk about causing someone or something to be a particular thing or to have a particular quality. *...James Bond, the role that made him a star... She made life very difficult for me... She's made it obvious that she's appalled by me.* **4** If you say that one thing or person **makes** another seem, for example, small, stupid, or good, you mean that they cause them to seem small, stupid, or good in comparison, even though they are not. *...a campaign of spite and revenge which makes Lady Sarah appear angelic by comparison.* **5** If you **make** yourself understood, heard, or known, you succeed in getting people to understand you, hear you, or know that you are there. *He almost had to shout to make himself heard above the music.* **6** If you **make** someone something, you appoint them to a particular job, role, or position. *Mr Major made him transport minister. ...if I am made chairman.* **7** If you **make** something into something else, you change it in some way so that it becomes that other thing. *Her bestseller 'Peachtree Road' is soon to be made into a television mini-series.* **8** If someone **makes** a friend or an enemy, someone becomes their friend or their enemy, often because of a particular thing they have done. *He was unruly in class and made an enemy of most of his teachers.* • to **make friends**: see **friend**. **9** To **make** a total or score a particular amount means to increase it to that amount. *This makes the total cost of the bulb and energy £27.*

◆◆◆◆◆
VERB
V n inf
be V-ed to-inf
VERB
V n inf
be V-ed to-inf
VERB
V n n
V n adj
V if adj that
Also V if adj
to-inf
VERB
V n inf adj/
prep/n

VERB
V pron-refl -ed

VERB
V n n

VERB
V n into n

VERB: V n
V n of n

VERB
V n amount

make 3 creating or producing

make /meɪk/ **makes, making, made. 1** To **make** something means to produce, construct, or create it. *Having curtains made professionally can be costly... Would you like me to make us all a coffee?... They make compost out of all kinds of waste.* ♦ **mak·ing** *...Salamon's book about the making of this movie. ...Ducks' eggs are particularly prized for cake making.* **2** If you **make** a note or list, you write something down in that form. *Mr Perry made a note in his book.* **3** If you **make** rules or laws, you decide what these should be. *The police don't make the laws, they merely enforce them.* **4** If something **makes** something else, it is responsible for the success of that thing. *What really makes the book are the beautiful designs.* **5** If you **make** money, you get it by working for it, by selling something, or by winning it. *I think every business's goal is to make money... Can it be moral to make so much money out of a commodity which is essential to life?.* **6** If you say that someone is **on the make**, you disapprove of them because they are trying to get a lot of money or power, possibly by illegal or immoral methods. **7** The **make** of something such as a car or radio is the name of the company that made it. *...a certain make of wristwatch.*

◆◆◆◆
VERB: V n
have n V-ed
V n n
V n from/out
of n
N-UNCOUNT:
with supp

VERB
V n

VERB
V n

VERB
V n

VERB
V n
V n out of/
from n
PHRASE
PRAGMATICS

N-COUNT:
supp N,
N of n

make 4 link verb uses

make /meɪk/ **makes, making, made. 1** You can use **make** to say that someone or something has the right qualities for a particular task or role. *She'll make a good actress, if she gets the right training.* **2** If people **make** a particular pattern such as a line or a circle, they arrange themselves in this way. *A group of people made a circle around the Pentagon.* **3** You can use **make** to say what two numbers add up to. *Four twos make eight.*

◆◆◆◆
V-LINK
V n
Also V n n

V-LINK
V n

V-LINK
V amount

make 5 achieving or reaching

make /meɪk/ **makes, making, made. 1** If someone **makes** a particular team or **makes** a particular high position, they do so well that they are put in

◆◆◆◆
VERB
V n

that team or get that position. *The athletes are just happy to make the British team.* **2** If you **make** a place in or by a particular time, you get there in or by that time, often with some difficulty. *The engine is gulping two tons of fuel an hour in order to make New Orleans by nightfall.* **3** If you **make it** somewhere, you succeed in getting there, especially in time to do something. *So you did make it to America, after all.* **4** If you **make it**, you are successful in achieving something difficult, or in surviving through a very difficult period. *You're brave and courageous. You can make it.* **5** If you cannot **make it**, you are unable to attend an event that you have been invited to. *He hadn't been able to make it to our dinner.*

VERB
V n prep

PHRASE

PHRASE

PHRASE

make 6 stating an amount or time

make /meɪk/ **makes, making, made. 1** You use **make** when saying what you calculate or guess an amount to be. *All I want to know is how many T-shirts Jim Martin has got. I make it three... I make the total for the year £69,599.* **2** You use **make** when saying what time your watch says it is. *I make it nearly 9.30.*

◆◆◆◆
VERB
V it amount
V n amount

VERB
V it n

make 7 phrasal verbs

make /meɪk/ **makes, making, made.**

◆◆◆◆

make for. 1 If you **make for** a place, you move towards it. *He rose from his seat and made for the door.* **2** If something **makes for** another thing, it causes or helps to cause that thing. *A happy parent makes for a happy child.*

PHRASAL VB
V P n
V P n
INFORMAL

make of. If you ask a person what they **make of** something, you want to know what their impression, opinion, or understanding of it is. *Nancy wasn't sure what to make of Mick's apology.*

PHRASAL VB
V P n

make off. If you **make off**, you leave somewhere as quickly as possible, often in order to escape. *They broke free and made off in a stolen car... Masked robbers broke in and made off with $8,000.*

PHRASAL VB
V P
V P with n

make out. 1 If you **make** something **out**, you manage with difficulty to see or hear it. *I could just make out a tall, pale, shadowy figure... I heard the voices, but couldn't make out what they were saying.* **2** If you try to **make** something **out**, you try to understand it or decide whether or not it is true. *It is hard to make out what criteria are used... As far as I can make out, the police consider that's unlikely.* **3** If you **make out** that something is true or **make** something **out** to be true, you try to cause people to believe that it is true. *They were trying to make out that I'd actually done it... He's more business-minded than he makes himself out to be.* **4** If you **make out** a case for something, you try to establish or prove that it is the best thing to do. *You could certainly make out a case for this point of view.* **5** When you **make out** a cheque, receipt, or order form, you write all the necessary information on it. *You can make a cheque out to Feed the Children... I'm going to make out a receipt for you.* **6** If you ask how someone **is making out**, you are asking how well they are doing with a particular task, or in their life in general. *Edgar made out well as a photographer.* **7** If two people **are making out**, they are engaged in sexual activity. *...pictures of the couple making out in their underwear on the beach.*

PHRASAL VB
V P noun
V P wh
Also V n P
V n P
V P wh
V P

V P that
V n P to-inf
Also V P

V P noun

V n P to n
V P noun

V P adv
INFORMAL

RECIP
pl-n V P
INFORMAL,
AMERICAN

make over. If you **make** something **over** to someone, you legally transfer the ownership of it to them. *John had made over to him most of the land... They moved on to a larger farm and in time made it over to Francis.*

PHRASAL VB
V P to n n
V n P to n

make up. 1 The people or things that **make up** something are the members or parts that form that thing. *Women officers make up 13 per cent of the police force... Insects are made up of tens of thousands of proteins.* **2** If you **make up** something such as a story or excuse, you invent it, sometimes in order to deceive people. *I think it's very unkind of you to make up stories about him... I'm not making it up.* **3** If you **make** yourself **up**, or if someone else **makes** you **up**, make-up is put on your face. *She spent too*

PHRASAL VB
V P noun
be V-ed P of n
Also V n P

V P noun
V n P

V pron-refl P
V P noun
Also V n P

M

much time making herself up... I can't be bothered to make up my face.

4 If you **make up** an amount, you add something to it so that it is as large as it should be. *Less than half of the money that students receive is in the form of grants, and loans have made up the difference... The team had six professionals and made the number up with five amateurs.* **5** If you **make up** time or hours, you work some extra hours to compensate for some time you have taken off work. *They'll have to make up time lost during the strike.*

6 If two people **make up** or **make it up** after a quarrel or disagreement, they become friends again. *She came back and they made up... They should make up with their ex-enemy in the West... I'll make it up with him again.*

7 If you **make up** something such as food or medicine, you prepare it by mixing or putting different things together. *Prepare the souffle dish before making up the souffle mixture.* **8** If you **make up** a bed or couch, you put sheets and blankets onto it so that someone can sleep there. *Her mother made up a bed in her old room.*

make up for. To **make up for** something that is lost, missing, or damaged means to replace it or compensate for it. *Ask for an extra compensation payment to make up for the stress you have been caused.*

make up to. If you say that you will **make it up to** someone for something, you are promising that you will do something for them to compensate for the fact that they have been upset or disappointed, especially by you. *I must make it up to him for the awful intrusion of last night.*

make-be'lieve. 1 If you say that someone is living in a **make-believe** world or is living in a world of **make-believe**, you disapprove of them because they are pretending that things are better or more exciting than they really are. *She squandered millions on a life of make-believe.* **2** When a child plays a game in which they pretend something, for example that they are someone else, you can refer to this activity as **make-believe**. **3** You use **make-believe** to describe things, for example in a play or film, that imitate or copy something real, but which are not what they appear to be. *The violence in those films was too unreal, it was make-believe.*

make·over /'meɪkəʊvə/ **makeovers.** If someone has a **makeover**, they have their make-up done by a beautician and their hair styled by a hair stylist, so that they feel they look as good as they possibly can.

mak·er /'meɪkə/ **makers. 1** The **maker** of something is the person or company that makes it. *...Japan's two largest car makers. ...the makers of chocolates, sweets and biscuits.* **2** See also **peacemaker.**

make·shift /'meɪkʃɪft/. **Makeshift** things are temporary and usually of poor quality, but they are used because there is nothing better available. *...a makeshift coffee table.*

'make-up; also spelled **makeup. 1 Make-up** consists of things such as lipstick, eye shadow, and powder which some women put on their faces to make themselves look more attractive or which actors use so that their faces can be clearly seen. *Normally she wore little make-up.* **2** Someone's **make-up** is their nature and the various qualities in their character. *His friends seem to see these tantrums as an inevitable part of his makeup.* **3** The **make-up** of something consists of its different parts and the way these parts are arranged. *...the chemical make-up of the oceans and atmosphere.*

mak·ing /'meɪkɪŋ/ **makings. 1** If you describe a person or thing as something **in the making**, you mean that they are going to become known or recognized as that thing. *Her drama teacher is confident Julie is a star in the making.* **2** If something **is the making of** a person or thing, it is the reason that they become successful or become very much better than they used to be. *This discovery may yet be the making of him.* **3** If someone or something has **the makings of** something, it seems possible or

likely that they will become that thing, as they have the necessary qualities. *Godfrey had the makings of a successful journalist.* **4** If something such as a problem you have is **of** your **own making**, you have caused or created it yourself. *The university's financial troubles are of its own making.*

5 See also **make.**

mal- /mæl-/. **Mal-** is added to words in order to form new words which describe things that are bad or unpleasant, or that are unsuccessful or imperfect. *The animals were seriously maltreated.*

mal·ad·just·ed /,mæləˈdʒʌstɪd/. If you describe a child as **maladjusted**, you mean that they have psychological problems and behave in a way which is not acceptable to society.

mal·ad·min·is·tra·tion /,mæləd,mɪnɪsˈtreɪʃən/. **Maladministration** is the act or process of administering a system or organization incorrectly.

mala·droit /,mæləˈdrɔɪt/. If you describe someone as **maladroit**, you mean that they are clumsy, awkward, or tactless.

mala·dy /'mælədi/ **maladies. 1** A **malady** is an illness or disease. *He was stricken at twenty-one with a crippling malady.* **2** People sometimes use **maladies** to refer to serious problems in a society or situation.

ma·laise /mæˈleɪz/. **1 Malaise** is a state in which there is something wrong with a society or group, for which there does not seem to be a quick or easy solution. *There is no easy short-term solution to Britain's chronic economic malaise.* **2** If someone is suffering from **malaise**, they feel tired, unwell, and lacking in energy. *He complained of depression, headaches and malaise.*

ma·laria /məˈleəriə/. **Malaria** is a serious disease carried by mosquitoes and which causes periods of fever. ♦ **ma·lar·ial** /məˈleəriəl/ *...malarial parasites.*

mal·con·tent /'mælkəntent/ **malcontents.** You describe people as **malcontents** when you disapprove of the way in which they are dissatisfied with a situation and want it to change.

male /meɪl/ **males. 1** A **male** is a person or animal that belongs to the sex that cannot give birth to babies or lay eggs. *A high proportion of crime is perpetrated by young males in their teens and twenties... Males and females take turns brooding the eggs.* ▶ Also an adjective. *...a deep male voice... Many women achievers appear to pose a threat to their male colleagues.* ♦ **male·ness** *...the solidarity among men which is part of maleness.* **2** A **male** flower or plant fertilizes the part that will become the fruit.

male 'chauvinist, male chauvinists. If you describe an attitude or remark as **male chauvinist**, you are critical of it because you think it is based on the belief that men are naturally superior to women. *The male chauvinist attitude of some people in the company could get you down.* ▶ A **male chauvinist** is a man who has male chauvinist views. ♦ **male chauvinism** *Insurance is a conservative profession, renowned for its male chauvinism.*

'male-dominated. A **male-dominated** society, organization, or area of activity is one in which men have most of the power and influence. *...the male-dominated world of journalism.*

mal·efac·tor /'mælɪfæktə/ **malefactors.** A **malefactor** is someone who has done something bad or illegal.

ma·levo·lent /məˈlevələnt/. A **malevolent** person deliberately tries to cause harm or evil. *Her stare was malevolent, her mouth a thin line, her eyes bright and glittering.* ♦ **ma·levo·lence** *...a rare streak of malevolence.*

mal·for·ma·tion /,mælfɔːˈmeɪʃən/ **malformations.** A **malformation** in a person's body is a part which does not have the proper shape or form, especially when it has been like this since birth.

mal·formed /,mælˈfɔːmd/. If people or parts of their body are **malformed**, they do not have the shape or form that they are supposed to, especially

when they have been like this since birth. *...premature births, malformed babies and mentally retarded babies.*

mal·func·tion /ˌmælˈfʌŋkʃən/ **malfunctions, malfunctioning, malfunctioned.** If a machine or part of the body **malfunctions**, it fails to work properly. *The radiation can damage microprocessors and computer memories, causing them to malfunction.* ▶ Also a noun. *...a computer malfunction.* ◆◇◇◇◇ VERB V FORMAL N-COUNT

mal·ice /ˈmælɪs/. **Malice** is behaviour that is intended to harm people or their reputations, or cause them embarrassment and upset. *There was no malice on his part.* ◆◇◇◇◇ N-UNCOUNT

ma·li·cious /məˈlɪʃəs/. If you describe someone's words or actions as **malicious**, you mean that they are intended to harm people or their reputations, or cause them embarrassment and upset. *...malicious gossip.* ♦ **ma·li·cious·ly** *...his maliciously accurate imitation of Hubert de Burgh.* ◆◇◇◇◇ ADJ-GRADED ADV-GRADED

ma·lign /məˈlaɪn/ **maligns, maligning, maligned.** 1 If you **malign** someone, you say unpleasant and untrue things about them. *We maligned him dreadfully when you come to think of it. We assumed the very worst about him.* 2 If something is **malign**, it causes harm. *...the malign influence jealousy had on their lives.* 3 See also **much-maligned**. ◆◇◇◇◇ VERB V n FORMAL ADJ-GRADED: ADJ n FORMAL

ma·lig·nan·cy /məˈlɪɡnənsi/ **malignancies.** When doctors talk about the **malignancy** of a tumour or disease, they mean that it is serious, is spreading to other parts of the body, and may cause death. N-VAR MEDICAL

ma·lig·nant /məˈlɪɡnənt/. 1 A **malignant** tumour or disease is serious, spreads rapidly to other parts of the body, and may cause death. *She developed a malignant breast tumour.* 2 If you say that someone is **malignant**, you think that they are cruel and like to cause harm. *He said that we were evil, malignant and mean.* ◆◇◇◇◇ ADJ MEDICAL ADJ-GRADED

ma·lin·ger /məˈlɪŋɡə/ **malingers, malingering, malingered.** If someone is **malingering**, they pretend to be ill in order to avoid working; used showing disapproval. *She was told by her doctor that she was malingering.* VERB PRAGMATICS V

mall /mɔːl, mæl/ **malls.** A **mall** is a very large enclosed shopping area. ◆◇◇◇◇ N-COUNT

mal·lard /ˈmælɑːd/ **mallards.** A **mallard** is a kind of wild duck which is very common. N-COUNT

mal·le·able /ˈmæliəbəl/. 1 If you say that someone is **malleable**, you mean that they are easily influenced or controlled by other people. 2 A substance that is **malleable** is soft and can easily be made into different shapes. *Silver is the most malleable of all metals.* ADJ-GRADED FORMAL ADJ-GRADED

mal·let /ˈmælɪt/ **mallets.** A **mallet** is a wooden hammer with a square head. See picture headed **tools**. N-COUNT

mal·nour·ished /ˌmælˈnʌrɪʃt/. If someone is **malnourished**, they are physically weak because they do not eat enough food or do not eat the right kind of food. ADJ-GRADED

mal·nu·tri·tion /ˌmælnjuːˈtrɪʃən, AM -nuː-/. If someone is suffering from **malnutrition**, they are physically weak and extremely thin because they have not eaten enough food. ◆◇◇◇◇ N-UNCOUNT

mal·odor·ous /mælˈəʊdərəs/. Something that is **malodorous** has an unpleasant smell. *...tons of malodorous garbage bags.* ADJ-GRADED LITERARY

mal·prac·tice /ˌmælˈpræktɪs/ **malpractices.** If you accuse someone of **malpractice**, you are accusing them of breaking the law or the rules of their profession in order to gain some advantage for themselves. *There were only one or two serious allegations of malpractice.* ◆◇◇◇◇ N-VAR FORMAL

malt /mɔːlt/ **malts.** 1 **Malt** is a substance made from grain that has been soaked in water and then dried in a hot oven. Malt is used in the production of whisky, beer, and other alcoholic drinks. 2 **Malt** is the same as **malt whisky**. ◆◇◇◇◇ N-UNCOUNT N-VAR

malt·ed /ˈmɔːltɪd/. **Malted** barley has been soaked in water and then dried in a hot oven. It is used in ADJ: ADJ n

the production of whisky, beer, and other alcoholic drinks.

mal·treat /ˌmælˈtriːt/ **maltreats, maltreating, maltreated.** If a person or animal **is maltreated**, they are treated badly, especially by being hurt. *He said that he was not tortured or maltreated during his detention.* VB: usu passive beV-ed

mal·treat·ment /ˌmælˈtriːtmənt/. **Maltreatment** is cruel behaviour, especially involving hurting a person or animal. *2,000 prisoners died as a result of torture and maltreatment.* N-UNCOUNT

malt '**whisky, malt whiskies.** **Malt whisky** or **malt** is whisky that is made from malt. *I got a bottle of my best malt out of the sideboard.* ▶ A **malt whisky** is a glass of malt whisky. N-VAR N-COUNT

mam /mæm/ **mams.** In some dialects of British English, **mam** is used to mean mother. *You sit here and rest, Mam.* ◆◇◇◇◇ N-FAMILY INFORMAL

mama /məˈmɑː, AM ˈmɑːmə/ **mamas. Mama** means the same as **mother**. ◆◇◇◇◇ N-FAMILY DATED

mam·ma /ˈmɑːmə/ **mammas. Mamma** means the same as **mother**. N-FAMILY AMERICAN, INFORMAL

mam·mal /ˈmæməl/ **mammals. Mammals** are animals such as humans, dogs, lions, and whales. ◆◇◇◇◇ N-COUNT

mam·ma·lian /mæˈmeɪliən/. **Mammalian** means relating to mammals. *Studies of mammalian behaviour.* ADJ: ADJ n TECHNICAL

mam·ma·ry /ˈmæməri/. **Mammary** means relating to the breasts. *...the mammary glands.* ADJ: ADJ n TECHNICAL

mam·mo·gram /ˈmæməɡræm/ **mammograms.** A **mammogram** is a test used to check whether women have breast cancer, using x-rays. N-COUNT

Mam·mon /ˈmæmən/. You can use **Mammon** to refer in a disapproving way to money and business activities in contrast to creative or spiritual activities. *...trendy bishops who had forsaken God for the Mammon of politics.* N-UNCOUNT PRAGMATICS

mam·moth /ˈmæməθ/ **mammoths.** 1 You can use **mammoth** to emphasize that a task or change is very great and needs a lot of effort to achieve. *...the mammoth task of relocating the library.* 2 A **mammoth** was a prehistoric animal like a large elephant with long curling tusks. ◆◇◇◇◇ ADJ-GRADED PRAGMATICS N-COUNT

mam·my /ˈmæmi/ **mammies.** In some dialects of English, **mammy** is used to mean mother. N-FAMILY INFORMAL

man /mæn/ **men; mans, manning, manned.** 1 A **man** is an adult male human being. *He was a very good looking young man.* 2 **Man** and **men** are sometimes used to refer to all human beings, including both males and females. Some people dislike this use. *Anxiety is modern man's natural state.* 3 Some people refer to a woman's husband, lover, or boyfriend as her **man**. *...if they see your man cuddle you in the kitchen or living room.* 4 If you say that a man is, for example, **a gambling man** or **an outdoors man**, you mean that he likes gambling or outdoor activities. 5 If you say that a man is, for example, **a London man** or **an Oxford man**, you mean that he comes from London or Oxford, or went to university there. 6 If you refer to a particular company's or organization's **man**, you mean a man who works for or represents that company or organization. *...the Daily Telegraph's man in Abu Dhabi.* 7 If you say that a man is someone's **man**, you mean that he always supports that person or does what they want. *At the time he was said to be very much Rajiv Gandhi's man.* ◆◆◆◆ N-COUNT N-VAR N-SING: poss N INFORMAL N-COUNT: supp N N-COUNT: n-proper N N-COUNT: poss N JOURNALISM N-COUNT: poss N

8 In the armed forces, the **men** are the ordinary soldiers, sailors, or airmen, but not the officers. 9 Male workers are sometimes referred to as **men**, especially if they do physical work or work for a more senior person. *The men voted by a four-to-one majority to accept the pay offer.* N-PLURAL N-PLURAL

10 **Man** is sometimes used as a greeting or form of address to a man. *Hey wow, man! Where d'you get those boots?* 11 People sometimes address a man as **my man**. *'Get the guy in the purple shirt.'—'All right, my man.'... Get in, and we'll take a little ride, my man.* N-VOC INFORMAL CONVENTION AMERICAN, INFORMAL

12 People sometimes address a man as **my man, my dear man**, or **my good man**. This is often friendly, but CONVENTION BRITISH, DATED

can also suggest that the speaker feels superior to the person being addressed. *My dear man, you are welcome to stay... It's not for you to say so, my man!*

13 If you **man** something such as a place, vehicle, or machine, you operate it or are in charge of it. *The station is seldom manned in the evening.* ♦ **manned** *...a manned spacecraft. ...manned exploration of the solar system.*   VERB / V n / ADJ

14 If you say that a man is **man enough** to do something, you mean that he has the necessary courage or ability to do it. *You can search me if you think you're man enough.*   PHRASE

15 If you describe a man as **a man's man**, you mean that he has qualities which make him popular with other men rather than with women.   PHRASE

16 If you say that a man **is his own man**, you approve of the fact that he makes his decisions and his plans himself, and does not depend on other people. *Be your own man.*   PHRASE PRAGMATICS

17 If you say that a group of men are, do, or think something **to a man**, you are emphasizing that every one of them is, does, or thinks that thing. *Economists, almost to a man, were sceptical.*   PHRASE PRAGMATICS

18 A **man-to-man** conversation or meeting takes place between two men, often to discuss a serious personal matter. *...a man-to-man talk... Me and Ben should sort this out man to man.*   PHRASE

19 See also **ladies' man**, **no-man's land**. **20** ● **the man in the street**: see **street**. ● **man about town**: see **town**. ● **man of the world**: see **world**.

-man /-mæn/. **-man** combines with numbers to make adjectives which indicate that something involves or is intended for that number of people. *The four-man crew. ...a two-man tent.*   COMB

mana·cle /'mænəkəl/ **manacles, manacling, manacled. 1 Manacles** are metal devices attached to a prisoner's wrists or legs in order to prevent him or her from moving or escaping. **2** If a prisoner is **manacled**, their wrists or legs are put in manacles. *His hands were manacled behind his back... He was manacled by the police.*   N-COUNT / VB: usu passive beV-ed / prep/adv beV-ed

man·age /'mænɪdʒ/ **manages, managing, managed. 1** If you **manage** an organization, business, or system, or the people who work in it, you are responsible for controlling them. *Within two years he was managing the store... Professors are notoriously difficult to manage.* **2** If you **manage** time, money, or other resources, you deal with them carefully and do not waste them. *In a busy world, managing your time is increasingly important.* **3** If you **manage** to do something, especially something difficult, you succeed in doing it. *Over the past 12 months the company has managed a 10 per cent improvement.* **4** If you **manage**, you succeed in coping with a difficult situation. *How did your mother manage when your father left?* ♦ **man·age·able** *He will now try to cut down the task to a manageable size.* **5** If you say that you can **manage** an amount of time or money for something, you mean that you can afford to spend that time or money on it. *'All right, I can manage a fiver,' McMinn said with reluctance.* **6** If you say that someone **managed** a particular response, such as a laugh or a greeting, you mean that it was difficult for them to do it because they were feeling sad or upset. *He looked dazed as he spoke to reporters, managing only a weak smile.* **7** You say **'I can manage'** or **'I'll manage'** as a way of refusing someone's offer of help and insisting on doing something by yourself. *I can manage by myself.*   VERB V n / VERB V n / VERB: V to-inf V / VERB V / ADJ-GRADED / VERB V n / VERB V n / CONVENTION PRAGMATICS

man·age·ment /'mænɪdʒmənt/ **managements. 1 Management** is the control and organizing of a business or other organization. *The zoo needed better management rather than more money.* **2** You can refer to the people who control and organize a business or other organization as the **management**. *The management is doing its best... We need to get more women into top management.* **3 Management** is the way people control different parts of their lives. *...the secret of time management.*   N-UNCOUNT / N-COLL-VAR / N-UNCOUNT

man·ag·er /'mænɪdʒə/ **managers. 1** A **manager** is a person who is responsible for running part of or the whole of a business organization. *...a retired*

bank manager. ♦ **mana·gerial** /ˌmænɪ'dʒɪəriəl/. *...his managerial skills.* **2** The **manager** of a pop star or other entertainer is the person who looks after their business interests. **3** The **manager** of a sports team is the person responsible for training the players and organizing the way they play.   ADJ / N-COUNT / N-COUNT

man·ag·er·ess /ˌmænɪdʒə'res/ **manageresses.** The **manageress** of a shop, restaurant, or other small business is the woman who is responsible for running it. Some women object to this word and prefer to be called a 'manager'. *...the manageress of a betting shop.*   N-COUNT

,managing di'rector, managing directors. The **managing director** of a company is the most important working director, and is in charge of the way the company is managed.   N-COUNT BRITISH

man·da·rin /'mændərɪn/ **mandarins. 1** Journalists sometimes use **mandarin** to refer to someone who has an important job in the Civil Service. *...Foreign Office mandarins.* **2 Mandarin** is the official language of China. **3** A **mandarin** was, in former times, an important government official in China. **4** A **mandarin** or a **mandarin orange** is a small orange which is easy to peel.   N-COUNT BRITISH / N-UNCOUNT / N-COUNT / N-COUNT

man·date /'mændeɪt/ **mandates, mandating, mandated. 1** If a government or other elected body has a **mandate** to carry out a particular policy or task, they have the authority to carry it out as a result of winning an election or vote. *A mandate for continued economic reform.* **2** When someone is **mandated** to carry out a particular policy or task, they are given the official authority to do it or are instructed to do it. *He'd now been mandated by the West African Economic Community to go in and to enforce a ceasefire.* ► If someone is given a **mandate** to carry out a particular policy or task, they are mandated to do it. *A mandate from the UN.* **3** You can refer to the fixed length of time that a country's leader or government remains in office as their **mandate**. *...his intention to leave politics once his mandate ends.* **4** To **mandate** something means to make it mandatory. *Sixteen years ago, Quebec mandated that all immigrants send their children to French schools. ...constitutionally mandated civil rights.*   N-COUNT / VB: usu passive beV-ed to-inf / N-COUNT / N-COUNT FORMAL / VERB: V n V that V-ed AMERICAN

man·da·tory /'mændətri, AM -tɔːri/. If an action or procedure is **mandatory**, people have to do it, because it is a rule or it is fixed by law. *...the mandatory retirement age of 65. ...the mandatory life sentence for murder.*   ADJ FORMAL

man·di·ble /'mændɪbəl/ **mandibles.** A **mandible** is a jawbone.   N-COUNT TECHNICAL

man·do·lin /ˌmændə'lɪn/ **mandolins.** A **mandolin** is a musical instrument that looks like a small guitar and has four pairs of strings. See picture headed **musical instruments.**   N-VAR

mane /meɪn/ **manes. 1** The **mane** on a horse or lion is the long thick hair that grows from its neck. **2** If you refer to a person's hair as their **mane**, you mean that they have a lot of hair. *He had a great mane of white hair.*   N-COUNT / N-COUNT LITERARY

'man-eating. A **man-eating** animal is one that has killed and eaten human beings, or that people think might do so. *...man-eating lions.*   ADJ: ADJ n

ma·neu·ver /mə'nuːvə/. See **manoeuvre**.

man·ful·ly /'mænfəli/. If you say that someone, especially a man, does something **manfully**, you mean that they do it in a very determined or brave way.   ADV-GRADED ADV with v

man·ga·nese /'mæŋgəniːz/. **Manganese** is a greyish-white metal that is used in making steel.   N-UNCOUNT

man·ger /'meɪndʒə/ **mangers.** A **manger** is a low open container which cows, horses, and other animals feed from in a stable or barn.   N-COUNT DATED

man·gle /'mæŋgəl/ **mangles, mangling, mangled. 1** If a physical object is **mangled**, it is crushed or twisted very forcefully, so that it is difficult to see what its original shape was. *...the mangled wreckage.* **2** If you say that someone **mangles**   VB: usu passive V-ed / VERB: V n

words or information, you are criticizing them for not speaking or writing clearly or correctly. **3** A **mangle** is an old-fashioned device for squeezing water from wet clothes after washing them. [PRAGMATICS] N-COUNT

man·go /'mæŋgəʊ/ **mangoes** or **mangos**. A **mango** is a large sweet yellowish fruit which grows on a tree in hot countries. ...*mango chutney*. ▶ A **mango** is the tree that this fruit grows on. ...*lime and mango trees*. ◆◇◇◇◇ N-VAR / N-COUNT

man·grove /'mæŋgrəʊv/ **mangroves**. A **mangrove** or **mangrove tree** is a tree with roots which are above the ground. It grows along coasts or river banks in hot countries. ...*mangrove swamps*. N-COUNT

man·gy /'meɪndʒi/ **mangier, mangiest**. A **mangy** animal looks dirty, uncared for, or ill. ADJ-GRADED

man·handle /'mænhændəl/ **manhandles, manhandling, manhandled**. **1** If someone is **manhandled**, they are physically held or pushed, for example when they are being taken somewhere. *They manhandled the old man along the corridor*. **2** If you **manhandle** something big or heavy somewhere, you move it there by hand. *The three of us manhandled the uncovered dinghy out of the shed*. VERB: be V-ed / V n prep/adv / Also V n / VERB / V n prep/adv

man·hole /'mænhəʊl/ **manholes**. A **manhole** is a hole in a road, leading down to a drain. It is covered by a metal plate which is removed when someone needs to go down into the drain. N-COUNT

man·hood /'mænhʊd/. **1 Manhood** is the state of being a man rather than a boy, or the period of a man's adult life. *They were failing lamentably to help their sons grow from boyhood to manhood*. **2** If you refer to **American manhood** or **French manhood**, for example, you are referring to American men or French men considered as a group. ◆◇◇◇◇ N-UNCOUNT / N-UNCOUNT: supp N

'man-hour, man-hours; also spelled **man hour**. A **man-hour** is the average amount of work that one person can do in an hour. **Man-hours** are used to estimate how long jobs take. Some people disapprove of this expression because it seems to exclude women. *The restoration took almost 4,000 man-hours over four years*. N-COUNT

man·hunt /'mænhʌnt/ **manhunts**. A **manhunt** is a major search for someone who has escaped or disappeared. N-COUNT

ma·nia /'meɪniə/ **manias**. **1** If you say that a person or group has a **mania** for something, you mean that they enjoy it very much or devote a lot of time to it. *The media have a mania about rugby*. **2 Mania** is a mental illness which causes the sufferer to become very worried or concerned about something. ...*the treatment of mania*. ◆◇◇◇◇ N-COUNT / N-UNCOUNT: also N in pl

ma·ni·ac /'meɪniæk/ **maniacs**. **1** A **maniac** is a mad person who is violent and dangerous. ...*a drug-crazed maniac*. **2** If you describe someone's behaviour as **maniac**, you are emphasizing that it is extremely foolish and reckless. ...*a maniac driver*. **3** If you call someone, for example, a religious **maniac** or a sports **maniac**, you are critical of them because they have an unnaturally strong and obsessive interest in religion or sport. ◆◇◇◇◇ N-COUNT / ADJ: ADJ n [PRAGMATICS] / N-COUNT: supp N

ma·nia·cal /mə'naɪəkəl/. If you describe someone's behaviour as **maniacal**, you mean that it is extreme, violent, or very determined. *He was almost maniacal in his pursuit of sporting records.* ♦ **ma·nia·cal·ly** /mə'naɪəkli/. *He was last seen striding maniacally to the hotel reception*. ADJ [PRAGMATICS] / ADV

man·ic /'mænɪk/. **1** If you describe someone as **manic**, you mean that they do things extremely quickly or energetically, often because they are very excited or anxious. *He was really manic. ...an almost manic energy*. ♦ **man·ic·al·ly** /'mænɪkli/. *We cleaned the house manically*. **2** If you describe someone's smile, laughter, or sense of humour as **manic**, you mean that it seems excessive or strange. ...*a manic grin*. ◆◇◇◇◇ ADJ-GRADED / ADV / ADJ-GRADED

manic-de'pressive, manic-depressives; also spelled **manic depressive**. If someone is **manic-depressive**, they have a medical condition in which they sometimes feel excited and confident and at other times very depressed. ...*manic depressive ill-* ADJ

ness. ▶ A **manic-depressive** is someone who is manic-depressive. *Her mother is a manic depressive.* N-COUNT

mani·cure /'mænɪkjʊə/ **manicures, manicuring, manicured**. If you **manicure** your hands or nails, you care for them by softening your skin and cutting and painting your nails. ▶ Also a noun. *I have a manicure occasionally*. ◆◇◇◇◇ VERB: V n / N-COUNT

mani·cured /'mænɪkjʊəd/. A **manicured** garden or lawn has very short neatly cut grass. ADJ

mani·cur·ist /'mænɪkjʊərɪst/ **manicurists**. A **manicurist** is a person whose job is manicuring people's hands and nails. N-COUNT

mani·fest /'mænɪfest/ **manifests, manifesting, manifested**. **1** If you say that something is **manifest**, you mean that it is clearly true and that nobody would disagree with it if they saw it or considered it. ...*the manifest failure of the policies.* ♦ **mani·fest·ly** *She manifestly failed to last the mile and a half of the race. ...the manifestly obvious health and social advantages of chastity.* **2** If you **manifest** a particular quality, feeling, or illness, or if it **manifests** itself, it becomes visible or obvious. *He manifested a pleasing personality on stage... The virus needs two weeks to manifest itself.* ▶ Also an adjective. *The same alarm is manifest everywhere*. ◆◆◇◇◇ ADJ-GRADED FORMAL / ADV-GRADED / V-ERG V n / V pron-refl FORMAL / ADJ-GRADED

mani·fes·ta·tion /,mænɪfe'steɪʃən/ **manifestations**. A **manifestation** of something is one of the different ways in which it can appear. ... *different manifestations of the disease*. N-COUNT: with supp FORMAL

mani·fes·to /,mænɪ'festəʊ/ **manifestos** or **manifestoes**. A **manifesto** is a statement published by a person or group of people, especially a political party, in which they say what their aims and policies are. ... *their election manifesto*. ◆◆◇◇◇ N-COUNT

mani·fold /'mænɪfəʊld/. Things that are **manifold** are of many different kinds. *The difficulties are manifold*. ADJ-GRADED FORMAL

ma·nila /mə'nɪlə/; also spelled **manilla**. A **manila** envelope or folder is made from a strong paper that is usually light brown. ADJ: ADJ n

ma·nipu·late /mə'nɪpjʊleɪt/ **manipulates, manipulating, manipulated**. **1** If you say that someone **manipulates** people, you disapprove of them because they skilfully force or persuade people to do what they want. *She's always borrowing my clothes and manipulating me to give her vast sums of money... They'll have kids who are two, three, who are manipulating them into buying toys.* ♦ **ma·nipu·la·tion** /mə,nɪpjʊ'leɪʃən/ **manipulations** *I don't like manipulations or lies.* **2** If you say that someone **manipulates** an event or situation, you disapprove of them because they use or control it for their own benefit. *They felt he had been cowardly in manipulating the system to avoid the draft.* ♦ **manipulation** ...*accusations of political manipulation*. **3** If you **manipulate** something that requires skill, such as a complicated piece of equipment or a difficult idea, you operate it or process it. *The technology uses a pen to manipulate a computer. ... people like journalists who manipulate ideas.* ♦ **manipulation** ...*the simplest of mathematical manipulations.* **4** If someone **manipulates** your bones or muscles, they skilfully move and press them with their hands in order to remove tension or push the bones into their correct position. *The way he can manipulate my leg has helped my arthritis so much.* ♦ **manipulation** ...*acupuncture, chiropractic or manipulation*. ◆◆◇◇◇ VERB: V n [PRAGMATICS] V n to-inf / V n into -ing / N-VAR / VERB [PRAGMATICS] V n / N-VAR / VERB V n / N-VAR / VERB V n / N-VAR

ma·nipu·la·tive /mə'nɪpjʊlətɪv/. If you describe someone as **manipulative**, you disapprove of them because they manipulate people. ...*aggressive and manipulative behaviour*. ◆◇◇◇◇ ADJ-GRADED [PRAGMATICS]

ma·nipu·la·tor /mə'nɪpjʊleɪtə/ **manipulators**. If you describe someone as a **manipulator**, you mean that they skilfully control events, situations, or people, often in a way that other people disapprove of. *Jean Brodie is a manipulator. She cons everybody. ...some of the best PR manipulators in the business*. N-COUNT

man·kind /,mæn'kaɪnd/. You can refer to all human beings as **mankind** when considering them as ◆◇◇◇◇ N-UNCOUNT

M

a group. Some people dislike this use. ...*the evolution of mankind.*

man·ly /ˈmænli/ **manlier, manliest.** If you describe a man's behaviour or appearance as **manly**, you approve of it because it shows qualities that are considered typical of a man, such as strength or courage. ...*he set himself manly tasks.* ♦ **man·li·ness** *He has no doubts about his manliness.* ◇◇◇◇ ADJ-GRADED PRAGMATICS   N-UNCOUNT: poss N

man-'made. **Man-made** things are created or caused by people, rather than occurring naturally. ...*man-made lakes.* ◇◇◇◇ ADJ

man·na /ˈmænə/. If you say that something unexpected is **manna from heaven** or **manna**, you mean that it is good and happened just at the time that it was needed. *The revealed documents were manna for journalists.* PHRASE

manned /mænd/. See **man**.

man·ne·quin /ˈmænɪkɪn/ **mannequins. 1** A **mannequin** is a life-sized model of a person which is used to display clothes, hats, or shoes, especially in shop windows. **2** A **mannequin** is a person who displays clothes, hats, or shoes by wearing them, especially in fashion shows or photographs. N-COUNT DATED   N-COUNT DATED

man·ner /ˈmænə/ **manners. 1** The **manner** in which you do something is the way that you do it. *She smiled again in a friendly manner.* **2** If something is done in the **manner** of something else, it is done in the style of that thing. *We kissed each other's cheeks in the European manner.* **3** Someone's **manner** is the way in which they behave and talk when they are with other people, for example whether they are polite, confident, or bad-tempered. *His manner was self-assured and brusque.* ♦ **-mannered** *Forrest was normally mild-mannered, affable, and untalkative.* **4** If someone has **good manners**, they are polite and observe social customs. If someone has **bad manners**, they are impolite and do not observe these customs. *He dressed well and had impeccable manners.* **5** See also **bedside manner, table manners.** ◆◆◆◇◇ N-SING: with supp   N-SING: with supp   N-SING   COMB   N-PLURAL

6 If you refer to **all manner of** objects or people, you are talking about objects or people of many different kinds. ...*pictures of all manner of wildlife.* **7** You say **in a manner of speaking** to indicate that what you have just said is not absolutely or literally true, but is true in a general way. *An attorney is your employee, in a manner of speaking.* **8** You use **what manner of** to suggest that the person or thing you are about to mention is of an unusual or unknown kind. *What manner of place is this?* PHRASE   PHRASE PRAGMATICS   PHRASE LITERARY

man·nered /ˈmænəd/. **1** If you describe someone's behaviour or a work of art as **mannered**, you dislike it because it is elaborate or formal, and therefore seems false or artificial. ...*Naomi's mannered voice.* **2** **Mannered** behaviour is polite and observes social customs. ...*perfectly polite and beautifully mannered.* ◇◇◇◇ ADJ-GRADED PRAGMATICS   ADJ-GRADED

man·ner·ism /ˈmænərɪzəm/ **mannerisms.** Someone's **mannerisms** are the gestures or ways of speaking which are very characteristic of them, and which they often use. N-COUNT

man·nish /ˈmænɪʃ/. If you describe a woman's appearance or behaviour as **mannish**, you mean it is more like a man's appearance or behaviour than a woman's. ...*a mannish trouser suit.* ADJ-GRADED

ma·noeu·vrable /məˈnuːvərəbəl/; spelled **maneuverable** in American English. Something that is **manoeuvrable** can be easily moved into different positions. *Ferries are very powerful and manoeuvrable compared to cargo ships.* ADJ-GRADED

ma·noeu·vre /məˈnuːvə/ **manoeuvres, ma·noeuvring, manoeuvred;** spelled **maneuver** in American English. **1** If you **manoeuvre** something into or out of an awkward position, you skilfully move it there. *We attempted to manoeuvre the canoe closer to him... I manoeuvred my way among the tables.* ► Also a noun. ...*a ship capable of high speed and rapid manoeuvre.* **2** If you **manoeuvre** a situation, you change it in a clever and skilful way so that you can benefit from it. *The authorities have to* ◆◆◇◇◇ VERB V n adv/prep V v prep/adv adv Also V   N-VAR   VERB: V n V n prep/adv Also V

manoeuvre the markets into demanding a cut in interest rates... He brilliantly manoeuvred himself back to power.* ► Also a noun. ...*manoeuvres to block the electoral process.* ♦ **ma·noeu·vring, manoeuvrings** ...*his unrivalled skill in political manoeuvring.* **3** Military **manoeuvres** are training exercises which involve the movement of soldiers and equipment over a large area. *Allied troops begin maneuvers tomorrow.* **4** ● **room for manoeuvre:** see **room.** N-VAR   N-PLURAL

man·or /ˈmænə/ **manors.** A **manor** is a large house in the country and the land and smaller buildings belonging to it, especially when the house was built in the Middle Ages or has replaced one that was built at that time. ◆◆◇◇◇ N-COUNT

'manor house, manor houses. A **manor house** is the main house that is or was on a medieval manor. ◆◇◇◇◇ N-COUNT

man·power /ˈmænpaʊə/. Workers are sometimes referred to as **manpower** when they are being considered as a part of the process of producing goods or providing services. ...*the shortage of skilled manpower in the industry.* ◆◇◇◇◇ N-UNCOUNT

man·qué /ˈmɒŋkeɪ, AM -ˈkeɪ/. You use **manqué** to describe someone who has never succeeded in becoming the kind of person mentioned, although they tried to or had the potential to. *He was, in a sense, an academic manqué.* ADJ: n ADJ

manse /mæns/ **manses.** In some Christian churches, a **manse** is the house provided for a clergyman to live in. ...*a Baptist manse in Monmouth.* N-COUNT BRITISH

man·servant /ˈmænsɜːvənt/ **manservants.** A **manservant** is a man who works as a servant in a private house. The American word is **houseman.** N-COUNT DATED, BRITISH

man·sion /ˈmænʃən/ **mansions. 1** A **mansion** is a very large house. ...*an eighteenth century mansion in Hampshire.* **2** In Britain, **Mansions** is often used in the names of blocks of flats. ...*Delaware Mansions, a block of 167 flats opposite the BBC Radio studios.* ◆◆◇◇◇ N-COUNT

man·slaughter /ˈmænslɔːtə/. **Manslaughter** is the unlawful killing of a person by someone who did not intend to kill them. ...*she was guilty of manslaughter, not murder.* ◆◇◇◇◇ N-UNCOUNT LEGAL

man·tel /ˈmæntəl/ **mantels.** A **mantel** is a mantelpiece. N-COUNT DATED

mantel·piece /ˈmæntəlpiːs/ **mantelpieces;** also spelled **mantlepiece.** A **mantelpiece** is a wood or stone shelf which is the top part of a border round a fireplace. *On the mantelpiece are a pair of bronze Ming vases.* N-COUNT

man·tle /ˈmæntəl/ **mantles. 1** If you take on the **mantle** of something such as a profession or an important job, you take on the responsibilities and duties which must be fulfilled by anyone who has this profession or job. *She has the intellectual form to take up the mantle of leadership.* **2** A **mantle** of something is a layer of it covering a surface, for example a layer of snow on the ground. ...*a mantle of soot and ash.* **3** A **mantle** is a piece of clothing without sleeves that people used to wear over their other clothes in former times. **4** See also **mantel.** ◆◇◇◇◇ N-SING: the N of n WRITTEN   N-COUNT: with supp WRITTEN   N-COUNT

mantle·piece /ˈmæntəlpiːs/. See **mantelpiece.**

,man-to-'man. See **man.**

man·tra /ˈmæntrə/ **mantras.** A **mantra** is a chant used by Buddhists and Hindus when they meditate, or to help them feel calm and deal with problems. ◆◇◇◇◇ N-COUNT

manu·al /ˈmænjuəl/ **manuals. 1** **Manual** work is work in which you use your hands or your physical strength rather than your mind. ...*skilled manual workers.* **2** **Manual** is used to talk about movements which are made by someone's hands. ...*toys designed to help develop manual dexterity.* **3** **Manual** means operated by hand, rather than by electricity or a motor. ♦ **manu·al·ly** *The device is manually operated, using a simple handle.* **4** A **manual** is a book which tells you how to do something or how a piece of machinery works. ...*the instruction manual.* ◆◆◇◇◇ ADJ   ADJ: ADJ n   ADJ: ADJ n   ADV: ADV with v   N-COUNT

manu·fac·ture /ˌmænjʊˈfæktʃə/ **manufactures, manufacturing, manufactured.** ◆◆◆◇◇ **1** To **manufacture** something means to make it in a factory, usually in large quantities. *They manufacture the class of plastics known as thermoplastic materials... We import foreign manufactured goods.* VERB V n V-ed ▶ Also a noun. *...the manufacture of nuclear weapons.* N-UNCOUNT: with supp ♦ **manu·fac·tur·ing** *...management headquarters for manufacturing in China.* N-UNCOUNT **2 Manufactures** are goods or products which have been made in a factory. N-COUNT TECHNICAL **3** If you say that someone **manufactures** information, you are criticizing them because they invent information that is not true. *According to the prosecution, the officers manufactured an elaborate story.* VERB PRAGMATICS V n

manu·fac·tur·er /ˌmænjʊˈfæktʃərə/ **manufacturers.** ◆◆◆◇◇ N-COUNT A **manufacturer** is a business or company which makes goods in large quantities to sell. *...the world's largest doll manufacturer.*

ma·nure /məˈnjʊə, AM -ˈnʊr/ **manures.** ◆◇◇◇◇ N-VAR **Manure** is animal faeces, sometimes mixed with chemicals, that is spread on the ground in order to make plants grow healthy and strong.

manu·script /ˈmænjʊskrɪpt/ **manuscripts.** ◆◆◇◇◇ **1** A **manuscript** is a handwritten or typed document, especially a writer's first version of a book before it is published. *He had seen a manuscript of the book... I am grateful to him for letting me read his early chapters in manuscript.* N-COUNT: also *in* N **2** A **manuscript** is an old document that was written by hand on paper or parchment before printing was invented. *...early printed books and rare manuscripts.* N-COUNT

many /ˈmeni/. ◆◆◆◆◆ **1** You use **many** to indicate that you are talking about a large number of people or things. *I don't think many people would argue with that... Not many films are made in Finland.* DET ▶ Also a pronoun. *We stood up, thinking through the possibilities. There weren't many.* PRON ▶ Also a quantifier. *In many of these neighborhoods a lot of people don't have telephones.* QUANT ▶ Also an adjective. *Among his many hobbies was the breeding of fine horses... The possibilities are many.* ADJ-GRADED: det ADJ, v-link ADJ **2** You use **many** to talk about numbers or quantities, and to ask and answer questions about numbers or quantities. *No-one knows how many people have been killed since the war began... How many people out here have ever been called by a pollster? Well, not very many.* DET ▶ Also a pronoun. *How many do you smoke a day?* PRON **3** You use **many** with 'as' when you are comparing numbers of things or people. *I've always entered as many photo competitions as I can.* DET ▶ Also a pronoun. *Let the child try on as many as she likes.* PRON **4** You use **many** followed by 'a' and a noun to emphasize that there are a lot of people or things involved in something. *Many a mother tries to act out her unrealized dreams through her daughter.* PREDET PRAGMATICS **5** You use **many** to mean 'many people'. *Iris Murdoch is regarded by many as a supremely good and serious writer.* PRON **6** The **many** means a large group of people considered as separate from a small minority. *The printing press gave power to a few to change the world for the many.* PRON

7 You use **as many as** before a number to suggest that it is surprisingly large. *New York City police say that as many as four and a half million people watched today's parade.* PHRASE **8** You use **a good many** or **a great many** to emphasize that you are referring to a large number of things or people. *We've both had a good many beers.* PHRASE PRAGMATICS **9** • **many happy returns**: see **return**. • **in so many words**: see **word**.

map /mæp/ **maps, mapping, mapped.** ◆◆◆◇◇ **1** A **map** is a drawing of a particular area such as a city, a country, or a continent, showing its main features as they would appear if you looked at them from above. *Have you got a map of the city centre?* N-COUNT **2** A **map** is a drawing that gives special information about an area. *...weather maps on television.* N-COUNT **3** To **map** an area means to make a map of it. *...a spacecraft which is using radar to map the surface of Venus.* VERB V n **4** If you say that someone or something **put** a person, thing, or place **on the map**, you mean that they made it become well-known and important. *...the attempts of the Edinburgh Festival's organisers to put C.P. Taylor firmly on the map.* PHRASE

map out. If you **map out** something that you are intending to do, you work out in detail how you will do it. *I cannot conceive of anybody writing a play by sitting down and mapping it out.* PHRASAL VB V P noun V n P

ma·ple /ˈmeɪpəl/ **maples.** ◆◇◇◇◇ A **maple** or a **maple tree** is a tree with large leaves which turn bright red or gold in autumn. N-VAR ▶ **Maple** is the wood of this tree. N-UNCOUNT

ˌmaple ˈsyrup. **Maple syrup** is a sweet sticky brown liquid made from the sap of maple trees, that can be eaten with pancakes or used to make puddings. N-UNCOUNT

mar /mɑː/ **mars, marring, marred.** ◆◆◇◇◇ To **mar** something means to spoil or damage it. *That election was marred by massive cheating.* VERB: V n *be* V-ed

Mar. ◆◆◇◇◇ **Mar.** is a written abbreviation for **March.**

mara·thon /ˈmærəθən, AM -θɒn/ **marathons.** ◆◆◇◇◇ **1** A **marathon** is a race in which people run a distance of 26 miles (about 42 km). N-COUNT ▶ **The marathon** is the sport of running marathon races. *I took up the marathon.* N-SING: *the* N **2** If you use **marathon** to describe an event or task, you are emphasizing that it takes a long time and is very tiring. *...a marathon session of talks. ...the medical team which successfully carried out the marathon operation.* ADJ: ADJ n PRAGMATICS

ma·raud·ing /məˈrɔːdɪŋ/. **Marauding** groups of people or animals are wandering around looking for opportunities to steal or kill. ADJ: ADJ n LITERARY ♦ **ma·raud·er** /məˈrɔːdə/ **marauders.** *Numb with terror, she stared at the departing marauders.* N-COUNT

mar·ble /ˈmɑːbəl/ **marbles.** ◆◆◇◇◇ **1 Marble** is a type of very hard rock which feels cold when you touch it and which shines when it is cut and polished. *He collected classical marble busts of Caesar.* N-UNCOUNT **2 Marbles** are sculptures made of marble. N-COUNT TECHNICAL **3 Marbles** is a children's game played with small balls, usually made of coloured glass. You roll a ball along the ground and try to hit an opponent's ball with it. *On the far side of the street, two boys were playing marbles.* N-UNCOUNT ▶ A **marble** is one of the small balls used in this game. N-COUNT **4** If you say that someone **has lost** their **marbles**, you mean that their ideas or behaviour are very strange, as if they have become insane. PHRASE INFORMAL

mar·bled /ˈmɑːbəld/. Something that is **marbled** has a pattern or colouring like that of marble. *If the meat is marbled with fat it should be tender.* ADJ

march /mɑːtʃ/ **marches, marching, marched.** ◆◆◆◇◇ **1** When soldiers **march** somewhere, or when a commanding officer **marches** them somewhere, they walk there with very regular steps, as a group. *Captain Ramirez called them to attention and marched them off to the main camp... We marched fifteen miles to Yadkin River.* V-ERG: V prep/adv V n adv/prep V n Also V ▶ Also a noun. *After a short march, the column entered the village.* N-COUNT • If a group of soldiers are **on the march**, they are marching somewhere. PHRASE **2** When a large group of people **march** for a cause, they walk somewhere together in order to express their ideas or to protest about something. *The demonstrators then marched through the capital chanting slogans.* VERB V prep/adv Also V ▶ Also a noun. *Organisers expect up to 300,000 protesters to join the march.* N-COUNT ♦ **march·er, marchers** *Fights between police and marchers lasted for three hours.* N-COUNT **3** If you say that someone **marches** somewhere, you mean that they walk there quickly and in a determined way, for example because they are angry. *He marched into the kitchen without knocking.* VERB V prep/adv **4** If you **march** someone somewhere, you force them to walk there with you, for example by holding their arm tightly. *I marched him across the room and out on to the doorstep.* VERB V n prep/adv

5 The **march** of something is its steady development or progress. *...the relentless march of technology.* N-SING **6** A **march** is a piece of music with a regular rhythm that you can march to. N-COUNT **7** If you give someone their **marching orders**, you tell them that you no longer want or need them, for example as your employee or as your PHRASE

M

lover. *They've had their marching orders.* **8** If you **steal a march** on someone, you start doing something before they do it in order to gain an advantage over them. *If its strategy succeeds, Mexico could even steal a march on its northern neighbour.* PHRASE

March, Marches. March is the third month of the year in the Western calendar. See Appendix headed Dates. *I flew to Milan in early March... She was born in Austria on March 6, 1920.* ◆◆◆◇ N-VAR

mar·chion·ess /ˌmɑːʃəˈnes/ **marchionesses.** A **marchioness** is the wife or widow of a marquis, or a woman with the same rank as a marquis. N-COUNT; N-TITLE

'march-past, march-pasts; also spelled **march past.** When soldiers take part in a **march-past,** they march in front of an important person as part of a ceremonial occasion. N-COUNT

mare /meə/ **mares.** A **mare** is an adult female horse. ◆◆◇◇ N-COUNT

mar·ga·rine /ˌmɑːdʒəˈriːn, AM -rɪn/ **margarines.** Margarine is a yellow substance made from vegetable oil and sometimes animal fats. It is similar to butter. ◆◇◇◇ N-VAR

mar·gin /ˈmɑːdʒɪn/ **margins. 1** A **margin** is the difference between two amounts, especially the difference in the number of votes or points between the winner and the loser in an election or other contest. *They could end up with a 50-point winning margin.* **2** The **margin** of a written or printed page is the blank space at the side of the page. **3** If there is a **margin** for something in a situation, there is some freedom to choose what to do or decide how to do it. *The money is collected in a straightforward way with little margin for error.* **4** The **margin** of a place or area is the extreme edge of it. *These islands are on the margins of human habitation.* **5** If you say that a person or thing is on the **margins** of a group, an idea, or a situation, you mean that they are among the least typical, least important, or least powerful parts of it. *...signs of the party's rapid retreat to the political margins.* **6** See also **profit margin.** ◆◆◆◇ N-COUNT: with supp / N-COUNT / N-VAR: with supp / N-COUNT: with supp / N-PLURAL:

mar·gin·al /ˈmɑːdʒɪnəl/ **marginals. 1** If you describe something as **marginal,** you mean that it is small or not very important. *This is a marginal improvement on October... The role of the Communist Party proved marginal.* **2** If you describe people as **marginal,** you mean that they are not involved in the main events or developments in society. *I don't want to call him marginal, but he's not a major character.* **3** In political elections, a **marginal** seat or constituency is one which is usually won or lost by only a few votes. ▶ A **marginal** is a marginal seat. *These are the key marginals which Labour must win.* **4 Marginal** activities, costs, or taxes are not the main part of a business or an economic system, but often make the difference between its success or failure. **5 Marginal** land is poor farming land which lies between fertile land and an area of completely infertile land such as a desert. ◆◆◇◇ ADJ-GRADED / ADJ-GRADED / ADJ-GRADED BRITISH / N-COUNT / ADJ TECHNICAL / ADJ-GRADED: ADJ n TECHNICAL

mar·gin·al·ize /ˈmɑːdʒɪnəlaɪz/ **marginalizes, marginalizing, marginalized;** also spelled **marginalise** in British English. To **marginalize** a group of people means to make them feel isolated and unimportant. *The effect of this has been to increasingly marginalize the local authority sector.* ◆ **mar·gin·ali·za·tion** *He spoke of his fears of the marginalization of Africa.* ◆◇◇◇ VERB V n / N-UNCOUNT

mar·gin·al·ly /ˈmɑːdʒɪnəli/. **Marginally** means to only a small extent. *Sales last year were marginally higher than in 1991.* ◆◇◇◇ ADV

mari·gold /ˈmærɪɡəʊld/ **marigolds.** A **marigold** is a type of yellow or orange flower. ◆◇◇◇ N-VAR

ma·ri·jua·na /ˌmærɪˈwɑːnə/. **Marijuana** is the dried leaves and flowers of the hemp plant which some people smoke or eat as a drug. Marijuana is illegal in many countries. ◆◇◇◇ N-UNCOUNT

ma·ri·na /məˈriːnə/ **marinas.** A **marina** is a small harbour for yachts and other small boats. ◆◇◇◇ N-COUNT

mari·nade /ˌmærɪˈneɪd/ **marinades, marinading, marinaded. 1** A **marinade** is a sauce of oil, vinegar, and seasonings, which you soak meat or fish in before you cook it, in order to add flavour or to make it more tender. **2** To **marinade** means the same as to **marinate.** ◆◇◇◇ N-COUNT / V-ERG

mari·nate /ˈmærɪneɪt/ **marinates, marinating, marinated.** If you **marinate** meat or fish, or if it **marinates,** you keep it in a mixture of oil, vinegar, and seasonings before cooking it, so that it can develop a special flavour. *Put it in a screw-top jar with French dressing and leave to marinate.* ◆◇◇◇ V-ERG: V n

ma·rine /məˈriːn/ **marines. 1** A **marine** is a soldier, for example in the US Marine Corps or the Royal Marines, who is specially trained for military duties at sea as well as on land. **2 Marine** is used to describe things relating to the sea or to the animals and plants that live in the sea. *...breeding grounds for marine life.* **3 Marine** is used to describe things relating to ships and their movement at sea. *...a solicitor specialising in marine law.* ◆◆◇◇ N-COUNT / ADJ: ADJ n / ADJ: ADJ n

mari·ner /ˈmærɪnə/ **mariners.** A **mariner** is a sailor. *...a master mariner.* ◆◇◇◇ LITERARY

mari·tal /ˈmærɪtəl/. **Marital** is used to describe things relating to marriage. *Caroline was keen to make her marital home in London.* ADJ: ADJ n

,marital 'status. Your **marital status** is whether you are married, single, or divorced. N-UNCOUNT FORMAL

mari·time /ˈmærɪtaɪm/. **Maritime** is used to describe things relating to the sea and to ships. *...the largest maritime museum of its kind.* ◆◇◇◇ ADJ: ADJ n

mar·jo·ram /ˈmɑːdʒərəm/. **Marjoram** is a kind of herb. N-UNCOUNT

mark /mɑːk/ **marks, marking, marked. 1** If something **marks** a surface, a small area of the surface is stained or damaged, for example because something has been spilled on it. *I have to be more careful with the work tops, as wood marks easily.* ▶ Also a noun. *The dogs are always rubbing against the wall and making dirty marks.* **2** If you **mark** something with a particular word or symbol, you write that word or symbol on it. *The bank marks the check 'certified'... For more details about these products, send a postcard marked HB/FF.* ▶ Also a noun. *He made marks with a pencil.* **3** A **mark** is a point that is given for a correct answer or for doing something well in an exam or competition. *Candidates who answered 'b' could be awarded half marks... He did well to get such a good mark.* **4** When a teacher **marks** a student's work, he or she decides how good it is and writes a number or letter on it to indicate this opinion. ▶ A **mark** is also a number or letter used in this way. ◆ **mark·ing** *For the rest of the lunchbreak I do my marking.* **5** If you say that someone gets good or high **marks** for doing something, you mean that they have done it well or deserve to be praised for doing it. If you say that they get poor or low **marks,** you mean that they have done it badly or do not deserve to be praised. *You have to give her top marks for moral guts.* **6** A particular **mark** is a particular number, point, or stage which has been reached or might be reached, especially a significant one. *Unemployment is rapidly approaching the one million mark.* **7** The **mark** of something is the characteristic feature that enables you to recognize it. *The mark of a civilized society is that it looks after its weakest members.* **8** If you say that a type of behaviour or an event is a **mark** of a particular quality, feeling, or situation, you mean it shows that that quality, feeling, or situation exists. *Shopkeepers closed their shutters as a mark of respect.* **9** If something **marks** a place or position, it shows where something else is or where it used to be. *...the river which marks the border with Thailand.* **10** An event that **marks** a particular stage or point is a sign that something different is about to happen. *The announcement marks the end of an extraordinary period in European history.* **11** If you do something to **mark** an event or occasion, you do it to show that you are aware of the importance of the event or occasion. *The* ◆◆◆◇ V-ERG: V n / V / N-COUNT / VERB: V n with n / V n quote / V-ed / N-COUNT / N-COUNT / VERB: V n / N-COUNT / N-UNCOUNT / N-PLURAL: supp N / N-COUNT / N-COUNT: N of n/-ing / N-SING: a N of n / VERB V n / VERB V n / VERB V n

four new stamps mark the 100th anniversary of the British Astronomical Association. **12** If a particular quality or feature **marks** something, it is a quality or feature which that thing often or typically has or shows. *The style is marked by simplicity, clarity, and candor.* **13** Something that **marks** someone as a particular type of person indicates that they are that type of person. *Her opposition to abortion and feminism mark her as a convinced traditionalist.*   VERB: Vn

14 In a team game, when a defender **is marking** an attacker, the defender is responsible for staying close to the attacker in order to try and prevent them from getting the ball and scoring goals. ♦ **marking** *They had stopped Ecuador from building up attacks with good marking.*   VERB: Vn   N-UNCOUNT

15 The **mark** is the unit of money that is used in Germany.   N-COUNT

16 **Mark** is used before a number to indicate a particular temperature level in a gas oven. *Set the oven at gas mark 4.* **17** **Mark** is used before a number to indicate a particular version or model of a vehicle, machine, or device. *...his Mark II Ford Cortina.* **18** See also **marked**, **marking**; **black mark**, **exclamation mark**, **full marks**, **high-water mark**, **punctuation mark**, **question mark**, **scuff mark**, **stretch marks**.   N-UNCOUNT: N num   N-UNCOUNT: N num

19 If something or someone **leaves** their **mark** or **leaves a mark**, they have a lasting effect on something or someone else. *Years of conditioning had left their mark on her, and she never felt inclined to talk to strange men.* **20** If you **make** your **mark** or **make a mark**, you become noticed or famous by doing something impressive or unusual. *She made her mark in the film industry in the 1960s.*   PHRASE   PHRASE

21 If you are **quick off the mark**, you are quick to understand or respond to something, or to take advantage of an opportunity. If you are **slow off the mark**, you are slow to understand or respond to something, or to take advantage of an opportunity. **22** If something is **off the mark**, it is inaccurate or incorrect. If it is **on the mark**, it is accurate or correct. *He's right on the mark about movies being out of step with American culture.* **23** If something such as a claim or estimate is **wide of the mark**, it is incorrect or inaccurate. *That comparison isn't as wide of the mark as it seems.* **24** ● to overstep the mark: see overstep. ● mark my words: see word.   PHRASE   PHRASE   PHRASE

mark down. 1 If you **mark** something **down**, you write it down. *As he marks down the prices, he stops now and then to pack things into a large bag.* **2** If you **mark** someone **down** as a particular type of person, especially a type that you do not like, you consider that they have the qualities which make them that type of person. *If he'd taken that five pounds, I would have marked him down as a greedy fool.* **3** To **mark** an item **down** or **mark** its price **down** means to reduce its price. *Clothes are the best bargain, with many items marked down.*   PHRASAL VB V n P / V P noun   V n P asn   V P noun V-ed P Also V n P

mark off. 1 If you **mark off** a piece or length of something, you make it separate, for example by putting a line on it or around it. *Read the text through and mark off the sections you find particularly applicable.* **2** If a particular quality or feature **marks** someone or something **off** from other people or things, it is unusual or special and makes them seem noticeably different. *The traditionalist influences within the navy marked it off as a rather old-fashioned institution.* **3** If you **mark off** a date on a calendar or an item on a list, you put a line through it or next to it, in order to show that it has been completed or dealt with. *Miss Hoare called out names and marked them off.*   PHRASAL VB V P noun   V n P from n V n P asn   V P noun V n P

mark out. 1 To **mark out** an area or shape means to show where it begins and ends. *When planting seedlings I prefer to mark out the rows in advance.* **2** If a particular quality or feature **marks** someone or something **out** from other people or things, it is unusual or special and makes them seem noticeably different from them. *There were several things about this evening that marked it out as very unusual.*   PHRASAL VB V P noun Also V n P   V n P from n V n P asad j/n Also V P noun

mark up. If you **mark** something **up**, you increase its   PHRASAL VB

price. *A typical warehouse club marks up its goods by only 10 to 15 percent.* ● See also **mark-up**.   V n P V P noun

marked /'mɑːkt/. **1** A **marked** change or difference is very obvious and easily noticed. *There has been a marked increase in crimes against property.* ♦ **mark-ed·ly** /'mɑːkɪdli/. *America's current economic downturn is markedly different from previous recessions.* **2** If you describe someone as a **marked** man or woman, you mean that they are in danger from someone who wants to harm or kill them.   ADJ-GRADED ♦♦♦◇◇   ADV-GRADED   ADJ: ADJ n

mark·er /'mɑːkə/ **markers. 1** A **marker** is an object which is used to show the position of something, or is used to help somebody remember something. *He put a marker in his book and followed her out.* **2** If you refer to something as a **marker** for a particular quality or feature, you mean that it demonstrates the existence or presence of that quality or feature. *Vitamin C is a good marker for the presence of other vitamins and nutrients in frozen food.* **3** A **marker** or a **marker pen** is a pen with a thick tip made of felt, used for drawing and colouring things.   ♦◇◇◇◇ N-COUNT   N-COUNT   N-COUNT

mar·ket /'mɑːkɪt/ **markets, marketing, marketed. 1** A **market** is a place where goods are bought and sold, usually in the open air. *He sold boots on a market stall.* **2** The **market** for a particular commodity or product is the number of people who want to buy it, or the area in the world in which it is sold. *The foreign market was increasingly crucial.* **3** The **market** refers to the total amount of a product that is sold each year, especially when you are talking about the competition between the companies who sell that product. *The two big companies control 72% of the market.* **4** If you talk about a **market** economy, or the **market** price of something, you are referring to an economic system in which the prices of things depend on how many are available and how many people want to buy them, rather than prices being fixed by governments. *He must sell the house for the current market value.* **5** To **market** a product means to organize its sale, by deciding on its price, where it should be sold, and how it should be advertised. *Touch-tone telephones have been marketed in America since 1963. ...if a soap is marketed as an anti-acne product.* ♦ **mar·ket·ing** *...Renault's marketing department.* **6** The **job market** or the **labour market** refers to the people who are looking for work and the jobs available for them to do. **7** The stock market is sometimes referred to as the **market**. *The market collapsed last October.* **8** See also **black market**, **market forces**, **open market**. **9** If you say that it is **a buyer's market**, you mean that it is a good time to buy something, because there is a lot of it available, and therefore its price is low. If you say that it is **a seller's market**, you mean that very little of it is available, so its price is high. **10** If you are in **the market for** something, you are interested in buying it. *...motorists in the market for a £10,000 car.* **11** If something is **on the market**, it is available for people to buy. If it comes **onto the market**, it becomes available for people to buy. *...new medicines that have just come onto the market.* **12** If you **price** yourself **out of the market**, you try to sell goods or services at a higher price than other people, with the result that nobody buys them from you.   ♦♦♦♦♦ N-COUNT   N-COUNT   N-SING: the N   ADJ: ADJ n   VERB: Vn be V-ed be V-ed asn   N-UNCOUNT   N-SING: the n N   N-SING: the N   PHRASE   PHRASE   PHRASE   PHRASE

mar·ket·able /'mɑːkɪtəbəl/. Something that is **marketable** is able to be sold because people want to buy it. ♦ **mar·ket·abil·ity** /,mɑːkɪtə'bɪlɪti/. *...a product that has sufficient marketability to enable them to recover their investment costs.*   ♦◇◇◇◇ ADJ-GRADED   N-UNCOUNT

mar·ket·eer /mɑːkɪ'tɪə/ **marketeers.** A **marketeer** is the same as a **marketer**. ● See also **free-marketeer**.   ♦◇◇◇◇ N-COUNT

mar·ket·er /'mɑːkɪtə/ **marketers.** A **marketer** is someone whose job involves marketing.   ♦◇◇◇◇ N-COUNT

market 'forces. When politicians and economists talk about **market forces**, they mean the economic factors that determine the price and availability of goods when there is no interference from the government.   ♦◇◇◇◇ N-PLURAL

,market 'garden, market gardens. A market garden is a small farm where vegetables and sometimes fruit and flowers are grown for sale.   N-COUNT BRITISH

market·place /'mɑːkɪtpleɪs/ **marketplaces;** also spelled **market place. 1** In business, the **marketplace** refers to the activity of buying and selling products. *It's our hope that we will play an increasingly greater role in the marketplace.* **2** A **marketplace** is a small area in a town or city where goods are bought and sold, often in the open air.   ◆◇◇◇ N-COUNT

,market re'search. Market research is the activity of collecting and studying information about what people want, need, and buy.   ◆◇◇◇ N-UNCOUNT

,market 'share, market shares. A company's **market share** in a product is the proportion of the total sales of that product that is produced by that company. *Ford has been gaining market share this year.*   ◆◆◇◇ N-VAR TECHNICAL

mark·ing /'mɑːkɪŋ/ **markings.** Markings are coloured lines, shapes, or patterns on an animal or object which help to identify it. *...identifying individual whales by the distinctive markings on their tails.* ● See also **mark**.   ◆◇◇◇ N-COUNT

marks·man /'mɑːksmən/ **marksmen. 1** A marksman is a person who can shoot very accurately. **2** A marksman is a football player who scores a lot of goals. *City's principal marksman was Joe Harvey who scored seventeen goals.*   ◇◇◇◇ N-COUNT N-COUNT

'mark-up, mark-ups. A mark-up is an increase in the price of something, for example the difference between its cost and the price that you sell it for.   N-COUNT

mar·ma·lade /'mɑːməleɪd/ **marmalades.** Marmalade is a food made from oranges, lemons, or grapefruit that is similar to jam.   ◆◇◇◇ N-VAR

ma·roon /mə'ruːn/ **maroons, marooning, marooned. 1** Something that is **maroon** is dark reddish-purple in colour. *...maroon velvet curtains.* **2** If someone **is marooned** somewhere, they are left in a place that is difficult for them to escape from. *Five couples were marooned in their caravans when the River Avon broke its banks.*   ◆◇◇◇ COLOUR / VB: usu passive beV-ed prep/adv

ma·rooned /mə'ruːnd/. If you say that you are **marooned**, you mean that you feel alone and helpless, because you are in an unpleasant situation that you cannot change. *...families marooned in decaying inner-city areas. ...temporarily marooned at home by my injured knee.*   ADJ

marque /mɑːk/ **marques.** A marque is a famous make or brand of a particular product. *...a marque long-associated with motor racing success, Alfa Romeo.*   ◆◇◇◇ N-COUNT

mar·quee /mɑː'kiː/ **marquees. 1** A marquee is a large tent which is used at a fair, garden party, or other outdoor event, usually for eating and drinking in. **2** A marquee is a cover over the entrance of a building, for example, a hotel or a theatre.   ◆◇◇◇ N-COUNT / N-COUNT AMERICAN

mar·quis /'mɑːkwɪs/ **marquises;** also spelled **marquess.** A marquis is a male member of the nobility who has the rank between duke and earl.   ◆◇◇◇ N-COUNT; N-TITLE

mar·riage /'mærɪdʒ/ **marriages. 1** A marriage is the relationship between a husband and wife. *In a good marriage, both husband and wife work hard to solve any problems that arise... When I was 35 my marriage broke up.* **2** A marriage is the act of marrying someone, or the ceremony at which this is done. *I opposed her marriage to Darryl.* **3** Marriage is the state of being married. *In twenty years of marriage he has only taken two proper vacations.* **4** See also **arranged marriage**.   ◆◆◆◆ N-COUNT / N-VAR / N-UNCOUNT

mar·ried /'mærɪd/. **1** If you are **married**, you have a husband or wife. *She is married to an Englishman. ...a married man with two children.* **2** Married means relating to marriage or to people who are married. *For the first ten years of our married life we lived in a farmhouse.* **3** If you say that someone is **married** to their work or another activity, you mean they are very involved with it and have little time or interest for anything else. *She was a very strict Christian who was married to her job.*   ◆◆◇◇ ADJ / ADJ: ADJ n / ADJ: v-link ADJ to n

mar·row /'mærəʊ/ **marrows. 1** A marrow is a long, thick, green vegetable with soft white flesh that is eaten cooked. The American term is 'vegetable marrow'. **2** Marrow is the same as **bone marrow**. *The marrow donor is her 14-month-old sister.* **3** The marrow of something is the most important and basic part of it. *We're getting into the marrow of the film.*   ◆◇◇◇ N-VAR BRITISH / N-UNCOUNT / N-SING: the N

mar·ry /'mæri/ **marries, marrying, married. 1** When two people **get married** or **marry**, they legally become husband and wife in a special ceremony. **Get married** is less formal and more commonly used than **marry**. *They married a month after they met... He wants to marry her... Laura just got married to Jake... I am getting married on Monday.* **2** When a priest or registrar **marries** two people, he or she conducts the ceremony in which the two people legally become husband and wife. *In July 1957, we were married in New York.*   ◆◆◆◆ V-RECIP: pl-n getV-ed pl-n V / V n / getV-ed to n getV-ed (non-recip) Also V (non-recip) / VERB / V n

marry off. If you **marry** someone **off**, you find a suitable person for them to marry. *They advised her mother to marry her off to the old man as he was very rich... He had the good fortune to marry off his daughter to the local chief... Tradition dictates that girls should be married off early.*   PHRASAL VB V n P / V n P n / V P noun to n be V-ed P

marsh /mɑːʃ/ **marshes.** A marsh is a wet muddy area of land.   ◆◇◇◇ N-VAR

mar·shal /'mɑːʃəl/ **marshals, marshalling, marshalled;** spelled **marshaling, marshaled** in American English. **1** If you **marshal** people or things, you gather them together and arrange them for a particular purpose. *Richard was marshalling the doctors and nurses, showing them where to go.* **2** A marshal is an official who helps to supervise a public event, especially a sports event. *The grand prix is controlled by well-trained marshals.* **3** In the United States and some other countries, a **marshal** is a police officer, often one who is responsible for a particular area. **4** A marshal is an officer who has the highest rank in an army or air force.   ◆◆◇◇ VERB V n / N-COUNT / N-COUNT

marsh·land /'mɑːʃlænd/ **marshlands.** Marshland is land that is covered in marshes.   N-UNCOUNT: also N in pl

marsh·mal·low /ˌmɑːʃ'mæləʊ, AM -mel-/ **marshmallows. 1** Marshmallow is a soft, sweet, spongy food that is used in some cakes, puddings, and sweets. **2** Marshmallows are sweets made from marshmallow.   N-UNCOUNT / N-COUNT

marshy /'mɑːʃi/. Marshy land is covered in marshes. *...the broad, marshy plain of the River Spey.*   ADJ-GRADED

mar·su·pial /mɑː'suːpiəl/ **marsupials.** A marsupial is an animal such as a kangaroo or an opossum. Female marsupials carry their babies in a pouch on their stomachs.   N-COUNT

mart /mɑːt/ **marts.** A mart is a place, such as a market, where things are bought and sold. *...the flower mart.*   N-COUNT AMERICAN

mar·tial /'mɑːʃəl/. Martial is used to describe things relating to soldiers or war. *The paper was actually twice banned under the martial regime.* ● See also **court-martial**.   ◆◆◇◇ ADJ FORMAL

,martial 'art, martial arts. A martial art is one of the techniques of self-defence that come from the Far East, for example kung fu, karate, or judo.   N-COUNT

,martial 'law. Martial law is control of an area that is established and maintained by soldiers instead of civilians.   ◆◇◇◇ N-UNCOUNT

Mar·tian /'mɑːʃən/ **Martians. 1** A Martian is an imaginary creature from the planet Mars. **2** Something that is **Martian** exists on or relates to the planet Mars. *...the Martian atmosphere.*   N-COUNT / ADJ

mar·ti·net /ˌmɑːtɪ'net/ **martinets.** If you say that someone is a **martinet**, you are criticizing them because they believe in strict discipline and they expect their orders to be obeyed immediately and not questioned. *He's a retired Lieutenant Colonel and a bit of a martinet.*   N-COUNT PRAGMATICS FORMAL

mar·tyr /'mɑːtə/ **martyrs, martyring, martyred. 1** A martyr is a person who is killed or made to suffer greatly, as a direct result of his or her reli- ◆◇◇◇ N-COUNT

gious or political beliefs, and therefore gives strength to people who share those beliefs. ...*a glorious martyr to the cause of liberty. ...a Christian martyr.* **2** If someone **is martyred**, they are killed or made to suffer very greatly, because of their religious or political beliefs. *St Pancras was martyred in 304 AD.* **3** If you refer to someone as a **martyr**, you disapprove of the fact that they pretend to suffer, or exaggerate their suffering, in order to get sympathy or praise from other people. *When are you going to quit acting like a martyr?* • See also **martyred**. **4** If you say that someone is a **martyr** to something, you mean that they suffer as a result of it. *Ellsworth was a martyr to his sense of honour.* `VB: usu passive beV-ed` `N-COUNT PRAGMATICS` `N-COUNT`

mar·tyr·dom /ˈmɑːtədəm/. **1** If someone suffers **martyrdom**, they are killed, tortured, or made to suffer because of their religious or political beliefs. **2** If you describe someone's behaviour as **martyrdom**, you are critical of them because they are showing that they are suffering in an exaggerated way, in order to gain sympathy or praise. *The air of patient martyrdom with which she greeted him.* `N-UNCOUNT` `N-UNCOUNT PRAGMATICS`

mar·tyred /ˈmɑːtəd/. If you describe a person or their behaviour as **martyred**, you are critical of them because they often exaggerate their suffering in order to get sympathy or praise from other people. *'As usual,' muttered his martyred wife.* `ADJ: ADJ n PRAGMATICS LITERARY`

mar·vel /ˈmɑːvəl/ **marvels, marvelling, marvelled;** spelled **marveling, marveled** in American English. **1** If you **marvel** at something, you express your great surprise, wonder, or admiration. *Her fellow members marveled at her seemingly infinite energy... 'That's the weirdest thing I've ever seen,' marveled Carl.* **2** You can describe something or someone as a **marvel** to indicate that you think that they are wonderful. *The whale, like the dolphin, has become a symbol of the marvels of creation.* **3** **Marvels** are things that people have done, or that have happened, which are very unexpected or surprising. *She almost died, but the hospital's skill achieved great marvels.* `◆◇◇◇◇` `VERB V at n V with quote Also V, V that` `N-COUNT` `N-COUNT`

mar·vel·lous /ˈmɑːvələs/; spelled **marvelous** in American English. If you describe someone or something as **marvellous**, you are emphasizing that they are very good. *He certainly is a marvellous actor... He looked marvellous.* ♦ **mar·vel·lous·ly** *He always painted marvellously.* `◆◆◇◇◇ ADJ-GRADED PRAGMATICS` `ADV-GRADED`

Marx·ism /ˈmɑːksɪzəm/. **Marxism** is a political philosophy based on the writings of Karl Marx which stresses the importance of the struggle between different social classes. `◆◇◇◇◇ N-UNCOUNT`

Marx·ist /ˈmɑːksɪst/ **Marxists. 1 Marxist** means based on Marxism or relating to Marxism. ...*a Marxist state. ...Marxist ideology.* **2** A **Marxist** is a person who believes in Marxism or who is a member of a Marxist party. `◆◆◇◇◇ ADJ` `N-COUNT`

mar·zi·pan /ˈmɑːzɪpæn/. **Marzipan** is a paste made of almonds, sugar, and egg which is sometimes put on top of cakes. `N-UNCOUNT`

masc. **Masc.** is a written abbreviation for the word **masculine**.

mas·cara /mæˈskɑːrə, AM -ˈkær-/ **mascaras. Mascara** is a substance used mainly by women, to colour their eyelashes. `◆◇◇◇◇ N-VAR`

mas·cot /ˈmæskɒt/ **mascots.** A **mascot** is an animal, toy, or symbol which is associated with a particular organization or event, and which is thought to bring good luck. ...*the official mascot of the Barcelona Games.* `◆◇◇◇◇ N-COUNT`

mas·cu·line /ˈmæskjʊlɪn/. **1 Masculine** qualities and things relate to or are considered typical of men, in contrast to women. ...*masculine characteristics like a husky voice and facial hair.* ♦ **mas·cu·lin·ity** /ˌmæskjʊˈlɪnɪti/ ...*a project on the link between masculinity and violence.* **2** If you say that someone or something is **masculine**, you mean that they have qualities such as strength or confidence which are considered typical of men. ...*her aggressive, masculine image.* ♦ **masculinity** ...*being unable to prove his masculinity.* **3** In some languages, `◆◇◇◇◇ ADJ` `N-UNCOUNT` `N-UNCOUNT ADJ-GRADED` `N-UNCOUNT` `ADJ`

a **masculine** noun, pronoun, or adjective has a different form from a feminine or neuter one, or behaves in a different way.

mash /mæʃ/ **mashes, mashing, mashed. 1** If you **mash** food that is solid but soft, you crush it so that it forms a soft mass. *Mash the bananas with a fork.* **2** **Mash** is mashed potato. *He only eats junk food like fish and chips or sausages and mash.* **3** A **mash** of food is a soft mass of food. It is often a mixture of several ingredients. *They ate a mash of 2 potatoes, 2 carrots & cabbage.* `◆◇◇◇◇ VERB V n` `N-UNCOUNT INFORMAL, BRITISH N-SING`

mask /mɑːsk, mæsk/ **masks, masking, masked. 1** A **mask** is something which you wear over your face in order to hide or protect it or to make yourself look different. *You must wear goggles and a mask that will protect you against the fumes.* • See also **gas mask, oxygen mask. 2** If you **mask** your feelings, you deliberately do not show them in your behaviour, so that people cannot know what you really feel. ► Also a noun. *His mask of detachment cracked.* **3** If one thing **masks** another, it prevents people from noticing or recognizing the other thing. *A thick grey cloud masked the sun.* `◆◆◆◇◇ N-COUNT` `VERB: V n` `N-COUNT` `VERB V n`

masked /mɑːskt, mæskt/. Someone who is **masked** is wearing a mask. `◆◇◇◇◇ ADJ`

'masking tape. Masking tape is plastic or paper tape which is sticky on one side and is used to protect part of a surface. `N-UNCOUNT`

maso·chism /ˈmæsəkɪzəm/. **1 Masochism** is behaviour in which someone gets sexual pleasure from their own pain or suffering. ♦ **maso·chist, masochists** ...*consensual sexual masochists.* ♦ **maso·chis·tic** /ˌmæsəˈkɪstɪk/ ...*his masochistic tendencies.* **2** If you describe someone's behaviour as **masochism**, you mean that they seem to be trying to get into a situation which causes them suffering or great difficulty. *It takes a peculiar kind of masochism to return to a British winter.* ♦ **maso·chist** *Anybody who enjoys this is a masochist.* ♦ **maso·chis·tic** *It seems masochistic, somehow.* **3** See also **sado-masochism**. `◆◇◇◇◇ N-UNCOUNT` `N-COUNT` `ADJ` `N-UNCOUNT` `N-COUNT` `ADJ-GRADED`

ma·son /ˈmeɪsən/ **masons. 1** A **mason** is a person who is skilled at making things or building things with stone. **2** A **Mason** is the same as a **Freemason**. `◆◇◇◇◇ N-COUNT` `N-COUNT`

Ma·son·ic /məˈsɒnɪk/. **Masonic** is used to describe things relating to the beliefs, traditions, or organization of Freemasons. ...*a Masonic lodge on Broughton Street.* `ADJ: ADJ n`

ma·son·ry /ˈmeɪsənri/. **Masonry** is bricks or pieces of stone which have been stuck together with cement as part of a wall or building. `N-UNCOUNT`

mas·quer·ade /ˌmæskəˈreɪd/ **masquerades, masquerading, masqueraded. 1** If someone or something **masquerades as** someone or something else, they pretend to be that person or thing. *He masqueraded as a doctor and fooled everyone.* **2** A **masquerade** is an attempt to deceive people about the true nature or identity of something. *He told a news conference that the elections would be a masquerade.* `◆◇◇◇◇ VERB V as n` `N-COUNT`

mass /mæs/ **masses, massing, massed. 1** A **mass** of something is a large quantity of it. *On his desk is a mass of books and papers... She had a mass of auburn hair.* **2 Masses** of something means a great deal of it. *There's masses of work for her to do.* **3 Mass** is used to describe something which involves or affects a very large number of people. ...*weapons of mass destruction.* **4** A **mass** of a solid substance, a liquid, or a gas is an amount of it, especially a large amount which has no definite shape. ...*a mass of rubble.* **5** If you talk about the **masses**, you mean the ordinary people in society, in contrast to the leaders or the highly educated people. *His music is commercial, it is aimed at the masses.* **6** The **mass** of people are most of the people in a country, society, or group. *The 1939-45 world war involved the mass of the population.* **7** A **mass** of people is a large crowd of them. ...*masses of excited people clogged the streets.* **8** When people or things **mass**, or when you **mass** them, they gather `◆◆◆◇ N-SING: N of n` `QUANT INFORMAL` `ADJ: ADJ n` `N-COUNT` `N-PLURAL: the N` `N-SING: the N of n` `N-COUNT: N of n` `V-ERG: V V n`

M

together into a large crowd or group. *The General was massing his troops for a counterattack.*

9 The **mass** of an object is the amount of physical matter that it has. `N-VAR TECHNICAL`

10 **Mass** is a Christian church ceremony during which people eat bread and drink wine in order to remember the last meal of Jesus Christ. **11** A **Mass** is a piece of music which uses the prayers from the Christian ceremony of Mass as the words that are sung. **12** See also **massed; critical mass, land mass.** `N-VAR` `N-COUNT`

mas·sa·cre /'mæsəkə/ **massacres, massacring, massacred.** **1** A **massacre** is the killing of a large number of people in a violent and cruel way. *...reports of massacre, torture and starvation.* **2** If people **are massacred**, a large number of them are killed in a violent and cruel way. *300 civilians are believed to have been massacred by the rebels.* `◆◇◇◇` `N-VAR` `VERB be V-ed Also V n`

mas·sage /'mæsɑ:ʒ, AM mə'sɑ:ʒ/ **massages, massaging, massaged.** **1** If you **massage** someone or a part of their body, you squeeze and rub their body, in order to make them relax or reduce their pain. *She continued massaging her right foot, which was bruised and aching.* ► Also a noun. *Massage isn't a long-term cure for stress.* **2** If you say that someone **massages** statistics, figures, or evidence, you are criticizing them for changing or rearranging the facts in such a way that other people are deceived. *Their governments have no reason to 'massage' the statistic.* `◆◆◇◇` `VERB V n` `N-VAR` `VERB PRAGMATICS V n`

masse. See **en masse.**

massed /mæst/. **Massed** is used to describe a large number of people who have been brought together for a particular purpose. *He could not escape the massed ranks of newsmen.* `ADJ: ADJ n`

mas·seur /mæ'sɜ:/ **masseurs.** A **masseur** is a person whose job is to give massages. `N-COUNT`

mas·seuse /mæ'sɜ:z/ **masseuses.** A **masseuse** is a woman whose job is to give massages. `N-COUNT`

mas·sif /'mæ'si:f/ **massifs.** A **massif** is a group of mountains or a high plateau. `N-COUNT`

mas·sive /'mæsɪv/. Something that is **massive** is very large in size, quantity, or extent. *There was evidence of massive fraud... The scale of the problem is massive.* ♦ **mas·sive·ly** *Interest rates will rise massively.* `◆◆◇◇` `ADJ-GRADED` `ADV-GRADED`

,mass 'media. The **mass media** are television, radio, and newspapers. *...mass media coverage of the issue.* `◆◇◇◇` `N-COLL-SING`

'mass noun, mass nouns. **1** A **mass noun** is a noun such as 'wine' which is usually uncount, but is used with an indefinite article or in the plural form when it refers to types or brands of a substance, as in 'a range of Australian wines'. **2** In some descriptions of grammar, a **mass noun** is the same as an **uncount noun.** `N-COUNT` `N-COUNT`

,mass-pro'duce, mass-produces, mass-producing, mass-produced. If someone **mass-produces** something, they make it in large quantities by repeating the process many times. *...machinery to mass-produce footwear.* ♦ **mass-produced** *...the first mass-produced mountain bike.* `◆◇◇◇` `VERB V n` `ADJ: ADJ n`

,mass pro'duction; also spelled **mass-production. Mass production** is the production of something in large quantities. `N-UNCOUNT`

mast /mɑ:st, mæst/ **masts.** **1** The **masts** of a boat are the tall upright poles that support its sails. **2** A **mast** is a long vertical pole that is used as an aerial to transmit sound or television pictures. **3** ♦ to **nail** your **colours to the mast:** see **colour.** ♦ to **nail** your **colours to a mast:** see **colour.** `◆◇◇◇` `N-COUNT` `N-COUNT`

mas·tec·to·my /mæ'stektəmi/ **mastectomies.** A **mastectomy** is a surgical operation to remove a woman's breast. `N-VAR`

mas·ter /'mɑ:stə, 'mæs-/ **masters, mastering, mastered.** **1** A servant's **master** is the man that he or she works for. *My master ordered me not to deliver the message except in private.* **2** A dog's **master** is the man or boy who owns it. **3** In the past, **Master** was used before a boy's name as a polite way of re- `◆◆◆◆` `N-COUNT DATED` `N-COUNT` `N-TITLE BRITISH`

ferring to him or addressing him. Nowadays, **Master** can be written before a boy's name when addressing a letter to him.

4 If you say that someone is a **master** of a particular activity, you mean that they are extremely skilled at it. *She was a master of the English language.* ● See also **old master, past master.** ► Also an adjective. *...a master craftsman.* **5** If you are **master** of a situation, you have complete control over it. *Jackson remained calm and always master of his passions.* **6** If you **master** something, you learn how to do it properly or you succeed in understanding it completely. *Students are expected to master a second language.* **7** If you **master** a difficult situation, you succeed in controlling it. *When you have mastered one situation you have to go on to the next.* `N-COUNT` `ADJ: ADJ n` `N-UNCOUNT: also N in pl` `VERB V n` `VERB V n`

8 A **master** is a male teacher, especially one in a British public school. ● See also **headmaster, housemaster.** `N-COUNT`

9 A **master** copy of something such as a film or a tape recording is an original copy that can be used to produce other copies. `ADJ: ADJ n`

10 A **master's degree** can be referred to as a **master's.** *I've a master's in economics.* `N-SING`

,master 'bedroom, master bedrooms. The **master bedroom** in a large house is the largest bedroom. `N-COUNT`

mas·ter·class /'mɑ:stəklɑ:s, 'mæstəklæs/ **masterclasses.** A **masterclass** is a lesson where someone who is an expert at something such as dancing or music gives advice to very talented students. `N-COUNT`

mas·ter·ful /'mɑ:stəfəl, 'mæs-/. **1** If you describe a man as **masterful**, you approve of him because he behaves in a way which shows that he is in control of a situation. *Big, successful moves need bold, masterful managers.* **2** If you describe someone's behaviour or actions as **masterful**, you mean that they show great skill. *...a masterful performance of boxing and punching skills.* `ADJ-GRADED PRAGMATICS` `ADJ-GRADED`

'master key, master keys. A **master key** is a key which will open all the locks in a set, even though each lock has its own different key. `N-COUNT`

mas·ter·ly /'mɑ:stəli, 'mæs-/. If you describe something as **masterly**, you admire it because it has been done extremely well or shows the highest level of ability and skill. *Malcolm Hebden gives a masterly performance.* `ADJ-GRADED PRAGMATICS`

master·mind /'mɑ:stəmaɪnd, 'mæs-/ **masterminds, masterminding, masterminded.** **1** If you **mastermind** a difficult or complicated activity, you plan it in detail and then make sure that it happens successfully. *The finance minister will continue to mastermind Poland's economic reform.* **2** The **mastermind** behind a difficult or complicated plan, often a criminal one, is the person who is responsible for planning and organizing it. *He was the mastermind behind the plan to acquire the explosives.* `◆◇◇◇` `VERB V n` `N-COUNT`

,master of 'ceremonies, masters of ceremonies. At events such as formal dinners, award ceremonies, and variety shows, the **master of ceremonies** is the person who introduces the speakers or performers, and who announces what is going to happen next. `N-COUNT`

master·piece /'mɑ:stəpi:s, 'mæs-/ **masterpieces.** **1** A **masterpiece** is an extremely good painting, novel, film, or other work of art. *His book, I must add, is a masterpiece.* **2** An artist's, writer's, or composer's **masterpiece** is the best work that they have ever produced. **3** A **masterpiece** is an extremely clever or skilful example of something. *The whole thing was a masterpiece of crowd management.* `◆◆◇◇` `N-COUNT` `N-COUNT: with poss` `N-COUNT`

'master plan, master plans. A **master plan** is a clever plan that is intended to help someone succeed in a very difficult or important task. *...the master plan for the reform of the economy.* `N-COUNT`

'master's degree, master's degrees; also spelled **Master's degree.** A **master's degree** is a `N-COUNT`

university degree which is of a higher level than a first degree. A master's degree, for example, an MA or an MSc, usually takes one or two years to complete.

mas·ter·stroke /'mɑːstəstrəʊk, 'mæs-/ **master-strokes.** A masterstroke is something you do which is unexpected but very clever and which helps you to achieve something. *To have convinced Hillsden that he would be justified in killing Calder was a masterstroke.* N-COUNT

mas·ter·work /'mɑːstəwɜːk, 'mæs-/ **masterworks.** If you describe something such as a book or a painting as a **masterwork**, it is your opinion that it is an excellent example of its type. *They endure as masterworks of American musical theatre.* N-COUNT

mas·tery /'mɑːstəri, 'mæs-/ **1** If you show **mastery** of a particular skill or language, you show you have learnt or understood it completely and have no difficulty using it. *He doesn't have mastery of the basic rules of grammar.* **2 Mastery** is power or control over something. *...his mastery over early, painful emotions.* ◆◇◇◇◇ N-UNCOUNT

mast·head /'mɑːsthed, 'mæst-/ **mastheads. 1** A ship's **masthead** is the highest part of its mast. **2** A newspaper's **masthead** is the part at the top of the front page where its name appears in big letters. N-COUNT

mas·ti·cate /'mæstɪkeɪt/ **masticates, masticating, masticated.** When you **masticate** food, you chew it. *Don't gulp everything down without masticating.* ♦ **mas·ti·ca·tion** /,mæstɪ'keɪʃən/ *...mastication of the food in the mouth.* VERB: V n | V | FORMAL | N-UNCOUNT

mas·tiff /'mæstɪf/ **mastiffs.** A mastiff is a large, powerful, short-haired dog. N-COUNT

mas·tur·bate /'mæstəbeɪt/ **masturbates, masturbating, masturbated.** If someone **masturbates**, they stroke or rub their own genitals in order to get sexual pleasure. ♦ **mas·tur·ba·tion** /,mæstə'beɪʃən/. ◆◇◇◇◇ VERB: V | N-UNCOUNT

mat /mæt/ **mats. 1** A **mat** is a small piece of something such as cloth, card, or plastic which you put on a table to protect the table against heat or spillages. *The food is served on polished tables with mats.* **2** A **mat** is a small piece of carpet or other thick material which is put on the floor for protection, decoration, or comfort. *Bring a sleeping bag and foam mat.* **3** A **mat** of something such as grass or moss is a thick untidy layer of it. *She touched the thick mat of sandy hair on his chest.* **4** See also **matt**, **place mat**. ◆◇◇◇◇ N-COUNT | N-COUNT | N-COUNT: with supp

mata·dor /'mætədɔː/ **matadors.** A matador is the person in a bullfight who is supposed to kill the bull. N-COUNT

match /mætʃ/ **matches, matching, matched. 1** A **match** is an organized game of football, tennis, cricket, or other sport. *He was watching a football match.* **2** A **match** is a small wooden stick with a substance on one end that produces a flame when you rub it along the rough side of a matchbox. **3** If one thing of a particular colour or design **matches** another, or if the two things **match**, they have the same colour or design, or have a pleasing appearance when they are used together. *'The shoes are too tight.'—'Well, they do match your dress.'... All the chairs matched... You don't have to match your lipstick exactly to your outfit.* ▶ **Match up** means the same as **match**. *The pillow cover can match up with the sheets... It's so easy to match them up with your own.* **4** If a combination of things or people is a good **match**, they have a pleasing effect when placed or used together. *Helen's choice of lipstick was a good match for her skin-tone.* **5** If something such as an amount or a quality **matches** with another, or if the two things **match**, they are both the same or equal. *Their strengths in memory and spatial skills matched... Our value system does not match with their value system. ...efforts to match demand with supply.* **6** If one thing **matches** another, or if the two things **match**, they are connected or suit each other in some way. *The students are asked to match the books with the authors... It can take time and effort to match buy-* ◆◆◆◆◆ N-COUNT BRITISH | N-COUNT | V-RECIP-ERG V n | pl-n V | V n to/with n | Also V pl-n | PHRASAL VB ERG V P with/ton V n P with/ton N-SING: adj N | V-RECIP-ERG pl-n V | V n with n | Also V pl-n | V-RECIP-ERG V n with/ton pl-n V | Also V with n

ers and sellers... The sale would only go ahead if the name and number matched. ▶ **Match up** means the same as **match**. *...to match up jobless professionals with small companies in need of expertise... My sister and I never really matched up... I'm going to hand your automatic over to the police so that they can match it up to the bullet taken from Siobhan's body.* PHRASAL VB RECIP-ERG V P noun with n | pl-n V P | V n P to/with n

7 If you **match** something, you are as good as it or equal to it, for example in speed, size, or quality. *They played some fine attacking football, but I think we matched them in every department.* **8** If you **meet** your **match**, you find that you are competing or fighting against someone or something that you cannot beat. *I had finally met my match in power and intellect.* **9** If one person or thing is **no match for** another, they are unable to compete successfully with the other person or thing. *Hand-held guns proved no match for heavy armor.* **10** See also **matched**, **matching**. VERB V n | PHRASE | PHRASE

match up. See **match** 3, 6. PHRASAL VB

match up to. If someone or something does not **match up to** what was expected, they are smaller, less impressive, or of poorer quality. *Her career never quite matched up to its promise.* PHRASAL VB V P P n

match·box /'mætʃbɒks/ **matchboxes.** A matchbox is a small box that you buy with matches in it. N-COUNT

matched /mætʃt/ **1** If you say that two people are well **matched**, you mean that they have qualities that will enable them to have a good relationship. *My parents were not very well matched.* **2** In sports and other competitions, if the two opponents or teams are well **matched**, they are both of the same standard in strength or ability. ◆◇◇◇◇ ADJ: adv ADJ | ADJ: adv ADJ

match·ing /'mætʃɪŋ/. **Matching** is used to describe things which are of the same colour or design. *...a coat and a matching handbag.* ◆◇◇◇◇ ADJ: ADJ n

match·less /'mætʃləs/. You can use **matchless** to emphasize that you think something is extremely good. *The Savoy provides a matchless hotel experience.* ADJ PRAGMATICS

match·making /'mætʃmeɪkɪŋ/. **Matchmaking** is the activity of encouraging people you know to form relationships or get married. ♦ **match·maker, matchmaker** *My services as a formal matchmaker aren't required.* N-UNCOUNT | N-COUNT

match 'point, match points. In a game of tennis, **match point** is the situation when the player who is in the lead can win the whole match if they win the next point. N-VAR

match·stick /'mætʃstɪk/ **matchsticks. 1** A **matchstick** is the wooden part of a match. **2** You can refer to something very small or thin as a **matchstick**. *...children with matchstick legs.* N-COUNT | N-COUNT

mate /meɪt/ **mates, mating, mated. 1** You can refer to someone's friends as their **mates**, especially when you are talking about a man and his male friends. *He's off drinking with his mates.* **2** Some men use **mate** as a way of addressing other men when they are talking to them. *Come on mate, things aren't that bad.* **3** Someone's wife, husband, or sexual partner can be referred to as their **mate**. **4** An animal's **mate** is its sexual partner. **5** When animals **mate**, a male and a female have sex in order to produce young. *This allows the pair to mate properly and stops the hen staying in the nest-box... They want the males to mate with wild females.* **6** On a commercial ship, **the mate** or **first mate** is the most important officer except for the captain. **7** A **mate** is an officer on a merchant ship. **8** In chess, **mate** is the same as **checkmate**. **9** See also **classmate, flatmate, playmate, roommate, running mate, schoolmate, shipmate, soul mate**. ◆◆◆◇◇ N-COUNT BRITISH, INFORMAL | N-VOC PRAGMATICS BRITISH, INFORMAL | N-COUNT | N-COUNT | V-RECIP pl-n V | V with n | Also V | N-COUNT | N-COUNT | N-UNCOUNT

ma·te·rial /mə'tɪəriəl/ **materials. 1** A **material** is a solid substance. *...a conducting material such as a metal.* **2 Material** is cloth. *...the thick material of her skirt.* **3 Materials** are the things that you need for a particular activity. *...sewing materials.* **4** Ideas or information that are used as a basis for a ◆◆◆◆◇ N-VAR | N-VAR | N-PLURAL | N-UNCOUNT

M

book, play, or film can be referred to as **material**. *In my version of the story, I added some new material.*

5 Material things are related to possessions or money, rather than to more abstract things such as ideas or values. ♦ **ma·teri·al·ly** *He has tried to help this child materially and spiritually.* ADV

6 If you say that someone is a particular kind of **material**, you mean that they have the qualities or abilities to do a particular job or task. *She was not university material.* N-UNCOUNT: supp N

7 Material information or evidence is directly relevant and important in a legal or academic argument. *The company failed to disclose material information.* ADJ: ADJ n TECHNICAL

ma·teri·al·ise /mə'tɪəriəlaɪz/. See **materialize.**

ma·teri·al·ism /mə'tɪəriəlɪzəm/. **1 Materialism** is the attitude of someone who attaches a lot of importance to money and wants to possess a lot of material things. ♦ **ma·teri·al·ist, materialists** *Leo is a materialist, living for life's little luxuries.* **2 Materialism** is the belief that only physical matter exists, and that there is no spiritual world. ♦ **materialist** *...the materialist view of nature and society.* N-UNCOUNT N-COUNT N-UNCOUNT ADJ

ma·teri·al·is·tic /mə,tɪəriəl'ɪstɪk/. If you describe a person or society as **materialistic**, you are critical of them because they attach too much importance to money and material possessions. ADJ-GRADED PRAGMATICS

ma·teri·al·ize /mə'tɪəriəlaɪz/ **materializes, materializing, materialized;** also spelled **materialise** in British English. **1** If a possible or expected event does not **materialize**, it does not happen. *A rebellion by radicals failed to materialize.* **2** If a person or thing **materializes**, they suddenly appear, after they have been invisible or in another place. *Tamsin materialized at her side, notebook at the ready.* ♦◇◇◇◇ VERB V VERB V

ma·ter·nal /mə'tɜ:nəl/. **1 Maternal** feelings or actions are typical of those of a mother towards her child. *She had little maternal instinct.* **2 Maternal** is used to describe things that relate to the mother of a baby. *Maternal smoking can damage the unborn child.* **3** A **maternal** relative is one who is related through a person's mother rather than their father. *...her maternal grandfather.* ♦◇◇◇◇ ADJ-GRADED ADJ: ADJ n ADJ: ADJ n

ma·ter·nity /mə'tɜ:nɪti/. **1 Maternity** is used to describe things relating to the help and medical care given to a woman when she is pregnant and when she gives birth. *...the city's maternity hospital.* **2 Maternity** is the state of being a mother. ♦◇◇◇◇ ADJ: ADJ n N-UNCOUNT

ma'ternity leave. Maternity leave is the period of time a mother is allowed to take off work when she has her baby. N-UNCOUNT

matey /'meɪti/. **1** If someone uses **matey** words or behaviour, they are being very friendly, usually insincerely. *...her irritatingly matey tone.* **2** You can address someone as **matey** when you are being friendly towards them. People sometimes also use **matey** when they are annoyed with someone. *Listen matey, just take a look at yourself in the mirror! You look awful!* ADJ-GRADED INFORMAL, BRITISH N-VOC PRAGMATICS INFORMAL, BRITISH

math /mæθ/. **Math** is the same as **mathematics.** The usual British word is **maths.** ♦◇◇◇◇ N-UNCOUNT AMERICAN

math·emati·cal /,mæθə'mætɪkəl/. **1** Something that is **mathematical** involves numbers and calculations. ♦ **math·emati·cal·ly** /,mæθə'mætɪkli/ *...a mathematically complicated formula... Mathematically, it made sense.* **2** If you have **mathematical** abilities or a **mathematical** mind, you are clever at doing calculations or understanding problems that involve numbers. *...a mathematical genius.* ♦ **mathematically** *Anyone can be an astrologer as long as they are mathematically minded.* ♦◇◇◇◇ ADJ: ADJ n ADV ADJ-GRADED ADV: ADV -ed/adj

math·ema·ti·cian /,mæθəmə'tɪʃən/ **mathematicians. 1** A **mathematician** is a person who is trained in the study of numbers and calculations. **2** A **mathematician** is a person who is good at doing calculations and using numbers. *I'm not a very good mathematician.* ♦◇◇◇◇ N-COUNT N-COUNT

math·emat·ics /,mæθə'mætɪks/. **1 Mathematics** is the study of numbers, quantities, or shapes. **2** The ♦◇◇◇◇ N-UNCOUNT

mathematics of a problem consists of the calculations that are involved in it. *...the mathematics of debt.* N-UNCOUNT

maths /mæθs/. **Maths** is the same as **mathematics.** The usual American word is **math.** ♦◇◇◇◇ BRITISH N-COUNT

mati·nee /'mætɪneɪ, AM -'neɪ/ **matinees;** also spelled **matinée.** A **matinee** is a performance of a play or a showing of a film which takes place in the afternoon. N-COUNT

ma·tri·arch /'meɪtriɑ:k/ **matriarchs. 1** A **matriarch** is a woman who rules in a society in which power passes from mother to daughter. ♦ **ma·tri·ar·chal** /,meɪtri'ɑ:kəl/. A **matriarchal** society or system is ruled by matriarchs. **2** A **matriarch** is an old and powerful female member of a family, for example a grandmother. ♦ **matriarchal.** If you describe a woman as **matriarchal**, you mean that she has authority and power within her family or group. N-COUNT ADJ N-COUNT ADJ

ma·tri·ar·chy /'meɪtriɑ:ki/ **matriarchies. 1** Matriarchy is a system of government in which the ruler is female and the power is passed from mother to daughter. **2** A **matriarchy** is a system of inheritance in which family property is traditionally inherited from women and not from men. N-VAR N-VAR

ma·tri·ces /'meɪtrɪsi:z/. **Matrices** is the plural of **matrix.**

ma·tricu·late /mə'trɪkjuleɪt/ **matriculates, matriculating, matriculated.** In some countries, if you **matriculate**, you complete a course of studies successfully, especially by passing examinations. ♦ **ma·tricu·la·tion** /mə,trɪkjʊ'leɪʃən/. *The head decided I should have another go at matriculation.* VERB: V N-UNCOUNT

mat·ri·mo·ny /'mætrɪməni, AM -məʊni/. **Matrimony** is marriage. *...the bonds of matrimony.* ♦ **mat·ri·mo·nial** /,mætrɪ'məʊniəl/ *...the matrimonial affairs of the royal family.* N-UNCOUNT FORMAL ADJ

ma·trix /'meɪtrɪks/ **matrices. 1** A **matrix** is the environment or context in which something such as a society develops and grows. *...the matrix of their culture.* **2** A **matrix** is a rectangular arrangement of numbers, symbols, or letters written in rows and columns and used in solving certain mathematical problems. ♦◇◇◇◇ N-COUNT with supp FORMAL N-COUNT TECHNICAL

ma·tron /'meɪtrən/ **matrons. 1** The **matron** in a nursing home is the woman who is in charge of all the nurses. **2** In some British schools, the **matron** is the woman who looks after the health and hygiene of the children. **3** The **matron** in a hospital or other institution is the woman who is in charge of domestic matters. **Matron** is also used to refer to a female officer in a prison. ♦◇◇◇◇ N-COUNT; N-TITLE; BRITISH N-TITLE; N-COUNT N-COUNT AMERICAN

4 People sometimes refer to middle-aged women as **matrons**, especially if they are fat. ♦ **ma·tron·ly** *...a matronly woman with an air of authority.* N-COUNT ADJ-GRADED

matt /mæt/; also spelled **matte.** American English also uses the spelling **mat.** A **matt** colour, paint, or surface is dull rather than shiny. ♦◇◇◇◇ ADJ

mat·ted /'mætɪd/. **Matted** hair has become a thick untidy mass, often because it is wet or dirty. ADJ-GRADED

mat·ter /'mætə/ **matters, mattering, mattered. 1** A **matter** is a task, situation, or event which you have to deal with or think about, especially one that involves problems. *She wanted to discuss some private matter... Until the matter is resolved the athletes will be ineligible to compete. ...business matters.* ♦♦♦♦ N-COUNT

2 You use **matters** to refer to the situation you are talking about, especially when something is affecting the situation in some way. *Retreating into a cosy ritual will not improve matters.* N-PLURAL: without det

3 If you say that something is **another matter** or a **different matter**, you mean that it is very different from the situation that you have just discussed or is an exception to a rule or general statement that you have just made. *Being responsible for one's own health is one thing, but being responsible for another person's health is quite a different matter.* **4** If something is **no easy matter**, it is difficult to do it. **5** If a person in authority says **that's the end of the matter** or **that's an end to the matter**, they mean that a decision that has been taken must not be changed or discussed any PHRASE PHRASE PHRASE PRAGMATICS

more. **6** If you say that something is **no laughing mat-** `PHRASE`
ter, you mean that it is very serious and not something that you should laugh or joke about. **7** If you say `PHRASE`
that something **makes matters worse**, you mean that
it makes a difficult situation even more difficult.

8 If you say that a situation is a **matter** of a particular `N-SING:`
thing, you mean that that is the most important thing `a N of n/-ing`
to be done or considered when you are involved in the
situation or explaining it. *History is always a matter of
interpretation.* **9** If you say that a statement is a **mat-** `PHRASE`
ter of opinion, you mean that it is not a fact, and that
other people, including yourself, do not agree with it.

10 Printed **matter** consists of books, newspapers, and `N-UNCOUNT:`
other texts that are printed. Reading **matter** consists `supp N`
of things that are suitable for reading, such as books
and newspapers. **11 Matter** is the physical part of the `N-UNCOUNT`
universe consisting of solids, liquids, and gases.
12 You use **matter** to refer to a particular type of sub- `N-UNCOUNT:`
stance. ...*decaying vegetable matter.* `with supp`

13 You use **matter** in expressions such as **'a matter of** `N-SING:`
weeks' when you are emphasizing how small an `a N of pl-n`
amount is or how short a period of time is. *Within a* `PRAGMATICS`
matter of days she was back at work. **14** If you say that `PHRASE`
something is just a **matter of time**, you mean that it is
certain to happen at some time in the future. *It would
be only a matter of time before he went through with it.*
15 You use **matter** in expressions such as **'What's the** `N-SING:`
matter?' or **'Is anything the matter?'** when you think `the N`
that someone has a problem and you want to know
what it is.

16 If you say that something does not **matter**, you `VB: no cont`
mean that it is not important to you because it does `V`
not have an effect on you or on a particular situation. `it V wh`
A lot of the food goes on the floor but that doesn't mat- `it V that`
ter... It does not matter how long their hair is... Does it `V to n`
matter that people don't know this?... Money is the `Also it V`
only thing that matters to them. **17** You say **'it doesn't** `CONVENTION`
matter' to tell someone who is apologizing to you that `PRAGMATICS`
you are not angry or upset, and that they should not
worry. **18** You say **'it doesn't matter'** when someone `CONVENTION`
offers you a choice between two or more things and
you do not mind which is chosen. *'Steve, what do you
want?'—'Coke, Pepsi, it doesn't matter.'* **19** You say `CONVENTION`
'no matter' after you have just asked a question or `PRAGMATICS`
mentioned an idea or doubt and you have decided
that it is not really important, interesting, or worth
discussing. *'Didn't you ever read the book?' Keating
shook his head. 'Well, no matter.'*

20 If you are going to do something **as a matter of** `PHRASE`
urgency or priority, you are going to do it as soon as
possible, because it is important.
21 You use **the fact of the matter is** or **the truth of the** `PHRASE`
matter is to introduce a fact which supports what you `PRAGMATICS`
are saying or which is not widely known, for example
because it is a secret. *The fact of the matter is that most
people consume far more protein than they actually
need.*

22 You can use **for that matter** to emphasize that the `PHRASE`
remark you are making is true in the same way as your `PRAGMATICS`
previous, similar remark. *The irony was that Shawn
had not seen her. Nor for that matter had anyone else.*
23 You use **no matter** in expressions like **'no matter** `PHRASE`
how' and **'no matter what'** to say that something is
true or happens in all circumstances. *No matter what
your age, you can lose weight.* **24** If you say that you `PHRASE`
are going to do something **no matter what**, you are `PRAGMATICS`
emphasizing that you are definitely going to do it,
whatever obstacles or difficulties you may face.

25 See also **subject matter**. ● **a matter of life and
death**: see **death**. ● **as a matter of course**: see **course**.
● **as a matter of fact**: see **fact**. ● **mind over matter**:
see **mind**.

matter-of-'fact. A **matter-of-fact** person shows `◆◇◇◇◇`
no emotions such as enthusiasm, anger, or surprise, `ADJ-GRADED`
especially in a situation where you would expect
them to be emotional. **♦ matter-of-factly** *'She* `ADV-GRADED:`
thinks you're a spy,' Scott said matter-of-factly. `ADV after v`
mat·ting /'mætɪŋ/. **Matting** is strong thick material, `N-UNCOUNT`
usually made from a material like rope, straw, or
rushes, which is used as a floor covering.

mat·tress /'mætrəs/ **mattresses.** A **mattress** is `◆◇◇◇◇`
the large flat layer of padding which is put on a bed `N-COUNT`
to make it comfortable to sleep on.
ma·ture /mə'tjʊə/ **matures, maturing, ma-** `◆◆◇◇◇`
tured; maturer, maturest. 1 When a child or `VERB: V`
young animal **matures**, it becomes an adult.
♦ matu·ra·tion /ˌmætjʊ'reɪʃən/. *Jessica takes pride* `N-UNCOUNT`
in the development and maturation of her son. **2** A `ADJ`
mature person is an adult. ...*when you are mature
and have all the experience, wisdom and confidence
that comes with age.* **♦ ma·tur·ity** /mə'tjʊərɪti/. `N-UNCOUNT`
Maturity is the state of being fully developed or
adult. **3** If you say that someone is **mature** or of `ADJ`
mature years, you are saying politely that they are `PRAGMATICS`
middle-aged or old. **4** If someone **matures**, they be- `VERB`
come more fully developed in their personality and `V`
emotional behaviour. *After three years at university I
will have matured.* **5** If you describe someone as `ADJ-GRADED`
mature, you think that they are fully developed and
balanced in their personality and emotional behav-
iour. **♦ maturity** *Her speech showed great maturity* `N-UNCOUNT`
and humanity.
6 When something **matures**, it reaches a state of com- `VERB`
plete development. *When the trees matured they were* `V`
cut. **7** If you describe someone's work of art or fiction `ADJ-GRADED:`
as **mature**, you mean they have created it thoughtful- `ADJ n`
ly and carefully and they have fully developed their
abilities and potential. *It is his most mature comedy
yet.*
8 If something such as wine or cheese **matures**, it is `V-ERG: V`
left for a time to allow its full flavour or strength to de- `be V-ed`
velop. ...*the cellars where the cheeses are matured.*
9 Mature cheese or wine has been left for a time to al- `ADJ-GRADED`
low its full flavour or strength to develop.
10 When an investment **matures**, the time comes `VERB: V`
when you stop paying money, and the bank, savings,
or insurance company pays you back the money you
have saved plus the interest. **11** A **mature** investment `ADJ`
is an investment which has matured. **♦ maturity** `N-UNCOUNT`
*Customers are told what their policies will be worth on
maturity.*
ma,ture 'student, mature students. A **mature** `N-COUNT`
student is a person who begins their studies at uni- `BRITISH`
versity or college a number of years after leaving
school, so that they are older than most of the people they are studying with.
maud·lin /'mɔːdlɪn/. **1** If you describe someone as `ADJ-GRADED`
maudlin, you mean that they are being sad and
sentimental in a foolish way. *Jimmy turned maudlin
after three drinks.* **2** If you describe a song, book, or `ADJ-GRADED`
film as **maudlin**, you are criticizing it for being very `PRAGMATICS`
sentimental.
maul /mɔːl/ **mauls, mauling, mauled. 1** If `◆◇◇◇◇`
someone **is mauled** by an animal, they are savagely `VERB:`
attacked by it and badly injured. *The dog went ber-* `be V-ed`
serk and mauled one of the girls. **2** If someone is `V n`
mauled, they are criticized or attacked fiercely and `VB: usu`
aggressively, and often harmed in some way. *The* `be V-ed`
*cable-TV and health-care industries are both being
mauled by government.*
mau·so·leum /ˌmɔːzə'liːəm/ **mausoleums.** A `N-COUNT`
mausoleum is a building which contains the grave
of a famous person or the graves of a rich family.
mauve /məʊv/ **mauves.** Something that is **mauve** `◆◇◇◇◇`
is pale purple. `COLOUR`
mav·er·ick /'mævərɪk/ **mavericks.** If you de- `◆◇◇◇◇`
scribe someone as a **maverick**, you mean that they `N-COUNT`
are unconventional and independent, and do not
think or behave in the same way as other people.
*He was too much of a maverick ever to hold high of-
fice. ...a maverick group of scientists.*
maw /mɔː/ **maws.** If you describe something as a `N-COUNT`
maw, you mean that it is like a huge mouth which `LITERARY`
swallows, consumes, or absorbs everything around
it. *Cale's best work has plunged fearlessly into the
dripping maw of emotional extremes.*
mawk·ish /'mɔːkɪʃ/. You can describe something `ADJ-GRADED`
as **mawkish** when it is sentimental and silly, and `PRAGMATICS`
you dislike it a lot. *A sordid, sentimental plot unwinds, with an inevitable mawkish ending.*

M

max /mæks/. **1 Max.** is an abbreviation for 'maximum' which is often used with numbers or amounts when you are giving measurements or ratings. *'Start small,' the man advised, 'Ten gallons, max.'* **2** If you do something **to the max**, you do it to the greatest degree possible. *Everyone involved is enjoying himself to the max.* `ADJ: num ADJ, ADJ n` `PHRASE INFORMAL`

max·im /'mæksɪm/ **maxims.** A **maxim** is a rule for good or sensible behaviour, especially one in the form of a saying or proverb. *I believe in the maxim 'if it ain't broke, don't fix it'.* `◆◇◇◇◇ N-COUNT`

max·im·ize /'mæksɪmaɪz/ **maximizes, maximizing, maximized;** also spelled **maximise** in British English. If you **maximize** something, you make it as great in amount or importance as you can. *In order to maximize profit the firm would seek to maximize output... How can you arrange the furniture to maximize the space in your living room?* ♦ **maxi·mi·za·tion** /ˌmæksɪmaɪ'zeɪʃən/ ...*a pricing policy that was aimed at profit maximisation.* `◆◇◇◇◇ VERB V n` `N-UNCOUNT`

maxi·mum /'mæksɪməm/. **1** You use **maximum** to describe an amount which is the largest that is possible, allowed, or required. ...*the maximum height for a fence or hedge is 2 metres... China headed the table with maximum points.* ▶ Also a noun. ...*a maximum of two years in prison.* **2** You use **maximum** to indicate how great an amount is. ...*the maximum amount of information... It was achieved with minimum fuss and maximum efficiency.* **3** If you say that something is a particular amount **maximum**, you mean that this is the greatest amount it should be or could possibly be, although a smaller amount is acceptable or very possible. *We need an extra 6g a day maximum.* **4** If someone does something **to the maximum**, they do it to the greatest degree possible. *You have to develop your capabilities to the maximum.* `◆◆◇◇◇ ADJ: ADJ n` `N-SING ADJ: ADJ n` `ADV: amount ADV` `PHRASE`

may /meɪ/. **May** is a modal verb. It is used with the base form of a verb. `◆◆◆◆◆`
1 You use **may** to indicate that something will possibly happen or be true in the future, but you cannot be certain. *We may have some rain today... I may be back... I don't know if they'll publish it or not. They may... Cancer may not show up for many years.* **2** You use **may** to indicate that there is a possibility that something is true, but you cannot be certain. *Throwing good money after bad may not be a good idea, they say.* **3** You use **may** to indicate that something is sometimes true or is true in some circumstances. *A vegetarian diet may not provide enough calories for a child's normal growth.* **4** You use **may have** with a past participle when suggesting that it is possible that something happened or was true, or when giving a possible explanation for something. *He may have been to some of those places... The chaos may have contributed to the deaths of up to 20 people.* **5** You use **may** in statements where you are accepting the truth of a situation, but contrasting it with something that is more important. *I may be almost 50, but there's not a lot of things I've forgotten.* **6** You use **may** when you are mentioning a quality or fact about something that people can make use of if they want to. *It may be worn over the shoulder or carried in the hand.* **7** If you do something so that a particular thing may happen, you do it so that there is an opportunity for it. ...*an increase in the numbers of surgeons so that patients may be treated as soon as possible.* **8** You use **may** to indicate that someone is allowed to do something or has the choice of doing something, usually because of a rule or law. You use **may not** to indicate that someone is not allowed to do something. *Any two persons may marry in Scotland provided that both persons are at least 16 years of age.* **9** You use **may** when you are giving permission to someone to do something, or when asking for permission to do something. *May we come in?... You may leave.* **10** You use **may** when you are making polite requests. *I'd like the use of your living room, if I may... May I come with you to Southampton?* **11** You use **may**, usually in `MODAL PRAGMATICS` `MODAL PRAGMATICS` `MODAL` `MODAL PRAGMATICS` `MODAL PRAGMATICS` `MODAL` `MODAL` `MODAL PRAGMATICS` `MODAL PRAGMATICS FORMAL` `MODAL PRAGMATICS` `MODAL`

questions, when you are politely making suggestions or offering to do something. *May we suggest you try one of our guest houses.* **12** You use **may** as a polite way of interrupting someone, asking a question, or introducing what you are going to say next. *'If I may interrupt for a moment,' Kenneth said.* **13** You use **may** when you are mentioning the reaction or attitude that you think someone is likely to have to something you are about to say. *Whatever you may think, I work hard for a living.* **14** You use **may** in expressions such as **I may add** and **I may say** in order to emphasize a statement that you are making. *Both of them, I may say, are thoroughly reliable men.* **15** People use **may** to express hopes and wishes. *Courage seems now to have deserted him. May it quickly reappear.* **16** ● **be that as it may**: see **be**. ● **may as well**: see **well**. `PRAGMATICS FORMAL` `MODAL PRAGMATICS FORMAL SPOKEN` `MODAL PRAGMATICS` `MODAL PRAGMATICS` `MODAL: MODAL n v PRAGMATICS FORMAL`

May /meɪ/ **Mays.** **May** is the fifth month of the year in the Western calendar. See Appendix headed **Dates.** `◆◆◆◇ N-VAR`

may·be /'meɪbi/. **1** You use **maybe** to express uncertainty, for example when you do not know that something is definitely true, or when you are mentioning something that may possibly happen in the future in the way you describe. *Maybe she is in love... I do think about having children, maybe when I'm 40.* **2** You can say **maybe** as a response to a question or remark, when you do not want to agree or disagree. *'Do you think that China and Japan will step in?'—'Maybe.'... 'Is she coming back?'—'Maybe.'* **3** You use **maybe** when you are making suggestions or giving advice. **Maybe** is also used to introduce polite requests. *Maybe we can go to the movies or something... Maybe you'd better tell me what this is all about.* **4** You use **maybe** to indicate that, although a comment is partly true, there is also another point of view that should be considered. *Maybe there is jealousy, but I think the envy is more powerful.* **5** You use **maybe** when you are making a rough guess at a number, quantity, or value, rather than stating it exactly. *The men were maybe a hundred feet away.* **6** People often use **maybe** to mean 'sometimes', particularly in a series of general statements about what someone does, or about something that regularly happens. *They'll come to the bar for a year, or maybe even two, then they'll find another favourite spot.* `◆◆◆◆ ADV: ADV with cl/group PRAGMATICS` `ADV PRAGMATICS` `ADV: ADV with cl/group PRAGMATICS` `ADV: ADV cl` `ADV: ADV amount PRAGMATICS` `ADV: ADV with cl/group`

May·day /'meɪdeɪ/ **Maydays.** A **Mayday** or a **Mayday** message is a radio message sent out by someone on a ship or plane to call for help because they are in serious difficulty. `N-COUNT`

may·hem /'meɪhem/. You use **mayhem** to refer to a situation that is not controlled or ordered, when people are behaving in a disorganized, confused, and often violent way. *Their arrival caused mayhem as crowds of refugees rushed towards them.* `◆◇◇◇◇ N-UNCOUNT`

mayn't /'meɪənt/. **Mayn't** is a spoken form of **may not.**

may·on·naise /ˌmeɪə'neɪz/. **Mayonnaise** is a thick pale sauce made from egg yolks, oil, and vinegar. It is eaten with salad. `◆◇◇◇◇ N-UNCOUNT`

mayor /meə, 'meɪə/ **mayors.** The **mayor** of a town or city is the person who has been elected to represent it for a fixed period of time. `◆◆◆◇ N-COUNT`

mayor·ess /'meərɛs, 'meɪərɛs/ **mayoresses.** **1** A woman who holds the office of mayor is sometimes referred to as a **mayoress.** **2** A **mayoress** is the wife of a mayor. `N-COUNT BRITISH` `N-COUNT BRITISH`

may've /'meɪəv/. **May've** is a spoken form of **may have**, especially when 'have' is an auxiliary verb.

maze /meɪz/ **mazes.** **1** A **maze** is a complex system of passages or paths separated by walls or hedges, which is designed to confuse people who try to find their way through it as a form of amusement. **2** A **maze** of streets, rooms, or tunnels is a large number of them that are connected in a complicated way, so that it is difficult to find your way through them. ...*a maze of dimly-lighted, brown-carpeted corridors.* **3** You can refer to a set of ideas, `◆◇◇◇◇ N-COUNT` `N-COUNT` `N-COUNT`

topics, or rules as a **maze** when a large number of them are related to each other in a complicated way that makes them difficult to understand. *The book tries to steer you through the maze of alternative therapies.*

MBA /ˌem biː ˈeɪ/ **MBAs. 1** An MBA is a master's degree in business administration. You can also refer to a person who has this degree as an **MBA**. MBA is an abbreviation for 'Master of Business Administration'. **2** MBA is written after someone's name to indicate that they have an MBA. ◆◇◇◇◇ N-COUNT

MC /ˌem ˈsiː/ **MCs.** An MC is the same as a **master of ceremonies**. N-COUNT; N-TITLE PHRASE

McCoy /məˈkɔɪ/. If you describe someone or something as **the real McCoy**, you mean that they are the genuine person or thing and not an imitation or fake. INFORMAL

MD /ˌem ˈdiː/ **MDs. 1** MD is an abbreviation for managing director. *He's going to be the MD of the Park Lane company.* **2** Some doctors have **MD** after their name. This indicates that they have obtained a higher degree in medicine. ◆◇◇◇◇ N-COUNT BRITISH

me /mi, STRONG miː/. A speaker or writer uses **me** to refer to himself or herself. **Me** is a first person singular pronoun. **Me** is used as the object of a verb or a preposition. *...decisions that would affect me for the rest of my life... She looked up at me.* ◆◆◆◆◇ PRON

mead /miːd/. In former times, **mead** was an alcoholic drink made of honey, spices, and water. N-UNCOUNT

mead·ow /ˈmedəʊ/ **meadows.** A **meadow** is a field which has grass and flowers growing in it. ◆◇◇◇◇ N-COUNT

mea·gre /ˈmiːɡə/; spelled **meager** in American English. If you describe an amount or quantity of something as **meagre**, you are critical of it because it is very small or not enough. *...a meagre 3.1% pay rise... Their food supply is meager.* ADJ-GRADED PRAGMATICS

meal /miːl/ **meals. 1** A **meal** is an occasion when people eat, at breakfast time, lunchtime, or dinnertime. *She sat next to him throughout the meal.* **2** A **meal** is the food you eat at breakfast time, lunchtime, or dinnertime. *The waiter offered him red wine or white wine with his meal.* **3** If you have a **square meal**, you have a large healthy meal. **4** Meal is a rough powder made of crushed grain. It is used to make flour or animal food. **5** If you think someone is taking more time and energy to do something than is necessary, you can say they are **making a meal of** it. **6** See also **bone meal**. ◆◆◆◇◇ N-COUNT / N-COUNT / PHRASE / N-UNCOUNT / PHRASE PRAGMATICS INFORMAL

meals on 'wheels; also spelled **Meals on Wheels. Meals on wheels** is a service provided by the local authority that delivers hot meals to people who are too old or too sick to cook for themselves. N-UNCOUNT

'meal ticket. If you say that something or someone is a **meal ticket**, you mean that they enable someone to have money or a rich lifestyle which they would not otherwise have. *His chosen field was unlikely to be a meal ticket for life.* N-SING

meal·time /ˈmiːltaɪm/ **mealtimes;** also spelled **meal time. Mealtimes** are occasions when you eat breakfast, lunch, or dinner. *At mealtimes he would watch her eat.* N-VAR

mealy /ˈmiːli/. Food that is dry and powdery can be described as **mealy**. ADJ-GRADED

mealy-mouthed /ˌmiːliˈmaʊðd/. If you say that someone is being **mealy-mouthed**, you are critical of them for being unwilling to speak in a simple or open way because they want to avoid talking directly about something unpleasant. *He did not intend to be mealy-mouthed with the country's leaders.* ADJ-GRADED PRAGMATICS

mean 1 verb uses

mean /miːn/ **means, meaning, meant. 1** If you want to know what a word, code, signal, or gesture **means**, you want to know what it refers to or what message it conveys. *In modern Welsh, 'glas' means 'blue'... What does 'evidence' mean?... The red signal means you can shoot.* **2** If you ask someone what they **mean**, you are asking them to explain exactly what or who they are referring to or what they are intending to say. *Do you mean me?... What do you* ◆◆◆◆◆ VB: no cont / V n / V that / VB: no cont / V n / V that

think he means by that?... He means that he does not want this marriage to turn out like his friend's. **3** You use **'you mean'** in a question to check that you have understood properly what someone has said. *What accident? You mean Christina's?* **4** You say **'I mean'** when making what you have just said clearer. *It was his idea. Gordon's, I mean.* **5** You can use **'I mean'** to introduce a statement, especially one that justifies something you have just said. *I'm sure he wouldn't mind. I mean, I was the one who asked him.* **6** You say **'I mean'** when correcting something that you have just said. *It was law or classics – I mean English or classics.* PHRASE PRAGMATICS (×4)

7 If something **means** something to you, it is important to you in some way. *It would mean a lot to them to win.* VERB: V amount to n / it V amount to n

8 If one thing **means** another, it shows that the second thing exists or is true. *An enlarged prostate does not necessarily mean cancer... Just because he has a beard doesn't necessarily mean he's a hippy.* **9** If one thing **means** another, it inevitably leads to the second thing happening. *Trade and product discounts can also mean big savings... The change will mean that Taiwan no longer has full diplomatic relations with any Middle Eastern state.* **10** If doing one thing **means** doing another, it involves doing the second thing. *Managing well means communicating well.* VB: no cont / V n / V that (×2), VERB V -ing

11 If you say that you **mean** what you are saying, you are telling someone that you are serious about it and are not joking, exaggerating, or just being polite. *He could see I meant what I said. So he took his fur coat and left.* **12** If you say that someone **meant** to do something, you are saying that they did it quite deliberately. *I didn't mean to hurt you... I can see why you believed my letters were threatening but I never meant them to be.* **13** If you **mean** to do something, you intend or plan to do it. *I mean to look after my body more.* **14** If you say that something **was meant to** happen, you believe it was made to happen by God or fate, and was not simply a coincidence or an accident. *John was constantly reassuring me that we were meant to be together.* VB: no cont / V n; V to-inf / V n to-inf; V to-inf; VB: usu passive, no cont beV-ed to-inf

15 If you say that someone did not **mean** any harm or disrespect, you are saying that they did not intend to upset people or to cause problems, even though they may in fact have done so. **16** If you say that someone **means well**, you mean they are trying to be kind and helpful, even though they might be causing someone problems or upsetting them. VERB: V n; PHRASE

17 If you say that you **know what it means** to do something, or that you **know what** something **means**, you mean that you know everything that is involved in a particular activity or experience, especially the effect that it has on you. *I know what it means to lose a child under such tragic circumstances.* **18** If a name, word, or phrase **means something to** you, you have heard it before and you know what it refers to. *Does the word 'Fareham' mean anything to anyone?* **19** ● to **mean business:** see **business.** ● **if you know what I mean:** see **know.** See also **meaning, meant.** PHRASE (×3)

mean 2 adjective uses

mean /miːn/ **meaner, meanest. 1** If you describe someone as **mean**, you are being critical of them because they are unwilling to spend much money or to use very much of a particular thing. *Don't be mean with fabric, otherwise curtains will end up looking skimpy.* ♦ **mean·ness** *This very careful attitude to money can sometimes border on meanness.* **2** If you describe an amount as **mean**, you are saying it is very small; used showing disapproval. *...the meanest grant possible from the local council.* **3** If you say that someone is being **mean**, you are saying they are being unkind to someone. *I'd feel mean saying no.* ♦ **mean·ly** *He had been behaving very meanly to his girlfriend.* **4** If you describe a person or animal as **mean**, you are saying they are very bad-tempered and cruel. **5** If you describe a place as **mean**, you think it looks poor, and perhaps dirty or violent. *He was raised on the mean streets of the central market district of Panama City.* ♦♦◇◇◇ ADJ-GRADED PRAGMATICS BRITISH / N-UNCOUNT PRAGMATICS / ADJ-GRADED PRAGMATICS BRITISH / ADJ-GRADED / ADV-GRADED / ADJ-GRADED AMERICAN / ADJ-GRADED

M

6 You can use **no mean** in expressions such as **'no mean writer'** to indicate that someone does something well, often when comparing them with someone else who also does it well. *She was no mean performer on a variety of other instruments.* **7** You can use **no mean** in expressions such as **'no mean achievement'** to indicate that someone has done something they deserve to be proud of. *To destroy 121 enemy aircraft is no mean record.* `PHRASE INFORMAL` `PHRASE`

mean 3 noun use

mean /miːn/. The **mean** is a number that is the average of a set of numbers. *...the mean score for 26-year-olds.* • See also **means**. `N-SING: the N`

me·ander /miˈændə/ **meanders, meandering, meandered.** **1** If a river or road **meanders**, it has a lot of bends in it. *A rural single railway track meanders through the valley. ...a meandering stream.* **2** A **meander** is a large bend in a river. *As we navigate the river, every meander brings some new surprise.* **3** If you **meander** somewhere, you move slowly and not in a straight line. *It's so restful to meander along Irish country roads.* **4** If a speech or piece of writing **meanders**, it seems to move from one topic to another without any order or purpose. *...a rich and meandering novel.* `◆◇◇◇◇` `VERB V prep/adv V-ing` `N-COUNT` `VERB V prep/adv` `VERB: V V-ing`

mean·ing /ˈmiːnɪŋ/ **meanings.** **1** The **meaning** of a word, expression, or gesture is the thing or idea that it refers to or represents and which can be explained using other words. *I became more aware of the symbols and their meanings.* **2** The **meaning** of what someone says or of something such as a book or film is the thoughts or ideas that are intended to be expressed by it. *Unsure of the meaning of this remark, Ryle chose to remain silent.* **3** If an activity or action has **meaning**, it has a purpose and is worthwhile. *...a challenge that gives meaning to life.* `◆◆◆◇◇` `N-VAR` `N-VAR` `N-UNCOUNT`

mean·ing·ful /ˈmiːnɪŋfʊl/. **1** If you describe something as **meaningful**, you mean that it is serious, important, or useful in some way. *He asked people to tell him about a meaningful event or period in their lives.* ♦ **mean·ing·ful·ly** *Marxist Yugoslavia thus contributed meaningfully to the formation of an international doctrine.* **2** A **meaningful** look or gesture is intended to express something, without anything being said. A **meaningful** remark is intend to express something which is not obvious but which is understood by a particular person. ♦ **meaningfully** *'Who's your publisher?'—'Lockett Press,' she said, and she raised an eyebrow meaningfully.* `◆◆◇◇◇` `ADJ-GRADED` `ADV-GRADED: ADV with v` `ADJ: ADJ n` `ADV-GRADED`

mean·ing·less /ˈmiːnɪŋləs/. **1** If something that someone says or writes is **meaningless**, it has no meaning, or appears to have no meaning. *The sentence 'kicked the ball the man' is meaningless.* **2** Something that is **meaningless** is of no importance or relevance. *Fines are meaningless to guys earning millions.* **3** If something that you do is **meaningless**, it has no purpose and is not at all worthwhile. *They seek strong sensations to dull their sense of a meaningless existence.* `◆◇◇◇◇` `ADJ-GRADED` `ADJ-GRADED` `ADJ-GRADED`

means /miːnz/. **1** A **means** of doing something is a method, instrument, or process which can be used to do it. **Means** is both the singular and the plural form for this use. *The move is a means to fight crime... Business managers are focused on increasing their personal wealth by any available means.* **2** If you do something **by means of** a particular method, instrument, or process, you do it using that method, instrument, or process. *This is a two year course taught by means of lectures and seminars.* **3** If you say that something is **a means to an end**, you mean it enables you to achieve what you want, and is not enjoyable or important in itself. *Marketing is only a means to an end.* **4** You can refer to the money that someone has as their **means**. *...a person of means... He did not have the means to compensate her.* **5** If someone is living **beyond** their **means**, they are spending more money than they can afford. If someone is living **within** their `◆◆◆◇` `N-COUNT: with supp` `PHR-PREP` `PHRASE` `N-PLURAL FORMAL` `PHRASE`

means, they are not spending more money than they can afford. **6** You can say **'by all means'** to tell someone that you are willing to allow them to do something. *'Can I come and have a look at your house?'—'Yes by all means'.* **7** You use expressions such as **'by no means'** and **'not by any means'** to emphasize that something is not true. *This is by no means out of the ordinary.* `CONVENTION PRAGMATICS` `PHRASE PRAGMATICS`

'means test, means tests. A **means test** is a test in which your income is assessed in order to see if you are eligible for certain state grants or benefits. If your income is above a certain amount, you are not eligible. ♦ **means-tested** *Many people entitled to means-tested benefits fail to make any claim.* `N-COUNT` `ADJ`

meant /mɛnt/. **1 Meant** is the past tense and past participle of **mean**. **2** If you say that something or someone **is meant** to be or do a particular thing, you mean that they are intended to be or do that thing, often when they have failed to be or do it. *I can't say any more, it's meant to be a big secret... I'm meant to be on holiday.* **3** If something **is meant for** particular people or for a particular situation, it is intended for those people or for that situation. *Fairy tales weren't just meant for children.* **4** If you say that something **is meant to** happen, you mean it is expected to happen or it ought to happen. *Parties are meant to be fun.* **5** If you say that something **is meant to** have a particular quality or characteristic, you mean it has a reputation for being like that. *Spurs are meant to be one of the top teams in the world.* `◆◆◇◇◇` `ADJ: v-link ADJ to-inf` `ADJ: v-link ADJ for n` `PHR-MODAL` `PHR-MODAL PRAGMATICS`

mean·time /ˈmiːntaɪm/. **1 In the meantime** or **meantime** means in the period of time between two events. *Eventually your child will leave home to lead her own life as a fully independent adult, but in the meantime she relies on your support.* **2 For the meantime** means for a period of time from now until something else happens. *The Prime Minister has, for the meantime, seen off the challenge of the opposition party.* `◆◆◇◇◇` `PHRASE` `PHRASE`

mean·while /ˈmiːnwaɪl/. **1 Meanwhile** means while a particular thing is happening. *Brush the aubergines with oil, add salt and pepper, and bake till soft. Meanwhile, heat the remaining oil in a heavy pan.* **2 Meanwhile** means in the period of time between two events. *You needn't worry; I'll be ready to greet them. Meanwhile I'm off to discuss the Fowlers' party with Felix.* • **In the meanwhile** means the same as **meanwhile**. **3** You use **meanwhile** to introduce a different aspect of a particular situation, especially one that is completely opposite to the one previously mentioned. *I somehow got through the meal. Christopher meanwhile never ate anything.* `◆◆◆◇` `ADV: ADV with cl` `ADV: ADV with cl` `PHRASE` `ADV: ADV with cl PRAGMATICS`

mea·sles /ˈmiːzəlz/. **Measles** is an infectious illness that gives you a high temperature and red spots on your skin. `◆◇◇◇◇` `N-UNCOUNT: also the N`

mea·sly /ˈmiːzli/. If you describe an amount, quantity, or size as **measly**, you are critical of it because it is very small or inadequate. *The average British bathroom measures a measly 3.5 square metres.* `ADJ-GRADED PRAGMATICS INFORMAL`

meas·ur·able /ˈmeʒərəbəl/. **1** If something is **measurable**, it is large enough to be noticed or to be significant. *Both leaders seemed to expect measurable progress.* ♦ **meas·ur·ably** *After this, the pace of events quickened measurably.* **2** Something that is **measurable** can be measured. `◆◇◇◇◇` `ADJ FORMAL` `ADV-GRADED` `ADJ-GRADED`

meas·ure /ˈmeʒə/ **measures, measuring, measured.** **1** If you **measure** the quality, value, or effect of something, you decide how great it is, by making observations or following particular procedures. *I continued to measure his progress against the charts in the doctor's office... It was difficult to measure the precise impact of the labor action.* **2** If you **measure** a quantity that can be expressed in numbers, such as the length of something, you discover it using a particular instrument, for example a ruler. *Measure the length and width of the gap.* **3** If something **measures** a particular length, width, or amount, that is its size or intensity, expressed in num- `◆◆◆◇` `VERB V n prep V n` `VERB V n` `VB: no cont V amount`

bers. *This hand-decorated plate measures 30cm across.* **4** A **measure** of a strong alcoholic drink such as whisky is an amount of it in a glass. In pubs, a **measure** is an official standard amount. N-COUNT

5 A **measure of** a particular quality, feeling, or activity is a fairly large amount of it. *Each attained a measure of success.* **6** If you say that something has changed or that it has affected you **beyond measure**, you are emphasizing that it has done this to a great extent. *She irritated him beyond measure.* **7** If something is true **in some measure** or **in large measure**, it is true in a partial or general way, although it is not completely true. *Power is in some measure an act of will.* N-SING: N of n; PHRASE; PRAGMATICS; PHRASE; FORMAL

8 If you say that something is done **for good measure**, you mean that it is done in addition to a number of other things. *I repeated my question for good measure.* PHRASE

9 If you **get** or **take the measure of** someone or something, you discover what they are like, so that you are able to control them or deal with them. If you **have the measure of** someone or something, you have succeeded in doing this. *The governments of the industrialized world had failed to get the measure of the crisis.* PHRASE; FORMAL

10 If you say that one aspect of a situation is a **measure** of that situation, you mean that it shows that the situation is very serious or has developed to a very great extent. *That is a measure of how bad things have become at the bank.* N-SING: N of n/wh

11 When someone, usually a government or other authority, takes **measures** to do something, they carry out particular actions in order to achieve a particular result. *The government warned that police would take tougher measures to contain the trouble.* **12** See also **measured**, **measuring**; **counter-measure**, **half measure**, **tape measure**. N-COUNT; FORMAL

measure out. If you **measure out** a certain amount of something, you measure that amount and take it or mark it because it is the amount that you want or need. *I'd already measured out the ingredients.* PHRASAL VB; V P noun; Also V n P

measure up. If you do not **measure up** to a standard or to someone's expectations, you are not good enough to achieve the standard or fulfil the person's expectations. *She's always comparing me to other people, and somehow I never measure up.* PHRASAL VB; V P to n; V P

meas·ured /'meʒəd/. A **measured** response or reaction is careful and deliberate. ADJ-GRADED

meas·ure·ment /'meʒəmənt/ **measurements.** **1** A **measurement** is a result, usually expressed in numbers, that you obtain by measuring something. *We took lots of measurements.* **2** Your **measurements** are the size of your waist, chest, hips, and other parts of your body, which you need to know when you are buying clothes. **3** **Measurement** of something is the process or activity of measuring it. ◆◆◇◇; N-COUNT; N-PLURAL: with poss; N-VAR

meas·ur·ing /'meʒərɪŋ/. A **measuring** jug or spoon is specially designed for measuring quantities, especially in cooking. ADJ: ADJ n

meat /miːt/ **meats.** **1** Meat is flesh taken from a dead animal that people cook and eat. *...a buffet of cold meats and salads.* **2** See also **luncheon meat**, **red meat**, **white meat**. **3** If you say something is **meat and drink** to someone, you mean that they enjoy it very much. *What normal people considered pressure was meat and drink to him.* ◆◆◇◇; N-VAR; PHRASE

meat·ball /'miːtbɔːl/ **meatballs.** Meatballs are small balls of chopped meat, breadcrumbs, and herbs. N-COUNT

meaty /'miːti/ **meatier, meatiest.** **1** Food that is **meaty** contains a lot of meat. **2** You can describe something such as a piece of writing or a part in a film as **meaty** if it contains a lot of interesting or important material. ADJ-GRADED; ADJ-GRADED

mec·ca /'mekə/ **meccas.** **1** Mecca is a city in Saudi Arabia, which is the holiest city in Islam because the Prophet Mohammed was born there. **2** If you describe a place as a **mecca** or Mecca for a particular thing or activity, you mean that many people who are interested in it go there. *Thailand has become the tourist mecca of Asia.* ◆◇◇◇; N-PROPER; N-COUNT

me·chan·ic /mɪ'kænɪk/ **mechanics.** **1** A **mechanic** is someone whose job is to repair and maintain ◆◆◇◇; N-COUNT

machines and engines, especially car engines. **2** The **mechanics** of a process, system, or activity are the way in which it works or the way in which it is done. *What are the mechanics of this new process?* **3** Mechanics is the part of physics that deals with the natural forces that act on moving or stationary objects. N-PLURAL; N-UNCOUNT

me·chani·cal /mɪ'kænɪkəl/. **1** A mechanical device has parts that move when it is working, often using power from an engine or from electricity. ♦ **me·chani·cal·ly** /mɪ'kænɪkli/. *The air was circulated mechanically.* **2** Mechanical means relating to machines and engines and the way they work. *The train had stopped due to a mechanical problem.* ♦ **mechanically** *The car was mechanically sound, he decided.* **3** If you describe a person as **mechanical**, you mean they are naturally good at understanding how machines work. ♦ **mechanically** *I'm not mechanically minded.* **4** If you describe someone's action as **mechanical**, you mean that they do it automatically, without thinking about it. ♦ **mechanically** *He nodded mechanically, his eyes fixed on the girl.* ◆◇◇◇; ADJ; ADV; ADJ: ADJ n; ADV; ADJ-GRADED; ADV-GRADED; ADJ-GRADED; ADV-GRADED

mecha·nise /'mekənaɪz/. See **mechanize**.

mecha·nism /'mekənɪzəm/ **mechanisms.** **1** In a machine or piece of equipment, a **mechanism** is a part, often consisting of a set of smaller parts, which performs a particular function. *...the locking mechanism.* **2** A **mechanism** is a special way of getting something done within a particular system. *There's no mechanism for punishing arms exporters who break the rules.* **3** See also **defence mechanism**. ◆◆◇◇; N-COUNT; N-COUNT: with supp

mecha·nis·tic /,mekə'nɪstɪk/. If you describe a view or explanation of something as **mechanistic**, you are criticizing it because it describes a natural or social process as if it were a machine. ADJ-GRADED; PRAGMATICS

mecha·nize /'mekənaɪz/ **mechanizes, mechanizing, mechanized**; also spelled **mechanise** in British English. If someone **mechanizes** a process, they cause it to be done by machines, when it was previously done by people. *Only gradually are technologies being developed to mechanize the task.* ♦ **mecha·nized** *...highly mechanised production methods.* ♦ **mecha·ni·za·tion** /,mekənaɪ'zeɪʃən/ *Mechanization happened years ago on the farms of Islay.* ◆◇◇◇; VERB; V n; ADJ-GRADED; N-UNCOUNT

med·al /'medəl/ **medals.** A **medal** is a small metal disc which is given as an award for bravery or as a prize in a sporting event. ◆◆◇◇; N-COUNT

me·dal·lion /mɪ'dæliən/ **medallions.** A medallion is a round metal disc which some people wear as an ornament, especially on a chain round their neck. N-COUNT

med·al·list /'medəlɪst/ **medallists.** A **medallist** is a person who has won a medal in sport. *...the Olympic gold medallists.* ◆◇◇◇; N-COUNT; JOURNALISM

med·dle /'medəl/ **meddles, meddling, meddled.** If you say that someone **meddles** in something, you are criticizing the fact they try to influence or change it without being asked. *If only you hadn't felt compelled to meddle. ...the inept and meddling bureaucrats.* ♦ **med·dler, meddlers** *They view activists as little more than meddlers.* VERB: V in/with n; PRAGMATICS; V; V-ing; N-COUNT

med·dle·some /'medəlsəm/. If you describe a person as **meddlesome**, you are criticizing them because they try to influence or change things that do not concern them. ADJ-GRADED; PRAGMATICS

me·dia /'miːdiə/. **1** You can refer to television, radio, newspapers, and magazines as the **media**. *It is hard work and not a glamorous job as portrayed by the media... Media coverage of cycling in July was pretty impressive.* ● See also **mass media**, **multimedia**. **2** Media is a plural of **medium**. ◆◆◆◇; N-COLL-SING

me·di·aeval /,medi'iːvəl, AM ,miːd-/. See **medieval**.

me·dian /'miːdiən/. The **median** value of a set of values is the middle one when they are arranged in order. For example, if five students take a test and their marks are 5, 7, 7, 8, and 10, the median mark is 7. ◆◇◇◇; ADJ: ADJ n; TECHNICAL

me·di·ate /'miːdieɪt/ **mediates, mediating, mediated.** **1** If someone **mediates** between two ◆◆◇◇; VERB:

M

groups of people, or **mediates** an agreement between them, they try to settle an argument between them by talking to both groups and trying to find things that they can both agree to. *United Nations officials have mediated a series of peace meetings between the two sides... The Vatican successfully mediated in a territorial dispute between Argentina and Chile in 1984.* ♦ **me·dia·tion** /ˌmiːdiˈeɪʃən/. *The agreement provides for United Nations mediation between the two sides.* ♦ **me·dia·tor, mediators** An archbishop has been acting as mediator between the rebels and the authorities. **2** If something **mediates** a particular process or event, it allows that process or event to happen and influences the way in which it happens. *...the thymus, the organ which mediates the response of the white blood cells.* ♦ **mediation** *This works through the mediation of the central nervous system.*

V between pl-n
V n between
V
Also V n

N-UNCOUNT

N-COUNT

VERB
V n
FORMAL

N-UNCOUNT

med·ic /ˈmedɪk/ **medics.** A **medic** is a doctor or medical student.
◆◇◇◇
INFORMAL

medi·cal /ˈmedɪkəl/ **medicals. 1 Medical** means relating to illness and injuries and to their treatment or prevention. *Several police officers received medical treatment for cuts and bruises.* ♦ **medi·cal·ly** /ˈmedɪkli/. *Therapists cannot prescribe drugs as they are not necessarily medically qualified.* **2** A **medical** is a thorough examination of your body by a doctor, for example before you start a new job.
◆◆◇◇
ADJ: ADJ n

ADV

N-COUNT

medical ex·am·iner, medical examiners. A **medical examiner** is a medical expert who is responsible for investigating the deaths of people who have died in a sudden, violent, or unusual way.
N-COUNT
AMERICAN

medi·cat·ed /ˈmedɪkeɪtɪd/. A **medicated** soap or shampoo contains substances which kill bacteria and therefore make your skin or hair healthier.
ADJ

medi·ca·tion /ˌmedɪˈkeɪʃən/ **medications. Medication** is medicine that is used to treat and cure illness. *When somebody comes for treatment I always ask them if they are on any medication.*
◆◆◇◇
N-VAR

me·dici·nal /meˈdɪsɪnəl/. **Medicinal** substances or substances with **medicinal** effects can be used to treat and cure illnesses. *...medicinal plants.* ♦ **me·dici·nal·ly** *Root ginger has been used medicinally for centuries.*
◆◇◇◇
ADJ

ADV:
ADV after v

medi·cine /ˈmedsən, AM ˈmedɪsɪn/ **medicines. 1 Medicine** is the treatment of illness and injuries by doctors and nurses. *He pursued a career in medicine.* **2 Medicine** is a substance, usually a liquid, tablets, or a powder, that you drink or swallow in order to cure an illness.
◆◆◇◇
N-UNCOUNT

N-VAR

me·di·eval /ˌmediˈiːvəl, AM ˌmiːd-/; also spelled **mediaeval.** Something that is **medieval** relates to or dates from the period in European history between the end of the Roman Empire in 476AD and about 1500AD. *...a medieval castle.*
◆◆◇◇
ADJ

me·dio·cre /ˌmiːdiˈəʊkə/. If you describe something as **mediocre**, you mean that it is of average quality but you think it should be better. *His school record was mediocre.*
◆◇◇◇
ADJ-GRADED
PRAGMATICS

me·di·oc·rity /ˌmiːdiˈɒkrɪti, ˌmed-/ **mediocrities. 1** If you refer to the **mediocrity** of something, you mean that it is of average quality but you think it should be better. **2** If you refer to someone as a **mediocrity**, you think that they are not very good at what they do.
◆◇◇◇
N-UNCOUNT
PRAGMATICS

N-COUNT
PRAGMATICS

medi·tate /ˈmedɪteɪt/ **meditates, meditating, meditated. 1** If you **meditate on** something, you think about it very deeply for a long time. **2** If you **meditate**, you remain in a silent and calm state for a period of time, as part of a religious training or so that you are more able to deal with the problems of everyday life. ♦ **meditation** *Many busy executives have begun to practice meditation.*
◆◆◇◇
VERB:
V on n

N-UNCOUNT:
also N in pl

VERB: V

N-UNCOUNT

medi·ta·tion /ˌmedɪˈteɪʃən/ **meditations.** A **meditation** on a particular subject is something such as a piece of writing or a speech which expresses deep thoughts about that subject.
N-COUNT

medi·ta·tive /ˈmedɪtətɪv, AM -teɪt-/. **Meditative** describes things that are related to the act of meditating or the act of thinking very deeply about something. *...moments of meditative silence.*
ADJ-GRADED:
ADJ n

Medi·ter·ra·nean /ˌmedɪtəˈreɪniən/. **1 The Mediterranean** is the sea which is between southern Europe and North Africa from north to south and the Straits of Gibraltar and western Asia from west to east. **2 The Mediterranean** refers to the southern part of Europe which borders the Mediterranean Sea. *...one of the most dynamic and prosperous cities in the Mediterranean.* **3** Something that is **Mediterranean** is characteristic of or belongs to the people or region around the Mediterranean Sea. *There was very little meat in the classic Mediterranean diet.*
◆◆◇◇
N-PROPER:
the N

N-PROPER:
the N

ADJ

me·dium /ˈmiːdiəm/ **mediums, media.** The plural of the noun can be either **mediums** or **media** for meanings 5 and 6. The form **mediums** is the plural for meaning 7. **1** If something is of **medium** size, it is neither large nor small, but approximately half way between the two. *He was of medium height.* **2** You use **medium** to describe something which is average in degree or amount, or approximately half way along a scale between two extremes. *...foods that contain only medium levels of sodium. ...a sweetish, medium-strength beer.* ► Also an adverb. *Cook under a medium-hot grill.* **3** If something is of a **medium** colour, it is neither light nor dark, but approximately half way between the two. *Andrea has medium brown hair.* **4** If you strike or find a **happy medium** between two extreme and opposite courses of action, you find a sensible way of behaving that is somewhere between the two extremes. **5** A **medium** is a way or means of expressing your ideas or of communicating with people. *In Sierra Leone, English is used as the medium of instruction for all primary education... But Artaud was increasingly dissatisfied with film as a medium.* **6** A **medium** is a substance or material which is used for a particular purpose or in order to produce a particular effect. *Blood is the medium in which oxygen is carried to all parts of the body.* **7** A **medium** is a person who claims to be able to contact and speak to people who are dead. **8** See also **media**.
◆◆◆◇
ADJ

ADJ

ADV

COMB

PHRASE

N-COUNT

N-COUNT

N-COUNT

medium-'dry; also spelled **medium dry. Medium-dry** wine or sherry is not very sweet.
ADJ

'medium-sized. The form **medium size** is also used. **Medium-sized** means neither large nor small, but approximately half way between the two. *...a medium-sized saucepan.*
◆◇◇◇
ADJ

'medium-term. The **medium-term** is the period of time which lasts a few months or years beyond the present time, in contrast with the short term or the long term. *The medium-term economic prospects remained poor.*
◆◇◇◇
N-SING

'medium wave. Medium wave is a range of radio waves which are used for broadcasting.
N-UNCOUNT

med·ley /ˈmedli/ **medleys. 1** In music, a **medley** is a collection of different tunes or songs that are played one after the other as a single piece of music. **2** In sport, a **medley** is a swimming race in which the four main strokes are used one after the other. **3** A **medley** of different foods or other things is a mixture of them. *...a medley of four fish in a cream sauce.*
◆◇◇◇
N-COUNT

N-COUNT

N-COUNT

meek /miːk/ **meeker, meekest.** If you describe a person as **meek**, you think that they are gentle and quiet, and likely to do what other people say. ► **The meek** are people who are meek. *The meek shall inherit the earth.* ♦ **meek·ly** *'Thank you, Peter', Amy said meekly.* ♦ **meek·ness** *She maintained a kind of meekness.*
◆◇◇◇
ADJ-GRADED

N-PLURAL:
the N

ADV-GRADED

N-UNCOUNT

meet /miːt/ **meets, meeting, met. 1** If you **meet** someone, either a stranger or someone you already know, you happen to be in the same place as them and start talking to them. *He's the kindest and sincerest person I've ever met... We met by chance.* ► **Meet up** means the same as **meet**. *Last night, when he was parking my automobile, he met up with a buddy he had at Oxford... They met up in*
◆◆◆◆◆
V-RECIP
V n
pl-n V

PHRASAL VB
RECIP
V P with n
pl-n V P

1956, when they were both young schoolboys. **2** If two or more people **meet**, they go to the same place, which they have earlier arranged to do, so that they can talk or do something together. *Meet me down at the beach tomorrow, at 6am sharp.* ► **Meet up** means the same as **meet**. *We tend to meet up for lunch once a week... My intention was to have a long holiday and meet up with old friends.* **3** If you **meet** someone, you are introduced to them and begin talking to them and getting to know them. *Hey, Terry, come and meet my Dad.* **4** You use **meet** in expressions such as **'Pleased to meet you'** and **'Nice to have met you'** when you want to politely say hello or goodbye to someone you have just met for the first time. V-RECIP: pl-n V, V n; PHRASAL VB RECIP pl-n V P, V P with n; VERB V n; VERB: V n PRAGMATICS

5 If you **meet** someone who is travelling, or if you **meet** someone off their train, plane, or bus, you go to the station, airport, or bus-stop in order to be there when they arrive. You can also say that you **meet** someone's train, plane, or bus. *Mama met me at the station... Lili and my father met me off the boat... Kurt's parents weren't able to meet our plane.* **6** When a group of people such as a committee **meet**, they gather together for a particular purpose. *Officials from the two countries will meet again soon to resume negotiations.* **7** If you **meet with** someone, you have a meeting with them. *Most of the lawmakers who met with the president said they backed the mission.* VERB V n prep/adv, V n off n, V n; VERB V; VERB V with n AMERICAN

8 If two sportsmen, teams, or armies **meet**, they compete or fight against one another. *England last met the French in 1984 when they lost 2-0.* **9** A **meet** is an event in which athletes come to a particular place in order to take part in a race or races. V-RECIP: pl-n V, V n; N-COUNT

10 If something such as a suggestion, proposal, or new book **meets with** a particular reaction, it gets that reaction from people. *The idea met with a cool response from various quarters... We hope today's offer will meet with your approval too... Reagan's speech was met with incredulity in the US.* **11** If you **meet** something such as a problem or challenge, you deal satisfactorily with it. *They had worked heroically to meet the deadline.* **12** If you **meet** a situation, attitude, or problem, you experience it or become aware of it. *Never had she met such spite and pettiness.* **13** You can say that someone **meets with** success or failure when they are successful or unsuccessful. *Attempts to find volunteers have met with embarrassing failure.* V-ERG V with n, V n with n; VERB V n; VERB V n; VERB V with n

14 If something **meets** a need, requirement, or condition, it is satisfactory or sufficiently large to fulfil it. *Out of the original 23,000 applications, 16,000 candidates meet the entry requirements.* **15** If you **meet** the cost of something, you provide the money that is needed for it. *The government said it will help meet some of the cost of the damage.* VERB V n; VERB V n

16 When a moving object **meets** another object, it hits or touches it. *You sense the stresses in the hull each time the keel meets the ground.* **17** If two areas **meet**, especially two areas of land or sea, they are next to one another. *It is one of the rare places in the world where the desert meets the sea.* **18** The place where two lines **meet** is the place where they join together. *The track widened as it met the road.* V-RECIP V n, Also pl-n V; V-RECIP: pl-n V, V n; V-RECIP: pl-n V, V n

19 If your eyes **meet** someone else's, you both look at each other at the same time. *Nina's eyes met her sisters' across the table.* **20** If you do not **meet** someone's **eyes** or **gaze**, you do not look at them although they are looking at you, for example because you are ashamed. *He hesitated, then shook his head, refusing to meet her eyes.* **21** If someone **meets** their **death** or **meets** their **end**, they die, especially in a violent or suspicious way. **22** • to **make ends meet**: see **end**. • **there's more to** this **than meets the eye**: see **eye**. • to **meet** someone's **eyes**: see **eye**. • to **meet** someone **halfway**: see **halfway**. • to **meet** your **match**: see **match**. V-RECIP V n WRITTEN; PHRASE; PHRASE WRITTEN

meet up. See meet 1, 2. PHRASAL VB

meet·ing /'mi:tɪŋ/ **meetings.** **1** A **meeting** is an event in which a group of people come together to discuss things or make decisions. *He still travels to London regularly for business meetings.* ► You can also refer to the people at a meeting as **the meeting**. *The meeting decided that further efforts were needed.* **2** When you meet someone, either intentionally or accidentally, you can refer to this event as a **meeting**. *Her life was changed by a chance meeting with her former art master a few years ago.* ◆◆◆◆◆ N-COUNT; N-SING: the N; N-COUNT

'meeting house, meeting houses. A **meeting house** is a building in which a group of nonconformist Christians, for example Quakers, meet in order to worship together. N-COUNT

'meeting place, meeting places. A **meeting place** is a place where people meet. ◆◇◇◇◇ N-COUNT

mega /'megə/. Young people sometimes use **mega** in front of adjectives in order to emphasize them. *He has become mega rich.* ► Also an adjective. *...her newly acquired mega salary.* ADV PRAGMATICS INFORMAL; ADJ: ADJ n

mega- /'megə-/. **1** **Mega-** is added to units of measurement in order to form nouns referring to units that are a million times bigger. *...a two thousand megawatt surge in electricity.* **2** **Mega-** combines with nouns and adjectives in order to emphasize the size, quality, or importance of something. *Now he can begin to earn the sort of mega-bucks he has always dreamed about. ...a Hollywood mega-star.* PREFIX; PREFIX PRAGMATICS INFORMAL

mega·byte /'megəbaɪt/ **megabytes.** In computing, a **megabyte** is one million bytes of data. ◆◇◇◇◇ N-COUNT

mega·hertz /'megəhɜ:ts/; **megahertz** is both the singular and the plural form. A **megahertz** is a unit of frequency which is used especially for radio frequencies. One megahertz equals one million cycles per second. N-COUNT

mega·lo·ma·nia /ˌmegələ'meɪniə/. **Megalomania** is the belief that you are more powerful and important than you really are. N-UNCOUNT

mega·lo·ma·ni·ac /ˌmegələ'meɪniæk/ **megalomaniacs.** If you describe someone as a **megalomaniac**, you are criticizing them because they enjoy being powerful, or because they believe that they are more powerful than they really are. N-COUNT PRAGMATICS

mega·phone /'megəfəʊn/ **megaphones.** A **megaphone** is a cone-shaped device for making your voice sound louder in the open air. N-COUNT

mega·ton /'megətʌn/ **megatons.** You can use **megaton** to refer to the power of a nuclear weapon. N-COUNT: num N

mega·watt /'megəwɒt/ **megawatts.** A **megawatt** is a unit of power. One megawatt is a million watts. N-COUNT

mel·an·cho·lia /ˌmelən'kəʊliə/. **Melancholia** is a feeling of great melancholy or depression. N-UNCOUNT LITERARY

mel·an·chol·ic /ˌmelən'kɒlɪk/ **melancholics.** If you describe someone or something as **melancholic**, you mean that they are very sad. *The night was as melancholic as his mood.* ► A **melancholic** is someone who is melancholic. ADJ-GRADED LITERARY; N-COUNT

mel·an·choly /'melənkɒli/. **1** You describe something that you see or hear as **melancholy** when it gives you an intense feeling of sadness. *The only sounds were the distant, melancholy cries of the sheep.* **2** **Melancholy** is an intense feeling of sadness which lasts for a long time and which strongly affects your behaviour and attitudes. **3** If someone feels or looks **melancholy**, they feel or look very sad. *...his melancholy smile.* ◆◇◇◇◇ ADJ-GRADED; N-UNCOUNT LITERARY; ADJ-GRADED LITERARY

me·lange /meɪ'lɒndʒ/ **melanges;** also spelled **mélange.** A **melange** of things is a mixture of them, especially when this is attractive or exciting. *...a successful melange of music styles, from soul and rhythm and blues to rap.* N-COUNT: with supp WRITTEN

mela·nin /'melənɪn/. **Melanin** is a dark substance in the skin, eyes, and hair of people and animals, which gives them colour and can protect them against strong sunlight. N-UNCOUNT

mela·no·ma /ˌmelə'nəʊmə/ **melanomas.** A **melanoma** is a tumour or type of cancer that forms in the skin. N-COUNT

me·lee /'meleɪ, AM meɪ-/ **melees;** also spelled **mêlée.** **1** A **melee** is a noisy confusing fight between the people in a crowd. *A policeman was killed and scores of people were injured in the melee.* **2** A **melee** of things is a large, disorganized group of them. *You* N-COUNT WRITTEN; N-SING WRITTEN

M

may want to wander through the melee of streets around the waterfront.

mel·lif·lu·ous /mɪˈlɪflʊəs/. A **mellifluous** voice or piece of music is smooth and gentle and very pleasant to listen to. `ADJ-GRADED FORMAL`

mel·low /ˈmeləʊ/ **mellower, mellowest; mellows, mellowing, mellowed. 1** Mellow is used to describe things that have a pleasant, soft, rich colour, usually red, orange, yellow, or brown. *...the softer, mellower light of evening.* **2** A **mellow** sound or flavour is pleasant, smooth, and rich. *...a delightfully mellow, soft and balanced wine.* **3** If someone **mellows**, they become kinder or less extreme in their behaviour, especially as a result of growing older. *Marriage had not mellowed him.* ► Also an adjective. *Is she more mellow and tolerant?* **4** If someone is **mellow**, they feel very relaxed and cheerful, especially as the result of alcohol or good food. `◆◇◇◇◇ ADJ-GRADED` `ADJ-GRADED` `V-ERG: V / Vn` `ADJ-GRADED` `ADJ-GRADED INFORMAL`

me·lod·ic /mɪˈlɒdɪk/. **1** Melodic means relating to melody. *...Schubert's effortless gift for melodic invention.* **2** Music that is **melodic** has beautiful tunes in it. `◆◇◇◇◇ ADJ TECHNICAL` `ADJ-GRADED`

me·lo·dious /mɪˈləʊdiəs/. A **melodious** sound is pleasant to listen to. `ADJ-GRADED FORMAL`

melo·dra·ma /ˈmelədrɑːmə/ **melodramas.** A **melodrama** is a story or play in which there are a lot of exciting or sad events and in which people's emotions are exaggerated. `◆◇◇◇◇ N-VAR`

melo·dra·mat·ic /ˌmelədrəˈmætɪk/. Melodramatic behaviour is behaviour in which someone treats a situation as much more serious than it really is. *She'd flung herself on the sofa in a pose of melodramatic exhaustion.* ♦ **melo·dra·mati·cal·ly** /ˌmelədrəˈmætɪkli/. *'For God's sake,' Michael said melodramatically, 'Whatever you do, don't look down.'* `◆◇◇◇◇ ADJ-GRADED` `ADV-GRADED: ADV with v`

melo·dy /ˈmelədi/ **melodies. 1** A melody is a tune. *He played me a melody and I said, 'I've heard that song before.'* **2** Melody is the quality of being tuneful. *Her voice was full of melody.* `◆◆◇◇◇ N-COUNT FORMAL` `N-UNCOUNT`

mel·on /ˈmelən/ **melons.** A melon is a large fruit which is sweet and juicy inside and has a hard green or yellow skin. See picture headed **fruit**. `◆◇◇◇◇ N-VAR`

melt /melt/ **melts, melting, melted. 1** When a solid substance **melts**, it changes to a liquid, usually because it has been heated. *Melt the white chocolate in a bowl suspended over simmering water. ...melted snow dripped from his boots.* **2** If a person or thing **melts into** something, they become difficult to see, for example because they are moving away from you or are the same colour as the background. *The youths dispersed and melted into the darkness.* **3** If something such as your feelings **melt**, they suddenly disappear and you no longer feel them. *He would have struggled but his strength had melted.* ► **Melt away** means the same as **melt.** *When he heard these words, Shinran felt his inner doubts melt away.* **4** If someone or something **melts** your heart, you start to feel loving or tender towards them. *When a bride walks down the aisle to a stirring tune, even the iciest of hearts melt.* `◆◆◇◇◇ V-ERG: V / Vn / V-ed` `VERB V into n LITERARY` `VERB V LITERARY` `PHRASAL VB V P` `V-ERG: V n V`

melt away. If a crowd of people **melts away**, members of the crowd gradually leave until there is nobody left. ● See also **melt** 3. `PHRASAL VB V P`

melt down. If an object **is melted down**, it is heated until it melts. *Some thieves do not even bother to melt down stolen silver for its scrap value.* `PHRASAL VB be V-ed P V P noun`

melt·down /ˈmeltdaʊn/ **meltdowns. 1** If there is **meltdown** in a nuclear reactor, a fault makes the core overheat and melt. This can cause radiation to escape. **2** The **meltdown** of an organization or system is its sudden and complete failure. *Urgent talks are going on to prevent the market going into financial meltdown during the summer.* `N-VAR` `N-UNCOUNT: with supp JOURNALISM`

melting point, melting points. The **melting point** of a substance is the temperature at which it melts when you heat it. `N-COUNT`

melting pot, melting pots. 1 A **melting pot** is a place or situation in which people or ideas of differ- `N-COUNT`

ent kinds gradually get mixed together. *The republic is a melting pot of different nationalities.* **2** If someone or something is **in the melting pot**, they are constantly changing, so that you don't know what will finally happen to them. *Their fate is still in the melting-pot.* `PHRASE BRITISH`

mem·ber /ˈmembə/ **members. 1** A **member** of a group is one of the people, animals, or things belonging to that group. *Their lack of training could put members of the public at risk. ...a sunflower or a similar member of the daisy family.* **2** A **member** of an organization such as a club or a political party is a person who has officially joined the organization. *Britain is a full member of NATO.* **3** A **member** country or **member state** is one of the countries that has joined an international organization or alliance. **4** A **member** is a Member of Parliament. *...the Member for Leeds North-East.* `◆◆◆◆◆ N-COUNT: with supp` `N-COUNT` `ADJ: ADJ n` `N-COUNT BRITISH`

Member of Parliament, Members of Parliament. A Member of Parliament is a person who has been elected by people to represent them in a country's parliament. It is usually abbreviated to 'MP'. `◆◆◇◇◇ N-COUNT`

mem·ber·ship /ˈmembəʃɪp/ **memberships. 1** Membership of an organization is the state of being a member of it. *...his membership of the Communist Party.* **2** The **membership** of an organization is the people who belong to it, or the number of people who belong to it. *The European Builders Confederation has a membership of over 350,000 building companies. ...organizations with huge memberships.* `◆◆◆◇◇ N-UNCOUNT: also N in pl` `N-COLL-VAR`

mem·brane /ˈmembreɪn/ **membranes.** A **membrane** is a thin piece of skin which connects or covers parts of a person's or animal's body. `◆◇◇◇◇ N-COUNT`

me·men·to /mɪˈmentəʊ/ **mementos** or **mementoes.** A memento is an object which you keep because it reminds you of a person or a special occasion. *They presented me with a superb wooden bowl as a memento of my visit.* `◆◇◇◇◇ N-COUNT`

memo /ˈmeməʊ/ **memos.** A memo is a short official note that is written from one person to another within the same company or organization. `◆◇◇◇◇ N-COUNT`

mem·oir /ˈmemwɑː/ **memoirs. 1** A person's **memoirs** are a written account of the people who they have known and events that they remember. **2** A **memoir** is a book or article that you write about someone who you have known well. `◆◇◇◇◇ N-PLURAL` `N-COUNT FORMAL`

memo·ra·bilia /ˌmemərəˈbɪliə/. Memorabilia are things that you collect because they are connected with a person or an organization in which you are interested. `◆◇◇◇◇ N-PLURAL`

memo·rable /ˈmemərəbəl/. Something that is **memorable** is worth remembering or likely to be remembered, because it is special or unique. *Annette's performance as Eliza Doolittle in 'Pygmalion' was truly memorable.* ♦ **memo·rably** *The National Theatre's production is memorably staged.* `◆◇◇◇◇ ADJ-GRADED` `ADV-GRADED`

memo·ran·dum /ˌmeməˈrændəm/ **memoranda** or **memorandums. 1** A **memorandum** is a written report that is prepared for a person or committee in order to provide them with information about a particular matter. **2** A **memorandum** is an informal diplomatic communication from one government to another. **3** A **memorandum** is a short official note that is written from one person to another within the same company or organization. `◆◇◇◇◇ N-COUNT` `N-COUNT` `N-COUNT FORMAL`

me·mo·rial /mɪˈmɔːrial/ **memorials. 1** A memorial is a structure built in order to remind people of a famous person or event. *Building a memorial to Columbus has been his lifelong dream... Every village had its war memorial.* **2** A **memorial** event, object, or prize is in honour of someone who has died, so that they will be remembered. *A memorial service is being held for her at St Paul's Church.* **3** If you say that something will be a **memorial to** someone who has died, you mean that it will continue to exist and remind people of them. *The museum will serve as a memorial to the millions who passed through Ellis Island.* `◆◆◇◇◇ N-COUNT` `ADJ: ADJ n` `N-COUNT`

me·mo·ri·al·ize /mɪˈmɔːriəlaɪz/ **memorializes,** VERB:
memorializing, memorialized; also spelled **me-** beV-ed
morialise in British English. If a person or event **is** Vn
memorialized, something is produced that will continue to exist and remind people of them. *When she
died in 1946, her friends wanted to memorialize her
in some significant way.*

memo·rize /ˈmeməraɪz/ **memorizes, memoriz-** ◆◇◇◇◇
ing, memorized; also spelled **memorise** in British VERB: Vn
English. If you **memorize** something, you learn it so
that you can remember it exactly.

memo·ry /ˈmeməri/ **memories. 1** Your **memory** is ◆◆◆◇◇
your ability to remember things. *All the details of* N-VAR
*the meeting are fresh in my memory... Two major
areas in which mentally retarded children require
help are memory and attention.* **2** If you do some- PHRASE
thing **from memory**, you do it without looking at
anything written or printed. *Many members of the
church sang from memory.* **3** If you **lose your** PHRASE
memory, you forget things that you used to know.
4 If you say that something is, for example, the best, PHRASE
worst, or first thing of its kind **in living memory** or [PRAGMATICS]
within living memory, you mean that it is the best,
worst, or only thing of that kind that people can remember happening. *The floods are the worst in living
memory.* **5 ●** to **commit** something **to memory**: see
commit.
6 A **memory** is something that you remember from N-COUNT
the past. *He had happy memories of his father.* **7** If you N-SING
talk about the **memory** of someone who has died, especially someone who was loved or respected, you are
referring to the thoughts, actions, and ceremonies by
which they are remembered. *The congress opened
with a minute's silence in memory of those who died in
the struggle.*
8 A computer's **memory** is the part of the computer N-COUNT
where information is stored, especially for a short
time before it is transferred to disks or magnetic
tapes.

mem·sa·hib /ˈmemsaːb/ **memsahibs.** Memsahib N-COUNT;
was used to refer to or address white women in In- N-TITLE;
dia, especially during the period of British rule, or N-VOC
sometimes to refer to or address upper-class Indian DATED
women.

men /men/. **Men** is the plural of **man.**

men·ace /ˈmenɪs/ **menaces, menacing, men-** ◆◇◇◇◇
aced. 1 If you say that someone or something is a N-COUNT
menace to other people or things, you mean that
person or thing is likely to cause serious harm. *In
my view you are a menace to the public. ...the menace of fascism.* **2** If you say that one thing **menaces** VERB
another, you mean that the first thing is likely to Vn
cause the second thing serious harm. *The European
states retained a latent capability to menace Britain's
own security.*
3 **Menace** is a quality or atmosphere that gives you N-UNCOUNT
the feeling that you are in danger or that someone
wants to harm you. *There is a pervading sense of menace.* **4** If you **are menaced** by someone, they threaten VERB
to harm you. *She's being menaced by her sister's latest* beV-ed
boyfriend. **5** If someone commits the crime of de- Also Vn
manding money **with menaces**, they threaten to PHRASE
cause harm unless they are given the money. **6** You BRITISH,
can refer to someone or something as a **menace** when LEGAL
you want to say that they cause you trouble or annoy- N-COUNT
ance. *Bad shoes are a menace.* INFORMAL

men·ac·ing /ˈmenɪsɪŋ/. If someone or something ◆◇◇◇◇
looks **menacing**, they give you a feeling that they ADJ-GRADED
are likely to cause you harm or put you in danger.
*The strong dark eyebrows give his face an oddly
menacing look.* **● men·ac·ing·ly** *A group of men* ADV-GRADED
*suddenly emerged from a doorway and moved men-
acingly forward to block her way.*

me·nage /meɪˈnɑːʒ/; also spelled **ménage.** A me- N-SING
nage is a group of people living together in one FORMAL
house.

me·nage a trois /meɪˌnɑːʒ ɑː ˈtwɑː/ **menages a** N-COUNT
trois; also spelled **ménage à trois.** A **menage a
trois** is a situation where three people live together,

especially when one of them is having a sexual relationship with both of the others.

me·nag·erie /məˈnædʒəri/ **menageries.** A menag- N-COUNT
erie is a collection of wild animals.

mend /mend/ **mends, mending, mended. 1** If ◆◇◇◇◇
you **mend** something that is broken or not working, VERB: Vn
you repair it, so that it works properly or can be haven V-ed
used. *I should have had the catch mended, but never
got round to it.* **2** If a person or a part of their body V-ERG: V
mends or **is mended**, they get better after they have Vn
been ill or have had an injury. *He must have a major operation on his knee to mend severed ligaments.*
3 If you are **on the mend** after an illness or injury, PHRASE
you are recovering from it. INFORMAL
4 If you try to **mend** divisions between people, you try VERB
to end the quarrels between them. *They will seek to* Vn
mend divisions that were caused by the Gulf conflict.
5 If a relationship or situation is **on the mend** after a PHRASE
difficult or unsuccessful period, it is improving. *More* INFORMAL
*evidence that the economy was on the mend was need-
ed.* **6** If someone who has been behaving badly **mends** PHRASE
their **ways**, they begin to behave well. **7 ●** to **mend
fences:** see **fence.**

men·da·cious /menˈdeɪʃəs/. A mendacious state- ADJ-GRADED
ment or remark is not truthful. FORMAL

men·dac·ity /menˈdæsɪti/. **Mendacity** is the quality N-UNCOUNT
of lying, rather than being truthful. *It was an aston-* FORMAL
ishing display of cowardice and mendacity.

mend·ing /ˈmendɪŋ/. **Mending** is the sewing and N-UNCOUNT
repairing of clothes that have got holes in them. DATED
● See also **mend.**

men·folk /ˈmenfəʊk/. When women refer to their N-PLURAL
menfolk, they mean the men in their family or society. *The majority of women are, like their menfolk,
rigidly typecast.*

me·nial /ˈmiːniəl/. Menial work is very boring and ADJ-GRADED
tiring, and the people who do it have a low status
and are usually poorly paid.

men·in·gi·tis /ˌmenɪnˈdʒaɪtɪs/. **Meningitis** is a seri- ◆◇◇◇◇
ous infectious illness which affects your brain and N-UNCOUNT
spinal cord.

meno·pause /ˈmenəpɔːz/. The **menopause** is the ◆◇◇◇◇
time during which a woman gradually stops men- N-SING:
struating, usually when she is about fifty years old. also no det
● meno·pau·sal *A menopausal woman of average* ADJ
build and height requires 1600 – 2400 calories daily.

'men's room, men's rooms. The **men's room** is N-COUNT
a toilet for men. AMERICAN

men·strual /ˈmenstruəl/. **Menstrual** means relat- ◆◇◇◇◇
ing to menstruation. *...the menstrual cycle.* ADJ: ADJ n

men·stru·ate /ˈmenstrueɪt/ **menstruates, men-** ◆◇◇◇◇
struating, menstruated. When a woman **men-** VERB: V
struates, a flow of blood comes from her womb. FORMAL
Women who are fertile menstruate once a month
unless they are pregnant. **● men·strua·tion** N-UNCOUNT
/ˌmenstruˈeɪʃən/. *Menstruation may cease when a
woman is anywhere between forty-five and fifty years
of age.*

mens·wear /ˈmenzweə/. **Menswear** is clothing for N-UNCOUNT
men. *...the menswear industry.* FORMAL

-ment. -ment is added to some verbs to form SUFFIX
nouns that refer to actions, processes, or states.
*...shortly after the commencement of the service.
...the enrichment of uranium.*

men·tal /ˈmentəl/. **1 Mental** means relating to the ◆◆◆◇◇
process of thinking. *The intellectual environment* ADJ: ADJ n
*has a significant influence on the mental develop-
ment of the children.* **● men·tal·ly** *I think you are* ADV
mentally tired. **2** A **mental** act is one that involves ADJ: ADJ n
only thinking and not physical action. *Practise men-
tal arithmetic when you go out shopping.*
● mentally *This technique will help people mental-* ADV:
ly organize information. **3** If you **make a mental** ADV with v
note of something, you make an effort to store it in PHRASE
your memory so that you will not forget it. *She
made a mental note to have his prescription refilled.*
4 **Mental** means relating to the state or the health of a ADJ: ADJ n
person's mind. *Most people know little about mental
health problems.* **● mentally** *...the needs of the men-* ADV
tally ill and the mentally handicapped. **5** If you say ADJ-GRADED

M

that someone is **mental**, you mean that you think they are mad; a use which some people find offensive. *INFORMAL, BRITISH*

mental 'age, mental ages. A person's **mental age** is the age which they are considered to have reached in their thinking ability. It is used especially when referring to people with learning difficulties. N-COUNT

'mental hospital, mental hospitals. A **mental hospital** is a hospital for people who are suffering from mental illness. N-COUNT

men·tal·ity /'men'tælɪti/ **mentalities.** Your **mentality** is your attitudes and your way of thinking. *Running a business requires a very different mentality from being a salaried employee.* ◆◇◇◇◇ N-COUNT

men·thol /'menθɒl, AM -θɔːl/. **Menthol** is a substance that smells a bit like peppermint. It is used in some medicinal products, especially for curing colds. N-UNCOUNT

men·tion /'menʃən/ **mentions, mentioning, mentioned. 1** If you **mention** something, you say something about it, usually briefly. *I may not have mentioned it to her... I had mentioned that I didn't really like contemporary music... She shouldn't have mentioned how heavy the dress was.* ▶ Also a noun. *At the community centre, mention of funds produces pained looks.* **2** People sometimes say **'don't mention it'** as a polite reply to someone who has just thanked them for doing something. **3** You use **not to mention** when you want to add extra information which emphasizes the point that you are making. *The audience, not to mention the bewildered cast, were not amused.* **4** If someone **is mentioned** in writing, a reference is made to them by name, often to criticize or praise something that they have done. *As for your father, he won't be mentioned in my will.* **5** A special or honourable **mention** is formal praise that is given for an achievement that is very good, although not usually the best of its kind. *Two of the losers deserve special mention: Caroline Swaithes, of Kings Norton, and Maria Pons.* **6 •** to **be mentioned in dispatches**: see **dispatch**. ◆◆◆◇◇ VERB: V n/-ing V n to n V that V wh ▷ N-VAR / CONVENTION PRAGMATICS / PHRASE PRAGMATICS / VB: usu passive be V-ed Also be V-ed as n/adj / N-VAR: with supp

men·tor /'mentɔː/ **mentors.** A person's **mentor** is someone who teaches them and gives them a lot of advice over a period of time. ◆◇◇◇◇ N-COUNT FORMAL

menu /'menjuː/ **menus. 1** In a restaurant or café, the **menu** is a list of the available meals and drinks. *Nothing on the menu costs more than $9.95.* **2** A **menu** is the food that you serve at a meal. *This menu uses some of the best produce available at this time of year.* **3** On a computer, a **menu** is a list of choices. Each choice represents something you can do using the computer. ◆◆◇◇ N-COUNT / N-COUNT / N-COUNT

MEP /ˌem iː 'piː/ **MEPs.** An **MEP** is a person who has been elected to the European Parliament. **MEP** is an abbreviation for 'Member of the European Parliament'. *...John Tomlinson, Labour MEP for Birmingham West.* ◆◇◇◇◇ N-COUNT

mer·can·tile /'mɜːkəntaɪl/. **Mercantile** means relating to merchants or trading. *The older noble families were eclipsed by the emergence of a new mercantile class.* ◆◇◇◇◇ ADJ: ADJ n FORMAL

mer·ce·nary /'mɜːsənri, AM -neri/ **mercenaries. 1** A **mercenary** is a soldier who is paid to fight by a country or group that he or she does not belong to. **2** If you describe someone as a **mercenary**, you are criticizing them because you think that they are only interested in the money that they can get from a particular person or situation. ◆◇◇◇◇ N-COUNT / ADJ-GRADED

mer·chan·dise /'mɜːtʃəndaɪz, -daɪs/. **Merchandise** is goods that are bought, sold, or traded. ◆◆◇◇ N-UNCOUNT FORMAL

mer·chan·dis·er /'mɜːtʃəndaɪzə/ **merchandisers.** A **merchandiser** is a person or company that sells goods to the public. The British word is **retailer**. *I trained to become a merchandiser.* N-COUNT AMERICAN

mer·chan·dis·ing /'mɜːtʃəndaɪzɪŋ/. **1 Merchandising** consists of goods such as toys and clothes that are produced in order to promote something such as a particular film, sports team, or pop group. *We are selling the full range of World Cup merchandising.* **2 Merchandising** is used to refer to the way shops and businesses organize the sale of their ◆◇◇◇◇ N-UNCOUNT / N-UNCOUNT

products, for example the way they are displayed and the prices that are chosen.

mer·chant /'mɜːtʃənt/ **merchants. 1** A **merchant** is a person whose business is buying, selling, or trading goods in large quantities. *...a wine merchant.* **2 Merchant** seamen or ships are involved in carrying goods for trade. *...the British merchant fleet.* ◆◆◆◇◇ N-COUNT / ADJ: ADJ n

merchant 'bank, merchant banks. A **merchant bank** is a bank that deals mainly with business firms, investment, and foreign trade. ◆◇◇◇◇ N-COUNT

mer·ci·ful /'mɜːsɪfʊl/. **1** If you describe someone in authority as **merciful**, you mean that they show kindness and forgiveness to people. *We can only hope the court is merciful. ...a merciful God.* **2** If you describe an event or situation as **merciful**, you mean that it seems fortunate, especially because it stops someone's suffering or discomfort. *We were told when he was taken to hospital that his injuries were so severe death would be merciful... Eventually the session came to a merciful end.* ADJ-GRADED / ADJ-GRADED

mer·ci·ful·ly /'mɜːsɪfʊli/. You can use **mercifully** to show that you are glad about something, because it avoids a dangerous or unpleasant situation, or puts an end to it. *Mercifully, a friend came to the rescue... Bolivia has been mercifully free of large-scale, drug-related violence.* ◆◇◇◇◇ ADV PRAGMATICS

mer·ci·less /'mɜːsɪləs/. If you describe a person or their behaviour as **merciless**, you mean that they are very cruel or determined and do not show any concern for the effect their actions have on other people. *...the merciless efficiency of a modern police state.* ♦ **mer·ci·less·ly** *We teased him mercilessly.* ◆◇◇◇◇ ADJ-GRADED / ADV-GRADED

mer·cu·rial /mɜː'kjʊəriəl/. If you describe someone as **mercurial**, you mean that they frequently change their mind or mood without warning. ADJ-GRADED LITERARY

mer·cu·ry /'mɜːkjʊri/. **Mercury** is a silver-coloured liquid metal, often used in thermometers. ◆◇◇◇◇ N-UNCOUNT

mer·cy /'mɜːsi/ **mercies. 1** If someone in authority shows **mercy**, they choose not to harm or punish someone they have power over. *Neither side took prisoners or showed any mercy... May God have mercy on your soul.* **2 Mercy** is used to describe a special journey to help someone in great need, such as sick people or refugees. *...a daring mercy mission to bring back refugees from Bosnia.* **3** If one person or thing is **at the mercy** of another, the first person or thing is in a situation where they cannot prevent themselves being harmed or affected by the second. *Buildings are left to decay at the mercy of vandals and the weather... He has us at his mercy.* **4** If you tell someone they should be **grateful for small mercies**, you mean that something relatively good or slightly less bad has happened to them, and they should be happy about it, instead of complaining. ◆◇◇◇◇ N-UNCOUNT / ADJ: ADJ n JOURNALISM / PHRASE / PHRASE

'mercy killing, mercy killings. A **mercy killing** is an act of killing someone who is very ill, in order to stop them suffering any more pain. N-VAR

mere /mɪə/ **merest. Mere** does not have a comparative form. The superlative form **merest** is used for emphasis, rather than in comparisons.
1 You use **mere** to emphasize how unimportant or insufficient something is. *She'd never received the merest hint of any communication from him... Sixty per cent of teachers are women, but a mere 5 percent of women are heads and deputies.* **2** You use **mere** to emphasize how small something is, in contrast to its great value or effect. *Tickets are a mere £7.50 at the door... Whenever there was a gap in the traffic the merest pressure on the accelerator was enough to close it.* ◆◆◆◇◇ / ADJ: ADJ n, a ADJ amount PRAGMATICS / ADJ: ADJ n, a ADJ amount PRAGMATICS

mere·ly /'mɪəli/. **1** You use **merely** to emphasize that something is only what you say and not better, more important, or more exciting. *Michael is now merely a good friend... Merely because you believe a thing is right, it isn't automatically so... They are offering merely technical assistance.* **2** You use **merely** to emphasize that a particular quantity is very small. *The brain accounts for merely three per cent of body weight.* **3** You use **not merely** before the less important of two contrasting statements, as a way ◆◆◇◇ ADV PRAGMATICS / ADV: ADV amount PRAGMATICS / PHRASE PRAGMATICS

of emphasizing the more important statement. *The team needs players who want to play cricket for England, not merely any country that will have them... His were not merely crimes of theft but of violence against elderly people.*

mer·et·ri·cious /ˌmerɪˈtrɪʃəs/. If you describe something as **meretricious**, you dislike it because although it looks attractive, it is in fact of little value. *...vulgar, meretricious and shabby souvenirs.*
   ADJ-GRADED PRAGMATICS FORMAL

merge /mɜːdʒ/ **merges, merging, merged.** **1** If one thing **merges** with another, or **is merged** with another, they combine or come together to make one whole thing. You can also say that two things **merge**, or **are merged**. *The rivers merge just north of a vital irrigation system... The two countries merged into one... He showed me how to merge the graphic with text on the same screen.* **2** If one sound, colour, or object **merges** into another, or they **merge**, the first changes so gradually into the second, or is so similar to it, that you do not notice the change or difference. *Night and day begin to merge.*
   ◆◆◇◇◇ V-RECIP-ERG: V *with* n pl-n V pl-n V *into* n V n *with* n Also V pl-n, V pl-n *into* n
   V-RECIP: V *into/with* n pl-n V

mer·ger /ˈmɜːdʒə/ **mergers.** A **merger** is the joining together of two separate companies or organizations so that they become one. *...the proposed merger of two Japanese banks.*
   ◆◆◆◇◇ N-COUNT

me·rid·ian /məˈrɪdiən/ **meridians.** A **meridian** is an imaginary line from the North Pole to the South Pole. Meridians are drawn on maps to help you describe the position of a place.
   N-COUNT

me·ringue /məˈræŋ/ **meringues.** A **meringue** is a very sweet cake that you make by whipping together sugar and the whites of eggs and then baking the mixture.
   ◆◇◇◇◇ N-VAR

mer·it /ˈmerɪt/ **merits, meriting, merited.** **1** If you refer to the **merit** or **merits** of something, you mean that it has good or useful qualities. *Box-office success mattered more than artistic merit... It was obvious that, whatever its merits, their work would never be used... Such an approach has the merit of precision.* **2** If someone or something **merits** a particular action or treatment, they are good, important, or serious enough for someone to treat them in this way. *He had done nothing wrong to merit a criminal investigation... Such ideas merit careful consideration.* **3** If you judge something or someone **on merit** or **on** their **merits**, your judgement is based on their actual qualities, rather than particular rules, traditions, or prejudices. *Everybody is selected on merit... Each case is judged on its merits.*
   ◆◆◇◇◇ N-VAR
   VERB V n FORMAL
   PHRASE

mer·it·oc·ra·cy /ˌmerɪˈtɒkrəsi/ **meritocracies.** A **meritocracy** is a social system in which people get rewards because of what they achieve, rather than because of their wealth or status.
   N-VAR

mer·it·o·crat·ic /ˌmerɪtəˈkrætɪk/. A **meritocratic** society gives people rewards because of what they achieve, rather than because of their wealth or social status.
   ADJ-GRADED

mer·it·o·ri·ous /ˌmerɪˈtɔːriəs/. If you describe something as **meritorious**, you approve of it for its good or worthwhile qualities. *I had been promoted for what was called gallant and meritorious service.*
   ADJ-GRADED PRAGMATICS FORMAL

mer·maid /ˈmɜːmeɪd/ **mermaids.** In fairy stories and legends, a **mermaid** is a woman with a fish's tail instead of legs, who lives in the sea.
   ◆◇◇◇◇ N-COUNT

mer·ri·ly /ˈmerɪli/. **1** If you say that something is happening **merrily**, you mean that it is happening fairly quickly, in a pleasant or satisfactory way. *A pan of potatoes was boiling away merrily on the gas stove.*
   ● See also **merry**.
   ADV: ADV with v

mer·ri·ment /ˈmerɪmənt/. **Merriment** means fun and laughter.
   N-UNCOUNT DATED

mer·ry /ˈmeri/ **merrier, merriest. 1** Someone or something that is **merry** is happy and cheerful. *He was much loved for his merry nature... Merry black eyes glinted at them... She was humming a merry little tune.* ♦ **mer·ri·ly** *Chris threw back his head and laughed merrily.* **2** In the days just before Christmas and on Christmas Day, you can use **'Merry Christmas'** as a friendly greeting or message to other people. *Merry Christmas, everyone... I just wanted to*
   ◆◆◇◇◇ ADJ-GRADED DATED
   ADV-GRADED: ADV after v
   CONVENTION

wish you a merry Christmas. **3** If you get **merry**, you get slightly drunk. *They went off to Glengarriff to get merry.*
   ADJ-GRADED: v-link ADJ BRITISH, INFORMAL

4 Merry is used to suggest, in a slightly disapproving way, that someone continues to do something confidently without thinking about the problems that it involves. *It hasn't stopped the British Navy proceeding on its merry way.* ♦ **merrily** *They knew they could not go merrily on as before.*
   ADJ: ADJ n PRAGMATICS
   ADV: ADV with v

5 See also **merrily**.

merry-go-round, merry-go-rounds. 1 At a fairground, a **merry-go-round** is a large, round rotating platform with model animals or vehicles on it which children can pretend to ride or drive when it turns round. **2** You can refer to a continuous series of activities as a **merry-go-round**. *...a merry-go-round of teas, fetes, musical events and the like.*
   N-COUNT
   N-COUNT

merry-making. Merry-making is the activities of people who are enjoying themselves together in a very lively way, for example by eating, drinking, or dancing.
   N-UNCOUNT

me·sa /ˈmeɪsə/ **mesas.** A **mesa** is a large hill with a flat top and steep sides, especially in the southwestern United States.
   N-COUNT

mesh /meʃ/ **meshes, meshing, meshed. 1 Mesh** is material like a net made from wire, thread, or plastic. *The ground-floor windows are obscured by wire mesh. ...a mesh small enough to exclude tiny insects.* **2** If two things or ideas **mesh** or **are meshed**, they go together well or fit together closely. *This of course meshes with the economic philosophy of those on the right... Meshing the research and marketing operations will be Mr. Furlaud's job.*
   ◆◇◇◇ N-VAR
   V-RECIP-ERG: pl-n V V *with* n pl-n V Also V n *with* n

mes·mer·ize /ˈmezməraɪz/ **mesmerizes, mesmerizing, mesmerized;** also spelled **mesmerise** in British English. If you **are mesmerized** by something, you are so interested in it or so attracted to it that you cannot think about anything else. *She stared mesmerized at all the green banknotes. ...a mesmerising smile.*
   ◆◇◇◇ VERB: be V-ed V-ed V-ing Also V n

mess /mes/ **messes, messing, messed. 1** If something is a **mess** or in a **mess**, it is in a dirty or untidy state. *Finally, making a dreadful mess, they devour the fruit... I'll clear up the mess later... The wrong shampoo can leave curly hair in a tangled mess.* **2** If you say that a situation is a **mess**, you mean that it is full of trouble or problems. You can also say that something is in a **mess**. *I've made such a mess of my life. ...the many reasons why the economy is in such a mess.* **3** The **mess** in an army barracks or on an airfield is the building in which members of the armed forces eat or relax. *...a party at the officers' mess.*
   ◆◆◆◇◇ N-SING: also no det
   N-VAR
   N-COUNT

mess about or **mess around.** The form **mess about** is mainly used in British English. **1** If you **mess about**, you spend time doing silly or casual things without any particular purpose or result. *...the ones who were not very bright and used to mess about in class... Boys and girls will enjoy messing about with any kind of machine.* **2** If you say that someone **is messing about with** something, you mean that they are interfering with it in a harmful way. *I'd like to know who's been messing about with the pram.* **3** If you **mess** someone **about**, you treat them badly, for example by not being honest with them, or by continually changing plans which affect them. *I think they've been messed around far too much.*
   PHRASAL VB V P V P *with* n
   V P *with* n
   V n P be V-ed P BRITISH

mess up. 1 If someone **messes** something **up**, or if they **mess up**, they cause something to fail or be spoiled. *He had messed up one career... If I messed up, I would probably be fired.* **2** If you **mess up** a place or a thing, you make it untidy or dirty. *I hope they haven't messed up your video tapes.* **3** If something **messes** someone **up**, it causes them to be very confused or worried, or to have psychological problems. *That really messed them up, especially the boys.*
   PHRASAL VB V n P V P V P noun INFORMAL
   V n P V P noun INFORMAL
   V n P INFORMAL

mess with. If you tell someone not to **mess with** someone or something, you are warning them not to
   PHRASAL VB PRAGMATICS V P n

M

get involved with that person or thing. *Do you know who you're messing with – do you know who I am?*

mes·sage /'mesɪdʒ/ **messages. 1** A message is a ◆◆◆◇ piece of information or a request that you send to N-COUNT someone or leave for them when you cannot speak to them directly. *I got a message you were trying to reach me... A message taped by the President was broadcast to US troops around the world.* **2** The N-COUNT message that someone is trying to communicate is the idea, argument, or opinion that they are trying to communicate. *The report's message was un-equivocal... I think they got the message that this is wrong.*

mes·sen·ger /'mesɪndʒə/ **messengers.** A mes- ◆◇◇◇ senger takes a message to someone, or takes mes- N-COUNT: sages regularly as their job. *He gave the instruction* also by N *for the document to be sent by messenger.*

mes·si·ah /mɪ'saɪə/ **messiahs. 1** For Jews, the ◆◇◇◇ Messiah is a king or leader who will be sent to them N-PROPER by God. **2** For Christians, the Messiah is Jesus N-PROPER Christ. **3** If people refer to someone as their **messi-** N-COUNT ah, they believe that he or she will do, or has done, wonderful things, especially rescuing them from se-rious trouble. *People see Mandela as their messiah.*

mes·si·an·ic /,mesi'ænɪk/. **1** Messianic means re- ADJ: ADJ n lating to the belief that a divine being has been born, or will be born, who will change the world. *The cult leader saw himself as a Messianic figure.* **2** Messianic means relating to the belief that there ADJ-GRADED will be a complete change in the social order in a country or in the world. *The defeated radicals of the French Revolution were the first to have this messi-anic vision in 1794.*

Messrs /'mesəz/. Messrs is used as the plural of ◆◇◇◇ Mr in front of the names of two or more men, for N-TITLE example as part of the name of a business. *...Messrs* FORMAL *Clegg & Sons of Balham.*

messy /'mesi/ **messier, messiest. 1** A messy ◆◆◇◇ person or activity makes things dirty or untidy. *She* ADJ-GRADED *was a good, if messy, cook... The work tends to be a bit messy.* **2** Something that is **messy** is dirty or un- ADJ-GRADED tidy. *This first coat of paint looks messy.* **3** If you de- ADJ-GRADED scribe a situation as **messy**, you dislike it because it PRAGMATICS is confused or complicated. *Negotiations would be messy and time-consuming.*

met /met/. Met is the past tense and past participle of **meet.**

meta·bol·ic /,metə'bɒlɪk/. **Metabolic** means relat- ◆◇◇◇ ing to a person's or animal's metabolism. *People* ADJ: ADJ n *who have inherited a low metabolic rate will gain* TECHNICAL *weight.*

me·tabo·lism /mɪ'tæbəlɪzəm/ **metabolisms.** ◆◇◇◇ Your **metabolism** is the way that chemical pro- N-VAR cesses in your body cause food to be used in an effi-cient way, for example to give you energy.

me·tabo·lize /mɪ'tæbəlaɪz/ **metabolizes, me-** VERB **tabolizing, metabolized;** also spelled **metabo-** V n **lise** in British English. When you **metabolize** a sub- TECHNICAL stance, it is broken down by chemical processes in your body, so that it can be absorbed and used. *Diabetics cannot metabolise glucose properly.*

met·al /'metəl/ **metals.** Metal is a hard substance ◆◆◆◇ such as iron, steel, copper, or lead. *...pieces of furni-* N-VAR *ture in wood, metal and glass... He hit his head against a metal bar.* ● See also **base metal.**

met·alled /'metəld/. A **metalled** road or path has a ADJ: ADJ n level surface made of many small pieces of stone.

me·tal·lic /mə'tælɪk/. **1** A **metallic** sound is like ◆◇◇◇ the sound of one piece of metal hitting another. *It* ADJ-GRADED *gave a metallic clang, like a cracked bell.* **2** Metallic ADJ paint or colours shine like metal. *...metallic silver paint.* **3** Metallic means consisting wholly or partly ADJ of metal. *Place the salmon in a nonstick metallic dish.*
4 A **metallic** voice has a harsh and unpleasant sound. ADJ-GRADED
5 A **metallic** taste is bitter and unpleasant. ADJ-GRADED

met·al·lur·gy /me'tælədʒi, AM 'metəlɜːrdʒi/. Metal- N-UNCOUNT lurgy is the science and technology of extracting metals from their ores and preparing them for use.
♦ **met·al·lur·gist** /me'tælədʒɪst, AM 'metəlɜːrdʒɪst/ N-COUNT

metallurgists. A **metallurgist** is an expert in metallurgy.

metal·work /'metəlwɜːk/. **1** Metalwork is the ac- N-UNCOUNT tivity of making objects out of metal in a skilful way. *...teachers of woodwork and metalwork.* **2** The N-UNCOUNT **metalwork** is the metal part of something. *Rust and flaking paint mean the metalwork is in very poor condition.*

meta·mor·phose /,metə'mɔːfəʊz/ **metamorpho-** V-ERG **ses, metamorphosing, metamorphosed.** To V *from/into* n metamorphose or be metamorphosed means to be V-ed develop and change into something completely dif- from/into n ferent. *The group is having to metamorphose from a* Also V n, *loose collection of businesses into a fully integrated* V n *from/into* multinational... The actors were metamorphosed n into a living tapestry of color at the dress rehearsal... FORMAL The tadpoles metamorphose and emerge onto land.

meta·mor·pho·sis /,metə'mɔːfəsɪs/ **metamor-** N-VAR **phoses.** When a **metamorphosis** occurs, a person FORMAL or thing develops and changes into something com-pletely different. *...his metamorphosis from Com-munist to nationalist.*

meta·phor /'metəfɔːr/ **metaphors. 1** A metaphor ◆◇◇◇ is an imaginative way of describing something by N-VAR referring to something else which has the qualities that you want to express. *...using a dinner party as a metaphor for life... She turned to a cricketing meta-phor to express her determination to beat off any challenge.* **2** If you mix your metaphors, you say PHRASE something that consists of parts of two well-known phrases or sayings. People do this accidentally, or sometimes deliberately as a joke. *To mix yet more metaphors, you were trying to run before you could walk, and I've clipped your wings.*

meta·phori·cal /,metə'fɒrɪkəl, AM -'fɔːr-/. You use ◆◇◇◇ the word **metaphorical** to indicate that you are not ADJ-GRADED using words with their ordinary meaning, but are describing something by means of an image or symbol. *The ship may be heading for the metaphori-cal rocks unless a buyer can be found.* ♦ **meta-phori·cal·ly** *You're speaking metaphorically, I* ADV *hope.*

meta·phys·ical /,metə'fɪzɪkəl/. **Metaphysical** ◆◇◇◇ means relating to metaphysics, or to difficult ab- ADJ stract problems. *...metaphysical questions like per-sonal responsibility for violence.*

meta·phys·ics /,metə'fɪzɪks/. **Metaphysics** is a N-UNCOUNT part of philosophy which is concerned with under-standing reality and developing theories about what exists and how we know that it exists.

mete /miːt/ **metes, meting, meted.** ◆◇◇◇
mete out. To **mete out** a punishment means to pun- PHRASAL VB ish someone. *...the two year sentence meted out to a* V P noun *convicted child molester.* V-ed P
FORMAL

me·teor /'miːtiə/ **meteors.** A meteor is a piece of ◆◇◇◇ rock flying through space, especially one that is N-COUNT shining or burning brightly.

me·teor·ic /,miːti'ɒrɪk, AM -'ɔːr-/. If you use **me-** ADJ-GRADED **teoric** to describe someone's career, you mean that they achieved success very quickly. *Let's hope that the meteoric rise to fame and fortune does not ad-versely affect him.*

me·teor·ite /'miːtiəraɪt/ **meteorites.** A meteorite ◆◇◇◇ is a large piece of rock or metal from space that has N-COUNT landed on Earth.

me·teoro·logi·cal /,miːtiərə'lɒdʒɪkəl/. Meteoro- ◆◇◇◇ logical means relating to meteorology. *...adverse* ADJ: ADJ n *meteorological conditions.*

me·teor·ol·ogy /,miːtiə'rɒlədʒi/. Meteorology is N-UNCOUNT the study of the processes in the Earth's atmosphere that cause particular weather conditions. Meteorol-ogy is used especially for giving weather forecasts.
♦ **me·teor·olo·gist** /,miːtiə'rɒlədʒɪst/ **meteorolo-** N-COUNT gists *Meteorologists have predicted mild rains for the next few days.*

me·ter /'miːtə/ **meters, metering, metered.** ◆◆◇◇
1 A meter is a device that measures and records N-COUNT something such as the amount of gas or electricity that you have used. *He was there to read the electric-ity meter.* **2** To meter something such as gas or VERB

electricity means to use a meter to measure how much of it people use, usually in order to calculate how much they have to pay. *Only a third of these households thought it reasonable to meter water. ...metered taxis.* **3** A **meter** is the same as a **parking meter**. **4** See also **metre**. `V n V-ed` `N-COUNT`

me·thane /ˈmiːθeɪn, AM ˈmeθ-/. Methane is a colourless gas that has no smell. Natural gas consists mostly of methane. `N-UNCOUNT`

meth·od /ˈmeθəd/ **methods.** A **method** is a particular way of doing something. *The pill is the most efficient method of birth control. ...new teaching methods.* `N-COUNT`

me·thodi·cal /məˈθɒdɪkəl/. If you describe someone as **methodical**, you mean that they do things carefully, thoroughly, and in order. *Da Vinci was methodical in his research, carefully recording his observations.* ♦ **me·thodi·cal·ly** /məˈθɒdɪkli/ *She methodically put the things into her suitcase.* `ADJ-GRADED` `ADV-GRADED: ADV with v`

meth·od·ol·ogy /ˌmeθəˈdɒlədʒi/ **methodologies.** A **methodology** is a system of methods and principles for doing something, for example for carrying out research. *The example used below concentrates on sexism; the methodology for the analysis of racism is exactly the same.* ♦ **meth·odo·logi·cal** /ˌmeθədəˈlɒdʒɪkəl/ *...theoretical and methodological issues raised by the study of literary texts.* `N-VAR FORMAL` `ADJ`

meths /meθs/. **Meths** is the same as **methylated spirits.** `N-UNCOUNT BRITISH`

meth·yl·at·ed spir·its /ˌmeθəleɪtɪd ˈspɪrɪts/. **Methylated spirits** is a liquid made from alcohol and other chemicals. It can be used for cleaning, and as a fuel in small lamps and heaters. `N-UNCOUNT BRITISH`

me·ticu·lous /məˈtɪkjʊləs/. If someone is **meticulous**, they do things very carefully and with great attention to detail. *He was so meticulous about everything, including safety at work.* ♦ **me·ticu·lous·ly** *The flat had been meticulously cleaned.* `ADJ-GRADED` `ADV-GRADED`

me·tier /ˈmetieɪ, AM ˈmetjeɪ/ **metiers;** also spelled **métier.** Your **metier** is the type of work that you have a natural talent for and do well. *It was as the magazine's business manager that he found his true metier.* `N-COUNT FORMAL`

me·tre /ˈmiːtə/ **metres;** spelled **meter** in American English. **1** A **metre** is a metric unit of length equal to 100 centimetres. *Chris Boardman won the Olympic 4,000 metres pursuit... The scarves are 2.3 metres long.* **2** **Metre** is the regular and rhythmic arrangement of syllables in poetry. *All of the poems are written in traditional metres and rhyme schemes.* `num N` `N-VAR TECHNICAL`

met·ric /ˈmetrɪk/. The **metric** system of measurement uses units such as metres, centimetres, grams, and litres. *...the metric system. ...oddities such as curtain material being sold in imperial widths but metric lengths.* `ADJ`

metric ton, metric tons. A metric ton is 1,000 kilograms. *The Wall Street Journal uses 220,000 metric tons of newsprint each year.* `N-COUNT`

Met·ro /ˈmetrəʊ/ **Metros.** The **Metro** is the underground railway system in some cities, for example in Paris. `N-COUNT`

met·ro·nome /ˈmetrənəʊm/ **metronomes.** A metronome is a device which is used to regulate the speed of a piece of music. It makes a clicking sound and can be adjusted to make the sound at different speeds. `N-COUNT`

me·tropo·lis /məˈtrɒpəlɪs/ **metropolises.** You can refer to a large, important, busy city as a **metropolis.** *...this booming metropolis... Shanghai aims to recapture its position as the metropolis of East Asia.* `N-COUNT`

met·ro·poli·tan /ˌmetrəˈpɒlɪtən/. **Metropolitan** means belonging to or typical of a large busy city. *...the metropolitan district of Miami. ...major metropolitan hospitals.* `ADJ: ADJ n`

met·tle /ˈmetəl/. Someone's **mettle** is their capability to do something well in difficult circumstances. *For both sides, it's the first real test of their mettle this season.* `N-UNCOUNT`

mew /mjuː/ **mews, mewing, mewed.** When a cat **mews**, it makes a soft high-pitched cry. `VERB: V`

mews /mjuːz/; **mews** is both the singular and the plural form. A **mews** is a yard or street surrounded by houses that were originally built as stables. *...her London mews house. ...his house in Stanhope Mews.* `N-COUNT BRITISH`

Mexican 'wave, Mexican waves. If a crowd of people do a **Mexican wave**, each person in the crowd stands up and puts their arms in the air after the person next to them, creating a continuous rolling motion through the crowd. The usual American term is **wave.** `N-COUNT BRITISH`

mez·za·nine /ˈmezəniːn/ **mezzanines.** A **mezzanine** is a small storey built between two main storeys in a building. *...the mezzanine floor.* `N-COUNT`

mezzo-so'prano /ˌmetsəʊ səˈprɑːnəʊ/ **mezzo-sopranos.** A mezzo-soprano, or a mezzo, is a woman singer who sings with a higher range than a contralto but a lower range than a soprano. `N-COUNT`

mg. Mg is a written abbreviation for **milligrams.** *...300 mg of calcium.*

MHz. MHz is a written abbreviation for **megahertz.**

miaow /miˈaʊ/ **miaows, miaowing, miaowed.** Miaow is used to represent the noise that a cat makes. *He made a frightened noise a little like the miaow of a cat.* ► Also a verb. *Cats miaow when they are unhappy.* `N-COUNT; SOUND` `VERB: V`

mi·as·ma /miˈæzmə/ **miasmas.** You can describe something bad or confused that seems to be in the air all around you as a **miasma.** *...a miasma of failure, stupidity, self-pity hovering all around him.* `N-VAR LITERARY`

mica /ˈmaɪkə/ **micas.** Mica is a hard mineral which splits easily into thin layers. `N-VAR`

mice /maɪs/. **Mice** is the plural of **mouse.**

mick·ey /ˈmɪki/. If you **take the mickey** out of someone or something, you make fun of them, usually in an unkind way. *He started taking the mickey out of this poor man just because he is bald.* `PHRASE BRITISH, INFORMAL`

Mickey 'Mouse. You use Mickey Mouse to show that you think something is silly, childish, easy, or worthless. *This is not a Mickey Mouse course.* `ADJ-GRADED PRAGMATICS`

micro- /ˈmaɪkrəʊ-/. **Micro-** is used to form nouns that refer to something that is a very small example or fraction of a particular type of thing. *...micro-organisms. ...micro-seconds.* `PREFIX`

mi·crobe /ˈmaɪkrəʊb/ **microbes.** A **microbe** is a very small living thing, which you can only see if you use a microscope. `N-COUNT`

micro·bi·ol·ogy /ˌmaɪkrəʊbaɪˈɒlədʒi/. Microbiology is the branch of biology which deals with the study of micro-organisms and their effects on people. ♦ **micro·bi·olo·gist, microbiologists** *...a microbiologist at Liverpool University.* ♦ **micro·bio·logi·cal** /ˌmaɪkrəʊbaɪəˈlɒdʒɪkəl/ *...microbiological testing.* `N-UNCOUNT` `N-COUNT` `ADJ`

micro·chip /ˈmaɪkrəʊtʃɪp/ **microchips.** A microchip is a very small piece of silicon inside a computer, on which electronic circuits are printed. `N-COUNT`

micro-co'mputer, micro-computers. A micro-computer is a small computer, often used for word-processing. `N-COUNT`

micro·cosm /ˈmaɪkrəʊkɒzəm/ **microcosms.** A place or event that is a **microcosm** of a much larger one has all the main features of the larger one and seems like a smaller version of it. *Mahan's story is that of the Asian community in microcosm.* `N-COUNT FORMAL`

micro·elec·tron·ics /ˌmaɪkrəʊelekˈtrɒnɪks/; the form **microelectronic** is used as a modifier. Microelectronics is the branch of electronics that deals with miniature electronic circuits. `N-UNCOUNT`

micro·fiche /ˈmaɪkrəʊfiːʃ/ **microfiches.** A microfiche is a small sheet of film on which writing or other information is stored, greatly reduced in size. `N-VAR`

micro·film /ˈmaɪkrəʊfɪlm/ **microfilms.** Microfilm is film that is used for photographing information and storing it in a reduced form. `N-VAR`

micro-'organism, micro-organisms; also spelled **microorganism.** A **micro-organism** is a very small living thing which you can only see if you use a microscope. `N-COUNT TECHNICAL`

micro·phone /ˈmaɪkrəfəʊn/ **microphones.** A ◆◆◇◇◇ N-COUNT
microphone is a device that is used to make sounds
louder or to record them on a tape recorder.

micro·pro·ces·sor /ˌmaɪkrəʊˈprəʊsesə/ **micro-** ◆◇◇◇◇
processors. A microprocessor is the central pro- N-COUNT TECHNICAL
cessing chip in a computer or in another piece of
equipment.

micro·scope /ˈmaɪkrəskəʊp/ **microscopes.** A ◆◇◇◇◇ N-COUNT
microscope is an instrument which magnifies very
small objects so that you can look at them and
study them.

micro·scop·ic /ˌmaɪkrəˈskɒpɪk/. **1 Microscopic** ◆◇◇◇◇ ADJ
objects are extremely small, and usually can be seen
only through a microscope. ...microscopic fibres of
protein. **2** A microscopic examination is done ADJ: ADJ n
using a microscope. Microscopic examination of a
cell's chromosomes can reveal the sex of the fetus.
3 If you say that something is done in microscopic ADJ PRAGMATICS
detail, you are emphasizing that it is done in a very
thorough, detailed way. ...the microscopic details of
those crucial minutes.

micro·sec·ond /ˈmaɪkrəʊsekənd/ **microseconds.** N-COUNT
A microsecond is one-millionth of a second.

micro·sur·gery /ˌmaɪkrəʊˈsɜːdʒəri/. Microsurgery N-UNCOUNT
is surgery that is done using a microscope and very
small instruments.

micro·wave /ˈmaɪkrəʊweɪv/ **microwaves,** ◆◆◇◇◇
microwaving, microwaved. 1 A microwave or N-COUNT
a microwave oven is an oven which cooks food very
quickly by electromagnetic radiation. **2** To micro- VERB: V n
wave food or drink means to cook or heat it in a
microwave oven.

mid- /mɪd-/. **Mid-** is used to form nouns or adjec- PREFIX
tives that refer to the middle part of a particular period of time, or the middle point of a particular
place. Davis is in her mid-thirties. ...the mid-west of
America.

mid-'air. If something happens in mid-air, it hap- N-UNCOUNT
pens in the air, rather than on the ground. The bird
stopped and hovered in mid-air.

mid·day /ˌmɪdˈdeɪ/. **1 Midday** is twelve o'clock in ◆◇◇◇◇ N-UNCOUNT
the middle of the day. At midday everyone would go
down to Reg's Cafe. **2 Midday** is the middle part of N-UNCOUNT
the day, from late morning to early afternoon. ...the
midday heat.

mid·dle /ˈmɪdəl/ **middles. 1** The middle of some- ◆◆◆◆◆ N-COUNT
thing is the part of it that is furthest from its edges,
ends, or outside surface. Howard stood in the middle of the room... Father told her to make sure the
roast potatoes weren't raw in the middle. ● the middle of nowhere: see nowhere.
2 The middle object in a row of objects is the one that ADJ: ADJ n
has an equal number of objects on each side. Around
the middle finger of her left hand, she wore a gold ring.
3 Your middle is the part of your body around your N-COUNT INFORMAL
stomach. The cook's apron covered her middle.
4 The middle of an event or period of time is the part N-SING:
that comes after the first part and before the last part. the N of n
I woke up in the middle of the night... She was born in
the middle of a rain storm. ▶ Also an adjective. The ADJ: ADJ n
middle fortnight saw nearly 100mm of rain fall
nationwide.
5 If someone is in their middle thirties, for example, ADJ: ADJ n
they are aged somewhere between thirty four and
thirty six. I went on competing till I was in my middle
forties.
6 The middle child in a family has equal numbers of ADJ: ADJ n
younger and older brothers and sisters. His middle
son died in a drowning accident.
7 The middle course or way is a moderate course of ADJ: ADJ n
action that lies between two opposite and extreme
courses. He favoured a middle course between free enterprise and state intervention.
8 If you divide or split something down the middle, PHRASE
you divide or split it into two equal halves or groups.
9 If you are in the middle of doing something, you are PHRASE
busy doing it. I'm in the middle of cooking for nine
people.

middle 'age; also spelled middle-age. Middle age ◆◇◇◇◇ N-UNCOUNT
is the period in your life between the ages of 45 and

60, when you are no longer young but have not yet
become old.

middle-'aged. Someone who is middle-aged is ◆◆◇◇◇ ADJ
between the ages of 45 and 60 and is neither young
nor old. ...middle-aged, married businessmen.
▶ The middle-aged are people who are middle- N-PLURAL: the N
aged.

Middle 'Ages. In European history, the Middle ◆◇◇◇◇
Ages was the period between the end of the Roman N-PLURAL: the N
Empire in 476 AD and about 1500 AD.

middle·brow /ˈmɪdəlbraʊ/; also **middle-brow.** ADJ-GRADED
Middlebrow entertainment is interesting and enjoyable but does not require much thought. ...a
middlebrow anti-war play.

middle 'class, middle classes. The middle ◆◆◇◇◇ N-COLL-COUNT
class or middle classes are the people in a society
who are not working class or upper class, for example managers, doctors, and lawyers. The President
may have secured some support from the middle
classes. ▶ Also an adjective. He is rapidly losing the ADJ
support of blue-collar voters and of middle-class
conservatives.

middle 'distance. 1 If you are looking into the N-SING:
middle distance, you are looking at a place that is the N
neither near nor far away. **2** A middle-distance run- ADJ: ADJ n
ner is someone who takes part in races that are
longer than a sprint, but not as long as a marathon.

Middle 'East. The Middle East is the area ◆◆◆◆◇
around the eastern Mediterranean that includes N-PROPER: the N
Iran and all the countries in Asia that are to the
west and south-west of Iran. ...the two great rivers of
the Middle East. ♦ **Middle 'Eastern** The US ADJ: ADJ n
economy depends on Middle Eastern oil.

middle·man /ˈmɪdəlmæn/ **middlemen. 1** A ◆◇◇◇◇ N-COUNT
middleman is a person or company which buys
things from the people who produce them and sells
them to other people at a profit. The CSO earns
huge profits as the middleman. **2** A middleman is a N-COUNT
person who helps in negotiations between people
who are unwilling to meet each other directly. The
two sides would only meet indirectly, through
middlemen.

middle name, middle names. Your middle N-COUNT
name is the name that comes between your first
name and your surname.

middle-of-the-'road. 1 Middle-of-the-road poli- ADJ-GRADED
ticians or opinions are moderate, not extreme. The
Archbishop is middle-of-the-road in politics. **2** If you ADJ-GRADED
describe something or someone as middle-of-the-
road, you mean that they have an ordinary or unadventurous nature or lifestyle. I actually don't want
to be a middle-of-the-road person.

middle-'ranking. A middle-ranking person has a ADJ: ADJ n
fairly important or responsible position in a particular organization, but is not one of the most important people in it.

middle school, middle schools. 1 In the Unit- N-VAR
ed States, a middle school is a school that children
go to between the ages of 10 or 11 and 14. ...Harlem
Park Middle School. **2** In Britain, a middle school is N-VAR
a state school that children go to between the ages
of 8 or 9 and 12 or 13.

Middle 'West. The Middle West is the central N-PROPER:
part of the United States of America. the N

mid·dling /ˈmɪdlɪŋ/. If you describe a quality such ADJ
as the size of something as middling, you mean
that it is average. The Beatles enjoyed only middling
success until 1963.

midge /mɪdʒ/ **midges.** Midges are very small in- N-COUNT
sects which fly in groups.

midg·et /ˈmɪdʒɪt/ **midgets. 1** People who are very N-COUNT
short are sometimes referred to as midgets; a use
which some people find offensive. **2** Midget is used ADJ: ADJ n
to describe something which is very small. ...midget
submarines.

Mid·lands /ˈmɪdləndz/. The Midlands is the region ◆◆◇◇◇
or area in the central part of a country, in particular N-COLL-PROPER:
the central part of England. the N

mid·night /ˈmɪdnaɪt/. **1 Midnight** is twelve o'clock ◆◆◆◇◇
in the middle of the night. The entrance gates were N-UNCOUNT

locked at midnight. **2 Midnight** is used to describe something which happens or appears at midnight or in the middle of the night. It is totally out of the question to postpone the midnight deadline. **3** If someone **is burning the midnight oil**, they are staying up very late in order to study or do some other work.   `ADJ: ADJ n` / `PHRASE`

midnight 'blue. Something that is **midnight blue** is a very dark blue colour, almost black.   `COLOUR`

mid·point /'mɪdpɔɪnt/; also spelled **mid-point**. **1** The **midpoint** between two things is the point that is the same distance from both things. ...the midpoint between Paris and Warsaw. **2** The **midpoint** of an event is the time halfway between the beginning and the end of it. She has not yet reached the midpoint of her life.   `N-SING`

mid·riff /'mɪdrɪf/ **midriffs.** Someone's **midriff** is the middle part of their body, between their waist and their chest.   `N-COUNT`

mid·sized /'mɪdsaɪzd/; also spelled **mid-sized**. The form **midsize** is also used. You use **midsized** or **midsize** to describe things, especially products and companies, that are of average size. ...a low-cost midsized car.   `ADJ: ADJ n` / `AMERICAN`

midst /mɪdst/. **1** If you are **in the midst of** doing something, you are doing it at the moment. Congress is in the midst of rewriting the nation's banking laws. **2** If something happens **in the midst of** an event, it happens during it. Eleanor arrived in the midst of a blizzard. **3** If someone or something is **in the midst of** a group of people or things, they are among them or surrounded by them. ...exposed like this in the midst of a large crowd. **4** You say that someone is **in** your **midst** when you are drawing attention to the fact that they are in your group. We're lucky to have such a man in our midst.   `PHR-PREP` / `PHR-PREP` / `PHR-PREP` / `PHRASE FORMAL`

mid·stream /ˌmɪd'striːm/; also spelled **mid-stream**. **1** Someone or something that is in **midstream** is in the middle of a river, where the current is strongest. Their boat had capsized in midstream. ► Also an adverb. Some of them got caught midstream by the tide. **2** If someone who has been doing something such as talking stops or pauses in **midstream**, they stop doing it, often before continuing. I was cut off in midstream. ► Also an adverb. ...to change course midstream.   `N-UNCOUNT` / `ADV` / `N-UNCOUNT` / `ADV: ADV after v`

mid·sum·mer /ˌmɪd'sʌmə/. **Midsummer** is the period in the middle of the summer.   `N-UNCOUNT`

Midsummer's 'Day. Midsummer's Day or **Midsummer Day** is the 24th of June.   `N-PROPER`

mid·way /ˌmɪd'weɪ/; also spelled **mid-way**. **1** If something is **midway** between two places, it is between them and the same distance from each of them. The studio is midway between his aunt's old home and his cottage. ► Also an adjective. ...the midway point between Gloucester, Hereford and Worcester. **2** If something happens **midway** through a period of time, it happens during the middle part of it. He returned midway through the afternoon. ► Also an adjective. ...the midway point of the first half of the game.   `ADV: ADV prep` / `ADJ: ADJ n` / `ADV: ADV after v` / `ADJ: ADJ n`

mid·week /ˌmɪd'wiːk/. **Midweek** describes something that happens in the middle of the week. ...midweek flights from Gatwick. ► Also an adverb. They'll be able to go up to London midweek.   `ADJ: ADJ n` / `ADV: ADV after v`

Mid·west /ˌmɪd'west/. The **Midwest** is the region in the north of the central part of the USA. ...farmers in the Midwest. ✦ **Mid·west·ern** /ˌmɪd'westən/ ...traditional Midwestern values.   `N-PROPER` / `ADJ`

mid·wife /'mɪdwaɪf/ **midwives.** A **midwife** is a nurse who is trained to deliver babies and to advise pregnant women.   `N-COUNT`

mid·wife·ry /ˌmɪd'wɪfəri/. **Midwifery** is the work of delivering babies and advising pregnant women.   `N-UNCOUNT`

mid·win·ter /ˌmɪd'wɪntə/; also spelled **mid-winter**. **Midwinter** is the period in the middle of winter.   `N-UNCOUNT`

mien /miːn/. Someone's **mien** is their general appearance and manner, especially the expression on their face, which shows what they are feeling or   `N-SING LITERARY`

thinking. It was impossible to tell from his mien whether he was offended.

miffed /mɪft/. If you are **miffed**, you are slightly annoyed and hurt because of something which someone has said or done to you. I was a bit miffed about that.   `ADJ-GRADED INFORMAL`

might 1 modal uses

might /maɪt/. **Might** is a modal verb. It is used with the base form of a verb.   ◆◆◆◆◆

1 You use **might** to indicate that something will possibly happen or be true in the future. Smoking might be banned totally in most buildings... I might well regret it later... He might not be back until tonight. **2** You use **might** to indicate that there is a possibility that something is true. They had not given up hope that he might be alive... You might be right... He might not be interested in her any more. **3** You use **might** to indicate that something has the potential for happening or being true in particular circumstances. ...the type of person who might appear in a fashion magazine.   `MODAL PRAGMATICS` / `MODAL PRAGMATICS` / `MODAL PRAGMATICS`

4 You use **might have** with a past participle to indicate that it is possible that something happened or was true, or when giving a possible explanation for something. I heard what might have been an explosion... She thought the shooting might have been an accident. **5** You use **might have** with a past participle to indicate that something was a possibility in the past, although it did not actually happen. The report might have been better written... I didn't give my name because if I did I thought you might not have come. **6** You use **might** in statements where you are accepting the truth of a situation, but contrasting it with something that is more important. He might be a bore, but he was as quick-witted as a weasel. **7** You use **might** when you are saying emphatically that someone ought to do the thing mentioned, especially when you are annoyed because they have not done it. You might have told me that before! **8** You use **might** to make a suggestion or to give advice in a very polite way. You might try the gas station down the street... I thought we might go for a drive on Sunday. **9** You use **might** as a polite way of interrupting someone, asking a question, making a request, or introducing what you are going to say next. Might I make a suggestion?... Might I trouble you for a drop more tea? **10** You use **might** in expressions such as **as you might expect** and **as you might imagine** in order to indicate that the statement you are making is not surprising. 'How's Jan?' she asked.—'Bad. As you might expect.' **11** You use **might** in expressions such as **I might add** and **I might say** in order to emphasize a statement that you are making. It didn't come as a great surprise to me, I might say. **12** You use **might** in expressions such as **I might have known** and **I might have guessed** to indicate that you are not surprised at a disappointing event or fact. 'I detest clutter, you know.'—'I didn't know, but I might have guessed.' **13** ● **might as well**: see **well**.   `MODAL PRAGMATICS` / `MODAL PRAGMATICS` / `MODAL PRAGMATICS` / `MODAL PRAGMATICS` / `MODAL PRAGMATICS` / `MODAL PRAGMATICS, SPOKEN` / `MODAL PRAGMATICS` / `MODAL PRAGMATICS` / `MODAL PRAGMATICS`

might 2 noun uses

might /maɪt/. **1 Might** is power or strength. The might of the army could prove a decisive factor... These symbols of Soviet power, represented the great might of the Soviet Union. **2** If you do something **with all** your **might**, you do it using all your strength and energy. She swung the hammer at his head with all her might.   ◆◇◇◇◇ `N-UNCOUNT FORMAL` / `PHRASE`

mighti·ly /'maɪtɪli/. **Mightily** means to a great extent or degree. He had given a mightily impressive performance.   `ADV-GRADED DATED`

mightn't /'maɪtənt/. **Mightn't** is a spoken form of **might not**.

might've /'maɪtəv/. **Might've** is the usual spoken form of **might have**, especially when 'have' is an auxiliary verb.

mighty /'maɪti/ **mightier, mightiest. 1** Mighty is used to describe something that is very large or powerful. There was a flash and a mighty bang. **2 Mighty** is used in front of adjectives and adverbs to emphasize the quality that they are describing. It's something you'll be mighty proud of.   ◆◆◇◇◇ `ADJ-GRADED LITERARY` / `ADV-GRADED PRAGMATICS AMERICAN, INFORMAL`

M

mi·graine /ˈmiːɡreɪn, AM ˈmaɪ-/ **migraines.** A migraine is an extremely painful headache that makes you feel very ill. ◆◇◇◇◇ N-VAR

mi·grant /ˈmaɪɡrənt/ **migrants.** 1 A migrant is a person who moves from one place to another, especially in order to find work. *...migrant workers following harvests northward.* 2 Migrants are birds, fish, or animals that migrate from one part of the world to another. ◆◆◆◇◇ N-COUNT / N-COUNT

mi·grate /maɪˈɡreɪt, AM ˈmaɪɡreɪt/ **migrates, migrating, migrated.** 1 If people migrate, they move from one place to another, especially in order to find work or to live somewhere for a short time. *People migrate to cities like Jakarta in search of work.* ♦ **mi·gra·tion** /maɪˈɡreɪʃən/ **migrations** *...the migration of Soviet Jews to Israel.* ♦ **mi·gra·tory** /ˈmaɪɡrətəri, AM -tɔːri/ *...migratory farm labour.* 2 When birds, fish, or animals migrate, they move at a particular time or season from one part of the world or from one part of a country to another. *...a dam system that kills the fish as they migrate from streams to the ocean.* ♦ **migration** *...the migration of animals in the Serengeti.* ♦ **migratory** *...the great migratory fish like swordfish, tuna and bluefish.* ◆◆◇◇ VERB / V prep/adv / Also V / N-VAR / ADJ / VERB / V prep/adv / Also V / N-VAR / ADJ: ADJ n

mike /maɪk/ **mikes.** A mike is the same as a microphone. *'One, two, three, four, testing,' Seaton said into a mike.* ◆◇◇◇◇ N-COUNT INFORMAL

mild /maɪld/ **milder, mildest.** 1 Mild is used to describe something such as a feeling, attitude, or illness that is not very strong or severe. *...a look of mild confusion... Anna put up a mild protest. ...if you have only mild symptoms.* ♦ **mild·ly** *I'm only mildly surprised.* 2 A mild person is gentle and does not get angry easily. *He is a mild man, who is reasonable almost to the point of blandness.* ♦ **mildly** *'I'm not meddling,' Kenworthy said mildly.* 3 Mild weather is pleasant because it is neither extremely hot nor extremely cold. 4 You describe food as mild when it does not taste or smell strong, sharp, or bitter. *This cheese has a soft, mild flavour. ...a mild curry powder.* 5 Mild soap or washing-up liquid does not contain anything which might damage the things you want to wash. 6 In Britain, mild is a clear, dark-coloured beer. ◆◆◆◇◇ ADJ-GRADED / ADV-GRADED / ADV-GRADED / ADV-GRADED: ADV after v / ADJ-GRADED / ADJ-GRADED / ADJ-GRADED / N-UNCOUNT

7 See also **mildly**.

mil·dew /ˈmɪldjuː, AM -duː/. Mildew is a powdery fungus that grows on things such as plants, books, and cloth in damp places. N-UNCOUNT

mil·dewed /ˈmɪldjuːd, AM -duːd/. Something that is mildewed has mildew growing on it. ADJ

mild·ly /ˈmaɪldli/. 1 See mild. 2 You use to put it mildly to indicate that you are describing something in language that is much less strong, direct, or critical than what you really think. *To say we are disappointed about this is putting it mildly.* PHRASE

mild-'mannered. If you describe someone as mild-mannered, you approve of them because they are gentle, kind, and polite. ADJ-GRADED PRAGMATICS

mile /maɪl/ **miles.** 1 A mile is a unit of distance equal to 1760 yards or approximately 1.6 kilometres. *They drove 600 miles across the desert... The hurricane is moving to the west at about 18 miles per hour.* 2 Miles is used, especially in the expression **miles away**, to refer to a long distance. *...if you enrol at a gym that's miles away... 'Shall I come to see you?'—'Are you kidding? It's miles.'* 3 If you say that someone is **miles away**, you mean that they are unaware of what is happening because they are thinking deeply about something else. *What were you thinking about? You were miles away.* 4 If you say that someone is willing to **go the extra mile**, you mean that they are willing to make a special effort to do or achieve something. 5 If you say that you can see or recognize something **a mile off**, you are emphasizing that it is very obvious and easy to recognize. *You can spot undercover cops a mile off.* 6 If you say that someone would **run a mile** when faced with a particular situation, you mean that they would be ◆◆◆◇ N-COUNT: num N / N-PLURAL / PHRASE INFORMAL / PHRASE / PHRASE PRAGMATICS INFORMAL / PHRASE INFORMAL

very frightened or unwilling to deal with it. *I'm very squeamish and when I see needles I run a mile.*

mile·age /ˈmaɪlɪdʒ/ **mileages.** 1 Mileage refers to the distance that you have travelled, measured in miles. *Most of their mileage may be in and around town.* 2 The mileage of a vehicle is the number of miles that it can travel using one gallon of petrol. *...cars that get better mileage.* 3 The mileage in a particular course of action is its usefulness in getting you what you want. *It's obviously very important to get as much mileage out of the convention as possible.* ◆◇◇◇◇ N-UNCOUNT: also N in pl / N-UNCOUNT: also N in pl / N-UNCOUNT

mile·stone /ˈmaɪlstəʊn/ **milestones.** 1 A milestone is an important event in the history or development of something or someone. *Starting school is a milestone for both children and parents.* 2 A milestone is a stone by the side of a road showing the distances to particular places. ◆◇◇◇◇ N-COUNT / N-COUNT

mi·lieu /ˈmiːljɜː, AM mɪˈljuː/ **milieux** or **milieus.** Your milieu is the group of people or activities that you live among or are familiar with. *They stayed, safe and happy, within their own social milieu.* ◆◇◇◇◇ N-COUNT FORMAL

mili·tant /ˈmɪlɪtənt/ **militants.** You use militant to describe people who believe in something very strongly and are very active in trying to bring about political or social change. *Militant mineworkers in the Ukraine have voted for a one-day stoppage.* ▶ Also a noun. *The militants were planning a series of terrorist acts.* ♦ **mili·tan·cy** *...the rise of trade union militancy.* ♦ **mili·tant·ly** *...Albania's militantly atheist authorities.* ◆◆◆◇◇ ADJ-GRADED / N-COUNT / N-UNCOUNT / ADV-GRADED

mili·ta·rism /ˈmɪlɪtərɪzəm/. Militarism is a country's desire to strengthen their armed forces in order to make themselves more powerful; used showing disapproval. *...a dangerous mixture of nationalism and militarism.* N-UNCOUNT PRAGMATICS

mili·ta·rist /ˈmɪlɪtərɪst/ **militarists.** 1 If you describe someone as a militarist, you mean that they are eager that their country's armed forces should be strengthened and used in order to make it more powerful; used showing disapproval. 2 Militarist means the same as militaristic. *...militarist policies.* N-COUNT PRAGMATICS / ADJ-GRADED

mili·ta·ris·tic /ˌmɪlɪtəˈrɪstɪk/. Militaristic is used to describe groups, ideas, or policies which support the strengthening and use of the armed forces of their country in order to make it more powerful; used showing disapproval. *...aggressive militaristic governments.* ADJ-GRADED PRAGMATICS

mili·ta·rized /ˈmɪlɪtəraɪzd/; also spelled **militarised** in British English. 1 A militarized area or region has members of the armed forces and military equipment in it. 2 You can use militarized to show disapproval of something that has many military characteristics. *...a militarized and confrontationist style of politics.* ADJ-GRADED / ADJ-GRADED PRAGMATICS

mili·tary /ˈmɪlɪtri, AM -teri/ **militaries.** 1 Military means relating to the armed forces of a country. *Military action may become necessary. ...military personnel to help with the relief efforts.* ♦ **mili·tari·ly** /ˌmɪlɪˈteərɪli/ *They remain unwilling to intervene militarily.* 2 Military means relating to or belonging to the army, rather than to the navy or the air force. *...American naval and military forces.* 3 The military are the armed forces of a country, especially officers of high rank. *Did you serve in the military?* ◆◆◆◆ ADJ / ADV / ADJ: ADJ n / N-COLL-COUNT the N

military po'lice. 1 The military police are the part of an army, navy, or air force that act as its police force. 2 Military police are men and women who are members of the military police. *The camp is surrounded by razor-wire fences and guarded by military police.* ◆◇◇◇◇ N-COLL-SING / N-PLURAL

military po'liceman, military policemen. A military policeman is a member of the military police. *Over by a newspaper stand was a military policeman.* N-COUNT

military 'service. Military service is a period of compulsory service in the armed forces of a country. *...young people refusing to do compulsory military service.* ◆◇◇◇◇ N-UNCOUNT

mili·tate /'mɪlɪteɪt/ **militates, militating, mili-**   VERB
tated. If something **militates against** something or   V against n
someone, it makes something less likely to happen   FORMAL
or someone less likely to achieve something. *Her*
background militates against her.

mi·li·tia /mɪ'lɪʃə/ **militias.** A militia is an organiza-   ◆◆◇◇◇
tion that operates like an army but whose members   N-COUNT
are not professional soldiers. *The troops will not at-*
tempt to disarm the warring militias.

mi·li·tia·man /mɪ'lɪʃəmən/ **militiamen.** A militia-   ◆◇◇◇◇
man is a member of a militia.   N-COUNT

milk /mɪlk/ **milks, milking, milked. 1** Milk is the   ◆◆◆◇◇
white liquid produced by cows, goats, and some   N-UNCOUNT
other animals. People drink milk, and use it to make
butter, cheese, and yoghurt. **2** If someone **milks** a   VERB: V n
cow or goat, they get milk from it by pulling its udders, using either their hands or a special machine.
♦ **milk·ing** ...*an automatic milking machine.*   N-UNCOUNT
3 Milk is the white liquid produced by women to   N-UNCOUNT
feed their babies.
4 If you say that someone **milks** something, you mean   VERB: V n
that they get as much benefit or profit as they can   PRAGMATICS
from it, without caring about the effects this has on   V n from n
other people; used showing disapproval. *The callous*
couple milked money from a hospital charity to fund a
lavish lifestyle. **5** See also **coconut milk, condensed**
milk, skimmed milk.

milk 'chocolate. Milk chocolate is chocolate   N-UNCOUNT
that has been made with milk. It is lighter in colour
and has a creamier taste than plain chocolate.

milk·man /'mɪlkmən, AM -mæn/ **milkmen.** A milk-   N-COUNT
man is a person who delivers milk to people's
homes.

'milk product, milk products. Milk products are   N-COUNT
foods made from milk, for example butter, cheese,
and yoghurt.

'milk round, milk rounds. 1 If someone has a   N-COUNT
milk round, they work as a milkman, going from   BRITISH
house to house delivering milk. **2** The **milk round** is   N-SING:
an annual event when employees from large com-   the N
panies visit colleges and universities and interview   BRITISH
students who are interested in working for them.

milk·shake /'mɪlkʃeɪk/ **milkshakes;** also spelled   N-VAR
milk shake. Milkshake is a cold drink made by mixing milk with a flavouring, and sometimes ice
cream or fruit, and then whisking it. ▶ A **milkshake**   N-COUNT
is a glass of milkshake.

'milk tooth, milk teeth. Your **milk teeth** are the   N-COUNT
first teeth that grow in your mouth, which later fall
out and are replaced by a second set.

milky /'mɪlki/ **1** If you describe something as   ◆◇◇◇◇
milky, you mean it is pale white in colour. You can   ADJ
describe other colours as **milky** when they are very
pale or have white streaks in them. ...*milky white*
paint... A milky mist filled the valley. **2** Drinks or   ADJ-GRADED
food that are **milky** contain a lot of milk. ...*a large*
bowl of milky coffee.

Milky 'Way. The Milky Way is the pale strip of   ◆◇◇◇◇
light consisting of many stars that you can see   N-PROPER:
stretched across the sky at night.   the N

mill /mɪl/ **mills, milling, milled. 1** A mill is a   ◆◆◆◇◇
building in which grain is crushed and ground to   N-COUNT
make flour. **2** A **mill** is a small device used for   N-COUNT:
grinding something such as coffee beans or pepper   supp N
into powder. ...*a pepper mill.* **3** To **mill** something   VERB: V n
such as wheat or pepper means to grind it in a mill.
♦ **mil·ler, millers** *The festival was a holiday for*   N-COUNT
millers and bakers. **4** A **mill** is a factory used for   N-COUNT
making and processing materials such as steel,
wool, or cotton. ...*a steel mill.* **5** See also **run-of-**
the-mill, watermill.

mill around; the form **mill about** is also used in   PHRASAL VB
British English. When a crowd of people **mill around**   V P
or **mill about**, they move around within a particular   V P n
place or area, so that the movement of the whole
crowd looks very confused. *Dozens of people milled*
around Charing Cross Road and Denmark Street.

mil·len·nium /mɪ'leniəm/ **millennia** or **millen-**   ◆◇◇◇◇
niums. 1 A millennium is a thousand years. *Their*   N-COUNT
creations survive half a millennium later. **2** A **mil-**   N-COUNT

lennium is one of the periods of a thousand years   FORMAL
before or after the birth of Jesus Christ. 1995 is in
the second millennium A.D. *Evidence exists that*
acupuncture was practised in China as long ago as
the third millennium BC.

mil·let /'mɪlɪt/ **millets.** Millet is a cereal crop that   ◆◇◇◇◇
is grown for its seeds or for hay.   N-VAR

milli- /'mɪli-/. **Milli-** is added to some nouns that re-   PREFIX
fer to units of measurement in order to form other
nouns referring to units a thousand times smaller.
...*a small current, around 5 milliamps.*

mil·li·gram /'mɪlɪgræm/ **milligrams;** also spelled   ◆◇◇◇◇
milligramme in British English. A **milligram** is a   N-COUNT:
unit of weight that is equal to one thousandth of a   num N
gramme. ...*0.5 milligrams of mercury.*

mil·li·li·tre /'mɪlɪliːtə/ **millilitres;** spelled **milliliter**   N-COUNT:
in American English. A **millilitre** is a unit of volume   num N
for liquids and gases that is equal to a thousandth
of a litre. ...*100 millilitres of blood.*

mil·li·metre /'mɪlɪmiːtə/ **millimetres;** spelled   ◆◇◇◇◇
millimeter in American English. A **millimetre** is a   N-COUNT:
metric unit of length that is equal to a tenth of a   num N
centimetre or a thousandth of a metre. ...*a tiny little*
transparent pill, about 20 millimetres long.

mil·li·ner /'mɪlɪnə/ **milliners.** A milliner is a per-   N-COUNT
son whose job is making or selling women's hats.

mil·li·nery /'mɪlɪnəri, AM -neri/. **Millinery** is used to   N-UNCOUNT
refer to hats made or sold by a milliner.

mil·lion /'mɪliən/ **millions.** The plural form is **mil-**   ◆◆◆◆◆
lion after a number, or after a word or expression
referring to a number, such as 'several' or 'a few'.
1 A **million** or one **million** is the number 1,000,000.   NUMBER
See Appendix headed **Numbers. 2** If you talk about   QUANT
millions of people or things, you mean that there is
a very large number of them but you do not know
or do not want to say exactly how many. *The pro-*
gramme was viewed on television in millions of
homes. ▶ Also a pronoun. *This wretched war has*   PRON
brought misery to millions.

mil·lion·aire /ˌmɪliə'neə/ **millionaires.** A million-   ◆◆◇◇◇
aire is a very rich person who has money or proper-   N-COUNT
ty worth at least a million pounds or dollars.

mil·lion·air·ess /ˌmɪliən'eərɛs/ **millionairesses.**   N-COUNT
A **millionairess** is a woman who has money or
property worth at least a million pounds or dollars.

mil·lionth /'mɪliənθ/ **millionths.** The **millionth**   ◆◆◆◇◇
item in a series is the one you count as number one
million. See Appendix headed **Numbers.**

mil·li·pede /'mɪlɪpiːd/ **millipedes.** A millipede is a   N-COUNT
small creature with a long, narrow body made of
small segments, each with two pairs of legs.

mil·li·sec·ond /'mɪlisekənd/ **milliseconds.** A mil-   N-COUNT
lisecond is a unit of time equal to one thousandth   TECHNICAL
of a second.

mill·stone /'mɪlstəʊn/ **millstones. 1** A millstone   N-COUNT
is a large, flat, round stone which is one of a pair of
stones used to grind grain into flour. **2** If you de-   PHRASE
scribe something as **a millstone** or **a millstone**
around your **neck**, you mean that it is a very unpleasant problem or responsibility that you cannot
escape from. *For today's politicians, the treaty is be-*
coming a millstone.

mime /maɪm/ **mimes, miming, mimed. 1** Mime   ◆◇◇◇◇
is the use of movements and gestures in order to   N-VAR
express something or tell a story without using
speech. ...*a mime artist.* **2** If you **mime** something,   VERB
you describe or express it using mime rather than   V n/-ing
speech. *I remember asking her to mime getting up in*   Also V
the morning. **3** If you **mime**, you pretend to be sing-   VERB: V
ing or playing an instrument, although the music is   V n
in fact coming from a record or cassette. *In concerts,*   V to n
the group mime their songs... The waiters mime to
records playing on the jukebox.

mim·ic /'mɪmɪk/ **mimics, mimicking, mim-**   ◆◇◇◇◇
icked. 1 If you **mimic** the actions or voice of a per-   VERB
son or animal, you imitate it, usually in a way that is   V n
meant to be amusing or entertaining. *He could*
mimic anybody. ▶ A **mimic** is a person who is able   N-COUNT
to mimic people or animals. **2** If someone or some-   VERB
thing **mimics** another person or thing, they try to be   V n

like them or are like them, although they are not really that person or thing. *The computer doesn't mimic human thought; it reaches the same ends by different means.*

mim·ic·ry /ˈmɪmɪkri/. **Mimicry** is the action of mimicking someone or something. N-UNCOUNT

min. **Min.** is a written abbreviation for **minimum**, or for **minutes** or **minute**. ◆◆◇◇

mina·ret /ˌmɪnəˈret/ **minarets.** A **minaret** is a tall thin tower which is part of a mosque. N-COUNT

mince /mɪns/ **minces, mincing, minced.** ◆◇◇◇
1 Mince is meat which has been cut into very small pieces by being forced through the small holes in a machine called a mincer. The usual American term is **hamburger meat. 2** If you **mince** food such as meat, you put it through a mincer. **3** If you say that someone **minces** somewhere, you mean that they walk there with quick small steps; often used to say disapprovingly that a man walks in an exaggeratedly effeminate way. *They minced in, in beach costumes and make-up.* **4** If you say someone does not **mince** their **words** or does not **mince words**, you mean they speak in a forceful direct way, especially when saying something unpleasant to someone. N-UNCOUNT BRITISH / VERB: V n / VERB V prep/adv / PHRASE

mince·meat /ˈmɪnsmiːt/. **Mincemeat** is a sweet mixture of currants, apple, sugar, and suet. It is usually cooked in pastry to make mince pies. N-UNCOUNT

mince 'pie, mince pies. **Mince pies** are small sweet pies containing mincemeat. They are usually eaten at Christmas. N-COUNT

mind 1 noun uses

mind /maɪnd/ **minds. 1** You refer to someone's **mind** when talking about their thoughts. For example, if you say that something is **in your mind**, you mean that you are thinking about it, and if you say that something is **at the back of your mind**, you mean that you are aware of it, although you are not thinking about it very much. *I'm trying to clear my mind of all this... He spent the next hour going over the trial in his mind.* **2** Your **mind** is your ability to think and reason. *You have a good mind.* **3** If you have a particular type of **mind**, you have a particular way of thinking which is part of your character, or a result of your education or professional training. *Andrew, you have a very suspicious mind.* ◆◆◆◇ N-COUNT: with poss / N-COUNT / N-COUNT
♦ **-minded** *These are evil-minded people. ...open-minded young people who are both productive and reflective.* **4** You can refer to someone as a particular kind of **mind** as a way of saying that they are clever, intelligent, or imaginative. *She moved to London, meeting some of the best minds of her time.* **5** See also **minded, -minded; frame of mind, state of mind.** COMB / N-COUNT: with supp
6 If you tell someone to **bear** something **in mind** or to **keep** something **in mind**, you are reminding or warning them about something important which they should remember. **7** If something **brings** another thing **to mind** or **calls** another thing **to mind**, it makes you think of that other thing, usually because it is similar in some way. *The word 'outing' probably brings to mind a trip to the seaside or the zoo.* **8** If you **cast** your **mind back** to a time in the past, you think about what happened then. *Cast your mind back to 1978, when Forest won the title.* **9** If you **change** your **mind**, or if someone or something **changes** your **mind**, you change a decision you have made or an opinion that you had. **10** If something **comes to mind** or **springs to mind**, you think of it without making any effort. *Integrity and honesty are words that spring to mind when talking of the man.* **11** If you say that an idea or possibility never **crossed** your **mind**, you mean that you did not think of it. **12** If you see something in your **mind's eye**, you imagine it and have a clear picture of it in your mind. **13** If you ask someone what they **have in mind**, you want to know in more detail about an idea or wish they have. *'Maybe we could celebrate tonight.'—'What did you have in mind?'* **14** If you do something **with a** particular thing **in mind**, you do it with that thing as your aim or as the reason or basis for your action. PHRASE / PRAGMATICS / PHRASE / PHRASE / PHRASE / PHRASE / PHRASE / PHRASE / PHRASE

15 If you say that something such as an illness is all **in the mind**, you mean that it relates to someone's feelings or attitude, rather than having any physical cause. *It could be a virus, or it could be all in the mind.* PHRASE
16 If you **know** your **own mind**, you are sure about your opinions, and are not easily influenced by other people. **17** If you say that someone **is losing** their **mind**, you mean that they are becoming mad. **18** If you **make up** your **mind** or **make** your **mind up**, you decide which of a number of possible things you will have or do. **19** You can use the expression **mind over matter** to describe situations in which a person seems to be able to control events, physical objects, or the condition of their own body using their mind. *Good health is simply a case of mind over matter.* PHRASE / PHRASE / PHRASE / PHRASE
20 If a number of people are **of one mind, of like mind,** or **of the same mind,** they all agree about something. **21** If something is **on** your **mind,** you are worried or concerned about it and think about it a lot. *This game has been on my mind all week.* **22** If your **mind is on** something or you **have** your **mind on** something, you are thinking about that thing rather than something else. **23** If you have **an open mind,** you avoid forming an opinion or making a decision until you know all the facts. **24** If you say that someone is **out of their mind,** you mean that they are mad or very foolish. **25** If you say that you have been **out of** your **mind** with a feeling such as worry, jealousy, or frustration, you are emphasizing that you have been extremely worried, jealous, or frustrated. PHRASE / PHRASE / PHRASE / PHRASE / PHRASE PRAGMATICS INFORMAL
26 If you say that someone is, for example, **bored out of** their **mind, scared out of** their **mind,** or **stoned out of** their **mind,** you are emphasizing that they are extremely bored, scared, or affected by drugs. **27** If you **put** your **mind to** something, you devote a lot of energy, effort, or attention to it. **28** If something **puts** you **in mind of** something else, it reminds you of it because it is similar to it or is associated with it. *This put me in mind of something Patrick said many years ago.* **29** If you can **read** someone's **mind,** you know what they are thinking without them saying anything. **30** To **put** someone's **mind at rest** or **set** their **mind at rest** means to stop them worrying about something. **31** If you say that nobody is in their **right mind** would do a particular thing, you are emphasizing that it is an irrational thing to do and you would be surprised if anyone did it. *No one in her right mind would make such a major purchase without asking questions.* **32** If you **set** your **mind on** something or **have** your **mind set on** it, you are determined to do it or obtain it. *When my wife sets her mind on something, she invariably finds a way to achieve it.* PHRASE PRAGMATICS INFORMAL / PHRASE / PHRASE / PHRASE / PHRASE / PHRASE PRAGMATICS / PHRASE
33 If something **slips** your **mind,** you forget it. *I was going to mention it, but it slipped my mind.* **34** If you **speak** your **mind,** you say firmly and honestly what you think about a situation, even if this may offend or upset people. **35** If something **sticks in** your **mind,** it remains firmly in your memory. **36** If something **takes** your **mind off** a problem or unpleasant situation, it helps you to forget about it for a while. **37** You say or write **to my mind** to indicate that the statement you are making is your own opinion. *There are scenes in this play which to my mind are incredibly violent.* **38** If you are **in two minds** or **of two minds,** you are uncertain about what to do, especially when you have to choose between two courses of action. **39** ● **presence of mind:** see **presence.** ● **out of sight, out of mind:** see **sight.** PHRASE / PHRASE / PHRASE / PHRASE / PHRASE / PHRASE

mind 2 verb uses

mind /maɪnd/ **minds, minding, minded. 1** If you do not **mind** something, you are not annoyed or bothered by it. *Do you mind being alone?... I hope you don't mind me calling in like this, without an appointment... It involved a little extra work, but nobody seemed to mind.* **2** You use **mind** in the expressions **'do you mind?'** and **'would you mind?'** as a polite way of asking permission or asking someone to do something. *You don't mind if they take a look round, do you?... Would you mind waiting outside for a moment?... 'Would you like me to read that* ◆◆◆◇◇ VERB V n/-ing V n -ing V / VERB PRAGMATICS V if V -ing V

for you?'—'If you wouldn't mind, please.' **3** If someone does not **mind** what happens or what something is like, they do not have a strong preference for any particular thing. *I don't mind what we play, really.* **4** If you tell someone to **mind** something, you are warning them to be careful so that they do not hurt themselves or other people, or damage something. *Mind that bike!* **5** You use **mind** when you are reminding someone that they must do something or telling them to be careful to not do something. *Mind you don't burn those sausages.* **6** If you **mind** a child or something such as a shop or luggage, you look after it, usually while the person who owns it or is usually responsible for it is elsewhere. *Jim Coulters will mind the store while I'm away.*

7 If you are offered something or offered a choice and you say **'I don't mind'**, you are saying politely that you will be happy with any of the things offered. **8** People use the expression **if you don't mind** when they are rejecting an offer or saying that they do not want to do something, especially when they are annoyed. *If you don't mind, we won't talk about it any more.* **9** You use **mind you** to emphasize a piece of information that you are adding, especially when the new information explains what you have said or contrasts with it. Some people use **mind** in a similar way. *They pay full rates. Mind you, they can afford it.* **10** If you tell someone, especially a child, to **mind** their **language**, **mind** their **tongue**, or **mind** their **manners**, you are telling them to speak or behave properly and politely. **11** You say **never mind** to someone to try and make them feel better when they have failed to do something or done something wrong, or when something unpleasant has happened to them. **12** You use **never mind** to tell someone that they need not do something or worry about something, because it is not important or because you will do it yourself. *'I'll go up in one second, I promise.'—'Never mind,' I said with a sigh. 'I'll do it.'... 'Was his name David?'—'No I don't think it was, but never mind, go on.'.* **13** You use **never mind** after a statement, often a negative one, to indicate that the statement is even more true of the person, thing, or situation that you are going to mention next. *I'm not going to believe it myself, never mind convince anyone else... Many of the potholes are a danger even to motor vehicles, never mind cyclists.* **14** If you say that you **wouldn't mind** something, you mean that you would quite like it. *I wouldn't mind a coffee... Anne wouldn't mind going to Italy or France to live.* **15 •** to **mind** your **own business**: see **business**.

VB: with brd- neg
V wh

VERB
PRAGMATICS
V n

VB: only imper
PRAGMATICS
V that

VERB
V n

CONVENTION
PRAGMATICS

PHRASE
PRAGMATICS

PHRASE
PRAGMATICS

PHRASE
PRAGMATICS

CONVENTION
PRAGMATICS

PHRASE
PRAGMATICS

PHR-CONJ
PRAGMATICS

PHRASE

¹mind-blowing; also spelled **mind blowing**. If you describe something as **mind-blowing**, you mean that it is extremely impressive or surprising. *...a mind-blowing array of treatments.*

ADJ-GRADED
INFORMAL

¹mind-boggling; also spelled **mind boggling**. If you say that something is **mind-boggling**, you mean that it is so enormous, complicated, or extreme that it is very hard to imagine. *The amount of paperwork involved is mind-boggling.*

ADJ-GRADED
INFORMAL

mind·ed /ˈmaɪndɪd/. If someone is **minded** to do something, they want or intend to do it. *The Home Office said at that time that it was minded to reject his application for political asylum.*

ADJ:
v-link ADJ,
ADJ to-inf,
so ADJ
FORMAL

-minded /-ˈmaɪndɪd/. **1** **-minded** combines with adverbs to form adjectives that indicate that someone is interested in a particular subject or is able to think in a particular way. *I am not an academically-minded person... He was not mechanically-minded.* **2** **-minded** combines with nouns to form adjectives that indicate that someone has a particular aim, priority, or interest. *We weren't career-minded like girls are today.* **3** See also **mind**.

COMB

COMB

mind·er /ˈmaɪndə/ **minders. 1** A **minder** is a person whose job is to protect someone such as a celebrity or businessman. **2** A **minder** is the same as a **childminder**.

◆◇◇◇
N-COUNT

N-COUNT
BRITISH

mind·ful /ˈmaɪndfʊl/. If you are **mindful** of something, you think about it and consider it when taking action. *We must be mindful of the consequences of selfishness.*

◆◇◇◇
ADJ-GRADED:
v-link ADJ
FORMAL

mind·less /ˈmaɪndləs/. **1** If you describe a destructive action as **mindless**, you mean it is not at all sensible and is done for no good reason. *...a plot that mixes blackmail, extortion and mindless violence.* **2** If you describe a person or group as **mindless**, you mean that they are stupid or do not think about what they are doing. *She wasn't at all the mindless little wife so many people perceived her to be.* **•** **mind·less·ly** *I was annoyed with myself for having so quickly and mindlessly lost thirty dollars.* **3** If you describe an activity as **mindless**, you mean that it is so dull that people do it or take part in it without thinking. *...the mindless repetitiveness of some tasks.* **•** **mindlessly** *I spent many hours in it mindlessly banging a tennis ball against the wall.*

◆◇◇◇
ADJ
BRITISH

ADJ-GRADED

ADV:
ADV with v

ADJ-GRADED

ADV:
ADV with v

'mind-numbing. If you describe an event or experience as **mind-numbing**, you mean that it is so bad, boring, or great in extent that you are unable to think about it clearly. *It was another day of mind-numbing tedium.*

ADJ-GRADED

mind·set /ˈmaɪndset/ **mindsets.** If you refer to someone's **mindset**, you mean their general attitudes and the way they typically think about things. *The greatest challenge for the Americans is understanding the mindset of Eastern Europeans.*

N-COUNT

mine 1 pronoun use

mine /maɪn/. **Mine** is the first person singular possessive pronoun. A speaker or writer uses **mine** to indicate that something belongs or relates to himself or herself. *Her right hand is inches from mine... That wasn't his fault, it was mine.*

◆◆◆◆
PRON-POSS

mine 2 noun and verb uses

mine /maɪn/ **mines, mining, mined. 1** A **mine** is a place where deep holes and tunnels are dug under the ground in order to obtain a mineral such as coal, diamonds, or gold. *...coal mines.* **2** When a mineral such as coal, diamonds, or gold **is mined**, it is obtained from the ground by digging deep holes and tunnels. *The pit is being shut down because it no longer has enough coal that can be mined economically.* **•** **min·ing** *...traditional industries such as coal mining and steel making.* **3** A **mine** is a bomb which is hidden in the ground or in water and which explodes when people or things touch it. **4** If an area of land or water **is mined**, mines are placed there which will explode when people or things touch them. *The approaches to the garrison have been heavily mined.* **5** If you say that someone is a **mine of information**, you mean that they know a great deal about something.

◆◆◇◇
N-COUNT

VB: usu
passive
be V-ed

N-UNCOUNT

N-COUNT

VERB
be V-ed
Also V n

PHRASE

mine·field /ˈmaɪnfiːld/ **minefields. 1** A **minefield** is an area of land or water where explosive mines have been hidden. **2** If you describe a situation as a **minefield**, you are emphasizing that there are a lot of hidden dangers or problems, and things could easily go wrong. *The whole subject is a political minefield.*

◆◇◇◇
N-COUNT

N-COUNT
PRAGMATICS

min·er /ˈmaɪnə/ **miners.** A **miner** is a person who works underground in mines in order to obtain minerals such as coal, diamonds, or gold.

◆◆◇◇
N-COUNT

min·er·al /ˈmɪnərəl/ **minerals.** A **mineral** is a substance such as tin, salt, uranium, or sulphur that is formed naturally in rocks and in the earth. Minerals are also found in small quantities in food and drink.

◆◆◇◇
N-COUNT

'mineral water, mineral waters. Mineral water is water that comes out of the ground naturally and is considered healthy to drink.

◆◇◇◇
N-VAR

min·estro·ne /ˌmɪnɪˈstrəʊni/. Minestrone soup is a type of soup made from meat stock that contains small pieces of vegetable and pasta.

N-UNCOUNT

mine·sweeper /ˈmaɪnswiːpə/ **minesweepers;** also spelled **mine sweeper**. A **minesweeper** is a ship that is used to clear away explosive mines in the sea.

N-COUNT

min·gle /ˈmɪŋgəl/ **mingles, mingling, mingled. 1** If things such as sounds, smells, or feelings **mingle**, they become mixed together but are usually still recognizable. *Foreboding mingled with his excite-*

◆◇◇◇
V-RECIP:
be V-ed
pl-n V
V with n

ment. **2** At a party, if you **mingle** with other people, you move around and chat to them. *Guests ate and mingled... Alison mingled for a while and then went to where Douglas stood with John.*

V-RECIP: V with pl-n pl-n V (non-recip)

mini /'mɪni/ **minis.** A **mini** is the same as a **mini-skirt.** *...a mini that has shocking-apricot flowers.*

N-COUNT

mini- /'mɪni-/. **Mini-** is used before nouns to form nouns which refer to something which is a smaller version of something else. *Provisions may be purchased from the mini-market... We were playing mini-golf.*

PREFIX

minia·ture /'mɪnɪtʃə, AM 'mɪniətʃʊr/ **miniatures.** **1 Miniature** is used to describe something which is very small, especially a smaller version of something which is normally much bigger. *Rosehill Farm has been selling miniature roses since 1979.* **2** If you describe one thing as another thing **in miniature**, you mean that it is much smaller in size or scale than the other thing, but is otherwise exactly the same. *Ecuador provides a perfect introduction to South America; it's a continent in miniature.* **3** A **miniature** is a very small detailed painting, often of a person. **4** A **miniature** is a very small bottle of alcoholic drink, usually containing enough for one or two servings.

◆◆◇◇◇ ADJ: ADJ n

PHRASE

N-COUNT

N-COUNT

minia·tur·ize /'mɪnɪtʃəraɪz/ **miniaturizes, miniaturizing, miniaturized;** also spelled **miniaturise** in British English. If you **miniaturize** something such as a machine, you produce a very small version of it. *...the problems of further miniaturizing the available technologies.* **✦ minia·turi·za·tion** /,mɪnɪtʃəraɪ'zeɪʃən/ *...increasing miniaturization in the computer industry.*

VERB V n

N-UNCOUNT

mini·bar /'mɪnibɑː/ **minibars.** In a hotel room, a **minibar** is a small fridge containing a selection of alcoholic drinks.

N-COUNT

mini·bus /'mɪnibʌs/ **minibuses;** also spelled **mini-bus.** A **minibus** is a large van which has seats in the back for passengers to sit on, and windows along its sides. *He was then taken by minibus to the military base.*

◆◇◇◇◇ N-COUNT: also by N

mini·cab /'mɪnikæb/ **minicabs;** also spelled **minicab.** A **minicab** is a taxi which you have to arrange to pick you up by telephone. *If you want a cheap ride, take a minicab.*

N-COUNT BRITISH

mini·mal /'mɪnɪməl/. Something that is **minimal** is very small in quantity, value, or degree. *The co-operation between the two is minimal.* **✦ mini·mal·ly** *He was paid, but only minimally.*

◆◆◇◇◇ ADJ

ADV

mini·mal·ist /'mɪnɪməlɪst/ **minimalists.** **Minimalist** ideas, artists, or designers are influenced by a style in which a small number of very simple things are used to create a particular effect. *The two designers settled upon a minimalist approach.* ▶ Also a noun. *...the minimalists in the 1970s.* **✦ mini·mal·ism** *She replaced austere minimalism with cosy warmth and colour.*

◆◇◇◇◇ ADJ-GRADED

N-COUNT N-UNCOUNT

mini·mize /'mɪnɪmaɪz/ **minimizes, minimizing, minimized;** also spelled **minimise** in British English. **1** If you **minimize** a risk, problem, or unpleasant situation, you reduce it to the lowest possible level. *Concerned people want to minimize the risk of developing cancer.* **2** If you **minimize** something, you make it seem smaller or less significant than it really is. *At his trial, he had tried to minimize his behavior.*

◆◆◇◇◇

VERB V n

VERB V n

mini·mum /'mɪnɪməm/. **1** You use **minimum** to describe an amount which is the smallest that is possible, allowed, or required. *...five feet nine, the minimum height for a policeman.* ▶ Also a noun. *This will take a minimum of one hour.* **2** You use **minimum** to state how small an amount is. *Neil and Chris try to spend the minimum amount of time on the garden.* ▶ Also a noun. *He goes about his job with a minimum of fuss.* **3** If you say that something is a particular amount **minimum**, you mean that this is the smallest amount it should be or could possibly be. *You're talking over a thousand pounds minimum for one course.* **4** You use **at a minimum**, or **at the minimum**, when you want to

◆◆◇◇◇ ADJ: ADJ n

N-SING

ADJ: ADJ n

N-SING

ADV: amount ADV

PHRASE

indicate that something is the very least which could or should happen. *This would take three months at a minimum.* **5** If you say that someone keeps something **to a minimum**, or **to the minimum**, you mean that they keep the amount of it as small as possible.

PHRASE

min·ing /'maɪnɪŋ/. See **mine.**

◆◆◇◇◇

min·ion /'mɪnjən/ **minions.** Someone's **minions** are the people who carry out unimportant or unrewarding jobs for them. *She delegated the job to one of her minions.*

N-COUNT

'mini-skirt, mini-skirts; also spelled **miniskirt.** A **mini-skirt** is a very short skirt.

N-COUNT

min·is·ter /'mɪnɪstə/ **ministers, ministering, ministered.** **1** A **minister** is a person who is in charge of a particular government department. *...minister of culture... The new Defence Minister.* **✦ min·is·terial** /,mɪnɪ'stɪəriəl/ *...the prime minister's initial ministerial appointments.* **2** A **minister** is a person who officially represents their government in a foreign country and has a lower rank than an ambassador. *He concluded a deal with the Danish minister.* **3** A **minister** is a member of the clergy, especially in Protestant churches. *...a Baptist minister.* **4** If you **minister to** people or **to** their needs, you serve them or help them, for example by making sure that they have everything they need or want. *For 44 years he had ministered to the poor.*

◆◆◆◆◆ N-COUNT

ADJ: ADJ n

N-COUNT

N-COUNT

VERB V to n FORMAL

mini·stra·tions /,mɪnɪ'streɪʃənz/. A person's **ministrations** are the things they do to help or care for someone, especially someone who is weak or ill. *...my increasing resistance to the ministrations of my friends.*

N-PLURAL LITERARY

min·is·try /'mɪnɪstri/ **ministries.** **1** A **ministry** is a government department that deals with a particular area of administration within a country. *...the Ministry of Justice. ...the Agriculture Ministry.* **2** The **ministry** of a religious person is the work that they do that is based on or inspired by their religious beliefs. *His ministry is among the poor.* **3** Members of the clergy belonging to some branches of the Christian church are referred to as **the ministry.** *So what prompted him to enter the ministry?*

◆◆◆◆◇ N-COUNT

N-COUNT

N-COLL-SING: the N

mink /mɪŋk/ **minks.** Mink can also be used as the plural form. **1** A **mink** is a small furry animal with highly valued fur. ▶ **Mink** is the fur of a mink. *...a mink coat.* **2** A **mink** is a coat or other garment made from the fur of a mink.

◆◇◇◇◇ N-COUNT N-UNCOUNT N-COUNT

min·now /'mɪnəʊ/ **minnows.** A **minnow** is a very small freshwater fish.

N-COUNT

mi·nor /'maɪnə/ **minors.** **1** You use **minor** when you want to describe something that is less important, serious, or significant than other things in a group or situation. *...a number of minor roles in films... The problem is minor, and should be quickly overcome.* **2** In European music, a **minor** scale is one in which the third note is one and a half tones higher than the first. *...the unfinished sonata movement in F minor.* **3** A **minor** is a person who is still legally a child.

◆◆◆◇◇ ADJ-GRADED

ADJ: n ADJ, ADJ n

N-COUNT

mi·nor·ity /mɪ'nɒrɪti, AM -'nɔːr-/ **minorities.** **1** If you talk about a **minority** of people or things in a larger group, you are referring to a number of them that forms less than half of the larger group, usually much less than half. *In a tiny minority of cases mistakes have been made. ...minority shareholders.* ● If people are **in a minority** or **in the minority**, they belong to a group of people or things that form less than half of a larger group. **2** A **minority** is a group of people of the same race, culture, or religion who live in a place where most of the people around them are of a different race, culture, or religion. *...the region's ethnic minorities.*

◆◆◆◇ N-SING

PHRASE

N-COUNT

min·strel /'mɪnstrəl/ **minstrels.** In medieval times, a **minstrel** was a singer and musician who travelled around and performed for noble families.

◆◇◇◇◇ N-COUNT

mint /mɪnt/ **mints, minting, minted.** **1** Mint is a fresh-tasting herb. **2** A **mint** is a sweet with a peppermint flavour.

◆◆◇◇◇ N-UNCOUNT

N-COUNT

3 The **mint** is the place where the official coins of a country are made. *In 1965 the mint stopped putting silver in dimes.* **4** To **mint** coins or medals means to make them in a mint. ◆ **mint·ing** *...the minting of new gold coins.*   N-COUNT / VERB: V n / N-UNCOUNT

5 If you say that someone makes a **mint**, you mean that they make a very large amount of money.   N-SING / INFORMAL

6 If you say that something is **in mint condition**, you mean that it is in perfect condition.   PHRASE

mint·ed /'mɪntɪd/. If you describe something as **newly minted** or **freshly minted**, you mean that it is very new, and that it has only just been produced or completed.   ADJ

mi·nus /'maɪnəs/ **minuses. 1** You use **minus** to show that one number or quantity is being subtracted from another. *One minus one is zero. ...their full July salary minus the hardship payment.* **2** You use **plus** or **minus** to give the amount by which a particular number may vary. *...a margin of error of plus or minus 5 per cent.*   ◆◆◇◇◇ CONJ / PHRASE

3 Minus before a number or quantity means that the number or quantity is less than zero. *...temperatures of minus 65 degrees.* **4** Teachers use **minus** in grading work in schools and colleges. 'B minus' is not as good as 'B', but is a better grade than 'C'.   ADJ: ADJ amount

5 If someone or something is **minus** something, they do not have that thing. *The film company collapsed, leaving Chris jobless and minus his life savings.*   PREP

6 A **minus** is a disadvantage. *The minuses far outweigh that possible gain.*   N-COUNT / INFORMAL

mi·nus·cule /'mɪnɪskjuːl/. If you describe something as **minuscule**, you mean that it is very small.   ADJ

minute 1 noun and verb uses

min·ute /'mɪnɪt/ **minutes, minuting, minuted. 1** A **minute** is one of the sixty parts that an hour is divided into. People often say **'a minute'** or **'minutes'** when they mean a short length of time. *The pizza will then take about twenty minutes to cook... See you in a minute... Within minutes we realized our mistake.*   ◆◆◆◆◆ N-COUNT

2 People often use expressions such as **wait a minute** or **just a minute** when they want to stop you doing or saying something. *Wait a minute, folks, something is wrong here.* **3** If you say that something will or may happen **at any minute** or **any minute now**, you are emphasizing that it is likely to happen very soon. **4** If you say that you do **not** believe **for a minute** or **for one minute** that something is true, you are emphasizing that you do not believe that it is true. **5** A **last-minute** action is done at the latest time possible. *He will probably wait until the last minute.* **6** You use the expression **the next minute** or expressions such as 'one minute he was there, **the next** he was gone' to emphasize that something happens suddenly, especially when it is very different from what was happening before. *The next minute my father came in.* **7** If you say that something happens **the minute** something else happens, you are emphasizing that it happens immediately after the other thing. *The minute you do this, you'll lose control.* **8** If you say that something must be done **this minute**, you are emphasizing that it must be done immediately. *Sit down this minute.*   CONVENTION / PRAGMATICS / PHRASE / PRAGMATICS / PHRASE / PRAGMATICS / PHRASE / PRAGMATICS / PHRASE / PRAGMATICS

9 The **minutes** of a meeting are the written records of the things that are discussed or decided at it. **10** When someone **minutes** something that is discussed or decided at a meeting, they make a written record of it.   N-PLURAL / VERB: V n

11 See also **up-to-the-minute**.

minute 2 adjective use

min·ute /maɪ'njuːt, AM -'nuːt/ **minutest.** If you say that something is **minute**, you mean that it is very small. *Only a minute amount is needed.* ◆ **mi·nute·ly** *The benefit of an x-ray far outweighs the minutely increased risk of cancer.*   ◆◇◇◇◇ ADJ-GRADED / ADV-GRADED

mi·nute·ly /maɪ'njuːtli, AM -'nuːt-/. You use **minutely** to indicate that something is done in great detail. *The metal is then minutely examined.*   ADV-GRADED: ADV with v

mi·nu·tiae /maɪ'njuːʃiiː, AM mɪ'nuːʃ-/. The **minutiae** of something such as someone's job or life are the very small details of it.   N-PLURAL / FORMAL

mira·cle /'mɪrəkəl/ **miracles. 1** If you say that an event, discovery, or invention is a **miracle**, you mean that it is very surprising and fortunate. *It is a miracle no one was killed.* **2** A **miracle** is a wonderful and surprising event that is believed to be caused by God. *...the miracle of the Virgin Birth.*   ◆◆◇◇◇ N-COUNT / N-COUNT

mi·racu·lous /mɪ'rækjʊləs/. **1** If you describe something as **miraculous**, you mean that it is very surprising and fortunate. *The horse made a miraculous recovery.* ◆ **mi·racu·lous·ly** *Miraculously, the guards escaped death or serious injury.* **2** If someone describes a wonderful event as **miraculous**, they believe the event has been caused by God. *...miraculous healing.* ◆ **miraculously** *He was miraculously healed of a severe fever.*   ◆◇◇◇◇ ADJ-GRADED / ADV-GRADED / ADJ / ADV

mi·rage /'mɪrɑːʒ/ **mirages. 1** A **mirage** is something which you see when it is extremely hot, for example in the desert, and which appears to be quite near but is actually a long way away or does not really exist. **2** If you describe something as a **mirage**, you mean that it is an illusion although it may seem real. *The girl was a mirage, cast up by his troubled mind.*   N-COUNT / N-COUNT

mire /maɪə/. **1** You can refer to an unpleasant or difficult situation as a **mire**. *...a mire of poverty and ignorance.* **2** **Mire** is dirt or mud. *...the muck and mire of sewers and farmyards.*   N-SING / LITERARY / N-UNCOUNT / LITERARY

mir·ror /'mɪrə/ **mirrors, mirroring, mirrored. 1** A **mirror** is an object made of glass in which you can see your reflection. ◆ **mir·rored** *...a mirrored ceiling.* **2** If something **mirrors** something else, it has similar features to it, and therefore seems like a copy or representation of it. *The book inevitably mirrors my own interests and experiences.* **3** If you see something reflected in water, you can say that the water **mirrors** it.   ◆◆◇◇◇ N-COUNT / ADJ / V n / VERB: V n / LITERARY

mirror 'image, mirror images; also spelled **mirror-image.** If something is a **mirror image** of something else, it is exactly the same as it or the same but reversed. *This is almost the mirror image of the situation in Scotland.*   ◆◇◇◇◇ N-COUNT

mirth /mɜːθ/. **Mirth** is amusement which you express by laughing. *That caused considerable mirth amongst pupils.*   N-UNCOUNT / LITERARY

mis- /mɪs-/. **Mis-** is added to some verbs and nouns to form new verbs and nouns which indicate that something is done badly or wrongly. *The local newspaper misreported the story. ...the misuse of official funds.*   PREFIX

mis·ad·ven·ture /ˌmɪsəd'ventʃə/ **misadventures.** A **misadventure** is an unfortunate incident. *...a verdict of death by misadventure.*   N-VAR / FORMAL

mis·an·thrope /'mɪzənθrəʊp/ **misanthropes.** A **misanthrope** is a person who does not like other people. ◆ **mis·an·throp·ic** /ˌmɪzən'θrɒpɪk/ *His father was a misanthropic but successful businessman.*   N-COUNT / FORMAL / ADJ-GRADED

mis·an·thro·py /mɪ'zænθrəpi/. **Misanthropy** is a general dislike of people.   N-UNCOUNT / FORMAL

mis·ap·ply /ˌmɪsə'plaɪ/ **misapplies, misapplying, misapplied.** If something **is misapplied**, it is used for a purpose for which it is not intended or not suitable. *The law had been misapplied.* ◆ **mis·ap·pli·ca·tion** /ˌmɪsæpli'keɪʃən/ **misapplications** *...a common misapplication of the law.*   VB: usu passive be V-ed / N-VAR

mis·ap·pre·hen·sion /ˌmɪsæprɪ'henʃən/ **misapprehensions.** A **misapprehension** is a wrong idea or impression that you have about something. *...the misapprehension that women want hairy, muscular men.*   N-VAR

mis·ap·pro·pri·ate /ˌmɪsə'prəʊprieɪt/ **misappropriates, misappropriating, misappropriated.** If someone **misappropriates** money which does not belong to them, they take it without permission and use it for their own purposes. ◆ **mis·ap·pro·pria·tion** /ˌmɪsəprəʊpri'eɪʃən/ *...charges of misappropriation of bank funds.*   VERB: V n / N-UNCOUNT

mis·be·have /ˌmɪsbɪ'heɪv/ **misbehaves, misbehaving, misbehaved.** If someone, especially a child, **misbehaves**, they behave in a way that is not acceptable to other people.   VERB: V

M

mis·be·hav·iour /ˌmɪsbɪˈheɪvjə/; spelled **misbehavior** in American English. **Misbehaviour** is behaviour that is not acceptable to other people. *...pupil misbehaviour in schools.* N-UNCOUNT FORMAL

mis·cal·cu·late /ˌmɪsˈkælkjʊleɪt/ **miscalculates, miscalculating, miscalculated.** If you **miscalculate**, you make a mistake in judging a situation or in making a calculation. *He has badly miscalculated the mood of the people.* ♦ **mis·cal·cu·la·tion** /ˌmɪskælkjʊˈleɪʃən/ **miscalculations** *The coup failed because of miscalculations by the plotters.* ◆◇◇◇◇ VERB: V V n; N-VAR

mis·carriage of justice, miscarriages of justice. A **miscarriage of justice** is a wrong decision made by a court, as a result of which an innocent person is punished. ◆◇◇◇◇ N-VAR

mis·car·ry /ˌmɪsˈkæri/ **miscarries, miscarrying, miscarried.** If a woman **miscarries**, she gives birth to a foetus before it is properly formed and it dies. *Many women who miscarry eventually have healthy babies.* ♦ **mis·car·riage** /ˌmɪsˈkærɪdʒ/ **miscarriages.** If a woman has a **miscarriage**, she miscarries. VERB V Also V n; N-VAR

mis·cast /ˌmɪsˈkɑːst, -ˈkæst/. If an actor or actress is **miscast**, the role that they have is not suitable for them, so that they appear silly or unconvincing to the audience. ADJ-GRADED

mis·cel·la·neous /ˌmɪsəˈleɪniəs/. A **miscellaneous** group consists of many different kinds of things or people that are difficult to put into a particular category. *....a hoard of miscellaneous junk.* ◆◇◇◇◇ ADJ-GRADED: ADJ n

mis·cel·la·ny /mɪˈseləni, AM ˈmɪsəleɪni/ **miscellanies.** A **miscellany** of things is a collection or group of many different kinds of things. *...glass cases filled with a miscellany of objects.* N-COUNT WRITTEN

mis·chief /ˈmɪstʃɪf/. **1 Mischief** is eagerness to have fun, especially by embarrassing people or by playing harmless tricks. *He was always up to mischief.* **2 Mischief** is behaviour that is intended to cause trouble for people. *...the mischief that young people get up to when they're not employed.* **3 Mischief** is the harm that someone or something does. *Voters have wisely never given him an overall parliamentary majority. There is no knowing what mischief he might have caused if they had.* ◆◇◇◇◇ N-UNCOUNT; N-UNCOUNT; N-UNCOUNT

'mischief-maker, mischief-makers. If you say that someone is a **mischief-maker**, you are criticizing them for saying or doing things which are intended to cause trouble between people. N-COUNT PRAGMATICS

mis·chie·vous /ˈmɪstʃɪvəs/. **1** A **mischievous** person likes to have fun by playing harmless tricks or embarrassing people. ♦ **mis·chie·vous·ly** *Kathryn winked mischievously.* **2** A **mischievous** act or suggestion is intended to cause trouble. *The Foreign Office dismissed the story as mischievous and false.* ♦ **mischievously** *That does not require 'massive' military intervention, as some have mischievously claimed.* ◆◇◇◇◇ ADJ-GRADED; ADV-GRADED; ADJ-GRADED; ADV-GRADED

mis·con·ceived /ˌmɪskənˈsiːvd/. If you describe a plan or method as **misconceived**, you mean it is not the right one for dealing with a particular problem or situation. *The teachers say the tests for 14-year-olds are misconceived.* ADJ-GRADED PRAGMATICS

mis·con·cep·tion /ˌmɪskənˈsepʃən/ **misconceptions.** A **misconception** is an idea that is not correct or which has been misunderstood. *There are many fears and misconceptions about cancer.* ◆◇◇◇◇ N-COUNT

mis·con·duct /ˌmɪsˈkɒndʌkt/. **Misconduct** is bad or unacceptable behaviour, especially by a professional person or someone who is normally respected by people. ◆◇◇◇◇ N-UNCOUNT

mis·con·strue /ˌmɪskənˈstruː/ **misconstrues, misconstruing, misconstrued.** If you **misconstrue** something that has been said or something that happens, you interpret it wrongly. *An outsider might misconstrue the nature of the relationship.* VERB V n FORMAL

mis·cre·ant /ˈmɪskriənt/ **miscreants.** A **miscreant** is someone who has done something illegal or behaved badly. *Local people demanded that the District Magistrate apprehend the miscreants.* N-COUNT LITERARY

mis·deed /ˌmɪsˈdiːd/ **misdeeds.** A **misdeed** is a bad or evil act. N-COUNT FORMAL

mis·de·mean·our /ˌmɪsdɪˈmiːnə/ **misdemeanours;** spelled **misdemeanor** in American English. **1** A **misdemeanour** is an act that some people consider to be wrong or unacceptable. *Emily knew nothing about her husband's misdemeanours.* **2** In countries where the legal system distinguishes between very serious crimes and less serious ones, a **misdemeanour** is a less serious crime. N-COUNT FORMAL; N-COUNT LEGAL

mis·di·rect /ˌmɪsdɪˈrekt, -daɪr-/ **misdirects, misdirecting, misdirected. 1** If resources or efforts **are misdirected**, they are used for or based upon wrong or inappropriate goals. *Many of the aid projects in the developing world have been misdirected.* ♦ **mis·di·rect·ed** *...a misdirected effort to mollify the bishop.* **2** If you **misdirect** someone, you send them in the wrong direction. VB: usu passive be V-ed; ADJ-GRADED; VERB: V n

mi·ser /ˈmaɪzə/ **misers.** If you say that someone is a **miser**, you disapprove of them because they are very mean and hate spending money. N-COUNT PRAGMATICS

mis·er·able /ˈmɪzərəbəl/. **1** If you are **miserable**, you are very unhappy. *She went to bed, miserable and depressed.* ♦ **mis·er·ably** /ˈmɪzərəbli/ *He looked miserably down at his plate.* **2** If you describe a place or situation as **miserable**, you mean that it makes you feel unhappy or depressed. *There was nothing at all in this miserable place to distract him.* **3** If you describe the weather as **miserable**, you mean that it makes you feel depressed, because it is raining or dull. *...a grey, wet, miserable day.* **4** If you describe someone as **miserable**, you mean that you do not like them because they are bad-tempered or unfriendly. *He always was a miserable man.* **5** You can describe a quantity as **miserable** when you think that it is much smaller than it ought to be. *Our speed over the ground was a miserable 2.2 knots.* ♦ **miserably** *...the miserably inadequate supply of books now provided for schools.* **6** A **miserable** failure is very disappointing or humiliating. ♦ **miserably** *Some manage it. Some seem to fail miserably.* ◆◆◇◇◇ ADJ-GRADED; ADV-GRADED; ADJ-GRADED; ADJ-GRADED; ADJ-GRADED: ADJ n; ADJ PRAGMATICS; ADV: ADV adj; ADJ: ADJ n; ADV: ADV with v

mi·ser·ly /ˈmaɪzəli/. **1** If you describe someone as **miserly**, you disapprove of them because they are very mean and hate spending money. **2** If you describe an amount of something as **miserly**, you are critical of it because it is very small. *Being a student today with miserly grants and limited career prospects is difficult.* ADJ-GRADED PRAGMATICS; ADJ-GRADED PRAGMATICS

mis·ery /ˈmɪzəri/ **miseries. 1 Misery** is great unhappiness. *All that money brought nothing but sadness and misery.* **2 Misery** is the way of life and unpleasant living conditions of people who are very poor. *A tiny, educated elite profited from the misery of their two million fellow countrymen.* **3** If someone **makes** your **life a misery**, they behave in an unpleasant way towards you over a period of time and make you very unhappy. **4** If you **put** someone **out of** their **misery**, you tell them something that they are very anxious to know. *Please put me out of my misery. How do you do it?* **5** If you **put** an animal **out of** its **misery**, you kill it because it is ill or injured and cannot be cured or healed. **6** If you say that someone is a **misery**, you are critical of them because they are always complaining. *I'm not such a misery now! I gave up drink a few years back and that has changed things a lot.* ◆◆◇◇◇ N-VAR; N-UNCOUNT; PHRASE; PHRASE INFORMAL; PHRASE; N-COUNT PRAGMATICS BRITISH, INFORMAL

mis·fire /ˌmɪsˈfaɪə/ **misfires, misfiring, misfired. 1** If a plan **misfires**, it goes wrong and does not have the results that you intend it to have. **2** If an engine **misfires**, it fails to ignite when it should. **3** If a gun **misfires**, the bullet is not sent out as it should be when the gun is fired. VERB: V; VERB: V; VERB: V

mis·fit /ˈmɪsfɪt/ **misfits.** A **misfit** is a person who is not easily accepted by other people, often because their behaviour is very different from that of everyone else. ◆◇◇◇◇ N-COUNT

mis·for·tune /ˌmɪsˈfɔːtʃuːn/ **misfortunes.** A misfortune is something unpleasant or unlucky that happens to someone. *She seemed to enjoy the misfortunes of others.* ◆◇◇◇◇ N-VAR

mis·giv·ing /ˌmɪsˈɡɪvɪŋ/ **misgivings.** If you have misgivings about something that is being proposed or done, you feel that it is not quite right, and you are worried that it may have undesirable consequences. *I have misgivings about going anywhere away from home.* ◆◇◇◇◇ N-VAR

mis·guid·ed /ˌmɪsˈɡaɪdɪd/. If you describe an opinion or plan as misguided, you are critical of it because you think it is based on a mistake or misunderstanding. *He is misguided in expecting honesty from her.* ◆◇◇◇◇ ADJ-GRADED PRAGMATICS

mis·han·dle /ˌmɪsˈhændəl/ **mishandles, mishandling, mishandled.** If you say that someone has mishandled something, you are critical of them because you think they have dealt with it badly or inefficiently. *The judge said the police had mishandled the siege.* ♦ **mis·han·dling** *...the Government's mishandling of the economy.* VERB PRAGMATICS V n — N-UNCOUNT

mis·hap /ˈmɪshæp/ **mishaps.** A mishap is an unfortunate but not very serious event that happens to someone. *After a number of mishaps she did manage to get back to Germany.* ◆◇◇◇◇ N-VAR

mis·hear /ˌmɪsˈhɪə/ **mishears, mishearing, misheard.** If you mishear what someone says, you hear it incorrectly, so that you think that they said something different. *You misheard me, Frank.* VERB V n Also V

mish·mash /ˈmɪʃmæʃ/; also spelled **mish-mash.** If you say that something is a mishmash, you are criticizing it because it is a confused mixture of different types of things. *...a bizarre mishmash of colours and patterns.* N-SING PRAGMATICS

mis·in·form /ˌmɪsɪnˈfɔːm/ **misinforms, misinforming, misinformed.** If you are misinformed, you are told something that is wrong or inaccurate. *...accusing the media of misinforming the people.* VERB: be V-ed V n

mis·in·for·ma·tion /ˌmɪsɪnfəˈmeɪʃən/. Misinformation is wrong information which is given to someone, often in a deliberate attempt to make them believe something which is not true. N-UNCOUNT

mis·in·ter·pret /ˌmɪsɪnˈtɜːprɪt/ **misinterprets, misinterpreting, misinterpreted.** If you misinterpret something, you understand it wrongly. *He was totally amazed that he'd misinterpreted the situation so completely.* ♦ **mis·in·ter·pre·ta·tion** /ˌmɪsɪnˌtɜːprɪˈteɪʃən/ **misinterpretations** *The message left no room for misinterpretation.* ◆◇◇◇◇ VERB V n — N-VAR

mis·judge /ˌmɪsˈdʒʌdʒ/ **misjudges, misjudging, misjudged.** If you say that someone has misjudged a person or situation, you mean that they have formed an incorrect idea or opinion about them, and often that they have made a wrong decision as a result of this. *Perhaps I had misjudged him, and he was not so predictable after all.* ◆◇◇◇◇ VERB V n

mis·judge·ment /ˌmɪsˈdʒʌdʒmənt/ **misjudgements**; also spelled **misjudgment.** A misjudgement is an incorrect idea or opinion that is formed about someone or something, especially when a wrong decision is made as a result of this. N-VAR

mis·lay /ˌmɪsˈleɪ/ **mislays, mislaying, mislaid.** If you mislay something, you put it somewhere and then forget where you have put it. VERB: V n

mis·lead /ˌmɪsˈliːd/ **misleads, misleading, misled.** If you say that someone has misled you, you mean that they have made you believe something which is not true, either by telling you a lie or by giving you a wrong idea or impression. ◆◇◇◇◇ VERB: V n

mis·lead·ing /ˌmɪsˈliːdɪŋ/. If you describe something as misleading, you mean that it gives you a wrong idea or impression. *It would be misleading to say that we were friends.* ♦ **mis·lead·ing·ly** *The data had been presented misleadingly.* ◆◆◇◇◇ ADJ-GRADED — ADV-GRADED

mis·led /ˌmɪsˈled/. Misled is the past tense and past participle of mislead.

mis·man·age /ˌmɪsˈmænɪdʒ/ **mismanages, mismanaging, mismanaged.** To mismanage something means to manage it badly. *75% of voters think* VERB V n

the President has mismanaged the economy. ♦ **mis·man·age·ment** /ˌmɪsˈmænɪdʒmənt/ *His gross mismanagement left the company desperately in need of restructuring.* N-UNCOUNT

mis·match, mismatches, mismatching, mismatched. The noun is pronounced /ˈmɪsmætʃ/. The verb is pronounced /mɪsˈmætʃ/. **1** If there is a mismatch between two or more things or people, they do not go together well or are not suitable for each other. *...a mismatch between the skills offered by people and the skills needed by industry.* **2** To mismatch things or people means to put them together although they do not go together well or are not suitable for each other. *She was deliberately mismatching articles of clothing.* ♦ **mis·matched** *The two opponents are mismatched.* N-COUNT ♦ VERB V pl-n — ADJ-GRADED

mis·named /ˌmɪsˈneɪmd/. If you say that something or someone is misnamed, you mean that they have a name that describes them badly or incorrectly. *...a high school teacher who was misnamed Mr. Witty.* V-PASSIVE: be V-ed be V-ed n

mis·no·mer /ˌmɪsˈnəʊmə/ **misnomers.** If you say that something is a misnomer, you mean that it is a word or name that describes something wrongly or inaccurately. *Herbal 'tea' is something of a misnomer because these drinks contain no tea at all.* N-COUNT

mi·sogy·nist /mɪˈsɒdʒɪnɪst, maɪs-/ **misogynists.** A misogynist is a man who hates women. ♦ **mi·sogy·ny** /mɪˈsɒdʒɪni/. Misogyny is a strong and irrational dislike of women. N-COUNT — N-UNCOUNT

mis·place /ˌmɪsˈpleɪs/ **misplaces, misplacing, misplaced.** If you misplace something, you lose it, usually only temporarily. VERB: V n

mis·placed /ˌmɪsˈpleɪst/. If you describe a feeling or action as misplaced, you are critical of it because you think it is inappropriate, or directed towards the wrong thing or person. *I think your concern is misplaced. Ackroyd is no threat to anyone.* ◆◇◇◇◇ ADJ-GRADED PRAGMATICS

mis·print /ˈmɪsprɪnt/ **misprints.** A misprint is a mistake in the way something is printed, for example a spelling mistake. N-COUNT

mis·pro·nounce /ˌmɪsprəˈnaʊns/ **mispronounces, mispronouncing, mispronounced.** If you mispronounce a word, you pronounce it wrongly. *He repeatedly mispronounced words and slurred his speech.* VERB V n

mis·quote /ˌmɪsˈkwəʊt/ **misquotes, misquoting, misquoted.** If someone is misquoted, something that they have said or written is repeated inaccurately. *...a psychoanalyst who says a journalist misquoted him in a series of magazine articles.* VERB: be V-ed V n

mis·read /ˌmɪsˈriːd/ **misreads, misreading.** The form misread is used in the present tense, and is the past tense and past participle, when it is pronounced /ˌmɪsˈred/. **1** If you misread a situation or someone's behaviour, you do not understand it properly. *The government largely misread the mood of the electorate.* ♦ **mis·read·ing, misreadings** *...a misreading of opinion in France.* **2** If you misread something that has been written or printed, you look at it and think that it says something that it does not say. *His chauffeur misread his route and took a wrong turning.* VERB V n — N-COUNT VERB V n

mis·rep·re·sent /ˌmɪsreprɪˈzent/ **misrepresents, misrepresenting, misrepresented.** If someone misrepresents a person or situation, they give a wrong or inaccurate account of what the person or situation is like. *The press had misrepresented him as arrogant and bullying.* ♦ **mis·rep·re·sen·ta·tion** /ˌmɪsˌreprɪzenˈteɪʃən/ **misrepresentations** *The programme's researchers are guilty of bias and misrepresentation.* ◆◇◇◇◇ VERB V n V n as adj Also V n as n — N-VAR

mis·rule /ˌmɪsˈruːl/. If you refer to someone's governing of a country as misrule, you are critical of them for governing their country in an unfair or inefficient way. N-UNCOUNT PRAGMATICS

miss 1 used as a title or a form of address

Miss, /mɪs/ **Misses.** You use Miss in front of the name of a girl or unmarried woman when you are speaking to her or referring to her. *The club was run by Miss Ivy Streeter.* ◆◆◆◇◇ N-TITLE PRAGMATICS

M

miss 2 verb and noun uses

miss /mɪs/ **misses, missing, missed. 1** If you ◆◆◆◇
are throwing, kicking, or shooting something, and VERB
you **miss**, you fail to hit something or reach your V n
target. *When I'd missed a few times, he suggested I
rest the rifle on a rock to steady it... She hurled the
ashtray across the room, narrowly missing my head.*
▶ Also a noun. *Striker Alan Smith was guilty of two* N-COUNT
glaring misses. **2** If you **miss** something, you fail to VERB
notice it. *From this vantage point he watched, his* V n
*searching eye never missing a detail... It's the first
thing you see as you come round the corner. You
can't miss it.* **3** If you **miss** the point or **miss** the VERB: V n
joke, you fail to understand or appreciate it. **4** If you VERB: V n
miss a chance or opportunity, you fail to take advantage of it. *It was too good an opportunity to miss.*
5 If you **miss** someone or something, you feel sad be- VERB
cause the person is no longer with you, or because V n/-ing
you no longer have the thing. *Your mama and I are
gonna miss you at Christmas... He missed having good
friends.*
6 If you **miss** something such as a plane or train, you VERB
arrive too late to catch it. *He missed the last bus home.* V n
7 If you **miss** an event or activity, you do not go to it or VERB
take part in it, because you are unable to or have for- V n
gotten to, or because you do not want to. *Makku and I
had to miss our lesson... 'Are you coming to the
show?'—'I wouldn't miss it for the world.'* **8** If you give PHRASE
something a **miss**, you decide not to do it or go to it. INFORMAL
9 See also **missing**; **hit and miss, near miss.** ● to **miss**
the boat: see **boat.** ● to **not miss a trick:** see **trick.**

miss out. 1 If you **miss out** on something that would PHRASAL VB
be beneficial or interesting to you, you are not in- V P on n
volved in it or do not take part in it. *We're missing out
on a tremendous opportunity.* **2** If you **miss out** some- V P noun
thing or someone, you do not include them in some- V n P
thing. *What about Sally? You've missed her out.* BRITISH

mis·shap·en /ˌmɪsˈʃeɪpən/. You can describe ADJ-GRADED
something as **misshapen** if it does not have a normal or natural shape.

mis·sile /ˈmɪsaɪl, AM -səl/ **missiles. 1** A **missile** is ◆◆◆◇◇
a tube-shaped weapon that moves long distances N-COUNT
through the air and explodes when it reaches its target. **2** Anything that is thrown as a weapon can be N-COUNT
called a **missile**. *The football supporters began* FORMAL
throwing missiles. **3** See also **cruise missile, guided
missile**.

miss·ing /ˈmɪsɪŋ/. **1** If something is **missing**, it is ◆◆◆◇
not in its usual place, and you cannot find it. *The* ADJ
playing cards had gone missing. **2** If a part of some- ADJ
thing is **missing**, it has been removed or has come
off. *Three buttons were missing from his shirt.* **3** If ADJ
you say that something is **missing**, you mean that it
has not been included, and you think that it should
have been. *She had given me an incomplete list. One
name was missing from it.* **4** Someone who is **miss-** ADJ
ing cannot be found, and it is not known whether
they are alive or dead. *Both pilots are listed as missing in action... She's tracked down over two hundred
missing persons, in many cases after the police have
given up.*

ˌmissing ˈlink, **missing links.** The **missing link** N-COUNT
in a situation is the thing, person, or idea you need
to know about in order to understand how the
situation has developed. *The discovery provides a
missing link in the evolution of the universe.*

mis·sion /ˈmɪʃən/ **missions. 1** A **mission** is an ◆◆◆◇
important task that people are given to do, especial- N-COUNT
ly one that involves travelling to another country.
*He has been on a mission to help end Lebanon's po-
litical crisis.* **2** A **mission** is a group of people, such N-COUNT
as diplomats or clergymen, who have been sent to a
foreign country to carry out their particular duties.
3 A **mission** is a special journey made by a military N-COUNT
aeroplane or spacecraft. *...a bomber that crashed
during a training mission.* **4** If you say that you N-SING
have a **mission**, you mean that you have a strong
commitment and sense of duty to do or achieve
something. *He viewed his mission in life as protecting the weak from the evil.*

5 A **mission** is a building or group of buildings in N-COUNT
which missionary work is carried out.

mis·sion·ary /ˈmɪʃənri, -neri/ **missionaries. 1** A ◆◇◇◇◇
missionary is a Christian who has been sent to a N-COUNT
foreign country to teach people about Christianity.
2 If you refer to someone's enthusiasm for an activ- ADJ: ADJ n
ity or belief as **missionary** zeal, you are emphasiz- PRAGMATICS
ing that they are very enthusiastic about it.

mis·sive /ˈmɪsɪv/ **missives.** A **missive** is a letter or N-COUNT
other message that someone sends. LITERARY

mis·spell /ˌmɪsˈspel/ **misspells, misspelling,** VERB: V n
misspelled or **misspelt**. If someone **misspells** a
word, they spell it wrongly. ♦ **mis·spell·ing, mis-** N-COUNT
spellings *...a misspelling of the writer's name.*

mis·spend /ˌmɪsˈspend/ **misspent.** If you say that VERB:
time or money **has been misspent**, you disapprove be V-ed
of the way in which it has been spent. *Ruby recalled* PRAGMATICS
getting stoned during her misspent youth. V-ed

mis·sus /ˈmɪsɪz/. Some people refer to a man's wife N-SING
as his **missus** or the **missus**. INFORMAL

mist /mɪst/ **mists, misting, misted. 1** Mist con- ◆◆◇◇
sists of a large number of tiny drops of water in the N-VAR
air, which make it difficult to see very far. *A bluish
mist hung in the air.* **2** If a piece of glass **mists**, it V-ERG: V
becomes covered with tiny drops of water, so that V n
you cannot see through it easily. *The temperature in
the car was misting the window.* ▶ **Mist over** and PHRASAL VB
mist up mean the same as **mist**. *The front wind-* ERG
shield was misting over. V P

mis·take /mɪˈsteɪk/ **mistakes, mistaking, mis-** ◆◆◆◇
took, mistaken. 1 If you make a **mistake**, you do N-COUNT:
something wrong, for example because you do not also by N
know what is right or because you are not thinking
clearly. *...spelling mistakes... The official who ignored the warning might have made a mistake... He
has been arrested by mistake.* **2** If you **mistake** one VERB
person or thing **for** another, you wrongly think that V n for n
they are the other person or thing. *I mistook you for
Carlos.* **3** You can say **there is no mistaking** some- PHRASE
thing when you are emphasizing that you cannot PRAGMATICS
fail to recognize or understand it. *There was no mistaking Magda's sincerity.*

mis·tak·en /mɪˈsteɪkən/. **1** If you are **mistaken**, or ◆◆◇◇
you have a **mistaken** belief, you are wrong about ADJ-GRADED
something. *You couldn't be more mistaken, Alex...
The dead men could have been the victims of mistaken identity.* ♦ **mis·tak·en·ly** *They mistakenly be-* ADV:
lieved the standard licenses they held were sufficient. ADV with v
2 You use expressions such as **if I'm not mistaken** PHRASE
and **unless I'm very much mistaken** as a polite way PRAGMATICS
of emphasizing a statement, especially when you
are confident that it is correct. *I think he wanted to
marry her, if I am not mistaken.*

mis·ter /ˈmɪstə/. Men are sometimes addressed as ◆◇◇◇
mister, especially by children, or when the person N-VOC
talking to them does not know their name. *Look,* PRAGMATICS
Mister, we know our job, so don't try to tell us what INFORMAL
to do.

mis·time /ˌmɪsˈtaɪm/ **mistimes, mistiming, mis-** VERB: V n
timed. If you **mistime** something, you do it at the V-ed
wrong time, so that it is not successful. *...a certain
mistimed comment.*

mis·tle·toe /ˈmɪsəltəʊ/. **Mistletoe** is a plant with N-UNCOUNT
white berries that grows on the branches of some
trees. It is used in Britain as a Christmas decoration.

mis·took /mɪˈstʊk/. **Mistook** is the past tense and
past participle of **mistake**.

mis·treat /ˌmɪsˈtriːt/ **mistreats, mistreating,** VERB: V n
mistreated. If someone **mistreats** a person or animal, they treat them cruelly or make them suffer.
♦ **mis·treat·ment** /ˌmɪsˈtriːtmənt/ *...issues like po-* N-UNCOUNT
lice brutality and mistreatment of people in prisons.

mis·tress /ˈmɪstrəs/ **mistresses. 1** If a married ◆◆◇◇
man has a **mistress**, he is having a sexual relation- N-COUNT
ship with a woman who is not his wife.
2 A **mistress** is a female teacher. *My history mistress* N-COUNT
was extremely helpful. She was a Cambridge graduate. DATED
3 A servant's **mistress** is the woman that he or she N-COUNT
works for. *The servant told me his mistress was gone* DATED

abroad. **4** A dog's **mistress** is the woman or girl who owns it.   N-COUNT

5 If you say that a woman is a **mistress of** a particular activity, you mean that she is very skilled at it. *She is a mistress of disguise.*   N-COUNT: N of n

mis·tri·al /ˈmɪstraɪəl, AM -ˈtraɪ-/ **mistrials. 1** A **mistrial** is a legal trial which is declared invalid, because one side has behaved improperly or because there has been a legal error. The trial usually has to be conducted again. **2** A **mistrial** is a legal trial which ends without a verdict, for example because the jury cannot agree on one. *The judge said he would declare a mistrial if the jury did not reach its verdict today.*   N-COUNT BRITISH / N-COUNT AMERICAN

mis·trust /ˌmɪsˈtrʌst/ **mistrusts, mistrusting, mistrusted. 1** Mistrust is the feeling that you have towards someone who you do not trust. *There was mutual mistrust between the two men.* **2** If you **mistrust** someone or something, you do not trust them.   ◆◇◇◇◇ N-UNCOUNT / VERB: V n

mis·trust·ful /ˌmɪsˈtrʌstfʊl/. If you are **mistrustful** of someone, you do not trust them.   ADJ-GRADED

misty /ˈmɪsti/. On a **misty** day, there is a lot of mist in the air. *It's a bit misty this morning.*   ◆◇◇◇◇ ADJ-GRADED

'misty-eyed. If you say that something makes you **misty-eyed**, you mean that it makes you feel very sentimental or nostalgic.   ADJ-GRADED

mis·under·stand /ˌmɪsʌndəˈstænd/ **misunderstands, misunderstanding, misunderstood. 1** If you **misunderstand** something or someone, you do not understand them properly. *She had misunderstood the word 'psychosomatic'... They have simply misunderstood what rock and roll is.* ◆ **mis·under·stand·ing, misunderstandings** *Tell your midwife what you want so she can make a note of it and avoid misunderstandings.* **2** See also **misunderstanding, misunderstood**.   ◆◆◇◇◇ VERB: V n / V wh / N-VAR

mis·under·stand·ing /ˌmɪsʌndəˈstændɪŋ/ **misunderstandings.** You can refer to a disagreement or slight quarrel as a **misunderstanding**. *...a little misunderstanding with the police.* ● See also **misunderstand**.   ◆◇◇◇◇ N-COUNT FORMAL

mis·under·stood /ˌmɪsʌndəˈstʊd/. **1** Misunderstood is the past tense and past participle of **misunderstand**. **2** If you describe someone as **misunderstood**, you mean that people have wrong ideas about them, and do not recognize their qualities or achievements. *...a misunderstood genius.*   ◆◇◇◇◇ ADJ-GRADED

mis·use, misuses, misusing, misused. The noun is pronounced /ˌmɪsˈjuːs/. The verb is pronounced /ˌmɪsˈjuːz/. If someone **misuses** something, they use it incorrectly, carelessly, or dishonestly. *...reports accusing the party boss of misusing his position to buy a Mercedes car.* ▶ Also a noun. *...the misuse of power and privilege. ...illness associated with drug misuse.*   ◆◇◇◇◇ VERB: V n / N-VAR

mite /maɪt/ **mites. 1** A **mite** means to a small extent or degree. It is sometimes used to make a statement less extreme. *I can't help feeling just a mite uneasy about it.* **2** Mites are very tiny creatures that live, for example, on plants or in animals' fur.   ◆◇◇◇◇ PHRASE / N-COUNT

miti·gate /ˈmɪtɪɡeɪt/ **mitigates, mitigating, mitigated.** To **mitigate** something means to make it less unpleasant, serious, or painful. *...ways of mitigating the effects of an explosion.* ◆ **miti·ga·tion** *...the mitigation or cure of a physical or mental condition.*   ◆◇◇◇◇ VERB: V n FORMAL / N-UNCOUNT

miti·gat·ing /ˈmɪtɪɡeɪtɪŋ/. **Mitigating** circumstances or factors make a bad action, especially a crime, easier to understand and excuse, and may result in the person responsible being punished less severely. *The judge found that in her case there were mitigating circumstances.*   ADJ: ADJ n FORMAL

miti·ga·tion /ˌmɪtɪˈɡeɪʃən/. If someone, such as a judge, is told something **in mitigation**, they are told something that makes a crime or fault easier to understand and excuse. *Kieran Coonan QC told the judge in mitigation that the offences had been at the lower end of the scale.* ● See also **mitigate**.   PHRASE FORMAL

mitt /mɪt/ **mitts. 1** You can refer to a person's hands as their **mitts**. *Joe also wants to get his mitts*   N-COUNT INFORMAL

on the lamp. **2** A baseball **mitt** is a large padded glove worn by baseball players.   N-COUNT

mit·ten /ˈmɪtən/ **mittens.** Mittens are gloves which have one section that covers your thumb and another section that covers your four fingers together.   N-COUNT

mix /mɪks/ **mixes, mixing, mixed. 1** If two substances **mix** or if you **mix** one substance with another, you stir or shake them together, or combine them in some other way, so that they become a single substance. *Oil and water don't mix... It mixes easily with cold or hot water... Mix the cinnamon with the rest of the sugar... Mix the ingredients together slowly.* **2** If you **mix** something, you prepare it by mixing two or more things together. *He had spent several hours mixing cement... Are you sure I can't mix you a drink?* **3** A **mix** is a powder containing all the ingredients you need in order to make something such as a cake or a sauce. When you want to use it, you add liquid. *For speed we used packets of pizza dough mix.*   ◆◆◆◇ V-RECIP-ERG pl-n V / V with n / V n with n / V pl-n together / VERB: V n / V n n / N-VAR

4 A **mix** of different things or people is two or more of them together. *The story is a magical mix of fantasy and reality... We get a very representative mix of people.* **5** If you say that two things or activities do not **mix** or that you cannot **mix** one thing or activity with another, you mean that it is not a good idea to have them or do them together, because the result would be unpleasant or harmful. *Politics and sport don't mix... Ted managed to mix business with pleasure.* **6** If you **mix** with other people, you meet them and talk to them. You can also say that people **mix**. *He has that rare ability to mix with people of any age... The two communities still find it difficult to mix beyond rather cursory social greetings.*   N-COUNT / V-RECIP-ERG pl-n V / V n with n / Also V with n, / V pl-n / V-RECIP V with n / pl-n V

7 When a record producer **mixes** a piece of music, he or she puts together the individual instrumental and vocal parts that have been recorded in order to make the finished sound. *They've been mixing tracks for a new album due out later this year.* ◆ **mix·ing** *Final mixing should be completed by the end of this week.*   VERB: V n / N-UNCOUNT

8 If someone **mixes it**, they deliberately start a fight or argument, or willingly take part in one. The usual American expression is **mix it up**. *Stewart has developed a tendency to mix it verbally with the opposition.*   PHRASE INFORMAL

9 See also **mixed; cake mix**. ● to **mix** your **metaphors**: see **metaphor**.

mix up. 1 If you **mix up** two things or people, you confuse them, so that you think that one of them is the other one. *People often mix me up with other actors... Depressed people may mix up their words... A lot of people mix the twins up.* **2** If you **mix up** a number of things, you put them together in a random way so that they are not in any particular order. *I like to mix up designer clothes... The plan was that the town should not fall into office, industrial and residential zones, but mix the three up together... This is music from a different era. I've taken those sounds from childhood and mixed them up with other things.* **3** See also **mixed up, mix-up**.   PHRASAL VB V n P with n / V P pl-noun / V pl-n P / V P pl-noun / V pl-n P / V n P with n

mixed /mɪkst/. **1** If you have **mixed** feelings about something or someone, you feel uncertain about them because you can see both good and bad points about them. *I came home from the meeting with mixed feelings... There has been a very mixed reaction to the decision.* ● a **mixed blessing**: see **blessing**. **2** A **mixed** group of people consists of people of many different types. *I found a very mixed group of individuals some of whom I could relate to and others with whom I had very little in common... The community is very mixed, not least because there are plenty of small industrial enterprises.* **3** Mixed is used to describe something that involves people from two or more different races or religions. *...a woman of mixed race. ...a racially mixed school. ...mixed marriages.* **4** Mixed education or accommodation is intended for both males and females. *...a mixed school... The spa has 6 indoor pools, 2 for women only, 2 for men only, and 2 for mixed bathing.* **5** Mixed is used to describe something which   ◆◆◇◇ ADJ-GRADED / ADJ-GRADED / ADJ / ADJ / ADJ: ADJ n

M

consists of different things of the same general kind. *...a small mixed salad. ...a teaspoon of mixed herbs.*

,mixed a'bility. In a **mixed ability** class or teaching system, pupils are taught together in the same class, even though their abilities are different. ADJ

,mixed 'bag. If you describe a situation or a group N-SING of things or people as a **mixed bag**, you mean that it contains some good items, features, or people and some bad ones. *...a mixed bag of results from banks and building societies.*

,mixed 'doubles. In sports such as tennis, **mixed** N-UNCOUNT **doubles** is a match in which a man and a woman play as partners against another man and a woman. *Vic Seixas and Doris Hart won the mixed doubles.*

,mixed e'conomy, mixed economies. If a N-COUNT country has a **mixed economy**, some companies there are owned by the state and some are owned privately.

,mixed 'up. 1 If you are **mixed up**, you are con- ◆◇◇◇◇ fused, often because of emotional or social prob- ADJ-GRADED lems. *I think he's a rather mixed up kid... I get mixed up about times and places.* 2 If you say that some- ADJ: one is **mixed up** with a person or in an activity that v-link ADJ you disapprove of, you mean they are involved with with/in n that person or activity. *Why did I ever get mixed up with you?... A scandal, I tell you, would mean dishonor for you, since you'd be mixed up in it.*

mix·er /'mɪksə/ **mixers.** 1 A **mixer** is a machine N-COUNT used for mixing things together. *...an electric mixer.* ● See also **food mixer.** 2 A **mixer** is a non-alcoholic N-COUNT drink such as fruit juice that you mix with strong alcohol such as gin.

'mixing bowl, mixing bowls. A **mixing bowl** is a N-COUNT large bowl used for mixing ingredients.

mix·ture /'mɪkstʃə/ **mixtures.** 1 A **mixture** of ◆◆◆◇◇ things consists of several different things together. N-SING *They looked at him with a mixture of horror, envy, and awe. ...a mixture of spiced, grilled vegetables.* 2 A **mixture** is a substance that consists of two or N-COUNT more substances which have been stirred or shaken together. *Prepare the gravy mixture. ...a mixture of water and sugar and salt.* ● See also **cough mixture.**

'mix-up, mix-ups. A **mix-up** is a mistake or a fail- N-COUNT ure in something that was planned. *...a mix-up over* INFORMAL *travel arrangements.*

Mk. Mk is a written abbreviation for **mark.** Mk is ◆◇◇◇◇ used to refer to a particular model or design of a car or machine. *...a 1974 white MG Midget Mk 3.*

ml. ml is a written abbreviation for **millilitre** or ◆◇◇◇◇ **millilitres.** *Boil the sugar and 100 ml of water.*

mm. mm is an abbreviation for **millimetre** or **mil-** ◆◆◇◇◇ **limetres.** *...a 135mm lens. ...0.25mm of rain.*

mne·mon·ic /nɪ'mɒnɪk/ **mnemonics.** A **mnemon-** N-COUNT ic is a word, short poem, or sentence that is intended to help you remember things such as scientific rules or spelling rules. *...mnemonic devices used to assist in remembering laws.*

mo /məʊ/. A **mo** is a very short length of time. *Hang* N-SING: *on a mo.* a N SPOKEN

moan /məʊn/ **moans, moaning, moaned.** 1 If ◆◇◇◇◇ you **moan**, you make a low sound, usually because VERB you are unhappy or in pain. *Tony moaned in his* V sleep and then turned over on his side. ● Also a Also V with noun. *Suddenly she gave a low, choking moan.* 2 To N-COUNT quote **moan** means to complain or speak in a way which VERB: V shows that you are very unhappy. *Voters moan* V prep/adv about the quality of their MPs... 'Look what he did,' Also V with quote she moaned. 3 A **moan** is a complaint or the act of N-COUNT complaining. *You can go see him and have a good* INFORMAL old moan. 4 A **moan** is a low noise. *...the occasional* N-COUNT moan of the wind. LITERARY

moan·er /'məʊnə/ **moaners.** If you refer to some- N-COUNT one as a **moaner**, you are criticizing them because PRAGMATICS they often complain about things. *Film critics are* INFORMAL dreadful moaners.

moat /məʊt/ **moats.** A **moat** is a deep wide ditch ◆◇◇◇◇ which used to be dug round a castle and then filled N-COUNT with water, in order to protect the castle from attack.

mob /mɒb/ **mobs, mobbing, mobbed.** 1 A mob ◆◆◇◇◇ is a large, disorganized, and often violent crowd of N-COLL- people. *Bottles and cans were hurled on the terraces* COUNT *by the mob. ...a growing mob of demonstrators.* 2 You can use **the mob** to refer disapprovingly to N-SING: the mass of people, especially when they are behav- the N, ing in a violent or threatening way. *There is a dan-* N n *ger of the mob taking over... They have been exercis-* PRAGMATICS ing what amounts to mob rule. 3 You can refer to N-SING the people involved in organized crime as the **Mob.** INFORMAL *...casinos that the Mob had operated. ...a Mob kill-* ing. 4 If someone **is being mobbed**, a crowd of VB: usu people is gathering very closely around that person passive in a disorderly way. *They are mobbed by fans wher-* beV-ed *ever they go.*

mo·bile /'məʊbaɪl, AM -bəl/ **mobiles.** 1 You use ◆◆◆◇◇ **mobile** to describe something that is able to move ADJ freely or be moved easily from place to place. *Mobi-* le units have been set up to get police quickly to an incident. *...the four hundred seat mobile theatre.* 2 If you are **mobile**, you can move or travel easily ADJ-GRADED from place to place, for example because you are not physically disabled or because you have your own transport. *He is now mobile thanks to a pow-* ered wheelchair. ● **mo·bil·ity** /məʊ'bɪlɪti/ *Two cars* N-UNCOUNT gave them the freedom and mobility to go their sepa-rate ways. 3 If someone has a **mobile** face, the ex- ADJ-GRADED pression on it changes quickly as their feelings change. 4 In a **mobile** society, people move easily from one ADJ-GRADED job, home, or social class to another. *...young, mobile professionals.* ● **mobility** *Prior to the nineteenth cen-* N-UNCOUNT tury, there were almost no channels of social mobility. 5 See also **upwardly mobile.** 6 A **mobile** is the same as a **mobile phone.** *They tried* N-COUNT to call me on the mobile yesterday. 7 A **mobile** is a INFORMAL decoration which you hang from a ceiling. It usually N-COUNT consists of several small objects which move as the air around them moves.

,mobile 'home, mobile homes. A mobile home ◆◇◇◇◇ is a caravan that people live in and that usually re- N-COUNT mains in the same place, but which can be pulled to another place using a car or van.

,mobile 'phone, mobile phones. A mobile ◆◇◇◇◇ phone is a telephone that you can carry with you N-COUNT and use to make or receive calls wherever you are.

mo·bi·lize /'məʊbɪlaɪz/ **mobilizes, mobilizing,** ◆◆◇◇◇ **mobilized;** also spelled **mobilise** in British Eng- lish. 1 If you **mobilize** support, you succeed in en- VERB couraging people to take action, especially political V n action. *The purpose of the journey is to mobilise* FORMAL public opinion on this controversial issue. ● **mo·bi-** **·li·za·tion** /,məʊbɪlaɪ'zeɪʃən/ *...the rapid mobiliza-* N-UNCOUNT tion of international opinion in support of the revo- lution. 2 If you **mobilize** resources, you organize VERB: V n them and make them available for use. FORMAL ● **mobilization** *...the mobilisation of resources for* N-UNCOUNT education. 3 If a country **mobilizes** its armed V-ERG: V n forces, or if the country or its armed forces mobi- V lize, they make preparations for a conflict. *Sudan* FORMAL even threatened to mobilize in response to the ulti- matums... It means that their whole army will mobi- lize. ● **mobilization** *...a demand for full-scale mo-* N-UNCOUNT bilisation to defend the republic.

mob·ster /'mɒbstə/ **mobsters.** A mobster is some- N-COUNT one who is a member of an organized group of vio- lent criminals.

moc·ca·sin /'mɒkəsɪn/ **moccasins.** Moccasins N-COUNT are soft leather shoes which have a low heel and a raised seam at the front.

mock /mɒk/ **mocks, mocking, mocked.** 1 If ◆◆◇◇◇ you **mock** someone or something, you laugh at VERB: V n them, tease them, or try to make them look foolish. beV-ed *Nigel was mocked by schoolmates about his protrud-* V with quote ing ears... 'I'm astonished, Benjamin,' she mocked. ● **mock·ing** *'It never really stops,' she complains in* ADJ-GRADED a mocking tone. ● **mock·ing·ly** *'Isn't that sweet?' he* ADV-GRADED says mockingly. 2 You use **mock** to describe some- ADJ: ADJ n thing which is not real or genuine, but which is in- tended to be very similar to the real thing. *'It's trag-*

ic!' swoons Jeffrey in mock horror... One of them was subjected to a mock execution. ...a mock Tudor mansion. **3** Mocks are practice exams that you take as part of your preparation for real exams. *She went from a D in her mocks to a B in the real thing.*   N-COUNT BRITISH

mock·ery /ˈmɒkəri/. **1** If someone mocks you, you can refer to their behaviour or attitude as **mockery**. *Was there a glint of mockery in his eyes?... There should be no snobbish mockery of catering or fashion design as university subjects.* **2** If something makes a **mockery** of something, it makes it appear worthless and foolish. *This action makes a mockery of the Government's continuing protestations of concern... The present system is a mockery of justice.*   ◆◇◇◇◇ N-UNCOUNT   N-SING

mock-up, mock-ups. A **mock-up** of something such as a machine or building is a model of it which is made to do tests on or to show people what it will look like. *...a mock-up of the high street.*   N-COUNT

mod /mɒd/ **mods.** Mods are young people who wear a special kind of neat clothes, ride motor-scooters, and like soul music. Mods first appeared in the early 1960s.   ◆◇◇◇◇ N-COUNT

mod·al /ˈməʊdəl/ **modals.** A **modal** or a **modal auxiliary** is a word such as 'can' or 'would' which is used with a main verb to express ideas such as possibility, intention, or necessity.   N-COUNT TECHNICAL

mod 'cons. If a house has all **mod cons**, it has all the modern facilities such as central heating and hot water that make it pleasant to live in.   N-PLURAL BRITISH INFORMAL

mode /məʊd/ **modes. 1** A **mode** of something is one of the different forms it can take or ways it can happen. *...the capitalist mode of production. ...a slightly more elegant and formal mode of dress.* **2** On some cameras or electronic devices, the different **modes** available are the different programs or functions that you can choose. *The camera is in manual mode.*   ◆◆◇◇◇ N-COUNT with supp FORMAL   N-COUNT

mod·el /ˈmɒdəl/ **models, modelling, modelled;** spelled **modeling, modeled** in American English. **1** A **model** of an object is a smaller copy of it that shows what it looks like or how it works. *...an architect's model of a wooden house.* ► Also an adjective. *...a model aeroplane that was the envy of the other students.* **2** If you **model** objects, you make them out of a substance such as clay or wood. *There she began to model in clay.* **3** A particular **model** of a machine is a particular type or version of it. *To keep the cost down, opt for a basic model.* **4** A **model** is a system that is being used and that people might want to copy in order to achieve similar results. *...the Chinese model of economic reform.* **5** If one thing **is modelled** on another, the first thing is made so that it is like the second thing in some way. *The quota system was modelled on those operated in America. She asked the author if she had modelled her hero on anybody in particular.* **6** A **model** of a system or process is a theoretical description of it that might help you understand how it works. *Darwin eventually put forward a model of biological evolution.* **7** If someone such as a scientist **models** a system or process, they make an accurate theoretical description of it in order to understand or explain how it works. *...the mathematics needed to model a nonlinear system like an atmosphere.* **8** If you say that someone or something is a **model** of a particular quality, you approve of them because they have that quality to a large degree. *His marriage and family life is a model of propriety.* **9** You use **model** to express approval of someone when you think that they give an excellent example by fulfilling their function very well. *She had been a model pupil.* **10** See also **role model.** **11** An artist's **model** is a person who is painted, drawn, or sculpted by them. **12** If someone **models** for an artist, they stay in a particular position so that the artist can paint, draw, or sculpt them. *Tullio has been modelling for Sandra for eleven years.* **13** A fashion **model** is a person whose job is to display clothes by wearing them. **14** If someone **models** clothes, they display them by wearing them. *She began modelling*   ◆◆◆◆◇   N-COUNT   ADJ: ADJ n   VERB: V n V in n   N-COUNT   N-COUNT: with supp FORMAL VERB be V-ed on n V n on n   N-COUNT TECHNICAL   N-COUNT: N of n PRAGMATICS   ADJ: ADJ n PRAGMATICS   N-COUNT   VERB V for n Also V   N-COUNT   VERB: V n V

in Paris when she was only 15. ◆ **mod·el·ling** *She was being offered a modelling contract.*   N-UNCOUNT

mo·dem /ˈməʊdem/ **modems.** A **modem** is a device which uses a telephone line to connect computers. *He sent his work to his publishers by modem.*   N-COUNT: also by N

mod·er·ate, moderates, moderating, moderated. The adjective and noun are pronounced /ˈmɒdərət/. The verb is pronounced /ˈmɒdəreɪt/. **1** Moderate political opinions or policies are not extreme. You can also use **moderate** to describe people or groups who have such opinions or policies. *...an easy-going man of very moderate views. ...a moderate Democrat.* ► A **moderate** is someone with moderate political opinions. **2** You use **moderate** to describe something that is neither large nor small in amount or degree. *While a moderate amount of stress can be beneficial, too much stress can exhaust you.* ◆ **mod·er·ate·ly** *...a moderately attractive woman.* **3** If you **moderate** something or if it **moderates**, it becomes less extreme or violent and more manageable or acceptable. *They are hoping that once in office he can be persuaded to moderate his views... The immediate sense of crisis has moderated somewhat.*   ◆◆◆◇◇   ADJ-GRADED   N-COUNT   ADJ-GRADED   ADV-GRADED   V-ERG V n V

mod·era·tion /ˌmɒdəˈreɪʃən/. If you say that someone's behaviour shows **moderation**, you approve of them because they act in a way that is reasonable and not extreme. *The United Nations Secretary General called on all parties to show moderation.* ● If you say that someone eats, drinks, or smokes **in moderation**, you approve of them because their eating, drinking, or smoking is not great or excessive. *Many adults are able to drink in moderation, but others become dependent on alcohol.*   ◆◇◇◇◇ N-UNCOUNT PRAGMATICS   PHRASE PRAGMATICS

mod·era·tor /ˈmɒdəreɪtə/ **moderators.** In some debates, the **moderator** is a neutral person who presides over the discussion and makes sure that it is conducted in an orderly way.   N-COUNT

mod·ern /ˈmɒdən/ **moderns. 1** Modern means relating to the present time, for example the present decade or present century. *...modern society. ...the risks facing every modern marriage.* **2** Something that is **modern** is new and involves the latest ideas or equipment. *...modern technology.* ◆ **mo·der·nity** /mɒˈdɜːnɪti/ *...an office block that astonished the city with its modernity.* **3** People are sometimes described as **modern** when they have opinions or ways of behaviour that have not yet been accepted by most people in a society. *They were very modern Tories... She is very modern in outlook.* **4** Modern is used to describe styles of art, dance, music, and architecture that have developed in recent times, in contrast to classical styles. *...the Museum of Modern Art.* ► The **moderns** are artists who follow modern styles.   ◆◆◆◆◇ ADJ: ADJ n   ADJ-GRADED   N-UNCOUNT   ADJ-GRADED   ADJ: ADJ n   N-COUNT

modern-'day. Modern-day is used to refer to the new or modern aspects of a place, activity, or society. *...modern-day America. ...modern-day living.*   ◆◇◇◇◇ ADJ: ADJ n

mod·ern·ise /ˈmɒdənaɪz/. See **modernize.**

mod·ern·ism /ˈmɒdənɪzəm/. In the first half of the 20th century, **modernism** was a tendency in the arts which was concerned with form, language, the mind, and the emotions, rather than with realism and narrative. ● See also **post-modernism**.   ◆◇◇◇◇ N-UNCOUNT

mod·ern·ist /ˈmɒdənɪst/ **modernists.** Modernist means relating to the ideas and methods of modernism or modern art. *The building is impeccably modernist: glass, aluminium and grey.* ● See also **post-modernist.** ► A **modernist** is an artist who uses modernist ideas and methods.   ◆◇◇◇◇ ADJ   N-COUNT

mod·ern·ize /ˈmɒdənaɪz/ **modernizes, modernizing, modernized;** also spelled **modernise** in British English. To **modernize** something such as a system or a factory means to change it by replacing old equipment or methods with new ones. *...plans to modernize the refinery.* ◆ **mod·erni·za·tion** /ˌmɒdənaɪˈzeɪʃən/ *...the modernization of the region. ...a five-year modernization programme.*   ◆◆◇◇◇ VERB V n   N-UNCOUNT

,**modern 'languages.** If you study **modern lan-** N-PLURAL
guages, you study foreign languages such as French,
German, and Russian which are widely used today.

mod·est /'mɒdɪst/. **1** A **modest** house or other ◆◆◆◇◇
building is not large or expensive. *A one-night stay* ADJ-GRADED
in a modest hotel costs around £35. **2** You use **mod-** ADJ-GRADED
est to describe something such as an amount, rate,
or improvement which is relatively small. *Swiss un-*
employment rose to the still modest rate of 0.7%...
She let him place two modest bets on the last two
races. ♦ **mod·est·ly** *Britain's balance of payments* ADV-GRADED
improved modestly last month. **3** A **modest** income ADJ
or success is not large, but is considered to be sufficient or satisfactory. *You don't get rich, but you can*
get a modest living out of it.
4 If you say that someone is **modest**, you approve of ADJ-GRADED
them because they do not talk much about their abil- PRAGMATICS
ities, qualities, or possessions. *Lord Carrington is*
modest about his achievements. ♦ **modestly** *'I have* ADV-GRADED
recently taken up playing the sax, but I'm not that ADV with v
good,' she said modestly. **5** You can describe a woman ADJ-GRADED
as **modest** when she avoids doing or wearing any-
thing that might cause men to have sexual feelings towards her. You can also describe her clothes or behaviour as **modest**. *Asian women are more modest and*
shy. ♦ **modestly** *She sat down cautiously on the red* ADV-GRADED
canvas cushions, knees modestly together.

mod·es·ty /'mɒdɪsti/. **1** Someone who shows ◆◇◇◇◇
modesty does not talk much about their abilities, N-UNCOUNT
achievements, or possessions; used showing ap- PRAGMATICS
proval. *I'm not good enough to play in Italy. That's*
not false modesty, I say it because it's true. **2** You can N-UNCOUNT
refer to the **modesty** of something such as a place,
an amount, or a plan when it is relatively small or
unambitious. *The modesty of the town itself comes*
as something of a surprise. **3** If a woman or girl N-UNCOUNT
shows **modesty**, she is cautious about the way she
dresses and behaves because she is aware that other
people may view her in a sexual way. *Mirella's skirt*
was drawn up much more than modesty allowed.

modi·cum /'mɒdɪkəm/. A **modicum** of something, QUANT
especially something that is good or desirable, is a FORMAL
reasonable but not large amount of it. *I'd like to*
think I've had a modicum of success.

modi·fi·er /'mɒdɪfaɪə/ **modifiers.** A **modifier** is a N-COUNT
word or group of words that modifies another word
or group. Sometimes, only words that are used before a noun are called **modifiers**.

modi·fy /'mɒdɪfaɪ/ **modifies, modifying, modi-** ◆◆◇◇◇
fied. **1** If you **modify** something, you change it VERB
slightly, often in order to improve it. *The club mem-* Vn
bers did agree to modify their recruitment policy.
♦ **modi·fi·ca·tion** /,mɒdɪfɪ'keɪʃən/ **modifications** N-VAR
Relatively minor modifications were required. **2** A VERB
word or group of words that modifies another word Vn
describes or classifies it, or restricts its meaning. *Ad-*
jectives generally precede the noun they modify.

mod·ish /'məʊdɪʃ/. Something or someone that is ADJ-GRADED
modish is fashionable. *...modish young women from* LITERARY
London society.*

modu·lar /'mɒdʒʊlə/. **1 Modular** is used to de- ADJ
scribe buildings or furniture consisting of separate TECHNICAL
parts or units that can be put together in different
ways. **2 Modular** means relating to the teaching of ADJ
college or university courses in units called mod- BRITISH
ules. *The course is modular in structure.*

modu·late /'mɒdʒʊleɪt/ **modulates, modulat-** VERB
ing, modulated. To **modulate** something means Vn
to alter or adjust it in order to make it more suitable FORMAL
or effective in particular circumstances. *These*
chemicals modulate the effect of potassium... He
carefully modulated his voice. ♦ **modu·la·tion** N-VAR
/,mɒdʒʊ'leɪʃən/ **modulations** *Even their voice*
modulations were similar.

mod·ule /'mɒdʒuːl/ **modules.** **1** In some college ◆◇◇◇◇
or university courses, a **module** is one of the units N-COUNT
that the course is divided into. *These courses cover a* BRITISH
twelve week period and are organised into three
four-week modules. **2** A **module** is part of a space- N-COUNT
craft which can operate independently of the main

part, often at a distance from it. *A rescue plan could*
be achieved by sending an unmanned module to the N-COUNT
space station. **3** A **module** is a part of a machine, es- TECHNICAL
pecially a computer, which performs a particular
function.

mo·dus op·eran·di /,məʊdəs ɒpə'rændiː, -daɪ/. A N-SING
modus operandi is a particular way of doing some- FORMAL
thing. *Serial killers sometimes change their methods,*
their modus operandi.

mo·dus vi·ven·di /,məʊdəs vɪ'vendiː, -daɪ/. A **mo-** N-SING
dus vivendi is an arrangement which allows people FORMAL
who have different attitudes to live or work together. *After 1940, a modus vivendi between church and*
state was achieved.

mo·gul /'məʊgəl/ **moguls.** A **mogul** is an impor- ◆◇◇◇◇
tant, rich, and powerful businessman. *...an interna-* N-COUNT
tional media mogul. ...Hollywood movie moguls. JOURNALISM

mo·hair /'məʊheə/. **Mohair** is a type of very soft N-UNCOUNT
wool. *...a brown mohair dress.*

moist /mɔɪst/. Something that is **moist** is slightly ◆◇◇◇◇
wet. *Wipe off any excess make-up with a clean,* ADJ-GRADED
moist cotton flannel.

mois·ten /'mɔɪsən/ **moistens, moistening,** VERB
moistened. To **moisten** something means to Vn
make it slightly wet. *She took a sip of water to mois-*
ten her dry throat.

mois·ture /'mɔɪstʃə/. **Moisture** is tiny drops of wa- ◆◆◇◇◇
ter in the air, on a surface, or in the ground. *...vari-* N-UNCOUNT
ations in the relative vigour of plants, as measured
by their level of moisture and chlorophyll.

mois·tur·ize /'mɔɪstʃəraɪz/ **moisturizes, mois-** ◆◇◇◇◇
turizing, moisturized; also spelled **moisturise** in VERB: V n
British English. If you use a substance to **moisturize** V
your skin, you rub it on your skin to make your skin V-ing
softer. *The lotion moisturizes while it cleanses.*
...moisturising cream. ♦ **moist·ur·iz·er, moistur-** N-VAR
izers. A **moisturizer** is a cream or other product
that you use to moisturize your skin.

mo·lar /'məʊlə/ **molars.** Your **molars** are the large N-COUNT
teeth towards the back of your mouth.

mo·las·ses /mə'læsɪz/. **Molasses** is a thick, dark N-UNCOUNT
brown syrup which is produced when sugar is re-
fined. It is used in cooking.

mold /məʊld/. See **mould**.

mold·ing /'məʊldɪŋ/. See **moulding**.

moldy /'məʊldi/. See **mouldy**.

mole /məʊl/ **moles.** **1** A **mole** is a natural dark ◆◇◇◇◇
spot or small dark lump on someone's skin. *... a* N-COUNT
smartly dressed man with a mole on his left cheek.
2 A **mole** is a small animal with black fur that lives N-COUNT
underground. **3** A **mole** is a member of a govern- N-COUNT
ment or organization who secretly reveals confidential information to the press or to a rival organization. *He had been recruited by the Russians as a*
mole.

mo,lecular bi'ology. **Molecular biology** is the ◆◇◇◇◇
study of the complex chemicals found in living N-UNCOUNT
things. ♦ **mo·lecu·lar bi·olo·gist, molecular bi-** N-COUNT
ologists *This substance has now been cloned by*
molecular biologists.

mol·ecule /'mɒlɪkjuːl/ **molecules.** A **molecule** is ◆◆◇◇◇
the smallest amount of a chemical substance which N-COUNT
can exist by itself. *...water molecules.* ♦ **mo·lecu-**
·lar /mə'lekjʊlə/. *...molecular genetics.* ADJ: ADJ n

mo·lest /mə'lest/ **molests, molesting, molest-** ◆◇◇◇◇
ed. A person who **molests** a woman or child inter- VERB: V n
feres with them in a sexual way against their will.
♦ **mo·les·ta·tion** /,mɒle'steɪʃən, AM ,məʊl-/ *Any* N-UNCOUNT
case of sexual molestation of a child should be re-
ported to the police. ♦ **mo·lest·er, molesters** *He'd* N-COUNT
been publicly labeled a child molester.

mol·li·fy /'mɒlɪfaɪ/ **mollifies, mollifying, molli-** VERB
fied. If you **mollify** someone, you do or say some- V n
thing to make them less upset or angry. *The investi-* FORMAL
gation was undertaken primarily to mollify pressure
groups. ♦ **mol·li·fied** *He looked first mollified and* ADJ-GRADED:
then relieved. v-link ADJ

mol·lusc /'mɒləsk/ **molluscs.** A **mollusc** is an ani- N-COUNT
mal such as a snail, clam, or octopus, which has a

soft body and no backbone. Many types of mollusc have shells to protect them.

molly·coddle /'mɒlikɒdəl/ **mollycoddles, molly- coddling, mollycoddled.** If you accuse someone of **mollycoddling** someone else, you are criticizing them for doing too many things for the other person and protecting them too much from unpleasant experiences. *VERB: V n* *PRAGMATICS*

Molo·tov cock·tail /ˌmɒlətɒv 'kɒkteɪl/ **Molotov cocktails.** A Molotov cocktail is a simple bomb made by putting petrol and cloth into a bottle. It is exploded by setting fire to the cloth. *N-COUNT*

mol·ten /'məʊltən/. Molten rock, metal, or glass has been heated to a very high temperature and has become a hot thick liquid. *ADJ*

mom /mɒm/ **moms.** Some people refer to or address their mother as **mom**. The usual British word is **mum**. *Mom, can you tell me how to do it?* *N-FAMILY AMERICAN, INFORMAL*

mo·ment /'məʊmənt/ **moments. 1** A moment or moments are a very short period of time, for example a few seconds. *She stared at him a moment, then turned away... In moments, I was asleep.* **2** A particular **moment** is the point in time at which something happens. *At this moment a car stopped at the house... Many people still remember the moment when they heard that President Kennedy had been assassinated.* **3** If you say that an ordinary person or thing **has** their **moments**, you mean that sometimes they are more successful or interesting than usual. *He's not the thoroughly outgoing character you'd predict, although he has his moments.* **4 • spur of the moment:** see **spur. 5** If someone does something at the **last moment**, they do it at the latest time possible. *They changed their minds at the last moment and refused to go.* **6** You use the expression **the next moment** or expressions such as **'one moment** he was there, **the next** he was gone' to emphasize that something happens suddenly, especially when it is very different from what was happening before. *He is unpredictable, weeping one moment, laughing the next.* *N-COUNT* *N-COUNT: with supp* *PHRASE* *PHRASE* *PHRASE* *PRAGMATICS*

7 If you say that something happens **the moment** something else happens, you are emphasizing that it happens immediately after the other thing. *The moment I closed my eyes, I fell asleep.* **8** If you say that you do not believe **for a moment** or **for one moment** that something is true, you are emphasizing that you do not believe that it could possibly be true. *I don't for a moment think there'll be a divorce.* *PHRASE* *PRAGMATICS* *PHRASE* *PRAGMATICS*

9 You use expressions such as **at the moment** and **at the present moment** to indicate that a particular situation exists at the time when you are speaking. *He's touring South America at this moment in time.* **10** You use **for the moment** to indicate that something is true now, even if it will not be true later or in the future. *For the moment, however, the government is happy to live with it.* **11** You use **of the moment** to describe someone or something that is especially popular at a particular time, especially when you want to suggest that their popularity is temporary. *He calls it a 'contraption', using his favourite word of the moment.* *PHRASE* *PHRASE* *PHRASE* *PRAGMATICS*

mo·men·tary /'məʊməntəri, AM -teri/. Something that is **momentary** lasts for a very short period of time, for example for a few seconds or less. *His hesitation was only momentary.* ♦ **mo·men·tari·ly** /ˌməʊmən'teərɪli/. *She paused momentarily.* *ADJ* *ADV*

moment of 'truth, moments of truth. If you refer to a time or event as the **moment of truth**, you mean that it is an important time when you must make a decision quickly, and whatever you decide will have important consequences in the future. *Both men knew the moment of truth had arrived.* *N-COUNT*

mo·men·tous /məʊ'mentəs/. If you refer to a decision, event, or change as **momentous**, you mean that it is very important, often because of the effects that it will have in the future. *The past three years have been among the most momentous in world history... It will be a momentous occasion.* *ADJ-GRADED*

mo·men·tum /məʊ'mentəm/. **1** If a process or movement gains **momentum**, it develops or progresses increasingly quickly, and becomes increasingly less likely to stop. *They are each anxious to maintain the momentum of the search for a solution.* **2 Momentum** is the mass of a moving object multiplied by its velocity. *N-UNCOUNT* *N-UNCOUNT TECHNICAL*

mom·ma /'mɒmə/ **mommas. Momma** means the same as **mommy**. *'Don't look so sad,' Momma advised. 'You are so pretty when you smile.'* *N-FAMILY AMERICAN, INFORMAL*

mom·my /'mɒmi/ **mommies.** Some children refer to or address their mother as **mommy**. The usual British word is **mummy**. *Mommy and I went in an aeroplane.* *N-FAMILY AMERICAN, INFORMAL*

Mon. Mon. is a written abbreviation for **Monday**. *...Mon Oct 19.*

mon·arch /'mɒnək/ **monarchs.** The **monarch** of a country or empire is the king, queen, or other hereditary ruler who reigns over it. *N-COUNT*

mo·nar·chi·cal /mɒ'nɑːkɪkəl/. **Monarchical** means relating to a monarch or monarchs. *...a monarchical system of government.* *ADJ*

mon·ar·chist /'mɒnəkɪst/ **monarchists.** If you have **monarchist** opinions, you believe that your country should have a hereditary ruler such as a king or queen. *...the tiny monarchist party.* ▶ A **monarchist** is someone with monarchist views. *ADJ-GRADED* *N-COUNT*

mon·ar·chy /'mɒnəki/ **monarchies. 1** A **monarchy** is a system in which a monarch reigns over a country. *...a serious debate on the future of the monarchy.* **2** A **monarchy** is a country that is ruled by a monarch. **3** The **monarchy** is used to refer to the monarch and his or her family. *The monarchy has to create a balance between its public and private lives.* *N-VAR* *N-COUNT* *N-COUNT*

mon·as·tery /'mɒnəstri, AM -teri/ **monasteries.** A **monastery** is a building or collection of buildings in which monks live. *N-COUNT*

mo·nas·tic /mə'næstɪk/. **Monastic** means relating to monks or to a monastery. *...the monastic life.* *ADJ*

Mon·day /'mʌndeɪ, -di/ **Mondays. Monday** is the day after Sunday. *N-VAR*

mon·etar·ism /'mʌnɪtərɪzəm, AM 'mɑːn-/. **Monetarism** is the control of a country's economy by regulating the total amount of money that is available. *N-UNCOUNT TECHNICAL*

mon·etar·ist /'mʌnɪtərɪst, AM 'mɑːn-/ **monetarists. Monetarist** economics is based on the theory that a country's economy should be controlled by regulating the total amount of money that is available. *...tough monetarist policies.* ▶ A **monetarist** is someone with monetarist views. *ADJ-GRADED TECHNICAL* *N-COUNT*

mon·etary /'mʌnɪtri, AM 'mɑːnɪteri/. **Monetary** means relating to money, or to the money supply. *Some countries tighten monetary policy to avoid inflation. ...the International Monetary Fund.* *ADJ: ADJ n FORMAL*

mon·ey /'mʌni/ **monies** or **moneys. 1 Money** consists of the coins or banknotes that you can spend, or a sum that can be represented by these. *Major Karnes took some money out of his pocket and handed it to the captain... Players should be allowed to earn money from advertising.* **2 Monies** is sometimes used to refer to an amount of money, or to separate amounts of money. *...the investment and management of monies by pension funds.* *N-UNCOUNT* *N-PLURAL FORMAL*

3 If you get your **money's worth** from something, you are satisfied because you think it is worth the amount of money you have spent on it. *The fans get their money's worth.* **4** If you are **in the money**, you have a lot of money to spend. *If you are one of the lucky callers chosen to play, you could be in the money.* **5** If you **make money**, you obtain money by earning it or by making a profit. *...the only bit of the firm that consistently made money.* **6** If you say that **money talks**, you mean that if someone has a lot of money, they also have a lot of power. *PHRASE* *PRAGMATICS* *PHRASE* *INFORMAL* *PHRASE* *PHRASE*

7 If a government or a central bank **prints money**, it provides the money for public spending by producing more banknotes, rather than by earning or borrowing what it needs. **8** If you say that someone is **throwing money at** a problem, you are criticizing them for try- *PHRASE* *PHRASE* *PRAGMATICS*

M

ing to solve it by spending money on it, instead of doing more thoughtful and imaginative things. **9** If you say that you want someone to put their **money where their mouth is**, you want them to spend money to improve a bad situation, instead of just talking about improving it. **10** If you say that the **smart money** is on a particular person or thing, you mean that people who know a lot about it think that this person will be successful, or this thing will happen. *A lot of smart money in Washington says that peace is nearly at hand.* **11** See also **pocket money**. ● a **licence to print money**: see **licence**. ● **give** someone **a run for their money**: see **run**. PHRASE / PHRASE JOURNALISM

mon·eyed /'mʌnid/; also spelled **monied**. A **moneyed** person has a lot of money. *...Japan's new monied classes.* ADJ FORMAL

money·lender /'mʌnilendə/ **moneylenders**; also spelled **money-lender**. A **moneylender** is a person who lends money which has to be paid back at a high rate of interest. N-COUNT DATED

'**money-maker, money-makers**. If you say that a business, product, or investment is a **money-maker**, you mean that it makes a big profit. N-COUNT

'**money market, money markets**. If you refer to the **money market**, you mean the lending of large amounts of money, and the buying and selling of foreign currencies by institutions such as large banks. *On the money markets the dollar was weaker against European currencies.* ◆◇◇◇ N-COUNT

'**money order, money orders**. A **money order** is a piece of paper representing a sum of money which you can buy at a post office and send to someone as a way of sending them money by post. The usual British term is **postal order**. N-COUNT AMERICAN

'**money-spinner, money-spinners**. If you say that something is a **money-spinner**, you mean that it earns a lot of money for someone. *The films have been fantastic money-spinners.* N-COUNT INFORMAL

'**money supply**. The **money supply** is the amount of money in circulation in a country's economy. *They believed that controlling the money supply would reduce inflation.* ◆◇◇◇ N-UNCOUNT TECHNICAL

mon·grel /'mʌŋgrəl/ **mongrels**. A **mongrel** is a dog which is not a pedigree but a mixture of different breeds. N-COUNT

mon·ied /'mʌnid/. See **moneyed**.

moni·tor /'mɒnitə/ **monitors, monitoring, monitored**. **1** If you **monitor** something, you regularly check its development or progress. *Officials had not been allowed to monitor the voting.* ◆ **moni·tor·ing** *...analysis and monitoring of the global environment.* **2** You can refer to a person who checks that something is done correctly, or that it is fair, as a **monitor**. *...UN monitors overseeing Namibian independence.* **3** If officials or journalists **monitor** radio broadcasts from other countries, they record them or listen carefully to them in order to obtain information. **4** A **monitor** is a machine that is used to check or record things, for example processes inside a person's body. *...a heart monitor.* **5** A **monitor** is a kind of television screen which is used to display information, for example in airports or television studios. ◆◆◆◇◇ VERB Vn / N-UNCOUNT / N-COUNT / VERB: Vn / N-COUNT / N-COUNT

monk /mʌŋk/ **monks**. A **monk** is a member of a male religious community that is usually separated from the outside world. ◆◆◇◇◇ N-COUNT

mon·key /'mʌŋki/ **monkeys**. A **monkey** is an animal with a long tail which lives in hot countries. Monkeys climb trees, and are related to gorillas and chimpanzees. ◆◆◇◇◇ N-COUNT

mono /'mɒnəʊ/. **Mono** is used to describe a system of playing music in which all the sound is directed through one speaker only. Compare **stereo**. ◆◇◇◇ ADJ

mono- /'mɒnəʊ-/. **Mono-** is used at the beginning of nouns and adjectives that have 'one' or 'single' as part of their meanings. *...monolingual teachers.* PREFIX

mono·chrome /'mɒnəkrəʊm/. **1** A **monochrome** film, photograph, or television shows black, white, and shades of grey, but no other colours. ADJ

2 A **monochrome** picture uses only one colour in various shades. ADJ

mono·cle /'mɒnəkəl/ **monocles**. A **monocle** is a glass lens which people wore in former times in front of one of their eyes to improve their ability to see with that eye. N-COUNT

mo·noga·my /mə'nɒgəmi/. **Monogamy** is used to refer to the state or custom of having a sexual relationship with only one partner or of being married to only one person. ◆ **mo·noga·mous** /mə'nɒgəməs/ *...a monogamous relationship.* N-UNCOUNT / ADJ

mono·gram /'mɒnəgræm/ **monograms**. A **monogram** is a design based on someone's initials, which is usually marked on things they own such as their clothes. ◆ **mono·grammed** *...a monogrammed handkerchief.* N-COUNT / ADJ

mono·graph /'mɒnəgrɑːf, -græf/ **monographs**. A **monograph** is a book or essay which is a detailed study of only one subject. N-COUNT FORMAL

mono·lin·gual /ˌmɒnəʊ'lɪŋgwəl/. **Monolingual** means involving, using, or speaking only one language. *...a largely monolingual country.* ADJ

mono·lith /'mɒnəlɪθ/ **monoliths**. **1** A **monolith** is a very large upright piece of stone that was erected in ancient times. **2** If you refer to an organization or system as a **monolith**, you are critical of it because it is very large and very slow to change, and it does not seem to have different parts with different characters. *In the past the USSR was a monolith under the control of the Communist Party.* ◆ **mono·lith·ic** *...an authoritarian and monolithic system.* N-COUNT / N-COUNT PRAGMATICS / ADJ-GRADED

mono·lith·ic /ˌmɒnə'lɪθɪk/. If you describe something such as a building as **monolithic**, you do not like it because it is very large and plain with no character. *...a huge monolithic concrete building.* ADJ-GRADED PRAGMATICS

mono·logue /'mɒnəlɒg, AM -lɔːg/ **monologues**. **1** If you refer to a long speech by one person during a conversation as a **monologue**, you mean it prevents other people from talking or expressing their opinions. *Morris ignored the question and continued his monologue.* **2** A **monologue** is a long speech which is spoken by one person in a play or other drama. ◆◇◇◇ N-COUNT / N-VAR

mo·nopo·lis·tic /məˌnɒpə'lɪstɪk/. If you refer to a business or its practices as **monopolistic**, you mean that it tries to control as much of an industry as it can and does not allow fair competition. ADJ-GRADED

mo·nopo·lize /mə'nɒpəlaɪz/ **monopolizes, monopolizing, monopolized**; also spelled **monopolise** in British English. **1** If someone **monopolizes** something, they have a very large share of it and prevent other people from having a share. *Johnson, as usual, monopolized the conversation.* ◆ **mo·nopo·li·za·tion** /məˌnɒpəlaɪ'zeɪʃən/ *...the monopolization of a market by a single supplier.* **2** If something or someone **monopolizes** you, they demand a lot of your time and attention, so that there is very little time left for anything else. ◆◇◇◇ VERB Vn / N-UNCOUNT / VERB: Vn

mo·nopo·ly /mə'nɒpəli/ **monopolies**. **1** If a company, person, or state has a **monopoly** on something such as an industry, they have complete control over it. *...a state monopoly on land ownership.* **2** A **monopoly** is a company which is the only provider of a particular product or service and which therefore has complete control over an industry, so that it is impossible for other companies to compete with it. *...the shift of state monopolies from government to private management.* **3** If you say that someone does not have a **monopoly** on something, you mean that they are not the only person who has that thing. *Women do not have a monopoly on feelings of betrayal.* ◆◆◇◇ N-VAR / N-COUNT / N-SING: with brd-neg

mono·rail /'mɒnəʊreɪl/ **monorails**. A **monorail** is a system of transport in which small trains travel along a single rail which is usually high above the ground. N-COUNT: also byN

mono·syl·la·ble /'mɒnəsɪləbəl/ **monosyllables**. If you say that someone speaks in **monosyllables**, you mean that they say very little. ◆ **mono·syl·lab·ic** /ˌmɒnəsɪ'læbɪk/. If you refer to someone or the ADJ-GRADED

way they speak as **monosyllabic**, you mean that they say very little.

mono·tone /'mɒnətəʊn/ **monotones. 1** If someone speaks in a **monotone**, their voice does not vary at all in tone or loudness and so it is not interesting to listen to. **2 Monotone** colours do not have any variations or shades. *On misty days, backgrounds fade to monotone blues and greys.* N-COUNT: also *in* N / ADJ

mo·noto·nous /mə'nɒtənəs/. Something that is **monotonous** is very boring because it has a regular repeated pattern which never changes. *It's monotonous work, like most factory jobs.* ♦ **mo·noto·nous·ly** *The rain dripped monotonously.* ◆◇◇◇◇ ADJ-GRADED / ADV-GRADED

mo·noto·ny /mə'nɒtəni/. The **monotony** of something is the fact that it never changes and is repetitive and boring. *A night on the town may help to break the monotony of the week.* N-UNCOUNT

mon·ox·ide /mə'nɒksaɪd/. See **carbon monoxide**.

mon·soon /mɒn'suːn/ **monsoons. 1** The **monsoon** is the season in Southern Asia when there is a lot of very heavy rain. **2** Monsoon rains are sometimes referred to as the **monsoons**. ◆◇◇◇◇ N-COUNT / N-PLURAL

mon·ster /'mɒnstə/ **monsters. 1** A **monster** is a large imaginary creature that looks very ugly and frightening. **2** If you describe someone as a **monster**, you mean that they are cruel, frightening, or evil. **3** A **monster** is something which is extremely large, especially something which is difficult to manage or which is unpleasant. *...the monster which is now the London marathon.* **4 Monster** means extremely and surprisingly large. *...a monster weapon... The film will be a monster hit.* ◆◆◇◇◇ N-COUNT / N-COUNT / N-COUNT / ADJ: ADJ n / PRAGMATICS / INFORMAL

mon·stros·ity /mɒn'strɒsɪti/ **monstrosities.** If you describe something, especially something large, as a **monstrosity**, you mean that you think it is extremely ugly. *The older buildings have been torn down and replaced by modern monstrosities.* PRAGMATICS

mon·strous /'mɒnstrəs/. **1** If you describe a situation or event as **monstrous**, you mean that it is extremely shocking and unfair. *She endured the monstrous behaviour for years.* ♦ **mon·strous·ly** *Your husband's family has behaved monstrously. ...a woman so monstrously treated.* **2** If you describe an unpleasant thing as **monstrous**, you mean that it is extremely large in size or extent. *...a monstrous copper edifice.* ♦ **monstrously** *...monstrously inflated prices. ...monstrously powerful engines.* **3** If you describe something as **monstrous**, you mean that it is extremely frightening because it appears unnatural or ugly. *...the film's monstrous fantasy figure.* ◆◇◇◇◇ ADJ-GRADED / PRAGMATICS / ADV-GRADED: ADV after v / ADJ-GRADED / PRAGMATICS / ADV-GRADED: ADV adj/-ed / ADJ-GRADED

mon·tage /mɒn'tɑːʒ, 'mɒntɑːʒ/ **montages.** A **montage** is a picture, film, or piece of music which consists of several different items that are put together, often in an unusual combination or sequence. N-COUNT

month /mʌnθ/ **months. 1** A **month** is one of the twelve periods of time that a year is divided into, for example January or February. *The trial is due to begin next month.* **2** A **month** is a period of about four weeks. *She was here for a month.* ◆◆◆◆◆ N-COUNT / N-COUNT

month·ly /'mʌnθli/ **monthlies. 1** A **monthly** event or publication happens or appears every month. *...their monthly house payments.* ▶ Also an adverb. *In some areas the property price can rise monthly.* **2** You can refer to a publication that is published monthly as a **monthly**. *...Scallywag, a London satirical monthly.* **3 Monthly** quantities or rates relate to a period of one month. *...the monthly rent for a two-bedroom flat.* ◆◆◇◇◇ ADJ: ADJ n / ADV: ADV after v / N-COUNT / ADJ: ADJ n

monu·ment /'mɒnjumənt/ **monuments. 1** A **monument** is a large structure, usually made of stone, which is built to remind people of an event in history or of a famous person. **2** A **monument** is something such as a castle or bridge which was built a very long time ago and is regarded as an important part of a country's history. **3** If you describe something as a **monument** to someone's qualities, you mean that it is a very good example of the results or effects of those qualities. *By his internation-* ◆◇◇◇◇ N-COUNT / N-COUNT / N-COUNT: N to n

al achievements he leaves a fitting monument to his beliefs.

monu·men·tal /ˌmɒnjʊ'mentəl/. **1** You can use **monumental** to emphasize the size or extent of something. *It had been a monumental blunder.* ♦ **monu·men·tal·ly** *...the most monumentally hideous night of my life! ...a task for which he is monumentally ill-equipped.* **2** If you describe a book or musical work as **monumental**, you are emphasizing that it is very large and impressive, and is likely to be important for a long time. *...his monumental work on Chinese astronomy.* ◆◇◇◇◇ ADJ-GRADED / PRAGMATICS / ADV-GRADED / ADJ-GRADED / PRAGMATICS

moo /muː/ **moos, mooing, mooed.** When cows **moo**, they make the long low sound that cattle typically make. ▶ Also a noun. *The cow says 'moo-moo'.* VERB: V / N-COUNT; SOUND

mooch /muːtʃ/ **mooches, mooching, mooched.**

mooch around; the form **mooch about** is also used in British English. If you **mooch around** or **mooch about** a place, you move around there slowly with no particular purpose. *Andrew was left to mooch around the house on his own.* PHRASAL VB / V P / V P n

mood /muːd/ **moods. 1** Your **mood** is the way you are feeling at a particular time. If you are in a good **mood**, you feel cheerful. If you are in a bad **mood**, you feel angry and impatient. *Lily was in one of her aggressive moods.* ● If you say that you are **in the mood** for something, you mean that you want to do it or have it. If you say that you are **in no mood to** do something, you mean that you do not want to do it or have it. **2** The **mood** of a group of people is the way that they think and feel about an idea, event, or question at a particular time. *They largely misread the mood of the electorate.* **3** If someone is in a **mood**, the way they are behaving shows that they are feeling angry and impatient. **4** The **mood** of a place is the general impression that you get of it. *First set the mood with music.* ◆◆◆◇◇ N-COUNT: with supp / PHRASE / PHRASE / N-SING / N-COUNT / N-COUNT

moody /'muːdi/ **moodier, moodiest. 1** A **moody** person often becomes depressed or angry without any warning. ♦ **mood·i·ly** /'muːdɪli/ *He sat and stared moodily out the window.* ♦ **mood·i·ness** *His moodiness may have been caused by his poor health.* **2** If you describe a picture, film, or piece of music as **moody**, you mean that it suggests particular emotions, especially sad ones. *...moody black and white photographs.* ◆◆◇◇◇ ADJ-GRADED / ADV-GRADED / N-UNCOUNT / ADJ-GRADED

moon /muːn/ **moons, mooning, mooned. 1** The **moon** is the object in the sky that goes round the Earth once every four weeks and that you can often see at night as a circle or part of a circle. *...the first man on the moon. ...the light of a full moon.* ● See also **new moon. 2** A **moon** is an object like a small planet that travels around a planet. *...Neptune's large moon.* **3** If you say that something happens **once in a blue moon**, you are emphasizing that it does not happen very often at all. **4** If you say that you are **over the moon**, you mean that you are very pleased about something. **5** If you **are mooning** around, you are spending time doing nothing in particular, for example because you feel unhappy or lazy, or are worried about something. ◆◆◆◇◇ N-SING / N-COUNT / PHRASE / PRAGMATICS / PHRASE / INFORMAL / VERB

moon·light /'muːnlaɪt/ **moonlights, moonlighting, moonlighted. 1** Moonlight is the light that comes from the moon at night. **2** If someone **moonlights**, they have a second job in addition to their main job, often without informing their main employers or the tax office. *...an engineer who was moonlighting as a taxi driver.* ◆◇◇◇◇ N-UNCOUNT / VERB: V / V as n

moon·lit /'muːnlɪt/. Something that is **moonlit** is lit by moonlight. ADJ

moon·shine /'muːnʃaɪn/. **1** Moonshine is whisky that is made illegally. **2** If you say that someone's thoughts, ideas, or comments are **moonshine**, you think they are foolish and not based on reality. *As Morison remarks, the story is pure moonshine.* N-UNCOUNT / AMERICAN / N-UNCOUNT / PRAGMATICS

moor /mʊə/ **moors, mooring, moored. 1** A **moor** is an area of open, uncultivated, and usually high land with poor soil that is covered mainly with grass and heather. *...265 square miles of moor.* ◆◆◇◇◇ N-VAR / BRITISH

2 If you **moor** a boat, you attach it to the land with a rope or cable so that it cannot drift away. *I decided to moor near some tourist boats.* **3** See also **mooring**. — VERB: V n, V

4 The **Moors** were a Muslim people who established a civilization in North Africa and Spain between the 8th and the 15th century A.D. ♦ **Moor·ish** *...a medieval Moorish palace.* — N-COUNT; ADJ

moor·ing /'mʊərɪŋ/ **moorings. 1** A **mooring** is a place or object on land to which a boat is tied so that it cannot drift away. **2 Moorings** are the rope, anchors, or chains used to moor a boat or ship. — N-COUNT; N-PLURAL

moor·land /'mʊələnd/ **moorlands. Moorland** is land which consists of moors. *...rugged Yorkshire moorland.* — N-UNCOUNT: also N in pl

moose /muːs/; **moose** is both the singular and the plural form. A **moose** is a large North American deer. — N-COUNT

moot /muːt/ **moots, mooting, mooted. 1** If a plan, idea, or subject **is mooted**, it is suggested or introduced for discussion. *...the scheme, which was first mooted in November.* **2** If something is a **moot** point or question, people cannot agree about it. — VB: usu passive FORMAL; ADJ-GRADED

mop /mɒp/ **mops, mopping, mopped. 1** A **mop** consists of a sponge or many pieces of string attached to a long handle and is used for washing floors. **2** If you **mop** a surface such as a floor, you clean it with a mop. *She wants the floors mopped every day.* **3** If you **mop** sweat from your forehead, you wipe it with a handkerchief. *The Inspector took out a handkerchief and mopped his brow.* **4** If someone has a **mop** of hair, they have a lot of hair and it looks rather untidy. — N-COUNT; VERB: V n; VERB: V n from n, V n; N-COUNT

mop up. 1 If you **mop up** a liquid, you clean it with a cloth so that the liquid is absorbed. *When the washing machine spurts out water at least we can mop it up. ...as the thunderstorms left homeowners mopping up.* **2** If you **mop up** something that you think is undesirable or dangerous, you remove it or deal with it so that it is no longer a problem. *The infantry divisions mopped up remaining centres of resistance.* — PHRASAL VB: V P noun, V n P, V P, V P noun, Also V n P

mope /məʊp/ **mopes, moping, moped.** If you **mope**, you feel miserable and do not feel interested in doing anything. — VERB: V

mope around; the form **mope about** is also used in British English. If you **mope around** or **mope about**, you wander around not doing anything, looking and feeling unhappy. *He moped around the office for a while, feeling bored.* — PHRASAL VB: V P, V P n

moped /'məʊped/ **mopeds.** A **moped** is a small motorcycle which you start by pedalling it like a bicycle. — N-COUNT

mor·al /'mɒrəl, AM 'mɔːr-/ **morals. 1 Morals** are principles and beliefs concerning right and wrong behaviour. *...Western ideas and morals... They have no morals.* **2 Moral** means relating to beliefs about what is right or wrong. *...the moral issues involved in 'playing God'.* ♦ **mor·al·ly** *When, if ever, is it morally justifiable to allow a patient to die?... Is there really morally any difference between slaughtering a cow for food and a horse for food?* **3 Moral** courage or duty is based on what you believe is right or acceptable, rather than on what the law says should be done. *The Government had a moral, if not a legal duty to pay compensation.* **4** A **moral** person behaves in a way that is believed by most people to be good and right. ♦ **morally** *Art is not there to improve you morally.* **5 ● moral victory:** see **victory**. **6** If you give someone **moral** support, you encourage them in what they are doing by expressing approval. **7** The **moral** of a story or event is what you learn from it about how you should or should not behave. *The moral of the story is let the buyer beware.* — N-PLURAL; ADJ: ADJ n; ADV-GRADED; ADJ: ADJ n; ADJ-GRADED; ADV: ADV with v; ADJ: ADJ n; N-COUNT

mo·rale /məˈrɑːl, -ˈræl/. **Morale** is the amount of confidence and optimism that people have. *Many pilots are suffering from low morale.* — N-UNCOUNT

moral 'fibre; spelled **moral fiber** in American English. **Moral fibre** is the quality of being determined to do what you think is right. *...the destruction of the moral fibre of the nation.* — N-UNCOUNT

mor·al·ise /'mɒrəlaɪz, AM 'mɔːr-/. See **moralize**.

mor·al·ist /'mɒrəlɪst, AM 'mɔːr-/ **moralists.** A **moralist** is someone who has strong ideas about right and wrong behaviour, and who tries to make other people behave according to these ideas. ♦ **mor·al·is·tic** /,mɒrəˈlɪstɪk, AM ,mɔːr-/ *He has become more moralistic.* — N-COUNT; ADJ-GRADED

mo·ral·ity /məˈrælɪti/ **moralities. 1 Morality** is the belief that some behaviour is right and acceptable and that other behaviour is wrong. *...standards of morality and justice.* **2** A **morality** is a system of principles and values concerning people's behaviour, which is generally accepted by a society or by a particular group of people. *...a morality that is sexist.* **3** The **morality** of something is how right or acceptable it is. *...the arguments about the morality of blood sports.* — N-UNCOUNT; N-COUNT; N-UNCOUNT

mor·al·ize /'mɒrəlaɪz, AM 'mɔːr-/ **moralizes, moralizing, moralized;** also spelled **moralise** in British English. If you say that someone **is moralizing**, you are critical of them for telling people what they think is right or wrong. *As a dramatist I hate to moralize.* ♦ **mor·al·iz·ing** *We have tried to avoid any moralising.* — VERB PRAGMATICS V; N-UNCOUNT

,moral ma'jority. If there is a large group in society that holds strong conservative opinions on matters of morality and religion, you can refer to these people as the **moral majority**. — N-COLL-SING; N-COLL-PROPER: the N

mo·rass /məˈræs/ **morasses.** If you describe an unpleasant or confused situation as a **morass**, you mean that it seems impossible to escape from or resolve, because it has become so serious or so complicated. *I tried to drag myself out of the morass of despair.* — N-COUNT

mora·to·rium /,mɒrəˈtɔːriəm, AM ,mɔːr-/ **moratoriums** or **moratoria.** A **moratorium** on a particular activity or process is the stopping of it for a fixed period of time, usually as a result of an official agreement. — N-COUNT

mor·bid /'mɔːbɪd/. A **morbid** person has a strange or unwise interest in unpleasant things, especially death. *Some people have a morbid fascination with crime.* ♦ **mor·bid·ly** *There's something morbidly fascinating about the thought.* — ADJ-GRADED; ADV-GRADED

mor·dant /'mɔːdənt/. **Mordant** humour or wit is sarcastic, sharp, and critical, but also very funny. — ADJ-GRADED FORMAL

more /mɔː/. **More** is often considered to be the comparative form of **much** and **many**. — ♦♦♦♦♦

1 You use **more** to indicate that there is a greater number of things or a greater amount of something than before or than average, or than something else. You can use 'a little', 'a lot', 'a bit', 'far' and 'much' in front of **more**. *...teaching more children foreign languages... Give adolescents a little more information than they ask for.* ► Also a pronoun. *He had four hundred dollars in his pocket. Billy had more.* ► Also a quantifier. *Employees may face increasing pressure to take on more of their own medical costs in retirement.* — DET; PRON; QUANT

2 You can use **more** to indicate that something continues to happen for a further period of time. *Things might have been different if I'd talked a bit more.* ● You can use **some more** to indicate that something continues to happen for a further period of time. *We walked some more.* **3** You use **more** to indicate that something is repeated. For example, if you do something 'once more', you do it again once. *This train would stop twice more.* **4** You use **more** to refer to an additional thing or amount. You can use 'a little', 'a lot', 'a bit', 'far' and 'much' in front of **more**. *They needed more time to consider whether to hold an inquiry.* ► Also an adjective. *We stayed in Danville two more days... Are you sure you wouldn't like some more wine?* ► Also a pronoun. *Oxfam has appealed to western nations to do more to help the refugees.* — ADV-COMPAR: ADV after v; PHRASE; ADV-COMPAR: adv ADV, n ADV; DET; ADJ-COMPAR: ADJ n; PRON

5 You use **more than** before a number or amount to say that the actual number or amount is even greater. *...a survey of more than 1,500 schools.* **6** You use **more than** to say that something is true to a greater degree than is necessary or than average. *Lithuania produces more than enough food to feed itself.* **7** You use **no** — PHR-PREP; PHRASE; PHRASE

more than or **not more than** when you want to emphasize how small a number or amount is. *Each box requires no more than a few hours of labor to build.* **8** You can use **more and more** to indicate that something is becoming greater in amount, extent, or degree all the time. *Bob became more and more furious... More and more women are wearing men's fragrances.* **9** You use **more** to indicate that something or someone has a greater amount of a quality than they used to or than is average or usual. *Prison conditions have become more brutal... We can satisfy our basic wants more easily than in the past.* **10** If you do something **more** than before or **more** than someone else, you do it to a greater extent or more often. *When we are tired, tense, depressed or unwell, we feel pain much more.* **11** You use **more** in conversations when you want to draw someone's attention to something interesting or important that you are about to say. *More seriously for him, there are members who say he is wrong.* **12** If you say that something is **more** one thing than another, you mean that it is like the first thing rather than the second. *He's more like a film star than a life-guard... It's not really an interview, it's more of a conversation.* **13** If something is **more than** a particular thing, it has greater value or importance than this thing. *He's more than a coach, he's a friend.* **14** You can use **more** in expressions like 'no more, no less' and 'neither more nor less' to indicate that what you are saying is exactly true or correct. *I told him the truth. No more, no less.* **15** If something is **more or less** true, it is true in a general way, but is not completely true. *The Conference is more or less over... He more or less started the firm.* **16** If you say that someone or something is **nothing more than** a particular thing, you are emphasizing that they are only that thing, and nothing more interesting or important. *Mr Urquhart was nothing more than a hard-working businessman.* **17** You can use **what is more** or **what's more** to introduce an extra piece of information which supports or emphasizes the point you are making. *You should remember it, and what's more, you should get it right.* **18** • **all the more**: see **all**. • **any more**: see **any**.

more·over /mɔːˈrəʊvə/. You use **moreover** to ◆◆◆◇◇ introduce a piece of information that adds to or ADV: supports the previous statement. *The young find* ADV with cl everything so simple. The young, moreover, see it as (not last in cl) *their duty to be happy and do their best to be so.* PRAGMATICS FORMAL

mo·res /ˈmɔːreɪz/. The **mores** of a particular place N-PLURAL or group of people are the customs and behaviour FORMAL that are typically found in that place or group. *...the accepted mores of British society.*

morgue /mɔːɡ/ **morgues. 1** A **morgue** is a build- N-COUNT ing or room where dead bodies are kept before being cremated or buried. **2** A **morgue** is a building or N-COUNT room where unidentified dead bodies or the bodies AMERICAN of murder victims are kept until they are identified or released for burial.

mori·bund /ˈmɒrɪbʌnd, AM ˈmɔːr-/. If you describe ◆◇◇◇◇ something as **moribund**, you mean that it is in a ADJ-GRADED very bad condition. *...the moribund economy.* FORMAL

Mor·mon /ˈmɔːmən/ **Mormons** are ◆◇◇◇◇ people who belong to the Christian religious group N-COUNT founded by Joseph Smith in the United States.

morn /mɔːn/. **Morn** means the same as morning. N-SING *...one cold February morn.* LITERARY

morn·ing /ˈmɔːnɪŋ/ **mornings. 1** The **morning** is ◆◆◆◆◆ the part of each day between the time that people N-VAR usually wake up and noon or lunchtime. *On Sunday morning Bill was woken by the telephone.* **2** If you N-SING: refer to a particular time in the **morning**, you mean *the*N a time during the part of a day between midnight and noon. *I often stayed up until two or three in the morning.* **3** If you say that something will happen **in** PHRASE **the morning**, you mean that it will happen during the morning of the following day. **4** If you say that PHRASE something happens **morning, noon and night**, you mean that it happens all the time. *You get fit by playing the game, day in, day out, morning, noon and night.*

'morning dress. Morning dress is a suit of N-UNCOUNT clothes that is worn by men for very formal or special occasions such as weddings.

'morning room, morning rooms. In some large N-COUNT old houses, the **morning room** is a sitting-room DATED which is sunny in the morning.

'morning sickness. Morning sickness is a feeling N-UNCOUNT of sickness that some women have, often in the morning, when they are pregnant.

,morning 'star. The **morning star** is the planet N-SING: Venus, which can be seen shining in the sky just af- *the*N ter sunrise.

mor·on /ˈmɔːrɒn/ **morons.** If you refer to someone N-COUNT as a **moron**, you think that they are very stupid. PRAGMATICS ◆ **mo·ron·ic** /məˈrɒnɪk/ *It was wanton, moronic* RUDE *vandalism.* ADJ-GRADED

mo·rose /məˈrəʊs/. A **morose** person is miserable, ADJ-GRADED bad-tempered, and not willing to talk very much to other people. ◆ **mo·rose·ly** *One elderly man sat* ADV-GRADED *morosely at the bar.*

mor·pheme /ˈmɔːfiːm/ **morphemes.** A **mor-** N-COUNT **pheme** is the smallest unit of meaning in a language. *In Tonga the morpheme ba is the prefix for a plural noun.*

mor·phine /ˈmɔːfiːn/. **Morphine** is a drug used to ◆◇◇◇◇ relieve pain. N-UNCOUNT

mor·phol·ogy /mɔːˈfɒlədʒi/. The **morphology** of N-UNCOUNT something is its form and structure. In linguistics, **morphology** refers to the way words are constructed with stems, prefixes, and suffixes.

mor·row /ˈmɒrəʊ, AM ˈmɔːr-/. **1** The **morrow** means N-SING tomorrow or the next day. *We do depart for Wales* DATED, *on the morrow.* **2 Good morrow** means the same as BRITISH 'good morning'. *Good morrow to you, my lord.* CONVENTION DATED

morse code /ˌmɔːs ˈkəʊd/; also spelled **Morse code.** N-UNCOUNT **Morse code** or **morse** is an international code which is used for sending messages.

mor·sel /ˈmɔːsəl/ **morsels.** A **morsel** is a very small N-COUNT amount of something, especially a very small piece of food. *...a delicious little morsel of meat.*

mor·tal /ˈmɔːtəl/ **mortals. 1** If you refer to the fact ◆◆◇◇◇ that people are **mortal**, you mean that they have to ADJ die and cannot live forever. *A man is deliberately designed to be mortal. He grows, he ages, and he dies.* ◆ **mor·tal·ity** *She has suddenly come face to face* N-UNCOUNT *with her own mortality.* **2** You can describe some- N-COUNT one as a **mortal** when you want to say that they are an ordinary person, rather than someone who has power or has achieved something. *Tickets seem un-obtainable to the ordinary mortal.* **3** You can use ADJ-GRADED: **mortal** to show that something is very serious or ADJ n may cause death. *The police were defending themselves and others against mortal danger.* ◆ **mor·tal-** ADV **·ly** *He falls, mortally wounded.* **4** You can use **mor-** ADJ: ADJ n **tal** to emphasize that a feeling is extremely great or PRAGMATICS severe. *When self-esteem is high, we lose our mortal fear of jealousy.* ◆ **mortally** *Candida admits to hav-* ADV: *ing been 'mortally embarrassed'.* ADV -ed/adj/ adv

mor·tal·ity /mɔːˈtælɪti/. The **mortality** in a particu- N-UNCOUNT lar place or situation is the number of people who die. *The nation's infant mortality rate has reached a record low.*

mor·tar /ˈmɔːtə/ **mortars. 1** A **mortar** is a short ◆◆◇◇◇ cannon which fires shells high into the air for a N-COUNT short distance. **2 Mortar** is a mixture of sand, water, N-UNCOUNT and cement or lime, which is put between bricks to make them stay firmly together when you are building walls. **3** A **mortar** is a bowl in which you can N-COUNT crush or grind things such as herbs, spices, or grain using a special rod called a pestle. **4** • **bricks and mortar**: see **brick**.

mort·gage /ˈmɔːɡɪdʒ/ **mortgages, mortgaging,** ◆◆◆◆◇ **mortgaged. 1** A **mortgage** is a loan of money N-COUNT which you get from a bank or building society in order to buy a house. **2** If you **mortgage** your house VERB: V n or land, you use it as a guarantee to a company in order to borrow money from them.

mor·ti·cian /mɔːˈtɪʃən/ **morticians.** A **mortician** is N-COUNT a person whose job is to deal with the bodies of AMERICAN

people who have died and to arrange funerals. The British word is **undertaker**.

mor·ti·fy /ˈmɔːtɪfaɪ/ **mortifies, mortifying, mortified.** If you say that something **mortifies** you, you mean that it offends, shames, or embarrasses you a great deal. *Jane mortified her family by leaving her husband.* ♦ **mor·ti·fied** *If I reduced somebody to tears I'd be mortified.* ♦ **mor·ti·fy·ing** *She felt it would be utterly mortifying to be seen in such company as his by anyone.* ♦ **mor·ti·fi·ca·tion** /ˌmɔːtɪfɪˈkeɪʃən/. *The chairman tried to disguise his mortification.*
`VB: no cont`
`Vn`
`ADJ-GRADED`
`ADJ-GRADED`
`N-UNCOUNT`

mor·tu·ary /ˈmɔːtʃʊəri, AM -eri/ **mortuaries.** A **mortuary** is a building or a room in a hospital where dead bodies are kept before they are buried or cremated.
`N-COUNT`

mo·sa·ic /məʊˈzeɪɪk/ **mosaics.** A **mosaic** is a design which consists of small pieces of coloured glass, tiles, or stone set in concrete or plaster.
`N-VAR`

mo·sey /ˈməʊzi/ **moseys, moseying, moseyed.** If you **mosey** somewhere, you go there slowly, often without any particular purpose. *He usually moseys into town for no special reason.*
`VERB`
`V adv/prep`
`INFORMAL`

Mos·lem /ˈmɒzləm, ˈmʊzlɪm/. See **Muslim.**

mosque /mɒsk/ **mosques.** A **mosque** is a building where Muslims go to worship.
`N-COUNT`

mos·qui·to /mɒˈskiːtəʊ/ **mosquitoes** or **mosquitos.** Mosquitos are small flying insects which bite people and animals and suck their blood. See picture headed **insects.**
`N-COUNT`

mos'quito net, mosquito nets. A mosquito net is a curtain made of very fine cloth which is hung round a bed in order to keep mosquitoes and other insects away.
`N-COUNT`

moss /mɒs, AM mɔːs/ **mosses. Moss** is a very small soft green plant which grows on damp soil, or on wood or stone. ♦ **mossy** /ˈmɒsi, AM ˈmɔːsi/. *...a mossy wall.*
`N-VAR`
`ADJ-GRADED`

most /məʊst/. **Most** is often considered to be the superlative form of **much** and **many.**
`♦♦♦♦♦`

1 You use **most** to refer to the majority of a group of things or people or the largest part of something. *Most of the houses in the capital don't have piped water... By stopping smoking you are undoing most of the damage smoking has caused.* ▶ Also a determiner. *Most people think the Queen has done a good job.* ▶ Also a pronoun. *All of the rooms have private baths, and most have radios and TV.* **2** You use **the most** to mean a larger amount than anyone or anything else, or the largest amount possible. *The President himself won the most votes... The skippers get the most money, and after them the cooks.* ▶ Also a pronoun. *The most they earn in a day is ten roubles.* **3** You use **most** to indicate that something is true or happens to a greater degree or extent than anything else. *What she feared most was becoming like her mother. ...Professor Morris, the person he most hated.* ● **Most of all** means the same as **most.** *She said she wanted most of all to be fair.* **4** You use **most** to indicate that someone or something has a greater amount of a particular quality than other things of its kind. *He was one of the most influential performers of modern jazz... If anything, swimming will appeal to her most strongly.* **5** If you do something **the most,** you do it to the greatest extent possible or with the greatest frequency. *What question are you asked the most?... Inevitably those who suffer the most are the mothers and children.* **6** You use **most** in conversations when you want to draw someone's attention to something very interesting or important that you are about to say. *Most surprisingly, quite a few said they don't intend to vote at all.* **7** You use **most** to emphasize an adjective or adverb. *I believe he is most painfully anxious about Diana.* **8** You use **at most** or **at the most** to say that a number or amount is the maximum that is possible or likely. *Poach the pears in apple juice or water and sugar for perhaps ten minutes at most.* **9** If you **make the most of** something, you get the maximum use or advantage from it. *Happiness is the ability to make the most of what you have.* **10** ● **for the most part:** see **part.**
`QUANT`
`DET`
`PRON`
`ADJ-SUPERL:`
`theADJ n`
`PRON`
`ADV-SUPERL:`
`ADV with v`
`PHRASE`
`ADV-SUPERL:`
`ADV adj/adv`
`ADV-SUPERL:`
`theADV after`
`v`
`ADV-SUPERL:`
`ADV adj/adj`
`PRAGMATICS`
`ADV-SUPERL:`
`ADV adj/adv`
`FORMAL`
`PHRASE`
`PHRASE`

-most /-məʊst/. **-most** is added to adjectives in order to form other adjectives that describe something as being further in a particular direction than other things of the same kind. *...the topmost branches of the trees. ...the northernmost suburbs of Chicago.*
`SUFFIX`

most·ly /ˈməʊstli/. You use **mostly** to indicate that a statement is generally true, for example true about the majority of a group of things or people, true most of the time, or true in most respects. *I am working with mostly highly motivated people... Cars are mostly metal.*
`♦♦♦◇◇`
`ADV:`
`ADV with cl/`
`group`

mo·tel /məʊˈtel/ **motels.** A **motel** is a hotel intended for people who are travelling by car.
`♦◇◇◇◇`
`N-COUNT`

moth /mɒθ, AM mɔːθ/ **moths.** A **moth** is an insect like a butterfly which usually flies about at night. See picture headed **insects.**
`♦◇◇◇◇`
`N-COUNT`

moth·ball /ˈmɒθbɔːl, AM ˈmɔːθ-/ **mothballs, mothballing, mothballed. 1** A **mothball** is a small white ball made of a special chemical, which you can put amongst clothes or blankets in order to keep moths away. **2** If someone in authority **mothballs** a plan, factory, or piece of equipment, they decide to stop developing or using it, perhaps temporarily. *The shuttle programme has now been mothballed to save money.*
`N-COUNT`
`VERB: V n`
`be V-ed`
`JOURNALISM`

'moth-eaten. 1 Moth-eaten clothes look very old and ragged and have holes in them. **2** If you describe something as **moth-eaten,** you mean that it seems unattractive or useless because it is old or has been used too much. *This strategy looks increasingly moth-eaten.*
`ADJ-GRADED`
`ADJ-GRADED`
`PRAGMATICS`

moth·er /ˈmʌðə/ **mothers, mothering, mothered. 1** Your **mother** is the woman who gave birth to you. *She's an English teacher and a mother of two children.* **2** If a woman **mothers** a child, she looks after it and brings it up, usually because she is its mother. *Colleen had dreamed of mothering a large family.* ♦ **moth·er·ing** *The reality of mothering is frequently very different from the romantic ideal.* **3** If you **mother** someone, you treat them with great care and affection, as if they were a small child. *She felt a great need to mother him.*
`♦♦♦♦♦`
`N-FAMILY`
`VERB`
`V n`
`N-UNCOUNT`
`VERB`
`V n`

'mother country, mother countries; also spelled **Mother Country. 1** Someone's **mother country** is the same as their **motherland. 2** If you refer to **the mother country** of a particular state or country, you are referring to the very powerful country that used to control its affairs. *Australia, New Zealand, and Canada, had no colonial conflict with the mother country.*
`N-COUNT`
`N-SING:`
`theN`

'mother figure, mother figures; also spelled **mother-figure.** If you regard someone as a **mother figure,** you think of them as having the role of a mother and being the person you can turn to for help, advice, or support.
`N-COUNT`

moth·er·hood /ˈmʌðəhʊd/. **Motherhood** is the state of being a mother. *...women who try to combine work and motherhood.*
`♦◇◇◇◇`
`N-UNCOUNT`

'mother-in-law, mothers-in-law. Someone's **mother-in-law** is the mother of their husband or wife.
`♦◇◇◇◇`
`N-COUNT`

moth·er·land /ˈmʌðəlænd/; also spelled **Motherland.** The **motherland** is the country in which you were born and to which you still feel emotionally linked. *Central to our belief is love for the motherland and a desire to serve.*
`♦◇◇◇◇`
`N-SING`

moth·er·ly /ˈmʌðəli/. **Motherly** feelings or actions are like those of a mother. *It was an incredible display of motherly love and forgiveness.*
`ADJ-GRADED`

Mother 'Nature. Mother Nature is sometimes used to refer to nature, especially when it is being considered as a force that affects human beings. *The gardener is convinced he can improve on Mother Nature's rather casual attitude to the plant kingdom.*
`N-UNCOUNT`

mother-of-'pearl; also spelled **mother of pearl. Mother-of-pearl** is the shiny layer on the inside of some shells. It is used to make buttons or to decorate things.
`N-UNCOUNT`

,mother-to-'be, mothers-to-be. A **mother-to-be** N-COUNT
is a woman who is pregnant, especially for the first
time.

'mother tongue, mother tongues; also spelled N-COUNT
mother-tongue. Your **mother tongue** is the language that you learn from your parents when you
are a baby.

mo·tif /məʊ'tiːf/ **motifs. 1** A **motif** is a design ◆◇◇◇◇
which is used as a decoration or as part of an artis- N-COUNT
tic pattern. ...*a rose motif.* **2** A **motif** is a theme or N-COUNT
idea that is frequently repeated throughout a piece
of literature or music.

mo·tion /'məʊʃən/ **motions, motioning, mo-** ◆◆◆◇◇
tioned. 1 Motion is the activity or process of con- N-UNCOUNT
tinually changing position or moving from one
place to another. *The wind from the car's motion
whipped her hair around her head.* **2** A **motion** is an N-COUNT
action, gesture, or movement. *Cover each part of the
body with long sweeping strokes or circular motions.*
3 If you **motion** to someone, you move your hand VERB:
or head as a way of telling them to do something or V ton
where to go. *She motioned for the locked front doors* V n prep/adv
to be opened... He stood aside and motioned Don to V n to-inf
the door... I motioned him to join us. **4** A **motion** is N-COUNT
a formal proposal or statement in a meeting, de-
bate, or trial, which is discussed and then voted on
or decided on. *Opposition parties are likely to bring
a no-confidence motion against the government.*
5 Some people, especially doctors or nurses, use N-COUNT
motion as a polite way of referring to a person's act BRITISH
of defecation or the faeces produced. *Try to make
sure your bowel motions are regular.*
6 See also **slow motion.**
7 If you say that someone **is going through the mo-** PHRASE
tions, you think they are only saying or doing some- PRAGMATICS
thing because it is expected of them without being interested, enthusiastic, or sympathetic. **8** If a process PHRASE
or event is **in motion,** it is happening. If it is **set in motion,** it is happening or beginning to happen.

mo·tion·less /'məʊʃənləs/. Someone or something ◆◇◇◇◇
that is **motionless** is not moving at all. *He remained* ADJ-GRADED
quite motionless behind his desk.

'motion picture, motion pictures. A **motion** ◆◇◇◇◇
picture is a film made for cinema. ...*the motion pic-* N-COUNT
ture industry. AMERICAN

mo·ti·vate /'məʊtɪveɪt/ **motivates, motivating,** ◆◆◆◇◇
motivated. 1 If you **are motivated** by something, VERB
especially an emotion, it causes you to behave in a beV-ed
particular way. *The crime was not politically moti-* V n to-inf
vated... What motivates athletes to take drugs? Also V n
♦ **mo·ti·vat·ed** ...*highly motivated employees.* ADJ-GRADED
♦ **mo·ti·va·tion** *His poor performance may be at-* N-UNCOUNT
tributed to lack of motivation. **2** If someone **moti-** VERB:
vates you to do something, they make you feel de- V n to-inf
termined to do it. *The manager doesn't know how to* V n
motivate his players. ♦ **motivation** *Given parental* N-UNCOUNT
*motivation we are optimistic about the ability of
people to change.*

mo·ti·va·tion /,məʊtɪ'veɪʃən/ **motivations.** Your ◆◆◇◇◇
motivation for doing something is what causes you N-COUNT
to want to do it. *The timing of the attack, and its
motivations, are unknown.*

mo·tive /'məʊtɪv/ **motives.** Your **motive** for doing ◆◆◇◇◇
something is your reason for doing it. *Police have* N-COUNT
ruled out robbery as a motive for the killing... His
motives are good, even if misguided.*

mot·ley /'mɒtli/. You can describe a group of ◆◇◇◇◇
things as a **motley** collection if you think they seem ADJ-GRADED
strange together because they are all very different. ADJ n
...*a motley collection of vans, old buses, cattle-trucks,
and even a fire engine.*

mo·tor /'məʊtə/ **motors, motoring, motored.** ◆◆◆◆◇
1 The **motor** in a machine, vehicle, or boat is the N-COUNT
part that uses electricity or fuel to produce movement, so that the machine, vehicle, or boat can
work. **2 Motor** vehicles and boats have a petrol or ADJ: ADJ n
diesel engine. **3 Motor** is used to describe activities ADJ: ADJ n
relating to motor vehicles. ...*the future of the British
motor industry.*
4 Some people refer to a car as a **motor.** *It's a lovely lit-* N-COUNT

tle motor. **5** If you **motor** somewhere, you travel there VERB
in a car, usually for pleasure. *I had motored down* V adv/prep
from Cheshire. **6** If the crew of a small sailing boat DATED
motor somewhere, they use the boat's motor rather V adv/prep
than the power of the wind to get the boat there. *Restarting the engine, we motored downriver.* **7** See also
motoring.

motor·bike /'məʊtəbaɪk/ **motorbikes;** also ◆◇◇◇◇
spelled **motor-bike.** A **motorbike** is the same as a N-COUNT
motorcycle.

motor·boat /'məʊtəbəʊt/ **motorboats;** also N-COUNT
spelled **motor boat.** A **motorboat** is a boat that is
driven by an engine.

motor·cade /'məʊtəkeɪd/ **motorcades.** A motor- N-COUNT
cade is a line of slowly-moving cars carrying important people, usually as part of a public ceremony.

'motor car, motor cars. A motor car is the same ◆◇◇◇◇
as a **car.** N-COUNT
DATED

motor·cycle /'məʊtəsaɪkəl/ **motorcycles.** A ◆◇◇◇◇
motorcycle is a two-wheeled vehicle which is driv- N-COUNT
en by an engine.

motor·cyclist /'məʊtəsaɪklɪst/ **motorcyclists.** A N-COUNT
motorcyclist is a person who rides a motorcycle.

mo·tor·ing /'məʊtərɪŋ/. Motoring means relating ◆◇◇◇◇
to cars and driving. ...*a three-month sentence for* ADJ: ADJ n
motoring offences. ...one of Britain's largest motoring organisations.*

mo·tor·ist /'məʊtərɪst/ **motorists.** A motorist is a ◆◆◇◇◇
person who drives a car. N-COUNT

mo·tor·ized /'məʊtəraɪzd/; also spelled **motorised.** ADJ
1 A **motorized** vehicle has an engine. *Motorized
carriages were beginning to replace horse-drawn
cabs.* **2** A **motorized** group of soldiers is equipped ADJ
with motor vehicles. ...*motorized infantry.*

,motor 'neurone disease. Motor neurone dis- N-UNCOUNT
ease is a disease which destroys the part of a person's nervous system that controls movement.

motor·way /'məʊtəweɪ/ **motorways.** A motor- ◆◆◇◇◇
way is a major road that has been specially built for N-VAR
fast travel over long distances. Motorways have sev- BRITISH
eral lanes and special places where traffic gets on
and leaves. The usual American word is **freeway.**
...*the M1 motorway.*

mott·led /'mɒtld/. Something that is **mottled** is ADJ-GRADED
covered with irregular patches of different colours.
...*mottled green and yellow leaves.*

mot·to /'mɒtəʊ/ **mottoes** or **mottos.** A motto is a ◆◇◇◇◇
short sentence or phrase that expresses the attitude N-COUNT
to life of a person or group. *The regiment's motto is
'Nemo nos impune lacessit' (No one provokes us with
impunity)... Aim high, that's my motto.*

mould /məʊld/ **moulds, moulding, moulded;** ◆◆◇◇◇
spelled **mold** in American English. **1** A **mould** is a N-COUNT
container that you use to make something into a
particular shape. You pour a soft or liquid substance such as melted metal or jelly into the mould,
and when it becomes solid, it has the same shape as
the mould. ...*jelly moulds.* **2** If a person fits into or N-COUNT
is cast in a **mould** of a particular kind, they have the
characteristics that are typical of that particular
type of person. *At first sight, Joe Pesci is not exactly
cast in the leading man mould.* ♦ If you say that PHRASE
someone **breaks the mould,** you mean that they do
completely different things from what has been
done before or from what is usually done.
3 If you **mould** a soft substance such as plastic or clay, VERB: V n
you make it into a particular shape or into an object. V n into n
Mould the cheese mixture into small balls. **4** To **mould** VERB: V n
someone or something means to change or influence V n into n
them over a period of time so that they develop in a
particular way. *Too often we try to mould our children
into something they do not wish to be.* **5** When some- V-ERG:
thing **moulds** to an object or when you **mould** it V prep
there, it round the object tightly so that the shape V n prep
of the object can still be seen. *She moulded her skirt
against her thighs.*
6 Mould is a soft grey, green, or blue substance that N-VAR
sometimes forms in spots on old food or damp walls.

mould·er /'məʊldə/ **moulders, mouldering,** VERB
mouldered; spelled **molder** in American English. V

If something **is mouldering**, it is decaying slowly where it has been left. *...one of your scripts that's been mouldering under the bed for ages.*

mould·ing /'mǝʊldɪŋ/ **mouldings;** spelled **molding** in American English. A **moulding** is a strip of plaster or wood along the top of a wall or round a door, which has been made into an ornamental shape or decorated with a pattern. ◆◇◇◇◇ N-COUNT

mouldy /'mǝʊldi/; spelled **moldy** in American English. Something that is **mouldy** is covered with mould. *Oranges can be kept for a long time without going mouldy.* ADJ-GRADED

moult /mǝʊlt/ **moults, moulting, moulted;** spelled **molt** in American English. When an animal or bird **moults**, it gradually loses its coat or feathers so that a new coat or feathers can grow. ◆◇◇◇◇ VERB:

mound /maʊnd/ **mounds.** A **mound** of things is a large heap or pile of them. *The bulldozers piled up huge mounds of dirt... The table was a mound of paper and books.* ◆◇◇◇◇ N-COUNT

mount /maʊnt/ **mounts, mounting, mounted.** **1** If you **mount** a campaign or event, you organize it and make it take place. *The ANC announced it was mounting a major campaign of mass political protests.* **2** If something **mounts**, it increases in intensity. *For several hours, tension mounted.* **3** If something **mounts**, it increases in quantity. *The uncollected garbage mounts in city streets.* ▶ To **mount up** means the same as to **mount**. *Her medical bills mounted up.* ◆◆◇◇◇ VERB / V n / VERB / V / VERB / V / PHRASAL VB / V P
4 If you **mount** the stairs or a platform, you go up the stairs or go up onto the platform. *The vehicle mounted the pavement.* **5** If you **mount** a horse or cycle, you climb on to it so that you can ride it. *They all mounted and rode off.* **6** A **mount** is a horse. *...the number of owners who care for older mounts.* VERB / V n / FORMAL / VERB: V n / V / N-COUNT / FORMAL
7 If you **mount** an object on something, you fix it there firmly. *Her husband mounts the work on velour paper.* ♦ **-mounted** *...a wall-mounted electric fan.* **8** If you **mount** an exhibition or display, you organize and present it. *The gallery has mounted an exhibition of art by Irish women painters.* VERB / V n on n / Also V n / COMB / VERB / V n
9 Mount is used as part of the name of a mountain. *...Mount Everest.* ● See also **mounted**.

mount up. See **mount** 3. PHRASAL VB

moun·tain /'maʊntɪn, AM -tən/ **mountains.** **1** A **mountain** is a very high area of land with steep sides. *...a lovely little mountain village.* **2** If you talk about a **mountain** of something or **mountains** of it, you are emphasizing that there is a large amount of it. *They are faced with a mountain of bureaucracy.* ◆◆◆◇ N-COUNT / QUANT / PRAGMATICS / INFORMAL

'mountain bike, mountain bikes. A **mountain bike** is a type of bicycle with a strong frame and thick tyres, suitable for riding over rough ground. ◆◇◇◇◇ N-COUNT

moun·tain·eer·ing /ˌmaʊntɪ'nɪərɪŋ/. **Mountaineering** is the activity of climbing the steep sides of mountains as a hobby or sport. ♦ **moun·tain·eer, mountaineers** *He is an experienced mountaineer.* N-UNCOUNT / N-COUNT

moun·tain·ous /'maʊntɪnəs/. **1** A **mountainous** place has a lot of mountains. *...the mountainous region of Campania.* **2** You use **mountainous** to emphasize that something is great in size, quantity, or degree. *...the company's mountainous debt.* ◆◇◇◇◇ ADJ-GRADED / ADJ: ADJ n / PRAGMATICS

moun·tain·side /'maʊntɪnsaɪd/ **mountainsides.** A **mountainside** is one of the steep sides of a mountain. *...the sheep on the mountainside.* ◆◇◇◇◇ N-COUNT

mount·ed /'maʊntɪd/. **Mounted** police or soldiers ride horses when they are on duty. ● See also **mount**. ◆◇◇◇◇ ADJ: ADJ n

mourn /mɔːn/ **mourns, mourning, mourned.** **1** If you **mourn** someone who has died, you are very sad that they have died and show your sorrow in the way that you behave. *He mourned for his valiant men.* ♦ **mourn·ing** *...the period of mourning and bereavement.* ● If you are **in mourning**, you are dressed or behaving in a particular way because someone you love or respect has died. **2** If you **mourn** something, you regret that you no longer have it and show your regret in the way that you behave. *She mourned for the beloved past.* VERB: V n / V forn / Also V / N-UNCOUNT / PHRASE / VERB: V n / V forn

mourn·er /'mɔːnə/ **mourners.** A **mourner** is a person who attends a funeral, especially as a relative or friend of the dead person. ◆◇◇◇◇ N-COUNT

mourn·ful /'mɔːnfʊl/. **1** If you are **mournful**, you are very sad. *He looked mournful, even near to tears.* ♦ **mourn·ful·ly** *He stood mournfully at the gate waving bye bye.* **2** A **mournful** sound seems very sad. *...the mournful wail of bagpipes.* ◆◇◇◇◇ ADJ-GRADED / ADV-GRADED / ADJ-GRADED

mourn·ing /'mɔːnɪŋ/. See **mourn**. ◆◇◇◇◇

mouse /maʊs/ **mice.** **1** A **mouse** is a small furry animal with a long tail. **2** A **mouse** is a hand-held device that you use with a computer system. By moving it and pressing its buttons, you can perform certain operations without using the keyboard. **3** ● game of cat and mouse: see cat. ◆◆◇◇◇ N-COUNT / N-COUNT

mouse·trap /'maʊstræp/ **mousetraps.** A **mousetrap** is a small device that catches or kills mice. N-COUNT

mous·ey /'maʊsi/. See **mousy**.

mousse /muːs/ **mousses.** **1** Mousse is a sweet light food made from eggs and cream. It is often flavoured with fruit or chocolate. **2** Mousse is a white foamy substance that you can put in your hair to make it easier to shape into a particular style. ◆◇◇◇◇ N-VAR / N-VAR

mous·tache /mə'stɑːʃ, AM 'mʌstæʃ/ **moustaches;** also spelled **mustache.** A man's **moustache** is the hair that grows on his upper lip. If it is very long, it is sometimes referred to as his **moustaches.** ♦ **mous·tached** *...three burly, moustached middle-aged men.* ◆◇◇◇◇ N-COUNT / ADJ

mous·ta·chi·oed /məs'tæʃiəʊd, AM -'tætʃəʊd/; also spelled **mustachioed.** A **moustachioed** man has a moustache, especially a thick, curly, or fancy one. ADJ / LITERARY

mousy /'maʊsi/; also spelled **mousey.** **1** Mousy hair is a dull light brown colour. **2** If someone is **mousy**, they are quiet and shy and people do not notice them. *The Inspector remembered her as a small, mousy woman.* ADJ-GRADED / ADJ-GRADED

mouth, **mouths, mouthing, mouthed.** The noun is pronounced /maʊθ/. The verb is pronounced /maʊð/. The plural of the noun and the third person singular of the verb are both pronounced /maʊðz/. **1** Your **mouth** is the area of your face where your lips are or the space behind your lips where your teeth and tongue are. *She clamped her hand against her mouth... His mouth was full of peas.* ♦ **-mouthed** /-maʊðd/ *He straightened up and looked at me, open-mouthed.* **2** You can say that someone has a particular kind of **mouth** to indicate that they speak in a particular kind of way or that they say particular kinds of things. *You've got such a crude mouth!* ♦ **-mouthed** *...Simon, their smart-mouthed teenage son.* **3** The **mouth** of a cave, hole, or bottle is its entrance or opening. ♦ **-mouthed** *Put the flowers in a wide-mouthed blue vase.* **4** If you have a number of **mouths to feed**, you have the responsibility of earning enough money to feed and look after that number of people. *My father had 11 mouths to feed.* **5** If you say that someone does not **open their mouth**, you are emphasizing that they never say anything at all. *He hasn't opened his mouth since he's been there.* **6** If you **keep your mouth shut** about something, you do not talk about it, especially because it is a secret. *You wouldn't be here now if she'd kept her mouth shut.* ◆◆◆◇ N-COUNT / COMB / N-COUNT: with supp / COMB / N-COUNT / COMB / PHRASE / PHRASE / PRAGMATICS / PHRASE
7 The **mouth** of a river is the place where it flows into the sea. **8** If you **mouth** something, you form words with your lips without making any sound. *'It's for you,' he mouthed.* **9** If you **mouth** something, you say it, especially without believing it or without understanding it. *I mouthed some sympathetic platitudes.* N-COUNT / VERB: V n / V with quote / VERB / V n
10 ● live hand to mouth: see hand. ● heart in your mouth: see heart. ● from the horse's mouth: see horse. ● to put your money where your mouth is: see money. ● shut your mouth: see shut. ● born with a silver spoon in your mouth: see spoon. ● word of mouth: see word. ● put words into someone's mouth: see word.

mouth·ful /'maʊθfʊl/ **mouthfuls.** **1** A **mouthful** of drink or food is the amount that you put or have in ◆◇◇◇◇ N-COUNT

your mouth. *Chew each mouthful fully before the next bite.* **2** If you describe a long word or phrase as **a mouthful**, you mean that it is difficult to say. *It's called the Pan-Caribbean Disaster Preparedness and Prevention Project, which is quite a mouthful.*

'mouth organ, mouth organs. A mouth organ is the same as a **harmonica**.

mouth·piece /'maʊθpiːs/ **mouthpieces. 1** The **mouthpiece** of a telephone is the part that you speak into. **2** The **mouthpiece** of a musical instrument or other device is the part that you put into your mouth. **3** The **mouthpiece** of an organization or person is someone who informs other people of the opinions and policies of that organization or person. *Their mouthpiece is the vice-president.*

mouth·wash /'maʊθwɒʃ/ **mouthwashes.** Mouthwash is a liquid that you rinse your mouth with, in order to clean and freshen it.

'mouth-watering; also spelled **mouthwatering. 1** Mouth-watering food looks or smells extremely delicious. *...more than 150 mouthwatering recipes.* **2** If you describe something as **mouth-watering**, you are emphasizing that it is very attractive. *...prizes worth a mouth-watering £9.6 million.*

mov·able /'muːvəbəl/; also spelled **moveable.** Something that is **movable** can be moved from one place or position to another. *It's a vinyl doll with movable arms and legs.*

move /muːv/ **moves, moving, moved. 1** When you **move** something or when it **moves**, its position changes and it does not remain still. *She moved the sheaf of papers into position... I could see the branches of the trees moving back and forth... The train began to move.* **2** When you **move**, you change your position or go to a different place. *She moved away from the window.* ▶ Also a noun. *Daniel's eyes followed her every move.* **3** If a person or company **moves**, they leave the building where they have been living or working, and go to live or work in a different place. *She had often considered moving to London... The London Evening Standard moved offices a few years ago.* ▶ Also a noun. *Modigliani announced his move to Montparnasse in 1909.* **4** If people in authority **move** someone, they make that person go from one place or job to another one. *His superiors moved him to another parish.* **5** If you **make a move**, you prepare or begin to leave one place and go somewhere else. *He glanced at his wristwatch. 'I suppose we'd better make a move.'* **6** If you are **on the move**, you are going from one place to another. *...they were always on the move.* **7** If you **move** from one job or interest to another, you change to it. *In the early days Christina moved jobs to get experience.* ▶ Also a noun. *...his move to the chairmanship.* **8** If you **move** to a new topic in a conversation, you start talking about something different. *Let's move to another subject, Dan.* **9** If you **move** an event to another date, you change the time at which it happens. *The band have moved forward their Leeds date to October 27.* **10** If you **move** towards a particular state, activity, or opinion, you start to be in that state, do that activity, or have that opinion. *The Labor Party has moved to the right and become like your Democrat Party.* ▶ Also a noun. *His move to the left was not a sudden leap but a natural working out of ideas.* **11** If you say that you will **not be moved**, you mean that you have come to a decision and nothing will change your mind. *Everyone thought I was mad to go back, but I wouldn't be moved.* **12** If a situation or process **is moving**, it is developing or progressing, rather than staying still. *...events are moving fast.* **13** A **move** is an act of putting a chess piece or other counter in a different position on a board when it is your turn to do so in a game. **14** A **move** is an action that you take in order to achieve something. *It may also be a good move to suggest she talks things over.* **15** If you **make a move**, you take a course of action. *...fifteen Japanese banks made a move to pull out.*

16 If you say that **one false move** will cause a disaster, you mean that you or someone else must not make even one mistake because the situation is so tricky or dangerous. *He knew one false move would end in death.* **17** If you **move**, you act or you begin to do something. *Industrialists must move fast to take advantage of new opportunities in Eastern Europe.* **18** If you tell someone to **get a move on**, you are telling them to hurry. **19** If something **moves** you to do something, it influences you and causes you to do it. *It was punk that first moved him to join a band seriously.* **20** If something **moves** you, it has an effect on your emotions and causes you to feel sadness or sympathy for another person. *His prayer moved me to tears.* ♦ **moved** *Walesa himself appeared to be deeply moved.* **21** If you **move** a motion or amendment, you formally propose it at a meeting so that everyone present can vote for or against it. *I move that the case be dismissed.* **22** You say that someone **moves in** a particular society, circle, or world when you mean that they know people in that social class or group and spend most of their time with them. *She moves in high-society circles in London.* **23** ● to **move the goalposts**: see **goalpost**. ● to **move heaven and earth**: see **heaven**. ● to **move a muscle**: see **muscle**.

move about or **move around.** The form **move about** is mainly used in British English. If you **move about** or **move around**, you keep changing your job or keep changing the place where you live. *He moved around the country working in orange groves.*

move along. 1 If someone, especially a police officer, tells you to **move along** or **move on**, they tell you to stop standing in a particular place and to go somewhere else. *The police were called to move them on.* **2** If a process **moves along** or if something **moves** it **along**, it progresses. *I hope we can move things along.*

move away. If you **move away**, you go and live in a different town or area of a country.

move down. If someone or something **moves down**, they go to a lower level, grade, or class. *Gold prices moved down.*

move in. 1 When you **move in** somewhere, you begin to live in a different house or place. *Her husband had moved in with a younger woman... He suggested we should move in together.* **2** If police, soldiers, or attackers **move in**, they go towards a place or person in order to deal with or attack them. *Forces were moving in on the town of Knin.* **3** If someone **moves in** on an area of activity which was previously only done by a particular group of people, they start becoming involved with it for the first time. *These black models are moving in on what was previously white territory: the lucrative cosmetic contracts.*

move into. If you **move into** a new house, you start living there. *I want you to move into my apartment.*

move off. When a vehicle or large group of people **moves off**, they start moving away from a place. *Gil waved his hand and the car moved off.*

move on. 1 When you **move on** somewhere, you leave the place where you have been staying or waiting and go or travel there. *What's wrong with his wanting to sell his land and move on?* **2** See **move along 1**. **3** If you **move on**, you finish or stop one activity and start doing something new. *His mother, Julia, soon moved on to a new relationship.*

move out. If you **move out**, you stop living in a particular house or place and you go to live somewhere else. *They had a huge row and Sally moved out of the house.*

move over. 1 If you **move over** to a new system or way of doing something, you change to it. *...moving over to a market economy.* **2** If you **move over**, you change your position in order to make room for someone else. *Move over and let me drive.*

move up. 1 If you **move up**, you change your position, especially in order to be nearer someone or to make room for someone else. *Move up, John, and let the lady sit down.* **2** If someone or something **moves**

up, they go to a higher level, grade, or class. *Children learn in mixed ability classes and move up a class each year.* `V P n`

move·able /'mu:vəbəl/. See **movable**.

move·ment /'mu:vmənt/ **movements. 1** A movement is a group of people who share the same beliefs, ideas, or aims. *...the women's movement.* `N-COUNT`

2 Movement involves changing position or going from one place to another. *They actually monitor the movement of the fish going up river... Her hand movements are becoming more animated.* **3** A **movement** is a planned change in position that an army makes during a battle or military exercise. *There are reports of fresh troop movements towards China.* **4 Movement** is a gradual development or change of an attitude, opinion, or policy. *...the movement towards democracy in Latin America.* **5** Your **movements** are everything which you do or plan to do during a period of time. *I want a full account of your movements the night Mr Gower was killed.* `N-VAR` `N-VAR` `N-VAR: with supp` `N-PLURAL: poss N`

6 A **movement** of a piece of classical music is one of its main sections. *...the first movement of Beethoven's 7th symphony.* `N-COUNT`

mov·er /'mu:və/ **movers.** If you describe a person or animal as a particular kind of **mover**, you mean that they move at that speed or in that way. *We found him a nice horse – a good mover who could gallop.* • See also **prime mover**. `N-COUNT: adj N`

movie /'mu:vi/ **movies. 1** A **movie** is a film. *...a horror movie.* **2** You can talk about the **movies** when you are talking about seeing a movie in a movie theater. The British term is **the cinema**. *He took her to the movies.* **3 The movies** are movies in general, or the business and art of making movies. The British term is **cinema**. *...sights I'd only ever seen in the movies.* `N-COUNT` `N-PLURAL: the N AMERICAN` `N-PLURAL: the N AMERICAN`

movie·goer /'mu:vigəʊə/ **moviegoers.** A **moviegoer** is a person who often goes to the movies. `N-COUNT AMERICAN`

'movie house, movie houses. A **movie house** is the same as a **movie theater**. `N-COUNT AMERICAN`

'movie theater, movie theaters. A **movie theater** is a place where people go to watch films for entertainment. The British word is **cinema**. `N-COUNT AMERICAN`

mov·ing /'mu:vɪŋ/. **1** If something is **moving**, it makes you feel a strong emotion such as sadness, pity, or sympathy. *It was a moving moment for Marianne.* ♦ **mov·ing·ly** *your sister Diana's suicide.* **2** A **moving** model or part of a machine moves or is able to move. **3** The **moving spirit** or **moving force** behind something is a person or thing that caused it to start and to keep going, or that influenced people to take part in it. *She alone must have been the moving spirit behind the lawsuit that lost me my position.* `ADJ-GRADED` `ADV-GRADED: ADV with v ADJ: ADJ n PHRASE`

moving 'picture, moving pictures. A **moving picture** is a film. `N-COUNT DATED`

mow /məʊ/ **mows, mowing, mowed, mown.** The past participle can be either **mowed** or **mown.** If you **mow** an area of grass, you cut it using a lawn mower. *...he continued to mow the lawn.* `VERB V n Also V`

mow down. If someone **is mown down**, they are killed violently by a vehicle or gunfire. *Gunmen mowed down 10 people in one attack.* `PHRASAL VB be V-ed P V P noun Also V n P`

mow·er /'məʊə/ **mowers. 1** A **mower** is the same as a **lawnmower. 2** A **mower** is a machine that has sharp blades for cutting something such as corn or wheat. `N-COUNT N-COUNT`

MP /ˌem 'pi:/ **MPs. 1** In Britain, an **MP** is a person who has been elected to represent the people from a particular area in the House of Commons. **MP** is an abbreviation for 'Member of Parliament'. *...Colin Pickthall, MP for West Lancashire.* **2 MP** is written after someone's name to indicate that they have been elected as an MP. `N-COUNT`

mpg /ˌem pi: 'dʒi:/. **mpg** is an abbreviation for 'miles per gallon'; it is written after a number to indicate how many miles a vehicle can travel using one gallon of fuel.

mph. **mph** is an abbreviation for 'miles per hour'; it is written after a number to indicate the speed of something such as a vehicle. `♦◊◊◊◊`

Mr /'mɪstə/; this abbreviation is usually followed by a full stop in American English. **1 Mr** is used before a man's name when you are speaking or referring to him. *Hello, Mr Simpson. ...Mr Bob Price.* **2 Mr** is sometimes used in front of words such as 'President' and 'Chairman' to address the man who holds the position mentioned. *Mr. President, you're aware of the system.* `♦♦♦♦♦ N-TITLE` `N-VOC: N n`

Mrs /'mɪsɪz/; this abbreviation is usually followed by a full stop in American English. **Mrs** is used before the name of a married woman when you are speaking or referring to her. *Hello, Mrs Miles. ...Mrs Anne Pritchard.* `♦♦♦♦♦ N-TITLE`

Ms /məz, mɪz/. **Ms** is used before a woman's name when you are speaking to her or referring to her. If you use **Ms**, you are not specifying if the woman is married or not. *...Ms Elizabeth Harman.* `♦♦♦♦♦ N-TITLE`

MS /ˌem 'es/. **1 MS** is a serious disease of the nervous system, which gradually makes a person weaker, and sometimes affects their sight or speech. **MS** is an abbreviation for **multiple sclerosis. 2** An **MS** is the same as an **MSc.** `N-UNCOUNT` `AMERICAN`

MSc /ˌem es 'si:/ **MScs. 1** An **MSc** is a master's degree in a science subject. **MSc** is an abbreviation for 'Master of Science'. **2 MSc** is written after someone's name to indicate that they have an MSc. `♦◊◊◊◊ N-COUNT`

Mt, Mts. **Mt** is a written abbreviation for **mount** or **mountain.** It is used as part of the name of a mountain or range of mountains. *...Mt Everest.* `♦◊◊◊◊`

much /mʌtʃ/. **1** You use **much** to indicate the great intensity, extent, or degree of something such as an action, feeling, or change. **Much** is usually used with 'so', 'too', and 'very', and in negative clauses with this meaning. *She laughs too much... Thank you very much... 'Can you hear it where you live?' He shook his head. 'Not much.'...* My hairstyle hasn't changed much since I was five. **2** You use **much** in front of 'too' or comparative adjectives and adverbs in order to emphasize that there is a large amount of a particular quality. *The skin is much too delicate... You'd be so much happier if you could see yourself the way I see you.* **3** If one thing is **much** the same as another thing, it is very similar to it. *The day ended much as it began... Sheep's milk is produced in much the same way as goat's milk.* **4** You use **so much so** to indicate that your previous statement is true to a very great extent, and therefore it has the result mentioned. *He himself believed in freedom, so much so that he would rather die than live without it.* **5** You use **very much** to emphasize that someone or something has a lot of a particular quality, or that the description you are about to give is particularly accurate. *Yorkshire is still very much a farming community.* `♦♦♦♦♦ ADV-GRADED` `ADV-GRADED: ADV compar, ADV too PRAGMATICS` `ADV: ADV as/like cl, ADV like n` `PHRASE PRAGMATICS` `PHRASE PRAGMATICS`

6 You use **much** to indicate that you are referring to a large amount of a substance, or of something else referred to by an uncount noun. *They are grown on the hillsides in full sun, without much water... Much crime goes unreported.* ▶ Also a pronoun. *There was so much to talk about.* ▶ Also a quantifier. *Joyce was tired and in pain much of the time... She does much of her work abroad.* **7** You use **much** in the expression **how much** to ask questions about amount or degree, and also in reported clauses and statements to give information about the amount or degree of something. *How much money can I afford?* ▶ Also an adverb. *She knows how much this upsets me.* ▶ Also a pronoun. *How much do you earn?* `DET` `PRON` `QUANT` `DET PRAGMATICS` `ADV-GRADED: how ADV PRON`

8 You use **much** in the expression **as much** when you are comparing amounts. *I shall try, with as much patience as is possible, to explain yet again.* **9** You use **as much as** before an amount to suggest that it is surprisingly large. *The organisers hope to raise as much as £6m for charity.* `DET` `PHRASE PRAGMATICS`

10 If something does not happen **much**, it does not happen very often. *His father never talked much* `ADV-GRADED`

about the war. **11** If you do not see **much of** someone, you do not see them very often.   QUANT

12 You say **nothing much** to refer to something that is not very interesting or important. *'What was stolen?'—'Oh, nothing much.'* **13** If you describe something as **not much of a** particular type of thing, you mean that it is small or of poor quality. *It hasn't been much of a holiday.* **14** If a situation or action is **too much** for you, it is so difficult, tiring, or upsetting that you cannot cope with it. *His inability to stay at one job for long had finally proved too much for her.*   PHRASE

15 You use **much less** after a statement, often a negative one, to indicate that the statement is even more true of the person, thing, or situation that you are going to mention next. *They are always short of water to drink, much less to bathe in.* **16** If you say that something is not **so much** one thing **as** another, you mean that it is more like the second thing than the first. *I don't really think of her as a daughter so much as a very good friend.*   PHRASE / PRAGMATICS

17 So much for is used to indicate that you have finished talking about a subject. *Well, so much for the producers. But what of the consumers?* **18** If you say **so much for** a particular thing, you mean that it has not been successful or helpful. *So much for all his damn theories!* **19** If you say that someone did not do **so much as** perform a particular action, you are emphasizing that they did not even do that, when you were expecting them to do more. *I didn't so much as catch sight of him all day long.* **20** You use **as much** in expressions such as **'I thought as much'** and **'I guessed as much'** after you have just been told something and you want to say that you already believed or expected it to be true. *You're waiting for a woman – I thought as much.*   PHRASE / PRAGMATICS

21 You use **much as** to introduce a fact which makes something else you have just said or will say rather surprising. *Much as they hope to go home tomorrow, they're resigned to staying on.*   PHR-CONJ / PRAGMATICS

22 • a bit much: see **bit. • not up to much:** see **up.**

much- /mʌtʃ-/. **Much-** combines with past participles to form adjectives which emphasize a particular quality of something or someone. *The resort will provide the tourist city with 150 much-needed rooms. ...a much-improved program.*   COMB / PRAGMATICS

much-ma'ligned. If you describe someone or something as **much-maligned**, you mean that they are often criticized by people, but you think the criticism is unfair or exaggerated. *...the much-maligned British Rail has a major expertise in electronic communications.*   ADJ-GRADED / PRAGMATICS

much-'travelled; spelled **much-traveled** in American English. A **much-travelled** person has travelled a lot in foreign countries.   ADJ

muck /mʌk/ **mucks, mucking, mucked.** **1** Muck is dirt or some other unpleasant substance. *This congealed muck was interfering with the filter and causing the flooding.* **2** Muck is manure. *...the smell of muck being spread.*   N-UNCOUNT INFORMAL / N-UNCOUNT

muck about or **muck around.** The form **muck about** is mainly used in British English. **1** If you **muck about** or **muck around**, you behave in a childish or silly way, often so that you waste your time and fail to achieve anything. *He'd spent his boyhood summers mucking about in boats.* **2** If you **muck about with** or **muck around with** something, you alter it, often making it worse than it already was. *The president's wife doesn't muck around with policy.*   PHRASAL VB / V P / V P prep/adv INFORMAL, BRITISH / V P with n INFORMAL

muck in. If someone **mucks in**, they join in with an activity or help other people with a job and do not consider themselves to be too important to do it. *Course residents are expected to muck in and be prepared to share rooms... She mucked in with the chores.*   PHRASAL VB / V P / V P with n INFORMAL, BRITISH

muck out. If you **muck out** a stable, pigsty, or other farm animal's home, you clean out all the manure and old hay. *He went to muck out the horses... Here's how to muck out.*   PHRASAL VB / V P noun / V P / Also V n P BRITISH

muck up. If you **muck up** or **muck** something **up**, you ruin something or do it very badly. *The people*   PHRASAL VB / V P / V P noun

who are mucking up the area come from outside... I've really managed to muck things up now.   V n P INFORMAL

'muck-raking; also spelled **muckraking.** If you accuse someone of **muck-raking**, you are criticizing them for finding and spreading scandal about someone, especially a public figure. *The allegations are disgraceful muck-raking.*   N-UNCOUNT PRAGMATICS

mucky /'mʌki/ **muckier, muckiest.** Something that is **mucky** is very dirty.   ADJ-GRADED INFORMAL

mu·cous mem·brane /ˌmjuːkəs 'membreɪn/ **mucous membranes.** A **mucous membrane** is a thin piece of skin that produces mucus to prevent itself from becoming dry. It covers delicate parts of the body such as the inside of your nose.   N-COUNT TECHNICAL

mu·cus /'mjuːkəs/. **Mucus** is a clear slimy liquid that is produced in some parts of your body, for example the inside of your nose.   ◆◇◇◇◇ N-UNCOUNT FORMAL

mud /mʌd/. **Mud** is a sticky mixture of earth and water. *Their lorry got stuck in the mud.*   ◆◆◇◇◇ N-UNCOUNT

mud·dle /'mʌdəl/ **muddles, muddling, muddled.** **1** If people or things are in a **muddle**, they are in a state of confusion or disorder. *My thoughts are all in a muddle.* **2** If you **muddle** things or people, you get them mixed up, so that you do not know which is which. *Already, one or two critics have begun to muddle the two names.* ► **Muddle up** means the same as **muddle**. *The question muddles up three separate issues... He sometimes muddles me up with other patients.* ♦ **mud·dled up** *I am getting my words muddled up.*   ◆◇◇◇ N-VAR / VERB V pl-n / PHRASAL VB V P pl-noun V n P with n Also V pl-n P / ADJ-GRADED

muddle through. If you **muddle through**, you manage to do something even though you do not have the proper equipment or do not really know how to do it. *The BBC may be able to muddle through the next five years like this.*   PHRASAL VB V P / V P n Also V way P

muddle up. See **muddle** 2.   PHRASAL VB

mud·dled /'mʌdəld/. If someone is **muddled**, they are confused about something. *This aim of wider share ownership is based on muddled thinking.*   ◆◇◇◇ ADJ-GRADED

mud·dy /'mʌdi/ **muddier, muddiest; muddies, muddying, muddied.** **1** Something that is **muddy** contains mud or is covered in mud. *...his muddy boots.* **2** If you **muddy** something, you cause it to be muddy. *His new grey jacket was torn and muddied.* **3** Muddy is used to describe a colour which is dull and brownish. *...a muddy green-brown.* **4** If someone or something **muddies** a situation or issue, they cause it to seem less clear and less easy to understand. *...the mixed motives that muddied Mr Crane's efforts.* ♦ **mud·died** *Overseas the legal issues are more muddied.* ● If someone or something **muddies the waters**, they cause a situation or issue to seem less clear and less easy to understand. *They keep on muddying the waters by raising other political issues.*   ◆◇◇◇ ADJ-GRADED / VERB: V n V-ed / VERB V n / ADJ-GRADED / PHRASE

mud·flats /'mʌdflæts/. **Mudflats** are areas of flat empty land at the coast which are covered by the sea only when the tide is in.   N-PLURAL

mud·guard /'mʌdɡɑːd/ **mudguards.** The **mudguards** on a bicycle or other vehicle are curved pieces of metal or plastic above the tyres, which stop the rider or vehicle from being splashed with mud. See picture headed **car and bicycle.**   N-COUNT

mud·slide /'mʌdslaɪd/ **mudslides.** A **mudslide** is a large amount of mud sliding down a mountain.   N-COUNT

'mud-slinging. If you accuse someone of **mud-slinging**, you are accusing them of making insulting, unfair, and damaging remarks about their opponents. *This political mud-slinging has left many ordinary Poles feeling confused.*   N-UNCOUNT PRAGMATICS

mues·li /'mjuːzli/ **mueslis.** Muesli is a breakfast cereal made from chopped nuts, dried fruit, and grains.   N-VAR

muff /mʌf/ **muffs, muffing, muffed.** **1** If you **muff** something, you do it badly or you make a mistake while you are doing it, so that it is not successful. *He muffed his opening speech.*   VERB V n INFORMAL

2 A **muff** is a piece of fur or thick cloth shaped like a short hollow cylinder, which you can put your hands   N-COUNT

M

in to warm them in cold weather. **3 Muffs** are the same as **earmuffs**.

muf·fin /'mʌfɪn/ **muffins. 1 Muffins** are small cakes, usually with fruit or some other flavouring in them. **2 Muffins** are small, flat, sweet bread rolls that you eat hot with butter.

muf·fle /'mʌfəl/ **muffles, muffling, muffled.** If something **muffles** a sound, it makes it quieter and more difficult to hear. *Blake held his handkerchief over the mouthpiece to muffle his voice.*

muf·fled /'mʌfəld/. If you are **muffled** or **muffled up**, you are wearing a lot of heavy clothes so that very little of your body or face is visible. *...children muffled in scarves and woolly hats.*

muf·fler /'mʌflə/ **mufflers. 1** A **muffler** is the same as a **scarf. 2** A **muffler** is a device on a car exhaust that makes it quieter. The British word is **silencer.**

mug /mʌg/ **mugs, mugging, mugged. 1** A **mug** is a large deep cup with straight sides and a handle, used for hot drinks. ▶ A **mug** of something is an amount of it contained in a cup.
2 If someone **mugs** you, they attack you in order to steal your money. *...a victim of mugging.* ♦ **mug·ger** /'mʌgə/, **muggers** *If you come face to face with a mugger, what do you do?*
3 If you say that someone is a **mug**, you mean that they are stupid and easily deceived or misled by other people. *He's a mug as far as women are concerned.*
4 Someone's **mug** is their face. *He managed to get his ugly mug on the telly.*

mug up. If you **mug up** a subject or **mug up** on it, you study it quickly, so that you can remember the main facts about it. *...visitors who want to mug up their knowledge in the shortest possible time... It is advisable to mug up on your Spanish.*

mug·gy /'mʌgi/. **Muggy** weather is unpleasantly warm and damp. *It was muggy and overcast.*

'mug shot, mug shots. A **mug shot** is a photograph of someone, especially a photograph of a criminal which has been taken by the police.

mul·berry /'mʌlbəri, AM -beri/ **mulberries.** A **mulberry** or a **mulberry tree** is a tree which has small purple or white berries. ▶ **Mulberries** are the fruit of a mulberry tree.

mulch /mʌltʃ/ **mulches, mulching, mulched.** To **mulch** plants means to put rotting leaves and twigs or manure on the ground around them to keep the soil moist and prevent weeds. ▶ Also a noun. *...thick mulches of decayed leaves.*

mule /mju:l/ **mules.** A **mule** is an animal whose parents are a horse and a donkey.

mull /mʌl/ **mulls, mulling, mulled.** If you **mull** something, you think about it for a long time before deciding what to do. *Do you know why he was mulling and hesitating?*

mull over. If you **mull** something **over**, you think about it for a long time before deciding what to do. *Mclaren had been mulling over an idea to make a movie.*

mul·lah /'mʊlə, 'mʌlə/ **mullahs.** A **mullah** is a Muslim who is a teacher, scholar, or religious leader.

mulled /mʌld/. **Mulled** wine has sugar and spice added to it and is then heated.

mul·let /'mʌlɪt/ **mullets; mullet** can also be used as the plural form. A **mullet** is a small sea fish that people cook and eat. ▶ **Mullet** is this fish eaten as food.

multi- /'mʌlti-/. **Multi-** is used to form adjectives indicating that something consists of many things of a particular kind. *...multi-party democracy.*

multi·col·oured /'mʌltikʌləd/; also spelled **multi-coloured**, and spelled **multicolored** in American English. A **multicoloured** object has many different colours. *...multicoloured umbrellas.*

multi·cul·tur·al /,mʌlti'kʌltʃərəl/; also spelled **multi-cultural. Multicultural** means consisting of or relating to people of many different nationalities and cultures. *...children growing up in a multicultural society.*

multi·cul·tur·al·ism /,mʌlti'kʌltʃərəlɪzəm/. **Multiculturalism** is the belief that all the different cultural or racial groups that make up a society should be given equal representation in areas such as education and the workplace.

multi-'faceted. Something that is **multi-faceted** has a variety of different and important features or elements. *Her job is multi-faceted.*

multi·fari·ous /,mʌlti'feəriəs/. If you describe things as **multifarious**, you mean that they are many in number and of many different kinds. *Spain is a composite of multifarious traditions and people.*

multi·lat·er·al /,mʌlti'lætərəl/. **Multilateral** means involving at least three different groups of people or nations. *...multilateral trade talks in Geneva.*

multi·lin·gual /,mʌlti'lɪŋgwəl/; also spelled **multi-lingual. 1 Multilingual** means involving several different languages. *...multilingual dictionaries.* **2** A **multilingual** person is able to speak more than two languages very well.

multi·media /,mʌlti'mi:diə/. **1** In computing, you use **multimedia** to refer to programs and products which involve the use of sound, pictures, and film, as well as ordinary text, to convey information. **2** In education, **multimedia** is the use of television and other different media in a lesson, instead of only textbooks. **3** In art, **multimedia** is the use of different kinds of material in a painting or sculpture.

multi·millio·naire, multi-millionaires; also spelled **multimillionaire.** A **multi-millionaire** is a very rich person who has money or property worth several million pounds or dollars.

multi·na·tion·al /,mʌlti'næʃənəl/ **multinationals;** also spelled **multi-national. 1** A **multinational** company has branches or subsidiary companies in many different countries. ▶ Also a noun. *...multinationals such as Ford and IBM.* **2 Multinational** armies, organizations, or other groups involve people from several different countries. *The US troops would be part of a multinational force.* **3 Multinational** countries or regions have a population that is made up of people of several different nationalities.

multi·ple /'mʌltɪpəl/ **multiples. 1** You use **multiple** to describe things that consist of many parts, involve many people, or have many uses. *He died of multiple injuries... The most common multiple births are twins.* **2** If one number is a **multiple** of a smaller number, it can be exactly divided by that smaller number. *We count the seconds, minutes and hours in multiples of six and ten.* **3** A **multiple** or a **multiple store** is a shop with a lot of branches in different towns.

multiple 'choice; also spelled **multiple-choice.** In a **multiple choice** test or question, you have to choose the answer that you think is right from several possible answers that are listed on the question paper.

multi·ple scle·ro·sis /,mʌltɪpəl sklə'rəʊsɪs/. **Multiple sclerosis** is a serious disease of the nervous system. The abbreviation 'MS' is also used.

multi·plex, multiplexes /'mʌltɪpleks/. A **multiplex** is a cinema complex with six or more screens.

multipli'cation table, multiplication tables. See **table.**

multi·plic·ity /,mʌltɪ'plɪsɪti/. A **multiplicity of** things is a large number or a large variety of them. *...a writer who uses a multiplicity of styles.*

multi·ply /'mʌltɪplaɪ/ **multiplies, multiplying, multiplied. 1** When something **multiplies**, it increases greatly in number or amount. *Her husband multiplied his demands on her time.* ♦ **multipli·ca·tion** /,mʌltɪplɪ'keɪʃən/ *Increasing gravity is known to speed up the multiplication of cells.* **2** When animals and insects **multiply**, they increase in number by giving birth to large numbers of young. **3** If you **multiply** one number by another, you calculate the total which you get when you add the first number to itself as many times as is indicated by the second number. *Twenty-five multiplied by one point one two is twenty-eight. ...the remark-*

able ability to multiply huge numbers correctly.
♦ **multiplication** *...simple tests in addition, sub-* N-UNCOUNT
traction, multiplication and division.

multi·racial /ˌmʌltiˈreɪʃəl/; also spelled **multi-** ADJ-GRADED
racial. **Multiracial** means consisting of or involving
people of many different nationalities and cultures.
We live in a multiracial society.

ˌmulti-ˈstorey. A **multi-storey** building has several ADJ
floors at different levels above the ground.

multi·tude /ˈmʌltɪtjuːd, AM -tuːd/ **multitudes.** ♦◇◇◇◇
1 A **multitude** of things or people is a very large QUANT
number of them. *There are a multitude of small qui-*
et roads to cycle along. **2** You can refer to a very N-COUNT
large number of people as a **multitude**. *...surround-* WRITTEN
ed by a noisy multitude. **3** **The multitude** or the N-COLL-
multitudes are the great majority of people in a COUNT:
particular country or situation. *The hideous truth* the N
was hidden from the multitude.

mum /mʌm/ **mums. 1** Your **mum** is your mother. N-FAMILY
He misses his mum. INFORMAL
2 If you **keep mum** about something, you do not tell PHRASE
anyone about it. *I'd be in trouble if I let on. So I kept* INFORMAL
mum.

mum·ble /ˈmʌmbəl/ **mumbles, mumbling,** ♦◇◇◇◇
mumbled. If you **mumble** something, you speak VERB: V n
very quietly and indistinctly so that the words are V with quote
difficult to understand. *'Today of all days,' she* Also V
mumbled. ▶ Also a noun. *He could hear the low* N-COUNT
mumble of Navarro's voice.

mumbo-jumbo /ˌmʌmbəʊ ˈdʒʌmbəʊ/. If you de- N-UNCOUNT
scribe an idea or belief as **mumbo-jumbo**, you are PRAGMATICS
criticizing it because you think it is unrealistic or INFORMAL
nonsensical. *It's all full of psychoanalytic mumbo-*
jumbo.

mum·mi·fy /ˈmʌmɪfaɪ/ **mummifies, mummify-** VERB:
ing, mummified. If a dead body **is mummified**, it beV-ed
is preserved, usually by rubbing it with special oils V-ed
and wrapping it in cloth. *...a mummified corpse sur-*
rounded by various artefacts.

mum·my /ˈmʌmi/ **mummies. 1** Some people, es- ♦◇◇◇◇
pecially children, call their mother **mummy**. N-FAMILY
INFORMAL
2 A **mummy** is a dead body which was preserved long N-COUNT
ago by being rubbed with special oils and wrapped in
cloth.

mumps /mʌmps/. **Mumps** is a disease usually N-UNCOUNT
caught by children in which the glands of the neck
swell up. *She's got mumps.*

munch /mʌntʃ/ **munches, munching,** ♦◇◇◇◇
munched. If you **munch** food, you eat it by chew- VERB: V n
ing it steadily, thoroughly, and rather noisily. *Across* V
the table, his son Benjie munched appreciatively... V way through
Sheep were munching their way through a yellow n
carpet of leaves. Also V away
at/on n

mun·dane /ˌmʌnˈdeɪn/. Something that is **mun-** ♦◇◇◇◇
dane is very ordinary and not at all interesting or ADJ-GRADED
unusual. *...the mundane realities of life.* ▶ You can N-SING:
refer to mundane things as **the mundane**. the N

mu·nic·i·pal /mjuːˈnɪsɪpəl/. **Municipal** means con- ♦♦◇◇◇
nected with the local government of a city or town. ADJ: ADJ n
...the municipal library.

mu·nic·i·pal·ity /mjuːˌnɪsɪˈpælɪti/ **municipalities.** ♦◇◇◇◇
A **municipality** is a city or town with its own local N-COUNT
council and officials. You can also refer to that city
or town's local government as the **municipality**.
...public woodlands, belonging to the municipality.

mu·ni·tions /mjuːˈnɪʃənz/. **Munitions** are military ♦◇◇◇◇
equipment and supplies, especially bombs and N-PLURAL
guns.

mu·ral /ˈmjʊərəl/ **murals.** A **mural** is a picture ♦◇◇◇◇
painted on a wall. N-COUNT

mur·der /ˈmɜːdə/ **murders, murdering, mur-** ♦♦♦♦◇
dered. 1 **Murder** is the deliberate and unlawful N-VAR
killing of a person. *...attempted murder... The mur-*
der charge was dismissed. **2** To **murder** someone VERB: V n
means to commit the crime of killing them deliber- V-ed
ately. *...the body of a murdered religious and politi-* Also V
cal leader. ♦ **mur·der·er, murderers** *...a notori-* N-COUNT
ous mass murderer. **3** If you say that someone **gets** PHRASE
away with murder, you are complaining that they PRAGMATICS
can do whatever they like without anyone trying to INFORMAL

control them or punish them. **4** If you say that PHRASE
someone **screams blue murder** or **screams bloody** PRAGMATICS
murder, you are emphasizing that they make a lot INFORMAL
of noise and fuss because something is happening
or has happened that they do not like.

mur·der·ess /ˈmɜːdərɪs/ **murderesses.** A **mur-** N-COUNT
deress is a woman who deliberately and unlawfully
kills another person.

mur·der·ous /ˈmɜːdərəs/. If you describe a person ♦◇◇◇◇
or their actions as **murderous**, you mean that they ADJ-GRADED
intend to kill someone or are likely to kill someone,
usually violently. *This murderous lunatic could kill*
them both.

mur·der·ous·ly /ˈmɜːdərəsli/. You use **murderous-** ADV
ly to indicate that something is extremely unpleasant or threatening. *The bags were murderously*
heavy.

murk /mɜːk/. The **murk** is darkness, dark water, or N-SING
thick mist that is very difficult to see through. *A tall*
old man in a black cloak loomed out of the murk.

murky /ˈmɜːki/ **murkier, murkiest. 1** A **murky** ♦◇◇◇◇
place or time of day is dark and rather unpleasant ADJ-GRADED
because there is not enough light. *...one murky No-*
vember afternoon. **2** **Murky** water or fog is so dark ADJ-GRADED
and dirty that you cannot see through it. **3** If you ADJ-GRADED
describe an activity or situation as **murky**, you sus- BRITISH
pect that it is dishonest or morally wrong. *...a*
murky conspiracy to keep them out of power. **4** If ADJ-GRADED
you describe something as **murky**, you mean that
the details of it are not clear or that it is difficult to
understand. *The law here is a little bit murky.*

mur·mur /ˈmɜːmə/ **murmurs, murmuring, mur-** ♦♦◇◇◇
mured. 1 If you **murmur** something, you say it VERB: V n
very quietly, so that not many people can hear what V n ton
you are saying. *He turned and murmured something* V with quote
to the professor... 'How lovely,' she murmured. Also V that
▶ Also a noun. *They spoke in low murmurs.* N-COUNT
2 A **murmur** is a continuous low sound, like the N-SING:
noise of a river or of distant voices. *I could hear the* with supp
murmur of the sea. **3** If there are **murmurs** of a par- N-COUNT:
ticular emotion, people are beginning to express with supp
that emotion. *Already there are murmurs of discon-*
tent. ♦ **mur·mur·ings** *There have been murmurings* N-PLURAL
of discontent over the government policy on infla-
tion. **4** A heart **murmur** is an abnormal sound N-COUNT
which is made by the heart and which shows that
there is probably something wrong with it. **5** If PHRASE
someone does something **without a murmur**, they
do it without complaining. *I explained what had*
happened and he accepted it without a murmur.

mus·cle /ˈmʌsəl/ **muscles, muscling, mus-** ♦♦♦◇◇
cled. 1 You **muscles** are the pieces of tissue inside N-VAR
your body which connect bones together and which
you use when you make a movement. You also refer
to the shapes which these make on your body as
your **muscles**. *Exercise will tone up your stomach*
muscles. **2** If you say that someone did not **move a** PHRASE
muscle, you mean that they stayed absolutely still.
3 If you say that someone has **muscle**, you mean N-UNCOUNT
that they have power and influence, which enables
them to do difficult things. *Eisenhower used his*
muscle to persuade Congress to change the law. **4** If PHRASE
a group, organisation, or country **flexes** its **muscles**,
it behaves in a way designed to show people that it
has power and is considering using it.

muscle in. If someone **muscles in** on something, PHRASAL VB
they force their way into a situation where they have V P onn
no right to be and where they are not welcome, in or- PRAGMATICS
der to gain some advantage for themselves; used V P
showing disapproval. *They are hoping to tie up the*
deal before any other rivals muscle in.

'muscle-bound. If you describe someone as ADJ-GRADED
muscle-bound, you mean that their muscles are
strongly developed, often in an exaggerated or unattractive way.

mus·cu·lar /ˈmʌskjʊlə/. **1** **Muscular** means involv- ♦♦◇◇◇
ing or affecting your muscles. *...muscular effort.* **2** If ADJ: ADJ n
a person or their body is **muscular**, they are very fit ADJ-GRADED
and strong, and have firm muscles which are not
covered with a lot of fat. *...his tanned muscular legs.*

M

mus·cu·lar dys·tro·phy /ˌmʌskjʊlə ˈdɪstrəfi/. Muscular dystrophy is a serious disease in which your muscles gradually weaken. N-UNCOUNT

mus·cu·la·ture /ˈmʌskjʊlətʃər/. Musculature refers to all the muscles in your body, or to a set of muscles that you use to perform a particular action. *He moved slowly and quietly, his musculature evident under his clothes.* N-UNCOUNT FORMAL

muse /mjuːz/ **muses, musing, mused. 1** If you muse on something, you think about it, usually saying or writing what you are thinking at the same time. *'When I was a child I was happy,' she mused.* ♦ **mus·ing, musings** *His musings were interrupted by Montagu.* **2** A muse is a person, usually a woman, who is believed to give inspiration and creative ideas to artists, writers, or musicians. ◆◇◇◇ VERB: V on/about/ overn V with quote WRITTEN N-COUNT N-COUNT

mu·seum /mjuːˈziːəm/ **museums.** A museum is a building where a large number of interesting and valuable objects, such as works of art or historical items, are kept, studied, and displayed to the public. *...the American Museum of Natural History.* ◆◆◆◇ N-COUNT

mu'seum piece, museum pieces. If you describe an object or building as a **museum piece**, you mean that it is old and unusual. N-COUNT

mush /mʌʃ/. Mush is a thick soft paste. *Be careful not to overcook them or they will turn to mush.* N-UNCOUNT: also a N

mush·room /ˈmʌʃruːm/ **mushrooms, mushrooming, mushroomed. 1** Mushrooms are fungi with short stems and round tops. Some types of mushrooms can be eaten. See picture headed **vegetables.** *...mushroom omelette.* **2** If something such as an industry or a place **mushrooms**, it grows or comes into existence very quickly. *A sleepy capital of a few hundred thousand people has mushroomed to a crowded city of 2 million.* ♦ **mush·room·ing** *...the mushrooming of commercial art galleries in Barcelona.* N-VAR VERB: V V to/into n N-UNCOUNT

'mushroom cloud, mushroom clouds. A mushroom cloud is an extremely large cloud caused by a nuclear explosion. N-COUNT

mushy /ˈmʌʃi/. **1** Vegetables and fruit that are mushy are soft and have lost most of their shape. **2** If you describe someone or something as **mushy**, you dislike them because they are very sentimental. *The film slides into mushy sentimentality.* ADJ-GRADED ADJ-GRADED PRAGMATICS

mu·sic /ˈmjuːzɪk/. **1** Music is the pattern of sounds produced by people singing or playing instruments. *...classical music. ...the music of George Gershwin.* **2** Music is the symbols written on paper which represent musical sounds. *He's never been able to read music.* ● See also **sheet music.** **3** If something that you hear or are told is **music to your ears**, you are very happy or pleased about it. *The slightest sound of conspiracy is music to the ears of journalists.* **4** If you **face the music**, you put yourself in a position where you will be criticized or punished for something you have done. ◆◆◆◆◆ N-UNCOUNT N-UNCOUNT PHRASE PHRASE

mu·si·cal /ˈmjuːzɪkəl/ **musicals. 1** Musical means connected with or relating to music. *We have a wealth of musical talent in this region. ...Stan Getz's musical career.* ♦ **mu·si·cal·ly** /ˈmjuːzɪkli/ *Musically there is a lot to enjoy. ...trying to communicate verbally what he can only communicate musically.* **2** A **musical** is a play or film that uses singing and dancing in the story. **3** Someone who is **musical** has a natural ability and interest in music. *My father was very musical.* ♦ **mu·si·cal·ity** /ˌmjuːzɪˈkælɪti/ *...a people of extraordinary musicality.* **4** Sounds that are **musical** are light and pleasant to hear. *He had a soft, almost musical voice.* ♦ **mu·si·cal·ly** *The voice was as musically soft as ever.* ◆◆◆◇ ADJ: ADJ n ADV N-COUNT ADJ-GRADED N-UNCOUNT ADJ-GRADED ADV-GRADED

musical 'chairs. 1 Musical chairs is a party game in which people run round a row of chairs while music plays and try to sit down on one when the music stops. **2** If you describe the situation within a particular organization or area of activity as **musical chairs**, you are critical of the fact that people in that organization or area exchange jobs or positions very often. N-UNCOUNT N-UNCOUNT PRAGMATICS

'musical comedy, musical comedies. Musical comedy is a type of play or film that has singing and dancing as part of the story, especially one written before the middle of the twentieth century. N-VAR

'musical director, musical directors. A musical director is the same as a **music director**. N-COUNT

,musical 'instrument, musical instruments. A musical instrument is an object such as a piano, guitar, or violin which you play in order to produce music. ◆◇◇◇◇ N-COUNT

'music box, music boxes. A music box is a box that contains a clockwork mechanism which plays a tune when you open the lid. N-COUNT

'music director, music directors. The music director of an orchestra or other group of musicians is the person who decides what they will play and where, and usually conducts them as well. N-COUNT

'music hall, music halls; also spelled **musichall. 1** Music hall consists of a series of performances by comedians, singers, and dancers. It was popular in the theatre in the nineteenth and early twentieth century. *...an old music hall song.* **2** A music hall was a theatre that presented popular entertainment. ◆◇◇◇◇ N-UNCOUNT BRITISH N-COUNT

mu·si·cian /mjuːˈzɪʃən/ **musicians.** A musician is a person who plays a musical instrument as their job or hobby. ◆◆◆◇ N-COUNT

mu·si·cian·ship /mjuːˈzɪʃənʃɪp/. Musicianship is the skill involved in performing music. *Her musicianship is excellent.* N-UNCOUNT

'music stand, music stands. A music stand is a device that holds pages of music in position while you play a musical instrument. N-COUNT

musk /mʌsk/. Musk is a substance with a strong smell which is used in making perfume. N-UNCOUNT

mus·ket /ˈmʌskɪt/ **muskets.** A musket was an early type of gun with a long barrel, which was used before rifles were invented. ◆◇◇◇◇ N-COUNT

musky /ˈmʌski/. A musky smell is strong, warm, and sweet. *...musky perfume.* ADJ-GRADED

Mus·lim /ˈmʊzlɪm, ˈmuːs-, AM ˈmʌz-/ **Muslims.** A Muslim is someone who believes in Islam and lives according to its rules. ▶ Also an adjective. *...Iran and other Muslim countries.* ◆◆◆◆ N-COUNT ADJ

mus·lin /ˈmʌzlɪn/ **muslins.** Muslin is very thin cotton cloth. N-VAR

mus·sel /ˈmʌsəl/ **mussels.** Mussels are a kind of shellfish which are cooked in their shells and eaten from them. The shells are oval and usually black. ◆◇◇◇◇ N-COUNT

must /məst, STRONG mʌst/ **musts.** The noun is pronounced /mʌst/. Must is a modal verb. It is followed by the base form of a verb. ◆◆◆◆◆

1 You use **must** to indicate that you think it is very important or necessary for something to happen. You use **must not** or **mustn't** to indicate that you think it is very important or necessary for something not to happen. *What you wear should be stylish and clean, and must definitely fit well... The doctor must not allow the patient to be put at risk.* **2** You use **must** to indicate that it is necessary for something to happen, usually because of a rule or law. *Candidates must satisfy the general conditions for admission.* **3** If you say that one thing **must have** happened in order for something else to happen, you mean that it is necessary for the first thing to have happened before the second thing can happen. *In order to take that job, you must have left another job.* MODAL PRAGMATICS MODAL PRAGMATICS MODAL PRAGMATICS

4 You use **must** to express your firm intention to do something. *I must be getting back.* **5** You use **must** to make forceful suggestions or invitations. *You must see a doctor, Frederick... You must see the painting Paul has given me.* **6** You use **must** in conversation in expressions such as **'I must say'** and **'I must admit'** in order to emphasize a point that you are making. *This came as a surprise, I must say... I must admit I like looking feminine.* **7** You use **must** in expressions such as **'it must be noted'** and **'it must be remembered'** in order to draw the reader's or listener's attention to what you are about to say. *It must be noted, however, that not all British and American officers carried out* MODAL PRAGMATICS MODAL PRAGMATICS MODAL PRAGMATICS MODAL PRAGMATICS

orders. **8** You use **must** in questions to express your anger or irritation about something that someone has done, usually because you do not understand their behaviour. *Why must you do everything as if you have to win?*   MODAL PRAGMATICS

9 You say **'if you must'** when you know that you cannot stop someone doing something that you think is wrong, stupid, or annoying. *If you must be in the sunlight, use the strongest filter cream you can get... 'Could I have a word?'—'Oh dear, if you must.'* **10** You say **'if you must know'** when you tell someone something that you did not want them to know and you want to suggest that you think they were wrong to ask you about it. *'Why don't you wear your jogging shorts Mum?'—'Well, my legs are too skinny, if you must know.'*   PHRASE PRAGMATICS

11 If you refer to something as a **must** you mean that it is very useful, important, or necessary. *A trip to this important religious monument is a must for all visitors.*   N-COUNT INFORMAL

12 You use **must** to indicate that you are fairly sure that something is the case. *At 29 Russell must be one of the youngest ever Wembley referees.* **13** You use **must**, or **must have** with a past participle, to indicate that you believe that something is the case, because of the available evidence. *'You must be Emma,' said the visitor... He must have brought them home in order to continue his work.* **14** You use **must** in remarks and comments where you are expressing sympathy. *This must be a very difficult job for you.* **15** You use **must** in exclamations to express surprise or shock. *You must have gone out of your mind!*   MODAL PRAGMATICS

must- /mʌst-/. **Must-** is added to verbs such as 'see', 'do', or 'read' to form adjectives and nouns which describe things that you consider that people must see, do, or read. For example, a **must-have** is something which you think people should get or which is very fashionable, and a **must-win** game is one which a team needs to win.   COMB INFORMAL

mus·tache /məˈstɑːʃ, AM ˈmʌstæʃ/. See **moustache**.

mus·tard /ˈmʌstəd/ **mustards**. **1** Mustard is a yellow or brown paste usually eaten with meat. It tastes hot and spicy. **2** Mustard is a small plant with yellow flowers and long seed pods. The seeds can be used to make mustard. **3** Mustard is used to describe things that are brownish yellow. *...a mustard coloured jumper.*   ◆◇◇◇◇ N-VAR   N-UNCOUNT   COLOUR

'mustard gas. Mustard gas is a gas used in chemical warfare. It burns and blisters the skin.   N-UNCOUNT

mus·ter /ˈmʌstə/ **musters, mustering, mustered**. **1** If you **muster** support, strength, or energy, you gather as much of it as you can in order to do something. *He travelled around West Africa trying to muster support for his movement.* **2** When soldiers **muster**, they gather together in one place in order to take part in a military action. *The general had mustered his troops north of the Hindu Kush.* **3** If someone or something **passes muster**, they are good enough for the thing they are needed for. *I could not pass muster in his language.*   ◆◇◇◇◇ VERB V n   V-ERG: V V n   PHRASE

mustn't /ˈmʌsənt/. **Mustn't** is the usual spoken form of **must not**.

must've /ˈmʌstəv/. **Must've** is the usual spoken form of **must have**, especially when 'have' is an auxiliary verb.

mus·ty /ˈmʌsti/. Something that is **musty** smells stale and damp. *...that terrible musty smell.*   ADJ-GRADED

mu·tant /ˈmjuːtənt/ **mutants**. A **mutant** is an animal or plant that is physically different from others of the same species as the result of a change in its genetic structure.   ◆◇◇◇◇ N-COUNT

mu·tate /mjuːˈteɪt, AM ˈmjuːteɪt/ **mutates, mutating, mutated**. **1** If an animal or plant **mutates**, it develops different characteristics as the result of a change in its genes. *HIV may have mutated into a new, as yet undetected virus... The technique has been to mutate the genes by irradiation.* ♦ **mu·ta·tion** /mjuːˈteɪʃən/ **mutations** *...a genetic mutation that appears to be the cause of Huntington's disease.*   ◆◇◇◇◇ V-ERG: V V into V V n   N-VAR

2 If something **mutates into** a very different thing, it changes into it. *Overnight, the gossip begins to mutate into headlines.*   VERB V into V

mute /mjuːt/ **mutes, muting, muted**. **1** Someone who is **mute** is silent and does not speak. *He was mute, distant, and indifferent.* ♦ **mute·ly** *I crouched by him and grasped his hand, mutely offering what comfort I could.* **2** Someone who is **mute** is unable to speak. *Marianna, the duke's daughter, became mute after a shock.* **3** If you **mute** a noise or sound, you lower its volume or make it less distinct. *They begin to mute their voices.* ♦ **mut·ed** *'Yes,' he muttered, his voice so muted I hardly heard his reply.* **4** If someone **mutes** something such as their feelings or their activities, they reduce the strength or intensity of them. *It accuses the Bush administration of muting its criticism of repression.* ♦ **muted** *Reaction to the news was muted.*   ◆◇◇◇◇ ADJ   ADV: ADV with v   ADJ DATED   VERB V n   ADJ-GRADED   VERB V n   ADJ-GRADED

mut·ed /ˈmjuːtɪd/. **Muted** colours are soft and gentle, not bright and strong.   ADJ-GRADED

mu·ti·late /ˈmjuːtɪleɪt/ **mutilates, mutilating, mutilated**. **1** If a person or animal **is mutilated**, their body is severely damaged, usually by someone who physically attacks them. *He tortured and mutilated six young men.* ♦ **mu·ti·la·tion** /ˌmjuːtɪˈleɪʃən/, **mutilations** *Amnesty International chronicles cases of torture and mutilation.* **2** If something **is mutilated**, it is deliberately damaged or spoiled. *I discovered a mutilated cassette stuffed in a wastebasket.*   ◆◇◇◇◇ VERB: be V-ed V n   N-VAR   VERB: be V-ed V-ed Also V n

mu·ti·nous /ˈmjuːtɪnəs/. If someone is **mutinous**, they are strongly dissatisfied with a person's authority and are likely to rebel against it. *His own army, stung by defeats, is mutinous.*   ADJ-GRADED

mu·ti·ny /ˈmjuːtɪni/ **mutinies, mutinying, mutinied**. **1** A **mutiny** is a rebellion by a group of people, usually soldiers or sailors, against a person in authority. ♦ **mu·ti·neer** /ˌmjuːtɪˈnɪə/, **mutineers**. A **mutineer** is a person who takes part in a mutiny. **2** If a group of people, especially soldiers or sailors, **mutiny**, they refuse to obey the person who has authority over them. *Sailors at a naval base had mutinied against their officers.*   ◆◇◇◇◇ N-VAR   N-COUNT   VERB: V V against n

mutt /mʌt/ **mutts**. A **mutt** is a dog, usually one that is a mixture of breeds.   N-COUNT INFORMAL

mut·ter /ˈmʌtə/ **mutters, muttering, muttered**. If you **mutter**, you speak very quietly so that you cannot easily be heard, often because you are complaining about something. *'God knows,' she muttered, 'what's happening in that madman's mind.'... She can hear the old woman muttering about consideration.* ▶ Also a noun. *They make no more than a mutter of protest.* ♦ **mut·ter·ing, mutterings** *He heard muttering from the front of the crowd.*   ◆◆◇◇◇ VERB V with quote V about n Also V to n   N-COUNT   N-VAR

mut·ton /ˈmʌtən/. **Mutton** is meat from an adult sheep.   N-UNCOUNT

mu·tu·al /ˈmjuːtʃuəl/. You use **mutual** to describe a situation, feeling, or action that is experienced, felt, or done by both of two people mentioned. *The East and the West can work together for their mutual benefit... It's plain that he adores his daughter, and the feeling is mutual.* ♦ **mu·tu·al·ly** *Attempts to reach a mutually agreed solution had been fruitless. ...a mutually convenient time.* ● **mutually exclusive**: see **exclusive**.   ◆◆◆◇◇ ADJ   ADV

'mutual fund, mutual funds. A **mutual fund** is an organization which invests money in many different kinds of business and which offers units for sale to the public as an investment. The British expression is **unit trust**.   ◆◇◇◇◇ N-COUNT AMERICAN

mu·zak /ˈmjuːzæk/. **1** Muzak is recorded music that is played as background music in shops or restaurants. Muzak is a trademark. **2** If you describe music as **muzak**, you dislike it because you think it is dull or unnecessary.   N-UNCOUNT   N-UNCOUNT PRAGMATICS

muz·zle /ˈmʌzəl/ **muzzles, muzzling, muzzled**. **1** The **muzzle** of an animal such as a dog is its nose and mouth. **2** The **muzzle** of a gun is the end where the bullets come out when it is fired. **3** A **muzzle** is a device that is put over a dog's nose and   ◆◇◇◇◇ N-COUNT   N-COUNT   N-COUNT

M

mouth so that it cannot bite people or bark. **4** If you muzzle a dog or other animal, you put a muzzle over its nose and mouth. **5** If you say that someone is **muzzled**, you are complaining that they are prevented from expressing their views freely. *She was opposed to new laws to muzzle the press.*

MW. 1 MW is a written abbreviation for **medium wave. 2** MW is a written abbreviation for **megawatt.**

my /maɪ/. My is the first person singular possessive determiner.

1 A speaker or writer uses **my** to indicate that something belongs or relates to himself or herself. *I invited him back to my flat... John's my best friend.* **2** In conversations or in letters, **my** is used in front of a name or a word like 'darling' to show affection. *Yes, all right, my dear.* **3** In spoken English, **my** is used in phrases such as '**My God**' and '**My goodness**' to express surprise or shock. *My goodness, Tim, you have changed!*

myo·pia /maɪˈəʊpiə/. **1** If someone suffers from **myopia**, they cannot see things properly when they are far away, because there is something wrong with their eyes. ♦ **my·op·ic** /maɪˈɒpɪk/. People who are **myopic** suffer from myopia. *She has wiry blonde hair and big myopic eyes.* **2** If you say that someone displays **myopia**, you disapprove of them because they seem to be unable or unwilling to recognize the true facts of a situation, especially the negative consequences of their own actions. *Only people with a bad dose of Utopian myopia could delude themselves that juvenile crime isn't an immensely serious problem.* ♦ **myopic** *The Government still has a myopic attitude to spending.*

myri·ad /ˈmɪriəd/; also spelled **myriads. 1** A **myriad** or **myriads** of people or things is a very large number or great variety of them. *They face a myriad of problems bringing up children.* **2 Myriad** means having a large number or great variety. *...British pop and culture in all its myriad forms.*

my·self /maɪˈself/. Myself is the first person singular reflexive pronoun.

1 A speaker or writer uses **myself** to refer to himself or herself. **Myself** is used as the object of a verb or preposition when the subject refers to the same person. *I asked myself what I would have done in such a situation... I looked at myself in the mirror.* **2** You use **myself** to emphasize a first person singular subject. Some speakers use **myself** instead of 'me' as the object of a verb or preposition. *I myself enjoy cinema, poetry, eating out and long walks. ...a complete beginner like myself.* **3** If you say something such as 'I did it **myself**', you are emphasizing that you did it, rather than anyone else. **4 ● by myself:** see **by.**

mys·teri·ous /mɪˈstɪəriəs/. **1** Someone or something that is **mysterious** is strange and is not known about or understood. *He died in mysterious circumstances... A mysterious illness confined him to bed.* ♦ **mys·teri·ous·ly** *A couple of messages had mysteriously disappeared.* **2** If someone is **mysterious** about something, they deliberately do not talk much about it, usually because they want people to be curious about it. *As for his job—well, he was very mysterious about it.* ♦ **mysteriously** *Asked what she meant, she said mysteriously: 'Work it out for yourself.'*

VERB: V n

VERB: be V-ed PRAGMATICS V n

DET-POSS

DET-POSS PRAGMATICS

DET-POSS PRAGMATICS

N-UNCOUNT FORMAL

ADJ-GRADED

N-UNCOUNT PRAGMATICS

ADJ-GRADED

QUANT

ADJ: ADJ n

♦♦♦♦◇

PRON-REFL v PRON, prep PRON

PRON-REFL PRAGMATICS

PRON-REFL PRAGMATICS

♦♦◇◇◇ ADJ-GRADED

ADV-GRADED

ADJ-GRADED: v-link ADJ

ADV-GRADED: ADV after v

mys·tery /ˈmɪstəri/ **mysteries. 1** A **mystery** is something that is not understood or known about. *The source of the gunshots still remains a mystery.* **2** If you talk about the **mystery** of someone or something, you are talking about how difficult they are to understand or know about, especially when this gives them a rather strange or magical quality. *She's a lady of mystery... It is an elaborate ceremony, shrouded in mystery.* **3** A **mystery** person or thing is one whose identity or nature is not known. *A mystery buyer purchased 1.5 million MGN shares last Friday.* **4** A **mystery** is a story in which strange things happen that are not explained until the end.

mys·tic /ˈmɪstɪk/ **mystics. 1** A **mystic** is a person who believes in religious practices in which people search for truth, knowledge, and unity with God through meditation and prayer. ♦ **mys·ti·cism** /ˈmɪstɪsɪzəm/. You can refer to the practices of mystics as **mysticism. 2 Mystic** means the same as **mystical.** *...mystic union with God.*

mys·ti·cal /ˈmɪstɪkəl/. Something that is **mystical** involves spiritual powers and influences that most people do not understand. *That was clearly a deep mystical experience.*

mys·ti·fy /ˈmɪstɪfaɪ/ **mystifies, mystifying, mystified.** If you **are mystified** by something, you find it impossible to explain or understand. *There was something strange in her attitude which mystified me.* ♦ **mys·ti·fi·ca·tion** /ˌmɪstɪfɪˈkeɪʃən/ *Some minerals, Pough explained to my mystification, are not truly black but only look so.* ♦ **mys·ti·fy·ing** *I find your attitude a little mystifying, Moira.*

mys·tique /mɪˈstiːk/. **Mystique** is a sense or atmosphere of mystery and secrecy which is associated with a particular person or thing. *...the mystique that surrounds fine art.*

myth /mɪθ/ **myths. 1** A **myth** is a well-known story which was made up in the past to explain natural events or to justify religious beliefs or social customs. *...a famous Greek myth in which Icarus flew too near to the Sun.* ♦ **myth·ic** *...the mythic figure of King Arthur.* ♦ **mythi·cal** /ˈmɪθɪkəl/ *...the Hydra, the mythical beast that had seven or more heads.* **2** If you describe a belief or explanation as a **myth**, you mean that many people believe it but it is actually untrue. *Contrary to the popular myth, women are not reckless spendthrifts.* ♦ **mythical** *...the mythical, romanticized West of cowboys and gunslingers.*

myth·ic /ˈmɪθɪk/. If you describe someone or something as **mythic**, you mean that they have become very famous or important. *...a team whose reputation has achieved mythic proportions.*

my·thol·ogy /mɪˈθɒlədʒi/ **mythologies. 1** Mythology is a group of myths, especially all the myths from a particular country, religion, or culture. *In Greek mythology she was the patroness of history.* ♦ **mytho·logi·cal** /ˌmɪθəˈlɒdʒɪkəl/ *...the mythological beast that was part lion and part goat.* **2** You can use **mythology** to refer to the beliefs or opinions that people have about something, when you think that they are false or untrue. *Altman strips away the pretence and mythology to expose the film industry as a business like any other.*

♦♦♦◇◇ N-COUNT

N-UNCOUNT

ADJ: ADJ n

N-COUNT

♦◇◇◇◇ N-COUNT

N-UNCOUNT

ADJ-GRADED: ADJ n

♦◇◇◇◇ ADJ-GRADED

♦◇◇◇◇ VERB: be V-ed V n

N-UNCOUNT

ADJ-GRADED

♦◇◇◇◇ N-UNCOUNT

♦♦♦◇◇ N-VAR

ADJ

ADJ-GRADED

N-VAR

...the ADJ

ADJ-GRADED

♦◇◇◇◇ N-VAR

ADJ

N-VAR

N n

N, n /en/ **N's, n's. 1** N is the fourteenth letter of the English alphabet. **2** N or n is used as an abbreviation for words beginning with N or n, such as 'north', 'northern', or 'noun'.   N-VAR

'n' /ən/. The word 'and' is sometimes written as **'n'** between certain pairs of words, for example 'rock 'n' roll' and 'fish 'n' chips'. *...a country 'n' western song.*   CONJ INFORMAL, WRITTEN

N.A.; also spelled **n/a. N.A.** is a written abbreviation for 'not applicable'. You use it when you are filling in a questionnaire when a question or category is not relevant to you.   ◆◇◇◇◇ CONVENTION

naan, naans /nɑːn/; also spelled **nan. Naan** or **naan bread** is a type of bread that comes in a large, round, flat piece and is usually eaten with Indian food.   N-VAR

nab /næb/ **nabs, nabbing, nabbed.** If people in authority such as the police **nab** someone who they think has done something wrong, they catch them or arrest them. *After a short spell in the masonry business he was back in the armed robbery business. Again, he got nabbed.*   ◆◇◇◇◇ VERB: V n getV-ed INFORMAL

na·dir /'neɪdɪə, AM -dər/. **1** The **nadir** of something such as someone's career or the history of an organization is its worst time. *1945 to 1946 was the nadir of Truman's presidency.* **2** In astronomy, **the nadir** is the point at which the sun or moon is directly below you, on the other side of the earth. Compare **zenith**.   ◆◆◇◇◇ N-SING: LITERARY / N-SING: the N

naff /næf/ **naffer, naffest.** If you say that something is **naff**, you mean it is very unfashionable or unsophisticated. *The music's really naff.*   ADJ-GRADED INFORMAL, BRITISH

nag /næg/ **nags, nagging, nagged. 1** If you say that someone **is nagging** you, you are annoyed with them because they are continuously asking you to do something, often something you do not want to do. *My girlfriend nagged me to cut my hair... She had stopped nagging him about never being home. ...children nagging their parents into buying things.* ✦ **nag·ging** *Her endless nagging drove him away from home.* **2** If something such as a doubt or worry **nags** at you, or **nags** you, it keeps worrying you. *...the anxiety that had nagged Amy all through lunch... Something was nagging in the back of his mind.* **3** People sometimes refer to a horse as a **nag**.   ◆◇◇◇◇ VERB: V n PRAGMATICS / V n to-inf / V n about n / V n into -ing / Also V / N-UNCOUNT VERB: V atn / V n / V / N-COUNT INFORMAL

nag·ging /'nægɪŋ/. A **nagging** pain is not very severe but is difficult to cure. *He complained of a nagging pain between his shoulder blades.*   ADJ: ADJ n

nail /neɪl/ **nails, nailing, nailed. 1** A **nail** is a thin piece of metal with one pointed end and one flat end. You hit the flat end with a hammer in order to push the nail into something such as a wall. See picture headed **tools**. *A mirror hung on a nail above the washstand.* **2** If you **nail** something somewhere, you fix it there using one or more nails. *The windows were all nailed shut.* **3** Your **nails** are the thin hard parts that grow at the ends of your fingers and toes. *Keep your nails short and your hands clean.* **4** To **nail** someone means to catch them and prove that they have been breaking the law. *The prosecution still managed to nail him for robberies at the homes of leading industrialists.* **5** If you say that someone **has hit the nail on the head**, you mean that you think their opinion about something is exactly right. *'I think it would civilize people a bit more if they had decent conditions.'—'I think you've hit the nail on the head.'* **6** ● **a nail in** something's **coffin**: see **coffin**. ● **to nail**   ◆◆◇◇◇ N-COUNT / VERB V n prep/adv / N-COUNT / VERB V n INFORMAL / PHRASE

your **colours to the mast**: see **colour**. ● **to fight tooth and nail**: see **tooth**.

nail down. 1 If you **nail down** something unknown or uncertain, you find out exactly what it is. *It would be useful if you could nail down the source of this tension.* **2** If you **nail down** an agreement, you manage to reach a firm agreement with a definite result. *The Secretary of State and his Russian counterpart met to try to nail down the elusive accord.* **3** If you **nail** something **down**, you fix it firmly onto something. *Lay strips of 4mm ply over the mesh and nail these down with panel pins.*   PHRASAL VB V P noun / Also V n P / V P noun / Also V n P / V n P / Also V P noun

'nail-biting. If you describe something such as a story or a sports match as **nail-biting**, you mean that it makes you feel very excited or nervous because you do not know how it is going to end. *...England's magnificent nail-biting 75-71 win over Russia.*   ADJ-GRADED

'nail file, nail files. A **nail file** is a small strip of metal or sandpaper that you rub on the ends of your nails to shorten them or shape them.   N-COUNT

'nail polish, nail polishes. Nail polish is the same as **nail varnish**.   N-VAR

'nail varnish, nail varnishes. Nail varnish is a thick liquid that some women paint on their nails. The usual American term is **nail polish**.   N-VAR BRITISH

na·ive /naɪ'iːv, AM nɑː-/; also spelled **naïve**. If you describe someone as **naive**, you think they lack experience, causing them to expect things to be uncomplicated or easy, or people to be honest or kind when they are not. *It's naive to think that teachers are always tolerant. ...naive idealists... Their view was that he had been politically naive.* ✦ **na·ive·ly** *...naively applying Western solutions to Eastern problems.* ✦ **na·ive·ty** /naɪ'iːvɪti/ *I was alarmed by his naivety and ignorance of international affairs.*   ◆◆◇◇◇ ADJ-GRADED / ADV-GRADED / N-UNCOUNT

na·ked /'neɪkɪd/. **1** Someone who is **naked** is not wearing any clothes. *Her naked body was found wrapped in a sheet in a field... They stripped me naked.* ✦ **na·ked·ness** *He had pulled the blanket over his body to hide his nakedness.* ● See also **stark naked. 2** If you say that someone is **naked** or feels **naked**, you mean they are helpless, unprotected, or powerless. *If the reports are accurate, the deal leaves the authorities and the President virtually naked.* **3** If an animal or part of an animal is **naked**, it has no fur or feathers on it. **4** You can describe an object as **naked** when it does not have its normal covering. *...a naked bulb dangling in a bare room.* **5** **Naked** emotions are easy to recognize, because they are very strongly felt. *The naked hatred in the woman's face shocked me.* ✦ **na·ked·ly** *She was embarrassed at showing her fear so nakedly.* **6** You can use **naked** to describe unpleasant or violent actions and behaviour which are not disguised or hidden in any way. *Naked aggression and an attempt to change frontiers by force could not go unchallenged. ...naked greed.* **7** If you say that something cannot be seen by the **naked eye**, you mean that it cannot be seen without the help of equipment such as a telescope or microscope. *The planet Mars will be visible to the naked eye all week.*   ◆◆◇◇◇ ADJ / N-UNCOUNT / ADJ / ADJ / ADJ / ADJ: ADJ n WRITTEN / ADV-GRADED / ADJ: ADJ n JOURNALISM / PHRASE

name /neɪm/ **names, naming, named. 1** The **name** of a person, place, or thing is the word or group of words that is used to identify them. *'What's his name?'—'Peter.'... They changed the name of the street.* **2** If something is **in** someone's **name**, it officially belongs to them or is reserved for them. *A*   ◆◆◆◆◆ N-COUNT / PHRASE

*double room had been reserved for him in the name
of Muller.* **3** When you mention someone or something **by name**, or address someone **by name**, you
use their name. *He greets customers by name and
enquires about their health.* **4** You can use **by name**
or **by the name of** when you are saying what someone is called. *This guy, Jack Smith, does he go by the
name of Jackal?* PHRASE

5 When you **name** someone or something, you give
them a name, usually at the beginning of their life. *My
mother insisted on naming me Horace. ...a man
named John T. Benson.* **6** If you **name** someone or
something **after** another person or thing, you give
them the same name as that person or thing. *Why
have you not named any of your sons after yourself?*
7 If you **name** someone, you identify them by stating
their name. *One of the victims of the weekend's snowstorm has been named as twenty-year-old John Barr.*
8 If you **name** someone as the person who will have a
particular job, you give them that job or appoint them
to it. *When the chairman of Campbell's retired,
McGovern was named as his successor... Early in 1941
he was named commander of the Afrika Korps.* **9** If you
name something such as a price, time, or place, you
say what you want it to be. *Call Marty, tell him to
name his price.* **10** You say **'You name it'**, usually after
or before a list, to indicate that you are talking about a
very wide range of things. *Pickled cucumbers, jam,
pickled berries, tomatoes; you name it, they've got it.*
11 You can refer to the reputation of a person or thing
as their **name**. *He had a name for good judgement...
She's never had any drug problems or done anything to
give jazz a bad name.* **12** If you **lend** your **name** to
something such as a project, a political programme,
or a charitable cause, you support it. *He had political
points of view and lent his name to a lot of causes.* **13** If
you **make a name for** yourself or **make** your **name** as
something, you become well-known for that thing. *He
made his name with several collections of short stories.*
14 You can refer to someone as, for example, a famous **name** or a great **name** when they are well-
known. *...some of the most famous names in model-
ling and show business.*
15 If someone **calls** you **names**, they insult you by
saying unpleasant things to you or about you. *They
had called her rude names.* **16** If you **name names**,
you identify the people who have done something, often something wrong. *Nobody was prepared to risk
prosecution by actually naming names.*
17 If someone does something **in the name of** a
group of people, they do it as the representative of
that group. *She accepted the gift in the name of the
Save the Children Fund.* **18** If you do something **in the
name of** an ideal or an abstract thing, you do it in order to preserve or promote that thing. *There had been
times when she had felt sickened by the things people
did in the name of business.* **19** People sometimes use
expressions such as **'in the name of'** heaven' or **'in the
name of'** humanity' to add emphasis to a question or
request. *What in the name of heaven's going on?*
20 If you say that a situation exists **in all but name**,
you mean that it is not officially recognized but that it
actually exists. *...the group, which is now a political
party in all but name.* **21** If you say that a situation exists **in name only**, you mean that it does not have the
status or position that it claims to have. *He is
commander-in-chief in name only.*
22 If you say that something is the **name of the game**,
you mean that it is the most important aspect of a
situation. *Family values are suddenly the name of the
game.*
23 See also **assumed name, big name, brand name,
Christian name, code name, first name, given name,
maiden name, middle name, pet name.**

'**name-drop, name-drops, name-dropping,
name-dropped.** If you say that someone is
name-dropping, you disapprove of them because
they are referring to famous people that they know,
or know about, in order to impress people. *The assistant carried on talking to his mate, name-*

PHRASE (right margin markers throughout left column)
VERB Vnn / V-ed / V-ed n
VERB Vn after n
VERB: Vn / Vn as n
VERB: Vn / be V-ed as n / be V-ed n / Also Vn as n, Vnn
VERB Vn
PHRASE
PHRASE
N-COUNT
PHRASE
PHRASE
N-COUNT JOURNALISM
PHRASE
PHRASE
PHRASE
PHRASE
PHRASE PRAGMATICS
PHRASE
PHRASE
PHRASE INFORMAL
PHRASE

VERB: V PRAGMATICS Vn

dropping all the famous riders he knew. ✦ **name-
dropping** *Her reminiscences of clients and friends
sometimes verge on name-dropping.* N-UNCOUNT

name·less /'neɪmləs/. **1** You describe people or
things as **nameless** when you do not know their
name or when they do not have a name. *They can
have their cases rejected, without reasons being giv-
en, by nameless officials.* **2** If you say that someone
or something will remain **nameless**, you mean that
you will not mention their name, often because you
do not want to embarrass them. *A local friend who
shall be nameless warned me that I was in for trouble soon.* ADJ / ADJ: v-link ADJ

name·ly /'neɪmli/. You use **namely** to introduce
detailed information about the subject you are discussing, or a particular aspect of it. *This shows how
little they were aware of the challenge facing them,
namely, to re-establish prosperity and the rule of
law.* ◆◆◇◇◇ ADV: ADV n/group PRAGMATICS

name·plate /'neɪmpleɪt/ **nameplates;** also spelled
name-plate. A **nameplate** is a sign on a door or wall
which shows the name of the person or organization that occupies that particular room or building. N-COUNT

name·sake /'neɪmseɪk/ **namesakes.** Your **namesake** is another person who has the same name as
you. *He is putting together a four-man team, including his son and namesake Tony O'Reilly Jnr.* N-COUNT WRITTEN

nan /næn/ **nans. 1** Some British people refer to
their grandmother as their **nan.** *I was brought up by
my nan.* ◆◇◇◇◇ N-COUNT INFORMAL
2 A **nan** is the same as a **naan.** N-VAR

nan·ny /'næni/ **nannies.** In some families, a **nanny**
is a woman who is paid by the parents to look after
their child or children. ◆◆◇◇◇ N-COUNT

,**nanny 'state.** If you refer to a government as the
nanny state, you disapprove of its system of providing certain social services which you think makes
people rely on the state rather than wanting to do
things for themselves. *The tussle to free the individ-
ual from the nanny state is still far from won.* N-SING PRAGMATICS BRITISH

nap /næp/ **naps, napping, napped. 1** If you **nap**,
you sleep for a short period of time, usually during
the day. *An elderly person may nap during the day
and then sleep only five hours a night.* ► Also a
noun. *I might take a little nap.* **2** If someone **is
caught napping**, something happens when they are
not prepared for it, although they should have been.
The security services were clearly caught napping.
3 The **nap** of a carpet or of a cloth such as velvet is
the top layer of short threads, which usually lie
smoothly in one direction. ◆◇◇◇◇ VERB V / N-COUNT / PHRASE INFORMAL / N-SING

na·palm /'neɪpɑːm/. **Napalm** is a substance containing petrol which is used to make bombs that
burn people, buildings, and plants. N-UNCOUNT

nape /neɪp/ **napes.** The **nape** of your neck is the
back of it. *...the way that his hair grew at the nape of
his neck.* N-COUNT

nap·kin /'næpkɪn/ **napkins.** A **napkin** is a square
of cloth or paper that you use when you are eating
to protect your clothes, or to wipe your mouth or
hands. ◆◇◇◇◇ N-COUNT

nap·py /'næpi/ **nappies.** A **nappy** is a piece of soft
thick cloth or paper which is fastened round a
baby's bottom in order to soak up its urine and faeces. The usual American word is **diaper**. ◆◇◇◇◇ N-COUNT BRITISH

nar·cis·si /nɑː'sɪsaɪ/. **Narcissi** is a plural form of
narcissus.

nar·cis·sism /'nɑːsɪsɪzəm/. **Narcissism** is the habit
of always thinking about yourself and admiring
yourself, often showing disapproval. *Those who suffer from narcissism become self-absorbed or chronic
show-offs.* ✦ **nar·cis·sis·tic** /,nɑːsɪ'sɪstɪk/. *...the
image of the vain, narcissistic man.* N-UNCOUNT PRAGMATICS FORMAL / ADJ-GRADED

nar·cis·sus /nɑː'sɪsəs/ **narcissi;** the plural can be
either **narcissi** or **narcissus**. **Narcissi** are trumpet-
shaped flowers, usually white or yellow, that bloom
in the spring. N-COUNT

nar·cot·ic /nɑː'kɒtɪk/ **narcotics. 1** **Narcotics** are
drugs such as opium or heroin which make you
sleepy and stop you feeling pain, but are also addic- ◆◇◇◇◇ N-COUNT

tive. *He appears to be high on some sort of narcotic.* **2** If something, especially a drug, has a **narcotic** effect, it makes the person who uses it feel sleepy and dazed. *...hormones that have a narcotic effect on the immune system.* ADJ

nar·rate /nə'reɪt, AM 'næreɪt/ **narrates, narrating, narrated. 1** If you **narrate** a story, you tell it from your own point of view. *The book is narrated by Richard Papen, a Californian boy.* ◆ **nar·ra·tion** /nə'reɪʃən/ *Its story-within-a-story method of narration is confusing.* ◆ **nar·ra·tor** /nə'reɪtə, AM 'næreɪt-/ **narrators** *Jules, the story's narrator, is an actress in her late thirties.* **2** The person who **narrates** a documentary film or programme speaks the words which accompany the pictures, but does not appear in it. *She also narrated a documentary about the Kirov Ballet School.* ◆ **narration** *As the crew gets back from lunch, we can put your narration on it right away.* ◆ **narrator** *Famous actors were narrators of some of the early shows.*
◆◇◇◇◇ VERB: V n
FORMAL
N-UNCOUNT
N-COUNT
VERB
V n
Also V
N-UNCOUNT
N-COUNT

nar·ra·tive /'nærətɪv/ **narratives. 1** A **narrative** is a story or an account of a series of events. *Sloan began his narrative with the day of the murder.* **2** Narrative is the description of a series of events, for example in a novel. *Neither author was very strong on narrative. ...Nye's simple narrative style.*
◆◆◇◇◇ N-COUNT
N-UNCOUNT

nar·row /'nærəʊ/ **narrower, narrowest; narrows, narrowing, narrowed. 1** Something that is **narrow** measures a very small distance from one side to the other, especially compared to its length or height. *...through the town's narrow streets... She had long, narrow feet.* ◆ **nar·row·ness** *...the narrowness of the river mouth.* **2** If something **narrows**, it becomes less wide. *The wide track narrows before crossing another stream.* **3** If your eyes **narrow** or if you **narrow** your eyes, you almost close them, for example because you are angry or thinking deeply. *He paused and narrowed his eyes in concentration.* **4** If you describe someone's ideas, attitudes, or beliefs as **narrow**, you disapprove of them because they are unimaginative, old-fashioned, or very strict, and often ignore the more important aspects of a situation. *...a narrow and outdated view of family life.* ◆ **nar·row·ly** *They're making judgments based on a narrowly focused vision of the world.* ◆ **nar·row·ness** *...the narrowness of their mental and spiritual outlook.* **5** If something **narrows** or if you **narrow** it, its extent, range, or scope becomes smaller. *The European Community and America had narrowed their differences over farm subsidies.* ◆ **nar·row·ing** *...a narrowing of the gap between rich members and poor.* **6** If you have a **narrow** victory, you succeed in winning but only by a small margin. *Delegates have voted by a narrow majority in favour of considering electoral reform.* ◆ **narrowly** *She narrowly failed to win enough votes.* **7** If you have a **narrow** escape, something unpleasant nearly happens to you. *Two police officers had a narrow escape when separatists attacked their vehicles.* ◆ **narrowly** *Five firemen narrowly escaped death when a staircase collapsed beneath their feet.* **8** ● **on the straight and narrow:** see **straight**.
◆◆◆◆◇ ADJ-GRADED
N-UNCOUNT
VERB
V
V-ERG: V
V n
WRITTEN
ADJ-GRADED
PRAGMATICS
ADV-GRADED
N-UNCOUNT
V-ERG: V
V n
N-SING
ADJ-GRADED
ADV
ADJ-GRADED
ADJ n
ADV-GRADED
ADV with v

narrow down. If you **narrow down** a range of things, you reduce the number of things included in it. *I've managed to narrow the list down to twenty-three.*
PHRASAL VB
V P noun
V n P ton
Also V n P

'narrow boat, narrow boats; also spelled **narrowboat.** A **narrow boat** is a long, low boat used on canals.
N-COUNT
BRITISH

,narrow-'minded. If you describe someone as **narrow-minded,** you are criticizing them because they are unwilling to consider new ideas or other people's opinion. *...a narrow-minded bigot.* ◆ **narrow-minded·ness** *It is unbelievable that as a result of this narrow-mindedness a group of people should suffer.*
ADJ-GRADED
PRAGMATICS
N-UNCOUNT

NASA /'næsə/. **NASA** is the American government organization concerned with the exploration of space. **NASA** is an abbreviation for 'National Aeronautics and Space Administration'.
◆◆◇◇◇ N-PROPER

na·sal /'neɪzəl/. **1** Nasal is used to describe things relating to the nose and the functions it performs. *...inflamed nasal passages. ...nasal decongestant sprays.* **2** If someone's voice is **nasal,** it sounds as if air is passing through their nose as well as their mouth while they are speaking. *She talked in a deep nasal monotone.*
◆◇◇◇◇ ADJ: ADJ n
ADJ

nas·cent /'næsənt/. **Nascent** things or processes are just beginning, and are expected to become stronger or to grow bigger. *Kenya's nascent democracy was threatened by conflict yesterday.*
ADJ: ADJ n
FORMAL

na·stur·tium /næ'stɜːʃəm/ **nasturtiums. Nasturtiums** are low plants which trail along the ground. They have orange, red, and yellow trumpet-shaped flowers.
N-COUNT

nas·ty /'nɑːsti, 'næsti/ **nasties; nastier, nastiest. 1** Something that is **nasty** is very unpleasant to see, experience, or feel. *...an extremely nasty murder... This divorce could turn nasty.* ◆ **nas·ti·ness** *...the nastiness of war.* **2** If you describe a person or their behaviour as **nasty,** you mean that they behave in an unkind and unpleasant way. *The guards looked really nasty... Mummy is so nasty to me when Daddy isn't here.* ◆ **nas·ti·ly** *She took the money and eyed me nastily.* ◆ **nastiness** *As the years went by his nastiness began to annoy his readers.* **3** If you describe something as **nasty,** you mean it is unattractive, undesirable, or in bad taste. *...Emily's nasty little house in Balham... That damned Farrel made some nasty jokes here about Mr. Lane.* **4** A **nasty** problem or situation is very worrying and difficult to deal with. *A spokesman said this firm action had defused a very nasty situation.* **5** If you describe an injury or a disease as **nasty,** you mean that it is serious or looks unpleasant. *Lili had a nasty chest infection.* **6 Nasties** are unpleasant or harmful people or things. *Decaffeinated coffee still contains some stimulants and other nasties linked with cancer.* **7** See also **video nasty.**
◆◆◇◇◇ ADJ-GRADED
N-UNCOUNT
ADJ-GRADED
ADV-GRADED
N-UNCOUNT
ADJ-GRADED
ADJ-GRADED
ADJ-GRADED
N-PLURAL
INFORMAL

natch /nætʃ/. **Natch** is used to indicate that something such as an idea or story is very obvious and predictable. *Ina is a bad girl so, natch, ends up in prison.*
ADV:
ADV with cl/
group
INFORMAL

na·tion /'neɪʃən/ **nations. 1** A **nation** is an individual country, especially when it is considered from the point of view of its cultural or ethnic identity. *Such policies would require unprecedented co-operation between nations... The Arab nations agreed to meet in Baghdad.* **2** The **nation** is sometimes used to refer to all the people who live in a particular country. *It was a story that touched the nation's heart.*
◆◆◆◆◇ N-COUNT
N-SING
JOURNALISM

na·tion·al /'næʃənəl/ **nationals. 1** National means relating to the whole of a country or nation rather than to part of it or to other nations. *Ruling parties have lost ground in national and local elections. ...major national and international issues.* ◆ **na·tion·al·ly** *...a nationally televised speech.* **2** National means typical of the people or customs of a particular country or nation. *...the national characteristics and history of the country... Baseball is the national pastime.* **3** When someone has citizenship of a particular country, you can refer to them as a **national** of that country. *...a Sri Lankanborn British national.*
◆◆◆◆◇ ADJ
ADV
ADJ: ADJ n
N-COUNT

,national 'anthem, national anthems. A national **anthem** is a nation's official song which is played or sung on public occasions.
◆◇◇◇◇ N-COUNT

,National Cur'riculum. The National Curriculum is the course of study that most school pupils in England and Wales are meant to follow between the ages of 5 and 16.
◆◆◇◇◇ N-PROPER:
the N

,national 'government, national governments. A **national government** is a coalition government, especially one that comes to power during a crisis.
◆◇◇◇◇ N-COUNT

,National 'Health Service. In the United Kingdom, **the National Health Service** is the state system for providing medical care. It is paid for by
◆◇◇◇◇ N-PROPER:
the N

taxes. *An increasing number of these treatments are now available on the National Health Service.*

,national in'surance. In the United Kingdom, **national insurance** is the state system of paying money to people who are ill, unemployed, or retired. It is financed by money that the government collects from people in employment and their employers. ◆◇◇◇◇ N-UNCOUNT

na·tion·al·ise /'næʃənəlaɪz/. See **nationalize**.

na·tion·al·ist /'næʃənəlɪst/. **1** Nationalist is used when describing the desire for political independence by people who have the same language, religion, or culture. *The crisis has set off a wave of nationalist feelings in Quebec.* ▶ A **nationalist** is someone with nationalist views. ♦ **na·tion·al·ism** /'næʃənəlɪzəm/ *The rising tide of Slovak nationalism may also help the SNP to win representation in parliament.* **2** Nationalist is used when describing people's great love for their nation, or their belief that their nation is better than others; often used showing disapproval. *Political life has been infected by growing nationalist sentiment.* ▶ A **nationalist** is someone with nationalist views. ♦ **nationalism** *This kind of fierce nationalism is a powerful and potentially volatile force.* ♦ **na·tion·al·is·tic** /,næʃənə'lɪstɪk/. *...Barcelona, a team who are a monument to the nationalistic pride of the Catalan people.* ◆◆◇◇ ADJ: ADJ n / N-COUNT / N-UNCOUNT / ADJ: ADJ n / N-COUNT / N-UNCOUNT / ADJ-GRADED

na·tion·al·ity /,næʃə'nælɪti/ **nationalities. 1** If you have the **nationality** of a particular country, you were born there or have the legal right to be a citizen of it. *Asked his nationality, he said British.* **2** You can refer to people who have the same racial origins as a **nationality**, especially when they do not have their own independent country. *...the many nationalities that comprise Ethiopia.* ◆◆◇◇ N-VAR / N-COUNT

na·tion·al·ize /'næʃənəlaɪz/ **nationalizes, nationalizing, nationalized;** also spelled **nationalise** in British English. If the government **nationalizes** a private company or industry, that company or industry becomes owned by the state and controlled by the government. *The coffee industry was nationalised at the time of independence.* ♦ **na·tion·ali·za·tion** /,næʃənəlaɪ'zeɪʃən/ **nationalizations** *...the campaign for the nationalization of the coal mines.* ◆◇◇◇ VERB: V n / be V-ed / N-VAR

,national 'park, national parks. A national **park** is a large area of land which is protected by the government because of its natural beauty, plants, or animals, and which the public can usually visit. ◆◆◇◇ N-COUNT

,national 'service. National service is service in the armed forces, which young people in some countries have to do by law. ◆◇◇◇ N-UNCOUNT

na·tion·hood /'neɪʃənhʊd/. A country's **nationhood** is its status as a nation. *To them, the monarchy is the special symbol of nationhood.* N-UNCOUNT

,nation 'state, nation states. A nation state is an independent state which consists of people from one particular national group. *Albania is a small nation state of around 3 million people.* ◆◇◇◇ N-COUNT

nation·wide /,neɪʃən'waɪd/. Nationwide activities or situations happen or exist in all parts of a country. *The rising number of car crimes is a nationwide problem.* ▶ Also an adverb. *...available from department stores nationwide... The figures show unemployment falling nationwide last month.* ◆◆◇◇ ADJ / ADV

na·tive /'neɪtɪv/ **natives. 1** Your native country or area is the country or area where you were born and brought up. *Mother Teresa visited her native Albania.* **2** A **native** of a particular country or region is someone who was born in that country or region. *Dr Aubin is a native of St Blaise.* ▶ Also an adjective. *...men and women native to countries such as Japan.* **3** Some European people use **native** to refer to a person who was born in or lives in a non-Western country and who belongs to the race or tribe that forms the majority of its inhabitants; some people consider this use offensive. *They used force to banish the natives from the more fertile land.* ▶ Also an ◆◆◇◇ ADJ: ADJ n / N-COUNT: N of n / ADJ / N-COUNT / ADJ: ADJ n

adjective. *Native people were allowed to retain some sense of their traditional culture and religion.* **4** Plants or animals that are **native to** a particular region live or grow there naturally rather than being brought there. *...a project to create a 50 acre forest of native Caledonian pines.* ▶ Also a noun. *The coconut palm is a native of Malaysia.* **5** Your **native** language or tongue is the first language that you learned to speak when you were a child. *French is not my native tongue.* **6** A **native** ability or quality is one that you possess naturally without having to learn it. *We have our native inborn talent, yet we hardly use it.* ADJ / N-COUNT: N of n / ADJ: ADJ n / ADJ: ADJ n

,Native A'merican, Native Americans. Native Americans are people from any one of the many tribes which were already living in North America before the Europeans arrived there. ▶ Also an adjective. *...a gathering of Native American elders.* ◆◇◇◇ N-COUNT / ADJ: ADJ n

,native 'speaker, native speakers. A native **speaker** of a language is someone who speaks that language as their first language rather than having learnt it as a foreign language. *Our programme ensures daily opportunities to practice your study language with native speakers.* N-COUNT

Na·tiv·ity /nə'tɪvɪti/. The Nativity is the birth of Jesus, which is celebrated by Christians at Christmas. *...the Nativity story.* N-SING: the N

na'tivity play, nativity plays. A nativity play is a play about the birth of Jesus, usually one performed by children at Christmas time. N-COUNT

NATO /'neɪtəʊ/. NATO is an international organization which consists of the USA, Canada, the UK, and other European countries who have agreed to support one another if they are attacked. It is an abbreviation for 'North Atlantic Treaty Organization'. ◆◆◇◇ N-PROPER

nat·ter /'nætə/ **natters, nattering, nattered.** When people **natter**, they talk casually for a long time about unimportant things. *There were several dozen people in the great hall, already nattering away to the music of a string quartet. ...a day of nattering with fellow farmers at the local market... You natter all day long at the hospital.* ▶ Also a noun. *...when a group of new mums get together for a natter.* V-RECIP: pl-n V / pl-n V adv/ prep / V with n / V / INFORMAL / N-SING: a N

nat·ty /'næti/ **nattier, nattiest. 1** If you describe a man as **natty**, you think that he dresses smartly and neatly. *Cliff was a natty dresser.* **2** If you describe something as **natty**, you think it is attractive and cleverly designed. *...natty little houses.* ADJ-GRADED INFORMAL / ADJ-GRADED INFORMAL

natu·ral /'nætʃərəl/ **naturals. 1** If you say that it is **natural** for someone to act in a particular way, you mean that it is reasonable in the circumstances. *It is only natural for youngsters to crave the excitement of driving a fast car... A period of depression can be a perfectly natural response to certain aspects of life.* **2** Natural behaviour or ability is instinctive and has not been learned. *...the insect's natural instinct to feed.* ♦ **natu·ral·ly** *Some individuals are naturally good communicators.* **3** If you say that someone is a **natural**, you mean that they do something very well and very easily. *He's a natural with any kind of engine.* **4** If someone's behaviour is **natural**, they appear to be relaxed and are not trying to hide anything. *Bethan's sister was as friendly and natural as the rest of the family.* ♦ **naturally** *You can talk quite naturally to her.* ♦ **natu·ral·ness** *...the naturalness of the acting.* **5** Natural things exist or occur in nature and are not made or caused by people. *...the worst natural disaster in South Korea in four years. ...the gigantic natural harbour of Poole.* ♦ **naturally** *Nitrates are chemicals that occur naturally in water... Honey is a naturally acidic substance.* **6** If someone dies of **natural causes**, they die because they are ill or old rather than because of an accident, murder, or suicide. **7** Someone's **natural** parent is their actual parent, as opposed to one who has adopted or fostered them. Someone's **natural** child is their actual child, rather than one they have adopted or fostered. ◆◆◆◇ ADJ-GRADED / ADJ / ADV / N-COUNT / ADJ-GRADED / ADV-GRADED: ADV after v / N-UNCOUNT / ADJ: ADJ n / ADV / PHRASE / ADJ: ADJ n

8 In music, a **natural** note is the ordinary note, not its `ADJ: n ADJ` sharp or flat form. *...B natural.*
9 See also **naturally**.

,natural 'childbirth. If a woman gives birth by `N-UNCOUNT` **natural childbirth**, she chooses not to be given any drugs to relieve her pain or to send her to sleep.

,natural 'gas. Natural gas is gas which is found `◆◇◇◇◇` underground or under the sea. It is collected and `N-UNCOUNT` stored, and piped into people's homes to be used for cooking and heating.

,natural 'history. Natural history is the study of `◆◇◇◇◇` animals, plants, and other living things. `N-UNCOUNT`

natu·ral·ise /ˈnætʃərəlaɪz/. See **naturalize**.

natu·ral·ism /ˈnætʃərəlɪzəm/. **Naturalism** is a theo- `N-UNCOUNT` ry in literature and art which states that people and objects should be shown as they actually are, rather than in an idealistic or unnatural way.

natu·ral·ist /ˈnætʃərəlɪst/ **naturalists.** A natural- `◆◇◇◇◇` ist is a person who studies plants, animals and oth- `N-COUNT` er living things.

natu·ral·is·tic /ˌnætʃərəˈlɪstɪk/. **1** Naturalistic is `ADJ-GRADED` used to describe the work of artists and writers who believe in and practice naturalism in their work. *These drawings are among his most naturalistic.*
2 Naturalistic means simulating the effects or char- `ADJ-GRADED` acteristics of nature. *Further research is needed un- der rather more naturalistic conditions.*

natu·ral·ize /ˈnætʃərəlaɪz/ **naturalizes, natural- izing, naturalized;** also spelled **naturalise** in Brit- ish English. **1** To **naturalize** a species of plant `V-ERG: V n` means to replant it in an area where it is not usually `V` found. *The plant naturalises well in grass.* **2** If the `VERB: V n` government of a country **naturalizes** someone, they allow a person who was not born in that country to become a citizen of it. ♦ **natu·rali·za·tion** `N-UNCOUNT` /ˌnætʃərəlaɪˈzeɪʃən/ *...their naturalization papers.*
♦ **natu·ral·ized** *We all became naturalized British* `ADJ: ADJ n` *citizens.*

natu·ral·ly /ˈnætʃərəli/. **1** You use **naturally** to in- `◆◆◆◇◇` dicate that you think something is very obvious and `ADV` not at all surprising in the circumstances. *When things go wrong, all of us naturally feel disappoint- ed... Naturally these comings and goings excited some curiosity.* **2** If one thing develops **naturally** `ADV:` from another, it develops as a normal consequence `ADV` or result of it. *A study of yoga leads naturally to meditation.* **3** If something **comes naturally** to you, `PHRASE` you find it easy to do and quickly become good at it. *With football, it was just something that came naturally to me.* **4** See also **natural**.

,natural re'sources. The **natural resources** of a `◆◇◇◇◇` place are all its land, forests, energy sources, and `N-PLURAL` minerals which exist naturally there and can be used by people. *...a country rich in natural resources.*

,natural se'lection. Natural selection is a pro- `N-UNCOUNT` cess by which species of animals and plants that are best adapted to their environment survive and re- produce, while those that are less well adapted die out.

,natural 'wastage. If a business or other organi- `N-UNCOUNT` zation reduces its workforce by **natural wastage**, it `BRITISH` does it by not replacing employees who leave or re- tire, rather than by sacking people or making them redundant. The usual American word is **attrition**.

na·ture /ˈneɪtʃə/. **1** Nature refers to all the ani- `◆◆◆◇` mals, plants, and other things in the world that are `N-UNCOUNT` not made by people, and all the events and pro- cesses that are not caused by people. *...grasses that grow wild in nature. ...the ecological balance of na- ture.* **2** If you say that something is **against nature**, `PHRASE` you disapprove of it because you think it is unnatu- `PRAGMATICS` ral or abnormal. **3** If you want to get **back to na- ture**, you want to return to a simpler way of living. `PHRASE` **4** Some people talk about a **call of nature** when re- `PHRASE` ferring politely to the need to go to the toilet. `PRAGMATICS`
5 The **nature** of something is its basic quality or char- `N-SING:` acter. *Mr Sharp would not comment on the nature of* `with supp,` *the issues being investigated. ...the ambitious nature of* `also by/in N` *the programme... The protests had been non-political*

by nature. **6** If you say that something has a particular `PHRASE` characteristic **by** its **nature** or **by** its **very nature**, you mean that things of that type always have that charac- teristic. *Peacekeeping, by its nature, makes pre- planning difficult.* **7** If you say that something is **in the** `PHRASE` **nature of things**, you mean that you would expect it to happen in the circumstances mentioned. *Many have already died, and in the nature of things many more will die.* **8** If you say that one thing is **in the na-** `PHRASE` **ture of** another, you mean that you think it is like the other thing. *It was in the nature of a debate rather than an argument.*
9 Someone's **nature** is their character, which they `N-SING:` show by the way they behave. *Her ambitious nature* `with poss,` *made her unsuitable for an arranged marriage... She* `also by N` *was by nature affectionate.* **10** If a way of behaving is `PHRASE` **second nature** to you, you do it almost without think- ing because it is easy or obvious to you. *Planning ahead had always come as second nature to her.*
11 See also **human nature, Mother Nature.**

'nature study. Nature study is the study of ani- `N-UNCOUNT` mals and plants at a very basic level by looking at them directly, for example as it is taught to young children.

'nature trail, nature trails. A **nature trail** is a `N-COUNT` route through an area of countryside which is sign- posted, pointing out things like animals, plants, and rocks.

na·tur·ism /ˈneɪtʃərɪzəm/. **Naturism** is the practice `N-UNCOUNT` of not wearing any clothes on beaches and other `BRITISH` areas specially set aside for this purpose. ♦ **na·tur- ·ist, naturists** *...a naturist beach.* `N-COUNT`

naught /nɔːt/. See **nought.**

naugh·ty /ˈnɔːti/ **naughtier, naughtiest. 1** If `◆◇◇◇◇` you say that a child is **naughty**, you think that he or `ADJ-GRADED` she is behaving badly or is disobedient. *Girls, you're being very naughty... You naughty boy!* ♦ **naugh·ti- ·ness** *...a young boy's natural naughtiness.* `N-UNCOUNT`
2 You can describe books, pictures, or words, as `ADJ-GRADED` **naughty** when they are slightly rude or related to sex. *...saucy TV shows, crammed full of naughty innuendo.*
♦ **naughtiness** *...a writer who shocked the bourgeoi- sie with his sexual naughtiness.* `N-UNCOUNT`

nau·sea /ˈnɔːziə/. **Nausea** is the feeling that you `◆◇◇◇` are going to vomit. *I was overcome with a feeling of* `N-UNCOUNT` *nausea.*

nau·seam /ˈnɔːziæm/. See **ad nauseam.**

nau·seate /ˈnɔːzieɪt/ **nauseates, nauseating,** `VERB: V n` **nauseated.** If something **nauseates** you, it makes you feel as if you are going to vomit.

nau·seat·ing /ˈnɔːzieɪtɪŋ/. If you describe `ADJ-GRADED` someone's attitude or behaviour as **nauseating**, you find it extremely unpleasant and feel disgusted by it. *The judge described the offences as nauseating and unspeakable.*

nau·seous /ˈnɔːziəs, AM -ʃəs/. If you feel **nauseous**, `ADJ-GRADED` you feel as if you want to vomit.

nau·ti·cal /ˈnɔːtɪkəl/. **Nautical** means relating to `◆◇◇◇` ships and sailing. *...a nautical chart of the region* `ADJ` *you sail.*

,nautical 'mile, nautical miles. A **nautical mile** `N-COUNT` is a unit of measurement used at sea. It is equal to 1852 metres.

na·val /ˈneɪvəl/. **Naval** means belonging to, relating `◆◆◆◇◇` to, or involving a country's navy. *He was the senior* `ADJ: ADJ n` *serving naval officer. ...the US naval base at Guanta- namo Bay.*

nave /neɪv/ **naves.** The **nave** of a church or ca- `N-COUNT` thedral is the long central part where people gather to worship.

na·vel /ˈneɪvəl/ **navels.** Your **navel** is the small `◆◇◇◇` hollow just below your waist at the front of your `N-COUNT` body.

'navel-gazing. If you refer to the way people ap- `N-UNCOUNT` proach a problem as **navel-gazing**, you are criticiz- `PRAGMATICS` ing them because they think about it for a long time but take no action on it. *She dismisses the reform process as an exercise in collective navel-gazing.*

N

navi·gable /'nævɪgəbəl/. Navigable rivers or waterways are wide and deep enough for a boat to travel along safely. — ADJ FORMAL

navi·gate /'nævɪgeɪt/ navigates, navigating, navigated. 1 When someone navigates a ship or an aircraft, they steer in the direction that has been decided upon. *The purpose of the visit was to navigate into an ice-filled fiord. ...the new navigation system which will enable aircraft to navigate with total pinpoint accuracy.* 2 When a ship or boat navigates an area of water, it sails on or across it. 3 If you say that someone navigates their way somewhere, you mean that they go there, often with some difficulty because the route is complicated or there are obstacles in the way. *They had just navigated their way through Maidstone... They had first to navigate around chairs in the middle of the room... Cars will navigate a maze of bridges, ramps and loops called 'Scheme Z'.* 4 If you manage to navigate a difficult situation, you deal with it successfully. *This outlook helped her to navigate through her later years with success.* 5 If a passenger in a car navigates, he or she tells the driver, often using a road map, what roads the car should be driven along in order to get somewhere. 6 When fish, animals, or insects navigate somewhere, they find the right direction to go and travel there. *In tests, the bees navigate back home after being placed in a field a mile away.* — ◆◇◇◇◇ V-ERG: V n; V prep/adv V; VERB: V n; VERB V way prep V prep/adv V n; VERB: V n V through n; VERB: V; VERB V adv/prep Also V

navi·ga·tion navigations /,nævɪ'geɪʃən/. 1 Navigation is the act of steering a ship or aircraft in a direction that has been decided upon. *The expedition was wrecked by bad planning and poor navigation.* ♦ navi·ga·tion·al /,nævɪ'geɪʃənəl/ *The crash was a direct result of inadequate navigational aids.* 2 You can refer to the movement of ships as navigation. *Pack ice around Iceland was becoming a threat to navigation.* — ◆◇◇◇◇ N-VAR; ADJ; N-UNCOUNT

navi·ga·tor /'nævɪgeɪtə/ navigators. The navigator on an aircraft or ship is the person whose job is to work out the direction in which the aircraft or ship should be travelling. — ◆◇◇◇◇ N-COUNT

nav·vy /'nævi/ navvies. A navvy is a person who is employed to do hard physical work, for example building roads or canals. — N-COUNT DATED, BRITISH

navy /'neɪvi/ navies. 1 A country's navy consists of the people it employs to fight at sea, and the ships they use. *Her own son was also in the Navy.* 2 Navy means the same as navy-blue. *...a navy sweater.* — ◆◆◇◇◇ N-COUNT; COLOUR

navy-blue. Navy-blue is very dark blue. *...a navy-blue blazer.* — COLOUR

nay /neɪ/. 1 You use nay in front of a stronger word or phrase which you feel is more correct than the one you have just used and helps to emphasize the point you are making. *...his son's remarkable, nay, unique performance.* 2 Nay is sometimes used to mean 'no' when people are talking about voting for or giving their consent for something. *The House of Commons can merely say yea or nay to the executive judgment.* 3 Nay is an old-fashioned, poetic, or religious word for 'no'. — ADV: ADV with cl/group PRAGMATICS FORMAL; CONVENTION; CONVENTION

Nazi /'nɑːtsi/ Nazis. The Nazis were members of the right-wing political party, led by Adolf Hitler, which held power in Germany from 1933 to 1945. ♦ Na·zism. Nazism was the political ideas and activities of the German Nazi Party. — ◆◆◆◇◇ N-COUNT; N-UNCOUNT

NB /,en 'biː/. You write NB to draw someone's attention to what you are about to say or write. NB is an abbreviation for the Latin expression 'nota bene'. *NB. Please watch the news for any announcement.* — ◆◇◇◇◇ PRAGMATICS

NCO /,en si: 'əʊ/ NCOs. An NCO is a soldier who has a rank such as sergeant or corporal. NCO is an abbreviation for 'non-commissioned officer'. — N-COUNT

NE. NE is a written abbreviation for north-east.

ne·an·der·thal /ni'ændətɑːl, -θɑːl/ neanderthals. 1 Neanderthal people lived in Europe between 35,000 and 70,000 years ago. *...neanderthal man.* ► You can refer to people from the Neanderthal period as Neanderthals. 2 If you describe people's, especially men's, ideas or ways of behaving as Neanderthal, you disapprove of them because they are very old-fashioned and uncivilized. *...his notoriously Neanderthal attitude to women.* ► Also a noun. *...drunken neanderthals.* — ADJ: ADJ n; N-COUNT; ADJ-GRADED PRAGMATICS; N-COUNT

near /nɪə/ nearer, nearest; nears, nearing, neared. 1 If something is near a place, thing, or person, it is a short distance from them. *Don't come near me. ...a farmhouse near the cottage... He drew his chair nearer the fire.* ► Also an adverb. *He crouched as near to the door as he could... She took a step nearer to the barrier... As we drew near, I saw that the boot lid was up.* ► Also a comparative and superlative adjective. *...the nearer of the two barges... He collapsed into the nearest chair.* ♦ near·ness *One of these gates is known as 'The Forest Gate' because of its nearness to woods bordering the lane.* 2 You can say that someone will not go near something or someone when you are emphasizing that they will not go somewhere, do something, or see someone. *He will absolutely not go near a hospital.* 3 The near one of two things is the one that is closer. *...a mighty beech tree on the near side of the little clearing.* 4 If you are nearing a place, you are getting quite near to it. *As he neared the stable, he slowed the horse.* 5 You use near and far to indicate that you are referring to a very large area or distance. *People would gather from near and far.* 6 If someone or something is near to a particular state, they have almost reached it. *The repairs to the Hafner machine were near to completion... He comes near to contradicting himself.* ► Near means the same as near to. *He was near tears.* 7 You use near to indicate that something is almost the thing mentioned. *She was believed to have died in near poverty.* ► Also an adverb. *...his near fatal accident.* 8 When someone or something nears a particular stage or point, they will soon reach that stage or point. *His age was hard to guess – he must have been nearing fifty.* 9 You use nowhere near and not anywhere near to emphasize that something is not the case. *They are nowhere near good enough.* 10 If something is similar to something else, you can say that it is near to it. *...a sickening sensation that was near to nausea.* ► Near means the same as near to. *Often her feelings were nearer hatred than love.* 11 You describe the thing most similar to something as the nearest thing to it when there is no example of the thing itself. *It would appear that the legal profession is the nearest thing to a recession-proof industry.* 12 If a time or event draws near, it will happen soon. *The time for my departure from Japan was drawing nearer every day. ...a person who knows or feels that death is near.* 13 If something happens near a particular time, it happens just before or just after that time. *Performance is lowest between 3 a.m. and 5 a.m. and reaches a peak near midday... I'll tell you nearer the day.* 14 You say that an important time or event nears when it is going to occur quite soon. *As half time neared, Hardyman almost scored twice.* 15 If you say that something will happen in the near future, you mean that it will happen quite soon. 16 You use near to say that something is a little more or less than an amount or number stated. *...to increase manufacturing from about 2.5 million cars a year to nearer 4.75 million. ...the pound, which ended last year near its annual low.* 17 In a contest, your nearest rival or challenger is the one that is most likely to defeat you. 18 People sometimes refer to their close relatives and friends as their nearest and dearest. 19 If you want to indicate that something is almost true, you can use the expressions near enough and damned near. In British English, you can also say as near as dammit. *I bought them for a pound apiece, near enough.* 20 If you want to indicate that something almost happened, you can use the expression damned near. In British English, you can also say as near as dammit. *He damned near fooled me.* — ◆◆◆◆◆ PREP; ADV-GRADED: ADV after v, be ADV; ADJ; N-UNCOUNT; PREP PRAGMATICS; ADJ-GRADED: det ADJ n; VERB V n WRITTEN PHRASE; PHR-PREP; PREP; ADJ: ADJ n WRITTEN; ADV: ADV adj; VB: no passive V n; PHRASE PRAGMATICS; PHR-PREP; PREP; ADJ-SUPER: the ADJ to n; ADJ-GRADED: ADV after v WRITTEN; PREP; VERB V; PHRASE; PREP; ADJ-SUPER: ADJ n; PHRASE; PHRASE INFORMAL; PHRASE INFORMAL

near·by /ˌnɪəˈbaɪ/. If something is **nearby**, it is only ◆◆◆◇◇ a short distance away. *...someone who lived nearby.* ADV *...a couple standing nearby... There is less expensive accommodation nearby.* ► Also an adjective. *At a* ADJ: ADJ n *nearby table a man was complaining in a loud voice.*

near death ex'perience, near death experi- N-COUNT **ences.** A **near death experience** is a strange experience that some people who have nearly died say they had when they were unconscious.

Near 'East. The **Near East** is the same as the N-PROPER: **Middle East.** the N

near·ly /ˈnɪəli/. **1 Nearly** is used to indicate that a ◆◆◆◆◇ quantity or time is a little smaller or a little less ADV-GRADED than the stated value. *Goldsworth stared at me in si-* ADV group, *lence for nearly twenty seconds... Hunter knew nearly* ADV before v *all of this already.* **2 Nearly** is used to indicate that ADV-GRADED something will soon be true. *It was already nearly* ADV group, *eight o'clock... I was nearly asleep... I've nearly fin-* ADV before v *ished the words for your song.* **3** You use **not nearly** PHRASE to emphasize that one thing or amount is much PRAGMATICS smaller or much less than another. *Father's flat in Paris wasn't nearly as grand as this... Minerals in general are not nearly so well absorbed as other nutrients.*

near 'miss, near misses; also spelled **near-** **miss. 1** A **near miss** is a bomb or shot that comes N-COUNT close to its target but misses it. *We've had a few near misses in the raids.* **2** You can say there is a N-COUNT **near miss** when a collision or accident nearly oc- curs. *...a near miss between two airliners over south-* *ern England.* **3** A **near miss** is an attempt to do N-COUNT something which fails by a very small margin. *...last Saturday's near miss against Ireland.*

near·side /ˈnɪəsaɪd/. The **nearside** of a vehicle is N-SING the side that is nearest the edge of the road when BRITISH the vehicle is being driven normally. *It hit the kerb on the nearside. ...the nearside front tyre.*

near-'sighted; also spelled **nearsighted.** If some- ADJ-GRADED one is **near-sighted**, they cannot see distant things DATED clearly.

neat /niːt/ **neater, neatest. 1** A **neat** place, thing, ◆◆◆◇◇ or person is tidy and smart, with everything ar- ADJ-GRADED ranged in an orderly way. *She undressed and put her wet clothes in a neat pile... Everything was neat and tidy.* ♦ **neat·ly** *He folded his paper neatly and* ADV-GRADED: *sipped his coffee.* ♦ **neat·ness** *The grounds were a* ADV with v *perfect balance between neatness and natural wild-* N-UNCOUNT *ness.* **2** Someone who is **neat** keeps their home or ADJ-GRADED possessions tidy, with everything arranged in an or- derly way. *'That's not like Alf,' he said, 'leaving pa-* *pers muddled like that. He's always so neat.'* ♦ **neatly** *I followed her into that room which her* ADV-GRADED: *mother had maintained so neatly.* ♦ **neatness** *...a* ADV with v *paragon of neatness, efficiency and reliability.* N-UNCOUNT **3** A **neat** object, part of the body, or shape is quite ADJ-GRADED small and has a smooth outline. *...a faded woman with neat features.* **4** A **neat** movement or action is ADJ-GRADED done accurately and skilfully, with no unnecessary movements. *A neat move between Black and Keane left Nigel Clough in the clear.* ♦ **neatly** *The experi-* ADV-GRADED: *enced favourite swerved neatly aside and surged for-* ADV with v *ward to beat two other younger horses by several lengths.* **5** A **neat** way of organizing, achieving, ex- ADJ-GRADED plaining, or expressing something is clever and con- venient. *It had been such a neat, clever plan.* ♦ **neatly** ADV-GRADED: *Real people do not fit neatly into these categories.* ADV with v ♦ **neatness** *He knew full well he had been out-* N-UNCOUNT *flanked, and he appreciated the neatness of it.* **6** If you say that something is **neat**, you like it or think ADJ-GRADED it is very good. *'Oh, those new apartments are really* INFORMAL, *neat,' the girl babbled on.* AMERICAN **7** If someone drinks strong alcohol **neat**, they do not ADJ add anything such as tonic or water to it. *He took a* BRITISH *mouthful of neat whisky.*

neb·u·la /ˈnebjələ/ **nebulae.** A **nebula** is a cloud of N-COUNT dust and gas in space. New stars are produced from nebulae.

neb·u·lous /ˈnebjələs/. If you describe something as ADJ-GRADED **nebulous**, you mean that it is vague and not clearly defined or not easy to describe. *The notions we chil-* *dren were able to form of the great world beyond were exceedingly nebulous.*

nec·es·sari·ly /ˌnesɪˈserɪli, -srɪli/. **1** If you say that ◆◆◆◇◇ something is not **necessarily** true, you mean that it ADV: may not be true or is not always true. *Anger is not* with neg *necessarily the most useful or acceptable reaction to such events.* ● If you reply **'Not necessarily'**, you CONVENTION mean that what has just been said or suggested may PRAGMATICS not be true. *'He was lying, of course.'—'Not neces- sarily.'* **2** If you say that something **necessarily** hap- ADV pens or is **necessarily** true, you mean that it has to happen or be true and cannot be any different. *Tourism is an industry that has a necessarily close connection with governments.*

nec·es·sary /ˈnesɪsəri/ **necessaries. 1** Some- ◆◆◆◆◇ thing that is **necessary** is needed in order for some- ADJ-GRADED thing to happen, especially something you want to happen. *It might be necessary to leave fast... We will do whatever is necessary to stop them.* **2** If you say CONVENTION **'That won't be necessary'** when someone has of- PRAGMATICS fered to do something for you, you are refusing their offer in a very definite way, often showing that you do not value their offer. *I offered to show him the video tape. 'Oh, that won't be necessary,' he said with a slight flutter of his fingers.* **3** If you say that PHRASE something will happen **if necessary, when neces- sary,** or **where necessary**, you mean that it will hap- pen if it is necessary, when it is necessary, or where it is necessary. *If necessary, the airship can stay up there for days.* **4** A **necessary** consequence or connection must hap- ADJ: ADJ n pen or exist, because of the nature of the things or events involved. *Wastage was no doubt a necessary consequence of war.* **5 Necessaries** are things, such as food or clothing, N-PLURAL that you need to have in order to live. *...a small parcel* DATED *of necessaries tied up in a handkerchief and carried on a stick.*

ne·ces·si·tate /nɪˈsesɪteɪt/ **necessitates, ne-** ◆◇◇◇◇ **cessitating, necessitated.** If something **neces-** VERB **sitates** an event, action, or situation, it makes it V n/-ing necessary. *A prolonged drought had necessitated the* FORMAL *introduction of water rationing.*

ne·ces·sity /nɪˈsesɪti/ **necessities. 1** The neces- ◆◆◇◇◇ sity of something is the fact that it must exist, hap- N-UNCOUNT pen, or be done. *There is agreement on the necessity of reforms... Most women, like men, work from eco- nomic necessity.* **2** If you say that something is of PHRASE **necessity** true, you mean that it is true because FORMAL nothing else is possible or imaginable in the cir- cumstances. **3** A **necessity** is something that you N-COUNT must have in order to live properly or do some- thing. *Water is a basic necessity of life.* **4** A situation N-COUNT or action that is a **necessity** is necessary and cannot be avoided. *The President pleaded that strong rule from the centre was a regrettable, but temporary necessity.*

neck /nek/ **necks, necking, necked. 1** Your ◆◆◆◇◇ **neck** is the part of your body which joins your head N-COUNT to the rest of your body. See picture headed **human body.** *She threw her arms round his neck and hugged him.* **2** The **neck** of an article of clothing N-COUNT such as a shirt, dress, jumper is the part which sur- rounds your neck. **3** The **neck** of something such as N-COUNT a bottle or a guitar is the long narrow part at one end of it. **4** If a racehorse wins **by a neck**, it wins by a very small N-SING distance. **5** If you say that someone **is breathing** PHRASE **down your neck**, you mean that they are watching you very closely and checking everything you do. *Most farmers have bank managers breathing down their necks.* **6** In a competition, especially an election, PHRASE if two or more competitors are **neck and neck**, they are level with each other and have an equal chance of winning. **7** If you say that you have something **round** your PHRASE **neck**, or **around** your **neck**, you mean that it is your responsibility and it causes you a lot of worry. *No-one should start working life with a debt round their neck.*

N

8 If you say that someone is in some sort of trouble or criminal activity **up to** their **neck**, you mean that they are deeply involved in it. *He is probably up to his neck in debt.* `PHRASE INFORMAL`

9 If you **stick** your **neck out**, you bravely say or do something that might be criticized or might turn out to be wrong. `PHRASE INFORMAL`

10 Someone or something that is from your **neck of the woods** is from the same part of the country as you are. `PHRASE INFORMAL`

11 If two people **are necking**, they are kissing each other passionately. You can also say that one person **is necking** with another. *I found myself behind a curtain, necking with my best friend's wife.* `V-RECIP V with n Also Also pl-n V INFORMAL`

12 • **a millstone round** your **neck**: see **millstone**. • **a pain in the neck**: see **pain**. • **the scruff of** your **neck**: see **scruff**.

neck·lace /'neklɪs/ **necklaces, necklacing, necklaced. 1** A **necklace** is a piece of jewellery such as a chain or a string of beads which someone, usually a woman, wears round their neck. *...a diamond necklace and matching earrings.* **2** To **necklace** someone means to kill them by putting a tyre soaked in petrol around their neck and then setting fire to it. `◆◇◇◇◇ N-COUNT` `VERB: V n`

neck·line /'neklaɪn/ **necklines.** The **neckline** of a dress, blouse, or other piece of clothing is the edge that goes around the neck, especially the front part of it. *...a short brown dress with a plunging neckline.* `N-COUNT`

neck·tie /'nektaɪ/ **neckties.** A **necktie** is a narrow piece of cloth that someone, usually a man, wears with a shirt. It is tied around the neck under the collar, with the ends hanging down in front. `N-COUNT AMERICAN`

nec·ro·philia /ˌnekrəˈfɪliə/. **Necrophilia** is the act of having sexual intercourse with a dead body, or the desire for it. `N-UNCOUNT`

ne·cropo·lis /neˈkrɒpəlɪs/ **necropolises.** A **necropolis** is a place where dead people were buried in ancient times. *...a small Etruscan museum and necropolis 3 km east of the village.* `N-COUNT FORMAL`

ne·cro·sis /neˈkrəʊsɪs/. **Necrosis** is the death of part of someone's body, for example because it is not getting enough blood. `N-UNCOUNT MEDICAL`

nec·tar /'nektə/. **1 Nectar** is a sweet liquid produced by flowers, which bees and other insects collect. **2** If you refer to a drink as **nectar**, you think it is delicious. `◆◇◇◇◇ N-UNCOUNT` `N-UNCOUNT LITERARY`

nec·tar·ine /'nektəriːn, -rɪn/ **nectarines.** A **nectarine** is a kind of peach with a smooth skin. `N-COUNT`

née /neɪ/. You use **née** after a married woman's name just before you mention the family surname she had before she got married. *...Lady Helen Taylor (née Windsor).* `FORMAL`

need /niːd/ **needs, needing, needed.** Need sometimes behaves like an ordinary verb, for example 'She needs to know' and 'She doesn't need to know' and sometimes like a modal, for example 'Need she know?', and 'She need not know'. 'Need not' has the contracted form 'needn't'. `◆◆◆◆◆`

1 If you **need** something, or **need** to do something, you cannot successfully achieve what you want or live properly without it. *He desperately needed money... I need to make a phone call... I need you to do something for me... I need you sane and sober... I need you here, Wally.* ► Also a noun. *Charles has never felt the need to compete with anyone. ...the child who never had his need for attention and importance satisfied.* **2** If an object or place **needs** something doing to it, that action must or should be done to improve the object or place, or to improve a situation. If a task **needs** doing, it must or should be done to improve a situation. *The building needs quite a few repairs... The taste of vitamins is not too nice so the flavour sometimes needs to be disguised.* **3** You can say **'Who needs** something?' as a way of emphasizing that you think that this thing is unnecessary or not useful. *Cigarettes, who needs them?* **4** If there is a **need** for something, that thing would improve a situation or something cannot happen `VB: no cont V n V to-inf V n to-inf V n adj V n adv/prep` `N-COUNT` `VB: no cont V n/-ing V to-inf` `PHRASE PRAGMATICS INFORMAL` `N-SING`

without it. *There is a need for other similar schools throughout Britain.* **5** If someone or something is **in need of** something, they need it or ought to have it. *I was all right but in need of rest.* **6** People **in need** do not have enough of essential things such as money, food, or good health. *When both of you were in need, I was the one who loaned you money.* **7** If you say that you will do something, especially an extreme action, **if need be**, or **if needs be**, you mean that you will do if it is necessary. *We can survive down here for three months, if need be.* `PHRASE` `PHRASE` `PHRASE`

8 If you say that someone **needn't** do something, you are telling them not to do it, or advising or suggesting that they should not do it. *Look, you needn't shout... She need not know I'm here.* ► Also a verb. *Well, for Heaven's sake, you don't need to apologize... Come along, Mother, we don't need to take up any more of Mr Kemp's time.* **9** You can tell someone that **there's no need** for them to do something as a way of telling them not to do it or telling them to stop doing it, for example because it is unnecessary or unjustified. *There's no need to call a doctor... There's no need for that kind of language in this magazine.* `MODAL: with neg PRAGMATICS` `VERB: no cont, with neg V to-inf` `PHRASE PRAGMATICS SPOKEN`

10 If you tell someone that they **needn't** do something, or that something **needn't** happen, you are reassuring them that it is not necessary or inevitable, because a situation is not as bad as they might think. *You needn't worry... This needn't take long, Simon... He need never drink again... All he need fear is a general postponement of Britain's economic recovery.* ► Also a verb. *He replied, with a reassuring smile, 'Oh, you don't need to worry about them.'... You don't need to be a millionaire to consider having a bank account in Switzerland.* **11** If someone **needn't** have done something, it was not necessary or useful for them to do it, although they did it. *I was a little nervous when I announced my engagement to Grace, but I needn't have worried.* ► If someone **didn't need to** do something, they needn't have done it. *You didn't need to give me any more money you know, but thank you.* **12** You use **needn't** when you are giving someone permission not to do something. *Well, you needn't tell me anything if you don't want to.* ► Also a verb. *You don't need to wait for me... Mommy, you don't need to stay while we talk.* **13** If something **need not** be true, it is not necessarily true or not always true. *What is right for us need not be right for others.* `MODAL: with brd-neg PRAGMATICS` `VERB: no cont, with neg V to-inf` `VERB: no cont, with neg V to-inf` `MODAL: with neg PRAGMATICS` `VERB: no cont V to-inf` `MODAL: with neg FORMAL`

14 You use **need** in expressions such as **I need hardly say** and **I needn't add** to emphasize to the person you are talking to that they should not be surprised by what you are about to say, because it is a natural consequence of what you have just said. *I needn't add that if you fail to do as I ask, you will suffer the consequences.* **15** You can use **need** in expressions such as **'Need I say more'** and **'Need I go on'** when you want to avoid stating an obvious consequence of something you have just said. *Mid-fifties, short black hair, grey moustache, distinctive Russian accent. Need I go on?* `MODAL PRAGMATICS` `MODAL PRAGMATICS`

need·ful /'niːdfʊl/. **Needful** means necessary. *...stoppages for needful rest and recreation.* `ADJ-GRADED DATED`

nee·dle /'niːdəl/ **needles, needling, needled. 1** A **needle** is a small very thin piece of metal with a sharp point which is used for sewing. **2** Knitting **needles** are thin metal or plastic sticks that are used for knitting. **3** A **needle** is a thin hollow metal rod with a sharp point, which forms part of a syringe. It is used to inject a drug into someone's body. **4** On a record player, the **needle** is the small pointed device that touches the record and picks up the sound signals. **5** On an instrument which measures something such as speed or weight, the **needle** is the long strip of metal or plastic on the dial that moves backwards and forwards, showing the measurement. **6** The **needles** of a fir or pine tree are its thin, hard, pointed leaves. **7** If someone **needles** you, they annoy you continual- `◆◆◇◇◇ N-COUNT` `N-COUNT` `N-COUNT` `N-COUNT` `N-COUNT` `N-COUNT` `VERB`

ly, especially by criticizing you. *He had needled* V n
Jerrold, which might be unwise.

8 • like looking for a needle in a haystack: see haystack. See also **pins and needles.**

'needle exchange, needle exchanges; also N-COUNT
spelled **needle-exchange.** A **needle exchange** is a
place where drug addicts are able to obtain new
hypodermic needles in exchange for used ones.

need·less /'niːdləs/. **1** Something that is **needless** ◆◇◇◇◇
is completely unnecessary. *...but his death was so* ADJ-GRADED
needless. ♦ **need·less·ly** *Half a million women die* ADV-GRADED
needlessly each year during childbirth... He said
something to me so mean, so needlessly cruel. **2** You PHRASE
use **needless to say** when you want to emphasize [PRAGMATICS]
that what you are about to say is obvious and to be
expected in the circumstances. *Needless to say, she*
awoke from anesthesia cold, crying, and in lots of
pain.

needle·work /'niːdəlwɜːk/. **1** Needlework is sew- N-UNCOUNT
ing or embroidery that is done by hand. *She did*
beautiful needlework. **2** Needlework is the activity N-UNCOUNT
of sewing or embroidering.

needn't /'niːdənt/. **Needn't** is the usual spoken
form of **need not.**

needy /'niːdi/ **needier, neediest. Needy** people ◆◇◇◇◇
do not have enough food, medicine, or clothing or ADJ-GRADED
an adequate house to live in. *...ensuring that food*
and medicine get to needy Somalis. ► **The needy** are N-PLURAL:
people who are needy. the N

ne·fari·ous /nɪ'feəriəs/. If you describe an activity ADJ-GRADED
as **nefarious,** you mean that it is wicked and im- LITERARY
moral. *Why make a whole village prisoner if it was*
not to some nefarious purpose?

neg. Neg. is a written abbreviation for 'negative'.

ne·gate /nɪ'geɪt/ **negates, negating, negated.** ◆◇◇◇◇
1 If one thing **negates** another, it causes that other VERB
thing to lose the effect or value that it had. *These* V n
weaknesses negated his otherwise progressive atti- FORMAL
tude towards the staff. **2** If someone **negates** some- VERB
thing, they say that it does not exist. *To negate the* V n
results of elections would only make things worse. FORMAL

ne·ga·tion /nɪ'geɪʃən/. **1** Negation is the act of N-UNCOUNT
causing something not to exist, or the state of not FORMAL
existing. *...an act of negation rather than creation.*
2 The **negation** of a quality or ideal is its complete N-SING:
opposite or its complete absence. *To do nothing* N of n
would seem to be a negation of what we stand for. FORMAL
3 Negation is a person's disagreement with some- N-UNCOUNT
one or refusal of something. *The editor grimaced,* FORMAL
gesturing in negation.

nega·tive /'negətɪv/ **negatives. 1** A fact, situa- ◆◆◆◇◇
tion, or experience that is **negative** is unpleasant, ADJ-GRADED
depressing, or harmful. *The news from China is*
overwhelmingly negative... All this had an extremely
negative effect on the criminal justice system.
♦ **nega·tive·ly** *This will negatively affect the result.* ADV-GRADED
2 If someone is **negative,** they consider only the ADJ-GRADED
bad aspects of a situation, rather than the good
ones. *Why does the media present such a negative*
view of this splendid city? ♦ **negatively** *Maybe he* ADV-GRADED:
viewed all his relationships rather negatively. ADV after v
♦ **nega·tiv·ity** /ˌnegə'tɪvɪti/ *I loathe negativity. I* N-UNCOUNT
can't stand people who moan.
3 A **negative** reply or decision indicates the answer ADJ
'no'. *...a vague but negative response.* ♦ **negatively** ADV
60 percent of the sample answered negatively. **4** A N-COUNT
negative is a word, expression, or gesture that means
'no' or 'not'. *In the past we have heard only negatives*
when it came to following a healthy diet. **5** If an an- PHRASE
swer is **in the negative,** it is 'no' or means 'no'.
6 In grammar, a **negative** clause contains a word such ADJ
as 'not', 'never', or 'nobody'. **7** If a sentence is **in the** PHRASE
negative, it contains a word such as 'not', 'never', or
'nobody'.
8 If a medical test or scientific test is **negative,** it ADJ
shows no evidence of the medical condition or substance that you are looking for. *So far 57 have taken*
the test and all have been negative.
9 In photography, a **negative** is the image that is first N-COUNT

produced when you use a camera, from which the
final photograph is developed.
10 A **negative** charge or current has the same electri- ADJ
cal charge as an electron. ♦ **negatively** *These elec-* ADV:
trons are negatively charged. ADV -ed
11 A **negative** number, quantity, or measurement is ADJ
less than zero.

,negative 'equity. If a person with a mortgage on N-UNCOUNT
their home has **negative equity,** the amount of
money they owe to the mortgage company is greater than the value of their home.

ne·glect /nɪ'glekt/ **neglects, neglecting, ne-** ◆◆◇◇◇
glected. 1 If you **neglect** someone or something, VERB
you fail to look after them properly. *The woman de-* V n
nied that she had neglected her child. ► Also a noun. N-UNCOUNT
The town's old quayside is collapsing after years of
neglect. **2** If you **neglect** someone or something, you VERB
fail to give them the degree of attention, recogni- V n
tion, or consideration that they deserve. *Children*
tend to neglect their homework. ♦ **ne·glect·ed** *The* ADJ-GRADED
fact that she is not coming today makes her grand-
mother feel lonely and neglected. **3** If you **neglect** to VERB:
do something you ought to do, you fail to do it. V to-inf
They never neglect their duties. **4 • benign neglect:** V n
see **benign.**

ne·glect·ful /nɪ'glektfʊl/. **1** If you describe some- ADJ-GRADED
one as **neglectful,** you think they fail to do everything they should do to look after someone or
something properly. *Children who are neglected*
tend to become neglectful parents. **2** If someone is ADJ-GRADED
neglectful of something, they do not give it the attention or consideration that it should be given.
Have I been neglectful of my friend, taking him for
granted?

neg·li·gee /'neglɪʒeɪ, AM -'ʒeɪ/ **negligees;** also N-COUNT
spelled **négligée.** A **negligee** is a woman's dressing
gown which is made of very thin fabric.

neg·li·gent /'neglɪdʒənt/. **1** If someone in a posi- ◆◇◇◇◇
tion of responsibility is **negligent,** they do not do ADJ-GRADED
something which they ought to do or they fail to
provide the care for someone or something they are
responsible for. *The jury determined that the airline*
was negligent in training and supervising the crew.
♦ **neg·li·gence** *The soldiers were ordered to appear* N-UNCOUNT
before a disciplinary council on charges of negli-
gence. ♦ **neg·li·gent·ly** *A manufacturer negligently* ADV:
made and marketed a car with defective brakes. ADV with v
2 If you describe a person's movements or manner as ADJ-GRADED
negligent, you mean they look relaxed and informal. LITERARY
Laura acknowledged this compliment with a negligent
wave of her left hand. ♦ **negligently** *He slouched,* ADV-GRADED
arms negligently spread over his papers.

neg·li·gible /'neglɪdʒɪbəl/. An amount or effect ◆◇◇◇◇
that is **negligible** is so small that it is not worth con- ADJ-GRADED
sidering or worrying about. *The pay that the soldiers*
received was negligible.

ne·go·tiable /nɪ'gəʊʃəbəl/. **1** Something that is ◆◇◇◇◇
negotiable can be changed or agreed when people ADJ
discuss it. *He warned that his economic programme*
for the country was not negotiable. **2** Contracts or ADJ
assets that are **negotiable** can be transferred to another person in exchange for money.

ne·go·ti·ate /nɪ'gəʊʃieɪt/ **negotiates, negotiat-** ◆◆◆◆◇
ing, negotiated. 1 If one person or group **negoti-** V-RECIP:
ates with another, they talk about a problem or a V with n
situation such as a business arrangement in order pl-n V n
to solve the problem or complete the arrangement. pl-n V n
You can also say that two people or groups **negoti-** V n
ate. *...when you have two adversaries negotiating...* V for n
The local government and the army negotiated a Also V to-inf
truce... Western governments have this week urged
him to negotiate... The South African president has
negotiated an end to white-minority rule... His pub-
lishing house had just begun negotiating for her next
books. ♦ **ne·go·tia·tor, negotiators** *Mr Clarke* N-COUNT
was a tough negotiator with the unions.
2 If you **negotiate** a place or an obstacle, you success- VERB: V n
fully travel across it or around it. *I negotiated my way* V way prep/
out of the airport and joined the flow of cars. adv

ne'gotiating table. If you say that people are at the **negotiating table**, you mean that they are having discussions in order to settle a dispute or reach an agreement. ◆◇◇◇◇ N-SING

ne·go·tia·tion /nɪ,gəʊʃiˈeɪʃən/ **negotiations. Ne**gotiations are formal discussions between people who have different aims or intentions, especially in business or politics, during which they try to reach an agreement. *The Mexican Senate has recommended the negotiation of a free trade agreement with the United States... Warren said, 'We have had meaningful negotiations.'* ◆◆◆◇ N-VAR

Ne·gro /ˈniːgrəʊ/ **Negroes. A Negro** is someone with dark skin who comes from Africa or whose ancestors came from Africa. Some people find this use offensive. ◆◇◇◇◇ N-COUNT DATED

neigh /neɪ/ **neighs, neighing, neighed.** When a horse **neighs**, it makes a loud sound with its mouth. ▶ Also a noun. *The horse gave a loud neigh.* VERB: V / N-COUNT

neigh·bour /ˈneɪbə/ **neighbours;** spelled **neighbor** in American English. **1** Your **neighbours** are the people who live near you, especially the people who live in the house or flat which is next to yours. *I got chatting with my neighbour in the garden.* **2** You can refer to the person who is standing or sitting next to you as your **neighbour**. *The woman prodded her neighbour.* **3** You can refer to something which stands next to something else of the same kind as its **neighbour**. *Each house was packed close behind its neighbour.* **4** A country's **neighbour** is another country which is near it or which borders on it. *Malaysia, unlike some of its neighbours, is a democracy.* ◆◆◆◇ N-COUNT / N-COUNT / N-COUNT / N-COUNT

neigh·bour·hood /ˈneɪbəhʊd/ **neighbourhoods;** spelled **neighborhood** in American English. **1** A **neighbourhood** is one of the parts of a town where people live. *...the Flatbush neighbourhood of Brooklyn.* **2** In the **neighbourhood of** a number means approximately that number. *He's won in the neighbourhood of four million dollars.* **3** A place **in the neighbourhood** of another place is near it. *...woodlands in the neighbourhood of large towns.* ◆◆◇◇ N-COUNT / PHR-PREP / PHRASE

neigh·bour·ing /ˈneɪbərɪŋ/; spelled **neighboring** in American English. **Neighbouring** places or things are near other things of the same kind. *Rwanda is to hold talks with leaders of neighbouring countries.* ◆◆◇◇ ADJ: ADJ n

neigh·bour·ly /ˈneɪbəli/; spelled **neighborly** in American English. If the people who live near you are **neighbourly**, they are friendly and helpful. If you live in a **neighbourly** place, it has a friendly atmosphere. *The noise would have provoked alarm and neighbourly concern. ...a small, neighbourly seaside resort.* ♦ **neigh·bour·li·ness** The head of state said his country had always attached great importance to good neighbourliness. ADJ-GRADED / N-UNCOUNT

nei·ther /ˈnaɪðə, ˈniːðə/. **1** You use **neither** in front of the first of two or more words or expressions when you are linking two or more things which are not true or do not happen. The other thing, or the last of the other things, is introduced by 'nor'. *Professor Hisamatsu spoke neither English nor German... The play is neither as funny nor as disturbing as Tabori thinks it is.* **2** You use **neither** to refer to each of two things or people, when you are making a negative statement that includes both of them. *At first, neither man could speak.* ▶ Also a quantifier. *Neither of us felt like going out.* ▶ Also a pronoun. *Neither seemed likely to be aware of my absence for long.* **3** If you say that one person or thing does not do something and **neither** does another, what you say is true of all the people or things that you are mentioning. *I never learned to swim and neither did they.* **4** You use **neither** after a negative statement to emphasize that you are introducing another negative statement. *I can't ever recall Dad hugging me. Neither did I sit on his knee.* ◆◆◆◇ CONJ PRAGMATICS / DET / QUANT / PRON / CONJ PRAGMATICS / CONJ PRAGMATICS FORMAL

5 If you say that something is **neither here nor there**, you mean that it does not matter because it is not a relevant point. *Whether or not he realised the fact was neither here nor there.* PHRASE

nemesis /ˈneməsɪs/. The **nemesis** of a person or thing is a situation, event, or person which causes it to be seriously harmed or destroyed, especially as a punishment or judgement. *Yet the imminent crisis in its balance of payments may be the President's nemesis.* N-UNCOUNT

neo- /ˈniːəʊ-/. **Neo-** is used with nouns to form adjectives and nouns that refer to modern versions of styles and political groups that existed in the past. *...10ft high neo-Victorian gates. ...the neo Socialists.* PREFIX

neo·clas·si·cal /,niːəʊˈklæsɪkəl/; also spelled **neoclassical. Neoclassical** architecture or art dates from the late 18th century and uses designs from Roman and Greek architecture and art. ◆◇◇◇◇ ADJ

neo·lith·ic /,niːəˈlɪθɪk/. **Neolithic** is used to describe things relating to the period of prehistory when people had started farming but still used stone for their weapons and tools. *...neolithic culture.* ADJ

ne·olo·gism /ˈniːələdʒɪzəm, niˈɒl-/ **neologisms.** A **neologism** is a new word or expression in a language, or a new meaning for an existing word or expression. N-COUNT FORMAL

neon /ˈniːɒn/. **1** Neon lights or signs are made from glass tubes filled with neon gas which produce a bright electric light. **2** Neon is a gas which occurs in very small amounts in the atmosphere. ◆◇◇◇◇ ADJ: ADJ n / N-UNCOUNT

neo·na·tal /,niːəʊˈneɪtəl/. **Neonatal** means relating to the first few days of life of a new born baby. *...the neonatal intensive care unit.* ADJ: ADJ n

neo·phyte /ˈniːəfaɪt/ **neophytes.** A **neophyte** is someone who is new to a particular activity. *...the self-proclaimed political neophyte Ross Perot.* N-COUNT FORMAL

neph·ew /ˈnefjuː, ˈnev-/ **nephews.** Someone's **nephew** is the son of their sister or brother. ◆◇◇◇◇ N-COUNT

nepo·tism /ˈnepətɪzəm/. **Nepotism** is using power unfairly in order to get jobs or other benefits for your family or friends; used showing disapproval. N-UNCOUNT PRAGMATICS

nerd /nɜːd/ **nerds.** If you say that someone is a **nerd**, you are saying in an unkind way that they are stupid or foolish, especially because they wear unfashionable clothes and behave awkwardly in social situations. N-COUNT INFORMAL

nerve /nɜːv/ **nerves. 1** Nerves are long thin fibres that transmit messages between your brain and other parts of your body. **2** If you refer to someone's **nerves**, you mean their ability to cope with problems such as emotional stress, tension, and danger. *Jill's nerves are stretched to breaking point.* **3** If someone or something **gets on** your **nerves**, they annoy or irritate you. **4** If you say that you have **touched a nerve** or **touched a raw nerve**, you mean that you have accidentally upset someone by talking about something that they feel strongly about or are very sensitive about. **5** You can refer to someone's feelings of anxiety or tension as **nerves**. *I just played badly. It wasn't nerves.* **6** Nerve is the courage that you need in order to do something difficult or dangerous. *He never got up enough nerve to meet me.* **7** If you **hold** your **nerve** or **keep** your **nerve**, you remain calm and determined in a difficult situation. If you **lose** your **nerve**, you suddenly panic and become too afraid to do something that you were about to do. **8** If you say that someone **has a nerve** or **has the nerve** to do something, you are criticizing them for doing something which you feel they had no right to do. *He had the nerve to ask me to prove who I was.* ◆◆◆◇ N-COUNT / N-PLURAL / PHRASE INFORMAL PHRASE / N-PLURAL / N-UNCOUNT / PHRASE / PHRASE PRAGMATICS INFORMAL

'nerve centre, nerve centres; spelled **nerve center** in American English. The **nerve centre** of an organization is the place from where its activities are controlled and where its leaders meet. *...the building that was once the nerve centre of the Communist party.* N-COUNT

'nerve ending, nerve endings. Your **nerve endings** are the millions of points on the surface of your body and inside it which send messages to your brain when you feel sensations such as heat, cold, and pain. N-COUNT

'nerve gas, nerve gases. Nerve gas is a poisonous gas that paralyses or kills people.   N-VAR

'nerve-racking; also spelled **nerve-wracking.** A nerve-racking situation or experience makes you feel very tense and worried. *It was more nerve-wracking than taking a World Cup penalty.*   ADJ-GRADED

ner·vo·sa /nɜːˈvəʊsə/. See **anorexia** and **bulimia**.

nerv·ous /ˈnɜːvəs/. **1** If someone is **nervous**, they are frightened or worried about something that is happening or might happen, and show this in their behaviour. *The party has become deeply nervous about its prospects of winning the next election.* ♦ **nerv·ous·ly** *Brunhilde stood up nervously as the men came into the room.* ♦ **nerv·ous·ness** *I smiled warmly so he wouldn't see my nervousness.* **2** A **nervous** person is very tense and easily upset. *She was apparently a very nervous woman, and that affected her career.*   ◆◆◇◇ ADJ-GRADED / ADV-GRADED: ADV with v / N-UNCOUNT / ADJ-GRADED

3 A **nervous** illness or condition is one that affects your emotions and your mental state.   ADJ: ADJ n

,nervous 'breakdown, nervous breakdowns. A **nervous breakdown** is an illness caused by mental stress. Sufferers become extremely depressed and anxious, and therefore have to be treated by a psychiatrist.   ◆◇◇◇ N-COUNT

'nervous system, nervous systems. Your **nervous system** consists of all the nerves in your body together with your brain and spinal cord. It controls your movements and reflexes as well as your thoughts and feelings.   ◆◇◇◇ N-COUNT

'nervous wreck, nervous wrecks. If you say that someone is a **nervous wreck**, you mean that they are extremely nervous or worried about something.   N-COUNT

nervy /ˈnɜːvi/. If someone is **nervy**, their behaviour shows that they are very tense or anxious, or they are the type of person who is easily upset. *Sometimes dad was nice to us, but sometimes he was bad-tempered and nervy.*   ADJ-GRADED

-ness /-nəs/. **-ness** is added to adjectives to form nouns which often refer to a state or quality. For example, 'sadness' is the state of being sad and 'kindness' is the quality of being kind.   SUFFIX

nest /nest/ **nests, nesting, nested. 1** A bird's **nest** is the home that it makes to lay its eggs in. **2** When a bird **nests** somewhere, it builds a nest and settles there to lay its eggs. **3** A **nest** is a home that a group of insects or other creatures make in order to live in and give birth to their young in. *Some solitary bees make their nests in burrows in the soil. ...a rat's nest.*   ◆◇◇◇ N-COUNT / VERB: V / N-COUNT

4 You can refer to a place as your **nest** when it is your home or where you feel comfortable and relaxed. *My wife seems to be building a nest of her own at Osborne House.* **5** If you accuse someone of **feathering their nest**, you are accusing them of taking advantage of their position in order to get a lot of money and lead a comfortable life. *Mary's much more interested in doing things for other people than feathering her own nest.*   N-COUNT / PHRASE PRAGMATICS

6 You can use **nest** to refer to a place where something bad is happening, or to the people there who are behaving in a bad or unpleasant way. *...Biarritz, notorious in those days as a nest of spies... You've got your own little nest of informers in the Police Department.* **7** See also **love nest ● a hornet's nest:** see **hornet**.   N-COUNT: N of n

'nest egg, nest eggs; also spelled **nest-egg.** A **nest egg** is a sum of money that you are saving for a particular purpose. *They have a little nest egg tucked away somewhere.*   N-COUNT INFORMAL

nes·tle /ˈnesəl/ **nestles, nestling, nestled. 1** If you **nestle** or **are nestled** somewhere, you move into a comfortable position, usually by pressing against someone or against something soft. *Jade nestled her first child in her arms.* **2** If a building, place, or thing **nestles** or **is nestled** somewhere, it is in that place or position and seems safe or sheltered. *She nestled eggs safely in the straw in Jim's basket.*   ◆◇◇◇ V-ERG: V pron Vn prep / V-ERG: Vpron Vn prep

nes·tl·ing /ˈnestlɪŋ/ **nestlings.** A **nestling** is a young bird that has not yet learnt to fly.   N-COUNT

---

net 1 noun and verb uses

net /net/ **nets, netting, netted. 1** Net is a kind of cloth that is made of very fine threads woven together so that there are small equal spaces between them. **2** A **net** is a piece of netting which is used as a protective covering for something, for example to protect vegetables from birds. **3** A **net** is a piece of netting which is used for catching fish, insects, or animals. *Several fishermen sat on wooden barrels, tending their nets.* **4** If you **net** a fish or other animal, you catch it in a net. *Poachers have been netting salmon.*   ◆◆◆◇◇ N-UNCOUNT / N-COUNT / N-COUNT / VERB: V n

5 In games such as tennis, the **net** is the piece of netting across the centre of the court which the ball has to go over. **6** The **net** on a football or hockey pitch is the framework with netting over it which is attached to the back of the goal. **7** When a football player **nets** a goal, he scores a goal.   N-COUNT / N-COUNT / VERB: V n JOURNALISM

8 If you **net** something, you manage to get it, especially by using skill. *They took to the water intent on netting the £250,000 reward offered for conclusive proof of the monster's existence.* **9** When a police operation **nets** a number of people or things, they catch those people or find those things. *The anti-drug sweep had netted nearly 900 kilogrammes of cocaine.* **10** If you **net** a particular amount of money, you gain it as profit after all expenses have been paid. *Last year he netted a cool 3 million pounds.*   VERB V n / VERB V n / VERB V n

11 The **net** is the same as the **Internet. 12** See also **netting; safety net.**   N-SING: the N

13 If criminals **slip through the net**, they avoid being caught by the system or trap that was meant to catch them. **14** You use **slip through the net** or **fall through the net** to describe a situation where people are not properly cared for by the system that is intended to help them. *...and a number of African countries, too, are slipping through the net.*   PHRASE / PHRASE

net 2 adjective and adverb uses

net /net/; also spelled **nett** in British English. **1** A net amount is one which remains when everything that should be subtracted from it has been subtracted. *...a rise in sales and net profit... What you actually receive is net of deductions for the airfare.* ▶ Also an adverb. *Balances of £5,000 and above will earn 11 per cent gross, 8.25 per cent net.* **2** The **net** weight of something is its weight without its container or the material that has been used to wrap it. **3** A **net** result is a final result after all the details have been considered or included. *We have a net gain of nearly 50 seats, the biggest for any party in Scotland.*   ◆◆◇◇ ADJ: ADJ n, v-link ADJ of n / ADV: amount ADV, ADV after v ADJ: ADJ n / ADJ: ADJ n

net·ball /ˈnetbɔːl/. In Britain and some other countries, **netball** is a game played by two teams of seven players, usually women. Each team tries to score goals by throwing a ball through a net on the top of a pole at each end of the court.   N-UNCOUNT

,net 'curtain, net curtains. In Britain, **net curtains** are pieces of lacy material that people hang in their windows.   N-COUNT

neth·er /ˈneðə/. **Nether** means the lower part of a thing or place. *He was escorted back to the nether regions of Main Street.*   ADJ: ADJ n DATED

nether·world /ˈneðəwɜːld/. If you refer to a place as a **netherworld**, you mean that it is gloomy and dangerous and full of poverty and deprivation. *...a London netherworld of criminals.*   N-SING

nett /net/. See **net.**

net·ting /ˈnetɪŋ/. **Netting** is a kind of material made of pieces of thread or metal wires. These are woven together so that there are equal spaces between them. *...wire netting.*   N-UNCOUNT

net·tle /ˈnetəl/ **nettles, nettling, nettled. 1** Nettles are wild plants that sting you when you touch them. **2** If you **grasp the nettle**, you deal with a problem, or do something that is unpleasant, quickly and in a determined way. *The government should grasp the nettle of devaluation before the referendum takes place.*   ◆◇◇◇ N-COUNT / PHRASE BRITISH

3 If you **are nettled** by something, you are annoyed or offended by it. *It was the suggestion that he might alter course to win an election that really nettled him.*   VERB: be V-ed V n

net·work /'netwɜːk/ **networks, networking, networked.** ◆◆◆◇◇ **1** A **network** of lines, roads, veins, or N-COUNT other long thin things is a large number of them which cross each other or meet at many points. *...Strasbourg, with its rambling network of medieval streets. ...a rich network of blood vessels and nerves.* **2** A **network** of people or institutions is a large num- N-COUNT ber of them that have a connection with each other and work together as a system. *Distribution of the food is going ahead using a network of local church people. ...the benefits which the family network can provide.* ● See also **old-boy network**. **3** A particular N-COUNT **network** is a system of things which are connected and which operate together. For example, a **comput- er network** consists of a number of computers that are part of the same system. *Huge sections of the rail network are out of action.* ● See also **neural network**. **4** A radio or television **network** is a company or group N-COUNT of companies that broadcasts the same radio or tele- vision programmes throughout an area. **5** When a VB: usu television or radio programme **is networked**, it is passive broadcast on different stations at the same time.

net·work·ing /'netwɜːkɪŋ/ **1 Networking** is the ◆◇◇◇◇ process of establishing business contacts, often N-UNCOUNT through social activities. *If executives fail to exploit the opportunities of networking they risk being left behind.* **2** You can refer to the things associated N-UNCOUNT with a computer system or the process of establish- ing such a system as **networking**. *...computer and networking equipment.*

neu·ral /'njʊərəl, AM 'nʊr-/. **Neural** means relating ◆◇◇◇◇ to a nerve or to the nervous system. *...neural path-* ADJ *ways in the brain.* TECHNICAL

neu·ral·gia /njʊə'rældʒə, AM nʊr-/. **Neuralgia** is se- N-UNCOUNT vere pain along the whole length of a nerve, espe- MEDICAL cially a nerve in the face or head.

neural 'network, neural networks. In comput- N-COUNT ing, a **neural network** is a program or system mod- elled on the human brain, and designed to imitate the brain's method of functioning.

neuro- /'njʊərəʊ-, AM 'nʊrəʊ-/. **Neuro** is used to PREFIX form words that refer or relate to a nerve or the nervous system. *...Karl Pribram, the well-known neuro-scientist. ...the neuromuscular system.*

neu·rol·ogy /njʊə'rɒlədʒi, AM nʊr-/. **Neurology** is N-UNCOUNT the study of the structure, function, and diseases of MEDICAL the nervous system. *He trained in neurology at the National Hospital for Nervous Diseases.* ◆ **neu·rolo- ·gist, neurologists** *His doctor sent him to a neu-* N-COUNT *rologist.* ◆ **neu·ro·logi·cal** /ˌnjʊərə'lɒdʒɪkəl, AM ADJ: ADJ n ˌnʊr-/. *...neurological disorders such as Parkinson's disease.*

neu·ron /'njʊərɒn, AM 'nʊr-/ **neurons;** also spelled ◆◇◇◇◇ **neurone.** A **neuron** is a cell which is part of the N-COUNT nervous system. Neurons send messages to and TECHNICAL from the brain. ● See also **motor neurone disease**.

neu·ro·sis /njʊə'rəʊsɪs, AM nʊr-/ **neuroses** ◆◇◇◇◇ /njʊə'rəʊsiːz, AM nʊr-/. **Neurosis** is a mental condi- N-VAR tion which causes people to have unreasonable fears and worries over a long period of time. *She got a neurosis about chemicals and imagined them everywhere killing her harm.* ◆ **neu·rot·ic** ADJ-GRADED /njʊə'rɒtɪk, AM nʊr-/ *He was almost neurotic about being followed.* ▶ A **neurotic** is someone who is N-COUNT neurotic.

neu·ter /'njuːtə, AM 'nuːt-/ **neuters, neutering, neutered.** **1** When an animal **is neutered**, its re- VB: usu productive organs are removed. *We ask the public to* passive *have their dogs neutered.* **2** To **neuter** an organiza- VERB: V n tion, group, or person means to make them power- beV-ed less and ineffective. *Their air force had been neu-* JOURNALISM, *tered before the work began.* **3** In some languages, a BRITISH **neuter** noun, pronoun, or adjective has a different ADJ form from a masculine or feminine one.

neu·tral /'njuːtrəl, AM 'nuːt-/ **neutrals. 1** If a per- ◆◆◇◇◇ son or country adopts a **neutral** position or remains ADJ-GRADED **neutral**, they do not support anyone in a disagree- ment, war, or contest. *Let's meet on neutral terri- tory... Iran has pledged to remain neutral if war breaks out.* ▶ A **neutral** is someone who is neutral. N-COUNT

It was a good game to watch for the neutrals. ◆ **neu- ·tral·ity** /nju:'trælɪti, AM 'nuːt-/ *...a reputation for* N-UNCOUNT *political neutrality and impartiality.* **2** If someone ADJ-GRADED speaks in a **neutral** voice or if their facial expression or language is **neutral**, they do not show what they are thinking or feeling, for example if they approve or disapprove of something. *He told her about the death, describing the events in as neutral a manner as he could... In our family, these people are referred to as scabs. The neutral term is strikebreakers.* ◆ **neutrality** *I noticed, behind the neutrality of his* N-UNCOUNT *gaze, a deep weariness.* **3** If you say that something ADJ-GRADED is **neutral**, you mean it does not have any effect on other things because it lacks any significant qual- ities of its own, or it is an equal balance of two or more different qualities, amounts, or ideas. *Three in every five interviewed felt that the Budget was neu- tral and they would be no better off.* **4 Neutral** is the position between the gears of a vehi- N-UNCOUNT cle such as car, in which the gears are not connected to the engine. *Graham put the van in neutral and jumped out.* **5** In an electrical device or system, the ADJ **neutral** wire is one of the three wires needed to com- plete the circuit so that the current can flow. **6** Neu- COLOUR **tral** is used to describe things that are a pale, indis- tinct colour such as light grey or beige, or things that contain no colour at all. *Mary suggests using a neutral lip pencil.* **7** In physics, **neutral** is used to describe ADJ things such as atomic particles that have neither a positive nor a negative charge. *A neutron is simply a neutral particle in the nucleus of an atom.* **8** In chem- ADJ-GRADED istry, **neutral** is used to describe things that are nei- ther acidic nor alkaline. *Pure water is neutral with a pH of 7.*

neu·tral·ize /'njuːtrəlaɪz, AM 'nuːt-/ **neutralizes,** ◆◇◇◇◇ **neutralizing, neutralized;** also spelled **neutral- ise** in British English. **1** To **neutralize** something VERB means to prevent it from having any effect or from V n working properly. *The intruder smashed a window to get in and then neutralized the alarm system.* ◆ **neu·trali·za·tion** /ˌnjuːtrəlaɪ'zeɪʃən, AM 'nuːt-/ N-UNCOUNT *...the sale or neutralization of the suspected nuclear site.* **2** When a chemical substance **neutralizes** an VERB acid, it reduces the acidic level. *Antacids are alka-* V n *line and they relieve pain by neutralizing acid in the contents of the stomach.*

neu·tron /'njuːtrɒn, AM 'nuːt-/ **neutrons.** A neu- ◆◇◇◇◇ **tron** is an atomic particle that has no electrical N-COUNT charge.

neutron 'star, neutron stars. A neutron star is N-COUNT a star that has collapsed under the weight of its own gravity.

nev·er /'nevə/. **1 Never** means at no time in the ◆◆◆◆◇ past or at no time in the future. *I have never lost the* ADV *weight I put on in my teens... Never say that. Never, do you hear?... This is never to happen again.* **2 Nev-** ADV **er** means not in any circumstances at all. *I would never do anything to hurt him... Divorce is never easy for children... The golden rule is never to clean a valuable coin.* **3 Never ever** is an emphatic expres- PHRASE sion for 'never'. *He's vowed never ever to talk about* PRAGMATICS *it.* **4 Never** is used to refer to the past and means ADV 'not'. *He never achieved anything... He waited until* SPOKEN *all the luggage was cleared, but Paula's never ap- peared.* **5** You say '**never!**' to indicate how surprised EXCLAM or shocked you are by something that someone has PRAGMATICS just said. **6** ● **never fear**: see **fear**. ● **never mind**: see **mind**.

never-'ending. If you describe something bad or ◆◇◇◇◇ unpleasant as **never-ending**, you are emphasizing ADJ that it seems to last a very long time. *The spiral of* PRAGMATICS *terrorism becomes never-ending.*

never-'never land. If you talk about a **never-** N-UNCOUNT **never land**, you mean an imaginary place where also a N everything is pleasant and people do not have any INFORMAL problems. *We became suspended in some stately never-never land of pleasure, luxury and idleness.*

never·the·less /ˌnevəðə'les/. You use **neverthe-** ◆◆◆◇◇ **less** when saying something that contrasts with ADV: what has just been said. *Although the market has* ADV with cl
PRAGMATICS

been flattened, residential property costs remain *FORMAL* high. Nevertheless, the fall-off in demand has had an impact on resale values.

new /njuː, AM nuː/ **newer, newest. 1** Something ♦♦♦♦ that is **new** has been recently created, built, or in- *ADJ-GRADED* vented or is in the process of being created, built, or invented. *They've just opened a new hotel in the Stoke area... Their epic fight is the subject of a new film... These ideas are nothing new in America.* ♦ **new·ness** *The board acknowledges problems* *N-UNCOUNT* *which arise from the newness of the approach.* **2** Something that is **new** has not been used or *ADJ* owned by anyone. *That afternoon she went out and bought a new dress... There are many boats, new and used, for sale.* **3** If you say that someone or some- *PHRASE* thing is as **good as new**, you mean that they are in a very good condition or state, especially after they have been damaged or ill. *In a day or so he will be as good as new.* **4** You use **new** to describe some- *ADJ* thing which has replaced another thing, for example because you no longer have the old one, or it is no longer useful. *I had to find somewhere new to live... They told me I needed a new battery.* **5** **New** is used to describe something that has only re- *ADJ* cently been discovered or noticed. *The new planet is about ten times the size of the earth.* **6** A **new** day or *ADJ: ADJ n* year is the beginning of the next day or year. *The next election is for the government to take us into the new century.* **7** **New** is used to describe someone or some- *ADJ: ADJ n* thing that has recently acquired a particular status or position. *...the usual exhaustion of a new mother.* **8** If *ADJ-GRADED:* you are **new** to a situation or place, or if the situation *v-link ADJ* or place is **new** to you, you have not previously seen it or had any experience of it. *His name was new to me then and it stayed in my mind... I'm new here and all I did was follow orders.* **9** **New** potatoes, carrots, or peas *ADJ: ADJ n* are produced early in the season for such vegetables and are usually small with a sweet flavour. **10** See also **brand-new.** ● **to turn over a new leaf**: see **leaf.** ● **a new lease of life**: see **lease.** ● **pastures new**: see **pasture.**

new- /njuː-, AM nuː-/. **New-** combines with the past *COMB* participle of some verbs to form adjectives which indicate that an action has been done or completed very recently. *He loved the smell of new-mown grass... Gerald treasures his new-won independence.*

ˌNew ˈAge. **New Age** is used to refer to activities ♦◇◇◇ such as meditation, astrology, and alternative medi- *N-UNCOUNT* cine, or to describe the people who are involved in them. *She was involved in many New Age activities such as yoga and healing.*

ˌNew Age ˈtraveller, New Age travellers.** In *N-COUNT* Britain, **New Age travellers** are people who travel around, living in tents and caravans, and who reject many of the values of modern society.

ˌnew ˈblood.** If people talk about bringing **new** *N-UNCOUNT* **blood** into an organization or sports team, they are referring to new people who are likely to improve it. *There should be major changes in the government to bring in new blood.*

new·born /ˈnjuːbɔːn, AM ˈnuː-/ **newborns;** also ♦◇◇◇ spelled **new-born** or **new born. 1** A **newborn** baby *ADJ* or animal is one that has just been born. *...new born lambs.* ▶ **The newborn** are babies or animals who *N-PLURAL:* are newborn. *Mild jaundice in the newborn is com-* *the N* *mon.* **2** A **newborn** is a baby that has just been *N-COUNT* born. *...an instrument for taking a sample of blood* *MEDICAL* *from a newborn.* **3** **Newborn** is sometimes used to *ADJ: ADJ n* describe things that have just come into existence. *LITERARY* *Microbiology was a newborn science.*

ˌnew ˈbroom, new brooms.** Someone who has *N-COUNT* just started a new job and who is expected to make *JOURNALISM* a lot of changes can be referred to as a **new broom.** *The company seemed set to make a fresh start under a new broom.*

new·comer /ˈnjuːkʌmə, AM ˈnuː-/ **newcomers.** ♦♦◇◇ **1** A **newcomer** is a person who has recently arrived *N-COUNT* in a place, joined an organization, or started a new activity. *The candidates are both relative newcomers to politics.* **2** A **newcomer** is something which has *N-COUNT*

not existed before or been available before. *The company's latest newcomer is a 4 x 4 estate with a 2.2 litre petrol engine.*

ˌnew ˈface, new faces.** Someone who is new in ♦◇◇◇ a particular situation or public role can be referred *N-COUNT* to as a **new face.** *All together there are six new faces in the cabinet.*

new-fangled /ˌnjuː ˈfæŋɡəld, AM ˌnuː -/; also spelled *ADJ: ADJ n* **newfangled.** If someone describes an idea or a *PRAGMATICS* piece of equipment as **new-fangled**, they dislike it *DATED,* because they find it too complicated or think it is *INFORMAL* unnecessary. *Mr Goss does not believe in any of this 'new-fangled nonsense' about lean meat.*

ˌnew-ˈfound;** also spelled **newfound.** A **new-found** ♦◇◇◇ quality, ability, or attribute is one that you have dis- *ADJ: ADJ n* covered recently. *Juliana was brimming over with new-found confidence.*

new·ly /ˈnjuːli, AM ˈnuːli/. **Newly** is used before a ♦♦♦◇◇ past participle or an adjective to indicate that a par- *ADV:* ticular action is very recent, or that a particular *ADV -ed/adj* state of affairs has very recently begun to exist. *...the newly independent countries of Africa and Asia.*

newly·wed /ˈnjuːliwed, AM ˈnuː-/ **newlyweds;** *N-COUNT* also spelled **newly-wed. Newlyweds** are a man and woman who have very recently got married to each other. *The newlyweds postponed their honeymoon.*

ˌnew ˈman, new men.** If you describe someone as *N-COUNT* a **new man**, you are saying, often humorously, that *BRITISH* he has modern ideas about relationships, and be- lieves that men should share in domestic tasks and caring for children. *Then we have the caring New Man, with a baby in one hand and a tea towel in the other.*

ˌnew ˈmoon, new moons.** A **new moon** is the *N-COUNT* moon when it appears as a thin crescent shape at the start of its four-week cycle of appearing to be- come larger and then smaller. *The new moon was the occasion of festivals of rejoicing in Egypt.*

news /njuːz, AM nuːz/. **1** **News** is information ♦♦♦♦♦ about a recently changed situation or a recent *N-UNCOUNT* event. *We waited and waited for news of him... I wish I had better news for you... He's thrilled to bits at the news.* **2** **News** is information that is published *N-UNCOUNT* in newspapers and broadcast on radio and televi- sion about recent events. *Foreign News is on Page 16... Those are some of the top stories in the news.* **3** **The news** is a television or radio broadcast which *N-SING:* consists of information about recent events. *I heard* *the N* *all about the bombs on the news. ...the six o'clock news.* **4** **News** is sometimes used in the names of *N-UNCOUNT* newspapers. *...the New York Daily News.* **5** If you *N-UNCOUNT* say that someone or something is **news**, you mean that they are considered to be interesting and im- portant at the moment, and that people want to hear about them on the radio and television and in newspapers. *For the first time since 1959, Tibet was headline news again.* **6** If you say that something is **bad news**, you mean *PHRASE* that it will cause you trouble or problems. If you say that something is **good news**, you mean that it will be useful or helpful to you. *The drop in travel is bad news for the airline industry.* **7** If you say that something **is** *PHRASE* **news to** you, you mean that you did not previously know what you have just been told, especially when you are surprised or annoyed about it. *I'd certainly tell you if I knew anything, but I don't. What you're saying is news to me.*

ˈnews agency, news agencies.** A **news agency** ♦♦♦◇◇ is an organization that gathers news stories from a *N-COUNT* particular country or from all over the world and supplies them to journalists.

news·agent /ˈnjuːzeɪdʒənt, AM ˈnuːz-/ **news-** ♦◇◇◇ **agents.** In Britain, a **newsagent** or a **newsagent's** *N-COUNT* is a shop where newspapers and magazines, as well as sweets, cigarettes, and stationery, are sold. You can also refer to the shopkeeper as a **newsagent.** *The newsagent said, 'Bye, Keith! See you later.'*

news·cast /ˈnjuːzkɑːst, AM ˈnuːzkæst/ **news-** ♦◇◇◇ **casts.** A **newscast** is a news programme that is *N-COUNT* broadcast on the radio or on television. ♦ **news-** *AMERICAN*

·**caster, newscasters.** *He became the most* N-COUNT *high-profile newscaster in Britain.*

'**news conference, news conferences.** A ◆◆◇◇◇ **news conference** is a meeting held by a famous or N-COUNT important person in which they answer journalists' questions.

news·flash /'njuːzflæʃ, AM 'nuːz-/ **newsflashes;** N-COUNT also spelled **news flash.** A **newsflash** is an important item of news that television or radio companies broadcast as soon as they receive it, often interrupting other programmes to do so.

news·letter /'njuːzletə, AM 'nuːz-/ **newsletters;** ◆◇◇◇◇ also spelled **news letter.** A **newsletter** is one or N-COUNT more printed sheets of paper containing information about an organization that is sent regularly to its members. *...a quarterly newsletter.*

news·man /'njuːzmən, AM 'nuːz-/ **newsmen.** A N-COUNT **newsman** is a reporter for a newspaper or a television or radio news programme.

news·paper /'njuːspeɪpə, AM 'nuːz-/ **news-** ◆◆◆◆◇ **papers. 1** A **newspaper** is a publication consisting N-COUNT of a number of large sheets of folded paper, on which news, advertisements, and other information is printed. *They read their daughter's allegations in the newspaper. ...a Sunday newspaper feature about AIDS in America.* **2** A **newspaper** is an organization N-COUNT that produces a newspaper. *It is Britain's fastest growing national daily newspaper.* **3** Newspaper N-UNCOUNT consists of pieces of old newspapers, especially when they are being used for another purpose such as wrapping things up. *He found two pots, each wrapped in newspaper.*

news·paper·man /'njuːspeɪpəmæn, AM 'nuːz-/ N-COUNT **newspapermen.** A **newspaperman** is a reporter, especially a man, who works for a newspaper.

news·print /'njuːzprɪnt, AM 'nuːz-/. **1** Newsprint is N-UNCOUNT the cheap fairly rough paper on which newspapers are printed. **2** Newsprint is the text that is printed N-UNCOUNT in newspapers. *The papers are still devoting pages of newsprint to the Gulf Crisis.* **3** Newsprint is the ink N-UNCOUNT which is used to print newspapers and magazines. *They get their hands covered in newsprint.*

news·read·er /'njuːzriːdə, AM 'nuːz-/ **newsread-** N-COUNT **ers.** A **newsreader** is a person who reads the news BRITISH on the radio or on television.

news·reel /'njuːzriːl, AM 'nuːz-/ **newsreels.** A ◆◆◇◇◇ **newsreel** is a short film of national or international N-COUNT news events. In the past newsreels were made for showing in cinemas.

'**news release, news releases.** A **news release** N-COUNT is a written statement about a matter of public in- AMERICAN terest which is given to the press by an organization concerned with the matter.

news·room /'njuːzruːm, AM 'nuːz-/ **newsrooms.** ◆◇◇◇◇ A **newsroom** is an office in a newspaper, radio, or N-COUNT television organization, where news reports are written and edited.

news·stand /'njuːzstænd, AM 'nuːz-/ **news-** N-COUNT **stands;** also spelled **news-stand.** A **newsstand** is a movable stall in the street, or a stall at a railway station, at which newspapers and magazines are sold. *Eight new national newspapers have appeared on the newsstands since 1981.*

news·worthy /'njuːzwɜːði, AM 'nuːz-/. An event, ADJ-GRADED fact, or person that is **newsworthy**, is considered to be interesting enough to be reported in newspapers or on the radio or television. *The number of deaths makes the story newsworthy.*

newt /njuːt, AM nuːt/ **newts.** A **newt** is a small N-COUNT creature which looks like a lizard and lives partly on land and partly in water.

,**New 'Testament.** The New Testament is the ◆◇◇◇◇ part of the Bible that deals with the life and teach- N-PROPER: ings of Jesus Christ and with Christianity in the ear- theN ly Church.

'**new town, new towns.** A **new town** is a town ◆◇◇◇◇ that has been planned and built as a single project, N-COUNT including houses, shops, and factories, rather than BRITISH one that has developed gradually. *...Basildon New Town.*

,**new 'wave, new waves.** In the arts or in poli- ◆◇◇◇◇ tics, a **new wave** is a group or movement that delib- N-COUNT erately introduces new or unconventional ideas instead of using traditional ones. *...the new wave of satirical comedy.*

,**New 'World.** The New World is used to refer to ◆◆◇◇◇ the continents of North and South America. *...wines* N-PROPER: *from the New World and Australasia.* theN

,**New 'Year. 1** New Year or the New Year is the ◆◆◇◇◇ time when people celebrate the start of a year. *Hap-* N-UNCOUNT *py New Year, everyone... The restaurant was closed over the New Year.* **2** The New Year is the first few N-SING: weeks of a year. *Isabel was expecting their baby in* theN *the New Year.*

,**New Year's reso'lution, New Year's resolu-** N-COUNT **tions;** also spelled **New Year resolution.** If you make a **New Year's resolution**, you make a decision at the beginning of a year to start doing something or to stop doing something. *She made a New Year's resolution to get fit.*

next /nekst/. **1** The **next** period of time, event, per- ◆◆◆◆◆ son, or thing is the one that comes immediately af- ORDINAL ter the present one or after the previous one. *I got up early the next morning... Many senior citizens have very few visitors from one week to the next... And then Captain Charles sings, 'Don't ever laugh when a hearse goes by or you will be the next to die.'* **2** You use **next** in expressions such as **next Friday,** DET **next day** and **next year** to refer, for example, to the Friday, day, or year which follows immediately after the present one or after the previous one. *Let's plan a big night next week... He retires next January.* ▶ Also an adjective. *I shall be 26 years old on Friday* ADJ: n ADJ *next.* ▶ Also a pronoun. *He predicted that the re-* PRON *gion's economy would grow by about six per cent both this year and next.* **3** You use **after next** in ex- PHRASE pressions such as **the week after next** to refer to a period of time after the next one. For example, when it is May, the month after next is July. **4** The **next** place or person is the one that is nearest to ADJ: det ADJ you or that is the first one that you come to. *Grace sighed so heavily that Trish could hear it in the next room... Stop at the next corner. I'm getting out.* **5** The ADV thing that happens **next** is the thing that happens immediately after something else. *Next, close your eyes then screw them up tight... The news is next.* **6** When ADV: you **next** do something, you do it for the first time ADV before v since you last did it. *I next saw him at his house in Berkshire.*

7 You use **next** to say that something has more of a ADV: particular quality than all other things except one. For ADV adj- example, the thing that is **next** best is the one that is superl the best except for one other thing. *At least three times more daffodils are grown than in Holland, the next largest grower.* **8** If you say that you do something or PHRASE experience something as much **as the next** person, you mean that you are no different from anyone else in the respect mentioned. *I'm as ambitious as the next man.* **9** You can say **the next thing** I knew to suggest PHRASE that a new situation which you are describing was INFORMAL, surprising because it happened very suddenly. *The* SPOKEN *next thing I knew, the bungalow was on fire.* **10** If one thing is **next to** another thing, it is at the other PHR-PREP side of it. *She sat down next to him on the sofa... The car was parked in the small weedy lot next to the hotel.* **11** You use **next to** in order to give the most important PHR-PREP aspect of something when comparing it with another aspect. *Her children were the number two priority in her life next to her career.* **12** You use **next to** before a PHRASE negative, or a word that suggests something negative, to mean almost, but not completely. *Most prepared weight loss products are next to useless.*

,**next 'door. 1** If a room or building is **next door,** ◆◆◇◇◇ it is the next one to the right or left. *She was next* ADV *door at the time... The flat next door was empty.* ▶ Also an adjective. *The wires trailed through other* ADJ: ADJ n *parts of the HQ into a next door building.* ▶ If a PHR-PREP room or building is **next door to** another one, it is the next one to the left or right. *The kitchen is right next door to the dining room.* **2** The people **next** ADV: n ADV

door are the people who live in the house to the right or left of yours. *The neighbors thought the family next door had moved.* ▶ Also an adjective. *Our next door neighbour knocked on the door to say that our car had been stolen.* **3** If you refer to someone as **the boy next door** or **the girl next door**, you mean that they are respectable and dependable but rather dull and boring. *He was dependable, straightforward, the boy next door.*

ADJ: ADJ n

PHRASE

next 'door's. You can use **next door's** to indicate that something belongs to the person or people who live in the house to the right or left of your own. *...next door's dog.*

DET-POSS

next of 'kin. Next of kin is sometimes used to refer to the person who is your closest relative, especially in official or legal documents. *We have notified the next of kin.*

N-COLL-UNCOUNT
FORMAL

nex·us /ˈnɛksəs/; **nexus** is both the singular and plural. A **nexus** is a connection or series of connections within a particular situation or system. *The Prayer Book has provided a flexible enough nexus of beliefs to hold together the different church parties.*

N-COUNT
FORMAL

NHS /ˌen eɪtʃ ˈɛs/. **NHS** is an abbreviation for **National Health Service.** *Three out of four NHS patients were given an appointment within three months.*

◆◇◇◇◇
N-SING:
the N,
N n

nia·cin /ˈnaɪəsɪn/. **Niacin** is a vitamin that occurs in milk, liver, yeast, and some other foods.

◆◇◇◇◇
N-UNCOUNT

nib /nɪb/ **nibs.** A **nib** is a small pointed piece of metal at the end of a fountain pen, which controls the flow of ink as you write.

N-COUNT

nib·ble /ˈnɪbəl/ **nibbles, nibbling, nibbled. 1** If you **nibble** food, you eat it by biting very small pieces of it, for example because you are not very hungry. *She nibbled at the corner of a piece of dry toast.* ▶ Also a noun. *We each took a nibble.* **2** When an animal **nibbles** something, it takes small bites of it quickly and repeatedly. *The birds cling to the wall and nibble at the brickwork.* ▶ **Nibble away** means the same as **nibble.** *The rabbits nibbled away on the herbaceous plants.* **3** If you **nibble** something, you bite it very gently. *Daniel Winter nibbled on his pen.* **4** If one thing **nibbles at** another, it gradually affects, harms, or destroys it. *It was all going to plan, yet small doubts kept nibbling at the edges of his mind.* ▶ **Nibble away** means the same as **nibble.** *Several manufacturers are also nibbling away at Ford's traditional customer base.* **5** Nibbles are small snacks such as biscuits, crisps, and peanuts, that are usually offered to you at parties. *Nibbles go down well with any age group.*

◆◇◇◇◇
VERB: V n
V at/on n
Also V

N-COUNT
VERB: V n
V at/on n
Also V

PHRASAL VB
V P on/at n

VERB: V n
V on/at n
VERB
V at n

PHRASAL VB
V P at n

N-COUNT
BRITISH

nice /naɪs/ **nicer, nicest. 1** If you say that something is **nice,** you mean that you find it attractive, pleasant, or enjoyable. *It's nice to be here together again... We had a nice meal with a bottle of champagne.* ◆ **nice·ly** *He's just written a book, nicely illustrated and not too technical.* **2** If you say that it is **nice of** someone to say or do something, you are saying that they are being kind and thoughtful. This is often used as a way of thanking someone. *It's awfully nice of you to come all this way to see me... 'How are your boys?' — 'How nice of you to ask.'* **3** If you say that someone is **nice,** you mean that you like them because they are friendly and pleasant. *He was a nice fellow, very quiet and courteous.* ◆ **nice·ness** *Mr Major quietly warned them not to mistake his niceness for weakness.* **4** If you are **nice** to people, you are friendly, pleasant, or polite towards them. *She met Mr and Mrs Ricciardi, who were very nice to her.* ◆ **nicely** *He treated you very nicely and acted like a decent guy.* **5** When the weather is **nice,** it is warm and pleasant. *He nodded to us and said, 'Nice weather we're having.'*

◆◆◆◆◇
ADJ-GRADED

ADV-GRADED
ADJ-GRADED
PRAGMATICS

ADJ-GRADED

◆ **nice·ness**
N-UNCOUNT
ADJ-GRADED:
v-link ADJ
ADV-GRADED:
ADV after v
ADJ-GRADED

6 You can use **nice** to emphasize a particular quality that you like. *People have got used to nice glossy magazines... Add the oats to thicken the mixture and stir until it is nice and creamy.* **7** A **nice** point or distinction is very clear, precise, and based on good reasoning. *Those are nice academic arguments, but what about*

ADJ
PRAGMATICS

ADJ

the immediate future? ◆ **nicely** *I think this puts the problem very nicely.* **8** You can use **nice** when you are greeting people. For example, you can say **Nice to meet you** when you meet someone for the first time and **Nice to have met you** when you are saying goodbye to them. You can also say **Nice to see you** when you meet someone you already know. **9** If someone says **nice one,** they are showing their approval of something clever or funny that they have just seen or heard. *Knowles became Torquay's manager. Nice one.* **10** See also **nicely.**

ADV-GRADED:
ADV after v

ADJ:
it-v-link ADJ
to-inf
PRAGMATICS

CONVENTION
INFORMAL

nice-'looking. Someone who is **nice-looking** is physically attractive. *I saw this nice-looking man in a gray suit.*

ADJ-GRADED

nice·ly /ˈnaɪsli/. **1** Something that is happening or working **nicely** is happening or working in a satisfactory way or in the way that you want it to. *She has a bit of private money, so they manage quite nicely.* ● See also **nice. 2** If you say that something will **do nicely,** you mean that it is adequate or satisfactory for the situation. *A shirt and jersey and an ordinary pair of trousers will do nicely, thank you.*

◆◆◇◇◇
ADV-GRADED:
ADV with v

PHRASE

ni·cety /ˈnaɪsɪti/ **niceties.** The **niceties** of a situation are its details, especially with regard to good manners or the appropriate behaviour for that situation. *He wasted no time with social niceties.*

N-COUNT

niche /niːʃ, AM nɪtʃ/ **niches. 1** In business, a **niche** in the market is a specific area which has its own particular requirements, customers, and products. *I think we have found a niche in the toy market.* **2** In business, **niche** marketing is the practice of dividing the market into specialized areas for which particular products are produced. A **niche** market is one of these specialized areas. *Many media experts see such all-news channels as part of a general move towards niche marketing.* **3** A **niche** is a hollow area in a wall which has been made to hold something such as a statue, or a natural hollow part in a hillside or cliff. *There was a niche in the rock where the path ended.* **4** Your **niche** is the job or activity which is exactly suitable for you. *Simon Lane quickly found his niche as a busy freelance model maker.* **5** If you **carve a niche** for yourself, you organize your work to create a secure position. *...a firm of solicitors that has carved a niche for itself in handling claims for investor compensation.*

◆◇◇◇◇
N-COUNT

ADJ: ADJ n

N-COUNT

N-COUNT

PHRASE

nick /nɪk/ **nicks, nicking, nicked. 1** If someone **nicks** something, they steal it. *He smashed a window to get in and nicked a load of silver cups... He'll think twice about nicking bags that aren't his again.* **2** If the police **nick** someone, they arrest them. *The police nicked me for carrying an offensive weapon... Keep quiet or we'll all get nicked.* **3** The **nick** is a prison, or a police station. *After several years banged up in the nick, even you might start to go mad.* **4** If you **nick** something or **nick** yourself, you accidentally make a small cut or scratch in the surface of the object or your skin. *When I pulled out of the space, I nicked the rear bumper of the car in front of me... He dropped a bottle in the kitchen and nicked himself on broken glass.* ▶ Also a noun. *The barbed wire had left only the tiniest nick just below my right eye.* **5** Nick is used in expressions such as **'in good nick'** or **'in bad nick'** to describe the physical condition of someone or something. *Tom's house is actually in better nick than mine.* **6** If you say that something happens **in the nick of time,** you are emphasizing that it happens at the last possible moment. *Seems we got here just in the nick of time.*

◆◆◇◇◇
VERB
V n
INFORMAL,
BRITISH
VERB: Vn
get/beV-ed
INFORMAL,
BRITISH
N-COUNT
INFORMAL,
BRITISH

VERB
V n
V pron-refl

N-COUNT
INFORMAL

PHRASE

PHRASE
PRAGMATICS
INFORMAL

nick·el /ˈnɪkəl/ **nickels. 1** Nickel is a silver-coloured metal that is used in making steel. **2** In the United States and Canada, a **nickel** is a coin worth five cents.

◆◇◇◇◇
N-UNCOUNT
N-COUNT

nick·name /ˈnɪkneɪm/ **nicknames, nicknaming, nicknamed.** If you **nickname** someone or something, you give them an informal name. *When he got older I nicknamed him Little Alf.* ▶ Also a noun. *Red got his nickname for his red hair.*

◆◇◇◇◇
VERB
V n n
N-COUNT

nico·tine /ˈnɪkətiːn/. **Nicotine** is an addictive substance contained in tobacco.

◆◇◇◇◇
N-UNCOUNT

N

niece /niːs/ **nieces.** Someone's **niece** is the daughter of their sister or brother. ◆◇◇◇◇ N-COUNT

nif·ty /'nɪfti/ **niftier, niftiest.** If you describe something as **nifty**, you think it is neat and pleasing or cleverly done. *Bridgeport was a pretty nifty place.* ADJ-GRADED INFORMAL

nig·gard·ly /'nɪɡədli/. If you describe someone or something as **niggardly**, you are critical of their meanness or lack of generosity. ...*a niggardly supply of hot water.* ADJ-GRADED PRAGMATICS

nig·gle /'nɪɡəl/ **niggles, niggling, niggled. 1** If something **niggles** you, it causes you to worry slightly over a long period of time. *It's been niggling at my mind ever since I met Neville in Nice... The puzzle niggled away in Arnold's mind.* ▶ Also a noun. *So why is there a little niggle at the back of my mind?* **2** If someone **niggles** you, they annoy you by continually criticizing you for what you think are small or insignificant details. *You tend to niggle at your partner, and get hurt when he doesn't hug you.* ▶ Also a noun. *The life we have built together is more important than any minor niggle either of us might have.* VERB: V n / V adj / V away / Also V / N-COUNT / VERB: V n / V adj / Also V, / V n that / N-COUNT

nig·gling /'nɪɡlɪŋ/. A **niggling** injury or worry is small but bothers you over a long period of time. ADJ-GRADED

nigh /naɪ/. **1** If an event **is nigh**, it is going to happen very soon. *The end of the world may be nigh, but do we really care?* ● See also **well-nigh**. ◆◇◇◇◇ ADV: be ADV DATED

2 Nigh on an amount, number, or age means almost that amount, number, or age. *I had to pay nigh on forty pounds for him.* PHRASE DATED

night /naɪt/ **nights. 1** The **night** is the part of each day when the sun has set and it is dark outside, especially the time when people are sleeping. *He didn't leave the house all night... Finally night fell.* **2** The **night** is the period of time between the end of the afternoon and the time that you go to bed. *So whose party was it last night?... Demiris took Catherine to dinner the following night.* **3** A particular **night** is a particular evening when a special event takes place, such as a show or a play. *The first night crowd packed the building. ...election night.* ◆◆◆◆ N-VAR / N-COUNT / N-COUNT: supp N

4 If it is a particular time **at night**, it is during the time when it gets dark and before midnight. *He works obsessively from 7.15 am to 9 or 10 at night.* **5** If something happens **at night**, it happens regularly during the evening or night. *He was going to college at night, in order to become an accountant.* PHRASE / PHRASE

6 If something happens **day and night** or **night and day**, it happens all the time without stopping. *He was at my door night and day, demanding my attention.* PHRASE

7 If you have **an early night**, you go to bed early. If you have **a late night**, you go to bed late. PHRASE

8 ● **morning, noon, and night**: see **morning**.

night·cap /'naɪtkæp/ **nightcaps.** A **nightcap** is a drink that you have just before you go to bed, usually an alcoholic drink. N-COUNT

night·clothes /'naɪtkləʊðz/. **Nightclothes** are clothes that you wear in bed. N-PLURAL

night·club /'naɪtklʌb/ **nightclubs;** also spelled **night club.** A **nightclub** is a place where people go late in the evening to drink and dance. ◆◆◇◇◇ N-COUNT

night·club·bing /'naɪtklʌbɪŋ/. **Nightclubbing** is the activity of going to nightclubs. N-UNCOUNT

night·dress /'naɪtdres/ **nightdresses.** A **nightdress** is a sort of loose dress that a woman or girl wears in bed. The usual American word is **nightgown.** N-COUNT BRITISH

night·fall /'naɪtfɔːl/. **Nightfall** is the time of day when it starts to get dark. *I need to get to Lyon by nightfall.* N-UNCOUNT

night·gown /'naɪtɡaʊn/ **nightgowns.** A **nightgown** is a **nightdress.** N-COUNT AMERICAN

nightie /'naɪti/ **nighties.** A **nightie** is a nightdress. *Carol was shivering in just her nightie.* N-COUNT INFORMAL

night·in·gale /'naɪtɪŋɡeɪl, AM -tən-/ **nightingales.** A **nightingale** is a small brown bird. The male's song, which can be heard at night, is very melodic. N-COUNT

night·life /'naɪtlaɪf/; also spelled **night-life. Night-life** is all the entertainment and social activities that are available at night in towns and cities, such as N-UNCOUNT

nightclubs and theatres. *Hamburg's energetic night-life is second to none.*

night·ly /'naɪtli/. A **nightly** event happens every night. *We watched the nightly news. ...air raids were a nightly occurrence.* ▶ Also an adverb. *She appears nightly on the television news.* ◆◇◇◇◇ ADJ: ADJ n / ADV

night·mare /'naɪtmeə/ **nightmares. 1** A **nightmare** is a very frightening dream. *All the victims still suffered nightmares.* **2** If you refer to a situation as a **nightmare**, you mean that it is very frightening and unpleasant. *The years in prison were a nightmare.* **3** If you refer to a situation as a **nightmare**, you are saying in a very emphatic way that it is irritating because it causes you a lot of trouble. *Taking my son Peter to a restaurant was a nightmare.* N-COUNT / N-COUNT / N-COUNT PRAGMATICS

night·mar·ish /'naɪtmeərɪʃ/. If you describe something as **nightmarish**, you mean that it is extremely frightening and unpleasant. *She described a nightmarish scene of dead bodies lying in the streets.* ADJ-GRADED

'night owl, night owls. A **night owl** is someone who regularly stays up late at night, or who prefers to work at night. *The late-night parties make the hotel a haven for night owls.* N-COUNT INFORMAL

'night porter, night porters. A **night porter** is a person whose job is to be on duty at the main reception desk of a hotel throughout the night. N-COUNT

'night school, night schools. Someone who goes to **night school** does an educational course in the evenings. *People can go out to work in the daylight hours and then come to night school in the evening.* N-VAR

night·shirt /'naɪtʃɜːt/ **nightshirts.** A **nightshirt** is a long, loose shirt worn in bed. N-COUNT

night·spot /'naɪtspɒt/ **nightspots.** A **nightspot** is a nightclub. ...*Harlem's most famous nightspot, the Cotton Club.* N-COUNT INFORMAL

night·stick /'naɪtstɪk/ **nightsticks.** A **nightstick** is a short thick club that is carried by policemen in the United States. N-COUNT

'night-time; also spelled **night time. Night-time** is the period of time between when it gets dark and when the sun rises. *A twelve hour night time curfew is in force.* ◆◇◇◇◇ N-UNCOUNT

night·watch·man /ˌnaɪt'wɒtʃmən/ **nightwatch-men;** also spelled **night-watchman.** A **nightwatch-man** is a person whose job is to guard buildings at night. N-COUNT

night·wear /'naɪtweə/. **Nightwear** is clothing that you wear in bed. N-UNCOUNT

ni·hil·ism /'naɪɪlɪzəm/. **Nihilism** is the belief that there is no justification for any existing authorities or institutions, and that they should all be rejected or destroyed. ♦ **ni·hil·ist, nihilists** *Why wasn't Weber a nihilist?* N-UNCOUNT / N-COUNT

ni·hil·is·tic /ˌnaɪɪ'lɪstɪk/. If you describe someone as **nihilistic**, you mean they do not trust political and religious authority and place their faith in the individual. ADJ-GRADED

nil /nɪl/. **1 Nil** means the same as nought or zero. It is usually used to say what the score is in sports such as rugby or football. *They beat the defending champions, Argentina, one-nil in the final.* **2** If you say that something is **nil**, you mean that it does not exist at all. *Their legal rights are virtually nil.* ◆◆◇◇◇ NUMBER / N-UNCOUNT

nim·ble /'nɪmbəl/ **nimbler, nimblest. 1** Someone who is **nimble** is able to move their fingers, hands, or legs quickly and easily. *Val, who was light and nimble on her feet, learnt to dance the tango.* ♦ **nim·bly** *Sabrina jumped nimbly out of the van.* **2** If you say that someone has a **nimble** mind, you mean they are clever and can think very quickly. *Elderly people are told that if they want to keep their minds nimble, they must use them.* ◆◇◇◇◇ ADJ-GRADED / ADV-GRADED: ADV with v / ADJ-GRADED

nim·bus /'nɪmbəs/. A **nimbus** is a large dark grey cloud that brings rain or snow. ...*layers of cold nimbus clouds.* N-SING TECHNICAL

nimby /'nɪmbi/; also spelled **Nimby.** If you say that someone has a **nimby** attitude, you are criticizing them because they do not want any new developments such as housing or roads near to where they ADJ PRAGMATICS INFORMAL

live. **Nimby** is an abbreviation for 'not in my backyard'. ...*the usual nimby protests from local residents.*

nine /naɪn/. **1 Nine** is the number 9. See Appendix headed **Numbers**. ◆◆◆◆ NUMBER

2 • **nine times out of ten:** see **time**.

nine·teen /ˌnaɪnˈtiːn/. **Nineteen** is the number 19. See Appendix headed **Numbers**. ◆◆◆◆◆ NUMBER

nine·teenth /ˌnaɪnˈtiːnθ/. The **nineteenth** item in a series is the one that you count as number nineteen. See Appendix headed **Numbers**. ◆◆◆◆◇ ORDINAL

nine·ti·eth /ˈnaɪntiəθ/. The **ninetieth** item in a series is the one that you count as number ninety. See Appendix headed **Numbers**. ◆◆◆◆◇ ORDINAL

nine·ty /ˈnaɪnti/ **nineties. 1 Ninety** is the number 90. See Appendix headed **Numbers**. **2** When you talk about the **nineties**, you are referring to numbers between 90 and 99. For example, if the temperature is **in the nineties**, the temperature is between 90 and 99 degrees. **3 The nineties** is the decade between 1990 and 1999. ◆◆◆◆◆ NUMBER N-PLURAL the N

nin·ny /ˈnɪni/ **ninnies.** If you refer to someone as a **ninny**, you think that they are foolish or silly. N-COUNT INFORMAL, DATED

ninth /naɪnθ/ **ninths. 1** The **ninth** item in a series is the one that you count as number nine. See Appendix headed **Numbers**. **2** A **ninth** is one of nine equal parts of something. ◆◆◆◇ ORDINAL FRACTION

nip /nɪp/ **nips, nipping, nipped. 1** If you **nip** somewhere, usually somewhere nearby, you go there quickly or for a short time. *Should I nip out and get some groceries?.* **2** If a person or an animal **nips** you, they pinch or bite you lightly. *He nipped Billy's cheek with two rough fingers... I have known cases where dogs have nipped babies.* ▶ Also a noun. *...a petty nip, which fails to break the skin or draw blood.* **3** A **nip** is a small sip or amount of strong alcoholic drink. *She had a habit of taking an occasional nip from a flask of cognac.* **4** • to **nip** something **in the bud:** see **bud**. ◆◇◇◇◇ VB: no passive V adv/prep INFORMAL, BRITISH VERB V n Also V a t n, V N-COUNT N-COUNT

nip·per /ˈnɪpə/ **nippers.** A **nipper** is a child. *I'm not ever going to forget what you've done for the nippers.* N-COUNT INFORMAL, BRITISH

nip·ple /ˈnɪpəl/ **nipples. 1** The **nipples** on someone's body are the two small pieces of slightly hard flesh on their chest. Babies suck milk from their mothers' breasts through the nipples. **2** A **nipple** is a piece of rubber or plastic which is fitted to the top of a baby's bottle. *...a white plastic bottle with a rubber nipple.* ◆◇◇◇◇ N-COUNT N-COUNT

nip·py /ˈnɪpi/. **1** If the weather is **nippy**, it is rather cold. *...it could get suddenly nippy in the evenings.* **2** If you describe something or someone as **nippy**, you mean they can move very quickly over short distances. *This nippy new car has fold-down rear seats.* ADJ-GRADED ADJ-GRADED BRITISH

nir·va·na /nɪəˈvɑːnə, nɜː-/. **1** In the Hindu and Buddhist religions, **Nirvana** is the ultimate state of spiritual enlightenment that can possibly be achieved. **2** People sometimes refer to a state of complete happiness and peace as **nirvana**. *Many businessmen think that a world where relative prices never varied would be nirvana.* N-UNCOUNT N-UNCOUNT

nit /nɪt/ **nits. 1** If someone has lice in their hair, the eggs of this insect are referred to as **nits**. **2** If you refer to someone as a **nit** or **nitwit**, you think they are a stupid person. N-PLURAL N-COUNT INFORMAL, BRITISH

nit·pick·ing /ˈnɪtpɪkɪŋ/; also spelled **nit-picking.** If you refer to someone's opinion as **nitpicking**, you disapprove of the fact that it concentrates on small and unimportant details, especially to try and find fault with something. *A lot of nit-picking was going on about irrelevant things... I can get down to nitpicking detail, I am pretty fussy about certain things.* N-UNCOUNT PRAGMATICS

ni·trate /ˈnaɪtreɪt/ **nitrates. Nitrates** are chemical compounds that consist of nitrogen, oxygen, and some other element or elements. They are used as fertilizers in agriculture. *High levels of nitrate occur in Eastern England because of the heavy use of fertilizers.* ◆◇◇◇◇ N-VAR

ˌnitric 'acid. **Nitric acid** is a strong colourless acid containing nitrogen, hydrogen, and oxygen. N-UNCOUNT

nitro- /ˈnaɪtrəʊ-/. **Nitro** combines with nouns to form other nouns referring to things which contain nitrogen and oxygen. *...highly corrosive substances such as nitro-phosphates.* COMB

ni·tro·gen /ˈnaɪtrədʒən/. **Nitrogen** is a colourless element that has no smell and is usually found as a gas. It forms about 78% of the earth's atmosphere, and is found in all living things. ◆◇◇◇◇ N-UNCOUNT

ni·tro·glyc·er·in /ˌnaɪtrəʊˈglɪsərɪn/; also spelled **ni·troglycerine. Nitroglycerin** is an explosive liquid that is used in making dynamite and also in some medicines. N-UNCOUNT

nitty-gritty /ˌnɪti ˈgrɪti/; also spelled **nitty gritty.** If people get down to the **nitty-gritty** of a matter, situation, or activity, they discuss the most important, basic parts of it or facts about it. *...the nitty gritty of everyday politics.* N-SING INFORMAL

nit·wit /ˈnɪtwɪt/. See **nit**.

no /nəʊ/ **noes** or **no's. 1** You use **no** to give a negative response to a question. *'Any problems?'—'No, I'm O.K.'* **2** You use **no** to say that something that someone has just said is not true. *'We thought you'd emigrated.'—'No, no.'... 'You're getting worse than me.'—'No I'm not.'* **3** You use **no** to refuse an offer or a request, or to refuse permission. *'Here, have mine.'—'No, this is fine.'... After all, the worst the boss can do is say no if you ask him.* **4** You use **no** to indicate that you do not want someone to do something. *No. I forbid it... 'No. It's not right. We mustn't.'* ◆◆◆◆ CONVENTION PRAGMATICS CONVENTION PRAGMATICS CONVENTION PRAGMATICS EXCLAM PRAGMATICS

5 You use **no** to acknowledge a negative statement or to show that you accept and understand it. *'I don't know him, do I?'—'No, you don't.'* **6** You use **no** as a way of introducing a correction to what you have just said. *...500 grams, no, a little less than that.* **7** You use **no** to express shock or disappointment at something you have just been told. *'We went with Sarah and the married man that she's currently seeing.'—'Oh no.'* CONVENTION PRAGMATICS CONVENTION PRAGMATICS EXCLAM PRAGMATICS

8 You use **no** to mean not any or not one person or thing. *He had no intention of paying the cash... No letters survive from this early period.* **9** You use **no** to emphasize that someone or something definitely does not have the characteristic or identity mentioned. *He is no singer... Kathryn was no beauty at the best of times.* **10** If you say **there is no** doing a particular thing, you mean that it is very difficult or impossible to do that thing. *There is no going back to the life she had.* **11** You use **no** when saying that something does not exceed a particular amount or number, or does not have more of a particular quality than something else. *...no later than the end of 1994. ...no fewer than thirty climbers reached the summit. ...he will be no more effective than his predecessors.* DET DET PRAGMATICS PHRASE ADV: ADV compar

12 You use **no** in front of an adjective and noun to make the noun group mean its opposite. *Today's elections in Peking are of no great importance in themselves.* **13 No** is used in notices or instructions to say that a particular activity or thing is forbidden. *...'no smoking' signs... No talking after lights out.* **14** A **no** is a person who has answered 'no' to a question or who has voted against something. **No** is also used to refer to their answer or vote. *According to the latest opinion polls, the noes have 50 percent, the yeses 35 percent.* DET DET PRAGMATICS N-COUNT

15 • to not **take no for an answer:** see **answer**. • **no doubt:** see **doubt**. • **no less:** see **less**. • **no less than:** see **less**. • **no longer:** see **long**. • **in no way:** see **way**. • **there's no way:** see **way**. • **no way:** see **way**.

No., Nos. No. is a written abbreviation for 'number'. *Mansell had two cars at his disposal and was the official No. 1.* ◆◇◇◇◇

nob /nɒb/ **nobs.** If you refer to a group of people as the **nobs**, you mean they are rich or come from a much higher social class than you do. *...the nobs who live in the Big House.* N-COUNT INFORMAL, DATED, BRITISH

nob·ble /ˈnɒbəl/ **nobbles, nobbling, nobbled. 1** If someone **nobbles** an important group of people such as a committee, they bribe or threaten them in order to make them do something. *...allegations of attempts to nobble the jury.* **2** If someone **nobbles** a V n INFORMAL, BRITISH VERB

racehorse, they deliberately harm it, often using drugs, in order to prevent it from winning a race. **3** If someone **nobbles** your plans or chances of succeeding, they prevent you from achieving what you want. *...an attempt to nobble Mr Heseltine's political progress.* INFORMAL, BRITISH VERB / V n / INFORMAL, BRITISH

no·bil·ity /nəʊˈbɪlɪti/. **1 The nobility** of a society are all the people who have titles and belong to a high social class. *They married into the nobility.* **2** A person's **nobility** is the noble and admirable quality of their behaviour and character. *She is not without some instincts of nobility and generosity.* ◆◇◇◇ N-COLL-SING: the N / N-UNCOUNT FORMAL

no·ble /ˈnəʊbəl/ **nobles; nobler, noblest. 1** If you say that someone is a **noble** person, you admire and respect their honesty, bravery, and unselfishness. *He was an upright and noble man who was always willing to help.* ♦ **no·bly** They have supported us nobly in this war. **2** If you say that something is a **noble** idea, goal, or action, you admire it because it is based on high moral principles. *He had implicit faith in the noble intentions of the Emperor... Their cause was noble.* **3** If you describe something as **noble**, you think that its appearance or quality is very impressive, making it superior to other things of its type. *...the great parks with their noble trees.* **4 Noble** means belonging to a high social class and having a title. *...rich and noble families.* **5** In former times, people who belonged to a high social class and had titles such as 'Baron' or 'Duke' were referred to as **nobles**. ◆◆◇◇ ADJ-GRADED PRAGMATICS / ADV-GRADED: ADV with v ADJ-GRADED PRAGMATICS / ADJ-GRADED / ADJ-GRADED / N-COUNT

noble·man /ˈnəʊbəlmən/ **noblemen.** In former times, a **nobleman** was a man who was a member of the nobility. N-COUNT

no·blesse oblige /nəʊˌbles əˈbliːʒ/. **Noblesse oblige** is the idea that privileged people, for example those of a high social class, should act honourably and use their privileges to help other people. *They did so without hope of further profit and out of a sense of noblesse oblige.* N-UNCOUNT FORMAL

noble·woman /ˈnəʊbəlwʊmən/ **noblewomen.** In former times, a **noblewoman** was a woman who was a member of the nobility. N-COUNT

no·body /ˈnəʊbɒdi/ **nobodies. 1 Nobody** or **no one** means not a single person, or not a single member of a particular group or set. *Nobody realizes how bad things are... Everyone wants to be a hero, but no one wants to die.* **2** If someone says that a person is a **nobody**, they are saying in an unkind way that the person is not at all important. *A man in my position has nothing to fear from a nobody like you.* ◆◆◆◇ PRON-INDEF / N-COUNT

no 'claims; also spelled **no-claims.** A **no claims** discount or bonus is a discount or bonus that you get on an insurance policy when you have not made any claims on it in the previous year. *Motorists could lose their no-claims discount.* ADJ: ADJ n

no-'confidence. 1 If members of an organization pass a vote or motion of **no-confidence** in someone, they take a vote which shows that they no longer support that person or their ideas. *The students passed a motion of no-confidence in the college principal.* **2** You can refer to something people say or do as **a vote of no-confidence** when it shows that they no longer support a particular person or organization. *Many police officers view this action as a vote of no-confidence in their service.* ◆◇◇◇ N-UNCOUNT / N-UNCOUNT

noc·tur·nal /nɒkˈtɜːnəl/. **1 Nocturnal** means occurring at night. *...the immensity of the nocturnal sky.* **2 Nocturnal** creatures are active mostly at night. *When there is a full moon, this nocturnal rodent is careful to stay in its burrow.* ◆◇◇◇ ADJ / ADJ

noc·turne /ˈnɒktɜːn/ **nocturnes.** A **nocturne** is a short gentle piece of music, often one written to be played on the piano. N-COUNT

nod /nɒd/ **nods, nodding, nodded. 1** If you **nod**, you move your head downwards and upwards to show that you are answering 'yes' to a question, or to show agreement, understanding, or approval. *'Are you okay?' I asked. She nodded and smiled...* ◆◆◆◇ VB: no passive V / V n / Also V with quote

Jacques tasted one and nodded his approval. ▶ Also a noun. *'Probably,' agreed Hunter, with a slow nod of his head... He gave Sabrina a quick nod of acknowledgement.* **2** If you **nod** in particular direction, you bend your head once in a that direction in order to indicate something or to give someone a signal to do something. *'Does it work?' he asked, nodding at the piano... He lifted the end of the canoe, nodding to me to take up mine.* **3** If you **nod**, you bend your head once, as a way of saying hello or goodbye. *All the girls nodded and said 'Hi'... Tom nodded a greeting but didn't say anything... Both of them smiled and nodded at friends.* **4** In football, if a player **nods** the ball in a particular direction, they hit the ball there with their head. *Taylor leapt up to nod the ball home... Brian McClair pulled United level, nodding in his twenty-third goal of the season.* **5** If you **give** someone **the nod** or if you **give the nod** to someone, you give them permission to do something. *'Keep him outside till I give you the nod.'* **6** If a proposal is accepted **on the nod**, it is accepted without being questioned or argued about. *Big issues are going through on the nod.* N-COUNT / VB: no passive V prep V n to-inf / VB: no passive V / V at/on ton Also V n ton / VERB V n adv/prep V adv / PHRASE INFORMAL / PHRASE INFORMAL, BRITISH

nod off. If you **nod off**, you fall asleep, especially when you had not intended to. *He was so tired that he started to nod off at work... He was nodding off to sleep in an armchair.* PHRASAL VB V P / V P ton INFORMAL

node /nəʊd/ **nodes.** A **node** is a point, especially in the form of lump or swelling, where one thing joins another. *Cut them off cleanly through the stem just below the node.* ◆◇◇◇ N-COUNT

nod·ule /ˈnɒdjuːl, AM -dʒuːl/ **nodules. 1** A **nodule** is a small lump or swelling that can appear on your skin or in your body and which may need medical treatment. *In a typical case, there is a small inflamed nodule just under the skin.* **2** A **nodule** is a small round lump which is found on the roots of certain plants. *...bacteria that live in root nodules on certain plants.* N-COUNT MEDICAL / N-COUNT

Noel /nəʊˈel/. **Noel** is sometimes printed on Christmas cards and Christmas wrapping paper to mean 'Christmas'. N-PROPER

no-'go area, no-go areas. 1 If you refer to a place as a **no-go area**, you mean it has a reputation for violence and crime which makes people frightened to go there. *...a subway system whose reputation for violence and lawlessness makes it a no-go area for many natives of the city.* **2** A **no-go area** is a place which is controlled by a group of people who use force to prevent other people from entering it. *The security forces entered the IRA's no-go areas.* N-COUNT BRITISH / N-COUNT

noise /nɔɪz/ **noises. 1 Noise** is a loud or unpleasant sound. *There was too much noise in the room and he needed peace... The noise of bombs and guns was incessant.* **2** A **noise** is a sound that someone or something makes. *...birdsong and other animal noises... She'd been working in her room till a noise had disturbed her.* **3** If someone **makes noises** of a particular kind about something, they say things that indicate their attitude to it in a rather indirect or vague way. *The President took care to make encouraging noises about the future... His mother had also started making noises about it being time for him to leave home.* **4** If you say that someone **makes the right noises** or **makes all the right noises**, you think that they are showing concern or enthusiasm about something because they feel they ought to rather than because they really want to. *He was making all the right noises about multi-party democracy and human rights.* **5** See also **big noise**. ◆◆◆◇ N-UNCOUNT / N-COUNT / N-PLURAL / PHRASE

noise·less /ˈnɔɪzləs/. Something or someone that is **noiseless** does not make any sound. *The snow was light and noiseless as it floated down.* ♦ **noise·less·ly** I shut the door noiselessly behind me. ADJ-GRADED / ADV-GRADED: ADV with v

noi·some /ˈnɔɪsəm/. If you describe something or someone as **noisome**, you mean that you find them extremely unpleasant. *His noisome reputation for corruption had already begun to spread.* ADJ-GRADED LITERARY

noisy /ˈnɔɪzi/ **noisier, noisiest. 1** A noisy person or thing makes a lot of loud or unpleasant noise. *...my noisy old typewriter.* ♦ **noisi·ly** The students on the grass bank cheered noisily. **2** A noisy place is full of a lot of loud or unpleasant noise. *...the crowded and noisy terrace of the cafe.* **3** If you describe someone as **noisy**, you are critical of them for trying to attract attention to their views by frequently and forcefully discussing them. *It might, at last, silence the small but noisy intellectual clique.* [ADJ-GRADED] [ADV-GRADED] [ADJ-GRADED] [ADJ-GRADED] [PRAGMATICS] ♦◇◇◇◇

no·mad /ˈnəʊmæd/ **nomads.** A **nomad** is a member of a tribe which travels from place to place rather than living in one place all the time. *...a country of nomads who raise cattle and camels.* [N-COUNT] ♦◇◇◇◇

no·mad·ic /nəʊˈmædɪk/. **1** Nomadic people travel from place to place rather than living in one place all the time. *...the great nomadic tribes of the Western Sahara.* **2** If someone has a **nomadic** way of life, they travel from place to place and do not have a settled home. *The daughter of a railway engineer, she at first had a somewhat nomadic childhood.* [ADJ] [ADJ-GRADED] ♦◇◇◇◇

'no-man's land. 1 No-man's land is an area of land that is not owned or controlled by anyone, for example the area of land between two opposing armies. *...the no-man's land between the Jordanian and Iraqi frontier posts.* **2** If you refer to a situation as a **no-man's land** between different things, you mean that it seems unclear because it does not fit into any of the categories. *This new play is set in the dangerous no-man's land between youth and adolescence.* [N-UNCOUNT also a N] [N-SING] ♦◇◇◇◇

nom de guerre /ˌnɒm də ˈgeə/ **noms de guerre.** A **nom de guerre** is a false name which is sometimes used by people who belong to an unofficial military organization. *...a Serb militia leader who goes by the nom de guerre Arkan.* [N-COUNT] [FORMAL]

no·men·cla·ture /nəˈmenklətʃə, ˈnəʊmənkleɪtʃər/ **nomenclatures.** The **nomenclature** of a particular set of things is the system of naming those things. *...the nomenclature of woody plants. ...the internationally agreed rules of chemical nomenclature.* [AM ˈnəʊmənkleɪtʃər] [N-UNCOUNT also N in pl] [FORMAL]

no·men·kla·tura /ˌnəʊmenklɑːˈtʊərə/. In former communist countries, **the nomenklatura** were the people the communist party approved of and appointed to positions of authority. *Ordinary people have always resented the nomenklatura's privileges.* [N-SING: the N]

nomi·nal /ˈnɒmɪnəl/. **1** You use **nominal** to indicate that someone or something is supposed to have a particular identity or status, but in reality does not have it. *As he was still not allowed to run a company, his wife became its nominal head.* ♦ **nomi·nal·ly** The Sultan was still nominally the Chief of Staff. ...South Africa's nominally independent homeland of Transkei. [ADJ] [ADV] ♦♦◇◇

2 A **nominal** price or sum of money is very small in comparison with the real cost or value of the thing that is being bought or sold. *All the ferries carry bicycles free or for a nominal charge.* [ADJ: ADJ n]

3 In economics, the **nominal** value, rate, or level of something is the one expressed in terms of current prices or figures, without taking into account the effects of changes in the level of prices over time. [ADJ: ADJ n]

nominal 'group, nominal groups. A **nominal group** is the same as a **noun group.** [N-COUNT]

nomi·nate /ˈnɒmɪneɪt/ **nominates, nominating, nominated. 1** If someone **is nominated** for a job or position, their name is formally suggested as a candidate for it. *The public will be able to nominate candidates for awards such as the MBE... The UN Secretary General has nominated Mrs Ogata as its next High Commissioner for Refugees.* ♦ **nomi·na·tion** /ˌnɒmɪˈneɪʃən/ **nominations** *...a list of nominations for senior lectureships.* **2** If you **nominate** someone to a job or position, you formally choose them to hold that job or position. *Voters will choose fifty of the seventy-five deputies. The Emir will nominate the rest... He was nominated by the African National Congress as one of its team at the Groote Schuur talks... Mr Gorbachev must nominate some-* [VERB: be V-ed V n for n V n asn Also V n, V n to-inf] [N-COUNT] [VERB: V n to n V n be V-ed asn V n to-inf Also V n asn, V n n] ♦♦◇◇

one to receive the award on his behalf. ♦ **nomination** There were two main candidates for nomination as his replacement. **3** If someone or something such as a book or film **is nominated** for an award, someone formally suggests that person or thing should be given that award. *...a campaign to nominate the twice World Champion as Sports Personality of the Year.* ♦ **nomination** He's certain to get a nomination for best supporting actor. [N-VAR] [VERB: be V-ed for n V n asn Also V n for n] [N-COUNT]

nomi·na·tive /ˈnɒmɪnətɪv/. In the grammar of some languages, **the nominative**, or **the nominative case** is the case used for a noun when it is the subject of a verb. In English, only the pronouns 'I', 'he', 'she', 'we', and 'they' are in the nominative. Compare **accusative.** [N-SING: the N]

nomi·nee /ˌnɒmɪˈniː/ **nominees.** A **nominee** is someone who is nominated for a job or position, or who is nominated for an award. *His nominee for vice president was elected only after a second ballot. ...nominees for the 1992 Nobel Peace Prize.* [N-COUNT] ♦♦◇◇

non- /nɒn-/. **1** Non- is used in front of adjectives and nouns to form adjectives that describe something as not having a particular quality or feature. *...non-nuclear weapons. ...non-verbal communication.* **2** Non- is used in front of nouns to form nouns which refer to situations where a particular action has not or will not take place. *He was disqualified from the council for non-attendance... Relations would be based on non-interference in each other's internal affairs.* **3** Non- is used in front of nouns to form nouns which refer to people who do not belong to a particular group or category. *How did these people, Chinese and non-Chinese, create the economic miracle Hong Kong is today?* [PREFIX] [PREFIX] [PREFIX]

non-ag'gression. If a country adopts a policy of **non-aggression**, it declares that it will not attack or try to harm a particular country. [N-UNCOUNT]

non-alco'holic. A **non-alcoholic** drink does not contain alcohol. [ADJ]

non-a'ligned. **Non-aligned** countries did not support or were in no way linked to groups of countries headed by the United States or the former Soviet Union. *...India's role as the most influential member of the non-aligned movement.* [ADJ] ♦◇◇◇

non·cha·lant /ˈnɒnʃələnt, AM -ˈlɑːnt/. If you describe someone as **nonchalant**, you mean that they appear not to worry or care about things and that they seem very calm. *Clark's mother is nonchalant about her role in her son's latest work.* ♦ **non·cha·lance** /ˈnɒnʃələns, AM -ˈlɑːns/ *Affecting nonchalance, I handed her two hundred dollar bills.* ♦ **non·cha·lant·ly** 'Does Will intend to return with us?' Joanna asked as nonchalantly as she could. [ADJ-GRADED] [N-UNCOUNT] [ADV-GRADED] ♦◇◇◇

non-'combatant, non-combatants. 1 Non-combatant troops are members of the armed forces whose duties do not include fighting. **2** In a war, **non-combatants** are people who are not members of the armed forces. [N-COUNT] [N-COUNT]

non-com·mit·tal /ˌnɒnkəˈmɪtəl/; also spelled **non-committal.** If someone is **noncommittal**, they deliberately do not express their opinion or intentions clearly. *Mr Hall is non-committal about the number of jobs that the development corporation has created.* ♦ **non-com·mit·tal·ly** 'I like some of his novels better than others,' I said noncommittally. [ADJ-GRADED] [ADV-GRADED: ADV after v]

non·con·form·ist /ˌnɒnkənˈfɔːmɪst/ **nonconformists;** also spelled **non-conformist. 1** If you say that someone's way of life or views are **nonconformist**, you mean that they behave or think in an unusual, original, or rebellious way, and not in the way that people in their society usually behave or think. ► A **nonconformist** is someone who is nonconformist. *Nureyev remained a rebel and a non-conformist.* ♦ **non·con·form·ity** /ˌnɒnkənˈfɔːmɪti/ *Lovelock's principled nonconformity can be traced to his childhood.* **2** In Britain, **nonconformist** churches are Protestant churches which are not part of the Church of England. ► A **nonconformist** is a member of a nonconformist church. [ADJ-GRADED] [N-COUNT] [N-UNCOUNT] [ADJ: ADJ n] [N-COUNT]

N

non·de·script /'nɒndɪskrɪpt/. If you describe ADJ-GRADED something or someone as **nondescript**, you mean that their appearance is rather dull, and not at all interesting or attractive. *...those hundreds of nondescript buildings along the Bath Road. ...a nondescript woman of uncertain age.*

none /nʌn/. **1** None of something means not even ◆◆◆◇ a small amount of it. **None of** a group of people or QUANT things means not even one of them. *She did none of the maintenance on the vehicle... None of us knew how to treat her.* ▶ Also a pronoun. *I turned to* PRON-INDEF *bookshops and libraries seeking information and found none... No one could imagine a great woman painter. None had existed yet.* **2** If you say that someone **will have none of** some- PHRASE thing, you mean that you refuse to tolerate it. *He knew* INFORMAL *his own mind and was having none of their attempts to keep him at home.* **3 None but** means only. *None* PHRASE *but God will ever know what I suffered.* **4** You use FORMAL **none too** in front of an adjective or adverb in order to PRAGMATICS emphasize that the quality mentioned is not present. FORMAL *He was none too thrilled to hear from me at that hour.* **5** You use **none** the to say that someone or something PHRASE does not have any more of a particular quality than they did before. *You could end up committed to yet another savings scheme and none the wiser about managing your finances.* **6 • it's none of** your busi- ness: see **business**. **• none other than**: see **other**. • **second to none**: see **second**.

non·en·ti·ty /nɒn'entɪti/ **nonentities.** If you refer N-COUNT to someone as a **nonentity**, you mean that they are not special or important in any way. *Amidst the current bunch of nonentities, he is a towering figure.*

non·es'sen·tial, **non-essentials.** **1** Non- ADJ **essential** means not absolutely necessary. *The crisis has led to the closure of a number of non-essential government services.* **2 Non-essentials** are things N-PLURAL that are not absolutely necessary. *Many consumers could be expected to cut down on non-essentials like toys.*

none·the·less /ˌnʌnðə'les/. **Nonetheless** means ◆◆◇◇◇ the same as **nevertheless**. *There was still a long way* ADV: to go. *Nonetheless, some progress had been made...* ADV with cl *His face is serious but nonetheless very friendly.* PRAGMATICS FORMAL

non-e'vent, non-events. If you say that some- N-COUNT thing was a **non-event**, you mean that it was disappointing or unexciting, especially when this was not what you had expected. *The whole affair was something of a non-event.*

non-e'xistent. If you say that something is **non-** ◆◇◇◇◇ **existent**, you mean that it does not exist when you ADJ feel that it should. *Hygiene was non-existent: no running water, no bathroom.* **• non-existence** N-UNCOUNT *The applause from the delegates was thin to the point of non-existence.*

non-'fiction; also spelled **nonfiction. Non-fiction** N-UNCOUNT is writing that gives information or describes real events, rather than telling a story. *...the author of thirteen novels and ten non-fiction books.*

non-'finite. A **non-finite** clause is based on an in- ADJ finitive or a participle and has no tense. Compare **finite**.

non-'human. **Non-human** means not human or ADJ not produced by humans. *Hostility towards outsiders is characteristic of both human and non-human animals.*

non-inte'rvention. Non-intervention is the prac- N-UNCOUNT tice or policy of not becoming involved in a dispute or disagreement between other countries or groups and of not helping either side.

non-'linear; also spelled **nonlinear.** If you describe ADJ something as **non-linear**, you mean that it does not progress or develop smoothly from one stage to the next in a logical way. *...non-linear trends in currency markets.*

non-'member, non-members. Non-members of N-COUNT a club or organization are people who are not members of it.

non-'nuclear. Non-nuclear means not using or ADJ involving nuclear weapons or nuclear power. *...the*

first postwar treaty to reduce non-nuclear weapons in Europe.

'no-no. If you say that something is **a no-no**, you N-SING: think it is undesirable or unacceptable. *We all know* aN *that cheating on our taxes is a no-no.* INFORMAL

no-'nonsense. If you describe someone as a **no-nonsense** person or something as a **no-** ADJ-GRADED **nonsense** thing, you approve of the fact that they PRAGMATICS are efficient and concentrate on important matters rather than trivial things. *She saw herself as a direct, no-nonsense modern woman... The decor is straightforward and no-nonsense.*

non-'payment. Non-payment is a failure to pay a sum of money that you owe. *...an eviction order* N-UNCOUNT *from the council for non-payment of rent.*

non·plussed /ˌnɒn'plʌst/. If you are **nonplussed**, ADJ-GRADED you feel confused and are not sure how to react. *She expected him to ask for a scotch and was rather nonplussed when he asked her to mix him a martini and lemonade.*

non-'profit-making. A **non-profit-making** or- ADJ ganization or a **non-profit** organization is run to make money for a cause or charity, rather than to make a profit for investors. *...the Film Theatre Foundation, a non-profit-making company which raises money for the arts.*

non-prolife'ration. Non-proliferation is the limiting of the production and spread of something N-UNCOUNT such as nuclear or chemical weapons. *...disarmament and the non-proliferation of nuclear weapons.*

non-'resident, non-residents. A **non-resident** is N-COUNT someone who is visiting a particular place but who does not live or stay there permanently. *100,000 non-resident workers would have to be sent back to their home villages.*

non·sense /'nɒnsəns/. **1** If you say that something ◆◆◇◇◇ spoken or written is **nonsense**, you mean that you N-UNCOUNT consider it to be untrue or silly. *...all that poetic nonsense about love... 'I'm putting on weight.'— 'Nonsense my dear.'* **2** You can use **nonsense** to re- N-UNCOUNT: fer to something that you think is foolish or that you also a N disapprove of. *Surely it is an economic nonsense to deplete the world of natural resources.* **3** You can re- N-UNCOUNT fer to spoken or written words that do not mean anything because they do not make sense as **nonsense**. *...a children's nonsense poem by Charles E Carryl.* **4** To **make a nonsense of** something or to PHRASE **make nonsense of** it means to make it seem ridiculous or pointless. *The fighting made a nonsense of peace pledges made in London last week.* **5** See also **no-nonsense**.

non·sen·si·cal /nɒn'sensɪkəl/. If you say that ADJ-GRADED something is **nonsensical**, you think it is stupid, ri- PRAGMATICS diculous, or untrue. *It seemed to me that Sir Robert's arguments were nonsensical.*

non se·qui·tur /ˌnɒn 'sekwɪtə/ **non sequiturs.** A N-VAR **non sequitur** is a statement, remark, or conclusion FORMAL that does not follow naturally or logically from what has just been said.

non-'smoker, non-smokers. A **non-smoker** is someone who does not smoke. N-COUNT

non-'smoking; also spelled **nonsmoking. 1** A ADJ **non-smoking** area in a public place is an area in which people are not allowed to smoke. **2** A **non-** ADJ **smoking** person is a person who does not smoke.

non-spe'cific; also spelled **nonspecific.** ADJ **1 Non-specific** diseases or symptoms have more than one cause or diagnosis. *...a 37 year old woman with a nine month history of non-specific headaches.* **2** Something that is **non-specific** is general rather ADJ than precise or exact. *I intend to use these terms in a deliberately non-specific and all-embracing way.*

non-'standard. Non-standard things are differ- ADJ ent from the usual version or type of that thing. *...non-standard window shapes.*

non-'starter, non-starters. If you describe a N-COUNT plan or idea as a **non-starter**, you mean that it has INFORMAL no chance of success. *The United States is certain to reject the proposal as a non-starter.*

non-'stick; also spelled **nonstick**. **Non-stick** cooking equipment such as saucepans, frying-pans, or baking tins has a special coating on the inside, which prevents food from sticking to it. ◆◇◇◇◇ ADJ

non-'stop; also spelled **nonstop**. Something that is **non-stop** continues without any pauses or interruptions. *Many US cities now have non-stop flights to Aspen. ...80 minutes of non-stop music.* ► Also an adverb. *The snow fell non-stop for 24 hours.* ◆◇◇◇◇ ADJ — ADV: ADV after v

non-'union; spelled **nonunion** in American English. **Non-union** workers do not belong to a trade union. A **non-union** company or organization does not employ workers who belong to a trade union. ADJ

non-'verbal; also spelled **nonverbal**. **Non-verbal** communication consists of things such as your facial expressions, arm movements, or tone of voice which show how you feel about a particular situation, as opposed to the words which you actually speak. ADJ

non-'violent; also spelled **nonviolent**. **1 Non-violent** methods of bringing about change do not involve hurting people or causing damage. ♦ **non-violence** *The Albanian opposition has made a firm public commitment to non-violence.* **2** You can refer to someone or something such as a crime as **non-violent** when that person or thing does not hurt or injure people. *The judiciary must think very hard before jailing non-violent offenders.* ◆◇◇◇◇ ADJ-GRADED — N-UNCOUNT — ADJ-GRADED

non-'white, non-whites. A **non-white** person is a member of a race of people who are not of European origin. ► Also a noun. *Not one non-white has ever been selected to play for the team.* ◆◇◇◇◇ ADJ — N-COUNT

noo·dle /'nuːdəl/ **noodles.** Noodles are long, thin strips of pasta used in Chinese and Italian cooking. ◆◇◇◇◇ N-COUNT

nook /nʊk/ **nooks.** A **nook** is a small and sheltered place. *We found a seat in a little nook, and had some lunch.* ● If you talk about every **nook and cranny** of a place or situation, you mean every part or every aspect of it. *Boxes are stacked in every nook and cranny at the factory.* N-COUNT — PHRASE PRAGMATICS

nookie /'nʊki/; also spelled **nooky**. You can refer to sexual intercourse as **nookie**. N-UNCOUNT INFORMAL

noon /nuːn/ **1 Noon** is twelve o'clock in the middle of the day. *The long day of meetings started at noon... He expected the transfer to go through by today's noon deadline.* ● See also **high noon**. **2** ● **morning, noon, and night**: see **morning**. ◆◆◇◇◇ N-UNCOUNT

noon·day /'nuːndeɪ/ **Noonday** means happening or appearing in the middle part of the day. *...the noonday sun.* ADJ: ADJ n

'no one; also spelled **no-one**. **No one** means the same as **nobody**. ◆◆◆◆◇

noose /nuːs/ **nooses. 1** A **noose** is a circular loop at the end of a piece of rope or wire that is used to trap animals or hang people. **2** You can refer to something that traps people in a difficult situation as a **noose**. *The rebels are tightening the noose around the capital.* ◆◇◇◇◇ N-COUNT — N-COUNT

nope /nəʊp/ **Nope** is sometimes used instead of 'no' as a response. *'Has the prisoner next door talked to you?'—'Nope,' the man answered.* ◆◇◇◇◇ CONVENTION INFORMAL, SPOKEN

nor /nɔː/ **1** You use **nor** after 'neither' in order to introduce the second alternative or the last of a number of alternatives in a negative statement. *Neither Mr Rose nor Mr Woodhead was available for comment... I can give you neither an opinion nor any advice.* **2** You use **nor** after a negative statement in order to indicate that the negative statement also applies to you or to someone or something else. *'None of us has any idea how long we're going to be here.'—'Nor do I.'... 'If my husband has no future,' she said, 'then nor do my children.'* **3** You use **nor** after a negative statement in order to introduce another negative statement which adds information to the previous one. *Cooking up a quick dish doesn't mean you have to sacrifice flavour. Nor does fast food have to be junk food.* ◆◆◆◇ CONJ PRAGMATICS — CONJ PRAGMATICS — CONJ PRAGMATICS

Nor·dic /'nɔːdɪk/ **Nordic** means relating to the countries of northern Europe, especially Scandina- ◆◇◇◇◇ ADJ: ADJ n

via. *The Nordic countries have been quick to assert their interest in the development of the Baltic States.*

norm /nɔːm/ **norms. 1 Norms** are ways of behaving that are considered normal in a particular society. *...the commonly accepted norms of democracy. ...a social norm that says drunkenness is inappropriate behaviour.* **2** If you say that a situation is the **norm**, you mean that it is usual and expected. *Families of six or seven are the norm in Borough Park.* **3** A **norm** is an official standard or level of achievement which people are expected to reach or conform to. *...a Europe-wide environmental protection agency which would establish European norms.* ◆◆◇◇◇ N-COUNT — N-SING: the N — N-COUNT

nor·mal /'nɔːml/ **1** Something that is **normal** is usual and ordinary, in accordance with what people expect. *He has occasional injections to maintain his good health but otherwise he lives a normal life... The two countries resumed normal diplomatic relations.* **2** A **normal** person is generally healthy in body and mind, without any major defects or problems. *Will the baby be normal?.* ◆◆◆◇ ADJ-GRADED — ADJ-GRADED

nor·mal·cy /'nɔːmlsi/ **Normalcy** is a situation in which everything is normal. *Underneath this image of normalcy, addiction threatened to rip this family apart.* N-UNCOUNT FORMAL

nor·mal·ity /nɔː'mælɪti/ **Normality** is a situation in which everything is normal. *A semblance of normality has returned.* ◆◇◇◇◇ N-UNCOUNT

nor·mal·ize /'nɔːməlaɪz/ **normalizes, normalizing, normalized;** also spelled **normalise** in British English. **1** When you **normalize** a situation or when it **normalizes**, it becomes normal. *...some deep-seated emotional reason which has to be dealt with before your eating habits normalize.* **2** If people, groups, or governments **normalize** relations or ties or when relations or ties **normalize**, they become normal or return to normal. *They are not prepared to join the EC in normalizing ties with Peking. ...if relations between Hanoi and Washington begin to normalise.* ♦ **nor·mali·za·tion** /,nɔːməlaɪ'zeɪʃən/ *The two sides would like to see the normalisation of diplomatic relations.* ◆◇◇◇◇ V-ERG: V n — V — V-RECIP-ERG: pl-n V n — V n with n — V — N-UNCOUNT

nor·mal·ly /'nɔːməli/ **1** If you say that something **normally** happens or that you **normally** do a particular thing, you mean that it is what usually happens or what you usually do. *All airports in the country are working normally today... Normally, the transportation system in Paris carries 950,000 passengers a day.* **2** If you do something **normally**, you do it in the usual or conventional way. *...failure of the blood to clot normally.* ◆◆◆◇ ADV — ADV: ADV after v

Nor·man /'nɔːmən/ **Normans. 1** The **Normans** were the people who came from northern France and conquered England in 1066, and their descendants. **2 Norman** is used to refer to the period of history in Britain from 1066 until around 1200, and in particular to the style of architecture of that period. *...a Norman castle.* ◆◇◇◇◇ N-COUNT — ADJ

nor·ma·tive /'nɔːmətɪv/ **Normative** means creating or stating particular rules of behaviour. *...a normative model of teaching.* ◆◇◇◇◇ ADJ FORMAL

Norse /nɔːs/ **1 Norse** means belonging or relating to medieval Scandinavia. *...Norse mythology.* **2 Norse** is the language that was spoken in medieval Scandinavia. ADJ — N-UNCOUNT

Norse·man /'nɔːsmən/ **Norsemen. Norsemen** were people who lived in Scandinavia during the medieval period. N-COUNT

north /nɔːθ/ **North** is one of the four points of the compass. See Appendix headed **Compass**. ◆◆◆◆◇

north·bound /'nɔːθbaʊnd/ See Appendix headed **Compass**.

north-'east. See Appendix headed **Compass**.

north-'easterly. See Appendix headed **Compass**.

north-'eastern. See Appendix headed **Compass**.

nor·ther·ly /'nɔːðəli/ See Appendix headed **Compass**.

north·ern /'nɔːðən/ See Appendix headed **Compass**.

north·ern·er /ˈnɔːðənə/. See Appendix headed **Compass**.

north·ern·most /ˈnɔːðənməʊst/. See Appendix headed **Compass**.

North 'Pole. The **North Pole** is the place on the surface of the earth which is farthest towards the north. N-PROPER

north·ward /ˈnɔːθwəd/. See Appendix headed **Compass**.

north-'west. See Appendix headed **Compass**.

north-'westerly. See Appendix headed **Compass**.

north-'western. See Appendix headed **Compass**.

nose /nəʊz/ **noses, nosing, nosed. 1** Your **nose** is the part of your face which sticks out above your mouth. You use it for smelling and breathing. See picture headed **human body. 2** You can refer to your sense of smell as your **nose**. *The river that runs through Middlesbrough became ugly on the eye and hard on the nose.* **3** See also **hard-nosed, toffee-nosed. 4** If a racehorse wins a race by a **nose**, it wins by the smallest possible distance. ◆◆◆◇◇ N-COUNT / N-COUNT / N-SING

5 If you **follow** your **nose**, you make decisions and behave in a particular way because you feel instinctively that this is what you should do. **6** If you say that someone **has a nose for** something, you mean that they have an instinctive ability to find it or recognize it. *He had a nose for trouble and a brilliant tactical mind.* **7** If you say that someone or something **gets up** your **nose**, you mean that they annoy you. *The guy I was living with was getting up my nose.* **8** If you say that someone **looks down** their **nose** at something or someone else, you mean that the first person believes they are superior to the other thing or person and treats them with disrespect; used showing disapproval. *I know what it's like when people look down their nose because you don't have nice things.* PHRASE / PHRASE / PHRASE INFORMAL / PHRASE PRAGMATICS

9 If you say that you **paid through the nose** for something, you mean that you had to pay too high a price for it. **10** If someone **pokes** their **nose into** something or **sticks** their **nose into** something, they try to interfere with it even though it does not concern them; used showing disapproval. *We don't like strangers who poke their noses into our affairs.* **11** To **rub** someone's **nose in** something that they do not want to think about, such as a mistake they have made, means to remind them repeatedly about it. *His enemies will attempt to rub his nose in past policy statements.* **12** If you say that someone **is cutting off** their **nose to spite** their **face**, you mean they do something that they think will hurt someone, without realizing or caring that it will hurt them as well. PHRASE INFORMAL / PHRASE PRAGMATICS INFORMAL / PHRASE INFORMAL / PHRASE PRAGMATICS

13 If you **thumb** your **nose at** someone, you behave in a way that shows that you do not care what they think. *He has always thumbed his nose at the media.* **14** If you **turn up** your **nose** at something, you reject it because you think that it is not good enough for you. *I'm not in a financial position to turn up my nose at several hundred thousand pounds.* **15** If you do something **under** someone's **nose**, you do it right in front of them, without trying to hide it from them. **16** ● **to put** someone's **nose out of joint**: see **joint**. PHRASE / PHRASE / PHRASE

17 The **nose** of a vehicle such as a car or aeroplane is the front part of it. **18** If vehicles are **nose to tail**, the front of one vehicle is close behind the back of another. **19** If a vehicle **noses** in a certain direction, you move it slowly and carefully in that direction. *A motorboat nosed out of the mist... Ben drove past them, nosing his car into the garage.* N-COUNT / PHRASE / V-ERG V adv/prep V n prep/adv

nose around; the form **nose about** is also used in British English. If you **nose around** or **nose about**, you look around a place that belongs to someone else, to see if you can find something interesting. *Accountants are nosing around the BBC at the moment, conducting an efficiency study.* PHRASAL VB VP VP n INFORMAL

nose·bleed /ˈnəʊzbliːd/ **nosebleeds;** also spelled **nose bleed**. If someone has a **nosebleed**, blood comes out from inside their nose. N-COUNT

nose·dive /ˈnəʊzdaɪv/ **nosedives, nosediving, nosedived;** also spelled **nose-dive. 1** If prices, profits, or exchange rates **nosedive**, they fall very VERB: V JOURNALISM

suddenly. ▶ Also a noun. *The bank yesterday revealed a 30 per cent nosedive in profits.* **2** If something such as someone's reputation or a particular situation **nosedives**, it gets worse very suddenly and dramatically. *Since the US invasion the president's reputation has nosedived.* ▶ Also a noun. *He told the tribunal his career had 'taken a nosedive' since his dismissal last year.* N-SING / VERB V JOURNALISM / N-SING

'nose job, nose jobs. A **nose job** is a surgical operation that some people have to improve the shape of their nose. N-COUNT INFORMAL

nos·ey /ˈnəʊzi/. See **nosy**.

nosh /nɒʃ/. Food can be referred to as **nosh**. *Fancy some nosh?* N-UNCOUNT INFORMAL

nos·tal·gia /nɒˈstældʒə/. **Nostalgia** is an affectionate feeling you have for the past, especially for a particularly happy time. ◆◇◇◇ N-UNCOUNT

nos·tal·gic /nɒˈstældʒɪk/. **1 Nostalgic** things cause you to think affectionately about the past. *Although we still depict nostalgic snow scenes on Christmas cards, winters are now very much warmer.* **2** If you feel **nostalgic**, you think affectionately about experiences you had in the past. *Many people were nostalgic for the good old days.* ◆ **nos·tal·gi·cal·ly** /nɒˈstældʒɪkli/ *People look back nostalgically on the war period, simply because everyone pulled together.* ◆◇◇◇ ADJ-GRADED / ADJ-GRADED / ADV

nos·tril /ˈnɒstrɪl/ **nostrils**. Your **nostrils** are the two openings at the end of your nose. See picture headed **human body**. ◆◇◇◇ N-COUNT

nos·trum /ˈnɒstrəm/ **nostrums**. You can refer to ideas or theories which are intended to solve a particular problem as **nostrums**, especially when you think that they are untrue, simplistic, or outdated. N-COUNT

nosy /ˈnəʊzi/ **nosier, nosiest;** also spelled **nosey**. If you describe someone as **nosy**, you mean that they are interested in things which do not concern them; used showing disapproval. ADJ-GRADED PRAGMATICS

not /nɒt/. In spoken English and informal written English, **not** is often contracted to **n't** and is added to the auxiliary or modal verb. For example, 'did not' is often contracted to 'didn't'. ◆◆◆◆◆

1 You use **not** with verbs to form negative statements. *The sanctions are not working the way they were intended... I was not in Britain at the time... I don't trust my father anymore.* **2** You use **not** to form questions to which you expect the answer 'yes'. *Haven't they got enough problems there already?... Didn't I see you at the party last week?* **3** You use **not**, usually in the form **n't**, in questions which imply that someone should have done something or should do something, or to express surprise that something is not the case. *Why didn't you do it months ago?... Why couldn't he listen to her?... Hasn't anyone ever kissed you before?* NEGATIVE / NEGATIVE PRAGMATICS / NEGATIVE PRAGMATICS

4 You use **not**, usually in the form **n't**, in question tags after a positive statement. *'It's a nice piece of jewellery though, isn't it?'... You will take me tomorrow, won't you?* **5** You use **not**, usually in the form **n't**, in polite suggestions. *Why don't you fill out our application?... Couldn't they send it by train?* **6** You use **not** to represent the negative of a word, group, or clause that has just been used. *'Have you found Paula?'—'I'm afraid not, Kate.'... At first I really didn't care whether he came or not.* **7** You can use **not** in front of 'all' or 'every' when you want to say something that applies only to some members of the group that you are talking about. *Not all the money, to put it mildly, has been used wisely... Not every applicant had a degree.* NEGATIVE / NEGATIVE PRAGMATICS / NEGATIVE / NEGATIVE

8 If something is **not** always the case, you mean that sometimes it is the case and sometimes it is not. *He didn't always win the arguments, but he often was right... She couldn't always afford a babysitter.* **9** You can use **not** or **not even** in front of 'a' or 'one' to emphasize that there is none at all of what is being mentioned. *The houses are beautiful, but there's no shop, not even a pub to go into... I sent report after report. But not one word was published.* **10** You can use **not** in front of a word referring to a distance, length of time, or other amount to say that the actual distance, time, or amount is less than the one mentioned. *The tug* NEGATIVE / NEGATIVE PRAGMATICS / NEGATIVE

crossed our stern not fifty yards away... They were here not five minutes ago.

11 You use **not** when you are contrasting something that is true with something that is untrue. You use this especially to indicate that people might think that the untrue statement is true. *Training is an investment not a cost.* **12** You use **not** in expressions such as 'not only', 'not just', 'not simply', and 'not merely' to emphasize that something is true, but it is not the whole truth. *These movies were not only making money; they were also perceived to be original... There is always a 'black market' not just in Britain but in Europe as a whole.* **13** You use **not that** to introduce a negative clause that contradicts something that the previous statement implies. *His death took me a year to get over; not that you're ever really over it.* *NEGATIVE* *PRAGMATICS*

NEGATIVE *PRAGMATICS*

PHR-CONJ *PRAGMATICS*

14 Not at all is an emphatic way of saying 'No' or of agreeing that the answer to a question is 'No'. *'Sorry. I sound like Abby, don't I?'—'No. Not at all.'... 'You don't think that you've betrayed your country.'—'No I don't. No, not at all.'* **15 Not at all** is a polite way of acknowledging a person's thanks. *'Thank you very much for speaking with us.'—'Not at all.'* **16 ● not half**: see **half**. ● **if not**: see **if**. ● **not least**: see **least**. ● **not to mention**: see **mention**. ● **nothing if not**: see **nothing**. ● **not for nothing**: see **nothing**. ● **more often than not**: see **often**. *CONVENTION* *PRAGMATICS*

CONVENTION *PRAGMATICS*

no·ta·ble /ˈnəʊtəbəl/ **notables.** **1** Someone or something that is **notable** is important or interesting. *The proposed new structure is notable not only for its height, but for its shape.* **2 Notables** are important or powerful people. ◆◆◇◇◇ *ADJ-GRADED*

N-COUNT *FORMAL*

no·ta·bly /ˈnəʊtəbli/ **1** You use **notably** to specify an important or typical example of something that you are talking about. *The divorce would be granted when more important problems, notably the fate of the children, had been decided.* **2** You can use **notably** to emphasize a particular quality that someone or something has. *A notably short, silver-haired man, he plays basketball with his staff several times a week.* ◆◆◇◇◇ *ADV-GRADED:* *ADV group/cl* *PRAGMATICS*

ADV: *ADV adj/adv* *PRAGMATICS*

no·ta·ry /ˈnəʊtəri/ **notaries.** A **notary** or a **notary public** is a person, usually a lawyer, who has legal authority to witness the signing of documents in order to make them legally valid. *N-COUNT*

no·ta·tion /nəʊˈteɪʃən/ **notations.** A **notation** is a set of written symbols that are used to represent a system such as music, logic, or mathematics. *N-VAR*

notch /nɒtʃ/ **notches, notching, notched.** **1** You can refer to a step on a scale of measurement or achievement as a **notch**. *Average earnings in the economy moved up another notch in August.* **2** If you **notch** a success, especially in sport, you achieve it. *Steve Bull notched his 200th goal for Wolves as they beat Leicester 3-0.* **3** A **notch** is a small V-shaped or circular cut in the surface or edge of something. *It is a myth that gunslingers in the American west cut notches in the handle of their pistol for each man they shot.* **4** See also **top-notch**. ◆◇◇◇◇ *N-COUNT* *JOURNALISM*

VERB *V n* *JOURNALISM*

N-COUNT

notch up. If you **notch up** something such as a score or total, you achieve it. *The economy is expanding, notching up high growth rates.* *PHRASAL VB* *Also V n P* *JOURNALISM*

note /nəʊt/ **notes, noting, noted.** **1** A **note** is a short letter. *I'll have to leave a note for Karen... Remember to write a note to say where you are.* **2** A **note** is something that you write down to remind yourself of something. *Take notes during the consultation as the final written report is very concise.* **3** When you **note** something, you write it down as a record of what has happened. *'He has had his tonsils out and has been ill, too,' she noted in her diary... One policeman was clearly visible noting the number plates of passing cars.* **4** If you tell someone to **note** something, you are drawing their attention to it. *Note the statue to Sallustio Bandini, a prominent Sienese... Please note that there are a limited number of tickets.* **5** If you **take note** of something, you pay attention to it because you think that it is important. *They took note that she showed no surprise at the news of the murder.* **6** If a piece of writ- ◆◆◆◇◇ *N-COUNT*

N-COUNT

VERB *V with quote* *V n* *Also V wh,* *V that*

VERB *V n* *V that*

PHRASE

VERB

ing **notes** something, it mentions it. *The report notes that many elderly people admitted to hospital suffer from inadequate nutrition.* *V that* *Also V n*

7 In a book or article, a **note** is a short piece of additional information. *See Note 16 on page p. 223.* **8** If you **compare notes** with someone on a particular subject, you talk to them and find out whether their opinion or information is the same as yours. You can also say that two people **compare notes**. *The women were busily comparing notes on the Queen's outfit.* **9** If you **note** a fact, you become aware of it. *Suddenly, I noted that the rain had stopped... At every stage people noted how painstaking he was about personal relations with constituents, party workers and civil servants.* *N-COUNT* *PHRASE*

VERB: V n *V that* *V wh*

10 A **note** is a short document that has to be signed by someone and that gives official information about something. *Since Mr Bennett was going to need some time off work, he asked for a sick note.* **11** You can refer to a banknote as a **note**. The usual American word is **bill**. *...a five pound note.* **12** In music, a **note** is the sound of a particular pitch, or a written symbol representing this sound. *She has a deep voice and doesn't even try for the high notes.* *N-COUNT:* *with supp*

N-COUNT *BRITISH*

N-COUNT

13 You can use **note** to refer to a particular quality in someone's voice that shows how they are feeling. *It was not difficult for him to catch the note of bitterness in my voice.* **14** You can use **note** to refer to a particular feeling, impression, or atmosphere. *He first came to national prominence in 1953 as the editor of Punch which he gave a note of aggressive radicalism.* **15** If someone or something **strikes** a particular **note** or **sounds** a particular **note**, they create a particular feeling, impression, or atmosphere. *Before his first round of discussions, Mr Baker sounded an optimistic note.* *N-SING:* *with supp*

N-SING: *with supp*

PHRASE

16 Someone or something that is **of note** is important, worth mentioning, or well-known. *He has published nothing of note in the last ten years.* *PHRASE*

17 See also **noted**, **promissory note**, **sleeve note**. ● to **make a mental note**: see **mental**.

note down. If you **note down** something, you write it down quickly, so that you have a record of it. *If you find a name that's on the list I've given you, note it down... Please note down what I'm about to say.* *PHRASAL VB* *V P noun* *V n P* *V P wh*

note·book /ˈnəʊtbʊk/ **notebooks.** **1** A **notebook** is a small book for writing notes in. *I'd already filled ten pages in my notebook.* **2** A **notebook** computer is a small portable personal computer. ◆◆◇◇◇ *N-COUNT*

N-COUNT

not·ed /ˈnəʊtɪd/ Someone or something that is **noted** for something they do or have is well-known and admired for it. *...a television programme noted for its attacks on organised crime.* ◆◆◆◇◇ *ADJ-GRADED*

note·pad /ˈnəʊtpæd/ **notepads.** A **notepad** is a pad of paper that you use for writing notes or letters on. *N-COUNT*

note·paper /ˈnəʊtpeɪpə/ **Notepaper** is paper that you use for writing letters on. *N-UNCOUNT*

note·worthy /ˈnəʊtwɜːði/. A fact or event that is **noteworthy** is interesting, remarkable, or significant in some way. *It is noteworthy that the Arabic words 'war', and 'javelin' or 'lance' are very similar.* *ADJ-GRADED* *FORMAL*

noth·ing /ˈnʌθɪŋ/ **nothings.** **1** **Nothing** means not a single thing, or not a single part of something. *I've done nothing much since coffee time... There's nothing else I can do for you.* **2** You use **nothing** to indicate that something or someone is not important or significant. *Because he had always had money it meant nothing to him... She kept bursting into tears over nothing at work.* ▶ Also a noun. *All it took was a word here, a word there, to convince him that he was a nothing.* **3** If you say that something cost **nothing** or is worth **nothing**, you are indicating that it cost or is worth a surprisingly small amount of money. *The furniture was threadbare; he'd obviously picked it up for nothing.* ◆◆◆◆◆ *PRON-INDEF*

PRON-INDEF

N-COUNT

PRON-INDEF

4 You use **nothing** before an adjective or 'to'-infinitive to mean that a situation or activity does not have the particular quality mentioned. *There is nothing wrong with the car... All kids her age do silly things; it's nothing to worry about.* **5** You can use **nothing** before 'so' and an adjective or adverb, or before a comparative, to em- *PRON-INDEF:* *PRON adj,* *PRON to-inf*

PRON-INDEF: *PRON so adj/* *adv,*

phasize how strong or great a particular quality is. *Youngsters learn nothing so fast as hòw to beat the system... There's nothing better than a good cup of hot coffee.* **6** You can use **all or nothing** to say that either something must be done fully and completely or else it cannot be done at all. *Either he went through with this thing or he did not; it was all or nothing.* **7** If you say that something is **better than nothing**, you mean that it is not what is required, but that it is better to have that thing than to have nothing at all. *15 minutes of exercise is better than nothing.* **8** You use **nothing but** in front of a noun, an infinitive without 'to', or an '-ing' form to mean 'only'. *All that money brought nothing but sadness and misery... It did nothing but make us ridiculous... They care for nothing but fighting.* **9** You can say **'Nothing doing'** when you want to say that something is not happening or cannot be done. *Pay now, or nothing doing.* **10** If you say that **there is nothing for it** but to take a particular course of action, you mean that it is the only possible course of action that you can take, even though it might be unpleasant. *Sleep was now impossible and there was nothing for it but to get up.* **11** You use **nothing if not** in front of an adjective to indicate that someone or something clearly has a lot of the particular quality mentioned. *Professor Fish has been nothing if not professional.* **12** People sometimes say **'It's nothing'** as a polite response after someone has thanked them for something they have done. *'Thank you for the wonderful dinner.'—'It's nothing,' Sarah said.* **13** If you say about an activity that there is **nothing to it** or **nothing in it**, you mean that it is extremely easy. *This device has a gripper that electrically twists off the jar top. Nothing to it... If you've shied away from making pancakes in the past, don't be put off – there's really nothing in it!* **14** You can use **nothing less than** to emphasize your next words, often indicating that something seems very surprising or important. *You're nothing less than a murderer!* **15** If you say that it was **not for nothing** that something happened, you are emphasizing that there was a very good reason for it to happen. *Not for nothing was the plane called 'the widow-maker'.* **16** If you say that someone is getting **something for nothing**, you disapprove of the fact that they are getting something that they want without having to give anything or do anything in return. **17** **Nothing of the sort** is used as an emphatic way of refusing permission or of denying something that someone has said. *'We're going to talk this over in my office.'—'We're going to do nothing of the sort.'* **18** See also **sweet nothings.** ● to **say nothing of**: see **say.** ● **nothing short of**: see **short.** ● to **stop at nothing**: see **stop.** ● to **think nothing of**: see **think.**

noth·ing·ness /ˈnʌθɪŋnəs/. **1** Nothingness is the N-UNCOUNT fact of not existing. *There might be something beyond the grave, you know, and not nothingness.* **2** Nothingness can refer to complete emptiness or a N-UNCOUNT complete absence of things or feelings. *Her eyes, glazed with the drug, stared with half closed lids at nothingness.*

no·tice /ˈnəʊtɪs/ **notices, noticing, noticed.** ◆◆◆◆ **1** If you **notice** something or someone, you become VERB: V n aware of them. *I noticed that most academics were V that writing papers during the summer... Luckily, I'd no- V wh ticed where you left the car... Mrs Shedden noticed a Also V bird sitting on the garage roof.* **2** If you **bring** some- PHRASE thing to someone's **notice**, you make them aware of it. If something **comes to** your **notice**, you become aware of it. *It was in 1982 that his name was first brought to our notice... As I write, a very interesting case has come to my notice.* **3** If you **take notice** of a particular fact or situation, PHRASE you behave in a way that shows that you are aware of it. *We want the government to take notice of what we think they should do for single parents.* **4** If you **take** PHRASE **no notice** of someone or something, you do not consider them to be important enough to affect what you think or what you do. *I tried not to take any notice at first but then I was offended by it.* **5** If something es-

PRON compar
PRAGMATICS

PHRASE

PHRASE

PHRASE

PHRASE

PHRASE

CONVENTION
PRAGMATICS
INFORMAL

PHRASE
BRITISH

PHRASE

CONVENTION
PRAGMATICS

PHRASE

PHRASE
PRAGMATICS

PHRASE
PRAGMATICS

PHRASE
PRAGMATICS

PHRASE
PRAGMATICS

capes your **notice**, you fail to recognize it or realize it. *From the smallest to the largest production unit, no one escaped notice.* **6** A **notice** is a written announcement in a place N-COUNT where everyone can read it. *A few guest houses had 'No Vacancies' notices in their windows.* **7** A **notice** is a for- N-COUNT mal announcement in a newspaper or magazine about something that has happened or is going to happen. *The request is published in notices in today's national newspapers.* **8** A **notice** is a written article in N-COUNT a newspaper or magazine in which someone gives their opinion of a play, film, or concert. **9** If you give **notice** about something that is going to N-UNCOUNT happen, you give a warning in advance that it is going to happen. *Interest is paid monthly. Three months' notice is required for withdrawals... She was transferred without notice.* **10** Notice is used in expressions such PHRASE as **'at short notice'**, **'at a moment's notice'** or **'at twenty-four hours' notice'**, to indicate that something can or must be done within a short period of time. *There's no one available at such short notice to take her class.* **11** If a situation is said to exist **until fur-** PHRASE **ther notice**, it will continue for an uncertain length of time until someone changes it. *All flights to Lanchow had been cancelled until further notice.* **12** If an employer **gives** an employee **notice**, the em- PHRASE ployer tells the employee that he or she must leave his or her job within a fixed period of time. **13** If you **hand** PHRASE **in** your **notice** or **give in** your **notice**, you tell your employer that you intend to leave your job soon within a set period of time.

no·tice·able /ˈnəʊtɪsəbəl/. Something that is no- ◆◆◇◇◇ ticeable is very obvious, so that it is easy to see, ADJ-GRADED hear, or recognize. *It is noticeable that women do not have the sort of rivalry that men have.* ♦ **no-** ADV-GRADED **·tice·ably** *Standards of living were deteriorating rather noticeably.*

not·ice·board /ˈnəʊtɪsbɔːd/ **noticeboards.** A N-COUNT noticeboard is a board which is attached to a wall BRITISH in order to display notices giving information about something. The usual American word is **bulletin board**.

no·ti·fi·ca·tion /ˌnəʊtɪfɪˈkeɪʃən/ **notifications.** If ◆◇◇◇◇ you are given **notification** of something, you are of- N-VAR ficially informed of it. *Payments should be sent with the written notification.*

no·ti·fy /ˈnəʊtɪfaɪ/ **notifies, notifying, notified.** ◆◇◇◇◇ If you **notify** someone of something, you officially VERB: inform them about it. *Earlier this year they were no-* V n of/about n *tified that their homes were to be cleared away... She* be V-ed that *confirmed that she would notify the police and the* V n *hospital.* Also V n that FORMAL

no·tion /ˈnəʊʃən/ **notions.** A notion is an idea or ◆◆◇◇◇ belief about something. *We each have a notion of* N-COUNT *just what kind of person we'd like to be. ...the notion that privatisation of our industry is now inevitable.*

no·tion·al /ˈnəʊʃənəl/. Something that is **notional** ADJ exists only in theory or as a suggestion or idea, but not in reality. ♦ **no·tion·al·ly** *Mr Deng, who is no-* ADV *tionally retired, has not appeared in public for three months now.*

no·to·ri·ety /ˌnəʊtəˈraɪɪti/. If someone or some- ◆◇◇◇◇ thing achieves **notoriety**, they become well-known N-UNCOUNT for something bad. *He had achieved notoriety as chief counsel to President Nixon in the Watergate break-in.*

no·to·ri·ous /nəʊˈtɔːriəs/. Someone or something ◆◇◇◇◇ that is **notorious** is well-known for something bad. ADJ-GRADED *West Berlin has long been notorious for its street violence.* ♦ **no·to·ri·ous·ly** *He worked mainly in New* ADV *York City where living space is notoriously at a premium... Doctors notoriously neglect their own health.*

not·with·stand·ing /ˌnɒtwɪðˈstændɪŋ/. If some- ◆◇◇◇◇ thing is true **notwithstanding** something else, it is PREP true in spite of that other thing. *He despised William* FORMAL *Pitt, notwithstanding the similar views they both held.* ► Also an adverb. *His relations with col-* ADV: n ADV *leagues, differences of opinion notwithstanding, were unfailingly friendly.*

nought /nɔːt/ **noughts;** also spelled **naught** for ◆◇◇◇◇
meaning 2. **1 Nought** is the number 0. See Appen- NUMBER
dix headed **Numbers**. **2** If you try to do something PHRASE
but your efforts are not successful, you can say that FORMAL
your efforts **come to naught**. *Numerous attempts to
persuade him to write his memoirs came to nought.*

noun /naʊn/ **nouns.** A noun is a word such as ◆◇◇◇◇
'woman', 'guilt', or 'Harry' which is used to refer to N-COUNT
a person or thing. ● See also **collective noun, count
noun, mass noun, proper noun, singular noun,
uncount noun.**

'**noun group, noun groups.** A noun group is a N-COUNT
noun or pronoun, or a group of words based on a
noun or pronoun. Noun groups can be the subject,
object, or complement in a clause, or the object of a
preposition. In the sentence, 'He put the bottle of
wine on the kitchen table', 'He', 'the bottle of wine',
and 'the kitchen table' are all noun groups.

'**noun phrase, noun phrases.** A noun phrase is N-COUNT
the same as a **noun group.**

nour·ish /ˈnʌrɪʃ, AM ˈnɜːrɪʃ/ **nourishes, nourish-** ◆◇◇◇◇
ing, nourished. 1 To **nourish** a person, animal, or VERB
plant means to provide them with the food that is V n
necessary for life, growth, and good health. *...mi-
crobes in the soil which nourish the plant.* ◆ **nour-**
·ish·ing *...sensible, nourishing food... The doctor* ADJ-GRADED
has ordered me to take a nourishing diet. **2** To **nour-** VERB
ish something such as a feeling or belief means to V n
allow or encourage it to grow. *Journalists on the
whole don't create public opinion. They can however
help to nourish it.*

-nourished /-ˈnʌrɪʃt, AM -ˈnɜːr-/. **-nourished** is COMB
used with adverbs such as 'well' or 'under' to indicate how much food someone eats or whether it is
the right kind of food. *To make sure the children are
well-nourished, vitamin drops are recommended.*

nour·ish·ment /ˈnʌrɪʃmənt, AM ˈnɜːr-/. **1** If some- ◆◇◇◇◇
thing provides a person, animal, or plant with N-UNCOUNT
nourishment, it provides them with the food that is
necessary for life, growth, and good health. *He was
unable to take nourishment for several days.* **2** The N-UNCOUNT
action of nourishing someone or something, or the
experience of being nourished, can be referred to as
nourishment. *Sugar gives quick relief to hunger but
provides no lasting nourishment.*

nous /naʊs/. **Nous** is intelligence or common sense. N-UNCOUNT
She may not have much political nous. BRITISH

nouveau-riche /ˌnuːvəʊ ˈriːʃ/ **nouveaux-riches.**
The plural can be either **nouveau-riche** or
nouveaux-riches. 1 The **nouveaux-riches** are peo- N-PLURAL
ple who have only recently become rich and who PRAGMATICS
have tastes and manners that some people consider
vulgar; used showing disapproval. **2 Nouveau-riche** ADJ-GRADED
means belonging or relating to the nouveaux-riches. PRAGMATICS
*He hit back at critics who did not appreciate his
nouveau-riche taste.*

nou·velle cui·sine /ˌnuːvel kwɪˈziːn/. **Nouvelle** N-UNCOUNT
cuisine is a style of cooking in which fresh foods are
lightly cooked and served in small amounts, attractively arranged. You can also refer to food that has
been cooked in this way as **nouvelle cuisine.**

Nov. Nov. is a written abbreviation for **November**. ◆◇◇◇◇

nov·el /ˈnɒvəl/ **novels. 1** A **novel** is a long written ◆◆◆◇◇
story about imaginary people and events. *...a novel* N-COUNT
by Herman Hesse. ...historical novels.
2 Novel things are unlike anything that has been ADJ-GRADED
done, experienced, or created before. *...a novel way of
demonstrating against steeply rising oil prices.*

nov·el·ist /ˈnɒvəlɪst/ **novelists.** A **novelist** is a ◆◆◇◇◇
person who writes novels. N-COUNT

no·vel·la /nəʊˈvelə/ **novellas.** A **novella** is a short N-COUNT
novel or a long short story.

nov·el·ty /ˈnɒvəlti/ **novelties. 1 Novelty** is the ◆◇◇◇◇
quality of being different, new, and unusual. *Rapid-* N-UNCOUNT
*ly changing styles cater to a desire for novelty and in-
dividualism.* **2** A **novelty** is something that is new N-COUNT
and therefore interesting. *...the days when a motor
car was a novelty.*
3 Novelties are cheap unusual objects that are sold as N-COUNT
gifts or souvenirs.

No·vem·ber /nəʊˈvembə/ **Novembers.** Novem- ◆◆◆◆◇
ber is the eleventh month of the year in the Western N-VAR
calendar. See Appendix headed **Dates**. *He arrived in
London in November 1939. ...what the voters will do
next November.*

nov·ice /ˈnɒvɪs/ **novices. 1** A **novice** is someone ◆◆◇◇◇
who has been doing a job or other activity for only a N-COUNT
short time and so is not experienced at it. *...a novice
writer.* **2** In a monastery or convent, a **novice** is a N-COUNT
person who is preparing to become a monk or nun.

now /naʊ/. **1** You use **now** to refer to the present ◆◆◆◆◆
time, often in contrast to a time in the past or the ADV
future. *She's a widow now... Beef now costs well over
30 roubles a pound... She should know that by now.*
► Also a pronoun. *Now is the time when we must all* PRON
live as economically as possible. **2** If you do some- ADV:
thing **now**, you do it immediately. *I must go now... If* ADV after v
*I don't write now I shall never have another oppor-
tunity to do so.* ► Also a pronoun. *Now is your* PRON
chance to talk to him.
3 You use **now** or **now that** to indicate that an event CONJ
has occurred and so as a result something else may or PRAGMATICS
will happen. *Now you're settled, why don't you take up
some serious study?* **4** You use **now** to indicate that a ADV
particular situation is the result of something that has
recently happened. *Mrs Chandra has received one
sweater for each of her five children and says that the
winter will not be so hard now... She told me not to repeat it, but now I don't suppose it matters.*
5 In stories and accounts of past events, **now** is used ADV
to refer to the particular time that is being written or
spoken about. *It was too late now for Blake to lock his
room door... By now it was completely dark outside.*
6 You use **now** in statements which specify the length ADV
of time up to the present that something has lasted.
*They've been married now for 30 years... They have
been missing for a long time now.*
7 You say **'Now'** or **'Now then'** to indicate to the per- ADV
son or people you are with that you want their atten- PRAGMATICS
tion, or that you are about to change the subject. *'Now* SPOKEN
*then,' Max said, 'to get back to the point.'... Now, can
we move on and discuss the vital business of the day,
please.* **8** Some people say **'Now'** when they are think- ADV
ing of what to say next. *Now, er, dogs can live to fifteen.* PRAGMATICS
9 You use **now** to give a slight emphasis to a request or ADV
command. *Come on now. You know you must be hun-* PRAGMATICS
gry... Come and sit down here, now. **10** You can say SPOKEN
'Now' to introduce information which is relevant to ADV cl
the part of a story or account that you have reached, PRAGMATICS
and which needs to be known before you can con- SPOKEN
tinue. *Now, I hadn't told him these details, so he
must have done some research on his own.* **11** You ADV:
say **'Now'** to introduce something which contrasts ADV cl
with what you have just said before. *Now, if it was* PRAGMATICS
me, I'd want to do more than just change the locks. SPOKEN
12 Just now means a very short time ago. *You looked* PHRASE
pretty upset just now. **13** You use **just now** when you PHRASE
want to say that a particular situation exists at the
time when you are speaking, although it may change
in the future. *I'm pretty busy just now.*
14 You can say **'now, now'** as a friendly way of trying CONVENTION
to comfort someone who is upset or distressed. *'I* PRAGMATICS
want to go with you, Daddy.'—'Now, now, sweetheart.' SPOKEN
15 You can say **'Now, then'** or **'Now, now'** when you CONVENTION
want to give someone you know well a friendly warn- PRAGMATICS
ing not to behave in a particular way. *Now then, no* SPOKEN
unpleasantness, please.
16 If you say that something happens **now and then** PHRASE
or **every now and again**, you mean that it happens
sometimes but not very often or regularly. *My father
has a collection of magazines to which I return every
now and then.* **17** If you say that something will hap- PHRASE
pen **any day now, any moment now,** or **any time
now,** you mean that it will happen very soon. **18** Peo- PHRASE
ple such as television presenters and entertainers PRAGMATICS
sometimes use **now for** when they are going to start
talking about a different subject or presenting a new
activity. *And now for something completely different.*
19 If you say **'It's now or never'**, you mean that some- PHRASE
thing must be done immediately, because if it is not

N

done immediately there will not be another chance to do it.

nowa·days /'navədeɪz/. **Nowadays** means at the present time, in contrast with the past. *I don't see much of Tony nowadays.*
ADV:
ADV with cl

no·where /'nəʊweə/. **1** You use **nowhere** to emphasize that a place has more of a particular quality than any other places, or that it is the only place where something happens or exists. *Nowhere is language a more serious issue than in Hawaii... This kind of forest exists nowhere else in the world.*
ADV
PRAGMATICS

2 You use **nowhere** when making negative statements to say that a suitable place of the specified kind does not exist. *There was nowhere to hide and nowhere to run... I have nowhere else to go, nowhere in the world... He had nowhere to call home.*
ADV

3 You use **nowhere** to indicate that something or someone cannot be seen or found. *Michael glanced anxiously down the corridor, but Wilfred was nowhere to be seen... The escaped prisoner was nowhere in sight.*
ADV

4 If you say that something or someone appears **from nowhere** or **out of nowhere**, you mean that they appear suddenly and unexpectedly. *A car came from nowhere, and I had to jump back into the hedge.*
ADV:
from/out of
ADV

5 You can use **nowhere** to refer in a general way to small, unimportant, or uninteresting places. *...endless paths that led nowhere in particular.*
ADV

6 You use **nowhere** to mean not in any part of a text, speech, or argument. *He nowhere offers concrete historical background to support his arguments.*
ADV

7 If you say that a place is **in the middle of nowhere**, you mean it is a long way from other places.
PHRASE

8 If you say that you **are getting nowhere**, or **getting nowhere fast**, or that something **is getting** you **nowhere**, you mean that you are not achieving anything or having any success. *My mind won't stop going round and round on the same subject and I seem to be getting nowhere.*
PHRASE

9 If you use **nowhere near** in front of a word or expression, you are emphasizing that the real situation is very different from, or has not yet reached, the state which that word or expression suggests. *He's nowhere near recovered yet from his experiences.*
PHRASE
PRAGMATICS

no-'win situation, no-win situations. If you are in a **no-win situation**, any action you take will fail to benefit you in any way. *It was a no-win situation. Either she pretended she hated Ned and felt awful or admitted she loved him and felt even worse!*
N-COUNT

nox·ious /'nɒkʃəs/. **1** A **noxious** gas or substance is poisonous or very harmful. *Many household products give off noxious fumes.* **2** If you refer to someone or something as **noxious**, you mean that they are extremely unpleasant. *Their behaviour was extremely noxious.*
ADJ-GRADED

ADJ-GRADED
FORMAL

noz·zle /'nɒzəl/ **nozzles.** The **nozzle** of a hose or pipe is a narrow piece fitted to the end to control the flow of liquid or gas.
N-COUNT

nr. In addresses, **nr** is used as a written abbreviation for **near**. *Brackhurst Agricultural College, Nr Southwell, Notts.*

-n't /-ənt/. See **not**.

nth /enθ/. **1** If you refer to the most recent item in a series of things as the **nth** item, you are emphasizing that it has happened many times. *The story was raised with me for the nth time two days before the article appeared.* **2** If something is done **to the nth degree**, it is done to an extreme degree. *Ned and I discussed everything to the nth degree.*
ADJ: ADJ n
PRAGMATICS

PHRASE

nu·ance /'njuːɑːns, AM 'nuː-/ **nuances.** A **nuance** is a small and subtle difference in sound, feeling, appearance, or meaning. *...every subtle nuance of emotion there is.*
N-VAR

nub /nʌb/. The **nub** of a situation, problem, or argument is the central and most basic part of it. *That, I think, is the nub of the problem.*
N-SING:
theN

nu·bile /'njuːbaɪl, AM 'nuːbɪl/. A **nubile** woman is young, physically mature, and sexually attractive.
ADJ-GRADED

nu·clear /'njuːkliə, AM 'nuːk-/. **Nuclear** means relating to the nuclei of atoms, or to the energy released when these nuclei are split or combined. *...a nuclear power station. ...nuclear weapons.*
ADJ: ADJ n

,nuclear 'family, nuclear families. A **nuclear family** is a family unit that consists of father, mother, and children.
N-COUNT

,nuclear-'free. A **nuclear-free** place is a place where the manufacture and transport of nuclear weapons, the building of nuclear reactors, and the disposal of nuclear waste are all forbidden. *...the idea of a nuclear-free world.*
ADJ

,nuclear re'actor, nuclear reactors. A **nuclear reactor** is a machine which is used to produce nuclear energy or the place where this machine and other related equipment is kept.
N-COUNT

,nuclear 'winter. **Nuclear winter** refers to the possible effects on the environment of a war in which large numbers of nuclear weapons are used. It is thought that there would be very low temperatures and very little light during a nuclear winter.
N-UNCOUNT:
also a N

nu·cleic acid /njuː,kleɪɪk 'æsɪd, AM ,nuː-/ **nucleic acids.** **Nucleic acids** are complex chemical substances, such as DNA, which are found in living cells.
N-VAR
TECHNICAL

nu·cleus /'njuːkliəs, AM 'nuː-/ **nuclei** /'njuːkliaɪ, AM 'nuː-/. **1** The **nucleus** of an atom or cell is the central part of it. **2** The **nucleus** of a group of people or things is the small number of members which form the most important part of the group. *The Civic Movement could be the nucleus of a centrist party.*
N-COUNT

N-COUNT

nude /njuːd, AM nuːd/ **nudes.** **1** A **nude** person is not wearing any clothes. *The occasional nude bather comes here... We are not allowed to perform nude.* **♦ nu·dity** /'njuːdɪti, AM 'nuː-/ *...constant nudity and bad language on TV.* ● If you do something **in the nude**, you are not wearing any clothes. If you paint or draw someone **in the nude**, they are not wearing any clothes. **2** A **nude** is a picture or statue of a person who is not wearing any clothes. A **nude** is also a person in a picture who is not wearing any clothes.
ADJ:
ADJ n,
ADJ after v
N-UNCOUNT
PHRASE

N-COUNT

nudge /nʌdʒ/ **nudges, nudging, nudged.** **1** If you **nudge** someone, you push them gently, usually with your elbow, in order to draw their attention to something or to show them that you want them to do something. *I nudged Stan and pointed again.* ► Also a noun. *She slipped her arm under his and gave him a nudge.* **2** If you **nudge** someone or something into a place or position, you gently push them there. *Edna Swinson nudged him into the sitting room.* ► Also a noun. *McKinnon gave the wheel another slight nudge to starboard.*
VERB
V n

N-COUNT
VERB
V n prep/adv

N-COUNT

3 If you **nudge** someone into doing something, you gently persuade them to do it. *Foreigners must use their power not simply to punish the country but to nudge it towards greater tolerance... British tour companies are nudging clients to travel further afield.* ► Also a noun. *I had a feeling that the challenge appealed to him. All he needed was a nudge.*
VERB:
V n into -ing/n
V n towards n
V n to-inf

N-COUNT

4 If someone or something **is nudging** a particular amount, level, or state, they have almost reached it. *The temperature when we were there was nudging 80°F.*
VERB
V n

5 If you refer to **a nudge and a wink** or to **nudge-nudge wink-wink**, you mean that the person who is writing or saying something is suggesting sexual misbehaviour without stating it openly. *...a series of nudge-nudge, wink-wink rumors that have appeared in newspapers over the last two years.*
PHRASE

nud·ism /'njuːdɪzəm, AM 'nuː-/. **Nudism** is the practice of not wearing any clothes on beaches and other areas specially set aside for this purpose. **♦ nud·ist, nudists** *There are no nudist class.*
N-UNCOUNT

N-COUNT

nug·get /'nʌgɪt/ **nuggets.** **1** A **nugget** is a small lump of something, especially gold. *...pure high-grade gold nuggets.* **2** A **nugget** of information is an interesting or useful piece of information.
N-COUNT

N-COUNT

nui·sance /'njuːsəns, AM 'nuː-/ **nuisances.** If you say that someone or something is a **nuisance**, you mean that they annoy you or cause you a lot of problems. *He could be a bit of a nuisance when he was drunk.* ● If someone **makes a nuisance of**
N-COUNT
PHRASE

themselves, they behave in a way that annoys other people.

nuke /njuːk, AM nuːk/ **nukes, nuking, nuked.**
1 A **nuke** is a nuclear weapon. *They have nukes, and* N-COUNT *if they're sufficiently pushed, they'll use them.* **2** If INFORMAL one country **nukes** another, it attacks it using nu- INFORMAL clear weapons. VERB: V n

null /nʌl/. If an agreement, a declaration, or the re- PHRASE sult of an election is **null and void**, it is not legally valid.

nul·li·fy /ˈnʌlɪfaɪ/ **nullifies, nullifying, nullified.** VERB
1 To **nullify** a legal decision or procedure means to V n declare that it is not legally valid. *He used his broad* FORMAL *executive powers to nullify decisions by local govern-ments.* **2** To **nullify** something means to make it VERB have no effect. *He may be able to nullify that disad-* V n *vantage by offering a wider variety of produce.* FORMAL

numb /nʌm/ **numbs, numbing, numbed. 1** If a ◆◇◇◇◇ part of your body is **numb**, you cannot feel any- ADJ-GRADED thing there. *He could feel his fingers growing numb at their tips.* ♦ **numb·ness** *I have recently been suf-* N-UNCOUNT *fering from pain and numbness in my hands.* **2** If VERB cold weather, a drug, or a blow **numbs** a part of V n your body, you can no longer feel anything in it. *The cold numbed my fingers.*
3 If you are **numb** with shock, fear, or grief, you are so ADJ-GRADED shocked, frightened, or upset that you cannot think clearly or feel any emotion. ♦ **numbness** *Many men* N-UNCOUNT *become more aware of emotional numbness in their 40s.* ♦ **numb·ly** /ˈnʌmli/ *He walked numbly into the* ADV *cemetery.* **4** If an event or experience **numbs** you, you VERB can no longer think clearly or feel any emotion. *The* V n *shock of Philippe's letter numbed her.* ● See also **mind-numbing.** ♦ **numbed** *I'm so numbed with* ADJ-GRADED *shock that I can hardly think.*

num·ber /ˈnʌmbə/ **numbers, numbering, num-** ◆◆◆◆◆ **bered. 1** A **number** is a word such as 'two', 'nine', N-COUNT or 'twelve', or a symbol such as 1, 3, or 47. You use numbers to say how many things you are referring to or where something comes in a series. *No, I don't know the room number. ...number 3, Argyll Street.*
2 A **number** is the series of digits that you dial N-COUNT when you are making a telephone call. *Sarah sat down and dialled a number... 'You must have a wrong number,' she said. 'There's no one of that name here.'* **3** If you **number** something, you mark VERB it with a number, usually starting at 1. *He cut his* V n *paper up into tiny squares, and he numbered each one.*
4 You use **number** with words such as 'large' or N-COUNT: 'small' to say approximately how many things or peo- adj N ple there are. *Quite a considerable number of inter-views are going on... I have had an enormous number of letters from single parents.* **5** If there are a **number** N-SING: of things or people, there are several of them. If there a/any N are any **number** of things or people, there is a large quantity of them. *Sam told a number of lies... There must be any number of people in my position.*
6 One of your **number** is a member of your group. *Sci-* PHRASE *entists like the idea that one of their number is close to the seat of power.*
7 You can refer to the position of someone or some- N-UNCOUNT: thing in a list of the most successful or most popular N num of a particular type of thing as, for example, number one or **number** two. *Martin now faces the world num-ber one, Jansher Khan of Pakistan.*
8 If a group of people or things **numbers** a particular VERB total, that is how many there are. *They told me that* V num *their village numbered 100... This time the dead were* be V-ed in *numbered in hundreds, not dozens.* num
9 You can refer to a short piece of music, a song, or a N-COUNT dance as a **number**. *...'Unforgettable', a number that was written and performed in 1951.*
10 If someone or something **is numbered** among a VERB: particular group, they are believed to belong in that be V-ed group. *He numbered several Americans among his* V n among n *friends.* FORMAL
11 If you say that someone's or something's **days are** PHRASE **numbered**, you mean that they will not survive or be successful for much longer.

12 See also **opposite number, prime number, serial number.** ● **safety in numbers:** see **safety.**

'number cruncher, number crunchers. If you N-COUNT refer to **number crunchers**, you mean people INFORMAL whose jobs involve dealing with numbers or math-ematical calculations.

'number crunching. If you refer to **number** N-UNCOUNT **crunching**, you mean activities or processes con- INFORMAL cerned with numbers or mathematical calculation, for example in finance, statistics, or computing.

num·ber·less /ˈnʌmbələs/. If there are **numberless** ADJ things, there are too many to be counted. *...num-* LITERARY *berless acts of personal bravery.*

number 'one, number ones. 1 Number one ◆◆◇◇◇ means better, more important, or more popular ADJ: ADJ n than anything else of its kind. *The economy is the* INFORMAL *number one issue by far.* **2** In popular music, the N-COUNT number one is the best selling record in any one INFORMAL week, or the group or person who has made that record.

'number plate, number plates; also spelled ◆◇◇◇◇ numberplate. A **number plate** is a sign on the front N-COUNT and back of a vehicle that shows its registration BRITISH number. The American term is **license plate.** See picture headed **car** and **bicycle.**

'numbers game. If you say that someone is play- N-SING ing the **numbers game**, you are criticizing them be-cause, when considering a particular situation, they mention only those aspects of it that can be ex-pressed in numbers, which may be misleading or dishonest.

,Number 'Ten. Number Ten is often used to refer N-PROPER to 10 Downing Street, London, the official home of the British Prime Minister.

numb·skull /ˈnʌmskʌl/ **numbskulls.** If you refer N-COUNT to someone as a **numbskull**, you mean that they are DATED, very stupid. *How were we to know that he was a* INFORMAL *numbskull?*

nu·mera·cy /ˈnjuːmərəsi, AM ˈnuː-/. **Numeracy** is N-UNCOUNT the ability to do arithmetic. *...literacy and numeracy skills.*

nu·mer·al /ˈnjuːmərəl, AM ˈnuː-/ **numerals.** Nu- N-COUNT **merals** are written symbols used to represent num-bers. *...a square wristwatch with classic Roman numerals.*

nu·mer·ate /ˈnjuːmərət, AM ˈnuː-/. Someone who is ADJ-GRADED **numerate** is able to do arithmetic. *Your children should be literate and numerate.*

nu·meri·cal /njuːˈmerɪkəl, AM ˈnuː-/. **Numerical** ◆◇◇◇◇ means expressed in numbers or relating to num- ADJ bers. *Put them in numerical order.* ♦ **nu·meri·cal·** ADV **·ly** *...a numerically coded colour chart.*

nu·mer·ol·ogy /ˌnjuːməˈrɒlədʒi, AM ˌnuː-/. **Numer-** N-UNCOUNT **ology** is the study of particular numbers, such as a person's date of birth, in the belief that they may have special significance in a person's life.

nu·mer·ous /ˈnjuːmərəs, AM ˈnuː-/. If people or ◆◆◆◇◇ things are **numerous**, they exist or are present in ADJ-GRADED large numbers. *Sex crimes were just as numerous as they are today.*

nu·mi·nous /ˈnjuːmɪnəs, AM ˈnuː-/. Things that ADJ-GRADED are **numinous** are holy, awe-inspiring, and mysteri- LITERARY ous. *...the galaxy's cold, numinous stars.*

nun /nʌn/ **nuns.** A **nun** is a member of a female re- ◆◆◇◇◇ ligious community who has taken religious vows N-COUNT and promised to spend her life serving God.

nun·cio /ˈnʌnsiəʊ/ **nuncios.** In the Roman Catholic N-COUNT church, a **nuncio** is an official who represents the Pope in a foreign country.

nun·nery /ˈnʌnəri/ **nunneries.** A **nunnery** is a N-COUNT group of buildings in which a community of nuns DATED live together.

nup·tial /ˈnʌpʃəl/ **nuptials. 1** Nuptial is used to re- ADJ fer to things relating to a wedding or to marriage. DATED *...the room which he had called the nuptial cham-ber.* **2** Someone's **nuptials** are their wedding cel- N-PLURAL ebrations. *I've heard of your impending nuptials, my* DATED *dear.*

nurse /nɜːs/ **nurses, nursing, nursed. 1** A ◆◆◆◇◇ **nurse** is a person whose job is to care for people N-COUNT

N

who are ill. **2** If you **nurse** someone, you care for
them when they are ill. *She rushed home to nurse
her daughter back to health.* ♦ **nurs·ing** *She had no
aptitude for nursing.* **3** A **nurse** is a person who is
trained to look after young children. *Every morning
she got up early with the children and the nurse.*
4 If you **nurse** an illness or injury, you allow it to get
better by resting as much as possible. *Botham continues to nurse a strained groin.*
5 If you **nurse** an emotion or desire, you feel it strongly for a long time. *Jane still nurses the pain of rejection.*
6 When a baby **nurses** or when its mother **nurses** it, it
feeds by sucking milk from its mother's breast.
...young women nursing babies.
7 See also **nursery nurse**.

nurse·maid /ˈnɜːsmeɪd/ **nursemaids.** A **nurse-
maid** is a woman or girl who is paid to look after
young children.

nurse·ry /ˈnɜːsəri/ **nurseries. 1** A **nursery** is a
place where children who are not old enough to go
to school are looked after. *Her company ran its own
workplace nursery.* ● See also **day nursery. 2** A
nursery or a **nursery school** is a school for young
children who are not yet old enough to go to primary school. *...an affordable nursery education.*
3 A **nursery** is a room in a family home in which the
young children of the family sleep or play. *He has
painted murals in his children's nursery.*
4 A **nursery** is a place where plants are grown in order
to be sold. *The garden, developed over the past 35
years, includes a nursery.*

nursery·man /ˈnɜːsərimən/ **nurserymen.** A
nurseryman is a man who works in a place where
young plants are grown in order to be sold.

nursery nurse, nursery nurses. A **nursery
nurse** is a person who has been trained to look after
very young children.

nursery rhyme, nursery rhymes. A **nursery
rhyme** is a poem or song for young children, especially one that is old or well known.

nursery school, nursery schools. See
nursery.

nursing home, nursing homes. A **nursing
home** is an institution, usually private, where people who need medical care are looked after, especially old people.

nur·ture /ˈnɜːtʃə/ **nurtures, nurturing, nurtured. 1** If you **nurture** something such as a young
child or a young plant, you care for it while it is
growing and developing. *Parents want to know the
best way to nurture and raise their child to adulthood.* ♦ **nur·tur·ing** *She was not receiving warm
nurturing care.* ♦ **nurturing** *Which adult in these
children's lives will provide the nurturing they need?*
2 **Nurture** is care and encouragement that is given
to someone while they are growing and developing.
*The human organism learns partly by nature, partly
by nurture.*
3 If you **nurture** plans, ideas, or people, you actively
encourage their development and success. *She had
always nurtured great ambitions for her son.*
♦ **nurturing** *...the nurturing of new talent.*

nut /nʌt/ **nuts. 1** The firm shelled fruit of some
trees and bushes are called **nuts.** ● See also **groundnut, hazelnut.**
2 A **nut** is a small piece of metal with a hole through
which you put a bolt. Nuts and bolts are used to hold
things together such as pieces of machinery. See picture headed **tools.**
3 If you think someone is extremely enthusiastic
about a subject or activity, you can say they are a **nut**
on it. *I was a nut on records and statistics. ...a football
nut.* **4** If someone is **nuts** about something or someone, they like that thing or person very much. *They're
nuts about the car.*
5 If you refer to someone as a **nut,** you mean they are
mad. *There's some nut out there with a gun... He
thought my father was a nut.* **6** If you say that someone is **nuts,** you think they are mad or very foolish.
They were either joking or completely nuts.

7 A man's testicles are sometimes referred to as his
nuts.
8 Your head is sometimes referred to as your **nut.**
9 If someone **does** their **nut,** they become extremely
angry. *We heard your sister doing her nut.* **10** If you
talk about the **nuts and bolts** of a subject or an activity, you are referring to the detailed practical aspects
of it rather than abstract ideas about it. *He's more concerned about the nuts and bolts of location work.* **11** If
you think someone is difficult to deal with, you can
say they are a **tough nut** or a **hard nut.** *The Daily Express describes Dr Carey as a pretty tough nut.* **12** If
you say that something is **a hard nut to crack** or a
tough nut to crack, you mean that it is difficult to do
or to understand.

nut·case /ˈnʌtkeɪs/ **nutcases;** also spelled **nut
case.** If you think that someone is mad or that their
behaviour is very strange, you can say they are a
nutcase. *The woman's a nutcase. She needs locking
up.*

nut·cracker /ˈnʌtkrækə/ **nutcrackers.** A **nut-
cracker** is a device used to crack the shell of a nut.
Nutcrackers can be used to refer to one or more of
these devices.

nut·meg /ˈnʌtmeg/. **Nutmeg** is a spice used to flavour sweet food.

nu·tra·sweet /ˈnjuːtrəswiːt, AM ˈnuː-/. **Nutrasweet**
is a low-calorie substance that is used instead of
sugar to sweeten food. **Nutrasweet** is a trademark.

nu·tri·ent /ˈnjuːtriənt, AM ˈnuː-/ **nutrients. Nutrients** are chemical substances that people and animals need from food, and plants need from soil.
...minerals and other essential nutrients.

nu·tri·tion /njuːˈtrɪʃən, AM ˈnuː-/. **Nutrition** is the
process of taking food into the body and absorbing
the nutrients in those foods. *There are alternative
sources of nutrition to animal meat.*

nu·tri·tion·al /njuːˈtrɪʃənəl, AM ˈnuː-/. The **nutri-
tional** content of food is all the proteins, vitamins,
and minerals that are in it which help you to remain
healthy. ♦ **nu·tri·tion·al·ly** *...a nutritionally balanced diet.*

nu·tri·tion·ist /njuːˈtrɪʃənɪst, AM nuː-/ **nutrition-
ists.** A **nutritionist** is a person whose job is to give
advice on what you should eat to remain healthy.

nu·tri·tious /njuːˈtrɪʃəs, AM nuː-/. **Nutritious** food
contains the proteins, vitamins, and minerals which
help your body to be healthy.

nu·tri·tive /ˈnjuːtrɪtɪv, AM ˈnuː-/. The **nutritive** content of food is all the proteins, vitamins, and minerals that are in it which help you to remain healthy.

nut·shell /ˈnʌtʃel/. You can use **in a nutshell** to indicate that what you are saying summarizes your
opinions or thoughts in a very brief and concise
way. *In a nutshell, the owners thought they knew
best.*

nut·ter /ˈnʌtə/ **nutters.** If you refer to someone as
a **nutter,** you think they are mad, or that their behaviour is very strange. *Is he a joker, is he a nutter,
or is he a genius?*

nut·ty /ˈnʌti/ **nuttier, nuttiest. 1** If you describe
food as **nutty,** you mean it tastes of nuts, has the
texture of nuts, or is made with nuts. *...nutty butter
cookies... Chick peas have a distinctive, delicious
and nutty flavour.*
2 If you describe someone as **nutty,** you think their
behaviour is very strange or foolish. *He looked like a
nutty professor.*

nuz·zle /ˈnʌzəl/ **nuzzles, nuzzling, nuzzled.** If
you **nuzzle** someone or something, you gently rub
your nose and mouth against them to show affection. *The dog came and nuzzled up against me.*

NW. NW is a written abbreviation for **north-west.**

ny·lon /ˈnaɪlɒn/ **nylons. 1 Nylon** is a strong flexible artificial fibre. *Green nylon nets were piled up
like a haystack on the rear deck.* **2 Nylons** are stockings made of nylon.

nymph /nɪmf/ **nymphs. 1** In Greek and Roman
mythology, **nymphs** were spirits of nature who took
the form of young women.

2 A **nymph** is the larva of an insect such as a dragonfly. It develops into an adult without going through the stage of being a pupa. [N-COUNT]

nym·pho·ma·ni·ac /ˌnɪmfəˈmeɪniæk/ **nymphomaniacs.** If someone refers to a woman as a **nympho-** [N-COUNT] [PRAGMATICS] maniac, they mean that she has sex or wants to have sex much more often than they consider normal or acceptable; used showing disapproval. *Madame Lucia was a known nymphomaniac in Paris in the Thirties.*

O o

O, o /əʊ/ **O's, o's. 1** O is the fifteenth letter of the English alphabet. **2** O is used to mean nought or zero, particularly when you are telling someone a telephone number. **3** O is used in exclamations, especially when you are expressing strong feelings. *O how mistaken you are!* ● See also **oh. 4** O is used as an abbreviation for words beginning with o, such as 'old' or 'organization'. [N-VAR] [NUMBER] [SPOKEN] [EXCLAM] [PRAGMATICS] [LITERARY]

o' /ə/. O' is used to represent the word 'of' pronounced in a particular way. *Can we have a cup o' coffee, please?* ● See also **o'clock.** [PREP] [WRITTEN]

oaf /əʊf/ **oafs.** If you refer to someone, especially a man or boy, as an **oaf**, you think that they are impolite, clumsy, or aggressive. *You drunken oaf!* ♦ **oaf·ish** /ˈəʊfɪʃ/ *The bodyguards, as usual, were brave but oafish.* [N-COUNT] [PRAGMATICS] [ADJ-GRADED]

oak /əʊk/ **oaks.** An **oak** or an **oak tree** is a large tree that often grows in woods and forests and has strong hard wood. ▶ **Oak** is the wood of this tree. ♦ **oak·en** /ˈəʊkən/. **Oaken** means made of the wood from an oak tree. *...an oaken door.* ◆◆◇◇◇ [N-VAR] [N-UNCOUNT] [ADJ: ADJ n]

OAP /ˌəʊ eɪ ˈpiː/ **OAPs.** OAP is an abbreviation for 'old age pensioner'. An **OAP** is a person who is old enough to receive an old age pension from the government. *Tickets for students and OAP's are £4.00.* [N-COUNT] [BRITISH]

oar /ɔː/ **oars.** Oars are long poles with a wide flat blade at one end which are used for rowing a boat. ◆◇◇◇◇ [N-COUNT]

oasis /əʊˈeɪsɪs/ **oases** /əʊˈeɪsiːz/. **1** An **oasis** is a small area in a desert where water and plants are found. **2** You can refer to a pleasant place or situation as an **oasis** when it is surrounded by unpleasant ones. *The gardens are an oasis in the midst of Cairo's urban sprawl.* ◆◇◇◇◇ [N-COUNT] [N COUNT]

oath /əʊθ/ **oaths. 1** An **oath** is a formal promise, especially a promise to be loyal to a person or country. *He took an oath of loyalty to the government.* **2** In a court of law, if someone takes the **oath**, they formally promise to tell the truth, and are then legally bound to do so. You can say that someone is **on oath** or **under oath** when they have made this promise. **3** An **oath** is an offensive expression or a swear-word. *William let out a foul oath.* ◆◇◇◇◇ [N-COUNT] [N-SING: the N, also on/under N] [N-COUNT] [WRITTEN]

oat·meal /ˈəʊtmiːl/. **1** Oatmeal is a coarse flour made by crushing oats. **2** Something that is **oatmeal** is a pale creamy brown colour. ◆◇◇◇◇ [N-UNCOUNT] [N-UNCOUNT COLOUR]

oats /əʊts/, the form **oat** is used as a modifier. **1** Oats are a cereal crop or its grains, used for making porridge or feeding animals. **2** If you say that someone, especially a young person, **sows** their **wild oats**, you mean they behave in a rather uncontrolled and irresponsible way, usually in their sexual activity. ◆◇◇◇◇ [N-PLURAL] [PHRASE]

ob·du·rate /ˈɒbdjʊrət, AM -dʊr-/. If you describe someone as **obdurate**, you think that they are being stubborn in their refusal to change their mind about something. *...a suspicious, obdurate and rebellious local administration.* ♦ **ob·du·ra·cy** /ˈɒbdjʊrəsi, AM -dʊr-/ *He is known for his obduracy in a crisis.* [ADJ-GRADED] [FORMAL] [N-UNCOUNT]

obedi·ent /əʊˈbiːdiənt/. A person or animal who is **obedient** does what they are told to do. *He was always very obedient to his parents.* ♦ **obedi·ence** [N-UNCOUNT] *...unquestioning obedience to the law.* ♦ **obedi·ent·ly** *He was looking obediently at Keith.* ◆◇◇◇◇ [ADJ-GRADED] [N-UNCOUNT] [ADV-GRADED: ADV with v]

obei·sance /əʊˈbeɪsəns/ **obeisances. 1** Obeisance to someone or something is respect for them and obedience towards them. *While he was still young and strong all paid obeisance to him.* **2** An **obeisance** is a physical gesture, especially a bow, that you make in order to show your respect for someone or something. [N-UNCOUNT] [FORMAL] [N-VAR] [FORMAL]

ob·elisk /ˈɒbəlɪsk/ **obelisks.** An **obelisk** is a tall stone pillar that has been built in honour of a person or an important event. [N-COUNT]

obese /əʊˈbiːs/. If someone is **obese**, they are extremely fat. *Obese people tend to have higher blood pressure than lean people.* ♦ **obesity** /əʊˈbiːsɪti/ *Excessive consumption of sugar leads to problems of obesity.* ◆◇◇◇◇ [ADJ-GRADED] [N-UNCOUNT]

obey /əʊˈbeɪ/ **obeys, obeying, obeyed.** If you **obey** a person, a command, or an instruction, you do what you are told to do. *It was Baker's duty to obey.* ◆◆◇◇◇ [VERB: V n] [V]

ob·fus·cate /ˈɒbfʌskeɪt/ **obfuscates, obfuscating, obfuscated.** To **obfuscate** something means to deliberately make it seem confusing and difficult to understand. *They are obfuscating the issue, as only insurance companies can.* ♦ **ob·fus·ca·tion** /ˌɒbfʌsˈkeɪʃən/ *...the general obfuscation of the navy's budget.* [VERB] [V n] [Also V] [FORMAL] [N-UNCOUNT]

obi·tu·ary /əʊˈbɪtʃʊəri, AM -ʃʊeri/ **obituaries.** Someone's **obituary** is an account of their character and achievements which is published or broadcast shortly after they have died. ◆◆◇◇◇ [N-COUNT]

ob·ject, objects, objecting, objected. The noun is pronounced /ˈɒbdʒɪkt/. The verb is pronounced /əbˈdʒekt/. **1** An **object** is anything that has a fixed shape or form, that you can touch or see, and that is not alive. *He squinted his eyes as though he were studying an object on the horizon. ...an object the shape of a coconut.* **2** The **object** of what someone is doing is their aim or purpose. *The object of the exercise is to raise money for the charity.* **3** The **object of** a particular feeling or reaction is the person or thing it is directed towards, or the person or thing that causes it. *The object of her hatred was 24-year-old Ros French.* ● See also **sex object. 4** In grammar, the **object** of a verb or a preposition is the word or phrase which completes the structure begun by the verb or preposition. ● See also **direct object, indirect object. 5** If you **object** to something, you express your dislike or disapproval of it. *Cullen objected that his staff would be unable to handle the added work... 'I don't know what you're talking about,' Russ objected.* ♦ **ob·ject·or** /əbˈdʒektə/ **objectors** *The district council agreed with the objectors and turned down the application.* **6** See also **conscientious objector. 7** If you say that **money is no object**, you are emphasizing that you are willing or able to spend as much money as necessary. ◆◆◆◆◇ [N-COUNT] [N-COUNT] [N-COUNT: N of n] [N-COUNT] [VERB: V to n] [V that] [V with quote] [N-COUNT] [PHRASE] [PRAGMATICS]

ob·jec·tion /əbˈdʒekʃən/ **objections. 1** If you make or raise an **objection** to something, you say that you do not like it or agree with it. *Two main objections to the proposal have been raised.* **2** If you say that you have no **objection** to something, you mean that you are not annoyed or bothered by it. *I have no objection to banks making money.* ◆◆◇◇◇ [N-VAR] [N-UNCOUNT: with brd-neg]

ob·jec·tion·able /əb'dʒekʃənəbəl/. If you describe someone or something as **objectionable**, you consider them to be extremely offensive and unacceptable. *Such power is politically dangerous and morally objectionable.* ADJ-GRADED FORMAL

ob·jec·tive /əb'dʒektɪv/ **objectives. 1** Your **objective** is what you are trying to achieve. *His objective was to win.* ◆◆◆◇◇ N-COUNT
2 Objective information is based on facts. *He had no objective evidence that anything extraordinary was happening.* ✦ **ob·jec·tive·ly** *We simply want to inform people objectively about events.* ✦ **ob·jec·tiv·ity** /ˌɒbdʒek'tɪvɪti/. **3** If someone is **objective**, they base their opinions on facts rather than on their personal feelings. *A journalist should be completely objective.* ✦ **ob·jec·tive·ly** *Try to view situations more objectively.* ✦ **ob·jec·tiv·ity.** ADJ: ADJ n / ADV-GRADED / N-UNCOUNT / ADJ-GRADED / ADV-GRADED / N-UNCOUNT

'object lesson, object lessons. If you describe an action, event, or situation as an **object lesson**, you think that it demonstrates the correct way to do something, or that it demonstrates the truth of a particular principle. *...an object lesson in how to use television as a means of persuasion.* N-COUNT

ob·jet d'art /ˌɒbʒeɪ 'dɑː/ **objets d'art.** Objet d'arts are small ornaments or objects that are considered to have artistic merit. N-COUNT

ob·li·gate /'ɒblɪgeɪt/ **obligates, obligating, obligated.** If something **obligates** you to do a particular thing, it creates a situation where you have to do it. *The ruling obligates airlines to release information about their flight delays... I felt obligated to let him read the letter.* VERB V n to-inf V-ed

ob·li·ga·tion /ˌɒblɪ'geɪʃən/ **obligations. 1** If you have an **obligation** to do something, it is your duty to do that thing. If you have an **obligation** to a person, it is your duty to look after them or protect their interests. *When teachers assign homework, students usually feel an obligation to do it... I have an ethical and a moral obligation to my client.* **2** If a product or a service is offered **without obligation**, you do not have to pay for that product or service until you have tried it and are satisfied with it. ◆◆◇◇◇ N-VAR / PHRASE

ob·liga·tory /ə'blɪgətri, AM -tɔːri/. **1** If something is **obligatory**, you must do it because of a rule or a law. *These rates do not include the charge for obligatory medical consultations.* **2** If you describe something as **obligatory**, you mean that it is done from habit or custom rather than any sense of enthusiasm. *His lips curved up in the obligatory smile, acknowledging the compliment.* ◆◇◇◇◇ ADJ / ADJ: ADJ n

oblige /ə'blaɪdʒ/ **obliges, obliging, obliged. 1** If you **are obliged** to do something, a situation, rule, or law makes it necessary for you to do that thing. *This decree obliges unions to delay strikes.* **2** To **oblige** someone means to be helpful to them by doing what they have asked you to do. *If you ever need help with the babysitting, I'd be glad to oblige... They obliged with very straightforward answers.* **3** People sometimes use **obliged** in expressions such as '**much obliged**' or '**I am obliged to you**' when they want to indicate that they are very grateful for something. *Thank you Doctor, I am extremely obliged to you.* **4** If you tell someone that you **would be obliged** or **should be obliged** if they would do something, you are telling them in a firm polite way that you want them to do it. *I would be obliged if you could read it to us.* ◆◆◇◇◇ VERB: be V-ed to-inf V n to-inf / VERB: V n V with n / CONVENTION PRAGMATICS / CONVENTION PRAGMATICS FORMAL

oblig·ing /ə'blaɪdʒɪŋ/. If you describe someone as **obliging**, you think that they are willing and eager to be helpful. *He is an extremely pleasant and obliging man.* ✦ **oblig·ing·ly** *Benedict obligingly held the door open.* ◆◇◇◇◇ ADJ-GRADED / ADV-GRADED: ADV with v

oblique /əʊ'bliːk/. **1** An **oblique** statement is not expressed directly or openly, making it difficult to understand. *Mr Golding delivered an oblique warning, talking of the danger of sudden action.* ✦ **oblique·ly** *He obliquely referred to the US and Saudi Arabia.* **2** An **oblique** line is a straight line that is not horizontal or vertical. An **oblique** angle is any angle other than a right angle. ✦ **oblique·ly.** ◆◇◇◇◇ ADJ-GRADED / ADV / ADJ / ADV

oblit·erate /ə'blɪtəreɪt/ **obliterates, obliterating, obliterated. 1** If something **obliterates** an object or place, it destroys it completely. *Their warheads are enough to obliterate the world several times over.* ✦ **oblit·era·tion** /əˌblɪtə'reɪʃən/ *...the obliteration of three rainforests.* **2** If you **obliterate** something such as a memory, emotion, or thought, you remove it completely from your mind. ◆◇◇◇◇ VERB V n / N-UNCOUNT / VERB: V n LITERARY

obliv·ion /ə'blɪviən/. **1 Oblivion** is the state of not being aware of what is happening around you, for example because you are asleep or unconscious. *He had slipped once again into deep and dreamless oblivion.* **2 Oblivion** is the state of having been forgotten or of no longer being considered important. *The Marxist-Leninist wing of the party looks set to sink into oblivion.* **3** If you say that something is bombed or blasted **into oblivion**, you are emphasizing that it is completely destroyed, so that it is unrecognizable and seems never to have existed. ◆◇◇◇◇ N-UNCOUNT / N-UNCOUNT / N-UNCOUNT: into N PRAGMATICS

obliv·ious /ə'blɪviəs/. If you are **oblivious** to something, you are not aware of it. *She lay motionless where she was, oblivious to pain.* ✦ **obliv·ious·ly** *Burke was sprawled obliviously against the window.* ◆◇◇◇◇ ADJ-GRADED / ADV-GRADED: ADV with v

ob·long /'ɒblɒŋ, AM -lɔːŋ/ **oblongs.** An **oblong** is a shape which has two long sides and two short sides and in which all the angles are right angles. See picture headed **shapes.** N-COUNT

ob·nox·ious /ɒb'nɒkʃəs/. If you describe someone as **obnoxious**, you think that they are very unpleasant. *One of the parents was a most obnoxious character. No-one liked him.* ◆◇◇◇◇ ADJ-GRADED

oboe /'əʊbəʊ/ **oboes.** An **oboe** is a wooden orchestral instrument that is shaped like a tube and played by blowing through a reed inserted at its top. See picture headed **musical instruments.** ✦ **obo·ist, oboists.** An **oboist** is someone who plays the oboe. N-VAR / N-COUNT

ob·scene /ɒb'siːn/. **1** If you describe something as **obscene**, you mean it offends you because it relates to sex or violence in an unpleasant and shocking way. *I think these photographs are obscene. ...obscene language.* **2** In law, books, pictures, or films which are judged **obscene** are illegal because they deal with sex or violence in a way that is offensive to the general public. *A city magistrate ruled that the novel was obscene.* **3** If you describe something as **obscene**, you disapprove of it very strongly and consider it to be offensive or immoral. *It was obscene to spend millions producing unwanted food.* ◆◇◇◇◇ ADJ-GRADED / ADJ / ADJ-GRADED PRAGMATICS

ob·scen·ity /ɒb'senɪti/ **obscenities. 1 Obscenity** is behaviour or things that offend people because they relate to sex in an unpleasant or indecent way. *He insisted the photographs were not art but obscenity.* **2** An **obscenity** is a very offensive word or expression. *They shouted obscenities at us.* **3** If you refer to an action or event as an **obscenity**, you disapprove of it very strongly and consider it to be offensive or immoral. *...the obscenities of civil war.* ◆◇◇◇◇ N-UNCOUNT / N-VAR / N-COUNT PRAGMATICS

ob·scur·ant·ism /ˌɒbskjʊ'ræntɪzəm, AM ɒb'skjʊrənt-/. **Obscurantism** is the practice or policy of deliberately making something vague and difficult to understand, especially in order to prevent people from finding out the truth. ✦ **ob·scu·rant·ist** /ˌɒbskjʊ'ræntɪst, AM ɒb'skjʊrənt-/. N-UNCOUNT / ADJ-GRADED

ob·scure /ɒb'skjʊə/ **obscurer, obscurest; obscures, obscuring, obscured. 1** If something or someone is **obscure**, they are unknown, or are known by only a few people. *The origin of the custom is obscure. ...an obscure Greek composer.* ✦ **ob·scu·rity** /ɒb'skjʊərɪti/ *The latter half of his life was spent in obscurity.* **2** If one thing **obscures** another, it prevents it from being seen or heard properly. *Trees obscured his vision; he couldn't see much of the square.* **3** Something that is **obscure** is difficult to understand or deal with, usually because it involves so many parts or details. *The contracts are written in obscure language.* ✦ **obscurity** *Hunt was irritated by the obscurity of Henry's reply.* **4** To **obscure** something means to make it difficult to understand. *...the jargon that obscures educational writing.* ◆◆◇◇◇ ADJ-GRADED / ADJ-GRADED / N-UNCOUNT / VERB V n / ADJ-GRADED / N-UNCOUNT / VERB V n

ob·se·qui·ous /ɒbˈsiːkwiəs/. If you describe some- ADJ-GRADED
one as **obsequious**, you think their eagerness to PRAGMATICS
help or agree with someone is based on how important they consider that person to be; used showing
disapproval. *Barrow was positively obsequious to me
until he learnt that I was the son of a labourer.* ♦ **ob-
·se·qui·ous·ness** *His tone quickly changed from* N-UNCOUNT
obsequiousness to outright anger.

ob·serv·able /əbˈzɜːvəbəl/. Something that is **ob-** ADJ
servable can be seen. *Coffee can, in some cases,
have an observable toxic effect.*

ob·ser·vance. See **observe**.

ob·ser·vant /əbˈzɜːvənt/. **1** Someone who is **obser-** ADJ-GRADED
vant pays a lot of attention to things and notices
more about them than most people do. *An observant doctor can often detect depression from posture,
and movement.* **2** An **observant** follower of a reli- ADJ: ADJ n
gion performs all the duties that his or her religion
requires. *...a profoundly observant Islamic country.*

ob·ser·va·tion /ˌɒbzəˈveɪʃən/ **observations.** ♦♦◇◇◇
1 Observation is the action or process of carefully N-UNCOUNT
watching someone or something. *...careful observation of the movement of the planets... In hospital
she'll be under observation all the time.* ♦ **ob·ser-
·va·tion·al** /ˌɒbzəˈveɪʃənəl/ *...observational studies* ADJ
*of the early emotional relationships of young chil-
dren.* **2** An **observation** is something that you have N-COUNT
learned by seeing or watching something and think-
ing about it. *This book contains observations about
the causes of addictions.* **3** If a person makes an **ob-** N-COUNT
servation, they make a comment about something
or someone, usually as a result of watching how
they behave. *Tom Lloyd makes the observation that
companies are living entities in their own right.*
4 Observation is the ability to pay a lot of attention N-UNCOUNT
to things and to notice more about them than most
people do. *My powers of observation and memory
had improved.*

ob·ser·va·tory /əbˈzɜːvətri, AM -tɔːri/ **observa-** ♦◇◇◇
tories. An **observatory** is a building with a large N-COUNT
telescope from which scientists study the stars and
planets.

ob·serve /əbˈzɜːv/ **observes, observing, ob-** ♦♦♦◇◇
served. 1 If you **observe** someone or something, VERB
you watch them carefully, especially in order to V n
learn something about them. *Professor Stern studies V n-ing
and observes the behaviour of babies... Our sniper* Also V,
teams observed them manning an anti-aircraft gun. V n inf
2 If you **observe** someone or something, you see or VERB
notice them. *Hooke observed a reddish spot on the* V n
surface of the planet. **3** If you **observe** that some- FORMAL
thing is the case, you make a remark or comment V that
about it, especially when it is something you have V with quote
noticed and thought about a lot. *We may observe* FORMAL
*that the government in a civilised country is much
more expensive than in a barbarous one... 'He is a
fine young man,' observed Stephen.* **4** If you **observe** VERB
something such as a law or custom, you obey it or V n
follow it. *Forcing motorists to observe speed restrictions is tricky.* ♦ **ob·ser·vance, observances** *Lo-* N-VAR
*cal councils should use their powers to ensure strict
observance of laws.*

ob·serv·er /əbˈzɜːvə/ **observers. 1** You can refer ♦♦♦◇◇
to someone who sees or notices something as an N-COUNT
observer. *Observers say the woman pulled a knife
out and stabbed him in the neck.* **2** An **observer** is N-COUNT
someone who studies current events and situations. JOURNALISM
*Political observers believe that a new cabinet may be
formed shortly.* **3** An **observer** is a person who is N-COUNT
sent to observe an important event or situation, especially in order to make sure it happens as it
should, or so that they can tell other people about
it. *The president suggested that a UN observer should
attend the conference.*

ob·sess /əbˈses/ **obsesses, obsessing, ob-** ♦♦◇◇◇
sessed. If something **obsesses** you, you keep V-ERG
thinking about it and find it difficult to think about V n
anything else. *I must admit that maps obsess me...* V about/over
She stopped drinking but began obsessing about her n
Also V that

weight. ♦ **ob·sessed** /əbˈsest/ *He was obsessed with* ADJ-GRADED
American gangster movies.

ob·ses·sion /əbˈseʃən/ **obsessions.** If you say ♦♦◇◇◇
that someone has an **obsession** with someone or N-VAR
something, you feel they are spending too much of
their time thinking about that person or thing. *She
would try to forget her obsession with Christopher.*
♦ **ob·ses·sion·al** *She became almost obsessional* ADJ-GRADED
about the way she looked.

ob·ses·sive /əbˈsesɪv/ **obsessives. 1** If ♦◇◇◇
someone's behaviour is **obsessive**, they cannot stop ADJ-GRADED
doing something or thinking about something.
Williams is obsessive about motor racing. ♦ **ob·ses-
·sive·ly** *He couldn't help worrying obsessively about* ADV
what would happen. **2** An **obsessive** is someone N-COUNT
who is obsessive about something or who behaves
in an obsessive way.

ob·so·les·cence /ˌɒbsəˈlesəns/. **Obsolescence** is N-UNCOUNT
the state of being no longer needed because something newer or more efficient has been invented.
The aircraft was nearing obsolescence by early 1942.
♦ **ob·so·les·cent** /ˌɒbsəˈlesənt/ *...outmoded, obso-* ADJ
lescent equipment.

ob·so·lete /ˌɒbsəˈliːt/. Something that is **obsolete** ♦◇◇◇
is no longer needed because something better has ADJ-GRADED
been invented. *So much equipment becomes obsolete almost as soon as it's made.*

ob·sta·cle /ˈɒbstəkəl/ **obstacles. 1** An **obstacle** is ♦♦◇◇◇
an object that makes it difficult for you to go where N-COUNT
you want to go, because it is in your way. *He left her
to navigate her own way round the trolleys and other
obstacles.* **2** You can refer to anything that makes it N-COUNT
difficult for you to do something as an **obstacle**.
*Overcrowding remains a large obstacle to improving
conditions.*

ˈobstacle course, obstacle courses. An obsta- N-COUNT
cle **course** is an area of land covered with obstacles AMERICAN
such as walls or ditches, which people, especially
soldiers, run over as an exercise to improve their
skills and strength. The usual British term is **assault
course**.

ob·stet·rics /ɒbˈstetrɪks/; the form **obstetric** is used N-UNCOUNT
as a modifier. **Obstetrics** is the branch of medicine MEDICAL
that is concerned with pregnancy and childbirth.
...modern obstetric medicine. ♦ **ob·ste·tri·cian** N-COUNT
/ˌɒbstəˈtrɪʃən/ **obstetricians.** An **obstetrician** is a
doctor who is specially trained to deal with childbirth and the care of pregnant women.

ob·sti·nate /ˈɒbstɪnət/. **1** If you describe someone ♦◇◇◇
as **obstinate**, you are critical of them because they ADJ-GRADED
are very determined to do what they want, and ref- PRAGMATICS
use to change their mind or be persuaded to do
something else. *He is obstinate and determined and
will not give up.* ♦ **ob·sti·nate·ly** *Smith obstinately* ADV-GRADED
refused to carry out the order. ♦ **ob·sti·na·cy** *She* N-UNCOUNT
*was capable of great obstinacy and occasional
selfishness.* **2** You can describe things as **obstinate** ADJ-GRADED
when they are difficult to move, change, or destroy.
...the obstinate weeds. ♦ **ob·sti·nate·ly** *...the door* ADV-GRADED:
of the shop which obstinately stayed closed. ADV with v

ob·strep·er·ous /ɒbˈstrepərəs/. If you say that ADJ-GRADED
someone is **obstreperous**, you think that they are PRAGMATICS
noisy and difficult to control. *I have no intention of
being awkward and obstreperous.*

ob·struct /əbˈstrʌkt/ **obstructs, obstructing,** ♦◇◇◇
obstructed. 1 If something **obstructs** a road or VERB
path, it blocks it, stopping people or vehicles getting V n
past. *Tractors and container lorries have completely
obstructed the road.* **2** To **obstruct** someone or VERB
something, means to make it difficult for them to V n
move forward by blocking their path. *A number of
local people have been arrested for trying to obstruct
lorries loaded with logs.* **3** To **obstruct** something VERB
such as justice or progress means to prevent it from V n
happening properly or from developing. *The
authorities are obstructing a United Nations investigation.* ♦ **ob·struc·tion** /əbˈstrʌkʃən/ *Mr Guest* N-UNCOUNT
faces a criminal charge of obstruction. **4** If someone VERB
or something **obstructs** your view, they are posi- V n
tioned between you and the thing you are trying to

look at, stopping you from seeing it properly. *Claire positioned herself so as not to obstruct David's line of sight.*

ob·struc·tion /ɒbˈstrʌkʃən/ **obstructions.** An obstruction is something that blocks a road, path, or passageway. *...drivers parking near his house and causing an obstruction.* ◆◇◇◇◇ N-VAR

ob·struc·tive /ɒbˈstrʌktɪv/. If you say that someone is being **obstructive**, you think that they are intentionally causing difficulties for other people. *Mr Smith was obstructive and refused to follow correct procedure.* ADJ-GRADED

ob·tain /ɒbˈteɪn/ **obtains, obtaining, obtained.** **1** To **obtain** something means to get it or achieve it. *Evans was trying to obtain a false passport and visa.* ◆ **ob·tain·able** /ɒbˈteɪnəbəl/ *...delicious cheeses which are obtainable anywhere in France.* **2** If a situation **obtains**, it exists. *The longer this situation obtains, the more extensive the problems become .* ◆◆◆◇ VERB V n FORMAL / ADJ / VERB V FORMAL

ob·tru·sive /ɒbˈtruːsɪv/. If you say that someone or something is **obtrusive**, you think that they are noticeable in an unpleasant way. *'You are rude and obtrusive, Mr Galbraith,' said Tommy.* ADJ-GRADED

ob·tuse /əbˈtjuːs, AM -ˈtuːs/. **1** Someone who is **obtuse** has difficulty understanding things, or makes no effort to understand them. *I've really been very obtuse and stupid.* ◆ **ob·tuse·ness** *Naivety bordering on obtuseness helped sustain his faith.* **2** In mathematics, an **obtuse** angle is between 90° and 180°. Compare **acute** angle. ADJ-GRADED FORMAL / N-UNCOUNT / ADJ TECHNICAL

ob·verse /ˈɒbvɜːs/. The **obverse** of an opinion, situation, or argument is its opposite. *The obverse of rising unemployment is gains in productivity.* N-SING FORMAL

ob·vi·ate /ˈɒbvieɪt/ **obviates, obviating, obviated.** To **obviate** something such as a problem or a need means to remove it or make it unnecessary. *The use of a solicitor trained as a mediator would obviate the need for independent legal advice.* VERB V n FORMAL

ob·vi·ous /ˈɒbviəs/. **1** If something is **obvious**, it is easy to see or understand. *...an elderly person with no obvious physical or mental ailments... Determining how the Democratic challenger would conduct his presidency isn't quite so obvious.* **2** If you describe something that someone says as **obvious**, you are being critical of it because you think it is unnecessary or shows lack of imagination. *There are some very obvious phrases that we all know.* ◆ **ob·vi·ous·ness** *He was irritated by the obviousness of this opinion.* ● If you say that someone **is stating the obvious**, you mean that they are saying something that everyone already knows and understands. *It may be stating the obvious, but most teleworking at present is connected with computers.* ◆◆◆◇ ADJ-GRADED / ADJ-GRADED PRAGMATICS / N-UNCOUNT / PHRASE

ob·vi·ous·ly /ˈɒbviəsli/. **1** You use **obviously** when you are stating something that you expect your listener to know already. *Obviously, they've had sponsorship from some big companies.* **2** You use **obviously** to indicate that something is easily noticed, seen, or recognized. *They obviously appreciate you very much.* ◆◆◆◇ ADV: ADV with cl / ADV-GRADED: ADV with cl group

oc·ca·sion /əˈkeɪʒən/ **occasions, occasioning, occasioned.** **1** An **occasion** is a time when something happens, or a case of it happening. *I often think fondly of an occasion some years ago at Covent Garden.* **2** An **occasion** is an important event, ceremony, or celebration. *...taking her with me on official occasions.* **3** An **occasion for** doing something is an opportunity for doing it. *Your baby's birthday is an occasion for all the family to celebrate.* ● See also **sense of occasion**. **4** To **occasion** something means to cause it. *He argued that the release of hostages should not occasion a change in policy.* **5** If you **have occasion** to do something, it is necessary for you to do it. *We have had occasion to deal with the group on a variety of charges.* **6** If something happens **on occasion**, it happens sometimes, but not very often. *He translated not only from the French but also, on occasion, from the Polish.* **7** If you say that someone **rose to the occasion**, you mean that they did ◆◆◆◇ N-COUNT / N-COUNT / N-COUNT: N for n/-ing FORMAL / VERB V n FORMAL / PHRASE / PHRASE / PHRASE

what was necessary to successfully overcome a difficult situation. *He rose to the occasion, and got me to the station with one minute to spare!*

oc·ca·sion·al /əˈkeɪʒənəl/. **Occasional** means happening sometimes, but not regularly or often. *I've had occasional mild headaches all my life.* ◆ **oc·ca·sion·al·ly** *He still misbehaves occasionally.* ◆◆◆◇ ADJ-GRADED / ADV-GRADED

oc·ci·den·tal /ˌɒksɪˈdentəl/. **Occidental** means relating to the countries of Europe and America. *...occidental culture.* ◆◇◇◇◇ ADJ: ADJ n FORMAL

oc·cult /ɒˈkʌlt, ˈɒkʌlt/. The **occult** is the knowledge and study of supernatural or magical forces. *...books dealing with the occult. ...paganism and occult practice.* ◆ **oc·cult·ist, occultists.** An **occultist** is a person who believes in the supernatural and the power of magic. ◆◇◇◇◇ N-SING / N-COUNT

oc·cu·pan·cy /ˈɒkjupənsi/. **Occupancy** is the act of using a room, building, or area of land, usually for a fixed period of time. *Hotel occupancy has been as low as 40%.* ◆◇◇◇◇ N-UNCOUNT FORMAL

oc·cu·pant /ˈɒkjupənt/ **occupants.** **1** The **occupants** of a building or room are the people who live or work there. *Most of the occupants had left before the fire broke out.* **2** You can refer to the people who are in a place such as a room, vehicle, or bed at a particular time as the **occupants**. *He wanted the occupants of the vehicle to get out.* ◆◇◇◇◇ N-COUNT / N-PLURAL

oc·cu·pa·tion /ˌɒkjuˈpeɪʃən/ **occupations.** **1** Your **occupation** is your job or profession. *What is your occupation?... Occupation: administrative assistant.* ◆ **oc·cu·pa·tion·al** /ˌɒkjuˈpeɪʃənəl/ *...occupational assistance in the form of low-interest loans.* ◆ **oc·cu·pa·tion·al·ly** *...an occupationally related skin problem.* **2** An **occupation** is something that you do for pleasure or as part of your daily life. *Parachuting is a dangerous occupation.* **3** The **occupation** of a country is its invasion and control by a foreign army. *The communist regime was established in Romania during the Soviet occupation.* **4** The **occupation** of a building is the act or fact of someone living or working in it. ◆◆◆◇ N-COUNT / ADJ-GRADED / ADV / N-COUNT / N-UNCOUNT / N-UNCOUNT

occupational 'hazard, occupational hazards. An **occupational hazard** is something unpleasant that you may suffer or experience as a result of doing your job or hobby. *Expense is an occupational hazard of being a cat lover.* N-COUNT

occupational 'therapy. Occupational therapy is a method of helping people who have been ill or injured to develop or regain skills by giving them certain activities to do. ◆ **'occupational th'erapist, occupational therapists.** N-UNCOUNT / N-COUNT

oc·cu·pi·er /ˈɒkjupaɪə/ **occupiers.** The **occupier** of a house, flat, or piece of land is the person who lives or works there. ● See also **owner-occupier**. ◆◇◇◇◇ N-COUNT FORMAL

oc·cu·py /ˈɒkjupaɪ/ **occupies, occupying, occupied.** **1** The people who **occupy** a building or a place are the people who live or work there. *Land is, in most instances, purchased by those who occupy it.* **2** If a room or something such as a seat **is occupied**, someone is using it, so that it is not available for anyone else. *I saw three camp beds, two of which were occupied.* **3** If something **occupies** a particular area or place, it fills or covers it, or exists there. *Bookshelves occupied most of the living room walls.* **4** If something **occupies** you, or if you **occupy** yourself, your time, or your mind with it, you are busy doing that thing or thinking about it. *Her parliamentary career has occupied all of her time... He occupied himself with packing the car.* ◆ **oc·cu·pied** *I had been so occupied with other things.* **5** If something **occupies** you, it requires your efforts, attention, or time. *I had other matters to occupy me, during the day at least.* **6** If something such as a journey **occupies** a particular period of time, it takes that amount of time to complete. **7** If a group of people or an army **occupies** a place or country, they move into it, using force in order to gain control of it. *U.S. forces now occupy a part of the country. ...the occupied territories.* **8** If someone or something **occupies** a particular place in a system, process, or plan, they have that ◆◆◆◇ VERB V n / V-PASSIVE be V-ed / VERB V n / VERB V n V pron-refl with n / ADJ-GRADED / VERB V n / VERB: V n / VERB V n

place. *Many men still occupy more positions of power than women.*

oc·cur /əˈkɜː/ **occurs, occurring, occurred.** ◆◆◆◇ **1** When something **occurs**, it happens. *If headaches only occur at night, lack of oxygen is often the cause... The crash occurred when the crew shut down the wrong engine.* **2** When something **occurs** in a particular place, it exists or is present there. *The cattle disease occurs more or less anywhere in Africa where the fly occurs.* **3** If a thought or idea **occurs** to you, you suddenly think of it or realize it. *It did not occur to me to check my insurance policy... It occurred to me that I could have the book sent to me.*

VERB
V
Also there V n

VERB
V adv/prep

VB: no passive, no cont
itV to n to-inf
itV to n that

oc·cur·rence /əˈkʌrəns, AM -ˈkɜːr-/ **occurrences.** **1** An **occurrence** is something that happens. *Complaints seemed to be an everyday occurrence.* **2** The **occurrence of** something is the fact that it happens or is present. *The greatest occurrence of coronary heart disease is in those over 65.*

◆◇◇◇◇
N-COUNT
FORMAL

N-COUNT:
the N of n

ocean /ˈəʊʃən/ **oceans.** **1** The **ocean** is the sea. *There were few sights as beautiful as the calm ocean.* ♦ **ocean·ic** /ˌəʊʃiˈænɪk/ *...oceanic islands. ...oceanic plants.* **2** An **ocean** is one of the five very large areas of sea on the Earth's surface. *...the Indian Ocean.* **3** If you say that there is an **ocean** of something, you are emphasizing that there is a very large amount of it. *I had cried oceans of tears.* **4** If you say that something is **a drop in the ocean**, you mean that it is a very small amount which is unimportant compared to the cost of other things or is so small that it has very little effect on something. *His fee is a drop in the ocean compared with the real cost of broadcasting.*

N-SING◇◇
the N
ADJ

N-COUNT:
with supp

N-COUNT
PRAGMATICS
INFORMAL
PHRASE

ocean-going. Ocean-going ships are designed for travelling on the sea rather than on rivers, canals, or lakes.

ADJ

ocean·og·ra·phy /ˌəʊʃəˈnɒgrəfi/. **Oceanography** is the scientific study of sea currents, the sea bed, and the fish and animals that live in the sea. ♦ **ocean·og·ra·pher, oceanographers** *...an oceanographer working on an environmental protection programme.* ♦ **oceano·graph·ic** /ˌəʊʃənəˈgræfɪk/ *...oceanographic research.*

N-UNCOUNT

N-COUNT

ADJ

ochre /ˈəʊkə/; also spelled **ocher**. **1** Something that is **ochre** is a yellowish orange colour. **2** Ochre is coloured earth, usually red or yellow, that is used to make dyes and paints.

COLOUR

N-UNCOUNT

o'clock /əˈklɒk/. You use **o'clock** after numbers from one to twelve to say what time it is. For example, if you say that it is 9 o'clock, you mean that it is nine hours after midnight or nine hours after midday. *...ten o'clock last night. ...two o'clock in the morning.*

◆◆◇◇◇
ADV:
num ADV

Oct. Oct. is a written abbreviation for **October**. *...Tuesday Oct. 25th.*

◆◆◇◇◇

oc·ta·gon /ˈɒktəgən/ **octagons.** An **octagon** is a geometrical shape that has eight straight sides. See picture headed **shapes**. ♦ **oc·tago·nal** /ɒkˈtægənəl/ *...a white octagonal box.*

N-COUNT

ADJ

oc·tane /ˈɒkteɪn/. **Octane** is a chemical substance that exists in petrol and that is used to measure the quality of petrol. *...high octane fuel for cars.*

N-UNCOUNT

oc·tave /ˈɒktɪv/ **octaves.** An **octave** is the musical interval between the first note and the eighth note of a scale.

N-COUNT

oc·tet /ɒkˈtet/ **octets.** An **octet** is a group of eight singers or musicians.

N-COUNT

Oc·to·ber /ɒkˈtəʊbə/ **Octobers.** October is the tenth month of the year in the Western calendar. See Appendix headed **Dates**. *Most seasonal hiring is done in early October... The first plane is due to leave on October 2.*

◆◆◆◇◇
N-VAR

oc·to·genar·ian /ˌɒktəʊdʒɪˈneəriən/ **octogenarians.** An **octogenarian** is a person who is between eighty and eighty-nine years old.

N-COUNT

oc·to·pus /ˈɒktəpəs/ **octopuses.** An **octopus** is a sea creature with eight tentacles which it uses to catch food. ▶ **Octopus** is this fish eaten as food.

N-VAR

N-UNCOUNT

OD /ˌəʊ ˈdiː/ **OD's, OD'ing, OD'd.** To OD means the same as to **overdose**. *The kid OD'd a year ago.* ▶ Also a noun. *I had a friend died of an OD.*

VERB
V
INFORMAL
N-COUNT

odd /ɒd/ **odder, oddest.** **1** If you say someone or something is **odd**, you think they are strange or unusual. *He'd always been odd, but not to this extent... What an odd coincidence.* ● See also **odd-looking**. ♦ **odd·ly** *...an oddly shaped hill... His own boss was behaving rather oddly.* ♦ **odd·ness.** **2** You use **odd** before a noun to indicate that you are not mentioning the type, size, or quality of something because it is not important. *I knew that Alan liked the odd drink.* **3** You use **odd** after a number to indicate that it is only approximate. *'How long have you lived here?' — 'Twenty odd years.'* **4** Odd numbers are those which cannot be divided exactly by the number two. **5** You say that two things are **odd** when they do not belong to the same set or pair. *I'm wearing odd socks.* **6** The **odd one out** in a particular situation is a person who is different from the other people in it. *The Prime Minister is the odd man out in a mainly university-educated government.* **7** See also **odds, odds and ends.**

◆◆◆◇
ADJ-GRADED

ADV-GRADED
N-UNCOUNT
ADJ: det ADJ

ADV:
num ADV
INFORMAL

ADJ

ADJ

PHRASE

odd·ball /ˈɒdbɔːl/ **oddballs.** If you refer to someone as an **oddball**, you think they behave in a strange or peculiar way. *Jim was a bit of an oddball.* ▶ Also an adjective. *He knew many fascinating oddball characters.*

N-COUNT
INFORMAL

ADJ-GRADED

odd·ity /ˈɒdɪti/ **oddities.** **1** An **oddity** is someone or something that is very strange. *Losing my hair made me feel an oddity.* **2** The **oddity** of something is the fact that it is very strange. *...the oddities of the Welsh legal system.*

♦◇◇◇◇
N-COUNT

N-COUNT

odd-'job man, odd-job men. An odd-job man is a man who is paid to do various manual jobs, usually in somebody's home.

N-COUNT

'odd-looking. Odd-looking people or things look unusual or peculiar. *...an odd-looking couple.*

ADJ-GRADED

odd·ly /ˈɒdli/. You use **oddly** to indicate that something you are saying is not what you expected. *He seemed oddly reluctant to talk about it... Oddly, Emma says she never considered her face was attractive.* ● See also **odd.**

♦◇◇◇◇
ADV
PRAGMATICS

odd·ment /ˈɒdmənt/ **oddments.** Oddments are unimportant objects of any kind, usually ones that are old or left over from a larger group of things. *...oddments of wool.*

N-COUNT

odds /ɒdz/. **1** You refer to the probability of something happening as the **odds** that it will happen. In gambling, if you bet one pound on a horse whose odds are '10 to 1', you will receive ten pounds if the horse wins. *What are the odds of finding a parking space?* ● See also **odds-on. 2** If you say that the **odds are against** something or someone, you mean that they are unlikely to succeed. *The odds are against the scheme going ahead.* **3** If something happens **against all odds**, it happens or succeeds although it seemed impossible or very unlikely. *Some women do manage to achieve business success against all odds.* **4** If you say that **the odds are in** someone's **favour**, you mean that they are likely to succeed in what they are doing. **5** To **lengthen the odds** on something happening means to make it less likely to happen. You can also say that **the odds are lengthening**. **6** If someone is **at odds** with someone else, or if two people are **at odds**, they are disagreeing or quarrelling with each other.

♦♦◇◇◇
N-PLURAL

PHRASE

PHRASE

PHRASE

PHRASE

PHRASE

'odds and 'ends. You can refer to a disorganized group of things of various kinds as **odds and ends**. *...some clothes, odds and ends, and make-up.*

N-PLURAL
INFORMAL

'odds-'on; also spelled **odds on**. If there is an **odds-on** chance that something will happen, it is very likely that it will happen. *Gerald was no longer the odds-on favourite to win.*

♦◇◇◇◇
ADJ
INFORMAL

ode /əʊd/ **odes.** An **ode** is a poem that is usually written in praise of a particular person, thing, or event.

N-COUNT
LITERARY

odi·ous /ˈəʊdiəs/. If you describe people or things as **odious**, you think that they are extremely unpleasant. ...*the most odious man I have ever met.* ADJ-GRADED

odium /ˈəʊdiəm/. **Odium** is the dislike, disapproval, or hatred that people feel for a particular person. N-UNCOUNT FORMAL

odour /ˈəʊdə/ **odours**; spelled **odor** in American English. An **odour** is a particular and distinctive smell. *The herb has a characteristic taste and odour.* ◆◇◇◇◇ N-VAR
● See also **body odour**.

odour·less /ˈəʊdələs/; spelled **odorless** in American English. An **odourless** substance has no smell. ADJ-GRADED

od·ys·sey /ˈɒdɪsi/ **odysseys**. An **odyssey** is a long exciting journey on which a lot of things happen. ◆◇◇◇◇ N-COUNT LITERARY N-SING

Oedipus com·plex /ˈiːdɪpəs kɒmpleks/. If a boy or man has an **Oedipus complex**, he feels sexual desire for his mother and is jealous of his father.

o'er /ɔː/. **O'er** means the same as 'over'; used mainly in poetry. PREP DATED

oesopha·gus /iːˈsɒfəgəs/ **oesophaguses**; also spelled **esophagus**. Your **oesophagus** is the part of your body that carries the food from the throat to the stomach. N-COUNT

oes·tro·gen /ˈiːstrədʒən, AM ˈe-/; also spelled **estrogen**. **Oestrogen** is a hormone produced in the ovaries of female animals. ◆◇◇◇◇ N-UNCOUNT

of /əv, STRONG ɒv, AM ʌv/. **1** You use **of** to combine two nouns when the first noun identifies the feature that the second noun has that you want to talk about. *The average age of the women interviewed was only 21.5. ...the population of this town.* **2** You use **of** to combine two nouns, or a noun and a present participle, when the second noun or present participle defines or gives more information about the first noun. *She let out a little cry of pain... He had little chance of winning.* **3** You use **of** after nouns referring to actions to specify the person or thing that is affected by the action or that performs the action. *...the assessment of future senior managers. ...the death of their father.* **4** You use **of** after a name to introduce the institution or place to which a person or thing belongs or with which they are connected. *...the Prince of Wales. ...the superb temples of India.* **5** You use **of** after words and phrases referring to quantities or groups to indicate the substance or thing that is being measured. *...dozens of people. ...billions of dollars. ...a collection of short stories.* **6** You use **of** after a noun referring to a container to form an expression referring to the container and its contents. *...a cup of tea. ...a roomful of people.* **7** You use **of** after a count noun and before an uncount noun to talk about an individual thing, when several such things are normally considered as a whole. *...a blade of grass. ...one slice of bread.* **8** You use **of** after a noun which specifies a particular part or feature, to introduce the thing that it belongs to. *...the other side of the square. ...on the 23rd of July.* **9** You use **of** to indicate the materials or things that form something. *...decorations of wood and straw. ...a mixture of paint-thinner and petrol.* **10** You use **of** after some verbs to indicate someone or something else involved in the action. *He'd been dreaming of her... The Americans cannot accuse him of ignoring the problem.* **11** You use **of** after some adjectives to indicate the person or thing that a feeling or quality relates to. *I have grown very fond of Alec... She would be guilty of betraying her mother.* **12** You use **of** before a word referring to the person who performed an action when saying what you think about the action. *That's very kind of you.* **13** You use **of** after a noun which describes someone or something, to introduce the person or thing you are talking about. *...an awkward, slow-moving giant of a man.* **14** If something is **more** or **less of** a particular thing, it is that thing to a greater or lesser degree. *Your extra fat may be more of a health risk than you realize.* **15** You use **of** to indicate a characteristic or quality that someone or something has or to introduce a person or thing that has a particular quality. PREP ◆◆◆◆◆

...*the worth of their music... The new deal was considered to be the most generous of its kind.* **16** You use **of** after the verb 'be' to indicate a characteristic or quality that someone or something has. *The crisis faced over the next few months is of an entirely different scale.* **17** You use **of** to specify an amount, value, or age. *...a rise of 13.8%... I feel like a girl of 18.* **18** You use **of** after a noun such as 'month' or 'year' to indicate how long some state or activity continues. *...eight years of war... The project has gone through a dozen years of planning.* **19** You use **of** to say what time it is by indicating how many minutes there are before the hour mentioned. *...a quarter of eight in the evening.* PREP FORMAL / PREP / PREP / PREP AMERICAN

of 'course. 1 You say **of course** to suggest that something is normal, obvious, or well-known, and should therefore not surprise the person you are talking to. *Of course there were lots of other interesting things at the exhibition.* **2** You use **of course** as a polite way of giving permission. '*Could I see these documents?'—'Of course.*' **3** You use **of course** in order to emphasize a statement that you are making, especially when you are agreeing or disagreeing with someone. *Of course I'm not afraid!... 'She doesn't have to know how things work.'—'Of course she does.'* **4 Of course not** is an emphatic way of saying no. '*You won't tell him, will you?'—'Of course not.*' ◆◆◆◆◆ ADV: ADV with cl [PRAGMATICS] / CONVENTION [PRAGMATICS] SPOKEN ADV [PRAGMATICS] SPOKEN / CONVENTION [PRAGMATICS] SPOKEN

off /ɒf, AM ɔːf/. **1** If something is taken **off** something else or moves **off** it, it is no longer touching that thing. *He took his feet off the desk... Hugh wiped the blood off his face.* ▶ Also an adverb. *Lee broke off a small piece of orange.* **2** When you get **off** a bus, train, or plane, you leave it after you have been travelling on it. *As he stepped off the aeroplane, he was shot dead.* ▶ Also an adverb. *At the next stop the man got off too and introduced himself.* **3** If you keep **off** a street or piece of land, you do not step on it or go there. *The police had warned visitors to keep off the beach. ...a sign saying 'Keep Off.'* **4** When you take **off** something that you are wearing, you remove it from your body. *He hastily stripped off his old uniform.* **5** If something is situated **off** a place such as a coast, room, or road, it is near to it or next to it, but not exactly in it. *The boat was anchored off the northern coast. ...a penthouse just off Park Avenue.* **6** If you go **off**, you leave a place. *He was just about to drive off... She was off again. Last year she had been to Kenya. This year it was Goa. ...when his master's off traveling.* **7 Off** is used in a number of informal phrasal verbs, such as **buzz off** or **clear off**, which are used to tell someone angrily to go away. **8** If you have time **off**, you do not go to work or school, for example because you are ill or it is a day when you do not usually work. *The rest of the men had the day off... The average Swede was off sick 27 days last year.* ▶ Also a preposition. *He could not get time off work.* **9** If you keep **off** a subject, you deliberately avoid talking about it. *Keep off the subject of politics.* **10** If something such as an agreement or a sporting event is **off**, it is cancelled. *The deal's off... Greenpeace refused to call off the event.* **11** If someone is **off** something harmful such as a drug, they have stopped taking or using it. *The psychiatrist took her off drug therapy.* **12** If you are **off** something, you have stopped liking it. *I'm off coffee at the moment.* **13** When something such as a machine or electric light is **off**, it is not functioning or in use. When you switch it **off**, you stop it functioning. *He saw her bedroom light was off... The microphones had been switched off.* **14** If there is money **off** something, its price is reduced by the amount specified. *...discounts offering thousands of pounds off the normal price of a car.* ▶ Also an adverb. *I'm prepared to knock five hundred pounds off but no more.* **15** If something is a long way **off**, it is a long distance away from you. *...animals that from a long way off* ◆◆◆◆◆ PREP / PREP / ADV / ADV / ADV: ADV after v / PREP / ADV / ADV: ADV after v / ADV / PREP / PREP / ADV / PREP / PREP / PREP / ADV / ADV: n/amount ADV

look like flies... Below you, though still 50 miles off, is the most treeless stretch of land imaginable. **16** If something is a long time **off**, it will not happen for a long time. *The required technology is probably still two years off.* | ADV: n/amount | ADV

17 If you get something **off** someone, you obtain it from them. *I don't really get a lot of information, and if I do I get it off Mark.* | PREP | SPOKEN

18 Off combines with adverbs such as 'well', 'badly', and 'worse' to form adjectives that indicate how poor or rich someone is. *He's very comfortably off.* | COMB

19 If food has gone **off**, it tastes and smells bad because it is no longer fresh enough to be eaten. | ADJ-GRADED: v-link ADJ BRITISH

20 If you live **off** a particular kind of food, you eat it in order to live. If you live **off** a particular source of money, you use it to live. *Paul had been living off the sale of his own paintings.* **21** If a machine runs **off** a particular kind of fuel or power, it uses that power in order to function. *The Auto Compact Disc Cleaner can run off batteries.* | PREP | PREP

22 If you say that someone's behaviour is a bit **off**, you mean that you find it unacceptable or wrong. | ADJ-GRADED: v-link adv ADJ INFORMAL

23 If something happens **on and off**, or **off and on**, it happens occasionally, or only for part of a period of time, not in a regular or continuous way. *I was still working on and off as a waitress.* | PHRASE

off-'air; also spelled **off air**. In radio or television, when a programme goes **off-air** or when something happens **off-air**, it is not broadcast. *The argument continued off air.* ▸ Also an adjective. *...a special off-air advice line.* | ADV | ADJ: ADJ n

of·fal /'ɒfəl, AM 'ɔːfəl/. **Offal** consists of the internal organs of animals, for example their hearts and livers, when they are cooked and eaten. | N-UNCOUNT

off-'balance; also spelled **off balance**. **1** If someone or something is **off-balance**, they can easily fall or be knocked over because they are not standing firmly. *The lunge had thrown him off-balance.* **2** If someone is caught **off-balance**, they are extremely surprised or upset by a particular event or piece of news they are not expecting. *He knocked me off-balance with his abrupt change of subject.* | ◆◇◇◇◇ ADJ-GRADED: v-link ADJ, v n ADJ v-link ADJ-GRADED

off 'balance sheet. In finance, an **off balance sheet** transaction is one that is not recorded in a company's balance sheets. | ADJ

off-'beam; also spelled **off beam**. If you describe something or someone as **off-beam**, you mean that they are wrong, mistaken, or inaccurate. *Everything she says is a little off beam.* | ADJ-GRADED INFORMAL

off·beat /ˌɒf'biːt, AM ˌɔːf-/; also spelled **off-beat**. If you describe something or someone as **offbeat**, you think that they are different from normal. *She adores old, offbeat antiques.* | ADJ-GRADED

off-Broadway /ˌɒf 'brɔːdweɪ, AM ˌɔːf -/. An **off-Broadway** play is less commercial and often more experimental than those usually staged in Broadway, the main theatre district in New York. *...adapted from the off-Broadway stage show.* | ADJ: ADJ n

off-'centre; spelled **off-center** in American English. **1** If something is **off-centre**, it is not exactly in the middle of a space or surface. *The pedals seem a bit off-centre.* **2** If you describe someone or something as **off-centre**, you mean that they are less conventional than other people or things. *Davies's writing is far too off-centre to be commercial.* | ADJ-GRADED ADJ-GRADED

'off-chance; also spelled **offchance**. If you do something **on the off-chance**, you do it because you hope that it will succeed, although you think that this is unlikely. *He had taken a flight to Paris on the off-chance that he might be able to meet her.* | PHRASE

off-'colour; spelled **off-color** in American English. **1** If you say that you are feeling **off-colour**, you mean that you are slightly ill. **2** If journalists say that someone's performance is **off-colour**, they mean that they are not performing as well as they usually do. | ADJ-GRADED: v-link ADJ BRITISH ADJ-GRADED BRITISH

'off day, off days; also spelled **off-day**. If someone has an **off day**, they do not perform as well as usual. | N-COUNT INFORMAL

off 'duty. When someone such as a soldier or policeman is **off duty**, they are not working. *Lisa's body was discovered by an off-duty policeman.* | ◆◇◇◇◇ ADJ

of·fence /ə'fens/ **offences**; spelled **offense** in American English. The pronunciation /'ɒfens/ is used for meaning 6. **1** An **offence** is a crime that breaks a particular law and requires a particular punishment. *It is a criminal offence to sell goods that are unsafe.* | ◆◆◆◇◇ N-COUNT

2 Offence or an **offence** is behaviour which causes people to be upset or embarrassed. *The book might be published without creating offense.* **3** If you **cause offence** or **give offence** to someone, you upset or embarrass them, for example by being rude or tactless. *The photograph is likely cause offence to the public.* **4** Some people say **'no offence'** to reassure you that they do not want to upset you, although what they are saying may seem rude. *No offence to her, but I know prettier girls than she.* **5** If someone **takes offence** at something you say or do, they feel upset, often unnecessarily, because they think you are being rude to them. *She never takes offence at anything.* | N-VAR PHRASE CONVENTION PRAGMATICS PHRASE

6 In sports such as American football, ice hockey, or basketball, **the offense** is the team which has possession of the ball and is trying to score. | N-SING: the N AMERICAN

of·fend /ə'fend/ **offends, offending, offended**. **1** If you **offend** someone, you upset or embarrass them by doing something rude or tactless. *Television censors are cutting out scenes which they claim may offend.* ◆ **of·fend·ed** *She is terribly offended, angered and hurt by this.* **2** To **offend** against a law, rule, or principle means to break it. *This bill offends against good sense and against justice.* **3** If someone **offends**, they commit a crime. *In Western countries girls are far less likely to offend than boys.* ◆ **of·fend·er, offenders** *...an open prison for young offenders.* | ◆◆◇◇◇ VERB: V n V ADJ-GRADED VERB V against n FORMAL VB: no cont V FORMAL N-COUNT

of·fend·er /ə'fendə/ **offenders**. You can refer to someone or something which you think is causing a problem as an **offender**. *The contraceptive pill is the worst offender, but it is not the only drug to deplete the body's vitamin levels.* | ◆◇◇◇ N-COUNT

of·fend·ing /ə'fendɪŋ/. You can use **offending** to describe something that is causing a problem that needs to be dealt with. *The dentist commenced to drill the offending tooth.* | ◆◇◇◇ ADJ-GRADED: the ADJ n

of·fense /ə'fens, 'ɒfens/. See **offence**.

of·fen·sive /ə'fensɪv/ **offensives**. **1** If you say that something is **offensive**, you mean that it upsets or embarrasses you because it is rude or insulting. *Some friends of his found the play horribly offensive.* ◆ **of·fen·sive·ly** *The group who had been shouting offensively opened to let her through.* **2** A military **offensive** is a carefully planned attack made by a large group of soldiers. **3** If you conduct an **offensive**, you take strong action to show how angry you are about something or how much you disapprove of something. *Republicans had little choice but to mount an all-out offensive on the Democratic nominee.* **4** If you **go on the offensive**, **go over to the offensive**, or **take the offensive**, you begin to take strong action against people who have been attacking you. | ◆◆◇◇◇ ADJ-GRADED ADV-GRADED N-COUNT N-COUNT PHRASE

of·fer /'ɒfə, AM 'ɔːfər/ **offers, offering, offered**. **1** If you **offer** something to someone, you ask them if they would like to have it or use it. *He has offered seats at the conference table to the Russian leader... Rhys offered him an apple.* **2** If you **offer** to do something, you say that you are willing to do it. *Peter offered to teach them water-skiing... 'Can I get you a drink?' she offered.* **3** An **offer** is something that someone says they will give you or do for you. *I ought to reconsider her offer to move in. ...several excellent job offers.* **4** If you **offer** someone information, advice, or praise, you give it to them, usually because you feel that they need it or deserve it. *...a company offering advice on mergers and acquisitions... Western leaders, who had been offering Yeltsin moral support.* **5** If you **offer** someone something such as love or friendship, you | ◆◆◆◆ VERB V n to n V n n Also V n VERB V to-inf V with quote N-COUNT VERB V n V n n Also V n to n VERB V n to n V n

show them that you feel that way towards them. *The President has offered his sympathy to the Georgian people... John's mother and sister rallied round offering comfort.* `Also V n n`

6 If people **offer** prayers, praise, or a sacrifice to a god, they worship a god in one of those ways. *Church leaders offered prayers... He will offer the first harvest of rice to the sun goddess.* ▶ **Offer up** means the same as **offer**. *He should consider offering up a prayer.* `VERB` `V n` `V n ton` `Also V n n` `PHRASAL VB` `V P noun`

7 If an organization **offers** something such as a service or product, it provides it. *We are offering a quality service... Sainsbury's is offering customers 1p for each shopping bag re-used.* `VERB` `V n` `V n n` `Also V n ton`

8 An **offer** in a shop is a specially low price for a specific product or something extra that you get if you buy a certain product. *Co-op prawn salad is on offer at £1.79.* `N-COUNT`

9 If you **offer** a particular amount of money for something, you say that you will pay that much to buy it. *They are offering farmers $2.15 a bushel for corn... He will offer her a fair price for the land.* 10 An **offer** is the amount of money that someone says they will pay to buy something. *No one else will make me an offer.* `VERB:` `V amount` `V n amount` `V n n` `N-COUNT`

11 If you are **open to offers**, you are willing to sell something or do something if someone will pay you an amount of money that you think is reasonable. *I am available for employment from July 1 and am open to offers.* `PHRASE`

12 If someone or something **has something to offer**, they have a particular quality or ability that makes them important, attractive, or useful. *Explore all that this incredible city has to offer.* 13 If there is something **on offer**, it is available to be used or bought. *Savings schemes are the best retail investment products on offer.* `PHRASE` `PHRASE`

offer up. See **offer** 6. `PHRASAL VB`

of·fer·ing /ˈɒfərɪŋ, AM ˈɔːf-/ **offerings.** 1 An **offering** is something that is specially produced to be sold. *...Provençal offerings such as aioli with salt cod.* 2 An **offering** is something that people offer to their God or gods as a sacrifice. `◆◆◇◇` `N-COUNT` `N-COUNT`

of·fer·tory /ˈɒfətri, AM ˈɔːfətɔːri/ **offertories.** In the Christian Mass, the **offertory** is the part of the service where the bread and wine of the Eucharist is offered to God by the priest. `N-COUNT`

off-'guard. If someone is caught **off-guard**, they are not expecting a surprise or danger that suddenly occurs. *He was caught completely off-guard.* `ADJ-GRADED` `v n ADJ,` `v-link ADJ`

off-'hand; also spelled **off hand.** 1 If you say that someone is being **off-hand**, you are critical of them for being unfriendly or impolite, and not showing any interest in what other people are doing or saying. *Consumers found the attitude of its staff off-hand and generally offensive.* 2 If you say something **off-hand**, you say it without checking the details or facts of it. *Were they at home or away, do you know off hand?* `ADJ-GRADED` `PRAGMATICS` `ADV:` `ADV after v`

of·fice /ˈɒfɪs, AM ˈɔːf-/ **offices.** 1 An **office** is a room or a part of a building where people work sitting at desks. *At about 4.30 p.m. Audrey arrived at the office.* 2 An **office** is a small building or room where people can go for information, tickets, or a service of some kind. *...the tourist office.* `◆◆◆◆◆` `N-COUNT` `N-COUNT`

3 An **office** is a department of an organization, especially the government, where people deal with a particular kind of administrative work. *...Downing Street's press office.* `N-COUNT`

4 If someone holds **office** in a government, they have an important job or position of authority. *...events to mark the President's ten years in office.* `N-UNCOUNT`

5 Someone's **good offices** are the help that they give to other people who are trying to achieve something. *She sought the good offices of the President for the smooth passage of the bill.* `PHRASE` `FORMAL`

6 See also **booking office**, **box office**, **post office**, **register office**, **registry office**.

office boy, office boys. An **office boy** is a young man, especially one who has just left school, who is employed in an office to do simple tasks. `N-COUNT` `DATED`

office-holder, office-holders; also spelled **office holder**. An **office-holder** is a person who has an important official position in an organization. *They appear to be in a mood to vote against office-holders in the elections.* `N-COUNT` `FORMAL`

office 'hours. Office hours are the times when an office or similar place of work is open for business. `N-PLURAL`

of·fic·er /ˈɒfɪsə, AM ˈɔːf-/ **officers.** 1 In the armed forces, an **officer** is a person in a position of authority. 2 An **officer** is a person who has a responsible position in an organization, especially a government organization. *...a local authority education officer.* 3 Members of the police force can be referred to as **officers**. *...senior officers in the West Midlands police force... Thank you, Officer.* 4 See also **petty officer**, **pilot officer**, **police officer**, **probation officer**, **returning officer**, **warrant officer**. `◆◆◆◆` `N-COUNT` `N-COUNT` `N-COUNT`

of·fi·cial /əˈfɪʃəl/ **officials.** 1 Official means approved by the government or by someone in authority. *According to the official figures, over one thousand people died.* ♦ **of·fi·cial·ly** *The election results have still not been officially announced.* 2 Official activities are carried out by a person in authority as part of their job. *The President is in Brazil for an official two-day visit.* 3 Official things are used by a person in authority as part of their job. *...the official residence of the Head of State.* `◆◆◆◆` `ADJ` `ADV` `ADJ: ADJ n` `ADJ: ADJ n`

4 An **official** is a person who holds a position of authority in an organization. *...a senior UN official.* `N-COUNT`

5 If you describe someone's explanation or reason for something as the **official** explanation, you are suggesting that it is probably not true, but is used because the real explanation is embarrassing. *The official reason given for the President's absence was sickness.* ♦ **officially** *Officially, the guard was to protect us. In fact, they were there to report on our movements.* `ADJ: ADJ n` `PRAGMATICS` `ADV`

of·fi·cial·dom /əˈfɪʃəldəm/. **Officialdom** is used to refer to government officials or officials in other organizations, especially when you think their rules and regulations make them slow and unhelpful. `N-UNCOUNT`

of·fi·ci·ate /əˈfɪʃieɪt/ **officiates, officiating, officiated.** 1 When someone **officiates** at a ceremony or formal occasion, he or she is in charge and performs the official part of the ceremony. *Bishop Silvester officiated at the funeral.* 2 When someone **officiates** at a sports match or competition, he or she acts as the referee or umpire. `VERB` `V` `VERB: V`

of·fi·cious /əˈfɪʃəs/. If you describe someone as **officious**, you are critical of them because they are eager to tell people what to do when you think they should not. *They wouldn't welcome any officious interference from the police.* ♦ **of·fi·cious·ly** *Lance Corporal Williams officiously ordered them out.* `ADJ-GRADED` `PRAGMATICS` `ADV:` `ADV with v`

of·fing /ˈɒfɪŋ, AM ˈɔːf-/. If you say that something is **in the offing**, you mean that it is likely to happen soon. *A general amnesty for political prisoners may be in the offing.* `PHRASE`

off-'key. When music is **off-key**, it is not in tune. *...wailing, off-key vocals and strangled guitars.* ▶ Also an adverb. *Laura couldn't sing off-key if she tried.* `ADJ-GRADED` `ADV-GRADED:` `ADV after v`

off-licence, off-licences. An **off-licence** is a shop which sells beer, wine, and other alcoholic drinks, as well as cigarettes. The usual American expression is **liquor store**. `N-COUNT` `BRITISH`

off 'limits; also spelled **off-limits.** 1 If a place is **off limits** to someone, they are not allowed to go there. *Downing Street has been off limits to the general public since 1982.* 2 If you say that an activity or a substance is **off limits** for someone, you mean that they are not allowed to do it or have it. *For Di, such pleasures are strictly off limits.* `ADJ` `ADJ-GRADED`

off·load /ˌɒfˈləʊd, AM ˌɔːf-/ **offloads, offloading, offloaded.** 1 If you **offload** something that you do not want, you get rid of it by giving it or selling it to someone else. *Prices have been cut by developers anxious to offload unsold apartments.* 2 When goods **are offloaded**, they are removed from a container or vehicle and put somewhere else. *The cargo was due to be offloaded in Singapore.* `VERB` `V n` `Also V n onto n` `VERB` `be V-ed` `Also V n`

off-'peak. You use **off-peak** to describe something that happens or that is used at times when there is least demand for it. Prices at off-peak times are often lower than at other times. ► Also an adverb. *Each tape lasts three minutes and costs 36p per minute off-peak.* `ADJ: ADJ n` `ADV: ADV after v`

off-'putting. If you describe someone as **off-putting**, you mean that they make you feel uneasy or uncomfortable. If you describe something as **off-putting**, you mean that it makes you dislike that thing. *I hope that you will not find my presence off-putting.* `ADJ-GRADED`

off-'screen; also spelled **offscreen**. You use **off-screen** to refer to the real lives of film or television actors, in contrast with the lives of the characters they play. *He was immensely attractive to women, onscreen and offscreen.* ► Also an adjective. *...an off-screen romance.* `ADV: ADV with cl` `ADJ: ADJ n`

'off season; also spelled **off-season. 1** The **off season** is the time of the year when not many people go on holiday and when things such as hotels and plane tickets are often cheaper. *It is possible to vacation at some of the more expensive resorts if you go in the off-season. ...off-season prices.* ► Also an adverb. *Times become more flexible off-season, especially in the smaller provincial museums.* **2** The **off season** is the time of the year when a particular sport is not played. *...intensive off-season training.* ► Also an adverb. *To stay fit off season, I play tennis or football.* `N-SING: also no det` `ADV` `N-SING` `ADV`

off·set /ˈɒfˌset, AM ˌɔːf-/ **offsets, offsetting.** The form **offset** is used in the present tense and is the past tense and past participle of the verb. If one thing **is offset** by another, the effect of the first thing is reduced or cancelled out, so that any advantage or disadvantage is cancelled out. *The increase in pay costs was offset by higher productivity.* `♦♦◇◇◇` `VERB` `be V-ed` `Also V n`

off·shoot /ˈɒfˌʃuːt, AM ˈɔːf-/ **offshoots.** If one thing is an **offshoot** of another, it has developed from that other thing. *Psychology began as a purely academic offshoot of natural philosophy.* `♦◇◇◇◇` `N-COUNT`

off·shore /ˌɒfˈʃɔː, AM ˌɔːf-/; also spelled **off-shore. 1 Offshore** means situated or happening in the sea, near to the coast. *...Britain's offshore oil industry.* ► Also an adverb. *One day a larger ship anchored offshore.* **2 Offshore** investments or companies are located in a place, usually an island, which has fewer tax regulations than most other countries. `♦♦◇◇◇` `ADJ: ADJ n` `ADV` `ADJ: ADJ n`

off·side /ˌɒfˈsaɪd, AM ˌɔːf-/; also spelled **off-side. 1** In games such as football or hockey, when an attacking player is **offside**, they have broken the rules by being nearer to the goal than a defending player when the ball is passed to them. ► Also an adverb. *Wise was standing at least ten yards offside.* ► Also a noun. *...a goal disallowed for offside.* **2** The **offside** of a vehicle is the side that is furthest from the edge of the road when you are driving. `♦◇◇◇◇` `ADJ` `ADV` `N-UNCOUNT` `N-SING` `BRITISH`

off·spring /ˈɒfsprɪŋ, AM ˈɔːf-/ **offspring** is both the singular and plural form. You can refer to a person's children or to an animal's young as their **offspring**. `♦◇◇◇◇` `N-COUNT` `FORMAL`

off·stage /ˌɒfˈsteɪdʒ, AM ˌɔːf-/; also spelled **off-stage. 1** When an actor or entertainer goes **offstage**, they go into the area behind or to the side of the stage, so that the audience no longer sees them. *She ran offstage in tears... There was a lot of noise offstage.* ► Also an adjective. *I was not alone in my reaction to the appalling, amateurish-sounding off-stage voices.* **2 Offstage** is used to describe the behaviour of actors or entertainers in real life, when they are not performing. *...the tragedies of their off-stage lives.* ► Also an adverb. *Off-stage they are close friends.* `ADV` `ADJ` `ADJ: ADJ n` `ADV: ADV with cl`

,off-the-'cuff. See **cuff**.
,off-the-'peg. See **peg**.
,off-the-'record. See **record**.
,off-the-'shelf. See **shelf**.
,off-the-'wall. 1 If you describe something as **off-the-wall**, you mean that it is unusual and rather strange but in an amusing or interesting way. *...surreal off-the-wall humor.* **2** If you say that a person, `♦◇◇◇◇` `ADJ-GRADED` `ADJ-GRADED`

their ideas, or their ways of doing something are **off-the-wall**, you are critical of them because you think they are mad or very foolish. *...some absurd, off-the-wall investment strategy.* `PRAGMATICS`

,off-'white. Something that is **off-white** is not pure white, but slightly grey or yellow. `COLOUR`

oft- /ɒft-, AM ɔːft-/. **Oft** combines with past participles to form adjectives that mean that something happens or is done often. *These were oft-repeated legal arguments.* `COMB` `LITERARY`

of·ten /ˈɒfən, AM ˈɔːf-/. **1** If something **often** happens, it happens many times or much of the time. *They often spent Christmas at Prescott Hill... They used these words freely, often in front of their parents too... That doesn't happen very often.* **2** You use **often** after 'how' to ask questions about frequency. You also use **often** in reported clauses and other statements to give information about the frequency of something. *How often do you brush your teeth?... They jog twice as often as the general population.* **3** If something happens **every so often**, it happens regularly, but with fairly long intervals between each occasion. *Every so often he would turn and look at her.* **4** If you say that something happens **as often as not**, or **more often than not**, you mean that it happens fairly frequently, and that this can be considered as typical of the kind of situation you are talking about. *As often as not it was something quite trivial that generated my worst rages.* `♦♦♦♦♦` `ADV-GRADED` `ADV` `PHRASE` `PHRASE`

often·times /ˈɒfənˌtaɪmz, AM ˈɔːf-/. If something **oftentimes** happens, it happens many times or much of the time. The usual British word is **often**. *Oftentimes, I wouldn't even return the calls... It was oftentimes difficult to discuss certain issues.* `ADV` `AMERICAN`

ogle /ˈəʊɡəl/ **ogles, ogling, ogled.** If you say that one person is **ogling** another, you disapprove of them continually staring at that person in a way that indicates a strong sexual interest. *All she did was hang around ogling the men... Paula is not used to everyone ogling at her while she undresses.* `VERB` `PRAGMATICS` `V n` `V at n` `Also V`

ogre /ˈəʊɡə/ **ogres. 1** If you refer to someone as an **ogre**, you are saying in a humorous way that they are very frightening. *Bank managers do not really like being thought of as ogres.* **2** In stories, an **ogre** is a cruel, frightening giant who often eats people. `N-COUNT` `N-COUNT`

oh /əʊ/. **1** You use **oh** to introduce a response or a comment on something that has just been said. *'Would you like me to phone and explain the situation?'—'Oh, would you?'* **2** You use **oh** to express a feeling such as surprise, pain, annoyance, or joy. *'Oh!' Kenny blinked. 'Has everyone gone?'... 'Oh, my God,' Korontzis moaned.* ● See also **o. 3** You use **oh** when you are hesitating while speaking, for example because you are trying to estimate something, or because you are searching for the right word. *I've been here, oh, since the end of June.* `♦♦♦♦♦` `CONVENTION` `PRAGMATICS` `SPOKEN` `EXCLAM` `SPOKEN` `CONVENTION` `PRAGMATICS` `SPOKEN`

ohm /əʊm/ **ohms.** An **ohm** is a unit which is used to measure electrical resistance. *...a resistance of 40 ohms.* `N-COUNT` `TECHNICAL`

OHMS /ˌəʊ eɪtʃ em 'es/. **OHMS** is the abbreviation for 'On Her Majesty's Service' or 'On His Majesty's Service'. It is used on official letters from British or Commonwealth government offices.

OHP /ˌəʊ eɪtʃ 'piː/ **OHPs.** An **OHP** is the same as an **overhead projector**. `N-COUNT`

oik /ɔɪk/ **oiks.** If you refer to someone as an **oik**, you think that they behave in a rude or uncivilized way. `N-COUNT` `BRITISH, INFORMAL`

oil /ɔɪl/ **oils, oiling, oiled. 1 Oil** is a smooth thick liquid that is used as a fuel and for lubricating machines. Oil is found underground. *The company buys and sells about 600,000 barrels of oil a day. ...a small oil-lamp.* **2** If you **oil** something, you put oil onto or into it, for example to make it work smoothly or to protect it. *A crew of assistants oiled and adjusted the release mechanism.* ♦ **oiled** *Oiled wood is water-resistant and won't flake.* ● See also **well-oiled. 3 Oil** is a smooth thick liquid made from plants or fish and used in cookery. *...olive oil.* **4 Oil** is a smooth thick liquid that is often scented and `♦♦♦♦♦` `N-VAR` `VERB` `V n` `ADJ-GRADED` `N-VAR` `N-VAR`

that you rub into your skin or add to your bath.

5 Oils are **oil paintings**. *Her colourful oils and* N-COUNT *works on paper have a naive, dreamlike quality.*

6 When an artist paints in **oils** he or she uses oil N-PLURAL paints.

7 See also **crude oil**, **olive oil**.

8 If you **pour oil on troubled waters**, you try to calm PHRASE down a difficult situation. **9** If someone or something PHRASE **oils the wheels** of a process or system, they help things to run smoothly and successfully. **10** ● to **burn the midnight oil**: see **midnight**.

oil·cloth /ˈɔɪlklɒθ, AM -klɔːθ/ **oilcloths**. **1** Oilcloth N-UNCOUNT is a cotton fabric with a shiny waterproof surface. **2** An **oilcloth** is a covering such as a tablecloth N-COUNT which has been made from oilcloth.

oil·field /ˈɔɪlfiːld/ **oilfields**; also spelled **oil field**. ◆◇◇◇◇ An **oilfield** is an area under which there is oil. N-COUNT

'oil-fired. **Oil-fired** heating systems and power sta- ADJ: ADJ n tions use oil as a fuel.

oil·man /ˈɔɪlmæn/ **oilmen**; also spelled **oil man**. An N-COUNT **oilman** is a man who owns an oil company or who works in the oil business, for example on an oil rig.

'oil paint, oil paints. Oil paint is a thick paint N-UNCOUNT: used by artists. also N in pl

'oil painting, oil paintings. An **oil painting** is a N-COUNT picture which has been painted using oil paints.

'oil platform, oil platforms. An **oil platform** is a N-COUNT structure that is used as a base when drilling for oil from the sea.

'oil rig, oil rigs. An **oil rig** is a structure on land or N-COUNT in the sea that is used as a base when drilling for oil.

oilseed rape /ˌɔɪlsiːd ˈreɪp/. **Oilseed rape** is a plant N-UNCOUNT with yellow flowers which is grown as a crop. Its seeds are crushed to make cooking oil.

oil·skins /ˈɔɪlskɪnz/. **Oilskins** consist of a coat and N-PLURAL a pair of trousers made from thick waterproof cotton cloth.

'oil slick, oil slicks. An **oil slick** is a layer of oil ◆◇◇◇◇ that floats on the sea or on a lake. It is formed when N-COUNT oil accidentally spills out of a ship or container.

'oil tanker, oil tankers. An **oil tanker** is a ship ◆◇◇◇◇ that is used for transporting oil. N-COUNT

'oil well, oil wells. An **oil well** is a hole which is ◆◇◇◇◇ drilled into the ground or the seabed in order to ex- N-COUNT tract oil.

oily /ˈɔɪli/ **oilier, oiliest**. **1** Something that is **oily** ◆◇◇◇◇ is covered with oil or contains oil. *...an oily rag...* ADJ-GRADED *Paul found the sauce too oily.* **2** Oily means looking, ADJ-GRADED feeling, tasting, or smelling like oil. **3** If you describe ADJ-GRADED someone as **oily**, you dislike them because you PRAGMATICS think they flatter people too much or are excessively but insincerely polite.

oint·ment /ˈɔɪntmənt/ **ointments**. **1** An **ointment** ◆◇◇◇◇ is a smooth thick substance that is put on sore skin N-VAR or a wound to help it heal. *A range of ointments and creams is available for the treatment of eczema.* **2** If PHRASE you describe someone or something as a **fly in the ointment**, you think they spoil a situation and prevent it being as successful as you had hoped.

okay /ˌəʊˈkeɪ/ **okays, okaying, okayed**; also ◆◆◆◆◇ spelled **OK**. **1** If you say that something is **okay**, you ADJ find it satisfactory or acceptable. *...a shooting range* INFORMAL *where it's OK to use weapons... Is it okay if I come by myself?* ▶ Also an adverb. *We seemed to manage* ADV *okay for the first year.* **2** You can say **'Okay'** to show CONVENTION that you agree to something. *'Shall I give you a ring* PRAGMATICS *on Friday?'—'Yeah okay.'* **3** You can say **'Okay?'** to INFORMAL check whether the person you are talking to under- CONVENTION stands what you have said and accepts it. *We'll get* INFORMAL *together next week, OK?* **4** If someone in authority VERB **okays** something, they officially agree to it or allow V n it to happen. *His doctor wouldn't OK the trip.* ▶ Also INFORMAL a noun. *Reluctantly, he gave the okay to issue a new* N-SING: *press release.* the N

5 If you say that someone is **okay**, you mean that they ADJ: are safe and well. *Check that the baby's okay.* v-link ADJ INFORMAL

6 You can use **okay** to indicate to someone that you CONVENTION want to start talking about something else or doing PRAGMATICS something else. *OK. Now, let's talk some business.* INFORMAL

7 You can use **okay** to stop someone arguing with you CONVENTION by showing that you accept the point they are mak- PRAGMATICS ing, though you do not necessarily regard it as very INFORMAL important. *Okay, so I'm forty-two.*

okra /ˈɒkrə/. **Okra** is a vegetable that consists of N-UNCOUNT long green pods.

old /əʊld/ **older, oldest**. **1** Someone who is **old** ◆◆◆◆ has lived for many years and is no longer young. *...a* ADJ-GRADED *white-haired old man... He was considered too old for the job.* ▶ **The old** are people who are old. N-PLURAL **2** Something that is **old** has existed for a long time. ADJ-GRADED *These books must be very old. ...an old Arab proverb.* ADJ-GRADED **3** Something that is **old** is no longer in good condi- tion because of its age or because it has been used a lot. *...an old toothbrush.* **4** You use **old** to talk or ask ADJ: about how many days, weeks, months, or years amount ADJ, someone or something has lived or existed. *The* how ADJ *paintings in the chapel were perhaps a thousand years old... How old are you now?*

5 You use **old** to refer to something that is no longer ADJ: ADJ n used, that no longer exists, or that has been replaced by something else. *The old road had disappeared un- der grass... In the old Liberal party the peace movement was a powerful voice.* **6** You use **old** to refer to some- ADJ: thing that used to belong to you, or to a person or poss ADJ n thing that used to have a particular role in your life. *I'll make up the bed in your old room. ...when Jane re- turned to her old boyfriend.*

7 An **old** friend, enemy, or rival is someone who has ADJ-GRADED: been your friend, enemy, or rival for a long time. *I* ADJ n *called my old friend John Horner.*

8 You can use **old** to express affection or familiarity ADJ: ADJ n when talking to or about someone you know. *Are you* PRAGMATICS *all right, old chap?.* INFORMAL

9 You use **any old** to emphasize that the quality or PHRASE type of something is not important. If you say that a PRAGMATICS particular thing is not **any old** thing, you are empha- sizing how special or famous it is. *Any old paper will do... This is not just any old front room.* **10** In the **old** PHRASE **days** means in the past, before things changed.

11 When people refer to **the good old days**, they are PHRASE referring to a time in the past when they think that life was better than it is now. **12** If you talk about people PHRASE or things **of old**, you are referring to people or things LITERARY that existed long ago but which no longer exist, or no longer exist in the same form. *...the warrior knights of old.*

13 ● **good old**: see **good**. ● **of the old school**: see **school**. ● to **settle an old score**: see **score**. ● **up to one's old tricks**: see **trick**.

old 'age. **1** Your **old age** is the period of years to- ◆◇◇◇◇ wards the end of your life. *They worry about how* N-UNCOUNT *they will support themselves in their old age.* **2** Old N-UNCOUNT **age** is the quality or state of being old and near the end of one's life. *We tend to consider old age as a so- cial problem.*

old age 'pension, old age pensions; also N-COUNT spelled **old-age pension**. An **old age pension** is a regular amount of money that people receive from the government when they have retired from work.

old age 'pensioner, old age pensioners; also N-COUNT spelled **old-age pensioner**. An **old age pensioner** is a person who is old enough to receive a pension from the government.

old 'bat, old bats. If someone refers to an elderly N-COUNT person as an **old bat**, they think that person is silly PRAGMATICS or unpleasant. RUDE

'old boy, old boys. **1** You can refer to a man who ◆◆◇◇◇ used to be a student at a particular school or uni- N-COUNT versity as an **old boy**. **2** If you refer to an old or BRITISH middle-aged man as an **old boy**, you are referring to N-COUNT him in a disrespectful informal way. BRITISH

'old-boy network, old-boy networks. The old- N-COUNT boy **network** is a situation in which people who PRAGMATICS went to the same public school or university use their positions of influence to help each other; used showing disapproval.

olde /əʊld/. **Olde** is used in names of places and in ADJ: ADJ n advertising to make people think that something is WRITTEN very old and interesting.

old·en /ˈəʊldən/. If you refer to a period in the past as the **olden** days, you are thinking or talking about it affectionately. • In the **olden days** or in **olden days** means in the past. *In the olden days the girls were married young.* `ADJ: ADJ n` `PHRASE`

old-ˈfashioned. Something that is **old-fashioned** is no longer used, done, or believed by most people, because it has been replaced by something that is more modern. *The house was dull, old-fashioned and in bad condition... They still make cheese the old-fashioned way... She has some old-fashioned values.* `◆◇◇◇◇` `ADJ-GRADED`

old ˈflame, old flames. An **old flame** is someone with whom you once had a romantic relationship. `N-COUNT`

old girl, old girls. 1 You can refer to a woman who used to be a student at a particular school or university as an **old girl**. **2** If you refer to an old or middle-aged woman as an **old girl**, you are referring to her in a disrespectful informal way. `◆◇◇◇◇` `N-COUNT` `BRITISH` `N-COUNT` `BRITISH`

old ˈguard. If you refer to a group of people as the **old guard**, you mean that they have worked in a particular organization for a very long time and are unwilling to accept new ideas or practices; used showing disapproval. `N-COLL-SING` `PRAGMATICS`

old ˈhand, old hands. If someone is an **old hand** at something, they are very skilled at it because they have been doing it for a long time. *She was something of an old hand at the game now.* `N-COUNT`

old ˈhat. See hat. `◆◇◇◇`

oldie /ˈəʊldi/ **oldies.** You can use **oldie** to refer affectionately to an old song, film, or person, especially when they are unfashionable or outdated but still seem interesting or relevant. *Radio Aire only plays Top 40 stuff and oldies... We'll be showing 13 classic oldie films.* `◆◇◇◇◇` `N-COUNT` `INFORMAL`

old ˈlady. Some men refer to their wife, girlfriend, or mother as their **old lady**. `◆◇◇◇◇` `N-SING` `INFORMAL`

old ˈmaid, old maids. People sometimes refer to an old or middle-aged woman as an **old maid** when she has never married and they think that it is unlikely that she ever will marry. `N-COUNT` `RUDE`

old ˈman. Some people refer to their father, husband, or boyfriend as their **old man**. `◆◇◇◇◇` `N-SING` `INFORMAL`

old ˈmaster, old masters. An **old master** is a painting by one of the famous European painters of the 16th, 17th, and 18th centuries. These painters can also be referred to as the **Old Masters**. `◆◇◇◇◇` `N-COUNT`

old people's ˈhome, old people's homes. An **old people's home** is a place where old people live and are cared for when they are too old to look after themselves. `N-COUNT`

old ˈschool. • of the old school: see school. `◆◇◇◇`

old school ˈtie. The old school tie is the situation in which people who attended the same public school use their positions of influence to help each other. `N-SING:` `the N` `BRITISH`

old-ˈstyle. You use **old-style** to describe something or someone of a type that was common in the past but is not common now. *...a proper barber shop with real old-style barber chairs.* `◆◇◇◇◇` `ADJ: ADJ n`

Old ˈTestament. The Old Testament is the first of the two main parts of the Bible. `◆◇◇◇◇` `N-PROPER:` `the N`

old-ˈtime. 1 You use **old-time** to refer to something that was common in the past but is not common now. *...an old-time dance hall.* **2** You can use **old-time** before the name of someone's job to show that they do their job in the way it was done in the past. *...like an old-time sailor climbing the rigging.* `◆◇◇◇◇` `ADJ: ADJ n` `◆◇◇◇◇` `ADJ: ADJ n`

old-timer, old-timers. 1 If you refer to someone as an **old-timer**, you mean that he or she has been living in a particular place or doing a particular job for a long time. *...an old timer who has been a villain all his life.* **2** An old man is sometimes referred to as an **old-timer**. *The old-timers used to recall how hot 1886 was.* `N-COUNT` `INFORMAL` `N-COUNT` `AMERICAN,` `INFORMAL`

old ˈwives' tale, old wives' tales. An **old wives' tale** is a commonly held belief that is based on traditional ideas which have since been proved to be incorrect. `N-COUNT`

old ˈwoman, old women. If you refer to someone, especially a man, as an **old woman**, you are critical of them because you think that they are very fussy or very timid. `N-COUNT` `PRAGMATICS` `INFORMAL`

ole /əʊl/. **Ole** is used to represent the word 'old' pronounced in a particular way. *I started fixin' up ole bicycles fer poor kids.* `ADJ: ADJ n` `WRITTEN`

olean·der /ˌəʊliˈændə/ **oleanders.** An **oleander** is a flowering evergreen tree or shrub which grows in hot countries. `N-VAR`

ˈO level, O levels. O levels are British educational qualifications which schoolchildren used to take at the age of fifteen or sixteen. `◆◇◇◇◇` `N-VAR`

ol·fac·tory /ɒlˈfæktəri/. **Olfactory** means concerned with the sense of smell. *This olfactory sense develops in the womb.* `ADJ: ADJ n` `FORMAL`

oli·gar·chy /ˈɒlɪɡɑːki/ **oligarchies. 1** An **oligarchy** is a small group of people who control and run a particular country or organization. You can also refer to a country which is governed in this way as an **oligarchy. 2 Oligarchy** is a situation in which a country or organization is run by an oligarchy. *...a protest against imperialism and oligarchy.* `N-COUNT` `N-UNCOUNT`

ol·ive /ˈɒlɪv/ **olives. 1** Olives are small green or black fruit with a bitter taste. Olives are often pressed to make olive oil. **2** An **olive tree** or an **olive** is a tree on which olives grow. **3** Something that is **olive** is yellowish-green in colour. *...glowing colours such as deep red, olive, saffron and ochre.* ► Also a combining form. *...an olive-green T-shirt.* **4** If someone has **olive** skin, the colour of their skin is light brown. `◆◆◇◇◇` `N-VAR` `N-VAR` `COLOUR` `COMB` `ADJ`

ˈolive branch, olive branches. If you offer an **olive branch** to someone, you say or do something in order to show or symbolize that you want to end a disagreement or quarrel. `N-COUNT`

ˈolive oil, olive oils. Olive oil is oil that is obtained by pressing olives. It is used for putting on salads or in cooking. `◆◆◇◇◇` `N-VAR`

-ological /-əˈlɒdʒɪkəl/. **-ological** is used to replace '-ology' at the end of nouns in order to form adjectives. These adjectives describe something as relating to a particular science or subject. For example, 'biological' means relating to biology. `SUFFIX`

-ologist /-ˈɒlədʒɪst/. **-ologist** is used to replace '-ology' at the end of nouns in order to form other nouns that refer to people who are concerned with a particular science or subject. For example, a 'biologist' is concerned with biology. `SUFFIX`

-ology /-ˈɒlədʒi/. **-ology** is used at the end of some nouns that refer to a particular science or subject, for example 'geology' or 'sociology'. `SUFFIX`

Olym·pian /əˈlɪmpiən/ **Olympians. 1** Olympian means very powerful, large, or impressive. *Getting his book into print has been an Olympian task.* **2** An **Olympian** is a competitor in the Olympic Games. `ADJ` `FORMAL` `N-COUNT`

Olym·pic /əˈlɪmpɪk/ **Olympics. 1** Olympic means relating to the Olympic Games. *...Gao, the reigning Olympic champion.* **2** The Olympics are the Olympic Games. `◆◆◆◇` `ADJ: ADJ n` `N-PROPER:` `the N`

O,lympic ˈGames. The Olympic Games are a set of international sports competitions which take place every four years, each time in a different country. `◆◆◇◇◇` `N-COLL-` `PROPER:` `the N`

om·buds·man /ˈɒmbʊdzmən/ **ombudsmen.** The **ombudsman** is an independent official who is appointed to investigate complaints that people make against the government or public organizations. `◆◇◇◇◇` `N-COUNT`

ome·lette /ˈɒmlət/ **omelettes;** spelled **omelet** in American English. An **omelette** is a type of food made by beating eggs and cooking them in a flat pan. `◆◇◇◇◇` `N-COUNT`

omen /ˈəʊmen/ **omens.** If you say that something is an **omen**, you think it indicates what is likely to happen in the future and whether it will be good or bad. *Her appearance at this moment is an omen of disaster.* `◆◇◇◇◇` `N-COUNT`

omi·nous /ˈɒmɪnəs/. If you describe something as **ominous**, you mean that it worries you because it makes you think that something unpleasant is going `◆◇◇◇◇` `ADJ-GRADED`

to happen. *The rolls of distant thunder were growing more ominous.* ♦ **omi·nous·ly** *The bar seemed ominously quiet... Ominously, car sales slumped in August.* ADV-GRADED

omis·sion /əʊˈmɪʃən/ **omissions. 1** An omission is something that has not been included or has not been done. *The duke was surprised by his wife's omission from the guest list.* **2** Omission is the act of not including someone or something or of not doing something. ...*the prosecution's seemingly malicious omission of recorded evidence.* ◆◇◇◇◇ N-COUNT / N-VAR

omit /əʊˈmɪt/ **omits, omitting, omitted. 1** If you omit something, you do not include it in an activity or piece of work, deliberately or accidentally. *Omit the salt in this recipe... Our apologies to David Pannick for omitting his name from last week's article.* **2** If you want to do something, you do not do it. *His new girlfriend had omitted to tell him she was married.* ◆◆◇◇◇ VERB / V n / V n from n / VERB / V to-inf / FORMAL

om·ni·bus /ˈɒmnɪbʌs/ **omnibuses. 1** An omnibus edition of a radio or television programme contains two or more similar programmes that were originally broadcast separately. **2** An omnibus is a book which contains a large collection of stories or articles, often by a particular person or about a particular subject. **3** Omnibus is an old-fashioned word for bus. N-COUNT BRITISH / N-COUNT / N-COUNT DATED

om·nip·o·tent /ɒmˈnɪpətənt/. An omnipotent person or thing has complete power over things or people. ...*his seemingly omnipotent father.* ♦ **om·nipo·tence** ...*the omnipotence of God.* ADJ FORMAL / N-UNCOUNT

om·ni·pres·ent /ˌɒmnɪˈprezənt/. Something that is omnipresent is present everywhere or seems to be always present. *The sound of sirens was an omnipresent background noise in New York.* ADJ-GRADED FORMAL

om·nis·ci·ent /ɒmˈnɪsiənt, AM -ˈnɪʃənt/. If you describe someone as omniscient, you mean they know or seem to know everything. *We all, long ago, expected teachers to be omniscient.* ♦ **om·nis·ci·ence** *Her open-mouthed amazement at his omniscience was sufficient reward for him.* ADJ FORMAL / N-UNCOUNT

om·niv·or·ous /ɒmˈnɪvərəs/. **1** An omnivorous person or animal eats all kinds of food, including both meat and plants. **2** An omnivorous person likes a wide variety of things of a particular type. *As a child, Coleridge seems to have developed omnivorous reading habits.* ADJ TECHNICAL / ADJ FORMAL

on /ɒn/. **1** If someone or something is on a surface or object, the surface or object is immediately below them and is supporting their weight. *He is sitting beside her on the sofa... On top of the cupboards are vast straw baskets. ...the Chinese rug on the floor.* **2** If something is on a surface or object, it is stuck to it or attached to it. ...*the peeling paint on the ceiling... There was a smear of gravy on his chin.* ▶ Also an adverb. ...*how to sew a button on.* **3** If you put something on a surface, you move it so that it is supported by the surface. *I dropped my bag on the floor.* **4** You use on to say what part of your body is supporting your weight. *He continued to lie on his back... She was on her hands and knees.* **5** You use on to say that someone or something is touching a part of someone's body. *He kissed her lightly on the mouth.* **6** If someone has a particular expression on their face, their face has that expression. *He had a big smile on his face.* **7** When you put a piece of clothing on, you place it over part of your body in order to wear it. If you have it on, you are wearing it. *He put his coat on... I had a hat on.* **8** You can say that you have something on you if you are carrying it in your pocket or in a bag. *I didn't have any money on me.* **9** If someone's eyes are on you, they are looking or staring at you. **10** If you hurt yourself on something, you accidentally hit a part of your body against it and that thing causes damage to you. *She cut her hand on a broken glass.* **11** If you are on an area of land, you are there. *He was able to spend only a few days at a time on the island.* ♦♦♦♦♦ PREP / PREP / ADV / PREP / PREP / PREP / PREP / ADV: ADV after v / PREP / PREP / PREP / PREP

...*a tall tree on a mountain.* **12** If something is situated on a place such as a road or coast, it forms part of it or is by the side of it. ...*a men's store on Fifth Avenue... The hotel is on the coast.* **13** If you get on a bus, train, or plane, you go into it in order to travel somewhere. If you are on it, you are travelling in it. *I never go on the bus into the town... I remember crying all the way up on the train.* ▶ Also an adverb. *He showed his ticket to the conductor and got on.* **14** If there is something on a piece of paper, it has been written or printed there. ...*the writing on the back of the card. ...the numbers she put on the chart.* **15** If something is on a list, it is included in it. *I've seen your name on the list... There are many controversial topics on the agenda.* **16** Books, discussions, or ideas on a particular subject are concerned with that subject. ...*any book on baby care. ...a free counselling service which can offer help and advice on legal matters.* **17** You use on to introduce the method, principle, or system which is used to do something. ...*a television that we bought on credit. ...a levelling system which acts on the same principle as a spirit level.* **18** If something is done on an instrument or a machine, it is done using that instrument or machine. ...*songs that I could just sit down and play on the piano... I could do all my work on the computer.* **19** If information is, for example, on tape or on computer, that is the way that it is stored. *Descriptions of the pieces have been logged on computer... A special version of 'Casablanca' is being released on video.* **20** If something is being broadcast, you can say that it is on the radio or television. ...*every sporting event on television and satellite... They're talking about it on Radio-Paris right now.* ▶ Also an adjective. ...*teenagers complaining there's nothing good on.* **21** When an activity is taking place, you can say that it is on. *Every year they put a play on.* **22** You use on in expressions such as 'have a lot on' and 'not have very much on' to indicate how busy someone is. **23** You use on to introduce an activity that someone is doing, particularly travelling. *I've always wanted to go on a cruise... They are on a fishing holiday.* **24** When something such as a machine or an electric light is on, it is functioning or in use. When you switch it on, it starts functioning. *The light was on and the door was open... The central heating's been turned off. I've turned it on again.* **25** If you are on a committee or council, you are a member of it. *Claire and Beryl were on the organizing committee.* **26** You can indicate when something happens by saying that it happens on a particular day or date. *This year's event will take place on June 19th... She travels to Korea on Monday.* **27** You use on when mentioning an event that was followed by another one. *She waited in her hotel to welcome her children on their arrival from London... On reaching Dubai the evacuees were taken straight to Dubai international airport.* **28** You use on to say that someone is continuing to do something. *They walked on in silence... Read on for further hints on leading successful relationships.* **29** If you say that someone goes on at you, you mean that they continually criticize you, complain to you, or ask you to do something. *She's been on at me for weeks to show her round the stables... He used to keep on at me about the need to win.* **30** You use on in expressions such as from now on and from then on to indicate that something starts to happen at the time mentioned and continues to happen afterwards. *We can expect trouble from this moment on.* **31** You often use on after the adverbs 'early', 'late', 'far', and their comparative forms, especially at the beginning or end of a sentence, or before a preposition. ...*early on in the morning... Later on I learned how to read music.* **32** Someone who is on a drug takes it regularly. *She was on antibiotics for an eye infection.* PREP / PREP / PREP / PREP / PREP / PREP / PREP / PREP / PREP / PREP / PREP / ADJ: v-link ADJ / ADJ / ADV SPOKEN / PREP / ADV / PREP / PREP / PREP / ADV: ADV after v / ADV / ADV: from n ADV / ADV: adv ADV / PREP

33 If you live **on** a particular kind of food, you eat it. If PREP a machine runs **on** a particular kind of power or fuel, it uses it in order to function. *The caterpillars feed on a wide range of trees, shrubs and plants... The system could be used to ensure that cars are converted to run on unleaded petrol.*

34 If you are **on** a particular income, that is the in- PREP come that you have. *...young people who are unemployed or on low wages.*

35 Taxes or profits that are obtained from something PREP are referred to as taxes or profits **on** it. *...a tax on food and medicine... The Church was to receive a cut of the profits on every record sold.*

36 When you buy something or pay for something, PREP you spend money **on** it. *I resolved not to waste money on a hotel... More money should be spent on education.*

37 When you spend time or energy **on** a particular ac- PREP tivity, you spend time or energy doing it. *People complain about how children spend so much time on computer games. ...the opportunity to concentrate more time and energy on America's domestic agenda.*

38 If you say that something is **not on** or is **just not** PHRASE **on**, you mean that it is unacceptable or impossible. BRITISH

39 If you say that something happens **on and on**, you PHRASE mean that it continues to happen for a very long time. *Lobell drove on and on through the dense and blowing snow. ...a desert of ice stretching on and on.* **40** If you PHRASE ask someone **what** they **are on about** or **what** they **are** INFORMAL **going on about**, you are puzzled because you cannot understand what they are talking about. **41** If you say PHRASE that someone **knows what** they **are on about**, you are INFORMAL confident that what they are saying is true or makes sense, for example because they are an expert.

42 ● on behalf of: see **behalf**. ● on and off: see **off**. ● and so on: see **so**. ● on top of: see **top**.

once /wʌns, wɒns/. **1** If something happens **once**, ◆◆◆◆ it happens one time only. *I met Wilma once,* ADV; *briefly... Since then I haven't once slept through the* ADV with v *night... Mary had only been to Manchester once before.* ► Also a pronoun. *'Have they been to visit you* PRON *yet?'—'Just the once yeah.'... Listen to us, if only this once.* **2** You use **once** with 'a' and words like 'day', ADV; 'week', and 'month' to indicate that something hap- ADV a n pens regularly, one time in each day, week, or month. *Lung cells die and are replaced about once a week... We arranged a special social event once a year.* **3** You use **once** with 'every' and words like ADV; 'day', 'week', and 'year' to indicate that something ADV every n, happens a specified number of times and on a regu- ADV every num n lar basis. *My daughter comes to visit me once every fortnight.* **4** If something was **once** true, it was true at some time ADV; in the past, but is no longer true. *The culture minister* ADV with v *once ran a theatre... The house where she lives was once the village post office.* **5** If someone **once** did ADV; something, they did it at an unspecified time in the ADV with v past. *I once went camping at Lake Darling with a friend... Diana had taken that path once.* **6** If something happens **once** another thing has hap- CONJ pened, it happens immediately afterwards. *The decision had taken about 10 seconds once he'd read a market research study... Once customers come to rely on these systems they almost never take their business elsewhere.* **7** If you do something **once or twice**, you do it a few PHRASE times, but not very often. *I popped my head round the door once or twice.* **8** If something happens **once in a** PHRASE **while**, it happens sometimes, but not very often. *Once in a while she phoned him.* **9** ● once in a blue moon: see **moon**. **10** If something happens **all at once**, it happens sud- PHRASE denly, often when you are not expecting it to happen. *I feel terribly sleepy all at once.* **11** If you do something PHRASE **at once**, you do it immediately. *I have to go, I really must, at once.* **12** If a number of different things hap- PHRASE pen **at once** or **all at once**, they all happen at the same time. *You can't be doing two things at once... She seems at once feminine and able to cope in a man's world.* **13 For once** is used to emphasize that something PHRASE happens on this particular occasion, especially if it

has never happened before, and may never happen again. *For once, dad is not complaining.* **14** If some- PHRASE thing happens **once again** or **once more**, it happens again. *Amy picked up the hairbrush and smoothed her hair once more... Once again an official inquiry has spoken of weak management.* **15** If something hap- PHRASE pens **once and for all**, it happens completely or finally. *We have to resolve this matter once and for all.*

16 Once upon a time is used to indicate that some- PHRASE thing happened or existed a long time ago or in an imaginary world. It is often used at the beginning of children's stories. *'Once upon a time,' he began, 'there was a man who had everything.'*

'once-over. If you **give** something or someone **the** PHRASE **once-over**, you quickly look at or inspect them. INFORMAL

on·coming /'ɒnkʌmɪŋ/. **Oncoming** means moving ADJ: ADJ n towards you. *She dashed across the road to avoid an oncoming car. ...the oncoming cold of winter.*

one /wʌn, wɒn/ **ones**. **1 One** is the number 1. See ◆◆◆◆ Appendix headed **Numbers**. *They had three sons* NUMBER *and one daughter. ...one thousand years ago. ...one of the children killed in the crash.* **2** You can use ex- PHRASE pressions such as **a hundred and one**, **a thousand** PRAGMATICS **and one**, and **a million and one** to emphasize that you are talking about a large number of things or people. *There are a hundred and one ways in which you can raise money.* **3** If a group of people does PHRASE something **as one**, all the people do the same thing WRITTEN at the same time or in the same way. *The 40,000 crowd rose as one.* **4** If you say that someone is **at** PHRASE **one with** the world, their feelings, or other people, you mean that they feel happy and at home in the situation they are in. *Take a stroll through the countryside and be at one with nature.* **5** You can PHRASE use **in one** to indicate that something is a single unit, but is made up of several different parts or has several different functions. *...a love story and an adventure all in one.* **6** You can use **in ones and twos** PHRASE to indicate that people do things or something happens gradually and in small groups. *They lose interest and start drifting away in ones and twos.* **7** You PHRASE can use **one by one** to indicate that people do things or that things happen in sequence, not all at the same time. *We went into the room one by one.*

8 If you say that someone or something is the **one** per- ADJ: det ADJ son or thing of a particular kind, you are emphasizing PRAGMATICS that they are the only person or thing of that kind. *His one regret is that he has never learned a language.* **9 One** can be used instead of 'a' to emphasize the fol- DET lowing noun. *One person I hate is Russ.* **10** You can PRAGMATICS use **one** instead of 'a' to emphasize the following ad- DET jective or expression. *It's like one enormous street car-* INFORMAL *nival here.* **11** You can use **for one** to emphasize that a PHRASE particular person is definitely reacting or behaving in PRAGMATICS a particular way, even if other people are not. *I, for one, hope you don't get the job.*

12 You can use **one** in front of someone's name to in- DET dicate that you have not met them or heard of them FORMAL before. *It seems that the fifth man is one John Cairncross.*

13 You can use **one** to refer to the first of two or more DET things that you are comparing. *Prices vary from one shop to another.* ► Also an adjective. *We ask why* ADJ: det ADJ *peace should have an apparent chance in the one territory and not the other.* ► Also a pronoun. *The twins* PRON *were dressed differently and one was thinner than the other.* **14** You use **one or other** to refer to one or more PHRASE things or people in a group, when it does not matter which particular one or ones are thought of or chosen. *One or other of the two women was wrong.*

15 You can use **one** or **ones** instead of a noun when it PRON is clear what type of thing or person you are referring to and you are describing them or giving more information about them. *They are selling their house to move to a smaller one.* **16** You use **ones** to refer to PRON people in general. *We are the only ones who know.* **17** You can use **one** instead of a noun group when PRON you have just mentioned something and you want to describe it or give more information about it. *His response is one of anger and frustration... The issue of*

land reform was one that dominated Hungary's parliamentary elections. **18** You can use **one** when you have been talking or writing about a group of people or things and you want to say something about a particular member of the group. *'A college degree isn't enough', said one honors student.* ► Also a pronoun. *Some of them couldn't eat a thing. One couldn't even drink.* **19** You use **one** in expressions such as '**one of the biggest airports**' or '**one of the most experienced players**' to indicate that something or someone is bigger or more experienced than most other things or people of the same kind. **20** If you say that someone is **one for** or is **a one for** something, you mean that they like or approve of it or enjoy doing it. *I'm not one for political discussions.* **21** If you say that someone is **not one** to do something, you think that it is very unlikely that they would do it because it is not their normal behaviour. *I'm not one to waste time on just anyone.* **22** You can use **one** when referring to a time in the past or in the future. For example, if you say that you did something **one day**, you mean that you did it on a day in the past. *How would you like to have dinner one night?* ● **one day**: see **day**.

23 You can use **one** to refer to a question, joke, remark, or subject of discussion. *This is a tricky one to answer.* **24** You can use **one** to refer to an alcoholic drink. *Other members of the committee drifted in for a quick one before closing time.*

25 You use **one** to make statements about people in general which also apply to themselves. **One** can be used as the subject or object of a sentence. *Where does one go from there?... Shares and bonds can bring one quite a considerable additional income.*

26 The one and only can be used in front of the name of an actor, singer, or other famous person when they are being introduced on a show. *...the one and only Tina Turner.* **27 One or two** means a few. *We may make one or two changes... I asked one or two of the stallholders about it.* **28** If you try to get **one up on** someone, you try to gain an advantage over them, usually by doing something they have not done or knowing something they do not know.

29 ● **one after the other**: see **after**. ● **one and all**: see **all**. ● **one another**: see **another**. ● **one thing after another**: see **another**. ● to **pull a fast one**: see **fast**. ● of **one mind**: see **mind**. ● **in one piece**: see **piece**.

‚one-armed 'bandit, one-armed bandits. A one-armed bandit is the same as a **fruit machine**.   N-COUNT

'one-horse. 1 If someone describes a town as a **one-horse** town, they mean it is very small, dull, and old-fashioned. **2** If a contest is described as a **one-horse** race, it is thought that one person or thing will obviously win it.   ADJ: ADJ n

‚one-'liner, one-liners. A one-liner is a funny remark or a joke told in one sentence, for example in a play or comedy programme.   N-COUNT INFORMAL

'one-man. 1 A one-man show is given by only one man rather than by several people. *...a modern one-man drama.* **2** A one-man organization, such as a business or type of government is controlled by one person, rather than by several people. *...a one-man cottage industry... He established one-man rule in his country.*   ADJ: ADJ n

‚one-man 'band, one-man bands. A one-man band is a street entertainer who plays a lot of different instruments at the same time.   N-COUNT

‚one-night 'stand, one-night stands. A one-night stand is a very brief sexual relationship, usually involving having sex with a particular person on only one occasion.   N-COUNT

‚one-of-a-'kind. You use one-of-a-kind to describe something that is special because there is nothing else exactly like it. *...a small one-of-a-kind publishing house.*   ADJ: ADJ n AMERICAN

'one-off, one-offs. If something is a one-off, it is made or happens only once. *Our survey revealed that these allergies were mainly one-offs. ...one-off cash benefits.*   N-COUNT BRITISH

‚one-parent 'family, one-parent families. A one-parent family is a family that consists of one parent and his or her children living together.   N-COUNT

'one-piece, one-pieces. 1 A one-piece article of clothing consists of one piece only, rather than two or more separate parts. *...a lined, one-piece suit.* **2** A one-piece is a type of woman's swimming costume that is not a bikini.   ADJ: ADJ n / N-COUNT

on·er·ous /'ɒunərəs, AM 'ɑːn-/. If you describe a task as **onerous**, you dislike having to do it because you find it difficult or unpleasant. *...the onerous task of bringing up a very difficult child.*   ADJ-GRADED FORMAL

one's /wʌnz/. **1** Speakers and writers use **one's** to indicate that something belongs or relates to people in general, or to themselves in particular. *...the welfare of others in one's community. ...to expect one's children simply to reproduce one's own views.* **2** One's can be used as a form of **one is** or **one has**, especially when 'has' is an auxiliary verb. See **one**. *No one's going to hurt you.*   DET-POSS FORMAL

one·self /wʌn'self/. Oneself is a third person singular reflexive pronoun. **1** A speaker or writer uses **oneself** as the object of a verb or preposition in a clause where 'oneself' meaning 'me' or 'any person in general' refers to the same person as the subject of the verb. *It is also a way of making oneself feel sophisticated... To work one must have time to oneself.* **2** Oneself can be used as the object of a verb or preposition, when 'one' is not present but is understood to be the subject of the verb. *It is a pleasant place to base oneself for summer vacations... It's so easy to feel sorry for oneself.* **3** To do something **oneself** means to do it without any help or interference from anyone else. *Some things one must do oneself.* **4** You use **oneself** to emphasize that something happens to you rather than to people in general. *It is better to die oneself than to kill.*   PRON-REFL

‚one-'sided. 1 If you say that an activity or relationship is **one-sided**, you think that one of the people or groups involved does much more than the other or is much stronger than the other. *The negotiating was completely one-sided. ...a very one-sided match.* **2** If you describe someone as **one-sided**, you are critical of what they say or do because you think it shows that they have considered only one side of an issue or event. *The organisation still believes the government is being one-sided. ...a very one-sided account of her problems.*   ADJ-GRADED / ADJ-GRADED PRAGMATICS

'one-time; also spelled onetime. One-time can be used to describe something such as a job, position, or role which someone used to have, or something which happened or existed in the past. *A one-time body builder, he now trains others for professional competition.*   ADJ: ADJ n JOURNALISM

‚one-to-'one. 1 In a one-to-one relationship, one person deals directly with only one other person. *...one-to-one training. ...one-to-one counselling is the answer.* ► Also an adverb. *She would like to talk to people one-to-one.* **2** In a one-to-one comparison, one thing is compared with another thing that is broadly equivalent or similar to it.   ADJ: ADJ n / ADV

one-upmanship /‚wʌn 'ʌpmənʃɪp/. One-upmanship is behaviour which someone uses to try to make other people feel inferior in order to make themselves appear more important; used showing disapproval.   N-UNCOUNT PRAGMATICS

‚one-'way. 1 In one-way streets or traffic systems, vehicles can only travel in one direction. **2** One-way describes journeys or tickets which go to just one place, rather than to that place and then back again. *...one-way trips.* **3** One-way glass or a one-way mirror is a device which acts as a mirror when looked at from one side, but acts as a window when looked through from the other side. They are used for watching people without their knowledge or consent.   ADJ

'one-woman. A one-woman performance or business is done by only one woman, rather than by several people. *She has already presented a one-woman show of her paintings.*   ADJ: ADJ n

on·going /ˌɒnˈɡəʊɪŋ/. An **ongoing** situation has been happening for quite a long time and seems likely to continue for some time in the future. *There is an ongoing debate on the issue.*   ◆◆◇◇◇ ADJ

on·ion /ˈʌnjən/ **onions**. An **onion** is a small round vegetable with a brown skin that grows underground. It has many white layers on its inside which have a strong sharp smell and taste. See picture headed **vegetables**.   ◆◆◇◇◇ N-VAR

on·line /ˌɒnˈlaɪn/; also spelled **on-line**. See **line**.

on·looker /ˈɒnlʊkə/ **onlookers**. An **onlooker** is someone who watches an event take place but does not take part in it. *A small crowd of onlookers were there to watch Mrs Thatcher.*   ◆◇◇◇◇ N-COUNT

only /ˈəʊnli/. **1** You use **only** to indicate the one thing that is true, appropriate, or necessary in a particular situation, in contrast to all the other things that are not true, appropriate, or necessary. *Only the President could authorize the use of the atomic bomb... A business can only be built on a sound financial base.* **2** You use **only** to introduce the thing which must happen before the thing mentioned in the main part of the sentence can happen. *The lawyer is paid only if he wins... The Bank insists that it will cut interest rates only when it is ready.* **3** If you talk about the **only** person or thing involved in a particular situation, you mean there are no others involved in it. *She was the only woman in the legal department... The only thing I have is television.* **4** An **only** child is a child who has no brothers or sisters. **5** You use **only** to indicate that something is no more important, interesting, or difficult, for example, than you say it is, especially when you want to correct a wrong idea that someone may get or has already got. *'I'm only a sergeant,' said Clements... Don't get defensive, Charlie. I was only joking.* **6** You use **only** to emphasize how small an amount is or how short a length of time is. *Child car seats only cost about £10 a week to hire... I've only recently met him.* **7** You use **only** to indicate that you are talking about a small part or sample, not the whole of an amount. *These are only a few of the possibilities... Teenagers typically earn only half the adult wage.* **8** **Only** is used after 'can' or 'could' to emphasize that it is impossible to do anything except the rather inadequate or limited action that is mentioned. *I could say nothing. I could only stand and look... The police can only guess at the scale of the problem.* **9** You can use **only** in the expressions **I only wish** or **I only hope** in order to emphasize what you are hoping or wishing. *We can only hope that she can recover.* **10** **Only** can be used to add a comment which slightly changes or limits what you have just said. *It's a bit like my house, only nicer. ...a sofa covered in the same fabric as covered her own sofa, only hers was green and this was brown.* **11** **Only** can be used after a clause with 'would' to indicate why something is not done. *I'd invite you to come with me, only it's such a long way.* **12** You can use **only** before an infinitive to introduce an event which happens immediately after one you have just mentioned, and which is rather surprising or unfortunate. *Ryle tried the Embassy, only to be told that Hugh was in a meeting.* **13** You can use **only** to emphasize how appropriate a certain course of action or type of behaviour is. *It's only fair to let her know that you intend to apply... She appeared to have changed considerably, which was only to be expected.* **14** You can use **only** in front of a verb to indicate that the result of something is unfortunate or undesirable and is likely to make the situation worse rather than better. *She says that legalising prostitution will only cause problems.* **15** If you say you **only have to** or **have only to** do one thing in order to achieve or prove a second thing, you are emphasizing how easily the second thing can be achieved or proved. *We have only to read the labels to know what ingredients are in foods.* **16** You can say that something has **only just** happened when you want to emphasize that it happened a very short time ago. *I've only just arrived... You're*   ◆◆◆◆◆ ADV; ADV with group, ADV before v / ADV cl/prep [PRAGMATICS] / ADJ: det ADJ / ADJ: ADJ n / ADV group, ADV before v / ADV n/adv [PRAGMATICS] / ADV: ADV n / modal ADV adv [PRAGMATICS] / ADV before v [PRAGMATICS] / CONJ [PRAGMATICS] INFORMAL / CONJ SPOKEN / ADV: ADV to-inf [PRAGMATICS] / ADV [PRAGMATICS] / ADV: ADV before v / PHRASE [PRAGMATICS] / PHRASE [PRAGMATICS]

only just back from leave. **17** You use **only just** to emphasize that something is true, but by such a small degree that it is almost not true at all. *For centuries farmers there have only just managed to survive.* **18** You can use **only too** to emphasize that something is true or exists to a much greater extent than you would expect or like. *I know only too well that plans can easily go wrong.* **19** You can say that you are **only too** happy to do something to emphasize how willing you are to do it. *I'll be only too pleased to help them out with any queries.* **20** ● **if only**: see **if**. ● **not only**: see **not**. ● **the one and only**: see **one**.   PHRASE [PRAGMATICS] / PHRASE [PRAGMATICS] / PHRASE [PRAGMATICS]

ono·mato·poeia /ˌɒnəmætəˈpiːə/. **Onomatopoeia** refers to the use of words which have been formed to sound like the noise of the thing that they are describing or representing. 'Hiss', 'buzz', and 'rat-a-tat-tat' are examples of onomatopoeia. ◆ **ono·mato·poe·ic** /ˌɒnəmætəˈpiːɪk/ *Japanese has three times as many onomatopoeic expressions as English.*   N-UNCOUNT / ADJ

on·rush /ˈɒnrʌʃ/. The **onrush** of something is its sudden development, which happens so quickly and forcefully that you are unable to control it. *She was screwing up her eyes against the onrush of air.*   N-SING

on·rush·ing /ˈɒnrʌʃɪŋ/. **Onrushing** describes something such as a vehicle that is moving forward so quickly or forcefully that it would be very difficult to stop. *He was killed by an onrushing train.*   ADJ: ADJ n

on-'screen; also spelled **onscreen**. **1** **On-screen** means appearing on the screen of a television, cinema, or computer. *...a clear and easy-to-follow menu-driven on-screen display.* **2** **On-screen** means relating to the roles being played by film or television actors, in contrast with their real life. *...her on-screen romance with Pierce Lawton.* ▶ Also an adverb. *He was immensely attractive to women, onscreen and offscreen.*   ◆◇◇◇◇ ADJ: ADJ n / ADJ: ADJ n / ADV: ADV with cl

on·set /ˈɒnset/. The **onset** of something, especially something unpleasant, is the beginning of it. *With the onset of war, oil prices climbed past $30 a barrel.*   ◆◇◇◇◇ N-SING: also no det

on·shore /ˌɒnˈʃɔː/. **Onshore** means happening or moving on or near land, rather than at sea. *...Western Europe's biggest onshore oilfield.* ▶ Also an adverb. *They missed the ferry and remained onshore.*   ADJ / ADV: ADV after v

on·slaught /ˈɒnslɔːt/ **onslaughts**. **1** An **onslaught** on someone or something is a very violent forceful attack against them. *The attackers launched another vicious onslaught on their victim. ...their relentless onslaught against spending plans.* **2** If you refer to an **onslaught** of something, you mean that there is a large amount of it, often so that it is very difficult to deal with. *The onslaught of orders should keep aircraft manufacturers busy.*   ◆◇◇◇◇ N-COUNT / N-COUNT

on·stage /ˌɒnˈsteɪdʒ/. When someone such as an actor or musician goes **onstage**, they go onto the stage in a theatre to give a performance. *You have to be onstage at eight o'clock.*   ◆◇◇◇◇ ADV

on-the-'job. See **job**.

on-the-'spot. See **spot**.

onto /ˈɒntuː/; also spelled **on to**. **1** If someone or something moves **onto** an object or surface, it is then on that object or surface. *I lowered myself onto the bed and switched on the TV... Smear cream on to your baby's skin.* **2** You can sometimes use **onto** to introduce the place that someone moves into or towards. When someone is already in that place, you would normally use the preposition 'on'. *The players emerged onto the field... Alex turned his car on to the Albert Quay.* **3** You can use **onto** to introduce the place towards which a light or someone's look is directed. *...the metal part of the door onto which the sun had been shining. ...the house with its view on to Regent's Park.* **4** You can use **onto** to introduce a place that you would immediately come to after leaving another place that you have just mentioned, because they are next to each other. *The door opened onto a lighted hallway. ...a strip of land that backs onto a large lake.* **5** When you change the position of your body, you use **onto** to introduce the part your body which is now supporting you. *I heaved myself over on to my back.*   ◆◆◆◇◇ PREP / PREP / PREP / PREP / PREP

O

6 When you get **onto** a bus, train, or plane, you en- `PREP` ter it in order to travel somewhere. **7 Onto** is used `PREP` after verbs such as 'hold', 'hang', and 'cling' to indicate what someone is holding firmly or where something is being held firmly. *She had to cling onto the door-handle until the pain passed.*

8 If people who are talking get **onto** a different sub- `PREP` ject, they begin talking about it. *Let's get on to more important matters.* . **9** You can sometimes use **onto** to `PREP` indicate that something or someone becomes included as a part of a list or system. When they are already included in this list or system, you would normally use the preposition 'on'. *Twelve-thousand workers will go onto a four-day week at their factory.*

10 If someone **is onto** something, they are about to `PREP` make a discovery. *Archaeologists knew they were onto* `INFORMAL` *something big when they started digging.* **11** If some- `PREP` one **is onto** you, they have discovered that you are do- `INFORMAL` ing something illegal or wrong. *I had told people what he had been doing, so now the police were onto him.*

on·tol·ogy /ɒnˈtɒlədʒi/. **Ontology** is the branch of `N-UNCOUNT` philosophy that deals with the nature of existence. ◆ **on·to·logi·cal** /ˌɒntəˈlɒdʒɪkəl/. *...feelings of onto-* `ADJ` *logical security.*

onus /ˈəʊnəs/. If you say that the **onus** is on some- ◆◇◇◇ one to do something, you mean it is their duty or `N-SING` responsibility to do it. *The onus is on the shopkeeper* `FORMAL` *to provide quality goods.*

on·ward /ˈɒnwəd/; also spelled **onwards**. In British ◆◇◇◇ English, **onwards** is an adverb and **onward** is an adjective. In American English and sometimes in formal British English, **onward** may also be an adverb.

1 Onward means moving forward or continuing a `ADJ` journey. *British Airways have two flights a day to Bangkok, and there are onward flights to Phnom Penh.* ▶ Also an adverb. *The bus continued onward...* `ADV` *She stumbled onward through the blackness.* **2 On-** `ADJ` **ward** means developing, progressing, or becoming more important over a period of time. *...the onward march of progress in the British aircraft industry.* ▶ Also an adverb. *The most important thing now is to* `ADV:` *move onwards... The White House feels no compulsion* `ADV after v` *to rush onwards to a new agreement.* **3** If something `ADV:` happens from a particular time **onwards** or **onward**, `from n ADV` it begins to happen at that time and continues to happen afterwards. *...from the turn of the century onward.*

onyx /ˈɒnɪks/. **Onyx** is a semi-precious stone which `N-UNCOUNT` can be various colours. It is used for making ornaments, jewellery, or furniture.

oo /uː/. See **ooh**.

oodles /ˈuːdəlz/. If you say that there is **oodles of** `QUANT` something, you are emphasizing that there is a very `PRAGMATICS` large quantity of it. *The recipe calls for oodles of* `INFORMAL` *melted chocolate.*

ooh /uː/; also spelled **oo**. People say **'ooh'** when ◆◇◇◇ they are surprised, looking forward to something, or `EXCLAM` find something pleasant or unpleasant. *'Red? Ooh* `PRAGMATICS` *how nice.'* `INFORMAL`

oomph /ʊmf/. If you say that someone or some- `N-UNCOUNT` thing has **oomph**, you mean that they are energetic `INFORMAL` and exciting. *'There's no buzz, there's no oomph about the place,' he complained.*

oops /ʊps, uːps/. You say **'oops'** to indicate that `EXCLAM` there has been a slight accident or mistake, or to `PRAGMATICS` apologize to someone for it. *Oops, we made a* `INFORMAL` *mistake.*

ooze /uːz/ **oozes, oozing, oozed**. **1** When a ◆◇◇◇ thick or sticky liquid **oozes** from something or when `V-ERG` something **oozes** it, the liquid flows slowly and in `V n` small quantities. *The wounds were still oozing* `V` *blood... He could see the cut now, still oozing slightly.* **2** If you say that someone or something **oozes** a `VERB` quality or characteristic, you mean that they show it `V n` very strongly. *The Elizabethan house oozes charm.* `V with n` *...a soundtrack oozing with the spirit of 18th century France.* **3** You can refer to any thick, sticky, liquid `N-UNCOUNT` substance as **ooze**, especially the mud at the bottom of a river, lake, or the sea.

op /ɒp/ **ops**. **1** An **op** is a medical operation. *Anna* ◆◇◇◇ *was recovering from a successful op to remove a tu-* `N-COUNT` `INFORMAL`

---

mour. **2 Ops** are military operations. *Flt Lt Beaumont* `N-COUNT` *had completed a 200 hour tour of ops in December 1941.*

op. In music, **op.** is a written abbreviation for **opus**. *...Beethoven's Op. 101 and 111 sonatas.*

opac·ity /əʊˈpæsɪti/. **1 Opacity** is the quality of be- `N-UNCOUNT` ing difficult to see through. *Opacity of the eye lens* `FORMAL` *can be induced by deficiency of certain vitamins.* **2** If `N-UNCOUNT` you refer to something's **opacity**, you mean that it `FORMAL` is difficult to understand. *His writing has an opacity to it.*

opal /ˈəʊpəl/ **opals**. An **opal** is a precious stone. `N-VAR` **Opals** are colourless or milky white.

opal·es·cent /ˌəʊpəˈlesənt/. **Opalescent** means `ADJ-GRADED` colourless or milky white like an opal, or changing `LITERARY` colour like an opal. *Elaine turned her opalescent eyes on him.*

opaque /əʊˈpeɪk/. **1** If an object or substance is ◆◇◇◇ **opaque**, you cannot see through it. *...opaque glass* `ADJ-GRADED` *windows.* **2** If you say that something is **opaque**, `ADJ-GRADED` you mean that it is difficult to understand. *...the opaque language of the inspector's reports.*

op. cit. /ˌɒp ˈsɪt/. In reference books, **op. cit.** is ◆◇◇◇ written after an author's name to refer to a book of theirs which has already been mentioned. *...quoted in Iyer, op. cit., p. 332.*

OPEC /ˈəʊpek/. **OPEC** is an organization of coun- ◆◆◇◇ tries that produce oil. **OPEC** is an abbreviation for `N-PROPER` 'Organization of Petroleum-Exporting Countries'.

open /ˈəʊpən/ **opens, opening, opened**. **1** If ◆◆◆◆ you **open** something such as a door, window, or lid, `V-ERG` or if it **opens**, its position is changed so that it no `V n` longer covers a hole or gap. *He opened the window* `V` *and looked out... The church doors would open and the crowd would surge out.* ▶ Also an adjective. *A* `ADJ` *door had been forced open. ...an open window.* **2** If `PHRASE` a door or window is **wide open**, it is open to its full extent. **3** If you **open** something such as a bottle, `VERB` box, parcel, or envelope, you move, remove, or cut `V n` part of it so you can take out what is inside. *The Inspector opened the packet of cigarettes.* ▶ Also an ad- `ADJ` jective. *I tore the letter open.* ▶ **Open up** means the `PHRASAL VB` same as **open**. *He opened up the jewelry case and* `V P n` took out a necklace... I opened this bag up; there `V n P` were five or six lamps in there.* **4** If people **open** `V-ERG` something such as a blocked road or a border, or if `V n` it opens, people can then pass along it or through it. `Also V` *The rebels have opened the road from Monrovia to the Ivory Coast.* ▶ Also an adjective. *...an entire regi-* `ADJ` *ment that had nothing else to do but to keep that highway open.* ▶ **Open up** means the same as `PHRASAL VB` **open**. *Rescue workers opened up roads today... It* `ERG` *wasn't just the roads that opened up but the water-* `V P noun` *ways too.* **5** If you **open** your shirt or coat, you un- `V P` fasten or unzip it. ▶ Also an adjective. *The top can* `ADJ` *be worn buttoned up or open... His open shirt revealed a fat gold chain.*

6 If you **open** something such as a book, an umbrella, `V-ERG` or your hand, or if it **opens**, the different parts of it `V n` move away from each other so that the inside of it can `V` be seen. *He opened the heavy Bible... The officer's mouth opened.* ▶ Also an adjective. *Bardo smacked* `ADJ-GRADED` *his fist into his open hand.* ▶ **Open out** means the `PHRASAL VB` same as **open**. *Keith took a map from the dashboard* `ERG` *and opened it out on his knees. ...oval tables which* `V n P` *open out... Opening out the bed couldn't be easier –* `V P` *just lift and pull.* **7** When you **open** your eyes or your `Also V P noun` eyes **open**, you move your eyelids upwards, for exam- `V-ERG` ple when you wake up, so that you can see. *When I* `V n` *opened my eyes I saw a man standing at the end of my* `V` *bed... His eyes were opening wide.* ▶ Also an adjective. `ADJ` *He saw that her eyes were open.* **8** If you **open** your `VERB: V n` arms, you stretch them wide apart in front of you, usually in order to hug someone. **9** If you stand or sit `ADJ-GRADED` in an **open** way, the front of your body is fully exposed and you are not hunched or at an angle to someone. *Good listeners sit in an open way: relaxed, arms loose.*

10 If you describe a person or their character as **open**, `ADJ-GRADED` you mean they are honest and do not want or try to hide anything or to deceive anyone. *He had always*

been open with her. ✦ **open·ness** *I was impressed by*   N-UNCOUNT
his openness and I felt he was being very sincere. **11** If   ADJ: ADJ n
you describe a situation, attitude, or way of behaving
as **open**, you mean it is not kept hidden or secret. *The
action is an open violation of the Vienna Convention.*
✦ **openness** *...the new climate of political openness.*   N-UNCOUNT
12 If something is **in the open** or **out in the open**,   PHRASE
people know about it and it is no longer kept secret.
You must bring this issue out in the open. **13** If you are   ADJ-GRADED:
open to suggestions or ideas, you are ready and will-   v-link ADJ to n
ing to consider or accept them. *They are open to suggestions on how working conditions might be
improved.*
14 If you say that a system, person, or idea is **open to**   ADJ:
something such as abuse or criticism, you mean they   v-link ADJ to n
might receive it because of the qualities they possess
or the effects they have had. *They left themselves wide
open to accusations of double standards.* **15** If you say   ADJ
that a fact or question is **open** to debate, interpretation, or discussion, you mean that people are uncertain whether it is true, what it means, or what the answer is. *The truth of the facts may be open to doubt.*
16 If a place **opens** into another, larger place, you can   VERB
move from one directly into the other. *The corridor*   V into/onto/
opened into a low smoky room. ▶ **Open out** means the   ton
same as **open**. *...narrow streets opening out into*   PHRASAL VB
charming squares.   V P into/
onto/to n
17 An **open** area is a large area that does not have   ADJ
many structures or obstructions in it. *Officers will
continue their search of nearby open ground.* **18** If you   PHRASE
do something **in the open**, you do it out of doors rather than in a house or other building. **19** An **open**   ADJ: ADJ n
structure or object is not covered or enclosed. *...a
room with an open fire.* **20** An **open** wound is one   ADJ
from which blood or pus is coming out.
21 When a shop, office, or public building **opens** or   V-ERG
when someone **opens** it, its doors are unlocked and   V
the people in it start working. *Banks closed on Friday*   Also V n
*afternoon and did not open again until Monday
morning.* ▶ Also an adjective. *His shop is open Mon-*   ADJ
day through Friday. **22** When a public building, facto-   V-ERG
ry, or company **opens** or when someone **opens** it, it   V
starts operating for the first time. *The original station*   V n
*opened in 1754... They are planning to open a factory
in Eastern Europe.* ✦ **open·ing, openings** *He was*   N-COUNT
there for the official opening. **23** If something such as   V-ERG
a meeting or series of talks **opens**, or if someone   V
opens it, it begins. *...an emergency session of Parlia-*   Also V n
ment due to open later this morning. ✦ **opening** *...a*   N-SING
communique issued at the opening of the talks. **24** If   V-ERG
an event such as a meeting or discussion **opens** or is   V with n
opened with a particular activity or topic, that activity   V n with n
or topic is the first thing that happens or is dealt with.
You can also say that someone such as a speaker or
singer **opens** in a particular way. *The service opened
with a hymn... Pollard opened the conversation with
some small talk.* **25** When a film, play, or other public   VERB
event **opens**, it begins to be shown or be performed,   V
or to take place for a limited period of time. *A photographic exhibition opens at the Royal College of Art on
Wednesday.* ✦ **open·ing** *...the opening of the Olympic*   N-SING:
Games.   the N of n
26 If you **open** an account with a bank or a commer-   VERB: V n
cial organization, you begin to use their services.
27 If an opportunity or choice is **open** to you, you are   ADJ:
able to do a particular thing if you choose to. *...a wide*   v-link ADJ to n
range of career opportunities open to young people.
28 To **open** opportunities or possibilities means the   V-ERG
same as to **open** them **up**. *The navy wants to open op-*   V n
portunities for women. **29** You can use **open** to de-   Also V
scribe something that anyone is allowed to take part   ADJ
in or accept. *...to keep entry into the managerial profession open and flexible.* **30** If something such as an   ADJ:
offer or vacancy is **open**, it is available for someone to   v-link ADJ
accept or apply for. *The offer will remain open until
further notice.* **31** See also **opening**. **32** If you say that   PHRASE
a competition, race, or election is **wide open**, you
mean that any of the participants could win it.
33 ● **with open arms**: see **arm**. ● **to open the door**:
see **door**. ● **to keep** your **eyes open**: see **eye**. ● **with**

your **eyes open**: see **eye**. ● **to open** your **eyes**: see **eye**.
● **to open fire**: see **fire**. ● **to open** your **heart**: see
heart. ● **the heavens open**: see **heaven**. ● **to keep**
your **options open**: see **option**.
open out. See **open** 6, 16, **open up** 6.   PHRASAL VB
open up. 1 See **open** 3, 4. **2** If a place, economy, or   PHRASAL VB
area of interest **opens up**, or if someone **opens** it **up**, it   ERG
becomes accessible to more people. *As the market*   V P
opens up, I think people are going to be able to spend   V P noun
more money on consumer goods... The money could   Also V n P
open up music to more children. **3** If something **opens**   ERG
up opportunities or possibilities, or if opportunities   V P noun
or possibilities **open up**, they are able to arise or de-   V P
velop. *The collapse of communism in Eastern Europe*   Also V n P
*opened up new possibilities... New opportunities are
opening up for investors.* **4** If you **open up** a lead in a   V P n
race or competition, you get yourself into a position
where you are leading, usually by quite a long way.
5 When you **open up** a building, you unlock and open   V P noun
the door so that people can get in. *The postmaster and*   Also V P
his wife arrived to open up the shop. **6** If someone   V P
opens up, or in British English **opens out**, they start to   V P to n
say exactly what they think or feel about something or
someone. *People were always willing to open up to
her.*
,open-'air; also spelled **open air. 1** An **open-air**   ◆◇◇◇◇
place or event is outside rather than in a building.   ADJ
...the Open Air Theatre in Regents Park. **2** If you are   N-SING:
in the **open air**, you are outside rather than in a   the N
building.
,open-and-'shut. If you describe a dispute or a le-   ADJ
gal case as **open-and-shut**, you mean that it is easily decided or solved because the facts are very clear.
...an open-and-shut murder charge.
open·cast /'əʊpənkɑːst, -kæst/; also spelled **open-**   ADJ: ADJ n
cast. At an **opencast** mine, the coal, metal, or minerals are near the surface and underground passages are not used.
'open day, open days. At a school, university, or   N-COUNT
other institution, an **open day** is a specific day   BRITISH
when the members of the public are encouraged to
visit the campus.
,open-'door; also spelled **open door**. If a country   ◆◇◇◇◇
or organization has an **open-door** policy towards   ADJ: ADJ n
people or goods, it allows them to come there
freely, without any restrictions. *...an open door economic policy.* ▶ Also a noun. *...an open door to for-*   N-SING
eign investment.
,open-'ended. When people begin an **open-**   ◆◇◇◇◇
ended discussion or activity, they do not start with   ADJ
any intention of achieving a particular decision or
result. *...open-ended questions about what passengers expect of an airline.*
open·er /'əʊpənə/ **openers**. An **opener** is a tool   ◆◇◇◇◇
which is used to open containers such as tins or   N-COUNT
bottles. *...a tin opener.* ● See also **eye-opener**.
,open 'house. If you say that someone keeps **open**   N-UNCOUNT
house, you mean that they welcome friends or visitors to their house whenever they arrive.
open·ing /'əʊpənɪŋ/ **openings. 1** The **opening**   ◆◆◆◇◇
event, item, day, or week in a series is the first one.   ADJ: ADJ n
*They returned to take part in the season's opening
game.* **2** The **opening** of something such as a book,   N-COUNT
play, or concert is the first part of it. *I've asked Mark
to write a piece for the opening of the film.* **3** An   N-COUNT
opening is a hole or empty space through which
things or people can pass. *...a narrow opening in the
fence.* **4** An **opening** is a good opportunity to do   N-COUNT
something, for example to show people how good
you are. *All she needed was an opening to show her
capabilities.* **5** An **opening** is a job that is available.   N-COUNT
We don't have any openings now. **6** See also **open**.
'opening hours. **Opening hours** are the times   N-PLURAL
during which a shop, bank, library, or pub is open
for business.
,opening 'night, opening nights. The **opening**   ◆◇◇◇◇
night of a play or an opera is the first night on   N-COUNT
which a particular production is performed.
'opening time, opening times. 1 You can refer   N-UNCOUNT
to the time that a shop, bank, library, or pub opens

for business as its **opening time**. **2** The **opening times** of a place such as a shop, a restaurant, or a museum is the period during which it is open. `N-PLURAL`

,open 'letter, open letters. An **open letter** is a letter that is published in a newspaper or magazine. It is addressed to a particular person but is intended for the general reader, usually in order to protest or give an opinion about something. `◆◇◇◇◇ N-COUNT`

open·ly /'əupənli/. If you do something **openly**, you do it without hiding any facts or hiding your feelings. *We can now talk openly about AIDS. ...a pair of nurses who were openly gay.* `◆◆◇◇ ADV-GRADED`

,open 'market. Goods that are bought and sold on **the open market** are advertised and sold publicly rather than privately. Compare **black market**. `◆◇◇◇◇ N-SING: the N`

,open-'minded. If you describe someone as **open-minded**, you approve of them because they are willing to listen to and consider other people's ideas. *He was very open-minded about other people's work.* ♦ **open-minded·ness** *...honesty, open-mindedness and willingness to learn.* `◆◇◇◇◇ ADJ-GRADED [PRAGMATICS] N-UNCOUNT`

,open-'mouthed. If someone is looking **open-mouthed**, they are staring at something with their mouth wide open because it has shocked, frightened, or excited them. *They watched open-mouthed as the two men came towards them.* `ADJ`

,open-'necked or **open-neck**. If you are wearing an **open-necked** shirt or blouse, you are wearing a shirt or blouse with the top button unfastened and no tie. `ADJ: ADJ n`

,open-'plan. An **open-plan** building or room has no internal walls dividing it into smaller areas. `ADJ`

,open 'question, open questions. If something is an **open question**, people have different opinions about it and nobody can say which opinion is correct. *It was an open question whether sanctions would do any good.* `N-COUNT`

,open 'secret, open secrets. If you refer to something as an **open secret**, you mean that it is supposed to be a secret, but many people know about it. *It's an open secret that the security service bugged telephones.* `N-COUNT`

,Open Uni'versity. In Britain, **the Open University** is a university that runs degree courses on the radio and television for students who do not have the qualifications necessary for ordinary universities, or who want to study part-time or mainly at home. `◆◇◇◇◇ N-PROPER: the N`

op·era /'ɒpərə/ **operas**. An **opera** is a musical entertainment. It is like a play but most of the words are sung. *...a one-act opera about contemporary women in America.* ● See also **soap opera**. ● **oper·at·ic** /ˌɒpə'rætɪk/ *He attended the local amateur operatic society.* `◆◆◇◇ N-VAR ADJ`

'opera house, opera houses. An **opera house** is a theatre that is specially designed for the performance of operas. `◆◇◇◇◇ N-COUNT`

op·eran·di /ˌɒpə'rændaɪ/. See **modus operandi**.

op·er·ate /'ɒpəreɪt/ **operates, operating, operated**. **1** If you **operate** a business or organization, you work to keep it running properly. If a business or organization **operates**, it carries out its work. *Greenwood owned and operated an enormous pear orchard. ...allowing commercial banks to operate in the country.* ♦ **op·era·tion** /ˌɒpə'reɪʃən/ *...funds for the everyday operation of the business.* **2** When you **operate** a machine or device, or when it **operates**, you make it work. *A massive rock fall trapped the men as they operated a tunnelling machine.* ♦ **operation**. **3** The way that something **operates** is the way that it works or has a particular effect. *Ceiling and wall lights can operate independently... The world of work doesn't operate that way.* ♦ **operation** *The operation of the new tax is being studied.* **4** When surgeons **operate** on a patient in a hospital, they cut open a patient's body in order to remove, replace, or repair a diseased or damaged part. *The surgeon who operated on the King released new details of his injuries.* **5** If military forces are `◆◆◆◆◆ V-ERG Vn V N-UNCOUNT V-ERG Vn Also V N-UNCOUNT VERB V adv/prep Vn N-UNCOUNT VERB V on n Also V VERB:`

operating in a particular region, they are in that place in order to carry out their orders. `V prep`

'operating system, operating systems. The **operating system** of a computer is its most basic program, which it needs in order to function and run other programs. `◆◇◇◇◇ N-COUNT`

'operating table, operating tables. An **operating table** is a table which a patient in a hospital lies on during a surgical operation. `N-COUNT`

'operating theatre, operating theatres; spelled **operating theater** in American English. An **operating theatre** is a special room in a hospital where surgeons carry out medical operations. The usual American term is **operating room**. `N-COUNT BRITISH`

op·era·tion /ˌɒpə'reɪʃən/ **operations**. **1** An **operation** is a highly organized activity that involves many people doing different things. *The rescue operation began on Friday afternoon. ...a military operation.* **2** A business or company can be referred to as an **operation**. *Thorn's electronics operation employs around 5,000 people.* **3** When a patient has an **operation**, a surgeon cuts open their body in order to remove, replace, or repair a diseased or damaged part. **4** If a system is in **operation**, it is being used. *Until the rail links are in operation, passengers can only travel through the tunnel by coach.* **5** When a rule, system, or plan **comes into operation** or you **put** it **into operation**, you begin to use it. *The Financial Services Act came into operation four years ago.* **6** If a machine or device is in **operation**, it is working. *There are three ski lifts in operation.* `◆◆◆◆◆ N-COUNT N-COUNT N-COUNT N-UNCOUNT: in/out of N PHRASE N-UNCOUNT: in/out of N`

op·era·tion·al /ˌɒpə'reɪʃənəl/. **1** A machine or piece of equipment that is **operational** is in use or is ready for use. *The whole system will be fully operational by December 1995.* **2 Operational** factors or problems relate to the working of a system, device, or plan. *The industry was required to prove that every operational aspect had been fully researched.* ♦ **op·era·tion·al·ly** *An all-female political section would have been operationally ineffective.* `◆◆◇◇◇ ADJ ADJ ADV`

op·era·tive /'ɒpərətɪv/ **operatives**. **1** A system or service that is **operative** is working or having an effect. *The Youth Training Scheme was operative by the end of 1983.* **2** An **operative** is a worker, especially one with a manual skill. *...the sufferings of the factory operative.* **3** An **operative** is someone who works for a government agency such as the intelligence service. **4** If you describe a word as **the operative word**, you want to draw attention to it because you think it is important or exactly true in a particular situation. *As long as the operative word is 'greed', you can't count on people keeping the costs down.* `◆◆◇◇◇ ADJ FORMAL N-COUNT FORMAL N-COUNT AMERICAN PHRASE`

op·era·tor /'ɒpəreɪtə/ **operators**. **1** An **operator** is a person who works at a telephone exchange or at the switchboard of an office or hotel. *He dialled the operator and put in a call for Rome.* **2** An **operator** is a person who is employed to operate or control a machine. **3** An **operator** is a person or a company that runs a business. *...the nation's largest cable TV operator.* **4** If you call someone a good **operator**, you mean that they are skilful at achieving what they want, often in a slightly dishonest way. *...one of the shrewdest political operators in the Arab world.* **5** See also **tour operator**. `◆◆◆◇◇ N-COUNT N-COUNT N-COUNT N-COUNT INFORMAL`

op·er·et·ta /ˌɒpə'retə/ **operettas**. An **operetta** is a light-hearted and often comic opera which has some of the words spoken rather than sung. `N-VAR`

oph·thal·mic /ɒf'θælmɪk/. **Ophthalmic** means relating to or concerned with the medical care of people's eyes and eyesight. *...ophthalmic surgeons.* `ADJ: ADJ n FORMAL`

oph·thal·mol·ogy /ˌɒfθæl'mɒlədʒi/. **Ophthalmology** is the branch of medicine concerned with people's eyes and eyesight and the problems that affect them. ♦ **oph·thal·m·olo·gist** /ˌɒfθæl'mɒlədʒɪst/ **ophthalmologists**. `N-UNCOUNT N-COUNT`

opi·ate /'əupiət/ **opiates**. **1** An **opiate** is a drug that contains opium. Opiates are used to reduce pain or to help people to sleep. **2** If you call `N-COUNT N-COUNT`

something an **opiate**, you disapprove of it because it makes people think less or spend less time on important activities. *He talked about the opiate of mass entertainment.* [PRAGMATICS]

opine /əʊˈpaɪn/ **opines, opining, opined.** To **opine** means to express your opinion. *'She's probably had a row with her boyfriend,' Charles opined... He opined that the navy would have to start again from the beginning.* VERB: V with quote; V that; Also V on/about n; FORMAL

opin·ion /əˈpɪnjən/ **opinions. 1** Your **opinion** about something is what you think or believe about it. *I wasn't asking for your opinion, Dick... He held the opinion that a government should think before introducing a tax.* **2** Your **opinion** of someone is your judgement of their character or ability. *That improved Mrs Goole's already favourable opinion of him.* **3** You can refer to the beliefs or views that people have as **opinion**. *There is a broad consensus of opinion about the policies which should be pursued.* **4** An **opinion** from an expert is the advice or judgement that they give you in the subject that they know a lot about. *Even if you have had a regular physical check-up recently, you should still seek a medical opinion.* **5** See also **public opinion, second opinion.** **6** You add expressions such as **'in my opinion'** or **'in their opinion'** to a statement in order to emphasize that it is what you or someone else thinks, and is not necessarily a fact. *Well he's not making a very good job of it in my opinion.* **7** If someone is **of the opinion** that something is the case, that is what they believe. *Frank is of the opinion that the 1934 yacht should have won.* **8 ● a matter of opinion:** see **matter.** N-COUNT; N-SING; N-UNCOUNT; N-COUNT; PHRASE [PRAGMATICS]; PHRASE FORMAL

opin·ion·at·ed /əˈpɪnjəneɪtɪd/. If you describe someone as **opinionated**, you mean that they have very strong opinions and refuse to accept that they may be wrong. ADJ-GRADED

o'pinion poll, opinion polls. An **opinion poll** involves asking people's opinions on a particular subject, especially one concerning politics. ◆◆◇◇◇ N-COUNT

opium /ˈəʊpiəm/. **Opium** is a powerful drug made from the seeds of a type of poppy. Opium is used in medicines that relieve pain or help someone sleep. ◆◇◇◇◇ N-UNCOUNT

opos·sum /əˈpɒsəm/ **opossums.** An **opossum** is a small animal that lives in America. It carries its young in a pouch on its body, and has thick fur and a long tail. N-VAR

op·po·nent /əˈpəʊnənt/ **opponents. 1** A politician's **opponents** are other politicians who belong to a different party or who have different aims or policies. *He described the detention without trial of political opponents as a cowardly act.* **2** In a sporting contest, your **opponent** is the person who is playing against you. **3** The **opponent** of an idea or policy do not agree with it and do not want it to be carried out. *...opponents of the spread of nuclear weapons.* ◆◆◇◇◇ N-COUNT; N-COUNT; N-COUNT

op·por·tune /ˈɒpətjuːn, AM -ˈtuːn/. If something happens at an **opportune** time or is **opportune**, it happens at the time that is most convenient for someone or most likely to lead to success. *I believe that I have arrived at a very opportune moment.* ADJ-GRADED FORMAL

op·por·tun·ism /ˌɒpəˈtjuːnɪzəm, AM -ˈtuːn-/. If you refer to someone's behaviour as **opportunism**, you are criticizing them for taking advantage of any opportunity that occurs in order to gain money or power, without thinking about whether their actions are right or wrong. *The most commanding jobs are still held by bureaucrats selected for their servility and political opportunism.* N-UNCOUNT [PRAGMATICS]

op·por·tun·ist /ˌɒpəˈtjuːnɪst, AM -ˈtuːn-/ **opportunists. 1** If you describe someone as **opportunist**, you are critical of them because they take advantage of any situation in order to gain money or power, without considering whether their actions are right or wrong. *...corrupt and opportunist politicians.* ▶ An **opportunist** is someone who is opportunist. **2 Opportunist** actions are not planned, but are carried out in order to take advantage of the im- ◆◇◇◇◇ ADJ-GRADED [PRAGMATICS]; N-COUNT; ADJ

mediate situation. *He made the game safe with a brilliant opportunist goal.*

op·por·tun·is·tic /ˌɒpətjuːˈnɪstɪk, AM -tuːn-/. If you describe someone's behaviour as **opportunistic**, you are critical of them because they take advantage of situations in order to gain money or power, without thinking about whether their actions are right or wrong. *Many of the party's members joined only for opportunistic reasons.* ♦ **op·por·tun·is·ti·cal·ly** *This nationalist feeling has been exploited opportunistically.* ◆◇◇◇◇ ADJ-GRADED [PRAGMATICS]; ADV-GRADED: ADV with v

op·por·tu·nity /ˌɒpəˈtjuːnɪti, AM -ˈtuːn-/ **opportunities.** An **opportunity** is a situation in which it is possible for you to do something that you want to do. *I had an opportunity to go to New York and study... The best reason for a trip to London is the super opportunity for shopping.* ● See also **photo opportunity.** ◆◆◆◆◇ N-VAR

op·pose /əˈpəʊz/ **opposes, opposing, opposed.** If you **oppose** someone or **oppose** their plans or ideas, you disagree with what they want to do and try to prevent them from doing it. *Many parents oppose bilingual education in schools.* ◆◆◆◇◇ VERB V n

op·posed /əˈpəʊzd/. **1** If you **are opposed to** something, you disagree with it or disapprove of it. *I am utterly opposed to any form of terrorism. ...an outspoken group of ministers opposed to drinking.* **2** You say that two ideas or systems are **opposed** when they are opposite to each other or very different from each other. *...people with policies almost diametrically opposed to his own.* **3** You use **as opposed to** when you want to make it clear that you are talking about one particular thing and not something else. *We ate in the restaurant, as opposed to the bistro.* ◆◆◇◇◇ ADJ-GRADED: v-link ADJ to n/-ing; ADJ; PHRASE

op·pos·ing /əˈpəʊzɪŋ/. **1** Opposing ideas or tendencies are totally different from each other. *I have a friend who has the opposing view and felt that the war was immoral.* **2** Opposing groups of people disagree about something or are in competition with one another. *He still favoured dialogue between the opposing sides.* ◆◇◇◇◇ ADJ: ADJ n; ADJ: ADJ n

op·po·site /ˈɒpəzɪt/ **opposites. 1** If one thing is **opposite** another, it is on the other side of a space from it. *Jennie had sat opposite her at breakfast.* ▶ Also an adverb. *He looked up at the buildings opposite. ...the little girl on the seat opposite... Her husband sat opposite.* **2** The **opposite** side or part of something is the side or part that is furthest away from you. *...the opposite corner of the room.* **3** Opposite is used to describe things of the same kind which are completely different in a particular way. *All the cars driving in the opposite direction had their headlights on... Everything he does is opposite to what is considered normal.* **4** The **opposite** of someone or something is the person or thing that is most different from them. *Ritter was a very complex man but Marius was the opposite, a simple farmer... The opposite of love is not hatred but indifference.* ◆◆◆◇◇ PREP; ADV; ADJ: ADJ n; ADJ; N-COUNT

opposite 'number, opposite numbers. Your **opposite number** is a person who has the same job or rank as you, but works in a different department, firm, or organization. *The French Defence Minister is to visit Japan later this month for talks with his Japanese opposite number.* ◆◇◇◇◇ N-COUNT JOURNALISM

opposite 'sex. If you are talking about men and refer to **the opposite sex**, you mean women. If you are talking about women and refer to **the opposite sex**, you mean men. ◆◇◇◇◇ N-SING: the N

op·po·si·tion /ˌɒpəˈzɪʃən/ **oppositions. 1** Opposition is strong, angry, or violent disagreement and disapproval. *The government is facing a new wave of opposition.* **2** The **opposition** consists of the political parties or groups that are opposed to a government. *...the main opposition parties.* **3** In a country's parliament, the **opposition** refers to the politicians or political parties that form part of the parliament but are not in the government. *...the Leader of the Opposition.* **4** The **opposition** is the ◆◆◆◇ N-UNCOUNT; N-COLL-COUNT; N-COLL-COUNT; N-COLL-SING

O

person or team you are competing against in a sports event.

op·press /ə'pres/ **oppresses, oppressing, oppressed.** 1 To **oppress** people means to treat them cruelly, or to prevent them from having the same opportunities, freedom, and benefits as others. *These people often are oppressed by their governments.* ♦ **op·pressed** /ə'prest/ *They felt oppressed by the white English speakers who controlled things.* ♦ **op·pres·sion** /ə'preʃən/ **oppressions** *...the oppression of the 19th-century poor by the rich.* ♦ **op·pres·sor, oppressors** *They could organise no defence against their oppressors.* 2 If something **oppresses** you, it makes you feel depressed, anxious, and uncomfortable. *It was not just the weather which oppressed her.*
VERB: V n
be V-ed
Also V,
V n with n

ADJ-GRADED

N-UNCOUNT:
also N in pl

N-COUNT

VERB
V n
LITERARY

op·pres·sive /ə'presɪv/. 1 If you describe a society, its laws, or customs as **oppressive**, you think they treat people cruelly and unfairly. *The new laws will be just as oppressive as those they replace.* 2 If you describe the weather or the atmosphere in a room as **oppressive**, you mean that it is uncomfortably hot and humid. *...the oppressive afternoon heat.* 3 An **oppressive** situation makes you feel depressed and uncomfortable. *...the oppressive sadness that weighed upon him like a physical chain.*
♦◇◇◇◇
ADJ-GRADED

ADJ-GRADED

ADJ-GRADED

op·pro·brium /ə'prəʊbriəm/. **Opprobrium** is open criticism or disapproval of something that someone has done. *His political opinions have attracted the opprobrium of the Left.*
N-UNCOUNT
FORMAL

opt /ɒpt/ **opts, opting, opted.** If you **opt** for something, you choose it or decide to do it in preference to anything else. *Our students can also opt to stay in residence.*
♦♦♦◇◇
VERB:
V for n
V to-inf

opt in. If you can **opt in**, you are able to choose to be part of an agreement or system. *Only those countries which were willing and able should opt in to phase three.*
PHRASAL VB
V P
V P to n

opt out. If you **opt out** of something, you choose to be no longer involved in it. *Under the agreement the Vietnamese can opt out at any time.*
PHRASAL VB
V P of n
V P

op·tic /'ɒptɪk/. **Optic** means relating to the eyes or to sight. *...the optic nerve.* ● See also **optics.**
♦◇◇◇◇
ADJ: ADJ n

op·ti·cal /'ɒptɪkəl/. 1 **Optical** instruments, devices, or processes are concerned with vision, light, or images. *...optical telescopes.* 2 **Optical** means relating to how people see things. *...the optical effects of volcanic dust.*
♦◇◇◇◇
ADJ

ADJ: ADJ n

optical 'fibre, optical fibres; spelled **optical fiber** in American English. An **optical fibre** is a very thin strand of glass used to transmit information in the form of light.
N-VAR

optical il'lusion, optical illusions. An **optical illusion** is something that tricks your eyes so that what you think you see is different from what is really there.
N-COUNT

op·ti·cian /ɒp'tɪʃən/ **opticians.** An **optician** is someone whose job involves testing people's eyesight, and making and selling glasses and contact lenses. You can refer to the shop where opticians work as an **optician** or an **optician's.**
N-COUNT

op·tics /'ɒptɪks/. **Optics** is the branch of science concerned with vision, sight, and light. ● See also **fibre optics.**
♦◇◇◇◇
N-UNCOUNT

op·ti·mal /'ɒptɪməl/. See **optimum.**

op·ti·mism /'ɒptɪmɪzəm/. **Optimism** is the feeling of being hopeful about the future or about the success of something. *The Indian Prime Minister has expressed optimism about India's future relations with the USA.* ♦ **op·ti·mist, optimists** *He has the upbeat manner of an eternal optimist.*
♦♦◇◇◇
N-UNCOUNT

N-COUNT

op·ti·mis·tic /,ɒptɪ'mɪstɪk/. If you feel **optimistic** about something, you think that it will turn out in the way you want. *She is optimistic that an agreement can be worked out soon.* ♦ **op·ti·mis·ti·cal·ly** *Both sides have spoken optimistically about the talks.*
♦◇◇◇◇
ADJ-GRADED

ADV-GRADED:
ADV with v

op·ti·mize /'ɒptɪmaɪz/ **optimizes, optimizing, optimized;** also spelled **optimise** in British English. 1 To **optimize** a plan, system, or machine
VERB

means to arrange or design it so that it operates as smoothly and efficiently as possible. *Doctors are concentrating on understanding the disease better, and on optimizing the treatment.* 2 To **optimize** a situation or opportunity means to get as much advantage or benefit from it as you can. *What can you do to optimize your family situation?*
V n
FORMAL

VERB
V n
FORMAL

op·ti·mum /'ɒptɪməm/ or **optimal.** The **optimum** level or state of something is the best level or state that it could achieve. *Aim to do some physical activity three times a week for optimum health. ...optimal conditions for farming.*
♦◇◇◇◇
ADJ
FORMAL

op·tion /'ɒpʃən/ **options.** 1 An **option** is something that you can choose to do in preference to one or more alternatives. *America and its allies are putting too much emphasis on the military option... What other options do you have?* 2 If you have the **option** to do something, you can choose whether to do it or not. *Several south-Asians were given the option of British citizenship... We had no option but to abandon the meeting.* 3 If you **keep** your **options open** or **leave** your **options open**, you avoid making an immediate decision about something. *She is keeping her options open, and has refused to leave her present job until the election is won.* 4 If you say that someone has taken a **soft option**, you mean that they have taken a course of action because it is the easiest thing to do or least likely to produce conflict rather than because it is the best thing to do in the circumstances. 5 In business, an **option** is an agreement or contract that gives someone the right to buy or sell something such as property or shares at a future date. 6 An **option** is one of a number of subjects which a student can choose to study as a part of his or her course. *Several options are offered for the student's senior year.*
♦♦♦♦◇
N-COUNT

N-SING

PHRASE

PHRASE

N-COUNT

N-COUNT

op·tion·al /'ɒpʃənəl/. If something is **optional**, you can choose whether or not you do it or have it. *Sex education is a sensitive area for some parents, and thus it should remain optional.*
♦◇◇◇◇
ADJ

'opt-out, opt-outs. 1 In Britain, you can refer to the action taken by a school or hospital in which they choose not to be controlled by a local government authority as an **opt-out**. *More freedom and choice will be given to parents, and the school opt-outs will be stepped up.* ► Also an adjective. *...a national funding council for opt-out schools. ...opt-out hospitals.* 2 An **opt-out** clause in an agreement gives participants the choice not to be involved in one part of that agreement. 3 You can refer to the action of choosing not to be involved in a particular part of an agreement as an **opt-out**. *...a list of demands, such as opt-outs from some parts of the treaty.*
♦◇◇◇◇
N-COUNT

ADJ: ADJ n

ADJ: ADJ n
BRITISH

N-COUNT

opu·lent /'ɒpjʊlənt/. 1 **Opulent** things or places look grand and expensive. *...an opulent office in London's West End.* ♦ **opu·lence** *...the opulence of Napoleon III's court.* 2 People who have an **opulent** lifestyle are very wealthy and spend a lot of money.
♦◇◇◇◇
ADJ-GRADED
FORMAL
N-UNCOUNT
ADJ-GRADED
FORMAL

opus /'əʊpəs, 'ɒpəs/ **opuses** or **opera.** 1 An **opus** is a musical composition. **Opus** is usually followed by a number which indicates when the composition was written. The abbreviation 'op.' is also used. 2 You can refer to an artistic work such as a piece of music or writing or a painting as an **opus.** ● See also **magnum opus.**
♦◇◇◇◇
N-COUNT

N-COUNT

or /ə, STRONG ɔː/. 1 You use **or** to link two or more alternatives. *'Tea or coffee?' John asked... Spread the inside of the loaf with olive paste or pesto sauce... He said he would try to write or call... Students are asked to take another course in English, or science, or mathematics.* 2 You use **or** to give another alternative, when the first alternative is introduced by 'either' or 'whether'. *Items like bread, milk and meat were either unavailable or could be obtained only on the black market... I don't know whether people will buy it or not.* 3 You use **or** between two numbers to indicate that you are giving an approximate amount. *...limiting*
♦♦♦♦♦
CONJ
PRAGMATICS

CONJ
PRAGMATICS

CONJ

*their intake of tea to just three or four cups a day.
...when I was nine or ten... Normally he asked questions, and had a humorous remark or two.* **4** You CONJ PRAGMATICS
use **or** to introduce a comment which corrects or
modifies what you have just said. *The man was a
fool, or at least incompetent... There was nothing
more he wanted, or so he thought.*

5 If you say that someone should do something or CONJ PRAGMATICS
something unpleasant will happen, you are warning
them that if they do not do it, the unpleasant thing
will happen. *She had to have the operation, or she
would die.* **6** You use **or** to introduce something which CONJ PRAGMATICS
is an explanation or justification for a statement you
have just made. *He must have thought Jane was worth
it or he wouldn't have wasted time on her.*

7 You use **or no** or **or not** to emphasize that a particu- PHRASE PRAGMATICS
lar thing makes no difference to what is going to happen. *Chairman or no, if I want to stop the project, I
can... Old-fashioned or not, it is very good.* **8** You use PHRASE
or no between two occurrences of the same noun in
order to say that whether something is true or not
makes no difference to a situation. *The next day, rain
or no rain, it was business as usual.*

9 ● **or else**: see **else**. ● **or other**: see **other**. ● **or so**: see
so. ● **or something**: see **something**.

-or /-ə/. **-or** is used at the end of nouns that refer to SUFFIX
people or things which perform a particular action.
...the translator. ...an electric generator.

ora·cle /ˈɒrəkəl, AM ˈɔːr-/ **oracles.** In ancient N-COUNT
Greece, an **oracle** was a priest or priestess who
made statements about future events or about the
truth.

oral /ˈɔːrəl/ **orals. 1** Oral communication is spo- ADJ ◆◆◇◇◇
ken rather than written. *...an oral agreement... They
had to give oral reports in school.* ♦ **oral·ly** *...their* ADV ADV after v
*ability to present ideas orally and in writing. ...the
tradition that is passed down orally.* **2** An **oral** is an N-COUNT
examination, especially in a foreign language, that is
spoken rather than written. **3** You use **oral** to indi- ADJ
cate that something is done with a person's mouth
or relates to a person's mouth. *...good oral hygiene.*
4 Oral medicines are taken by mouth. *...a single* ADJ: ADJ n
oral dose of vitamin B. ♦ **orally** *...tablets taken* ADV
orally.

,oral 'sex. Oral sex is sexual activity involving con- N-UNCOUNT
tact between a person's mouth and their partner's
genitals.

or·ange /ˈɒrɪndʒ, AM ˈɔːr-/ **oranges. 1** Something ◆◆◆◇◇ COLOUR
that is **orange** is of a colour between red and yellow. **2** An **orange** is a round juicy fruit with a thick N-VAR
orange coloured skin. See picture headed **fruit**.
3 Orange is a drink that is made from or tastes of N-UNCOUNT
oranges.

orang-utang /ɒˌræŋuːˈtæn/ **orang-utangs;** also N-COUNT
spelled **orang-utan**. An **orang-utang** is a type of ape
with long reddish hair that comes from Borneo and
Sumatra.

ora·tion /əˈreɪʃən, AM ɔːr-/ **orations.** An oration is N-COUNT FORMAL
a formal speech made in public.

ora·tor /ˈɒrətə, AM ˈɔːr-/ **orators.** An **orator** is N-COUNT
someone who is skilled at making formal speeches
in public which strongly affect people's feelings and
beliefs. *Lenin was the great orator of the Russian
Revolution.*

ora·to·rio /ˌɒrəˈtɔːriəʊ, AM ˈɔːr-/ **oratorios.** An ora- N-COUNT
torio is a long piece of music with a religious theme
which is written for singers and an orchestra.

ora·tory /ˈɒrətəri, AM ˈɔːrətɔːri/ **oratories. 1** Ora- N-UNCOUNT FORMAL
tory is the art of making formal speeches. *He dis-
played determination as well as powerful oratory.*
2 An **oratory** is a small room or private place where N-COUNT
Christians go to pray.

orb /ɔːb/ **orbs.** An **orb** is something that is shaped N-COUNT LITERARY
like a ball, for example the sun or moon. *...a glow-
ing orb of light.*

or·bit /ˈɔːbɪt/ **orbits, orbiting, orbited. 1** An or- N-COUNT: ◇◇◇◇◇ also in/intoN
bit is the curved path in space that is followed by an
object going round and round a planet, moon, or
star. *Mars and Earth have orbits which change with
time.* **2** If something such as a satellite **orbits** a VERB: V

planet, moon, or sun, it moves around it in a con-
tinuous curving path. **3** The **orbit** of a particular N-SING: with supp
person, group, or institution is the area over which
they have influence. *Laos fell within the orbit of Vietnam and the Soviet Union.*

or·bit·al /ˈɔːbɪtəl/. **1** An **orbital** road goes all the ◆◇◇◇◇
way round a large city. *...the M25 London orbital* ADJ: ADJ n
motorway. **2** Orbital describes things relating to ADJ: ADJ n
the orbit of an object in space. *...an orbital path unlike that of any other planet.*

or·chard /ˈɔːtʃəd/ **orchards.** An **orchard** is an ◆◇◇◇◇ N-COUNT
area of land on which fruit trees are grown.

or·ches·tra /ˈɔːkɪstrə/ **orchestras.** An orchestra ◆◆◇◇◇ N-COUNT
is a large group of musicians who play a variety of
different instruments together. Orchestras usually
play classical music. ● See also **chamber orchestra**,
symphony orchestra. ♦ **or·ches·tral** /ɔːˈkestrəl/ ADJ: ADJ n
...an orchestral concert.

'orchestra pit. In a theatre, the **orchestra pit** is N-SING
the space reserved for the orchestra immediately in
front of or below the stage.

or·ches·trate /ˈɔːkɪstreɪt/ **orchestrates, or-** ◆◇◇◇◇
chestrating, orchestrated. 1 If you say that VERB
someone **orchestrates** an event or situation, you V n Also V-ed
mean that they carefully organize it in a way that
will produce the particular result that they want.
*The colonel was able to orchestrate a rebellion from
inside an army jail.* ♦ **or·ches·tra·tion** *...the* N-UNCOUNT
orchestration of criminal justice policy. **2** When VERB
someone **orchestrates** a piece of music, they write V n
the individual parts to be played by the different instruments of an orchestra. *He was orchestrating the
second act of his opera.* ♦ **orchestration** *...lessons* N-UNCOUNT
in orchestration.

or·ches·tra·tion /ˌɔːkɪsˈtreɪʃən/ **orchestrations.** N-COUNT
An **orchestration** is a piece of music that has been
rewritten so that it can be played by an orchestra.

or·chid /ˈɔːkɪd/ **orchids.** Orchids are plants with N-COUNT
brightly coloured, unusually shaped flowers.

or·dain /ɔːˈdeɪn/ **ordains, ordaining, ordained.** ◆◇◇◇◇
1 When someone is **ordained**, they are made a VERB
member of the clergy in a religious ceremony. *He* be V-ed n V n
was ordained a Catholic priest in 1982... He or- V n as n
dained his own priests... The church's ruling body Also V n to n
voted to ordain women as priests. ♦ **or·di·na·tion** N-VAR
/ˌɔːdɪˈneɪʃən/ **ordinations** *...the ordination of wom-
en... selecting candidates for ordination.* **2** If some VERB
authority or power **ordains** something, they decide V that
that it should happen or be in existence. *Nehru or-* V n FORMAL
*dained that socialism should rule... The recession
may already be severe enough to ordain structural
change.*

or·deal /ɔːˈdiːl/ **ordeals.** If you describe an experi- ◆◆◇◇◇ N-COUNT
ence or situation as an **ordeal**, you think it is difficult and unpleasant. *...the painful ordeal of the last
eight months... She described her agonising ordeal.*

order 1 subordinating conjunction uses

or·der /ˈɔːdə/. **1** If you do something **in order to** ◆◆◆◆◇
achieve a particular thing or **in order that** some- PHR-CONJ
thing can happen, you do it because you want to
achieve that thing. *Most schools are extremely unwilling to cut down on staff in order to cut costs... No
agenda was drawn up, in order that all matters
could be raised.* **2** If someone must be in a particu- PHR-CONJ
lar situation **in order to** achieve something they
want, they cannot achieve that thing if they are not
in that situation. *We need to get rid of the idea that
we must be liked all the time in order to be worthwhile.* **3** If something must happen **in order for** PHR-CONJ
something else to happen, the second thing cannot
happen if the first thing does not happen. *In order
for their computers to trace a person's records, they
need both the name and address of the individual.*

order 2 commands and requests

or·der /ˈɔːdə/ **orders, ordering, ordered. 1** If ◆◆◆◆◆
someone in authority **orders** someone to do some- VERB
thing, they tell them to do it. *He ordered the women* V n to-inf
out of the car... 'Let him go!' he ordered... 'Stay here!', V n prep/adv V with quote
she ordered him. **2** If someone in authority **orders** VERB
something, they give instructions that it should be V n

done. *The President has ordered a full investiga-* V n to-inf
tion... The prime minister had ordered price controls V that
to be introduced... He ordered that all party property Also V n -ed
be confiscated. **3** If someone in authority gives you N-COUNT
an **order**, they tell you to do something. *I don't take*
orders from him any more. **4** A court **order** is a legal N-COUNT
instruction stating that something must be done.
...a court order banning her from keeping animals.
5 If you are **under orders** to do something, you PHRASE
have been told to do it by someone in authority. *I*
am under orders not to discuss his mission. **6** ● your
marching orders: see **march.** ● **a tall order**: see **tall.**
7 When you **order** something that you are going to VERB
pay for, you ask for it to be brought to you, sent to you, V n
or obtained for you. *Iris finally ordered coffees for her-* V n n
self and Tania... The waitress appeared. 'Are you ready
to order?'... We ordered him a beer. **8** An **order** is a re- N-COUNT
quest for something to be brought, made, or obtained
for you in return for money. *British Rail are going to*
place an order for a hundred and eighty-eight trains.
9 Someone's **order** is what they have asked to be N-COUNT:
brought, made, or obtained for them in return for poss N
money. *The waiter returned with their order.*
10 Something that is **on order** at a shop or factory has PHRASE
been asked for but has not yet been supplied. **11** If PHRASE
you do something **to order**, you do it whenever you
are asked to do it. *She makes wonderful dried flower*
arrangements to order. **12** If something is done **in** PHRASE
short order, it is done quickly and without any delay.
Constitutional rule was restored in short order. **13** See
also **holy orders, mail order, postal order, standing**
order.

order around or **order about.** The form **order** PHRASAL VB
about is mainly used in British English. If you say that ⟨PRAGMATICS⟩
someone **is ordering you around** or **is ordering you** V n P
about, you mean they are telling you what to do as if Also V P noun
they have authority over you, and you dislike this. *He*
gets really bossy and starts ordering me around.

order 3 arrangements, situations, and groupings

or·der /'ɔːdə/ **orders, ordering, ordered. 1** If a ◆◆◆◆◇
set of things are arranged or done in a particular **or-** N-UNCOUNT:
der, they are arranged or done so that one thing fol- also a N
lows another, often according to a particular factor
such as importance. *Write down (in order of prior-*
ity) the qualities you'd like to have... Sort them into a
logical order... The chairman re-arranged the order
of the speakers. **2 Order** is the situation that exists N-UNCOUNT
when everything is in a correct or predictable place,
or happens at a correct or predictable time. *Making*
lists can create order and control. **3** If you put or PHRASE
keep something **in order**, you make sure that it is
tidy or properly organized. *It was her job to keep the*
room in order... Now he has a chance to put his life
back in order. **4 Order** is the situation that exists N-UNCOUNT
when people obey the law and do things peacefully,
rather than fighting or rioting. *Troops were sent to*
the islands to restore order. **5** The chairman or CONVENTION
chairwoman of a meeting or tribunal can say **'Or-** ⟨PRAGMATICS⟩
der!' to tell people to stop causing a disturbance.
6 When people talk about a particular **order**, they N-SING:
mean the way society is organized at a particular time. with supp
Some feminists sought reforms within the existing so-
cial order. **7** The way that something **is ordered** is the VERB
way that it is organized and structured. *We know the* V n
French order things differently.
8 If you refer to something of a particular **order**, you N-COUNT:
mean something of a particular kind. *Gorillas are ani-* with supp
mals of high intelligence, capable of problem-solving FORMAL
of a high order.
9 A religious **order** is a group of monks or nuns who N-COUNT
live according to a particular set of rules. **10** People N-COUNT
who belong to a particular **order** have been given a
particular honour or rank by the head of their country
as a reward for their services or achievements. *...the*
Order of the Garter.
11 See also **ordered; law and order, pecking order,**
point of order.
12 If you think something is **in order**, you think it PHRASE
should happen or be provided. *It's great to have you*
back. Congratulations are surely in order! **13** If a par-
PHRASE

ticular way of behaving or doing something is **the or-**
der of the day, it is very common. *Chaos and the pur-*
suit of power are rapidly becoming the order of the day
in political life.
14 You use **in the order of** or **of the order of** when PHR-PREP
mentioning an approximate figure. *They borrowed*
something in the order of £10 million.
15 If something is **in good order**, it is in good condi- PHRASE
tion. *The vessel's safety equipment was not in good or-*
der. **16** A machine or device that is **in working order** PHRASE
is functioning properly and is not broken. *...a ten-*
year-old car that is in perfect working order. **17** A ma- PHRASE
chine or device that is **out of order** is broken and does
not work. *Their phone's out of order.*
18 If you say that someone or their behaviour is **out of** PHRASE
order, you mean that their behaviour is unacceptable INFORMAL
or unfair. *You don't think the paper's a bit out of order*
in publishing it?
19 ● to **put your house in order**: see **house.** ● **order**
of magnitude: see **magnitude.**

'order book, order books. When you talk about N-COUNT
the state of a company's **order book** or **order** BRITISH
books, you are talking about how many orders for
their goods the company has.

or·dered /'ɔːdəd/. An **ordered** society or system is ADJ-GRADED
well-organized and has a clear structure.

or·der·ly /'ɔːdəli/ **orderlies. 1** If something is ◆◇◇◇◇
done in an **orderly** fashion or manner, it is done in ADJ-GRADED
a well organized and controlled way. *The organizers*
guided them in an orderly fashion out of the build-
ing. **2** Something that is **orderly** is neat and well- ADJ-GRADED
arranged. *It's a beautiful, clean and orderly city.*
♦ or·der·li·ness *...the rather sterile orderliness of* N-UNCOUNT
temples in Japan. **3** An **orderly** is a person who N-COUNT
works in a hospital and does jobs that do not require any special training.

or·di·nal num·ber /ˌɔːdɪnəl 'nʌmbə/ **ordinal num-** N-COUNT
bers. An **ordinal number** or an **ordinal** is a word
such as 'first', 'third', and 'tenth' that tells you
where a particular thing occurs in a sequence of
things. Compare **cardinal number.**

or·di·nance /'ɔːdɪnəns/ **ordinances.** An **ordi-** ◆◇◇◇◇
nance is an official rule or order. N-COUNT
FORMAL

or·di·nand /'ɔːdɪnænd/ **ordinands.** An **ordinand** is N-COUNT
someone who is being trained to be a priest.

or·di·nari·ly /'ɔːdɪnərəli, AM -'nerɪli/. If you say ◆◇◇◇◇
what is **ordinarily** the case, you are saying what is ADV
normally the case. *The streets would ordinarily have*
been full of people. ...places where the patient does
not ordinarily go.

or·di·nary /'ɔːdɪnri, AM -neri/. **1 Ordinary** people ◆◆◆◇◇
or things are normal and not special or different in ADJ-GRADED
any way. *Most ordinary people would agree with*
me... It was just an ordinary weekend. **2** If you de- ADJ-GRADED
scribe someone or something as **ordinary**, you
mean they are not special or interesting in any way
and may be rather dull. *I'm just a very ordinary,*
boring normal guy. **3** Something that is **out of the** PHRASE
ordinary is unusual or different. *The boy's knowl-*
edge was out of the ordinary.

or·di·na·tion. See **ordain.**

ord·nance /'ɔːdnəns/. **Ordnance** refers to military ◆◇◇◇◇
supplies, especially weapons. *...lorries loaded with* N-UNCOUNT
green boxes of ordnance.

ore /ɔː/ **ores. Ore** is rock or earth from which met- ◆◇◇◇◇
al can be obtained. *...a huge iron ore mine.* N-VAR

orega·no /ˌprɪ'gɑːnəʊ, AM ə'regənəʊ/. **Oregano** is a N-UNCOUNT
herb that is used in cooking.

or·gan /'ɔːgən/ **organs. 1** An **organ** is a part of ◆◆◆◇◇
your body that has a particular purpose or function, N-COUNT
for example your heart or lungs. *...damage to the*
muscles and internal organs. **2** An **organ** is a large N-COUNT
musical instrument with pipes of different lengths
through which air is forced. It has keys and pedals
rather like a piano. ● See also **mouth organ. ♦ or-**
·gan·ist, organists. An **organist** is someone who N-COUNT
plays the organ. **3** You refer to a newspaper or or- N-COUNT
ganization as the **organ** of the government or another group when it is used by them as a means of
giving information or getting things done. *The most*

powerful organ of government in Scotland is the Scottish Office.

or·gan·ic /ɔːˈgænɪk/. **1 Organic** methods of farming and gardening use only natural animal and plant products to fertilize the land and control pests and diseases, rather than using chemicals. ♦ **or·gani·cal·ly** *Organically grown vegetables taste totally different.* **2 Organic** substances are of the sort produced by or found in living things. *...incorporating organic material into chalky soils.* **3 Organic** change or development happens gradually and naturally rather than suddenly. *...to manage the company and supervise its organic growth.* **4** If a community or structure is an **organic** whole, each part of it is necessary and is in harmony with the other parts. *City planning treats the city as an organic whole.*
◆◇◇◇ ADJ
♦ ADV: ADV with v
ADJ
ADJ FORMAL
ADJ: ADJ n FORMAL

or·gani·sa·tion /ˌɔːgənaɪˈzeɪʃən/. See **organization**.

or·gani·sa·tion·al /ˌɔːgənaɪˈzeɪʃənəl/. See **organizational**.

or·gan·ise /ˈɔːgənaɪz/. See **organize**.

or·gan·is·er /ˈɔːgənaɪzə/. See **organize**.

or·gan·ism /ˈɔːgənɪzəm/ **organisms**. An **organism** is an animal or plant, especially one that is so small that you cannot see it without using a microscope. *Not all chemicals normally present in living organisms are harmless.*
♦♦◇◇ N-COUNT

or·gani·za·tion /ˌɔːgənaɪˈzeɪʃən/ **organizations**; also spelled **organisation**. **1** An **organization** is an official group of people, for example a political party, a business, a charity, or a club. *Most of these specialized schools are provided by voluntary organizations. ...the International Labour Organisation.* ♦ **or·gani·za·tion·al** *This problem needs to be dealt with at an organizational level.* **2** The **organization** of an event or activity involves making all the necessary arrangements for it. *Several of the projects have been delayed by poor organisation.* ♦ **organizational** *Evelyn's excellent organisational skills were soon spotted by her employers.* **3** The **organization** of something is the way in which its different parts are arranged or relate to each other. *The organization of the book leaves something to be desired.* ♦ **organizational** *The police now recognise that big organisational changes are needed.*
♦♦♦♦ N-COUNT
ADJ: ADJ n
N-UNCOUNT
ADJ: ADJ n
N-UNCOUNT
ADJ: ADJ n

or·gan·ize /ˈɔːgənaɪz/ **organizes, organizing, organized**; also spelled **organise** in British English. **1** If you **organize** an event or activity, you make sure that the necessary arrangements are made. *We all decided to organize a concert for Easter. ...a two-day meeting organised by the United Nations.* ♦ **-organized** *...student-organized seminars.* ♦ **or·gan·iz·er** /ˈɔːgənaɪzə/ **organizers** *...Jack Cunningham, Labour's campaign organiser... She was a good organiser.* **2** See also **personal organizer**. **3** If you **organize** something that someone wants or needs, you make sure that it is provided. *He rang his wife and asked her to organize coffee and sandwiches.* **4** If you **organize** a set of things, you arrange them in an ordered way or give them a structure. *He began to organize his materials.* **5** If you **organize** yourself, you plan your work and activities in an ordered efficient way. *...changing the way you organize yourself... I'm sure you don't need me to organize you.* **6** If someone **organizes** workers or if workers **organize**, they form a group or society such as a trade union in order to have more power. *...helping to organize women working abroad.*
♦♦♦♦ VERB Vn
COMB
♦ N-COUNT
VERB Vn
VERB Vn
VERB V pron-refl Vn
V-ERG Vn Also V

or·gan·ized /ˈɔːgənaɪzd/; also spelled **organised**. **1** An **organized** activity or group involves a number of people doing something together in a structured way, rather than doing it by themselves. *...organised groups of art thieves. ...organised religion.* **2** Someone who is **organized** plans their work and activities efficiently. *These people are very efficient, very organized and excellent time managers.*
♦♦♦◇ ADJ: ADJ n
ADJ-GRADED

,organized 'crime; also spelled **organised crime**. **Organized crime** is criminal activity such as the
♦◇◇◇ N-UNCOUNT

production and sale of illegal drugs which involves large numbers of people and is centrally organized.

or·gan·za /ɔːˈgænzə/. **Organza** is a thin stiff fabric made of silk, cotton, or an artificial fibre.
N-UNCOUNT

or·gasm /ˈɔːgæzəm/ **orgasms**. An **orgasm** is the moment of greatest pleasure and excitement in sexual activity. ♦ **or·gas·mic** /ɔːˈgæzmɪk/ *...deep orgasmic pleasure.*
♦◇◇◇ N-VAR
ADJ

or·gi·as·tic /ˌɔːdʒiˈæstɪk/. An **orgiastic** event is one in which people enjoy themselves in an extreme uncontrolled way.
ADJ: ADJ n

orgy /ˈɔːdʒi/ **orgies**. **1** An **orgy** is a party in which people behave in a very uncontrolled way, especially one involving sexual activity. *...a drunken orgy.* **2** You can refer to an activity as an **orgy** to emphasize that it is done to an excessive extent. *The rioters were engaged in an orgy of destruction.*
♦◇◇◇ N-COUNT
N-COUNT: with supp PRAGMATICS

ori·ent /ˈɔːriənt/ **orients, orienting, oriented**; the form **orientate** is also used. **1** When you **orient** yourself to a new situation or course of action, you learn about it and prepare to deal with it. *...orienting students to new ways of thinking... Anxiety comes from not being able to orient yourself in your own existence.* **2** When you **orient** yourself, you find out exactly where you are and which direction you are facing in. *She lay still for a few seconds, trying to orient herself.* **3** See also **oriented**.
♦◇◇◇ VERB V n towards/ to n/-ing V pron-refl FORMAL
VERB V pron-refl

Ori·ent /ˈɔːriənt/. The eastern part of Asia was sometimes referred to as **the Orient**. *I found my schedule no longer permitted my frequent visits to the Orient.*
♦◇◇◇ N-PROPER: the N LITERARY

ori·en·tal /ˌɔːriˈentəl/ **orientals**. **1 Oriental** means coming from or associated with eastern Asia, especially China and Japan. *...oriental carpets.* **2** Some people refer to people from eastern Asia, especially China or Japan as **Orientals**; a use which some people find offensive.
♦♦◇◇ ADJ
N-COUNT

ori·en·tal·ist /ˌɔːriˈentəlɪst/ **orientalists**. An **orientalist** is someone from the West who studies the language, culture, history, or customs of countries in eastern Asia.
N-COUNT

ori·en·tate /ˈɔːriənteɪt/. See **orient**.

ori·en·tat·ed /ˈɔːriənteɪtɪd/. See **oriented**.

-orientated /-ɔːriənteɪtɪd/. **-orientated** means the same as **-oriented**.
COMB

ori·en·ta·tion /ˌɔːriənˈteɪʃən/ **orientations**. **1** If you talk about the **orientation** of an organization or country, you are talking about the kinds of aims and interests it has. *...a marketing orientation.* **2** Someone's **orientation** is their basic beliefs or preferences. *...discrimination on the basis of sexual orientation.* **3 Orientation** is basic information or training that is given to people starting a new job or course. *...a one-day orientation session.* **4** The **orientation** of a structure or object is the direction it faces.
♦◇◇◇ N-VAR: with supp
N-VAR: supp N
N-UNCOUNT
N-COUNT

ori·ent·ed /ˈɔːrientɪd/; the form **orientated** is also used. If someone **is oriented towards** or **oriented to** a particular thing or person, they are mainly concerned with that thing or person. *Most students here are oriented to computers.*
♦♦◇◇ ADJ-GRADED: v-link ADJ towards/to n

-oriented /-ɔːrientɪd/; the form **-orientated** is also used. **-oriented** is added to nouns and adverbs to form adjectives which describe what someone or something is primarily interested in or concerned with. *...a market-oriented economy.*
COMB

ori·ent·eer·ing /ˌɔːrienˈtɪərɪŋ/. **Orienteering** is a sport in which people run from one place to another, using a compass and a map to guide them between points that are marked along the route.
N-UNCOUNT

ori·fice /ˈɒrɪfɪs, AM ˈɔːr-/ **orifices**. An **orifice** is an opening, especially one in your body such as your mouth.
N-COUNT FORMAL

ori·ga·mi /ˌɒrɪˈgɑːmi, AM ˌɔːr-/. **Origami** is the craft of folding paper to make models.
N-UNCOUNT

ori·gin /ˈɒrɪdʒɪn, AM ˈɔːr-/ **origins**. **1** You can refer to the beginning, cause, or source of something as its **origin** or **origins**. *...theories about the origin of life. ...many drugs which have their origins in herbs.* **2** Your **origin** or **origins** is the country, race, or
♦♦♦◇ N-COUNT
N-COUNT:

social class of your parents or ancestors. *...people of Asian origin. ...their country of origin.* also of/in N

origi·nal /əˈrɪdʒɪnəl/ **originals.** 1 You use **original** ◆◆◆◇ when referring to something that existed at the be- ADJ: det ADJ ginning of a process or activity, or the characteristics that something had when it began or was made. *The original plan was to hold an indefinite stoppage.* 2 If something such as a document, work of art, or N-COUNT piece of writing is an **original**, it is not a copy or a later version. *Copy the questionnaire and send the original to your employer.* 3 An **original** piece of ADJ writing or music was written recently and has not been published or performed before. *...its policy of commissioning original work.* 4 If you describe ADJ-GRADED someone or their work as **original**, you mean that they are very imaginative and have new ideas. *...a chef with an original touch.* ♦ **origi·nal·ity** N-UNCOUNT /əˌrɪdʒɪˈnælɪti/ *He was capable of writing things of startling originality.* 5 If you read or sing something PHRASE **in the original** or, for example, **in the original French**, you read or sing it in the language it was written in, rather than a translation.

origi·nal·ly /əˈrɪdʒɪnəli/. When you say what hap- ◆◆◆◇ pened **originally**, you are saying what happened ADV: when something began or came into existence, of- ADV with v, ten to contrast it with what happened later. *France* ADV with cl/ *originally refused to sign the treaty.* group

o,riginal 'sin. According to some Christians, **origi-** N-UNCOUNT **nal sin** is the wickedness that all human beings are born with.

origi·nate /əˈrɪdʒɪneɪt/ **originates, originating,** ◆◆◇◇ **originated.** When something **originates** or when V-ERG someone **originates** it, it begins to happen or exist. V prep/adv *All carbohydrates originate from plants... I suppose* V n *no one has any idea who originated the story?* FORMAL ♦ **origi·na·tor, originators** *...Mick Jagger, one of* N-COUNT *the originators of National Music Day.*

or·na·ment /ˈɔːnəmənt/ **ornaments.** 1 An orna- ◆◇◇◇ ment is an attractive object that you display in your N-COUNT home or garden. ♦ **or·na·men·tal** *...ornamental* ADJ *trees.* 2 Decorations and patterns on a building or a N-UNCOUNT piece of furniture can be referred to as **ornament** or FORMAL **ornamentation.** ♦ **ornamental** *...ornamental plas-* ADJ-GRADED ter mouldings.

or·na·men·ta·tion /ˌɔːnəmənˈteɪʃən/. See **ornament.**

or·na·ment·ed /ˈɔːnəmentɪd/. If something is **or-** ADJ-GRADED **namented** with attractive objects or patterns, it is decorated with them. *It had a high ceiling, orna-mented with plaster fruits and flowers.*

or·nate /ɔːˈneɪt/. An **ornate** building or object is ◆◇◇◇ decorated with complicated patterns or carvings. ADJ-GRADED *...an ornate iron staircase.* ♦ **or·nate·ly** *...the or-* ADV *nately carved doors.*

or·ni·thol·ogy /ˌɔːnɪˈθɒlədʒi/. **Ornithology** is the N-UNCOUNT study of birds. ♦ **or·ni·tho·logi·cal** FORMAL /ˌɔːnɪθəˈlɒdʒɪkəl/ *...the Hampshire Ornithological* ADJ: ADJ n *Society.* ♦ **or·ni·tholo·gist, ornithologists.** *That* N-COUNT *area is an ornithologist's paradise.*

or·phan /ˈɔːfən/ **orphans, orphaned.** 1 An **or-** ◆◇◇◇ **phan** is a child whose parents are dead. *He was left* N-COUNT *an orphan at the age of twelve.* 2 If a child is **or-** V-PASSIVE: **phaned**, their parents die, or their remaining parent no cont dies. *Jones was orphaned at the age of ten.* be V-ed

or·phan·age /ˈɔːfənɪdʒ/ **orphanages.** An **or-** ◆◇◇◇ **phanage** is a place where orphans live and are N-COUNT looked after.

ortho·dox /ˈɔːθədɒks/. 1 **Orthodox** beliefs, meth- ◆◆◇◇ ods, or systems are ones which are accepted or used ADJ-GRADED by most people. *Payne gained a reputation for sound, if orthodox, views. ...orthodox police meth-ods.* 2 If you describe someone as **orthodox**, you ADJ mean that they hold the older and more traditional ideas of their religion or party. *...orthodox Jews.* 3 The **Orthodox** churches are Christian churches in ADJ Eastern Europe which separated from the western church in the eleventh century.

ortho·doxy /ˈɔːθədɒksi/ **orthodoxies.** 1 An ◆◇◇◇ **orthodoxy** is an accepted view about something. N-VAR *These ideas rapidly became the new orthodoxy in*

linguistics. 2 The old traditional beliefs of a religion, N-UNCOUNT: political party, or philosophy can be referred to as also N in pl **orthodoxy.** *...a return to Marxist orthodoxy.*

ortho·paedic /ˌɔːθəˈpiːdɪk/; also spelled **ortho-** ADJ: ADJ n **pedic. Orthopaedic** means relating to problems af- MEDICAL fecting people's joints and spines.

os·cil·late /ˈɒsɪleɪt/ **oscillates, oscillating, os-** ◆◇◇◇ **cillated.** 1 If an object **oscillates**, it moves repeat- VERB edly from one position to another and back again, V or keeps getting bigger and smaller. *I checked to see* TECHNICAL *if the needle indicating volume was oscillating.* ♦ **os-** **·cil·la·tion** /ˌɒsɪˈleɪʃən/ **oscillations** *Some oscilla-* N-VAR *tion of the fuselage had been noticed on early flights.* 2 If something **oscillates** between one amount or VB: no passive value and another, there is a frequent or regular in- V between pl-crease or decrease in its value. *The lira oscillated be-* amount *tween 840 and 850 lire to the mark.* ♦ **oscillation** Also V *...oscillations in world temperature.* 3 If you **oscil-** TECHNICAL **late** between two moods, attitudes, or types of be- N-VAR haviour, you keep changing from one to the other VB: no passive and back again. *Kelly just stood there, suddenly os-* V between n *cillating between anger and guilt.* ♦ **oscillation** FORMAL *...his own oscillation between hope and despair.* N-UNCOUNT

os·mo·sis /ɒsˈməʊsɪs/. **Osmosis** is the process by N-UNCOUNT which a liquid passes through a thin piece of solid TECHNICAL substance such as the roots of a plant.

os·si·fy /ˈɒsɪfaɪ/ **ossifies, ossifying, ossified.** If V-ERG: V an idea, system, or organization **ossifies** or if some- PRAGMATICS thing **ossifies** it, it becomes fixed and difficult to V n change; used showing disapproval. *It reckons that* FORMAL *rationing would ossify the farm industry.*

os·ten·sible /ɒˈstensɪbəl/. **Ostensible** is used to ◆◇◇◇ describe something that seems to be true or is offi- ADJ: ADJ n cially stated to be true, but about which you or oth- FORMAL er people have doubts. *The ostensible purpose of these meetings was to gather information.* ♦ **os·ten-** **·sibly** /ɒˈstensɪbli/ *...such ostensibly independent* ADV *organisations.*

os·ten·ta·tion /ˌɒstenˈteɪʃən/. If you describe N-UNCOUNT someone's behaviour as **ostentation**, you are criti- PRAGMATICS cizing them for doing things or buying things purely FORMAL in order to impress people. *...the excess and ostenta-tion of the 1980s.*

os·ten·ta·tious /ˌɒstenˈteɪʃəs/. 1 If you describe ◆◇◇◇ something or someone as **ostentatious**, you disap- ADJ-GRADED prove of them because their content, appearance, PRAGMATICS or behaviour is intended to impress people with its wealth and importance. *...an ostentatious wedding reception.* ♦ **os·ten·ta·tious·ly** *Her servants were* ADV-GRADED *similarly, if less ostentatiously attired.* 2 You can de- ADJ-GRADED scribe an action or behaviour as **ostentatious** when it is done in an exaggerated way to attract people's attention. ♦ **ostentatiously** *Harry stopped under a* ADV-GRADED *street lamp and ostentatiously began inspecting the contents of his bag.*

os·teo·path /ˈɒstiəpæθ/ **osteopaths.** An **osteo-** N-COUNT **path** is a person who treats illnesses by massaging people's bodies and bending them in different ways, especially in order to reduce pain or stiffness.

os·teo·po·ro·sis /ˌɒstiəʊpəˈrəʊsɪs/. **Osteoporosis** ◆◇◇◇ is a condition in which your bones lose calcium and N-UNCOUNT become more likely to break.

os·tra·cize /ˈɒstrəsaɪz/ **ostracizes, ostracizing,** VB: usu **ostracized;** also spelled **ostracise** in British Eng- passive lish. If someone **is ostracized**, people deliberately be V-ed behave in an unfriendly way towards them and do FORMAL not allow them to take part in any of their social ac-tivities. *She claims she's being ostracized by some members of her local community.* ♦ **os·tra·cism** N-UNCOUNT *...incurring ostracism from their families.*

os·trich /ˈɒstrɪtʃ, AM ˈɔːst-/ **ostriches.** An **ostrich** ◆◇◇◇ is a very large African bird that cannot fly. N-COUNT

oth·er /ˈʌðə/ **others.** When **other** follows the de- ◆◆◆◆◆ terminer **an**, it is written as one word: see **another.** 1 You use **other** to refer to an additional thing or per- ADJ: son of the same type as one that has been mentioned det ADJ, or is known about. *They were just like any other young* ADJ n *couple... The communique gave no other details.* ▶ Also a pronoun. *Four crewmen were killed, one oth-* PRON *er was injured.* 2 You use **other** to indicate that some- ADJ:

thing is not the thing already mentioned, but something else. *Calls cost 36p per minute cheap rate and 48p per minute at all other times.* ▶ Also a pronoun. *Some of these methods will work. Others will not.* `det ADJ, ADJ n` `PRON`

3 You use **other** to refer to the second of two things or people when the identity of the first is already known or understood, or has already been mentioned. *The Captain was at the other end of the room.* ▶ Also a pronoun. *Almost everybody had a cigarette in one hand and a martini in the other.* **4** You use **other** at the end of a list or a group of examples, to refer generally to people or things like the ones just mentioned. *...shops, restaurants and other amenities.* ▶ Also a pronoun. *...the new physics and astronomy of Copernicus, Galileo, and others.* **5** You use **other** to refer to the rest of the people or things in a group, when you are talking about one particular person or thing. *When the other pupils were taken to an exhibition, he was left behind.* ▶ Also a pronoun. *Aubrey's on his way here, with the others.* **6 Other** people are people in general, excluding yourself or the particular person you have mentioned. *She likes to be with other people.* ▶ **Others** means the same as **other people**. `ADJ: det ADJ, ADJ n` `PRON` `ADJ: det ADJ, ADJ n` `PRON` `ADJ: det ADJ, ADJ n` `PRON` `ADJ: ADJ n` `PRON`

7 You use expressions like **among other** things or **among others** to indicate that there are several more facts, things, or people like the one or ones mentioned, but that you do not intend to mention them all. *His travels took him to Dublin, among other places.* `PHRASE` `PRAGMATICS`

8 You use **every other** to emphasize that you are referring to all the rest of the people or things in a group. *The same will apply in every other country.* **9** You use **other than** after a negative statement to say that the person, item, or thing that follows is the only exception to the statement. *She makes no reference to any feminist work other than her own.* `PHRASE` `PRAGMATICS` `PHRASE`

10 You use **other** in informal expressions of time such as **the other day**, **the other evening**, or **the other week** to refer to a day, evening, or week in the recent past. *I rang her the other day... The other evening we had a party.* **11** If something happens, for example, **every other day** or **every other month**, it does not happen every day or month, but on one day or in one month and then every second day or month after that. `ADJ: the ADJ n` `PHRASE`

12 You use expressions like **none other than** and **no other than** to emphasize the name of a person or thing when something about that person or thing is surprising in a particular situation. *The manager was none other than his son.* **13** You use **nothing other than** and **no other than** to emphasize that a course of action, decision, or description is the only one possible in a particular situation. *Nothing other than an immediate custodial sentence could be justified.* **14** You use **or other** in expressions like **somehow or other** and **someone or other** to indicate that you cannot or do not want to be more precise about the information that you are giving. *I was going to have him called away from the house on some pretext or other.* **15** ● **one after the other**: see **after**. ● **each other**: see **each**. ● **your other half**: see **half**. ● **one or other**: see **one**. ● **this, that, and the other**: see **this**. ● **in other words**: see **word**. `PHRASE` `PRAGMATICS` `PHRASE` `PRAGMATICS` `PHRASE`

oth·er·ness /'ʌðənəs/. **Otherness** is the quality that someone or something has which is different from yourself or from the things that you have experienced. *I like the otherness of men's minds and bodies.* `N-UNCOUNT`

other·wise /'ʌðəwaɪz/. **1** You use **otherwise** after stating a situation or fact, in order to say what the result or consequence would be if this situation or fact was not the case. *I'm lucky that I'm interested in school work, otherwise I'd go mad... She must not think of them, otherwise she would cry.* **2** You use **otherwise** before stating the general condition or quality of something, when you are also mentioning an exception to this general condition or quality. *...a blue and gold caravan, slightly travel-stained but otherwise in good condition.* **3** You use **otherwise** to refer in a general way to actions or situations that are very different from, or the opposite to, your main statement. *Take approximately 60mg up to four times a day, unless advised otherwise by a doc-* `ADV: ADV with cl` `ADV: ADV group` `ADV: ADV with v WRITTEN`

tor. **4** You use **otherwise** to indicate that other ways of doing something are possible in addition to the way already mentioned. *Do your best to avoid bruising or otherwise damaging them.* **5** You use **or otherwise** and **and otherwise** to refer to something which contrasts with the preceding word. *It was for the police to assess the validity or otherwise of the evidence.* `ADV: ADV before v` `PHRASE`

,other-'worldly. **Other-worldly** means more concerned with spiritual matters than with daily life. *They encourage an image of Tibet as an other-worldly sort of place.* `ADJ-GRADED`

OTT /,əʊ tiː 'tiː/. If you describe something as **OTT**, you mean that it is exaggerated and extreme. **OTT** is an abbreviation for 'over the top'. *...an OTT comedy cabaret revue.* `ADJ-GRADED` `INFORMAL`

ot·ter /'ɒtə/ **otters.** An **otter** is a small animal with brown fur, short legs, and a long tail. Otters swim well and eat fish. `◆◇◇◇◇` `N-COUNT`

ouch /aʊtʃ/. People say '**ouch**' when they suddenly feel pain. *She was barefoot and stones dug into her feet. 'Ouch, ouch,' she cried.* `EXCLAM`

ought /ɔːt/. **1** You use **ought to** to say that you think that it is morally right to do a particular thing or behave in a particular way or that it is morally right for a situation to exist, especially when giving or asking for advice or opinions. *You've got a good wife. You ought to take care of her... Do you think I ought to stay with him?* **2** You use **ought to** when saying that you think it is a good idea and important for you or someone else to do a particular thing, especially when giving or asking for advice or opinions. *You ought to ask a lawyer's advice.* **3** You use **ought to have** with a past participle to indicate that although it was best or correct for someone to do something in the past, they did not actually do it. *I realize I ought to have told you about it.* **4** You use **ought to** when politely telling someone that you must do something, for example that you must leave. *I think I ought to go.* `◆◆◇◇` `PHR-MODAL` `PRAGMATICS` `PHR-MODAL` `PRAGMATICS` `PHR-MODAL` `PHR-MODAL` `PRAGMATICS`

5 You use **ought to** to indicate that you expect something to be the case or you expect something to happen. You use **ought to have** to indicate that you expect something to have happened already. *'This ought to be fun,' he told Alex, eyes gleaming.* **6** You use **ought to** to indicate that you think that something should be the case, but might not be. *This news ought to send a shiver down John Major's spine.* **7** You use **ought to** to indicate that you think that something has happened because of what you know about the situation, but you are not certain. *He ought to have reached the house some time ago.* **8** You use **ought to have** with a past participle to indicate that something was expected to happen or be the case, but it did not happen or was not the case. *Basically the system ought to have worked.* `PHR-MODAL` `PHR-MODAL` `PHR-MODAL` `PHR-MODAL`

oughtn't /'ɔːtənt/. **Oughtn't** is a spoken form of **ought not**.

ounce /aʊns/ **ounces.** **1** An **ounce** is a unit of weight used in Britain and the USA. There are sixteen ounces in a pound and one ounce is equal to 28.35 grams. **2** You can refer to a very small amount of something, such as a quality or characteristic, as an **ounce**. *I spent every ounce of energy trying to hide.* **3** See also **fluid ounce**. `◆◆◇◇◇` `N-COUNT: num N` `N-SING`

our /aʊə/. **1** A speaker or writer uses **our** to indicate that something belongs or relates both to himself or herself and to one or more other people. *We're expecting our first baby... I locked myself out of our apartment.* **2** A speaker or writer sometimes uses **our** to indicate that something belongs or relates to people in general. *The quality of our life depends on keeping well.* **3** In non-standard English, speakers sometimes use **our** with the name of a member of their family or a very close friend. *Our Barry had a habit of doing that sort of thing.* `◆◆◆◆◆` `DET-POSS` `DET-POSS` `DET-POSS` `SPOKEN`

ours /aʊəz/. A speaker or writer uses **ours** to refer to something that belongs or relates both to himself or herself and to one or more other people. *There are few strangers in a town like ours.* `◆◆◇◇◇` `PRON-POSS`

our·self /auəˈself/. **Ourself** is sometimes used instead of 'ourselves' when it clearly refers to a singular subject. Some people consider this use to be incorrect. ...*the way we think of ourself and others.*

PRON-REFL:
v PRON,
prep PRON

our·selves /auəˈselvz/. **1** A speaker or writer uses **ourselves** to refer to himself or herself and one or more other people as a group. **Ourselves** is used as the object of a verb or preposition when the subject refers to the same people. *We sat round the fire to keep ourselves warm... It was the first time we admitted to ourselves that we were tired.* **2** A speaker or writer sometimes uses **ourselves** to refer to people in general. **Ourselves** is used as the object of a verb or preposition when the subject refers to the same people. *When we exert ourselves our heart rate increases.* **3** You use **ourselves** to emphasize a first person plural subject. In more formal English, **ourselves** is sometimes used instead of 'us' as the object of a verb or preposition, for emphasis. *Others are feeling just the way we ourselves would feel in the same situation.* **4** If you say something such as 'We did it **ourselves**', you are indicating that the people you are referring to did it, rather than anyone else.

PRON-REFL:
v PRON,
prep PRON

PRON-REFL:
v PRON,
prep PRON

PRON-REFL
PRAGMATICS

PRON-REFL

oust /aust/ **ousts, ousting, ousted.** If someone **is ousted** from a position of power or from a job or place, they are forced to leave it. *They tried to oust him in a parliamentary vote of no confidence.* ♦ **oust·ing** ...*the ousting of Mr Perez.*

♦♦♢♢♢
VERB:
be V-ed
V n
FORMAL

N-UNCOUNT

out 1 adverb uses

out /aut/. **1** When something is in a particular place and you take it **out**, you remove it from that place. *Carefully pull out the centre pages... He took out his notebook.* **2** You can use **out** to indicate that you are talking about the situation outside, rather than inside buildings. *It's hot out.* **3** If you are **out**, you are not at home or not at your usual place of work. *I tried to get in touch with you yesterday evening, but I think you were out... She had to go out.* **4** If you say that someone is **out** in a particular place, you mean that they are in a different place, usually one far away. *The police tell me they've finished their investigations out there... Rosie's husband was now out East.* **5** When the sea or tide goes **out**, the sea moves away from the shore.

♦♦♦♦♦
ADV:
ADV after v

ADV:
ADV after v

ADV:
be ADV,
ADV after v

ADV:
ADV adv/prep

ADV:
ADV after v,
be ADV

out 2 adjective uses

out /aut/. **1** If a light or fire is **out** or goes **out**, it is no longer shining or burning. **2** If flowers are **out**, their petals have opened. *The cherry blossom was out early in Washington this year.* ► Also an adverb. ...*when I see the wild flowers coming out.* **3** If something such as a book or record is **out**, it is available for people to buy. ...*cover versions of 40 British Number Ones – out now.* ► Also an adverb. *The HMSO edition came out a week later, priced £13.30.* **4** If workers are **out**, they are on strike. *We've been out for two and a half months and we're not going back until we get what we're asking for.* ► Also an adverb. *26 people came out on strike.* **5** In a game or sport, if someone is **out**, they can no longer take part either because they are unable to or because they have been defeated. *Becker is out of the World Championships in Frankfurt, beaten in straight sets by Agassi.* **6** If you say that a proposal or suggestion is **out**, you mean that it is unacceptable. **7** If you say that a particular fashion or method is **out**, you mean that it is unfashionable. *Romance is making a comeback. Reality is out.* **8** If you say that a calculation or measurement is **out**, you mean that it is incorrect. *They were only a few inches out.* **9** If someone is **out** to do something, they intend to do it. *Most companies these days are just out to make a quick profit.*

♦♦♦♦♦
ADJ:
v-link ADJ

ADJ:
v-link ADJ

ADV:
ADV after v

ADJ:
v-link ADJ

ADV:
ADV after v

ADJ:
v-link ADJ
INFORMAL
ADV:
ADV after v

ADJ:
v-link ADJ

ADJ:
v-link ADJ

ADJ:
v-link ADJ

ADJ-GRADED:
v-link ADJ

ADJ:
v-link ADJ to-
inf
INFORMAL

out 3 verb use

out /aut/ **outs, outing, outed.** If a group of people **out** a public figure or famous person, they reveal

VERB: V n

that person's homosexuality against their wishes. ♦ **out·ing** *The gay and lesbian rights group, Stonewall, sees outing as completely unhelpful.*

N-UNCOUNT

out 4 preposition uses

out of. **1** If you go **out of** a place, you leave it. *She let him out of the house.* **2** If you take something **out of** the container or place where it has been, you remove it. *I always took my key out of my bag and put it in my pocket.* **3** If you look or shout **out of** a window, you look or shout away from the room where you are towards the outside. *He went on staring out of the window.* **4** If you are **out of** the sun, the rain, or the wind, you are sheltered from it. **5** If someone or something gets **out of** a situation, especially an unpleasant one, they are then no longer in it. If they keep **out of** it, they do not start being in it. *In the past army troops have relied heavily on air support to get them out of trouble.* **6** You can use **out of** to say that someone leaves an institution. *You come out of university and find there are no jobs available.* **7** If you are **out of** range of something, you are beyond the limits of that range. *Shaun was in the bedroom, out of earshot... By then she was out of sight.* **8** You use **out of** to say what emotion or motive causes someone to do something. For example, if you do something **out of** pity, you do it because you pity someone. *He took up office out of a sense of duty.* **9** If you get something such as information or work **out of** someone, you manage to make them give it to you, usually when they are unwilling to give it. *'Where is she being held prisoner?' I asked. 'Did you get it out of him?'* **10** If you get pleasure or an advantage **out of** something, you get it as a result of being involved with that thing or making use of it. *To get the most out of your money, you have to invest.* **11** If you are **out of** something, you no longer have any of it. *We're out of milk.* **12** If something is made **out of** a particular material, it consists of that material because it has been formed or constructed from it. **13** You use **out of** to indicate what proportion of a group of things something is true of. For example, if something is true of one **out of** five things, it is true of one fifth of all things of that kind. *Two out of five thought the business would be sold privately.*

♦♦♦♦♢
PHR-PREP
PHR-PREP

PHR-PREP

PHR-PREP
PHR-PREP

PHR-PREP

PHR-PREP

PHR-PREP

PHR-PREP

PHR-PREP

PHR-PREP

PHR-PREP

PHR-PREP

out- /aut-/. You can use **out-** to form verbs that describe an action as being done better by one person than by another. For example, if you can outswim someone, you can swim further or faster than they can. ...*a younger brother who always outperformed him.*

PREFIX

out·age /ˈautɪdʒ/ **outages.** An **outage** is a period of time when the electricity supply to a building or area is interrupted, for example because of damage to the cables. The British term is **power cut.**

N-COUNT
AMERICAN

,out-and-'out. You use **out-and-out** to emphasize that someone or something has all the characteristics of a particular type of person or thing. *The Olympic theme tune 'Amigos para Siempre' proved an out-and-out success.*

ADJ: ADJ n

out·back /ˈautbæk/. The remote parts of Australia where very few people live are referred to as **the outback.**

N-SING:
the N

out·bid /ˌautˈbɪd/ **outbids, outbidding.** If you **outbid** someone, you offer more money than they do for something that you both want to buy. *A developer outbid them at the auction.*

VERB
V n

out·board /ˈautbɔːd/. An **outboard** motor is one that you can fix to the back of a small boat.

♦♢♢♢♢
ADJ: ADJ n

out·bound /ˈautbaund/. An **outbound** flight is one that is leaving or one that is due to leave its place of departure.

ADJ

out·break /ˈautbreɪk/ **outbreaks.** If there is an **outbreak** of something unpleasant, such as violence or a disease, it suddenly starts to happen. ...*the outbreak of war in the Middle East.*

♦♦♢♢♢
N-COUNT

out·build·ing /ˈautbɪldɪŋ/ **outbuildings. Outbuildings** are small buildings such as barns or stables that are part of a larger property.

N-COUNT

out·burst /'aʊtbɜːst/ **outbursts. 1** An outburst of an emotion, especially anger, is a sudden strong expression of that emotion. ...*a spontaneous outburst of cheers and applause... There has been another angry outburst against the new local tax.* **2** An **outburst** of violent activity is a sudden period of this activity. *Five people were reported killed today in a fresh outburst of violence.* ◆◇◇◇ N-COUNT

out·cast /'aʊtkɑːst, -kæst/ **outcasts.** An outcast is someone who is not accepted by a group of people or by society. *All of us felt like social outcasts.* ◆◇◇◇ N-COUNT

out·class /,aʊt'klɑːs, -'klæs/ **outclasses, outclassing, outclassed. 1** If you **are outclassed** by someone, they are a lot better than you are at a particular activity. *Mason was outclassed by Lennox Lewis in his tragic last fight at Wembley.* **2** If one thing **outclasses** another thing, the first thing is of a much higher quality than the second thing. *These planes are outclassed by the most recent designs from the former Soviet Union.* VERB be V-ed Also V n / VERB be V-ed Also V n

out·come /'aʊtkʌm/ **outcomes.** The outcome of an activity, process, or situation is the situation that exists at the end of it. *It's too early to know the outcome of her illness... I am confident of a successful outcome to the negotiations.* ◆◆◇◇ N-COUNT

out·crop /'aʊtkrɒp/ **outcrops;** spelled **outcropping** in American English. An **outcrop** is a large area of rock sticking out of the ground. ...*an outcrop of rugged granite.* N-COUNT

out·cry /'aʊtkraɪ/ **outcries.** An outcry is a reaction of strong disapproval and anger shown by the public or media about a recent event. *The killing caused an international outcry.* ◆◇◇◇ N-VAR

out·dat·ed /,aʊt'deɪtɪd/. If you describe something as **outdated**, you mean that you think it is old-fashioned and no longer useful or relevant to modern life. ...*outdated and inefficient factories.* ◆◇◇◇ ADJ-GRADED

out·did /,aʊt'dɪd/. **Outdid** is the past tense of **outdo**.

out·dis·tance /,aʊt'dɪstəns/ **outdistances, outdistancing, outdistanced. 1** If you **outdistance** someone, you are a lot better and more successful than you are at a particular activity over a period of time. *Ingrid had far outdistanced them as a movie star.* **2** If you **outdistance** your opponents in contest of some kind, you beat them easily. ...*a millionaire businessman who easily outdistanced his major rivals for the nomination.* VERB V n / VERB V n

out·do /,aʊt'duː/ **outdoes, outdoing, outdid, outdone. 1** If you **outdo** someone, you are a lot more successful than they are at a particular activity. *It was important for me to outdo them, to feel better than they were.* **2** You use **not to be outdone** to introduce an action which someone takes in response to a previous action. *The guys hire a stripper for the bachelor party. Not to be outdone, Hope and the girls organise their own night out.* ◆◇◇◇ VERB V n / PHRASE

out·door /,aʊt'dɔː/. **Outdoor** activities or things happen or are used outside and not in a building. *If you enjoy outdoor activities, this is the trip for you.* ...*outdoor cafes.* ◆◆◇◇ ADJ: ADJ n

out·doors /,aʊt'dɔːz/. **1** If something happens **outdoors**, it happens outside in the fresh air rather than in a building. *It was warm enough to be outdoors all afternoon.* **2** You refer to **the outdoors** when talking about work or leisure activities which take place outside away from buildings. *Life in the great outdoors isn't supposed to be luxurious.* ◆◇◇◇ ADV: beADV, ADV after v / N-SING: the N

out·er /'aʊtə/. The **outer** parts of something are the parts which contain or enclose the other parts, and which are furthest from the centre. *He heard a voice in the outer room.* ...*the outer suburbs of the city.* ◆◆◇◇ ADJ: ADJ n

outer·most /'aʊtəməʊst/. The **outermost** thing in a group is the one that is furthest from the centre. ...*the outermost corners of each room.* ADJ: ADJ n

,outer 'space. Outer space is the area outside the earth's atmosphere where the other planets and stars are situated. ◆◇◇◇ N-UNCOUNT

outer·wear /'aʊtəweə/. **Outerwear** is clothing that is not worn underneath other clothing. ...*colorful tops designed as outerwear.* N-UNCOUNT

out·fall /'aʊtfɔːl/ **outfalls.** An **outfall** is a place where water or waste flows out of a drain, often into the sea. N-COUNT

out·field /'aʊtfiːld/. In baseball and cricket, the **outfield** is the part of the field that is furthest from the batting area. N-SING: the N

out·field·er /'aʊtfiːldə/ **outfielders.** In baseball and cricket, the **outfielders** are the players in the part of the field that is furthest from the batting area. N-COUNT

out·fit /'aʊtfɪt/ **outfits, outfitting, outfitted. 1** An **outfit** is a set of clothes. *I spent lots of money on smart new outfits for work.* **2** You can refer to an organization as an **outfit**. *We are a professional outfit and we do require payment for our services.* **3** To **outfit** someone or something means to provide them with equipment for a particular purpose. *I outfitted an attic bedroom as a studio.* ◆◆◇◇ N-COUNT / N-COUNT JOURNALISM / VERB: V n V n with/as n AMERICAN

out·fit·ter /'aʊtfɪtə/ **outfitters;** also spelled **outfitters.** An **outfitter** or an **outfitters** is a shop that sells clothes and equipment for a specific purpose. N-COUNT BRITISH

out·flank /,aʊt'flæŋk/ **outflanks, outflanking, outflanked. 1** In a battle, when one group of soldiers **outflanks** another, it succeeds in moving past the other group in order to be able to attack it from the side. **2** If you **outflank** someone, you succeed in getting into a position where you can defeat them, for example in an argument. *He outflanked Mr Shamir by promising to be no less tough on security matters.* VERB: V n / VERB V n

out·flow /'aʊtfləʊ/ **outflows.** When there is an **outflow** of money or people, a large amount of money or people move from one place to another. *There was a net outflow of about £650m in short-term capital.* ◆◇◇◇ N-COUNT

out·fox /,aʊt'fɒks/ **outfoxes, outfoxing, outfoxed.** If you **outfox** someone, you defeat them in some way because you are cleverer or more cunning than they are. *He made a worldwide name outfoxing Franco's censors in the '60s.* VERB V n

out·going /,aʊt'gəʊɪŋ/. **1** An **outgoing** president, chairman, or minister is one who is going to leave. ...*the outgoing director of the Edinburgh International Festival.* **2 Outgoing** things such as planes, mail, and passengers are leaving or being sent somewhere. *All outgoing flights were grounded.* **3** Someone who is **outgoing** is very friendly and likes meeting and talking to people. ◆◇◇◇ ADJ: ADJ n / ADJ: ADJ n / ADJ-GRADED

out·goings /'aʊtgəʊɪŋz/. Your **outgoings** are the regular amounts of money which you have to spend every week or every month, for example in order to pay your rent or bills. N-PLURAL BRITISH

out·grow /,aʊt'grəʊ/ **outgrows, outgrowing, outgrew, outgrown. 1** If you **outgrow** a piece of clothing, you can no longer wear it because you have grown and are now too big for it. *She outgrew her clothes so rapidly that Patsy was always having to buy new ones.* **2** If you **outgrow** a particular way of behaving or thinking, you change and become more mature, so that you no longer behave or think in that way. *The girl may or may not outgrow her interest in fashion.* ◆◇◇◇ VERB V n / VERB V n

out·growth /'aʊtgrəʊθ/ **outgrowths.** Something that is an **outgrowth** of another thing has developed naturally as a result of it. *Her first book is an outgrowth of an art project she began in 1988.* N-COUNT

out·gun /,aʊt'gʌn/ **outguns, outgunning, outgunned. 1** In a battle, if one army is **outgunned**, they are in a very weak position because the opposing army has more or better weapons. **2** If you **are outgunned** in a contest, you are beaten because your rival is stronger or better than you. *He soon hit top speed to outgun all his rivals in the opening qualifying session.* VERB: be V-ed / VERB: be V-ed V n

out·house /'aʊthaʊs/ **outhouses. 1** An **outhouse** is a small building attached to a house or very close to the house, used, for example, for storing things N-COUNT

O

in. *A police appeal for people to search outhouses and gardens came to nothing.* **2** An **outhouse** is an outside toilet. N-COUNT AMERICAN

out·ing /'aʊtɪŋ/ **outings. 1** An **outing** is a short enjoyable trip, usually with a group of people, away from your home, school, or place of work. *...families on a Sunday afternoon outing.* **2** In sport, an **outing** is an occasion when a player competes in a particular contest or competition. *Bedford were beaten at Wakefield in their first league outing since returning to the Second Division.* **3** See also **out** section 3. ◆◇◇◇ N-COUNT   N-COUNT

out·land·ish /aʊt'lændɪʃ/. If you describe something as **outlandish**, you disapprove of it because you think it is very unusual, strange, or unreasonable. *They appeared at parties in outlandish clothes.* ◆◇◇◇ ADJ-GRADED

out·last /ˌaʊt'lɑːst, -'læst/ **outlasts, outlasting, outlasted.** If one thing **outlasts** another thing, the first thing lives or exists longer than the second. *These naturally dried flowers will outlast a bouquet of fresh blooms.* VB: no passive Vn

out·law /'aʊtlɔː/ **outlaws, outlawing, outlawed. 1** When something **is outlawed**, it is made illegal. *In 1975, the track was closed down and gambling was outlawed.* **2** An **outlaw** is a criminal who is hiding from the authorities. ◆◆◇◇ VERB be V-ed Also V n N-COUNT DATED

out·lay /'aʊtleɪ/ **outlays. Outlay** is the amount of money that you have to spend in order to buy something or start a project. *Apart from the capital outlay of buying the machine, dishwashers can actually save you money.* N-VAR

out·let /'aʊtlet/ **outlets. 1** An **outlet** is a shop or organization which sells the goods made by a particular manufacturer. *...the largest retail outlet in the city.* **2** If someone has an **outlet** for their feelings or ideas, they have a means of expressing and releasing them. *Her father had found an outlet for his ambition in his work.* **3** An **outlet** is a hole or pipe through which liquid or air can flow away. **4** An **outlet** is a place, usually in a wall, where you can connect electrical devices to the electricity supply. ◆◆◇◇ N-COUNT   N-COUNT   N-COUNT   N-COUNT AMERICAN

out·line /'aʊtlaɪn/ **outlines, outlining, outlined. 1** If you **outline** an idea or a plan, you explain it in a general way. *The mayor outlined his plan to clean up the town's image.* **2** An **outline** is a general explanation or description of something. *Following is an outline of the survey findings.* ◆◆◇◇ VERB Vn   N-COUNT: also in N

3 You say that an object **is outlined** when you can see its general shape because there is light behind it. *The Ritz hotel was outlined against the lights.* **4** The **outline** of something is its general shape, especially when it cannot be clearly seen. *He could see only the hazy outline of the goalposts.* V-PASSIVE be V-ed   N-COUNT

out·live /ˌaʊt'lɪv/ **outlives, outliving, outlived.** If one person **outlives** another, they are still alive after the second person has died. If one thing **outlives** another thing, the first thing continues to exist after the second has disappeared or been replaced. *I'm sure Rose will outlive many of us... Khrushchev predicted that Communism would outlive Capitalism.* ● If something **outlives its usefulness**, it has existed for too long, and is no longer useful or necessary. *He argued in his memoirs that the organisation had outlived its usefulness.* ◆◇◇◇ VERB Vn   PHRASE

out·look /'aʊtlʊk/ **outlooks. 1** Your **outlook** is your general attitude towards life. *We were quite different in outlook, Philip and I.* **2** The **outlook** for something is whether or not it is going to be prosperous, successful, or safe. *Has motherhood changed your career outlook?* ◆◆◇◇ N-COUNT   N-SING

out·ly·ing /'aʊtlaɪɪŋ/. **Outlying** places are far away from the main cities of a country. *Tourists can visit outlying areas like the Napa Valley Wine Country.* ◆◇◇◇ ADJ: ADJ n

out·ma·noeu·vre /ˌaʊtmə'nuːvə/ **outmanoeuvres, outmanoeuvring, outmanoeuvred;** spelled **outmaneuver** in American English. When you **outmanoeuvre** someone, you gain an advantage over them in a particular situation by behaving in a clever and skilful way. *He has shown once again that he's able to outmanoeuvre the military.* VERB Vn

out·mod·ed /ˌaʊt'məʊdɪd/. If you describe something as **outmoded**, you mean that you think it is old-fashioned and no longer useful or relevant to modern life. *Romania badly needs aid to modernise its outmoded industries.* ADJ-GRADED

out·num·ber /ˌaʊt'nʌmbə/ **outnumbers, outnumbering, outnumbered.** If one group of people or things **outnumbers** another, the first group has more people or things in it than the second group. *...a town where men outnumber women four to one.* ◆◇◇◇ VERB v-link ADJ

'out of. See **out.**

,out-of-'body. An **out-of-body** experience is one in which you feel as if you are outside your own body, watching it and what is going on around it. ADJ

,out of 'date; also spelled **out-of-date**. Something that is **out of date** is old-fashioned and no longer useful. *Think how rapidly medical knowledge has gone out of date.* ◆◇◇◇ ADJ-GRADED

,out of 'doors; also spelled **out-of-doors**. If you are **out of doors**, you are outside a building rather than inside it. *Sometimes we eat out of doors.* ADV: ADV after v, be ADV

,out-of-'pocket. Out-of-pocket expenses are those which you pay out of your own money on behalf of someone else, and which are often paid back to you later. ● See also **pocket**. ADJ: ADJ n

,out-of-the-'way; also spelled **out of the way**. **Out-of-the-way** places are difficult to reach and are therefore not often visited. ◆◇◇◇ ADJ-GRADED

,out of 'touch. 1 Someone who is **out of touch** with a situation is not aware of recent changes in it. *Washington politicians are out of touch with the American people.* **2** If you are **out of touch** with someone, you have not been in contact with them recently and are not familiar with their present situation. *James wasn't invited. We've been out of touch for years.* ◆◇◇◇ ADJ-GRADED: v-link ADJ   ADJ: v-link ADJ

,out-of-'town. 1 Out-of-town shops or facilities are situated away from the centre of a town or city. **2** Out-of-town is used to describe people who do not live in a particular town or city, but have travelled there for a particular purpose. *...a deluxe hotel for out-of-town visitors.* ◆◇◇◇ ADJ: ADJ n   ADJ: ADJ n

,out of 'work. Someone who is **out of work** does not have a job. ◆◇◇◇ ADJ

out·pace /ˌaʊt'peɪs/ **outpaces, outpacing, outpaced.** To **outpace** someone or something means to perform a particular action faster or better than they can. *These hovercraft can easily outpace most boats.* ◆◇◇◇ VERB Vn

out·pa·tient /'aʊtpeɪʃənt/ **outpatients;** also spelled **out-patient**. An **outpatient** is someone who receives treatment at a hospital but does not stay there overnight. *...the outpatient clinic.* ◆◇◇◇ N-COUNT

out·per·form /ˌaʊtpə'fɔːm/ **outperforms, outperforming, outperformed.** If one thing **outperforms** another, the first is more successful or efficient than the second. *In recent years the Austrian economy has outperformed most other industrial economies.* ◆◇◇◇ VERB Vn JOURNALISM

out·place·ment /'aʊtpleɪsmənt/. An **outplacement** agency gives advice to managers and other professional people who have recently become unemployed, and helps them find new jobs. N-UNCOUNT

out·play /ˌaʊt'pleɪ/ **outplays, outplaying, outplayed.** In sport, if one person or team **outplays** an opposing person or team, they play much better than their opponents. VERB: Vn

out·point /ˌaʊt'pɔɪnt/ **outpoints, outpointing, outpointed.** In boxing, if one boxer **outpoints** another, they win the match by getting more points then their opponent. VERB: Vn

out·post /'aʊtpəʊst/ **outposts.** An **outpost** is a small settlement in a foreign country or a distant part of your own country which is used for trading or military purposes. *...a remote mountain outpost.* ◆◇◇◇ N-COUNT

out·pour·ing /'aʊtpɔːrɪŋ/ **outpourings.** An **outpouring** of something such as an emotion or a reaction is the expression of it in an uncontrolled way. N-COUNT

The news of his death produced an instant outpouring of grief.

out·put /'aʊtpʊt/ **outputs. 1 Output** is used to refer to the amount of something that a person or thing produces. *Government statistics show the largest drop in industrial output for ten years.* **2** The **output** of a computer or word processor is the information that it displays on a screen or prints on paper as a result of a particular program. ◆◆◆◇◇ N-VAR / N-VAR

out·rage, outrages, outraging, outraged. The verb is pronounced /,aʊt'reɪdʒ/. The noun is pronounced /'aʊtreɪdʒ/. **1** If you **are outraged** by something, it makes you extremely shocked and angry. *Many people have been outraged by some of the things that have been said.* ◆ **out·raged** *He is truly outraged about what's happened to him.* **2 Outrage** is an intense feeling of anger and shock. *The decision provoked outrage from women.* **3** You can refer to an act or event which you find very shocking as an **outrage.** *Tom, this is an outrage!* ◆◆◇◇◇ VERB be V-ed Also V n / ADJ-GRADED / N-UNCOUNT / N-COUNT

out·ra·geous /aʊt'reɪdʒəs/. If you describe something as **outrageous**, you are emphasizing that it is unacceptable or very shocking. *Charges for local telephone calls are particularly outrageous... He was thrown out of a hotel for his outrageous drunken behaviour.* ◆ **out·ra·geous·ly** *Car-parks are few, crammed, and outrageously expensive.* ◆◆◇◇◇ ADJ-GRADED PRAGMATICS / ADV

out·ran /,aʊt'ræn/. **Outran** is the past tense of **outrun.**

out·rank /,aʊt'ræŋk/ **outranks, outranking, outranked.** If one person **outranks** another person, he or she has a higher position or grade within an organization than the other person. VERB: V n

outré /'uːtreɪ, AM uːt'reɪ/. Something that is **outré** is very unusual and strange. ADJ-GRADED FORMAL

out·reach /'aʊtriːtʃ/. **Outreach** programmes or schemes try to find people who need help or advice rather than waiting for those people to come and ask for help. N-UNCOUNT

out·rid·er /'aʊtraɪdə/ **outriders. Outriders** are people such as policemen who ride on motorcycles or horses beside or in front of an official vehicle, in order to protect the people in the vehicle. N-COUNT

out·right /,aʊt'raɪt/. The adjective is pronounced /'aʊtraɪt/. The adverb is pronounced /,aʊt'raɪt/. **1** You use **outright** to describe behaviour and actions that are open and direct, rather than indirect. *Kawaguchi finally resorted to an outright lie. ...outright condemnation.* ► Also an adverb. *Why are you so mysterious? Why don't you tell me outright?* **2 Outright** means complete and total. *She had failed to win an outright victory.* ► Also an adverb. *The peace plan wasn't rejected outright.* ● If someone **is killed outright,** they die immediately, for example in an accident. ◆◆◇◇◇ ADJ: ADJ n / ADV: ADV after v / ADJ: ADJ n / ADV: ADV after v / PHRASE

out·run /,aʊt'rʌn/ **outruns, outrunning, outran.** The form **outrun** is used in the present tense and is also the past participle of the verb. **1** If you **outrun** someone, you run faster than they do, and therefore are able to escape from them or to arrive somewhere before they do. *There are not many players who can outrun me.* **2** If one thing **outruns** another thing, the first thing develops faster than the second thing. *Spending could outrun the capacity of businesses to produce the goods.* VERB V n / VERB V n

out·sell /,aʊt'sel/ **outsells, outselling, outsold.** If one product **outsells** another product, the first product is sold more quickly or in larger quantities than the second. *Hexagonal pencils outsell round ones by ten to one.* VERB V n

out·set /'aʊtset/. If something happens **at the outset** of an event, process, or period of time, it happens at the beginning of it. If something happens **from the outset** it happens from the beginning and continues to happen. *Decide at the outset what kind of learning programme you want to follow.* ◆◆◇◇◇ PHRASE

out·shine /,aʊt'ʃaɪn/ **outshines, outshining, outshone.** If you **outshine** someone at a particular activity, you are much better at it than they are. *Jesse has begun to outshine me in sports.* VERB V n

out·side /,aʊt'saɪd/ **outsides.** The form **outside of** can also be used as a preposition. This form is more usual in American English. ◆◆◆◆◆

1 The **outside** of something is the part which surrounds or encloses the rest of it. *...the outside of the building... Cook over a fairly high heat until the outsides are browned.* ► Also an adjective. *...high up on the outside wall.* **2** If you are **outside,** you are not inside a building but are quite close to it. *'Was the car inside the garage?'—'No, it was still outside.'... The shouting outside grew louder.* ► Also a preposition. *The victim was outside a shop when he was attacked.* ► Also an adjective. *...a house with no bathroom and an outside lavatory.* **3** If you are **outside** a room, you are not in it but are in the hall or corridor next to it. ► Also an adverb. *They heard voices coming from outside in the corridor.* **4** People or things **outside** a country, town, or region are not in it. *...an old castle outside Budapest. ...warships stationed outside European waters.* ► Also a noun. *Peace cannot be imposed from the outside by the United States.* **5** When you talk about the **outside** world, you are referring to things that happen or exist in places other than your own home or community. *...a side of Morris's character she hid carefully from the outside world.* ► Also an adverb. *That was good for the prisoners because it brought them outside into the community.* **6 Outside** people or organizations are not part of a particular organization or group. *The company now makes much greater use of outside consultants.* ► Also a preposition. *He is hoping to recruit a chairman from outside the company.* **7 Outside** a particular institution or field of activity means in other fields of activity or in general life. *The condition is practically unknown outside psychiatry clinics.* **8** Something that is **outside** a particular range of things is not included within it. *She is a beautiful boat, but way, way outside my price range.* **9** Something that happens **outside** a particular period of time happens at a different time from the one mentioned. *They are open outside normal daily banking hours.* **10** On a wide road, the **outside** lanes are the ones which are closest to its centre. ► Also a noun. *...coming up on the outside.* **11 Outside of** is used to introduce the only thing or person that prevents your main statement from being completely true. *Outside of a few cuts and mosquito bites, few of the campers would require his services as a doctor.* **12** You use **at the outside** to say that you think that a particular amount is the largest possible in a particular situation, or that a particular time is the latest possible time for something to happen. *Give yourself forty minutes at the outside.* N-COUNT / ADJ: ADJ n / ADV / PREP / ADJ: ADJ n / PREP / ADV / PREP / ADJ: ADJ n / ADV: ADV after v / ADJ: ADJ n / PREP / PREP / PREP / PREP / ADJ: ADJ n / N-SING: the N / N-SING: the N / PHR-PREP PRAGMATICS / PHRASE / N-SING: the N

outside 'broadcast, outside broadcasts. An **outside broadcast** is a radio or television programme that is not recorded or filmed in a studio, but in another building or in the open air. N-COUNT

out·sid·er /,aʊt'saɪdə/ **outsiders. 1** An **outsider** is someone who does not belong to a particular group or organization. *The most likely outcome may be to subcontract much of the work to an outsider.* **2** An **outsider** is someone who is not accepted by a particular group, or who feels that they do not belong in it. *Malone, a cop, felt as much an outsider as any of them.* **3** In a competition, an **outsider** is a competitor who is unlikely to win. ◆◆◇◇◇ N-COUNT / N-COUNT / N-COUNT

out·size /,aʊt'saɪz/ or **outsized. 1** Outsize or outsized things are much larger than usual or much larger than you would expect. *...an outsize pair of scissors.* **2** Outsize clothes are clothes for very large people. ADJ BRITISH / ADJ BRITISH

out·skirts /'aʊtskɜːts/. The **outskirts** of a city or town are the parts of it that are farthest away from its centre. *Hours later we reached the outskirts of New York.* ◆◆◇◇◇ N-PLURAL: the N

out·smart /,aʊt'smɑːt/ **outsmarts, outsmarting, outsmarted.** If you **outsmart** someone, you defeat them or gain an advantage over them in a clever VERB V n

and sometimes dishonest way. *He claims that the smugglers are just outsmarting the border patrols.*

out·sold /ˌaʊtˈsəʊld/. **Outsold** is the past tense and past participle of **outsell**.

out·spo·ken /ˌaʊtˈspəʊkən/. Someone who is **outspoken** gives their opinions about things openly and honestly, even if they are likely to shock or offend people. *...his outspoken criticism of the prime minister.* ♦ **out·spo·ken·ness** *Her outspokenness had alienated many voters.* ◆◆◇◇◇ ADJ-GRADED / N-UNCOUNT

out·stand·ing /ˌaʊtˈstændɪŋ/. **1** If you describe someone or something as **outstanding**, you think that they are very remarkable and impressive. *Derartu is an outstanding athlete.* **2 Outstanding** means very important or obvious. *...an outstanding example of a small business that grew into a big one.* **3** Money that is **outstanding** has not yet been paid and is still owed to someone. *The total debt outstanding is $70 billion.* **4 Outstanding** issues or problems have not yet been resolved. ◆◆◆◇◇ ADJ-GRADED / ADJ / ADJ / ADJ

out·stand·ing·ly /ˌaʊtˈstændɪŋli/. You use **outstandingly** to emphasize how good something is. *Salzburg is an outstandingly beautiful place to visit.* ADV-GRADED: ADV adj/adv PRAGMATICS

out·stay /ˌaʊtˈsteɪ/ **outstays, outstaying, outstayed.** ● to outstay your **welcome**: see **welcome**.

out·stretched /ˌaʊtˈstretʃt/. If a part of the body of a person or animal is **outstretched**, it is stretched out as far as possible. *...an eagle with outstretched wings.* ◆◇◇◇◇ ADJ

out·strip /ˌaʊtˈstrɪp/ **outstrips, outstripping, outstripped.** If one thing **outstrips** another, the first thing becomes larger in amount, or more successful or important, than the second thing. *In the mid-eighteenth century the production of food far outstripped the rise in population.* ◆◇◇◇◇ VERB V n

'out-take, out-takes; also spelled **outtake.** An **out-take** is a song on an album or part of a film or programme that is removed before the album is released or the film or programme is shown. N-COUNT

'out tray, out trays; also spelled **out-tray.** An **out tray** is a tray or shallow basket used in offices to put letters and documents in when they have been dealt with and are ready to be sent out of the office. N-COUNT

out·vote /ˌaʊtˈvəʊt/ **outvotes, outvoting, outvoted.** If you **are outvoted**, more people vote against what you are proposing than vote for it, so that your proposal is defeated. *Twice his colleagues have outvoted him.* VERB: be V-ed V n

out·ward /ˈaʊtwəd/. **1** An **outward** journey is a journey that you make away from a place that you are intending to return to later. *Tickets must be bought in advance, with outward and return dates specified.* **2** The **outward** feelings, qualities, or attitudes of someone or something are the ones they appear to have rather than the ones that they actually have. *What the military rulers have done is to restore the outward appearance of order.* **3** The **outward** features of something are the ones that you can see from the outside. *Mark was lying unconscious but with no outward sign of injury.* **4** See also **outwards**. ◆◇◇◇◇ ADJ: ADJ n / ADJ: ADJ n / ADJ: ADJ n

out·ward·ly /ˈaʊtwədli/. You use **outwardly** to indicate the feelings or qualities that a person or situation may appear to have, rather than the ones that they actually have. *Outwardly this looked like the beginning of a terrific programme.* ◆◇◇◇◇ ADV

out·wards /ˈaʊtwədz/; the form **outward** is also used. In American English, **outward** is more usual. **1** If something moves or faces **outwards**, it moves or faces away from the place you are in or the place you are talking about. *The top door opened outwards.* **2** If you say that a person or a group of people, such as a government, looks **outwards**, you mean that they turn their attention to another group that they are interested in or would like greater involvement with. *Other poor countries looked outward, strengthening their ties to the economic superpowers.* ◆◇◇◇◇ ADV: ADV after v / ADV: ADV after v

out·weigh /ˌaʊtˈweɪ/ **outweighs, outweighing, outweighed.** If one thing **outweighs** another, the ◆◇◇◇◇ VERB V n

first thing is of greater importance, benefit, or significance than the second thing. *The medical benefits of x-rays far outweigh the risk of having them.* FORMAL

out·wit /ˌaʊtˈwɪt/ **outwits, outwitting, outwitted.** If you **outwit** someone, you use your intelligence or a clever trick to defeat them or to gain an advantage over them. *To win the presidency he had first to outwit his rivals.* VERB V n

out·worn /ˌaʊtˈwɔːn/. If you describe a belief or custom as **outworn**, you mean that it is old-fashioned and no longer has any meaning or usefulness. *...an ancient nation sunk in an outworn culture.* ADJ

ouzo /ˈuːzəʊ/ **ouzos. Ouzo** is a strong aniseed-flavoured alcoholic drink that is made in Greece. ▶ A glass of ouzo can be referred to as an **ouzo**. N-UNCOUNT / N-COUNT

ova /ˈəʊvə/. **Ova** is the plural of **ovum**.

oval /ˈəʊvəl/ **ovals. Oval** things have a shape that is like a circle but is wider in one direction than the other. See picture headed **shapes**. *...a pale oval face.* ▶ Also a noun. *Mould the cheese into small ovals.* ◆◆◇◇◇ ADJ / N-COUNT

ovar·ian /əʊˈveəriən/. **Ovarian** means relating to or coming from the ovaries. *...ovarian cancer.* ◆◇◇◇◇ ADJ: ADJ n

ova·ry /ˈəʊvəri/ **ovaries.** A woman's **ovaries** are the two organs in her body that produce eggs. ◆◇◇◇◇ N-COUNT

ova·tion /əʊˈveɪʃən/ **ovations.** An **ovation** is a long burst of applause from an audience for a particular performer or speaker. ● See also **standing ovation**. ◆◇◇◇◇ N-COUNT FORMAL

oven /ˈʌvən/ **ovens.** An **oven** is a cooker or part of a cooker that is like a box with a door. You cook food inside an oven. ◆◆◇◇◇ N-COUNT

oven·proof /ˈʌvənpruːf/. An **ovenproof** dish is one that has been specially made to be used in an oven without being damaged by the heat. ADJ

over 1 position and movement

over /ˈəʊvə/. In addition to the uses shown below, **over** is used after some verbs, nouns, and adjectives in order to introduce extra information. **Over** is also used in phrasal verbs such as 'hand over' and 'glaze over'. ◆◆◆◆◆

1 If one thing is **over** another thing or is moving **over** it, the first thing is directly above the second, either resting on it, or with a space between them. *He looked at himself in the mirror over the table... We were crossing the small iron bridge over the stream... I also noted Blackhawk helicopters flying low over the crowd.* ▶ Also an adverb. *...planes flying over every 10 or 15 minutes.* **2** If one thing is **over** another thing, it is supported by it and its ends are hanging down on each side of it. *Joe's clothing was flung over the back of a chair.* **3** If one thing is **over** another thing, it covers part or all of it. *Mix the ingredients and pour over the mushrooms... He was wearing a light-grey suit over a shirt.* ▶ Also an adverb. *Heat this syrup and pour it over... The workers decided it would be too difficult to recover it so they covered it over.* **4** If you lean **over** an object, you bend your body so that the top part of it is above the object. *They stopped to lean over a gate... She bent over the table, frowning.* ▶ Also an adverb. *Sam leant over to open the door of the car.* **5** If you look **over** or talk **over** an object, you look or talk across the top of it. *I went and stood beside him, looking over his shoulder.* **6** If a window has a view **over** an area of land or water, you can see the land or water through the window. *...a wonderful view over the River Amstel.* **7** If someone or something goes **over** a barrier or boundary, they get to the other side of it by going across it, or across the top of it. *Policemen jumped over the wall in pursuit... She stepped over his shoes.* ▶ Also an adverb. *I climbed over into the back seat.* **8** If someone or something moves **over** an area or surface, they move across it, from one side to the other. *She ran swiftly over the lawn to the gate.* **9** If something is on the opposite side of a road or river, you can say that it is **over** the road or river. *...Richard Garrick, who lived in the house over the road.* **10** If you go **over** to a place, you go to that place. *I got out the car and drove over to Dervaig... I thought you might have invited her over.* **11** You can use **over** PREP / ADV / PREP / PREP / ADV: ADV after v / ADV / PREP / PREP / PREP / ADV / PREP / ADV / PREP / ADV

to indicate a particular position or place a short distance away from someone or something. *He noticed Rolfe standing silently over by the window.* **12 Over here** means near you, or in the country you are in. *Why don't you come over here tomorrow evening... My father was in the U.S. army over here.* **13 Over there** means in a place a short distance away from you, or in another country. *The cafe is just across the road over there... She'd married some American and settled down over there.*

14 You use **over** to say that someone or something falls towards or onto the ground, often suddenly or violently. *He was knocked over by a bus and broke his leg.* **15** If something rolls **over** or is turned **over**, its position changes so that the part that was facing upwards is now facing downwards. *His car rolled over after a tyre was punctured.*

16 All over a place means in every part of it. *...the letters she received from people all over the world.* **17 ● the world over:** see **world.**

over 2 amounts and occurrences

over /ˈəʊvə/. **1** If something is **over** a particular amount, measurement, or age, it is more than that amount, measurement, or age. *Cigarettes kill over a hundred thousand Britons every year. ...equipment costs of over £100m.* ► Also an adverb. *...people aged 65 and over... The catalogue costs $5, refundable against orders of $30 and over.* **2 Over and above** an amount, especially a normal amount, means more than that amount or in addition to it. *Expenditure on education has gone up by seven point eight per cent over and above inflation.* **3** If you say that you have some food or money **over**, you mean that it remains after you have used all that you need. *Larsons pay me well enough, but there's not much over for luxuries.*

4 If you do something **over**, you do it again or start doing it again from the beginning. *She said if she had the chance to do it over, she would.* **5** If you say that something happened **twice over**, **three times over** and so on, you are stating the number of times that it happened and emphasizing that it happened more than once. **6** If you say that something is happening **all over again**, you are emphasizing that it is happening again, and you are suggesting that it is tiring, boring, or unpleasant. *The whole process started all over again.* **7** If you say that something happened **over and over** or **over and over again**, you are emphasizing that it happened many times. *He plays the same songs over and over.*

over 3 other uses

over /ˈəʊvə/ **overs. 1** If an activity is **over** or all **over**, it is completely finished. *The bad times were over... I am glad it's all over.* **2** If you are **over** an illness or an experience, it has finished and you have recovered from its effects. *I'm glad that you're over the flu.*

3 If you have control or influence **over** someone or something, you are able to control them or influence them. *The oil companies have lost their power over oil prices.* **4** You use **over** to indicate what a disagreement or feeling relates to or is caused by. *...concern over recent events in Burma... Staff at some air and sea ports are beginning to protest over pay.*

5 If something happens **over** a period of time or **over** a meal or a drink, it happens during that time or during that meal or drink. *Many strikes over the last few years have not ended successfully. ...discussing the problem over a glass of wine.* **6** You use **over** to indicate that you give or receive information using a telephone, radio, or other piece of electrical equipment. *I'm not prepared to discuss this over the telephone.*

7 The presenter of a radio or television programme says **'over to someone'** to indicate the person who will speak next. *With the rest of the sports news, over to Colin Maitland.* **8** When people such as the police or the army are using a radio to communicate, they say **'Over'** to indicate that they have finished speaking and are waiting for a reply.

9 In cricket, an **over** consists of six correctly bowled balls.

over- /ˈəʊvə-/. You can add **over-** to an adjective or verb to indicate that a quality exists or an action is done to too great an extent. For example, if you say that someone is being over-cautious, you mean that they are being too cautious.

over·act /ˌəʊvərˈækt/ **overacts, overacting, overacted.** If you say that someone **overacts**, you mean they exaggerate their emotions and movements, usually when acting in a play. *Sometimes he had overacted in his role as Prince.*

over·all, overalls. The adjective and adverb are pronounced /ˌəʊvərˈɔːl/. The noun is pronounced /ˈəʊvərɔːl/. **1** You use **overall** to indicate that you are talking about a situation in general or about the whole of something. *Cut down your overall amount of physical activity.* ► Also an adverb. *...the quality of education overall.* **2 Overalls** consist of a single piece of clothing that combines trousers and a jacket. You wear overalls over your clothes in order to protect them from dirt while you are working. **3 Overalls** are trousers that are attached to a piece of cloth which covers your chest and which has straps going over your shoulders. The British word is **dungarees. 4** An **overall** is a piece of clothing shaped like a coat that you wear over your clothes in order to protect them from dirt while you are working.

overall ma'jority, overall majorities. If a political party wins an **overall majority** in an election or vote, they get more votes than the total number of votes or seats won by all their opponents.

over·arch·ing /ˌəʊvərˈɑːtʃɪŋ/. You use **overarching** to indicate that you are talking about something that includes or affects everything or everyone. *Home ownership has been an overarching and innate desire of the British.*

over·arm /ˈəʊvərɑːm/. You use **overarm** to describe actions, such as throwing a ball, in which you stretch your arm over your shoulder.

over·awe /ˌəʊvərˈɔː/ **overawes, overawing, overawed.** If you **are overawed** by something or someone, you are very impressed by them and a little afraid of them. *Don't be overawed by people in authority, however important they are.* ♦ **over·awed** *He had been rather overawed to meet one of the Billington family.*

over·bal·ance /ˌəʊvəˈbæləns/ **overbalances, overbalancing, overbalanced.** If you **overbalance**, you fall over or nearly fall over, because you are not standing properly.

over·bear·ing /ˌəʊvəˈbeərɪŋ/. An **overbearing** person tries to make other people do what he or she wants in an unpleasant and forceful way. *My husband can be quite overbearing with our son.*

over·blown /ˌəʊvəˈbləʊn/. Something that is **overblown** makes something seem larger, more important, or more significant than it really is. *The reporting of the hostage story was fair, if sometimes a little overblown.*

over·board /ˈəʊvəbɔːd/. **1** If you fall **overboard**, you fall over the side of a boat into the water. **2** If you say that someone **goes overboard**, you mean that they do something to a greater extent than is necessary or reasonable. *What do you think causes the police to go overboard, to use excessive violence?* **3** If you **throw** something **overboard**, for example an idea or suggestion, you reject it completely.

over·book /ˌəʊvəˈbʊk/ **overbooks, overbooking, overbooked.** If an organization such as an airline or a theatre company **overbooks**, they sell more tickets than they have places for. *Planes are crowded, airlines overbook, and departures are almost never on time.*

over·booked /ˌəʊvəˈbʊkt/. If something such as a hotel or a coach is **overbooked**, more people have booked than the number of places that are available. *He was left behind in Auckland because the much-delayed flight was overbooked.*

over·bur·dened /ˌəʊvəˈbɜːdənd/. **1** If a system or ADJ-GRADED
organization is **overburdened**, it has too many people or things to deal with and so does not function
properly. *The city's hospitals are overburdened by
casualties.* **2** If you are **overburdened** with something such as work or problems, you have more of it
than you can cope with. *The Chief Inspector disliked
being overburdened with insignificant detail.*

over·came /ˌəʊvəˈkeɪm/. **Overcame** is the past
tense of **overcome**.

over·cast /ˌəʊvəˈkɑːst, -ˈkæst/. If it is **overcast**, or if ADJ
the sky or the day is **overcast**, the sky is completely
covered with cloud and there is not much light. *The
weather forecast is for showers and overcast skies.*

over·charge /ˌəʊvəˈtʃɑːdʒ/ **overcharges, over-** ◆◇◇◇
charging, overcharged. If someone **over-** VERB: V n
charges you, they charge you too much for their
goods or services. **♦ over·charg·ing.** N-UNCOUNT

over·coat /ˈəʊvəkəʊt/ **overcoats.** An overcoat is ◆◇◇◇
a thick warm coat that you wear in winter. N-COUNT

over·come /ˌəʊvəˈkʌm/ **overcomes, overcom-** ◆◆◇◇
ing, overcame. 1 If you **overcome** a feeling or VERB
problem, you successfully deal with it and control V n
it. *Molly had fought and overcome her fear of flying.*
2 If you **are overcome** by something, it makes you feel VERB
so helpless, surprised, or embarrassed that you can- be V-ed
not think clearly. *The night before the test I was over-* Also V n
come by fear and despair. **3** If you **are overcome** by VERB:
smoke or a poisonous gas, you become very ill or die be V-ed
from breathing it in.

over·crowd·ed /ˌəʊvəˈkraʊdɪd/. An **overcrowded** ◆◇◇◇
place has too many things or people in it. *...one of* ADJ-GRADED
the most overcrowded prisons in the country.

over·crowd·ing /ˌəʊvəˈkraʊdɪŋ/. If there is a ◆◇◇◇
problem of **overcrowding**, there are more people N-UNCOUNT
living in a place than it was designed for.

over·do /ˌəʊvəˈduː/ **overdoes, overdoing, over-** ◆◇◇◇
did, overdone. 1 If you **overdo** it, you behave in VERB
an exaggerated or extreme way. *He thought Dan* V n
was overdoing the charity bit. **♦ over·done** *The* Also V it
gloom about a never-ending recession was somewhat ADJ-GRADED
overdone. **2** If you **overdo** an activity, you try to do VERB
more than you can physically manage. *Satisfy your* V it
urge to take exercise but don't overdo it. Also V n

over·done /ˌəʊvəˈdʌn/. If food is **overdone**, it has ADJ-GRADED
been spoiled by being cooked for too long.

over·dose /ˈəʊvədəʊs/ **overdoses, overdosing,** ◆◇◇◇
overdosed. 1 If someone takes an **overdose** of a N-COUNT
drug, they take more of it than is safe. *Guitarist Jimi
Hendrix died of a drug overdose.* **2** If someone **over-** VERB
doses, they take more of a drug than is safe. *He'd* V on n
overdosed on heroin. **3** You can refer to an excess of Also V
something, especially something harmful, as an N-COUNT
overdose. *An overdose of chlorine can give lighter
hair a green tinge.* **4** You can say that someone VERB
overdoses on something if they have or do too V on n
much of it. *The city, he concluded, had overdosed on* Also V
design.

over·draft /ˈəʊvədrɑːft, -dræft/ **overdrafts.** If you ◆◇◇◇
have an **overdraft**, you have spent more money N-COUNT
than you have in your bank account, and so you are
in debt to the bank.

over·drawn /ˌəʊvəˈdrɔːn/. If a person or their bank ADJ-GRADED
account is **overdrawn**, they have spent more money
than they have in their account, and so are in debt
to the bank. *He was £100 overdrawn.*

over·dressed /ˌəʊvəˈdrest/. If you say that some- ADJ-GRADED
one is **overdressed**, you think that they are wearing
clothes that are too formal or too smart for a particular occasion.

over·drive /ˈəʊvədraɪv/ **overdrives. 1** The **over-** N-COUNT
drive in a vehicle is a very high gear that is used
when you are driving at high speeds. **2** If you go PHRASE
into overdrive, you begin to work very hard or perform a particular activity in a very intense way.

over·due /ˌəʊvəˈdjuː, -ˈduː/. **1** If you say that a ◆◇◇◇
change or an event is **overdue**, you mean that you ADJ-GRADED
think it should have happened before now. *This debate is long overdue.* **2 Overdue** sums of money ADJ-GRADED
have not been paid, even though it is later than the

date on which they should have been paid. **3** An ADJ-GRADED
overdue library book has not been returned to the
library, even though the date on which it should
have been returned has passed.

over·eat /ˌəʊvəˈiːt/ **overeats, overeating,** ◆◇◇◇
overate, overeaten. If you **overeat**, you eat more VERB
than you need to or more than is healthy. *...if you* V
tend to overeat because of depression. **♦ over-** Also V n
·eater, overeaters *She eats in secret like most* N-COUNT
compulsive overeaters. **♦ over·eat·ing** *Certain seg-* N-UNCOUNT
*ments of the food industry do actively promote
overeating.*

over·em·pha·size /ˌəʊvərˈemfəsaɪz/ **overempha-**
sizes, overemphasizing, overemphasized;
also spelled **overemphasise** in British English. **1** If VERB
you say that someone **overemphasizes** something, be V-ed
you mean that they give it more importance than it Also V n
deserves or than you consider appropriate. *Drugs
have been overemphasized in explaining the increase
in violence.* **♦ over·em·pha·sis** *...an overemphasis* N-SING
on ideology and ideas. **2** If you say that something VB: with brd-
cannot **be overemphasized**, you are emphasizing neg
that you think it is very important. *The importance* be V-ed
of education cannot be overemphasised. Also V n

over·es·ti·mate /ˌəʊvərˈestɪmeɪt/ **overesti-** ◆◇◇◇
mates, overestimating, overestimated. 1 If VERB
you say that someone **overestimates** something, V n
you mean that they think it is greater in amount or Also V
importance than it really is. *With hindsight, he was
overestimating their desire for peace.* **2** If you say VB: with brd-
that something cannot **be overestimated**, you are neg
emphasizing that you think it is very important. *The* PRAGMATICS
benefits of this cannot be overestimated. **3** If you be V-ed
overestimate someone, you think that they have VERB
more of a skill or quality than they really have. *I* V n
think you overestimate me, Fred.

over-e·xcited. If you say that someone is **over-** ADJ-GRADED
excited, you mean that they are more excited than
you think is desirable. *Provide continuous, organised entertainment or children may get over-excited.*

over·ex·posed /ˌəʊvərɪksˈpəʊzd/. An **overexposed** ADJ-GRADED
photograph is of poor quality because the film has
been exposed to too much light.

over·ex·tend·ed /ˌəʊvərɪksˈtendɪd/. If someone is ADJ-GRADED
overextended, they have become involved in more
activities than they can financially or physically
manage. *The UN budget for peacekeeping operations
already is overextended.*

over·flight /ˈəʊvəflaɪt/ **overflights.** An **overflight** N-VAR
is the passage of an aircraft from one country over
another country's territory.

over·flow, overflows, overflowing, over- ◆◇◇◇
flowed. The verb is pronounced /ˌəʊvəˈfləʊ/. The
noun is pronounced /ˈəʊvəfləʊ/. **1** If a liquid or a VB: no passive
river **overflows**, it flows over the edges of the con- V
tainer or place it is in. *The sewers were overflowing* Also V n
and the river was bursting its banks. **2** If a place or
container **is overflowing** with people or things, V with n
there are too many of them in it. *The great hall was* Also V
overflowing with people. **3** If someone **is overflow-** VERB
ing with a feeling or if the feeling **overflows**, the V with n
person is experiencing it very strongly and shows Also V
this in their behaviour. *Kenneth overflowed with
friendliness and hospitality.* **4** The **overflow** is the N-COUNT
extra people or things that something cannot contain or deal with because it is not large enough.
*Tents have been set up next to hospitals to handle
the overflow.* **5** An **overflow** is a hole or pipe N-COUNT
through which liquid can flow out of a container
when it gets too full. **6** If a place or container is PHRASE
filled **to overflowing**, it is so full of people or things
that no more can fit in.

over·fly /ˌəʊvəˈflaɪ/ **overflies, overflying, over-** VERB: V n
flew, overflown. When an aircraft **overflies** an
area, it flies over it.

over·ground /ˈəʊvəɡraʊnd/. In an **overground** ADJ: ADJ n
transport system, vehicles run on the surface of the
ground, rather than below it. ▶ Also an adverb. ADV:
There are plans to run the line overground. ADV after v

over·grown /ˌəʊvəˈɡrəʊn/. **1** If a place is **overgrown**, it is thickly covered with plants because it has not been looked after. ...*a courtyard overgrown with weeds.* **2** If you describe an adult as an **overgrown** child, you mean that their behaviour and attitudes are like those of a child, and that you dislike this.
◆◇◇◇◇ ADJ-GRADED
ADJ: ADJ n
PRAGMATICS

over·hang, overhangs, overhanging, overhung. The verb is pronounced /ˌəʊvəˈhæŋ/. The noun is pronounced /ˈəʊvəhæŋ/. **1** If one thing **overhangs** another, it sticks out over and above it. *Part of the rock wall overhung the path.* **2** An **overhang** is the part of something that sticks out over and above something else. ...*a sharp overhang of rock.*
◆◇◇◇◇ VERB Vn
N-COUNT

over·haul, overhauls, overhauling, overhauled. The verb is pronounced /ˌəʊvəˈhɔːl/. The noun is pronounced /ˈəʊvəhɔːl/. **1** If a piece of equipment **is overhauled**, it is cleaned, checked thoroughly, and repaired if necessary. *He had had his little Fiat car overhauled three times.* ▶ Also a noun. ...*the overhaul of aero engines.* **2** If you **overhaul** a system or method, you examine it carefully and make many changes in it in order to improve it. *The government said it wanted to overhaul the employment training scheme.* ▶ Also a noun. ...*a complete overhaul of air traffic control systems.*
◆◇◇◇◇ VERB: beV-ed haveV-ed
N-COUNT VERB Vn
N-COUNT

over·head The adjective is pronounced /ˈəʊvəhed/. The adverb is pronounced /ˌəʊvəˈhed/. You use **overhead** to indicate that something is above you or above the place that you are talking about. ...*the overhead light.* ...*overhead cables.* ▶ Also an adverb. *Helicopters have been seen flying overhead.*
◆◆◇◇◇ ADJ: ADJ n
ADV

overhead pro·jector, overhead projectors. An **overhead projector** is a machine that projects writing or pictures from a transparency onto a screen or wall. The abbreviation 'OHP' is also used.
N-COUNT

over·heads /ˈəʊvəhedz/. The **overheads** of a business are its regular and essential expenses, such as salaries, rent, electricity, and telephone bills.
◆◇◇◇◇ N-PLURAL

over·hear, overhears, overhearing, overheard. If you **overhear** someone, you hear what they are saying when they are not talking to you and they do not know that you are listening. *I overheard two doctors discussing my case.*
◆◇◇◇◇ VERB Vn

over·heat, overheats, overheating, overheated. **1** If something **overheats** or if you **overheat** it, it becomes hotter than is necessary or desirable. *The engine was overheating and the car was not handling well.* ◆ **over·heat·ed** ...*that stuffy, overheated apartment.* **2** If a country's economy **overheats** or if conditions **overheat** it, it grows so rapidly that inflation and interest rates rise very quickly. *The private sector is increasing its spending so sharply that the economy is overheating.* ◆ **overheated** ...*the disastrous consequences of an overheated market.*
◆◇◇◇◇ V-ERG V Also Vn
ADJ-GRADED V-ERG V Also Vn
ADJ-GRADED

over·heat·ed /ˌəʊvəˈhiːtɪd/. Someone who is **overheated** is very angry about something. *I think the reaction has been a little exaggerated.*
ADJ-GRADED

over·hung /ˌəʊvəˈhʌŋ/. **Overhung** is the past tense and past participle of **overhang**.

over·kill /ˈəʊvəkɪl/. You can say that something is **overkill** when you think that there is more of it than is necessary or appropriate. *Such security measures may well be overkill.*
N-UNCOUNT

over·land /ˈəʊvəlænd/. An **overland** journey is made across land rather than by ship or aeroplane. *The overland route is across some really tough mountains.* ▶ Also an adverb. *They're travelling to Baghdad overland.*
◆◇◇◇◇ ADJ: ADJ n
ADV: ADV after v

over·lap, overlaps, overlapping, overlapped. The verb is pronounced /ˌəʊvəˈlæp/. The noun is pronounced /ˈəʊvəlæp/. **1** If one thing **overlaps** another, or if you **overlap** them, a part of the first thing occupies the same area as a part of the other thing. You can also say that two things **overlap**. *The upper layer of felt should overlap the lower... Overlap the slices carefully so there are no gaps... The* edges must overlap each other. **2** If one idea or activity **overlaps** another, or **overlaps** with another, they involve some of the same subjects, people, or periods of time. You can also say that two ideas or activities, **overlap**. *Elizabeth met other Oxford intellectuals, some of whom overlapped Naomi's world... Christian holy week overlaps with the beginning of the Jewish holiday of Passover.* ▶ Also a noun. ...*the overlap between civil and military technology.*
◆◆◇◇◇ V-RECIP-ERG Vn V pl-n pl-n Vn Also pl-n V
V-RECIP Vn V with n Also pl-n V
N-VAR

over·lay, overlays, overlaying, overlaid. The verb is pronounced /ˌəʊvəˈleɪ/. The noun is pronounced /ˈəʊvəleɪ/. **1** If something **is overlaid** with something else, it is covered by it. *The floor was overlaid with rugs of oriental design.* **2** You can use **overlay** to refer to a substance which covers the surface of something. ...*an overlay of snow on the tops of the iron fences.* **3** If something **is overlaid** with a feeling or quality, that feeling or quality is the most noticeable one, but there may be deeper and more important ones involved. *The party had been overlaid with a certain nervousness.* ▶ Also a noun. *There can be an emotional overlay to the frustration of solving real problems.*
◆◇◇◇◇ VB: usu passive beV-ed with n
N-VAR
VERB beV-ed with n Also Vn
N-COUNT

over·leaf /ˌəʊvəˈliːf/. **Overleaf** is used in books and magazines to say that something is on the other side of the page you are reading. *Answer the questionnaire overleaf.*
ADV

over·load, overloads, overloading, overloaded. **1** If you **overload** a vehicle, you put more things or people into it than it was designed to carry. *Don't overload the boat or it will sink.* ◆ **over·load·ed** *Some trains were so overloaded that their suspension collapsed.* **2** To **overload** someone **with** work, problems, or information means to give them more work, problems, or information than they can cope with. ...*an effective method that will not overload staff with yet more paperwork.* ▶ Also a noun. *57 per cent complained of work overload.* ◆ **overloaded** *The bar waiter was already overloaded with orders.* **3** If you **overload** an electrical system, you cause too much electricity to flow through it, and so damage it.
◆◇◇◇◇ VERB Vn
ADJ-GRADED
VERB Vn with n
N-UNCOUNT ADJ-GRADED VERB: Vn

over·look, overlooks, overlooking, overlooked. **1** If a building or window **overlooks** a place, you can see the place clearly from the building or window. *Pretty and comfortable rooms overlook a flower-filled garden.* **2** If you **overlook** a fact or problem, you do not notice it, or do not realize how important it is. *We overlook all sorts of warning signals about our own health.* **3** If you **overlook** someone's faults or bad behaviour, you forgive them and take no action. ...*satisfying relationships that enable them to overlook each other's faults.*
◆◆◇◇◇ VERB Vn
VERB Vn
VERB Vn

over·lord /ˈəʊvəlɔːd/ overlords. **1** If you refer to someone as an **overlord**, you mean that they have great power which they exercise in an unjust way. *The West has a huge job to defeat the cocaine and heroin overlords.* **2** In former times, an **overlord** was someone who had power over many people.
N-COUNT
N-COUNT

over·ly /ˈəʊvəli/. **Overly** means more than is normal, necessary, or reasonable. *Employers may become overly cautious about taking on new staff.*
◆◇◇◇◇ ADV: ADV adj/ adv/-ed

over·manned /ˌəʊvəˈmænd/. If you say that a place or an industry is **overmanned**, you mean that you think there are more people working there or doing the work than is really necessary.
ADJ-GRADED

over·man·ning /ˌəʊvəˈmænɪŋ/. If there is a problem of **overmanning** in an industry, there are more people working there or doing the work than is really necessary.
N-UNCOUNT

over·much /ˌəʊvəˈmʌtʃ/. If something happens **overmuch**, it happens too much or very much. *He was not a man who thought overmuch about clothes.*
ADV FORMAL

over·night /ˌəʊvəˈnaɪt/. **1** If something happens **overnight**, it happens throughout the night or at some point during the night. *The weather remained calm overnight.* ▶ Also an adjective. *Travel and overnight accommodation are included.* **2** You can
◆◆◆◇◇ ADV: ADV after v
ADJ: ADJ n
ADV:

say that something happens **overnight** when it happens very quickly and unexpectedly. *The rules are not going to change overnight.* ▶ Also an adjective. *He became an overnight success.* **3 Overnight** bags or clothes are ones that you take when you go and stay somewhere for one or two nights. [ADV after v] [ADJ: ADJ n] [ADJ: ADJ n]

over·paid /ˌəʊvəˈpeɪd/. If you say that someone is **overpaid**, you think they are paid more than they deserve for the work they do. ● See also **overpay**. [ADJ-GRADED]

over·pass /ˈəʊvəpɑːs, -pæs/ **overpasses.** An **overpass** is a structure which carries one road over the top of another one. The British word is **flyover**. [N-COUNT AMERICAN]

over·pay /ˌəʊvəˈpeɪ/ **overpays, overpaying, overpaid.** If you **overpay** someone, or if you **overpay** for something, you pay more than is necessary or reasonable. *The council is said to have been overpaying for repairs made by its housing department... The scheme will overpay some lawyers and underpay others.* ● See also **overpaid**. [VERB V for n] [V n] [Also V]

over·play /ˌəʊvəˈpleɪ/ **overplays, overplaying, overplayed.** If you say that someone is **overplaying** something such as a problem, you mean that they are making it seem more important than it really is. *...overplaying the depth of the economic crisis.* [VERB V n]

over·pop·u·lat·ed /ˌəʊvəˈpɒpjʊleɪtɪd/. If an area is **overpopulated**, there are problems because it has too many people living there. [ADJ-GRADED]

over·pop·u·la·tion /ˌəʊvəpɒpjʊˈleɪʃən/. If there is a problem of **overpopulation** in an area, there are more people living there than can be supported properly. [N-UNCOUNT]

over·pow·er /ˌəʊvəˈpaʊə/ **overpowers, overpowering, overpowered. 1** If you **overpower** someone, you seize them despite their struggles because you are stronger than they are. *It took ten guardsmen to overpower him.* **2** If a feeling **overpowers** you, it suddenly affects you very strongly. *A sudden dizziness overpowered him.* ♦ **over·pow·er·ing** *The desire for revenge can be overpowering.* **3** In a sports match, when one team or player **overpowers** the other, they play much better than them and beat them easily. [VERB V n] [VERB V n] [ADJ-GRADED] [VERB: V n]

over·pow·er·ing /ˌəʊvəˈpaʊərɪŋ/. An **overpowering** person makes other people feel uncomfortable because they have such a strong personality. *...an overpowering manner.* [ADJ-GRADED]

over·priced /ˌəʊvəˈpraɪst/. If you say that something is **overpriced**, you think it costs much more than it should. *I went and had an overpriced cup of coffee in the hotel cafeteria.* [ADJ-GRADED]

over·ran /ˌəʊvəˈræn/; also spelled **over-ran**. **Over-ran** is the past tense of **overrun**.

over·rate /ˌəʊvəˈreɪt/ **overrates, overrating, overrated;** also spelled **over-rate**. If you say that something or someone is **overrated**, you mean that people have a higher opinion of them than they deserve. *More men are finding out that the joys of work have been overrated.* ♦ **over·rat·ed** *Life in the wild is vastly overrated.* [VERB be V-ed Also V n] [ADJ-GRADED]

over·reach /ˌəʊvəˈriːtʃ/ **overreaches, overreaching, overreached;** also spelled **over-reach**. If you say that someone **overreaches** themselves, you mean that they fail at something because they are trying to do more than they are able to. *He overreached himself and lost much of his fortune.* [VERB V pron-refl]

over·react /ˌəʊvəriˈækt/ **overreacts, overreacting, overreacted;** also spelled **over-react**. If you say that someone **overreacts** to something, you mean that they have and show more of an emotion than is necessary or appropriate. *I overreact to anything sad.* ♦ **over·reac·tion** /ˌəʊvəriˈækʃən/ **overreactions** *The use of tear gas and rubber bullets was a monstrous overreaction.* [VERB V to n Also V] [N-VAR]

over·ride /ˌəʊvəˈraɪd/ **overrides, overriding, overrode, overridden;** also spelled **over-ride**. **1** If one thing in a situation **overrides** other things, it is more important than them. *The welfare of a child should always override the wishes of its parents.* ♦ **over·rid·ing** *...the overriding need to cut the budget deficit.* **2** If someone in authority **overrides** [VERB V n] [ADJ] [VERB]

a person or their decisions, they cancel their decisions. *I'm applying in advance for the authority to override him.* **3** An **override** is an attempt to cancel someone's decisions by using your authority over them or by gaining more votes than them in an election or contest. [V n] [N-COUNT AMERICAN]

over·rule /ˌəʊvəˈruːl/ **overrules, overruling, overruled;** also spelled **over-rule**. If someone in authority **overrules** a person or their decision, they officially decide that the decision is incorrect or not valid. [◆◇◇◇ VERB: V n]

over·run /ˌəʊvəˈrʌn/ **overruns, overrunning, overran;** also spelled **over-run**. **1** If an army or an armed force **overruns** a place, it succeeds in occupying it very quickly. *A group of rebels overran the port area.* **2** If you say that a place is **overrun** with things that you consider undesirable, you mean that there are a large number of them there. *The flower beds were overrun with grasses.* **3** If an event or meeting **overruns** by, for example, ten minutes, it continues for ten minutes longer than it was intended to. *Tuesday's lunch overran by three-quarters of an hour... The talks overran their allotted time.* **4** If costs **overrun**, they are higher than was planned or expected. *Costs overran the budget by about 30%.* ▶ Also a noun. *...cost overruns of at least $1 billion.* [◆◇◇◇ VERB V n] [ADJ-GRADED: v-link ADJ] [VERB V by n V n Also V] [VERB Also V N-COUNT]

over·seas /ˌəʊvəˈsiːz/. **1** You use **overseas** to describe things that happen or exist abroad. *He has returned to South Africa from his long overseas trip.* ▶ Also an adverb. *...if you're staying for more than three months or working overseas.* **2** An **overseas** student or visitor comes from abroad. [◆◆◇◇ ADJ: ADJ n] [ADV] [ADJ: ADJ n]

over·see /ˌəʊvəˈsiː/ **oversees, overseeing, oversaw, overseen.** If someone in authority **oversees** a job or an activity, they make sure that it is done properly. *...a commission to oversee the peace process.* ♦ **over·seer, overseers** *...overseer of oil production and safety.* [◆◆◇◇ VERB V n] [N-COUNT]

over·sell /ˌəʊvəˈsel/ **oversells, overselling, oversold.** If you say that something or someone is **oversold**, you mean that people say they are better or more useful than they really are. *He thinks that DNA fingerprinting has been badly oversold... I think the reformers have at times oversold the reforms.* [VERB be V-ed Also V n]

over·sexed /ˌəʊvəˈsekst/. If you say someone is **oversexed**, you mean that they are more interested in sex or more involved in sexual activities than you think they should be; used showing disapproval. [ADJ-GRADED PRAGMATICS]

over·shad·ow /ˌəʊvəˈʃædəʊ/ **overshadows, overshadowing, overshadowed. 1** If an unpleasant event or feeling **overshadows** something, it makes it less happy or enjoyable. *Fears for the President's safety could overshadow his peace-making mission.* **2** If someone or something is **overshadowed** by another person or thing, they are less successful, important, or impressive than the other person or thing. *Hester is overshadowed by her younger and more attractive sister.* **3** If one building, tree, or large structure **overshadows** another, it stands near it, is much taller than it, and casts a shadow over it. *...one of the Edinburgh University towers that overshadows George Square.* [◆◇◇◇ VERB V n] [VB: usu passive be V-ed] [VERB V n]

over·shoot /ˌəʊvəˈʃuːt/ **overshoots, overshooting, overshoot. 1** If you **overshoot** a place that you want to get to, you go past it by mistake. *The plane apparently overshot the runway after landing.* **2** If an organization **overshoots** its budget, it spends more than it had planned to. [VERB V n Also V VERB: V n]

over·sight /ˈəʊvəsaɪt/ **oversights. 1** If there has been an **oversight**, someone has forgotten to do something which they should have done. *By an unfortunate oversight, full instructions do not come with the product.* **2** If someone has **oversight** of a process or system, they are responsible for making sure that it works efficiently and correctly. *Mr Yeltsin entrusted Mr Rutskoi with the oversight of agricultural reform.* [◆◇◇◇ N-COUNT] [N-UNCOUNT]

over·sim·pli·fy /ˌəʊvəˈsɪmplɪfaɪ/ **oversimplifies, oversimplifying, oversimplified.** If you say that someone is **oversimplifying** something, you mean [VERB V n]

that they are describing or explaining it so simply that what they say is no longer true or reasonable. *To judge trips as if they're successes or failures may be oversimplifying things.* ♦ **over·sim·pli·fied** ...*an oversimplified view of mathematics and the sciences.* ADJ-GRADED

♦ **over·sim·pli·fi·ca·tion** /ˌəʊvəsɪmplɪfɪˈkeɪʃən/ **oversimplifications** *To say that peer relationships affect self-esteem, is an oversimplification.* N-VAR

over·size /ˈəʊvəsaɪz/ or **oversized. Oversize** or **oversized** things are too big, or much bigger than usual. ...*the oversize white sweater she had worn at school.* ...*an oversized bed.* ADJ-GRADED

over·sleep /ˌəʊvəˈsliːp/ **oversleeps, oversleeping, overslept.** If you **oversleep**, you sleep longer than you should have done. *I forgot to set my alarm and I overslept.* VERB V

over·spend /ˌəʊvəˈspend/ **overspends, overspending, overspent. 1** If you **overspend**, you spend more money than you can afford to. *Don't overspend on your home and expect to get the money back when you sell... I overspent by £1 on your shopping.* **2** In business, if an organization or business has an **overspend**, it spends more money than was planned or allowed in its budget. The usual American term is **overrun**. VERB / V by amount / Also V / N-COUNT BRITISH

over·spill /ˈəʊvəspɪl/. **1 Overspill** is used to refer to people who live near a city because there is no room in the city itself. ...*new towns built to absorb overspill from nearby cities.* **2** You can use **overspill** to refer to something or someone which is extra and cannot be accommodated in the usual place. *The overspill could stand at the back of the court.* N-UNCOUNT: also a N BRITISH / N-UNCOUNT: also a N

over·staffed /ˌəʊvəˈstɑːft, -ˈstæft/. If you say that a place is **overstaffed**, you think there are more people working there than is necessary. ADJ-GRADED

over·state /ˌəʊvəˈsteɪt/ **overstates, overstating, overstated.** If you say that someone is **overstating** something, you mean they are describing it in a way that makes it seem more important or serious than it really is. *The authors no doubt overstated their case with a view to catching the public's attention... Many scientists think this method overstates the dangers.* ♦ **over·state·ment, overstatements** *This may have been an improvement, but 'breakthrough' was an overstatement.* ◆◇◇◇◇ VERB V n / N-VAR

over·stay /ˌəʊvəˈsteɪ/ **overstays, overstaying, overstayed.** If you **overstay** your time, you stay somewhere for longer than you have permission to stay. *Up to forty per cent of the students who overstayed their visas.* ● to **overstay** your **welcome:** see **welcome.** VB: no passive V n / Also V

over·step /ˌəʊvəˈstep/ **oversteps, overstepping, overstepped.** If you say that someone **oversteps** the limits of a system or situation, you mean that they do something that is not permissible or acceptable. *The Commission is sensitive to accusations that it is overstepping its authority.* ● If someone **oversteps the mark**, they behave in a way that is considered unacceptable. VERB V n / PHRASE

over·stretch /ˌəʊvəˈstretʃ/ **overstretches, overstretching, overstretched.** If you **overstretch** something or someone or if they **overstretch**, you force them to do something they are not really capable of, and may do them harm as a result. *Do what you know you can do well and don't overstretch yourself.* ♦ **over·stretched** *The police force is overstretched.* V-ERG: V n / V pron-refl / Also V / ADJ-GRADED

over·sub·scribed /ˌəʊvəsəbˈskraɪbd/. If something such as an event or a service is **oversubscribed**, too many people apply to attend the event or use the service. *The popular schools tend to be heavily oversubscribed.* ADJ-GRADED

overt /əʊˈvɜːt/. An **overt** action or attitude is done or shown in an open and obvious way. *Although there is no overt hostility, black and white students do not mix much.* ♦ **overt·ly** *He's written a few overtly political lyrics over the years.* ◆◇◇◇◇ ADJ-GRADED / ADV-GRADED

over·take /ˌəʊvəˈteɪk/ **overtakes, overtaking, overtook, overtaken. 1** If you **overtake** a vehicle or a person that is ahead of you and moving in the same direction, you pass them. *When he eventually overtook the last truck he pulled over to the inside lane.* **2** If someone or something **overtakes** a competitor, they become more successful than them. *It's the first time at these games that the Americans have overtaken the Cubans.* **3** If an event **overtakes** you, it happens unexpectedly or suddenly. *Tragedy was shortly to overtake him, however.* **4** If a feeling **overtakes** you, it affects you very strongly. *Something like panic overtook me in a flood.* ◆◆◇◇◇ VERB V n / VERB V n / VERB V n / VERB V n LITERARY

over·tax /ˌəʊvəˈtæks/ **overtaxes, overtaxing, overtaxed. 1** If you **overtax** someone or something, you force them to work harder than they can really manage. ...*a contralto who has overtaxed her voice.* **2** If you say that a government **is overtaxing** its people, you mean that it is making them pay more tax than you think they should pay. VERB V n / VERB: V n

over-the-counter. See **counter.**

over-the-top. See **top.**

over·throw /ˌəʊvəˈθrəʊ/ **overthrows, overthrowing, overthrew, overthrown.** The verb is pronounced /ˌəʊvəˈθrəʊ/. The noun is pronounced /ˈəʊvəθrəʊ/. When a government or leader **is overthrown**, they are removed from power by force. *That government was overthrown in a military coup.* ...*an attempt to overthrow the president.* ► Also a noun. ...*the overthrow of the Communists.* ◆◇◇◇◇ VERB be V-ed / N-SING

over·time /ˈəʊvətaɪm/. **1 Overtime** is time that you spend doing your job in addition to your normal working hours. *He would work overtime, without pay, to finish a job.* **2** If you say that someone **is working overtime** to do something, you mean that they are using a lot of energy, effort, or enthusiasm trying to do it. *Our defence worked overtime to keep us in the game.* **3 Overtime** is an additional period of time that is added to the end of a sports match in which the two teams are level, as a way of allowing the teams more time to produce a conclusive result. The British expression is **extra time.** ◆◇◇◇◇ N-UNCOUNT / PHRASE INFORMAL / N-UNCOUNT AMERICAN

over·tired /ˌəʊvəˈtaɪəd/. If you are **overtired**, you are so tired that you feel unhappy or irritable, or feel that you cannot do things properly. ADJ-GRADED

over·tone /ˈəʊvətəʊn/ **overtones.** If something has **overtones** of a particular thing or quality, it suggests that thing or quality but does not openly express it. *The strike has taken on overtones of a civil rights campaign.* ◆◇◇◇◇ N-COUNT

over·took /ˌəʊvəˈtʊk/. **Overtook** is the past tense of **overtake.**

over·ture /ˈəʊvətʃʊə/ **overtures. 1** An **overture** is a piece of music, often one that is the introduction to an opera or play. **2** If you make **overtures** to someone, you behave in a friendly or romantic way towards them. ...*clumsy yet endearing overtures of friendship.* ◆◇◇◇◇ N-COUNT / N-COUNT

over·turn /ˌəʊvəˈtɜːn/ **overturns, overturning, overturned. 1** If something **overturns** or if you **overturn** it, it turns upside down or on its side. *The lorry veered out of control, overturned and smashed into a wall... Alex jumped up so violently that he overturned his glass of sherry.* **2** If someone in authority **overturns** a legal decision, they officially decide that that decision is incorrect or not valid. **3** To **overturn** a government or system means to remove it or destroy it. *He accused his opponents of wanting to overturn the government.* ◆◆◇◇◇ V-ERG V n / VERB: V n / VERB V n

over·use, overuses, overusing, overused. The verb is pronounced /ˌəʊvəˈjuːz/. The noun is pronounced /ˌəʊvəˈjuːs/. **1** If someone **overuses** something, they use more of it than necessary, or use it more often than necessary. *Don't overuse heated appliances on your hair.* ► Also a noun. *The record player packed up from overuse.* **2** If you say that people **overuse** a word or idea, you mean that they use it so often that it no longer has any real meaning or effect. *Which words or phrases do you most overuse?* ♦ **over·used** *'Just Do It' has become one of the most overused catch phrases in recent memory.* VERB V n / N-UNCOUNT / VERB V n / ADJ-GRADED

over·value /ˌəʊvəˈvæljuː/ **overvalues, over-valuing, overvalued.** To **overvalue** something such as a currency or a share means to fix its value at too high a level as compared to other similar things. *He was wrong to overvalue sterling in the first place.* ◆ **over·valu·ation** /ˌəʊvəvæljuˈeɪʃən/ *...the overvaluation of the pound.* ◆ **over·valued** *Japanese shares are overvalued in terms of the return they offer.*

over·view /ˈəʊvəvjuː/ **overviews.** An **overview** of a situation is a general understanding or description of it as a whole. *...a historical overview of drug use.*

over·ween·ing /ˌəʊvəˈwiːnɪŋ/. If you want to emphasize your disapproval of someone's very great ambition or arrogance, you can refer to their **overweening** ambition or their **overweening** arrogance.

over·weight /ˌəʊvəˈweɪt/. Someone who is **overweight** weighs more than is considered healthy or attractive.

over·whelm /ˌəʊvəˈwelm/ **overwhelms, over-whelming, overwhelmed.** **1** If you are **overwhelmed** by a feeling or event, it affects you very strongly, and you do not know how to deal with it. *The need to talk to someone, anyone, overwhelmed her.* ◆ **over·whelmed** *Sightseers may be a little overwhelmed by the crowds and noise.* **2** If a group of people **overwhelm** a place or another group, they gain complete control or victory over them. *One massive Allied offensive would overwhelm the weakened enemy.*

over·whelm·ing /ˌəʊvəˈwelmɪŋ/. **1** If something is **overwhelming**, it affects you very strongly, and you do not know how to deal with it. *She felt an overwhelming desire to have another child.* ◆ **over·whelm·ing·ly** *Women found him overwhelmingly attractive.* **2** You can use **overwhelming** to emphasize that an amount or quantity is much greater than other amounts or quantities. *The overwhelming majority of small businesses go broke within the first twenty-four months.* ◆ **overwhelmingly** *The House of Commons has overwhelmingly rejected calls to bring back the death penalty.*

over·work /ˌəʊvəˈwɜːk/ **overworks, overworking, overworked.** If you **overwork** or if someone **overworks** you, you work too hard, and are likely to become very tired or ill. *He overworks and underpays the poor clerk whom he employs.* ◆ Also a noun. *...a heart attack brought on by overwork.* ◆ **over·worked** *...an overworked doctor.*

over·worked /ˌəʊvəˈwɜːkt/. If you describe a word, expression, or idea as **overworked**, you mean it has been used so often that it is no longer effective or meaningful. *'Ecological' has become one of the most overworked adjectives among manufacturers of garden supplies.*

over·wrought /ˌəʊvəˈrɔːt/. Someone who is **overwrought** is very upset and is behaving in an uncontrolled way.

ovu·late /ˈɒvjʊleɪt/ **ovulates, ovulating, ovulated.** When a woman or female animal **ovulates**, she produces eggs from her ovary. ◆ **ovu·la·tion** /ˌɒvjʊˈleɪʃən/ *By noticing these changes, the woman can tell when ovulation is about to occur.*

ovum /ˈəʊvəm/ **ova.** An **ovum** is one of the reproductive cells of a woman or female animal.

ow /aʊ/. **'Ow!'** is used in writing to represent the noise that people make when they suddenly feel pain. *Ow! Don't do that!*

owe /əʊ/ **owes, owing, owed.** **1** If you **owe** money to someone, they have lent it to you and you have not yet paid it back. You can also say that the money **is owing.** *The company owes money to more than 60 banks... Blake already owed him nearly £50... He could take what was owing for the rent.* **2** If someone or something **owes** a particular quality, their success, or their existence to a person or thing, they only have it because of that person or thing. *I always suspected she owed her first job to her friendship with Roger... I owe him my life.* **3** If you say that you **owe** a great deal to someone or something, you mean

that they have helped you or influenced you a lot, and you feel very grateful to them. *As a professional composer I owe much to Radio 3... He's been fantastic. I owe him a lot.* **4** If you say that something **owes** a great deal to someone or something, you mean that it exists, is successful, or has its particular form largely because of them. *The island's present economy owes a good deal to whisky distilling.* **5** If you say that you **owe** someone gratitude, respect, or loyalty, you mean that they deserve it from you. *I owe you an apology... I owe a big debt of gratitude to her.* **6** If you say that you **owe it to** someone to do something, you mean that you should do that thing because they deserve it. *I can't go. I owe it to him to stay.*

7 You use **owing to** when you are introducing the reason for something. *He was out of work owing to a physical injury.*

owl /aʊl/ **owls.** An **owl** is a bird with a flat face, large eyes, and a small sharp beak. Most owls obtain their food by hunting small animals at night. ● See also **night owl.**

own /əʊn/ **owns, owning, owned.** **1** You use **own** to indicate that something belongs to a particular person or thing. *My wife decided I should have my own shop... His office had its own private entrance.* ▶ Also a pronoun. *He saw the Major's face a few inches from his own.* **2** You use **own** to indicate that something is used by, or is characteristic of, only one person, thing, or group. *Jennifer insisted on her own room... I let her tell me about it in her own way.* ▶ Also a pronoun. *...a sense of style that is very much her own.* **3** If you say that someone has something they can **call** their **own**, you mean it belongs to them personally, rather than, for example, being controlled by or shared with someone else. *I would like a place I could call my own.* **4** If you **make** something your **own**, you become involved in it in such a way that people think of it as being related only to you or belonging only to you, rather than to anyone else. *Here again is the song that Pavarotti has made his own.* **5** If you say that someone has a particular thing of their **own**, you mean that that thing belongs or relates to them, rather than to other people. *He set out in search of ideas for starting a company of his own.* **6** If you say that someone or something has a particular quality or characteristic **of** their **own** or **all** of their **own**, you mean that that quality or characteristic is especially theirs, rather than being shared by other things or people of that type. *The cries of the seagulls gave this part of the harbour a fascinating character all of its own.*

7 You use **own** to indicate that someone does something without any help from other people. *He'll have to make his own arrangements.* ▶ Also a pronoun. *There's no career structure, you have to create your own.* **8** If you do something **on** your **own**, you do it without any help from other people. *I work best on my own.* **9** When you are **on** your **own**, you are alone. *I told him how scared I was of being on my own.* **10** If you **own** something, it is your property. *His father owns a local pub.* **11** If you say that someone does something **as if** they **own the place** or **like** they **own the place**, you are critical of them because they do it in a very arrogant way. *He struts around town like he owns the place.*

12 If someone or something **comes into** their **own**, they become very successful or start to perform very well because the circumstances are right. *The goalkeeper came into his own with a series of brilliant saves.* **13** If you **get** your **own back** on someone, you have your revenge on them because of something bad that they have done to you. *...ways in which women have got their own back on former loved ones.*

14 ● to **hold** your **own**: see **hold.**

own up. If you **own up** to something wrong that you have done, you admit that you did it. *Last year my husband owned up to an affair with his secretary.*

-owned /-əʊnd/. **-owned** combines with nouns, adjectives, and adverbs to form adjectives that

indicate who owns something. ...*state-owned companies.* ...*the Japanese-owned Bel Air Hotel.*

own·er /'əʊnə/ **owners.** The **owner** of something is the person to whom it belongs. *The owner of the store was sweeping his floor when I walked in... Every pet owner knows their animal has its own personality.* ● See also **home owner, landowner.** N-COUNT

owner-'occupier, **owner-occupiers.** An **owner-occupier** is a person who owns the house or flat that they live in. N-COUNT BRITISH

own·er·ship /'əʊnəʃɪp/. **Ownership** of something is the state of owning it. ...*the growth of home ownership in Britain.* N-UNCOUNT

own 'goal, **own goals. 1** In sport, if someone scores an **own goal**, they accidentally score a goal for the team they are playing against. **2** If a course of action that someone takes harms their own interests, you can refer to it as an **own goal**. *Women have made themselves unemployable. They have scored an own goal.* N-COUNT BRITISH N-COUNT BRITISH

ox /ɒks/ **oxen** /'ɒksən/. An **ox** is a bull that has been castrated. Oxen are used in some countries for pulling vehicles or carrying things. N-COUNT

Ox·bridge /'ɒksbrɪdʒ/. **Oxbridge** is used to refer to the universities of Oxford and Cambridge together. N-PROPER BRITISH

ox·cart /'ɒkskɑːt/ **oxcarts;** also spelled **ox-cart**. An **oxcart** is a cart pulled by an ox or oxen. N-COUNT

ox·ide /'ɒksaɪd/ **oxides.** An **oxide** is a compound of oxygen and another chemical element. ...*nitrogen oxide.* N-VAR

oxi·dize /'ɒksɪdaɪz/ **oxidizes, oxidizing, oxidized;** also spelled **oxidise** in British English. When a substance **is oxidized** or when it **oxidizes**, it changes chemically because of the effect of oxygen on it. *Aluminium is rapidly oxidized in air.* ♦ **oxi·da·tion** /ˌɒksɪ'deɪʃən/ *Carbon dioxide is a necessary result of the oxidation of carbon compounds.* V-ERG be V-ed Also V N-UNCOUNT

ox·tail /'ɒksteɪl/ **oxtails. Oxtail** is meat from the tail of a cow. It is used for making soups and stews. N-VAR

oxy·gen /'ɒksɪdʒən/. **Oxygen** is a colourless gas that exists in large quantities in the air. All plants and animals need oxygen in order to live. N-UNCOUNT

oxy·gen·ate /'ɒksɪdʒɪneɪt/ **oxygenates, oxygenating, oxygenated.** To **oxygenate** something means to mix or dissolve oxygen into it. *Previous attempts at filtering and oxygenating aquarium water had failed.* VERB V n

'oxygen mask, oxygen masks. An **oxygen mask** is a device that is connected to a cylinder of oxygen by means of a tube. It is placed over the nose and mouth of someone who is having difficulty in breathing. N-COUNT

oxy·mo·ron /ˌɒksi'mɔːrɒn/ **oxymorons.** If you describe a phrase as an **oxymoron**, you mean that what it refers to combines two contradictory qualities or ideas and therefore seems impossible. *This has made many Americans conclude that business ethics is an oxymoron.* N-COUNT

oys·ter /'ɔɪstə/ **oysters. 1** An **oyster** is a large flat shellfish. Some oysters can be eaten and others produce pearls. **2** If you say that **the world is** someone's **oyster**, you mean that they can do anything or go anywhere that they want to. *You're young, you've got a lot of opportunity. The world is your oyster.* N-COUNT PHRASE

'oyster bed, oyster beds. An **oyster bed** is a place where oysters breed and grow naturally or are cultivated for food or pearls. N-COUNT

oyster·catcher /'ɔɪstəkætʃə/ **oystercatchers.** An **oystercatcher** is a black and white wading bird with a long red beak. N-COUNT

oz. Oz is a written abbreviation for **ounce.**

ozone /'əʊzəʊn/. **Ozone** is a colourless gas which is a form of oxygen. There is a layer of ozone high above the earth's surface. ...*ozone depletion.* N-UNCOUNT

'ozone layer. The **ozone layer** is the part of the Earth's atmosphere that has the highest number of ozone molecules. The ozone layer protects living things from the harmful radiation of the sun. N-SING

P p

P, p /piː/ **P's, p's. 1** P is the sixteenth letter of the English alphabet. **2** p is an abbreviation for 'pence' or 'penny'. *They cost 5p each.* **3** You write **p.** before a number as an abbreviation for 'page'. The plural form is 'pp.'. ...*examined in Chapter 4 (pp. 109-13).* **4** P or p is used as an abbreviation for words beginning with p, such as 'per' or 'parking'. N-VAR

pa /pɑː/ **pas.** Some people address or refer to their father as **pa**. *'Pa,' he said, 'I don't feel well.'* N-FAMILY INFORMAL

p.a. p.a. is a written abbreviation for **per annum.** ... *a yield of 10.5% p.a.*

PA /ˌpiː 'eɪ/ **PAs. 1** A **PA** is the same as a **personal assistant. 2** PA or PA system is an abbreviation for 'public address system'. *A voice came booming over the PA.* N-COUNT N-COUNT

pace /peɪs/ **paces, pacing, paced. 1** The **pace** of something is the speed at which it happens or is done. *Many people were not satisfied with the pace of change.* **2** Your **pace** is the speed at which you walk. *He moved at a brisk pace down the rue St Antoine.* **3** A **pace** is the distance that you move when you take one step. *I took a pace backwards.* **4** If you **pace** a small area, you keep walking up and down it, because you are anxious or impatient. *He found John pacing around the flat, unable to sleep.* **5** If you **pace** yourself when doing something, you do it at a steady rate. **6** If something **keeps pace** with something else that is changing, it changes quickly in response to it. ...*a world changing far too fast for her to* N-SING N-SING N-COUNT VERB: V n V pep/adv Also V VERB: V pron-refl PHRASE

keep pace. **7** If you **keep pace** with someone who is walking or running, you succeed in going as fast as them. **8** If you do something **at** your **own pace**, you do it at a speed that is comfortable for you. **9** If you **put** someone **through** their **paces** or make them **go through** their **paces**, you get them to show you how well they can do something. *The eleven boxers are in the hands of the British coach, who is putting them through their paces.* **10** ● **at a snail's pace:** see **snail.** PHRASE PHRASE PHRASE

pace out. If you **pace out** a distance, you measure it by walking from one end of it to the other. *I marked the ground and then paced it out to be sure.* PHRASAL VB V P noun V n P

paced /peɪst/. If you talk about the way that something such as a film or book is **paced**, you are referring to the way in which the story is revealed and the speed at which the narrative moves along. *This excellent thriller is fast paced and believable.* ADJ: adv ADJ

pace·maker /'peɪsmeɪkə/ **pacemakers. 1** A **pacemaker** is a device that is placed inside someone's body in order to help their heart beat in the right way. **2** A **pacemaker** is a competitor in a race whose task is to start the race very quickly in order to help the other runners achieve a very fast time. N-COUNT N-COUNT

pace·setter /'peɪssetə/ **pacesetters;** also spelled **pace-setter. 1** A **pacesetter** is someone who is in the lead during part of a race or competition and therefore decides the speed or standard of the race or competition for that time. *Real's victory keeps them five points behind the pacesetters, Barcelona.* N-COUNT

2 A **pacesetter** is a person or a company that is considered to be the leader in a particular field or activity. *Mongolia seemed an unlikely candidate as the pacesetter for political change in Asia.* `N-COUNT`

pa·cif·ic /pə'sɪfɪk/. A **pacific** person, country, or course of action is peaceful or has the aim of bringing about peace. *The Liberals were traditionally seen as the more pacific party.* `ADJ-GRADED FORMAL`

paci·fist /'pæsɪfɪst/ **pacifists.** If someone has **pacifist** views, they believe that war and violence are always wrong. ♦ A **pacifist** is someone with pacifist views. ♦ **paci·fism.** Pacifism is the belief that war and violence are always wrong. `◇◇◇◇ ADJ-GRADED` `N-COUNT` `N-UNCOUNT`

paci·fy /'pæsɪfaɪ/ **pacifies, pacifying, pacified.** **1** If you **pacify** someone who is angry, upset, or dissatisfied, you succeed in making them calm or satisfied. *She shrieked again, refusing to be pacified.* **2** If the army or the police **pacify** a group of people, they use force to overcome their resistance or protests. *They were eventually pacified by officers of the local police.* `◇◇◇◇ VERB: V n` `VERB: V n be V-ed`

pack /pæk/ **packs, packing, packed. 1** When you **pack** a bag, you put your belongings into it, because you are leaving a place or going on holiday. *When I was 17, I packed my bags and left home.* ♦ **pack·ing** *She left Frances to finish her packing.* **2** When people **pack** things, for example in a factory, they put them into containers or parcels so that they can be transported and sold. *Machines now exist to pack olives in jars.* ♦ **pack·er, packers** *She is a meat packer.* ♦ **pack·ing** *His onions cost 9p a lb wholesale; packing and transport costs 10p.* **3** If people or things **pack into** a place or if they **pack** a place, there are so many of them that the place is full. *Seventy thousand people will pack the stadium.* ♦ **packed** *The streets were packed with men, women and children.* **4** A **pack** of things is a collection of them in one packet. *...a free information pack. ...a pack of cigarettes.* **5** A **pack** is a bag containing your belongings that you carry on your back when you are travelling. *I hid the money in my pack.* **6** You can refer to a group of people who go around together as a **pack**, especially when it is a large group that you feel threatened by. *...a pack of journalists eager to question him.* **7** A **pack** of wolves or dogs is a group of them that hunt together. **8** A **pack** of playing cards is a complete set of playing cards. The usual American word is **deck**. **9** If someone **packs** a jury, committee, or meeting, they make sure that it includes people who support them. *Opposition parties have boycotted the proceedings, saying the government has packed the conference with its own supporters.* **10** If you say that an account is **a pack of lies**, you mean that it is completely untrue. **11** If something **packs a punch**, it has a very powerful effect. *W. Somerset Maugham's novel still packs an emotional punch.* **12** If you **send** someone **packing**, you make them go away. **13** You can say that someone is **ahead of the pack**, if they are ahead of everyone else in a race or competition. *The Socialists may still finish ahead of the pack.* **14** See also **fanny pack, packed, packing.** `◇◇◇◇ VERB V n Also V` `N-UNCOUNT VERB: V n V n in n` `N-COUNT` `N-UNCOUNT` `VERB: V into n V n` `ADJ-GRADED` `N-COUNT` `N-COUNT` `N-COUNT PRAGMATICS` `N-COUNT` `N-COUNT BRITISH` `VERB: V n V n with n` `PHRASE` `PHRASE` `PHRASE INFORMAL` `PHRASE`

pack in. 1 If someone **packs in** things or people, they fit a lot of them into a limited space or time. *It's kind of a referendum, though a lot of issues are packed in.* ● If a play, film or event **packs them in**, lots of people go to see it. **2** If you **packed** something **in**, you stop doing it. *I'd just packed in a job the day before.* `PHRASAL VB V n P V P noun INFORMAL PHRASE INFORMAL V P noun be V-ed P`

pack into. 1 If someone **packs** a lot of something **into** a limited space or time, they fit a lot into it. *...packing more events or tasks into less time... I have tried to pack a good deal into a few words.* **2** If people or things **are packed into** a place, so many of them are put in there that the place becomes very full. `PHRASAL VB V n P n usu passive`

pack off. If you **pack** someone **off** somewhere, you send them there to stay for a period of time. *Malcolm packed off Vivienne and the two children to stay in a caravan.* `PHRASAL VB V n P noun V n P noun to-inf`

pack up. 1 If you **pack up** or if you **pack up** your belongings, you tidy everything away and put all your `PHRASAL VB V P V P noun`

belongings in a case or bag, because you are leaving. *He began packing up his things.* **2** If a machine or a part of the body **packs up**, it stops working. *In the end it was his stomach and lungs that packed up.* `V P BRITISH, INFORMAL`

pack·age /'pækɪdʒ/ **packages, packaging, packaged. 1** A **package** is a small parcel. **2** A **package** is a small container in which a quantity of something is sold. The usual British word is **packet**. *...a package of doughnuts.* **3** A **package** is a set of proposals that are made by a government or organization and which must be accepted or rejected as a group. *...a Western economic aid package for Moscow.* **4** When a product **is packaged**, it is put into packets to be sold. **5** If something such as an idea, place, or politician **is packaged**, advertisers try to make it seem attractive or interesting. *...entertainment packaged as information.* `◆◆◆◇ N-COUNT N-COUNT AMERICAN N-COUNT VB: usu passive VB: usu passive be V-ed as n`

'package deal, package deals. A package deal is a set of offers or proposals which is made by a government or an organization, and which must be accepted or rejected as a whole. `N-COUNT`

package 'holiday, package holidays. A package holiday or a package tour is a holiday arranged by a travel company in which your travel and your accommodation are booked for you. `N-COUNT`

pack·ag·ing /'pækɪdʒɪŋ/. Packaging is the container or wrappings that something is sold in. `◆◆◇◇ N-UNCOUNT`

packed /pækt/. **1** See **pack. 2** Something that is **packed with** things contains a very large number of them. *The Encyclopedia is packed with clear illustrations and over 250 recipes.* `◆◆◇◇ ADJ-GRADED: v-link ADJ with n`

packed 'lunch, packed lunches. A packed lunch is food, for example sandwiches, which you take to work, to school, or on an outing and eat as your lunch. `N-COUNT BRITISH`

packed 'out. If a place is **packed out**, it is very full of people. `ADJ BRITISH, INFORMAL`

pack·et /'pækɪt/ **packets. 1** A **packet** is a small container in which a quantity of something is sold. Packets are either small boxes made of thin cardboard, or bags or envelopes made of paper or plastic. *Cook the rice according to instructions on the packet. ...a cigarette packet.* ▶ A **packet** of something is an amount of it contained in a packet. *Elinor bought her a packet of biscuits.* **2** A **packet** is a small flat parcel. *...a packet of photographs.* **3** You can refer to a lot of money as a **packet**. *It'll cost you a packet.* **4** See also **pay packet, wage packet.** `◆◆◇◇ N-COUNT BRITISH N-COUNT N-COUNT N-SING: a N BRITISH`

pack·ing /'pækɪŋ/. Packing is the paper, plastic, or other material which is put round things that are being sent somewhere. ● See also **pack.** `◆◆◇◇ N-UNCOUNT`

'packing case, packing cases. A packing case is a large wooden box in which things are put so that they can be stored or taken somewhere. `N-COUNT`

pact /pækt/ **pacts.** A **pact** is a formal agreement between two or more people, organizations, or governments. *Last month he signed a new non-aggression pact with Germany.* `◆◆◇◇ N-COUNT`

pad /pæd/ **pads, padding, padded. 1** A **pad** is a fairly thick flat piece of a material such as cloth or rubber. Pads are used, for example, to clean things, to protect things, or to change their shape. *He withdrew the needle and placed a pad of cotton-wool over the spot.* **2** If you **pad** something, you put something soft in it or over it in order to make it less hard, to protect it, or to give it a different shape. *Pad the back of a car seat with a pillow.* ♦ **pad·ded** *...a man in a padded jacket.* **3** A **pad** of paper is a number of pieces of paper which are fixed together along the top or the side, so that each piece can be torn off when it has been used. **4** A **pad** is a platform or an area of flat, hard ground where helicopters take off and land or rockets are launched. *...a landing pad on the back of the ship.* ● See also **launch pad. 5** People can refer to the place where they live as their **pad**, especially if it is a flat. *It wouldn't have occurred to me to get myself a bachelor pad.* **6** The **pads** of a person's fingers and toes or of an animal's paws are the soft, fleshy parts of them. **7** When `◆◆◇◇ N-COUNT VERB: V n V n with n ADJ N-COUNT N-COUNT N-COUNT INFORMAL, DATED N-COUNT VERB:`

someone **pads** somewhere, they walk there with steps that are fairly quick, light, and quiet. *Kissinger rages as he pads the corridors.* **8** See also **padding**. [V prep/adv, V n]

pad out. If you **pad out** a piece of writing or a speech with unnecessary words or pieces of information, you include them in it to make it longer and hide the fact that you have not got very much to say. *If I wanted to pad out my sermon a little, I might offer my congregation one of my favourite quotations.* [PHRASAL VB, V P noun, Also V n P, V n P with n, BRITISH]

pad·ding /'pædɪŋ/. **1** Padding is soft material which is put on something or inside it in order to make it less hard, to protect it, or to give it a different shape. *Players must wear padding to protect them from injury.* **2** Padding is unnecessary words or information used to make a piece of writing or a speech longer. *...the kind of subject that politicians put in their speeches for a bit of padding.* [N-UNCOUNT, N-UNCOUNT]

pad·dle /'pædəl/ **paddles, paddling, paddled.** **1** A **paddle** is a short pole with a wide flat part at one end or at both ends. You hold it in your hands and use it as an oar to move a small boat through water. **2** If you **paddle** a boat, you move it through water using a paddle. *...paddling around the South Pacific in a kayak.* **3** If you **paddle**, you walk or stand in shallow water, for example at the edge of the sea, for pleasure. *...a lovely little stream that you can paddle in.* ▶ Also a noun. *Ruth enjoyed her paddle.* [N-COUNT, VERB: V prep/adv, VERB: V, V prep, N-SING]

'paddling pool, paddling pools. A **paddling pool** is a shallow artificial pool for children to paddle in. The usual American terms is **wading pool**. [N-COUNT, BRITISH]

pad·dock /'pædək/ **paddocks.** **1** A **paddock** is a small field where horses are kept. **2** In horse racing or motor racing, the **paddock** is the place where the horses or cars are kept just before each race. [N-COUNT, N-COUNT]

pad·dy /'pædi/ **paddies.** **1** A **paddy** or a **paddy field** is a field that is kept flooded with water and is used for growing rice. **2** Some people use the word **paddy** to refer to an Irishman; an offensive word. [N-COUNT, N-COUNT, INFORMAL]

pad·lock /'pædlɒk/ **padlocks, padlocking, padlocked.** **1** A **padlock** is a lock which is used for fastening two things or two parts of something together. It consists of a block of metal with a U-shaped bar attached to it. One end of the bar is released when the padlock is unlocked with a key. **2** If you **padlock** something, you lock it or fasten it to something else using a padlock. *An old mailbox has been padlocked shut.* [N-COUNT, VERB: V n, be V-ed, Also V n to n]

pa·dre /'pɑːdreɪ/ **padres.** A **padre** is a Christian priest, especially a chaplain to the armed forces. *Could I speak to you in private a moment, padre.* [N-COUNT; N-VOC, INFORMAL]

paean /'piːən/ **paeans.** A **paean** is a piece of music, writing, or film that expresses praise, admiration, or joy. *...a paean to deep, passionate love.* [N-COUNT, LITERARY]

pae·di·at·rics /ˌpiːdiˈætrɪks/; spelled **pediatrics** in American English. The form **paediatric** is used as a modifier. **Paediatrics** is the area of medicine that is concerned with the treatment of children's illnesses. ♦ **pae·dia·tri·cian** /ˌpiːdiəˈtrɪʃən/ **paediatricians.** *Only an experienced paediatrician can tell the difference.* [N-UNCOUNT, N-COUNT]

pae·do·philia /ˌpiːdəˈfɪliə/; spelled **pedophilia** in American English. **Paedophilia** is sexual activity with children or the condition of being sexually attracted to children. ♦ **pae·do·phile** /'piːdəfaɪl/ **paedophiles.** *...a convicted paedophile.* [N-UNCOUNT, N-COUNT]

pa·el·la /paɪˈelə/ **paellas.** Paella is a dish cooked especially in Spain, which consists of rice mixed with small pieces of vegetables, fish, and chicken. [N-VAR]

paeo·ny /'piːəni/. See **peony**.

pa·gan /'peɪɡən/ **pagans.** **1** Pagan beliefs and activities do not belong to any of the main religions of the world and take nature and a belief in many gods as a basis. They are older, or are believed to be older, than other religions. **2** In former times, **pagans** were people who did not believe in Christianity and who many Christians considered to be inferior. [ADJ, N-COUNT]

pa·gan·ism /'peɪɡənɪzəm/. **Paganism** is the belief in pagan ideas and activities. *The country swayed precariously between Christianity and paganism.* [N-UNCOUNT]

page /peɪdʒ/ **pages, paging, paged.** **1** A page is one side of one of the pieces of paper in a book, magazine, or newspaper. Each page usually has a number printed at the top or bottom. *Where's your book? Take it out and turn to page 4.* **2** The pages of a book, magazine, or newspaper are the pieces of paper it consists of. *He turned the pages of his notebook.* **3** You can refer to an important event or period of time as a **page** of history. *...a new page in the country's political history.* **4** If someone who is in a public place **is paged**, they receive a message, often over a speaker, telling them that someone is trying to contact them. *I'll have them paged and tell them you're here.* **5** A **page** is a small boy who is one of the bride's attendants at a wedding. The British word is **pageboy**. [N-COUNT, N-COUNT, N-COUNT: with supp, LITERARY, VERB: be V-ed, have V-ed, N-COUNT, AMERICAN]

pag·eant /'pædʒənt/ **pageants.** A **pageant** is a colourful public parade, show, or ceremony, often organized to celebrate a historic event. [N-COUNT]

pag·eant·ry /'pædʒəntri/. **Pageantry** is the colour and formality associated with royal celebrations and other official occasions, for example, when people dress in special clothes and bands play. [N-UNCOUNT]

page·boy /'peɪdʒbɔɪ/ **pageboys;** also spelled **page-boy.** A **pageboy** is a small boy who is one of the bride's attendants at a wedding. The American word is **page**. [N-COUNT, BRITISH]

pager /'peɪdʒə/ **pagers.** A **pager** is a small electronic device which you can carry around with you and which can receive signals from a telephone. The pager gives you a number or a message when someone is trying to telephone you. [N-COUNT]

pa·go·da /pəˈɡəʊdə/ **pagodas.** A **pagoda** is a tall building, often highly decorated, which is used for religious purposes, especially by Buddhists, in China, Japan, and South-East Asia. [N-COUNT]

paid /peɪd/. **1** Paid is the past tense and past participle of **pay**. **2** Paid workers receive money for the work that they do. If you do **paid** work or are in **paid** employment, you receive money for the work that you do. **3** If you are given **paid** holiday, you get your wages or salary even though you are not at work. **4** If you are well **paid**, you receive a lot of money for the work that you do. If you are badly **paid**, you do not receive much money. **5** If an unexpected event **puts paid to** someone's hopes, chances, or plans, it completely ends or destroys them. *Only six months ago I ran my own business. The recession put paid to that.* [ADJ: ADJ n, ADJ: ADJ n, ADJ: ADJ n, ADJ: adv ADJ, PHRASE, BRITISH]

'paid-up; also spelled **paid up.** **1** If a person or country is a **paid-up** member of a group, they are an enthusiastic member or are recognized by most people as being a member of it. *...our future as an independent nation lies as a fully paid-up member of Europe.* **2** If someone is a **paid-up** member of a political party or other organization, they have paid the money needed to become an official member. [ADJ: ADJ n, ADJ: ADJ n]

pail /peɪl/ **pails.** A **pail** is a bucket, usually made of metal or wood. [N-COUNT, AMERICAN]

pain /peɪn/ **pains, pained.** **1** Pain is the feeling of great discomfort you have, for example when you have been hurt or when you are ill. *...a bone disease that caused excruciating pain... I felt a sharp pain in my lower back.* ● If you are **in pain**, you feel pain in a part of your body, because you are injured or ill. **2** Pain is the feeling of unhappiness that you have when something unpleasant or upsetting happens. *...grey eyes that seemed filled with pain.* **3** If a fact or idea **pains** you, it makes you feel upset and disappointed. *It pains me to think of you struggling all alone.* **4** If you think that a person, job, or situation is very annoying or irritating, you can say that they are **a pain** or **a pain in the neck.** **5** If someone **is at pains to** do something, they are very eager and anxious to do it. *Mobil is at pains to point out that the chances of an explosion at the site are remote.* **6** You say that something was all you got **for** your **pains** when you are mentioning the disappointing result of a situation into which you put a lot of effort. *All Corfield got for his pains was a bullet in the* [N-VAR, PHRASE, N-UNCOUNT, VB: no cont: V n, it V n to-inf, Also it V n that, PHRASE, PHRASE, INFORMAL, PHRASE, JOURNALISM, PHRASE, PRAGMATICS]

head. **7** If someone is ordered not to do something **on pain of** or **under pain of** death, imprisonment, or arrest, they must not do it and if they do it they will be killed, put in prison, or arrested. **8** If you **take pains** to do something or **go to great pains** to do something, you try hard to do it, because you think it is important. — PHR-PREP / PHRASE

'pain barrier. If you say that a sports player has gone through **the pain barrier**, you mean that he or she is continuing to make a great effort in spite of being injured or exhausted. — N-SING: *the N* JOURNALISM

pained /peɪnd/. If you have a **pained** expression or look, you look upset, worried, or slightly annoyed. — ◆◇◇◇◇ ADJ-GRADED

pain·ful /'peɪnfʊl/. **1** If a part of your body is **painful**, it hurts because it is injured or because there is something wrong with it. *Her glands were swollen and painful.* ♦ **pain·ful·ly** *His tooth had started to throb painfully again.* **2** If something such as an illness, injury, or operation is **painful**, it causes you a lot of physical pain. *...a painful back injury.* ♦ **painfully** *...cracking his head painfully against the cupboard.* **3** Situations, memories, or experiences that are **painful** are difficult and unpleasant to deal with, and often make you feel sad and upset. *She finds it too painful to return there without him.* ♦ **painfully** *...their old relationship, which he had painfully broken off.* **4** If a performance or interview is **painful**, it is so bad that it makes you feel embarrassed for the people taking part in it. *It was a joint interview with the BBC and ITV and was painful both to watch and to listen to.* — ◆◇◇◇◇ ADJ-GRADED / ADV-GRADED: ADV with v / ADJ-GRADED / ADV-GRADED: ADV with v / ADJ-GRADED / ADV-GRADED: ADV with v / ADJ-GRADED

pain·ful·ly /'peɪnfʊli/. You use **painfully** to emphasize a quality or situation that is undesirable. *Things are moving painfully slowly... I am painfully aware that staff have a heavy work schedule.* — ◆◇◇◇◇ ADV: ADV adv/adj [PRAGMATICS]

pain·killer /'peɪnkɪlə/ **painkillers.** A **painkiller** is a pill or other form of drug which reduces or stops physical pain. — ◆◇◇◇◇ N-COUNT

pain·less /'peɪnləs/. **1** Something such as a treatment that is **painless** causes no physical pain. *Acupuncture treatment is gentle, painless, and, invariably, most relaxing.* ♦ **pain·less·ly** *...a technique to eliminate unwanted facial hair quickly and painlessly.* **2** If a process or activity is **painless**, you do not have to make a great effort or suffer in any way. *There are no easy or painless solutions to the nation's economic ills.* ♦ **painlessly** *...a game for children which painlessly teaches essential pre-reading skills.* — ◆◇◇◇◇ ADJ-GRADED / ADV-GRADED: ADV with v / ADJ-GRADED / ADV-GRADED: ADV with v

pains·taking /'peɪnsteɪkɪŋ/. A **painstaking** search, examination, or investigation is done extremely carefully and thoroughly. ♦ **pains·taking·ly** *Broken bones were painstakingly pieced together.* — ◆◇◇◇◇ ADJ-GRADED; usu ADJ n / ADV-GRADED

paint /peɪnt/ **paints, painting, painted. 1** Paint is a coloured liquid that you put onto a surface with a brush in order to protect the surface or to make it look nice, or that you use to produce a picture. *They saw some large letters in white paint... The paint was peeling on the window frames.* **2** If you **paint** a wall or an object, you cover it with paint. *I made a guitar and painted it red.* **3** If you **paint** something or **paint** a picture of it, you produce a picture of it using paint. *I had come here to paint.* **4** When you **paint** a design or message on a surface, you put it on the surface using paint. *...a machine for painting white lines down roads.* **5** If a woman **paints** her lips or nails, she puts lipstick or nail varnish on them. *She painted her fingernails bright red.* **6** If you **paint** a grim or vivid picture of something, you give a description of it that is grim or vivid. **7** See also **painting; gloss paint, oil paint, war paint.** — ◆◆◆◇ N-VAR / VERB: V n / V n colour / VERB: V n / V / VERB / V n prep / VERB: V n / V n colour / VERB: V n

paint·brush /'peɪntbrʌʃ/ **paintbrushes;** also spelled **paint brush** or **paint-brush.** A **paintbrush** is a brush which you use for painting. See picture headed **tools.** — N-COUNT

paint·er /'peɪntə/ **painters. 1** A **painter** is an artist who paints pictures. **2** A **painter** is someone who paints walls, doors, and some other parts of buildings as their job. — ◆◆◇◇◇ N-COUNT / N-COUNT

paint·er·ly /'peɪntəli/. **Painterly** means relating to or characteristic of painting or painters. *...his painterly talents... The film has a painterly eye.* — ADJ

paint·ing /'peɪntɪŋ/ **paintings. 1** A **painting** is a picture which someone has painted. *...a large oil-painting of Queen Victoria.* **2 Painting** is the activity of painting pictures. *...two hobbies she really enjoyed, painting and gardening.* **3 Painting** is the activity of painting doors, walls, and some other parts of buildings. *...painting and decorating.* — ◆◆◆◇ N-COUNT / N-UNCOUNT / N-UNCOUNT

paint·work /'peɪntwɜːk/. The **paintwork** of a building, room, or vehicle is the covering of paint on it, or the parts of it that are painted. *The paintwork, the wardrobes and the bedside cupboards were coffee-cream.* — N-UNCOUNT BRITISH

pair /peə/ **pairs, pairing, paired. 1** A **pair** of things are two things of the same size and shape that are intended to be used together, for example shoes, earrings, or parts of the body. *...a pair of socks... 72,000 pairs of hands clapped in unison to the song.* **2** Some objects that have two main parts of the same size and shape are referred to as a **pair**, for example **a pair of trousers** or **a pair of scissors.** *...a pair of faded jeans. ...a pair of binoculars.* **3** You can refer to two people as a **pair** when they are standing or walking together or when they have some kind of relationship with each other. *A pair of teenage boys were smoking cigarettes... He and Paula made an unlikely pair.* **4** If one thing **is paired with** another, it is put with it or considered with it. *The trainees will then be paired with experienced managers.* ♦ **pair·ing** *...the pairing of these two fine musicians.* **5** See also **au pair. 6** If you say that someone is or has a **safe pair of hands**, you mean that they are reliable and will not make any serious mistakes. *He has now held five cabinet posts and remains a safe pair of hands.* — ◆◆◆◇ N-COUNT / N-COUNT / N-SING / VB: usu passive be V-ed with n / PAIRING N-UNCOUNT / PHRASE BRITISH

pair off. When people **pair off** or **are paired off,** they form a pair, often in order to become girlfriend and boyfriend. *I knew she wouldn't be able to resist pairing me off with someone.* — PHRASAL VB RECIP-ERG: pl-n V P / V n P / V n P with n

pair up. If people **pair up** or **are paired up,** they form a pair, in order to do something together. *They asked us to pair up with the person next to us and form teams... Smokers and non-smokers are paired up as roommates.* — PHRASAL VB RECIP-ERG: pl-n V P / V P with n / pl-n be V-ed

pair·ing /'peərɪŋ/ **pairings.** Two people, especially sportspeople, actors, or musicians, who are working together as a pair can be referred to as a **pairing.** *In first place we now find the Belgian pairing of Nancy Feber and Laurence Courtois.* — ◆◇◇◇◇ N-COUNT

pais·ley /'peɪzli/ **paisleys. Paisley** is a special pattern of curving shapes and colours, used especially on fabric. See picture headed **patterns.** *He was elegantly dressed in a grey suit, blue shirt and paisley tie.* — N-VAR

pa·jam·as /pə'dʒɑːməz/. See **pyjamas.**

pal /pæl/ **pals.** Your **pals** are your friends. *This time, they were going out to a nightclub with a mixed party of college pals.* — ◆◆◇◇◇ N-COUNT INFORMAL

pal·ace /'pælɪs/ **palaces. 1** A **palace** is a very large splendid house, especially the home of a king, queen, or president. **2** When the members of a royal palace make an announcement through an official spokesperson, journalists refer to them as **the Palace. 3** You can refer to any large splendid house or other building as a **palace.** *...a barn Maxwell bought and turned into a palace.* — ◆◆◆◇ N-COUNT / N-SING: the N / N-COUNT

palae·on·tol·ogy /ˌpæliɒn'tɒlədʒi/ AM ˌpeɪl-/; also spelled **paleontology. Palaeontology** is the study of fossils as a guide to the history of life on earth. ♦ **palae·on·tolo·gist, palaeontologists.** — N-UNCOUNT / N-COUNT

pal·at·able /'pælətəbəl/. **1** If you describe food or drink as **palatable**, you mean that it tastes pleasant. **2** If you describe something such as an idea or method as **palatable**, you mean that people are willing to accept it. *...a palatable way of sacking staff.* — ADJ-GRADED FORMAL / ADJ-GRADED

pal·ate /'pælɪt/ **palates. 1** Your **palate** is the top part of the inside of your mouth. **2** You can refer to — ◆◇◇◇◇ N-COUNT / N-COUNT

someone's **palate** as a way of talking about their ability to judge good food or drink. *...fresh pasta sauces to tempt more demanding palates.*

pa·la·tial /pə'leɪʃəl/. A **palatial** house, hotel, or office building is large and splendid like a palace. ADJ-GRADED

pa·la·ver /pə'lɑːvə, -'læv-/. **Palaver** is unnecessary fuss about the way something is done. N-UNCOUNT INFORMAL

pale /peɪl/ **paler, palest; pales, paling, paled.** 1 If something is **pale**, it is very light in colour or almost white. ► Also a combining form. *In the background, dressed in pale green, stood Eunice.* 2 If someone looks **pale**, their face looks a lighter colour than usual, usually because they are ill, frightened, or shocked. ♦ **pale·ness** *...his paleness when he realized that he was bleeding.* 3 If one thing **pales** in comparison with another, it is made to seem much less important, serious, or good by it. *...a soap opera against which other soaps pale into insignificance.* 4 If you think that someone's actions or behaviour are not acceptable, you can say that they are **beyond the pale.** ♦♦♦◇◇ ADJ-GRADED; COMB; ADJ-GRADED; N-UNCOUNT; VERB: V; V prep; PHRASE

pal·ette /'pælɪt/ **palettes.** 1 A **palette** is a flat piece of wood or plastic on which an artist mixes paints. 2 You can refer to the range of colours that are used by a particular artist or group of artists as their **palette**. *David Fincher paints from a palette consisting almost exclusively of grey and mud brown.* ♦◇◇◇ N-COUNT; N-COUNT

pali·mo·ny /'pælɪməʊni/. **Palimony** is money that a person pays to a partner they have lived with for a long time and are now separated from. Compare **alimony**. N-UNCOUNT

pal·in·drome /'pælɪndrəʊm/ **palindromes.** A **palindrome** is a word or a phrase that is the same whether you read it backwards or forwards, for example the word 'refer'. N-COUNT

pali·sade /ˌpælɪ'seɪd/ **palisades.** A **palisade** is a fence of wooden posts which are driven into the ground in order to protect people from attack. N-COUNT

pall /pɔːl/ **palls, palled.** 1 If something **palls**, it becomes less interesting or less enjoyable after a period of time. *Already the allure of meals in restaurants had begun to pall.* 2 If something unpleasant **casts a pall over** an event or occasion, it makes it less enjoyable than it should be. 3 If a **pall** of smoke hangs over a place, there is a thick cloud of smoke above it. ♦◇◇◇ VB: no cont V; PHRASE; N-COUNT

pall·bearer /'pɔːlbeərər/ **pallbearers.** A **pallbearer** is a person who helps to carry the coffin or walks beside it at a funeral. N-COUNT

pal·let /'pælɪt/ **pallets.** 1 A **pallet** is a narrow mattress filled with straw which is put on the floor for someone to sleep on. 2 A **pallet** is a hard narrow bed. 3 A **pallet** is a flat wooden or metal platform on which goods are stacked and stored so that they can be lifted and moved using a fork-lift truck. N-COUNT; N-COUNT; N-COUNT

pal·lia·tive /'pæliətɪv, AM -eɪt-/ **palliatives.** 1 A **palliative** is a drug or medical treatment that relieves suffering without treating the cause of the suffering. 2 A **palliative** is an action that is intended to make the effects of a problem less severe but does not actually solve the problem. *The society's board realised that the loan was a palliative, not a cure, for ever-increasing financial troubles.* N-COUNT; N-COUNT

pal·lid /'pælɪd/. 1 Someone or something that is **pallid** is unattractively or unnaturally pale in appearance. 2 You can describe something as **pallid** if it is weak and unexciting. *...a pallid account of the future of transport.* ADJ-GRADED; ADJ-GRADED

pal·lor /'pælə/. If you refer to the **pallor** of someone's face or skin, you mean that it is pale and unhealthy. N-SING

palm /pɑːm/ **palms, palming, palmed.** 1 A **palm** or a **palm tree** is a tree that grows in hot countries. It has long leaves growing at the top, and no branches. 2 The **palm** of your hand is the inside part. See picture headed **human body.** 3 If you have someone or something **in the palm of** your hand, you have control over them. *They held his fate in the palms of their ancient hands.* ♦♦◇◇ N-COUNT; N-COUNT; PHRASE

palm off. If you say that someone **has palmed** something or someone **off** on you or that they **have palmed** you **off** with something, you feel annoyed because they have made you accept something which is not valuable or which is not your responsibility. *Joseph Smith made sure that he was never palmed off with such inferior stuff.* PHRASAL VB V n P on n; PRAGMATICS; be V-ed P with n

palm off with. If you say that you **are palmed off with** a lie or an excuse, you are annoyed because you are told something in order to stop you asking any more questions. PHRASAL VB be V-ed P with n; PRAGMATICS; BRITISH

'palm oil. **Palm oil** is a yellow oil which comes from the fruit of certain palm trees and is used in making soap and sometimes as a fat in cooking. N-UNCOUNT

palo·mi·no /ˌpælə'miːnəʊ/ **palominos.** A **palomino** is a horse which is golden or cream in colour and has a white mane and tail. N-COUNT

pal·pable /'pælpəbəl/. You describe something as **palpable** when it is obvious or intense and easily noticed. *There is an almost palpable feeling of hopelessness.* ♦ **pal·pably** /'pælpəbli/ *The scene was palpably intense to watch.* ♦◇◇◇ ADJ-GRADED; ADV-GRADED

pal·pi·tate /'pælpɪteɪt/ **palpitates, palpitating.** If something **palpitates**, it trembles or moves quickly backwards and forwards, or seems to move in this way. VERB: V; LITERARY

pal·pi·ta·tion /ˌpælpɪ'teɪʃən/ **palpitations.** When someone has **palpitations**, their heart beats very fast and with an irregular beat. N-VAR

pal·sy /'pɔːlzi/. See **cerebral palsy.**

pal·try /'pɔːltri/. 1 A **paltry** amount of money or something else is very small. *They suffered an electoral catastrophe, winning a paltry 3 seats.* 2 You can use **paltry** to describe something that you consider to be small or unimportant. *The parents had little interest in paltry domestic concerns.* ♦◇◇◇ ADJ-GRADED; ADJ-GRADED: usu ADJ n

pam·pas /'pæmpəs, -əz/. The **pampas** is the large area of flat grassy land in South America. N-SING: the N

pam·per /'pæmpə/ **pampers, pampering, pampered.** If you **pamper** someone, you make them feel comfortable by doing things for them or giving them expensive or luxurious things, sometimes in a way which has a bad effect on their character. ♦ **pam·pered** *...today's pampered superstars.* ♦◇◇◇ VERB: V n; ADJ-GRADED

pam·phlet /'pæmflət/ **pamphlets.** A **pamphlet** is a very thin book, with a paper cover, which gives information about something. ♦◇◇◇ N-COUNT

pan /pæn/ **pans, panning, panned.** 1 A **pan** is a round metal container with a long handle, which is used for cooking things in, usually on top of a cooker. 2 A **pan** is a shallow metal container used for baking foods. The British term is **baking tin.** 3 If something such as a film or a book **is panned** by critics, they say it is very bad. 4 If you **pan** a film or television camera or if it **pans** somewhere, it moves slowly across an area in a wide sweep. *The camera panned along the line of players.* 5 If someone **pans** for gold or **pans** gold, they use a shallow pan to sift gold from a river. *Every year they panned about a ton and a half of gold.* ♦♦♦◇◇ N-COUNT; N-COUNT AMERICAN; VERB: be V-ed; INFORMAL V-ERG: V n V prep/adv Also V; VERB: V for n n

pan out. If something, for example a project or some information, **pans out**, it produces something useful or valuable. *None of Morgan's proposed financings panned out.* PHRASAL VB V P; INFORMAL

pan- /pæn-/. **pan-** is added to the beginning of adjectives and nouns to form other adjectives and nouns that describe something as being connected with all places or people of a particular kind. *...a pan-European culture system.* PREFIX

pana·cea /ˌpænə'siːə/ **panaceas.** If you say that something is not a **panacea** for a particular set of problems, you mean that it will not solve all those problems. *Western aid may help but will not be a panacea.* ♦◇◇◇ N-COUNT; PRAGMATICS

pa·nache /pə'næʃ/. If you do something with **panache**, you do it in a confident, stylish, and elegant way. ♦◇◇◇ N-UNCOUNT

pana·ma hat /ˌpænəmɑː 'hæt/ **panama hats.** A **panama hat** or a **panama** is a straw hat with a N-COUNT

rounded crown and quite a wide brim, worn especially by men.

pan·cake /'pænkeɪk/ **pancakes.** A **pancake** is a thin, flat, circular piece of cooked batter made of milk, flour, and eggs. Pancakes can be folded and eaten hot with a sweet or savoury filling inside. ◆◇◇◇ N-COUNT

'Pancake Day. **Pancake Day** is the popular name for the day before the beginning of Lent, when people traditionally make pancakes. N-UNCOUNT BRITISH

,pancake 'roll, pancake rolls. A **pancake roll** is an item of Chinese food consisting of a small fried roll of thin pastry filled with vegetables and sometimes meat. N-COUNT BRITISH

pan·cre·as /'pæŋkriəs/ **pancreases.** Your **pancreas** is an organ in your body that is situated behind your stomach. It produces insulin and enzymes that help in the digestion of food. ◆◇◇◇ N-COUNT

pan·cre·at·ic /,pæŋkri'ætɪk/. **Pancreatic** means relating to or involving the pancreas. *...pancreatic juices.* ADJ: ADJ n

pan·da /'pændə/ **pandas.** A **panda** or a **giant panda** is a large animal rather like a bear, which has black and white fur and lives in the bamboo forests of China. ◆◇◇◇ N-COUNT

'panda car, panda cars. A **panda car** is a small police patrol car. N-COUNT BRITISH

pan·dem·ic /pæn'demɪk/ **pandemics.** A **pandemic** is an occurrence of a disease that affects many people over a very wide area. *One pandemic of Spanish flu took nearly 22 million lives worldwide.* N-COUNT FORMAL

pan·de·mo·nium /,pændɪ'məʊniəm/. If there is **pandemonium** in a place, the people there are behaving in a very noisy and uncontrolled way. *Pandemonium broke out as they ran into the street shouting.* N-UNCOUNT

pan·der /'pændə/ **panders, pandering, pandered.** If you **pander to** someone or to their wishes, you do everything that they want, often to get some advantage for yourself; used showing disapproval. *He said the government had pandered to the terrorists for too long.* ◆◇◇◇ VERB PRAGMATICS V to n

Pan·do·ra /pæn'dɔːrə/. If someone or something **opens Pandora's box** or **opens a Pandora's box,** they take an action which unintentionally causes a lot of problems that did not exist or were not known about before. PHRASE

p & p; also spelled **p and p.** In Britain, **p & p** is a written abbreviation for 'postage and packing'. It is used when stating the cost of packing goods in a parcel and sending them through the post to a customer. *The guide costs £9.95 (inc. p&p).*

pane /peɪn/ **panes.** A **pane** of glass is a flat sheet of glass in a window or door. ◆◇◇◇ N-COUNT

pan·el /'pænəl/ **panels.** 1 A **panel** is a small group of people who are chosen to do something, for example to discuss something in public. *The advisory panel disagreed with the decision.* 2 A **panel** is a flat rectangular piece of wood or other material that forms part of a larger object such as a door. 3 A control **panel** or instrument **panel** is a board which contains switches and controls to operate a machine or piece of equipment. ◆◇◇◇ N-COLL-COUNT / N-COUNT / N-COUNT: n N

pan·elled /'pænəld/; spelled **paneled** in American English. If something such as a room or door is **panelled,** its walls or surface are covered in decorative wooden panels. ► **-panelled** combines with nouns to form adjectives that describe the way a room or wall is decorated or the way a door or window is made. *The walls are oak-panelled.* ◆◇◇◇ ADJ / COMB

pan·el·ling /'pænəlɪŋ/; spelled **paneling** in American English. **Panelling** consists of boards or strips of wood covering a wall inside a building. ◆◇◇◇ N-UNCOUNT

pan·el·list /'pænəlɪst/ **panellists;** spelled **panelist** in American English. A **panellist** is a person who is a member of a panel and speaks in public, especially on a radio or television programme. N-COUNT

pang /pæŋ/ **pangs.** A **pang** is a sudden strong feeling or emotion. *For a moment she felt a pang of guilt about the way she was treating him.* ◆◇◇◇ N-COUNT

pan·han·dle /'pænhændəl/ **panhandles, panhandling, panhandled.** 1 A **panhandle** is a narrow strip of land joined to a larger area of land. *Thunderstorms caused flooding in the Texas panhandle early today.* 2 If someone **panhandles,** they stop people in the street and ask them for food or money. The usual British word is **beg.** *There was also a guy panhandling for quarters.* ♦ **pan·han·dling** *Arrests for panhandling take place every day.* N-COUNT AMERICAN / VERB: V / V for n AMERICAN, INFORMAL / N-UNCOUNT

pan·han·dler /'pænhændlə/ **panhandlers.** A **panhandler** is a person who stops people in the street and asks them for food or money. The usual British word is **beggar.** N-COUNT AMERICAN, INFORMAL

pan·ic /'pænɪk/ **panics, panicking, panicked.** 1 **Panic** is a very strong feeling of anxiety or fear, which makes you act without thinking carefully. *I phoned the doctor in a panic, crying that I'd lost the baby.* 2 **Panic** or a **panic** is a situation in which people are affected by a strong feeling of anxiety. *There was a moment of panic in Britain as it became clear just how vulnerable the nation was.* 3 If you **panic** or if someone **panics** you, you suddenly feel anxious or afraid, and act quickly and without thinking carefully. *The unexpected and sudden memory briefly panicked her... The Government has been panicked into giving us a promise to abolish it.* ◆◆◆◇◇ N-VAR / N-VAR / V-ERG: V / V n / be V-ed into / -ing/n / Also V n into n

pan·icky /'pænɪki/. A **panicky** feeling or **panicky** behaviour is characterized by panic. *...yesterday's panicky decision by the Bank of Ireland.* ADJ-GRADED

'panic-stricken. If someone is **panic-stricken** or is behaving in a **panic-stricken** way, they are so anxious or afraid that they may act without thinking carefully. ADJ-GRADED

pan·ni·er /'pæniə/ **panniers.** A **pannier** is one of two bags, boxes, or baskets for carrying things in, which are put either side of a bicycle, motorbike, or animal. N-COUNT

pano·ply /'pænəpli/. A **panoply** of things is a wide range of them, especially one that is considered impressive. *...the marvellous panoply of exhibitions laid on this year.* N-SING FORMAL

pano·ra·ma /,pænə'rɑːmə, -'ræmə/ **panoramas.** 1 A **panorama** is a view over a wide area of land. *...a panorama of fertile valleys and gentle hills.* 2 A **panorama** is a broad view of a state of affairs or of a constantly changing series of events. *...a panorama of the history of communism.* ◆◇◇◇ N-COUNT / N-COUNT

pano·ram·ic /,pænə'ræmɪk/. If you have a **panoramic** view, you can see a long way over a wide area. ◆◇◇◇ ADJ-GRADED

pan·sy /'pænzi/ **pansies.** A **pansy** is a small brightly coloured garden flower with large round petals. N-COUNT

pant /pænt/ **pants, panting, panted.** If you **pant,** you breathe quickly and loudly with your mouth open, because you have been doing something energetic. ● See also **pants.** ◆◇◇◇ VERB: V

pan·ta·loons /,pæntə'luːnz/. **Pantaloons** are long trousers with wide legs, gathered at the ankle. N-PLURAL

pan·the·ism /'pænθiɪzəm/. 1 **Pantheism** is the religious belief that God is in everything in nature and the universe. 2 **Pantheism** is a willingness to worship and believe in all gods. N-UNCOUNT / N-UNCOUNT

pan·theis·tic /,pænθi'ɪstɪk/. **Pantheistic** religions involve the acceptance of the idea that God is in everything in nature and the universe. ADJ

pan·the·on /'pænθiɒn/ **pantheons.** You can refer to a group of gods or a group of important people as a **pantheon.** *...the Communist Party's pantheon of Marx, Engels, Lenin and Stalin.* ◆◇◇◇ N-COUNT

pan·ther /'pænθə/ **panthers.** A **panther** is a large wild animal that belongs to the cat family. Panthers are usually black. See picture headed **animals.** ◆◇◇◇ N-COUNT

panties /'pæntiz/. In Britain, some people use the word **panties** to refer to the close-fitting underpants worn by women or girls. **Panties** is the usual American word for women's'underpants. N-PLURAL: also a pair of N

pan·to /'pæntəʊ/ **pantos.** A **panto** is the same as a **pantomime.** N-VAR INFORMAL, BRITISH

pan·to·mime /'pæntəmaɪm/ **pantomimes.** 1 A **pantomime** is a funny musical play for children. N-COUNT BRITISH

Pantomimes are usually based on fairy stories and are performed at Christmas. **2 Pantomime** is the form of entertainment which involves producing a pantomime. *He is currently starring in pantomime in Weston-super-Mare.* **3 Pantomime** is acting something out without speaking. *Chaplin feared that the art of pantomime was under threat.* **4** If you say that a situation or a person's behaviour is a **pantomime**, you mean that it is silly or exaggerated and that there is something false about it. *They were made welcome with the usual pantomime of exaggerated smiles and gestures.*   N-UNCOUNT BRITISH / N-UNCOUNT / N-SING BRITISH

pan·try /ˈpæntri/ **pantries.** A pantry is a small room or large cupboard where food is kept.   N-COUNT

pants /pænts/. **1 Pants** are a piece of underwear which have two holes to put your legs through and elastic around the top to hold them up round your waist or hips. See picture headed **clothes. 2 Pants** are a piece of clothing that covers the lower part of your body and each leg. The British word is **trousers**. See picture headed **clothes. 3** If someone bores or scares **the pants off** you, for example, they bore or scare you a lot. **4** If you **fly by the seat of** your **pants** or do something **by the seat of** your **pants**, you use your instincts to tell you what to do rather than following a plan or relying on equipment. **5 ●** to **be caught with** one's **pants down**: see **catch. ●** to **wear the pants**: see **wear**.   ◆◇◇◇ N-PLURAL: also a pair of N BRITISH / N-PLURAL: also a pair of N AMERICAN / PHRASE INFORMAL / PHRASE

pan·ty·hose /ˈpæntihəʊz/; also spelled **panty hose. Pantyhose** are nylon tights worn by women. The usual British word is **tights**.   N-PLURAL: also a pair of N AMERICAN

pap /pæp/. If you describe something such as writing or entertainment as **pap**, you mean that it is of no worth or serious interest.   N-UNCOUNT

papa /pəˈpɑː, AM ˈpɑːpə/ **papas.** Some people refer to or address their father as **papa**.   ◆◇◇◇ N-FAMILY

pa·pa·cy /ˈpeɪpəsi/; also spelled **Papacy**. The **papacy** is the position, power, and authority of the Pope, including the period of time that a particular person holds this position. *Throughout his papacy, John Paul has called for a second evangelization of Europe.*   N-SING

pa·pal /ˈpeɪpəl/. **Papal** is used to describe things relating to the Pope. *...the doctrine of papal infallibility. ...a papal visit to Japan.*   ◆◇◇◇ ADJ: ADJ n

pa·pa·raz·zo /ˌpæpəˈrætsəʊ/ **paparazzi** /ˌpæpəˈrætsi/. The **paparazzi** are photographers who follow rich or famous people around, hoping to take interesting or shocking photographs of them that they can sell to a newspaper.   N-COUNT

pa·pa·ya /pəˈpaɪə/ **papayas.** A papaya is a fruit with a green skin, sweet yellow flesh, and small black seeds. Papayas grow in hot countries such as the West Indies.   N-COUNT

pa·per /ˈpeɪpə/ **papers, papering, papered. 1 Paper** is a material that you write on or wrap things with. The pages of this book are made of paper. *He wrote his name down on a piece of paper for me. ...a paper bag.*   ◆◆◆◆◆ N-UNCOUNT

2 If you put your thoughts down **on paper**, you write them down. *It is important to get something down on paper.* **3** If something seems to be the case **on paper**, it seems to be the case from what you read or hear about it, but it may not really be the case. *On paper, their country is a multi-party democracy.* **4** If you say that a promise or an agreement **is not worth the paper it's written on**, you mean that although it has been written down and seems to be official, it is in fact worthless because what has been promised or agreed will not be done. **5 Paper** agreements, qualifications, or profits are ones that are stated by official documents to exist, although they may not really be effective or useful. *We're looking for people who have experience rather than paper qualifications.*   PHRASE / PHRASE / PHRASE / ADJ: ADJ n

6 A **paper** is a newspaper. **7** You can refer to newspapers in general as **the paper** or **the papers**. *You can't believe everything you read in the paper... There's been a lot in the papers about the problems facing stepchildren.*   N-COUNT / N-COUNT: the N

8 Your **papers** are sheets of paper with writing or information on them, which you might keep in a safe place at home. *After her death, her papers – including unpublished articles and correspondence – were deposited at the library.* **9** Your **papers** are official documents, for example your passport or identity card, which prove who you are or which give you official permission to do something. *A young Moroccan stopped by police refused to show his papers.*   N-PLURAL / N-PLURAL

10 A **paper** is a long essay written on an academic subject. **11** A **paper** prepared by a government or a committee is a report on a question they have been considering or a set of proposals for changes in the law. *...a new government paper on European policy.* **●** See also **green paper, white paper. 12** A **paper** is a part of a written examination in which you answer a number of questions in a particular period of time. *...the applied mathematics paper.*   N-COUNT / N-COUNT / N-COUNT

13 If you **paper** a wall, you put wallpaper on it. *We papered all four bedrooms.*   VERB V n

paper over. If people **paper over** a disagreement between them, they find a temporary solution to it in order to give the impression that things are going well. *...his determination to paper over the cracks in his party and avoid confrontation.*   PHRASAL VB V P n

paper·back /ˈpeɪpəbæk/ **paperbacks.** A paperback is a book with a thin cardboard or paper cover. Compare **hardback** and **softback**. *She said she would buy the book when it comes out in paperback.*   ◆◆◇◇ N-COUNT: also in N

paper·boy /ˈpeɪpəbɔɪ/ **paperboys;** also spelled **paper boy**. A **paperboy** is a boy who delivers newspapers to people's homes.   N-COUNT

paper clip, /ˈpeɪpə/ **paper clips;** also spelled **paper-clip** or **paperclip**. A **paper clip** is a small piece of bent wire that is used to fasten papers together.   N-COUNT

paper·girl /ˈpeɪpəgɜːl/ **papergirls;** also spelled **paper girl**. A **papergirl** is a girl who delivers newspapers to people's homes.   N-COUNT

paper knife, paper knives; also spelled **paper-knife**. A **paper knife** is a tool shaped like a blunt knife, which is used for opening envelopes. The usual American term is **letter opener**.   N-COUNT BRITISH

paper·less /ˈpeɪpələs/. **Paperless** is used to describe transactions or office activities which are done by computer and telephone, rather than by writing things down and exchanging pieces of paper. *Paperless trading can save time and money.*   ADJ: ADJ n

paper 'money. Paper money is money which is made of paper.   N-UNCOUNT

paper round, paper rounds. In Britain, a **paper round** is a job of delivering newspapers to houses along a certain route. Paper rounds are usually done by children before or after school. In the united States, it is called a **paper route**.   N-COUNT

paper shop, paper shops. A **paper shop** is a shop that sells newspapers, tobacco, sweets, and stationery.   N-COUNT BRITISH

paper-'thin; also spelled **paper thin**. If something is **paper-thin**, it is very thin.   ADJ

paper 'tiger, paper tigers. If you say that an institution, a country, or a person is a **paper tiger**, you mean that although they seem powerful they do not really have any power.   N-COUNT

paper trail. Documentary evidence of someone's activities can be referred to as a **paper trail**. *Criminals are very reluctant to leave a paper trail.*   N-SING AMERICAN

paper·weight /ˈpeɪpəweɪt/ **paperweights.** A **paperweight** is a small heavy object which you place on papers to prevent them from being disturbed or blown away.   N-COUNT

paper·work /ˈpeɪpəwɜːk/. **Paperwork** is things like letters, reports, and records which have to be dealt with as the routine part of a job.   ◆◇◇◇ N-UNCOUNT

pa·pery /ˈpeɪpəri/. Something that is **papery** is thin and dry like paper.   ADJ

papier-mâché /ˌpæpieɪ ˈmæʃeɪ, AM ˌpeɪpə məˈʃeɪ/. **Papier-mâché** is a mixture of pieces of paper and glue. It can be made, while still damp, into objects such as ornaments and models.   N-UNCOUNT

pap·ri·ka /pəˈpriːkə, ˈpæprɪkə/. **Paprika** is a mild-tasting red powder that is used for flavouring food.   N-UNCOUNT

P

pa·py·rus /pəˈpaɪrəs/ **papyri.** **1** Papyrus is a tall N-UNCOUNT
water plant that grows in Africa. **2** Papyrus is a type N-UNCOUNT
of paper made from papyrus stems that was used in
ancient Egypt, Rome, and Greece. **3** A **papyrus** is an N-COUNT
ancient document that is written on papyrus.

par /pɑː/. **1** If you say that someone or something ◆◆◇◇◇
is **on a par with** someone or something else, you PHRASE
mean that the two people or things are equally good
or bad, or equally important. *Parts of Glasgow are
on a par with the worst areas of London and Liverpool for burglaries.* **2** If you say that someone or PHRASE
something is **below par** or **under par**, you mean
that they are below the standard you expected.
*Duffy's primitive guitar playing is well below par. ...a
below par effort.* **3** If you say that someone or PHRASE
something is not **up to par**, you mean that they are
below the standard you expected. **4** If you say that PHRASE
something that happens is **par for the course**, you PRAGMATICS
mean that you are not pleased with it but it is what
you expected to happen. *He said long hours are par
for the course.*
5 In golf, **par** is the number of strokes that a good golf- N-UNCOUNT:
er should take to get the ball into a hole or into all the N with num,
holes on a particular golf course. *He was five under under/overN*
par after the first round.*

para /ˈpærə/ **paras.** A para is a **paratrooper.** N-COUNT

para. /ˈpærə/ **paras.** Para. is a written abbreviation N-COUNT
for **paragraph.** INFORMAL

par·a·ble /ˈpærəbəl/ **parables.** A **parable** is a short ◆◇◇◇◇
story, which is told in order to make a moral or reli- N-COUNT
gious point, like those in the Bible.

pa·rab·o·la /pəˈræbələ/ **parabolas.** A **parabola** is a N-COUNT
type of curve such as the path of something that is
thrown up into the air and comes down in a different place.

para·bol·ic /ˌpærəˈbɒlɪk/. A **parabolic** object or ADJ
curve is shaped like a parabola.

pa·ra·ceta·mol /ˌpærəˈsiːtəmɒl/; **paracetamol** is N-VAR
both the singular and the plural form. **Paracetamol**
is a mild drug which reduces pain and fever. It is
sold in the form of tablets.

para·chute /ˈpærəʃuːt/ **parachutes, parachut-** ◆◇◇◇◇
ing, parachuted. **1** A **parachute** is a device which N-COUNT:
enables a person to jump from an aircraft and float also byN
safely to the ground. It consists of a large piece of
thin cloth attached to your body by strings. **2** If a V-ERG
person **parachutes** or someone **parachutes** them V prep/adv
somewhere, they jump from an aircraft using a beV-ed
parachute. *He was a courier for the Polish under- prep/adv
ground and parachuted into Warsaw... He was parachuted in.* **3** If someone **parachutes** something, VERB
they drop it somewhere by parachute. *Supplies were Vn prep/adv
parachuted into the mountains.*

para·chut·ing /ˈpærəʃuːtɪŋ/. **Parachuting** is the ac- N-UNCOUNT
tivity or sport of jumping from an aircraft with a
parachute. ♦ **para·chut·ist, parachutists.** N-COUNT

pa·rade /pəˈreɪd/ **parades, parading, paraded.** ◆◆◇◇◇
1 A **parade** is a procession of people or vehicles N-COUNT
moving through a public place in order to celebrate
an important day or event. **2** When people **parade**, VERB
they walk together in a formal group or in a line, V prep/adv
usually in front of spectators. *Soldiers, sailors and
airmen paraded down the Champs Elysee.* **3** Parade N-VAR
is a formal occasion when soldiers stand in lines in
order to be inspected, or march in formation. **4** If VB: usu
flags or statues **are paraded**, they are carried in a passive
procession. *Banners were paraded from church to beV-ed prep
church.*
5 If prisoners **are paraded** through the streets of a VERB:
town or on television, their captors show them to the beV-ed prep
public in order to show their power. **6** If you say that VB: usu
someone **parades** a person, you mean that they show passive
that person to others only in order to gain some ad- beV-ed
vantage for themselves. *Children have been paraded
alongside the party leaders to publicise the latest issue.*
7 If people **parade** something, they show it in public VERB
so that they can be admired or envied. *Valentino is Vn
keen to see celebrities parading his clothes at big occasions.* **8** If someone **parades**, they walk about some- VERB

where in order to be seen and admired. *They danced V prep/adv
and paraded around.*
9 If someone **parades** a real or pretended feeling or VERB
quality, they draw attention to themselves by display- Vn
ing it. *They parade their virtuous beliefs and hide their
vices.* **10** If you say that something **parades** as or is V-ERG:
paraded as a good or important thing, you mean that V asn
some people say that it is good or important but you PRAGMATICS
think it probably is not. *The Chancellor will be able to Vn asn
parade his cut in interest rates as a small victory.* **11** If N-COUNT:
you talk about a **parade of** people or things, you mean N ofn
that there is a series of them that seems never to end.
...an endless parade of advertisements.
12 A **parade** is a short row of shops, usually set back N-COUNT
from the main street. **13** Parade is used as part of the BRITISH
name of a street. *Queens Hotel, Clarence Parade.*
14 See also **hit parade, identity parade.**

'parade ground, parade grounds. A **parade** N-COUNT
ground is an area of ground where soldiers practise
marching and where they hold parades.

para·digm /ˈpærədaɪm/ **paradigms.** **1** A **para-** ◆◇◇◇◇
digm is a model for something which explains it or N-VAR
shows how it can be produced. *...a new paradigm of FORMAL
production.* **2** A **paradigm** is a clear and typical ex- N-COUNT
ample of something. *...he had become the paradigm
of the successful man.*

para·dig·mat·ic /ˌpærədɪgˈmætɪk/. You can de- ADJ
scribe something as **paradigmatic** if it acts as a FORMAL
model or example for something. *Their great academic success was paraded as paradigmatic.*

para·dise /ˈpærədaɪs/ **paradises.** **1** According to ◆◆◇◇◇
some religions, **paradise** is a wonderful place where N-PROPER
people go after they die, if they have led good lives.
2 You can refer to a place or situation that seems N-VAR
beautiful or perfect as **paradise** or **a paradise.** *...one
of the world's great natural paradises.* **3** You can N-COUNT:
also use **paradise** to say that a place is very attrac- suppN
tive to a particular kind of person and has everything they need for a particular activity. *The Algarve
is a golfer's paradise.*

para·dox /ˈpærədɒks/ **paradoxes.** **1** You describe ◆◇◇◇◇
a situation as a **paradox** when it involves two or N-COUNT
more facts or qualities which seem to contradict
each other. *The paradox is that the region's most dynamic economies have the most primitive financial
systems.* ♦ **para·doxi·cal** *Some sedatives produce ADJ-GRADED
the paradoxical effect of making the person more
anxious.* ♦ **para·doxi·cal·ly** /ˌpærəˈdɒksɪkli/ *Para- ADV-GRADED
doxically, the less you have to do the more you may
resent the work that does come your way.* **2** A **para-** N-VAR
dox is a statement in which it seems that if one part
of it is true, the other part of it cannot be true. *Although I'm so successful I'm really rather a failure.
That's a paradox, isn't it?*

par·af·fin /ˈpærəfɪn/. **Paraffin** is a strong-smelling N-UNCOUNT
liquid which is used as a fuel in heaters, lamps, and
engines. The usual American word is **kerosene.**

para·gon /ˈpærəgɒn/ **paragons.** If you refer to ◆◇◇◇◇
someone as a **paragon**, you mean that you think N-COUNT
they are perfect. If you say that they are a **paragon**
of virtue, or some other good quality, you mean that
they have a lot of that quality. *...a paragon of neatness, efficiency and reliability.*

para·graph /ˈpærəgrɑːf, -græf/ **paragraphs.** A ◆◆◇◇◇
paragraph is a section of a piece of writing. A para- N-COUNT
graph always begins on a new line and contains at
least one sentence.

para·keet /ˈpærəkiːt/ **parakeets;** also spelled **par-** N-COUNT
rakeet. A **parakeet** is a small parrot with a long tail.

par·al·lax /ˈpærəlæks/ **parallaxes.** Parallax is the N-VAR
effect whereby an object appears to change its posi- TECHNICAL
tion because the person or instrument observing it
has changed their position.

par·al·lel /ˈpærəlel/ **parallels, parallelling,** ◆◆◇◇◇
parallelled; spelled **paralleling, paralleled** in
American English. **1** If something has a **parallel**, it N-COUNT
is similar to something else, but exists or happens
in a different place or at a different time. If it has **no
parallel** or is **without parallel**, it is not similar to
anything else. *Readers familiar with English history*

will find a vague parallel to the suppression of the monasteries. **2** If there are **parallels** between two things, they are similar in some ways. *Detailed study of folk music from a variety of countries reveals many close parallels.* N-COUNT

3 If one thing **parallels** another, they happen at the same time or are similar, and often seem to be connected. *His remarks paralleled those of the president.* VERB / V n

4 Parallel events or situations happen at the same time as one another, or are similar to one another. *...parallel talks between the two countries' Foreign Ministers.* **5** Something that occurs **in parallel** with something else occurs at the same time as it. ADJ / PHRASE

6 If two lines, two objects, or two lines of movement are **parallel**, they are the same distance apart along their whole length. **7** A **parallel** is an imaginary line round the earth that is parallel to the equator. Parallels are shown on maps. ADJ / N-COUNT

ˌparallel 'bars. Parallel bars consist of a pair of bars on posts which are used for doing gymnastic exercises. N-PLURAL

par·al·lel·ism /'pærəlelɪzəm/. When there is **parallelism** between two things, there are similarities between them. *...parallelism between the priorities of the European Community and the United States.* N-UNCOUNT / FORMAL

par·al·lelo·gram /ˌpærə'leləgræm/ **parallelograms.** A parallelogram is a four-sided geometrical figure in which every side is parallel to the side opposite it. N-COUNT

para·lyse /'pærəlaɪz/ **paralyses, paralysing, paralysed;** spelled **paralyze** in American English. **1** If someone **is paralysed** by an accident or an illness, they have no feeling in their body, or in part of their body, and are unable to move. *...a virus which paralysed his legs.* ♦ **para·lysed** *...a paralysed right arm.* **2** If a person, place, or organization **is paralysed** by something, they become unable to act or function properly. *The government has been paralysed by indecision.* ♦ **paralysed** *...a paralysed civil service.* ♦ **para·lys·ing** *...paralysing shyness.* ◆◇◇◇◇ VERB: be V-ed / V n / ADJ / VERB be V-ed Also V n / ADJ / ADJ-GRADED

pa·raly·sis /pə'ræləsɪs/. **1 Paralysis** is the loss of feeling in all or part of your body, and the inability to move. *...paralysis of the leg.* **2 Paralysis** is the state of being unable to act or function properly. *...the paralysis of the leadership.* ◆◇◇◇◇ N-UNCOUNT / N-UNCOUNT

para·lyt·ic /ˌpærə'lɪtɪk/. **1 Paralytic** means suffering from or related to paralysis. *...paralytic disease in laboratory animals.* **2** Someone who is **paralytic** is very drunk indeed. *By the end of the evening they were all absolutely paralytic.* ADJ / ADJ-GRADED INFORMAL, BRITISH

para·med·ic /ˌpærə'medɪk, AM -medɪk/ **paramedics.** A paramedic is a person whose training is similar to that of a nurse and who helps to do medical work. ♦ **para·medi·cal** /ˌpærə'medɪkəl/ *...doctors and paramedical staff.* N-COUNT / ADJ: ADJ n

pa·ram·eter /pə'ræmɪtə/ **parameters.** Parameters are factors or limits which affect the way that something can be done or made. *...the parameters of our loan agreement.* ◆◇◇◇◇ N-COUNT

para·mili·tary /ˌpærə'mɪlɪtri, AM -teri/ **paramilitaries. 1** A **paramilitary** organization is organized like an army and performs either civil or military functions in a country. ► **Paramilitaries** are members of a paramilitary organization. **2** A **paramilitary** organization is an illegal group that is organized like an army. *...paramilitary activity supported from abroad.* ► **Paramilitaries** are members of an illegal paramilitary organization. ◆◇◇◇◇ ADJ: ADJ n / ADJ: ADJ n / N-COUNT

para·mount /'pærəmaʊnt/. Something that is **paramount** or of **paramount** importance is more important than anything else. *The child's welfare must be seen as paramount.* ◆◇◇◇◇ ADJ

par·amour /'pærəmʊə/ **paramours.** Someone's **paramour** is their lover. N-COUNT DATED

para·noia /ˌpærə'nɔɪə/. **1** If you say that someone suffers from **paranoia**, you mean that they are too suspicious, distrustful, and afraid of other people. *...the mounting paranoia with which he viewed the world.* **2** If someone suffers from **paranoia**, they ◆◇◇◇◇ N-UNCOUNT / N-UNCOUNT

wrongly believe that other people are trying to harm them. MEDICAL

para·noi·ac /ˌpærə'nɔɪæk/. **Paranoiac** means the same as **paranoid.** ADJ-GRADED

para·noid /'pærənɔɪd/. **1** If you say that someone is **paranoid**, you mean that they are extremely suspicious, distrustful, and afraid of other people. *I'm not going to get paranoid about it.* **2** Someone who is **paranoid** suffers from the mental illness of paranoia. *...a paranoid schizophrenic.* ◆◇◇◇◇ ADJ-GRADED PRAGMATICS / ADJ MEDICAL

para·nor·mal /ˌpærə'nɔːməl/. A **paranormal** event or power, for example the appearance of a ghost, cannot be explained by scientific laws and is thought to involve strange, unknown forces. *...paranormal phenomena.* ► You can refer to paranormal events and matters as **the paranormal.** ADJ / N-SING: the N

para·pet /'pærəpɪt/ **parapets.** A parapet is a low wall along the edge of a bridge, roof, or balcony. N-COUNT

para·pher·na·lia /ˌpærəfə'neɪliə/. **1** You can refer to a large number of objects that someone has with them or that are connected with a particular activity as **paraphernalia.** *...a large courtyard full of builders' paraphernalia.* **2** If you disapprove of the things and events that are involved in a particular system or activity, and you think they are unnecessary, you can refer to them as **paraphernalia.** *The public don't necessarily want the paraphernalia of a full hearing.* ◆◇◇◇◇ N-UNCOUNT / N-UNCOUNT PRAGMATICS

para·phrase /'pærəfreɪz/ **paraphrases, paraphrasing, paraphrased.** If you **paraphrase** someone or **paraphrase** something that they have said or written, you express what they have said or written in a different way. *Baxter paraphrased the contents of the press release.* ► Also a noun. *...a paraphrase of Proust's novel.* VERB V n Also V / N-COUNT

para·plegia /ˌpærə'pliːdʒə/. **Paraplegia** is paralysis of the lower half of the body. N-UNCOUNT MEDICAL

para·plegic /ˌpærə'pliːdʒɪk/ **paraplegics.** A **paraplegic** is someone whose lower body is paralysed. ► Also an adjective. *He will be paraplegic for the rest of his life.* N-COUNT / ADJ

para·psy·chol·ogy /ˌpærəsaɪ'kɒlədʒi/. **Parapsychology** is the study of strange mental abilities that seem to exist but cannot be explained by accepted scientific theories. N-UNCOUNT

para·site /'pærəsaɪt/ **parasites. 1** A parasite is a small animal or plant that lives on or inside a larger animal or plant, and gets its food from it. ♦ **para·sit·ic** /ˌpærə'sɪtɪk/ *...tiny parasitic insects.* **2** If you disapprove of someone because you think that they get money or other things from other people but do not do anything in return, you can call them a **parasite.** ♦ **parasitic** *She is not self-sufficient, she is parasitic.* ◆◇◇◇◇ N-COUNT / ADJ / N-COUNT PRAGMATICS / ADJ

para·sol /'pærəsɒl, AM -sɔːl/ **parasols.** A parasol is an object like an umbrella that provides shade from the sun. N-COUNT

para·troop·er /'pærətruːpə/ **paratroopers.** Paratroopers are soldiers who are trained to be dropped by parachute into battle or into enemy territory. ◆◇◇◇◇ N-COUNT

para·troops /'pærətruːps/; the form **paratroop** is used as a modifier. **Paratroops** are soldiers who are trained to be dropped by parachute into battle or into enemy territory. N-PLURAL

par·boil /ˌpɑː'bɔɪl/ **parboils, parboiling, parboiled.** If you **parboil** food, especially vegetables, you boil it until it is partly cooked. VERB: V n

par·cel /'pɑːsəl/ **parcels, parcelling, parcelled;** spelled **parceling, parceled** in American English. **1** A **parcel** is something wrapped in paper, usually so that it can be sent to someone by post. The more usual American word is **package.** *...a large brown paper parcel.* **2** A **parcel of** land is a piece of land. *These small parcels of land were purchased for the most part by local people.* **3** A **parcel of** things or people is a quantity of them. *...a run-down house and a parcel of financial worries.* **4** If you say that something is **part and parcel** of something else, you mean that it is involved or included in it. *Payment* ◆◆◇◇◇ N-COUNT / N-COUNT: N of n / N-COUNT: N of n BRITISH / PHRASE

was part and parcel of carrying on insurance business within the UK.

parcel out. If you **parcel out** something, you divide it into several parts or amounts and give them to different people. *...an agreement that parcelled out the Middle East into several spheres of influence.* PHRASAL VB / V P noun / Also V n P

parched /pɑːtʃt/. **1** If something, especially the ground or a plant, is **parched**, it is very dry, because there has been no rain. *...a hill of parched brown grass.* **2** If your mouth, throat, or lips are **parched**, they are unpleasantly dry. **3** If you say that you are **parched**, you mean that you are very thirsty. ADJ-GRADED / ADJ-GRADED / v-link ADJ

parch·ment /'pɑːtʃmənt/ **parchments. 1** In former times, **parchment** was the skin of a sheep or goat that was used for writing on. **2 Parchment** is a kind of thick yellowish paper. *...an old lamp with a parchment shade.* **3** A **parchment** is a document written on parchment. N-UNCOUNT / N-UNCOUNT / N-COUNT

par·don /'pɑːdən/ **pardons, pardoning, pardoned. 1** You say **'Pardon'** or **'I beg your pardon?'** or, in American English, **'Pardon me?'** when you want someone to repeat what they have just said because you have not heard or understood it. *'Will you let me open it?'—'Pardon?'—'Can I open it?'.* **2** People say **'I beg your pardon!'** when they are surprised or offended by something that someone has just said. *'Would you get undressed, please?'—'I beg your pardon?'* **3** You say **'I beg your pardon'** or **'I do beg your pardon'** as a way of apologizing for accidentally doing something wrong, such as disturbing someone or making a mistake. *I was impolite and I do beg your pardon.* **4** Some people say **'Pardon me'** instead of 'Excuse me' when they want to politely get someone's attention or interrupt them. *Pardon me, are you finished, madam?* **5** You can say things like **'Pardon me for asking'** or **'Pardon my frankness'** as a way of showing you understand that what you are going to say may sound rude. *That, if you'll pardon my saying so, is neither here nor there.* **6** Some people say things like **'If you'll pardon the expression'** or **'Pardon my French'** just before or after saying something which they think might offend people. *It's enough to make you wet yourself, if you'll pardon the expression.* **7** If someone who has been found guilty of a crime **is pardoned**, they are officially allowed to go free and are not punished. ▶ Also a noun. *...he was granted a presidential pardon.* ◆◆◇◇◇ CONVENTION PRAGMATICS / CONVENTION PRAGMATICS / CONVENTION PRAGMATICS / CONVENTION PRAGMATICS / CONVENTION PRAGMATICS / CONVENTION PRAGMATICS / VERB: be V-ed / N-COUNT

pare /peə/ **pares, paring, pared. 1** When you **pare** something, or **pare** part of it off or away, you cut off its skin or its outer layer. *He took out a slab of cheese, pared off a slice and ate it hastily.* ♦ See also **paring. 2** If you **pare** something **down** or **back**, or if you **pare** it, you reduce it. *The number of Ministries has been pared down by a third... The luxury tax won't really do much to pare down the budget deficit.* ◆◇◇◇◇ VERB / V n with adv / Also V n from n / VERB: V n / be V-ed adv / V n with adv

'pared-down. If you describe something as **pared-down**, you mean that it has no unnecessary features, and has been reduced to a very simple form. *...a pared-down military organization.* ADJ-GRADED

par·ent /'peərənt/ **parents. 1** Your **parents** are your mother and father. ♦ See also **one-parent family, single parent.** ♦ **pa·ren·tal** /pə'rentəl/. *Parental attitudes vary widely.* **2** An organization's **parent** organization is the organization that created it and usually still controls it. **3** The **parent** animal, plant, or organism of a particular animal, plant or organism is the one that it comes from or is produced by. *Parent birds began to hunt for food for their young.* ◆◆◆◆◇ N-COUNT / ADJ / ADJ: ADJ n / ADJ: ADJ n

par·ent·age /'peərəntɪdʒ/. Your **parentage** is the identity and origins of your parents. For example, if you are of Greek **parentage**, your parents are Greek. *We are all the result of our parentage and upbringing.* ◆◇◇◇◇ N-UNCOUNT

pa·ren·thesis /pə'renθəsɪs/ **parentheses** /pə'renθəsiːz/. **1 Parentheses** are brackets used in writing. (This sentence is in parentheses). **2** A pa- N-COUNT / N-COUNT

renthesis is a remark that is made in the middle of a piece of speech or writing, and which gives a little more information about the subject being discussed. **3** You say **'in parenthesis'** to indicate that you are about to add something before going back to the main topic. *In parenthesis, I'd say that there were two aspects to writing you must never lose sight of.* PHRASE PRAGMATICS

par·en·the·ti·cal /,pærən'θetɪkəl/. A **parenthetical** remark or section is put into something written or spoken but is not essential to it. *Fox was making a long parenthetical remark about his travels on the border of Tibet.* ♦ **par·en·the·ti·cal·ly** Well, parenthetically, I was trying to quit smoking at the time. ADJ / ADV

par·ent·hood /'peərənthʊd/. **Parenthood** is the state of being a parent. ◆◇◇◇◇ N-UNCOUNT

par·ent·ing /'peərəntɪŋ/. **Parenting** is the activity of bringing up and looking after your child. ◆◇◇◇◇ N-UNCOUNT

,parent-'teacher association, parent-teacher associations. A parent-teacher association is the same as a PTA. N-COUNT

par ex·cel·lence /,pɑː 'eksəlɑːns, AM - 'lɑːns/. You say that something is a particular kind of thing **par excellence** in order to emphasize that it is a very good example of that kind of thing. *Mr Yeltsin is the populist par excellence.* ▶ Also an adverb. *Bresson is par excellence the Catholic film-maker.* ADJ: n ADJ PRAGMATICS / ADV: ADV after v

pa·ri·ah /pə'raɪə/ **pariahs.** If you describe someone as a **pariah**, you mean that other people dislike them so much that they refuse to associate with them. *His landlady had treated him like a dangerous criminal, a pariah.* N-COUNT

par·ing /'peərɪŋ/ **parings. Parings** are thin pieces that have been cut off things such as a fingernails, fruit, or vegetables. N-COUNT

par·ish /'pærɪʃ/ **parishes. 1** A **parish** is a village or part of a town which has its own church and clergyman. **2** A **parish** is a small country area in England which has its own elected council. *...County and Parish Councillors.* ◆◆◇◇◇ N-COUNT / N-COUNT

pa·rish·ion·er /pə'rɪʃənə/ **parishioners.** A clergyman's **parishioners** are the people who live in his parish, especially the ones who go to his church. N-COUNT

par·ity /'pærɪti/ **parities. 1** If there is **parity** between two things, they are equal. *Women have yet to achieve wage or occupational parity in many fields.* **2** If there is **parity** between the units of currency of two countries, the exchange rate is such that the units are equal to each other. ◆◇◇◇◇ N-UNCOUNT FORMAL / N-VAR TECHNICAL

park /pɑːk/ **parks, parking, parked. 1** A **park** is a public area of land with grass and trees, usually in a town, where people go in order to relax and enjoy themselves. **2** In Britain, a private area of grass and trees around a large country house is referred to as a **park. 3** Some people refer to a football or rugby field as **the park.** *Chris was also the best player on the park.* **4** You can refer to a place where a particular activity is carried out as a **park.** *...a business park.* **5** When you **park** a vehicle or **park** somewhere, you drive the vehicle into a position where it can stay for a period of time, and leave it there. *Ben parked across the street.* ♦ See also **double-park. 6** See also **parked; amusement park, ballpark, car park, national park, safari park, theme park.** ◆◆◆◆◇ N-COUNT / N-VAR / N-SING BRITISH, JOURNALISM / N-COUNT: supp N / VERB: V n / V prep/adv / Also V

par·ka /'pɑːkə/ **parkas.** A **parka** is a jacket or coat which has a quilted lining and a hood with fur round the edge. N-COUNT

parked /pɑːkt/. If you are **parked** somewhere, you have parked your car there. *My sister was parked down the road.* ◆◇◇◇◇ ADJ: v-link ADJ

park·ing /'pɑːkɪŋ/. **1 Parking** is the action of moving a vehicle into a place in a car park or by the side of the road where it can be left. *...parking is allowed only on one side of the street.* **2 Parking** is space for parking a vehicle in. *...parking is limited.* ◆◆◇◇◇ N-UNCOUNT / N-UNCOUNT

'parking garage, parking garages. A **parking garage** is a building where people can leave their cars. The usual British term is **car park.** N-COUNT AMERICAN

'**parking light, parking lights.** The **parking lights** on a vehicle are the small lights at the front that help other drivers to notice the vehicle and to judge its width. The British word is **sidelights**.   N-COUNT AMERICAN

'**parking lot, parking lots.** A **parking lot** is an area of ground where people can leave their cars. The usual British word is **car park**.   ♦◇◇◇◇ N-COUNT AMERICAN

'**parking meter, parking meters.** A **parking meter** is a device which you have to put money into when you park in a parking space.   N-COUNT

'**parking ticket, parking tickets.** A **parking ticket** is a piece of paper with instructions to pay a fine which a traffic warden puts on your car when you have parked it somewhere illegally.   N-COUNT

'**park-keeper, park-keepers;** also spelled **park keeper**. A **park-keeper** is a person whose job is to look after a park.   N-COUNT BRITISH

park·land /ˈpɑːklænd/ **parklands. Parkland** is land with grass and trees on it. ...*extensive national and regional parklands*.   ♦◇◇◇◇ N-UNCOUNT: also N in pl

park·way /ˈpɑːkweɪ/ **parkways.** A **parkway** is a wide road with trees and grass on both sides.   N-COUNT AMERICAN

par·lance /ˈpɑːləns/. You use **parlance** when indicating that the expression you are using is normally used by a particular group of people. *Local councils became, in official parlance, 'agencies of the state authority'.*   N-UNCOUNT: supp N FORMAL

par·ley /ˈpɑːli/ **parleys, parleying, parleyed.** **1** A **parley** is a discussion between two opposing people or groups in which both sides try to come to an agreement. **2** When two opposing people or groups **parley**, they meet to discuss something in order to come to an agreement. ...*a place where we meet and parley*.   N-VAR DATED / V-RECIP V Also V with n INFORMAL

par·lia·ment /ˈpɑːləmənt/ **parliaments;** also spelled **Parliament**. **1** The **parliament** of a country is the group of people who make or change its laws. ● See also **Member of Parliament, Houses of Parliament**. **2** A particular **parliament** is a particular period of time in which a parliament is doing its work, between two elections or between two periods of holiday. *The legislation is expected to be passed in the next parliament.*   ♦♦♦♦◇ N-COUNT; N-PROPER / N-COUNT

par·lia·men·tar·ian /ˌpɑːləmenˈteəriən/ **parliamentarians. 1 Parliamentarians** are members of a parliament; used especially to refer to a group of Members of Parliament who are dealing with a particular task. **2** A **parliamentarian** is a Member of Parliament who is an expert on the rules and procedures of Parliament and takes an active part in debates.   ♦◇◇◇◇ N-COUNT / N-COUNT

par·lia·men·ta·ry /ˌpɑːləˈmentəri/. **Parliamentary** is used to describe things that are connected with a parliament or with Members of Parliament. ...*a parliamentary candidate*.   ♦♦◇◇◇ ADJ: ADJ n

par·lour /ˈpɑːlə/ **parlours;** spelled **parlor** in American English. **1** A **parlour** is a sitting-room. **2 Parlour** is used in the names of some types of shops which provide a service, rather than selling things. ...*a funeral parlour*.   ♦◇◇◇◇ N-COUNT / DATED N-COUNT: n N

'**parlour game, parlour games;** spelled **parlor game** in American English. A **parlour game** is a game that is played indoors by families or at parties, for example a guessing game or word game.   N-COUNT

par·lous /ˈpɑːləs/. If something is in a **parlous** state, it is in a bad or dangerous condition. ...*the parlous state of our economy*.   ADJ-GRADED FORMAL

Par·me·san /ˈpɑːmɪzæn/; also spelled **parmesan**. **Parmesan** or **Parmesan cheese** is a hard cheese with a strong flavour.   ♦◇◇◇◇ N-UNCOUNT

pa·ro·chial /pəˈrəʊkiəl/. **1** If you describe someone as **parochial**, you are critical of them because you think that they are too concerned with their own local affairs and interests. **2 Parochial** is used to describe things that relate to the parish connected with a particular church. ...*the local parochial church council*.   ♦◇◇◇◇ ADJ-GRADED PRAGMATICS / ADJ: ADJ n

pa·ro·chi·al·ism /pəˈrəʊkiəlɪzəm/. **Parochialism** is the quality of being parochial and self-centred; used showing disapproval.   N-UNCOUNT PRAGMATICS

paro·dy /ˈpærədi/ **parodies, parodying, parodied. 1** A **parody** is a humorous piece of writing, drama, or music which imitates the style of a well-known person or represents a familiar situation in an exaggerated way. **2** When someone **parodies** a particular work, thing, or person, they imitate it in an amusing or exaggerated way. ...*a brilliant job of parodying a number of television and film genres.* **3** When you say that something is a **parody** of a particular thing, you are criticizing it because you think it is a very poor example or bad imitation of that thing. *After the first trial, a parody of justice, defence lawyers are now allowed a bit of a say.*   ♦◇◇◇◇ N-VAR / VERB V n / N-COUNT PRAGMATICS

pa·role /pəˈrəʊl/ **paroles, paroling, paroled. 1** When prisoners are given **parole**, they are released before their prison sentence is due to end, on condition that they behave well. ● If someone is **on parole**, they will stay out of prison if they behave well. **2** If a prisoner **is paroled**, they are released before their prison sentence is due to end, on condition that they behave well.   ♦◇◇◇◇ N-UNCOUNT / PHRASE / VB: usu passive: be V-ed

par·ox·ysm /ˈpærəksɪzəm/ **paroxysms. 1** A **paroxysm** of emotion is a sudden, very strong occurrence of it. ...*a paroxysm of rage.* **2** A **paroxysm** is a series of sudden, violent, uncontrollable movements that your body makes because you are coughing, laughing, or in great pain. ...*a paroxysm of coughing.*   N-COUNT / N-COUNT

par·quet /ˈpɑːkeɪ, AM -ˈkeɪ/. **Parquet** is a floor covering made of small rectangular blocks of wood fitted together in a pattern.   N-UNCOUNT

par·ra·keet. See parakeet.

par·rot /ˈpærət/ **parrots, parroting, parroted. 1** A **parrot** is a tropical bird with a curved beak and brightly-coloured or grey feathers. Parrots can be kept as pets. **2** If you think that someone is just repeating what someone else has said without really understanding it, you can say that they are **parroting** it. *Generations of students have learnt to parrot the standard explanations.*   ♦◇◇◇◇ N-COUNT / VERB PRAGMATICS V n

par·ry /ˈpæri/ **parries, parrying, parried. 1** If you **parry** a question or argument, you cleverly avoid answering it or dealing with it. **2** If you **parry** a blow from someone who is attacking you, you push aside their arm or weapon so that you are not hurt. *I parried, and that's when my sword broke.*   VERB: V n / VERB: V n V

parse /pɑːz/ **parses, parsing, parsed.** In grammar, if you **parse** a sentence, you examine each word and clause in order to work out what grammatical type each one is.   V n

par·si·mo·ny /ˈpɑːsɪməni, AM -ˈməʊni/. **Parsimony** is extreme unwillingness to spend money; used showing disapproval. ● **par·si·mo·ni·ous** /ˌpɑːsɪˈməʊniəs/. *The president's parsimonious economic programme is not loved by his army.*   N-UNCOUNT PRAGMATICS FORMAL / ADJ-GRADED

pars·ley /ˈpɑːsli, AM -zli/. **Parsley** is a small plant with curly leaves that are used for flavouring or decorating food.   ♦♦◇◇◇ N-UNCOUNT

pars·nip /ˈpɑːsnɪp/ **parsnips.** A **parsnip** is a long cream-coloured root vegetable. See picture headed **vegetables.**   N-COUNT

par·son /ˈpɑːsən/ **parsons.** A **parson** is a vicar in the Church of England, or any clergyman. ● **par·son·age** /ˈpɑːsənɪdʒ/ **parsonages.** A **parsonage** is the house where a parson lives.   ♦♦◇◇◇ N-COUNT / DATED N-COUNT

part 1 noun uses, quantifier uses, and phrases

part /pɑːt/ **parts. 1** A **part** of something is one of the pieces, sections, or elements that it consists of. *I like that part of Cape Town... Respect is a very important part of any relationship.* **2** A **part** for a machine or vehicle is one of the smaller pieces that is used to make it. ...*spare parts for military equipment.* **3 Part of** something is some of it. *Mum and he were able to walk part of the way together... Woodhead spent part of his childhood in Rhodesia.* **4** If you say that something is **part** one thing, **part** another, you mean that it is to some extent the first thing and to some extent the second thing. *The television producer today has to be part news person, part educator.* **5** You can use **part** when you are talking about the   ♦♦♦♦♦ N-COUNT / N-COUNT / QUANT / ADV / N-COUNT

proportions of substances in a mixture. For example, if some instructions say that you should use two **parts** disinfectant to three **parts** water, you should mix two measures of disinfectant with three measures of water. **6** If something or someone is **part of** a group or organization, they belong to it or are included in it. ...*voting on whether to remain part of the Union or become independent.* ● **part and parcel**: see **parcel**. **7** See also **private parts**.

8 For the most part means mostly or usually. *For the most part the Germans kept out of local disputes.* **9** You use **in part** to indicate that something exists or happens to some extent but not completely. *The levels of blood glucose depend in part on what you eat and when you eat.* **10** If you say that something happened for **the best part** or **the better part** of a period of time, you mean that it happened for most of that time. *We spent the better part of an hour searching for her.*

11 A **part** in a play or film is one of the roles in it which an actor or actress can perform.

12 If something or someone **plays a** large or important **part** in something, they are very involved in it and have an important effect on what happens. *These days work plays an important part in a single woman's life.* **13** Your **part** in something that happens is your involvement in it. *If only he could conceal his part in the accident.* **14** If you **take part in** an activity, you do it together with other people. **15** If you say that you **want no part of** something, you mean that you do not want to be involved in it at all.

16 When you are describing people's thoughts or actions, you can say **for** her **part** or **for** my **part**, for example, to introduce what a particular person thinks or does. *The soldiers, for their part, agreed not to disrupt the election campaign.* **17** If you talk about a feeling or action **on** someone's **part**, you are referring to something that they feel or do. *There is no need for any further instructions on my part.* ...*instances of excessive force on the part of security police.*

part 2 verb uses

part /pɑːt/ **parts, parting, parted.** **1** If things that are next to each other **part** or if you **part** them, they move in opposite directions, so that there is a space between them. *He crossed to the window of the sitting-room and parted the curtains.* **2** If you **part** your hair in the middle or at one side, you comb it in two different directions so that there is a straight line running from the front of your head to the back. *His hair was slicked back and neatly parted.* **3** When two people **part**, they leave each other. *He has confirmed he is parting from his Swedish-born wife Eva.* ● **to part company**: see **company**. **4** If you **are parted from** someone you love, you are prevented from being with them. *I don't believe Lotte and I will ever be parted.* **5** See also **parting**.

part with. If you **part with** something that is valuable or that you would prefer to keep, you give it or sell it to someone else. *He parted with much of his collection to pay his gardening bills.*

part- /pɑːt-/. **Part-** combines with adjectives, nouns, and verbs to mean partly but not completely the thing mentioned. ...*part-baked breads and rolls.* ...*a part-human part-ape fossil... Some associations provide homes to buy or part-buy.*

par·take /pɑːˈteɪk/ **partakes, partaking, partook, partaken.** **1** If you **partake of** food or drink, you eat or drink some of it. *Miss Janie Keane? Did you partake of the crisps?* **2** If you **partake in** an activity, you take part in it. *He decided to partake in a little morning exercise.*

,**part ex'change;** also spelled **part-exchange.** If you give an old item in **part exchange** for something you are buying, the seller accepts the old item as a partial payment, so reducing the amount of money you have to pay.

par·tial /ˈpɑːʃəl/. **1** You use **partial** to refer to something that is not complete or whole. ...*a partial ban on the use of cars in the city.* **2** If you are **partial to** something, you like it. *I am partial to baking cookies.* ♦ **par·tial·ity** /ˌpɑːʃiˈælɪti/ *He has a great*

partiality for chocolate biscuits. **3** Someone who is **partial** supports a particular person or thing, for example in a competition or dispute, when they should be completely fair and unbiased. ♦ **partiality** *She is criticized by some others for her one-sidedness and partiality.*

par·tial·ly /ˈpɑːʃəli/. If something happens or exists **partially**, it happens or exists to some extent, but not completely. *Lisa is deaf in one ear and partially blind.*

par·tici·pant /pɑːˈtɪsɪpənt/ **participants.** The **participants** in an activity are the people who take part in it.

par·tici·pate /pɑːˈtɪsɪpeɪt/ **participates, participating, participated.** If you **participate** in an activity, you take part in it. ...*special contracts at lower rates for participating corporations.* ♦ **par·tici·pa·tion** /pɑːˌtɪsɪˈpeɪʃən/ ...*participation in religious activities.*

par·tici·pa·tive /pɑːˈtɪsɪpətɪv/. **Participative** management or decision-making involves the participation of all the people engaged in an activity or affected by certain decisions.

par·tici·pa·tory /pɑːˌtɪsɪˈpeɪtəri, AM -tɔːri/. A **participatory** system, activity, or role involves a particular person or group of people taking part in it. *Fishing is said to be the most popular participatory sport in the U.K.*

par·ti·ci·ple /ˈpɑːtɪsɪpəl/ **participles.** In grammar, a **participle** is a form of a verb that can be used in compound tenses of the verb. There are two participles in English: the past participle, which usually ends in '-ed', and the present participle, which usually ends in '-ing'.

par·ti·cle /ˈpɑːtɪkəl/ **particles.** **1** A **particle** of something is a very small piece or amount of it. *There is a particle of truth in his statement.* **2** In physics, a **particle** is a piece of matter smaller than an atom, for example an electron or a proton. **3** In grammar, a **particle** is a preposition such as 'into' or an adverb such as 'out' which can combine with a verb to form a phrasal verb.

'**particle accelerator, particle accelerators.** A **particle accelerator** is a machine used for research in nuclear physics which can make subatomic particles go very fast.

'**particle physics. Particle physics** is the study of the qualities of atoms and molecules and the way they behave and react.

par·ticu·lar /pəˈtɪkjʊlə/. **1** You use **particular** to emphasize that you are talking about one thing or one kind of thing rather than other similar ones. *I remembered a particular story about a postman.* **2** You use **in particular** to indicate that what you are saying applies especially to one thing or person. *Why should he notice her car in particular?* **3** You use **nothing in particular** or **nobody in particular** to mean nothing or nobody important or special, or no one thing or person more than any other. ...*a conversation about nothing in particular.* **4** If a person or thing has a **particular** quality or possession, it is distinct and belongs only to them. *I have a particular responsibility to ensure that I make the right decision.*

5 You can use **particular** to emphasize that something is greater or more intense than usual. *Particular emphasis will be placed on oral language training.* **6** If you say that someone is **particular**, you mean that they choose things and do things very carefully, and are not easily satisfied. *Ted was very particular about the colors he used.* **7** See also **particulars**.

par·ticu·lar·ity /pəˌtɪkjʊˈlærɪti/ **particularities. Particularity** is the quality of being unusual or unique. The **particularities** of something are the unusual features that characterize it. *The values professionals bring to their work are every bit as crucial as the particularities of the work itself.*

par·ticu·lar·ly /pəˈtɪkjʊləli/. **1** You use **particularly** to indicate that what you are saying applies especially to one thing or situation. *Keep your office*

N-UNCOUNT: also a N, N of n
PHRASE
PHRASE FORMAL
N-COUNT
PHRASE
N-SING: poss N in n
PHRASE
PHRASE
PHRASE
PRAGMATICS FORMAL
PHRASE
V-ERG: V n
VERB: V n V-ed
V-RECIP: pl-n V V from n FORMAL
V-RECIP: be V-ed from n pl-n be V-ed
PHRASAL VB V P n
PREFIX
VERB: V of n FORMAL V in n
N-UNCOUNT BRITISH
♦♦♢♢ ADJ
ADJ-GRADED: v-link ADJ to n/-ing
N-UNCOUNT

ADJ: v-link ADJ
N-UNCOUNT
♦♦♢♢ ADV: ADV with cl/ group
♦♦♢♢ N-COUNT
♦♦♢♢ VERB: V in n V-ing
N-UNCOUNT
ADJ-GRADED FORMAL
ADJ
N-COUNT
♦♦♢♢ N-COUNT
N-COUNT TECHNICAL
N-COUNT
N-COUNT
N-UNCOUNT
♦♦♦♢ ADJ: ADJ n
PHRASE
PHRASE
ADJ: ADJ n
ADJ: ADJ n
ADJ-GRADED
N-UNCOUNT: also N in pl FORMAL
♦♦♦♢ ADV: ADV with cl/ group

space looking good, particularly your desk... I often do absent-minded things, particularly when I'm worried. **2 Particularly** means more than usual or more than other things. *I particularly liked the wooden chests and chairs.* ADV: ADV with cl/ group

par·ticu·lars /pəˈtɪkjʊləz/. The **particulars** of something or someone are facts or details about them which are kept as a record. *The nurses at the admission desk asked her for particulars.* N-PLURAL

part·ing /ˈpɑːtɪŋ/ **partings. 1 Parting** is the act of leaving a particular person or place. A **parting** is an occasion when this happens. **2** Your **parting** words or actions are the things that you say or do as you are leaving a place or person. *...his bold parting kiss.* **3** When there is **a parting of the ways**, two or more people or groups of people stop working together or travelling together. **4** The **parting** in someone's hair is the line running from the front to the back of their head where their hair has been combed in opposite directions. The usual American word is **part**. ◇◇◇◇◇ N-VAR / ADJ: ADJ n / PHRASE / N-COUNT BRITISH

'parting shot, parting shots. If someone makes a **parting shot**, they make an unpleasant or forceful remark at the end of a conversation, and then leave so that nobody has the chance to reply. N-COUNT

par·ti·san /ˌpɑːtɪˈzæn, AM -zən/ **partisans. 1** Someone who is **partisan** strongly supports a particular person or cause, often without thinking carefully about the matter. ► A **partisan** is someone who is partisan. **2 Partisans** are ordinary people who join together to fight enemy soldiers who are occupying their country. ◇◇◇◇◇ ADJ-GRADED / N-COUNT / N-COUNT

par·ti·san·ship /ˌpɑːtɪˈzænʃɪp, AM -zən-/. **Partisanship** is support for a person or group without fair consideration of the facts and circumstances. N-UNCOUNT

par·ti·tion /pɑːˈtɪʃən/ **partitions, partitioning, partitioned. 1** A **partition** is a wall or screen that separates one part of a room or vehicle from another. **2** If you **partition** a room, you separate one part of it from another by means of a partition. **3** If a country **is partitioned**, it is divided into two or more independent countries. *Britain was accused of trying to partition the country 'because of historic enmity'.* ► Also a noun. *...fighting which followed the partition of India.* ◇◇◇◇◇ N-COUNT / VERB: V n / VERB: be V-ed / V n / N-UNCOUNT

part·ly /ˈpɑːtli/. You use **partly** to indicate that something happens or exists to some extent, but not completely. *It's partly my fault... I have not worried so much this year, partly because I have had other things to think about.* ◇◇◇◇ ADV: ADV with cl/ group

part·ner /ˈpɑːtnə/ **partners, partnering, partnered. 1** Your **partner** is the person you are married to or are having a romantic or sexual relationship with. **2** Your **partner** is the person you are doing something with, for example dancing with or playing with in a game against two other people. *...a partner in crime.* **3** If you **partner** someone, you are their partner in a game or in a dance. *He will be partnered by Ian Baker, the defending champion... He partnered Andre Agassi to victory.* **4** The **partners** in a firm or business are the people who share the ownership of it. **5** The **partner** of a country or organization is another country or organization with which they have an alliance or agreement. ◇◇◇◇ N-COUNT / N-COUNT / VERB: V n / be V-ed by/ with n / V n to n / N-COUNT / N-COUNT

part·ner·ship /ˈpɑːtnəʃɪp/ **partnerships. Partnership** or a **partnership** is a relationship in which two or more people, organizations, or countries work together as partners. ◇◇◇◇◇ N-VAR

,part of 'speech, parts of speech. A **part of speech** is a particular grammatical class of word, for example noun, adjective, or verb. N-COUNT

par·took /pɑːˈtʊk/. **Partook** is the past tense of **partake**.

par·tridge /ˈpɑːtrɪdʒ/ **partridges.** A **partridge** is a wild bird with brown feathers, a round body, and a short tail. N-COUNT

,part-'time. If someone is a **part-time** worker or has a **part-time** job, they work for only part of each day or week. *I'm part-time. I work three days a week.* ► Also an adverb. *I want to work part-time.* ◇◇◇◇ ADJ / ADV

,part-'timer, part-timers. A **part-timer** is a person who works part-time. N-COUNT

,part 'way; also spelled **part-way. Part way** means part of the way or partly. *She was on the hillside, part way up... It might go part way to repaying the debt.* ADV: ADV after v, ADV prep/adv

par·ty /ˈpɑːti/ **parties, partying, partied. 1** A **party** is a political organization whose members have similar aims and beliefs. Usually the organization tries to get its members elected to the government of a country. *...a member of the Labour party. ...her resignation as party leader.* **2** A **party** of people is a group of people who are doing something together, for example travelling together. *They became separated from their party... She was with a party of sightseers.* **3** A **party** is a social event, often in someone's home, at which people enjoy themselves doing things such as eating, drinking, dancing, talking, or playing games. **4** If you **party**, you enjoy yourself doing things such as going out to parties, drinking, dancing, and talking to people. *After a long evening of partying he looked tired.* **5** One of the people involved in a legal agreement or dispute can be referred to as a particular **party**. *It has to be proved that they are the guilty party.* **6** Someone who **is a party to** or **is party to** an action or agreement is involved in it, and therefore partly responsible for it. *Crook had resigned his post rather than be party to such treachery.* **7** See also **dinner party, garden party, hen party, search party, stag party, third party, working party.** ◆◆◆◆◆ N-COUNT / N-COUNT / N-COUNT / VERB V / N-COUNT LEGAL / PHRASE

party·goer /ˈpɑːtigəʊə/ **partygoers.** A **partygoer** is someone who likes going to parties or someone who is at a particular party. N-COUNT

,party 'line. The **party line** on a particular issue is the official view taken by a political party, which its members are expected to support. *They ignored the official party line.* ◆◇◇◇◇ N-SING

'party piece, party pieces. Someone's **party piece** is something that they often do to entertain people, especially at parties, for example singing a particular song. N-COUNT INFORMAL, BRITISH

,party po'litical. Party political matters relate to political parties. *The debate is being conducted almost exclusively on party political lines.* ◆◇◇◇◇ ADJ: ADJ n

,party political 'broadcast, party political broadcasts. In Britain, a **party political broadcast** is a short broadcast on radio or television made by a political party, especially before an election. N-COUNT

,party 'politics. 1 Party politics is political activity involving political parties. *He had decided to retire from party politics.* **2** If politicians are accused of playing **party politics**, they are criticized for doing something only because they are trying to improve people's opinion of their party, rather than doing it for the benefit of the country. ◆◇◇◇◇ N-UNCOUNT / N-UNCOUNT PRAGMATICS

party pooper /ˈpɑːti puːpə/ **party poopers.** You describe someone as a **party pooper** when you think that they spoil other people's fun and their enjoyment of something; used showing disapproval. N-COUNT PRAGMATICS INFORMAL

pass /pɑːs, pæs/ **passes, passing, passed. 1** To **pass** someone or something means to go past them without stopping. *Jane stood aside to let her pass... I sat in the garden and watched the passing cars.* **2** When someone or something **passes** in a particular direction, they move in that direction. *He passed through the doorway into Ward B... He passed down the tunnel.* **3** A **pass** is a narrow way between two mountains. **4** If something such as a road **passes** along a particular route, it goes along that route. *The route passes through St-Paul-sur-Ubaye... The road passes a farmyard.* **5** If you **pass** something through, over, or round something else, you move or push it through, over, or round that thing. *She passed the needle through the rough cloth... He passed a hand wearily over his eyes.* **6** If you **pass** something to someone, you take it in your hand and give it to them. *he found what he was looking for, and, bending forward, passed the book to* ◆◆◆◆◆ VERB: V n / V-ing / VERB V prep/adv / N-COUNT / VERB V prep/adv / V n / VERB V n prep/adv / VERB V n to n / V n n

Jessica... Pass me that bottle. **7** If something **passes** V-ERG:
from one person to another, the second person then be V-ed from n
has it instead of the first. *His mother's small estate had* to n
passed to him after her death... These powers were be V-ed to n
eventually passed to municipalities. **8** If you **pass** in- VERB
formation **to** someone, you give it to them because it V n to
concerns them. *He passed the letters to the Depart-*
ment of Trade and Industry. ▶ **Pass on** means the PHRASAL VB
same as **pass**. *I do not know what to do with the infor-* V n P
mation if I cannot pass it on... From time to time he V P noun
passed on confidential information to him... He has
written a note asking me to pass on his thanks. **9** If you VERB
pass the ball to someone in your team in a game such V n adv/prep
as football, hockey, or rugby, you kick, hit, or throw it Also V prep/
to them. *Your partner should then pass the ball back to* adv
you. ▶ Also a noun. *Hirst rolled a short pass to Merson.* N-COUNT
10 When a period of time **passes**, it happens and fin- VERB
ishes. *Several minutes passed before the girls were no-* V
ticed. **11** If you **pass** a period of time in a particular VERB
way, you spend it in that way. *The children passed the* V n -ing/adv
time playing in the streets... To pass the time they sang
songs and played cards. **12** If you **pass through** a stage VERB
of development or a period of time, you experience it. V through n
The country was passing through a grave crisis. **13** If VERB
an amount **passes** a particular total or level, it be- V n
comes greater than that total or level. *...the first com-*
pany in their field to pass the £2 billion turn-over
mark.
14 If someone or something **passes** a test, they are VERB
considered to be of an acceptable standard. *Kevin has* V n
just passed his driving test... I didn't pass. ▶ Also a V
noun. *An A-level pass in Biology is preferred for all* N-COUNT
courses. **15** If an examiner or someone in authority VERB: V n
passes something or someone, they declare that they V n adj
are of an acceptable standard. *The medical board*
would not pass him fit for General Service. **16** A **pass** is N-COUNT
a document that allows you to do something. *I got my-*
self a pass into the barracks.
17 When people in authority **pass** a new law or a pro- VERB
posal, they formally agree to it or approve it. *The Esto-* V n
nian parliament has passed a resolution declaring the
republic fully independent. **18** When a judge **passes** VERB
sentence on someone, he or she says what their pun- V n
ishment will be. *Passing sentence, the judge said it all*
had the appearance of a con trick.
19 If you **pass** comment or **pass** a comment, you say VERB
something. *We passed a few remarks about the weath-* V n
er. **20** If something **passes** without comment, or VERB:
passes unnoticed, nobody comments on it, reacts to V without n
it, or notices it. *The cocktails were so sweet that the* V adj
strength of them might pass unnoticed until it was too
late.
21 If someone or something **passes for** or **passes as** VERB
something that they are not, they are accepted as that V for/as n
thing or mistaken for that thing. *Childrens' toy guns*
now look so realistic that they can often pass for the
real thing. ...a woman passing as a man. **22** If some- VERB: V n
one **passes** water or **passes** urine, they urinate.
23 If someone **makes a pass at** you, they try to begin a PHRASE
romantic or sexual relationship with you. INFORMAL
24 See also **passing**. ● to **pass the buck**: see **buck**.
● to **pass judgment**: see **judgment**. ● to **pass the time**
of day: see **time**.
pass around or **pass round**. If a group of people PHRASAL VB
pass something **around** or **pass** it **round**, they each V n P
take it and then give it to the next person. *Serve the* be V-ed P
pudding, and pass around a bowl of yogurt to go with
it... A bottle of whisky was passed around.
pass away. You can say that someone **passed away** PHRASAL VB
to mean that they died, if you want to avoid using the V P
word 'die' because you think it is too blunt.
pass by. If you **pass by** something, you go past it or PHRASAL VB
near it on your way to another place. *A parked car ex-* V P n
ploded as their convoy passed by. V P
pass off. If an event **passes off** without any trouble, PHRASAL VB
it happens and ends without any trouble. *The main* V P adv/prep
demonstration passed off peacefully. BRITISH
pass off as. If you **pass** something **off as** another PHRASAL VB
thing, you convince people that it is that other thing. V n P P n
V P noun P n

I've tried to pass off my accent as a posh convent school
accent.
pass on. **1** If you **pass** something **on** to someone, PHRASAL VB
you give it to them so that they have it instead of you. V n P
There is a risk of passing the virus on... The late Earl V P noun to n
passed on much of his fortune to the Princess. **2** If you V P noun
pass on costs or savings to someone else, you make V n P to n
them pay for your costs or allow them to benefit from Also V n P,
your savings. *It is right to pass the savings on to the* V P noun to n
customer. **3** See also **pass** 8.
pass out. **1** If you **pass out**, you faint or collapse. *A* PHRASAL VB
drink of creme de menthe invariably made her sick. In V P
fact, she passed out on several occasions when trying to
drink it. **2** When a police, army, navy, or air force ca- V P
det **passes out**, he or she satisfactorily finishes his or BRITISH
her training.
pass over. **1** If someone **is passed over** for a job, PHRASAL VB
they do not get the job and someone younger or less usu passive
experienced is chosen instead. *She claimed she was* be V-ed P for n
repeatedly passed over for promotion. **2** If you **pass** Also be V-ed P
over a topic in a conversation or speech, you do not V P n
talk about it. *He largely passed over the government's*
record.
pass round. **Pass round** means the same as **pass** PHRASAL VB
around. BRITISH
pass up. If you **pass up** a chance or an opportunity, PHRASAL VB
you do not take advantage of it. *'I can't pass this up.'* V P noun
She waved the invitation. V n P
pass·able /ˈpɑːsəbəl, ˈpæs-/. **1** If something is a ADJ-GRADED
passable effort or or of **passable** quality, it is satisfactory or quite good. *Ms Campbell speaks passable*
French. ♦ **pass·ably** /ˈpɑːsəbli, ˈpæs-/ *She has al-* ADV-GRADED
ways been quick to pick things up, doing passably
well in school without really trying. **2** If a **road** is ADJ
passable, it is not completely blocked, and people
can still use it.
pas·sage /ˈpæsɪdʒ/ **passages.** **1** A **passage** is a ◆◆◆◇◇
long narrow space with walls or fences on both N-COUNT
sides, which connects one place or room with an-
other. **2** A **passage** is a long narrow hole or tube in N-COUNT
your body, which air or liquid can pass along.
...blocked nasal passages. **3** A **passage** through a N-COUNT
crowd of people or things is an empty space that allows you to move through them. *He cleared a pas-*
sage for himself through the crammed streets.
4 The **passage** of someone or something is their N-UNCOUNT
movement from one place to another. *Yugoslavia*
would not permit the passage of German troops
through its territory. **5** If you are granted **passage** N-UNCOUNT
through a country or area of land, you are given permission to go through it. *Mr Thomas would be given*
safe passage to and from Jaffna.
6 The **passage** of someone or something is their pro- N-UNCOUNT
gress from one situation or one stage in their development to another. *...to ease their passage from Socialist*
to market economies. **7** The **passage** of a bill or act is N-UNCOUNT
the official acceptance of it by a parliament. *It's been*
200 years since the passage of the Bill of Rights. **8** The N-SING:
passage of a period of time is its passing. *...after the* the N of n
passage of eighteen months. **9** A **passage** is a journey N-COUNT
by ship.
10 A **passage** in a book, speech, or piece of music is a N-COUNT
section of it that you are considering separately from
the rest. *He reads a passage from Milton.*
passage·way /ˈpæsɪdʒweɪ/ **passageways.** A ◆◇◇◇◇
passageway is a long narrow space with walls or N-COUNT
fences on both sides, which connects one place or
room with another.
pass·book /ˈpɑːsbʊk, ˈpæs-/ **passbooks.** A **pass-** N-COUNT
book is a small book recording the amount of money you pay in or take out of a savings account at a
bank or building society.
pas·sé /ˈpæˈseɪ/. If you describe something as **passé**, ADJ-GRADED
you think that it is no longer fashionable or that it is PRAGMATICS
no longer effective. *She has publicly proclaimed that*
the Socialist Party is passé and that it is time to cre-
ate a new party.
pas·sen·ger /ˈpæsɪndʒə/ **passengers.** **1** A **pas-** ◆◆◆◇◇
senger in a vehicle such as a bus, boat, or plane is a N-COUNT
person who is travelling in it, but who is not driving

it or working on it. **2 Passenger** is used to describe
something that is designed for travellers, rather
than drivers or goods. ...*a passenger train.* `ADJ: ADJ n`

,passer-'by, passers-by; also spelled **passerby.** ◆◇◇◇
A **passer-by** is a person who is walking past some- `N-COUNT`
one or something. *A passer-by described what he
saw moments after the car bomb had exploded.*

pas·sim /'pæsɪm/. In indexes and notes, **passim** indicates that a particular name or subject occurs frequently throughout a piece of writing or section of a
book. ...*The Theories of their Relation (London,
1873), p. 8 and passim.*

pass·ing /'pɑːsɪŋ, 'pæs-/. **1** A **passing** fashion, ac- ◆◆◇◇
tivity, or feeling lasts for only a short period of time `ADJ: ADJ n`
and is not worth taking very seriously. *He had never
taken more than a passing interest in the girl.*
2 The **passing** of an empire, era, or custom is the fact `N-SING`
of its coming to an end. *East Germany as a state is on* `with poss`
the point of disappearing. Few will mourn its passing.
3 Someone's **passing** is their death. ...*the passing of* `N-SING`
one of this century's great artists, Miles Davis. **4** The `N-SING:`
passing of a period of time is the fact or process of its `the N of n`
going by. *The passing of time brought a sense of empti-
ness.* **5** If something changes **with each passing year** `PHRASE`
or **with every passing day,** it changes continuously.
6 A **passing** mention or reference is brief and is made `ADJ: ADJ n`
while you are talking or writing about something else.
It was just a passing comment. ● If you mention `PHRASE`
something **in passing,** you mention it briefly while
you are talking or writing about something else. *The
army is only mentioned in passing.* **7** See also **pass.**

pas·sion /'pæʃən/ **passions.** **1** Passion is a feeling ◆◆◇◇
of very strong attraction for someone. ...*my* `N-UNCOUNT`
passion for a dark-haired, slender boy named James.
2 Passion is a very strong feeling about something `N-UNCOUNT:`
or a strong belief in something. *He spoke with great* `also N in pl`
passion. **3** If you have a **passion** for something, you `N-COUNT`
have a very strong interest in it and like it very
much.

pas·sion·ate /'pæʃənət/. **1** A **passionate** person ◆◆◇◇
has very strong feelings about something or a strong `ADJ-GRADED`
belief in something. *I'm a passionate believer in
public art. ...his passionate commitment to peace.*
♦ **pas·sion·ate·ly** *I am passionately opposed to the* `ADV-GRADED`
death penalty. **2** A **passionate** person has strong ro- `ADV-GRADED`
mantic or sexual feelings and expresses them in
their behaviour. ♦ **passionately** *He was passion-* `ADV-GRADED`
ately in love with her.

'passion fruit; passion fruit is both the singular `N-VAR`
and the plural form. A **passion fruit** is a small,
round, brown fruit that is produced by certain types
of tropical flower.

pas·sive /'pæsɪv/. **1** If you describe someone as ◆◆◇◇
passive, you mean that they do not take action but `ADJ-GRADED`
instead let things happen to them; used showing `[PRAGMATICS]`
disapproval. *His passive attitude made things easier
for me.* ♦ **pas·sive·ly** *He sat there passively, content* `ADV`
to wait for his father to make the opening move.
♦ **pas·siv·ity** /pæ'sɪvɪti/ ...*the passivity of the public* `N-UNCOUNT`
under communism. **2** A **passive** activity involves `ADJ: ADJ n`
watching, looking at, or listening to things rather
than doing things. ...*the passive enjoyment one gets
from looking at a painting or sculpture.* **3 Passive** `ADJ: ADJ n`
resistance involves showing opposition to the peo-
ple in power in your country by not co-operating
with them and protesting in non-violent ways.
4 In grammar, **the passive** or **the passive voice** is `N-SING:`
formed using 'be' and the past participle of a verb. `the N`
The subject of a passive clause does not perform the
action expressed by the verb but is affected by it. For
example, in 'He's been murdered', the verb is in the
passive. Compare **active.**

,passive 'smoking. Passive smoking involves `N-UNCOUNT`
breathing in the smoke from other people's cigarettes because you happen to be near them.

pas·siv·ize /'pæsɪvaɪz/ **passivizes, passivizing,** `VERB: V n`
passivized; also spelled **passivise** in British English. If you can **passivize** a verb or clause, you can
put the verb in the passive voice.

Pass·over /'pɑːsəʊvə, 'pæs-/. **Passover** is a Jewish `N-UNCOUNT:`
festival beginning in March or April and lasting for `also the N`
seven or eight days.

pass·port /'pɑːspɔːt, 'pæs-/ **passports.** **1** Your ◆◆◇◇
passport is an official document which you need to `N-COUNT`
show when you enter or leave a country. **2** If you `N-COUNT:`
say that a thing is a **passport to** success or happi- `N to n`
ness, you mean that this thing makes success or
happiness possible.

pass·word /'pɑːswɜːd, 'pæs-/ **passwords.** A pass- `N-COUNT`
word is a secret word or phrase that you must know
in order to be allowed to enter a place such as a
military base, or to be allowed to use a computer
system.

past /pɑːst, pæst/ **pasts.** **1 The past** is the time be- ◆◆◆◆◆
fore the present, and the things that have hap- `N-SING:`
pened. *In the past, about a third of the babies born* `the N`
to women with diabetes were lost. ● If you accuse `PHRASE`
someone of **living in the past,** you mean that they
think too much about the past or believe that things
are the same as they were in the past. **2 Past** events `ADJ: ADJ n`
and things happened or existed before the present
time. In literary English, **years past, months past,**
and **days past** are sometimes referred to. *I knew
from past experience that alternative therapies could
help. ...the exploitation of Africa in centuries past.*
3 Your **past** consists of all the things that you have `N-COUNT`
done or that have happened to you. ...*revelations
about his past. ...Germany's recent past.*
4 You use **past** to talk about a period of time that has `ADJ:`
just finished. For example, if you talk about the **past** `det ADJ n`
five years, you mean the period of five years that has
just finished. ...*the momentous events of the past few
days.*
5 If a situation is **past,** it has ended and no longer ex- `ADJ:`
ists. *The worst of the economic downturn is past.* `v-link ADJ`
`LITERARY`
6 The **past tenses** of a verb are the ones used to talk `ADJ: ADJ n`
about things that happened at some time before the
present. In English, the simple past tense is sometimes called the **past tense.** The past tense uses the
past form of a verb, which for regular verbs ends in
'-ed', as in 'They walked back to the car'. See also **past
perfect.**
7 You use **past** when you are stating a time which is `PREP`
thirty minutes or less after a particular hour. For example, if it is **twenty past six,** it is twenty minutes after
six o'clock. ► Also an adverb. *I have my lunch at half* `ADV`
past. **8** If it is **past** a particular time, it is later than that `PREP`
time. *It was past midnight... It's past your bedtime.*
9 If you go **past** someone or something, you go near `PREP`
them and keep moving, so that they are then behind
you. *I dashed past him... A steady procession of people
filed past the coffin.* ► Also an adverb. *An ambulance* `ADV`
drove past. **10** If you look or point **past** someone or `PREP`
something, you look or point at something behind
them. *She stared past Christine at the bed.* **11** If some- `PREP`
thing is **past** a place, it is on the other side of it. *Just
past the Barlby roundabout there's temporary traffic
lights.*
12 If someone or something is **past** a particular point `PREP`
or stage, they are no longer at that point or stage. *He
was well past retirement age.* **13** If you are **past** doing `PREP`
something, you are no longer able to do it, often because you have undergone so much. In particular, if
you are **past caring,** you do not care about something
because so many bad things have happened to you.
*Often by the time they do accept the truth they are past
being able to put words to feelings.* ● If you say that `PHRASE`
someone or something is **past it,** they are no longer `[PRAGMATICS]`
able to do what they used to do. `INFORMAL`
14 If you say that you **would not put it past** someone `PHRASE`
to do something bad, you mean that you would not be
surprised if they did it because you think their character is bad.

pas·ta /'pæstə, AM 'pɑːstə/ **pastas.** Pasta is a type ◆◆◇◇
of food made from a mixture of flour, eggs, and wa- `N-VAR`
ter that is formed into different shapes and then
boiled. Spaghetti, macaroni, and noodles are types
of pasta.

paste /peɪst/ **pastes, pasting, pasted. 1** Paste   ◆◇◇◇
 is a soft, wet, sticky mixture of a substance, which   N-VAR <br> can be spread easily. *...wallpaper paste.*
2 If you **paste** something on a surface, you put glue or   VERB: <br> paste on it and stick it on the surface. *Activists pasted*   V n prep
 up posters criticizing the leftist leaders.   V n with adv
3 Paste is a hard shiny glass that is used for making   N-UNCOUNT <br> imitation jewellery. *...paste emeralds.*
4 See also **pasting**.

pas·tel /'pæstəl, AM pæ'stel/ **pastels. 1** Pastel col-   ◆◇◇◇
 ours are pale rather than dark or bright. *...delicate*   ADJ,
 pastel shades. ...pastel pink. ► Also a noun. *The*   ADJ n,
 lobby is decorated in pastels.   ADJ colour
 N-COUNT
2 Pastels are small sticks of different coloured chalks   N-COUNT <br> that are used for drawing pictures. **3** A **pastel** is a pic-   N-COUNT <br> ture that has been done using pastels.

pas·teur·ized /'pɑːstʃəraɪzd, 'pæs-/; also spelled   ADJ
 pasteurised. Pasteurized milk, cream, or cheese has <br> had bacteria removed from it by a heating process <br> to make it safer to drink or eat.

pas·tiche /pæ'stiːʃ/ **pastiches**. A pastiche is a   ◆◇◇◇
 piece of writing or music in which the style is   N-VAR <br> copied from someone or something else, often in an   FORMAL <br> amusing way. *...an amusing seven-page pastiche of*
 Nabokov's 'Lolita' entitled 'Granita'.
pas·tille /'pæstəl, pæ'stiːl/ **pastilles**. A pastille   N-COUNT <br> is a small round sweet with a fruit flavour.   BRITISH
pas·time /'pɑːstaɪm, 'pæs-/ **pastimes**. A pastime   ◆◇◇◇
 is something that you do in your spare time be-   N-COUNT <br> cause you enjoy it or are interested in it.
past·ing /'peɪstɪŋ/. **1** If something or someone   N-SING <br> takes a **pasting**, they are severely criticized. *John*   INFORMAL,
 Major and Neil Kinnock took a pasting on live TV   BRITISH
 last night. ...the critical pasting that the film re-
 ceived. **2** If a sports team or political party is given   N-SING <br> a **pasting**, they are heavily defeated.   INFORMAL,
 BRITISH
,past 'master, past masters. If you are a **past**   N-COUNT
 master at something, you are very skilful at it be-
 cause you have had a lot of experience doing it.
pas·tor /'pɑːstə, 'pæstə/ **pastors**. In some Protest-   N-COUNT <br> ant churches, a **pastor** is a member of the clergy.
pas·to·ral /'pɑːstərəl, 'pæst-/. **1** The **pastoral**   ◆◇◇◇
 duties of a religious leader are their responsibilities   ADJ: ADJ n <br> to the members of their religious group, especially <br> for members' personal problems rather than mem-
 bers' religious needs. *...the pastoral care of the sick.*
2 If a school offers **pastoral** care, it is concerned   ADJ: ADJ n <br> with the personal needs and problems of its pupils, <br> not just with their schoolwork.
3 A **pastoral** place, atmosphere, or idea is characteris-   ADJ-GRADED: <br> tic of peaceful country life and scenery. *...the pastoral*   ADJ n
 beauty of a park. **4** A **pastoral** way of life is one in   ADJ: ADJ n <br> which people keep animals such as cows and sheep <br> that feed off the land.
,past 'participle, past participles. The **past**   N-COUNT
 participle of a verb is a form which is usually the <br> same as the past form and so ends in '-ed'. A num-
 ber of verbs have irregular past participles, for <br> example 'come' (past participle 'come'). Past <br> participles are used to form perfect tenses and the <br> passive voice, and many of them can be used like <br> an adjective in front of a noun.
'past perfect. The **past perfect** tenses of a verb   ADJ: ADJ n <br> are the ones used to talk about things that hap-
 pened at some time before a specific time. The <br> simple past perfect tense uses 'had' and the past <br> participle of the verb, as in 'She had seen him be-
 fore'. It is sometimes called the **pluperfect**.
pas·tra·mi /pæ'strɑːmi/. Pastrami is strongly sea-   N-UNCOUNT <br> soned smoked beef.
pas·try /'peɪstri/ **pastries. 1** Pastry is a food   ◆◆◇◇
 made of flour, fat, and water that is mixed into a   N-UNCOUNT <br> dough, rolled flat, and baked in the oven. It is used <br> for making pies and flans. **2** A **pastry** is a small cake   N-COUNT <br> made with sweet pastry.
pas·ture /'pɑːstʃə, 'pæs-/ **pastures. 1** Pasture is   ◆◇◇◇
 land that has grass growing on it and that is used   N-VAR <br> for farm animals to graze on. *...three acres of pasture*
 and woodland. ...mountain pastures. **2** If someone   PHRASE <br> leaves for **greener pastures**, or in British English

pastures new, they leave their job, their home, or <br> the situation they are in for something they think <br> will be much better. *Michael decided he wanted to*
 move on to pastures new for financial reasons.
pasty, pasties. The adjective is pronounced   ◆◇◇◇
 /'peɪsti/. The noun is pronounced /'pæsti/. **1** If you   ADJ-GRADED <br> have a **pasty** face, you look pale and unhealthy.
2 A **pasty** is a small pie consisting of pastry folded   N-COUNT <br> around meat, vegetables, or cheese. *...meat pasties.*   BRITISH
pat /pæt/ **pats, patting, patted. 1** If you **pat**   ◆◆◇◇
 something or someone, you tap them lightly,   VERB: V n <br> usually with your hand held flat. *'Don't you worry*   V n on n
 about any of this,' she said patting me on the knee.
 ► Also a noun. *...an encouraging pat on the shoul-*   N-COUNT
 der. **2** If you **give** someone **a pat on the back** or if   PHRASE <br> you **pat** them **on the back**, you show them that you <br> think they have done well and deserve to be <br> praised. *The players deserve a pat on the back.*
3 If you say that an answer or explanation is **pat**, you   ADJ-GRADED <br> disapprove of it because it is too simple and sounds as   PRAGMATICS <br> if it has been prepared in advance.
patch /pætʃ/ **patches, patching, patched. 1** A   ◆◆◇◇
 patch on a surface is a part of it which is different   N-COUNT <br> in appearance from the area around it. *...the bald*
 patch on the top of his head. ...two big damp
 patches on the carpet. **2** A **patch** of land is a small   N-COUNT: <br> area of land where a particular plant or crop grows.   with supp
 ...a patch of land covered in forest.
3 A **patch** is a piece of material which you use to cover   N-COUNT <br> a hole in something. **4** If you **patch** something that   VERB <br> has a hole in it, you mend it by fastening a patch over   V n <br> the hole. *He and Walker patched the barn roof.*
5 A **patch** or an **eye patch** is a small piece of material   N-COUNT <br> which you wear to cover an injured eye.
6 If you have or go through **a bad patch** or **a rough**   PHRASE
 patch, you have a lot of problems for a time.   BRITISH
7 If you say that someone or something is **not a patch**   PHRASE
 on someone or something else, you mean that they   INFORMAL, <br> are not nearly as good as the other person or thing.   BRITISH
patch together. If you **patch** something **together**,   PHRASAL VB <br> you form it from a number of parts in a quick hurried   V P noun <br> way. *...to avoid an election by patching together a new*   Also V n P
 government.
patch up. 1 If you **patch up** a quarrel or relation-   PHRASAL VB <br> ship, you try to be friendly again and not to quarrel   RECIP <br> any more. *He has now patched up his differences with*   V P noun
 the Minister... France patched things up with New   V n P
 Zealand. **2** If you **patch up** something which is dam-   V P noun <br> aged, you mend it with a patch. *We can patch up those*   Also V n P
 holes. **3** If doctors **patch** someone **up**, they treat their   V n P <br> injuries, for example by putting bandages on them.   V P noun
 Emergency surgery patched up his face. **4** If people or   INFORMAL <br> countries **patch up** a deal, they manage to agree on it   V P noun <br> after difficult discussions. *Trade ministers patched up*   Also V n P
 a compromise.
patch·work /'pætʃwɜːk/. **1** A **patchwork** quilt or   ◆◇◇◇
 cushion is made by sewing together small pieces of   ADJ: ADJ n <br> material of different colours. ► Also a noun. *For*   N-UNCOUNT
 centuries, quilting and patchwork have been popular
 needlecrafts. **2** If you refer to something as a **patch-**   N-SING
 work, you mean that it is made up of many differ-
 ent parts, pieces or colours. *The low mountains*
 were a patchwork of green and brown.
patchy /'pætʃi/. **1** A **patchy** substance or colour is   ◆◇◇◇
 not spread evenly, but is scattered around in small   ADJ-GRADED <br> quantities. *...thick patchy fog.*
2 If something is **patchy**, it is not completely reliable   ADJ-GRADED <br> or satisfactory because it is not always good. *The evi-*
 dence is patchy.
pate /peɪt/ **pates**. Your **pate** is the top of your   N-COUNT <br> head. *...Bryan's bald pate.*   DATED
pâté /'pæteɪ, AM pɑː'teɪ/ **pâtés**. Pâté is a mixture   ◆◇◇◇
 of meat, fish, or vegetables with various flavourings,   N-VAR <br> which is blended into a paste and eaten cold.
pa·tent /'peɪtənt, AM pæt-/ **patents, patenting,**   ◆◆◇◇
 patented. The pronunciation /'pætənt/ is also used <br> for meanings 1 and 2 in British English. **1** A **patent**   N-COUNT <br> is an official right to be the only person or company <br> allowed to make or sell a new product for a certain

period of time. **2** If you **patent** something, you obtain a patent for it. VERB: V n

3 If you use **patent** to describe something, especially something bad, you are emphasizing that you think its nature or existence is clear and obvious. *This was patent nonsense.* ♦ **pa·tent·ly** *He made his displeasure patently obvious.* ADJ-GRADED PRAGMATICS / ADV-GRADED

patent 'leather. Patent leather is leather or plastic with a shiny surface. It is used to make shoes, handbags, and belts. N-UNCOUNT

pa·ter·nal /pə'tɜːnəl/. **1 Paternal** is used to describe feelings or actions which are typical of those of a father towards his child. *...paternal love.* **2** Your **paternal** relatives are related to you through your father rather than your mother. ♦◇◇◇◇ ADJ-GRADED / ADJ: ADJ n

pa·ter·nal·ism /pə'tɜːnəlɪzəm/. **Paternalism** means taking all the decisions for the people you govern, employ, or are responsible for, thus taking away their own personal responsibility. ♦ **pa·ter·nal·ist, paternalists** *Primo de Rivera himself was a benevolent and sincere paternalist. ...a paternalist policy of state welfare for the deserving poor.* ♦ **pa·ter·nal·is·tic** /pə,tɜːnə'lɪstɪk/ *The doctor is being paternalistic. He's deciding what information the patient needs to know.* N-UNCOUNT / N-COUNT / ADJ-GRADED

pa·ter·nity /pə'tɜːnɪti/. **Paternity** is the state or fact of being the father of a particular child. *He was tricked into the marriage by a false accusation of paternity.* N-UNCOUNT FORMAL

pa'ternity leave. If a man has **paternity leave**, his employer allows him some time off work because his child has just been born. N-UNCOUNT

pa'ternity suit, paternity suits. If a woman starts or takes out a **paternity suit**, she asks a court of law to help her to prove that a particular man is the father of her child, often in order to claim financial support from him. N-COUNT

path /pɑːθ, pæθ/ **paths. 1** A **path** is a strip of ground, usually covered with concrete or gravel, which people walk on. See picture headed **house and flat.** *He went up the garden path.* ♦♦♦◇◇ N-COUNT

2 Your **path** is the space ahead of you as you move along. *A group of reporters blocked his path.* **3** The **path** of something is the line which it moves along in a particular direction. *He stepped without looking into the path of a reversing car.* N-COUNT / N-COUNT: with poss

4 A **path** that you take is a particular course of action or way of achieving something. *The opposition appear to have chosen the path of cooperation rather than confrontation.* **5** You can say that something is in your **path** or blocking your **path** to mean that it is preventing you from doing or achieving what you want. *The Church of England put a serious obstacle in the path of women who want to become priests.* N-COUNT

6 If you **cross** someone's **path** or if your **paths cross**, you meet them by chance. PHRASE

pa·thet·ic /pə'θetɪk/. **1** If you describe a person or animal as **pathetic**, you mean that they are sad and weak and helpless, and they make you feel very sorry for them. *...a pathetic little dog with a curly tail.* ♦ **pa·theti·cal·ly** *She was pathetically thin.* **2** If you describe someone or something as **pathetic**, you mean that they make you feel impatient or angry, often because they are very bad or weak. *What pathetic excuses. ...the pathetic attempts at public speaking made by members of all parties.* ♦ **pathetically** *Five women in a group of 18 people is a pathetically small number.* ♦♦◇◇ ADJ-GRADED / ADV-GRADED / ADJ-GRADED / ADV-GRADED: ADV adj

path·finder /'pɑːfaɪndə, 'pæθ-/ **pathfinders.** A **pathfinder** is someone whose job is to find routes across areas. N-COUNT

patho·gen /'pæθədʒen/ **pathogens.** A **pathogen** is any organism which can cause disease in a person, animal, or plant. ♦ **patho·gen·ic** /,pæθə'dʒenɪk/ *...pathogenic bacteria.* N-COUNT TECHNICAL / ADJ

patho·logi·cal /,pæθə'lɒdʒɪkəl/. **1** You describe a person as **pathological** when they behave in an extreme and unacceptable way, and have very powerful feelings which they cannot control. *He experiences chronic, almost pathological jealousy.* ♦◇◇◇ ADJ-GRADED / ADJ

2 Pathological also means relating to pathology. *...pathological conditions in animals.* MEDICAL

pa·thol·ogy /pə'θɒlədʒi/. **Pathology** is the study of the way diseases and illnesses develop, and examining dead bodies in order to find out the cause of death. ♦ **pa·tholo·gist** /pə'θɒlədʒɪst/ **pathologists.** A **pathologist** is someone whose job is pathology. ♦◇◇◇ N-UNCOUNT MEDICAL / N-COUNT

pa·thos /'peɪθɒs/. **Pathos** is a quality in a situation, film, or play that makes people feel sadness and pity. *...the pathos of man's isolation.* ♦◇◇◇ N-UNCOUNT

path·way /'pɑːθweɪ, 'pæθ-/ **pathways. 1** A **pathway** is a path which you can walk along or a route which you can take. *Richard was coming up the pathway.* **2** A **pathway** is a particular course of action or a way of achieving something. *Diplomacy will smooth your pathway to success.* ♦◇◇◇ N-COUNT / N-COUNT

pa·tience /'peɪʃəns/. **1** If you have **patience**, you are able to stay calm and not get annoyed, for example when something takes a long time, or when someone is not doing what you want them to do. *He doesn't have the patience to wait.* **2** If someone **tries** your **patience** or **tests** your **patience**, they annoy you so much that it is very difficult for you to stay calm. ♦♦◇◇ N-UNCOUNT / PHRASE

3 Patience is also a card game for only one player; the American word is **solitaire**. N-UNCOUNT BRITISH

pa·tient /'peɪʃənt/ **patients. 1** A **patient** is a person who is receiving medical treatment from a doctor or hospital. A **patient** is also someone who is registered with a particular doctor. *The earlier the treatment is given, the better the patient's chances.* ♦♦♦◇ N-COUNT

2 If you are **patient**, you stay calm and do not get annoyed, for example when something takes a long time, or when someone is not doing what you want them to do. *Please be patient – your cheque will arrive.* ♦ **pa·tient·ly** *She waited patiently for Frances to finish talking.* ADJ-GRADED / ADV-GRADED: ADV with v

pati·na /'pætɪnə/. **1** A **patina** is a thin layer of something that has formed on the surface of something. *He allowed a fine patina of old coffee to develop around the inside of the mug.* **2** The **patina** on an antique or other old object is a soft shine that develops on its surface as it grows older. **3** If you say that someone has a **patina** of a quality or characteristic, you mean that they have a small amount of this quality or characteristic. *...a superficial patina of knowledge.* N-SING: with supp WRITTEN / N-SING: with supp / N-SING: with supp LITERARY

pa·tio /'pætiəʊ/ **patios.** A **patio** is an area of paving or concrete in a garden, where people can sit to eat or relax. ♦◇◇◇ N-COUNT

patio 'door, patio doors. Patio doors are glass doors that lead onto a patio. N-COUNT

pa·tis·serie /pə'tiːsəri, AM -'tɪs-/ **patisseries. 1** A **patisserie** is a shop where cakes and pastries are sold. **2 Patisserie** refers to cakes and pastries. *Blois is famous for patisserie.* N-COUNT / N-UNCOUNT: also N in pl

pat·ois /'pætwɑː/; **patois** is both the singular and the plural form. The singular form is pronounced /'pætwɑː/, the plural form is pronounced /'pætwɑːz/. **1** A **patois** is an unwritten form of a language, especially French, that is spoken in a particular area of a country. **2** A **patois** is a language that has developed from a mixture of other languages. N-VAR / N-VAR

pa·tri·arch /'peɪtriɑːk/ **patriarchs. 1** A **patriarch** is the male head of a family or tribe. *The patriarch of the house, Mr Jawad, rules it with a ferocity renowned throughout the neighbourhood.* **2** A **patriarch** is the head of one of a number of Eastern Christian Churches. *...the new head of the Russian Orthodox church, Patriarch Alexei the Second.* ♦◇◇◇ N-COUNT / N-COUNT; N-TITLE

pa·tri·ar·chal /,peɪtriˈɑːkəl/. A **patriarchal** society, family, or system is one in which the men have all or most of the power and importance. *She is a classic victim of the patriarchal society.* ♦◇◇◇ ADJ-GRADED

pa·tri·ar·chy /'peɪtriɑːki/ **patriarchies. 1 Patriarchy** is a system in which men have all or most of the power and importance in a society or group. **2** A **patriarchy** is a patriarchal society. ♦◇◇◇ N-UNCOUNT / N-COUNT

P

pa·tri·cian /pəˈtrɪʃən/ **patricians. 1** A **patrician** is ◆◇◇◇◇
a person who comes from a family of high social   N-COUNT
rank. **2** If you describe someone as **patrician**, you   FORMAL
mean that they behave in a sophisticated way, and   ADJ-GRADED
look as though they are from a high social rank. *He
was a lean, patrician gent in his early sixties.*

pat·ri·mo·ny /ˈpætrɪməni, AM -məʊni/ **1** Someone's   N-SING
patrimony is the possessions that they have inherit-   FORMAL
ed from their father or ancestors. *I left my parents'
house, relinquished my estate and my patrimony.*
2 A country's **patrimony** is its national treasures   N-SING
and works of art.   FORMAL

pa·tri·ot /ˈpætriət, ˈpeɪt-/ **patriots.** Someone who ◆◇◇◇
is a **patriot** loves their country and feels very loyal   N-COUNT
towards it. ◆ **pat·ri·ot·ic** /ˌpætriˈɒtɪk, ˌpeɪt-/   ADJ-GRADED
Woosnam is fiercely patriotic.

pat·ri·ot·ism /ˈpætriətɪzəm, ˈpeɪt-/. **Patriotism** is ◆◇◇◇◇
love for your country and loyalty towards it. *...a*   N-UNCOUNT
*country boy who had joined the army out of a sense
of patriotism.*

pa·trol /pəˈtrəʊl/ **patrols, patrolling, patrolled.** ◆◆◇◇◇
1 When soldiers, police, or guards **patrol** an area or   VERB: V n
building, they move around it in order to make sure
that there is no trouble there. ► Also a noun. *He*   N-COUNT
failed to return from a patrol. **2** Soldiers, police, or   PHRASE
guards who are **on patrol** are patrolling an area. **3** A   N-COUNT
patrol is a group of soldiers or vehicles that are patrolling an area.

pa·trol car, patrol cars. A **patrol car** is a police   N-COUNT
car used for patrolling streets and highways.

patrol·man /pəˈtrəʊlmən/ **patrolmen. 1** A **patrol-**   N-COUNT
man is a uniformed policeman who patrols a par-   AMERICAN
ticular area. **2** A **patrolman** is a person employed   N-COUNT
by a motorists' association who is based in a par-   BRITISH
ticular area and goes to help motorists when, for example, their cars break down.

pa·tron /ˈpeɪtrən/ **patrons. 1** A **patron** is a person ◆◆◇◇◇
who supports and gives money to artists, writers, or   N-COUNT:
musicians. *Catherine the Great was a patron of the*   with supp
arts and sciences. **2** The **patron** of a charity, group,   N-COUNT:
or campaign is an important person who allows his   with supp
or her name to be used for publicity. *The Princess is
patron of the National AIDS Trust.*
3 The **patrons** of a place such as a pub or a hotel are   N-COUNT
its customers. *He spent the night at the Savoy: like so*   FORMAL
*many of its patrons, he could not resist the exclusively
English cooking.*

pat·ron·age /ˈpætrənɪdʒ, ˈpeɪt-/. **Patronage** is the ◆◇◇◇◇
support and money given by someone to a person   N-UNCOUNT
or a group such as a charity. *...government patronage of the arts.*

pa·tron·ess /ˈpeɪtrənəs/ **patronesses.** A woman   N-COUNT
who is a patron of something can be described as a
patroness.

pat·ron·ise /ˈpætrənaɪz/. See **patronize.**

pat·ron·is·ing /ˈpætrənaɪzɪŋ/. See **patronizing.**

pat·ron·ize /ˈpætrənaɪz, AM ˈpeɪt-/ **patronizes,** ◆◇◇◇◇
patronizing, patronized; also spelled **patronise**
in British English. **1** If someone **patronizes** you,   VERB
they speak or behave towards you in a way which   PRAGMATICS
seems friendly, but which shows that they think   V n
they are superior to you in some way; used showing
disapproval. *Don't you patronize me!.*
2 Someone who **patronizes** artists, writers, or musi-   VERB
cians supports them and gives them money. *The*   V n
Japanese Imperial family patronises the Japanese Art   FORMAL
Association.
3 If someone **patronizes** a place such as a pub or a ho-   VERB
tel, they are one of its customers. *The ladies of Berne*   V n
liked to patronize the Palace for tea and little cakes.   FORMAL

pat·ron·iz·ing /ˈpætrənaɪzɪŋ, AM ˈpeɪt-/; also ◆◇◇◇◇
spelled **patronising.** If someone is **patronizing,** they   ADJ-GRADED
speak or behave towards you in a way that seems   PRAGMATICS
friendly, but which shows that they think they are
superior to you; used showing disapproval. *The tone
of the interview was unnecessarily patronizing.*
◆ **pat·ron·iz·ing·ly** *Schneider patted the girl pat-*   ADV-GRADED
ronizingly on the cheek.

ˌpatron ˈsaint, patron saints. The **patron saint**   N-COUNT
of a place, an activity, or a group of people is a saint
who is believed to give them special help and protection. *...St Nicholas, patron saint of sailors.*

pat·sy /ˈpætsi/ **patsies.** If you describe someone as   N-COUNT
a **patsy,** you mean that they are rather stupid and   PRAGMATICS
are easily cheated or misled by other people, or that   AMERICAN,
they take the blame for other people's actions.   INFORMAL
Davis was nobody's patsy.

pat·ter /ˈpætə/ **patters, pattering, pattered.** ◆◇◇◇◇
1 If something **patters** on a surface, it hits it quickly   VERB
several times, making quiet tapping sounds. *Rain*   V adv/prep
pattered gently outside. **2** A **patter** is a series of   N-SING
quick, quiet, tapping sounds. *...the patter of the
driving rain on the roof.*
3 Someone's **patter** is a series of things that they say   N-SING
quickly and easily, usually in order to entertain peo-
ple or to persuade them to buy or do something. *Fran
began her automatic patter about how Jon had been
unavoidably detained.*

pat·tern /ˈpætən/ **patterns. 1** A **pattern** is the re- ◆◆◆◆◇
peated or regular way in which something happens   N-COUNT
or is done. *All three attacks followed the same pattern... A change in the pattern of his breathing became apparent.* **2** A **pattern** is an arrangement of   N-COUNT
lines or shapes, especially a design in which the
same shape is repeated at regular intervals. *...a
snaking three-dimensional pattern of colored dots.*
3 A **pattern** is a diagram or shape that you can use   N-COUNT
as a guide when you are making something such as
a model or a piece of clothing. *...sewing patterns.*

pat·terned /ˈpætənd/. **1** Something that is **pat-** ◆◇◇◇◇
terned is covered with a pattern or design. *...a*   ADJ
strange bird with beautiful patterned plumage. **2** If   V-PASSIVE:
something new **is patterned** on something else that   be V-ed on/
already exists, it is deliberately made so that it has   aftern
similar features. *My intimate relationships were pat-*   AMERICAN
terned on what I had had with my mother.

pat·tern·ing /ˈpætənɪŋ/. **1 Patterning** is the form-   N-UNCOUNT
ing of fixed ways of behaving or of doing things by   FORMAL
constantly repeating an action or by copying other
people. **2** You can refer to lines, spots, or other pat-   N-UNCOUNT
terns as **patterning.**

pau·ci·ty /ˈpɔːsɪti/. If you say that there is a **paucity**   N-SING:
of something, you mean that there is an insufficient   N of n
amount of it. *Even the film's impressive finale can't*   FORMAL
hide the first hour's paucity of imagination.

paunch /pɔːntʃ/ **paunches.** If a man has a   N-COUNT
paunch, he has a fat stomach.

pau·per /ˈpɔːpə/ **paupers.** A **pauper** is a very poor   N-COUNT
person.   FORMAL

pause /pɔːz/ **pauses, pausing, paused. 1** If ◆◆◆◇◇
you **pause** while you are doing something, you stop   VERB
for a short period and then continue. *'It's rather em-*   V
barrassing,' he began, and paused... He talked for   V forn
two hours without pausing for breath. ► Also a   N-COUNT
noun. *There was a pause while the barmaid set
down two plates in front of us.* **2** If something **gives**   PHRASE
you **pause for thought,** it makes you think carefully
about something, or think about it in a different
way.

pave /peɪv/ **paves, paving, paved. 1** If a road or ◆◆◇◇◇
an area of ground **has been paved,** it has been cov-   VERB:
ered with blocks of stone or concrete. **2** If one thing   be V-ed
paves the way for another, it makes the other thing   PHRASE
possible or more likely. *...a new proposal intended*   JOURNALISM
*to pave the way for the signing of a chemical weap-
ons reduction agreement.*

pave·ment /ˈpeɪvmənt/ **pavements. 1** A **pave-** ◆◆◇◇◇
ment is a path with a hard surface, usually by the   N-COUNT
side of a road. The usual American word is **side-**   BRITISH
walk. 2 The **pavement** is the hard surface of a road.   N-COUNT
The car spun on the slippery pavement.   AMERICAN

pa·vil·ion /pəˈvɪliən/ **pavilions. 1** A **pavilion** is a ◆◇◇◇◇
building on the edge of a sports field where players   N-COUNT
can change their clothes and wash. **2** A **pavilion** is a   BRITISH
large temporary structure such as a tent, which is   N-COUNT
used at outdoor public events. *...the United States
pavilion at the Expo '70 exhibition in Japan.* **3** A   N-COUNT
pavilion is an ornamental building in a garden or
park.

pav·ing /ˈpeɪvɪŋ/. **Paving** is a paved area or surface. N-UNCOUNT

'paving stone, paving stones. Paving stones N-COUNT
are flat pieces of stone, usually square in shape, that BRITISH
are used for making pavements.

pav·lo·va /pævˈləʊvə/ **pavlovas**. A **pavlova** is a N-VAR
dessert that consists of a meringue base with fruit
and whipped cream on top.

paw /pɔː/ **paws, pawing, pawed. 1** The **paws** of ◆◇◇◇
an animal such as a cat, dog, or bear are its feet. N-COUNT
The falling cat instinctively spreads its paws and tail.
2 If an animal **paws** something, it rubs or hits it VERB: V n
with its paw or hoof. *The dogs continued to paw and* V at n
claw frantically at the chain mesh. **3** You can de- N-COUNT
scribe someone's hand as their **paw**, especially if it
is very large or if they are very clumsy. **4** If one per- VERB: V n
son **paws** another, they touch or stroke them in a PRAGMATICS
way that the other person finds offensive. *He pawed* V at n
at my jacket with his free hand.

pawn /pɔːn/ **pawns, pawning, pawned. 1** If ◆◇◇◇
you **pawn** something that you own, you leave it VERB: V n
with a pawnbroker, who gives you money for it and
who can sell it if you do not pay back the money
before a certain time. **2** In chess, a **pawn** is the N-COUNT
smallest and least valuable playing piece. Each player has eight pawns at the start of the game. **3** If you N-COUNT
say that someone is using you as a **pawn**, you mean
that they are using you for their own advantage.
They are the pawns in the power game played by
their unseen captors.

pawn·broker /ˈpɔːnbrəʊkə/ **pawnbrokers**. A N-COUNT
pawnbroker is a person who will lend you money if
you give them something that you own. The pawnbroker can sell that thing if you do not pay back the
money before a certain time.

'pawn shop, pawn shops; also **pawnshop**. A N-COUNT
pawn shop is a pawnbroker's shop.

paw·paw /ˈpɔːpɔː/ **pawpaws;** also spelled **paw-** N-VAR
paw. A **pawpaw** is a fruit with green skin, sweet yellow flesh, and black seeds that grows in the West
Indies.

pay /peɪ/ **pays, paying, paid. 1** When you **pay** an ◆◆◆◆
amount of money to someone, you give it to them VERB:
because you are buying something from them or V n to n
because you owe it to them. When you **pay** some- V for n
thing such as a bill or a debt, you pay the amount V n
that you owe. *Accommodation is free – all you pay* V adv/prep
for is breakfast and dinner... She paid £300,000 for Also V to-inf,
the 34-room mansion... The wealthier may have to V n to-inf
pay a little more in taxes... You can pay by credit
card. **2** When you are **paid**, you get your wages or VERB
salary from your employer. *The lawyer was paid a* be/get V-ed n
huge salary... I get paid monthly... They could wan- get/be V-ed
der where they wished and take jobs from who paid adv
best. **3** Your **pay** is the money that you get from V adv
your employer as wages or salary. *...the workers' de-* N-UNCOUNT
mand for a twenty per cent pay rise. **4** If you **are** VERB:
paid to do something, someone gives you some be V-ed to-inf
money so that you will do it. *If you help me, I'll pay* V n n
you anything.
5 If a government or organization makes someone VERB
pay for something, it makes them responsible for pro- V for n
viding the money for it, for example by increasing Also V
prices or taxes. *...a legally binding international treaty*
that establishes who must pay for environmental
damage. **6** If a job, deal, or investment **pays**, it brings VERB: V n
you a profit or some money. *We're stuck in jobs that* V adv
don't pay very well. **7** When you **pay** money into a VERB:
bank account, you put the money in the account. V n into n
There is nothing more annoying than queueing when V n with adv
you only want to pay in a few cheques.
8 If a course of action **pays**, it results in some advan- VERB:
tage or benefit for you. *It pays to invest in protective* it V to-inf
clothing. **9** If you **pay** for something that you do or VERB:
have, you suffer as a result of it. *Why should I pay the* V n for n
penalty for somebody else's mistake?... It's a small price Also V
to pay for the pleasure of living in this delightful house.
10 You use **pay** with some nouns, for example in the VERB
expressions **pay a visit** and **pay attention**, to indicate V n n
that something is given or done. *Do pay us a visit next* V n to n
time you're in Birmingham... He felt a heavy bump, Also V n

but paid no attention to it. **11 Pay television** consists ADJ: ADJ n
of programmes and channels which are not part of an
ordinary public broadcasting system, and for which
viewers have to pay a special fee or subscription.
12 If something that you buy or invest in **pays for it-** PHRASE
self after a period of time, the money you gain from it,
or save because you have it, is greater than the
amount you originally spent or invested. **13** If you say PHRASE
that someone is **in the pay of** a certain person or PRAGMATICS
group, you disapprove of the fact that they are being
paid by and are working for that person or group, often secretly or illegally. *He was murdered at a presi-*
dential rally by gunmen in the pay of drug traffickers.
14 If you **pay** your **way**, you have or earn enough PHRASE
money to pay for what you need, without needing
other people to give or lend you money. *I went to col-*
lege anyway, as a part-time student, paying my own
way.
15 See also **paid; sick pay. ●** to **pay dividends**: see
dividend. ● to **pay through the nose**: see **nose.**

pay back. 1 If you **pay back** some money that you PHRASAL VB
have borrowed or taken from someone, you give them V P n
an equal sum of money at a later time. *I'll pay you* V n P n
back that two quid tomorrow. **2** If you **pay** someone V P for n
back for doing something unpleasant to you, you take Also V n P
your revenge on them. *Some day I'll pay you back for*
this!

pay off. 1 If you **pay off** a debt, you give someone all PHRASAL VB
the money that you owe them. *It would take him the* V P noun
rest of his life to pay off that loan.* **2** If you **pay** some- V P n
one **off**, you give them the amount of money that you V P noun
owe them or that they are asking for, so that they will
not take action against you or cause you any trouble.
There was no point in paying off the boy if he was going
to give evidence to police. **3** If an action **pays off**, it is V P
successful or profitable after a period of time. *Sandra*
was determined to become a doctor and her persistence
paid off. **4** See also **payoff.**

pay out. 1 If you **pay out** money, especially a large PHRASAL VB
amount, you spend it on something. *...football clubs* V P n for/to n
who pay out millions of pounds for players. **2** When an Also V P n
insurance policy **pays out**, the holder of the policy re- V P
ceives the money that he or she is entitled to receive.
3 See also **payout.**

pay up. If you **pay up**, you give someone the money PHRASAL VB
that you owe them or that they are entitled to, even V P
though you would prefer not to give it.

pay·able /ˈpeɪəbəl/. **1** If an amount of money is ◆◇◇◇
payable, it has to be paid or it can be paid. *Pur-* ADJ
chase tax was not payable on goods for export. **2** If a ADJ:
cheque or postal order is made **payable to** you, it v n ADJ,
has your name written on it to indicate that you are n ADJ,
the person who will receive the money. ADJ to n

pay·back /ˈpeɪbæk/ **paybacks;** also **pay-back.** You N-COUNT
can use **payback** to refer to the profit or benefit that AMERICAN
you obtain from something that you have spent
money, time, or effort on. *There is always a substan-*
tial payback in terms of employee and union rela-
tions.

'pay cheque, pay cheques; spelled **paycheck** in N-COUNT
American English. Your **pay cheque** is a piece of paper that your employer gives you as your wages or
salary, and which you can then cash at a bank. You
can also use **pay cheque** as a way of referring to
your wages or salary.

'pay day, pay days; also spelled **payday. Pay day** N-UNCOUNT
is the day of the week or month on which you re- also N in pl
ceive your wages or salary.

PAYE /ˌpiː eɪ waɪ ˈiː/. In Britain, **PAYE** is a system of N-UNCOUNT
paying income tax in which your employer deducts
tax from your wages and pays it directly to the government; PAYE is an abbreviation for 'pay as you
earn'.

payee /peɪˈiː/ **payees**. The **payee** of a cheque, or of N-COUNT
a document authorizing payment, is the person FORMAL
who receives the cheque or payment.

pay·er /ˈpeɪə/ **payers. 1** You can refer to someone ◆◇◇◇
as a **payer** if they pay a particular kind of bill or fee. N-COUNT
For example, a mortgage **payer** is someone who
pays a mortgage. **●** See also **ratepayer, taxpayer.**

2 A good **payer** pays you quickly or pays you a lot of money. A bad **payer** takes a long time to pay you, or does not pay you very much. `N-COUNT: adj N`

paying 'guest, paying guests. A paying guest is a person who pays to stay with someone in their home, usually for a short time. `N-COUNT`

pay·load /ˈpeɪləʊd/ **payloads. 1** The **payload** of an aircraft or spaceship is the amount of things or people that it is carrying. *With these very large passenger payloads one question looms above all others – safety.* **2** The **payload** of a missile or similar weapon is the quantity of explosives it contains. `N-VAR TECHNICAL` `N-VAR TECHNICAL`

pay·master /ˈpeɪmɑːstə, -mæst-/ **paymasters. 1** A **paymaster** is a person or organization that pays and therefore controls another person or organization; used showing disapproval. *...the ruling party's paymasters in business and banking.* **2** A **paymaster** is an official in the armed forces who is responsible for the payment of wages and salaries. `N-COUNT PRAGMATICS` `N-COUNT TECHNICAL`

pay·ment /ˈpeɪmənt/ **payments. 1** A **payment** is an amount of money that is paid to someone, or the act of paying this money. *Thousands of its customers are in arrears with loans and mortgage payments.* **2** **Payment** is the act of paying money to someone or of being paid. **3** See also **balance of payments, down payment.** `◆◆◆◆◇ N-COUNT` `N-UNCOUNT`

pay·off /ˈpeɪɒf/ **payoffs;** also spelled **pay-off. 1** The **payoff** from an action is the advantage or benefit that you get from it. *The payoffs from such a breakthrough would be enormous.* **2** A **payoff** is a payment which is made to someone, often secretly or illegally, so that they will not cause trouble. **3** A **payoff** is a payment made to someone when they have been dismissed from their job. `◆◇◇◇◇ N-COUNT` `N-COUNT` `N-COUNT`

pay·out /ˈpeɪaʊt/ **payouts;** also spelled **pay-out.** A **payout** is a sum of money, especially a large one, that is paid to someone, for example by an insurance company or as a prize. `◆◇◇◇◇ N-COUNT`

'pay packet, pay packets. Your **pay packet** is the envelope containing your wages, which your employer gives you at the end of every week. **Pay packet** can also be used to refer to someone's wages or salary. The American term is **pay envelope.** `N-COUNT BRITISH`

pay-per-'view. A **pay-per-view** television station charges viewers for each film or programme that they watch. `ADJ: ADJ n`

pay·phone /ˈpeɪfəʊn/ **payphones;** also spelled **pay phone.** A **payphone** is a telephone which you need to put coins or a card in before you can make a call. `N-COUNT`

pay·roll /ˈpeɪrəʊl/ **payrolls.** The people on the **payroll** of a company or an organization are the people who work for it and are paid by it. `◆◇◇◇◇ N-COUNT`

PC /ˌpiːˈsiː/ **PCs. 1** In Britain, a **PC** is a male police officer of the lowest rank. **PC** is an abbreviation for **police constable. 2** A **PC** is a small computer that is usually used by one person in a small business, a school, or in their own home. **PC** is an abbreviation for **personal computer. 3** If you say that someone is **PC,** you mean that their attitudes and language are typical of people who hold left-wing or liberal views; used showing disapproval. **PC** is an abbreviation for 'politically correct'. `◆◇◇◇◇ N-COUNT` `N-COUNT` `ADJ-GRADED PRAGMATICS`

PE /ˌpiːˈiː/. In schools, **PE** is a lesson in which pupils do physical exercises or sport. **PE** is an abbreviation for 'physical education'. `◆◇◇◇◇ N-UNCOUNT`

pea /piː/ **peas.** Peas are small, round, green seeds which grow in pods and are eaten as a vegetable. See picture headed **vegetables.** `◆◆◇◇◇ N-COUNT`

peace /piːs/. **1** If countries or groups involved in a war or violent conflict are discussing **peace,** they are talking to each other in order to try to end the conflict. *Leaders of the two rival factions signed a peace agreement last week.* **2** If there is **peace** in a country or in the world, there are no wars or violent conflicts going on. *The President spoke of a shared commitment to world peace and economic development.* **3** If you approve of disarmament, especially nuclear disarmament, you can use **peace** to refer to cam- `◆◆◆◆◆ N-UNCOUNT` `N-UNCOUNT` `N-UNCOUNT PRAGMATICS`

paigns and other activities designed to promote it. *...two peace campaigners accused of causing damage to an F1-11 nuclear bomber.* **4** If you have **peace,** you are not being disturbed, and you are in calm, quiet surroundings. *One more question and I'll leave you in peace.* **5** If you have a feeling of **peace,** you feel contented and calm and not at all worried. *I know you will never be at peace until you have discovered where your brother is.* **6** If there is **peace** among a group of people, they live or work together in a friendly way and do not quarrel. You can also say that people live or work **in peace with** each other. *...a period of relative peace in the country's industrial relations.* **7** See also **breach of the peace, Justice of the Peace.** `N-UNCOUNT` `N-UNCOUNT` `N-UNCOUNT`

8 If you **hold** or **keep** your **peace,** you do not speak, even though there is something you want or ought to say. **9** If someone **keeps the peace,** they make sure that people behave in an orderly way and do not fight or quarrel with each other. *How did your mother succeed in keeping the peace between these two very different men?* **10** If the law requires you **to keep the peace,** you must behave in an orderly way and not cause any trouble in public. *The demonstrators were bound over to keep the peace.* **11** If you **make peace** with someone or **make** your **peace** with them, you put an end to your quarrel with them, often by apologizing. **12** If something gives you **peace of mind,** it stops you from worrying about a particular problem or difficulty. *He began to insist upon a bullet-proof limousine, just for peace of mind.* **13** If you express the wish that a dead person may **rest in peace,** you are showing respect and sympathy for him or her. *'Rest in peace'* is also sometimes written on gravestones. **14** If you are **at peace with** yourself or **at peace with the world,** you feel calm and contented, and you have no emotional conflicts within yourself or with other people. **15** ● to **disturb the peace:** see **disturb.** `PHRASE FORMAL` `PHRASE` `PHRASE LEGAL` `PHRASE` `PHRASE` `PHRASE PRAGMATICS FORMAL` `PHRASE`

peace·able /ˈpiːsəbəl/. Someone who is **peaceable** tries to avoid quarrelling or fighting with other people. ◆ **peace·ably** *The rival guerrilla groups had agreed to stop fighting and settle their differences peaceably.* `ADJ-GRADED WRITTEN` `ADV-GRADED: ADV with v`

'Peace Corps; also spelled **peace corps.** The **Peace Corps** is an American organization that sends young people as volunteers to help with projects in developing countries. The British equivalent is **VSO.** `◆◇◇◇◇ N-PROPER: the N`

peace 'dividend, peace dividends. The **peace dividend** is the economic benefit that was expected in the world after the end of the Cold War, as a result of money previously spent on defence and arms becoming available for other purposes. `N-COUNT`

peace·ful /ˈpiːsfʊl/. **1** Peaceful activities and situations do not involve war. *They emphasised that their equipment was for peaceful and not military purposes.* ◆ **peace·ful·ly** *The US military expects the matter to be resolved peacefully.* **2** Peaceful occasions happen without violence or serious disorder. *Despite the violence that preceded the elections, reports say that polling was orderly and peaceful.* ◆ **peacefully** *Ten thousand people are reported to have taken part in the protest which passed off peacefully.* **3** Peaceful people are not violent and try to avoid quarrelling or fighting with other people. *...warriors who killed or enslaved the peaceful farmers.* ◆ **peacefully** *They've been living and working peacefully with members of various ethnic groups.* **4** A peaceful place or time is quiet, calm, and free from disturbance. *Mornings are usually quiet and peaceful in Hueytown.* ◆ **peacefully** *Except for traffic noise the night passed peacefully.* **5** Someone who **feels** or **looks peaceful** feels or looks calm and free from worry. *I feel relaxed and peaceful.* ◆ **peacefully** *Would she wake to find Gaston sleeping peacefully at her side?* `◆◆◆◇◇ ADJ-GRADED` `ADV-GRADED` `ADJ-GRADED` `ADV-GRADED: ADV with v` `ADJ-GRADED` `ADV-GRADED: ADV with v` `ADJ-GRADED` `ADV-GRADED: ADV after v` `ADJ-GRADED` `ADV-GRADED`

peace·ful·ly /ˈpiːsfʊli/. If you say that someone died **peacefully,** you mean that they suffered no pain or violence when they died. *He died peacefully on 10th December after a short illness.* `◆◇◇◇◇ ADV: ADV after v PRAGMATICS`

peace·keep·er /'piːskiːpə/ **peacekeepers;** also ◆◇◇◇◇
peace-keeper. **1** Peacekeepers are soldiers who are N-COUNT
members of a peacekeeping force. **2** If you describe N-COUNT
a country or an organization as a **peacekeeper,** you
mean that it often uses its influence or armed forces
to try to prevent wars or violent conflicts in the
world.

peace·keep·ing /'piːskiːpɪŋ/; also **peace-keeping.** ◆◆◇◇◇
A **peacekeeping** force is a group of soldiers, usually N-UNCOUNT
from several different countries, that is sent to a
country where there is war or fighting, in order to
try to prevent more violence. ...*Nigerian warplanes
involved in peace-keeping operations in Liberia.* ...*a
UN peacekeeping mission.*

'peace-loving. If you describe someone as ADJ-GRADED
peace-loving, you mean that they try to avoid quarrelling or fighting with other people. *By and large,
these people are peace-loving, law-abiding citizens.*

peace·mak·er /'piːsmeɪkə/ **peacemakers;** also N-COUNT
spelled **peace-maker** or **peace maker.** You can describe an organization, a country or a person as a
peacemaker when they try to persuade countries or
people to stop fighting or quarrelling. *She was a
powerful peace-maker in local feuds.*

peace·mak·ing /'piːsmeɪkɪŋ/; also **peace-making.** N-UNCOUNT
Peacemaking efforts are attempts to persuade
countries or groups to stop fighting with each other.
*The United States is more than ever the prime mover
in Middle East peace-making.*

peace·nik /'piːsnɪk/ **peaceniks.** If you describe N-COUNT
someone as a **peacenik,** you mean that they are PRAGMATICS
strongly opposed to war and support such causes as INFORMAL
nuclear disarmament.

'peace offering, peace offerings. You can use N-COUNT
peace offering to refer to something that is given or
said to someone as a kind of apology in order to
end a quarrel. *'A peace offering,' Roberts said as he
handed the box of cigars to Cohen.*

peace·time /'piːstaɪm/; also spelled **peace-time.** ◆◇◇◇◇
Peacetime is a period of time during which a coun- N-UNCOUNT
try is not at war. *He served during peace-time as an
intelligence officer in the Navy.* ...*one of the greatest
peacetime Prime Ministers of this country.*

peach /piːtʃ/ **peaches. 1** A **peach** is a soft, round, ◆◆◇◇◇
juicy fruit with sweet yellow flesh and pinky-orange N-COUNT
skin. Peaches grow in warm countries. **2** Something
that is **peach** is pale pinky-orange in colour. ...*a COLOUR
peach silk blouse.* **3** If you describe someone or N-SING
something as a **peach,** you find them very pleasing INFORMAL
or attractive. ...*a peach of a goal from Beardsley.*

peachy /'piːtʃi/ **1** If you describe something as ADJ-GRADED
peachy, you mean that it tastes or smells like a
peach or is similar in colour to a peach. ...*a rich,
peachy dessert wine.* ...*peachy pink.* **2** If you say ADJ-GRADED
that something is **peachy** or **peachy keen,** you AMERICAN,
mean that it is very nice. *Everything in her life is just* INFORMAL
peachy.

pea·cock /'piːkɒk/ **peacocks. 1** A **peacock** is a ◆◇◇◇◇
large bird of the pheasant family. The male has a N-COUNT
very large tail which it can spread out like a fan and
which is marked with beautiful blue and green
spots. **2** If you describe someone as a **peacock,** you N-COUNT
think that they behave in a vain and arrogant way. PRAGMATICS
*He introduced himself as 'the leader' and strutted up
and down like a peacock.*

peak /piːk/ **peaks, peaking, peaked. 1** The ◆◆◆◇◇
peak of a process or an activity is the point at which N-COUNT
it is at its strongest, most successful, or most fully
developed. *The bomb went off in a concrete dustbin
at the peak of the morning rush hour.* ...*a flourishing
career that was at its peak at the time of his death...
Economies have peaks and troughs.* **2** When some- VERB
thing **peaks,** it reaches its highest value or its high- V atn
est level. *Temperatures have peaked at over thirty* V
degrees Celsius... The crisis peaked in July 1974.
3 The **peak** level or value of something is its highest ADJ: ADJ n
level or value. *Calls cost 36p (cheap rate) and 48p
(peak rate) per minute.* **4** Peak times are the times ADJ: ADJ n
when there is most demand for something or most
use of something. *During peak periods, reservations*

are difficult to make at some of the hotels. ● See also
peak time.

5 A **peak** is a mountain or the top of a mountain. ...*the* N-COUNT
snow-covered peaks. **6** The **peak** of a cap is the part at N-COUNT
the front that sticks out above your eyes.

peaked /piːkt/. A **peaked cap** has a pointed or ADJ: ADJ n
rounded part that sticks out above your eyes. ...*a
man in a blue-grey uniform and peaked cap.*

'peak time. Programmes which are broadcast at N-UNCOUNT
peak time are broadcast when the greatest number BRITISH
of people are watching television or listening to the
radio. The usual American term is **prime time.**
...*peak-time television drama.*

peal /piːl/ **peals, pealing, pealed. 1** When bells VERB
peal, they ring one after another, making a musical V
sound. *Church bells pealed at the stroke of midnight.*
▶ Also a noun. ...*the great peal of the Abbey bells.* N-COUNT
2 A **peal** of laughter or thunder consists of a long, N-COUNT
loud series of sounds. ...*great peals of thunder.*

pea·nut /'piːnʌt/ **peanuts. 1** Peanuts are small ◆◇◇◇◇
oval-shaped nuts that grow under the ground. Pea- N-COUNT
nuts are often eaten as a snack, especially roasted
and salted. **2** If you say that a sum of money is **pea-** N-PLURAL
nuts, you mean that it is very small. *The jobs they* PRAGMATICS
offer pay peanuts. INFORMAL

,peanut 'butter. Peanut butter is a brown paste ◆◇◇◇◇
made out of crushed peanuts which you can spread N-UNCOUNT
on bread and eat.

pear /peə/ **pears.** A **pear** is a sweet, juicy fruit ◆◇◇◇◇
which is narrow near its stalk, and wider and N-COUNT
rounded at the bottom. Pears have white flesh and
thin green or yellow skin. See picture headed **fruit.**

pearl /pɜːl/ **pearls. 1** A **pearl** is a hard round ob- ◆◆◇◇◇
ject which is shiny and creamy white in colour. N-COUNT
Pearls grow inside the shell of an oyster and are
used for making expensive jewellery. *I put on the
pearl earrings Daddy had bought me.* ● See also
mother-of-pearl. 2 Pearl is used to describe some- ADJ
thing which looks like a pearl. ...*tiny pearl buttons.*
3 You can describe someone's wise remarks as PHRASE
pearls of wisdom. However, people are usually be- PRAGMATICS
ing insincere when they use this expression; they
are usually indicating that what someone has said is
not wise or helpful at all. *And what is that pearl of
wisdom supposed to mean?*

pearly /'pɜːli/. Something that is **pearly** has a soft, ADJ
smooth, shiny appearance, like a pearl. ...*the pearly
light of early morning.* ▶ Also a combining form. COMB
...*pearly pink lipstick.*

'pear-shaped. 1 Something that is **pear-shaped** ADJ
has a shape like a pear. ...*her pear-shaped diamond
earrings.* **2** If one person describes another person, ADJ
especially a woman as **pear-shaped,** they mean that
they are wider around their hips than around the
top half of their body.

peas·ant /'pezənt/ **peasants.** A peasant is a poor ◆◆◇◇◇
person of low social status who works on the land; N-COUNT
used of people who live in countries where farming
is still a common way of life.

peas·ant·ry /'pezəntri/. You can refer to all the ◆◇◇◇◇
peasants in a particular country as the **peasantry.** N-COLL-SING:
The Communists may have won power largely also no det
through support among the peasantry.

peat /piːt/. Peat is decaying plant material which is ◆◇◇◇◇
found under the ground in some cool, wet regions. N-UNCOUNT
Peat can be added to soil to help plants grow, or
can be burnt on fires instead of coal.

peaty /'piːti/. Peaty soil or land contains a large ADJ-GRADED
quantity of peat.

peb·ble /'pebəl/ **pebbles.** A **pebble** is a small, ◆◇◇◇◇
smooth, round stone which is found on seashores N-COUNT
and river beds.

peb·bly /'pebəli/. A **pebbly** beach or river bed is ADJ-GRADED
covered in pebbles.

pec /pek/ **pecs.** Your pecs are the main muscles in N-COUNT
your chest. INFORMAL

pe·can /'piːkən, AM pɪ'kɑːn/ **pecans.** Pecans are N-COUNT
nuts with a thin, smooth shell that grow on pe-
can nuts are nuts with a thin, smooth shell and
grow on trees in the southern United States and
central America.

pec·ca·dil·lo /ˌpekəˈdɪləʊ/ **peccadilloes** or **pec-**   N-COUNT
cadilloes. Peccadilloes are small, unimportant sins   WRITTEN
or faults. *People are prepared to be tolerant of
extra-marital peccadilloes by public figures.*

peck /pek/ **pecks, pecking, pecked. 1** If a bird   ◆◇◇◇◇
pecks something, it moves its beak forward quickly   VERB: V n
and bites at it. *It was winter and the sparrows were*   V a t n
pecking at whatever they could find... Chickens   V prep/adv
pecked in the dust... These birds peck off all the red   V n with adv
flowers. **2** If you **peck** someone on the cheek, you   Also V
give them a quick, light kiss. ▶ Also a noun. *He gave*   VERB:
me a little peck on the cheek.   V n on n
  N-COUNT

'pecking order, pecking orders. The **pecking**   N-COUNT
order of a group is the order of seniority or power
within the group. *They both came from families fairly far down the social pecking order.*

peck·ish /ˈpekɪʃ/. If you say that you are feeling   ADJ-GRADED
peckish, you mean that you are slightly hungry.   INFORMAL,
  BRITISH

pec·tin /ˈpektɪn/ **pectins. Pectin** is a substance   N-VAR
that is found in ripe fruit. It is used in the manufacture of jam to help it set.

pec·to·ral /ˈpektərəl/ **pectorals.** Your **pectorals**   N-COUNT
are the large chest muscles that help you to move
your shoulders and your arms.

pe·cu·liar /pɪˈkjuːliə/. **1** If you describe someone   ◆◆◇◇◇
or something as **peculiar**, you think that they are   ADJ-GRADED
strange or unusual, sometimes in an unpleasant
way. *Rachel thought it tasted peculiar.* ◆ **pe·cu·liar-
·ly** *His face had become peculiarly expressionless.*   ADV-GRADED
2 If something is **peculiar** to a particular thing, person, or situation, it belongs or relates only to that
thing, person, or situation. *Punks, soldiers, hippies,
and Sumo wrestlers all have distinct hair styles, pe-
culiar to their group.* ◆ **peculiarly** *But cricket, sure-*   ADV-GRADED
*ly, is so peculiarly English that the continentals will
never catch on.* **3** If you say that you **feel peculiar**,   ADJ-GRADED:
you mean that you feel slightly ill or dizzy.   v-link ADJ

pe·cu·li·ar·ity /pɪˌkjuːliˈærɪti/ **peculiarities. 1** A   N-COUNT:
peculiarity that someone or something has is a   with supp
strange or unusual characteristic or habit. **2** A **peculiarity** is a characteristic or quality which belongs or   N-COUNT:
relates only to one person or thing. *...a strange pe-*   with supp
culiarity of the Soviet system.

pe·cu·ni·ary /pɪˈkjuːniəri/, AM -nieri/ **Pecuniary**   ADJ
means concerning or involving money. *She denies*   FORMAL
obtaining a pecuniary advantage by deception.

peda·gog·ic /ˌpedəˈɡɒdʒɪk/. **Pedagogic** means the
same as **pedagogical**.

peda·gogi·cal /ˌpedəˈɡɒdʒɪkəl/. **Pedagogical**   ADJ: ADJ n
means concerning the methods and theory of   FORMAL
teaching. *...teachers' pedagogical skills.*

peda·gogue /ˈpedəɡɒɡ/ **pedagogues.** If you de-   N-COUNT
scribe someone as a **pedagogue**, you mean that   FORMAL
they like to teach people things in a firm way as if
they know more than anyone else.

peda·go·gy /ˈpedəɡɒdʒi/, AM -ɡəʊdʒi/. **Pedagogy** is   N-UNCOUNT
the study and theory of the methods and principles   FORMAL
of teaching.

ped·al /ˈpedəl/ **pedals, pedalling, pedalled;**   ◆◇◇◇◇
spelled **pedaling, pedaled** in American English.
1 The **pedals** on a bicycle are the two parts that you   N-COUNT
push with your feet in order to make the bicycle
move. See picture headed **car and bicycle. 2** When   VERB
you **pedal** a bicycle, you push the pedals around   V n
with your feet to make it move. *She climbed on her*   V adv/prep
*bike with a feeling of pride and pedalled the five mi-
les home... She was too tired to pedal back.* ● See
also **back-pedal, soft-pedal. 3** A **pedal** in a car or   N-COUNT
on a machine is a lever that you press with your
foot in order to control the car or machine. *...the
brake or accelerator pedals.*

'pedal bin, pedal bins. A **pedal bin** is a waste bin   N-COUNT
that has a lid controlled by a pedal.   BRITISH

ped·ant /ˈpedənt/ **pedants.** If you say that some-   N-COUNT
one is a **pedant**, you mean that they are too con-   PRAGMATICS
cerned with unimportant details or traditional rules,
especially in connection with academic subjects;
used showing disapproval. ◆ **ped·ant·ry.** If you ac-   N-UNCOUNT
cuse someone of **pedantry**, you mean that they are
a pedant.

pe·dan·tic /pɪˈdæntɪk/. If you think someone is **pe-**   ADJ-GRADED
dantic, you mean that they are too concerned with
unimportant details or traditional rules, especially
in connection with academic subjects.

ped·dle /ˈpedəl/ **peddles, peddling, peddled.**   ◆◇◇◇◇
1 Someone who **peddles** things goes from place to   VERB: V n
place trying to sell them. **2** Someone who **peddles**   DATED
drugs sells illegal drugs. ◆ **ped·dling** *The war*   VERB: V n
against drug peddling is all about cash. **3** If some-   N-UNCOUNT
one **peddles** an idea or piece of information, they   VERB
try very hard to get people to accept it. Used show-   PRAGMATICS
ing disapproval. *They even set up their own news*   V n
agency to peddle anti-isolationist propaganda.

ped·dler /ˈpedlə/ **peddlers.** British English also
uses the spelling **pedlar** for meanings 1 and 3. **1** A   N-COUNT
peddler is someone who goes from place to place in   AMERICAN
order to sell something. **2** A **drug peddler** is a per-   N-COUNT
son who sells illegal drugs. **3** A **peddler** of informa-   N-COUNT
tion or ideas is someone who frequently expresses   PRAGMATICS
such ideas to other people; used showing disapproval. *...the peddlers of fear.*

ped·es·tal /ˈpedɪstəl/ **pedestals. 1** A **pedestal** is   ◆◇◇◇◇
the base on which something such as a statue   N-COUNT
stands. **2** If you **put** someone **on a pedestal**, you   N-COUNT
admire them very much and think that they cannot
be criticized. If someone is knocked off a **pedestal**
they are no longer admired.

pe·des·trian /pɪˈdestriən/ **pedestrians. 1** A **pe-**   ◆◇◇◇◇
destrian is a person who is walking, especially in a   N-COUNT
town or city, rather than travelling in a vehicle. **2** If   ADJ-GRADED
you describe something as **pedestrian**, you mean   PRAGMATICS
that it is ordinary and not at all interesting; used
showing disapproval. *I drove home contemplating
my own more pedestrian lifestyle.*

pe,destrian 'crossing, pedestrian crossings.   N-COUNT
A **pedestrian crossing** is a place where pedestrians   BRITISH
can cross a street and where motorists must stop to
let them cross. The American word is **crosswalk.**

pe·des·tri·an·ized /pɪˈdestriənaɪzd/; also spelled   ADJ
pedestrianised. A **pedestrianized** area has been   BRITISH
made into an area for pedestrians, not vehicles.

pe,destrian 'precinct, pedestrian precincts.   N-COUNT
A **pedestrian precinct** is a street or part of a town   BRITISH
where vehicles are not allowed.

pe·dia·tri·cian /ˌpiːdiəˈtrɪʃən/. See **paediatrics.**

pe·di·at·rics /ˌpiːdiˈætrɪks/. See **paediatrics.**

pedi·cure /ˈpedɪkjʊə/ **pedicures.** If you have a   N-COUNT
pedicure, you have your toenails cut and the skin
on your feet softened by a medical expert or by a
beautician.

pedi·gree /ˈpedɪɡriː/ **pedigrees. 1** If a dog, cat, or   ◆◇◇◇◇
other animal has a **pedigree**, its ancestors are   N-COUNT
known and recorded. **2** A **pedigree** animal is de-   ADJ
scended from animals which have all been of a particular type, and is therefore considered to be of
good quality. *...pedigree horses.* **3** Someone's **pedi-**   N-COUNT
gree is their background or ancestry. *She had an
impeccable aristocratic pedigree.*

pedi·ment /ˈpedɪmənt/ **pediments.** A **pediment** is   N-COUNT
a large triangular structure built over a doorway or
window as a decoration.

ped·lar /ˈpedlə/ **pedlars.** See **peddler.**

pe·do·phile /ˈpiːdəfaɪl/ **pedophiles.** See **paedophilia.**

pe·do·philia /ˌpiːdəˈfɪliə/. See **paedophilia.**

pee /piː/ **pees, peeing, peed.** When someone   ◆◇◇◇◇
pees, they urinate. ▶ Also a noun. *The driver was*   VERB: V
probably having a pee.   INFORMAL
  N-SING: a N

peek /piːk/ **peeks, peeking, peeked.** If you   VERB:
peek at something or someone, you have a quick   V at n
look at them, often secretly. ▶ Also a noun. *Ameri-*   N-COUNT
*can firms have been paying outrageous fees for a
peek at the technical data.*

peel /piːl/ **peels, peeling, peeled. 1** The **peel** of   ◆◆◇◇◇
a fruit such as a lemon or an apple is its skin. In   N-UNCOUNT
American English, you can also refer to a **peel.**
...grated lemon peel. ...a banana peel. **2** When you   VERB: V n
peel fruit or vegetables, you remove their skins. **3** If   V-ERG
you **peel off** something that has been sticking to a   V n with off/
surface or if it **peels off**, it comes away from the sur-   away
  V off/away

face. *It took me two days to peel off the labels... Most*   V off/from n
of the gold paint had tarnished and was peeling   V-ing
away... Paint was peeling off the walls. ...peeling
blue paint. **4** If a surface **is peeling**, the paint, plas-   VERB
ter, or paper on it is coming away. *The walls were*   V
peeling, the pictures were damp. **5** If you **are peeling**   VERB
or if your skin **is peeling**, small pieces of skin are
coming off your body, usually because you are
sunburnt.

peel off. If you **peel off** a tight piece of clothing, you   PHRASAL VB
take it off, especially by turning it inside out. *She*   V P
peeled off her gloves.   Also V n P

peel·er /'piːlə/ **peelers.** A **peeler** is a tool used for   N-COUNT
removing the skin from fruit and vegetables. See
picture headed **kitchen utensils**. *...a potato peeler.*

peel·ings /'piːlɪŋz/. **Peelings** are pieces of skin   N-PLURAL
peeled from vegetables and fruit.

peep /piːp/ **peeps, peeping, peeped. 1** If you   ◆◇◇◇◇
peep, or **peep at** something, you have a quick look   VERB:
at it, often secretly and quietly. *Now and then she*   V at n
peeped to see if he was noticing her. ▶ Also a noun.   V
'Fourteen minutes,' Chris said, taking a peep at his   N-SING:
watch. **2** If something **peeps** out from behind or un-   a N
der something, a small part of it is visible or be-   VERB
comes visible. *Purple and yellow flowers peeped up*   V prep/adv
between rocks.

peep·hole /'piːphəʊl/ **peepholes.** A **peephole** is a   N-COUNT
small hole in a door or wall through which you can
look secretly at what is happening on the other side.

Peeping 'Tom, Peeping Toms. A **Peeping Tom**   N-COUNT
is someone who secretly watches other people, es-   PRAGMATICS
pecially when those people are undressing; used
showing disapproval.

peep·show /'piːpʃəʊ/ **peepshows.** A **peepshow** is   N-COUNT
a form of entertainment which consists of watching
something, for example moving pictures or a person
dancing or stripping, through a small hole or
window.

peer /pɪə/ **peers, peering, peered. 1** If you **peer**   ◆◆◇◇
at something, you look at it very hard, usually be-   VERB
cause it is difficult to see clearly. *He watched the*   V prep
Customs official peer into the driver's window. **2** A   N-COUNT
peer is a member of the nobility, either by being a   BRITISH
child of aristocratic parents, or by being appointed
by a King or Queen. **3** Your **peers** are the people   N-COUNT
who are the same age as you or who have the same
status as you. *...children who are much cleverer than*
their peers.

peer·age /'pɪərɪdʒ/ **peerages. 1** If someone has a   ◆◇◇◇◇
peerage, they have the rank of a peer. **2** The peers   N-COUNT
of a particular country are sometimes referred to as   N-SING:
the peerage.   the N

peer·ess /'pɪəres/ **peeresses.** A **peeress** is a wom-   N-COUNT
an who is a member of the nobility.

'peer group, peer groups. Your **peer group** is   N-COUNT
the group of people you know who are the same age
as you or who have the same social status as you.

peer·less /'pɪələs/. Something that is **peerless** is so   ADJ-GRADED
beautiful or wonderful that you feel that nothing   FORMAL
can equal it. *...two days of clear sunshine under*
peerless blue skies.

peer of the 'realm, peers of the realm. A **peer**   N-COUNT
of the realm is a member of the nobility who has   BRITISH
the right to sit in the House of Lords.

peeved /piːvd/. If you are **peeved** about something,   ADJ-GRADED
you are annoyed about it.   INFORMAL

peev·ish /'piːvɪʃ/. Someone who is **peevish** is bad-   ADJ-GRADED
tempered.

peg /peg/ **pegs, pegging, pegged. 1** A **peg** is a   ◆◆◇◇
small hook or knob that is attached to a wall or   N-COUNT
door and is used for hanging things on. **2** A **peg** is a   N-COUNT
small device which you use to fasten clothes to a   BRITISH
washing line. The usual American word is
clothespin. 3 A **peg** is a small piece of wood or met-   N-COUNT
al that is used for fastening something to something
else. *He builds furniture using wooden pegs instead*
of nails. **4** If you **peg** something somewhere or **peg**   VERB:
it down, you fix it there with pegs. *Peg down netting*   V n prep/adv
over the top to keep out leaves. ...a tent pegged to the   V n with adv
ground nearby for the kids.   V-ed prep

5 If you say that someone should **be brought down a**   PHRASE
peg or **be taken down a peg**, you mean that they
should be made to realize that they are not as impor-
tant or wonderful as they think they are. **6** Off-the-   PHRASE
peg clothes or other items are bought ready-made   BRITISH
from a shop, and not made specially for a particular
person. *Off-the-peg knitwear never gives a perfect fit...*
Instead of buying bikes off the peg we buy all the bits
and make them up ourselves.

7 If a price or amount of something **is pegged** at a par-   VERB:
ticular level, it is fixed at that level. *The Bank wants to*   be V-ed at n
peg rates at 9%. ● See also **level pegging.**   V n at amount
  JOURNALISM

pe·jo·ra·tive /pə'dʒɒrətɪv, AM -'dʒɔːr-/. A **pejora-**   ADJ-GRADED
tive word or expression is one that expresses criti-   FORMAL
cism of someone or something. *Isn't there a sugges-*
tion that 'poetess' is slightly pejorative?

pe·kin·ese /ˌpiːkɪ'niːz/ **pekineses;** also spelled   N-COUNT
pekingese. A **pekinese** is a type of small dog with
long hair, short legs, and a short, flat nose.

peli·can /'pelɪkən/ **pelicans.** A **pelican** is a type of   N-COUNT
large water bird. It catches fish and keeps them in
the bottom part of its beak which is shaped like a
large bag.

pelican 'crossing, pelican crossings. A peli-   N-COUNT
can crossing is a place where pedestrians can cross   BRITISH
a busy road by pressing a button at the side of the
road, which operates traffic lights to stop the traffic.

pel·let /'pelɪt/ **pellets.** A **pellet** is a small ball of   ◆◇◇◇◇
paper, mud, lead, or other material. *He was shot in*   N-COUNT
the head by an air gun pellet.

pell-mell /ˌpel 'mel/. If you move **pell-mell** some-   ADV:
where, you move there in a hurried, uncontrolled   ADV after v
way. *All three of us rushed pell-mell into the kitchen.*

pel·met /'pelmɪt/ **pelmets.** A **pelmet** is a long, nar-   N-COUNT
row piece of wood or fabric which is fitted at the   BRITISH
top of a window for decoration and to hide the cur-
tain rail. The usual American word is **valance.**

pelt /pelt/ **pelts, pelting, pelted. 1** The **pelt** of   ◆◇◇◇◇
an animal is its skin which can be used to make   N-COUNT
clothing or rugs. **2** If you **pelt** someone **with** things,   VERB
you throw things at them. *Crowds started to pelt po-*   V n with n
lice cars with stones. **3** If the rain **is pelting down**, it   VERB
is raining very hard. *The rain now was pelting*   V adv
down... We drove through pelting rain. **4** If you do   V-ing
something **full pelt** or **at full pelt**, you do it very   INFORMAL
quickly indeed. *He drove his car through the gates at*   PHRASE
full pelt.   INFORMAL

pel·vic /'pelvɪk/. **Pelvic** means near or relating to   ◆◇◇◇◇
your pelvis.   ADJ: ADJ n

pel·vis /'pelvɪs/ **pelvises.** Your **pelvis** is the wide,   ◆◇◇◇◇
curved group of bones at the level of your hips.   N-COUNT

pen /pen/ **pens, penning, penned. 1** A **pen** is a   ◆◆◇◇
long thin object which you use to write in ink.   N-COUNT
● **ballpoint pen:** see **ballpoint.** ● **felt-tip pen:** see
felt-tip. ● See also **fountain pen. 2** If someone **pens**   VERB
a letter, article, or book, they write it. *She penned a*   V n to n
short memo to his private secretary. **3** If you **put pen**   Also V n n
to paper, you write something.   PHRASE

4 A **pen** is a small area with a fence round it in which   N-COUNT
farm animals are kept for a short time. ● See also
playpen. 5 If people or animals **are penned** some-   VB: usu
where, they have to remain in a very small area. *The*   passive
men drove the cattle back to the house so they could be   be V-ed
milked and penned for the night... The goats are   be V-ed in/up
penned in... I don't have to stay in my room penned up   V-ed
like a prisoner.

pe·nal /'piːnəl/. **1 Penal** means relating to the pun-   ◆◇◇◇◇
ishment of criminals. *...penal and legal systems.* **2** A   ADJ
penal institution or colony is one where criminals   ADJ: ADJ n
are imprisoned or kept.

'penal code, penal codes. The **penal code** of a   N-COUNT
country consists of all the laws that are related to   FORMAL
crime and punishment.

pe·nal·ize /'piːnəlaɪz/ **penalizes, penalizing,**   ◆◇◇◇◇
penalized; also spelled **penalise** in British English.   VB: usu
If someone **is penalized** for something, they are   passive
made to suffer some disadvantage because of it.   be V-ed
Some of the players may, on occasion, break the rules   V n
and be penalized... Don't penalize those who have
come on time by waiting for those who are late.

pen·al·ty /ˈpenəlti/ **penalties.** **1** A **penalty** is a ◆◆◆◇◇
punishment for doing something which is against a   N-COUNT
law or rule. *The penalty for travelling without a ticket was one month in prison.* ● See also **death penal-**
ty. **2** In sports such as football, rugby, and hockey, a   N-COUNT
penalty is a free kick or hit at a goal, which is given
to the attacking team if the defending team commit
a foul near their own goal. *Jonathan Davies scored a*
penalty goal. **3** The **penalty** that you pay for some-   N-COUNT
thing you have done is something unpleasant that
you experience as a result. *Their countries are now*
paying the penalty for the neglect into which their
water supply systems have fallen.

penalty area, **penalty areas.** On a football   ◆◇◇◇◇
pitch, the **penalty area** is the rectangular area in   N-COUNT
front of the goal where certain rules apply.   BRITISH

penalty box, penalty boxes. **1** In football, the   N-COUNT
penalty box is the same as the **penalty area.** **2** In   BRITISH
ice hockey, the **penalty box** is an area in which   N-COUNT
players who have been penalized have to sit for a
period of time.

penalty 'shoot-out, penalty shoot-outs. In   N-COUNT
football, a **penalty shoot-out** is a way of deciding   BRITISH
the results of a game that has ended in a draw. Each
team takes penalty kicks in turn until one of them
misses and loses the game.

pen·ance /ˈpenəns/ **penances.** If you do **penance**   N-VAR
for something wrong that you have done, you do
something that you find unpleasant to show that
you are sorry. *The Koran recommends fasting as a*
penance before pilgrimages.

pen and 'ink. A **pen and ink** drawing is done   ADJ
using a pen rather than a pencil.

pence /pens/. See **penny.**

pen·chant /ˈpɒnʃɒn, ˈpentʃənt/. If someone has a   ◆◇◇◇◇
penchant for something, they have a special liking   N-SING:
for it or a tendency to do it. *...a stylish woman with*   N for n/-ing
a penchant for dark glasses.   FORMAL

pen·cil /ˈpensəl/ **pencils, pencilling, pencilled.**   ◆◆◇◇◇
1 A **pencil** is an object that you write or draw with.   N-COUNT:
It consists of a thin piece of wood with a rod of   also in N
graphite in the middle. If you write or draw something in **pencil**, you do it using a pencil. **2** If you   VERB
pencil a letter or a note, you write it using a pencil.   V n
He pencilled a note to Joseph Daniels. ◆ **pen·cilled.**   ADJ
...folded notepaper with the pencilled block letters on
the outside.

pencil in. If an event or appointment **is pencilled in,**   PHRASAL VB
it has been agreed that it should take place, but it will   usu passive
have to be confirmed later. *He told us that the tour*   be V-ed P
was pencilled in for the following March.

pen·dant /ˈpendənt/ **pendants.** A **pendant** is an   N-COUNT
ornament on a chain that you wear round your
neck.

pend·ing /ˈpendɪŋ/. **1** If something such as a legal   ◆◆◇◇◇
procedure is **pending,** it is waiting to be dealt with   ADJ
or settled. *In 1989, the court had 600 pending cases...*   FORMAL
She had a libel action against the magazine pending.
2 If something is done **pending** a future event, it is   PREP
done until that event happens. *A judge has suspend-*   FORMAL
ed a ban on the magazine pending a full inquiry.
3 Something that is **pending** is going to happen   ADJ
soon. *A growing number of customers have been in-*   FORMAL
quiring about the pending price rises.

pen·du·lous /ˈpendʒʊləs/. Something that is **pen-**   ADJ
dulous hangs downwards and moves loosely,
usually in an unattractive way. *...a stout, gloomy*
man with a pendulous lower lip.

pen·du·lum /ˈpendʒʊləm/ **pendulums.** **1** The   ◆◇◇◇◇
pendulum of a clock is a rod with a weight at the   N-COUNT
end which swings from side to side in order to make
the clock work. **2** You can talk about a **pendulum**   N-SING
and the way it swings regularly to express the idea
of regular changes in a situation or in people's
opinions. *The pendulum has swung back and the*
American car companies have made dramatic ad-
vances in safety.

pen·etrate /ˈpenɪtreɪt/ **penetrates, penetrat-**   ◆◆◇◇◇
ing, penetrated. **1** If something or someone **pen-**   VERB
etrates a physical object or an area, they succeed in   V n

getting into it or passing through it. *His men had*
been ordered to shoot on sight anyone trying to pen-
etrate the area. ◆ **pen·etra·tion** /ˌpenɪˈtreɪʃən/   N-UNCOUNT:
penetrations *The water has become clearer, per-*   also N in pl
mitting deeper penetration by the heat of the sun.
2 If someone **penetrates** an organization, a group,   VERB
or a profession, they succeed in entering it although   V n
it is difficult to do so. *...the continuing failure of*
women to penetrate the higher levels of engineering.
3 If someone **penetrates** an enemy group or a rival   VERB: V n
organization, they succeed in joining it in order to
get information or cause trouble. ◆ **penetration**   N-UNCOUNT:
...the successful penetration by the KGB of the French   with supp
intelligence service. **4** If a company or country **pen-**   VERB: V n
etrates a market or area, they succeed in selling
their products there. ◆ **penetration** *...import pen-*   N-UNCOUNT:
etration across a broad range of heavy industries.   with supp

pen·etrat·ing /ˈpenɪtreɪtɪŋ/. **1** A **penetrating**   ◇◇◇◇◇
sound is loud and usually high-pitched. **2** If some-   ADJ-GRADED
one gives you a **penetrating** look, it makes you   ADJ-GRADED
think that they know what you are thinking. *...dark*
penetrating eyes. **3** Someone who has a **penetrating**   ADJ-GRADED
mind understands and recognizes things quickly
and thoroughly. *He never stopped asking penetrat-*
ing questions.

pen-friend, pen-friends; also spelled **penfriend.**   N-COUNT
A **pen-friend** is the same as a **pen pal.**   BRITISH

pen·guin /ˈpeŋgwɪn/ **penguins.** A **penguin** is a   ◆◆◇◇◇
type of large black and white sea bird found mainly   N-COUNT
in the Antarctic. Penguins cannot fly.

peni·cil·lin /ˌpenɪˈsɪlɪn/. **Penicillin** is an antibiotic.   N-UNCOUNT

pe·nile /ˈpiːnaɪl/. **Penile** means relating to a penis.   ADJ: ADJ n
...penile cancer.   FORMAL

pen·in·su·la /pəˈnɪnsjʊlə/ **peninsulas.** A **penin-**   ◆◆◇◇◇
sula is a long narrow piece of land that is joined at   N-COUNT
one part to the mainland and is almost completely
surrounded by water.

pe·nis /ˈpiːnɪs/ **penises.** A man's **penis** is the part   ◆◆◇◇◇
of his body that he uses when urinating and when   N-COUNT
having sex.

peni·tent /ˈpenɪtənt/. Someone who is **penitent**   ADJ-GRADED
shows sincere sorrow and regret about something   LITERARY
wrong that they have done. ◆ **peni·tent·ly** *He sat*   ADV-GRADED:
penitently in his chair by the window. ◆ **peni·tence**   ADV after v
He caused a worldwide sensation by his gesture of   N-UNCOUNT
penitence for past Nazi atrocities.

peni·ten·tia·ry /ˌpenɪˈtenʃəri/ **penitentiaries.** A   N-COUNT
penitentiary is a prison.   FORMAL,
   AMERICAN

pen·knife /ˈpennaɪf/ **penknives.** A **penknife** is a   N-COUNT
small knife with a blade that folds back into the
handle.

pen name, pen names; also spelled **pen-name.**   N-COUNT
A writer's **pen name** is the name that he or she uses
on books and articles instead of his or her real
name.

pen·nant /ˈpenənt/ **pennants.** **1** A **pennant** is a   ◆◇◇◇◇
long, narrow, triangular flag. **2** In baseball, a **pen-**   N-COUNT
nant is a flag that is given to the team that wins a   N-COUNT
league championship.   AMERICAN

pen·nies /ˈpeniz/. **Pennies** is the plural of **penny.**
In Britain, **pennies** is used to refer only to coins.

pen·ni·less /ˈpenɪləs/. Someone who is **penniless**   ◆◇◇◇◇
has hardly any money at all.   ADJ

penn'orth /ˈpenəθ/. During a discussion about   PHRASE
something, if you have your **two penn'orth** or put   BRITISH
in your **two penn'orth,** you add your own opinion,
even when it is unwelcome.

pen·ny /ˈpeni/ **pennies, pence.** The form **pence**   ◆◆◇◇◇
is used for the plural of meaning 1. **1** In Britain, a   N-COUNT
penny is a coin which is worth one hundredth of a
pound, or the amount of money which it is worth.
Cider also goes up by a penny a pint while sparkling
wine will cost another eight pence a bottle. **2** In Brit-   N-COUNT
ain, a **penny** was a coin used before 1971 and was
worth one twelfth of a shilling. **3** In America, a **pen-**   N-COUNT
ny is a coin or an amount that is worth one cent.   INFORMAL
4 If you say, for example, that you do not have a **pen-**   N-SING:
ny, or that something does not cost a **penny,** you are   a N
emphasizing that you do not have any money at all, or   PRAGMATICS
that something did not cost you any money at all. *The*

Brilliantons paid their rent on time and did not owe him a penny. **5** Things that are said to be **two a penny** or **ten a penny** are not valuable or interesting because they are very common and easy to find; used showing disapproval. *Leggy blondes are two a penny in Hollywood.* **6** If you say that something or someone is **worth every penny**, you mean that they are worth all the money that is spent on them. *If you say* **the penny dropped**, you mean that someone suddenly understood or realized something. *'Did he know who you are?'—'I think so. I think the penny dropped.'*   PHRASE PRAGMATICS BRITISH / PHRASE / PHRASE BRITISH

penny 'farthing, penny farthings. A penny farthing was a bicycle that had a very large front wheel and a small back wheel.   N-COUNT BRITISH

'penny-pinching. 1 Penny-pinching is the practice of trying to spend as little money as possible; used showing disapproval. *The bridges have not been painted regularly and this penny-pinching has exposed them to the corroding effects of salt and water.* **2** Penny-pinching people spend as little money as possible; used showing disapproval.   N-UNCOUNT PRAGMATICS / ADJ PRAGMATICS

'pen pal; pen pals; also spelled **pen-pal.** A pen pal is someone you write friendly letters to and receive letters from, although the two of you may never have met.   ◇◇◇◇ N-COUNT

'pen-pusher, pen-pushers; also **penpusher.** If you call someone a **pen-pusher**, you mean that their work consists of writing or dealing with letters, reports, and records, and that it seems pointless or boring to you; used showing disapproval. The American expression is **pencil-pusher.**   N-COUNT PRAGMATICS BRITISH

pen·sion /ˈpenʃən/ **pensions, pensioning, pensioned.** A **pension** is a sum of money which a retired, widowed, or disabled person regularly receives from the state or from a former employer. *I wonder how she would manage on a pension. ...a company pension scheme.*   ◆◆◇◇ N-COUNT

pension off. If someone **is pensioned off**, they are made to retire from work and are given a pension. *When his employees were no longer of use to him, he pensioned them off.*   PHRASAL VB beV-ed P V n P Also V P noun

pen·sion·able /ˈpenʃənəbəl/. **Pensionable** means relating to someone's right to receive a pension. *...civil servants who were nearing pensionable age.*   ADJ: ADJ n

pen·sion·er /ˈpenʃənə/. A **pensioner** is someone who receives a pension, especially a pension paid by the state to retired people. ● See also **old age pensioner.**   ◆◆◇◇ N-COUNT

pen·sive /ˈpensɪv/. If someone is **pensive**, they are thinking deeply about something, especially something that worries them slightly. *He looked suddenly sombre, pensive.* ♦ **pen·sive·ly** *Angela stared pensively out of the window.*   ADJ-GRADED / ADV: ADV with v

pen·ta·gon /ˈpentəgən, AM -gɑːn/ **pentagons.** A **pentagon** is a shape with five sides. See picture headed **shapes.**   N-COUNT

Pen·ta·gon. The **Pentagon** is the headquarters of the US Defense Department in Washington. The US Defense Department itself can also be referred to as the **Pentagon**. *The defence budget has been cut this year and the Pentagon needs to save money.*   ◆◆◇◇ N-PROPER

pen·tam·eter /penˈtæmɪtə/ **pentameters.** A **pentameter** is a line of poetry that has five strong beats in it.   N-COUNT TECHNICAL

pen·tath·lon /penˈtæθlɒn/ **pentathlons.** The **pentathlon** is an athletics competition in which each person must compete in five different events.   N-COUNT

pent·house /ˈpenthaʊs/ **penthouses.** A **penthouse** is a luxurious flat or set of rooms at the top of a tall building. *...his penthouse flat in Chelsea.*   N-COUNT

pent-up /ˌpent ˈʌp/. **Pent-up** emotions have been held back and not expressed. *He still had a lot of pent-up anger to release.*   ◆◇◇◇ ADJ

pe·nul·ti·mate /peˈnʌltɪmət/. The **penultimate** thing in a series of things is the one before the final one. *...in the penultimate chapter.*   ◆◇◇◇ ADJ: det ADJ FORMAL

penu·ry /ˈpenjʊri/. **Penury** is extreme poverty. *He was brought up in penury, without education.*   N-UNCOUNT FORMAL

peo·ny /ˈpiːəni/ **peonies.** A **peony** is a medium-sized garden plant which has large round flowers.   N-COUNT

peo·ple /ˈpiːpəl/ **peoples, peopling, peopled. 1** People are men, women, and children. **People** is normally used as the plural of **person**, instead of 'persons'. *Millions of people have lost their homes. ...the people of Angola.* **2** The **people** is sometimes used to refer to ordinary men and women, in contrast to the government or the upper classes. *...a tremendous rift between the people and their leadership.* **3** A **people** is all the men, women, and children of a particular country or race. *...the native peoples of Central and South America.* **4** If a place or country **is peopled by** a particular group of people, that group of people live there. *It was peopled by a fiercely independent race of peace-loving Buddhists.* **5** If something such as a story or a time in history **is peopled** with people of a particular kind, those people occur or exist in it. *Grass's novels are peopled with outlandish characters.*   ◆◆◆◆ N-PLURAL / N-PLURAL: the N / N-COLL-COUNT / VB: usu passive beV-ed by/ with n / VERB beV-ed with/ by n Also V n LITERARY

pep /pep/ **peps, pepping, pepped.** Pep is liveliness and energy. *...a holiday to put the pep back in their lives.*   ◆◇◇◇ N-UNCOUNT INFORMAL

pep up. If you try to **pep** something **up**, you try to make it more lively, more interesting, or stronger. *...some ideas about pepping up trade in the region.*   PHRASAL VB V n P V P noun INFORMAL

pep·per /ˈpepə/ **peppers, peppering, peppered. 1** Pepper is a hot-tasting spice which is used to flavour food. *...salt and pepper.* **2** A **pepper** is a hollow green, red, or yellow vegetable with seeds. See picture headed **vegetables. 3** If something **is peppered with** small objects, a lot of those objects hit it. *He was wounded in both legs and severely peppered with shrapnel.* **4** If something **is peppered** with things, it has a lot of those things in it or on it. *Yachts peppered the tranquil waters of Botafogo Bay.*   ◆◆◆◇ N-UNCOUNT / N-COUNT / VB: usu passive beV-ed with n / VERB: beV-ed with n V n

pep·per·corn /ˈpepəkɔːn/ **peppercorns.** Peppercorns are the small berries which are dried and crushed to make pepper.   N-COUNT

pep·per·mill /ˈpepəmɪl/ **peppermills.** A peppermill is a container in which peppercorns are ground to make pepper.   N-COUNT

pep·per·mint /ˈpepəmɪnt/ **peppermints. 1** Peppermint is a strong fresh-tasting flavouring that is obtained from the peppermint plant or made artificially. **2** A **peppermint** is a peppermint-flavoured sweet.   ◆◇◇◇ N-UNCOUNT / N-COUNT

pep·per·oni /ˌpepəˈrəʊni/. Pepperoni is a spicy sausage which is often sliced and put on pizzas.   N-UNCOUNT

pep·pery /ˈpepəri/. Food that is **peppery** has a strong hot taste like pepper.   ADJ-GRADED

'pep talk, pep talks. If you give someone a **pep talk**, you say things to them that are intended to encourage them to make more effort or feel more confident.   N-COUNT INFORMAL

pep·tic ul·cer /ˌpeptɪk ˈʌlsə/ **peptic ulcers.** A peptic ulcer is an ulcer that occurs in the digestive system.   N-COUNT

per /pɜː/. **1** You use **per** to express rates and ratios. For example, if something costs £50 **per** year, you must pay £50 each year for it. If a vehicle is travelling at 40 miles **per** hour, it travels 40 miles each hour. ● **per head:** see **head. 2** If something happens or is done **as per** a particular plan or suggestion, it happens or is done in the way planned or suggested. *They are not being paid as per the agreement.*   PREP / PHR-PREP FORMAL

per·am·bu·late /pəˈræmbjʊleɪt/ **perambulates, perambulating, perambulated.** When someone **perambulates**, they walk about for pleasure. ♦ **per·am·bu·la·tion** /pəˌræmbjʊˈleɪʃən/ **perambulations** *It was time now to end our perambulation round Paris.*   VERB DATED / N-COUNT

per an·num /pər ˈænəm/. A particular amount **per annum** means that amount each year. *...a fee of £35 per annum.*   ◆◇◇◇ ADV: amount ADV

per capi·ta /pə ˈkæpɪtə/. The **per capita** amount of something is the total amount of it in a country or area divided by the number of people in that country or area. *They have the world's largest per capita income.* ► Also an adverb. *Ethiopia has almost the lowest oil consumption per capita in the world.*   ◆◇◇◇ ADJ: ADJ n / ADV: n ADV

P

per·ceive /pə'siːv/ **perceives, perceiving, perceived.** 1 If you **perceive** something, especially something that is not obvious, you see, notice, or realize it. *...to get pupils to perceive for themselves the relationship between success and effort.* 2 If you **perceive** someone or something **as** doing or being a particular thing, it is your opinion that they do this thing or that they are that thing. *He didn't perceive what I was doing as important... A woman cannot succeed if she is perceived as being too feminine.*
VERB
V n

VERB
V n as n/-ing

per cent /pə 'sent/; also spelled **percent. Per cent** is both the singular and the plural form. You use **per cent** to talk about amounts. For example, if an amount is 10 per cent (10%) of a larger amount, it is equal to 10 hundredths of the larger amount. *20 to 40 per cent of the voters are undecided.* ► Also an adjective. *...a ten per cent increase in the number of new students.* ► Also an adverb. *...its prediction that house prices will fall 5 per cent over the year.*
N-COUNT:
num N

ADJ: ADJ n

ADV:
ADV with v

per·cent·age /pə'sentɪdʒ/ **percentages.** A **percentage** is a fraction of an amount expressed as a particular number of hundredths of that amount. *Only a few vegetable-origin foods have such a high percentage of protein.*
N-COUNT

per·cep·tible /pə'septɪbəl/. Something that is **perceptible** can be seen or noticed. *No perceptible change had taken place... Pasternak gave him a barely perceptible smile.* ♦ **per·cep·tibly** /pə'septɪbli/ *The tension was mounting perceptibly.*
ADJ-GRADED

ADV-GRADED:
ADV with v

per·cep·tion /pə'sepʃən/ **perceptions.** 1 Your **perception** of something is the way that you think about it or the impression you have of it. *Our perceptions of death affect the way we live.* 2 Someone who has **perception** realizes or notices things that are not obvious. *It did not require a great deal of perception to realise the interview was over.* 3 **Perception** is the recognition of things using your senses, especially the sense of sight.
N-COUNT

N-UNCOUNT

N-COUNT

per·cep·tive /pə'septɪv/. If you describe a person as **perceptive**, you think that they are good at noticing or realizing things, especially things that are not obvious. *...one of the most perceptive US political commentators.* ♦ **per·cep·tive·ly** *The stages in her love affair with Harry are perceptively written.* ♦ **per·cep·tive·ness** *The task I have in mind requires little more than perceptiveness and a good memory.*
ADJ-GRADED

ADV-GRADED

N-UNCOUNT

per·cep·tual /pə'septʃuəl/. Your **perceptual** skills are the mental abilities that you use in order to interpret and understand what you perceive. *Some children come to school with more finely trained perceptual skills than others.*
ADJ: ADJ n
FORMAL

perch /pɜːtʃ/ **perches, perching, perched.** 1 If you **perch** on something, you sit down lightly on the very edge or tip of it. *I walked across the bridge, and perched on the narrow railing there... He perched himself on the side of the bed.* ♦ **perched** *She was perched on the edge of the sofa.* 2 If something **perches** somewhere, it is on the top or edge of something. *...the vast slums that perch precariously on top of the hills.* ♦ **perched** *...a small college perched high up in the hills.* 3 If you **perch** something on something else, you put or balance it on the top or edge of that thing. *He picked up one of the baseball caps and perched it on his head.* 4 When a bird **perches** on something such as a branch or a wall, it lands on it and stays there. ♦ **perched** *Are there any birds perched in the branches?* 5 A **perch** is a short rod for a bird to stand on. 6 You can refer to a high place where someone is sitting as their **perch**. *I watched him discreetly from my perch on a boulder.*
♦♦♦◇◇
VERB
V prep/adv
V pron-refl

prep/adv

ADJ:
v-link ADJ
prep/adv
VERB
V prep/adv

ADJ:
v-link ADJ
prep/adv
VERB
V n on n

VERB:
V prep/adv

ADJ:
v-link ADJ
prep/adv
N-COUNT
N-COUNT

7 A **perch** is an edible fish. The form **perch** is used for both singular and plural.
N-COUNT

per·chance /pə'tʃɑːns, -'tʃæns/. **Perchance** means perhaps. *Would you, perchance, have made any phone calls since these events unfolded?*
ADV:
ADV with
group/cl
DATED,
LITERARY

per·co·late /'pɜːkəleɪt/ **percolates, percolating, percolated.** 1 If an idea, feeling, or piece of information **percolates** through a group of people or a
VERB
V prep/adv

thing, it spreads slowly through it. *New fashions took a long time to percolate down.* 2 If something **percolates** somewhere, it passes slowly through something that has very small holes or gaps in it. *Rain water will only percolate through slowly.* 3 When you **percolate** coffee or when coffee **percolates**, you prepare it in a special piece of equipment. *...freshly percolated coffee.* ♦ **per·co·la·tor, percolators.** A **percolator** is a special piece of equipment for percolating coffee.
VERB
V prep/adv

V-ERG: V n
V-ed
Also V
N-COUNT

per·cus·sion /pə'kʌʃən/. Percussion instruments are musical instruments that you hit, such as drums and cymbals. ♦ **per·cus·sion·ist, percussionists.** A **percussionist** is a person who plays percussion instruments.
◇◇◇◇◇
N-UNCOUNT

N-COUNT

per·cus·sive /pə'kʌsɪv/. Percussive sounds are like the sound of drums. *...strange South American percussive instruments.*
ADJ-GRADED

per·di·tion /pɜː'dɪʃən/. If you say that someone is on the road to **perdition**, you mean that their behaviour is likely to lead them to failure and disaster.
N-UNCOUNT
LITERARY

per·emp·tory /pə'remptəri/. If you describe an action as **peremptory**, you mean it is done in a way that suggests someone expects to be obeyed immediately, and you think this is rather rude. *With a brief, almost peremptory gesture he pointed to a chair.* ♦ **per·emp·to·ri·ly** /pə'remptərɪli/ *'Hello!' the voice said, more peremptorily. 'Who is it? Who do you want?'*
ADJ-GRADED
PRAGMATICS
FORMAL

ADV-GRADED:
ADV with v

per·en·nial /pə'reniəl/ **perennials.** 1 You use **perennial** to describe problems or situations that keep occurring or which seem to exist all the time. *...the perennial urban problems of drugs and homelessness.* ♦ **per·en·ni·al·ly** *Both services are perennially short of staff.* 2 A **perennial** plant lives for several years and has flowers each year. ► Also a noun. *...a low-growing perennial.*
♦♦◇◇◇
ADJ-GRADED

ADV
ADJ

N-COUNT

per·fect, perfects, perfecting, perfected. The adjective is pronounced /'pɜːfɪkt/. The verb is pronounced /pə'fekt/. 1 Something that is **perfect** is as good as it could possibly be. *He spoke perfect English... Hiring a nanny has turned out to be the perfect solution.* ● **practice makes perfect**: see **practice**. ♦ **per·fec·tion** /pə'fekʃən/ *...fresh fish, cooked to perfection.* ♦ **per·fect·ly** *The system worked perfectly.* 2 If you say that something is **perfect** for a particular person, thing, or activity, you are emphasizing that it is very suitable for them or for that activity. *Carpet tiles are perfect for kitchens because they're easy to take up and wash.* 3 If an object or surface is **perfect**, it does not have any marks on it, or have any lumps, cracks, or dents in it. *...their perfect white teeth.* 4 If you **perfect** something, you improve it so that it becomes as good as it can possibly be. *We perfected a hand-signal system.* ♦ **perfection** *Madame Clicquot is credited with the perfection of this technique.* 5 You can use **perfect** to give emphasis to the noun following it. *Some people are always coming up to perfect strangers and asking them what they do... What he had said to her made perfect sense.* 6 The **perfect** tenses of a verb are the ones used to talk about things that happened or began before a particular time, as in 'He's already left' and 'They had always liked her'. The present perfect tense is sometimes called the **perfect** tense. ● See also **future, past perfect, present perfect.** 7 See also **perfectly.**
♦♦♦♦◇

ADJ-GRADED

N-UNCOUNT
ADV-GRADED:
ADV with v
ADJ-GRADED

ADJ

VERB
V n

N-UNCOUNT

ADJ: ADJ n
PRAGMATICS

ADJ: ADJ n

per·fec·tion·ist /pə'fekʃənɪst/ **perfectionists.** Someone who is a **perfectionist** refuses to do or accept anything that is not as good as it could possibly be. *I'm trying to cope with my perfectionist tendencies better.* ♦ **per·fec·tion·ism** *...the author's literary perfectionism.*
◆◇◇◇◇
N-COUNT

N-UNCOUNT

per·fect·ly /'pɜːfɪktli/. 1 You can use **perfectly** to emphasize an adjective or adverb, especially when you think the person you are talking to might doubt what you are saying. *There's no reason why you can't have a perfectly normal child... They made it perfectly clear that it was pointless to go on.* 2 If you de-
♦♦♦◇◇
ADV:
ADV adj/adv
PRAGMATICS

ADV:

scribe something as **perfectly** good or acceptable, you are emphasizing that there is no reason to use or get something else, although someone else has a different opinion. *Bunbury, ignoring a perfectly good pedestrian crossing twenty yards further along, marched boldly out into the traffic.* **3** See also **perfect.**

ADV adj/adv
PRAGMATICS

,perfect 'pitch. Someone who has **perfect pitch** is able to identify or sing musical notes correctly.

N-UNCOUNT

per·fid·i·ous /pə'fɪdiəs/. If someone is **perfidious**, they are dishonest or untrustworthy.

ADJ-GRADED
LITERARY

per·fi·dy /'pɜːfɪdi/. **Perfidy** is treacherous behaviour or actions.

N-UNCOUNT
LITERARY

per·fo·rate /'pɜːfəreɪt/ **perforates, perforating, perforated.** To **perforate** something means to pierce it or cause it to have a hole or holes in it. *I refused to wear headphones because they can perforate your eardrums.* ♦ **per·fo·rat·ed** *...perforated polythene bags.* ♦ **per·fo·ra·tion** /,pɜːfə'reɪʃən/, **perforations.** Perforations are small holes that are found in perforated things.

VERB
V n

ADJ: ADJ n
N-COUNT

per·force /pə'fɔːs/. **Perforce** is used to indicate that something happens or is the case because it is unavoidable or inevitable, rather than because it is intended or desired. *The war in 1939 perforce ushered in an era of more grime and drabness.*

ADV
DATED

per·form /pə'fɔːm/ **performs, performing, performed.** **1** When you **perform** a task or action, especially a complicated one, you do it. *...people of all ages who have performed outstanding acts of bravery... His council had had to perform miracles on a tiny budget.* ♦ **per·form·ance** *He devoted in excess of seventy hours a week to the performance of his duties.* **2** If something **performs** a particular function, it has that function. *A complex engine has many separate components, each performing a different function.* **3** If someone or something **performs well**, they work well or achieve a good result. If they **perform badly**, they work badly or achieve a poor result. *The point of the tables is to get a picture of how schools are performing.* ♦ **performance, performances** *That study looked at the performance of 18 surgeons.* ♦ **per·form·er, performers** *Until 1987, Canada's industry had been the star performer.* **4** If you **perform** a play, a piece of music, or a dance, you do it in front of an audience. *Dominique Gallery performed Tchaikovsky's Violin Concerto in D Major... He began performing in the early fifties.* ♦ **performer** *A performer in evening dress plays classical selections on the violin.*

♦♦♦♦◊
VERB
V n

N-SING

VERB
V n

VERB
V adv

N-VAR

N-COUNT:
supp N

VERB
V n
V

N-COUNT

per·for·mance /pə'fɔːməns/ **performances.** **1** A **performance** involves entertaining an audience by doing something such as singing, dancing, or acting. *Inside the theatre, they were giving a performance of Bizet's Carmen.* **2** You can describe something that is or looks complicated or difficult to do as a **performance.** *The whole process is quite a performance.* **3** A car's **performance** is its ability to go fast and accelerate quickly. A **performance** car is one that can go very fast and accelerate very quickly. *At £14,900 the Sabre offers a lot of performance for the money.* ♦ See also **high-performance.** **4** See also **perform.** ● **a repeat performance:** see **repeat.**

♦♦♦♦◊
N-COUNT

N-SING
INFORMAL

N-UNCOUNT

per'formance art. **Performance art** is a theatrical presentation that includes various art forms such as dance, music, painting, and sculpture.

N-UNCOUNT

per'formance-related. **Performance-related** pay is related to the quality of a person's work or to the amount that they produce, so that if their work improves or they produce more, they receive more money. *All of the firm's 14,000 employees are offered performance-related financial rewards.*

ADJ
BRITISH

per,forming 'arts. Dance, drama, music, and other forms of entertainment that are usually performed live in front of an audience are referred to as the **performing arts.**

N-PLURAL

per·fume /'pɜːfjuːm, pə'fjuːm/ **perfumes, perfuming, perfumed.** **1** Perfume is a pleasant-smelling liquid which women put on their necks and wrists to make themselves smell nice. *The hall*

♦♦◊◊◊
N-VAR

smelled of her mother's perfume. **2** **Perfume** is the ingredient that is added to some products to make them smell nice. *...a delicate white soap without perfume.* **3** If something is used to **perfume** a product, it is added to the product to make it smell nice. *...shower gel perfumed with the popular Paris fragrance.* **4** The **perfume** of something is the pleasant smell it has. *...the perfume of roses.* **5** If the smell of something **perfumes** a place or area, it makes it smell nice. *As they bake, they perfume the whole house with the aroma of apples and spices.*

N-VAR

VERB: V n
be V-ed with n

N-COUNT
LITERARY
VERB: V n
V n with n
LITERARY

per·fumed /'pɜːfjuːmd, pə'fjuːmd/. Perfumed things have a sweet pleasant smell, either naturally or because perfume has been added to them. *She opened the perfumed envelope. ...perfumed roses.*

♦◊◊◊◊
ADJ

per·fum·ery /pə'fjuːməri/ **perfumeries.** **1** Perfumery is the activity or business of producing perfume. **2** A **perfumery** is a shop or a department in a shop where perfume is the main product that is sold.

N-UNCOUNT

N-COUNT

per·func·tory /pə'fʌŋktəri, AM -tɔːri/. A **perfunctory** action is done quickly and carelessly, and shows a lack of interest in what you are doing. *She gave the list only a perfunctory glance.* ♦ **per·func·to·ri·ly** /pə'fʌŋktərɪli, AM -'tɔːr-/ *Melina was perfunctorily introduced to the men.*

ADJ-GRADED

ADV-GRADED:
ADV with v

per·go·la /'pɜːgələ/ **pergolas.** In a garden, a **pergola** is an arch or a structure with a roof over which climbing plants can be grown.

N-COUNT

per·haps /pə'hæps, præps/. **1** You use **perhaps** to express uncertainty, for example when you do not know that something is definitely true, or when you are mentioning something that may possibly happen in the future in the way you describe. *In the end they lose millions, perhaps billions... It was bulky, perhaps three feet long and almost as high... Perhaps, in time, the message will get through.* **2** You use **perhaps** in opinions and remarks to make them appear less definite or more polite. *Perhaps the most important lesson to be learned is that you simply cannot please everyone... His very last paintings are perhaps the most puzzling.* **3** You use **perhaps** when you are making suggestions or giving advice. *Perhaps is also used in formal English to introduce requests. Perhaps I may be permitted a few suggestions... Well, perhaps you'll come and see us at our place?* **4** You can say **perhaps** as a response to a question or remark, when you do not want to agree or accept, but think that it would be rude to disagree or refuse. 'I'm sure we can make it,' he says. Perhaps, but it will not be easy.*

♦♦♦♦◊
ADV:
ADV with cl/
group
PRAGMATICS

ADV:
ADV with cl/
group
PRAGMATICS

ADV:
ADV with cl
PRAGMATICS

ADV
PRAGMATICS

per·il /'perɪl/ **perils.** **1** Perils are great dangers. *...the perils of the sea... In spite of great peril, I have survived.* **2** The **perils** of a particular activity or course of action are the dangers or problems that can arise from doing it. *...the perils of starring in a television commercial.* **3** If you say that someone does something **at their peril**, you are warning them that they will probably suffer as a result of doing it. *Education and training are not optional extras and you ignore them at your peril.* **4** If someone or something is **in peril**, they are in great danger.

♦◊◊◊◊
N-VAR
FORMAL
N-PLURAL:
with poss

PHRASE

PHRASE

per·il·ous /'perɪləs/. Something that is **perilous** is very dangerous. *...a perilous journey across the war-zone.* ♦ **per·il·ous·ly** *The track snaked perilously upwards.*

♦◊◊◊◊
ADJ-GRADED
LITERARY
ADV-GRADED

pe·rim·eter /pə'rɪmɪtə/ **perimeters.** The **perimeter** of an area of land is the whole of its outer edge or boundary. *...the perimeter of the airport.*

♦◊◊◊◊
N-COUNT

peri·na·tal /,peri'neɪtəl/. Perinatal deaths, complications, or experiences happen at the time of birth or soon after the time of birth. *Premature birth is the main cause of perinatal mortality.*

ADJ: ADJ n
MEDICAL

pe·ri·od /'pɪəriəd/ **periods.** **1** A **period** is a length of time. *This crisis might last for a long period of time. ...a period of a few months.* **2** A **period** in the life of a person, organization, or society is a length of time which is has a particular quality. *...a period of economic good health and expansion... He went through a period of wanting to be accepted.* **3** A par-

♦♦♦♦◊
N-COUNT

N-COUNT:
with supp

N-COUNT

ticular length of time in history is sometimes called a **period**. For example, you can talk about the Victorian period or the Elizabethan period in Britain. *No reference to their existence appears in any literature of the period.* **4 Period** costumes, furniture, and instruments were made at an earlier time in history, or look as if they were made then. ADJ: ADJ n

5 Exercise, training, or study **periods** are lengths of time that are set aside for exercise, training, or study. N-COUNT

6 At a school or college, a **period** is one of the parts that the day is divided into during which lessons or private study take place. *...periods of private study.* N-COUNT

7 When a woman has a **period**, she bleeds from her womb. This usually happens once a month, unless she is pregnant. N-COUNT

8 A **period** is the punctuation mark (.) which you use at the end of a sentence when it is not a question or an explanation. The British expression is **full stop**. N-COUNT AMERICAN

9 Some people say **period** after stating a fact or opinion when they want to emphasize that they are definite about something and do not want to discuss it further. *I don't want to do it, period.* ADV: cl ADV PRAGMATICS

pe·ri·od·ic /ˌpɪəriˈɒdɪk/. **Periodic** events or situations happen occasionally, at fairly regular intervals. *Periodic checks with a dentist can prevent infection in the mouth. ...periodic bouts of illness.* ADJ ◇◇◇◇

pe·ri·od·i·cal /ˌpɪəriˈɒdɪkəl/ **periodicals. 1** A **periodical** is a magazine, especially a serious or academic one, that is published at regular intervals. ◆◇◇◇ N-COUNT ADJ **2 Periodical** events or situations happen occasionally, at fairly regular intervals. *She made periodical visits to her dentist.* ♦ **pe·ri·od·i·cal·ly** /ˌpɪəriˈɒdɪkli/ *Meetings are held periodically to monitor progress.* ADV: ADV with v

periodic 'table. In chemistry, the **periodic table** is a table showing the chemical elements arranged according to their atomic numbers. N-SING: the N

'period piece, period pieces. A **period piece** is a play, book, or film that is set at a particular time in history and describes life at that time. N-COUNT

peri·pa·tet·ic /ˌperɪpəˈtetɪk/. If someone has a **peripatetic** life or career, they travel around a lot, living or working in places for short periods of time. *Her father was in the army and the family led a peripatetic existence.* ADJ-GRADED FORMAL

pe·riph·er·al /pəˈrɪfərəl/ **peripherals. 1** A **peripheral** activity or issue is one which is not very important compared with other activities or issues. *Companies are increasingly keen to contract out peripheral activities like training.* ♦ **pe·riph·er·al·ly** *The Marshall Plan did not include Britain, except peripherally.* **2 Peripheral** areas of land are ones which are on the edge of a larger area. *...peripheral regions beyond the reach of powerful rulers.* **3 Peripherals** are devices that can be attached to computers. ◆◇◇◇ ADJ-GRADED ADV-GRADED ADJ N-COUNT TECHNICAL

pe·riph·ery /pəˈrɪfəri/ **peripheries. 1** If something is on the **periphery** of an area, place, or thing, it is on the edge of it. *...the republics on the periphery of the Soviet Union.* **2** The **periphery** of a subject or area of interest is the part of it that is not considered to be as important or basic as the main part. *The sociological study of religion moved from the centre to the periphery of sociology.* ◆◇◇◇ N-COUNT FORMAL N-COUNT

peri·scope /ˈperɪskəʊp/ **periscopes**. A **periscope** is a vertical tube used to see above the surface of the water from inside a submarine. N-COUNT

per·ish /ˈperɪʃ/ **perishes, perishing, perished. 1** If people or animals **perish**, they die as a result of very harsh conditions or of an accident. *...the ferry disaster in which 193 passengers perished.* **2** If something **perishes**, it comes to an end or is destroyed for ever. *Buddhism had to adapt to the new world or perish.* **3** If a substance or material **perishes** or **is perished**, it starts to fall to pieces and becomes useless. *...their tyres are slowly perishing.* ♦ **perished** *...tattered pieces of ancient, perished leather.* **4** If someone says **perish the thought**, they mean that they think that a suggestion or possibility is unpleasant or ridiculous. ◆◇◇◇ VERB WRITTEN V WRITTEN V-ERG: V n V ADJ CONVENTION PRAGMATICS

per·ish·able /ˈperɪʃəbəl/. Goods such as food that are **perishable** go bad after quite a short length of time. *...perishable food like fruit, vegetables and meat.* ADJ

per·ished /ˈperɪʃt/. If someone is **perished**, they are extremely cold. ADJ INFORMAL, BRITISH

peri·to·ni·tis /ˌperɪtəˈnaɪtɪs/. **Peritonitis** is a disease in which the inside wall of your abdomen becomes swollen and very painful. N-UNCOUNT MEDICAL

per·jure /ˈpɜːdʒə/ **perjures, perjuring, perjured.** If someone **perjures** themselves in a court of law, they lie, even though they have promised to tell the truth. ♦ **per·jured**. **Perjured** evidence or testimony is a false statement of events. VERB: V pron-refl ADJ

per·jury /ˈpɜːdʒəri/. If someone who is giving evidence in a court of law commits **perjury**, they lie. N-UNCOUNT LEGAL

perk /pɜːk/ **perks, perking, perked. Perks** are special benefits that are given to people who have a particular job or belong to a particular group. *One of the perks of being a student is cheap travel.* ◇◇◇◇ N-COUNT

perk up. 1 If something **perks** you **up** or if you **perk up**, you become cheerful and lively, after feeling tired, bored, or depressed. *He perks up and jokes with them.* **2** If you **perk** something **up** or it **perks up**, it becomes more interesting, lively, or successful. *Psychological twists perk up an otherwise predictable story line... The economy perked up in July.* PHRASAL VB ERG: V n P V P V P Also V P noun ERG: V n P V P noun V P

perky /ˈpɜːki/ **perkier, perkiest.** If someone is **perky**, they are cheerful and lively. ADJ-GRADED

perm /pɜːm/ **perms, perming, permed.** When a hair stylist **perms** someone's hair, they curl it and treat it with chemicals so that it stays curly or wavy for several months. The usual American expression is 'to give someone a **permanent**'. *She had her hair permed.* ▶ If you have a **perm**, you have your hair permed. ♦ **permed** *...dry, damaged or permed hair.* ◆◇◇◇ VERB: V n haven V-ed BRITISH N-COUNT ADJ

per·ma·frost /ˈpɜːməfrɒst/. **Permafrost** is land that is permanently frozen to a great depth. N-UNCOUNT

per·ma·nent /ˈpɜːmənənt/ **permanents. 1** Something that is **permanent** lasts for ever. *...permanent damage to the brain... The ban is intended to be permanent.* ♦ **per·ma·nent·ly** *The only way to lose weight permanently is to completely change your attitudes toward food.* ♦ **per·ma·nence** *Anything which threatens the permanence of the treaty is a threat to stability and to peace.* **2** You use **permanent** to describe problems or situations that keep occurring or which seem to exist all the time. *...a permanent state of tension.* ♦ **permanently** *...the heavy, permanently locked gate.* **3** A **permanent** employee is one who is employed for an unlimited length of time. *...a permanent job.* ♦ **permanently** *...permanently employed registered dockers.* **4** Your **permanent** home or address is the one at which you spend most of your time or the one that you return to after having stayed in other places. **5** A **permanent** is a treatment where a hairstylist curls your hair and treats it with a chemical so that it stays curly or wavy for several months. The British word is a **perm**. ◆◆◇◇ ADJ ADV N-UNCOUNT ADJ ADV ADJ: ADJ n ADV: ADV with v ADJ: ADJ n N-COUNT AMERICAN

per·me·able /ˈpɜːmiəbəl/. If a substance is **permeable**, something such as water or gas can pass through it or soak into it. *...permeable to air and water.* ♦ **per·me·abil·ity** /ˌpɜːmiəˈbɪlɪti/ *...ingenious devices for adjusting the permeability of the exterior wall.* ADJ-GRADED N-UNCOUNT

per·me·ate /ˈpɜːmieɪt/ **permeates, permeating, permeated. 1** If an idea, feeling, or attitude **permeates** a system or **permeates** society, it affects every part of it or is present throughout it. *An obvious change of attitude at the top will permeate through the system.* **2** If a substance **permeates** a place, it spreads throughout it. *Eventually, the water will permeate through the surrounding concrete.* ◆◇◇◇ VERB: V n V through n VERB: V n V through n

per·mis·si·ble /pəˈmɪsəbəl/. If something is **permissible**, it is considered to be acceptable because it does not break any laws or rules. *Religious practices are permissible under the Constitution.* ◆◇◇◇ ADJ

per·mis·sion /pəˈmɪʃən/ **permissions. 1** If someone who has authority over you gives you **permis-** ◆◆◇◇ N-UNCOUNT

sion to do something, they say that they will allow you to do it. *Permission for the march had not been granted... They cannot leave the country without permission.* **2** A **permission** is a formal, written statement from an official group or place allowing you to do something. *...oil exploration permissions.* ● see also **planning permission**.   N-COUNT

per·mis·sive /pə'mɪsɪv/. A **permissive** person, society, or way of behaving allows or tolerates things which other people disapprove of. *...the 'permissive tolerance' of the 1960s.* ♦ **per·mis·sive·ness** *Permissiveness and democracy go together.*   ADJ-GRADED   N-UNCOUNT

per·mit, permits, permitting, permitted. The verb is pronounced /pə'mɪt/. The noun is pronounced /'pɜːmɪt/. **1** If someone **permits** something, they allow it to happen. If they **permit** you to do something, they allow you to do it. *The guards permitted me to bring my camera and tape recorder... No outside journalists have been permitted into the country.* **2** If a situation **permits** something, it makes it possible for that thing to exist, happen, or be done or it provides the opportunity for it. *Try to go out for a walk at lunchtime, if the weather permits... This method of cooking also permits heat to penetrate evenly from both sides.* **3** If you **permit** yourself something, you allow yourself to have or do something that you do not normally have or do, or that you think you probably should not have or do. *Only once in his life had Douglas permitted himself to lose control of his emotions.* **4** You can use **permit me** when you are about to say something or to make a suggestion. *Permit me to give you some advice.*   ♦♦♦◇◇   VERB: V n / V n to-inf / be V-ed into n / Also V n n   VERB: V n / V / V n to-inf / FORMAL   VERB: V pron-refl n / V pron-refl to-inf   PHRASE / PRAGMATICS / FORMAL

5 A **permit** is an official document which says that you may do something. For example you usually need a **permit** to work in a foreign country. *She hasn't got a work permit.*   N-COUNT

per·mu·ta·tion /,pɜːmjuː'teɪʃən/ **permutations.** A **permutation** is one of the ways in which a number of things can be ordered or arranged. *He was turning over several permutations in his mind.*   N-COUNT

per·ni·cious /pə'nɪʃəs/. If you describe something as **pernicious**, you mean that it is very harmful. *Her mother's influence was pernicious.*   ♦◇◇◇ ADJ-GRADED

per·nick·ety /pə'nɪkɪti/. If you describe someone as **pernickety**, you think that they pay too much attention to small, unimportant details; used showing disapproval.   ADJ-GRADED / PRAGMATICS / INFORMAL

pero·ra·tion /,perə'reɪʃən/ **perorations. 1** A **peroration** is the last part of a speech, especially the part where the speaker sums up his or her argument. **2** If someone describes a speech as a **peroration**, they mean that they dislike it because they think it is very long and not worth listening to.   N-COUNT / FORMAL   N-COUNT / PRAGMATICS / INFORMAL

per·ox·ide /pə'rɒksaɪd/ **peroxides. Peroxide** is a chemical that is often used for making hair lighter in colour. It can also be used as an antiseptic. ● See also **hydrogen peroxide**.   N-VAR

per·pen·dic·u·lar /,pɜːpən'dɪkjulə/. **1** A **perpendicular** line or surface points straight up, rather than being sloping or horizontal. *The sides of the loch are almost perpendicular.* **2** If one thing is **perpendicular** to another, it is at an angle of 90 degrees to it. *The left wing dipped until it was perpendicular to the ground.*   ADJ-GRADED   ADJ / FORMAL

per·pe·trate /'pɜːpɪtreɪt/ **perpetrates, perpetrating, perpetrated.** If someone **perpetrates** a crime or any other immoral or harmful act, they commit it. *A high proportion of crime in any country is perpetrated by young males... Tremendous wrongs were being perpetrated on the poorest and least privileged human beings.* ♦ **per·pe·tra·tion** /,pɜːpɪ'treɪʃən/ *...a very small minority who persist in the perpetration of these crimes.* ♦ **per·pe·tra·tor, perpetrators** *It's time the death penalty was used for perpetrators of terrorist acts.*   ♦◇◇◇ VERB: V n / be V-ed / be V-ed on/ against n   N-SING   N-COUNT

per·pet·ual /pə'petʃuəl/. **1** A **perpetual** feeling, state, or quality is one that never ends or changes. *...the creation of a perpetual union.* ♦ **per·pet·ual·ly** *They were all perpetually starving.* **2** A **perpetual**   ♦◇◇◇ ADJ   ADV   ADJ

act, situation, or state is one that happens again and again and so seems never to end. *I thought her perpetual complaints were going to prove too much for me.* ♦ **perpetually** *He perpetually interferes in political affairs.*   N-COUNT   ADV

per·petu·al 'motion. The idea of **perpetual motion** is the idea of something continuing to move for ever without getting energy from anything else.   N-UNCOUNT

per·petu·ate /pə'petʃueɪt/ **perpetuates, perpetuating, perpetuated.** If someone or something **perpetuates** a situation, system, or belief, especially one that is bad or wrong, they cause it to continue. *This image is a myth perpetuated by the media.* ♦ **per·petua·tion** /pə,petʃu'eɪʃən/ *That is why the perpetuation of nuclear deployments is morally unacceptable.*   ♦◇◇◇◇ VERB: V n / V-ed   N-SING

per·pe·tu·ity /,pɜːpɪ'tjuːɪti/. If something is done **in perpetuity**, it is intended to last for ever. *The US Government gave the land to the tribe in perpetuity.*   PHRASE / FORMAL

per·plex /pə'pleks/ **perplexes, perplexing, perplexed.** If something **perplexes** you, you find it confusing, worrying, or difficult to understand. *...an aspect of modern science that has always perplexed me.* ♦ **per·plexed** *She is perplexed about what to do for her daughter.* ♦ **per·plex·ing** *British Parliamentary procedure is perplexing at the best of times.*   VERB V n   ADJ-GRADED   ADJ-GRADED

per·plex·ity /pə'pleksɪti/ **perplexities. 1** Perplexity is a feeling of being confused and frustrated because you don't completely understand something. *He began counting them and then, with growing perplexity, counted them a second time.* **2** The **perplexities** of something are those things about it which are complicated and difficult to understand. *...the perplexities of quantum mechanics.*   N-UNCOUNT   N-COUNT

per·se·cute /'pɜːsɪkjuːt/ **persecutes, persecuting, persecuted. 1** If someone is **persecuted**, they are treated cruelly and unfairly, often because of their race or beliefs. *The Communists began by brutally persecuting the Catholic Church.* ♦ **per·se·cu·tion** /,pɜːsɪ'kjuːʃən/ *...victims of political persecution.* ♦ **per·se·cu·tor, persecutors** *People of all races had their own persecutors and their own problems.* **2** If you say that someone is **persecuting** you, you mean that they are deliberately making your life difficult. *Vic was bullied by his father and persecuted by his sisters.*   ♦◇◇◇◇ VERB: be V-ed / V n / Also V-ed   N-UNCOUNT: also N in pl   N-COUNT   VERB: V n

per·se·vere /,pɜːsɪ'vɪə/ **perseveres, persevering, persevered.** If you **persevere** with something, you keep trying to do it and do not give up, even though it is difficult. *This ability to persevere despite obstacles and setbacks is the quality people most admire in others... She persevered in her idea despite obvious objections raised by friends.* ♦ **per·sever·ance** *Adam's perseverance eventually proved worthwhile.* ♦ **per·sever·ing** *He is a persevering, approachable family man.*   ♦◇◇◇◇ VERB: V with n / V / V prep   N-UNCOUNT   ADJ-GRADED

Per·sian /'pɜːʒən/ **Persians. 1** Something that is **Persian** belongs or relates to the ancient kingdom of Persia. *...the Persian Empire.* **2 Persians** were the people who came from the ancient kingdom of Persia.   ♦♦♦◇◇ ADJ   N-COUNT

Persian 'Gulf. The **Persian Gulf** is the area of sea between Saudi Arabia and Iran.   ♦♦♦◇◇ N-PROPER

per·sim·mon /pɜː'sɪmən/ **persimmons.** A **persimmon** is a soft, orange fruit that looks similar to a large tomato.   N-COUNT

per·sist /pə'sɪst/ **persists, persisting, persisted. 1** If something undesirable **persists**, it continues to exist. *Contact your doctor if the cough persists.* **2** If you **persist** in doing something, you continue to do it, even though it is difficult or other people are against it. *He urged the United States to persist with its efforts to bring about peace... 'You haven't answered me,' she persisted.*   ♦♦◇◇◇ VERB V   VERB: V in-ing / V with/in n / V with quote / Also V

per·sis·tent /pə'sɪstənt/. **1** Something bad or undesirable that is **persistent** continues to exist or happen for a long time. *His cough grew more persistent. ...persistent rain.* ♦ **per·sis·tence** *...an expression of concern at the persistence of inflation*   ♦♦◇◇◇ ADJ-GRADED   N-UNCOUNT

P

and high interest rates. ♦ **per·sis·tent·ly** *The alle-* ADV-GRADED
gations have been persistently denied by ministers.
2 Someone who is **persistent** continues trying to do ADJ-GRADED
something, even though it is difficult or other peo-
ple are against it. *He phoned again this morning.*
He's very persistent. ♦ **persistence** *Chandra was* N-UNCOUNT
determined to become a doctor and her persistence
paid off. ♦ **persistently** *Rachel gently but persis-* ADV-GRADED:
tently imposed her will upon Douglas. ADV with v

per·son /ˈpɜːsən/ **people, persons.** The usual ♦♦♦♦♦
plural of person is **people**. The form **persons** is used
as the plural in formal or legal language. **1** A **person** N-COUNT
is a man or a woman. *The amount of sleep we need*
varies from person to person... At least fifty-four peo-
ple have been killed. ...the right of accused persons to
remain silent. **2** Your **person** is your body. *An Ira-* N-COUNT:
nian passport was found on his person. poss N
FORMAL
3 If you talk about someone **as a person**, you are con- N-COUNT
sidering them from the point of view of their real nature. *Robin didn't feel good about herself as a person.*
4 If someone says, for example, **'I'm an outdoor per-** N-COUNT
son' or **'I'm not a coffee person'**, they are saying
whether or not they like that particular activity or
thing. *They tend to be cat rather than dog people.*
5 If you do something **in person**, you do it yourself ra- PHRASE
ther than letting someone else do it for you. **6** If you PHRASE
meet, hear, or see someone **in person**, you are in the
same place as them, rather than, for example, speaking to them on the telephone, writing to them, or seeing them on television. **7** You can use **in the person of** PHRASE
when mentioning the name of someone you have just
referred to in a more general or indirect way. *We had a*
knowledgeable guide in the person of George Adams.
8 A **person-to-person** conversation takes place di- PHRASE
rectly between two people, and often involves private
or individual matters. *In the end, overcoming people's*
prejudice will be done locally, person to person.
9 In grammar, the term **first person** is used when re- N-COUNT
ferring to 'I' and 'we', **second person** when referring
to 'you', and **third person** when referring to 'he',
'she', 'it', 'they', and all other noun groups. **Person** is
also used like this when referring to the verb forms
that go with these pronouns and noun groups. ● See
also **first person, second person, third person**.

-person /-pɜːsən/ **-people** or **-persons. 1** -person COMB
is added to numbers to form adjectives which indicate how many people are involved in something or
can use something. **People** is not used in this way.
...two-person households. ...the spa's 32-person staff.
2 -person is used to form nouns which refer to COMB
someone who does a particular job or is in a particular group. -person is used to avoid indicating
whether someone is a man or a woman, or to avoid
referring to a woman as, for example, a 'chairman'.
-people can also be used in this way. *...Mrs. Sahana*
Pradhan, chairperson of the United Leftist Front...
He had a staff of six salespeople working for him.

per·so·na /pəˈsəʊnə/ **personas** or **personae** ♦♦♦♦♦
/pəˈsəʊnaɪ/. Someone's **persona** is the aspect of N-COUNT
their character or nature that they present to other FORMAL
people, perhaps in contrast to their real character or
nature. *...the contradictions between her private life*
and the public persona. ● See also **persona non**
grata.

per·son·able /ˈpɜːsənəbəl/. Someone who is **per-** ADJ-GRADED
sonable has a pleasant appearance and character.

per·son·age /ˈpɜːsənɪdʒ/ **personages. 1** A **per-** N-COUNT
sonage is a famous or important person. *...MPs, film* FORMAL
stars and other important personages. **2** A **person-** N-COUNT
age is also a character in a play or book, or in histo- FORMAL
ry. *...Shakespeare's famous personages.*

per·son·al /ˈpɜːsənəl/. **1** A **personal** opinion, qual- ♦♦♦♦♦
ity, or thing belongs or relates to one particular per- ADJ: ADJ n
son rather than to other people. *That's my personal*
opinion. ...books, furniture, and other personal be-
longings. **2** If you give something your **personal** ADJ
care or attention, you deal with it yourself rather
than letting someone else deal with it. *...a personal*
letter from the President's secretary. **3 Personal** care ADJ: ADJ n
involves looking after your body and appearance.

...men who take as much time and trouble over per- ADJ
sonal hygiene as the women in their lives. **4 Person-**
al matters relate to your feelings, relationships, and
health. *Mr Knight said that he had resigned for per-* ADJ-GRADED
sonal reasons. **5 Personal** comments refer to
someone's appearance or character in an offensive
way. *Newspapers resorted to personal abuse... There's*
no need to get personal. Calm down. **6** A **personal** ADJ
relationship is one that is not connected with your
job or public life. *Mr Gamsakhurdia said he had a*
good personal relationship with Boris Yeltsin.

personal as·sistant, personal assistants. A N-COUNT
personal assistant is a person who does secretarial
and administrative work for someone. The abbreviation 'PA' is also used.

personal 'best, personal bests. A sports play- ♦♦♦♦♦
er's **personal best** is the highest score or fastest N-COUNT
time that they have ever achieved.

personal com'puter, personal computers. A ♦♦♦♦♦
personal computer is a computer which is used by N-COUNT
one person, normally independently. The abbreviation 'PC' is also used.

per·son·al·ity /ˌpɜːsəˈnælɪti/ **personalities.** ♦♦♦♦♦
1 Your **personality** is your whole character and na- N-VAR
ture. *She has such a kind, friendly personality... The*
contest was as much about personalities as it was
about politics. **2** If someone has **personality** or is a N-VAR
personality, they have a strong and lively character.
...a woman of great personality. **3** You can refer to a N-COUNT
famous person, especially in entertainment, broadcasting, or sport, as a **personality**. *...the radio and*
television personality, Jimmy Saville.

per·son·al·ize /ˈpɜːsənəlaɪz/ **personalizes, per-** ♦♦♦♦♦
sonalizing, personalized; also spelled **personal-**
ise in British English. **1** If an object **is personalized**, VB: usu
it is marked with the name or initials of its owner. passive
The clock has easy-to-read numbers and is personal- be V-ed
ised with the child's name and birth date. ...a Rolls- V-ed
Royce with a personalised number plate. **2** If you VERB: V n
personalize something, you do or design it specially V-ed
according to the needs of an individual or to your
own needs. *...professional men or women who need*
intensive, personalised French courses. **3** If you **per-** VERB: V n
sonalize an argument, discussion, idea, or issue, V-ed
you consider it from the point of view of individual Also V
people and their characters or relationships, rather
than considering the facts in a general or objective
way. *The contest has become personalised, if not*
bitter.

per·son·al·ly /ˈpɜːsənəli/. **1** You use **personally** to ♦♦♦♦♦
emphasize that you are giving your own opinion. ADV:
Personally I think it's a waste of time. **2** If you do ADV with cl
something **personally**, you do it yourself rather PRAGMATICS
than letting someone else do it. *The minister is re-* ADV:
turning to Paris to answer the allegations personally. ADV with v
3 If you meet or know someone **personally**, you ADV:
meet or know them in real life, rather than knowing ADV with v
about them or knowing their work. *He did not know*
them personally, but he was familiar with their
reputation.
4 You can use **personally** to say that something refers ADV
to an individual person rather than to other people. *In*
order for me to spend three months on something it has
to interest me personally. **5** You can use **personally** to ADV
show that you are talking about someone's private life
rather than their professional or public life. *He is bet-*
ter liked personally, if less respected professionally,
than Emmott. **6** If you **take** someone's remarks **per-** PHRASE
sonally, you are upset because you think that they are
criticizing you in particular.

personal 'organizer, personal organizers; N-COUNT
also spelled **personal organiser**. A **personal organ-**
izer is a kind of diary which you can add pages to or
remove pages from to keep the information up to
date. Small computers with a similar function are
also called **personal organizers**.

personal 'pronoun, personal pronouns. A N-COUNT
personal pronoun is a pronoun such as 'I', 'you',
'she', or 'they' which is used to refer to the speaker
or the hearer, or to a person or thing whose identity

is clear, usually because they have already been mentioned.

,personal 'space. 1 If someone invades your **personal space**, they stand or lean too close to you, so that you feel uncomfortable. 2 If you need your **personal space**, you need time on your own, with the freedom to do something that you want to do or to think about something. N-UNCOUNT

,personal 'stereo, personal stereos. A **personal stereo** is a small cassette player with very light headphones, which people carry round so that they can listen to music while doing something else. N-COUNT

per·so·na non gra·ta /pəˌsəʊnə nɒn ˈgrɑːtə/ **personae non gratae.** If someone is **persona non grata**, they have become unwelcome or unacceptable because of something they have said or done. *As a Ku Klux Klan member he was declared persona non grata on a visit to Britain.* PHRASE

per·soni·fi·ca·tion /pəˌsɒnɪfɪˈkeɪʃən/ **personifications.** 1 A **personification** of something abstract is its representation in the form of a person. *...personifications of the attributes of Justice, Prudence and Truth.* 2 See also **personify.** N-VAR

per·soni·fy /pəˈsɒnɪfaɪ/ **personifies, personifying, personified.** If you say that someone **personifies** a particular thing or quality, you mean that they seem to be a perfect example of that thing, or to have that quality to a very large degree. *She can be charm personified.* ♦ **per·soni·fi·ca·tion** *Janis Joplin was the personification of the '60s female rock singer.* ◆◇◇◇◇ VERB: V n V-ed / N-SING

per·son·nel /ˌpɜːsəˈnel/. 1 The **personnel** of an organization are the people who work for it. *All remaining American military personnel are scheduled to leave the country. ...personnel problems.* 2 **Personnel** is the department in a large company or organization that deals with employees, keeps their records, and helps with any problems they might have. *Her first job was in personnel.* ◆◆◆◇◇ N-PLURAL / N-UNCOUNT

,person-to-'person. See **person.**

per·spec·tive /pəˈspektɪv/ **perspectives.** 1 A particular **perspective** is a particular way of thinking about something, especially one that is influenced by your beliefs or experiences. *He says the death of his father 18 months ago has given him a new perspective on life.* 2 If you get something **in perspective** or **into perspective**, you judge its real importance by considering it in relation to everything else. If you get something **out of perspective**, you fail to judge its real importance in relation to everything else. 3 **Perspective** is the art of making some objects or people in a picture look further away than others. ◆◆◆◇◇ N-COUNT / PHRASE / N-UNCOUNT

per·spex /ˈpɜːspeks/; also spelled **Perspex.** In Britain, **perspex** is a strong clear plastic which is sometimes used instead of glass. **Perspex** is a trademark. N-UNCOUNT

per·spi·cac·ity /ˌpɜːspɪˈkæsɪti/. **Perspicacity** is the ability to notice and understand things quickly. N-UNCOUNT FORMAL

per·spire /pəˈspaɪə/ **perspires, perspiring, perspired.** When you **perspire**, a liquid comes out on the surface of your skin, because you are hot or frightened. ♦ **per·spi·ra·tion** /ˌpɜːspɪˈreɪʃən/. **Perspiration** is the liquid which is produced when you perspire. *His hands were wet with perspiration.* VERB: V FORMAL / N-UNCOUNT

per·suade /pəˈsweɪd/ **persuades, persuading, persuaded.** 1 If you **persuade** someone to do something, you cause them to do it by giving them good reasons for doing it. *My husband persuaded me to come... Some new acquaintances persuaded us into spending the summer near Kiev.* ♦ **per·suad·er, persuaders** *All great persuaders and salesmen are the same.* 2 If you **persuade** someone to take a particular course of action, it causes them to take that course of action because it is a good reason for doing so. *The Conservative Party's victory in April's general election persuaded him to run for President again.* 3 If you **persuade** someone that something is true, you say things that eventually make them believe that it is true. *Derek persuaded me of the feasibility of the idea.* ♦ **per·suad·ed** *He* ◆◆◆◇◇ VERB V n to-inf V n into n/-ing Also V n / N-COUNT / VERB V n to-inf / VERB: V n that V n of n / ADJ-GRADED:

is not persuaded of the need for electoral reform... Most seemed to have been completely persuaded that the result is reliable.

per·sua·sion /pəˈsweɪʒən/ **persuasions.** 1 **Persuasion** is the act of persuading someone to do something or to believe that something is true. *She was using all her powers of persuasion to induce the Griffins to remain in Rollway.* 2 If you are of a particular **persuasion**, you have a particular belief or set of beliefs. *...people of all political persuasions.* ◆◇◇◇◇ N-UNCOUNT / N-COUNT FORMAL

per·sua·sive /pəˈsweɪsɪv/. Someone or something that is **persuasive** is likely to persuade someone to believe or do a particular thing. *...some of the more persuasive arguments on the other side.* ♦ **per·sua·sive·ly** *...a trained lawyer who can present arguments persuasively.* ♦ **per·sua·sive·ness** *He was convinced that his eloquence and persuasiveness would tip them into supporting him.* ◆◇◇◇◇ ADJ-GRADED / ADV-GRADED: ADV with v / N-UNCOUNT

pert /pɜːt/. 1 If someone describes a young woman as **pert**, they mean that they like her because she is lively and cheeky. Some women find this use offensive. 2 If you say that someone has, for example, a **pert** bottom or nose, you mean that it is quite small and neat, and you think it is attractive. ADJ-GRADED PRAGMATICS / ADJ PRAGMATICS

per·tain /pəˈteɪn/ **pertains, pertaining, pertained.** If one thing **pertains** to another, it relates, belongs, or applies to it. *The restrictions he imposed pertained to the type and height of buildings.* ◆◇◇◇◇ VERB V to n Also V / FORMAL

per·ti·nent /ˈpɜːtɪnənt/. Something that is **pertinent** is relevant to a particular subject. *She had asked some pertinent questions. ...knowledge and skills pertinent to classroom teaching.* ♦ **per·ti·nent·ly** *Where had they learned all this, or, more pertinently, why had they remembered it?* ◆◇◇◇◇ ADJ-GRADED FORMAL / ADV-GRADED

per·turb /pəˈtɜːb/ **perturbs, perturbing, perturbed.** If something **perturbs** you, it worries you quite a lot. ♦ **per·turbed** *He apparently was not perturbed by the prospect of a policeman coming to call.* ♦ **per·tur·ba·tion** *This message caused perturbation in the Middle East Headquarters.* VERB: V n FORMAL / ADJ-GRADED / N-UNCOUNT

per·tur·ba·tion /ˌpɜːtəˈbeɪʃən/ **perturbations.** A **perturbation** is a small change in the movement, quality, or behaviour of something, especially an unusual change. *...perturbations in Jupiter's gravitational field.* N-VAR TECHNICAL

pe·ruse /pəˈruːz/ **peruses, perusing, perused.** If you **peruse** something such as a letter, article, or document, you read it. *In making our decision we perused the company's financial statements for the past five years.* ♦ **pe·rus·al** *Peter Cooke undertook to send each of us a sample contract for perusal.* VERB V n FORMAL / N-UNCOUNT: also a N

per·vade /pəˈveɪd/ **pervades, pervading, pervaded.** If something **pervades** a place or thing, it is a noticeable feature throughout it. *The smell of sawdust and glue pervaded the factory.* ◆◇◇◇◇ VERB V n FORMAL

per·va·sive /pəˈveɪsɪv/. Something, especially something bad, that is **pervasive** is present or felt throughout a place or thing. *...the pervasive influence of the army in national life.* ♦ **per·va·sive·ness** *...the pervasiveness of computer technology.* ◆◇◇◇◇ ADJ-GRADED FORMAL / N-UNCOUNT

per·verse /pəˈvɜːs/. Someone who is **perverse** deliberately does things that are unreasonable or that result in harm for themselves. *It would be perverse to stop this healthy trend.* ♦ **per·verse·ly** *She was perversely pleased to be causing trouble.* ♦ **per·ver·sity** *Undoubtedly it would be wrong to continue out of perversity.* ◆◇◇◇◇ ADJ-GRADED PRAGMATICS / ADV-GRADED / N-UNCOUNT

per·ver·sion /pəˈvɜːʃən, -ʒən/ **perversions.** 1 You can refer to a sexual desire or action that you consider to be abnormal and unacceptable as a **perversion.** 2 A **perversion** of something is a form of it that is bad or wrong, or the changing of it into this form. *What monstrous perversion of the human spirit leads a sniper to open fire on a bus carrying children?* ◆◇◇◇◇ N-VAR / N-VAR

per·vert, perverts, perverting, perverted. The verb is pronounced /pəˈvɜːt/. The noun is pronounced /ˈpɜːvɜːt/. 1 If you **pervert** something such as a process or society, you interfere with it so that it is not as good as it used to be or as it should ◆◇◇◇◇ VERB V n FORMAL

be. *Any reform will destroy and pervert our constitution.* ♦ **per·vert·ed** *...a perverted form of knowledge.* **2** If someone **perverts the course of justice,** they commit the offence of deliberately trying to make it difficult to discover who committed a particular crime, for example by destroying evidence or lying to the police. **3** If you say that someone is a **pervert,** you mean that you consider their behaviour, especially their sexual behaviour, to be immoral or unacceptable. ♦ **perverted** *You've been protecting sick and perverted men.*
ADJ-GRADED
PHRASE
LEGAL

N-COUNT

ADJ-GRADED

pes·sa·ry /'pesəri/ **pessaries.** A **pessary** is a small block of a medicine or a contraceptive chemical that a woman puts in her vagina.
N-COUNT

pes·si·mism /'pesɪmɪzəm/. **Pessimism** is the belief that bad things are going to happen. *...universal pessimism about the economy.* ♦ **pes·si·mist** /'pesɪmɪst/, **pessimists** *I'm a natural pessimist; I usually expect the worst.* ♦ **pes·si·mis·tic** /ˌpesɪ'mɪstɪk/ *Hardy has often been criticised for an excessively pessimistic view of life.*
♦◇◇◇◇
N-UNCOUNT
N-COUNT

ADJ-GRADED

pest /pest/ **pests. 1** **Pests** are insects or small animals which damage crops or food supplies. *...new and innovative methods of pest control.* **2** You can describe someone, especially a child, as a **pest** if they keep bothering you. *He climbed on the table, pulled my hair, and was generally a pest.*
♦♦◇◇◇
N-COUNT
N-COUNT
PRAGMATICS
INFORMAL

pes·ter /'pestə/ **pesters, pestering, pestered.** If you say that someone **is pestering** you, you mean that they keep asking you to do something, or keep talking to you, and you find this annoying. *He gets fed up with people pestering him for money. ...that creep who's been pestering you to go out with him.*
♦◇◇◇◇
VERB: V n
PRAGMATICS
V n prep
V n to-inf
Also V

pes·ti·cide /'pestɪsaɪd/ **pesticides. Pesticides** are chemicals which farmers put on their crops to kill harmful insects.
♦♦◇◇◇
N-VAR

pes·ti·lence /'pestɪləns/ **pestilences. Pestilence** is any disease that spreads quickly and kills large numbers of people.
N-VAR
LITERARY

pes·tle /'pesəl/ **pestles.** A **pestle** is a short rod with a thick round end. It is used for crushing things such as herbs, spices, or grain in a bowl called a mortar.
N-COUNT

pes·to /'pestəʊ/. **Pesto** is an Italian sauce made from basil, garlic, pine nuts, cheese, and olive oil.
N-UNCOUNT

pet /pet/ **pets, petting, petted. 1** A **pet** is an animal that you keep in your home to give you company and pleasure. *It is plainly cruel to keep turtles as pets.* **2** Someone's **pet** theory, project, or subject is one that they particularly support or like. Someone's **pet** hate is something that they particularly dislike. *Three of my pet hates are estate agents, politicians and pompous people.* **3** Some people call the person they are talking to **'pet'** to show affection or friendliness. *It's all right, pet, let me do it.* **4** If you **pet** a person or animal, you pat or stroke them affectionately.
♦♦♦◇◇
N-COUNT

ADJ: ADJ n

N-VOC
PRAGMATICS

VERB: V n

pet·al /'petəl/ **petals.** The **petals** of a flower are the thin coloured or white parts which together form the flower.
♦◇◇◇◇
N-COUNT

pe·ter /'piːtə/ **peters, petering, petered.**
peter out. If something **peters out,** it gradually comes to an end. *The six-month strike seemed to be petering out.*
♦◇◇◇◇
PHRASAL VB
V P

pethi·dine /'peθɪdiːn/. **Pethidine** is a drug given to people to stop them feeling pain. Women who are giving birth are often given pethidine.
N-UNCOUNT

pet·it bour·geois /ˌpeti 'bʊəʒwɑː/; also spelled **pet·ty bourgeois.** Someone or something that is **petit bourgeois** belongs or relates to the lower middle class; used showing disapproval. ♦ **pet·it bour·geoi·sie** /ˌpeti bʊəʒwɑː'ziː/. The **petit bourgeoisie** are people in the lower middle class.
ADJ
PRAGMATICS
FORMAL

N-COLL-SING

pe·tite /pə'tiːt/. If you say that a woman is **petite,** you are politely saying that she is small and slim. *...a petite and attractive blond woman.*
ADJ-GRADED
PRAGMATICS

pet·it four /ˌpeti 'fɔː/ **petits fours** or **petit fours.** **Petits fours** are very small sweet cakes or biscuits.
N-COUNT

pe·ti·tion /pə'tɪʃən/ **petitions, petitioning, petitioned. 1** A **petition** is a document signed by a lot
♦♦◇◇◇
N-COUNT

of people which asks a government or other official group to do a particular thing. ♦ **pe·ti·tion·er, pe·titioners** *The petitioners were unable to see the Serbian president.* **2** A **petition** is an application to a court of law for some legal action to be taken. *His lawyers filed a petition for all charges to be dropped.* **3** If you **petition** someone in authority, you make a formal request to them. *...couples petitioning for divorce... Twenty-five of his supporters petitioned him to restore the monarchy... She's petitioning to regain custody of the child.* ♦ **pe·ti·tion·er** *...a legal process that treated petitioners for divorce with insensitive cruelty.*
N-COUNT

N-COUNT
FORMAL

VERB: V n
V forn
V n to-inf
V to-inf
Also V n forn
N-COUNT

'pet name, pet names. A **pet name** is a special name that you use for a close friend or a member of your family instead of using their real name. *His pet name for her was Bird.*
N-COUNT

pet·rel /'petrəl/. **petrels.** A **petrel** is a type of seabird which often flies a long way out from land. There are many varieties of petrel.
N-COUNT

pet·ri·fied /'petrɪfaɪd/. A **petrified** plant or animal has died and has gradually turned into stone.
ADJ: ADJ n

pet·ri·fy /'petrɪfaɪ/ **petrifies, petrifying, petrified. 1** If something **petrifies** you, it makes you feel very frightened indeed. ♦ **pet·ri·fied** *I've always been petrified of being alone.* ♦ **pet·ri·fy·ing** *It was absolutely petrifying.* **2** If something such as a society or institution **petrifies,** it ceases to change and develop. *...the fear that a political deadlock may petrify economic initiatives.*
VERB: V n
ADJ-GRADED
ADJ-GRADED
V-ERG: V
V n
FORMAL

pet·ro·chemi·cal /ˌpetrəʊ'kemɪkəl/ **petrochemicals;** also spelled **petro-chemical. Petrochemicals** are chemicals that are obtained from petroleum or natural gas.
♦◇◇◇◇
N-COUNT

pet·rol /'petrəl/. **Petrol** is a liquid which is used as a fuel for motor vehicles. The usual American word is **gas** or **gasoline.**
♦♦◇◇◇
N-UNCOUNT
BRITISH

'petrol bomb, petrol bombs. A **petrol bomb** is a simple bomb consisting of a bottle full of petrol with a cloth in it that is lit just before the bottle is thrown.
N-COUNT
BRITISH

pe·tro·leum /pə'trəʊliəm/. **Petroleum** is oil which is found under the surface of the earth or under the sea bed. Petrol and paraffin are obtained from petroleum.
♦♦◇◇◇
N-UNCOUNT

pe'troleum jelly. **Petroleum jelly** is a soft, clear, jelly-like substance obtained from petroleum and used as a lubricant.
N-UNCOUNT

'petrol station, petrol stations. A **petrol station** is a garage by the side of the road where petrol is sold and put into vehicles. The usual American expression is **gas station.**
♦◇◇◇◇
N-COUNT
BRITISH

'petrol tank, petrol tanks. The **petrol tank** In a motor vehicle is the container for petrol. The usual American word is **gas tank.**
N-COUNT
BRITISH

pet·ti·coat /'petikəʊt/ **petticoats.** A **petticoat** is a piece of clothing like a thin skirt, which is worn under a skirt or dress.
N-COUNT

pet·ting /'petɪŋ/. **Petting** is the activity of kissing and stroking another person in a sexual way, but without having sexual intercourse.
N-UNCOUNT

pet·ty /'peti/ **pettier, pettiest. 1** You can use **petty** to describe things such as rules, problems, or arguments which you think are trivial or unimportant. *...endless rules and petty regulations.* **2** If you describe someone's behaviour as **petty,** you disapprove of it because you think it shows that they care too much about small, unimportant things. ♦ **pet·ti·ness** *Never had she met such spite and pettiness.* **3** **Petty** is used of people or actions that are comparatively low in importance, rank, seriousness, or scale. *...petty crime, such as handbag-snatching.*
♦♦◇◇◇
ADJ-GRADED
PRAGMATICS
ADJ-GRADED
PRAGMATICS
N-UNCOUNT
ADJ: ADJ n

petty 'bourgeois. See petit bourgeois.

petty 'cash. **Petty cash** is money that is kept in the office of a company, to be used for making small payments when necessary.
N-UNCOUNT

'petty officer, petty officers. A **petty officer** is an officer in the navy.

petu·lant /'petʃʊlənt/. Someone who is **petulant** is unreasonably angry and upset in a childish way.
ADJ-GRADED

♦ **petu·lance** /'petʃʊləns/. *His petulance made her* N-UNCOUNT
impatient. ♦ **petu·lant·ly** *He petulantly threatened* ADV-GRADED
to quit tennis if he was fined.

pe·tu·nia /pɪ'tjuːniə, AM -tuː-/ **petunias**. A petunia N-COUNT
is a type of garden plant with pink, white or purple
trumpet-shaped flowers.

pew /pjuː/ **pews**. A pew is a long wooden seat with ♦◇◇◇◇
a back, which people sit on in church. N-COUNT

pew·ter /'pjuːtə/. **Pewter** is a grey metal which is ♦◇◇◇◇
made by mixing tin and lead. Pewter was often used N-UNCOUNT
in former times to make ornaments or containers
for eating and drinking.

PG /,piː 'dʒiː/. Films that are labelled **PG** are not ♦◇◇◇◇
considered suitable for younger children to see ADJ
without an adult being with them. **PG** is an abbreviation for 'parental guidance'.

PGCE /,piː dʒiː siː 'iː/ **PGCEs**. In Britain, a PGCE N-COUNT
is a teaching qualification that qualifies graduates to
teach in a state school. PGCE is an abbreviation of
'Postgraduate Certificate of Education'. Compare
BEd.

pH /,piː 'eɪtʃ/. The **pH** of a solution indicates how ♦◇◇◇◇
acid or alkaline the solution is. A pH of less than 7 N-UNCOUNT
indicates that it is an acid, and a pH of more than 7
indicates that it is an alkali.

phal·anx /'fælæŋks/ **phalanxes** or **phalanges**
/fə'lændʒiːz/. **1**A **phalanx** is a group of soldiers or N-COUNT
police who are standing or marching close together FORMAL
ready to fight. **2**A **phalanx** of people is a large N-COUNT
group who are brought together for a particular FORMAL
purpose. *...a phalanx of waiters with silver dishes.*

phal·lic /'fælɪk/. Something that is **phallic** is ADJ-GRADED
shaped like an erect penis, or symbolic of male sexual powers. *Cars are phallic symbols.*

phal·lus /'fæləs/ **phalluses** or **phalli** /'fælaɪ/. **1**A N-COUNT
phallus is a model of an erect penis, especially one
used as a symbol in ancient religions. **2**A **phallus** is N-COUNT
a penis. TECHNICAL

phan·ta·sy /'fæntəzi/ **phantasies**. See fantasy.

phan·tom /'fæntəm/ **phantoms**. **1**A **phantom** is ♦◇◇◇◇
a ghost. **2**You use **phantom** to describe something N-COUNT
which does not really exist, but which someone be- ADJ: ADJ n
lieves or pretends does exist. *She was always taking
regular days off for what her colleagues considered
phantom illnesses. ...phantom companies run by her
relations.* **3**Phantom can refer to something that is ADJ: ADJ n
done by an unknown person, especially something
criminal. *...the people who claim they have suffered
phantom withdrawals from automatic cash
dispensers.*

phar·ma·ceu·ti·cal /,fɑːmə'suːtɪkəl/ **pharma-** ♦♦◇◇◇
ceuticals. **1**Pharmaceutical means connected ADJ: ADJ n
with the industrial production of medicine. *They
claim about 50 percent of the school's research
is funded by pharmaceutical companies.* N-PLURAL
2Pharmaceuticals are medicines.

phar·ma·cist /'fɑːməsɪst/ **pharmacists**. A phar- ♦◇◇◇◇
macist is a person who is qualified to prepare and N-COUNT
sell medicines. The shop where a pharmacist works
can also be called a **pharmacist** or a **pharmacist's**.

phar·ma·col·ogy /,fɑːmə'kɒlədʒi/. **Pharmacology** N-UNCOUNT
is the branch of science relating to drugs and medicines. ♦ **phar·ma·co·logi·cal** /,fɑːməkə'lɒdʒɪkəl/ ADJ: ADJ n
*As little as 50mg of caffeine can produce pharmaco-
logical effects.* ♦ **phar·ma·colo·gist**, **pharma-** N-COUNT
cologists *...a pharmacologist from the University
of California.*

phar·ma·cy /'fɑːməsi/ **pharmacies**. **1**A pharma- ♦◇◇◇◇
cy is a shop or a department in a shop where medi- N-COUNT
cines are sold or given out. **2**Pharmacy is the job N-UNCOUNT
or the science of preparing medicines.

phase /feɪz/ **phases, phasing, phased**. **1**A ♦♦♦◇◇
phase is a particular stage in a process or in the N-COUNT
gradual development of something. *Most kids will
go through a phase of being faddy about what they
eat.* **2**If an action or change **is phased** over a period VB: usu
of time, it is done in stages. *The redundancies will* passive
be phased over two years. ...the phased introduction V-ed
of environmental taxes. **3**If one thing is **out of** PHRASE
phase with another, the two things are not working

or happening together as they should be, or are not
in harmony with each other. If two things are **in
phase**, they are happening or working together as
they should be, or are in harmony with each other.
*The British and German economies were out of
phase.*

phase in. If a new way of doing something **is phased** PHRASAL VB
in, it is introduced gradually. *...the government's poli-* beV-ed P
cy of phasing in Arabic as the official academic lan- V P noun
guage. Also V n P

phase out. If something **is phased out**, people PHRASAL VB
gradually stop using it or doing it. *They phased out my* beV-ed P
job in favor of a computer. V P noun
Also V n P

PhD /,piː eɪtʃ 'diː/ **PhDs**. **1**A **PhD** is a degree ♦◇◇◇◇
awarded to people who have done advanced re-
search into a particular subject. **PhD** is an abbreviation for 'Doctor of Philosophy'. **2**PhD is written
after someone's name to indicate that they have a
PhD. *...R.D. Combes, PhD.*

pheas·ant /'fezənt/ **pheasants; pheasant** can ♦◇◇◇◇
also be used as the plural form. A **pheasant** is a N-COUNT
long-tailed bird. Pheasants are often shot as a sport
and then eaten. ▶ **Pheasant** is this bird eaten as N-UNCOUNT
food. *...roast pheasant.*

phe·nom·ena /fɪ'nɒmɪnə/. **Phenomena** is the plural of phenomenon.

phe·nom·enal /fɪ'nɒmɪnəl/. Something that is ♦◇◇◇◇
phenomenal is so great or good that it is very un- ADJ-GRADED
usual indeed. *Exports of Australian wine are growing at a phenomenal rate.* ♦ **phe·nom·enal·ly** ADV-GRADED
...her phenomenally successful singing career.

phe·nom·enol·ogy /fɪ,nɒmɪ'nɒlədʒi/. **Phenom-** N-UNCOUNT
enology is a branch of philosophy which deals with TECHNICAL
consciousness, thought, and experience. ♦ **phe-**
·nom·eno·logi·cal /fɪ,nɒmɪnə'lɒdʒɪkəl/ *...a phe-* ADJ
nomenological approach to the definition of 'reality'.

phe·nom·enon /fɪ'nɒmɪnən, AM -nɑːn/ **phenom-** ♦◇◇◇◇
ena. A **phenomenon** is something that is observed N-COUNT
to happen or exist. *...scientific explanations of natu-* FORMAL
*ral phenomena... This form of civil disobedience
isn't a particularly new phenomenon.*

phero·mone /'ferəməʊn/ **pheromones**. Some ♦◇◇◇◇
animals and insects produce chemicals called N-COUNT
pheromones which affect the behaviour of other TECHNICAL
animals and insects of the same type, for example
by attracting them sexually.

phew /fjuː/. **Phew** is used in writing to represent EXCLAM
the soft whistling sound that you make when you
breathe out quickly, for example when you are relieved or shocked about something or when you are
very hot. *Phew, what a relief!*

phial /faɪəl/ **phials**. A **phial** is a small tube-shaped N-COUNT
glass bottle used, for example, to hold medicine. BRITISH

phi·lan·der·er /fɪ'lændərə/ **philanderers**. If you N-COUNT
say that a man is a **philanderer**, you disapprove of PRAGMATICS
him because he flirts a lot or has a lot of casual love FORMAL
affairs with women.

phi·lan·der·ing /fɪ'lændərɪŋ/ **philanderings**. Phi- N-UNCOUNT:
landering means having casual affairs with women; also N in pl
used showing disapproval. *She intended to leave her* PRAGMATICS
husband because of his philandering. ▶ Also an ad- ADJ: ADJ n
jective. *...her philandering husband.*

phi·lan·thro·py /fɪ'lænθrəpi/. **Philanthropy** is the N-UNCOUNT
giving of money to people who need it, without
wanting anything in return. *...a retired banker well
known for his philanthropy.* ♦ **phil·an·throp·ic** ADJ-GRADED
/,fɪlən'θrɒpɪk/. *Some of the best services for the ageing are sponsored by philanthropic organizations...
He said his involvement in Arsenal isn't purely philanthropic.* ♦ **phi·lan·thro·pist** /fɪ'lænθrəpɪst/ **phi-** N-COUNT
lanthropists. *Dr Hammer was also known as a
philanthropist.*

phi·lat·ely /fɪ'lætəli/. **Philately** is the hobby of col- N-UNCOUNT
lecting and learning about postage stamps. ♦ **phi-** FORMAL
·lat·elist /fɪ'lætəlɪst/, **philatelists** *More than 300* N-COUNT
*British philatelists belong to the Society of Olympic
collectors.*

-phile /-faɪl/ or **-ophile** /-əfaɪl/ **-philes** or **-** SUFFIX
ophiles. **-phile** or **-ophile** occurs in words which
refer to someone who has a very strong liking for

people or things of a particular kind. For example, an **Anglophile** is someone who has a strong liking for England and English culture.

phil·har·mon·ic /ˌfɪlɑːˈmɒnɪk/. A **philharmonic** ◆◇◇◇◇ orchestra is a large orchestra which plays classical ADJ: ADJ n music. *The Lithuanian Philharmonic Orchestra played Beethoven's Ninth Symphony.*

phil·is·tine /ˈfɪlɪstaɪn, AM -stiːn/ **philistines.** If you N-COUNT call someone a **philistine**, you mean that they do PRAGMATICS not care about or understand good art, music, or literature, and do not think that they are important; used showing disapproval. ▶ Also an adjective. *...a* ADJ-GRADED: *philistine government that is blamed for allowing* ADJ n *the arts to decline.* ◆ **phil·is·tin·ism** /ˈfɪlɪstɪnɪzəm/. N-UNCOUNT *What horrified him was her philistinism.*

phi·lol·ogy /fɪˈlɒlədʒi/. **Philology** is the study of N-UNCOUNT words, especially the history and development of the words in a particular language or group of languages. ◆ **phi·lolo·gist, philologists.** N-COUNT

phi·loso·pher /fɪˈlɒsəfə/ **philosophers.** 1 A phi- ◆◇◇◇◇ losopher is a person who studies or writes about N-COUNT philosophy. *...the Greek philosopher Plato.* 2 If you N-COUNT refer to someone as a **philosopher**, you mean that they think deeply and seriously about life and other basic matters.

philo·soph·ic /ˌfɪləˈsɒfɪk/. **Philosophic** means the ADJ-GRADED same as **philosophical**.

philo·sophi·cal /ˌfɪləˈsɒfɪkəl/. 1 Philosophical ◆◆◇◇◇ means concerned with or relating to philosophy. *He* ADJ *was more accustomed to cocktail party chatter than to political or philosophical discussions.* ◆ **philo·sophi·cal·ly** /ˌfɪləˈsɒfɪkli/ *Wiggins says he's not a* ADV *coward, but that he's philosophically opposed to war.* 2 Someone who is **philosophical** does not get ADJ-GRADED upset when disappointing or disturbing things hap- PRAGMATICS pen; used showing approval. *Lewis has grown philosophical about life.* ◆ **philosophically** *She says* ADV-GRADED: *philosophically: 'It could have been far worse.'* ADV after v

phi·loso·phize /fɪˈlɒsəfaɪz/ **philosophizes, phi-** VERB: V **losophizing, philosophized;** also spelled **phi-** V about/on n **losophise** in British English. If you say that Also V with someone **is philosophizing**, you mean that they are quote talking or thinking about important subjects such as life, often in a boring or pointless way. *...a tendency to philosophize about racial harmony.* ◆ **phi·loso·phiz·ing** *She loved all the sitting around at table* N-UNCOUNT *and philosophising.*

phi·loso·phy /fɪˈlɒsəfi/ **philosophies.** 1 Philoso- ◆◆◆◇◇ phy is the study or creation of theories about basic N-UNCOUNT things such as the nature of existence, knowledge, thought, or about how people should live. *He was a professor of philosophy. ...traditional Chinese philosophy.* 2 A **philosophy** is a particular set of ideas N-COUNT that a philosopher has. *...the philosophies of Socrates, Plato, and Aristotle.* 3 A **philosophy** is a N-COUNT particular theory that someone has about how to live or how to deal with a particular situation. *The best philosophy is to change your food habits to a low-sugar, high-fibre diet... Annie's work reflects her philosophy that life is full of mysteries.*

phlegm /flem/. **Phlegm** is the thick yellowish sub- N-UNCOUNT stance that develops in your throat and at the back of your nose when you have a cold.

phleg·mat·ic /flegˈmætɪk/. Someone who is **phleg-** ADJ-GRADED **matic** stays calm even when upsetting or exciting FORMAL things happen. *...a most phlegmatic man, steadily working on as the rain splashed down.*

-phobe /-fəʊb/ or **-ophobe** /-əfəʊb/ **-phobes** or – SUFFIX **ophobes.** **-phobe** or **-ophobe** occurs in words which refer to someone who has a very strong, irrational fear or hatred of people or things of a particular kind. *Its design makes it suitable for the computerphobe who just wants to type and see something come out looking right.*

pho·bia /ˈfəʊbiə/ **phobias.** A phobia is a very ◆◇◇◇◇ strong irrational fear or hatred of something. *The* N-COUNT *man had a phobia about flying.* ▶ Also a suffix. *The* SUFFIX *place seethed with Europhobia... Technophobia increases with age.*

pho·bic /ˈfəʊbɪk/ **phobics.** 1 A **phobic** feeling or ADJ reaction results from or is related to a strong, irrational fear or hatred of something. *Many children acquire a phobic horror of dogs.* 2 Someone who is ADJ-GRADED **phobic** has a strong, irrational fear or hatred of something. *In Victorian times people were phobic about getting on trains. They weren't used to it.* ▶ Also a noun. *Social phobics quake at the thought* N-COUNT *of meeting strangers.* ▶ Also a suffix. *Curtiz seemed* SUFFIX *to have a particular taste for Anglophobic items.*

phoe·nix /ˈfiːnɪks/ **phoenixes.** 1 A phoenix is an N-COUNT imaginary bird which, according to ancient myths, burns itself to ashes every five hundred years and is then born again. 2 If you describe someone or N-SING something as a **phoenix**, you mean that they return again after seeming to disappear or be destroyed. *Out of the ashes of the economic shambles, a phoenix of recovery can arise.*

phone /fəʊn/ **phones, phoning, phoned.** 1 The ◆◆◆◇ **phone** is an electrical system that you use to talk to N-SING someone else in another place, by dialling a number on a piece of equipment and speaking into it. *She looked forward to talking to her daughter by phone... Do you have an address and phone number for him?* 2 The **phone** is the piece of equipment N-COUNT that you use when you dial someone's phone number and talk to them. *Jamie answered the phone.* ● See also **mobile phone.** 3 If you say that someone N-SING picks up or puts down **the phone**, you mean that they lift or replace the receiver. 4 When you **phone** someone, you dial their phone VERB: V n number and speak to them by phone. *I got more and* V *more angry as I waited for her to phone.* 5 If someone PHRASE is **on the phone**, they are speaking to someone else by phone. 6 If you are **on the phone**, you have a phone in PHRASE your home or place of work, so that you can be con- BRITISH tacted by phone.

phone up. When you **phone** someone **up**, you dial PHRASAL VB their phone number and speak to them by phone. V n P *Phone him up and tell him to come and have dinner* Also V P noun *with you.* BRITISH

phone book, phone books. A phone book is a N-COUNT book that contains an alphabetical list of the names, addresses, and telephone numbers of the people in a town or area.

phone booth, phone booths. 1 A phone booth N-COUNT is a place in a station, hotel, or other public building where there is a public telephone. 2 A phone N-COUNT booth is a small shelter in the street in which there AMERICAN is a public telephone. The British term is **phone box** or **call box.**

phone box, phone boxes. A phone box is a N-COUNT small shelter in the street in which there is a public BRITISH telephone. The American term is **phone booth.**

phone call, phone calls. If you **make a phone** ◆◆◇◇◇ **call**, you dial somebody's phone number and speak N-COUNT to them by phone.

phone-in, phone-ins. A phone-in is a pro- ◆◇◇◇◇ gramme on radio or television in which people tele- N-COUNT phone with questions or opinions and their calls are BRITISH broadcast.

phone-tapping. Phone-tapping is the activity of N-UNCOUNT listening secretly to someone's phone conversations using special electronic equipment. ● See also **tap.**

pho·net·ics /fəˈnetɪks/; the form **phonetic** is used as a modifier. 1 **Phonetics** is the study of speech N-UNCOUNT sounds. 2 **Phonetic** means relating to the sound of TECHNICAL a word or to the sounds that are used in languages. ADJ *...the Japanese phonetic system, with its relatively few, simple sounds.*

pho·ney /ˈfəʊni/ **phoneys;** also spelled **phony.** ◆◇◇◇◇ 1 If you describe something as **phoney**, you disap- ADJ-GRADED prove of it because it is false rather than genuine. PRAGMATICS *He'd telephoned with some phoney excuse she didn't* INFORMAL *believe for a minute.* 2 If you say that someone is ADJ-GRADED **phoney**, you disapprove of them because they are PRAGMATICS pretending to be someone that they are not in order INFORMAL to deceive people. ▶ Also a noun. *'He's false, a pho-* N-COUNT *ney,' Harry muttered.*

ˌphoney ˈwar. A **phoney war** is when two oppos- N-SING
ing groups are openly hostile towards each other or BRITISH
are in competition with each other, as if they were
at war, but there is no real fighting.

pho·no·graph /ˈfəʊnəgrɑːf, -græf/ **phonographs.** N-COUNT
A **phonograph** is a record player. DATED

pho·ny /ˈfəʊni/. See **phoney.**

phos·phate /ˈfɒsfeɪt/ **phosphates.** A phosphate ◆◇◇◇◇
is a chemical compound that contains phosphorus. N-VAR
Phosphates are often used in fertilizers.

phos·pho·res·cent /ˌfɒsfəˈresənt/. A **phosphores-** ADJ
cent object or colour glows in the dark with a soft
light, but gives out little or no heat. ...*phosphores-*
cent paint. ◆ **phos·pho·res·cence.** Phosphores- N-UNCOUNT
cence is a glow or soft light produced by a phos-
phorescent object.

phos·pho·rus /ˈfɒsfərəs/. **Phosphorus** is a chemi- ◆◇◇◇◇
cal element which glows faintly, and it burns on N-UNCOUNT
contact with air.

pho·to /ˈfəʊtəʊ/ **photos.** A photo is the same as a ◆◆◆◆◇
photograph. *We must take a photo!* N-COUNT

photo- /ˈfəʊtəʊ-/. **Photo-** is added to nouns and ad- PREFIX
jectives in order to form other nouns and adjectives
which refer or relate to photography or photographic processes, or to light. ...*an eight-day photo-trip to*
northern Greece. ...*a photo-sensitive detector system.*

photo·copi·er /ˈfəʊtəʊkɒpɪə/ **photocopiers.** A N-COUNT
photocopier is a machine which quickly copies
documents onto paper by photographing them.

photo·copy /ˈfəʊtəʊkɒpi/ **photocopies, photo-** ◆◇◇◇◇
copying, photocopied. If you **photocopy** a VERB: V n
document, you make a copy of it using a photocopier. ► Also a noun. ...*photocopies of newspaper* N-COUNT
cuttings.

ˌphoto-ˈfinish, photo-finishes. If the end of a N-COUNT
race is a **photo-finish**, two or more of the competitors cross the finishing line so close together that a
photograph of the finish has to be examined to decide who has won.

Photo·fit /ˈfəʊtəʊfɪt/ **Photofits.** A Photofit is a pic- N-COUNT
ture of someone wanted by the police which is BRITISH
made up of several photographs or drawings of different facial features. Photofit is a trademark.

photo·gen·ic /ˌfəʊtəʊˈdʒenɪk/. Someone who is ADJ-GRADED
photogenic looks nice in photographs.

photo·graph /ˈfəʊtəgrɑːf, -græf/ **photographs,** ◆◆◆◆◇
photographing, photographed. 1 A **photo-** N-COUNT
graph is a picture that is made using a camera. *Her*
photograph appeared on the front page of The New
York Times. 2 When you **photograph** someone or VERB: V n
something, you use a camera to obtain a picture of beV-ed-ing
them. *They were photographed kissing on the plat-*
form. ◆ **pho·tog·ra·pher** /fəˈtɒgrəfə/ **photogra-** N-COUNT
phers. A **photographer** is someone who takes
photographs as a job or hobby.

photo·graph·ic /ˌfəʊtəˈgræfɪk/. 1 Photographic ◆◆◇◇◇
means connected with photographs or photogra- ADJ
phy. ...*photographic equipment.* ◆ **photo·graphi-**
·cal·ly /ˌfəʊtəˈgræfɪkli/ ...*photographically repro-* ADV
duced copies of his notes. 2 If you have a **photo-** ADJ
graphic memory, you are able to remember things
in great detail after you have seen them.

pho·tog·ra·phy /fəˈtɒgrəfi/. **Photography** is the ◆◆◇◇◇
skill, job, or process of producing photographs. N-UNCOUNT
...*some of the top names in fashion photography.*

photo·jour·nal·ism /ˌfəʊtəʊˈdʒɜːnəlɪzəm/; also N-UNCOUNT
spelled **photo-journalism. Photojournalism** is a
form of journalism in which stories are presented
mainly through photographs rather than words.
◆ **photo·jour·nal·ist, photojournalists.** N-COUNT

pho·ton /ˈfəʊtɒn/ **photons.** A photon is a particle ◆◇◇◇◇
of light. N-COUNT
TECHNICAL

ˈphoto opportunity, photo opportunities. If a N-COUNT
politician or other public figure arranges a **photo**
opportunity, they invite the newspapers and television to photograph them doing something which
they think will interest or impress the public.

photo·syn·the·sis /ˌfəʊtəʊˈsɪnθəsɪs/. Photosyn- N-UNCOUNT
thesis is the way that green plants make their food TECHNICAL
using sunlight.

phras·al verb /ˌfreɪzəl ˈvɜːb/ **phrasal verbs.** A N-COUNT
phrasal verb is a combination of a verb and an adverb or preposition, for example 'shut up' or 'look
after', which together have a particular meaning.

phrase /freɪz/ **phrases, phrasing, phrased.** ◆◆◆◇◇
1 A **phrase** is a short group of words that people of- N-COUNT
ten use as a way of referring to something or saying
something. The meaning of a phrase is often not
obvious from the meaning of the individual words
in it. In this dictionary, phrases are labelled PHRASE
in the grammar notes beside the entries. *He used a*
phrase I hate: 'You have to be cruel to be kind.' 2 A N-COUNT
phrase is a small group of words which forms a
unit, either on its own or within a sentence. *A writer*
spends many hours going over and over a scene –
changing a phrase here, a word there. 3 If you VERB
phrase something in a particular way, you express it V n adv
in words in that way. *I would have phrased it quite* V n as n
differently... *They phrased it as a question.* 4 If PHRASE
someone has a particular **turn of phrase**, they have
a particular way of expressing themselves in words.
Rose's stories weren't bad; she had a nice turn of
phrase. ● to **coin a phrase**: see **coin.**

ˈphrase book, phrase books. A **phrase book** is a N-COUNT
book for travellers to a foreign country. It contains
useful words and expressions, with translations.

phra·seol·ogy /ˌfreɪziˈɒlədʒi/. If something is ex- N-UNCOUNT
pressed using a particular type of **phraseology**, it is
expressed in words and expressions of that type.
This careful phraseology is clearly intended to appeal
to various sides of the conflict.

phras·ing /ˈfreɪzɪŋ/. 1 The **phrasing** of something N-UNCOUNT
that is said or written is the exact words that are
chosen to express the ideas in it. ...*a letter to the*
Pope, which necessitates careful phrasing. 2 The N-UNCOUNT
phrasing of someone who is singing, playing a
piece of music, or acting is the way in which they
divide up the work by pausing slightly in appropriate places.

phre·nol·ogy /frɪˈnɒlədʒi/. **Phrenology** is the study N-UNCOUNT
of the size and shape of people's skulls in the belief
that it can reveal what their characters and abilities
are. *He has submitted to a cranial phrenology*
examination.

physi·cal /ˈfɪzɪkəl/ **physicals.** 1 Physical qual- ◆◆◆◆◇
ities, actions, or things are connected with a per- ADJ-GRADED
son's body, rather than with their mind. *Physical*
activity promotes good health... *The attraction be-*
tween them is physical. ◆ **physi·cal·ly** ...*disabled* ADV
people who cannot physically use a telephone. 2 ADJ: ADJ n
Physical is used in expressions such as **physical**
love and **physical relationships** to refer to sexual
relationships between people. 3 Someone who is ADJ-GRADED
physical touches people a lot, either in an affectionate way or in a rough way. 4 A **physical** is a medical N-COUNT
examination, done in order to see if someone is fit
and well enough to do a particular job or to join the
army.
5 **Physical** things are real things that can be touched ADJ
and seen, rather than ideas or concepts. *Physical and*
ideological barriers had come down in Eastern Europe.
◆ **physically** ...*physically cut off from every other* ADV
country. 6 **Physical** means relating to the structure, ADJ: ADJ n
size, or shape of something that can be touched and
seen. ...*the physical properties (weight, volume, hard-*
ness, etc.) of a substance. 7 **Physical** means connected ADJ: ADJ n
with physics or the laws of physics. ...*the physical laws*
of combustion and thermodynamics.

ˌphysical edu· cation. Physical education is the N-UNCOUNT
school subject in which children do physical exercises or take part in physical games and sports.

ˌphysical ˈscience, physical sciences. The N-COUNT
physical sciences are branches of science such as
physics, chemistry, and geology that are concerned
with natural forces and with things that do not have
life.

phy·si·cian /fɪˈzɪʃən/ **physicians.** A physician is ◆◆◇◇◇
a doctor. *Be sure to consult your physician before* N-COUNT
making a major change in your physical activity. FORMAL,
AMERICAN

P

phys·i·cist /'fɪzɪsɪst/ **physicists.** A **physicist** is a person who does research connected with physics or who studies physics. ◆◆◇◇◇ N-COUNT

phys·ics /'fɪzɪks/. **Physics** is the scientific study of forces such as heat, light, sound, pressure, gravity, and electricity, and the way that they affect objects. ◆◆◇◇◇ N-UNCOUNT

physio /'fɪziəʊ/ **physios.** 1 A **physio** is a **physio·therapist.** 2 **Physio** is physiotherapy. *At the start of the week, nine of the 18 players were having physio for niggling problems.* N-COUNT INFORMAL N-UNCOUNT INFORMAL, BRITISH

physi·og·no·my /ˌfɪzi'ɒnəmi/ **physiognomies.** Your **physiognomy** is your face, especially when it is considered to show your real character. N-COUNT FORMAL

physi·ol·ogy /ˌfɪzi'ɒlədʒi/. 1 **Physiology** is the scientific study of how people's and animals' bodies function, and of how plants function. ♦ **physi·olo·gist, physiologists** ... *a retired plant physiologist.* 2 The **physiology** of a human or animal's body or of a plant is the way that it functions. ... *the physiology of respiration.* ♦ **physio·logi·cal** /ˌfɪzi'lɒdʒɪkəl/ ...*the physiological effects of stress.* ♦ **physio·logi·cal·ly** *Camels are among the most physiologically resilient creatures on Earth.* ◆◇◇◇◇ N-UNCOUNT N-COUNT N-UNCOUNT ADJ ADV

physio·thera·pist /ˌfɪziəʊ'θerəpɪst/ **physiothera·pists.** A **physiotherapist** is a person who treats people using physiotherapy. ◆◇◇◇◇ N-COUNT

physio·thera·py /ˌfɪziəʊ'θerəpi/. **Physiotherapy** is medical treatment for problems of the joints, muscles, or nerves, which involves doing exercises or having part of your body massaged or warmed. N-UNCOUNT

phy·sique /fɪ'ziːk/ **physiques.** Someone's **physique** is the shape and size of their body. ◆◇◇◇◇ N-COUNT

pi /paɪ/. **Pi** is a number, approximately 3.142, which is equal to the circumference of a circle divided by its diameter. It is usually represented by the Greek letter π. NUMBER

pia·nist /'piːənɪst, AM pi'æn-/ **pianists.** A **pianist** is a person who plays the piano. ◆◇◇◇◇ N-COUNT

pi·ano, /pi'ænəʊ/ **pianos.** A **piano** is a large musical instrument with a row of black and white keys. When you press these keys with your fingers, little hammers hit wire strings inside the piano which vibrate to produce musical notes. *I taught myself how to play the piano.* ● See also **grand piano.** ◆◆◇◇◇ N-VAR

pi·ano·for·te /pi,ænəʊ'fɔːteɪ/ **pianofortes.** A **pianoforte** is a piano. N-COUNT DATED

pi·az·za /pi'ætsə/ **piazzas.** A **piazza** is a large open square in a town or city, especially in Italy. ◆◇◇◇◇ N-COUNT

pic /pɪk/ **pics.** 1 A **pic** is a film. *'Angels with Dirty Faces' is a Cagney gangster pic.* 2 A **pic** is a photograph. *All you have to do is identify the location and the city from the pic on page 9.* ◆◇◇◇◇ N-COUNT INFORMAL N-COUNT INFORMAL

pica·resque /ˌpɪkə'resk/. A **picaresque** story is one in which a dishonest but likeable hero travels around and has lots of exciting adventures. ADJ LITERARY

pic·co·lo /'pɪkələʊ/ **piccolos.** A **piccolo** is a small musical instrument that is like a flute but produces higher notes. N-VAR

pick /pɪk/ **picks, picking, picked.** 1 If you **pick** a particular person or thing, you choose that one. *I had deliberately picked a city with a tropical climate.* 2 If you **pick and choose,** you carefully choose only things that you really want and reject the others. *We, the patients, cannot pick and choose our doctors.* ◆◆◆◆◇ VERB V n PHRASE

3 You can refer to the best things or people in a particular group as the **pick** of that group. *The boys here are the pick of the under-15 cricketers in the country.* N-SING: theN

4 If you **have** your **pick of** a group of things, you are able to choose any of them that you want. *Here is an actress who could have her pick of any part.* 5 If you are told to **take** your **pick,** you can choose any one that you like from a group of things. *Take your pick from ten luxury hotels.* PHRASE PHRASE

6 When you **pick** flowers, fruit, or leaves, you break them off the plant or tree and collect them. ♦ **pick·er, pickers.** ...*travelling fruit pickers.* 7 If you **pick** something from a place, you remove it from there with your fingers or your hand. *He picked the telephone off the wall bracket.* 8 If you **pick your nose** or VERB: V n N-COUNT VERB V n prep VERB: V n

teeth, you remove dried mucus from your nostrils or food from your teeth.

9 If you **pick** a fight or quarrel with someone, you deliberately cause one. *He picked a fight with a waiter and landed in jail.* 10 If you **pick** your **way** across an area, you walk across it very carefully in order to avoid obstacles or dangerous things. 11 If someone such as a thief **picks** a lock, they open it without a key, for example by using a piece of wire. 12 ● to **pick** someone's **brains:** see brain. ● to **pick holes in** something: see hole. ● to **pick** someone's **pocket:** see pocket. VERB w th n Also V n PHRASE VERB: V n

13 A **pick** is the same as a pickaxe. ● See also **handpick, ice pick.** N-COUNT

pick at. If you **pick at** the food that you are eating, you eat only very small amounts of it. PHRASAL VB V P n

pick off. If someone **picks off** people or aircraft, they shoot them down one by one. *Any decent shot with telescopic sights could pick us off at random.* PHRASAL VB V P noun V n P

pick on. 1 If someone **picks on** you, they repeatedly criticize you unfairly or treat you unkindly. *Bullies pick on younger children.* 2 If someone **picks on** a particular person or thing, they choose them for special attention or treatment. *Pick on a day when you will not be under much stress.* PHRASAL VB V P n BRITISH V P n

pick out. 1 If you **pick out** someone or something, you recognize them when it is difficult to see them, for example because they are among a large group. *Steven describes himself as 'a regular guy – you couldn't pick me out of a crowd'.* 2 If you **pick out** someone or something, you choose them from a group of people or things. *There are so many great newscasters it's difficult to pick one out.* 3 If part of something **is picked out** in a particular colour, it is painted in that colour so that it can be seen clearly beside the other parts. *The name is picked out in gold letters over the shop-front.* PHRASAL VB V P noun V n P V P noun V n P usu passive beV-ed P

pick over. If you **pick over** a quantity of things, you examine them carefully, for example to reject the ones you do not want. PHRASAL VB V P noun

pick up. 1 When you **pick** something **up,** you lift it up. *Ridley picked up a pencil and fiddled with it.* 2 When you **pick** yourself **up** after you have fallen or been knocked down, you stand up rather slowly. 3 When you **pick up the pieces** after a disaster, you do what you can to get the situation back to normal again. PHRASAL VB V n P V P noun V pron-refl P PHRASE

4 When you **pick up** someone or something that is waiting to be collected, you go to the place where they are and take them away, often in a car. *We drove to the airport the next morning to pick up Susan.* 5 If someone **is picked up** by the police, they are arrested and taken to a police station. *The police picked him up within the hour.* 6 If you **pick up** someone you do not know, you talk to them and try to start a sexual relationship with them. V P noun Also V n P beV-ed P V n P Also V P noun V n P INFORMAL

7 If you **pick up** something such as a skill or an idea, you acquire it without effort over a period of time. *Where did you pick up your English?* 8 If you **pick up** something, such as a feature or a pattern, you discover or identify it. *Consumers in Europe are slow to pick up trends in the use of information technology.* 9 If you **pick up** an illness, you get it from somewhere or something. *They've picked up a really nasty infection from something they've eaten.* 10 If a piece of equipment, for example a radio or a microphone, **picks up** a signal or sound, it receives it or detects it. *We can pick up Italian television.* Also V n P INFORMAL V P noun Also V n P V P noun

11 If someone **picks up** a point or topic that has already been mentioned, or if they **pick up on** it, they refer to it or develop it. *Can I just pick up that gentleman's point?... I'll pick up on what I said a couple of minutes ago.* 12 If you **pick** someone **up on** something that they have said or done, you mention it and tell them that you think it is wrong. *If I may pick you up on that point.* V P noun V P P n Also V n P V n P P n BRITISH

13 If trade or the economy of a country **picks up,** it improves. 14 When a vehicle **picks up speed,** it begins to move more quickly. 15 See also **pick-up.** V P PHRASE

pick·axe /'pɪkæks/ **pickaxes;** also spelled **pickax** N-COUNT
in American English. A **pickaxe** is a large tool consisting of a curved, pointed piece of metal with a
long handle joined to the middle. Pickaxes are used
for breaking up rocks or the ground. See picture
headed **tools.**

pick·et /'pɪkɪt/ **pickets, picketing, picketed.** ◆◇◇◇◇
1 When a group of people, usually trade union VERB
members, **picket** a place of work, they stand outside V n
it in order to protest about something, to prevent Also V
people from going in, or to persuade the workers to
join a strike. *The miners went on strike and picketed
the power stations.* ► Also a noun. ...*forty demon-* N-COUNT
strators who have set up a twenty four hour picket.
♦ **pick·et·ing** *There was widespread picketing of* N-UNCOUNT
mines where work was continuing. **2 Pickets** are N-COUNT
people who are picketing a place of work.

'picket fence, picket fences. A **picket fence** is a N-COUNT
fence made of pointed wooden sticks fixed into the
ground, supported by pieces of wood nailed horizontally across.

'picket line, picket lines. A **picket line** is a ◆◇◇◇◇
group of pickets outside a place of work. N-COUNT

pick·ings /'pɪkɪŋz/. You can refer to the money N-PLURAL
that can be made easily in a particular place or area
of activity as the **pickings**. *Traditional hiding places
are easy pickings for experienced burglars.*

pick·le /'pɪkəl/ **pickles, pickling, pickled.** ◆◇◇◇◇
1 Pickles are vegetables or fruit which have been N-PLURAL
kept in vinegar or salt water for a long time so that
they have a strong, sharp taste. **2 Pickle** is a spicy N-VAR
fruity sauce that is made by boiling chopped vegetables and fruit with spices for several hours and
then left to cool. **3** When you **pickle** food, you keep VERB: V n
it in vinegar or salt water so that it does not go bad
and it develops a strong, sharp taste. ♦ **pick·led** ...*a* ADJ
jar of pickled fruit. ♦ **pick·ling** *Small pickling on-* N-UNCOUNT
ions can be used instead of sliced ones.
4 If you are in **a pickle**, you are in a difficult situation. N-SING:
Companies find themselves in a pickle when their a N
markets change. INFORMAL

pick·led /'pɪkəld/. If you say that someone is **pick-** ADJ-GRADED
led, you mean that they are drunk. BRITISH,
INFORMAL

'pick-me-up, pick-me-ups. A **pick-me-up** is N-COUNT
something that you have or do when you are tired INFORMAL
or depressed in order to make you feel better. *This
is an ideal New Year pick-me-up – a five day holiday
in the Bahamas.*

,pick 'n' 'mix; also spelled **pick and mix. Pick 'n'** ADJ: ADJ n
mix is used to describe a way of assembling a col- BRITISH
lection of things by choosing a lot of different elements and putting them together. *It is, as some
senior officials conceded, a pick'n'mix approach to
policy.*

pick·pocket /'pɪkpɒkɪt/ **pickpockets.** A **pick-** N-COUNT
pocket is a person who steals things from people's
pockets or handbags in public places.

'pick-up, pick-ups; also spelled **pickup. 1** A ◆◆◇◇◇
pick-up or a **pick-up truck** is a small truck with low N-COUNT
sides that can be easily loaded and unloaded. **2** A N-SING
pick-up in trade or in a country's economy is an
improvement in it. ...*a pick-up in the housing market.* **3** A **pick-up** takes place when someone picks N-COUNT
up a person or thing that is waiting to be collected.
*Trains will operate from Waterloo with a pick-up
stop at Ashford.*

picky /'pɪki/. Someone who is **picky** is difficult to ADJ-GRADED
please and only likes a small range of things. INFORMAL

pic·nic /'pɪknɪk/ **picnics, picnicking, pic-** ◆◆◇◇◇
nicked. 1 When people have a **picnic**, they eat a N-COUNT
meal out of doors, usually in a field or a forest, or at
the beach. *We'll take a picnic lunch.* **2** When people VERB
picnic somewhere, they have a picnic. *Afterwards,* V
we picnicked on the riverbank. ♦ **pic·nick·er, pic-** N-COUNT
nickers ...*fires started by careless picnickers.* **3** If PHRASE
you say that an experience, task, or activity **is no** INFORMAL
picnic, you mean that it is quite difficult or unpleasant. *Emigrating is no picnic.*

pic·to·rial /pɪk'tɔːriəl/. **Pictorial** means using or ◆◇◇◇◇
relating to pictures. ...*a pictorial history of the Spe-* ADJ

cial Air Service. ♦ **pic·to·ri·al·ly** *Each section is ex-* ADV
plained pictorially.

pic·ture /'pɪktʃə/ **pictures, picturing, pictured.** ◆◆◆◇
1 A **picture** consists of lines and shapes which are N-COUNT
drawn, painted, or printed on a surface and show a
person, thing, or scene. *A picture of Rory O'Moore
hangs in the dining room.* **2** A **picture** is also a N-COUNT
photograph. *The Observer carries a big front-page
picture of rioters.* **3** Television **pictures** are the N-COUNT
scenes which you see on a television screen. **4** If VERB:
someone or something **is pictured** somewhere, be V-ed
usually in a newspaper or magazine, they appear in be V-ed -ing
a photograph or picture. ...*a woman who claimed V-ed
she had been pictured dancing with a celebrity in
Stringfellows nightclub... The rattan and wrought-
iron chair pictured here costs £125.*
5 You can refer to a film as a **picture**. ...*a director of* N-COUNT
epic action pictures. **6** If you go to **the pictures**, you go N-PLURAL:
to a cinema to see a film. The American word is the N
movies. BRITISH
7 If you have a **picture** of something in your mind, N-COUNT
you have a clear idea or memory of it in your mind as
if you were actually seeing it. **8** If you **picture** some- VERB
thing in your mind, you think of it and have such a V n prep
clear memory or idea of it that you seem to be able to V n -ing
see it. *He pictured her with long black braided hair...* Also V n adj
*She pictured herself working with animals... I tried to
picture the place, but could not.* **9** A **picture** of some- N-COUNT
thing is a description of it or an indication of what it is
like. *I'll try and give you a better picture of what the
boys do... Her book paints a bleak picture of the problems women now face.*
10 When you refer to the **picture** in a particular place, N-SING
you are referring to the situation there. *It's a similar
picture across the border in Ethiopia.* **11** If you **get the** PHRASE
picture, you understand the situation, especially one
which someone is describing to you. **12** If you **put** PHRASE
someone **in the picture**, you tell them about a situation which they need to know about. **13** If you say that PHRASE
someone is **in the picture**, you mean that they are involved in the situation that you are talking about. If
you say that they are **out of the picture**, you mean
that they are not involved in the situation. *Sometimes
security was so tight that people who might have had
something important to offer were left out of the
picture.*
14 You use **picture** to describe what someone looks PHRASE
like. For example, if you say that someone is **a picture
of health** or **the picture of misery**, you mean that they
look extremely healthy or extremely miserable.

'picture book, picture books; also spelled N-COUNT
picture-book. A **picture book** is a book with a lot of
pictures in and not much writing, usually for
children.

,picture 'postcard, picture postcards; also N-COUNT
spelled **picture-postcard** for meaning 2. **1** A **picture** N-COUNT
postcard is a postcard with a photograph of a place
on it. People often buy picture postcards of places
they visit when on holiday. **2** You can use **picture** ADJ: ADJ n
postcard to describe a place that is attractive and
unspoiled. ...*picture-postcard Normandy villages.*

'picture rail, picture rails; also spelled **picture-** N-COUNT
rail. A **picture rail** is a continuous narrow piece of
wood which is fixed round a room just below the
ceiling that pictures can be hung from.

pic·tur·esque /,pɪktʃə'resk/. **1** A **picturesque** ◆◇◇◇◇
place is attractive, interesting, and unspoiled. ► You ADJ-GRADED
can refer to picturesque things as the **picturesque.** N-SING:
...*lovers of the picturesque.* **2 Picturesque** words the N
and expressions are unusual or poetical. ADJ-GRADED

'picture window, picture windows. A **picture** N-COUNT
window is a window containing one large sheet of
glass, so that people have a good view of what is
outside.

pid·dle /'pɪdəl/ **piddles, piddling, piddled.** To VERB: V
piddle means to urinate. INFORMAL

pid·dling /'pɪdlɪŋ/. **Piddling** means small or unim- ADJ-GRADED
portant. ...*piddling amounts of money.* INFORMAL

pidg·in /'pɪdʒɪn/. **1 Pidgin** is a language which is a N-UNCOUNT
mixture of two other languages. **Pidgin** is not

anyone's native language but is used when people who speak different languages communicate with each other. *Wu talked pidgin to her.* **2** If someone is speaking in, for example, **pidgin** English or **pidgin** Italian, they may be speaking in a mixture of two languages. Or, they may be speaking another language badly or their own language simply, in an attempt to communicate.

ADJ: ADJ n

pie /paɪ/ **pies. 1** A **pie** consists of meat, vegetables, or fruit baked in pastry. *...apple pie and custard.* ● See also **shepherd's pie. 2** If you describe a plan or promise of something good as **pie in the sky,** you think that it is very unlikely to happen. ● to **eat humble pie:** see **humble.**

◆◆◇◇◇
N-VAR
PHRASE

piece /piːs/ **pieces, piecing, pieced. 1** A **piece** of something is an amount of it that has been broken off, torn off, or cut off. *...a few words scrawled on a piece of paper... Cut the ham into pieces.* **2** A **piece** of an object is one of the individual parts which it is made of, especially a part that can be removed. *The equipment was taken down the shaft in pieces.* **3** If someone or something is still **in one piece** after a dangerous journey or experience, they are safe and not damaged or hurt. **4** If something is smashed **to pieces,** is taken **to pieces,** or falls **to pieces,** it is broken or comes apart so that it is in separate pieces. *If the shell had hit the boat, it would have blown it to pieces.*

◆◆◆◇
N-COUNT

N-COUNT

PHRASE

PHRASE

5 If you **go to pieces,** you are so upset or nervous that you lose control of yourself and cannot do what you should do. **6** If someone **tears** you **to pieces** or **pulls** your work **to pieces,** they criticize you or your work very severely. **7** If something with several different parts is **all of a piece,** each part is consistent with the others. If one thing is **of a piece** with another, it is consistent with it. *At its peak in the Thirties, Underground design and architecture was all of a piece.*

PHRASE
INFORMAL
PHRASE
INFORMAL

PHRASE

8 A **piece** of land is an area of land. **9** You can use **piece** with many uncount nouns to refer to an individual thing of a particular kind. For example, you can refer to some advice as a **piece of advice.** *It is a highly complex piece of legislation. ...a sturdy piece of furniture.* **10** You can refer to a work of art or a high-quality decorative object as a **piece.** *None of the pieces is insured.*

N-COUNT
N-COUNT:
N of n

N-COUNT
FORMAL

11 You can refer to specific coins as **pieces.** For example, a 10p **piece** is a coin that is worth 10p. **12** The **pieces** which you use when you play a board game such as chess are the specially shaped objects which you move around on the board. **13** A **piece** of something is part of it or a share of it. *They got a small piece of the net profits.*

N-COUNT:
supp N
N-COUNT

QUANT
AMERICAN

14 You can refer to an article in a newspaper or magazine, a musical composition, a broadcast, or a play as a **piece.** *There was a piece about him on television.* **15** If you **say** your **piece,** you say everything you want to say about a particular matter without being interrupted, although people may be wanting to express opposing views. *I'll answer your questions when I've said my piece.* **16** If you say that someone is **a nasty piece of work,** you mean that they are very unkind or unpleasant.

N-COUNT

PHRASE

PHRASE
PRAGMATICS
INFORMAL,
BRITISH

17 See also **museum piece, party piece, set piece. 18** ● **a piece of the action:** see **action.** ● **bits and pieces:** see **bit.** ● **a piece of cake:** see **cake.** ● to **pick up the pieces:** see **pick up.**

piece together. 1 If you **piece together** the truth about something, you gradually discover it. *Francis was able to piece together what had happened.* **2** If you **piece** something **together,** you gradually make it by joining several things or parts together. *Doctors painstakingly pieced together the broken bones.*

PHRASAL VB
V P noun
V P what
V P noun
Also V n P

-piece /-piːs/. **-piece** combines with numbers to form adjectives indicating that something consists of a particular number of items. *...his well-cut three-piece suit. ...a four-piece band.*

COMB

pièce de ré·sis·tance /piˌes də reɪˈzɪstɒns, AM -zɪˈstɑːns/. The **pièce de résistance** of a collection or series of things is the most impressive thing in it.

N-SING
FORMAL

piece·meal /ˈpiːsmiːl/. If you describe a change or process as **piecemeal,** you disapprove of it because it happens gradually and usually at irregular intervals, although this may not be satisfactory. *Instead of the government's piecemeal approach, what is needed is a radical shake-up of 16-19 education.* ► Also an adverb. *It was built piecemeal over some 130 years.*

◆◇◇◇◇
ADJ-GRADED
PRAGMATICS

ADV:
ADV after v

piece·work /ˈpiːswɜːk/; also spelled **piece-work.** If you do **piecework,** you are paid according to the amount of work that you do rather than the length of time that you work.

N-UNCOUNT

'pie chart, pie charts. A **pie chart** is a circle divided into sections to show the relative proportions of a set of things.

N-COUNT

pied-à-terre /piˌeɪd ɑː ˈteə/ **pieds-à-terre.** A **pied-à-terre** is a small house or flat, especially in a town, which you own or rent but only use occasionally. *...a pied-à-terre in Manhattan.*

N-COUNT

pier /pɪə/ **piers.** A **pier** is a platform sticking out into water, usually the sea, which people walk along or use when getting onto or off boats.

◆◇◇◇◇
N-COUNT

pierce /pɪəs/ **pierces, piercing, pierced. 1** If a sharp object **pierces** something, or if you **pierce** something with a sharp object, the object goes into it and makes a hole in it. *Pierce the skin of the potato with a fork.* **2** If you have your ears or some other part of your body **pierced,** you have a small hole made through them so that you can wear a piece of jewellery in them. *...her pierced ears with their tiny gold studs.* **3** If a light or sound **pierces** something or **pierces through** it, it is suddenly seen or heard very strongly or clearly. *The clock striking the hour pierced through his thoughts.* **4** If someone **pierces** something that acts as a barrier, they manage to get through it. *German armoured divisions pierced the Russian lines.*

◆◇◇◇
VERB
V n

VERB:
have n V-ed
V-ed
Also V n

VERB: V n
V through n
LITERARY

VERB
V n
Also V through
n

pierc·ing /ˈpɪəsɪŋ/. **1** A **piercing** sound or voice is high-pitched and clear in an unpleasant way. **2** If someone has **piercing** eyes or a **piercing** stare, they seem to look at you very intensely. **3** If you describe a quality or feeling as **piercing,** you mean that it makes you experience a feeling, especially sadness, very strongly. *She was aware of a sharp piercing regret.* **4** A **piercing** wind makes you feel very cold.

◆◇◇◇◇
ADJ-GRADED

ADJ-GRADED
WRITTEN
ADJ-GRADED:
ADJ n
LITERARY

ADJ-GRADED

pi·eties /ˈpaɪɪtiz/. You refer to statements about what is morally right as **pieties** when you think they are insincere or unrealistic. *...politicians who constantly intone pieties about respect for the rule of law.*

N-PLURAL
PRAGMATICS

pi·ety /ˈpaɪɪti/. **Piety** is strong religious belief, or religious or dutiful behaviour. *Her piety earned her a personal missive from Pope Gregory VII.*

N-UNCOUNT

pif·fle /ˈpɪfəl/. If you describe what someone says as **piffle,** you think that it is nonsense.

N-UNCOUNT
INFORMAL

pif·fling /ˈpɪfəlɪŋ/. If you describe something as **piffling,** you are critical of it because it is very small or unimportant.

ADJ-GRADED
PRAGMATICS
INFORMAL

pig /pɪg/ **pigs, pigging, pigged. 1** A **pig** is a pink or black animal with short legs and not much hair on its skin. Pigs are often kept on farms for their meat, which is called pork, ham, bacon, or gammon. ● See also **guinea pig. 2** If you call someone a **pig,** you think that they are unpleasant in some way, especially that they are greedy or unkind; an offensive use. **3** If you **make a pig's ear of** something, you do it very badly.

◆◆◇◇◇
N-COUNT

N-COUNT
RUDE

PHRASE
INFORMAL,
BRITISH

pig out. If you say that people **are pigging out,** you are criticizing them for eating a very large amount at one meal.

PHRASAL VB
V P
INFORMAL

pi·geon /ˈpɪdʒɪn/ **pigeons.** A **pigeon** is a bird, usually grey in colour, which has a fat body. Pigeons often live in towns. ● See also **clay pigeon, homing pigeon.**

◆◇◇◇◇
N-COUNT

'pigeon-hole, pigeon-holes, pigeon-holing, pigeon-holed; also spelled **pigeonhole. 1** A **pigeon-hole** is one of the sections in a frame on a wall where letters and messages can be left for someone, or one of the sections in a writing desk where you can keep documents. **2** To **pigeon-hole** someone or something means to decide that they

N-COUNT

VERB: V n
be V-ed as n

belong to a particular class or category, often without considering all their qualities or characteristics. *I don't want to be pigeonholed as a kids' presenter.* **3** If you put someone in a particular **pigeon-hole**, N-COUNT you decide that they belong in a particular category. *Because I had an unusual accent people were not able to put me into a pigeon-hole.*

pig·gery /'pɪgəri/ **piggeries.** A **piggery** is a farm or N-COUNT building where pigs are kept. BRITISH

pig·gy /'pɪgi/ **piggies. 1** A **piggy** is a pig or a piglet; N-COUNT used by children. **2** If someone has **piggy** eyes, their ADJ: ADJ n eyes are small and unattractive.

piggy·back /'pɪgibæk/ **piggybacks, piggyback- ing, piggybacked;** also spelled **piggy-back. 1** If N-COUNT you give someone a **piggyback**, you carry them high on your back, supporting them under their knees. ▶ Also an adverb. *My father carried me up the hill,* ADV *piggyback.* **2** If you **piggyback** on something that VERB someone else has thought of or done, you use it to V on your advantage. *I was just piggybacking on Stokes's* Also V *idea.*

piggy bank, piggy banks; also spelled N-COUNT **piggybank.** A **piggy bank** is a small container shaped like a pig, with a slot in it to put coins in. Children use piggy banks to save money in.

piggy-in-the-middle; also spelled **pig-in-the-** N-SING: **middle.** If someone is **piggy-in-the-middle** or **pig-** also no det **in-the-middle**, they are unwillingly involved in a BRITISH dispute between two other people or groups.

pig-'headed. If you describe someone as **pig-** ADJ-GRADED **headed**, you are critical them because they refuse to PRAGMATICS change their mind about things, and you think they are unreasonable.

pig·let /'pɪglət/ **piglets.** A **piglet** is a young pig. N-COUNT

pig·ment /'pɪgmənt/ **pigments.** A **pigment** is a ◆◇◇◇ substance that gives something a particular colour. N-VAR *The Romans used natural pigments on their fabrics* FORMAL *and walls.*

pig·men·ta·tion /,pɪgmen'teɪʃən/. The **pigmenta-** N-UNCOUNT **tion** of a person's or animal's skin is its natural FORMAL colouring.

pig·ment·ed /pɪg'mentɪd/. **Pigmented** skin has a ADJ-GRADED lot of natural colouring. *...deeply pigmented areas on* FORMAL *the skin.*

pig·my /'pɪgmi/. See **pygmy**.

pig·pen /'pɪgpen/ **pigpens.** A **pigpen** is a hut with N-COUNT a yard where pigs are kept on a farm. AMERICAN

pig·skin /'pɪgskɪn/. **Pigskin** is leather made from N-UNCOUNT the skin of a pig.

pig·sty /'pɪgstaɪ/ **pigsties. 1** A **pigsty** is a hut with N-COUNT a yard where pigs are kept on a farm. **2** If you de- N-COUNT scribe a room as a **pigsty**, you are criticizing the fact PRAGMATICS that it is very dirty and untidy. INFORMAL

pig·tail /'pɪgteɪl/ **pigtails.** If someone has a **pigtail** N-COUNT or **pigtails**, their hair is tied into one or two bunches and then plaited. The usual American word is **braid**.

pike /paɪk/ **pikes;** the form **pike** can be used as ◆◇◇◇◇ the plural for meaning 1. **1** A **pike** is a large fish that N-VAR lives in rivers and lakes and eats other fish. ▶ **Pike** N-UNCOUNT is a piece of this fish eaten as food. **2** In former N-COUNT times, a **pike** was a weapon consisting of a pointed blade on the end of a long pole.

pil·af /'pɪlæf, AM pɪ'lɑːf/ **pilafs;** also spelled **pilaff**. N-VAR **Pilaf** is the same as **pilau**.

pi·las·ter /pɪ'lɑːstə/ **pilasters. Pilasters** are shal- N-COUNT low decorative pillars attached to a wall.

pi·lau /'pɪlaʊ, AM pɪ'ləʊ/ **pilaus. Pilau** or **pilau rice** N-VAR is rice flavoured with spices, often mixed with pieces of meat or fish.

pil·chard /'pɪltʃəd/ **pilchards. Pilchards** are small N-COUNT fish that live in the sea. Pilchards can be eaten as food.

pile /paɪl/ **piles, piling, piled. 1** A **pile** of things is ◆◆◆◇◇ a mass of them that is high in the middle and has N-COUNT sloping sides. *The leaves had been swept into huge piles.* **2** A **pile** of things is a quantity of things that N-COUNT have been put neatly somewhere so that each thing is on top of the one below. *...a pile of boxes.* **3** If VERB you **pile** things somewhere, you put them there so V n adv/prep

that they form a pile. *He was piling clothes into the* suitcase. **4** If something **is piled with** things, it is VB: usu covered or filled with piles of things. *Tables were* passive *piled high with local produce.* beV-ed with n

5 If you talk about a **pile** of something or **piles** of QUANT something, you mean a large amount of it. *I've got a* INFORMAL *pile of questions afterwards for you.* **6** Someone who is PHRASE **at the bottom of the pile** is low down in society or low INFORMAL down in an organization. Someone who is **at the top of the pile** is high up in society or high up in an or- ganization. **7** If a group of people **pile into** or **out of** a VERB: vehicle, they all get into it or out of it in a disorganized V into/out of n way. *A fleet of police cars suddenly arrived. Dozens of* V in/out *officers piled out.*

8 You can refer to a large impressive building as a **pile**, N-COUNT especially when it is the home of a rich important per- BRITISH son. **9 Piles** are wooden, concrete, or metal posts N-COUNT which are pushed into the ground and on which buildings or bridges are built. **10 Piles** are painful N-PLURAL swellings that can appear in the veins inside a per- son's anus. **11** The **pile** of a carpet or of a fabric such N-SING as velvet is its soft surface. It consists of a lot of little threads standing on end.

pile up. 1 If you **pile up** a quantity of things or if they PHRASAL VB **pile up**, they gradually form a pile. *Mail was still pil-* ERG: *ing up at the office.* **2** If you **pile up** work, problems, or V P noun losses or if they **pile up**, you get more and more of V P them. *Problems were piling up at work... He piled up* V P *huge debts.* V P noun

pile-up, pile-ups; also spelled **pileup** in Ameri- ◆◇◇◇◇ can English. A **pile-up** is a road accident in which a N-COUNT lot of vehicles crash into each other.

pil·fer /'pɪlfə/ **pilfers, pilfering, pilfered.** If VERB someone **pilfers**, they steal things, usually small in- V n expensive things. *When food stores close, they go to work, pilfering food for resale on the black market.* ♦ **pil·fer·ing** *Precautions had to be taken to prevent* N-UNCOUNT *pilfering.*

pil·grim /'pɪlgrɪm/ **pilgrims. Pilgrims** are people ◆◆◇◇◇ who make a journey to a holy place for a religious N-COUNT reason.

pil·grim·age /'pɪlgrɪmɪdʒ/ **pilgrimages. 1** If you ◆◇◇◇◇ make a **pilgrimage** to a holy place, you go there for N-COUNT a religious reason. **2** A **pilgrimage** is a journey that N-COUNT someone makes to a place that is very important to them. *...a private pilgrimage to family graves.*

pil·ing /'paɪlɪŋ/ **pilings. Pilings** are wooden, con- N-COUNT crete, or metal posts which are pushed into the ground and on which buildings or bridges are built.

pill /pɪl/ **pills. 1 Pills** are small solid round masses ◆◆◆◇◇ of medicine or vitamins that you swallow without N-COUNT chewing. **2** If a woman is on **the pill**, she takes a N-SING: special pill that prevents her becoming pregnant. the N **3** If a person or group has to accept a failure or an PHRASE unpleasant piece of news, you can say that it was a **bitter pill** or **a bitter pill to swallow. 4** If someone PHRASE does something to **sweeten the pill** or **sugar the** BRITISH **pill**, they do it to make some unpleasant news or an unpleasant measure more acceptable. American English uses the expression **sugar-coat the pill**.

pil·lage /'pɪlɪdʒ/ **pillages, pillaging, pillaged.** If ◆◇◇◇◇ a group of people **pillage** a place, they steal proper- VERB: V n ty from it using violent methods. *...the boldness to* V *pillage and rape.* ▶ Also a noun. *There were no signs* N-UNCOUNT *of violence or pillage.* ♦ **pil·lag·ing** *...pillaging by* N-UNCOUNT *people looking for something to eat.*

pil·lar /'pɪlə/ **pillars. 1** A **pillar** is a tall solid struc- ◆◆◇◇◇ ture, which is usually used to support part of a N-COUNT building. **2** If something is the **pillar** of a system or N-COUNT agreement, it is the most important part of it or what makes it strong and successful. *The pillar of her economic policy was keeping tight control over money supply.* **3** If you describe someone as a **pillar** N-COUNT: **of** society or as a **pillar** of the community, you ap- N of n prove of them because they play an important and PRAGMATICS active part in society or in the community.

pillar box, pillar boxes; also spelled **pillar-box.** N-COUNT A **pillar box** is a tall red box in the street in which BRITISH you put letters that you are sending by post.

pil·lared /'pɪləd/. A **pillared** building is a building that is supported by pillars. ADJ

pill·box /'pɪlbɒks/ **pillboxes**; also spelled **pill box**. A **pillbox** is a small tin or box in which you can keep pills. N-COUNT

pil·lion /'pɪliən/ **pillions. 1** If someone rides **pillion** on a motorcycle or bicycle, they sit behind the person who is controlling it. **2** On a motorcycle, the **pillion** is the seat or part behind the rider. *As a learner rider you must not carry a pillion passenger.* ADV: ADV after v BRITISH / N-COUNT

pil·lo·ry /'pɪləri/ **pillories, pillorying, pilloried. 1** If someone **is pilloried**, a lot of people, especially journalists, criticize them and make them look stupid. **2** A **pillory** is a wooden frame with holes for the head and hands. In Europe in former times criminals were sometimes locked in a pillory as a form of punishment. VB: usu passive / N-COUNT

pil·low /'pɪləʊ/ **pillows.** A **pillow** is a rectangular cushion which you rest your head on when you are in bed. ◆◇◇◇ N-COUNT

pillow·case /'pɪləʊkeɪs/ **pillowcases**; also spelled **pillow case**. A **pillowcase** is a cover for a pillow, which can be removed and washed. ◆◇◇◇ N-COUNT

'pillow slip, pillow slips. A **pillow slip** is the same as a **pillowcase**. N-COUNT

'pillow talk. Conversations that people have when they are in bed together can be referred to as **pillow talk**. These conversations are often about secret or intimate subjects. N-UNCOUNT

pi·lot /'paɪlət/ **pilots, piloting, piloted. 1** A **pilot** is a person who is trained to fly an aircraft. **2** A **pilot** is a person who steers a ship through a difficult stretch of water, for example the entrance to a harbour. **3** If someone **pilots** an aircraft or ship, they act as its pilot. ◆◆◇◇ N-COUNT / N-COUNT / VERB: V n

4 See also **automatic pilot, test pilot.**

5 A **pilot scheme** or a **pilot project** is one which is used to test an idea before deciding whether to introduce it on a larger scale. **6** If a government or organization **pilots a programme** or a **scheme**, they test it, before deciding whether to introduce it on a larger scale. *The trust is looking for 50 schools to pilot a programme aimed at teenage pupils preparing for work.* **7** If a government minister **pilots** a new law or bill through parliament, he or she makes sure that it is introduced successfully. *...Mr Mellor's likely role in piloting possible privacy legislation through Parliament.* N-COUNT / VERB V n / VERB V n through n Also V n

8 A **pilot** is the pilot light on a gas cooker, boiler, or fire. N-COUNT

'pilot light, pilot lights. A **pilot light** is a small gas flame in a cooker, boiler, or fire. It burns all the time and lights the main large flame when the gas is turned fully on. N-COUNT

'pilot officer, pilot officers. A **pilot officer** is an officer in the Royal Air Force. N-COUNT

pi·men·to /pɪ'mentəʊ/ **pimentos.** A **pimento** is a mild-tasting red pepper. N-VAR

pimp /pɪmp/ **pimps.** A **pimp** is a man who gets clients for prostitutes and takes a large part of the money the prostitutes earn. ◆◇◇◇ N-COUNT

pim·per·nel /'pɪmpənel/ **pimpernels.** A **pimpernel** is a small wild plant that usually has red flowers. N-VAR

pim·ple /'pɪmpəl/ **pimples. Pimples** are small red spots. They appear especially on the face. N-COUNT

pim·ply /'pɪmpli/. If someone is **pimply** or has a **pimply** face, they have a lot of pimples on their face. ADJ-GRADED

pin /pɪn/ **pins, pinning, pinned. 1 Pins** are very small thin pieces of metal with points at one end. They are used in needlework to fasten pieces of material together. **2** You can say **you could have heard a pin drop** when a place is extremely quiet, especially because everyone is waiting for someone to say something or when someone has said something shocking. **3** If you **pin** something on something or if you **pin** it to something, you attach it with a pin, a drawing pin, or a safety pin. *They pinned a notice to the door... He had pinned up a map of Finland.* ◆◆◇◇ N-COUNT / PHRASE / VERB V n prep V n with adv

4 You can refer to any long narrow piece of metal or N-COUNT

wood with a blunt end, especially one that is used to fasten two things together, as a **pin**. *...the 18-inch steel pin holding his left leg together.* **5** A **pin** is a small brooch or badge. **6** A **pin** is the clip on a hand grenade that prevents it from exploding and that is pulled out when you want the grenade to explode. N-COUNT / N-COUNT

7 See also **pins and needles, drawing pin, rolling pin, safety pin.**

8 If someone **pins** you to something or **pins** you against something, they press you against a surface so that you cannot move. *I pinned him against the wall... She fought at the bulk that pinned her.* **9** If someone tries to **pin** something **on** you or to **pin the blame on** you, they say, often unfairly, that you were responsible for something bad or illegal. *The trade unions are pinning the blame for the violence on the government.* **10** If you **pin** your hopes **on** something or **pin** your faith **on** something, you hope very much that it will produce the result you want. VERB V n adv/prep V n / VERB V n on n / VERB: V n on n

pin down. 1 If you try to **pin** something **down**, you try to discover exactly what, where, or when it is. *It has taken until now to pin down its exact location... I can only pin it down to between 1936 and 1942... If we cannot pin down exactly what we are supposed to be managing, how can we manage it?* **2** If you **pin** someone **down**, you force them to make a decision or to tell you what their decision is, when they have been trying to avoid doing this. *She couldn't pin him down to a date... If you pin people down, they will tell you some puzzling things about stress.* PHRASAL VB V P noun V n P to n V P wh Also V n P / V n P V n P to/on n Also V P noun

PIN /pɪn/. Someone's **PIN** or **PIN number** is the secret number they use with a bank card to withdraw money from a cash machine. **PIN** is an abbreviation for 'personal identification number'. N-SING

pina·fore /'pɪnəfɔː/ **pinafores.** A **pinafore** or a **pinafore dress** is a sleeveless dress. It is worn over a blouse or sweater. The usual American word is **jumper**. See picture headed **clothes**. N-COUNT

pin·ball /'pɪnbɔːl/. **Pinball** is a game in which a player presses two buttons on each side of a pinball machine in order to flick a small ball to the top of the machine. The aim of the game is to prevent the ball reaching the bottom of the machine by pressing the buttons. N-UNCOUNT

'pinball machine, pinball machines. A **pinball machine** is a games machine consisting of a sloping table with obstructions, on which pinball is played. The obstructions are often electrically wired so that they light up and a bell rings when the ball touches them. N-COUNT

pince-nez /ˌpæns 'neɪ/. **Pince-nez** are an old-fashioned kind of spectacles that consist of two lenses that fit tightly onto the top of the nose. N-UNCOUNT: also a N

pin·cer /'pɪnsə/ **pincers. 1 Pincers** consist of two pieces of metal that are hinged in the middle. They are used as a tool for gripping things or for pulling things out. See picture headed **tools. 2** The **pincers** of an animal such as a crab or a lobster are its front claws. N-PLURAL: also a pair of N / N-COUNT

'pincer movement, pincer movements. A **pincer movement** is an attack by an army or other group in which they attack their enemies in two places at once with the aim of surrounding them. N-COUNT

pinch /pɪntʃ/ **pinches, pinching, pinched. 1** If you **pinch** a part of someone's body, you take a piece of their skin between your thumb and first finger and give it a short squeeze. ► Also a noun. *She gave him a little pinch.* **2** A **pinch of** an ingredient such as salt is the amount of it that you can hold between your thumb and your first finger. *...a pinch of nutmeg.* ● to **take something with a pinch of salt**: see **salt. 3** If someone **pinches** something, especially something of little value, they steal it. ◆◆◇◇ VERB: V n / N-COUNT / N-COUNT / VERB: V n INFORMAL

4 If something is possible **at a pinch** it would be possible if it was absolutely necessary and if there was no alternative. In American English the expression is **in a pinch**. *Six people, and more at a pinch, could be seated comfortably at the table.* **5** If a person or company is **feeling the pinch**, they do not have as much money as PHRASE BRITISH / PHRASE

they used to, and so they cannot buy the things they would like to buy.

pinched /pɪntʃt/. If someone's face is **pinched**, it looks thin and pale, usually because they are ill or old. ADJ-GRADED

pin·cushion /'pɪnkuʃən/ **pincushions;** also spelled **pin-cushion**. A **pincushion** is a very small cushion that you stick pins and needles into so that you can get them easily when you need them. N-COUNT

pine /paɪn/ **pines, pining, pined. 1** A **pine** tree or a **pine** is a tall tree which has needle-like leaves and a fresh smell. Pine trees keep their leaves all year round. ▶ **Pine** is the wood of this tree. *...a big pine table.* **2** If you **pine** for someone who has died or gone away, you want them to be with you very much and feel sad because they are not there. *Make sure your pet won't pine while you're away.* **3** If you **pine for** something, you want it very much, especially when it is unlikely that you will be able to have it. *...the democracy they have pined for since 1939.* N-VAR / N-UNCOUNT / VERB: V for n V / VERB V for n

pine·apple /'paɪnæpəl/ **pineapples**. A **pineapple** is a large oval fruit that grows in hot countries. It is sweet, juicy, and yellow inside. It has a thick, brownish skin. See picture headed **fruit**. N-VAR

'pine cone, pine cones. A **pine cone** is the seed case produced by a pine tree. It is small, brown, and oval-shaped. N-COUNT

'pine needle, pine needles. **Pine needles** are very thin, sharp leaves that grow on pine trees. N-COUNT

'pine nut, pine nuts. **Pine nuts** are small cream-coloured seeds that grow on pine trees. They can be used in salads and other dishes. N-COUNT

pine·wood /'paɪnwʊd/ **pinewoods;** also spelled **pine wood**. A **pinewood** is a wood which consists mainly of pine trees. N-COUNT

ping /pɪŋ/ **pings, pinging, pinged**. If a bell or a piece of metal **pings**, it makes a short, high-pitched noise. ▶ Also a noun. *...a metallic ping.* VERB: V / N-COUNT

'ping-pong. **Ping-pong** is the game of **table tennis**. *Another pair played a vigorous game of Ping-Pong on a nearby table.* N-UNCOUNT INFORMAL

pin·head /'pɪnhed/ **pinheads**. A **pinhead** is the small metal or plastic part on the top of a pin. *It may even be possible to make computers the size of a pinhead one day.* N-COUNT

pin·hole /'pɪnhəʊl/ **pinholes**. A **pinhole** is a tiny hole. N-COUNT

pin·ion /'pɪnjən/ **pinions, pinioning, pinioned**. If you **are pinioned**, someone prevents you from moving or escaping, especially by holding or tying your arms. *At nine the next morning Bentley was pinioned, hooded and hanged.* VERB be V-ed Also V n

pink /pɪŋk/ **pinker, pinkest; pinks**. **1** Pink is the colour between red and white. ♦ **pink·ish** *Her nostrils and eyelids were always a little pinkish, as though she had a cold.* **2** Pinks are small plants that people grow in their gardens. They have sweet-smelling pink, white, or red flowers. COLOUR ADJ / N-COUNT

pinkie /'pɪŋki/ **pinkies;** also spelled **pinky**. In American and Scottish English, your **pinkie** is the smallest finger on your hand. N-COUNT INFORMAL

pinko /'pɪŋkəʊ/ **pinkos** or **pinkoes**. If someone says they are a Socialist, but you think that their beliefs are too moderate, you can call them a **pinko**. N-COUNT INFORMAL

pinky /'pɪŋki/. See **pinkie**.

'pin money. **Pin money** is small amounts of extra money that someone earns or gets in order to buy things that they want but that they do not really need. N-UNCOUNT

pin·na·cle /'pɪnɪkəl/ **pinnacles**. **1** A **pinnacle** is a pointed piece of stone or rock that is high above the ground. **2** If someone reaches the **pinnacle of** their career or the **pinnacle of** a particular area of life, they are at the highest point of it. *John Major has reached the pinnacle of British politics.* N-COUNT / N-COUNT

pin·ny /'pɪni/ **pinnies**. A **pinny** is an apron. *The waiters and waitresses wear black jeans, off-white shirts and white pinnies.* N-COUNT BRITISH

pin·point /'pɪnpɔɪnt/ **pinpoints, pinpointing, pinpointed. 1** If you **pinpoint** the cause of something, you discover or explain the cause exactly. *...if you can pinpoint exactly what the anger is about... The commission pinpoints inadequate housing as a basic problem threatening village life.* **2** If you **pinpoint** something or its position, you discover or show exactly where it is. *Computers pinpointed where the shells were coming from.* **3** If something is placed with **pinpoint** accuracy, it is placed in exactly the right place or position. VERB: V n / V wh / V n as n / VERB: V n V wh / ADJ: ADJ n

pin·prick /'pɪnprɪk/ **pinpricks;** also spelled **pin-prick** or **pin prick**. A very small spot of something can be described as a **pinprick**. *She looked up at me with pinpricks of sweat along her hairline.* N-COUNT: with supp

,pins and 'needles. If you have **pins and needles** in a part of your body, you feel sharp tingling pains there for a short period of time. It usually happens when the part of your body has been in an awkward or uncomfortable position. N-UNCOUNT

pin·stripe /'pɪnstraɪp/ **pinstripes;** also spelled **pin-stripe**. **Pinstripes** are very narrow vertical stripes found on certain types of clothing. Businessmen's suits often have pinstripes. See picture headed **patterns**. ♦ **pin-striped** *I'm wearing a gray pinstriped suit.* N-COUNT / ADJ

pint /paɪnt/ **pints**. **1** A **pint** is a unit of measurement for liquids. In Britain, it is equal to 568 cubic centimetres or one eighth of an imperial gallon. In America, it is equal to 473 cubic centimetres or one eighth of an American gallon. *...a pint of milk. ...glasses which can hold a full pint.* **2** In Britain, if you go for a **pint**, you go to the pub to drink a pint of beer or more. N-COUNT / N-COUNT

'pint-sized. If you describe someone or something as **pint-sized**, you think they are smaller than is normal or smaller than they should be. *...two pint-sized kids.* ADJ INFORMAL

'pin-up, pin-ups; also spelled **pinup**. A **pin-up** is an attractive man or woman who appears on posters, often wearing very few clothes. *She was already a famous model and pin-up.* N-COUNT

pio·neer /,paɪə'nɪə/ **pioneers, pioneering, pioneered. 1** Someone who is referred to as a **pioneer** in a particular area of activity is one of the first people to be involved in it and develop it. *...one of the leading pioneers of British photo journalism.* **2** Someone who **pioneers** a new activity, invention, or process is one of the first people to do it. *...Professor Alec Jeffreys, who invented and pioneered DNA tests.* **3 Pioneers** are people who leave their own country, go to a new one, and settle in a part of it that has not been settled in before. *...early European pioneers.* N-COUNT / VERB V n Also V / N-COUNT

pio·neer·ing /,paɪə'nɪərɪŋ/. **Pioneering** work or a **pioneering** individual does something that has not been done before. *The school has won awards for its pioneering work with the community.* ADJ

pi·ous /'paɪəs/. **1** Someone who is **pious** is very religious and moral. *He was brought up by pious female relatives.* ♦ **pi·ous·ly** *Conti kneeled and crossed himself piously.* **2** If you describe someone's words as **pious**, you disapprove of them because their words are full of good intentions but do not lead to anything useful. *What we need is not manifestos of pious intentions, but real action.* ♦ **piously** *The groups at the conference spoke piously of their fondness for democracy.* **3** If you describe someone as **pious**, you disapprove of the fact that they pretend to be very religious without being sincere. *...an expression of pious innocence.* ♦ **piously** *'Life,' said Dr Holly piously, 'is the only wealth.'* ADJ-GRADED / ADV-GRADED: ADV with v / ADJ-GRADED: ADJ n PRAGMATICS / ADV-GRADED: ADV with v / ADJ-GRADED PRAGMATICS / ADV-GRADED: ADV with v

pip /pɪp/ **pips, pipping, pipped**. **1** Pips are the small hard seeds in a fruit such as an apple, orange, or pear. **2** In Britain, the pips on the radio are a series of short, high-pitched sounds that are used as a time signal. **3** In Britain, when you make a telephone call from a public telephone, the pips are a signal that you need to put in more money. **4** If someone **is pipped** to something, such as a prize N-COUNT / N-PLURAL / N-PLURAL / VERB

or an award, they are narrowly defeated. *It's still possible for the losers to be pipped by West Germany for a semi-final place.* **5** If someone **is pipped at the post** or **pipped to the post** they are just beaten in a competition or in a race to achieve something. `be V-ed prep` `Also V n prep` `BRITISH,` `INFORMAL` `PHRASE` `BRITISH,` `INFORMAL`

pipe /paɪp/ **pipes, piping, piped. 1** A **pipe** is a long, round, hollow object, usually made of metal or plastic, through which a liquid or gas can flow. *The plant makes plastic covered steel pipes for the oil and gas industries.* **2** If liquid or gas **is piped** somewhere, it is transferred from one place to another through a pipe. *The heated gas is piped through a coil surrounded by water.* ◆◆◆◇ `N-COUNT` `VERB` `be V-ed prep` `Also V n with` `adv`

3 A **pipe** is an object which is used for smoking tobacco. **4** If someone, especially a child, **pipes** something, they say it in a high-pitched voice. *'But I want to help,' Bessie piped.* **5** A **pipe** is a simple musical instrument in the shape of a tube with holes in it. **6 Pipes** are the same as **bagpipes. 7** See also **piping, piping hot.** `N-COUNT` `VERB` `V with quote` `N-COUNT` `N-PLURAL`

pipe down. If you tell someone who is talking a lot or talking too loudly to **pipe down**, you are telling them to stop talking. *Just pipe down and I'll tell you what I want.* `PHRASAL VB` `no cont` `V P` `INFORMAL`

pipe up. If someone who has been silent for a while **pipes up**, they say something, especially something surprising or strange. *'That's right, mister,' another child piped up.* `PHRASAL VB` `no cont` `V P with quote` `Also V P`

'pipe cleaner, pipe cleaners. A **pipe cleaner** is a piece of wire covered with a soft woolly substance which is used to clean a tobacco pipe. `N-COUNT`

,piped 'music. Piped music is music which is played through loudspeakers in some supermarkets, restaurants, and other public places. `N-UNCOUNT`

'pipe dream, pipe dreams; also spelled **pipe-dream.** A **pipe dream** is a hope or plan that you have which you know will never really happen. `N-COUNT`

pipe·line /ˈpaɪplaɪn/ **pipelines. 1** A **pipeline** is a large pipe which is used for carrying oil or gas over a long distance. **2** If something is **in the pipeline**, it has already been planned or begun. *Mr Major said some changes and modifications were already in the pipeline.* ◆◆◇◇ `N-COUNT` `PHRASE`

pip·er /ˈpaɪpə/ **pipers.** A **piper** is a musician who plays the bagpipes. ◆◇◇◇ `N-COUNT`

pipe·work /ˈpaɪpwɜːk/. **Pipework** is the pipes that are part of a machine or construction. `N-UNCOUNT`

pip·ing /ˈpaɪpɪŋ/. **1 Piping** is metal, plastic, or another substance made in the shape of a pipe or tube. *...rolls of bright yellow plastic piping.* **2 Piping** is cloth made into a narrow tube. Piping is used to decorate the edges of clothing and things such as cushions. ◆◇◇◇ `N-UNCOUNT` `N-UNCOUNT`

,piping 'hot; also spelled **piping-hot.** Food or water that is **piping hot** is very hot. *...large cups of piping-hot coffee.* `ADJ`

pi·quant /ˈpiːkənt, -kɑːnt/. **1** Food that is **piquant** has a pleasantly spicy taste. *...a crisp mixed salad with an unusually piquant dressing.* ◆ **pi·quan·cy** /ˈpiːkənsi/ *A little mustard is served on the side to add further piquancy.* **2** Something that is **piquant** is interesting and exciting. *There may well have been a piquant novelty about her books.* ◆ **piquancy** *The debate is given added piquancy by a new mood of unusual self-doubt.* `ADJ-GRADED` `N-UNCOUNT` `ADJ-GRADED` `FORMAL` `N-UNCOUNT`

pique /piːk/ **piques, piquing, piqued. 1 Pique** is the feeling of anger and resentment that you have when your pride is hurt. *Mimi had gotten over her pique at Susan's refusal to accept the job.* **2** If something **piques** your interest or curiosity, it arouses your interest or curiosity. **3** If someone does something **in a fit of pique**, they do it because they are angry and resentful that their pride has been hurt. *Lawrence, in a fit of pique, left the Army and took up a career in the City.* `N-UNCOUNT` `VERB: V n` `PHRASE`

piqued /piːkt/. If someone is **piqued**, they are offended or annoyed, often by something that is not very important. *She wrinkled her nose, piqued by his total lack of enthusiasm.* `ADJ-GRADED`

pi·ra·cy /ˈpaɪrəsi/. **1 Piracy** is robbery at sea carried out by pirates. **2** You can refer to the illegal copying `N-UNCOUNT` `N-UNCOUNT`

of things such as video tapes and computer programs as **piracy.**

pi·ra·nha /pɪˈrɑːnə/ **piranhas; piranha** can also be used as the plural form. A **piranha** is a small, fierce fish which is found in South America. `N-COUNT`

pi·rate /ˈpaɪrət/ **pirates, pirating, pirated.** **1 Pirates** are sailors who attack other ships and steal property from them. **2** Someone who **pirates** video tapes, cassettes, books, or computer programs copies and sells them when they have no right to do so. *A school technician pirated anything from video nasties to computer games.* ▶ A **pirate** version of something is an illegal copy of it. ◆ **pi·rat·ed** *...a pirated edition of the book.* ◆◆◇◇ `N-COUNT` `VERB` `V n` `ADJ: ADJ n` `ADJ`

,pirate 'radio, pirate radios. In Britain, **pirate radio** is the broadcasting of radio programmes illegally. `N-VAR`

pirou·ette /ˌpɪruˈet/ **pirouettes, pirouetting, pirouetted. 1** In ballet, a **pirouette** is a fast turn of the dancer's body while standing. **2** If someone **pirouettes**, they perform one or more pirouettes. `N-COUNT` `VERB: V`

piss /pɪs/ **pisses, pissing, pissed. Piss** is a very informal and rude word which many people find offensive. ◆◆◇◇

1 To **piss** means to urinate. **2** If someone has **a piss**, they urinate. **3 Piss** is urine. **4** If you **take the piss out of** someone, you tease them and make fun of them. `VERB: V` `N-SING` `N-UNCOUNT` `PHRASE` `BRITISH`

piss about. If you say that someone **pisses about**, you mean they waste a lot of time doing things that do not really need doing. `PHRASAL VB` `V P` `INFORMAL`

piss off. 1 If someone or something **pisses** you **off**, they annoy you. *It pisses me off when they start moaning.* ◆ **pissed off** *I was really pissed off.* **2** If someone tells a person to **piss off**, they are telling the person in a rude way to go away. `PHRASAL VB` `V n P` `INFORMAL` `ADJ-GRADED` `V P` `PRAGMATICS`

pissed /pɪst/. **1** Someone who is **pissed** is drunk. Some people find this use offensive. *He was just lying there completely pissed.* **2** If you say that someone is **pissed**, you mean that they are annoyed. Some people find this use offensive. *You know Molly's pissed at you.* `ADJ-GRADED` `BRITISH,` `INFORMAL` `ADJ-GRADED` `v-link ADJ` `AMERICAN,` `INFORMAL`

'piss-take, piss-takes. A **piss-take** is an act of making fun of someone or something. `N-COUNT` `BRITISH`

pis·ta·chio /pɪˈstætʃiəʊ/ **pistachios. Pistachios** or **pistachio nuts** are small, green, edible nuts. `N-VAR`

piste /piːst/ **pistes.** A **piste** is a track of firm snow for skiing on. `N-COUNT`

pis·tol /ˈpɪstəl/ **pistols.** A **pistol** is a small handgun. ◆◆◇◇ `N-COUNT`

pis·ton /ˈpɪstən/ **pistons.** A **piston** is a cylinder or metal disc that is part of an engine. ◆◇◇◇ `N-COUNT`

pit /pɪt/ **pits, pitting, pitted. 1** A **pit** is a coal mine. **2** A **pit** is a large hole that is dug in the ground. *Eric lost his footing and began to slide into the pit.* **3** In motor racing, the **pits** are the areas at the side of the track where drivers stop to get more fuel and to repair their cars during races. ◆ See also **pit stop. 4** If you have a feeling **in the pit of** your **stomach**, you have an unpleasant feeling inside your body because you are afraid or anxious. *I had a funny feeling in the pit of my stomach.* **5** If two opposing things or people **are pitted against** one another, they are in conflict. *You will be pitted against two, three, or four people who are every bit as good as you are.* **6** If you describe someone or something as the **pits**, you mean that it is really awful. *Mary Ann asked him how dinner had been. 'The pits,' he replied.* **7** See also **pitted; orchestra pit, sandpit.** ◆◆◇◇ `N-COUNT` `N-COUNT` `N-COUNT` `PHRASE` `VB: usu` `passive` `be V-ed` `against n` `N-PLURAL:` `the N` `SPOKEN`

pita /ˈpiːtə/ **pitas.** See **pitta.**

'pit bull terrier, pit bull terriers. A **pit bull terrier** or **pit bull** is a very fierce kind of dog. `N-COUNT`

pitch /pɪtʃ/ **pitches, pitching, pitched. 1** A **pitch** is an area of ground that is marked out and used for playing a game such as football, cricket, or hockey. The more usual American word is **field.** *There was a swimming-pool, cricket pitches, playing fields.* **2** In the game of baseball or rounders, when you **pitch** the ball, you throw it to the batsman for ◆◆◆◇ `N-COUNT` `BRITISH` `VERB: V n`

him to hit. ♦ **pitch·ing** *His pitching was a legend* N-UNCOUNT *among major league hitters.* **3** If you **pitch** some- VERB thing somewhere, you throw it forcefully but aiming V n prep carefully. *Simon pitched the empty bottle into the lake.* **4** If someone or something **pitches** some- VERB where, they fall forwards suddenly and with a lot of V adv force. *The movement took him by surprise, and he* beV-ed *pitched forward... I was pitched into the water and* prep/adv *swam ashore.*

5 The **pitch** of a sound is how high or low it is. *He* N-UNCOUNT *raised his voice to an even higher pitch.* ● See also **per-fect pitch. 6** If a sound **is pitched at** a particular level, VB: usu it is produced at the level indicated. *His cry is pitched* passive *at a level that makes it impossible to ignore.* ● See also beV-ed **high-pitched, low-pitched. 7** If something **is pitched** VERB: at a particular level or degree of difficulty, it is set at beV-ed that level. *The government has pitched High Street in-* V n prep *terest rates at a new level.* **8** If something such as a feel- N-SING ing or a situation rises to a high **pitch,** it rises to a high level. *...the competitors who have all worked them-selves up to a very high pitch.* ● See also **fever pitch.**

9 If you **pitch your tent,** or **pitch camp,** you put up VERB: V n your tent in a place where you are going to stay.

10 If a boat **pitches,** it moves violently up and down VERB: V with the movement of the waves when the sea is rough.

11 Pitch is a black substance that is sticky when it is N-UNCOUNT hot and very hard when it is dry. Pitch is used on the bottoms of boats and on the roofs of houses to pre-vent water getting in. ● See also **pitch-black.**

12 If someone **makes a pitch** for something, they try PHRASE to persuade people to do or buy that thing. *Prue invit-ed the magazine's editor to lunch and made her pitch.* ● See also **sales pitch.**

13 See also **pitched.**

pitch for. If someone is **pitching for** something, PHRASAL VB they are trying to persuade other people to give it to them. *It was middle-class votes they were pitching for.*

pitch in. If you **pitch in,** you join in and help with an PHRASAL VB activity. *The entire company pitched in to help.* V P
V P to-inf
,pitch-'black. If a place or the night is **pitch-** ADJ•NORMAL **black,** it is completely dark.

,pitch-'dark; also spelled **pitch dark. Pitch-dark** ADJ means the same as **pitch-black.**

pitched /pɪtʃt/. A **pitched roof** is one that slopes ADJ-GRADED quite steeply as opposed to one that is flat. ● See also **high-pitched, low-pitched.**

,pitched 'battle, pitched battles. A pitched bat- N-COUNT tle is a very fierce and violent fight involving a large number of people. *For the next three nights pitched battles were fought with the police.*

pitch·er /'pɪtʃə/ **pitchers. 1** A **pitcher** is a jug. *I* ◇◇◇◇ *flinched, almost knocking over the milk pitcher.* **2** A N-COUNT **pitcher** is a large jug made of clay. **3** In baseball, N-COUNT the **pitcher** is the person who throws the ball to the N-COUNT batsman, who tries to hit it.

pitch·fork /'pɪtʃfɔːk/ **pitchforks.** A pitchfork is a N-COUNT large fork with a long handle and two prongs that is used for lifting hay or cut grass.

pit·eous /'pɪtiəs/. Something that is **piteous** is so ADJ-GRADED sad that you feel great pity for the person involved. WRITTEN *As they pass by, a piteous wailing is heard.* ♦ **pit-·eous·ly** *'I can't bear to face anyone,' she said* ADV-GRADED: *piteously.* ADV after v

pit·fall /'pɪtfɔːl/ **pitfalls.** The pitfalls involved in a ◇◇◇◇◇ particular activity or situation are the things that N-COUNT may go wrong or may cause problems. *The pitfalls of working abroad are numerous.*

pith /pɪθ/. The **pith** of an orange, lemon, or other N-UNCOUNT citrus fruit is the white substance between the peel and the inside of the fruit.

pit·head /'pɪthed/ **pitheads.** The **pithead** at a coal N-COUNT mine is all the buildings and machinery which are BRITISH above ground.

pithy /'pɪθi/ **pithier, pithiest.** A **pithy** comment or ADJ-GRADED piece of writing is short, direct, sensible, and WRITTEN memorable. *Many of them made a point of praising the film's pithy dialogue.*

piti·able /'pɪtiəbəl/. Someone who is **pitiable** is in ADJ-GRADED such a sad or weak state that you feel pity for them. WRITTEN

Her grandmother seemed to her a pitiable figure. ♦ **piti·ably** /'pɪtiəbli/. *She found Frances lying on* ADV-GRADED *the bed crying pitiably.*

piti·ful /'pɪtiful/. **1** Someone or something that is ◇◇◇◇ **pitiful** is so sad, weak, or small that you feel pity for ADJ-GRADED them. *It was the most pitiful sight I had ever seen.* ♦ **piti·ful·ly** *His legs were pitifully thin.* **2** If you de- ADV-GRADED scribe something as **pitiful,** you mean that it is ADJ-GRADED completely inadequate. *The farmers pay pitiful wages, often in the form of food and clothes.* ♦ **pitifully** *State help for the mentally handicapped* ADV-GRADED *is pitifully inadequate.* **3** If you describe something ADJ-GRADED as **pitiful,** you mean that it does not deserve respect or consideration. *This argument seems to show a pitiful lack of confidence in the capabilities of our juries.*

piti·less /'pɪtiləs/. Someone or something that is ADJ-GRADED **pitiless** shows no pity or mercy. *He saw the pitiless eyes of his enemy.*

'pit stop, pit stops. 1 In motor racing, if a driver N-COUNT makes a **pit stop,** he stops in a special place at the side of the track to get more fuel and to make re-pairs. **2** A **pit stop** is a brief stop for rest and re- N-COUNT freshment, especially when you are on a journey. *They went around the world in a week without a pit stop.*

pit·ta /'pɪtə/ **pittas;** spelled **pita** and pronounced N-VAR /'piːtə/ in American English. **Pitta** or **pitta bread** is a type of bread in the shape of a flat oval.

pit·tance /'pɪtəns/ **pittances.** If you say that you N-COUNT receive a **pittance,** you are emphasizing that you get PRAGMATICS only a very small amount of money. *Her secretaries work tirelessly for a pittance.*

pit·ted /'pɪtɪd/. **1** Pitted fruits have had their stones ADJ: ADJ n removed. *...green and black pitted olives.* **2** If the ADJ surface of something is **pitted,** it is covered with a lot of small, shallow holes. *...the pitted surface of the moon.*

pi·tui·tary gland /pɪˌtjuːɪtri 'glænd, AM -ˌtuːɪteri -/ N-COUNT **pituitary glands.** The **pituitary gland** or the **pi-tuitary** is a gland that is attached to the base of the brain. It produces hormones which affect growth, sexual development, and other functions of the body.

pity /'pɪti/ **pities, pitying, pitied. 1** If you feel ♦♦◇◇◇ **pity** for someone, you feel sorry for them. *He* N-UNCOUNT *felt a sudden tender pity for her.* ● See also **self-pity.** VERB **2** If you **pity** someone, you feel very sorry for them. V n *I don't know whether to hate or pity him.* **3** If you PHRASE **take pity on** someone, you feel sorry for them and help them. *No woman had ever felt the need to take pity on him.* **4** If someone shows **pity,** they show N-UNCOUNT mercy and forgiveness. *Non-communist forces have some pity towards people here.*

5 If you say that something is **a pity,** that is the case, N-SING: you mean that you feel disappointment or regret a N about it. *It is a great pity that all pupils in the city can-* PRAGMATICS *not have the same chances... Pity you haven't got your car, isn't it.* **6** If you add **more's the pity** to a comment, PHRASE you are expressing your disappointment or regret PRAGMATICS about something. *But my world isn't your world, more's the pity.* **7** If you say **the pity is that,** or **the pity** PHRASE **of it is that,** before a comment, you are emphasizing PRAGMATICS your disappointment or regret about something. *The pity is that it was all completely unnecessary.*

pity·ing /'pɪtiɪŋ/. A **pitying** look shows that some- ADJ one feels pity and perhaps slight contempt. *She gave him a pitying look.*

piv·ot /'pɪvət/ **pivots, pivoting, pivoted. 1** The ◇◇◇◇ **pivot** in a situation is the most important thing N-COUNT which everything else is based on or arranged around. *Forming the pivot of the exhibition is a large group of watercolours.* **2** If something **pivots,** it VERB balances or turns on a central point. *The boat pivot-* V prep/adv *ed on its central axis and pointed straight at the har-* Also V n prep *bour entrance.* **3** A **pivot** is the pin or the central N-COUNT point on which something balances or turns.

pivot on. If one thing **pivots on** another, it depends PHRASAL VB on it. *...the economic problems that pivoted on over-* V P n *seas trade.*

piv·ot·al /'pɪvətəl/. A **pivotal** role, point, or figure in something is one that is very important and affects the success of that thing. *The Court of Appeal has a pivotal role in the English legal system.* ◆◇◇◇◇ ADJ

pix·el /'pɪksəl/ **pixels.** A **pixel** is the smallest size of spot on a computer screen which can be independently controlled by the computer. N-COUNT TECHNICAL

pixie /'pɪksi/ **pixies.** A **pixie** is an imaginary little creature like a fairy. Pixies have pointed ears and wear pointed hats. N-COUNT

piz·za /'piːtsə/ **pizzas.** A **pizza** is a flat round piece of dough covered with tomatoes, cheese, and other savoury food, and then baked in an oven. ◆◆◇◇◇ N-VAR

piz·zazz /pɪ'zæz/; also spelled **pzazz** or **pizazz**. If you say that someone or something has **pizzazz**, you approve of the fact that they are exceptionally exciting, energetic, and stylish. *...a young woman with a lot of energy and pizzazz.* N-UNCOUNT PRAGMATICS INFORMAL

piz·ze·ria /ˌpiːtsə'riːə/ **pizzerias.** A **pizzeria** is a place where pizza is made, sold, and eaten. N-COUNT

pkt. Pkt is used in recipes as a written abbreviation for **packet**.

pl. 1 In addresses and on maps and signs, **Pl** is often used as a written abbreviation for **Place**. *27 Queensdale Pl, London W11, England.* **2** In grammar, **pl** is often used as a written abbreviation for **plural**. ◆◇◇◇◇

plac·ard /'plækɑːd/ **placards.** A **placard** is a large notice that is carried in a march or demonstration or is displayed in a public place. *The protesters sang songs and waved placards.* ◆◇◇◇◇ N-COUNT

pla·cate /plə'keɪt, AM 'pleɪkeɪt/ **placates, placating, placated.** If you **placate** someone, you stop them feeling angry or resentful by doing or saying things that will please them. *He smiled, and made a gesture intended to placate me... 'I didn't mean to upset you,' Agnew said in a placating voice.* ◆◇◇◇◇ VERB V n V-ing Also V

placa·tory /plə'keɪtəri, AM 'pleɪkətɔːri/. A **placatory** remark or action is intended to stop someone feeling angry or resentful by doing or saying things that will please them. *When next he spoke he was more placatory.* ADJ-GRADED

place /pleɪs/ **places, placing, placed. 1** When something **takes place**, it happens, especially in a controlled or organized way. *The discussion took place in a famous villa.* ◆◆◆◆◆ PHRASE

2 A **place** is any point, building, area, town, or country. *...Temple Mount, the place where the Temple actually stood... The snow along the roadside was five or six feet deep in places.* **3** You can use **the** to refer to the point, building, area, town, or country that you have already mentioned. *Except for the remarkably tidy kitchen, the place was a mess.* **4 Place** can be used after 'any', 'no', 'some', or 'every' to mean 'anywhere', 'nowhere', 'somewhere', or 'everywhere'. *The poor guy obviously didn't have any place to go for Easter... Why not go out and see if there's some place we can dance?* **5** Your **place** is the house or flat where you live. *Let's all go back to my place!... Did she say she didn't want to stay at your place?* ● See also **meeting place**. N-COUNT; N-SING: the N; N-SING: det N AMERICAN, INFORMAL; N-COUNT INFORMAL

6 If you go **places**, you visit pleasant or interesting places. *People were talking to him, listening to him, taking him places.* **7** If you say that someone **is going places**, you mean that they are showing a lot of talent or ability and are likely to become very successful. ADV; ADV after v AMERICAN PHRASE

8 You can refer to the position where something belongs, or where it is supposed to be, as its **place**. *He returned the album to its place on the shelf.* **9** A **place** is a seat or position that is available for someone to occupy. *I found a place to park beside a station wagon.* N-COUNT: poss N; N-COUNT

10 If something is **in place**, it is in its correct or usual position. If it is **out of place**, it is not in its correct or usual position. *Geoff hastily pushed the drawer back into place.* PHRASE

11 Someone's or something's **place** in a society, system, or situation is their position or role in relation to other people or things. *They want to see more women take their place higher up the corporate or professional ladder.* **12** If you **change places** with another person, you change situations or roles in life with them. *When* N-COUNT: with poss; PHRASE

he has tried to identify all the items, you can change places, and he can test you. **13** People **in high places** are people who have powerful and influential positions in a government, society, or organization. **14** If you say what you would have done **in** someone else's **place**, you say what you would have done if you had been in their situation. *In her place I wouldn't have been able to resist it.* **15** If you say that **it is not** your **place** to do something, you mean that it is not right or appropriate for you to do it. *It's not my place to do their job.* **16** If someone or something seems **out of place** in a particular situation, they do not seem to belong there or to be suitable for that situation. *I felt out of place in my suit and tie.* PHRASE

17 Your **place** in a race or competition is your position in relation to the other competitors. If you are in first place, you are ahead of all the other competitors. **18** If a competitor **is placed** first, second, or last, for example, that is their position at the end of a race or competition. *Second-placed Auxerre suffered a surprising 2-0 home defeat.* N-COUNT; VB: usu passive, be V-ed ord V-ed

19 If you get a **place** in a team, on a committee, on a course, or on a trip, for example, you are accepted as a member of the team or committee or as a participant on the course or trip. *I eventually got a place at York University.* N-COUNT

20 A good **place** to do something in a situation or activity is a good time or stage at which to do it. *It seemed an appropriate place to end somehow.* **21** Your **place** in a book or speech is the point you have reached in reading the book or making the speech. *...her finger marking her place in the book.* N-SING: with supp; N-COUNT

22 If you say how many decimal **places** there are in a number, you are saying how many numbers there are to the right of the decimal point. N-COUNT

23 If you **place** something somewhere, you put it in a particular position, especially in a careful, firm, or deliberate way. *Brand folded it in his handkerchief and placed it in the inside pocket of his jacket.* **24** If an agency or organization **places** someone, it finds them a job or somewhere to live. *They managed to place fourteen women in paid positions in the colonies.* VERB V n prep/adv; VERB: V n V n in n

25 To **place** a person or thing in a particular state means to cause them to be in it. *The remaining 30 per cent of each army will be placed under UN control.* VERB: V n V-ed prep; be V-ed prep

26 You can use **place** instead of 'put' or 'lay' in certain expressions where the meaning is carried by the associated noun. For example, if you **place emphasis** on something, you emphasize it. *His government is placing its faith in international diplomacy.* VERB: V n on/upon n V n in n

27 If you **place** someone or something in a particular class or group, you classify them in that way. *The authorities have placed the drug in Class A.* **28** If you **place** one thing **above**, **before**, or **over** another, you think that the first thing is more important than the second and you show this in your behaviour. *He continued to place security above all other objectives.* VERB V n prep; PHRASE

29 If you **place an order** for some goods or for a meal, you ask a company to send you the goods or a waiter to bring you the meal. **30** If you **place an advertisement** in a newspaper, you arrange for the advertisement to appear in the newspaper. *They placed an advertisement in the local paper for a secretary.* **31** If you **place a telephone call** to a particular place, you give the operator the number of the person you want to speak to and ask them to connect you. *I'd like to place an overseas call.* **32** If you **place a bet** with a bookmaker, you bet on the result of a future event. *He had already placed a bet on one of the horses.* VERB: V n; VERB V n in n Also V n; VERB V n; VERB V n on n Also V n

33 If you say that you cannot **place** someone, you mean that you recognize them but cannot remember exactly who they are or where you have met them before. *He felt he should know him, but could not quite place him.* VERB V n

34 If something is happening **all over the place**, it is happening in many different places. *Businesses are closing down all over the place.* **35** If things are **all over the place**, they are spread over a very large area, usually in a disorganized way. *Our fingerprints are probably all over the place.* **36** If you say that someone PHRASE

is **all over the place**, you mean that they are confused or disorganized, and unable to think clearly or act properly.

37 If you have been trying to understand something PHRASE puzzling and then everything **falls into place** or **clicks into place**, you suddenly understand how different pieces of information are connected and everything becomes clearer. **38** If things **fall into place**, events PHRASE happen naturally to produce a situation you want. *Once the decision was finally made, things fell into place rapidly.*

39 If something such as a law, a policy, or an adminis- PHRASE trative structure is **in place**, it is working or able to be used. *Similar legislation is already in place in Wales.*

40 If one thing or person is used or appears **in place** PHRASE **of** another or in another's **place**, they replace the other thing or person. *Cooked kidney beans can be used in place of French beans.* **41** If one thing or person **takes** PHRASE **the place of** another or **takes** another's **place**, they replace the other thing or person. *Optimism was gradually taking the place of pessimism.*

42 You say **in the first place** when you are talking PHRASE about the beginning of a situation or about the situa- PRAGMATICS tion as it was before a series of events. *What brought you to Washington in the first place?*.

43 You say **in the first place** and **in the second place** PHRASE to introduce the first and second in a series of points PRAGMATICS or reasons. **In the first place** can also be used to emphasize a very important point or reason. *In the first place you are not old, Norman. And in the second place, you are a very strong and appealing man.*

44 If you say that someone has found their **place in** PHRASE **the sun**, you mean that they are in a job or a situation where they will be happy and have everything that they want.

45 If you **put** someone **in** their **place**, you show them PHRASE that they are less important or clever than they think they are. *In a few words she had not only put him in his place but delivered a precise and damning assessment of his movie.* **46** If you say that someone should be PHRASE **shown** their **place** or **be kept in** their **place**, you mean BRITISH that they should be made aware of the fact that they are not important. *...an uppity publican who needs to be shown his place.*

47 If one thing **takes second place** to another, it is PHRASE considered to be less important and is given less attention than the other thing.

48 ● **pride of place**: see **pride**.

Place. Place is used as part of the name of a ◆◆◇◇◇ square or short street in a town. *...15 Portland Place.*

pla·ce·bo /pləˈsiːbəʊ/ **placebos.** A placebo is a ◆◇◇◇◇ harmless inactive substance that a doctor gives to a N-COUNT patient instead of a drug. Placebos are used when testing new drugs or when a patient has imagined their illness.

pla'cebo effect, placebo effects. The placebo N-COUNT effect is the fact that some patients' health improves after taking what they believe is an effective drug but which is in fact only a placebo.

-placed /-pleɪst/. **1 -placed** combines with adverbs COMB to form adjectives which describe how well or badly someone is able to do a particular task. *You were better-placed than most to know the truth... Fund managers are poorly placed to monitor firms.* **2 -placed** combines with adverbs to form adjectives COMB which indicate how good or bad the position of a building or area is considered to be. *Chicago is perfectly-placed for exploring the US by rail.*

place·man /ˈpleɪsmən/ **placemen.** If you refer to a N-COUNT public official as a **placeman**, you disapprove of the PRAGMATICS fact that they use their position for their own per- BRITISH sonal benefit, or that they have been given their position because those who appointed them know that they will give them political support.

'**place mat, place mats.** Place mats are mats N-COUNT that are put on a table before a meal for people to put their plates or bowls on.

place·ment /ˈpleɪsmənt/ **placements. 1** The ◆◇◇◇◇ **placement** of something or someone is the act of N-COUNT: putting them in a particular place or position. *The* with supp

treatment involves the placement of twenty-two electrodes in the inner ear. **2** The **placement** of some- N-UNCOUNT: one in a job, home, or school is the act or process of with supp finding them a job, home, or school. *The children were waiting for placement in a foster care home.*

3 If someone who is training gets a **placement**, they N-COUNT get a job for a period of time which is intended to give BRITISH them experience in the work they are training for.

4 You can refer to a home that is found for someone N-COUNT who is unable to look after themselves, for example a child, as a **placement**. *This home seemed like a good placement for Sarah.*

pla·cen·ta /pləˈsentə/ **placentas.** The **placenta** is N-COUNT the mass of veins and tissue inside the womb of a pregnant woman or animal, which the foetus is attached to.

'**place setting, place settings. 1** A place setting N-COUNT is an arrangement of knives, forks, spoons, and glasses that has been laid out on a table for the use of one person at a meal. **2** A **place setting** of cutlery N-COUNT or crockery is a complete set of all the cutlery or crockery that one person might use at a meal.

plac·id /ˈplæsɪd/. **1** A **placid** person or animal is ◆◇◇◇◇ calm and does not easily become excited, angry, or ADJ-GRADED upset. *She was a placid child who rarely cried.* ♦ **plac·id·ly** *'No matter, we will pay the difference,'* ADV-GRADED *Helena said placidly.* **2** A **placid** place, area of water, ADJ-GRADED or life is calm and peaceful. *...the placid waters of Lake Erie.*

plac·ings /ˈpleɪsɪŋz/. The **placings** in a competi- ◆◇◇◇◇ tion are the relative positions of the competitors at N-PLURAL the end or at a particular stage of the competition. *The placings remained unaltered.*

pla·gia·rize /ˈpleɪdʒəraɪz/ **plagiarizes, plagiariz-** VERB: V n **ing, plagiarized;** also spelled **plagiarise** in British V from n English. If someone **plagiarizes** another person's Also V idea or work, they use it or copy it and pretend that they thought of it or created it. *...a verse plagiarized from a billboard.* ♦ **pla·gia·rism** *He was nervous* N-UNCOUNT *about being accused of plagiarism.*

plague /pleɪg/ **plagues, plaguing, plagued. 1** A ◆◆◇◇◇ **plague** is a very infectious disease that spreads N-COUNT quickly and kills large numbers of people. *A cholera plague had been killing many prisoners of war.* **2 Plague** or **the plague** is a very infectious and N-UNCOUNT: usually fatal disease, in which the patient has a se- also the N vere fever and swellings on his or her body. **3** If you PHRASE say that you **avoid** someone or something **like the** PRAGMATICS **plague**, you are emphasizing that you deliberately avoid them completely. *The athlete must avoid all extra sugar like the plague.* **4** A **plague of** unpleas- N-COUNT: ant things is a large number of them that arrive or N of n happen at the same time. *The city is under threat from a plague of rats.* **5** If you describe something N-COUNT as a **plague**, you mean that it causes a great deal of trouble or harm. *Inflation will remain a recurrent plague.*

6 If you are **plagued** by unpleasant things, they con- VERB: tinually cause you a lot of trouble or suffering. *Fears* be V-ed by n *about job security plague nearly half the workforce.* V n

7 If someone **plagues** you, they keep bothering you or VERB: V n asking you for something. *I'm not going to plague you* V n with n *with a lot more questions.*

plaice /pleɪs/. **plaice** is both the singular and the ◆◇◇◇◇ plural form. **Plaice** are a type of flat sea fish. N-VAR ▶ **Plaice** is this fish eaten as food. N-UNCOUNT

plaid /plæd/ **plaids. 1 Plaid** is material with a ◇◇◇◇◇ check design on it. **Plaid** is also the design itself. **2** A N-VAR **plaid** is a long piece of tartan material that is worn N-COUNT over the shoulder as part of the Scottish Highland national dress.

plain /pleɪn/ **plainer, plainest; plains. 1** A plain ◆◆◆◇◇ object, surface, or fabric is entirely in one colour ADJ and has no pattern, design, or writing on it. *In general, a plain carpet makes a room look bigger. ...a plain envelope.* **2** Something that is **plain** is very ADJ-GRADED simple in style. *Bronwen's dress was plain but it hung well on her.* ♦ **plain·ly** *He was very tall and* ADV-GRADED: *plainly dressed.* **3** If a police officer is in plain ADV -ed clothes, he or she is wearing ordinary clothes PHRASE

P

instead of a police uniform. *He was arrested by plain-clothes detectives.*
4 If a fact, situation, or statement is **plain**, it is easy to recognize or understand. *It was plain to him that I was having a nervous breakdown.* **5** If you describe someone as **plain**, you think they look ordinary and not at all beautiful. *...a shy, rather plain girl with a pale complexion.* **6** A **plain** is a large flat area of land with very few trees on it. **7** You can use **plain** before an adjective in order to emphasize it. *The food was just plain terrible.* ▶ also used before a noun. *Is it love of publicity or plain stupidity on her part?* — ADJ-GRADED / ADJ-GRADED / N-COUNT / ADV: ADV adj [PRAGMATICS] / ADJ: ADJ n
8 ● **plain sailing**: see **sailing**.

,plain 'chocolate. **Plain chocolate** is dark brown chocolate that has a stronger and less sweet taste than milk chocolate. — N-UNCOUNT BRITISH

,plain 'flour. **Plain flour** is flour that does not make cakes and biscuits rise when they are cooked. — N-UNCOUNT

plain·ly /'pleɪnli/. **1** You use **plainly** when stating something that you believe cannot be doubted or denied. *The judge's conclusion was plainly wrong... Plainly, a more objective method of description must be adopted.* **2** You use **plainly** to indicate that something is easily seen, noticed, or recognized. *He was plainly annoyed... I could plainly see him turning his head to the right and left.* **3** If you say something **plainly**, you say it in a direct and honest way, without trying to hide the facts. *'You're a coward,' Mark said very plainly and soberly.* — ADV-GRADED: ADV with cl, not last in cl [PRAGMATICS] / ADV-GRADED: ADV adj, ADV with v, / ADV-GRADED: ADV with v

plain·tiff /'pleɪntɪf/ **plaintiffs**. A **plaintiff** is a person who brings a legal case against someone in a court of law. — N-COUNT

plain·tive /'pleɪntɪv/. A **plaintive** sound or voice is sad and mournful. *...the plaintive cry of the seagulls.* ♦ **plain·tive·ly** *'Why don't we do something?' Davis asked plaintively.* — ADJ-GRADED / ADV-GRADED

plait /plæt, AM pleɪt/ **plaits, plaiting, plaited.**
1 If you **plait** three or more lengths of hair, rope, or other material together, you twist them over and under each other to make one thick length. **2** A **plait** is a length of hair that has been plaited. — VERB: V n / N-COUNT

plan /plæn/ **plans, planning, planned. 1** A **plan** is a method of achieving something that you have worked out in detail beforehand. *The three leaders had worked out a peace plan. ...a detailed plan of action for restructuring the group... Everything is going according to plan.* **2** If you **plan** what you are going to do, you decide in detail what you are going to do, and you intend to do it. *He planned to leave Baghdad on Monday... It would be difficult for schools to plan for the future.* **3** If you have **plans**, you are intending to do a particular thing. *'I'm sorry,' she said. 'I have plans for tonight.'*
4 When you **plan** something that you are going to make, build, or create, you decide what the main parts of it will be and do a drawing of how it should be made. *It is no use trying to plan an 18-hole golf course on a 120-acre site if you have to ruin the environment to do it.* **5** A **plan** of something that is going to be built or made is a detailed diagram or drawing of it. *...when you have drawn a plan of the garden.*
6 See also **planning**. — N-COUNT: also according to N / VERB: V wh, V to-inf, V for n, Also V n / N-PLURAL / VERB: V n / N-COUNT

plan on. If you **plan on** doing something, you intend to do it. *They were planning on getting married.* — PHRASAL VB V P -ing/n

plan out. If you **plan out** the future, you decide in detail what you are going to do. *Tony spent the next week with his marketing people planning out the production and sale of portrait dolls.* — PHRASAL VB V P noun Also V n P

plane /pleɪn/ **planes, planing, planed. 1** A **plane** is a vehicle with wings and one or more engines, which can fly through the air. You have plenty of time to catch his plane. **2** A **plane** is a flat level surface which may be sloping at a particular angle. *...a building with angled planes.* **3** If a number of points are in the same **plane**, one line or one flat surface could pass through them all. **4** If you say that something is **on a higher plane**, you mean that it is more spiritual or less concerned with worldly things.
5 A **plane** is a tool that has a flat bottom with a sharp — N-COUNT / N-COUNT TECHNICAL / N-SING TECHNICAL / N-COUNT: adj N / N-COUNT

blade in it. You move the plane over a piece of wood in order to remove thin pieces of its surface. See picture headed **tools**. **6** If you **plane** a piece of wood, you make it smaller or smoother by using a plane. *Again I planed the surface flush.* ▶ **Plane down** means the same as **plane**. *The piece was reduced in size by planing down the four corners.* — VERB: V n / V n adj / PHRASAL VB V P noun Also V n P

7 If something such as a boat **planes** across water, it moves quickly across the water, just touching the surface. *All four of the boats planed across the Solent with the greatest of ease.* — VERB V across n Also V

plane down. See **plane 6**. — PHRASAL VB

plane·load /'pleɪnləʊd/ **planeloads**. A **planeload** of people or goods is as many people or goods as a plane can carry. — N-COUNT

plan·et /'plænɪt/ **planets**. A **planet** is a large round object in space that moves around a star. *...the nine planets in the solar system.* ♦ **plan·etary** /'plænɪtri, AM -teri/ *There are probably tens of thousands of planetary systems.* — N-COUNT / ADJ: ADJ n

plan·etar·ium /,plænɪ'teəriəm/ **planetariums**. A **planetarium** is a building where lights are shone on the ceiling to represent the planets and the stars and to show how they appear to move. — N-COUNT

plan·gent /'plændʒənt/. A **plangent** sound is a deep loud sound, which may be sad. *...plangent violins supported by soft chords on violas.* — ADJ-GRADED LITERARY

plank /plæŋk/ **planks. 1** A **plank** of wood is a long, thin, rectangular piece of wood. **2** The main **plank** of the policy of a particular group or political party is the main principle on which it bases its policy, or its main aim. — N-COUNT / N-COUNT: with supp JOURNALISM

plank·ing /'plæŋkɪŋ/. **Planking** is wood that has been cut into planks. — N-UNCOUNT

plank·ton /'plæŋktən/. **Plankton** is a mass of tiny animals and plants that live in the surface layer of the sea. — N-UNCOUNT

plan·ner /'plænə/ **planners. Planners** are people whose job is to make decisions about what is going to be done in the future. *...James, a 29-year-old town planner.* — N-COUNT

plan·ning /'plænɪŋ/. **1 Planning** is the process of deciding in detail how to do something before you actually start to do it. *The trip needs careful planning... The new system is still in the planning stages.*
● See also **family planning**. **2 Planning** is control by the local government of the way that land is used in an area and of what new buildings are built there. — N-UNCOUNT / N-UNCOUNT

'planning permission, planning permissions. In Britain, **planning permission** is official permission that you must get from the local authority before a new building can be built or before an extension can be made to an existing building. — N-COUNT

plant /plɑːnt, plænt/ **plants, planting, planted.**
1 A **plant** is a living thing that grows in the earth and has a stem, leaves, and roots. *Water each plant as often as required. ...exotic plants.* ● See also **bedding plant, pot plant, rubber plant**. **2** When you **plant** a seed, plant, or young tree, you put it into the ground so that it will grow there. ♦ **plant·ing** *Extensive flooding in the country has delayed planting.* **3** When someone **plants** land with a particular type of plant or crop, they put plants, seeds, or young trees into the land to grow them there. *Much of their energy has gone into planting a large vegetable garden.* — N-COUNT / VERB: V n / N-UNCOUNT / VERB: V n with n, V n
4 A **plant** is a factory or a place where power is generated. *...Ford's British car assembly plants.* **5 Plant** is large machinery that is used in industrial processes. — N-COUNT / N-UNCOUNT
6 If you **plant** something somewhere, you put it there firmly. *She planted her feet wide and bent her knees slightly.* **7** If someone **plants** something such as a bomb somewhere, they hide it in the place where they want it to function. *So far no one has admitted planting the bomb.* **8** If something such as a weapon or drugs **is planted** on someone, it is put amongst their belongings or in their house or office so that they will be wrongly accused of a crime. **9** If an organization **plants** an informer or a spy somewhere, they send — VERB V n adv/prep / VERB V n / VERB / VERB V n

that person there so that they can do something secretly. *Journalists informed police who planted an
undercover detective to trap Smith.* **10** If you **plant a**
kiss on someone, you give them a kiss. *She rushed forward to plant a kiss on his cheek.* **11** If you **plant an**
idea in someone's mind, they begin to accept the idea
without realizing that it has originally come from you
and not from them.
VERB
V n on n
VERB: V n

plant out. When you **plant out** young plants, you
plant them in the ground in the place where they are
to be left to grow. *Plant out the spring cabbage when-
ever opportunities arise.*
PHRASAL VB
V P noun
Also V n P
BRITISH

plan·tain /'plæntɪn/ **plantains. 1** A **plantain** is a
type of green banana which can be cooked and eat-
en as a vegetable. **2** A **plantain** is a wild plant with
broad leaves and a head of tiny green flowers on a
long stem.
N-VAR
N-VAR

plan·ta·tion /plɑːn'teɪʃən, plæn-/ **plantations.**
1 A **plantation** is a large piece of land, especially in
a tropical country, where crops such as rubber, coffee, tea, or sugar are grown. **2** A **plantation** is a
large number of trees that have been planted together. *...a plantation of almond trees.*
◆◆◇◇
N-COUNT
N-COUNT

plant·er /'plɑːntə, plæn-/ **planters. 1 Planters** are
people who own or manage plantations in tropical
countries. **2** A **planter** is a container for plants that
people keep in their homes.
◆◇◇◇
N-COUNT
N-COUNT

'plant pot, plant pots. A **plant pot** is a container
that is used for growing plants.
N-COUNT
BRITISH

plaque /plæk, plɑːk/ **plaques. 1** A **plaque** is a flat
piece of metal, wood, or stone, which is fixed to a
wall or monument in memory of a famous person
or event. **2 Plaque** is a substance that forms on the
surface of your teeth.
◆◇◇◇
N-COUNT
N-UNCOUNT

plas·ma /'plæzmə/. **Plasma** is the clear fluid part of
blood which contains the corpuscles and cells.
◆◇◇◇
N-UNCOUNT

plas·ter /'plɑːstə, 'plæs-/ **plasters, plastering,**
plastered. 1 Plaster is a smooth paste made of
sand, lime, and water which dries and forms a hard
layer. Plaster is used to cover walls and ceilings, and
is also used to make sculptures. *There were huge
cracks in the plaster, and the green shutters were
faded. ...a sculpture in plaster.* **2** If you **plaster a**
wall or **ceiling**, you cover it with a layer of plaster.
♦ **plas·ter·er, plasterers 3** If you have a leg or
arm **in plaster**, you have a cast made of plaster of
Paris around your leg or arm, in order to protect a
broken bone and allow it to mend. **4** If you **plaster**
a surface or a place with posters or pictures, you
stick a lot of them all over it. *His room is plastered
with pictures of Porsches and Ferraris.* **5** If you **plaster** yourself in some kind of sticky substance, you
cover yourself in it. *She plasters herself from head to
toe in Factor 7 sun lotion.*
6 A **plaster** is a strip of sticky material used for covering small cuts or sores on your body. The usual American word is **Band-Aid**. **7** See also **plastered**, **sticking**
plaster.
◆◇◇◇
N-UNCOUNT
VERB: V n
N-COUNT
PHRASE
VERB:
V n with n
VERB
V pron-refl in
n
N-COUNT
BRITISH

plaster·board /'plɑːstəbɔːd, 'plæs-/. **Plasterboard**
consists of sheets of cardboard which are held together with plaster, and is used for covering walls
and ceilings instead of using plaster.
N-UNCOUNT

'plaster cast, plaster casts. A **plaster cast** is a
case made of plaster of Paris, which is used for protecting broken bones by keeping part of the body
stiff and rigid, and can also be used as a mould for
sculptures.
N-COUNT

plas·tered /'plɑːstəd, 'plæs-/. **1** If something is
plastered to a surface, it is sticking to the surface.
*His hair was plastered down to his scalp... My shirt
was plastered to my body with sweat.* **2** If something
or someone is **plastered with** a sticky substance,
they are covered with it. *My hands, boots and trousers were plastered with mud.* **3** If a story or a set of
photos is **plastered all over** the front page of a
newspaper, it is given a lot of space on the page and
is printed or displayed in a very prominent way. **4** If
someone's arm or leg is **plastered**, it has a hard cast
of plaster of Paris around it to protect the broken
bone whilst it is mending.
◆◇◇◇
ADJ:
v-link ADJ
prep/adv
ADJ:
v-link ADJ
ADJ:
v-link ADJ
prep/adv
ADJ

5 If someone gets **plastered**, they get very drunk. *With
gin at 9p a tot, getting plastered was cheap and easy...
He's absolutely plastered, lying in the gutter with his
mouth open.*
ADJ:
v-link ADJ
INFORMAL,
BRITISH

plas·ter of Par·is /ˌplɑːstər əv 'pærɪs, ˌplæs-/. **Plaster of Paris** is a type of plaster made from white
powder and water which dries quickly.
N-UNCOUNT

plas·tic /'plæstɪk/ **plastics. 1 Plastic** is a light but
strong material which is produced by a chemical
process and which is used to make many objects.
...a black plastic bag. **2** If you describe something
as **plastic**, you mean that you think it looks or tastes
unnatural or false because it is man-made; used
showing disapproval. *...plastic hotel decor and airline
food.* **3** If you use **plastic** to pay for something, you
pay for it with a credit card instead of using cash.
4 Something that is **plastic** is soft and can easily be
made into different shapes.
◆◆◇◇
N-VAR
ADJ-GRADED
PRAGMATICS
N-UNCOUNT
INFORMAL
ADJ

plastic 'bullet, plastic bullets. A **plastic bullet**
is a bullet made of plastic, which is intended to disperse crowds in riots, rather than to kill.
N-COUNT

plastic ex'plosive, plastic explosives. Plastic
explosive is a substance which explodes and which
is used in making small bombs.
N-VAR

Plas·ti·cine /'plæstɪsiːn/. **Plasticine** is a soft coloured substance which children use for making
models. **Plasticine** is a trademark.
N-UNCOUNT

plastic 'surgeon, plastic surgeons. A **plastic**
surgeon is a doctor who performs operations to repair or replace skin which has been damaged, or to
improve people's appearance. ♦ **pl'astic s'urgery.**
Plastic surgery is the practice of performing operations of this type.
N-COUNT
N-UNCOUNT

plastic 'wrap. Plastic wrap is a thin, clear,
stretchy plastic which you use to cover food to keep
it fresh. The British word is **clingfilm**.
N-UNCOUNT
AMERICAN

plate /pleɪt/ **plates. 1** A **plate** is a round or oval
flat dish that is used to hold food. *...a set of white
dinner plates.* ▶ A **plate** of food is the amount of
food on the plate. *...a huge plate of bacon and eggs.*
♦ **plate·ful** /'pleɪtfʊl/ **platefuls** *Jacques came back
with a plateful of sandwiches.* **2** If you **have enough**
on your **plate** or **have a lot on** your **plate**, you have
a lot of work to do or a lot of things to deal with.
3 If you say that someone has things **handed to**
them on a plate, you disapprove of them because
they get good things easily. *Even the presidency was
handed to him on a plate.*
4 A **plate** is a flat piece of metal, for example part of a
machine. **5** On a road vehicle, the **plates** are the panels at the front and back which display the license
number or registration number. *...cars with New Jersey plates.* ● See also **number plate, license plate.**
6 Plate is dishes, bowls, and cups that are made of
precious metal, especially silver, gold, or pewter.
7 In printing, a **plate** is a sheet of metal which is
carved or specially treated with chemicals so that it
can be used to print text or pictures. **8** In photography, a **plate** is a thin sheet of glass that is covered with
a layer of chemicals which react to the light and on
which an image can be formed. **9** A **plate** in a book is a
picture or photograph which takes up a whole page
and is usually printed on better quality paper than the
rest of the book. *Fermor's book has 55 colour plates.*
10 A dental **plate** is a piece of plastic which a set of
false teeth is attached to. **11** In geology, a **plate** is a
large piece of the earth's surface, which moves very
slowly.
◆◆◇◇
N-COUNT
N-COUNT
N-COUNT
PHRASE
PHRASE
PRAGMATICS
N-COUNT
N-PLURAL
N-UNCOUNT
N-COUNT
N-COUNT
N-COUNT
N-COUNT
N-COUNT
TECHNICAL

plat·eau /'plætəʊ, AM plæ'təʊ/ **plateaus** or **plat-
eaux. 1** A **plateau** is a large area of high fairly flat
land. **2** If an activity or process has reached a **plateau**, it is going through a stage where there is no
change or development.
◆◇◇◇
N-COUNT
N-COUNT

plat·ed /'pleɪtɪd/. If something made of metal is
plated with a thin layer of another type of metal, it
is covered with it. *...solid brass, plated with 24-carat
gold.* ♦ **-plated** *...a gold-plated watch.*
◆◇◇◇
ADJ:
v-link ADJ
with n
COMB

plate 'glass; also spelled **plate-glass.** Plate glass
is thick glass made in large flat pieces, which is used
especially to make large windows and doors.
N-UNCOUNT

P

plate·let /'pleɪtlət/ **platelets.** Platelets are a kind N-COUNT
of blood cell which help your blood to clot if you TECHNICAL
are bleeding.

plate tec'tonics. Plate tectonics is the study of N-UNCOUNT
the way that large pieces of the earth's surface move TECHNICAL
slowly around.

plat·form /'plætfɔːm/ **platforms. 1** A platform is ◆◆◇◇◇
a flat raised structure, usually made of wood, which N-COUNT
people stand on when they make speeches or give a
performance. **2** A **platform** is a flat raised structure N-COUNT
or area, usually one which something can stand on
or land on. *They found a spot on a rocky platform
where they could pitch their tents.* **3** A **platform** is a N-COUNT
structure built for people to work and live on when
drilling for oil or gas at sea. **4** A **platform** in a rail- N-COUNT
way station is the area beside the rails where you
wait for or get off a train. *He was waiting on platform five.*
5 The **platform** of a political party is what they say N-COUNT:
they will do if they are elected. *The Socialist Party won* with supp
a landslide victory on a nationalist platform. **6** If N-COUNT
someone has a **platform**, they have an opportunity to
tell people what they think or want. *The demonstration provided a platform for a broad cross section of
speakers.*

plat·ing /'pleɪtɪŋ/. **Plating** is a thin layer of metal N-UNCOUNT
on something, or a covering of metal plates.

plati·num /'plætɪnəm/. **1 Platinum** is a very valu- ◆◇◇◇◇
able silvery-grey metal. **2 Platinum** hair is very fair, N-UNCOUNT
almost white. *...a platinum blonde.* COLOUR

plati·tude /'plætɪtjuːd, AM -tuːd/ **platitudes.** A N-COUNT
platitude is a statement which is considered meaningless and boring because it has been made many
times before in similar situations. *I had told her the
truth, while everyone else was mouthing platitudes.*

pla·ton·ic /plə'tɒnɪk/. **1 Platonic** relationships or ADJ-GRADED
feelings of affection do not involve sex. *She maintains their relationship was purely platonic.* **2** You ADJ
use **Platonic** to describe things relating to the ideas
of the Greek philosopher Plato.

pla·toon /plə'tuːn/ **platoons.** A **platoon** is a small ◆◇◇◇◇
group of soldiers commanded by a lieutenant. N-COUNT

plat·ter /'plætə/ **platters. 1** A **platter** is a large flat ◆◇◇◇◇
plate used for serving food. *Waiters would feed her* N-COUNT
shrimps off a silver platter. **2** A **platter** is a selection N-COUNT
of different kinds of the same food on a large flat
plate. *...a cheese platter.*

plau·dits /'plɔːdɪts/. If someone or something re- N-PLURAL
ceives **plaudits**, people express admiration or praise FORMAL
for them. *They won plaudits and prizes for their accomplished films.*

plau·sible /'plɔːzɪbəl/. **1** A **plausible** explanation ◆◇◇◇◇
or statement seems likely to be true or valid. *Is it* ADJ-GRADED
*plausible that the President did not know what was
going on?* ♦ **plau·sibly** /'plɔːzɪbli/ *He is the charac-* ADV-GRADED:
ter who could plausibly have been in contact with all ADV with v
these people. ♦ **plau·sibil·ity** /ˌplɔːzɪ'bɪlɪti/ *...the* N-UNCOUNT
plausibility of the theory. **2** If you say that someone ADJ-GRADED
is **plausible**, you mean that although they seem to
be telling the truth and they seem to be sincere and
honest, they may be deceiving people. *...a plausible,
articulate young man.*

play /pleɪ/ **plays, playing, played. 1** When peo- ◆◆◆◆◆
ple, especially children, or animals **play**, they spend VERB: V
time doing enjoyable things, such as using toys and V with n
taking part in games. *Polly was playing with her teddy bear.* ▶ Also a noun. *...a few hours of play until* N-UNCOUNT
the baby-sitter takes them off to bed. **2** When you VERB
play a sport, game, or match, you take part in it. V n with n
Alain was playing cards with his friends... I used to V n
play basketball... I want to play for my country. V forn
▶ Also a noun. *Both sides adopted the Continental* Also V
style of play. **3** When one person or team **plays** an- N-UNCOUNT
other or **plays against** them, they compete against VERB
them in a sport or game. *Northern Ireland will play* Also V against
Latvia. **4** In sport, when you **play** the ball, or **play** a VERB: V n
shot or stroke, you kick or hit the ball. *I played the* V n adv
ball back slightly. **5** If you ask **what** someone **is** PHRASE
playing at, you are angry because you think they PRAGMATICS
are doing something stupid or wrong. **6** When INFORMAL
PHRASE

something **comes into play** or **is brought into play**,
it begins to be used or to have an effect. *The real existence of a military option will come into play...* PHRASE
Breathing brings many muscles into play. **7** If something or someone **plays a part** or **plays a role** in a
situation, they are involved in it and have an effect
on it. *The UN would play a major role in monitoring
a ceasefire.*
8 A **play** is a piece of writing which is performed in a N-COUNT
theatre, on the radio, or on television. *...a play about
the homeless... It's my favourite Shakespeare play.* **9** If VERB
an actor **plays** a role or character in a play or film, he V n
or she performs as that character. *...Dr Jekyll and Mr
Hyde, in which he played Hyde.* **10** You can use **play** V-LINK:
to describe how someone behaves, when they are de- V n
liberately behaving in a certain way or like a certain V adj
type of person. For example, if someone **plays the in-** V it adj/adv
nocent, they pretend to be innocent. *I already knew
what was going on, but I played stupid... Mary Ann
made no attempt at playing it cool.*
11 If you **play** a musical instrument or **play** a tune on V-ERG
it, music is produced from it. *Nina had been playing* V n
the piano... Play her a lullaby... The guitars played. V n n
12 If you **play** a record, CD, or tape, you put it onto a V-ERG
record player or into a tape recorder and sound is pro- V n
duced. *Every evening in those days the BBC played* Also V n n
*'God Save The King'... There is classical music playing
in the background.* **13** If a musician or group of musi- VERB: V
cians **plays**, they perform music for people to listen or V n
dance to. *He will play concerts in Amsterdam.*
14 If you **play** a joke or a trick on someone, you de- VERB:
ceive them or give them a surprise in a way that you V n on n
think is funny, but that often causes problems for
them or annoys them. *I thought: 'This cannot be happening, somebody must be playing a joke'.*
15 If you **play with** an object or with your hair, you VERB:
keep moving it or touching it with your fingers, often V with n
because you are bored or nervous. **16** When light VERB
plays somewhere, it moves about on a surface in an V prep
unsteady way. *The sun played on the frosty roofs.* LITERARY
17 Play is used in a large number of expressions
which are explained under other words in this dictionary. For example, the expression **to play fair** is explained at **fair**.

play along. If you **play along** with a person, you ap- PHRASAL VB
pear to agree with them and do what they want, even no passive
though you are not sure whether they are right. *My* V P with n
mother has learnt to play along with the bizarre con- V P
*versations begun by father... He turned and led the way
to the lift. Fox played along, following him.*
play at. 1 If you say that someone is **playing at** PHRASAL VB
something, you disapprove of the fact that they are no passive
doing it casually and not very seriously. *We were still* PRAGMATICS
playing at war – dropping leaflets instead of bombs. V P n/-ing
2 If someone, especially a child, **plays at** being some- no passive,
one or doing something, they pretend to be that per- V P n/-ing
son or do that thing as a game.
play around. 1 If you **play around**, you behave in a PHRASAL VB
silly way to amuse yourself or other people. *Stop play-* V P
ing around and eat!... Had he taken the keys and V P with n
played around with her car? **2** If you **play around with** INFORMAL
a problem or an arrangement of objects, you try dif- V P with n
ferent ways of organizing it in order to find the best INFORMAL
solution or arrangement. **3** If someone **plays around**, V P
they have sex with people other than the person they V P with n
are married to or having a serious relationship with. INFORMAL
Robert was playing around with another woman.
play back. When you **play back** a tape or film, you PHRASAL VB
listen to the sounds or watch the pictures after rec- V P noun
ording them. *I played the tape back... Ted might ben-* V n P
efit from hearing his own voice recorded and played V-ed P
back. ● See also **playback**.
play down. If you **play down** something, you try to PHRASAL VB
make people believe that it is not particularly impor- V P noun
tant. *Western diplomats have played down the signifi-* Also V n P
cance of the reports.
play off against. If you **play** people **off against** PHRASAL VB
each other, you make them compete or argue, so that V n P P n
you gain some advantage. *Gregory would interview* Also V P noun
them, and would play one off against the other. P n

play on. If you **play on** someone's fears, weaknesses, or faults, you deliberately use them in order to persuade that person to do something, or to achieve what you want. ...*an election campaign which plays on the population's fear of change.* PHRASAL VB / V P n

play out. If a tragic or dramatic event **is played out**, it gradually continues. *The film has eerie parallels with the drama being played out in real life.* PHRASAL VB / be V-ed P / Also V P n

play up. 1 If you **play up** something, you emphasize it and try to make people believe that it is important. *The media played up the prospects for a settlement.* **2** If something such as a machine or a part of your body **is playing up** or **is playing** you **up**, it is causing you problems because it is not working properly. *The engine had been playing up... It was his back playing him up.* PHRASAL VB / V P noun / Also V P n / V P / INFORMAL, BRITISH

play-acting. **Play-acting** is behaviour in which someone pretends to have attitudes or feelings that they do not really have. *Some of the supposed conflict between them may have been play-acting.* N-UNCOUNT

play-back /'pleɪbæk/ **playbacks.** The **playback** of a tape is the operation of playing it on a machine in order to listen to the sound or watch the pictures recorded on it. N-COUNT

play-boy /'pleɪbɔɪ/ **playboys.** You can refer to a rich man who spends most of his time enjoying himself as a **playboy.** N-COUNT

play-er /'pleɪə/ **players. 1** A **player** in a sport or game is a person who takes part, either as a job or for fun. ...*his greatness as a player... She was a good golfer and tennis player.* **2** You can use **player** to refer to a musician. ...*a professional trumpet player.* **3** If a person, country, or organization is a **player** in something, they are involved in it and important in it. *Big business has become a major player in the art market... Mr Lafontant has re-emerged as a player in Haiti's affairs.* **4** A **player** is an actor. *Oscar nominations went to all five leading players.* **5** See also **cassette player, CD player, record player.** ♦♦♦♦♦ N-COUNT / N-COUNT / N-COUNT / N-COUNT

play-ful /'pleɪfʊl/ A **playful** gesture is friendly and cheerful. ...*a playful kiss on the tip of his nose.* ♦ **play-ful-ly** *She pushed him away playfully.* ♦ **play-ful-ness** ...*the child's natural playfulness.* ♦◇◇◇◇ ADJ-GRADED / ADV-GRADED / N-UNCOUNT

play-ground /'pleɪgraʊnd/ **playgrounds. 1** A **playground** is a piece of land, at school or in a public area, where children can play. ● See also **adventure playground. 2** If you describe a place as a **playground** for a certain group of people, you mean that those people like to enjoy themselves there or go on holiday there. ...*St Tropez, playground of the rich and famous.* ♦◇◇◇◇ N-COUNT / N-COUNT

play-group /'pleɪgruːp/ **playgroups.** A **playgroup** is an informal kind of school for very young children, where they learn things by playing. ♦◇◇◇◇ N-COUNT: also prep N BRITISH

play-house /'pleɪhaʊs/ **playhouses. 1** A **playhouse** is a theatre. ...*two shows at the Edinburgh Playhouse.* **2** A **playhouse** is a small house made for children to play in. ♦◇◇◇◇ N-COUNT / N-COUNT

playing card, playing cards. Playing cards are thin pieces of cardboard with numbers or pictures printed on them, which are used to play games. N-COUNT

playing field, playing fields. 1 A **playing field** is a large area of grass where people play sports. **2** You talk about a **level playing field** to mean a situation that is fair, because no competitor or opponent has an advantage over another. *American businessmen ask for a level playing field when they compete with foreign companies.* ♦◇◇◇◇ N-COUNT / PHRASE

play-mate /'pleɪmeɪt/ **playmates.** A child's **playmate** is another child who he or she often plays with. N-COUNT

play-off, play-offs; also spelled **playoff.** A **play-off** is an extra game which is played to decide the winner of a sports competition when two or more people have got the same score. *Nick Faldo was beaten by Peter Baker in a play-off.* ♦◇◇◇◇ N-COUNT

play on words, plays on words. A **play on words** is the same as a **pun.** N-COUNT

play-pen /'pleɪpen/ **playpens.** A **playpen** is a small structure for a baby or young child to play in, which has bars or a net at the sides and is open at the top. N-COUNT

play-room /'pleɪruːm/ **playrooms.** A **playroom** is a room in a house for children to play in. N-COUNT

play-school /'pleɪskuːl/ **playschools.** A **playschool** is an informal kind of school for very young children where they learn things by playing. N-COUNT: also prep N BRITISH

play-thing /'pleɪθɪŋ/ **playthings. 1** A **plaything** is a toy or other object that a child plays with. **2** If you say that someone is treating you as a **plaything**, you think that they are using you for their amusement or advantage, and do not care about you. N-COUNT / N-COUNT PRAGMATICS

play-time /'pleɪtaɪm/. In a school for young children, **playtime** is the period of time between lessons when they can play outside. *Any child who is caught will be kept in at playtime.* N-UNCOUNT

play-wright /'pleɪraɪt/ **playwrights.** A **playwright** is a person who writes plays. ♦♦◇◇◇ N-COUNT

pla-za /'plɑːzə, AM 'plæzə/ **plazas.** A **plaza** is an open square in a city. ♦◇◇◇◇ N-COUNT

plc /,piː el 'siː/ **plcs;** also spelled **PLC.** In Britain, **plc** is an abbreviation for 'public limited company', meaning a company whose shares can be bought by the public. ...*British Telecommunications plc.* ♦♦◇◇◇ N-COUNT

plea /pliː/ **pleas. 1** A **plea** is an appeal or request for something, made in an intense or emotional way. *Mr Nicholas made his emotional plea for help in solving the killing.* **2** In a court of law, a person's **plea** is the answer that they give when they have been charged with a crime, saying whether or not they are guilty of that crime. *The judge questioned him about his guilty plea... We will enter a plea of not guilty.* **3** A **plea** is a reason which is given, to a court or to other people, as an excuse for doing something or for not doing something. *Mr Dunn's pleas of poverty are only partly justified.* ♦♦◇◇◇ N-COUNT JOURNALISM / N-COUNT / N-COUNT

plea bargain, plea bargains, plea bargaining, plea bargained. In some legal systems, a **plea bargain** is an agreement that, if the defendant pleads guilty, he or she will be charged with a less serious crime or receive a lighter punishment. ► Also a verb. *More and more criminals will agree to plea-bargain.* ♦ **plea bar-gain-ing** ...*the introduction of a system of plea bargaining.* N-COUNT / VERB: V / N-UNCOUNT

plead /pliːd/ **pleads, pleading, pleaded. 1** If you **plead** with someone to do something, you ask them in an intense emotional way to do it. *He was kneeling on the floor pleading for mercy... 'Do not say that,' she pleaded... I pleaded to be allowed to go.* **2** When someone charged with a crime **pleads** guilty or not guilty in a court of law, they officially state that they are guilty or not guilty of the crime. **3** If someone **pleads the case** or **cause** of someone or something, they speak out in their support or defence. *He would plead the cause of Russian unity.* **4** If you **plead** a particular thing as the reason for doing or not doing something, you give it as your excuse. *Mr Giles pleads ignorance as his excuse.* ♦♦◇◇◇ VERB: V with n to-inf / V for n / V with quote / V to-inf-passive / VERB: V adj / VERB V n / VERB V n Also V that

plead-ing /'pliːdɪŋ/ **pleadings. 1** A **pleading** expression or gesture shows someone that you want something very much. ...*his pleading eyes.* ♦ **plead-ing-ly** *He looked at me pleadingly... 'I'm thirsty,' she said pleadingly.* **2 Pleading** is asking someone for something you want very much, in an intense or emotional way. *He simply ignored Sid's pleading.* ● See also **special pleading.** ♦◇◇◇◇ ADJ / ADV-GRADED: ADV after v / N-UNCOUNT: also N in pl

pleas-ant /'plezənt/ **pleasanter, pleasantest. 1** Something that is **pleasant** is nice, enjoyable, or attractive. *It's always pleasant to do what you're good at doing.* ♦ **pleas-ant-ly** *We talked pleasantly of old times... The room was pleasantly warm.* **2** Someone who is **pleasant** is friendly and likeable. ♦♦♦◇◇ ADJ-GRADED / ADV-GRADED / ADJ-GRADED

pleas-ant-ry /'plezəntri/ **pleasantries. Pleasantries** are casual friendly remarks which you make in order to be polite. *He exchanged pleasantries about his hotel and the weather.* N-COUNT

please /pliːz/ **pleases, pleasing, pleased. 1** You say **please** when you are politely asking or inviting someone to do something, or when you are ♦♦♦♦◇ ADV: ADV with cl PRAGMATICS

asking someone for something. *Can you help us please?... Please come in... 'May I sit here?'—'Please do.'* **2** You say **please** when you are accepting something politely. *'Tea?'—'Yes, please.'... 'You want an apple with your cheese?'—'Please.'* **3** You can say **please** to indicate that you want someone to stop doing something or stop speaking. *Please, Mary, this is all so unnecessary.* **4** You can say **please** in order to attract someone's attention politely. *Please sir, can we have some more?*
ADV: ADV with cl / PRAGMATICS
CONVENTION PRAGMATICS
CONVENTION PRAGMATICS

5 If someone or something **pleases** you, they make you feel happy and satisfied. *Much of the food pleases rather than excites... It pleased him to talk to her.* **6** You use **please** in expressions such as **as she pleases, whatever you please**, and **anything he pleases** to indicate that someone can do or have whatever they want. *Women should be free to dress and act as they please.* **7** You can use **as you please** in expressions such as **casually as you please** or **charming as you please** in order to emphasize what you are saying. *Bold as you please, she grabbed me by the sleeve.* **8** If **you please** is sometimes used as a very polite and formal way of attracting someone's attention or of asking someone to do something. *Take your seats, if you please.* **9** You say **'please yourself'** to indicate in a rather rude way that you do not mind or care whether the person you are talking to does a particular thing or not. **10** ● **please God:** see **God**.
VERB: V n / V / it V n to-inf
PHRASE
PHRASE PRAGMATICS INFORMAL
CONVENTION PRAGMATICS FORMAL
CONVENTION PRAGMATICS INFORMAL

pleased /pliːzd/. **1** If you are **pleased**, you are happy about something or satisfied with something. *Felicity seemed pleased at the suggestion... I think he's going to be pleased that we identified the real problems... They're pleased to be going home.* **2** If you say you will be **pleased** to do something, you are saying in a polite way that you are willing to do it. *We will be pleased to answer any questions you may have.* **3** You can tell someone that you are **pleased** with something they have done in order to express your approval. *I'm pleased with the way things have been going... We were very pleased to hear this encouraging news.* **4** When you are about to give someone some news you know will please them you can say that you are **pleased** to tell them the news or that they will be **pleased** to hear it. *I'm pleased to say that he is now doing well.* **5** In letters, people sometimes say they will be **pleased** to do something, in order to state politely that they are going to do it. *We will be pleased to delete the charge from the original invoice.* **6** If someone seems very satisfied with something they have done, you can say that they are **pleased with** themselves, especially if you think they are more satisfied than they should be.
ADJ-GRADED
ADJ-GRADED: v-link ADJ to-inf PRAGMATICS
ADJ-GRADED: v-link ADJ PRAGMATICS
ADJ-GRADED: v-link ADJ to-inf PRAGMATICS
ADJ-GRADED: v-link ADJ to-inf PRAGMATICS FORMAL
PHRASE

7 You can say **'Pleased to meet you'** as a polite way of greeting someone who you are meeting for the first time.
CONVENTION PRAGMATICS

pleas·ing /pliːzɪŋ/. Something that is **pleasing** gives you pleasure and satisfaction. *This area of France has a pleasing climate... It's pleasing to see some criminals have a conscience.* ♦ **pleas·ing·ly** *The interior design is pleasingly simple.*
ADJ-GRADED
ADV-GRADED

pleas·ur·able /pleʒərəbəl/. **Pleasurable** experiences or sensations are pleasant and enjoyable. *He found sailing more pleasurable than skiing.*
ADJ-GRADED

pleas·ure /pleʒə/ **pleasures. 1** If something gives you **pleasure**, you get a feeling of happiness, satisfaction, or enjoyment from it. *Everybody takes pleasure in eating... He gets huge pleasure from ballet.* **2 Pleasure** is the activity of enjoying yourself, especially rather than working or doing something you have a duty to do. *He mixed business and pleasure... I read for pleasure.* **3** A **pleasure** is an activity, experience or aspect of something that you find very enjoyable or satisfying. *Watching TV is our only pleasure. ...the pleasure of seeing a smiling face.* **4** If you meet someone for the first time, you can say, as a way of being polite, that it is **a pleasure to meet them**. You can also ask for the **pleasure of** someone's **company** as a polite and formal way of inviting them. **5** You can say **'It's a pleasure'** or **'My pleasure'** as a polite way of replying to someone who has just
N-UNCOUNT
N-UNCOUNT
N-COUNT
CONVENTION PRAGMATICS
CONVENTION PRAGMATICS

thanked you for doing something. *'Thanks very much anyhow.'—'It's a pleasure.'* **6** You can say **'With pleasure'** as a polite way of saying that you are very willing to do something. *'Could you photocopy the advert and put it in the post to us?'—'With pleasure, John.'*
CONVENTION PRAGMATICS FORMAL

'pleasure boat, pleasure boats. A **pleasure boat** or **pleasure craft** is a large boat which takes people for trips on rivers, lakes, or on the sea for pleasure. The plural form of pleasure craft is **pleasure craft**.
N-COUNT

pleat /pliːt/ **pleats.** A **pleat** in a piece of clothing is a permanent fold that is made in the cloth by folding one part over the other and sewing across the top end of the fold. ♦ **pleat·ed** /pliːtɪd/. A **pleated** piece of clothing has pleats in it.
◆◇◇◇ N-COUNT
ADJ

pleb /pleb/ **plebs.** If someone refers to people as **plebs**, they think that they are ignorant and uncultured; used showing disapproval.
N-COUNT PRAGMATICS BRITISH, INFORMAL

ple·beian /pləbiːən/; also spelled **plebian. 1** A person who is **plebeian** comes from a low social class. **2** If someone describes something as **plebeian**, they disapprove of it because they think it is connected with or typical of people from a low social class.
ADJ
ADJ-GRADED PRAGMATICS INFORMAL

plebi·scite /plebɪsaɪt, -sɪt/ **plebiscites.** A **plebiscite** is a direct vote by the people of a country or region in which they say whether they agree or disagree with a particular policy.
◆◇◇◇ N-COUNT

pledge /pledʒ/ **pledges, pledging, pledged. 1** When someone makes a **pledge**, they make a solemn promise that they will do something or provide something. *The meeting ended with a pledge to step up cooperation between the six states of the region.* **2** When someone **pledges** to do something, they promise solemnly that they will do it or provide it. *Britain pledged $36 million to the refugees... Both sides pledged that a nuclear war must never be fought.* **3** If you **pledge** yourself to something, you commit yourself to following a particular course of action or to supporting a particular person, group, or idea. *The President pledged himself to increase taxes for the rich... The treaties renounce the use of force and pledge the two countries to co-operation.*
◆◆◇◇ N-COUNT
VERB: V to-inf / V n / V that
VERB: V pron-refl to / V pron-refl / to-inf / V n to n

ple·na·ry /pliːnəri, plen-/ **plenaries.** A **plenary** or **plenary session** is a meeting that is attended by all members of a committee or conference.
N-COUNT

plen·ti·ful /plentɪfʊl/. Things that are **plentiful** exist in such large amounts or numbers that there is enough for people's wants or needs. *...a plentiful supply of vegetables and salads and fruits.* ♦ **plen·ti·ful·ly** *Nettle grows plentifully on any rich waste ground.*
◆◇◇◇ ADJ-GRADED
ADV-GRADED

plen·ty /plenti/. **1** If there is **plenty of** something, there is a large amount of it, often more than is needed. If there are **plenty of** things, there are many of them, often more than needed. *There was still plenty of time to take Jill out for pizza.* ► Also a pronoun. *I don't believe in long interviews. Fifteen minutes is plenty.* **2 Plenty** is a situation in which people have a lot to eat or a lot of money to live on. *You are all fortunate to be growing up in a time of peace and plenty.* **3** You use **plenty** in front of adjectives or adverbs to emphasize the degree of the quality they are describing. *The compartment is plenty big enough.* **4** If there are things **in plenty**, those things exist or happen in large amounts or numbers. *He did have talent in plenty.*
◆◆◇◇ QUANT
PRON
N-UNCOUNT FORMAL
ADV: ADV adj/adv PRAGMATICS INFORMAL PHRASE

ple·num /pliːnəm/ **plenums.** A **plenum** is a meeting that is attended by all the members of a committee or conference.
◆◇◇◇ N-COUNT

pletho·ra /pleθərə/. A **plethora** of something is a large amount of it, especially an amount of it that is greater than you need, want, or can cope with. *A plethora of new operators will be allowed to enter the market.*
◆◇◇◇ N-SING: N of n FORMAL

pleu·ri·sy /plʊərɪsi/. **Pleurisy** is a serious illness in which a person's lungs are inflamed and breathing is difficult.
N-SING

plex·us /pleksəs/. See **solar plexus**.

pli·able /plaɪəbəl/. **1** If something is **pliable**, you can bend it easily without cracking or breaking it.
ADJ-GRADED

2 Someone who is **pliable** can be easily influenced and controlled by other people. [ADJ-GRADED]

pli·ant /ˈplaɪənt/. **1** A **pliant** person can be easily influenced and controlled by other people. [ADJ-GRADED] **2** If something is **pliant**, you can bend it easily without breaking it. [ADJ-GRADED]

pli·ers /ˈplaɪəz/. **Pliers** are a tool with two handles at one end and two hard, flat, metal parts at the other. **Pliers** are used to hold or pull out things such as nails, or to bend or cut wire. See picture headed **tools**. [N-PLURAL]

plight /plaɪt/ **plights**. If you refer to someone's **plight**, you mean that they are in a difficult or distressing situation. *...the worsening plight of Third World countries.* [◆◆◇◇ N-COUNT]

plim·soll /ˈplɪmsəʊl/ **plimsolls**. Plimsolls are canvas shoes with flat rubber soles. [N-COUNT BRITISH]

plinth /plɪnθ/ **plinths**. A **plinth** is a rectangular block of stone on which a statue or pillar stands. [N-COUNT]

plod /plɒd/ **plods, plodding, plodded. 1** If someone **plods** somewhere, they walk there slowly and heavily. *Crowds of French and British families plodded around.* **2** If you say that someone **plods on** or **plods along** with a job, you mean that the job is taking a long time. *He is plodding on with negotiations.* ♦ **plod·ding** *The plot unfolds at a plodding pace.* [◆◇◇◇ VERB V adv/prep] [VERB V adv] [ADJ-GRADED]

plod·der /ˈplɒdə/ **plodders**. If you say that someone is a **plodder**, you have a low opinion of them because you think they work steadily but slowly and without inspiration. [N-COUNT PRAGMATICS INFORMAL]

plonk /plɒŋk/ **plonks, plonking, plonked. 1** If you **plonk** something somewhere, you put it or drop it there heavily and carelessly. *She plonked the beer on the counter.* **2** If you **plonk** yourself somewhere, you sit down carelessly without paying attention to the people around you. *Steve plonked himself down on a seat and stayed motionless as the bus moved away.* **3** Plonk is cheap or poor quality wine. *I don't want plonk. It has to be exquisite wine.* **4** A **plonk** is a heavy hollow sound. *Then plonk, down went the fork... She hated that kind of music. Plonk-plonk, it went.* [VERB V n prep/adv INFORMAL, BRITISH] [VERB V pron-refl adv/prep INFORMAL, BRITISH] [N-VAR INFORMAL, BRITISH] [N-SING; SOUND BRITISH]

plonk·er /ˈplɒŋkə/ **plonkers**. If someone calls a person, especially a man, a **plonker**, they think that he is stupid and incompetent; a word which some people find offensive. [PRAGMATICS INFORMAL, BRITISH]

plop /plɒp/ **plops, plopping, plopped. 1** A plop is a soft gentle sound, like the sound made by something light dropping into water without a splash. **2** If something **plops** somewhere, or you **plop** it there, it drops there with a soft gentle sound. *The ice cream plopped to the ground.* [N-COUNT; SOUND] [V-ERG V prep Also V n prep/adv]

plot /plɒt/ **plots, plotting, plotted. 1** A plot is a secret plan by a group of people to do something that is illegal or wrong, usually against a person or a government. *...a plot to overthrow the government.* **2** If people **plot** to do something that is illegal or wrong, they plot it secretly to do it. *The military were plotting a coup... They are awaiting trial on charges of plotting against the state.* ♦ **plot·ter, plotters**. *Coup plotters tried to seize power in Moscow.* **3** When people **plot** a strategy or a course of action, they carefully plan each step of it. **4** The plot of a film, novel, or play is the connected series of events which make up the story. ● see also **sub-plot. 5** A plot of land is a small piece of land, especially one that is intended for a special purpose, such as building houses or growing vegetables. **6** When someone **plots** something on a graph, they mark certain points on it and then join the points up. **7** To **plot** the position, course, or progress of something means to follow its position, course, or progress and show it on a map or diagram. ♦ **plot·ter**. A plotter is a person or instrument that does this. [◆◆◇◇ N-COUNT] [VERB: V to-inf V n V against n] [N-COUNT] [VERB: V n] [N-VAR] [N-COUNT] [VERB: V n] [VERB: V n] [N-COUNT]

plough /plaʊ/ **ploughs, ploughing, ploughed;** spelled **plow** in American English. **1** A plough is a large farming tool with sharp blades, which is attached to a tractor or an animal and used to turn over the soil before planting. ● See also **snow-** [◆◆◇◇ N-COUNT]

plough. 2 When someone **ploughs** an area of land, they turn over the soil using a plough. *...a carefully ploughed field.* ♦ **plough·ing** *In Roman times November was a month of hard work in ploughing and sowing.* **3** ● **to plough a furrow:** see **furrow.** [VERB: V n V-ed] [N-UNCOUNT]

plough back. If profits **are ploughed back** into a business, they are invested in it in order to expand it or improve it. [PHRASAL VB be V-ed P into n]

plough into. 1 If something, for example a car, **ploughs into** something else, it crashes violently into it. **2** If you say that money **is ploughed into** something such as a business or a service, you are emphasizing that the amount of money which is invested in it or spent on it is very large. *He claimed he ploughed all his money into his antique business.* [PHRASAL VB V P n] [be V-ed P n/-ing PRAGMATICS V n P n/-ing]

plough on. If you **plough on**, you continue moving or trying to complete something, even though it takes a lot of effort. *The Chancellor has opted to plough on with policies that could run his coalition on to the rocks.* [PHRASAL VB V P V P with n]

plough through. 1 If you **plough through** something such as a large meal or a long piece of work, you finally finish it although it takes a lot of effort. *Researchers have ploughed through 16,000 different pieces of classical, rock and jazz music.* **2** If a person or vehicle **ploughs through** a place or substance, they move through it with great force or effort. [PHRASAL VB no passive V P n] [V P n, no passive]

plough up. If someone **ploughs up** an area of land, they plough the land, usually in order to turn grassland into land used for growing crops. [PHRASAL VB V P n]

plough·share /ˈplaʊʃeə/ **ploughshares;** spelled **plowshare** in American English. To **turn swords into ploughshares** or **beat swords into ploughshares** means to replace warlike activities with peaceful ones. [PHRASE JOURNALISM]

plov·er /ˈplʌvə/ **plovers**. A **plover** is a bird with a rounded body, a short tail, and a short beak. [◆◇◇◇ N-COUNT]

plow /plaʊ/ **plows, plowing, plowed.** See **plough.**

plow·share /ˈplaʊʃeə/ **plowshares**. See **ploughshare.**

ploy /plɔɪ/ **ploys**. A **ploy** is a way of behaving that someone plans carefully and secretly in order to gain an advantage for themselves. *Christmas should be a time of excitement and wonder, not a cynical marketing ploy.* [◆◇◇◇ N-COUNT]

pluck /plʌk/ **plucks, plucking, plucked. 1** If you **pluck** a fruit, flower, or leaf, you take it between your fingers and pull it from its stalk. *I plucked a lemon from the tree.* **2** If you **pluck** something from somewhere, you take it in your fingers or hands and pull it sharply from where it is. *He plucked the cigarette from his mouth and tossed it out into the street.* **3** If you **pluck** a guitar or other musical instrument, you pull the strings with your fingers and let them go, so that they make a sound. **4** If you **pluck** a chicken or other dead bird, you pull its feathers out to prepare it for cooking. **5** If a woman **plucks her eyebrows**, she pulls out some of the hairs using tweezers. **6** If someone unknown is given an important job or role and quickly becomes famous because of it, you can say that they **have been plucked from** obscurity. **7** If someone is rescued from a dangerous situation, you can say that they **are plucked from** it or are **plucked to** safety. *A workman was plucked from the roof of a burning power station.* **8** If you say that someone has **pluck**, you mean that they show great courage and determination. **9** If you **pluck up the courage** to do something that you feel nervous about, you make an effort to be brave enough to do it. **10** If you say that someone **plucks** a figure, name, or date **out of the air**, you mean that they say it without thinking much about it before they speak. [◆◇◇◇ VERB: V n WRITTEN] [VERB V n from/out of/off n] [VERB: V n] [VERB: V n] [VERB: V n] [VERB: be V-ed from n WRITTEN] [VB: usu passive be V-ed from/to n] [N-UNCOUNT] [PHRASE] [PHRASE]

pluck at. If you **pluck at** something, you take it between your fingertips and pull it sharply but gently. *The boy plucked at Adam's sleeve.* [PHRASAL VB V P n]

plucky /ˈplʌki/. If you describe someone as **plucky**, you mean that they face their difficulties with courage, although they may be weak. [ADJ-GRADED JOURNALISM]

plug /plʌg/ **plugs, plugging, plugged. 1** A plug ◆◆◇◇◇
on a piece of electrical equipment is a small plastic N-COUNT
object with two or three metal pins which fit into
the holes of an electric socket in order to connect
the equipment to the electrical supply. **2** A **plug** is N-COUNT
an electric socket. **3** A **plug** is a thick circular piece N-COUNT
of rubber or plastic that you use to block the hole in
a bath or sink when it is filled with water. **4** A **plug** N-COUNT
is a small round piece of wood, plastic, or wax
which is used to block holes. **5** If you **plug** a hole, a VERB
gap, or a leak, you block it with something. *Crews* V n
are working to plug a major oil leak. **6** See also **ear-
plug, spark plug.**
7 If someone **plugs** a commercial product, especially VERB
a book or a film, they praise it in order to encourage V n
people to buy it or see it because they have an interest
in it doing well. *We did not want people on the show
who are purely interested in plugging a book or film.*
▶ Also a noun. *Let's do this show tonight and it'll be a* N-COUNT
great plug, a great promotion. **8** If someone in a posi- PHRASE
tion of power **pulls the plug on** a project or on
someone's activities, they use their power to stop
them continuing. *The banks have the power to pull the
plug on the project.*
plug away. If you **plug away**, you keep trying very PHRASAL VB
hard to do something or achieve something even V P
though you find it difficult. *My confidence is still there
and I'll just keep plugging away.*
plug in or **plug into. 1** If you **plug** a piece of electri- PHRASAL VB
cal equipment **into** an electricity supply or if you **plug** V n P
it **in**, you push its plug into an electric socket. *They* V P noun
plugged in their tape-recorders... I filled the kettle V n P
while she was talking and plugged it in. **2** If you **plug** V n P
one piece of electrical equipment **into** another or if V P noun
you **plug** it **in**, you make it work by connecting the
two. *He plugged in his guitar.* **3** If one piece of electri- V P n
cal equipment **plugs in** or **plugs into** another piece of V P
electrical equipment, it works by being connected to
the other piece of equipment. *A CD-I deck looks like a
video recorder and plugs into the home television and
stereo system... They've found out where the other
speaker plugs in.* **4** If you **plug** something **into** a hole, V n P n
you push it into the hole. *Her instructor plugged live
bullets into the gun's chamber.*
plug into. 1 If you **plug into** a computer system, you PHRASAL VB
get access to the information on it. *It is possible to plug* V P n
into remote databases to pick up information. **2** If you INFORMAL
plug into a group of people or their ideas, you find out
about them and try to understand them. *The Centre
for European Policy Studies is plugged into the thinking of the people who matter.*
plug·hole /plʌghəʊl/ **plugholes. 1** A plughole is a N-COUNT
small hole in a bath or sink which allows the water BRITISH
to flow away and into which you can put a plug.
The usual American word is **drain. 2** If you say that PHRASE
something has gone **down the plughole**, you mean BRITISH
that it has failed or has been lost or wasted. *Millions
of pounds have gone down the plughole.*
plum /plʌm/ **plums. 1** A plum is a small sweet fruit ◆◇◇◇◇
with a smooth red or yellow skin and a stone in the N-COUNT
middle. See picture headed **fruit. 2** Something that COLOUR
is plum or plum-coloured is a dark reddish-purple
colour. *...plum-coloured silk.* **3** A **plum** job, con- ADJ: ADJ n
tract, or role is a very good one that a lot of people JOURNALISM
would like. *Laura landed a plum job with a smart
art gallery.*
plum·age /pluːmɪdʒ/. A bird's **plumage** consists of ◆◇◇◇◇
all the feathers on its body. N-UNCOUNT
plumb /plʌm/ **plumbs, plumbing, plumbed.** ◆◇◇◇◇
1 If you **plumb** something mysterious or difficult to VERB
understand, you succeed in understanding it. *She* V n
never abandoned her attempts to plumb my inner- LITERARY
most emotions. **2** If something is **plumb** in a par- ADV:
ticular place, it is exactly in that place. *The hotel is* ADV prep
set plumb in the middle of the high street. **3** When INFORMAL
someone **plumbs** a building, they connect all the VERB
water and drainage pipes and make sure they are all V n
working properly. *She learned to wire and plumb
the house herself.* **4** If someone **plumbs the depths** PHRASE
of an unpleasant emotion or quality, they experi-

ence it or show it to an extreme degree. *They frequently plumb the depths of loneliness, humiliation
and despair.* **5** If you say that something **plumbs** PHRASE
new depths, you mean that it is worse than all the
bad things of its kind that have existed before. *Relations between the two countries have plumbed new
depths.*
plumb in. When someone **plumbs in** a device such PHRASAL VB
as a washing machine, toilet, or bath, they connect it V P noun
to the water and drainage pipes in a building. *He had* haven V-ed P
a washing machine plumbed in. Also V n P
BRITISH
plumb·er /plʌmə/ **plumbers.** A plumber is a per- ◆◇◇◇◇
son whose job is to connect and repair things such N-COUNT
as water and drainage pipes, baths, and toilets.
plumb·ing /plʌmɪŋ/. **1** The **plumbing** in a build- ◆◇◇◇◇
ing consists of the water and drainage pipes, baths, N-UNCOUNT
and toilets in it. *The electrics and the plumbing were
sound but everything else had to be cleaned up.*
2 Plumbing is the work of connecting and repairing N-UNCOUNT
things such as water and drainage pipes, baths, and
toilets. *She learned the rudiments of brick-laying,
wiring and plumbing.*
plume /pluːm/ **plumes. 1** A plume of smoke, dust, ◆◇◇◇◇
fire, or water is a large quantity of it that rises into N-COUNT
the air in a column. *The rising plume of black smoke
could be seen all over Kabul.* **2** A **plume** is a large N-COUNT
soft bird's feather. **3** A **plume** is a bunch of long, N-COUNT
thin strands of material, tied at one end and flowing
loosely at the other. Plumes are usually attached to
soldiers' helmets and horses' heads as decoration.
♦ **plumed** *...a young man wearing a plumed hat.* ADJ
plum·met /plʌmɪt/ **plummets, plummeting,** ◆◇◇◇◇
plummeted. If an amount, rate, or price **plum-** VERB: V
mets, it decreases quickly by a large amount. *The* V to n
Prime Minister's popularity has plummeted to an V from/to/by
all-time low in recent weeks... The shares have plum- n
meted from 130p to 2.25p in the past year. JOURNALISM
plum·my /plʌmi/. If you say that someone has a ADJ-GRADED
plummy voice or **accent**, you mean that they sound PRAGMATICS
snobbish or upper-class. BRITISH
plump /plʌmp/ **plumper, plumpest; plumps,** ◆◆◇◇◇
plumping, plumped. 1 You can describe some- ADJ-GRADED
one or something as **plump** to indicate, usually in PRAGMATICS
an affectionate or appreciative way, that they are rather fat or rounded. *Maria was a pretty little thing,
small and plump with a mass of curly hair. ...red
pears, ripe peaches and plump nectarines.*
♦ **plump·ness** *There was a sturdy plumpness about* N-UNCOUNT
her hips. **2** If you **plump a pillow** or **cushion**, you VERB
shake and pat it so that it goes back into a rounded V n
shape. *Michael plumped the pillow next to him.*
▶ **Plump up** means the same as **plump**. *'You need* PHRASAL VB
to rest,' she told her reassuringly as she moved to V P noun
plump up her pillows. **3** If you **plump for** someone Also V n P
or something, you choose them, often after hesitat- V forn
ing or thinking carefully. *I think Tessa should play it
safe and plump for Malcolm, her long-suffering admirer.*
plum to'mato, plum tomatoes. Plum tomatoes N-VAR
are long egg-shaped tomatoes.
plun·der /plʌndə/ **plunders, plundering, plun-** ◆◇◇◇◇
dered. 1 If someone **plunders** a place or **plunders** VERB: V n
things from a place, they steal things from it. *She* V n of n
faces charges of helping to plunder her country's V n from n
treasury of billions of dollars... This has been done by LITERARY
plundering £4 billion from the Government reserves.
▶ Also a noun. *...a guerrilla group infamous for tor-* N-UNCOUNT
ture and plunder. **2 Plunder** is property that is stol- N-UNCOUNT
en. *The thieves are often armed and in some cases* LITERARY
have killed for their plunder.
plunge /plʌndʒ/ **plunges, plunging, plunged.** ◆◆◆◇◇
1 If something or someone **plunges** in a particular VERB
direction, especially into water, they fall, rush, or V prep/adv
throw themselves in that direction. *At least 50 people died when a bus plunged into a river.* ▶ Also a N-COUNT
noun. *...a plunge into cold water.* **2** If you **plunge** VERB
an object into something, you push it quickly or V n into n
violently into it. *She plunged her face into a bowl of* V n with n
cold water... I plunged in my knife and fork. **3** If V-ERG
something **plunges** someone or something into a V n into n
V into n

particular state or situation, or if they **plunge into** it, they are suddenly in that state or situation. *8,000 homes were plunged into darkness as electricity cables crashed down... The economy is plunging into recession.* ▶ Also a noun. *That peace often looked like a brief truce before the next plunge into war.* **4** If you **plunge into** an activity or **are plunged into** it, you suddenly get very involved in it. *The prince should be plunged into work... Take the opportunity to plunge yourself into your career.* ▶ Also a noun. *His sudden plunge into the field of international diplomacy is a major surprise.* **5** If an amount or rate **plunges**, it decreases quickly and suddenly. *The Pound plunged to a new low on the foreign exchange markets yesterday... Shares have plunged from £17 to £7.55... The bank's profits plunged by 87 per cent.* ▶ Also a noun. *Japan's banks are in trouble because of bad loans and the stock market plunge.* **6** If you **take the plunge**, you decide to do something that you consider difficult or risky. *If you have been thinking about buying shares, now could be the time to take the plunge.*

N-COUNT
V-ERG:
V into n
beV-ed into n
V pron-refl
into n

N-COUNT

VERB: V
V into n
V from/to
amount
V by amount
Also V amount

N-COUNT
PHRASE

plung·er /ˈplʌndʒə/ **plungers.** A **plunger** is a device for unblocking pipes and sinks, consisting of a rubber cup on the end of a stick.

◆◇◇◇◇
N-COUNT

plunk /plʌŋk/ **plunks, plunking, plunked.** **1** If you **plunk** something down, you put it down without great care. *She swept up a hat from where it had fallen on the ground, and plunked it on her hair.* **2** If you **plunk down**, you sit down heavily and clumsily. *I watched them go and plunked down on one of the small metal chairs.*

VERB:
V n with down
V n on n
INFORMAL,
AMERICAN
VERB
V down
INFORMAL,
AMERICAN

plu·ral /ˈplʊərəl/ **plurals.** **1** The **plural** form of a word is the form that is used when referring to more than one person or thing. *...his use of the plural pronoun 'we'.* **2** The **plural** of a noun is the form of it that is used to refer to more than one person or thing. *What is the plural of 'person'? ...irregular plurals.* **3** A **plural** society or system involves different kinds of people. *Britain is a plural society in which the secular predominates.*

◆◇◇◇◇
ADJ

N-COUNT

ADJ-GRADED
ADJ n
FORMAL

plu·ral·ism /ˈplʊərəlɪzəm/. If there is **pluralism** within a society, it has many different groups and political parties. *...as the country shifts towards political pluralism.* ♦ **plu·ral·ist** *...an attempt to create a pluralist democracy.*

◆◇◇◇◇
N-UNCOUNT
FORMAL
ADJ-GRADED

plu·ral·ist·ic /ˌplʊərəˈlɪstɪk/. **Pluralistic** means the same as **pluralist**.

ADJ-GRADED
FORMAL

plu·ral·ity /plʊəˈrælɪti/. **1** If there is a **plurality of** things, a number of them exist. *Federalism implies a plurality of political authorities, each with its own powers.* **2** If a candidate, political party, or idea has the support of a **plurality of** people, they have more support than any other candidate, party, or idea. *The Conservative party retained a plurality of the votes.*

QUANT
FORMAL

QUANT
FORMAL

plus /plʌs/ **pluses** or **plusses.** **1** You say **plus** to show that one number or quantity is being added to another. *Send a cheque for £18.99 plus £2 for postage and packing.* **2 Plus** before a number or quantity means that the number or quantity is greater than zero. *The aircraft was subjected to temperatures of minus 65 degrees and plus 120 degrees.* ● **plus or minus**: see **minus**. **3** You can use **plus** when mentioning an additional item or fact. *There's easily enough room for two adults and three children, plus a dog in the boot.* **4** You use **plus** after a number or quantity to indicate that the actual number or quantity is greater than the one mentioned. *There are only 35 staff to serve 30,000-plus customers.* **5** Teachers use **plus** in grading work in schools and colleges. 'B plus' is a better grade than 'B', but it is not as good as 'A'. **6** A **plus** is an advantage or benefit. *Experience of any career in sales is a big plus.*

◆◆◆◇
CONJ

ADJ:
ADJ amount

CONJ
INFORMAL

ADJ:
amount ADJ

N-COUNT
INFORMAL

plush /plʌʃ/ **plusher, plushest.** **1** If you describe something as **plush**, you mean that it is very smart, comfortable, or expensive. *...a plush, four-storey, Georgian house in Mayfair.* **2 Plush** is a thick soft material like velvet. *All the seats were in red plush.*

◆◇◇◇◇
ADJ-GRADED

N-UNCOUNT

plu·to·ni·um /pluːˈtəʊniəm/. **Plutonium** is a radioactive element used especially in nuclear weapons and as a fuel in nuclear power stations.

◆◇◇◇◇
N-UNCOUNT

ply /plaɪ/ **plies, plying, plied. 1** If you **ply** someone with food or drink, you keep giving them more of it in an insistent way. *The poor priest was plied with drink at a dinner party.* **2** If you **ply** someone with questions, you keep asking them questions in an insistent way. *Giovanni plied him with questions and comments with the deliberate intention of prolonging his stay.* **3** If you **ply** a trade, you do a particular kind of work regularly as your job, especially a kind of work that involves trying to sell goods or services to passers-by. *It's illegal for unmarked mini-cabs to ply for hire.* **4** If a ship, aircraft, or vehicle **plies** a route, it makes regular journeys along that route. *The brightly-coloured boats ply between the islands.*

◆◇◇◇◇
VERB
V n with n

VERB
V n with n

VERB: V n
V for n

VERB: V n
V prep

-ply /-plaɪ/. You use **-ply** after a number to indicate how many strands a type of wool, thread, or rope is made from. *...any 4-ply knitting wool.*

COMB

ply·wood /ˈplaɪwʊd/. **Plywood** is wood that consists of thin layers of wood stuck together. *...a sheet of plywood.*

◆◇◇◇◇
N-UNCOUNT

PM /ˌpiː ˈem/ **PMs. PM** is an abbreviation for **Prime Minister**. *Michael Heseltine said he welcomed the PM's decision.*

◆◆◆◇◇
N-COUNT:
the N
BRITISH

p.m. /ˌpiː ˈem/; also spelled **pm. p.m.** is used after a number to show that you are referring to a particular time between noon and midnight. *The spa is open from 7:00 am to 9:00 pm every day of the year.*

◆◆◇◇◇
ADV:
num ADV

PMS /ˌpiː em ˈes/. **PMS** is an abbreviation for **premenstrual syndrome**.

◆◇◇◇◇
N-UNCOUNT

PMT /ˌpiː em ˈtiː/. **PMT** is an abbreviation for **premenstrual tension**.

N-UNCOUNT

pneu·mat·ic /njuːˈmætɪk/. **1** A **pneumatic drill** is operated by compressed air and is very powerful. **2 Pneumatic** means filled with air. *Use a bicycle pump to keep the pneumatic tyres full of air.*

ADJ: ADJ n

ADJ: ADJ n

pneu·mo·nia /njuːˈməʊniə/. **Pneumonia** is a serious disease which affects your lungs and makes it difficult for you to breathe.

◆◇◇◇◇
N-UNCOUNT:
also a N

PO /ˌpiː ˈəʊ/. **PO** is an abbreviation for **Post Office** or **postal order**.

poach /pəʊtʃ/ **poaches, poaching, poached. 1** If someone **poaches** fish, animals, or birds, they illegally catch them on someone else's property. *Many national parks set up to provide a refuge for wildlife are regularly invaded by people poaching game.* ♦ **poach·er, poachers.** *Security cameras have been installed to guard against poachers.* ♦ **poach·ing** *...the poaching of elephants for their tusks.* **2** If an organization or team **poaches** members or customers from another organization or team, they secretly or dishonestly persuade them to join them or become their customers. *...allegations that it had poached members from other unions.* ♦ **poaching** *The union was accused of poaching.* **3** If someone **poaches** an idea, they dishonestly or illegally use the idea. **4** When you **poach an egg**, you cook it gently in boiling water without its shell. **5** If you **poach** food such as fish, you cook it gently in boiling water, milk, or other liquid.

◆◇◇◇◇
VERB
V n
Also V

N-COUNT

N-UNCOUNT
VERB: V n
V n from n

N-UNCOUNT
VERB: V n

VERB: V n
VERB: V n

PO Box /ˌpiː ˈəʊ bɒks/. **PO Box** is used before a number as a kind of address. The Post Office keeps letters addressed to the PO Box until they are collected by the person who has paid for the service.

◆◆◇◇◇

pocked /pɒkt/. **Pocked** means the same as **pockmarked**. *...a bus pocked with bullet holes.*

ADJ-GRADED

pock·et /ˈpɒkɪt/ **pockets, pocketing, pocketed. 1** A **pocket** is a kind of small bag which forms part of a piece of clothing, and which is used for carrying small things such as money. *He took his flashlight from his jacket pocket.* **2** You can use **pocket** in a lot of different ways to refer to money that people have, get, or spend. For example, if someone gives or pays a lot of money, you can say that they **dig deep into their pocket**. If something is very cheap to buy, you can say that it **suits people's**

◆◆◆◇◇
N-COUNT

N-COUNT

P

pockets. *We don't believe that they have the economic reforms in place which would justify putting huge sums of Western money into their pockets.* **3** You use **pocket** to describe something that is small enough to fit into a pocket, often something that is a smaller version of a larger item. *...a pocket calculator.* `ADJ: ADJ n`

4 If someone who is in possession of something valuable such as a sum of money **pockets** it, they steal it or take it for themselves, even though it does not belong to them. **5** If someone **pockets** something, they put it in their pocket, for example because they want to steal it or hide it. **6** If you say that someone **is lining** their own or someone else's **pockets**, you disapprove of them because they are making money dishonestly or unfairly for themselves or for someone else. `VERB: V n` `VERB: V n` `PHRASE`

7 If you say that some money **is burning a hole in** someone's **pocket**, you mean that they want to spend it as soon as possible. **8** If you are **out of pocket**, you have less money than you should have or than you intended. ● See also **out-of-pocket**. **9** If someone **picks** your **pocket**, they steal something from your pocket, usually without you noticing. *Somebody picks his pocket and he decides it's time the city was cleaned up.* `PHRASE` `PHRASE` `PHRASE`

10 If you say that someone **pockets** something such as a prize or sum of money, you mean that they win or obtain it, often without needing to make much effort or in a way that seems unfair. *He pocketed more money from this tournament than in his entire three years as a professional.* **11** If you say that someone is **in** someone else's **pocket**, you disapprove of the fact that the first person is willing to do whatever the second person tells them. *The board of directors must have been in Johnstone's pocket.* `VERB V n JOURNALISM` `PHRASE` `PRAGMATICS`

12 A **pocket** of something is a small area where something is happening, or a small area which has a particular quality, and which is different from the other areas around it. *The newly established government controls the bulk of the city apart from a few pockets of resistance.* `N-COUNT`

pocket·book /'pɒkɪtbʊk/ **pocketbooks. 1** You can use **pocketbook** to refer to people's concerns about the money they have or hope to earn. *People feel pinched in their pocketbooks and insecure about their futures.* **2** A **pocketbook** is a small bag which a woman uses to carry things such as her money and keys in. The usual British word is **handbag**. `N-COUNT AMERICAN, JOURNALISM` `N-COUNT AMERICAN`

'pocket knife, pocket knives; also spelled **pocketknife.** A **pocket knife** is a small knife with several blades which fold into the handle so that you can carry it around with you safely. `N-COUNT`

'pocket money; also spelled **pocket-money. 1 Pocket money** is money which children are given by their parents, usually every week. **2 Pocket money** is a small amount of money which you earn, and which you can use for buying the things that you want. *Volunteers receive £21 pocket money each week, accommodation and expenses.* `N-UNCOUNT` `N-UNCOUNT`

'pocket-sized; also spelled **pocket-size.** Something that is **pocket-sized** is small enough to fit in your pocket. *...a handy pocket-sized reference book.* `ADJ`

pock·mark /'pɒkmɑːk/ **pockmarks;** also spelled **pock mark. Pockmarks** are small hollows on the surface of something. *The pockmarks made by her bullets are still on the wall.* ◆ **pock·marked** *The living room is pockmarked with bullet holes.* `N-COUNT` `ADJ-GRADED`

pod /pɒd/ **pods.** A **pod** is a seed container that grows on plants such as peas or beans. `N-COUNT`

podgy /'pɒdʒi/. If you describe someone as **podgy**, you think that they are a little overweight but not fat. The usual American word is **pudgy**. `ADJ-GRADED INFORMAL, BRITISH`

po·dia·try /pə'daɪətri/. **Podiatry** is the professional care and treatment of people's feet. **Podiatry** is a more modern term for **chiropody** and also deals with correcting foot problems relating to the way people stand and walk. ◆ **po·dia·trist, podia·trists.** *Ingrown toenails are also a common complaint podiatrists see a lot of.* `N-UNCOUNT` `N-COUNT`

po·dium /'pəʊdiəm/ **podiums.** A **podium** is a small platform on which someone stands in order to give a lecture or conduct an orchestra. `N-COUNT`

poem /'pəʊɪm/ **poems.** A **poem** is a piece of writing in which the words are chosen for their beauty and sound and are carefully arranged. `N-COUNT`

poet /'pəʊɪt/ **poets.** A **poet** is a person who writes poems. `N-COUNT`

po·et·ess /'pəʊɪtes/ **poetesses.** A **poetess** is a female poet. Most female poets prefer to be called poets. `N-COUNT PRAGMATICS`

po·et·ic /pəʊ'etɪk/. **1** Something that is **poetic** is very beautiful, expressive, and sensitive. *...an exciting yet poetic performance.* ◆ **po·eti·cal·ly** *The speech was as poetically written as any he'd ever heard.* **2 Poetic** means relating to poetry. *There's a very rich poetic tradition in Gaelic.* `ADJ-GRADED` `ADV-GRADED` `ADJ`

po·eti·cal /pəʊ'etɪkəl/. **Poetical** means the same as **poetic.** `ADJ-GRADED`

po,etic 'justice. If you describe something bad that happens to someone as **poetic justice,** you mean that it is exactly what they deserve because of the things that that person has done. `N-UNCOUNT`

poet lau·reate /ˌpəʊɪt 'lɒriət, AM - 'lɔːr-/ **poet laureates** or **poets laureate.** The **poet laureate** of a particular country is the poet who has been chosen to write poems for special occasions. `N-COUNT`

po·et·ry /'pəʊɪtri/. **1** Poems, considered as a form of literature, are referred to as **poetry.** *Lawrence Durrell wrote a great deal of poetry.* **2** You can refer to the beauty or greatness that people see or experience in something as **poetry.** *His music is purer poetry than a poem in words.* `N-UNCOUNT` `N-UNCOUNT`

po-faced /ˌpəʊ 'feɪst/. If you describe someone as **po-faced,** you think that they are being unnecessarily serious about something. `ADJ-GRADED PRAGMATICS BRITISH`

pog·rom /'pɒgrəm, AM pə'grɑːm/ **pogroms.** A **pogrom** is an organized, official persecution, for racial or religious reasons, which usually leads to mass killing of a group of people. `N-COUNT`

poign·an·cy /'pɔɪnjənsi/. **Poignancy** is the quality that something has when it affects you deeply and makes you feel very sad. *The fact that he had been talking to the victims only minutes before their deaths gave the tragedy greater poignancy.* `N-UNCOUNT`

poign·ant /'pɔɪnjənt/. Something that is **poignant** makes you feel very sad because it reminds you of something that has happened in the past, or because something that you wanted to happen did not happen. *...a poignant combination of beautiful surroundings and tragic history.* ◆ **poign·ant·ly** *Naomi's mothering experiences are poignantly described in her fiction.* `ADJ-GRADED` `ADV-GRADED`

poin·set·tia /pɔɪn'setiə/ **poinsettias.** A **poinsettia** is a plant with groups of bright red or pink leaves that grows in Central and South America. Poinsettias are very popular in Britain as house plants. `N-COUNT`

point /pɔɪnt/ **points, pointing, pointed. 1** You use **point** to refer to something that someone has said or written. *We disagree with every point Mr Blunkett makes.* **2** If you say that someone **has a point,** or if you **take their point,** you mean that you accept that what they have said is important and should be considered. *'If he'd already killed once, surely he'd have killed Sarah?' She had a point there.* **3 The point** of what you are saying or discussing is the most important part that provides a reason or explanation for the rest. *The American Congress and media mostly missed the point about all this.* **4** When someone **comes to the point** or **gets to the point,** they start talking about the thing that is most important to them. **5** If you say that something is **beside the point,** you mean that it is not relevant to the subject that you are discussing. **6** Something that is **to the point** is relevant to the subject that you are discussing, or is expressed neatly without wasting words or time. *The description which he had been given was brief and to the point.* **7** If you **make** your **point** or **prove** your **point,** you prove that something is true. **8** If you say that `N-COUNT` `N-SING: a N, poss N` `N-SING: the N` `PHRASE` `PHRASE` `PHRASE` `PHRASE` `PHRASE`

something is true **up to a point**, you mean that it is partly but not completely true. *It worked up to a point.* **9** If you ask what the **point** of something is, or say that there is **no point** in it, you are indicating that a particular action has no purpose or would not be useful. *There was no point in staying any longer.* **10** If you **make a point of** doing something, you do it in a deliberate or obvious way. *She made a point of spending as much time as possible away from Osborne House.* **N-SING**

11 A **point** is a detail, aspect, or quality of something or someone. *Many of the points in the report are correct... Science was never my strong point at school.* **N-COUNT**

12 A **point** is a particular place or position where something happens. *The pain originated from a point in his right thigh.* **13** You use **point** to refer to a particular time, or to a particular stage in the development of something. *At this point Diana arrived... It got to the point where he had to leave.* **14** If you are **on the point of** doing something, you are about to do it. *He was on the point of saying something when the phone rang.* **N-SING: with supp / PHRASE**

15 The **point** of something such as a pin, needle, or knife is the thin, sharp end of it. **16** You use **point** to refer to the dot or mark in a decimal number that separates the whole numbers from the fractions. *This is FM stereo one oh three point seven.* **17** In some sports and games, a **point** is one of the single marks that are added together to give the total score. **N-COUNT / SPOKEN / N-COUNT**

18 The **points** of a compass are the marks on it that show the directions, such as North, South, East, and West. **19** On a railway track, the **points** are the levers and rails at a place where two tracks join or separate. The points enable a train to move from one track to another. **20** A **point** is an electric socket. **N-COUNT / N-PLURAL BRITISH / N-COUNT**

21 If you **point at** someone, you hold out your finger towards them in order to show someone else where they are. If you **point** at something, you hold out your finger towards it to make someone notice it. *He pointed to a chair, signalling for her to sit.* **22** If you **point** something **at** someone, you aim the tip or end of it towards them. *A man pointed a gun at them.* **23** If something **points** to a place or **points** in a particular direction, it shows where that place is or it faces in that direction. *An arrow pointed to the toilets.* **VERB: V at n / V to n / VERB V n at n / VERB V prep/adv**

24 If something **points to** a particular situation, it suggests that the situation exists or is likely to occur. *Private polls and embassy reports pointed to a no vote.* **25** If you **point to** something that has happened or that is happening, you are using it as proof that a particular situation exists. *Gooch last night pointed to their bowling as the key to World Cup success.* **VERB V to n / VERB V to n**

26 When builders **point** a wall, they put mortar or cement into the gaps between the bricks or stones so that the surface becomes sealed. **VERB: V n**

27 See also **pointed**; **breaking point, focal point, power point, sticking point, vantage point**. ● **a case in point**: see **case**. ● **in point of fact**: see **fact**. ● **to point the finger at** someone: see **finger**. ● **a sore point**: see **sore**.

point out. 1 If you **point out** an object or place, you make people look at it or show them where it is. *They kept standing up to take pictures and point things out to each other.* **2** If you **point out** a fact or mistake, you tell someone about it or draw their attention to it. *Critics point out that the prince, on his income, should be paying tax.* **PHRASAL VB / V P noun / V n P / V P noun / V P that / Also V n P**

point·blank. 1 If you say something **point-blank**, you say it very directly or rudely, without explaining or apologizing. *Mr Mellor was asked point blank if he would resign.* ► Also an adjective. *...a point-blank refusal.* **2** If someone or something is shot **point-blank**, they are shot when the gun is touching them or extremely close to them. ► Also an adjective. *He had been shot at point-blank range.* **◆◇◇◇◇ ADV: ADV after v / ADJ: ADJ n / ADV: ADV after v / ADJ: ADJ n**

point·ed /'pɔɪntɪd/. **1** Something that is **pointed** has a point at one end. *...pointed shoes. ...a wooden house, sheltered by a low pointed roof.* **2 Pointed** comments or behaviour express criticism in a clear and direct way. *...the pointed remarks slung in my* **◆◆◇◇◇ ADJ-GRADED / ADJ-GRADED**

direction. ♦ **point·ed·ly** *They were pointedly absent from the news conference.* **ADV-GRADED**

point·er /'pɔɪntə/ **pointers. 1** A **pointer** is a piece of advice or information which helps you to understand a situation or to find a way of making progress. *Here are a few pointers to help you make a choice.* **2** A **pointer** to something suggests that it exists or gives an indication of what it is like. *Sunday's elections should be a pointer to the public mood.* **3** A **pointer** is also a long thin stick that is used to point at something such as a chart on a wall. **4** The **pointer** on a measuring instrument is the long, thin piece of metal that points to the numbers. **◆◇◇◇◇ N-COUNT: with supp / N-COUNT: N to/towards n / N-COUNT / N-COUNT**

point·ing /'pɔɪntɪŋ/. **1 Pointing** is a way of filling in the gaps between the bricks or stones on the outside of a building so that the surface becomes sealed. **2 Pointing** is the cement between the bricks or stones in a wall. **N-UNCOUNT / N-UNCOUNT**

point·less /'pɔɪntləs/. If you say that something is **pointless**, you are criticizing it because it has no sense or purpose. *Violence is always pointless.* ♦ **point·less·ly** *Chemicals were pointlessly poisoning the soil.* ♦ **point·less·ness** *You cannot help wondering about the pointlessness of it all.* **◆◇◇◇◇ ADJ-GRADED PRAGMATICS / ADV / N-UNCOUNT**

point of 'order, points of order. In a formal debate, a **point of order** is an objection that someone makes because the rules of behaviour or organization have been broken. *The postponement was demanded and won on a point of order.* **N-COUNT FORMAL**

point of 'reference, points of reference. A **point of reference** is something which you use to help you understand a situation or communicate with someone. *Do we still have any fixed point of reference in the teaching of English?* **N-COUNT**

point of 'view, points of view. 1 You can refer to the opinions or attitudes that you have about something as your **point of view**. **2** If you consider something from a particular **point of view**, you are using one aspect of a situation in order to judge that situation. *Do you think that, from the point of view of results, this exercise was worth the cost?* **◆◆◇◇◇ N-COUNT / N-COUNT**

pointy /'pɔɪnti/ **pointier, pointiest.** Something that is **pointy** has a point at one end. **ADJ-GRADED INFORMAL**

poise /pɔɪz/. **1** If someone has **poise**, they are calm, dignified, and self-controlled. *It took a moment for Mark to recover his poise.* **2 Poise** is a graceful, very controlled way of standing and moving. *Ballet classes are important for poise and grace.* **N-UNCOUNT / N-UNCOUNT**

poised /pɔɪzd/. **1** If a part of your body is **poised**, it is completely still but ready to move at any moment. *He studied the keyboard carefully, one finger poised.* **2** If someone is **poised** to do something, they are ready to take action at any moment. *US forces are poised for a massive air, land and sea assault.* **3** If you are **poised**, you are calm, dignified, and self-controlled. **◆◆◇◇◇ ADJ / ADJ: v-link ADJ / ADJ-GRADED**

poi·son /'pɔɪzən/ **poisons, poisoning, poisoned. 1 Poison** is a substance that harms or kills people or animals if they swallow it or absorb it. *Mercury is a known poison.* **2** If someone **poisons** another person, they kill the person or make them ill by giving them poison. ♦ **poi·son·ing** *She was sentenced to twenty years' imprisonment for poisoning.* **3** If you **are poisoned** by a substance, it makes you very ill and sometimes kills you. *Toxic waste could endanger lives and poison fish.* ♦ **poisoning** *His illness was initially diagnosed as food poisoning.* **4** If someone **poisons** a food, drink, or weapon, they add poison to it so that it can be used to kill someone. ♦ **poi·soned** *...a poisoned dart.* **5** To **poison** water, air, or land means to damage it with harmful substances such as chemicals. *...industries that taint the air, poison the water and use vast amounts of natural resources.* **6** Something that **poisons** a good situation or relationship spoils it or destroys it. *The whole atmosphere has really been poisoned.* **◆◆◇◇◇ N-VAR / VERB: V n / N-UNCOUNT / VERB: be V-ed by n / V n / N-UNCOUNT / VERB: V n / ADJ / VERB V n / VERB: V n / be V-ed**

poi·son·er /'pɔɪzənə/ **poisoners.** A **poisoner** is someone who has killed or harmed another person by using poison. **N-COUNT**

'**poison gas.** Poison gas is a gas that is poisonous N-UNCOUNT
and is usually used to kill people in war or to execute criminals.

poi·son·ous /ˈpɔɪzənəs/. **1** Something that is **poi-** ◆◇◇◇◇
sonous will kill you or make you ill if you swallow ADJ-GRADED
or absorb it. *A chemical plant dumped poisonous
liquid into the local water-supply system.* **2** A **poi-** ADJ-GRADED
sonous animal produces a poison that will kill you
or make you ill if the animal bites you. *...poisonous
spiders and snakes.* **3** If you describe something as ADJ-GRADED
poisonous, you mean that it is extremely unpleasant and likely to spoil or destroy a good relationship
or situation. *...lying awake half the night tormented
by poisonous suspicions.*

'**poison-'pen letter, poison-pen letters.** A N-COUNT
poison-pen letter is an anonymous letter which is
sent in order to upset someone or to cause trouble.

poke /pəʊk/ **pokes, poking, poked. 1** If you ◆◇◇◇◇
poke someone or something, you quickly push VERB: V n
them with your finger or with a sharp object. ▶ Also N-COUNT
a noun. *John smiled at them and gave Richard a
playful poke.* **2** If you **poke** one thing **into** another, VERB
you push the first thing into the second thing. *He* V n into n
poked his finger into the hole. **3** If something **pokes** VERB:
out of or **through** another thing, you can see part of V out of n
it appearing from behind or underneath the other V through n
thing. *His fingers poked through the worn tips of his
gloves.* **4** If you **poke** your head through an opening, V-ERG
you push it through, often so that you can see V n adv/prep
something more easily. *Raymond's head poked* V prep/adv
through the doorway. **5** ● to **poke fun at**: see **fun.**
● to **poke** your **nose into** something: see **nose.**

poke around. If you **poke around** for something, PHRASAL VB
you search for it, usually by moving a lot of objects V P
around. If you **poke through** a lot of objects, you V P n
search for something among them. *We opened up the* INFORMAL
*car bonnet and he started poking around in my en-
gine... In a nearby neighborhood police and onlookers
were poking through broken glass and debris.*

poke at. If you **poke at** something, you make lots of PHRASAL VB
little pushing movements at it with a sharp object. V P n

pok·er /ˈpəʊkə/ **pokers. 1 Poker** is a card game ◆◇◇◇◇
that people usually play in order to win money. *Bar-* N-UNCOUNT
ry loves a good game of poker. **2** A **poker** is a metal N-COUNT
bar which you use to move coal or wood in a fire in
order to make it burn better.

'**poker-'faced.** If you are **poker-faced**, you have a ADJ-GRADED
calm expression on your face which shows none of INFORMAL
your thoughts or feelings.

poky /ˈpəʊki/ **pokier, pokiest.** A room or house ADJ-GRADED
that is **poky** is uncomfortably small. INFORMAL

po·lar /ˈpəʊlə/. **1 Polar** means near the North and ◆◇◇◇◇
South Poles. *...the polar regions of the Soviet Union.* ADJ: ADJ n
2 Polar is used to describe things which are com- ADJ: ADJ n
pletely opposite in character, quality, or type. FORMAL
*...economists at polar ends of the politico-economic
spectrum.*

'**polar bear, polar bears.** A polar bear is a large N-COUNT
white bear which is found near the North Pole.

po·lar·ise /ˈpəʊləraɪz/. See **polarize.**

po·lar·ity /pəʊˈlærɪti/ **polarities.** If there is a **polar-** N-VAR
ity between two people or things, they are com- FORMAL
pletely different from each other in some way. *...the
polarities of good and evil.*

po·lar·ize /ˈpəʊləraɪz/ **polarizes, polarizing, po-** ◆◇◇◇◇
larized; also spelled **polarise** in British English. If V-ERG
something **polarizes** people, two separate groups V n
are formed with opposite opinions or positions. Also V into n
*Missile deployment did much to further polarize
opinion in Britain... As the car rental industry polarizes, business will go to the bigger companies.* ♦ **po-**
·**larized** *Since Independence the electorate has been* ADJ-GRADED
polarized equally between two parties. ♦ **po·lari·za·**
·**tion** /ˌpəʊləraɪˈzeɪʃən/ *There is increasing polariza-* N-UNCOUNT
tion between the blacks and whites in the US.

Po·lar·oid /ˈpəʊlərɔɪd/ **Polaroids. 1** A **Polaroid** ◆◇◇◇◇
camera is a small camera that can take, develop, ADJ: ADJ n
and print a photograph in a few seconds. **Polaroid**
is a trademark. **2** A **Polaroid** is a photograph taken N-COUNT
with a Polaroid camera. **3 Polaroid** sunglasses have ADJ: ADJ n

been treated with a special substance in order to reduce the glare of the sun.

pole /pəʊl/ **poles. 1** A **pole** is a long thin piece of ◆◆◆◇◇
wood or metal, used especially for supporting N-COUNT
things. *...a telegraph pole.* **2** The earth's **poles** are N-COUNT
the two opposite ends of its axis. ● See also **North
Pole, South Pole. 3** The two **poles** of a range of N-COUNT
qualities or beliefs are the completely opposite
qualities or beliefs at either end of the range. *...op-
posite poles of the political spectrum.* **4** If you say PHRASE
that two people or things are **poles apart**, you mean
that they have completely different beliefs or qualities. *Physically, my husband and I are poles apart.*

'**pole-axed;** also spelled **poleaxed.** If someone is ADJ
pole-axed, they are so surprised or shocked that INFORMAL,
they do not know what to say or do. BRITISH

po·lem·ic /pəˈlemɪk/ **polemics. 1** A **polemic** is a ◆◇◇◇◇
fierce written or spoken attack on, or defence of, a N-VAR
particular belief or opinion. **2 Polemics** is the skill N-UNCOUNT
or practice of arguing passionately for or against a
belief or opinion. ♦ **po·lemi·cal** /pəˈlemɪkəl/. ADJ-GRADED
...Kramer's biting polemical novel.

po·lemi·cist /pəˈlemɪsɪst/ **polemicists.** A **polemi-** N-COUNT
cist is someone who is skilled at arguing passionate- FORMAL
ly for or against an opinion or belief.

'**pole po'sition, pole positions.** When a racing ◆◇◇◇◇
car is in **pole position**, it is in front of the other cars N-UNCOUNT:
at the start of a race. also N in pl

'**pole vault.** The **pole vault** is an athletics event in N-SING:
which athletes jump over a high bar, using a long the N
flexible pole to help lift themselves up. ♦ '**pole
vaulter, pole vaulter.** A **pole vaulter** is an athlete N-COUNT
who performs the pole vault.

po·lice /pəˈliːs/ **polices, policing, policed.** ◆◆◆◆◆
1 The **police** are the official organization that is re- N-COLL-SING
sponsible for making sure that people obey the law.
*Police say they have arrested twenty people following
the disturbances.* **2 Police** are men and women who N-PLURAL
are members of the official organization that is responsible for making sure that people obey the law.
More than one hundred police have ringed the area.
3 If the police or military forces **police** an area or VERB: V n
event, they make sure that law and order is pre-
served in that area or at that event. ♦ **po·lic·ing** N-UNCOUNT
...the policing of public places. **4** If a person or VERB: V n
group in authority **polices** a law or an area of public
life, they make sure that what is done is fair and legal. ♦ **policing** *Policing of business courses varies* N-UNCOUNT
widely. **5** See also **community policing, secret
police.**

po'lice dog, police dogs. A **police dog** is a work- N-COUNT
ing dog which is owned by the police.

po'lice force, police forces. A **police force** is ◆◆◇◇◇
the police organization in a particular country or N-COUNT
area.

police·man /pəˈliːsmən/ **policemen.** A **police-** ◆◆◆◇◇
man is a man who is a member of the police force. N-COUNT

po'lice officer, police officers. A **police officer** ◆◇◇◇◇
is a member of the police force. N-COUNT

po,lice 'state, police states. A **police state** is a N-COUNT
country in which the government controls people's PRAGMATICS
freedom by means of the police, especially secret
police; used showing disapproval.

po'lice station, police stations. A **police sta-** ◆◆◇◇◇
tion is the local office of a police force in a particu- N-COUNT
lar area.

police·woman /pəˈliːswʊmən/ **policewomen.** A ◆◇◇◇◇
policewoman is a woman who is a member of the N-COUNT
police force.

poli·cy /ˈpɒlɪsi/ **policies. 1** A **policy** is a set of ◆◆◆◆◇
ideas or plans that is used as a basis for making de- N-VAR
cisions, especially in politics, economics, or business. *...the evolution of British foreign policy under
Thatcher.* **2** An official organization's **policy** on a N-COUNT
particular issue or towards a country is their attitude and actions regarding that issue or country.
*...the organisation's future policy towards South Afri-
ca.* **3** An **insurance policy** is a document which N-COUNT
shows the agreement that you have made with an
insurance company.

pol·i·cy·hold·er /'pɒlɪsihəʊldə/ **policyholders;** also
spelled **policy-holder.** A **policyholder** is a person
who has an insurance policy with an insurance
company. ◆◇◇◇◇ N-COUNT

pol·i·cy·mak·er /'pɒlɪsimeɪkə/ **policymakers;** also
spelled **policy-maker.** In politics, **policymakers** are
people who are involved in making policies and
policy decisions. N-COUNT

'pol·i·cy-mak·ing; also spelled **policymaking.**
Policy-making is the making of policies. ◆◇◇◇◇ N-UNCOUNT

po·lio /'pəʊliəʊ/. **Polio** is a serious infectious disease caused by a virus. It often causes paralysis. ◆◇◇◇◇ N-UNCOUNT

po·lio·my·eli·tis /,pəʊliəʊmaɪə'laɪtɪs/. **Poliomyeli-
tis** is the same as **polio.** N-UNCOUNT MEDICAL

pol·ish /'pɒlɪʃ/ **polishes, polishing, polished.**
1 Polish is a substance that you put on the surface
of an object in order to clean it, protect it, and make
it shine. *...furniture polish.* **2** If you **polish** something, you put polish on it or rub it with a cloth to
make it shine. *He removed his glasses and began
polishing them with his handkerchief.* ◆ **pol·ished**
...a highly polished floor. ◆◆◇◇◇ N-VAR / VERB V n Also V / ADJ-GRADED

3 If you say that a person, performance, or piece of
work has **polish,** you mean that they show confidence
and sophistication. *The opera lacks the polish of his
later work.* ◆ **polished** *He is polished, charming, articulate.* **4** If you **polish** your technique, performance,
or skill at doing something, you work on improving it. N-UNCOUNT / ADJ-GRADED / VERB: V n

▶ **Polish up** means the same as **polish.** *Polish up your
writing skills on a one-week professional course.* PHRASAL VB V P noun
5 See also **nail polish.**

polish off. If you **polish off** food or drink, you finish
it. *He polished off his scotch and slammed the glass
down.* PHRASAL VB V P noun INFORMAL

polish up. See **polish** 4. PHRASAL VB

Pol·it·bu·ro /'pɒlɪtbjʊərəʊ/ **Politburos.** In communist countries the **Politburo** is the chief committee that formulates policy and makes decisions. ◆◇◇◇◇ N-COUNT

po·lite /pə'laɪt/ **politer, politest. 1** Someone who
is **polite** has good manners and behaves in a way
that is socially correct and not rude to other
people. *I hate having to make polite conversation.* ◆◆◇◇◇ ADJ-GRADED

◆ **po·lite·ly** *'Your home is beautiful,' I said politely.* ADV-GRADED
◆ **po·lite·ness** *She listened to him, but only out of
politeness.* **2** You can refer to people who consider
themselves to set standards of behaviour for every-
one else as **polite society** or **polite company.** N-UNCOUNT / ADJ: ADJ n

po·li·tic /'pɒlɪtɪk/. If it seems **politic** to do a particular thing, that seems to be the most sensible thing
to do in the circumstances. *I didn't feel it was politic
to mention it to the police.* ● See also **politics; body
politic.** ADJ-GRADED FORMAL

po·liti·cal /pə'lɪtɪkəl/. **1 Political** means relating to
the way power is achieved and used in a country or
society. *All other political parties there have been
completely banned... Abortion is once again a controversial political and moral issue.* ● See also **party
political.** ◆ **po·liti·cal·ly** *They do not believe the killings were politically motivated.* **2** Someone who is **political** is interested or involved in
politics and holds strong beliefs about it. *Oh I'm not
political, I have no interest in politics.* ◆◆◆◆◆ ADJ / ADV / ADJ-GRADED

po,litical a'sylum. Political asylum is the right
to live in a country which is given by the government to foreigners who have to leave their own
country for political reasons. *...a university teacher
who is seeking political asylum in Britain.* ◆◇◇◇◇ N-UNCOUNT

po,litical cor'rectness. Political correctness is
behaviour and beliefs that reflect the attitudes
and language that are typical of people who hold
left-wing or liberal views; often used showing disapproval. ◆ **po·liti·cal·ly cor·rect** *The politically-
correct woman can no longer wear fur.* ◆◇◇◇◇ N-UNCOUNT / ADJ-GRADED

po,litical e'conomy. Political economy is the
study of the way in which a government influences
or organizes a nation's wealth. N-UNCOUNT

po,litical 'prisoner, political prisoners. A po-
litical prisoner is someone who has been imprisoned for criticizing or disagreeing with their own
government. ◆◇◇◇◇ N-COUNT

po,litical 'science. Political science is the study
of the ways in which political power is acquired and
used in a country. ◆ **po·liti·cal sci·en·tist, political scientists.** ◆◇◇◇◇ N-UNCOUNT / N-COUNT

poli·ti·cian /,pɒlɪ'tɪʃən/ **politicians.** A politician
is a person whose job is in politics, especially a
member of parliament. ◆◆◆◇ N-COUNT

po·liti·cize /pə'lɪtɪsaɪz/ **politicizes, politicizing,
politicized;** also spelled **politicise** in British English. If you **politicize** someone or something, you
make them more interested in politics or more involved with politics. *...ideas which might politicize
the labouring classes.* ◆ **po·liti·cized** *...the highly
politicized nature of China's legal system.* ◆ **po·liti-
·ci·za·tion** /pəlɪtɪsaɪ'zeɪʃən/ *There has been increas-
ing politicization of the civil service.* ◆◇◇◇◇ VERB V n / ADJ-GRADED / N-UNCOUNT

poli·tick·ing /'pɒlɪtɪkɪŋ/. If you describe someone's
political activity as **politicking,** you think that they
are engaged in it to gain votes or personal advan-
tage for themselves; used showing disapproval. N-UNCOUNT PRAGMATICS

po·liti·co /pə'lɪtɪkəʊ/ **politicos.** You can describe a
politician as a **politico,** especially if you do not like
them or approve of what they do. N-COUNT PRAGMATICS

politico- /pə'lɪtɪkəʊ-/. **Politico-** is used to form adjectives that describe something as being both political and the other thing that is mentioned. *...the
capitalist politico-economic system.* COMB

poli·tics /'pɒlɪtɪks/. **1 Politics** are the actions or
activities concerned with achieving and using power in a country or society. The verb that follows
politics may be either singular or plural. *He quickly
involved himself in local politics... Politics is by no
means the only arena in which women are excelling.*
● See also **party politics. 2** Your **politics** are your
beliefs about how a country ought to be governed.
My politics are well to the left of centre. **3 Politics** is
the study of the ways in which countries are governed. *...young politics graduates.* **4 Politics** can be
used to talk about the ways that power is shared in
an organization and the ways it is affected by personal relationships between people who work together. The verb that follows **politics** may be either
singular or plural. *Office politics influence the working environment.* ◆◆◆◇ N-PLURAL / N-PLURAL / N-UNCOUNT / N-PLURAL

pol·ity /'pɒlɪti/ **polities.** A **polity** is an organized
society, such as a nation, city, or church, together
with its government and administration. N-COUNT FORMAL

pol·ka /'pɒlkə, AM 'pəʊlkə/ **polkas.** A **polka** is a
lively dance that was very popular in the nineteenth
century. ◆◇◇◇◇ N-COUNT

'polka dots; the form **polka-dot** is used as a modifier. **Polka dots** are very small spots printed on a
piece of cloth. See picture headed **patterns.** N-PLURAL

poll /pəʊl/ **polls, polling, polled. 1** A **poll** is a
survey in which people are asked their opinions
about something, usually in order to find out how
popular something is or what people intend to do
in the future. *Polls show that the European treaty
has gained support in Denmark.* **2** If you **are polled**
on something, you are asked what you think about
it as part of a survey. *Audiences were going to be
polled on which of these pieces of contemporary music they liked best.* **3 The polls** means an election for
a country's government, or the place where people
go to vote in an election. *In 1945, Winston Churchill
was defeated at the polls... Voters are due to go to the
polls on Sunday.* **4** If a political party or a candidate
polls a particular number or percentage of votes,
they get that number or percentage of votes in an
election. **5** See also **deed poll, opinion poll, polling,
straw poll.** ◆◆◆◇ N-COUNT / VERB: be V-ed be V-ed on wh/n / N-PLURAL: the N / VERB: V n

pol·len /'pɒlən/ **pollens. Pollen** is a very fine powder produced by flowers in order to fertilize other
flowers. ◆◇◇◇◇ N-VAR

'pollen count, pollen counts. The **pollen count**
is a measure of how much pollen is in the air at a
particular place and time. N-COUNT

pol·li·nate /'pɒlɪneɪt/ **pollinates, pollinating,
pollinated.** When an insect **pollinates** a plant or
tree, it fertilizes it with pollen. ◆ **pol·li·na·tion** VERB: V n / N-UNCOUNT

/ˌpɒlɪ'neɪʃən/ *Without sufficient pollination, the growth of the corn is stunted.*

poll·ing /'pəʊlɪŋ/. Polling is the act of voting in an election. *There has been a busy start to polling in today's local elections.* ◆◇◇◇◇ N-UNCOUNT

'polling booth, polling booths. 1 Polling booths are the places where people go to vote in an election. **2** A polling booth is one of the compartments in a polling station where people vote. N-COUNT

'polling day. Polling day is the day on which people vote in an election. N-UNCOUNT

'polling station, polling stations. A polling station is a place, often a school or other public building, where people go to vote at an election. ◆◇◇◇◇ N-COUNT

poll·ster /'pəʊlstə/ **pollsters.** A pollster is a person or organization that conducts opinion polls. ◆◇◇◇◇ N-COUNT

'poll tax. In Britain, many people refer to local taxes as the poll tax. ◆◆◇◇◇ N-UNCOUNT

pol·lu·tant /pə'luːtənt/ **pollutants.** Pollutants are substances that pollute the environment, especially poisonous chemicals that are produced as waste by vehicles and by industrial processes. ◆◇◇◇◇ N-VAR

pol·lute /pə'luːt/ **pollutes, polluting, polluted.** To pollute water, air, or land means to make it dirty and dangerous to live in or to use, especially with poisonous chemicals or sewage. ♦ **pol·lut·ed** *The police have warned the city's inhabitants not to bathe in the polluted river.* ♦ **pol·lut·er, polluters.** *Governments decide what penalties to impose on polluters.* ◆◆◇◇◇ VERB: V n / ADJ-GRADED / N-COUNT

pol·lu·tion /pə'luːʃən/. **1** Pollution is poisonous or dirty substances that are polluting water, air, or land. *The level of pollution in the river was falling.* **2** Pollution is the process of polluting water, air, or land, especially with poisonous chemicals. ◆◆◇◇◇ N-UNCOUNT / N-UNCOUNT

polo /'pəʊləʊ/. Polo is a game played between two teams of players. The players ride horses and use wooden hammers with long handles to hit a ball. ● See also **water polo.** ◆◇◇◇◇ N-UNCOUNT

'polo neck, polo necks; also spelled **polo-neck.** A polo neck or a polo neck sweater is a sweater with a high neck which folds over. N-COUNT

'polo shirt, polo shirts. A polo shirt is a T-shirt with a collar. N-COUNT

pol·ter·geist /'pɒltəɡaɪst, AM 'pəʊl-/ **poltergeists.** A poltergeist is a ghost or supernatural force which is believed to move objects. N-COUNT

poly /'pɒli/ **polys.** A poly is the same as a **polytechnic.** *He wants to go to Manchester Poly to do Communication Studies.* ◆◇◇◇◇ N-COUNT BRITISH, INFORMAL

poly- /'pɒli-/. Poly- is used to form adjectives and nouns which indicate that many things or types of things are involved in something. For example, a **polysyllabic** word contains many syllables. PREFIX

poly·es·ter /'pɒli'estə, AM -es-/ **polyesters.** Polyester is a type of synthetic cloth used especially to make clothes. ◆◇◇◇◇ N-VAR

poly·eth·yl·ene /ˌpɒli'eθɪliːn/. Polyethylene is the same as **polythene.** N-UNCOUNT

po·lyga·mous /pə'lɪɡəməs/. In a **polygamous** society, people can be legally married to more than one person at the same time. A **polygamous** person, especially a man, is married to more than one person. ♦ **po·lyga·my** *Though polygamy is a dying practice, it is not yet dead.* ADJ / N-UNCOUNT

poly·glot /'pɒliɡlɒt/ **polyglots.** A polyglot is a person who speaks or understands many languages. ▶ Also an adjective. *...Chicago's polyglot population.* N-COUNT / ADJ

poly·graph /'pɒliɡrɑːf, -ɡræf/ **polygraphs.** A polygraph or a polygraph test is a test in which someone asks you questions and a machine records any changes in your blood pressure, temperature, or breathing in order to find out if you are telling the truth when you answer. N-COUNT

poly·mer /'pɒlimə/ **polymers.** A polymer is a chemical compound with large molecules made of many smaller molecules of the same kind. ◆◇◇◇◇ N-COUNT

pol·yp /'pɒlɪp/ **polyps. 1** A polyp is a small growth on a surface inside your body. **2** A polyp is a small N-COUNT

animal that lives in the sea. It has a hollow body like a tube and tentacles around its mouth.

poly·pro·py·lene /ˌpɒli'prɒpɪliːn/. Polypropylene is a strong, flexible synthetic material used to make things such as rope, carpet, and pipes. N-UNCOUNT

poly·sty·rene /ˌpɒli'staɪriːn/. Polystyrene is a very light, plastic substance used especially to make containers or as an insulating material. The usual American word is **styrofoam.** N-UNCOUNT BRITISH

poly·tech·nic /ˌpɒli'teknɪk/ **polytechnics.** In Britain, a **polytechnic** is a college where you can go after leaving school in order to study academic subjects at various levels up to degree level or to train for particular jobs. In 1992, all the polytechnics in Britain became universities. ♦♦◇◇◇ N-VAR

poly·thene /'pɒliθiːn/. Polythene is a type of plastic made into thin sheets or bags and used especially to keep food fresh or to keep things dry. *...a polythene bag.* ◆◇◇◇◇ N-UNCOUNT

poly·un·satu·rate /ˌpɒliʌn'sætʃərət/ **polyunsaturates.** Polyunsaturates are types of animal or vegetable fats which are used to make cooking oil and margarine. They are thought to be less harmful to your body than other fats. ♦ **poly·un·satu·rat·ed** /ˌpɒliʌn'sætʃəreɪtɪd/. *Use polyunsaturated spread instead of butter.* ◆◇◇◇◇ N-COUNT / ADJ

poly·urethane /ˌpɒli'jʊərəθeɪn/ **polyurethanes.** Polyurethane is a plastic material used especially to make paint or types of foam and rubber. N-VAR

pom /pɒm/ **poms.** A pom is the same as a **pommy.** N-COUNT

pom·egran·ate /'pɒmɪɡrænɪt/ **pomegranates.** A pomegranate is a round fruit with a thick reddish skin. It contains lots of small seeds with juicy flesh around them. N-VAR

pom·mel /'pʌməl, 'pɒm-/ **pommels.** A pommel is the part of a saddle that rises up at the front, or a knob that is fixed there. N-COUNT

pom·my /'pɒmi/ **pommies;** also spelled **pommie.** A **pommy** is an English person; a slightly offensive word. N-COUNT PRAGMATICS AUSTRALIAN

pomp /pɒmp/. Pomp is the use of a lot of ceremony, fine clothes, and decorations, especially on a special occasion. *...the coronation of a British monarch, with all its pomp and grandeur.* ◆◇◇◇◇ N-UNCOUNT

pomp·ous /'pɒmpəs/. **1** If you describe someone as **pompous,** you mean that they behave or speak in a very serious way because they think they are more important than they really are; used showing disapproval. ♦ **pom·pos·ity** /pɒm'pɒsɪti/ *Einstein was a scientist who hated pomposity.* ♦ **pomp·ous·ly** *Robin told me firmly and pompously that he had an important business appointment.* **2** A pompous building or ceremony is very grand and elaborate. ◆◇◇◇◇ ADJ-GRADED PRAGMATICS / N-UNCOUNT / ADV-GRADED / ADJ-GRADED

pon·cho /'pɒntʃəʊ/ **ponchos.** A poncho is a piece of clothing that consists of a long piece of material, usually wool, with a hole cut in the middle through which you put your head. N-COUNT

pond /pɒnd/ **ponds.** A pond is a small area of water that is smaller than a lake. *...a bench beside the duck pond. ...a garden pond.* ◆◆◇◇◇ N-COUNT

pon·der /'pɒndə/ **ponders, pondering, pondered.** If you ponder a question, you think about it carefully. *The Prime Minister pondered on when to go to the polls... I'm continually pondering how to improve the team.* ◆◆◇◇◇ V on/over n / V wh / Also V

pon·der·ous /'pɒndərəs/. **1** Ponderous writing or speech is very serious, uses more words than necessary, and is rather dull. ♦ **pon·der·ous·ly** *...the rather ponderously titled 'Recommendation for National Reconciliation and Salvation'.* **2** A movement or action that is ponderous is very slow or clumsy. ♦ **ponderously** *Wilson shifted ponderously in his chair.* ◆◇◇◇◇ ADJ-GRADED / ADV with v / ADJ-GRADED WRITTEN / ADV-GRADED ADV with v

pong /pɒŋ, AM pɔːŋ/ **pongs.** A pong is an unpleasant smell. *...the pong of milk and sick and nappies.* N-COUNT BRITISH, INFORMAL

pon·tiff /'pɒntɪf/ **pontiffs.** The Pontiff is the Pope. N-COUNT

pon·tifi·cate /pɒn'tɪfɪkeɪt/ **pontificates, pontificating, pontificated.** If someone pontificates about something, they state their opinions as if they are the only correct ones and nobody could VERB V about/on n Also V

possibly argue against them. *Politicians like to pontificate about falling standards.*

pon·toon /ˌpɒnˈtuːn/ **pontoons.** A **pontoon** is a N-COUNT floating platform, often one used to support a bridge.

pony /ˈpəʊni/ **ponies, ponying, ponied.** A **pony** ◆◇◇◇◇ is a type of small horse. N-COUNT

pony·tail /ˈpəʊniteɪl/ **ponytails;** also spelled N-COUNT **pony-tail.** A **ponytail** is a hairstyle in which someone's hair is tied up at the back of the head and hangs down like a tail.

poo /puː/ **poos. Poo** is excrement; a word used by ◆◇◇◇◇ children. N-VAR
INFORMAL

pooch /puːtʃ/ **pooches.** A **pooch** is a dog; a word N-COUNT used by journalists. INFORMAL

poo·dle /ˈpuːdəl/ **poodles.** A **poodle** is a type of ◆◇◇◇◇ dog with thick curly hair. N-COUNT

poof /pʊf/ **poofs;** also spelled **pouf.** Some people EXCLAM say **poof** to indicate that something happened very suddenly. *Poof! they disappear in a blinding flash of light.*

pooh-pooh /ˌpuː ˈpuː/ **pooh-poohs, pooh-** VERB: V n **poohing, pooh-poohed.** If someone **pooh-poohs** an idea or suggestion, they say or imply that it is foolish, impractical, or unnecessary.

pool /puːl/ **pools, pooling, pooled. 1** A **pool** is ◆◆◇◇ the same as a **swimming pool.** *...a heated indoor* N-COUNT *pool.* **2** A **pool** is a fairly small area of still water. N-COUNT *...beautiful gardens filled with pools, fountains and rare birds.* ● See also **rock pool. 3** A **pool** of liquid N-COUNT: or light is a small area of it on the ground or on a N of n surface. *She was found lying in a pool of blood.*

4 A **pool** of people, money, or things is a quantity or N-COUNT: number of them that is available for an organization with supp or group to use. *The new proposal would create a reserve pool of cash.* ● See also **car pool. 5** If a group of VERB people or organizations **pool** their money, knowledge, or equipment, they share it or put it together so that it can be used for a particular purpose. *Philip and I pooled our savings to start up my business.*

6 Pool is a game played on a large cloth-covered ta- N-UNCOUNT ble. Players use a long stick called a cue to hit a white ball so that it knocks coloured balls into six holes around the edge of the table. **7** If you do **the pools,** N-PLURAL: you take part in a gambling competition in which the N people try to win money by guessing correctly the re- BRITISH sults of football matches. *The odds of winning the pools are about one in 20 million.*

poop /puːp/ **poops.** The **poop** of an old-fashioned N-COUNT sailing ship is the raised structure at the back end of it. *...the poop deck.*

pooped /puːpt/. If you are **pooped**, you are very ADJ-GRADED tired. *No. I am not angry. It's just that I'm pooped.* v-link ADJ
INFORMAL

poor /pʊə, pɔː/ **poorer, poorest. 1** Someone who ◆◆◆◇ is **poor** has very little money and few possessions. ADJ-GRADED *He was one of thirteen children from a poor family.* ▶ **The poor** are people who are poor. *Even the poor* N-PLURAL *have their pride.* **2** A **poor** country or area is inhab- ADJ-GRADED ited by people with very little money and few pos- sessions. *...children in a poor neighborhood.*

3 You use **poor** to express your sympathy for some- ADJ: ADJ n one. *Poor Gordon!* PRAGMATICS

4 If you describe something as **poor**, you mean that it ADJ-GRADED is of a low quality or standard or that it is in bad condi- tion. *The flat was in a poor state of repair... The wine was poor.* ◆ **poor·ly** *Some are living in poorly built* ADV-GRADED *dormitories, even in tents.* **5** If you describe an ADJ-GRADED amount, rate, or number as **poor**, you mean that it is less than expected or less than is considered reason- able. *...poor wages and working conditions.* ◆ **poorly** ADV-GRADED *The evening meetings were poorly attended.* **6** You use ADJ-GRADED **poor** to describe someone who is not very skilful in a particular activity. *He was a poor actor... Hospitals are poor at collecting information.* ◆ **poorly** *Today I* ADV-GRADED *played as poorly as I ever have.* **7** If something is **poor** ADJ-GRADED in a particular quality or substance, it contains very v-link ADJ in n little of the quality or substance. *...soil that is poor in zinc.*

poor·house /ˈpʊəhaʊs, ˈpɔː-/ **poorhouses;** also N-COUNT spelled **poor-house.** In former times, a **poorhouse** was an institution in which poor people could live.

poor·ly /ˈpʊəli, ˈpɔː-/. If someone is **poorly,** they ◆◇◇◇◇ are ill. The American word is **sick.** *Miss Cartwright* ADJ-GRADED *looks very poorly.* ● See also **poor.** BRITISH
INFORMAL

poor re·lation, poor relations. If you describe N-COUNT one thing as a **poor relation** of another, you mean that it is similar to or part of the other thing, but is considered to be inferior to it. *Watercolour still seems to be the poor relation of oil painting.*

pop /pɒp/ **pops, popping, popped. 1 Pop** is ◆◆◆◇ modern music that usually has a strong rhythm and N-UNCOUNT uses electronic equipment. *...a life-size poster of a pop star... I know nothing about pop music.*

2 You can refer to fizzy drinks such as lemonade as N-UNCOUNT **pop.** *...a massive beef sandwich washed down by a bot- tle of pop.* **3 Pop** is used to represent a short sharp N-COUNT; sound, for example the sound made by bursting a bal- SOUND loon or by pulling a cork out of a bottle. *Each corn ker- nel will make a loud pop when cooked... His back tyre just went pop on a motorway.* **4** If something **pops**, it VERB makes a short sharp sound. *The cork popped and shot* V *to the ceiling.* **5** If your eyes **pop** or **pop out**, you look VERB very surprised or excited when you see something. *My* V *eyes popped at the sight of the rich variety of food on* Also V out *show.* INFORMAL

6 If you **pop** something somewhere, you put it there VERB quickly. *Marianne got a couple of mugs from the dress-* V n prep/adv *er and popped a teabag into each of them.* **7** If you **pop** INFORMAL *somewhere,* you go there for a short time. *He's just* VERB *popped out to the shops. He won't be a minute.* V adv/prep
INFORMAL

8 Some people call their father **Pop.** *We got so worried* N-FAMILY *but Pop didn't want to take her to the doctors.* AMERICAN,
INFORMAL

9 ● to **pop the question:** see **question.**

pop up. If someone or something **pops up,** they ap- PHRASAL VB pear in a place or situation unexpectedly. *You solved* V P one problem and another would immediately pop up.* INFORMAL ● See also **pop-up.**

pop. /pɒp/. **pop.** is an abbreviation for 'popula- tion'. *...Somalia, pop. 7.9 million.*

'pop art. Pop art is a style of modern art which be- N-UNCOUNT gan in the 1960s. It uses bright colours and takes a lot of its techniques and subject matter from every- day modern life.

pop·corn /ˈpɒpkɔːn/. **Popcorn** is a snack which ◆◇◇◇◇ consists of grains of maize that have been heated N-UNCOUNT until they have burst and become large and light.

pope /pəʊp/ **popes.** The **Pope** is the head of the ◆◆◇◇ Roman Catholic Church. *...Pope John Paul II.*

pop·lar /ˈpɒplə/ **poplars.** A **poplar** is a type of tall ◆◇◇◇◇ thin tree. N-VAR

pop·pa·dom /ˈpɒpədɒm/ **poppadoms.** A **poppa-** N-COUNT **dom** is a very thin circular crisp made from a mixture of flour and water, which is fried in oil. Poppadoms are usually eaten with Indian food.

pop·per /ˈpɒpə/ **poppers.** A **popper** is a device for N-COUNT fastening clothes. It consists of two pieces of plastic BRITISH or metal which you press together.

pop·py /ˈpɒpi/ **poppies.** A **poppy** is a plant with a ◆◇◇◇◇ large, delicate flower, usually red. Opium is ob- N-COUNT tained from one type of poppy.

popu·lace /ˈpɒpjʊləs/. The **populace** of a country ◆◇◇◇◇ is its people, especially its working-class people. *The* N-UNCOUNT *President was much-loved among a large section of* FORMAL *Pakistan's populace.*

popu·lar /ˈpɒpjʊlə/. **1** Something that is **popular** is ◆◆◆◇ enjoyed or liked by a lot of people. *This is the most* ADJ-GRADED *popular ball game ever devised... Chocolate sauce is always popular with youngsters.* ◆ **popu·lar·ity** N-UNCOUNT /ˌpɒpjʊˈlærɪti/ *Golf increased in popularity during the 1980s.* **2** Someone who is **popular** is liked by ADJ-GRADED most people, or by most people in a particular group. *He was the most popular politician in France.* ◆ **popularity** *...his popularity with ordinary* N-UNCOUNT *people.* **3 Popular** newspapers, television pro- ADJ: ADJ n grammes, or forms of art are aimed at ordinary peo- ple and not at experts or intellectuals. *...one of the classics of modern popular music. ...the popular cul- ture of his native Mexico.* **4 Popular** ideas, feelings, ADJ

or attitudes are approved of or held by most people. *Contrary to popular belief, the oil companies can't control the price of crude... The military government has been unable to win popular support.* ♦ **popularity** *Over time, though, Watson's views gained in popularity.* N-UNCOUNT

5 Popular is used to describe political activities which involve the ordinary people of a country. *President Ferdinand Marcos was overthrown by a popular uprising.* ADJ: ADJ n

popu·lar·ize /'pɒpjʊləraɪz/ **popularizes, popularizing, popularized;** also spelled **popularise** in British English. **1** To **popularize** something means to make a lot of people interested in it and able to enjoy it. ♦ **popu·lari·za·tion** /ˌpɒpjʊləraɪˈzeɪʃən/ *...the popularisation of sport through television.* ◆◇◇◇◇
VERB: V n
N-UNCOUNT

2 To **popularize** an academic subject or scientific idea means to make it more easily understandable to ordinary people. ♦ **popularization** *He became world famous for his popularisation of science.* VERB: V n
N-UNCOUNT

popu·lar·ly /'pɒpjʊləli/. **1** If something or someone is **popularly** known as something, most people call them that, although it is not their official name or title. *...the Mesozoic era, more popularly known as the age of dinosaurs. ...an infection popularly called mad cow disease.* **2** If something is **popularly** believed or supposed to be the case, most people believe or suppose it to be the case, although it may not be true. *Schizophrenia is not a 'split mind' as is popularly believed.* **3** A **popularly** elected leader or government has been elected by a majority of the people in a country. ◆◇◇◇◇
ADV-GRADED:
ADV with -ed
ADV:
ADV -ed
ADV:
ADV -ed

popu·late /'pɒpjʊleɪt/ **populates, populating, populated. 1** If an area **is populated** by certain people or animals, those people or animals live there, often in large numbers. *Before all this the island was populated by native American Arawaks.* ♦ **popu·lat·ed** *The southeast is the most densely populated area.* ♦ **-populated** *Army tanks razed half the houses in the Croat-populated part of Glina.* **2** To **populate** an area means to cause people to live there. *Successive regimes annexed the region and populated it with lowland people.* **3** The people or characters who **populate** an area of public life or a piece of entertainment are the people or characters in it. *...the sort of low-life characters who populate the film.* ◆◇◇◇◇
VERB
be V-ed
Also V n
ADJ-GRADED
COMB
VERB
V n with n
Also V n
VERB
V n

popu·la·tion /ˌpɒpjʊˈleɪʃən/ **populations. 1** The **population** of a country or area is all the people who live in it. *Bangladesh now has a population of about 110 million.* **2** If you refer to a particular type of **population** in a country or area, you are referring to all the people or animals of that type there. *...75.6 per cent of the male population over sixteen.* ◆◆◆◇
N-COUNT
N-COUNT
FORMAL

popu·lism /'pɒpjʊlɪzəm/. **Populism** refers to political activities or ideas that claim to promote the interests and opinions of ordinary people. N-UNCOUNT
FORMAL

popu·list /'pɒpjʊlɪst/ **populists.** If you describe a politician or an artist as **populist**, you mean that they behave according to the principles of populism. *...Jose Sarney, the current populist president.* ▶ A **populist** is someone who expresses populist views. ◆◇◇◇◇
ADJ-GRADED
FORMAL
N-COUNT

popu·lous /'pɒpjʊləs/. A **populous** country or area has a lot of people living in it. *Indonesia, with 185 million people, is the fifth most populous country in the world.* ◆◇◇◇◇
ADJ-GRADED
FORMAL

pop-up. 1 A **pop-up book**, usually a children's book, has pictures that stand up when you open the pages. **2** A **pop-up toaster** has a mechanism that pushes slices of bread up when they are toasted. ◆◇◇◇◇
ADJ: ADJ n
ADJ: ADJ n

porce·lain /'pɔːsəlɪn/ **porcelains. 1** Porcelain is a hard, shiny substance made by heating clay. It is used to make delicate cups, plates, and ornaments. *...tall white porcelain vases.* **2** A **porcelain** is an ornament that is made of porcelain. You can refer to a number of such ornaments as **porcelain**. ◆◇◇◇◇
N-UNCOUNT
N-VAR

porch /pɔːtʃ/ **porches. 1** A **porch** is a sheltered area at the entrance to a building. It has a roof and sometimes has walls. See picture headed **house and** ◆◇◇◇◇
N-COUNT

flat. 2 A **porch** is a raised platform built along the outside wall of a house and often covered with a roof. The British word is **veranda**. N-COUNT
AMERICAN

por·cine /'pɔːsaɪn/. If you describe someone as **porcine**, you mean that they look like a pig. *...a porcine countenance.* ADJ-GRADED
LITERARY

por·cu·pine /'pɔːkjʊpaɪn/ **porcupines.** A **porcupine** is an animal with many long, thin, sharp spikes on its back that stick out as protection when it is attacked. N-COUNT

pore /pɔː/ **pores, poring, pored. 1** Your **pores** are the tiny holes in your skin. **2** The **pores** of a plant are the tiny holes on its surface. **3** If you **pore over** or **through** information, you look at it and study it very carefully. *We spent hours poring over travel brochures.* ◆◇◇◇◇
N-COUNT
N-COUNT
VERB
V over/
through n

pork /pɔːk/. **Pork** is meat from a pig, usually fresh and not smoked or salted. ◆◆◇◇
N-UNCOUNT

'pork barrel; also spelled **pork-barrel.** If you say that someone is using **pork barrel** politics, you mean that they are spending a lot of government money on a local project in order to win the votes of the people who live in that area; used showing disapproval. N-SING
PRAGMATICS

pork 'pie, pork pies. A **pork pie** is a round pie with cooked pork inside. N-VAR

porn /pɔːn/. **Porn** is the same as **pornography**. *...a porn cinema.* ● See also **soft porn, hard porn.** ◆◇◇◇◇
N-UNCOUNT
INFORMAL
ADJ
INFORMAL

por·no /'pɔːnoʊ/. **Porno** is the same as **pornographic**. *...porno mags.*

por·nog·ra·pher /pɔːˈnɒɡrəfə/ **pornographers.** A **pornographer** is a person who produces or sells pornography; used showing disapproval. N-COUNT
PRAGMATICS

por·nog·ra·phy /pɔːˈnɒɡrəfi/. **Pornography** refers to books, magazines, and films that are designed to cause sexual excitement by showing naked people or referring to sexual acts; used showing disapproval. *...a new campaign against pornography in China.* ♦ **por·no·graph·ic** /ˌpɔːnəˈɡræfɪk/ *I found out he'd been watching pornographic videos.* ◆◆◇◇
N-UNCOUNT
PRAGMATICS
ADJ-GRADED

po·ros·ity /pɔːˈrɒsɪti/. **Porosity** is the state of being porous. *...the porosity of the coal.* N-UNCOUNT
FORMAL

po·rous /'pɔːrəs/. Something that is **porous** has many small holes in it, which water and air can pass through. *...a porous material like sand or charcoal.* ◆◇◇◇◇
ADJ-GRADED

por·poise /'pɔːpəs/ **porpoises.** A **porpoise** is a sea animal that looks similar to a dolphin. N-COUNT

por·ridge /'pɒrɪdʒ, AM 'pɔːr-/. **Porridge** is a thick sticky food made from oats cooked in water or milk and eaten hot, especially for breakfast. ◆◇◇◇◇
N-UNCOUNT

port /pɔːt/ **ports. 1** A **port** is a town by the sea or on a river, which has a harbour. *...the Mediterranean port of Marseilles.* **2** A **port** is a harbour area with docks and warehouses, where ships load or unload goods or passengers. ◆◆◆◇
N-COUNT
N-COUNT

3 The **port** side of a ship is the left side when you are on it and facing towards the front. *Her official number is carved on the port side of the forecabin.* ▶ Also a noun. *USS Ogden turned to port.* ADJ
N-UNCOUNT

4 Port is a type of strong, sweet red wine. N-UNCOUNT

port·able /'pɔːtəbəl/ **portables. 1** A **portable** machine or device is designed to be easily carried or moved. *I always carry a portable computer with me.* ♦ **port·abil·ity** /ˌpɔːtəˈbɪlɪti/ *Portability was as important as reliability.* **2** A **portable** is something such as a television, radio, or computer which can be easily carried or moved. *We bought a colour portable for the bedroom.* ◆◆◇◇
ADJ-GRADED
N-UNCOUNT
N-COUNT

por·tal /'pɔːtəl/ **portals.** A **portal** is a large impressive doorway at the entrance to a building. *I went in through the royal portal.* N-COUNT
LITERARY

port·cul·lis /pɔːtˈkʌlɪs/ **portcullises.** A **portcullis** is a strong gate above an entrance to a castle or fort, which used to be lowered to the ground in order to keep out enemies. N-COUNT

por·tend /pɔːˈtend/ **portends, portending, portended.** If something **portends** an event or occurrence, it indicates that it is likely to happen in the future. *The change did not portend a basic improvement in social conditions.* VERB
V n
FORMAL

por·tent /'pɔːtent/ **portents.** A **portent** is some- N-COUNT
thing that indicates what is likely to happen in the FORMAL
future. *The savage civil war there could be a portent
of what's to come in the rest of the region.*

por·ten·tous /pɔː'tentəs/. **1** If someone's way of ADJ-GRADED
speaking, writing, or behaving is **portentous**, they PRAGMATICS
speak, write, or behave more seriously than neces- FORMAL
sary because they want to impress other people;
used showing disapproval. *There was nothing portentous or solemn about him.* **2** Something that is ADJ-GRADED
portentous is important in indicating or affecting FORMAL
future events. *'This film has been made at the right
time,' she says. 'It has proved horribly portentous.'*

por·ter /'pɔːtə/ **porters. 1** A **porter** is a person ◆◆◇◇◇
whose job is to be in charge of the entrance of a N-COUNT
building such as a hotel. The usual American word BRITISH
is **doorman. 2** A **porter** is a person whose job is to N-COUNT
carry things, for example people's luggage at a rail-
way station or in a hotel. **3** In a hospital, a **porter** is N-COUNT
someone whose job is to move patients around.

port·fo·lio /pɔːt'fəʊliəʊ/ **portfolios. 1** A **portfolio** ◆◆◇◇◇
is a set of pictures by someone, or photographs of N-COUNT
examples of their work, which they use when entering competitions or applying for work. *After dinner
that evening, Edith showed them a portfolio of her
own political cartoons.* **2** In finance, a **portfolio** is N-COUNT
the combination of shares or other investments that
a particular investor or company has. **3** In politics, a N-COUNT
portfolio is a minister's responsibility for a particular area of a government's activities. *He has held the
defence portfolio since the first free elections in 1990.*
● In Britain, a **minister without portfolio** is a poli- PHRASE
tician who is given the rank of minister without being given responsibility for any particular area of a
government's activities.

port·hole /'pɔːthəʊl/ **portholes.** A **porthole** is a N-COUNT
small round window in the side of a ship or aircraft.

por·ti·co /'pɔːtɪkəʊ/ **porticoes** or **porticos.** A N-COUNT
portico is a large covered area at the entrance to a FORMAL
building, with pillars supporting the roof.

por·tion /'pɔːʃən/ **portions. 1** A **portion** of some- ◆◆◇◇◇
thing is a part of it. *Damage was confined to a small* N-COUNT:
portion of the castle... I have spent a fairly consider- N of n
able portion of my life here. **2** A **portion** is the N-COUNT
amount of food that is given to one person at a
meal. *Desserts can be substituted by a portion of
fresh fruit.*

port·ly /'pɔːtli/ **portlier, portliest.** A **portly** per- ADJ-GRADED
son, especially a man, is rather fat. *...a portly* FORMAL
middle-aged man.

‚port of 'call, ports of call. 1 A **port of call** is a N-COUNT
place where a ship stops during a journey. *Their
first port of call will be Cape Town.* **2** A **port of call** N-COUNT
is any place where you stop for a short time when INFORMAL
you are visiting several places, shops, or people. *The
local tourist office should be your first port of call in
any town.*

por·trait /'pɔːtreɪt/ **portraits.** A **portrait** is a ◆◆◆◇◇
painting, drawing, or photograph of a particular N-COUNT
person. *...a portrait of the Queen.*

por·trait·ist /'pɔːtreɪtɪst/ **portraitists.** A portrait- N-COUNT
ist is an artist who paints people's portraits. FORMAL

por·trai·ture /'pɔːtrɪtʃə/. **Portraiture** is the art of N-UNCOUNT
painting or drawing portraits. FORMAL

por·tray /pɔː'treɪ/ **portrays, portraying, por-** ◆◆◇◇◇
trayed. 1 When an actor or actress **portrays** some- VERB
one, he or she plays that person in a play or film. *He* V n
*portrayed the king in a Los Angeles revival of 'Cam-
elot'.* ◆ **por·tray·al** /pɔː'treɪəl/ **portrayals** *Mr Ying* N-COUNT
*is well-known for his portrayal of a prison guard in
the film 'The Last Emperor'.* **2** When a writer or art- VERB
ist **portrays** something, he or she writes a descrip- V n
tion or produces a painting of it. *...this northern
novelist, who accurately portrays provincial domestic
life.* ◆ **portrayal** *...a moving portrayal of St John* N-COUNT
the Evangelist. **3** If a film, book, or television pro- VERB
gramme **portrays** someone in a certain way, it rep- V n asn
resents them in that way. *The programme portrayed
her as a 'lady of easy virtue'.* ◆ **portrayal** *...a sensi-* N-COUNT

tive and often funny portrayal of a friendship between two 11-year-old boys.

pos. Pos. is the written abbreviation for **positive.**

pose /pəʊz/ **poses, posing, posed. 1** If some- ◆◆◆◇◇
thing **poses** a problem or a danger, it is the cause of VERB
that problem or danger. *His ill health poses serious* V n
problems for the future. **2** If you **pose** a question, VERB
you ask it. If you **pose** an issue that needs consider- V n
ing, you mention the issue. *When I finally posed the* FORMAL
question, 'Why?' he merely shrugged.
3 If you **pose as** someone, you pretend to be that per- VERB
son in order to deceive people. *The team posed as* V as n
drug dealers to trap the ringleaders. **4** If you **pose for** a VERB: V
photograph or painting, you stay in a particular posi-
tion so that someone can photograph you or paint
you. ▶ Also a noun. *We have had several preliminary* N-COUNT
sittings in various poses. **5** You can say that people **are** VERB
posing when they are behaving in an insincere or ex- PRAGMATICS
aggerated way because they want to make a particular V
impression on other people; used showing disapproval. *He criticized them for dressing outrageously
and posing pretentiously.* ▶ Also a noun. *In many* N-COUNT
writers modesty is a pose.

pos·er /'pəʊzə/ **posers. 1** A **poser** is the same as a N-COUNT
poseur. 2 A **poser** is a difficult problem or puzzle. N-COUNT
Here is a little poser for you. DATED

po·seur /pəʊ'zɜː/ **poseurs.** You can describe N-COUNT
someone as a **poseur** when you think that they be- PRAGMATICS
have in an insincere or exaggerated way because
they want to make a particular impression on other
people; used showing disapproval. *I am sometimes
accused of being an inveterate poseur.*

posh /pɒʃ/ **posher, poshest. 1** If you describe ◆◇◇◇◇
something as **posh**, you mean that it is smart, fash- ADJ-GRADED
ionable, and expensive. *I took her to a posh hotel for* INFORMAL
a cocktail. ...a posh car. **2** If you describe a person ADJ-GRADED
as **posh**, you mean that they belong to or behave as INFORMAL
if they belong to the upper classes. *He sounded so
posh on the phone.*

pos·it /'pɒzɪt/ **posits, positing, posited.** If you VERB
posit something, you suggest or assume it as the V n
basis for an argument or calculation. *Several writers* Also V that
have posited the idea of a universal consciousness. FORMAL

po·si·tion /pə'zɪʃən/ **positions, positioning,** ◆◆◆◆◆
positioned. 1 The **position** of someone or some- N-COUNT
thing is the place where they are in relation to other
things. *The ship was identified, and its name and
position were reported to the coastguard.* **2** If some- PHRASE
one or something is **in position**, they are in their
correct or usual place or arrangement. *Some 28,000
US troops are moving into position.* **3** When some- N-COUNT
one or something is in a particular **position**, they
are sitting, lying, or arranged in that way. *It is crucial that the upper back and neck are held in an
erect position... Mr Dambar raised himself to a
sitting position.* **4** If you **position** something some- VERB
where, you put it there carefully, so that it is in the V n prep
right place or position. *Position trailing plants near
the edges.*
5 Your **position** in society is the role and the impor- N-COUNT
tance that you have in it. *Adjustment to their changing
role and position in society can be painful for some old
people.* **6** A **position** in a company or organization is a N-COUNT
job. *He left a career in teaching to take up a position* FORMAL
with the Arts Council. **7** Your **position** in a race or N-COUNT
competition is how well you did in relation to the other competitors or how well you are doing. *By the ninth
hour the car was running in eighth position.*
8 You can describe your situation at a particular time N-COUNT
by saying that you are in a particular **position**. *He's going to be in a very difficult position indeed if things go
badly for him.* **9** If you are **in a position** to do some- N-SING:
thing, you are able to do it. If you are **in no position** to N to-inf
do something, you are unable to do it. *I am not in a
position to comment.*
10 Your **position** on a particular matter is your atti- N-COUNT
tude towards it or your opinion of it. *The former Soviet* FORMAL
*Union has been reluctant to state a clear position on
the crisis.*

posi·tive /ˈpɒzɪtɪv/. **1** If you are **positive** about things, you are hopeful and confident, and think of the good aspects of a situation rather than the bad ones. *Be positive about your future and get on with living a normal life.* ♦ **posi·tive·ly** *Try thinking positively about yourself.* **2** A **positive** fact, situation, or experience is pleasant and helpful to you in some way. *Working abroad should be an exciting and positive experience.* ▶ **The positive** in a situation is the good and pleasant aspects of it. **3** If you make a **positive** decision or take **positive** action, you do something definite in order to deal with a task or problem. *He was expected to make a very positive contribution to the 1996 Games organisation.* **4** A **positive** response to something indicates agreement, approval, or encouragement. *There's been a positive response to the UN Secretary-General's recent peace efforts.* ♦ **positively** *This shows voters would respond positively to a good campaign argument.* **5** If you are **positive** about something, you are completely sure about it. *I'm as positive as I can be about it.* **6 Positive** evidence gives definite proof of the truth or identity of something. *There was no positive evidence that any birth defects had arisen.* ● **proof positive**: see **proof.** ♦ **positively** *He has positively identified the body.* **7** If a medical or scientific test is **positive**, it shows that something has happened or is present. *If the test is positive, a course of antibiotics may be prescribed.* ● **HIV positive**: see **HIV. 8** You can use **positive** to emphasize a noun. *Good day to you, Bernard! It's a positive delight to see you.* ● See also **positively. 9** A **positive number** is greater than zero. *...a simple numbers game with negative and positive numbers.*

ADJ-GRADED

ADV-GRADED:
ADV after v
ADJ-GRADED

N-SING:
the N
ADJ-GRADED

ADJ-GRADED

ADV:
ADV after v
ADJ-GRADED:
v-link ADJ

ADJ: ADJ n

ADV:
ADV with v
ADJ

ADJ
PRAGMATICS
DATED

ADJ: ADJ n

,positive discrimi'nation. Positive discrimination means making sure that members of disadvantaged groups, such as racial minorities or women, get an appropriate share of the opportunities available. The American term is **affirmative action.**

N-UNCOUNT
BRITISH

posi·tive·ly /ˈpɒzɪtɪvli/. **1** You use **positively** to emphasize that something really is the case, although it may sound surprising or extreme. *He's changed since he came back—he seems positively cheerful.* **2** You use **positively** to emphasize that you really mean what you are saying. *This is positively the worst thing that I can even imagine.*

♦◇◇◇◇
ADV
PRAGMATICS

ADV:
ADV adj-
superl
PRAGMATICS

posi·tiv·ism /ˈpɒzɪtɪvɪzm/. **Positivism** is a philosophical system which accepts only things that can be seen or proved. ♦ **posi·tiv·ist, positivists** *By far the most popular idea is the positivist one that we should keep only the facts.*

N-UNCOUNT

N-COUNT

poss /pɒs/. **Poss** is an abbreviation for 'possible'. *Tell them I'll be there as soon as poss.*

INFORMAL,
BRITISH

pos·se /ˈpɒsi/ **posses. 1** A **posse of** people is a group of people with the same job or purpose. *He refused to engage in conversation with a posse of reporters.* **2** In former times, in the United States, a **posse** was a group of men who were brought together by the local sheriff to help him chase and capture a criminal.

♦◇◇◇◇
N-COUNT:
N of n
INFORMAL
N-COUNT

pos·sess /pəˈzes/ **possesses, possessing, possessed. 1** If you **possess** something, you have it or own it. *He is said to possess a fortune of more than two and a half thousand-million dollars.* **2** If someone or something **possesses** a particular quality, ability, or feature, they have it. *...individuals who are deemed to possess the qualities of sense, loyalty and discretion.* **3** If a feeling or belief **possesses** you, it strongly influences your thinking or behaviour. *Absolute terror possessed her.* **4** See also **possessed. 5** If you ask **what possessed** someone to do something, you are emphasizing your great surprise that they have done something which you consider foolish or dangerous. *What on earth had possessed her to agree to marry him?*

♦♦◇◇◇
VB: no
passive,
no cont
V n
VB: no cont
V n
FORMAL

VERB
V n
LITERARY

PHRASE
PRAGMATICS

pos·sessed /pəˈzest/. **1** If someone is described as being **possessed** by the devil or by an evil spirit, it is believed that their mind and body are controlled by the devil or by the evil spirit. *She even*

♦◇◇◇◇
ADJ:
v-link ADJ

claimed the couple's daughter was possessed by the devil. **2** If someone or something is **possessed of** a particular quality, ability, or feature, they have that quality, ability, or feature. If someone is **possessed of** a particular feeling or belief, they have that feeling or belief. *He is possessed of the most brilliant talents.* **3** See also **possess.**

ADJ:
v-link ADJ of n
FORMAL

pos·ses·sion /pəˈzeʃən/ **possessions. 1** If you are in **possession** of something, you have it, because you have obtained it or because it belongs to you. *Those documents are now in the possession of the Guardian. ...illegal possession of firearms.* **2** Your **possessions** are the things that you own or have with you at a particular time. *People had lost their homes and all their possessions.* **3** A belief in **possession** by the devil or by an evil spirit is the belief that a person's mind and body can be controlled or are being controlled by the devil or by an evil spirit.

♦♦◇◇◇
N-UNCOUNT
FORMAL

N-COUNT

N-UNCOUNT

pos·ses·sive /pəˈzesɪv/ **possessives. 1** Someone who is **possessive** about another person wants all that person's love and attention. *Danny could be very jealous and possessive about me.* ♦ **pos·ses·sive·ness** *I've ruined every relationship with my possessiveness.* **2** Someone who is **possessive** about things that they own does not like other people to use them. *People were very possessive about their coupons.* **3** In grammar, a **possessive determiner** or **possessive adjective** is a word such as "my" or "his" which shows who or what something belongs to or is connected with. The **possessive** form of a name or noun has 's added to it, as in "Jenny's" or "cat's". ▶ A **possessive** is a possessive determiner or the possessive form of a name or noun.

♦◇◇◇◇
ADJ-GRADED

N-UNCOUNT
ADJ-GRADED

ADJ: ADJ n

N-COUNT

pos,sessive 'pronoun, possessive pronouns. A **possessive pronoun** is a pronoun such as 'mine', 'yours', or 'theirs' which is used to refer to something that belongs to someone.

N-COUNT

pos·ses·sor /pəˈzesə/ **possessors.** The **possessor** of something is the person who has it. *Ms Nova is the proud possessor of a truly incredible voice.*

N-COUNT
FORMAL

pos·sibil·ity /ˌpɒsɪˈbɪlɪti/ **possibilities. 1** If you say there is a **possibility** that something is the case or that something will happen, you mean that it might be the case or it might happen. *Tax on food has become a very real possibility.* **2** A **possibility** is one of several different things that could be done. *The government now owns a lot of our land – one possibility would be to compensate us with other property.*

♦♦♦♦◇
N-COUNT

N-COUNT

pos·sible /ˈpɒsɪbəl/ **possibles. 1** If it is **possible** to do something, it can be done. *If it is possible to find out where your brother is, we shall... Everything is possible if we want it enough... He had tried every way possible to contact her.* **2 The possible** is everything that can be done in a situation. *He is a democrat with the skill, nerve, and ingenuity to push the limits of the possible.* **3** If you do something as soon **as possible**, you do it as soon as you can. If you get as much **as possible** of something, you get as much of it as you can. *Please make your decision as soon as possible... Mrs. Pollard decided to learn as much as possible about the People's Republic of China.* **4** A **possible** event is one that might happen. *Her family is discussing a possible move to America.* **5** If you say that it is **possible** that something is true or correct, you mean that you do not know whether it is true or correct, but you accept that it might be. *It is possible that there's an explanation for all this.* **6** If you describe someone as, for example, a **possible** Prime Minister, you mean that he or she may become the Prime Minister. *Mr Lukanov is thought of as a possible successor to the president.* ▶ Also a noun. *Kennedy, who divorced wife Joan in 1982, was tipped as a presidential possible.* **7** You use **possible** with superlative adjectives to emphasize that something has more or less of a quality than anything else of its kind. *They have joined the job market at the worst possible time... He is doing the best job possible.*

♦♦♦♦♦
ADJ

N-SING:
the N

ADJ:
as adv/pron
as ADJ

ADJ

ADJ-GRADED:
v-link ADJ
PRAGMATICS

ADJ: ADJ n

N-COUNT

ADJ:
adj-superl ADJ
n,
adj-superl n
ADJ
PRAGMATICS

8 You use **possible** in expressions such as **'if possible'** and **'if at all possible'** when stating a wish or intention, to show that although this is what you really want, you may have to accept something less, or something slightly different. *I need to see you, right away if possible.* — ADJ PRAGMATICS

pos·sibly /'pɒsɪbli/. **1** You use **possibly** to indicate that you are not sure whether something is true or might happen. *Exercise will not only lower blood pressure but possibly protect against heart attacks.* **2** You use **possibly** to emphasize that you are surprised, puzzled, or shocked by something that you have seen or heard. *How could they possibly eat that stuff?... What could this possibly mean?* **3** You use **possibly** to emphasize that someone has tried their hardest to do something, or has done it as well as they can. *They've done everything they can possibly think of.* **4** You use **possibly** with a negative and a modal, to emphasize that something definitely cannot happen or definitely cannot be done. *No I really can't possibly answer that!... There's nothing more they can possibly do.* — ◆◆◆◆ PRAGMATICS; ADV; ADV before v PRAGMATICS; ADV; ADV before v PRAGMATICS; ADV; with brd-neg, ADV before v PRAGMATICS

pos·sum /'pɒsəm/ **possums**. A **possum** is the same as an **opossum**. — N-COUNT AMERICAN

post 1 letters, parcels, and information

post /pəʊst/ **posts, posting, posted**. **1** The **post** is the public service by which letters and parcels are collected and delivered. The American word is **mail**. *The winner will be notified by post... The cheque is in the post.* **2** You can use **post** to refer to letters and parcels that are delivered to you. The American word is **mail**. *He flipped through the post without opening any of it.* **3** In Britain, **post** is used to refer to a particular delivery of letters or parcels. For example, **first post** is the first delivery on a particular day. **4** If you **post** a letter or parcel, you send it to someone by putting it in a post box or taking it to a post office. The American word is **mail**. *I'm posting you a cheque tonight.* ▶ **Post off** means the same as **post**. *Simply fill in the coupon on the right and post it off to the address shown.* **5** If you **post** notices, signs, or information somewhere, you fix them to a wall or noticeboard so that everyone can see them. *Officials began posting warning notices.* ▶ **Post up** means the same as **post**. *He has posted a sign up that says 'No Fishing'... The results of this year's exams, are being posted up on school noticeboards today.* **6** If you **keep** someone **posted** on a situation, you keep giving them the latest information about it. — ◆◆◆◇ N-SING; also by N BRITISH; N-UNCOUNT BRITISH; N-UNCOUNT: supp N; VERB: V n, V n n, Also V n to n BRITISH; PHRASAL VB V n P, Also V P noun; VERB: V n prep/adv, V n; PHRASAL VB V n P, V P noun; PHRASE

post 2 jobs and places

post /pəʊst/ **posts, posting, posted**. **1** A **post** in a company or organization is a job or official position in it. *She had earlier resigned her post as President Menem's assistant.* **2** If you **are posted** somewhere, you are sent there to work by your employers, usually for several years. *Eric was posted to the South Seas for a year.* ♦ **post·ing, postings** Relevant work experience is required for overseas postings. **3** If a soldier, guard, or other person **is posted** somewhere, they are told to stand there, in order to supervise an activity or guard a place. *British Rail had to post a signalman at the entrance to the tunnel.* ▶ The place where they stand is called their **post**. *Quick men, back to your post!* **4** See also **staging post**. — ◆◆◆◆ N-COUNT FORMAL; VB: usu passive be V-ed; N-COUNT: with supp; VERB be V-ed prep/adv V n prep/adv Also be V-ed; N-COUNT

post 3 poles

post /pəʊst/ **posts**. **1** A **post** is a strong upright pole made of wood or metal that is fixed into the ground. *The device is fixed to a post.* **2** A **post** is the same as a **goalpost**. **3** On a horse-racing track, the **post** is a pole which marks the finishing point. **4** See also **first-past-the-post**. ● to **pip** someone **at the post**: see **pip**. — ◆◆◇◇ N-COUNT; N-COUNT; N-SING: the N

post- /pəʊst-/. **Post-** is used to form words that indicate that something takes place after a particular date, period, or event. *...post-election euphoria.* — PREFIX

post·age /'pəʊstɪdʒ/. **Postage** is the money that you pay for sending letters and parcels by post. — ◆◆◇◇ N-UNCOUNT

'postage stamp, postage stamps. A **postage stamp** is the small piece of gummed paper that you buy from the post office and stick on an envelope or parcel before you post it. — N-COUNT FORMAL

post·al /'pəʊstəl/. **1 Postal** is used to describe things or people connected with the public service of collecting and delivering letters and parcels. *Include your full postal address. ...postal workers.* **2 Postal** is used to describe activities that involve sending things by post. *Trust members voted by postal ballot.* — ◆◆◇◇ ADJ: ADJ n; ADJ: ADJ n

'postal order, postal orders. A **postal order** is a piece of paper representing a sum of money which you can buy at a post office and send to someone as a way of sending them money by post. The usual American term is **money order**. — N-COUNT BRITISH

post·bag /'pəʊstbæg/ **postbags**; also spelled **post-bag**. In Britain, the letters that are received by an important person, a newspaper, or a television or radio company can be referred to as the **postbag**. The American word is **mailbag**. *Here's another selection of recent letters from our postbag.* — N-COUNT

'post box, post boxes. A **post box** is a metal box with a hole in it, which you put letters into to be collected. The usual American word is **mailbox**. — N-COUNT BRITISH

post·card /'pəʊstkɑːd/ **postcards**; also spelled **post card**. A **postcard** is a piece of thin card, often with a picture on one side, which you can write on and send to people without using an envelope. ● See also **picture postcard**. — ◆◆◇◇ N-COUNT

post·code /'pəʊstkəʊd/ **postcodes**. Your **postcode** is a short sequence of numbers and letters at the end of your address, which helps the post office to sort the mail. The American term is **zip code**. — N-COUNT BRITISH

post-'dated. On a **post-dated** cheque the date is a later one than the date when the cheque was written, so that it cannot be cashed straight away. — ADJ

post·er /'pəʊstə/ **posters**. A **poster** is a large notice or picture that you stick on a wall or noticeboard, often in order to advertise something. — ◆◆◇◇ N-COUNT

pos·teri·or /pɒ'stɪəriə/ **posteriors**. **1** Someone's buttocks can be referred to as their **posterior**. **2 Posterior** describes something that is situated at the back of something else. *...the posterior leg muscles.* — N-COUNT; ADJ: ADJ n MEDICAL

pos·ter·ity /pɒ'stɛrɪti/. You can refer to everyone who will be alive in the future as **posterity**. *A photographer recorded the scene on video for posterity.* — ◆◇◇◇ N-UNCOUNT FORMAL

post·gradu·ate /ˌpəʊst'grædʒʊət/ **postgraduates**; also spelled **post-graduate**. A **postgraduate** or a **postgraduate student** is a student with a first degree from a university who is studying or doing research at a more advanced level. The American term is **graduate**. ▶ Also an adjective. *Dr Hoffman did his postgraduate work at Leicester University.* — ◆◇◇◇ N-COUNT BRITISH; ADJ: ADJ n

post·hu·mous /'pɒstjʊməs/. **Posthumous** is used to describe something that happens after someone's death but that relates to something that they did before they died. *...the posthumous publication of his first novel.* ♦ **post·hu·mous·ly** *She was posthumously awarded the George Cross.* — ◆◇◇◇ ADJ; ADV: ADV with v

post-i'ndustrial. **Post-industrial** is used to describe many Western societies, whose economies are no longer based on heavy industry but are based on service industries and the production of consumer goods. — ADJ: ADJ n

post·ing /'pəʊstɪŋ/. See **post**. — ◆◇◇◇

post·man /'pəʊstmən/ **postmen**. A **postman** is a man whose job is to collect and deliver the post. The usual American word is **mailman**. — ◆◇◇◇ N-COUNT BRITISH

post·mark /'pəʊstmɑːk/ **postmarks**. A **postmark** is a mark which is printed on letters and parcels at a post office. It shows the time and place at which something was posted. ♦ **post·marked** /'pəʊstmɑːkt/. *The third and last letter was post-marked Window Rock, Arizona.* — N-COUNT; ADJ

post·master /'pəʊstmɑːstə, -mæs-/ **postmasters**. A **postmaster** is a man who is in charge of a local post office. — N-COUNT

post·mis·tress /ˈpəʊstmɪstrəs/ **postmistresses.** A N-COUNT
postmistress is a woman who is in charge of a local
post office.

post-ˈmodern; also spelled **postmodern. Post-** ◆◇◇◇◇
modern is used to describe something or someone ADJ
that is strongly influenced by post-modernism.
...post-modern architecture.

post-ˈmodernism; also spelled **postmodernism.** ◆◇◇◇◇
In late 20th-century culture, **post-modernism** is a N-UNCOUNT
general tendency in which there is an increased
awareness of the artificial nature of all means of expression and systems of thought. ♦ **post-**
mˈodernist, post-modernists. *...the post-* N-COUNT
modernist suspicion of grand ideological narratives.

post-mortem /ˌpəʊst ˈmɔːtəm/ **post-mortems;** ◆◇◇◇◇
also spelled **post mortem** or **postmortem.** 1 A N-COUNT
post-mortem is a medical examination of a dead
person's body to find out how they died. 2 A **post-** N-COUNT
mortem is an examination of something that has
recently happened, especially something that has
failed or gone wrong. *Almost every postmortem on*
the Los Angeles riots lists unemployment among the
urban poor as an underlying cause.

post·na·tal /ˌpəʊstˈneɪtəl/; also spelled **post-natal.** ADJ: ADJ n
Postnatal means happening after and relating to
the birth of a baby. *...postnatal depression.*

ˈ**post office, post offices.** 1 In Britain, the **Post** ◆◆◇◇◇
Office is the national organization that is respon- N-PROPER
sible for postal services. *The Post Office has con-*
firmed that up to fifteen thousand jobs could be lost. N-COUNT
2 A **post office** is a building where you can buy
stamps, post letters and parcels, and use other services provided by the postal service.

ˈ**post office box, post office boxes.** A **post of-** N-COUNT
fice box is a numbered box in a post office where a
person's mail is kept for them until they collect it.

post·op·er·a·tive /ˌpəʊstˈɒpərətɪv/; also spelled ADJ: ADJ n
post-operative. Postoperative means occurring after and relating to a medical operation. *...post-*
operative pain.

post·pone /pəʊsˈpəʊn/ **postpones, postponing,** ◆◆◇◇◇
postponed. If you **postpone** an event, you arrange VERB:
for it to take place at a later time than was originally V n/-ing
planned. *The visit has now been postponed indefi-* be V-ed
nitely. ♦ **post·pone·ment, postponements.** *The* N-VAR
postponement was due to a dispute over where the
talks should be held.

post·script /ˈpəʊstskrɪpt/ **postscripts.** 1 A **post-** N-COUNT
script is something written at the end of a letter after you have signed your name. You usually write
'PS' in front of it. 2 A **postscript** is an addition to a N-COUNT
finished story, account, or statement, which gives
further information. *I should like to add a postscript*
to your obituary for John Cage.

pos·tu·late, postulates, postulating, postu- ◆◇◇◇◇
lated. The verb is pronounced /ˈpɒstʃʊleɪt/. The V that
noun is pronounced /ˈpɒstʃʊlət/. If you **postulate** FORMAL
something, you suggest it as the basis for a theory,
argument, or calculation, or assume that it is the
basis. *Freud postulated that we all have a death in-*
stinct as well as a life instinct.

pos·ture /ˈpɒstʃə/ **postures, posturing, pos-** ◆◆◇◇◇
tured. 1 Your **posture** is the position in which you N-VAR
stand or sit. *You can make your stomach look flatter*
instantly by improving your posture. ♦ **pos·tur·al** ADJ
/ˈpɒstʃərəl/. *...bad postural habits.* 2 A **posture** is N-COUNT
an attitude that you have towards something. *None* FORMAL
of the banks changed their posture on the deal.
3 You can say that someone **is posturing** when you VERB
disapprove of their behaviour because you think PRAGMATICS
they are trying to give a particular impression in or- FORMAL
der to deceive people. ♦ **pos·tur·ing** *Any calls for a* N-UNCOUNT
new UN resolution are largely political posturing.

ˌ**post·war;** also spelled **postwar. Post-war** is used ◆◇◇◇◇
to describe things that happened, existed, or were ADJ
made in the period immediately after a war, especially the Second World War (1939-45). *...postwar*
architecture.

posy /ˈpəʊzi/ **posies.** A **posy** is a small bunch of N-COUNT
flowers.

pot /pɒt/ **pots, potting, potted.** 1 A **pot** is a deep ◆◆◆◇◇
round container used for cooking stews, soups, and N-COUNT
other food. *...metal cooking pots.* 2 You can use **pot** N-COUNT
to refer to a teapot or coffee pot. *There's tea in the*
pot. 3 A **pot** is a cylindrical container for jam, paint, N-COUNT
or some other thick liquid. *...jam pots.* 4 A **pot** of BRITISH
something is an amount of it contained in a pot. *...a* N-COUNT
pot of coffee.
5 If you **pot** a young plant, or part of a plant, you put it VERB: V n
into a flowerpot filled with soil. 6 A **pot** is the same as N-COUNT
a **flowerpot.** 7 **Pot** is sometimes used to refer to can- N-UNCOUNT
nabis. 8 In a card game, **the pot** is a sum of money to INFORMAL
which each player has contributed and which the N-SING:
winner of the game takes as a prize. 9 You can refer to the N
a fund of money to which several people contribute as N-SING:
the pot. *I've taken some money from the pot for wrap-* the N
ping paper. 10 In the games of snooker and billiards, VERB: V n
if you **pot** a ball, you succeed in hitting it into one of BRITISH
the pockets. 11 See also **potted; chamber pot, chim-**
ney pot, coffee pot, melting pot, plant pot.
12 If you take **pot luck,** you decide to do something PHRASE
even though you do not know what you will get as a
result. *If you haven't made an appointment, take pot*
luck and knock on the door.

pot·ash /ˈpɒtæʃ/. **Potash** is a white powdery sub- N-UNCOUNT
stance, obtained from the ashes of burnt wood. It
can be used as a fertilizer.

po·tas·sium /pəˈtæsiəm/. **Potassium** is a soft ◆◇◇◇◇
silvery-white chemical element.

po·ta·to /pəˈteɪtəʊ/ **potatoes.** 1 Potatoes are ◆◆◆◇◇
roundish vegetables with brown or red skins and N-VAR
white insides. See picture headed **vegetables.** ● See
also **sweet potato.** 2 You can refer to a difficult sub- PHRASE
ject that people disagree on as a **hot potato.** *Anoth-*
er political hot potato is animal rights.

po·ta·to chip, potato chips. Potato chips are N-COUNT
very thin slices of potato that have been fried until AMERICAN
they are hard, dry, and crispy. The British word is
crisps.

po·ta·to crisp, potato crisps. Potato crisps are N-COUNT
the same as **crisps.** BRITISH, FORMAL

ˌ**pot ˈbelly, pot bellies.** Someone who has a **pot** N-COUNT
belly has a round fat stomach which sticks out.
♦ **pot-bellied** *...a pot-bellied man in his 50s.* ADJ-GRADED

po·ten·cy /ˈpəʊtənsi/. 1 **Potency** is the power and ◆◇◇◇◇
influence that a person, action, or idea has to affect N-UNCOUNT
or change people's lives, feelings, or beliefs. *They*
testify to the extraordinary potency of his personality.
2 The **potency** of a drug, poison, or other chemical is N-UNCOUNT
its strength. *Sunscreen can lose its potency if left over*
winter in the bathroom cabinet. 3 **Potency** is the abil- N-UNCOUNT
ity of a man to have sex. *Alcohol abuse in men can*
cause loss of sex drive and reduced potency.

po·tent /ˈpəʊtənt/. Something that is **potent** is very ◆◆◇◇◇
effective and powerful. *The drug is extremely potent,* ADJ-GRADED
but causes unpleasant side effects.

po·ten·tate /ˈpəʊtənteɪt/ **potentates.** A potentate N-COUNT
is a ruler who has absolute power over his people. FORMAL

po·ten·tial /pəˈtenʃəl/ **potentials.** 1 You use po- ◆◆◆◇◇
tential to say that someone or something is capable ADJ: ADJ n
of developing into the particular kind of person or
thing mentioned. *The firm has identified 60 poten-*
tial customers. ♦ **po·ten·tial·ly** *This is a potentially* ADV
dangerous situation. 2 If you say that someone or N-UNCOUNT:
something has **potential,** you mean that they have also N in pl
the necessary abilities or qualities to become successful or useful in the future. *The boy has great po-*
tential. 3 If you say that someone or something has N-UNCOUNT:
potential for doing something, you mean that it is with supp
possible that they may do it. If there is **the potential**
for something, it may happen. *John seemed as hor-*
rified as I about his potential for violence.

po·ten·ti·al·ity /pəˌtenʃiˈæliti/ **potentialities.** If N-VAR
something has **potentialities** or **potentiality,** it is FORMAL
capable of being used or developed in particular
ways. *...immense potentialities for resolving the most*
complex problems.

pot·hole /ˈpɒthəʊl/ **potholes;** also spelled **pot-**
hole. 1 A **pothole** is a large hole in the surface of a N-COUNT
road, which is caused by traffic and bad weather.

2 A **pothole** is a deep hole in the ground in a lime- N-COUNT
stone area. Potholes often lead to networks of
underground caves and tunnels.

pot·holed; also spelled **potholed**. A **pot-holed** ADJ-GRADED
road has a lot of potholes in it.

po·tion /'pəʊʃən/ **potions**. A **potion** is a drink that ◆◇◇◇◇
contains medicine, poison, or something that is N-COUNT
supposed to have magic powers.

pot·'luck. See pot.

pot plant, pot plants. A **pot plant** is a plant in a N-COUNT
flowerpot which is grown indoors. The usual Ameri- BRITISH
can term is **house plant**.

pot·pour·ri /ˌpəʊ'pʊəri, AM -pu'riː/ **potpourris;**
also spelled **pot-pourri** or **pot pourri**. **1** Potpourri N-VAR
is a mixture of dried petals and leaves from different
flowers, used to make rooms smell pleasant. **2** A N-SING
potpourri of things is a collection of various different items which were not originally intended to
form a group. ...*a potpourri of architectural styles
from all over the world.*

pot shot, pot shots; also spelled **pot-shot**. **1** If N-COUNT
someone takes a **pot shot** at something or someone, INFORMAL
they shoot at them without taking the time to aim
carefully. **2** A **pot shot** is a criticism of someone N-COUNT
which may be unexpected and unfair. *Their cam-* INFORMAL
paign was taking pot shots at Clinton's personal life.

pot·ted /'pɒtɪd/. **1** Potted meat or fish is cooked ADJ: ADJ n
meat or fish, usually in the form of a paste, which BRITISH
has been put into a small sealed container. ...*potted
shrimps.* **2** A potted history or biography contains ADJ: ADJ n
the main facts about someone or something in a BRITISH
short and simplified form. *The film is a potted history of the band.* **3** See also pot.

pot·ter /'pɒtə/ **potters, pottering, pottered.** A ◆◆◇◇◇
potter is someone who makes pottery. N-COUNT

potter around or **potter about**. If you **potter** PHRASAL VB
around or **potter about**, you pass the time in a gentle, V P
unhurried way, doing pleasant but unimportant PRAGMATICS
things. The American term is **putter around**. *At week-* V P n
ends he would potter around the garden. BRITISH

pot·tery /'pɒtəri/ **potteries**. **1** You can use **pot-** ◆◇◇◇◇
tery to refer to pots, dishes, and other objects which N-UNCOUNT
are made from clay and then baked in an oven until
they are hard. **2** You can use **pottery** to refer to the N-UNCOUNT
hard clay that some pots, dishes, and other objects
are made of. *Some bowls were made of pottery and
wood.* **3** Pottery is the craft or activity of making N-UNCOUNT
objects out of clay. **4** A **pottery** is a factory or work- N-COUNT
shop where pottery is made.

potting compost, potting composts. Potting N-VAR
compost is soil that is specially prepared to help BRITISH
young plants to grow. The American term is **potting
soil.**

potting shed, potting sheds. A **potting shed** is N-COUNT
a shed in a garden, in which you can keep seeds or
garden tools.

pot·ty /'pɒti/ **potties**. **1** A **potty** is a deep bowl N-COUNT
which a small child uses instead of a toilet. **2** If you ADJ-GRADED
say that someone is **potty**, you think that they are PRAGMATICS
crazy or foolish. BRITISH, INFORMAL

pouch /paʊtʃ/ **pouches**. **1** A pouch is a flexible ◆◇◇◇◇
container like a small bag. **2** The pouch of an ani- N-COUNT
mal such as a kangaroo or a koala bear is the pocket N-COUNT
of skin on its stomach in which its baby grows.

pouf /puf/. See **poof**.

poul·tice /'pəʊltɪs/ **poultices**. A **poultice** is a N-COUNT
bandage with a soft substance such as clay or a mixture of herbs or plants on it, which is heated and
applied to someone's body in order to reduce pain
or swelling.

poul·try /'pəʊltri/. You can refer to chickens, ◆◇◇◇◇
ducks, and other birds that are kept for their eggs N-PLURAL
and meat as **poultry**. *Most poultry farmers have to
rely on commercially manufactured feeds.* ▶ Meat N-UNCOUNT
from these birds is also referred to as **poultry**.

pounce /paʊns/ **pounces, pouncing, pounced.** ◆◇◇◇◇
1 If someone **pounces** on you, they come up to- VERB:
wards you suddenly and take hold of you. *Fraud* V on/upon n
squad officers had bugged the phone and were ready V
to pounce. **2** If someone **pounces** on something VERB

such as a mistake, they draw attention to it, usually V on/upon n
in order to gain an advantage for themselves. *The* Also V
*Democrats were ready to pounce on any Republican
failings or mistakes.* **3** When an animal or bird VERB:
pounces on something, it leaps on it and grabs it, in V on/upon n
order to kill it. *Before I could get the pigeon the cat* V
pounced.

pound /paʊnd/ **pounds, pounding, pounded.** ◆◆◆◆◆
1 The **pound** is the unit of money which is used in N-COUNT:
Britain. It is represented by the symbol £. One Brit- num N
ish pound is divided into a hundred pence. Some
other countries, for example Egypt, also have a unit
of money called a **pound**. *Beer cost three pounds a
bottle. ...a thousand pounds worth of jewellery and
silver.* **2** The **pound** is used to refer to the British N-SING:
currency system, and sometimes to the currency the N
systems of other countries which use pounds. *The
pound is expected to continue to increase against
most other currencies.*

3 A **pound** is a unit of weight used mainly in Britain, N-COUNT:
America, and other countries where English is spo- num N,
ken. One pound is equal to 0.454 kilograms. A **pound** N of n
of something is a quantity of it that weighs one
pound. *Her weight was under ninety pounds. ...a
pound of cheese.*

4 A **pound** is a place where stray dogs and cats are tak- N-COUNT
en and kept until they are claimed by their owners.

5 A **pound** is a place where cars that have been parked N-COUNT
illegally are taken by the police and kept until they
have been claimed by their owners.

6 If you **pound** something or **pound on** it, you hit it VERB: V n
with great force, usually loudly and repeatedly. *Some-* V prep/adv
body began pounding on the front door... She came at V n prep
him, pounding her fists against his chest. **7** If you VERB
pound something, you crush it into a paste or a pow- V n
der or into very small pieces. *She paused as she
pounded the maize grains.* **8** If your heart **is pound-** VERB
ing, it is beating with an unusually strong and fast V
rhythm, usually because you are afraid. *I'm sweating,
my heart is pounding. I can't breathe.* ♦ **pound·ing** N-UNCOUNT
...*the fast pounding of her heart.* **9** See also **pounding**.

10 If you say that someone demands their **pound of** PHRASE
flesh, you mean that they insist on getting something PRAGMATICS
they are entitled to, even though they do not really
need it and it may cause distress to the person it is demanded from; used showing disapproval. *Banks are
quick to demand their pound of flesh when overdrafts
run a little over the limit.*

-pounder /-'paʊndə/ **-pounders**. **1** -pounder can COMB
be added to numbers to form nouns that refer to
animals or fish that weigh a particular number of
pounds. *My fish average 2 lb 8 oz and I've had two
eight-pounders.* **2** -pounder can be added to num- COMB
bers to form nouns that refer to guns that fire shells
weighing a particular number of pounds. *The guns
were twelve-pounders.*

pound·ing /'paʊndɪŋ/ **poundings**. **1** If someone or N-COUNT
something takes a **pounding**, they are severely in- BRITISH,
jured or damaged. *Sarajevo took one of its worst* INFORMAL
poundings in weeks. **2** If a person or team gets a N-COUNT
pounding, they are severely defeated. *The prospects* BRITISH,
are that he will give opponents a thorough pound- INFORMAL
ing. **3** See also **pound**.

pour /pɔː/ **pours, pouring, poured.** **1** If you ◆◆◆◇◇
pour a liquid or other substance, you make it flow VERB
steadily out of a container by holding the container V n prep
at an angle. *Pour a pool of sauce on two plates and
arrange the meat neatly.* **2** If you **pour** someone a VERB: V n n
drink, you put some of the drink in a cup or glass so V n for n
that they can drink it. *Quietly Mark poured and* Also V n
served drinks for all of them. **3** When a liquid or VERB
other substance **pours** somewhere, it flows quickly V
and in large quantities. *There was dense smoke* V adv
*pouring from all four engines... Tears poured down
both our faces.*

4 When it rains very heavily, you can say that **it is** VERB
pouring. *The rain was pouring down.* V down

5 If people **pour** into or out of a place, they go there VERB
quickly and in large numbers. *Any day now, the* V prep/adv
Northern forces may pour across the new border. **6** If VERB

information or correspondence **pours** into a place, a lot of it is obtained or given. *As the results poured in, Labour chiefs were forced to admit the scale of their defeat.* — V adv/prep

7 If someone **pours cold water on** a plan or idea, they criticize it so much that people lose their enthusiasm for it. *The education secretary poured cold water on the recommendations.* ● to **pour scorn on** something: see **scorn**. — PHRASE

pour into. If you **pour** money or supplies **into** an activity or organization, or if it **pours in**, a lot of money or supplies are given in order to do the activity or help the organization. *Food donations have poured in from all over the country.* — PHRASAL VB / ERG: V n P n / V P

pour out. 1 If you **pour out** a drink, you put some of it in a cup or glass. *Carefully and slowly he poured the beer out.* **2** If you **pour out** your thoughts, feelings, or experiences, you tell someone all about them. *I poured my thoughts out on paper in an attempt to rationalize my feelings.* — PHRASAL VB / V P noun / V n P / V P noun / V n P

pout /paʊt/ **pouts, pouting, pouted. 1** If someone **pouts**, they stick out their lips, usually in order to show that they are annoyed or to make themselves sexually attractive. *Like one of the kids, he whined and pouted when he did not get what he wanted.* ► Also a noun. *She shot me a reproachful pout.* **2** If someone **pouts**, they say something with a pout. *'You're no fun,' she pouted.* — ◆◇◇◇◇ VERB V / N-COUNT / VERB V with quote

pov·er·ty /ˈpɒvəti/. **1 Poverty** is the state of being extremely poor. *According to World Bank figures, 41 per cent of Brazilians live in absolute poverty.* **2** You can use **poverty** to refer to any situation in which there is not enough of something or its quality is poor. *Britain has suffered from a poverty of ambition. ...a poverty of ideas.* — ◆◆◇◇◇ N-UNCOUNT / N-SING: also no det, N of n FORMAL

'poverty line. If someone is on **the poverty line**, they have just enough income to buy the things they need in order to live. — N-SING: the N

'poverty-stricken. **Poverty-stricken** people or places are extremely poor. *The Pope is visiting some of the most poverty-stricken areas of the city.* — ADJ

'poverty trap, poverty traps. If someone is in a **poverty trap**, they are in a situation where they are very poor, but cannot improve their income because they depend on government benefits which decrease as their earnings increase. — N-COUNT

POW /ˌpiː əʊ ˈdʌbəljuː/ **POWs.** A **POW** is the same as a **prisoner of war**. — ◆◇◇◇◇ N-COUNT

pow·der /ˈpaʊdə/ **powders, powdering, powdered. 1 Powder** consists of many tiny particles of a solid substance. *Put a small amount of the powder into a container and mix with water... Her face was covered with white powder.* **2 Powder** is the same as **face powder. 3** If a woman **powders** her face or some other part of her body, she puts face powder or talcum powder on it. *She powdered her face and applied her lipstick and rouge.* **4 Powder** is the same as **gunpowder**. *The smell of powder was in the air.* **5 Powder** is very fine snow. *...a day's powder skiing.* **6** See also **baking powder, chilli powder, curry powder, talcum powder, washing powder**. — ◆◆◇◇◇ N-VAR / N-VAR / VERB V n / N-UNCOUNT DATED / N-UNCOUNT

'powder blue; also spelled **powder-blue.** Something that is **powder blue** is a very pale blue colour. — COLOUR

pow·dered /ˈpaʊdəd/. A **powdered** substance is one which is in the form of a powder although it can come in a different form. *There are only two tins of powdered milk left.* — ◆◇◇◇◇ ADJ

'powder keg, powder kegs; also spelled **powder-keg.** If you describe a situation or a place as a **powder keg**, you mean that it could easily become very dangerous. *Unless these questions are solved, the region will remain a powder keg.* — N-COUNT

pow·dery /ˈpaʊdəri/. Something that is **powdery** looks or feels like powder. *A couple of inches of dry, powdery snow had fallen.* — ADJ-GRADED

pow·er /ˈpaʊə/ **powers, powering, powered. 1** If someone has **power**, they have a lot of control over people and activities. *...positions of great power and influence. ...a power struggle at the top of Albania's ruling Communist Party.* **2** Your **power** to — ◆◆◆◆◆ N-UNCOUNT / N-UNCOUNT

do something is your ability to do it. *Fathers have the power to dominate children and young people.* **3** If it is **in** or **within** your **power** to do something, you are able to do it or you have the resources to deal with it. *We must do everything in our power to ensure the success of the conference.* — N-UNCOUNT: poss N

4 If someone in authority has the **power** to do something, they have the legal right to do it. *The Prime Minister has the power to dismiss and appoint senior ministers. ...the legal powers of British Customs officers.* **5** You can refer to people in authority as **the powers that be**, especially when you want to say that you disagree with them or do not understand what they say or do. *The powers that be may keep us from building a house just where we want to.* **6** If people take **power** or come to **power**, they take charge of a country's affairs. If a group of people are in **power**, they are in charge of a country's affairs. **7** You can use **power** to refer to a country that is very rich or important, or has strong military forces. *...the emergence of the new major economic power, Japan.* — N-UNCOUNT: also N in pl / PHRASE PRAGMATICS / N-UNCOUNT / N-COUNT

8 The **power** of something is the physical strength or the electronic capability it has to move or affect things. *The Roadrunner had better power, better tyres, and better brakes. ...massive computing power.* **9 Power** is energy, especially electricity, that is obtained in large quantities from a fuel source and used to operate lights, heating, and machinery. *Nuclear power is cleaner than coal... Power has been restored to most parts that were hit last night by high winds.* **10** The device or fuel that **powers** a machine provides the energy that the machine needs in order to work. *The 'flywheel' battery, it is said, could power an electric car for 600 miles on a single charge.* ♦ **-powered** *...nuclear-powered submarines.* ● See also **high-powered. 11 Power** tools are operated by electricity. *...a power drill.* — N-UNCOUNT / N-UNCOUNT / VERB V n / COMB / ADJ: ADJ n

'power base, power bases; also spelled **power-base.** The **power base** of a politician or other leader is the area or the group of people from which they get most support, and which enables him or her to become powerful. — ◆◇◇◇◇ N-COUNT

'power·boat /ˈpaʊəbəʊt/ **powerboats.** A **powerboat** is a very fast, powerful motorboat. — N-COUNT

'power cut, power cuts. A **power cut** is a period of time when the electricity supply to a particular building or area is interrupted. The American term is **power outage**. — N-COUNT BRITISH

'power failure, power failures. A **power failure** is a period of time when the electricity supply to a particular building or area is interrupted, for example because of damage to the cables. — N-VAR

pow·er·ful /ˈpaʊəfʊl/. **1** A **powerful** person or organization is able to control or influence people and events. *...Russia and India, two large, powerful countries.* ● See also **all-powerful. 2** You say that someone's body is **powerful** when it is physically strong. *...his powerful muscles.* ♦ **pow·er·ful·ly** *He is described as a strong, powerfully-built man of 60.* **3** A **powerful** machine or substance is effective because it is very strong. *...powerful computer systems.* ♦ **powerfully** *Crack is a much cheaper, smokable form of cocaine which is powerfully addictive.* **4** A **powerful** smell is very strong. ♦ **powerfully** *The railway station smelt powerfully of cats and drains.* **5** A **powerful** voice is loud and can be heard from a long way away. **6** You describe a piece of writing, speech, or work of art as **powerful** when it has a strong effect on people's feelings or beliefs. *...one of the world's most powerful and moving operas, Verdi's 'Otello'.* ♦ **powerfully** *It's a play – painful, funny and powerfully acted.* — ◆◆◆◇ ADJ-GRADED / ADJ-GRADED / ADV-GRADED: ADV with v / ADJ-GRADED / ADV: ADV adj / ADJ-GRADED / ADV-GRADED: ADV after v / ADJ-GRADED / ADJ-GRADED / ADV-GRADED

'power game, power games. You can refer to a situation in which different people or groups are competing for power as a **power game**, especially if you disapprove of the methods they are using in order to try to win power. *...the dangerous power games in the Kremlin following Stalin's death.* — N-COUNT PRAGMATICS

power·house /ˈpaʊəhaʊs/ **powerhouses. 1** A **powerhouse** is a country or organization that has a — ◆◇◇◇ N-COUNT

lot of power or influence. ...*Shanghai, China's industrial powerhouse.* **2** If you say that someone is a **powerhouse**, you mean that they are very energetic. `N-COUNT` `INFORMAL`

pow·er·less /ˈpaʊələs/. **1** Someone who is **powerless** is unable to control or influence events. ♦ **pow·er·less·ness** *If we can't bring our problems under control, feelings of powerlessness and despair often ensue.* **2** If you are **powerless** to do something, you are completely unable to do it. *He was sympathetic, but powerless to help.* `◆◇◇◇◇` `ADJ-GRADED` `N-UNCOUNT` `ADJ-GRADED: ADJ to-inf`

'power line, power lines. A **power line** is a cable, especially above ground, along which electricity passes to an area or building. `◆◇◇◇◇` `N-COUNT`

,power of at'torney. **Power of attorney** is a legal document which allows you to appoint someone, for example a lawyer, to act on your behalf in specified matters. `N-UNCOUNT`

'power plant, power plants. A **power plant** is a place where electricity is generated. `◆◇◇◇◇` `N-COUNT`

'power point, power points. A **power point** is a place in a wall where you can connect electrical devices such as televisions to the electricity supply. The American word is **socket** or **outlet.** `N-COUNT` `BRITISH`

'power-sharing. also spelled **power sharing.** **Power-sharing** is a type of political arrangement which allows different or opposing groups all to participate in government. `◆◇◇◇◇` `N-UNCOUNT`

'power station, power stations. A **power station** is a place where electricity is generated. `◆◆◇◇◇` `N-COUNT`

,power 'steering. In a vehicle, **power steering** is a system for steering which uses power from the engine so that it is easier for the driver to steer. `N-UNCOUNT`

pow-wow /ˈpaʊ waʊ/ **pow-wows;** also spelled **powwow.** **1** A **pow-wow** is a meeting or conference of Native Americans. **2** People sometimes refer to a meeting or discussion as a **pow-wow.** `N-COUNT` `INFORMAL`

poxy /ˈpɒksi/. If you describe something or someone as **poxy**, you think that they are pathetic and insignificant; a word which some people find offensive. `ADJ: ADJ n` `PRAGMATICS` `BRITISH, INFORMAL`

pp. pp is written before a person's name at the bottom of a letter in order to indicate that they have signed the letter on behalf of the person whose name appears before theirs. ...*J.R. Adams, pp D. Philips.*

pp. pp. is the plural of 'p.' and means 'pages'. See *chapter 6, pp. 137-41.* `◆◆◆◇◇`

PPS /ˌpiː piː 'es/ **PPS's.** A **PPS** is an MP who is appointed by a more senior MP to help them with their duties. **PPS** is an abbreviation for 'parliamentary private secretary'. `N-COUNT` `BRITISH`

PR /ˌpiː 'ɑː/. **1 PR** is an abbreviation for **public relations.** *It will be good PR.* **2 PR** is an abbreviation for **proportional representation.** `◆◆◇◇◇` `N-UNCOUNT` `N-UNCOUNT`

prac·ti·cable /ˈpræktɪkəbəl/. If a task, plan, or idea is **practicable**, people are able to do it or carry it out. *Teachers can only be expected to do what is reasonable and practicable.* ♦ **prac·ti·cabil·ity** /ˌpræktɪkəˈbɪlɪti/ *Knotman and I first thought of the idea and discussed the practicability of it one night in March.* `ADJ-GRADED` `FORMAL` `N-UNCOUNT`

prac·ti·cal /ˈpræktɪkəl/ **practicals. 1** The **practical** aspects of something involve real situations and events, rather than just ideas and theories. *We can offer you practical suggestions on how to increase the fibre in your daily diet.* **2** You describe people as **practical** when they make sensible decisions and deal effectively with problems. *He lacked any of the practical common sense essential in management.* **3 Practical** ideas and methods are likely to be effective or successful in a real situation. *Although the causes of cancer are being uncovered, we do not yet have any practical way to prevent it.* **4** You can describe clothes and things in your house as **practical** when they are suitable for a particular purpose rather than just being fashionable or attractive. *Our clothes are lightweight, fashionable, practical for holidays.* **5** A **practical** is an examination or a lesson in which you make things or do experiments rather than simply writing answers to questions. `◆◆◆◇◇` `ADJ` `ADJ-GRADED` `ADJ-GRADED` `ADJ-GRADED` `N-COUNT`

prac·ti·cal·ity /ˌpræktɪˈkælɪti/ **practicalities.** The **practicalities** of a situation are the practical aspects of it, as opposed to its theoretical aspects. *Decisions about your children should be based on the practicalities of everyday life.* `◆◇◇◇◇` `N-VAR`

,practical 'joke, practical jokes. A **practical joke** is a trick that is intended to embarrass someone or make them look ridiculous. `N-COUNT`

prac·ti·cal·ly /ˈpræktɪkəli/. **1 Practically** means almost, but not completely or exactly. *He'd known the old man practically all his life.* **2** You use **practically** to describe something which involves real actions or events rather than ideas or theories. *The course is essentially more practically based than the Masters degree.* `◆◆◇◇◇` `ADV: ADV with group/cl` `ADV: ADV adj/-ed`

prac·tice /ˈpræktɪs/ **practices. 1** You can refer to something that people do regularly as a **practice.** *Gordon Brown has demanded a public inquiry into bank practices.* **2** If something such as a procedure is **normal practice** or **standard practice**, it is the usual thing that is done in a particular situation. *It is normal practice not to reveal details of a patient's condition.* **3** If you **put** a belief or method **into practice**, you behave or act in accordance with it. *Now that he is back, the prime minister has another chance to put his new ideas into practice.* **4** What happens **in practice** is what actually happens, in contrast to what is supposed to happen. ...*the difference between foreign policy as presented to the public and foreign policy in actual practice.* **5 Practice** means doing something regularly in order to be able to do it better. A **practice** is a session of this. ...*basketball practice... The defending world racing champion recorded the fastest time in a final practice today.* **6** If you are **out of practice** at doing something, you have not had much experience of it recently, although you used to do it a lot or be quite good at it. **7** If you say **'practice makes perfect'**, you mean that it is possible to learn something or develop a skill if you practise enough. People often say this to encourage someone to keep practising something. **8** The work done by doctors and lawyers is referred to as the **practice** of medicine and law. People's religious activities are referred to as the **practice** of a religion. *I had to change my attitude toward medical practice. ...a law guaranteeing the people freedom of conscience and religious practice.* **9** A doctor's or lawyer's **practice** is his or her business, often shared with other doctors or lawyers. **10** See also **practise.** `◆◆◆◇` `N-COUNT` `PHRASE` `PHRASE` `PHRASE` `N-VAR` `PHRASE` `PHRASE` `PRAGMATICS` `N-UNCOUNT: with supp` `N-COUNT`

prac·tise /ˈpræktɪs/ **practises, practising, practised;** spelled **practice** in American English. **1** If you **practise** something, you keep doing it regularly in order to be able to do it better. *Lauren practises the piano every day.* ● See also **practised.** **2** When people **practise** something such as a custom, craft, or religion, they take part in the activities associated with it. *He was brought up in a family which practised traditional Judaism... Acupuncture was practised in China as long ago as the third millennium BC.* ♦ **prac·tis·ing** *All employees must be practising Christians.* **3** Someone who **practises** medicine or law works as a doctor or a lawyer. *He was born in Hong Kong where he subsequently practised as a lawyer until his retirement. ...a practising architect.* **4** ● to **practise what** you **preach:** see **preach.** `◆◆◇◇◇` `VERB` `V n` `Also V` `VERB` `V n` `ADJ: ADJ n` `VERB: V n` `V as n` `V-ing` `Also V`

prac·tised /ˈpræktɪst/; spelled **practiced** in American English. Someone who is **practised** at doing something is good at it because they have had experience and have developed their skill at it. ...*a practised and experienced surgeon.* `ADJ-GRADED`

prac·ti·tion·er /prækˈtɪʃənə/ **practitioners.** Doctors are sometimes referred to as **practitioners** or **medical practitioners.** ● See also **GP.** `◆◆◇◇◇` `N-COUNT` `FORMAL`

prae·sid·ium /prɪˈsɪdiəm, praɪ-/. See **presidium.**

prae·to·rian guard /prɪˌtɔːriən ˈgɑːd/. You can use **praetorian guard** to refer to a group of people who `N-COLL-SING` `FORMAL`

are close associates and loyal supporters of someone important.

prag·mat·ic /præg'mætɪk/. A **pragmatic** way of
dealing with something is based on practical considerations, rather than theoretical ones. A **pragmatic** person deals with things in a practical way.
Robin took a pragmatic look at her situation.
♦ **prag·mati·cal·ly** /præg'mætɪkli/ *'I can't ever see
us doing anything else,' states Brian pragmatically.*

prag·mat·ics /præg'mætɪks/. **Pragmatics** is the
branch of linguistics that deals with the meanings
and effects which come from the use of language in
particular situations. Compare **semantics**. In this
dictionary, the word 'pragmatics' appears in the extra column to show that a word, meaning, or phrase
is being used to convey a particular evaluation or to
carry out a particular function. This use is explained
in the introductory section of the dictionary.

prag·ma·tism /'prægmətɪzm/. **Pragmatism**
means thinking of or dealing with problems in a
practical way, rather than by using theory or abstract principles. ♦ **prag·ma·tist, pragmatists**
He is a political pragmatist, not an idealist.

prai·rie /'preəri/ **prairies.** A **prairie** is a large area
of flat, grassy land in North America.

prairie dog, prairie dogs. A **prairie dog** is a type
of small furry animal that lives underground in the
prairies of North America.

praise /preɪz/ **praises, praising, praised.** 1 If
you **praise** someone or something, you express approval for their achievements or qualities. *The
American president praised Turkey for its courage...
He praised the excellent work of the UN weapons inspectors.* ▶ Also a noun. *I have nothing but praise
for the police.* 2 If you **sing** someone's **praises**, you
praise them in an enthusiastic way. 3 If someone
damns something **with faint praise**, they say something about it which sounds quite nice but which
shows that they do not have a high opinion of it.
4 If you **praise** God, you express your respect, honour,
and thanks to God. 5 **Praise** is the expression of respect, honour, and thanks to God. *Hindus were singing hymns in praise of the god Rama.*

praise·worthy /'preɪzwɜːði/. If you say that something is **praiseworthy**, you mean that you approve
of it and it deserves to be praised. *...the government's praiseworthy efforts to improve efficiency in
health and education.*

pra·line /'prɑːliːn, 'preɪ-/. **Praline** is a sweet substance made from nuts cooked in boiling sugar. It is
used in desserts and as a filling for chocolates.

pram /præm/ **prams.** A **pram** is a baby's cot which
has wheels so that you can push it along when you
want to take a baby somewhere. The usual American term is **baby carriage**.

prance /prɑːns, præns/ **prances, prancing,
pranced.** 1 If someone **prances** around, they walk
or move around with exaggerated movements,
usually because they want people to look at them
and admire them; used showing disapproval. *He
was horrified at the thought of any son of his prancing about on a stage in tights.* 2 When a horse
prances, it moves with quick, high steps. *...as the
carriage horses pranced through the bustling
thoroughfares.*

prank /præŋk/ **pranks.** A **prank** is a childish trick.
...laddish pranks.

prank·ster /'præŋkstə/ **pranksters.** A **prankster** is
someone who plays tricks and practical jokes on
people.

prat /præt/ **prats.** If you describe someone as a
prat, you are saying in an unkind way that you
think that they are very stupid or foolish.

prat·fall /'prætfɔːl/ **pratfalls.** If someone takes a
pratfall, they make an embarrassing mistake.

prat·tle /'prætəl/ **prattles, prattling, prattled.** If
you say that someone **prattles on** about something,
or that someone **prattles**, you are showing that you
disapprove of them or are annoyed by them because they are talking a great deal without saying

anything important. *She prattled on as she drove out
to the Highway... Archie, shut up. You're prattling.*
▶ Also a noun. *What a bore it was to listen to the
woman's prattle!*

prawn /prɔːn/ **prawns.** A **prawn** is a small shellfish, similar to a shrimp, which can be eaten. The
usual American word is **shrimp**.

prawn 'cocktail, prawn cocktails. A **prawn
cocktail** is a dish that consists of prawns, salad, and
a sauce. It is usually eaten at the beginning of a
meal. The American term is **shrimp cocktail**.

pray /preɪ/ **prays, praying, prayed.** 1 When
people **pray**, they speak to God in order to give
thanks or to ask for his help. *Now all we have to do
is help ourselves and to pray to God... Kelly prayed
that God would judge her with mercy.* 2 When
someone is hoping very much that something will
happen, you can say that they **are praying** that it
will happen. *By the time it came to vote, many of the
centrists were secretly praying for a compromise.* 3 In
former times, **pray** was used to add sarcasm to a
question. *'And what, pray, do you buy and sell, Major?'* 4 In former times, **pray** was used to add politeness to a command. *I beg your pardon, pray
continue.*

prayer /preə/ **prayers.** 1 **Prayer** is the activity of
speaking to God. *The night was spent in prayer.* 2 A
prayer is the words a person says when they speak
to God. 3 A short religious service at which people
gather to pray can be referred to as **prayers**. *...Mus-
lims attending prayers in the main mosque.*
4 You can refer to a strong hope that you have as your
prayer. *This drug could be the answer to our prayers.*
5 If you say that someone **hasn't got a prayer**, you
mean that it is impossible for them to succeed in what
they are trying to do.

'prayer book, prayer books. A **prayer book** is a
book which contains the prayers which are used in
church or at home.

'prayer meeting, prayer meetings. A **prayer
meeting** is a religious meeting where people say
prayers to God.

pre- /priː-/. **Pre-** is used to form words that indicate
that something takes place before a particular date,
period, or event. *...pre-1971 cars. ...life in pre-
industrial England.*

preach /priːtʃ/ **preaches, preaching,
preached.** 1 When a member of the clergy
preaches a sermon, he or she gives a talk on a religious or moral subject during a religious service.
*The bishop preached to a crowd of several hundred
local people... He denounced the decision to invite
his fellow archbishop to preach.* 2 When people
preach a belief or a course of action, they try to persuade other people to accept the belief or to take
the course of action. *Health experts are now preaching that even a little exercise is far better than none
at all... For many years I have preached against war.*
3 If you say that someone **practises what** they
preach, you mean that they behave in the way that
they encourage other people to behave in. 4 If you say
that someone **is preaching to the converted**, you
mean that they are wasting their time because they
are trying to persuade people to think or believe in
things that they already think or believe in.

preach·er /'priːtʃə/ **preachers.** A **preacher** is a
person, often a member of the clergy, who preaches
sermons as part of a church service.

pre·am·ble /'priːæmbəl/ **preambles.** A preamble
is an introduction that comes before something you
say or write. *The controversy has arisen over the text
of the preamble to the unification treaty.*

pre·ar·ranged /ˌpriːə'reɪndʒd/; also spelled **pre-
arranged**. You use **prearranged** to indicate that
something has been planned or arranged before the
time when it actually happens. *He had an urgent
pre-arranged meeting in London.*

pre·cari·ous /prɪ'keəriəs/. 1 If your situation is
precarious, you are not in complete control of
events and might fail in what you are doing at any

moment. ...*the Government's precarious position.*
♦ **pre·cari·ous·ly** *She remains, though more and*   ADV-GRADED
more precariously, in power. **2** Something that is   ADJ-GRADED
precarious is not securely held in place and seems
likely to fall or collapse at any moment. *They looked*
rather comical as they crawled up precarious lad-
ders. ♦ **precariously** *One of my grocery bags was*   ADV-GRADED
still precariously perched on the car bumper.

pre·cau·tion /prɪ'kɔːʃən/ **precautions.** A precau-   ♦♦◇◇
tion is an action that is intended to prevent some-   N-COUNT
thing dangerous or unpleasant from happening. *I*
had taken the precaution of doing a little research
before I left London. ...safety precautions.

pre·cau·tion·ary /prɪ'kɔːʃənri, AM -neri/. Precau-   ADJ
tionary actions are taken in order to prevent some-   FORMAL
thing dangerous or unpleasant from happening. *The*
local administration says the curfew is a precaution-
ary measure.

pre·cede /prɪ'siːd/ **precedes, preceding, pre-**   ♦♦◇◇
ceded. 1 If one event or period of time **precedes**   VERB: V n
another, it happens before it. *The earthquake was*   be V-ed by n
preceded by a loud roar and lasted 20 seconds... In-   V-ing
dustrial orders had already fallen in the preceding   FORMAL
months. **2** If you **precede** someone somewhere, you   VERB: V n
go in front of them. *They were preceded by mounted*   be V-ed by n
cowboys. **3** A sentence or chapter that **precedes** an-   VERB
other one occurs just before it in, for example, a   Also V-ing
book or magazine. *Look at the information that pre-*
cedes the paragraph in question.

prec·edence /'presɪdəns/. If one thing takes **prec-**   ♦◇◇◇
edence over another, it is regarded as more impor-   N-UNCOUNT
tant than the other thing. *He took precedence over*
everyone else.

prec·edent /'presɪdənt/ **precedents.** If there is a   ♦♦◇◇
precedent for an action or event, it has happened   N-VAR
before, and this can be regarded as an argument for   FORMAL
doing it again. *There are plenty of precedents in Hol-*
lywood for letting people out of contracts.

pre·cept /'priːsept/ **precepts.** A **precept** is a gen-   N-COUNT
eral rule that helps you to decide how you should   FORMAL
behave in particular circumstances. ...*the precepts of*
Buddhism.

pre·cinct /'priːsɪŋkt/ **precincts. 1** A shopping   ♦◇◇◇
precinct is an area in the centre of a town in which   N-COUNT
cars are not allowed. *The Centre was a pedestrian*   BRITISH
precinct with a bandstand in the middle. **2** In the   N-COUNT
United States a **precinct** is a part of a city which has   AMERICAN
its own police force and fire service. **3** The **pre-**   N-PLURAL
cincts of an institution are its buildings and land.   FORMAL

pre·cious /'preʃəs/. **1** If you say that something   ♦♦◇◇
such as a resource is **precious**, you mean that it is   ADJ-GRADED
valuable and should not be wasted or used badly. *A*
family break allows you to spend precious time to-
gether. **2 Precious** objects and materials are worth a   ADJ-GRADED
lot of money because they are rare. **3** If something   ADJ-GRADED
is **precious** to you, you regard it as important and
do not want to lose it. *Her family's support is par-*
ticularly precious to Josie. **4** If you say that there is   PHRASE
precious little of something, you are emphasizing   PRAGMATICS
that there is very little of it, and that it would be
better if there were more. **Precious few** has a similar meaning. *Precious few home-buyers will notice*
any reduction in their monthly repayments.

precious 'metal, precious metals. A **precious**   ♦◇◇◇
metal is a valuable metal such as gold or silver.   N-VAR

precious 'stone, precious stones. A **precious**   N-COUNT
stone is a valuable stone, such as a diamond or a
ruby, that is used for making jewellery.

preci·pice /'presɪpɪs/ **precipices.** A **precipice** is a   N-COUNT
very steep cliff on a mountain.

pre·cipi·tate,   **precipitates, precipitating,**   ♦◇◇◇
precipitated. The verb is pronounced
/prɪ'sɪpɪteɪt/. The adjective is pronounced
/prɪ'sɪpɪtət/. **1** If something **precipitates** an event   VERB
or situation, usually a bad one, it causes it to hap-   V n
pen suddenly or sooner than normal. *A slight mis-*   FORMAL
take could precipitate a disaster. **2** A **precipitate** ac-   ADJ-GRADED
tion or decision happens or is made more quickly   FORMAL
or suddenly than most people think is sensible.

♦ **pre·cipi·tate·ly** *I fled precipitately in the oppo-*   ADV-GRADED:
site direction.   ADV with v

pre·cipi·ta·tion /prɪ,sɪpɪ'teɪʃən/. **Precipitation** is   N-UNCOUNT
rain, snow, or hail.   TECHNICAL

pre·cipi·tous /prɪ'sɪpɪtəs/. A **precipitous** slope or   ♦◇◇◇
drop is very steep and often dangerous. ♦ **pre·cipi-**   ADJ-GRADED
·tous·ly *The road and seemed to fall precipitously*   ADV-GRADED
away.

pré·cis /'preɪsi, AM preɪ'siː/. The form **précis** is both   N-COUNT
the singular and the plural. It is pronounced   FORMAL
/'preɪsiz/ when it is the plural. A **précis** is a short
written or spoken account of something, which
gives the important points but not the details.

pre·cise /prɪ'saɪs/. **1** You use **precise** to emphasize   ♦♦◇◇
that you are referring to an exact thing, rather than   ADJ-GRADED:
something vague. *The precise location of the wreck*   ADJ n
was discovered in 1988... We will never know the
precise details of his death. **2** Something that is **pre-**   ADJ-GRADED
cise is exact and accurate in all its details. *They*
speak very precise English. **3** You say '**to be precise**'   PHRASE
to indicate that you are giving more detailed or ac-
curate information than you have just given. *More*
than a week ago, Thursday evening to be precise,
Susanne was at her evening class.

pre·cise·ly /prɪ'saɪsli/. **1 Precisely** means accu-   ♦♦◇◇
rately and exactly. *The meeting began at precisely*   ADV-GRADED
4.00 p.m. **2** You can use **precisely** to emphasize that   ADV-GRADED:
a reason or fact is the only important one there is,   ADV with cl/
or that it is obvious. *That is precisely the result the*   group
system is designed to produce. **3** You can say '**pre-**   PRAGMATICS
cisely' to confirm in an emphatic way that what   ADV
someone has just said is true. *'So, you're trying to*   PRAGMATICS
put trained, responsible people in every place where
you think they might be able to help?'—'Precisely.'

pre·ci·sion /prɪ'sɪʒən/. If you do something with   ♦♦◇◇
precision, you do it exactly as it should be done.   N-UNCOUNT
The choir sang with precision.

pre·clude /prɪ'kluːd/ **precludes, precluding,**   ♦◇◇◇
precluded. 1 If something **precludes** an event or   VERB
action, it prevents the event or action from happen-   V n/-ing
ing. *At 84, John feels his age precludes too much*   FORMAL
travel. **2** If something **precludes** you **from** doing   VERB
something or going somewhere, it prevents you   V n from
from doing it or going there. *In some cases poor*   -ing/n
English precluded them from ever finding a job.   FORMAL

pre·co·cious /prɪ'kəʊʃəs/. A **precocious** child is   ♦◇◇◇
very clever, talented, or mature, often in a way that   ADJ-GRADED
you usually only expect to find in an adult. ♦ **pre-**
·co·cious·ly *He was a precociously bright school*   ADV-GRADED
boy. ♦ **pre·coc·ity** /prɪ'kɒsɪti/. *Their sexual precoc-*   N-UNCOUNT
ity is not matched by emotional maturity.

pre·con·ceived /,priːkən'siːvd/. If you have **pre-**   ADJ: ADJ n
conceived ideas about something, you have already
formed an opinion about it before you have enough
information or experience. *I had abandoned my*
preconceived ideas about boxers.

pre·con·cep·tion /,priːkən'sepʃən/ **preconcep-**   ♦◇◇◇
tions. Your **preconceptions** about something are   N-COUNT
beliefs formed about it before you have enough information or experience. ...*preconceptions about the*
sort of people who did computing.

pre·con·di·tion /,priːkən'dɪʃən/ **preconditions.**   ♦◇◇◇
If one thing is a **precondition** for another, it must   N-COUNT
happen or be done before the second thing can   FORMAL
happen or exist. *The new government has set pre-*
conditions for dialogue with the Palestinians.

pre-'cooked; also spelled **precooked. Pre-cooked**   ADJ
food has been prepared and cooked in advance so
that it only needs to be heated before you eat it.

pre·cur·sor /prɪ'kɜːsə/ **precursors.** A **precursor**   ♦◇◇◇
of something is a similar thing that happened or ex-   N-COUNT
isted before it, often something which led to the existence or development of that thing. ...*real tennis,*
an ancient precursor of the modern game.

pre·date /,priː'deɪt/ **predates, predating, pre-**   VERB
dated. If you say that one thing **predated** another,   V n
you mean that the first thing happened or existed   FORMAL
some time before the second thing. *His troubles pre-*
dated the recession.

preda·tor /ˈpredətə/ **predators. 1** A predator is ◆◇◇◇◇ an animal that hunts and eats other animals. N-COUNT ♦ **preda·tory** /ˈpredətri, AM -tɔːri/. ...*predatory* ADJ *birds like the eagle.* **2** People sometimes refer to N-COUNT people or organizations as **predators** when they are eager to benefit from the weakness of other people or organizations. ♦ **predatory** *People will not set* ADJ-GRADED: *up new businesses while they are frightened by the* ADJ n *predatory behaviour of the banks.*

pre·de·cease /ˌpriːdɪˈsiːs/ **predeceases, prede-** VERB: V n **ceasing, predeceased.** If one person **prede-** FORMAL **ceases** another, they die before them.

pre·de·ces·sor /ˈpriːdɪsesə, AM ˈpred-/ **predeces-** ◆◆◇◇◇ **sors. 1** Your **predecessor** is the person who had N-COUNT your job before you. *He learned everything he knew from his predecessor.* **2** The **predecessor** of an object N-COUNT or machine is the object or machine that came before it in a sequence or process of development. *The car is some 40mm shorter than its predecessor.*

pre·des·ti·na·tion /ˌpriːdestɪˈneɪʃən, AM priːˈdest-/. N-UNCOUNT If you believe in **predestination,** you believe that people have no control over events because they have already been decided by God or by fate.

pre·des·tined /ˌpriːˈdestɪnd/. If you say that some- ADJ thing was **predestined,** you mean that it seems that it could not have been prevented or altered because it had already been decided by God or by fate. *His was not a political career predestined from birth.*

pre·de·ter·mined /ˌpriːdɪˈtɜːmɪnd/. If you say that ADJ something is **predetermined,** you mean that its form or nature was decided by previous events or by people rather than by chance. *The capsules can be made to release the pesticides at a predetermined time.*

pre·dica·ment /prɪˈdɪkəmənt/ **predicaments.** If ◆◇◇◇◇ you are in a **predicament,** you are in an unpleasant N-COUNT situation that is difficult to get out of. *The decision will leave her in a peculiar predicament.*

predi·cate, predicates, predicating, predi- **cated.** The noun is pronounced /ˈpredɪkət/. The verb is pronounced /ˈpredɪkeɪt/. **1** In some systems N-COUNT of grammar, the **predicate** of a clause is the part of it that is not the subject. For example, in 'I decided what to do', 'decided what to do' is the predicate. **2** If you say that one idea or situation **is predicated on** VB: usu another, you mean that the first idea or situation can passive be true or real only if the second one is true or real. *Fi-* beV-ed on n/ *nancial success is usually predicated on having money.* FORMAL

pre·dict /prɪˈdɪkt/ **predicts, predicting, pre-** ◆◆◆◇◇ **dicted.** If you **predict** an event, you say that it will VERB: V n happen. *He predicted that my hair would grow back* V that *'in no time'... It's very difficult to predict how long it's* V wh *going to take.*

pre·dict·able /prɪˈdɪktəbəl/. If you say that an ◆◆◇◇◇ event is **predictable,** you mean that it is obvious in ADJ-GRADED advance that it will happen. *The result was entirely predictable.* ♦ **pre·dict·ably** *His article is, predict-* ADV-GRADED *ably, a scathing attack on communism.* ♦ **pre·dict-** **·abil·ity** /prɪˌdɪktəˈbɪlɪti/ *Your mother values the* N-UNCOUNT *predictability of your Sunday calls.*

pre·dic·tion /prɪˈdɪkʃən/ **predictions.** If you ◆◆◇◇◇ make a **prediction** about something, you say what N-VAR you think will happen. *Predictions that the recession will be short are small comfort to those already affected.*

pre·dic·tive /prɪˈdɪktɪv/. You use **predictive** to de- ADJ-GRADED scribe something such as a test, science, or theory FORMAL that is concerned with determining what will happen in the future. *There is a wealth of research confirming the predictive validity of these methods.*

pre·dic·tor /prɪˈdɪktə/ **predictors.** You can refer to N-COUNT: something that helps you predict something that with supp will happen in the future as a **predictor** of that thing. *Opinion polls are an unreliable predictor of election outcomes.*

pre·di·lec·tion /ˌpriːdɪˈlekʃən, AM ˌpred-/ **predilec-** N-COUNT **tions.** If you have a **predilection** for something, FORMAL you have a strong liking for it.

pre·dis·pose /ˌpriːdɪˈspəʊz/ **predisposes, pre-** VERB **disposing, predisposed. 1** If something **predis-**

poses you to think or behave in a particular way, it makes it likely that you will think or behave in that V n ton/-ing way. ...*people whose personalities predispose them to* FORMAL *serve customers well... Factors such as personality and attitude predispose some individuals to criminal behaviour.* ♦ **pre·dis·posed** *Franklin was predis-* ADJ-GRADED: *posed to believe him.* ♦ **pre·dis·po·si·tion,** v-link ADJ /ˌpriːdɪspəˈzɪʃən/ **predispositions.** ...*a woman's* N-COUNT *predisposition to use the right side of her brain.* **2** If VERB: something **predisposes** you **to** a disease or condi- V n ton tion, it makes it likely that you will suffer from that FORMAL disease or condition. ♦ **pre·dis·posed** *Some people* ADJ-GRADED: *are genetically predisposed to diabetes.* ♦ **pre·dis-** v-link ADJ **·po·si·tion** *People with the gene have a predisposi-* N-COUNT *tion to alcoholism.*

pre·domi·nance /prɪˈdɒmɪnəns/. **1** If there is a N-SING **predominance** of one type of person or thing, there FORMAL are many more of that type than of any other type. *There's a predominance of women in the profession.* **2** If someone or something has **predominance,** they N-UNCOUNT have the most power or importance among a group of FORMAL people or things. ...*their economic predominance.*

pre·domi·nant /prɪˈdɒmɪnənt/. If something is ◆◇◇◇◇ **predominant,** it is more important or noticeable ADJ-GRADED than anything else in a set of people or things. *Amanda's predominant emotion was that of confu- sion.* ♦ **pre·domi·nant·ly** *The landscape has re-* ADV-GRADED *mained predominantly rural in appearance. ...a pre- dominantly female profession.*

pre·domi·nate /prɪˈdɒmɪneɪt/ **predominates,** ◆◇◇◇◇ **predominating, predominated. 1** If one type of VERB person or thing **predominates** in a group, there is V more of that type of person or thing in the group FORMAL than of any other. *In older age groups women pre- dominate because men tend to die younger.* **2** When VERB something or someone **predominates,** they have V the most power or importance among a group of FORMAL people or things. ...*a society where Islamic principles predominate.*

pre·domi·nate·ly /prɪˈdɒmɪnətli/. **Predominately** ADV means the same as **predominantly.**

pre-'eminent. If someone or something is **pre-** ◆◇◇◇◇ **eminent** in a group, they are more important, pow- ADJ-GRADED erful, or successful than other people or things in FORMAL the group. *For a decade 'X' was the pre-eminent punk band in Los Angeles.* ♦ **pre-eminence** N-UNCOUNT ...*London's continuing pre-eminence among Euro- pean financial centres.*

pre-'eminently. **Pre-eminently** means to a very ADV great extent. *The party was pre-eminently the party of the landed interest.*

pre-empt /priː ˈempt/ **pre-empts, pre-empting,** ◆◇◇◇◇ **pre-empted.** If you **pre-empt** an action, you pre- VERB vent it from happening by doing something before V n it can happen, which makes it pointless or impos- sible. *You can pre-empt pain by taking a painkiller at the first warning sign.* ♦ **pre-emption** N-UNCOUNT /priːˈempʃən/ ...*strategic plans which demanded pre-emption as the only method of averting defeat.*

pre-emptive /priː ˈemptɪv/. A **pre-emptive** attack ADJ or strike is intended to weaken or damage an en- emy or opponent, for example by destroying their weapons before they can do any harm.

preen /priːn/ **preens, preening, preened. 1** If VERB someone **preens** themselves, they admire their own V pron-refl appearance or make gestures designed to improve V n their appearance, such as touching their hair. *50%* Also V *of men under 35 spend at least 20 minutes preening themselves every morning... Bill turned to preen his beard.* **2** When birds **preen** their feathers or **preen,** VERB: they clean and arrange their feathers using their V n, beaks. V

pre-e'xisting; also spelled **preexisting.** A **pre-** ADJ: ADJ n **existing** situation or thing exists already or existed before something else. ...*the pre-existing tensions between the two countries.*

pre·fab /ˈpriːfæb/ **prefabs.** A **prefab** is a house N-COUNT built with parts which have been made in a factory BRITISH and then quickly put together.

pre·fab·ri·cat·ed /priːˈfæbrɪkeɪtɪd/. **Prefabricated** ADJ
buildings are built with parts which have been
made in a factory so that they can be easily carried
and put together.

pref·ace /ˈprefɪs/ **prefaces, prefacing, pref-** ◆◇◇◇◇
aced. 1 A **preface** is an introduction at the begin- N-COUNT
ning of a book, which explains what the book is
about or why it was written. **2** If you **preface** an ac- VERB:
tion or speech with something else, you do or say V n with n
this other thing first. *The president prefaced his re-* V n by -ing
marks by saying he has supported unemployment
benefits all along.

pre·fect /ˈpriːfekt/ **prefects. 1** In some British ◆◇◇◇◇
schools, a **prefect** is an older pupil who does special N-COUNT
duties and helps the teachers to control the younger
pupils. **2** In some countries, a **prefect** is the head of N-COUNT
the local government administration or of a local
government department.

pre·fec·ture /ˈpriːfektʃə/ **prefectures.** In some N-COUNT
countries, local government administrative areas
are called **prefectures**.

pre·fer /prɪˈfɜː/ **prefers, preferring, preferred.** ◆◆◆◇
If you **prefer** someone or something, you like that VB: no cont
person or thing better than another, and so you are V n /-ing
more likely to choose them if there is a choice. *Does* V to-inf
he prefer a particular sort of music?... I became a Also V that
teacher because I preferred books and people to poli-
tics... I prefer to go on self-catering holidays... I
would prefer him to be with us next season.

pref·er·able /ˈprefrəbəl/. If you say that one thing ◆◆◇◇
is **preferable** to another, you mean that it is more ADJ-GRADED
desirable or suitable. *The hazards of the theatre*
seemed preferable to joining the family paint busi-
ness... It is preferable to use only vegetable oil for
cooking. ◆ **pref·er·ably** /ˈprefrəbli/. *Take exercise,* ADV-GRADED
preferably in the fresh air.

pref·er·ence /ˈprefərəns/ **preferences. 1** If you ◆◆◇◇
have a **preference** for something, you would like to N-VAR
have or do that thing rather than something else.
The Bill will allow parents the right to express a pref-
erence for the school their child attends... Many of
these products were bought in preference to their
own. **2** If you **give preference** to someone with a N-UNCOUNT
particular qualification or feature, you choose them
rather than someone else. *They also give preference*
to companies with good environmental records.

pref·er·en·tial /ˌprefəˈrenʃəl/. If you get **preferen-** ◆◇◇◇
tial treatment, you are treated better than other ADJ-GRADED
people and therefore have an advantage over them.
Despite her status, the Duchess will not be
given preferential treatment. ◆ **pref·er·en·tial·ly** ADV-GRADED:
Those who sign up with a bank will be treated ADV with v
preferentially.

pre·fer·ment /prɪˈfɜːmənt/ **preferments.** Prefer- N-VAR
ment is promotion to a better and more influential FORMAL
job.

pre·fig·ure /ˌpriːˈfɪɡə, AM -ɡjər/ **prefigures, pre-** VERB
figuring, prefigured. If one thing **prefigures** an- V n
other, it is a first indication which suggests or determines that the second thing will happen. *...Max*
Linder, the French cinematic pioneer whose comic
shorts prefigured the work of Chaplin.

pre·fix /ˈpriːfɪks/ **prefixes. 1** A **prefix** is a letter or N-COUNT
group of letters which is added to the beginning of a
word in order to form a different word. For example, the prefix 'un-' is added to 'happy' to form 'unhappy'. Compare **affix** and **suffix**. ◆ **pre·fixed** ADJ-GRADED:
Sulphur-containing compounds are often prefixed by v-link ADJ
the term 'thio'. **2** A **prefix** is one or more numbers with/by n
or letters added to the beginning of a code number N-COUNT
to indicate, for example, what area something belongs to. *To telephone from the US use the prefix 011*
33 before the numbers given here. ◆ **prefixed** *Calls* ADJ-GRADED:
to Dublin should now be prefixed with 010 3531. v-link ADJ
with/by n

preg·nant /ˈpreɡnənt/. **1** If a woman or female ◆◆◇◇
animal is **pregnant**, she has a baby or babies devel- ADJ-GRADED
oping in her body. *Lena got pregnant... Tina was*
pregnant with their first daughter. ◆ **preg·nan·cy** N-VAR
/ˈpreɡnənsi/ **pregnancies.** *It would be wiser to cut*
out all alcohol during pregnancy... She was exhaust-

ed by eight pregnancies in 13 years. **2** A **pregnant** si- ADJ:
lence or moment has a special meaning which is ADJ n,
not obvious but which people are aware of. v-link ADJ
with n

pre·heat /ˌpriːˈhiːt/ **preheats, preheating, pre-** ◆◇◇◇
heated. If you **preheat** an oven, you switch it on VERB: V n
and allow it to reach a certain temperature before V-ed
you put food inside it. *Bake in the preheated oven*
for 25 minutes.

pre·his·tor·ic /ˌpriːhɪˈstɒrɪk, AM -ˈtɔːr-/. **Prehistor-** ◆◇◇◇
ic people and things existed at a time before infor- ADJ
mation was written down. *...the famous prehistoric*
cave paintings of Lascaux. ◆ **pre·his·to·ry** N-UNCOUNT
/ˌpriːˈhɪstəri/. *...the island's prehistory.*

pre·judge /ˌpriːˈdʒʌdʒ/ **prejudges, prejudging,** VERB
prejudged. If you **prejudge** a situation, you form V n
an opinion about it before you know all the facts. Also V
They tried to prejudge the commission's findings. FORMAL

preju·dice /ˈpredʒʊdɪs/ **prejudices, prejudic-** ◆◆◇◇
ing, prejudiced. 1 Prejudice is an unreasonable N-VAR
dislike of a group of people or things, or an unreasonable preference for one group over another.
There was a deep-rooted racial prejudice... There is
widespread prejudice against workers over 45.
◆ **preju·diced** /ˈpredʒʊdɪst/. *Some landlords and* ADJ-GRADED
landladies are racially prejudiced. **2** To **prejudice** VERB
someone or something is to influence them in such V n
a way that they are no longer fair and unbiased. *I*
think your South American youth has prejudiced
you... The report was held back for fear of prejudic-
ing his trial. **3** If someone **prejudices** another per- VERB
son's situation, they do something which makes it V n
worse than it should be. *Her study was not in any* FORMAL
way intended to prejudice the future development of
the college.

preju·di·cial /ˌpredʒʊˈdɪʃəl/. If an action or situa- ADJ-GRADED
tion is **prejudicial** to someone or something, it is FORMAL
harmful to them. *He has the right to ban a film, a*
demonstration or a procession if he feels it is likely to
be prejudicial to public order.

prel·ate /ˈprelɪt/ **prelates.** A **prelate** is a clergyman N-COUNT
of high rank, for example a bishop or an arch- TECHNICAL
bishop.

pre·limi·nary /prɪˈlɪmɪnri, AM -neri/ **prelimi-** ◆◆◇◇
naries. 1 Preliminary activities or discussions take ADJ
place at the beginning of an event, often as a form
of preparation. *Preliminary results show the Repub-*
lican party with 11 percent of the vote. **2** A **prelimi-** N-COUNT
nary is something that you do at the beginning of
an activity, often as a form of preparation. *A back-*
ground check is normally a preliminary to a presi-
dential appointment. **3** A **preliminary** is the first N-COUNT
part of a competition to see who will go on to the
main competition.

prel·ude /ˈpreljuːd, AM ˈpreɪluːd/ **preludes. 1** You ◆◇◇◇
can describe an event as a **prelude** to a more im- N-COUNT
portant event when it happens before it and acts as
an introduction to it. *The protests in Brasov in 1987*
are today seen as the prelude to last year's uprising.
2 A **prelude** is a short piece of music for the piano or N-COUNT
organ.

pre·mari·tal /ˌpriːˈmærɪtəl/; also spelled **pre-** ADJ: ADJ n
marital. Premarital means happening at some time
before someone gets married. *I rejected the teaching*
that premarital sex was immoral.

prema·ture /ˌpreməˈtʃʊə, AM ˌpriː-/. **1** Something ◆◆◇◇
that is **premature** happens earlier than usual or ear- ADJ-GRADED
lier than people expect. *Accidents are still the num-*
ber one cause of premature death for Americans...
His career was brought to a premature end by a suc-
cession of knee injuries. ◆ **prema·ture·ly** *The years* ADV-GRADED
in the harsh mountains had prematurely aged him.
2 You can say that something is **premature** when it ADJ-GRADED
happens too early and is therefore inappropriate. *It*
now seems their optimism was premature... I think
it's premature for restaurants to come out with that
advice. ◆ **prematurely** *Holmgren is careful not to* ADV-GRADED
celebrate prematurely. **3** A **premature** baby is one ADJ-GRADED
that was born before the date when it was due to be
born. ◆ **prematurely** *Miles was born three months* ADV-GRADED:
prematurely. ADV after v

P

pre·medi·tat·ed /priːˈmedɪteɪtɪd/. A **premeditated** ADJ
crime is planned or thought about before it is done.
♦ **pre·medi·ta·tion** /priːˌmedɪˈteɪʃən/. *There was* N-UNCOUNT
insufficient evidence of premeditation.

pre·men·stru·al /priːˈmenstruəl/. **Premenstrual** is ADJ: ADJ n
used to refer to the time immediately before menstruation and a woman's behaviour and feelings at
this time. *...a common symptom of premenstrual
syndrome... Her premenstrual tension became worse
after the birth of her baby .*

prem·ier /ˈpremiə, AM prɪˈmɪr/ **premiers. 1** The ♦♦♦◇◇
leader of the government of a country is sometimes N-COUNT
referred to as the country's **premier**. *...Australian
premier Mr Paul Keating.* ♦ **prem·ier·ship** N-SING
/ˈpremiəʃɪp, AM prɪˈmɪr-/. *...the final years of
Margaret Thatcher's premiership.* **2 Premier** is used ADJ: ADJ n
to describe something that is considered to be the
best or most important thing of a particular type.
...the country's premier opera company.

premi·ere /ˈpremiə, AM prɪˈmjer/ **premieres,** ♦♦◇◇◇
premiering, premiered. 1 The **premiere** of a N-COUNT
new play or film is the first public performance of it.
2 When a film or show **premieres** or **is premiered**, V-ERG
it is shown to an audience for the first time. *The* be V-ed
*documentary premiered at the Jerusalem Film Festi-
val... The opera is due to be premiered by ENO next
year.*

prem·ise /ˈpremɪs/ **premises;** also spelled ♦♦◇◇◇
premiss in British English for meaning 2. **1** The N-PLURAL
premises of a business or an institution are all the
buildings and land that it occupies on one site.
*There is a kitchen on the premises... The business
moved to premises in Brompton Road.* **2** A **premise** N-COUNT
is something that you suppose is true and that you FORMAL
use as a basis for developing an idea. *The programme started from the premise that men and
women are on equal terms in this society.* ♦ **prem-
·ised** /ˈpremɪst/. *All our activities are premised on* ADJ:
the basis of 'Quality with Equality'. ADJ on n

prem·iss /ˈpremɪs/. See **premise**.

pre·mium /ˈpriːmiəm/ **premiums. 1** A **premium** is ♦♦♦◇◇
money that you pay regularly to an insurance com- N-COUNT
pany for an insurance policy. **2** A **premium** is a sum N-COUNT
of money that you have to pay for something in addition to the normal cost. *Even if customers want
'solutions', most are not willing to pay a premium
for them... Callers are charged a premium rate of 48p
a minute.* **3 Premium** goods are of a higher than ADJ: ADJ n
usual quality and are often expensive. *...the most
popular premium ice cream in this country.* **4** If PHRASE
something is **at a premium**, it is wanted or needed,
but is difficult to get or achieve. *If space is at a premium, choose adaptable furniture.* **5** If you buy or PHRASE
sell something **at a premium**, you buy or sell it at a
higher price than usual, for example because it is in
short supply. **6** If you **place a high premium on** a PHRASE
quality or characteristic or **put a high premium on**
it, you regard it as very important.

premium bond, premium bonds. In Britain, N-COUNT
premium bonds are numbered tickets sold by the
government. Each month, ticket numbers are randomly selected and the people who have them win
money.

premo·ni·tion /ˌpremoˈnɪʃən, AM ˌpriː-/ **premoni-** ♦◇◇◇◇
tions. If you have a **premonition**, you have a N-COUNT
feeling that something is going to happen, often
something unpleasant. *He had an unshakable
premonition that he would die.*

pre·na·tal /ˌpriːˈneɪtəl/. **Prenatal** is used to de- ADJ
scribe things relating to the period during a woman's pregnancy, before a baby is born.

pre·oc·cu·py /priːˈɒkjʊpaɪ/ **preoccupies, preoc-** ♦◇◇◇◇
cupying, preoccupied. If something **is preoccu-** VERB
pying you, you are thinking about it a lot. *The* V n
*Persian Gulf crisis is preoccupying both American
citizens and their leaders.* ♦ **pre·oc·cu·pied** Tom ADJ-GRADED
*Banbury was preoccupied with the missing Shepherd
child.* ♦ **pre·oc·cu·pa·tion** /priːˌɒkjuˈpeɪʃən/ **pre-** N-VAR
·cupations. *In his preoccupation with Robyn,
he had neglected everything.*

pre·or·dained /ˌpriːɔːˈdeɪnd/. If you say that some- ADJ
thing is **preordained**, you mean you believe it to be FORMAL
happening in the way that has been decided by God
or by fate.

prep /prep/. In some British private schools, **prep** ♦◇◇◇◇
is the name given to school work that children do in N-UNCOUNT
the evening after school has finished.

pre-'packaged. Pre-packaged foods have been ADJ
prepared in advance and put in plastic or cardboard
packages before they are sold.

pre-'packed. Pre-packed goods are packed or ADJ
wrapped before they are sent to the shop where
they are sold. *...pre-packed bacon.*

pre-paid /ˌpriːˈpeɪd/; also spelled **pre-paid. Prepaid** ADJ
items are paid for in advance, before the time when
you would normally pay for them. *Return the enclosed Donation Form today in the prepaid envelope
provided.*

prepa·ra·tion /ˌprepəˈreɪʃən/ **preparations.** ♦♦♦◇◇
1 Preparation is the process of getting something N-UNCOUNT
ready for use or for a particular purpose, or making
arrangements for something. *Rub the surface of the
wood in preparation for the varnish... Behind any
successful event lay months of preparation.* **2 Prepa-** N-PLURAL
rations are all the arrangements that are made for a
future event. *Final preparations are under way for
celebrations to mark German unification.* **3** A **prepa-** N-COUNT
ration is a mixture that has been prepared for use FORMAL
as food, medicine, or a cosmetic. *...sensitive-skin
preparations.*

pre·para·tory /prɪˈpærətri, AM -tɔːri/. **1 Prepara-** ♦◇◇◇◇
tory actions are done before doing something else ADJ
as a form of preparation or as an introduction. *At FORMAL
least a year's preparatory work will be necessary be-
fore building can start.* **2** If one action is done **pre-** PHR-PREP
paratory to another, it is done before the other ac- FORMAL
tion, usually as preparation for it. *Sloan cleared his
throat preparatory to speaking.*

pre'paratory school, preparatory schools. A N-VAR
preparatory school is the same as a **prep school**.

pre·pare /prɪˈpeə/ **prepares, preparing, pre-** ♦♦♦♦◇
pared. 1 If you **prepare** something, you make it VERB
ready for something that is going to happen. *Two* V n
technicians were preparing a videotape recording of V n for n
last week's programme... The crew of the Iowa has Also V n to-inf
been preparing the ship for storage. **2** If you **prepare** VERB
for an event or action that will happen soon, you V for n
get yourself ready for it or make the necessary ar- V to-inf
rangements. *He told the deputies that they needed to* V pron-refl for
*prepare for new elections... He had to go back to his n
hotel and prepare to catch a train... His doctor had* Also V,
told him to prepare himself for surgery. **3** When you V n to-inf
prepare food, you get it ready to be eaten, for ex- VERB: V n
ample by cooking it.

pre·pared /prɪˈpeəd/. **1** If you are **prepared** to do ♦♦♦♦◇
something, you are willing to do it if necessary. *Are* v-link ADJ to-
you prepared to take industrial action? **2** If you are inf
prepared for something that you think is going to ADJ:
happen, you are ready for it. *Police are prepared for* v-link ADJ for
large numbers of demonstrators. ♦ **pre·par·ed-** n
·ness *The situation in the capital forced them to* N-UNCOUNT
maintain military preparedness. **3** You can describe ADJ: ADJ n
something as **prepared** when it has been done or
made beforehand, so that it is ready when it is
needed. *He ended his prepared statement by thanking the police.*

pre·pon·der·ance /prɪˈpɒndərəns/. If there is a N-SING
preponderance of one type of person or thing in a
group, there is more of that type than of any other.

prepo·si·tion /ˌprepəˈzɪʃən/ **prepositions.** A N-COUNT
preposition is a word such as 'by', 'for', 'into', or
'with' which usually has a noun group as its object.

pre·pos·ter·ous /prɪˈpɒstərəs/. If you describe ♦◇◇◇◇
something as **preposterous**, you mean that it is ex- ADJ-GRADED
tremely unreasonable and foolish. ♦ **pre·pos·ter-
·ous·ly** *Some prices are preposterously high.* ADV-GRADED

prep·py /ˈprepi/ **preppies.** Preppies are young N-COUNT
people, especially American people who have been
to a prep school or Ivy League University, who are
conventional and conservative in their behaviour

and style of dress. ▶ Also an adjective. *I couldn't be-* ADJ-GRADED
lieve how straight-looking he was, how preppy.

pre-prandial /ˌpriː ˈprændiəl/. You use **pre-** ADJ: ADJ n
prandial to refer to things you do or have before a FORMAL
meal. *...pre-prandial drinks.*

'**prep school, prep schools. 1** In Britain, a **prep** ◆◇◇◇◇
school is a private school where children are edu- N-VAR
cated until the age of 11 or 13. **2** In the United N-VAR
States, a **prep school** is a private secondary school
for students who intend to go to college after they
leave.

pre·pu·bes·cent /ˌpriːpjuːˈbesənt/. **Prepubescent** ADJ
means relating to the time just before someone FORMAL
reaches puberty.

pre·quel /ˈpriːkwəl/ **prequels.** A **prequel** is a film N-COUNT
that is made about an earlier stage of a story or a
character's life when the later part of it has already
been made into a successful film.

Pre-Raphael·ite /ˌpriː ˈræfəlaɪt/ **Pre-**
Raphaelites. 1 The **Pre-Raphaelites** were a group N-COUNT
of British painters in the nineteenth century who
concentrated on themes from medieval history, romantic myth, and folklore. **2 Pre-Raphaelite** art ADJ: ADJ n
was created by the Pre-Raphaelites. *...a number of*
pre-Raphaelite murals.

,**pre-re'corded.** Something that is **pre-recorded** ADJ
has been recorded in advance so that it can be
broadcast or played later.

pre·req·ui·site /ˌpriːˈrekwɪzɪt/ **prerequisites.** If ◆◇◇◇◇
one thing is a **prerequisite** for another, it must hap- N-COUNT:
pen or exist before the other thing is possible. *Good* N for/ofn
self-esteem is a prerequisite for a happy life.

pre·roga·tive /prɪˈrɒgətɪv/ **prerogatives.** If ◆◇◇◇◇
something is the **prerogative** of a particular person N-COUNT
or group, it is a privilege or a power that only they FORMAL
have. *Constitutional changes are exclusively the pre-*
rogative of the parliament.

pres·age /ˈpresɪdʒ/ **presages, presaging, pres-** VERB
aged. If something **presages** a situation or event, it V n
is considered to be a warning or sign of what is FORMAL
about to happen. *...the dawn's loud chorus that*
seemed to presage a bright hot summer's day.

pre-school /ˌpriː ˈskuːl/. **Pre-school** is used to de- ADJ: ADJ n
scribe things relating to the care and education of WRITTEN
children before they reach the age when they have
to go to school. *Looking after pre-school children is*
very tiring. ♦ **pres·chooler, pre-schoolers.** Chil- N-COUNT
dren who are no longer babies but are not yet old
enough to go to school are sometimes referred to as
preschoolers.

pres·ci·ent /ˈpresiənt, AM ˈpreʃ-/. If you say that ADJ-GRADED
someone or something was **prescient**, you mean FORMAL
that they were able to know or predict what was going to happen in the future. *Hadley's idea appears*
remarkably prescient. ♦ **pres·ci·ence** *He's demon-* N-UNCOUNT
strated a certain prescience in foreign affairs.

pre·scribe /prɪˈskraɪb/ **prescribes, prescrib-** ◆◆◇◇◇
ing, prescribed. 1 If a doctor **prescribes** medi- VERB
cine or treatment for you, he or she tells you what V n
medicine or treatment to have. *Our doctor diag-* Also V n n
nosed a throat infection and prescribed antibiotic.
2 If a person or set of laws or rules **prescribes** an VERB
action or duty, they state that it must be carried out. V n
...article II of the constitution, which prescribes the FORMAL
method of electing a president.

pre·scrip·tion /prɪˈskrɪpʃən/ **prescriptions. 1** A ◆◆◇◇◇
prescription is a medicine which a doctor has told N-COUNT
you to take, or the form on which the doctor has
written the details of that medicine. ● If a medicine PHRASE
is available **on prescription**, you can get it from a
chemist if a doctor gives you a prescription for it.
2 A **prescription** is a proposal or a plan which gives N-COUNT
ideas about how to solve a problem or improve a
situation. *...President Clinton's proposed prescription*
for reform.

pre·scrip·tive /prɪˈskrɪptɪv/. A **prescriptive** ap- ADJ-GRADED
proach to something involves telling people what FORMAL
they should do, rather than simply giving suggestions or describing what is done. *...prescriptive atti-*
tudes to language on the part of teachers.

pres·ence /ˈprezəns/ **presences. 1** Someone's ◆◆◆◆◇
presence in a place is the fact that they are there. N-SING:
His presence in the village could only stir up trouble. with poss
2 If you refer to the **presence** of a substance in an- N-UNCOUNT:
other thing, you mean that it is in that thing. *The* with poss
somewhat acid flavour is caused by the presence of
lactic acid. **3** If someone or something **makes** their PHRASE
presence felt, they do something which forces people to pay attention to them. **4** If you are **in** PHRASE
someone's **presence**, you are in the same place as
that person, and are close enough to them to be
seen or heard. **5** A **presence** is a person or creature N-COUNT
that you cannot see, but that you are aware of. *The* LITERARY
forest was dark and silent, haunted by shadows and
unseen presences.
6 If you say that someone has **presence**, you mean N-UNCOUNT
that they impress people by their appearance and
manner. *They do not seem to have the vast, authorita-*
tive presence of those great men. **7** If you say that PHRASE
someone had the **presence of mind** to do something, PRAGMATICS
you admire the fact that they were able to think and
act calmly in a difficult situation.

present 1 existing or happening now

pres·ent /ˈprezənt/. **1** You use **present** to describe ◆◆◆◆◇
things and people that exist now, rather than those ADJ: ADJ n
that existed in the past or those that may exist in
the future. *...the government's present economic dif-*
ficulties... No statement can be made at the present
time. **2 The present** is the period of time that we N-SING:
are in now and the things that are happening now. the N
...his struggle to reconcile the past with the present.
3 The **present** tenses of a verb are the ones used to ADJ: ADJ n
talk about things that happen regularly or situations
that exist at this time.
4 A situation that exists **at present** exists now, al- PHRASE
though it may change. **5 The present day** is the period PHRASE
of history that we are in now. *...Western European art*
from the period of Giotto to the present day. **6** Some- PHRASE
thing that exists or will be done **for the present** exists
now or will continue for a while, although the situation may change later.

present 2 being somewhere

pres·ent /ˈprezənt/. **1** If someone is **present** at an ◆◆◆◆◇
event, they are there. *The president was not present* ADJ:
at the meeting... The whole family was present. **2** If v-link ADJ
something, especially a substance or disease, is **pre-** ADJ:
sent in something else, it exists within that thing. v-link ADJ
This special form of vitamin D is naturally present in
breast milk.

present 3 gift

pres·ent /ˈprezənt/ **presents.** A **present** is some- ◆◆◇◇◇
thing that you give to someone, for example at N-COUNT
Christmas or when you visit them. *This book would*
make a great Christmas present.

present 4 verb uses

pres·ent /prɪˈzent/ **presents, presenting, pre-** ◆◆◆◆◇
sented. 1 If you **present** someone **with** something VERB:
such as a prize or document, or if you **present** it to V n with n
them, you formally give it to them. *Prince Michael* V n
of Kent presented the prizes. ♦ **pres·en·ta·tion** Also V n to n
Then came the presentation of the awards. **2** When N-UNCOUNT
you **present** information, you give it to people in a VERB: V n
formal way. *We presented three options to the unions* V n to n
for discussion. ♦ **pres·en·ta·tion, presentations** Also V n with n
...a fair presentation of the facts to a jury. N-VAR
3 If something **presents** a difficulty, challenge, or op- VERB: V n
portunity, it causes it or provides it. *Public policy on* V n with n
the family presents liberals with a dilemma. **4** If an op- Also V n to n
portunity or problem **presents** itself, it occurs, often VERB:
when you do not expect it. V pron-refl
5 If you **present** someone or something in a particular VERB
way, you describe them in that way. *The British like to* V n asn
present themselves as a nation of dog-lovers. **6** The Also V n in n
way you **present yourself** is the way you speak and act VERB
when meeting new people. *...tricks which would help* V pron-refl
him to present himself in a more confident way. **7** If prep/adv
someone or something **presents** a particular appear- VERB: V n
ance or image, that is how they appear or try to ap- V n to n
pear. *...presenting a calm and dignified face to the*
world at large.

P

8 If you **present yourself** somewhere, you officially arrive there. *She was told to present herself at the Town Hall at 11.30 for the induction ceremony.* **9** If you **present** someone **to** someone else, often someone important, you formally introduce them. *Fox stepped forward, welcomed him in Malay, and presented him to Jack.* VERB V pron-refl prep/adv VERB V n to n Also V n

10 If someone **presents** a programme on television or radio, they introduce each item in it. ◆ **pre·sent·er**, **presenters** ...*the presenter of the BBC radio programme Law in Action.* **11** When someone **presents** something such as a production of a play or an exhibition, they organize it. **12** See also **presentation**. VERB: V n N-COUNT VERB: V n

pre·sent·able /prɪˈzentəbəl/. **1** If you say that someone looks **presentable**, you mean that they look fairly tidy or attractive. ...*wearing his most presentable suit.* **2** If you describe something as **presentable**, you mean that it is acceptable or quite good. *His score of 29 had helped Leicestershire reach a presentable total.* ADJ-GRADED ADJ-GRADED

pre·sen·ta·tion /ˌprezənˈteɪʃən, AM ˌpriːzen-/ **presentations**. **1** Presentation is the appearance of something, which someone has worked to create. ...*traditional French food cooked in a lighter way, keeping the presentation simple.* **2** A **presentation** is a formal event at which someone is given a prize or award. ...*after receiving his award at a presentation in London yesterday.* **3** When someone gives a **presentation**, they give a formal talk, often in order to sell something or get support for a proposal. ...*a slide and video presentation.* **4** A **presentation** is something that is performed in front of an audience, for example a play or a ballet. ...*Blackpool Opera House's presentation of Buddy, the musical.* **5** See also **present**. ◆◆◇◇◇ N-UNCOUNT N-COUNT N-COUNT N-COUNT FORMAL

present-'day; also spelled **present day**. **Present-day** things, situations, and people exist at the time in history we are now in. *Even by present-day standards these were large aircraft.* ◆◇◇◇◇ ADJ: ADJ n

pre·sen·ti·ment /prɪˈzentɪmənt/ **presentiments**. A **presentiment** is a feeling that a particular event, for example someone's death, will soon take place. *I had a presentiment that he represented a danger to me.* N-COUNT FORMAL

pres·ent·ly /ˈprezəntli/. **1** If you say that something is **presently** happening, you mean that it is happening now. *She is presently developing a number of projects... The island is presently uninhabited.* **2** You use **presently** to indicate that something happened quite a short time after the time or event that you have just mentioned. *He was shown to a small office. Presently, a young woman in a white coat came in.* **3** If you say that something will happen **presently**, you mean that it will happen quite soon. *'Who's Agnes?'—'You'll be meeting her presently.'* ◆◇◇◇◇ ADV ADV: ADV with cl WRITTEN ADV: ADV after v FORMAL

present 'participle, **present participles**. The **present participle** of a verb is the form which ends in '-ing'. N-COUNT

present 'perfect. The **present perfect** tenses of a verb are the ones used to talk about things which happened before the time you are speaking or writing but are relevant to the present situation or are still happening. ADJ: ADJ n

pres·er·va·tion·ist /ˌprezəˈveɪʃənɪst/ **preservationists**. A preservationist is someone who takes action to preserve something such as historic buildings or an area of countryside. N-COUNT

pre·serva·tive /prɪˈzɜːvətɪv/ **preservatives**. A **preservative** is a chemical that prevents things from decaying. *Nitrates are used as preservatives in food manufacture.* ◆◇◇◇◇ N-VAR

pre·serve /prɪˈzɜːv/ **preserves, preserving, preserved**. **1** If you **preserve** a situation or condition, you make sure that it remains as it is, and does not change or end. *We will do everything to preserve peace.* ◆ **pres·er·va·tion** /ˌprezəˈveɪʃən/ ...*the preservation of the status quo.* **2** If you **preserve** something, you take action to save it or protect it from ◆◆◆◇◇ VERB V n V-ed N-UNCOUNT VERB V n V-ed

damage or decay. *We need to preserve the forest. ...perfectly preserved medieval houses.* ◆ **preservation** ...*the preservation of buildings of architectural or historic interest.* **3** A nature **preserve** is an area of land or water where animals are protected from hunters. **4** If you **preserve** food, you treat it in order to prevent it from decaying so that you can store it for a long time. *I like to make puree, using only enough sugar to preserve the plums.* **5 Preserves** are foods such as jam and marmalade that are made by cooking fruit with a large amount of sugar so that they can be stored for a long time. **6** If you say that a job or activity is the **preserve of** a particular person or group of people, you mean that they are the only ones who take part in it. *The making and conduct of foreign policy is largely the preserve of the president.* N-UNCOUNT N-COUNT VERB V n N-PLURAL N-COUNT

pre·set /ˌpriːˈset/ **presets, presetting**; also spelled **pre-set**. The form **preset** is used in the present tense and is the past tense and past participle. If a piece of equipment **is preset**, its controls have been set in advance of the time you want it to work. ...*a computerised timer that can be preset to a variety of programs.* VB: usu passive be V-ed

pre·side /prɪˈzaɪd/ **presides, presiding, presided**. If you **preside over** a meeting or an event, you are in charge or act as the chairperson. *The PM returned to Downing Street to preside over a meeting of his inner Cabinet.* ◆◆◇◇◇ VERB V over/at n

presi·den·cy /ˈprezɪdənsi/ **presidencies**. The **presidency** of a country or organization is the position of being the president or the period of time during which someone is president. ...*a candidate for the presidency of the organisation... Poverty had declined during his presidency.* ◆◆◇◇◇ N-COUNT

presi·dent /ˈprezɪdənt/ **presidents**. **1** The **president** of a country that has no king or queen is the person who has the highest political position and is the leader of the country. ...*President Mubarak... The White House says the president would veto the bill.* ◆ **presi·den·tial** /ˌprezɪˈdenʃəl/ ...*campaigning for Peru's presidential election.* **2** The **president** of an organization is the person who has the highest position in it. ...*Alexandre de Merode, the president of the medical commission.* ◆◆◆◆◆ N-TITLE; N-COUNT ADJ: ADJ n N-COUNT

president-e'lect. The **president-elect** is the person who has been elected as an organization or country's president, but who has not yet taken office. ...*the difficulties which face the president-elect.* ◆◆◇◇◇ N-SING

pre·sid·ium /prɪˈsɪdiəm/; also spelled **praesidium**. In Communist countries, a **presidium** is a committee which takes policy decisions on behalf of a larger group such as a parliament. N-SING

press /pres/ **presses, pressing, pressed**. **1** If you **press** something somewhere, you push it firmly against something else. *He pressed his back against the door... They pressed the silver knife into the cake.* **2** If you **press** a button or switch, you push it with your finger in order to make a machine or device work. *Drago pressed a button and the door closed.* ▶ Also a noun. ...*a TV which rises from a table at the press of a button.* **3** If you **press** something or **press down on** it, you push hard against it with your foot or hand. *The engine stalled. He pressed the accelerator hard... She leaned forward with her hands pressing down on the desk.* **4** If you **press** clothes, you iron them in order to get rid of the creases. **5** If you **press** fruits or vegetables, you squeeze them or crush them, usually in order to extract the juice. **6** If you **press for** something, you try hard to persuade someone to give it to you or to agree to it. *Police might now press for changes in the law... They had pressed for their children to be taught French.* **7** If you **press** someone, you try hard to persuade them to do something or to tell you something. *Trade unions are pressing him to stand firm... Mr King seems certain to be pressed for further details.* **8** If something or someone is **pressed into service** as something or to do something, they are used temporarily as that thing or to do that thing. *The local bar has been pressed into service* ◆◆◆◆◆ VERB V n against n V n prep VERB V n N-COUNT VERB V n V adv Also V on n VERB: V n VERB: V n VERB V for n V for n to-inf VERB V n to-inf be V-ed for/about n PHRASE

as a school. **9** If someone **presses** their claim, de- VERB
mand, or point, they state it in a very forceful way. *Of-* V n
ficials have visited Washington to press their case for
economic aid.

10 If an unpleasant feeling such as guilt, sadness, or VERB
anxiety **presses on** you, it worries you very much and V on n
you are always thinking about it. *Right now, I've got*
other problems that are pressing on me. **11** If you VERB
press something **on** someone, you give it to them and V n on n
insist that they take it. *All I had was money, which I*
pressed on her reluctant mother.

12 Newspapers and journalists are referred to as **the** N-COLL-SING:
press. *Today the British press is full of articles on* theN
India's new prime minister... Christie looked relaxed
and calm as he faced the press. **13** When a newspaper PHRASE
or magazine **goes to press**, an edition of it starts to be
printed.

14 A **press** or a **printing press** is a machine used for N-COUNT
printing books, newspapers, and leaflets. **15** If you PHRASE
press charges against someone, you make an official
accusation against them which has to be decided in a
court of law. *Police have announced they will not be*
pressing charges. **16** See also **pressed, pressing**.

press ahead. See press on **1**.

press on or **press ahead. 1** If you **press on** or PHRASAL VB
press ahead, you continue with a task or activity in a V P
determined way, and do not allow any problems or V P with n
difficulties to delay you. *Poland pressed on with eco-*
nomic reform. **2** If you **press on**, you continue with a V P
journey, even though it is becoming more difficult or
more dangerous. *I considered turning back, but it was*
getting late, so I pressed on.

'press agency, press agencies. A country's N-COUNT
press agency is an organization that gathers news
from that country and supplies it to journalists from
all over the world.

'press agent, press agents. A **press agent** is a N-COUNT
person who is employed by a famous person to give
information about that person to the press.

'press box, press boxes. The **press box** at a N-COUNT
sports ground is a room or area which is reserved
for journalists to watch sporting events.

'press conference, press conferences. A ◆◆◇◇◇
press conference is a meeting held by a famous or N-COUNT
important person in which they answer journalists'
questions. *Botham called a Press conference and an-*
nounced his resignation.

'press corps; press corps. is both the singular and N-COLL-
plural form. The **press corps** is a group of reporters COUNT
who are all working in the same place. *...the White* AMERICAN
House press corps.

pressed /prest/. If you say that you are **pressed for** ADJ-GRADED:
time or **pressed for money**, you mean that you do v-link ADJ
not have enough time or money at the moment.
● See also **hard-pressed**.

'press gallery, press galleries. The **press gal-** N-COUNT
lery is the area in a parliament which is reserved for
journalists who report on the parliament's activities.

'press-gang, press-gangs, press-ganging,
press-ganged. 1 If you **are press-ganged into** VB: usu
doing something, you are made or persuaded to do passive
it, even though you do not really want to. *I was* beV-ed into
press-ganged into working in that business... She was -ing/n
a volunteer, she hadn't had to be press-ganged. **2** If VB: usu
civilians **are press-ganged**, they are captured and passive
forced to join the army or navy. *They left their vil-* beV-ed into n
lages to evade being press-ganged into the army. Also beV-ed
♦ press-ganging *...the press-ganging of young* N-SING:
people into the country's armed forces. **3** In former theN of n
times, a **press-gang** was a group of men who used N-COUNT
to capture boys and men and force them to join the
navy.

press·ing /'presɪŋ/. **1** A **pressing** problem, need, ◆◇◇◇◇
or issue has to be dealt with immediately. *It is one* ADJ-GRADED
of the most pressing problems facing this country.
2 See also **press.**

press·man /'presmæn/ **pressmen.** A **pressman** is N-COUNT
a reporter, especially a man, who works for a news- BRITISH
paper or magazine.

'press officer, press officers. A **press officer** is ◆◇◇◇◇
a person who is employed by an organization to N-COUNT
give information about that organization to the
press.

'press release, press releases. A **press release** ◆◇◇◇◇
is a written statement about a matter of public in- N-COUNT
terest which is given to the press by an organization
concerned with the matter. *The government had put*
out a press release naming the men.

'press stud, press studs. A **press stud** is a small N-COUNT
metal fastener for clothes, made up of two parts BRITISH
which can be pressed together. The American term
is **snap fastener** or **snap.**

'press-up, press-ups. Press-ups are exercises N-COUNT
which are done by lying with your face towards the BRITISH
floor and pushing with your hands to raise your
body until your arms are straight. *He made me do*
30 press-ups.

pres·sure /'preʃə/ **pressures, pressuring,** ◆◆◆◆◇
pressured. 1 Pressure is force that you produce N-UNCOUNT
when you press hard on something. *The pressure of*
his fingers had relaxed... The best way to treat such
bleeding is to apply firm pressure. **2** The **pressure** in N-UNCOUNT:
a place or container is the force produced by the also N in pl
quantity of gas or liquid in that place or container.
...another high pressure area over the North Sea.
3 See also **blood pressure.**

4 If there is **pressure** on someone to do something, N-UNCOUNT:
someone is trying to persuade or force them to do it. also N in pl
He may have put pressure on her to agree... Its govern-
ment is under pressure from the European Commis-
sion. **5** If you are experiencing **pressure**, you feel that N-UNCOUNT:
you must do a lot of tasks or make a lot of decisions in also N in pl
very little time, or that people expect a lot from you.
Can you work under pressure?... The pressures of mod-
ern life are great. **6** If you **pressure** someone to do VERB
something, you try forcefully to persuade them to do V n to-inf
it. *He will never pressure you to get married... The Gov-* beV-ed into
ernment should not be pressured into making hasty -ing
decisions... Don't pressure me. **♦ pres·sured** *You're* Also V n for n
likely to feel anxious and pressured. ADJ-GRADED

'pressure cooker, pressure cookers. A **pres-** N-COUNT
sure cooker is a large saucepan with a lid that fits
tightly, in which you can cook food quickly using
steam at high pressure. See picture headed **kitchen**
utensils.

'pressure group, pressure groups. A pressure ◆◇◇◇◇
group is an organized group of people who are try- N-COUNT
ing to persuade a government or other authority to
do something. *...the environmental pressure group*
Greenpeace.

pres·sur·ize /'preʃəraɪz/ **pressurizes, pressuriz-** VERB
ing, pressurized; also spelled **pressurise** in Brit- beV-ed into
ish English. If you are **pressurized into** doing some- -ing
thing, you are forcefully persuaded to do it. *Do not* V n
be pressurized into making your decision immedi- Also V n to-inf
ately... He thought she was trying to pressurize him.
● See also **pressurized.**

pres·sur·ized /'preʃəraɪzd/; also spelled **pressur-** ◆◇◇◇◇
ised in British English. In a **pressurized** container or ADJ
area, the pressure inside is different from the pressure outside. *Supplementary oxygen is rarely needed*
in pressurized aircraft.

pres·tige /pre'stiːʒ/. **1** If a person, a country, or an ◆◆◇◇◇
organization has **prestige**, they are admired and re- N-UNCOUNT
spected because of the position they hold or the
things they have achieved. *...efforts to build up the*
prestige of the United Nations. ...high prestige jobs.
2 Prestige is used to describe products, places, or ADJ: ADJ n
activities which people admire because they are associated with being rich or having a high social position. *...such prestige cars as Cadillac, Mercedes.*

pres·tig·ious /pre'stɪdʒəs/. A **prestigious** institu- ◆◆◇◇◇
tion, job, or activity is respected and admired by ADJ-GRADED
people. *It's one of the best equipped and most pres-*
tigious schools in the country.

pre·sum·ably /prɪ'zjuːməbli, AM -'zuːm-/. If you ◆◆◆◇◇
say that something is **presumably** the case, you ADV
mean that you think it is very likely to be the case,
although you are not certain. *Presumably the front*

door was locked?... The spear is presumably the murder weapon... He had gone to the reception desk, presumably to check out.

pre·sume /prɪˈzjuːm, AM -ˈzuːm/ **presumes, presuming, presumed. 1** If you **presume** that something is the case, you think that it is the case, although you are not certain. I presume you're here on business... 'Had he been home all week?'—'I presume so.' ...areas that have been presumed to be safe... The missing person is presumed dead. **2** If you say that someone **presumes** to do something, you mean that they do it even though they have no right to do it. They're resentful that outsiders presume to meddle in their affairs. **3** If an idea, theory, or plan **presumes** certain facts, it regards them as true so that they can be used as a basis for further ideas and theories. The legal definition of 'know' often presumes mental control.

◆◆◇◇
VERB
V that
V so
be V-ed to-inf
be V-ed adj

VERB
V to-inf
FORMAL

VERB
V n
Also V that
FORMAL

pre·sump·tion /prɪˈzʌmpʃən/ **presumptions. 1** A **presumption** is something that is accepted as true but is not certain to be true. ...the presumption that a defendant is innocent until proved guilty. **2** If you describe someone's behaviour as **presumption**, you disapprove of it because they are doing something that they have no right to do. They were angered by his presumption.

◆◇◇◇
N-COUNT

N-UNCOUNT
PRAGMATICS
FORMAL

pre·sump·tu·ous /prɪˈzʌmptʃuəs/. If you describe someone or their behaviour as **presumptuous**, you disapprove of them because they are doing something that they have no right or authority to do. It would be presumptuous to judge what the outcome will be.

ADJ-GRADED
PRAGMATICS

pre·sup·pose /ˌpriːsəˈpəʊz/ **presupposes, presupposing, presupposed.** If one thing **presupposes** another, the first thing cannot be true or exist unless the second thing is true or exists. All your arguments presuppose that he's a rational, intelligent man.

VERB
V that
Also V n

pre·sup·po·si·tion /ˌpriːsʌpəˈzɪʃən/ **presuppositions.** A presupposition is something that you assume to be true, especially something which you must assume is true in order to continue with what you are saying or thinking. ...the presupposition within medical science that human life must be sustained for as long as possible.

N-COUNT
FORMAL

pre·tax; also spelled **pretax. Pre-tax** profits or losses are the total profits or losses made by a company before tax has been deducted. ▶ Also an adverb. Last year it made £2.5m pre-tax.

◆◆◇◇
ADJ: ADJ n

ADV:
ADV after v

pre·teen, pre-teens; also spelled **preteen.** A **pre-teen** is a child who is not yet a teenager, usually a child aged between nine and thirteen.

N-COUNT

pre·tence /prɪˈtens, AM ˈpriːtens/ **pretences;** spelled **pretense** in American English. **1** A **pretence** is an action or way of behaving that is intended to make people believe something that is not true. Welland made a pretence of writing a note in his pad... We have to go along with the pretence that things are getting better. **2** If you do something under **false pretences**, you do it when people do not know the truth about you and your intentions. Conrad had been imprisoned for a year for gaining money by false pretences.

◆◇◇◇
N-VAR

PHRASE

pre·tend /prɪˈtend/ **pretends, pretending, pretended. 1** If you **pretend** that something is the case, you act in a way that is intended to make people believe that it is the case, although in fact it is not. Sometimes the boy pretended to be asleep... I had no option but to pretend ignorance. **2** If you **pretend** that you are doing something, you imagine that you are doing it, for example as part of a game. She can sunbathe and pretend she's in Spain. **3** You use **pretend** to describe something which you know is not genuine but which you treat as genuine, for example as part of a game. They are only too glad to share the stage with a pretend crocodile or polar bear. **4** If you say you **do not pretend** that something is the case, you mean that you do not claim that it is the case. We do not pretend that the past six years have been without problems.

◆◆◇◇
VERB
V that
V to-inf
V n

VERB
Also V that
Also V to-inf

ADJ: ADJ n

VB: with neg
V that
Also V to-inf

pre·tend·er /prɪˈtendə/ **pretenders.** A pretender to a position is someone who claims the right to that position, and whose claim is disputed by others. ...the Comte de Paris, pretender to the French throne.

◆◇◇◇
N-COUNT

pre·ten·sion /prɪˈtenʃən/ **pretensions. 1** If you say that someone has **pretensions**, you disapprove of them because they claim or pretend that they are more important than they really are. We like him for his honesty, his lack of pretension. **2** If someone has **pretensions to** something, they claim to be or do that thing. It will remain as a pressure group, but no longer has any pretension to be a political party.

◆◇◇◇
N-VAR
PRAGMATICS

N-UNCOUNT:
also N in pl

pre·ten·tious /prɪˈtenʃəs/. If you say that someone or something is **pretentious**, you mean that they try to seem important or significant, but you do not think that they are; used showing disapproval. His response was full of pretentious nonsense. ♦ **pre·ten·tious·ness** He has a tendency towards pretentiousness.

◆◇◇◇
ADJ-GRADED
PRAGMATICS

N-UNCOUNT

pre·text /ˈpriːtekst/ **pretexts.** A **pretext** is a reason which you pretend has caused you to do something. They would now find some dubious pretext to restart the war.

◆◇◇◇
N-COUNT

pret·ty /ˈprɪti/ **prettier, prettiest. 1** If you describe someone, especially a girl, as **pretty**, you mean that they look nice and are attractive in a delicate way. ♦ **pret·ti·ly** /ˈprɪtɪli/. She was laughing prettily at me. ♦ **pret·ti·ness** Her prettiness had been much admired. **2** A place or a thing that is **pretty** is attractive and pleasant, in a charming but not particularly unusual way. ♦ **pret·ti·ly** The living-room was prettily decorated. ♦ **pret·ti·ness** ...shells of quite unbelievable prettiness. **3** You can use **pretty** before an adjective or adverb to mean 'quite' or 'rather'. Pretty soon after my arrival I found lodgings. **4 Pretty much** or **pretty well** means 'almost'. His new government looks pretty much like the old one... I travel pretty well every week. **5** If you say that someone **is sitting pretty**, you mean that they are in a good, safe, or comfortable position. **6** ● **not a pretty sight**: see **sight**.

◆◆◆◇
ADJ-GRADED

ADV-GRADED
N-UNCOUNT

ADJ-GRADED

ADV-GRADED
N-UNCOUNT

ADV:
ADV adj/adv
INFORMAL
PHRASE
INFORMAL

PHRASE
INFORMAL

pret·zel /ˈpretsl/ **pretzels.** A **pretzel** is a small, glazed, crisp biscuit, which has salt on the outside. Pretzels are usually shaped like knots or sticks.

N-COUNT

pre·vail /prɪˈveɪl/ **prevails, prevailing, prevailed. 1** If a proposal, principle, or opinion **prevails**, it gains influence or is accepted, often after a struggle or argument. Political and personal ambitions are starting to prevail over economic interests. **2** If a situation, attitude, or custom **prevails** in a particular place at a particular time, it is normal or most common in that place at that time. ...the confusion which had prevailed at the time of the revolution. **3** If one side in a battle, contest, or dispute **prevails**, it overcomes the other side and is victorious. I do hope he will prevail over the rebels. **4** If you **prevail upon** someone or **prevail on** someone to do something, you succeed in persuading them to do it. We must, each of us, prevail upon our congressman to act.

◆◆◇◇
VERB: V
V over n

VERB
V

VERB: V
V over/
against n
VERB
V upon/on n
to-inf
FORMAL

pre·vail·ing /prɪˈveɪlɪŋ/. The **prevailing wind** in an area is the type of wind that blows over that area most of the time.

ADJ: ADJ n

preva·lent /ˈprevələnt/. A condition or belief that is **prevalent** is common. This condition is more prevalent in women than in men. ♦ **preva·lence** Not much is known about the prevalence of AIDS in the general population.

◆◇◇◇
ADJ-GRADED

N-UNCOUNT

pre·vari·cate /prɪˈværɪkeɪt/ **prevaricates, prevaricating, prevaricated.** If you **prevaricate**, you avoid giving a direct answer or making a firm decision. ♦ **pre·vari·ca·tion** /prɪˌværɪˈkeɪʃən/ **prevarications.** After months of prevarication, the political decision had at last been made.

VERB: V

N-UNCOUNT:
also N in pl

pre·vent /prɪˈvent/ **prevents, preventing, prevented. 1** To **prevent** something means to ensure that it does not happen. Further treatment will prevent cancer from developing... We recognized the possibility and took steps to prevent it happening.

◆◆◆◆
VERB
V n
V n from -ing
V n -ing

♦ **pre·ven·tion** ...*crime prevention.* **2** To **prevent** someone **from** doing something means to make it impossible for them to do it. *The police have been trying to prevent them carrying weapons.*
<small>N-UNCOUNT VERB: V n from-ing V n -ing Also V n</small>

pre·vent·able /prɪˈventəbəl/. **Preventable** diseases or deaths could be stopped from occurring.
<small>ADJ</small>

pre·ven·ta·tive /prɪˈventətɪv/. **Preventative** means the same as **preventive**.
<small>ADJ: ADJ n</small>

pre·ven·tive /prɪˈventɪv/. **Preventive** actions are intended to help prevent things such as disease or crime. *People accused the ministry of failing to take adequate preventive measures.*
<small>♦◇◇◇◇ ADJ</small>

pre·view /ˈpriːvjuː/ **previews, previewing, previewed. 1** A **preview** is an opportunity to see something such as a film or invention before it is open or available to the public. *...a sneak preview of the type of car that could be commonplace within ten years.* **2** If a journalist or critic **previews** something such as a film or invention, they see it and describe it to the public before the public see it for themselves.
<small>♦♦◇◇◇ N-COUNT</small>
<small>VERB: V n</small>

pre·vi·ous /ˈpriːviəs/. **1** A **previous** event or thing is one that happened or came before the one that you are talking about. *She has a teenage daughter from a previous marriage.* **2** You refer to the period of time or the thing immediately before the one that you are talking about as the **previous** one. *...the rain of the previous week.*
<small>♦♦♦♦◇ ADJ: ADJ n</small>
<small>ADJ: det ADJ</small>

pre·vi·ous·ly /ˈpriːviəsli/. **1 Previously** means at some time before the period that you are talking about. *The contract was awarded to a previously unknown company... Previously she had very little time to work.* **2** You can use **previously** to say how much earlier one event was than another event. *He had first entered the House 12 years previously.*
<small>♦♦♦◇◇ ADV</small>
<small>ADV: n ADV</small>

pre-'war; also spelled **prewar. Pre-war** is used to describe things that happened, existed, or were made in the period immediately before a war, especially the Second World War (1939-45). *...Poland's pre-war leader.*
<small>♦◇◇◇◇ ADJ</small>

prey /preɪ/ **preys, preying, preyed. 1** A creature's **prey** are the creatures that it hunts and eats in order to live. ● See also **bird of prey.** A creature that **preys on** other creatures lives by catching and eating them. *The larvae prey upon small aphids.* **3** You can refer to people as someone's **prey** when they are the victims of criminals or other dishonest people. *This burglar thought old people are easy prey.* **4** If someone **preys on** other people, especially people who are unable to protect themselves, they take advantage of them or harm them in some way. *Loan companies prey on weak families already in debt.* **5** If something **preys on** your mind, you cannot stop thinking and worrying about it. **6** If someone or something is **prey** to something bad, they have a tendency to let themselves be affected by it. *He was prey to a growing despair.* **7** To **fall prey** to something bad means to be taken over or affected by it. *Children in evacuation centres are falling prey to disease.*
<small>♦♦◇◇◇ N-COLL-UNCOUNT VERB V on/upon n</small>
<small>N-UNCOUNT</small>
<small>VERB V on n</small>
<small>VERB: V on n N-UNCOUNT: also a N, N ton</small>
<small>PHRASE</small>

price /praɪs/ **prices, pricing, priced. 1** The **price** of something is the amount of money that you have to pay in order to buy it. *They expected house prices to rise... They haven't come down in price.* **2** See also **retail price index, selling price. 3** If something **is priced at** a particular amount, the price is set at that amount. *Digital will price the new line at less than half the cost of comparable IBM mainframes.* ♦ **pric·ing** *It's hard to maintain competitive pricing.* **4** If you can buy something that you want **at a price**, it is for sale, but it is extremely expensive. *Most goods are available, but at a price.* **5** ● to **price** yourself **out of the market**: see **market. 6** The **price** that you pay for something that you want is an unpleasant thing that you have to do or suffer in order to get it. *Slovenia will have to pay a high price for independence.* **7** If you want something **at any price**, you are determined to get it, even if unpleasant things happen as a result. **8** If you get something that you
<small>♦♦♦♦♦ N-COUNT</small>
<small>VERB: be V-ed at n V n at n</small>
<small>N-UNCOUNT</small>
<small>PHRASE</small>
<small>N-SING</small>
<small>PHRASE</small>
<small>PHRASE</small>

want **at a price**, you get it but something unpleasant happens as a result. *Fame comes at a price.* **9** You use **what price** in front of a word or expression that refers to something happening when you want to ask how likely it is to happen. You usually do this to emphasize either that it is very likely or that it is very unlikely to happen. *What price a glorious repeat of last week's triumph?* **10** You use 'at **what price?**' to comment on the fact that the consequences of doing something are unpleasant. *Yes, they are free of him, but at what price to themselves, their families, those left behind?*
<small>PHRASE PRAGMATICS</small>
<small>PHRASE</small>

price·less /ˈpraɪsləs/. **1** If you say that something is **priceless**, you are emphasizing that it is worth a very large amount of money. **2** If you say that something is **priceless**, you mean that it is extremely useful. *They are a priceless record of a brief period in British history.*
<small>♦◇◇◇◇ ADJ-GRADED</small>
<small>PRAGMATICS ADJ-GRADED</small>

'price tag, price tags; also spelled **price-tag. 1** If something has a **price tag** of a particular amount, that is the amount that you must pay in order to buy it. *I can't say it justifies the price tag of £100.* **2** In a shop, the **price tag** on an article is a small piece of card or paper which is attached to the article and which has the price written on it.
<small>♦◇◇◇◇ N-COUNT WRITTEN</small>
<small>N-COUNT</small>

'price war, price wars. If competing companies are involved in a **price war**, they each try to gain an advantage by lowering their prices as much as possible in order to sell more of their products and damage their competitors financially.
<small>♦◇◇◇◇ N-COUNT</small>

pricey /ˈpraɪsi/ **pricier, priciest.** If something is **pricey**, it is expensive.
<small>ADJ-GRADED INFORMAL</small>

prick /prɪk/ **pricks, pricking, pricked. 1** If you **prick** something, you make small holes in it with a sharp object such as a pin. **2** If something sharp **pricks** you or if you **prick** yourself with something sharp, it sticks into you or presses your skin and causes you pain. *She had just pricked her finger with the needle.* ► Also a noun. *At the same time she felt a prick on her neck.* **3** If something **pricks your conscience**, you are suddenly aware of your conscience. *Most were sympathetic once we pricked their consciences.*
<small>♦◇◇◇◇ VERB: V n</small>
<small>VERB V n Also V pron-refl</small>
<small>N-COUNT</small>
<small>VERB V n</small>

prick up. If someone **pricks up their ears** or if their **ears prick up**, they listen eagerly when they suddenly hear an interesting sound or an important piece of information. *Ears which prick up at the mention of royalty are sure to be disappointed.*
<small>PHRASAL VB ERG: V P noun V P</small>

prick·le /ˈprɪkəl/ **prickles, prickling, prickled. 1** If your skin **prickles**, it feels as if a lot of small sharp points are being stuck into it, either because of something touching it or because you feel a strong emotion. *He paused, feeling his scalp prickling under his hair.* ► Also a noun. *I felt a prickle of disquiet.* **2 Prickles** are small sharp points that stick out from leaves or from the stalks of plants.
<small>VERB V</small>
<small>N-COUNT</small>
<small>N-COUNT</small>

prick·ly /ˈprɪkli/. **1** Something that is **prickly** feels rough and uncomfortable, as if it has a lot of prickles. **2** Someone who is **prickly** loses their temper or gets upset very easily. **3** A **prickly** issue or subject is one that is rather complicated and difficult to discuss or resolve.
<small>♦◇◇◇◇ ADJ-GRADED</small>
<small>ADJ-GRADED</small>
<small>ADJ-GRADED</small>

,prickly 'pear, prickly pears. A **prickly pear** is a kind of cactus that has round fruit with prickles on it. The fruit from the cactus, which you can eat, is also called a **prickly pear.**
<small>N-COUNT</small>

pride /praɪd/ **prides, priding, prided. 1 Pride** is a feeling of satisfaction which you have because you or people close to you have done something good or possess something good. *...the sense of pride in a job well done... They can look back on their endeavours with pride.* **2** If you **pride** yourself **on** a quality or skill that you have, you are very proud of it. *Smith prides himself on being able to organise his own life.* **3** Someone or something that is your **pride and joy** is very important to you and makes you feel very happy. *The bike soon became his pride and joy.* **4 Pride** is a sense of dignity and self-respect. *It was a severe blow to Kendall's pride.* **5** Someone's **pride** is the feeling that they have that
<small>♦♦♦◇◇ N-UNCOUNT</small>
<small>VERB V pron-refl on -ing/n</small>
<small>PHRASE</small>
<small>N-UNCOUNT</small>
<small>N-UNCOUNT</small>

they are better or more important than other people; used showing disapproval. *His pride may still be his downfall.* **6** If you **swallow** your **pride**, you decide to do something even though you think it will cause you to lose some of your dignity and self-respect. [PRAGMATICS] [PHRASE]

7 If something takes **pride of place**, it is treated as the most important thing in a group of things. *The manifesto gives pride of place to job creation.* [PHRASE]

priest /priːst/ **priests. 1** A **priest** is a member of the Christian clergy in the Catholic, Anglican, or Orthodox church. **2** In many non-Christian religions a **priest** is a man who has particular duties and responsibilities in a place where people worship. **3** See also **high priest**. ◆◆◇◇ N-COUNT N-COUNT

priest·ess /ˈpriːstes/ **priestesses.** A **priestess** is a woman in a non-Christian religion who has particular duties and responsibilities in a place where people worship. ● See also **high priestess**. ◆◇◇◇ N-COUNT

priest·hood /ˈpriːsthʊd/ **1 Priesthood** is the position of being a priest or the period of time during which someone is a priest. *He spent the first twenty-five years of his priesthood as an academic.* **2 The priesthood** is all the members of the Christian clergy, especially in a particular Church. *Should the General Synod vote women into the priesthood?* ◆◇◇◇ N-UNCOUNT N-SING: the N

priest·ly /ˈpriːstli/. **Priestly** is used to describe things that belong or relate to a priest. *...his priestly duties.* ADJ

prig /prɪg/ **prigs.** If you call someone a **prig**, you disapprove of them because they behave in a very moral way and disapprove of other people's behaviour as though they were superior. ◆ **prig·gish** *He hated the kid's priggish tone.* N-COUNT [PRAGMATICS] ADJ-GRADED

prim /prɪm/ **1** If you describe someone as **prim**, you disapprove of them because they behave too correctly and are too easily shocked by anything rude or improper. *We tend to imagine that the Victorians were very prim and proper.* ◆ **prim·ly** *We sat primly at either end of a long settee.* **2** If you describe something as **prim**, you mean that it is very neat, tidy, or sensible. ADJ-GRADED [PRAGMATICS] ADV-GRADED: ADV with v ADJ-GRADED

pri·ma·cy /ˈpraɪməsi/. The **primacy** of something is the fact that it is the most important or most powerful thing in a particular situation. *...the primacy of the individual.* ◆◇◇◇◇ N-UNCOUNT FORMAL

pri·ma don·na /ˌpriːmə ˈdɒnə/ **prima donnas. 1** A **prima donna** is the main female singer in an opera. **2** If you describe someone as a **prima donna**, you disapprove of them because they think they can behave badly or get what they want because they have a particular talent. N-COUNT N-COUNT [PRAGMATICS]

pri·mae·val /praɪˈmiːvəl/. See **primeval**.

pri·ma fa·cie /ˌpraɪmə ˈfeɪʃi/. **Prima facie** is used to describe something which appears to be true when you first consider it. *There was a prima facie case that a contempt of court had been committed.* ADJ FORMAL

pri·mal /ˈpraɪməl/. **Primal** is used to describe something that relates to the origins of things or that is very basic. *Jealousy is a primal emotion. ...the primal mysteries of the earth.* ◆◇◇◇◇ ADJ-GRADED FORMAL

pri·mari·ly /ˈpraɪmərɪli, AM praɪˈmeərɪli/. You can use **primarily** to say what is mainly true in a particular situation. *Public order is primarily an urban problem.* ◆◆◇◇◇ ADV: ADV with v, ADV with cl/group

pri·ma·ry /ˈpraɪməri, AM -meri/ **primaries. 1** You use **primary** to describe something that is extremely important or most important for someone or something. *That's the primary reason the company's share price has held up so well... The family continues to be the primary source of care and comfort for people as they grow older.* **2 Primary** education is given to pupils between the ages of 5 and 11. The American equivalent is **elementary** education. *...primary pupils.* **3 Primary** is used to describe something that occurs first. *It is not the primary tumour that kills, but secondary growths elsewhere in the body.* **4** A **primary** or a **primary election** is an election in an American state in which people vote for someone to become a candidate for a political office. ◆◆◆◇◇ ADJ: ADJ n FORMAL ADJ: ADJ n BRITISH ADJ: ADJ n N-COUNT

primary 'colour, primary colours; spelled **primary color** in American English. **Primary colours** are basic colours that can be mixed together to produce other colours. They are usually considered to be red, yellow, blue, and sometimes green. N-COUNT

'primary school, primary schools. A **primary school** is a school for children between the ages of 5 and 11. The American equivalent is an **elementary school.** ◆◆◇◇◇ N-VAR BRITISH

pri·mate /ˈpraɪmət/ **primates.** The pronunciation /ˈpraɪmeɪt/ is also used for meaning 2. **1** A **primate** is a member of the group of mammals which includes humans, monkeys, and apes. **2 The Primate** of a particular country or region is the archbishop of that country or region. ◆◇◇◇◇ N-COUNT N-COUNT

prime /praɪm/ **primes, priming, primed. 1** You use **prime** to describe something that is most important in a situation. *Political stability, meanwhile, will be a prime concern... The police will see me as the prime suspect!* **2** You use **prime** to describe something that is of the best possible quality. *It was one of the City's prime sites, giving a clear view of the Stock Exchange and the Bank of England.* **3** You use **prime** to describe an example of a particular kind of thing that is absolutely typical. *New York is a prime example of a city where crime strangles small-business development.* **4** If someone or something is in their **prime**, they are at the stage in their existence when they are at their strongest, most active, or most successful. *She was in her intellectual prime.* **5** If you **prime** someone to do something, you prepare them to do it, for example by giving them information about it beforehand. *Marianne had not known until Arnold primed her for her duties that she was to be the sole female... The White House press corps has been primed to leap to the defense of the fired officials.* **6** If someone **primes a bomb** or **a gun**, they prepare it so that it is ready to explode or fire. ◆◆◆◇◇ ADJ: ADJ n ADJ: ADJ n ADJ: ADJ n N-UNCOUNT VERB: V n V n for n be V-ed to-inf VERB: V n

Prime 'Minister, Prime Ministers. The leader of the government in some countries is called the **Prime Minister.** ◆◆◆◆◆ N-COUNT

prime 'mover, prime movers. The **prime mover** behind a plan, idea, or situation is someone who has an important influence in starting it. *He was the prime mover behind the coup.* N-COUNT

prime 'number, prime numbers. In mathematics, a **prime number** is a whole number greater than 1 that cannot be divided exactly by any whole number except itself and the number 1, for example 17. N-COUNT

pri·mer /ˈpraɪmə/ **primers. 1 Primer** is a type of paint that is put onto wood in order to prepare it for the main layer of paint. **2** A **primer** is a book containing basic facts about a subject, which is used by someone who is beginning to study that subject. N-VAR N-COUNT DATED

'prime rate, prime rates. A bank's **prime rate** is the lowest rate of interest which it charges at a particular time and which is offered only to certain customers. ◆◇◇◇◇ N-COUNT

'prime time; also spelled **primetime. Prime time** television or radio programmes are broadcast when the most viewers or listeners are watching television or listening to the radio. ◆◇◇◇◇ N-UNCOUNT

pri·meval /praɪˈmiːvəl/; also spelled **primaeval** in British English. **1** You use **primeval** to describe things that belong to a very early period in the history of the world. *...a vast expanse of primeval swamp.* **2** You use **primeval** to describe feelings and emotions that are instinctive. *...a primeval urge to hit out at that which causes him pain.* ADJ FORMAL ADJ

primi·tive /ˈprɪmɪtɪv/. **1 Primitive** means belonging to a society in which people live in a very simple way, usually without industries or a writing system. *...primitive tribes.* **2 Primitive** means belonging to a very early period in the development of an animal or plant. *...primitive whales... It is a primitive instinct to flee a place of danger.* **3** If you describe something as **primitive**, you mean that it is very ◆◆◇◇◇ ADJ-GRADED ADJ-GRADED ADJ-GRADED

simple in style or very old-fashioned. *It's using some rather primitive technology.*

pri·mor·dial /praɪˈmɔːdiəl/. You use **primordial** to describe things that belong to a very early time in the history of the world. *Twenty million years ago, Idaho was populated by dense primordial forest.* — ADJ FORMAL

prim·rose /ˈprɪmrəʊz/ **primroses.** A **primrose** is a wild plant which has pale yellow flowers. — ◆◇◇◇◇ N-VAR

primu·la /ˈprɪmjʊlə/ **primulas.** A **primula** is a type of primrose with very brightly coloured flowers. — N-VAR

Pri·mus /ˈpraɪməs/. A **Primus** or a **Primus stove** is a small cooker that burns paraffin and is often used in camping. Primus is a trademark. — N-SING BRITISH

prince /prɪns/ **princes.** 1 A **prince** is a male member of a royal family, especially the son of the king or queen of a country. 2 A **prince** is the male royal ruler of a small country or state. 3 If someone describes a man as the **prince** of a particular type of work, they mean that he is the best man doing that type of work. *To his 19th-century peers, Robert Brown was the prince of botany.* — ◆◆◆◇ N-TITLE; N-COUNT N-TITLE; N-COUNT N-COUNT LITERARY

prince·ly /ˈprɪnsli/. 1 A **princely** sum of money is a large sum of money. 2 **Princely** means belonging to a prince or suitable for a prince. *It was the embodiment of princely magnificence.* — ADJ-GRADED ADJ

prin·cess /ˌprɪnˈses, AM -ˈsəs/ **princesses.** A **princess** is a female member of a royal family, usually the daughter of a king or queen or the wife of a prince. — ◆◆◆◇ N-TITLE; N-COUNT

prin·ci·pal /ˈprɪnsɪpəl/ **principals.** 1 **Principal** means first in order of importance. *Their principal concern is bound to be that of winning the next general election.* 2 The **principal** of a school or college is the person in charge of it. — ◆◆◆◇◇ ADJ: ADJ n N-COUNT

prin·ci·pal·i·ty /ˌprɪnsɪˈpæliti/ **principalities.** A **principality** is a country that is ruled by a prince. — N-COUNT

prin·ci·pal·ly /ˈprɪnsɪpəli/. **Principally** means more than anything else. *This is principally because the major export markets are slowing.* — ◆◇◇◇◇ ADV; ADV with cl/ group

prin·ci·ple /ˈprɪnsɪpəl/ **principles.** 1 A **principle** is a belief that you have about the way you should behave, which influences your behaviour. *Buck never allowed himself to be bullied into doing anything that went against his principles. ...a man of principle.* 2 If you refuse to do something **on principle**, you refuse to do it because of a particular belief that you have. *He would vote against it on principle.* 3 The **principles** of a particular theory or philosophy are its basic rules or laws. 4 Scientific **principles** are general scientific laws which explain how something happens or works. 5 If you agree with something **in principle**, you agree in general terms to the idea of it, although you do not know the details or know if it will be possible. *The conference approved in principle a new policy-making process.* 6 If something is possible **in principle**, there is no known reason why it should not happen, even though it has not happened before. *Even assuming this to be in principle possible, it will not be achieved soon.* — ◆◆◆◇ N-VAR PHRASE N-COUNT N-COUNT PHRASE PHRASE

prin·ci·pled /ˈprɪnsɪpəld/. If you describe someone as **principled**, you approve of them because they have strong moral principles. — ADJ-GRADED PRAGMATICS

print /prɪnt/ **prints, printing, printed.** 1 If someone **prints** something such as a book, newspaper, or leaflet, they produce it in large quantities by a mechanical process. *Our brochure is printed on environmentally-friendly paper.* ▶ **Print up** means the same as **print.** *Community workers here are printing up pamphlets for peace demonstrations.* ♦ **print·ing** *...a printing and publishing company.* 2 The **print** media consists of newspapers and magazines, but not television or radio. 3 If a newspaper or magazine **prints** a piece of writing, it includes it or publishes it. *...a questionnaire printed in the magazine recently.* 4 If you or your words appear **in print**, or get **into print**, what you say or write is published in a book, newspaper, or other printed text. 5 If a book is **in print**, it is available from a publisher. If it is **out of print** it is no longer — ◆◆◆◆ VERB: V n beV-ed prep/adv PHRASAL VB V P noun N-UNCOUNT ADJ: ADJ n VERB: V n V-ed Also beV-ed in n PHRASE PHRASE

available from a publisher. 6 See also **printing.** 7 ● to **print money**: see **money.** 8 If numbers or letters **are printed** on an object, they appear on it. You can also say that an object **is printed** with letters or numbers. *The company has for some time printed its phone number on its products.* 9 If a text or a picture **is printed**, a copy of it is produced by means of a computer printer or some other type of equipment. *'Ecu' was printed in lower case rather than capital letters. ...machines that can print on both sides of a page.* 10 If material or clothing **is printed** with a pattern, or a pattern **is printed** on it, the pattern is reproduced on the material, usually by means of dye and special machinery. *She hand-paints and prints scarves.* 11 A **print** is a piece of clothing or material with a pattern printed on it. You can also refer to the pattern itself as a **print.** *Her mother wore one of her dark summer prints.* 12 When you **print** a photograph, you produce it from a negative. *...printing a black-and-white negative on to colour paper.* 13 A **print** is a photograph from a film that has been developed. 14 A **print** is a picture that is copied from a painting by photography or made mechanically from specially prepared surfaces and dyes. 15 **Print** is used to refer to letters and numbers as they appear on the pages of a book, newspaper, or printed document. *...columns of tiny print.* 16 The **small print** or the **fine print** of something such as an advertisement or a contract consists of the technical details and legal conditions, which are often printed in much smaller letters than the rest of the text. 17 If you **print** words, you write in letters that are not joined together and that look like the letters in a book or newspaper. 18 You can refer to a footprint as a **print.** 19 You can refer to someone's fingerprints as their **prints.** — VERB V n on n Also beV-ed with n VERB beV-ed prep/adv Also V n VERB: beV-ed with n V n N-COUNT VERB: V n V n onto/from N-COUNT N-COUNT N-UNCOUNT PHRASE VERB: V n N-COUNT N-COUNT

print out. If a computer or a machine attached to a computer **prints** something **out**, it produces a copy of it on paper. *Enter measurements and the computer will print out the pattern.* ● See also **printout.** — PHRASAL VB V n P V P noun

print up. See **print** 1. — PHRASAL VB

print·able /ˈprɪntəbəl/. If you say that someone's words or remarks are not **printable**, you mean that they are likely to offend people, and are therefore not suitable to be repeated in writing or speech. — ADJ-GRADED JOURNALISM

printed 'circuit board, printed circuit boards. A **printed circuit board** is an electronic circuit in which some of the components and connections are formed by fine metallic lines and shapes on a thin insulating board. — N-COUNT

printed 'word. The **printed word** is the same as the written word. — N-SING: the N

print·er /ˈprɪntə/ **printers.** 1 A **printer** is a machine that can be connected to a computer in order to make copies on paper of documents or other information held by the computer. ● See also **laser printer.** 2 A **printer** is a person or firm whose job is printing books, leaflets, or similar material. — ◆◆◇◇ N-COUNT N-COUNT

print·ing /ˈprɪntɪŋ/ **printings.** If copies of a book are printed and published on a number of different occasions, you can refer to each of these occasions as a **printing.** ● See also **print.** — N-COUNT

'printing press, printing presses. A **printing press** is a machine used for printing, especially one that can print books, newspapers, or leaflets in large numbers. — N-COUNT

print·out /ˈprɪntaʊt/ **printouts;** also spelled **print-out.** A **printout** is a piece of paper on which information from a computer or similar device has been printed. — N-COUNT

'print run, print runs. A **print run** of something such as a book or a newspaper is the number of copies of it that are printed and published at one time. *...an initial print run of 7,000 copies.* — N-COUNT TECHNICAL

'print shop, print shops. A **print shop** is a small business which prints and copies things such as documents, letters, and cards for customers. — N-COUNT

pri·or /ˈpraɪə/ **priors.** 1 You use **prior** to indicate that something has already happened, or must — ◆◆◇◇ ADJ: ADJ n

happen, before another event takes place. *He had no prior knowledge of the protest... The Constitution requires the president to seek the prior approval of Congress for military action.* **2** A **prior** claim or duty is more important than other claims or duties and needs to be dealt with first. *The firm I wanted to use had prior commitments.* **3** If something happens **prior to** a particular time or event, it happens before that time or event. *...a man seen hanging around the area prior to the shooting.* **4** A **prior** is a monk who is in charge of a priory or a monk who is an abbot's deputy in a monastery. `ADJ: ADJ n` `PHR-PREP FORMAL` `N-COUNT; N-TITLE`

pri·or·ess /'praɪərəs/ **prioresses.** A **prioress** is a nun who is in charge of a convent. `N-COUNT; N-TITLE`

pri·ori·tize /praɪ'ɒrɪtaɪz, AM -'ɔːr-/ **prioritizes, prioritizing, prioritized;** also spelled **prioritise** in British English. **1** If you **prioritize** something, you treat it as more important than other things. *The government is prioritising the service sector, rather than investing in industry and production.* **2** If you **prioritize** the tasks you have to do, you decide which are the most important and do them first. *Make lists of what to do and prioritize your tasks.* `VERB Vn` `VERB Vn Also V`

pri·or·ity /praɪ'ɒrɪti, AM -'ɔːr-/ **priorities.** **1** If something is a **priority**, it is the most important thing you have to do or deal with, or must be done or dealt with before everything else you have to do. *Being a parent is her first priority... The government's priority is to build more power plants.* **2** If you **give priority** to something or someone, you treat them as more important than anything or anyone else. *The school will give priority to science.* **3** If something **takes priority** or **has priority** over other things, it is regarded as being more important than them and is dealt with first. *The fight against inflation took priority over measures to combat the deepening recession.* `◆◆◆◇ N-COUNT` `PHRASE` `PHRASE`

pri·ory /'praɪəri/ **priories.** A **priory** is a place where a small group of monks live and work together. *...Lindisfarne Priory on Holy Island.* `◆◇◇◇ N-COUNT`

prise /praɪz/. See **prize.** `◆◇◇◇`

prism /'prɪzəm/ **prisms.** **1** A **prism** is an object made of clear glass or plastic which has many straight sides. It separates the light which passes through it into the colours of the rainbow. **2** If you see something through a **prism of** something such as time or memory, your perception is distorted by that thing. *Through the smoky prism of time, I could just barely make out my father as a young man.* `N-COUNT` `N-COUNT LITERARY`

pris·on /'prɪzən/ **prisons.** A **prison** is a building where criminals are kept in order to punish them or where people awaiting trial are kept. *...the gas chamber at San Quentin Prison.* `◆◆◆◆ N-VAR`

'prison camp, prison camps. A **prison camp** is a guarded camp where prisoners of war or political prisoners are kept. `N-COUNT`

pris·on·er /'prɪzənə/ **prisoners.** **1** A **prisoner** is a person who is kept in a prison as a punishment for a crime that they have committed. *The committee is concerned about the large number of prisoners sharing cells.* **2** A **prisoner** is a person who has been captured by an enemy, for example in war. *...wartime hostages and concentration-camp prisoners... He was held prisoner in Vietnam.* **3** If you say that you are a **prisoner of** a situation, you mean that your are trapped by it. *She was a prisoner of her own ego.* `◆◆◆◆ N-COUNT` `N-COUNT: also hold/take n N` `N-COUNT N of n`

prisoner of 'conscience, prisoners of conscience. **Prisoners of conscience** are people who have been put into prison for their political or social beliefs or for breaking the law while protesting against a political or social system. `N-COUNT`

prisoner of 'war, prisoners of war. Prisoners of war are soldiers who have been captured by their enemy during a war and kept as prisoners until the end of the war. `◆◇◇◇ N-COUNT`

pris·sy /'prɪsi/ **prissier, prissiest.** If you say that someone is **prissy**, you are critical of them because they are very easily shocked by anything rude or improper. `ADJ-GRADED` `PRAGMATICS` `INFORMAL`

pris·tine /'prɪstiːn/. **Pristine** things are extremely clean or new. *Now the house is in pristine condition.* `◆◇◇◇ ADJ`

pri·va·cy /'prɪvəsi, AM 'praɪ-/. **1** If you have **privacy**, you are in a place or situation which allows you to do things without other people seeing you or disturbing you. *...shady retreats for relaxing and reading in privacy. ...a collection of over 60 designs to try on in the privacy of your own home.* **2** If someone or something **invades your privacy**, they interfere in your life without your permission. *The press invaded people's privacy unfairly and unjustifiably.* `◆◆◇◇ N-UNCOUNT` `PHRASE`

pri·vate /'praɪvɪt/ **privates.** **1** **Private** industries and services are owned or controlled by an individual person or a commercial company, rather than by the state or an official organization. *...a joint venture with private industry... Bupa runs private hospitals in Britain.* ♦ **pri·vate·ly** *...privately owned businesses.* **2** **Private** individuals are acting only for themselves, and are not representing any group, company, or organization. *The family tried to bring a private prosecution against him for assault.* **3** Your **private** things belong only to you, or may only be used by you. *The landowners have had to sell their private aircraft. ...communists, who want more State control over private property.* **4** **Private** places or gatherings may be attended only by a particular group of people, rather than by the general public. *...private golf clubs... The door is marked 'Private'.* **5** **Private** meetings, discussions, and other activities involve only a small number of people, and very little information about them is given to other people. *Don't bug private conversations, and don't buy papers that reprint them.* ♦ **privately** *I had not talked to Winnette privately for weeks.* **6** If you do something **in private**, you do it without other people being present, often because it is something that you want to keep secret. *Some of what we're talking about might better be discussed in private.* **7** If you describe a place as **private**, or as somewhere where you can be **private**, you mean that it is a quiet place and you can be alone there without being disturbed. *It was the only reasonably private place they could find.* **8** Your **private** life is that part of your life that is concerned with your personal relationships and activities, rather than with your work or business. *My private affairs are no one's business but my own.* **9** Your **private** thoughts or feelings are ones that you do not talk about to other people. *We all felt as if we were intruding on his private grief... It's something very private, and I simply can't talk about it.* ♦ **privately** *Privately, she worries about whether she's really good enough... He had privately resolved he would buy her the dress.* **10** If you describe someone as a **private** person, you mean that they are very quiet by nature and do not reveal their thoughts and feelings to other people. *Gould was an intensely private individual.* **11** You can use **private** to describe situations or activities that are understood only by the people involved in them, and not by anybody else. *Chinese waiters stood in a cluster, sharing a private joke... Twins have a private language that excludes the rest of the family.* **12** **Private** lessons are not part of ordinary school activity, and are given by a teacher to an individual pupil or a small group, usually in return for payment. **13** A **private** is a soldier of the lowest rank in an army. *...Private Wilcox.* **14** Your **privates** are your genitals. *You should wash your feet and your privates every day.* **15** See also **privately.** `◆◆◆◇ ADJ` `ADV: ADV with v` `ADJ: ADJ n` `ADJ` `ADJ` `ADJ` `ADV` `PHRASE` `ADJ-GRADED` `ADJ` `ADJ-GRADED` `ADV` `ADJ-GRADED` `ADJ: ADJ n` `ADJ` `N-COUNT: N-TITLE` `N-PLURAL INFORMAL`

private de'tective, private detectives. A **private detective** is a detective who is not in the police, and who you can hire to find missing people or do other kinds of investigation for you. `N-COUNT`

private 'enterprise. **Private enterprise** is industry and business which is owned by individual people or commercial companies, and not by the government or an official organization. `◆◇◇◇ N-UNCOUNT`

private 'eye, private eyes. You can refer to a private detective as a **private eye**, especially when `◆◇◇◇ N-COUNT INFORMAL`

he or she is a character in a film or story. *Harmon plays a private eye hired by Mimi Rogers to investigate her husband's disappearance.*

private in·ves·ti·ga·tor, private investigators. N-COUNT
A **private investigator** is the same as a **private detective.**

pri·vate·ly /ˈpraɪvɪtli/. If you buy or sell something ◆◇◇◇◇
privately, you buy it from or sell it to another person directly, rather than, for example, going to a shop or asking a dealer to act for you. *The whole process makes buying a car privately as painless as buying from a garage.* ● See also **private**.
ADV: ADV after v

Private 'Member's Bill, Private Members' Bills. In Britain, a **Private Member's Bill** is a law that is proposed by a Member of Parliament acting as an individual rather than as a member of his or her political party.
N-COUNT

private 'parts. You can refer to your genitals as N-PLURAL INFORMAL
your **private parts.**

private 'school, private schools. A private N-VAR
school is a school which is not supported financially by the government and which parents have to pay for their children to go to.

private 'sector. The **private sector** is the part of ◆◆◇◇◇
a country's economy which consists of industries and commercial companies that are not owned or controlled by the government.
N-SING: the N, N n

private 'soldier, private soldiers. A private N-COUNT FORMAL
soldier is a soldier of the lowest rank in an army.

pri·va·tion /praɪˈveɪʃən/ **privations.** If you suffer N-UNCOUNT: also N in pl FORMAL
privation or **privations**, you have to live without many of the things that are thought to be necessary in life, such as food, clothing, or comfort. *They endured five years of privation during the second world war.*

pri·vat·ize /ˈpraɪvətaɪz/ **privatizes, privatizing,** ◆◆◇◇◇
privatized; also spelled **privatise** in British English. If a company or industry that is owned or controlled by the state **is privatized**, the government sells it or transfers control of it to one or more private companies. *...a pledge to privatise the rail and coal industries within three years.* ♦ **pri·vati·za·tion** /ˌpraɪvətaɪˈzeɪʃən/ **privatizations** *...the privatisation of British Rail.*
VERB: be V-ed V n

N-VAR

priv·et /ˈprɪvɪt/. **Privet** is a type of bush with small N-UNCOUNT
leaves that stay green all year round. It is often grown in gardens to form hedges.

privi·lege /ˈprɪvɪlɪdʒ/ **privileges, privileging,** ◆◆◇◇◇
privileged. 1 A **privilege** is a special right or advantage that only one person or group has. *...a decree abolishing special privileges for government officials.* **2** If you talk about **privilege**, you are talking about the power and advantage that only a small group of people have, usually because of their wealth or their high social class. *Pironi was the son of privilege and wealth, and it showed.* You can use **privilege** in expressions such as **be a privilege** or **have the privilege** when you want to show your appreciation of someone or something or to show your respect. *It must be a privilege to know such a man.* **4** To **privilege** someone or something means to treat them better or differently than other people or things rather than treat them all equally. *They are privileging a tiny number to the disadvantage of the rest.*
N-COUNT

N-UNCOUNT

N-SING PRAGMATICS

VERB V n

privi·leged /ˈprɪvɪlɪdʒd/. **1** Someone who is **privi-** ◆◆◇◇◇
leged has an advantage or opportunity that most other people do not have, often because of their wealth or high social class. *...a very wealthy, privileged elite.* ► Also a noun. *...preserving the power of the privileged and the well off.* **2** Privileged information is known by only a small group of people who are not legally required to disclose it.
ADJ-GRADED

N-PLURAL: the N ADJ

privy /ˈprɪvi/. If you **are privy to** something secret, ◆◇◇◇◇
you have been allowed to know about it. *Only three people, including a policeman, will be privy to the facts.*
ADJ: v-link ADJ to n FORMAL

Privy 'Council. In Britain, **the Privy Council** is a N-PROPER:
group of people who are appointed to advise the the N
king or queen on political affairs.

prize /praɪz/ **prizes, prizing, prized;** also spelled ◆◆◆◇
prise in British English for meanings 5 and 6. **1** A N-COUNT
prize is something valuable, for example money or a trophy, that is given to someone who has the best results in a competition or game, or as a reward for doing good work. *You must claim your prize by telephoning our claims line... He won first prize. ...the Nobel Prize for Physics.* **2** You use **prize** to describe ADJ: ADJ n
things that are of such good quality that they. win prizes or deserve to win prizes. *...a prize bull.* **3** You N-COUNT
can refer to someone or something as a **prize** when people consider them to be of great value or importance. *With no lands of his own, he was no great matrimonial prize.*
4 Something that **is prized** is wanted and admired be- VB: usu
cause it is considered to be very valuable or very good passive,
quality. be V-ed
5 If you **prize** something open or **prize** it away from a VERB:
surface, you force it to open or force it to come away V n with adj
from the surface. *I prised off the metal rim surround-* V n with adv
ing one of the dials... Your dad would prise bullets out from n
of old dead trees. **6** If you **prize** something such as in- VERB
formation **out of** someone, you persuade them to tell V n out of n
you although they may be very unwilling to do. *Alison* out
and I had to prize conversation out of him.

'prize fighter, prize fighters. A **prize fighter** is a N-COUNT
boxer who fights to win money.

'prize-giving, prize-givings. In Britain, a **prize-** N-COUNT
giving is a ceremony where prizes are awarded to people who have produced a very high standard of work.

pro /proʊ/ **pros. 1** A **pro** is a professional. *I have* ◆◆◇◇◇
enjoyed playing with some of the top pros from N-COUNT
Europe and America. **2** A **pro** player is a profession- INFORMAL
al sportsman or woman. You can also use **pro** AMERICAN
to refer to sports that are played by professional sportsmen or women. *...a former college and pro basketball player.*
3 If you are **pro** a particular course of action or belief, PREP
you agree with it or support it. *They're still very pro the Communist party.* **4** The **pros and cons** of something PHRASE
are its advantages and disadvantages, which you consider carefully so that you can make a sensible decision. *They sat for hours debating the pros and cons of setting up their own firm.*

pro- /proʊ-/. You can add **pro-** to adjectives and PREFIX
nouns in order to form adjectives that describe people who support or admire a particular person, system, or idea. *...the pro-democracy campaign.*

pro·ac·tive /proʊˈæktɪv/. **Proactive** actions are in- ADJ-GRADED
tended to cause changes, rather than just reacting to change. *In order to survive the competition a company should be proactive not reactive.*

pro-'am, pro-ams; also spelled **pro am.** A **pro-am** N-COUNT
is a tournament where professional and amateur players compete together in the same event.

prob·abil·is·tic /ˌprɒbəbɪˈlɪstɪk/. **Probabilistic** ac- ADJ
tions, methods, or arguments are based on the idea that you cannot be certain about results or future events but you can judge whether or not they are probable, and act or formulate beliefs on the basis of this judgement.

prob·abil·ity /ˌprɒbəˈbɪlɪti/ **probabilities. 1** The ◆◇◇◇◇
probability of something happening is how likely it N-VAR
is to happen, sometimes expressed as a fraction or a percentage. *Without a transfusion, the victim's prob-*
ability of dying was 100%. **2** You say that there is a N-VAR
probability that something will happen when it is PRAGMATICS
likely to happen. *There's an excellent probability that unless action is quickly taken, pipes will freeze.*
3 If you say that something will happen **in all prob-** PHRASE
ability, you mean that you think it is very likely to PRAGMATICS
happen.

prob·able /ˈprɒbəbəl/. **1** If you say that something ◆◇◇◇◇
is **probable**, you mean that it is likely to be true or ADJ-GRADED
likely to happen. *It is probable that the medication* PRAGMATICS
will suppress the symptom without treating the condition... A bomb was the incident's most probable cause. **2** You can use **probable** to describe a role or ADJ: ADJ n
function that someone or something is likely to

have. *The Socialists united behind their probable presidential candidate, Michel Rocard.*

prob·ab·ly /'prɒbəbli/. **1** If you say that something is **probably** the case, you think that it is likely to be the case, although you are not sure. *The White House probably won't make this plan public until July... Van Gogh is probably the best-known painter in the world.* **2** You can use **probably** when you want to make your opinion sound less forceful or definite, so that you do not offend people. *He'd probably think she and Lenny were both crazy!*　◆◆◆◆ ADV-GRADED: ADV with cl/ group PRAGMATICS

pro·bate /'prəʊbeɪt/. **Probate** is the act or process of officially proving a will to be valid.　N-UNCOUNT

pro·ba·tion /prə'beɪʃən, AM 'prəʊ-/. **1 Probation** is a period of time during which a person who has committed a crime is supervised by a probation officer to ensure that they do not break the law again, rather than being sent to prison. *A young woman admitted three theft charges and was put on probation for two years.* ◆ **pro·ba·tion·er, probationers.** A **probationer** is someone who has been found guilty of committing a crime but is on probation rather than in prison. **2 Probation** is a period of time during which someone is judging your character and ability while you work, in order to see if you are suitable for that type of work. *Employee appointment to the Council will be subject to a term of probation of 6 months.* ◆ **pro·ba·tion·er.** A **probationer** is someone who is still being trained to do a job and is on trial.　◆◇◇◇ N-UNCOUNT N-COUNT N-UNCOUNT N-COUNT

pro·ba·tion·ary /prə'beɪʃənəri, AM prəʊ'beɪʃəneri/. A **probationary** period is a period during which someone is assessed at the beginning of a new job before they are allowed to continue.　ADJ: ADJ n

pro'bation officer, probation officers. A **probation officer** is a person whose job is to supervise and help people who have committed crimes and been put on probation.　◆◇◇◇ N-COUNT

probe /prəʊb/ **probes, probing, probed. 1** If you **probe** into something, you ask questions or make enquiries in order to discover facts about it. *For three years, I have probed for understanding... The Office of Fair Trading has been probing banking practices.* ▶ Also a noun. *...a federal grand-jury probe into corruption within the FDA.* ◆ **prob·ing, probings** *He'll be away from the press and their probings.* **2** If a doctor or dentist **probes**, he or she uses a special instrument to examine delicate parts of a patient's body. *Dr Amid probed around the sensitive area.* **3** A **probe** is a long thin instrument that doctors and dentists use to examine delicate parts of the body. *...a fibre-optic probe.* **4** If you **probe** a place, you search it in order to find someone or something that you looking for. *I probed around for some time in the bushes.* **5** In a conflict such as a war, if one side **probes** another side's defences, they try to find their weaknesses, for example by attacking them in specific areas using a small number of troops. ▶ Also a noun. *Small probes would give the allied armies some combat experience before the main battle started.* **6** A **space probe** is an unmanned spacecraft which travels deep into space in order to study the planets and send information about them back to earth.　◆◆◇◇ VERB: V into n V forn V n N-COUNT N-COUNT VERB: V V prep/adv N-COUNT VERB: V n V adv/prep VERB JOURNALISM N-COUNT N-COUNT

pro·bity /'prəʊbɪti/. **Probity** is a high standard of correct moral behaviour. *He asserted his innocence and his financial probity.*　N-UNCOUNT FORMAL

prob·lem /'prɒbləm/ **problems. 1** A **problem** is a situation that is unsatisfactory and causes difficulties for people. *...the economic problems of the inner city... The main problem is unemployment. ...solving the energy problem.* **2 Problem** children or **problem** families cause a lot of difficulties for themselves or for other people, often because they come from a deprived background or because they have had a lot of bad experiences. **3** 'No problem' is an expression that people say to show their willingness to do what they have been asked. *'Can you repair it?' 'No problem. .* **4** 'No prob-　◆◆◆◆ N-COUNT ADJ: ADJ n CONVENTION PRAGMATICS INFORMAL CONVENTION

lem' is an expression that you can use to let someone else know that you do not mind them doing something they have said they are going to do. *If they don't want to speak to me, fine. No problem.* **5** A **problem** is a puzzle that requires logical thought or mathematics to solve it. *With mathematical problems, you can save time by approximating.*　PRAGMATICS INFORMAL N-COUNT

prob·lem·at·ic /ˌprɒblə'mætɪk/. Something that is **problematic** involves problems and difficulties. *Some places are more problematic than others for women traveling alone.*　◆◇◇◇ ADJ-GRADED FORMAL

prob·lem·at·i·cal /ˌprɒblə'mætɪkəl/. **Problematical** means the same as **problematic**.　ADJ-GRADED FORMAL

pro·ced·ur·al /prə'siːdʒərəl/. **Procedural** means involving a formal procedure. *A Spanish judge rejected the suit on procedural grounds.*　◆◇◇◇ ADJ FORMAL

pro·ce·dure /prə'siːdʒə/ **procedures.** A **procedure** is a way of doing something, especially the usual or correct way. *A biopsy is usually a minor surgical procedure... Michael did not follow the correct procedure in applying for a visa.*　◆◆◇◇ N-VAR

pro·ceed, proceeds, proceeding, proceeded. The verb is pronounced /prə'siːd/. The plural noun in meaning 5 is pronounced /'prəʊsiːdz/. **1** If you **proceed** to do something, you do it, often after doing something else first. *He proceeded to tell me of my birth.* **2** If you **proceed with** a course of action, you continue with it. *The trial has been delayed until November because the defence is not ready to proceed.* **3** If an activity, process, or event **proceeds**, it goes on and does not stop. *The ideas were not new. Their development had proceeded steadily since the war.* **4** If you **proceed** in a particular direction, you go in that direction. *The freighter was allowed to proceed after satisfying them that it was not breaking sanctions.* **5** The **proceeds** of an event or activity are the money that has been obtained from it. *The proceeds from the concert will go towards famine relief.*　◆◆◇◇ VERB V to-inf VERB: V with n VERB V VERB: V prep/adv FORMAL N-PLURAL: the N

pro·ceed·ing /prə'siːdɪŋ/ **proceedings. 1** Legal **proceedings** are legal action taken against someone. *...criminal proceedings against the former prime minister.* **2 The proceedings** are an organized series of events that take place in a particular place. *The proceedings of the enquiry will take place in private.* **3** You can refer to a written record of the discussions at a meeting or conference as **the proceedings**.　◆◆◇◇ N-COUNT FORMAL N-COUNT FORMAL N-PLURAL: the N

pro·cess /'prəʊses, AM 'prɑːses/ **processes, processing, processed. 1** A **process** is a series of actions which are carried out in order to achieve a particular result. *They decided to spread the building process over three years. ...a process of elimination.* **2** A **process** is a series of things which happen naturally and result in a biological or chemical change. *...factors that accelerate the ageing process.* **3** When raw materials or foods **are processed**, they are treated by a chemical or industrial process before they are used or sold. *The material will be processed into plastic pellets. ...diets high in refined and processed foods.* ◆ **pro·cess·ing** *...nuclear fuel processing plant.* ◆ **pro·ces·sor, processors** *...baby-food manufacturers and other processors.* **4** When a person or computer **processes** information, it is dealt with by being put through a system or into a computer. ◆ **pro·cess·ing** *...data processing.* ● See also **word processing.** **5** When people **are processed** by officials, their case is dealt with in stages and they pass from one stage of the process to the next. **6** If you are **in the process of** doing something, you have started to do it and are still doing it. **7** If you are doing something and you do something else **in the process**, you do the second thing as part of doing the first thing. *You have to let us struggle for ourselves, even if we must die in the process.*　◆◆◆◆◆ N-COUNT N-COUNT VERB: be V-ed be V-ed into n Also V n N-UNCOUNT N-COUNT VERB: V n N-UNCOUNT: supp N VERB: be V-ed PHRASE PHRASE

pro·ces·sion /prə'seʃən/ **processions.** A **procession** is a group of people who are walking, riding, or driving in a line as part of a public event. *...a funeral procession.* ◆ **pro·ces·sion·al** *...the processional route along the town's main streets.*　◆◆◇◇ N-COUNT ADJ: ADJ n

pro·ces·sor /ˈprəʊsesə, AM ˈprɑːs-/ **processors.** ◆◆◇◇◇
1 A processor is the part of a computer that inter- N-COUNT TECHNICAL
prets commands and performs the processes the
user has requested. **2** See also **process**.

pro·claim /prəʊˈkleɪm/ **proclaims, proclaiming,** ◆◆◇◇◇
proclaimed. 1 If people **proclaim** something, they VERB: V n
formally make it known to the public. *Britain* V that
proudly proclaims that it is a nation of animal lov- Also V n n,
ers... He still proclaims himself a believer in the V n as n
Revolution. **2** If you **proclaim** something such as an VERB
opinion, you state it emphatically. *'I think we have* V with quote
been heard today,' he proclaimed... He confidently V that
proclaims that he is offering the best value.

proc·la·ma·tion /ˌprɒkləˈmeɪʃən/ **proclama-** ◆◇◇◇◇
tions. A proclamation is a public announcement N-COUNT
about something important. *The proclamation of*
independence was broadcast over the radio.

pro·cliv·ity /prəˈklɪvɪti, AM prəʊ-/ **proclivities.** A N-COUNT
proclivity is a tendency to behave in a particular FORMAL
way or to like a particular thing, often a bad way or
thing. *He was indulging his own sexual proclivities.*

pro·cras·ti·nate /prəʊˈkræstɪneɪt/ **procrasti-** VERB: V
nates, procrastinating, procrastinated. If FORMAL
you **procrastinate**, you keep postponing things that
you should do, often because you do not want to do
them. ◆ **pro·cras·ti·na·tion** /prəʊˌkræstɪˈneɪʃən/. N-UNCOUNT
He hates delay and procrastination.

pro·cre·ate /ˈprəʊkrieɪt/ **procreates, procreat-** VERB: V
ing, procreated. When animals or people **procre-** FORMAL
ate, they produce young or babies. ◆ **pro·crea-**
·tion /ˌprəʊkriˈeɪʃən/. *Early marriage and procrea-* N-UNCOUNT
tion are no longer discouraged.

procurator 'fiscal, procurators fiscal. In the N-COUNT
Scottish legal system, the **procurator fiscal** performs the functions of a public prosecutor.

pro·cure /prəˈkjʊə/ **procures, procuring, pro-** ◆◇◇◇◇
cured. 1 If you **procure** something, especially VERB
something that is difficult to get, you obtain it. *It re-* V n
mained very difficult to procure food, fuel and other FORMAL
daily necessities. ◆ **pro·cure·ment** *Russia was cut-* N-UNCOUNT
ting procurement of new weapons. **2** If someone VERB: V n
procures a prostitute, they introduce the prostitute
to a client.

prod /prɒd/ **prods, prodding, prodded. 1** If you ◆◇◇◇◇
prod someone or something, you give them a quick VERB: V n
push with your finger or with a pointed object. *He* V n with n
prodded Murray with the shotgun... Cathy was prod- V at n
ding at a boiled egg. ► Also a noun. *He gave the* N-COUNT
donkey a mighty prod. **2** If you **prod** someone **into** VERB:
doing something, you remind or persuade them to V n into n/-ing
do it. *One had to prod him to show the range of his* V n to-inf
paranormal abilities. ◆ **prod·ding** *She did her* N-UNCOUNT
chores without prodding. **3** See also **cattle prod**.

prodi·gal /ˈprɒdɪɡəl/ **prodigals. 1** You can de- ADJ
scribe someone as **prodigal** if they leave their family LITERARY
or friends but later return as a better person. *...the*
parable of the prodigal son. ► A **prodigal** is some- N-COUNT
one who is prodigal. **2** Someone who behaves in a ADJ
prodigal way spends a lot of money carelessly; used PRAGMATICS
showing disapproval.

pro·di·gious /prəˈdɪdʒəs/. Something that is **pro-** ◆◇◇◇◇
digious is very large or impressive. *This business* ADJ-GRADED
generates cash in prodigious amounts. ◆ **pro·di-** LITERARY
·gious·ly *She are prodigiously.* ADV-GRADED

prodi·gy /ˈprɒdɪdʒi/ **prodigies.** A prodigy is ◆◇◇◇◇
someone who has a great natural talent for some- N-COUNT
thing such as music or mathematics which shows
itself at an early age.

pro·duce, produces, producing, produced. ◆◆◆◆◆
The verb is pronounced /prəˈdjuːs, AM -ˈduːs/. The
noun is pronounced /ˈprɒdjuːs, AM -duːs/. **1** To VERB
produce something means to cause it to happen. V n
The drug is known to produce side-effects in women.
2 If you **produce** something, you make or create it. VERB
The company produced circuitry for communica- V n
tions systems. ◆ **pro·duc·er, producers** /*...Saudi* N-COUNT
Arabia, the world's leading oil producer. **3** When VERB
things or people **produce** something, it comes from V n
them or slowly forms from them. *These plants are*

then pollinated and allowed to mature and produce
seed.
4 If you **produce** evidence or an argument, you show VERB
it or explain it in order to make people agree with you. V n
They challenged him to produce evidence to support
his allegations. **5** If you **produce** an object from some- VERB
where, you show it or bring it out so that it can be V n
seen. *To hire a car you must produce a passport and a*
current driving licence. **6** If someone **produces** some- VERB: V n
thing such as a film, a magazine, or a record, they
organize it and decide how it should be done. ◆ **pro-**
·duc·er. *Vanya Kewley is a freelance film producer.* N-COUNT
7 Produce is food or other things that are grown in N-UNCOUNT
large quantities to be sold.

prod·uct /ˈprɒdʌkt/ **products. 1** A product is ◆◆◆◆
something that is produced and sold in large quan- N-COUNT
tities. **2** If you say that someone or something is a N-COUNT:
product of a situation or process, you mean that N of n
the situation or process made that person or thing
what they are. *The bank is the product of a 1971*
merger of two Japanese banks.

pro·duc·tion /prəˈdʌkʃən/ **productions. 1** Pro- ◆◆◆◇
duction is the process of manufacturing or growing N-UNCOUNT
something in large quantities. *That model won't go*
into production before late 1990. **2 Production** is N-UNCOUNT
the amount of goods manufactured or grown by a
company or country. *We needed to increase the vol-*
ume of production. **3** The **production of** something N-UNCOUNT
is its creation as the result of a natural process.
These proteins stimulate the production of blood
cells.
4 Production is the process of organizing and prepar- N-UNCOUNT
ing a play, film, programme, or record. *She is head of*
the production company. **5** A **production** is a play, op- N-COUNT
era, or other show that is performed in a theatre. *...a*
critically proclaimed production of Othello. **6** When PHRASE
you can do something **on production of** or **on the**
production of documents, you need to show someone those documents in order to be able to do that
thing. *Entry to the show is free to members on produc-*
tion of their membership cards.

pro'duction line, production lines. A produc- ◆◇◇◇◇
tion line is an arrangement of machines in a factory N-COUNT
where the products pass from machine to machine
until they are finished.

pro·duc·tive /prəˈdʌktɪv/. **1** Someone or some- ◆◆◇◇◇
thing that is **productive** is very efficient at produc- ADJ-GRADED
ing a particular thing or result. *Training makes*
workers highly productive. ◆ **pro·duc·tive·ly** The ADV-GRADED:
company is certain to reinvest its profits productive- ADV with v
ly. **2** If you say that a relationship between people is ADJ-GRADED
productive, you mean that a lot of good or useful
things happen as a result of it. ◆ **productively** ADV:
They feel they are interacting productively with el- ADV with v
derly patients.

prod·uc·tiv·ity /ˌprɒdʌkˈtɪvɪti/. **Productivity** is the ◆◆◇◇◇
rate at which goods are produced. *...continued im-* N-UNCOUNT
provements in productivity.

Prof. /prɒf/ **Profs;** also spelled **prof. 1 Prof.** is an ◆◇◇◇◇
abbreviation for **professor**. *...Prof. Richard Joyner of* N-TITLE
Liverpool University. **2** People sometimes refer to a WRITTEN
professor as **prof** or the **Prof**. *Write a note to my* N-VOC;
prof and tell him why I missed an exam this PRAGMATICS
morning. INFORMAL

pro·fane /prəˈfeɪn, AM prəʊ-/ **profanes, profan-**
ing, profaned. 1 Profane behaviour shows disre- ADJ-GRADED
spect for a religion or religious things. *...profane* FORMAL
language. ◆ **pro·fan·ity** *To desecrate a holy spring* N-UNCOUNT
is considered profanity. **2** Something that is **profane** ADJ
is concerned with everyday life rather than religion
and spiritual things. *Churches should not be used for*
profane or secular purposes. **3** If someone **profanes** VERB: V n
a religious belief or institution, they treat it with
disrespect.

pro·fan·ity /prəˈfænɪti, AM prəʊ-/ **profanities.** Pro- N-COUNT
fanities are swear words. FORMAL

pro·fess /prəˈfes/ **professes, professing, pro-** ◆◇◇◇◇
fessed. 1 If you **profess** to do or have something, VERB:
you claim that you do it or have it, often when you V to-inf
do not. *Why do organisations profess that they* V that
V n

care?... 'I don't know,' Pollard replied, professing in- `FORMAL`
nocence. **2** If you **profess** a feeling, opinion, or be- `VERB: V n`
lief, you express it. *He professed to be content with* `V to-inf`
the arrangement... Bacher professed himself pleased `V pron-refl adj`
with the Indian tour. `FORMAL`

pro·fes·sion /prə'feʃən/ **professions. 1** A profes- ◆◆◆◇
sion is a type of job that requires advanced educa- `N-COUNT:`
tion or training. **2** You can use **profession** to refer `also by N`
to all the people who have the same profession. *The* `N-COLL-`
attitude of the medical profession is very much more `COUNT`
liberal now.

pro·fes·sion·al /prə'feʃənəl/ **professionals.** ◆◆◆◆
1 Professional means relating to a person's work, `ADJ: ADJ n`
especially work that requires special training. *His*
professional career started at Liverpool University.
♦ **pro·fes·sion·al·ly** ...*a professionally-qualified* `ADV`
architect. **2 Professional** people have jobs that re- `ADJ: ADJ n`
quire advanced education or training. ► Also a `N-COUNT`
noun. *My father wanted me to become a professional*
and have more stability.
3 You use **professional** to describe people who do a `ADJ`
particular thing to earn money rather than as a hobby.
...a professional footballer. ► Also a noun. *He had* `N-COUNT`
been a professional since March 1985.
♦ **professionally** *By age 16 he was playing profes-* `ADV:`
sionally with bands in Greenwich Village. **4 Profes-** `ADV after v`
sional sports are played for money rather than as a `ADJ: ADJ n`
hobby. **5** If you say that something that someone does `ADJ-GRADED`
or produces is **professional**, you approve of it because `PRAGMATICS`
you think it shows skill and high standards. *They run it*
with a truly professional but personal touch. ► Also a `N-COUNT`
noun. *...a dedicated professional who worked harmo-*
niously with the cast and crew. ♦ **pro·fes·sion·al-**
·ism *American companies pride themselves on their* `N-UNCOUNT`
professionalism. ♦ **pro·fes·sion·al·ly** *These tickets* `ADJ-GRADED:`
have been produced very professionally. **6** See also `ADV with v`
semi-professional.

pro,fessional 'foul, professional fouls. In foot- `N-COUNT`
ball, if a player commits a **professional foul**, he or `BRITISH`
she deliberately does something which is against
the rules in order to prevent another player from
scoring a goal.

pro·fes·sion·al·ize /prə'feʃənəlaɪz/ **profession-** `VERB: V n`
alizes, professionalizing, professionalized;
also spelled **professionalise** in British English. To
professionalize an organization, an institution, or
an activity means to make it more professional.
♦ **pro·fes·sion·ali·za·tion** /prə,feʃənəlaɪ'zeɪʃən/ `N-UNCOUNT`
The professionalisation of politics is a major source
of our ills.

pro·fes·sor /prə'fesə/ **professors. 1** A professor ◆◆◆◆
in a British university is the most senior teacher in a `N-TITLE;`
department. *In 1979, only 2% of British professors* `N-COUNT;`
were female. **2** A professor in an American or Cana- `N-VOC`
dian university or college is a teacher there. `N-COUNT;`
`N-TITLE;`
`N-VOC`
prof·es·so·rial /,prɒfɪ'sɔːriəl/. **1** If you describe `ADJ-GRADED`
someone as **professorial**, you mean that they look
or behave like a professor. **2 Professorial** means re- `ADJ: ADJ n`
lating to the work of a professor. *...the cuts which*
have led to 36 per cent of professorial posts remain-
ing unfilled.

pro·fes·sor·ship /prə'fesəʃɪp/ **professorships.** A `N-COUNT`
professorship is the post of professor in a university. *In 1839 he accepted a full professorship at Kiel.*

prof·fer /'prɒfə/ **proffers, proffering, prof-** ◇◇◇◇◇
fered. 1 If you **proffer** something to someone, you `VERB:`
hold it towards them so that they can take it or `V n to n`
touch it. *He rose and proffered a silver box full of* `V n`
cigarettes. **2** If you **proffer** something such as advice `FORMAL`
to someone, you offer it to them. *The army has not* `V n`
yet proffered an explanation of how and why the ac- `Also V n to n,`
cident happened. `V n n`
`FORMAL`

pro·fi·cient /prə'fɪʃənt/. If you are **proficient** in `ADJ-GRADED`
something, you can do it very well. *A great number*
of Egyptians are proficient in foreign languages.
♦ **pro·fi·cien·cy** /prə'fɪʃənsi/. *Evidence of basic* `N-UNCOUNT`
proficiency in English is part of the admission
requirement.

pro·file /'prəʊfaɪl/ **profiles, profiling, profiled.** ◆◆◆◇
1 Your **profile** is the outline of your face as it is seen `N-COUNT`

when someone is looking at you from the side. **2** If `N-UNCOUNT:`
you see someone **in profile**, you see them from the `in N`
side. **3** If a journalist **profiles** someone, they give an `VERB`
account of that person's life and character. *Tamar* `V n`
Golan, a Paris-based journalist, profiles the rebel
leader. ► Also a noun. *A Washington newspaper* `N-COUNT:`
published comparative profiles of the candidates' `with supp`
wives. **4** If someone has a **high profile**, people no- `PHRASE`
tice them and what they do. If you keep a **low pro-**
file, you avoid doing things that will make people
notice you. *Football is a high profile business.* ● See
also **high-profile, low-profile.**

prof·it /'prɒfɪt/ **profits, profiting, profited. 1** A ◆◆◆◆◇
profit is an amount of money that you gain when `N-VAR`
you are paid more for something than it cost you to
make, get, or do it. *The bank made pre-tax profits of*
£3.5 million. **2** If you **profit** from something, you `VERB:`
earn a profit from it. *The dealers profited shamefully* `V from/by n/`
at the expense of my family. **3** If you **profit** from `-ing`
something, or it **profits** you, you gain some advan- `V-ERG:`
tage or benefit from it. *So far the French alliance* `V from/by n`
had profited the rebels little... Whom would it profit `V n`
to terrify or to kill James Sinclair? ► Also a noun. `it V to n-inf`
The artist found more to his profit in the sculpture `FORMAL`
collections. `N-UNCOUNT`

prof·it·able /'prɒfɪtəbəl/. **1** A **profitable** organiza- ◆◇◇◇◇
tion or practice makes a profit. *It was profitable for* `ADJ-GRADED`
them to produce large amounts of food. ♦ **prof·it-**
·ably /'prɒfɪtəbli/. *The 28 French stores are trading* `ADV-GRADED:`
profitably. ♦ **prof·it·abil·ity** /,prɒfɪtə'bɪlɪti/ *Changes* `ADV with v`
were made in operating methods in an effort to in- `N-UNCOUNT with v`
crease profitability. **2** Something that is **profitable** `ADJ-GRADED`
results in some benefit for you. *...close collaboration*
with industry which leads to a profitable exchange of
personnel and ideas. ♦ **prof·it·ably** *In fact he could* `ADV-GRADED:`
scarcely have spent his time more profitably. `ADV with v`

profi·teer·ing /,prɒfɪ'tɪərɪŋ/. If someone makes `N-UNCOUNT`
large profits by charging high prices for goods that `PRAGMATICS`
are hard to get, you can say that they are engaged in
profiteering; used showing disapproval. *There's*
been a wave of profiteering and corruption. ♦ **profi-**
·teer, profiteers. *...a new social class composed* `N-COUNT`
largely of war profiteers and gangsters.

'**profit-making.** A **profit-making** business or or- `ADJ`
ganization makes a profit. *He wants to set up a*
profit-making company, owned mostly by the uni-
versity. ● See also **non-profit-making.**

'**profit margin, profit margins.** A profit margin ◆◇◇◇◇
is the difference between the selling price of a prod- `N-COUNT`
uct and the cost of producing and marketing it.

'**profit-sharing.** Profit-sharing is a system by `N-UNCOUNT`
which all the people who work in a company have a
share in its profits.

'**profit-taking.** Profit-taking is the selling of ◆◇◇◇◇
stocks and shares at a profit after their value has ris- `N-UNCOUNT`
en or just before their value falls.

prof·li·gate /'prɒflɪgɪt/. **Profligate** means extrava- `ADJ-GRADED`
gant and wasteful. *...the most profligate consumer of* `FORMAL`
energy in the world. ♦ **prof·li·ga·cy** /'prɒflɪgəsi/. `N-UNCOUNT`
...the continuing profligacy of certain states.

pro forma /,prəʊ 'fɔːmə/; also spelled **pro-forma.** `ADJ`
In banking, a company's **pro forma** balance or
earnings are their expected balance or earnings.

pro·found /prə'faʊnd/ **profounder, profound-** ◆◆◇◇◇
est. 1 You use **profound** to emphasize that some- `ADJ-GRADED`
thing is very great or intense. *...discoveries which*
had a profound effect on many areas of medicine...
Anna's patriotism was profound. ♦ **pro·found·ly** `ADV-GRADED`
This has profoundly affected my life. **2** A **profound** `ADJ-GRADED`
idea, work, or person shows great intellectual depth
and understanding. *...one of the country's most pro-*
found minds.

pro·fun·dity /prə'fʌndɪti/ **profundities. 1 Profun-** `N-UNCOUNT`
dity is great intellectual depth and understanding.
The profundity of this book is achieved with breath-
taking lightness. **2** If you refer to the **profundity** of a `N-UNCOUNT`
feeling, experience, or change, you mean that it is
deep, powerful, or serious. *...the profundity of the*
structural problems besetting the country. **3** A **pro-** `N-COUNT`
fundity is a remark that shows great intellectual

871 projectile

depth and understanding. *His work is full of profundities and asides concerning the human condition.*

pro·fuse /prə'fju:s/. **1** Profuse sweating, bleeding, or vomiting is sweating, bleeding, or vomiting large amounts. ♦ **pro·fuse·ly** *He was bleeding profusely.* **2** If you offer profuse apologies or thanks, you apologize or thank someone a lot. ♦ **profusely** *They were very grateful to be put right and thanked me profusely.* — ADJ-GRADED; ADV-GRADED: ADV after v; ADJ; ADV-GRADED: ADV after v

pro·fu·sion /prə'fju:ʒən/. If there is a profusion of something or if it occurs in profusion, there is a very large quantity or variety of it. *The Dart is a delightful river with a profusion of wild flowers along its banks.* — ◆◇◇◇ N-COLL-SING: also in N FORMAL

pro·geni·tor /prəʊ'dʒenɪtə/ progenitors. **1** A progenitor of someone is a direct ancestor of theirs. *He was also a progenitor of seven presidents of Nicaragua.* **2** The progenitor of an idea or invention is the person who first thought of it. *...Clive Sinclair, progenitor of the C5 electric car.* — N-COUNT FORMAL; N-COUNT FORMAL

prog·eny /'prɒdʒəni/. **1** You can refer to a person's children or to an animal's young as their progeny. **2** The progeny of a particular thing are the things that develop from it. *Among its many progeny, the 1944 Education Act gave birth to the modern youth service.* — N-PLURAL FORMAL; N-PLURAL

pro·ges·ter·one /prəʊ'dʒestərəʊn/. Progesterone is a hormone produced in the ovaries of women and female animals. Progesterone helps prepare the body for pregnancy. — ◆◇◇◇ N-UNCOUNT

prog·no·sis /prɒg'nəʊsɪs/ prognoses /prɒg'nəʊsi:z/. A prognosis is an estimate of the future of someone or something. *The hospital physiotherapist's prognosis was that Laurence might walk within 12 months.* — ◆◇◇◇ N-COUNT FORMAL

prog·nos·ti·ca·tion /prɒg,nɒstɪ'keɪʃən/ prognostications. A prognostication is a prediction about something. *The country is currently obsessed with gloomy prognostications about its future.* — N-VAR FORMAL

pro·gram /'prəʊgræm/ programs, programming, programmed. **1** A program is a set of instructions that a computer follows in order to perform a particular task. **2** When you program a computer, you give it a set of instructions to make it able to perform a particular task. *He programmed his computer to compare the 1431 possible combinations of pairs in this population.* ♦ **pro·gram·ming** *...programming skills.* ♦ **pro·gram·mer, pro·grammers.** *Mike found a challenging job as a computer programmer.* **3** See also programme. — ◆◆◆◇ N-COUNT; VERB: V n V n to-inf; N-UNCOUNT; N-COUNT

pro·gram·ma·ble /'prəʊgræməbəl/. A programmable machine can be programmed, so that for example it will switch on and off automatically. — ADJ

pro·gram·mat·ic /,prəʊgrə'mætɪk/. Programmatic ideas or policies follow a particular programme. *He gave up on programmatic politics and turned his back on public life.* — ADJ

pro·gramme /'prəʊgræm/ programmes, programming, programmed; spelled program in American English. **1** A programme of actions or events is a series of actions or events that are planned to be done. *The general argued that the nuclear programme should still continue.* **2** A television or radio programme is something that is broadcast on television or radio. *...local news programmes.* **3** A theatre or concert programme is a booklet or sheet of paper which gives information about a play or concert. **4** When you programme a machine or system, you set its controls so that it will work in a particular way. *Parents can programme the machine not to turn on at certain times.* **5** If a living creature is programmed to behave in a particular way, they are likely to behave in that way because of social or biological factors that they cannot control. *We are all genetically programmed to develop certain illnesses.* — ◆◆◆◆◆; N-COUNT; N-COUNT; N-COUNT; VERB V n to-inf Also V n; VB: usu passive be V-ed to-inf Also be V-ed

pro·gress, progresses, progressing, progressed. The noun is pronounced /'prəʊgres, AM 'prɑ:-/. The verb is pronounced /prə'gres/. **1** Progress is the process of gradually improving or getting nearer to achieving or completing something. *The medical community continues to make progress in the fight against cancer.* **2** The progress of a situation or action is the way in which it develops. *The Chancellor is reported to have been delighted with the progress of the first day's talks.* **3** To progress means to move over a period of time to a stronger, more advanced, or more desirable state. *He started only five years ago, sketching first and then progressing to painting.* **4** If events progress, they continue to happen gradually over a period of time. *Life was hard, and it became harder as the war progressed.* **5** If something is in progress, it has started and is still continuing. — ◆◆◆◇ N-UNCOUNT; N-SING: the N; VERB: V V to n; VERB V; PHRASE

pro·gres·sion /prə'greʃən/ progressions. A progression is a gradual development from one state to another. *Both drugs slow the progression of AIDS, but neither cures the disease.* — ◆◇◇◇ N-COUNT

pro·gres·sive /prə'gresɪv/ progressives. **1** Someone who is progressive or has progressive ideas has modern ideas about how things should be done, rather than traditional ones. *...a progressive businessman who had voted for Roosevelt in 1932 and 1936.* ▶ A progressive is someone who is progressive. **2** A progressive change happens gradually over a period of time. *One prominent symptom of the disease is progressive loss of memory.* ♦ **pro·gres·sive·ly** *Her symptoms became progressively worse... It's got progressively more difficult to light up a cigarette without breaking a law.* — ◆◆◇◇ ADJ-GRADED; N-COUNT; ADJ; ADV

pro·hib·it /prə'hɪbɪt, AM prəʊ-/ prohibits, prohibiting, prohibited. If a law or someone in authority prohibits something, they forbid it or make it illegal. *Federal law prohibits foreign airlines from owning more than 25% of any U.S. airline.* ♦ **pro·hi·bi·tion** /,prəʊhɪ'bɪʃən/. *The Air Force and the Navy retain and codify their prohibition of women on air combat missions.* — ◆◆◇◇ VERB: V n V n from -ing FORMAL; N-UNCOUNT

pro·hi·bi·tion /,prəʊɪ'bɪʃən/ prohibitions. A prohibition is a law or rule forbidding something. *...a prohibition on discrimination.* — ◆◇◇◇ N-COUNT

Pro·hi·bi·tion. In the United States, Prohibition was the official banning of alcoholic drinks between 1920 and 1933. — N-UNCOUNT

pro·hibi·tive /prə'hɪbɪtɪv, AM prəʊ-/. If the cost of something is prohibitive, it is so high that many people cannot afford it. *...the prohibitive prices charged for seats at the opera.* ♦ **pro·hibi·tive·ly** *Meat and butter were prohibitively expensive.* — ◆◇◇◇ ADJ-GRADED FORMAL; ADV: ADV adj

proj·ect, projects, projecting, projected. The noun is pronounced /'prɒdʒekt/. The verb is pronounced /prə'dʒekt/. **1** A project is a task that requires a lot of time and effort. *Money will also go into local development projects in Vietnam.* **2** A project is a detailed study of a subject by a pupil or student. **3** If something is projected, it is planned or expected. *Africa's mid-1993 population is projected to more than double by 2025... The government had been projecting a 5% consumer price increase for the entire year.* **4** If you project a particular feeling or quality, you show it in your behaviour. If you project someone or something in a particular way, you try to make people see them in that way. *He just hasn't been able to project himself as the strong leader... His first job will be to project Glasgow as a friendly city.* **5** If you project feelings or ideas on to other people, you imagine that they have the same ideas or feelings as you. *He projects his own thoughts and ideas onto her.* **6** If you project a film or picture onto a screen or wall, you make it appear there. *The team tried projecting the maps with two different projectors onto the same screen.* **7** If something projects, it sticks out above or beyond a surface or edge. *...the remains of a war-time defence which projected out from the shore.* **8** See also housing project. — ◆◆◆◇; N-COUNT; N-COUNT; VERB be V-ed to-inf V n; VERB: V n V pron-refl as n V n as n; VERB V n on/onto/ upon n; VERB V n; VERB V prep/adv FORMAL

pro·jec·tile /prə'dʒektaɪl, AM -təl/ projectiles. A projectile is an object that is fired from a gun or other weapon. — N-COUNT FORMAL

P

pro·jec·tion /prəˈdʒekʃən/ **projections. 1** A projection is an estimate of a future amount. *...sales projections.* **2** The **projection** of a film or picture is the act of projecting it onto a screen or wall. *They took me into a projection room to see a picture.*
◆◆◇◇◇
N-COUNT

N-UNCOUNT

pro·jec·tion·ist /prəˈdʒekʃənɪst/ **projectionists.** A **projectionist** is someone whose job is to work a projector at a cinema.
N-COUNT

pro·jec·tor /prəˈdʒektə/ **projectors.** A **projector** is a machine that projects films or slides onto a screen or wall. • See also **overhead projector**.
◆◇◇◇◇
N-COUNT

pro·lapse /ˈprəʊlæps, AM prəʊˈlæps/ **prolapses, prolapsing, prolapsed.** The verb is also pronounced /prəˈlæps/. If an organ in someone's body **prolapses**, it sags or falls within the body. *Sometimes the original abortion was done so badly that the uterus prolapses.* ▶ Also a noun. *...the causes and treatment of uterine prolapse.*
VERB
V
MEDICAL

N-VAR

prole /prəʊl/ **proles.** A **prole** is a working-class person. Some people find this word offensive. *We had proles working alongside university types as equals.*
N-COUNT
PRAGMATICS
BRITISH,
INFORMAL

pro·letar·ian /ˌprəʊlɪˈteəriən/ **proletarians. 1** In socialist theory, **proletarian** means relating to the proletariat. *...a proletarian revolution.* **2** A **proletarian** is a member of the proletariat.
ADJ

N-COUNT

pro·letari·at /ˌprəʊlɪˈteəriæt/. In socialist theory, the **proletariat** is a term used to refer to working-class people, especially industrial workers.
N-COLL-SING:
theN

pro-'life. The **pro-life** movement consists of people who campaign against legalized abortion, euthanasia, and experiments using human embryos.
◆◇◇◇◇
ADJ

pro·lif·er·ate /prəˈlɪfəreɪt/ **proliferates, proliferating, proliferated.** If things **proliferate**, they increase in number very quickly. *Computerized data bases are proliferating fast.* ♦ **pro·lif·era·tion** /prəˌlɪfəˈreɪʃən/ *...the proliferation of nuclear weapons.*
◆◆◇◇◇
VERB
V
FORMAL
N-UNCOUNT

pro·lif·ic /prəˈlɪfɪk/. **1** A **prolific** writer, artist, or composer produces a large number of works. **2** A **prolific** sports player scores a lot of goals or wins a lot of matches or races. *Another prolific scorer is Dean Saunders.*
◆◇◇◇◇
ADJ-GRADED
ADJ-GRADED

3 A **prolific** animal or person produces a large number of young. A **prolific** plant produces a large number of fruit or new plants. *They are prolific breeders, with many hens laying up to six eggs.*
ADJ-GRADED

pro·logue /ˈprəʊlɒg, AM -lɔːg/ **prologues. 1** A **prologue** is a speech or section of text that introduces a play or book. **2** If one event is a **prologue to** another event, it leads to it. *I am convinced that it was a prologue to today's bloodless revolution.*
◆◇◇◇◇
N-COUNT

N-COUNT
FORMAL

pro·long /prəˈlɒŋ, AM -lɔːŋ/ **prolongs, prolonging, prolonged.** To **prolong** something means to make it last a longer period of time. *Mr Chesler said foreign military aid was prolonging the war.*
◆◇◇◇◇
VERB
V n

pro·longed /prəˈlɒŋd, AM -lɔːŋd/. A **prolonged** event or situation continues for a long time. *...a prolonged period of low interest rates.*
◆◇◇◇◇
ADJ-GRADED

prom /prɒm/ **proms. 1** In the United States, a **prom** is a formal dance at school or college which is usually held at the end of the academic year. **2** In Britain, **the prom** is the same as the **promenade**.
◆◇◇◇◇
N-COUNT

N-SING

prom·enade /ˌprɒməˈnɑːd, AM -ˈneɪd/ **promenades, promenading, promenaded. 1** In a seaside town, the **promenade** is the road by the sea where people go for a walk. **2** If someone **promenades** somewhere, for example along a main street, they go for a walk there. *People came out in smarter clothes to promenade along the front.*
◆◇◇◇◇
N-COUNT

VERB
V prep
DATED

promi·nence /ˈprɒmɪnəns/. If someone or something is in a position of **prominence**, they are well-known and important. *Crime prevention had to be given more prominence.*
◆◇◇◇◇
N-UNCOUNT

promi·nent /ˈprɒmɪnənt/. **1** A **prominent** person is important. *...the children of very prominent or successful parents.* **2** Something that is **prominent** is very noticeable or is an important part of something else. *...Romania's most prominent independent*
◆◆◇◇◇
ADJ-GRADED

ADJ-GRADED

newspaper. ♦ **promi·nent·ly** *Entries will be prominently displayed in the exhibition hall.*
ADV-GRADED:
ADV with v

pro·mis·cu·ous /prəˈmɪskjuəs/. **1** A **promiscuous** person has sex with many different people; used showing disapproval. *You know the risks of promiscuous sex.* ♦ **promis·cu·ity** /ˌprɒmɪˈskjuːɪti/ *...an attempt to limit promiscuity.* **2 Promiscuous** means including a wide range of different things. *...the dazzling, promiscuous display of new styles.*
◆◇◇◇◇
ADJ-GRADED
PRAGMATICS

N-UNCOUNT

ADJ-GRADED
FORMAL

prom·ise /ˈprɒmɪs/ **promises, promising, promised. 1** If you **promise** that you will do something, you say to someone that you will definitely do it. *He promised to wait till I came back... Promise me you will not waste your time... 'We'll be back next year,' he promised.* **2** If you **promise** someone something, you tell them that you will definitely give it to them or make sure that they have it. *In 1920 the great powers promised them an independent state... Mr Fujimori has promised a national unity government.* **3** A **promise** is a statement which you make to someone in which you say that you will definitely do something or give them something. *The program has lived up to its promise to promote family welfare.* **4** If a situation or event **promises** to have a particular quality or to be a particular thing, it shows signs that it will have that quality or be that thing. *The seminar also promises to be most instructive.* **5** If someone or something shows **promise**, they seem likely to be very good or successful.
◆◆◆◇
VERB:
V that
V to-inf
V n that
V n
Also V
VERB
V n n

V n

N-COUNT

VERB
V to-inf

N-UNCOUNT

promised 'land, promised lands. If you refer to a place or a state as a **promised land**, you mean that people desire it and expect to find happiness or success there.
N-COUNT

prom·is·ing /ˈprɒmɪsɪŋ/. Someone or something that is **promising** seems likely to be very good or successful. *...one of the most promising poets of his generation.*
◆◆◇◇◇
ADJ-GRADED

prom·is·ing·ly /ˈprɒmɪsɪŋli/. If something or someone starts **promisingly**, they begin well but often fail in the end. *It all started so promisingly when Speed scored a tremendous first goal.*
ADV-GRADED

prom·is·sory note /ˈprɒmɪsəri nəʊt, AM -sɔːri/ **promissory notes.** A **promissory note** is a written promise to pay a specific sum of money to a particular person.
N-COUNT
AMERICAN

pro·mo /ˈprəʊməʊ/ **promos.** A **promo** is something such as a short video film which is used to promote a product.
N-COUNT
INFORMAL,
JOURNALISM

prom·on·tory /ˈprɒməntri, AM -tɔːri/ **promontories.** A **promontory** is a cliff stretching out into the sea.
N-COUNT

pro·mote /prəˈməʊt/ **promotes, promoting, promoted. 1** If people **promote** something, they help or encourage it to happen, increase, or spread. *In many ways, our society actively promotes alcoholism.* ♦ **pro·mo·tion** *...disease prevention and health promotion.* **2** If a firm **promotes** a product, it tries to increase the sales or popularity of that product. *...a full British tour to promote his second solo album... The island could be promoted as a tourist destination.* ♦ **promotion, promotions** *Remington spent a lot of money on advertising and promotion.*
◆◆◆◇
VERB
V n

N-UNCOUNT
VERB
V n
be V-ed as n

N-VAR

3 If someone **is promoted**, they are given a more important job in the organization they work for. *I was promoted to editor and then editorial director.* ♦ **promotion** *Consider changing jobs or trying for promotion.* **4** If a team that competes in a league **is promoted**, it starts competing in a higher division in the next season. ♦ **promotion** *...their team's promotion to the first division.*
VERB:
be V-ed

N-VAR

VERB:
be V-ed
N-UNCOUNT

pro·mot·er /prəˈməʊtə/ **promoters. 1** A **promoter** is a person who helps organize and finance an event, especially a sports event. **2** The **promoter of** a cause or idea tries to make it become popular. *...the most energetic promoter of American music.*
◆◆◇◇◇
N-COUNT

N-COUNT

pro·mo·tion /prəˈməʊʃən/. See **promote**.

pro·mo·tion·al /prə'məʊʃənəl/. **Promotional** ma- ◆◇◇◇◇
terial, events, or ideas are designed to advertise a ADJ
product or service and increase its sales.

prompt /prɒmpt/ **prompts, prompting,** ◆◆◆◇◇
prompted. **1** If something **prompts** someone to VERB
do something, it makes them decide to do it. *Ja-* V n to-inf
pan's recession has prompted consumers to cut back Also V n
on buying cars. **2** If you **prompt** someone when VERB: V n
they stop speaking, you encourage or help them to V with quote
continue. *'Well, Daniels?' Wilson prompted.* ▶ Also a N-COUNT
noun. *Her blushes were saved by a prompt from one*
of her hosts. **3** A **prompt** action is done without any ADJ-GRADED
delay. *It is not too late, but prompt action is needed.*
4 If you are **prompt** to do something, you do it ADJ-GRADED:
without delay or you are not late. *They were always* v-link ADJ
so prompt with their rental payment.

prompt·ing /'prɒmptɪŋ/ **promptings.** If you re- ◆◇◇◇
spond to **prompting**, you do what someone encour- N-UNCOUNT:
ages or reminds you to do. *She telephoned* also N in pl
Wychwood House at your prompting yesterday.

prompt·ly /'prɒmptli/. **1** If you do something ◆◆◇◇◇
promptly, you do it immediately. *Sister Francesca* ADV-GRADED:
entered the chapel, took her seat, and promptly fell ADV with v
asleep. **2** If you do something **promptly at** a par- ADV
ticular time, you do it at exactly that time. *Promptly*
at a quarter past seven, we left the hotel.

prom·ul·gate /'prɒməlgeɪt/ **promulgates,** ◆◇◇◇
promulgating, promulgated. **1** If people **prom-** VERB
ulgate information or a new idea, they make it V n
widely known. *The oil and shipping industries* FORMAL
undertook to promulgate a voluntary code. **2** If a VERB:
new law or a country's constitution **is promulgated** be V-ed
by a government or national leader, it is publicly FORMAL
approved or made official. ◆ **prom·ul·ga·tion** N-UNCOUNT
/ˌprɒməl'geɪʃən/ ...*the promulgation of a military*
decree.

prone /prəʊn/. **1** If someone or something is **prone** ◆◆◇◇◇
to something, usually something bad, they have a ADJ-GRADED:
tendency to be affected by it or to do it. *People with* v-link ADJ,
fair skin who sunburn easily are very prone to devel- ADJ to n,
op skin cancer. ▶ Also a combining form. ...*the most* ADJ to-inf
injury-prone rider on the circuit. ● See also **acci-** COMB
dent prone. **2** If you are lying **prone** or if you are in ADJ:
a **prone** position, you are lying flat with the front of ADJ after v,
your body facing downwards. ADJ n
FORMAL

prong /prɒŋ, AM prɔːŋ/ **prongs.** **1** The **prongs** of N-COUNT
something such as a fork are the long thin pointed
parts. **2** The **prongs** of something such as a policy N-COUNT
or strategy are the separate stages or parts of it. *The*
shareholder rights movement has two prongs.
◆ **-pronged** *The bank has a three-pronged strategy* COMB
for recovery.

pro·nomi·nal /prəʊ'nɒmɪnəl/. **Pronominal** means ADJ
relating to pronouns or like a pronoun.

pro·noun /'prəʊnaʊn/ **pronouns.** A **pronoun** is a N-COUNT
word which is used instead of a noun or noun
group to refer to someone or something. Examples
are 'she', 'something', and 'myself'. ● See also **in-**
definite pronoun, personal pronoun, reflexive pro-
noun, relative pronoun.

pro·nounce /prə'naʊns/ **pronounces, pro-** ◆◆◇◇◇
nouncing, pronounced. **1** To **pronounce** a word VERB: V n
means to say it by making sounds that are right or V n n
understandable. *He pronounced it Per-sha, the way*
the English do. **2** If you **pronounce** something, you VERB
state it formally or publicly. *The Communist author-* V n
ities took time to pronounce their verdicts... I now V n n/adj
pronounce you man and wife... Ingrid pronounced Also V that
herself 'really happy'. FORMAL

pro·nounced /prə'naʊnst/. Something that is **pro-** ◆◇◇◇
nounced is very noticeable. *Most of the art exhibi-* ADJ-GRADED
tions have a pronounced Scottish theme.

pro·nounce·ment /prə'naʊnsmənt/ **pronounce-** ◆◇◇◇
ments. Pronouncements are public or official N-COUNT
statements on an important subject.

pron·to /'prɒntəʊ/. If you say that something must ADV:
be done **pronto**, you mean that it must be done ADV after v
quickly and at once. *Get down to the post office* INFORMAL
pronto!

pro·nun·cia·tion /prəˌnʌnsi'eɪʃən/ **pronuncia-** ◆◇◇◇
tions. The **pronunciation** of a word or language is N-VAR
the way in which it is pronounced.

proof /pruːf/ **proofs.** **1** Proof is a fact, argument, ◆◆◆◇◇
or piece of evidence which shows that something is N-VAR
definitely true or definitely exists. *You have to have*
proof of residence in the state of Texas, such as a
Texas ID card... This is not necessarily proof that he
is wrong. **2** If someone is **living proof** of something, PHRASE
their actions or personal qualities show that a particular fact is true or that a particular quality exists.
He is living proof that some players just get better
with age. **3** If something or someone is **proof posi-** PHRASE
tive of a certain fact or quality, their existence or actions prove that it is true or that it exists. *The Win-*
dermere Golf Club is proof positive that golf and
ecology can co-exist.
4 The **proofs** of a book or article are a first copy of it N-COUNT
that is printed so that mistakes can be corrected be- TECHNICAL
fore more copies are printed and published. ▶ Also an ADJ: ADJ n
adjective. ...*an uncorrected proof copy of the book.*
5 Proof is used after a number of degrees or a per- ADJ:
centage, when indicating the strength of a strong al- amount ADJ
coholic drink. ...*Wild Turkey bourbon: 101 degrees*
proof.
6 If something or someone is **proof against** some- ADJ:
thing, they cannot be damaged, harmed, or affected v-link ADJ
by that thing. *The fortress was proof against the tech-* against n
niques of attack then in use. WRITTEN
7 ● **burden of proof:** see burden. ● **the proof of the**
pudding is in the eating: see pudding.

-proof /-pruːf/ **-proofs, -proofing, -proofed.** COMB
1 -proof combines with nouns and verbs to form
adjectives which indicate that something cannot be
damaged or badly affected by the thing or action
mentioned. ...*a bomb-proof aircraft.* ...*a large*
microwave-proof dish. **2** -proof combines with COMB
nouns to form verbs which refer to protecting V n
something against being damaged or badly affected
by the thing mentioned. ...*the cost of draught-*
proofing your home. **3** See also **bullet-proof,**
childproof, fireproof, ovenproof, soundproof,
waterproof, weatherproof.

proof·read /'pruːfriːd/ **proofreads, proofread-** ◆◇◇◇
ing. The form **proofread** is pronounced /ˌpruːf'riːd/ VERB:
when it is the present tense, and /ˌpruːf'red/ when it V n,
is the past tense and past participle. When someone V
proofreads something such as a book or an article, TECHNICAL
they read it before it is published in order to find
and mark mistakes that need to be corrected.

prop /prɒp/ **props, propping, propped.** **1** If you ◆◆◇◇◇
prop an object **on** or **against** something, you sup- VERB
port it by putting something underneath it or by V n adv/prep
resting it against something. *He rocked back in the*
chair and propped his feet on the desk. ▶ **Prop up** PHRASAL VB
means the same as **prop.** *Sam slouched back and* V n P prep
propped his elbows up on the bench behind him... V P noun prep
Prop up your back against a wall. **2** A **prop** is a stick N-COUNT
or other object that you use to support something. N-COUNT
3 Someone or something that is a **prop** for a system, institution, or person is the main thing that
keeps that system or person strong or helps them
survive. *The army is one of the main props of the*
government. **4** The **props** in a play or film are all the N-COUNT
objects or pieces of furniture that are used in it.

prop up. **1** To **prop up** something means to support PHRASAL VB
it or help it to survive. *Investments in the U.S. money* V P noun
market have propped up the American dollar. **2** See Also V n P
prop 1.

propa·gan·da /ˌprɒpə'gændə/. **Propaganda** is in- ◆◆◇◇◇
formation, often inaccurate or biased information, N-UNCOUNT
which a political organization publishes or broad- PRAGMATICS
casts in order to influence people; used showing
disapproval. ...*anti-communist propaganda movies.*

propa·gan·dist /ˌprɒpə'gændɪst/ **propagandists.** N-COUNT
A **propagandist** is a person who tries to persuade PRAGMATICS
people to support a particular idea or group; often
used showing disapproval.

propa·gate /'prɒpəgeɪt/ **propagates, propagat-** ◆◇◇◇
ing, propagated. **1** If people **propagate** an idea VERB

or piece of information, they spread it and try to make people believe it or support it. *They propagated political doctrines which promised to tear apart the fabric of British society.* ♦ **propa·ga·tion** /ˌprɒpəˈɡeɪʃən/ *...the propagation of true Buddhism.* **2** To **propagate** plants means to grow more of them from the original ones. *The pasque flower can be propagated from seed.* ♦ **propagation** *...the successful propagation of a batch of plants.*

pro·pane /ˈprəʊpeɪn/. **Propane** is a gas that comes from petroleum and is used for cooking and heating. *...a propane gas cylinder.*

pro·pel /prəˈpel/ **propels, propelling, propelled. 1** To **propel** something in a particular direction means to cause it to move in that direction. *Rebecca took Steve's elbow and propelled him towards the staircase. ...a single-stage rocket propelled by liquid fuel.* ♦ **-propelled** *...the first jet-propelled aeroplane.* **2** If something **propels** you into a particular activity, it causes you to do it. *It was a shooting star that propelled me into astronomy in the first place.*

pro·pel·lant /prəˈpelənt/ **propellants. 1** Propellant is fuel used in spacecraft and missiles. **2** Propellant is a gas used in aerosol cans to force the contents out of the can when you press the button.

pro·pel·ler /prəˈpelə/ **propellers.** A **propeller** is a device with blades which is attached to a boat or aircraft. The engine makes the propeller spin round and causes the boat or aircraft to move.

pro·pen·sity /prəˈpensɪti/ **propensities.** A **propensity** to do something or a **propensity for** something is a natural tendency that you have to behave in a particular way. *Mr Bint has a propensity to put off decisions to the last minute.*

prop·er /ˈprɒpə/. **1** You use **proper** to describe things that you consider to be real and satisfactory rather than inadequate in some way. *Two out of five people lack a proper job. ...a proper evening meal.* ♦ **prop·er·ly** *You're too thin. You're not eating properly.* **2** The **proper** thing is the one that is correct or most suitable. *The proper procedures have been followed.* **3** If you say that a way of behaving is **proper**, you mean that it is considered socially acceptable and right. *It was not thought entirely proper for a woman to be on the stage.* ♦ **properly** *It's about time he learnt to behave properly.* **4** You can add **proper** after a word to emphasize that you are referring to the main, central, and most important part of a place, event, or object. *A distinction must be made between archaeology proper and science-based archaeology.*

ˌproper ˈnoun, proper nouns. A **proper noun** is the name of a particular person, place, or organization. Proper nouns begin with a capital letter.

prop·er·tied /ˈprɒpətid/. **Propertied** people own land or property. *...the propertied classes.*

prop·er·ty /ˈprɒpəti/ **properties. 1** Someone's **property** is all the things that belong to them or something that belongs to them. *Richard could easily destroy her personal property to punish her for walking out on him. ...confiscating weapons and stolen property.* **2** A **property** is a building and the land belonging to it. *Cecil inherited a family property near Stamford.* **3** The **properties** of a substance or object are the ways in which it behaves in particular conditions. *A radio signal has both electrical and magnetic properties.*

proph·ecy /ˈprɒfɪsi/ **prophecies.** A **prophecy** is a statement in which someone says they strongly believe that a particular thing will happen. *...Biblical prophecy.*

proph·esy /ˈprɒfɪsaɪ/ **prophesies, prophesying, prophesied.** If you **prophesy** that something will happen, you say that you strongly believe that it will happen. *He prophesied that within five years his opponent would either be dead or in prison.*

proph·et /ˈprɒfɪt/ **prophets.** A **prophet** is a person who is believed to be chosen by God to say the

things that God wants to tell people. *...the sacred name of the Holy Prophet of Islam.*

pro·phet·ic /prəˈfetɪk/. **1** If something was **prophetic**, it described or suggested something that did actually happen later. *This ominous warning soon proved prophetic.* **2** Prophetic means related to a prophecy or a prophet. *...a charming romance intermingled with scientific fact and prophetic vision.*

prophy·lac·tic /ˌprɒfɪˈlæktɪk/ **prophylactics. 1** Prophylactic means concerned with preventing disease. *Vaccination and other prophylactic measures can be carried out.* **2** A **prophylactic** is a substance or device used for preventing disease or pregnancy. *The region began to use quinine successfully as a prophylactic.*

pro·pi·ti·ate /prəˈpɪʃieɪt/ **propitiates, propitiating, propitiated.** If you **propitiate** someone, you stop them being angry or impatient by doing something to please them. *I've never gone out of my way to propitiate people.*

pro·pi·tious /prəˈpɪʃəs/. If something is **propitious**, it is likely to lead to success. *They should wait for the most propitious moment.*

pro·po·nent /prəˈpəʊnənt/ **proponents.** If you are a **proponent** of a particular idea or course of action, you actively support it. *...a leading proponent of the values of progressive education.*

pro·por·tion /prəˈpɔːʃən/ **proportions. 1** A **proportion of** a group or an amount is a part of it. *A large proportion of the dolphins in that area will eventually die.* **2** The **proportion of** one kind of person or thing in a group is the number of people or things of that kind compared to the total number in the group. *The proportion of women in the profession had risen to 17.3%.* **3** The **proportion of** one amount **to** another is the relationship between the two amounts in terms of how much there is of each thing. *Women's bodies tend to have a higher proportion of fat to water.* **4** If you refer to the **proportions** of something, you are referring to its size, usually when this is extremely large. *In the tropics plants grow to huge proportions.*

5 If you refer to the **proportions** in a work of art or design, you are referring to the relative sizes of its different parts. *You can vary the relative proportions of things in a picture very simply.* **6** If one thing increases or decreases **in proportion to** another thing, it increases or decreases to the same degree as that thing. **7** If something is small or large **in proportion to** something else, it is small or large when compared with that thing.

8 If you say that something is **out of all proportion to** something else, you think that it is far greater or more serious than it should be. *The punishment was out of all proportion to the crime.* **9** If you get something **out of proportion**, you think it is more important or worrying than it really is. If you keep something **in proportion**, you have a realistic view of how important it is. *We've got to keep this in proportion.* **10** If someone has a **sense of proportion**, they know what is really important and what is not. *We must not lose our sense of proportion.*

pro·por·tion·al /prəˈpɔːʃənəl/. If one amount is **proportional** to another, the two amounts increase and decrease at the same rate so there is always the same relationship between them. *Loss of weight is directly proportional to the rate at which the disease is progressing.* ♦ **pro·por·tion·al·ly** *You have proportionally more fat on your thighs and hips than anywhere else on your body.*

pro·por·tion·al·ity /prəˌpɔːʃəˈnælɪti/. The principle of **proportionality** is the idea that an action should not be more severe than is necessary, especially in a war or when punishing someone for a crime.

proˌportional represenˈtation. Proportional **representation** is a system of voting in which each political party is represented in parliament in proportion to the number of people who vote for it in an election.

pro·por·tion·ate /prə'pɔːʃənət/. **Proportionate** ◆◇◇◇◇ means the same as **proportional**. *Republics will* ADJ *have voting rights proportionate to the size of their economies.* ♦ **pro·por·tion·ate·ly** *Proportionately* ADV *more Americans are married nowadays than before.*

-proportioned /-prə'pɔːʃənd/. **-proportioned** is COMB added to adverbs to form adjectives that indicate that the proportions of the different parts of something or someone are good or bad. *...a perfectly-proportioned young woman.*

pro·po·sal /prə'pəʊzəl/ **proposals. 1** A **proposal** ◆◆◆◇ is a plan or an idea, often a formal or written one, N-COUNT which is suggested for people to think about and decide upon. *...the government's proposals to abolish free health care.* **2** A **proposal** is the act of ask- N-COUNT ing someone to marry you.

pro·pose /prə'pəʊz/ **proposes, proposing, pro-** ◆◆◆◇ **posed. 1** If you **propose** something such as a plan VERB or an idea, you suggest it for people to think about V n/-ing and decide upon. *Britain is about to propose* V -ing *changes to European Community institutions.* **2** If VERB you **propose** to do something, you intend to do it. V to-inf *It's still far from clear what action the government* V -ing *proposes to take over the affair... And where do you* Also V n *propose building such a huge thing?* **3** If you **pro-** VERB **pose** a theory or an explanation, you state that it is V n possibly or probably true. *This highlights a problem* Also V that *faced by people proposing theories of ball lightning.* **4** If you **propose** a motion for debate, or a candi- VERB date for election, you begin the debate or the elec- V n tion procedure by formally stating your support for Also V that that motion or candidate. *I asked Robert Balfour and Dawyck Haig to propose and second me.* ♦ **pro-** **·pos·er, proposers** *...Mr Ian Murch, the proposer* N-COUNT *of the motion.* **5** If you **propose a toast** to someone VERB: V n or something, you ask people to drink a toast to them. **6** If you **propose to** someone, or **propose** VERB **marriage** to them, you ask them to marry you. *He* Also V, *had proposed to Isabel the day after taking his seat* V n, *in Parliament.* V n to n

propo·si·tion /ˌprɒpə'zɪʃən/ **propositions,** ◆◆◇◇ **propositioning, propositioned. 1** If you de- N-COUNT scribe something such as a task or an activity as, for example, a difficult **proposition** or an attractive **proposition**, you mean that it is difficult or pleasant to do. *Making easy money has always been an attractive proposition.* **2** A **proposition** is a statement N-COUNT or an idea which people can consider or discuss to FORMAL decide whether it is true. *The proposition that democracies do not fight each other is based on a tiny historical sample.* **3** In the United States, a **proposi-** N-COUNT **tion** is a question or statement which appears on a ballot paper, and which people can vote for or against. **4** A **proposition** is an offer or a suggestion N-COUNT that someone makes to you, usually concerning some work or business. *You came to see me at my office the other day with a business proposition.* **5** If VERB someone who you do not know very well **proposi-** V n **tions** you, they suggest that you have sex with them. *Mr Whitfield had allegedly tried to proposition Miss Hawes.* ► Also a noun. *...unwanted sexual* N-COUNT *propositions.*

pro·pound /prə'paʊnd/ **propounds, propound-** VERB: V n **ing, propounded.** If someone **propounds** an idea FORMAL or theory, they suggest it for people to consider.

pro·pri·etary /prə'praɪətri, AM -teri/. **1** Propri- ◆◇◇◇ **etary** substances or products are sold under a trade ADJ: ADJ n name. *...some proprietary brands of dog food.* **2** If FORMAL someone has a **proprietary** attitude towards some- ADJ-GRADED thing, they behave as if they own it. FORMAL

pro·pri·eties /prə'praɪɪtiz/. The **proprieties** are the N-PLURAL standards of social behaviour which most people DATED consider socially or morally acceptable. *...respectable couples who observe the proprieties but loathe each other.*

pro·pri·etor /prə'praɪətə/ **proprietors.** The **pro-** ◆◇◇◇ **prietor** of a hotel, shop, newspaper, or other busi- N-COUNT ness is the person who owns it. ♦ **pro·pri·etorial** FORMAL /prəˌpraɪə'tɔːriəl/. If you have a **proprietorial** atti- ADJ-GRADED tude to something, you feel or behave as if you own

it. *Fundraisers are justified in feeling a touch propri-etorial about the city.*

pro·pri·ety /prə'praɪɪti/. **Propriety** is the quality of N-UNCOUNT being socially or morally acceptable. *...their sense of* FORMAL *social propriety.*

pro·pul·sion /prə'pʌlʃən/. **Propulsion** is the power ◆◇◇◇ that moves something, especially a vehicle, in a for- N-UNCOUNT ward direction. *...jet propulsion. ...the submarine's propulsion system.*

pro rata /ˌprəʊ 'rɑːtə, AM -'reɪtə/; also spelled **pro-** ADV: **rata.** If something is distributed **pro rata**, it is dis- ADV after v tributed in proportion to the amount or size of something. *All part-timers should be paid the same, pro rata, as full-timers.* ► Also an adjective. *He was* ADJ: ADJ n *prepared to contribute on a pro-rata basis.*

pro·sa·ic /prəʊ'zeɪɪk/. Something that is **prosaic** is ◆◇◇◇ dull and unimaginative. *The truth is more prosaic.* ADJ-GRADED ♦ **pro·sai·cal·ly** /prəʊ'zeɪɪkli/. *Arabian jam is also* FORMAL *known as angels' hair preserve, or more prosaically* ADV-GRADED *as carrot jam.*

pro·sce·ni·um /prəʊ'siːniəm/ **prosceniums.** A pro- N-COUNT **scenium** or a **proscenium arch** is an arch in a thea- tre which separates the stage from the audience.

pro·scribe /prəʊ'skraɪb/ **proscribes, proscrib-** VERB: **ing, proscribed.** If something is **proscribed** by beV-ed people in authority, the existence or the use of that beV-ed from thing is forbidden. *They are proscribed by federal* -ing *law from owning guns.* ♦ **pro·scrip·tion** N-VAR /prəʊ'skrɪpʃən/ **proscriptions.** *...the proscription against any religious service.*

prose /prəʊz/. **Prose** is ordinary written language, ◆◆◇◇ in contrast to poetry. *...a novel in prose with a sec-* N-UNCOUNT *tion in verse.*

pros·ecute /'prɒsɪkjuːt/ **prosecutes, prosecut-** ◆◆◆◇◇ **ing, prosecuted. 1** If the authorities **prosecute** V n someone, they charge them with a crime and put V them on trial. *The police have decided not to pros-ecute because the evidence is not strong enough.* ♦ **pros·ecu·tion** /ˌprɒsɪ'kjuːʃən/ **prosecutions.** N-VAR *The head of government called for the prosecution of those responsible.* **2** When a lawyer **prosecutes** a VERB: V n case, he or she tries to prove that the person who is V-ing on trial is guilty. *...the prosecuting attorney.* ♦ **pros-** **·ecu·tion.** The prosecuting lawyers in a trial are N-SING: called **the prosecution.** *Colonel Pugh, for the pros-* the N *ecution, said that the offences occurred over a six-year period.*

pros·ecu·tor /'prɒsɪkjuːtə/ **prosecutors.** In ◆◆◇◇ some countries, a **prosecutor** is a lawyer or official N-COUNT who brings charges against alleged criminals or tries to prove in a trial that they are guilty.

pros·elyt·ize /'prɒsɪlɪtaɪz/ **proselytizes, pros-** VERB: V **elytizing, proselytized;** also spelled **proselytise** V n in British English. If you **proselytize**, you try to per- BRITISH suade someone to share your beliefs, especially reli-gious or political beliefs. *Christians were arrested for trying to convert people, to proselytise them.*

pros·pect, prospects, prospecting, pro- ◆◆◆◇ **spected.** The noun is pronounced /'prɒspekt/. The verb is pronounced /prə'spekt, AM 'prɑːspekt/. **1** If there is some **prospect** of something happen- N-VAR: ing, there is a possibility that it will happen. *Unfor-* with supp *tunately, there is little prospect of seeing these big questions answered... The prospects for peace in the country's eight-year civil war are becoming brighter.* **2** A particular **prospect** is something that you ex- N-SING pect or know is going to happen. *They now face the prospect of having to wear a cycling helmet by law... After supper he'd put his feet up and read. It was a pleasant prospect.* **3** Someone's **prospects** are their N-PLURAL chances of being successful, especially in their career. *I chose to work abroad to improve my career prospects.* **4** When people **prospect for** oil, gold, or VERB: some other valuable substance, they look for it in V for n the ground or under the sea. *The oil companies are already prospecting not far from here.* ♦ **pro·spect-** **·ing** *He was involved in oil, zinc and lead prospect-* N-UNCOUNT *ing.* ♦ **pro·spec·tor, prospectors.** N-COUNT

pro·spec·tive /prə'spektɪv, AM prɑː-/. **1** You use ◆◆◇◇ **prospective** to describe someone who wants to be ADJ: ADJ n

the thing mentioned or who is likely to be the thing mentioned. *The story should act as a warning to other prospective buyers... When his prospective employers learned that he smoked, they said they wouldn't hire him.* **2** You use **prospective** to describe something that is likely to happen soon. *The terms of the prospective deal are most clearly spelt out in the Financial Times.* ADJ: ADJ n

pro·spec·tus /prə'spektəs, AM prɑː-/ **prospec-tuses.** A **prospectus** is a detailed document produced by a college, school, or company, which gives details about it. ◆◇◇◇ N-COUNT

pros·per /'prɒspə/ **prospers, prospering, pros-pered.** If people or businesses **prosper**, they are successful and do well. ◆◇◇◇ VERB: V FORMAL

pros·per·ity /prɒ'sperɪti/. **Prosperity** is a condition in which a person or community is doing well financially. *...a new era of peace and prosperity.* ◆◆◇◇ N-UNCOUNT

pros·per·ous /'prɒspərəs/. **Prosperous** people, places, and economies are rich and successful. ◆◇◇◇ ADJ-GRADED FORMAL

pros·tate /'prɒsteɪt/ **prostates.** The **prostate** or the **prostate gland** is an organ in the body of male mammals which is situated at the neck of the bladder and produces a liquid which forms part of the semen. ◆◇◇◇ N-COUNT

pros·the·sis /prɒs'θiːsɪs/ **prostheses.** A **prosthesis** is an artificial external body part. *Was it possible that he had had a false finger, a prosthesis of some kind?* ◆ **pros·thet·ic** /prɒs'θetɪk/. *...a prosthetic hand.* N-COUNT MEDICAL / ADJ: ADJ n

pros·ti·tute /'prɒstɪtjuːt, AM -tuːt/ **prostitutes, prostituting, prostituted.** **1** A **prostitute** is a person, usually a woman, who has sex with men in exchange for money. **2** If someone **prostitutes** a woman or if a woman **prostitutes** herself, she has sex with men for money. *...a woman who's forced to prostitute herself in order to get food. ...prostituting his beautiful daughters.* ◆ **pros·ti·tu·tion** /ˌprɒstɪ'tjuːʃən, AM -'tuː-/. *She eventually drifts into prostitution.* **3** If you **prostitute** yourself or your talents, you use your talents for unworthy purposes, usually for money. *Higher education is being forced to prostitute itself to market forces.* ◆◆◇◇ N-COUNT / VERB V pron-refl V n / N-UNCOUNT / VERB V pron-refl Also V n

pros·trate, prostrates, prostrating, prostrated. The verb is pronounced /prɒ'streɪt, AM 'prɑːstreɪt/. The adjective is pronounced /'prɒstreɪt/. **1** If you **prostrate** yourself, you lie down stretched out flat on the ground with your face downwards, usually as an act of worship or submission. **2** If you are lying **prostrate**, you are lying flat on the ground with your face downwards. **3** If someone is **prostrate**, they are so distressed or affected by a very bad experience that they are unable to do anything at all. *I was prostrate with grief.* VERB: V pron-refl / ADJ: ADJ after v / ADJ FORMAL

pro·tago·nist /prə'tægənɪst, AM prəʊ-/ **protago-nists. 1** A **protagonist** in a play, novel, or real event is one of the main people in it. *...the leading protagonists in the Gulf crisis.* **2** A **protagonist** of an idea or movement is a supporter of it. ◆◇◇◇ N-COUNT FORMAL / N-COUNT FORMAL

pro·tean /'prəʊtiən/. If you describe someone or something as **protean**, you mean that they have the ability to continually change their nature, appearance, or behaviour. ADJ-GRADED LITERARY

pro·tect /prə'tekt/ **protects, protecting, pro-tected. 1** To **protect** someone or something means to prevent them from being harmed or damaged. *What can women do to protect themselves from heart disease?... A purple headscarf protected her against the wind... The government is committed to protecting the interests of tenants.* **2** If an insurance policy **protects** you against a particular event such as death, injury, fire, or theft, it states that it will give money to you or your family if that event occurs. *...coverage that protects against the loss of personal belongings.* ◆◆◆◆ VERB V n from/against n / Also V against n / VERB: V n against n V against n

pro·tect·ed /prə'tektɪd/. **Protected** is used to describe animals, plants, and areas of land which are not allowed to be destroyed, harmed, or damaged. *In England, thrushes are a protected species.* ADJ

pro·tec·tion /prə'tekʃən/ **protections. 1** If something gives or is **protection** against something unpleasant, it prevents people or things from being harmed or damaged by it. *Such a diet is widely believed to offer protection against a number of cancers.* **2** If an insurance policy gives you **protection** against a particular event, it states that it will give money to you or your family if that event happens. **3 Protections** are laws and other official measures intended to protect people's rights and freedoms. **4** If a government has a policy of **protection**, it helps its own industries by putting a tax on imported goods or by restricting imports in some other way. *Over the same period trade protection has increased in the rich countries.* ◆ **pro·tec·tion·ism** /prə'tekʃənɪzəm/. *Reagan was for free trade and against protectionism.* ◆ **pro·tec·tion·ist, protec-tionists.** *...protectionist agricultural policies.* **5** If gangsters offer people **protection**, they demand money from them and in return promise not to hurt them or damage their property. *A businessman who refused to pay protection money was shot.* ◆◆◆◇ N-VAR / N-UNCOUNT / N-COUNT / N-UNCOUNT / N-UNCOUNT / N-COUNT / N-UNCOUNT

pro·tec·tive /prə'tektɪv/. **1 Protective** means designed or intended to protect something or someone from harm. *Protective measures are necessary if the city's monuments are to be preserved. ...protective gloves.* **2** If someone is **protective** towards you, they show a strong desire to look after you and keep you safe. *Glynis was beside her, putting a protective arm around her shoulders.* ◆ **pro·tec·tive·ly** *Simon drove me to the airport, gave me a bear-hug and protectively told me to look after myself.* ◆ **pro·tec·tive·ness** *What she felt now was protectiveness towards her brothers.* ◆◆◇◇ ADJ / ADJ-GRADED / ADV: ADV with v / N-UNCOUNT

pro·tec·tor /prə'tektə/ **protectors. 1** If you refer to someone as your **protector**, you mean that they protect you from being harmed. **2** A **protector** is a device that protects someone or something from physical harm. *He was the only National League umpire to wear an outside chest protector.* ◆◇◇◇ N-COUNT / N-COUNT

pro·tec·tor·ate /prə'tektərət/ **protectorates.** A **protectorate** is a country that is controlled and protected by a more powerful country. N-COUNT

pro·té·gé /'prɒtɪʒeɪ, AM 'prəʊt-/ **protégés;** sometimes spelled **protégée** when referring to a woman. The **protégé** of an older and more experienced person is a young person who is helped and guided by them over a period of time. *...Klimt's young protége, Egon Schiele.* ◆◇◇◇ N-COUNT

pro·tein /'prəʊtiːn/ **proteins. Protein** is a substance which the body needs and which is found in food and drink such as meat, eggs, and milk. *Fish was a major source of protein for the working man. ...a high protein diet.* ◆◆◇◇ N-VAR

pro tem /ˌprəʊ 'tem/. If someone has a particular position **pro tem**, they have it temporarily. *...the president pro tem of the California State Senate.* ADV: n ADV FORMAL

pro·test, protests, protesting, protested. The verb is pronounced /prə'test/. The noun is pronounced /'prəʊtest/. **1** To **protest** means to say or show publicly that you object to something. In British English, you **protest about** something or **against** something. In American English, you **protest** something. *Groups of women took to the streets to protest against the arrests... They were protesting soaring prices... He picked up the cat before Rosa could protest.* ◆ **pro·test·er, protesters;** also spelled **protestor.** *...anti-abortion protesters.* **2** A **protest** is the act of saying or showing publicly that you object to something. *The opposition now seems too weak to stage any serious protests against the government... The unions called a two-hour strike in protest at the railway authority's announcement.* **3** If you **protest** that something is the case, you insist that it is the case, when other people think that it may not be. *'I never said any of that to her,' he protested... He has always protested his innocence.* ▶ Also a noun. *For once she did not make the usual protest that her name was Trish.* ◆◆◆◇ VERB V about/against/at n V n / V / N-COUNT / N-VAR / VERB: V that V with quote V n / N-COUNT

Pro·test·ant /'prɒtɪstənt/ **Protestants.** A Protestant is a Christian who belongs to the branch of the Christian church which separated from the Catholic church in the sixteenth century. ▶ Also an adjective. ADJ *Most Protestant churches now have women ministers.* ♦ **Prot·es·tant·ism** *Catholic leaders are* N-UNCOUNT *alarmed at the spread of Protestantism.*

pro·tes·ta·tion /ˌprɒtɪ'steɪʃən/ **protestations.** A N-COUNT *protestation* is a strong declaration that something FORMAL is true or not true. *Despite his constant protestations of devotion and love, her doubts persisted.*

proto- /'prəʊtəʊ-/. **Proto-** is used to form adjectives PREFIX and nouns which indicate that something is in the early stages of its development. *...the proto-fascist tendencies of some of its supporters.*

pro·to·col /'prəʊtəkɒl, AM -kɔːl/ **protocols.** ♦◇◇◇◇ **1** *Protocol* is a system of rules about the correct N-VAR way to act in formal situations. *...minor breaches of protocol.* **2** A *protocol* is a written record of a treaty N-COUNT or agreement that has been made by two or more FORMAL countries. *There are also protocols on the testing of nuclear weapons.* **3** A *protocol* is a course of medi- N-COUNT cal treatment for someone who is ill or has an ad- AMERICAN, diction. *...the detoxification protocol.* MEDICAL

pro·ton /'prəʊtɒn/ **protons.** A *proton* is an atomic ♦◇◇◇◇ particle that has a positive electrical charge. N-COUNT

proto·type /'prəʊtətaɪp/ **prototypes.** **1** A *proto-* N-COUNT *type* is an experimental model of something new which has not yet been produced commercially. **2** If N-COUNT you say that someone or something is a *prototype* **of** a type of person or thing, you mean that they are the first or most typical one of that type. *He was the prototype of the elder statesman.* ♦ **proto·typ·ical** ADJ /ˌprəʊtə'tɪpɪkəl/. *Park Ridge is the prototypical American suburb.*

proto·zoan /ˌprəʊtə'zəʊən/ **protozoa** or **proto-** N-COUNT **zoans.** *Protozoa* are very small life forms which of- TECHNICAL ten live inside larger animals.

pro·tract·ed /prə'træktɪd, AM prəʊ-/. Something, ♦◇◇◇◇ usually something unpleasant, that is *protracted* ADJ-GRADED lasts a long time, especially longer than usual or FORMAL longer than you hoped. *After protracted negotiations Ogden got the deal he wanted. ...a protracted civil war.*

pro·trude /prə'truːd, AM prəʊ-/ **protrudes, pro-** ♦◇◇◇◇ **truding, protruded.** If something *protrudes* from VERB somewhere, it sticks out. *...a huge round mass of* V prep *smooth rock protruding from the water... The tip of* FORMAL *her tongue was protruding slightly.* ♦ **pro·trud·ing** ADJ-GRADED *...protruding ears.* ♦ **pro·tru·sion** /prə'truːʒən, AM N-VAR prəʊ-/ **protrusions.** *He grabbed at a protrusion of rock.*

proud /praʊd/ **prouder, proudest.** **1** If you feel ♦♦◇◇◇ *proud*, you feel glad about something good that you ADJ-GRADED possess or have done, or about something that someone close to you possesses or has done. *I felt proud of his efforts... They are proud that she is doing well at school... He is the proud father of a 5-month-old baby son.* ♦ **proud·ly** *'That's the first* ADV-GRADED *part finished,' he said proudly.* **2** Your *proudest* mo- ADJ-GRADED: ments or achievements are the ones that you are ADJ n most proud of. **3** Someone who is *proud* has dignity ADJ-GRADED and self-respect. *He was too proud to ask his family for help.* **4** Someone who is *proud* feels that they ADJ-GRADED are better or more important than other people. **5** If PHRASE someone **does you proud**, they do something very INFORMAL well, so that you can feel proud of them or pleased with them. *His team did him proud.*

prove /pruːv/ **proves, proving, proved, prov-** ♦♦♦♦◇ **en.** The forms *proved* and *proven* can both be used as a past participle. **1** If something *proves* to V-LINK be true or to have a particular quality, it becomes V to-inf clear after a period of time that it is true or has that V adj quality. *Unfortunately all our reports proved to be* V n *true... In the past this process of transition has often proven difficult. ...an experiment which was to prove a source of inspiration for many years to come.* **2** If VERB: you *prove* that something is true, you show by V that means of argument or evidence that it is definitely V n true. *Professor Cantor set out to prove his theory.* V wh V n adj V n to-inf

...trying to prove how groups of animals have evolved... That made me hopping mad and determined to prove him wrong... History will prove him VERB: *to have been right all along.* **3** If you *prove* yourself V pron-refl to have a certain good quality, you show by your ac- to-inf tions that you have it. *As a composer he proved him-* V pron-refl adj *self adept at large dramatic forms... A man needs* V pron-refl *time to prove himself.*

prov·enance /'prɒvɪnəns/ **provenances.** The N-VAR *provenance* of something is the place that it comes FORMAL from or that it originally came from. *He had no idea of its provenance.*

prov·erb /'prɒvɜːb/ **proverbs.** A *proverb* is a short N-COUNT sentence that people often quote, which gives advice or tells you something about life. *An old Arab proverb says, 'The enemy of my enemy is my friend'.*

pro·ver·bial /prə'vɜːbiəl/. You use *proverbial* to ♦◇◇◇◇ show that you know the way you are describing ADJ: ADJ n something is one that is often used or is part of a popular saying. *My audience certainly isn't the proverbial man in the street.*

pro·vide /prə'vaɪd/ **provides, providing, pro-** ♦♦♦♦♦ **vided. 1** If you *provide* something that someone VERB needs or wants, or if you *provide* them **with** it, you V n give it to them or make it available to them. *They* V n with n *would not provide any details... The government was not in a position to provide them with food.* ♦ **pro-** **·vid·er, providers.** *They remain the main provid-* N-COUNT *ers of sports facilities.* **2** If a law or agreement *pro-* VERB *vides* that something will happen, it states that it V that will happen. *The treaty provides that, by the end of* FORMAL *the century, the United States must have removed its bases.* **3** See also **provided, providing.**

provide for. 1 If you *provide for* someone, you sup- PHRASAL VB port them financially and make sure that they have V P n the things that they need. *Elaine wouldn't let him provide for her... Her father always ensured she was well provided for.* **2** If you *provide for* something that V P n might happen or that might need to be done, you make arrangements to deal with it. *James had provided for just such an emergency.* **3** If a law or agreement V P n *provides for* something, it makes it possible. *The bill* FORMAL *also provides for the automatic review by the appeal court of all death sentences.*

pro·vid·ed /prə'vaɪdɪd/. If you say that something ♦♦◇◇◇ will happen *provided* or *provided that* something CONJ else happens, you mean that the first thing will happen only if the second thing also happens. *Provided they are fit I see no reason why they shouldn't go on playing.*

provi·dence /'prɒvɪdəns/. *Providence* is God, or a ♦◇◇◇◇ force which is believed by some people to arrange N-UNCOUNT the things that happen to us. *These women regard* LITERARY *his death as an act of providence.*

provi·den·tial /ˌprɒvɪ'denʃəl/. A *providential* event ADJ-GRADED is lucky because it happens at exactly the right time. FORMAL ♦ **provi·den·tial·ly** *Providentially, he had earlier* ADV *made friends with a Russian Colonel.*

pro·vid·ing /prə'vaɪdɪŋ/. If you say that something ♦◇◇◇◇ will happen *providing* or *providing that* something CONJ else happens, you mean that the first thing will happen only if the second thing also happens. *I do believe in people being able to do what they want to do, providing they're not hurting someone else.*

prov·ince /'prɒvɪns/ **provinces. 1** A *province* is a ♦♦♦◇◇ large section of a country which has its own admin- N-COUNT istration. **2** The *provinces* are all the parts of a N-PLURAL country except the part where the capital is situated. *The government plans to transfer some 30,000 government jobs from Paris to the provinces.* **3** If you N-SING: say that a subject or activity is a particular person's with poss *province*, you mean that this person has a special interest in it, a special knowledge of it, or a special responsibility for it. *Industrial research is the province of the Department of Trade and Industry.*

pro·vin·cial /prə'vɪnʃəl/ **provincials. 1** *Provin-* ♦♦◇◇◇ *cial* means connected with the parts of a country ADJ: ADJ n outside the capital. **2** If you describe someone or ADJ-GRADED something as *provincial*, you disapprove of them PRAGMATICS because you think that they are narrow-minded and

unsophisticated. *The audience was dull and very provincial.* ▶ Also a noun. *...uncouth provincials.* N-COUNT
♦ **pro·vin·cial·ism** /prə'vɪnʃəlɪzəm/. *...the stifling* N-UNCOUNT *bourgeois provincialism of Buxton.*

'**proving ground, proving grounds.** If you de- N-COUNT scribe a place as a **proving ground**, you mean that new things or ideas are tried out or tested there. *New York is a proving ground today for the Demo-cratic presidential candidates.*

pro·vi·sion /prə'vɪʒən/ **provisions. 1** The provi- ♦♦♦◊◊ sion of something is the act of giving it or making it N-UNCOUNT: available to people who need or want it. *The depart- also a N ment is responsible for the provision of residential care services.* **2** If you make **provision for** something N-VAR or someone, you make arrangements to deal with anything that is needed in connection with them, especially money. *Mr King asked if it had ever oc-curred to her to make provision for her own pen-sion... There are very generous provisions for the mother.* **3** A **provision** in a law or an agreement is N-COUNT an arrangement which is included in it. **4** Provi- N-PLURAL **sions** are supplies of food. DATED

pro·vi·sion·al /prə'vɪʒənəl/. You use **provisional** ♦◊◊◊◊ to describe something that has been arranged or ADJ appointed for the present, but may be changed in the future. *...the possibility of setting up a provision-al coalition government.* ♦ **pro·vi·sion·al·ly** *The* ADV: *European Community has provisionally agreed to* ADV with v *increase the quotas.*

pro·vi·so /prə'vaɪzəʊ/ **provisos.** A **proviso** is a N-COUNT condition in an agreement. *I told Norman I would invest in his venture as long as he agreed to one pro-viso... Okay, with the proviso that Jane agrees, I accept.*

pro·vo·ca·teur /prəʊˌvɒkə'tɜ:/ **provocateurs.** See **agent provocateur.**

provo·ca·tion /ˌprɒvə'keɪʃən/ **provocations.** If ♦◊◊◊◊ you describe something that someone does as N-VAR **provocation** or a **provocation**, you mean that it is a reason for someone to react angrily, violently, or emotionally. *He denies murder on the grounds of provocation... The soldiers fired without provocation.*

pro·voca·tive /prə'vɒkətɪv/. **1** If you describe ♦◊◊◊◊ something as **provocative**, you mean that it is in- ADJ-GRADED tended to make people react angrily or argue against it. *He has made a string of outspoken and sometimes provocative speeches.* ♦ **pro·voca·tive-ly** *The soldiers fired into the air when the demon-* ADV-GRADED *strators behaved provocatively.* **2** If you describe ADJ-GRADED someone's clothing or behaviour as **provocative**, you mean that it is intended to make someone feel sexual desire. ♦ **provocatively** *She smiled at him* ADV-GRADED *provocatively.*

pro·voke /prə'vəʊk/ **provokes, provoking, pro-** ♦♦♦◊◊ **voked. 1** If you **provoke** someone, you deliberately VERB annoy and try to make them behave aggres- V n into-ing/n sively. *He started beating me when I was about fifteen but I didn't do anything to provoke him... I provoked him into doing something really stupid.* VERB **2** If something **provokes** a reaction, it causes it. *The* V n destruction of the mosque has provoked anger throughout the Muslim world.*

prov·ost /'prɒvɒst, AM 'prəʊvəʊst/ **provosts. 1** A N-COUNT **provost** is the head of a university college in Britain. **2** In the United States, a **provost** is an important N-COUNT administrator in a university. **3** A **provost** is the N-COUNT chief magistrate of a Scottish borough. **4** In the Ro-man Catholic and Anglican Churches, a **provost** is N-COUNT the person who is in charge of the administration of a cathedral.

prow /praʊ/ **prows.** The **prow** of a ship or boat is N-COUNT the front part of it.

prow·ess /'praʊɪs/. Someone's **prowess** is their ♦◊◊◊◊ outstanding ability at doing a particular thing. *He's* N-UNCOUNT *always bragging about his prowess as a cricketer.* FORMAL

prowl /praʊl/ **prowls, prowling, prowled. 1** If ♦◊◊◊◊ an animal or a person **prowls** around, they move V prep/adv around quietly, for example when they are hunting. Also V, *He prowled around the room, not sure what he was* V n *looking for.* **2** If an animal is **on the prowl**, it is PHRASE

hunting. If a person is **on the prowl**, they are hunt-ing for something such as a sexual partner or a business deal.

prowl·er /'praʊlə/ **prowlers.** A **prowler** is an un- N-COUNT known man who creeps around, especially at night, following women and children or hiding near their houses in order to steal something, frighten them, or perhaps harm them.

prox·im·ity /prɒk'sɪmɪti/. **Proximity** to a place or ♦◊◊◊◊ person is nearness to that place or person. *Families* N-UNCOUNT *are no longer in close proximity to each other.* FORMAL

proxy /'prɒksi/ **proxies. 1** If you do something **by** ♦◊◊◊◊ **proxy**, you arrange for someone else to do it for N-UNCOUNT you. *Those not attending the meeting may vote by proxy.* **2** A **proxy** is a person or thing that is acting N-COUNT or being used in the place of someone or something else.

prude /pru:d/ **prudes.** If you call someone a **prude**, N-COUNT you think that they are easily shocked and embar- PRAGMATICS rassed by things relating to nudity or sex; used showing disapproval. ♦ **prud·ish** *I'm not prudish* ADJ-GRADED *but I think these photographs are obscene.* ♦ **prud-** **·ish·ness** *Older people will have grown up in a* N-UNCOUNT *time of greater sexual prudishness.*

pru·dent /'pru:dənt/. Someone who is **prudent** is ♦◊◊◊◊ sensible and careful. *It is always prudent to start* ADJ-GRADED *any exercise programme gradually at first.* ♦ **pru-** **·dent·ly** *Prudently, Joanna spoke none of this* ADV-GRADED *aloud.* ♦ **pru·dence** /'pru:dəns/. *A lack of prudence* N-UNCOUNT *may lead to financial problems.*

prune /pru:n/ **prunes, pruning, pruned. 1** A ♦♦◊◊◊ **prune** is a dried plum. *...iron-rich foods such as lean* N-COUNT *meat, liver, prunes, and kidney beans.* **2** When you VERB: V n **prune** a tree or bush, you cut off some of the branches so that it will grow better the next year. ▶ **Prune back** means the same as **prune**. *Apples,* PHRASAL VB *pears and cherries can be pruned back when they've* V P noun *lost their leaves.* **3** If you **prune** something, you cut VERB out all the parts that you do not need. *Firms are* V n *cutting investment and pruning their product ranges.*

prune back. See **prune** 2. PHRASAL VB

pru·ri·ent /'prʊəriənt/. If you describe someone as ADJ-GRADED **prurient**, you are criticizing them for showing too PRAGMATICS much interest in sexual matters. *We read the gossip* FORMAL *written about them with prurient interest.* ♦ **pru·ri-** **·ence** *Nobody ever lost money by overestimating the* N-UNCOUNT *public's prurience.*

pry /praɪ/ **pries, prying, pried. 1** If someone ♦◊◊◊◊ **pries**, they try to find out about someone else's pri- V n vate affairs, or look at their personal possessions. V into n *We do not want people prying into our affairs... She* V-ing *thought she was safe from prying eyes.* **2** If you **pry** VERB something **open** or **pry** it away from a surface, you V n with adj force it open or away from a surface. *She pried open* V n prep *his jaws... I pried the top off a can of chilli... Prying* V n with adv *off the plastic lid, she took out a small scoop.*

PS /ˌpi:'es/. You write **PS** before a comment or ♦◊◊◊◊ note you add at the end of a letter, after you have signed it. *PS. Please show your friends this letter and the enclosed leaflet.*

psalm /sɑːm/ **psalms.** The **Psalms** are the 150 N-COUNT songs, poems, and prayers which together form the Book of Psalms in the Bible.

pseud /sju:d/ **pseuds.** If you say that someone is a N-COUNT **pseud**, you mean that they are trying to appear very PRAGMATICS well-educated or artistic but you think that they are INFORMAL, being pretentious; used showing disapproval. BRITISH

pseudo- /'sju:dəʊ-, AM 'su:dəʊ-/. **Pseudo-** is used to PREFIX form adjectives and nouns that indicate that some-thing is not the thing it is claimed to be. For example, if you describe a country as a pseudo-democracy, you mean that it is not really a democ-racy, although its government claims that it is. *...pseudo-intellectual images.*

pseudo·nym /'sju:dənɪm, AM 'su:-/ **pseudonyms.** N-COUNT A **pseudonym** is a name which someone, usually a writer, uses instead of his or her real name.

pso·ria·sis /sə'raɪəsɪs/. **Psoriasis** is a skin disease N-UNCOUNT that causes red scaly patches.

psst /psst/. **Psst** is used in writing to represent the short hissing sound that someone makes when they want to attract another person's attention secretly or quietly. *'Psst! Come over here!' one youth hissed furtively.*

psych /saɪk/ **psychs, psyching, psyched;** also spelled **psyche.**

psych up. If you **psych** yourself **up** before a contest or a difficult task, you prepare yourself for it mentally, especially by telling yourself that you can win or succeed. *Before the game everyone gets psyched up and starts shouting.*
PHRASAL VB V pron-refl P get V-ed P INFORMAL

psyche /'saɪki/ **psyches.** Your **psyche** is your mind and your deepest feelings and attitudes. *...art which gives expression to disturbing elements of the human psyche.*
◆◇◇◇◇ N-COUNT TECHNICAL

psychedelia /ˌsaɪkəˈdiːliə/. **Psychedelia** refers to psychedelic objects, clothes, and music.
N-UNCOUNT

psychedel·ic /ˌsaɪkəˈdelɪk/. **1 Psychedelic** means relating to drugs such as LSD which have a strong effect on your mind, often producing hallucinations and visions. *...his first real, full-blown psychedelic experience.* **2 Psychedelic** art has bright colours and strange patterns. **3 Psychedelic** music is pop music, especially of the late 1960s and early 1970s, which is closely associated with hallucinogenic drugs.
◆◇◇◇◇ ADJ-GRADED
ADJ-GRADED
ADJ

psy·chia·try /saɪˈkaɪətri, AM sɪ-/. **Psychiatry** is the branch of medicine concerned with the treatment of mental illness. ♦ **psy·chi·at·ric** /ˌsaɪkiˈætrɪk/ *We finally insisted that he seek psychiatric help... About 4% of the prison population have chronic psychiatric illnesses.* ♦ **psy·chia·trist** /saɪˈkaɪətrɪst, AM sɪ-/, **psychiatrists** *A colleague urged him to see a psychiatrist.*
◆◇◇◇◇ N-UNCOUNT
ADJ
N-COUNT

psy·chic /'saɪkɪk/ **psychics. 1** If you believe that someone is **psychic** or has **psychic powers,** you believe that they have strange mental powers, such as being able to read the minds of other people or to see into the future. *You don't need to be psychic to see she needs comfort and kind words.* ▶ A **psychic** is someone who seems to be psychic. **2 Psychic** means relating to ghosts and the spirits of the dead. *He declared his total disbelief in psychic phenomena.* **3 Psychic** means relating to the mind rather than the body. *These truths cause individuals much psychic pain.*
◆◆◇◇◇ ADJ-GRADED
N-COUNT
ADJ
ADJ FORMAL

psy·cho /'saɪkəʊ/ **psychos.** A **psycho** is someone who has serious mental problems and who may act in a violent way without feeling sorry for what they have done.
◆◇◇◇◇ N-COUNT INFORMAL

psycho- /'saɪkəʊ-/. **Psycho-** is used to form words which describe or refer to things connected with the mind or with mental processes. *...the psycho-social aspects of youth unemployment.*
PREFIX

psycho·ac·tive /ˌsaɪkəʊˈæktɪv/. **Psychoactive** drugs or stimulants affect your mind.
ADJ

psycho·ana·lyse /ˌsaɪkəʊˈænəlaɪz/ **psychoanalyses, psychoanalysing, psychoanalysed;** spelled **psychoanalyze** in American English. When a psychotherapist or psychiatrist **psychoanalyses** someone who has mental problems, he or she examines or treats them using psychoanalysis.
VERB: V n

psycho·analy·sis /ˌsaɪkəʊəˈnælɪsɪs/. **Psychoanalysis** is the treatment of someone who has mental problems by asking them about their feelings and their past in order to try to discover what may be causing their condition. *...the methods of strict Freudian psychoanalysis.* ♦ **psycho·ana·lyst,** **psychoanalysts.** *Jane is seeing a psychoanalyst.* ♦ **psycho·ana·lyt·ic** /ˌsaɪkəʊænəˈlɪtɪk/. *...psychoanalytic therapy.*
◆◇◇◇◇ N-UNCOUNT
N-COUNT
ADJ

psycho·ana·lyze /ˌsaɪkəʊˈænəlaɪz/. See **psychoanalyse.**

psycho·bab·ble /'saɪkəʊbæbəl/. You can use **psychobabble** to refer to complicated or pretentious language, especially language relating to psychoanalysis, which is used in a meaningless way.
N-UNCOUNT INFORMAL

psycho·logi·cal /ˌsaɪkəˈlɒdʒɪkəl/. **1 Psychological** means concerned with a person's mind and
◆◆◇◇ ADJ

thoughts. *Robyn's loss of memory is a psychological problem, rather than a physical one.* ♦ **psycho·logi·cal·ly** /ˌsaɪkəˈlɒdʒɪkli/ *It was very important psychologically for us to succeed, and I'm delighted.* **2** See also **psychology.**
ADV

psychological 'warfare. Psychological warfare consists of attempts to make your enemy lose confidence, give up hope, or feel afraid, so that you can win.
N-UNCOUNT

psy·chol·ogy /saɪˈkɒlədʒi/. **1 Psychology** is the scientific study of the human mind and the reasons for people's behaviour. *...Professor of Psychology at Bedford College.* ♦ **psycho·logi·cal** *...psychological testing.* ♦ **psy·cholo·gist, psychologists.** *She'd taken her daughter to several child psychologists.* **2** The **psychology** of a person is the kind of mind that they have, which makes them think or behave in the way that they do. *...a fascination with the psychology of murderers.*
◆◆◇◇ N-UNCOUNT
ADJ: ADJ n
N-COUNT
N-UNCOUNT

psycho·met·ric /ˌsaɪkəˈmetrɪk/. **Psychometric** tests are designed to test a person's mental state, personality, and thought processes.
ADJ: ADJ n

psycho·path /'saɪkəʊpæθ/ **psychopaths.** A **psychopath** is someone who has serious mental problems and who may act in a violent way without feeling sorry for what they have done. ♦ **psycho·path·ic** /ˌsaɪkəʊˈpæθɪk/. Someone who is **psychopathic** is a psychopath.
N-COUNT
ADJ

psy·cho·sis /saɪˈkəʊsɪs/ **psychoses. Psychosis** is severe mental illness which can make people lose contact with reality.
◆◇◇◇◇ N-VAR MEDICAL

psycho·so·mat·ic /ˌsaɪkəʊsəˈmætɪk/. If someone has a **psychosomatic** illness, their symptoms are caused by worry or unhappiness rather than by a physical problem.
ADJ

psycho·thera·py /ˌsaɪkəʊˈθerəpi/. **Psychotherapy** is the use of psychological methods in treating people who are mentally ill, rather than using physical methods such as drugs or surgery. ♦ **psycho·thera·pist, psychotherapists** *He arranged for him to see a psychotherapist.*
◆◆◇◇◇ N-UNCOUNT
N-COUNT

psy·chot·ic /saɪˈkɒtɪk/ **psychotics.** Someone who is **psychotic** is suffering from a psychosis. ▶ Also a noun. *A religious psychotic in Las Vegas has killed four people.*
◆◇◇◇◇ ADJ MEDICAL N-COUNT

pt, pts. 1 pt is a written abbreviation for 'pint'. The plural is either 'pt' or 'pts'. **2 pt** is the written abbreviation for 'point'. *3 pts for a correct result.*
◆◇◇◇

PTA /ˌpiː tiː ˈeɪ/ **PTAs.** A **PTA** is a school association run by some of the parents and teachers to discuss matters that affect the children and to organize fund-raising and social events. **PTA** is an abbreviation for 'parent-teacher association'.
N-COUNT

Pte. Pte is a written abbreviation for the military title 'Private'. The American abbreviation is **Pvt.**
BRITISH

ptero·dac·tyl /ˌterəˈdæktɪl/ **pterodactyls.** A **pterodactyl** was a flying reptile that existed in prehistoric times.
N-COUNT

PTO /ˌpiː tiː ˈəʊ/. **PTO** is a written abbreviation for 'please turn over'. You write it at the bottom of a page to indicate that there is more writing on the other side.

pub /pʌb/ **pubs.** In Britain, a **pub** is a building where people can buy and drink alcoholic drinks, and talk to their friends.
◆◆◆◇◇ N-COUNT

'pub crawl, pub crawls. If people go on a **pub crawl,** they go from one pub to another having drinks in each one.
N-COUNT BRITISH, INFORMAL

pu·ber·ty /'pjuːbəti/. **Puberty** is the stage in someone's life when their body starts to become physically mature.
◆◇◇◇◇ N-UNCOUNT

pu·bes·cent /pjuːˈbesənt/. A **pubescent** girl or boy has reached the stage in their life when their bodies are becoming physically like an adult.
ADJ FORMAL

pu·bic /'pjuːbɪk/. **Pubic** means relating to the area just above a person's genitals. *...pubic hair.*
ADJ: ADJ n

pub·lic /'pʌblɪk/. **1** You can refer to people in general, or to all the people in a particular country or community, as the **public.** *Lauderdale House is now open to the public... Pure alcohol is not for sale to*
◆◆◆◆◆ N-COLL-SING: the N

the general public. **2 Public** means relating to all the people in a country or community. *The President is attempting to drum up public support for his economic program.* **3** You can refer to a set of people in a country who share a common interest, activity, or characteristic as a particular kind of **public**. *...the American voting public.* **4 Public** is used to describe statements, actions, and events that are made or done in such a way that any member of the public can see them or be aware of them. *The comments were the ministry's first detailed public statement on the subject... Marilyn made her last public appearance at Madison Square Garden.* ♦ **pub·lic·ly** *He never spoke publicly about the affair.*

5 If someone is a **public figure** or in **public life**, many people know who they are because they serve the public in their job, for example as a politician, and are often mentioned on television or in the newspapers. **6** If someone is **in the public eye**, many people know who they are, because they are famous or because they are often mentioned on television or in the newspapers. *He has kept his wife and daughter out of the public eye.* **7** If a fact is **made public** or **becomes public**, it becomes known to everyone rather than being kept secret.

8 Public means relating to the government or state, or things that are done by the state for the people. *The social services account for a substantial part of public spending.* ♦ **publicly** *...publicly funded legal services.* **9 Public** buildings and services are provided for everyone to use. *...the New York Public Library. ...public transport.* **10** A **public** place is one where people can go about freely and where you can easily be seen and heard. *...the heavily congested public areas of international airports.* **11** If a company **goes public**, it starts selling its shares on the stock exchange. **12** If you say or do something **in public**, you say or do it when a group of people are present. *By-laws are to make it illegal to smoke in public.* **13** ● to **wash** your **dirty linen in public**: see **dirty**.

public ad'dress system, public address systems. A **public address system** is an electrical system including a microphone, amplifier, and loudspeakers which is used so that someone's voice, or music, can be heard by a large number of people. The abbreviation 'PA' is also used.

pub·li·can /ˈpʌblɪkən/ **publicans.** A **publican** is a person who owns or manages a pub. N-COUNT BRITISH, FORMAL

pub·li·ca·tion /ˌpʌblɪˈkeɪʃən/ **publications.** **1** The **publication** of a book or magazine is the act of printing it and sending it to shops to be sold. *The guide is being translated into several languages for publication near Christmas.* **2** A **publication** is a book or magazine that has been published. *The US Golf Association sponsored a publication entitled Golf Course Management.* **3** The **publication** of something such as information is the act of making it known to the public, for example by informing journalists or by publishing a government document. *A spokesman said: 'We have no comment regarding the publication of these photographs.'*

public 'bar, public bars. In a British pub, a **public bar** is a room where the furniture is plain and the drinks are cheaper than in the pub's other bars. N-COUNT

public 'company, public companies. A **public company** is a company whose shares can be bought by the general public. N-COUNT

public con'venience, public conveniences. A **public convenience** is a toilet in a public place for everyone to use. N-COUNT BRITISH, FORMAL

public do'main. If information is **in the public domain**, it is not secret or copyright and can be used or discussed by anybody. *It is outrageous that the figures are not in the public domain.* N-SING

public 'house, public houses. A **public house** is the same as a **pub**. N-COUNT BRITISH, FORMAL

pub·li·cise /ˈpʌblɪsaɪz/. See **publicize**.

pub·li·cist /ˈpʌblɪsɪst/ **publicists.** A **publicist** is a person who publicizes things, especially as part of a job in advertising or journalism. N-COUNT

pub·lic·ity /pʌˈblɪsɪti/. **1 Publicity** is information or actions intended to attract the public's attention to someone or something. *Peking is to give unprecedented advance publicity to the talks... They dismissed the truce as a publicity stunt.* **2** When the news media and the public show a lot of interest in something, you can say that it is receiving **publicity**. *The case has generated enormous publicity in Brazil.* N-UNCOUNT

pub·li·cize /ˈpʌblɪsaɪz/ **publicizes, publicizing, publicized;** also spelled **publicise** in British English. If you **publicize** a fact or event, you make it widely known to the public. *The author appeared on television to publicize her latest book.* VERB V n

public limited 'company, public limited companies. A **public limited company** is the same as a **public company**. The abbreviation 'plc' is used after such companies' names. N-COUNT

public 'nuisance, public nuisances. If something or someone is or causes a **public nuisance**, they harm or annoy members of the public. *Back in the 1980s drug users were a public nuisance in Zurich.* N-COUNT LEGAL

public o'pinion. **Public opinion** is the opinion or attitude of the public regarding a particular matter. *He mobilized public opinion all over the world against hydrogen-bomb tests.* N-UNCOUNT

public 'property. **1 Public property** is land and other assets that belong to the general public and not to a private owner. **2** If you describe a person or thing as **public property**, you mean that information about them is known and discussed by everybody. *She complained that intimate aspects of her personal life had been made public property.* N-UNCOUNT

public 'prosecutor, public prosecutors. A **public prosecutor** is an official who carries out criminal prosecutions on behalf of the government and people of a particular country. N-COUNT

public re'lations. **1 Public relations** is the part of an organization's work that is concerned with obtaining the public's approval for what it does. The abbreviation 'PR' is also used. *The chairman's statement is merely a public relations exercise... I used to work in public relations.* **2 Public relations** are the state of the relationship between an organization and the public. *His behaviour was not good for public relations.* N-PLURAL

public 'school, public schools. **1** In Britain, a **public school** is a private school that provides secondary education which parents have to pay for. The pupils often live at the school during the school term. **2** In the USA, Australia, and some other parts of the world, a **public school** is a school that is supported financially by the government and usually provides free education. N-VAR

public 'sector. The **public sector** is the part of a country's economy which is controlled or supported financially by the government. N-SING the N

public 'servant, public servants. A **public servant** is a person who is appointed or elected to a public office, for example working for a local or state government. N-COUNT

public 'service, public services. **1** A **public service** is something such as health care, transport, or waste disposal which is organized by the government or an official body in order to benefit all the people in a particular society or community. **2 Public service** broadcasting consists of television and radio programmes supplied by an official or government organization, rather than by a commercial company. Such programmes often provide information or education, as well as entertainment. **3** A **public service** is an activity or type of work which is concerned with helping people in a particular community, rather than making a profit. *...an egalitarian society based on cooperation and public service.* N-COUNT / ADJ: ADJ n / N-VAR

public-'spirited. A **public-spirited** person tries to help the community that they belong to. ADJ-GRADED

public u'tility, public utilities. Public utilities N-COUNT
are services provided by the state, such as the supply of electricity and gas, or the train network.

public 'works. Public works are buildings, ◆◇◇◇◇
roads, and other projects that are built by the gov- N-PLURAL
ernment for the public.

pub·lish /'pʌblɪʃ/ **publishes, publishing, pub-** ◆◆◆◇
lished. 1 When a company **publishes** a book or VERB
magazine, it prints copies of it, which are sent to V n
shops to be sold. *The English Tourist Board publishes a book called 'Activity and Hobby Holidays'.*
2 When the people in charge of a newspaper or VERB: V n
magazine **publish** a piece of writing or a photo- V
graph, they print it in their newspaper or magazine.
*I don't encourage people to take photographs like
this without permission, but by law we can publish.*
3 If someone **publishes** a book or an article that VERB
they have written, they arrange to have it published. V n
He has published two collections of poetry. **4** If you VERB
publish information or an opinion, you make it V n
known to the public by having it printed in a newspaper, magazine, or official document. *The demonstrators called on the government to publish a list of
registered voters.*

pub·lish·er /'pʌblɪʃə/ **publishers.** A publisher is ◆◆◇◇◇
a person or a company that publishes books, news- N-COUNT
papers, or magazines.

pub·lish·ing /'pʌblɪʃɪŋ/. Publishing is the profes- ◆◆◆◇◇
sion of publishing books. *They work in publishing...* N-UNCOUNT
The future lay in electronic publishing.

'publishing house, publishing houses. A pub- ◆◇◇◇◇
lishing house is a company which publishes books. N-COUNT

puce /pjuːs/. Something that is **puce** is dark purple. COLOUR

puck /pʌk/ **pucks.** In the game of ice hockey, the N-COUNT
puck is the small rubber disc that is used instead of
a ball.

puck·er /'pʌkə/ **puckers, puckering, puck-** V-ERG: V
ered. When a part of your face **puckers**, it becomes V n
wrinkled, often because you are frowning or trying
not to cry. *She puckered her lips into a rosebud and
kissed him on the nose.* ♦ **puck·ered** ...a long puck- ADJ-GRADED
ered scar.

puck·ish /'pʌkɪʃ/. If you describe someone as ADJ
puckish, you mean that they are mischievous and DATED,
enjoy playing tricks on people. *He had a puckish* WRITTEN
sense of humour.

pud /pʊd/ **puds. Pud** is the same as **pudding.** ...rice N-VAR
pud. BRITISH,
INFORMAL

pud·ding /'pʊdɪŋ/ **puddings. 1** A pudding is a ◆◆◇◇◇
cooked sweet food, often made with flour, fat, and N-VAR
eggs, and usually served hot. **2** Some people refer to N-VAR
the sweet course of a meal as the **pudding.** *I tend to* BRITISH
stick to fresh fruit for pudding. **3** If you say that the PHRASE
proof of the pudding is in the eating, you mean
that something new can only be judged to be good
or bad after it has been tried or used. **4** See also
Yorkshire pudding.

'pudding basin, pudding basins. A pudding ba- N-COUNT
sin is a deep round bowl that is used in the kitchen, BRITISH
especially for mixing or for cooking puddings.

pud·dle /'pʌdəl/ **puddles.** A puddle is a small, ◆◇◇◇◇
shallow pool of rain or other liquid that has spread N-COUNT
on the ground.

pudgy /'pʌdʒi/. If you describe someone as pudgy, ADJ-GRADED
you mean that they are unpleasantly plump. PRAGMATICS

pu·er·ile /'pjʊəraɪl, AM -rəl/. If you describe some- ADJ-GRADED
one or something as **puerile**, you mean that they
are silly and childish.

puff /pʌf/ **puffs, puffing, puffed. 1** If someone ◆◇◇◇◇
puffs at a cigarette, cigar, or a pipe, they smoke it. VERB
He nodded and puffed on a stubby pipe as he lis- V at/on n
tened. ► Also a noun. *She was taking quick puffs at* V
her cigarette. **2** If you **puff** smoke or moisture from N-COUNT
your mouth, you breathe it out. *The weather was* V-ERG: V n
dry and cold; wisps of steam puffed from their lips. V prep
► **Puff out** means the same as **puff.** *He drew heavily* PHRASAL VB
on his cigarette and puffed out a cloud of smoke. **3** A V P noun
puff of something such as air or smoke is a small Also V n P
amount of it that is blown out from somewhere. N-COUNT
4 If you **are puffing**, you are breathing loudly and VERB: V

quickly with your mouth open because you are out of
breath after a lot of physical effort. **5** A **puff** is the N-COUNT
same as a **poof. 6** See also **puffed.**

puff out. If you **puff out your cheeks**, you make PHRASAL VB
them larger and rounder by filling them with air. V P noun
● See also **puff 2.**

puff up. If part of your body **puffs up** as a result of an PHRASAL VB
injury or illness, it becomes swollen. V P

puffed /pʌft/. **1** If a part of your body **is puffed**, it is ADJ-GRADED:
swollen because of an injury or because you are un- v-link ADJ
well. *Her eyes were puffed and red from weeping.* **2** If ADJ-GRADED:
you are **puffed**, you are breathing with difficulty be- v-link ADJ
cause you have been using a lot of energy. *Taking* INFORMAL
exercise means making an effort and getting puffed.

puffed 'up. If someone is **puffed up**, they are feel- ADJ-GRADED
ing very proud of themselves. *He came home all
puffed up with pride at having won a gold medal.*

puf·fin /'pʌfɪn/ **puffins.** A puffin is a black and N-COUNT
white sea bird with a large, brightly-coloured beak.

puff 'pastry. Puff pastry is a type of pastry which N-UNCOUNT
is very light and flaky.

puffy /'pʌfi/ **puffier, puffiest.** If part of someone's ADJ-GRADED
body, especially their face, is **puffy**, it has has a
round, swollen appearance. ♦ **puffi·ness** *He no-* N-UNCOUNT
ticed some slight puffiness beneath her eyes.

pug /pʌg/ **pugs.** A pug is a small, fat, short-haired N-COUNT
dog with a flat nose.

pu·gi·list /'pjuːdʒɪlɪst/ **pugilists.** A pugilist is a N-COUNT
boxer. DATED

pug·na·cious /pʌg'neɪʃəs/. Someone who is pug- ADJ-GRADED
nacious is always ready to quarrel or start a fight. FORMAL

puke /pjuːk/ **pukes, puking, puked.** When V
someone **pukes**, they vomit. *It makes me want to* INFORMAL
puke, just thinking about it. ► **Puke** is vomit. N-UNCOUNT

puk·ka /'pʌkə/. If you describe something or some- ADJ-GRADED
one as **pukka**, you mean that they are real or genu- BRITISH,
ine, and of good quality. *He considered himself a* DATED
pukka English gentleman.

pull /pʊl/ **pulls, pulling, pulled. 1** When you **pull** ◆◆◆◇
something, you hold it firmly and use force in order VERB: V n
to move it towards you or away from its previous V n with adv
position. *He pulled on a jersey... Erica was solemn,* V prep
pulling at her blonde curls... I helped pull him out of V
the water... Pull as hard as you can. ► Also a noun. Also V n adj
The feather must be removed with a straight, firm N-COUNT
pull. **2** When a vehicle, animal, or person **pulls** a VERB
cart or piece of machinery, they are attached to it or V n
hold it, so that it moves along behind them when
they move forward. *He pulls a rickshaw.* **3** If you VERB
pull yourself or **pull** a part of your body in a par- V pron-refl
ticular direction, you move your body or a part of prep/adv
your body with effort or force. *Hughes pulled him-* V n prep/adv
self slowly to his feet... He pulled his arms out of the V n adj
sleeves... She tried to pull her hand free. **4** If you **pull** Also V adv
a muscle, you injure it by straining it. VERB: V n

5 When you **pull** an object from a bag, pocket, or cup- VERB:
board, you put your hand in and bring the object out. V n prep
Wade walked quickly to the refrigerator and pulled out V n with adv
another beer. **6** If someone **pulls** a gun or a knife on VERB:
someone else, they take out a gun or knife and threat- V n on n
en the other person with it. *I pulled a knife and threat-* INFORMAL
ened her. **7** If you **pull** something **apart**, you break or VERB:
divide it into small pieces, often in order to put them V n with adv
back together again in a different way.

8 A **pull** is a strong physical force which causes things N-COUNT
to move in a particular direction. ...*the pull of gravity.*
9 In a race or contest, if you **pull ahead** of or **pull away** VERB
from an opponent, you gradually increase the margin V adv
by which you are ahead of them. *He pulled away, extending his lead to 15 seconds.* **10** To **pull** crowds or VERB: V n
viewers means to attract them or attract their sup- INFORMAL
port. ► **Pull in** means the same as **pull.** *They provided* PHRASAL VB
a far better news service and pulled in many more V P noun
viewers. **11** If something **pulls** you or your thoughts or Also V n P
feelings in a particular direction, it strongly attracts VERB
you or influences you in a particular way. *Joe felt there* V n adv
*was little he could do to help Betty, and his heart was
pulling him elsewhere.* ► Also a noun. *No matter how* N-COUNT
*much you feel the pull of the past, make a determined
effort to look to the future.*

12 If someone **pulls a stunt** or a **trick** on someone, they do something dramatic or silly to fool them, or to get their attention. *Everyone saw the stunt you pulled on me.* **13** If someone **pulls** someone else, they succeed in attracting them sexually and in spending the rest of the evening or night with them. **14 ●** to **pull** oneself **up** by one's **bootstraps**: see **bootstraps**. **●** to **pull** a **face**: see **face**. **●** to **pull** someone's **leg**: see **leg**. **●** to **pull** your **punches**: see **punch**. **●** to **pull rank**: see **rank**. **●** to **pull** your **socks up**: see **sock**. **●** to **pull out all** the **stops**: see **stop**. **●** to **pull strings**: see **string**. **●** to **pull** your **weight**: see **weight**. **●** to **pull** the **wool over** someone's **eyes**: see **wool**.

VERB
PRAGMATICS
V n on n
Also V n
INFORMAL
VERB:
V n,
v
INFORMAL,
BRITISH

pull away. 1 When a vehicle or driver **pulls away**, the vehicle starts moving forward. **2** If you **pull away from** someone that you have had close links with, you deliberately become less close to them. *The Soviet Union began pulling away from Cuba.*

PHRASAL VB
V P
V P from n
Also V P

pull back. 1 If someone **pulls back from** an action, they decide not to continue or persist with it, because it could have bad consequences. *The British government threatened to make public its disquiet but then pulled back.* **2** If troops **pull back**, they retreat some or all of the way to their own territory. *The president pulled back forces from Mongolia, and he withdrew from Afghanistan.*

PHRASAL VB
V P from n

ERG:
V P
V P noun
Also V n P

pull down. To **pull down** a building or statue means to deliberately destroy it. *They'd pulled the registry office down which then left an open space.*

PHRASAL VB
V P noun
V n P

pull in. 1 When a vehicle or driver **pulls in** somewhere, the vehicle stops there. *He pulled in at the side of the road.* **2** If the police **pull** someone **in**, they arrest them and take them to the police station. *'Brady looks like a suspect.'—'I'd pull him in.'* **3** If someone or something **pulls in** an amount of money, they earn or collect that amount. *In the nine months to March 31, gambling taxes pulled in $210 million.* **4** See **pull 10**.

PHRASAL VB
V P prep/adv
Also V P
V n P
Also V n P noun
INFORMAL
V P amount
INFORMAL

pull into. When a vehicle or driver **pulls into** a road or driveway, the vehicle makes a turn into the road or driveway and stops there. *She pulled the car into a tight parking space on a side street.*

PHRASAL VB
V P n
V n P n

pull off. 1 If you **pull off** something very difficult, you manage to achieve it successfully. *It will be a very, very fine piece of mountaineering if they pull it off.* **2** If a vehicle or driver **pulls off** the road, the vehicle stops by the side of the road. *He pulled the truck off the road.*

PHRASAL VB
V P noun
V P n
V P n
V n P n

pull out. 1 When a vehicle or driver **pulls out**, the vehicle moves out into the road or nearer the centre of the road. *She pulled out into the street.* **2** If you **pull out of** an agreement, a contest, or an organization, you withdraw from it. *A racing injury forced Stephen Roche to pull out.* **3** If troops **pull out of** a place, they leave it. *Economic sanctions will be lifted once two-thirds of their forces have pulled out... His government decided to pull its troops out of Cuba.* **4** If a country **pulls out of recession** or if someone **pulls** it **out**, it begins to recover from it. *The government finally has a chance to pull Britain out of recession.* **5** See also **pull-out**.

PHRASAL VB
V P
V P prep
V P ofn
V P

ERG:
V P ofn
V P
V n P ofn
V P noun
ERG:
V P ofn
V n P ofn
Also V P

pull over. 1 When a vehicle or driver **pulls over**, the vehicle moves closer to the side of the road and stops there. **2** If the police **pull** someone **over**, they make them stop their car at the side of the road, usually because they have been driving dangerously. *Police pulled over his Mercedes near Dieppe.* **3** See also **pullover**.

PHRASAL VB
V P

V n P
V P noun

pull through. If someone with a serious illness or in a very difficult situation **pulls through**, they recover. *It is only our determination to fight that has pulled us through... Finding ways of helping Russia pull through its upheavals will be the most pressing task.*

PHRASAL VB
ERG:
V P
V n P
V P n

pull together. 1 If people **pull together**, they cooperate with each other in order to get through a difficult period. *The nation was urged to pull together to avoid a slide into complete chaos.* **2** If you are upset or depressed and someone tells you to **pull** yourself **together**, they are telling you in a rather unsympathetic way to control your feelings and behave calmly. **3** If you **pull together** different facts or ideas, you link

PHRASAL VB
V P

V pron-refl P
PRAGMATICS

V P noun
V P
Also V n P

them to form a single theory or story. *Data exists but it needs pulling together.*

pull up. 1 When a vehicle or driver **pulls up**, the vehicle slows down and stops. **2** If you **pull up** a chair, you move it closer to something or someone and sit on it. *He pulled up a chair behind her.*

PHRASAL VB
V P
V P n
Also V n P

pul·ley /'poli/ **pulleys.** A pulley is a device which is used for lifting or lowering heavy objects. It consists of one or more wheels which a rope is passed over.

N-COUNT

Pull·man /'pulmən/ **Pullmans. 1** A Pullman is a type of train or railway carriage which is extremely comfortable and luxurious. **2** A **Pullman** or a **Pullman car** is a railway carriage that provides beds for passengers to sleep in. The usual British expression is **sleeping car**.

N-COUNT
BRITISH
N-COUNT
AMERICAN

'pull-out, pull-outs. 1 In a newspaper or magazine, a **pull-out** is a section which you can remove easily and keep. **2** When there is a **pull-out** of armed forces from a place, troops which have occupied an area of land withdraw from it.

N-COUNT

N-SING

pull·over /'pulouvə/ **pullovers.** A pullover is a woollen piece of clothing that covers the upper part of your body and your arms. You put it on by pulling it over your head. The usual American word is **sweater**. See picture headed **clothes**.

N-COUNT
BRITISH

pul·mo·nary /'pʌlmənəri, AM -neri/. Pulmonary means relating to your lungs.

ADJ
MEDICAL

pulp /pʌlp/ **pulps, pulping, pulped. 1** If an object is pressed into a **pulp**, it is crushed or beaten until it is soft, smooth, and wet. *The olives are crushed to a pulp by stone rollers.* **2** If paper, vegetables, or fruit are **pulped**, they are crushed into a smooth, wet paste. **3** In fruit or vegetables, the **pulp** is the soft inner part. **4 Pulp** fiction refers to cheap, poor quality books, usually written in a sensational way.

◆◇◇◇◇
N-SING:
also no det

VERB:
be V-ed

N-SING

ADJ: ADJ n

pul·pit /'pulpit/ **pulpits.** A pulpit is a small raised platform in a church with a rail or barrier around it, where a member of the clergy stands to preach.

◆◇◇◇◇
N-COUNT

pul·sate /pʌl'seɪt, AM 'pʌlseɪt/ **pulsates, pulsating, pulsated.** If something **pulsates**, it beats, moves in and out, or shakes with strong, regular movements *...a pulsating blood vessel.* **♦ pul·sa·tion** /pʌl'seɪʃən/ **pulsations** *...the pulsations of the Pole Star.*

◆◇◇◇◇
VERB: V
V-ing

N-VAR

pulse /pʌls/ **pulses, pulsing, pulsed. 1** Your **pulse** is the regular beating of blood through your body, which you can feel when you touch particular parts of your body, especially your wrist. *Mahoney's pulse was racing, and he felt confused.* **2** When someone **takes** your **pulse** or **feels** your **pulse**, they find out the speed of your heartbeat by feeling the pulse in your wrist. **3** If something **pulses**, it has a strong regular tempo. *His temples pulsed a little, threatening a headache.* ► Also a noun. *...the repetitive pulse of the music.* **4** If you have your **finger on the pulse** of something, you know all the latest opinions or developments. *He claims to have his finger on the pulse of the industry.* **5** Some seeds which can be cooked and eaten are called **pulses**, for example peas, beans, and lentils.

◆◆◇◇◇
N-COUNT

PHRASE

VERB
V

N-COUNT
PHRASE

N-PLURAL

pul·ver·ize /'pʌlvəraɪz/ **pulverizes, pulverizing, pulverized;** also spelled **pulverise** in British English. **1** To **pulverize** something means to do great damage to it or to destroy it completely. *...the economic policies which pulverised the economy during the 1980s.* **2** If someone **pulverizes** an opponent in an election or competition, they thoroughly defeat them. **3** If you **pulverize** something, you make it into a powder by crushing it.

VERB
V n

VERB: V n
INFORMAL

VERB: V n

puma /'pjuːmə/ **pumas.** A puma is a brownish-grey wild animal that is a member of the cat family. Pumas live in mountain regions of North and South America.

N-COUNT

pum·ice /'pʌmɪs/. Pumice is a kind of lightweight grey volcanic stone that can be used for cleaning or for softening the skin. *Scrub rough spots with a pumice stone.*

N-UNCOUNT

pum·mel /'pʌməl/ **pummels, pummelling, pummelled;** spelled **pummeling, pummeled** in

American English. If you **pummel** someone or something, you hit them again and again using your fists. `VERB: V n`

pump /pʌmp/ **pumps, pumping, pumped. 1** A **pump** is a machine which is used to force a liquid or gas to flow in strong regular movements in a particular direction. **2** To **pump** a liquid or gas in a particular direction means to force it to flow in that direction, using a pump. *It's not enough to get rid of raw sewage by pumping it out to sea... A windmill is used to pump water into the Fen.* **3** A **pump** is a device for bringing water to the surface from below the ground. **4** To **pump** water, oil, or gas means to get a supply of it from below the surface of the ground, using a pump. *She pumps drinking water from a well... The country is trying very hard to pump out more oil.* **5** A **pump** is a device that you use to force air into something, for example a tyre. See picture headed **car and bicycle**. *...a bicycle pump.* **6** A **petrol pump** is a machine with a hose attached to it from which you can fill a car with petrol. The American term is **gas pump. 7** If someone has their stomach **pumped**, doctors use a special pump to remove the contents of their stomach. *She was released from hospital yesterday after having her stomach pumped.*

8 If you **pump** money or other resources into something such as a project or an industry, you invest a lot of money or resources in it. *West Germany is set to pump huge amounts of resources into East Germany.*

9 If you **pump** someone about something, you keep asking them questions in order to get information. *He ran in every five minutes to pump me about the case.*

10 Pumps are canvas shoes with flat rubber soles which people wear for sports and leisure. **11 Pumps** are ladies' shoes that do not cover the top part of the foot and are usually made of plain leather with no design. The British expression is **court shoes.**

12 • to **pump iron:** see **iron.**

pump out. To **pump out** something means to produce or supply it continually and in large amounts. *Japanese companies have been pumping out plenty of innovative products.* `PHRASAL VB / V P noun / Also V n P`

pump up. If you **pump up** something such as a tyre, you fill it with air using a pump. *I tried to pump up my back tyre.* `PHRASAL VB / V P noun / Also V n P`

pumped-up. When sports competitors are **pumped up**, they are in a state of great excitement about the match or competition that they are involved in. *I was really pumped up for this one and I knew whatever happened I was going to ride as though my life depended on it.* `ADJ-GRADED`

pum·per·nick·el /pʌmpənɪkəl/. **Pumpernickel** is a dark brown, heavy bread made from rye. `N-UNCOUNT`

pump·kin /pʌmpkɪn/ **pumpkins.** A **pumpkin** is a large, round, orange-coloured vegetable with a thick skin. *...pumpkin pie.* `N-VAR`

pun /pʌn/ **puns, punning, punned. 1** A **pun** is a clever and amusing use of a word with more than one meaning, or a word that sounds like another word, so that what you say has two different meanings. *...the revolutionary (for boxing) knock-down (pardon the pun) prices with tickets at £5:00.* **2** If you **pun**, you try to amuse people by making a pun. *He is constantly punning, constantly playing with language. ...punning headlines.* `VERB V`

punch /pʌntʃ/ **punches, punching, punched. 1** If you **punch** someone or something, you hit them hard with your fist. *If anyone tried to stop me I'd punch him on the nose.* ► Also a noun. *He was hurting Johansson with body punches in the fourth round.* ♦ **punch·er, punchers** *...boxing's hardest puncher.* **2** If you **punch** something such as the buttons on a keyboard, you touch them in order to store information on a machine such as a computer or to give the machine a command to do something. *Mrs. Baylor strode to the elevator and punched the button.* **3** If you **punch holes** in something, you make holes in it by pushing or pressing it with something sharp. *I took a ballpoint pen and* `VERB V n / N-COUNT / VERB V n / VERB V n in n`

punched a hole in the carton. **4** A **punch** is a tool that you use for making holes in something. *Make two holes with a hole punch.* `N-COUNT`

5 If you say that something has **punch**, you mean that it has force or effectiveness. *Patterned tiles obviously have much more punch than plain.* `N-UNCOUNT`

6 If you say that someone does not **pull** their **punches** when they are criticizing someone or something, you mean that they say exactly what they think and do not moderate their criticism. • to **pack a punch:** see **pack.** `PHRASE`

7 Punch is a drink made from wine or spirits mixed with things such as sugar, lemons, and spices. `N-VAR`

punch in. If you **punch in** a number on a machine or **punch** numbers **into** it, you push the machine's numerical keys in order to give it a command to do something. *You can bank by phone in the USA, punching in account numbers on the phone.* `PHRASAL VB / V P noun / Also V n P`

punch·bag /pʌntʃbæg/ **punchbags;** also spelled **punch bag.** A **punchbag** is a heavy leather bag hanging on a rope, which is punched hard by boxers and other sportsmen for training and exercise. The American term is **punching bag.** `N-COUNT BRITISH`

punch-drunk; also spelled **punch drunk. 1** A **punch-drunk** boxer shows signs of brain damage after suffering too many blows on their head. **2** If you say that someone **is punch-drunk**, you mean that they are dazed and confused, for example because they have been working too hard. *He was punch-drunk with fatigue.* `ADJ / ADJ-GRADED`

punching bag, punching bags. A **punching bag** is the same as a **punchbag.** `N-COUNT AMERICAN`

punch-line /pʌntʃlaɪn/ **punchlines;** also spelled **punch line** or **punch-line.** The **punchline** of a joke or funny story is its last sentence or phrase, which gives it its humour. `N-COUNT`

punch-up, punch-ups. A **punch-up** is a fight in which people hit each other. *He was involved in a punch-up with Sarah's former lover.* `N-COUNT BRITISH, INFORMAL`

punchy /pʌntʃi/ **punchier, punchiest.** If you describe something as **punchy**, you mean it conveys a meaning or creates an effect in a forceful or effective way. *A good way to sound confident is to use short punchy sentences.* `ADJ-GRADED`

punc·til·ous /pʌŋktɪliəs/. Someone who is **punctilious** is very careful to behave correctly. *He was punctilious about being ready.* `ADJ-GRADED FORMAL`

punc·tu·al /pʌŋktʃuəl/. Someone who is **punctual** arrives somewhere or does something at the right time and is not late. *He's always very punctual.* ♦ **punc·tu·al·ly** *My guest arrived punctually.* ♦ **punc·tu·al·ity** /ˌpʌŋktʃuˈælɪti/ *I'll have to have a word with them about punctuality.* `ADJ-GRADED / ADV-GRADED / N-UNCOUNT`

punc·tu·ate /pʌŋktʃueɪt/ **punctuates, punctuating, punctuated.** If an activity or situation **is punctuated** by particular things, it is interrupted by them at intervals. *The silence of the night was punctuated by the distant rumble of traffic.* `VB: usu passive be V-ed by/ with n`

punc·tua·tion /ˌpʌŋktʃuˈeɪʃən/. **Punctuation** is the system of signs such as full stops, commas, or question marks that you use in writing to divide words into sentences and clauses. `N-UNCOUNT`

punctu·ation mark, punctuation marks. A **punctuation mark** is a sign such as a full stop, comma, or question mark. `N-COUNT`

punc·ture /pʌŋktʃə/ **punctures, puncturing, punctured. 1** A **puncture** is a small hole in a car or bicycle tyre that has been made by a sharp object. *Somebody helped me mend the puncture.* **2** If a car tyre or bicycle tyre **punctures** or something **punctures** it, a hole is made in the tyre. *The tyre is guaranteed never to puncture or go flat.* **3** A **puncture** is a small hole in someone's skin that has been made by or with a sharp object. **4** If a sharp object **punctures** something, it makes a hole in it. *The bullet punctured the skull.* `N-COUNT / V-ERG V / Also V n / N-COUNT TECHNICAL / VERB V n`

pun·dit /pʌndɪt/ **pundits.** A **pundit** is a person who knows a lot about a subject and is often asked to give information or opinions about it to the public. *...a well known political pundit.* `N-COUNT`

pun·gent /ˈpʌndʒənt/. **1** Something that is **pungent** has a smell or taste that is very sharp and strong, sometimes so strong that it is unpleasant. *The more herbs you use, the more pungent the sauce will be.* ♦ **pun·gen·cy** *...the spices that give Jamaican food its pungency.* **2** If you describe something someone has said or written as **pungent**, you approve of it because it has a direct and powerful effect, and often criticizes something very cleverly. *He particularly enjoyed the play's shrewd and pungent social analysis.*
◆◇◇◇◇ ADJ-GRADED
N-UNCOUNT
ADJ-GRADED
PRAGMATICS
FORMAL

pun·ish /ˈpʌnɪʃ/ **punishes, punishing, punished.** **1** To **punish** someone means to make them suffer in some way because they have done something wrong. *I don't believe that George ever had to punish the children... Don't punish your child for being honest.* **2** To **punish** a crime means to punish anyone who commits that crime. *The government voted to punish corruption in sport.*
◆◆◇◇◇
VERB
V n
V n for n
VERB
V n

pun·ish·able /ˈpʌnɪʃəbəl/. If a crime is **punishable** in a particular way, anyone who is found to have committed can be punished in that way. *Treason in this country is still punishable by death.*
ADJ

pun·ish·ing /ˈpʌnɪʃɪŋ/. A **punishing** schedule, activity, or experience requires a lot of physical effort and makes you very tired or weak. *His punishing work schedule had made him resort to taking the drug.*
◆◇◇◇◇ ADJ-GRADED

pun·ish·ment /ˈpʌnɪʃmənt/ **punishments.** **1** **Punishment** is the act of punishing someone or of being punished. *The man is guilty and he deserves punishment.* **2** A **punishment** is a particular way of punishing someone. *The usual punishment is a fine.* **3** You can use **punishment** to refer to severe physical treatment of any kind. *Don't expect these types of boot to take the punishment that gardening will give them.* **4** See also **capital punishment, corporal punishment.**
◆◆◇◇◇
N-UNCOUNT
N-VAR
N-UNCOUNT

pu·ni·tive /ˈpjuːnɪtɪv/. **Punitive** actions are intended to punish people. *Any punitive measures against foreign companies would hurt US interests.*
◆◇◇◇◇ ADJ-GRADED
FORMAL

punk /pʌŋk/ **punks.** **1** Punk or punk rock is rock music that is played in a fast, loud, and aggressive way and is often a protest against conventional attitudes and behaviour. Punk rock was particularly popular in the late 1970s. **2** Punk clothes or styles are associated with punk music. *...a punk hairdo.* **3** A **punk** or a **punk rocker** is a young person who likes punk music and dresses in a very noticeable and unconventional way. **4** A **punk** is a young person who behaves in an unruly, aggressive, or anti-social manner. *He is fast getting a reputation as a young punk.*
◆◆◇◇◇
N-UNCOUNT
ADJ: ADJ n
N-COUNT
N-COUNT
AMERICAN, INFORMAL

pun·net /ˈpʌnɪt/ **punnets.** A **punnet** is a small, light, square box in which soft fruits such as strawberries or raspberries are often sold. ▶ A **punnet of** fruit is the amount of fruit that a punnet contains.
N-COUNT
BRITISH
N-COUNT

punt /pʌnt/ **punts, punting, punted.** **1** A **punt** is a long boat with a flat bottom. You move the boat along by standing at one end and pushing a long pole against the bottom of the river. **2** When you **punt**, you travel along a river in a punt. *We punted up towards Grantchester.* ♦ **punt·ing** *The one thing I look forward to is going punting in Cambridge.* **3** The **punt** is the unit of money used in the Irish Republic.
◆◇◇◇◇
N-COUNT
BRITISH
VERB: V
V prep/adv
BRITISH
N-UNCOUNT
N-COUNT

punt·er /ˈpʌntə/ **punters.** **1** A **punter** is a person who bets money, especially on horse races. *Punters are expected to gamble £50m on the Grand National.* **2** People sometimes refer to their customers or clients as **punters.** *Is the show funny? The punters seem to think so.*
◆◇◇◇◇
N-COUNT
BRITISH, INFORMAL
N-COUNT
BRITISH, INFORMAL

puny /ˈpjuːni/ **punier, puniest.** Someone or something that is **puny** is very small or weak. *Our Kevin was a very puny lad.*
ADJ-GRADED

pup /pʌp/ **pups.** **1** A **pup** is a young dog. *...an Alsatian pup.* **2** The young of some other animals, for example seals, are called **pups.**
◆◇◇◇◇
N-COUNT
N-COUNT

pupa /ˈpjuːpə/ **pupae** /ˈpjuːpiː/. A **pupa** is an insect that is in the stage of development between a larva and a fully grown adult.
N-COUNT
TECHNICAL

pu·pil /ˈpjuːpɪl/ **pupils.** **1** The **pupils** of a school are the children who go to it. *Eleanor was a reluctant, anxious pupil.* **2** A **pupil** of a painter, musician, or other expert is someone who studies with him or her and learns his or her skills. *Goldschmidt became a pupil of the composer Franz Schreker.* **3** The **pupils** of your eyes are the small, round, black holes in the centre of them.
◆◆◆◇◇
N-COUNT
N-COUNT:
with poss
N-COUNT

pup·pet /ˈpʌpɪt/ **puppets.** **1** A **puppet** is a doll that you can move, either by pulling strings which are attached to it or by putting your hand inside its body and moving your fingers. **2** You can refer to a person or country as a **puppet** when you mean their actions are controlled by a more powerful person or government, even though they may appear to be independent. *The radical students say Seoul is a puppet of the Washington government.*
◆◇◇◇◇
N-COUNT
N-COUNT
PRAGMATICS

pup·pet·eer /ˌpʌpɪˈtɪə/ **puppeteers.** A **puppeteer** is a person who gives shows using puppets.
N-COUNT

pup·py /ˈpʌpi/ **puppies.** A **puppy** is a young dog.
◆◇◇◇◇
N-COUNT

'puppy fat; also spelled **puppy-fat. Puppy fat** is fat that some children have on their bodies when they are young but that disappears when they grow older and taller.
N-UNCOUNT

pur·chase /ˈpɜːtʃɪs/ **purchases, purchasing, purchased.** **1** When you **purchase** something, you buy it. *He purchased a ticket and went up on the top deck.* ▶ Also a noun. *This week he is to visit China to discuss the purchase of military supplies.* ♦ **pur·chas·er, purchasers** *The group is the second largest purchaser of fresh fruit in the US.* ● See also **hire purchase.** **2** A **purchase** is something that you buy. *She opened the tie box and looked at her purchase.* **3** If someone or something is able to get a **purchase** on something, they manage to get a firm grip on it. *I got a purchase on the rope and pulled.*
◆◆◆◇
VERB
FORMAL
N-COUNT
FORMAL
N-COUNT
N-COUNT
FORMAL
N-UNCOUNT:
also a N
FORMAL

pur·dah /ˈpɜːdə/. **Purdah** is a custom practised in some Muslim and Hindu societies, in which women keep apart from male strangers by remaining in a special part of a house or by covering their faces and the whole of their bodies to avoid being seen.
N-UNCOUNT

pure /pjʊə/ **purer, purest.** **1** A **pure** substance is not mixed with anything else. *...a carton of pure orange juice.* **2** Something that is **pure** is clean and does not contain any harmful substances. *...demands for purer and cleaner river water.* ♦ **pu·rity** /ˈpjʊərɪti/ *They worried about the purity of tap water.* **3** People who are **pure** have not done anything bad or sinful. *She was baptized and she was pure and clean of sin.* ♦ **purity** *...sexual purity.* **4** If you describe something such as a colour, a sound, or a type of light as **pure**, you mean that it is very clear and represents a perfect example of its type. *This traditional cheese is almost pure white in colour.* ♦ **purity** *...the soaring purity of her voice.* **5** A **pure** form of an art or philosophy is produced or practised exactly according to an accepted standard, form, or pattern. *A true prince of the ballet has a pure classical technique.* ♦ **purity** *...the purity of their artistic vision.* **6** Pure science or **pure** research is concerned only with theory. *Physics isn't just about pure science with no immediate applications.* **7** Pure means complete and total. *The old man turned to give her a look of pure surprise.* **8** You use **pure and simple** to emphasize that the thing you are mentioning is the only thing that is involved or that should be considered. *It's blackmail, pure and simple.*
◆◆◆◇◇
ADJ-GRADED
ADJ-GRADED
N-UNCOUNT:
with poss
ADJ-GRADED
LITERARY
N-UNCOUNT
ADJ-GRADED
N-UNCOUNT
ADJ-GRADED
FORMAL
N-UNCOUNT
N-UNCOUNT
ADJ: ADJ n
ADJ-GRADED
PRAGMATICS
PHRASE
PRAGMATICS

'pure-bred; also spelled **purebred.** A **pure-bred** animal is one whose parents and ancestors all belong to the same breed.
ADJ: ADJ n

pu·ree /ˈpjʊəreɪ, AM pjʊˈreɪ/ **purees, pureeing, pureed.** **1** Puree is food which has been mashed, sieved, or blended so that it forms a thick, smooth sauce. *...a can of tomato puree.* **2** If you puree food, you make it into a puree. *Puree the apricots in a liquidiser.*
◆◇◇◇◇
N-VAR
VERB
V n

pure·ly /'pjʊəli/. **1** You use **purely** to emphasize that the thing you are mentioning is the most important feature or that it is the only thing which should be considered. *It is a racing machine, designed purely for speed.* **2** You use **purely and simply** to emphasize that the thing you are mentioning is the only thing involved. *John came down here purely and simply to make money.*
◆◆◇◇◇ ADV: ADV with cl/group PRAGMATICS PHRASE PRAGMATICS

pur·ga·tive /'pɜːgətɪv/ **purgatives.** A **purgative** is a medicine that causes you to defecate and so to get rid of unwanted substances from your body.
N-COUNT FORMAL

pur·ga·tory /'pɜːgətri, AM -tɔːri/. **1 Purgatory** is the place where Roman Catholics believe the spirits of dead people are sent to suffer for their sins before they go to heaven. **2** You can describe a very unpleasant experience as **purgatory**. *Every step of the last three miles was purgatory.*
N-PROPER
N-UNCOUNT

purge /pɜːdʒ/ **purges, purging, purged. 1** To **purge** an organization of its unacceptable members means to remove them from it. You can also talk about **purging** people from an organization. *The leadership voted to purge the party of 'hostile and anti-party elements'... He recently purged the armed forces, sending hundreds of officers into retirement.* ▶ Also a noun. *The army have called for a more thorough purge of people associated with the late President.* **2** If you **purge** something of undesirable things, you get rid of them. *He closed his eyes and lay still, trying to purge his mind of anxiety.*
◆◇◇◇◇ VERB V n ofn V n Also V n from n
N-COUNT
VERB V n ofn Also V n

pu·ri·fy /'pjʊərɪfaɪ/ **purifies, purifying, purified.** To **purify** a substance means to make it pure by removing any harmful, dirty, or inferior substances from it. *I take wheat and yeast tablets daily to purify the blood.* ♦ **pu·ri·fi·ca·tion** /pjʊərɪfɪ'keɪʃən/ *...a water purification plant.* ♦ **pu·ri·fi·er, purifiers** *...an air purifier.*
◆◇◇◇◇ VERB V n
N-UNCOUNT
N-COUNT

pur·ist /'pjʊərɪst/ **purists.** A **purist** is someone who believes in absolute correctness, especially concerning a particular subject which they know a lot about. *This version of 'The Marriage Of Figaro' may not satisfy opera purists.* ▶ Also an adjective. *The drawing room is late 17th century, but Derek is not purist about the contents.*
N-COUNT
ADJ-GRADED

pu·ri·tan /'pjʊərɪtən/ **puritans;** spelled **Puritan** in sense 2. **1** You describe someone as a **puritan** when you think they disapprove of pleasure, especially physical pleasure, often because they are strictly religious; used showing disapproval. *He condemned frivolous living as vehemently as any puritan.* ▶ Also an adjective. *It is a part of our puritan culture to believe that medicine is only effective if it is nasty.* **2** The **Puritans** were a group of English Protestants who lived in the sixteenth and seventeenth centuries. They lived according to very strict religious rules.
N-COUNT PRAGMATICS
ADJ-GRADED
N-COUNT

pu·ri·tani·cal /pjʊərɪ'tænɪkəl/. If you describe someone as **puritanical**, you mean that they disapprove of pleasure, especially physical pleasure, for example because they are strictly religious; used showing disapproval. *...a puritanical attitude towards sex.*
ADJ-GRADED PRAGMATICS

pu·ri·tan·ism /'pjʊərɪtənɪzəm/; spelled **Puritanism** in sense 2. **1 Puritanism** is behaviour or beliefs that are based on strict moral or religious principles, especially the principle that people should avoid physical pleasures; often used showing disapproval. *...the tight-lipped puritanism of the Scottish literary world.* **2 Puritanism** is the set of beliefs that were held by the Puritans.
N-UNCOUNT PRAGMATICS
N-UNCOUNT

pur·loin /pɜː'lɔɪn/ **purloins, purloining, purloined.** If someone **purloins** something, they steal it or borrow it without asking permission. *Each side purloins the other's private letters.*
VERB V n FORMAL

pur·ple /'pɜːpəl/ **purples.** Something that is **purple** is of a reddish-blue colour.
◆◆◇◇◇ COLOUR

pur·plish /'pɜːpəlɪʃ/. **Purplish** means slightly purple. *...large, purplish blue flowers.*
ADJ

pur·port /pə'pɔːt/ **purports, purporting, purported.** If something or someone **purports** to do
◆◇◇◇◇ VERB V to-inf

or be a particular thing, they claim to do or be that thing. *...a book that purports to tell the whole truth.*
FORMAL

pur·port·ed·ly /pə'pɔːtɪdli/. If something has **purportedly** been done, someone claims that it has been done but you cannot be sure. *He was given a letter purportedly signed by the Prime Minister.*
ADV FORMAL

pur·pose /'pɜːpəs/ **purposes. 1** The **purpose** of something is the reason for which it is made or done. *The purpose of the occasion was to raise money for medical supplies. ...the use of nuclear energy for military purposes... Most of them are destroyed because they've served their purpose.* **2** Your **purpose** is the thing that you want to achieve. *His purpose was to make a profit by improving the company's performance.* **3 Purpose** is the feeling of having a definite aim and of being determined to achieve it. *The teachers are enthusiastic and have a sense of purpose.* **4** You use **for all practical purposes** or **to all intents and purposes** to suggest that a situation is not exactly as you describe it, but the effect is the same as if it were. *For all practical purposes the treaty has already ceased to exist.* **5** If you do something **on purpose**, you do it deliberately. *Was it an accident or did David do it on purpose?* **6** See also **cross-purposes.**
◆◆◆◇ N-COUNT: with supp
N-COUNT: with poss
N-UNCOUNT
PHRASE
PHRASE

purpose-'built. A **purpose-built** building has been specially designed and built for a particular use. *...a new purpose-built factory.*
◆◇◇◇◇ ADJ BRITISH

pur·pose·ful /'pɜːpəsfʊl/. If someone is **purposeful**, they show that they have a definite aim and a strong desire to achieve it. *She had a purposeful air.* ♦ **pur·pose·ful·ly** *He strode purposefully towards the barn.*
ADJ-GRADED
ADV-GRADED

pur·pose·less /'pɜːpəsləs/. If an action is **purposeless**, it does not seem to have a sensible purpose. *Time may also be wasted in purposeless meetings.*
ADJ-GRADED

pur·pose·ly /'pɜːpəsli/. If you do something **purposely**, you do it deliberately. *They are purposely withholding information.*
ADV FORMAL

purr /pɜː/ **purrs, purring, purred. 1** When a cat **purrs**, it makes a low vibrating sound with its throat. **2** When an engine **purrs**, it is working and making a quiet, continuous, vibrating sound. *Both boats purred out of the cave mouth and into open water.* ▶ Also a noun. *...the purr of a motor-cycle coming up the drive.* **3** When someone **purrs**, they speak in a soft gentle voice because they are pleased about something or because they want to persuade you to do something for them. *'You can tell me the truth,' she purred.*
◆◇◇◇◇ VERB: V
VERB: V V prep
N-SING
VERB V with quote

purse /pɜːs/ **purses, pursing, pursed. 1** A **purse** is a very small bag that people, especially women, keep their money in. The usual American expression is **change purse**. **2** A **purse** is a small bag that women carry. The usual British word is **handbag**. **3** The word **purse** is used to refer to the total amount of money that a country, family, or group has. *The money could simply go into the public purse, helping to lower taxes.* **4** If you **purse your lips**, you move them into a small rounded shape, usually because you disapprove of something or when you are thinking.
◆◆◇◇◇ N-COUNT BRITISH
N-COUNT AMERICAN
N-SING: with supp
PHRASE

purs·er /'pɜːsə/ **pursers.** On a ship, the **purser** is an officer who deals with the accounts and official papers. On a passenger ship, the purser is also responsible for the welfare of the passengers.
N-COUNT

'purse strings. If you say that someone holds **the purse strings,** you mean that they control the way that money is spent in a particular family, group, or country. *This new research might help loosen the purse strings of those hesitant to provide food aid.*
N-PLURAL: the N

pur·su·ant /pə'sjuːənt, AM -'suː-/. If something is done **pursuant to** a law or regulation, it is done in agreement or conformity with it. *He should continue to act pursuant to the United Nations Security Council resolutions.*
PHR-PREP FORMAL

pur·sue /pə'sjuː, -'suː/ **pursues, pursuing, pursued. 1** If you **pursue** a particular aim or result, you make efforts to achieve it or to progress in it, often over a long period of time. *It is impossible to*
◆◆◇◇◇ VERB V n FORMAL

pursue economic reform and democracy simulta-neously. **2** If you **pursue** a particular topic, you try to find out more about it by asking questions. *If your original request is denied, don't be afraid to pursue the matter.* **3** If you **pursue** a person, vehicle, or animal, you follow them, usually in order to catch them. *She pursued the man who had stolen a woman's bag.* ♦ **pur·su·er, pursuers** They had shaken off their pursuers. [VERB Vn FORMAL] [VERB Vn FORMAL] [N-COUNT]

pur·suit /pəˈsjuːt, AM -ˈsuːt/ **pursuits. 1** Your **pur-suit** of something refers to your attempts to achieve it. If you do something **in pursuit of** a particular re-sult, you do it in order to achieve that result. *...a young man whose relentless pursuit of excellence is conducted with single-minded determination. ...in-dividuals who impoverish their families in pursuit of some dream.* **2** The **pursuit** of an activity, interest, or plan consists of all the things that you do when you are carrying it out. *The vigorous pursuit of poli-cies is no guarantee of success.* **3** If you are **in pur-suit of** a person, vehicle, or animal you are chasing them. **4** If you are **in hot pursuit** of someone, you are chasing after them with great determination. *I rushed through, with Sue in hot pursuit.* **5** Your **pursuits** are your activities, usually activities that you enjoy when you are not working. *They both love outdoor pursuits.* [♦♦◇◇◇ N-UNCOUNT: N of n] [N-UNCOUNT N of n FORMAL] [N-UNCOUNT FORMAL] [PHRASE] [N-COUNT FORMAL]

pur·vey /pəˈveɪ/ **purveys, purveying, pur-veyed. 1** If you **purvey** something such as infor-mation, you tell it to people. *He accused me of purveying 'silly gossip' about practices in schools.* **2** If someone **purveys** goods or services, they provide them. *...two restaurants that purvey dumplings.* ♦ **pur·vey·or, purveyors** ...*purveyors of gourmet foods.* [VERB Vn FORMAL] [VERB Vn FORMAL] [N-COUNT]

pur·view /ˈpɜːvjuː/. The **purview** of an organiza-tion or operation is the scope of its powers or influ-ence. *That, however, was beyond the purview of the court.* [N-SING FORMAL]

pus /pʌs/. **Pus** is a thick yellowish liquid that forms in wounds when they are infected. [N-UNCOUNT]

push /pʊʃ/ **pushes, pushing, pushed. 1** When you **push** something, you use force to make it move away from you or away from its previous position. *The woman pushed back her chair and stood up... They pushed him into the car... He put both hands flat on the door and pushed as hard as he could... When there was no reply, he pushed the door open.* ▶ Also a noun. *He gave me a sharp push.* **2** If you **push through** things that are blocking your way or **push** your way **through** them, you use force in or-der to move past them. *Dix pushed forward carrying a glass... He pushed his way towards her, laughing.* **3** If an army **pushes into** a country or area that it is attacking or invading, it moves further into it. *The army may push southwards into the Kurdish areas.* ▶ Also a noun. *...the allied push into occupied Kuwait.* **4** To **push** a value or amount **up** or **down** means to cause it to increase or decrease. *Interest had pushed the loan up to $27,000.* **5** If someone or something **pushes** an idea or project in a particular direction, they cause it to develop or progress in a particular way. *The coming of new members is bound to push the EC towards a more flexible structure... China would use its influence to help push forward the peace process.* **6** If you **push** someone to do something or **push** them into doing it, you urge, encourage, or force them to do it. *James did not push her into stealing the money... I knew he was pushing himself to the limit.* ▶ Also a noun. *We need a push to take the first step.* **7** If you **push for** something, you try very hard to achieve it or to persuade someone to do it. *Germany is pushing for direct flights to be established.* ▶ Also a noun. *They urged negotiators to make a final push to arrive at an agreement.* **8** If someone **pushes** an idea, a point, or a product, they try in a forceful way to convince people to accept it or buy it. *Ministers will push the case for opening the* [♦♦♦♦◇ VERB: Vn Vn with adv Vn prep V Vn adj] [N-COUNT VERB Vprep/adv V way prep/ adv] [VERB: Vinto n Vadv into n] [N-COUNT] [VERB: Vn with adv Vn prep VERB Vn prep/adv Vn with adv] [VERB: Vn to-inf Vn into-ing Vn prep/adv Also Vn N-COUNT VERB: V for n V for n to-inf] [VERB Vn]

plant. **9** When someone **pushes** drugs, they sell them illegally. ♦ **push·er, pushers** ...*acting as a carrier for some drug pushers.* [VERB: Vn INFORMAL] [N-COUNT]

10 If you say that someone **is pushing it**, you mean that their actions or claims are excessive or risky. *He was pushing it a bit when he said it was the best sta-dium in the world.* [VERB V it INFORMAL]

11 See also **pushed, pushing.** ● to **push the boat out**: see **boat.** ● to **push** your **luck**: see **luck.**

push ahead or **push forward.** If you **push ahead** or **push forward** with something, you make progress with it. *The government intends to push ahead with its reform programme.* [PHRASAL VB VP with n Also VP]

push around. If someone **pushes** you **around**, they give you orders in a rude and insulting way. *We don't like somebody coming in with lots of money and trying to push people around.* [PHRASAL VB VnP INFORMAL]

push aside. If you **push** something **aside**, you ig-nore it or refuse to think about it. *By pushing aside un-pleasant thoughts they merely repress these thoughts.* [PHRASAL VB VnP VP noun]

push forward. See **push ahead.** [PHRASAL VB]

push in. When someone **pushes in**, they join a queue in front of other people when they have no right to do so; used showing disapproval. *Nina pushed in next to Liddie.* [PHRASAL VB PRAGMATICS VP]

push off. If you tell someone to **push off**, you are telling them rather rudely to go away. *Push off, Bob.* [VP INFORMAL]

push on. When you **push on**, you continue with a journey or task. *Although the journey was a long and lonely one, Tumalo pushed on.* [PHRASAL VB VP]

push over. If you **push** someone or something **over**, you push them so that they fall onto the ground. *We have had trouble with people damaging hedges, uprooting trees and pushing over walls.* ● See also **pushover.** [PHRASAL VB VnP VP noun]

push through. If someone **pushes through** a law, reform, or policy, they succeed in getting it accepted, often despite opposition. *He tried to push the amend-ment through Parliament.* [PHRASAL VB VP noun VnPn Also VnP]

ˈpush bike, push bikes. A **push bike** is a bicycle which you move by turning the pedals with your feet. [N-COUNT BRITISH, DATED]

ˈpush-button. A **push-button** machine or process is controlled by means of buttons or switches. *...push-button phones.* [ADJ: ADJ n]

push·chair /ˈpʊʃtʃeə/ **pushchairs.** A **pushchair** is a small chair on wheels, in which a baby or small child can sit and be wheeled around. The usual American word is **stroller.** [N-COUNT BRITISH]

pushed /pʊʃt/. **1** If you are **pushed for** something such as time or money, you do not have enough of it. *He's going to be a bit pushed for money.* **2** If you **are hard pushed to do** something, you find it very difficult to do it. **3** See also **push.** [ADJ-GRADED: v-link ADJ INFORMAL PHRASE]

push·ing /ˈpʊʃɪŋ/. If you say that someone is **push-ing** a particular age, you mean that they are nearly that age. *Pushing 40, he was an ageing rock star.* [PREP INFORMAL]

push·over /ˈpʊʃəʊvə/ **pushovers. 1** You say that someone is a **pushover** when you find it easy to persuade them to do what you want. **2** You say that something is a **pushover** when it is easy to do or easy to get. *You might think Hungarian a pushover to learn. It is not.* [N-COUNT INFORMAL] [N-COUNT]

ˈpush-up, push-ups. A **push-up** is the same as a **press-up.** [♦◇◇◇◇ N-COUNT]

pushy /ˈpʊʃi/ **pushier, pushiest.** If you describe someone as **pushy**, you mean that they try in a forceful way to get things done as they would like or to increase their status or influence; used showing disapproval. *Pushy parents get their children into the best schools.* [ADJ-GRADED PRAGMATICS INFORMAL]

puss /pʊs/. People sometimes call a cat by saying 'Puss'. [N-VOC]

pussy /ˈpʊsi/ **pussies.** Children, or people talking to children, often refer to a cat as a **pussy.** [♦◇◇◇◇ N-COUNT]

pussy·cat /ˈpʊsikæt/ **pussycats. 1** Children or people talking to children often refer to a cat as a **pussycat. 2** If you describe someone as a **pussycat**, you think that they are kind and gentle. [N-COUNT] [N-COUNT]

pussy·foot /ˈpusifut/ **pussyfoots, pussyfoot-** | VERB
ing, pussyfooted. If you say that someone **is** | PRAGMATICS
pussyfooting around, you are criticizing them for | V around/
behaving in a cautious way because they are afraid | about
to act or commit themselves. *Why don't they stop* | Also V
pussyfooting around and say what they really mean?

pus·tule /ˈpʌstʃuːl/ **pustules.** A **pustule** is a pim- | N-COUNT
ple on the skin which contains pus. | MEDICAL

put /put/ **puts, putting.** The form **put** is used in | ◆◆◆◆
the present tense and is the past tense and past par-
ticiple. **1** When you **put** something in a particular | VERB
place or position, you move it into that place or po- | V n prep/adv
sition. *Leaphorn put the photograph on the desk...*
Mishka put down a heavy shopping bag. **2** If you | VERB
put someone somewhere, you cause them to go | V n prep/adv
there and to stay there for a period of time. *I'd put*
the children to bed. **3** To **put** someone or something | VERB
in a particular state or situation means to cause | V n prep/adv
them to be in that state or situation. *This is going to*
put them out of business... He was putting himself at
risk. **4** If you say that something is bigger or better | PHRASE
than several other things **put together**, you mean
that it is bigger or has more good qualities than all
of those other things together. *...more tanks than in*
the rest of the world put together.
5 To **put** something **on** people or things means to | VERB
cause them to have it, or to cause them to be affected | V n on n
by it. *Mr Wapenhans's comments put additional pres-*
sure on the Polish government. **6** If you **put** your trust, | VERB
faith, or confidence **in** someone or something, you | V n in n
trust them or have faith or confidence in them. *How*
much faith should we put in anti-ageing products? **7** If | VERB
you **put** time, strength, or energy **into** an activity, you | V n into n/-ing
use it in doing that activity. *Eleanor did not put much*
energy into the discussion. **8** If you **put** money **into** a | VERB:
business or project, you invest money in it. | V n into n
9 When you **put** an idea or remark in a particular way, | VERB
you express it in that way. You can use expressions | V it adv/prep
like **to put it simply** and **to put it bluntly** before say- | V it
ing something, to explain that you are going to ex- | V n into
press it in a simple way or in a blunt way. *I had already*
met Pete a couple of times through – how should I put
it – friends in low places... The security forces might
have made some mistakes, as he put it... You can't put
that sort of fear into words. **10** When you **put a ques-** | VERB:
tion to someone, you ask them the question. *Some* | V n
workers may be afraid to put questions publicly. **11** If | VERB: V
you **put** a case, opinion, or proposal, you explain it | V n to n
and list the reasons why you support or believe it. *He*
put the case to the Saudi Foreign Minister. **12** If you | PHRASE
put it to someone **that** something is true, you suggest | BRITISH
that it is true, especially when you think that they will
be unwilling to admit this. *But I put it to you that*
they're useless.
13 If you **put** something **at** a particular value or **in** a | VERB
particular category, or **put** a particular value or cat- | V n at amount
egory label **on** it, you estimate it to have that value or | V n on n
to be in that category. *I would put her age at about 50* | V n into n
or so... All the more technically advanced countries put | Also V n adj-
a high value on science... It is not easy to put the guilty | compar
and innocent into clear-cut categories.
14 If you **put** written information somewhere, you | VERB
write, type, or print it there. *They put an announce-* | V n prep/adv
ment in the local paper... He crossed out 'Screenplay' | V n
and put 'Written by' instead.
15 **Put** is used in a large number of expressions which
are explained under other words in this dictionary.
For example, the expression **to put** someone **in the**
picture is explained at **picture**.

put about. If you **put** something **about**, you tell it to | PHRASAL VB
people that you meet and cause it to become well- | V n P
known. *They put it about that he was unreliable.* | V it P that
| BRITISH

put across or **put over.** When you **put** something | PHRASAL VB
across or **put** it **over**, you succeed in describing or ex- | V n P
plaining it to someone. *He really enjoys putting across* | V P noun
a technical argument.

put aside. 1 If you **put** something **aside**, you keep it | PHRASAL VB
to be dealt with or used at a later time. *She took up a* | V n P
slice of bread, broke it nervously, then put it aside. **2** If | Also V P noun
you **put** a feeling or disagreement **aside**, you forget | V P noun
| Also V n P

about it or ignore it in order to solve a problem or argument. *We should put aside our differences and dis-*
cuss the things we have in common.

put away. 1 If you **put** something **away**, you put it | PHRASAL VB
into the place where it is normally kept when it is not | V n P
being used, for example in a drawer. *She finished putt-* | Also V P noun
ing the milk away. **2** If someone **is put away**, they are | be V-ed P
sent to prison or to a mental hospital for a long time. | V n P
His testimony could put Drago away for life. | INFORMAL

put back. To **put** something **back** means to delay it | PHRASAL VB
or postpone it. *News conferences due to be held by both* | V n P
men have been put back... They put back the date of his | be V-ed P
court appearance. | V P noun

put by. If you **put** money **by**, you save it so that you | PHRASAL VB
can use it at a later time. *There was enough put by for* | V n P
her fare. | V-ed P
| Also V P noun

put down. 1 If you **put** something **down** some- | PHRASAL VB
where, you write or type it there. *Never put anything* | V n P in/on n
down on paper which might be used in evidence | V P that
against you... We've put down on our staff develop- | V P wh
ment plan for this year that we would like some tech- | Also V P noun
nology courses... I had prepared for the meeting by put-
ting down what I wanted from them.
2 If you **put down** some money, you pay part of the | V P noun
price of something as a deposit. *He bought an invest-* | Also V n P
ment property for $100,000 and put down $20,000.
3 When soldiers, police, or the government **put down** | V P noun
a riot or rebellion, they stop it by using force. *Soldiers* | Also V n P
went in to put down a rebellion.
4 If someone **puts** you **down**, they treat you in an un- | V n P
pleasant way by criticizing you in front of other peo- | V P noun
ple or making you appear foolish. *Racist jokes come* | INFORMAL
from wanting to put down other kinds of people we feel
threatened by. ● See also **put-down**.
5 When an animal **is put down**, it is killed because it is | be V-ed P
dangerous or very ill. *They think that any legislation* | V P noun
that involved putting down dogs was wrong. | Also V n P

put down as. If you **put** someone or something | PHRASAL VB
down as a particular type of person or thing, you con- | V n P P n/-ing
sider that they are that thing. *They'll put her down as*
being one of our best Prime Ministers.

put down for. If you **put** someone **down for** an ac- | PHRASAL VB
tivity, donation, or purchase, you record their name | V n P P n
and the fact that they intend to do that activity or
make that donation or purchase. *Put her down for a*
'yes' vote.

put down to. If you **put** something **down to** a par- | PHRASAL VB
ticular thing, you believe that it is caused by that | V n P P n
thing. *You may be a sceptic and put it down to life's in-*
equalities.

put forth. If someone **puts forth** a plan or proposal, | PHRASAL VB
they suggest it. | V P noun
| FORMAL

put forward. If you **put forward** a plan, proposal, or | PHRASAL VB
name, you suggest that it should be considered for a | V P noun
particular purpose or job. *Mr Ryzhkov put his name* | V n P for n
forward for the presidency. | Also V n P

put in. 1 If you **put in** an amount of time or effort do- | PHRASAL VB
ing something, you spend that time or effort doing it. | V P noun
They've put in time and effort to keep the strike going. | V P noun
2 If you **put in a request** or **put in for** something, you | V P noun
make a formal request or application. *I decided to put* | V P for n
in for a job as deputy secretary. **3** If you **put in** a re-
mark, you interrupt someone or add to what they | V P with quote
have said with the remark. *'He was a lawyer before*
that,' Mary Ann put in. **4** When a ship **puts in** or **puts** | V P adv/prep
into a port, it goes into the port for a short stop.

put off. 1 If you **put** something **off**, you delay doing | PHRASAL VB
it. *He'll have to make a definite decision, he can't put it* | V n P
off any longer. ...women who put off having a baby. | V P -ing/-noun
2 If you **put** someone **off**, you make them wait for | V n P
something that they want. *The old priest insisted on*
them off, saying that the hour was late. **3** If something | V n P n/-ing
puts you **off** something, it makes you dislike it, or de- | V n P
cide not to do or have it. *His personal habits put them* | Also V P noun
off. **4** If someone or something **puts** you **off**, they dis- | V n P
tract you from what you are trying to do and make it | V n P -ing/-noun
more difficult for you to do it. *He's putting me off... It* | Also V n P
put her off revising for her exams. | BRITISH

put on. 1 When you **put on** clothing or make-up, you | PHRASAL VB
place it on your body in order to wear it. *I haven't even* | V P noun
| V n P

put any lipstick on. **2** If you **put on** a way of behaving, you behave in a way that is not natural to you or that does not express your real feelings. *It was hard to believe she was ill, she was putting it on.* `V P noun` `V itP` `Also V n P`

3 When people **put on** a show, exhibition, or service, they perform it or organize it. *We put it on and everybody said 'Oh it's a brilliant production'.* `V P noun` `V n P`

4 If someone **puts on** weight, they become heavier. *Luther's put on three stone.* **5** To **put** a particular amount **on** the cost or value of something means to add that amount to it. *The proposal could put 3p on a loaf of bread.* `V P noun` `Also V n P` `V n P` `BRITISH`

6 If you **put on** a piece of equipment or a device, you make it start working, for example by pressing a switch or turning a knob. *I put the radio on.* **7** If you **put** a record, tape, or CD **on**, you place it in a record, tape, or CD player and listen to it. *Let's go into the study and put on some music.* **8** If you **put** something **on**, you begin to cook or heat it. *Put on a pan of water to simmer.* `V P noun` `V n P` `V P noun` `V n P` `V n P` `V P noun`

9 If you **put** a sum of money **on** something, you make a bet about it. For example, if you put £10 on a race-horse, you bet £10 that it will win. *I'll put a bet on for you.* `V n P n/-ing` `V n P` `Also V P noun`

put onto. If you **put** someone **onto** something useful, you tell them about it. *This elastic is a powerful variety which a friend in the clothing trade put me onto.* `PHRASAL VB` `V n P n`

put out. 1 If you **put out** an announcement or story, you make it known to a lot of people. *The French news agency put out a statement from the Trade Minister.* `PHRASAL VB` `V P noun` `Also V n P`

2 If you **put out** a fire, candle, or cigarette, you make it stop burning. *He lit a half-cigarette and almost immediately put it out again.* **3** If you **put out** an electric light, you make it stop shining by pressing a switch. *He crossed to the bedside table and put out the light.* `V P noun` `V n P` `V P noun` `Also V n P`

4 If you **put out** things that will be needed, you place them somewhere ready to be used. *I slowly unpacked the teapot and put it out on the table.* `V P noun` `V n P`

5 If you **put out** your **hand**, you move it forward, away from your body. *She put her hand out and tried to touch her mother's arm.* `V P noun` `V n P`

6 If you **put** someone **out**, you cause them trouble or inconvenience because they have to do something for you. *I've always put myself out for others.* ● See also **put out.** `V n P`

7 In a sporting competition, to **put out** a player or team means to defeat them and eliminate them from the competition. *...the debatable goal that put Villa out of the UEFA Cup.* `V P noun` `V n P of n` `Also V n P`

put over. See **put across.** `PHRASAL VB`

put through. 1 When someone **puts through** a telephone call or a caller, they make the connection that allows the caller to speak to the person they are phoning. *The operator will put you through.* **2** If someone **puts** you **through** an unpleasant experience, they make you experience it. *She wouldn't want to put them through the ordeal of a huge ceremony.* `PHRASAL VB` `V P noun` `V n P n`

put together. 1 If you **put** something **together**, you join its different parts to each other so that it can be used. *The factories no longer relied upon a mechanic to put together looms within the plant.* **2** If you **put together** a group of people or things, you form them into a team or collection. *He is trying to put a team together for next season.* **3** If you **put together** an agreement, plan, or product, you design and create it. *We got to work on putting the book together.* `PHRASAL VB` `V n P` `V P noun` `V n P` `V n P`

put up. 1 If people **put up** a wall, building, tent, or other structure, they construct it so that it is upright. *Protesters have been putting up barricades across a number of major intersections.* **2** If you **put up** a poster or notice, you fix it to a wall or board. *They're putting new street signs up.* `PHRASAL VB` `V P noun` `Also V n P` `V P n` `V n P`

3 If you **put up** resistance to something means to resist it. *He was old and very frail. He couldn't have put up a fight.* `V P noun`

4 If you **put up** money for something, you provide the money that is needed to pay for it. *The merchant banks raise capital for industry. They don't actually put it up themselves.* `V P noun` `V n P`

5 To **put up** the price of something means to cause it to increase. *They know he would put their taxes up.* `V P noun` `V n P`

6 If a person or hotel **puts** you **up** or if you **put up** somewhere, you stay at the person's home or at the hotel for one or more nights. *He would drive back to town instead of putting up for the night at the hotel.* `ERG:` `V n P` `V P prep`

7 If a political party **puts up** a candidate in an election or if the candidate **puts up**, the candidate fights the election. *He put up as a candidate.* `ERG:` `V P noun` `V P as n`

put up for. If you **put** something **up for** sale, review, or auction, you make it available to be sold, reviewed, or auctioned. *She put up her daughter for adoption in 1967.* `PHRASAL VB` `V P noun` `V n P n`

put up to. If you **put** someone **up to** something wrong or foolish or something that they would not normally do, you suggest that they do it and you encourage them to do it; used showing disapproval. *Matthew put you up to this, didn't he?* `PHRASAL VB` `PRAGMATICS` `V n P P n`

put up with. If you **put up with** something, you tolerate or accept it, even though you find it unpleasant or unsatisfactory. *You're late, Shelly, and I'll tell you, I won't put up with it.* `PHRASAL VB` `V P P n`

pu·ta·tive /'pjuːtətɪv/. If you describe someone or something as **putative** you mean that they are generally thought to be the thing mentioned. *...a putative father.* `ADJ: ADJ n` `FORMAL`

'put-down, put-downs; also spelled **put down.** A **put-down** is something that you say or do to criticize someone or make them appear foolish. *Treat one another with some respect; avoid put-downs.* `◆◇◇◇` `N-COUNT` `INFORMAL`

,put 'out. If you feel **put out**, you feel rather annoyed or upset. *He was plainly very put out at finding her there.* `◆◆◇◇` `ADJ-GRADED:` `v-link ADJ`

pu·tre·fy /'pjuːtrɪfaɪ/ **putrefies, putrefying, putrefied.** When something **putrefies**, it rots and produces a disgusting smell. *...putrefying corpses.* `VERB: V` `V-ing` `FORMAL`

pu·trid /'pjuːtrɪd/. Something that is **putrid** is rotten and beginning to smell disgusting. *...a foul, putrid stench.* `ADJ-GRADED` `FORMAL`

putsch /pʊtʃ/ **putsches.** A **putsch** is a sudden attempt to get rid of a government by force. `N-COUNT`

putt /pʌt/ **putts, putting, putted.** In golf, when you **putt** the ball, you hit it a short distance. *Turner, however, putted superbly.* ▶ Also a noun. *...a 5-foot putt.* `◆◆◇◇` `VERB: V n` `V` `N-COUNT`

putt·er /'pʌtə/ **putters, puttering, puttered. 1** A **putter** is a club used for hitting a golf ball a short distance once it is on the green. **2** If you **putter around**, you pass the time in a gentle unhurried way, doing pleasant but unimportant things. The usual British word is **potter**. *She liked to putter in the kitchen.* `◆◇◇◇` `N-COUNT` `VERB:` `V around` `V` `AMERICAN`

put·ting green /'pʌtɪŋ griːn/ **putting greens.** A **putting green** is a very small golf course on which the grass is kept very short and on which there are no obstacles. `N-COUNT`

put·ty /'pʌti/. **Putty** is a stiff paste used to fix glass panes into frames. `N-UNCOUNT`

'put-upon; also spelled **put upon.** If you are **put-upon**, you are treated badly by someone who takes advantage of your willingness to help them. *...Bernard's put-upon wife Maud.* `ADJ-GRADED` `INFORMAL`

puz·zle /'pʌzəl/ **puzzles, puzzling, puzzled. 1** If something **puzzles** you, you do not understand it and find it confusing. *My sister puzzles me and causes me anxiety... It puzzles me that people in Britain are willing to pay any taxes at all to this Government.* ♦ **puz·zled** *Critics remain puzzled by the British election results.* ♦ **puz·zling** *...a number of puzzling questions.* **2** If you **puzzle over** something, you try hard to think of the answer to it or the explanation for it. *She puzzled over his behavior for a moment.* **3** A **puzzle** is a question, game, or toy which you have to think about carefully in order to answer it correctly or put it together properly. *...a word puzzle.* **4** You can describe a person or thing that is hard to understand as **a puzzle.** *'Women are a puzzle,' he said.* `◆◆◇◇` `VERB` `V n` `it V n that` `ADJ-GRADED` `ADJ-GRADED` `VERB` `V over/about` `N-COUNT` `N-SING:` `a N`

puzzle out. If you **puzzle out** a problem, you find the answer to it by thinking hard about it. *He left for* `PHRASAL VB` `V P noun` `V P wh`

his summer cottage to puzzle out what he might try next. *Also V n P*

puz·zle·ment /ˈpʌzəlmənt/. Puzzlement is the confusion that you feel when you do not understand something. *He frowned in puzzlement.* N-UNCOUNT

PVC /ˌpiː viː ˈsiː/. PVC is a plastic material used for making things such as tiles, shoes, and clothing. N-UNCOUNT

Pvt. Pvt. is a written abbreviation for the military title 'Private'. The British abbreviation is **Pte**. AMERICAN

pw. pw is the written abbreviation for 'per week'. BRITISH

pyg·my /ˈpɪgmi/ **pygmies**; also spelled **pigmy**. 1 Pygmy means belonging to a species of animal which is the smallest of a group of related species. ...*the pygmy goat.* 2 A pygmy is a member of a tribal group of very small people. ...*the pygmy tribes of Papua New Guinea.* ADJ: ADJ n / N-COUNT

py·ja·mas /pɪˈdʒɑːməz/; spelled **pajamas** in American English. The form **pyjama** is used as a modifier. A pair of **pyjamas** consists of loose trousers and a loose jacket that are worn in bed. See picture headed **clothes**. ◆◇◇◇◇ N-PLURAL

py·lon /ˈpaɪlɒn/ **pylons**. Pylons are very tall metal structures which hold electric cables high above the ground so that electricity can be transmitted over long distances. N-COUNT

pyr·a·mid /ˈpɪrəmɪd/ **pyramids**. 1 A pyramid is a shape, object, or pile of things with a flat base and ◆◇◇◇◇ N-COUNT sloping triangular sides that meet at a point. See picture headed **shapes**. *On a plate in front of him was piled a pyramid of flat white biscuits.* ◆ **py·rami·dal** /ˌpɪrəˈmɪdəl, pɪˈræm-/ ...*a black pyramidal tent.* 2 You can describe something as a pyramid when it is organized so that there are fewer people at each level as you go towards the top. ...*the top of the social pyramid.* ADJ / N-COUNT

pyre /ˈpaɪə/ **pyres**. A pyre is a high pile of wood which is built outside to ceremonially burn dead bodies or religious offerings. N-COUNT

pyro·ma·ni·ac /ˌpaɪərəʊˈmeɪniæk/ **pyromaniacs**. A pyromaniac is a person who has an uncontrollable desire to start fires. N-COUNT

pyro·tech·nics /ˌpaɪərəʊˈtekniks/. 1 Pyrotechnics is the making or displaying of fireworks. *The festival will feature pyrotechnics, live music, and sculptures.* 2 Amazing displays of skill are sometimes referred to as **pyrotechnics**. ...*the soaring pyrotechnics of the singer's voice.* N-UNCOUNT / N-PLURAL

pyr·rhic vic·to·ry /ˌpɪrɪk ˈvɪktəri/ **pyrrhic victories**. If you describe something as a pyrrhic victory, you mean that although someone has won or gained something, it was not worth the sacrifices that they had to make. N-COUNT

py·thon /ˈpaɪθən/ **pythons**. A python is a type of large snake. ◆◇◇◇◇ N-COUNT

Q q

Q, q /kjuː/ **Q's, q's**. 1 Q is the seventeenth letter of the English alphabet. 2 Q or q is used as an abbreviation for words beginning with q, such as 'question' or 'queen'. *Q: Should I dress up or dress down on the first date? A: It depends..* N-VAR

QC /ˌkjuː ˈsiː/ **QCs**. 1 In Britain, a QC is a senior barrister. QC is an abbreviation for 'Queen's Counsel'. *The Sun hired a top QC to defend Kay.* 2 QC is written after someone's name to indicate that they are qualified as a QC. ...*Channel 4's counsel, George Carman QC.* ◆◆◇◇◇ N-COUNT

quack /kwæk/ **quacks, quacking, quacked**. 1 If you call someone a **quack** or a **quack doctor**, you mean that they claim to be skilled in medicine but are not. *I went everywhere for treatment, tried all sorts of quacks.* 2 **Quack remedies** or **quack cures** are ones that you think are unlikely to work because they have been suggested by a quack doctor. *Why do intelligent people find quack remedies so appealing?* 3 When a duck **quacks**, it makes the noise that ducks typically make. *There are plenty of ducks and geese quacking on the lawn.* ▶ Also a noun. *Suddenly he heard a quack.* N-COUNT / ADJ: ADJ n / VERB V / N-COUNT; SOUND

quad /kwɒd/ **quads**. A quad is the same as a **quadrangle**. N-COUNT INFORMAL

quad·ran·gle /ˈkwɒdræŋgəl/ **quadrangles**. A quadrangle is an open square area with buildings round it, especially in a college or school. N-COUNT

quad·rant /ˈkwɒdrənt/ **quadrants**. A quadrant is one of four equal parts into which a circle or other shape has been divided. *The player appears in an upper quadrant of the screen.* N-COUNT

quad·ri·ceps /ˈkwɒdriseps/; **quadriceps** is both the singular and the plural form. Your **quadriceps** are the groups of four muscles at the front of your thighs. N-COUNT

quad·ri·ple·gic /ˌkwɒdrɪˈpliːdʒɪk/ **quadriplegics**. A quadriplegic is a person who is permanently unable to use their arms and legs. ▶ Also an adjective. *He is now quadriplegic and permanently confined to a wheelchair.* N-COUNT / ADJ

quad·ru·ple /ˈkwɒdrʊpəl, kwɒˈdruː-/ **quadruples, quadrupling, quadrupled**. 1 If someone quadruples an amount or if it **quadruples**, it becomes four times bigger. *The price has quadrupled in the last few years.* 2 If one amount is **quadruple** another amount, it is four times bigger. *Fifty-nine percent of its residents have attended graduate school – quadruple the national average.* 3 You use **quadruple** to indicate that something has four parts or happens four times. *The quadruple murder has replaced property prices as the sole topic of interest.* ◆◇◇◇◇ / V-ERG: V n / V / PREDET / ADJ: ADJ n

quaff /kwɒf/ **quaffs, quaffing, quaffed**. If you **quaff** an alcoholic drink, you drink a lot of it in a short space of time. *The customers mumble into their salads and quaff their beer.* VERB V n DATED

quag·mire /ˈkwægmaɪə/ **quagmires**. 1 A quagmire is a difficult, complicated, or unpleasant situation which is not easy to avoid or escape from. *We have no intention of being drawn into a political quagmire.* 2 A quagmire is a soft, wet area of land which your feet sink into if you try to walk across it. ◆◇◇◇◇ N-COUNT / N-COUNT

quail /kweɪl/ **quails**; **quail** can also be used as the plural form. A quail is a type of small bird which is often shot and eaten. ▶ **Quail** is the meat of this bird eaten as food. ◆◇◇◇◇ N-COUNT / N-UNCOUNT

quaint /kweɪnt/ **quainter, quaintest**. Something that is quaint is attractive because it is unusual and rather old-fashioned. ...*a small, quaint town with narrow streets and traditional half-timbered houses.* ◆ **quaint·ly** *This may seem a quaintly old-fashioned idea.* ◆ **quaint·ness** ...*the quaintness of the rural north.* ◆◇◇◇◇ ADJ-GRADED / ADV-GRADED / N-UNCOUNT

quake /kweɪk/ **quakes, quaking, quaked**. 1 A quake is the same as an **earthquake**. ...*fires that start from broken gas lines after a quake.* 2 If you **quake**, you tremble or shake, usually because you are very afraid. *I just stood there quaking with fear.* ◆◇◇◇◇ N-COUNT / VERB: V / V with n

quali·fi·ca·tion /ˌkwɒlɪfɪˈkeɪʃən/ **qualifications**. 1 Your qualifications are the examinations that you have passed. *They will be encouraged to mix academic A-levels with vocational qualifications.* 2 The **qualifications** you need for an activity or task are ◆◆◇◇◇ N-COUNT / N-COUNT

the qualities and skills that you need to be able to do it. *Responsibility and reliability are necessary qualifications.* **3** A **qualification** is a detail or explanation that you add to a statement to make it less strong or less generalized. *The empirical evidence considered here is subject to many qualifications.* N-VAR

quali·fied /'kwɒlɪfaɪd/. **1** Someone who is **qualified** has passed the examinations that they need to pass in order to work in a particular profession. *Demand has far outstripped supply of qualified teachers.* **2** If you give someone or something **qualified** support, acceptance, or approval, you give support, acceptance, or approval that is not total and suggests that you have some doubts. *Mr Wade answers both questions with a qualified yes.* **3** If you describe something as a **qualified success**, you mean that it is only partly successful. *Even as a humanitarian mission it has been only a qualified success.* ◆◆◆◇◇ ADJ   ADJ: ADJ n   PHRASE

quali·fi·er /'kwɒlɪfaɪə/ **qualifiers.** **1** A qualifier is an early round or match in some competitions. The players or teams who are successful are able to continue to the next round or to the main competition. *Last week Wales lost 5-1 to Romania in a World Cup qualifier.* **2** See also **qualify.** ◆◆◇◇◇ N-COUNT

quali·fy /'kwɒlɪfaɪ/ **qualifies, qualifying, qualified.** **1** When someone **qualifies**, they pass the examinations that they need to be able to work in a particular profession. *I qualified as a doctor from London University over 30 years ago.* ♦ **quali·fi·ca·tion** *Following qualification, he worked as a social worker.* **2** If someone **qualifies** for something or if something **qualifies** them for it, they have the right to do it or have it. *The basic course does not qualify you to practise as a therapist... A few useful skills – English-teaching, for example – qualified foreigners for work visas.* **3** To **qualify** as something or to **be qualified** as something means to have all the features that are needed to be that thing. *These people seem to think that reading a few books on old age qualifies them as experts.* **4** If you **qualify** in a competition, you are successful in one part of it and go on to the next stage. *Nottingham Forest qualified for the final by beating Tranmere on Tuesday.* ♦ **quali·fi·er, qualifiers** *Kenya's Robert Kibe was the fastest qualifier for the 800 metres final.* **5** If you **qualify** a statement, you make it less strong or less general by adding a detail or explanation to it. *I would qualify that by putting it into context.* **6** See also **qualified.** ◆◆◆◇◇ VERB: V   V as/inn   Also V to-inf   N-UNCOUNT   V-ERG: V forn   V to-inf   V n forn   Also V   V-ERG: V as n   V n as n   Also V   VERB: V   V forn   N-COUNT   VERB   V n

quali·ta·tive /'kwɒlɪtətɪv, AM -teɪt-/. **Qualitative** means relating to the nature or standard of something, rather than to its quantity. *There are qualitative differences in the way children of different ages and adults think.* ♦ **quali·ta·tive·ly** *The new media are unlikely to prove qualitatively different from the old.* ◆◇◇◇◇ ADJ FORMAL   ADV

qual·ity /'kwɒlɪti/ **qualities.** **1** The quality of something is how good or bad it is. *Everyone can greatly improve the quality of life. ...high quality paper and plywood.* **2** Something of **quality** is of a high standard. *...a college of quality... We have been successful because we are offering a quality service.* **3** Someone's **qualities** are the good characteristics which are part of their nature. *He wanted to introduce mature people with leadership qualities.* **4** You can describe a particular characteristic of a person or thing as a **quality**. *...a childlike quality... Thyme tea can be used by adults for its antiseptic qualities.* **5** In Britain, the **quality papers** or the **quality press** are the more serious newspapers which give detailed accounts of world events, as well as reports on business, culture, and society. ◆◆◆◆◇ N-UNCOUNT   N-UNCOUNT   N-COUNT   N-COUNT   ADJ: ADJ n

quality con'trol. **Quality control** is the activity of checking that goods or services are of an acceptable standard. ◆◇◇◇◇ N-UNCOUNT

qualm /kwɑːm/ **qualms.** If you have no **qualms** about doing something, you are not worried that it may be wrong in some way. *I have no qualms about recommending the same approach to other doctors.* ◆◇◇◇◇ N-COUNT

quan·da·ry /'kwɒndəri/ **quandaries.** If you are in a **quandary**, you have to make a decision but cannot decide what to do. *The government appears to be in a quandary about what to do with so many people.* N-COUNT

quango /'kwæŋgəʊ/ **quangos.** In Britain, a **quango** is a committee appointed by the government, but which works independently. A quango has responsibility for a particular area of activity. N-COUNT

quan·ti·fi·able /'kwɒntɪfaɪəbəl/. Something that is **quantifiable** can be measured or counted in a scientific way. *A clearly quantifiable measure of quality is not necessary.* ADJ-GRADED

quan·ti·fi·er /'kwɒntɪfaɪə/ **quantifiers.** In grammar, a **quantifier** is a word or phrase like 'plenty' or 'a lot', which allows you to refer to the quantity of something without being absolutely precise. It is often followed by 'of', as in 'a lot of money'. N-COUNT

quan·ti·fy /'kwɒntɪfaɪ/ **quantifies, quantifying, quantified.** If you try to **quantify** something, you try to calculate how much of it there is. *It is difficult to quantify an exact figure as firms are reluctant to declare all of their losses.* ♦ **quan·ti·fi·ca·tion** /ˌkwɒntɪfɪ'keɪʃən/. *Others are more susceptible to attempts at quantification.* ◆◇◇◇◇ VERB V n   N-UNCOUNT

quan·ti·ta·tive /'kwɒntɪtətɪv, AM -teɪt-/. **Quantitative** means relating to different sizes or amounts of things. *...the quantitative analysis of migration.* ♦ **quan·ti·ta·tive·ly** *We cannot predict quantitatively the value or the cost of a new technology.* ◆◇◇◇◇ ADJ FORMAL   ADV

quan·tity /'kwɒntɪti/ **quantities.** **1** A quantity is an amount that you can measure or count. *...a small quantity of water. ...vast quantities of food... Cheap goods are available, but not in sufficient quantities to satisfy demand.* **2** Things that are produced or available in **quantity** are produced or available in large amounts. *After some initial problems, acetone was successfully produced in quantity.* **3** You can use **quantity** to refer to the amount of something that there is, especially when you want to contrast it with its quality. *...the less discerning drinker who prefers quantity to quality.* **4** If you say that someone or something is an **unknown quantity**, you mean that not much is known about what they are like or how they will behave. *She had known Max for some years now, but he was still pretty much an unknown quantity.* N-VAR   N-UNCOUNT   N-UNCOUNT   PHRASE

quan·tum /'kwɒntəm/. **1** In physics, **quantum** theory and **quantum** mechanics are concerned with the behaviour of atomic particles. **2** You can use **quantum** in the expressions **quantum leap** and **quantum jump**, which mean a very great and sudden increase in size, amount, or quality. *A vaccine which can halt this suffering represents a quantum leap in healthcare in this country.* ◆◆◇◇◇ ADJ: ADJ n   ADJ: ADJ n

quar·an·tine /'kwɒrəntiːn, AM 'kwɔːr-/ **quarantines, quarantining, quarantined.** **1** If a person or animal is in **quarantine**, they are being kept separate from other people or animals for a set period of time, usually because they have or may have a disease. *No mammals other than people may enter the country without lengthy quarantine.* **2** If people or animals **are quarantined**, they are stopped from having contact with other people or animals. If a place **is quarantined**, people and animals are prevented from entering or leaving it. *Dogs have to be quarantined for six months before they'll let them in.* ◆◇◇◇◇ N-UNCOUNT   VB: usu passive be V-ed

quark /kwɑːk, AM kwɔːrk/ **quarks.** In physics, a **quark** is one of the basic units of matter. ◆◇◇◇◇ N-COUNT

quar·rel /'kwɒrəl, AM 'kwɔːr-/ **quarrels, quarrelling, quarrelled;** spelled **quarreling, quarreled** in American English. **1** A **quarrel** is an angry argument between two or more friends or family members. *I had a terrible quarrel with my other brothers.* **2** **Quarrels** between countries or groups of people are disagreements which may be diplomatic or include fighting. *New Zealand's quarrel with France over the Rainbow Warrior incident was formally ended.* **3** When two or more people **quarrel**, they have an angry argument. *My brother quarrelled with* ◆◆◇◇◇ N-COUNT   N-COUNT JOURNALISM   V-RECIP: pl-n V   V with n

my father. **4** If you say that you have no **quarrel** N-SING: with someone or something, you mean that you do with neg not disagree with them. *She had no quarrel with much of what had been said at dinner.* **5** If you say VERB that you would **quarrel** with someone or with V with n something that they have said, you mean that you disagree with them. *I would quarrel with you on that figure.*

quar·rel·some /ˈkwɒrəlsəm, AM ˈkwɔːr-/. A **quar-** ADJ-GRADED **relsome** person often gets involved in arguments. *Benedict had been a wild boy and a quarrelsome young man.*

quar·ry /ˈkwɒri, AM ˈkwɔːri/ **quarries, quarrying,** ◆◇◇◇◇ **quarried. 1** A **quarry** is an area that is dug out N-COUNT from a piece of land or mountainside in order to extract stone, slate, or minerals. *...an old limestone quarry.* **2** When stone or minerals **are quarried** or VERB when an area **is quarried** for them, they are re- be V-ed moved from the area by digging, drilling, or using explosives. *The large limestone caves are also quarried for cement.* ♦ **quar·ry·ing** *Farming, quarrying* N-UNCOUNT *and other local industries have declined.* **3** A per- N-SING son's or animal's **quarry** is the person or animal that they are hunting.

quart /kwɔːt/ **quarts.** A **quart** is a unit of volume N-COUNT: that is equal to two pints. num N

quar·ter /ˈkwɔːtə/ **quarters, quartering, quar-** ◆◆◆◆ **tered. 1** A **quarter** is one of four equal parts of FRACTION something. *A quarter of the residents are over 55 years old... I've got to go and collect my son in about a quarter of an hour... Cut the peppers into quarters.* ▶ Also a predeterminer. *The largest asteroid is Ceres* PREDET *which is about a quarter the size of the moon.* ▶ Also ADJ: ADJ n an adjective. *...the past quarter century.* **2** A **quarter** N-COUNT is a fixed period of three months. Companies often divide their financial year into four quarters. *The group said results for the third quarter are due on October 29.* **3** When you are telling the time, you use N-UNCOUNT: **quarter** to talk about the fifteen minutes before or also a N after the hour. For example, 8.15 is **quarter past** eight, and 8.45 is **quarter to** nine. In American English you can also say that 8.15 is a **quarter after** eight and 8.45 is a **quarter of** nine. **4** If you **quarter** something, you cut it into four rough- VERB ly equal parts. *Chop the mushrooms and quarter the* V n *tomatoes.* **5** If the number or size of something **is** VB: usu **quartered**, it is reduced to about 25 per cent of its pre- passive vious number or size. *The doses I suggested for adults* be V-ed *could be halved or quartered.* **6** A **quarter** is an Ameri- N-COUNT can or Canadian coin worth 25 cents. **7** A particular **quarter** of a town is a part where a par- N-COUNT: ticular group of people traditionally live or work. *We* supp N *wandered through the Chinese quarter.* **8** To refer to a N-COUNT person or group you may not want to name, you can talk about the reactions or actions from a particular **quarter.** *There are fears in some quarters that the republic would have little chance of surviving on its own.* **9** The rooms provided for soldiers, sailors, or servants N-PLURAL: to live in are called their **quarters.** *Mckinnon went* poss N *down from deck to the officers' quarters.* **10** If people VB: usu **are quartered** somewhere, they are provided with ac- passive commodation for a short time. *Our soldiers are quar-* be V-ed *tered in Peredelkino.* prep/adv **11** If you do something **at close quarters**, you do it PHRASE from a place that is very near to someone or something. *You can watch aircraft take off or land at close quarters.* **12** If you say that someone was given **no** PHRASE **quarter**, you mean that they were not shown any mercy or forgiveness by someone who has power over them. *This is not war as you learned it. It is brutal work, with no quarter given.*

quarter-'final, quarter-finals; spelled **quarter-** ◆◆◇◇◇ **final** in American English. A **quarter-final** is one of N-COUNT the four matches in a competition which decides which four players or teams will compete in the semi-final. *The very least I'm looking for at Wimbledon is to reach the quarter-finals.*

quar·ter·ly /ˈkwɔːtəli/ **quarterlies. 1** A **quarterly** ◆◆◇◇◇ event happens four times a year, at intervals of ADJ three months. *...the latest Bank of Japan quarterly*

survey of 5,000 companies. ▶ Also an adverb. *It* ADV: *makes no difference whether dividends are paid* ADV after v *quarterly or annually.* **2** A **quarterly** is a magazine N-COUNT or journal that is published four times a year, at intervals of three months. *...'Foreign Policy', a quarterly journal published in Paris.*

quar·tet /kwɔːˈtet/ **quartets. 1** A **quartet** is a ◆◆◇◇◇ group of four people who play musical instruments N-COLL- or sing together. *...a string quartet.* **2** A **quartet** is a COUNT piece of music for four instruments or four singers. **3** A **quartet** of people or things is a group or set of N-COUNT four people or things. *...a quartet of local women in* WRITTEN *their mid-forties.*

quartz /kwɔːts/. **Quartz** is a mineral usually found N-UNCOUNT in the form of hard clear crystals. It is used in making electronic equipment and very accurate watches and clocks.

qua·sar /ˈkweɪzɑː/ **quasars.** A **quasar** is an object ◆◇◇◇◇ in space that has a very bright centre and is often a N-COUNT very strong source of radio waves. TECHNICAL

quash /kwɒʃ/ **quashes, quashing, quashed.** ◆◇◇◇◇ **1** If a court or someone in authority **quashes** a deci- VERB sion or conviction, they officially reject it and make V n it no longer legally valid. *The Appeal Court has quashed the convictions of all eleven people.* **2** If VERB someone **quashes** rumours, they say or do some- V n thing to demonstrate that the rumours are not true. *Graham attempted to quash rumours of growing discontent in the dressing room.* **3** To **quash** rebel- VERB lion or protest is to stop it, often in a violent way. V n *Troops were displaying an obvious reluctance to get involved in quashing demonstrations.*

quasi- /ˈkweɪzaɪ-/. **Quasi-** is used to form adjectives COMB and nouns that describe something as being in many ways like something else, without actually being that thing. *The flame is a quasi-religious emblem of immortality.*

qua·ver /ˈkweɪvə/ **quavers, quavering, qua-** ◆◇◇◇◇ **vered.** If someone's voice **quavers**, it sounds un- VERB steady. *Her voice quavered and she fell silent.* ▶ Also V a noun. *There was a quaver in Beryl's voice.* N-COUNT

quay /kiː/ **quays.** A **quay** is a long platform beside ◆◇◇◇◇ the sea or a river where boats can be tied up and N-COUNT loaded or unloaded.

quay·side /ˈkiːsaɪd/ **quaysides.** A **quayside** is the N-COUNT same as a **quay.** *...an old quayside warehouse.*

quea·sy /ˈkwiːzi/ **queasier, queasiest. 1** If you ADJ-GRADED feel **queasy** or if you have a **queasy** stomach, you INFORMAL feel rather ill, as if you are going to be sick. *He was very prone to seasickness and already felt queasy.* ♦ **quea·si·ness** *The food did nothing to stifle her* N-UNCOUNT *queasiness.* **2** If you feel **queasy** about something, ADJ-GRADED you are a little worried about it. *Some people feel* INFORMAL *queasy about how their names and addresses have been obtained.*

queen /kwiːn/ **queens. 1** A **queen** is a woman ◆◆◆◇ who rules a country as its monarch. *...Queen Victo-* N-TITLE *ria. ...the time she met the Queen.* **2** A **queen** is a N-COUNT woman who is married to a king. *The king and queen had fled.* **3** If you refer to a woman as the N-COUNT: **queen** of a particular activity, you are referring to with supp, the fact that she is well-known for being very good N of n at it. *...the queen of crime writing.* ● See also **beauty queen.** **4** A **queen** is a male homosexual who dresses and N-COUNT speaks rather like a woman. INFORMAL **5** In chess, the **queen** is the most powerful piece. It N-COUNT can be moved in any direction. **6** A **queen** is a playing N-COUNT card with a picture of a queen on it. *...the queen of spades.* **7** A **queen** or a **queen bee** is a very large fe- N-COUNT male bee. The queen is the only bee in a hive which lays eggs.

queer /kwɪə/ **queerer, queerest; queers.** ◆◇◇◇◇ **1** Something that is **queer** is strange. *If you ask me,* ADJ-GRADED *there's something a bit queer going on.* **2** A man who DATED is **queer** is homosexual; some people find this use ADJ offensive. ▶ A **queer** is a man who is queer. **3** Queer N-COUNT means relating to homosexual people; used by ADJ: ADJ n some homosexuals. *Contemporary queer culture is*

allowed to rub shoulders with the lesbian feminist camps.

quell /kwel/ **quells, quelling, quelled. 1** To **quell** opposition or violent behaviour means to put an end to it using persuasion or force. *Troops eventually quelled the unrest.* **2** If you **quell** unpleasant feelings, you stop yourself or other people having these feelings. *The Information Minister is trying to quell fears of a looming oil crisis.* ◆◇◇◇◇ VERB V n / VERB V n

quench /kwentʃ/ **quenches, quenching, quenched.** When you are thirsty, you can **quench** your thirst by having a drink. *He stopped to quench his thirst at a stream.* VERB V n

queru·lous /ˈkwerʊləs/. Someone who is **querulous** often complains about things; used showing disapproval. *A querulous male voice said, 'Look, are you going to order, or what?'* ADJ-GRADED PRAGMATICS FORMAL

que·ry /ˈkwɪəri/ **queries, querying, queried. 1** A **query** is a question, especially one that you ask an organization, publication, or expert. *If you have any queries about this insurance, please contact Travel Insurance Services Limited.* **2** If you **query** something, you check it by asking about it because you are not sure if it is correct. *No one queried my decision.* **3** To **query** means to ask a question. *'Is there something else?' Ryle queried as Helen stopped speaking... One of the journalists queried whether sabotage could have been involved.* ◆◆◇◇◇ N-COUNT / VERB V n / VERB V with quote Also V n

quest /kwest/ **quests.** A **quest** is a long and difficult search for something. *My quest for a better bank continues.* ● If you go **in quest of** something, you try to find or obtain it. *The Puritans became fugitives in quest of liberty.* ◆◆◇◇◇ N-COUNT / PHRASE

quest·ing /ˈkwestɪŋ/. If you **are questing** for something, you are searching for it; a literary word. *The knights searching for the Holy Grail were questing for vision and wisdom.* VB: only cont V for n

ques·tion /ˈkwestʃən/ **questions, questioning, questioned. 1** A **question** is something which you say or write in order to ask someone about something. *They asked a great many questions about England... The President refused to answer further questions on the subject.* **2** If you **question** someone, you ask them questions about something. *This led the therapist to question Jim about his parents and their marriage.* ♦ **ques·tion·er, questioners** *He told the questioner: 'I don't know about their activities.'* ♦ **ques·tion·ing** *The police have detained thirty-two people for questioning.* **3** If you **question** something, you have or express doubts about whether it is true, reasonable, or worthwhile. *It never occurs to them to question the doctor's decisions.* **4** If you say that there is some **question** about something, you mean that there is doubt or uncertainty about it. If something is **in question** or has been called **into question**, doubt or uncertainty has been expressed about it. *There's no question about their success... As a footballer, Le Saux's ability was beyond question... Why Marlowe was killed may be open to question, but where he is buried is not.* **5** A **question** is a problem, matter, or point which needs to be considered. *But the whole question of aid is a tricky political one. ...the security question... It was just a question of having the time to re-adjust.* **6** The **questions** in an examination are the problems or topics which are set in order to test your knowledge or ability. *That question did come up in the examination.* **7** If you say **'Good question'** in reply to a question, you mean that it is a difficult one to answer, or perhaps that you are embarrassed about the answer or do not know the answer. *'Why didn't you appoint Ron twelve months ago?'—'Good question.'* **8** The person, thing, or time **in question** is one which you have just been talking about or which is relevant. *The player in question is Mark Williams.* **9** If you say that something is **out of the question**, you are emphasizing that it is completely impossible or unacceptable. *For the homeless, private medical care is simply out of the question.* **10** If you **pop the question**, you ask someone to mar- ◆◆◆◆◆ N-COUNT / VERB V n / N-COUNT / N-UNCOUNT / VERB V n / N-SING: with supp, also prep N / N-COUNT / N-COUNT / CONVENTION PRAGMATICS / PHRASE / PHRASE PRAGMATICS / PHRASE

ry you; an expression used by journalists. **11** If you say **there is no question of** something happening, you are emphasizing that it is not going to happen. *As far as he was concerned there was no question of betraying his own comrades.* **12** If you do something **without question**, you do it without arguing or asking why it is necessary. **13** You use **without question** to emphasize the opinion that you are expressing. *He was our greatest storyteller, without question.* INFORMAL PHRASE PRAGMATICS / PHRASE / PHRASE PRAGMATICS

14 See also **questioning; cross-question; leading question.**

ques·tion·able /ˈkwestʃənəbəl/. If you say that something is **questionable**, you do not consider it to be completely honest, reasonable, or acceptable. *...allegations of questionable business practices... It is questionable whether the expenditure on this project is really justified.* ◆◇◇◇◇ ADJ-GRADED FORMAL

ques·tion·ing /ˈkwestʃənɪŋ/. If someone has a **questioning** expression on their face, they look as if they want to know the answer to a question. ♦ **ques·tion·ing·ly** *Brenda looked questioningly at Daniel.* ● See also **question.** ADJ: ADJ n WRITTEN / ADV: ADV with v

'question mark, question marks. 1 A **question mark** is the punctuation mark (?) which is used in writing at the end of a question. **2** If there is doubt or uncertainty about something, you can say that there is a **question mark** over it. *There's now a big question mark hanging over the success of the negotiations.* ◆◇◇◇◇ N-COUNT / N-COUNT

ques·tion·naire /ˌkwestʃəˈneə, ˌkes-/ **questionnaires.** A **questionnaire** is a written list of questions which are answered by a lot of people in order to provide information for a report or a survey. *Headteachers will be asked to fill in a questionnaire.* ◆◇◇◇◇ N-COUNT

'question tag, question tags. A **question tag** is a very short clause at the end of a statement which changes the statement into a question. For example, in 'She said half price, didn't she?', the words 'didn't she' are a question tag. N-COUNT

queue /kjuː/ **queues, queuing, queued; queueing** can also be used as the continuous form. **1** A **queue** is a line of people or vehicles that are waiting for something. The American word is **line**. *He got a tray and joined the queue... There was still a queue for tickets on the night.* **2** If you say there is a **queue** of people who want to do or have something, you mean that a lot of people are waiting for an opportunity to do it or have it. *Single parents got priority in the housing queue... The queue for places at the school has never been longer.* **3** When people **queue**, they stand in a line waiting for something. The American expression is **line up**. *...a line of women queueing for bread.* ▶ **Queue up** means the same as **queue**. *We all had to queue up for our ration books.* ● See also **queue** 3. ◆◆◇◇◇ N-COUNT BRITISH / N-COUNT BRITISH / VERB: V V for n BRITISH / PHRASAL VB V P

queue up. If you say that people **are queuing up** to do or have something, you mean that a lot of them want the opportunity to do it or have it. *People are queuing up to work for me!... There are a growing number of countries queuing up for membership.* PHRASAL VB V P to-inf V P for n BRITISH

quib·ble /ˈkwɪbəl/ **quibbles, quibbling, quibbled. 1** When people **quibble** over a small matter, they argue about it even though it is not important. *Council members spent the day quibbling over the final wording of the resolution... Let's not quibble.* **2** A **quibble** is a small and unimportant objection to something. *These are minor quibbles.* V-RECIP pl-n V over/ about n pl-n V Also V with n / N-COUNT

quiche /kiːʃ/ **quiches.** A **quiche** is a tart filled with a savoury mixture of eggs, cheese, and other foods or flavourings. N-VAR

quick /kwɪk/ **quicker, quickest. 1** Someone or something that is **quick** moves or does things with great speed. *You'll have to be quick. The flight leaves in about three hours... I think I'm a reasonably quick learner.* ♦ **quick·ly** *Stop me if I'm speaking too quickly.* ♦ **quick·ness** *...the natural quickness of his mind.* **2** **Quicker** is sometimes used to mean 'at a greater speed'. In non-standard English, **quick** is used to mean 'with great speed'. *Warm the sugar* ◆◆◆◆◆ ADJ-GRADED / ADV-GRADED / N-UNCOUNT / ADV-GRADED: ADV after v INFORMAL

slightly first to make it dissolve quicker. **3** Something `ADJ-GRADED` that is **quick** takes or lasts only a short time. *He took one last quick look about the room... Although this recipe looks long, it is actually very quick to prepare.* ◆ **quickly** *You can become fitter than you are quite* `ADV-GRADED` *quickly and easily.* **4 Quick** means happening with- `ADJ-GRADED` out delay or with very little delay. *These investors feel the need to make quick profits... As Gervaise was quick to point out, Mr Scully was not a detective.* ◆ **quick·ly** *We need to get it back as quickly as pos-* `ADV-GRADED:` *sible... 'Not me,' Robarts said quickly.* **5 Quick** is `ADV with v` sometimes used to mean 'with very little delay'. *I* `INFORMAL` *got away as quick as I could.* **6** If someone has a `ADJ-GRADED:` **quick** temper, they are easily made angry. `ADJ n` **7** If someone **bites** their nails **to the quick**, they bite `PHRASE` off so much of their fingernails that the flesh under- neath them is exposed. **8** If something **cuts** you **to the** `PHRASE` **quick**, it makes you feel very upset. `LITERARY` **9** ● **quick as a flash**: see **flash**. ● **quick off the mark**: see **mark**. ● **quick on the uptake**: see **uptake**.

quick- /kwɪk-/. **quick-** is used to form adjectives `COMB` which indicate that someone or something does something quickly. *Quick-thinking young Alice shut the cupboard. ...quick-drying paint.*

quick·en /ˈkwɪkən/ **quickens, quickening,** ◆◇◇◇ **quickened.** If something **quickens** or if you `V-ERG` **quicken** it, it becomes faster or moves at a greater `V` speed. *Ainslie's pulse quickened in alarm... He* `V n` *quickened his pace a little.*

quick·fire /ˈkwɪkfaɪə/; also spelled **quick-fire.** `ADJ: ADJ n` **Quickfire** speech or action is very fast with no pauses in it.

,**quick 'fix, quick fixes.** If you refer to a solution `N-COUNT` or a problem as a **quick fix**, you disapprove of it be- `PRAGMATICS` cause, although it seems easy, it is only temporary or inadequate.

quickie /ˈkwɪki/ **quickies.** You can refer to some- `N-COUNT` thing as a **quickie** if it takes a very short time. For `INFORMAL` example, sex that happens without being planned and takes a short time is often called a **quickie**. *...a quickie divorce.*

quick·sand /ˈkwɪksænd/ **quicksands. 1 Quick-** `N-UNCOUNT:` **sand** is deep, wet sand that you sink into if you try `also N in pl` to walk on it. **2** You can refer to a situation as **quicksand** when you want to suggest that it is dan- `N-UNCOUNT:` gerous or difficult to escape from, or does not pro- `also N in pl` vide a strong basis for what you are doing. *I was about to sink into the quicksand of sin.*

quick·silver /ˈkwɪksɪlvə/. **1 Quicksilver** is the `N-UNCOUNT` same as **mercury**. *With half-closed eyes he looked at* `DATED` *the quicksilver in the glass.* **2 Quicksilver** move- `ADJ: ADJ n` ments or changes are very fast and unpredictable.

,**quick-'tempered.** Someone who is **quick-** `ADJ-GRADED` **tempered** often gets angry without having a good reason.

,**quick-'witted.** Someone who is **quick-witted** is `ADJ-GRADED` intelligent and good at thinking quickly.

quid /kwɪd/; **quid** is both the singular and the plural ◆◇◇◇ form. A **quid** is a pound in British money. *It cost* `N-COUNT` *him five hundred quid.* `BRITISH, INFORMAL`

,**quid pro 'quo, quid pro quos.** A **quid pro quo** is `N-COUNT` a gift or advantage that is given to someone in re- `FORMAL` turn for something that they have done. *They share a great deal of information on a quid pro quo basis.*

qui·es·cent /kwiˈesənt, AM kwaɪ-/. Someone or `ADJ-GRADED` something that is **quiescent** is quiet and inactive. `LITERARY` *...a society which was politically quiescent.* ◆ **qui** **·es·cence** *...the quiescence of the workforce.* `N-UNCOUNT`

qui·et /ˈkwaɪət/ **quieter, quietest; quiets, qui-** ◆◆◆◇ **eting, quieted. 1** Someone or something that is `ADJ-GRADED` **quiet** makes only a small amount of noise. *Tania kept the children reasonably quiet and contented.* ◆ **qui·et·ly** *'This is goodbye, isn't it?' she said quiet-* `ADV-GRADED` *ly.* ◆ **qui·et·ness** *...the smoothness and quietness of* `N-UNCOUNT` *the flight.* **2** If a place is **quiet**, there is very little `ADJ-GRADED` noise there. *The street was unnaturally quiet.* ◆ **quietness** *I really miss the quietness of the* `N-UNCOUNT` *countryside.* **3** If a place, situation, or time is **quiet**, `ADJ-GRADED` there is no excitement, activity, disturbance, or trouble. *...a quiet rural backwater... She wanted a*

quiet life... The Bosnian capital is reported relatively quiet this morning. ◆ **quietly** *They have asked peo-* `ADV-GRADED` *ple to stay quietly at home and not join demonstra-* *tions.* ◆ **quietness** *I do very much appreciate the* `N-UNCOUNT` *quietness and privacy here.* **4** If you are **quiet**, you `ADJ-GRADED:` are not saying anything. *I told them to be quiet and* `v-link ADJ` *go to sleep... I just went quiet, embarrassed, and couldn't answer.* ► Also a noun. *He called for quiet.* `N-UNCOUNT` ◆ **quietly** *Amy stood quietly in the doorway watch-* `ADV` *ing him.* **5** If you refer, for example, to someone's **quiet** confi- `ADJ: ADJ n` dence or **quiet** despair, you mean that they do not say much about the way they are feeling. *All through his life he has shown a quiet determination to get things done.* ◆ **quietly** *The publisher is quietly confident* `ADV: ADV adj` *about the magazine's chances.* **6** You describe activ- `ADJ: ADJ n` ities as **quiet** when they happen in secret or in such a way that people do not notice. *The Swedes had sought his freedom through quiet diplomacy... Can I have a quiet word with you, son?* ◆ **qui·et·ly** *I slipped away* `ADV` *quietly... The goal of shifting freight from road to rail has been quietly abandoned.* **7** If someone or something **quiets** or if you **quiet** `V-ERG` them, they become less noisy, less active, or silent. `V` The British word is **quieten**. *The wind dropped and* `AMERICAN` *the sea quieted... A gesture from her husband quieted her at once.* ► **Quiet down** means the same as **quiet**. `PHRASAL VB` *Once the vote was taken, things quieted down quick-* `ERG` *ly... Try gradually to quiet them down as bedtime ap-* `V P` *proaches.* **8** In American English, to **quiet** fears or `VERB: V n` complaints means to say or show that they are unjus- tified. The British word is **quieten**. **9** If someone does not **go quietly**, they do not volun- `PHRASE` tarily leave a job or a place without complaining or re- sisting. **10** If you **keep quiet about** something or **keep** `PHRASE` something **quiet**, you do not say anything about it. *I found it easier than Nell to keep our engagement quiet.* **11** If something is done **on the quiet**, it is done secret- `PHRASE` ly or in such a way that people do not notice. *She'd* `BRITISH` *promised to give him driving lessons, on the quiet.*

qui·et·en /ˈkwaɪətən/ **quietens, quietening, qui-** **etened. 1** If you **quieten** someone or something, `V-ERG` or if they **quieten**, you make them become less `V n` noisy, less active, or silent. The usual American `V` word is **quiet**. *She tried to quieten her breathing... A* `BRITISH` *man shouted and the dogs suddenly quietened.* ► **Quieten down** means the same as **quieten**. *The* `PHRASAL VB` *labour unrest which swept the country last week has* `ERG` *quietened down... Somehow I managed to quieten* `V P` *her down.* **2** To **quieten** fears or complaints means `V n P` to say or show that they are unjustified. The usual `VERB: V n` American word is **quiet**. `BRITISH`

quiff /kwɪf/ **quiffs.** If a man has a **quiff**, he has his `N-COUNT` hair swept upwards and backwards from his fore- `BRITISH` head.

quill /kwɪl/ **quills. 1** A **quill** is a pen made from a `N-COUNT` bird's feather. **2** A bird's **quills** are large, stiff feath- `N-COUNT` ers on its wings and tail. **3** The **quills** of a porcupine `N-COUNT` are the stiff, sharp points on its body.

quilt /kwɪlt/ **quilts. 1** A **quilt** is a thin bed-cover ◆◇◇◇ filled with some warm, soft material, which is often `N-COUNT` decorated with lines of stitching. *...an old patch- work quilt.* **2** A **quilt** is the same as a **duvet**. `N-COUNT`

quilt·ed /ˈkwɪltɪd/. Something that is **quilted** con- `ADJ` sists of two layers of fabric with a layer of warm, soft material between them, often decorated with lines of stitching which form a pattern.

quince /kwɪns/ **quinces.** A **quince** is a hard yellow `N-VAR` fruit that looks like a large pear.

qui·nine /kwɪˈniːn, AM ˈkwaɪnaɪn/. **Quinine** is a `N-UNCOUNT` drug that is used to treat fevers such as malaria.

quin·tes·sence /kwɪnˈtesəns/. **1** The **quintes-** ◆◇◇◇ **sence** of something is the most perfect or typical ex- `N-UNCOUNT:` ample of it. *Jonathan was the quintessence of all* `with supp` *that Eva most deeply loathed.* ◆ **quin·tes·sen·tial** `FORMAL` /ˌkwɪntɪˈsenʃəl/. *This was quintessential Midwestern* `ADJ-GRADED` *farming country.* ◆ **quin·tes·sen·tial·ly** *It is a fa-* `ADV-GRADED` *miliar, and quintessentially British, ritual.* **2** The `N-UNCOUNT:` **quintessence** of something is the aspect of it which `with supp` seems to represent its central nature. *He succeeds in* `FORMAL`

Q

capturing that quintessence of the Greeks' life.
♦ **quin·tes·sen·tial** ...*the quintessential charm of*   ADJ
his songs.

quin·tet /kwɪn'tet/ **quintets. 1** A **quintet** is a   N-COUNT
group of five singers or musicians singing or playing
together. **2** A **quintet** is a piece of music written for   N-COUNT
five instruments or five singers.

quip /kwɪp/ **quips, quipping, quipped. 1** A **quip**   ◆◇◇◇◇
is a remark that is intended be amusing or clever.   N-COUNT
The commentators make endless quips about the fe-   WRITTEN
male players' appearance. **2** To **quip** means to say
something that is intended to be amusing or clever.   V with quote
'He'll have to go on a diet,' Ballard quipped.   Also V that
  WRITTEN

quirk /kwɜːk/ **quirks. 1** A **quirk** is a strange acci-   N-COUNT
dental occurrence that is difficult to explain. *By a*
tantalising quirk of fate, the pair have been drawn to
meet in the first round of the championship. **2** A   N-COUNT
quirk is a habit or aspect of a person's character
which is odd or unusual.

quirky /kwɜːki/ **quirkier, quirkiest.** Someone or   ◆◇◇◇◇
something that is **quirky** is rather odd or unpredict-   ADJ-GRADED
able in their appearance, character, or behaviour.
The judges liked her quirky and original style.
♦ **quirki·ness** *You will probably notice an element*   N-UNCOUNT
of quirkiness in his behaviour.

quis·ling /kwɪzlɪŋ/ **quislings.** A **quisling** is a trai-   N-COUNT
tor who helps the enemy army that has invaded his   DATED
or her own country.

quit /kwɪt/ **quits, quitting.** The form **quit** is used   ◆◆◇◇◇
in the present tense and is the past tense and past
participle. **1** If you **quit** your job, you resign from it.   VERB: V n
He quit his job and headed back to the hills of North   V n
Carolina... He figured he would quit before Johnson   INFORMAL
fired him. **2** If you **quit** an activity or **quit** doing   VERB
something, you stop doing it. *A nicotine spray can*   V n/-ing
help smokers quit the habit. **3** If you **quit** a place,   VERB
you leave it completely and do not go back to it. *Po-*   V n
lice were called when he refused to quit the building.
4 If you say that you are going to **call it quits**, you   PHRASE
mean that you have decided to stop doing some-
thing or being involved in something.

quite /kwaɪt/. **1** You use **quite** to indicate that   ◆◆◆◆◆
something is the case to a fairly great extent. **Quite**   ADV
is less emphatic than 'very' and 'extremely'. *I felt*   PRAGMATICS
quite bitter about it at the time... I was doing quite
well, but I wasn't earning a lot of money... I was
quite a long way away, on the terrace... I quite enjoy
living here. **2** You use **quite** to indicate certainty or   ADV
to emphasize that something is definitely the case.   PRAGMATICS
It is quite clear that we were firing in self defence...
This was a serious breach of trust quite apart from
the gravity of any offence... It's difficult to know quite
how much to tell them... I quite agree with you.
3 You use **quite** after a negative to weaken the force   ADV
of your statement. *Something here is not quite*   PRAGMATICS
right... It is still good after that, but not quite the
same... At the beginning, I didn't quite understand
what all this was about. **4** You use **quite** in front of   PREDET
a noun group to emphasize that a person or thing is   PRAGMATICS
very impressive or unusual. *He's quite a character.*
5 You can say **'quite'** to express your agreement   ADV
with someone. *'And if you buy the record it's your*   PRAGMATICS
choice isn't it.'—'Quite.'   SPOKEN

quit·ter /kwɪtə/ **quitters.** If you say that someone   N-COUNT
is not a **quitter**, you mean that they continue doing
something even though it is very difficult.

quiv·er /kwɪvə/ **quivers, quivering, quivered.**   ◆◇◇◇◇
1 If something **quivers**, it shakes with very small   VERB
movements. *Her bottom lip quivered.* **2** If you say   V
that someone **is quivering with** an emotion such as   VERB
rage or happiness, you mean that their appearance   V with n
or voice clearly shows this emotion. *Cooper arrived,*
quivering with rage. ▶ Also a noun. *I recognized it*   N-COUNT
instantly and felt a quiver of panic. **3** A **quiver** is a   N-COUNT
container for carrying arrows in.

quix·ot·ic /kwɪk'sɒtɪk/. If you describe someone's   ADJ-GRADED
ideas or plans as **quixotic**, you mean that they are   FORMAL
imaginative or hopeful but unrealistic.

quiz /kwɪz/ **quizzes, quizzing, quizzed. 1** A   ◆◇◇◇◇
quiz is a game or competition in which someone   N-COUNT

tests your knowledge by asking you questions. **2** If   VERB:
you **are quizzed** by someone about something, they   be V-ed about
ask you questions because they want to get infor-   V n about n
mation from you. *Sybil quizzed her about life as a*
working girl.

quiz·mas·ter /kwɪzmɑːstə, -mæs-/ **quizmasters.** A   N-COUNT
quizmaster is the person who asks the questions in   BRITISH
a game or quiz on the television or radio. The
American word is **host**.

quiz·zi·cal /kwɪzɪkəl/. If you give someone a **quiz-**   ADJ-GRADED
zical look or smile, you look at them in a way that
shows that you are surprised or amused by their be-
haviour. ♦ **quiz·zi·cal·ly** *She looked at him slightly*   ADV-GRADED:
quizzically.   ADV after v

quo /kwəʊ/. See **quid pro quo, status quo.**

quor·ate /kwɔːreɪt/. When a committee is **quorate,**   ADJ:
there are enough people present for it to conduct   v-link ADJ
official business and make decisions.   BRITISH

quor·um /kwɔːrəm/. A **quorum** is the minimum   N-SING
number of people that a committee needs in order
to carry out its business officially. *It's not certain*
enough deputies will show up to make a quorum.

quo·ta /kwəʊtə/ **quotas. 1** A **quota** is the limited   ◆◆◇◇◇
number or quantity of something which is officially   N-COUNT
allowed. *The quota of four tickets per person had*
been reduced to two. **2** A **quota** is a fixed maximum   N-COUNT
or minimum proportion of people from a particular
group who are permitted to do something, such as
come and live in a country or work for the government. *The bill would force employers to adopt a*
quota system when recruiting workers. **3** Someone's   N-COUNT
quota of something is their expected or deserved
share of it. *They have the usual quota of human*
weaknesses, no doubt.

quot·able /kwəʊtəbəl/. **Quotable** comments are   ADJ-GRADED
written or spoken comments that people think are
interesting and worth quoting.

quo·ta·tion /kwəʊ'teɪʃən/ **quotations. 1** A **quota-**   ◆◇◇◇◇
tion is a sentence or phrase taken from a book,   N-COUNT
poem, or play, which is repeated by someone else.
He illustrated his argument with quotations from
Pasternak. **2** When someone gives you a **quotation,**   N-COUNT
they tell you how much they will charge to do a par-   BRITISH
ticular piece of work. The American word is **esti-**
mate.

quo·'tation mark, quotation marks. Quotation   N-COUNT
marks are punctuation marks that are used in writing to show where speech or a quotation begins and
ends. They are usually written or printed as '...' and
"...".

quote /kwəʊt/ **quotes, quoting, quoted. 1** If   ◆◆◆◇
you **quote** someone as saying something, you re-   VERB
peat what they have written or said. *He quoted Mr*   V n as-ing
Polay as saying that peace negotiations were already   V n
underway... She quoted a great line from a book by   V from n
Romain Gary... I gave the letter to our local press and
they quoted from it. **2** A **quote** from a book, poem,   N-COUNT
play, or speech is a passage or phrase from it. *There*
is a Groucho Marx quote that he is fond of using. **3** If   VERB
you **quote** something such as a law or a fact, you   V n
state it because it supports what you are saying. *Mr*
Meacher quoted statistics saying that the standard of
living of the poorest people had fallen.
4 If someone **quotes** a price for doing something, they   VERB
say how much money they would charge you for a ser-   V n
vice they are offering or a for a job that you want them
to do. *British Telecom quoted him £50 to put in a tele-*
phone... Lantz quoted a price for trucking in water. **5** A   N-COUNT
quote for a piece of work is the price that someone
says they will charge you to do the work. **6** If a   V-PASSIVE:
company's shares, a substance, or a currency **is quot-**   be V-ed at
ed at a particular price, that is its current market   amount
price. *Heron is a private company and is not quoted on*   TECHNICAL
the Stock Market.
7 Quotes are the same as **quotation marks.** *The word*   N-PLURAL
'remembered' is in quotes. **8** You can say **'quote'** to   CONVENTION
show that you are about to quote someone's words.   PRAGMATICS
William Schneider predicts the Democrats will have,   SPOKEN
quote, 'an awful lot of explaining to do.'

quoth /kwəʊθ/. **Quoth** is an old-fashioned word that means 'said', which is now mainly used for humorous effect. *'I blame the selectors,' quoth he.* — VERB V with quote

quo·tid·ian /kwəʊ'tɪdiən/. **Quotidian** activities or experiences are basic, everyday activities or experiences. *...puzzled and disturbed by the quotidian ordinariness of her married life with Jack.* — ADJ-GRADED ADJ n FORMAL

quo·tient /'kwəʊʃənt/ **quotients.** Quotient is used when indicating the presence or degree of a characteristic in someone or something. *Being rich doesn't actually increase your happiness quotient.* — N-COUNT

• **intelligence quotient:** see **IQ**.

Quran /kɔː'rɑːn/; also spelled **Koran** or **Qur'an. The Quran** is the sacred book on which the religion of Islam is based. — N-PROPER: the N

Quran·ic /kɔː'rænɪk/; also spelled **Koranic** or **Qur'anic. Quranic** is used to describe something which belongs or relates to the Quran. — ADJ: ADJ n

Qwer·ty /'kwɜːti/. A **Qwerty** keyboard on a typewriter or computer is the standard English language keyboard, on which the top line of keys begins with the letters q, w, e, r, t, and y. — ADJ: ADJ n

R r

R, r /ɑː/ **R's, r's. 1 R** is the eighteenth letter of the English alphabet. • See also **three Rs. 2 R** is a written abbreviation meaning king or queen. It is short for the Latin words 'rex' and 'regina'. *...Elizabeth R.* **3 R** is used as a written abbreviation for words beginning with r, for example 'river' on maps. — N-VAR / N-TITLE: n N

rab·bi /'ræbaɪ/ **rabbis.** A **rabbi** is a Jewish religious leader, usually one who is in charge of a synagogue, one who is qualified to teach Judaism, or one who is an expert on Jewish law. — ◆◇◇◇◇ N-COUNT; N-TITLE

rab·bini·cal /ræ'bɪnɪkəl/ or **rabbinic** /ræ'bɪnɪk/. **Rabbinical** or **rabbinic** refers to the teachings of Jewish religious teachers and leaders. — ADJ

rab·bit /'ræbɪt/ **rabbits, rabbiting, rabbited.** A **rabbit** is a small furry animal with long ears. Rabbits are sometimes kept as pets. ▶ **Rabbit** is the flesh of this animal eaten as food. *...rabbit stew.* — ◆◆◇◇◇ N-COUNT / N-UNCOUNT

rabbit on. If you say that someone is **rabbiting on** about something, you do not like the way they keep talking for a long time about something that is not very interesting. *Jane was rabbiting on about her current inquiry into computer based maths teaching.* — PHRASAL VB [PRAGMATICS] V P about n BRITISH, INFORMAL

rab·ble /'ræbəl/. **1** A **rabble** is a crowd of noisy, disorderly people; used showing disapproval. *...a rabble of men, women, and children.* **2** People sometimes refer to ordinary people in general as **the rabble** when they consider them to be superior to them. *...trying to keep the rabble out of athletic competition.* — N-SING [PRAGMATICS] / N-SING: the N [PRAGMATICS]

'rabble-rouser, rabble-rousers. A **rabble-rouser** is a clever speaker who can persuade a group of people to behave violently or aggressively, often for his or her own political advantage; used showing disapproval. ♦ **rabble-rousing** *Critics have accused him of rabble-rousing and opportunism.* — N-COUNT [PRAGMATICS] / N-UNCOUNT

rab·id /'ræbɪd, 'reɪb-/. **1** You can use **rabid** to describe someone who has very strong or extreme opinions which you do not like. ♦ **rab·id·ly** *Mead calls the group 'rabidly right-wing'.* **2** A **rabid** dog or other animal is infected with rabies. — ADJ-GRADED [PRAGMATICS] / ADV / ADJ

ra·bies /'reɪbiːz/. **Rabies** is a serious disease which causes people and animals, especially dogs, to go mad and die. — ◆◇◇◇◇ N-UNCOUNT

rac·coon /ræ'kuːn/ **raccoons;** also spelled **racoon. Raccoon** can also be used as the plural form. A **raccoon** is a small animal from North America and the West Indies. It has long grey fur, patches round its eyes, and a long striped tail. — N-COUNT

race /reɪs/ **races, racing, raced. 1** A **race** is a competition to see who is the fastest, for example in running, swimming, or driving. **2** If you **race**, you take part in a race. *Morris is the only other horse in the land who could race him.* **3** If you **race** a vehicle or animal that you own, you use it to take part in races. **4 The races** are a series of horse races that are held at a racecourse on a particular day. *...a day at the races.* — ◆◆◆◆◆ N-COUNT / VERB: V / VERB: V n / N-PLURAL: the N

5 A **race** is a situation in which people or organiza-

tions compete with each other for power or control. *The race for the White House begins in earnest today.* **6** If you **race** somewhere, you go there as quickly as possible. *He raced across town to the State House building.* **7** If something **races** towards a particular state or position, it moves very fast towards that state or position. *Do they realize we are racing towards complete economic collapse?* **8** If your mind **races**, or thoughts **race** through your mind, you think very fast about something. *Already her mind was racing ahead to the hundred and one things she had to do.* **9** If your heart **races**, it beats very quickly because you are excited or afraid. **10** You describe a situation as a **race against time** when you have to work very fast in order to do something before a particular time. — VERB V adv/prep / VERB V prep/adv / VERB: V adv/prep / VERB: V / PHRASE

11 A **race** is one of the major groups which human beings can be divided into according to their physical features, such as the colour of their skin. *Discrimination by employers on the grounds of race and nationality was illegal.* **12** See also **arms race, human race, race relations, racing, rat race.** — N-VAR

race·course /'reɪskɔːs/ **racecourses;** also spelled **race course.** A **racecourse** is a track on which horses race. The American word is **racetrack.** — ◆◇◇◇◇ N-COUNT BRITISH

race·go·er /'reɪsgəʊə/ **racegoers;** also spelled **race-goer.** Journalists refer to people who regularly go to watch horse races as **racegoers.** — N-COUNT BRITISH

race·horse /'reɪshɔːs/ **racehorses;** also spelled **race horse.** A **racehorse** is a horse that is trained to run in races. — ◆◇◇◇◇ N-COUNT

'race meeting, race meetings. A **race meeting** is an occasion when a series of horse races are held at the same racecourse, often during a period of several days. — N-COUNT BRITISH

rac·er /'reɪsə/ **racers. 1** A **racer** is a person or animal that takes part in races. *...a former champion powerboat racer.* **2** A **racer** is a vehicle such as a car or bicycle that is designed to be used in races and therefore travels fast. — N-COUNT / N-COUNT

,race re'lations. Race relations are the ways in which people of different races living together in the same community behave towards one another. — ◆◇◇◇◇ N-PLURAL

'race riot, race riots. Race riots are violent fights between people of different races living in the same community. — N-COUNT

race·track /'reɪstræk/ **racetracks;** also spelled **race track.** A **racetrack** is a track for races. — N-COUNT

ra·cial /'reɪʃəl/. **Racial** describes things relating to people's race. *...racial discrimination.* ♦ **ra·cial·ly** *...children of racially mixed marriages.* — ◆◆◇◇◇ ADJ / ADV

ra·cial·ism /'reɪʃəlɪzəm/. **Racialism** means the same as **racism.** *Eurasians are constantly being hurt by the outside world's uncomprehending racialism.* ♦ **ra·cial·ist** *...racialist groups.* — N-UNCOUNT BRITISH / ADJ

rac·ing /'reɪsɪŋ/. **Racing** refers to races between animals, especially horses, or between vehicles. *I'm not a big fan of horse racing. ...a terrific racing car.* — ◆◆◆◇◇ N-UNCOUNT

R

rac·ism /'reɪsɪzəm/. Racism is the belief that people of some races are inferior to others, and the behaviour which is the result of this belief. ♦ **rac·ist,** racists *He has a hard core of support among white racists.* ▶ Also an adjective. *...dealing with a racist society.*
◆◇◇◇◇ N-UNCOUNT PRAGMATICS N-COUNT
ADJ-GRADED

rack /ræk/ **racks, racking, racked.** The verb is also spelled **wrack** in American English. **1** A **rack** is a piece of equipment, usually with bars, hooks, or pegs, that is used for holding things or for hanging things on. *...a luggage rack. ...racks of clothes.* **2** If someone **is racked** by something such as illness or anxiety, it causes them great suffering or pain. *...a teenager racked with guilt and anxiety.*
♦♦◇◇◇
N-COUNT
VERB: be V-ed by/ with n V-ed Also V n

3 If you **rack** your **brains**, you try very hard to think of something. **4** If you say that someone is **on the rack,** you mean that they are suffering very much, either physically or mentally. **5** If you say that a place **is going to rack and ruin,** you are emphasizing that it is decaying and falling to pieces because nobody is looking after it.
PHRASE PHRASE JOURNALISM PHRASE PRAGMATICS

6 See also **nerve-racking, roof rack.**

rack up. If a business **racks up** profits, losses, or sales, it makes a lot of them. If a sportsperson **racks up** wins, they win a lot of matches or races.
PHRASAL VB V P noun JOURNALISM

rack·et /'rækɪt/ **rackets;** also spelled **racquet** for meaning 3. **1** A **racket** is a loud unpleasant noise. *He makes such a racket.* **2** You can refer to an illegal activity used to make money as a **racket.** *A reporter posed as a junkie to uncover a drugs racket.* **3** A **racket** is an oval-shaped bat with strings across it. Rackets are used in tennis, squash, and badminton.
N-SING N-COUNT INFORMAL N-COUNT

rack·et·eer /ˌrækɪ'tɪə/ **racketeers.** A racketeer is someone who makes money from illegal activities such as selling worthless, immoral, or illegal goods or services. ♦ **rack·et·eer·ing** *Edwards was indicted on racketeering charges.*
N-COUNT N-UNCOUNT

rac·on·teur /ˌrækɒn'tɜː/ **raconteurs.** A raconteur is someone, usually a man, who can tell stories in an interesting or amusing way.
N-COUNT

ra·coon /ræ'kuːn/. See **raccoon.**

rac·quet /'rækɪt/. See **racket.**

racy /'reɪsi/ **racier, raciest.** Racy writing or behaviour is lively, amusing, and slightly shocking.
ADJ-GRADED

ra·dar /'reɪdɑː/ **radars.** Radar is a way of discovering the position or speed of objects such as aircraft or ships by using radio signals.
♦♦◇◇◇ N-VAR

ra·dial /'reɪdiəl/ **radials. 1** A **radial** pattern is the pattern formed when straight lines are drawn from the centre of a circle to a number of points round the edge. **2** A **radial** or a **radial tyre** is a tyre which is strengthened inside by cords that point towards the centre of the wheel.
ADJ
N-COUNT

ra·di·ant /'reɪdiənt/. **1** Someone who is **radiant** is so happy that their joy shows in their face and makes them look very attractive. *On her wedding day the bride looked truly radiant.* ♦ **ra·di·ant·ly** *He smiled radiantly and embraced her.* ♦ **ra·di·ance** *A sort of radiance envelops her.* **2** Something that is **radiant** glows brightly. ♦ **ra·di·ant·ly** *The sun was still shining radiantly.* ♦ **ra·di·ance** *The sun shone with such radiance it was obviously going to be a perfect day.* **3** Radiant heat or energy is sent out in the form of rays.
♦◇◇◇◇ ADJ-GRADED
ADV-GRADED N-UNCOUNT ADJ-GRADED
N-UNCOUNT: also a N
ADJ: ADJ n

ra·di·ate /'reɪdieɪt/ **radiates, radiating, radiated. 1** If things **radiate** out from a place, they form a pattern that is like lines drawn from the centre of a circle to various points on its edge. *...the various walks which radiate from the Heritage Centre.* **2** If you **radiate** an emotion or quality or if it **radiates** from you, people can see it very clearly in your face and in your behaviour. *She radiates happiness... I felt the anger that radiated from her.* **3** If something **radiates** heat or light, heat or light comes from it.
♦◇◇◇◇ VERB V prep/adv
VERB V n V from n
VERB: V n

ra·dia·tion /ˌreɪdi'eɪʃən/. **1** Radiation is very small particles of a radioactive substance. Large amounts of radiation can cause illness and death. **2** Radiation is energy, often in waves of heat or light, that comes from a particular source.
♦♦◇◇◇ N-UNCOUNT: also N in pl N-UNCOUNT: also N in pl

ra·dia·tor /'reɪdieɪtə/ **radiators. 1** A **radiator** is a hollow metal device, usually connected by pipes to a central heating system, that is used to heat a room. **2** The **radiator** in a car is the part of the engine which is filled with water in order to cool the engine.
◆◇◇◇◇ N-COUNT
N-COUNT

radi·cal /'rædɪkəl/ **radicals. 1** Radical changes and differences are very important and great in degree. *He wants to continue the radical economic reforms begun under Mr Mazowiecki.* ♦ **radi·cal·ly** /'rædɪkli/. *...two large groups of people with radically different beliefs.* **2** Radical people believe that there should be great changes in society and try to bring about these changes. *...political tension between radical and conservative politicians.* ▶ A **radical** is someone who has radical views. ♦ **radi·cal·ism** *Jones himself was a curious mixture of radicalism and conservatism.*
♦♦♦♦◇ ADJ-GRADED
ADV-GRADED
ADJ-GRADED
N-COUNT
N-UNCOUNT

radi·cal·ize /'rædɪkəlaɪz/ **radicalizes, radicalizing, radicalized;** also spelled **radicalise** in British English. If something **radicalizes** a process, situation, or person, it makes them more radical. *...women radicalized by feminism.* ♦ **radi·cali·za·tion** /ˌrædɪkəlaɪ'zeɪʃən/. *...the radicalization of conservative right.*
VERB: V n V-ed
N-UNCOUNT

ra·dic·chio /ræ'dɪkiəʊ, AM rɑː'diː-/. Radicchio is a vegetable with purple and white leaves that is usually eaten raw in salads.
N-UNCOUNT

ra·dii /'reɪdiaɪ/. Radii is the plural of **radius.**

ra·dio /'reɪdiəʊ/ **radios, radioing, radioed. 1** Radio is the broadcasting of programmes for the public to listen to, by sending out signals from a transmitter. You can refer to the programmes broadcast in this way as **the radio.** *The last 12 months have been difficult ones for local radio... He's been on the radio a lot recently.* **2** A **radio** is a piece of equipment that you use in order to listen to radio programmes. **3** Radio is a system of sending sound over a distance by transmitting electrical signals. *They are in twice daily radio contact with the rebel leader. ...radio waves.* **4** A **radio** is a piece of equipment that is used for sending and receiving messages. **5** If you **radio** someone, you send a message to them by radio. *The officer radioed for advice.*
♦♦♦♦◇ N-UNCOUNT: also the N
N-COUNT
N-UNCOUNT
N-COUNT
VERB: V n V adv/prep

radio·ac·tive /ˌreɪdiəʊ'æktɪv/. Something that is **radioactive** contains a substance that produces energy in the form of powerful and often harmful rays. *...radioactive waste material.* ♦ **radio·ac·tiv·ity** /ˌreɪdiəʊæk'tɪvɪti/. *...waste which is contaminated with low levels of radioactivity.*
♦♦◇◇◇ ADJ-GRADED
N-UNCOUNT

radio·car·bon /ˌreɪdiəʊ'kɑːbən/; also spelled **radio carbon.** Radiocarbon is a type of carbon which is radioactive, and which therefore breaks up slowly at a steady rate. *...radiocarbon dating.*
N-UNCOUNT

,radio cas'sette, radio cassettes. A radio cassette is a radio and a cassette player together in a single machine.
N-COUNT BRITISH

,radio-con'trolled. A radio-controlled device works by receiving radio signals which operate it.
ADJ

ra·di·og·ra·phy /ˌreɪdi'ɒɡrəfi/. Radiography is the process of taking X-rays. ♦ **ra·di·og·ra·pher, radiographers** *She qualified as a radiographer.*
N-COUNT BRITISH N-COUNT

radio·logi·cal /ˌreɪdiə'lɒdʒɪkəl/. **1** Radiological means relating to radiology. **2** Radiological means relating to radioactive materials.
ADJ: ADJ n ADJ: ADJ n

ra·di·ol·ogy /ˌreɪdi'ɒlədʒi/. Radiology is the branch of medicine that uses X-rays and radioactive substances to treat diseases. ♦ **ra·di·olo·gist, radiologists** *This injection will be given by the resident radiologist.*
N-UNCOUNT
N-COUNT

,radio 'telephone, radio telephones. A radio telephone is a telephone which carries sound by sending radio signals rather than by using wires.
N-COUNT

,radio 'telescope, radio telescopes. A radio telescope is a very large outdoor telescope which finds the position of stars and other objects in space by their radio waves.
N-COUNT

radio·thera·py /ˌreɪdiəʊ'θerəpi/. Radiotherapy is the treatment of diseases such as cancer by using
N-UNCOUNT

radiation. **radio·thera·pist, radiotherapists** N-COUNT
Your radiotherapist will be able to advise you.

rad·ish /'rædɪʃ/ **radishes. Radishes** are small red N-VAR or white vegetables that are the roots of a plant.

ra·dium /'reɪdiəm/. **Radium** is a radioactive el- N-UNCOUNT ement which used to be used in the treatment of cancer.

ra·dius /'reɪdiəs/ **radii** /'reɪdiaɪ/. **1** The **radius** N-SING: with supp around a point is the distance from it in any direc- tion. *Nigel has searched for work in a ten-mile ra- dius around his home.* **2** The **radius** of a circle is the N-COUNT distance from its centre to its outside edge. *...a ra- dius of about thirty miles.*

ra·don /'reɪdɒn/. **Radon** is a radioactive element in N-UNCOUNT the form of a gas.

RAF /ˌɑːr eɪ 'ef, ræf/. The **RAF** is the air force of the N-PROPER: theN United Kingdom. **RAF** is an abbreviation for 'Royal Air Force'.

raf·fia /'ræfiə/. **Raffia** is a fibre made from palm N-UNCOUNT leaves. It is used to make mats and baskets.

raff·ish /'ræfɪʃ/. **Raffish** people and places are not ADJ-GRADED WRITTEN very respectable but are attractive and stylish. *There seemed something raffish and ungentlemanly about dealing in used cars.*

raf·fle /'ræfəl/ **raffles.** A **raffle** is a competition in N-COUNT which you buy tickets with numbers on them. After- wards some numbers are chosen, and if your ticket has one of these numbers on it, you win a prize.

raft /rɑːft, ræft/ **rafts. 1** A **raft** is a floating plat- N-COUNT form made from large pieces of wood or other ma- terials tied together. **2** A **raft** is a small inflatable N-COUNT rubber or plastic boat. ● See also **life raft. 3** A **raft** N-COUNT **of** people or things is a lot of them. *He has sur- rounded himself with a raft of advisers.*

raft·er /'rɑːftə, 'ræf-/ **rafters. Rafters** are the slop- N-COUNT ing pieces of wood that support a roof.

raft·ing /'rɑːftɪŋ, 'ræf-/. **Rafting** is the sport of trav- N-UNCOUNT elling down a river on a raft.

rag /ræg/ **rags. 1** A **rag** is a piece of old cloth which N-VAR you can use to clean or wipe things. *...a small oil- can wrapped in a rag.* **2 Rags** are old torn clothes. N-PLURAL *...small children, some dressed in rags.* **3** People re- N-COUNT fer to a newspaper as a **rag** when they have a low INFORMAL opinion of it. *I carried on writing for the local rag for another two years.* ● See also **ragged.**

4 You use **rags to riches** to describe the way in which PHRASE someone quickly becomes very rich after they have been quite poor.

rag·bag /'rægbæg/; also spelled **rag-bag.** A **ragbag** of N-SING things is a group of things which do not have much in common with each other, but which are being considered together at the same time. *The govern- ment was still in effect a ragbag of ex-Communists, Social Democrats and Liberals.*

rag doll, rag dolls. A **rag doll** is a soft doll made N-COUNT of cloth.

rage /reɪdʒ/ **rages, raging, raged. 1 Rage** is N-VAR strong anger that is difficult to control. *I flew into a rage. ...a fit of rage.* **2** You say that something pow- VERB erful or unpleasant **rages** when it continues with V on great force or violence. *The fire raged for more than four hours... The war rages on and the time has come to take sides.* **rag·ing** *The field trip involved* ADJ: ADJ n *crossing a raging torrent.* **3** If you **rage** about some- VERB thing, you speak or think very angrily about it. *He* V about/ against/at n *began to rage against his bad luck... Inside, Frannie* V *was raging.* **4** When something is popular and fash- N-SING: theN ionable, you can say that it is **the rage.** *Badges are all the rage in France.*

ragged /'rægɪd/. **1** Someone who is **ragged** is ADJ-GRADED wearing clothes that are old and torn. **2 Ragged** ADJ-GRADED clothes are old and torn. **3** You can say that some- ADJ-GRADED thing is **ragged** when it is uneven or untidy. *She could hear his ragged breathing, as if he had been running... O'Brien formed the men into a ragged line.* **rag·ged·ly** *Their voices soon died raggedly* ADV-GRADED *away.* **4** If someone **runs** you **ragged,** they make PHRASE you do so much that you become exhausted. *They'd* INFORMAL *always send me here, there and everywhere and I'd run myself ragged.*

rag·gedy /'rægɪdi/. People and things that are **rag-** ADJ-GRADED **gedy** are dirty and untidy. **Raggedy** clothes are old INFORMAL and torn.

rag rug, rag rugs. A **rag rug** is a small carpet N-COUNT made of old pieces of cloth stitched or woven to- gether.

rag·tag /'rægtæg/; also spelled **rag-tag.** If a group or ADJ: ADJ n organization is not very smart or not very well or- INFORMAL ganized, you can describe it as a **ragtag** group or organization.

rag·time /'rægtaɪm/. **Ragtime** is a kind of jazz pia- N-UNCOUNT no music that was invented in America in the early 1900s.

rag trade. The **rag trade** is the business and in- N-SING: theN dustry of making and selling clothes. INFORMAL

raid /reɪd/ **raids, raiding, raided. 1** When sol- VERB diers **raid** a place, they make a sudden armed attack V n against it, with the aim of causing damage rather than occupying any of the enemy's land. *Warplanes raided the capital of Croatia.* ► Also a noun. *The re- bels attempted a surprise raid on a military camp.* ● See also **air raid.** **raid·er, raiders** *The raiders* N-COUNT *continued on their mission – to seek out and destroy American air and sea forces.* **2** If the police **raid** a VERB: V n building, they enter it suddenly and by force in or- der to look for dangerous criminals or for evidence of something illegal. ► Also a noun. *...a raid on a* N-COUNT *house by thirty armed police.* **3** If someone **raids** a VERB building or place, they enter it by force in order to V n BRITISH steal something. *A 19-year-old man has been found guilty of raiding a bank.* ► Also a noun. *...an armed* N-COUNT *raid on a small Post Office.* **raid·er** *The raiders* N-COUNT *escaped with cash and jewellery.*

rail /reɪl/ **rails, railing, railed. 1** A **rail** is a hori- N-COUNT zontal bar attached to posts or fixed round the edge of something as a fence or support. *She gripped the hand rail in the lift.* **2** A **rail** is a horizontal bar that N-COUNT you hang things on. *...frocks hanging from a rail.* **3 Rails** are the steel bars which trains run on. *The* N-COUNT *train left the rails.* **4** If you travel or send something N-UNCOUNT by **rail,** you travel or send it on a train. *...the electric rail link between Manchester and Sheffield.*
5 If you **rail** against something, you criticize it loudly VERB and bitterly. *I'd cursed him and railed at him.* **6** If V against/at n something is **back on the rails,** it is beginning to be PHRASE successful again after a period when it almost failed. JOURNALISM *They are keen to get the negotiating process back on the rails.* **7** If someone **goes off the rails,** they start to be- PHRASE have in a way that other people think is unacceptable or strange, for example they start taking drugs or breaking the law.

rail·card /'reɪlkɑːd/ **railcards.** In Britain, a **rail- card** is an identity card that allows people to buy train tickets cheaply.

rail·ing /'reɪlɪŋ/ **railings.** A fence made from metal N-COUNT bars is called a **railing** or **railings.**

rail·road /'reɪlrəʊd/ **railroads, railroading, rail- roaded. 1** A **railroad** is the same as a **railway. 2** If N-COUNT you **railroad** someone into doing something, you AMERICAN make them do it although they do not really want VERB: V n into n/-ing to, by hurrying them and putting pressure on them. V n through *He railroaded the reforms through.*

rail·way /'reɪlweɪ/ **railways. 1** A **railway** is a route N-COUNT between two places along which trains travel on BRITISH steel rails. The American word is **railroad. 2** A **rail-** N-COUNT **way** is a company or organization that operates rail- BRITISH way routes. The American word is **railroad.** *...the state-owned French railway. ...the privatisation of the railways.*

rail·way·man /'reɪlweɪmæn/ **railwaymen.** Rail- N-COUNT **waymen** are men who work for the railway. The BRITISH usual American term is **rail workers** or **railroad workers.**

rain /reɪn/ **rains, raining, rained. 1 Rain** is water N-UNCOUNT that falls from the clouds in small drops. *I hope you didn't get soaked standing out in the rain.* **2** In N-PLURAL countries where rain only falls in certain seasons, this rain is referred to as **the rains.** *The rains have failed again in the Horn of Africa.* **3** When rain falls, VERB you can say that **it is raining.** *It rained the whole* it V

weekend. **4** If someone does something **rain or shine**, they do it regularly, without being affected by the weather or other circumstances. *Frances took her daughter walking every day, rain or shine.*
5 If someone **rains** blows, kicks, or bombs **on** a person or place, the person or place is heavily attacked. *Rockets, mortars and artillery rounds rained on buildings.* ▶ **Rain down** means the same as **rain.** *Fighter aircraft rained down high explosives... Grenades and mortars rained down on Dubrovnik.* **6** A **rain of** things is a large number of things that fall from the sky at the same time. *A rain of stones descended on the police.*
rain off. If a sports match **is rained off**, it has to stop, or it is not able to start, because of rain. The usual American expression is **be rained out.**
rain·bow /ˈreɪnbəʊ/ **rainbows. 1** A **rainbow** is an arch of different colours that you can sometimes see in the sky when it is raining. **2** A **rainbow** of colours is a wide range of bright colours. *...a rainbow of coloured cushions.* **3** If you say that something is at **the end of the rainbow**, you mean that people want it but it is almost impossible to obtain or achieve. *The promise of a cure – the pot of gold at the end of the rainbow – often makes sensible people do irrational things.*
'**rain check.** If you say you will **take a rain check on** an offer or suggestion, you mean that you do not want to accept it straight away, but you might accept it at another time.
rain·coat /ˈreɪnkəʊt/ **raincoats.** A **raincoat** is a waterproof coat.
rain·drop /ˈreɪndrɒp/ **raindrops.** A **raindrop** is a single drop of rain.
rain·fall /ˈreɪnfɔːl/ **rainfalls. Rainfall** is the amount of rain that falls in a place during a particular period. *There have been four years of below average rainfall.*
rain·for·est /ˈreɪnfɒrɪst, AM -fɔːr-/ **rainforests.** A **rainforest** is a thick forest of tall trees which is found in tropical areas where there is a lot of rain.
rain·storm /ˈreɪnstɔːm/ **rainstorms.** A **rainstorm** is a fall of very heavy rain.
'**rain-swept;** also spelled **rainswept.** A **rain-swept** place is a place where it is raining heavily. *...rain-swept streets.*
rain·water /ˈreɪnwɔːtə/. **Rainwater** is water that has fallen as rain.
rainy /ˈreɪni/ **rainier, rainiest. 1** During a **rainy** day, season, or period it rains a lot. **2** If you say that you are saving something, especially money, **for a rainy day**, you mean that you are saving it until a time in the future when you might need it.
raise /reɪz/ **raises, raising, raised. 1** If you **raise** something, you move it so that it is in a higher position. *She went to the window and raised the blinds... Milton raised the glass to his lips. ...a small raised platform.* **2** If you **raise** a flag or banner, you display it by moving it into a high place. **3** If you **raise** yourself, you lift your body so that you are standing up straight, or so that you are no longer lying flat. *He raised himself into a sitting position.*
4 If you **raise** the rate or level of something, you increase it. *The Republic of Ireland is expected to raise interest rates. ...a raised body temperature.* **5** To **raise** the standard of something means to improve it.
6 If you **raise** your voice, you speak more loudly. **7** If an event **raises** a particular emotion or question, it makes people feel the emotion or consider the question. *The agreement has raised hopes that the war may end soon... The accident again raises questions about the safety of the plant.* **8** If you **raise** a subject, an objection, or a question, you mention it or bring it to someone's attention. *In the meeting Mrs. Ashrawi raised the three main concerns that the Palestinians have.*
9 A **raise** is an increase in your wages or salary. The British word is **rise.** *Within two months Kelly got a raise.* **10** If you **raise** money for a charity or an institution, you ask people for money which you collect on its behalf. **11** If a person or company **raises** money

that they need, they manage to get it. *They raised the money to buy the house.*
12 Someone who **raises** a child looks after it until it is grown up. **13** If someone **raises** a particular type of animal or crop, they breed that type of animal or grow that type of crop.
14 ● to **raise the alarm**: see **alarm.** ● to **raise** your **eyebrows**: see **eyebrow.** ● to **raise hell**: see **hell.** ● to **raise a laugh**: see **laugh.**
rai·sin /ˈreɪzən/ **raisins. Raisins** are dried grapes. *...a large plate of roast pork stuffed with apples and raisins.*
rai·son d'etre /ˌreɪzɒn ˈdetrə/; also spelled **raison d'être.** A person's or organization's **raison d'etre** is the most important reason for them existing in the way that they do. *The armed forces are caught up in a debate about their raison d'etre.*
Raj /rɑːʒ/. **The Raj** was the period of British rule in India which ended in 1947.
rake /reɪk/ **rakes, raking, raked. 1** A **rake** is a garden tool consisting of a row of metal or wooden teeth attached to a long handle. You can use a rake, for example, to gather leaves together. See picture headed **tools. 2** If you **rake** a surface, you move a rake across it in order to make it smooth and level.
3 If you **rake** leaves or ashes, you move them somewhere using a rake or a similar tool. *I watched the men rake leaves into heaps... She raked out the ashes from the boiler.*
4 If someone **rakes** an area with gunfire or with light, they cover it thoroughly by moving the gun or the light across from one side of the area to another. *The headlights raked across a painted sign.* **5** If you call a man a **rake**, you mean that he is rather immoral, for example because he gambles, drinks, or has sexual relationships with many women.
rake in. If you say that someone **is raking in** money, you mean that they are making a lot of money more easily than you think they should. *The privatisation allowed companies to rake in huge profits.*
rake over. If you say that someone **is raking over** something that has been said or done in the past, you mean that they are examining and discussing it, in a way that you do not think is very pleasant or useful. *Let's not rake over old quarrels.*
rake up. If you say that someone **is raking up** something unpleasant or embarrassing that happened in the past, you mean they are talking about it or reminding someone about it, and you do not think they should. *All this trial is doing is raking up the pain of the last year.*
raked /reɪkt/. A **raked** surface is sloping.
'**rake-off, rake-offs.** If someone who has helped to arrange a business deal takes or gets a **rake-off**, they illegally or unfairly take a share of the profits.
rak·ish /ˈreɪkɪʃ/. A **rakish** person or appearance is stylish in a confident, daring way.
ral·ly /ˈræli/ **rallies, rallying, rallied. 1** A **rally** is a large public meeting that is held in order to show support for something such as a political party.
2 When people **rally** to something or when something **rallies** them, they unite to support it. *Her cabinet colleagues have continued to rally to her support... He rallied his own supporters for a fight.*
3 When someone or something **rallies**, they begin to recover or improve after having been weak. *Markets began to rally worldwide.* ▶ Also a noun. *After a brief rally the shares returned to 126p.* **4** A **rally** is a competition in which vehicles are driven over public roads. *He was an accomplished rally driver.* **5** A **rally** in tennis, badminton, or squash is a continuous series of shots that players exchange without stopping.
rally around or **rally round.** When people **rally around** or **rally round**, they work as a group in order to support someone or something at a difficult time. *Connie's friends rallied round her.*
'**rallying cry, rallying cries.** A **rallying cry** or **rallying call** is something such as a slogan, event, or

belief which inspires people to unite and to act in support of a group or ideal.

'rallying point, rallying points. A **rallying point** N-COUNT is a place, event, or person that people are attracted to as a symbol of a political group or ideal. *Students used the death of political activists as a rallying point for anti-government protests.*

ram /ræm/ **rams, ramming, rammed. 1** If a ve- ◆◇◇◇◇ hicle **rams** something such as another vehicle, it VERB: V n crashes into it with a lot of force. **2** If you **ram** VERB something somewhere, you push it there with great V n adv/prep force. *He rammed the key into the lock and kicked the front door open.* **3** If something **rams home** a PHRASE message or a point, it makes it clear in a forceful way that people are likely to listen to. *Railway lines are dangerous places and it is up to parents to ram home the dangers to their children.* **4** A **ram** is an N-COUNT adult male sheep.
5 See also **battering ram**. • to **ram** something **down** someone's **throat**: see **throat**.

RAM /ræm/. **RAM** is the part of a computer in which N-UNCOUNT information is kept temporarily for immediate use. TECHNICAL It is an abbreviation for 'Random Access Memory'.

Rama·dan /'ræmədæn/. **Ramadan** is the ninth ◆◇◇◇◇ month of the Muslim year, when Muslims do not N-UNCOUNT eat between sunrise and sunset. During Ramadan, Muslims celebrate the fact that it was in this month that God first revealed the words of the Quran to Mohammed.

ram·ble /'ræmbəl/ **rambles, rambling, ram-** ◆◇◇◇◇ **bled. 1** If you **ramble**, you go on a long walk in the VERB countryside. ▶ Also a noun. *...an hour's ramble through the* N-COUNT *woods.* **2** If you say that a person **rambles** in their VERB: V speech or writing, you mean they keep going off the subject in a confused way.
ramble on. If you say that someone **is rambling on,** PHRASAL VB you mean that they have been talking for a long time V P in a boring and rather confused way. *He stood in my* V P about n *kitchen drinking beer, rambling on about Lillian.*

ram·bler /'ræmblə/ **ramblers.** A **rambler** is a per- ◆◇◇◇◇ son whose hobby is going on long walks in the N-COUNT countryside. BRITISH

ram·bling /'ræmblɪŋ/. **1** A **rambling** building is big ◆◇◇◇◇ and old with an irregular shape. *...the rambling,* ADJ *ranch-style building.* **2** If you describe a speech or ADJ-GRADED piece of writing as **rambling**, you are criticizing it for being too long and confused.

ram·blings /'ræmblɪŋz/. If you describe a speech or N-PLURAL piece of writing as someone's **ramblings**, you mean it is meaningless or unimportant because the person who said or wrote it was confused or perhaps even slightly insane. *The official dismissed the speech as the ramblings of a desperate lunatic.*

ram·bunc·tious /ræm'bʌŋkʃəs/. A **rambunctious** ADJ-GRADED person is energetic in a cheerful, noisy way. The AMERICAN usual British word is **rumbustious**.

ram·ekin /'ræmɪkɪn/ **ramekins.** A **ramekin** or a N-COUNT **ramekin dish** is a small dish in which a portion of food for one person can be baked in the oven.

rami·fi·ca·tion /ˌræmɪfɪ'keɪʃən/ **ramifications.** ◆◇◇◇◇ The **ramifications** of a decision or event are all its N-COUNT consequences and effects, especially ones which are not obvious at first. *...the social and political ramifications of AIDS for the gay community.*

ramp /ræmp/ **ramps. 1** A **ramp** is a sloping surface ◆◇◇◇◇ between two places that are at different levels. *...a* N-COUNT *ramp to facilitate entry into the pool from a wheelchair.* **2** An **entrance ramp** is a road which cars use N-COUNT to drive onto an expressway, and an **exit ramp** is AMERICAN one which cars use to drive off. The usual British expression for both of these roads is **slip road**.

ram·page, rampages, rampaging, ram- ◆◇◇◇◇ **paged.** Pronounced /ræm'peɪdʒ/ for meaning 1, and /'ræmpeɪdʒ/ for meaning 2. **1** When people or VERB: animals **rampage** through a place, they rush about V adv/prep there in a wild or violent way, causing damage or V-ing destruction. *...a rampaging mob.* **2** If people go **on** PHRASE **the rampage**, they rush about in a wild or violent way, causing damage or destruction.

ram·pant /'ræmpənt/. If you describe something ◆◇◇◇◇ bad, such as a crime or disease, as **rampant**, you ADJ-GRADED mean that it is very widespread and is growing in an uncontrolled way. *...the rampant corruption of the administration.*

ram·part /'ræmpɑːt/ **ramparts.** The **ramparts** of a N-COUNT castle or city are the earth banks, often with walls on them, that were built to protect it.

'ram-raid, ram-raids, ram-raiding, ram- VERB **raided.** If people **ram-raid**, they carry out a rob- V bery on a shop or other building using a stolen car Also V n to smash their way into the building. *The kids who* BRITISH *are joyriding and ramraiding are unemployed.* ▶ Also a noun. *He was out to do a ram-raid.* N-COUNT **♦ ram-raider, ram-raiders** *Ram-raiders smashed* N-COUNT *their way into a high-class store.*

ram·rod /'ræmrɒd/. **Ramrod** is used to describe ADJ: ADJ n someone who has a very straight back and appears rather stiff and formal. *I don't have the ramrod posture I had when I was in the Navy.* ▶ Also an adverb. ADV: ADV adj *At 75, she's still ramrod straight.*

ram·shack·le /'ræmʃækəl/. **1** A **ramshackle** build- ◆◇◇◇◇ ing is badly made or in bad condition, and looks as ADJ-GRADED if it is likely to fall down. **2** A **ramshackle** system, ADJ-GRADED coalition, or collection has been put together without much thought and is not likely to work or last very well. *...the ramshackle economic policies of the government.*

ran /ræn/. **Ran** is the past tense of **run**.

ranch /rɑːntʃ, ræntʃ/ **ranches.** A **ranch** is a large ◆◇◇◇◇ farm used for raising animals, especially cattle, N-COUNT horses, or sheep. • See also **dude ranch**.

ranch·ing /'rɑːntʃɪŋ, 'ræn-/. **Ranching** is the activ- N-UNCOUNT ity of running a large farm, especially one used for raising cattle, horses, or sheep. **♦ ranch·er, ranch-** N-COUNT **ers** *...a cattle rancher.*

ran·cid /'rænsɪd/. If butter or other fatty foods are ADJ-GRADED **rancid**, they have gone bad and taste unpleasant.

ran·cor /'ræŋkɔː/. See **rancour**.

ran·cor·ous /'ræŋkərəs/. A **rancorous** argument or ADJ-GRADED person is full of bitterness and resentment. FORMAL

ran·cour /'ræŋkə/; spelled **rancor** in American Eng- N-UNCOUNT lish. **Rancour** is a strong feeling of bitterness and FORMAL resentment.

R&B /ˌɑː bɔ 'biː/. **R&B** is a style of popular music ◆◇◇◇◇ developed in the 1940's from blues music, but using N-UNCOUNT electrically amplified instruments. **R&B** is an abbreviation for 'rhythm and blues'.

R&D /ˌɑː ən 'diː/; also spelled **R and D. R&D** refers ◆◇◇◇◇ to the research and development work or depart- N-UNCOUNT ment within a large company. **R&D** is an abbrevia- TECHNICAL tion for 'Research and Development'.

ran·dom /'rændəm/. **1** A **random** sample or meth- ◆◆◇◇◇ od is one in which all the people or things involved ADJ have an equal chance of being chosen. *The competitors will be subject to random drug testing.* **♦ ran-** **·dom·ly** *...a randomly selected sample of thirty girls.* ADV **2** If you choose people or things **at random**, you do PHRASE not use any particular method, so they all have an equal chance of being chosen. **3** If you describe ADJ-GRADED events as **random**, you mean that they do not seem to follow a definite plan or pattern. *...random violence against innocent victims.* **♦ randomly** ADV-GRADED *...drinks and magazines left scattered randomly around.* **♦ ran·dom·ness** *...the randomness of life.* N-UNCOUNT **4** If something happens **at random**, it happens PHRASE without a definite plan or pattern. *Three black people were killed by shots fired at random from a minibus.*

ran·dom·ize /'rændəmaɪz/ **randomizes, random-** VERB: V n **izing, randomized;** also spelled **randomise** in V-ed British English. If you **randomize** the events or peo- TECHNICAL ple in scientific experiments or academic research, you use a method that gives them all an equal chance of happening or being chosen. *Properly randomized studies are only now being completed.*

randy /'rændi/. Someone who is **randy** is sexually ADJ-GRADED excited and eager to have sex. The usual American INFORMAL, word is **horny**. BRITISH

R

rang

rant

rang /ræŋ/. **Rang** is the past tense of **ring**.

range /reɪndʒ/ **ranges, ranging, ranged.** **1** A ◆◆◆◆◇
range of things is a number of different things of N-COUNT
the same general kind. *...a range of issues... The
range includes chests of drawers, tables and wardrobes.* **2** A **range** is the complete group that is N-COUNT
included between two points on a scale of measurement or quality. *The average age range is between 35
and 55. ...properties available in the price range they
are looking for.* **3** If things **range** between two VERB:
points or **range** from one point to another, they V from n to n
vary within these points on a scale of measurement V from
or quality. *They range in price from $3 to $15. ...tem-* amount to
peratures ranging between 5°C and 20°C. amount
4 The **range** of something is the maximum area in N-COUNT
which it can reach things or detect things. *The 120mm
mortar has a range of 18,000 yards... The trees on the
mountains within my range of vision had all been
felled.* **5** If something is **in range** or **within range**, it is PHRASE
near enough to be reached or detected. If it is **out of
range**, it is too far away to be reached or detected.
*...within range of their aircraft... The fish stayed 50
yards offshore, well out of range.* **6** If you see or hit PHRASE
something **at close range**, or **from close range**, you
are very close to it when you see it or hit it. If you do
something **at a range of** half a mile, for example, you
are half a mile away from it when you do it. *He was
shot in the head at close range. ...photographing wild
animals from close range... The enemy opened fire at a
range of only 20 yards.*
7 A **range** of mountains or hills is a line of them. N-COUNT
8 A rifle **range** or a shooting **range** is a place where N-COUNT
people can practise shooting at targets. **9** A **range** is N-COUNT
an old-fashioned metal cooking stove.
10 If people or things **are ranged** somewhere, they VB: usu
are arranged in a row or in lines. *Some 300 trees have* passive
been ranged along the perimeter hedge. **11** See also be V-ed prep
free-range. FORMAL

range·finder /'reɪndʒfaɪndə/ **rangefinders.** A N-COUNT
rangefinder is an instrument, usually part of a cam- TECHNICAL
era or a piece of military equipment, that measures
the distance between things that are far away from
each other.

rang·er /'reɪndʒə/ **rangers.** A **ranger** is a person ◆◇◇◇◇
whose job is to look after a forest or large park. N-COUNT

rangy /'reɪndʒi/. A **rangy** person or animal has long, ADJ
slim, powerful legs.

rank /ræŋk/ **ranks, ranking, ranked.** ◆◆◆◇◇
1 Someone's **rank** is the position or grade that they N-VAR:
have in an organization. *He eventually rose to the* with supp
*rank of captain. ...officers of equivalent rank in the
other branches.* ♦ **-ranking** /-ræŋkɪŋ/ *...a low-* COMB
ranking civil servant. **2** Someone's **rank** is the so- N-VAR
cial class, especially the high social class, that they FORMAL
belong to. *Each rank of the peerage was represented... He must be treated as a hostage of high rank,
not as a common prisoner.* **3** If you say that some- PHRASE
one in authority **pulls rank**, you mean that they PRAGMATICS
unfairly force other people to do what they want
because of their higher rank or position; used showing disapproval.
4 If an official organization **ranks** someone or some- V-ERG
thing 1st or 50th, for example, they calculate that the V n ord
person or thing has that position in their list or scale. V in/among n
The report ranks the UK 20th out of 22 advanced na- Also be V-ed in
tions... Mr Short does not even rank in the world's top n
ten. ♦ **-ranked** /-ræŋkt/ *...the world's ten highest-* COMB
ranked players. **5** If you say that someone or some- V-ERG
thing **ranks** high or low, or **ranks** as important, for V adj
example, you are saying how good, important, or V n adj
useful you think they are. *His prices rank high among* V as adj
those of other contemporary photographers... Investors
ranked South Korea high among Asian nations... St
Petersburg's night life ranks as more exciting than the
capital's.* **6** If you say that someone or something VERB
ranks with a group of famous people or things, you V with n
mean that they are extremely good and should be included in that group. *...a remarkable scientist whose
work ranked with that of Einstein.*
7 The **ranks** of a group or organization are the people N-PLURAL:

who belong to it. *There were some misgivings within* with supp
the ranks of the media too. **8** The **ranks** are the ordi- N-PLURAL:
nary members of an organization, especially of the the N
armed forces. *Most store managers have worked their
way up through the ranks.* **9** A **rank** of people or things N-COUNT
is a row of them.
10 If a member of a group or organization **breaks** PHRASE
ranks, they disobey the instructions of their group or
organization. *China appears unlikely to break ranks
with other members of the United Nations Security
Council.* **11** If the members of a group **close ranks**, PHRASE
they support each other totally and oppose any attacks from outside on individual members or any
criticism of them. *Most institutions tend to close ranks
when a member has been accused of misconduct.* **12** If PHRASE
you experience something, usually something bad,
that other people have experienced, you can say that
you have **joined** their **ranks**. *Last month, more than
370,000 Americans joined the ranks of the unemployed.*
13 A taxi **rank** is a part of a city street where taxis park N-COUNT
when they are available for hire. BRITISH
14 You can use **rank** to emphasize a bad or undesir- ADJ: ADJ n
able quality that exists in an extreme form. *He called it* PRAGMATICS
'rank hypocrisy' that the government was now promot- FORMAL
ing equal rights. **15** You can describe something as ADJ
rank when it has a strong and unpleasant smell. **16** If LITERARY
one of the people in a competition is described as a PHRASE
rank outsider, they are considered to have very little
chance of winning.

,rank and 'file. The **rank and file** are the ordinary ◆◇◇◇
members of an organization or workers in a compa- N-SING
ny, as opposed to its leaders or managers. *The rank
and file of the party hadn't been consulted.*

rank·ing /'ræŋkɪŋ/ **rankings. 1** In many sports, ◆◆◇◇◇
the list of the best players made by an official or- N-PLURAL:
ganization is called the **rankings.** *...the 25 leading* the N
teams in the world rankings.* **2** Someone's **ranking** N-COUNT
is their position in an official list of the best players
of a sport. **3** The **ranking** member of a group, ADJ: ADJ n
usually a political group, is the most senior person AMERICAN
in it. *...the ranking American diplomat in Baghdad.*

ran·kle /'ræŋkəl/ **rankles, rankling, rankled. 1** If VERB: V
an event or situation **rankles**, it makes you feel an- V with n
gry or bitter afterwards, because you think it was V n
unfair or wrong. *Britain's refusal to sell Portugal
arms in 1937 still rankled with him... The only thing
that rankles me is what she says about Ireland.*

ran·sack /'rænsæk/ **ransacks, ransacking, ran-** ◆◇◇◇◇
sacked. If people **ransack** a building, they make a VERB: V n
mess and damage things in it, often because they V-ed
are looking for something. *...the wrecked schools
and churches, the ransacked embassies and homes.*
♦ **ran·sack·ing** *Nor did he explicitly denounce the* N-SING:
ransacking of the opposition parties' offices. the N of n

ran·som /'rænsəm/ **ransoms, ransoming, ran-** ◆◇◇◇◇
somed. 1 A **ransom** is the money that has to be N-VAR
paid to someone so that they will set free a person
they have kidnapped. *The ransom demand was
made by telephone.* **2** If a kidnapper **holds** a person PHRASE
to ransom or **for ransom**, or **holds** a person **ransom**, they keep that person prisoner until they are
given what they want. **3** If you **ransom** someone VERB: V n
who has been kidnapped, you pay the money to set V n
them free. *The same system was used for ransoming
or exchanging captives.*
4 If you say that someone **is holding** you **to ransom** or PHRASE
for ransom, you mean that they are using their power PRAGMATICS
to force you to do something you do not want to do;
used showing disapproval. **5** If you refer to a sum of PHRASE
money as **a king's ransom**, you are emphasizing that DATED
it is very large. *...clients happy to pay a king's ransom
for a good haircut.*

rant /rænt/ **rants, ranting, ranted. 1** If you say ◆◇◇◇◇
that someone **rants**, you mean that they talk loudly VERB: V
or angrily, and exaggerate or say foolish things. V about/at/
...the mentally ill patient we heard ranting about de- against n
mons... Even their three dogs got bored and fell V on
asleep as he ranted on. ▶ Also a noun. *Part I is a* N-COUNT
rant against organised religion. ♦ **rant·ing,**

rantings ...*listening to Goldstone's rantings all night.* **2** If you say that someone **rants and raves**, you mean that they talk loudly and angrily in an uncontrolled way; used showing disapproval.   N-VAR   PHRASE   PRAGMATICS

rap /ræp/ **raps, rapping, rapped. 1** Rap is a type of music in which the words are not sung but are spoken in a rapid, rhythmic way. **2** Someone who **raps** performs rap music. *New Yorkers rap about parties and clubs.* **3** A **rap** is a piece of music performed in rap style, or the words that are used in it. **4** If you **rap** on something, you hit it with a series of quick blows. *...rapping the glass with the knuckles of his right hand... A guard raps his stick on a metal hand rail.* ▶ Also a noun. *There was a sharp rap on the door.* **5** A **rap** is a criminal conviction. *You'll be facing a Federal rap for aiding and abetting.* **6** The **rap** about someone or something is their reputation. *The rap on this guy is that he doesn't really care.* **7** A **rap** is an act of criticizing or blaming someone. *Timeshare companies also come in for a rap as they continue to flout the rules.* **8** If you **rap** someone for something, you criticize or blame them for it. *The minister rapped banks over their treatment of small businesses.* **9** If someone in authority **raps** your **knuckles** or **raps** you **on the knuckles**, they criticize you or blame you for doing something they think is wrong. *I joined the workers on strike and was rapped over the knuckles.* **10** If someone in authority gives you a **rap on the knuckles**, they criticize you or blame you for doing something they think is wrong. *Britain gave them a diplomatic rap over the knuckles.* **11** If you **take the rap**, you are blamed or punished for something, especially something that is not your fault or for which other people are equally guilty. *When the client was murdered, his wife took the rap, but did she really do it?*   ◆◆◇◇◇   N-UNCOUNT   VERB: V   V about n   N-COUNT   VERB: V on n   V on   V n on n   N-COUNT   N-COUNT   INFORMAL   N-SING   INFORMAL, AMERICAN   N-COUNT   JOURNALISM   VERB   V n for/over n   JOURNALISM   PHRASE   JOURNALISM   PHRASE   JOURNALISM   PHRASE

ra·pa·cious /rə'peɪʃəs/. If you describe a person or their behaviour as **rapacious**, you disapprove of their greedy or uncaring behaviour. *Oil fields have already been depleted by a rapacious exploitation policy.*   ADJ-GRADED   PRAGMATICS   FORMAL

rape /reɪp/ **rapes, raping, raped. 1** If someone **is raped**, they are forced to have sex, usually by violence or threats of violence. *They'd held him down and raped him.* **2** Rape is the crime of forcing someone to have sex. *Almost ninety per cent of all rapes and violent assaults went unreported.* **3** The **rape of** an area or a country is the destruction or spoiling of it. **4** See also **date rape, oilseed rape**.   ◆◆◆◇◇   VERB: be V-ed   V n   N-VAR   N-SING: the N of n   LITERARY

rap·id /'ræpɪd/. **1** A **rapid** change is one that happens very quickly. *...the country's rapid economic growth in the 1980's.* ◆ **rap·id·ly** *'Operating profit is rising more rapidly,' he said.* ◆ **ra·pid·ity** /rə'pɪdɪti/. *...the rapidity with which the weather can change.* **2** A **rapid** movement is one that is very fast. *Breathing becomes more rapid and sweating starts.* ◆ **rap·id·ly** *He was moving rapidly around the room.* ◆ **ra·pid·ity** *The water rushed through the holes with great rapidity.*   ◆◆◆◇◇   ADJ-GRADED   ADV-GRADED   N-UNCOUNT   ADJ-GRADED   ADV-GRADED: ADV with v   N-UNCOUNT

rapid-'fire. A **rapid-fire** conversation or speech is one in which people talk or reply very quickly. *...arguing a point in rapid-fire Spanish.*   ADJ: ADJ n

rap·ids /'ræpɪdz/. **Rapids** are a section of a river where the water moves very fast, often over rocks.   ◆◇◇◇◇   N-PLURAL

rapid 'transit. A **rapid transit** system is a transport system in a city which allows people to travel quickly, using trains that run underground or above the streets.   ADJ: ADJ n

ra·pi·er /'reɪpiə/ **rapiers. 1** A **rapier** is a very thin sword with a long sharp point. **2** If you say that someone has a **rapier** wit, you mean that they are very intelligent and quick at making clever comments or jokes in a conversation.   N-COUNT   ADJ: ADJ n

rap·ist /'reɪpɪst/ **rapists.** A **rapist** is a man who has raped someone.   ◆◇◇◇◇   N-COUNT

rap·per /'ræpə/ **rappers.** A **rapper** is a person who performs rap music.   ◆◇◇◇◇   N-COUNT

rap·port /ræ'pɔ:/. If two people or groups have a **rapport**, they have a good relationship in which they are able to understand each other's ideas or   ◆◇◇◇◇   N-SING: also no det

feelings very well. *The success depends on good rapport between interviewer and interviewee.*

rap·por·teur /ˌræpɔ:'tɜ:/ **rapporteurs.** A **rapporteur** is a person who is officially appointed by an organization to investigate a problem or attend a meeting and to report on it. *...UN human rights rapporteurs.*   N-COUNT   TECHNICAL

rap·proche·ment /ræ'prɒʃmɒn, AM -'prəʊʃ-/. A **rapprochement** is an increase in friendliness between two countries, groups, or people, especially after a period of unfriendliness. *...the process of political rapprochement between the two former foes.*   ◆◇◇◇◇   N-SING: also no det   JOURNALISM

rapt /ræpt/. If someone watches or listens with **rapt** attention, they are extremely interested or fascinated. *Delegates sat in rapt silence as Mrs Fisher spoke.* ◆ **rapt·ly** *...listening raptly to stories.*   ADJ-GRADED   WRITTEN   ADV

rap·tor /'ræptə/ **raptors. Raptors** are birds of prey, such as eagles and hawks.   N-COUNT   TECHNICAL

rap·ture /'ræptʃə/. **Rapture** is a feeling of extreme joy or pleasure.   N-UNCOUNT   LITERARY

rap·tures /'ræptʃəz/. If you are **in raptures** or go **into raptures** about something, you are extremely impressed by it and enthusiastic about it. *His goal sent the crowd into raptures.*   PHRASE   WRITTEN, BRITISH

rap·tur·ous /'ræptʃərəs/. A **rapturous** feeling or reaction is one of extreme happiness or enthusiasm. *...rapturous applause.* ◆ **rap·tur·ous·ly** *He was rapturously received by the American Congress.*   ADJ   JOURNALISM   ADV: ADV with v

rare /reə/ **rarer, rarest. 1** Something that is **rare** is not common and is therefore interesting or valuable. *...the black-necked crane, one of the rarest species in the world... She collects rare plants.* **2** An event or situation that is **rare** does not occur very often. *...on those rare occasions when he did eat alone... It's very rare to have big families nowadays.* **3** You use **rare** to emphasize an extremely good or remarkable quality. *It was a rare pleasure to see him in action.* **4** Meat that is **rare** is cooked very lightly so that the inside is still red. *Thick tuna steaks are eaten rare, like beef.*   ◆◆◆◇◇   ADJ-GRADED   ADJ-GRADED   ADJ: ADJ n   PRAGMATICS   ADJ-GRADED

rar·efied /'reərɪfaɪd/. **1** If you talk about the **rarefied** atmosphere of a place or institution, you are expressing your disapproval of it, because it has a special social or academic status that makes it very different from ordinary life. *They are plunged into the rarefied atmosphere of university.* **2** **Rarefied** air is air that does not contain much oxygen, for example in mountain areas.   ADJ-GRADED   PRAGMATICS   ADJ-GRADED

rare·ly /'reəli/. If something **rarely** happens, it does not happen very often. *I very rarely wear a raincoat... Rarely did anyone seem very bothered about levels of expenditure... Adolescent suicide is rarely an impulsive reaction to immediate distress.*   ◆◆◆◇◇   ADV

rar·ing /'reərɪŋ/. **1** If you say that you **are raring to go**, you mean that you are very eager to start doing something. *After a good night's sleep, Paul said he was raring to go.* **2** If you are **raring** to do something or are **raring** for it, you are very eager to do it or very eager that it should happen. *Sarah's here and raring to meet you.*   PHRASE   ADJ: v-link ADJ

rar·ity /'reərɪti/ **rarities. 1** If someone or something is a **rarity**, they are interesting or valuable because they are so unusual. *He was a rarity among Wall Street lawyers... Signatures on 18th century Irish furniture are a rarity.* **2** The **rarity** of something is the fact that it is very uncommon. *It was a real prize due to its rarity and good condition.*   ◆◇◇◇◇   N-COUNT   PRAGMATICS   JOURNALISM   N-UNCOUNT

ras·cal /'rɑːskəl, 'ræs-/ **rascals.** If you call a man or child a **rascal**, you mean that they are mischievous, rude, or dishonest. *What's that old rascal been telling you?*   N-COUNT   DATED

rash /ræʃ/ **rashes. 1** If someone is **rash** or does **rash** things, they act without thinking carefully first, and therefore make mistakes or behave foolishly. *It would be rash to rely on such evidence... Mr. Major is making no rash promises.* ◆ **rash·ly** *I made quite a lot of money, but I rashly gave most of it away.* ◆ **rash·ness** *...the rashness of youth.* **2** A **rash** is an area of red spots that appear on your skin when you   ◆◆◇◇◇   ADJ-GRADED   ADV-GRADED   N-UNCOUNT   N-COUNT

R

are ill or have an allergy. **3** A **rash of** unpleasant events or things is a large number of them which happen or appear within a short period of time. *This confusion is responsible for a rash of suicides this spring.* [N-SING: N ofn PRAGMATICS]

rash·er /ˈræʃə/ **rashers.** A **rasher** of bacon is a slice of bacon. [N-COUNT BRITISH]

rasp /rɑːsp, ræsp/ **rasps, rasping, rasped. 1** If someone **rasps**, their voice or breathing is harsh and unpleasant to listen to. *'Where've you put it?' he rasped.* ► Also a noun. *...the rasp of Rennie's voice.* **2** If something **rasps**, or if you **rasp** it on something, it makes a harsh, unpleasant sound as it rubs against something hard or rough. *Foden rasped a hand across his chin.* ► Also a noun. *...the rasp of something being drawn across the sand.* **3** A **rasp** is a long metal tool with rough surfaces, used to rub on solid objects and give them smooth surfaces. [VERB: V, V with quote; N-SING; V-ERG: V, V n prep; N-SING; N-COUNT]

rasp·berry /ˈrɑːzbri, AM ˈræzberi/ **raspberries. 1** Raspberries are small, soft, red fruit that grow on bushes. **2** If you blow a **raspberry**, you make a sound by putting your tongue out and blowing, in order to insult someone. [N-COUNT; N-COUNT BRITISH, INFORMAL]

raspy /ˈrɑːspi, ˈræs-/. If someone has a **raspy** voice, they make rough sounds as if they have a sore throat or have difficulty in breathing. *Her voice was raspy with nicotine and whiskey.* [ADJ LITERARY]

Ras·ta /ˈræstə/ **Rastas.** A **Rasta** is the same as a **Rastafarian.** ► Also an adjective. *...Rasta singer Pablo Moses.* [N-COUNT INFORMAL; ADJ]

Ras·ta·far·ian /ˌræstəˈfeəriən/ **Rastafarians. 1** A **Rastafarian** is a member of a religious group which began in Jamaica. Rastafarians consider Haile Selassie, the former Emperor of Ethiopia, to be God. **2** Rastafarian is used to describe Rastafarians and their beliefs and lifestyle. *...Rastafarian poet Benjamin Zephaniah.* [N-COUNT; ADJ: ADJ n]

rat /ræt/ **rats. 1** A **rat** is an animal which has a long tail and looks like a large mouse. **2** If you call someone a **rat**, you mean that you are angry with them or dislike them, often because they have cheated you or betrayed you. *What did you do with the gun you took from that little rat Turner?* **3** If you **smell a rat**, you begin to suspect or realize that something is wrong in a particular situation, for example that someone is trying to deceive you or harm you. *Though Lloyd George's behaviour seemed curious, Haig still did not smell a rat.* [N-COUNT; N-COUNT RUDE; PHRASE]

ra·ta /ˈrɑːtə/. See **pro rata**.

ra·ta·touille /ˌrætəˈtuːi/. **Ratatouille** is a cooked vegetable dish, usually made with onions, tomatoes, aubergines, courgettes, and peppers. [N-UNCOUNT: also a N]

ratch·et /ˈrætʃɪt/ **ratchets. 1** In a tool or machine, a **ratchet** is a wheel or bar with sloping teeth, which can move only in one direction, because a piece of metal stops the teeth from moving backwards. *The chair has a ratchet below it to adjust the height.* **2** If you describe a situation as a **ratchet**, you think that it is bad and can only become worse. *...another raising of the ratchet of violence in the conflict.* [N-COUNT; N-SING: with supp PRAGMATICS]

rate /reɪt/ **rates, rating, rated. 1** The **rate** at which something happens is the speed with which it happens. *The rate at which hair grows can be agonisingly slow.* **2** The **rate** at which something happens is the number of times it happens over a period of time. *New diet books appear at a rate of nearly one a week.* **3** A **rate** is the amount of money that is charged for goods or services. *...specially reduced rates for travellers using Gatwick Airport.* **4** The **rate** of taxation or interest is the amount of tax or interest that needs to be paid. It is expressed as a percentage of the amount that is earned, gained as profit, or borrowed. **5** In Britain, the **rates** were a local tax which you paid if you owned property or rented unfurnished property. **6** If you **rate** someone or something as good or bad, you consider them to be good or bad. *The film was rated excellent by 90 per cent of children... Most rated it a hit... We rate him as one of the best.* **7** If you **rate** someone or something, you think that they are good. [N-COUNT: with supp; N-COUNT: with supp; N-COUNT: with supp; N-COUNT: with supp; N-PLURAL; V-ERG: no cont V n adj/adv V n n; V n asn/adj VERB V n]

It's flattering to know that other clubs have shown interest and seem to rate me. **8** If someone or something **is rated** at a particular position or rank, they are calculated or estimated to be at that position in a table or list. *He is generally rated Italy's No. 3 industrialist.* **9** If you say that someone or something **rates** a particular reaction, you mean that is the reaction you consider to be appropriate. *This is so extraordinary, it rates a medal.* [INFORMAL V-PASSIVE: no cont be V-ed n; VB: no cont V n]

10 You use **at any rate** to indicate that what you have just said might be incorrect or unclear in some way, and that you are now being more precise. *He is the least appealing character, to me at any rate.* **11** You use **at any rate** to indicate that the important thing is what you are saying now, and not what was said before. *Well, at any rate, let me thank you for all you did.* **12** If you say that **at this rate** something bad or extreme will happen, you mean that it will happen if things continue to develop as they have been doing. *At this rate they'd be lucky to get home before eight.* **13** See also **exchange rate, rating**. [PHRASE PRAGMATICS; PHRASE PRAGMATICS; PHRASE PRAGMATICS]

rate·able value /ˌreɪtəbəl ˈvæljuː/ **rateable values.** In Britain, the **rateable value** of a building was a value based on its size and facilities, which was used in calculating local taxes called rates. [N-COUNT]

'rate-cap, rate-caps, rate-capping, rate-capped. 1 In Britain, when a local council **was rate-capped**, the government prevented it from increasing local taxes called rates, in order to force the council to reduce its spending or improve its efficiency. ♦ **rate-capping** *The project is seriously threatened by rate-capping.* **2** In America, a **rate cap** is a limit placed by the government on the amount of interest that banks or credit card companies can charge their customers. [VERB: be V-ed; N-UNCOUNT; N-COUNT]

,rate of ex'change, rates of exchange. A **rate of exchange** is the same as an **exchange rate**. [N-COUNT]

rate·payer /ˈreɪtpeɪə/ **ratepayers. 1** In Britain, a **ratepayer** is a person who owns or rents property and therefore has to pay local taxes. **2** In the United States, a **ratepayer** is a person whose property is served by an electricity, water, or telephone company, and who pays for these services. [N-COUNT; N-COUNT]

ra·ther /ˈrɑːðə, ˈræð-/. **1** You use **rather than** when you are contrasting two things or situations. **Rather than** introduces the thing or situation that is not the case or that you do not want or approve of. *The problem was psychological rather than physiological... When I'm going out in the evening I use the bike if I can rather than the car.* ► Also a conjunction. *She made students think for themselves, rather than telling them what to think.* **2** You use **rather** when you are correcting the thing that you have just said, especially when you are describing the true situation after saying what it is not. *Twenty million years ago, Idaho was not the arid place it is now. Rather, it was warm and damp, populated by dense primordial forest.* **3** If you **would rather** do something, you would prefer to do it. If you **would rather not** do something, you do not want to do it. *Kids would rather play than study... Sorry. I'd rather not talk about it.* **4** You use **rather** to indicate that something is true to a fairly great extent. *I grew up in rather unusual circumstances... The reality is rather more complex.* **5** You use **rather** before verbs that introduce your thoughts and feelings, in order to express your opinion politely, especially when a different opinion has been expressed. *I rather think he was telling the truth... I rather like the decorative effect.* **6** People sometimes say **rather** to express agreement or acceptance. *'Well, he did have a sort of family connection with it, didn't he.'—'Oh yes. Rather.'* [PHR-PREP; PHR-CONJ; ADV: ADV with cl/ group PRAGMATICS; PHR-MODAL; ADV; ADV: ADV before v PRAGMATICS BRITISH; CONVENTION BRITISH, FORMAL]

rati·fi·ca·tion /ˌrætɪfɪˈkeɪʃən/ **ratifications.** The **ratification** of a treaty or written agreement is the process of ratifying it. *...the ratification of the Maastricht Treaty.* [N-COUNT]

rati·fy /ˈrætɪfaɪ/ **ratifies, ratifying, ratified.** When national leaders or organizations **ratify** a treaty or written agreement, they make it official by [VERB V n]

giving their formal approval to it, usually by signing it or voting for it. *The parliaments of Australia and Indonesia have yet to ratify the treaty.*

rat·ing /ˈreɪtɪŋ/ **ratings. 1** A **rating** of something is a score or assessment of how good or popular it is. *...a value-for-money rating of ten out of ten.* ● See also **credit rating. 2** The **ratings** are the statistics published each week which show how popular each television programme is. *CBS's ratings again showed huge improvement over the previous year.* **3 Ratings** are the sailors in national navies who are not officers or who have no rank.
◆◆◆◇◇ N-COUNT
N-PLURAL
N-COUNT BRITISH

ra·tio /ˈreɪʃɪəʊ, AM -ʃəʊ/ **ratios.** The **ratio** of something is the relationship between two things expressed in numbers or amounts, to show how much greater one is than the other. *The adult to child ratio is 1 to 6.*
◆◆◇◇◇ N-COUNT

ra·tion /ˈræʃən/ **rations, rationing, rationed. 1** When there is a shortage of something, your **ration** of it is the amount that you are allowed to have. *The meat ration was down to one pound per person per week.* **2** When something **is rationed** by a person or government, you are only allowed to have a limited amount of it, usually because there is a shortage. *The decision to ration food comes as Muscovites will have overrun bakeries... Motorists will be rationed to thirty litres of petrol a month.* **3 Rations** are the food which is given to people with food shortages or to soldiers. **4** See also **rationing.**
◆◇◇◇◇ N-COUNT
VERB: be V-ed V n be V-ed to amount
N-PLURAL

ra·tion·al /ˈræʃənəl/ **1 Rational** decisions and thoughts are based on reason rather than on emotion. *Look at both sides of the case and come to a rational decision.* ◆ **ra·tion·al·ly** *It can be very hard to think rationally when you're feeling so vulnerable.* ◆ **ra·tion·al·ity** /ˌræʃəˈnælɪti/. *We live in an era of rationality.* **2** A **rational** person is someone who thinks clearly and is not emotionally or mentally unbalanced. *Rachel looked calmer and more rational now.*
◆◆◇◇◇ ADJ-GRADED
ADV-GRADED
N-UNCOUNT
ADJ-GRADED

ra·tion·ale /ˌræʃəˈnɑːl, -ˈnæl/ **rationales.** The **rationale** for a course of action, practice, or belief is the set of reasons on which it is based. *Wilson explained his rationale for refusing Sims' request.*
◆◇◇◇◇ N-COUNT FORMAL

ra·tion·al·ism /ˈræʃənəlɪzəm/. **Rationalism** is the belief that your life should be based on reason and logic, rather than emotions or religious beliefs.
N-UNCOUNT

ra·tion·al·ist /ˈræʃənəlɪst/ **rationalists.** If you describe someone as **rationalist,** you mean that their beliefs are based on reason and logic rather than emotion or religion. ▶ A **rationalist** is someone who bases their life on rationalist beliefs.
ADJ
N-COUNT

ra·tion·al·ize /ˈræʃənəlaɪz/ **rationalizes, rationalizing, rationalized;** also spelled **rationalise** in British English. **1** If you try to **rationalize** attitudes or actions that are difficult to accept, you think of reasons to justify them or to explain them. *I poured all my thoughts out on paper in an attempt to rationalize my feelings.* ◆ **ra·tion·ali·za·tion** /ˌræʃənəlaɪˈzeɪʃən/ **rationalizations** *...this rationalization of his bedside grief.* **2** When a company, system, or industry **is rationalized,** it is made more efficient, usually by getting rid of staff and equipment that are not essential. ◆ **rationalization** *...the rationalization of the textile industry.*
◆◇◇◇◇ VERB V n
N-VAR
VERB: be V-ed
N-UNCOUNT

ra·tion·ing /ˈræʃənɪŋ/. **Rationing** is the system of limiting the amount of food or other necessary substances that each person is permitted to have or buy when there is a shortage of them.
◆◇◇◇◇ N-UNCOUNT

'rat race. If you talk about getting out of **the rat race,** you mean leaving a job or way of life in which people compete aggressively with each other to be successful.
N-SING the N

rat·tan /ræˈtæn/. **Rattan** furniture is made from the woven strips of stems of a plant which grows in South East Asia.
N-UNCOUNT

rat·tle /ˈrætəl/ **rattles, rattling, rattled. 1** When something **rattles** or when you **rattle** it, it makes short sharp knocking sounds because it is being shaken or it keeps hitting against something hard. *He gently rattled the cage... Somewhere close at hand*
◆◆◇◇◇ V-ERG: V V n V adv

a train rattled by. ▶ Also a noun. *There was a rattle of rifle-fire.* ◆ **rat·tling** *At that moment, there was a rattling at the door.* **2** A **rattle** is a baby's toy with loose bits inside which make a noise when the baby shakes it. **3** If something or someone **rattles** you, they make you nervous. *The news from Body Shop rattled the rest of the retail sector.* ◆ **rat·tled** *He swore in Spanish, another indication that he was rattled.*
N-COUNT
N-SING
N-COUNT
VERB V n
ADJ-GRADED

rattle around. If you say that someone **rattles around** in a room or other space, you mean that the space is too large for them. *We don't want to move, but we're rattling around in our large house.*
PHRASAL VB V P in Also V P n

rattle off. If you **rattle off** something, you say it or do it very quickly and without much effort. *Asked what English he knew, Mr Semko rattled off 'One, two, three'.*
PHRASAL VB V P noun Also V n P

rattle on. When you say that someone **rattles on** about something, you mean that they talk about it for a long time in a way that annoys you. *I heard my mother rattling on and on about the day I get married.*
PHRASAL VB V P about n Also V P

rattle through. If you **rattle through** something, you deal with it quickly in order to finish it. *She rattled through a translation from Virgil's Aeneid.*
PHRASAL VB V P n BRITISH

rattle·snake /ˈrætəlsneɪk/ **rattlesnakes.** A **rattlesnake** is a poisonous American snake which can make a rattling noise with its tail.
N-COUNT

ˌrattling 'good. If you describe a story as a **rattling** yarn or tale, you mean that it is very good and very exciting. *He tells a rattling good yarn.*
ADJ: ADJ n BRITISH, DATED

rat·ty /ˈræti/ **rattier, rattiest. 1** If someone is **ratty,** they get angry and irritated easily. *I was beginning to get a bit ratty and fed up.* **2 Ratty** clothes and objects are frayed or tattered, especially because they are old.
ADJ-GRADED BRITISH, INFORMAL
ADJ-GRADED AMERICAN

rau·cous /ˈrɔːkəs/. A **raucous** sound is loud, harsh, and rather unpleasant. *...the raucous cries of the sea-birds. ...a raucous crowd.* ◆ **rau·cous·ly** *They laughed together raucously.*
◆◇◇◇◇ ADJ-GRADED [PRAGMATICS]
ADV-GRADED

raun·chy /ˈrɔːntʃi/ **raunchier, raunchiest.** If you describe a film, a person, or the way that someone is dressed as **raunchy,** you mean that they are sexually exciting or sexually explicit. *...her raunchy new movie.*
◆◇◇◇◇ ADJ-GRADED INFORMAL

rav·age /ˈrævɪdʒ/ **ravages, ravaging, ravaged.** A town, country, or economy that **has been ravaged** has been damaged so much that it is almost completely destroyed. *For two decades the country has been ravaged by civil war.*
◆◇◇◇◇ VB: usu passive be V-ed

rav·ages /ˈrævɪdʒɪz/. The **ravages** of time, war, or the weather are the damaging effects that they have. *...a hi-tech grass pitch that can survive the ravages of a cold, wet climate.*
N-PLURAL

rave /reɪv/ **raves, raving, raved. 1** If someone **raves,** they talk in an excited and uncontrolled way. *'What is wrong with you, acting like that,' she raved.* **2** If you **rave** about something, you speak or write about it with great enthusiasm. *Rachel raved about the new foods she ate while she was there.* **3** A **rave** is a large event at which young people dance to loud music in a warehouse or in the open air. ▶ Also an adjective. *...the rave scene.* **4** A **rave** is the same as a **rave review.** *'Only the Truth is Funny', has drawn raves from the critics.* **5** See also **raving.** ● to **rant and rave:** see **rant.**
◆◆◇◇◇ VERB: V V with quote
VERB V about n
N-COUNT
ADJ: ADJ n
N-COUNT INFORMAL

ra·ven /ˈreɪvən/ **ravens. 1** A **raven** is a large bird with shiny black feathers and a deep harsh call. **2 Raven** hair is black, shiny, and smooth. *...a striking woman with long raven hair.*
◆◇◇◇◇ N-COUNT
ADJ WRITTEN

rav·en·ous /ˈrævənəs/. If you are **ravenous,** you are extremely hungry. *...a pack of ravenous animals.* ◆ **rav·en·ous·ly** *She began to eat ravenously.*
ADJ
ADV

rav·er /ˈreɪvə/ **ravers.** A **raver** is a young person who has a busy social life and goes to a lot of parties, raves, or nightclubs.
N-COUNT INFORMAL

ˌrave re'view, rave reviews. When journalists write **rave reviews,** they praise something such as a play or book in a very enthusiastic way.
N-COUNT

ra·vine /rəˈviːn/ **ravines.** A **ravine** is a very deep narrow valley with steep sides.
◆◇◇◇◇ N-COUNT

R

rav·ing /ˈreɪvɪŋ/. **1** You use **raving** to describe someone who you think is completely mad. *Malcolm looked at her as if she were a raving lunatic.* ▶ Also an adverb. *Jean-Paul has gone raving mad.* **2** See also **rave**. [ADJ INFORMAL] [ADV: ADV adj]

rav·ings /ˈreɪvɪŋz/. If you describe what someone says or writes as their **ravings**, you mean that it makes no sense because they are mad or very ill. *...the lunatic ravings of a mad politician.* [N-PLURAL]

ra·vio·li /ˌrævɪˈəʊli/ **raviolis**. Ravioli is a type of pasta which is shaped like very small pillows and usually filled with minced meat or cheese. [N-VAR]

rav·ish /ˈrævɪʃ/ **ravishes, ravishing, ravished.** If a woman **is ravished** by a man, she is raped by him. [VERB: be V-ed LITERARY]

rav·ish·ing /ˈrævɪʃɪŋ/. If you describe someone or something as **ravishing**, you mean that they are very beautiful. *...the ravishing scenery of Cumbria and Yorkshire.* ♦ **rav·ish·ing·ly** *The Beaujolais hills are ravishingly pretty.* [ADJ-GRADED LITERARY] [ADV-GRADED: ADV adj]

raw /rɔː/ **rawer, rawest. 1** Raw materials or substances are in their natural state before being processed or used in manufacturing. *...two ships carrying raw sugar from Cuba.* **2** Raw food is food that is eaten uncooked, that has not been cooked, or that has not been cooked enough. *...a popular dish made of raw fish.* **3** Raw data is facts or information that has not yet been sorted, analysed, or prepared for presentation. **4** Raw sewage is sewage that has been disposed of without being treated. **5** If a part of your body is **raw**, it is red and painful, perhaps because the skin has come off or has been burnt. *Her hands were rubbed raw from unaccustomed work.* **6** Raw emotions are strong basic feelings or responses to something. *...the raw passions of nationalism.* ♦ **raw·ness** *The rawness of his greed was frank and uninhibited.* **7** If you describe someone in a new job as **raw**, or as a **raw** recruit, you mean that they lack experience in that job. *Davies is still raw but his potential shows.* **8** If you say that you are getting **a raw deal**, you mean that you are being treated unfairly. *I think women have a raw deal.* **9** You use **in the raw** to describe something in its true unsophisticated state. *He also wanted to see Bangladesh in the raw.* **10** ● to **touch a raw nerve**; see **nerve**. [ADJ] [ADJ] [ADJ] [ADJ: ADJ n] [ADJ-GRADED] [ADJ-GRADED] [N-SING] [ADJ-GRADED] [PHRASE INFORMAL] [PHRASE]

raw·hide /ˈrɔːhaɪd/. **Rawhide** is stiff untreated leather from cows or buffaloes. [N-UNCOUNT]

ray /reɪ/ **rays. 1** Rays of light are narrow beams of light. *...the first rays of light spread over the horizon.* **2** A **ray** of hope, comfort, or other positive quality is a small amount of it that you welcome because it makes a bad situation seem less bad. *The one ray of sunlight in this depressing history is her meeting and falling in love with Martin.* **3** A **ray** is a large sea fish which has a flat body, eyes on the top of its body, and a long tail. **4** See also **cosmic rays, gamma rays, X-ray.** [N-COUNT] [N-COUNT: N of n] [N-COUNT]

ray·on /ˈreɪɒn/. **Rayon** is a smooth man-made fabric that is made from cellulose. [N-UNCOUNT]

raze /reɪz/ **razes, razing, razed.** If buildings, villages or towns are **razed**, or are **razed** to the ground, they are completely destroyed. *Towns such as Mittelwihr and Bennwihr were virtually razed to the ground.* [VERB: be V-ed / be V-ed to n]

ra·zor /ˈreɪzə/ **razors.** A razor is a tool that people use for shaving. [N-COUNT]

'razor blade, razor blades. A razor blade is a small flat piece of metal with a very sharp edge that is put into a razor and used for shaving. [N-COUNT]

,razor-'sharp. 1 A cutting tool that is **razor-sharp** is extremely sharp. *...a razor sharp butcher's knife.* **2** If you describe someone or their mind as **razor-sharp**, you mean that they have a very precise and clear understanding of things. *...his razor-sharp intelligence.* [ADJ] [ADJ]

'razor wire. Razor wire is strong wire with sharp blades sticking out of it. In wars or civil conflict it is sometimes used to prevent people from entering or leaving buildings or areas of land. [N-UNCOUNT]

razz·a·ma·tazz /ˌræzəməˈtæz/. **Razzamatazz** is the same as **razzmatazz**. [N-UNCOUNT]

razzle-dazzle /ˌræzəl ˈdæzəl/. **Razzle-dazzle** is the same as **razzmatazz**. *...a razzle-dazzle marketing man.* [N-UNCOUNT]

razz·ma·tazz /ˌræzməˈtæz/. **Razzmatazz** is a noisy and showy display. *...the colour and razzmatazz of a US election.* [N-UNCOUNT]

RC /ˌɑː ˈsiː/. **RC** is an abbreviation for **Roman Catholic**. *...St Mary's RC Cathedral.* [ADJ]

Rd. **Rd** is a written abbreviation for 'road'. It is used especially in addresses and on maps or signs. *St Pancras Library, 100 Euston Rd, London, NW1.*

re /riː/. You use **re** in business letters, faxes, or memos to introduce a subject or item which you are going to refer to in detail. *Dear Mrs Cox, Re: Household Insurance. We note from our files that we have not yet received your renewal instructions.*

re-. Usually pronounced /ˈriː-/ for meaning 1, and before an unstressed syllable for meanings 2 and 3. Otherwise the pronunciation is /rɪ-/ before a vowel sound and /rɪ-/ before a consonant sound. **1** Re- is added to verbs and nouns to form new verbs and nouns that refer to the repeating of an action or process. For example, to 're-read' something means to read it again. **2** Re- is added to verbs and nouns to form new verbs and nouns that refer to a process opposite to one that has already taken place. For example, to 'reappear' means to appear after disappearing. **3** Re- is added to verbs and nouns to form new verbs and nouns which describe a change in the position or state of something. For example, to 'relocate' something means to locate it in a different place. [PREFIX] [PREFIX] [PREFIX]

R.E. /ˌɑː ˈiː/. **R.E.** is a school subject in which children learn about religion and other social matters. R.E. is an abbreviation for 'religious education'. [N-UNCOUNT BRITISH]

-'re /ə/. **-'re** is a shortened form of 'are'. It is added to the end of the pronoun or noun which is the subject of the verb. *We're not, are we?... What're you going to do with all that money?* [SPOKEN, INFORMAL WRITTEN]

reach /riːtʃ/ **reaches, reaching, reached. 1** When someone or something **reaches** a place, they arrive there. *He did not stop until he reached the door.* **2** If someone or something has **reached** a certain stage, level, or amount, they are at that stage, level, or amount. *We're told the figure could reach 100,000 next year.* **3** If something **reaches** a place, point, or level, it extends as far as that place, point, or level. *...a nightshirt which reached to his knees.* **4** When people **reach** an agreement, compromise, or settlement, they succeed in achieving it. *They are meeting in Lusaka in an attempt to reach a compromise.* **5** If you **reach** somewhere, you move your arm and hand to take or touch something. *Judy reached into her handbag.* **6** If you can **reach** something, you are able to touch it by stretching out your arm or leg. *Can you reach your toes with your fingertips?* **7** The **reach** of something or someone is the distance or limit to which they can stretch, extend, or travel. *Isabelle placed a wine cup on the table within his reach.* **8** If you try to **reach** someone, you try to contact them, usually by telephone. *Has the doctor told you how to reach him or her in emergencies?* **9** If a place or thing is within **reach**, it is possible to have it or get to it because of its position or price. If it is beyond your **reach** or out of **reach**, you are not able to have it or get to it. [VERB V n] [VERB V n] [VERB: V n / V to n] [VERB V n] [VERB V prep/adv] [VERB V n] [N-UNCOUNT] [VERB V n] [N-UNCOUNT]

reaches /ˈriːtʃɪz/. **1** The upper, middle, or lower **reaches** of a river are parts of a river. The upper **reaches** are nearer to the river's source and the lower **reaches** are nearer to the sea. **2** You can refer to the distant or outer parts of a place or area as the far, farthest, or outer **reaches**. *...the outer reaches of the solar system.* **3** You can refer to the higher or lower levels of an organization as its upper or lower **reaches**. *...the upper reaches of the legal profession.* [N-PLURAL] [N-PLURAL FORMAL] [N-PLURAL FORMAL]

re·act /riˈækt/ **reacts, reacting, reacted. 1** When you **react** to something that has happened [VERB: V to n]

to you, you behave in a particular way because of it. *It's natural to react with disbelief if your child is accused of bullying.* **2** If you **react against** someone's way of behaving, you deliberately behave in a different way because you do not like the way they behave. *My father never saved and perhaps I reacted against that.* **3** If you **react** to a treatment or substance, you are affected unpleasantly or made ill by it. *He reacted very badly to the radiation therapy.* ♦ **re·ac·tion, reactions** *Every year, 5000 people have life-threatening reactions to anaesthetics.* **4** When one chemical substance **reacts** with another, or when two chemical substances **react**, they combine chemically to form another substance. *These two gases react readily to produce carbon dioxide and water.* ♦ **re·ac·tion** *Ozone is produced by the reaction between oxygen and ultra-violet light.*
V adv/prep Also V
VERB V against n
VERB V to n Also V
N-COUNT
V-RECIP: V with n pl-n V
N-COUNT

re·ac·tion /ri'ækʃən/ **reactions. 1** Your **reaction** to something that has happened or something that you have experienced is what you feel, say, or do because of it. *Reaction to the visit is mixed... He was surprised that his answer should have caused such a strong reaction.* **2** A **reaction against** something is a way of behaving or doing something that is deliberately different from what has been done before. *All new fashion starts out as a reaction against existing convention.* **3** If there is a **reaction against** something, it becomes unpopular. *...a strong reaction against socialism.* **4** Your **reactions** are your ability to move quickly in response to something. *The sport requires very fast reactions.* **5** Reaction is the belief that the political or social system of your country should not change; used showing disapproval. *...their victory against the forces of reaction and censorship.*
♦♦♦♦♢ N-VAR
N-COUNT: N against n
N-SING: also n o det, N against n
N-PLURAL
N-UNCOUNT

re·ac·tion·ary /ri'ækʃnri, AM -neri/ **reaction·aries.** A **reactionary** person or group tries to prevent changes in the political or social system of their country; used showing disapproval. *The Minister was too reactionary, too blinkered.* ▶ A **reactionary** is someone with reactionary views.
♦♢♢♢♢ ADJ-GRADED PRAGMATICS
N-COUNT

re·ac·ti·vate /ri'æktɪveɪt/ **reactivates, reactivating, reactivated.** If people **reactivate** a system or organization, they make it work again after a period in which it has not been working. *It was also finally agreed to reactivate two joint committees on negotiations.*
VERB V n

re·ac·tive /ri'æktɪv/. **1** Something that is **reactive** is able to react chemically with a lot of different substances. *Ozone is a highly reactive form of oxygen gas.* **2** If someone is **reactive**, they behave in response to what happens to them, rather than deciding in advance how they want to behave. *I want our organization to be less reactive and more proactive.*
♦♢♢♢♢ ADJ-GRADED
ADJ-GRADED

re·ac·tor /ri'æktə/ **reactors.** A **reactor** is the same as a **nuclear reactor**.
♦♦♢♢♢ N-COUNT

read, reads, reading. The form **read** is pronounced /riːd/ when it is the present tense of the verb and when it is the noun, and /red/ when it is the past tense and past participle of the verb. **1** When you **read** something such as a book or article, you look at and understand the words that are written there. *I read about it in the paper... He read through the pages slowly and carefully.* ▶ Also a noun. *I settled down to have a good read.* **2** When you **read** a piece of writing to someone, you say the words aloud. *Jay reads poetry so beautifully... I like it when she reads to us... I sing to the boys or read them a story before tucking them in.* **3** People who can **read** have the ability to look at and understand written words. *He could read words at 18 months.* **4** If you can **read** music, you have the ability to look at and understand the symbols that are used in written music to represent musical sounds. **5** You can use **read** when saying what is written on something. For example, if a notice **reads** 'Exit', the word 'Exit' is written on it. **6** If you refer to how a piece of writing **reads**, you are referring to its style. *It reads very awkwardly.* **7** If you say that a book or magazine is a good **read**, you mean that it is very enjoyable to
VERB: V n V about n V through n Also V n V that N-SING: a N VERB: V n V n to n V n to n V n n VERB: V V n VB: no cont: V with quote VERB V prep/adv N-COUNT: adj N

read. **8** If something **is read** in a particular way, it is understood or interpreted in that way. *The play is being widely read as an allegory of imperialist conquest... Now how do you read his remarks on that subject?* **9** If you **read** someone's mind or thoughts, you know exactly what they are thinking without them telling you. **10** If you can **read** someone or you can **read** their gestures, you can understand what they are thinking or feeling by the way they behave or the things they say. **11** When you **read** a measuring device, you look at it to see what the figure or measurement on it is. *It is essential that you are able to read a thermometer.* **12** If a measuring device **reads** a particular amount, it shows that amount. *The fuel gauge reads below zero.* **13** If you **read** a subject at university, you study it. *He is now reading for a maths degree at Surrey University.* **14** See also **reading**. ● to **read between the lines:** see **line.**
VERB beV-ed as n V n adv/prep
VERB: V n
VERB: V n
VERB V n
VERB V amount
VERB: V n V for n BRITISH, FORMAL

read into. If you **read** a meaning **into** something, you think it is there although it may not actually be there. *It would be wrong to try to read too much into such a light-hearted production.*
PHRASAL VB V n P n V amount P n Also V P n n

read out. If you **read out** a piece of writing, you say it aloud. *Shall I read them out?*
PHRASAL VB V P noun V n P

read up on. If you **read up on** a subject, you read a lot about it so that you become informed about it.
PHRASAL VB V P P n

read·able /'riːdəbəl/. If you say that a book or article is **readable**, you mean that it is enjoyable and easy to read. *This is an impeccably researched and very readable book.*
♦♢♢♢♢ ADJ-GRADED

read·er /'riːdə/ **readers. 1** The **readers** of a newspaper, magazine, or book are the people who read it. **2** A **reader** is a person who reads, especially one who reads for pleasure. *Their books are loved by young readers the world over.* **3** A **reader** is a person who reads books for a publisher in order to give an opinion on whether they should be published or not. **4** In Britain, a **reader** is a senior lecturer at a university, with a rank just below that of a professor. **5** A **reader** is a book of simplified literature, selected passages, and exercises used for teaching at school.
♦♦♦♢ N-COUNT
N-COUNT
N-COUNT
N-COUNT
N-COUNT

read·er·ship /'riːdəʃɪp/ **readerships. 1** The **readership** of a book, newspaper, or magazine is the number or type of people who read it. *A new format would alienate its ageing readership.* **2** In Britain, a **readership** is the post of a reader at a university.
♦♢♢♢♢ N-COUNT
N-COUNT

read·ily /'redɪli/. **1** If you do something **readily**, you do it willingly and eagerly. *When I was invited to the party, I readily accepted.* **2** You use **readily** to say that something can be done or obtained quickly and easily. *I don't readily make friends.*
♦♦♢♢♢ ADV-GRADED: ADV with v ADV-GRADED

readi·ness /'redɪnəs/. **1** Your **readiness** to do something is your willingness or eagerness to do it. *...his apparent readiness to improve relations with the West.* **2** Readiness is the state of being prepared for something. *A bowl of water lies in readiness for the dogs.* ● If you do something **in readiness** for a particular event, you do it so that you will be prepared for that event. *A considerable time was occupied in refuelling and inspection in readiness for an early start on the following morning.*
♦♢♢♢♢ N-UNCOUNT: N to-inf
N-UNCOUNT
PHRASE

read·ing /'riːdɪŋ/ **readings. 1** Reading is the activity of reading books. *I have always loved reading.* **2** A **reading** is an event at which poetry or extracts from books are read to an audience. *This year's event consisted of readings, lectures and workshops.* **3** Your **reading** of a word, text, or situation is the way in which you understand or interpret it. *Local public housing authorities disagree with this reading of the law.* **4** The **reading** on a measuring device is the figure or measurement that it shows. **5** In the British Parliament or the US Congress, a **reading** is one of the three stages of presentation and discussion of a new bill before it can be passed as law. *The bill is expected to pass its second reading with a comfortable majority.* **6** If you say that a book or an article **makes** interesting **reading** or **makes for** interesting **reading**, you mean that it is interesting to read.
♦♦♦♢ N-UNCOUNT
N-COUNT
N-COUNT: with supp
N-COUNT
N-COUNT
PHRASE

R

'reading glasses. Reading glasses are spectacles that are worn by people who cannot see things close to them very well, when they want to see properly, for example when they are reading. *N-PLURAL: also a pair of N*

'reading list, reading lists. A reading list is a list of books that students are encouraged to read for a particular course of study. *Salter supplied us with reading lists on our subject.* *N-COUNT*

'reading room, reading rooms. A reading room is a quiet room in a library or museum where you can read and study. *N-COUNT*

re·ad·just /ˌriːəˈdʒʌst/ **readjusts, readjusting, readjusted. 1** When you **readjust** to a new situation, usually one you have been in before, you adapt to it. *They are bound to take time to readjust after a holiday.* ♦ **re·ad·just·ment** The next few weeks will be a period of re-adjustment. **2** If you **readjust** the way you do something, your attitude to something, or the level of something, you change it so that it is more effective or appropriate. *The rebel army has readjusted its strategy.* ♦ **re·ad·just·ment** The organization denies that it is seeking any readjustment of state borders. **3** If you **readjust** something such as a piece of clothing or a mechanical device, you correct or alter its position or setting. *Readjust your watch. You are now on Moscow time.* *VERB: V to n V* / *N-VAR* / *VERB V n* / *N-VAR* / *VERB V n*

read·out /ˈriːdaʊt/ **readouts.** If an electronic measuring device gives you a **readout**, it displays information about the level of something such as a speed, height, or sound. *...a digital readout of the vehicle's speed.* *N-COUNT*

ready /ˈredi/ **readier, readiest; readies, readying, readied. 1** If someone is **ready**, they are properly prepared for something. If something is **ready**, it has been properly prepared and is now able to be used. *It took her a long time to get ready for church... Are you ready to board, Mr. Daly?... Your breakfast's ready.* **2** If you are **ready** for something or **ready** to do something, you have enough experience to do it or you are old enough and sensible enough to do it. *She says she's not ready for marriage.* **3** If you are **ready** to do something, you are willing to do it. *She was always ready to give interviews.* **4** If you are **ready for** something, you need it or want it. *After five days in the heat of Bangkok, we were ready for the beach.* **5** If someone or something is **ready** to do something, they are about to do it or likely to do it. *He says it's like a volcano ready to erupt.* *ADJ: v-link ADJ / ADJ: v-link ADJ / ADJ-GRADED: v-link ADJ to-inf / ADJ: v-link ADJ for n / ADJ: v-link ADJ to-inf*

6 You use **ready** to describe things that are able to be used very quickly and easily. *...a ready supply of well-trained and well-motivated workers.* **7 Ready** money is in the form of notes and coins rather than cheques or credit cards. *ADJ-GRADED: ADJ n / ADJ: ADJ n*

8 When you **ready** something, you prepare it for a particular purpose. *John's soldiers were readying themselves for the final assault.* **9** **ready** combines with past participles to indicate that something has already been done, and that therefore you do not have to do it yourself. *...ready-printed forms.* **10** If you have something **at the ready**, you have it in a position where it can be quickly and easily used. *Soldiers came charging through the forest, guns at the ready.* **11** If you want to emphasize that someone is properly prepared for something, or that something is now able to be used, you can say that they are **ready and waiting**. *VERB: V n V n form FORMAL COMB / PHRASE / PHRASE PRAGMATICS*

ready-'made. 1 If something that you buy is **ready-made**, you can use it immediately, because the work you would normally have to do has been done by the producer of the product. *You can buy it ready-made at Chinese groceries... The ready-made bedcovers cost from £200.* **2 Ready-made** means extremely convenient or useful for a particular purpose. *It provides perfect strangers with a ready-made and infinitely adaptable topic of conversation.* *♦◇◇◇◇ ADJ / ADJ*

ready-to-'wear. **Ready-to-wear** clothes are bought ready-made from a shop and not made specially for a particular person. *ADJ: ADJ n*

re·affirm /ˌriːəˈfɜːm/ **reaffirms, reaffirming, reaffirmed.** If you **reaffirm** something, you state it again clearly and firmly. *The government has reaffirmed that it will take any steps necessary to maintain law and order.* *♦◇◇◇◇ V n V that FORMAL*

re·agent /riˈeɪdʒənt/ **reagents.** A **reagent** is a substance that is used to cause a chemical reaction. Reagents are often used in order to indicate the presence of another substance. *N-COUNT TECHNICAL*

real /rɪəl/ **1** Something that is **real** actually exists and is not imagined, invented, or theoretical. *No, it wasn't a dream. It was real... Legends grew up around a great many figures, both real and fictitious.* **2** If something is **real** to someone, they experience it as though it really exists or happens, even though it does not. *Whitechild's life becomes increasingly real to the reader.* **3** A material or object that is **real** is natural or functioning, and not artificial or an imitation. *...the smell of real leather... Who's to know if they're real guns or not?* **4** You can use **real** to describe someone or something that has all the characteristics or qualities that such a person or thing typically has. *...his first real girlfriend.* **5** You can use **real** to describe something that is the true or original thing of its kind, in contrast to one that someone wants you to believe is true. *This was the real reason for her call... Her real name had been Miriam Pinckus.* **6** You can use **real** to describe something that is the most important or typical part of a thing. *When he talks, he only gives glimpses of his real self... The smart executive has people he can trust doing all the real work.* **7** You can use **real** when you are talking about a situation or feeling to emphasize that it exists and is important or serious. *Global warming is a real problem.* *♦♦♦♦♦ ADJ / ADJ-GRADED / ADJ / ADJ: ADJ n / ADJ: ADJ n / ADJ: ADJ n / ADJ-GRADED PRAGMATICS*

8 You can use **real** to emphasize a quality that is genuine and sincere. *You've been drifting from job to job without any real commitment.* **9** You can use **real** before nouns to emphasize your description of something or someone. *It's a fabulous deal, a real bargain.* **10** The **real** cost or value of something is its cost or value after other amounts have been added or subtracted and when factors such as the level of inflation have been considered. **11** You can use **real** to emphasize an adjective or adverb. *He is finding prison life 'real tough'.* **12** If you say that someone does something **for real**, you mean that they actually do it and do not just pretend to do it. *The sex scenes were just good acting. We didn't do it for real.* **13** The cost or value of something **in real terms** is the same as its real cost. *Pensions have increased in real terms over the last twenty years.* **14** If you say that a thing or event is **the real thing**, you mean that it is the actual thing or event, and not an imitation or rehearsal. *The counterfeits sell for about $20 less than the real thing.* *ADJ-GRADED: ADJ n PRAGMATICS / ADJ: ADJ n PRAGMATICS SPOKEN / ADJ: ADJ n / ADV PRAGMATICS INFORMAL, AMERICAN PHRASE / PHRASE / PHRASE / PHRASE*

,real 'ale, real ales. **Real ale** is beer which is stored in a barrel and is pumped from it without the use of carbon dioxide. *N-VAR BRITISH*

'real estate. 1 **Real estate** is property in the form of land and buildings, rather than personal possessions. **2** **Real estate** businesses or **real estate** agents sell houses, buildings, and land. In British English, real estate agents are called **estate agents**. *♦♦◇◇◇ N-UNCOUNT AMERICAN N-UNCOUNT AMERICAN*

re·align /ˌriːəˈlaɪn/ **realigns, realigning, realigned. 1** If you **realign** your ideas, policies, or plans, you organize them in a different way in order to take account of new circumstances. *She has, almost single-handedly, realigned British politics.* ♦ **re·align·ment** /ˌriːəˈlaɪnmənt/ **realignments** *...a realignment of the existing political structure.* **2** If you **realign** objects, you move them in order to make them into a particular pattern. *He carefully realigned his silverware.* *VERB V n Also V / N-VAR / VERB V n*

re·al·ise /ˈriːəlaɪz/. See **realize.**

re·al·ism /ˈriːəlɪzəm/. **1** When people show **realism** in their behaviour, they recognize and accept the true nature of a situation and try to deal with it in a practical way; used showing approval. ♦ **re·al·ist, realists** *I see myself not as a cynic but as a* *♦◇◇◇◇ N-UNCOUNT PRAGMATICS / N-COUNT*

realist. 2 If things and people are presented with **realism** in painting, novels, or films, they are presented in a way that is like real life; used showing approval. N-UNCOUNT PRAGMATICS

re·al·ist /ˈriːəlɪst/. A **realist** painter or writer is one who represents things and people in a way that is like real life. ADJ: ADJ n

re·al·is·tic /ˌriːəˈlɪstɪk/. **1** If you are **realistic** about a situation, you recognize and accept its true nature and try to deal with it in a practical way. *It's only realistic to acknowledge that something, some time, will go wrong.* ♦ **re·al·is·ti·cal·ly** *As an adult, you can assess the situation realistically.* **2** Something such as a goal, target, or deadline that is **realistic** is one which you can sensibly expect to achieve. *Is EC membership a realistic goal for Eastern European countries?* **3** You say that a painting, story, or film is **realistic** when the people and things in it are like people and things in real life. ♦ **realistically** *The film starts off realistically and then develops into a ridiculous fantasy.* ADJ-GRADED ADV-GRADED ADJ-GRADED ADJ-GRADED ADV-GRADED

re·al·is·ti·cal·ly /ˌriːəˈlɪstɪkəli/. You use **realistically** when you want to emphasize that what you are saying is true, even though you would prefer it not to be true. *Realistically, there is never one right answer.* ● See also **realistic**. ADV: ADV with cl PRAGMATICS

re·al·ity /riˈæləti/ **realities. 1** You use **reality** to refer to real things or the real nature of things rather than imagined, invented, or theoretical ideas. *Psychiatrists become too caught up in their theories to deal adequately with reality.* ● See also **virtual reality. 2** The **reality** of a situation is the truth about it, especially when it is unpleasant or difficult to deal with. *...the harsh reality of top international competition.* **3** You say that something has become a **reality** when it actually exists or is happening. *...the whole procedure that made this book become a reality... The reality is that they are poor.* **4** You can use **in reality** to introduce a statement about the real nature of something, when it contrasts with something incorrect that has just been described. *He came across as streetwise, but in reality he was not.* N-UNCOUNT N-COUNT N-SING PHRASE

re·al·iz·able /ˌriːəˈlaɪzəbl/; also spelled **realisable** in British English. **1** If your hopes or aims are **realizable**, there is a possibility that the things that you want to happen will happen. *...the reasonless assumption that one's dreams and desires were realizable.* **2** **Realizable** wealth can be easily obtained by selling something. *...£250,000 of realisable assets.* ADJ FORMAL ADJ TECHNICAL

re·al·ize /ˈriːəlaɪz/ **realizes, realizing, realized;** also spelled **realise** in British English. **1** If you **realize** that something is true, you become aware of that fact or understand it. *People don't realize how serious this recession has actually been... Once they realised their mistake the phone was reconnected again.* ♦ **re·ali·za·tion** /ˌriːəlaɪˈzeɪʃən/ **realizations** *There is now a growing realisation that things cannot go on like this for much longer.* **2** If your hopes, desires, or fears **are realized**, the things that you hope for, desire, or fear actually happen. *All his worst fears have now been realised.* ♦ **realization** *In Kravis's venomous tone he recognized the realization of his worst fears.* **3** When someone **realizes** a design or an idea, they make or organize something based on that design or idea. *The kaleidoscopic quality of the book is brilliantly realised on stage.* **4** If someone or something **realizes** their potential, they do everything they are capable of doing. *All of us can improve ourselves and realize our full potential.* **5** If something **realizes** a particular amount of money when it is sold, that amount of money is paid for it. *A selection of correspondence from P G Wodehouse realised £1,232.* VERB: V that V wh V n Also V N-VAR VB: usu passive be V-ed N-UNCOUNT VERB: V n be V-ed FORMAL VERB V n VERB V n TECHNICAL

,real 'life. If something happens in **real life**, it actually happens and is not just in a story or in someone's imagination. *In real life men like Richard Gere don't marry street girls.* ► Also an adjective. *...a real-life horror story.* N-UNCOUNT ADJ: ADJ n

re·allo·cate /ˌriː ˈæləkeɪt/ **reallocates, reallocating, reallocated.** When organizations **reallocate** money or resources, they decide to change the VERB: V n V n to n

way they spend the money or use the resources. *The Treasury would not reallocate the funds to other transport schemes.*

re·al·ly /ˈriːəli/. **1** You can use **really** to emphasize a statement. *I'm very sorry. I really am... It really is best to manage without any medication if you possibly can... I really do feel that some people are being unfair.* **2** You can use **really** to emphasize an adjective or adverb. *It was really good... They were really nice people.* **3** You use **really** when you are discussing the real facts about something, in contrast to the ones someone wants you to believe. *My father didn't really love her... What was really going on?* **4** People use **really** in questions and negative statements when they want you to answer 'no'. *Do you really think he would be that stupid?* **5** If you say when something **really** begins to happen, you are emphasizing that it starts to happen then to a much greater extent and much more seriously than before. *That's when the pressure really started... He only really started going out with girls at college.* **6** People sometimes use the word **really** to slightly reduce the force of a negative statement. *I'm not really surprised... 'Did they hurt you?'—'Not really'.* **7** People sometimes add **really** to statements in order to make them less definite and more hesitant. *She is a quiet girl really... I'm happy most of the time, really.* **8** People use the word **really** to show they are surprised or that the speaker may be surprised about something. *Actually it was quite good really... I was really rather fond of Arthur.* **9** You can say **really** to express surprise or disbelief at what someone has said. *'We saw a very bright shooting star.'—'Did you really?'* **10** You can say '**really**' in a conversation to show that you are interested in what someone is saying. *'We had a very interesting chat.'—'Really? About what?'* **11** Some people say **really** when they are slightly annoyed or offended by something someone has said or done. *Really, Mr Riss, I expected better of you.* ADV SPOKEN ADV: ADV adj/adv SPOKEN ADV ADV: ADV before v SPOKEN ADV: ADV before v ADV: ADV after neg SPOKEN ADV: ADV with cl SPOKEN ADV: ADV with cl SPOKEN, BRITISH CONVENTION CONVENTION EXCLAM SPOKEN, BRITISH

realm /relm/ **realms. 1** You can use the word **realm** to refer to any area of activity, interest, or thought. *...the realm of politics.* **2** A **realm** is a country that has a king or queen. *Defence of the realm is crucial.* **3** If you say that something is not beyond the **realms of possibility**, or that it is **within the realms of possibility**, you mean that it is possible. N-COUNT FORMAL N-COUNT FORMAL PHRASE

,real 'property. Real property is property in the form of land and buildings, rather than personal possessions. N-UNCOUNT AMERICAN

'real time. If something is done in **real time**, there is no noticeable delay between the action and its effect or consequence. *...umpires, who have to make every decision in real time.* N-UNCOUNT

'real-time. Real-time processing is a type of computer programming or data processing in which the information received is processed by the computer almost immediately. ADJ: ADJ n

re·al·tor /ˈriːəltɔːr/ **realtors.** A **realtor** is a person whose job is to sell houses, buildings, and land. The usual British term is **estate agent**. N-COUNT AMERICAN

,real 'world. If you talk about the **real world**, you are referring to the world and life in general, in contrast to a particular person's own life, experience, and ideas. *When they eventually leave the school they will be totally ill-equipped to deal with the real world.* N-SING the N

ream /riːm/ **reams.** If you say that there are **reams** of paper or **reams** of writing, you mean that there are large amounts of it. *Their specific task is to sort through the reams of information.* N-COUNT INFORMAL

reap /riːp/ **reaps, reaping, reaped. 1** If you **reap** the benefits or the rewards of something, you enjoy the good things that happen as a result of it. *You'll soon begin to reap the benefits of being fitter.* **2** To **reap** crops means to cut them down and gather them. VERB V n VERB: V n

reap·er /ˈriːpə/ **reapers.** A **reaper** is a machine that is used to cut and gather crops. ● See also **Grim Reaper**. N-COUNT

re·appear /ˌriːəˈpɪə/ **reappears, reappearing,** ◆◇◇◇◇ **reappeared.** When people or things **reappear,** VERB they return again after they have been away or out V of sight for some time. *Thirty seconds later she re-appeared and beckoned them forward.* ♦ **re·appear·ance** /ˌriːəˈpɪərəns/ **reappearances** N-COUNT ...*the reappearance of Cossack culture in Russia.*

re·appraise /ˌriːəˈpreɪz/ **reappraises, re-** VERB **appraising, reappraised.** If you **reappraise** V n something such as an idea or a plan, you think FORMAL carefully about it and decide whether it needs to be changed. *This prompted them to reappraise their political strategy.* ♦ **re·apprais·al** /ˌriːəˈpreɪzəl/ **re-** N-VAR **appraisals** ...*a fundamental reappraisal of prison policy.*

rear /rɪə/ **rears, rearing, reared. 1** The **rear** of ◆◆◆◇◇ something such as a building or vehicle is the back N-SING: part of it. *He settled back in the rear of the taxi. ...the* theN *rear of the building.* ▶ Also an adjective. *Manufac-* ADJ: ADJ n *turers have been obliged to fit rear seat belts in all new cars.* **2** If you are at the **rear** of a queue or of a N-SING: moving line of people, you are the last person in it. theN **3** If a person or vehicle is **bringing up the rear,** they FORMAL are the last person or vehicle in a moving line of PHRASE them. **4** You can refer to someone's buttocks as N-COUNT their **rear.** INFORMAL **5** If you **rear** children, you bring them up until they VERB: V n are old enough to look after themselves. The usual beV-ed prep American word is **raise.** *I was reared in east Texas.* **6** If VERB: V n you **rear** a young animal, you keep and look after it until it is old enough to be used for work or food, or until it can look after itself. **7** When a horse **rears,** it moves the front part of its VERB: V body upwards, so that its front legs are high in the air and it is standing on its back legs. ▶ **Rear up** means PHRASAL VB the same as **rear.** ...*an army pony that didn't rear up at* V P *the sound of gunfire.* **8** If you say that something such VERB as a building or mountain **rears** above you, you mean V prep/adv that is very tall and close to you. *The mountains reared up on each side, steep and white.* **9** If something un- PHRASE pleasant **rears its head** or **rears its ugly head,** it be-gins to become apparent. *The threat of strikes reared its head again this summer.*

rear up. See **rear** 7 PHRASAL VB

'Rear Admiral, Rear Admirals. A **Rear Admiral** N-TITLE is a senior officer in the Navy.

rear·guard /ˈrɪəɡɑːd/. **1** The **rearguard** is a group N-SING: of soldiers who protect the back part of an army in theN a battle, especially when the army is retreating. **2** If PHRASE someone is **fighting a rearguard action** or **mount-ing a rearguard action,** they are trying very hard to prevent something from happening, even though it is probably too late for them to succeed.

re·arm /riːˈɑːm/ **rearms, rearming, rearmed;** V-ERG: V also spelled **re-arm.** If a country **rearms** or **is re-** V n **armed,** it starts to build up a new stock of military weapons. ...*NATO's decision to rearm West Germany.*

re·arma·ment /riːˈɑːməmənt/. **Rearmament** is N-UNCOUNT the process of building up a new stock of military weapons.

re·arrange /ˌriːəˈreɪndʒ/ **rearranges, rearrang-** ◆◇◇◇◇ **ing, rearranged. 1** If you **rearrange** things, you VERB change the way they are organized or ordered. *A* V n *waiter was rapidly rearranging tables for the big group.* ♦ **re·arrange·ment** /ˌriːəˈreɪndʒmənt/ **re-** N-VAR **arrangements** ...*a rearrangement of the job structure.* **2** If you **rearrange** a meeting or an VERB: V n appointment, you arrange for it to take place at a different time from that originally intended.

'rear-view mirror, rear-view mirrors. Inside a N-COUNT car, the **rear-view mirror** is the mirror that enables you to see the traffic behind when you are driving. See picture headed **car and bicycle.**

rear·ward /ˈrɪəwəd/. If something moves or faces ADV: **rearward,** it moves or faces backwards. ...*a rear-* ADV with v *ward facing infant carrier.* ▶ Also an adjective. ...*the* ADJ: ADJ n *rearward window.*

rea·son /ˈriːzən/ **reasons, reasoning, rea-** ◆◆◆◆◆ **soned. 1** The **reason** for something is a fact or N-COUNT situation which explains why it happens or what

causes it to happen. *Who would have a reason to want to kill her? ...the reason why Italian tomatoes have so much flavour. ...reasons of security.* **2** If you PHRASE do not know why someone did something, you can PRAGMATICS say that they did it **for reasons best known to** themselves. You usually use this expression when you do not agree with what they did. *For reasons best known to himself, Algie changed his name.* **3** If PHRASE you say that something happened or was done **for no reason, for no good reason,** or **for no reason at all,** you mean that there was no obvious reason why it happened or was done. **4** If you say that some- PHRASE thing happened or is true **for some reason,** you mean that you know it happened or is true, but you do not know why. **5** If you say that you have **reason** to believe something N-UNCOUNT or to have a particular emotion, you mean that you have evidence for your belief or there is a definite cause of your feeling. *He had every reason to be upset.* **6** The ability that people have to think and to make N-UNCOUNT sensible judgements can be referred to as **reason.** ...*a conflict between emotion and reason.* **7** If you **reason** VERB that something is true, you decide that it is true after V that thinking carefully about all the facts. *I reasoned that* Also V with changing my diet would lower my cholesterol level. quote ● See also **reasoned, reasoning. 8** If you try to make PHRASE someone **listen to reason,** you try to persuade them to listen to sensible arguments and be influenced by them. **9** If one thing happens **by reason of** another, it hap- PHRASE pens because of it. *The boss retains enormous influ-* INFORMAL ence by reason of his position. **10** If you say that someone or something is PHRASE someone's **reason for living** or their **reason for being,** you mean that it is the most important thing in their life. **11** If you say that you will do anything **within reason,** PHRASE you mean that you will do anything that is fair or rea-sonable and not too extreme. *I will take any job that comes along, within reason.* **12** ● **rhyme or reason:** see **rhyme.** ● **to see reason:** see **see.** ● **it stands to reason:** see **stand.**

reason with. If you try to **reason with** someone, PHRASAL VB you try to persuade them to do something or to accept V P n something by using sensible arguments.

rea·son·able /ˈriːzənəbəl/. **1** If you think that ◆◆◆◇◇ someone is fair and sensible you can say they are ADJ-GRADED **reasonable.** ...*a perfectly reasonable decision.* ♦ **rea-** **·son·ably** /ˈriːzənəbli/. *'I'm sorry, Andrew,' she said* ADV *reasonably.* ♦ **rea·son·able·ness** ...*the sincerity* N-UNCOUNT *and reasonableness of what he had to say.* **2** If you ADJ-GRADED say that an expectation or explanation is **reason-able,** you mean that there are good reasons why it may be correct. *It seems reasonable to expect rapid urban growth.* ♦ **reasonably** *Property owners may* ADV *not reasonably expect refunds.* **3** If you say that the ADJ-GRADED price of something is **reasonable,** you mean that it is fair and not too high. *His fees were quite reason-able.* ♦ **reasonably** ...*reasonably priced accommo-* ADV-GRADED dation. **4** You can use the word **reasonable** to ADJ-GRADED describe something that is fairly good, but not very good. *The boy answered him in reasonable French.* ♦ **reasonably** *I can dance reasonably well.* ADV-GRADED **5** A **reasonable** amount of something is a fairly large ADJ-GRADED amount of it. *They will need a reasonable amount of desk area.* ♦ **rea·son·ably** *From now on events* ADV: moved reasonably quickly. ADV adj/adv

rea·soned /ˈriːzənd/. A **reasoned** discussion or ar- ADJ-GRADED gument is based on sensible reasons, rather than on PRAGMATICS an appeal to people's emotions; used showing ap-proval. *Younger Japanese want decisions justified by reasoned argument.*

rea·son·ing /ˈriːzənɪŋ/ **reasonings. Reasoning** is ◆◇◇◇◇ the process by which you reach a conclusion after N-VAR thinking about all the facts. ...*the reasoning behind the decision.*

re·as·sem·ble /ˌriːəˈsembəl/ **reassembles, reas-** **sembling, reassembled. 1** If you **reassemble** VERB: V n something, you put it back together after it has been taken apart. **2** If a group of people **reassem-** V-ERG

bles or if you **reassemble** them, they gather together again in a group. *We shall reassemble in the car park in thirty minutes.*　V Also V n

re·as·sert /ˌriːəˈsɜːt/ **reasserts, reasserting, reasserted.** **1** If you **reassert** your control or authority, you make it clear that you are still in a position of power, or you strengthen the power that you had. *...the government's continuing effort to reassert its control.* **2** If something such as an idea or habit **reasserts** itself, it becomes noticeable again. *His sense of humour was beginning to reassert itself.*　◆◇◇◇◇ VERB V n / VERB V pron-refl

re·as·sess /ˌriːəˈses/ **reassesses, reassessing, reassessed.** If you **reassess** something, you think about it and decide whether you need to change your opinion about it. *You should reassess the situation after a month.* ♦ **re·as·sess·ment** /ˌriːəˈsesmənt/ **reassessments** *A reassessment of the UN's role is overdue.*　◆◇◇◇◇ VERB V n / N-VAR

re·assur·ance /ˌriːəˈʃʊərəns/ **reassurances.** **1** If someone needs **reassurance**, they are very worried about something and need someone to help them stop worrying by saying kind or helpful things. *She needed reassurance that she belonged somewhere.* **2** **Reassurances** are things that you say to help people stop worrying about something.　◆◇◇◇◇ N-UNCOUNT / N-COUNT

re·assure /ˌriːəˈʃʊə/ **reassures, reassuring, reassured.** If you **reassure** someone, you say or do things to make them stop worrying about something. *She just reassured me that everything was fine.*　◆◆◇◇◇ VERB: V n / V n that / Also V n about

re·assured /ˌriːəˈʃʊəd/. If you feel **reassured**, you feel less worried about something. *I feel much more reassured when I've been for a health check.*　◆◇◇◇◇ ADJ-GRADED

re·assur·ing /ˌriːəˈʃʊərɪŋ/. If you find someone's words or actions **reassuring**, they make you feel less worried about something. *It was reassuring to hear John's familiar voice.* ♦ **re·assur·ing·ly** *'It's okay now,' he said reassuringly.*　◆◇◇◇◇ ADJ-GRADED / ADV-GRADED

re·awak·en /ˌriːəˈweɪkən/ **reawakens, reawakening, reawakened.** If something **reawakens** an issue, or an interest or feeling that you used to have, it makes you think about it or feel it again. *The food reawakens memories of dishes that their mothers once cooked.* ▶ Also a noun. *...a reawakening of interest in stained glass.*　VERB V n / N-UNCOUNT

re·bate /ˈriːbeɪt/ **rebates.** A **rebate** is an amount of money which is paid to you when you have paid more tax, rent, or rates than you needed to. *...a tax rebate... Customers are to benefit from a rebate on their electricity bills.*　◆◇◇◇◇ N-COUNT

re·bel, rebels, rebelling, rebelled. The noun is pronounced /ˈrebəl/. The verb is pronounced /rɪˈbel/. **1** **Rebels** are people who are fighting against their own country's army in order to change the political system there. **2** If politicians **rebel** against one of their own party's policies, they show that they oppose it. *More than forty Conservative MPs rebelled against the government.* ▶ Politicians who oppose some of their party's policies can be referred to as **rebels**. **3** When someone **rebels**, they start to behave differently from other people and reject the values of society or of their parents. *I was very young and rebelling against everything.* ▶ Someone who rebels can be referred to as a **rebel**.　◆◆◆◇ N-COUNT / VERB V against n / Also V / N-COUNT / VERB: V V against n / N-COUNT

re·bel·lion /rɪˈbeliən/ **rebellions.** **1** A **rebellion** is a violent organized action by a large group of people who are trying to change their country's political system. *...the ruthless and brutal suppression of rebellion.* **2** A situation in which politicians show their opposition to their own party's policies can be referred to as **rebellion**.　◆◆◇◇◇ N-VAR / N-VAR

re·bel·lious /rɪˈbeliəs/. **1** If you think someone behaves in an unacceptable way and does not do what they are told, you can say they are **rebellious**. *...a rebellious teenager.* ♦ **re·bel·lious·ness** *...the normal rebelliousness of youth.* **2** A **rebellious** group of people is a group involved in taking violent action against the rulers of their own country, usually in order to change the system of government there.　◆◇◇◇◇ ADJ-GRADED / N-UNCOUNT / ADJ: ADJ n

re·birth /ˌriːˈbɜːθ/. You can refer to a change that leads to a new period of growth and improvement in something as its **rebirth**. *...the rebirth of democracy in Latin America.*　◆◇◇◇◇ N-UNCOUNT

re·born /ˌriːˈbɔːn/. If you say that someone or something **has been reborn**, you mean that they have become active again after a period of inactivity. *Shilling has been reborn as an artist.*　◆◇◇◇◇ V-PASSIVE be V-ed as n

re·bound, rebounds, rebounding, rebounded. The verb is pronounced /rɪˈbaʊnd/. The noun is pronounced /ˈriːbaʊnd/. **1** If something **rebounds** from a solid surface, it bounces or springs back from it. *His shot in the 21st minute of the game rebounded from a post.* **2** If an action or situation **rebounds** on you, it has an unpleasant effect on you, especially when this effect was intended for someone else. *Mia realised her trick had rebounded on her.* **3** If you say that someone is **on the rebound**, you mean that they have just ended a relationship with a girlfriend or boyfriend. This often makes them do things they would not normally do.　◆◇◇◇◇ VERB V prep Also V / VERB V on/upon n Also V / PHRASE

re·buff /rɪˈbʌf/ **rebuffs, rebuffing, rebuffed.** If you **rebuff** someone or **rebuff** a suggestion that they make, you refuse to do what they suggest. *He wanted sex with Julie but she rebuffed him.* ▶ Also a noun. *The results of the poll dealt a humiliating rebuff to Mr Jones.*　◆◇◇◇◇ VERB V n / N-VAR

re·build /ˌriːˈbɪld/ **rebuilds, rebuilding, rebuilt.** **1** When people **rebuild** something such as a building or a city, they build it again after it has been damaged or destroyed. **2** When people **rebuild** something such as an institution, a system, or an aspect of their lives, they take action to restore it to its previous condition. *The East Europeans want aid to help rebuild their economies.*　◆◆◇◇◇ VERB: V n / VERB V n Also V

re·buke /rɪˈbjuːk/ **rebukes, rebuking, rebuked.** If you **rebuke** someone, you speak severely to them because they have said or done something that you do not approve of. ▶ Also a noun. *The Prime Minister delivered a tough rebuke to Tory Euro-rebels.*　◆◇◇◇◇ VERB: V n FORMAL / N-VAR

re·but /rɪˈbʌt/ **rebuts, rebutting, rebutted.** If you **rebut** a charge or criticism that is made against you, you give reasons why it is untrue or unjustified. *He spent most of his speech rebutting criticisms of his foreign policy.* ♦ **re·but·tal** /rɪˈbʌtəl/ **rebuttals** *Pakistan has still not issued an official rebuttal to the latest Indian statements.*　◆◇◇◇◇ VERB: V n / N-COUNT

re·cal·ci·trant /rɪˈkælsɪtrənt/. If you describe someone or something as **recalcitrant**, you mean that they are stubborn, unco-operative, or unwilling to obey orders. *He had a knack for coaxing even the most recalcitrant engine to life.*　ADJ-GRADED FORMAL

re·call, recalls, recalling, recalled. The verb is pronounced /rɪˈkɔːl/. The noun is pronounced /ˈriːkɔːl/. **1** When you **recall** something, you remember it and tell others about it. *Henderson recalled that he first met Pollard during a business trip... Her teacher recalled: 'She was always on about modelling.'... They recalled how they came to be missionaries.* **2** You can say **as I recall**, you might **recall**, or **you will recall** to someone that you are talking to when you want to mention something that you are both already aware of which is relevant to the discussion. *As I recall, you're not on the board, Joe; you're only a minor shareholder.* **3** **Recall** is the ability to remember something that has happened in the past or the act of remembering it. *He had a good memory, and total recall of her spoken words.* **4** If you are **recalled** to your home, country, or the place where you work, you are ordered to return there. *Spain has recalled its Ambassador after a row over refugees.* ▶ Also a noun. *...the recall of ambassador Alan Green.* **5** If a company **recalls** a product, they ask the shops or the people who have bought that item to return it because there is something wrong with it. **6** If something is **beyond recall**, it is no longer possible to recreate it. *The ground has been polluted beyond recall.*　◆◆◆◇ VERB V that V with quote V wh Also V n, V / VERB PRAGMATICS V Also V that / N-UNCOUNT / VERB V n / N-SING: the N of n VERB: V n / PHRASE

re·cant /rɪ'kænt/ **recants, recanting, recanted.** VERB: V
If you **recant**, you say publicly that you no longer Vn
hold a set of beliefs that you had in the past. *Luther* FORMAL
was asked to recant his teachings.

re·cap /ˌriː'kæp/ **recaps, recapping, recapped.** VERB: V
You can say that you are going to **recap** when you PRAGMATICS
want to draw people's attention to the fact that you Vn
are going to repeat the main points of an explanation, argument, or description, as a summary of it.
Can you recap the points included in the regional
conference proposal? ▶ Also a noun. *...a recap of La-* N-SING
bour's defence policies.

re·capi·tal·ize /riː'kæpɪtəlaɪz/ **recapitalizes, re-** VERB
capitalizing, recapitalized. If a company re- V
capitalizes, they alter the way the company manages Also Vn
its financial affairs, for example by borrowing AMERICAN
money or reissuing shares. *Mr Warnock resigned as*
the company abandoned a plan to recapitalize. ♦ **re-**
·capi·tali·za·tion /riːˌkæpɪtəlaɪ'zeɪʃən/ **recapi-** N-COUNT
talizations *...a recapitalization of the company.*

re·ca·pitu·late /ˌriːkə'pɪtʃuleɪt/ **recapitulates,** VERB
recapitulating, recapitulated. Recapitulate PRAGMATICS
means the same as **recap.** *Let's just recapitulate the* Vn
essential points. Also V

re·cap·ture /ˌriː'kæptʃə/ **recaptures, recaptur-** ◆◇◇◇◇
ing, recaptured. 1 When soldiers **recapture** an VERB: Vn
area of land or a place, they win control of it again
from an opposing army who had taken it from
them. ▶ Also a noun. *...the recapture of the city.* **2** N-SING
When people **recapture** something that they have VERB
lost to a competitor, they win it back again. *One poll* Vn
shows that Labour is recapturing the voters who
helped the Tories to victory. **3** To **recapture** a person VERB: Vn
or animal which has escaped from somewhere
means to catch them again. ▶ Also a noun. *...the re-* N-SING
capture of a renegade police chief in Panama.
4 When you **recapture** something such as an experi- VERB
ence, emotion, or a quality you had in the past, you Vn
experience it again. When something **recaptures** an
experience for you, it makes you remember it. *These*
cookies seem to recapture all the textures and flavors
we remember from childhood.

re·cast /ˌriː'kɑːst, -'kæst/ **recasts, recasting.** The
form **recast** is used in the present tense and is also
the past tense and past participle. **1** If you **recast** VERB
something, you change it by organizing it in a dif- Vn
ferent way. *The shake-up aims to recast IBM as a*
federation of flexible and competing subsidiaries.
♦ **re·cast·ing** *...the recasting of the political map of* N-SING
Europe. **2** If the producers of a play or a film **recast** VERB: Vn
an actor's role, they give the role to another actor.

rec·ce /'reki/ **recces, recceing, recced.** If you VERB
recce an area, you visit that place in order to be- Vn
come familiar with it. *The first duty of a director is to* BRITISH
recce his location. ▶ Also a noun. *Uncle Jim took the* N-COUNT
air rifle and went on a recce to the far end of the
quarry.

recd. Recd. can be used as a written abbreviation WRITTEN
for 'received'.

re·cede /rɪ'siːd/ **recedes, receding, receded.** ◆◇◇◇◇
1 If something **recedes** from you, it moves away. VERB
Luke's footsteps receded into the night... As she reced- V prep
ed he waved goodbye. **2** When something such as a V
quality, problem, or illness **recedes**, it becomes VERB
weaker, smaller, or less intense. *Just as I started to* V
think that I was never going to get well, the illness Also V prep
began to recede. **3** If a man's hair starts to **recede**, VERB: V
no longer grows on the front of his head. **4** If your VERB: V
gums start to **recede**, they begin to cover less of
your teeth, usually as the result of an infection.

re·ceipt /rɪ'siːt/ **receipts. 1** A **receipt** is a piece of ◆◆◇◇◇
paper that you get from someone as confirmation N-COUNT
that they have received money or goods from you. *I*
wrote her a receipt for the money. **2 Receipts** are the N-PLURAL
amount of money received during a particular peri-
od, for example by a shop or theatre. *He was tally-*
ing the day's receipts. **3** The **receipt** of something is N-UNCOUNT
the act of receiving it. *Goods should be supplied* FORMAL
within 28 days after the receipt of your order. **4** If PHRASE

you are **in receipt of** something, you have received FORMAL
it or you receive it regularly.

re·ceive /rɪ'siːv/ **receives, receiving, re-** ◆◆◆◆◆
ceived. 1 When you **receive** something, you get it VERB
after someone gives it to you or sends it to you. Vn
They will receive their awards at a ceremony in FORMAL
Stockholm. **2** You can use **receive** to say that certain VERB
kinds of thing happen to someone. For example if Vn
they are injured, you can say that they **received** an FORMAL
injury. *He received more of the blame than anyone*
when the plan failed to work. **3** If you **are on the re-** PHRASE
ceiving end or **at the receiving end** of something
unpleasant, you are the person that it happens to.
4 When you **receive** a visitor or a guest, you greet VERB
them. *The following evening the duchess was again re-* Vn
ceiving guests. FORMAL
5 If you say that something **is received** in a particular VB: usu
way, you mean that people react to it in that way. *The* passive
resolution had been received with great disappoint- be V-ed
ment within the PLO... The proposals have been well prep/adv
received by many deputies. be V-ed with
6 When a radio or television **receives** signals that are VERB: Vn
being transmitted, it picks them up and converts
them into sound or pictures.
7 If someone **receives** stolen goods, they buy or are VERB: Vn
given things that have been stolen. BRITISH,
LEGAL

re·ceived /rɪ'siːvd/. The **received** opinion about ADJ: ADJ n
something or the **received** way of doing something FORMAL
is generally accepted by people as being correct. *He*
was among the first to question the received wisdom
of the time.

Re·ceived Pronunci·ation. Received Pronun- N-UNCOUNT
ciation is a way of pronouncing British English that
is often considered to be the standard accent. The
abbreviation **RP** is also used.

re·ceiv·er /rɪ'siːvə/ **receivers. 1** A telephone's **re-** ◆◆◇◇◇
ceiver is the part that you hold near to your ear and N-COUNT
speak into. **2** A **receiver** is the part of a radio or N-COUNT
television that picks up incoming signals and con-
verts them into sound or pictures. **3** The **receiver** is N-COUNT
someone who is officially appointed to manage the
affairs of a business, usually when it has gone into
bankruptcy.

re·ceiv·er·ship /rɪ'siːvəʃɪp/ **receiverships.** If a ◆◇◇◇◇
company goes into **receivership**, it becomes bank- N-VAR
rupt and the administration of its business is handled by the receiver.

re·cent /'riːsənt/. A **recent** event or period of time ◆◆◆◆◆
happened only a short while ago. *In the most recent* ADJ-GRADED
attack one man was shot dead... Sales have fallen by
more than 75 percent in recent years.

re·cent·ly /'riːsəntli/. If you have done something ◆◆◆◇
recently or if something happened **recently**, it hap- ADV-GRADED
pened only a short time ago. *The bank recently*
opened a branch in Germany... He was until very re-
cently the most powerful banker in the city.

re·cep·ta·cle /rɪ'septɪkəl/ **receptacles.** A **recep-** N-COUNT
tacle is an object which you use to put or keep FORMAL
things in.

re·cep·tion /rɪ'sepʃən/ **receptions. 1** The **recep-** ◆◆◇◇◇
tion in a hotel, office, or hospital is the part of the N-SING:
building where people are received and their reser- theN,
vations, appointments, or enquiries are dealt with. also at N
2 A **reception** is a formal party which is given to N-COUNT
welcome someone or to celebrate a special event.
...a glittering wedding reception.
3 If you get good **reception** from your radio or televi- N-UNCOUNT
sion, the sound or picture is clear because the signal is
strong.
4 If someone or something has a particular kind of **re-** N-COUNT
ception, that is the way people react to them. *He re-*
ceived a cool reception to his speech. **5** The **reception** N-SING
of guests is the act of formally welcoming them. FORMAL

re·ception centre, reception centres; spelled N-COUNT
reception center in American English. A **reception** BRITISH
centre is a place which provides temporary accommodation for people who are homeless, for example
because they are refugees or because their own
homes have been destroyed.

re·cep·tion class, reception classes. In Britain, a **reception class** is a class that children go into when they first start infant school.   N-COUNT

re·cep·tion·ist /rɪ'sepʃənɪst/ **receptionists.** In a hotel, office, or hospital, the **receptionist** is the person whose job is to answer the telephone, arrange reservations or appointments, and deal with people when they first arrive.   ◆◇◇◇ N-COUNT

re·cep·tion room, reception rooms. A **reception room** is a room in a house, for example a living room or a dining room, where people can sit.   N-COUNT BRITISH

re·cep·tive /rɪ'septɪv/. **1** Someone who is **receptive** to new ideas or suggestions is prepared to consider them or accept them. *The voters had seemed very receptive to his ideas.* ♦ **re·cep·tiv·ity** /ˌriːsep'tɪvɪti/. *There was a lack of receptivity to the advances in science.* **2** If someone who is ill is **receptive** to treatment, they start to get better when they are given treatment.   ◆◇◇◇ ADJ-GRADED / N-UNCOUNT / ADJ-GRADED: v-link ADJ to n

re·cep·tor /rɪ'septə/ **receptors.** Receptors are nerve endings in your body which react to changes and stimuli and make your body respond in a particular way.   ◆◇◇◇ N-COUNT TECHNICAL

re·cess /rɪ'ses, 'riːses/ **recesses, recessing, recessed. 1** A **recess** is a break between the sessions of work of an official body such as a committee, a court of law, or a government. *The conference broke for a recess... Congress is now in recess.* **2** When formal proceedings **recess**, they stop temporarily. *The hearings have now recessed for dinner.* **3** In a room, a **recess** is part of a wall which is built further back than the rest of the wall. **4** The **recesses** of something or somewhere are the parts of it which are hard to see because light does not reach them or they are hidden from view. *He emerged from the dark recesses of the garage.* **5** If you refer to the **recesses** of the someone's mind or soul, you are referring to thoughts or feelings they have which are hidden or difficult to describe.   ◆◇◇◇ N-COUNT: also in/from N / VERB: V / V for n / N-COUNT / N-COUNT / N-COUNT

re·cessed /'riːsest/. A **recessed** window or door is set into the wall surrounding it so that it is further back than the wall.   ADJ

re·ces·sion /rɪ'seʃən/ **recessions.** A **recession** is a period when the economy of a country is doing badly, for example because industry is producing less and more people are unemployed. *The oil price increases sent Europe into deep recession.* ♦ **re·ces·sion·ary** /rɪ'seʃənri/. *He said the recessionary trend in Germany was growing stronger.*   ◆◆◆◇ N-VAR / ADJ-GRADED: ADJ n

re·charge /ˌriː'tʃɑːdʒ/ **recharges, recharging, recharged. 1** If you **recharge** a battery, you put an electrical charge back into the battery by connecting it to a machine that draws power from another source of electricity such as the mains. ♦ **re·charge·able** ...*rechargeable batteries. ...a rechargeable drill.* **2** If you **recharge your batteries**, you take a break from activities which are tiring or stressful in order to relax and be refreshed when you return to them.   ◆◇◇◇ VERB: V n / ADJ / PHRASE

re·cher·ché /rə'ʃeəʃeɪ/. If you describe something as **recherché**, you mean that it is very sophisticated or is associated with people who like things which are unusual and expensive.   ADJ-GRADED FORMAL

re·cidi·vist /rɪ'sɪdɪvɪst/ **recidivists.** A **recidivist** is someone who has committed crimes in the past and commits crimes again. ♦ **re·cidi·vism** /rɪ'sɪdɪvɪzəm/. *Prisons do not reduce the crime rate, they cause recidivism.*   N-COUNT / N-UNCOUNT

reci·pe /'resɪpi/ **recipes. 1** A **recipe** is a list of ingredients and a set of instructions that tell you how to cook something. **2** If you say that something is a **recipe for** a particular situation, you mean that it is likely to result in that situation. *Large-scale inflation is a recipe for disaster.*   ◆◆◇◇ N-COUNT / N-SING: a N for n

re·cipi·ent /rɪ'sɪpiənt/ **recipients.** The **recipient** of something is the person who receives it.   ◆◆◇◇ N-COUNT

re·cip·ro·cal /rɪ'sɪprəkəl/. A **reciprocal** action or agreement involves two people or groups who do the same thing to each other or agree to help each another in a similar way. *They expected a reciprocal*   ◇◇◇◇ ADJ FORMAL

gesture before more hostages could be freed. ♦ **re·cip·ro·cal·ly** *The object of her desires did not act reciprocally.*   ADV

re·cip·ro·cate /rɪ'sɪprəkeɪt/ **reciprocates, reciprocating, reciprocated.** If your feelings or actions towards someone **are reciprocated**, the other person feels or behaves in the same way towards you as you have felt or behaved towards them. *I hope they reciprocate by coming to support us.* ♦ **re·cip·ro·ca·tion** /rɪ,sɪprə'keɪʃən/. *There was no reciprocation of esteem, let alone affection.*   ◆◇◇◇ VERB: be V-ed / V by-ing / Also V n / N-UNCOUNT

reci·proc·ity /ˌresɪ'prɒsɪti/. **Reciprocity** is the exchange of something between people or groups, when each person or group gives or allows something to the other. *They would press for reciprocity with Greece in the issuing of visas.*   N-UNCOUNT FORMAL

re·cit·al /rɪ'saɪtl/ **recitals. 1** A **recital** is a performance of music or poetry, usually given by one person. **2** If someone speaks for a long time, especially if what they say is boring or has been heard many times before, you can describe it as a **recital**. *I finished my recital of the past hour's happenings.*   ◆◇◇◇ N-COUNT / N-COUNT WRITTEN

reci·ta·tion /ˌresɪ'teɪʃən/ **recitations. 1** When someone does a **recitation**, they say aloud a piece of poetry or other writing that they have learned. *The transmission began with a recitation from the Koran.* **2** A **recitation** of something is a statement of it. *The letter was short – a simple recitation of their problem.*   N-VAR / N-COUNT WRITTEN

re·cite /rɪ'saɪt/ **recites, reciting, recited. 1** When someone **recites** a poem or other piece of writing, they say it aloud after they have learned it. **2** If you **recite** something such as a list, you say it aloud. *All he could do was recite a list of Government failings.*   ◆◇◇◇ VERB: V n / VERB V n

reck·less /'rekləs/. If you say that someone is **reckless**, you mean that they act in a way which shows that they do not care about danger or the effect their behaviour will have on other people. *He is charged with causing death by reckless driving.* ♦ **reck·less·ly** *He was leaning recklessly out of the unshuttered window.* ♦ **reck·less·ness** ...*the headstrong recklessness of youth.*   ◆◇◇◇ ADJ-GRADED / ADV-GRADED / N-UNCOUNT

reck·on /'rekən/ **reckons, reckoning, reckoned. 1** If you **reckon** that something is true, you think that it is true. *Toni reckoned that it must be about three o'clock.* **2** If you say that something is **reckoned** to be true, you mean that people think that it is true. *The sale has been held up because the price is reckoned to be too high.* **3** If you say that someone **reckons** to do something, you mean that they expect to do it. *The merged banks want to raise 4 billion dollars.* **4** If something **is reckoned** to be a particular figure, it is calculated to be roughly that amount. *The amount being poured into East Germany was reckoned at 140 billion marks.*   ◆◆◆◇ VERB / V that INFORMAL / VB: usu passive / be V-ed to-inf INFORMAL / VERB V to-inf INFORMAL / VERB: be V-ed to-inf / be V-ed at n

reckon on. If you **reckon on** something happening, you feel certain that it will happen and therefore make your plans based on it. *He reckons on being world heavyweight champion.*   PHRASAL VB V P -ing/n

reckon with. 1 If you say that you had not **reckoned with** something, you mean that you had not expected it and so were not prepared for it. *Giles had not reckoned with the strength of Sally's feelings for him.* **2** If you refer to a person or force as someone or something **to be reckoned with**, you mean they will be difficult to deal with because they are quite powerful or skilful. *This act was a signal to his victim's friends that he was someone to be reckoned with.*   PHRASAL VB with brd-neg V P n / PHRASE

reckon without. If you say that you had **reckoned without** something, you mean that you had not expected it and so were not prepared for it.   PHRASAL VB V P n

reck·on·ing /'rekənɪŋ/ **reckonings. 1** Someone's **reckoning** is a calculation they make about something, especially a calculation that is not very exact. *By my reckoning we were seven or eight kilometres from Borj Mechaab.* **2** See also **day of reckoning**.   ◆◇◇◇ N-VAR

re·claim /rɪ'kleɪm/ **reclaims, reclaiming, reclaimed. 1** If you **reclaim** something that you   ◆◇◇◇ VERB

have lost or had taken away from you, you succeed in getting it back. *In 1986, they got the right to reclaim South African citizenship.* **2** If you **reclaim** an amount of money, for example tax that you have paid, you ask for it to be returned to you.   VERB: V n

3 When people **reclaim** land, they make it suitable for a purpose such as farming or building, for example by draining it. *...1,100 acres of reclaimed land in Tokyo Bay.* ♦ **rec·la·ma·tion** /ˌreklə'meɪʃən/. *...the reclamation of dry land from the marshes.* **4** If a piece of land that was used for farming or building **is reclaimed** by a desert, or forest, or by the sea, it turns back into desert, forest, or sea.   VERB: V-ed / N-UNCOUNT / VERB: be V-ed

re·cline /rɪ'klaɪn/ **reclines, reclining, reclined.** ♦◊◊◊◊ **1** If you **recline** on something, you sit or lie on it with the upper part of your body supported at an angle. *Move to a reclining position.* **2** If a seat **reclines**, you can lower the back so that it is more comfortable to sit in. *First-class seats recline almost like beds. ...a soft reclining chair.*   VERB V prep V-ing / VERB V-ing

re·cluse /rɪ'kluːs, AM 'rekluːs/ **recluses.** A **recluse** is a person who lives alone and deliberately avoids other people. ♦ **re·clu·sive** /rɪ'kluːsɪv/. *...a reclusive millionaire.*   N-COUNT / ADJ-GRADED

rec·og·nise /'rekəgnaɪz/. See **recognize**.

rec·og·ni·tion /ˌrekəg'nɪʃən/. **1 Recognition** is the act of recognizing someone or identifying something when you see it. *He searched for a sign of recognition on her face.* • If you say that someone or something has changed **beyond recognition** or **out of all recognition**, you mean that person or thing has changed so much that you can no longer recognize them. **2 Recognition** of something is an understanding and acceptance of it. *The CBI welcomed the Chancellor's recognition of the recession.* **3** When a government gives diplomatic **recognition** to another country, they officially accept that its status is valid. **4** When a person receives **recognition** for the things that they have done, people acknowledge the value or skill of their work. *He is an outstanding goalscorer who doesn't get the recognition he deserves.* • If something is done **in recognition of** someone's achievements, it is done as a way of showing official appreciation of them. *He had just received a doctorate in recognition of his contributions to seismology.*   ♦♦♦◊ N-UNCOUNT / PHRASE / N-UNCOUNT: with supp / N-UNCOUNT: with supp / N-UNCOUNT: with supp / PHR-PREP

rec·og·niz·able /ˌrekəg'naɪzəbəl/; also spelled **recognisable** in British English. If something can be easily recognized or identified, you can say it is easily **recognizable**. ♦ **rec·og·niz·ably** /ˌrekəg'naɪzəbli/. *He was playing a popular song, not very well, but recognizably.*   ♦◊◊◊ ADJ-GRADED / ADV-GRADED

re·cog·ni·zance /rɪ'kɒgnɪzəns, -'kɒn-/; also spelled **recognisance**. If someone who has been charged with a crime is released on their own **recognizance**, they are allowed to leave the courtroom after promising to return on a specified date. **Recognizance** also refers to an amount of money that is pledged as a guarantee of someone's return after they are released.   N-UNCOUNT LEGAL, AMERICAN

rec·og·nize /'rekəgnaɪz/ **recognizes, recognizing, recognized;** also spelled **recognise** in British English. **1** If you **recognize** someone or something that you have seen before or had described to you, you know who that person is or what that thing is. *The receptionist recognized him at once... A man I easily recognized as Luke's father sat with a newspaper on his lap.* **2** If someone says that they **recognize** something, they realize or acknowledge that it exists or that it is true. *I recognize my own shortcomings... Of course I recognize that evil exists... They have been slow to recognize AIDS as a problem.* **3** If people or organizations **recognize** something as valid, they officially accept it or approve of it. *Russia has recognized Ukraine independence. ...a nationally recognized expert on psychology.* **4** When people **recognize** the work someone has done, they show their appreciation of it, often by giving that person an award of some kind.   ♦♦♦♦ VB: no cont V n V n as n / VB: no cont V n V that V n as n / VERB V n V-ed Also V n as n / VERB: V n

re·coil, recoils, recoiling, recoiled. The verb is pronounced /rɪ'kɔɪl/. The noun is pronounced /'riːkɔɪl/. **1** If something makes you **recoil**, you move your body quickly away from it because it frightens, offends, or hurts you. *I thought he was going to kiss me. I recoiled in horror.* **2** If you say that someone **recoils** from doing something or **recoils** at the idea of something, you mean that they are reluctant to do it because they dislike it so much. *People used to recoil from the idea of getting into debt.* **3** The **recoil** of a gun is the quick backward movement that it makes when it is fired.   ♦◊◊◊◊ VERB V Also V from n / VERB V from/at n / N-SING: also no det

rec·ol·lect /ˌrekə'lekt/ **recollects, recollecting, recollected.** If you **recollect** something, you remember it. *She recollected that Shirley was not the most reliable of informants.* ♦ **rec·ol·lec·tion** /ˌrekə'lekʃən/ **recollections** *Pat has vivid recollections of the trip... He had no recollection of the crash.*   VERB: V n V that / N-VAR

re·com·mence /ˌriːkə'mens/ **recommences, recommencing, recommenced.** If you **recommence** something or if it **recommences**, it begins again after having stopped. *He recommenced work on his novel.*   V-ERG V n Also V WRITTEN

rec·om·mend /ˌrekə'mend/ **recommends, recommending, recommended. 1** If someone **recommends** something or someone to you, they suggest that you would find them good or useful. *I have just spent a holiday there and would recommend it to anyone... I'll recommend you for a promotion... Ask your doctor to recommend a suitable therapist.* ▶ Also an adjective. *This book is highly recommended.* ♦ **rec·om·men·da·tion** /ˌrekəme'ndeɪʃən/ **recommendations** *On O'Leary's recommendation, they started with tortellini.* **2** If you **recommend** that something is done, you advise that it should be done. *We strongly recommend reporting the incident to the police... It is recommended that you should consult your doctor... The recommended daily dose is 12 to 24 grams.* ♦ **recommendation** *The committee's recommendations are unlikely to be made public.* **3** If something or someone has a particular quality to **recommend** it, that quality makes it attractive or gives it an advantage over similar things. *La Noblesse restaurant has much to recommend it... These qualities recommended him to Olivier.*   ♦♦♦♦◊ V n to/for/as n V n / ADJ-GRADED / N-VAR / VERB: V that V n/-ing it be V-ed that V-ed Also V n to-inf / N-VAR / VERB V n V n to n

rec·om·pense /'rekəmpens/ **recompenses, recompensing, recompensed. 1** If you are given something, usually money, in **recompense**, you are given it as a reward or because you have suffered. *He demands no financial recompense for his troubles.* **2** If you **recompense** someone for their efforts or their loss, you give them something, usually money, as a payment or reward. *The fees offered by the NHS do not recompense dental surgeons for their professional time.*   N-UNCOUNT FORMAL / VERB V n for n FORMAL

rec·on·cile /'rekənsaɪl/ **reconciles, reconciling, reconciled. 1** If you **reconcile** two beliefs, facts, or demands that seem to be opposed or completely different, you find a way in which they can both be true or both be fulfilled. *It's difficult to reconcile the demands of my job and the desire to be a good father... How do you reconcile your ideals with your lifestyle?* ♦ **rec·on·cilia·tion** /ˌrekənsɪli'eɪʃən/. *...the ideal of democracy based upon a reconciliation of the values of equality and liberty.* **2** If you **are reconciled** with someone or another person **reconciles** the two of you, you become friendly with them again after a quarrel or disagreement. *He never believed he and Susan would be reconciled... Devlin was reconciled with the Catholic Church in his last few days. ...my attempt to reconcile him with Toby.* ♦ **rec·on·cilia·tion, reconciliations** *...an appeal for reconciliation between Catholics and Protestants... The couple have separated but he wants a reconciliation.* **3** If you **reconcile** yourself to an unpleasant situation, you accept it, although it makes you unhappy to do so. *She had reconciled herself to never seeing him again.* ♦ **rec·on·ciled** *Ferraro seemed reconciled to defeat.*   ♦♦◊◊◊ VERB V pl-n V n with n / N-SING / V-RECIP pl-n be V-ed be V-ed with n V n within Also V pl-n / N-VAR / VERB V pron-refl to n/-ing / ADJ-GRADED: v-link ADJ to n/-ing

re·con·dite /rɪ'kɒndaɪt, 'rekən-/. **Recondite** areas of knowledge or learning are difficult to understand, and not many people know about them. `ADJ-GRADED FORMAL`

re·con·di·tion /ˌriːkən'dɪʃən/ **reconditions, reconditioning, reconditioned.** To **recondition** a machine or piece of equipment means to repair or replace all the parts that are damaged or broken. *They sell used and reconditioned motorcycle parts.* `VERB: V n V-ed`

re·con·firm /ˌriːkən'fɜːm/ **reconfirms, reconfirming, reconfirmed.** **Reconfirm** means the same as **confirm.**

re·con·nais·sance /rɪ'kɒnɪsəns/. **Reconnaissance** is the activity of obtaining military information about a place by sending soldiers or planes there, or by the use of satellites. ♦♦♦♦♦ `N-UNCOUNT`

re·con·nect /ˌriːkə'nekt/ **reconnects, reconnecting, reconnected.** If a company **reconnects** you or **reconnects** your electricity, water, gas, or telephone, they provide you with that service once again after it has been stopped. ♦ **re·con·nec·tion** /ˌriːkə'nekʃən/. *The cost of reconnection after supplies are cut off is high.* `VERB: V n` `N-UNCOUNT`

rec·on·noi·tre /ˌrekə'nɔɪtə/ **reconnoitres, reconnoitring, reconnoitred;** spelled **reconnoiter** in American English. To **reconnoitre** an area means to obtain information about its geographical features or about the size and position of an army there. `VERB: V n, V`

re·con·sid·er /ˌriːkən'sɪdə/ **reconsiders, reconsidering, reconsidered.** If you **reconsider** a decision or opinion, you think about it and try to decide whether it should be changed. *This has forced the United States to seriously reconsider its position... The judge initially dismissed the suit but said he will reconsider his decision.* ♦ **re·con·sid·era·tion** /ˌriːkənsɪdə'reɪʃən/. *The report urges reconsideration of the decision.* ♦♦♦♦♦ `VERB V` `N-UNCOUNT`

re·con·sti·tute /ˌriː'kɒnstɪtjuːt, AM -tuːt/ **reconstitutes, reconstituting, reconstituted. 1** If an organization or state **is reconstituted**, it is formed again in a different way. *The reconstituted Communist party remains the third most popular party.* ♦ **re·con·sti·tu·tion** /ˌriːkɒnstɪ'tjuːʃən, AM -'tuːʃ-/. *They oppose any sort of reconstitution of the Soviet Union.* **2** To **reconstitute** dried food means to add water to it so that it can be eaten. *Try eating reconstituted dried prunes.* ♦♦♦♦♦ `VERB: be V-ed V-ed Also V n` `N-UNCOUNT` `VERB: V n V-ed`

re·con·struct /ˌriːkən'strʌkt/ **reconstructs, reconstructing, reconstructed. 1** If you **reconstruct** something that has been destroyed or badly damaged, you build it and make it work again. *The government must reconstruct the shattered economy... He has had plastic surgery to help reconstruct his badly damaged face.* ♦ **re·con·struc·tion** /ˌriːkən'strʌkʃən/. *...America's part in the post-war reconstruction of Germany.* **2** To **reconstruct** something such as a system means to change its construction so that it works in a different way. *She actually wanted to reconstruct the state and transform society.* **3** If you **reconstruct** an event that happened in the past, you try to get a complete understanding of it by combining a lot of small pieces of information. *Efforts were made to reconstruct what had happened.* ♦ **re·con·struc·tion, reconstructions** *Mrs Kerr was too upset to take part in a reconstruction of her ordeal.* ♦♦♦♦♦ `VERB V n` `N-UNCOUNT` `VERB V n` `VERB: V n V wh` `N-COUNT`

re·con·struc·tive /ˌriːkən'strʌktɪv/. **Reconstructive** surgery or treatment involves rebuilding a part of someone's body that has been badly damaged. `ADJ: ADJ n`

re·con·vene /ˌriːkən'viːn/ **reconvenes, reconvening, reconvened.** If a parliament, court, or conference **reconvenes**, it meets again after a break. *It was certainly serious enough for him to reconvene Parliament.* ♦♦♦♦♦ `V-ERG: V`

rec·ord, records, recording, recorded. The noun is pronounced /'rekɔːd, AM -kərd/. The verb is pronounced /rɪ'kɔːd/. **1** If you keep a **record of** something or keep something **on record**, you keep an account of it in writing, photographs, or on a computer so that it can be referred to later. *There's* ♦♦♦♦♦ `N-COUNT: also on N`

no record of any marriage or children... The result will go on your medical records... The practice is to keep on record any analysis of samples. **2** Someone's **record** is the facts that are known about their achievements or character. *He had a distinguished record as a chaplain... His country is making a big effort to improve its human rights record.* **3** If someone has a criminal **record**, it is officially known that they have committed crimes in the past. **4** If you **record** a piece of information or an event, you write it down, photograph it, or put it into a computer so that in the future people can refer to it. *Her letters record the domestic and social details of diplomatic life in China. ...a place which has rarely suffered a famine in its recorded history.* **5** If a dial, gauge, or other measuring device **records** a certain measurement or value, it shows that measurement or value. *An EEG records the electrical activity of the brain... The index of the performance of leading shares recorded a 16 per cent fall.* ♦ **re·cord·er, recorders** *...data recorders.* ● See also **flight recorder.** **6** If you **record** something such as a speech or performance, you put it on tape or film. *The call was answered by a recorded message.* **7** If a musician or performer **records** a piece of music or a television or radio show, they perform the music or show so that it can be put onto record, tape, or film. *She has recently recorded a programme for television.* **8** A **record** is a round, flat piece of black plastic on which sound, especially music, is stored, and which can be played on a record player. You can also refer to the music stored on this piece of plastic as a **record**. *This is one of my favourite records.* **9** A **record** is the best result that has ever been achieved in a particular sport or activity, for example the fastest time or the furthest distance. *...the 800 metres, where she is the world record holder.* **10** You use **record** to say that something is higher, lower, better, or worse than ever before. *Profits were at record levels.* **11** See also **recording; track record. 12** If you say that what you are going to say next is **for the record**, you mean that you are saying it publicly and officially and you want it to be written down and remembered. *We're willing to state for the record that it has enormous value.* **13** If you give some information **for the record**, you give it in case people might find it useful at a later time, although it is not a very important part of what you are talking about. *For the record, most Moscow girls leave school at about 18.* **14** If you say something **off the record**, you do not intend what you say to be taken as official, or published with your name attached to it. *...some off-the-record comments.* **15** If you are **on record** as saying something, you have said it publicly and officially and it has been written down. *The Italians are also on record as backing the use of force.* **16** If you **set the record straight** or **put the record straight**, you show that something which has been regarded as true is in fact not true. `N-COUNT: with supp` `N-COUNT` `VERB V n V-ed` `VERB V n` `N-COUNT` `VERB: V n V-ed` `VERB V n` `N-COUNT` `N-COUNT` `ADJ: ADJ n` `PHRASE` `PHRASE` `PHRASE` `PHRASE` `PHRASE`

'record-breaker, record-breakers; also spelled **record breaker.** A **record-breaker** is someone or something who beats the previous best result in a sport or other activity. ♦ **record-breaking** *Australia's rugby union side enjoyed a record-breaking win over France.* `N-COUNT` `ADJ: ADJ n`

re·cord·er /rɪ'kɔːdə/ **recorders. 1** You can refer to a cassette recorder, a tape recorder, or a video recorder as a **recorder. 2** A **recorder** is a musical instrument in the shape of a wooden or plastic pipe. You play it by blowing into the mouthpiece and covering and uncovering the holes with your fingers. See picture headed **musical instruments. 3** In the legal system of England and Wales, a **recorder** is a barrister or solicitor who is appointed as a part-time judge in the Crown Court. **4** See also **record.** ♦♦♦♦♦ `N-COUNT` `N-VAR` `N-COUNT; N-TITLE`

rec·ord·ing /rɪ'kɔːdɪŋ/ **recordings. 1** A **recording** of something is a record, CD, tape, or video of it. *...a video recording of a police interview.* **2** **Recording** is the process of making records, tapes, or videos. *...the recording industry.* ♦♦♦♦♦ `N-COUNT` `N-UNCOUNT`

R

'**record player, record players;** also spelled N-COUNT
record-player. A **record player** is a machine on
which you can play a record in order to listen to the
music or other sounds on it.

re·count, recounts, recounting, recounted. ◆◇◇◇◇
The verb is pronounced /rɪˈkaʊnt/. The noun is pronounced /ˈriːkaʊnt/. **1** If you **recount** a story or VERB: V n
event, you tell or describe it to people. *He recounted* V wh
how heavily armed soldiers forced him from the Also V that
presidential palace. **2** A **recount** is a second count N-COUNT
of votes in an election when the result is very close.

re·coup /rɪˈkuːp/ **recoups, recouping, re-** ◆◇◇◇◇
couped. If you **recoup** a sum of money that you VERB
have spent or lost, you get it back. *Insurance com-* V n
*panies are trying to recoup their losses by increasing
premiums.*

re·course /rɪˈkɔːs/. If you say that you can achieve ◆◇◇◇◇
something without **recourse** to something you N-UNCOUNT
would rather not do, you mean that you can succeed without having to do it. *The public believes its
only recourse is to take to the streets... He urged the
Union to settle the issue without recourse to court
action.*

re·cov·er /rɪˈkʌvə/ **recovers, recovering, re-** ◆◆◆◇◇
covered. 1 When you **recover** from an illness or VERB:
an injury, you become well again. *A policeman was* V from/-ing
recovering in hospital last night after being stabbed.
2 If you **recover** from an unhappy or unpleasant ex- VERB:
perience, you stop being upset by it. *Her plane* V from n
*broke down and it was 18 hours before she got there.
It took her three days to recover.* **3** If something **re-** VERB:
covers from a period of weakness or difficulty, it V from n
improves or gets stronger again. *The stockmarket
index fell by 80% before it began to recover.*
4 If you **recover** something that has been lost or stol- VERB: V n
en, you find it or get it back. **5** If you **recover** a mental VERB: V n
or physical state, it comes back again. For example, if
you **recover** consciousness, you become conscious
again. **6** If you **recover** money that you have spent, in- VERB
vested, or lent to someone, you get the same amount V n
back. *The British market alone was not large enough to
recover their costs of production.*

re·cov·er·able /rɪˈkʌvərəbəl/. If something is **re-** ADJ
coverable, it is possible for you to get it back. *If you
decide not to buy, the money you have spent on the
survey is not recoverable.*

re·cov·ery /rɪˈkʌvəri/ **recoveries. 1** If a sick per- ◆◆◆◇◇
son makes a **recovery,** he or she becomes well N-VAR
again. *He had been given less than a one in 500
chance of recovery.* **2** When there is a **recovery** in a N-VAR
country's economy, it improves.
3 You talk about the **recovery** of something when you N-UNCOUNT
get it back after it has been lost or stolen. *A substantial
reward is being offered for the recovery of a painting by
Turner.* **4** You talk about the **recovery** of someone's N-UNCOUNT:
physical or mental state when they return to this N of n
state. *...the abrupt loss and recovery of consciousness.*

rec·re·ate /ˌriːkriˈeɪt/ **recreates, recreating,** ◆◇◇◇◇
recreated. If you **recreate** something, you suc- VERB
ceed in making it exist or seem to exist in a different V n
time or place to its original time or place. *I am trying to recreate family life far from home.*

rec·rea·tion, recreations. Pronounced ◆◆◇◇◇
/ˌrekriˈeɪʃən/ for meaning 1, and /ˌriːkriˈeɪʃən/ for
meaning 2. **1 Recreation** consists of things that you N-VAR
do in your spare time to relax. *All the family members need to have their own interests and recreations.*
♦ **rec·rea·tion·al** /ˌrekriˈeɪʃənəl/. *...parks and other* ADJ
recreational facilities. **2** A **recreation** of something N-COUNT
is an act or process of making it exist or seem to exist again in a different time or place to its original
time or place. *...a faithful recreation of the original
Elizabethan theatre.*

re·crimi·na·tion /rɪˌkrɪmɪˈneɪʃən/ **recrimina-** ◆◇◇◇◇
tions. Recriminations are accusations that two N-UNCOUNT:
people or groups make about each other. *The war* also N in pl
sweeps up everyone in hatred and recrimination.

re·cruit /rɪˈkruːt/ **recruits, recruiting, recruit-** ◆◆◆◇◇
ed. 1 If you **recruit** people for an organization, you VERB:
select them and persuade them to join it or work for V n to/for n
V n

it. *The police are trying to recruit more black and* V n to-inf
*Asian officers... He helped to recruit volunteers to go
to Pakistan to fight.* ♦ **re·cruit·er, recruiters** *...a* N-COUNT
Marine recruiter. ♦ **re·cruit·ing** *...an army recruit-* N-UNCOUNT
ing office. ♦ **re·cruit·ment** *...a crisis in teacher re-* N-UNCOUNT
cruitment. **2** A **recruit** is a person who has recently N-COUNT
joined an organization or an army.

rec·tal /ˈrektəl/. **Rectal** means relating to the rec- ADJ: ADJ n
tum. *...rectal cancer.* MEDICAL

rec·tan·gle /ˈrektæŋgəl/ **rectangles.** A **rectangle** ◆◇◇◇◇
is a four-sided shape whose corners are all ninety N-COUNT
degree angles. Each side of a rectangle is the same
length as the one opposite to it. See picture headed
shapes. ♦ **rec·tan·gu·lar** /rekˈtæŋgjʊlə/. *...a rec-* ADJ
tangular table.

rec·ti·fy /ˈrektɪfaɪ/ **rectifies, rectifying, recti-** ◆◇◇◇◇
fied. If you **rectify** something that is wrong, you VERB
change it so that it becomes correct or satisfactory. V n
Only an act of Congress could rectify the situation.

rec·ti·tude /ˈrektɪtjuːd, AM -tuːd/. **Rectitude** is the N-UNCOUNT
quality that makes people behave honestly and vir- FORMAL
tuously according to accepted standards.

rec·tor /ˈrektə/ **rectors. 1** A **rector** is an Anglican ◆◇◇◇◇
priest who is in charge of a parish. **2** A **rector** is a N-COUNT
high-ranking official in some universities. N-COUNT

rec·tory /ˈrektəri/ **rectories.** A **rectory** is a house N-COUNT
in which a rector and his family live.

rec·tum /ˈrektəm/ **rectums.** Someone's **rectum** is N-COUNT
the bottom end of the tube down which waste food MEDICAL
passes out of their body.

re·cum·bent /rɪˈkʌmbənt/. A **recumbent** figure or ADJ
person is lying down. FORMAL

re·cu·per·ate /rɪˈkuːpəreɪt/ **recuperates, recu-** ◆◇◇◇◇
perating, recuperated. When you **recuperate,** VERB: V
you recover your health or strength after you have V from n
been ill or injured. *He is recuperating from a serious
back injury.* ♦ **re·cu·pera·tion** /rɪˌkuːpəˈreɪʃən/. N-UNCOUNT
Sleep is necessary for recuperation.

re·cur /rɪˈkɜː/ **recurs, recurring, recurred.** If ◆◇◇◇◇
something **recurs,** it happens more than once. VERB: V

re·cur·rence /rɪˈkʌrəns, AM -ˈkɜːr-/ **recurrences.** ◆◇◇◇◇
If there is a **recurrence** of something, it happens N-VAR
again.

re·cur·rent /rɪˈkʌrənt, AM -ˈkɜːr-/. A **recurrent** ◆◇◇◇◇
event or feeling happens or is experienced more ADJ
than once. *...buildings in which staff suffer recurrent
illness.*

re·cy·clable /riːˈsaɪkələbəl/. **Recyclable** waste or ADJ-GRADED
materials can be processed and used again.

re·cy·cle /ˌriːˈsaɪkəl/ **recycles, recycling, recy-** ◆◆◇◇◇
cled. If you **recycle** things that have already been VERB: V n
used, such as bottles or sheets of paper, you process
them so that they can be used again. ♦ **re·cy·cling** N-UNCOUNT
...a recycling scheme.

red /red/ **reds; redder, reddest. 1** Something ◆◆◆◆◆
that is **red** is the colour of blood or of a ripe tomato. COLOUR
2 You describe someone's hair as **red** when it is be- ADJ
tween red and brown in colour. **3** Your **red** blood ADJ: ADJ n
cells or **red** corpuscles are the cells in your blood
which carry oxygen around your body.
4 If you refer to someone as a **red** or a **Red,** you disap- N-COUNT
prove of the fact that they are a communist, a socialist PRAGMATICS
or have left-wing ideas. **5** If a person or company is **in** INFORMAL
the red or if their bank account is **in the red,** they have PHRASE
spent more money than they have in their account
and therefore they owe money to the bank. **6** If you PHRASE
see red, you suddenly become very angry.

,**red a'lert, red alerts.** If a hospital, a police force, N-VAR
or a military force is on **red alert,** they have been
warned that an emergency may happen soon, and
they are ready to deal with it.

,**red-'blooded.** If a man is described as **red-** ADJ: ADJ n
blooded, he is considered to be strong and healthy INFORMAL
and have a strong interest in sex.

red·brick /ˈredbrɪk/. A **redbrick** university is one of ADJ: ADJ n
the universities that were established in large cities BRITISH
outside London in the late 19th and early 20th centuries, as opposed to much older universities such
as Oxford and Cambridge.

,red 'cabbage, red cabbages. A red cabbage is N-VAR a round vegetable with dark red leaves.

,red 'carpet, red carpets. The red carpet is spe- N-COUNT cial treatment given to an important or honoured guest, for example the laying of a strip of red carpet for them to walk on.

,Red 'Crescent. The Red Crescent is an organiza- N-PROPER: tion in Muslim countries that helps people who are theN suffering due to war, famine, or natural disaster.

,Red 'Cross. The Red Cross is an international ◆◆◇◇◇ organization that helps people who are suffering N-PROPER: due to war, famine, or natural disaster. theN

red·cur·rant /ˌred'kʌrənt, AM -'kɜːr-/ **redcurrants.** N-COUNT Redcurrants are very small bright red berries that can be eaten. The bush on which they grow can also be called a **redcurrant.**

red·den /ˈredən/ **reddens, reddening, red-** VERB: V dened.** If someone **reddens** or their face **reddens,** WRITTEN their face turns pink or red, often because they are embarrassed or angry.

red·dish /ˈredɪʃ/. **Reddish** means slightly red in ◆◇◇◇◇ colour. ADJ

re·deco·rate /ˌriː'dekəreɪt/ **redecorates, re-** ◆◇◇◇◇ decorating, redecorated.** If you **redecorate** a VERB: V n room or a building, you put new paint or wallpaper V on it. *I've just been waiting for an excuse to redeco-rate.* ✦ **re·deco·ra·tion** /ˌriːˌdekəˈreɪʃən/. *The* N-UNCOUNT *house is in desperate need of redecoration.*

re·deem /rɪ'diːm/ **redeems, redeeming, re-** ◆◇◇◇◇ deemed.** **1** If you **redeem** yourself or your reputa- VERB: V n tion, you do something that makes people have a good opinion of you again after you have behaved or performed badly. **2** When something **redeems** an VERB unpleasant thing or situation, it prevents it from be- V n ing completely bad. *Work is the way that people seek to redeem their lives from futility.* **3** If you **redeem** a VERB: V n debt or an obligation, you pay money that you owe or that you promised to pay. **4** If you **redeem** an VERB object you possess, you get it back from someone V n by repaying them money that you have borrowed from them, using the object as a guarantee. *Make sure you know exactly what you will be paying back at the date upon which you plan to redeem the item.* **5** In religions such as Christianity, to **redeem** some- VERB: V n one means to save them by freeing them from sin and evil.

re·deem·able /rɪ'diːməbəl/. If something is **re-** ADJ deemable,** it can be exchanged for a particular sum of money or for goods worth a particular sum. *Tick-ets cost $10, which is redeemable against any Chanel purchase.*

Re·deem·er /rɪ'diːmə/. In the Christian religion, N-PROPER: the **Redeemer** is Jesus Christ. theN

re·de·fine /ˌriːdɪ'faɪn/ **redefines, redefining, re-** ◆◇◇◇◇ defined.** If you **redefine** something, you cause VERB people to consider it in a new way. *Feminists have* V n *redefined the role of women.* ✦ **re·defi·ni·tion** N-UNCOUNT /ˌriːdefɪ'nɪʃən/. *...the redefinition of socialism.*

re·demp·tion /rɪ'dempʃən/ **redemptions. 1** Re-** ◆◇◇◇◇ demption** is the act of redeeming something or of N-VAR being redeemed by something. *He craves redemp-tion for his sins.* **2** If you say that someone or some- PHRASE thing is **beyond redemption,** you mean that they are so bad it is unlikely that anything can be done to improve them. *We are polluting the environment beyond redemption.*

re·demp·tive /rɪ'demptɪv/. In Christianity, a **re-** ADJ demptive** act or quality is something which leads to freedom from the consequences of sin and evil.

re·deploy /ˌriːdɪ'plɔɪ/ **redeploys, redeploying, redeployed. 1** If troops are redeployed, they go V-ERG: to new positions so that they are ready for action. beV-ed *We were forced urgently to redeploy our forces... US* V troops are redeploying to positions held earlier.* **2** If VERB: resources or workers **are redeployed,** they are used beV-ed for a different purpose or task. *It would give us an* V n *opportunity to redeploy our resources.*

re·deploy·ment /ˌriːdɪ'plɔɪmənt/ **redeploy-** N-VAR ments.** The **redeployment** of forces, troops, work-ers, or resources involves putting them in a different

place from where they were before, or using them for a different task or purpose.

re·design /ˌriːdɪ'zaɪn/ **redesigns, redesigning,** ◆◇◇◇◇ redesigned.** If a building, vehicle, or system **is re-** VERB: designed,** it is rebuilt according to a new design in beV-ed order to improve it. *The second step is to redesign* V n *the school system so that it produces a well-educated population.*

re·devel·op /ˌriːdɪ'veləp/ **redevelops, redevel-** VERB: oping, redeveloped.** When an area **is redevel-** beV-ed oped,** existing buildings and roads are removed and new ones are built in their place.

re·devel·op·ment /ˌriːdɪ'veləpmənt/. When re-** ◆◇◇◇◇ development** takes place, the buildings in one area N-UNCOUNT of a town are knocked down and new ones are built in their place.

,red-'faced. A **red-faced** person has a face that ADJ-GRADED looks red, often because they are embarrassed or angry. *A red-faced Mr Jones was led away by police.*

,red 'flag, red flags. A **red flag** is a flag that is red N-COUNT in colour and is used as a symbol to represent com-munism and socialism or to indicate danger or as a symbol to stop. *Then the rain came and the red flag went up to signal a halt.*

,red-'handed. If someone **is caught red-handed,** PHRASE they are caught while they are in the act of doing something wrong.

red·head /ˈredhed/ **redheads.** A **redhead** is a per- N-COUNT son, especially a woman, whose hair is a colour that is between red and brown. ✦ **red-headed** ADJ /ˌred'hedɪd/. *He ran off with a redheaded divorcee.*

,red 'herring, red herrings. If you say that some- N-COUNT thing is a **red herring,** you mean that it is irrelevant and takes your attention away from the main sub-ject or problem you are considering.

,red-'hot. 1 Red-hot** metal or rock has been heat- ◆◇◇◇◇ ed to such a high temperature that it has turned ADJ red. **2** A **red-hot** object is too hot to be touched ADJ safely or comfortably. **3** The **red-hot** favourite in a ADJ: ADJ n race or contest is the person who is most definitely INFORMAL expected to win.

,Red 'Indian, Red Indians. The Native Ameri- N-COUNT cans who were living in North America when the DATED Europeans arrived there used to be called **Red In-dians;** an offensive term.

re·di·rect /ˌriːdɪ'rekt, -daɪ-/ **redirects, redirect-** ◆◇◇◇◇ ing, redirected. 1** If you **redirect** your energy, VERB: V n resources, or ability, you begin doing something different or trying to achieve something different. ✦ **re·di·rec·tion** /ˌriːdɪ'rekʃən, -daɪ-/. *A redirection* N-UNCOUNT: *of resources would be required.* **2** If you **redirect** also aN someone or something, you change their course or VERB destination. *She redirected them to the men's depart-* V n *ment.* ✦ **redirection** *...the Royal Mail redirection* N-UNCOUNT *service.*

re·dis·cov·er /ˌriːdɪ'skʌvə/ **rediscovers, redis-** ◆◇◇◇◇ covering, rediscovered.** If you **rediscover** VERB: V n something good or valuable that you had forgotten or lost, you become aware of it again or find it again.

re·dis·cov·ery /ˌriːdɪ'skʌvəri/ **rediscoveries.** The N-VAR: rediscovery** of something good or valuable that you N of n had forgotten or lost is the fact or the process of be-coming aware of it again or finding it again. *The best part of his expedition had been the rediscovery of his natural passion for making things.*

re·dis·trib·ute /ˌriːdɪ'strɪbjuːt/ **redistributes, re-** ◆◇◇◇◇ distributing, redistributed.** If something such VERB: as money or property **is redistributed,** it is shared beV-ed among people or organizations in a different way V n from the way that it was previously shared. *Taxes could be used to redistribute income.* ✦ **re·dis·tri·** **·bu·tion** /ˌriːdɪstrɪ'bjuːʃən/. *Labour will still be* N-UNCOUNT *committed to a redistribution of wealth.*

,red-'letter day, red-letter days. A **red-letter** N-COUNT day** is a day that you will always remember because something good happens to you then.

,red 'light, red lights. 1 A **red light** is a traffic ◆◇◇◇◇ signal which shines red to indicate that drivers must N-COUNT

red meat

916

stop. **2** The **red-light** district of a city is the area where prostitutes work.

red 'meat, red meats. Red meat is meat such as beef or lamb, which is dark brown in colour after it has been cooked.

red·neck /'rednek/ **rednecks.** If someone describes a white man, especially a lower class, rural American, as a **redneck**, they disapprove of him because they think he is ignorant and has strong, unreasonable opinions; a use that is often considered offensive.

red·ness /'rednəs/. **Redness** is the quality of being red. *Slowly the redness left Sophie's face.*

redo /ˌriː'duː/ **redoes, redoing, redid, redone.** If you **redo** a piece of work, you do it again in order to improve it or change it.

redo·lent /'redələnt/. **1** If something is **redolent** of something else, it has features that make you think of that other thing. *...percussion instruments, redolent of Far Eastern cultures.* **2** If something is **redolent** of something else, it smells strongly of that other thing.

re·dou·ble /ˌriː'dʌbəl/ **redoubles, redoubling, redoubled.** If you **redouble** your efforts, you try much harder to achieve something. If something **re-doubles**, it increases in volume or intensity. *The applause redoubled.*

re·doubt /rɪ'daʊt/ **redoubts.** A **redoubt** is a place or situation in which someone feels safe because they know that nobody can attack them or spoil their peace. *...the last redoubt of hippy culture.*

re·doubt·able /rɪ'daʊtəbəl/. If you describe someone as **redoubtable**, you respect them because they have a very strong character, even though you are slightly afraid of them.

re·dound /rɪ'daʊnd/ **redounds, redounding, redounded.** If an action or situation **redounds** to your benefit or advantage, it gives people a good impression of you or brings you something that can improve your situation. *The success in the Middle East redounds to his benefit.*

red 'pepper, red peppers. 1 Red peppers are ripe peppers which are sweet-tasting and can be used in cooking or eaten raw in salads. **2** Red pepper is a hot-tasting spicy powder made from the flesh and seeds of small, dried, red peppers. It is used for flavouring food.

re·draft /ˌriː'drɑːft, -'dræft/ **redrafts, redrafting, redrafted.** If you **redraft** something you have written, you write it again in order to improve it or change it.

re·draw /ˌriː'drɔː/ **redraws, redrawing, redrew, redrawn. 1** If people in a position of authority **redraw** the boundaries or borders of a country or region, they change the borders so that the country or region covers a slightly different area than before. **2** If people **redraw** something, for example an arrangement or plan, they change it because circumstances have changed.

re·dress /rɪ'dres/ **redresses, redressing, redressed.** The noun is also pronounced /'riːdres/ in American English. **1** If you **redress** something such as a wrong or a grievance, you do something to correct it or to improve things for the person who has been badly treated. *More and more victims turn to litigation to redress wrongs done to them.* **2** If you **redress** the balance or the imbalance between two things that have become unequal, you make them equal again. *...to redress the economic imbalance between the developed countries and the developing countries.* **3** Redress is compensation for something wrong that has been done.

red 'tape. You refer to official rules and procedures as **red tape** when they seem unnecessary and cause delay. *The little money that was available was tied up in bureaucratic red tape.*

re·duce /rɪ'djuːs, AM -'duːs/ **reduces, reducing, reduced. 1** If you **reduce** something, you make it smaller in size or amount, or less in degree. *It reduces the risks of heart disease.* **2** If someone is re-

duced to a weaker or inferior state, they become weaker or inferior as a result of something that happens to them. *They were reduced to extreme poverty.* **3** If something is changed to a different or less complicated form, you can say that it **is reduced** to that form. *All the buildings in the town have been reduced to rubble.* **4** If you say that someone **is reduced** to doing something, you mean that they have to do it, although it is unpleasant or humiliating. *He was reduced to begging for a living.* **5** If someone or something **reduces** you to **tears**, they make you feel so sad that you cry. **6** If you say that someone is living in **reduced circumstances**, you mean that they do not have as much money as they used to have.

re·duc·ible /rɪ'djuːsɪbəl, AM -'duːs-/. If you say that an idea, problem, or situation is not **reducible** to something simple, you mean that it is complicated and cannot be described in a simple way. *The structure of the universe may not be reducible to a problem in physics.*

re·duc·tion /rɪ'dʌkʃən/ **reductions. 1** When there is a **reduction** in something, it is made smaller. *Many companies have announced dramatic reductions in staff.* **2** Reduction is the act of making something smaller in size or amount, or less in degree. *...a new strategic arms reduction agreement.*

re·duc·tion·ist /rɪ'dʌkʃənɪst/. **Reductionist** describes a way of analysing problems and things by dividing them into simpler parts. *This encourages reductionist explanations of fascist ideology.*

re·duc·tive /rɪ'dʌktɪv/. If you describe something such as a theory or a work of art as **reductive**, you disapprove of it because it reduces complex things to simple elements.

re·dun·dan·cy /rɪ'dʌndənsi/ **redundancies. 1** When there are **redundancies**, an organization dismisses some of its employees because their jobs are no longer necessary or because the organization can no longer afford to pay them. The usual American word is **layoff. 2** Redundancy means being made redundant. *Thousands of bank employees are facing redundancy.*

re·dun·dant /rɪ'dʌndənt/. **1** If you are made **re-dundant**, you are dismissed by your employer because your job is no longer necessary or because your employer cannot afford to keep paying you. The usual American expression is **laid off.** *...a redundant miner.* **2** Something that is **redundant** is no longer needed because its job is being done by something else or because its job is no longer necessary or useful. *Changes in technology may mean that once-valued skills are now redundant.*

red·wood /'redwʊd/ **redwoods.** A **redwood** is an extremely tall tree which grows in California.

reed /riːd/ **reeds. 1** Reeds are tall plants that grow in large groups in shallow water or marshy ground. They have strong stems that can be used for making things such as mats or baskets. **2** A **reed** is a small piece of cane or metal inserted into the mouthpiece of a woodwind instrument. The reed vibrates when you blow through it and makes a sound.

re·'educate, re-educates, re-educating, re-educated. If an organization such as a government tries to **re-educate** a group of people, they try to make them adopt new attitudes, beliefs, or types of behaviour. ♦ **re-education** *...a programme of punishment and re-education of political dissidents.*

reedy /'riːdi/. If someone has a **reedy** voice, their voice is unpleasant because it is high and unclear.

reef /riːf/ **reefs.** A **reef** is a long line of rocks or sand, the top of which is just above or just below the surface of the sea.

reef·er /'riːfə/ **reefers. 1** A **reefer** or **reefer coat** is a type of short thick coat which used to be worn by sailors. **2** A **reefer** is a cigarette containing marijuana and tobacco.

reek /riːk/ **reeks, reeking, reeked. 1** If something **reeks** of something else, usually something unpleasant, it smells very strongly of it. *The entire*

house reeked for a long time. ▶ Also a noun. *He* N-SING
smelt the reek of whisky. **2** If you say that something
reeks of unpleasant ideas, feelings, or practices, you [PRAGMATICS]
disapprove of it because it gives a firm impression V ofn
that it involves those ideas, feelings, or practices.
The whole thing reeks of hypocrisy.

reel /riːl/ **reels, reeling, reeled. 1** A reel is a cy- ◆◆◆◇◇
lindrical object around which you wrap something N-COUNT
such as cinema film, fishing line, or cotton thread.
American English usually uses the term **spool** to refer to thicker reels. **2** You can talk about a **reel** as a N-COUNT
way of referring to all the scenes in a film which fit
onto one reel of film. *I shall not reveal the movie's
final reel.*
3 If someone **reels**, they move about unsteadily as if VERB: V
they were going to fall. *He lost his balance and reeled* V adv/prep
back. **4** If you are **reeling** from a shock, you are feeling VERB:
extremely surprised or upset because of it. *It left us* V prep
reeling with disbelief. **5** If you say that your brain or VERB: V
your mind is **reeling**, you mean that you are very confused because you have too many things to think
about.
6 A **reel** is a type of fast Scottish dance. N-COUNT

reel in. If you **reel in** something such as a fish, you PHRASAL VB
pull it towards you by winding around a reel the wire V P noun
or line that it is attached to. *Gleacher reeled in the first* Also V n P
fish.

reel off. If you **reel off** information, you repeat it PHRASAL VB
from memory quickly and easily. *She reeled off the ti-* V P noun
tles of a dozen or so of the novels. Also V n P

re-e'lect, re-elects, re-electing, re-elected. ◆◆◇◇◇
When someone such as a politician is **re-elected**, VERB:
they win a new election and are therefore able to beV-ed
continue in their position as, for example, a mem- beV-ed n
ber of parliament. *Juan Peron was re-elected presi-* Also beV-ed
dent of Argentina in 1973. ◆ **re-election** N-UNCOUNT
/ˌriːɪˈlekʃən/. *I would like to see him stand for re-
election.*

re-en'act, re-enacts, re-enacting, re- VERB
enacted. If you **re-enact** a scene or incident, you V n
repeat the actions that occurred in the scene or incident. *He re-enacted scenes from his TV series.*
◆ **re-enactment, re-enactments.** When a **re-** N-COUNT
enactment of a scene or incident takes place, people re-enact it.

re-'enter, re-enters, re-entering, re-entered. ◆◇◇◇◇
If you **re-enter** a place, organization, or area of ac- VERB: V n
tivity that you have left, you return to it.

re-'entry. 1 Re-entry is the act of returning to a N-UNCOUNT:
place, organization, or area of activity that you have also a N
left. *The military men are contemplating a re-entry
into politics.* **2** Re-entry is used to refer to the mo- N-UNCOUNT:
ment when a spacecraft comes back into the earth's also a N
atmosphere after being in space. *The station would
burn up on re-entry into the earth's atmosphere.*

re-ex'amine, re-examines, re-examining, ◆◇◇◇◇
re-examined. If a person or group of people **re-** VERB
examines their ideas, beliefs, or attitudes, they V n
think about them carefully because they are no
longer sure if they are correct. *The European Community is to re-examine its policy towards South Africa.* ◆ **re-examina·tion, re-examinations** *It* N-VAR
was time for a re-examination of the situation.

ref /ref/ **refs. 1** Ref. is an abbreviation for 'refer- ◆◇◇◇◇
ence'. It is written in front of a code at the top of
letters and documents. The code refers to a file
where all the letters and documents about the same
matter are kept. *Our Ref: JAH/JW.* **2** The **ref** in a N-COUNT
sports match, such as football or boxing, is the
same as the **referee.**

re·fec·tory /rɪˈfektəri/ **refectories.** A refectory is N-COUNT
a large dining hall in a monastery, university, or
other institution.

re·fer /rɪˈfɜː/ **refers, referring, referred. 1** If ◆◆◆◆◇
you **refer** to a particular subject or person, you VERB
mention them. *In his speech, he referred to a recent* V to n
trip to Canada. **2** If you **refer** to someone or something as a particular thing, you use a particular VERB
word or expression to mention or describe them. *He* V to n as n
simply referred to him as Ronnie. **3** If a word refers VERB

to a particular thing, situation, or idea, it describes V to n
it. *The term electronics refers to electrically-induced
action.*
4 If a person who is ill is **referred** to a hospital or a VERB:
specialist, they are sent there by a doctor in order to beV-ed n
be treated. **5** If you **refer** a task or a problem to a per- VERB
son or an organization, you formally tell them about V n to n
it, so that they can deal with it. *He could refer the matter to the high court.* **6** If you **refer** someone to a per- VERB
son or organization, you send them there for the help V n to n
they need. *Now and then I referred a client to him.*
7 If you **refer** to a book or other source of information, VERB:
you look at it in order to find something out. **8** If you V to n
refer someone to a source of information, you tell VERB
them the place where they will find the information. V n to n
*Mr Bryan also referred me to a book by the American
journalist Anthony Scaduto.*

ref·er·ee /ˌrefəˈriː/ **referees, refereeing, ref-** ◆◆◇◇◇
ereed. 1 The **referee** is the official who controls a N-COUNT
sports match. **2** When someone **referees** a sports V
match or contest, they act as referee. *It's been years
and years and years since I've refereed.* **3** A **referee** is N-COUNT
a person who gives you a reference, for example
when you are applying for a job. In American English, this person is called a **reference.**

ref·er·ence /ˈrefərəns/ **references, referenc-** ◆◆◆◇◇
ing, referenced. 1 Reference to someone or N-VAR
something is the act of talking about them or mentioning them. A **reference** to someone or something
is an instance of this. *He made no reference to any
agreement.* **2** Reference means consulting someone N-UNCOUNT
or something for information or advice. *Please keep
this sheet in a safe place for reference.* **3** Reference ADJ: ADJ n
books are ones you look at when you need specific
information about a subject.
4 A **reference** is a word, phrase, or idea which comes N-COUNT
from something such as a book, poem, or play. *...a reference from the Quran.* **5** A **reference** is something N-COUNT
such as a number or a name that tells you where you
can obtain the information you want. *...a map refer-
ence.* **6** A **reference** is a letter written by someone who N-COUNT
knows you which describes your character and abil-
ities. When you apply for a job, an employer might ask
for **references. 7** See also **cross-reference, frame of
reference, point of reference, terms of reference.**
8 You use **with reference to** or **in reference to** in or- PHR-PREP
der to indicate what something relates to. *I am writ-
ing with reference to your article on salaries.*

'reference library, reference libraries. A ref- N-COUNT
erence library is a library that contains books
which you can look at in the library itself but which
you cannot borrow.

ref·er·en·dum /ˌrefəˈrendəm/ **referendums** or ◆◆◆◇◇
referenda /ˌrefəˈrendə/. If a country holds a **refer-** N-COUNT
endum on a particular policy, they ask the people
to vote on whether or not they agree with the policy. *Estonia said today it too plans to hold a referendum on independence.*

re·fer·ral /rɪˈfɜːrəl/ **referrals.** Referral is the act of ◆◇◇◇◇
officially sending someone to a person or authority N-VAR
that is authorized or better qualified to deal with
them. A **referral** is an instance of this.

re·fill, refills, refilling, refilled. The verb is pro- ◆◇◇◇◇
nounced /ˌriːˈfɪl/. The noun is pronounced /ˈriːfɪl/. VERB
If you **refill** something, you fill it again after it has V n
been emptied. *I refilled our wine glasses.* ▶ Also a N-COUNT
noun. *Max held out his cup for a refill.*

re·fi·nance /ˌriːfaɪˈnæns/ **refinances, refinanc-** ◆◇◇◇◇
ing, refinanced. If a person or a company VERB: V n
refinances a debt, they borrow some money in or- V
der to pay the debt. *At the end of the term the borrower must pay in full or refinance.*

re·fine /rɪˈfaɪn/ **refines, refining, refined.** ◆◇◇◇◇
1 When a substance is **refined**, it is made pure by VB: usu
having all other substances removed from it. *Oil is* passive
refined to remove naturally occurring impurities. beV-ed
◆ **re·fined** *...refined sugar.* ◆ **re·fin·ing** *...oil refin-* ADJ-GRADED
ing. **2** If something such as a process, a theory, or a N-UNCOUNT
machine is **refined**, it is improved by having small VB: usu
passive

alterations made to it. *Surgical techniques are constantly being refined.* be V-ed

re·fined /rɪˈfaɪnd/. **1** If you say that someone is **refined**, you mean that they are very polite and well-mannered and have good taste. **2** If you describe a machine or a process as **refined**, you mean that it has been carefully developed and is therefore very efficient or elegant. ◆◇◇◇ ADJ-GRADED / ADJ-GRADED

re·fine·ment /rɪˈfaɪnmənt/ **refinements. 1 Refinements** are small alterations or additions that you make to something in order to improve it. **Refinement** is the process of making refinements. *Older cars inevitably lack the latest safety refinements.* **2 Refinement** is politeness and good manners, combined with a way of behaving which shows that you dislike anything vulgar. ◆◇◇◇ N-VAR / N-UNCOUNT

re·fin·er /rɪˈfaɪnə/ **refiners. Refiners** are people or organizations that refine substances such as oil or sugar. N-COUNT

re·fin·ery /rɪˈfaɪnəri/ **refineries. A refinery** is a factory which refines substances such as oil or sugar. ◆◇◇◇ N-COUNT

re·fit, refits, refitting, refitted. The verb is pronounced /ˌriːˈfɪt/. The noun is pronounced /ˈriːfɪt/. When a ship **is refitted**, it is repaired or is given new parts, equipment, or furniture. ◆ Also a noun. *The ship finished an extensive refit last year.* ◆◇◇◇ VERB: be V-ed / N-COUNT

re·flect /rɪˈflekt/ **reflects, reflecting, reflected. 1** If something **reflects** an attitude or situation, it shows that the attitude or situation exists. *Concern at the economic situation was reflected in the government's budget.* **2** When light, heat or other rays **reflect** off a surface or when a surface **reflects** them, they are sent back from the surface and do not pass through it. *The glass appears to reflect light naturally.* ◆ **re·flec·tion** ...*the reflection of a beam of light off a mirror.* **3** When something **is reflected** in a mirror or in water, you can see its image there. **4** When you **reflect**, you think deeply about something. *I reflected on the child's future.* **5** You can use **reflect** to indicate that a particular thought occurs to someone. *Things were very much changed since before the war, he reflected.* **6** If an action or situation **reflects** in a particular way on someone or something, it gives people a good or bad impression of them. *The affair hardly reflected well on the British.* ◆◆◆◇ VERB V n / V-ERG: V prep / V n / N-UNCOUNT / VERB: be V-ed / VERB: V / V on/upon n / VERB V that / VERB V adv on n / Also V on n

re·flec·tion /rɪˈflekʃən/ **reflections. 1** A **reflection** is an image that you can see in a mirror or in glass or water. **2** If you say that something is a **reflection** of a person's attitude or a situation, you mean that it is caused by that attitude or situation and therefore reveals something about it. *Inhibition in adulthood seems to be very clearly a reflection of a person's experiences as a child.* **3** If you say that something is a **reflection** on someone or a **sad reflection** on someone, you mean that it gives a bad impression of them. *Infection with head lice is no reflection on personal hygiene.* **4 Reflection** is careful thought about a particular topic. Your **reflections** are your thoughts about a particular topic. ● If someone admits or accepts something **on reflection**, they admit or accept it after having thought carefully about it. *On reflection, he says, he very much regrets the comments.* ◆◆◇◇ N-COUNT / N-COUNT / N-SING / N-UNCOUNT / PHRASE

re·flec·tive /rɪˈflektɪv/. **1** If you are **reflective**, you think deeply about things. *Mike is a quiet, reflective man.* ◆ **re·flec·tive·ly** *He gazed reflectively at his companion.* **2** If something is **reflective** of a particular situation or attitude, it is typical of that situation or attitude. *The German government's support of the US is not entirely reflective of German public opinion.* **3** A **reflective** surface or material sends back light or heat. ◆◇◇◇ ADJ-GRADED WRITTEN / ADV-GRADED: ADV with v / ADJ-GRADED: v-link ADJ of n / ADJ-GRADED FORMAL

re·flec·tor /rɪˈflektə/ **reflectors. 1** A **reflector** is a small piece of specially patterned glass or plastic which glows when light shines on it. **2** A **reflector** is a type of telescope which has a curved mirror. N-COUNT / N-COUNT

re·flex /ˈriːfleks/ **reflexes. 1** A **reflex** or a **reflex action** is something that you do automatically and without thinking. *Walsh fumbled in his pocket, a re-* ◆◇◇◇ N-COUNT

flex from his smoking days. **2** A **reflex** or a **reflex action** is a normal, uncontrollable reaction of your body to something that you feel, see, or experience. ...*the stress hormone adrenaline, released by reflex action from the adrenal glands.* **3** Your **reflexes** are your ability to react quickly with your body when something unexpected happens. ...*skill, cool nerves, and the reflexes of an athlete.* N-COUNT / N-PLURAL

re·flex·ive /rɪˈfleksɪv/. A **reflexive** reaction or movement occurs immediately in response to something that happens. ...*that reflexive urge for concealment.* ADJ FORMAL

re,flexive 'pronoun, reflexive pronouns. A **reflexive pronoun** is a pronoun such as 'myself' which refers back to the subject of a sentence or clause. N-COUNT

re,flexive 'verb, reflexive verbs. A **reflexive verb** is a transitive verb whose subject and object always refer to the same person or thing, so the object is always a reflexive pronoun. An example is 'to enjoy yourself', as in 'Did you enjoy yourself?'. N-COUNT

re·flex·ol·ogy /ˌriːflekˈsɒlədʒi/. **Reflexology** is the practice of massaging a person's feet, and sometimes their hands, in the belief that it can heal particular organs in other parts of the body. ◆ **re·flex·olo·gist, reflexologists** *Reflexologists don't use any oils on the feet.* ◆◇◇◇ N-UNCOUNT / N-COUNT

re·for·est /ˌriːˈfɒrɪst/ **reforests, reforesting, reforested.** To **reforest** an area where there used to be a forest means to plant trees over it. ◆ **re·for·esta·tion** /ˌriːfɒrɪˈsteɪʃən/. ...*the reforestation of the Apennine Mountains.* VERB: V n / N-UNCOUNT

re·form /rɪˈfɔːm/ **reforms, reforming, reformed. 1 Reform** consists of changes and improvements to a law, social system, or institution. A **reform** is an instance of this. *He has urged reform of the welfare system.* **2** If someone **reforms** something such as a law, social system, or institution, they change or improve it. ◆ **ref·or·ma·tion** ...*the reformation of science.* ◆ **re·form·er, reformers** *Tarasas is another leading reformer.* **3** When someone **reforms** or when something **reforms** them, they stop doing something that society does not approve of. *We will try to reform him within the community.* ◆ **re·formed** ...*a reformed alcoholic.* **4** See also **re-form**. ◆◆◆◇ N-VAR / VERB: V n / N-UNCOUNT / N-COUNT / V-ERG: V n / ADJ

,re-'form, re-forms, re-forming, re-formed; also spelled **reform**. When an organization, group, or shape **re-forms**, or when someone **re-forms** it, it is created again after a period during which it did not exist. *The 40-year-old singer reformed his band.* V-ERG: V n

ref·or·ma·tion /ˌrefəˈmeɪʃən/. **The Reformation** is the movement to reform the Catholic Church in the sixteenth century, which led to the Protestant church being set up. ◆◇◇◇ N-PROPER: the N

re·form·ism /rɪˈfɔːmɪzəm/. **Reformism** is the belief that a system or law should be reformed. ◆ **re·form·ist, reformists** ...*the growing split between reformists and conservatives.* ► Also an adjective ...*a strong supporter of reformist policies.* N-UNCOUNT / N-COUNT / ADJ-GRADED

re·fract /rɪˈfrækt/ **refracts, refracting, refracted.** When a ray of light or a sound wave **refracts** or **is refracted**, the path it follows bends at a particular point. *As we age the lenses of the eyes thicken, and thus refract light differently.* V-ERG: V n

re·frain /rɪˈfreɪn/ **refrains, refraining, refrained. 1** If you **refrain** from doing something, you deliberately do not do it. *He appealed to all factions to refrain from violence.* **2** A **refrain** is a short, simple part of a song, which is repeated many times. **3** A **refrain** is a comment or saying that people often repeat. *Rosa's constant refrain is that she doesn't have a life.* ◆◇◇◇ VERB V from-ing/n / N-COUNT / N-COUNT

re·fresh /rɪˈfreʃ/ **refreshes, refreshing, refreshed. 1** If something **refreshes** you when you have become hot, tired, or thirsty, it makes you feel cooler or more energetic. *The lotion cools and refreshes the skin.* ◆ **re·freshed** *He awoke feeling completely refreshed.* ◆ **re·fresh·ing** ...*refreshing drinks.* **2** If you **refresh** something old or faded, ◆◇◇◇ VERB V n / ADJ-GRADED / ADJ-GRADED / VERB

you make it as strong or fresh as it was when it was V n
new. ...*an occasion to share new ideas and refresh
friendship.* **3** If someone **refreshes** your memory, VERB: V n
they tell you something that you had forgotten.

re·fresher course, refresher courses. A **re-** N-COUNT
fresher course is a training course in which people
improve their knowledge or skills and learn about
new developments that are related to their job.

re·fresh·ing /rɪˈfreʃɪŋ/. You say that something is ◆◇◇◇
refreshing when it is pleasantly different from what ADJ-GRADED
you are used to. *It's refreshing to hear somebody
speaking common sense.* ♦ **re·fresh·ing·ly** *He was* ADV-GRADED
refreshingly honest.

re·fresh·ment /rɪˈfreʃmənt/ **refreshments.** ◆◇◇◇
1 Refreshments are drinks and small amounts of N-PLURAL
food that are provided, for example, during a meeting or a journey. **2** You can refer to food and drink N-UNCOUNT
as **refreshment**. *May I offer you some refreshment?* FORMAL

re·frig·er·ate /rɪˈfrɪdʒəreɪt/ **refrigerates, refrig-** ◆◇◇◇
erating, refrigerated. If you **refrigerate** food, VERB: V n
you make it cold, for example by putting it in a
fridge. ♦ **re·frig·era·tion** /rɪˌfrɪdʒəˈreɪʃən/. *Refrig-* N-UNCOUNT
eration will make olive oil cloudy.

re·frig·era·tor /rɪˈfrɪdʒəreɪtə/ **refrigerators.** A ◆◇◇◇
refrigerator is a large container which is kept cool N-COUNT
inside, usually by electricity, so that the food and
drink in it stays fresh.

re·fu·el /ˌriːˈfjuːəl/ **refuels, refuelling, refu-** ◇◇◇◇
elled; spelled **refueling, refueled** in American Eng- V-ERG: V
lish. When an aircraft or other vehicle **refuels** or V n
when someone **refuels** it, it is filled with more fuel
so that it can continue its journey. *The airline's crew
refuelled the plane.* ♦ **re·fu·el·ling** *It will make two* N-UNCOUNT
refuelling stops.

ref·uge /ˈrefjuːdʒ/ **refuges. 1** If you take **refuge** ◆◇◇◇
somewhere, you try to protect yourself from physi- N-UNCOUNT
cal harm by going there. *His home became a place of
refuge for the believers.* **2** A **refuge** is a place where N-COUNT
you go for safety and protection. ...*a refuge for battered women.* **3** If you take **refuge** in a particular N-UNCOUNT
way of behaving or thinking, you try to protect
yourself from unhappiness or unpleasantness by
behaving or thinking in that way. *They get bored,
and seek refuge in drink and drugs.*

refu·gee /ˌrefjuˈdʒiː/ **refugees. Refugees** are ◆◆◆◇
people who have been forced to leave their homes N-COUNT
or their country, either because there is a war there
or because of their political or religious beliefs.

re·fund, refunds, refunding, refunded. The ◆◆◇◇
noun is pronounced /ˈriːfʌnd/. The verb is pronounced /rɪˈfʌnd/. **1** A **refund** is a sum of money N-COUNT
which is returned to you, for example because you
have returned goods to a shop. **2** If you give some- VERB: V n
funds your money, they return it to you. *Take the* V n n
*goods back to your retailer who will refund you the
purchase price.*

re·fund·able /rɪˈfʌndəbəl/. A **refundable** deposit or ADJ
charge will be paid back in certain circumstances.

re·fur·bish /ˌriːˈfɜːbɪʃ/ **refurbishes, refurbish-** ◆◇◇◇
ing, refurbished. To **refurbish** a building or room VERB: V n
means to clean it and decorate it and make it more
attractive or better equipped. ♦ **re·fur·bish·ment** N-UNCOUNT:
/ˌriːˈfɜːbɪʃmənt/ **refurbishments** *The boat has* also N in pl
undergone extensive refurbishment.

re·fus·al /rɪˈfjuːzəl/ **refusals. 1** Someone's **refusal** ◆◆◇◇
to do something or **refusal** of something is the fact N-VAR
of them showing or saying that they will not do it,
allow it, grant it, or accept it. ...*the Council's refusal
of planning permission.* **2** If someone has **first re-** PHRASE
fusal on something, they have the right to decide
whether or not to buy it or take it before it is offered
to anyone else.

re·fuse, refuses, refusing, refused. The verb is ◆◆◆◇
pronounced /rɪˈfjuːz/. The noun is pronounced
/ˈrefjuːs/. **1** If you **refuse** to do something, you de- VERB:
liberately do not do it, or you say firmly that you V to-inf
will not do it. *He expects me to stay on here and I* V
can hardly refuse. **2** If someone **refuses** you some- VERB: V n n
thing, they do not give it to you or do not allow you V n
to have it. *The town council had refused permission*

for the march. **3** If you **refuse** something that is of- VERB
fered to you, you do not accept it. *The patient has* V n
the right to refuse treatment.

4 Refuse consists of all the rubbish and all the things that N-UNCOUNT
are not wanted in a house, shop, or factory, and that FORMAL
are regularly thrown away.

re·fute /rɪˈfjuːt/ **refutes, refuting, refuted. 1** If ◆◇◇◇
you **refute** an allegation, an argument, or a theory, VERB
you prove that it is wrong or untrue. *It was the kind* V n
of rumour that it is impossible to refute. ♦ **refu·ta-** FORMAL
·tion /ˌrefjuˈteɪʃən/ **refutations** ...*a complete refu-* N-VAR
tation of the Republicans' most serious charges. **2** If VERB: V n
you **refute** an allegation or accusation, you deny FORMAL
that it is true.

re·gain /rɪˈgeɪn/ **regains, regaining, regained.** ◆◆◇◇
1 If you **regain** something that you have lost, you VERB
get it back again. *Troops have regained control of the* V n
city. **2** If you **regain** a place that you have left, you VERB: V n
succeed in getting back there. FORMAL

re·gal /ˈriːgəl/. If you describe something as **regal**, ◆◇◇◇
you mean that it is suitable for a king or queen, be- ADJ-GRADED
cause it is very splendid or dignified. ♦ **re·gal·ly** *He* ADV-GRADED
inclined his head regally.

re·gale /rɪˈgeɪl/ **regales, regaling, regaled.** If VERB
someone **regales** you with stories or jokes, they tell V n with n
you a lot of them, whether you want to hear them
or not. *He was constantly regaled with tales of woe.*

re·ga·lia /rɪˈgeɪliə/. **Regalia** consists of the tradi- N-UNCOUNT
tional clothes and items which someone such as a
king or a judge wears and carries on official
occasions.

re·gard /rɪˈgɑːd/ **regards, regarding, regard-** ◆◆◆◇
ed. 1 If you **regard** someone or something as being VERB:
a particular thing or as having a particular quality, V n as n
you believe that they are that thing or have that be V-ed as n
quality. *He was regarded as the most successful
Chancellor of modern times.* **2** If you **regard** some- VERB
thing or someone with a feeling such as dislike or V n with n
respect, you have that feeling about them. *He re-
garded drug dealers with loathing.* **3** If you **regard** VERB: V n
someone or something in a certain way, you look at V n with n
them in that way. *The clerk regarded him with be-* LITERARY
nevolent amusement.

4 If you have **regard** for someone or something, you N-UNCOUNT
respect them and care about them. If you hold some-
one in high **regard**, you have a lot of respect for them.
5 Regards are greetings. You use **regards** in expres- N-PLURAL
sions like **best regards** and **with kind regards** as a way PRAGMATICS
of expressing friendly feelings towards someone, especially in a letter.
6 You can use **as regards, with regard to,** or **in regard** PHR-PREP
to to indicate the subject that is being talked or writ- PRAGMATICS
ten about. *As regards the war, Haig believed in victory
at any price.* **7** You can use **in this regard** or **in that re-** PHRASE
gard to refer back to something you have just said. *In* PRAGMATICS
this regard nothing has changed.

re·gard·ing /rɪˈgɑːdɪŋ/. You can use **regarding** to ◆◆◇◇
indicate the subject that is being talked or written PREP
about. *He refused to divulge any information regard-* PRAGMATICS
ing the man's whereabouts.

re·gard·less /rɪˈgɑːdləs/. **1** If something happens ◆◆◇◇
regardless of something else, it is not affected or in- PHR-PREP
fluenced at all by that other thing. *Regardless of
whether he is right or wrong, we have to abide by his
decisions.* **2** If you say that someone did something ADV:
regardless, you mean that they did it even though ADV after v
there were problems or factors that could have
stopped them, or perhaps should have stopped
them. *Despite her recent surgery she has been carrying on regardless.*

re·gat·ta /rɪˈgætə/ **regattas.** A **regatta** is a sports ◆◇◇◇
event consisting of races between yachts or rowing N-COUNT
boats.

re·gen·cy /ˈriːdʒənsi/ **regencies;** usually spelled
Regency for meaning 1. **1 Regency** is used to refer ADJ
to the period in Britain at the beginning of the nineteenth century, and to the style of architecture, literature, and furniture that was popular at the time.
2 A **regency** is a period of time when a country is N-COUNT
governed by a regent.

re·gen·er·ate /rɪ'dʒenəreɪt/ **regenerates, re-** ◆◇◇◇◇
generating, regenerated. 1 To **regenerate** VERB
something means to develop and improve it to Vn
make it more active, successful, or important. *The*
government will continue to try to regenerate inner
city areas. ♦ **re·gen·er·a·tion** /rɪ,dʒenə'reɪʃən/. N-UNCOUNT
...the physical and economic regeneration of the
area. **2** If organs or tissues **regenerate**, they heal V-ERG: V
and grow again after they have been damaged. *The* Vn
rays then stimulate the natural metabolic processes
to regenerate damaged tissue. ♦ **regeneration** N-UNCOUNT
...red-blood-cell regeneration.
re·gen·era·tive /rɪ'dʒenərətɪv/. **Regenerative** pow- ADJ
ers or processes cause something to heal or become
active again after it has declined or been damaged.
...the regenerative power of nature.
re·gent /'riːdʒənt/ **regents.** A **regent** is a person N-COUNT
who rules a country when the king or queen is un-
able to rule.
reg·gae /'regeɪ/. **Reggae** is a kind of West Indian ◆◆◇◇◇
popular music with a very strong beat. N-UNCOUNT
re·gime /reɪ'ʒiːm/ **regimes. 1** If you refer to a ◆◆◆◇◇
government or system of running a country as a **re-** N-COUNT
gime, you are critical of it because you think it is PRAGMATICS
not democratic and uses unacceptable methods.
Pujol was imprisoned and tortured under the Franco
regime. **2** A **regime** is the way that something such N-COUNT
as an institution, company, or economy is run, especially when it involves tough or restrictive action.
...a drastic regime of economic reform. **3** A **regime** is N-COUNT
the same as a **regimen**.
regi·men /'redʒɪmen/ **regimens.** A **regimen** is a N-COUNT
set of rules about food and exercise that some people follow in order to stay healthy.
regi·ment /'redʒɪmənt/ **regiments. 1** A **regiment** ◆◆◇◇◇
is a large group of soldiers that is commanded by a N-COUNT
colonel. **2** A **regiment of** people is a large number N-COUNT:
of them. N of n
regi·men·tal /,redʒɪ'mentəl/. **Regimental** means ◆◇◇◇◇
belonging to a particular regiment. ADJ: ADJ n
regi·men·ta·tion /,redʒɪmen'teɪʃən/. **Regimenta-** N-UNCOUNT
tion is very strict control over the way a group of
people behave or the way something is done. *...bu-*
reaucratic regimentation of social life.
regi·ment·ed /'redʒɪmentɪd/. Something that is ADJ-GRADED
regimented is very strictly controlled. *...the regi-*
mented atmosphere of the orphanage.
re·gion /'riːdʒən/ **regions. 1** A **region** is a large ◆◆◆◆◇
area of land that is different from other areas of N-COUNT
land, for example because it has a particular geographical feature. *...Barcelona, capital of the autono-*
mous region of Catalonia. **2** The **regions** are the N-PLURAL:
parts of a country that are not the capital city and theN
its surrounding area. *Tax incentives would be used* BRITISH
to attract firms to the regions.* **3** You can refer to a N-COUNT:
part of your body as a **region**. *...the pelvic region.* with supp
4 You say **in the region of** to indicate that an PHRASE
amount that you are stating is approximate. *The*
scheme will cost in the region of six million pounds.
re·gion·al /'riːdʒənəl/. **Regional** is used to describe ◆◆◆◆◇
things which relate to a particular area of a country ADJ
or of the world. *...the autonomous regional govern-*
ment of Andalucia. ♦ **re·gion·al·ly** *The impact of* ADV
these trends has varied regionally.
re·gion·al·ism /'riːdʒənəlɪzəm/. **Regionalism** is a N-UNCOUNT
strong feeling of pride or loyalty that people in a region have for that region.
reg·is·ter /'redʒɪstə/ **registers, registering,** ◆◆◆◇◇
registered. 1 A **register** is an official list or record N-COUNT
of things. *She calls the register for her class of thirty*
12 year olds. **2** If you **register** to do something, you VERB:
put your name on an official list, in order to be able V to-inf
to do that thing or to receive a service. *Have you* V
come to register at the school? **3** If you **register** VERB: V n
something, such as a birth or a death, you have the
fact recorded on an official list.
4 When something **registers** on a scale or measuring V-ERG: V
instrument or when a scale or measuring instrument Vn
registers it, it shows on the scale or instrument. *The*
earthquake registered 5.3 points on the Richter scale.

5 If you **register** your feelings or opinions about VERB
something, you do something that makes them clear Vn
to other people. *Workers stopped work to register their*
protest. **6** If a feeling **registers** on someone's face, VERB
their expression shows clearly that they have that V
feeling. *Surprise again registered on Rodney's face.* V-ERG: V
7 If a piece of information does not **register** or if Also V that
you do not **register** it, you do not really pay attention to it, and so you do not remember it or react to
it. *The sound was so familiar that she didn't register*
it. **8** See also **cash register**, **electoral register**.
reg·is·tered /'redʒɪstəd/. A **registered** letter or ◆◇◇◇◇
parcel is sent by a special postal service, for which ADJ
you pay extra money to insure it in case it is lost.
'register office, register offices. A **register of-** N-COUNT
fice is a place where births, marriages, and deaths BRITISH
are officially recorded, and where people can get
married without a religious ceremony.
reg·is·trar /,redʒɪ'strɑː, AM -'strɑːr/ **registrars.** ◆◇◇◇◇
1 In Britain, a **registrar** is a person whose job is to N-COUNT
keep official records, especially of births, marriages,
and deaths. **2** A **registrar** is a senior administrative N-COUNT
official in a British college or university.
reg·is·tra·tion /,redʒɪ'streɪʃən/. The **registration** ◆◆◇◇◇
of something such as a person's name or the details N-UNCOUNT
of an event is the recording of it in an official list.
,regis'tration number, registration numbers. N-COUNT
The **registration number** or the **registration** of a BRITISH
car or other road vehicle is the series of letters and
numbers that are shown at the front and back of it.
The American expression is **license plate number**.
reg·is·try /'redʒɪstri/ **registries.** A **registry** is a ◆◇◇◇◇
collection of all the official records relating to some- N-COUNT
thing, or the place where they are kept.
'registry office, registry offices. A **registry of-** N-COUNT
fice is the same as a **register office**. BRITISH
re·gress /rɪ'gres/ **regresses, regressing, re-** ◆◇◇◇◇
gressed. When people or things **regress**, they VERB:
return to an earlier and less advanced stage of V to/into n
development. *...if your child regresses to babyish be-* FORMAL
haviour. ♦ **re·gres·sion** /rɪ'greʃən/ **regressions** N-VAR
...regression in a pupil's learning process.
re·gres·sive /rɪ'gresɪv/. **Regressive** behaviour, ac- ADJ-GRADED
tivities, or processes involve a return to an earlier FORMAL
and less advanced stage of development.
re·gret /rɪ'gret/ **regrets, regretting, regretted.** ◆◆◆◇◇
1 If you **regret** something that you have done, you V n /-ing
wish that you had not done it. *I simply gave in to* V that
him, and I've regretted it ever since... Ellis seemed to
be regretting that he had asked the question. **2** Re- N-VAR
gret is a feeling of sadness or disappointment,
which is caused by something that has happened or
something that you have done or not done. *My*
great regret in life is that I didn't bring home the
America's Cup. **3** You can say that you **regret** some- VERB: V n
thing as a polite way of saying that you are sorry PRAGMATICS
about it. You use expressions such as **I regret to say** V that
or **I regret to inform you** to show that you are sorry Also V to-inf
about something. *I regret that the United States has* FORMAL
added its voice to such protests. **4** If someone ex- N-UNCOUNT
presses **regret** about something, they say that they FORMAL
are sorry about it.
re·gret·ful /rɪ'gretful/. If you are **regretful**, you ADJ-GRADED
show that you regret something. ♦ **re·gret·ful·ly** ADV-GRADED
He shook his head regretfully.
re·gret·table /rɪ'gretəbəl/. You describe some- ◆◇◇◇◇
thing as **regrettable** when you think that it is bad ADJ-GRADED
and that it should not happen or have happened. *It* PRAGMATICS
is regrettable that strike leaders seem intent on spoil-
ing holidays. ♦ **re·gret·tably** *Regrettably we could* ADV-GRADED
find no sign of the man.
re·group /,riː'gruːp/ **regroups, regrouping, re-** ◆◇◇◇◇
grouped. When people, especially soldiers, **re-** V-ERG
group, they form an organized group again, in order Also V n
to continue fighting. *Now the rebel army has re-*
grouped and reorganised.
regu·lar /'regjulə/ **regulars. 1** Regular events ◆◆◆◆◇
have equal amounts of time between them, so that ADJ-GRADED
they happen, for example, at the same time each
day or each week. *Take regular exercise... We're*

going to be meeting there on a regular basis. ♦ **regu·**
·lar·ly *He also writes regularly for 'International* ADV-GRADED
Management magazine. ♦ **regu·lar·ity** N-UNCOUNT
/ˌreɡjʊ'lærɪti/. *The overdraft arrangements had been*
generous because of the regularity of the half-yearly
payments. **2** A **regular** rhythm consists of a series of ADJ-GRADED
sounds or movements with equal periods of time
between them. ♦ **regularly** *Remember to breathe* ADV-GRADED
regularly. ♦ **regularity** *...the rate and regularity of* N-UNCOUNT
the heartbeat.
3 Regular events happen often. *...a morning punctu-* ADJ-GRADED
ated by regular volleys of gunfire. ♦ **regu·lar·ly** *Fox,* ADV-GRADED:
badger, weasel and stoat are regularly seen here. ADV with v
♦ **regularity** *Job losses are again being announced* N-UNCOUNT
with monotonous regularity. **4** If you are, for example, ADJ-GRADED:
a **regular** customer at a shop or a **regular** visitor to a ADJ n
place, you go there often. *...people who are not regular*
churchgoers. **5** The **regulars** at a place or in a team are N-COUNT
the people who often go to the place or are often in
the team. *...regulars at his local pub.*
6 You use **regular** when referring to the thing, person, ADJ:
time, or place that is usually used by someone or in- det ADJ n
volved in something. For example, someone's **regular**
place is the place where they usually sit. *...samples*
from one of their regular suppliers. **7 Regular** is used ADJ: ADJ n
to mean 'normal'. *The product looks and burns like a*
regular cigarette. **8** In some restaurants, a **regular** ADJ: ADJ n
drink or portion of food is of medium size. *...a cheese-*
burger and regular fries.
9 A **regular** pattern or arrangement consists of a se- ADJ-GRADED
ries of things with equal spaces between them. *...regu-*
lar rows of wooden huts. **10** If something has a **regu-** ADJ-GRADED
lar shape, both halves are the same and it has straight
edges or a smooth outline. ♦ **regu·lar·ity** *...the chess-* N-UNCOUNT
board regularity of their fields.
11 Regular troops are professional soldiers who are a ADJ: ADJ n
permanent part of an official national army.
► **Regulars** are regular troops. N-COUNT
12 In grammar, a **regular** verb, noun, or adjective in- ADJ
flects in the same way as most verbs, nouns, or adjectives in the language.

regu·lar·ity /ˌreɡjʊ'lærɪti/ **regularities. 1** A **regu-** ◆◇◇◇◇
larity is the fact that the same thing always happens N-COUNT
in the same circumstances. *Children seek out regu-* FORMAL
larities and rules in acquiring language. **2** See also
regular.

regu·lar·ize /'reɡjʊləraɪz/ **regularizes, regular-** VERB: V n
izing, regularized; also spelled **regularise** in Brit- FORMAL
ish English. If someone **regularizes** a situation or
system, they make it officially acceptable or put it
under a system of rules.

regu·late /'reɡjʊleɪt/ **regulates, regulating,** ◆◆◇◇◇
regulated. To **regulate** an activity or process VERB: V n
means to control it, especially by means of rules.
♦ **regu·lat·ed** *It's a treatment that can carry risks,* ADJ-GRADED
and in Britain it's strictly regulated. ♦ **regu·la·tion,** N-COUNT
regulations *Social services also have responsibility*
for the regulation of nurseries.

regu·la·tion /ˌreɡjʊ'leɪʃən/ **regulations. Regula-** ◆◆◆◇◇
tions are rules made by a government or other N-COUNT
authority in order to control the way something is
done or the way people behave. *...the new safety*
regulations. ► Also an adjective. *...a noisy cheerful* ADJ: ADJ n
group of people in regulation black parade tunics.

regu·la·tor /'reɡjʊleɪtə/ **regulators. 1** A **regula-** ◆◆◆◇◇
tor is a person or organization appointed by a gov- N-COUNT
ernment to regulate the activities of private companies who provide a service to the public. *...why it*
took so long for government regulators to shut the
plant down. ♦ **regu·la·tory** /ˌreɡjʊ'leɪtəri/. *...the* ADJ: ADJ n
UK's financial regulatory system. **2** A **regulator** is a N-COUNT
device or mechanism that automatically controls
something, such as the temperature in a room or
the growth of a body. *An automatic voltage regula-*
tor ensured a constant output from the generator.

re·gur·gi·tate /rɪ'ɡɜːdʒɪteɪt/ **regurgitates, regur-**
gitating, regurgitated. 1 If you say that some- VERB
one is **regurgitating** ideas or facts, you mean that PRAGMATICS
they are repeating them without understanding V n
them properly; used showing disapproval. *You can*

get sick to death of a friend regurgitating her part-
ner's opinions. **2** If a person or animal **regurgitates** VERB: V n
food, they bring it back up from the stomach before FORMAL
they digest it.

re·hab /'riːhæb/. **Rehab** is the process of helping N-UNCOUNT
someone to lead a normal life again after they have INFORMAL
been ill, or when they are addicted to drugs or alcohol. **Rehab** is short for rehabilitation.

re·ha·bili·tate /ˌriːhə'bɪlɪteɪt/ **rehabilitates, re-** ◆◆◇◇◇
habilitating, rehabilitated. 1 To **rehabilitate** VERB
someone who has been ill or in prison means to V n
help them to live a normal life again. To **rehabili-**
tate someone who is addicted to drugs or alcohol
means to help them stop using drugs and alcohol
and to live without them. *Considerable efforts have*
been made to rehabilitate patients who have suffered
in this way. ♦ **re·ha·bili·ta·tion** /ˌriːhəbɪlɪ'teɪʃən/. N-UNCOUNT
...an alcohol and drug rehabilitation centre. **2** If VERB:
someone **is rehabilitated**, they begin to be consid- be V-ed
ered acceptable again after a period during which V n
they have been rejected or severely criticized. *His*
candidacy has divided the Republican Party; while
most have scorned him, others have sought to reha-
bilitate him. ♦ **rehabilitation** *...an important step* N-UNCOUNT
towards Peking's rehabilitation in the West. **3** To **re-** VERB
habilitate a building or an area means to improve V n
its condition so that it can be used again. *...a pro-*
gram for rehabilitating low-income housing.
♦ **rehabilitation** *We have to support the rehabilita-* N-UNCOUNT
tion and reconstruction of Cambodia.

re·hash, rehashes, rehashing, rehashed. The VERB
noun is pronounced /'riːhæʃ/. The verb is pro- PRAGMATICS
nounced /riː'hæʃ/. If you say that someone **re-** V n
hashes old ideas, facts, or accusations, you disapprove of the fact that they present them in a slightly
different way so that they seem new or original.
They've taken some of the best bits out of the best
things and rehashed them. ► Also a noun. *The Ob-* N-COUNT
server found the play 'a feeble rehash of familiar Mil-
ler themes'. ♦ **re·hash·ing** *...the embarrassing re-* N-SING
hashing of past scandal.

re·hears·al /rɪ'hɜːsəl/ **rehearsals. 1** A **rehearsal** ◆◆◇◇◇
of a play, dance, or piece of music is a practice of it N-VAR
in preparation for a performance. *The band was*
scheduled to begin rehearsals for a concert tour.
● See also **dress rehearsal. 2** You can describe an N-COUNT:
event or object which is a preparation for a more N for n
important event or object as a **rehearsal for** it. *The*
sketch should be a kind of rehearsal for the eventual
painting.

re·hearse /rɪ'hɜːs/ **rehearses, rehearsing, re-** ◆◇◇◇◇
hearsed. 1 When people **rehearse** a play, dance, VERB: V
or piece of music, they practise it in order to pre- V for n
pare for a performance. *Tens of thousands of people* Also V
have been rehearsing for the opening ceremony. **2** If VERB: V n
you **rehearse** something that you are going to say or V wh
do, you silently practise it by imagining that you are
saying or doing it. *We encouraged them to rehearse*
what they were going to say. **3** If you **rehearse** VERB
something, you repeat it in detail. *Yesterday's speech* V n
to the Scottish party conference rehearsed the argu- FORMAL
ments again.

re·house /ˌriː'haʊz/ **rehouses, rehousing, re-** VERB:
housed. If someone **is rehoused**, their council or be V-ed
another authority provides them with a different V n
house to live in. *The council has agreed to rehouse* BRITISH
the family.

reign /reɪn/ **reigns, reigning, reigned. 1** If you ◆◆◇◇◇
say, for example, that silence **reigns** in a place or VERB: V
confusion **reigns** in a situation, you mean that the V over n
place is silent or the situation is confused. *A relative*
calm reigned over the city. **2** When a king or queen VERB: V
reigns, he or she rules a country. *...George III,* V-ing
Britain's longest reigning monarch. ► Also a noun. N-COUNT:
...Queen Victoria's reign. **3** If you say that a person with poss
reigns in a situation or area, you mean that they are VERB: V
very powerful or successful. *Coco Chanel reigned* V over n
over fashion for half a century. ► Also a noun. N-COUNT:
...Giles Havergal's reign as artistic director of the with poss
Citizens' Theatre. **4** Someone or something that PHRASE

reigns supreme is the most important or powerful element in a situation or period of time. *The bicycle reigned supreme as Britain's most popular mode of transport.* **5** A **reign of terror** is a period during which there is a lot of violence and killing, especially by people who are in a position of power. PHRASE

reign·ing /ˈreɪnɪŋ/. The **reigning** champion is the most recent winner of a contest or competition at the time you are talking about. ◆◇◇◇◇ ADJ: ADJ n

re·im·burse /ˌriːɪmˈbɜːs/ **reimburses, reimbursing, reimbursed.** If you **reimburse** someone for something, you pay them back the money that they have spent or lost because of it. *The funds are supposed to reimburse policyholders in the event of insurer failure.* ◆ **re·im·burse·ment, reimbursements** *She is demanding reimbursement for medical and other expenses.* ◆◇◇◇◇ VERB: V n for n / V n FORMAL / N-VAR

rein /reɪn/ **reins, reining, reined. 1 Reins** are the thin leather straps attached to a horse's bridle which are used to control the horse. **2** Journalists sometimes use the expression **the reins** or **the reins of power** to refer to the control of a country or organization. *Mr Castro, who is sixty-five today, shows no sign of handing over the reins of power.* **3** If you **give a free rein to** someone, you give them a lot of freedom to do what they want. **4** If you **keep a tight rein on** someone, you control them firmly. *Her parents had kept her on a tight rein with their narrow and inflexible views.* ◆◆◇◇◇ N-PLURAL / N-PLURAL / PHRASE / PHRASE

rein back. To **rein back** something such as spending means to control it strictly. *The government would try to rein back inflation.* PHRASAL VB / V P noun / Also V P

rein in. 1 To **rein in** something means to control it. *His administration's economic policy would focus on reining in inflation.* **2** If you **rein in** a horse, you stop it or cause it to go more slowly by pulling its reins. *The horsemen reined in and shouted at the men behind to turn back.* PHRASAL VB / V P noun / Also V n P / V P noun / V P / Also V n P

re·in·car·nate /ˌriːɪnˈkɑːneɪt/ **reincarnates, reincarnating, reincarnated.** If people believe that they will be **reincarnated** when they die, they believe that their spirit will be born again and will live in the body of another person or animal. VB: usu passive

re·in·car·na·tion /ˌriːɪnkɑːˈneɪʃən/ **reincarnations. 1** If you believe in **reincarnation**, you believe that you will be reincarnated after you die. **2** A **reincarnation** is a person or animal whose body is believed to contain the spirit of a dead person. ◆◇◇◇◇ N-UNCOUNT / N-COUNT

rein·deer /ˈreɪndɪə/. **Reindeer** is both the singular and the plural form. A **reindeer** is a deer with large antlers that lives in northern areas of Europe, Asia, and America. N-COUNT

re·in·force /ˌriːɪnˈfɔːs/ **reinforces, reinforcing, reinforced. 1** If something **reinforces** a feeling, situation, or process, it makes it stronger or more intense. *A stronger European Parliament would, they fear, only reinforce the power of the larger countries.* ◆ **re·in·force·ment,** /ˌriːɪnˈfɔːsmənt/ **reinforcements** *What the teacher now has to do is remove the reinforcement for this bad behaviour.* **2** If something **reinforces** an idea or point of view, it provides more evidence or support for it. *The delegation hopes to reinforce the idea that human rights are not purely internal matters.* **3** To **reinforce** an object means to make it stronger or harder. *They had to reinforce the walls with exterior beams.* ◆ **re·in·forced** *Its windows were of reinforced glass.* **4** To **reinforce** an army or a group of police means to make it stronger by increasing its size or providing it with more weapons. To **reinforce** a position or place means to make it stronger by sending more soldiers or weapons. *Both sides have been reinforcing their positions after yesterday's fierce fighting.* ◆ **re·in·force·ments.** **Reinforcements** are soldiers or policemen who are sent to join an army or group of police in order to make it stronger. ◆◆◇◇◇ VERB / V n / N-VAR / VERB / V n / VERB: V n / V n with n / ADJ / VERB / V n / N-PLURAL

reinforced 'concrete. Reinforced concrete is concrete that is made with pieces of metal inside it to make it stronger. N-UNCOUNT

re·instate /ˌriːɪnˈsteɪt/ **reinstates, reinstating, reinstated. 1** If you **reinstate** someone, you give them back a job or position which had been taken away from them. *The governor is said to have agreed to reinstate five senior workers who were dismissed.* ◆ **re·instate·ment** /ˌriːɪnˈsteɪtmənt/. *Parents campaigned in vain for her reinstatement.* **2** To **reinstate** a law, facility, or practice means to start having it again. *...the decision to reinstate the grant.* ◆ **reinstatement** *He welcomed the reinstatement of the 10 per cent bank base rate.* ◆◇◇◇◇ VERB / V n / N-UNCOUNT / VERB / V n / N-UNCOUNT

re·is·sue /ˌriːˈɪʃuː/ **reissues, reissuing, reissued. 1** A **reissue** is a book, record, or film that has not been available for some time but is now published or produced again. *...this welcome reissue of a 1955 Ingmar Bergman classic.* **2** If something such as a book, record, or film is **reissued** after it has not been available for some time, it is published or produced again. ◆◇◇◇◇ N-COUNT / VB: usu passive; be V-ed

re·it·er·ate /riːˈɪtəreɪt/ **reiterates, reiterating, reiterated.** If you **reiterate** something, you say it again or emphasize it. *I want to reiterate that our conventional weapons are superior.* ◆ **re·it·era·tion** /riːˌɪtəˈreɪʃən/ **reiterations** *...a reiteration of the same old entrenched positions.* ◆◇◇◇◇ VERB: V n / V that / Also V quote / N-VAR FORMAL

re·ject, rejects, rejecting, rejected. The verb is pronounced /rɪˈdʒekt/. The noun is pronounced /ˈriːdʒekt/. **1** If you **reject** something such as a proposal or request, you do not accept it or you do not agree to it. *The British government is expected to reject the idea of state subsidy for a new high speed railway.* ◆ **re·jec·tion** /rɪˈdʒekʃən/ **rejections** *The rejection of such initiatives by no means indicates that voters are unconcerned about the environment.* **2** If you **reject** a belief or a political system, you refuse to believe in it or to live by its rules. *...the children of Eastern European immigrants who had rejected their parents' political and religious beliefs.* ◆ **rejection** *His rejection of our values is far more complete than that of D. H. Lawrence.* **3** If someone **is rejected** for a job or course of study, it is not offered to them. *One of my most able students was rejected by another university.* ◆ **rejection** *Be prepared for lots of rejections before you land a job.* **4** If someone **rejects** another person who expects affection from them, they are cold and unfriendly towards them. *You make friends with people and then make unreasonable demands so that they reject you.* ◆ **rejection** *...feelings of rejection and hurt.* **5** If a person's body **rejects** something such as a new heart that has been transplanted into it, it tries to attack and destroy it. ◆ **rejection** *...a special drug which stops rejection of transplanted organs.* **6** If a machine **rejects** a coin that you put in it, the coin comes out and the machine does not work. **7** A **reject** is a product that has not been accepted for use or sale, because there is something wrong with it. ◆◆◆◇ VERB / V n / N-VAR / VERB / V n / N-VAR / VERB / is V-ed / Also V n / N-COUNT / VERB / V n / N-VAR VERB: V n / N-VAR VERB: V n / N-COUNT

re·jig /ˌriːˈdʒɪg/ **rejigs, rejigging, rejigged.** If someone **rejigs** an organization or a piece of work, they completely rearrange it. VERB: V n BRITISH

re·joice /rɪˈdʒɔɪs/ **rejoices, rejoicing, rejoiced. 1** If you **rejoice**, you are very pleased about something and you show it in your behaviour. *Garbo plays the Queen, rejoicing in the love she has found with Antonio.* ◆ **re·joic·ing** *There was general rejoicing at the news.* **2** If you say that someone or something **rejoices in the name of** something, you mean that they are called that and you find it amusing. *...their tortoise, who rejoiced in the name of Carruthers.* ◆◇◇◇◇ VERB / V in/at n / Also V that / N-UNCOUNT / PHRASE PRAGMATICS

re·join, rejoins, rejoining, rejoined. Pronounced /ˌriːˈdʒɔɪn/ for meanings 1, 2, and 3, and /rɪˈdʒɔɪn/ for meaning 4. **1** If you **rejoin** a group, club, or organization, you become a member of it again after not being a member for a period of time. *He rejoined Sadler's Wells Royal Ballet as Assistant Administrator in 1988.* **2** If you **rejoin** someone, you go back to them after a short time away from them. *Mimi and her family went off to Tunisia to rejoin her father.* **3** If you **rejoin** a route, you go back to it ◆◇◇◇◇ VERB / V n / Also V / VERB / V n / VERB

after travelling along a different route for a time. *At* `V n`
Dorset Wharf go left to rejoin the river.
4 To **rejoin** means to answer quickly what someone `VB: no cont`
has said, usually in a witty or critical manner. *'I dare* `V with quote`
say they do,' rejoined his wife drily. `Also V that`
`WRITTEN`
re·join·der /rɪ'dʒɔɪndə/ **rejoinders.** A rejoinder is `N-COUNT`
a reply, especially a quick, witty, or critical one. `FORMAL`

re·ju·ve·nate /rɪ'dʒuːvəneɪt/ **rejuvenates, reju-** ◆◇◇◇◇
venating, rejuvenated. 1 If something **reju-** `VERB`
venates you, it makes you feel or look young again. `V n`
The Italian climate would rejuvenate him. **♦ re·ju**
·venat·ing *The hotel's new Spa offers every kind of* `ADJ`
rejuvenating treatment. **2** If you **rejuvenate** an or- `VERB`
ganization or system, you make it more lively and `V n`
more efficient, for example by introducing new
ideas. *...schemes to rejuvenate the inner cities.* **♦ re·**
·ju·vena·tion /rɪ,dʒuːvə'neɪʃən/. *The way Britain* `N-UNCOUNT`
organises its politics needs rejuvenation.

re·kin·dle /,riː'kɪndəl/ **rekindles, rekindling, re-** ◆◇◇◇◇
kindled. 1 If something **rekindles** an interest, feel- `VERB`
ing, or thought that you used to have, it makes you `V n`
think about it or feel it again. *Ben Brantley's article*
on Sir Ian McKellen rekindled many memories. **2** If `VERB`
something **rekindles** an unpleasant situation, it `V n`
makes the unpleasant situation happen again. *The*
continuing disintegration of the Soviet empire is re-
kindling old national and ethnic tensions.

re·lapse, relapses, relapsing, relapsed. The ◆◇◇◇◇
verb is pronounced /rɪ'læps/; the noun can be pronounced /rɪ'læps/ or /'riːlæps/. **1** If you say that `VERB`
someone **relapses into** a way of behaving that is `V into n`
undesirable, you mean that they start to behave in
that way again. *'I wish I did,' said Phil Jordan, re-*
lapsing into his usual gloom. ▶ Also a noun. *...a re-* `N-COUNT`
lapse into the nationalism of the nineteenth century.
2 If a sick person **relapses**, their health suddenly `VERB: V`
gets worse after it had been improving. ▶ Also a `N-VAR`
noun. *...women with a high risk of relapse after*
surgery.

re·late /rɪ'leɪt/ **relates, relating, related. 1** If ◆◆◇◇◇
something **relates** to a particular subject, it con- `VERB`
cerns that subject. *Other recommendations relate to* `V to n`
the details of how such data is stored. **♦ -related** `COMB`
...drug-related offences. ...smoking-related diseases.
2 The way that two things **relate**, or the way that `V-RECIP-ERG:`
one thing **relates** to another, is the sort of connec- `pl-n V`
tion that exists between them. *...a course that inves-* `V to n`
tigates how language relates to particular cultural `Also V pl-n,`
codes. `V n to n`
3 If you can **relate** to someone, you can understand `V-RECIP:`
how they feel or behave so that you are able to com- `V to n`
municate with them or deal with them easily. *When* `pl-n V`
people are cut off from contact with others for any
length of time, they lose all ability to relate.
4 If you **relate** a story, you tell it. *...Tibetan-speaking* `VERB: V n`
officials to whom he could relate the whole story. `V n to n`
`FORMAL`
re·lat·ed /rɪ'leɪtɪd/. **1** If two or more things are **re-** ◆◆◇◇◇
lated, there is a connection between them. *The* `ADJ`
philosophical problems of chance and of free will are
closely related. ...diving and related activities.
2 People who are **related** belong to the same family. `ADJ:`
There are two families of Elwoods in Galway, and `v-link ADJ`
we're not related. **3** If you say that different types of `ADJ`
animal or different languages are **related**, you mean
that they have developed from the same type of animal or language.

re·la·tion /rɪ'leɪʃən/ **relations. 1** Relations be- ◆◆◆◇
tween people, groups, or countries are contacts `N-COUNT`
between them and the way in which they behave
towards each other. *Greece has established full dip-*
lomatic relations with Israel.
2 If you talk about the **relation** of one thing to anoth- `N-COUNT`
er, you are talking about the ways in which they are
connected. *...the relation of ethics to economics.* **3** You `PHR-PREP`
can talk about something **in relation to** something
else when you want to compare the size, condition, or
position of the two things. *The money he'd been or-*
dered to pay was minimal in relation to his salary. **4** If `PHR-PREP`
something is said or done **in relation to** a subject, it is
said or done in connection with that subject. *...a ques-*

tion which has been asked many times in relation to
Irish affairs.
5 Your **relations** are the members of your family. `N-COUNT`
...visits to friends and relations.
6 See also **industrial relations, poor relation, public**
relations, race relations.

re·la·tion·al /rɪ'leɪʃənəl/. **Relational** means con- `ADJ: ADJ n`
cerning relationships and connections. *...in the* `FORMAL`
middle of a relational crisis... Language, for exam-
ple, is a relational whole.

re·la·tion·ship /rɪ'leɪʃənʃɪp/ **relationships.** ◆◆◆◇
1 The **relationship** between two people or groups is `N-COUNT:`
the way in which they feel and behave towards each `with supp`
other. *China will maintain its traditional friendly*
relationship with Bangladesh. ...close family rela-
tionships. **2** A **relationship** is a close friendship `N-COUNT`
between two people, especially one involving roman-
tic or sexual feelings. *Both of us felt the relationship*
wasn't really going anywhere. **3** The **relationship** `N-COUNT:`
between two things is the way in which they are `N between/`
connected. *...a relationship between diet and cancer.* `to/of n`

rela·tive /'relətɪv/ **relatives. 1** Your **relatives** are ◆◆◇◇◇
the members of your family. *Get a relative to look* `N-COUNT`
after the children. **2** If one animal, plant, language, `N-COUNT`
or invention is a **relative** of another, they have both
evolved or developed from the same type of animal,
plant, language, or invention. *The pheasant is a*
close relative of the Guinea hen.
3 You use **relative** to say that something is true to a `ADJ: ADJ n`
certain degree, especially when compared with other
things of the same kind. *The fighting resumed after a*
period of relative calm. **♦ rela·tive·ly** *The sums need-* `ADV`
ed are relatively small. **4** You use **relative** when you `ADJ: ADJ n`
are comparing the quality or size of two things. *...the*
relative merits of London and Paris as places to live.
5 Relative to something means with reference to it or `PHR-PREP`
in comparison with it. *Japanese interest rates rose rela-*
tive to America's. **6** If you say that something is **rela-** `ADJ-GRADED`
tive, you mean that it needs to be considered and
judged in relation to other things. *Fitness is relative;*
one must always ask 'Fit for what?'.

relative 'clause, relative clauses. A **relative** `N-COUNT`
clause is a subordinate clause which specifies or
gives information about a person or thing. Relative
clauses come after a noun or pronoun and, in English, often begin with a relative pronoun such as
'who', 'which', or 'that'.

relative 'pronoun, relative pronouns. A **rela-** `N-COUNT`
tive pronoun is a word such as 'who', 'that', or
'which' that is used to introduce a relative clause.
'Whose', 'when', 'where', and 'why' are generally
called **relative pronouns**, though they are actually
adverbs.

rela·tiv·ism /'relətɪvɪzəm/. **Relativism** is the belief `N-UNCOUNT`
that what is right or wrong is not always the same
but varies according to circumstances. **♦ rela·tiv·**
·ist, relativists *Bonger advocated a relativist posi-* `N-COUNT`
tion. In his view, what is considered immoral de-
pends on the social structure.

rela·tiv·ity /,relə'tɪvɪti/. **Relativity** is Einstein's ◆◇◇◇◇
theory concerning space, time, and motion. `N-UNCOUNT`
`TECHNICAL`
re·lax /rɪ'læks/ **relaxes, relaxing, relaxed. 1** If ◆◆◇◇◇
you **relax** or if something **relaxes** you, you feel more `V-ERG`
calm and less worried or tense. *I ought to relax and* `V`
stop worrying about it... Do something that you `V n`
know relaxes you. **♦ re·laxa·tion** /,riːlæk'seɪʃən/. `N-UNCOUNT`
...relaxation techniques. **♦ re·laxed** *Try to adopt a* `ADJ-GRADED`
more relaxed manner... The atmosphere at lunch
was relaxed. **♦ re·lax·ing** *...a quiet, relaxing holi-* `ADJ-GRADED`
day. **2** When a part of your body **relaxes**, or when `V-ERG: V`
you **relax** it, it becomes less stiff or firm. *Massage is* `V n`
used to relax muscles, relieve stress and improve the
circulation. **3** If you **relax** your grip or hold on `VERB: V n`
something, you hold it less tightly than before. **4** If `V-ERG: V n`
you **relax** a rule or your control over something, or `V`
if it **relaxes**, it becomes less firm or strong. *Rules*
governing student conduct have relaxed somewhat
in recent years. **♦ re·laxa·tion** *...the relaxation of* `N-UNCOUNT`
travel restrictions.

re·lay, relays, relaying, relayed. The noun is pronounced /ˈriːleɪ/. The verb is pronounced /rɪˈleɪ/. ◆◆◇◇◇
1 A **relay** or a **relay race** is a race between two or more teams, for example teams of runners or swimmers. Each member of the team runs or swims one section of the race. **2** To **relay** television or radio signals means to send them on or broadcast them. *This system continuously monitors levels of radiation and relays the information to a central computer.* ► Also a noun. *More than a thousand people outside listened to a relay of the proceedings.* **3** A **relay** is a piece of equipment that receives television or radio signals from one place and sends them on to another place. *...a security system with satellite relays.* **4** If you **relay** something that has been said to you, you repeat it to another person. *The decision will be relayed to Iraq's ambassador at the UN.*
N-COUNT / VERB: V n, V n to/from n / N-COUNT / N-COUNT / VERB: V n, be V-ed to/from n FORMAL

re·lease /rɪˈliːs/ **releases, releasing, released.** ◆◆◆◆◆
1 If a person or animal **is released** from somewhere where they have been imprisoned or looked after, they are set free or allowed to go. ► Also a noun. *He called for the immediate release of all political prisoners.* **2** If someone or something **releases** you from an obligation, task, or feeling, they free you from it. *Divorce releases both the husband and wife from all marital obligations to each other.* ► Also a noun. *Our therapeutic style offers release from stored tensions.* **3** To **release** feelings or abilities means to allow them to be expressed. *Humour is wonderful for releasing tension.* ► Also a noun. *She felt the sudden sweet release of her own tears.* **4** If something **releases** gas, heat, or a substance, it causes it to leave its container or the substance that it was part of and enter the surrounding atmosphere or area. ► Also a noun. *...releases of cancer-causing chemicals.* **5** If you **release** someone or something, you stop holding them. *He stopped and faced her, releasing her wrist.* **6** If you **release** a device, you move it so that it stops holding something. *Wade released the hand brake.* **7** If someone in authority **releases** something such as a document or information, they make it available. ► Also a noun. *Action had been taken to speed up the release of cheques.* **8** When an entertainer or company **releases** a new record, video, or film, it becomes available so that people can buy it or see it. **9** A new **release** is a new record, video, or film that has just become available for people to buy or see. **10** If a film or video is **on release** or **on general release**, it is available for showing in public cinemas or for people to buy.
11 See also **day release, news release, press release**.
VB: usu passive / N-COUNT: with supp / VERB: V n from n Also V n FORMAL / N-COUNT: also a N / VERB V n / N-UNCOUNT / VERB: V n / N-COUNT: with supp VERB V n FORMAL / VERB V n / VERB: V n / N-COUNT / VERB: V n / N-COUNT / N-UNCOUNT: on N BRITISH

rel·egate /ˈreləɡeɪt/ **relegates, relegating, relegated.** ◆◆◇◇◇
1 If you **relegate** someone or something to a less important or less prominent position, you give them this position. *Other newspapers relegated the item to the middle pages.* **2** If a team that competes in a league **is relegated**, it has to compete in a lower division in the next competition, because it was one of the least successful teams in the higher division. *...a team about to be relegated to the second division.* ◆ **rel·ega·tion** /ˌreləˈɡeɪʃən/. *Relegation to the Third Division would prove catastrophic.*
VERB V n to n / VERB: be V-ed be V-ed to n BRITISH / N-UNCOUNT

re·lent /rɪˈlent/ **relents, relenting, relented.** If you **relent**, you allow someone to do something that you had previously refused to allow them to do. *Finally his mother relented and gave permission for her youngest son to marry.* ◆◇◇◇◇ VERB V

re·lent·less /rɪˈlentləs/. **1** Something bad that is **relentless** never stops or never becomes less intense. *The pressure now was relentless.* ◆ **relent·less·ly** *The sun is beating down relentlessly.* **2** Someone who is **relentless** is determined to do something and refuses to give up, even if what they are doing is unpleasant or cruel. *Relentless in his pursuit of quality, his technical ability was remarkable.* ◆ **relentlessly** *She always questioned me relentlessly.*
◆◆◇◇◇ ADJ-GRADED / ADV-GRADED ADJ-GRADED / ADV-GRADED

rel·evant /ˈreləvənt/. **1** Something that is **relevant** to a situation or person is important or significant in that situation or to that person. *We have passed ◆◆◆◇◇ ADJ-GRADED all relevant information on to the police.* ◆ **rel·evance** *...publications of special relevance to new graduates.* **2** The **relevant** thing of a particular kind is the one that is appropriate. *Make sure you enclose all the relevant certificates.*
N-UNCOUNT: with supp / ADJ: the ADJ n

re·li·able /rɪˈlaɪəbəl/. **1** People or things that are **reliable** can be trusted to work well or to behave in the way that you want them to. ◆ **re·li·ably** /rɪˈlaɪəbli/. *It's been working reliably for years.* ◆ **re·li·abil·ity** /rɪˌlaɪəˈbɪlɪti/. *He's not at all worried about his car's reliability.* **2** Information that is **reliable** or that is from a **reliable** source is very likely to be correct. ◆ **re·li·ably** *Sonia, we are reliably informed, loves her family very much.* ◆ **re·li·abil·ity** *Both questioned the reliability of recent opinion polls.*
◆◆◆◇◇ ADJ-GRADED / ADV-GRADED / N-UNCOUNT / ADJ-GRADED / ADV-GRADED / N-UNCOUNT

re·li·ant /rɪˈlaɪənt/. A person or thing that is **reliant** on something needs it and often cannot live or work without it. *These people are not wholly reliant on Western charity.* ● See also **self-reliant.** ◆ **re·li·ance** *...the country's increasing reliance on foreign aid.*
◆◆◇◇◇ ADJ-GRADED: v-link ADJ on/upon n / N-UNCOUNT

rel·ic /ˈrelɪk/ **relics. 1** If you refer to something or someone as a **relic** of an earlier period, you mean that they belonged to that period but have survived into the present. *The tower is a relic of grim days when big houses had to be fortified against invaders.* **2** A **relic** is something which was made or used a long time ago and which is kept for its historical significance. *...a museum of war relics.* **3** A **relic** is the body of a saint or something else associated with a saint, which some people regard as holy.
◆◇◇◇◇ N-COUNT / N-COUNT / N-COUNT

re·lief /rɪˈliːf/ **reliefs. 1** If you feel a sense of **relief**, you feel glad because something unpleasant has not happened or is no longer happening. *I breathed a sigh of relief... The news will come as a great relief to the French authorities.* **2** If something provides **relief** from pain or distress, it stops the pain or distress. **3** **Relief** is money, food, or clothing that is provided for people who are very poor or hungry, or who have been affected by war or a natural disaster. *...relief agencies.* **4** A **relief** worker is someone who does your work when you go home, or who is specially employed to do it instead of you when you are sick. **5** A **relief** is a sculpture that is carved out of a flat vertical surface. **6** See also **bas-relief, tax relief.**
◆◆◆◇ N-UNCOUNT: also a N / N-UNCOUNT / N-UNCOUNT / N-COUNT / N-COUNT TECHNICAL

re·lieve /rɪˈliːv/ **relieves, relieving, relieved. 1** If something **relieves** an unpleasant feeling or situation, it makes it less unpleasant or causes it to disappear completely. *Drugs can relieve much of the pain.* **2** If someone or something **relieves** you of an unpleasant feeling or difficult task, they take it from you. **3** If someone **relieves** you of something, they take it away from you. *A porter relieved her of the three large cases.* **4** If you **relieve** someone, you take their place and continue to do the job or duty that they have been doing. *At seven o'clock the night nurse came in to relieve her.* **5** If someone is **relieved** of their duties or **is relieved** of their post, they are told that they are no longer required to continue in their job. **6** If people or animals **relieve** themselves, they urinate or defecate.
◆◆◇◇◇ VERB V n / VERB: V n of n / VERB V n of n FORMAL / VERB V n / VERB: be V-ed of n FORMAL / VERB: V pron-refl

re·lieved /rɪˈliːvd/. If you are **relieved**, you feel glad because something unpleasant has not happened or is no longer happening.
◆◆◇◇ ADJ-GRADED

re·li·gion /rɪˈlɪdʒən/ **religions. 1** **Religion** is belief in a god or gods and the activities that are connected with this belief. *...Indian philosophy and religion.* **2** A **religion** is a particular system of belief in a god or gods and the activities that are connected with this system. *...the Christian religion.*
◆◆◇◇ N-UNCOUNT / N-COUNT

re·ligi·os·ity /rɪˌlɪdʒiˈɒsɪti/. If you refer to a person's **religiosity**, you are referring to the fact that they are religious in a way which seems exaggerated and insincere.
N-UNCOUNT FORMAL

re·li·gious /rɪˈlɪdʒəs/. **1** You use **religious** to describe things that are connected with religion or with one particular religion. *...different religious beliefs.* ◆ **re·li·gious·ly** *...one of the most religiously*
◆◆◆◇ ADJ: ADJ n / ADV

diverse countries. **2** Someone who is **religious** has a ADJ-GRADED
strong belief in a god or gods.

re·li·gious·ly /rɪ'lɪdʒəsli/. If you do something **reli-** ADV-GRADED:
giously, you do it very regularly because you feel ADV with v
you have to. *Do these exercises religiously every day.*

re·lin·quish /rɪ'lɪŋkwɪʃ/ **relinquishes, relin-** ◆◇◇◇◇
quishing, relinquished. If you **relinquish** some- VERB: V n
thing such as power or control, you give it up. FORMAL
I relish the challenge of doing jobs that oth-

rel·ish /'relɪʃ/ **relishes, relishing, relished. 1** If ◆◆◇◇◇
you **relish** something, you get a lot of enjoyment VERB
from it. *I relish the challenge of doing jobs that oth-* V n
ers turn down. ► Also a noun. *The three men ate* N-UNCOUNT
with relish. **2** If you **relish** the thought or prospect VERB
of something, you are looking forward to it very V n
much. *He relished the idea of getting some cash.*
3 Relish is a sauce or a pickle that you eat with oth- N-VAR
er food in order to give it more flavour.

re·live /,ri:'lɪv/ **relives, reliving, relived.** If you ◆◇◇◇◇
relive something that has happened to you in the VERB
past, you remember it and imagine that you are ex- V n
periencing it again. *Last night he relived his terrify-*
ing ordeal.

re·load /,ri:'ləʊd/ **reloads, reloading, reloaded.** VERB: V n
If someone **reloads** a gun, they load it again by put- V
ting in more bullets or explosive. If you **reload** a
container, you fill it again. *He reloaded and nodded*
to the gamekeeper.

re·lo·cate /,ri:ləʊ'keɪt, AM -'ləʊkeɪt/ **relocates,** ◆◇◇◇◇
relocating, relocated. If people or businesses V-ERG: V
relocate, they move to a different place. *There will*
be the problem of where to relocate the returning
troops. ♦ **re·lo·ca·tion** /,ri:ləʊ'keɪʃən/ **relocations** N-UNCOUNT:
...the cost of relocation. also N in pl

re·luc·tant /rɪ'lʌktənt/. If you are **reluctant** to do ◆◆◆◇◇
something, you are unwilling to do it and hesitate ADJ-GRADED
before doing it, or do it slowly and without enthusiasm. ♦ **re·luc·tant·ly** *We have reluctantly agreed to* ADV-GRADED
let him go. ♦ **re·luc·tance** *Ministers have shown* N-UNCOUNT
extreme reluctance to explain their position.

rely /rɪ'laɪ/ **relies, relying, relied. 1** If you **rely** ◆◆◆◇◇
on someone or something, you need them and de- VERB:
pend on them in order to live or work properly. *The* V on/upon n
Association relies on member subscriptions for most for n
of its income. **2** If you can **rely** on someone to work VERB:
well or to behave as you want them to, you can V on/upon n
trust them to do this. *The Red Cross are relying on* to-inf
us. V on/upon n

REM /,ɑː i: 'em/. **REM** sleep is a period of sleep ADJ: ADJ n
that is very deep, during which your eyes and mus-
cles make many small movements. **REM** is an abbreviation of 'rapid eye movement'.

re·main /rɪ'meɪn/ **remains, remaining, re-** ◆◆◆◆◆
mained. 1 If someone or something **remains** in a V-LINK
particular state or condition, they stay in that state V adj
or condition and do not change. *The three men re-* V prep
mained silent... The government remained in V n
control... He remained a formidable opponent... It V adj that/
remains possible that bad weather could tear more to-inf/wh
holes in the tanker's hull. **2** If you **remain** in a place, V prep
you stay there and do not move away. *From time to* Also V
time, James remained at home with his family.
3 You can say that something **remains** when it still VERB
exists. *The wider problem remains... There remains* V
deep mistrust of his government. there V n
4 If something **remains** to be done, it has not yet been V-LINK
done and still needs to be done. *Major questions re-* V to-inf-
main to be answered about his work. **5** You can use **re-** passive
main in expressions such as **the fact remains that** or V-LINK
the question remains whether to introduce and em- PRAGMATICS
phasize something that you want to talk about. *The* V that
fact remains that inflation is unacceptably high... The V wh
question remains whether he was fully aware of the
claims. **6** If you say that it **remains to be seen** whether PHRASE
something will happen, you mean that nobody knows PRAGMATICS
whether it will happen. *It remains to be seen whether*
her parliamentary colleagues will agree.
7 The **remains** of something are the parts of it that are N-PLURAL
left after most of it has been taken away or destroyed.
...the charred remains of a tank. **8** The **remains** of a N-PLURAL
person or animal are the parts of their body that are

left after they have died, sometimes after they have
been dead for a long time. **9 Remains** are things N-PLURAL
that have been found from an earlier period of history, usually buried in the ground. *There are Roman*
remains all around us. **10** See also **remaining.**

re·main·der /rɪ'meɪndə/ **remainders, remain-** ◆◆◇◇◇
dering, remaindered. 1 The **remainder** of some- QUANT
thing is the part of it that remains after the other
parts have gone or been dealt with. *He gulped down*
the remainder of his coffee. ► Also a pronoun. *Only* PRON
5.9 per cent of the area is now covered in trees. Most
of the remainder is farmland. **2** In arithmetic, **the** N-SING:
remainder is the amount that remains when one the N
amount cannot be exactly divided by another. For
example, if you divide 22 by 7, the answer is 3 and
the remainder is 1. **3** If a book **is remaindered**, it is VB: usu
sold at a reduced price because it has not been sell- passive
ing very well and the publishers have decided not to
produce any more copies of it.

re·main·ing /rɪ'meɪnɪŋ/. **1** The **remaining** things ADJ: ADJ n
or people out of a group are the things or people
that still exist, are still present, or have not yet been
dealt with. *Stir in the remaining ingredients.* **2** See
also **remain.**

re·make, remakes, remaking, remade. The ◆◇◇◇◇
noun is pronounced /'ri:meɪk/. The verb is pronounced /,ri:'meɪk/. **1** A **remake** is a film that has N-COUNT
the same story, and often the same title, as a film
that was made earlier. **2** If a film **is remade**, a new VB: usu
film is made that has the same story, and often the passive
same title, as a film that was made earlier. **3** If you VERB
have something **remade**, you ask someone to make have n V-ed
it again, especially in a way that is better than be- Also V n
fore. *He had paid hundreds of pounds to have all the*
window frames in the room remade.

re·mand /rɪ'mɑːnd, -'mænd/ **remands, remand-** ◆◇◇◇◇
ing, remanded. 1 If a person who is accused of a VB: usu
crime **is remanded** in custody, they are kept in pris- passive
on until their trial. If they **are remanded** on bail,
they are told to return to the court at a later date,
when their trial will take place. **2 Remand** is used to N-UNCOUNT:
refer to the process of remanding someone in cus- also N in pl
tody or on bail, or to the period of time until their
trial begins. *...remand prisoners being held in police*
cells... She has already served a year on remand.

re'mand centre, remand centres. A remand N-COUNT
centre is an institution where people who are ac- BRITISH
cused of a crime are sent until their trial begins or
until a decision about their punishment has been
made.

re·mark /rɪ'mɑːk/ **remarks, remarking, re-** ◆◆◆◇◇
marked. 1 If you **remark** that something is the VERB:
case, you say that it is the case. *On several occasions* V that
she had remarked on the boy's improvement... 'It V on/upon n/
was a queer sensation,' remarked Eddie afterward. wh
2 If you make a **remark** about something, you say V with quote
something about it. N-COUNT:
with supp

re·mark·able /rɪ'mɑːkəbəl/. Someone or some- ◆◆◇◇◇
thing that is **remarkable** is unusual or exceptional ADJ-GRADED
in some way that causes people to notice them and
be surprised or impressed. *It was a remarkable*
achievement. ♦ **re·mark·ably** /rɪ'mɑːkəbli/. *Re-* ADV-GRADED
markably, the system continued until as recently as
1817.

re·mar·ry /,ri:'mæri/ **remarries, remarrying, re-** ◆◇◇◇◇
married. If someone **remarries**, they marry again VERB: V
after they have obtained a divorce from their previous husband or wife, or after their previous husband or wife has died. ♦ **re·mar·riage** /,ri:'mærɪdʒ/ N-VAR
remarriages *The question of divorce and remar-*
riage in church remains highly contentious.

re·mas·ter /,ri:'mɑːstə, -'mæstə/ **remasters, re-** VERB: be V-ed
mastering, remastered. If a film or musical recording **is remastered**, a new recording is made of
the old version, using modern technology to improve the quality.

re·match /'ri:mætʃ/ **rematches.** In sport, a **re-** N-COUNT
match is a second match that is played between
two people or teams, either because their first

match was a draw or because there was a dispute about it.

re·me·di·al /rɪˈmiːdiəl/. **1 Remedial** education involves special teaching for young people who find it difficult to learn as quickly as most others. **2** Remedial action is intended to correct something that has been done wrong or that has not been successful. *Some authorities are now having to take remedial action.* ◆◇◇◇◇ ADJ

ADJ FORMAL

rem·e·dy /ˈremədi/ **remedies, remedying, remedied. 1** A **remedy** is a successful way of dealing with a problem. *...a remedy for economic ills.* **2** If you **remedy** something that is wrong or harmful, you correct it or improve it. *Action has been taken to remedy temporary shortages of supplies.* **3** A **remedy** is something that is intended to cure you when you are ill or in pain. ◆◆◇◇◇ N-COUNT / VERB / V n / N-COUNT

re·mem·ber /rɪˈmembə/ **remembers, remembering, remembered. 1** If you **remember** people or events from the past, you still have an idea of them in your mind and you are able to think about them. *I certainly don't remember talking to you at all... I remember her being a dominant figure... I remembered that we had drunk the last of the coffee the week before.* **2** If you **remember** that something is the case, you become aware of it again after a time when you did not think about it. *She remembered that she was going to the social club that evening... Then I remembered the cheque, which cheered me up.* **3** If you cannot **remember** something, you are not able to bring it back into your mind when you make an effort to do so. *I couldn't remember ever having felt so safe and secure... I don't remember you asking me about that.* **4** If you **remember** to do something, you do it when you intend to. *Please remember to enclose a stamped addressed envelope when writing.* **5** You tell someone to **remember** that something is the case when you want to emphasize its importance. *It may be something that they already know about. It is important to remember that each person reacts differently... It should be remembered that this loss of control can never be regained.* **6** If you say that someone will **be remembered** for something that they have done, you mean that people will think of this whenever they think about the person. *He will always be remembered as one of the great Chancellors of the Exchequer.* **7** If you ask someone to **remember** you to a person who you have not seen for a long time, you are asking them to pass your greetings on to that person. *'Remember me to Lyle, won't you?' I said.* **8** If you make a celebration an occasion to **remember**, you make it very enjoyable for all the people involved. *I'll make it a birthday to remember.* ◆◆◆◆◇ VERB / V n/-ing / V n-ing / Also V, / V wh / VERB / V that / V n / VERB / V n/-ing / V n-ing / Also V wh, / V / VERB / V to-inf / VERB / PRAGMATICS / V that / it modal be V- / ed that / VERB: / be V-ed for / n/-ing / be V-ed as n / VB: no cont / V n to n / VB: / only to-inf / V

re·mem·brance /rɪˈmembrəns/ **remembrances. 1** If you do something in **remembrance** of a dead person, you do it as a way of showing that you want to remember them and that you respect them. *They wore black in remembrance of those who had died.* **2** A **remembrance** is a memory that you have of someone or something. *...happier remembrances of family holidays.* ◆◇◇◇◇ N-UNCOUNT FORMAL / N-VAR FORMAL

Re·mem·brance Day. Remembrance Day or **Remembrance Sunday** is the Sunday nearest to the 11th of November, when people honour the memory of those who died in the two world wars. N-UNCOUNT BRITISH

re·mind /rɪˈmaɪnd/ **reminds, reminding, reminded. 1** If someone **reminds** you of a fact or event that you already know about, they say something which makes you think about it. *He reminded Mrs Thatcher of an interview she had given five years ago... I had to remind myself that being confident is not the same as being perfect!* **2** You use **remind** in expressions such as **Let me remind you that** and **May I remind you that** to introduce a piece of information that you want to emphasize. It may be something that the hearer already knows about. Sometimes these expressions can sound unfriendly. *'Let me remind you,' said Marianne, 'that Manchester is also my home town.'... Need I remind you who* ◆◆◆◇◇ VERB / V n of n / V n that / VERB / PRAGMATICS / V n that / V n wh / SPOKEN

the enemy is? **3** If someone **reminds** you to do something, they say something which makes you remember to do it. *The note was to remind him about something he had to explain to one of his students.* **4** If you say that someone or something **reminds** you **of** another person or thing, you mean that they are similar to the other person or thing and that they make you think about them. *This reminds me of Christmas parties.* VERB / V n to-inf / V n about n / VERB / V n of n

re·mind·er /rɪˈmaɪndə/ **reminders. 1** Something that serves as a **reminder** of another thing makes you think about the other thing. *Violence has broken out in the capital, a stark reminder that the religious tensions are refusing to go away.* **2** A **reminder** is a letter or note that is sent to tell you that you have not done something such as pay a bill. *...the final reminder for the gas bill.* ◆◆◇◇◇ N-COUNT WRITTEN / N-COUNT BRITISH

rem·i·nisce /ˌremɪˈnɪs/ **reminisces, reminiscing, reminisced.** If you **reminisce** about something from your past, you write or talk about it, often with pleasure. *I don't like reminiscing because it makes me feel old.* ◆◇◇◇◇ VERB / V about n / Also V with / quote / FORMAL

rem·i·nis·cence /ˌremɪˈnɪsəns/ **reminiscences.** Someone's **reminiscences** are things that they remember from the past, and which they talk or write about. **Reminiscence** is the process of remembering these things and talking or writing about them. *A faint smile of reminiscence appeared on her face..* ◆◇◇◇◇ N-VAR FORMAL

rem·i·nis·cent /ˌremɪˈnɪsənt/. If you say that one thing is **reminiscent of** another, you mean that it reminds you of it. *...a gesture somehow reminiscent of royalty.* ◆◆◇◇◇ ADJ-GRADED: / v-link ADJ of n / FORMAL

re·miss /rɪˈmɪs/. If someone is **remiss**, they are careless about doing things which ought to be done. ADJ-GRADED: / v-link ADJ / FORMAL

re·mis·sion /rɪˈmɪʃən/ **remissions. 1** If someone who has had a serious disease such as cancer is in **remission** or if the disease is in **remission**, the disease has been controlled so that they are not as ill as they were. **2** If someone in prison gets **remission**, their prison sentence is reduced, usually because they have behaved well. N-VAR / N-UNCOUNT BRITISH

re·mit, remits, remitting, remitted. The noun is pronounced /ˈriːmɪt/. The verb is pronounced /rɪˈmɪt/. **1** Someone's **remit** is the area of activity which they are expected to deal with, or which they have authority to deal with. *The centre has a remit to advise Asian businesses and entrepreneurs.* **2** If you **remit** money to someone, you send it to them. ◆◇◇◇◇ N-COUNT BRITISH / VERB / V n to n / FORMAL

re·mit·tance /rɪˈmɪtəns/ **remittances.** A **remittance** is a sum of money that you send to someone. ◆◇◇◇◇ N-VAR FORMAL

re·mix, remixes, remixing, remixed. The noun is pronounced /ˈriːmɪks/. The veb is pronounced /ˌriːˈmɪks/. If a record producer **remixes** a piece of music, he or she makes a new version of it by putting together the individual instrumental and vocal parts in a different way. ► A **remix** of a piece of music is a new version created in this way. ◆◇◇◇◇ VERB: V n / N-COUNT

rem·nant /ˈremnənt/ **remnants.** The **remnants** of something are small parts of it that are left over when the main part has disappeared or been destroyed. *Beneath the present church were remnants of Roman flooring.* ◆◇◇◇◇ N-COUNT

re·mod·el /ˌriːˈmɒdəl/ **remodels, remodelling, remodelled;** spelled **remodeling, remodeled** in American English. To **remodel** something such as a building or a room is to give it a different form or shape. ♦ **re·mod·el·ling** *...the remodelling of Barcelona's airport.* VERB: V n / N-UNCOUNT

re·mon·strate /ˈremənstreɪt, AM rɪˈmɒnstreɪt/ **remonstrates, remonstrating, remonstrated.** If you **remonstrate** with someone, you protest to them about something you do not approve of or disagree with, and you try to get it changed or stopped. *I jumped in the car and went to remonstrate.* ♦ **re·mon·stra·tion** /ˌremənˈstreɪʃən/ **remonstrations** *There had been remonstrations from the Town Clerk.* VERB: / V with n / V / Also V prep / FORMAL / N-VAR

re·morse /rɪˈmɔːs/. **Remorse** is a strong feeling of guilt and regret about something wrong that you have done. ◆◇◇◇◇ N-UNCOUNT

re·morse·ful /rɪ'mɔːsfʊl/. If you are **remorseful**, ADJ-GRADED you feel very guilty and sorry about something wrong that you have done. ♦ **re·morse·ful·ly** 'My ADV-GRADED: poor wife!' he said, remorsefully. ADV with v

re·morse·less /rɪ'mɔːsləs/. **1** If you describe some- ADJ-GRADED thing, especially something unpleasant, as **remorseless**, you mean that it continues in a persistent way and cannot be stopped. ...the remorseless pressure of recession and financial constraint. ♦ **re·morse·less·ly** ...remorselessly rising unemployment. ADV-GRADED **2** Someone who is **remorseless** is prepared to be ADJ-GRADED cruel to other people and feels no pity for them. ♦ **remorselessly** They remorselessly beat up any- ADV-GRADED: one they suspected of supporting the opposition. ADV with v

re·mote /rɪ'məʊt/ **remoter, remotest**. **1** Remote ♦♦♦◇◇ areas are far away from cities and places where ADJ-GRADED most people live, and are therefore difficult to get to. ♦ **re·mote·ness** ...the remoteness of the island. N-UNCOUNT **2** The **remote** past or **remote** future is a time that is ADJ-GRADED many years distant from the present. **3** If something ADJ-GRADED is **remote** from a particular subject or area of experience, it is not relevant to it because it is very different. Teenagers are forced to study subjects that seem remote from their daily lives. **4** If you say that ADJ-GRADED there is a **remote** possibility or chance that some- PRAGMATICS thing will happen, you are emphasizing that there is only a very small chance that it will happen. I use a sunscreen whenever there is even a remote possibility that I will be in the sun. **5** If you describe someone ADJ-GRADED as **remote**, you mean that they behave as if they do not want to be friendly or closely involved with other people. ♦ **remoteness** His remoteness was N-UNCOUNT resented.

re·mote con'trol, remote controls. **1** Remote ♦◇◇◇◇ **control** is a system of controlling a machine or a ve- N-UNCOUNT hicle from a distance by using radio or electronic signals. ♦ **remote-controlled** ...a remote- ADJ controlled bomb. **2** The **remote control** for a televi- N-COUNT sion or video recorder is the device that you use to control the machine from a distance.

re·mote·ly /rɪ'məʊtli/. **1** You use **remotely** with a ♦◇◇◇◇ negative statement to emphasize the statement. No- ADV: body was remotely interested. ...a reluctance to say or with brd-neg, do anything that might remotely provoke or offend. also ADV **2** If someone or something is **remotely** placed or PRAGMATICS situated, they are a long way from other people or ADV-GRADED: places. ADV -ed

re·mote 'sensing. Remote sensing is the gather- N-UNCOUNT ing of information about something by observing it from space or from the air.

re·mould, remoulds, remoulding, remoulded; spelled **remold** in American English. The noun is pronounced /'riːməʊld/. The verb is pronounced /ˌriː'məʊld/. **1** A **remould** is an old tyre which has N-COUNT been given a new surface and can be used again. BRITISH The usual American term is **retread**. **2** To **remould** VERB something such as an idea or an economy is to V n change it so it has a new structure or is based on new principles. ...the crusade by Chairman Mao to remould the world view of the people.

re·mount /ˌriː'maʊnt/ **remounts, remounting,** VERB: **remounted**. When you **remount** a bicycle or V n, horse, you get back on it after you have got off it or V fallen off it.

re·mov·able /rɪ'muːvəbəl/. A **removable** part of ADJ something is a part that can easily be moved from its place or position. ...a cake tin with a removable base.

re·mov·al /rɪ'muːvəl/ **removals**. **1** Removal is the ♦♦◇◇◇ process of transporting furniture from one building N-VAR to another. Home removals are best done in cool BRITISH weather. ...a removal van. **2** See also **remove**.

re·move /rɪ'muːv/ **removes, removing, re-** ♦♦♦◇◇ **moved**. **1** If you **remove** something from a place, VERB you take it away or cause it to disappear. As soon as V n from n the cake is done, remove it from the oven... At least Also V n three bullets were removed from his wounds. ♦ **re-** WRITTEN **·mov·al** ...popular methods of hair removal. **2** If N-UNCOUNT you **remove** clothing, you take it off. He removed his VERB jacket. **3** If people **remove** someone from power or WRITTEN V n

from something such as a committee, they stop VERB: them being in power or being a member of the V n from n committee. All senior officers involved in the coup be V-ed will have to be removed. ♦ **removal** Parliament had N-UNCOUNT decided that his removal from power was illegal. **4** If VERB you **remove** an obstacle, a restriction, or a problem, V n you get rid of it. The agreement removes the last serious obstacle to the signing of the arms treaty. ♦ **removal** The Treaty provided for the removal of N-UNCOUNT trade restrictions between member countries.

re·moved /rɪ'muːvd/. **1** If you say that an idea or ◆◇◇◇◇ situation is far **removed from** something, you mean ADJ: that it is very different from it. The country had wit- v-link adv ADJ nessed scenes of tumult not far removed from civil from n war. **2** If someone is your cousin once **removed**, ADJ: n ADJ they are your cousin's child or your parent's cousin.

re·mov·er /rɪ'muːvə/ **removers**. Remover is a sub- N-VAR stance that you use for removing an unwanted stain or coating from a surface. ...paint remover.

re·mu·ner·ate /rɪ'mjuːnəreɪt/ **remunerates, re-** VERB: **munerating, remunerated**. If you **are** remuner- be V-ed **ated** for work that you do, you are paid for it. ...an Also V n adequately remunerated job. ♦ **re·mu·nera·tion** FORMAL /rɪˌmjuːnə'reɪʃən/ **remunerations** $31,000 is a gen- N-VAR erous remuneration.

re·mu·nera·tive /rɪ'mjuːnərətɪv/. Remunerative ADJ-GRADED work is work that you are paid for. FORMAL

re·nais·sance /rɪ'neɪsɒns, AM ˌrenɪ'sɑːns/. **1 The** ♦♦◇◇◇ Renaissance was the period in Europe, especially N-PROPER: Italy, in the 14th, 15th, and 16th centuries, when the N there was a great revival of interest in art, literature, science, and learning. **2** If something experiences a N-SING **renaissance**, it becomes popular or successful again after a time when people were not interested in it.

re·nal /'riːnəl/. Renal describes things that concern ADJ: ADJ n or are related to the kidneys. ...acute renal failure. MEDICAL

re·name /ˌriː'neɪm/ **renames, renaming, re-** ◆◇◇◇◇ **named**. If you **rename** something, you change its VERB name to a new name. The Prime Minister is now be- V n n ing pressed to rename child benefit 'child allowance'. V-ed ...the former Communist party, now renamed Socialists.

rend /rend/ **rends, rending, rent**. **1** If something VERB or someone **rends** something, they tear it. ...pain V n that rends the heart. ● See also **heart-rending**. **2** If LITERARY a loud sound **rends** the air, it is heard suddenly and VERB: V n violently. LITERARY

ren·der /'rendə/ **renders, rendering, rendered.** ◆◇◇◇◇ **1** You can use **render** with an adjective that de- VERB scribes a particular state to say that someone or V n adj something is changed into that state. For example, if someone or something makes a thing harmless, you can say that they **render** it harmless. It contained so many errors as to render it worthless. **2** If VERB you **render** someone help or assistance, you help V n to n them. He had a chance to render some service to his V n n country... Any assistance you can render him will be FORMAL appreciated. **3** When a jury or authority **renders** a VERB: V n verdict, decision, or response, they announce it. FORMAL **4** To **render** something in a particular language or VERB in a particular way means to translate it into that V n as/in/into language or in that way. ...'Zensho shimasu,' which n the translator rendered literally as, 'I will do my FORMAL best.' ♦ **ren·der·ing, renderings** This phrase may N-COUNT well have been a rendering of a popular Arabic expression.

ren·dez·vous /'rɒndeɪvuː/ **rendezvousing, ren-** ◆◇◇◇◇ **dezvoused**. The form **rendezvous** is pronounced /'rɒndeɪvuːz/ when it is the plural of the noun or the third person singular of the verb. **1** A **rendezvous** is N-COUNT a meeting, often a secret one, that you have arranged with someone for a particular time and place. I had decided to keep my rendezvous with Tony. **2** A **rendezvous** is the place where you N-COUNT have arranged to meet someone, often secretly. **3** If V-RECIP you **rendezvous** with someone or if the two of you V with n **rendezvous**, you meet at a time and place that you Also pl-n V have arranged. The plan was to rendezvous with him on Sunday afternoon.

R

ren·di·tion /renˈdɪʃən/ **renditions.** A rendition of a play, poem, or piece of music is a performance of it. *The musicians burst into a rousing rendition of 'Paddy Casey's Reel'.* ◆◇◇◇◇ N-COUNT

ren·egade /ˈrenɪɡeɪd/ **renegades. 1** A renegade is a person who abandons the religious, political, or philosophical beliefs that he or she used to have, and accepts opposing or different beliefs. **2 Ren·egade** is used to describe a member of a group who does or believes things which go against the normal behaviour or beliefs of that group. *Three men were shot dead by a renegade policeman.* ◆◇◇◇◇ N-COUNT · ADJ: ADJ n

re·nege /rɪˈniːɡ, AM -ˈnɪɡ/ **reneges, reneging, reneged.** If someone **reneges** on a promise or an agreement, they do not do what they have promised or agreed to do. *He reneged on a promise to leave his wife.* ◆◇◇◇◇ VERB · V on n · Also V

re·new /rɪˈnjuː, AM -ˈnuː/ **renews, renewing, renewed. 1** If you **renew** an activity, you begin it again. *He renewed his attack on government policy towards Europe... There was renewed fighting yesterday.* ♦ **re·new·al** /rɪˈnjuːəl, -ˈnuː-/. *Is he really considering a renewal of hostilities at this stage?* **2** If you **renew** a relationship with someone, you start it again after you have not seen them or have not been friendly with them for some time. *When the two men met again after the war they renewed their friendship... In December 1989 Syria renewed diplomatic relations with Egypt.* ♦ **renewal** *They will discuss the possible renewal of diplomatic relations.* **3** When you **renew** something such as a licence or a contract, you extend the period of time for which it is valid. *Larry's landlord threatened not to renew his lease.* ♦ **re·new·able** *A formal contract is signed which is renewable annually.* ♦ **re·new·al, renewals** *His contract came up for renewal.* **4** You can say that something **is renewed** when it grows or succeeds again after a time when it was destroyed, lost, or failing. *...a renewed interest in public transport systems.* ♦ **renewal** *...a political lobbyist concentrating on urban renewal and regeneration.* ◆◆◇◇◇ VERB · V n · V-ed · N-UNCOUNT · V-RECIP · pl-n V n · V n with n · N-UNCOUNT · VERB · V n · ADJ · N-VAR · VERB: be V-ed · V-ed · Also V n · N-UNCOUNT

re·new·able /rɪˈnjuːəbəl, AM -ˈnuː-/. **1 Renewable** resources are ones such as wind, water, and sunlight, which are constantly replacing themselves and therefore do not become used up. **2** See also **renew.** ◆◇◇◇◇ ADJ-GRADED

re·nounce /rɪˈnaʊns/ **renounces, renouncing, renounced. 1** If you **renounce** a belief or a way of behaving, you decide and declare publicly that you no longer have that belief or will no longer behave in that way. *After a period of imprisonment she renounced terrorism.* **2** If you **renounce** an official post, rank, or title, you formally give it up. *He renounced his claim to the French throne.* ◆◇◇◇◇ VERB · V n · VERB · V n

reno·vate /ˈrenəveɪt/ **renovates, renovating, renovated.** If someone **renovates** an old building, they repair and improve it and get it back into good condition. *She lives in a large, renovated farmhouse.* ♦ **reno·va·tion** /ˌrenəˈveɪʃən/ **renovations** *...a property which will need extensive renovation.* ◆◇◇◇◇ VERB: V n · V-ed · N-VAR

re·nown /rɪˈnaʊn/. A person or thing of **renown** is well known, usually for something good. *She used to be a singer of some renown.* ♦ **re·nowned** *The area is renowned for its Romanesque churches.* N-UNCOUNT · ADJ-GRADED

rent /rent/ **rents, renting, rented. 1** If you **rent** something, you regularly pay its owner a sum of money in order to be able to have it and use it yourself. *She rents a house with three other girls... He left his hotel in a rented car.* **2** If you **rent** something to someone, you let them have it and use it in exchange for a sum of money which they pay you regularly. *She rented rooms to university students.* ▶ **Rent out** means the same as **rent.** *Williams rented out his house and went camping... He bought the boat, and rented it out for $150.* **3 Rent** is the amount of money that you pay regularly to use a house, flat, or piece of land. *She worked to pay the rent while I went to college.* **4 Rent** is the past tense and past participle of **rend.** ● See also **ground rent.** ◆◆◆◇◇ VERB · V n · V-ed · VERB · V n to n · PHRASAL VB · V P noun · V n P · N-VAR

rent out. See rent 2. PHRASAL VB

rent·al /ˈrentəl/ **rentals. 1** The **rental** of something such as a car or television is the fact of paying an amount of money in order to have and use it. *We can organise car rental.* **2** The **rental** is the amount of money that you have to pay to use something such as a television, telephone, car, or property. **3** You use **rental** to describe things that are connected with the renting out of goods, properties, and services. *She picked up a rental car.* ◆◆◇◇◇ N-UNCOUNT: also N in pl, with supp · N-COUNT BRITISH · ADJ: ADJ n

'rent boy, rent boys. A **rent boy** is a boy or young man who has sex with men for money. N-COUNT BRITISH

,rent-'free. If you have a **rent-free** house or office, you do not have to pay anything to use it. ▶ Also an adverb. *They told James he could no longer live rent-free.* ADJ · ADV: ADV after v

re·nun·cia·tion /rɪˌnʌnsiˈeɪʃən/ **renunciations. 1** The **renunciation** of a belief or a way of behaving is the public declaration that you reject it. **2** The **renunciation** of a claim, title, or privilege is the act of officially giving it up. *...the renunciation of territory in the Mediterranean.* **3 Renunciation** is the act of denying yourself certain pleasures for moral or religious reasons. N-UNCOUNT: also N in pl · N-UNCOUNT · N-UNCOUNT

re·open /riːˈəʊpən/ **reopens, reopening, reopened. 1** If someone **reopens** a public building such as a factory, airport, or school, it opens and starts working again after it has been closed for some time. *The Theatre Royal, Norwich, will reopen in November.* **2** If police or the courts **reopen** a legal case, they investigate it again because it has never been solved or because there was something wrong in the way it was investigated before. **3** If people or countries **reopen** talks or relations, they begin again after they have stopped for some time. *US and Soviet negotiators reopened talks in Geneva... He reopened ties with Moscow earlier this year... Middle East peace talks reopen in Washington on Wednesday.* **4** If something **reopens** a question or debate, it makes the question or debate relevant again and causes people to start discussing it again. **5** If a country **reopens** a border or route, it becomes possible to cross or travel along it again. *The important Peking Shanghai route has reopened.* ◆◆◇◇◇ V-ERG: V n · V · VERB: V n · V-RECIP-ERG · pl-n V n · V n with n · V · VERB: V n · V-ERG: V n

re·or·gan·ize /riːˈɔːɡənaɪz/ **reorganizes, reorganizing, reorganized;** also spelled **reorganise** in British English. To **reorganize** something means to change the way in which it is organized, arranged, or done. *It is the mother who is expected to reorganize her busy schedule. ...a proposal to reorganize Bosnia into semi-autonomous provinces.* ♦ **re·or·gani·za·tion** /riːˌɔːɡənaɪˈzeɪʃən/ **reorganizations** *...the reorganization of the legal system... David was worried about major reorganisations taking place at work.* ◆◆◇◇◇ V-ERG · V n into n · Also V · N-VAR

rep /rep/ **reps. 1** A **rep** is a person whose job is to sell a company's products or services, especially by travelling round and visiting other companies. *I'd been working as a sales rep for a photographic company.* **2** A **rep** is a person who acts as a representative for a group of people, usually a group of colleagues. *...the health and safety rep at your union.* **3** In the theatre, **rep** is the same as **repertory.** ◆◇◇◇◇ N-COUNT · N-COUNT · N-UNCOUNT

Rep. In the United States, **Rep.** is a written abbreviation for **Representative.** *...Rep. Barbara Boxer.* ◆◆◇◇◇

re·paid /riːˈpeɪd/. **Repaid** is the past tense and past participle of **repay.**

re·pair /rɪˈpeə/ **repairs, repairing, repaired. 1** If you **repair** something that has been damaged or is not working properly, you mend it. *The cost of repairing earthquake damage could be more than $7,000 million... A woman drove her car to the garage to have it repaired.* ♦ **re·pair·er, repairers** *...builders, plumbers and TV repairers.* **2** If you **repair** something such as a relationship that has been damaged, you do something to improve it. *The government continued to try to repair the damage caused by the minister's interview.* **3** A **repair** is something that you do to mend a machine, building, piece of clothing, or other thing that has been damaged or is not working properly. *Many women* ◆◆◇◇◇ VERB · V n · have n V-ed · N-COUNT · VERB · V n · N-VAR

know how to carry out repairs on their cars... Many of the buildings are in need of repair... Her marriage is beyond repair. ● If something such as a building is **in good repair**, it is in good condition. If it is in **bad repair**, it is in bad condition.   PHRASE

4 If someone **repairs to** a particular place, they go there.   VERB: V to n FORMAL

re·pair·man /rɪˈpeəmæn/ **repairmen**. A repairman is a man who mends broken machines such as televisions.   N-COUNT

rep·a·ra·tion /ˌrepəˈreɪʃən/ **reparations. 1** Reparations are sums of money that are paid after a war by the defeated country for the damage and injuries it caused in other countries. *Israel accepted billions of dollars in war reparations.* **2** If you make **reparation** for something wrong that you have done to someone, you give them something or do something to help them because you have made them suffer.   ◆◇◇◇◇ N-UNCOUNT: also N in pl / N-UNCOUNT

rep·ar·tee /ˌrepɑːˈtiː, AM -pərˈteɪ/. Repartee is conversation that consists of quick witty comments and replies.   N-UNCOUNT

re·past /rɪˈpɑːst, -ˈpæst/ **repasts**. A repast is a meal.   N-COUNT LITERARY

re·pat·ri·ate /ˌriːˈpætrieɪt, AM -ˈpeɪt-/ **repatriates, repatriating, repatriated. 1** If a country repatriates someone, it sends them back to their home country. *It was not the policy of the government to repatriate genuine refugees.* ♦ **re·pat·ria·tion** /ˌriːpætriˈeɪʃən, AM -ˈpeɪt-/ **repatriations** *Today they begin the forced repatriation of Vietnamese boat people.* **2** If a company **repatriates** profits that it has made in another country, it brings them back into its home country. ♦ **repatriation** *...penalties on the repatriation of profits.*   ◆◆◇◇◇ VERB V n / N-VAR / VERB: V n / N-VAR

re·pay /rɪˈpeɪ/ **repays, repaying, repaid. 1** If you **repay** a loan or a debt, you pay back the money that you owe to the person who you borrowed or took it from. *He advanced funds of his own to his company, which was unable to repay him.* ♦ **re·pay·ment** *He failed to meet last Friday's deadline for repayment of a £114m loan.* **2** If you **repay** a favour that someone did for you, you do something or give them something in return. *It was very kind. I don't know how I can ever repay you.*   ◆◆◇◇◇ VERB V n / N-UNCOUNT / VERB V n

re·pay·able /rɪˈpeɪəbəl/. A loan that is **repayable** within a certain period of time must be paid back within that time. The usual American word is **payable**. *The loan is repayable over twenty years.*   ADJ BRITISH

re·pay·ment /rɪˈpeɪmənt/ **repayments. 1** Repayments are amounts of money which you pay at regular intervals to a person or organization who you owe money to. *They were unable to meet their mortgage repayments.* **2** See also **repay.**   ◆◆◇◇◇ N-COUNT

re·peal /rɪˈpiːl/ **repeals, repealing, repealed.** If the government **repeals** a law, it officially ends it, so that it is no longer valid. ► Also a noun. *...the 60th anniversary of the repeal of Prohibition.*   ◆◇◇◇◇ VERB: V n / N-UNCOUNT: N of n

re·peat /rɪˈpiːt/ **repeats, repeating, repeated. 1** If you **repeat** something, you say or write it again. You can say **I repeat** or **repeat** to emphasize that you are repeating something because it is important. *He repeated that he had been misquoted... He has repeated his call for the release of hostages... This is your last warning. I repeat: This is your last warning.* **2** If you **repeat** something that someone else has said or written, you say or write the same thing, or tell it to someone else. *Williams only repeated what General Colin Powell said yesterday... I trust you not to repeat that to anyone else... Repeat after me, 'All praise to Allah'.* **3** If you **repeat** yourself, you say something which you have said before, usually by mistake. **4** If you **repeat** an action, you do it again. *He said Japan would never repeat its mistakes... Hold this position for 30 seconds, release and repeat on the other side.* **5** If an event or series of events **repeats** itself, it happens again. *The UN will have to work hard to stop history repeating itself.* **6** If there is a **repeat** of an event, usually an undesirable event, it happens again.   ◆◆◆◇ VERB V that / V with quote / VERB V n / V n to n / V after n with quote / VERB: V pron-refl / VERB V n / VERB V pron-refl Also V / N-COUNT

There might be a repeat of last year's campaign of strikes. **7** A **repeat** is a television or radio programme that has been broadcast before. *There's nothing except sport and repeats on TV.* **8** If there is a **repeat performance** of something, usually an undesirable event, it happens again. *This year can only see a repeat performance of the decline.*   N-COUNT / PHRASE

re·peat·ed /rɪˈpiːtɪd/. Repeated actions or events are ones which happen many times. *Mr Lawssi apparently did not return the money, despite repeated reminders.* ♦ **re·peat·ed·ly** /rɪˈpiːtɪdli/. *Both men have repeatedly denied the allegations.*   ◆◆◇◇◇ ADJ: ADJ n / ADV: ADV with v

re·pel /rɪˈpel/ **repels, repelling, repelled. 1** When an army **repels** an attack or an invasion, they successfully fight and drive back soldiers from another army. **2** When a magnetic pole **repels** another magnetic pole, it exerts a force that pushes the opposite pole away. *Like poles repel, unlike poles attract.* **3** If something **repels** you, you find it unattractive or disgusting. *She was very striking but in some way I felt repelled.* ♦ **re·pel·lent** *...a very large, very repellent toad.*   ◆◇◇◇◇ VERB: V n FORMAL / V-RECIP pl-n V Also V n TECHNICAL VB: no cont, V n / ADJ-GRADED / ADJ-GRADED

re·pel·lent /rɪˈpelənt/ or **repellant, repellents.** Insect **repellent** is a product containing chemicals that you spray into the air or spray or rub on your body in order to keep insects away.   ◆◇◇◇◇ N-VAR

re·pent /rɪˈpent/ **repents, repenting, repented.** If you **repent**, you show or say that you are sorry for something wrong you have done. *Those who refuse to repent, he said, will be punished... Did he repent of anything in his life?* ♦ **re·pent·ance** /rɪˈpentəns/. *They showed no repentance during their trial.* ♦ **re·pent·ant** *...a repentant criminal.*   VERB V / V of/for n / Also V n / N-UNCOUNT / ADJ-GRADED

re·per·cus·sion /ˌriːpəˈkʌʃən/ **repercussions.** If an action or event has **repercussions**, it causes unpleasant things to happen some time after the original action or event. *Members of congress were warned of possible repercussions if their vote went through.*   ◆◇◇◇◇ N-COUNT FORMAL

rep·er·toire /ˈrepətwɑː/ **repertoires. 1** A performer's **repertoire** is all the pieces of music or parts in plays that he or she has learned and can perform. You can also refer to all the things of a particular kind that a person can do as their **repertoire**. *This has been one of the most successful desserts in my repertoire.* **2** You can refer to all the plays or music of a particular kind as, for example, the classical **repertoire** or the cello's **repertoire**.   ◆◇◇◇◇ N-COUNT / N-SING: with supp

rep·er·tory /ˈrepətri, AM -tɔːri/. **1** A **repertory** company is a group of actors and actresses who perform plays for just a few weeks at a time. *He was in repertory in Dundee.* **2** **Repertory** means the same as **repertoire**.   ◆◇◇◇◇ N-UNCOUNT / N-SING

rep·e·ti·tion /ˌrepɪˈtɪʃən/ **repetitions. 1** If there is a **repetition** of an event, usually an undesirable event, it happens again. *The city government has taken measures to prevent a repetition of last year's confrontation.* **2** **Repetition** means using the same words again. *He could also have cut much of the repetition and thus saved many pages.*   ◆◇◇◇◇ N-VAR / N-VAR

rep·e·ti·tious /ˌrepɪˈtɪʃəs/. Something that is **repetitious** involves actions or elements that are repeated many times and is therefore boring.   ADJ-GRADED PRAGMATICS

re·peti·tive /rɪˈpetɪtɪv/. **1** Something that is **repetitive** involves actions or elements that are repeated many times and is therefore boring. *...factory workers who do repetitive jobs.* **2** **Repetitive** movements or sounds are repeated many times.   ◆◇◇◇◇ ADJ-GRADED PRAGMATICS / ADJ

re·petitive 'strain injury. People who suffer from **repetitive strain injury** have pain in their hands and arms as a result of performing many similar movements over a long period of time, usually as part of their job. The abbreviation **RSI** is also used.   N-UNCOUNT

re·phrase /ˌriːˈfreɪz/ **rephrases, rephrasing, rephrased.** If you **rephrase** a question or statement, you ask it or say it again in a different way.   VERB: V n

re·place /rɪˈpleɪs/ **replaces, replacing, replaced. 1** If one thing or person **replaces** another, the first is used or acts instead of the second. *The*   ◆◆◆◇ VERB V n V n as n

R

council tax replaces the poll tax next April. ...the city lawyer who replaced Bob as chairman. ♦ **re·place·** V n
·ment, replacements. One thing or person that N-COUNT
replaces another can be referred to as their **replace-**
ment. *Taylor has nominated Adams as his replace-*
ment. **2** If you **replace** one thing or person with VERB
another, you put something or someone else in their V n with/by n
place to do their job. *I clean out all the grease and* V n
replace it with oil... The BBC decided it could not re-
place her. ♦ **replacement** *...a gradual replacement* N-UNCOUNT
of staff with less experienced contractors. **3** If you VERB: V n
replace something that is broken, damaged, or lost,
you get a new one to use instead. ♦ **re·place·ment**
...the replacement of damaged or lost books. ● See N-UNCOUNT
also **hormone replacement. 4** If you **replace** some- VERB
thing, you put it back where it was before. *Whitlock* V n
replaced the receiver. Also V n
prep/adv

re·place·able /rɪˈpleɪsəbəl/. **1** If something is **re-** ADJ
placeable, you can throw it away when it is finished
and put a new one in its place. *...replaceable butane*
gas cartridges. **2** If you say that someone is **replace-** ADJ-GRADED
able, you mean that they are not so important that
someone else could not take their place.

re·play, replays, replaying, replayed. The ♦♦◇◇◇
verb is pronounced /ˌriːˈpleɪ/. The noun is pronounced /ˈriːpleɪ/. **1** If a match between two sports VERB:
teams is **replayed**, the two teams play it again, be- be V-ed
cause neither team won the first time. ▶ You can BRITISH
refer to a match that is replayed as a **replay.** *If there* N-COUNT
has to be a replay we are confident of victory. **2** If VERB: V n
you **replay** something that you have recorded on
film or tape, you play it again in order to watch it or
listen to it. ▶ Also a noun. *I watched a slow-motion* N-COUNT
videotape replay of his fall. ● See also **action replay.**
3 If you **replay** an event in your mind, you think VERB: V n
about it again and again.

re·plen·ish /rɪˈplenɪʃ/ **replenishes, replenish-** ◆◇◇◇◇
ing, replenished. If you **replenish** something, VERB
you make it full or complete again. *Three hundred* V n
thousand tons of cereals are needed to replenish FORMAL
stocks. ♦ **re·plen·ish·ment** *...cell replenishment.* N-UNCOUNT

re·plete /rɪˈpliːt/. **1** To be **replete with** something ADJ-GRADED
means to be full of it. *History is replete with exam-* FORMAL
ples of populations out of control. **2** If you are **re-** ADJ
plete, you are pleasantly full of food and drink. FORMAL

rep·li·ca /ˈreplɪkə/ **replicas.** A **replica** of some- ◆◇◇◇◇
thing is an accurate copy of it. *...a human-sized rep-* N-COUNT
lica of the Statue of Liberty. ...a replica gun.

rep·li·cate /ˈreplɪkeɪt/ **replicates, replicating,** ◆◇◇◇◇
replicated. 1 If you **replicate** someone's experi- VERB: V n
ment, work, or research, you do it yourself in exact- FORMAL
ly the same way. **2** If a molecule **replicates**, it VERB: V
divides into smaller molecules which are exact TECHNICAL
copies of itself. ♦ **rep·li·ca·tion** /ˌreplɪˈkeɪʃən/. The N-UNCOUNT
process of replication is very quick and efficient.

re·ply /rɪˈplaɪ/ **replies, replying, replied.** ◆◆◆◆◇
1 When you **reply** to something that someone has VERB
said or written to you, you say or write something V with quote
as an answer. *'That's a nice dress,' said Michael.* V that
'Thanks,' she replied... He replied that this was abso- V to n
lutely impossible... I've not replied to Lee's letter yet. Also V
2 A **reply** is something that you say or write when N-COUNT:
you answer someone or answer a letter or advertise- also n N
ment. *I called out a challenge, but there was no*
reply... David has had 12 replies to his ad. **3** If you VERB
reply to something such as an attack, you do some- V with n
thing in response. *Farmers threw eggs and empty* Also V to n
bottles at police, who replied with tear gas.

re·port /rɪˈpɔːt/ **reports, reporting, reported.** ◆◆◆◆◆
1 If you **report** something that has happened, you VERB: V n
tell people about it. *I reported the theft to the po-* V n to n
lice... The officials also reported that two more ships V that
were apparently heading for Malta... 'He seems to be V with quote
all right now,' reported a relieved Taylor... The for- be V-ed as
eign secretary is reported as saying that force will -ing/-ed
have to be used... She reported him missing the next V adj
day. **2** If you **report** on an event or subject, you tell Also be V-ed
people about it, because it is your job or duty to do to-inf
so. *I'll now call at the vicarage and report to you in* VERB:
due course. V on n
V to n

3 If you give someone a **report** on something, you tell N-COUNT
them what has been happening. *...a progress report on*
how the project is going. **4** If you say that there are **re-** N-COUNT
ports that something has happened, you mean that PRAGMATICS
some people say it has happened but you have no direct evidence of it. *There are unconfirmed reports that*
two people have been shot.

5 A **report** is a news article or broadcast which gives N-COUNT
information about something that has just happened.
6 A **report** is an official document which a group of N-COUNT
people issue after investigating a situation or event.
The education committee will today publish its report
on the supply of teachers for the 1990's. **7** A school **re-** N-COUNT
port is an official written account of how well or how BRITISH
badly a pupil has done during the term or year that
has just finished. The American term is **report card.**
8 If someone **reports** you to a person in authority, VERB:
they tell that person about something wrong that you V n to n
have done. *The Princess was reported for speeding.* be V-ed for
9 If you **report** to a person or place, you go to that per- -ing/n
son or place and say that you are ready to start work or VERB:
say that you are present. *None of the men had reported* V to n
for duty. **10** If you say that one employee **reports** to V to n
another, you mean that the first employee is told what VB: no cont,
to do by the second one and is responsible to them. FORMAL
11 See also **reporting.**

report back. 1 If you **report back** to someone, you PHRASAL VB
tell them about something that they asked you to find V P to n
out about. *I'll report back the moment I have located* V P
him... He would, of course, report back on all delibera- V P on n
tions... The repairman reported back that the comput- V P that
er had a virus. **2** If you **report back** to a place, you go Also V n P,
back there and say that you are ready to start work or V P noun
say that you are present. *They were sent home and told* V P to n
to report back in the afternoon. **3** If you **report back** a V P
comment or remark, often a critical one, you repeat it Also V P for n
to the person it was about. *We reported this back to* V n P to n
Krajicek.

re·port·age /rɪˈpɔːtɪdʒ, ˌrepɔːˈtɑːʒ/. **Reportage** is N-UNCOUNT
news reporting or documentary. *...the magazine's* FORMAL
acclaimed mix of reportage, fashion/beauty, and hu-
man interest stories.

re·port card, report cards. 1 A **report card** is an N-COUNT
official written account of how well or how badly a AMERICAN
pupil has done during the term or year that has just
finished. The British word is **report. 2** A **report card** N-COUNT
is a report on how well a person, organization, or AMERICAN,
country has been doing recently. *...his final report* JOURNALISM
card on the state of the economy.

re·port·ed clause, reported clauses. A **report-** N-COUNT
ed clause is a clause which indicates what someone
said. For example, in 'She said that she was hungry',
'she was hungry' is a reported clause.

re·port·ed·ly /rɪˈpɔːtɪdli/. If you say that some- ◆◆◇◇◇
thing is **reportedly** true, you mean that someone ADV
has said that it is true, but you have no direct evi- FORMAL
dence of it. *More than two hundred people have re-*
portedly been killed.

re·ported 'question, reported questions. A **re-** N-COUNT
ported question is a question which is reported
using a clause beginning with a word such as 'why'
or 'whether', as in 'I asked her why she'd done it'.

re·ported 'speech. Reported speech is speech N-UNCOUNT
which is reported using a report structure rather
than the actual words used by the speaker, as in
'They said you didn't like it'.

re·port·er /rɪˈpɔːtə/ **reporters.** A **reporter** is ◆◆◆◆◇
someone who writes news articles or who broad- N-COUNT
casts news reports. *...a TV reporter.*

re·port·ing /rɪˈpɔːtɪŋ/. **Reporting** is the presenting ◆◆◆◆◇
of news in newspapers, on radio, and on television. N-UNCOUNT
...honest and impartial political reporting.

re·porting clause, reporting clauses. A **re-** N-COUNT
porting clause is a clause which indicates that you
are talking about what someone said or thought.
For example, in 'She said that she was hungry', 'She
said' is a reporting clause.

re·port structure, report structures. A **report** N-COUNT
structure is a structure containing a reporting
clause and a reported clause or a quote.

re·pose /rɪ'pəʊz/ **reposes, reposing, reposed.** N-UNCOUNT
1 Repose is a state in which you are resting and LITERARY
feeling calm. **2** If something **reposes** somewhere, it VERB
is there. *Exquisite china soup dishes reposed on sil-* V prep/adv
ver plates. FORMAL

re·pos·i·tory /rɪ'pɒzɪtri, AM -tɔːri/ **repositories.** ◆◇◇◇◇
1 A **repository** is a place where something is kept N-COUNT
safely. *A church in Moscow became a repository for* FORMAL
police files. **2** A **repository** of information is a N-COUNT
person or group of people who know a lot of LITERARY
information about a particular place or subject. *The*
repository of all important knowledge in a small
town was the chief barman of the local pub.

re·pos·sess /,riːpə'zes/ **repossesses, repos-** ◆◇◇◇◇
sessing, repossessed. If your car or house **is** VB: usu
repossessed, the people who supplied it take it back passive
because they are still owed money for it.

re·pos·ses·sion /,riːpə'zeʃən/ **repossessions.** ◆◇◇◇◇
1 The **repossession** of someone's house is the act of N-VAR
repossessing it. **2** You can refer to a house or car N-COUNT
that has been repossessed as a **repossession**. *Many*
of the cars you will see at auction are repossessions.

rep·re·hen·si·ble /,reprɪ'hensɪbəl/. If you think that ADJ-GRADED
a type of behaviour or an idea is very bad and mor- FORMAL
ally wrong, you can say that it is **reprehensible**.

rep·re·sent /,reprɪ'zent/ **represents, represent-** ◆◆◆◇
ing, represented. 1 If someone such as a lawyer VERB
or a politician **represents** a person, they act on be- V n
half of that person. *...the politicians we elect to rep-*
resent us. **2** If you **represent** a person or group at VERB
an official event, you go there on their behalf. *The* V n
general secretary may represent the president at offi-
cial ceremonies. **3** If you **represent** your country or VERB: V n
town in a competition or event, you take part in it
on behalf of the country or town where you live.
4 If a group of people or things **is** well **represented** in V-PASSIVE:
a particular activity or in a particular place, a lot of beadv V-ed
them can be found there. *In New Mexico all kinds of* beV-ed
cuisines are represented.
5 If you say that something **represents** a change, V-LINK:
achievement, or victory, you mean that it is a change, V n
achievement, or victory.
6 If a sign or symbol **represents** something, it is ac- VB: no cont
cepted as meaning that thing. *...a black dot in the* V n
middle of the circle is supposed to represent the source
of the radiation.
7 If you say that something or someone **represents** an VB: no cont,
idea or quality, you mean that they are a symbol or an no passive
expression of that idea or quality. *You represent every-*
thing British racing needs.
8 If you **represent** a person or thing as a particular VERB
thing, you describe them as being that thing. *The* V n as n
popular press tends to represent him as an environ-
mental guru.

rep·re·sen·ta·tion /,reprɪze'nteɪʃən/ **representa-** ◆◆◇◇◇
tions. 1 If a group or person has **representation** in N-UNCOUNT
a parliament or on a committee, someone in parlia-
ment or on the committee will vote or make decisions on their behalf. *Puerto Ricans are U.S. citizens*
but they have no representation in Congress. ● See
also **proportional representation**.
2 You can describe a picture, model, or statue of a N-COUNT
person or thing as a **representation** of them. *...a life-* FORMAL
like representation of Christ.
3 If you make **representations** to a government or N-PLURAL
other official group, you make formal complaints or
requests to them.

rep·re·sen·ta·tion·al /,reprɪze'nteɪʃənəl/. In a **rep-** ADJ-GRADED
resentational painting, the artist attempts to show FORMAL
things as they really are.

rep·re·sen·ta·tive /,reprɪ'zentətɪv/ **representa-** ◆◆◆◇
tives. 1 A **representative** is a person who has been N-COUNT
chosen to act or make decisions on behalf of anoth-
er person or a group of people. *...trade union repre-*
sentatives. **2** A **representative** is someone whose N-COUNT
job is to sell a company's products or services, BRITISH
usually by travelling round other companies and
organizations. *...a sales representative.* **3** A **repre-** ADJ: ADJ n
sentative group consists of a small number of peo-

ple who have been chosen to make decisions on behalf of a larger group.
4 Someone who is typical of the group to which they ADJ-GRADED
belong can be described as **representative**. *He was in*
no way representative of dog-trainers in general.
5 See also **House of Representatives**.

re·press /rɪ'pres/ **represses, repressing, re-** ◆◇◇◇◇
pressed. 1 If you **repress** a feeling, you make a VERB
deliberate effort not to show it or to have this feel- PRAGMATICS
ing; used showing disapproval. *People who repress* V n
their emotions risk having nightmares. ♦ **re·pres-**
·sion, /rɪ'preʃən/. *...the repression of his feelings* N-UNCOUNT
about men. **2** If you **repress** a smile, sigh, or moan, VERB: V n
you try hard not to smile, sigh, or moan. **3** If a sec- VERB
tion of society **is repressed**, their freedom is re- PRAGMATICS
stricted by the people who have authority over V n
them; used showing disapproval. *...a UN resolution*
banning him from repressing his people.
♦ **repression, repressions** *...a society condi-* N-UNCOUNT:
tioned by violence and repression. also N in pl

re·pressed /rɪ'prest/. A **repressed** person is some- ADJ-GRADED
one who does not allow themselves to have natural PRAGMATICS
feelings and desires, especially sexual ones; used
showing disapproval.

re·pres·sive /rɪ'presɪv/. A **repressive** government ◆◇◇◇◇
is one that restricts people's freedom and controls ADJ-GRADED
them by using force; used showing disapproval. PRAGMATICS
♦ **re·pres·sive·ly** *...the country, which had been re-* ADV-GRADED:
pressively ruled for ten years. ADV with v

re·prieve /rɪ'priːv/ **reprieves, reprieved. 1** If ◆◇◇◇◇
someone who has been sentenced in a court **is re-** VB: usu
prieved, their punishment is officially postponed or passive,
cancelled. **2** A **reprieve** is a delay before a very un- no cont
pleasant or difficult situation which may or may not N-COUNT
take place. *Ministers agreed to postpone the aboli-*
tion of duty-free sales in Europe. The reprieve may
only be temporary, however.

rep·ri·mand /'reprɪmɑːnd, -'mænd/ **reprimands,** ◆◇◇◇◇
reprimanding, reprimanded. If someone in VERB: V n
authority, **reprimands** you, they speak to you angri- beV-ed for
ly or seriously for doing something wrong. *He was* -ing/n
reprimanded by a teacher for talking in the corridor. FORMAL
▶ Also a noun. *He has been fined five thousand* N-VAR
pounds and given a severe reprimand.

re·print, reprints, reprinting, reprinted. The ◆◇◇◇◇
verb is pronounced /,riː'prɪnt/. The noun is pro-
nounced /'riːprɪnt/. **1** If a book **is reprinted**, further VB: usu
copies of it are printed when all the other ones have passive
been sold. **2** A **reprint** is a process in which new N-COUNT
copies of a book or article are printed because all
the other ones have been sold. **3** A **reprint** is a new N-COUNT
copy of a book or article, printed because all the
other ones have been sold or because minor
changes have been made to the original. *...a reprint*
of a 1962 novel.

re·pris·al /rɪ'praɪzəl/ **reprisals.** If you do some- ◆◇◇◇◇
thing to someone in **reprisal**, you do something N-VAR
violent or unpleasant to them because they have
done something similar to you. *Witnesses are un-*
willing to testify through fear of reprisals.

re·prise /rɪ'priːz/ **reprises, reprising, reprised.** ◆◇◇◇◇
1 In music, if there is a **reprise**, an earlier section of N-COUNT
music is repeated. **2** If someone **reprises** a role or a VERB: V n
song, they play or sing it again. WRITTEN

re·proach /rɪ'prəʊtʃ/ **reproaches, reproach-** ◆◇◇◇◇
ing, reproached. 1 If you **reproach** someone, VERB: V n
you say or show that you are disappointed, upset, V n for-ing/n
or angry because they have done something wrong.
She had not even reproached him for breaking his
promise. **2** If you look at or speak to someone with N-VAR
reproach, you show or say that you are disappointed, upset, or angry because they have done something wrong. *Women in public life must be beyond*
reproach. **3** If you **reproach** yourself, you think with VERB:
regret about something you have done wrong. *We* V pron-refl
begin to reproach ourselves for not having been more V pron-refl for
careful. **4** If you consider someone's actions or be- -ing/n
haviour to be a **reproach** to a group of people, you N-SING
consider them to be harmful or insulting to that

R

group. *The shootings and bombings were 'a scandal and reproach to all of us in Europe'.*

re·proach·ful /rɪˈprəʊtʃfʊl/. **Reproachful** expressions or remarks show that you are disappointed, upset, or angry because someone has done something wrong. ♦ **re·proach·ful·ly** *Luke's mother stopped smiling and looked reproachfully at him.* ADJ-GRADED / ADV-GRADED: ADV after v

rep·ro·bate /ˈreprəbeɪt/ **reprobates.** If you think someone behaves in a foolish and immature way you can say they are a **reprobate.** N-COUNT

re·pro·duce /ˌriːprəˈdjuːs, AM -ˈduːs/ **reproduces, reproducing, reproduced. 1** If you **reproduce** something, you copy it. *I shall not try to reproduce the policemen's English.* **2** If you **reproduce** a picture, speech, or a piece of writing, you make a photograph or printed copy of it. *We are grateful to you for permission to reproduce this article.* **3** If you **reproduce** an action or an achievement, you repeat it. *...if we can reproduce the form we have shown in the last couple of months.* **4** When people, animals, or plants **reproduce**, they produce young. *We are reproducing ourselves at such a rate that our numbers threaten the ecology of the planet.* ♦ **re·pro·duc·tion** /ˌriːprəˈdʌkʃən/. *...sexual reproduction.* ◆◆◇◇◇ VERB: V n / VERB: V n / VERB: V n / VERB: V / V pron-refl / N-UNCOUNT

re·pro·duc·tion /ˌriːprəˈdʌkʃən/ **reproductions. 1** A **reproduction** is a copy of something such as an antique or a painting. **2** Sound **reproduction** is the recording of sound onto cassettes, records, or films so that it can be heard by a large number of people. ◆◇◇◇◇ N-COUNT / N-UNCOUNT

re·pro·duc·tive /ˌriːprəˈdʌktɪv/. **Reproductive** processes and organs are concerned with the reproduction of living things. ◆◇◇◇◇ ADJ

re·proof /rɪˈpruːf/ **reproofs.** If you say or do something in **reproof**, you say or do it to show that you disapprove of what someone has done or said. N-VAR / FORMAL

re·prove /rɪˈpruːv/ **reproves, reproving, reproved.** If you **reprove** someone, you speak angrily or seriously to them because they have behaved wrongly or foolishly. *'There's no call for talk like that,' Mrs Evans reproved him.* VERB: V n / V with quote / FORMAL

rep·tile /ˈreptaɪl, AM -tɪl/ **reptiles.** Reptiles are a group of animals which have scaly skins and lay eggs. Snakes, lizards, and crocodiles are reptiles. ♦ **rep·til·ian** /repˈtɪlɪən/. *...a prehistoric jungle occupied by reptilian creatures.* ◆◇◇◇◇ N-COUNT / ADJ

re·pub·lic /rɪˈpʌblɪk/ **republics.** A **republic** is a country that has a president or whose system of government is based on the idea that every citizen has equal status. *In 1918 Austria became a republic. ...the Republic of Ireland.* ● See also **banana republic.** ◆◆◆◇◇ N-COUNT

re·pub·li·can /rɪˈpʌblɪkən/ **republicans. 1** A **republican** government has a president or is based on the idea that every citizen has equal status. ♦ **re·pub·li·can·ism** /rɪˈpʌblɪkənɪzəm/. **Republicanism** is the belief that the best system of government is a republic. **2** A **republican** is someone who is a member or supporter of a particular political party which has the word 'republican' in its title, for example the Republican Party in the United States. *What made you decide to become a Republican?* ► Also an adjective *Some families have been republican for generations.* ♦ **re·pub·li·can·ism. Republicanism** is support for a republican political party. **3** In Northern Ireland, if someone is **Republican**, they believe that Northern Ireland should not be ruled by Britain but should become part of the Republic of Ireland. *...a Republican paramilitary group.* ► A **Republican** is someone who has Republican views. ◆◆◆◇◇ ADJ / N-UNCOUNT / ADJ / ADJ / N-UNCOUNT / ADJ / N-COUNT

re·pu·di·ate /rɪˈpjuːdieɪt/ **repudiates, repudiating, repudiated.** If you **repudiate** something or someone, you show that you strongly disagree with them and do not want to be connected with them in any way. *Leaders urged people to turn out in large numbers to repudiate the violence.* ♦ **re·pu·dia·tion** /rɪˌpjuːdiˈeɪʃən/ **repudiations** *...his public repudiation of the conference decision.* ◆◇◇◇◇ VERB / V n / N-VAR

re·pug·nant /rɪˈpʌgnənt/. If you think that something is horrible and disgusting, you can say that it ADJ-GRADED / FORMAL

is **repugnant.** ♦ **re·pug·nance** *She felt a deep sense of shame and repugnance.* N-UNCOUNT

re·pulse /rɪˈpʌls/ **repulses, repulsing, repulsed. 1** If you **are repulsed** by something, you think that it is horrible and disgusting and you want to avoid it. *Evil has charisma. Though people are repulsed by it, they also are drawn to its power.* **2** If an army or other group **repulses** a group of people, they drive it back using force. VB: usu passive beV-ed / VERB: V n

re·pul·sion /rɪˈpʌlʃən/. **1 Repulsion** is an extremely strong feeling of disgust. *She gave a dramatic shudder of repulsion.* **2 Repulsion** is a force that pushes two things apart, such as the force that there is in magnets. N-UNCOUNT / N-UNCOUNT TECHNICAL

re·pul·sive /rɪˈpʌlsɪv/. **1** If you find something or someone **repulsive**, you find them horrible and disgusting and you want to avoid them. *...repulsive fat white slugs.* **2** A **repulsive** force is a force which pushes away what is around it. ADJ-GRADED / ADJ TECHNICAL

repu·table /ˈrepjʊtəbl/. A **reputable** company or person is reliable and trustworthy. ◆◇◇◇◇ ADJ-GRADED

repu·ta·tion /ˌrepjʊˈteɪʃən/ **reputations. 1** To have a **reputation** for something means to be known or remembered for it. *Alice Munro has a reputation for being a very depressing writer.* **2** Something's or someone's **reputation** is the opinion that people have about how good they are. *The stories ruined his reputation.* ◆◆◆◇◇ N-COUNT / N-COUNT

re·pute /rɪˈpjuːt/. **1** A person or thing **of repute** or of high **repute** is respected and known to be good. **2** A person's or organization's **repute** is their reputation, especially when this is good. *Under his stewardship, the UN's repute has risen immeasurably.* PHRASE FORMAL / N-UNCOUNT FORMAL

re·put·ed /rɪˈpjuːtɪd/. If you say that something **is reputed** to be true, you mean that people say it is true, but you do not know if it is definitely true. *He is reputed to earn ten million pounds a year.* ♦ **re·put·ed·ly** /rɪˈpjuːtɪdli/. *Both women have dramatic dark looks and, reputedly, fiery temperaments.* ◆◇◇◇◇ V-PASSIVE PRAGMATICS beV-ed to-inf / FORMAL / ADV

re·quest /rɪˈkwest/ **requests, requesting, requested. 1** If you **request** something, you ask for it politely or formally. *She had requested that the door to her room be left open.* **2** If you **request** someone to do something, you politely or formally ask them to do it. *They requested him to leave.* **3** If you make a **request**, you politely ask for something or ask someone to do something. **4** A **request** is a song or piece of music which someone has asked a performer or disc jockey to play. **5** If you do something **at** someone's **request**, you do it because they have asked you to. **6** If something is given or done **on request**, it is given or done whenever you ask for it. *Leaflets giving details are available on request.* ◆◆◆◆◇ VERB: V n / V that / VERB / V n to-inf / FORMAL / N-COUNT / N-COUNT / PHRASE / PHRASE

requi·em /ˈrekwiem/ **requiems. 1** A **requiem** or a **requiem mass** is a Catholic church service in memory of someone who has recently died. **2** A **requiem** is a piece of music for singers and musicians that can be performed either as part of a requiem mass or as part of a concert. ◆◇◇◇◇ N-COUNT / N-COUNT

re·quire /rɪˈkwaɪə/ **requires, requiring, required. 1** If you **require** something or if something **is required**, you need it or it is necessary. *...the kind of crisis that requires us to drop everything else.* **2** If a law or rule **requires** you to do something, you have to do it. *...a law requiring prompt reporting of such malfunctions... Then he'll know exactly what's required of him.* **3** If you say that something is **required reading** for a group of people, you mean that you think it is essential for them to read it because it will give them information which they should have. ◆◆◆◆◇ VERB: V n / V n to-inf / VERB: V n to-inf / beV-ed ofn / Also V that / FORMAL / PHRASE

re·quire·ment /rɪˈkwaɪəmənt/ **requirements. 1** A **requirement** is a quality or qualification that you must have in order to be allowed to do something or to be suitable for something. *Its products met all legal requirements.* **2** Your **requirements** are the things that you need. *Variations of this programme can be arranged to suit your requirements.* ◆◆◆◇◇ N-COUNT / N-COUNT

requi·site /'rekwɪzɪt/ **requisites. 1** You can use **requisite** to describe something that is necessary for a particular purpose. *She filled in the requisite paperwork.* **2** A **requisite** is something which is necessary for a particular purpose. *An understanding of accounting techniques is a major requisite for the work.* ◆◇◇◇◇ ADJ FORMAL / N-COUNT FORMAL

requi·si·tion /,rekwɪ'zɪʃən/ **requisitions, requisitioning, requisitioned. 1** If people in authority **requisition** a vehicle, building, or food, they formally demand it and take it for official use. **2** A **requisition** is a written document which allows a person or organization to obtain goods. *...a requisition for a replacement typewriter.* VERB: V n FORMAL / N-COUNT

re·'route, re-routes, re-routing, re-routed; also spelled **reroute.** If vehicles **are re-routed**, they are directed along a different route because the usual route cannot be used. *They rerouted the planes at La Guardia airport.* VERB V n

re-run, re-runs, re-running, re-ran. The form **re-run** is used in the present tense and is also the past participle of the verb. The noun is pronounced /'riː rʌn/. The verb is pronounced /,riː 'rʌn/. **1** If you say that something is a **re-run of** a particular event or experience, you mean that what happens now is very similar to what happened in the past. **2** If someone **re-runs** a process or event, they do it or organize it again. *Edit the input text and re-run the software.* ▶ Also a noun. *In the re-run he failed to make the final at all.* **3** If an election **is re-run**, it is organized again, for example because the correct procedures were not followed or because no candidate got an overall majority. ▶ Also a noun. *The opposition has demanded a re-run of parliamentary elections held yesterday.* **4** If a theatre company or cinema **re-runs** a play or a film, it puts it on or shows it again. **5** A **re-run** is a film, play, or television programme, that is broadcast or put on again. ◆◇◇◇◇ N-SING N of n / VERB V n / N-COUNT / VB: usu passive BRITISH / N-COUNT / VERB: V n / N-COUNT

re·sat /,riː'sæt/. **Resat** is the past tense and past participle of **resit**.

re·sched·ule /,riː'ʃedjuːl, AM -'skedʒuːl/ **reschedules, rescheduling, rescheduled. 1** If someone **reschedules** an event, they change the time at which it is due to happen. *They've rescheduled the vigil for February 14th.* ♦ **re·sched·ul·ing, reschedulings** *...a rescheduling of the trip to Asia.* **2** To **reschedule** a debt means to arrange for the person, organization, or country that owes money to pay it back over a longer period because they are in financial difficulty. ♦ **re·sched·ul·ing** *...a rescheduling of loan repayments.* ◆◇◇◇◇ VERB: V n V n for/ton / N-VAR / VERB: V n / N-VAR

re·scind /rɪ'sɪnd/ **rescinds, rescinding, rescinded.** If a government or a group of people in power **rescind** a law or agreement, they officially withdraw it and state that it is no longer valid. *Trade Union leaders have demanded the government rescind the price rise.* ◆◇◇◇◇ VERB V n FORMAL

res·cue /'reskjuː/ **rescues, rescuing, rescued. 1** If you **rescue** someone, you get them out of a dangerous or unpleasant situation. ▶ Also a noun. *...a major air-sea rescue... Lights clipped onto life jackets improve the chances of rescue.* ♦ **res·cu·er, rescuers** *It took rescuers 90 minutes to reach the trapped men.* **2** If you **go to** someone's **rescue** or **come to** their **rescue**, you help them when they are in danger or difficulty. ◆◆◆◇◇ VERB: V n / N-VAR / N-COUNT / PHRASE

re·search /rɪ'sɜːtʃ/ **researches, researching, researched.** If you **research** something, you try to discover facts about it. *She spent two years in South Florida researching and filming her documentary.* ▶ Also a noun. *...cancer research. ...his researches into which kinds of flowers bees can detect their best honey from.* ♦ **re·search·er, researchers** *He chose to join the company as a market researcher.* ◆◆◆◆◆ VERB V n Also V / N-UNCOUNT: also N in pl / N-COUNT

re·sell /,riː'sel/ **resells, reselling, resold.** If you **resell** something that you have bought, you sell it again. *Shopkeepers buy them in bulk and resell them for £150 each.* VERB V n Also V

re·sem·blance /rɪ'zembləns/ **resemblances.** If there is a **resemblance** between two people or things, they are similar to each other. ◆◇◇◇◇ N-VAR

re·sem·ble /rɪ'zembəl/ **resembles, resembling, resembled.** If one thing or person **resembles** another, they are similar to each other. *She so resembles her mother.* ◆◆◇◇◇ VB: no cont V n

re·sent /rɪ'zent/ **resents, resenting, resented.** If you **resent** someone or something, you feel bitter and angry about them. *She resents her mother for being so tough on her.* ◆◆◇◇◇ VERB V n/-ing

re·sent·ful /rɪ'zentful/. If you are **resentful**, you feel resentment. *I felt very resentful and angry about losing my job.* ♦ **re·sent·ful·ly** *She continued to look at him resentfully.* ◆◇◇◇◇ ADJ-GRADED / ADV-GRADED

re·sent·ment /rɪ'zentmənt/ **resentments. Resentment** is bitterness and anger that someone feels about something. *She expressed resentment at being interviewed by a social worker.* ◆◆◇◇◇ N-UNCOUNT: also N in pl

res·er·va·tion /,rezə'veɪʃən/ **reservations. 1** If you have **reservations** about something, you are not sure that it is entirely good or right. *My main reservation about his film was the ending.* **2** If you make a **reservation**, you arrange for something such as a table in a restaurant or a room in a hotel to be kept for you. **3** A **reservation** is an area of land that is kept separate for a particular group of people to live in. *Sixty percent of the 700 Native Americans who live on the reservation are unemployed.* **4** See also **central reservation.** ◆◇◇◇◇ N-VAR / N-COUNT / N-COUNT

re·serve /rɪ'zɜːv/ **reserves, reserving, reserved. 1** If something **is reserved** for a particular person or purpose, it is kept specially for that person or purpose. *A double room with a balcony overlooking the sea had been reserved for him.* **2** If you **reserve** something such as a table, ticket, or magazine, you arrange for it to be kept specially for you. **3** A **reserve** is a supply of something that is available for use when it is needed. *...the world's oil reserves.* **4** If you have something **in reserve**, you have it available for use when it is needed. *...the bottle of whisky that he kept in reserve.* **5** In sport, a **reserve** is someone who is available to play as part of a team if one of the members is ill or cannot play. **6** A nature **reserve** is an area of land where the animals, birds, and plants are officially protected. **7** If someone shows **reserve**, they keep their feelings hidden. *I do hope that you'll overcome your reserve and let me know.* **8** ● to **reserve judgment**: see **judgment.** ● to **reserve the right**: see **right.** ◆◆◆◇ VB: usu passive be V-ed for n / VERB: V n / N-COUNT / PHRASE / N-COUNT BRITISH / N-COUNT / N-UNCOUNT

re·served /rɪ'zɜːvd/. **1** Someone who is **reserved** keeps their feelings hidden. **2** A table in a restaurant or a seat in a theatre that is **reserved** is being kept for someone. ◆◆◇◇◇ ADJ-GRADED / ADJ

re·serve price, reserve prices. A **reserve price** is the lowest price which is acceptable to the owner of property being auctioned or sold. N-COUNT BRITISH

re·serv·ist /rɪ'zɜːvɪst/ **reservists. Reservists** are soldiers who are not serving in the regular army of a country, but who can be called to serve whenever they are needed. ◆◇◇◇◇ N-COUNT

res·er·voir /'rezəvwɑː/ **reservoirs. 1** A **reservoir** is a lake that is used for storing water before it is supplied to people. **2** A **reservoir** of something is a large quantity of it that is available for use when needed. *...the huge oil reservoir beneath the Kuwaiti desert.* ◆◆◇◇◇ N-COUNT / N-COUNT: with supp

re·set /,riː'set/ **resets, resetting.** The form **reset** is used in the present tense and is also the past tense and past participle. **1** If you **reset** a machine or device, you adjust or set it, so that it is ready to work again or ready to perform a particular function. *The remote control key resets the electrically adjusted seats.* **2** If a doctor **resets** a broken bone, they put it back into its correct position. ◆◇◇◇◇ VERB V n / VERB: V n

re·set·tle /riː'setəl/ **resettles, resettling, resettled.** If people **are resettled** by a government or organization, or if people **resettle**, they move to a ◆◇◇◇◇ V-ERG: be V-ed V

different place to live because they are no longer able or allowed to stay in the area where they used to live. *In 1990, 200,000 Soviet Jews resettled on Israeli territory.* ♦ **re·set·tle·ment** /ˌriːˈsetəlmənt/. N-UNCOUNT *Only refugees are eligible for resettlement abroad.*

re·shape /ˌriːˈʃeɪp/ **reshapes, reshaping, re-** ◆◇◇◇ **shaped.** To reshape something means to change VERB its structure or organization. *...changes that have been reshaping the industry.* ♦ **re·shap·ing** *...a* N-SING: *radical reshaping of Labour policies.* also no det

re·shuf·fle, reshuffles, reshuffling, reshuf- ◆◇◇◇ **fled.** The noun is pronounced /ˈriːʃʌfəl/. The verb VERB is pronounced /ˌriːˈʃʌfəl/. When a political leader V n **reshuffles** the ministers in a government, he or she changes their jobs so that some of the ministers change their responsibilities. *He plans to reshuffle his entire cabinet.* ▶ Also a noun. *...a partial cabinet* N-COUNT *reshuffle.*

re·side /rɪˈzaɪd/ **resides, residing, resided. 1** If ◆◇◇◇ someone **resides** somewhere, they live there or are VERB staying there. *Margaret resides with her invalid* V prep/adv *mother in a London suburb.* **2** If a quality **resides** in VB: no cont something, it is in that thing. *Happiness does not re-* V n *side in strength or money.* FORMAL

resi·dence /ˈrezɪdəns/ **residences. 1** A residence ◆◆◇◇ is a house where people live. *...Mr Kohl's private* N-COUNT *residence.* **2** Your place of **residence** is the place FORMAL where you live. **3** If someone is **in residence** in a N-COUNT particular place, they are living there. **4** Someone's FORMAL **residence** in a place is the fact that they live there PHRASE or that they are officially allowed to live there. *They* N-UNCOUNT *had entered the country and had applied for permanent residence.* **5** See also **hall of residence.**

6 An artist or writer **in residence** is one who teaches in PHRASE an institution such as a university or a theatre company.

resi·den·cy /ˈrezɪdənsi/. Someone's **residency** in a ◆◇◇◇ place is the fact that they live there or that they are N-UNCOUNT officially allowed to live there. *He applied for British residency.*

resi·dent /ˈrezɪdənt/ **residents. 1** The residents ◆◆◆◇ of a house or area are the people who live there. N-COUNT **2** Someone who is **resident** in a country or a town ADJ: lives there. *He had been resident in Brussels since* v-link ADJ *1967.* **3** A **resident** doctor or tutor lives in the place ADJ where he or she works. *...the resident physician.* **4** If an institution has a **resident** specialist, that spe- ADJ: ADJ n cialist works for the institution. *She stayed there as resident designer for seven years.*

resi·den·tial /ˌrezɪˈdenʃəl/. **1** A residential area ◆◇◇◇ contains houses rather than offices or factories. **2** A ADJ **residential** institution is one where people live ADJ while they are studying there or being cared for there.

'residents' association, residents' associa- N-COUNT **tions.** A **residents' association** is an organization BRITISH of people who live in a particular area. Residents' associations take action to make the area more pleasant to live in. The usual American term is **neighborhood association.**

re·sid·ual /rɪˈzɪdjuəl/. **Residual** is used to describe ◆◇◇◇ what remains of something when most of it has ADJ gone. *Allow the residual heat to keep the mixture simmering.*

resi·due /ˈrezɪdjuː, AM -duː/ **residues.** A residue ◆◇◇◇ of something is a small amount that remains after N-COUNT most of it has gone. *Using the same shampoo means that a residue can build up on the hair.*

re·sign /rɪˈzaɪn/ **resigns, resigning, resigned.** ◆◆◆◇ **1** If you **resign** from a job or position, you formally VERB: announce that you are leaving it. *A hospital admin-* V from v *istrator has resigned over claims that he lied to get* V as n *the job... In 1980, he resigned as chairman of the* Also V n *Electricity Council.* **2** If you **resign** yourself to an un- VERB pleasant situation or fact, you accept it because you V pron-refl to realize that you cannot change it. *Pat and I resigned* n/-ing *ourselves to yet another summer without a boat.* **3** See also **resigned.**

res·ig·na·tion /ˌrezɪgˈneɪʃən/ **resignations.** ◆◆◇◇ **1** Your **resignation** is a formal statement of your in- N-VAR

tention to leave a job or position. **2 Resignation** is N-UNCOUNT the acceptance of an unpleasant situation or fact because you realize that you cannot change it. *He sighed with profound resignation.*

re·signed /rɪˈzaɪnd/. If you are **resigned** to an un- ◆◆◇◇ pleasant situation or fact, you accept it without ADJ complaining because you realize that you cannot change it. *He is resigned to the noise, the mess, the constant upheaval.* ♦ **re·sign·ed·ly** /rɪˈzaɪnɪdli/. *'I* ADV: *know you don't believe me,' I said resignedly.* ADV with v

re·sili·ent /rɪˈzɪliənt/. **1** Something that is resilient ◆◇◇◇ is strong and not easily damaged by being hit, ADJ-GRADED stretched, or squeezed. *Cotton is more resistant to being squashed and polyester is more resilient.* ♦ **re- ·sili·ence** *Your muscles do not have the strength* N-UNCOUNT *and resilience that they should have.* **2** People and ADJ-GRADED things that are **resilient** are able to recover easily and quickly from unpleasant or damaging events. *Fraser was clearly a good soldier, calm and resilient.* ♦ **resilience** *...the resilience of human beings to* N-UNCOUNT: *fight after they've been attacked.* also a N

res·in /ˈrezɪn/ **resins. 1** Resin is a sticky substance ◆◇◇◇ that is produced by some trees. **2** Resin is a sub- N-VAR stance that is produced chemically and used to N-VAR make plastics.

res·in·ous /ˈrezɪnəs/. Something that is resinous is ADJ-GRADED like resin or contains resin. *...a hard resinous substance made by bees from the juices of plants.*

re·sist /rɪˈzɪst/ **resists, resisting, resisted. 1** If ◆◆◆◇ you **resist** something such as a change, you refuse VERB: V n to accept it and try to prevent it. *The Prime Minister* V n -ing *says she will resist a single European currency being imposed.* **2** If you **resist** someone or **resist** an attack VERB by them, you fight back against them. *The man was* V n *shot outside his house as he tried to resist arrest.* **3** If Also V VERB you **resist** doing something, you **resist** the temptation V n/-ing to do something, you stop yourself from doing it although you would like to do it. *She cannot resist giving him advice.* **4** If someone or something **resists** VERB damage of some kind, they remain unharmed or V n undamaged by it. *...bodies trained and toughened to resist the cold.*

re·sist·ance /rɪˈzɪstəns/ **resistances. 1** Resist- ◆◆◆◇ **ance** to something such as a change or a new idea N-UNCOUNT is a refusal to accept it. *The US wants big cuts in European agricultural export subsidies, but this is meeting resistance.*

2 Resistance to an attack consists of fighting back N-UNCOUNT against the people who have attacked you. *...the troops are encountering stiff resistance.* **3** In a country N-SING: which is occupied by the army of another country, or the N which has a dictatorship, **the resistance** is an organized group of people who are involved in illegal activities against the people in power. **4** The **resistance** of N-UNCOUNT your body to germs or diseases is its power to remain unharmed or unaffected by them.

5 Wind or air **resistance** is a force which slows down a N-UNCOUNT moving object or vehicle. **6** In electrical engineering N-VAR or physics, **resistance** is the ability of a substance or an electrical circuit to obstruct the flow of an electrical current through it.

re·sist·ant /rɪˈzɪstənt/. **1** Someone who is **resist- ◆◆◇◇ ant** to something is opposed to it and wants to pre- ADJ-GRADED vent it. *Some people are very resistant to the idea of exercise.* **2** If something is **resistant** to a particular ADJ-GRADED thing, it is not harmed by it. *...how to improve plants to make them more resistant to disease.*

-resistant /-rɪzɪstənt/. **-resistant** is added to nouns COMB to form adjectives that describe something as not being harmed or affected by the thing mentioned. *...bullet-resistant glass.*

re·sis·tor /rɪˈzɪstə/ **resistors.** A resistor is a device N-COUNT in an electric circuit which can slow down or con- TECHNICAL trol the flow of electricity through the circuit.

re·sit, resits, resitting, resat. The verb is pro- VERB: V n nounced /ˌriːˈsɪt/. The noun is pronounced /ˈriːsɪt/. V If someone **resits** a test or examination, they take it BRITISH again, usually because they failed the first time. The usual American word is **retake.** *If they fail, they can*

often resit the next year. ▶ Also a noun. *He failed his* N-COUNT
First Year exams and didn't bother about the resits.

re·sold /ˌriːˈsəʊld/. **Resold** is the past tense and
past participle of **resell**.

reso·lute /ˈrezəluːt/. If you describe someone as ◆◇◇◇◇
resolute, you approve of them because they are ab- ADJ-GRADED
solutely determined not to change their mind or not PRAGMATICS
to give up a course of action. *Voters perceive him as* FORMAL
a decisive and resolute international leader. ♦ **reso-**
·lute·ly *He resolutely refused to speak English unless* ADV-GRADED
forced to.

reso·lu·tion /ˌrezəˈluːʃən/ **resolutions. 1** A reso- ◆◆◆◇
lution is a formal decision taken at a meeting by N-COUNT
means of a vote. *The UN had passed two major reso-*
lutions calling for a complete withdrawal. **2** If you N-COUNT
make a **resolution**, you decide to try very hard to do
something. *They made a resolution to lose all the*
weight gained during the Christmas period. ● See
also **New Year's resolution. 3** Resolution is deter- N-UNCOUNT
mination to do or do something. *'I think I'll try*
a hypnotist,' I said with sudden resolution.
4 The **resolution** of a problem or difficulty is the final N-SING
solving of it. *...a peaceful resolution to the crisis.* FORMAL
5 The **resolution** of an image is how clear the image N-UNCOUNT
is. *This machine gives us such high resolution that we* TECHNICAL
can see very small specks of calcium.

re·solve /rɪˈzɒlv/ **resolves, resolving, re-** ◆◆◇◇
solved. 1 To **resolve** a problem, argument, or diffi- VERB
culty means to find a solution to it. *We must find a* V n
way to resolve these problems before it's too late. FORMAL
2 If you **resolve** to do something, you make a firm de- VERB:
cision to do it. *She resolved that, if Mimi forgot this* V to-inf
promise, she would remind her. **3** Resolve is absolute N-VAR
determination to do what you have decided to do. FORMAL
This will strengthen the American public's resolve to go
to war if necessary.
4 If you **resolve** something into a clearer form, or if it V-ERG
resolves into a clearer form, its shape or the different V n into n
parts it contains become clear. *...like a musician re-* Also V into n
solving a confused mass of sound into melodic or har- FORMAL
monic order.

re·solved /rɪˈzɒlvd/. If you are **resolved** to do ◆◇◇◇◇
something, you are determined to do it. *Most folk* ADJ-GRADED:
with property to lose were resolved to defend it. v-link ADJ to-
inf

reso·nance /ˈrezənəns/ **resonances. 1** If some- ◆◇◇◇◇
thing has a **resonance** for someone, it has a special N-VAR
meaning or is particularly important to them, for
example because it reminds them of something
else. *The ideas of order, security, family, religion and*
country had the same resonance for them as for
Michael. ♦ **reso·nant** /ˈrezənənt/. *It is a country* ADJ
resonant with cinematic potential, from its architec-
ture to its landscape. **2** If a sound has **resonance**, it N-UNCOUNT
is deep, clear, and echoing. ♦ **resonant** *His voice* ADJ-GRADED
sounded oddly resonant in the empty room. **3** A N-VAR
resonance is the sound which is produced by an TECHNICAL
object when it vibrates at the same rate as the
sound waves from another object.

reso·nate /ˈrezəneɪt/ **resonates, resonating,** ◆◇◇◇◇
resonated. 1 If something **resonates**, it vibrates VERB
and produces a deep, strong sound. *The bass guitar* V
began to thump so loudly that it resonated in my
head. **2** You say that something **resonates** when it VERB
has a special meaning or when it is particularly im- V with n
portant to someone, for example because they
agree with it or because it reminds them of something else. *London is confident and alive, resonating*
with all the qualities of a civilised city.

re·sort /rɪˈzɔːt/ **resorts, resorting, resorted.** ◆◆◆◇
1 If you **resort** to a course of action that you do not VERB
really approve of, you adopt it because you cannot V to n/-ing
see any other way of achieving what you want to
achieve. *His punishing work schedule had made*
him resort to drugs. **2** If you say that you can N-UNCOUNT:
achieve something without **resort** to a particular N to n
course of action, you mean that you can succeed in
what you are trying to do without carrying out that
action. *...a responsibility to ensure that all peaceful*
options are exhausted before resort to war. **3** If you PHRASE
do something **as a last resort**, you do it because you

can find no other way of getting out of a difficult
situation or of solving a problem. *Nuclear weapons*
should be used only as a last resort. **4** You use **in the** PHRASE
last resort when stating the most basic or impor-
tant fact that will still be true in a situation whatever else happens. *...the British would in the last resort*
support them whatever they did.
5 A **resort** is a place where a lot of people spend their N-COUNT
holidays. *...ski resorts.*

re·sound /rɪˈzaʊnd/ **resounds, resounding, re-**
sounded. 1 When a noise **resounds**, it is heard VERB
very loudly and clearly. *The soldiers' boots resound-* V prep
ed in the street. **2** If a place **resounds** with particular LITERARY
noises, it is filled with them. *The whole place re-* VERB
sounded with music. V with/to n
LITERARY

re·sound·ing /rɪˈzaʊndɪŋ/. **1** A resounding sound ◆◇◇◇◇
is loud and echoing. *There was a resounding slap as* ADJ
Andrew struck him violently across the face. ♦ **re-**
·sound·ing·ly *Leatherdale was hit resoundingly on* ADV
the side of the head. **2** You can refer to a very great ADJ
success as a **resounding** success. *The good weather*
helped to make the occasion a resounding success.
♦ **resoundingly** *They resoundingly support govern-* ADV-GRADED
ment programs for the poor.

re·source /rɪˈzɔːs, AM ˈriːsɔːrs/ **resources. 1** The ◆◆◆◇
resources of an organization or person are the ma- N-COUNT
terials, money, and other things that they have and
can use in order to function properly. *Some families*
don't have the resources to feed themselves properly.
2 A country's **resources** are the things that it has N-COUNT
and can use to increase its wealth, such as coal, oil,
or land.

re·sourced /rɪˈzɔːst, AM ˈriːsɔːrst/. If an organiza- ADJ
tion is **resourced**, it has all the things, such as mon- BRITISH
ey and materials, that it needs to function properly.

re·source·ful /rɪˈzɔːsfʊl/. Someone who is re- ◆◇◇◇◇
sourceful is good at finding ways of dealing with ADJ-GRADED
problems. ♦ **re·source·ful·ness** *He is a person of* N-UNCOUNT
far greater experience and resourcefulness.

re·spect /rɪˈspekt/ **respects, respecting, re-** ◆◆◆◇
spected. 1 If you **respect** someone, you have a VERB
good opinion of their character or ideas. *I want him* V n
to respect me as a career woman. **2** If you have re- N-UNCOUNT
spect for someone, you have a good opinion of
them. See also **self-respect. 3** If you **respect** VERB
someone's wishes, rights, or customs, you avoid do- V n
ing things that they would dislike or regard as
wrong. *Finally, trying to respect her wishes, I said I'd*
leave. **4** If you show **respect** for someone's wishes, N-UNCOUNT
rights, or customs, you avoid doing anything they
would dislike or regard as wrong. **5** If you **respect** a VERB
law or moral principle, you agree not to break it. *It* V n
is about time tour operators respected the law and
their own code of conduct. ▶ Also a noun. *...respect* N-UNCOUNT
for the law and the rejection of the use of violence.
6 You can say **with respect** when you are politely dis- PHRASE
agreeing with someone or criticizing them. *With re-* PRAGMATICS
spect, I hardly think that's the point.
7 If you **pay your respects** to someone, you go to see PHRASE
them or speak to them in order to be polite. *Carl had* FORMAL
asked him to visit the hospital and to pay his respects to
Francis. **8** If you **pay** your **last respects** to someone PHRASE
who has just died, you show your respect or affection
for them by coming to see their body or their grave.
9 You use expressions like **in this respect** and **in** PHRASE
many respects to indicate that what you are saying PRAGMATICS
applies to the feature you have just mentioned or to
many features of something. *In many respects Asian*
women see themselves as equal to their men. **10** You PHRASE
use **with respect to**, or in British English **in respect of**, FORMAL
to say what something relates to. *Parents often have*
little choice with respect to the way their child is medi-
cally treated.

re·spect·able /rɪˈspektəbəl/. **1** Someone or some- ◆◆◇◇◇
thing that is **respectable** is approved of by society ADJ-GRADED
and considered to be morally correct. ♦ **re·spect-**
·ably /rɪˈspektəbli/. *The juror was respectably* ADV-GRADED
dressed in a beige suit. ♦ **re·spect·abil·ity** N-UNCOUNT
/rɪˌspektəˈbɪlɪti/. *If she divorced Tony, she would lose*
the respectability she had. **2** You can say that ADJ-GRADED

something is **respectable** when you mean that it is adequate or acceptable. *At last I have something respectable to wear!*

re·spect·ed /rɪ'spektɪd/. Someone or something that is **respected** is admired and considered important by many people. *She is a well respected member of the international community.* ◆◆◇◇◇ ADJ-GRADED

re·spect·er /rɪ'spektə/ **respecters.** If you say that someone or something is **no respecter** of a rule or tradition, you mean that the rule or tradition is not important to them or does not affect to them. *Accidents and sudden illnesses are no respecters of age.* PHRASE

re·spect·ful /rɪ'spektfʊl/. If you are **respectful**, you show respect for someone. *The children in our family are always respectful.* ◆ **re·spect·ful·ly** *'You are an artist,' she said respectfully.* ◆◇◇◇◇ ADV-GRADED

re·spec·tive /rɪ'spektɪv/. **Respective** means relating or belonging separately to the individual people you have just mentioned. *They went into their respective bedrooms to pack.* ◆◇◇◇◇ ADJ: ADJ n

re·spec·tive·ly /rɪ'spektɪvli/. **Respectively** means in the same order as the items that you have just mentioned. *Their sons, Ben and Jonathan, were three and six respectively.* ◆◆◇◇◇ ADV: ADV with cl/ group

res·pi·ra·tion /ˌrespɪ'reɪʃən/. Your **respiration** is your breathing. ● See also **artificial respiration.** N-UNCOUNT MEDICAL

res·pi·ra·tor /'respɪreɪtə/ **respirators. 1** A **respirator** is a device that allows people to breathe when they cannot breathe naturally, for example because they are ill or have been injured. **2** A **respirator** is a device you wear over your mouth and nose in order to breathe when you are surrounded by smoke or poisonous gas. N-COUNT

res·pi·ra·tory /'respərətri, AM -tɔːri/. **Respiratory** means relating to breathing. *If you smoke then the whole respiratory system is constantly under attack.* ◆◇◇◇◇ ADJ: ADJ n MEDICAL

res·pite /'respaɪt, -pɪt/. **1** A **respite** is a short period of rest from something unpleasant. *It was some weeks now since they had had any respite from shellfire.* **2** A **respite** is a short delay before a very unpleasant or difficult situation which may or may not take place. *Devaluation would only give the economy a brief respite.* ◆◇◇◇◇ N-SING: also no det FORMAL / N-SING: also no det FORMAL

re·splend·ent /rɪ'splendənt/. If you describe someone or something as **resplendent**, you mean that their appearance is very impressive and expensive-looking. *...the resplendent hotel banqueting-room.* ADJ-GRADED FORMAL

re·spond /rɪ'spɒnd/ **responds, responding, responded. 1** When you **respond** to something that is done or said, you react to it by doing or saying something yourself. *They are likely to respond positively to the President's request for aid... The army responded with gunfire and tear gas.* **2** When you **respond** to a need, crisis, or challenge, you take the necessary or appropriate action. *This modest group size allows our teachers to respond to the needs of each student.* **3** If a patient or their injury or illness **is responding** to treatment, the treatment is working and they are getting better. ◆◆◆◆◇ VERB V to n / Also V that, V with quote / VERB V to n / VERB: V to n

re·spond·ent /rɪ'spɒndənt/ **respondents. 1** The **respondents** to a survey or questionnaire are the people who answer the questions in it. **2** A **respondent** is someone who is summoned to a court to answer an accusation. *The respondent disclosed professional confidences to one of the patients.* ◆◇◇◇◇ N-COUNT / N-COUNT LEGAL

re·sponse /rɪ'spɒns/ **responses.** Your **response** to an event or to something that is said is your reply or reaction to it. *The meeting was called in response to a request from Venezuela.* ◆◆◆◆◇ N-VAR: also in N

re·spon·sibil·ity /rɪˌspɒnsɪ'bɪlɪti/ **responsibilities. 1** If you have **responsibility** for something or someone, or if they are your **responsibility**, it is your job or duty to deal with them. *Each manager had responsibility for just under 600 properties.* **2** Your **responsibilities** are the duties that you have because of your job or position. *...programmes to help employees balance work and family responsibilities.* **3** If someone is given **responsibility**, they are given the right or opportunity to make important decisions or to take action without having to get ◆◆◆◆◇ N-UNCOUNT / N-PLURAL / N-UNCOUNT

permission from anyone else. *She would have loved to have a better-paying job with more responsibility.* **4** If you think that you have a **responsibility** to someone or to do something, you feel that you ought to do it because it is morally right or your duty to do it. *As a doctor she had a responsibility to her fellow creatures.* N-SING

5 If you accept **responsibility** for something that has happened, you agree that you were to blame for it. *British Rail has admitted responsibility for the accident.* N-UNCOUNT

re·spon·sible /rɪ'spɒnsɪbəl/. **1** If someone or something is **responsible** for a particular event or situation, they are the cause of it or they can be blamed for it. *He still felt responsible for her death.* **2** If you are **responsible** for something, it is your job or duty to deal with it and make decisions relating to it. *...the minister responsible for the environment.* **3** If you are **responsible to** a person or group, they have authority over you and you have to report to them about what you do. *I'm responsible to my board of directors.* **4 Responsible** people behave properly and sensibly, without needing to be supervised. *The media should be more responsible in what they report.* ◆ **re·spon·sibly** *He urged everyone to act responsibly.* **5 Responsible** jobs involve making important decisions or carrying out important tasks. ◆◆◆◇ ADJ: v-link ADJ / ADJ: v-link ADJ / ADJ: v-link ADJ to n / ADJ-GRADED / ADV-GRADED / ADJ-GRADED: ADJ n

re·spon·sive /rɪ'spɒnsɪv/. **1** A **responsive** person is quick to react to people or events and to show emotions such as pleasure and affection. ◆ **re·spon·sive·ness** *This condition decreases sexual desire and responsiveness.* **2** If someone or something is **responsive**, they react quickly and favourably. ◆ **responsive·ness** *Such responsiveness to public pressure is extraordinary.* ◆◇◇◇◇ ADJ-GRADED / N-UNCOUNT / ADJ-GRADED / N-UNCOUNT

rest 1 quantifier uses

rest /rest/. **1 The rest** is used to refer to all the parts of something or all the things in a group that remain or that you have not already mentioned. *It was an experience I will treasure for the rest of my life... He was unable to travel to Barcelona with the rest of the team.* ▶ Also a pronoun. *Only 55 per cent of the raw material is canned. The rest is thrown away.* **2** You can add **and the rest** or **all the rest of it** to the end of a statement or list when you want to refer vaguely to other things like or associated with the ones you have already mentioned. *And what about racism and all the rest of it?* ◆◇◇◇◇ QUANT / PRON / PHRASE PRAGMATICS INFORMAL, SPOKEN

rest 2 verb and noun uses

rest /rest/ **rests, resting, rested. 1** If you **rest** or if you **rest** your body, you do not do anything active for a time. *Try to rest the injured limb as much as possible.* ◆ **rest·ed** *He looked tanned and well rested after his vacation.* **2** If you get some **rest** or have a **rest**, you do not do anything active for a time. **3** If something such as a theory or someone's success **rests** on a particular thing, it depends on that thing. *Such a view rests on a number of incorrect assumptions.* **4** If authority, a responsibility, or a decision **rests** with you, you have that authority or responsibility, or you are the one who will make that decision. *The final decision rested with the President.* **5** If you **rest** something somewhere, you put it there so that its weight is supported. *He rested his arms on the back of the chair... His head was resting on her shoulder.* **6** If you **rest** on or against someone or something, you lean on them so that they support the weight of your body. *He rested on his pickaxe for a while.* **7** A **rest** is an object that is used to support something. *Keep your elbow on the arm rest.* **8** If your eyes **rest** on a particular person or object, you look directly at them. **9** When an object that has been moving **comes to rest**, it finally stops. *The ball came to rest four feet from the hole.* **10** If you say that someone can **rest easy**, you mean that they don't need to worry about a particular situation. **11** If someone tells you to **give** something a **rest**, they want you to stop doing it because it annoys them or because they think it is harming you. *Give it a rest, will you? We're trying to get some sleep.* ◆◆◆◆◇ VERB: V n / ADJ-GRADED / N-VAR / VERB V on/upon n/ wh FORMAL / VERB V with n FORMAL / V-ERG V n prep/adv V prep/adv / VERB V prep / N-COUNT / VERB V on/upon n WRITTEN / PHRASE FORMAL / PHRASE / PHRASE PRAGMATICS INFORMAL

12 If you say that someone who has died is **laid to rest**, you mean that they are buried. **13** If you **lay** something such as fears or rumours **to rest** or you **put** them **to rest**, you succeed in proving that they are not true. *His speech should lay those fears to rest.* **14** If someone refuses to **let** a subject **rest**, they refuse to stop talking about it. *I am not prepared to let this matter rest.* **15** If someone or something **puts** your **mind at rest** or **sets** your **mind at rest**, they tell you something that stops you worrying. *A brain scan last Friday finally set his mind at rest.* **16 • rest assured**: see **assured. •** to **rest on** your **laurels**: see **laurel. •** to **rest in peace**: see **peace.**

re·start /ˌriːˈstɑːt/ **restarts, restarting, restarted.** If you **restart** something that has been interrupted or stopped, it starts to happen or function again. *The trial will restart today with a new jury.* ▶ Also a noun. *Australia took the lead within a minute of the restart.* ◆◇◇◇◇ V-ERG: V n V N-COUNT

re·state /ˌriːˈsteɪt/ **restates, restating, restated.** If you **restate** something, you say it again in words or writing, usually in a slightly different way. ◆◇◇◇◇ VERB: V n FORMAL **• re·state·ment** /ˌriːˈsteɪtmənt/ **restatements** *I hope this book is not yet another restatement of the prevailing wisdom.* N-COUNT

res·tau·rant /ˈrestərɒnt, AM -rənt/ **restaurants.** A **restaurant** is a place where you can pay for and eat a meal. In restaurants your food is usually served to you at your table by a waiter or waitress. ◆◆◆◇ N-COUNT

res·tau·ra·teur /ˌrestərəˈtɜː/ **restaurateurs.** A **restaurateur** is a person who owns and manages a restaurant. ◆◇◇◇◇ N-COUNT FORMAL

rest·ful /ˈrestfʊl/. Something that is **restful** helps you to feel calm and relaxed. ADJ-GRADED

rest home, rest homes. A **rest home** is the same as an **old people's home.** N-COUNT

resting place, resting places. You can refer to the place where a dead person is buried as their **resting place** or their final **resting place.** N-COUNT

res·ti·tu·tion /ˌrestɪˈtjuːʃən, AM -ˈtuː-/. **Restitution** is the act of giving back to a person something that was lost or stolen, or of paying them money for the loss. *The victims are demanding full restitution.* N-UNCOUNT FORMAL

res·tive /ˈrestɪv/. If you are **restive**, you are impatient, bored, or dissatisfied. ADJ-GRADED FORMAL

rest·less /ˈrestləs/. **1** If you are **restless**, you are bored, impatient, or dissatisfied, and you want to do something else. **• rest·less·ness** *From the audience came increasing sounds of restlessness.* **2** If someone is **restless**, they keep moving around because they find it difficult to keep still. **• restlessness** *Karen complained of hyperactivity and restlessness.* **• rest·less·ly** *He paced up and down restlessly.* **3** If you have a **restless** night, you do not sleep properly and when you wake up you feel tired and uncomfortable. ◆◆◇◇◇ N-UNCOUNT ADJ-GRADED N-UNCOUNT ADV ADJ-GRADED: ADJ n

re·stock /ˌriːˈstɒk/ **restocks, restocking, restocked.** **1** If you **restock** something such as a shelf, fridge, or shop, you fill it with food or other goods to replace what has been used or sold. **2** To **restock** a lake means to put more fish in it because there are very few left. VERB: V n VERB: V n

Res·to·ra·tion /ˌrestəˈreɪʃən/. **1 The Restoration** was the event in 1660 when Charles the Second became King of England, Scotland, Wales, and Ireland after a period when there had been no King or Queen. **2 Restoration** is used to refer to the style of drama and architecture that were popular in England during and just after the reign of Charles the Second. *...a Restoration comedy.* ◆◆◇◇◇ N-PROPER: the N ADJ: ADJ n

re·stora·tive /rɪˈstɔːrətɪv/. Something that is **restorative** makes you feel healthier, stronger, or more cheerful after you have been feeling tired, weak, or miserable. ADJ-GRADED

re·store /rɪˈstɔː/ **restores, restoring, restored.** **1** To **restore** a situation or practice means to cause it to exist again. *The army has recently been brought in to restore order.* **• res·to·ra·tion** /ˌrestəˈreɪʃən/. *His visit is expected to lead to the restoration of diplomatic relations.* **2** To **restore** someone or some- ◆◆◆◇ VERB N-UNCOUNT VERB

thing to a previous condition means to cause them to be in that condition once again. *His country desperately needs Western aid to restore its ailing economy.* **• restoration** *I owe the restoration of my hearing to this remarkable new technique.* **3** When someone **restores** something such as an old building, painting, or piece of furniture, they repair and clean it, so that it looks like it did when it was new. **• re·stor·er, restorers** *...an antiques restorer.* **• res·to·ra·tion, restorations** *The bones were 'mislaid' during the seventeenth-century restorations.* **4** If something that was lost or stolen **is restored** to its owner, it is returned to them. *The looted property was restored.* V n to n V n N-UNCOUNT VERB: V n N-COUNT N-VAR VERB: be V-ed to n be V-ed FORMAL

re·strain /rɪˈstreɪn/ **restrains, restraining, restrained.** **1** If you **restrain** someone, you stop them from doing what they intended or wanted to do, usually by using your physical strength. *Wally gripped my arm, partly to restrain me and partly to reassure me.* **2** If you **restrain** an emotion or impulse, you prevent yourself from showing that emotion or doing what you wanted or intended to do. *Nancy restrained herself from bringing up the subject.* **• re·strained** *In the circumstances he felt he'd been very restrained.* **3** To **restrain** something that is growing or increasing means to prevent it from getting too large. *The radical 500-day plan was very clear on how it intended to try to restrain inflation.* ◆◆◇◇◇ VERB V n VERB: V n V pron-refl from -ing/n ADJ-GRADED VERB V n

re·strained /rɪˈstreɪnd/. **1** If you describe something as **restrained**, you approve of it because it is subtle and tasteful. *She chose restrained earrings.* **2** See also **restrain.** ◆◇◇◇◇ ADJ-GRADED PRAGMATICS

re·straint /rɪˈstreɪnt/ **restraints. 1 Restraints** are rules or conditions that limit or restrict someone or something. *The Prime Minister is calling for new restraints on trade unions.* **2 Restraint** is calm, controlled, and unemotional behaviour. *They behaved with more restraint than I'd expected.* ◆◆◇◇◇ N-VAR N-UNCOUNT

re·strict /rɪˈstrɪkt/ **restricts, restricting, restricted.** **1** If you **restrict** something, you put a limit on it in order to reduce it or prevent it from becoming too great. *The French, I believe, restrict Japanese imports to a maximum of 3 per cent of their market.* **• re·stric·tion** /rɪˈstrɪkʃən/, **restrictions** *The restriction of carbohydrates helps to curb the craving for them.* **2** To **restrict** the movement or actions of someone or something means to prevent them from moving or acting freely. *These dams have restricted the flow of the river downstream.* **• restriction** *The relaxation of travel restrictions means they are free to travel.* **3** If you **restrict** someone or their activities to one thing, they can only do, have, or deal with that thing. If you **restrict** them to one place, they cannot go anywhere else. *He was, however, allowed to stay on at the temple as long as he restricted himself to his studies.* **4** If you **restrict** something to a particular group, only that group can do it or have it. If you **restrict** something to a particular place, it is allowed only in that place. *The International Shooting Union is to restrict the competition to men from 1996.* ◆◆◇◇◇ VERB: V n V n to amount N-VAR VERB V n Also V n from -ing N-VAR VERB V n to n VERB V n to n

re·strict·ed /rɪˈstrɪktɪd/. **1** Something that is **restricted** is quite small or limited. *Plants, like animals, often have restricted habitats.* **2** If something is **restricted to** a particular group, only members of that group have it. If it is **restricted** to a particular place, it exists only in that place. *The problem is not restricted to the southeast.* **3 Restricted** is used to describe something like an area or document which only people with special permission can have access to. ◆◆◇◇◇ ADJ-GRADED ADJ: v-link ADJ to n ADJ-GRADED

re·stric·tive /rɪˈstrɪktɪv/. Something that is **restrictive** prevents people from doing what they want to do, or from moving freely. *...increasingly restrictive immigration laws... Do not wear restrictive clothing.* ◆◇◇◇◇ ADJ-GRADED

re,strictive 'practice, restrictive practices. **Restrictive practices** are ways in which people in an industry, trade, or profession protect their own N-COUNT BRITISH

interests, rather than having a system which is fair to the public, employers, and other workers.

rest·room /'restruːm/ **restrooms**; also spelled **rest** N-COUNT **room**. A **restroom** is a toilet in a public place such AMERICAN as a restaurant or theatre. The usual British word is **ladies** or **gents**.

re·struc·ture /ˌriːˈstrʌktʃə/ **restructures, re-** ◆◆◇◇◇ **structuring, restructured**. To **restructure** an VERB organization or system means to change the way it Vn is organized, usually in order to make it work more Also V effectively. *The President called on educators and politicians to help him restructure American education.* ♦ **re·struc·tur·ing, restructurings** *The* N-VAR *company is to lay off 1,520 workers as part of a restructuring.*

re·sult /rɪˈzʌlt/ **results, resulting, resulted. 1** A ◆◆◆◆ **result** is something that happens or exists because N-COUNT of something else that has happened. *...people who have developed asthma as a direct result of their work... A real pizza oven gives better results.* **2** If VERB something **results** in a particular situation or event, V inn it causes that situation or event to happen. *Fifty per cent of road accidents result in head injuries.* **3** If VERB: something **results** from a particular event or action, V from n it is caused by that event or action. *Ignore the early* V *warnings and illness could result.*
4 A **result** is the situation that exists at the end of a N-COUNT contest. *The final election results will be announced on Friday. ...the football results.* **5** A **result** is the num- N-COUNT ber that you get when you do a calculation. *They found their computers producing different results from exactly the same calculation.* **6** Your **results** are N-COUNT the marks or grades that you get for examinations you BRITISH have taken. The usual American term is **scores**. *Kate's exam results were excellent.*

re·sult·ant /rɪˈzʌltənt/. **Resultant** means caused ◆◇◇◇◇ by the event just mentioned. *At least a quarter of a* ADJ: ADJ n *million people have died in the fighting and the re-* FORMAL *sultant famines.*

re·sume /rɪˈzjuːm, AM -ˈzuːm/ **resumes, resum-** ◆◆◇◇◇ **ing, resumed. 1** If you **resume** an activity or if it V-ERG: Vn **resumes**, it begins again. *The search is expected to* V *resume early today.* ♦ **re·sump·tion** /rɪˈzʌmpʃən/. FORMAL *It is premature to speculate about the resumption of* N-UNCOUNT *negotiations.* **2** If you **resume** your seat or position, VERB you return to the seat or position you were in before Vn you moved. *'I changed my mind,' Blanche said, re-* FORMAL, *suming her seat.* **3** If someone **resumes**, they begin VERB speaking again after they have stopped for a short V with quote time. *'Hey, Judith,' he resumed, 'tell me all about* WRITTEN *yourself.'*

ré·su·mé /'rezjʊmeɪ, AM -zʊm-/ **résumés;** also ◆◇◇◇◇ spelled **resumé. 1** A **résumé** is a short account, N-COUNT either spoken or written, of something that has happened or that someone has said or written. *I will leave with you a resumé of his most recent speech.* **2** Your **résumé** is a brief account of your personal N-COUNT details., your education, and the jobs you have had. AMERICAN The usual British term is **curriculum vitae**.

re·sur·face /ˌriːˈsɜːfɪs/ **resurfaces, resurfac-** ◆◇◇◇◇ **ing, resurfaced. 1** If something such as an idea VERB or problem **resurfaces**, it becomes important or no- V ticeable again. *The disease was said to have resurfaced in three countries.* **2** If someone who has not VERB been seen for a long time **resurfaces**, they suddenly V reappear. *It was at this time that Jennifer's lover re-* INFORMAL *surfaced.* **3** If someone or something that has been VERB under water **resurfaces**, they come back to the sur- V face of the water again. *George struggled wildly, going under and resurfacing at regular intervals.* **4** To VERB **resurface** something such as a road means to put a Vn new surface on it. *Meanwhile the race is on to resurface the road before next Wednesday.*

re·sur·gence /rɪˈsɜːdʒəns/. If there is a **resur-** ◆◇◇◇◇ **gence** of an attitude or activity, it reappears and N-SING: grows. *Police say drugs traffickers are behind the re-* also n det *surgence of violence.* FORMAL

re·sur·gent /rɪˈsɜːdʒənt/. You use **resurgent** to say ADJ-GRADED that something is becoming stronger and more popular after a period when it has been weak and

unimportant. *...the threat from the resurgent nationalist movement.*

res·ur·rect /ˌrezəˈrekt/ **resurrects, resurrect-** ◆◇◇◇◇ **ing, resurrected.** If you **resurrect** something, you VERB cause it to exist again after it had disappeared or Vn ended. *Attempts to resurrect the ceasefire have already failed once.* ♦ **res·ur·rec·tion** /ˌrezəˈrekʃən/. N-UNCOUNT *...a resurrection of an old story from the mid-70s.*

Res·ur·rec·tion /ˌrezəˈrekʃən/. In Christian belief, ◆◇◇◇◇ the **Resurrection** is the event in which Jesus Christ N-PROPER: came back to life after he had been killed. the N

re·sus·ci·tate /rɪˈsʌsɪteɪt/ **resuscitates, resus-** ◆◇◇◇◇ **citating, resuscitated. 1** If you **resuscitate** VERB someone who has stopped breathing, you cause Vn them to start breathing again. *A policeman and then a paramedic tried to resuscitate her.* ♦ **re·sus·ci·ta-** N-UNCOUNT **·tion** /rɪˌsʌsɪˈteɪʃən/. *Despite attempts at resuscitation, Mr Lynch died a week later in hospital.* **2** If you VERB **resuscitate** something, you cause it to become ac- Vn tive or successful again. *He has submitted a bid to resuscitate the weekly magazine, which closed in April.* ♦ **resuscitation** *The economy needs vigorous* N-UNCOUNT *resuscitation.*

re·tail, retails, retailing, retailed. The pronun- ◆◆◇◇◇ ciation is /'riːteɪl/ for meanings 1 to 3, and /riːˈteɪl/ for meaning 4. **1 Retail** is the activity of selling N-UNCOUNT goods direct to the public, usually in small quantities. Compare **wholesale**. *Retail sales grew just 3.8 percent last year.* **2** If something is sold **retail**, it is ADV: sold in ordinary shops direct to the public. **3** If an ADV after v item in a shop **retails** at or for a particular price, it VERB is for sale at that price. *It originally retailed at* V at/for n £23.50. **4** If someone **retails** a story or event, they VERB tell it to someone else. *Mr Hastings gleefully retailed* Vn the story to Mr Anderson over lunch. LITERARY

re·tail·er /'riːteɪlə/ **retailers.** A **retailer** is a person ◆◆◇◇◇ or business that sells goods to the public. N-COUNT

re·tail·ing /'riːteɪlɪŋ/. **Retailing** is the activity of ◆◇◇◇◇ selling goods direct to the public, usually in small N-UNCOUNT quantities. *...the car retailing industry.*

retail 'price index. In Britain, the **retail price in-** N-PROPER: **dex** is a list of prices of typical goods which shows the N how much the cost of living changes from one month to the next.

re·tain /rɪˈteɪn/ **retains, retaining, retained.** ◆◆◇◇◇ **1** To **retain** something means to continue to have VERB that thing. *If left covered in a warm place, this rice* FORMAL *will retain its heat for a good hour.* **2** If you **retain** a VERB lawyer, you pay him or her a fee to make sure that Vn he or she will represent you when you go to court. LEGAL *He decided to retain him for the trial.*

re·tain·er /rɪˈteɪnə/ **retainers. 1** A **retainer** is a ◆◇◇◇◇ fee that you pay to someone in order to make sure N-COUNT that they will be available to do work for you if you need them to. *Liz was being paid a regular monthly retainer.* **2** A servant who has been with one family N-COUNT for a long time can be referred to as a **retainer**. DATED

re·taining 'wall, retaining walls. A **retaining** N-COUNT **wall** is a wall that is built to prevent the earth behind it from moving.

re·take, retakes, retaking, retook, retaken. ◆◇◇◇◇ The verb is pronounced /riːˈteɪk/. The noun is pronounced /'riːteɪk/. **1** If a military force **retakes** a VERB place or building which it has lost in a war or battle, Vn it captures it again. *Residents were moved 30 miles away as the rebels retook the town.* **2** If during the N-COUNT making of a film there is a **retake** of a particular scene, that scene is filmed again because it needs to be changed or improved. **3** If you **retake** an exam, VERB you take it again because you failed it the first time. Vn *I had one year in the sixth form to retake my O levels.*

re·tali·ate /rɪˈtælieɪt/ **retaliates, retaliating, re-** ◆◆◇◇◇ **taliated.** If you **retaliate** when someone harms or VERB: V annoys you, you do something which harms or an- V by-ing noys them in return. *Christie retaliated by sending* V against/for n *his friend a long letter detailing Carl's utter incom-* Also V with n *petence... The militia responded by saying it would retaliate against any attacks.* ♦ **re·talia·tion** N-UNCOUNT

/rɪˌtæliˈeɪʃən/. *Police said they believed the attack was in retaliation for the death of the drug trafficker.*

re·tal·ia·to·ry /rɪˈtæliətəri, AM -tɔːri/. If you take **re-taliatory** action, you try to harm or annoy someone who has harmed or annoyed you. *There's talk of a retaliatory blockade to prevent supplies getting through.*   ADJ FORMAL

re·tard, retards, retarding, retarded. The verb is pronounced /rɪˈtɑːd/. The noun is pronounced /ˈriːtɑːd/. **1** If something **retards** a process, or the development of something, it makes it happen more slowly. *Continuing violence will retard nego-tiations over the country's future.* ♦ **re·tar·da·tion** /ˌriːtɑːˈdeɪʃən/. *She carries a defective gene which causes mental and physical retardation.* **2** If you de-scribe someone as a **retard**, you mean that they have not developed normally, either mentally or so-cially; an offensive use. *What the hell do I want with an emotional retard?*   VERB Vn FORMAL   N-UNCOUNT   N-COUNT PRAGMATICS

re·tard·ed /rɪˈtɑːdɪd/. Someone who is **retarded** is much less advanced mentally than most people of their age. *...a special school for mentally retarded children.*   ◆◇◇◇◇ ADJ-GRADED DATED

retch /retʃ/ **retches, retching, retched.** If you **retch**, your stomach moves as if you are vomiting. *The smell made me retch.*   VERB V

re·tell /ˌriːˈtel/ **retells, retelling, retold.** If you **retell** a story, you write it, tell it, or present it again, often in a different way from its original form. *It is a tale which has often been retold within West Indian literature.* ♦ **re·tell·ing, retellings** *...this briskly attractive retelling of the Biblical creation story.*   VERB: Vn be V-ed   N-COUNT

re·ten·tion /rɪˈtenʃən/. The **retention** of some-thing is the keeping of it. *His call for the retention of sanctions will be well received.*   ◆◇◇◇◇ N-UNCOUNT FORMAL

re·ten·tive /rɪˈtentɪv/. If you have a **retentive** memory, you are able to remember things very well.   ADJ-GRADED

re·think /ˌriːˈθɪŋk/ **rethinks, rethinking, re-thought.** If you **rethink** something such as a prob-lem, a plan, or a policy, you think about it again and change it. *I think all of us need to rethink our atti-tudes toward health and sickness.* ▶ Also a noun. *There must be a rethink of government policy to-wards this vulnerable group.* ♦ **re·think·ing** *...some fundamental rethinking of the way in which pilots are trained.*   ◆◇◇◇◇ VERB Vn Also V   N-SING   N-UNCOUNT

reti·cent /ˈretɪsənt/. Someone who is **reticent** does not tell people about things. *Mrs. Smith, normally a reticent woman, took it upon herself to write to the President.* ♦ **reti·cence** *Pearl didn't mind his reti-cence; in fact she liked it.*   ◆◇◇◇◇ ADJ-GRADED   N-UNCOUNT

reti·na /ˈretɪnə/ **retinas.** Your **retina** is the part of your eye at the back of your eyeball. It receives the image that you see and then sends the image to your brain.   ◆◇◇◇◇ N-COUNT

reti·nal /ˈretɪnəl/. **Retinal** means relating to a per-son's retina. *...retinal blood vessels.*   ADJ: ADJ n TECHNICAL

reti·nue /ˈretɪnjuː, AM -nuː/ **retinues.** An impor-tant person's **retinue** is the group of servants, friends, or assistants who go with them and look af-ter their needs. *Mind trainers are now as much a part of a tennis star's retinue as the body trainers.*   N-COUNT

re·tire /rɪˈtaɪə/ **retires, retiring, retired. 1** When older people **retire**, they leave their job and stop working. *Although their careers are important many said they plan to retire at 50... In 1974 he retired from the museum.* **2** When a sports player **retires** from their sport, they stop playing competitively. When they **retire** from a race or a match, they stop competing in it. *I have decided to retire from For-mula One racing at the end of the season.* **3** If you **retire** to another room or place, you go there. *Eisenhower left the White House and retired to his farm in Gettysburg.* **4** When you **retire**, you go to bed. *Some time after midnight, he retired to bed.* **5** See also **retiring**.   ◆◆◇◇◇ VERB V V from n   VERB V from n Also V   VERB V to n FORMAL   VERB V to n FORMAL

re·tired /rɪˈtaɪəd/. A **retired** person is an older per-son who has left his or her job and has usually stopped working altogether. *...a seventy-three-year-old retired teacher from Florida.*   ◆◇◇◇◇ ADJ

re·tiree /rɪˌtaɪəˈriː/ **retirees.** A **retiree** is a retired person.   N-COUNT AMERICAN

re·tire·ment /rɪˈtaɪəmənt/ **retirements. 1** Retire-ment is the time when a worker retires. *The Gover-nor of the prison and another official are to take ear-ly retirement.* **2** A person's **retirement** is the period in their life after they have retired. *General Charles de Gaulle died in retirement in 1970.*   ◆◆◇◇◇ N-VAR   N-UNCOUNT

re·tir·ing /rɪˈtaɪərɪŋ/. **1** Someone who is **retiring** is shy and avoids meeting other people. *She was a shy and retiring person off-stage.* **2** See also **retire**.   ADJ-GRADED

re·told /ˌriːˈtəʊld/. **Retold** is the past tense and past participle of **retell**.

re·took /ˌriːˈtʊk/. **Retook** is the past tense of **retake**.

re·tool /ˌriːˈtuːl/ **retools, retooling, retooled.** If the machines in a factory or the items of equipment used by a firm **are retooled**, they are replaced or changed so that they can do new tasks. *Each time the product changes, the machines have to be retooled.*   VERB be V-ed Also V n, V

re·tort /rɪˈtɔːt/ **retorts, retorting, retorted.** To **retort** means to reply angrily to someone. *Was he afraid, he was asked. 'Afraid of what?' he retorted... Others retort that strong central power is a danger-ous thing in Russia.* ▶ Also a noun. *His sharp retort clearly made an impact.*   ◆◆◇◇◇ VERB V with quote V that Also V WRITTEN N-COUNT

re·touch /ˌriːˈtʌtʃ/ **retouches, retouching, re-touched.** If something such as a painting or a photograph **is retouched**, it is restored, changed, or improved by painting over parts of it. *She put on fresh clothes and retouched her make-up.*   VERB: be V-ed Vn

re·trace /rɪˈtreɪs/ **retraces, retracing, re-traced.** If you **retrace** your steps or **retrace** your way, you return to the place you started from by go-ing back along the same route. *He retraced his steps to the spot where he'd left the case.*   ◆◇◇◇◇ VERB Vn

re·tract /rɪˈtrækt/ **retracts, retracting, retract-ed. 1** If you **retract** something that you have said or written, you say that you did not mean it. *He's hoping that if he makes me feel guilty, I'll retract.* ♦ **re·trac·tion** /rɪˈtrækʃən/ **retractions** *Miss Pearce said she expected an unqualified retraction of his comments.* **2** When a part of a machine, or a part of a person's or animal's body **retracts** or is **re-tracted**, it moves inwards or back. *...when the aircraft's wheels were retracted.*   ◆◇◇◇◇ V FORMAL   N-COUNT   V-ERG: V Also V n FORMAL

re·tract·able /rɪˈtræktəbəl/. A **retractable** part of a machine or a building can be moved inwards or backwards. *A 20,000-seat arena with a retractable roof is planned.*   ADJ

re·train /ˌriːˈtreɪn/ **retrains, retraining, re-trained.** If you **retrain**, or if someone **retrains** you, you learn new skills. *Union leaders have called upon the government to help retrain workers.* ♦ **re·train-ing** *...retraining programmes.*   ◆◇◇◇◇ V-ERG: V V n   N-UNCOUNT

re·treat /rɪˈtriːt/ **retreats, retreating, retreat-ed. 1** If you **retreat**, you move away from some-thing or someone. *'I've already got a job,' I said quickly, and retreated from the room.* **2** When an army **retreats**, it moves away from enemy forces in order to avoid fighting them. *The French, suddenly outnumbered, were forced to retreat.* ▶ Also a noun. *In June 1942, the British 8th Army was in full retreat.* **3** If you **retreat** from something such as a plan or a way of life, you give it up, usually in order to do something safer or less extreme. *From bouncing confidence she had retreated into self-pity.* ▶ Also a noun. *The President's remarks appear to signal that there will be no retreat from his position.* **4** A **retreat** is a quiet, secluded place that you go to in order to rest or to do things in private. *...hidden away in his country retreat.* **5** If you **beat a retreat**, you leave a place quickly in order to avoid an embarrassing or dangerous situation. *It was time to beat a hasty retreat.*   ◆◆◆◇◇ VERB Also V   VERB V   N-VAR   VERB V from/into n   N-VAR   N-COUNT   PHRASE

re·trench /rɪˈtrentʃ/ **retrenches, retrenching, retrenched.** If a person or organization **retrenches**, they spend less money. *Shortly after-wards, cuts in defence spending forced the aerospace industry to retrench.* ♦ **re·trench·ment**   VERB V FORMAL   N-VAR

/rɪ'trentʃmənt/ **retrenchments** *Defense planners predict an extended period of retrenchment.*

re·tri·al /ˌriː'traɪəl/ **retrials.** A **retrial** is a second N-COUNT trial of someone for the same offence.

ret·ri·bu·tion /ˌretrɪ'bjuːʃən/. **Retribution** is pun- ◆◇◇◇◇ ishment for a crime, especially punishment which is N-UNCOUNT carried out by someone other than the official FORMAL authorities. *He didn't want any further involvement for fear of retribution.*

re·trieve /rɪ'triːv/ **retrieves, retrieving, re-** ◆◆◇◇◇ **trieved. 1** If you **retrieve** something, you get it VERB back from the place where you left it. *He reached* V n *over and retrieved his jacket from the back seat.* ◆ **re·triev·al** /rɪ'triːvəl/. **2** If you manage to **re-** N-UNCOUNT **trieve** a situation, you succeed in bringing it back VERB into a more acceptable state. *He, the one man who* V n *could retrieve that situation, might receive the call.* **3** To **retrieve** information from a computer or from VERB: V n your memory means to get it back. ◆ **retrieval** N-UNCOUNT *...electronic storage and retrieval systems.*

re·triev·er /rɪ'triːvə/ **retrievers.** A **retriever** is a N-COUNT kind of dog, traditionally used by hunters to bring back birds and animals which they have shot.

ret·ro /'retrəʊ/. **Retro** clothes, music, and objects ◆◇◇◇◇ are based on the styles of the past. *...original ver-* ADJ *sions of many of today's retro looks.*

retro- /'retrəʊ-/. **Retro-** is used to form adjectives PREFIX and nouns which indicate that something goes back or goes backwards. *...retro-style photography.*

retro·ac·tive /ˌretrəʊ'æktɪv/. If a decision or law is ADJ **retroactive**, it is intended to take effect from a date FORMAL in the past. ◆ **retro·ac·tive·ly** *It isn't yet* ADV: clear whether the new law can actually be applied ADV with v *retroactively.*

retro·fit /'retrəʊfɪt/ **retrofits, retrofitting, retro-** V n **fitted.** To **retrofit** a machine or a building means AMERICAN to put a new part or new equipment in it after it has been in use for some time, especially to improve its safety or efficiency. *Much of this business involves retrofitting existing planes.*

retro·grade /'retrəgreɪd/. A **retrograde** action is ADJ-GRADED one that you think makes a situation worse rather FORMAL than better. *The Prime Minister described transfer- ring education to central government funding as 'a retrograde step'.*

retro·gres·sion /ˌretrə'greʃən/. **Retrogression** N-UNCOUNT means moving back to an earlier and less efficient also a N stage of development. *There has been a retrogression* FORMAL *in the field of human rights since 1975.*

retro·gres·sive /ˌretrə'gresɪv/. If you describe an ADJ action or idea as **retrogressive**, you disapprove of it [PRAGMATICS] because it returns to old ideas or beliefs and does FORMAL not take advantage of recent progress. *...the often retrogressive policies of the National parties.*

retro·spect /'retrəspekt/. When you consider ◆◇◇◇◇ something **in retrospect**, you think about it after- PHRASE wards, and often have a different opinion about it from the one that you had at the time. *In retrospect, I wish that I had thought about alternative courses of action.*

retro·spec·tive /ˌretrə'spektɪv/ **retrospectives.** ◆◇◇◇◇ **1** A **retrospective** is an exhibition or showing of N-COUNT work done by an artist over many years, rather than his or her most recent work. **2 Retrospective** feel- ADJ ings or opinions concern things that happened in the past. *Afterwards, retrospective fear of the respon- sibility would make her feel almost faint.* ◆ **retro·spec·tive·ly** *Retrospectively, it seems as if they* ADV *probably were negligent.* **3 Retrospective** laws or le- ADJ gal actions take effect from a date before the date when they are officially approved. *...retrospective tax legislation.* ◆ **retrospectively** *...a decree which* ADV: *retrospectively changes the electoral law.* ADV with v

re·turn /rɪ'tɜːn/ **returns, returning, returned.** ◆◆◆◆◇ **1** When you **return** to a place, you go back there af- VERB ter you have been away. *Our correspondent Stephen* V to/from n *Sackur has just returned from the camps on the bor-* V adv *der... So far more than 350,000 people have returned* Also V *home.* ► Also a noun. *...his sudden return to Lon-* N-SING: *don.* **2** A **return** ticket is a ticket for a journey from with poss ADJ

one place to another and then back again. The BRITISH American term is **round trip.** ► Also a noun. *BA and* N-COUNT *Air France charge more than £400 for a return to* ADJ: ADJ n *Nice.* ● See also **day return. 3** The **return** trip or BRITISH journey is the part of a journey that takes you back to where you started from.

4 If you **return** something that you have borrowed or VERB taken, you give it back or put it back. *I enjoyed the* V n *book and said so when I returned it.* ► Also a noun. N-SING *The main demand of the Indians is for the return of one-and-a-half-million acres of forest to their com- munities.* **5** If you **return** something somewhere, you VERB put it back where it was. *He returned the notebook to* V n to n *his jacket.*

6 If you **return** someone's action, you do the same VERB thing to them as they have just done to you. If you **re-** V n **turn** someone's feeling, you feel the same way to- wards them as they feel towards you. *The Chief In- spector returned the call.* **7** If you do something **in re-** PHRASE **turn** for what someone else has done for you, you do it because they did that thing for you. *You pay regular premiums and in return the insurance company will pay out a lump sum.*

8 If a feeling or situation **returns**, it comes back or VERB happens again after a period of absence. *The pain re-* V *turned in waves.* ► Also a noun. *It was like the return* N-SING: *of his youth.* **9** If you **return** to a state that you were in with supp before, you start being in that state again. *Life has im-* VERB *proved and returned to normal.* ► Also a noun. *He* N-SING: *made an uneventful return to normal health.* **10** If you V n return to a subject that you have mentioned before, VERB you begin talking about it again. *The power of the* V to n Church is one theme all these writers return to. **11** If VERB you **return** to an activity that you were doing before, V to n you start doing it again. *He will be 52, young enough to return to politics if he wishes to do so.* ► Also a noun. N-SING: *He has not ruled out the shock possibility of a return to* N to n *football.* **12** If you say that you have reached **the point** PHRASE **of no return,** you mean that you now have to con- tinue with what you are doing and it is too late to stop.

13 When a judge or jury **returns** a verdict, they an- VERB: V n nounce whether they think the person on trial is guilty or not.

14 The **return** on an investment is the profit that you N-COUNT get from it. ● See also **tax return.**

15 Returns are the results of votes in various places as N-PLURAL part of an election or ballot. *Early returns show Bulgaria's opposition party may have won.*

16 When it is someone's birthday, people sometimes CONVENTION say **'Many happy returns'** to them as a way of con- gratulating them.

re·turn·able /rɪ'tɜːnəbəl/. **1 Returnable** containers ADJ are intended to be taken back to the place they came from so that they can be used again. **2** If ADJ something such as a sum of money or a document is **returnable,** it will eventually be given back to the person who provided it.

re·turnee /ˌrɪtɜː'niː/ **returnees.** A **returnee** is a N-COUNT person who returns to the country where they were born after they have been away for a long time.

re·turn·er /rɪ'tɜːnə/ **returners.** A **returner** is some- N-COUNT one who returns to work after a period when they BRITISH did not work, especially a woman who returns after having children.

re'turning officer, returning officers. In Brit- N-COUNT ain, the **returning officer** for a town or district is an official who is responsible for arranging an election and who formally announces the result.

re'turn match, return matches. A **return match** N-COUNT is the second of two matches that are played by two BRITISH sports teams or two players.

re,turn 'visit, return visits. If you make a **return** N-COUNT **visit,** you visit someone who has already visited you, or you go back to a place where you have al- ready been once.

re·uni·fi·ca·tion /ˌriːjuːnɪfɪ'keɪʃən/. The **reunifica-** ◆◇◇◇◇ **tion** of a country or city that has been divided into N-UNCOUNT: two or more parts for some time is the joining of it with supp together again.

re·union /ˌriːˈjuːniən/ **reunions. 1** A **reunion** is a party attended by members of the same family, school, or other group who have not seen each other for a long time. ...*this big family reunion.* **2** A **reunion** is a meeting between people who have been separated for some time. *It was a very emotional reunion.* ◆◇◇◇◇ N-COUNT / N-VAR

re·unite /ˌriːjuːˈnaɪt/ **reunites, reuniting, reunited. 1** If people **are reunited**, or if they **reunite**, they meet each other again after they have been separated for some time. *She spent the post-war years of her marriage trying to reunite father and son.* **2** If a divided organization or country **is reunited**, or if it **reunites**, it becomes one united organization or country again. *His first job will be to reunite the army.* ◆◇◇◇◇ V-ERG: be V-ed V n Also V / V-ERG: be V-ed V n Also V

re·us·able /ˌriːˈjuːzəbəl/; also spelled **re-usable.** Things that are **reusable** can be used more than once. ...*re-usable plastic containers.* ADJ

re·use, reuses, reusing, reused. The verb is pronounced /riːˈjuːz/. The noun is pronounced /riːˈjuːs/. When you **reuse** something, you use it again instead of throwing it away. ...*the pressure to reuse paper.* ► Also a noun. *Copper, brass and aluminium are separated and re-melted for reuse.* VERB V n / N-UNCOUNT

rev /rev/ **revs, revving, revved. 1** When the engine of a vehicle **revs**, or when you **rev** it, the engine speed is increased as the accelerator is pressed. *The old bus was revving its engine.* ► **Rev up** means the same as **rev.** ...*drivers revving up their engines.* **2** If you talk about the **revs** of an engine, you are referring to its speed, which is measured in revolutions per minute. ◆◇◇◇◇ V-ERG: V V n / PHRASAL VB ERG: V P V P noun / N-PLURAL

rev up. 1 See **rev** sense 1. **2** If you **rev** something **up**, or if it **revs up**, it becomes more intense or more active. ...*the temptation to rev up the arms race with high-tech weapons... Now he plans to rev up publicity with a regional media campaign.* PHRASAL VB ERG V P noun Also V n P INFORMAL

Rev. Rev is a written abbreviation for **Reverend.** ◆◆◇◇◇

re·value /ˌriːˈvæljuː/ **revalues, revaluing, revalued. 1** When a country **revalues** its currency, it increases the currency's value so that it can buy more foreign currency than before. ♦ **re·valua·tion** /riːˌvæljuːˈeɪʃən/ **revaluations** ...*a general revaluation of other currencies.* **2** To **revalue** something means to increase the amount that you calculate it is worth so that its value stays roughly the same in comparison with other things, even if there is inflation. *It is now usual to revalue property assets on a more regular basis.* ♦ **revaluation** ...*doubtful property revaluations.* ◆◇◇◇◇ VERB: V n / N-VAR / VERB / N-VAR

re·vamp /ˌriːˈvæmp/ **revamps, revamping, revamped.** If someone **revamps** something, they make changes to it in order to try and improve it. *It is time to revamp the system.* ► Also a noun. *The revamp includes replacing the old navy uniform.* ♦ **re·vamp·ing** ...*a revamping of the courts.* ◆◇◇◇◇ VERB VERB / N-SING / N-SING: with supp

Revd. Revd is a written abbreviation for **Reverend.**

re·veal /rɪˈviːl/ **reveals, revealing, revealed. 1** To **reveal** something means to make people aware of it. *A survey of the British diet has revealed that a growing number of people are overweight... It was revealed that North Carolina officials had never inspected the factory... No test will reveal how much of the drug was taken.* **2** If you **reveal** something that has been out of sight, you uncover it so that people can see it. *A grey carpet was removed to reveal the original pine floor.* ◆◆◆◇ VERB: V n V that it be V-ed that V wh Also be V-ed as n / VERB V n

re·veal·ing /rɪˈviːlɪŋ/ **1** A **revealing** statement, account, or action tells you something that you did not know, especially about the person doing it or making it. ...*a revealing interview.* ♦ **re·veal·ing·ly** *Even more revealingly, he says: 'There's no such thing as failure.'* **2 Revealing** clothes allow more of the wearer's body to be seen than is usual. ...*a tight and revealing gold dress.* ◆◆◇◇◇ ADJ-GRADED / ADV-GRADED / ADJ-GRADED

re·veil·le /rɪˈvæli, AM ˈrevəli/. **Reveille** is the time when soldiers have to get up in the morning. *Soon would be reveille and the end of the night's rest.* N-UNCOUNT

rev·el /ˈrevəl/ **revels, revelling, revelled;** spelled **reveling, reveled** in American English. **1** If you **revel** in a situation or experience, you enjoy it very much. *Cats positively revel in heat.* **2 Revels** are noisy celebrations. *The revels often last until dawn.* ◆◇◇◇◇ VERB V in n / N-COUNT

rev·ela·tion /ˌrevəˈleɪʃən/ **revelations. 1** A **revelation** is a surprising or interesting fact that is made known to people. ...*revelations about his private life.* **2** The **revelation** of something is the act of making it known. ...*the revelation of his affair with a former secretary.* **3** If you say that something you experienced was **a revelation**, you are emphasizing that it was very surprising or very good. *Degas's work had been a revelation to her.* **4** A divine **revelation** is a sign or explanation from God about his nature or purpose. ◆◆◇◇◇ N-COUNT / N-VAR / N-SING: a N PRAGMATICS / N-VAR

rev·ela·tory /ˈrevələtəri, AM -tɔːri/. A **revelatory** account or statement tells you a lot that you did not know. ...*Barbara Stoney's revelatory account of the author's life.* ADJ-GRADED

rev·el·ler /ˈrevələ/ **revellers;** spelled **reveler** in American English. **Revellers** are people who are enjoying themselves in a noisy and often drunken way. *Many of the revellers are tourists.* N-COUNT

rev·el·ry /ˈrevəlri/. **Revelry** is people enjoying themselves in a noisy and often drunken way. *We heard the sounds of revelry getting louder and louder.* N-UNCOUNT LITERARY

re·venge /rɪˈvendʒ/ **revenges, revenging, revenged. 1 Revenge** involves hurting or punishing someone who has hurt or harmed you. *The killings were said to have been in revenge for the murder of her lover.* **2** If you **revenge** yourself on someone who has hurt you, you hurt them in return. ...*the relatives of murdered villagers wanting to revenge the dead.* ◆◆◇◇◇ N-UNCOUNT / VERB: V pron-refl on V n WRITTEN

rev·enue /ˈrevənjuː/ **revenues. Revenue** is money that a company, organization, or government receives from people. ...*a boom year at the cinema, with record advertising revenue.* ● See also **Inland Revenue.** ◆◆◇◇ N-UNCOUNT: also N in pl

re·ver·ber·ate /rɪˈvɜːbəreɪt/ **reverberates, reverberating, reverberated. 1** When a loud sound **reverberates** through a place, it echoes through it. *A woman's shrill laughter reverberated in the courtyard.* **2** You can say that an event or idea **reverberates** when it has a powerful effect which lasts a long time. *The controversy surrounding the take-over yesterday continued to reverberate around the television industry.* ◆◇◇◇◇ VERB: V prep / VERB: V V prep

re·ver·bera·tion /rɪˌvɜːbəˈreɪʃən/ **reverberations. 1 Reverberations** are serious effects that follow a sudden dramatic event. *The move by the two London colleges is sending reverberations through higher education.* **2** A **reverberation** is the shaking and echoing effect that you hear after a loud sound has been made. ...*the reverberation of the slammed door.* N-COUNT / N-VAR

re·vere /rɪˈvɪə/ **reveres, revering, revered.** If you **revere** someone or something, you respect and admire them greatly. *The Chinese revered corn as a gift from heaven.* ♦ **re·vered** ...*some of the country's most revered institutions.* ◆◇◇◇◇ VERB V n FORMAL / ADJ-GRADED

rev·er·ence /ˈrevərəns/. **Reverence** for someone or something is a feeling of great respect for them. ◆◇◇◇◇ N-UNCOUNT

Rev·er·end /ˈrevərənd/. **Reverend** is a title used before the name or rank of an officially appointed religious leader. The abbreviation 'Rev' or 'Revd' is also used. ...*the Reverend Jim Simons.* ◆◇◇◇◇ N-TITLE

rev·er·ent /ˈrevərənt/. If you describe someone's behaviour as **reverent**, you mean that it shows great respect for someone or something. ...*the reverent hush of a rapt audience.* ♦ **rev·er·ent·ly** *He got up and took the book out almost reverently.* ADJ / ADV

rev·er·en·tial /ˌrevəˈrenʃəl/. Something that is **reverential** has the qualities of respect, admiration, and awe. *'That's the old foresters' garden,' she said in reverential tones.* ♦ **rev·er·en·tial·ly** *He reverentially returned the novel to a glass-fronted bookcase.* ADJ-GRADED FORMAL / ADV-GRADED: ADV with v

R

rev·erie /'revəri/ **reveries.** A reverie is a kind of short pleasant daydream. *The announcer's voice brought Holden out of his reverie.*   N-COUNT FORMAL

re·verse /rɪ'vɜːs/ **reverses, reversing, reversed. 1** When someone or something **reverses** a decision, policy, or trend, they change it to the opposite decision, policy, or trend. *They will not reverse the decision to increase prices.* ♦ **re·ver·sal** /rɪ'vɜːsəl/ **reversals** *The move represents a complete reversal of previous US policy.*   ♦♦♦◇◇ VERB V n   N-COUNT

2 If you **reverse** the order of a set of things, you arrange them in the opposite order, so that the first thing comes last.   VERB: V n

3 If you **reverse** the positions or functions of two things, you change them so that each thing has the position or function that the other one had. *He reversed the position of the two stamps.* ♦ **reversal** *When children end up taking care of their parents, it is a strange role reversal indeed.* **4** If you **reverse the charges** when you make a telephone call, the person who is phoning pays the cost of the call and not you. The usual American term is to **call collect.**   VERB V n   N-COUNT: n N, N of n PHRASE BRITISH

5 When a car **reverses** or when you **reverse** a car, the car is driven backwards. The usual American expression is **back up.** *He reversed his car straight at the umpire.* **6** If your car is in **reverse,** you have changed gear so that you can drive it backwards.   V-ERG: V V n BRITISH   N-UNCOUNT

7 Reverse means opposite to what you expect or to what has just been described. *The wrong attitude will have exactly the reverse effect.* **8** If you say that one thing is **the reverse** of another, you are emphasizing that the first thing is the exact opposite of the second thing. *There is absolutely no evidence at all that spectators want longer cricket matches. Quite the reverse.*   ADJ   N-SING: the N PRAGMATICS

9 If something happens **in reverse** or goes **into reverse,** it happens in the opposite way to usual or to what has been happening. *Amis tells the story in reverse, from the moment the man dies.*   PHRASE

10 A **reverse** is a serious failure or setback. *It's clear that the party of the former Prime Minister has suffered a major reverse.*   N-COUNT FORMAL

11 The reverse or **the reverse** side of a flat object which has two sides is the less important or the other side. *Cheques should be made payable to Country Living and your address written on the reverse.*   N-SING: the N

re,verse discrimi'nation. Reverse discrimination is the same as **positive discrimination.**   N-UNCOUNT

re·vers·ible /rɪ'vɜːsɪbəl/ **1** If a process or an action is **reversible,** its effects can be reversed so that the original situation is restored. *Heart disease is reversible in some cases, according to a study published last summer.*   ADJ

2 Reversible clothes, bedclothes, or materials have been made so that either side can be worn or shown.   ADJ

re·ver·sion /rɪ'vɜːʃən/ **reversions. 1** A **reversion** to a previous state, system, or kind of behaviour is a change back to it. *...a reversion to the emotions of her baby years.* **2** In law, the **reversion** of land or property to a person, family, or country is the return to them of the ownership or control of the land or property.   N-SING: also no det, N to n   N-VAR

re·vert /rɪ'vɜːt/ **reverts, reverting, reverted. 1** When people or things **revert** to a previous state, system, or type of behaviour, they go back to it. *Jackson said her boss became increasingly depressed and reverted to smoking heavily.* **2** When someone **reverts** to a previous topic, they start talking or thinking about it again. *She reverted to the subject uppermost in her mind.* **3** If you **revert** to your usual language, you start using that language again. *She had reverted to her Veneto dialect and nobody could understand what she was saying.* **4** In law, if property, rights, or money **reverts** to someone, it becomes theirs again after someone else has had it for a period of time.   ♦◇◇◇◇ VERB V to n   VERB V to n   VERB V to n   VERB V to n

re·view /rɪ'vjuː/ **reviews, reviewing, reviewed. 1** If you **review** a situation or system, you consider it carefully to see what is wrong with it or how it could be improved. *The Prime Minister reviewed the situation with his Cabinet yesterday.*   ♦♦♦♦◇ VERB V n

▶ Also a noun. *The president ordered a review of US economic aid to Jordan.*   N-COUNT

2 A **review** is a report in a newspaper or magazine, or on television or radio, in which someone gives their opinion of a new book, film, television programme, record, play, or concert. **3** If someone **reviews** something such as a new book or play, they write a report or give a talk on television or radio in which they express their opinion of it. *Richard Coles reviews all of the latest video releases.* ♦ **re·view·er, reviewers** *...the reviewer for the Times Literary Supplement.*   N-COUNT   VERB V n   N-COUNT

4 When a military or political leader **reviews** troops, they inspect or watch the troops in a military parade.   VERB: V n

re'viewing stand, reviewing stands. A **reviewing stand** is a raised platform from which military and political leaders watch military parades.   N-COUNT

re·vile /rɪ'vaɪl/ **reviles, reviling, reviled.** If someone or something **is reviled,** people hate them intensely or show their hatred of them. *He was just as feared and reviled as his tyrannical parents.* ♦ **re·viled** *...the most reviled man in contemporary theatre.*   VERB be V-ed FORMAL   ADJ-GRADED

re·vise /rɪ'vaɪz/ **revises, revising, revised. 1** If you **revise** the way you think about something, you adjust your thoughts, usually in order to make them better or more suited to how things are. *He fairly soon came to revise his opinion of the profession.*   ♦♦◇◇◇ VERB V n

2 If you **revise** a price, amount, or estimate, you change it to make it more realistic, competitive, or accurate. **3** When you **revise** an essay, a book, a law, or a piece of music, you change it in some way to improve it, update it, or adapt it for a particular purpose. *Three editors handled the work of revising the articles for publication.* ♦ **re·vi·sion** /rɪ'vɪʒən/ **revisions** *The phase of writing that is actually most important is revision.*   VERB: V n   VERB: V n V n for n   N-VAR

4 When you **revise** for an examination, you read things again and make notes in order to be prepared for the examination. *After Friday 17th May all girls may stay at home to revise.* ♦ **revision** *Some girls prefer to do their revision at home.*   VERB: V for n V BRITISH   N-UNCOUNT

re·vi·sion·ism /rɪ'vɪʒənɪzəm/. **Revisionism** is any theory of socialism that is more moderate than orthodox Marxist theory, and is therefore considered to be wrong and dangerous by orthodox Marxists. ♦ **re·vi·sion·ist, revisionists** *...the revisionist interpretation of the French Revolution.*   N-UNCOUNT PRAGMATICS   N-COUNT

re·vis·it /,riː'vɪzɪt/ **revisits, revisiting, revisited.** If you **revisit** a place, you return there for a visit after you have been away for a long time.   ♦◇◇◇◇ VERB: V n

re·vi·tal·ize /riː'vaɪtəlaɪz/ **revitalizes, revitalizing, revitalized;** also spelled **revitalise** in British English. To **revitalize** something that has lost its activity or its health means to make it active or healthy again. *This hair conditioner is excellent for revitalizing dry, lifeless hair.*   ♦◇◇◇◇ VERB V n

re·viv·al /rɪ'vaɪvəl/ **revivals. 1** When there is a **revival** of something, it becomes active or popular again. *This return to realism has produced a revival of interest in a number of artists.* **2** A **revival** is a new production of a play, an opera, or a ballet. *...John Clement's revival of Chekhov's 'The Seagull'.*   ♦♦◇◇◇ N-COUNT   N-COUNT

re·viv·al·ism /rɪ'vaɪvəlɪzəm/. **Revivalism** is a movement whose aim is to make a religion more popular and more influential. ♦ **re·viv·al·ist, revivalists** *...the Hindu revivalist party.*   N-UNCOUNT   N-COUNT

re·vive /rɪ'vaɪv/ **revives, reviving, revived. 1** When something such as the economy, a business, a trend, or a feeling **is revived** or when it **revives,** it becomes active, popular, or successful again. *...an attempt to revive the British economy.* ▶ Also an adjective. *Habib grimaced at the revived memories.* **2** When someone **revives** a play, opera, or ballet, they present a new production of it. **3** If you manage to **revive** someone who has fainted or if they **revive,** they become conscious again. *With a glazed stare she revived for one last instant.*   ♦♦◇◇◇ V-ERG: V V n   ADJ   V-ERG: V n   V

re·vivi·fy /riː'vɪvɪfaɪ/ **revivifies, revivifying, revivified.** To **revivify** a situation, event, or activity   VERB V n FORMAL

means to make it more active, lively, or efficient. *They've revivified rhythm and blues singing.*

re·voke /rɪ'vəʊk/ **revokes, revoking, revoked.** When people in authority **revoke** something such as a licence, a law, or an agreement, they cancel it. *The government revoked her husband's license to operate migrant labor crews.* ♦ **revo·ca·tion** /ˌrevə'keɪʃən/. *Now the Montserrat government has announced its revocation of 311 banking licences.*
◆◇◇◇◇
VERB
V n
FORMAL

N-UNCOUNT

re·volt /rɪ'vəʊlt/ **revolts, revolting, revolted.** **1** A **revolt** is an illegal and often violent attempt by a group of people to change their country's political system. *...a revolt by ordinary people against their leaders.* **2** When people **revolt**, they make an illegal and often violent attempt to change their country's political system. *The islanders revolted against the sultanate.* **3** A **revolt** by a person or group against someone or something is a rejection of the authority of that person or thing. *The prime minister is facing a revolt by Conservative party activists over his refusal to hold a referendum.* **4** When people **revolt**, they reject the authority of someone or something. *Caroline revolted against her ballet training at sixteen.*
◆◆◇◇◇
N-VAR

VERB:
V against n

N-VAR

VERB: V
V against n

re·volt·ing /rɪ'vəʊltɪŋ/. If you say that something or someone is **revolting**, you mean that they are horrible and disgusting. *The smell in the cell was revolting.*
◆◇◇◇◇
ADJ-GRADED

revo·lu·tion /ˌrevə'luːʃən/ **revolutions. 1** A **revolution** is a successful attempt by a large group of people to change the political system of their country by force. *The period since the revolution has been one of political turmoil.* **2** A **revolution** in a particular area of human activity is an important change in that area. *...the industrial revolution.*
◆◆◆◇◇
N-COUNT

N-COUNT:
with supp

revo·lu·tion·ary /ˌrevə'luːʃənri, AM -neri/ **revolutionaries. 1 Revolutionary** activities, organizations, or people have the aim of causing a political revolution. *...the Cuban revolutionary leader, Jose Marti.* **2** A **revolutionary** is a person who tries to cause a revolution or who takes an active part in one. **3 Revolutionary** ideas and developments involve great changes in the way that something is done or made. *...a revolutionary concept in internal combustion.*
◆◆◇◇◇
ADJ

N-COUNT

ADJ-GRADED

revo·lu·tion·ize /ˌrevə'luːʃənaɪz/ **revolutionizes, revolutionizing, revolutionized;** also spelled **revolutionise** in British English. When something **revolutionizes** an activity, it causes great changes in the way that it is done. *Plastics have revolutionised the way we live.*
◆◇◇◇◇
VERB
V n

re·volve /rɪ'vɒlv/ **revolves, revolving, revolved. 1** If you say that one thing **revolves** around another thing, you mean that the second thing is the main feature or focus of the first thing. *Since childhood, her life has revolved around tennis.* **2** If a discussion or conversation **revolves** around a particular topic, it is mainly about that topic. *The conversation revolved around the terrible condition of the road.* **3** If one object **revolves** around another object, the first object turns in a circle around the second object. *The satellite revolves around the Earth once every hundred minutes.* **4** When something **revolves** or when you **revolve** it, it moves or turns in a circle around a central point or line. *Monica picked up her Biro and revolved it between her teeth.*
◆◇◇◇◇
VERB
V around n

VERB
V around n

VERB
V around n

V-ERG: V
V n

re·volv·er /rɪ'vɒlvə/ **revolvers.** A **revolver** is a kind of hand gun.
◆◇◇◇◇
N-COUNT

re·volv·ing 'door, revolving doors. 1 Revolving doors consist of four glass doors which turn together around a vertical post. **2** In business, when you talk about a **revolving door**, you mean a situation in which the employees or owners of an organization keep changing; used showing disapproval.
N-COUNT

N-COUNT
PRAGMATICS

re·vue /rɪ'vjuː/ **revues.** A **revue** is a light theatrical entertainment consisting of songs, dances, and jokes about recent events.
◆◇◇◇◇
N-COUNT

re·vul·sion /rɪ'vʌlʃən/. Someone's **revulsion** at something is the strong feeling of disgust or disap-
◆◇◇◇◇
N-UNCOUNT:
also a N

proval they have towards it. *His voice was filled with horror and revulsion.*

revved 'up. If someone is **revved up**, they are prepared for an important or exciting activity. *The crowd is revved up for the game.*
ADJ-GRADED:
v-link ADJ
INFORMAL

re·ward /rɪ'wɔːd/ **rewards, rewarding, rewarded. 1** A **reward** is something that you are given, for example because you have behaved well, worked hard, or provided a service to the community. *He was given the job as a reward for running a successful leadership bid.* **2** A **reward** is a sum of money offered to anyone who can give information about lost or stolen property or about someone who is wanted by the police. **3** If you do something and **are rewarded** with a particular benefit, you receive that benefit as a result of doing that thing. *Impress the buyer and you will be rewarded with a quicker sale.* **4** The **rewards** of something are the benefits that you receive as a result of doing or having that thing. *The company is only just starting to reap the rewards of long-term investments.*
◆◆◆◇◇
N-COUNT

N-COUNT

VERB
be V-ed
Also V n

N-COUNT

re·ward·ing /rɪ'wɔːdɪŋ/. An experience or action that is **rewarding** gives you satisfaction or brings you benefits. *...a career which she found stimulating and rewarding.*
◆◇◇◇◇
ADJ-GRADED

re·wind, rewinds, rewinding, rewound. The verb is pronounced /ˌriː'waɪnd/. The noun is pronounced /'riːwaɪnd/. **1** When the tape in a video or tape recorder **rewinds** or when you **rewind** it, the tape goes backwards so that you can play it again. Compare **fast forward.** *Waddington rewound the tape and played the message again.* **2** If you put a video or cassette tape on **rewind**, you make the tape go backwards. Compare **fast forward.**
V-ERG: V
V n

N-UNCOUNT

re·wire /ˌriː'waɪə/ **rewires, rewiring, rewired.** If someone **rewires** a building or an electrical appliance, a new system of electrical wiring is put into it. *I have had to spend a lot of money having my house re-plumbed and rewired.* ♦ **re·wir·ing** *...the re-plumbing and rewiring of the flat.*
VERB: V n
have n V-ed

N-UNCOUNT

re·word /ˌriː'wɜːd/ **rewords, rewording, reworded.** When you **reword** something that is spoken or written, you try to express it in a way that is more accurate, more acceptable, or more easily understood. *All right, I'll reword my question.*
VERB
V n

re·work /ˌriː'wɜːk/ **reworks, reworking, reworked.** If you **rework** something such as an idea or a piece of writing, you reorganize it and make changes to it in order to improve it or bring it up to date. *She reworked a lot of her compositions to make them more danceable.* ♦ **re·work·ing, reworkings** *...a reworking of similar themes.*
◆◇◇◇◇
VERB
V n

N-COUNT

re·wound /ˌriː'waʊnd/. **Rewound** is the past tense and past participle of **rewind.**

re·write, rewrites, rewriting, rewrote, rewritten. The verb is pronounced /ˌriː'raɪt/. The noun is pronounced /'riːraɪt/. **1** If someone **rewrites** a piece of writing such as a book, a script, or a law, they write it in a different way in order to improve it. *Students rewrite their papers and submit them for final evaluation.* **2** In the film industry, a **rewrite** is the writing of parts of a script again to improve it. **3** If governments **rewrite** history, they select and present historical events in a way that suits their own purposes; used showing disapproval. **4** When journalists say that a sports player **has rewritten** the record books or the history books, they mean that he or she has broken a record or several records.
◆◇◇◇◇
VERB
V n

N-COUNT

VERB: V n
PRAGMATICS

VERB: V n

rhap·so·dize /'ræpsədaɪz/ **rhapsodizes, rhapsodizing, rhapsodized;** also spelled **rhapsodise** in British English. If you **rhapsodize** about someone or something, you express great delight or enthusiasm about them. *The critics rhapsodized over her performance in 'Autumn Sonata'.*
VERB
V over/about n
Also V with
quote
FORMAL

rhap·so·dy /'ræpsədi/ **rhapsodies.** A **rhapsody** is a piece of music which has an irregular form and is full of feeling.
N-COUNT

rhet·o·ric /'retərɪk/. **1** If you refer to fine-sounding speech or writing as **rhetoric**, you disapprove of it because it is meant to convince and impress people
◆◆◇◇◇
N-UNCOUNT
PRAGMATICS

but may lack sincerity or honesty. ...*political rheto-ric rather than social reality.* **2 Rhetoric** is the skill or art of using language effectively. N-UNCOUNT FORMAL

rhe·tori·cal /rɪ'tɒrɪkəl, AM -'tɔːr-/. **1** A **rhetorical** question is one which is asked in order to make a statement rather than to get an answer. ♦ **rhe·tori·cal·ly** /rɪ'tɒrɪkli, AM -'tɔːr-/. *'Do these kids know how lucky they are?' Jackson asked rhetorically.* **2 Rhetorical** language is intended to be grand and impressive. ♦ **rhetorically** *Suddenly, the narrator speaks in his most rhetorically elevated mode.* ◆◇◇◇◇ ADJ | ADV: ADV with v | ADJ-GRADED FORMAL ADV

rheu·mat·ic /ruː'mætɪk/. **1 Rheumatic** is used to describe conditions and pains that are related to rheumatism. ...*new treatments for a range of rheu-matic diseases.* **2** Someone who is **rheumatic** suf-fers from rheumatism. ADJ: ADJ n | ADJ-GRADED

rheu·ma·tism /'ruːmətɪzəm/. **Rheumatism** is an illness that makes your joints or muscles stiff and painful. N-UNCOUNT

rheu·ma·toid ar·thri·tis /,ruːmətɔɪd ɑː'θraɪtɪs/. **Rheumatoid arthritis** is a long-lasting disease that causes your joints to swell up and become painful. ◆◇◇◇◇ N-UNCOUNT

rheu·ma·tol·ogy /,ruːmə'tɒlədʒi/. **Rheumatology** is the area of medicine that is concerned with rheu-matism, arthritis, and related diseases. ♦ **rheu·ma·tolo·gist, rheumatologists** ...*consultant rheu-matologist at the Royal Hampshire Hospital.* N-COUNT

rheumy /'ruːmi/. If someone has **rheumy** eyes, their eyes are moist and watery, usually because they are very ill or old. ADJ LITERARY

rhine·stone /'raɪnstəʊn/ **rhinestones.** **Rhine-stones** are shiny, glass jewels that are used in cheap jewellery and to decorate clothes. N-COUNT

rhi·ni·tis /raɪ'naɪtɪs/. If you suffer from **rhinitis**, you have a constantly sore and runny nose. N-UNCOUNT MEDICAL

rhi·no /'raɪnəʊ/ **rhinos.** A **rhino** is the same as a **rhinoceros**; an informal word. ◆◇◇◇◇ N-COUNT

rhi·noc·er·os /raɪ'nɒsərəs/ **rhinoceroses.** A **rhi-noceros** is a large Asian or African animal with thick grey skin and a horn, or two horns, on its nose. See picture headed **animals**. N-COUNT

rhi·zome /'raɪzəʊm/ **rhizomes.** **Rhizomes** are the horizontal stems from which some plants, such as irises, grow. N-COUNT

rho·do·den·dron /,rəʊdə'dendrən/ **rhododen-drons.** A **rhododendron** is a large bush with groups of flowers which are usually pink, red, or purple. ◆◇◇◇◇ N-VAR

rhom·bus /'rɒmbəs/ **rhombuses.** A **rhombus** is a geometrical shape which has four equal sides but is not a square. N-COUNT TECHNICAL

rhu·barb /'ruːbɑːb/. **Rhubarb** is a plant with large leaves and long red stems. You can cook the stems with sugar to make jam or puddings. N-UNCOUNT

rhyme /raɪm/ **rhymes, rhyming, rhymed. 1** If one word **rhymes** with another or if two words **rhyme**, they have a very similar sound. *June always rhymes with moon in old love songs.* ...*names that rhyme: Donnie, Ronnie, Connie.* ...*a singer rhyming 'eyes' with 'realise'.* **2** A **rhyme** is a word which rhymes with another word, or a set of lines which rhyme. *The one rhyme for passion is fashion.* **3** A **rhyme** is a short poem which has rhyming words at the ends of its lines. *He was teaching Helen a little rhyme.* ● See also **nursery rhyme. 4 Rhyme** is the use of rhyming words as a technique in poetry. If something is written **in rhyme**, it is written as a poem in which the lines rhyme. **5** If something happens or is done **without rhyme or reason**, there seems to be no logical reason for it to happen or be done. ◆◇◇◇◇ V-RECIP-ERG V with n pl-n V V n with n Also V n (non-recip) | N-COUNT | N-COUNT | N-UNCOUNT | PHRASE

'rhyming slang. Rhyming slang is a colloquial form of language in which you do not use the nor-mal word for something, but say a word or phrase that rhymes with it instead. In Cockney rhyming slang, for example, people say 'apples and pears' to mean 'stairs'. N-UNCOUNT

rhythm /'rɪðəm/ **rhythms. 1** A **rhythm** is a regular series of sounds or movements. *She could hear the constant rhythm of his breathing.* **2** A **rhythm** is a ◆◆◇◇◇ N-VAR | N-COUNT

regular pattern of changes, for example changes in your body, in the seasons, or in the tides. ...*the sea-sonal rhythm of the agricultural year.*

,rhythm and 'blues. Rhythm and blues is a style of popular music developed in the 1940's from blues music. N-UNCOUNT

rhyth·mic /'rɪðmɪk/ or **rhythmical** /'rɪðmɪkəl/. A **rhythmic** movement or sound is repeated at regular intervals, forming a regular pattern or beat. *Good breathing is slow, rhythmic and deep.* ♦ **rhyth·mi·cal·ly** /'rɪðmɪkli/. *She stood, swaying her hips, moving rhythmically.* ◆◇◇◇◇ ADJ-GRADED | ADV-GRADED: ADV after v

'rhythm method. The **rhythm method** is a form of contraception in which a couple try to prevent pregnancy by having sex only at times when the woman is not likely to become pregnant. N-SING

'rhythm section. The **rhythm section** of a band is the musicians whose main job is to supply the rhythm. N-SING

rib /rɪb/ **ribs, ribbing, ribbed. 1** Your **ribs** are the curved bones that go from your backbone around your chest. **2 Rib** or **ribbing** is a method of knitting that makes a raised pattern of parallel lines. **3** If you **rib** someone about something, you tease them about it in a friendly way. *The guys in my local pub used to rib me about drinking 'girly' drinks.* ♦ **rib·bing** *I got quite a lot of ribbing from my team-mates.* ◆◆◇◇◇ N-COUNT | N-UNCOUNT | VERB V n INFORMAL | N-UNCOUNT

rib·ald /'rɪbəld/. A **ribald** remark or sense of hu-mour is rather rude and refers to sex in a humorous way. ...*her ribald comments about a fellow guest's body language.* ADJ-GRADED

ribbed /rɪbd/. A **ribbed** surface, material, or gar-ment has a raised pattern of parallel lines on it. ...*ribbed cashmere sweaters.* ADJ

rib·bon /'rɪbən/ **ribbons. 1** A **ribbon** is a long, nar-row piece of cloth that you use for tying things to-gether or as a decoration. *She had tied back her hair with a peach satin ribbon.* **2** A typewriter or printer **ribbon** is a long, narrow piece of cloth containing a special ink that you put into a typewriter or printer. ◆◆◇◇◇ N-VAR | N-COUNT

'rib cage, rib cages; also spelled **ribcage.** Your **rib cage** is the structure of ribs in your chest. N-COUNT

ri·bo·fla·vin /,raɪbəʊ'fleɪvɪn/. **Riboflavin** is a vita-min that occurs in green vegetables, milk, fish, eggs, liver, and kidney. N-UNCOUNT

rice /raɪs/ **rices. Rice** consists of white or brown grains taken from a cereal plant. ...*a meal consisting of chicken, rice and vegetables.* ● See also **brown rice.** ◆◆◆◇◇ N-VAR

'rice paper. Rice paper is a type of very thin paper which you can eat. It is used in baking. N-UNCOUNT

rich /rɪtʃ/ **richer, richest; riches. 1** A **rich** per-son has a lot of money or valuable possessions. *Their one aim in life is to get rich.* ▶ **The rich** are rich people. ...*a gossip page featuring the rich and famous.* **2 Riches** are valuable possessions or large amounts of money. *Some people want fame or riches – I just wanted a baby.* **3** A **rich** country has a strong economy and produces a lot of wealth, so many people who live there have a high standard of living. **4** If you say that someone is **filthy rich** or **stinking rich**, you mean that they have a lot of money. ...*a handful of filthy rich young men.* **5** If you talk about the earth's **riches**, you are referring to things that exist naturally in large quantities and that are useful and valuable. ...*the oil riches of the Mid-dle East.* **6** If something is **rich in** a useful or valuable sub-stance or is a **rich source** of it, it contains a lot of that substance. *Fish is a rich source of protein.* ▶ Also a combining form. ...*Angola's northern oil-rich coast-line.* **7 Rich** soil contains large amounts of substances that make it good for growing crops or flowers in. *Farmers grow rice in the rich soil.* **8** A **rich** deposit of a mineral or other substance consists of a large amount of it. ...*the country's rich deposits of the metal, lithium.* ♦ **rich·ness** ...*the richness of Tibet's mineral deposits.* **9** A **rich** life or history is one that is interesting be-cause it is full of different events and activities. ...*the* ◆◆◆◆◇ ADJ-GRADED | N-PLURAL: the N | N-PLURAL | ADJ-GRADED | PHRASE PRAGMATICS INFORMAL | N-PLURAL | ADJ-GRADED | COMB | ADJ-GRADED | ADJ-GRADED | N-UNCOUNT | ADJ-GRADED

rich history of the island. ♦ **richness** *...the richness of human life.* `N-UNCOUNT`

10 Rich food contains a lot of fat or oil. *Additional cream would make it too rich.* ♦ **richness** *...the richness of the pudding.* **11 Rich** smells are strong and very pleasant. **Rich** colours and sounds are deep and very pleasant. *...a rich and luxuriously perfumed bath essence. ...an attractive, glossy rich red colour.* ♦ **richness** *...the richness of colour in Gauguin's paintings.* `ADJ-GRADED` `N-UNCOUNT` `ADJ-GRADED` `N-UNCOUNT`

12 If you say that something someone says or does is **rich**, you are making fun of it because you think it is a surprising and inappropriate thing for them to say or do. *Gil says that women can't keep secrets. That's rich, coming from him, the professional sneak.* `ADJ-GRADED` `v-link ADJ` `PRAGMATICS` `INFORMAL`

rich·ly /ˈrɪtʃli/ **1** If something is **richly** coloured, flavoured, or scented, it has a pleasantly strong colour, flavour, or scent. *...an opulent display of richly coloured fabrics.* **2** If something is **richly** decorated, patterned, or furnished, it has a lot of elaborate and beautiful decoration, patterns, or furniture. *Coffee steamed in the richly decorated silver pot.* `ADV-GRADED` `ADV-GRADED`

3 If you say that someone **richly** deserves an award, success, or victory, you approve of what they have done and feel very strongly that they deserve it. *He achieved the success he so richly deserved.* **4** If a person or place is **richly** endowed or supplied with something, they have a lot of it. *...a boy richly endowed with courage.* **5** If someone is **richly** rewarded for doing something, they get something very valuable or pleasurable in return for doing it. *It is a difficult book to read, but it richly rewards the effort.* `ADV-GRADED` `ADV before v` `PRAGMATICS` `ADV-GRADED` `ADV -ed` `ADV-GRADED` `ADV before v`

Richter scale /ˈrɪktə skeɪl/. **The Richter scale** is a scale which is used for measuring how severe an earthquake is. `N-SING:` `theN`

rick /rɪk/ **ricks, ricking, ricked. 1** If you **rick** your neck, you hurt it by pulling or twisting it in an unusual way. **2** A **rick** is a large pile of hay or straw that is built in a regular shape with a thatched top. `VERB: V n` `BRITISH` `N-COUNT`

rick·ets /ˈrɪkɪts/. **Rickets** is a disease that children can get when their food does not contain enough Vitamin D. It makes their bones soft, and can cause their legs to become deformed. `N-UNCOUNT`

rick·ety /ˈrɪkɪti/. A **rickety** structure or piece of furniture is not very strong or well made, and seems likely to collapse or break. *Mona climbed the rickety wooden stairway.* `ADJ-GRADED`

rick·shaw /ˈrɪkʃɔː/ **rickshaws.** A **rickshaw** is a cart, often pulled by hand, that is used in parts of Asia for carrying passengers. `N-COUNT`

rico·chet /ˈrɪkəʃeɪ, AM -ˈʃeɪ/ **ricochets, ricocheting, ricocheted.** If a bullet **ricochets**, it hits a surface or object and bounces away from it. *The bullets ricocheted off the bonnet and windscreen.* ► Also a noun. *He was wounded in the shoulder by a ricochet.* `VERB` `V prep/adv` `Also V` `N-COUNT`

rid /rɪd/ **rids, ridding.** The form **rid** is used in the present tense and is the past tense and past participle of the verb. **1** When you **get rid of** something that you do not want or do not like, you take action so that you no longer have it. *The owner needs to get rid of the car for financial reasons... She will have to get rid of the excess weight on her hips.* **2** If you **get rid of** someone who is causing problems for you, you make them leave. *His manager wanted to get rid of him for personal reasons.* **3** If you **rid** a place or person **of** something undesirable or unwanted, you succeed in removing it completely. *The proposals are an attempt to rid the country of political corruption... Why couldn't he ever rid himself of those thoughts?* `PHRASE` `PHRASE` `VERB` `V n of n`

4 If you **are rid of** someone or something that you did not want or that caused problems for you, they are no longer with you or causing problems for you. *The family had sought a way to be rid of her.* **5** If you say that someone is **well rid of** someone, you think it is good that the person has gone because you did not like them or you think they caused a lot of problems. *Your wife was a shallow woman and you're well rid of her.* `ADJ:` `v-link ADJ of n` `PHRASE`

rid·dance /ˈrɪdəns/. You say **'good riddance'** to indicate that you are glad that someone has left or that something has gone. *He's gone back to London in a huff and good riddance.* `PHRASE` `PRAGMATICS`

rid·den /ˈrɪdən/. **Ridden** is the past participle of **ride.**

-ridden /-rɪdən/. **-ridden** combines with nouns to form adjectives that describe something as having a lot of a particular undesirable thing or quality. *...the debt-ridden economies of Latin America.* `COMB`

rid·dle /ˈrɪdəl/ **riddles, riddling, riddled. 1** A **riddle** is a puzzle or joke in which you ask a question that seems to be nonsense but which has a clever or amusing answer. **2** You can describe something as a **riddle** if people have been trying to understand or explain it but have not been able to. *...the riddle of the birth of the Universe.* **3** If someone **riddles** something **with** bullets or bullet holes, they fire a lot of bullets into it. *Unknown attackers riddled two homes with gunfire.* `N-COUNT` `N-COUNT` `VERB` `V n with n`

rid·dled /ˈrɪdəld/. **1** If something **is riddled with** bullets or bullet holes, it is full of bullet holes. *The bodies of four people were found riddled with bullets.* **2** If something **is riddled with** undesirable qualities or features, it is full of them. *The report was riddled with errors.* ► Also a combining form. *It is a dangerous, crime-riddled, filthy city.* `ADJ-GRADED` `ADJ-GRADED:` `v-link ADJ` `with n` `COMB`

ride /raɪd/ **rides, riding, rode, ridden. 1** If you **ride** a horse, you sit on it and control its movements. *Can you ride?... He was riding on his horse looking for the castle... The French horsemen were turning and riding away.* ● See also **riding. 2** If you **ride** a bicycle or a motorcycle, you sit on it, control it, and travel along on it. *Two men riding on motorcycles opened fire on him... He rode to work on a bicycle.* **3** If you **ride** in a vehicle such as a car, you travel in it. *He prefers travelling on the Tube to riding in a limousine. ...American servicemen riding around in jeeps.* **4** A **ride** is a journey on a horse or bicycle, or in a vehicle. `VERB: V n` `V` `V adv/prep` `VERB: V n` `V o n n` `V prep/adv` `VERB` `V in/on n` `V adv/prep` `N-COUNT`

5 If you say that one thing **is riding on** another, you mean that the first thing is dependent on the other. *Billions of pounds are riding on the outcome of the election.* `VERB` `V on n`

6 If you say that someone or something **is riding high**, you mean that they are popular or successful at the present time. *He was riding high in the public opinion polls.* **7** If you say that someone faces **a rough ride**, you think that things are going to be difficult for them. *The Chancellor could face a rough ride unless the plan works.* **8** If you say that someone has **been taken for a ride**, you mean that they have been deceived or cheated. *You've been taken for a ride. Why did you give him five thousand francs?* **9** ● to **ride roughshod over** something: see **roughshod.** `PHRASE` `PHRASE` `INFORMAL` `PHRASE` `INFORMAL`

ride out. If someone **rides out** a difficult period or a crisis, they manage to survive it without suffering serious harm. *The ruling party think they can ride out the political storm.* `PHRASAL VB` `V P noun` `Also V n P`

ride up. If a garment **rides up**, it moves upwards, out of its proper position. *My underskirt had ridden up into a thick band around my hips.* `PHRASAL VB` `V P`

rid·er /ˈraɪdə/ **riders.** A **rider** is someone who rides a horse, a bicycle, or a motorcycle. *She is a very good and experienced rider.* `N-COUNT`

ridge /rɪdʒ/ **ridges. 1** A **ridge** is a long, narrow piece of raised land. **2** A **ridge** is a raised line on a flat surface. *...the bony ridge of the eye socket.* `N-COUNT` `N-COUNT:` `with supp`

ridged /rɪdʒd/. A **ridged** surface has raised lines on it. *...boots with thick, ridged soles for walking.* `ADJ-GRADED`

ridi·cule /ˈrɪdɪkjuːl/ **ridicules, ridiculing, ridiculed. 1** If you **ridicule** someone or **ridicule** their ideas or beliefs, you make fun of them in an unkind way. *...allowing them to ridicule her and never striking back.* **2** If someone or something is an object of **ridicule** or is held up to **ridicule**, someone makes fun of them in an unkind way. *As a heavy child, she became the object of ridicule from classmates.* `VERB` `V n` `N-UNCOUNT`

ri·dicu·lous /rɪˈdɪkjələs/. If you say that something or someone is **ridiculous**, you mean that they `ADJ-GRADED`

are very foolish. *It is ridiculous to suggest we are having a romance.*

ri·dic·u·lous·ly /rɪˈdɪkjʊləsli/. You use **ridiculously** to emphasize the fact that you think something is unreasonable or very surprising. *She looked ridiculously young to be a mother.* ◆◇◇◇ ADV-GRADED PRAGMATICS

rid·ing /ˈraɪdɪŋ/. **Riding** is the activity or sport of riding horses. *The next morning we went riding.* ◆◆◇◇ N-UNCOUNT

rife /raɪf/. If you say that something, usually something bad, is **rife** in a place or that the place is **rife** with it, you mean that it is very common. *Bribery and corruption were rife in the industry... Hollywood soon became rife with rumors.* ◆◇◇◇ ADJ-GRADED: v-link ADJ

riff /rɪf/ **riffs.** In jazz and rock music, a **riff** is a short repeated tune. ◆◇◇◇ N-COUNT

rif·fle /ˈrɪfəl/ **riffles, riffling, riffled.** If you **riffle** through the pages of a book, you turn them over quickly, without reading everything that is on them. *I riffled through the pages until I reached the index.* VERB V through n Also V n

riff-raff /ˈrɪf ræf/; also spelled **riffraff.** If you refer to a group of people as **riff-raff**, you disapprove of them because you think they are not respectable. N-UNCOUNT PRAGMATICS

ri·fle /ˈraɪfəl/ **rifles, rifling, rifled.** **1** A **rifle** is a gun with a long barrel. *They shot him at point blank range with an automatic rifle.* **2** If you **rifle** through things or **rifle** them, you make a quick search among them in order to find something or steal something. *The men rifled through his clothing and snatched the wallet.* ◆◇◇◇ N-COUNT VERB V through n Also V n

rifle·man /ˈraɪfəlmæn/ **riflemen.** A **rifleman** is a person, especially a soldier, who is skilled in the use of a rifle. N-COUNT

'rifle range, rifle ranges. A **rifle range** is a place where you can practise shooting with a rifle. N-COUNT

rift /rɪft/ **rifts. 1** A **rift** between people or countries is a serious quarrel that stops them having a co-operative relationship. *The serious rifts within the country could lead to civil war... They hope to heal the rift with their father.* **2** A **rift** is a split that appears in something solid, especially in the ground. ◆◇◇◇ N-COUNT N-COUNT

rig /rɪɡ/ **rigs, rigging, rigged. 1** If someone **rigs** an election, a job appointment, or a game, they dishonestly arrange it to get the result they want or to give someone an unfair advantage. *They rig their domestic markets in favour of local businesses.* **2** A **rig** is a large structure that is used for looking for oil or gas and for taking it out of the ground or the sea bed. **3** See also **rigging.** ◆◆◇◇ VERB V n N-COUNT

rig out. If you **rig** yourself **out** or **are rigged out** in a particular way, you are wearing a particular kind of clothes. *I rigged myself out in thick jeans and heavy belt.* PHRASAL VB V pron-refl P INFORMAL

rig up. If you **rig up** a device or structure, you make it or fix it in place using any materials that are available. *I rigged up a partial shelter with a tarpaulin.* PHRASAL VB V P noun Also V n P

rig·ging /ˈrɪɡɪŋ/. **1** Vote or ballot **rigging** is the act of dishonestly organizing an election to get a particular result. *...vote rigging on a massive scale.* **2** On a ship, the **rigging** is the ropes which support the ship's masts and sails. ◆◇◇◇ N-UNCOUNT N-UNCOUNT

right 1 correct, appropriate, or acceptable

right /raɪt/ **rights, righting, righted. 1** If something is **right**, it is correct and agrees with the facts. *That's absolutely right... Clocks never told the right time... The barman tells me you saw Ann on Tuesday morning. Is that right?* ▶ Also an adverb. *He guessed right about some things.* **2** If you do something in the **right** way or in the **right** place, you do it as or where it should be done or was planned to be done. *They have computerized systems to ensure delivery of the right pizza to the right place.* ▶ Also an adverb. *To make sure I did everything right, I bought a fat instruction book... I was pleased with my performance on Saturday – everything went right.* **3** If you say that someone is seen in all the **right** places or knows all the **right** people, you mean that they go to places which are socially acceptable or know people who are socially acceptable. **4** If someone is **right** about something, they are correct in what they say or think about it. *Am I right in* ◆◆◆◆ ADJ ADV: ADV after v ADJ ADV: ADV after v ADJ ADJ

thinking you're the only person in the club who's actually played at Wembley? **5** If something such as an action or decision is the **right** one, it is the best or most suitable one. *They decided the time was right for their escape.* **6** If something is not **right**, there is something unsatisfactory about the situation or thing that you are talking about. *The name Sue Anne never seemed quite right to Molly... He went into hospital and came out after a week. But he still wasn't right.* ADJ ADJ: v-link ADJ with brd-neg

7 If you **right** something or if it **rights** itself, it returns to its normal or correct state, after being in an undesirable state. *They recognise the urgency of righting the economy.* **8** If you **put** something **right**, you correct something that was wrong or that was causing problems. **9** If you **right** a wrong, you do something to make up for a mistake or something bad you did in the past. **10** If you **right** something that has fallen or rolled over or if it **rights** itself, it returns to its normal upright position. *The helicopter turned at an awful angle before righting itself.* VERB V n Also V pron-refl PHRASE VERB: V n VERB: V n V pron-refl

11 If you think that someone was **right** to do something, you think that there were good moral reasons why they did it. *I was right to issue that order and you were wrong to refuse.* **12** If someone has behaved in a way which is morally or legally right, you can say that they are **in the right**. You usually use this expression when the person is involved in an argument or dispute. *Legally, the local tax office is in the right.* **13 Right** is used to refer to activities or actions that are considered to be morally good and acceptable. *The BBC thought it was right and proper not to show the film.* ▶ Also a noun. *At least he knew right from wrong.* ♦ **right·ness** Many people have very strong opinions about the rightness or wrongness of abortion. **14** The **right** side of a material is the side that is intended to be seen and that faces outwards when it is made into something. **15 ● heart in the right place**: see **heart. ● it serves** you **right**: see **serve. ● on the right side** of someone: see **side**. ADJ: v-link ADJ PHRASE ADJ N-UNCOUNT N-UNCOUNT ADJ: ADJ n

right 2 direction and political groupings

right /raɪt/; also written **Right** for meaning 3. **1** The **right** is one of two opposite directions, sides, or positions. If you are facing north and you turn to the right, you will be facing east. In the word 'to', the 'o' is to the right of the 't'. *Ahead of you on the right will be a lovely garden... To her right was an orange grove.* ▶ Also an adverb. *Turn right into the street... He looked left. He looked right. He looked above him.* **2** Your **right** arm, leg, or ear, for example, is the one which is on the right side of your body. Your **right** shoe or glove is the one which is intended to be worn on your right foot or hand. **3** You can refer to people who support the political ideals of capitalism and conservatism as **the right**. *The Tory Right despise him... They see the shift to the Right as a worldwide phenomenon.* ◆◆◆◇ N-SING ADV: ADV after v ADJ: ADJ n N-COLL-SING: the N

right 3 entitlement

right /raɪt/ **rights. 1** Your **rights** are what you are morally or legally entitled to do or to have. *...voting rights.* **2** If you have a **right** to do or to have something, you are morally or legally entitled to do it or to have it. *People have the right to read any kind of material they wish.* **3** If you say that someone is **within their rights** to do something, you mean that they are morally or legally entitled to do it. *You were quite within your rights to refuse to co-operate with him.* **4** If you say that you **reserve the right** to do something, you mean that you will do it if you feel that it is necessary. *He reserved the right to change his mind.* ◆◆◆◇ N-COUNT N-SING PHRASE PHRASE

5 If someone has the **rights** to a story or book, they are legally allowed to publish it or reproduce it in another form, and nobody else can do so without their permission. *He'd tried to buy the film rights of all George Bernard Shaw's plays.* **6** If something is not the case but you think that it should be, you can say that **by rights**, it should be the case. *She did work which by rights should be done by someone else.* **7** If someone is a successful or respected person **in their own right**, they are successful or respected because of their own N-PLURAL: the N PHRASE PHRASE

efforts and talents rather than those of the people they are closely connected with.

right /raɪt/. **1** You use **right** in order to attract someone's attention or to indicate that you have dealt with one thing so you can go on to another. *Wonderful. Right, let's go to our next caller.* **2** You can use **right** to check whether what you have just said is right. *They have a small plane, right?* **3** You can say **'right'** to show that you are listening to what someone is saying and that you accept it or understand it. *'Your children may well come away speaking with a bit of a broad country accent'— 'Right.'—'because they're mixing with country children.'* **4** See also **all right**.
♦♦♦♦◇ ADV: ADV cl
CONVENTION PRAGMATICS
ADV PRAGMATICS

5 In informal English, you say **'right on'** to express your support, encouragement, or approval. **6** If someone says **'right you are'**, they are agreeing to do something very willingly. *'I want a word with you when you stop.'—'Right you are.'*
CONVENTION PRAGMATICS
PHRASE PRAGMATICS

right /raɪt/. **1** You can use the word **right** to emphasize the precise place, position, or time of something. *The back of a car appeared right in front of him... I had to decide right then.* **2** You can use the word **right** to emphasize how far something moves or extends or how long it continues. *She was kept very busy right up to the moment of her departure... It was taken right there on a conveyor belt.* **3** You can use the word **right** to emphasize the completeness of an action or of a state. *The candle had burned right down.* **4** You can use the word **right** to emphasize a noun, usually referring to something bad. *England's European Championship plans are in a right mess.*
♦♦♦♦◇ ADV: ADV adv/prep PRAGMATICS
ADV: ADV prep/adv PRAGMATICS
ADV: ADV adv/prep PRAGMATICS
ADJ: ADJ n PRAGMATICS INFORMAL, BRITISH

5 If you say that something happened **right** after a particular time or event or **right** before it, you mean that it happened immediately after or before it. *She then decided right before the opening to make a dramatic announcement.* **6** If you say **I'll be right there** or **I'll be right back**, you mean that you will get to a place or get back to it in a very short time. **7** If you do something **right away** or **right off**, you do it immediately. *He wants to see you right away... Right off I want to confess that I was wrong.* **8** You can use the expression **right now** to emphasize that you are referring to the present moment in time. *I'm warning you; stop it right now!*
ADV: ADV prep/adv PRAGMATICS
ADV PRAGMATICS SPOKEN PHRASE
PRAGMATICS SPOKEN
PHRASE PRAGMATICS SPOKEN

Right /raɪt/. The word **Right** is used in some British titles. It indicates high rank or status. *...The Right Reverend John Baker.*
ADV: ADV adj

'right angle, right angles; also spelled **right-angle. 1** A **right angle** is an angle of ninety degrees. A square has four right angles. **2** If two things are at **right angles**, they are situated so that they form an angle of 90° where they touch each other. You can also say that one thing is **at right angles** to another.
♦◇◇◇◇ N-COUNT PHRASE

'right-angled. A **right-angled** bend is a sharp bend that turns through approximately 90 degrees.
ADJ: ADJ n

right·eous /'raɪtʃəs/. If you think that someone behaves or lives in a way that is morally good you can say that they are **righteous**. People sometimes use **righteous** to express their disapproval when they think someone is only behaving in this way so that others will admire or support them. *He was full of righteous indignation.* ♦ **right·eous·ly** *They righteously maintain that they do not practise rationing.* ♦ **right·eous·ness** *Both sides in the dispute have been adopting a tone of moral righteousness.*
♦◇◇◇◇ ADJ-GRADED PRAGMATICS FORMAL
ADV-GRADED
N-UNCOUNT

right·ful /'raɪtfʊl/. If you say that someone or something has returned to its **rightful** place or position, they have returned to the place or position that you think they should have. *The Baltics' own democratic traditions would help them to regain their rightful place in Europe.* ♦ **right·ful·ly** *She's inherited the money which is rightfully hers.*
♦◇◇◇◇ ADJ: ADJ n PRAGMATICS
ADV

'right-hand. If something is on the **right-hand** side of something, it is positioned on the right of it. *...the upper right-hand corner of the picture.*
♦♦◇◇◇ ADJ: ADJ n

,right-hand 'drive. A **right-hand drive** vehicle has its steering wheel on the right side. It is designed to be driven in countries such as Britain and Japan where people drive on the left side of the road.
ADJ

,right-'handed. Someone who is **right-handed** uses their right hand rather than their left hand for activities such as writing and for picking things up. ▶ Also an adverb. *I batted left-handed and bowled right-handed.* ♦ **,right-'hander, right-handers** *Clothes, as everything else, were designed for right-handers.*
♦◇◇◇◇ ADJ
ADV: ADV after v
N-COUNT

'right-hand man, right-hand men. Someone's **right-hand man** is the person who acts as their chief assistant and helps them a lot in their work.
N-COUNT

right·ist /'raɪtɪst/ **rightists.** If someone is described as a **rightist**, they are politically conservative and traditional and support the ideals of capitalism. ▶ Also an adjective. *A rightist coup ousted him from power.*
N-COUNT
ADJ-GRADED

right·ly /'raɪtli/. **1** **Rightly** is used to indicate that what someone says or thinks is correct or accurate. *She attended one meeting only, if I remember rightly... He rightly assumed that the boy was hiding.* **2** If you say that someone **rightly** does something, you approve of the fact that they do it. *The crowd screamed for a penalty but the referee rightly ignored them.*
ADV
ADV PRAGMATICS

'right-minded. If you think that someone's opinions or beliefs are sensible and you agree with them, you can describe them as a **right-minded** person.
ADJ PRAGMATICS

righto /,raɪ'təʊ/; also spelled **right oh.** Some people say **righto** to show that they have heard what someone has said and are willing to do what they want. *Righto, Harry. I'll put Russ Clements in charge.*
EXCLAM PRAGMATICS BRITISH, INFORMAL

,right-of-'centre. You can describe a person or political party as **right-of-centre** if they have political views which are closer to capitalism and conservatism than to socialism but which are not very extreme.
ADJ

'right of way, rights of way. 1 A **right of way** is a public path across private land. **2** When someone has **right of way** or the **right of way**, they have the right to continue along a particular route, and other people must stop for them.
N-COUNT
N-UNCOUNT

'right-on. You can describe someone as **right-on** if they have modern, liberal, or left-wing ideas, especially if you disagree with them or want to make fun of them. ● See also **right**.
♦♦◇◇◇ ADJ-GRADED PRAGMATICS

'right-thinking. If you think that someone's opinions or beliefs are sensible and you agree with them, you can describe them as a **right-thinking** person.
ADJ PRAGMATICS

right·ward /'raɪtwəd/; the form **rightwards** is also used. If there is a **rightward** trend in the politics of a person or party, their views become more right-wing. ▶ Also an adverb. *The last-minute switching was strongly rightwards, from Labour to Liberal Democrat.*
ADJ: ADJ n
ADV: ADV after v

,right-'wing; also spelled **right wing** for meaning 2. **1** A **right-wing** person or group has conservative or capitalist views. ♦ **right-winger, right-wingers** *Many civilian right-wingers endorse this policy.* **2** The **right wing** of a political party consists of the members who have the most conservative or the most capitalist views.
♦♦♦◇◇ ADJ-GRADED
N-COUNT
N-SING: the N

rig·id /'rɪdʒɪd/. **1** Laws or systems that are **rigid** cannot be changed or varied, and are therefore considered to be rather severe; used showing disapproval. *Hospital routines for nurses are very rigid.* ♦ **ri·gid·ity** /rɪ'dʒɪdɪti/. *...the rigidity of government policy.* ♦ **rig·id·ly** *The caste system was so rigidly enforced that non-Hindus were not even allowed inside a Hindu house.* **2** If you disapprove of someone because you think they are not willing to change their way of thinking or behaving, you can describe them as **rigid**. **3** A **rigid** substance or object is stiff
♦♦◇◇◇ ADJ-GRADED PRAGMATICS
N-UNCOUNT
ADV-GRADED
ADJ-GRADED PRAGMATICS
ADJ-GRADED

R

and does not bend, stretch, or twist easily. ♦ **ri·gid·ity** ...*the strength and rigidity of glass.* **4** If someone goes **rigid**, their body becomes very straight and stiff, usually as a result of shock or fear. ♦ **rig·id·ly** *She stood rigidly and stared into the room.*

rig·ma·role /'rɪgmərəʊl/ **rigmaroles.** You can describe a long and complicated process as a **rigmarole**; used showing disapproval. *I couldn't be bothered to go through the rigmarole of changing clothes.*

rig·or mor·tis /ˌrɪgə 'mɔːtɪs/. In a dead body, when **rigor mortis** sets in, the joints and muscles become very stiff.

rig·or·ous /'rɪgərəs/. **1** A test, system, or procedure that is **rigorous** is very thorough and strict. *...rigorous military training.* ♦ **rig·or·ous·ly** *...rigorously conducted research.* **2** If someone is **rigorous** in the way that they do something, they are very careful and thorough in the way that they do it.

rig·our /'rɪgə/ **rigours;** spelled **rigor** in American English. **1** If you refer to the **rigours** of an activity or job, you mean the difficult or unpleasant things that are associated with it. *...the rigours of childbirth.* **2** If something is done with **rigour**, it is done in a strict, thorough way.

rile /raɪl/ **riles, riling, riled.** If something **riles** you, it makes you angry. ♦ **riled** *He saw I was riled.*

rim /rɪm/ **rims. 1** The **rim** of a container such as a cup is the edge that goes all the way round the top. **2** The **rim** of a circular object is its outside edge. *...a round mirror with white metal rim.* **3** See also **rimmed.**

rim·less /'rɪmləs/. **Rimless** glasses have no frame around the lenses or have a frame only along the top of the lenses.

rimmed /rɪmd/. If something is **rimmed** with a substance or colour, it has that substance or colour around its border. ► Also a combining form. *...horn-rimmed spectacles.*

rind /raɪnd/ **rinds. 1** The **rind** of a fruit such as a lemon or orange is its thick outer skin. **2** The **rind** of cheese or bacon is the hard outer edge which you do not usually eat.

ring 1 telephoning or making a sound

ring /rɪŋ/ **rings, ringing, rang, rung. 1** When you **ring** someone, you phone them. In American English you **call** someone. *If you'd like more information, ring the Hotline on 414 3929... She has rung home just once... Could someone ring for a taxi?* ► **Ring up** and **call up** mean the same as **ring.** *You can ring us up anytime... John rang up and invited himself over for dinner... A few months ago I rang up about some housing problems.* **2** If you **give** someone **a ring**, you phone them. *We'll give him a ring as soon as we get back.* **3** When a telephone **rings**, it makes a sound, to let you know that someone is phoning you. ► Also a noun. *After at least eight rings, an ancient-sounding maid answered the phone.* **4** When you **ring** a bell or when a bell **rings**, it makes a metallic sound. *He heard the school bell ring... The door was opened before she could ring the bell.* ► Also a noun. *There was a ring at the bell.* **5** If you **ring** for something, you ring a bell to call someone to bring it to you. If you **ring** for someone, you ring a bell so that they come to you. *He rang for the guard to let him out.* **6** If you say that a place is **ringing** with sound, usually pleasant sound, you mean that it is completely filled with it. *The whole place was ringing with music.* **7** If you say that someone's words **ring in** your **ears**, you mean that you remember them vividly, usually when you would rather forget them. *She shivered as the sound of that man's abuse rang in her ears.* **8** You can use the word **ring** to describe a quality that something such as a statement or argument seems to have. For example, if an argument **has a plausible ring**, it seems quite plausible. **9** If a statement **rings true**, it seems to be true or genuine. If it **rings hollow**, it does not seem to be true or genuine. **10** ● to **ring a bell**: see **bell**. **11** If you say that someone **rings the changes**, you

mean that they make alterations or improvements to the way something is organized or done.

ring around. See **ring round.**

ring back. If you **ring** someone **back**, you phone them either because they phoned you earlier and you were not there or because you did not finish an earlier telephone conversation. In American English, you **call** someone **back**. *Tell her I'll ring back in a few minutes.*

ring in. If you **ring in**, you phone a place where you regularly go or the place where you work, for example to tell the people there that you will not be coming to work that day. The American expression is **call in**.

ring off. When you **ring off**, you put down the receiver at the end of a telephone call. The American expression is **hang up**.

ring out. If a sound **rings out**, it can be heard loudly and clearly. *A single shot rang out.*

ring round. If you **ring round** or **ring around**, you phone several people, usually when you are trying to organize something or to find out some information. The American expression is **call round**. *She immediately started ringing round her friends and relatives.*

ring up. 1 See **ring 1. 2** If a shop assistant **rings up** a sale on a cash register, he or she presses the keys in order to record the amount that is being put into it. **3** If a company **rings up** an amount of money, usually a large amount, it makes that amount of money in sales or profits.

ring 2 shapes and groups

ring /rɪŋ/ **rings, ringing, ringed. 1** A **ring** is a small circle of metal that you wear on your finger. You wear it as an ornament or to show that you are engaged or married. **2** An object or substance that is in the shape of a circle can be described as a **ring**. *...a ring of blue smoke.* **3** A group of people or things arranged in a circle can be described as a **ring**. *...grilled fish surrounded by a ring of thinly cut carrots.* **4** If you say that someone **runs rings round** you or **runs rings around** you, you mean that they are a lot better or a lot more successful than you at a particular activity. *Mentally, he can still run rings round men half his age!* **5** If a building or place **is ringed** with something, it is surrounded by it. *The areas are sealed off and ringed by troops.* **6** A gas or electric **ring** is a small plate, usually on a cooker, that heats up. You heat up saucepans of food or water on it. **7** At a boxing match or circus, the **ring** is the place where the contest or performance takes place. It is an enclosed space with seats round it. **8** You can refer to an organized group of people who are involved in an illegal activity as a **ring**. *...an international spy ring.*

ring·er /'rɪŋə/ **ringers. 1** If you say that one person is **a dead ringer** for another, you mean that they look exactly like each other. **2** A bell **ringer** is someone who rings church bells or hand bells as a hobby.

'ring-fence, ring-fences, ring-fencing, ring-fenced. To **ring-fence** a grant or fund means to put restrictions on it, so that it can only be used for a particular purpose. *There should be ring-fenced funding for local crime prevention initiatives.*

'ring finger, ring fingers. Your **ring finger** is the third finger of your left or right hand. In some countries, people wear a wedding ring or engagement ring on this finger.

ring·ing /'rɪŋɪŋ/. **1** A **ringing** sound is loud and can be heard very clearly. *He hit the metal steps with a ringing crash.* **2** **Ringing** is a continuous sound made by a telephone, a bell, or several bells. *She was jolted out of her sleep by the ringing of the telephone. ...the ringing of church bells.* **3** A **ringing** statement or declaration is one that is made forcefully and is intended to make a very powerful impression.

ring·leader /'rɪŋliːdə/ **ringleaders.** The **ringleaders** in a quarrel, disturbance, or illegal activity

are the people who started it and who cause the most trouble; used showing disapproval.

ring·let /'rɪŋlət/ **ringlets. Ringlets** are long curls of hair that hang down. N-COUNT

ring·master /'rɪŋmɑːstə, -mæst-/ **ringmasters.** A circus **ringmaster** is the person who introduces the performers and the animals. N-COUNT

'**ring-pull, ring-pulls.** A **ring-pull** is a metal strip that you pull off the top of a can of drink in order to open it. The American term is **tab.** N-COUNT BRITISH

'**ring road, ring roads.** A **ring road** is a road that goes all the way round the edge of a town so that traffic does not have to go through the town centre. N-COUNT BRITISH

ring·side /'rɪŋsaɪd/. **1** The **ringside** is the area immediately around the edge of a circus ring, boxing ring, or show jumping ring. **2** If you have a **ringside** seat or a **ringside** view, you have a clear and uninterrupted view of an event. N-SING / ADJ: ADJ n

rink /rɪŋk/ **rinks.** A **rink** is a large area where people go to ice-skate or roller-skate. ◆◇◇◇◇ N-COUNT

rinse /rɪns/ **rinses, rinsing, rinsed. 1** When you **rinse** something, you wash it in clean water in order to remove dirt or soap from it. ► Also a noun. *Clean skin means plenty of lather followed by a rinse with water.* **2** If you **rinse** your mouth, you wash it with a mouthful of water or an antiseptic mouthwash. ► **Rinse out** means the same as **rinse.** *After her meal she invariably rinsed out her mouth.* **3** A hair **rinse** is a dye which gradually fades after you have washed your hair a number of times rather than being permanent. VERB: V n / N-COUNT / VERB: V n / PHRASAL VB V P noun Also V n P / N-COUNT

riot /'raɪət/ **riots, rioting, rioted. 1** When there is a **riot**, a crowd of people behave violently in a public place. For example, they fight or damage buildings and vehicles. **2** If people **riot**, they behave violently in a public place. ♦ **ri·ot·er, rioters** *The militia dispersed the rioters.* ♦ **riot·ing** *At least fifteen people are now known to have died in three days of rioting.* **3** If people **run riot**, they behave in a wild and uncontrolled manner. **4** If someone in authority **reads** you **the riot act**, they tell you that you will be punished unless you start behaving as they would like you to. **5** If you say that there is **a riot of** something pleasant such as colour, you mean that there is a large amount of various types of it. *With Indian cuisine, you expect a riot of tastes and spices.* **6** If something such as imagination or speculation **runs riot**, it expresses itself or spreads in an uncontrolled way. *We have no proof and when there is no proof, rumour runs riot.* ♦♦♦◇◇ N-COUNT / VERB: V / N-COUNT / N-UNCOUNT / PHRASE / PHRASE / N-SING: a N of n PRAGMATICS / PHRASE

ri·ot·ous /'raɪətəs/. If you describe someone's behaviour or lifestyle as **riotous**, you mean that they behave in an excessive and uncontrolled way, for example by drinking or celebrating a lot, or making a lot of noise. ADJ-GRADED FORMAL

ri·ot·ous·ly /'raɪətəsli/. If you describe something as **riotously** funny, you mean that it is extremely funny and makes you laugh a lot. *...a slapstick affair which I found riotously amusing.* ADV

'**riot police.** The **riot police** are the section of a police force that is trained to deal with rioters. ◆◇◇◇◇ N-COLL-SING

'**riot shield, riot shields. Riot shields** are seethrough shields used by police officers to control crowds and protect themselves from attack. N-COUNT

rip /rɪp/ **rips, ripping, ripped. 1** If you **rip** something, you tear it forcefully with your hands or with a tool such as a knife. If something **rips**, it is torn forcefully. *I tried not to rip the paper as I unwrapped it... I felt the banner rip as we were pushed in opposite directions.* **2** A **rip** is a long cut or split in something made of cloth or paper. **3** If you **rip** something away, you remove it quickly and forcefully. *He ripped away a wire that led to the alarm button... She ripped off her dress and let it fall to the floor.* **4** If something **rips** into someone or something or **rips** through them, it enters that person or thing so quickly and forcefully that it often goes completely through them before heading in another direction. *A volley of bullets ripped into the facing* ♦♦◇◇◇ V-ERG V / N-COUNT / VERB V n with adv / VERB V prep/adv

wall... A violent streak of pain ripped through her whole body. **5** If you **let rip**, you do something forcefully and without restraint. *Turn the guitars up full and let rip.* PHRASE INFORMAL

rip apart. If something **rips** people **apart**, it causes them to quarrel or fight very bitterly, so that they can no longer be friends. *Communal carnage was ripping the country apart.* PHRASAL VB V n P Also V P n

rip off. If someone **rips** you **off**, they cheat you by charging you too much money for something or by selling you something that is faulty. *Ticket touts ripped off soccer fans to the tune of £138,000 in the FA Cup Final.* ● See also **rip-off.** PHRASAL VB V n P V P noun INFORMAL

rip up. If you **rip** something **up**, you tear it into small pieces. *I think he would rip up the letter.* PHRASAL VB V n P V P noun

R.I.P /,ɑːr aɪ 'piː/. **R.I.P.** is often written or engraved on gravestones. It is an abbreviation for 'rest in peace'. CONVENTION

rip·cord /'rɪpkɔːd/ **ripcords.** A **ripcord** is the cord that you pull to open a parachute. N-COUNT

ripe /raɪp/ **riper, ripest. 1 Ripe** fruit or grain is fully grown and ready to eat. *...a large, yellowy-brown ripe banana.* ♦ **ripe·ness** *Test the figs for ripeness.* **2** If a situation is **ripe for** a particular development or event, you mean that development or event is likely to happen soon. *This society is ripe for change.* **3** If someone lives to a **ripe old age**, they live until they are very old. *He lived to the ripe old age of 95.* **4** If you say **the time is ripe** for something, you mean that a suitable time has arrived for it to happen or be done. *The time is ripe to send its first female ambassador to the region.* ♦♦◇◇◇ ADJ-GRADED / N-UNCOUNT / ADJ-GRADED: v-link ADJ for n/-ing / PHRASE / PHRASE

rip·en /'raɪpən/ **ripens, ripening, ripened.** When crops **ripen**, they become ripe. *I'm waiting for the apples to ripen... You can ripen the tomatoes on a sunny windowsill.* ♦◇◇◇◇ V-ERG V V n

'**rip-off, rip-offs. 1** If you say that something that you bought was a **rip-off**, you mean that you have been cheated, because you were charged too much money or because the item was faulty. **2** If you say that something is a **rip-off** of something else, you mean that it is a copy of that thing and has no original features of its own. ♦◇◇◇◇ N-COUNT INFORMAL / N-COUNT INFORMAL

ri·poste /rɪ'pɒst, AM -'pəʊst/ **ripostes. 1** A **riposte** is a quick, clever reply to something that someone has said. **2** You can refer to an action as a **riposte** to something when it is a reaction to that thing. *The operation is being seen as a swift riposte to the killing of a senior army commander.* N-COUNT WRITTEN / N-COUNT JOURNALISM

rip·ple /'rɪpəl/ **ripples, rippling, rippled. 1 Ripples** are little waves on the surface of water caused by the wind or by something moving in or on the water. **2** When the surface of an area of water **ripples**, a number of little waves appear on it. *I could see the dawn breeze rippling the shining water.* **3** When the wind **ripples** plants or trees, they move in a wave-like motion. *The tops of the trees rippled in the breeze.* **4** If something such as a feeling **ripples** through a person or group, it gradually spreads across them. *Murmurs of admiration rippled through the crowd of guests.* **5** If an event causes **ripples**, its effects gradually spread, causing several other events to happen one after the other. *The ripples of Europe's currency crisis continue to be felt in most of the ERM's member states.* ♦◇◇◇◇ N-COUNT / V-ERG: V V n / V-ERG: V n / V LITERARY VERB V prep/adv across/overn LITERARY / N-COUNT

'**rip-roaring.** If you describe something as **rip-roaring**, you mean that it is very exciting and full of energy. *...a rip-roaring movie with a great array of special effects.* ADJ: ADJ n INFORMAL

rip·tide /'rɪptaɪd/ **riptides;** also spelled **rip-tide.** A **riptide** is a rough, dangerous area of sea where two different currents meet or where the water is extremely deep. N-COUNT

rise /raɪz/ **rises, rising, rose, risen. 1** If something **rises**, it moves upwards. *Wilson's ice-cold eyes watched the smoke rise from his cigarette.* ► **Rise up** means the same as **rise.** *Spray rose up from the surface of the water.* **2** If the level of something such as the water in a river **rises**, it becomes higher. **3** If land **rises**, it slopes upwards. *He looked up the slope* ♦♦♦♦ VERB: V V from/ton PHRASAL VB: V P V P from/ton VERB: V VERB V prep/adv V

*of land that rose from the house... The ground begins
to rise some 20 yards away.* **4** You can say that
something **rises** when it appears as a large tall
shape. *The building rose before him, tall and stately.*
▶ **Rise up** means the same as **rise**. *The White
Mountains rose up before me.*
5 A **rise** is an area of ground that slopes upwards.
6 When the sun or moon **rises**, it appears from below
the horizon.
7 When you **rise**, you stand up. *Luther rose slowly
from the chair... He looked at Livy and Mark, who had
risen to greet him.* **8** When you **rise**, you get out of bed.
Tony had risen early.
9 If an amount **rises**, it increases. *Pre-tax profits rose
from £842,000 to £1.82m... Tourist trips of all kinds in
Britain rose by 10.5% between 1977 and 1987... Exports
in June rose 1.5% to a record £30.91 billion.* **10** A **rise in**
the amount of something is an increase in it. *...the
prospect of another rise in interest rates.* **11** A **rise** is an
increase in your wages or your salary. *The American
word is* **raise**. *He will get a pay rise of nearly £4,000.*
12 The **rise of** something or someone is an increase in
their popularity, success, power, or influence. *The rise
of racism in America is a serious concern. ...the ruthlessness that explains his rise.* **13** If someone **rises** to a
higher position or status, they become more important, successful, or powerful. *He has risen rapidly
through the ranks of government.* ▶ **Rise up** means
the same as **rise**. *I started with Hoover 26 years ago in
sales and rose up through the ranks.*
14 If the wind **rises**, it becomes stronger. **15** If a
sound **rises** or if someone's voice **rises**, it becomes
louder or higher. *His voice rose almost to a scream.*
16 If a sound **rises** from a group of people, it comes
from them. *There were low, muffled voices rising from
the hallway.* ▶ **Rise up** means the same as **rise**. *From
the people, a cheer rose up.* **17** If an emotion **rises** in
someone, they suddenly feel it very intensely so that it
affects their behaviour. *A tide of emotion rose and
clouded his judgement.* **18** If your colour **rises** or if a
blush **rises** in your cheeks, you turn red because you
feel angry, embarrassed, or excited.
19 When the people in a country **rise**, they rebel
against the people in authority and start fighting
them. *The National Convention has promised armed
support to any people who wish to rise against armed
oppression.* ▶ **Rise up** means the same as **rise**. *A woman called on the population to rise up against the government.* ♦ **ris·ing, risings** *...popular risings against
tyrannical rulers.*
20 If something **gives rise to** an event or situation, it
causes that event or situation to happen. *Low levels of
choline in the body can give rise to high blood-
pressure.* **21** ● to **rise to the bait**: see **bait**. ● to **rise to
the challenge**: see **challenge**. ● to **rise to the occasion**: see **occasion**.

rise above. If you **rise above** a difficulty or problem,
you manage not to let it affect you. *It tells the story of
an aspiring young man's attempt to rise above the
squalor of the street.*

rise up. See **rise**.

ris·en /'rɪzən/. **Risen** is the past participle of **rise**.

ris·er /'raɪzə/ **risers.** An early **riser** is someone who
likes to get up early in the morning. A late **riser** is
someone who likes to get up late.

ris·ible /'rɪzɪbəl/. If you describe something as **ris-
ible**, you mean that it is ridiculous and does not deserve to be taken seriously.

risk /rɪsk/ **risks, risking, risked. 1** If there is a
risk of something unpleasant, there is a possibility
that it will happen. *There is a small risk of brain
damage from the procedure... In all the confusion,
there's a serious risk that the main issues will be forgotten. ...mentally disordered women who pose a serious risk to the public.* **2** If you say that something
or someone is a **risk**, you mean they are likely to
cause harm. *It's being overfat that constitutes a
health risk... He was not seen as a risk to national security.* **3** If someone or something is put **at risk**,
they are put in a situation where something un-

VERB
V prep/adv
LITERARY

PHRASAL VB
V P prep/adv

N-COUNT
VERB: V

VERB
V from n
V
FORMAL
VERB: V

VERB
V from/to/by
amount
V amount
N-COUNT:
N in n
N-COUNT
BRITISH

N-SING:
the N of n

VERB
V prep
PHRASAL VB
V P prep

VERB: V
VERB: V
V to n
VERB
V from n
PHRASAL VB
V P
VERB
V

VERB: V

VERB: V
V against n

PHRASAL VB:
V P
V P against n
N-COUNT

PHRASE

PHRASAL VB
V P n

PHRASAL VB

N-COUNT:
supp N

ADJ-GRADED
PRAGMATICS
FORMAL

◆◆◆◇
N-VAR

N-COUNT

PHRASE

*pleasant might happen to them. Up to 25,000 jobs
are still at risk... An estimated seven million people
are at risk of starvation.*
4 If something that you do is a **risk**, it might have unpleasant or undesirable results. *You're taking a big
risk showing this to Kravis.* **5** If you **run the risk** of doing or experiencing something undesirable, you do
something knowing that the undesirable thing might
happen as a result. *The officers had run the risk of being dismissed... I knew I was running a great many
risks.* **6** If you do something **at the risk of** something
unpleasant happening, you do it even though you
know that the unpleasant thing might happen as a result. *At the risk of being repetitive, I will say again that
statistics are only a guide.* **7** If you tell someone that
they are doing something **at their own risk**, you are
warning them that, if they are harmed, it will be their
own responsibility.
8 If you **risk** something unpleasant, you do something which might result in that thing happening or
affecting you. *Those who fail to register risk severe penalties... Pregnant women who are heavy drinkers risk
damaging the unborn foetus.* **9** If you **risk** doing
something, you do it, even though you know that it
might have undesirable consequences. *The skipper
was not willing to risk taking his ship through the
straits... At the top, I risked a glance back.* **10** If you **risk**
someone's life or something that is worth having, you
do something which might result in it being lost or
harmed. *She risked her own life to help a disabled
woman.*
11 If you are considered a good **risk**, a bank or shop
thinks that it is safe to lend you money or let you have
goods without paying for them at the time.

'risk-taking. Risk-taking means choosing to act in
a bold way, possibly with unpleasant or undesirable
results.

risky /'rɪski/ **riskier, riskiest.** If an activity or action is **risky**, it is dangerous or likely to fail. *Investing in airlines is a very risky business... It's risky to
assume that we know what voters will be thinking in
a year's time.*

ri·sot·to /rɪ'zɒtəʊ/ **risottos. Risotto** is an Italian
dish consisting of rice cooked with ingredients such
as tomatoes, meat, or fish.

ris·qué /'rɪskeɪ, AM rɪ'skeɪ/. If you describe something as **risqué**, you mean that it is slightly rude because it refers to sex. *...risqué dance routines.*

rite /raɪt/ **rites.** A **rite** is a traditional ceremony
that is carried out in a particular group or society.
...a fertility rite. ● See also **last rites**.

ritu·al /'rɪtʃʊəl/ **rituals. 1** A **ritual** is a religious
service or other ceremony which involves a series of
actions performed in a fixed order. ♦ **ritu·al·is·tic**
/ˌrɪtʃʊə'lɪstɪk/. *...a ritualistic celebration upon the
successful harvesting of rice.* **2 Ritual** activities happen as part of a ritual or tradition. *...fastings and
ritual dancing.* ♦ **ritu·al·ly** *The statue was ritually
bathed and purified.* **3** A **ritual** is a way of behaving
or a series of actions which people regularly carry
out in a particular situation, because it is their custom to do so. *Cocktails at the Plaza was a nightly
ritual of their sophisticated world... After the ritual
courtesies, I took a few steps.* ♦ **ritu·al·is·tic** *Each
evening she bursts into her apartment with a ritualistic shout of 'Honey I'm home!'*

ritu·al·ized /'rɪtʃʊəlaɪzd/; also spelled **ritualised** in
British English. **Ritualized** acts are carried out in a
fixed, structured way rather than being spontaneous. *...highly ritualised courtship displays.*

ritzy /'rɪtsi/ **ritzier, ritziest.** If you describe something as **ritzy**, you mean that it is fashionable, glamorous, or expensive. *Palm Springs has a lot of ritzy
restaurants.*

ri·val /'raɪvəl/ **rivals, rivalling, rivalled;** spelled
rivaling, rivaled in American English. **1** Your **rival**
is a person, business, or organization who you are
competing against in the same area or for the same
things. *The world champion finished more than two
seconds ahead of his nearest rival. ...a dispute be-*

N-COUNT

N-COUNT

PHRASE

PHRASE

PHRASE
PRAGMATICS

VERB
V n/-ing

VERB
V -ing/n

VERB
V n

N-COUNT:
supp N

N-UNCOUNT

◆◆◇◇◇
ADJ-GRADED

N-VAR

ADJ-GRADED

◆◆◇◇◇
N-COUNT

◆◆◇◇◇
N-VAR
ADJ-GRADED

ADJ: ADJ n

ADV

N-VAR

ADJ

ADJ-GRADED

ADJ-GRADED
INFORMAL

◆◆◆◇
N-COUNT

tween *rival teenage gangs.* **2** If you say that some- N-COUNT:
one or something has no **rivals** or is without **rival**, with brd-neg
you mean that it is best of its type. *He is a pastry
chef without rival.* **3** If you say that one thing **rivals** VERB
another, you mean that they are both of the same V n
standard or quality. *An epidemic to rival that which
killed 26,000 in 1989 may hit the UK.*

ri·val·ry /ˈraɪvəlri/ **rivalries.** Rivalry is competi- ◆◆◇◇◇
tion or conflict between people, businesses, or or- N-VAR
ganizations who are in the same area or want the
same things.

riv·en /ˈrɪvən/. If a country or organization is **riven** ADJ
by conflict, its unity is torn apart by a violent disagreement between its people. *The Communist
movement has been riven with factional fighting.*

riv·er /ˈrɪvə/ **rivers. 1** A **river** is a large amount of ◆◆◆◆◇
fresh water flowing continuously in a long line N-COUNT
across the land. *...a chemical works on the banks of
the river. ...boating on the River Danube.* **2** ● **to sell**
someone **down the river:** see **sell.**

'river bank, river banks; also spelled **riverbank.** N-COUNT
A **river bank** is the land along the edge of a river.

'river basin, river basins. A **river basin** is the N-COUNT
area of land which is drained of water by a river and
its tributaries.

'river bed, river beds; also spelled **riverbed.** A N-COUNT
river bed is the ground which a river flows over.

riv·er·boat /ˈrɪvəbəʊt/ **riverboats.** A **riverboat** is a N-COUNT:
large boat that carries passengers along a river. also by N

riv·er·front /ˈrɪvəfrʌnt/. The **riverfront** is an area N-SING
of land next to a river with buildings such as
houses, shops, or restaurants on it.

river·side /ˈrɪvəsaɪd/. The **riverside** is the area of ◆◇◇◇◇
land by the banks of a river. N-SING

riv·et /ˈrɪvɪt/ **rivets, riveting, riveted. 1** If you ◆◇◇◇◇
are riveted by something, it fascinates you and VERB
holds your interest completely. *As a child I remem-* beV-ed
ber being riveted by my grandfather's appearance... beV-ed to n
He was riveted to the John Wayne movie. ♦ **riv·et-** ADJ-GRADED
·ing *I find snooker riveting.* **2** A **rivet** is a short met- N-COUNT
al pin with a flat head which is used to fasten flat
pieces of metal together.

rivu·let /ˈrɪvjʊlɪt/ **rivulets.** A **rivulet** is a small N-COUNT
stream. FORMAL

RN /ˌɑːr ˈen/. **RN** is a written abbreviation for 'Royal BRITISH
Navy', the navy of the United Kingdom.

RNA /ˌɑːr en ˈeɪ/. **RNA** is an acid in the chromo- ◆◇◇◇◇
somes of the cells of living things, and plays a vital N-UNCOUNT
part in passing information about a cell's protein TECHNICAL
structure between different cells. **RNA** is an abbreviation for 'ribonucleic acid'.

RNAS. RNAS is a written abbreviation for 'Royal
Naval Air Services', one of the units which make up
the United Kingdom's armed forces.

roach /rəʊtʃ/ **roaches.** The form **roach** can be ◆◆◇◇◇
used as the plural for meaning 2. **1** A **roach** is the N-COUNT
same as a **cockroach.** *...a seedy, roach-infested* AMERICAN
apartment. **2** A **roach** is a fish that lives in Euro- N-COUNT
pean rivers and lakes.

road /rəʊd/ **roads. 1** A **road** is a long piece of hard ◆◆◆◆◇
ground which is built between two places so that N-COUNT:
people can drive or ride easily from one place to the also by N
other. *There was very little traffic on the roads... We
just go straight up the Bristol Road... Buses carry 30
per cent of those travelling by road.* **2** In informal PHRASE
English, if you **hit the road,** you set out on a jour- INFORMAL
ney. **3** If you are **on the road,** you are going on a PHRASE
long journey or a series of journeys by road. **4** The N-COUNT
road to a particular result is the means of achieving
it or the process of achieving it. *We are bound to see
some ups and downs along the road to recovery.* **5** If PHRASE
you say that someone is **on the road** to something,
you mean that they are likely to achieve it. *The government took another step on the road to political
reform.* **6** ● **the end of the road:** see **end.**

road·block /ˈrəʊdblɒk/ **roadblocks;** also spelled ◆◇◇◇◇
road block. When the police or the army set up a N-COUNT
roadblock, they stop all the traffic on a particular
road, for example because they are looking for a
criminal.

road·hog /ˈrəʊdhɒg/ **roadhogs;** also spelled **road** N-COUNT
hog. If you describe someone as a **roadhog,** you INFORMAL
mean that they drive in an inconsiderate way which
is dangerous to other people.

road·house /ˈrəʊdhaʊs/ **roadhouses.** A **road-** N-COUNT
house is a bar or restaurant on a road outside a city. AMERICAN

road·ie /ˈrəʊdi/ **roadies.** A **roadie** is a person who N-COUNT
transports and sets up equipment for a pop band.

'road pricing. In Britain, **road pricing** is a system N-UNCOUNT
of making motorists pay money for driving on cer-
tain roads.

road·show /ˈrəʊdʃəʊ/ **roadshows.** A **roadshow** is ◆◇◇◇◇
a travelling show organized by a radio station, N-COUNT
magazine, or company.

road·side /ˈrəʊdsaɪd/ **roadsides.** The **roadside** is ◆◇◇◇◇
the area at the edge of a road. *Bob was forced to* N-COUNT
leave the car at the roadside. ...roadside cafes.

road·ster /ˈrəʊdstə/ **roadsters.** A **roadster** is a car N-COUNT
with no roof and only two seats.

'road tax. In Britain, **road tax** is a tax paid every N-UNCOUNT
year by the owners of every motor vehicle which is
being used on the roads.

road·way /ˈrəʊdweɪ/ **roadways.** The **roadway** is N-COUNT
the part of a road that is used by traffic. *Marks in
the roadway seem to indicate that he skidded.*

road·works /ˈrəʊdwɜːks/. **Roadworks** are repairs N-PLURAL
or other work being done on a road.

roam /rəʊm/ **roams, roaming, roamed.** If you ◆◇◇◇◇
roam an area or **roam around** it, you wander or VERB
travel around it without having a particular pur- V n
pose. *Barefoot children roamed the streets... He was* V adv/prep
able to roam around and explore places. Also V

roan /rəʊn/ **roans.** A **roan** is a horse that is brown N-COUNT
or black with some white hairs.

roar /rɔː/ **roars, roaring, roared. 1** If something, ◆◇◇◇◇
usually a vehicle, **roars** somewhere, it goes there VERB
very fast, making a loud noise. *A police car roared* V adv/prep
past... The plane roared down the runway for take- WRITTEN
off. **2** If something **roars,** it makes a very loud noise. VERB
Her heart was pounding and the blood roared in her V
ears. ► Also a noun. *...the roar of traffic.* N-COUNT
3 If someone **roars** with laughter, they laugh in a very
noisy way. ► Also a noun. *There were roars of laughter* V with n
as he stood up. **4** If someone **roars,** they shout some- N-COUNT
thing in a very loud voice. *'I'll kill you for that,' he* VERB: V
roared... The general was roaring for his dinner... The V for n
audience roared its approval. ► Also a noun. *There* WRITTEN
was a roar of approval. N-COUNT
5 When a lion **roars,** it makes the loud sound that VERB: V
lions typically make. ► Also a noun. *...the roar of lions* N-COUNT
in the distance.

roar·ing /ˈrɔːrɪŋ/. **1** A **roaring** fire has large flames ◆◇◇◇◇
and is sending out a lot of heat. ADJ: ADJ n
2 If something is a **roaring** success, it is very success- ADJ: ADJ n
ful indeed. **3** If someone **does a roaring trade** in a PHRASE
type of goods, they sell a lot of them. *Salesmen of unofficial souvenirs have also been doing a roaring trade.*

roast /rəʊst/ **roasts, roasting, roasted. 1** When ◆◆◇◇◇
you **roast** meat or other food, you cook it by dry VERB: V n
heat in an oven or over a fire, often adding fat or oil.
2 **Roast** meat has been cooked by roasting. *...deli-* ADJ: ADJ n
cious roast beef. **3** A **roast** is a piece of meat that is N-COUNT
cooked by roasting.

rob /rɒb/ **robs, robbing, robbed. 1** If someone **is** ◆◆◇◇◇
robbed, they have had money or property stolen from VERB
them. *Mrs Yacoub was robbed of her £3,000 designer* beV-ed ofn
watch. **2** If someone **is robbed** of something that Also V n
they deserve, have, or need, it is taken away from VERB
them. *When Miles Davis died last September, jazz* beV-ed ofn
was robbed of its most distinctive voice... Bad luck V n ofn
robbed him of victory.

rob·ber /ˈrɒbə/ **robbers.** A **robber** is someone ◆◇◇◇◇
who steals money or property from a bank, a shop, N-COUNT
or a vehicle, often by using force. *Armed robbers
broke into a jeweller's.* ♦ **rob·bery, robberies.** N-VAR
Robbery is the crime committed by a robber. *The
gang members committed dozens of armed robberies.*

robe /rəʊb/ **robes. 1** A **robe** is a long, loose piece ◆◇◇◇◇
of clothing, usually worn in religious or official cer- N-COUNT
emonies. You can describe someone as wearing a

robe or as wearing **robes**. ♦ **-robed** ...*a brown-* COMB
robed monk. **2** A **robe** is a piece of clothing, usually N-COUNT
made of towelling, which people wear in the house,
especially when they have just got up or had a bath.

rob·in /'rɒbɪn/ **robins**. **1** A **robin** is a small, brown N-COUNT
European bird. The male has an orangey-red neck
and breast. **2** A **robin** is a North American bird, N-COUNT
similar to a blackbird in size and shape. The male
has a reddish-brown breast. **3** See also **round-
robin**.

ro·bot /'rəʊbɒt, AM -bət/ **robots**. A **robot** is a ma- ◆◇◇◇
chine, often shaped like a person, which is pro- N-COUNT
grammed to move and perform certain tasks automatically.

ro·bot·ic /rəʊ'bɒtɪk/. **1** Robotic equipment can ADJ: ADJ n
move and perform certain tasks automatically. **2** If ADJ-GRADED
you describe someone as **robotic**, you mean that
they speak or move in a stiff and mechanical way
like a robot.

ro·bot·ics /rəʊ'bɒtɪks/. Robotics is the science of N-UNCOUNT
designing and building robots.

ro·bust /rəʊ'bʌst, 'rəʊbʌst/. **1** Someone or some- ◆◆◇◇◇
thing that is **robust** is very strong or healthy. ♦ **ro-** ADJ-GRADED
·bust·ly *He became robustly healthy.* ♦ **ro·bust·** ADV-GRADED
·ness *The robustness of diesel engines is another at-* N-UNCOUNT
tractive quality. **2** Robust views or opinions are
strongly held and forcefully expressed. ♦ **ro·bust·ly** ADV-GRADED
We have to defend our position very robustly indeed.
♦ **ro·bust·ness** ...*a prominent industrialist re-* N-UNCOUNT
nowned for the robustness of his right-wing views.

rock /rɒk/ **rocks, rocking, rocked**. **1** Rock is ◆◆◆◇◇
the hard substance which the Earth is made of. *The* N-UNCOUNT
hills above the valley are bare rock. **2** A **rock** is a N-COUNT
large piece of rock that sticks up out of the ground
or the sea, or that has broken away from a moun-
tain or a cliff. **3** A **rock** is a piece of rock that is N-COUNT
small enough for you to pick up. **4** If you are caught PHRASE
between a rock and a hard place, you are in a difficult situation where you have to choose between
two equally unpleasant courses of action. **5** If you PHRASE
have an alcoholic drink such as whisky **on the
rocks**, you have it with ice cubes in it. **6** If some- PHRASE
thing such as a marriage or a business is **on the
rocks**, it is experiencing very severe difficulties and
looks likely to end very soon.
7 When something **rocks** or when you **rock** it, it V-ERG
moves slowly and regularly backwards and forwards V prep/adv
or from side to side. *His body rocked from side to side* V n
with the train... She sat on the porch and rocked the Also V
baby. **8** If an explosion or an earthquake **rocks** a V-ERG: V n
building or an area, it causes the building or area to V
shake. *The buildings rocked under heavy shell-fire*. **9** If VERB
an event or a piece of news **rocks** a group or society, it V n
shocks them or makes their position less secure. ...*the* JOURNALISM
latest scandal to rock the monarchy. **10** ● to **rock the
boat**: see **boat**.
11 Rock or **rock music** is loud music with a strong N-UNCOUNT
beat that is usually played and sung by a small group
of people using a variety of instruments including
electric guitars and drums.

rocka·bil·ly /ˌrɒkə'bɪli/. Rockabilly is a kind of fast N-UNCOUNT
rock music which developed in the southern United
States in the 1950s.

rock and 'roll; also spelled **rock'n'roll**. Rock and ◆◇◇◇◇
roll is a kind of popular music developed in the N-UNCOUNT
1950s which has a strong beat and is played on
electrical instruments.

rock 'bottom; also spelled **rock-bottom**. **1** If ◆◇◇◇◇
something has reached **rock bottom**, it is at such a N-UNCOUNT
low level that it cannot go any lower. *Morale in the
armed forces was at rock bottom... Prices have hit
rock bottom*. **2** A **rock-bottom** price is very low; ADJ
used mainly in advertisements.

rock climber, rock climbers. A **rock climber** is N-COUNT
a person whose hobby or sport is climbing cliffs or
large rocks. ♦ **rock climbing** *He liked outdoor ac-* N-UNCOUNT
tivities like sailing and rock-climbing.

rock·er /'rɒkə/ **rockers**. **1** A **rocker** is a chair that ◆◇◇◇◇
is built on two curved pieces of wood so that you N-COUNT
can rock backwards and forwards while you are sit- AMERICAN

ting in it. The British term is **rocking chair**. **2** A N-COUNT
rocker is someone who performs rock music.

rock·ery /'rɒkəri/ **rockeries**. A **rockery** is a raised N-COUNT
part of a garden which is built of stones and soil, BRITISH
with small plants growing between the rocks.

rock·et /'rɒkɪt/ **rockets, rocketing, rocketed.** ◆◆◆◇
1 A **rocket** is a space vehicle that is shaped like a N-COUNT
long tube. **2** A **rocket** is a missile containing explo- N-COUNT
sive and powered by gas. **3** A **rocket** is a firework N-COUNT
that quickly goes high into the air and then explodes. **4** If things such as prices or social problems VERB: V
rocket, they increase very quickly and suddenly. V-ing
Rocketing crime forces inner city communities to live JOURNALISM
in terror.

rocket launcher, rocket launchers. A **rocket** N-COUNT
launcher is a cylindrical device that can be carried
and used by soldiers for firing rockets.

rock garden, rock gardens. A **rock garden** is ◆◇◇◇◇
the same as a **rockery**. N-COUNT

rock-'hard; also spelled **rock hard**. Something ADJ
that is **rock-hard** is very hard indeed. *During the
dry season the land is rock hard*.

rocking chair, rocking chairs. A **rocking chair** N-COUNT
is a chair that is built on two curved pieces of wood
so that you can rock backwards and forwards when
you are sitting in it.

rocking horse, rocking horses. A **rocking** N-COUNT
horse is a toy horse which a child can sit on and
rock backwards and forwards.

rock-like. Something that is **rock-like** is very ADJ
strong or firm, and is unlikely to change. *He affected
fellow writers with his rock-like integrity*.

rock'n'roll /ˌrɒkən'rəʊl/. See **rock and roll**.

rock pool, rock pools. A **rock pool** is a small N-COUNT
pool between rocks on the seashore. BRITISH

rock salt. Rock salt is salt that is formed in the N-UNCOUNT
ground. It is obtained by mining.

rock-'solid; also spelled **rock solid**. **1** Something ADJ
that is **rock-solid** is extremely hard. **2** If you de- ADJ
scribe someone or something as **rock-solid**, you ap- PRAGMATICS
prove of them because they are extremely reliable
or unlikely to change. *Mayhew is a man of rock-
solid integrity... I'll need rock solid proof... The firm
is rock-solid financially*.

rock 'steady; also spelled **rock-steady**. Something ADJ
that is **rock steady** is very firm and does not shake
or move about.

rocky /'rɒki/. **1** A **rocky** place is covered with rocks ◆◇◇◇◇
or consists of large areas of bare rock. ...*a rocky* ADJ-GRADED
headland. **2** A **rocky** situation or relationship is un- ADJ-GRADED
stable and full of difficulties. *Their relationship had
gotten off to a rocky start*.

ro·co·co /rə'kəʊkəʊ, AM ˌrəʊkə'kəʊ/. Rococo is a N-UNCOUNT
decorative style featuring complicated curly decoration that was popular in Europe in the eighteenth
century.

rod /rɒd/ **rods**. A **rod** is a long, thin metal or wood- ◆◆◇◇◇
en bar. ● See also **fishing rod**, **lightning rod**. N-COUNT

rode /rəʊd/. **Rode** is the past tense of **ride**.

ro·dent /'rəʊdənt/ **rodents**. Rodents are small ◆◇◇◇◇
mammals which have sharp front teeth. Rats, mice, N-COUNT
and squirrels are rodents.

ro·deo /'rəʊdiəʊ, rəʊ'deɪəʊ/ **rodeos.** In the United ◆◇◇◇◇
States, a **rodeo** is a public entertainment in which N-COUNT
cowboys show different skills, including riding wild
horses and catching calves with ropes.

roe /rəʊ/ **roes**. Roe is the eggs or sperm of a fish, N-VAR
which is eaten as food. ...*smoked cod's roe*.

roe deer; **roe deer** is both the singular and the N-COUNT
plural form. A **roe deer** is a small deer which lives in
woods in Europe and Asia.

rogue /rəʊg/ **rogues**. **1** A **rogue** is a man who be- ◆◇◇◇◇
haves in a dishonest or criminal way. *He declares* N-COUNT
that all politicians are rogues. **2** If a man behaves in
a way that you do not approve of but you like him PRAGMATICS
anyway, you can refer to him as a **rogue**. ...*Falstaff,
the loveable rogue*. **3** A **rogue** element is someone ADJ: ADJ n
or something that behaves differently from others of
its kind, often causing damage. *The rogue male is
not a twentieth-century phenomenon*.

ro·guish /ˈrəʊgɪʃ/. If someone has a **roguish** expression or manner, they look as though they are about to do or say something mischievous. ...*a roguish grin.*　ADJ-GRADED

role /rəʊl/ **roles. 1** If you have a **role** in a situation or in society, you have a particular position and function in it. ...*clear evidence about the drug's role in preventing more serious effects of infection... Both sides have roles to play.* **2** A **role** is one of the characters that an actor or singer can play in a film, play, or opera. *The lead role of Princess Ida has been given to soprano Lesley Garrett.*　◆◆◆◆◆ N-COUNT: with supp　N-COUNT

'role model, role models. A **role model** is someone you admire and try to imitate. *Five out of the ten top role models for British teenagers are black.*　◆◇◇◇◇ N-COUNT

'role play, role plays, role playing, role played; also spelled **role-play. 1 Role play** is the act of imitating the character and behaviour of someone who is different from yourself, for example as a training exercise. *Use role-play to practise making your request.* **2** If people **role play**, they do a role play. *Rehearse and role-play the interview with a friend beforehand.* ♦ **role play·ing** *We did a lot of role playing.*　◆◇◇◇◇ N-VAR　VERB V n Also V N-UNCOUNT

roll /rəʊl/ **rolls, rolling, rolled. 1** If something **rolls** or if you **roll** it, it moves along a surface, turning over many times. *The ball rolled into the net... Their car went off the road and rolled over... When I was a little kid I rolled down a hill and broke my leg... Roll the meat in coarsely ground black pepper to season it.* **2** When vehicles **roll** along, they move along slowly. *More than 100 tanks rolled into eastern Croatia.* **3** If a machine **rolls**, it is operating. *He slipped and fell on an airplane gangway as the cameras rolled.* **4** If drops of liquid **roll** down a surface, they move quickly down it. *She looked at Ginny and tears rolled down her cheeks.*　◆◆◆◇ V-ERG V prep/adv V n prep　VERB V　VERB V prep/adv　VERB V　VERB V down n

5 If you **roll** something flexible into a cylinder or a ball, you form it into a cylinder or a ball by wrapping it several times around itself or by shaping it between your hands. *He rolled and lit another cigarette.* ▶ **Roll up** means the same as **roll**. *Stein rolled up the paper bag with the money inside.* **6** A **roll** of paper, plastic, cloth, or wire is a long piece of it that has been wrapped many times around itself or around a tube. *The photographers had already shot a dozen rolls of film.* **7** If you **roll** something such as a car window or a blind up or down, you cause it to move upwards or downwards by turning a handle. *In mid-afternoon, shopkeepers began to roll down their shutters.* **8** If you **roll** your eyes or if your eyes **roll**, they turn up or turn from one side to another because you are very frightened or upset, or because you disapprove of something. *His eyes rolled and he sobbed.*　VERB: V n into n V n　PHRASAL VB V P noun Also V n P N-COUNT　VERB V n with adv　V-ERG: V n V WRITTEN

9 A **roll** is a very small loaf of bread that is eaten by one person. **10** A **roll** of drums is a long, rumbling sound made by drums. *He made a roll on the drums.* **11** A **roll** is an official list of people's names. *Pro-democracy activists say a new electoral roll should be drawn up.*　N-COUNT　N-COUNT　N-COUNT: with supp

12 If someone is **on a roll**, they are having great success which seems likely to continue. *I made a name for myself and I was on a roll.* **13** If you say **roll on** something, you mean that you are looking forward to it, and would like it to come soon. *Roll on the day someone develops an effective vaccine against malaria.* **14** If something is several things **rolled into one**, it combines the main features or qualities of those things. *This is our kitchen, sitting and dining room all rolled into one.*　PHRASE INFORMAL　PHRASE PRAGMATICS INFORMAL, BRITISH　PHRASE

15 See also rolling; **drum roll, rock and roll, sausage roll, toilet roll.** ● to **start the ball rolling:** see **ball.** ● **heads will roll:** see **head.**

roll back. To **roll back** a change or the power of something means to gradually reduce it or bring it to an end. *Most major political reforms of the past five years would be rolled back.* ● See also **rollback.**　PHRASAL VB V P noun Also V n P

roll in or **roll into. 1** If something such as money **is rolling in**, it is being received in large quantities. *Don't forget, I have always kept the money rolling in.*　PHRASAL VB V P Also V P n INFORMAL

2 If someone **rolls into** a place or **rolls in**, they arrive in a casual way, often late. *'I've made you late.'—'No that's all right. I can roll in when I feel like it.'.*　V P n V P

roll up. 1 If you **roll up** your sleeves or trouser legs, you fold the ends back several times, making them shorter. *Walking in the surf, she had to roll her pants up to her knees.* ● See also **rolled-up. 2** If people **roll up** somewhere, they arrive there, especially in large numbers, to see something interesting. *Roll up, come and join The Greatest Show on Earth.* **3** See also **roll 5, rolled-up.**　PHRASAL VB V P noun V n P　V P prep/adv V P

roll·back /ˈrəʊlbæk/ **rollbacks.** A **rollback** of taxes, wages, or prices is a reduction in them. A **rollback** of a change is a reversal of it.　N-COUNT AMERICAN

'roll call, roll calls; also spelled **roll-call. 1** If you take a **roll call**, you check which of the members of a group are present by reading their names out. **2** A **roll call of** a particular type of people or things is a list of them. *Her list of pupils reads like a roll-call of the great and good.*　N-VAR　N-SING: N of n JOURNALISM

,rolled-'up. 1 Rolled-up objects have been folded or wrapped into a cylindrical shape. ...*a rolled-up newspaper.* **2 Rolled-up** sleeves or trouser legs have been made shorter by being folded over at the lower edge.　◆◇◇◇◇ ADJ: ADJ n　ADJ: ADJ n

roll·er /ˈrəʊlə/ **rollers. 1** A **roller** is a cylinder that turns round in a machine or device. **2 Rollers** are hollow tubes that women roll their hair round in order to make it curly.　◆◆◇◇◇ N-COUNT　N-COUNT

'roller-coaster, roller-coasters; also spelled **roller coaster** or **rollercoaster. 1** At a fairground, a **roller-coaster** is a small railway that goes up and down steep slopes fast and that people ride on for pleasure. **2** If you say that someone or something is on a **roller coaster**, you mean that they go through many dramatic changes in a short time. *Japan's socialists have seen their electoral popularity take a roller-coaster ride.*　◆◇◇◇◇ N-COUNT　N-COUNT JOURNALISM

'roller-skate, roller-skates, roller-skating, roller-skated. 1 Roller-skates are shoes with four small wheels on the bottom. **2** If you **roller-skate**, you move over a flat surface wearing roller-skates. *My son Gary was roller-skating outside our house.* ♦ **roller-skating** *The craze for roller skating spread throughout the U.S.*　N-COUNT　VERB V　N-UNCOUNT

rol·lick·ing /ˈrɒlɪkɪŋ/. A **rollicking** occasion is lighthearted, jolly, and usually noisy. A **rollicking** book or film is entertaining and enjoyable, and not very serious. *I'm having a rollicking good time.*　ADJ: ADJ n

roll·ing /ˈrəʊlɪŋ/. **Rolling** hills are small hills with gentle slopes that extend a long way into the distance. ...*the rolling countryside of south western France.*　◆◇◇◇◇ ADJ: ADJ n

'rolling pin, rolling pins. A **rolling pin** is a cylinder that you roll backwards and forwards over uncooked pastry to flatten it.　N-COUNT

'rolling stock. Rolling stock is the engines, carriages, and wagons that are used on a railway.　N-UNCOUNT

,roll of 'honour. A **roll of honour** is a list of the names of people who are admired or respected for something they have done, such as doing very well in a sport or exam. The American term is **honor roll.**　N-SING BRITISH

'roll-on, roll-ons. A **roll-on** is a deodorant or cosmetic that you apply to your body by means of a ball which rotates in the neck of the container. *I use unperfumed roll-on deodorant.*　N-COUNT

,roll-on roll-'off. A **roll-on roll-off** ship is designed so that cars and lorries can drive on at one end before the ship sails, and then drive off at the other end after the voyage.　ADJ: ADJ n BRITISH

roly-poly /ˌrəʊli ˈpəʊli/. **Roly-poly** people are pleasantly fat and round.　ADJ: ADJ n INFORMAL

ROM /rɒm/. **ROM** is the permanent part of a computer's memory. The information stored there can be used but not changed. **ROM** is an abbreviation for 'read-only memory'. ● See also **CD-ROM.**　◆◇◇◇ N-UNCOUNT

Ro·man /ˈrəʊmən/ **Romans. 1 Roman** means related to or connected with ancient Rome and its empire. ...*the remains of a Roman fort.* ▶ A **Roman**　◆◆◇◇ ADJ　N-COUNT

was a citizen of ancient Rome or its empire. **2 Ro-** ADJ
man means related to or connected with modern
Rome. ▶ A **Roman** is someone who lives in or N-COUNT
comes from Rome. **3 Roman** is the most common N-UNCOUNT
style of printing in books and magazines. It consists
of upright letters. The definitions in this dictionary
are printed in roman.

Roman 'Catholic, Roman Catholics. 1 The ◆◆◇◇◇
Roman **Catholic** Church is the same as the **Catholic** ADJ
Church. ...*a Roman Catholic priest.* **2** A **Roman** N-COUNT
Catholic is the same as a **Catholic**.

Roman Ca'tholicism. Roman Catholicism is N-UNCOUNT
the same as **Catholicism**.

ro·mance /rə'mæns, 'rəʊmæns/ **romances, ro-** ◆◆◇◇◇
mancing, romanced. 1 A **romance** is a relation- N-COUNT
ship between two people who are in love with each
other. *After a whirlwind romance the couple announced their engagement in July.* **2 Romance** refers N-UNCOUNT
to the actions and feelings of people who are in
love, especially behaviour which is very caring, impulsive, or extravagant. *He still finds time for romance by cooking candlelit dinners for his girlfriend.*
3 If a man **romances** a woman, he takes her out VERB
and treats her tenderly, because, or as if, he is in V n
love with her. *He has romanced some of the world's* JOURNALISM
most eligible women. **4** You can refer to the pleasure N-UNCOUNT
and excitement of doing something new or exciting
as **romance**. *We want to recreate the romance and
excitement that used to be part of rail journeys.*
5 A **romance** is a novel or film about a love affair. N-COUNT
6 Romance is used to refer to novels about love af- N-UNCOUNT
fairs. *Since taking up writing romance in 1967 she has
brought out over fifty books.* **7** A medieval **romance** is N-VAR
a story about someone's adventures, for example the
battles they fought. ...*Arthurian Romances.* **8 Ro-** ADJ: ADJ n
mance languages are languages such as French, TECHNICAL
Spanish, and Italian, which are derived from Latin.

Ro·man·esque /ˌrəʊmə'nesk/. **Romanesque** archi- ADJ
tecture is in the style that was common in western
Europe around the eleventh century. It is characterized by rounded arches and thick pillars.

Roman 'numeral, Roman numerals. Roman N-COUNT
numerals are the letters used by the ancient Romans to represent numbers, for example I, IV, VIII,
and XL, which represent 1, 4, 8, and 40. Roman numerals are still sometimes used today.

ro·man·tic /rəʊ'mæntɪk/ **romantics. 1** Someone ◆◆◆◇◇
who is **romantic** or does **romantic** things says and ADJ-GRADED
does things that make their wife, husband, girl-
friend, or boyfriend feel special and loved. ...*a romantic dinner for two.* ♦ **ro·man·ti·cal·ly** ADV-GRADED
/rəʊ'mæntɪkli/. *He lived with his pretty wife
Helga—his barge was romantically called after her.*
2 Romantic means connected with love. *He was not* ADJ: ADJ n
interested in a romantic relationship with Ingrid.
♦ **romantically** *We are not romantically involved.* ADV
3 A **romantic** play, film, or story describes or repre- ADJ: ADJ n
sents a love affair. *It is a lovely romantic comedy,
well worth seeing.*
4 If you say that someone has a **romantic** view or idea ADJ-GRADED
of something, you are criticizing them because their PRAGMATICS
view of it is unrealistic and they think that thing is better or more exciting than it really is. *He has a romantic
view of rural society.* ▶ A **romantic** is a person who N-COUNT
has romantic views. ♦ **romantically** *They suffered* ADV-GRADED
*from tuberculosis, then still romantically called con-
sumption.* **5** Something that is **romantic** is beautiful ADJ-GRADED
in a way that strongly affects your feelings. *Seacliff
House is one of the most romantic ruins in Scotland.*
♦ **romantically** ...*the romantically named, but very* ADV-GRADED
muddy, Cave of the Wild Horses. **6 Romantic** means ADJ: ADJ n
connected with the artistic movement of the eighteenth and nineteenth centuries which was concerned
with the expression of the individual's feelings and
emotions. ...*the poems and prose of the English romantic poets.*

ro·man·ti·cism /rəʊ'mæntɪsɪzəm/. **1 Romanticism** ◆◇◇◇◇
is thoughts and feelings which are idealistic and ro- N-UNCOUNT
mantic, rather than realistic. **2 Romanticism** is the N-UNCOUNT
artistic movement of the eighteenth and nineteenth

centuries which was concerned with the expression
of the individual's feelings and emotions.

ro·man·ti·cize /rəʊ'mæntɪsaɪz/ **romanticizes, ro-** VERB
manticizing, romanticized; also spelled **roman-** V n
ticise in British English. If you **romanticize** someone or something, you think or talk about them in a
way which is not at all realistic and which makes
them seem better than they really are. *I am not generally one to romanticize the past.* ♦ **ro·man·ti-
·cized** ...*a highly romanticized view of life on the* ADJ-GRADED
streets.

Roma·ny /'rəʊməni/ **Romanies. 1** A **Romany** is N-COUNT
the same as a **gypsy**. **2 Romany** means related or ADJ
connected to the Romany people. ...*the Romany
community.*

Romeo /'rəʊmiəʊ/ **Romeos.** You can describe a N-COUNT
man as a **Romeo** if you want to indicate in a hu- PRAGMATICS
morous way that he is very much in love with a INFORMAL
woman, or that he frequently has sexual relationships with women.

romp /rɒmp/ **romps, romping, romped. 1** ◆◇◇◇◇
Romp is used in expressions like **romp home, romp** VERB
in, or **romp to victory**, to say that a person or horse V adv / prep
has won a race or competition very easily. *Mr Foster* JOURNALISM
romped home with 141 votes. **2** When children or VERB: V
animals **romp**, they play noisily and happily. **3** If N-COUNT
two people have a **romp**, they have sex in a light- BRITISH
hearted and very casual way. **4** A book, film, or play N-COUNT
can be described as a **romp** when it is funny, light- JOURNALISM
hearted, and full of action. ...*a riveting, readable
romp.*

romp through. If you **romp through** something, PHRASAL VB
you do it or deal with it quickly and easily. *He had* V P n
romped through the maze of questions. BRITISH

roof /ruːf/ **roofs.** The plural can be pronounced ◆◆◆◇◇
/ruːfs/ or /ruːvz/. **1** The **roof** of a building is the N-COUNT
covering on top of it that protects the people and
things inside from the weather. See picture headed
house and flat. ...*a small stone cottage with a red
slate roof.* ♦ **roofed** /ruːft, ruːvd/. ...*a peasant hut* ADJ
roofed with branches. ♦ **-roofed** ...*a huge flat-* COMB
roofed concrete and glass building. **2** The **roof** of a N-COUNT
car or other vehicle is the top part of it, which protects passengers or goods from the weather. See
picture headed **car and bicycle**. **3** The **roof** of your N-COUNT:
mouth is the highest part of the inside of your the N of n
mouth. **4** The **roof** of an underground space such as N-COUNT
a cave or mine is the highest part of it. *The cave roof
collapsed.*
5 If the level or price of something **goes through the** PHRASE
roof, it suddenly increases very rapidly indeed. *Prices* INFORMAL
for Korean art have gone through the roof. **6** If you **hit** PHRASE
the roof or **go through the roof**, you become very an- INFORMAL
gry indeed. *Sergeant Long will hit the roof when I tell
him you've gone off.* **7** If you have a **roof over** your PHRASE
head, you have somewhere to live. *I am just thankful
that we have a roof over our heads.* **8** If a number of PHRASE
things or people are **under one roof** or **under the
same roof**, they are in the same building. *The firms intend to open either together under one roof or alongside each other in shopping malls.*

roof·er /'ruːfə/ **roofers.** A **roofer** is a person whose N-COUNT
job is to build or repair roofs.

'roof garden, roof gardens. A **roof garden** is a N-COUNT
garden on the flat roof of a building.

roof·ing /'ruːfɪŋ/. **1 Roofing** is material used for N-UNCOUNT
making or covering roofs. *Stone began to be used as
a roofing material.* **2 Roofing** is the work of putting N-UNCOUNT:
new roofs on houses. ...*a roofing company.*

'roof rack, roof racks; also spelled **roof-rack**. A N-COUNT
roof rack is a metal frame that is fixed on top of a
car and used for carrying large objects. See picture
headed **car and bicycle**.

roof·top /'ruːftɒp/ **rooftops;** also spelled **roof-top**. ◆◇◇◇◇
1 A **rooftop** is the outside part of the roof of a N-COUNT
building. **2** If you shout something **from the roof-** PHRASE
tops, you say it or announce it in a very public way.

rook /rʊk/ **rooks. 1** A **rook** is a large black bird. N-COUNT
Rooks are members of the crow family. **2** In chess, a N-COUNT

rook is one of the chess pieces which stand in the corners of the board at the beginning of a game.

rookie /ˈrʊki/ **rookies.** A **rookie** is a person who is new to a particular job, activity, or sport, and who does not have much experience. ◆◇◇◇◇ N-COUNT AMERICAN, INFORMAL

room /ruːm, rʊm/ **rooms, rooming, roomed.** ◆◆◆◆ N-COUNT **1** A **room** is one of the separate sections in a building. Rooms have their own walls, ceiling, floor, and door. *The largest conference room could seat 5,000 people.* ▶ You can refer to all the people in a room as the **room**. *The whole room roared with laughter.* N-COLL-SING **2** If you talk about your **room**, you are referring to the room that you alone use, especially your bedroom at home or your office at work. *Go to my room and bring down my sweater, please.* **3** A **room** is a bedroom in a hotel. *Toni booked a room in an hotel not far from Arzfeld.* **4** If you **room** with someone, you share a rented room, apartment, or house with them. *I had roomed with him in New Haven when we were both at Yale Law School.* N-COUNT: poss N / N-COUNT / VERB V with n Also V together AMERICAN **5** If there is **room** somewhere, there is enough empty N-UNCOUNT space there for people or things to be fitted in, or for people to move freely or do what they want to. *The old artist's studio is a brilliant place for a party with a high ceiling and plenty of room.* **6** If there is **room** for a particular kind of behaviour or action, people are able to behave in that way or to take that action. *The intensity of the work left little room for personal grief or anxiety.* N-UNCOUNT **7** If you have **room for manoeuvre**, you have the opportunity to change your plans if it becomes necessary or desirable. *With an election looming, he has little room for manoeuvre.* PHRASE **8** Room is also used in the names of many of the different kinds of room that are found in houses and buildings. These are explained at other places in the dictionary. See, for example, **consulting room**, **dining room**, **locker room**. See also **elbow room**, **leg room**, **standing room**.

-roomed /-ruːmd/. **-roomed** combines with numbers to form adjectives which tell you how many rooms a house or flat contains. *They found a little two-roomed flat to rent.* COMB

room·ful /ˈruːmfʊl/ **roomfuls.** A **roomful** of things N-COUNT or people is a room that is full of them. You can also refer to the amount or number of things or people that a room can contain as a **roomful**. *It was like a teacher disciplining a roomful of second-year pupils... I accumulated a roomful of documents and tape recordings.*

room·mate /ˈruːmmeɪt, ˈrʊm-/ **roommates;** also spelled **room-mate. 1** Your **roommate** is the person N-COUNT you share a rented room, apartment, or house with. **2** Your **roommate** is the person you share a rented room with. AMERICAN N-COUNT BRITISH

ˈroom service. Room service is a service in a hotel by which meals or drinks are provided for guests in their rooms. *The hotel did not normally provide room service.* N-UNCOUNT

roomy /ˈruːmi/ **roomier, roomiest. 1** If you describe a place as **roomy**, you mean that you like it because it is large inside and you can move around freely and comfortably. **2** If you describe a piece of clothing as **roomy**, you mean that you like it because it is large and fits loosely. *...roomy jackets.* ADJ-GRADED PRAGMATICS / ADJ-GRADED PRAGMATICS

roost /ruːst/ **roosts, roosting, roosted. 1** A ◆◇◇◇ **roost** is a place where birds or bats rest or sleep. N-COUNT **2** When birds or bats **roost** somewhere, they rest or VERB sleep there. *The peacocks roost in nearby shrubs.* **3** If V prep/adv bad or wrong things that someone has done in the PHRASE past **have come home to roost**, or if their **chickens have come home to roost**, they are now experiencing the unpleasant effects of these actions. **4** If you PHRASE say that someone **rules the roost** in a particular INFORMAL place, you mean that they have control and authority over the people there.

roost·er /ˈruːstə/ **roosters.** A **rooster** is an adult N-COUNT male chicken. See picture headed **animals**. AMERICAN

root /ruːt/ **roots, rooting, rooted. 1** The **roots** of ◆◆◆◇ a plant are the parts of it that grow under the N-COUNT ground. **2** Root vegetables or **root** crops are grown ADJ: ADJ n

for their roots which are large and can be eaten. **3** The **root** of a hair or tooth is the part of it beneath the skin. *...wax strips which remove hairs cleanly from the root.* N-COUNT **4** You can refer to the place or culture that a person or N-PLURAL their family comes from as their **roots**. *I am proud of my Brazilian roots.* **5 Roots** is used to refer to types of N-UNCOUNT pop music, especially types of reggae, that are strongly influenced by the traditional music of their culture of origin. *...superb roots reggae by the likes of Little Roy and Wailing Souls.* **6** You can refer to the cause of a N-COUNT problem or of an unpleasant situation as the **root** of it or the **roots** of it. *We got to the root of the problem... They were treating symptoms and not the root cause.* **7** The **root** of a word is the part that contains its N-COUNT meaning and that does not change. *The word 'secretary' comes from the same Latin root as the word 'secret'.* **8** See also **rooted; cube root, grass roots, square root.** TECHNICAL

9 If something has been completely changed or destroyed, you can say that it has been changed or destroyed **root and branch**. *Some prison practices are in need of root and branch reform.* **10** If someone **puts down roots**, they make a place their home, for example by making a lot of friends there. **11** If an idea, belief, or custom **takes root**, it becomes established among a group of people. *Time would be needed for democracy to take root.* **12** If you **root** through something or **root** in something, you look for something in it, moving things around as you search. PHRASE WRITTEN / PHRASE / PHRASE / VERB: V prep

root around; the form **root about** is also used in PHRASAL VB British English. If you **root around** or **root about** in V P prep something, you look for something there, moving Also V P things around as you search. *'It's in here somewhere,' he said, rooting about in his desk.*

root for. If you **are rooting for** someone, you are giving them your support while they are doing something difficult or trying to defeat someone else. PHRASAL VB V P n INFORMAL

root out. 1 If you **root out** a person, you find them and force them from the place they are in, usually in order to punish them. *It shouldn't take too long to root him out.* **2** If you **root out** a problem or an unpleasant situation, you find out who or what is the cause of it and put an end to it. *There would be a major drive to root out corruption.* PHRASAL VB V P noun V n P / V P noun Also V pron P

root·ed /ˈruːtɪd/. **1** If you say that one thing is ◆◇◇◇ **rooted in** another, you mean that it is strongly influenced by it or has developed from it. *The crisis is rooted in deep rivalries between the two groups.* **2** If someone has deeply **rooted** opinions or feelings, they believe or feel something extremely strongly and are unlikely to change. *Racism is a deeply rooted prejudice.* ● See also **deep-rooted.** ADJ: v-link ADJ in n / ADJ-GRADED **3** If you are **rooted to the spot**, you are unable to PHRASE move because you are very frightened or shocked.

root·less /ˈruːtləs/. If someone has no permanent ADJ-GRADED home or job and is not settled in any community, you can describe them as **rootless.**

rope /rəʊp/ **ropes, roping, roped. 1** A **rope** is a ◆◆◇◇ very thick cord or wire that is made by twisting together several thinner cords or wires. Ropes are used for jobs such as towing cars, mooring boats, or tying large things together. *He tied the rope around his waist.* **2** If you **rope** one thing to another, you tie the two things together with a rope. *I roped myself to the chimney.* **3** The **ropes** refers to the fence made of ropes that surrounds a boxing or wrestling ring. *He was knocked through the ropes by Tafer.* N-VAR / VERB V n to n / N-PLURAL the N **4** If you **are learning the ropes**, you are learning how PHRASE a particular task or job is done. **5** If you **know the** INFORMAL **ropes**, you know how a particular job or task should PHRASE be done. **6** If you **show** someone **the ropes**, you show INFORMAL them how to do a particular job or task. **7** If you say PHRASE that someone is **on the ropes**, you mean that they are INFORMAL very near to giving up or being defeated. PHRASE

rope in. If you say that you **were roped in** to do a PHRASAL VB particular task, you mean that someone persuaded beV-ed P to- you to help them do that task. *Visitors were roped in* inf for potato picking. beV-ed P for n INFORMAL

rope off. If you **rope off** an area, you tie ropes be- PHRASAL VB

tween posts around its edges so that people cannot enter it without permission. ...*a large roped-off area.* `V P noun` `V-ed P` `Also V n P`

'**rope ladder, rope ladders;** also spelled **rope-ladder**. A **rope ladder** is a ladder made of two long ropes connected by short pieces of rope, wood, or metal. `N-COUNT`

ropey /'rəʊpi/ **ropier, ropiest.** If you say that something is **ropey**, you mean that its quality is poor or unsatisfactory. *Your spelling's a bit ropey.* `ADJ-GRADED` `INFORMAL, BRITISH`

ro·sary /'rəʊzəri/ **rosaries.** A **rosary** is a string of beads that members of certain religions, especially Catholics, use for counting prayers. A series of prayers counted in this way is also called a **rosary.** *He's saying three rosaries a day.* `N-COUNT`

rose /rəʊz/ **roses. 1 Rose** is the past tense of **rise.** `♦♦♦◇◇`
2 A **rose** is a flower which grows on a bush with thorny stems. **3** If you say that a situation is not a **bed of roses**, you mean that it is not all pleasant, and that there are some unpleasant aspects to it as well. `N-COUNT` `PHRASE`
4 Something that is **rose** is reddish-pink in colour. `COLOUR`

rosé /'rəʊzeɪ, AM rəʊ'zeɪ/ **rosés. Rosé** is wine which is pink in colour. *The vast majority of wines produced in this area are reds or rosés.* `♦◇◇◇◇` `N-VAR`

rose·bud /'rəʊzbʌd/ **rosebuds.** A **rosebud** is a young rose whose petals have not yet opened fully. `N-COUNT`

'**rose-coloured;** spelled **rose-colored** in American English. If you say that someone is looking at a person or situation through **rose-coloured spectacles** or **rose-coloured glasses**, you mean that they are only noticing the pleasant things about that person or situation and that therefore their view is unrealistic. `PRAGMATICS`

rose·hip /'rəʊzhɪp/ **rosehips.** A **rosehip** is a bright red or orange fruit that grows on some kinds of rose bushes. `N-COUNT`

rose·mary /'rəʊzməri, AM -meri/. **Rosemary** is a herb used in cooking. `♦◇◇◇◇` `N-UNCOUNT`

'**rose-tinted. Rose-tinted** means the same as **rose-coloured.**

ro·sette /rəʊ'zet/ **rosettes. 1** A **rosette** is a large circular badge made from coloured ribbons which is worn to show support for a political party or sports team, or is given as a prize in a competition. `♦◇◇◇◇` `N-COUNT`
2 A **rosette** is a decoration or design that looks rather like a rose. ...*intricately carved wood rosettes.* `N-COUNT`

rose·water /'rəʊzwɔːtə/. **Rosewater** is a liquid which is made from roses and which has a pleasant smell. It is used as a perfume and in cooking. `N-UNCOUNT`

'**rose window, rose windows.** A **rose window** is a large round stained glass window in a church. `N-COUNT`

rose·wood /'rəʊzwʊd/. **Rosewood** is a hard dark-coloured wood that is used for making furniture. `N-UNCOUNT`

ros·ter /'rɒstə/ **rosters. 1** A **roster** is a list which gives details of the order in which different people have to do a particular job. ...*new roster for domestic chores.* **2** A **roster** is a list, especially a list of the people employed by a particular organization, or available to do a particular job. You can also refer to the people or things mentioned in a list as a **roster** of people or things. ...*the Amateur Softball Association's roster of umpires.* `♦◇◇◇◇` `N-COUNT`

ros·trum /'rɒstrəm/ **rostrums** or **rostra** /'rɒstrə/. A **rostrum** is a raised platform on which someone stands when they are speaking to an audience, receiving a prize, or conducting an orchestra. `N-COUNT`

rosy /'rəʊzi/ **rosier, rosiest. 1** If you say that someone has a **rosy** face, you mean that they have pink cheeks and look very healthy. **2** Something that is **rosy** is reddish-pink in colour. ...*the rosy brick buildings.* **3** If you say that a situation looks **rosy** or that the picture looks **rosy**, you mean that the situation seems likely to be good or successful. `♦◇◇◇◇` `ADJ` `ADJ` `ADJ-GRADED`

rot /rɒt/ **rots, rotting, rotted. 1** When food, wood, or other substances **rot**, or when something **rots** them, they decay and fall apart. *Sugary canned drinks rot your teeth.* **2** If there is **rot** in something, especially something that is made of wood, parts of it have decayed and fallen apart. ...*extensive rot in the main beams.* **3** See also **dry rot.** `♦♦◇◇◇` `V-ERG: V` `V n` `N-UNCOUNT`
4 You can use **the rot** to refer to a gradual worsening `N-SING`

of something. For example, if you are talking about the time when **the rot** set in, you are talking about the time when a situation began to get steadily worse and worse. *The country's leaders are unwilling to take unpopular measures to stop the rot.* `the N` `BRITISH`
5 If you say that someone is being left to **rot** in a particular place, especially in a prison, you mean that they are being left there and their physical and mental condition is being allowed to get worse and worse. *Most governments simply leave the long-term jobless to rot on the dole.* `VERB` `V prep` `Also V`
6 If you say that what someone is saying is **rot**, you mean that they are saying very silly things. *What a load of pompous, pseudo-intellectual rot.* `N-UNCOUNT` `INFORMAL, BRITISH`

rot away. When something **rots away**, it decays until it falls to pieces or none of it remains. *The pillars rotted away and were replaced.* `PHRASAL VB` `V P`

rota /'rəʊtə/ **rotas.** A **rota** is a list which gives details of the order in which different people have to do a particular job. *Work out a careful rota which will make it clear who tidies the room on which day.* `N-COUNT` `BRITISH`

ro·ta·ry /'rəʊtəri/. **1 Rotary** means turning or able to turn round a fixed point. **2 Rotary** is used in the names of some machines that have parts that turn round a fixed point. ...*a rotary engine.* `♦◇◇◇◇` `ADJ: ADJ n` `ADJ: ADJ n`

ro·tate /rəʊ'teɪt, AM 'rəʊteɪt/ **rotates, rotating, rotated. 1** When something **rotates** or when you **rotate** it, it turns with a circular movement. *Gently rotate your hips.* ♦ **ro·ta·tion** /rəʊ'teɪʃən/ **rotations** ...*the daily rotation of the earth upon its axis.* **2** If people or things **rotate**, or if someone **rotates** them, they take it in turns to do a particular job or serve a particular purpose. *They will swap posts in a year's time, according to new party rules which rotate the leadership.* ♦ **rotation** ...*crop rotation...* *In rotation each one led the group.* `♦♦◇◇◇` `V-ERG: V` `V n` `N-VAR` `V-ERG: V` `V n` `N-UNCOUNT`

rote /rəʊt/. **Rote** learning is learning things by repeating them without thinking about them or trying to understand them; used showing disapproval. *You are merely reciting facts that you have learned by rote.* `N-UNCOUNT: N n, by N` `PRAGMATICS`

ro·tor /'rəʊtə/ **rotors.** The **rotors** or **rotor blades** of a helicopter are the four long, flat, thin pieces of metal on top of it which go round and lift it off the ground. `♦◇◇◇◇` `N-COUNT`

rot·ten /'rɒtən/. **1** If food, wood, or another substance is **rotten**, it has decayed and can no longer be used. *The front bay window is rotten.* `♦♦◇◇◇` `ADJ`
2 If you describe something as **rotten**, you think it is very unpleasant or of very poor quality. *I personally think it's a rotten idea.* **3** If you describe someone as **rotten**, you are insulting them or criticizing them because you think that they are very unpleasant or unkind. *You rotten swine!.* **4** If you feel **rotten**, you feel bad, either because you are ill or because you are sorry about something. *She woke up feeling rotten.* **5** You use **rotten** to emphasize your dislike for something or your anger or frustration about it. *Keep your rotten mouth shut.* `ADJ-GRADED` `INFORMAL` `ADJ-GRADED` `INFORMAL` `ADJ-GRADED` `INFORMAL` `ADJ: ADJ n` `PRAGMATICS` `INFORMAL`

rot·ter /'rɒtə/ **rotters.** If you call someone a **rotter**, you are criticizing them because you think that they have behaved in a very unkind or selfish way. `N-COUNT` `INFORMAL, BRITISH`

rott·wei·ler /'rɒtvaɪlə/ **rottweilers.** A **rottweiler** is a large, black, and very muscular breed of dog. `N-COUNT`

ro·tund /rəʊ'tʌnd/. If someone is **rotund**, they are round and fat. ...*a rotund figure with silver hair.* `ADJ-GRADED` `FORMAL`

ro·tun·da /rəʊ'tʌndə/ **rotundas.** A **rotunda** is a round building or room, especially one with a dome. `N-COUNT`

rou·ble /'ruːbəl/. The **rouble** is the unit of currency in Russia, and in some other countries. `♦♦◇◇◇` `N-COUNT`

rouge /ruːʒ/ **rouges, rouging, rouged. 1** Rouge is a red powder or cream which women and actors can put on their cheeks in order to give them more colour. **2** If a woman or an actor **rouges** their cheeks or lips, they put red powder or cream on them to give them more colour. `♦♦◇◇◇` `N-UNCOUNT` `DATED` `VERB: V n`

rough /rʌf/ **rougher, roughest; roughs, roughing, roughed. 1** If a surface is **rough**, it is uneven and not smooth. *His hands were rough and* `♦♦♦◇◇` `ADJ-GRADED`

calloused. ♦ **rough·ness** *...the roughness of his jacket.* `N-UNCOUNT`

2 You say that people or their actions are **rough** when they use too much force and not enough care or gentleness. *Rugby's a rough game.* ♦ **rough·ly** *A hand roughly pushed him aside.* ♦ **rough·ness** *He regretted his roughness.* **3** A **rough** area, city, school, or other place is unpleasant and dangerous because there are a lot of violence or crime there. *...quite a rough part of our town.* `ADJ-GRADED`

4 If you say that someone has had a **rough** time, you mean that they have had some difficult or unpleasant experiences. *Tomorrow, he knew, would be a rough day.* **5** If you feel **rough**, you feel ill. *The virus won't go away and the lad is still feeling a bit rough.* `ADJ-GRADED` `v-link ADJ` `INFORMAL`

6 A **rough** calculation or guess is approximately correct, but not exact. *...a rough estimate of how much fuel would be required.* ♦ **roughly** *Gambling and tourism pay roughly half the entire state budget.* **7** If you give someone a **rough** idea, description, or drawing of something, you indicate only the most important features, without much detail. *I've got a rough idea of what he looks like. ...a rough sketch showing where the vehicles were.* ♦ **roughly** *He knew roughly what was about to be said.* `ADV-GRADED`

8 You can say that something is **rough** when it is not neat and well made. *The bench had a rough wooden table in front of it.* ♦ **rough·ly** *Roughly chop the tomatoes and add them to the casserole.* `ADJ-GRADED` `ADV-GRADED:` `ADV with v`

9 If the sea or the weather at sea is **rough**, the weather is windy or stormy and there are very big waves. `ADJ-GRADED`

10 When people sleep or live **rough**, they sleep in unusual places, often out of doors, usually because they have no home. **11** If you have to **rough** it, you have to live without the possessions and comforts that you normally have. *You won't be roughing it; each room comes equipped with a telephone and a radio.* `ADV:` `ADV after v` `BRITISH` `VERB` `V it`

12 ◆ **rough justice**: see **justice**.

rough out. If you **rough out** a drawing or an idea, you draw or write the main features of it before you do it in detail. *Wood roughed out a possible framework for their story.* `PHRASAL VB` `V P noun` `Also V n P`

rough up. If someone **roughs** you **up**, they attack you and hit or beat you. *He was fired from his job after roughing up a colleague.* `PHRASAL VB` `V n P` `V P noun` `INFORMAL`

rough·age /'rʌfɪdʒ/. **Roughage** consists of substances in food such as bran or fibre. `N-UNCOUNT`

rough and 'ready; also spelled **rough-and-ready**. `ADJ-GRADED` **1** A **rough and ready** solution or method is one that is rather simple and not very exact because it has been thought of or done in a hurry. **2** A **rough and ready** person is not very polite or gentle. `ADJ-GRADED`

rough and 'tumble; also spelled **rough-and-tumble. 1** You can use **rough and tumble** to refer to a situation in which the people involved try hard to get what they want, and do not worry about upsetting or harming others, and you think this is acceptable and normal. *All this is part of the rough-and-tumble of political combat.* **2 Rough and tumble** is physical playing that involves noisy and slightly violent behaviour. *He enjoys rough and tumble play.* `N-UNCOUNT` `N-UNCOUNT`

rough·en /'rʌfən/. **roughens, roughening, roughened.** If something has **been roughened**, its surface has become less smooth. *...complexions that have been roughened by long periods in the hot sun.* `VB: usu` `passive` `be V-ed`

'rough-hewn. Rough-hewn wood or stone has been cut into a shape but has not yet been smoothed or finished off. *...a rough-hewn carving of a cat's head.* `ADJ-GRADED`

rough·neck /'rʌfnek/. **roughnecks. 1** A **roughneck** is a man who works on an oil rig or oil well. **2** If you describe a man as a **roughneck**, you disapprove of him because you think he is not gentle or polite, and can be violent. `N-COUNT` `INFORMAL,` `AMERICAN` `N-COUNT` `PRAGMATICS` `INFORMAL`

rough·shod /'rʌfʃɒd/. If you say that someone **is riding roughshod over** a person or their views, you disapprove of them because they are using their power or authority to do what they want, completely ignoring that person's wishes. `PHRASE` `PRAGMATICS`

rou·lette /ruː'let/. **Roulette** is a gambling game in which a ball is dropped onto a revolving wheel with numbered holes in it. The players bet on which hole the ball will be in when the wheel stops spinning. ● See also **Russian roulette**. `N-UNCOUNT`

round 1 preposition and adverb uses

round /raʊnd/. **Round** is an adverb and preposition that has the same meanings as 'around'. **Round** is often used with verbs of movement, such as 'walk' and also in phrasal verbs such as 'get round'. **Round** is commoner in British English than American English. ◆◆◆◇

1 To be positioned **round** a place or object means to surround it or be on all sides of it. To move **round** a place means to go along its edge, back to your starting-point. *They were sitting round the kitchen table... The nightdress has handmade lace round the armholes... He tramped hurriedly round the lake towards the garden.* ► Also an adverb. *Visibility was good all round... The goldfish swam round and round in their tiny bowls.* **2** If you say that something **is going round and round** in your head, you mean that you can't stop thinking about it. `PREP` `ADV:` `ADV after v` `PHRASE`

3 If you move **round** a corner or obstacle, you move to the other side of it. If you look **round** a corner or obstacle, you look to see what is on the other side. *Suddenly a car came round a corner... One of his men tapped and looked round the door.* `PREP`

4 You use **round** to say that something happens in or relates to different parts of a place or area, or is near a place or area. *He happens to own half the land round here... He has earned the respect of leaders all round the world.* ► Also an adverb. *Shirley found someone to show them round.* `PREP` `ADV`

5 If a wheel or object spins **round**, it turns on its axis. **6** If you turn **round**, you turn so that you are facing or going in the opposite direction. *The wind veered round to the east... Tricia looked round in surprise.* **7** If you move things **round**, you move them so they are in different places. *He will be glad to refurnish where possible, change things round and redecorate.* `ADV` `ADV:` `ADV after v` `ADV:` `ADV after v`

8 If you hand or pass something **round**, it is passed from person to person in a group. *John handed round the plate of sandwiches.* ► Also a preposition. *They started handing the microphone out round the girls at the front.* `ADV:` `ADV after v` `PREP`

9 If you go **round** to someone's house, you visit them. *He came round with a bottle of champagne.* ► Also a preposition in non-standard English. *I went round my wife's house.* `ADV:` `ADV after v` `PREP`

10 You use **round** in expressions such as **sit round** or **hang round** when you are saying that someone is spending time in a place and not doing anything very important. *I was running round all hyped up.* ► Also a preposition. *She would spend the day hanging round street corners.* `ADV:` `ADV after v` `INFORMAL` `PREP`

11 If something is built or based **round** a particular idea, that idea is the basis for it. *...a design built round an existing American engine.* `PREP`

12 If you get **round** a problem or difficulty, you find a way of dealing with it. *There are ways of getting round most things!* **13** If you win someone **round**, or if they come **round**, they change their mind about something and start agreeing with you. *He did his best to talk me round.* `PREP` `ADV:` `ADV after v`

14 You use **round** in expressions such as **this time round** or **to come round** when you are describing something that has happened before or things that happen regularly. *Of course, it isn't the same first time round... We were very keen when the 1954 Rally came round.* `ADV:` `n ADV,` `ADV after v`

15 When you are giving measurements, you can use **round** to mention the circumference of something. *...forty-eight inches round the hips.* ► Also an adverb. *It's six feet high and five feet round.* `PREP` `ADV`

16 You use **round** in front of times or amounts to indicate that they are approximate. *I go to bed round 11:00 at night.* **17 Round about** means approximately. *Round about one and a half million people died.* `ADV:` `ADV amount` `PHR-PREP` `SPOKEN`

18 You say **all round** to emphasize that something `PHRASE`

R

affects all parts of a situation or all members of a group. *It ought to make life much easier all round.* **BRITISH**

19 • **round the corner**: see **corner**. • **the other way round**: see **way**. • **all year round**: see **year**.

round 2 noun uses

round /raʊnd/ **rounds. 1** A **round** of events is a series of related events, especially one which comes after or before a similar series of events. *Another round of preliminary talks would be held in Peking. ...the latest round of job cuts.* **2** In sport, a **round** is a series of games in a competition. The winners of these games go on to play in the next round, and so on, until only one player or team is left. *...in the third round of the Pilkington Cup.* **3** In a boxing or wrestling match, a **round** is one of the periods during which the boxers or wrestlers fight. **4** A **round** of golf is one game, usually including 18 holes. **N-COUNT**
5 A **round** is a circular shape. *...small fresh rounds of goats' cheese... A cucumber was sliced into rounds.* **6** A **round** of bread is a slice of bread. A **round** of sandwiches is a sandwich made from two slices of bread. *...four rounds of toast.* **N-COUNT BRITISH**
7 If you do your **rounds** or your **round**, you make a series of visits to different places or people, for example as part of your job. *The consultants still did their morning rounds.* **N-COUNT**
8 If you buy a **round** of drinks, you buy a drink for each member of the group of people that you are with. **N-COUNT**
9 A **round** of ammunition is the bullet or bullets that are released when a gun is fired. **N-COUNT**
10 If there is a **round** of applause, everyone claps. *Sue got a sympathetic round of applause.* **N-COUNT: N of n**
11 In music, a **round** is a simple tune sung by several people in which each person sings a different part of the song at the same time. **N-COUNT**
12 If a story, idea, or joke **is going the rounds** or **doing the rounds**, a lot of people have heard it and are passing it on. *This story was going the rounds 20 years ago.* **PHRASE BRITISH**
13 If you **make the rounds** or **do the rounds**, you visit a series of different places. *We could do the rounds of the galleries.* **PHRASE BRITISH**

round 3 adjective uses

round /raʊnd/ **rounder, roundest. 1** Something that is **round** is shaped like a circle or ball. *She had small feet and hands and a flat, round face. ...large round loaves dusted with flour.* **2** If someone has **round** eyes, their eyes are open wide, for example because they are surprised, excited, or afraid. **ADJ-GRADED**
3 A **round** number is a whole number, especially a multiple of 10, 100, 1000, and so on. Round numbers are used instead of precise ones to give the general idea of a quantity or proportion. *I asked how much silver could be bought for a million pounds, which seemed a suitably round number.* **ADJ: ADJ n**

round 4 verb uses

round /raʊnd/ **rounds, rounding, rounded. 1** If you **round** a place or obstacle, you move in a curve past the edge or corner of it. *The house disappeared from sight as we rounded a corner.* **VERB: V n**
2 If you **round** an amount up or down, or if you **round** it off, you change it to the nearest whole number or nearest multiple of a number. *The fraction was then multiplied by 100 and rounded to the nearest half or whole number... I'll round it off to about £30.* **VERB: V n with adv be V-ed to n amount V n adv to amount**
3 See also **rounded.**

round off. If you **round off** an activity with something, you end the activity by doing something that provides a clear or satisfactory conclusion to it. *This rounded the afternoon off perfectly... He rounds off by proposing a toast to the attendants.* **PHRASAL VB V P n V n P V P by-ing**

round on. If someone **rounds on** you, they criticize you fiercely and attack you with aggressive words. The usual American expression is **turn on**. *The Conservative Party rounded angrily on him for damaging the Government.* **PHRASAL VB V P n BRITISH**

round up. 1 If the police or army **round up** a number of people, they arrest or capture them. *The patrolmen rounded them up at the village school and beat them with rifle butts.* **2** If you **round up** animals or **PHRASAL VB V P noun V n P V P noun**

things, you gather them together. *He had sought work as a cowboy, rounding up cattle.* **3** See also **roundup.**

round·about /ˈraʊndəbaʊt/ **roundabouts. 1** A **roundabout** is a circular structure in the road at a place where several roads meet. You drive round it until you come to the road that you want. **◆◇◇◇◇ N-COUNT BRITISH**
2 A **roundabout** at a funfair is a large circular mechanical device with seats, often in the shape of animals or cars, on which children sit and go round and round. The American word is **carousel**. **3** A **roundabout** in a playground is a circular platform that children sit or stand on. People push the platform to make it spin round. **N-COUNT BRITISH**
4 If you go somewhere by a **roundabout** route, you do not go there by the shortest and quickest route. **5** If you do or say something in a **roundabout** way, you do not do or say it in a simple, clear, and direct way. **ADJ-GRADED ADJ-GRADED**
6 • **round about**: see **round**. • **swings and roundabouts**: see **swing**.

round·ed /ˈraʊndɪd/ **1** Something that is **rounded** is curved in shape, without any points or sharp edges. *...a low rounded hill.* **◆◇◇◇◇ ADJ-GRADED**
2 You describe something or someone as **rounded** or **well-rounded** when you are expressing approval of them because they are balanced, with no single aspect or characteristic dominating the others. *...a well-rounded, well-educated and highly intelligent man.* **ADJ-GRADED PRAGMATICS**

roun·del /ˈraʊndəl/ **roundels.** A **roundel** is a circular design, for example one painted on an aircraft to identify it. **N-COUNT**

round·ers /ˈraʊndəz/. In Britain, **rounders** is a game played by two teams of schoolchildren, in which a player scores points by hitting a ball thrown by a member of the other team and then running round all four sides of a square. **N-UNCOUNT**

round·ly /ˈraʊndli/. If you are **roundly** condemned or criticized, you are condemned or criticized forcefully or by many people. If you are **roundly** defeated, you are defeated completely. **ADV-GRADED**

ˈround-robin, round-robins; also spelled **round robin.** A **round-robin** is a sports competition in which each player or team plays against every other player or team. **N-COUNT**

ˈround table, round tables; also spelled **round-table** or **roundtable.** A **round table** discussion is one where people meet in order to discuss something on equal terms. *...a round-table conference.* **◆◇◇◇◇ N-COUNT**

ˈround-the-clock. See **clock.**

ˌround ˈtrip, round trips; also spelled **round-trip. 1** If you make a **round trip**, you travel to a place and then back again. **2** A **round-trip** ticket is a ticket for a train, bus, or plane that allows you to travel to a particular place and then back again. The usual British term is **return ticket**. **◆◇◇◇◇ N-COUNT ADJ: ADJ n AMERICAN**

round·up /ˈraʊndʌp/ **roundups;** also spelled **round-up. 1** A **roundup** of news is a summary of the main events that have happened; used especially for radio and television. *First, we have this roundup of the day's news.* **◆◇◇◇◇ N-COUNT JOURNALISM**
2 When there is a **roundup** of people, they are arrested or captured by the police or army and brought to one place. *There are reports that round-ups of westerners are still taking place.* **3** A **roundup** is an occasion when cattle, horses, or other animals are collected together so that they can be counted or sold. **N-COUNT N-COUNT AMERICAN**

rouse /raʊz/ **rouses, rousing, roused. 1** If someone **rouses** you when you are sleeping or if you **rouse**, you wake up. *When I put my hand on his, he stirs but doesn't quite rouse.* **2** If you **rouse** yourself to do something, you stop being inactive and start doing something. *Hong Kong's voters did not rouse themselves from their traditional political apathy.* **3** If something or someone **rouses** you, they make you very emotional or excited. *...a man not quickly roused to anger or harsh opinions.* ◆ **rousing** *...a rousing speech.* **4** If something **rouses** a feeling in you, it causes you to have that feeling. *It roused a feeling of rebellion in him.* **◆◇◇◇◇ V-ERG: V n V LITERARY VERB: V pron-refl to-inf V pron-refl from n VERB: V n be V-ed to n ADJ-GRADED VERB V n**

roust·about /ˈraʊstəbaʊt/ **roustabouts.** A **roustabout** is an unskilled labourer, especially one who works in the docks or on an oil rig. *N-COUNT AMERICAN*

rout /raʊt/ **routs, routing, routed.** If an army, sports team, or other group **routs** its opponents, it defeats them completely and easily. ...*the Battle of Hastings at which the Norman army routed the English opposition.* ► Also a noun. *One after another the Italian bases in the desert fell as the retreat turned into a rout.* *◆◇◇◇◇ VERB: V n*   *N-COUNT*

route /ruːt/ **routes, routing, routed.** Also pronounced /raʊt/ in American English. **1** A **route** is a way from one place to another. ...*the most direct route to the town centre.* **2** A bus, air, or shipping **route** is the way between two places along which buses, planes, or ships travel regularly. **3** If vehicles, goods, or passengers **are routed** in a particular direction, they are made to travel in that direction. **4** Route is used in front of a number in the names of main roads between major cities. *Take the freeway to the Broadway-Webster exit on Route 580.* **5** You can refer to a way of achieving something as a **route.** *Researchers are trying to get at the same information through an indirect route.* **6** If telephone calls or other electronic signals **are routed** in a particular way, the signals are sent through a particular series of connections. ...*plans to route every emergency call in Britain through just three telephone exchanges.* **7** En route to a place means on the way to that place. En route is sometimes spelled on route in non-standard English. *One of the bags was lost en route.* **8** Journalists sometimes use en route when they are mentioning an event that happened as part of a longer process or before another event. *The German set three tournament records and equalled two others en route to grabbing golf's richest prize.* *◆◆◆◇ N-COUNT*   *N-COUNT*   *VERB: be V-ed*   *AMERICAN*   *N-COUNT*   *VERB V n prep/adv TECHNICAL*   *PHRASE*   *PHRASE*

rou·tine /ruːˈtiːn/ **routines. 1** A **routine** is the usual series of things that you do at a particular time. A **routine** is also the practice of regularly doing things in a fixed order. *The players had to change their daily routine and lifestyle... He checked up on you as a matter of routine.* **2** You use **routine** to describe activities that are done as a normal part of a job or process. ...*a series of routine medical tests.* ♦ **rou·tine·ly** *Vitamin K is routinely given in the first week of life to prevent bleeding.* **3** A **routine** situation, action, or event is one which seems completely ordinary, rather than interesting, exciting, or different; used showing disapproval. *So many days are routine and uninteresting, especially in winter.* ♦ **routinely** *Any outside criticism is routinely dismissed as interference.* **4** You use **routine** to refer to a way of life that is uninteresting and ordinary, or hardly ever changes; used showing disapproval. ...*the mundane routine of her life.* **5** A **routine** is a short sequence of jokes, remarks, actions, or movements that forms part of a longer performance. ...*an athletic dance routine.* *◆◆◆◇◇ N-VAR*   *ADJ*   *ADV*   *ADJ-GRADED PRAGMATICS*   *ADV*   *N-VAR PRAGMATICS*   *N-COUNT*

rove /rəʊv/ **roves, roving, roved. 1** If someone **roves** about an area or **roves** an area, they wander around there. ...*organised anti-foreign bands called the Boxers who roved the countryside and the provinces.* ♦ **rov·ing** ...*a roving reporter.* **2** If you say that someone's eyes **roved** round a place, you mean that they are looking around to see what is interesting. *His eyes roved to see how many of the group appreciated his heavy humour.* ● If you say that a man has **a roving eye**, you are criticizing him for continually paying attention to different women. *VERB: V prep/adv V n*   *ADJ: ADJ n VERB: V prep V*   *PHRASE*

row 1 arrangement or sequence

row /rəʊ/ **rows. 1** A **row** of things or people is a number of them arranged in a line. ...*a row of pretty little cottages.* **2** In a theatre or cinema, each line of seats is called a **row.** *She was sitting in the front row.* **3** Row is sometimes used in the names of streets. ...*the house at 236 Larch Row.* **4** If something happens several times **in a row**, it happens that number of times without a break. If something happens several days **in a row**, it happens on each *◆◆◆◇◇ N-COUNT*   *N-COUNT*   *PHRASE*

of those days. *They have won five championships in a row.* **5** See also **death row**, **skid row**.

row 2 making a boat move

row /rəʊ/ **rows, rowing, rowed.** When you **row,** you sit in a boat and make it move through the water by using oars. If you **row** someone somewhere, you take them there in a boat, using oars. *We could all row a boat and swim... The boatman refused to row him back.* ► Also a noun. *I took Daniel for a row.* ● See also **rowing.** *◆◆◇◇◇ VERB: V prep V n V n adv/prep*   *N-COUNT*

row 3 disagreement or noise

row /raʊ/ **rows, rowing, rowed. 1** A **row** is a serious disagreement between people or organizations. *They risked what could be a major diplomatic row with France.* **2** If two people **row** or if one person **rows** with another, they have a noisy argument. *They rowed all the time and thought it couldn't be good for the baby... He had earlier rowed with his girlfriend.* ► Also a noun. *They had a terrible row on their wedding day.* **3** If you say that someone is making a **row,** you mean that they are making a loud, unpleasant noise. '*Whatever is that row?*' she demanded. *◆◆◇◇◇ N-COUNT BRITISH, INFORMAL*   *V-RECIP V with n V with n INFORMAL*   *N-COUNT*   *N-SING BRITISH, INFORMAL*

ro·wan /ˈrəʊən/ **rowans.** A **rowan** or a **rowan** tree is a tree that has red berries in autumn. ► **Rowan** is the wood of this tree. *N-VAR*   *N-UNCOUNT*

row·boat /ˈrəʊbəʊt/ **rowboats.** A **rowboat** is a small boat that you move through the water by using oars. The usual British term is **rowing boat.** *N-COUNT AMERICAN*

row·dy /ˈraʊdi/ **rowdier, rowdiest; rowdies. 1** When people are **rowdy,** they are noisy, rough, and likely to cause trouble. *He has complained to the police about rowdy neighbours.* ♦ **row·di·ness** ...*adolescent behaviour like vandalism and rowdiness.* **2** If you describe people as **rowdies,** you mean that they are noisy, rough, and likely to cause trouble. *◆◇◇◇◇ ADJ-GRADED*   *N-UNCOUNT*   *N-PLURAL INFORMAL*

row·er /ˈrəʊə/ **rowers.** A **rower** is a person who rows a boat, especially as a sport. *N-COUNT*

row house /ˈrəʊ haʊs/ **row houses;** also spelled **rowhouse.** A **row house** is one of a row of similar houses joined together by their side walls. The usual British term is **terraced house.** *N-COUNT AMERICAN*

row·ing /ˈrəʊɪŋ/ **Rowing** is a sport in which people or teams race against each other in boats with oars. *◆◇◇◇◇ N-UNCOUNT*

'rowing boat, rowing boats; also spelled **rowing-boat.** A **rowing boat** is a small boat that you move through the water by using oars. The usual American word is **rowboat.** *N-COUNT BRITISH*

'rowing machine, rowing machines. A **rowing machine** is an exercise machine with moving parts which you move as if you were rowing a boat. *N-COUNT*

row·lock /ˈrɒlək, ˈrəʊlɒk/ **rowlocks.** The **rowlocks** on a rowing-boat are the U-shaped pieces of metal that keep the oars in position. *N-COUNT BRITISH*

roy·al /ˈrɔɪəl/ **royals. 1** Royal is used to indicate that something is connected with a king, queen, or emperor, or their family. A **royal** person is a king, queen, or emperor, or a member of their family. ...*the Japanese royal couple.* **2** Royal is used in names of institutions or organizations that are officially appointed or supported by a member of a royal family. ...*the Royal Academy of Music.* **3** Members of the royal family are sometimes referred to as the **royals.** *◆◆◆◇ ADJ*   *ADJ: ADJ n*   *N-COUNT INFORMAL*

,royal 'blue. Something that is **royal blue** is deep blue in colour. *COLOUR*

,royal 'family, royal families. The **royal family** of a country is the king, queen, or emperor, and all the members of their family. *◆◆◇◇◇ N-COUNT*

,Royal 'Highness, Royal Highnesses. Expressions such as **Your Royal Highness** and **Their Royal Highnesses** are used to address or refer to members of royal families who are not kings or queens. *◆◇◇◇◇ N-VOC: PRON*

roy·al·ist /ˈrɔɪəlɪst/ **royalists.** A **royalist** is someone who supports their country's royal family or who believes that their country should have a king or queen. *◆◇◇◇◇ N-COUNT*

R

,royal 'jelly. Royal jelly is a substance that bees N-UNCOUNT
make in order to feed young bees and queen bees.

roy·al·ly /ˈrɔɪəli/. If you say that something is done ADV
royally, you are emphasizing that it is done impres- PRAGMATICS
sively or grandly, or that it is very great in degree.
They were royally received in every aspect.

roy·al·ty /ˈrɔɪəlti/ **royalties. 1** The members of ◆◆◇◇◇
royal families are sometimes referred to as **royalty.** N-UNCOUNT
...a ceremony attended by royalty. **2 Royalties** are N-PLURAL
payments made to authors and musicians when
their work is sold or performed. They usually receive a fixed percentage of the profits from these
sales or performances. **3** Payments made to some- N-COUNT
one whose invention, idea, or property is used by a
commercial company is referred to as **royalties.**

RP /ˌɑː ˈpiː/. **RP** is an abbreviation for 'received pronunciation'. It is a way of pronouncing British English that is considered to be the standard accent.

rpm /ˌɑː piː ˈem/. **rpm** is an abbreviation for 'revo- ◆◇◇◇◇
lutions per minute'. It is used to indicate the speed
of something by saying how many times per minute
it will go round in a circle.

RSI /ˌɑːr es ˈaɪ/. **RSI** is an abbreviation for **repetitive** N-UNCOUNT
strain injury.

RSVP /ˌɑːr es viː ˈpiː/. **RSVP** is an abbreviation for
'répondez s'il vous plaît', which means 'please reply'. It is written on the bottom of invitations.

Rt Hon. /ˌraɪt ˈɒn/. **Rt Hon.** is an abbreviation for ADJ:
'Right Honourable'. It is used in Britain as part of theADJ n
the formal title of some members of the Privy Council and some judges. *...the leader of the Liberal
Democrats, the Rt. Hon Paddy Ashdown.*

rub /rʌb/ **rubs, rubbing, rubbed. 1** If you **rub** a ◆◆◇◇◇
part of your body, you move your hand or fingers VERB: V n
backwards and forwards over it while pressing firm- V prep/adv
ly. *'I fell in a ditch,' he said, rubbing at a scrape on
his hand.* **2** If you **rub** against a surface or **rub** a VERB
part of your body against a surface, you move it V prep
backwards and forwards while pressing it against V n prep
the surface. *A cat was rubbing against my leg... He
kept rubbing his leg against mine.* **3** If you **rub** an VERB
object or a surface, you move a cloth backward and V n
forward over it in order to clean or dry it. *She took* Also V
off her glasses and rubbed them hard. **4** If you **rub** a VERB
substance into a surface or **rub** something such as V n prep
dirt from a surface, you spread it over the surface or
remove it from the surface using your hand or
something such as a cloth. *He rubbed oil into my
back.* **5** If you **rub** two things together or if they **rub** V-ERG
together, they move backwards and forwards, press- V n together
ing against each other. *He rubbed his hands together* Also V
a few times. together

6 If something you are wearing or holding **rubs**, it VERB
makes you sore because it keeps moving backwards V
and forwards against your skin. *Smear cream on to* Also V n
*your baby's skin at the edges of the plaster to prevent it
from rubbing.*

7 Rub is used in expressions such as **there's the rub** N-SING:
and **the rub is** when you are mentioning a difficulty theN
that makes something hard or impossible to achieve. FORMAL
*'What do you want to write about?'. And there was the
rub, because I didn't yet know.*

8 A massage can be referred to as a **rub.** N-COUNT

9 See also **rubbing.** ● to **rub** someone's **nose in** it: see
nose. ● to **rub salt into the wound:** see **salt.** ● to **rub**
shoulders: see **shoulder.**

rub along. If two people **rub along** or if one person PHRASAL VB
rubs along with another, they are able to live or work RECIP
together in a fairly friendly way. *North and South had* pl-n V P
officials at the meeting and they rubbed along toler- Also V P with n
ably well. BRITISH,
INFORMAL

rub down. 1 If you **rub down** a rough surface, you PHRASAL VB
make it smooth by rubbing it with something such as V P noun
sandpaper. *They were settling to their work, rubbing* Also V P n
down the woodwork with sandpaper. **2** If you **rub** V n P
someone **down,** you dry them or massage them with Also V P noun
something such as a towel or cloth. *He set him on the
bed and rubbed him down with a coarse towel.*

rub in. 1 If you **rub** a substance **in,** you press it into PHRASAL VB
something by continuously moving it over its surface. V P noun
Also V n P

When hair is dry, rub in a little oil to make it smooth V n P
and glossy. **2** If someone keeps reminding you of V P noun
something you would rather forget you can say that
they **are rubbing** it **in.** *It was by way of rubbing in his
brother's inadequacy that Noel took the lead part for
himself.*

rub off. If someone's qualities or habits **rub off** on PHRASAL VB
you, you develop some of their qualities or habits af- V P on n
ter spending time with them. *He was a tremendously* Also V P
*enthusiastic teacher and that rubbed off on all the chil-
dren he taught.*

rub out. If you **rub out** something that you have PHRASAL VB
written on paper or a blackboard, you remove it by V P noun
rubbing it with a rubber or cloth. *She began rubbing* Also V n P
out the pencilled marks in the margin.

rub·ber /ˈrʌbə/ **rubbers. 1 Rubber** is a strong, ◆◆◇◇◇
waterproof, elastic substance made from the sap of N-UNCOUNT
a tropical tree or produced chemically. It is used for
making tyres, boots, and other products. **2 Rubber** ADJ
things are made of rubber. *...rubber gloves. ...a rubber ball.* **3** A **rubber** is a small piece of rubber or N-COUNT
other material used to rub out mistakes that you BRITISH
have made while writing, drawing, or typing. The
American word is **eraser. 4** A **rubber** is a condom. N-COUNT
I'm very well and taking care of myself; wearing rub- AMERICAN,
bers, brushing my teeth etc. **5** In some card games, INFORMAL
for example bridge or whist, a **rubber** is a match of N-COUNT
three games.

,rubber 'band, rubber bands. A rubber band is N-COUNT
a thin circle of very elastic rubber. You put it
around things such as papers in order to keep them
together.

,rubber 'boot, rubber boots. Rubber boots are N-COUNT
long boots made of rubber that you wear to keep AMERICAN
your feet dry. The British word is **wellington.**

,rubber 'bullet, rubber bullets. A rubber bullet N-COUNT
is a bullet made of rubber. It is intended to injure
people rather than kill them.

'rubber plant, rubber plants. A rubber plant is a N-COUNT
type of plant with shiny leaves. It grows naturally in
Asia but is also grown as a house plant in other
parts of the world.

,rubber 'stamp, rubber stamps, rubber ◆◇◇◇◇
stamping, rubber stamped; also spelled
rubber-stamp. 1 A **rubber stamp** is a small device N-COUNT
with a name, date, or symbol on it. You press it on
to an ink pad and then on to a document in order
to show that the document has been officially dealt
with. **2** When someone in authority **rubber-stamps** VERB
a decision, plan, or law, they agree to it. *Nearly 60* V n
banks have rubber-stamped a refinancing deal.

rub·bery /ˈrʌbəri/. **1** Something that is **rubbery** ADJ-GRADED
looks or feels soft or elastic like rubber. *She had the
most rubbery face.* **2** Food such as meat that is **rub-** ADJ-GRADED
bery is difficult to chew.

rub·bing /ˈrʌbɪŋ/ **rubbings. 1** A **rubbing** is a pic- N-COUNT
ture that you make by putting a piece of paper over
a carved surface and rubbing crayon, charcoal, or
chalk over it. **2** See also **rub.**

rub·bish /ˈrʌbɪʃ/ **rubbishes, rubbishing, rub-** ◆◆◇◇◇
bished. Rubbish is used mainly in British English.
1 Rubbish consists of unwanted things or waste ma- N-UNCOUNT
terial such as used paper, empty tins and bottles, and
waste food. The usual American word is **garbage** or
trash.

2 If you think that something is of very poor quality N-UNCOUNT
you can say that it is **rubbish.** *He described her book as* INFORMAL
absolute rubbish. **3** If you think that an idea or a state- N-UNCOUNT
ment is foolish or wrong you can say that it is **rubbish.** INFORMAL
These reports are total and utter rubbish. **4** If you think
that someone is not very good at something, you can V-link ADJ
say that they are **rubbish** at it. *I tried playing golf, but I* INFORMAL
was rubbish. **5** If you **rubbish** a person, their ideas or VERB
their work, you say that they are of little value. *Five whole* V n
*pages of script were devoted to rubbishing her political
opponents.*

rub·bishy /ˈrʌbɪʃi/. If you describe something as ADJ
rubbishy, you think it is of very poor quality. *...some* BRITISH,
old rubbishy cop movie. INFORMAL

rub·ble /'rʌbəl/. **1** When a building is destroyed, the pieces of brick, stone, or other materials that remain are referred to as **rubble**. **2** The word **rubble** is used to refer to the small pieces of stone that are used to build the foundations of roads, paths, and houses. ◆◇◇◇◇ N-UNCOUNT / N-UNCOUNT

ru·bel·la /ruː'belə/. **Rubella** is a disease. The symptoms are a cough, a sore throat, and red spots on your skin. N-UNCOUNT MEDICAL

ru·ble /'ruːbəl/. See **rouble**.

ru·bric /'ruːbrɪk/ **rubrics**. **1** A **rubric** is a set of rules or instructions, for example the rules at the beginning of an examination paper. **2** A **rubric** is a title or heading under which something operates or is studied. *The aid comes under the rubric of technical co-operation between governments.* N-COUNT FORMAL / N-COUNT FORMAL

ruby /'ruːbi/ **rubies**. **1** A **ruby** is a red jewel. *...earrings set with diamonds, rubies, and sapphires.* **2** Something that is **ruby** is dark red in colour. ◆◇◇◇◇ N-COUNT COLOUR

ruck /rʌk/ **rucks, rucking, rucked**. **1** A **ruck** is a situation where a group of people are fighting or struggling. *There'll be a huge ruck with the cops as they try to take photographs.* **2** A **ruck** is a fold or crease in cloth or clothing. *There was a small ruck in the office carpet.* ◆◇◇◇◇ N-COUNT BRITISH / N-COUNT BRITISH

ruck up. If cloth or someone's clothing **rucks up** or if someone or something **rucks** it **up**, it forms folds and covers a smaller area than it did before. *His shoe had rucked up one corner of the pale rug.* PHRASAL VB ERG: V P / V P noun BRITISH

ruck·sack /'rʌksæk/ **rucksacks**. A **rucksack** is a bag with straps that go over your shoulders, so that you can carry things on your back, for example when you are walking or climbing. The usual American word is **pack** or **backpack**. ◆◇◇◇◇ N-COUNT BRITISH

ruck·us /'rʌkəs/. If someone or something causes a **ruckus**, they cause a great deal of noise, argument, or confusion. N-SING AMERICAN, INFORMAL

ruc·tion /'rʌkʃən/ **ructions**. If someone or something causes **ructions**, they cause strong protests, quarrels, or other trouble. N-COUNT INFORMAL

rud·der /'rʌdə/ **rudders**. **1** A **rudder** is a device for steering a boat. It consists of a vertical piece of wood or metal at the back of the boat. **2** An aeroplane's **rudder** is a vertical piece of metal at the back which is used to make the plane turn to the right or to the left. ◆◇◇◇◇ N-COUNT / N-COUNT

rud·dy /'rʌdi/ **ruddier, ruddiest**. **1** If you describe someone's face as **ruddy**, you mean that their face is a reddish colour, usually because they are healthy or have been working hard. *He had a naturally ruddy complexion.* **2** Something that is **ruddy** is reddish in colour. **3 Ruddy** is used as a mild swear word to add emphasis or to express anger. *Why are you being so ruddy mysterious?.* ◆◇◇◇◇ ADJ-GRADED / ADJ-GRADED LITERARY / ADJ: ADJ n BRITISH, DATED

rude /ruːd/ **ruder, rudest**. **1** When people are **rude**, they act in an impolite way towards other people or say impolite things about them. *He's rude to her friends and obsessively jealous... People were quite often rude about him.* ♦ **rude·ly** *...why she felt compelled to behave so rudely to a friend.* ♦ **rude·ness** *Mother is cross at Caleb's rudeness.* **2 Rude** is used to describe words and behaviour that are likely to embarrass or offend people, because they relate to sex or to bodily functions. *Luke made a rude gesture with his finger.* **3** If someone receives a **rude** shock, something unpleasant happens unexpectedly. *It will come as a rude shock when their salary or income-tax refund cannot be cashed.* ♦ **rude·ly** *People were awakened rudely by a siren just outside their window.* ● a **rude awakening**: see **awakening**. **4** Objects can be described as **rude** when they are very simply and roughly made. *Roden had already constructed a rude cabin for himself.* ◆◆◇◇◇ ADJ-GRADED / ADV-GRADED / N-UNCOUNT / ADJ-GRADED / ADJ-GRADED: ADJ n / ADV-GRADED: ADV with v / ADJ: ADJ n LITERARY

ru·di·men·ta·ry /ˌruːdɪ'mentri/. **1 Rudimentary** things are very basic or undeveloped and therefore unsatisfactory. *...a kind of rudimentary kitchen.* **2 Rudimentary** knowledge includes only the simplest and most basic facts. *...a rudimentary grasp of economics.* ◆◇◇◇◇ ADJ-GRADED FORMAL / ADJ-GRADED FORMAL

ru·di·ments /'ruːdɪmənts/. When you learn the **rudiments** of something, you learn the simplest or most essential things about it. *...learning the rudiments of brick-laying.* N-PLURAL

rue /ruː/ **rues, ruing, rued**. If you **rue** something that you have done, you are sorry that you did it, because it has had unpleasant results. *Tavare was probably ruing his decision.* ◆◆◇◇◇ VERB V n LITERARY

rue·ful /'ruːfʊl/. If someone is **rueful**, they feel or express regret or sorrow in a quiet and gentle way. *He shook his head and gave me a rueful smile.* ♦ **rue·ful·ly** *He grinned at her ruefully.* ◆◇◇◇◇ ADJ-GRADED LITERARY / ADV-GRADED

ruff /rʌf/ **ruffs**. **1** A **ruff** is a stiff strip of cloth or other material with many small folds in it, which some people wore round their neck in former times. **2** A **ruff** is a thick band of feathers or fur round the neck of a bird or animal. N-COUNT / N-COUNT

ruf·fian /'rʌfiən/ **ruffians**. A **ruffian** is a man who behaves violently and is involved in crime. N-COUNT DATED

ruf·fle /'rʌfəl/ **ruffles, ruffling, ruffled**. **1** If you **ruffle** someone's hair, you move your hand backwards and forwards through it as a way of showing your affection towards them. **2** When the wind **ruffles** something such as the surface of the sea, it causes it to move gently in a wave-like motion. *The evening breeze ruffled the pond.* **3** If a bird **ruffles** its feathers or if its feathers **ruffle**, they stand out on its body, for example when it is cleaning itself or when it is frightened. *Tame birds, when approached, will stretch out their necks and ruffle their neck feathering.* **4 Ruffles** are folds of cloth at the neck or cuffs of a piece of clothing. **5** If something **ruffles** someone, it causes them to panic and lose their confidence or to become angry or upset. *Nothing could ruffle the perfect composure with which she casually greets members of staff.* **6** If someone or something **ruffles** some **feathers** or **ruffles** someone's **feathers**, they cause people to become very angry, nervous, or upset. ◆◇◇◇◇ VERB: V n / VERB V n LITERARY / V-ERG V n Also V / N-COUNT / VERB V n / PHRASE

ruf·fled /'rʌfəld/. **1** Something that is **ruffled** is no longer smooth or neat. *Her short hair was oddly ruffled.* **2 Ruffled** clothes are decorated with small folds of material. ● See also **ruffle**. ADJ-GRADED / ADJ: ADJ n

rug /rʌg/ **rugs**. **1** A **rug** is a piece of thick material that you put on a floor. It is like a carpet but covers a smaller area. *A Persian rug covered the hardwood floors.* **2** A **rug** is a small blanket which you use to cover your shoulders or your knees to keep them warm. ◆◆◇◇◇ N-COUNT / N-COUNT BRITISH

rug·by /'rʌgbi/. **Rugby** or **rugby football** is a game played by two teams using an oval ball. Players try to score points by carrying the ball to their opponents' end of the pitch, or by kicking it over a bar fixed between two goalposts. ◆◆◇◇◇ N-UNCOUNT

rug·ged /'rʌgɪd/. **1** A **rugged** area of land is rocky and uneven, with few trees or plants. *...a rugged mountainous terrain.* ♦ **rug·ged·ly** *...a ruggedly beautiful wilderness.* ♦ **rug·ged·ness** *...the island's ruggedness.* **2** If you describe a man as **rugged**, you mean that he has strong, masculine features; used showing approval. *A look of pure disbelief crossed Shankly's rugged face.* ♦ **rug·ged·ly** *He was six feet tall and ruggedly handsome.* **3** If you describe someone's character as **rugged**, you mean that they are strong and determined; used showing approval. *Rugged individualism forged America's frontier society.* **4** A **rugged** piece of equipment is made of strong material and is designed to last a long time, even if it is treated roughly. *The camera combines rugged reliability with unequalled performance.* ◆◇◇◇◇ ADJ-GRADED LITERARY / ADV: ADV adj / N-UNCOUNT / ADJ-GRADED PRAGMATICS / ADV / ADJ-GRADED PRAGMATICS / ADJ-GRADED

rug·ger /'rʌgə/. **Rugger** is the same as **rugby**. *...a rugger match.* N-UNCOUNT BRITISH, INFORMAL

ruin /'ruːɪn/ **ruins, ruining, ruined**. **1** To **ruin** something means to severely harm, damage, or spoil it. *My wife was ruining her health through worry.* ▶ Also a noun. *She wasn't going to let her plans go to ruin.* **2** If something is **in ruins**, it is completely spoiled. *Its heavily-subsidized economy is in ruins.* **3** To **ruin** someone means to cause them to no longer have any money. *She accused* ◆◆◇◇◇ VERB V n / N-UNCOUNT / PHRASE / VERB V n

him of ruining her financially with his taste for the high life. ► Also a noun. *The family faced financial ruin.* N-UNCOUNT

4 The **ruins of** something are the parts of it that remain after it has been severely damaged or weakened. *The new Turkish republic he helped to build emerged from the ruins of a great empire.* **5** The **ruins of** a building are the parts of it that remain after the rest has fallen down or been destroyed. ● See also **ruined.** N-PLURAL: the N of n

6 If a building or place is **in ruins**, most of it has been destroyed and only parts of it remain. PHRASE N-COUNT

ru·ina·tion /ˌruːɪˈneɪʃən/. The **ruination** of someone or something is the act of ruining them or the process of being ruined. *Money was the ruination of him.* N-UNCOUNT

ruined /ˈruːɪnd/. A **ruined** building or place has been very badly damaged or has gradually fallen down because of neglect. ...*a ruined church.* ADJ: ADJ n

ru·in·ous /ˈruːɪnəs/. **1** If you describe the cost of something as **ruinous**, you mean that it costs far more money than you can afford or than is reasonable. ...*the potentially ruinous costs of their legal system.* ♦ **ru·in·ous·ly** ...*a ruinously expensive court case.* **2** A **ruinous** process or course of action is one that is likely to lead to ruin. *The economy of the state is experiencing the ruinous effects of the conflict.* ADJ ADV: ADV adj ADJ-GRADED

♦ **ruinously** ...*cities ruinously choked by uncontrolled traffic.* ADV

rule /ruːl/ **rules, ruling, ruled. 1** Rules are instructions that tell you what you are allowed to do and what you are not allowed to do. ...*a thirty-two-page pamphlet explaining the rules of basketball... This was against the rules.* ...*the amendment to Rule 22.* **2** If someone in authority **bends the rules** or **stretches the rules,** they do something or allow something to happen, even though it is against the rules. *There was a time when a minority of officers were prepared to bend the rules.* **3** If workers **work to rule,** or if they go on a **work to rule,** they protest by working strictly according to the rules of their job but doing no extra work and taking no new decisions. **4** A **rule** is a statement telling people what they should do in order to achieve success or a benefit of some kind. *The rules for healthy eating are the same during pregnancy as at any other time.* **5** The **rules** of something such as a language or a science are statements that describe the way that things usually happen in a particular situation. ...*according to the rules of quantum theory.* N-COUNT PHRASE PHRASE BRITISH N-COUNT N-COUNT

6 If something is **the rule,** it is the normal state of affairs. *For many Americans today, weekend work has unfortunately become the rule.* **7** If you say that something happens **as a rule,** you mean that it usually happens. *As a rule she eats dinner with us.* **8** A **rule of thumb** is a rule or principal that you follow which is not based on exact calculations but rather on experience. *As a rule of thumb, a cup of filter coffee contains about 80mg of caffeine.* N-SING: the N PHRASE PHRASE

9 The person or group that **rules** a country controls its affairs. *For four centuries, he says, foreigners have ruled Angola.* ...*demands for an end to one-party rule.* **10** If something **rules** your life, it influences or restricts your actions in a way that is not good for you. *Scientists have always been aware of how fear can rule our lives.* **11** When someone in authority **rules** that something is true or should happen, they state that they have officially decided that it is true or should happen. *The Israeli court has not yet ruled on the case... A provincial magistrates' court last week ruled it unconstitutional.* VERB: V n Also V N-UNCOUNT VERB V n VERB: V that V onn V n adj/n FORMAL

12 See also **golden rule, ground rule, ruling, slide rule.**

rule out. 1 If you **rule out** a course of action, an idea, or a solution, you decide that it is impossible or unsuitable. *The Prime Minister is believed to have ruled out cuts in child benefit or pensions.* **2** If something **rules out** a situation, it prevents it from happening or from being possible. *A serious car accident in 1986 ruled out a permanent future for him in farming.* PHRASAL VB V P noun Also V n P V P noun

'rule book, rule books. A **rule book** is a book containing the official rules for a particular game, job, or organization. ...*one of the most serious offences mentioned in the Party rule book.* N-COUNT

rule of 'law. The **rule of law** refers to a situation in which the people in a society obey its laws and enable it to function properly. ...*peace, stability and respect for the rule of law.* ◆◇◇◇ N-SING FORMAL

rul·er /ˈruːlə/ **rulers. 1** The **ruler** of a country is the person who rules the country. *He was a weak-willed and indecisive ruler.* **2** A **ruler** is a long flat piece of wood, metal, or plastic with straight edges marked in centimetres or inches. Rulers are used to measure things and to draw straight lines. ◆◆◇◇◇ N-COUNT N-COUNT

rul·ing /ˈruːlɪŋ/ **rulings. 1** The **ruling** group of people in a country or organization is the group that controls its affairs. ...*the Mexican voters' growing dissatisfaction with the ruling party.* **2** A **ruling** is an official decision made by a judge or court. *Goodwin tried to have the court ruling overturned.* **3** Someone's **ruling** passion or emotion is the feeling they have most strongly, which influences their actions. *Even my love of literary fame, my ruling passion, never soured my temper.* ◆◆◇◇◇ ADJ: ADJ n N-COUNT ADJ: ADJ n

rum /rʌm/ **rums. 1** Rum is an alcoholic drink made from sugar cane juice. ...*a rum punch.* **2** If you describe people or things as **rum,** you mean that they are rather strange. *It was a joke, of course, but surely a rum sort of joke?* ◆◇◇◇◇ N-VAR ADJ-GRADED ADJ n BRITISH DATED

rum·ba /ˈrʌmbə/ **rumbas.** The **rumba** is a type of ballroom dance that comes from Cuba, or the music that the dance is performed to. N-COUNT

rum·ble /ˈrʌmbəl/ **rumbles, rumbling, rumbled. 1** If something **rumbles,** it makes a low, throbbing noise. *Speeches rumbled within the walls of the churches.* ► Also a noun. ...*the distant rumble of traffic.* **2** If your stomach **rumbles,** it makes a vibrating noise, usually because you are hungry. **3** If someone **is rumbled,** the truth about them or something they were trying to conceal is discovered. *When his fraud was rumbled he had just £20.17 in the bank.* ◆◇◇◇◇ VERB N-COUNT VERB: V VB: usu passive be V-ed BRITISH, INFORMAL

rumble on. If you say that something such as an argument **rumbles on,** you mean that it continues long after it should have been settled. *And still the row rumbles on over who is to blame.* PHRASAL VB V P BRITISH, JOURNALISM

rum·bling /ˈrʌmblɪŋ/ **rumblings. 1** A **rumbling** is a low, continuous, throbbing noise. ...*the rumbling of an empty stomach.* **2** Rumblings are signs that a bad situation is developing or that people are becoming dissatisfied. *There were rumblings of discontent within the ranks.* ◆◇◇◇◇ N-COUNT N-COUNT

rum·bus·tious /rʌmˈbʌstʃəs/. A **rumbustious** person is energetic in a cheerful, noisy way. The usual American word is **rambunctious.** ...*the flamboyant and somewhat rumbustious prime minister.* ADJ-GRADED BRITISH

ru·mi·nate /ˈruːmɪneɪt/ **ruminates, ruminating, ruminated. 1** If you **ruminate** on something, you think about it very carefully. *He ruminated on the terrible wastage that typified American life... Obsessional personalities commonly ruminate excessively about death.* **2** When animals **ruminate,** they bring food back from their stomach into their mouth and chew it again. VERB V on/about/ overn Also V FORMAL VERB: V TECHNICAL

ru·mi·na·tion /ˌruːmɪˈneɪʃən/ **ruminations.** Your **ruminations** are your careful thoughts about something. ...*profound ruminations about life.* N-COUNT FORMAL

ru·mi·na·tive /ˈruːmɪnətɪv, AM -neɪt-/. If you are **ruminative,** you are thinking very deeply and carefully about something. *He was uncharacteristically depressed and ruminative.* ♦ **ru·mi·na·tive·ly** *He stared ruminatively into the distance.* ADJ FORMAL ADV: ADV with v

rum·mage /ˈrʌmɪdʒ/ **rummages, rummaging, rummaged. 1** If you **rummage** through something, you search for something you want by moving things around in a careless or hurried way. *They rummage through piles of second-hand clothes for something that fits.* ► Also a noun. ...*a rummage through his wardrobe for some tennis whites.* ► **Rummage about** and **rummage around** mean ◆◇◇◇◇ VERB V prep Also V N-SING: a N PHRASAL VB

the same as **rummage**. *I opened the fridge and rummaged about.* **2 Rummage** is old or unwanted things that people give away to charities. The British word is **jumble**.

rum·my /'rʌmi/. Rummy is a card game in which players try to collect cards of the same value or cards in a sequence in the same suit.

ru·mour /'ruːmə/ **rumours;** spelled **rumor** in American English. A **rumour** is a story or piece of information that may or may not be true, but that people are talking about. *Simon denied rumours that he was planning to visit Bulgaria. ...persistent rumours of quarrels within the movement.*

ru·moured /'ruːməd/; spelled **rumored** in American English. If something **is rumoured** to be the case, people are suggesting that it is the case, but they do not know for certain. *Her parents are rumoured to be on the verge of splitting up... It was rumoured that he had been interned in an asylum for a while.*

'rumour mill; spelled **rumor mill** in American English. You can refer to a group of people who spread rumours as the **rumour mill**. *The Washington rumor mill suggests that the president secured his narrow majority only by promising all sorts of concessions on the BTU tax.*

rump /rʌmp/ **rumps. 1** The **rump** of a group, organization, or country consists of the members who remain in it after the rest have left. *The rump of the party does in fact still have considerable assets.* **2** An animal's **rump** is its rear end. **3 Rump** is the same as **rump steak. 4** A person's **rump** is his or her buttocks. *...jeans stretching across her rump.*

rum·ple /'rʌmpəl/ **rumples, rumpling, rumpled.** If you **rumple** someone's hair, you move your hand backwards and forwards through it as your way of showing affection to them.

rum·pled /'rʌmpəld/. **Rumpled** means creased, untidy, or disordered. *I hurried to the tent and grabbed a few clean, if rumpled, clothes. ...a sprawl of white, rumpled sheets.*

,rump 'steak, rump steaks. Rump steak or **rump** is meat from the top back part of a cow's leg.

rum·pus /'rʌmpəs/ **rumpuses.** If someone or something causes a **rumpus**, they cause a lot of noise or argument. *He had actually left the company a year before the rumpus started.*

run /rʌn/ **runs, running, ran.** The form **run** is used in the present tense and is also the past participle of the verb. **1** When you **run**, you move quickly, leaving the ground during each stride. *I excused myself and ran back to the telephone... Neighbouring shopkeepers ran after the man and caught him... He ran the last block to the White House... Antonia ran to meet them.* ► Also a noun. *After a six-mile run, Jackie returns home for a substantial breakfast.* ♦ **run·ning** *We chose to do cross-country running. ...running shoes.* ● If you **make a run for it** or if you **run for it**, you run away in order to escape from someone or something. **2** When someone **runs** in a race, they run in competition with other people. *I was running in the New York Marathon... She ran a great race to finish second.* **3** When a horse **runs** in a race or when its owner **runs** it, it competes in a race. *Cecil could also run Armiger in the Derby.*

4 If someone is **on the run**, they are trying to escape or hide from someone such as the police or an enemy. *Fifteen-year-old Danny is on the run from a local authority home.* ● If someone is **on the run**, they are being severely defeated in a contest or competition. *I knew I had him on the run.* **6** If you say that a person or group **is running scared**, you mean that they are frightened of what someone might do to them or what might happen. **7** If you **run someone close**, **run them a close second**, or **run a close second**, you almost beat them in a race or competition. **8** If you say that someone could **give** someone else **a run for their money**, you mean you think they are almost as good

as the other person. *...a youngster who even now could give Meryl Streep a run for her money.*

9 If you say that something long, such as a road, **runs** in a particular direction, you are describing its course or position. You can also say that something **runs** the length or width of something else. *...the sun-dappled trail which ran through the beech woods... The hallway ran the length of the villa.* **10** If you **run** a wire or tube somewhere, you install it or arrange it so that it is in a particular position. *He ran a wire under his bedroom carpet.* **11** If you **run** your hand or an object over something or through something, you move your hand or the object over it or through it. *It hurt to breathe, and he winced as he ran his hand over his ribs... Fumbling, he ran her card through the machine.* **12** If you **run** something through a machine, process, or series of tests, you make it undergo a process. *They have gathered the best statistics they can find and run them through their own computers.* **13** If someone **runs** for office in an election, they take part as a candidate. The usual British word is **stand**. *He announced he would run for president... It is no easy job to run against John Glenn... Women are running in nearly all the contested seats in Los Angeles.* ► Also a noun. *He was already preparing his run for the presidency.*

14 If you **run** something such as a business or an activity, you are in charge of it or you organize it. *Is this any way to run a country? ...a well-run, profitable organisation.* ♦ **running** *...the committee in charge of the day-to-day running of the party... The aim is to cut running costs by £90 million per year.* **15** If you talk about how a system, an organization, or someone's life **is running**, you are saying how well it is operating or progressing. *The system is now running extremely smoothly. ...the staff who have kept the bank running.* **16** If you **run** an experiment, computer program, or other process, you start it and let it continue. *He ran a lot of tests and it turned out I had an infection called mycoplasma... The program runs on a standard personal computer.* **17** When a machine **is running** or when you **are running** it, it is switched on and operating. *We told him to wait out front with the engine running... She ran the tape and found a message from Charles.* **18** A machine that **runs** on or off a particular source of energy functions using that source of energy. *Black cabs run on diesel.* **19** If you **run** a car or a piece of equipment, you have it and use it. *I ran a 1960 Rover 100 from 1977 until 1983... Always buy a heater with thermostat control to save on running costs.* **20** If something such as a system or place is **up and running**, it is operating normally. *We're trying to get the medical facilities up and running again.*

21 When you say that vehicles such as trains and buses **run** from one place to another, you mean they regularly travel along that route. *A shuttle bus runs frequently between the Inn and the Country Club. ...a government which can't make the trains run on time.* **22** If you **run** somewhere in a car, you drive there. *I'll run over to Short Mountain and check on Mrs Adams... Could you run me up to Baltimore?* ► Also a noun. *...doing the morning school run.*

23 If a liquid **runs** in a particular direction, it flows in that direction. *Tears were running down her cheeks... Wash the rice in cold water until the water runs clear.* **24** If you **run** water, you cause it to flow from a tap. *They heard him running the kitchen tap... I threw off my clothing quickly and ran a warm bath.* ♦ **running** *Wash the lentils under cold running water.* **25** If a tap **is running**, water is coming out of it. *You must have left a tap running in the bathroom.* ♦ **run·ning**. If a house has **running** water, water is supplied to it through pipes and taps. **26** If your nose **is running**, mucus is flowing out of it, usually because you have a cold. **27** If a surface **is running** with a liquid, that liquid is flowing down it. *He was completely running with sweat.* **28** If the dye in some cloth or the ink on some paper **runs**, it comes off or spreads when the cloth or paper gets wet. **29** If a river or well **runs dry**, it

Right column grammar labels:

VP / Also VP noun / N-UNCOUNT / AMERICAN

N-UNCOUNT

N-VAR / ◆◆◇◇

V-PASSIVE / be V-ed to-inf / it be V-ed that / ◆◇◇◇

N-SING / JOURNALISM

N-SING: with supp / BRITISH / N-COUNT / N-UNCOUNT / N-COUNT / INFORMAL

VERB: V n

ADJ-GRADED

N-VAR

N-COUNT

◆◆◆◆ / VERB: V / V adv/prep / V n/amount / V to-inf / N-COUNT / N-UNCOUNT / PHRASE / VERB / V / V n / V-ERG: V / V n / PHRASE / PHRASE / PHRASE / PHRASE / PHRASE

VERB / V prep/adv / V n / VERB / V n prep/adv / VERB / V n prep / VERB / V n through n / VERB / V for n / V against n / V / AMERICAN / N-SING: / N for n / VERB / V n / V-ed / N-SING / VERB / V adv / V / V-ERG / V n / V / V-ERG / V n / V / VERB / V on/off n / VERB / V n / V-ing / BRITISH / PHRASE / VERB / V prep / V / VERB / V adv / V n prep/adv / INFORMAL / N-COUNT / VERB / V prep/adv / V adj / VERB / VERB / running ADJ: ADJ n / VB: only cont / ADJ: ADJ n / VERB: V / VERB / V with n / VERB: V / PHRASE

R

ceases to have any water in it. If an oil well **runs dry**, it no longer produces any oil.

30 If a feeling **runs** through your body or a thought **runs** through your mind, you experience it or think it quickly. *She felt a surge of excitement run through her.* `VERB V through n`

31 If a feeling or noise **runs** through a group of people, it spreads among them. *A buzz of excitement ran through the crowd.* **32** If a theme or feature **runs** through something such as someone's actions or writing, it is present in all of it. *Another thread running through this series is the role of doctors in the treatment of the mentally ill.* `VERB V through n` `VERB V through/ throughout n`

33 When newspapers or magazines **run** a particular item or story, or if it **runs**, it is published or printed. *...an editorial that ran this weekend entitled 'Mr. Cuomo Backs Out.'* `V-ERG: V n V`

34 You can use **run** to indicate that you are quoting someone else's words or ideas. *'Whoa, I'm goin' to Barbay-dos!' ran the jaunty lyrics of a 1970s hit song.* `VERB V with quote BRITISH`

35 If an amount **is running** at a particular level, it is at that level. *Today's RPI figure shows inflation running at 10.9 per cent.* **36** If you **are running short** of something or **running low** on something, you do not have much of it left. *Time is running short.* **37** If people's feelings **are running high**, they are very angry, concerned, or excited. **38** If someone or something **is running** late, they have taken more time than had been planned. If they **are running** to time or ahead of time, they have taken the time planned or less than the time planned. *Tell her I'll call her back later, I'm running late again.* **39** If you **are running** a temperature or a fever, you have a high temperature because you are ill. `VERB V at n` `PHRASE` `PHRASE` `VERB V adv/prep` `VERB: V n`

40 If a play, event, or legal contract **runs** for a particular period of time, it lasts for that period of time. *It pleased critics but ran for only three years in the West End... The contract was to run from 1992 to 2020... I predict it will run and run.* ▶ Also a noun. *The show will transfer to the West End on October 9, after a month's run in Birmingham.* **41** If you talk about what will happen **in the long run**, you are saying what you think will happen over a long period of time in the future. If you talk about what will happen **in the short run**, you are saying what you think will happen in the near future. **42** A **run** of successes or failures is a series of successes or failures. *The England skipper is haunted by a run of low scores... The Scottish Tories' run of luck is holding.* **43** If something happens **against the run of** play or **against the run of** events, it is not what you would expect given what is generally happening in a game or situation. **44** A **run** of a product is the amount that a company or factory decides to produce at one time. *Wayne plans to increase the print run.* **45** If you say that someone or something is different from the average **run** or common **run** of people or things, you mean that they are different from ordinary people or things. `VERB V for amount V` `N-COUNT: with supp` `PHRASE` `N-SING` `PHRASE BRITISH` `N-COUNT` `N-SING: with supp`

46 In cricket or baseball, a **run** is a score of one, which is made by players running between marked places on the pitch after hitting the ball. `N-COUNT`

47 If someone gives you **the run of** a place, they give you permission to go where you like in it and use it as you wish. *He had the run of the house and the pool.* `N-SING: the N of n`

48 If there is a **run on** something, a lot of people want to buy it or get it at the same time. *A run on sterling has killed off hopes of a rate cut.* `N-SING: N on n TECHNICAL`

49 See also **running**; **dummy run**, **test run**, **trial run**. **50 Run** is used in a large number of expressions which are explained under other words in this dictionary. For example, the expression **to run amok** is explained at **amok**.

run across. If you **run across** someone or something, you meet them or find them unexpectedly. *We ran across some old friends in the village.* `PHRASAL VB V P n`

run after. If you **are running after** someone, you are trying to start a sexual relationship with them; used showing disapproval. *Maria was already running after men twice her age.* `PHRASAL VB PRAGMATICS V P n`

run along. If you tell a child to **run along**, you mean that you want them to go away. `PHRASAL VB V P INFORMAL`

run around. If you **run around**, you go to a lot of places and do a lot of things, often in a rushed or disorganized way. *We had been running around emptying bins and cleaning up... I spend all day running around after the family... I will not have you running around the countryside without my authority.* `PHRASAL VB V P V P after/with n V P noun`

run away. 1 If you **run away** from a place, you secretly leave it. *I ran away from home when I was sixteen... Colin ran away and hasn't been heard of since... She ran away with a man called McTavish last year.* **2** If you **run away** from something unpleasant or new, you try to avoid dealing with it or thinking about it. *You can't run away for ever.* **3** See also **runaway**. `PHRASAL VB V P from/to n V P V P with n` `V P from n`

run away with. 1 If you let your imagination or your emotions **run away with** you, you fail to control them and cannot think sensibly. **2** If someone **runs away with** a competition, race, or prize, they win it easily. **3** If you **run away with** a particular idea, you accept it without thinking about it carefully, even though it is wrong. *It's very easy for us to run away with the idea that we can control everything.* `PHRASAL VB V P P pron` `V P P n` `V P P n`

run by. If you **run** an idea **by** someone, you tell them about it or mention it, to see if they think it is a good idea, or can understand or recognize it. *I'm definitely interested, but I'll have to run it by Larry Estes.* `PHRASAL VB V n P`

run down. 1 If you **run** people or things **down**, you criticize them strongly. *He last night denounced the British 'genius for running ourselves down'.* **2** If a vehicle or its driver **runs** someone **down**, the vehicle hits them and injures them. *Lozano claimed that motorcycle driver Clement Lloyd was trying to run him down.* **3** If people **run down** an organization or the amount of its activity, they deliberately reduce it or allow it to decrease. *The government is cynically running down Sweden's welfare system... Firms are running down stocks instead of making new products.* **4** If a machine or device **runs down**, it gradually loses power or works more slowly. *The batteries are running down.* **5** See also **run-down**. `PHRASAL VB V n P Also V P noun V n P Also V P noun` `V P noun BRITISH` `V P`

run into. 1 If you **run into** problems or difficulties, you unexpectedly begin to experience them. *The government's plans have run into strong opposition from civil rights campaigners.* **2** If you **run into** someone, you meet them unexpectedly. *He ran into Krettner in the corridor.* **3** If a vehicle **runs into** something, it accidentally hits it. *The driver failed to negotiate a bend and ran into a tree.* **4** You use **run into** when indicating that the cost or amount of something is very great. *...punitive civil penalties running into millions of pounds.* `PHRASAL VB V P noun` `V P n` `V P n` `V P amount`

run off. 1 If you **run off** with someone, you secretly go away with them in order to live with them or marry them. *She fell in love with someone and ran off with him... We could run off together.* **2** If you **run off** copies of a piece of writing, you produce them using a machine. *If you want to run off a copy sometime today, you're welcome to.* `PHRASAL VB V P with n pl-n V P together V P noun Also V n P n`

run out. 1 If you **run out** of something or it **runs out**, you have no more of it left. *They have run out of ideas... We had lots before but now we've run out... Time is running out.* ● to **run out of steam**: see **steam**. **2** When a legal document **runs out**, it becomes no longer valid. *When the lease ran out the family moved to Campigny.* `PHRASAL VB V P of n V P` `V P`

run over. If a vehicle or its driver **runs** someone **over**, it knocks them down or rolls over them. *He ran over a six-year-old child as he was driving back from a party.* `PHRASAL VB V n P V P n`

run past. To **run** something **past** someone means the same as to **run** it **by** them. `PHRASAL VB V n P n`

run through. 1 If you **run through** a list of items, you read or mention all the items quickly. *I ran through the options with him.* **2** If you **run through** a performance or a series of actions, you rehearse it or practise it. **3** See also **run-through**. `PHRASAL VB V P n` `V P n`

run to. 1 If you **run to** someone, you go to them for help or to tell them something. *When danger threatens he runs to his mother.* **2** If something **runs to** a particular amount or size, it is that amount or size. *The list of suppliers runs to 683 pages.* **3** If you cannot `PHRASAL VB V P n` `V P noun` `V P n`

run to a particular item, you cannot afford to buy it or pay for it.   BRITISH

run up. 1 If someone **runs up** bills or debts, they acquire them by buying a lot of things or borrowing money. *He ran up a £1,400 bill at the Britannia Adelphi Hotel.* **2** See also **run-up.**   PHRASAL VB V P noun

run up against. If you **run up against** problems, you suddenly begin to experience them. *He ran up against a solid wall of opposition when it came to the sensitive issue of party privileges.*   PHRASAL VB V P P n

run·around /ˈrʌnəraʊnd/; also spelled **run-around.** If someone **gives** you **the runaround**, they deliberately do not give you all the information or help that you want, and send you to another person or place to get it.   PHRASE INFORMAL

run·away /ˈrʌnəweɪ/ **runaways. 1** You use **runaway** to describe a situation in which something increases or develops very quickly and cannot be controlled. *Our Grand Sale in June was a runaway success. ...an era of runaway inflation.* **2** A **runaway** is someone, especially a child, who leaves home without telling anyone or without permission. *...a teenage runaway. ...a runaway slave.* **3** A **runaway** vehicle or animal is moving forward quickly, and its driver or rider has lost control of it. *The runaway car careered into a bench.*   ◆◇◇◇ ADJ: ADJ n   N-COUNT   ADJ: ADJ n

run-down; also spelled **rundown.** The adjective is pronounced /ˌrʌn ˈdaʊn/. The noun is pronounced /ˈrʌn daʊn/. **1** If you are **run-down**, they are tired or slightly ill. **2** A **run-down** building or area is in very poor condition. *...a run-down block of flats.* **3** A **run-down** piece of business has reduced its size or activity. *...a run-down slate quarry.* ► Also a noun. *...the rundown of the coal industry.* **4** If you give someone a **run-down** of a group of things or a **run-down** on something, you give them details about it. *Here's a rundown of the options.*   ◆◇◇◇ ADJ-GRADED INFORMAL ADJ-GRADED   ADJ-GRADED   N-SING   N-SING INFORMAL

rune /ruːn/ **runes. Runes** are letters from an ancient alphabet that were carved in wood or stone by people in Northern Europe in former times. They were believed to have magical properties.   ◆◇◇◇ N-COUNT

rung /rʌŋ/ **rungs. 1 Rung** is the past participle of **ring. 2** The **rungs** on a ladder are the wooden or metal bars that form the steps. **3** If you reach a particular **rung** in your career, in an organization, or in a process, you reach that level in it. *There has never been a better time to get on the first rung of the property ladder.*   ◆◇◇◇ N-COUNT   N-COUNT with supp

run-in, run-ins. 1 If you have a **run-in** with someone, you have an argument or quarrel with them. **2** The **run-in** to an event is the period of time or series of events leading up to it.   ◆◆◇◇ N-COUNT INFORMAL N-SING

run·ner /ˈrʌnə/ **runners. 1** A **runner** is a person who runs, especially for sport or pleasure. *...a marathon runner... I am a very keen runner.* **2** The **runners** in a horse race are the horses taking part. **3** A drug **runner** or gun **runner** is someone who illegally takes drugs or guns into a country. **4** Someone who is a **runner** for a particular person or company is employed to take messages, collect money, or do other small errands for them. *...a bookie's runner.* **5 Runners** are thin strips of wood or metal underneath something which help it to move smoothly. **6** On a plant, **runners** are long shoots that grow from the main stem and put down roots to form a new plant. **7** If someone **does a runner**, they leave a place hurriedly, for example in order to escape arrest or to avoid paying for something.   ◆◆◇◇ N-COUNT   N-COUNT   N-COUNT n N   N-COUNT   N-COUNT   N-COUNT   PHRASE INFORMAL, BRITISH

runner bean, runner beans. Runner beans are long green beans that are eaten as a vegetable. See picture headed **vegetables.**   N-COUNT

runner-up, runners-up. A **runner-up** is someone who has finished in second place in a race or competition.   ◆◆◇◇ N-COUNT

run·ning /ˈrʌnɪŋ/. **1** You use **running** to describe things that continue or keep occurring over a period of time. *The song turned into a running joke between him and the press.* **2** You use **running** to describe something that keeps being changed or added-   ◆◆◆◇ ADJ: ADJ n   ADJ: ADJ n

ed to as something progresses. *He kept a running tally of who had called him... John gave the police control room a running commentary on the driver's antics.* **3** You can use **running** when indicating that something keeps happening. For example, if something has happened every day for three days, you can say that it has happened for the third day **running** or for three days **running.** **4** If someone is **in the running** for something, they have a good chance of winning or obtaining it. If they are **out of the running**, they have no chance of winning or obtaining it. **5** If someone **is making the running** in a situation, they are more active than the other people involved. *Republicans are furious that the Democrats currently seem to be making all the running.* **6** See also **run.**   ADJ: n ADJ   PHRASE   PHRASE BRITISH

-running /-ˈrʌnɪŋ/. **-running** is used to form nouns which refer to the illegal importing of drugs or guns. *...a serviceman suspected of drug-running.*   COMB

running battle, running battles. When two groups of people fight a **running battle**, they keep attacking each other in various parts of a place. *They fought running battles in the narrow streets with police.*   N-COUNT

running mate, running mates. In an election campaign, a candidate's **running mate** is the person that they have chosen to be their deputy if they win.   ◆◇◇◇ N-COUNT

running order. The **running order** of the items in a broadcast, concert, or show is the order in which the items will come.   N-SING BRITISH

run·ny /ˈrʌni/ **runnier, runniest. 1** Something that is **runny** is more liquid than usual or than was intended. *Warm the honey until it becomes runny.* **2** If someone has a **runny** nose or **runny** eyes, liquid is flowing from their nose or eyes.   ◆◇◇◇ ADJ-GRADED   ADJ-GRADED

run-off, run-offs; also spelled **runoff. 1** A **run-off** is an extra vote or contest which is held in order to decide the winner of an election or competition, because nobody has yet clearly won. **2 Run-off** is rainwater that forms a stream rather than being absorbed by the ground.   N-COUNT   N-UNCOUNT

run-of-the-mill; also spelled **run of the mill.** A **run-of-the-mill** person or thing is very ordinary, with no special or interesting features; used showing disapproval. *I was just a very average run-of-the-mill kind of student.*   ADJ-GRADED PRAGMATICS

runt /rʌnt/ **runts. 1** The **runt** of a group of animals born to the same mother at the same time is the smallest and weakest of them. *Animals reject the runt of the litter.* **2** If you call a small person a **runt**, you are expressing your dislike for them. *He actually started out as a failure, as the runt of a brilliant athletic home.*   N-COUNT   N-COUNT PRAGMATICS BRITISH, INFORMAL

run-through, run-throughs. A **run-through** for a show or event is a rehearsal or practice for it. *Charles and Eddie are getting ready for their final run-through before the evening's recording.*   N-COUNT

run-up, run-ups. 1 The **run-up** to an event is the period of time just before it. *The issue of the monarchy is complicating politics in the run-up to the elections.* **2** In sport, a **run-up** is a running approach made by a player or athlete.   ◆◆◇◇ N-SING BRITISH   N-COUNT

run·way /ˈrʌnweɪ/ **runways.** At an airport, the **runway** is the long strip of ground with a hard surface which an aeroplane takes off from or lands on.   ◆◇◇◇ N-COUNT

ru·pee /ruːˈpiː/ **rupees.** A **rupee** is a unit of money that is used in India, Pakistan, and some other countries. *He earns 20 rupees a day.*   ◆◇◇◇ N-COUNT

rup·ture /ˈrʌptʃə/ **ruptures, rupturing, ruptured. 1** A **rupture** is a severe injury in which an internal part of your body tears or bursts open, especially the part between the bowels and the abdomen. **2** If an organ or animal **ruptures** or if you rupture part of their body, it tears or bursts open. *His stomach might rupture from all the acid. ...a ruptured appendix.* **3** If an object **ruptures**, it bursts open. *Gasoline tanks can rupture and burn in a collision.* **4** If someone or something **ruptures** relations between people, they damage them, causing them to be-   ◆◇◇◇ N-COUNT   V-ERG: V n V V-ed   V-ERG V VERB: V n

come worse or to end. ▶ Also a noun. ...*a rupture of the family unit.* `N-COUNT`

ru·ral /ˈrʊərəl/. **1 Rural** places are far away from large towns or cities. ...*the closure of rural schools.* **2 Rural** means having features which are typical of areas that are far away from large towns or cities. *He spoke with a heavy rural accent.* `◆◆◆◇◇ ADJ-GRADED` `ADJ-GRADED: ADJ n`

ruse /ruːz, AM ruːs/ **ruses.** A **ruse** is an action or plan which is intended to deceive someone. *It is now clear that this was a ruse to divide them.* `◆◇◇◇◇ N-COUNT FORMAL`

rush /rʌʃ/ **rushes, rushing, rushed. 1** If you **rush** somewhere, you go there quickly. *A schoolgirl rushed into a burning flat to save a man's life... I've got to rush. Got a meeting in a few minutes... Shop staff rushed to get help.* **2** If people **rush** to do something, they do it as soon as they can, because they are very eager to do it. *Russian banks rushed to buy as many dollars as they could.* **3** A **rush** is a situation in which you need to go somewhere or do something very quickly. *The men left in a rush... Then there was the mad rush not to be late for school.* **4** If there is a **rush** for something, many people suddenly try to get it or do it. ...*the rush for contracts.* `◆◆◆◇◇ VERB` `V prep/adv` `V` `V to-inf` `VERB` `V to-inf` `N-SING` `N-SING`

5 The **rush** is a period of time when many people go somewhere or do something. *The shop's opening coincided with the Christmas rush.* **6** If you **rush** something, you do it in a hurry, often too quickly and without much care. *Chew your food well and do not rush meals.* **♦ rushed** *The report had all the hallmarks of a rushed job.* **7** If you **rush** someone or something to a place, you take them there quickly. *We got an ambulance and rushed her to hospital... We'll rush it round today if possible.* **8** If you **rush** into something or are **rushed** into it, you do it without thinking about it for long enough. *He will not rush into any decisions... They had rushed in without adequate appreciation of the task... Ministers won't be rushed into a response.* **♦ rushed** *At no time did I feel rushed or under pressure.* `N-SING: theN` `VERB` `V n` `Also V a tn` `ADJ-GRADED` `VERB` `V n prep` `V n with adv` `V-ERG` `V into n` `V in` `be V-ed into n` `Also V n` `ADJ-GRADED`

9 If you are **rushed off your feet**, you are extremely busy. *We have a cut-back in staff in this department, and I'm rushed off my feet.* **10** If you **rush** something or someone, you move quickly and forcefully at them, often in order to attack them. *They rushed the entrance and forced their way in.* **11** If air or liquid **rushes** somewhere, it flows there suddenly and quickly. *The air was rushing past us all the time. ...the sound of rushing water.* ▶ Also a noun. *A rush of air on my face woke me.* **12** If you experience a **rush** of a feeling, you suddenly experience it very strongly. *A rush of pure affection swept over him.* `PHRASE INFORMAL` `VERB` `Also V at n` `VERB` `V prep/adv` `V-ing` `N-COUNT` `N-COUNT`

13 Rushes are plants with long thin stems that grow near water. **14** The **rushes** of a film are the parts of it that have been filmed but have not yet been edited. `N-PLURAL` `N-PLURAL TECHNICAL`

rush out. If a document or product is **rushed out**, it is produced very quickly. *A statement was rushed out... Studios are rushing out monster movies.* `PHRASAL VB be V-ed P` `V P noun`

rush through. If you **rush** something **through**, you deal with it quickly so that it is ready in a shorter time than usual. *The government rushed through legislation aimed at Mafia leaders.* `PHRASAL VB V P noun` `Also V n P`

'rush hour, rush hours; also spelled **rush-hour.** The **rush hour** is one of the periods of the day when most people are travelling to or from work. *Try to avoid rush-hour traffic.* `◆◇◇◇◇ N-COUNT: also at/during N`

rusk /rʌsk/ **rusks. Rusks** are hard, dry biscuits that are given to babies and young children. `N-VAR BRITISH`

rus·set /ˈrʌsɪt/ **russets. Russet** is used to describe things that are reddish-brown. ...*a russet apple.* `COLOUR`

Russian rou'lette. 1 If you say that someone is playing **Russian roulette**, you mean that what they are doing is very dangerous because it involves unpredictable risks. **2** If someone plays **Russian roulette**, they fire a gun with only one bullet at their head without knowing whether it will release the bullet. `N-UNCOUNT` `N-UNCOUNT`

rust /rʌst/ **rusts, rusting, rusted. 1 Rust** is a brown substance that forms on iron or steel when it `◆◇◇◇◇ N-UNCOUNT`

comes into contact with water. **2** When a metal object **rusts**, it becomes covered in rust and often loses its strength. **3 Rust** is sometimes used to describe things that are reddish-brown. **4 Rust** is a disease, caused by a fungus, which affects plants. `VERB: V` `COLOUR` `N-UNCOUNT`

rust away. When a metal object **rusts away**, it is gradually weakened and destroyed by rust. `PHRASAL VB V P`

'Rust Belt. The **Rust Belt** refers to a region which used to have a lot of manufacturing industry, but which is now in economic decline. `N-SING: theN AMERICAN`

rus·tic /ˈrʌstɪk/ **rustics. 1** You can use **rustic** to describe things or people that you approve of because they are simple or unsophisticated in a way that is typical of the countryside. ...*the rustic charm of a country lifestyle.* **♦ rus·tic·ity** /ˌrʌˈstɪsɪti/. ...*growing up here in deep rusticity.* **2** You can refer to someone who comes from the countryside as a **rustic** if you find their behaviour amusing or very different from that of people who live in towns and cities. `◆◇◇◇◇ ADJ-GRADED` `PRAGMATICS` `N-UNCOUNT` `N-COUNT`

rus·tle /ˈrʌsəl/ **rustles, rustling, rustled.** When something thin and dry **rustles**, it makes soft sounds as it moves. *The leaves rustled in the wind... She rustled her papers impatiently... A snake rustled through the dry grass.* ▶ Also a noun. ...*a rustle of her frilled petticoats.* **♦ rus·tling, rustlings** *There was a rustling of paper.* `◆◇◇◇◇ V-ERG` `V` `V n` `V prep` `N-COUNT` `N-VAR`

rustle up. If you **rustle** something **up**, you provide, obtain, or prepare it quickly, with very little planning. *He managed to rustle up a couple of blankets.* `PHRASAL VB V P noun` `Also V n P` `INFORMAL`

rus·tler /ˈrʌslə/ **rustlers. Rustlers** are thieves who steal farm animals, especially cattle. **♦ rus·tling** ...*cattle rustling and horse stealing.* `N-COUNT AMERICAN` `N-UNCOUNT`

rusty /ˈrʌsti/ **rustier, rustiest. 1** A **rusty** metal object such as a car or a machine has a lot of rust on it. *We spent years travelling around in a rusty old van.* **2** If a skill that you have or your knowledge of something is **rusty**, it is not as good as it used to be, because you have not used it for a long time. *You may be a little rusty, but past experience and teaching skills won't have been lost.* **3 Rusty** is sometimes used to describe things that are reddish-brown. *Her hair was rusty brown.* `◆◇◇◇◇ ADJ-GRADED` `ADJ-GRADED` `ADJ`

rut /rʌt/ **ruts. 1** If you say that someone is in a **rut**, you disapprove of the fact that they have become fixed in their way of thinking and doing things, and find it difficult to change. You can also say that someone's life or career is in a **rut**. **2** A **rut** is a deep, narrow mark made in the ground by the wheels of a vehicle. **♦ rut·ted** ...*deeply rutted roads.* **3** The **rut** is the period of the year when some animals such as deer are sexually active. ...*a stag in rut.* `◆◇◇◇◇ N-COUNT` `PRAGMATICS` `N-COUNT` `ADJ-GRADED` `N-SING: also in N`

ru·ta·ba·ga /ˌruːtəˈbeɪgə/ **rutabagas.** A **rutabaga** is a round yellow root vegetable with a brown or purple skin. The usual British word is **swede**. `N-VAR AMERICAN`

ruth·less /ˈruːθləs/. **1** If you say that someone is **ruthless**, you disapprove of them because they are very harsh or cruel, and will do anything that is necessary to achieve what they want. *The late newspaper tycoon is condemned for his ruthless treatment of employees.* **♦ ruth·less·ly** *The Party has ruthlessly crushed any sign of organised opposition.* **♦ ruth·less·ness** ...*a powerful political figure with a reputation for ruthlessness.* **2** A **ruthless** action or activity is done forcefully and thoroughly, without much concern for its effects on other people. *Her lawyers have been ruthless in thrashing out a divorce settlement.* **♦ ruth·less·ly** ...*the ruthlessly efficient woman her father wanted her to be.* **♦ ruth·less·ness** ...*a certain healthy ruthlessness.* `◆◆◇◇◇ ADJ-GRADED` `PRAGMATICS` `ADV-GRADED: ADV with v` `N-UNCOUNT` `ADJ-GRADED` `ADV-GRADED` `N-UNCOUNT`

RV /ˌɑː ˈviː/ **RVs.** An **RV** is a van which is equipped with such things as beds and cooking equipment, so that people can live in it, usually when they are on holiday. RV is an abbreviation for 'recreational vehicle'. The usual British term is **camper**. `N-COUNT AMERICAN`

rye /raɪ/. **1 Rye** is a cereal grown in cold countries. Its grains can be used to make flour, bread, or other foods. **2** You can refer to rye bread as **rye**. *I was eating ham and Swiss cheese on rye.* `◆◇◇◇◇ N-UNCOUNT` `N-UNCOUNT AMERICAN`

S s

S, s /es/ **S's, s's.** **1** S is the nineteenth letter of the N-VAR English alphabet. **2** S or s is an abbreviation for words beginning with s, such as 'south' and 'seconds'.

-s; also spelled **-es.** The suffix **-s** is pronounced /-s/ after the consonant sounds /p, t, k, f/ or /θ/. After other sounds **-s** is pronounced /-z/. The suffix **-es** is pronounced /-z/ after vowel sounds, and /-ɪz/ after consonant sounds. **1 -s** or **-es** is added to a noun to SUFFIX form a plural. ...*a few problems.* ...*new houses and flats.* **2 -s** or **-es** is added to a verb to form the third SUFFIX person singular, present tense. *She likes her job... No-one wishes to see that.*

-'s. Pronounced /-s/ after the consonant sounds /p, t, k, f/ or /θ/, and the consonant sounds /s, z, ʃ, ʒ, tʃ/ or /dʒ/. After other sounds **-'s** is pronounced /-z/. A final **-s'** is pronounced in the same way as a final **-s**. **1 -'s** is added to nouns to form possessives. However, with plural nouns ending in '-s', and sometimes with names ending in '-s', you form the possessive by adding -'. ...*Britain's coal mines.* ...*a boys' boarding-school.* ...*Sir Charles' car.* INFORMAL, **2 -'s** is the shortened form of 'is'. For example, 'he SPOKEN is' can be shortened to 'he's'. *She's a counselor... It's a disaster... That's right.* **3 -'s** is the shortened form INFORMAL, of 'has', especially where 'has' is an auxiliary verb. SPOKEN For example, 'It has gone' can be shortened to 'It's gone'. *He's got a four year contract... There's been a lot of rewriting.* **4 -'s** is sometimes added to numbers, letters, and abbreviations to form plurals, although many people think you should just add '-s'. ...*new strategies for the 1990's.* ...*p's and q's.*

sab /sæb/ **sabs.** Some people refer to the people N-COUNT who try to stop blood sports such as fox hunting as INFORMAL, **sabs. Sab** is short for saboteur. BRITISH

Sab·bath /'sæbəθ/. The **Sabbath** is the day of the N-PROPER: week when members of some religious groups do theN not work. The Jewish Sabbath is on Saturday and the Christian Sabbath is on Sunday.

sab·bati·cal /sə'bætɪkəl/ **sabbaticals.** A sabbati- N-COUNT: cal is a period of time during which someone such also onN as a teacher or university lecturer can leave their ordinary work and travel or study.

sa·ber /'seɪbə/. See **sabre**.

sa·ble /'seɪbəl/ **sables.** A **sable** is a small furry N-COUNT animal with valued fur. ▶ **Sable** is the fur of a sable. N-UNCOUNT

sabo·tage /'sæbɒtɑːʒ/ **sabotages, sabotaging,** ◆◇◇◇ **sabotaged.** **1** If a machine, railway line, or bridge **is sabotaged**, it is deliberately damaged or de- be V-ed stroyed, for example in a war or as a protest. ▶ Also N-UNCOUNT a noun. *The bombing was a spectacular act of sabotage.* **2** If someone **sabotages** a plan or a meeting, VERB they deliberately prevent it from being successful. V n *My ex-wife deliberately sabotages my access to the children.*

sabo·teur /ˌsæbə'tɜː/ **saboteurs.** A saboteur is a ◆◇◇◇ person who deliberately damages or destroys things N-COUNT such as machines and railway lines in order to weaken the enemy or to make a protest. People who try to stop blood sports such as fox hunting are also referred to as **saboteurs**.

sa·bre /'seɪbə/ **sabres;** spelled **saber** in American ◆◇◇◇ English. A **sabre** is a heavy sword with a curved N-COUNT blade that was formerly used by soldiers on horseback.

'sabre-rattling. If you refer to a threat, especially N-UNCOUNT a threat of military action, as **sabre-rattling**, you do PRAGMATICS not believe that the threat will actually be carried out.

sac /sæk/ **sacs.** A sac is a small part of an animal's ◆◇◇◇ body, shaped like a little bag. It contains air, liquid, N-COUNT or some other substance. *The lungs consist of millions of tiny air sacs.*

sac·cha·rin /'sækərɪn/; also spelled **saccharin**. N-UNCOUNT **1 Saccharine** is a very sweet chemical substance that some people use instead of sugar, especially when they are trying to lose weight. **2** You describe ADJ-GRADED something as **saccharine** when you find it unpleasantly sweet and sentimental. *She smiled with saccharine sweetness.*

sa·chet /'sæʃeɪ, AM sæ'ʃeɪ/ **sachets.** A sachet is a N-COUNT small closed plastic or paper packet, containing a very small quantity of something. ...*individual sachets of instant coffee.*

sack /sæk/ **sacks, sacking, sacked.** **1** A sack is ◆◆◇◇ a large bag made of rough woven material. **2** If your N-COUNT employers **sack** you, they tell you that you can no VERB: V n longer work for them because you have done something that they did not like or because your work was not good enough. ▶ Also a noun. *People who* N-SING: *make mistakes can be given the sack the same day.* theN **3** When an army **sacks** a town or city, they destroy VERB: V n it, taking away all valuable things. **4** Some people N-SING: refer to bed as **the sack.** theN
INFORMAL

sack·ful /'sækfʊl/ **sackfuls.** A **sackful** is the N-COUNT amount of something held by a sack.

sack·ing /'sækɪŋ/ **sackings.** **1** Sacking is rough ◆◇◇◇ woven material that is used to make sacks. **2** A N-UNCOUNT **sacking** is the dismissal of a person from their job. N-COUNT

sac·ra·ment /'sækrəmənt/ **sacraments.** A sacra- N-COUNT **ment** is a Christian religious ceremony such as communion, baptism, or marriage. ♦ **sac·ra·men-** ADJ **·tal** /ˌsækrə'mentəl/. ...*the sacramental wine.*

sa·cred /'seɪkrɪd/. **1** Something that is **sacred** is ◆◆◇◇ believed to be holy and to have a special connec- ADJ-GRADED tion with God. ♦ **sa·cred·ness** ...*the sacredness of* the site. **2** Something connected with religion or ADJ: ADJ n used in religious ceremonies is described as **sacred.** ...*sacred songs or music.* **3** You can describe some- ADJ-GRADED thing as **sacred** when it is regarded as too important to be changed or interfered with. *He said the unity of the country was sacred.* ♦ **sacredness** ...*the sa-* N-UNCOUNT credness of his given word.

,sacred 'cow, sacred cows. If you describe a N-COUNT belief, custom, or institution as a **sacred cow**, you disapprove of people treating it with too much respect and being afraid to criticize or question it. ...*the sacred cow of monetarism.*

sac·ri·fice /'sækrɪfaɪs/ **sacrifices, sacrificing,** ◆◆◇◇ **sacrificed.** **1** To **sacrifice** an animal or person VERB means to kill them in a special religious ceremony V n as an offering to a god. *The priest sacrificed a chick-* Also V n to n en. ▶ Also a noun. ...*animal sacrifices to the gods.* N-COUNT ♦ **sac·ri·fi·cial** /ˌsækrɪ'fɪʃəl/. ...*the sacrificial altar.* ADJ: ADJ n **2** If you **sacrifice** something that is valuable or im- VERB: V n portant, you give it up, usually to obtain something V n to/for n else for yourself or for other people. *She sacrificed* V to/for n *family life to her career... Her husband's pride was a* Also V pron- *small thing to sacrifice for their children's security.* refl ▶ Also a noun. *He was willing to make any sacrifice* N-VAR *for peace.* ● See also **self-sacrifice**.

,sacrificial 'lamb, sacrificial lambs. If you refer N-COUNT to someone as a **sacrificial lamb**, you mean that PRAGMATICS they have been blamed unfairly for something they did not do or for which they are only partly responsible, usually in order to protect another more powerful person or people.

sac·ri·lege /'sækrɪlɪdʒ/. **1 Sacrilege** is behaviour that shows great disrespect for a holy place or object. *Stealing from a place of worship was regarded as sacrilege.* **2** You can use **sacrilege** to refer to disrespect that is shown for someone who is widely admired or for a belief that is widely accepted. *It is a sacrilege to offend democracy.* — N-UNCOUNT: also a N

sac·ri·legious /ˌsækrɪ'lɪdʒəs/. If someone's behaviour or actions are **sacrilegious**, they show great disrespect towards something holy or towards something that people think should be respected. — ADJ-GRADED

sac·ro·sanct /'sækrəʊsæŋkt/. If you describe something as **sacrosanct**, you consider it to be special and are unwilling to see it criticized or changed. *Freedom of the press is sacrosanct and should remain so.* — ADJ-GRADED

sad /sæd/ **sadder, saddest. 1** If you are **sad**, you feel unhappy, usually because something has happened that you do not like. *I'm sad that Julie's marriage is on the verge of splitting up.* ♦ **sad·ly** *...a gallant man who will be sadly missed by all his comrades.* ♦ **sad·ness** *It is with a mixture of sadness and joy that I say farewell.* **2 Sad** stories and **sad** news make you feel sad. **3** A **sad** event or situation is unfortunate or undesirable. *It's a sad truth that children are the biggest victims of passive smoking.* ♦ **sad·ly** *Sadly, bamboo plants die after flowering.* **4** You can use the expression **sad to say** when you are describing a situation which you find unfortunate. *The results, sad to say, are disappointing... He died five or six years ago I'm sad to say.* **5** If you describe someone as **sad**, you do not have any respect for them and think their behaviour or ideas are ridiculous. — ADJ-GRADED / ADV-GRADED / N-UNCOUNT / ADJ-GRADED / ADJ-GRADED / ADV / PHRASE / PRAGMATICS / ADJ-GRADED INFORMAL

sad·den /'sædən/ **saddens, saddening, saddened.** If something **saddens** you, it makes you feel sad. ♦ **sad·dened** *He was disappointed and saddened that legal argument had stopped the trial.* ♦ **sad·den·ing** *...a saddening experience.* — VERB: V n, no cont / ADJ-GRADED: v-link ADJ / ADJ-GRADED

sad·dle /'sædəl/ **saddles, saddling, saddled. 1** A **saddle** is a leather seat that you put on the back of an animal so that you can ride the animal. ● See also **side-saddle. 2** If you **saddle** a horse or pony, you put a saddle on it so that you can ride it. ▶ **Saddle up** means the same as **saddle**. *I want to be gone from here as soon as we can saddle up... She saddled up a horse.* **3** A **saddle** is a seat on a bicycle or motorcycle. See picture headed **car and bicycle. 4** A **saddle** of lamb, hare, or venison is a large joint of meat taken from the middle of the animal's back. **5** If you **saddle** someone with a problem or with a responsibility, you put them in a position where they have to deal with it. *The war devastated the economy and saddled the country with a huge foreign debt.* **6** If you are **in the saddle**, you are riding a horse. **7** If you are **in the saddle**, you are in power or in control of a situation. *The armed forces and the hardliners are now going to be in the saddle.* — N-COUNT / VERB: V n / PHRASAL VB V P, V P noun / N-COUNT / N-COUNT / VERB V n with n / PHRASE, PHRASE

saddle up. See **saddle** 2. — PHRASAL VB

saddle·bag /'sædəlbæg/ **saddlebags.** A **saddlebag** is a bag fastened to the saddle of a bicycle or motorcycle. — N-COUNT

sad·dler /'sædlə/ **saddlers.** A **saddler** is a person who makes, repairs, and sells saddles and other equipment for riding horses. — N-COUNT

sad·ism /'seɪdɪzəm/. **Sadism** is a type of behaviour in which a person obtains pleasure from hurting other people and making them suffer physically or mentally. ♦ **sad·ist** /'seɪdɪst/ **sadists** *The man was a sadist who tortured animals and people.* — N-UNCOUNT / N-COUNT

sa·dis·tic /sə'dɪstɪk/. A **sadistic** person enjoys hurting other people and making them suffer physically or mentally. ♦ **sa·dis·ti·cal·ly** /sə'dɪstɪkli/. *Many were killed, often most sadistically.* — ADJ-GRADED / ADV-GRADED

sado-masochism /ˌseɪdəʊ 'mæsəkɪzəm/; also spelled **sadomasochism. Sado-masochism** is the enjoyment by a person of both sadism and masochism. *...the sado-masochism of the Marquis de Sade.* ♦ **sado-masochist, sado-masochists** — N-UNCOUNT / N-COUNT

♦ **sado-masochistic** /ˌseɪdəʊ mæsə'kɪstɪk/. *...a sado-masochistic relationship.* — ADJ-GRADED

s.a.e. /ˌes eɪ 'iː/ **s.a.e.s.** An **s.a.e.** is an envelope on which you have stuck a stamp and written your own name and address. You send it to a person or organization so that they can send you something such as information in it. s.a.e. is an abbreviation for 'stamped addressed envelope' or 'self addressed envelope'. — N-COUNT BRITISH

sa·fa·ri /sə'fɑːri/ **safaris.** A **safari** is an expedition for observing or hunting wild animals, especially in East Africa. — N-COUNT: also on N

sa'fari park, safari parks. A **safari park** is a large enclosed area of land where wild animals, such as lions and elephants, live freely. People can pay to drive through the park and look at the animals. — N-COUNT BRITISH

safe /seɪf/ **safer, safest; safes. 1** Something that is **safe** does not cause physical harm or danger. *Officials arrived to assess whether it is safe to bring emergency food supplies into the city... Most foods that we eat are safe for birds.* ♦ **safe·ly** *The waste is safely locked away until it is no longer radioactive... 'Drive safely,' he said and waved goodbye.* **2** If someone or something is **safe** from something, they cannot be harmed or damaged by it. *In the future people can go to a football match knowing that they are safe from hooliganism... Crime Prevention Officers can visit your home and suggest ways to make it safer.* **3** If you are **safe**, you have not been harmed, or you are not in danger of being harmed. *Where is Sophy? Is she safe?... A baby boy is safe after rescue workers pulled him from a 12-foot-deep construction hole.* ♦ **safely** *All 140 guests were brought out of the building safely by firemen.* **4** You say that someone is **safe and sound** when they are still alive or unharmed after being in danger. **5** A **safe** place is one where it is unlikely that any harm, damage, or unpleasant things will happen to the people or things that are there. *The elimination of all nuclear weapons would make the world a safer place.* ♦ **safely** *The banker keeps the money tucked safely under his bed.* **6** If people or things have a **safe** journey, they reach their destination without harm, damage, or unpleasant things happening to them. *'I'm heading back to Ireland again for another weekend.'—'Have a safe journey.' ...the UN plan to deploy 500 troops to ensure the safe delivery of food and other supplies.* ♦ **safely** *Once Mrs Armsby was safely home, she called the police again.* **7** If you are at a **safe** distance from something or someone, you are far enough away from them to avoid any danger, harm, or unpleasant effects. **8** If you say that someone or something is **in safe hands**, or is **safe in** someone's **hands**, you mean that they are being looked after by a reliable person and will not be harmed or damaged. **9** If you say you are doing something **to be on the safe side**, you mean that you are doing it as a precaution, in case something unexpected or unpleasant happens. *You might still want to go for an X-ray, however, just to be on the safe side.* **10** If you say **'it's better to be safe than sorry'**, you are advising someone to take precautions in order to avoid possible unpleasant consequences later, even if these precautions might seem a waste of time. *Don't be afraid to have this checked by a doctor – better safe than sorry!* **11** ● **safe in the knowledge**: see **knowledge. 12** If something you have or expect to obtain is **safe**, you cannot lose it or be prevented from having it. *Is the National Health Service safe with the Conservative party?* ♦ **safely** *The number two seed is safely through to the second round of the tournament.* **13** A **safe** course of action is one in which there is very little risk of loss or failure. *Electricity shares are still a safe investment.* ♦ **safely** *We reveal only as much information as we can safely risk at a given time.* **14** If you **play safe** or **play it safe**, you do not take any risks. *If you want to play safe, cut down on the amount of salt you eat... The pilot decided that Christchurch was too far away, and played it safe and landed at Wellington.* **15** If it is **safe** to say or assume something, you can say — ADJ-GRADED / ADV-GRADED / ADJ-GRADED: v-link ADJ / ADJ-GRADED: v-link ADJ / ADV PHRASE / PHRASE / ADJ-GRADED / ADV-GRADED / ADJ: ADJ n / ADV / ADJ: ADJ n / PHRASE / PHRASE / PHRASE / ADJ-GRADED / ADV / ADJ-GRADED / ADV / PHRASE / ADJ-GRADED

it with very little risk of being wrong. *I think it is safe to* [PRAGMATICS]
say that very few students expend the effort to do qual-
ity work in school. ♦ **safely** *If I go to a grocer I know* ADV-GRADED:
and trust, I can safely assume the eggs will be fresh. **16** ADV before v
If you disapprove of something that someone chooses ADJ-GRADED
to do because you think it is not very adventurous, in- [PRAGMATICS]
teresting, or original, you can describe it as **safe**.
...frustrated artists who became lawyers at an early age
because it seemed a safe option.
17 A **safe** is a strong metal cupboard with special N-COUNT
locks, in which you keep money, jewellery, or other
valuable things. **18** See also **safe seat**.

'safe area, safe areas. If part of a country that is ♦◇◇◇◇
involved in a war is declared a **safe area**, neutral N-COUNT
forces will try to keep peace there so that it is safe
for people.

,safe 'conduct. If you are given **safe conduct**, the N-UNCOUNT:
authorities officially allow you to travel somewhere, also a N
guaranteeing that you will not be arrested or
harmed while doing so.

,safe de'posit box, safe deposit boxes. A **safe** N-COUNT
deposit box is a small box, usually kept in a special
room in a bank, in which you can store valuable
objects.

safe·guard /'seɪfgɑːd/ **safeguards, safeguard-** ♦♦◇◇◇
ing, safeguarded. 1 To **safeguard** something or VERB: V n
someone means to protect them from being V n from v
harmed, lost, or badly treated. *...precautionary* FORMAL
measures to safeguard their forces from the effects of
chemical weapons. **2** A **safeguard** is a law, rule, or N-COUNT
measure intended to prevent someone or some-
thing from being harmed. *...civil rights legislation*
that offers safeguards against discrimination in the
workplace.

,safe 'haven, safe havens. 1 If part of a country ♦◇◇◇◇
is declared a **safe haven**, people who need to escape N-COUNT
from a dangerous situation such as a war can go
there and be protected. **2** If a country provides **safe** N-UNCOUNT
haven for refugees or other people in difficulties, it
allows them to stay there under its official protection. *Some Democrats support granting the Haitians*
temporary safe haven in the US. **3** A **safe haven** is a N-COUNT
place, a situation, or an activity which provides people with an opportunity to escape from things that
they find unpleasant or worrying. *...the idea of the*
family as a safe haven from the brutal outside world.

'safe house, safe houses. You can refer to a N-COUNT
building as a **safe house** when it is used as a place
where someone can stay and be protected. Safe
houses are often used by spies, criminals, or the
police.

safe·keeping /,seɪf'kiːpɪŋ/. If something is given N-UNCOUNT
to you for **safekeeping**, it is given to you so that you
will make sure that it is not harmed or stolen.

,safe 'passage. If someone is given **safe passage**, N-UNCOUNT:
they are allowed to go somewhere safely, without also a N
being attacked or arrested. *We try to negotiate a safe*
passage for relief convoys.

,safe 'seat, safe seats. In politics a **safe seat** is a N-COUNT
constituency in which the candidate from one par-
ticular party nearly always wins with a large majority of votes.

,safe 'sex or **safer sex**. **Safe sex** is sexual activity ♦◇◇◇◇
in which people protect themselves against the risk N-UNCOUNT
of AIDS and other sexually transmitted diseases,
usually by using condoms.

safe·ty /'seɪfti/. **1 Safety** is the state of being safe ♦♦♦♦◇
from harm or danger. *...a number of recommenda-* N-UNCOUNT
tions to improve safety on aircraft. **2** If you reach N-UNCOUNT
safety, you reach a place where you are safe from
danger. *Guests ran for safety as the device went off in*
a ground-floor men's toilet. ...the safety of one's own
home. **3** If you are concerned about the **safety** of N-SING:
something, you are concerned that it might be with poss
harmful or dangerous. *Three reactors at Chernobyl*
have continued to operate even though there is con-
cern about the safety of their design. **4** If you are N-SING:
concerned for someone's **safety**, you are concerned with poss
that they might be in danger. *There is grave concern*
for the safety of witnesses. **5 Safety** features or meas- ADJ: ADJ n

ures are intended to make something less dangerous. *The built-in safety device compensates for a fall*
in water pressure. **6** If you say that there is **safety in** PHRASE
numbers, you mean that you are safer doing some-
thing if there are a lot of people doing it rather than
doing it alone. *Many people still feel there is safety in*
numbers when belonging to a union.

'safety belt, safety belts. A **safety belt** is a strap N-COUNT
attached to a seat in a car or aeroplane. You fasten
it round your body and it stops you being thrown
forward if there is an accident.

'safety catch, safety catches. The **safety catch** N-COUNT
on a gun is a device that stops you firing the gun
accidentally.

'safety glass. **Safety glass** is very strong glass that N-UNCOUNT
does not splinter if it breaks.

'safety net, safety nets. 1 A **safety net** is some- ♦◇◇◇◇
thing that you can rely on to help you if you get into N-COUNT
a difficult situation. *Welfare is the only real safety*
net for low-income workers. **2** In a circus, a **safety** N-COUNT
net is a large net that is placed below performers on
a high wire or trapeze in order to catch them and
prevent them being injured if they fall off.

'safety pin, safety pins. A **safety pin** is a bent N-COUNT
metal pin used for fastening things together. The
point of the pin has a cover so that when the pin is
closed it cannot hurt anyone.

'safety valve, safety valves. 1 A **safety valve** is N-COUNT
a device which allows liquids or gases to escape
from a machine when the pressure inside it be-
comes too great. **2** A **safety valve** is something that N-COUNT
allows you to release strong feelings without hurting
yourself or others. *...crying is a natural safety valve.*

saf·fron /'sæfrən/. **1 Saffron** is a yellowish-orange ♦◇◇◇◇
powder obtained from a flower and used to give fla- N-UNCOUNT
vour and colouring to some foods. **2 Saffron** is a COLOUR
yellowish-orange colour.

sag /sæg/ **sags, sagging, sagged. 1** When ♦◇◇◇◇
something **sags**, it hangs down loosely or sinks VERB: V
downwards in the middle. *...the sagging armchair.* V-ing
2 When someone's body begins to **sag**, it starts to V-ing
lose its firmness, because of old age. *...flabby thighs*
and sagging bottoms. **3** To **sag** means to become VERB
weaker. *The pound continued to sag despite four* Also V-ing
interventions by the Bank of England.

saga /'sɑːgə/ **sagas.** A **saga** is a long story, ac- ♦◇◇◇◇
count, or sequence of events. *The continuing saga of* N-COUNT
unexpected failures by leading companies.

sa·ga·cious /sə'geɪʃəs/. A **sagacious** person is in- ADJ-GRADED
telligent and has the ability to make good decisions. FORMAL

sa·gac·ity /sə'gæsɪti/. **Sagacity** is the quality of be- N-UNCOUNT
ing sagacious. *...a man of great sagacity and im-* FORMAL
mense experience.

sage /seɪdʒ/ **sages. 1** A **sage** is a person who is re- ♦◇◇◇◇
garded as being very wise. **2 Sage** means wise and N-COUNT
knowledgeable, especially as the result of a lot of ex- ADJ-GRADED
perience. *He was famous for his intellectual integrity* LITERARY
and sage advice to younger painters. ♦ **sage·ly** ADV
Susan nodded sagely. **3 Sage** is a herb.

sag·gy /'sægi/ **saggier, saggiest.** If you describe ADJ-GRADED
something as **saggy**, you mean that it has lost its
firmness over a period of time and become unattractive.

sago /'seɪgəʊ/. **Sago** is a white starchy substance N-UNCOUNT
obtained from the trunk of some palm trees, used
for making sweet puddings.

sa·hib /'sɑːb, 'sɑːhɪb/ **sahibs. Sahib** is a term used N-TITLE;
by some people in India to address or to refer to a N-COUNT
man in a position of authority. Sahib was used es- [PRAGMATICS]
pecially of white government officials in the period
of British rule.

said /sed/. **Said** is the past tense and past participle
of **say**.

sail /seɪl/ **sails, sailing, sailed. 1 Sails** are large ♦♦♦◇◇
pieces of material attached to the mast of a ship. N-COUNT
The wind blows against the sails and pushes the
ship along. **2** When a ship **sets sail**, it leaves a port. PHRASE
3 If you cross the sea **under sail**, you cross it in a PHRASE
ship that has sails rather than an engine. **4** You say VERB
a ship **sails** when it moves over the sea. *The trawler* V prep/adv

S

had sailed from the port of Zeebrugge. **5** If you **sail** a boat or if a boat **sails**, it moves across water using its sails. *I shall get myself a little boat and sail her around the world... For nearly two hundred miles she sailed on, her sails hard with ice.* **6** If someone or something **sails** somewhere, they move there steadily and fairly quickly. *We got into the lift and sailed to the top floor.* **7** See also **sailing**. `V-ERG: V` `V n prep` `V adv/prep`

sail through. If someone or something **sails through** a difficult situation or experience, they deal with it easily and successfully. *While she sailed through her maths exams, he struggled.* `PHRASAL VB` `V P n` `Also V P`

sail·boat /ˈseɪlbəʊt/ **sailboats.** A **sailboat** is the same as a **sailing boat**. `N-COUNT` `AMERICAN`

sail·ing /ˈseɪlɪŋ/ **sailings. 1** Sailings are voyages made by a ship carrying passengers. *We'll get the next sailing.* **2** Sailing is the activity or sport of sailing boats. **3** If you say that a task was not all **plain sailing**, you mean that it was not very easy. The American expression is **clear sailing**. *We know it won't be plain sailing at Wembley because there are no easy games at this level.* `◆◆◇◇◇` `N-COUNT` `PHRASE` `BRITISH`

'sailing boat, sailing boats; also spelled **sailing-boat.** A **sailing boat** is a boat with sails. `N-COUNT`

'sailing ship, sailing ships. A **sailing ship** is a large ship with sails, especially of the kind that were used to carry passengers or cargo. `N-COUNT`

sail·or /ˈseɪlə/ **sailors.** A **sailor** is a man who works on a ship as a member of its crew. `◆◆◇◇◇` `N-COUNT`

saint /seɪnt/ **saints;** the title is usually pronounced /sənt/. **1** A **saint** is someone who has died and been officially recognized and honoured by the Christian church because his or her life was a perfect example of the way Christians should live. *The Church of Saint Lawrence.* **2** If you refer to a living person as a **saint**, you mean that they are extremely kind, patient, and unselfish. *I would have to be a saint to put up with your resentments.* ♦ **saint·ly** *He is supported by his saintly wife and three children.* `◆◆◇◇◇` `N-COUNT;` `N-TITLE` `N-COUNT` `ADJ-GRADED`

saint·hood /ˈseɪnthʊd/. **Sainthood** is the state of being a saint. *His elevation to sainthood is entirely justified.* `N-UNCOUNT`

sake /seɪk/ **sakes. 1** If you do something **for the sake of** something, you do it for that purpose or in order to achieve that result. *Let's assume for the sake of argument that we manage to build a satisfactory database.* **2** Something that is done or obtained **for** its **own sake** is done or obtained because someone wants to do it or have it, and not because it is expected to bring any other benefit. *...a love of truth and learning for its own sake.* **3** When you do something **for** someone's **sake**, you do it in order to help them or make them happy. *Linda knew that for both their sakes she must take drastic action.* **4** Some people use expressions such as **for God's sake** or **for heaven's sake** in order to express annoyance or impatience, or to add force to a question or request. Some people find 'for God's sake' and 'for Christ's sake' offensive. *For goodness sake, why didn't you ring me?* `◆◆◇◇◇` `PHRASE` `PHRASE` `PHRASE` `PHRASE` `PRAGMATICS` `INFORMAL`

saké /ˈsɑːki, -keɪ/; also spelled **sake.** Saké is a Japanese alcoholic drink that is made from rice. `N-UNCOUNT`

sa·la·cious /səˈleɪʃəs/. If you describe something as **salacious**, you think that it deals with sexual matters in an unnecessarily detailed way. `ADJ-GRADED`

sal·ad /ˈsæləd/ **salads.** A **salad** is a mixture of raw vegetables or cold cooked vegetables. ● See also **fruit salad.** `◆◆◇◇◇` `N-VAR`

'salad cream, salad creams. Salad cream is a yellow creamy sauce that you eat with salad. `N-VAR` `BRITISH`

,salad 'dressing, salad dressings. Salad dressing is a mixture of oil, vinegar, herbs, and other flavourings, which you pour over a salad. `N-VAR`

sala·man·der /ˈsæləmændə/ **salamanders.** A **salamander** is an animal that looks rather like a lizard, and that can live both on land and in water. `N-COUNT`

sa·la·mi /səˈlɑːmi/ **salamis.** Salami is a type of strong-flavoured sausage made from chopped meat and spices. `N-VAR`

sala·ried /ˈsælərɪd/. **Salaried** people receive a salary from their job. `◆◇◇◇◇` `ADJ`

sala·ry /ˈsæləri/ **salaries.** Your **salary** is the money that you are paid each month by your employer. `◆◆◇◇` `N-VAR`

sale /seɪl/ **sales. 1** The **sale** of goods is the act of selling of them for money. *Efforts were made to limit the sale of alcohol.* **2** The **sales** of a product are the quantity of it that is sold. *The newspaper has sales of 1.72 million.* **3** The part of a company that deals with **sales** deals with selling the company's products. *He worked in sales and marketing.* **4** A **sale** is an occasion when a shop sells things at less than their normal price. *...a pair of jeans bought half-price in a sale.* **5** A **sale** is an event when goods such as paintings or antiques are sold to the person who offers the highest price. **6** See also **car boot sale**, **jumble sale.** **7** If something is **for sale**, it is being offered to people to buy. *His former home is for sale at £495,000.* **8** Products that are **on sale** can be bought in shops. *All tickets go on sale this Friday.* **9** If products in a shop are **on sale**, they can be bought for less than their normal price. *He bought a sports jacket on sale at Gowings Men's Store.* **10** If a property or company is **up for sale**, its owner is trying to sell it. *The castle has been put up for sale.* `◆◆◆◆` `N-SING` `N-PLURAL` `N-PLURAL` `N-COUNT` `N-COUNT` `PHRASE` `PHRASE` `PHRASE` `AMERICAN` `PHRASE`

sale·able /ˈseɪləbl/; also spelled **salable.** Something that is **saleable** is easy to sell to people. *Vouchers are very saleable items in a pub.* `ADJ-GRADED`

sale·room /ˈseɪlruːm/ **salerooms.** A **saleroom** is a place where things are sold by auction. `N-COUNT` `BRITISH`

'sales clerk, sales clerks. A **sales clerk** is a person who works in a shop selling things to customers and helping them to find what they want. The British expression is **shop assistant.** `N-COUNT` `AMERICAN`

'sales force, sales forces; also spelled **salesforce.** A company's **sales force** consists of all the people that work for that company selling its products. `N-COUNT`

sales·man /ˈseɪlzmən/ **salesmen.** A **salesman** is a man whose job is to sell things, especially directly to businesses on behalf of a company. `◆◆◇◇◇` `N-COUNT`

sales·man·ship /ˈseɪlzmənʃɪp/. **Salesmanship** is the skill of persuading people to buy things. `N-UNCOUNT`

sales·person /ˈseɪlzpɜːsən/ **salespeople** or **salespersons.** A **salesperson** is a person who sells things, either in a shop or directly to customers on behalf of a company. `◆◇◇◇◇` `N-COUNT`

'sales pitch, sales pitches. Someone's **sales pitch** is what they say in order to persuade someone to buy something. `N-COUNT`

'sales tax, sales taxes. A **sales tax** is an amount of money which people pay to the government when they buy something. `◆◇◇◇◇` `N-VAR`

sales·woman /ˈseɪlzwʊmən/ **saleswomen.** A **saleswoman** is a woman who sells things, in a shop or directly to customers on behalf of a company. `N-COUNT`

sa·li·ent /ˈseɪliənt/ **salients. 1** The **salient** points or facts of a situation are the most important ones. **2** A **salient** is a narrow area where an army has pushed its front line forward into enemy territory. `◆◇◇◇◇` `ADJ-GRADED` `N-COUNT`

sa·line /ˈseɪlaɪn, AM -liːn/. A **saline** substance or liquid contains salt. ♦ **sa·lin·ity** /səˈlɪnɪti/. *...a problem of soil salinity.* `ADJ` `N-UNCOUNT`

sa·li·va /səˈlaɪvə/. **Saliva** is the watery liquid that forms in your mouth and helps you to chew and digest food. `◆◇◇◇◇` `N-UNCOUNT`

sali·vate /ˈsælɪveɪt/ **salivates, salivating, salivated. 1** When people or animals **salivate**, they produce a lot of saliva in their mouth. **2** If someone is **salivating** over something such as the chance to make a lot of money, they are excited about it; used showing disapproval. `VERB: V` `VERB:` `V over/atn` `PRAGMATICS`

sal·low /ˈsæləʊ/. If a person has **sallow** skin, their skin is a pale yellowish colour and may look unhealthy. `ADJ-GRADED`

sal·ly /ˈsæli/ **sallies, sallying, sallied. 1** Sallies are clever and amusing remarks. *She responded to stories and sallies with original comments.* **2** If someone **sallies** forth or **sallies** somewhere, they go `N-COUNT` `LITERARY` `VERB:` `V forth` `V prep/adv`

there quickly or energetically, without any fear or hesitation. *Tamara would sally out on a bitterly cold night to keep her appointments.* ► Also a noun. *...their first sallies outside the student world.* LITERARY N-COUNT

salm·on /ˈsæmən/; **salmon** is both the singular and the plural form. A **salmon** is a large silver-coloured fish. ► **Salmon** is the pink flesh of this fish which is eaten as food. ◆◆◇◇◇ N-COUNT N-UNCOUNT

sal·mo·nel·la /ˌsælməˈnelə/. **Salmonella** is a disease caused by bacteria in food. You can also refer to the bacteria itself as **salmonella**. N-UNCOUNT

salmon 'pink. Something that is **salmon pink** or **salmon** is the orange-pink colour of a salmon's flesh. COLOUR

sa·lon /ˈsælɒn, AM səˈlɑːn/ **salons**. **1** A **salon** is a place where hairdressers or beauticians work. *...a new hair salon.* **2** A **salon** is a shop where smart expensive clothes are sold. **3** A literary **salon** is an informal meeting of fashionable writers or artists, which is held at the house of someone who is well-known. Salons were more common in former times. ◆◆◇◇◇ N-COUNT N-COUNT N-COUNT

sa·loon /səˈluːn/ **saloons**. **1** A **saloon** or a **saloon car** is a car with seats for four or more people, a fixed roof, and a boot that is separated from the rear seats. The American word is **sedan**. **2** A **saloon** is a place where alcoholic drinks are sold and drunk. **3** In Britain, the **saloon** or **saloon bar** in a pub or hotel is a comfortable bar. ◇◇◇◇ N-COUNT BRITISH N-COUNT AMERICAN N-COUNT DATED

sal·sa /ˈsælsə, AM ˈsɑːlsə/ **salsas**. **1** Salsa is a hot spicy sauce made from onions and tomatoes, usually eaten with Mexican or Spanish food. **2** Salsa is a type of dance music especially popular in Latin America. ◆◇◇◇ N-VAR N-UNCOUNT

salt /sɔːlt/ **salts, salting, salted**. **1** Salt is a strong-tasting substance, in the form of white powder or crystals, which is used to improve the flavour of food or to preserve it. Salt occurs naturally in sea water. **2** When you **salt** food, you add salt to it. ◆ **salt·ed** *...lightly salted butter.* **3** Salts are substances like salt that are formed when an acid reacts with an alkaline. *The rock is rich in mineral salts.* **4** See also epsom salts, smelling salts. **5** If you describe someone as the **salt of the earth**, you have a lot of respect for them because you think they are ordinary and dependable, and deal with situations without making any unnecessary fuss. **6** If you take something **with a pinch of salt**, you do not believe that it is completely accurate or true. *He's inclined to take tales of the supernatural with a liberal pinch of salt.* **7** If you say, for example, that any doctor or parent **worth** his or her **salt** would do something, you mean that any good doctor or parent would do it. **8** If someone or something **rubs salt into the wound**, they make the unpleasant situation that you are in even worse, often by reminding you of your failures or faults. ◆◆◇◇◇ N-UNCOUNT VERB: V n ADJ-GRADED N-COUNT PHRASE PHRASE PHRASE PHRASE

salt away. If someone **salts away** sums of money, they save the money for the future, often illegally. *Senior party functionaries have illegally salted away money abroad.* PHRASAL VB V P noun Also V n P

'salt marsh, salt marshes. A **salt marsh** is an area of flat ground where a lot of salt water lies. N-VAR

,salt 'water; also spelled **saltwater**. **Salt water** is water from the sea, which has salt in it. N-UNCOUNT

salty /ˈsɔːlti/ **saltier, saltiest**. Something that is **salty** contains salt or tastes of salt. ◆◇◇◇◇ ADJ-GRADED

sa·lu·bri·ous /səˈluːbriəs/. A place that is **salubrious** is pleasant and healthy or respectable. *...London's less salubrious quarters.* ADJ-GRADED FORMAL

salu·tary /ˈsæljʊtəri, AM -teri/. A **salutary** experience is good for you, even though it may seem difficult or unpleasant at first. ADJ-GRADED

salu·ta·tion /ˌsæljʊˈteɪʃən/ **salutations**. Salutation or a **salutation** is a greeting to someone. N-COUNT also in/ofN

sa·lute /səˈluːt/ **salutes, saluting, saluted**. **1** If you **salute** someone, you greet them or show your respect with a formal sign. *I stood to attention and saluted.* ► Also a noun. *The soldier gave the clenched-fist salute... He stood to attention, lifted his arm in salute.* **2** To **salute** a person or their achieve- ◆◆◇◇◇ VERB: V n V N-COUNT also in N VERB: V n

ments means to publicly show or state your admiration for them.

sal·vage /ˈsælvɪdʒ/ **salvages, salvaging, salvaged**. **1** If something **is salvaged**, someone manages to save it, for example from a ship that has sunk. ► **Salvage** is the act of salvaging things from somewhere. **2** The **salvage** from somewhere such as a wrecked ship or destroyed building is the things that are saved from it. **3** If you manage to **salvage** a difficult situation, you manage to get something useful from it so that it is not a complete failure. *Diplomats are still hoping to salvage something from the meeting.* **4** If you **salvage** something such as your pride or your reputation, you manage not to lose it even though it seems likely that you will, or you regain it after losing it. ◆◆◇◇◇ VERB: be V-ed N-UNCOUNT N-UNCOUNT VERB: V n V n from n VERB: V n

sal·va·tion /sælˈveɪʃən/. **1** In Christianity, salvation is the fact that Christ has saved a person from evil. **2** The **salvation** of someone or something is the act of saving them from harm, destruction, or an unpleasant situation. *...those whose marriages are beyond salvation.* **3** If someone or something is your **salvation**, they are responsible for saving you from something. *The country's salvation lies in forcing through democratic reforms.* ◆◆◇◇◇ N-UNCOUNT N-UNCOUNT N-SING with poss

salve /sælv, AM sæv/ **salves, salving, salved**. **1** If you do something to **salve** your conscience, you do it in order to feel less guilty or worried. **2** Salve is an oily substance that is put on sore skin or a wound to help it heal. VERB: V n N-VAR

sal·ver /ˈsælvə/ **salvers**. A **salver** is a tray or large plate, usually made of silver. N-COUNT

sal·vo /ˈsælvəʊ/ **salvoes**. **1** A **salvo** is the firing of several guns or missiles at the same time. *They were to fire a salvo of blanks, after the national anthem.* **2** A **salvo** of activity such as laughing or shouting is a sudden outburst of it. *His testimony, however, was only one in a salvo of new attacks.* ◆◇◇◇◇ N-COUNT N-COUNT with supp

Sa·mari·tan /səˈmærɪtən/ **Samaritans**. You refer to someone as a good **Samaritan** if they help you when you are in difficulty. N-COUNT

sam·ba /ˈsæmbə/ **sambas**. A **samba** is a lively Brazilian dance. N-COUNT

same /seɪm/. **1** If two or more things, actions, or qualities are the **same**, or if one is the **same** as another, the two are very similar or exactly like each other in some way. *The houses were all the same – square, close to the street, needing paint... Driving a boat is not the same as driving a car... I want my son to wear the same clothes as everyone else at the school.* **2** If something is happening **the same as** something else, the two things are happening in a similar or identical way to each other. *I mean, it's a relationship, the same as a marriage is a relationship... He just wanted the war to end, the same as Wally did.* **3** You use **same** to indicate that you are referring to only one place, time, or thing, and not to different ones. *It's impossible to get everybody together at the same time... John just told me that your birthday is on the same day as mine.* **4** Something that is still the **same** has not changed in any way. *Only 17% said the economy would improve, but 25% believed it would stay the same.* **5** You use the **same** to refer to something that has previously been mentioned or suggested. *We made the decision which was right for us. Other parents must do the same... In the United States small specialised bookshops survive quite well. The same applies to small publishers.* ► Also an adjective. *Eisenhower possessed much the same ability to appear likeable.* **6** You use **same** to refer to the exact thing that has already been mentioned in a document such as a business letter, bill, or receipt. *Wrist watches: £5. Inscription of same: £25.* **7** You say **'same here'** in order to suggest that you feel the same way about something as the person who has just spoken to you, or that you have done the same thing. *'I hate going into stores.'—'Same here.'* **8** You say **'same to you'** in response to someone who wishes you well with something. *'Have a nice Easter.'—'And the same to you Bridie.'* **9** You can say **all the same** or ◆◆◆◆◆ ADJ: the ADJ PHR-CONJ ADJ: the ADJ ADJ: the ADJ PRON ADJ: the ADJ PRON FORMAL, WRITTEN CONVENTION PRAGMATICS INFORMAL CONVENTION PRAGMATICS PHRASE

S

just the same to introduce a statement which indicates that a situation or your opinion has not changed, in spite of what has happened or what has just been said. *Matt is weak and dependent, but you love him all the same.* **10** If you say **'It's all the same to me'**, you mean that you do not care which of several things happens or is chosen. [PRAGMATICS] [PHRASE]

11 When two or more people or things are thought to be distinct or separate and you say that they are **one and the same**, you mean that they are in fact one single person or thing. *Luckily, Nancy's father and her attorney were one and the same person.* **12** You say **'the same'** or **'the very same'** in reply to someone's question when you are saying that they have identified a person or thing correctly. *'This Sawtry guy, he is John Sawtry?'—'Yes, sir. The very same.'* **13** • **at the same time**: see **time**. [PHRASE] [PHRASE FORMAL]

same·ness /'seɪmnəs/. The **sameness** of something is its lack of variety. *He grew bored by the sameness of the speeches.* [N-UNCOUNT]

sam·ple /'sɑːmpəl, 'sæm-/ **samples, sampling, sampled.** **1** A **sample** of a substance or product is a small quantity of it that shows you what it is like. *We're giving away 2000 free samples.* **2** A **sample** of a substance is a small amount of it that is examined and analysed scientifically. *They took samples of my blood.* **3** A **sample** of people or things is a number of them chosen out of a larger group and then used in tests or used to provide information about the whole group. *We based our analysis on a random sample of more than 200 males.* **4** If you **sample** food or drink, you taste a small amount of it in order to find out if you like it. *We sampled a selection of different bottled waters.* **5** If you **sample** a place or situation, you experience it for a short time in order to find out about it. *...the chance to sample a different way of life.* **6** When musicians or pieces of their music **are sampled**, parts of their music are used by other musicians in their own work. [♦♦♦◇◇] [N-COUNT] [N-COUNT] [N-COUNT] [VERB Vn] [VERB Vn] [VERB: be V-ed]

sam·pler /'sɑːmplə, 'sæm-/ **samplers.** **1** A **sampler** is a piece of cloth embroidered with various patterns, which is intended to show the skill of the person who made it. **2** A **sampler** is a piece of equipment that is used for copying and remixing a piece of music into a new piece of music. [♦◇◇◇◇] [N-COUNT] [N-COUNT]

samu·rai /'sæmjʊraɪ, AM -mʊr-/; **samurai** is both the singular and the plural form. In former times a **samurai** was a member of a powerful class of warriors in Japan. [N-COUNT]

sana·to·rium /ˌsænə'tɔːriəm/ **sanatoriums** or **sanatoria** /ˌsænə'tɔːriə/; also spelled **sanitarium**. A **sanatorium** is an institution that provides medical treatment and rest for people who have been ill for a long time. [N-COUNT]

sanc·ti·fy /'sæŋktɪfaɪ/ **sanctifies, sanctifying, sanctified.** **1** If someone or something is **sanctified** by a priest or other holy person, the priest or holy person officially blesses them and declares that they should be considered holy. **2** If an organization such as the Church **sanctifies** an activity, they approve of it, support it, and want it to remain exactly as it is. *The Church sanctified these sordid property rights.* [VERB: be V-ed] [VERB Vn]

sanc·ti·mo·ni·ous /ˌsæŋktɪ'məʊniəs/. If you disapprove of someone because you think that they try-ing to appear virtuous and morally better than other people, you can say that they are **sanctimonious**. [ADJ-GRADED PRAGMATICS]

sanc·tion /'sæŋkʃən/ **sanctions, sanctioning, sanctioned.** **1** If someone in authority **sanctions** an action or practice, they officially approve of it and allow it to be done. *He may now be ready to sanction the use of force.* ▶ Also a noun. *The king could not enact laws without the sanction of Parliament.* **2** **Sanctions** are measures taken by countries to restrict trade and official contact with a country that has broken international law. *He expressed his opposition to the lifting of sanctions.* **3** If a country or an authority **sanctions** another country or a person for doing something, it declares that the country or person is guilty of doing it and imposes sanc- [♦♦♦♦◇] [VERB Vn] [N-UNCOUNT: with supp] [N-PLURAL] [VERB Vn]

tions on them. *...their failure to sanction Japan for butchering whales in violation of international conservation treaties.* **4** A **sanction** is a severe course of action which is intended to make people obey instructions, customs, or laws. *As an ultimate sanction, they can sell their shares if they disagree with the company's investment policy.* [N-COUNT]

sanc·tity /'sæŋktɪti/. If you talk about the **sanctity** of something, you mean that it is very important and must be treated with respect. *...the sanctity of human life.* [N-UNCOUNT]

sanc·tu·ary /'sæŋktʃʊəri, AM -tʃueri/ **sanctuaries.** **1** A **sanctuary** is a place of safety and refuge for people, especially people who are being persecuted. *His church became a sanctuary for thousands of people.* **2** **Sanctuary** is the safety provided in a sanctuary. *Some of them have sought sanctuary in the church.* **3** A **sanctuary** is a place where birds or animals are protected and allowed to live freely. *...a wildlife sanctuary.* [♦♦◇◇◇] [N-COUNT] [N-UNCOUNT] [N-COUNT]

sanc·tum /'sæŋktəm/ **sanctums.** **1** A **sanctum** is a holy place inside a temple or mosque. **2** If you refer to someone's **inner sanctum**, you mean a place which is private and sometimes secret, in which they can be quiet and alone. *...His bedroom's his inner sanctum.* [N-COUNT] [N-COUNT]

sand /sænd/ **sands, sanding, sanded.** **1** **Sand** is a powdery substance that consists of extremely small pieces of stone. *They all walked barefoot across the damp sand to the water's edge. ...grains of sand.* **2** **Sands** are a large area of sand, for example a beach. *...miles of golden sands.* **3** If you **sand** a wood or metal surface, you rub sandpaper over it in order to make it smooth or clean. *Sand the surface softly and carefully.* ▶ **Sand down** means the same as **sand**. *I was going to sand down the chairs and repaint them... Simply sand them down with a fine grade of sandpaper.* [♦♦♦◇◇] [N-UNCOUNT] [N-PLURAL] [VERB Vn] [PHRASAL VB V P noun V n P]

san·dal /'sændəl/ **sandals.** **Sandals** are light shoes that you wear in warm weather, which have straps instead of a solid part over the top of your foot. [♦◇◇◇◇] [N-COUNT]

sandal·wood /'sændəlwʊd/. **1** **Sandalwood** is the sweet-smelling wood of a tree that is found in South Asia and Australia. It is also the name of the tree itself. **2** **Sandalwood** is the oil extracted from the wood of the tree. It is used to make perfume. [N-UNCOUNT] [N-UNCOUNT]

sand·bag /'sændbæg/ **sandbags, sandbagging, sandbagged.** **1** A **sandbag** is a sack filled with sand. Sandbags are usually used to build a wall for protection against floods or explosions. **2** To **sandbag** something means to protect or strengthen it using sandbags. *Residents sandbagged their homes to keep out flood waters.* [N-COUNT] [VERB Vn]

sand·bank /'sændbæŋk/ **sandbanks.** A **sandbank** is a bank of sand below the surface of the sea or a river. [N-COUNT]

sand·box /'sændbɒks/ **sandboxes.** A **sandbox** is a shallow hole or box in the garden with sand in it where small children can play. The usual British word is **sandpit**. [N-COUNT AMERICAN]

'sand castle, sand castles. A **sand castle** is a heap of sand, usually shaped roughly like a castle, which children make when they are playing on the beach. [N-COUNT]

'sand dune, sand dunes. A **sand dune** is a hill of sand near the sea or in a sand desert. [N-COUNT]

sand·er /'sændə/ **sanders.** A **sander** is a machine for making wood or metal surfaces smoother. [N-COUNT]

sand·paper /'sændpeɪpə/. **Sandpaper** is strong paper that has a coating of sand on it. It is used for rubbing wood or metal surfaces to make them smoother. [N-UNCOUNT]

sand·pit /'sændpɪt/ **sandpits.** A **sandpit** is a shallow hole or box in the ground with sand in it where small children can play. The usual American word is **sandbox**. [N-COUNT BRITISH]

sand·stone /'sændstəʊn/ **sandstones.** **Sandstone** is a type of rock which contains a lot of sand. It is often used for building houses and walls. *...sandstone cliffs.* [♦◇◇◇◇] [N-VAR]

sand·storm /'sændstɔːm/ **sandstorms**. A sandstorm is a strong wind in a desert area, which creates a mass of swirling sand.   N-COUNT

sand·wich /'sænwɪdʒ, -wɪtʃ/ **sandwiches, sandwiching, sandwiched**. **1** A **sandwich** consists of two slices of bread with a layer of food such as cheese or meat between them. *...a ham sandwich.* **2** If you **sandwich** two things together with something else, you put that other thing between them. If you **sandwich** one thing between two other things, you put it between them. *When you write, avoid sandwiching the bad news between an irrelevant, indirect, or overly cushioned beginning and end.*   ◆◆◇◇◇   N-COUNT   VERB: V pl-n together   V n between pl-n

sand·wiched /'sænwɪdʒd, -wɪtʃt/. If something is **sandwiched between** two other things, it is in a narrow space between them. *The original kitchen was sandwiched between the breakfast room and the toilet.*   ADJ: v-link ADJ between pl-n

sandy /'sændi/. **1** A **sandy** area is covered with sand. *...long, sandy beaches.* **2 Sandy** hair is light orange-brown in colour.   ◆◆◇◇◇   ADJ-GRADED   ADJ-GRADED

sane /seɪn/ **saner, sanest**. **1** Someone who is **sane** is able to think and behave normally and reasonably, and is not mentally ill. *It wasn't the act of a sane person.* **2** If you refer to a **sane** person, action, or system, you mean one that you think is reasonable and sensible. *No sane person wishes to see conflict or casualties.*   ◆◇◇◇◇   ADJ-GRADED   ADJ-GRADED

sang /sæŋ/. **Sang** is the past tense of **sing**.

sang-froid /ˌsɒŋ ˈfrwɑː/; also spelled **sangfroid**. A person's **sang-froid** is their ability to remain calm in a dangerous or difficult situation. *He behaves throughout with a certain sang-froid.*   N-UNCOUNT FORMAL

san·gria /sæŋˈgriːə/. **Sangria** is a Spanish drink made of red wine, orange or lemon juice, soda, and brandy.   N-UNCOUNT

san·guine /'sæŋgwɪn/. If you are **sanguine** about something, you are cheerful and confident that things will happen in the way you want them to. *They have begun to take a more sanguine view.*   ◆◇◇◇◇   ADJ-GRADED

sani·ta·rium /ˌsænɪˈteəriəm/ **sanitariums**. See **sanatorium**.

sani·tary /'sænɪtri, AM -teri/. **1 Sanitary** means concerned with keeping things clean and hygienic, especially by providing a sewage system and a clean water supply. *Sanitary conditions are appalling.* **2** If you say that a place is not **sanitary**, you mean that it is not very clean. *It's not the most sanitary place one could swim.*   ◆◇◇◇◇   ADJ: ADJ n   ADJ-GRADED

'sanitary napkin, sanitary napkins. A **sanitary napkin** is the same as a **sanitary towel**.   N-COUNT AMERICAN

ˌsanitary pro'tection. **Sanitary protection** refers to sanitary towels or tampons.   N-UNCOUNT

'sanitary towel, sanitary towels. A **sanitary towel** is a pad of thick soft material which women wear to absorb the blood during their periods. The usual American expression is **sanitary napkin**.   N-COUNT BRITISH

sani·ta·tion /ˌsænɪˈteɪʃən/. **Sanitation** is the process of keeping places clean and hygienic, especially by providing a sewage system and a clean water supply. *...the hazards of contaminated water and poor sanitation.*   ◆◇◇◇◇   N-UNCOUNT

sani·tize /'sænɪtaɪz/ **sanitizes, sanitizing, sanitized**; also spelled **sanitise** in British English. If someone **sanitizes** an activity or a situation that is unpleasant or unacceptable, they describe it in a way that makes it seem more pleasant or acceptable. *...the cosy English school of crime writers who sanitise violence and make it respectable.*   VERB V n

san·ity /'sænɪti/. **1** A person's **sanity** is their ability to think and behave normally and reasonably. *He and his wife finally had to move from their apartment just to preserve their sanity.* **2** If there is **sanity** in a situation or activity, there is a purpose and a regular pattern, rather than confusion and worry. *Rafsanjani has been considering various ways of introducing some sanity into the currency market.*   ◆◇◇◇◇   N-UNCOUNT   N-UNCOUNT

sank /sæŋk/. **Sank** is the past tense of **sink**.

San·skrit /'sænskrɪt/. **Sanskrit** is an ancient language which used to be spoken in India and is now used only in religious writings and ceremonies.   N-UNCOUNT

Santa Claus /ˌsæntə ˈklɔːz/. **Santa Claus** or **Santa** is an imaginary old man with a long white beard and a red coat. Traditionally, young children in many countries are told that he brings their Christmas presents.   ◆◇◇◇◇   N-PROPER

sap /sæp/ **saps, sapping, sapped**. **1** If something **saps** your strength or confidence, it gradually weakens or destroys it. *The recession in Japan has sapped investor confidence.* **2 Sap** is the watery liquid in plants and trees.   ◆◇◇◇◇   VERB V n   N-UNCOUNT

sa·pi·ens /'sæpienz/. See **homo sapiens**.

sap·ling /'sæplɪŋ/ **saplings**. A **sapling** is a young tree.   N-COUNT

sap·per /'sæpə/ **sappers**. A **sapper** is a soldier whose job is to carry out building, digging, and engineering work.   N-COUNT

sap·phire /'sæfaɪə/ **sapphires**. A **sapphire** is a precious stone which is blue in colour.   ◆◇◇◇◇   N-VAR

sar·casm /'sɑːkæzəm/. **Sarcasm** refers to speech or writing which actually means the opposite of what it seems to say. Sarcasm is usually intended to mock or insult someone. *'May I,' he went on with heavy sarcasm, 'be the last to welcome you aboard the ship.'*   ◆◇◇◇◇   N-UNCOUNT

sar·cas·tic /sɑːˈkæstɪk/. Someone who is **sarcastic** says the opposite of what they really mean in order to mock or insult someone. *She poked fun at people's shortcomings with sarcastic remarks.* ♦ **sar·cas·ti·cal·ly** /sɑːˈkæstɪkli/. *'What a surprise!' Caroline murmured sarcastically.*   ◆◇◇◇◇   ADJ-GRADED   ADV-GRADED: ADV with v

sar·co·ma /sɑːˈkəʊmə/ **sarcomas**. **1 Sarcoma** is one of two general forms of cancer. It affects tissues such as muscle and bone. Compare **carcinoma**. **2 Sarcomas** are malignant tumours.   N-UNCOUNT   N-COUNT

sar·copha·gus /sɑːˈkɒfəgəs/ **sarcophagi** or **sarcophaguses**. A **sarcophagus** is a large decorative coffin that was used in ancient times.   N-COUNT

sar·dine /sɑːˈdiːn/ **sardines**. **Sardines** are a kind of small sea fish, often eaten as food.   ◆◇◇◇◇   N-COUNT

sar·don·ic /sɑːˈdɒnɪk/. If you describe someone or their behaviour as **sardonic**, you mean that they are mocking or scornful, often in a rather calm, quiet way. *...a sardonic sense of humour.* ♦ **sar·doni·cal·ly** /sɑːˈdɒnɪkli/. *He grinned sardonically.*   ◆◇◇◇◇   ADJ-GRADED   ADV-GRADED

sarge /sɑːdʒ/. A sergeant is sometimes addressed as **sarge**. *Good luck, sarge.*   N-VOC; N-SING INFORMAL

sari /'sɑːri/ **saris**. A **sari** is a piece of clothing worn especially by Indian women. It consists of a long piece of thin material wrapped around the body.   N-COUNT

sar·nie /'sɑːni/ **sarnies**. A **sarnie** is a sandwich. *...two crates of beer and a plate of sarnies.*   N-COUNT BRITISH, INFORMAL

sa·rong /səˈrɒŋ, AM -rɔːŋ/ **sarongs**. A **sarong** is a piece of clothing worn especially by Malaysians. It consists of a long piece of cloth attached around the waist or under the arms.   N-COUNT

sar·to·rial /sɑːˈtɔːriəl/. **Sartorial** means relating to clothes and to the way they are made or worn. *James gave him some sartorial advice.*   ADJ: ADJ n FORMAL

SAS /ˌes eɪ ˈes/. The **SAS** is a group of highly trained British soldiers who work on secret or very difficult military operations. SAS is an abbreviation for 'Special Air Service'.   N-PROPER: the N

sash /sæʃ/ **sashes**. A **sash** is a long piece of cloth which people wear round their waist or over one shoulder, especially with formal or official clothes. *She wore a white dress with a thin blue sash.*   N-COUNT

sas·sy /'sæsi/. **1** If an older person describes a younger person as **sassy**, they mean that they are cheeky and disrespectful. *Are you that sassy with your parents, young lady?* **2 Sassy** is used to describe people or things that are fashionable and attractive. *...colourful and sassy fashion accessories.*   ADJ-GRADED AMERICAN, INFORMAL   ADJ-GRADED AMERICAN, INFORMAL

sat /sæt/. **Sat** is the past tense and past participle of **sit**.

Sat. **Sat**. is a written abbreviation for **Saturday**.   ◆◆◇◇◇

SAT /sæt/ **SATs**. **1** In the United States, the **SAT** is an examination which is often taken by students   N-PROPER

who wish to enter a college or university as undergraduates. **SAT** is an abbreviation for 'Scholastic Aptitude Test'. **2** In Britain, **SATs** are a set of tasks given to seven-year old school children in order to test their ability. **SAT** is an abbreviation for 'Standard Assessment Task'. N-COUNT

Satan /'seɪtən/. Satan is a name sometimes given to the Devil. *It was like Satan had risen from hell.* ♦ **sa·tan·ic** /sə'tænɪk/. *...satanic rituals.* ◆◇◇◇ N-PROPER ADJ

Sa·tan·ism /'seɪtənɪzəm/. Satanism is worship of the devil. *...witchcraft and Satanism.* ♦ **Sa·tan·ist** /'seɪtənɪst/ **Satanists**. A Satanist is a person who worships the Devil. N-UNCOUNT N-COUNT

sa·tay /'sæteɪ, AM 'saːteɪ/. Satay consists of pieces of meat cooked on skewers and served with a peanut sauce. N-UNCOUNT

satch·el /'sætʃəl/ **satchels**. A satchel is a bag with a long strap that schoolchildren use for carrying books. N-COUNT

sat·ed /'seɪtɪd/. If you are **sated** with something, you have had more of it than you can enjoy at one time. *...children happily sated with ice cream.* ADJ-GRADED: v-link ADJ

sat·el·lite /'sætəlaɪt/ **satellites**. **1** A satellite is an object which has been sent into space in order to collect information or to be part of a communications system. Satellites move continuously round the earth or through space. *The rocket launched two communications satellites... President Bush spoke by satellite last night to 34 campaign rallies across the country.* **2 Satellite** television is broadcast using a satellite. *They have four satellite channels.* **3** A **satellite** is a natural object in space that moves round a planet or star. *...the satellites of Jupiter.* **4** You can refer to a country, area, or organization as a **satellite** when you mean that it has no real power of its own, but is dependent on a larger and more powerful country, area, or organization. *...China's satellite territories.* ◆◆◇◇ N-COUNT: also byN / ADJ: ADJ n / N-COUNT / N-COUNT

'**satellite dish, satellite dishes.** A satellite dish is a piece of equipment which people need to have on their house in order to receive satellite television. N-COUNT

sa·ti·ate /'seɪʃieɪt/ **satiates, satiating, satiated.** If something such as food or pleasure **satiates** you, you have all that you need or all that you want of it, often so much that you become tired of it. *The Edinburgh International Festival offers enough choice to satiate most appetites.* VERB FORMAL

sat·in /'sætɪn, AM -tən/ **satins. 1** Satin is a smooth shiny kind of cloth, usually made from silk. **2** If something such as a paint, wax, or cosmetic gives something a **satin** finish, it reflects light to some extent but is not very shiny. ◆◇◇◇ N-VAR ADJ: ADJ n

sat·ire /'sætaɪə/ **satires. 1** Satire is the use of humour to mock or criticize aspects of society or politics. *The commercial side of the Christmas season is an easy target for satire.* **2** A satire is a play, film, or story that uses satire. *...a sharp satire on the American political process.* ◆◇◇◇ N-UNCOUNT / N-COUNT

sa·tir·ic /sə'tɪrɪk/. Satiric means the same as **satirical**. ADJ-GRADED

sa·tir·i·cal /sə'tɪrɪkəl/. A **satirical** drawing, piece of writing, or comedy show uses satire to criticize something. *...a satirical novel about London life.* ◆◇◇◇ ADJ-GRADED

sati·rist /'sætɪrɪst/ **satirists**. A satirist is someone who writes or uses satire. N-COUNT

sati·rize /'sætɪraɪz/ **satirizes, satirizing, satirized**; also spelled **satirise** in British English. If you **satirize** a person or group of people, you use satire to criticize or mock them in something such as a novel or a film. *...Robert Altman, whose film 'The Player' so painfully satirised the movie business.* VERB V n

sat·is·fac·tion /ˌsætɪs'fækʃən/. **1 Satisfaction** is the pleasure that you feel when you do something or get something that you wanted or needed to do or get. *Both sides expressed satisfaction with the progress so far. ...job satisfaction.* **2** If you get **satisfaction** from someone, you get money or an apology from them because of some harm or injustice which has been done to you. *If you can't get any satisfac-* ◆◆◇◇ N-UNCOUNT / N-UNCOUNT FORMAL

tion, complain to the park owner. **3** If you do something to someone's **satisfaction**, they are happy with the way that you have done it. PHRASE

sat·is·fac·tory /ˌsætɪs'fæktəri/. Something that is **satisfactory** is acceptable to you or fulfils a particular need or purpose. *I never got a satisfactory answer.* ♦ **sat·is·fac·to·ri·ly** /ˌsætɪs'fæktərɪli/. *Their motives have never been satisfactorily explained.* ◆◆◆◇◇ ADJ-GRADED ADV-GRADED: ADV with v

sat·is·fied /'sætɪsfaɪd/. If you are **satisfied** with something, you are happy because you have got what you wanted or needed. *We are not satisfied with these results. ...satisfied customers.* ◆◆◇◇ ADJ-GRADED

sat·is·fy /'sætɪsfaɪ/ **satisfies, satisfying, satisfied**. **1** If someone or something **satisfies** you, they give you enough of what you want or need to make you pleased or contented. *The pace of change has not been quick enough to satisfy everyone.* **2** If someone or something **satisfies** you that something is true or has been done properly, they convince you by giving you more information or by showing you what has been done. *He has to satisfy the environmental lobby that real progress will be made to cut emissions.* **3** If you **satisfy** the requirements for something, you are good enough or have the right qualities to fulfil these requirements. *Candidates must satisfy the general conditions for admission.* ◆◆◇◇ VERB V n / VERB V n that / VERB V n

sat·is·fy·ing /'sætɪsfaɪɪŋ/. Something that is **satisfying** gives you a feeling of pleasure and fulfilment. *...a satisfying and enriching task.* ♦ **sat·is·fy·ing·ly** *...a series of satisfyingly detailed and painstakingly constructed documentaries.* ◆◆◇◇ ADJ-GRADED ADV-GRADED

sat·su·ma /sæt'suːmə/ **satsumas**. A satsuma is a small type of orange. N-COUNT

satu·rate /'sætʃʊreɪt/ **saturates, saturating, saturated. 1** If people or things **saturate** a place or object, they fill it completely so that no more can be added. *In the last days before the vote, both sides are saturating the airwaves.* ♦ **satu·ra·tion** *...the saturation of the market with various kinds of goods.* **2** If someone or something is **saturated**, they become extremely wet. *His work clothes, having become saturated with oil, had to be cleaned.* ◆◇◇◇ VERB Also be V-ed / N-UNCOUNT / VERB: be V-ed V-ed Also V n

satu·rat·ed /'sætʃʊreɪtɪd/. Saturated fats are types of fat that are found in some foods, especially dairy products, eggs, and meat. ◆◇◇◇ ADJ-GRADED

satu·ra·tion /ˌsætʃʊ'reɪʃən/. Saturation is used to describe a campaign or other activity that is carried out very thoroughly, so that nothing is missed. *Newspapers, television and radio are all providing saturation coverage.* ● See also **saturate**. ◆◇◇◇ ADJ: ADJ n

Sat·ur·day /'sætədeɪ, -di/ **Saturdays**. Saturday is the day after Friday and before Sunday. *She had a call from him on Saturday morning... Every Saturday dad made a beautiful pea and ham soup.* ◆◆◆◇ N-VAR

sauce /sɔːs/ **sauces**. A sauce is a thick liquid which is served with other food. *...pasta cooked in a sauce of garlic, tomatoes, and cheese.* ◆◆◆◇ N-VAR

sauce·pan /'sɔːspən, AM -pæn/ **saucepans**. A saucepan is a deep metal cooking pot, usually with a long handle and a lid. See picture headed **kitchen utensils**. ◆◇◇◇ N-COUNT

sau·cer /'sɔːsə/ **saucers**. A saucer is a small curved plate on which you stand a cup. ● See also **flying saucer**. ◆◇◇◇ N-COUNT

saucy /'sɔːsi/ **saucier, sauciest**. Someone or something that is **saucy** refers to sex in a light-hearted amusing way. *...a saucy joke.* ADJ-GRADED

sau·er·kraut /'saʊəkraʊt/. Sauerkraut is cabbage which has been cut into very small pieces and pickled. It is eaten mainly in Germany. N-UNCOUNT

sau·na /'sɔːnə/ **saunas. 1** If you have a **sauna**, you sit or lie in a room that is so hot that it makes you sweat. People have saunas in order to relax and to clean their skin thoroughly. **2** A **sauna** is a room or building where you can have a sauna. ◆◇◇◇ N-COUNT / N-COUNT

saun·ter /'sɔːntə/ **saunters, sauntering, sauntered**. If you **saunter** somewhere, you walk there in a slow casual way. *He sauntered along the river to the mill.* ◆◇◇◇ VERB V prep/adv

sau·sage /ˈsɒsɪdʒ, AM ˈsɔːs-/ **sausages.** A sausage consists of minced meat, mixed with other ingredients, inside a thin casing like a tube. ◆◆◇◇◇ N-VAR

sausage 'roll, sausage rolls. A sausage roll consists of a small amount of sausage meat which has been covered with pastry and cooked. N-COUNT BRITISH

sau·té /ˈsəʊteɪ, AM sɔːˈteɪ/ **sautés, sautéing, sautéed.** When you sauté food, you fry it quickly in hot oil or butter. ◆◇◇◇ VERB: V n

sav·age /ˈsævɪdʒ/ **savages, savaging, savaged. 1** Someone or something that is **savage** is extremely cruel, violent, and uncontrolled. *This was a savage attack on a defenceless young girl.* ♦ **sav·age·ly** *He was savagely beaten.* **2** If you refer to people as **savages**, you dislike them because you think that they are cruel, violent, or uncivilized. *...their conviction that the area was a frozen desert peopled with uncouth savages.* **3** If someone **is savaged** by a dog or other animal, the animal attacks them violently. **4** If someone or something that they have done **is savaged** by another person, that person criticizes them severely. *The show had already been savaged by critics.* ◆◆◇◇◇ ADJ-GRADED / ADV-GRADED / N-COUNT [PRAGMATICS] / VB: usu passive / VERB beV-ed Also V n

sav·age·ry /ˈsævɪdʒri/. **Savagery** is extremely cruel and violent behaviour. *...the sheer savagery of war.* N-UNCOUNT

sa·van·nah /səˈvænə/ **savannahs;** also spelled **savanna.** A **savannah** is an open flat stretch of grassland, usually in Africa. ◆◇◇◇ N-VAR

save /seɪv/ **saves, saving, saved. 1** If you save someone or something, you help them to avoid harm or to escape from a dangerous or unpleasant situation. *...a final attempt to save 40,000 jobs... The national health system saved him from becoming a cripple.* **2** If a goalkeeper **saves** a shot, they succeed in preventing the ball from going into the goal. ▶ Also a noun. *Spurs could have had several goals but for some brilliant saves from John Hallworth.* **3** If you **save** something, you keep it because it will be needed later. *Drain the beans thoroughly and save the stock for soup.* **4** If you **save**, you gradually collect money by spending less than you get, usually in order to buy something that you want. *Tim and Barbara are now saving for a house in the suburbs... They could not find any way to save money.* ▶ **Save up** means the same as **save**. *People often put money aside in order to save up enough to make one major expenditure.* ♦ **sav·er, savers** *Low interest rates are bad news for savers.* **5** If you **save** something such as time or money, you prevent the loss or waste of it. *It saves time in the kitchen to have things you use a lot within reach... I got the fishmonger to skin the fish which helped save on the preparation time.* ♦ **-saver, -savers** *These potatoes are sold ready sorted and washed, and can prove a great time-saver for the busy cook... These zip-top bags are great space-savers if storage is limited.* ♦ **sav·ing, savings** *...a program of household savings on energy use.* ♦ **-saving** *...money-saving special offers on the latest products.* **6** If you save someone an unpleasant task or experience, you do something which helps or enables them to avoid it. *He arranges to collect the payment from the customer, thus saving the client the paperwork... The scanner will reduce the need for exploratory operations which will save risk and pain for patients.* **7** You can use **save** to introduce the only things, people, or ideas that your main statement does not apply to. *There is almost no water at all in Mochudi save that brought up from bore holes.* ▶ **Save for** means the same as **save**. *The parking lot was virtually empty save for a few cars.* **8** ● to save someone's **bacon**: see **bacon**. ● to save **the day**: see **day**. ◆◆◆◆◆ VERB V n / V n from n/-ing / VERB: V n / N-COUNT / VERB V n / Also V on V n / VERB: V / V for n / V n / PHRASAL VB V P noun Also V P for n / VERB / COMB / VERB V n n / COMB / VERB V n n / V n / PREP FORMAL / PHR-PREP

save up. see save 4. PHRASAL VB

saving 'grace, saving graces. A **saving grace** is a good quality or feature in a person or thing that prevents them from being completely bad or worthless. *He's funny, which is probably his greatest saving grace.* N-COUNT: with supp

savings /ˈseɪvɪŋz/. Your **savings** are the money that you have saved, especially in a bank or a build- ◆◆◇◇ N-PLURAL

ing society. *Her savings were in the Post Office Savings Bank.* ● See also **save**.

sav·iour /ˈseɪvjə/ **saviours;** spelled **savior** in American English. **1** A **saviour** is a person who saves someone or something from danger, ruin, or defeat. *...the saviour of English football... She regarded him as her saviour.* **2** In the Christian religion, **the Saviour** is Jesus Christ. ◆◇◇◇◇ N-COUNT / N-PROPER: the N

sa·vour /ˈseɪvə/ **savours, savouring, savoured;** spelled **savor** in American English. If you **savour** something pleasant, you enjoy it as much as you can or for as long as possible. *Savour the flavour of each mouthful, and chew your food well... There's something about the Loire Valley that makes you want to savour every moment... We won't pretend we savour the prospect of a month in prison.* VERB V n

sa·voury /ˈseɪvəri/ **savouries;** spelled **savory** in American English. **1 Savoury** food has a salty or spicy flavour rather than a sweet one. *Italian cooking is best known for savoury dishes.* **2 Savouries** are small portions of savoury food, usually eaten as a snack. ◆◇◇◇ ADJ / N-COUNT BRITISH

sav·vy /ˈsævi/. If you describe someone as **savvy**, you think that they show a lot of practical knowledge and instinctive understanding. *She was a pretty savvy woman.* ▶ Also a noun. *He is known for his political savvy.* ADJ-GRADED INFORMAL / N-UNCOUNT

saw /sɔː/ **saws, sawing, sawed, sawn. 1** Saw is the past tense of **see**. **2** A **saw** is a tool for cutting wood. It has a blade with sharp teeth along one edge. Some saws are pushed and pulled by hand, and others are powered by electricity. See picture headed **tools**. ● See also **chain saw**. **3** If you **saw** something, you cut it with a saw. *He escaped by sawing through the bars of his cell.* ◆◇◇◇ / N-COUNT / VERB: V n V prep/adv

saw·dust /ˈsɔːdʌst/. **Sawdust** is dust and very small pieces of wood which are produced when you saw wood. N-UNCOUNT

sawed-off 'shotgun, sawed-off shotguns. A **sawed-off shotgun** is the same as a **sawn-off shotgun.** N-COUNT AMERICAN

saw·mill /ˈsɔːmɪl/ **sawmills.** A **sawmill** is a factory where wood is sawn into planks using a power-driven saw. N-COUNT

sawn /sɔːn/. **Sawn** is the past participle of **saw**.

sawn-off 'shotgun, sawn-off shotguns. A **sawn-off shotgun** is a shotgun whose barrel has been cut short. They are often used by criminals. N-COUNT

sax /sæks/ **saxes.** A **sax** is the same as a **saxophone.** N-COUNT INFORMAL

Sax·on /ˈsæksən/ **Saxons.** Saxons were members of a West Germanic tribe. ▶ Also an adjective. *...a seventh-century Saxon church.* ◆◇◇◇ N-COUNT / ADJ

saxo·phone /ˈsæksəfəʊn/ **saxophones.** A **saxophone** is a musical instrument in the shape of a curved metal tube with keys and a curved mouthpiece. See picture headed **musical instruments**. ♦ **sax·opho·nist,** /ˈsæksəfənɪst, AM ˈsæksəfəʊn-/ **saxophonists.** A **saxophonist** is someone who plays the saxophone. ◆◇◇◇ N-VAR / N-COUNT

say /seɪ/ **says** /sez/ **saying, said** /sed/. **1** When you **say** something, you speak words. You can also use **say** to signal that you are stating a fact or your opinion. *'I'm sorry,' he said... She said they were very impressed... I would just like to say that this is the most hypocritical thing I have ever heard in my life... Forty-one people are said to have been seriously hurt... I packed and said goodbye to Charlie... Did he say where he was going?... It doesn't sound exactly orthodox, if I may say so.* **2** You can mention the contents of a piece of writing by mentioning what it **says** or what someone **says** in it. *The report says there is widespread and routine torture of political prisoners in the country... Auntie Winnie wrote back saying Mam wasn't well enough to write... 'Highly inflammable,' it says on the spare canister.* **3** If you **say** something to yourself, you think it. *Perhaps I'm still dreaming, I said to myself... 'Keep your temper,' he said to himself.* **4** You indicate the information given by something such as a clock, dial, or map by ◆◆◆◆◆ VERB V with quote V that beV-ed to-inf V n to n V wh V so Also V n, V to-inf / VERB V that itV with quote Also V quote, V so / VERB V to pron-refl with quote / VERB V n V that

S

mentioning what it **says**. *The clock said four minutes past eleven... The map says there's six of them.*

5 If you state that you **can't say** something or you **wouldn't say** something, you are indicating in a polite or indirect way that it is not true or that it is not your opinion. *Dead? Well, I can't say I'm sorry... I wouldn't say it's a great success.* **6** You use **shall I say** and **shall we say** in order to warn someone that what you are about to say may cause offence or be surprising. *My involvement has not been altogether, shall we say, ethical.* **7** You can use **'You can say that again'** to express strong agreement with what someone has just said. *'Must have been a fiddly job.'—'You can say that again.'*

8 If something **says** something about a person, situation, or thing, it reveals something about them. *I think that says a lot about how well Seles is playing... The appearance of the place and the building says something about the importance of the project.* **9** If something **says** a lot for a person or thing, it shows that this person or thing is very good or has a lot of good qualities. *That the Escort is still the nation's bestselling car in 1992 says a lot for the power of Ford's marketing people... It says much for Brookner's skill that while the book is suffused with sadness, it is never depressing.* **10** If you say there is a lot **to be said for** something, you think it has a lot of good qualities or aspects. *There's a lot to be said for being based in the country.* **11** You use **say** in expressions such as **I'll say that for** them and **you can say this for them** after or before you mention a good quality that someone has, usually when you think they do not have many good qualities. *He's usually smartly-dressed, I'll say that for him.*

12 If you say that something **says it all**, you mean that it shows you very clearly the truth about a situation or someone's feelings. *This is my third visit in a week, which says it all.* **13** If something **goes without saying**, it is obvious or definitely true. *It goes without saying that if someone has lung problems they should not smoke.* **14** You use **to say nothing of** when you mention an additional thing which gives even more strength to the point you are making. *Unemployment leads to a sense of uselessness, to say nothing of financial problems.* **15** You can use **not to say** when adding a stronger or more extreme description than the one you have just used. *To those who've never received million dollar royalty cheques, this sounded a little odd, not to say offensive.* **16** You use **that is to say** to indicate that you are about to express the same idea more clearly or precisely. *We're basically talking about an independent state in the territories that were occupied in 1967, that is to say, in the West Bank and Gaza.* ● **to say the least**: see **least**. ● **needless to say**: see **needless**.

18 You can use **say** or **let's say** to introduce an example or hypothetical situation that you want to refer to. *Say you lived in Boston, Massachusetts, and dug straight down through the center of the Earth, what country would you come out nearest to?... Someone with, say, between 300 and 500 acres could be losing thousands of pounds a year.* **19 Say** can be used to attract someone's attention or to express surprise, pleasure, or admiration. *Say, Leo, how would you like to have dinner one night, just you and me?*

20 If you have a **say** in something, you have the right to give your opinion and influence decisions relating to it. When you have your **say**, you use this right or give your opinion. *It's time the people of Glasgow had a say in the future of Europe... The Football Association have had their say and so have the Football League.*

say·ing /ˈseɪɪŋ/ **sayings**. A saying is a famous or profound sentence that gives advice or information about human life and experience. *We also realize the truth of that old saying: Charity begins at home.*

'say-so. If you do something on someone's **say-so**, they tell you to do it or they give you permission to do it. *Directors call the shots and nothing happens on set without their say-so.*

scab /skæb/ **scabs**. **1** A scab is a hard dry covering that forms over the surface of a wound. **2** People

who continue to work during a strike are called **scabs** by the people who are on strike. ► Also an adjective. *The mill was started up with scab labor.*

scab·bard /ˈskæbəd/ **scabbards**. A scabbard is a holder for a sword which hangs from a belt.

sca·bies /ˈskeɪbiːz/. Scabies is a very infectious and itchy skin disease caused by a parasite.

sca·brous /ˈskeɪbrəs, ˈskæb-/. If you describe something as **scabrous**, you mean that it deals with sex or describes sex in a shocking way; used showing disapproval. *...the scabrous lower reaches of the film business.*

scaf·fold /ˈskæfəʊld/ **scaffolds**. **1** A scaffold is a temporary raised platform which is used by house decorators. **2** A scaffold is a raised platform on which criminals used to be hanged or beheaded. *Ascending the shaky ladder to the scaffold, More addressed the executioner.*

scaf·fold·ing /ˈskæfəldɪŋ/. Scaffolding is a temporary framework of poles and boards that is used by workers to stand on while they are building, repairing, or painting the outside walls of a building.

scald /skɔːld/ **scalds, scalding, scalded**. **1** If you **scald** yourself, you burn yourself with very hot liquid or steam. *A patient jumped into a bath being prepared by a member of staff and scalded herself.* **2** A **scald** is a burn caused by very hot liquid or steam.

scald·ing /ˈskɔːldɪŋ/. Scalding or scalding hot liquids are extremely hot. *I tried to sip the tea but it was scalding. ...scalding hot water.*

scale /skeɪl/ **scales, scaling, scaled**. **1** If you refer to the **scale** of something, you are referring to its size or extent, especially when it is very big. *You may feel dwarfed by the sheer scale of the place... The break-down of law and order could result in killing on a massive scale... The British aid programme is small in scale.* ● See also **full-scale, large-scale, small-scale**. **2** A **scale** is a set of levels or numbers which are used in a particular system of measuring things or are used when comparing things. *...an earthquake measuring five-point-five on the Richter scale... On a scale of 1 to 10, voters rated their lives at an average of 6.1... The higher up the social scale they are, the more the men have to lose.* **3** A pay **scale** or **scale** of fees is a list of amounts of money which indicates how much someone should be paid, depending, for example, on their age or what work they do. *...those on the high end of the pay scale.* **4** In music, a **scale** is a fixed sequence of musical notes, each one higher than the next, which begins at a particular note. *...the scale of C major.*

5 The **scale** of a map, plan, or model is the relationship between the size of something in the map, plan, or model and its size in the real world. *The map, on a scale of 1:10,000, shows over 5,000 individual paths.* **6** A **scale** model of something is smaller than the original, but the sizes of all the parts are in the same, exact relation to each other. *Franklin made his mother an intricately detailed scale model of the house.* **7** If the different parts of a map, drawing, or model are **to scale**, they are the right size in relation to each other. *...a miniature garden, with little pagodas and bridges all to scale.* **8** If something is **out of scale** with the things near it, it is too big or too small in relation to them. *...the tower surmounted by its enormous golden statue of the Virgin, utterly out of scale with the building.*

9 Scales are a piece of equipment used for weighing things or people. *...kitchen scales... I step on the scales practically every morning.* **10** The **scales** of a fish or reptile are the small flat pieces of hard skin that cover its body. **11** If you **scale** something such as a mountain or a wall, you climb up it or over it. *...the first British woman to scale Everest.* **12** See also **sliding scale, time scale, full-scale, large-scale.**

scale back. To **scale back** means the same as to **scale down**. *UK manufacturers are still having to scale back production.*

scale down. If you **scale down** something, you make it smaller in size, amount, or extent than it used to be. *One Peking factory has had to scale down its workforce from six hundred to only six... The air rescue operation has now been scaled down.* PHRASAL VB / V P noun / Also V n P

scale up. If you **scale up** something, you make it greater in size, amount, or extent than it used to be. *Wellcome has been scaling up production to prepare for clinical trials.* PHRASAL VB / V P noun / Also V n P

scal·lion /'skæljən/ **scallions.** A **scallion** is a small onion with long green leaves. The British expression is **spring onion**. N-COUNT / AMERICAN

scal·lop /'skɒləp, 'skæl-/ **scallops. 1** Scallops are large shellfish with two flat fan-shaped shells. Scallops can be eaten. **2** Scallops are a series of small curves that form an ornamental border on things such as clothes, tablecloths, or handkerchiefs. ♦ **scal·loped** /'skɒləpt, 'skæl-/. *The quilt has pretty, scalloped edges.* ◆◇◇◇ N-COUNT / N-COUNT / ADJ

scalp /skælp/ **scalps, scalping, scalped. 1** Your **scalp** is the skin under the hair on your head. **2** To **scalp** someone means to remove the skin and hair from the top of their head. *He pretended to scalp me with his sword.* **3** A **scalp** is the piece of skin and hair that is removed when someone is scalped. ◆◇◇◇ N-COUNT / VERB / V n

scal·pel /'skælpəl/ **scalpels.** A **scalpel** is a knife with a short, thin, sharp blade. Scalpels are used by surgeons during operations. N-COUNT

scalp·er /'skælpə/ **scalpers.** A **scalper** is someone who sells tickets outside a sports ground or theatre, usually for more than their original value. The British word is **tout**. N-COUNT / AMERICAN

scaly /'skeɪli/. **Scaly** skin is covered in small dry patches of hard or flaking skin. ADJ-GRADED

scam /skæm/ **scams.** A **scam** is a large-scale illegal trick, usually with the purpose of getting money from people or avoiding paying tax. *The duo set up a scam to settle their respective debts.* ◆◇◇◇ N-COUNT / INFORMAL

scamp·er /'skæmpə/ **scampers, scampering, scampered.** When people or small animals **scamper** somewhere, they move there quickly with small light steps. *Children scampered off the yellow school bus.* VERB / V prep/adv

scam·pi /'skæmpi/. **Scampi** is a dish of large prawns that have been fried in batter. N-UNCOUNT

scan /skæn/ **scans, scanning, scanned. 1** When you **scan** written material, you look through it quickly in order to find important or interesting information. *She scanned the advertisement pages of the newspapers.* ▶ Also a noun. *I just had a quick scan through your book again.* **2** When you **scan** a place or group of people, you look at it carefully, usually because you are looking for something or someone. *She was nervous and kept scanning the crowd for Paul.* **3** If a machine **scans** luggage or other items, it examines it, for example by moving X-rays over it. ♦ **scan·ning** *The gun was not revealed in routine scanning of luggage.* **4** If a picture or document **is scanned** into a computer, a machine passes a beam of light over it to make a copy of it in the computer. *The entire paper contents of all libraries will eventually be scanned into computers.* **5** If a radar or sonar machine **scans** an area, it examines or searches it by sending radar or sonar beams over it. **6** A **scan** is a medical test in which a machine sends a beam of X-rays over a part of your body in order to check that your organs are healthy and working normally. **7** If a pregnant woman has a **scan**, a machine using sound waves produces an image of her womb on a screen so that a doctor can see if her baby is developing normally. **8** In a poem, if a line does not **scan**, it does not fit into the poem's regular rhythmic pattern. ◆◆◇◇ VERB / V n / Also V through n / N-SING / VERB: / V n, / no passive / V n for n / VERB: V n / N-UNCOUNT / VB: usu / passive / be V-ed into/ / on to n / VERB: V n / N-COUNT / N-COUNT / VERB: V

scan·dal /'skændl/ **scandals. 1** A **scandal** is a situation or event that a lot of people think is very shocking and immoral and that everybody knows about. *...a financial scandal.* **2** Scandal is talk about the shocking and immoral aspects of someone's behaviour or something that has happened. *He loved* ◆◆◇◇ N-COUNT / N-UNCOUNT

gossip and scandal. **3** If you say that something is a **scandal**, you are angry about it and think that the people responsible for it should be ashamed. *It is a scandal that a person can be stopped for no reason by the police.* N-SING / PRAGMATICS

scan·dal·ize /'skændəlaɪz/ **scandalizes, scandalizing, scandalized;** also spelled **scandalise** in British English. If something **scandalizes** people, they are shocked or offended by it. *She scandalized her family by falling in love with a married man.* VERB / V n

scan·dal·ous /'skændələs/. **1** Scandalous behaviour or activity is considered immoral and shocking. *They would be sacked for criminal or scandalous behaviour.* ♦ **scan·dal·ous·ly** *He asked only that Ingrid stop behaving so scandalously.* **2** Scandalous stories or remarks are concerned with the immoral and shocking aspects of someone's behaviour or something that has happened. *A jealous colleague could spread scandalous gossip about you.* **3** You can describe something as **scandalous** if it makes you very angry and you think the people responsible for it should be ashamed. *...a scandalous waste of money.* ♦ **scandalously** *...scandalously overpriced Beaujolais Nouveau.* ◆◇◇◇ ADJ-GRADED / ADV with v / ADJ-GRADED / ADJ / PRAGMATICS / ADV

scan·ner /'skænə/ **scanners.** A **scanner** is a machine which is used to examine, identify, or record things, for example by moving a beam of light, sound, or X-rays over them. *...brain scanners. ...an optical scanner.* ◆◇◇◇ N-COUNT

scant /skænt/. **1** You use **scant** to indicate that there is very little of something or not as much of something as there should be. *She began to berate the police for paying scant attention to the theft from her car.* **2** If you describe an amount as **scant**, you are emphasizing that it is small. *Richard Savage had known Edward Bellamy a scant five hours.* ◆◇◇◇ ADJ-GRADED / ADJ: / a ADJ amount / PRAGMATICS

scanty /'skænti/ **scantier, scantiest. 1** You describe something as **scanty** when there is less of it than you think there should be. *What scanty evidence we have points to two suspects.* **2** If someone is wearing **scanty** clothing, he or she is wearing clothes which are sexually revealing. *...a model in scanty clothing.* ♦ **scanti·ly** *...pictures of scantily dressed women.* ADJ-GRADED / ADJ-GRADED / ADV-GRADED: / ADV -ed/adj

scape·goat /'skeɪpɡəʊt/ **scapegoats, scapegoating, scapegoated. 1** If someone is made a **scapegoat** for something bad that has happened, people blame them and may punish them for it although it may not be their fault. *I don't think I deserve to be messed about and made the scapegoat for a couple of bad results.* **2** To **scapegoat** someone means to blame them publicly for something bad that has happened, even though it was not their fault. ♦ **scape·goating** *The teachers are fair and avoid favouritism and scapegoating.* ◆◇◇◇ N-COUNT / VERB: V n / N-UNCOUNT

scapu·la /'skæpjʊlə/ **scapulae.** Your **scapula** is your shoulder bone. N-COUNT / MEDICAL

scar /skɑː/ **scars, scarring, scarred. 1** A **scar** is a mark on the skin which is left after a wound has healed. *...facial injuries which leave soft permanent scars.* **2** If your skin **is scarred**, it is badly marked as a result of a wound. *He was scarred for life during a pub fight.* **3** If a surface **is scarred**, it is damaged and there are ugly marks on it. *The arena was scarred by deep muddy ruts.* ▶ Also a combining form. *...a bullet-scarred bus.* **4** If an unpleasant physical or emotional experience leaves a **scar** on someone, it has a permanent effect on their mind. *...emotional scars that come from having been abused.* **5** If an unpleasant physical or emotional experience **scars** you, it has a permanent effect on your mind. ▶ Also a combining form. *...a war-scarred orphan.* ◆◆◇◇ N-COUNT / VB: usu / passive / VB: usu / passive / COMB / N-COUNT / VERB: V n / COMB

scarce /skeəs/ **scarcer, scarcest. 1** If something is **scarce**, there is not enough of it. *Jobs are becoming increasingly scarce.* **2** If you **make** yourself **scarce**, you quickly leave the place you are in, usually in order to avoid a difficult or embarrassing situation. ◆◆◇◇ ADJ-GRADED / PHRASE / INFORMAL

S

scarce·ly /ˈskeəsli/. **1** You use **scarcely** to emphasize that something is only just true or only just the case. *He could scarcely breathe... Scarcely a week goes by without the news providing fresh examples of police racism.* **2** You can use **scarcely** to say that something is certainly not true or is certainly not the case. *It was scarcely in their interest to let too many people know.* **3** If you say **scarcely** had one thing happened when something else happened, you mean that the first event was followed immediately by the second. *Bruce had scarcely shaken our hands when the phone rang.*
*ADV:
ADV before v,
ADV group
PRAGMATICS*
*ADV:
ADV before v,
ADV group
PRAGMATICS*
*ADV:
ADV before v
PRAGMATICS*

scar·city /ˈskeəsiti/ **scarcities**. If there is a **scarcity** of something, there is not enough of it for the people who need it or want it. *...an ever increasing scarcity of water.*
*◆◇◇◇◇
N-VAR
FORMAL*

scare /skeə/ **scares, scaring, scared**. **1** If something **scares** you, it frightens or worries you. *The prospect of failure scares me rigid... It scared him to realise how close he had come to losing everything.* • If you want to emphasize that something scares you a lot, you can say that it **scares the hell out of** you or **scares the life out of** you. **2** If a sudden unpleasant experience gives you a **scare**, it frightens you. *Don't you realize what a scare you've given us all?* **3** A **scare** is a situation in which many people are afraid or worried because they think something dangerous is happening which will affect them all. *...the doctor at the centre of an Aids scare.* **4** A bomb **scare** or a security **scare** is a situation in which there is believed to be a bomb in a place. **5** See also **scared**.
*◆◆◇◇◇
VERB:
V n,
V n adj
it V n to-inf
PHRASE
PRAGMATICS
INFORMAL
N-SING
N-COUNT
N-COUNT*

scare away. See **scare off** 1. *PHRASAL VB*

scare into. If something **scares** you **into** doing something, it makes you do it, because you are frightened of what will happen if you do not do it. *An 80% fall in Taipei's stock market scared consumers into cutting spending.*
*PHRASAL VB
V n P -ing/n*

scare off. **1** If you **scare off** or **scare away** a person or animal, you frighten them so that they go away. *...an alarm to scare off an attacker.* **2** If you **scare** someone **off**, you accidentally discourage them from becoming involved with you. *I don't think that revealing your past to your boyfriend scared him off.*
*PHRASAL VB
V P noun
Also V P
V n P
Also V P noun*

scare·crow /ˈskeəkrəʊ/ **scarecrows**. A **scarecrow** is an object in the shape of a person, which is put in a field where crops are growing in order to frighten birds away.
N-COUNT

scared /skeəd/. **1** If you are **scared** of someone or something, you are frightened of them. *I'm certainly not scared of him... I was too scared to move.* **2** If you are **scared** that something unpleasant might happen, you are nervous and worried because you think that it might happen. *I was scared that I might be sick... He was scared of letting us down.* **3** If you are **scared to death** or **scared stiff**, you are extremely scared.
*◆◆◇◇◇
ADJ-GRADED
ADJ-GRADED
PHRASE*

scare·monger·ing /ˈskeəmʌŋɡərɪŋ/. If one person or group accuses another of **scaremongering**, they accuse them of deliberately spreading worrying stories to try and frighten people.
N-UNCOUNT

'**scare story, scare stories**. A **scare story** is something that is said or written to make people feel frightened and think that a situation is much more unpleasant or dangerous than it really is.
N-COUNT

scarf /skɑːf/ **scarfs** or **scarves**. A **scarf** is a piece of cloth that you wear round your neck or head, usually to keep yourself warm. See picture headed **clothes**.
*◆◇◇◇◇
N-COUNT*

scar·let /ˈskɑːlət/ **scarlets**. **1** Something that is **scarlet** is bright red. **2** If someone with pale skin turns or goes **scarlet**, their face becomes redder than usual because they are very embarrassed or angry. *Her face went bright scarlet.*
*◆◇◇◇◇
COLOUR
COLOUR*

,**scarlet 'fever**. **Scarlet fever** is an infectious disease which causes a painful throat, a high temperature, and a red rash.
N-UNCOUNT

scarp·er /ˈskɑːpə/ **scarpers, scarpering, scarpered**. If someone **scarpers**, they leave a place
*VERB
V
BRITISH,*

quickly. *He owed Vince money for drugs, which is perhaps the reason he scarpered.*
INFORMAL

-scarred /-skɑːd/. See **scar**.

scarves /skɑːvz/. **Scarves** is a plural of **scarf**.

scary /ˈskeəri/ **scarier, scariest**. Something that is **scary** is rather frightening. *There's something very scary about him... We watched scary movies.*
*◆◇◇◇◇
ADJ-GRADED
INFORMAL*

scath·ing /ˈskeɪðɪŋ/. If you say that someone is being **scathing** about something, you mean that they are being very critical and scornful of it. *He then launched a scathing attack on previous leaders.* ♦ **scath·ing·ly** *'Oh, they want to be excused,' the other girl said scathingly.*
*◆◇◇◇◇
ADJ-GRADED
ADV-GRADED*

scat·ter /ˈskætə/ **scatters, scattering, scattered**. **1** If you **scatter** things over an area, you throw or drop them so that they spread all over the area. *She tore the rose apart and scattered the petals over the grave.* **2** If a group of people **scatter** or if you **scatter** them, they suddenly separate and move in different directions. *The cavalry scattered them and chased them off the field.* **3** A **scatter** of things is a number of them spread over an area in an irregular way. *...a scatter of papers.*
*◆◆◇◇◇
V n prep/adv
Also V n
V-ERG: V
V n
N-SING
LITERARY*

scat·tered /ˈskætəd/. **1** Scattered things are spread over an area in an untidy or irregular way. *He picked up the scattered toys... Food was scattered across the floor.* **2** If something is **scattered with** a lot of small things, they are spread all over it. *Every surface is scattered with photographs.*
*◆◆◇◇◇
ADJ
ADJ:
v-link ADJ
with n*

scat·ter·ing /ˈskætərɪŋ/ **scatterings**. A **scattering** of things or people is a small number of them spread over an area. *...the scattering of houses east of the village.*
*◆◇◇◇◇
N-COUNT*

scat·ty /ˈskæti/. If you describe someone as **scatty**, you mean that they are dreamy and often forget things or behave in a silly way. *Her mother is scatty and absent-minded.*
*ADJ-GRADED
BRITISH,
INFORMAL*

scav·enge /ˈskævɪndʒ/ **scavenges, scavenging, scavenged**. If people or animals **scavenge** for things, they collect them by searching among waste or unwanted objects. *Many are orphans, their parents killed as they scavenged for food... Children scavenge through garbage.* ♦ **scav·en·ger, scavengers** *...scavengers such as rats.*
*◆◇◇◇◇
VERB
V for n
V prep/adv
Also V,
V n
N-COUNT*

sce·nario /sɪˈnɑːriəʊ, AM -ˈner-/ **scenarios**. **1** If you talk about a likely or possible **scenario**, you are talking about the way in which a situation may develop. *In the worst-case scenario, you could become a homeless person.* **2** The **scenario** of a film is a piece of writing that gives an outline of the story.
*◆◆◇◇◇
N-COUNT
N-COUNT*

scene /siːn/ **scenes**. **1** A **scene** in a play, film, or book is part of it in which a series of events happen in the same place. *...the opening scene of 'A Christmas Carol'... Act I, scene 1.* **2** You refer to a place as a **scene** when you are describing its appearance and indicating what impression it makes on you. *It's a scene of complete devastation.* **3** You can describe an event that you see, or that is broadcast or shown in a picture, as a **scene** of a particular kind. *There were emotional scenes as the refugees enjoyed their first breath of freedom.* **4** The **scene** of an event is the place where it happened. *The area has been the scene of fierce fighting for three months.* **5** You can refer to an area of activity as a particular type of **scene**. *...a youth guide to London's club scene.* **6** If you say that an activity or place **is not** your **scene**, you mean that you do not like it or enjoy it. *Lying on the beach all week isn't my scene.* **7** Paintings and drawings of places are sometimes called **scenes**. *...James Lynch's country scenes.* **8** If you make a **scene**, you embarrass people by publicly showing your anger about something. **9** If something is done **behind the scenes**, it is done secretly rather than publicly. *But behind the scenes Mr Cain will be working quietly to try to get a deal done.* **10** If you refer to what happens **behind the scenes**, you are referring to what happens during the making of a film, play, or radio or television programme. **11** If you have a **change of scene**, you go somewhere
*◆◆◆◇
N-COUNT
N-COUNT
N-COUNT:
with supp
N-COUNT
N-SING:
supp N
PHRASE
INFORMAL
N-COUNT
N-COUNT
PHRASE
PHRASE
PHRASE*

different after being in a particular place for a long time.

12 Something that **sets the scene for** a particular event creates the conditions in which the event is likely to happen. *Mr Yeltsin's declaration set the scene for a further confrontation with Mr Gorbachev.* PHRASE

13 When someone or something appears **on the scene**, they come into being or become involved in something. When they disappear **from the scene**, they are no longer there or are no longer involved. *He could react rather jealously when and if another child comes on the scene.* PHRASE

scen·ery /'siːnəri/. **1** The **scenery** in a country area is the land, water, or plants that you can see around you. *...the island's spectacular scenery.* **2** In a theatre, the **scenery** consists of the structures and painted backcloths that give an indication of where the action in the play takes place. **3** If you have a **change of scenery**, you go somewhere different after being in a particular place for a long time. ◆◇◇◇◇ N-UNCOUNT / N-UNCOUNT / PHRASE

sce·nic /'siːnɪk/. **1** A **scenic** place has attractive scenery. *...a 2-hour drive through scenic country.* **2** A **scenic** route goes through attractive scenery and has nice views. *Take the scenic road into Macon.* **3** If a place has **scenic** beauty, its scenery is attractive. *...a land of unparalleled scenic beauty.* ◆◇◇◇◇ ADJ-GRADED / ADJ-GRADED / ADJ: ADJ n

scent /sent/ **scents, scenting, scented. 1** The **scent** of something is the pleasant smell that it has. *Flowers are chosen for their scent as well as their look.* **2** If something **scents** a place or thing, it makes it smell pleasant. *Scent your drawers and wardrobe with your favourite aromas.* **3 Scent** is a pleasant-smelling liquid which women put on their necks and wrists to make themselves smell nice. **4** The **scent** of a person or animal is the smell that they leave and that other people sometimes follow when looking for them. *A police dog picked up the murderer's scent.* **5** When an animal **scents** something, it becomes aware of it by smelling it. *...dogs which scent the hidden birds.* **6** If you **scent** a situation, you feel that it is going to happen. *Republicans from Pennsylvania and New York are scenting victory.* ◆◆◇◇◇ N-COUNT / VERB: V n, V n with n / N-VAR BRITISH / N-VAR / VB: no cont V n / VERB V n

scent·ed /'sentɪd/. **Scented** things have a pleasant smell, either naturally or because perfume has been added to them. ◆◇◇◇◇ ADJ

scep·ter /'septə/ **scepters.** See sceptre.

scep·tic /'skeptɪk/ **sceptics;** spelled **skeptic** in American English. A **sceptic** is a person who has doubts about things that other people believe. *He now has to convince sceptics that he has a serious plan.* ◆◇◇◇◇ N-COUNT

scep·ti·cal /'skeptɪkəl/; spelled **skeptical** in American English. If you are **sceptical** about something, you have doubts about it. *...scientists who are sceptical of global warming.* ◆ **scep·ti·cal·ly** /'skeptɪkli/. *'What's your point?' demanded the old man sceptically.* ◆◆◇◇◇ ADJ-GRADED / ADV-GRADED: ADV after v

scep·ti·cism /'skeptɪsɪzəm/; spelled **skepticism** in American English. **Scepticism** is great doubt about whether something is true or useful. *The report has inevitably been greeted with scepticism.* ◆◇◇◇◇ N-UNCOUNT

scep·tre /'septə/ **sceptres;** spelled **scepter** in American English. A **sceptre** is an ornamental rod that a king or queen carries on ceremonial occasions as a symbol of his or her power. N-COUNT

sched·ule /'ʃedjuːl, AM 'skedʒuːl/ **schedules, scheduling, scheduled. 1** A **schedule** is a plan that gives a list of events or tasks and the times at which each one should happen or be done. *He has been forced to adjust his schedule.* **2** You can use the word **schedule** to refer to the time or way something is planned to be done. For example, if something is completed **on schedule**, it is completed at the time planned. *The jet arrived in Johannesburg two minutes ahead of schedule.* **3** If something **is scheduled** to happen at a particular time, arrangements are made for it to happen at that time. *The space shuttle had been scheduled to blast off at 04:38... No new talks are scheduled.* ◆◆◆◆◇ N-COUNT / N-UNCOUNT: prep N / VB: usu passive be V-ed to-inf

4 A **schedule** is a written list of things, for example a list of prices, details, or conditions. **5** A **schedule** is a list of all the times when trains, boats, buses, or aircraft are supposed to arrive or depart from a particular place. N-COUNT / N-COUNT

sche·ma /'skiːmə/ **schemas** or **schemata** /'skiːmətə/. A **schema** is an outline of a plan or theory. *...a definite position in the schema of the economic process.* N-COUNT FORMAL

sche·mat·ic /ski'mætɪk/. A **schematic** diagram or picture shows in a simplified way how something works. *...a schematic picture of the solar system.* ◆ **sche·mati·cal·ly** /ski'mætɪkli/. *Let me schematically show what happens.* ADJ-GRADED / ADV-GRADED: ADV with v

scheme /skiːm/ **schemes, scheming, schemed. 1** A **scheme** is a large-scale plan or arrangement produced by a government or other organization. *...schemes to help combat unemployment. ...a private pension scheme.* **2** A **scheme** is someone's plan for achieving something. *...a quick money-making scheme to get us through the summer.* **3** If you say that people **are scheming**, you mean that they are making secret plans in order to gain something for themselves; used showing disapproval. *The bride's family were scheming to prevent a wedding.* ◆ **schem·ing** *...their favourite pastimes of scheming and gossiping.* **4** See also **colour scheme. 5** The **scheme of things** is the way that everything in the world or in a particular situation seems to be organized. *He did not quite know how to place women in his scheme of things.* ◆◆◆◇ N-COUNT / N-COUNT / VERB: V, V to-inf, Also V against / N-UNCOUNT / PHRASE

schem·er /'skiːmə/ **schemers.** If you refer to someone as a **schemer**, you mean that they make secret plans in order to get some benefit for themselves; used showing disapproval. *...office schemers, thinking of nothing but our own advancement.* N-COUNT PRAGMATICS

scher·zo /'skeətsəʊ/ **scherzos.** A **scherzo** is a short, lively piece of classical music which is usually part of a longer piece of music such as a symphony or a sonata. N-COUNT

schism /'skɪzəm, 'sɪz-/ **schisms.** When there is a **schism**, a group or organization divides into two groups as a result of differences in thinking and beliefs. *The church seems to be on the brink of schism.* N-VAR FORMAL

schiz·oid /'skɪtsɔɪd/. **1** If you describe someone as **schizoid**, you mean that they seem to have very different opinions and purposes at different times. **2** Someone who is **schizoid** suffers from schizophrenia. ADJ-GRADED INFORMAL / ADJ

schizo·phre·nia /ˌskɪtsə'friːniə/. **Schizophrenia** is a serious mental illness. People who suffer from it are unable to relate their thoughts and feelings to what is happening around them and often withdraw from society. ◆◇◇◇◇ N-UNCOUNT

schizo·phren·ic /ˌskɪtsə'frenɪk/ **schizophrenics. 1** A **schizophrenic** is a person who is suffering from schizophrenia. ▶ Also an adjective. *...schizophrenic tendencies.* **2** Someone's attitude or behaviour can be described as **schizophrenic** when they seem to have very different opinions or purposes at different times. *...the schizophrenic mood of the American public.* ◆◇◇◇◇ N-COUNT / ADJ / ADJ-GRADED INFORMAL

schlock /ʃlɒk/. If you refer to films, pop songs, or books as **schlock**, you mean that they have no artistic or social value. *...a showman with a good eye for marketable schlock.* N-UNCOUNT INFORMAL

schmaltz /ʃmælts, AM ʃmɑːlts/. If you describe a play, film, or book as **schmaltz**, you do not like it because it is very sentimental. N-UNCOUNT PRAGMATICS

schmaltzy /'ʃmæltsi, AM 'ʃmɑːltsi/. If you describe songs, films, or books as **schmaltzy**, you do not like them because they are very sentimental. ADJ-GRADED PRAGMATICS

schmooze /ʃmuːz/ **schmoozes, schmoozing, schmoozed.** If you **schmooze**, you talk casually and socially with someone. *...those coffee houses where you can schmooze for hours.* VERB V AMERICAN, INFORMAL

schnapps /ʃnæps/. **Schnapps** is a strong alcoholic drink made from potatoes. ▶ A **schnapps** is a glass of schnapps. N-UNCOUNT / N-SING

S

schol·ar /ˈskɒlə/ **scholars. 1** A **scholar** is a person who studies an academic subject and knows a lot about it. *...an influential Islamic scholar.* **2** You can use the word **scholar** to refer to someone who learns things at school in a particular way. For example, if someone is a good **scholar**, they are good at learning things. **3** A **scholar** is a student who has obtained a scholarship. *He came to Oxford as a Rhodes scholar and studied law.*

schol·ar·ly /ˈskɒləli/. **1** A **scholarly** person spends a lot of time studying and knows a lot about academic subjects. *He was an intellectual, scholarly man.* **2** A **scholarly** book or article contains a lot of academic information and is intended for academic readers. **3** **Scholarly** matters and activities relate to scholars or their work. *...scholarly research.*

schol·ar·ship /ˈskɒləʃɪp/ **scholarships. 1** If you get a **scholarship** to a school or university, your studies are paid for by the school or university or by some other organization. **2** **Scholarship** is serious academic study and the knowledge that is obtained from it. *I want to take advantage of your lifetime of scholarship.*

scho·las·tic /skəˈlæstɪk/. Your **scholastic** achievement or ability is your academic achievement or ability while you are at school. *...the values which encouraged her scholastic achievement.*

school /skuːl/ **schools, schooling, schooled. 1** A **school** is a place where children are educated. You usually refer to this place as **school** when you are talking about the time that children spend there. *...a boy who was in my class at school. ...a school built in the Sixties. ...two boys wearing school uniform.* **2** A **school** is the pupils or staff at a school. *Deirdre, the whole school's going to hate you.* **3** A privately-run place where a particular skill or subject is taught can be referred to as a **school**. *...a riding school and equestrian centre.* **4** A university, college, or university department specializing in a particular type of subject can be referred to as a **school**. *...a lecturer in the school of veterinary medicine at the University of Pennsylvania.* **5** **School** is used to refer to university or college. *Bill Clinton's an Oxford man – he went to school in England.* **6** A particular **school** of writers, artists, or thinkers is a group of them whose work, opinions, or theories are similar. *...the Chicago school of economists.* **7** A **school of** fish or dolphins is a large group of them moving through water together. **8** If you **school** someone in something, you train or educate them to have a certain skill, type of behaviour, or way of thinking. *Many mothers schooled their daughters in the myth of female inferiority... He is schooled to spot trouble.* **9** In American English and in formal British English, to **school** a child means to educate him or her. *She's been schooling her kids herself.* ♦ **schooled** *...Indian children, both schooled and unschooled.* **10** If you **school** a horse, you train it so that it can be ridden in competitions. *She bought him as a £1,000 colt of six months and schooled him.* **11** If you approve of someone because they have good qualities that used to be more common in the past, you can describe them as one **of the old school**. *...an elderly gentleman of the old school.* **12** **School** is used in a large number of expressions which are explained at other places in this dictionary.

'school age. When a child reaches **school age**, he or she is old enough to go to school. *...young children below school age.* ▶ Also an adjective. *...families with school-age children.*

school·bag /ˈskuːlbæg/ **schoolbags;** also spelled **school bag.** A **schoolbag** is a bag such as a satchel or a holdall that children use to carry books and other things to and from school.

'school board, school boards. In the United States, a **school board** is a committee in charge of education in a particular city or area, or in a particular school.

school·boy /ˈskuːlbɔɪ/ **schoolboys. 1** A **schoolboy** is a boy who goes to school. *...a group of ten-*

year-old schoolboys. **2** If you think a man's sense of humour is silly or immature, you can describe it as **schoolboy** humour. *...tiresome schoolboy jokes.*

school·child /ˈskuːltʃaɪld/ **schoolchildren.** **Schoolchildren** are children who go to school.

school·days /ˈskuːldeɪz/; also spelled **school days.** Your **schooldays** are the period of your life when you were at school. *...a girl he had known since his schooldays.*

,school 'dinner, school dinners. School dinners are midday meals provided for children at a school.

schooled /skuːld/. If you are **schooled** in something, you have learned about it as the result of training or experience. *They were both well schooled in the ways of the Army.* ● See also **school.**

'school friend, school friends; also spelled **schoolfriend.** A **school friend** is a friend of yours who is at the same school as you, or who used to be at the same school when you were children.

school·girl /ˈskuːlɡɜːl/ **schoolgirls.** A **schoolgirl** is a girl who goes to school. *...half a dozen giggling schoolgirls.*

school·house /ˈskuːlhaʊs/ **schoolhouses.** A **schoolhouse** is a small building used as a school.

school·ing /ˈskuːlɪŋ/. **Schooling** is education that children receive at school. *...a voucher scheme to help poorer families pay for private schooling.*

'school kid, school kids; also spelled **schoolkid.** **School kids** are schoolchildren; see **schoolchild.** *...young school kids in short pants.*

,school 'leaver, school leavers; also spelled **school-leaver. School leavers** are young people who have just left school, because they have completed their time there.

school·master /ˈskuːlmɑːstə, -mæst-/ **schoolmasters.** A **schoolmaster** is a man who teaches children in a school.

school·mate /ˈskuːlmeɪt/ **schoolmates.** A **schoolmate** is a child who goes to the same school as you, especially one who is your friend.

school·mistress /ˈskuːlmɪstrəs/ **schoolmistresses.** A **schoolmistress** is a woman who teaches children in a school.

school·room /ˈskuːlruːm/ **schoolrooms.** A **schoolroom** is a classroom, especially the only classroom in a small school.

school·teacher /ˈskuːltiːtʃə/ **schoolteachers.** A **schoolteacher** is a teacher in a school.

'school teaching. School teaching is the work that schoolteachers do.

school·work /ˈskuːlwɜːk/. **Schoolwork** is the work that a child does at school or as homework.

school·yard /ˈskuːljɑːd/ **schoolyards;** also spelled **school yard.** The **schoolyard** is the large open area with a hard surface just outside a school building, where the schoolchildren can play and do other activities.

schoon·er /ˈskuːnə/ **schooners.** A **schooner** is a medium-sized sailing ship.

schwa /ʃwɑː/ **schwas.** In the study of language, **schwa** is the name of the neutral vowel sound represented by the symbol /ə/ in this dictionary.

sci·ati·ca /saɪˈætɪkə/. **Sciatica** is a severe pain in the long nerve in your legs or the lower part of your back.

sci·ence /ˈsaɪəns/ **sciences. 1** **Science** is the study of the nature and behaviour of natural things and the knowledge that we obtain about them. **2** A **science** is a particular branch of science such as physics, chemistry, or biology. **3** A **science** is the study of some aspect of human behaviour, for example sociology or anthropology. *...the modern science of psychology.* **4** See also **domestic science, exact science, political science, social science.**

,science 'fiction. Science fiction consists of stories in books, comics, and films about events that take place in the future or in other parts of the universe.

'science park, science parks. A **science park** is an area, usually linked to a university, where there are a lot of private companies, especially ones concerned with high technology.   N-COUNT

sci·en·tif·ic /ˌsaɪən'tɪfɪk/. **1 Scientific** is used to describe things that relate to science or to a particular science. *Scientific research is widely claimed to be the source of the high standard of living in the US. ...scientific instruments.* ♦ **sci·en·tif·i·cal·ly** /ˌsaɪən'tɪfɪkli/. *...scientifically advanced countries.* **2** If you do something in a **scientific** way, you do it carefully and thoroughly, using experiments or tests. *It's not a scientific way to test their opinions.* ♦ **scientifically** *Efforts are being made to research it scientifically.*   ♦♦♦◇◇ ADJ   ADV   ADJ-GRADED   ADV-GRADED

sci·en·tist /'saɪəntɪst/ **scientists.** A **scientist** is someone who has studied science and whose job is to teach or do research in science. ● See also **social scientist.**   ♦♦♦♦◇ N-COUNT

sci-fi /'saɪ faɪ/. **Sci-fi** is science fiction. *...low-budget sci-fi films.*   ♦◇◇◇◇ N-UNCOUNT

scimi·tar /'sɪmɪtə/ **scimitars.** A **scimitar** is a sword with a curved blade that was used in former times in some Eastern countries.   N-COUNT

scin·til·la /sɪn'tɪlə/. If you say that there is **not** a **scintilla** of evidence, hope, or doubt about something, you are emphasizing that there is none at all.   QUANT   PRAGMATICS   LITERARY

scin·til·lat·ing /'sɪntɪleɪtɪŋ/. A **scintillating** conversation or performance is very lively and interesting.   ADJ-GRADED

sci·on /'saɪən/ **scions.** A **scion** of a rich or famous family is one of its younger or more recent members. *Nabokov was the scion of an aristocratic family.*   N-COUNT   LITERARY

scis·sors /'sɪzəz/; the form **scissor** is used as a modifier. **Scissors** are a small cutting tool with two sharp blades that are screwed together. You use scissors for cutting things such as paper and cloth. See picture headed **kitchen utensils.** *He told me to get some scissors.*   ♦◇◇◇◇ N-PLURAL: also a pair of N

scle·ro·sis /sklə'rəʊsɪs/. **Sclerosis** is a medical condition in which the tissue in a part of your body becomes abnormally hard. ● See also **multiple sclerosis.**   ♦◇◇◇◇ N-UNCOUNT MEDICAL

scoff /skɒf/ **scoffs, scoffing, scoffed. 1** If you **scoff** at something, you speak in a scornful, mocking way about it because you think it is ridiculous or inadequate. *'You'll have to do better than that,' Joanna scoffed.* **2** If you **scoff** food, you eat it quickly and greedily. *The pancakes were so good that I scoffed the lot.*   ♦◇◇◇◇ VERB: V at n V with quote Also V   VERB V n INFORMAL, BRITISH

scold /skəʊld/ **scolds, scolding, scolded.** If you **scold** someone, you speak angrily to them because they have done something wrong. *Later she scolded her daughter for having talked to her father like that.*   ♦◇◇◇◇ VERB: V n V n for n Also V, V with quote FORMAL

sconce /skɒns/ **sconces.** A **sconce** is a decorated bracket that holds candles or an electric light, and that is attached to the wall of a room.   N-COUNT

scone /skɒn, skəʊn/ **scones.** A **scone** is a small cake made from flour and fat, usually eaten with butter.   ♦◇◇◇◇ N-COUNT BRITISH

scoop /skuːp/ **scoops, scooping, scooped. 1** If you **scoop** someone or something somewhere, you put your hands or arms under or round them and quickly move them there. *Michael knelt next to her and scooped her into his arms.* **2** If you **scoop** something from a container, you remove it with something such as a spoon. **3** A **scoop** is an object like a spoon which is used for picking up a quantity of a food such as ice cream or an ingredient such as flour. ▶ A **scoop** of food is the amount that a scoop will hold. **4** A **scoop** is an exciting news story which is reported in one newspaper or on one television programme before it appears anywhere else. **5** If you **scoop** a prize or award, you win it.   ♦◇◇◇◇ VERB V n prep/adv Also V n   VERB: V n prep/adv   N-COUNT   N-COUNT   N-COUNT   VERB: V n JOURNALISM

scoop out. If you **scoop out** part of something, you remove it using a spoon or other tool. *Cut a marrow in half and scoop out the seeds.*   PHRASAL VB V P noun Also V n P

scoop up. If you **scoop** something **up**, you put your   PHRASAL VB

hands or arms under it and lift it in a quick movement. *Use both hands to scoop up the leaves.*   V n P V P noun

scoot /skuːt/ **scoots, scooting, scooted.** If you **scoot** somewhere, you go there very quickly. *Sam said, 'I'm going to hide,' and scooted up the stairs.*   VERB V prep/adv Also V INFORMAL

scoot·er /'skuːtə/ **scooters. 1** A **scooter** is a small light motorcycle. **2** A **scooter** is a type of child's bicycle which has two wheels joined by a board and a handle on a long pole attached to the front wheel. The child stands on the board with one foot, and uses the other foot to move forwards.   N-COUNT   N-COUNT

scope /skəʊp/. **1** If there is **scope** for a particular kind of behaviour or activity, people have the opportunity to behave in this way or do that activity. *Banks had increased scope to develop new financial products.* **2** The **scope** of an activity, topic, or piece of work is the whole area which it deals with or includes. *Mr Chavis promised to widen the organisation's scope of activity.*   ♦♦◇◇◇ N-UNCOUNT   N-SING

scorch /skɔːtʃ/ **scorches, scorching, scorched. 1** To **scorch** something means to burn it slightly. *The bomb scorched the side of the building.* ♦ **scorched** *...scorched black earth.* **2** If something **scorches** it becomes marked or discoloured by too much heat or by a chemical. *If any of the spray goes onto the lawn it will scorch the grass.* ♦ **scorched** *...the lamp with its scorched plastic shade.*   ♦◇◇◇◇ VERB V n   ADJ-GRADED V-ERG: V V n   ADJ-GRADED

,scorched 'earth. A **scorched earth** policy is the deliberate burning, destruction, and removal by an army of everything that would be useful to an enemy that might invade the area.   N-UNCOUNT

scorch·ing /'skɔːtʃɪŋ/. **Scorching** or scorching hot weather or temperatures are very hot indeed.   ♦◇◇◇◇ ADJ

score /skɔː/ **scores, scoring, scored;** in meaning 13, the plural form is **score. 1** In a sport or game, if a player **scores** a goal or a point, they gain a goal or point. *England scored 282 in their first innings... Gascoigne almost scored in the opening minute.* **2** The **score** in a game is the result of it or the current situation, as indicated by the number of goals, runs, or points obtained by the two teams or players. *4-1 was the final score.* **3** If you **score** a particular number or amount, for example as a mark in a test, you achieve that number or amount. *Kelly had scored an average of 147... Congress as an institution scores low in public opinion polls.* **4** Someone's **score** in a game or test is a number, for example, a number of points or runs, which shows what they have achieved or what level they have reached. *The U.S. Open golf tournament was won by Ben Hogan, with a score of 287.* **5** If you **score** a success, a victory, or a hit, you are successful in what you are doing. *Soldiers using a multiple rocket launcher scored a direct hit on the steeple of a church.* **6** If you **keep score** of the number of things that are happening in a certain situation, you count them and record them. *Keep score of your baby's movements before birth by recording them on a kick chart.* **7** If you **know the score**, you know what the real facts of a situation are and how they affect you, even though you may not like them. *I don't feel sorry for Carl. He knew the score, he knew what he had to do.* **8** If you **settle a score** or **settle an old score** with someone, you take revenge on them for something they have done in the past. **9** The **score** of a film, play, or similar production is the music which is written or used for it. **10** The **score** of a piece of music is the written version of it. **11 Scores of** things or people means a large number of them. ▶ Also a pronoun. *Two people were killed and scores were injured.* **12** If things happen or exist **by the score**, they happen or exist in large numbers. *The companies brought out new products by the score.* **13** A **score** is twenty or approximately twenty. *It's thought a score of countries may be either producing or planning to obtain chemical weapons.* **14** You can use **on that score** or **on this score** to refer to something that has just been mentioned, especially an area of difficulty or concern. *I became pregnant*   ♦♦♦♦◇ VERB V n V   N-COUNT   VERB V n V adv   N-COUNT   VERB V n WRITTEN   PHRASE   PHRASE SPOKEN   PHRASE   N-COUNT   N-COUNT   QUANT PRAGMATICS   PRON PHRASE   NUMBER   PHRASE PRAGMATICS

S

easily. *At least I've had no problems on that score.* **15** If someone **scores** drugs, they buy them illegally. *My mate went to score a kilo of amphetamine down in London.* **16** If you **score** a surface with something sharp, you cut or scratch a line in it.
VERB
V n
Also V
INFORMAL
VERB: V n

score·board /'skɔːbɔːd/ **scoreboards.** A **score-board** is a large board, for example at a sports ground, which shows how many goals, runs, or points have been scored in a match or competition.
N-COUNT

score·card /'skɔːkɑːd/ **scorecards. 1** A **score-card** is a printed card which tells you who is in a match or race, and on which you can record the scores of the players. **2** A **scorecard** is a system or procedure that is used for checking or testing something. *This commission would keep environmental scorecards on UN member nations.*
N-COUNT

N-COUNT:
with supp
AMERICAN

score·less /'skɔːləs/. In football, baseball, and some other sports, a **scoreless** game is one in which neither team has scored any goals, runs, or points.
ADJ
JOURNALISM

score·line /'skɔːlaɪn/ **scorelines.** The **scoreline** of a football, rugby, or tennis match is the score or the final result of it. *The scoreline was 2-nil.*
N-COUNT
BRITISH,
JOURNALISM

scor·er /'skɔːrə/ **scorers. 1** In football, cricket, and many other sports and games, a **scorer** is a player who scores a goal, runs, or points. **2** A **scorer** is an official who writes down the score of a match or competition as it is being played. **3** You can refer to someone as a **scorer** when you are talking about what mark they achieved in a test. *...the top 2 per cent of scorers in IQ tests.*
◆◇◇◇
N-COUNT

N-COUNT

N-COUNT

score·sheet /'skɔːʃiːt/; also spelled **score sheet**. In football, rugby, and some other sports, if a player **gets on the scoresheet**, he scores one or more goals, tries, or points.
PHRASE
JOURNALISM

scorn /skɔːn/ **scorns, scorning, scorned. 1** If you treat someone or something with **scorn**, you show contempt for them. **2** If you **scorn** someone or something, you feel or show contempt for them. *People scorn me as a single parent.* **3** If you **pour scorn on** someone or something or **heap scorn on** them, you say that you think they are stupid and worthless. **4** If you **scorn** something, you refuse to have it or accept it because you think it is not good enough or suitable for you. *...people who scorned traditional methods.*
◆◇◇◇
N-UNCOUNT

VERB: V n
V n asn
PHRASE

VERB
V n

scorn·ful /'skɔːnfəl/. If you are **scornful** of someone or something, you show contempt for them. **♦ scorn·ful·ly** *'I didn't think so,' the judge said scornfully.*
◆◇◇◇
ADJ-GRADED

ADV-GRADED

scor·pi·on /'skɔːpiən/ **scorpions.** A **scorpion** is a small creature which looks like a large insect. Scorpions have a long curved tail, and some of them are poisonous.
N-COUNT

scotch /skɒtʃ/ **scotches, scotching, scotched.** If you **scotch** a rumour, plan, or idea, you put an end to it before it can develop any further. *Mr Major is taking every opportunity to scotch any notion that he sympathises with the rebels.*
◆◇◇◇
VERB
V n

Scotch /skɒtʃ/ **Scotches. 1** Scotch or Scotch whisky is whisky made in Scotland. ▶ A **Scotch** is a glass of Scotch. **2** Scotch means the same as **Scottish**. This use is considered incorrect by many people.
◆◇◇◇
N-VAR
N-COUNT
ADJ

Scotch 'tape. Scotch tape is a clear sticky tape that is sold in rolls and that you use to stick paper or card together or onto a wall. The British word is **Sellotape**. Scotch tape and **Sellotape** are trademarks.
N-UNCOUNT
AMERICAN

scot-'free. If you say that someone got away **scot-free**, you are emphasizing that they escaped punishment for something that you believe they should have been punished for.
ADV:
ADV after v
PRAGMATICS

Scots /skɒts/. Scots is a dialect of the English language that is spoken in Scotland.
◆◆◇◇

scoun·drel /'skaʊndrəl/ **scoundrels.** If you refer to a man as a **scoundrel**, you mean that he behaves very badly towards other people.
N-COUNT
DATED

scour /skaʊə/ **scours, scouring, scoured. 1** If you **scour** something such as a place or book, you make a thorough search of it for someone or some-
◆◇◇◇
VERB: V n
V n forn

thing. *We scoured the telephone directory for clues.* **2** If you **scour** something such as a sink, floor, or pan, you clean its surface by rubbing it hard with something rough.
VERB: V n

scourge /skɜːdʒ/ **scourges, scourging, scourged. 1** A **scourge** is something that causes a lot of trouble or suffering to a group of people. *Drugs are a scourge that is devastating our society.* **2** If something **scourges** a place or group of people, it causes great pain and suffering to people. *Economic anarchy scourged the post-war world.*
◆◇◇◇
N-COUNT

VERB
V n

scout /skaʊt/ **scouts, scouting, scouted. 1** A **scout** is someone who is sent to an area of country-side to find out the position of an enemy army. **2** A **scout** is the same as a **talent scout**. **3** If you **scout** somewhere for something, you go through that area searching for it. *A team of four was sent to scout for a nuclear test site... I have people scouting the hills.*
◆◇◇◇
N-COUNT

N-COUNT
VERB:
V n forn
V forn
V n

Scout, Scouts. 1 The Scouts is an organization for children and young people which teaches them to become disciplined, practical, and self-sufficient. **2** A **Scout** is a member of the Scouts.
◆◇◇◇
N-COLL-
PROPER:
the N
N-COUNT

scout·master /'skaʊtmɑːstə, -mæs-/ **scout-masters.** A **scoutmaster** is a man who is in charge of a troop of Scouts.
N-COUNT

scowl /skaʊl/ **scowls, scowling, scowled.** When someone **scowls**, they frown to show that they are angry or displeased. *She scowled at the two men.* ▶ Also a noun. *Chris met the remark with a scowl.*
◆◇◇◇
VERB: V
V atn

N-COUNT

scrab·ble /'skræbəl/ **scrabbles, scrabbling, scrabbled. 1** If you **scrabble** for something, especially something that you cannot see, you move your hands or your feet about quickly and wildly in order to find it. *He grabbed his jacket and scrabbled in his desk drawer for some loose change... I hung there, scrabbling with my feet to find a foothold.* ▶ **Scrabble around** or **scrabble about** means the same as **scrabble**. *Alberg scrabbled around for pen and paper.* **2** If you say that someone **is scrabbling** to do something, you mean that they are having difficulty because they are in too much of a hurry, or because the task is almost impossible. *The banks are now desperately scrabbling to recover their costs.*
VERB
V forn
V to-inf

PHRASAL VB
V P forn

VERB
V to-inf

scrag·gy /'skrægi/ **scraggier, scraggiest.** If you describe a person or animal as **scraggy**, you mean that they look unattractive because they are so thin and bony.
ADJ-GRADED
PRAGMATICS
BRITISH

scram·ble /'skræmbəl/ **scrambles, scrambling, scrambled. 1** If you **scramble** over rocks or up a hill, you move quickly over them or up it using your hands to help you. **2** If you **scramble** to a different place or position, you move there in a hurried, un-dignified way. *Ann threw back the covers and scram-bled out of bed.* **3** If a number of people **scramble** for something, they compete with each other for it, in a rough and undignified way. *Business is booming and foreigners are scrambling to invest.* ▶ Also a noun. *...the scramble for jobs.* **4** If you **scramble** eggs, you mix the whites and yolks of the eggs, then cook the mixture by stirring and heating it in a pan. **♦ scram·bled** *...scrambled eggs and bacon.*
◆◆◇◇
VERB
V prep/adv

VERB
V prep/adv

VERB:
V forn
V to-inf

N-COUNT
VERB: V n

ADJ

scram·bler /'skræmblə/ **scramblers.** A **scrambler** is an electronic device which alters the sound of a radio or telephone message so that it can only be understood by someone who has special equipment.
N-COUNT

scrap /skræp/ **scraps, scrapping, scrapped. 1** A **scrap** of something is a very small piece or amount of it. *...a fire fueled by scraps of wood... They need every scrap of information they can get.* **2** Scraps are pieces of unwanted food which are thrown away or given to animals. **3** If you **scrap** something, you get rid of it or cancel it. *President Hussein called on all countries in the Middle East to scrap nuclear or chemical weapons.* **4** Scrap metal or paper is no longer wanted for its original purpose, but may have some other use. **5** Scrap is metal from old or damaged machinery or cars. *Thousands of tanks, artillery pieces and armored*
◆◆◇◇
N-COUNT

N-PLURAL

VERB
V n

ADJ: ADJ n

N-UNCOUNT

vehicles will be cut up for scrap. **6** You can refer to a [N-COUNT INFORMAL] fight or a quarrel as a **scrap**.

scrap·book /'skræpbʊk/ **scrapbooks.** A **scrap-** [N-COUNT] **book** is a book with blank pages. People stick things such as pictures or newspaper articles into scrapbooks in order to make a collection.

scrape /skreɪp/ **scrapes, scraping, scraped.** ◆◆◇◇◇ **1** If you **scrape** something from a surface, you re- [VERB: V n with adv] move it, especially by pulling a sharp object over the surface. *She went round the car scraping the frost off the windows.* **2** If something **scrapes** [V-ERG: V prep, V n prep, V n] against something else it rubs against it, making a noise or causing slight damage. *The cab driver struggled with her luggage, scraping a bag against the door as they came in... The car hurtled past us, scraping the wall and screeching to a halt.* ► Also a [N-SING] noun. *From the other side of the door came the scrape of a guard's boot.* ◆ **scrap·ing** *The house was* [N-SING: N of n] *silent but for the scraping of a branch on the slates.* **3** If you **scrape** a part of your body, you accidentally [VERB: V n] rub it against something hard and rough, and damage it slightly. **4** If you are in a **scrape**, you are in a [N-COUNT DATED] difficult situation. **5** ● to **scrape the barrel:** see **barrel.** ● to **scrape a living:** see **living.**

scrape by. If someone **scrapes by**, they earn just [PHRASAL VB V P] enough money to live on.

scrape through. If you **scrape through** an exami- [PHRASAL VB V P n, V P] nation, you just succeed in passing it. If you **scrape through** a competition or a vote, you just succeed in winning it. *As a student he always did the minimum amount of work necessary to scrape through.*

scrape together. If you **scrape together** an [PHRASAL VB V P noun, V n P] amount of money or a number of things, you succeed in obtaining it with difficulty. *They only just managed to scrape the money together.*

scrap·er /'skreɪpə/ **scrapers.** A **scraper** is a tool [N-COUNT] with a small handle and a metal or plastic blade which can be used for scraping a surface clean, for example, to scrape old paint off a wall.

scrap·heap /'skræphiːp/; also spelled **scrap heap.** [N-SING PRAGMATICS] **1** If you say that someone has been thrown on the **scrapheap**, you strongly disapprove of the way that their employers have dismissed them from their jobs without any concern for their future welfare. **2** If things such as machines or weapons are thrown [N-SING] on the **scrapheap**, they are thrown away because they are no longer needed.

scrap·ings /'skreɪpɪŋz/. **Scrapings** are small [N-PLURAL] amounts or pieces of something that have been scraped or scratched off a surface.

scrap·py /'skræpi/. If you describe something as [ADJ-GRADED PRAGMATICS] **scrappy**, you are critical of the fact that it seems to be badly planned or untidy.

scrap·yard /'skræpjɑːd/ **scrapyards;** also spelled [N-COUNT BRITISH] **scrap yard.** A **scrapyard** is a place where old machines such as cars or ships are destroyed and where useful parts are saved. The usual American word is **junkyard.**

scratch /skrætʃ/ **scratches, scratching,** ◆◆◇◇◇ **scratched. 1** If you **scratch** yourself, you rub your [VERB: V pron-refl, V n, VERB: V n] fingernails against your skin because it is itching. *The old man lifted his cardigan to scratch his side... I had to wear long sleeves to stop myself scratching.* **2** If a sharp object **scratches** someone or something, it makes small shallow cuts on their skin or surface. *Knives will scratch the worktop.* **3** **Scratches** [N-COUNT] on someone or something are small shallow cuts.

4 If you say that someone is **scratching** their **head**, [PHRASE] you mean that they are thinking hard and trying to solve a problem or puzzle. **5** If you only **scratch the** [PHRASE] **surface** of a subject or problem, you deal with it in a superficial way, without understanding or solving it fully. *We had only two weeks to tour Malaysia, which was hardly enough time to scratch the surface.* **6** If you [PHRASE] do something **from scratch**, you do it without making use of anything that has been done before. *...building a home from scratch.* **7** If you say that someone or [PHRASE] something is not **up to scratch**, you mean that they are not good enough.

scratchy /'skrætʃi/. **1 Scratchy** sounds are thin [ADJ-GRADED] and harsh. **2 Scratchy** clothes or fabrics are rough [ADJ-GRADED] and make you itch.

scrawl /skrɔːl/ **scrawls, scrawling, scrawled.** ◆◇◇◇◇ **1** If you **scrawl** something, you write it in a careless [VERB: V n prep, V with quote] and untidy way. *He scrawled a hasty note to his wife... Someone had scrawled 'Scum' on his car.* **2** You can refer to writing that looks careless and [Also V n, N-VAR] untidy as **scrawl.**

scrawny /'skrɔːni/ **scrawnier, scrawniest.** If [ADJ-GRADED PRAGMATICS] you describe a person or animal as **scrawny**, you mean that they look unattractive because they are so thin and bony.

scream /skriːm/ **screams, screaming,** ◆◆◆◇◇ **screamed. 1** When someone **screams**, they make [VERB: V inn, V-ing] a very loud, high-pitched cry, for example because they are in pain or are very frightened. *He staggered around the playground, screaming in agony... To play in front of 40,000 screaming fans was a great experience.* ► Also a noun. *...screams of terror.* **2** If [N-COUNT] you **scream** something, you shout it in a loud, [V with quote, V atn to-inf] high-pitched voice. *'Brigid!' she screamed. 'Get up!'... I was screaming at them to get out of my house.* [V: V, V prep/adv] **3** When something makes a loud, high-pitched noise, you can say that it **screams**. *An airforce jet screamed over the town.* ► Also a noun. *There was a* [N-COUNT] *scream of brakes from the carriageway outside.*

scree /skriː/ **screes.** **Scree** is a mass of loose [N-VAR] stones on the side of a mountain.

screech /skriːtʃ/ **screeches, screeching,** ◆◇◇◇◇ **screeched. 1** If a vehicle **screeches** somewhere or [VERB: V, V prep/adv] if its tyres **screech**, its tyres make an unpleasant high-pitched noise on the road. *A black Mercedes screeched to a halt beside the helicopter.* **2** When you [VERB: V with quote, V n] **screech** something, you shout it in a loud, unpleasant, high-pitched voice. *'Get me some water, Jeremy!' I screeched.* ► Also a noun. *The figure gave a screech.* [Also V, N-COUNT] **3** When a bird, animal, or thing **screeches**, it makes [VERB: V atn] a loud, unpleasant, high-pitched noise. *A macaw screeched at him from its perch.* ► Also a noun. *He* [N-COUNT] *heard the screech of brakes.*

screen /skriːn/ **screens, screening, screened.** ◆◆◆◆◇ **1** A **screen** is a flat vertical surface on which pic- [N-COUNT] tures or words are shown. Television sets and computer terminals have screens, and films are shown on a screen in cinemas. ● See also **big screen, small screen. 2** You can refer to film or television as [N-SING: the N, also on/offN] **screen.** *Many viewers have strong opinions about violence on the screen.* **3** When a film or a television [VERB: be V-ed] programme **is screened**, it is shown in the cinema or broadcast on television. *TV firms were later banned from screening any pictures of the demo.* ◆ **screen·ing, screenings** *The film-makers will* [N-COUNT] *be present at the screenings to introduce their works.*

4 A **screen** is a vertical panel which can be moved [N-COUNT] around. It is used to keep cold air away from part of a room, or to create a smaller area within a room. **5** If [VB: usu passive, be V-ed by n] something **is screened** by another thing, it is behind it and hidden by it. *Most of the road behind the hotel was screened by a block of flats.*

6 To **screen** for a disease means to examine people to [VERB: V for n, Also V n] make sure that they do not have it. *...a quick saliva test that would screen for people at risk of tooth decay.* ◆ **screen·ing** *Britain has an enviable record on* [N-VAR] *breast screening for cancer.* **7** When an organization [VERB: V n, V-ing] **screens** people, it investigates them to make sure that they are not likely to be dangerous or disloyal. *...screening procedures for the regiment.* **8** To **screen** [VERB: V n] people or luggage means to check them using special equipment to make sure they are not carrying a weapon or a bomb.

screen out. If an organization or country **screens** [PHRASAL VB V P noun] **out** certain people, it keeps them out because it thinks they may cause problems. *The company screened out applicants motivated only by money.*

screen·play /'skriːnpleɪ/ **screenplays.** A **screen-** ◆◇◇◇◇ **play** is a script for a film including instructions for [N-COUNT] the cameras.

S

'screen test, screen tests. When a film studio N-COUNT
gives an actor a **screen test**, they film a short scene
in order to test how good he or she would be.

screen·writer /'skriːraɪtə/ **screenwriters.** ◆◇◇◇◇
A **screenwriter** is a person who writes screenplays.

screen·writing /'skriːraɪtɪŋ/. **Screenwriting** is the N-UNCOUNT
process of writing screenplays.

screw /skruː/ **screws, screwing, screwed. 1** A ◆◆◇◇◇
screw is a metal object similar to a nail, with a spi- N-COUNT
ral ridge around it, which is used to fix one thing to
another. See picture headed **tools**. *Each bracket is
fixed to the wall with just three screws.* **2** If you V-ERG
screw something somewhere or if it **screws** some- Vn prep
where, you fix it in place by means of a screw or Also V prep/
screws. *I had screwed the shelf on the wall myself...* adv
Screw down any loose floorboards. **3** A **screw** lid or ADJ: ADJ n
fitting is one that has a spiral ridge on the inside or
outside of it, so that it can be fixed in place by twisting. **4** If you **screw** something somewhere or if it V-ERG
screws somewhere, you fix it in place by twisting it Vn prep
round and round. *'Yes, I know that,' Kelly said,* Vn with adv
screwing the silencer onto the pistol... Screw down Also V prep/
the lid fairly tightly. adv

5 If you **screw** something such as a piece of paper **into** VERB:
a ball, you squeeze it or twist it tightly so that it is in Vn into n
the shape of a ball. ► **Screw up** means the same as PHRASAL VB
screw. *He would start writing to his family and would* Vn P
screw the letter up in frustration. **6** If you **screw** your VERB
face or your eyes **into** a particular expression, you Vn into n
tighten the muscles of your face to form that expression. *He screwed his face into an expression of mock
pain.* ► **Screw up** means the same as **screw**. *She had* PHRASAL VB
screwed up her eyes, as if she found the sunshine too V P noun
bright. Also V n P

7 If someone **screws** someone else or if two people V-RECIP
screw, they have sex together; an offensive use. RUDE

8 Some people use **screw** in expressions such as VB: only imper
screw you or **screw that** to show that they are not PRAGMATICS
concerned about someone or something or that they RUDE
feel contempt for them; an offensive use.

9 If someone says that they **have been screwed**, they VERB:
mean that someone else has cheated them, especially be/getV-ed
by getting money from them dishonestly; some peo- INFORMAL
ple find this use offensive. **10** If someone **screws** VERB
something, especially money, **out of** you, they get it Vn out of n
from you by putting strong pressure on you. *...rich na-* BRITISH,
tions screwing money out of poor nations. **11** If you INFORMAL
turn or **tighten the screw** on someone, you increase PHRASE
the pressure which is already on them in order to
force them to do a particular thing. *...a blockade to
turn the screw on the government.* **12** You can refer to PHRASE
each of a series of threats or actions which are intended to force someone to do a particular thing as another **turn of the screw**.

13 Prisoners sometimes refer to prison officers as N-COUNT
screws. INFORMAL

screw up. 1 See **screw** sense 5, 6. **2** If someone PHRASAL VB
screws something **up**, or if they **screw up**, they cause V P
something to fail or be spoiled. *You can't open the* V P noun
window because it screws up the air conditioning. INFORMAL

screw·ball /'skruːbɔːl/. **Screwball** comedy is silly ADJ: ADJ n
and eccentric in an amusing and harmless way.

screw·driver /'skruːdraɪvə/ **screwdrivers.** A N-COUNT
screwdriver is a tool that is used for turning screws.
See picture headed **tools**.

,screwed 'up. If you say that someone is **screwed** ◆◇◇◇◇
up, you mean that they are very confused or wor- ADJ-GRADED
ried, or that they have psychological problems. INFORMAL

'screw-top. A **screw-top** bottle or jar has a lid that ADJ: ADJ n
is secured by being twisted on.

scrib·ble /'skrɪbəl/ **scribbles, scribbling,** ◆◇◇◇◇
scribbled. 1 If you **scribble** something, you write VERB: Vn
it quickly and roughly. *As I scribbled in my diary the* V prep/adv
light went out. ► **Scribble down** means the same as PHRASAL VB
scribble *I attempted to scribble down the names.* V P noun
2 To **scribble** means to make meaningless marks or VERB
rough drawings using a pencil or pen. *When Caro-* V prep/adv
line was five she scribbled on a wall. **3 Scribble** is N-VAR
something that has been written or drawn quickly
and roughly.

scrib·bler /'skrɪbələ/ **scribblers.** People some- N-COUNT
times refer to writers as **scribblers** when they think PRAGMATICS
they are not very good writers.

scribe /skraɪb/ **scribes.** In the days before printing N-COUNT
was common, a **scribe** was a person who wrote
copies of things such as letters or documents.

scrimp /skrɪmp/ **scrimps, scrimping,** VERB
scrimped. If you **scrimp** on things, you live V on n
cheaply and spend as little money as possible. *...a* Also V
*debt-ridden airline that may be tempted to scrimp
on maintenance.*

script /skrɪpt/ **scripts, scripting, scripted.** ◆◆◆◇◇
1 The **script** of a play, film, or television pro- N-COUNT
gramme is the written version of it. **2** The person VERB: Vn
who **scripts** a film or a radio or television play
writes it. **3** You can refer to a particular system of N-VAR
writing as a particular **script**. *...written in Arabic
script.*

script·ed /'skrɪptɪd/. A **scripted** speech has been ADJ
written in advance.

scrip·tur·al /'skrɪptʃərəl/. **Scriptural** is used to de- ADJ: ADJ n
scribe things that are written in or based on the
Christian Bible. *...scriptural accounts of the process
of salvation.*

scrip·ture /'skrɪptʃə/ **scriptures. Scripture** or the ◆◇◇◇◇
scriptures refers to writings that are regarded as sa- N-VAR
cred in a particular religion, for example the Bible
in Christianity.

script·writer /'skrɪptraɪtə/ **scriptwriters.** N-COUNT
A **scriptwriter** is a person who writes scripts for
films or for radio or television programmes.

scroll /skrəʊl/ **scrolls, scrolling, scrolled. 1** A ◆◇◇◇◇
scroll is a long roll of paper, parchment, or other N-COUNT
material with writing on it. *Ancient scrolls were
found in caves by the Dead Sea.* **2** If you **scroll** VERB
through text on a computer screen, you move V prep/adv
the text up or down to find the information that you
need. *I scrolled down to find 'United States of
America'.*

Scrooge /skruːdʒ/ **Scrooges.** If you call someone N-VAR
a **Scrooge**, you disapprove of them because they are PRAGMATICS
very mean and hate spending money.

scro·tum /'skrəʊtəm/ **scrotums.** A man's **scrotum** N-COUNT
is the bag of skin that contains his testicles.

scrounge /skraʊndʒ/ **scrounges, scrounging,** VERB
scrounged. If you say that someone **scrounges** PRAGMATICS
something such as food or money, you mean they V n
get it by asking someone for it, rather than by Also V for n
buying it or earning it, and you think this is wrong. INFORMAL
*...tales of Williams having to scrounge enough
money to get his car out of the long-term car park.*
♦ **scroung·er, scroungers** *They are just* N-COUNT
scroungers.

scrub /skrʌb/ **scrubs, scrubbing, scrubbed.** ◆◆◇◇◇
1 If you **scrub** something, you rub it hard in order VERB: Vn
to clean it, using a stiff brush and water. *The corri-* be V-ed adj
dors are scrubbed clean. ► Also a noun. *That floor* N-SING:
needs a jolly good scrub. **2** If you **scrub** dirt or stains aN
off something, you remove them by rubbing hard. *I* VERB
started to scrub off the dirt... Matthew scrubbed the Vn with off/
coal dust from his face. **3 Scrub** consists of low trees away
and bushes, especially in an area that has very little N-UNCOUNT
rain.

scrub·by /'skrʌbi/. **Scrubby** land is rough and dry ADJ
and covered with scrub.

scrub·land /'skrʌblænd/ **scrublands. Scrubland** N-VAR
is an area of land which is covered with low trees
and bushes.

scruff /skrʌf/. If someone grabs you **by the scruff** PHRASE
of the neck, they take hold of the back of your neck
or collar suddenly and roughly.

scruffy /'skrʌfi/ **scruffier, scruffiest.** Someone ◆◇◇◇◇
or something that is **scruffy** is dirty and untidy. *...a* ADJ-GRADED
scruffy basement flat in London.

scrum /skrʌm/ **scrums. 1** In rugby, a **scrum** is a ◆◇◇◇◇
formation in which players from each side form a N-COUNT
tight group and push against each other with their
heads down in an attempt to get the ball. **2** A **scrum** N-COUNT
is a confused, disorderly group of people. *She
pushed through the scrum of photographers.*

scrum·mage /'skrʌmɪdʒ/ **scrummages.** In rugby, a **scrummage** is the same as a **scrum.** `N-COUNT`

scrump·tious /'skrʌmpʃəs/. If you describe food as **scrumptious,** you mean that it tastes extremely good. ...*a scrumptious apple pie.* `ADJ-GRADED` `INFORMAL`

scrunch /skrʌntʃ/ **scrunches, scrunching, scrunched. 1** If something **scrunches,** it makes a loud sound as it is pressed or crushed or as it presses or crushes something else. *The sand on the floor scrunched under our feet.* **2** If you **scrunch** something, you squeeze it or bend it so that it is no longer in its natural shape. ...*sitting bolt upright, scrunching her white cotton gloves into a ball.* ▸ **Scrunch up** means the same as **scrunch.** *She scrunched up two pages of notes.* `VERB: V` `V prep` `VERB: V n` `V n into n` `PHRASAL VB` `V P means n`

scru·ple /'skru:pəl/ **scruples.** Scruples are moral principles or beliefs that make you reluctant to do something that seems wrong. ...*a man with no moral scruples.* `N-VAR`

scru·pu·lous /'skru:pjʊləs/. **1** Someone who is **scrupulous** takes great care to do what is fair, honest, or morally right. *I have been scrupulous about telling them the dangers.* ♦ **scru·pu·lous·ly** *He is scrupulously fair.* **2 Scrupulous** means thorough, exact, and careful about details. ...*his scrupulous attention to detail.* ♦ **scrupulously** *The streets and parks were scrupulously clean.* `◆◇◇◇◇` `ADJ-GRADED` `ADV-GRADED` `ADJ-GRADED` `ADV-GRADED`

scru·ti·nize /'skru:tɪnaɪz/ **scrutinizes, scrutinizing, scrutinized;** also spelled **scrutinise** in British English. If you **scrutinize** something, you examine it very carefully, often to find out some information from it or about it. *Her purpose was to scrutinize his features to see if he was an honest man.* `◆◇◇◇◇` `VERB` `V n`

scru·ti·ny /'skru:tɪni/. If a person or thing is under **scrutiny,** they are being studied or observed very carefully. *His private life came under media scrutiny.* `◆◆◇◇◇` `N-UNCOUNT`

scuba diving /'sku:bə daɪvɪŋ/. **Scuba diving** is the activity of swimming under water using a special type of breathing equipment. `N-UNCOUNT`

scud /skʌd/ **scuds, scudding, scudded.** If clouds **scud** along, they move quickly and smoothly through the sky. ...*clouds scudding across the south-west.* `VERB` `V adv/prep` `LITERARY`

scuff /skʌf/ **scuffs, scuffing, scuffed. 1** If you **scuff** something or if it **scuffs,** you mark the surface by scraping it against other things or by scraping other things against it. *Constant wheelchair use will scuff almost any floor surface.* ♦ **scuffed** ...*scuffed brown shoes.* **2** If you **scuff** your feet, you drag them along the ground as you walk. `V-ERG` `V n` `Also V adv` `ADJ-GRADED` `VERB: V n`

scuf·fle /'skʌfəl/ **scuffles, scuffling, scuffled.** If people **scuffle,** they fight for a short time in a disorganized way. *Police scuffled with some of the protesters.* ▸ Also a noun. *Violent scuffles broke out between rival groups.* `◆◇◇◇◇` `V-RECIP` `V with n` `Also pl-n V` `N-COUNT`

scuf·fling /'skʌfəlɪŋ/. A **scuffling** noise is a noise made by someone or something moving about, usually someone or something that you cannot see. `ADJ: ADJ n`

'scuff mark, scuff marks. Scuff marks are marks made on a smooth surface when something is rubbed against it. `N-COUNT`

scull /skʌl/ **sculls, sculling, sculled. 1** Sculls are small oars which are held by one person and used to move a boat through water. **2** A **scull** is a small light racing boat which is rowed with two sculls. **3** To **scull** a boat means to row it using sculls. `N-COUNT` `N-COUNT` `VERB: V n`

scul·lery /'skʌləri/ **sculleries.** A **scullery** is a small room next to a kitchen where washing and other domestic work is done. `N-COUNT` `BRITISH,` `DATED`

sculpt /skʌlpt/ **sculpts, sculpting, sculpted. 1** When an artist **sculpts** something, they carve or shape it out of a hard material such as stone or clay. **2** If something **is sculpted,** it is made into a particular shape. *Michael smoothed and sculpted Jane's hair into shape.* `◆◇◇◇◇` `VERB: V n` `VERB:` `be V-ed` `V n into n`

sculp·tor /'skʌlptə/ **sculptors.** A **sculptor** is someone who creates sculptures. `◆◇◇◇◇` `N-COUNT`

sculp·tur·al /'skʌlptʃərəl/. **Sculptural** means relating to sculpture. ...*working with clay as a sculptural form.* `ADJ`

sculp·ture /'skʌlptʃə/ **sculptures. 1** A **sculpture** is a work of art that is produced by carving or shaping stone, wood, clay, or other materials. **2 Sculpture** is the art of creating sculptures. `◆◆◇◇◇` `N-VAR` `N-UNCOUNT`

sculp·tured /'skʌlptʃəd/. **Sculptured** objects have been carved or shaped from something. ...*a beautifully sculptured bronze horse.* `ADJ`

scum /skʌm/. **1** If you refer to people as **scum,** you are expressing your feelings of dislike and disgust for them; an offensive use. **2 Scum** is a layer of a dirty or unpleasant-looking substance on the surface of a liquid. ...*scum marks around the bath.* `◆◇◇◇◇` `N-PLURAL` `PRAGMATICS` `N-UNCOUNT`

scup·per /'skʌpə/ **scuppers, scuppering, scuppered.** To **scupper** a plan or attempt means to spoil it completely. *Any increase in the female retirement age would scupper the plans of women like Gwen Davis.* `◆◇◇◇◇` `VERB` `V n` `BRITISH,` `JOURNALISM`

scur·ril·ous /'skʌrɪləs, AM 'skɜːrɪ-/. **Scurrilous** accusations or stories are untrue and unfair, and are likely to damage the reputation of the person that they relate to. ...*scurrilous rumours.* `ADJ-GRADED`

scur·ry /'skʌri, AM 'skɜːri/ **scurries, scurrying, scurried. 1** When people or small animals **scurry** somewhere, they move quickly and hurriedly, especially because they are frightened. *The attack began, sending residents scurrying for cover.* **2** If people **scurry** to do something, they do it as soon as they can. *Pictures of starving children have sent many people scurrying to donate money.* `◆◇◇◇◇` `VERB` `V prep/adv` `WRITTEN` `VERB` `V to-inf` `WRITTEN`

scur·vy /'skɜːvi/. **Scurvy** is a disease that is caused by a lack of vitamin C. `N-UNCOUNT`

scut·tle /'skʌtəl/ **scuttles, scuttling, scuttled. 1** When people or small animals **scuttle** somewhere, they run there with short quick steps. *Two very small children scuttled away in front of them.* **2** To **scuttle** a plan or a proposal means to make it fail or cause it to stop. *Such threats could scuttle the peace conference.* **3** To **scuttle** a ship means to sink it deliberately. **4** A **scuttle** is a kind of bucket for keeping coal in. ...*an antique brass scuttle.* `◆◇◇◇◇` `VERB` `V adv/prep` `VERB` `V n` `VERB: V n` `N-COUNT` `BRITISH`

scythe /saɪð/ **scythes, scything, scythed. 1** A **scythe** is a tool with a long curved blade at right angles to a long handle. It is used to cut long grass or grain. **2** If you **scythe** grass or grain, you cut it with a scythe. `N-COUNT` `VERB: V n`

SE. SE is a written abbreviation for **south-east.**

sea /siː/ **seas. 1** The **sea** is the salty water that covers about three-quarters of the earth's surface. *Most of the kids have never seen the sea.* **2** You use **seas** when you are describing the sea at a particular time or in a particular area. *The seas are warm further south.* **3** A **sea** is a large area of salty water that is part of an ocean or is surrounded by land. ...*the North Sea.* **4 At sea** means on or under the sea, far away from land. *The boats remain at sea for an average of ten days.* **5** If you go or look out **to sea,** you go or look across the sea. **6** A **sea of** people or things is a very large number of them together. ...*the sea of bottles and glasses on the table.* `◆◆◆◇` `N-SING:` `the N,` `also by N` `N-PLURAL` `LITERARY` `N-COUNT` `PHRASE` `PHRASE` `N-SING:` `N of n`

sea·bed /'siːbed/; also spelled **sea bed.** The **seabed** is the ground under the sea. `N-SING`

sea·bird /'siːbɜːd/ **seabirds;** also spelled **sea-bird.** Seabirds are birds that live near the sea and get their food from it. `N-COUNT`

sea·board /'siːbɔːd/ **seaboards.** The **seaboard** is the part of a country that is next to the sea; used especially of the coasts of North America. ...*the Eastern seaboard of the USA.* `N-COUNT`

sea·borne /'siːbɔːn/; also spelled **sea-borne.** Seaborne actions or events take place on the sea in ships. ...*seaborne trade.* `ADJ: ADJ n`

,sea 'breeze, sea breezes. A **sea breeze** is a light wind blowing from the sea towards the land. `N-COUNT`

'sea captain, sea captains. A **sea captain** is a person in command of a ship, usually a ship that carries goods for trade. `N-COUNT`

S

'**sea change, sea changes;** also spelled **sea-change.** A **sea change** in someone's attitudes or behaviour is a complete change. *A sea change has taken place in young people's attitudes.* — N-COUNT

'**sea dog, sea dogs;** also spelled **seadog.** A **sea dog** is a sailor is who has spent many years at sea. — N-COUNT DATED

sea·far·er /ˈsiːfeərə/ **seafarers.** Seafarers are people who work on ships or people who travel regularly on the sea. — N-COUNT WRITTEN

sea·far·ing /ˈsiːfeərɪŋ/. Seafaring means working as a sailor or travelling regularly on the sea. *The Lebanese were a seafaring people.* — ADJ: ADJ n

sea·floor /ˈsiːflɔː/. The **seafloor** is the ground under the sea. — N-SING

sea·food /ˈsiːfuːd/ **seafoods.** Seafood is shellfish such as lobsters, mussels, and crabs. — ◆◇◇◇◇ N-UNCOUNT: also N in pl

sea·front /ˈsiːfrʌnt/ **seafronts.** The **seafront** is the part of a seaside town that is next to the sea. It usually consists of a road with buildings facing the sea. — N-COUNT BRITISH

sea·go·ing /ˈsiːɡəʊɪŋ/; also spelled **sea-going.** Seagoing boats and ships are designed for travelling on the sea. — ADJ: ADJ n

,**sea-'green;** also spelled **sea green.** Something that is **sea-green** is a bluish-green colour. — COLOUR

sea·gull /ˈsiːɡʌl/ **seagulls.** A seagull is a common kind of seabird with white or grey feathers. — ◆◇◇◇◇ N-COUNT

sea·horse /ˈsiːhɔːs/ **seahorses;** also spelled **sea horse.** A seahorse is a type of small fish which appears to swim in a vertical position and whose head looks a little like the head of a horse. — N-COUNT

seal 1 *closing*

seal /siːl/ **seals, sealing, sealed. 1** When you **seal** an envelope, you close it by sticking down the flap, so that it cannot be opened without being torn. If you **seal** something **in** an envelope, you put it inside and then seal the envelope. *Write your letter and seal it in a blank envelope.* **2** If you **seal** a container or an opening, you cover it with something in order to prevent air, liquid, or other material getting in or out. If you **seal** something **in** a container, you put it inside and then seal the container. *...a lid to seal in heat and keep food moist.* **3** The **seal** on a container or opening is the part where it has been sealed. *Wet the edges where the two crusts join, to form a seal.* **4** A **seal** is a device or a piece of material, for example in a machine or a system of pipes, which closes an opening tightly so that air, liquid or other substances cannot get in or out. *Check seals on fridges and freezers regularly.* **5** A **seal** is something such as a piece of sticky paper or wax that is fixed to a container or door and must be broken before the container or door can be opened. *The seal on the box broke when it fell from its hiding-place.* **6** A **seal** is a special mark or design, for example on a document, representing someone or something. It may be used to show that something is genuine or officially approved. *...the Presidential seal.* **7** If someone in authority **seals** an area, they stop people entering or passing through it, for example by placing barriers in the way. *The soldiers were deployed to help paramilitary police seal the border.* ▶ **Seal off** means the same as **seal.** *Police and troops sealed off the area after the attack.* **8** If something or someone **seals** something, they make it definite or confirm how it is going to be. *British Aerospace is close to sealing a deal with Taiwan Aerospace.* **9** If something **sets** or **puts the seal on** something, it makes it definite or confirms how it is going to be. *Such a visit may set the seal on a new relationship between the two governments.* **10** • **seal of approval:** see **approval.** • **to seal someone's fate:** see **fate.** • **my lips are sealed:** see **lip.** • **signed and sealed:** see **sign.** — ◆◆◇◇ VERB: V n V n in n / VERB: V n V n with in / N-COUNT / N-COUNT / N-COUNT / N-COUNT / VERB V n / PHRASAL VB V P noun / VERB V n WRITTEN / PHRASE WRITTEN

seal in. If something **seals in** a smell or liquid, it prevents it from getting out of a food. *The coffee is freeze-dried to seal in all the flavour.* — PHRASAL VB V P noun Also V n P

seal off. 1 If one object or area **is sealed off** from another, there is a physical barrier between them, so — PHRASAL VB be V-ed P V P noun

nothing can pass between them. *...the anti-personnel door that sealed off the chamber.* **2** See **seal** 7. — Also V n P

seal up. If you **seal** something **up,** you close it completely so that nothing can get in or out. *The paper was used for sealing up holes in walls and roofs.* — PHRASAL VB V P noun Also V n P

seal 2 *animal*

seal /siːl/ **seals.** A **seal** is a large animal with flippers, which eats fish and lives partly on land and partly in the sea. — ◆◇◇◇◇ N-COUNT

'**sea lane, sea lanes.** Sea lanes are particular routes which ships regularly use in order to cross a sea or ocean. — N-COUNT

seal·ant /ˈsiːlənt/ **sealants.** A **sealant** is a substance that is used to seal holes, cracks, or gaps. — N-VAR

seal·er /ˈsiːlə/ **sealers.** A **sealer** is the same as a **sealant.** — N-VAR

'**sea level;** also spelled **sea-level.** Sea level is the average level of the sea with respect to the land. *The stadium was 2275 metres above sea level.* — ◆◇◇◇◇ N-UNCOUNT

'**sealing wax.** Sealing wax is a hard, usually red, substance that melts quickly and is used for putting seals on documents or letters. — N-UNCOUNT

'**sea lion, sea lions.** A **sea lion** is a type of large seal. — N-COUNT

seal·skin /ˈsiːlskɪn/. Sealskin is the fur of a seal, used to make coats and other clothing. — N-UNCOUNT

seam /siːm/ **seams. 1** A **seam** is a line of stitches which joins two pieces of cloth together. **2** A **seam** of coal is a long, narrow layer of it beneath the ground. **3** If something **is coming apart at the seams** or **is falling apart at the seams,** it is no longer working properly and may soon stop working completely. *Britain's university system is in danger of falling apart at the seams.* **4** If a place is very full, you can say that it is **bursting at the seams.** — ◆◇◇◇◇ N-COUNT N-COUNT PHRASE PHRASE

sea·man /ˈsiːmən/ **seamen.** A **seaman** is a sailor, especially one who is not an officer. — ◆◇◇◇◇ N-COUNT

sea·man·ship /ˈsiːmənʃɪp/. Seamanship is skill in managing a boat and controlling its movement through the sea. — N-UNCOUNT

seam·less /ˈsiːmləs/. You use **seamless** to describe something that has no breaks or gaps in it or which continues without stopping. *...the seamless blue sky.* — ◆◇◇◇◇ ADJ

♦ **seam·less·ly** *...allowing new and old to blend seamlessly.* — ADV-GRADED ADV with v

seam·stress /ˈsiːmstrəs, ˈsem-/ **seamstresses.** A **seamstress** is a woman who sews and makes clothes as her job. — N-COUNT

seamy /ˈsiːmi/ **seamier, seamiest.** If you describe something as **seamy,** you mean that it involves unpleasant aspects of life such as crime, sex, or violence. *...the seamier side of life.* — ADJ-GRADED

se·ance /ˈseɪɒns/ **seances.** A **seance** is a meeting in which people try to make contact with people who have died. — N-COUNT

sea·plane /ˈsiːpleɪn/ **seaplanes.** A **seaplane** is a type of aeroplane that can take off from or land on water. — N-COUNT

sea·port /ˈsiːpɔːt/ **seaports.** A **seaport** is a town with a large harbour that is used by ships. — N-COUNT

'**sea power, sea powers. 1** Sea power is the size and strength of a country's navy. *The transformation of American sea power began in 1940.* **2** A **sea power** is a country that has a large navy. — N-UNCOUNT N-COUNT

sear /sɪə/ **sears, searing, seared. 1** To **sear** something means to burn its surface with a sudden intense heat. *Grass fires have seared the land near the farming village of Basekhai.* **2** If something **sears** a part of your body, it causes a painful burning feeling there. *I distinctly felt the heat start to sear my throat.* **3** See also **searing.** — VERB V n / VERB V n LITERARY

search /sɜːtʃ/ **searches, searching, searched. 1** If you **search** for something or someone, you look carefully for them. *The Turkish security forces have started searching for the missing men.* **2** If you **search** a place, you look carefully for something or someone there. *She searched her desk for the necessary information.* **3** A **search** is an attempt to find something or someone by looking for them carefully. *The search was abandoned.* **4** If a — ◆◆◆◆ VERB V n Also V / VERB: V n V n for n Also V prep / N-COUNT / VERB: V n

police officer or someone else in authority **searches** you, they look and feel carefully to see whether you have something hidden on you. **5** See also **searching**, **strip-search**. **6** If you go **in search of** something or someone, you try to find them. ...*people in search of better economic opportunities.* **7** You say **'search me'** when someone asks you a question and you want to emphasize that you do not know the answer. *'So why did he get interested all of a sudden?'—'Search me.'* · PHRASE · CONVENTION · PRAGMATICS · INFORMAL

search out. If you **search** something **out**, you keep looking for it until you find it. *Many people want jobs. They try to search them out every day.* · PHRASAL VB · V n P · Also V P noun

search·er /ˈsɜːtʃə/ **searchers. 1 Searchers** are people who are looking for someone or something that is missing. *Searchers have found three mountain climbers missing since Saturday.* **2** A **searcher** is someone who is trying to find something such as the truth or the answer to a problem. · N-COUNT · N-COUNT

search·ing /ˈsɜːtʃɪŋ/. A **searching** question or look is intended to discover the truth about something. *They asked her some searching questions on moral philosophy.* · See also **soul-searching**. · ADJ-GRADED

search·light /ˈsɜːtʃlaɪt/ **searchlights.** A **searchlight** is a large powerful light that can be turned to shine a long way in any direction. · N-COUNT

'search party, search parties. A **search party** is an organized group of people who are searching for someone who is missing. · N-COUNT

'search warrant, search warrants. A **search warrant** is a special document that gives the police permission to search a house or other building. · N-COUNT

sear·ing /ˈsɪərɪŋ/. **1 Searing** is used to indicate that something such as pain or heat is very intense. *...the searing heat of the Saudi Arabian desert.* **2** A **searing** speech or piece of writing is very critical. *...searing criticism.* · ADJ: ADJ n · ADJ-GRADED: ADJ n

sea·scape /ˈsiːskeɪp/ **seascapes.** A **seascape** is a painting or photograph of a scene at sea. · N-COUNT

sea·shell /ˈsiːʃel/ **seashells;** also spelled **sea shell**. **Seashells** are the empty shells of small sea creatures. · N-COUNT

sea·shore /ˈsiːʃɔː/ **seashores.** The **seashore** is the part of a coast where the land slopes down into the sea. · N-COUNT

sea·sick /ˈsiːsɪk/. If someone is **seasick** when they are travelling in a boat, they vomit or feel sick because of the way the boat is moving. ◆ **sea·sick·ness** *He was very prone to seasickness.* · ADJ-GRADED · N-UNCOUNT

sea·side /ˈsiːsaɪd/. You can refer to an area that is close to the sea, especially one where people go for their holidays, as the **seaside**. · N-SING: the N · BRITISH

sea·son /ˈsiːzən/ **seasons, seasoning, seasoned. 1** The **seasons** are the main periods into which a year can be divided and which each have their own typical weather conditions. *Autumn's my favourite season. ...the rainy season.* **2** You can use **season** to refer to a particular period during each year when something usually happens. *...birds arriving for the breeding season. ...the baseball season.* **3** You can use **season** to refer to the period when a particular fruit, vegetable, or other food is ready for eating and is widely available. *Now British asparagus is in season.* **4** A **season** is a period in which a play or show, or a series of plays or shows, is performed in one place. *...a season of three new plays.* **5** A **season** of films is several of them shown as a series because they are connected in some way. *...a brief season of films in which Artaud appeared.* **6** If you **season** food with salt, pepper, or spices, you add them to it in order to improve its flavour. *Season the meat with salt and pepper.* · See also **seasoning**. **7** If wood **is seasoned**, it is made suitable for making into furniture or for burning, usually by being allowed to dry out gradually. **8** If a female animal is **in season**, she is in a state where she is ready for mating. **9** See also **seasoned**, **seasoning**. · N-COUNT · N-COUNT · N-COUNT: n N, also in/out of N · N-COUNT: with supp · N-COUNT · VERB V n with n · VERB: be V-ed · PHRASE

sea·son·al /ˈsiːzənəl/. A **seasonal** factor, event, or change occurs during one particular time of the year. *The EC's jobless rate is adjusted for seasonal factors.* ◆ **sea·son·al·ly** *...the seasonally adjusted unemployment figures.* · ADJ: ADJ n · ADV

sea·soned /ˈsiːzənd/. You can use the word **seasoned** to describe someone who has a lot of experience of something. *...the confidence of a seasoned performer.* · ADJ-GRADED

sea·son·ing /ˈsiːzənɪŋ/ **seasonings. Seasoning** is salt, pepper, or other spices that are added to food to improve its flavour. · N-VAR

'season ticket, season tickets. A **season ticket** is a ticket that you can use repeatedly during a certain period, without having to pay each time. · N-COUNT

seat /siːt/ **seats, seating, seated. 1** A **seat** is an object that you can sit on, for example a chair. *Ann could remember sitting in the back seat of their car.* **2** If you **take a seat**, you sit down. *'Take a seat,'* he said in a bored tone. **3** If you **seat** yourself somewhere, you sit down. *...a portrait of one of his favourite models seated on an elegant sofa.* **4** If you **take a back seat**, you allow other people to have all the power and to make all the decisions. **5** A building or vehicle that **seats** a particular number of people has enough seats for that number. *The Theatre seats 570.* **6** The **seat** of a chair is the part that you sit on. **7** The **seat** of a piece of clothing is the part that covers your bottom. **8** When someone is elected to parliament, you can say that they, or their party, have won a **seat**. **9** If someone has a **seat** on the board of a company or on a committee, they are a member of it. **10** The **seat** of an organization, a wealthy family, or an activity is its base. *Gunfire broke out early this morning around the seat of government in Lagos.* **11** See also **deep-seated**, **hot seat**. **12** · **bums on seats**: see **bum**. · **in the driving seat**: see **driver's seat**. · **by the seat of** your **pants**: see **pants**. · N-COUNT · PHRASE FORMAL · VERB: V pron-refl · V-ed prep/adv PHRASE · VERB V amount · N-COUNT · N-SING · N-COUNT · N-COUNT · N-COUNT: with supp

'seat belt, seat belts; also spelled **seatbelt**. A **seat belt** is a strap attached to a seat in a car or aircraft. You fasten it round your body and it stops you being thrown forward if there is a sudden movement. See also **car** and **bicycle**. · N-COUNT

-seater /-ˈsiːtə/ **-seaters.** **-seater** combines with numbers to form adjectives and nouns which indicate how many people something such as a car has seats for. *...a three-seater sofa.* · See also **all-seater**. · COMB

seat·ing /ˈsiːtɪŋ/. **1** You can refer to the seats in a place as the **seating**. *The stadium has been fitted with seating for over eighty thousand spectators.* **2** The **seating** at a public place or a formal occasion is the arrangement of where people will sit. · N-UNCOUNT · N-UNCOUNT

,seat of 'learning, seats of learning. People sometimes refer to a university or a similar institution as a **seat of learning**. · N-COUNT

'sea turtle, sea turtles. A **sea turtle** is a large reptile which has a thick shell covering its body and which lives in the sea most of the time. The usual British word is **turtle**. · N-COUNT AMERICAN

'sea urchin, sea urchins. A **sea urchin** is a small round sea creature that has a hard shell covered with sharp points. · N-COUNT

'sea wall, sea walls. A **sea wall** is a wall built along the edge of the sea to stop the sea flowing over the land or eroding it. · N-COUNT

sea·ward /ˈsiːwəd/; the form **seawards** can be used for meaning 1. **1** Something that moves or faces **seaward** or **seawards** moves or faces in the direction of the sea or further out to sea. **2** The **seaward** side of something faces in the direction of the sea or further out to sea. · ADV · ADJ

sea·weed /ˈsiːwiːd/ **seaweeds. Seaweed** is a plant that grows in the sea. There are many kinds of seaweed. · N-VAR

sea·worthy /ˈsiːwɜːði/. A ship or boat which is **seaworthy** is fit to travel at sea. · ADJ-GRADED

se·bum /ˈsiːbəm/. **Sebum** is an oily substance produced by glands in your skin. · N-UNCOUNT

S

sec /sek/ **secs.** If you ask someone to wait a **sec**, N-COUNT you are asking them to wait for a very short time. *Be* INFORMAL *with you in a sec.*

sec., secs. 1 Sec. is a written abbreviation for **second** or **seconds. 2 Sec.** is a written abbreviation for **Secretary**, especially when it is used as part of a person's title.

seca·teurs /ˌsekəˈtɜːz/. **Secateurs** are a gardening N-PLURAL tool that look like a pair of strong, heavy scissors. *also a pair of N* Secateurs are used for cutting the stems of plants. BRITISH The American term is **pruning shears**. See picture headed **tools**.

se·cede /sɪˈsiːd/ **secedes, seceding, seceded.** ◆◇◇◇ If a region or group **secedes** from the country or VERB: larger group to which it belongs, it formally be- V *from v* comes a separate country or stops being a member V of the larger group. *On 20 August 1960 Senegal seceded.*

se·ces·sion /sɪˈseʃən/. The **secession** of a region ◆◇◇◇ or group from the country or larger group to which N-UNCOUNT it belongs is its formal separation from it.

se·ces·sion·ist /sɪˈseʃənɪst/ **secessionists.** Se- ◆◇◇◇ **cessionists** are people who want their region or N-COUNT group to become separate from the country or larg- er group to which it belongs.

se·clud·ed /sɪˈkluːdɪd/. A **secluded** place is quiet, ◆◇◇◇ private, and undisturbed. ADJ-GRADED

se·clu·sion /sɪˈkluːʒən/. If you are living in **seclu-** N-UNCOUNT **sion**, you are in a quiet place away from other peo- ple. *They love the seclusion of their garden.*

second 1 part of a minute

sec·ond /ˈsekənd/ **seconds.** A **second** is one of ◆◆◆◆◆ the sixty parts that a minute is divided into. People N-COUNT often say **'a second'** or **'seconds'** when they simply mean a very short length of time. *It only takes forty seconds... Seconds later, firemen reached his door.*

second 2 coming after something else

sec·ond /ˈsekənd/ **seconds, seconding, sec-** ◆◆◆◆◆ **onded. 1** The **second** item in a series is the one ORDINAL that you count as number two. See Appendix head- ed **Numbers. 2 Second** is used before superlative ORDINAL adjectives to indicate that there is only one thing better or larger than the thing you are referring to. *The party is still the second strongest in Italy.* **3** You ADV: say **second** when you want to make a second point ADV cl or give a second reason for something. *First, the* PRAGMATICS *weapons should be intended for use only in retalia- tion after a nuclear attack. Second, the possession of the weapons must be a temporary expedient.* **4** If you say that something is **second to none**, you are PHRASE emphasizing that it is very good indeed or the best PRAGMATICS that there is. **5** If you say that something is **second** PHRASE **only to** something else, you mean that it is exceeded or excelled only by that thing. *As a major health risk hepatitis is second only to tobacco.* **6** In Britain, an upper **second** is a good honours de- N-COUNT gree and a lower **second** is an average honours de- gree. **7 Seconds** are goods that are sold cheaply in N-COUNT shops because they are slightly faulty. **8** The **seconds** N-COUNT of someone who is taking part in a boxing match or chess tournament are the people who assist and en- courage them. **9** If you **second** a proposal in a meeting or debate, you VERB: V n formally express your agreement with it so that it can then be discussed or voted on. ◆ **sec·ond·er, sec-** N-COUNT **onders** *The names of Mr Heseltine's proposer and seconder will be revealed this morning.* **10** If you **sec-** VERB **ond** what someone has said, you say that you agree V n with them or say the same thing yourself. *The Prime Minister seconded the call for discipline and austerity.* **11 ● second nature:** see **nature. ● in the second place:** see **place.**

second 3 sending someone to do a job

sec·ond /sɪˈkɒnd/ **seconds, seconding, sec-** VERB: **onded.** If you **are seconded** somewhere, you are be V-ed sent there temporarily by your employer in order to prep/adv do special duties. *Several hundred soldiers have* be V-ed to-inf *been seconded to help farmers.* ◆ **se·cond·ment,** BRITISH **secondments** *We have two full-time secretaries,* N-VAR *one of whom is on secondment from the Royal Navy.*

sec·ond·ary /ˈsekəndri, AM -deri/. **1** If you de- ◆◆◇◇◇ scribe something as **secondary**, you mean that it is ADJ less important than something else. *They argue that human rights considerations are now of only second- ary importance.* **2 Secondary** diseases or infections ADJ happen as a result of another disease or infection that has already happened. **3 Secondary** education ADJ is given to pupils between the ages of 11 or 12 and 18.

,secondary 'modern, secondary moderns. N-COUNT **Secondary moderns** were schools which existed un- til recently in Britain for children aged between about eleven and sixteen, which were more practi- cal and less academic than grammar schools.

'secondary school, secondary schools. A ◆◇◇◇ **secondary school** is a school for pupils between the N-VAR ages of 11 or 12 and 18.

,second 'best; also spelled **second-best. 1 Sec-** ◆◇◇◇ **ond best** is used to describe something that is not ADJ as good as the best thing of its kind but is better than all the other things of that kind. *He put on his second best suit.* **2** You can use **second best** to de- ADJ scribe something that you have to accept even though you would have preferred something else. *He refused to settle for anything that was second best.* ▶ Also a noun. *Oatmeal is a good second best.* N-SING

,second 'chamber. The **second chamber** is one N-SING of the two bodies that a parliament is divided into. In Britain, the second chamber is the House of Lords.

,second-'class; also spelled **second class. 1** If ◆◇◇◇ someone treats you as a **second-class** citizen, they ADJ: ADJ n treat you as if you are less valuable and less impor- tant than other people. *He was not prepared to see Uzbekistan become a second class republic.* **2** If you ADJ describe something as **second-class**, you mean that it is of poor quality. **3** In the past, **second-class** was N-UNCOUNT the ordinary accommodation on a train or ship, which was cheaper and less luxurious than the first-class accommodation. Nowadays, this type of accommodation is usually called 'standard class'. ▶ Also an adverb. *I recently travelled second class* ADV: *from Pisa to Ventimiglia.* **4** In Britain, **second-class** ADV after v postage is the slower and cheaper type of postage. ADJ: ADJ n In the United States, **second-class** postage is the type of postage that is used for sending newspapers and magazines. *...a second-class stamp.* ▶ Also an ADV: adverb. *They're going to send it second class.* **5** In ADV after v Britain, a **second-class** degree is a good university ADJ: ADJ n degree, but not as good as a first-class degree.

,second 'coming. When Christians refer to the N-SING: **second coming**, they mean the expected return to *the N* earth of Jesus Christ.

,second 'cousin, second cousins. Your **second** N-COUNT **cousins** are the children of your parents' first cousins.

,second-de'gree. 1 In the United States, ADJ: ADJ n **second-degree** is used to describe crimes that are considered to be less serious than first-degree crimes. *...second-degree murder.* **2** A **second-degree** ADJ: ADJ n burn is more severe than a first-degree burn but less severe than a third-degree burn.

,second-'guess, second-guesses, second- VERB **guessing, second-guessed.** If you try to V n **second-guess** something, you try to guess in ad- Also V vance what someone will do or what will happen. *Editors and contributors are trying to second-guess the future.*

,second-'hand. 1 Second-hand things are not ◆◇◇◇ new and have been owned by someone else. ▶ Also ADJ an adverb. *Far more boats are bought second-hand* ADV: *than are bought brand new.* **2** A **second-hand** shop ADV after v sells second-hand goods. **3 Second-hand** informa- ADJ: ADJ n tion or opinions are those you learn about from ADJ other people rather than directly or from your own experience.

,second-in-com'mand; also spelled **second in** N-SING **command.** A **second-in-command** is someone who is next in rank to the leader of a group.

,second 'language, second languages. N-COUNT
Someone's **second language** is a language which is
not their native language but which they use at
work or at school.

,second lieu'tenant, second lieutenants. A N-COUNT
second lieutenant is a junior officer in the army.

sec·ond·ly /'sekəndli/. You say **secondly** when you ◆◇◇◇◇
want to make a second point or give a second rea- ADV: ADV with cl (not last in cl)
son for something. *The problems were numerous.*
Firstly, I didn't know exactly when I was going to PRAGMATICS
America; secondly, who was going to look after
Doran and Lili?

se·cond·ment /sɪ'kɒndmənt/ secondments. See
second.

,second o'pinion, second opinions. If you seek N-COUNT
a **second opinion**, you ask another qualified person
for their opinion about something such as your
health.

,second 'person. A statement in **the second per-** N-SING: theN
son is a statement about the person or people you
are talking to. The subject of a statement like this is
'you'.

,second-'rate. If you describe something as ◆◇◇◇◇
second-rate, you mean that it is of poor quality. ADJ-GRADED

,second 'sight. If you say that someone has **sec-** N-UNCOUNT
ond sight, you mean that they seem to have the
ability to know about things that will happen in the
future, or are happening in a different place.

,second 'string; also spelled **second-string**. If you N-SING
describe a person or thing as someone's **second**
string, you mean that they are a substitute and only
used if someone or something else is not available.
...a second string team.

,second 'thought, second thoughts. 1 If you ◆◇◇◇◇
do something without **a second thought**, you do it N-SING: with brd-neg, aN
without thinking about it carefully, usually because
you do not have enough time or you do not care
very much. *Roberto didn't give a second thought to*
borrowing $2,000 from him. 2 If you have **second** N-PLURAL
thoughts about a decision that you have made, you
begin to doubt whether it was the best thing to do.
3 You can say **on second thoughts** when you sud- PHRASE BRITISH
denly change your mind about something that you
are saying or something that you have decided to
do. In American English, you say **on second**
thought. *'On second thoughts,' he said, 'I guess I'll*
come with you.'

,second 'wind. When you get your **second wind**, N-SING
you become able to continue doing a difficult or
strenuous task after you have been tired or out of
breath.

,Second World 'War. The **Second World War** is ◆◆◇◇◇
the major war that was fought between 1939 and N-PROPER: theN
1945.

se·cre·cy /'si:krəsi/. **Secrecy** is the act of keeping ◆◆◇◇◇
something secret, or the state of being kept secret. N-UNCOUNT
He shrouds his business dealings in secrecy.

se·cret /'si:krɪt/ secrets. 1 If something is **secret**, ◆◆◆◆◇
it is known about by only a small number of people, ADJ-GRADED: ADJ n,
and is not told or shown to anyone else. *The police* v n ADJ, v-link ADJ
have been trying to keep the documents secret. ● See
also **top secret**. ♦ se·cret·ly *He wore a hidden* ADV-GRADED
microphone to secretly tape-record conversations.
2 A **secret** is a fact that is known by only a small N-COUNT
number of people, and is not told to anyone else. *I*
think he enjoyed keeping our love a secret. 3 If you PHRASE
do something **in secret**, you do it without anyone
else knowing. 4 If you say that someone can **keep a** PHRASE
secret, you mean that they can be trusted not to tell
other people a secret that you have told them. 5 If PHRASE
you **make no secret** of something, you tell others
about it openly and plainly. *His wife made no secret*
of her hatred for formal occasions.
6 If you say that a particular way of doing things is **the** N-SING: theN
secret of achieving something, you mean that it is the
best or only way to achieve it. *The secret of success is*
honesty and fair dealing. 7 Something's **secrets** are N-COUNT
the things about it which have never been fully explained. *...the secrets of the universe.*

,secret 'agent, secret agents. A **secret agent** is N-COUNT
a person who is employed by a government to find
out the secrets of other governments.

sec·re·tar·ial /,sekrə'teəriəl/. **Secretarial** work or ◆◇◇◇◇
training involves the work of a secretary. ADJ: ADJ n

sec·re·tari·at /,sekrə'teəriæt/ secretariats. A ◆◇◇◇◇
secretariat is a department that is responsible for N-COUNT
the administration of an international political organization. *...the UN secretariat.*

sec·re·tary /'sekrətri, AM -teri/ secretaries. 1 A ◆◆◆◆◆
secretary is a person who is employed to do office N-COUNT
work, such as typing letters or answering phone
calls. 2 The **secretary** of an organization such as a N-COUNT
trade union or a club is its official manager. 3 The N-COUNT
secretary of a company is the person who has the
legal duty of keeping the company's records. 4 **Sec-** N-COUNT
retary is used in the titles of ministers and officials
who are in charge of main government departments. *...the British Foreign Secretary.*

,secretary-'general, secretaries-general; ◆◆◆◇◇
also spelled **Secretary General**. The **secretary-** N-COUNT
general of an international political organization is
the person in charge of its administration.

,Secretary of 'State, Secretaries of State. ◆◆◆◇◇
1 In the United States, **the Secretary of State** is the N-COUNT
head of the government department which deals
with foreign affairs. 2 In Britain, **the Secretary of** N-COUNT
State for a particular government department is the
head of that department. *...the Secretary of State for*
Education.

se·crete /sɪ'kri:t/ secretes, secreting, secret- ◆◇◇◇◇
ed. 1 If part of a plant, animal, or human **secretes** a VERB: V n
liquid, it produces it. ♦ se·cre·tion /sɪ'kri:ʃən/ se- N-UNCOUNT: also N in pl
cretions *...insulin secretion.* 2 If you **secrete** VERB: V n prep/adv
something somewhere, you hide it there so that no- LITERARY
body will find it.

se·cre·tive /'si:krətɪv, sɪ'kri:t-/. If you are **secre-** ◆◇◇◇◇
tive, you like to have secrets and to keep your ADJ-GRADED
knowledge, feelings, or intentions hidden. ♦ se-
·cre·tive·ness *He was evasive, to the point of se-* N-UNCOUNT
cretiveness.

,secret po'lice. The **secret police** is a police ◆◇◇◇◇
force, especially in a non-democratic country, that N-UNCOUNT
works secretly and is concerned with political
crimes.

,secret 'service, secret services. A country's ◆◇◇◇◇
secret service is a government department whose N-COUNT
job is to find out enemy secrets and to prevent its
own government's secrets from being discovered.

sect /sekt/ sects. A **sect** is a group of people that ◆◇◇◇◇
has separated from a larger group and has a par- N-COUNT
ticular set of religious or political beliefs.

sec·tar·ian /sek'teəriən/. **Sectarian** means result- ◆◇◇◇◇
ing from the differences between different religions. ADJ
The police said the murder was sectarian.

sec·tari·an·ism /sek'teəriənɪzəm/. **Sectarianism** is N-UNCOUNT
strong support for a particular sect and its beliefs.

sec·tion /'sekʃən/ sections, sectioning, sec- ◆◆◆◆◇
tioned. 1 A **section** of something is one of the N-COUNT
parts into which it is divided or from which it is
formed. *He said it was wrong to single out any sec-*
tion of society for Aids testing. 2 If something **is sec-** VERB:
tioned, it is divided into sections. 3 A **section** of an beV-ed N-COUNT
official document such as a report or a law is one of
the parts into which it is divided. *...section 14 of the*
Trade Descriptions Act 1968. 4 A **section** is a dia- N-COUNT
gram of something such as a building or a part of
the body. It shows how the object would appear to
you if it were cut from top to bottom and looked at
from the side. 5 See also **cross-section**.
● Caesarean section: see Caesarean.

section off. If an area **is sectioned off**, it is separat- PHRASAL VB
ed by a wall, fence, or other barrier from the sur- beV-ed P
rounding area.

sec·tion·al /'sekʃənəl/. **Sectional** interests are ADJ: ADJ n
those of a particular group within a community or
country.

sec·tor /'sektə/ sectors. 1 A particular **sector** of a ◆◆◆◆◇
country's economy is the part connected with that N-COUNT: supp N
specified type of industry. *...the nation's manufac-*

turing sector. **2** A **sector** of a large group is a smaller group which is part of it. *...the poorest sectors of Pakistani society.* **3** A **sector** is an area of a city or country which is controlled by a military force. N-COUNT

4 See also **private sector, public sector.**

sec·tor·al /'sektərəl/. **Sectoral** means relating to the various economic sectors of a society or to a particular economic sector; used in economics. *...sectoral differences within social classes.* ADJ: ADJ n TECHNICAL

secu·lar /'sekjʊlə/. You use **secular** to describe things that have no connection with religion. *He spoke about preserving the country as a secular state.* ◆◇◇◇◇ ADJ-GRADED

secu·lar·ism /'sekjʊlərɪzəm/. **Secularism** is a system of social organization and education where religion is not allowed to play a part in civil affairs. N-UNCOUNT

♦ **secu·lar·ist, secularists** *...conflict between fundamentalists and secularists.* N-COUNT

secu·lar·ized /'sekjʊləraɪzd/; also spelled **secularised.** **Secularized** societies are no longer under the control or influence of religion. ADJ-GRADED

se·cure /sɪ'kjʊə/ **secures, securing, secured.** **1** If you **secure** something that you want or need, you obtain it after a lot of effort. *Graham's achievements helped secure him the job.* ◆◆◆◆◇ VERB: V n V n n Also V n for n FORMAL

2 If you **secure** a place, you make it safe from harm or attack. *Staff withdrew from the main part of the prison but secured the perimeter.* **3** A **secure** place is tightly locked or well protected, so that people cannot enter it or leave it. ♦ **se·cure·ly** *He locked the heavy door securely.* **4** If you **secure** an object, you fasten it firmly to another object. **5** If an object is **secure**, it is fixed firmly in position. *Shelves are only as secure as their fixings.* ♦ **securely** *Builders must fasten down roofs of newly-built homes more securely.* VERB V n FORMAL ADJ-GRADED ADV VERB: V n ADJ-GRADED ADV-GRADED: ADV with v

6 If you describe something such as a job as **secure**, it is safe and certain not to be lost. *...the failure of financial institutions once thought to be secure.* **7** A **secure** base or foundation is strong and reliable. *For many young blacks, the only jobs that offer a secure future are in the armed forces.* **8** If you feel **secure**, you feel safe and happy and are not worried about life. **9** If a loan **is secured**, it is guaranteed by assets such as a house which becomes the property of the lender if the borrower fails to repay the loan. *The loan is secured against your home.* ADJ-GRADED ADJ-GRADED ADJ-GRADED VB: usu passive be V-ed adv/ prep

se·cur·ity /sɪ'kjʊərɪti/ **securities. 1 Security** refers to all the measures that are taken to protect a place, or to ensure that only authorized people enter it or leave it. *They are now under a great deal of pressure to tighten their airport security. ...a top security jail.* **2** A feeling of **security** is a feeling of being safe and free from worry. *He loves the security of a happy home life.* ● If something gives you **a false sense of security**, it makes you believe that you are safe when you are not. **3** If you pledge something as **security** for a loan, you promise to give it to the person who lends you money, if you fail to pay the money back. *The banks will pledge the land as security.* **4 Securities** are stocks, shares, bonds, or other certificates that you buy in order to earn regular interest from them or to sell them later for a profit. **5** See also **social security.** ◆◆◆◆◇ N-UNCOUNT: with supp N-UNCOUNT PHRASE N-UNCOUNT N-PLURAL TECHNICAL

se'curity blanket, security blankets. If you refer to something as a **security blanket**, you mean that it provides someone with a feeling of safety and comfort when they are in a situation that worries them. *Alan sings with shy intensity, hiding behind the security blanket of his guitar.* N-COUNT

Se'curity Council. The **Security Council** is the committee which governs the United Nations. ◆◆◆◇◇ N-PROPER

se'curity guard, security guards. A **security guard** is someone whose job is to protect a building or to collect and deliver large amounts of money. ◆◇◇◇◇ N-COUNT

se'curity risk, security risks. A person who may be a threat to the safety of a country or organization can be described as a **security risk**. N-COUNT

se·dan /sɪ'dæn/ **sedans.** A **sedan** is a car with seats for four or more people, a fixed roof, and a boot that is separate from the part of the car that you sit in. The British word is **saloon.** ◆◇◇◇◇ N-COUNT AMERICAN

se,dan 'chair, sedan chairs. A **sedan chair** is an enclosed chair for one person carried on two poles by two men, one in front and one behind. **Sedan chairs** were used in the 17th and 18th centuries. N-COUNT

se·date /sɪ'deɪt/ **sedates, sedating, sedated.** **1** If you describe someone as **sedate**, you mean that they are quiet and rather dignified, though perhaps dull. ♦ **se·date·ly** *He saw her come out of the lift alone and walk sedately across the carpeting.* **2 Sedate** places are peaceful and rather dignified, though unexciting. **3** If you describe something such as a car or an event as **sedate**, you mean that it is slow and unexciting. ♦ **sedately** *He pulled sedately out of the short driveway.* ◆◇◇◇◇ ADJ-GRADED ADV-GRADED ADJ-GRADED ADJ-GRADED ADV-GRADED

4 If someone **is sedated**, they are given a drug to calm them or to make them sleep. *Doctors have been told not to sedate children with an anaesthetic that may be linked to five deaths.* ♦ **se·dat·ed** *Grace was asleep, lightly sedated.* VERB: be V-ed V n ADJ-GRADED: v-link ADJ

se·da·tion /sɪ'deɪʃən/. If someone is under **sedation**, they have been given medicine or drugs in order to calm them or make them sleep. N-UNCOUNT

seda·tive /'sedətɪv/ **sedatives.** A **sedative** is a medicine or drug that calms you or makes you sleep. ◆◇◇◇◇ N-COUNT

sed·en·tary /'sedəntəri, AM -teri/. Someone who has a **sedentary** lifestyle or job, sits down a lot of the time and does not take much exercise. ADJ-GRADED

sedge /sedʒ/ **sedges.** **Sedge** is a grass-like plant that grows in wet, marshy ground. ◆◇◇◇◇ N-VAR

sedi·ment /'sedɪmənt/ **sediments. Sediment** is solid material that settles at the bottom of a liquid, especially earth and pieces of rock that have been carried along and then left somewhere by water, ice, or wind. ◆◇◇◇◇ N-VAR

sedi·men·tary /,sedɪ'mentəri, AM -teri/. **Sedimentary** rocks are formed from sediment left by water, ice, or wind. ADJ: ADJ n

se·di·tion /sɪ'dɪʃən/. **Sedition** is speech, writing, or behaviour intended to encourage rebellion or resistance against the government. N-UNCOUNT

se·di·tious /sɪ'dɪʃəs/. A **seditious** act, utterance, or piece of writing encourages rebellion or resistance against the government. ADJ-GRADED

se·duce /sɪ'djuːs, AM -'duːs/ **seduces, seducing, seduced.** **1** If something **seduces** you, it is so attractive that it tempts you into doing something that you would not otherwise do. *The clever advertising employed by U.S. cigarette companies would seduce more people into smoking.* ♦ **se·duc·tion** /sɪ'dʌkʃən/ **seductions** *The country had resisted the seductions of mass tourism.* **2** If someone **seduces** another person, they use their charm to persuade that person to have sex with them. ♦ **seduction** *Her methods of seduction are subtle.* ◆◆◇◇◇ VERB: V n V n into -ing/n N-VAR VERB: V n N-VAR

se·duc·er /sɪ'djuːsə, AM -'duːs-/ **seducers.** A **seducer** is a man who seduces someone. N-COUNT

se·duc·tive /sɪ'dʌktɪv/. **1** Something that is **seductive** is very attractive or tempting. *It's a seductive argument.* ♦ **se·duc·tive·ly** *The film opens seductively.* **2** A person who is **seductive** is very attractive sexually. ♦ **seductively** *Her mouth is seductively large and full.* ◆◇◇◇◇ ADJ-GRADED ADV-GRADED ADV-GRADED

se·duc·tress /sɪ'dʌktrəs/ **seductresses.** A **seductress** is a woman who seduces someone. N-COUNT

see /siː/ **sees, seeing, saw, seen.** **1** When you **see** something, you notice it using your eyes. *I saw a man making his way towards me... Passengers saw him punch the dog in the face and kick it... She can see, hear, touch, smell, and taste... Did you see what happened?* **2** If you **see** someone, you visit them or meet them. *You need to see a doctor.* **3** If you **see a** lot **of** someone, you often meet each other or visit each other. **4** '**See you**', '**be seeing you**', and '**see you later**' are ways of saying goodbye to someone when you expect to meet them again soon. **5** If you **are seeing** someone, you spend time with them socially, and are having a romantic or sexual relationship with them. ◆◆◆◆◆ VB: no cont V n V n-ing V n inf V n V wh VERB V n VERB: V amount of n CONVENTION INFORMAL VERB: V n

6 If you **see** an entertainment such as a film, concert, VB: no cont

or sports game, you watch it. *It was one of the most* `V n`
amazing films I've ever seen. **7 See** is used in books to `VB: only imper` `PRAGMATICS`
indicate to readers that they should look at another `V n`
part of the book, or at another book, because more information is given there. *See Chapter 7 below for fur-*
ther comments on the textile industry. **8** Some writers `VERB`
use **see** in expressions such as **we saw** and **as we have** `PRAGMATICS`
seen to refer to something that has already been ex- `V wh`
plained or described. *We saw in Chapter 16 how an-*
nual cash budgets are produced.

9 If you **see** that something is true or exists, you real- `VB: no cont,`
ize by observing it that it is true or exists. *We saw what* `V that`
happened to Labour in the 1980s... You've just been `V wh`
cleaning it, I see... The army must be seen to be taking `V` `be V-ed to-inf`
firm action. **10** You can use **seeing that** or **seeing as** to `PHR-CONJ`
introduce a reason for what you are saying or a reason `PRAGMATICS`
why you think something is the case. *Seeing as Mr*
Moreton is a doctor, I would assume he has a modicum
of intelligence.

11 If you **see** what someone means or **see** why some- `VB: no cont,`
thing happened, you understand what they mean or `no passive`
why it happened. *Oh, I see what you're saying... I don't* `V wh` `V n`
see why you're complaining... I really don't see any rea- `Also V that`
son for changing it. **12** You can say '**I see**' to indicate `CONVENTION`
that you understand what someone is telling you. *'He* `PRAGMATICS`
came here in my car.'—'I see.' **13** You can say '**you** `CONVENTION`
see' when you are explaining something to someone, `PRAGMATICS`
to encourage them to listen and understand. *She was*
a prime target for blackmail, don't you see? **14** People `CONVENTION`
say '**let me see**' or '**let's see**' when they are trying to re- `PRAGMATICS`
member something, or are trying to find something.
Let's see, they're six – no, make that five hours ahead of
us.

15 If you **see** someone or something as a certain `VERB:`
thing, you have the opinion that they are that thing. `V n as n/-ing`
Others saw it as a betrayal... I don't see it as my duty to `V it as n to-inf`
take sides... As I see it, Llewelyn has three choices open `V it`
to him. **16** If you **see** a particular quality in someone, `VB: no cont,`
you believe they have that quality. *Frankly, I don't* `no passive`
know what Paul sees in her... Young and old saw in `V n inn`
him an implacable opponent of apartheid. **17** If you `PHRASE`
try to make someone **see sense** or **see reason**, you try
to make them realize that they are wrong because you
think they are behaving stupidly.

18 If you **see** something happening in the future, you `VB: no cont,`
imagine it, or predict that it will happen. *We can see a* `V n -ing`
day where all people live side by side. **19** You can say `CONVENTION`
'**You'll see**' to someone if they do not agree with you `PRAGMATICS`
about what you think will happen in the future, and
you believe that you will be proved right. *The thrill*
wears off after a few years of marriage. You'll see. **20** If `VB: no passive`
you say that a period of time or a person **sees** a par- `V n`
ticular change or event, you mean that the change or `V n inf`
event takes place during that period of time or while `Also V n -ed`
that person is alive. *Yesterday saw the resignation of*
the acting Interior Minister... He had worked with the
General for three years and was sorry to see him go.

21 You can use **see** in expressions to do with finding `VERB`
out information. For example, if you say '**I'll see** `V wh`
what's happening', you mean that you intend to find
out what is happening. *Let me just see what the next*
song is. **22** You can use **see** to promise to try and help `VERB`
someone. For example, if you say '**I'll see if I can do** `PRAGMATICS`
it', you mean that you will try to do the thing con- `V what`
cerned. *We'll see what we can do, miss.* **23** People say `CONVENTION`
'**I'll see**' or '**We'll see**' to indicate that they do not in- `PRAGMATICS`
tend to make a decision immediately, and will decide
later. *We'll see. It's a possibility.* **24** If you **see** that `VERB`
something is done or if you **see** to it that it is done, you `V that`
make sure that it is done. *See that you take care of* `V to it that`
him... Catherine saw to it that the information went
directly to Walter.

25 If you **see** someone to a particular place, you ac- `VERB`
company them to make sure that they get there safely, `V n prep/adv`
or to show politeness. *'Goodnight.'—'I'll see you out.'*
26 See is used in a number of expressions which can
be found at other places in this dictionary. For example, the expression **wait and see** can be found at **wait**.

see about. When you **see about** something, you `PHRASAL VB`

arrange for it to be done or provided. *I must see about* `V P n/-ing`
selling the house.

see off. 1 If you **see off** an opponent, you defeat `PHRASAL VB`
them. *There is no reason why they cannot see off the* `V P noun`
Socialist challenge. **2** When you **see** someone **off**, you `Also V n P`
go with them to the station, airport, or port that they `V n P`
are leaving from, and say goodbye to them there. *Ben* `Also V P noun`
had planned a steak dinner for himself after seeing
Jackie off on her plane.

see through. If you **see through** someone or their `PHRASAL VB`
behaviour, you realize what their intentions are, even `V P n`
though they are trying to hide them. *I saw through*
your little ruse from the start. ● See also **see-through**.

see to. If you **see to** something that needs attention, `PHRASAL VB`
you deal with it. *While Franklin saw to the luggage,* `V P n`
Sara took Eleanor home.

seed /siːd/ **seeds, seeding, seeded. 1** A **seed** is ◆◆◆◇
the small hard part of a plant from which a new `N-VAR`
plant grows. *...sunflower seeds.* **2** If you **seed** a piece `VERB: V n`
of land, you plant seeds in it. *The primroses should* `V pron-refl`
begin to seed themselves down the steep hillside. **3** If `PHRASE`
vegetable plants **go to seed** or **run to seed**, they
produce flowers and seeds as well as leaves.

4 You can refer to the **seeds of** something when you `N-PLURAL:`
want to talk about the beginning of a feeling or pro- `N of n`
cess that gradually develops and becomes stronger or `LITERARY`
more important. *...questions meant to plant seeds of*
doubts in the minds of jurors.

5 In sports such as tennis or badminton, a **seed** is a `N-COUNT`
player who has been ranked according to his or her `TECHNICAL`
ability. *...Pete Sampras, Wimbledon's top seed.* **6** In `VERB:`
competitive sporting events, when a player or a team `be V-ed`
is seeded, they are ranked according to their ability. `TECHNICAL`

7 If you say that someone or something has **gone to** `PHRASE`
seed or **run to seed**, you mean that their health, `PRAGMATICS`
strength, or efficiency has started to diminish or decay. *He says the economy has gone to seed.*

seed·bed /ˈsiːdbed/ **seedbeds;** also spelled **seed-**
bed. 1 A **seedbed** is an area of specially prepared `N-COUNT`
ground where young plants are grown from seed.
2 You can refer to a place or a situation as a **seed-** `N-COUNT`
bed when it seems likely that rebellion or conflict
will develop there easily. *My region is a seedbed of*
crime.

seed·less /ˈsiːdləs/. A **seedless** fruit has no seeds in `ADJ`
it.

seed·ling /ˈsiːdlɪŋ/ **seedlings.** A **seedling** is a ◆◇◇◇◇
young plant that has been grown from a seed. `N-COUNT`

seedy /ˈsiːdi/ **seedier, seediest.** If you describe ◆◇◇◇◇
a person or place as **seedy**, you disapprove of them `ADJ-GRADED`
because they look dirty and untidy, or they have a `PRAGMATICS`
bad reputation. *...a seedy hotel close to the red light*
district. ♦ **seedi·ness** *...the atmosphere of seedi-* `N-UNCOUNT`
ness and decay about the city.

seek /siːk/ **seeks, seeking, sought. 1** If you ◆◆◆◆◆
seek something, you try to find or obtain it. *They* `VERB`
have had to seek work as labourers... Candidates are `V n` `be V-ed for n`
urgently sought for the post of Conservative party `FORMAL`
chairman. ♦ **seek·er, seekers** *I am a seeker after* `N-COUNT`
truth... The beaches draw sun-seekers from all over
Europe. ● See also **job seeker.** **2** If you **seek** `VERB: V n`
someone's help or advice, you contact them in or- `V n from n`
der to ask for it. *The couple have sought help from* `FORMAL`
marriage guidance counsellors. **3** If you **seek** to do `VERB`
something, you try to do it. *He also denied that he* `V to-inf`
would seek to annex the country. `FORMAL`

seek out. If you **seek out** someone or something, `PHRASAL VB`
you keep looking for them until you find them. *Ellen* `V P noun`
spent the day in the hills and sought me out when she `V n P`
returned.

seem /siːm/ **seems, seeming, seemed. 1** You ◆◆◆◆◆
use **seem** to say that someone or something gives `V-LINK: no`
the impression of having a particular quality, or that `cont`
something gives the impression of happening in the `V adj/prep`
way you describe. *Everyone seems busy except us...* `V n`
They seemed an ideal couple... The calming effect `V to-inf`
seemed to last for about ten minutes... It seems that `it V that`
the attack this morning was very carefully planned... `it V as if`
It seemed as if she'd been gone forever... There seems `there V to-inf`
to be a lot of support in Congress for this move.

S

2 You use **seem** when you are describing your own feelings or thoughts, or describing something that has happened to you, in order to make your statement less forceful. *I seem to have lost all my self-confidence... I seem to remember giving you very precise instructions.* **3** If you say that you **cannot seem** or **could not seem** to do something, you mean that you have tried to do it and were unable to. *Kim's mother couldn't seem to stop crying.* **4** See also **seeming**.
V-LINK: no cont
V to-inf

PHRASE

seem·ing /'si:mɪŋ/. **Seeming** means appearing to be the case, but not necessarily the case. *...the company's seeming inability to control costs.* ♦ **seem·ing·ly** *A seemingly endless line of trucks waits in vain to load up... He has moved to Spain, seemingly to enjoy a slower style of life.*
ADJ: ADJ n
PRAGMATICS
FORMAL

ADV

seem·ly /'si:mli/. **Seemly** behaviour or dress is appropriate in the particular circumstances. *It wasn't seemly for a boy still in school to be courting a young woman who worked.*
ADJ-GRADED
DATED

seen /si:n/. **Seen** is the past participle of **see**.

seep /si:p/ **seeps, seeping, seeped. 1** If liquid or gas **seeps** somewhere, it leaks slowly and in small amounts into a place where it should not go. ► Also a noun. *...an oil seep.* ♦ **seep·age** /'si:pɪdʒ/. **Seepage** is the slow flow of a liquid into something. **2** If something such as an unpleasant emotion **seeps** into an area, it gradually spreads into it. *Competition can seep into areas of our lives where we may not want it.*
♦◇◇◇
VERB:
V prep/adv
N-COUNT
N-UNCOUNT
VERB
V prep/adv

seer /'si:ə/ **seers.** A **seer** is a person who tells people what will happen in the future.
N-COUNT
LITERARY

see·saw /'si:sɔ:/ **seesaws, seesawing, seesawed;** also spelled **see-saw. 1** A seesaw consists of a long board which is balanced on a fixed part in the middle. Children play on seesaws by making the board tilt up and down when one child sits on each end. **2** In a **seesaw** situation, something continually changes from one state to another and back again. *Marriage, however, is an emotional seesaw.* **3** If someone's emotions **see-saw**, or a particular situation **see-saws**, they continually change from one state to another and back again. *The Tokyo stock market see-sawed up and down.*
N-COUNT

N-COUNT

VERB
V

seethe /si:ð/ **seethes, seething, seethed. 1** When you **are seething**, you are very angry about something but do not express your feelings about it. *I seethed with rage.* **2** If you say that a place **is seething** with people or things, you are emphasizing that it is very full of them and that they are all moving about. *The forest below him seethed and teemed with life.*
♦◇◇◇
VERB:
V prep

VERB
PRAGMATICS
V with n
Also V

'see-through. See-through clothes are made of thin cloth, so that you can see a person's body or underclothes through them.
ADJ-GRADED

seg·ment /'segmənt/ **segments. 1** A segment of something is one part of it, considered separately from the rest. *...the poorer segments of society.* **2** A segment of fruit such as an orange or grapefruit is one of the sections into which it is easily divided. See picture headed **fruit. 3** A segment of a circle is one of the two parts into which it is divided when you draw a straight line through it.
♦◇◇◇
N-COUNT:
N of n
N-COUNT

N-COUNT

seg·men·ta·tion /,segmen'teɪʃən/. **Segmentation** is the dividing of something into loosely-connected parts.
N-UNCOUNT
TECHNICAL

seg·ment·ed /'seg'mentɪd/. **Segmented** means divided into parts that are loosely connected to each other. *...segmented oranges.*
ADJ: ADJ n

seg·re·gate /'segrɪgeɪt/ **segregates, segregating, segregated.** To **segregate** two groups of people or things means to keep them physically apart from each other. *They segregate you from the rest of the community.* ♦ **seg·re·ga·tion** /,segrɪ'geɪʃən/. *...its segregation of prison inmates suffering from AIDS.*
VERB: V n
V n prep

N-UNCOUNT

seg·re·gat·ed /'segrɪgeɪtɪd/. **Segregated** buildings or areas are kept for the use of one group of people who are the same race, sex, or religion, and no oth-
♦◇◇◇
ADJ

er group is allowed to use them. *...racially segregated schools.*

seg·re·ga·tion·ist /,segrɪ'geɪʃənɪst/ **segregationists.** A **segregationist** is someone who thinks people of different races should be segregated.
N-COUNT

segue /'segweɪ/ **segues, segueing, segued.** If something such as a piece of music or conversation **segues into** another piece of music or conversation, it changes into it or is followed by it without a break. *The piece segues into his solo with the strings.* ► Also a noun. *...a neat segue into an arrangement of 'Eleanor Rigby'.*
VERB
V into n
Also V from n,
V
FORMAL
N-COUNT

seis·mic /'saɪzmɪk/. **Seismic** means caused by or relating to an earthquake. *...seismic waves.*
♦◇◇◇
ADJ: ADJ n
TECHNICAL

seis·mol·ogy /saɪz'mɒlədʒi/. **Seismology** is the scientific study of earthquakes. ♦ **seis·molo·gist,** **seismologists** *...a seismologist with the US Geological Survey.*
N-UNCOUNT
N-COUNT

seize /si:z/ **seizes, seizing, seized. 1** If you **seize** something, you take hold of it quickly, firmly, and forcefully. *'Leigh,' he said seizing my arm to hold me back.* **2** When a group of people **seize** a place or **seize** control of it, they take control of it quickly and suddenly, using force. *Troops have seized the airport.* **3** If a government or other authority **seize** someone's property, they take it from them, often by force. *Police were reported to have seized all copies of this mornings edition of the newspaper.* **4** When someone **is seized**, they are arrested or captured. *Men carrying submachine guns seized the five soldiers and drove them away.* **5** When you **seize** an opportunity, you take advantage of it and do something that you want to do.
♦♦◇◇
VERB
V n

VERB
V n

VERB
V n

VERB
V n

VERB: V n

seize on. If you **seize on** an event or **seize upon** it, you show great interest in it, because it is useful to you or confirms what you believe. *People will seize upon it as evidence of Australians lacking cultural depth.*
PHRASAL VB
V P n

seize up. If an engine or a part of your body **seizes up,** it stops working.
PHRASAL VB
V P

sei·zure /'si:ʒə/ **seizures. 1** If someone has a **seizure,** they have a sudden violent attack of an illness, especially a heart attack or an epileptic fit. *...a mild cardiac seizure.* **2** If there is a **seizure** of power or a **seizure** of an area of land, a group of people suddenly take control of the place, using force. *...the seizure of territory through force.* **3** When an organization such as the police or customs service makes a **seizure** of illegal goods, they confiscate them. **4** If a financial institution or a government makes a **seizure** of someone's assets, they take their money or property from them because they have not paid money that they owe. *A Greek court has ordered the seizure of two ships in compensation for non-payment of a debt.*
♦◇◇◇
N-COUNT

N-COUNT

N-COUNT

N-COUNT

sel·dom /'seldəm/. If something **seldom** happens, it happens only occasionally. *They seldom speak... I've seldom felt so happy... We were seldom at home.*
♦♦◇◇
ADV

se·lect /sɪ'lekt/ **selects, selecting, selected. 1** If you **select** something, you choose it from a number of things of the same kind. *Voters are selecting candidates for both US Senate seats.* **2** A **select** group is a small group of some of the best people or things of their kind. *...a select band of illustrious sportsmen.* **3** If you describe something as **select,** you mean it has many desirable features, but is available only to people who have a lot of money or who belong to a high social class. *...a very lavish and very select party.*
♦♦◇◇
VERB
V n
Also V n for/
from n
ADJ-GRADED:
ADJ n

ADJ-GRADED

se,lect com'mittee, select committees. A **select committee** is composed of members of a parliament, senate, or other elected assembly, and is set up to investigate and report back on a particular matter.
♦◇◇◇
N-COLL-
COUNT

se·lec·tion /sɪ'lekʃən/ **selections. 1** Selection is the act of selecting one or more people or things from a group. *Dr. Sullivan's selection to head the Department of Health was greeted with satisfaction... The children have to sit a tough selection test.* **2** A **selection** of people or things is a set of them that
♦♦♦◇◇
N-UNCOUNT:
with supp

N-COUNT

have been selected from a larger group. ...*this selection of popular songs.* **3** The **selection** of goods in a shop is the particular range of goods that it has available and from which you can choose what you want. ...*the widest selection of antiques of every description in a one day market.*

se·lec·tive /sɪˈlektɪv/. **1** A **selective** process applies only to a few things or people. ...*selective education.* ♦ **se·lec·tive·ly** *Trees are selectively cut on a 25-year rotation.* ♦ **se·lec·tiv·ity** /sɪˌlekˈtɪvɪti/. *The soldiers specialized in going out in small groups, to kill with a very high degree of selectivity.* **2** When someone is **selective**, they choose things carefully, for example the things that they buy or do. *Sales still happen, but buyers are more selective.* ♦ **selectively** ...*people on small incomes who wanted to shop selectively.* **3** If you say that someone has a **selective** memory, you disapprove of the fact that they remember certain facts about something and deliberately forget others, often because it is convenient for them to do so. ♦ **selectively** ...*a tendency to remember only the pleasurable effects of the drug and selectively forget all the adverse effects.*
(margin: ◆◆◇◇◇ ADJ-GRADED: ADJ n ADV N-UNCOUNT ADJ-GRADED ADV-GRADED ADJ-GRADED PRAGMATICS ADV-GRADED: ADV with v)

se·lec·tor /sɪˈlektə/ **selectors.** **1** The **selectors** are the people who choose the members of a sports team for a particular match or tour. *The selectors have made seven changes to the side beaten by Argentina earlier this year.* **2** A **selector** is a device which enables you to determine in advance which way a system or machine will operate. *During the attempt the bomb-door selector was operated... His thumb went down on the selector switch.*
(margin: ◆◆◇◇◇ N-COUNT N-COUNT)

self /self/ **selves.** **1** Your **self** is your basic personality or nature, especially considered in terms of what you are really like as a person. *You're looking more like your usual self.* **2** A person's **self** is the essential part of their nature which makes them different from everyone and everything else. ...*my inner self.*
(margin: ◆◆◆◇◇ N-COUNT N-COUNT)

self- /self-/. **1** Self- is used to form words which indicate that you do something to yourself or by yourself. *He is a self-proclaimed racist.* ...*self-destructive behaviour.* **2** Self- is used to form words which describe something such as a device that does something automatically by itself. ...*a self-loading pistol.*
(margin: COMB COMB)

self-ab·sorbed. Someone who is **self-absorbed** thinks so much about things concerning themselves that they do not notice other people or the things around them.
(margin: ADJ-GRADED)

self-ad·dressed. A **self-addressed** envelope is an envelope which you have written your own address on.
(margin: ADJ)

self-ad·hesive. Something that is **self-adhesive** is covered on one side with a sticky substance like glue, so that it will stick to surfaces. ...*self-adhesive labels.*
(margin: ADJ)

self-aggran·dize·ment /ˌself əˈgrændɪzmənt/; also spelled **self-aggrandisement.** If you say that someone is guilty of **self-aggrandizement**, you mean that they do certain things in order to make themselves more powerful, wealthy, or important; used showing disapproval. *He wanted to serve rather than use his position for self-aggrandizement.*
(margin: N-UNCOUNT PRAGMATICS)

self-ap·pointed. A **self-appointed** leader has taken the position of leader without anyone else asking them or choosing them to have it.
(margin: ADJ)

self-as·sembly. Self-assembly goods are bought in parts and have to be put together.
(margin: ADJ)

self-as·sertion. Self-assertion is confidence that you have in speaking firmly about your opinions and demanding the rights that you believe you should have. ...*her silence and lack of self-assertion.*
(margin: N-UNCOUNT)

self-as·sured. Someone who is **self-assured** shows confidence in what they say and do because they are sure of their own abilities. ...*a self-assured, confident negotiator.* ♦ **self-assurance.** Someone who has **self-assurance** is self-assured.
(margin: ADJ-GRADED N-UNCOUNT)

self-·catering. If you go on a **self-catering** holiday or you stay in **self-catering** accommodation,
(margin: N-UNCOUNT BRITISH)

you stay in a place where you have to provide your own meals.

self-·centred; spelled **self-centered** in American English. Someone who is **self-centred** is only concerned with their own wants and needs and never thinks about other people. *He was self-centred, he was stingy, but he wasn't cruel.*
(margin: ADJ-GRADED)

self-con·fessed. If you describe someone as a **self-confessed** murderer or a **self-confessed** perfectionist, for example, you mean that they admit openly that they are a murderer or a perfectionist. *She is a self-confessed workaholic.*
(margin: ADJ: ADJ n)

self-·confident. Someone who is **self-confident** behaves confidently because they feel sure of their abilities or value. ...*a self-confident young woman.* ♦ **self-confidence** *I've developed a lot of self-confidence.*
(margin: ADJ-GRADED N-UNCOUNT)

self-congratu·lation. If someone keeps emphasizing how well they have done or how good they are, you can refer to their behaviour as **self-congratulation.** *This is not a matter for self-congratulation.* ♦ **self-congratula·tory** *Foreign ministers were in self-congratulatory mood about co-operation in the UN Security Council.*
(margin: N-UNCOUNT ADJ-GRADED)

self-·conscious. **1** Someone who is **self-conscious** is easily embarrassed and nervous because they feel that everyone is looking at them and judging them. *I felt a bit self-conscious in my swimming costume.* ♦ **self-conscious·ly** *I glanced down at my dress jacket a little self-consciously.* ♦ **self-conscious·ness** ...*her painful self-consciousness.* **2** If you describe someone or something as **self-conscious**, you mean that they are strongly aware of who or what they are. *Putting the work together is a very self-conscious process.* ♦ **self-consciously** *The place is as self-consciously trendy as they come.*
(margin: ◆◇◇◇◇ ADJ-GRADED ADV-GRADED: ADV with v N-UNCOUNT ADJ-GRADED FORMAL ADV-GRADED: ADV adj)

self-con·tained. **1** You can describe someone or something as **self-contained** when they are complete and separate and do not need help or resources from outside. *He seems completely self-contained and he doesn't miss you when you're not there.* **2** Self-contained accommodation such as a flat has all its own facilities, so that a person living there does not have to share rooms such as a kitchen or bathroom with other people.
(margin: ◆◇◇◇◇ ADJ-GRADED ADJ-GRADED)

self-con·trol. Your **self-control** is your ability to control your feelings so that you do not show the emotions that you feel or do the things you instinctively want to do. *I began to wish I'd shown more self-control.* ♦ **self-con·trolled** *My father, who had always been very self-controlled, became bad-tempered and unpredictable.*
(margin: ◆◇◇◇◇ N-UNCOUNT ADJ-GRADED)

self-de·feating. A plan or action that is **self-defeating** is likely to cause problems or difficulties instead of producing useful results. *Dishonesty is ultimately self-defeating.*
(margin: ADJ-GRADED)

self-de·fence; spelled **self-defense** in American English. **1** Self-defence is the use of force to protect yourself against someone who is attacking you. *He acted in self-defence.* **2** Self-defence involves taking action to protect yourself from someone or something that you feel is threatening you. *Jokes were a natural self-defence mechanism against the tedium of communism.*
(margin: ◆◇◇◇◇ N-UNCOUNT N-UNCOUNT)

self-de·lusion. Self-delusion is the state of having a false idea about yourself or the situation you are in. ...*the grandiose self-delusion of the addict.*
(margin: N-UNCOUNT)

self-de·nial. Self-denial is the habit of refusing to do or have things that you would like, either because you cannot afford them, or because you believe it is morally good for you not to do them or have them. *Should motherhood necessarily mean sacrifice and self-denial?*
(margin: N-UNCOUNT)

self-·deprecating. If you describe someone's behaviour as **self-deprecating**, you mean that they criticize themselves or represent themselves as foolish in a light-hearted way. *Sharon tells the story of that night with self-deprecating humour.*
(margin: ADJ-GRADED)

S

self-de'struct, self-destructs, self- VERB
destructing, self-destructed. If someone V
self-destructs, they do something that seriously
damages their chances of success. *The Democrats
self-destructed in their primary.*

self-determi'nation. Self-determination is the ◆◇◇◇◇
right of a country to be independent, instead of be- N-UNCOUNT
ing controlled by a foreign country, and to choose
its own form of government.

self-'discipline. Self-discipline is the ability to N-UNCOUNT
control yourself and to make yourself work hard or
behave in a particular way without needing anyone
else to tell you what to do. ♦ **self-'disciplined.** ADJ-GRADED
Someone who is **self-disciplined** has self-discipline.

self-'doubt. Self-doubt is a lack of confidence in N-UNCOUNT
yourself and your abilities.

'self-drive. A self-drive car is one which you hire ADJ: ADJ n
and drive yourself. The usual American expression BRITISH
is **rental** car.

self-ef'facing. Someone who is **self-effacing** is ADJ-GRADED
modest and does not like talking about themselves
or drawing attention to themselves. *...the slightly
self-effacing manner adopted by many diplomats.*
♦ **self-e'ffacement.** Self-effacement is self- N-UNCOUNT
effacing behaviour.

self-em'ployed. If you are **self-employed**, you ◆◇◇◇◇
organize your own work and taxes and are paid by ADJ
people for a service you provide, rather than being
paid a regular salary by a person or a firm. ▶ Also a N-PLURAL:
noun. *We want more support for the self-employed.* the N

self-es'teem. Your self-esteem is how you feel ◆◇◇◇◇
about yourself. For example, if you have low **self-** N-UNCOUNT
esteem, you do not like yourself, you do not think
that you are a valuable person, and therefore you
do not behave confidently.

self-'evident. A fact or situation that is **self-** ◆◇◇◇◇
evident is so obvious that there is no need for proof ADJ-GRADED
or explanation. *It is self-evident that we will never
have enough resources to meet the demand.* ♦ **self-**
evident·ly The task was self-evidently impossible... ADV-GRADED
Self-evidently a handful of companies will benefit.

self-exami'nation. **1** Self-examination is N-UNCOUNT:
thought that you give to your own character and ac- also a N
tions, for example in order to judge whether you
have been behaving in a way that is acceptable to
your own set of values. *Once you've picked a company that seems right for you, you have to make sure
you're right for it. This is a time for some more self-
examination.* **2** Self-examination is the act of ex- N-UNCOUNT
amining your own body to check whether or not
you have any signs of a particular disease or illness.
...breast self-examination.

self-ex'planatory. Something that is **self-** ADJ-GRADED
explanatory is clear and easy to understand without
needing any extra information or explanation.

self-ex'pression. A person's **self-expression** is N-UNCOUNT
the expression of their own personality, feelings, or
opinions, for example through a creative activity
such as drawing or dancing.

self-ful'filling. If you describe a statement or be- ADJ
lief about the future as **self-fulfilling**, you mean that
what is said or believed comes true because people
expect it to come true.

self-'governing. A self-governing region or or- ◆◇◇◇◇
ganization is governed or run by its own people ra- ADJ
ther than by the people of another region or organization. ♦ **self-'government.** If there is **self-** N-UNCOUNT
government in a region or organization, it is self-
governing.

self-'help. **1** Self-help consists of people provid- ◆◇◇◇◇
ing support and help for each other in an informal N-UNCOUNT
way, rather than relying on the authorities or other
official organizations. *...a self-help group for parents
with over-weight children.* **2** Self-help consists of N-UNCOUNT
doing things yourself to try and solve your own
problems without depending on other people. *...a
society that encourages competitiveness and self-help
among the very young.*

self-'image, self-images. Your self-image is ◆◇◇◇◇
your opinion of yourself. *You must strive constantly* N-COUNT
to improve your self-image.

self-'im'portant. If you say that someone is **self-** ADJ-GRADED
important, you disapprove of them because they PRAGMATICS
behave as if they are more important than they really are. *He was self-important, vain and ignorant.*
♦ **self-import·ance** Many visitors complained of N-UNCOUNT
his bad manners and self-importance.

self-im'posed. A **self-imposed** restriction, task, ◆◇◇◇◇
or situation is one that you have deliberately creat- ADJ
ed or accepted for yourself. *...eleven years of self-
imposed exile.*

self-in'dulgence, self-indulgences. Self- N-VAR
indulgence is the act of allowing yourself to have or
do the things that you enjoy very much. *Going to
the movies in the afternoon is one of my big self-
indulgences.*

self-in'dulgent. If you say that someone is **self-** ADJ-GRADED
indulgent, you mean that they allow themselves to
have or do the things that they enjoy very much. *To
buy flowers for myself seems wildly self-indulgent.*

self-in'flicted. A **self-inflicted** wound or injury is ADJ
one that you do to yourself deliberately.

self-'interest. If you accuse someone of **self-** ◆◇◇◇◇
interest, you disapprove of them because they al- PRAGMATICS
ways want to do what is best for themselves rather
than for anyone else. ♦ **self-'interested.** Narrow- ADJ
ly self-interested behaviour is ultimately self-
defeating.

self·ish /'selfɪʃ/. If you say that someone is **selfish**, ◆◆◇◇◇
you mean that they care only about themselves, and ADJ-GRADED
not about other people. *...the selfish interests of a
few people.* ♦ **self·ish·ly** Ministers are selfishly pur- ADV
suing their own vested interests. ♦ **self·ish·ness.** N-UNCOUNT

self-'knowledge. Self-knowledge is knowledge N-UNCOUNT
that you have about your own character and nature.
*The more self-knowledge we have, the more control
we can exert over our feelings and behaviour.*

self·less /'selfləs/. If you say that someone is ◆◇◇◇◇
selfless, you approve of them because they care ADJ-GRADED
about other people more than themselves. *Her gen-
erosity to me was entirely selfless.* ♦ **self·less·ly** I've ADV-GRADED
never known anyone who cared so selflessly about
children. ♦ **self·less·ness.** N-UNCOUNT

self-'loathing. If someone feels **self-loathing**, N-UNCOUNT
they feel great dislike and disgust for themselves.

self-'made. Self-made is used to describe people ADJ
who have become successful and rich through their
own efforts, especially if they started life without
money, education, or high social status. *...a self-
made millionaire.*

self-'pity. Self-pity is a feeling of unhappiness ◆◇◇◇◇
and depression that you have about yourself and N-UNCOUNT
your problems, especially when this is unnecessary
or greatly exaggerated. *I was unable to shake off my
self-pity.* ♦ **self-'pitying.** Someone who is **self-** ADJ-GRADED
pitying is full of self-pity.

self-'portrait, self-portraits. A self-portrait is a N-COUNT
drawing, painting, or written description that you
do of yourself.

self-pos'sessed. Someone who is **self-possessed** ADJ-GRADED
is calm and confident and in control of their own
emotions.

self-preser'vation. Self-preservation is the in- N-UNCOUNT
stinctive behaviour that makes you keep yourself
safe from injury or death in a dangerous situation.
*The police have the same human urge for self-
preservation as the rest of us.*

self-'raising flour. Self-raising flour is flour that N-UNCOUNT
makes cakes rise when they are cooked. The Ameri- BRITISH
can term is **self-rising flour.**

self-re'liant. If you are **self-reliant**, you are able ADJ-GRADED
to do things and make decisions by yourself, with- PRAGMATICS
out needing other people to help you; used showing
approval. *Colleges should help students become independent, self-reliant human beings.* ♦ **self-**
re'liance People learned self-reliance because they N-UNCOUNT
had to.

self-re'spect. Self-respect is a feeling of confidence and pride in your own ability and worth. *I'd lost all my self-respect.* ◆◇◇◇◇ N-UNCOUNT

self-re'specting. If you say what any self-respecting person of a particular type would do, you are saying what is a typical, normal, or necessary thing for that type of person to do. *...things that any self-respecting thief would have taken.* ADJ: ADJ n

self-'righteous. If you describe someone as self-righteous, you disapprove of them because they are convinced that they are right in their beliefs, attitudes, and behaviour and that other people are wrong. *...self-righteous reformers.* ◆ self-righteous·ness *Her aggressiveness and self-righteousness caused prickles of anger at the back of his neck.* ADJ-GRADED PRAGMATICS / N-UNCOUNT

self-'rising flour. Self-rising flour is flour that makes cakes rise when they are cooked. The British term is **self-raising flour.** N-UNCOUNT AMERICAN

self-'rule. Self-rule is the same as self-government. N-UNCOUNT

self-'sacrifice. Self-sacrifice is the giving up of what you want so that other people can have what they need or want. *I thanked my parents for all their self-sacrifice on my behalf.* ◆ **self-'sacrificing.** Someone who is self-sacrificing shows self-sacrifice. N-UNCOUNT / ADJ-GRADED

'self-same; also spelled **selfsame.** You use self-same when you want to emphasize that the person or thing mentioned is exactly the same as the one mentioned previously. *If I find myself consistently noticing and condemning certain behaviours in other people, I can be quite certain that I possess those very self-same traits of character.* ADJ: ADJ n PRAGMATICS

self-'satisfied. If you describe someone as self-satisfied, you mean that they are so pleased and proud about their achievements or their situation that they do not feel they need to do anything more; used showing disapproval. *You were too self-satisfied to pay attention to what I was doing.* ◆ **self-'satisfaction** is the feeling you have when you are self-satisfied. ADJ-GRADED PRAGMATICS / N-UNCOUNT

self-'seeking. If you describe someone as self-seeking, you disapprove of them because they are interested only in doing things which give them an advantage over other people. *He said that democracy would open the way for self-seeking politicians to abuse the situation.* ADJ-GRADED PRAGMATICS

self-'service. A self-service shop, restaurant, or garage is one where you serve yourself rather than being served by another person. ADJ

self-'serving. If you describe someone or their motives as self-serving, you are critical of them because they are only interested in their own advantage or profit. *...corrupt, self-serving politicians.* ADJ-GRADED PRAGMATICS

self-'styled. If you describe someone as a self-styled leader or expert, you disapprove of them because they claim to be a leader or expert but they do not actually have the right to call themselves this. *Two of these arrested are said to be self-styled area commanders.* ◆◇◇◇◇ ADJ: ADJ n PRAGMATICS

self-suf'ficient. 1 If a country or group is self-sufficient, it is able to produce or make everything that it needs. *This enabled the country to become self-sufficient in sugar.* ◆ **self-su'fficiency** 2 Someone who is self-sufficient is able to live happily without anyone else. *He'd created a tiny, self-sufficient world for himself.* ◆◇◇◇◇ ADJ-GRADED / N-UNCOUNT ADJ-GRADED

self-sup'porting. Self-supporting is used to describe organizations, schemes, and people who earn enough money to not need financial help from anyone else. *The income from visitors makes the museum self-supporting.* ADJ

self-sus'taining. A self-sustaining process or system is able to continue without any intervention from outside. *Asia's emerging economies will be on a self-sustaining cycle of growth.* ADJ

self-'taught. If you are self-taught, you have learnt a skill by yourself rather than being taught it by someone else such as a teacher at school. ADJ

self-'will. Someone's self-will is their determination to do what they want without caring what other people think. *She had a little core of self-will that gave her a sparkle lacking in Isabel.* N-UNCOUNT

self-'willed. Someone who is self-willed is determined to do the things that they want to do and will not take advice from other people. ADJ-GRADED

sell /sel/ **sells, selling, sold.** 1 If you sell something that you own, you let someone have it in return for money. *His heir sold the painting to the London art dealer Agnews... The directors sold the business for £14.8 million.* 2 If a shop sells a particular thing, it is available for people to buy there. *It sells everything from hair ribbons to oriental rugs.* 3 If something sells for a particular price, that price is paid for it. *...a brand-new Yamaha moped, which sells at £1,374.* 4 If something sells, it is bought by the public, usually in fairly large quantities. *The products will sell well in the run-up to Christmas.* 5 Something that sells a product makes people want to buy the product. *...car manufacturers' long-held maxim that safety doesn't sell.* 6 If you sell someone an idea or proposal, you convince them that it is a good one. *She is hoping she can sell the idea to clients... An employee sold him on the notion that cable was the medium of the future.* 7 If someone sells their body, they have sex for money. 8 If someone sells you down the river, they betray you for some personal advantage. *The Government has sold us down the river.* 9 If you someone short, you do not point out their good qualities or help them as much as you should. *They need to improve their image – they are selling themselves short.* 10 ● to sell one's soul: see soul. ● to sell like hot cakes: see cake. ◆◆◆◆◇ VERB / V n / Also V / VERB / V n / VERB / V for/at n / VERB: V / V adv / VERB: V n / VERB: V n n / V n to n / V n on n / PHRASE / PHRASE / PHRASE

sell off. If you sell something off, you sell it because you need the money. *He announced plans to sell off more than half the company.* ● See also **sell-off.** PHRASAL VB V n P / V P noun

sell on. If you buy something and then sell it on, you sell it to someone else soon after buying it, usually to make a profit. *She'd buy old cars, paint them an unusual purple, and sell them on for an extra £100.* PHRASAL VB V n P

sell out. 1 If a shop sells out of something, it sells all its stocks of it. *Yesterday there were long queues at shops, which reported selling out of many items... The next day the bookshops sold out.* 2 If a performance, sports event, or other entertainment sells out, all the tickets for it are sold. *Tickets for the show sold out in 70 minutes.* 3 When things sell out, all of them that are available are sold. 4 If you accuse someone of selling out, you disapprove of the fact that they do something which used to be against their principles. *Critics have accused the trust of selling out to foreigners.* 5 Sell out also means the same as sell up. *I hear she's going to sell out and move to the city.* 6 See also sell-out, sold out. PHRASAL VB V P of n / V P / V P / V P / PRAGMATICS V P to n / V P / AMERICAN

sell up. If you sell up, you sell everything you have, because you need the money. The usual American expression is **sell out.** *He advised Evans to sell up his flat and move away to the country.* PHRASAL VB V P / V P noun BRITISH

'sell-by date, sell-by dates. 1 The sell-by date on a food container is the date by which the food should be sold or eaten, before it starts to deteriorate. 2 If you say that someone or something is past their sell-by date, you mean they are no longer effective, interesting, or useful. *When you get to my age you start to feel past your sell-by date.* N-COUNT / PHRASE

sell·er /'selə/ **sellers.** 1 A seller of a type of thing is a person or company that sells that type of thing. *...Kraft, the largest seller of cheese in the United States.* 2 In a business deal, the seller is the person who is selling something to someone else. *Housing became a seller's market, and prices zoomed up.* 3 If you describe a product as, for example, a big seller, you mean that large numbers of it are being sold. ● See also best seller. ◆◆◇◇◇ N-COUNT: n N, N of n / N-COUNT / N-COUNT: adj N

'selling point, selling points. A selling point is a desirable quality or feature that something has which makes it likely that people will want to buy it. N-COUNT

'selling price, selling prices. The **selling price** N-COUNT
of something is the price for which it is sold.

'sell-off, sell-offs; also spelled **selloff**. The **sell-off** ◆◇◇◇◇
of something, for example a state-owned industry, N-COUNT
is the selling of it. *Labour yesterday set out its alter-*
native to the rail sell-off.

Sel·lo·tape /'seləteɪp/. **Sellotape** is a clear sticky N-UNCOUNT
tape that you use to stick paper or card together or BRITISH
onto a wall. The American term is **Scotch tape**. **Sel-**
lotape and **Scotch tape** are trademarks.

'sell-out, sell-outs; also spelled **sellout**. **1** If a ◆◇◇◇◇
play, sports event, or other entertainment is a **sell-** N-COUNT
out, all the tickets for it are sold. *Their concert there*
was a sell-out. **2** If you describe someone's behav- N-COUNT
iour as a **sell-out**, you disapprove of the fact that PRAGMATICS
they have done something which used to be against
their principles. *He denounced the summit agree-*
ment as a sell-out.

selves /selvz/. **Selves** is the plural of **self**.

se·man·tic /sɪ'mæntɪk/. **Semantic** is used to de- ADJ
scribe something which concerns the meaning of
words and sentences. *He did not want to enter into*
a semantic debate.

se·man·tics /sɪ'mæntɪks/. The form **semantic** is N-UNCOUNT
used as a modifier. **Semantics** is the branch of linguistics that deals with the meaning of words or
sentences in isolation. Compare **pragmatics**.

sem·blance /'semblans/. If there is a **semblance** ◆◇◇◇◇
of a particular condition or quality, it appears to ex- N-COUNT:
ist, even though in fact it may not. *A semblance of* N of n
normality has been restored to parts of the country.

se·men /'siːmen/. **Semen** is the liquid containing ◆◇◇◇◇
sperm that is produced by the male sex organs. N-UNCOUNT

se·mes·ter /sɪ'mestə/ **semesters.** In colleges and N-COUNT
universities in some countries, a **semester** is one of
the two periods into which the year is divided.

semi /'semɪ/ **semis.** **1** A **semi** is a semi-detached ◆◇◇◇◇
house. *The properties range from council flats and* N-COUNT
suburban semis to stately homes. **2** In a sporting BRITISH
competition, the **semis** are the semi-finals. *He* INFORMAL
reached the semis after beating Lendl.

semi- /'semi-/. **Semi-** combines with adjectives and PREFIX
nouns to form other adjectives and nouns that describe someone or something as being partly, but
not completely, in a particular state. *He found*
Isabel's room in semi-darkness.

'semi-circle, semi-circles; also **semicircle**. A N-COUNT
semi-circle is one half of a circle, or something having the shape of half a circle.

,semi-'circular; also spelled **semicircular**. Some- ADJ
thing that is **semi-circular** has the shape of a semi-
circle. *...a semi-circular amphitheatre.*

'semi-colon, semi-colons. A **semi-colon** is the N-COUNT
punctuation mark (;) which is used in writing to
separate different parts of a sentence or list or to indicate a pause.

semi·con·duc·tor /ˌsemikən'dʌktə/ **semicon-** ◆◇◇◇◇
ductors; also spelled **semi-conductor**. A **semicon-** N-COUNT
ductor is a substance used in electronics whose
ability to conduct electricity increases with greater
heat.

,semi-de'tached. A **semi-detached** house is a ADJ
house that is joined to another house on one side BRITISH
by a shared wall. See picture headed **house and flat**.

'semi-final, semi-finals. A **semi-final** is one of ◆◆◇◇◇
the two matches or races in a competition that are N-COUNT
held to decide who will compete in the final. ▶ The N-PLURAL
semi-finals is the round of a competition in which
these two matches or races are held. *He was beaten*
in the semi-finals by Chris Dittmar.

,semi-'finalist, semi-finalists. A **semi-finalist** is N-COUNT
a player, athlete, or team that is competing in a
semi-final.

semi·nal /'semɪnəl/. **Seminal** is used to describe ◆◇◇◇◇
things such as books or events that have a great in- ADJ
fluence in a particular field. *...author of the seminal* SEMINAL
book 'Animal Liberation'.

semi·nar /'semɪnɑː/ **seminars.** **1** A **seminar** is a ◆◆◇◇◇
meeting where a group of people discuss a problem N-COUNT
or topic. *We run a lot of seminars and training*

courses for women. **2** A **seminar** is a class at a col- N-COUNT
lege or university in which the teacher and a small
group of students discuss a topic.

semi·nary /'semɪnəri, AM -neri/ **seminaries.** A N-COUNT
seminary is a college where priests or rabbis are
trained.

,semi-'precious. **Semi-precious** stones are stones ADJ
such as turquoises and agates that are used in jewellery but that are less valuable than precious stones
such as diamonds and rubies.

,semi-pro'fessional. **Semi-professional** sports ADJ
players, musicians, and singers receive some money
for playing their sport or for performing but they
also have an ordinary job as well.

,semi-'skilled; also spelled **semiskilled**. A **semi-** ADJ
skilled worker has some training and skills, but not
enough to do specialized work.

Se·mit·ic /sɪ'mɪtɪk/. **1** Semitic languages are a ◆◇◇◇◇
group of languages that include Arabic and Hebrew. ADJ
2 Semitic people belong to one of the groups of ADJ
people who speak a Semitic language. **3** Semitic is ADJ
sometimes used to mean Jewish. ● **anti-Semite:** see
anti-Semite.

semi·tone /'semitəʊn/ **semitones.** In Western N-COUNT
music, a **semitone** is the smallest interval between
two musical notes. Two semitones are equal to one
tone.

semo·li·na /ˌsemə'liːnə/. **Semolina** consists of N-UNCOUNT
small hard grains of wheat that are used for making
foods such as spaghetti and for making sweet puddings with milk.

Sen·ate /'senɪt/ **Senates.** **1** The Senate is the ◆◆◆◇
smaller and more important of the two councils in N-COLL:
the government of some countries, for example in PROPER
the United States and Australia. **2** The Senate is the N-COLL:
governing council at some universities. PROPER

sena·tor /'senɪtə/ **senators.** A **senator** is a mem- ◆◇◇◇◇
ber of a law-making Senate. N-COUNT

sena·to·rial /ˌsenɪ'tɔːriəl/. **Senatorial** means be- ADJ: ADJ n
longing to or relating to a Senate. *He has senatorial* FORMAL
experience in defence and foreign policy.

send /send/ **sends, sending, sent. 1** When you ◆◆◆◆
send someone something, you arrange for it to be VERB: V n n
taken and delivered to them. *I sent a copy to the* V n to n
minister for transport... Sir Denis took one look and be V-ed from n
sent it back... More than half a million sheep are Also V n
sent from Britain to Europe for slaughter every year.*
2 If you **send** someone somewhere, you tell them to VERB
go there. *Inspector Banbury came up to see her, but* V n with adv
she sent him away. ...the government's decision to V n to/for n
send troops to the region... I suggested that he rest, Also be V-ed
and sent him for an X-ray.* **3** If you **send** someone to from n
an institution such as a school or a prison, you ar- VERB:
range for them to stay there for a period of time. V n to n

4 To **send** a signal means to cause it to go to a place by VERB: V n
means of radio waves or electricity. *The transmitters* V n to n
will send a signal automatically to a local base sta-* V n with adv
tion... Luna II sent back the first pictures of the dark Also V n
side of the moon.* **5** If something **sends** things or peo- VERB
ple in a particular direction, it causes them to move in V n -ing
that direction. *The explosion sent shrapnel flying* Also V n prep
through the sides of cars.* **6** If something **sends** some- VERB:
one or something into a particular state, it causes V n into n
them to be in that state. *...before civil war and famine* V n -ing
sent the country plunging into anarchy.* **7** ● to **send** Also V n adj
someone **packing:** see **pack.**

send away for. To **send away for** something PHRASAL VB
means the same as to **send for** something. *She sent* V P P n
away for a collection of china birds.*

send down. If someone who is on trial **is sent** PHRASAL VB
down, they are convicted and sent to prison. be V-ed P
BRITISH

send for. 1 If you **send for** someone, you send them PHRASAL VB
a message asking them to come and see you. *I've sent* V P n
for the doctor.* **2** If you **send for** something, you write
and ask for it to be sent to you. *Send for your free cata-*
logue today.*

send in. 1 If you **send in** something such as a com- PHRASAL VB
petition entry, you post it to the organization con- V P noun
cerned. *Applicants are asked to send in a CV and a cov-* Also V P n
ering letter.* **2** When a government **sends in** troops or V P noun

police officers, it orders them to deal with a crisis or problem somewhere. *He has asked the government to send in troops to end the fighting.* | Also V n P

send off. 1 When you **send off** a letter or parcel, you send it somewhere by post. *He sent off copies to various people for them to read.* **2** If a footballer **is sent off**, the referee makes him or her leave the field during a game, as a punishment for seriously breaking the rules. ● See also **sending-off**. | PHRASAL VB / V P noun / Also V n P / be V-ed P / BRITISH

send off for. To **send off for** something means the same as to **send for** something. *I sent off for the Hoseasons catalogue.* | PHRASAL VB / V P P n

send on. If you **send on** something you have received, you send it to another place or person. *We co-ordinate the reports from the overseas divisions, and send them on to headquarters.* | PHRASAL VB / V n P

send out. 1 If you **send out** things such as leaflets or bills, you send them to a large number of people at the same time. *She had sent out well over four hundred invitations.* **2** To **send out** a signal, sound, light, or heat means to produce it. *The crew did not send out any distress signals.* **3** When a plant **sends out** roots or shoots, they grow. | PHRASAL VB / V P noun / Also V n P / V P noun / V P noun

send out for. If you **send out for** food, you phone and ask for it to be delivered to you. *Let's send out for a pizza.* | PHRASAL VB / V P P n

send up. If you **send** someone or something **up**, you imitate them amusingly in a way that makes them appear foolish. *...a spoof that sends up the macho world of fighter pilots.* ● See also **send-up**. | PHRASAL VB / V n P / V P noun / INFORMAL

send·er /'sendə/ **senders.** The **sender** of a letter, parcel, or radio message is the person who sent it. | ◆◇◇◇ / N-COUNT

sending-'off, sendings-off. If there is a **sending-off** during a football match, a player is told to leave the field by the referee, as a punishment for seriously breaking the rules. | N-COUNT / BRITISH

'send-off, send-offs. If a group of people give someone who is going away a **send-off**, they come together to say goodbye to them. *All the people in the buildings came to give me a rousing send-off.* | N-COUNT / INFORMAL

'send-up, send-ups. A **send-up** is a piece of writing or acting in which someone or something is amusingly imitated in a way that makes them appear foolish. *...his classic send-up of sixties rock, 'Get Crazy'.* | N-COUNT / INFORMAL, / BRITISH

se·nile /'si:naɪl/. If old people become **senile**, they become confused, and are unable to look after themselves. **♦ se·nil·ity** /sɪ'nɪlɪti/. *Alzheimer's disease causes premature senility.* | ◆◇◇◇ / ADJ-GRADED / N-UNCOUNT

senile de'mentia. Senile dementia is a mental illness that affects some old people and that causes them to become confused and to forget things. | N-UNCOUNT

sen·ior /'si:njə/ **seniors. 1** The **senior** people in an organization or profession have the highest and most important jobs. *...senior officials in the Israeli government.* **2** If someone is **senior** to you in an organization or profession, they have a more important job than you or they are considered to be superior to you. *The position had to be filled by an officer senior to Haig.* ▶ Your **seniors** are the people who are senior to you. **3 Senior** is used when indicating how much older one person is than another. For example, if someone is ten years your **senior**, they are ten years older than you. **4 Seniors** are the oldest students in a school or college who have reached an advanced level in their studies. | ◆◆◆◇ / ADJ-GRADED: / ADJ n / ADJ / N-PLURAL / N-SING: / poss N / N-COUNT / AMERICAN

senior 'citizen, senior citizens. A **senior citizen** is a person who is old enough to receive an old-age pension. | ◆◇◇◇ / N-COUNT

sen·ior·ity /ˌsi:ni'ɒrɪti, AM -'ɔːrɪti/. A person's **seniority** in an organization is the degree of importance and power that they have. *He has said he will fire editorial employees without regard to seniority.* | N-UNCOUNT

sen·sa·tion /sen'seɪʃən/ **sensations. 1** A **sensation** is a physical feeling. *...a sensation of burning or tingling.* **2 Sensation** is your ability to feel things physically, especially through your sense of touch. *The pain was so bad that she lost all sensation.* **3** You can use **sensation** to refer to the general feeling or impression caused by a particular experience. | ◆◆◇◇ / N-COUNT: / with supp / N-UNCOUNT: / supp N / N-COUNT

It's a funny sensation to know someone's talking about you. **4** If a person, event, or situation is a **sensation**, it causes great excitement or interest. *...the film that turned her into an overnight sensation.* **5** If a person, event, or situation causes **a sensation**, they cause great interest or excitement. *She was just 14 when she caused a sensation at the Montreal Olympics.* | N-COUNT / N-SING: / a N

sen·sa·tion·al /sen'seɪʃənəl/. **1** A **sensational** result, event, or situation is so remarkable that it causes great excitement and interest. *The world champions suffered a sensational defeat.* **♦ sen·sa·tion·al·ly** *The rape trial was sensationally halted yesterday.* **2** You can describe stories or reports as **sensational** if you disapprove of them because they present facts in a way that is intended to cause feelings of shock, anger, or excitement. *...sensational tabloid newspaper reports.* **3** You can describe something as **sensational** when you think that it is extremely good. *Her voice is sensational.* **♦ sensationally** *...sensationally good food.* | ◆◇◇◇ / ADJ-GRADED / ADV-GRADED / ADJ-GRADED / PRAGMATICS / ADJ / INFORMAL / ADV

sen·sa·tion·al·ism /sen'seɪʃənəlɪzəm/. **Sensationalism** is the presentation of facts or stories in a way that is intended to produce strong feelings of shock, anger, or excitement; used showing disapproval. *The report criticises the newspaper for errors and sensationalism.* **♦ sen·sa·tion·al·ist** *...sensationalist headlines.* | N-UNCOUNT / PRAGMATICS / ADJ-GRADED

sen·sa·tion·al·ize /sen'seɪʃənəlaɪz/ **sensationalizes, sensationalizing, sensationalized;** also spelled **sensationalise** in British English. If someone **sensationalizes** a situation or event, they make it seem worse or more shocking than it really is; used showing disapproval. *Local news organizations are being criticized for sensationalizing the story.* | VERB / PRAGMATICS / V n

sense /sens/ **senses, sensing, sensed. 1** Your **senses** are the physical abilities of sight, smell, hearing, touch, and taste. *...a keen sense of smell.* **2** If you **sense** something, you become aware of it or you realize it, although it is not very obvious. *She probably sensed that I wasn't telling her the whole story... Prost had sensed what might happen.* **3** If you have a **sense** that something is the case, you think that it is the case, although you may not have firm, clear evidence for this belief. *Suddenly you got this sense that people were drawing themselves away from each other.* **4** If you have a **sense of** guilt or shame, for example, you feel guilty or ashamed. *Lulled into a false sense of security, we eagerly awaited their return.* **5** If you have a **sense of** something such as duty or justice, you are aware of it and believe it is important. *She needs to regain a sense of her own worth.* **6** Someone who has a **sense** of timing or style has a natural ability with regard to timing or style. You can also say that someone has a bad **sense** of timing or style. *Her dress sense is appalling.* **7 Sense** is the ability to make good judgements and to behave sensibly. *When that doesn't work they sometimes have the sense to seek help.* **8** If you say that there is no **sense** or little **sense** in doing something, you mean that nothing useful would be gained by doing it. *There's no sense in pretending this doesn't happen.* **9** A **sense** of a word or expression is one of its possible meanings. *...a noun which has two senses.* **10 Sense** is used in several expressions to indicate how true your statement is. For example, if you say that something is true **in a sense**, you mean that it is partly true, or that it is true in one way. *He's not the leader in a political sense.* **11** If something **makes sense**, you can understand it. *He was sitting there saying, 'Yes, the figures make sense.'.* **12** When you **make sense of** something, you succeed in understanding it. *This is to help her to come to terms with her early upbringing and make sense of past experiences.* **13** If a course of action **makes sense**, it seems sensible. *It makes sense to look after yourself.* **14** If you say that someone **has come to** their **senses** or **has been brought to** their **senses**, you mean that | ◆◆◆◆◆ / N-COUNT / VERB: V n / V that / V wh / N-SING: / N that, / N of n / N-SING: / N of n / N-SING: / N of n / N-SING: / N of n / N-UNCOUNT / N-SING: / with neg, / N in -ing, / N -ing / N-COUNT / PHRASE / PRAGMATICS / PHRASE / PHRASE / PHRASE / PHRASE

S

they have stopped being foolish and are being sensible again. **15** If you say that someone **talks sense**, you mean that what they say is sensible. PHRASE

16 See also **common sense, sense of humour, sense of occasion, sixth sense. ●** to **see sense**: see **see**.

sense·less /'sensləs/. **1** If you describe an action as **senseless**, you think it is wrong because it has no purpose and produces no benefit. *...acts of senseless violence.* **2** If someone is **senseless**, they are unconscious. *They were knocked to the ground, beaten senseless and robbed.* ◆◇◇◇◇ ADJ-GRADED ADJ: ADJ after v, v-link ADJ

sense of di'rection. 1 Your **sense of direction** is your ability to know roughly where you are, or which way to go, even when you are in an unfamiliar place. *He had absolutely no sense of direction.* **2** If you say that someone has a **sense of direction**, you mean that they seem to have clear ideas about what they want to do or achieve; used showing approval. *This helped to bring new life to NATO and a new sense of direction.* N-SING / N-SING PRAGMATICS

sense of 'humour; spelled **sense of humor** in American English. Someone who has a **sense of humour** often finds things amusing, rather than being serious all the time. *He had enormous charm and a great sense of humour.* ◆◆◇◇◇ N-SING

sense of oc'casion. If there is a **sense of occasion** when a planned event takes place, people feel that something special and important is happening. *There is a great sense of occasion and a terrific standard of musicianship.* N-SING

sen·sibil·ity /ˌsensɪ'bɪlɪti/ **sensibilities. 1** Sensibility is the ability to experience deep feelings. *Everything he writes demonstrates the depth of his sensibility.* **2** Someone's **sensibility** is their tendency to be influenced or offended by things. *The challenge offended their sensibilities.* ◆◇◇◇◇ N-UNCOUNT / N-VAR

sen·sible /'sensɪbəl/. **1 Sensible** actions or decisions are good because they are based on reasons rather than emotions. *It might be sensible to get a solicitor.* ◆ **sen·sibly** /'sensɪbli/. *They have very sensibly adjusted their diet.* **2 Sensible** people behave in a sensible way. *Oh come on, let's be sensible about this.* **3 Sensible** shoes or clothes are practical and strong rather than fashionable and attractive. *Wear loose clothing and sensible footwear.* ◆ **sensibly** *They were not sensibly dressed.* ◆◆◇◇◇ ADJ-GRADED / ADV-GRADED / ADJ-GRADED / ADV-GRADED

sen·si·tive /'sensɪtɪv/. **1** If you are **sensitive** to other people's needs, problems, or feelings, you show understanding and awareness of them. *He was always so sensitive and caring.* ◆ **sen·si·tive·ly** *The abuse of women needs to be treated seriously and sensitively.* ◆ **sen·si·tiv·ity** /ˌsensɪ'tɪvɪti/. *...concern and sensitivity for each other's feelings.* **2** If you are **sensitive** about something, you are easily worried and offended when people talk about it. *Young people are very sensitive about their appearance.* ◆ **sensitivity, sensitivities** *...American political sensitivities about their country's role.* **3** A **sensitive** subject or issue needs to be dealt with carefully because it is likely to cause disagreement or make people angry or upset. *Employment is a very sensitive issue.* ◆ **sensitivity** *Due to the obvious sensitivity of the issue he would not divulge any details.* **4 Sensitive** documents or reports contain information that needs to be kept secret and dealt with carefully. *He instructed staff to shred sensitive documents.* **5** Something that is **sensitive** to a physical force, substance, or treatment is easily affected by it and often harmed by it. *...a chemical which is sensitive to light.* ◆ **sensitivity** *...the sensitivity of cells to damage by chemotherapy.* **6** A **sensitive** piece of scientific equipment is capable of measuring or recording very small changes. *...an extremely sensitive microscope.* ◆◆◆◇◇ ADJ-GRADED / ADV-GRADED / N-UNCOUNT / ADJ-GRADED / N-VAR / ADJ-GRADED / N-UNCOUNT / ADJ-GRADED / ADJ-GRADED / N-UNCOUNT / ADJ-GRADED

sen·si·tize /'sensɪtaɪz/ **sensitizes, sensitizing, sensitized;** also spelled **sensitise** in British English. **1** If you **sensitize** people to a particular problem or situation, you make them aware of it. *It seems important to sensitize people to the fact that depression is more than the blues.* **2** If a substance is VERB V n to n Also V n VB: usu passive

sensitized to something such as light or touch, it is made sensitive to it. *Skin is easily irritated, chapped, chafed, and sensitized.* be V-ed

sen·sor /'sensə/ **sensors.** A **sensor** is an instrument which reacts to certain physical conditions or impressions such as heat or light, and which is used to provide information. *...vacuum cleaners contain sensors that detect the amount of dust and type of floor.* ◆◇◇◇◇ N-COUNT

sen·so·ry /'sensəri/. **Sensory** means relating to the physical senses. *...our body's sensory system.* ◆◇◇◇◇ ADJ: ADJ n FORMAL

sen·sual /'senʃuəl/. **1** Someone or something that is **sensual** shows or suggests a great liking for physical pleasures, especially sexual pleasures. *He was a very sensual person.* ◆ **sen·su·al·ity** /ˌsenʃu'ælɪti/ *...sensuality and youth.* **2** Something that is **sensual** gives pleasure to your physical senses rather than to your mind. *...sensual dance rhythms.* ◆ **sensuality** *These perfumes have warmth and sensuality.* ◆◇◇◇◇ ADJ-GRADED / N-UNCOUNT / ADJ-GRADED / N-UNCOUNT

sen·su·ous /'senʃuəs/. **1** Something that is **sensuous** gives pleasure to the mind or body through the senses. *The film is ravishing to look at and boasts a sensuous musical score.* ◆ **sen·su·ous·ly** *She lay in the deep bath for a long time, enjoying its sensuously perfumed water.* **2** Someone or something that is **sensuous** shows or suggests a great liking for sexual pleasure. *His voice was deep but gentle, almost sensuous.* ◆ **sensuously** *The nose was straight, the mouth sensuously wide and full.* ◆◇◇◇◇ ADJ-GRADED / ADV-GRADED / ADJ-GRADED / ADV-GRADED

sent /sent/. **Sent** is the past tense and past participle of **send**.

sen·tence /'sentəns/ **sentences, sentencing, sentenced. 1** A **sentence** is a group of words which, when they are written down, begin with a capital letter and end with a full stop, question mark, or exclamation mark. Most sentences contain a subject and a verb. **2** In a law court, a **sentence** is the punishment that a person receives after they have been found guilty of a crime. *They are already serving prison sentences for their part in the assassination.* **3** When a judge **sentences** someone, he or she states in court what their punishment will be. *A military court sentenced him to death in his absence... He has admitted the charge and will be sentenced later.* **4** See also **death sentence, life sentence, suspended sentence.** ◆◆◆◇ N-COUNT / N-VAR / VERB V n to n be V-ed Also V n to-inf

sen·ti·ent /'sentiənt, -ʃənt/. A **sentient** being is capable of experiencing things through its senses. *...sentient creatures human and nonhuman alike.* ADJ FORMAL

sen·ti·ment /'sentɪmənt/ **sentiments. 1** A sentiment that people have is an attitude which is based on their thoughts and feelings. *...nationalist sentiments that threaten to split the country.* **2** A **sentiment** is an idea or feeling that someone expresses in words. *I must agree with the sentiments expressed by John Prescott.* **3** Sentiment is an emotion such as tenderness, romance, or sadness, which influences a person's behaviour. *Laura kept that letter out of sentiment.* ◆◆◇◇◇ N-VAR: supp N / N-COUNT / N-UNCOUNT

sen·ti·men·tal /ˌsentɪ'mentəl/. **1** Someone or something that is **sentimental** feels or arouses emotions such as tenderness, romance, or sadness, sometimes to an extent that is considered exaggerated and foolish. *I'm trying not to be sentimental about the past.* ◆ **sen·ti·men·tal·ly** *Childhood had less freedom and joy than we sentimentally attribute to it.* ◆ **sen·ti·men·tal·ity** /ˌsentɪmen'tælɪti/. *In this book there is no sentimentality.* **2** You use **sentimental** to describe things relating to or affecting a person's emotions. *Our paintings and photographs are of sentimental value only.* ◆◆◇◇◇ ADJ-GRADED / ADV-GRADED / N-UNCOUNT / ADJ

sen·ti·men·tal·ize /ˌsentɪ'mentəlaɪz/ **sentimentalizes, sentimentalizing, sentimentalized;** also spelled **sentimentalise** in British English. If you **sentimentalize** something, you make it seem sentimental or think about it in a sentimental way. *He's the kind of filmmaker who doesn't hesitate to over sentimentalize.* VERB: V n V

sen·ti·nel /'sentɪnəl/ **sentinels.** A sentinel is a N-COUNT sentry. DATED

sen·try /'sentri/ **sentries.** A sentry is a soldier ◆◇◇◇◇ who guards a camp or a building. *Aren't you sup-* N-COUNT *posed to be on sentry duty?*

Sep. Sep. is a written abbreviation for **September.** ◆◆◇◇◇ The more usual abbreviation is **Sept.**

sep·a·rate, separates, separating, separat- ◆◆◆◆◇ **ed.** The adjective and noun are pronounced /'sepərət/. The verb is pronounced /'sepəreɪt/. **1** If ADJ one thing is **separate** from another, there is a partition, space, or division between them, so that they are clearly two things. *Each villa has a separate sitting-room... Business bank accounts were kept separate from personal ones.* ♦ **sepa·rate·ness** N-UNCOUNT *...establishing Australia's cultural separateness from Britain.* **2** If you refer to **separate** things, you mean ADJ several different things, rather than just one thing. *Use separate chopping boards for raw meats, cooked meats, vegetables and salads... Six civilians have been killed in two separate attacks.* ♦ **sepa·rate·ly** ADV: *Cook each vegetable separately until just tender.* ADV with v PHRASE

3 When two or more people who have been together for some time **go** their **separate ways**, they go to different places or end their relationship.

4 If you **separate** people or things that are together, or V-RECIP-ERG: if they **separate**, they move apart. *...a chemical factory* V pl-n *for separating the plutonium from by-products... The* V n from n *front end of the car separated from the rest of the vehi-* V from n *cle... They separated. Stephen returned to the square.* pl-n V

5 If you **separate** people or things that have been con- V-RECIP-ERG: nected, or if one **separates** from another, the connec- V pl-n tion between them is ended. *They want to separate* V n from n *teaching from research. ...Quebec's threat to separate* V from n *from Canada.* ♦ **sepa·ra·tion** /,sepə'reɪʃən/ **sepa-** N-VAR **rations** *...a clear separation between church and state.* **6** An object, obstacle, distance, or period of VERB: time which **separates** two people, groups, or things V pl-n exists between them. *...the white-railed fence that* V n from n *separated the yard from the paddock... But a group of* getV-ed *six women and 23 children got separated from the oth-ers.* ♦ **sepa·rat·ed** *...trying their best to bring together* ADJ *those separated families.*

7 If a couple who are married or living together **sepa-** V-RECIP: **rate,** they decide to live apart. *Since I separated from* pl-n V *my husband I have gone a long way.* ♦ **separated** V from n *Most single parents are either divorced or separated.* ADJ: ♦ **separation** *They agreed to a trial separation.* v-link ADJ N-VAR

8 If you **separate** one idea or fact from another, you VERB: consider them individually and see or show the dis- V n from n tinction between them. *It is difficult to separate the* V pl-n *two aims.* ▶ **Separate out** means the same as **sepa-** PHRASAL VB **rate.** *How can one ever separate out the act from the* V P n from n *attitudes that surround it?* **9** A quality or factor that VERB *separates* one thing from another is the reason why V n from n the two things are different from each other. *What separates terrorism from other acts of violence?*

10 If a particular number of points **separate** two VERB teams or competitors, one of them is winning or has V pl-n won by that number of points. *Only three points sepa-rated the two teams.*

11 If you **separate** a group of people or things into V-ERG: smaller groups or elements, or if a group **separates**, V n into n the group is divided into smaller groups or elements. V into n *Let's separate into smaller groups... So all the colours* V *that make up white light are sent in different direc-tions and they separate.* ▶ **Separate out** means the PHRASAL VB same as **separate.** *If prepared many hours ahead, the* V P *mixture may separate out.*

12 Separates are clothes such as skirts, trousers, and N-PLURAL shirts which cover just the top half or the bottom half of your body.

separate out. If you **separate out** something from PHRASAL VB the other things it is with, you take it out. *...the ability* V P n from n *to separate out reusable elements from other waste.* Also V P noun ● See also **separate** 8, 11.

sepa·ra·tist /'sepərətɪst/ **separatists. Separatists** ◆◇◇◇ are people of an ethnic or cultural group within a N-COUNT country who want to establish their own separate government. *...the Basque separatist movement.*

♦ **sepa·ra·tism.** Separatism refers to the beliefs N-UNCOUNT and activities of separatists.

se·pia /'siːpiə/. Something that is **sepia** is deep COLOUR brown in colour, like the colour of old photographs.

Sept. Sept. is the usual written abbreviation for ◆◆◇◇◇ **September.**

Sep·tem·ber /sep'tembə/ **Septembers.** Septem- ◆◆◆◆◇ ber is the ninth month of the year in the Western N-VAR calendar. See Appendix headed **Dates.** *They re-turned to Moscow on 22 September 1930... They spent a couple of nights here last September.*

sep·tic /'septɪk/. If a wound or a part of your body ADJ becomes **septic,** it becomes infected.

sep·ti·cae·mia /,septɪ'siːmiə/. **Septicaemia** is N-UNCOUNT blood poisoning. MEDICAL

septic 'tank, septic tanks. A septic tank is an N-COUNT underground tank where faeces, urine, and other waste matter is made harmless using bacteria.

sep·tua·gen·ar·ian /,septʃuədʒɪ'neəriən/ **septua-** N-COUNT **genarians.** A septuagenarian is a person between FORMAL 70 and 79 years old.

se·pul·chral /sɪ'pʌlkrəl/. Something that is **sepul-** ADJ-GRADED **chral** is gloomy and solemn. *'He's gone,' Rory whis-* LITERARY *pered in sepulchral tones.*

sep·ul·chre /'sepəlkə/ **sepulchres;** spelled **sepul-** N-COUNT **cher** in American English. A **sepulchre** is a large LITERARY tomb in which a dead person is buried.

se·quel /'siːkwəl/ **sequels. 1** A book or film which ◆◇◇◇ is a **sequel** to an earlier one continues the story of N-COUNT the earlier one. **2** The **sequel** to something that has N-COUNT happened is an event or situation that happens af-ter it or as a result of it. *The clash was a sequel to yesterday's nationwide strike.*

se·quence /'siːkwəns/ **sequences. 1** A sequence ◆◆◇◇ of events or things is a number of them that come N-COUNT one after another in a particular order. *...the se-quence of events which led to the murder.* **2** A par- N-COUNT ticular **sequence** is a particular order in which things happen or are arranged. *...the colour se-quence yellow, orange, purple, blue, green and white.* **3** A film **sequence** is a part of a film that shows a N-COUNT single set of actions.

se·quenc·er /'siːkwənsə/ **sequencers.** A se- N-COUNT **quencer** is an electronic instrument that can be used for recording and storing sounds so that they can be replayed as part of a new piece of music.

se·quen·tial /sɪ'kwenʃəl/. Something that is **se-** ADJ **quential** follows a fixed order and therefore forms a FORMAL pattern. *...the sequential story of the universe.*

se·ques·ter /sɪ'kwestə/ **sequesters, sequester-** VERB **ing, sequestered. 1 Sequester** means the same VERB as **sequestrate.** *Everything he owned was seques-* be V-ed *tered.* **2** If someone **is sequestered** somewhere, they Also V n are isolated from other people. *This jury is expected* VERB *to be sequestered for at least two months.* be V-ed

se·ques·tered /sɪ'kwestəd/. A **sequestered** place is ADJ-GRADED quiet, undisturbed, and far away from other people LITERARY and places.

se·ques·trate /'siːkwestreɪt/ **sequestrates, se-** VERB: **questrating, sequestrated.** When property is be V-ed **sequestrated,** it is taken officially from someone who has debts, usually after a decision in a court of law. If the debts are paid off, the property is re-turned to its owner. ♦ **se·ques·tra·tion** N-UNCOUNT /,siːkwe'streɪʃən/. *...the sequestration of large areas of land.*

se·quin /'siːkwɪn/ **sequins. Sequins** are small N-COUNT shiny discs that are sewn on clothes to decorate them. ♦ **se·quinned** *...a sequinned dress.* ADJ

Serbo-Croat /,sɜːbəʊ'krəʊæt/. **Serbo-Croat** is one N-UNCOUNT of the languages spoken in the former Yugoslavia.

ser·enade /,serɪ'neɪd/ **serenades, serenading,** ◆◇◇◇ **serenaded. 1** If one person **serenades** another, VERB they sing or play a piece of music for them. *A blond* V n *boy dressed in white serenaded the company on the flute.* ▶ Also a noun. *Placido Domingo sang his ser-* N-COUNT *enade of love.* **2** In classical music, a **serenade** is a N-COUNT piece in several parts written for a small orchestra.

ser·en·dip·ity /,seren'dɪpɪti/. **Serendipity** is the N-UNCOUNT luck some people have in finding or creating inter- LITERARY

S

esting or valuable things by chance. *Some of the best effects in my garden have been the result of serendipity.* ♦ **ser·en·dipi·tous** /ˌserenˈdɪpɪtəs/. *...her serendipitous choice of careers as an antique dealer.* ADJ-GRADED

se·rene /sɪˈriːn/. Someone or something that is **serene** is calm and quiet. *He didn't speak much, he just smiled with that serene smile of his.* ♦ **se·rene·ly** *She carried on serenely sipping her gin and tonic.* ♦ **se·ren·ity** /sɪˈrenɪti/. *I had a wonderful feeling of peace and serenity when I saw my husband.* ◆◇◇◇◇ ADJ-GRADED / ADV-GRADED / N-UNCOUNT

serf /sɜːf/ **serfs.** In former times, **serfs** were a class of people who had to work on their master's land and could not leave without his permission. ♦ **serf·dom** /ˈsɜːfdəm/. The system of **serfdom** was the social and economic system by which the land was cultivated by serfs. N-COUNT / N-UNCOUNT

serge /sɜːdʒ/. **Serge** is strong woollen cloth. N-UNCOUNT

ser·geant /ˈsɑːdʒənt/ **sergeants. 1** A **sergeant** is an officer of middle rank in the army or air force. **2** A **sergeant** is an officer in the police force. *Sergeant Wright pulled out his gun.* ◆◆◇◇◇ N-TITLE; N-VOC / N-TITLE; N-VOC

'sergeant major, sergeant majors. A **sergeant major** is a high-ranking army officer. N-TITLE; N-VOC

se·rial /ˈsɪəriəl/ **serials. 1** A **serial** is a story which is broadcast on television or radio or published in a magazine in a number of parts over a period of time. **2 Serial** killings or attacks are a series of killings or attacks committed by the same person. This person is known as a **serial** killer or attacker. ◆◆◇◇◇ N-COUNT / ADJ: ADJ n

se·rial·ize /ˈsɪəriəlaɪz/ **serializes, serializing, serialized;** also spelled **serialise** in British English. If a book is **serialized**, it is broadcast on the radio or television or published in a magazine in a number of parts. ♦ **se·riali·za·tion** /ˌsɪəriəlaɪˈzeɪʃən/. *...the serialization of Andrew Morton's book about Princess Di.* VERB: be V-ed / N-UNCOUNT

'serial number, serial numbers. The **serial number** of an object is a number on that object which identifies it. N-COUNT

se·ries /ˈsɪəriːz/. **series** is both the singular and plural form. **1** A **series** of things or events is a number of them that come one after the other. *...a series of explosions.* **2** A radio or television **series** is a set of programmes of a particular kind which have the same title. ◆◆◆◇ N-COUNT / N-COUNT

se·ri·ous /ˈsɪəriəs/. **1 Serious** problems or situations are very bad and cause people to be worried or afraid. *Crime is an increasingly serious problem in Russian society... His condition was serious but stable.* ♦ **se·ri·ous·ly** *They are not thought to be seriously hurt.* ♦ **se·ri·ous·ness** *...the seriousness of the crisis.* **2 Serious** matters are important and deserve careful and thoughtful consideration. *Don't laugh boy. This is serious.* **3** When important matters are dealt with in a **serious** way, they are given careful and thoughtful consideration. *It was a question which deserved serious consideration.* ♦ **seriously** *The management will have to think seriously about their positions.* **4 Serious** music or literature requires concentration to understand or appreciate it. *...serious classical music. ...a serious newspaper.* **5** If someone is **serious** about something, they are sincere about what they are saying, doing, or intending to do. *You really are serious about this, aren't you?.* ♦ **seriously** *Are you seriously jealous of Erica?* ♦ **seriousness** *In all seriousness, there is nothing else I can do.* **6 Serious** people are thoughtful and quiet, and do not laugh very often. ♦ **seriously** *They spoke to me very seriously but politely.* **7 Serious** money is a very large amount of money. *He started earning serious money only in the sixties.* ♦ **seriously** *What's it like to be seriously rich at 15?* ◆◆◆◆◆ ADJ-GRADED / ADV-GRADED / N-UNCOUNT / ADJ-GRADED / ADV-GRADED: ADV with v / ADJ: ADJ n / ADJ-GRADED / ADV / N-UNCOUNT / ADJ-GRADED / ADV-GRADED: ADV with v / ADJ: ADJ n; INFORMAL / ADV: ADV adj

se·ri·ous·ly /ˈsɪəriəsli/. **1** You use **seriously** to indicate that you are not joking and that you really mean what you say. *Seriously, I only smoke in the evenings.* **2** You say **'seriously'** when you are surprised by what someone has said, as a way of asking ◆◆◇◇◇ ADV; ADV with cl / CONVENTION SPOKEN

them if they really mean it. *'I tried to chat him up at the general store.' He laughed. 'Seriously?'* **3** See also **serious. 4** If you **take** someone or something **seriously**, you believe that they are important and deserve attention. *The phrase was not meant to be taken seriously.* PHRASE

ser·mon /ˈsɜːmən/ **sermons.** A **sermon** is a talk on a religious or moral subject that is given by a member of the clergy as part of a church service. ◆◇◇◇◇ N-COUNT

ser·pent /ˈsɜːpənt/ **serpents.** A **serpent** is a snake. *...the serpent in the Garden of Eden.* ◆◇◇◇◇ N-COUNT LITERARY

ser·pen·tine /ˈsɜːpəntaɪn/. Something that is **serpentine** is curving and winding in shape, like a snake when it moves. *...serpentine woodland pathways.* ADJ-GRADED LITERARY

ser·rat·ed /seˈreɪtɪd/. A **serrated** knife or blade has a row of V-shaped points along the edge. ADJ

ser·ried /ˈserid/. **Serried** things or people are closely crowded together in rows. *...serried rows of law books.* ADJ: ADJ n LITERARY

se·rum /ˈsɪərəm/ **serums. 1** A **serum** is a liquid that is injected into someone's blood to protect them against a poison or disease. **2 Serum** is the watery pale yellow part of blood. ◆◇◇◇◇ N-VAR / N-UNCOUNT

serv·ant /ˈsɜːvənt/ **servants. 1** A **servant** is someone who is employed to work in another person's house, for example as a cleaner or a gardener. **2** You can use the word **servant** to refer to someone or something that provides a service for people or can be used by them. *Like any other public servants, police must respond to public demand.* ● See also **civil servant.** ◆◆◆◇ N-COUNT / N-COUNT

serve /sɜːv/ **serves, serving, served. 1** If you **serve** your country, an organization, or a person, you do useful work for them. *...soldiers who have served their country well... I would serve the Party in any way it felt appropriate.* **2** If you **serve** in a particular place or as a particular official, you perform official duties, especially in the armed forces, as a civil servant, or as a politician. *During the second world war he served with RAF Coastal Command.* **3** If something **serves** as a particular thing or **serves** a particular purpose, it performs a particular function, which is often not its intended function. *I really do not think that an inquiry would serve any useful purpose... Their brief visit has served to underline the deep differences between the two countries.* **4** If something **serves** people or an area, it provides them with something that they need. *...small businesses which serve the community. ...the public water-supply system serving the Nairobi area.* **5** Something that **serves** someone's interests benefits them. *The economy should be organized to serve the interests of all the people.* **6** When you **serve** food and drink, you give it to people. *Serve it with French bread. ...the pleasure of having someone serve you champagne and caviar in bed... She's been helping to serve food to hostage families.* ► **Serve up** means the same as **serve.** *He served it up on delicate white plates.* **7 Serve** is used to indicate how much food a recipe produces. For example, a recipe that **serves** six provides enough food for six people. ● See also **serving. 8** Someone who **serves** customers in a shop or a bar helps them and provides them with what they want to buy. *They wouldn't serve me in any pubs because I looked too young.* **9** When the police or other officials **serve** someone with a legal order, they give or send the legal order to them. *Police said they had been unable to serve a summons on 25-year-old Lee Jones.* **10** If you **serve** something such as a prison sentence or an apprenticeship, you spend a period of time doing it. *...Leo, who is currently serving a life sentence for murder.* **11** When you **serve** in games such as tennis and badminton, you throw up the ball or shuttlecock and hit it to start play. *He served 17 double faults.* ► Also a noun. *His second serve clipped the net.* ♦ **serv·er, servers** *...a brilliant server and volleyer.* **12** When you describe someone's **serve,** you are indicating how ◆◆◆◆◇ VERB: V n / VERB: V prep/adv / VERB: V as/for n; V n; V to-inf; Also V n as/for n / VERB: V n / VERB: V n / VERB: V n; V n prep/adj; V n to n / PHRASAL VB: V n P; VB: no cont; V n / VERB: V n; Also V / VERB: V n with n; V n on n; Also V n; LEGAL / VERB: V n / VERB: V; V n / N-COUNT / N-COUNT / N-COUNT

well or how fast they serve a ball or shuttlecock. *She has the most powerful serve in women's tennis.*

13 If you say **it serves** someone **right** when something unpleasant happens to them, you mean that it is their own fault and you have no sympathy for them. *Serves her right for being so stubborn.* PHRASE PRAGMATICS

serve out. If someone **serves out** their term of office, contract, or prison sentence, they do not leave before the end of the agreed period of time. *I was resigned to serving out the sentence.* PHRASAL VB V P noun

serve up. See serve 6. PHRASAL VB

serv·er /'sɜːvə/ **servers. 1** A **server** is something such as a fork or spoon that is used for serving food. *...salad servers.* ◆◇◇◇◇ N-COUNT

2 A **server** is part of a computer network which does a particular task, for example storing or processing information, for all or part of the network. N-COUNT

serv·ice /'sɜːvɪs/ **services, servicing, serviced. 1** A **service** is something that the public needs, such as transport, communications facilities, hospitals, or energy supplies, which is provided in a planned and organized way by the government or an official body. *Britain still boasts the cheapest postal service... They will attempt to maintain essential services.* **2** You can sometimes refer to an organization or private company as a particular **service** when it provides something for the public or acts on behalf of the government. *...the BBC World Service. ...Careers Advisory Services.* **3 Services** are activities such as tourism, banking, and which contribute to a country's economy, but which are not directly concerned with producing or manufacturing goods. *Mining rose by 9.1%, manufacturing by 9.4% and services by 4.3%.* **4** If an organization or company provides a particular **service**, they can do a particular job or a type of work for you. *The kitchen maintains a twenty-four hour service.* **5** Your **services** are the things that you do or the skills that you use in your job, which other people find useful and are usually willing to pay you for. *I have obtained the services of a top photographer.* **6** If someone or something is **at the service of** a person or organization, they are fully available to help or to be used by that person or organization. *The intellectual and moral potential of the world's culture must be put at the service of politics.* **7** You can use '**at your service**' after your name as a way of introducing yourself to someone and saying that you are willing to help them in any way you can. *She bowed dramatically. 'Anastasia Krupnik, at your service,' she said.* **8** If someone or something is **of service** to you, they help you or are useful to you. *That is, after all, the primary reason we live – to be of service to others.* ◆◆◆◆◆ N-COUNT / N-COUNT / N-PLURAL / N-COUNT / N-PLURAL: with poss / PHRASE / CONVENTION PRAGMATICS FORMAL / PHRASE

9 The level or standard of **service** provided by an organization or company is the amount or quality of the work it can do for you. *Taking risks is the only way employees can provide effective and efficient customer service.* N-UNCOUNT

10 A bus or train **service** is a route or regular journey that is part of a transport system. N-COUNT

11 If you refer to someone's **service** or **services** to a particular organization or activity, you mean that they have done a lot of work for it or devoted a lot of their time to it. *More than half his long service in parliament has been as a cabinet minister.* N-UNCOUNT: also N in pl

12 The **Services** are the army, the navy, and the air force. **13 Service** is the work done by people or equipment in the army, navy, or air force, for example during a war. *...an aircraft carrier that saw service in World War II.* N-COUNT / N-UNCOUNT

14 When you receive **service** in a restaurant, hotel, or shop, an employee asks you what you want or gives you what you have ordered. *A five-course meal including coffee, service and VAT is £25.* N-UNCOUNT

15 A **service** is a religious ceremony that takes place in a church with a congregation present. N-COUNT: also no det

16 A dinner **service** or a tea **service** is a complete set of plates, cups, saucers, and other pieces of china. N-COUNT

17 A **services** is a place where you can stop on a motorway and where there is a petrol station, a res- N-COUNT BRITISH

taurant, a shop, and toilets. The plural **services** can be used to refer either to one or to more than one of these places. *...a motorway services.*

18 In tennis, badminton, and some other sports, when it is your **service**, it is your turn to serve. N-COUNT

19 Service is used to describe parts of a building or structure that are used by people such as technical and maintenance staff, and not usually by the public. *...the service lift.* ADJ: ADJ n

20 If someone is in **service**, they are working as a servant. *If a young woman did not have a dowry, she went into domestic service.* N-UNCOUNT

21 If you have a vehicle or machine **serviced**, you arrange for someone to examine, adjust, and clean it so that it will keep working efficiently and safely. *Make sure that all gas fires and central heating boilers are serviced annually.* ▶ Also a noun. *The car is nearly due for a service.* VERB: have n V-ed be V-ed Also V n / N-COUNT

22 If a country or organization **services** its debts, it pays the interest on them. *Almost a quarter of the country's export earnings go to service a foreign debt of $29 billion.* VERB V n

23 If someone or something **services** something such as an organization, a project or a group of people, they provide it with things that it needs in order to function properly or effectively. *There are now 400 staff at headquarters, servicing our regional and overseas work.* VERB V n

24 If you **do** someone **a service**, you do something that helps or benefits them. *You are doing me a great service, and I'm very grateful to you.* **25** If a piece of equipment or a vehicle is **in service**, it is being used or is able to be used. If it is **out of service**, it is not being used, usually because it is not working properly. PHRASE / PHRASE

26 ● **be pressed into service**: see **press.**

27 See also **active service, Civil Service, community service, emergency services, in-service, National Health Service, national service, public service, room service.**

serv·ice·able /'sɜːvɪsəbəl/. If you describe something as **serviceable**, you mean that it is good enough to be used and to perform its function adequately. *His Arabic was not as good as his English, but serviceable enough.* ADJ-GRADED

'**service area, service areas.** A **service area** is an area beside a motorway where you can stop and buy petrol and something to eat. N-COUNT

'**service charge, service charges.** A **service charge** is an amount that is added to your bill in a restaurant to pay for the work of the waiter or waitress who serves you. N-COUNT BRITISH

'**service industry, service industries.** A **service industry** is an industry such as banking or insurance that provides a service but does not produce anything. ◆◇◇◇◇ N-COUNT

ser·vice·man /'sɜːvɪsmən/ **servicemen.** A **serviceman** is a man who is in the army, navy, or air force. ◆◆◇◇◇ N-COUNT

'**service station, service stations.** A **service station** is a garage that sells things such as petrol, oil, spare parts, and sometimes things to eat. N-COUNT

ser·vi·ette /ˌsɜːviˈet/ **serviettes.** A **serviette** is a square of cloth or paper that you use to protect your clothes or to wipe your mouth when you are eating. The usual American term is **table napkin.** N-COUNT BRITISH

ser·vile /'sɜːvaɪl, AM -vəl/. If you say that someone is **servile**, you disapprove of them because they are too eager to obey someone or do things for them. *He was subservient and servile.* ♦ **ser·vil·ity** /sɜːˈvɪlɪti/. *She's a curious mixture of stubbornness and servility.* ADJ-GRADED PRAGMATICS / N-UNCOUNT

serv·ing /'sɜːvɪŋ/ **servings.** A **serving** is an amount of food that is given to one person at a meal. *Each serving contains 240 calories.* ◆◇◇◇◇ N-COUNT

ser·vi·tude /'sɜːvɪtjuːd, AM -tuːd/. **Servitude** is the condition of being a slave or of being completely under the control of someone else. *None will be held in slavery or servitude.* N-UNCOUNT

S

sesa·me /'sesəmi/. **Sesame** is a plant grown for its seeds and oil which are used in cooking. *...sesame seeds.*
◆◇◇◇◇ N-UNCOUNT

ses·sion /'seʃən/ **sessions. 1** A **session** is a meeting of a court, parliament, or other official group. *...an emergency session of parliament... The court was in session.* **2** A **session** is a period during which the meetings of a court, parliament, or other official group are regularly held. *From September until December, Congress remained in session.* **3** A **session** of a particular activity is a period of that activity. *The two leaders emerged for a photo session.*
◆◆◆◇ N-COUNT: also *in* N

N-COUNT: also *in* N

N-COUNT

4 Musicians are employed to play backing music in recording studios.
ADJ: ADJ n

set 1 noun uses

set /set/ **sets. 1** A **set** of things is a number of things that belong together or that are thought of as a group. *There must be one set of laws for the whole of the country... Only she and Mr Cohen had complete sets of keys to the shop. ...a chess set.* **2** You can refer to a group of people as a **set** if they meet together socially or have the same interests and lifestyle. *...what the press called 'The Chelsea Set' – upper-class rakes forced by lack of cash to fraternise with criminals. ●* See also **jet set. 3** In tennis, a **set** is one of the groups of six or more games that form part of a match. **4** A band's or musician's **set** is the group of songs or tunes that they perform at a concert. **5** The **set** for a play, film, or television show is the furniture and scenery that is on the stage when the play is being performed or in the studio where filming takes place. *...stars who behave badly on set.* **6** The **set** of someone's face or part of their body is the way that it is fixed in a particular expression or position, especially one that shows determination. *Matt looked at Hugh and saw the stubbornness in the set of his shoulders.* **7** A **set** is an appliance. For example, a television set is a television.
◆◆◆◆ N-COUNT

N-SING supp N

N-COUNT

N-COUNT

N-COUNT: also *on/offN*

N-SING

N-COUNT

set 2 verb and adjective uses

set /set/ **sets, setting.** The form **set** is used in the present tense and is the past tense and past participle of the verb. **1** If you **set** something somewhere, you put it there, especially in a careful or deliberate way. *He took the case out of her hand and set it on the floor... When he set his glass down he spilled a little drink.* **2** If something is **set** in a particular place or position, it is in that place or position. *The castle is set in 25 acres of beautiful grounds.* **3** If something is **set** into a surface, it is fixed there and does not stick out. *...a gate set in a high wall.* **4** You can use **set** to say that a person or thing causes something to be in a particular condition or situation. For example, if something **sets** someone free, it causes them to be free, and if someone **sets** something doing something, they cause it to do that thing. *A phrase from the conference floor set my mind wandering... Dozens of people have been injured and many vehicles set on fire... Churchill immediately set into motion a daring plan.* **5** When you **set** a clock or control, you adjust it to a particular point or level. *Set the volume as high as possible.* **6** If you **set** a date, price, goal, or level, you decide what it will be. *The conference chairman has set a deadline of noon tomorrow... The German government has set a tight budget for next year... The pass mark is set at 50 per cent.* **7** To **set** an examination or a question paper means to decide what questions will be asked in it. **8** When someone **sets** a trap, they prepare it to catch someone or something. *He seemed to think I was setting some sort of trap for him.* **9** When someone **sets** the table, they prepare it for a meal by putting plates and cutlery on it. **10** If you **set** something such as a record, an example, or a precedent, you create it for people to copy or to try to achieve. *They set the pace in cutting ozone-damaging emissions... If you are smoking in front of the children then you are setting them a bad example.* **11** If someone **sets** you a task or aim or if you **set** yourself a task or aim, you have to do that task or achieve
◆◆◆◆◆

VERB V n prep V n with adv

ADJ: v-link ADJ prep/adv ADJ: v-link ADJ prep/adv

VERB V n -ing *be* V-ed adj/ adv V n with prep

VERB: V n V n adv/prep

VERB V n *be* V-ed adv

VERB: V n

VERB: V n V n for n

VERB: V n

VERB V n V n n

VERB V pron-refl n Also V n n

that aim. *The secret to happiness is to keep setting yourself new challenges.*

12 If a play, film, or story is **set** in a particular place or period of time, the events in it take place in that place or period. *The play is set in a small Midwestern town.* **13** If someone **sets** a poem or a piece of writing **to** music, they write music for the words to be sung to. **14** If someone **sets the scene** or **sets the stage** for an event to take place, they make preparations so that it can take place. *The company has been setting the stage recently for progress in the US.* **15** You use **set** to describe something which is fixed and cannot be changed. *Investors can apply for a package of shares at a set price... There is a set menu from £24.00 for two courses with coffee.* **16** A **set** book must be studied by students taking a particular course.
ADJ: v-link ADJ prep/adv VERB: V n to n

V n ton

PHRASE

ADJ

ADJ: ADJ n

17 If you are **set** to do something, you are ready to do it or are likely to do it. If something is **set** to happen, it is about to happen or likely to happen. *Roberto Baggio is set to become one of the greatest players of all-time... The talks are set to continue through the week.* **18** If you are **set on** something, you are strongly determined to do or have it. If you are **set against** something, you are strongly determined not to do or have it. *She was set on going to an all-girls school.* **19** If you **set** your face or jaw, you put on a fixed expression of determination. *He came insolently towards Mr. Won, his features set in a scowl.* **20** When something such as jelly or cement **sets**, it becomes firm or hard. *The material requires higher temperatures and pressures to set hard.* **21** When the sun **sets**, it goes below the horizon. *...the setting sun.* **22** See also **setting, set-to. 23 ●** to **set eyes on** something: see **eye. ●** to **set fire** to something: see **fire. ●** to **set foot** somewhere: see **foot. ●** to **set** your **heart on** something: see **heart. ●** to **set sail**: see **sail. ●** to **set out** one's **stall**: see **stall. ●** to **set great store by** or **on** something: see **store. ●** to **be set in** your **ways**: see **way. ●** to **set to work**: see **work.**
ADJ: v-link ADJ to-inf

ADJ: v-link ADJ on/against n/-ing

VERB V n

VERB: V V adj

VERB: V V-ing

set against. 1 If one argument or fact **is set against** another, it is considered in relation to it. *£1,000 was a considerable sum in those days and particularly when set against the maximum wage.* **2** To **set** one person **against** another means to cause them to become enemies or rivals. *The case has set neighbour against neighbour in the village.*
PHRASAL VB *be* V-ed P n Also V n P n

V n P n

set apart. If a characteristic **sets** you **apart** from other people, it makes you different from the others in a noticeable way. *Li blends right into the crowd of teenagers. Only his accent sets him apart.*
PHRASAL VB V P *from* n V n P

set aside. 1 If you **set** something **aside** for a special use or purpose, you keep it available for that use or purpose. *Some doctors advise setting aside a certain hour each day for worry.* **2** If you **set aside** a belief, principle, or feeling, you decide that you will not be influenced by it. *He urged the participants to set aside minor differences.*
PHRASAL VB V n P V P noun

V P noun Also V n P

set back. 1 If something **sets** you **back** or **sets back** a project or scheme, it causes a delay. *There will be a risk of public protest that could set back reforms.* **2** If something **sets** you **back** a certain amount of money, it costs you that much money. *In 1981 dinner for two in New York would have set you back £5.* **3** See also **setback.**
PHRASAL VB V n P V P noun V n P amount

set down. If a committee or organization **sets down** rules or guidelines for doing something, they decide what they should be and officially record them. *The Dublin Convention of June 1990 sets down rules for deciding which EC country should deal with an asylum request.*
PHRASAL VB V P noun Also V n P

set forth. 1 If you **set forth** a number of facts, beliefs, or arguments, you explain them in writing or speech in a clear, organized way. *Dr. Mesibov set forth the basis of his approach to teaching students.* **2** If you **set forth**, you start a journey.
PHRASAL VB V P noun FORMAL

V P LITERARY

set in. If something unpleasant **sets in**, it begins and seems likely to continue or develop. *Despondency is setting in.*
PHRASAL VB V P

set off. 1 When you **set off**, you start a journey. *Nichols set off for his remote farmhouse in Connecti-*
PHRASAL VB V P V P prep/adv

cut. **2** If something **sets off** something such as an alarm or a bomb, it activates it so that the alarm rings or the bomb explodes. *Someone set off a fire extinguisher.* **3** If something **sets off** an event or a series of events, it causes it to start happening. *If he attended a party without the Princess, it set off a storm of speculation.* **4** If something **sets** someone **off**, they start talking a lot because it makes them angry, or makes them remember something. *The smallest thing sets him off, and he can't stop talking about his childhood.* **5** If one colour, flavour, or object **sets off** another, it makes it look more attractive, often by providing a contrast. *Blue suits you, sets off the colour of your hair.*

   V P noun
   Also V n P

   V P noun
   Also V n P

   V n P
   Also V P noun

   V P noun
   Also V n P

set out. 1 When you **set out**, you start a journey. *When setting out on a long walk, always wear suitable boots.* **2** If you **set out** to do something, you start trying to do it. *We set out to find the truth behind the mystery.* **3** If you **set** things **out**, you arrange or display them somewhere. *She set out the cups and saucers, milk jug and sugar bowl.* **4** If you **set out** a number of facts, beliefs, or arguments, you explain them in writing or speech in a clear, organized way. *You will be given a Back To Work plan which sets out how you can best help yourself.*

   PHRASAL VB
   V P prep/adv

   V P prep/adv
   V P to-inf

   V P noun
   Also V n P

   V P noun
   V P wh
   Also V n P

set up. 1 If you **set** something **up**, you make the preparations that are necessary for it to start. *The two sides agreed to set up a commission to investigate claims.* ♦ **set·ting up** *The British government announced the setting up of a special fund.* **2** If you **set up** a temporary structure, you place it or build it somewhere. *They took to the streets, setting up roadblocks of burning tyres.* **3** If you **set up** a device or piece of machinery, you make the preparations and adjustments that are necessary for it to start working. *Setting up the camera can be tricky.*

   PHRASAL VB
   V n P
   V P noun

   N-UNCOUNT

   V P noun

   V P noun
   Also V n P

4 If you **set up** somewhere or **set** yourself **up** somewhere, you establish yourself in a new business or in a new area. *The Hong Kong-based Bank of East Asia is thinking of setting up in Canada... He worked as a dance instructor in London before setting himself up in Bucharest.* **5** If you **set up** home or **set up** shop, you buy a house or business of your own and start living or working there. *...20 businessmen hoping to set up shop in Japan.* **6** If something **sets** you **up** for something, it puts you in a good condition or position to deal with it. *The win sets you up perfectly for the match in Belgium.* **7** If you **are set up** by someone, they make it seem that you have done something wrong when you have not. *He claimed yesterday that he had been set up after drugs were discovered at his home.* **8** See also **set-up.**

   V P prep/adv
   V pron-refl P
   prep/adv
   Also V n P
   prep/adv

   V P n

   V n P

   be V-ed P
   Also V n P
   INFORMAL

set upon. If you **are set upon** by people, they make a sudden and unexpected physical attack on you.

   PHRASAL VB
   be V-ed

'set-aside. In the European Union, **set-aside** is a scheme in which an area of land is taken out of production in order to reduce surpluses or maintain the price of a specific crop. *...set-aside land.*

   N-UNCOUNT

set·back /'setbæk/ **setbacks;** also spelled **set-back.** A **setback** is an event that delays your progress or reverses some of the progress that you have made. *He has suffered a serious setback in his political career.*

   ♦◆◇◇◇
   N-COUNT

set 'piece,   set pieces; also spelled **set-piece.** **1** A **set piece** is an occasion such as a battle or a move in a football match that is planned and carried out in an ordered way. *The first three Oldham goals came from set-pieces.* **2** A **set piece** is a part of a film or novel which has a strong dramatic effect and which is often not an essential part of the main story.

   ◆◇◇◇◇
   N-COUNT

   N-COUNT

sett /set/ **setts.** A **sett** is the place where a badger lives.

   N-COUNT

set·tee /se'tiː/ **settees.** A **settee** is a long comfortable seat with a back and arms, which two or more people can sit on.

   ◆◇◇◇◇
   N-COUNT

set·ter /'setə/ **setters.** A **setter** is a long-haired dog that can be trained to show hunters where birds and animals are.

   ◆◇◇◇◇
   N-COUNT

set·ting /'setɪŋ/ **settings. 1** A particular **setting** is a particular place or type of surroundings where something is or takes place. *Perth was the setting for the SNP's conference this year... The house is in a lovely setting in the Malvern hills.* **2** A **setting** is one of the positions to which the controls of a device such as a cooker or heater can be adjusted. *You can boil the fish fillets on a high setting.* **3** A table **setting** is the complete set of equipment that one person needs to eat a meal, including knives, forks, spoons, and glasses.

   N-COUNT

   N-COUNT

set·tle /'setəl/ **settles, settling, settled. 1** If two people **settle** an argument or problem, or if someone or something **settles** it, they solve it by making a decision about who is right or about what to do. *Both sides are looking for ways to settle their differences... Tomorrow's vote is unlikely to settle the question of who will replace their leader..* **2** If people **settle** a legal dispute or if they **settle**, they agree to end the dispute without going to a court of law, for example by paying some money or by apologizing. *She got much less than she would have done if she had settled out of court... His company settled with the American authorities by paying a $200 million fine.* **3** If you **settle** a bill or debt, you pay the amount that you owe. *They settled with Colin at the end of the evening.* **4** If something **is settled**, it has all been decided and arranged. *That's settled then. We'll exchange addresses tonight.* **5** When people **settle** a place or in a place, or when a government **settles** them there, they start living there permanently. *He visited Paris and eventually settled there... Paris was one of the first areas to be settled by Europeans... Thirty-thousand-million dollars is needed to settle the immigrants.* **6** If you **settle** yourself somewhere or **settle** somewhere, you sit down or make yourself comfortable. *Jessica settled into her chair with a small sigh of relief.* **7** If something **settles**, it sinks slowly down and becomes still. *A black dust settled on the walls... Tap each one firmly on your work surface to settle the mixture.* **8** If your eyes **settle** on something, you stop looking around and look at that thing for some time. **9** When birds or insects **settle on** something, they land on it from above. **10** See also **settled.** **11** ● **when the dust settles:** see **dust.** ● **to settle a score:** see **score.**

   ♦♦♦♦◇
   VERB
   V n

   VERB: *V n*
   V
   V with n

   VERB: *V n*
   V with n

   VB: usu
   passive
   be V-ed

   V-ERG
   V prep/adv
   V n
   Also V n
   prep/adv,
   V

   VERB:
   V pron-refl
   prep/adv
   V prep/adv
   V-ERG: *V*
   V n
   V prep/adv

   VERB:
   V on/upon n
   VERB:
   V on n

settle down. 1 When someone **settles down**, they start living a quiet life in one place, especially when they get married or buy a house. *Before she settled down in Portugal, she had run her own antiques shop in London.* **2** If a situation or a person that has been **settles down**, they become calm. *We saw the therapist four times, and the children have now settled down.* **3** If you **settle down** to do something or to something, you prepare to do it and concentrate on it. *They settled down to some serious work.* **4** If you **settle down** for the night, you get ready to lie down and sleep.

   PHRASAL VB
   V P
   V P prep/adv

   V p

   V P to-inf
   V P to n

   V p

settle for. If you **settle for** something, you choose or accept it, especially when it is not what you really want but there is nothing else available. *England will have to settle for third or fourth place.*

   PHRASAL VB
   V P n

settle into. If you **settle into** a new place, job, or routine, or **settle in**, you become used to it. *I'm sure they will settle in very well.*

   PHRASAL VB
   V P n
   V P

settle on. If you **settle on** a particular thing, you choose it after considering other possible choices.

   PHRASAL VB
   V P n

settle up. When you **settle up**, you pay a bill or a debt.

   PHRASAL VB
   V P

set·tled /'setəld/. **1** If you have a **settled** way of life, you stay in one place, in one job, or with one person, rather than moving around or changing. *His house was the only settled home I had as a child.* **2** A **settled** situation or system stays the same all the time. *...a period of settled weather.* **3** If you feel **settled**, you have been living or working in a place long enough to feel comfortable there.

   ♦♦◇◇◇
   ADJ-GRADED

   ADJ-GRADED

   ADJ-GRADED:
   v-link ADJ

set·tle·ment /'setəlmənt/ **settlements. 1** A **settlement** is an official agreement between two sides who were involved in a conflict or argument. *Our objective must be to secure a peace settlement.* **2** A **settlement** is an agreement to end a disagreement

   ♦♦♦♦◇
   N-COUNT

   N-COUNT

or dispute without going to a court of law, for example by offering someone money. ...*a libel settlement.* **3** A **settlement** is a place where people have come to live and have built homes. **4** The **settlement of a** group of people is the process in which they settle in a place where people from their country or ethnic group have never lived before. ...*the settlement of immigrants in the occupied territories.* — N-COUNT / N-UNCOUNT: N ofn

set·tler /ˈsetələ/ **settlers.** Settlers are people who go to live in a new country. — ◆◆◇◇◇ N-COUNT

,set·'to, set·tos A **set-to** is a dispute or fight. *This was the subject of a bit of a set-to between Smith and his record company.* — N-COUNT INFORMAL

'set-up, set-ups; also spelled **setup. 1** A particular **set-up** is a particular system or way of organizing something. *I gradually got rather disillusioned with the whole setup of the university.* **2** If you describe a situation as a **set-up**, you mean that people have planned it in order to deceive you or to make it look as if you have done something wrong. *He was asked to pick somebody up and bring them to a party, not realizing it was a setup.* — ◆◆◇◇◇ N-COUNT INFORMAL / N-COUNT INFORMAL

sev·en /ˈsevən/ **sevens. Seven** is the number 7. See Appendix headed **Numbers**. — ◆◆◆◆◆ NUMBER

sev·en·teen /ˌsevənˈtiːn/ **seventeens. Seventeen** is the number 17. See Appendix headed **Numbers**. — ◆◆◆◆◆ NUMBER

sev·en·teenth /ˌsevənˈtiːnθ/ **seventeenths. 1** The **seventeenth** item in a series is the one that you count as number seventeen. See Appendix headed **Numbers**. **2** A **seventeenth** is one of seventeen equal parts of something. See Appendix headed **Numbers**. — ◆◆◆◇ ORDINAL / FRACTION

sev·enth /ˈsevənθ/ **sevenths. 1** The **seventh** item in a series is the one that you count as number seven. See Appendix headed **Numbers**. **2** A **seventh** is one of seven equal parts of something. — ◆◆◆◆◇ ORDINAL / FRACTION

,seventh 'heaven. If you say that you are **in seventh heaven**, you mean that you are very happy. — N-UNCOUNT: in N

sev·en·ti·eth /ˈsevəntiəθ/ **seventieths. 1** The **seventieth** item in a series is the one that you count as number seventy. See Appendix headed **Numbers**. **2** A **seventieth** is one of seventy equal parts of something. — ◆◆◆◇ ORDINAL / FRACTION

sev·en·ty /ˈsevənti/ **seventies. Seventy** is the number 70. See Appendix headed **Numbers**. — ◆◆◆◆◆ NUMBER

sev·er /ˈsevə/ **severs, severing, severed. 1** To **sever** something means to cut completely through it or to cut it completely off. ...*oil still gushing from a severed fuel line.* **2** If you **sever** a relationship or connection that you have with someone, you end it suddenly and completely. *She severed her ties with England.* — VERB: V n V-ed / VERB V n

sev·er·al /ˈsevrəl/ **Several** is used to refer to an imprecise number of people or things that is not large but is greater than two. *I had lived two doors away from this family for several years... Several hundred students gathered on campus.* ▶ Also a quantifier. *According to several of their friends, their 25-year marriage has suffered some difficulties.* ▶ Also a pronoun. *No one drug will suit or work for everyone and sometimes several may have to be tried.* — ◆◆◆◆◆ DET / QUANT / PRON

sev·er·ance /ˈsevərəns/ **1 Severance** from a person or group, or the severance of a connection, involves the ending of a relationship or connection. ...*the complete severance of diplomatic relations.* **2 Severance** pay is money that a firm pays its employees as compensation when it has to stop employing them. — N-UNCOUNT FORMAL / ADJ: ADJ n

se·vere /sɪˈvɪə/ **severer, severest. 1** You use **severe** to indicate that something bad or undesirable is great or intense. *I suffered from severe bouts of depression... Shortages of professional staff are very severe in some places.* ♦ **se·vere·ly** *An aircraft overshot the runway and was severely damaged.* ♦ **se·ver·ity** /sɪˈverɪti/ *Several drugs are used to lessen the severity of the symptoms.* **2 Severe** punishments or actions are harsh and show an unforgiving attitude. *Before she could reply, my mother launched into a severe reprimand.* ♦ **severely** ...*a campaign* — ◆◆◆◆◇ ADJ-GRADED / ADV-GRADED / N-UNCOUNT / ADJ-GRADED / ADV-GRADED:

to try to change the law to punish dangerous drivers more severely. ♦ **severity** *The Bishop said he was sickened by the severity of the sentence.* **3** If you describe the appearance of someone or something as **severe**, you do not like its plain appearance and lack of decoration. *The cushions add a touch of colour in a room that might otherwise look severe.* — ADV with v / N-UNCOUNT / ADJ-GRADED PRAGMATICS

sew /səʊ/ **sews, sewing, sewed, sewn. 1** When you **sew** something such as clothes, you make them or repair them by joining pieces of cloth together by passing thread through them with a needle. *Anyone can sew on a button, including you... She taught her daughter to sew.* **2** When something such as a hand or finger **is sewn** back by a doctor, it is joined with the patient's body using a needle and thread. *Surgeons at Odstock Hospital, Wilts, sewed the thumb on.* ● See also **sewing**. — ◆◇◇◇◇ VERB: V n V n with on V / Also V n prep / VERB: be V-ed adv V n with adv

sew up. If someone **sews up** something such as a business deal, an election, or a game, they make sure that they will get the result they want. *If they didn't move fast, Johnson could sew this deal up within days.* — PHRASAL VB V n P Also V P noun INFORMAL

sew·age /ˈsuːɪdʒ/. **Sewage** is waste matter such as faeces or dirty water from homes and factories, which flows away through sewers. — ◆◇◇◇◇ N-UNCOUNT

sew·er /ˈsuːə/ **sewers.** A **sewer** is a large underground channel that carries waste matter and rain water away, usually to a place where it is treated and made harmless. — ◆◇◇◇◇ N-COUNT

sew·er·age /ˈsuːərɪdʒ/. **Sewerage** is the system by which waste matter is carried away in sewers and made harmless. ...*without access to any services such as water or sewerage.* — N-UNCOUNT

sew·ing /ˈsəʊɪŋ/. **1 Sewing** is the activity of making or mending clothes or other things using a needle and thread. **2 Sewing** is clothes or other things that are being sewn. *We all got out our own sewing and sat in front of the log fire.* — ◆◇◇◇◇ N-UNCOUNT / N-UNCOUNT

'sewing machine, sewing machines. A **sewing machine** is a machine that you use for sewing. — ◆◇◇◇◇ N-COUNT

sewn /səʊn/. **Sewn** is the past participle of **sew**.

sex /seks/ **sexes. 1** The two **sexes** are the two groups, male and female, into which people and animals are divided according to the function they have in producing young. *She found it hard to form relationships with the opposite sex.* ● See also **fair sex. 2** The **sex** of a person or animal is their characteristic of being either male or female. *She continually failed to gain promotion because of her sex.* ...*sex discrimination.* **3 Sex** is the physical activity by which people can produce young. *We have a very active sex life.* **4** If two people **have sex**, they perform the act of sex. — ◆◆◆◇ N-COUNT / N-COUNT / N-UNCOUNT / PHRASE

'sex appeal. Someone's **sex appeal** is their sexual attractiveness. — ◆◇◇◇◇ N-UNCOUNT

-sexed /-sekst/. **-sexed** is used after adverbs such as 'over' and 'under' to form adjectives which indicate that someone wants to have sex too often or not often enough. *My husband has always been a bit over-sexed.* — COMB

'sex education. Sex education is education in schools on the subject of sexual activity and sexual relationships. — ◆◇◇◇◇ N-UNCOUNT

'sex goddess, sex goddesses. If you refer to a woman, especially a film star, as a **sex goddess**, you mean that many people consider her to be sexually attractive. — N-COUNT JOURNALISM

sex·ism /ˈseksɪzəm/. **Sexism** is the belief that the members of one sex, usually women, are less intelligent or less capable than those of the other sex and need not be treated equally. It is also the behaviour which is the result of this belief. — ◆◇◇◇◇ N-UNCOUNT

sex·ist /ˈseksɪst/ **sexists.** If you describe people, things, or behaviour as **sexist**, you mean that they are influenced by the belief that the members of one sex, usually women, are less intelligent or less capable than those of the other sex and need not be treated equally; used showing disapproval. *Old-fashioned sexist attitudes are still common.* ▶ A **sexist** is someone with sexist views or behaviour. — ◆◇◇◇◇ ADJ-GRADED PRAGMATICS / N-COUNT

sex·less /'seksləs/. If you describe a person as **sex-** ADJ-GRADED
less, you mean that they have no sexual feelings or
that they are not sexually active. A **sexless** relationship does not involve sex.

'sex object, sex objects. If someone is described N-COUNT
as a **sex object**, he or she is considered only in
terms of their physical attractiveness and not their
character or abilities.

sex·olo·gist /sek'sɒlədʒɪst/ **sexologists.** A **sex-** N-COUNT
ologist is a person who studies sexual relationships
and gives advice or makes reports.

'sex shop, sex shops. A **sex shop** is a shop that N-COUNT
sells products that are associated with sexual pleasure, for example magazines, videos, and clothing.

'sex symbol, sex symbols. A **sex symbol** is a fa- N-COUNT
mous person, especially an actor or a singer, who is
considered by many people to be extremely sexually
attractive.

sex·tant /'sekstənt/ **sextants.** A **sextant** is an in- N-COUNT
strument used for measuring angles, for example
between the sun and the horizon, so that the position of a ship or aeroplane can be calculated.

sex·tet /,seks'tet/ **sextets. 1** A **sextet** is a group of N-COUNT
six musicians who play or sing together. **2** A **sextet** N-COUNT
is a piece of music written for six performers.

sex·ual /'sekʃuəl/. **1 Sexual** feelings or activities ◆◆◆◆◇
are connected with the act of sex or with people's ADJ
desire for sex. *This was the first sexual relationship I*
had had. ♦ **sex·ual·ly** *...sexually transmitted dis-* ADV
eases. **2 Sexual** means relating to the differences ADJ
between male and female people. *Womens groups*
denounced sexual discrimination. ♦ **sexually** *If* ADV:
you're sexually harassed, you ought to do something ADV with v
about it. **3 Sexual** means relating to the differences ADJ
between heterosexuals and homosexuals. *...dis-*
crimination based on sexual orientation. **4 Sexual** ADJ
means relating to the biological process by which
people and animals produce young. *Girls generally*
reach sexual maturity two years earlier than boys.
♦ **sexually** *The first organisms that reproduced sex-* ADV
ually were free-floating plankton.

,sexual 'harassment. Sexual harassment is re- ◆◇◇◇◇
peated unwelcome sexual comments, looks, or N-UNCOUNT
physical contact, usually by men against women.
This usually occurs in the workplace or in public
places.

,sexual 'intercourse. Sexual intercourse is the ◆◇◇◇◇
physical act of sex between two people. N-UNCOUNT
FORMAL

sexu·al·ity /,sekʃu'ælɪti/. **1** A person's **sexuality** is ◆◆◇◇◇
their sexual feelings. *The growing discussion of* N-UNCOUNT
women's sexuality raised its own disquiet. **2** You can N-UNCOUNT
refer to a person's **sexuality** when you are talking
about whether they are heterosexual, homosexual,
or bisexual. *He believes he has been discriminated*
against because of his sexuality.

sexy /'seksi/ **sexier, sexiest.** You can describe ◆◆◇◇◇
people and things as **sexy** if you think they are sex- ADJ-GRADED
ually exciting or sexually attractive. ♦ **sexi·ly** *He* ADV-GRADED
says I don't dress sexily enough. ♦ **sexi·ness** *Our* N-UNCOUNT
image of sexiness is changing.

SF /,es 'ef/. **SF** is the same as **science fiction.** *...SF* N-UNCOUNT
writer Ray Bradbury.

Sgt. Sgt is the written abbreviation for 'Sergeant' N-TITLE
when it is used as a title.

sh /ʃ/; also spelled **shh.** You can say **'Sh!'** to tell ◆◇◇◇◇
someone to be quiet. *Sh! You want to listen or don't* CONVENTION
you? PRAGMATICS
INFORMAL

shab·by /'ʃæbi/ **shabbier, shabbiest. 1** Shabby ◆◇◇◇◇
things or places look old and in bad condition. ADJ-GRADED
♦ **shab·bi·ly** /'ʃæbɪli/. *...a shabbily dressed young* ADV-GRADED
man. ♦ **shab·bi·ness** *...the shabbiness of the* N-UNCOUNT
building. **2** A person who is **shabby** is wearing old, ADJ-GRADED
worn clothes. **3** If you describe someone's behav- ADJ-GRADED
iour as **shabby**, you think they behave in an unfair PRAGMATICS
or unacceptable way. ♦ **shabbily** *I feel I behaved* ADV-GRADED
shabbily.

shack /ʃæk/ **shacks, shacking, shacked.** A ◆◇◇◇◇
shack is an old or flimsy hut built from tin, wood, N-COUNT
or other materials.

shack up. If you say that someone **has shacked up** PHRASAL VB

with someone else or that two people **have shacked** RECIP:
up together, you disapprove of the fact that they have V P with n
started living together as lovers. *The Government was* PRAGMATICS
keen for people to get married rather than shack up. pl-n V P
Also be V-ed P
INFORMAL

shack·le /'ʃækəl/ **shackles, shackling, shack-** ◆◇◇◇◇
led. 1 If you **are shackled** by something, it prevents VERB
you from doing what you want to do. *Many, in the* be V-ed by/to
Nineties, find themselves shackled to a high-stress n
job and a large mortgage. **2** If you throw off the FORMAL
shackles of something, you reject it or free yourself N-PLURAL:
from it because it was preventing you from doing with supp
what you wanted to do. *He had not yet thrown off* LITERARY
the intellectual shackles of Marxism. **3 Shackles** are N-PLURAL
two metal rings joined by a chain which are fas-
tened around someone's wrists or ankles in order to
prevent them from moving or escaping. **4** To **shack-** VERB: V n
le someone means to put shackles on them. *She* V-ed to n
was shackled to a wall.

shade /ʃeɪd/ **shades, shading, shaded. 1** A ◆◆◆◇◇
shade of a particular colour is any of its different N-COUNT
forms. For example, emerald green and olive green
are shades of green.
2 Shade is an area of darkness under or next to an ob- N-UNCOUNT
ject, where sunlight does not reach. *Alexis resumed his*
reading in the shade of an overhanging cliff. **3** If a VERB:
place **is shaded** by something, that thing prevents be V-ed
light from falling on it. *Most plants prefer to be lightly* be V-ed by/from n
shaded from direct, hot sunlight. ♦ **shad·ed** *These* Also V n
plants will grow happily in a sunny or partially shaded ADJ-GRADED
spot. ♦ **-shaded** *...the winding, tree-shaded driveway* COMB
of the mansion. **4** If you **shade** your eyes, you put your VERB: V n
hand or an object partly in front of your face in order
to prevent a bright light from shining into your eyes.
5 Shade is darkness or shadows as they are shown in a N-UNCOUNT
picture. *...Rembrandt's skilful use of light and shade.*
6 The **shades** of something abstract are its many, N-COUNT
slightly different forms. *...newspapers of every shade of*
opinion.
7 If something **shades** into something else, there is no VERB
clear division between the two things. *The dusk shad-* V into/to n
ed into night. LITERARY
8 Shades is an informal word for sunglasses. N-PLURAL
9 A **shade** is the same as a **lampshade. 10** A **shade** is a N-COUNT
piece of stiff cloth or heavy paper that you can pull N-COUNT
down over a window in order to prevent sunlight from AMERICAN
coming into a room. The usual British word is **blind.**
11 If you say that something is, for example, **a shade** PHRASE
unusual or **a shade** disappointing, you mean that it is
slightly unusual or disappointing. **12** If someone or PHRASE
something **puts** someone or something else **in the**
shade, they are so impressive that they make the other person or thing seem unimportant by comparison.
13 See also **shaded, shading.**

shad·ed /'ʃeɪdɪd/. A **shaded** area on something ◆◇◇◇◇
such as a map is one that is coloured darker than ADJ
the surrounding areas, so that it can be distinguished from them.

shad·ing /'ʃeɪdɪŋ/ **shadings. 1** Shading is material N-UNCOUNT
that provides shade, especially for plants. **2** Dark N-UNCOUNT
areas or patches in a picture can be referred to as
shading. 3 You can refer to very small changes or N-UNCOUNT:
differences between things as **shading** or **shadings.** also N in pl,
Their language is particularly difficult to teach be- with supp
cause of its subtle shading of tone and emphasis.
4 See also **shade.**

shad·ow /'ʃædəʊ/ **shadows, shadowing, shad-** ◆◆◆◇◇
owed. 1 A **shadow** is a dark shape on a surface N-COUNT
that is made when something stands between a
light and the surface. *An oak tree cast its shadow*
over a tiny round pool. **2 Shadow** is darkness in a N-UNCOUNT
place caused by something preventing light from
reaching it. *Most of the lake was in shadow.* **3** If VERB
something **shadows** a thing or place, it covers it V n
with a shadow. *The hood shadowed her face.*
4 If someone **shadows** you, they follow you very VERB
closely wherever you go. *Soviet spies had been shad-* V n
owing him for some time.
5 In Britain, the **Shadow** Cabinet consists of the lead- ADJ: ADJ n
ers of the main opposition party. *...the shadow chan-*

cellor. ► A cabinet member's **shadow** is the politician who has the equivalent job in the shadow cabinet. N-COUNT poss N

6 If you say that something is true without a **shadow of a doubt** or without **a shadow of doubt**, you are emphasizing that there is no doubt at all that it is true. *It was without a shadow of a doubt the best we've played.* PHRASE PRAGMATICS

7 If you live **in the shadow** of someone or **in their shadow**, their achievements and abilities are so great that you are not noticed or valued. **8** If you say that someone is **a shadow** of their **former self**, you mean that they are much less strong or capable than they used to be. PHRASE PHRASE

shad·ow·y /ˈʃædəʊi/. **1** A **shadowy** figure or shape is someone or something that you can hardly see because they are in a dark or misty place. **2** A **shadowy** place is dark or full of shadows. **3** You describe activities and people as **shadowy** when very little is known about them. ...*the shadowy world of spies.* ◆◇◇◇◇ ADJ-GRADED: ADJ n ADJ-GRADED ADJ

shady /ˈʃeɪdi/ **shadier, shadiest**. **1** You can describe a place as **shady** when you like the fact that it is sheltered from bright sunlight. **2 Shady** trees provide a lot of shade. **3** You can describe activities as **shady** when you think that they might be dishonest or illegal. *I knew that John was a bit of a shady character, but I was desperate for money.* ◆◇◇◇◇ ADJ-GRADED PRAGMATICS ADJ ADJ-GRADED

shaft /ʃɑːft, ʃæft/ **shafts**. **1** A **shaft** is a long vertical passage. ...*a lift shaft.* ...*a disused mine shaft.* **2** In a machine, a **shaft** is a rod that turns round continually in order to transfer movement in the machine. ...*a drive shaft.* ...*the propeller shaft.* **3** A **shaft** is a long thin piece of wood or metal that forms part of a spear, axe, golf club, or other object. **4** A **shaft** of light is a beam of light. ◆◆◇◇◇ N-COUNT N-COUNT N-COUNT N-COUNT

shag /ʃæg/ **shags**. A **shag** is a black seabird with a yellow beak, found in Europe and North Africa. ◆◇◇◇◇ N-COUNT

shag·gy /ˈʃægi/ **shaggier, shaggiest**. Shaggy hair or fur is long and untidy. ◆◇◇◇◇ ADJ-GRADED

shaikh /ʃeɪk/ **shaikhs**. See **sheikh**.

shake /ʃeɪk/ **shakes, shaking, shook, shaken**; the form **shook** can be used as the past participle for meaning 2 of the phrasal verb **shake up**. **1** If you **shake** something, you hold it and move it quickly backwards and forwards or up and down. You can also **shake** a person, for example, because you are angry with them or because you want them to wake up. *Shake the rugs well... As soon as he got inside, the dog shook himself.* ► Also a noun. *She picked up the cellophane bag of salad and gave it an angry shake.* **2** If you **shake** your fist or an object such as a stick at someone, you wave it in the air in front of them because you are angry with them. *The protesters burst through police lines into the cathedral square, shaking clenched fists.* **3** If a force **shakes** something, or if something **shakes**, it moves from side to side or up and down with quick, small, but sometimes violent movements. ...*an explosion that shook buildings several kilometers away.* **4** To **shake** something into a certain place or state means to bring it into that place or state by moving it quickly up and down or from side to side. *She frees her mass of hair from a rubber band and shakes it off her shoulders... Shake off any excess flour.* **5** If you **shake** your head, you turn it from side to side in order to say 'no' or to show disgust or sadness. *'Anything else?' Colum asked. Kathryn shook her head wearily.* ► Also a noun. *'The elm trees are all dying,' said Palmer, with a sad shake of his head.* **6** If you **shake hands** with someone, you hold their right hand in your own for a few moments, often moving it up and down slightly, when you are meeting them, saying goodbye to them, or congratulating them. You can also say that two people **shake hands**. *He nodded greetings to Mary Ann and Michael and shook hands with Burke.* **7** If you **shake** someone's **hand** or **shake** someone **by the hand**, you shake hands with them. **8** If you **are shaking**, or a part of your body **is shaking**, you are making quick, small movements that you cannot control, for example because you are cold or afraid. *I stood there, crying and shaking with fear.* **9** If you have **the shakes**, your body is shaking uncontrol- ◆◆◆◆◇ VERB V n V pron-refl N-COUNT VERB: V n at n V n V-ERG V n Also V VERB V n prep V n with adv Also V n adj VERB V n N-COUNT PHRASE PHRASE VERB: V V with n N-PLURAL: the N INFORMAL

lably because you are afraid or ill, or because you have drunk too much alcohol. **10** If your voice **is shaking**, you cannot control it properly and it sounds very unsteady, for example because you are nervous or angry. VERB: V

11 If an event or a piece of news **shakes** you, or **shakes** your confidence, it makes you feel shocked or upset, and unable to think calmly or clearly. *The news of Tandy's escape had shaken them all.* ► **Shake up** means the same as **shake**. *The jockey was shaken up when he was thrown twice from his horse yesterday... He was in the car when those people died. That really shook him up.* ♦ **shak·en** Unhurt, but a bit shaken, she was trying not to cry. **12** If an event **shakes** a group of people or their beliefs, it causes great uncertainty and makes them question their beliefs. *When events happen that shake these beliefs, our fear takes control.* **13** If you **shake** someone **out of** an attitude or belief that you dislike or disapprove of, you cause them to change their attitude or belief to one that is more responsible or sensible. *Many businessmen still find it hard to shake themselves out of the old state-dependent habit.* VERB V n PHRASAL VB be V-ed P V n P Also V-ed P, V P noun ADJ-GRADED VERB V n VERB V n out of n

14 A **shake** is the same as a **milkshake**. *He sent his driver to fetch him a strawberry shake.* **15** A **shake** of a liquid or a powder is a small amount of it that comes out of something such as a bottle when you shake it. *Serve with an aromatic shake of ground cinnamon added to each.* N-COUNT N-COUNT

16 ● to **shake the foundations of** something: see **foundation**.

shake down. If someone **shakes** you **down**, they use threats or search you physically in order to obtain something from you. ...*police checkpoints on highways, which were being used to shake down motorists for bribes.* PHRASAL VB V P noun Also V n P AMERICAN

shake off. 1 If you **shake off** something that you do not want such as an illness or a bad habit, you manage to recover from it or get rid of it. *Businessmen are frantically trying to shake off the bad habits learned under six decades of a protected economy.* **2** If you **shake off** someone who is following you, you manage to get away from them, for example by running faster than them. *It seems that he was unaware that they had shaken off their pursuers.* **3** If you **shake off** someone who is touching you, you move your arm or body sharply so that they are no longer touching you. *He grabbed my arm. I shook him off... She shook off his restraining hand.* PHRASAL VB V P noun Also V n P V P noun Also V n P V n P V P noun

shake out. If you **shake out** a cloth or a piece of clothing, you hold it by one of its edges and move it up and down one or more times, in order to open it out, make it flat, or remove dust. *While the water was heating she decided to shake out the carpet.* ● See also **shake-out**. PHRASAL VB V P noun Also V n P

shake up. 1 If someone **shakes up** something such as an organization, an institution, or a profession, they make major changes to it. *Directors and shareholders are preparing to shake things up in the corporate boardrooms of America.* ● See also **shake-up**. **2** See **shake** sense 11. PHRASAL VB V n P Also V P noun

shak·en /ˈʃeɪkən/. Shaken is the past participle of **shake**.

ˈshake-out, shake-outs; spelled **shakeout** in American English. A **shake-out** is a major set of changes in a system or an organization which results in a large number of companies closing or a large number of people losing their jobs. N-COUNT JOURNALISM

ˈshake-up, shake-ups; spelled **shakeup** in American English. A **shake-up** is a major set of changes in an organization or a system. ...*an unexpectedly radical shake-up of the secondary education system.* ◆◇◇◇◇ N-COUNT JOURNALISM

shaky /ˈʃeɪki/ **shakier, shakiest**. **1** If you describe a situation as **shaky**, you mean that it is weak or unstable, and seems unlikely to last long or be successful. *The Prime Minister's political position is becoming increasingly shaky.* **2** If your body or your voice is **shaky**, you cannot control it properly and it trembles, for example because you are ill or nervous. You can also describe someone's movements ◆◇◇◇◇ ADJ-GRADED ADJ-GRADED

as **shaky**. *Even small operations can leave you feeling a bit shaky.* ◆ **shaki·ly** /'ʃeɪkɪli/. *'I'm okay,' she said shakily.*

ADV-GRADED: ADV with v

shale /ʃeɪl/ **shales**. Shale is smooth soft rock that breaks easily into thin layers. ◆◇◇◇◇ N-VAR

shall /ʃəl, STRONG ʃæl/. Shall is a modal verb. It is used with the base form of a verb. ◆◆◆◆◇

1 You use **shall** with 'I' and 'we' in questions in order to make offers or suggestions, or to ask for advice. *Shall I get the keys?... Well, shall we go?... Let's have a nice little stroll, shall we?... What shall I do?*

MODAL PRAGMATICS

2 You use **shall**, usually with 'I' and 'we', when you are referring to something that you intend to do, or when you are referring to something that you are sure will happen to you in the future. *We shall be landing in Paris in sixteen minutes, exactly on time... I shall miss him terribly.*

MODAL

3 You use **shall** with 'I' or 'we' during a speech or piece of writing to say what you are going to discuss or explain later. *In Chapter 3, I shall describe some of the documentation that I gathered.*

MODAL

4 You use **shall** to indicate that something must happen, usually because of a rule or law. You use **shall not** to indicate that something must not happen. *The president shall hold office for five years... If you want to pry into other people's business you shall not do it here, young man.*

MODAL PRAGMATICS

5 You use **shall**, usually with 'you', when you are assuring someone that they will be able to do something or that something will happen. *Very well, if you want to go, go you shall... 'I want to hear all the gossip, all the scandal.'—'You shall, dearie, you shall!'.*

MODAL PRAGMATICS

6 You use **shall** with verbs such as 'look forward to' and 'hope' to say politely that you are looking forward to something or hoping to do something. *Well, we shall look forward to seeing him tomorrow.*

MODAL FORMAL

7 You use **shall** when you are referring to the likely result or consequence of a particular action or situation. *This is our last chance and we shall need to take it if we are to compete and survive.*

MODAL

8 ● **shall I say**: see **say**.

shal·lot /ʃə'lɒt/ **shallots**. Shallots are small round vegetables that are the roots of a crop and are similar to onions. They have a strong taste and are used for flavouring other food. ◆◇◇◇◇ N-VAR

shal·low /'ʃæləʊ/ **shallower, shallowest. 1** A shallow container, hole, or area of water measures only a short distance from the top to the bottom. *Put the milk in a shallow dish... The water is quite shallow for some distance.* **2** If you describe a person, piece of work, or idea as **shallow**, you disapprove of them because they do not show or involve any serious or careful thought. *The evening news is often criticized for being shallow.* ◆ **shal·low·ness** *...intellectual shallowness.* **3** If your breathing is shallow, you take only a very small amount of air into your lungs at each breath. ◆ **shal·low·ly** *He was breathing, quickly and shallowly.*

◆◇◇◇◇ ADJ-GRADED

ADJ-GRADED PRAGMATICS

N-UNCOUNT

ADJ-GRADED

ADV-GRADED

shal·lows /'ʃæləʊz/. The shallows are the shallow part of an area of water. *At dusk more fish come into the shallows.*

◆◇◇◇◇ N-PLURAL: the N

shalt /ʃəlt, STRONG ʃælt/. Shalt is an old-fashioned form of **shall**. *Thou shalt not kill.* MODAL

sham /ʃæm/ **shams**. Something that is a **sham** is not real or is not really what it seems to be; used showing disapproval. *The government's promises were exposed as a hollow sham. ...sham marriages.*

◆◇◇◇◇ N-COUNT PRAGMATICS

sham·an /'ʃeɪmən/ **shamans. 1** In some North American tribes, a **shaman** is a person who is believed to have powers to heal sick people or to rid them of evil spirits. **2** A **shaman** is a priest or priestess in shamanism.

◆◇◇◇◇ N-COUNT

N-COUNT

sham·an·ism /'ʃeɪməmɪzəm/. Shamanism is a religion based on the belief that the world is controlled by good and evil spirits, and that these spirits can be directed by people with special powers. N-UNCOUNT

sham·ble /'ʃæmbəl/ **shambles, shambling, shambled. 1** If a place, event, or situation is a **shambles** or is **in a shambles**, everything is in disorder. *The ship's interior was an utter shambles.* **2** If ◆◇◇◇◇ N-SING

VERB

you **shamble** somewhere, you walk clumsily, dragging your feet. *The conductor shambled to the next carriage.*

V prep/adv

sham·bol·ic /ʃæm'bɒlɪk/. If you describe a situation, person, or place as **shambolic**, you mean that they are very disorganized. *John lived in a stylishly shambolic artist's studio.*

ADJ-GRADED BRITISH

shame /ʃeɪm/ **shames, shaming, shamed. 1** Shame is an uncomfortable feeling that you get when you have done something wrong or embarrassing, or when someone close to you has. *She felt a deep sense of shame... I was, to my shame, a coward.* **2** If someone brings **shame** on you, they make other people lose their respect for you. *I don't want to bring shame on the family name.* **3** If something shames you, it causes you to feel shame. *Her son's affair had humiliated and shamed her.* **4** If you shame someone close to you, you make people lose their respect for that person, by behaving in an unacceptable way. *I wouldn't shame my father by trying that.* **5** You can use **shame** in expressions such as **shame on you** and **shame on him** to indicate that someone ought to feel shame for something they have said or done. *He tried to deny it. Shame on him!*

◆◆◇◇◇ N-UNCOUNT

N-UNCOUNT

VERB V n

VERB V n

CONVENTION PRAGMATICS

6 If you **shame** someone into doing something, you force them to do it by making them feel ashamed not to. *Museums have now been shamed out of selling the treasures from their collections.*

VERB V n into/out of n/-ing

7 If you say that something is a **shame**, you are expressing your regret about it and indicating that you wish it had happened differently. *It's a crying shame that police have to put up with these mindless attacks.*

N-SING: a N PRAGMATICS

8 If someone **puts** you **to shame**, they make you feel ashamed because they do something much better than you do. *His playing really put me to shame.*

PHRASE

shame·faced /'ʃeɪmfeɪst/. If you are **shamefaced**, you feel embarrassed because you have done something that you know you should not have done. *There was a long silence, and my father looked shamefaced.*

ADJ-GRADED FORMAL

shame·ful /'ʃeɪmfʊl/. If you describe a person's action or attitude as **shameful**, you think that it is so bad that the person ought to be ashamed. *...the most shameful episode in US naval history.* ◆ **shame·ful·ly** *At times they have been shamefully neglected.*

◆◇◇◇◇ ADJ-GRADED PRAGMATICS

ADV-GRADED

shame·less /'ʃeɪmləs/. If you describe someone as **shameless**, you mean that they should be ashamed of their behaviour, which is unacceptable to other people. *...a shameless hustler and dealer in stolen goods.* ◆ **shame·less·ly** *...a shamelessly lazy week-long trip.*

◆◇◇◇◇ ADJ-GRADED PRAGMATICS

ADV-GRADED

sham·poo /ʃæm'puː/ **shampoos, shampooing, shampooed. 1** Shampoo is a soapy liquid that you use for washing your hair. **2** When you **shampoo** your hair, you wash it using shampoo.

◆◇◇◇◇ N-VAR

VERB: V n

sham·rock /'ʃæmrɒk/ **shamrocks**. A shamrock is a small plant with three round leaves on each stem. The shamrock is the national emblem of Ireland.

N-COUNT

shan·dy /'ʃændi/ **shandies**. Shandy is a drink which is made by mixing beer and lemonade. *...half a pint of shandy.* ▶ A glass of shandy can be referred to as a **shandy**.

N-UNCOUNT BRITISH

N-COUNT

shank /ʃæŋk/ **shanks. 1** The shank of an object is the long, thin, straight part of the object. *These hooks are sharp with long shanks.* **2** Shanks are the lower parts of the legs; used with reference to meat. *Turn the shanks and baste them once or twice as they cook.*

◆◇◇◇◇ N-COUNT

N-COUNT

shan't /ʃɑːnt, ʃænt/. 'Shall not' is usually said or written as **shan't**.

INFORMAL

shan·ty /'ʃænti/ **shanties. 1** A shanty is a small rough hut which poor people live in, built from tin, cardboard, or other materials that are not very strong. **2** A shanty is a song which sailors used to sing while they were doing work on a ship.

◆◇◇◇◇ N-COUNT

N-COUNT

'shanty town, shanty towns; also spelled **shantytown**. A **shanty town** is a collection of rough

N-COUNT

huts which poor people live in, usually in or near a large city.

shape /ʃeɪp/ **shapes, shaping, shaped.** 1 The ◆◆◆◆◇
shape of an object, a person, or an area is the appearance of their outside edges or surfaces, for example whether they are round, square, curved, or
fat. *The glass bottle is the shape of a woman's torso...
The buds are conical or pyramidal in shape... These
bras should be handwashed to help them keep their
shape.* 2 You can refer to something that you can N-COUNT
see as a **shape** if you cannot see it clearly, or if its
outline is the clearest or most striking aspect of it.
*The great grey shape of a tank rolled out of the vil-
lage.* 3 A **shape** is a space enclosed by an outline, N-COUNT
for example a circle, a square, or a triangle. *...if you
imagine a sort of a kidney shape.* 4 If something is PHRASE
out of shape, it is no longer in its proper or original
shape. *Once most wires are bent out of shape, they
don't return to the original position.* 5 If you **shape** VERB: V n
an object, you give it a particular shape, using your V n into n
hands or a tool. *Cut the dough in half and shape
each half into a loaf.* ● See also **shaped.**

6 The **shape** of something that is planned or organ- N-SING
ized is its structure and character. *Leaders are meeting
in Dublin to plan the future shape of Western Europe.*

7 You can use **in the shape of** to state exactly who or PHRASE
what you are referring to, immediately after referring
to them in a general way. *What industry needed now
was a little hope in the shape of an interest-rate cut.*

8 If you say that something is **the shape of things to** PHRASE
come, you mean that it is the start of a new trend or
development, and in future things will be like this.
*British Rail says its new Liverpool Street station is the
shape of things to come.* 9 Someone or something that VERB
shapes a situation or an activity has a very great influ- V n
ence on the way it develops. *Like it or not, our families
shape our lives and make us what we are.* 10 When PHRASE
something **takes shape,** it develops or starts to appear
in such a way that it becomes fairly clear what its final
form will be. *In 1912 women's events were added, and
the modern Olympic programme began to take shape.*

11 If you say, for example, that you will not accept PHRASE
something in **any shape or form,** or in **any way,** [PRAGMATICS]
shape or form, you are emphasizing that you will not
accept it for any reason or in any circumstances. *I
don't condone violence in any shape or form.*

12 If someone or something is **in shape,** or **in good** PHRASE
shape, they are in a good state of health or in a good
condition. If they are **in bad shape,** they are in a bad
state of health or in a bad condition. *He was still in
better shape than many young men.* 13 If you **lick,** PHRASE
knock, or **whip** someone or something **into shape,**
you use whatever methods are necessary to change or
improve them so that they are in the condition that
you want them to be in. *Few people doubt his ability to
whip the economy into shape.* 14 If you are **out of** PHRASE
shape, you are unhealthy and unable to do a lot of
physical activity without getting tired.

shape up. 1 If something **is shaping up,** it is starting PHRASAL VB
to develop or seems likely to happen. *The accident is* V P
already shaping up as a significant environmental dis- V P as n
aster... This is shaping up to be the closest governor's V P to-inf
race in recent memory. 2 If you ask how someone or V P as n
something **is shaping up,** you want to know how well Also V P adv
they are doing in a particular situation or activity. *I
did have a few worries about how Hugh and I would
shape up as parents.* 3 If you tell someone to **shape** V P
up, you are telling them to start behaving in a sensible
and responsible way.

shaped /ʃeɪpt/. Something that is **shaped** like a ◆◆◇◇◇
particular object or in a particular way has the ADJ:
shape of that object or a shape of that type. *...a bot-* v-link ADJ like
tle shaped like a tank. ...oddly shaped little pack- n,
ages. ▶ Also a combining form. *...large, heart-* adv ADJ
shaped leaves. COMB

shape·less /ʃeɪpləs/. Something that is **shapeless** ADJ-GRADED
does not have a distinct or attractive shape.
...shapeless black dresses.

shape·ly /ʃeɪpli/. If you describe a woman as ADJ-GRADED
shapely, you mean that she has an attractive shape.
...her shapely legs.

shard /ʃɑːd/ **shards.** Shards are pieces of broken N-COUNT
glass, pottery, or metal. *Eyewitnesses spoke of rocks
and shards of glass flying in the air.*

share /ʃeə/ **shares, sharing, shared.** 1 A ◆◆◆◆◆
company's **shares** are the many equal parts into N-COUNT
which its ownership is divided. Shares can be
bought by people as an investment. *...a period of
some months when the share price would remain
fairly static.*

2 If you **share** something with another person, you V-RECIP
both have it, use it, or occupy it. You can also say that V n with n
two people **share** something. *...the small income he* pl-n V n
had shared with his brother... Two Americans will be V-ed
share this year's Nobel Prize for Medicine... Scarce wa- between pl-n
ter resources are shared between states. 3 If you **share** a V-RECIP
task, duty, or responsibility with someone, you each V n with n
carry out or accept part of it. You can also say that two Also pl-n V n
people **share** something. *You can find out whether
they are prepared to share the cost of the flowers with
you.*

4 If you **share** an experience with someone, you have V-RECIP
the same experience, often because you are with V n with n
them at the time. You can also say that two people pl-n V n
share something. *Yes, I want to share my life with
you... I felt we both shared the same sense of loss.* 5 If V-RECIP: no
one person or thing **shares** a quality or characteristic cont
with another, they have the same quality or charac- V n with n
teristic. You can also say that two people or things Also pl-n V n
share something. *...politically independent newspapers which share similar characteristics with certain British newspapers.* 6 If you **share** someone's VB: no cont
opinion, you agree with them. *The forum's members* V n
share his view.

7 If you **share** something that you have with some- VERB
one, you give some of it to them or let them use it. *The* V n with n
village tribe is friendly and they share their water sup- V n among pl-
ply with you... Scientists now have to compete for fund- n
ing, and do not share information among themselves. Also V n,
V

8 If you **share** something personal such as a thought VERB
or a piece of news with someone, you tell them about V n with n
it. *It can be beneficial to share your feelings with some-* Also V n
one you trust.

9 If something is divided or distributed among a N-COUNT
number of different people or things, each of them
has, or is responsible for, a **share** of it. *Sara also pays a
share of the gas, electricity and phone bills.* 10 If you N-COUNT
have or do your **share** of something, you have or do
the amount that it is reasonable or fair. *Women must
receive their fair share of training for good-paying jobs.*

11 See also **lion's share, market share, power-
sharing.**

share in. If you **share in** something such as a suc- PHRASAL VB
cess or a responsibility, you are one of a number of V P n
people who achieve or accept it. *Everybody shares in
the cooking chores.*

share out. If you **share out** an amount of some- PHRASAL VB
thing, you give each person in a group an equal or fair V n P
part of it. *Warsaw Pact members have failed to agree* V P noun
on how to share out proposed cuts in tank numbers. V P n among/
...a formula for sharing out power among the various between pl-n
clans. ● See also **share-out.**

share·crop·per /ʃeəkrɒpə/ **sharecroppers.** A N-COUNT
sharecropper is a farmer who pays the rent for his
land with some of the crops they produce.

share·hold·er /ʃeəhəʊldə/ **shareholders.** A ◆◆◆◇◇
shareholder is a person who owns shares in a com- N-COUNT
pany. *...a shareholders' meeting.*

share index, share indices or **share in-** ◆◇◇◇◇
dexes. A share index is an indicator of the state of N-COUNT
a stock market. It is based on the combined share
prices of a set of companies.

'share-out, share-outs. If there is a **share-out** of N-COUNT
something, several people are given equal or fair BRITISH
parts of it. *...a referendum on independence and the
share-out of seats in the transitional government.*

share·ware /ˈʃeəweə/; also spelled **Shareware.** **Shareware** is computer software that you can try before you buy the legal right to use it. `N-UNCOUNT` `TECHNICAL`

shark /ʃɑːk/ **sharks.** The form **shark** can also be used as the plural form for meaning 1. **1** A **shark** is a very large fish. Some sharks have very sharp teeth and may attack people. **2** If you refer to a person as a **shark**, you disapprove of them because they trick people out of their money by giving bad financial advice. *Beware the sharks when you are making up your mind how to invest.* ● See also **loan shark.** `◆◇◇◇` `N-VAR` `N-COUNT` `PRAGMATICS` `INFORMAL`

sharp /ʃɑːp/ **sharper, sharpest. 1** A **sharp** point or edge is very small or thin and can cut through things very easily. *The other end of the twig is sharpened into a sharp point.* **2** You can describe a shape or an object as **sharp** if part of it or one end of it comes to a point or forms an angle. *His nose was thin and sharp.* **3** A **sharp** bend or turn is one that changes direction suddenly. ● Also an adverb. *Do not cross the bridge but turn sharp left.* ♦ **sharp·ly** *Downstream the canyon bent sharply to the north.* **4** If you describe someone as **sharp**, you are praising them because they are quick to notice, hear, understand, or react to things. *He is very sharp, a quick thinker.* ♦ **sharp·ness** *I liked their enthusiasm and sharpness of mind.* **5** If someone says something in a **sharp** way, they say it suddenly and rather firmly or angrily. *'Don't contradict your mother,' was Charles's sharp reprimand.* ♦ **sharply** *Environmentalists were sharply critical of the policy.* ♦ **sharpness** *'Let them find their own way out,' said his father with unaccustomed sharpness.* **6** A **sharp** change, movement, or feeling occurs suddenly, and is great in amount, force, or degree. *There's been a sharp rise in the rate of inflation.* ♦ **sharply** *Unemployment among the over forties has risen sharply in recent years.* **7** A **sharp** difference, image, or sound is very easy to see, hear, or distinguish. *Many people make a sharp distinction between humans and other animals.* ♦ **sharply** *The woman's figure is sharply brought out by the intense Provençal light.* ♦ **sharpness** *Scientists said they were amazed at the sharpness of the first picture.* **8** A **sharp** taste or smell is rather strong or bitter, but is often also clear and fresh. ♦ **sharpness** *The pesto vinaigrette added a stimulating sharpness.* **9** A **sharp** wind, or **sharp** cold, is so strong or intense that it almost hurts you. **10** **Sharp** clothes are neat, elegant, and fashionable. **11** **Sharp** is used after stating a particular time to show that something happens at exactly that time. *She planned to unlock the store at 8.00 sharp.* **12** **Sharp** is used after a letter representing a musical note to show that the note should be played or sung half a tone higher than the note which otherwise corresponds to that letter. **Sharp** is often represented by the symbol ♯. *A solitary viola plucks a lonely, soft F sharp.* **13** If you say that someone is **at the sharp end** of a particular activity or type of work, you mean that they are involved in the most difficult or dangerous aspects of it. *These men are at the sharp end of law enforcement.* ● **short sharp shock**: see **shock. 14** See also **razor-sharp.** `◆◆◆◇` `ADJ-GRADED` `ADJ-GRADED` `ADJ-GRADED` `ADV: ADV adv` `ADV-GRADED: ADV after v` `ADJ-GRADED` `PRAGMATICS` `N-UNCOUNT` `ADJ-GRADED` `ADV-GRADED` `N-UNCOUNT` `ADJ-GRADED` `ADV-GRADED` `ADV-GRADED` `N-UNCOUNT` `ADJ-GRADED` `N-UNCOUNT` `ADJ-GRADED` `ADJ-GRADED` `ADV: n ADV` `ADJ: n ADJ` `PHRASE` `BRITISH`

sharp·en /ˈʃɑːpən/ **sharpens, sharpening, sharpened. 1** If your senses, understanding, or skills **sharpen** or **are sharpened**, you become better at noticing things, thinking, or doing something. *You can sharpen your skills with rehearsal.* **2** If you **sharpen** an object, you make its edge very thin or you make its end pointed. ♦ **sharp·en·er, sharpeners.** A **sharpener** is a tool or machine used for sharpening pencils or knives. *...a pencil sharpener.* **3** If disagreements or differences between people **sharpen**, or if they **are sharpened**, they become bigger or more important. *The case of Harris has sharpened the debate over capital punishment.* `◆◇◇◇` `V-ERG: V` `V n` `VERB: V n` `N-COUNT` `V-ERG: V` `V n`

sharpen up. If you **sharpen** something **up**, or if it **sharpens up**, it becomes smarter or better than it was. *The fashion designers have sharpened up their act in* `PHRASAL VB` `ERG:` `V n P` `V P n`

the last few years... *We have got to sharpen up and get it right.* `V P` `INFORMAL`

'sharp-eyed. A **sharp-eyed** person is good at noticing and observing things. `ADJ-GRADED`

,sharp 'practice. You can use **sharp practice** to refer to an action or a way of behaving that you think is clever but dishonest. *He accused some solicitors of sharp practice in quoting low fees which were later increased.* `N-UNCOUNT`

sharp·shooter /ˈʃɑːpʃuːtə/ **sharpshooters.** A **sharpshooter** is a person who can fire a gun very accurately. `N-COUNT` `AMERICAN`

shat·ter /ˈʃætə/ **shatters, shattering, shattered. 1** If something **shatters** or if something or someone **shatters** it, it breaks into a lot of small pieces. *The car shattered into a thousand burning pieces in a 200mph crash... One bullet shattered his skull.* ♦ **shat·ter·ing** *...the shattering of glass.* **2** If something **shatters** your dreams, hopes, or beliefs, it completely destroys them. **3** If someone **is shattered** by an event, it shocks and upsets them very much. *...the tragedy which had shattered his life.* ♦ **shattering** *Yesterday's decision was another shattering blow.* **4** See also **shattered, earth-shattering.** `◆◇◇◇` `V-ERG: V` `V into n` `V n` `Also V n into n` `N-UNCOUNT` `VERB: V n` `VERB:` `be V-ed` `ADJ-GRADED`

shat·tered /ˈʃætəd/. **1** If you are **shattered** by something, you are extremely shocked and upset about it. *It is desperately sad news and I am absolutely shattered to hear it.* **2** If you say you are **shattered**, you mean you are extremely tired and have no energy left. *He was shattered and too tired to concentrate on schoolwork.* `◆◆◇◇` `ADJ-GRADED` `ADJ-GRADED` `BRITISH`

shave /ʃeɪv/ **shaves, shaving, shaved. 1** If you **shave**, you cut hair from a part of your body using a razor or shaver. *He had shaved his face until it was smooth... If you have long curly hair, don't shave it off.* ► Also a noun. *He never seemed to need a shave.* ♦ **shav·ing** *...a range of shaving products.* **2** If you **shave off** part of a piece of wood or other material, you cut very thin pieces from it. *She was shaving thin slices off a courgette.* **3** If you **shave** a small amount off something such as a record, cost, or price, you reduce it by that amount. *She's already shaved four seconds off the national record for the mile.* **4** If you describe a situation as a **close shave**, you mean that there was nearly an accident or a disaster but that it was avoided. **5** See also **shaving.** `◆◆◇◇` `VERB: V` `V n` `V n with off` `N-COUNT` `N-UNCOUNT` `VERB:` `V n with off` `V n off n` `VERB` `V n off/from n` `PHRASE`

shav·en /ˈʃeɪvən/. If a part of someone's body is **shaven**, it has been shaved. *...a small boy with a shaven head.* ● See also **clean-shaven.** `ADJ`

shav·er /ˈʃeɪvə/ **shavers.** A **shaver** is an electric device, used for shaving hair from the face and body. `◆◇◇◇` `N-COUNT`

shav·ing /ˈʃeɪvɪŋ/ **shavings.** **Shavings** are small very thin pieces of wood or other material which have been cut from a larger piece. *...metal shavings.* ● See also **shave.** `◆◇◇◇` `N-COUNT`

'shaving cream, shaving creams. **Shaving cream** is soap or foam which men put on their face before they shave. `N-VAR`

shawl /ʃɔːl/ **shawls.** A **shawl** is a large piece of woollen cloth which a woman wears over her shoulders or head, or which is wrapped around a baby to keep it warm. `◆◇◇◇` `N-COUNT`

she /ʃi, STRONG ʃiː/. **She** is a third person singular pronoun. **She** is used as the subject of a verb. **1** You use **she** to refer to a woman, girl, or female animal who has already been mentioned or whose identity is clear. *She was seventeen... She was a little fluffy baby duck.* **2** Some writers may use **she** to refer to a person who is not identified as either male or female, to avoid using the pronoun 'he' all the time. Some people dislike this use and prefer to use 'he or she' or 'they'. *Very early in life when the baby feels the pangs of hunger, she learns to scream.* **3** **She** is sometimes used to refer to a country or nation. *Now Britain needs new leadership if she is to play a significant role shaping Europe's future development.* **4** Some people use **she** to refer to a car, ship, or other vehicle. *Hundreds of small boats clustered round the yacht as she sailed into Southampton docks.* `◆◆◆◆` `PRON` `PRON` `WRITTEN` `PRON` `PRON`

s/he. Some writers use **s/he** instead of either 'he' or 'she' when they are referring to someone who might exist but who has not been identified. By using 's/he', the writer does not need to say whether the person is male or female. *Talk to your doctor and see if s/he knows of any local groups.* — PRON WRITTEN

sheaf /ʃiːf/ **sheaves. 1** A **sheaf** of papers is a bundle of papers. **2** A **sheaf** is a bundle of ripe corn plants tied together. — N-COUNT / N-COUNT

shear /ʃɪə/ **shears, shearing, sheared, shorn. 1** To **shear** a sheep means to cut its wool off. ◆◇◇◇ VERB: V n
♦ **shear·ing** ...*a display of sheep shearing.* **2** A pair of **shears** is a tool like a very large pair of scissors, used especially for cutting hedges. See picture headed **tools.** — N-UNCOUNT / N-PLURAL

shear off. If something such as a piece of metal **shears off,** or if it **is sheared off,** it breaks. *The aircraft's wings were sheared off in the crash.* — PHRASAL VB ERG: be V-ed P / V P

sheath /ʃiːθ/ **sheaths. 1** A **sheath** is a covering for the blade of a knife. **2** A **sheath** is a rubber covering for a man's penis that is used as a contraceptive. — ◆◇◇◇◇ N-COUNT / N-COUNT

sheathe /ʃiːð/ **sheathes, sheathing, sheathed. 1** If something is **sheathed** in a material or other covering, it is closely covered with it. *The television was sheathed in a snug coverlet.* **2** When someone **sheathes** a knife, they put it in its sheath. — VB: usu passive LITERARY / VERB: V n LITERARY

sheaves /ʃiːvz/. **Sheaves** is the plural of **sheaf.**

she·bang /ʃɪˈbæŋ/. The **whole shebang** is the whole situation or business that you are describing. — PHRASE INFORMAL

shed /ʃed/ **sheds, shedding.** The form **shed** is used in the present tense and in the past tense and past participle of the verb. **1** A **shed** is a small building that is used for storing things such as garden tools. **2** A **shed** is a large shelter or building, for example at a railway station, port, or factory. ◆◆◆◇◇ — N-COUNT / N-COUNT

3 When a tree **sheds** its leaves, its leaves fall off in the autumn. When an animal **sheds** hair or skin, some of its hair or skin drops off. **4** To **shed** something means to get rid of it. *The firm is to shed 700 jobs.* **5** If a lorry **sheds** its load, the goods that it is carrying accidentally fall onto the road. **6** If you **shed** tears, you cry. *I don't think any of us would shed tears if that happened.* **7** To **shed** blood means to kill people in a violent way. If someone **sheds** their blood, they are killed in a violent way, usually when they are fighting in a war. *Gunmen in Ulster shed the first blood of the new year.* **8** ● to **shed light on** something: see **light.** — VERB: V n / VERB: V n FORMAL / VERB: V n / VERB V n / VERB V n

she'd /ʃiːd, ʃɪd/. **1** **She'd** is the usual spoken form of 'she had', especially when 'had' is an auxiliary verb. *She would go for a swim when she'd unpacked.* **2** **She'd** is a spoken form of 'she would'. *She'd do anything for a bit of money.*

sheen /ʃiːn/. If something has a **sheen,** it has a smooth and gentle brightness on its surface. *The carpet had a silvery sheen to it.* — ◆◇◇◇◇ N-SING

sheep /ʃiːp/; **sheep** is both the singular and plural form. **1** A **sheep** is a farm animal with a thick woolly coat, kept for its wool or its meat. See picture headed **animals. 2** If you say that a group of people are like **sheep,** you disapprove of them because if one person does something, all the others copy them. **3** See also **black sheep.** — ◆◆◇◇◇ N-COUNT / N-PLURAL PRAGMATICS

sheep·dog /ʃiːpdɒg/ **sheepdogs.** A **sheepdog** is a breed of dog often used for controlling sheep. — N-COUNT

sheep·ish /ʃiːpɪʃ/. If you look **sheepish,** you look slightly embarrassed because you feel foolish. ◆◇◇◇◇ — ADJ-GRADED
♦ **sheep·ish·ly** *He grinned sheepishly.* — ADV-GRADED

sheep·skin /ʃiːpskɪn/ **sheepskins.** Sheepskin is the skin of a sheep with the wool still attached to it, used especially for making coats and rugs. *...a sheepskin coat.* — N-VAR

sheer /ʃɪə/ **sheerer, sheerest. 1** You can use **sheer** to emphasize that a state or situation is complete and does not involve anything else. *...acts of sheer desperation.* **2** A **sheer** cliff or drop is extremely steep or completely vertical. **3** **Sheer** material is very thin, light, and delicate. *...sheer black tights.* — ◆◆◇◇◇ ADJ: ADJ n PRAGMATICS / ADJ-GRADED / ADJ-GRADED

sheet /ʃiːt/ **sheets. 1** A **sheet** is a large rectangular piece of cotton or other cloth that you sleep on ◆◆◆◇◇ N-COUNT

or cover yourself with in a bed. **2** A **sheet** of paper is a rectangular piece of paper. **3** You can use **sheet** to refer to a piece of paper which gives information about something. *...information sheets on each country in the world.* **4** A **sheet** of glass, metal, or wood is a large, flat, thin piece of it. **5** A **sheet** of something is a thin wide layer of it over the surface of something else. *...a sheet of ice.* **6** A **sheet** of fire or water is a fast-moving mass of it that is difficult to see through. **7** See also **balance sheet, charge sheet, fact sheet, scoresheet, spreadsheet.** — N-COUNT / N-COUNT / N-COUNT / N-COUNT / N-COUNT / N-COUNT

sheet·ing /ʃiːtɪŋ/. **Sheeting** is metal, plastic, or other material that is made in the form of sheets. — N-UNCOUNT

'sheet metal. Sheet metal is metal which is made into thin sheets rather than being made into solid bars or cast in moulds. — N-UNCOUNT

'sheet music. Sheet music is music that is printed on sheets of paper without a hard cover. — N-UNCOUNT

sheikh /ʃeɪk, AM ʃiːk/ **sheikhs;** also spelled **sheik** or **shaikh.** A **sheikh** is a male Arab chief or ruler. ◆◆◇◇◇ — N-TITLE; N-COUNT

shelf /ʃelf/ **shelves. 1** A **shelf** is a flat piece of wood, metal, or glass which is attached to a wall or to the sides of a cupboard. *He took a book from the shelf.* **2** A **shelf** is a section of rock on a cliff or mountain or underwater that sticks out like a shelf. *The house stands on a shelf of rock among pines.* ● See also **continental shelf. 3** If you buy something **off the shelf,** you buy something that is not specially made for you. *...off-the-shelf software.* **4** If you say that someone or something is **on the shelf,** you mean that no one wants them. *I was afraid of getting left on the shelf.* — ◆◆◇◇◇ N-COUNT / N-COUNT / PHRASE / PHRASE INFORMAL

'shelf life, shelf lives. The **shelf life** of a product, especially food, is the length of time that it can be kept before it becomes too old to use. — N-COUNT

shell /ʃel/ **shells, shelling, shelled. 1** The **shell** of a nut or egg is the hard covering which surrounds it. ► **Shell** is the substance that a shell is made of. *...beads made from ostrich egg shell.* **2** The **shell** of a tortoise, snail, or crab is the hard protective covering that it has on its back. **3** **Shells** are hard objects found on beaches. They are usually pink, white, or brown and are the covering which surrounds, or used to surround, small sea creatures. **4** If you **shell** nuts, peas, prawns, or other food, you remove their natural outer covering. **5** If someone comes out of their **shell,** they become more friendly and less quiet, shy, and reserved. **6** The **shell** of a building, boat, car, or other structure is the outside frame of it. *...the shells of burned buildings.* — ◆◆◆◇◇ N-COUNT / N-UNCOUNT / N-COUNT / N-COUNT / VERB: V n / N-COUNT / N-COUNT

7 A **shell** is a weapon consisting of a metal container filled with explosives that can be fired from a large gun over long distances. **8** To **shell** a place means to fire explosive shells at it. ♦ **shell·ing, shellings** *Out on the streets, the shelling continued.* — N-COUNT / VERB: V n / N-VAR

shell out. If you **shell out** for something, you spend a lot of money on it. *You won't have to shell out a fortune for it... Nearly half are shelling out 50 percent of their income or more... The very fact that you shelled out money to come and see us is a good sign.* — PHRASAL VB V P for/on n / V P n for/on n / V P n to-inf / Also V P to-inf

she'll /ʃiːl, ʃɪl/. **She'll** is the usual spoken form of 'she will'. *Sharon was a wonderful lady and I know she'll be greatly missed.*

shell·fish /ʃelfɪʃ/; **shellfish** is both the singular and plural form. **Shellfish** are small creatures that live in the sea and have a shell. *Fish and shellfish are the specialities.* — ◆◇◇◇◇ N-VAR

'shell-shocked; also spelled **shell shocked. 1** If you say that someone is **shell-shocked,** you mean that they are very shocked, usually because something bad has happened. *We were shell-shocked when Chelsea took the lead.* **2** If someone is **shell-shocked,** they have a confused or nervous mental condition as a result of a shocking experience such as being in a war or an accident. *...a shell-shocked war veteran.* — ADJ-GRADED INFORMAL / ADJ-GRADED

'shell suit, shell suits; also spelled **shell-suit.** A **shell suit** is a casual suit made of thin nylon. — N-COUNT BRITISH

shel·ter /ʃeltə/ **shelters, sheltering, sheltered. 1** A **shelter** is a small building or covered ◆◆◇◇◇ N-COUNT

place which is made to protect people from bad weather or danger. ...*a bus shelter.* **2** If a place provides **shelter**, it provides you with a place to stay or live. *The number of families seeking shelter rose by 17 percent.* **3** A **shelter** is a building where homeless people can sleep and get food. ...*a shelter for homeless women.* **4** If you **shelter** in a place, you stay there and are protected from bad weather or danger. ...*a man sheltering in a doorway.* **5** If a place or thing **is sheltered** by something, it is protected by that thing from wind and rain. **6** If you **shelter** someone, usually someone who is being hunted by police or other people, you provide them with a place to stay or live. *A neighbor sheltered the boy for seven days.*

N-UNCOUNT

N-COUNT

VERB
V prep/adv

VB: usu
passive

VERB
V n

shel·tered /ˈʃeltəd/. **1** A **sheltered** place is protected from wind and rain. ...*a shallow-sloping beach next to a sheltered bay.* **2** If you say that someone has led a **sheltered** life, you mean that they have not experienced things that most people of their age have experienced, and that as a result they are rather naive. *My mother, who had a sheltered upbringing, has fantastic memories of childhood.* **3 Sheltered** accommodation or work is designed for old or disabled people. It allows them to be independent but also gives them supervision when they need it. ...*sheltered employment for people with severe disabilities.*

◆◇◇◇◇
ADJ-GRADED

ADJ-GRADED

ADJ: ADJ n

shelve /ʃelv/ **shelves, shelving, shelved. 1** If someone **shelves** a plan or project, they decide not to continue with it at that time. *Sadly, the project has now been shelved.* **2** If a stretch of land **shelves**, it slopes or drops downwards. *The shoreline shelves away steeply.* **3 Shelves** is the plural of **shelf**.

◆◇◇◇◇
VERB: V n

VERB
V adv/prep

shelv·ing /ˈʃelvɪŋ/. **Shelving** is a set of shelves, or material which is used for making shelves. ...*a pyramid-shaped shelving unit.*

N-UNCOUNT

she·nani·gans /ʃɪˈnænɪɡənz/. You can use **shenanigans** to refer to rather dishonest or immoral behaviour, especially when you think it is amusing or interesting. *Media people knew about the private shenanigans of public figures.*

N-PLURAL
INFORMAL

shep·herd /ˈʃepəd/ **shepherds, shepherding, shepherded. 1** A **shepherd** is a person, especially a man, whose job is to look after sheep. **2** If you are **shepherded** somewhere, someone takes you there to make sure that you arrive at the right place safely. *She was shepherded by her guards up the rear ramp of the aircraft.*

◆◆◇◇◇

VB: usu
passive
beV-ed
prep/adv

shep·herd·ess /ˈʃepədes/ **shepherdesses.** A **shepherdess** is a woman whose job is to look after sheep.

N-COUNT

,**shepherd's 'pie, shepherd's pies.** In Britain, **shepherd's pie** is a dish consisting of minced meat, usually lamb, covered with mashed potato.

N-VAR

sher·bet /ˈʃɜːbət/ **sherbets. 1 Sherbet** is a type of ice cream made with fruit juices, sugar, and water. **2 Sherbet** is a sweet dry powder that tastes fizzy and is eaten as a sweet.

N-VAR
AMERICAN
N-UNCOUNT
BRITISH

sher·iff /ˈʃerɪf/ **sheriffs. 1** In the United States, a **sheriff** is a person who is elected to make sure that the law is obeyed in a particular county. ...*Sheriff Bob Cahill.* **2** In Scotland, a **sheriff** is a legal officer whose chief duty is to act as judge in a Sheriff Court. These courts deal with all but the most serious crimes and with most civil actions. ...*the presiding judge, Sheriff John Mowatt.* **3** In England and Wales, the **Sheriff** of a city or county is a person who is elected or appointed to carry out mainly ceremonial duties. ...*the Sheriff of Oxford.*

◆◇◇◇◇
N-COUNT;
N-TITLE

N-COUNT;
N-TITLE

N-COUNT

sher·ry /ˈʃeri/ **sherries.** Sherry is a type of strong wine that is made in south-western Spain. *He sipped his sherry.* ▶ A glass of sherry can be referred to as a **sherry**.

◆◆◇◇◇
N-VAR

N-COUNT

she's /ʃiːz, ʃɪz/. **1 She's** is the usual spoken form of 'she is'. *Have they told you, she's having a baby in October?* **2 She's** is a spoken form of 'she has', especially when 'has' is an auxiliary verb. *She's been married for seven years.*

shh /ʃ/. See **sh**.

shib·bo·leth /ˈʃɪbəleθ/ **shibboleths.** If you describe a popular idea or belief as a **shibboleth**, you mean that it may be meaningless or wrong although many people believe it. *It is time to go beyond the shibboleth that conventional forces, unlike nuclear ones, cannot deter.*

N-COUNT
FORMAL

shield /ʃiːld/ **shields, shielding, shielded. 1** Something or someone which is a **shield** against a particular danger or risk provides protection from it.' ...*asbestos heat shields.* **2** If something or someone **shields** you **from** a danger or risk, they protect you from it. *He shielded his head from the sun with an old sack.* **3** If you **shield** your eyes, you put your hand above your eyes to protect them from direct sunlight. *He squinted and shielded his eyes.* **4** A **shield** is a large piece of metal or leather which soldiers used to carry to protect their bodies while they were fighting. **5** A **shield** is a sports trophy or a badge that is shaped like a shield.

◆◇◇◇◇
N-COUNT

VERB
V n from n

VERB
V n

N-COUNT

N-COUNT

shift /ʃɪft/ **shifts, shifting, shifted. 1** If you **shift** something or if it **shifts**, it moves slightly. *He stopped, shifting his cane to his left hand... He shifted from foot to foot.* **2** If someone's opinion, a situation, or a policy **shifts** or **is shifted**, it changes slightly. *The emphasis should be shifted more towards Parliament.* ▶ Also a noun. ...*a shift in government policy.* **3** If someone **shifts** the responsibility or blame for something onto you, they unfairly make you responsible or make people blame you for it, instead of them; used showing disapproval. *Their husbands try to shift the blame by accusing them of having 'suspicious minds'.* **4** If a shop or company **shifts** goods, they sell goods that are difficult to sell. *Some suppliers were selling at a loss to shift stock.*

◆◆◇◇◇
V-ERG: V n
V n prep/adv
V prep/adv

V-ERG: V
beV-ed
prep/adv

N-COUNT

VERB:
V n prep
PRAGMATICS
V n

VERB
V n

5 If you **shift** gears in a car or if you **shift up** or **shift down**, you put the car into a different gear. In British English, you **change** gears, or **change up** or **change down**. **6** If a group of factory workers, nurses, or other people work **shifts**, they work for a set period before being replaced by another group, so that there is always a group working. Each of these set periods is called a **shift**. You can also use **shift** to refer to a group of workers who work together on a particular shift. *His father worked shifts in a steel mill. ...workers coming home from the afternoon shift.*

VERB:
V n,
V up/down
AMERICAN

N-COUNT

shift·ing /ˈʃɪftɪŋ/. **Shifting** is used to describe something which is made up of parts that are continuously moving and changing position in relation to other parts. ...*the shifting sand beneath their feet.* ● See also **shift**.

◆◆◇◇◇
ADJ: ADJ n

shifty /ˈʃɪfti/. Someone who looks **shifty** gives the impression of being dishonest. *He had a shifty face and previous convictions.*

ADJ-GRADED
INFORMAL

shil·ling /ˈʃɪlɪŋ/ **shillings.** A **shilling** was a unit of money used in Britain until 1971. There were 20 shillings in a pound, and there were 12 pence in a shilling.

◆◇◇◇◇
N-COUNT

shim·mer /ˈʃɪmə/ **shimmers, shimmering, shimmered.** If something **shimmers**, it shines with a faint unsteady light or has an unclear unsteady appearance. *The lights shimmered on the water.* ▶ Also a noun. ...*a shimmer of starlight.*

◆◇◇◇◇
VERB
V

N-SING

shim·my /ˈʃɪmi/ **shimmies, shimmying, shimmied.** If you **shimmy**, you dance or move in a way that involves shaking your hips and shoulders from side to side. *Tina Turner shimmied across the stage in an incredibly sexy dress.*

VERB: V
V prep/adv

shin /ʃɪn/ **shins. 1** Your **shins** are the front parts of your legs between your knees and your ankles. See picture headed **human body**. **2 Shin** of beef or veal is the meat from the lower foreleg of a cow.

◆◇◇◇◇
N-COUNT

N-UNCOUNT
BRITISH

shin·dig /ˈʃɪndɪɡ/ **shindigs.** A **shindig** is a large, noisy, enjoyable party.

N-COUNT
INFORMAL

shine /ʃaɪn/ **shines, shining, shined, shone.** The past tense and past participle of the verb is **shone**, except for meaning 5 when it is **shined**. **1** When the sun or a light **shines**, it gives out bright light. *It is a mild morning and the sun is shining.*

◆◆◇◇◇

VERB
V

S

2 If you **shine** a torch or other light somewhere, you point it there, so that you can see something when it is dark. *One of the men shone a torch in his face... The man walked slowly towards her, shining the flashlight.* **3** Something that **shines** is very bright and clear because it is reflecting light. *Her blue eyes shone and caught the light.* **4** Something that has a **shine** is bright and clear because it is reflecting light. *This gel gives a beautiful shine to the hair.* **5** If you **shine** a wooden, leather, or metal object, you make it bright by rubbing or polishing it. *His high black boots had been shined to a gleaming finish.*
VERB
V n prep
V n

VERB
V

N-SING

VERB
V n

6 Someone who **shines** at a skill or activity does it extremely well. *He failed to shine academically.* **7** If you say that someone has **taken a shine to** another person, you mean that he or she liked them very much at their first meeting. *Seems to me you've taken quite a shine to Miss Richmond.* **8** See also **shining**. **9 • rain or shine:** see **rain**.
VERB
V
PHRASE
INFORMAL

shin·gle /ˈʃɪŋɡəl/ **shingles. 1 Shingle** is a mass of small rough pieces of stone on the shore of a sea or a river. *...a beach of sand and shingle.* **2 Shingles** are thin rectangular tiles, especially ones made of wood, which are laid in overlapping rows to cover a roof or wall. **3 Shingles** is a disease which causes a rash of painful red spots which spread in bands over a person's body, especially around their waist.
◆◇◇◇◇
N-UNCOUNT

N-COUNT

N-UNCOUNT

shin·ing /ˈʃaɪnɪŋ/. A **shining** achievement or quality is a very good one which should be greatly admired. *She is a shining example to us all.* **•** See also **shine**.
◆◇◇◇
ADJ

shiny /ˈʃaɪni/ **shinier, shiniest. Shiny** things are bright and reflect light. *...a shiny new sports car.*
◆◆◇◇◇
ADJ-GRADED

ship /ʃɪp/ **ships, shipping, shipped. 1** A **ship** is a large boat which carries passengers or cargo. *He will then go by ship to England.* **2** If people or things **are shipped** somewhere, they are sent there on a ship or by some other means of transport. **3** See also **shipping**.
N-COUNT:
also by N
VERB:
be V-ed
prep/adv

ship·board /ˈʃɪpbɔːd/. **Shipboard** means taking place on a ship. *...a shipboard romance.*
ADJ: ADJ n

ship·builder /ˈʃɪpbɪldə/ **shipbuilders.** A **shipbuilder** is a company or a person that builds ships.
N-COUNT

ship·building /ˈʃɪpbɪldɪŋ/. **Shipbuilding** is the industry of building ships.
◆◇◇◇◇
N-UNCOUNT

ship·load /ˈʃɪpləʊd/ **shiploads.** A **shipload** of people or goods is as many people or goods as a ship can carry.
N-COUNT

ship·mate /ˈʃɪpmeɪt/ **shipmates.** Sailors who work together on the same ship are **shipmates.**
N-COUNT

ship·ment /ˈʃɪpmənt/ **shipments. 1** A **shipment** is an amount of a particular kind of cargo that is sent to another country on a ship, train, aeroplane, or other vehicle. **2** The **shipment** of a cargo somewhere is the sending of it there by ship, train, aeroplane, or some other vehicle. *The furniture was ready for shipment.*
◆◆◇◇◇
N-COUNT

N-UNCOUNT

ship·owner /ˈʃɪpəʊnə/ **shipowners.** A **shipowner** is someone who owns a ship or ships or who has shares in a shipping company.
N-COUNT

ship·per /ˈʃɪpə/ **shippers. Shippers** are people or companies who ship cargo as a business.
N-COUNT

ship·ping /ˈʃɪpɪŋ/. **1 Shipping** is the transport of cargo as a business, especially on ships. *...the international shipping industry.* **2** You can refer to the amount of money that you pay to a company to transport cargo as **shipping**. **3** You can refer to ships as **shipping** when considering them as a group. *They sent naval forces to protect merchant shipping.*
◆◆◇◇◇
N-UNCOUNT

N-UNCOUNT

N-UNCOUNT

ship·shape /ˈʃɪpʃeɪp/. If something is **shipshape**, it looks tidy and in good condition.
ADJ-GRADED

ship·wreck /ˈʃɪprek/ **shipwrecks; shipwrecked. 1** If there is a **shipwreck**, a ship is destroyed in an accident at sea. *...the perils of storm and shipwreck.* **2** A **shipwreck** is a ship which has been destroyed in an accident at sea. **3** If someone **is shipwrecked**, their ship is destroyed in an accident at sea but they survive and manage to reach
N-VAR

N-COUNT

V-PASSIVE:
be V-ed
V-ed

land. *The shipwrecked couple were rescued by two fishermen.*

ship·wright /ˈʃɪpraɪt/ **shipwrights.** A **shipwright** is a person who builds or repairs ships as a job.
N-COUNT

ship·yard /ˈʃɪpjɑːd/ **shipyards.** A **shipyard** is a place where ships are built and repaired.
◆◇◇◇◇
N-COUNT

shire /ʃaɪə/ **shires. 1** The **Shires** or the **shire counties** are the mainly rural counties of England. **2** A **shire** or **shire horse** is a large heavy horse used for pulling loads.
◆◇◇◇◇
N-COUNT
N-COUNT
BRITISH

shirk /ʃɜːk/ **shirks, shirking, shirked.** If someone does not **shirk** their responsibility or duty, they do what they have a responsibility to do. *The Government will not shirk from considering the need for further action.*
VERB
V from -ing/n
Also V

shirt /ʃɜːt/ **shirts. 1** A **shirt** is a piece of clothing that you wear on the upper part of your body. Shirts have a collar, sleeves, and buttons down the front. See picture headed **clothes.** **♦ -shirted** *...white-shirted men.* **2** See also **dress shirt, sweatshirt, T-shirt.**
◆◆◇◇◇
N-COUNT

COMB

shirt·sleeve /ˈʃɜːtsliːv/ **shirtsleeves. Shirtsleeves** are the sleeves of a shirt. If a man is **in shirtsleeves** or **in his shirtsleeves**, he is wearing a shirt but not a jacket.
N-COUNT

'shirt-tail, shirt-tails; also spelled **shirttail. Shirt-tails** are the long parts of a shirt below the waist.
N-COUNT

shirty /ˈʃɜːti/. If someone gets **shirty**, they behave in a bad-tempered and rude way because they are annoyed about something.
ADJ-GRADED
BRITISH,
INFORMAL

shiv·er /ˈʃɪvə/ **shivers, shivering, shivered.** When you **shiver**, your body shakes slightly because you are cold or frightened. ► Also a noun. *The emptiness here sent shivers down my spine.*
VERB: V

N-COUNT

shiv·ery /ˈʃɪvəri/. If you are **shivery**, you cannot stop shivering because you feel cold, frightened, or ill.
ADJ-GRADED

shoal /ʃəʊl/ **shoals.** A **shoal** of fish is a large group of them swimming together.
◆◇◇◇◇
N-COUNT

shock /ʃɒk/ **shocks, shocking, shocked. 1** If you have a **shock**, something suddenly happens which is unpleasant, upsetting, or very surprising. *The extent of the violence came as a shock.* **2 Shock** is a person's emotional and physical condition when something very frightening or upsetting has happened to them. *She's still in a state of shock.* **3** A **short sharp shock** is a punishment that is fairly severe but only lasts for a short time. **4** If someone is **in shock**, they are suffering from a serious physical condition in which their blood cannot circulate properly, for example because they have had a bad injury.
◆◆◆◇◇
N-COUNT

N-UNCOUNT

PHRASE
BRITISH

N-UNCOUNT

5 If something **shocks** you, it makes you feel very upset, because it involves death or suffering and because you had not expected it. **♦ shocked** *This was a nasty attack and the woman is still very shocked.* **6** A **shock** announcement or event is one which shocks people because it is unexpected. *...a shock defeat.* **7** If someone or something **shocks** you, it upsets or offends you because you think it is rude or morally wrong. *They were easily shocked in those days.* **♦ shocked** *Don't look so shocked... I'm shocked and dismayed by your mis-statement.* **8** A **shock** is something sudden and unexpected that threatens the economy, traditions, or way of life of a group of people. *This is the latest in a series of shocks to the Scandinavian banking system.*
VERB: V n
ADJ-GRADED

ADJ: ADJ n

VERB: V n
V-ed
Also V

ADJ-GRADED

N-COUNT

9 A **shock** is a slight movement in something when it is hit or jerked by something else. *Steel barriers can bend and absorb the shock.* **10** A **shock** is the same as an **electric shock. 11** A **shock** of hair is a very thick mass of hair on a person's head. **12** See also **shocking; culture shock, electric shock, shell-shocked.**
N-VAR

N-COUNT
N-COUNT:
N of n

'shock absorber, shock absorbers; also spelled **shock-absorber.** A **shock absorber** is a device fitted near the wheels of a vehicle to reduce the effects of travelling over bumpy surfaces.
N-COUNT

shock·er /ˈʃɒkə/ **shockers.** A **shocker** is something such as a story, a piece of news, or a film that shocks people or that is intended to shock them.
N-COUNT
INFORMAL

shock 'horror. **1** A **shock horror** story is present- ADJ: ADJ n
ed in a way that is intended to cause shock or INFORMAL
anger. *...shock-horror headlines about under-age
crime.* **2** You can say **shock horror!** in reaction to EXCLAM
something that other people may find shocking or PRAGMATICS
surprising, to indicate in a humorous way that you INFORMAL
do not find it shocking or surprising at all. *I have
felt intellectually superior to most of them despite –
shock, horror – my total lack of educational
qualifications.*

shock·ing /'ʃɒkɪŋ/. **1** You can say that something ♦♦◇◇◇
is **shocking** if you think that it is very bad. ADJ-GRADED
♦ **shock·ing·ly** *His memory was becoming shock-* INFORMAL
ingly bad. **2** You can say that something is **shocking** ADJ-GRADED
if you think that it is morally wrong. *This was a
shocking invasion of privacy.* ♦ **shockingly** *Shock-* ADV
*ingly, this useless and dangerous surgery did not end
until the 1930s.* **3** See also **shock**.

shocking 'pink. Something that is **shocking pink** COLOUR
is very bright pink.

shock tactic, shock tactics. **Shock tactics** are N-COUNT
a way of trying to influence people's attitudes to a
particular matter by shocking them. *We must use
shock tactics if we are to stop Aids becoming another
accepted 20th-century disease.*

shock therapy. **1** You can refer to the use of ex- N-UNCOUNT
treme policies or actions to solve a particular problem quickly as **shock therapy**. *...Prague's policy of
economic shock therapy.* **2 Shock therapy** is a way N-UNCOUNT
of treating mentally ill patients by passing an electric current through their brain.

shock treatment, shock treatments. **Shock** N-UNCOUNT:
treatment is the same as shock therapy. also N in pl

shock troops. **Shock troops** are soldiers who are N-PLURAL
specially trained to carry out a quick attack.

shock wave, shock waves; also spelled ♦◇◇◇◇
shockwave. **1** A **shock wave** is an area of very high N-COUNT
pressure moving through the air, earth, or water. It
is caused by an explosion or an earthquake, or by
an object travelling faster than sound. **2** A **shock** N-COUNT
wave is the effect of something surprising, such as a
piece of unpleasant news, that causes strong reactions when it spreads through a place. *The crime
sent shock waves throughout the country.*

shod /ʃɒd/. **1** You can use **shod** when you are de- ADJ
scribing the kind of shoes that a person is wearing. FORMAL
...her stoutly shod feet. **2 Shod** is the past participle
of **shoe**.

shod·dy /'ʃɒdi/ **shoddier, shoddiest.** Shoddy ♦◇◇◇◇
work or a **shoddy** product has been done or made ADJ-GRADED
carelessly or badly. ♦ **shod·di·ly** *...shoddily-built* ADV-GRADED
cars.

shoe /ʃuː/ **shoes, shoeing, shoed, shod.** ♦♦♦◇◇
1 Shoes are objects which you wear on your feet. N-COUNT
They cover most of your foot and you wear them
over socks or stockings. See picture headed **clothes**.
...a pair of shoes. ● See also **training shoe.** **2** If you PHRASE
fill someone's **shoes** or **step into** their **shoes**, you
take their place by doing the job they were doing.
3 If you talk about being **in** someone's **shoes**, you PHRASE
talk about what you would do or how you would
feel if you were in their situation. *I wouldn't want to
be in his shoes.* **4** A **shoe** is the same as a **horseshoe.** N-COUNT
5 When a blacksmith **shoes** a horse, he or she fixes VERB: V n
horseshoes onto its hooves. **6** See also **shod**.

shoe·horn /'ʃuːhɔːn/ **shoehorns, shoehorning,
shoehorned.** **1** A **shoehorn** is a piece of metal or N-COUNT
plastic with a slight curve that you put in the back
of your shoe so that your heel will go into the shoe
easily. **2** If you **shoehorn** something into a tight VERB:
place, you manage to get it in there even though it V n into n
is difficult. *Their cars are shoehorned into tiny* be V-ed into n
spaces.

shoe·lace /'ʃuːleɪs/ **shoelaces.** **Shoelaces** are N-COUNT
long narrow pieces of material like pieces of string
that you use to fasten your shoes.

shoe·maker /'ʃuːmeɪkə/ **shoemakers.** A **shoe-** N-COUNT
maker is a person whose job is making shoes and
boots.

shoe·string /'ʃuːstrɪŋ/ **shoestrings.** **1 Shoe-** N-COUNT
strings are long narrow pieces of material like AMERICAN
pieces of string that you use to fasten your shoes;
the British word is **shoelace. 2** A **shoestring** budget ADJ: ADJ n
is one where you have very little money to spend.
3 If you do something or make something **on a** PHRASE
shoestring, you do it using very little money.

shone /ʃɒn, AM ʃoʊn/. **Shone** is the past tense and
past participle of **shine**.

shoo /ʃuː/ **shoos, shooing, shooed.** If you **shoo** VERB:
an animal or a person away, you make them go V n with adv
away by waving your hands or arms at them. *I* V n prep
shooed him out of the room.

'shoo-in, shoo-ins. A **shoo-in** is a person or thing N-COUNT
that seems sure to succeed. *George Bush looked like* AMERICAN,
a shoo-in for a second term in the White House. INFORMAL

shook /ʃʊk/. **Shook** is the past tense of **shake**.

shoot /ʃuːt/ **shoots, shooting, shot.** **1** If some- ♦♦♦♦◇
one **shoots** a person or an animal, they kill them or VERB: V n
injure them by firing a bullet or arrow at them. V n with adj
Gunmen shot dead the brother of the minister... Her V n in n
father shot himself in the head. **2** To **shoot** means to VERB: V
fire a bullet from a weapon such as a gun. *They* V at n
started shooting at us... She had never been able to V adv/prep
shoot straight. **3** If you **shoot** yourself **in the foot**, PHRASE
something you say or do causes you harm.
4 If someone or something **shoots** in a particular di- VERB
rection, they move in that direction quickly and sud- V adv/prep
denly. *Another car shot out of a junction and smashed
into the back of them.* **5** If you **shoot** something some- V-ERG
where, you move it there quickly and suddenly. *Mas-* V n prep/adv
ters shot a hand across the table and gripped his V adv/prep
*wrist... You'd turn on the water, and it would shoot
straight up in the air.* **6** If you **shoot** a glance at some- VERB:
one, you look at them quickly and briefly, often in a V n at n
way that expresses your feelings. *Mary Ann shot him a* V n n
rueful look. **7** If someone **shoots** to fame, they be- VERB
come famous or successful very quickly. *She shot to* V to n
stardom on Broadway in a Noel Coward play.
8 When people **shoot** a film or **shoot** photographs, VERB: V n
they make a film or take photographs using a camera.
▶ Also a noun. *...a barn presently being used for a* N-COUNT
video shoot. **9** In sports such as football or basketball, VERB
when someone **shoots**, they try to score by kicking, V adv/prep
throwing, or hitting the ball towards the goal. *A time* Also V n
limit was set for a team to shoot at the basket. **10** When VERB: V n
someone **shoots** pool, they play a game of pool. AMERICAN
11 See also **shooting, shot**.
12 Shoots are plants that are beginning to grow, or N-COUNT
new parts growing from a plant or tree.

shoot down. **1** If someone **shoots** **down** an aircraft PHRASAL VB
or a missile, they make it fall to the ground by hitting it V P noun
with a bullet or missile. *They claimed to have shot* Also V n P
down one incoming missile. **2** If one person **shoots** V P noun
down another, they shoot them with a gun. *They shot* V n P
him down in cold blood. **3** If you **shoot** someone V P noun
down or **shoot down** their ideas, you ridicule that per- Also V n P
son or their ideas. *So far America has shot down proposals for an Asia-wide security conference.*

shoot up. **1** If something **shoots** up, it grows or in- PHRASAL VB
creases very quickly. *Sales shot up by 9% last month.* V P
2 If a drug addict **shoots up**, they inject drugs into V P by/to n
their body. V P

shoot·er /'ʃuːtə/ **shooters.** A **shooter** is a person ♦◇◇◇◇
who shoots a gun. N-COUNT

shoot·ing /'ʃuːtɪŋ/ **shootings.** **1** A **shooting** is an ♦♦◇◇◇
occasion when someone is killed or injured by be- N-COUNT
ing shot with a gun. *Two more bodies were found
nearby after the shooting.* **2 Shooting** is hunting ani- N-UNCOUNT
mals with a gun as a form of sport or recreation. BRITISH
The usual American word is **hunting**. *Grouse shoot-
ing begins in August.* **3** The **shooting** of a film is the N-UNCOUNT
act of filming it.

'shooting gallery, shooting galleries. A **shoot-** N-COUNT
ing gallery is a place where people use rifles to
shoot at targets, especially in order to win prizes.

'shooting star, shooting stars. A **shooting star** N-COUNT
is a piece of rock or metal that burns very brightly
when it enters the earth's atmosphere from space,

and is seen from earth as a bright star travelling very fast across the sky.

'shooting war, shooting wars. When two countries engage in a **shooting war**, they fight each other with weapons rather than opposing each other by diplomatic or other means.   N-COUNT JOURNALISM

'shoot-out, shoot-outs. A **shoot-out** is a fight in which people shoot at each other with guns. ● See also **penalty shoot-out.**   ◆◇◇◇◇ N-COUNT

shop /ʃɒp/ **shops, shopping, shopped. 1** A **shop** is a building or part of a building where things are sold. The more usual American word is **store.** *It's not available in the shops.* **2** You can refer to a place where a particular service is offered as a particular type of **shop.** *...your local video shop.* **3** You can refer to a place where things are made or done as a particular kind of **shop.** *...the blacksmith's shop. ...a repair shop.* **4** When you **shop**, you go to shops and buy things. *He always shopped at the Co-op.* ♦ **shop·per, shoppers** *...crowds of Christmas shoppers.* **5** See also **shopping; chip shop, coffee shop, corner shop, paper shop, pawn shop, print shop, sex shop, tea shop, talking shop, thrift shop. 6** When a shop, office, or firm **shuts up shop**, it stops doing business and closes, either at the end of the day or permanently. **7** If something is happening **all over the shop**, it is happening in many different places or throughout a wide area. **8** If you say that people are **talking shop**, you mean that they are talking about their work, and this is boring for other people who do not do the same work. **9** ● to **set up shop**: see **set up. 10** If you **shop** someone, you report them to the police for doing something illegal. *His father was so disgusted to discover his son was dealing drugs he shopped him to police.*   ◆◆◆◇ N-COUNT BRITISH / N-COUNT: n N / N-COUNT: n N / VERB: V V prep/adv / N-COUNT / PHRASE BRITISH / PHRASE INFORMAL, BRITISH / PHRASE PRAGMATICS / VERB V n to n Also be V-ed INFORMAL, BRITISH

shop around. If you **shop around**, you go to different shops or companies in order to compare the prices and quality of goods or services before you decide to buy them. *He shopped around for a firm that would be flexible.*   PHRASAL VB V P V P for n

shop·a·ho·lic /ˌʃɒpəˈhɒlɪk/ **shopaholics.** A **shopaholic** is a person who cannot stop spending money.   N-COUNT INFORMAL

'shop assistant, shop assistants. A **shop assistant** is a person who works in a shop selling things to customers. The usual American word is **sales clerk.**   ◆◇◇◇◇ N-COUNT BRITISH

,shop 'floor; also spelled **shop-floor** or **shopfloor.** The **shop floor** is used to refer to all the workers in a factory or the area where they work, especially in contrast to the management or the area where the management work. *Cost must be controlled, not just on the shop floor but in the boardroom too.*   N-SING

'shop front, shop fronts; also spelled **shopfront.** A **shop front** is the outside part of a shop which faces the street, including the door and windows; the usual American term is **storefront.**   N-COUNT BRITISH

shop·keep·er /ˈʃɒpkiːpə/ **shopkeepers.** A **shopkeeper** is a person who owns or manages a small shop; the usual American term is **storekeeper.**   ◆◇◇◇◇ N-COUNT BRITISH

shop·lift /ˈʃɒplɪft/ **shoplifts, shoplifting, shoplifted.** If someone **shoplifts**, they steal goods from a shop by hiding them in a bag or in their clothes. *They had shoplifted thousands of dollars' worth of merchandise.* ♦ **shop·lifter, shoplifters** *A persistent shoplifter has been banned from every Marks & Spencer store in Britain.* ♦ **shop·lifting** *The grocer accused her of shoplifting.*   ◆◇◇◇◇ VERB: V n / N-COUNT / N-UNCOUNT

shop·ping /ˈʃɒpɪŋ/ **1** When you do the **shopping**, you go to shops and buy things. ● See also **window shopping. 2** Your **shopping** consists of the things that you have bought from shops, especially food and groceries.   ◆◆◆◇ N-UNCOUNT / N-UNCOUNT

'shopping cart, shopping carts. A **shopping cart** is the same as a **shopping trolley.**   N-COUNT AMERICAN

'shopping centre, shopping centres; also spelled **shopping center. 1** A **shopping centre** is a covered area where many shops have been built and where cars are not allowed. The American term is **shopping mall. 2** A **shopping centre** is an area in   ◆◇◇◇◇ N-COUNT BRITISH / N-COUNT

a town where a lot of shops have been built close together.   BRITISH

'shopping list, shopping lists. A **shopping list** is a list of the things that you want to buy when you go shopping, which you write on a piece of paper.   ◆◇◇◇◇ N-COUNT

'shopping mall, shopping malls. A **shopping mall** is a covered area where many shops have been built and where cars are not allowed.   ◆◇◇◇◇ N-COUNT

'shopping trolley, shopping trolleys. A **shopping trolley** is a large metal basket on wheels which is provided by shops such as supermarkets for customers to use while they are in the shop. The American word is **shopping cart.**   N-COUNT BRITISH

,shop 'steward, shop stewards. A **shop steward** is a trade union member who is elected by the other members in a factory or office to speak for them at official meetings.   N-COUNT

shore /ʃɔː/ **shores, shoring, shored. 1** The **shores** or the **shore** of a sea, lake, or wide river is the land along the edge of it. Someone who is **on shore** is on the land rather than on a ship. *I decided to head back to shore.* **2** When someone or something reaches or leaves the **shores** of a country or continent, they arrive in or depart from that country or continent. *This youngster is another destined to leave these shores.*   ◆◆◆◇ N-COUNT: also prep N / N-PLURAL: with supp LITERARY

shore up. If you **shore up** something that is weak or about to fail, you do something in order to strengthen it or support it. *The democracies of the West may find it hard to shore up their defences.*   PHRASAL VB V P noun Also V n P

shore·line /ˈʃɔːlaɪn/ **shorelines.** A **shoreline** is the edge of a sea, lake, or wide river.   ◆◇◇◇◇ N-COUNT

shorn /ʃɔːn/ **1** If hair is **shorn**, it has been cut very short. **2** If someone or something is **shorn** of something that is an important part of them, it has been removed from them. *She looks terrible, shorn of all her beauty and dignity.* **3** **Shorn** is the past participle of **shear.**   ADJ LITERARY / ADJ: v-link ADJ of n LITERARY

short 1 adjective and adverb uses

short /ʃɔːt/ **shorter, shortest. 1** If something is **short** or lasts for a **short** time, it does not last very long. *The announcement was made a short time ago... Mr Mandela took a short break before resuming his schedule... Kemp gave a short laugh.* **2** If you talk about a **short** hour, day, or year, you mean that it seems to have passed very quickly or will seem to pass very quickly. *Only five short years later, your money will have grown by $94,000.* **3** If something is cut **short** or stops **short**, it is stopped before people expect it or before it has finished. *Jackson cut short his trip to Africa.* **4** If workers are put on **short time**, they are asked to work fewer hours than the normal working week, because their employer can not afford to pay them a full time wage. **5** Someone who is **short** is not as tall as most people are. **6** Something that is **short** measures only a small amount from one end to the other. *The city centre and shops are only a short distance away... His black hair was very short.* **7** A **short** speech, letter, or book does not have many words or pages in it. **8** You use the expression **in short** when you have been giving a lot of details and you want to give a conclusion or summary. *Try tennis, badminton or windsurfing. In short, anything challenging.* **9** If you are **short of** something or if it is **short**, you do not have enough of it. If you are running **short** of something or if it is running **short**, you do not have much of it left. *Her father's illness left the family short of money... Time is running short.* **10** If you say that someone is, for example, **several cards short of a full deck** or **one sandwich short of a picnic**, you think they are stupid, foolish, or crazy. **11** If you **go short** or **run short** of something, especially food, you do not have as much of it as you want or need. *He probably never went short of anything.* **12** If someone or something **is short on** a particular good quality, they do not have as much of it as you think they should have; used showing disapproval. *The proposals were short on detail.*   ◆◆◆◆◆ ADJ-GRADED / ADJ-GRADED / ADV: ADV after v / PHRASE / ADJ-GRADED / ADJ-GRADED / ADJ-GRADED / PHRASE / ADJ-GRADED: v-link ADJ / PHRASE INFORMAL / PHRASE / PHRASE PRAGMATICS

13 If someone or something is or stops **short of** a place, they have not quite reached it. If they are or fall **short of** an amount, they have not quite achieved it. *They were still 91 short of their target.* **14** If someone **stops short of** doing something, they come close to doing it but do not actually do it. **15 Short of** a particular thing means except for that thing or without actually doing that thing. *Short of climbing railings four metres high, there was no way into the garden from this road.* **16** You use **nothing short of** or **little short of** to emphasize how great or extreme something is. For example, if you say that something is **nothing short of** a miracle, you mean that it is a miracle. **17** If a name or abbreviation is **short for** another name, it is the short version of that name. *Her friend Kes (short for Kesewa) was in tears.* **18** If a person or thing is called something **for short**, that is the short version of their name. *This condition is called seasonal affective disorder, or SAD for short.* **19** If you have a **short** temper, you get angry very easily. ● See also **short-tempered**. **20** If something **pulls** you **up short** or **brings** you **up short**, it makes you suddenly stop what you are doing. *The name on the gate pulled me up short.* **21** If you **make short work of** someone or something, you deal with them or defeat them very quickly. **22** ● **short of breath**: see **breath**. ● **at short notice**: see **notice**. ● **to sell** someone **short**: see **sell**. ● **to get short shrift**: see **shrift**. ● **to cut a long story short**: see **story**. ● **in short supply**: see **supply**. ● **in the short term**: see **term**.

ADJ: v-link ADJ of n
PHRASE
PHR-PREP
PHRASE
PRAGMATICS
ADJ: v-link ADJ for n
PHRASE
ADJ-GRADED
PHRASE
PHRASE
INFORMAL

short 2 noun uses

short /ʃɔːt/ **shorts. 1 Shorts** are trousers with very short legs, that people wear in hot weather or for taking part in sport. **2 Shorts** are men's underpants that usually reach to mid-thigh. **3** A **short** is a small, strong alcoholic drink of a spirit such as whisky or gin, rather than a weaker alcoholic drink like beer or wine that you can drink in larger quantities. **4** A **short** is a short film, especially one that is shown before the main film at the cinema.

N-PLURAL
N-PLURAL
N-COUNT AMERICAN BRITISH
N-COUNT

short·age /ˈʃɔːtɪdʒ/ **shortages.** If there is a **shortage** of something, there is not enough of it. *Vietnam is suffering from food shortage... There's no shortage of ideas when it comes to improving the education of children.*

N-VAR

short back and 'sides; also spelled **short-back-and-sides.** A **short back and sides** is a haircut in which the hair is cut very short at the back and sides with slightly thicker, longer hair on the top of the head.

N-SING

short·bread /ˈʃɔːtbred/ **shortbreads.** Shortbread is a biscuit made from flour, sugar, and butter.

N-VAR

short-'change, short-changes, short-changing, short-changed. 1 If someone **short-changes** you, they do not give you enough change after you have bought something from them. **2** If you **are short-changed**, you are treated unfairly or dishonestly, often because you are given less of something than you deserve. *Women are in fact still being short-changed in the press.* ♦ **short-changed** *Theatre-goers may feel short-changed when they arrive expecting to see an international superstar.*

VERB: V n
VB: usu passive be V-ed
ADJ-GRADED: v-link ADJ

short-'circuit, short-circuits, short-circuiting, short-circuited. 1 If an electrical system or device **short-circuits** or is **short-circuited**, a wrong connection or damaged wire causes electricity to travel along the wrong route and damage the system or device. *Once inside they short-circuited the electronic security.* ▶ Also a noun. *Ensure that any electrical gadgets are fitted expertly to eliminate the risk of a short-circuit.* **2** If someone or something **short-circuits** a process or system, they avoid long or difficult parts of it and use a quicker, more direct method to achieve their aim. *The approach was intended to short-circuit normal complaints procedures.*

V-ERG: V n
N-COUNT
VERB V n

short·coming /ˈʃɔːtkʌmɪŋ/ **shortcomings.** The **shortcomings** of a person or thing are the faults

N-COUNT

or weaknesses which they have. *His book has its shortcomings.*

short 'cut, short cuts; also spelled **short-cut** or **shortcut. 1** A **short cut** is a quicker way of getting somewhere than the usual route. *I tried to take a short cut and got lost.* **2** A **short cut** is a method of achieving something more quickly or more easily than if you use the usual methods. *Fame can be a shortcut to love and money.*

N-COUNT
N-COUNT

short·en /ˈʃɔːtən/ **shortens, shortening, shortened. 1** If you **shorten** an event or the length of time that something lasts, or if it **shortens**, it does not last as long as it would otherwise do or as it used to do. *Smoking can shorten your life. ...when the days shorten in winter.* **2** If you **shorten** an object or if it **shortens**, it becomes smaller in length. *...an operation to shorten her nose.* **3** If you **shorten** a name or other word, you change it by removing some of the letters. *Originally called Lili, she eventually shortened her name to Lee.*

V-ERG: V n, V
V-ERG: V n, Also V
VERB: V n

short·en·ing /ˈʃɔːtnɪŋ/ **shortenings.** Shortening is cooking fat that you use with flour in order to make pastry or dough.

N-VAR AMERICAN

short·fall /ˈʃɔːtfɔːl/ **shortfalls.** If there is a **shortfall** in something, there is less of it than you need. *The government has refused to make up a £30,000 shortfall in funding.*

N-COUNT

short·hand /ˈʃɔːthænd/. **1** Shorthand is a way of writing, used especially by secretaries, which uses signs to represent words or syllables. **2** You can use **shorthand** to mean a quick or simple way of referring to something. *...the fiction that 'he' is a neutral shorthand for 'he or she'.*

N-UNCOUNT
N-UNCOUNT: also a N

short-'handed. If a company or organization is **short-handed**, it does not have enough people to work on a particular job.

ADJ-GRADED

'short-haul. Short-haul is used to describe things that involve transporting passengers or goods over short distances. *...short-haul flights.*

ADJ: ADJ n

short·list /ˈʃɔːtlɪst/ **shortlists, shortlisting, shortlisted;** also spelled **short list. 1** If someone is on a **shortlist**, for example for a job or a prize, they are one of a small group of people who have been chosen from a larger group. The successful person is then chosen from the small group. **2** If someone or something **is shortlisted** for a job or a prize, they are put on a shortlist. *He was shortlisted for the Nobel Prize for literature.*

N-COUNT
VB: usu passive be V-ed for/as n BRITISH

short-'lived. Something that is **short-lived** does not last very long.

ADJ-GRADED

short·ly /ˈʃɔːtli/. **1** If something happens **shortly** after or before something else, it happens not long after or before it. If something is going to happen **shortly**, it is going to happen soon. *Their trial will shortly begin.* **2** If you speak to someone **shortly**, you speak to them in a cross or impatient way. *'I don't know you,' he said shortly.*

ADV-GRADED
ADV-GRADED: ADV after v

short-'range. Short-range weapons or missiles are designed to be fired across short distances.

ADJ-GRADED: ADJ n

short-'sighted; also spelled **shortsighted. 1** If you are **short-sighted**, you cannot see things properly when they are far away, because there is something wrong with your eyes. ♦ **short-sighted·ness** *Radical eye surgery promises to cure short-sightedness.* **2** If someone is **short-sighted** about something, they do not make proper or careful judgements about the future. *This is a short-sighted approach to the problem of global warming.* ♦ **short-sightedness** *The government now recognises the short-sightedness of this approach.*

ADJ-GRADED
N-UNCOUNT
ADJ-GRADED
N-UNCOUNT

short-'staffed. A company or place that is **short-staffed** does not have enough people working in there.

ADJ-GRADED

short 'story, short stories. A short story is a piece of prose fiction that is only a few pages long.

N-COUNT

short-'tempered. Someone who is **short-tempered** gets angry very quickly.

ADJ-GRADED

'short-term. Short-term is used to describe things that will last for a short time, or things that will have an effect soon rather than in the distant future. *...a cynical manipulation of the situation for*

ADJ-GRADED

S

short-term political gain... The short-term outlook for employment remains gloomy.

'short-wave; also spelled **short wave** or **shortwave. Short-wave** is a range of short radio wavelengths used for broadcasting. *I use the short-wave radio to get the latest war news.* N-UNCOUNT

shot /ʃɒt/ **shots. 1 Shot** is the past tense and past participle of **shoot. 2** A **shot** is an act of firing a gun. *A man fired a volley of shots at them.* **3** Someone who is a good **shot** can shoot well. Someone who is a bad **shot** cannot shoot well. **4** In sports such as football, golf, or tennis, a **shot** is an act of kicking, hitting, or throwing the ball, especially in an attempt to score a point. *He had only one shot at goal.* ◆◆◆◇ N-COUNT N-COUNT: adj N N-COUNT

5 A **shot** is a photograph or a particular sequence of pictures in a film. *I decided to try for a more natural shot of a fox peering from the bushes.* N-COUNT

6 If you have a **shot at** something, you attempt to do it. *The heavyweight champion will be given a shot at Holyfield's world title.* **7** If you **give** something your **best shot**, you do it as well as you possibly can. **8** If you describe something as a **long shot**, you mean that it is unlikely to succeed, but is worth trying. N-COUNT INFORMAL INFORMAL PHRASE

9 A **shot** of a drug is an injection of it. **10** A **shot** of a strong alcoholic drink is a small glass of it. N-COUNT N-COUNT

11 The person who **calls the shots** is in a position to tell others what to do. **12** If you do something **like a shot**, you do it without any delay or hesitation. **13** People sometimes use the expression **by a long shot** to emphasize the opinion they are giving. **14** If something **is shot through with** an element or feature, it contains a lot of that element or feature. *This is an argument shot through with inconsistency.* **15 • a shot in the dark**: see **dark.** PHRASE PHRASE INFORMAL PHRASE PRAGMATICS PHRASE

shot·gun /'ʃɒtɡʌn/ **shotguns.** A **shotgun** is a gun which fires a lot of small metal balls at one time. ◆◇◇◇◇ N-COUNT

'shot put. In athletics, the **shot put** is a competition in which the contestants throw a heavy metal ball as far as possible. **♦ shot putt·er, shot putt·ers** *...Canadian shot-putter Georgette Reed.* N-SING N-COUNT

should /ʃəd, STRONG ʃʊd/. **Should** is a modal verb. It is used with the base form of a verb. ◆◆◆◆◆

1 You use **should** or **should not** when you are giving advice or recommendations. You also use **should** when you are mentioning things that are not the case but that you think ought to be. *I should exercise more... He's never going to be able to forget it. And I don't think he should... Should our children be taught to swim at school?* **2** You use **should** or **should not** to tell someone what to do or to report a rule or law which tells someone what to do. *A High Court judge has ruled that the two men should stand trial.* **3** You use **should** in questions when you are asking someone for advice, permission, or information. *Should I or shouldn't I go to university?... Please could you advise me what I should do?.* MODAL PRAGMATICS MODAL PRAGMATICS MODAL PRAGMATICS

4 If you say that something **should have** happened, you mean that it did not happen, but that you wish it had happened or that you expected it to happen. If you say that something **should not have** happened, you mean that it did happen, but that you wish it had not. *I should have gone this morning but I was feeling a bit ill... I shouldn't have said what I did.* MODAL

5 You use **should** when you are saying that something is probably the case or will probably happen in the way you are describing. If you say that something **should have** happened by a particular time, you mean that it will probably have happened by that time. *You should have no problem with reading this language... We should have finished by a quarter past two and the bus doesn't leave till half past.* MODAL

6 You use **should** in conditional clauses when you are talking about things that might happen. *Should you buy a home from Lovell, the company promises to buy it back at the same price after three years.* MODAL FORMAL

7 You use **should** in 'that' clauses after certain verbs, nouns, and adjectives when you are talking about a future event or situation. In formal English the subjunctive is used instead of this structure. *He raised his* MODAL

glass and indicated that I should do the same... I insisted that we should have a look at every car.

8 You use **should** in expressions such as **I should think** and **I should imagine** to indicate that you think something is true but you are not sure. *I should think it's going to rain soon... 'I suppose that was the right thing to do.'—'I should imagine so.'.* MODAL PRAGMATICS

9 You say **'I should'**, usually with the expression 'if I were you', when you are giving someone advice by telling them what you would do if you were in their position. *I should look out if I were you!.* MODAL PRAGMATICS FORMAL, BRITISH

10 You use **should** in expressions such as **I should like** and **I should be happy** to show politeness when you are saying what you want to do, or when you are requesting, offering, or accepting something. *I should like to know anything you can tell me.* MODAL PRAGMATICS BRITISH

11 You use **should have** with 'you' when reporting an event to emphasize how funny, shocking, or impressive it was. *You should have heard him last night!.* MODAL PRAGMATICS SPOKEN

12 You use **should** in interrogative structures with words like 'who' and 'what' when you are reporting an event, to emphasize how surprising or shocking it was. *Who should I meet but this blonde guy and John?* MODAL PRAGMATICS SPOKEN

shoul·der /'ʃəʊldə/ **shoulders, shouldering, shouldered. 1** Your **shoulders** are between your neck and the tops of your arms. See picture headed **human body.** *He glanced over his shoulder.* **2** If two or more people stand **shoulder to shoulder,** they are standing next to each other, with their shoulders touching. *They fell into step, walking shoulder to shoulder.* **3** The **shoulders** of a piece of clothing are the parts that cover your shoulders. *...extravagant fashions with padded shoulders.* **4** If you **shoulder** something heavy, you put it across one of your shoulders so that you can carry it more easily. *He shouldered his bike and walked across the finish line.* **5** If you **shoulder** someone aside or if you **shoulder** your way somewhere, you push past people roughly using your shoulder. *She could do nothing to stop him as he shouldered his way into the house.* ◆◆◆◇ N-COUNT PHRASE N-COUNT VERB V n VERB: V n with aside V way prep/ adv Also V past/ through n

6 When you talk about someone's problems or responsibilities, you can say that they carry them on their **shoulders.** *I fervently hope he recognizes and understands the burden that's on his shoulders.* **7** If you **shoulder** the responsibility or the blame for something, you accept it. *He has had to shoulder the responsibility of his father's mistakes.* N-PLURAL: poss N VERB V n

8 A **shoulder** is a joint of meat from the upper part of the front leg of an animal. *...shoulder of lamb.* N-VAR

9 See also **cold-shoulder, hard shoulder.**

10 If someone offers you a **shoulder to cry on** or is a **shoulder to cry on,** they listen sympathetically to all your troubles. **11** If you say that someone or something stands **head and shoulders** above other people or things, you mean that they are a lot better than them. **12** If you say that someone is **looking over** their **shoulder,** you mean that they feel anxious or insecure about someone or something that threatens them. *When a company keeps making people redundant, those who are left behind might start looking over their shoulder.* **13** If you **rub shoulders with** famous or notorious people, you meet them and talk to them. **14** If people work **shoulder to shoulder,** they work cooperatively together in order to achieve a common aim. *They could fight shoulder-to-shoulder against a common enemy.* **15 • a chip on** one's **shoulder:** see **chip.** PHRASE PHRASE PHRASE PHRASE PHRASE

'shoulder-bag, shoulder-bags. A **shoulder-bag** is a bag that has a long strap so that it can be carried on a person's shoulder. N-COUNT

'shoulder blade, shoulder blades. Your **shoulder blades** are the two large, flat, triangular bones that you have in the upper part of your back, below your shoulders. N-COUNT

'shoulder-length. Shoulder-length hair is long enough to reach your shoulders. ADJ

'shoulder pad, shoulder pads. Shoulder pads are small pads that are put inside the shoulders of clothing in order to raise and widen them. N-COUNT

'**shoulder-strap, shoulder-straps.** **1** The `N-COUNT` **shoulder-straps** on a piece of clothing such as a dress are two narrow straps that go over the shoulders. **2** A **shoulder-strap** on a bag is a long strap `N-COUNT` that you put over your shoulder to carry the bag.

shouldn't /ˈʃʊdənt/. 'Should not' is usually said or `INFORMAL` written as **shouldn't**.

should've /ˈʃʊdəv/. **Should've** is the usual form of `SPOKEN` 'should have', especially when 'have' is an auxiliary verb.

shout /ʃaʊt/ **shouts, shouting, shouted. 1** If ◆◆◆◇◇ you **shout**, you say something very loudly, usually `VERB: V` because you want people a long distance away to `V with quote` hear you or because you are angry. *'She's alive!' he* `V for n` *shouted triumphantly... Andrew rushed out of the* `V at n` *house, shouting for help... You don't have to shout at* `Also V n,` *me... I shouted at mother to get the police.* ► Also a `V that` noun. *I heard a distant shout.* ♦ **shout·ing** One of `N-UNCOUNT` *my grandchildren heard the shouting first.* **2** If you `CONVENTION` are in a pub and someone you are with says '**It's** `INFORMAL,` **your shout**' or '**It's my shout**', they mean that it is `BRITISH` your turn or their turn to buy a round of drinks.

shout down. If people **shout down** someone who is `PHRASAL VB` trying to speak, they prevent that person from being `V P noun` heard by shouting at them. *They shouted him down* `V n P` *when he tried to explain why Zaire needed an interim government.*

shout out. If you **shout** something **out**, you say it `PHRASAL VB` very loudly so that people can hear you clearly. *They* `V n P` *shouted out the names of those detained... I shouted* `V P noun` *out 'I'm OK'.* `V P with quote`

'**shouting match, shouting matches.** A shout- `N-COUNT` **ing match** is an angry quarrel in which people shout at each other. *We had a real shouting match with each other.*

shove /ʃʌv/ **shoves, shoving, shoved. 1** If you ◆◆◇◇◇ **shove** someone or something, you push them with `VERB: V n` a quick violent movement. *He shoved her out of the* `V n prep/adv` *way... She shoved as hard as she could.* ► Also a `V` noun. *She gave Gracie a shove towards the house.* `N-COUNT` **2** If you **shove** something somewhere, you push it `VERB` there quickly and carelessly. *He shoved a cloth in* `V n prep/adv` *my hand.* **3** If you talk about what you think will `PHRASE` happen if **push comes to shove**, you are talking `INFORMAL` about what you think will happen in a situation becomes very bad or difficult. *If push comes to shove, if you should lose your case in the court, what will you do?.*

shov·el /ˈʃʌvəl/ **shovels, shovelling, shov-** ◆◇◇◇◇ **elled;** spelled **shoveling, shoveled** in American English. **1** A **shovel** is a tool like a spade, used for `N-COUNT` lifting and moving earth, coal, or snow. See picture headed **tools. 2** If you **shovel** earth, coal, or snow, `VERB: V n` you lift and move it with a shovel. *Pendergood had* `V n prep/adv` *shovelled the sand out of the caravan.* **3** If you shov- `VERB` el something somewhere, you push a lot of it quick- `V n prep/adv` ly into that place. *There was silence, except for Randall, who was obliviously shoveling food into his mouth.*

show /ʃəʊ/ **shows, showing, showed, shown.** ◆◆◆◆◆ **1** If something **shows** that a state of affairs exists, it `VERB:` gives information that proves it or makes it clear to `V that` people. *These figures show an increase of over one* `V n` million in unemployment... It was only later that the `be V-ed to-inf` drug was shown to be addictive... You'll be given `V wh` regular blood tests to show whether you have been infected.* **2** If a picture, chart, film, or piece of writ- `VERB` ing **shows** something, it represents it or gives `V n` information about it. *Figure 4.1 shows the respira-* `V n -ing` *tory system... Much of the film shows the painter* `V wh` *simply going about his task... Our photograph shows how the plants will turn out.* **3** If you say **it just goes** `PHRASE` **to show** or **it just shows** that something is the case, you mean that what you have just said or experienced demonstrates that it is the case. *It's crazy and just shows the inconsistency of refereeing.*

4 If you **show** someone something, you give it to `VERB: V n n` them, take them to it, or point to it, so that they can `V n to n` see it or know what you are referring to. *Cut out this* `V n wh` *article and show it to your bank manager... I showed*

them where the gun was.* **5** If you **show** someone to a `VERB:` room or seat, you lead them there. *Your office is ready* `V n prep/adv` *for you. I'll show you the way.* **6** If you **show** someone `V n` how to do something, you do it yourself so that they `VERB` can watch you and learn how to do it. *Claire showed* `V n wh` *us how to make a chocolate roulade... Dr. Reichert has* `V n n` *shown us a new way to look at those behavior problems.* **7** You can say **'I'll show you'** to threaten or warn `PHRASE` someone that you are going to make them admit that `PRAGMATICS` they are wrong. *She shook her fist. 'I'll show you,' she said.*

8 If something **shows** or if you **show** it, it is visible or `V-ERG` noticeable. *He showed his teeth in a humourless grin...* `V n` *Faint glimmers of daylight were showing through the* `V` *treetops.* **9** If a question is decided by a **show of hands**, `PHRASE` people vote on it by raising their hands to indicate whether they vote yes or no.

10 If you **show** a particular attitude, quality, or feel- `V-ERG: V n` ing, or if it **shows**, you behave in a way that makes this `V` attitude, quality, or feeling clear to other people. *`V n n` Ferguson was unhappy and it showed... You show me* `V n to-inf` *respect... Mr Clarke has shown himself to be resolutely* `V that` *opposed to compromise... The baby was tugging at his coat to show that he wanted to be picked up.* **11** If `VERB` something **shows** a quality or characteristic or if that `V n` quality or characteristic **shows** itself, the quality or characteristic can be noticed or observed. *Peace talks in Washington showed signs of progress yesterday... How else did his hostility to women show itself?* **12** A `N-COUNT` **show** of a feeling or quality is an attempt by someone to make it clear that they have that feeling or quality. *Miners gathered in the centre of Bucharest in a show of support for the government.* **13** If you say that some- `N-UNCOUNT` thing is for **show**, you mean that it has no real purpose and is done just to give a good impression. *'It's all show,' said Linus. 'The girls don't take it seriously.'*

14 If you **have** something **to show for** your efforts, `PHRASE` you have achieved something as a result of what you have done. *I'm nearly 31 and it's about time I had something to show for my time in my job.*

15 If a company **shows** a profit or a loss, its accounts `VERB: V n` indicate that it has made a profit or a loss.

16 If a person you are expecting to meet does not `VERB: V` **show**, they do not arrive at the place where you expect to meet them. ► **Show up** means the same as **show**. `PHRASAL VB` *He always shows up in a fancy car... If I don't show up* `V P` *for class this morning, I'll be kicked out.* `V P for/to n`

17 A television or radio **show** is a programme on tele- `N-COUNT` vision or radio. **18** A **show** in a theatre is an entertain- `N-COUNT` ment or concert, especially one that includes different items such as music, dancing, and comedy. *How about going shopping and seeing a show in London?* **19** If someone **shows** a film or television programme, `V-ERG` it is broadcast or appears on television or in the cine- `V n` ma. *The BBC World Service Television news showed* `V` *the same film clip... American films are showing at Moscow's cinemas.* ♦ **show·ing, showings** I gave `N-COUNT` *him a private showing of the film.* **20** A **show** is a pub- `N-COUNT:` lic exhibition of things, such as works of art, fashion- `also on N` able clothes, or things that have been entered in a competition. **21** To **show** things such as works of art `VERB` means to put them in an exhibition where they can be `V n` seen by the public. *50 dealers will show oils, water-colours, drawings and prints.*

22 If you say that someone **is running the show**, you `PHRASE` mean that they are in control or in charge of a situation. *They made it clear who is now running the show.* **23** If you say that someone **steals the show**, you mean `PHRASE` that they get a lot of attention or praise because they perform better than anyone else in a show or other event. *It was Chinese women who stole the show on the first day of competition.*

24 A **show** home is one of a group of newly-built `ADJ: ADJ n` homes. It is decorated and furnished by the building company, and people who want to buy one of the homes come and look round it.

25 ● to **show** someone **the door**: see **door**. ● to **show** your **face**: see **face**.

show around or **show round.** If you **show** some- `PHRASAL VB` one **around** or **show** them **round**, you go with them to `V n P`

show them all the interesting, useful, or important features of a place when they first visit it. *Spear showed him around the flat.* `V n P n`

show off. 1 If you say that someone is **showing off**, you are criticizing them for trying to impress people by showing in a very obvious way what they can do or what they own. *All right, there's no need to show off.* **2** If you **show off** something that you own or an attribute that you have, you show it to a lot of people or make it obvious, because you are proud of it. *He actually enjoys his new hair-style and has decided to start showing it off.* **3** If something **shows** something **off**, it emphasizes its good features so that it looks especially attractive. *...a dress which showed off her tiny waist.* **4** See also **show-off**. `PHRASAL VB` `PRAGMATICS` `V P` `V P noun` `V n P` `V n P` `V P noun`

show round. See **show around**. `PHRASAL VB`

show up. 1 If an object or phenomenon **shows up** or if something **shows** it **up**, it can be clearly seen or noticed. *...a telescope so powerful that it can show up galaxies billions of light years away.* **2** See **show** 16. **3** If someone or something **shows** you **up**, they make you feel embarrassed or ashamed of them. *We expected every drawing exercise to show us up as hopeless artists.* `PHRASAL VB` `ERG:` `V P` `V P noun` `Also V n P` `V n P` `V n P asn`

show·biz /'ʃəʊbɪz/. **Showbiz** is the same as **show business**. `N-UNCOUNT` `INFORMAL`

'show business. **Show business** is the entertainment industry of film, theatre, and television. `♦◇◇◇◇` `N-UNCOUNT`

show·case /'ʃəʊkeɪs/ **showcases, showcasing, showcased. 1** A **showcase** is a glass container with valuable objects inside it, for example at an exhibition or in a museum. **2** You use **showcase** to refer to a situation or setting in which something is displayed or presented to its best advantage. *The festival remains a valuable showcase for new talent.* **3** If something **is showcased**, it is displayed or presented to its best advantage. *Restored films are being showcased this month at a festival in Paris.* `♦◇◇◇◇` `N-COUNT` `N-COUNT:` `with supp` `VB: usu` `passive` `be V-ed` `JOURNALISM`

show·down /'ʃəʊdaʊn/ **showdowns**; also spelled **show-down**. A **showdown** is a big argument or conflict which is intended to settle a dispute that has lasted for a long time. *They may be pushing the Prime Minister towards a final showdown with his party.* `♦◇◇◇◇` `N-COUNT`

show·er /ʃaʊə/ **showers, showering, showered. 1** A **shower** is a device used for washing yourself. It consists of a pipe or hose which ends in a flat piece with a lot of holes in it so that water comes out in a spray. You can also describe a cubicle which contains one of these devices as a **shower**. *She heard him turn on the shower.* **2** The **showers** or the **shower** in a place such as a sports centre is the area containing showers. *The showers are a mess.* **3** If you **shower**, you wash yourself by standing under a spray of water from a shower. *There wasn't time to shower or change clothes.* ▶ Also a noun. *I think I'll have a shower before dinner... She took two showers a day.* **4** A **shower** is a short period of rain, especially light rain. *There'll be bright or sunny spells and scattered showers this afternoon.* **5** You can refer to a lot of things that are falling as a **shower** of them. *Showers of sparks flew in all directions.* **6** If you **are showered with** a lot of small objects or pieces, they are scattered over you. *They were showered with rice in the traditional manner.* **7** If you **shower** a person **with** presents or kisses, you give them a lot of presents or kisses in a very generous and extravagant way. `♦♦◇◇◇` `N-COUNT` `N-COUNT` `VERB` `V` `N-COUNT` `N-COUNT` `N-COUNT` `VB: usu` `passive` `be V-ed with n` `VERB:` `V n with n`

show·ery /'ʃaʊəri/. If the weather is **showery**, there are showers of rain but it does not rain all the time. `ADJ-GRADED`

show·girl /'ʃəʊɡɜːl/ **showgirls**. A **showgirl** is a young woman who sings and dances as part of the chorus in a musical show. `N-COUNT`

show·ground /'ʃəʊɡraʊnd/ **showgrounds**. A **showground** is a large open-air area where events such as agricultural shows or competitions are held. `N-COUNT`

'show jumping; also spelled **showjumping. Show jumping** is a sport in which horses are ridden in competitions to demonstrate their skill in jumping `♦◇◇◇◇` `N-UNCOUNT`

over fences and walls. ♦ **'show jumper, show jumpers** *...the Canadian show jumper Ian Miller.* `N-COUNT`

show·man /'ʃəʊmæn/ **showmen.** A **showman** is a person who is very entertaining and dramatic in the way that they perform, or the way that they present things. ♦ **show·man·ship** /'ʃəʊmənʃɪp/. **Showmanship** is a person's skill at performing or presenting things in an entertaining and dramatic way. `N-COUNT` `N-UNCOUNT`

shown /ʃəʊn/. **Shown** is the past participle of **show**.

'show-off, show-offs. If you say that someone is a **show-off**, you are criticizing them for trying to impress people by showing in a very obvious way what they can do or what they own. `◆◇◇◇` `N-COUNT` `PRAGMATICS` `INFORMAL`

show·piece /'ʃəʊpiːs/ **showpieces**; also spelled **show-piece**. A **showpiece** is something that is admired as a fine example of its type, especially something which is intended to make people admire its owner or creator. *The factory was to be a showpiece of Western investment in the East.* `◆◇◇◇` `N-COUNT:` `with supp`

show·room /'ʃəʊruːm/ **showrooms.** A **showroom** is a shop in which goods are displayed for sale, especially goods such as cars or electrical or gas appliances. `◆◇◇◇` `N-COUNT`

'show-stopper, show-stoppers; also spelled **showstopper.** If something is a **show-stopper**, it is very impressive. *Her natural creativity and artistic talent make her home a real show stopper.* `N-COUNT` `INFORMAL`

show·time /'ʃəʊtaɪm/. **Showtime** is the time when a particular stage or television show is due to begin. *It's close to showtime now, so you retire into the dressing room.* `N-UNCOUNT`

'show trial, show trials. People describe a trial as a **show trial** if they believe that the trial is unfair and is held for political reasons rather than in order to find out the truth; used showing disapproval. *Amnesty International has denounced the show trials of political dissidents.* `N-COUNT` `PRAGMATICS`

showy /'ʃəʊi/ **showier, showiest.** Something that is **showy** is very noticeable because it is large, colourful, or bright. *Since he was color blind, he favored large, showy flowers.* `ADJ-GRADED`

shrank /ʃræŋk/. **Shrank** is the past tense of **shrink**.

shrap·nel /'ʃræpnəl/. **Shrapnel** consists of small pieces of metal which are scattered from exploding bombs and shells. `◆◇◇◇` `N-UNCOUNT`

shred /ʃred/ **shreds, shredding, shredded. 1** If you **shred** something such as food or paper, you cut it or tear it into very small narrow pieces. *Finely shred the carrots, cabbage and cored apples.* ♦ **shred·der, shredders.** A **shredder** is a machine for shredding things such as documents or twigs. *...a document shredder.* **2** If you cut or tear food or paper into **shreds**, you cut or tear it into small narrow pieces. **3** If there is not a **shred** of something, there is not even a small amount of it. *He said there was not a shred of evidence to support such remarks.* **4** If you **tear** someone **to shreds** or **rip** them **to shreds**, you criticize them very severely. `◆◇◇◇` `VERB` `V n` `N-COUNT` `N-COUNT` `N-COUNT:` `N of n` `PHRASE`

shrew /ʃruː/ **shrews.** A **shrew** is a small brown animal like a mouse with a long pointed nose. `N-COUNT`

shrewd /ʃruːd/ **shrewder, shrewdest.** A **shrewd** person is able to understand and judge a situation quickly and to use this understanding to their own advantage. ♦ **shrewd·ly** *She looked at him shrewdly.* ♦ **shrewd·ness** *His natural shrewdness tells him what is needed to succeed.* `◆◇◇◇` `ADJ-GRADED` `ADV-GRADED` `N-UNCOUNT`

shriek /ʃriːk/ **shrieks, shrieking, shrieked.** When someone **shrieks**, they make a short very loud cry, for example because they are startled or in pain, or are laughing. *She shrieked and leapt from the bed... 'Stop it! Stop it!' shrieked Jane.* ▶ Also a noun. *Sue let out a terrific shriek.* `◆◇◇◇` `VERB` `V` `V with quote` `N-COUNT`

shrift /ʃrɪft/. If someone or something gets **short shrift**, they are paid very little attention. *The idea has been given short shrift by philosophers.* `PHRASE`

shrill /ʃrɪl/ **shriller, shrillest; shrills, shrilling, shrilled. 1** A **shrill** sound is high-pitched, piercing, and unpleasant to listen to. *...the shrill whistle of the engine.* ♦ **shril·ly** *'What are you doing?' she demanded shrilly.* ♦ **shrill·ness** *...that ugly shrillness* `◆◇◇◇` `ADJ-GRADED` `ADV-GRADED` `N-UNCOUNT`

in her voice. **2** If you describe a demand, protest, or statement as **shrill**, you disapprove of it and do not like the strong forceful way it is said. *...shrill protests from groups closely associated with the terrorists.* **3** If a bell or whistle **shrills**, it makes a loud, high-pitched sound. **4** If someone with a high-pitched voice **shrills** something, they say it loudly. *'No, no, no,' she shrilled.*
ADJ-GRADED PRAGMATICS
VERB: V
VERB V with quote WRITTEN

shrimp /ʃrɪmp/ **shrimps; shrimp** can also be used as the plural form. **Shrimps** are small shellfish with long tails and many legs.
◆◇◇◇◇ N-COUNT

shrine /ʃraɪn/ **shrines. 1** A **shrine** is a holy place of worship which is associated with a sacred person or object. *...the holy shrine of Mecca.* **2** A **shrine** is a place that people visit and treat with respect because it is connected with a dead person who they want to remember.
◆◇◇◇◇ N-COUNT
N-COUNT

shrink /ʃrɪŋk/ **shrinks, shrinking, shrank, shrunk. 1** If cloth or clothing **shrinks**, it becomes smaller in size, usually as a result of being washed. **2** If something **shrinks** or if something else **shrinks** it, it becomes smaller. *The vast forests of West Africa have shrunk.* **3** If you **shrink** away from someone or something, you move away from them because you are frightened or horrified by them. *She shrank back with an involuntary gasp.* **4** If you do not **shrink** from a task or duty, you do it even though it is unpleasant or dangerous. *They didn't shrink from danger.* **5** A **shrink** is a psychiatrist. *I've seen a shrink already.* **6** ● **no shrinking violet**: see **violet**.
◆◆◇◇◇ VERB: V
V-ERG: V n V
VERB V prep/adv
VERB V from n
N-COUNT INFORMAL

shrink·age /ʃrɪŋkɪdʒ/. **Shrinkage** is a decrease in the size or amount of something. *Allow for some shrinkage in both length and width.*
N-UNCOUNT

'shrink-wrapped. A **shrink-wrapped** product is sold in a tight-fitting polythene cover.
ADJ

shriv·el /ʃrɪvəl/ **shrivels, shrivelling, shrivelled;** spelled **shriveling, shriveled** in American English. When something **shrivels** or when something else **shrivels** it, it becomes dry and wrinkled. *...dry weather that shrivelled this summer's crops.* ▶ **Shrivel up** means the same as **shrivel**. *The leaves started to shrivel up. ...as if her face shrivelled up and she became an old woman.* ♦ **shriv·elled** *It looked old and shrivelled.*
◆◇◇◇◇ V-ERG: V n
PHRASAL VB V P
ADJ-GRADED

shroud /ʃraʊd/ **shrouds, shrouding, shrouded. 1** A **shroud** is a cloth which is used for wrapping a dead body. **2** You can refer to something that surrounds an object or situation as a **shroud** of something. *...a parked car huddled under a shroud of grey snow.* **3** If something **has been shrouded** in mystery or secrecy, very little information about it has been made available. *For years the teaching of acting has been shrouded in mystery.* ♦ **shroud·ed** *His demise is as shrouded in mystery as ever.* **4** If darkness, fog, or smoke **shrouds** an area, it covers it so that it is difficult to see. ♦ **shrouded** *The area is shrouded in smoke.*
◆◇◇◇◇ N-COUNT
N-COUNT: N of n
VERB be V-ed in n Also V n
ADJ-GRADED VERB: V n
ADJ-GRADED: v-link ADJ in n

shrub /ʃrʌb/ **shrubs. Shrubs** are low plants like small trees with several woody stems instead of a trunk.
◆◇◇◇◇ N-COUNT

shrub·bery /ʃrʌbəri/ **shrubberies. 1** A **shrubbery** is a part of a garden where a lot of shrubs are growing. **2** You can refer to a lot of shrubs or to shrubs in general as **shrubbery**.
N-COUNT
N-UNCOUNT

shrub·by /ʃrʌbi/. A **shrubby** plant is like a shrub. *...a shrubby tree.*
ADJ

shrug /ʃrʌg/ **shrugs, shrugging, shrugged.** If you **shrug**, you raise your shoulders to show that you are not interested in something or that you do not know or care about something. *The man shrugged his shoulders.* ▶ Also a noun. *'I suppose so,' said Anna with a shrug.*
◆◆◇◇◇ VERB: V V n
N-COUNT

shrug off. If you **shrug** something **off**, you ignore it or treat it as if it is not really important or serious. *He shrugged off the criticism.*
PHRASAL VB V n P V P noun

shrunk /ʃrʌŋk/. **Shrunk** is the past participle of **shrink**.

shrunk·en /ʃrʌŋkən/. Someone or something that is **shrunken** has become smaller than they used to be. *She now looked small, shrunken and pathetic.*
ADJ-GRADED

shuck /ʃʌk/ **shucks, shucking, shucked. 1** The **shuck** of something is its outer covering, for example the husk of an ear of maize, or the shell of an oyster or clam. **2** If you **shuck** something such as maize or shellfish, you remove it from its outer covering. **3** If you **shuck** something that you are wearing, you take it off. *He shucked his coat and set to work.* **4 Shucks** is an exclamation that is used to express embarrassment, disappointment, or annoyance. *Terry actually says 'Oh, shucks!' when complimented on her singing.*
N-COUNT AMERICAN
VERB: V n AMERICAN
VERB: V n AMERICAN, INFORMAL
EXCLAM PRAGMATICS AMERICAN, INFORMAL

shud·der /ʃʌdə/ **shudders, shuddering, shuddered. 1** If you **shudder**, you tremble with fear, horror, or disgust, or with cold. *Lloyd had urged her to eat caviar. She had shuddered at the thought.* ▶ Also a noun. *She gave a violent shudder.* **2** If something such as a machine or vehicle **shudders**, it shakes suddenly and violently. *The train began to pull out of the station – then suddenly shuddered to a halt.* **3** If you say that you **shudder to think** what would happen in a particular situation, you mean that you expect it to be so awful or disastrous that you do not really want to think about it.
◆◇◇◇◇ VERB: V V prep/adv
N-COUNT V prep/adv
PHRASE

shuf·fle /ʃʌfəl/ **shuffles, shuffling, shuffled. 1** If you **shuffle** somewhere, you walk there without lifting your feet properly off the ground. ▶ Also a noun. *She noticed her own proud walk had become a shuffle.* **2** If you **shuffle** around, you move your feet about while standing or you move your bottom about while sitting, often because you feel uncomfortable or embarrassed. *He grinned and shuffled his feet.* **3** If you **shuffle** things such as pieces of paper or cards in a pack, you move them around so that they are in a different order.
◆◆◇◇◇ VERB: V V prep/adv N-SING
VERB: V prep/adv V n
VERB: V n

shun /ʃʌn/ **shuns, shunning, shunned.** If you **shun** someone or something, you deliberately avoid them or keep away from them. *From that time forward everybody shunned him.*
◆◇◇◇◇ VERB V n

shunt /ʃʌnt/ **shunts, shunting, shunted. 1** If someone or something **is shunted** somewhere, they are moved or sent there, usually because someone finds them inconvenient; used showing disapproval. *He has spent most of his life being shunted between his mother, father and various foster families.* **2** When railway engines **shunt** wagons or carriages, they push or pull them from one railway line to another.
◆◇◇◇◇ VB: usu passive PRAGMATICS be V-ed prep/adv
VERB: V n

shush /ʃʊʃ, ʃʌʃ/ **shushes, shushing, shushed. 1** You say **shush** when you are telling someone to be quiet. *Shush! Here he comes. I'll talk to you later.* **2** If you **shush** someone, you tell them to be quiet by saying 'shush' or 'sh', or by indicating in some other way that you want them to be quiet. *Frannie shushed her with a forefinger to the lips.*
CONVENTION PRAGMATICS
VERB V n Also V

shut /ʃʌt/ **shuts, shutting.** The form **shut** is used in the present tense and is the past tense and past participle. **1** If you **shut** something such as a door or if it **shuts**, it moves so that it fills a hole or a space. *Just make sure you shut the gate after you... The screen door shut gently.* ▶ Also an adjective. *The exit doors were locked shut.* **2** If you **shut** your eyes, you lower your eyelids so that you cannot see anything. ▶ Also an adjective. *His eyes were shut.* **3** If your mouth **shuts** or if you **shut** your mouth, you place your lips firmly together. *He opened and shut his mouth, unspeaking.* ▶ Also an adjective. *She was silent for a moment, lips tight shut.* **4** If someone tells you to **shut** your **mouth** or **shut** your **face**, they are telling you very rudely to stop talking. **5** When a shop or pub **shuts** or when someone **shuts** it, it is closed and you cannot go into it until the next time that it is open. *What time do the pubs shut?* ▶ Also an adjective. *The local shop may be shut.*
◆◆◆◇◇ V-ERG V n V
ADJ
VERB: V n
ADJ
V-ERG: V V n
ADJ: v-link ADJ PHRASE
PRAGMATICS INFORMAL
V-ERG: V n V
ADJ: v-link ADJ

6 ● **keep** your **mouth shut**: see **mouth**. ● **shut up shop**: see **shop**.

shut away. If you **shut** yourself **away**, you avoid go-
PHRASAL VB

ing out and seeing other people, usually because you are feeling depressed. `V pron-refl P`

shut down. If a factory or business **shuts down** or if someone **shuts** it **down**, work there stops or it no longer trades as a business. *Smaller contractors had been forced to shut down.* ● See also **shutdown.** `PHRASAL VB ERG: V P noun V P`

shut in. 1 If you **shut** someone or something **in** a room, you close the door so that they cannot leave it. **2** If you **shut** yourself **in** a room, you stay in there and make sure nobody else can get in. `PHRASAL VB V n P n` `V pron-refl P n`

shut off. 1 If you **shut off** something such as an engine or an electrical item, you turn it off to stop it working. *They pulled over and shut off the engine.* **2** If you **shut** yourself **off**, you avoid seeing other people, usually because you are feeling depressed. **3** If an official organization **shuts off** the supply of something, they no longer send it to the people they supplied in the past. `PHRASAL VB V P noun Also V n P` `V pron-refl P` `V P noun`

shut out. 1 If you **shut** something or someone **out**, you prevent them from getting into a place, for example by closing the doors. *'I shut him out of the bedroom,' says Maureen.* **2** If you **shut out** a thought or a feeling, you prevent yourself from thinking or feeling it. *I shut out the memory which was too painful to dwell on.* **3** If you **shut** someone **out** of something, you prevent them from having anything to do with it. *She is very reclusive, to the point of shutting me out of her life.* `PHRASAL VB V P noun V n P ofn Also V n P` `V P noun Also V n P` `V n P ofn Also V n P`

shut up. If someone **shuts up** or if someone or something **shuts** them **up**, they stop talking. You can say **'shut up'** to someone to tell them to stop talking. *...the only way he knew of shutting her up.* `PHRASAL VB ERG: V P V n P`

shut·down /ˈʃʌtdaʊn/ **shutdowns.** A **shutdown** is the closing of a factory, shop, or other business, either for a short time or for ever. `◆◇◇◇◇ N-COUNT`

'shut-eye; also spelled **shuteye.** **Shut-eye** is sleep. *Go home and get some shut-eye, Craig.* `N-UNCOUNT INFORMAL`

shut·ter /ˈʃʌtə/ **shutters. 1** The **shutter** in a camera is the part which opens to allow light through the lens when a photograph is taken. **2 Shutters** are wooden or metal covers fitted on the outside of a window. They can be opened to let in the light, or closed to keep out the sun or the cold or to protect the windows from damage. `◆◇◇◇◇ N-COUNT` `N-COUNT`

shut·tered /ˈʃʌtəd/. **1** A **shuttered** window, room, or building has its shutters closed. *Many shops remain shuttered.* **2** A **shuttered** window, room, or building has shutters fitted to it. *...green-shuttered colonial villas.* `ADJ` `ADJ: ADJ n`

shut·tle /ˈʃʌtəl/ **shuttles, shuttling, shuttled.** **1** A **shuttle** is the same as a **space shuttle.** **2** A **shuttle** is a plane, bus, or train which makes frequent journeys between two places. **3** If someone or something **shuttles** or **is shuttled** from one place to another place, they frequently go from one place to the other. *Machine parts were also being shuttled across the border without authorisation.* **4** A **shuttle** is a piece of equipment used in weaving. It takes a thread backwards and forwards over the other threads in order to make a piece of cloth. `◆◆◇◇◇ N-COUNT N-COUNT` `V-ERG: V prep/adv be V-ed prep/adv` `N-COUNT`

shuttle·cock /ˈʃʌtəlkɒk/ **shuttlecocks.** A **shuttlecock** is the small object that you hit over the net in a game of badminton. `N-COUNT`

,shuttle di'plomacy. **Shuttle diplomacy** is the movement of diplomats between countries whose leaders refuse to talk directly to each other, in order to try to settle the argument between them. `N-UNCOUNT`

shy /ʃaɪ/ **shyer, shyest; shies, shying, shied.** **1** A **shy** person is nervous and uncomfortable in the company of other people. *She was a shy, quiet-spoken girl... He is painfully shy of women.* ◆ **shy·ly** *The children smiled shyly.* ◆ **shy·ness** *Eventually he overcame his shyness.* **2** If you are **shy** of doing something, you are unwilling to do it because you are afraid of what might happen. *You should not be shy of having your say in the running of the school.* **3** When a horse **shies**, it moves away suddenly, because something has frightened it. **4** If you **fight shy** of something, you try very hard to avoid it. *It is no use fighting shy of publicity.* `◆◆◇◇◇ ADJ-GRADED` `ADV-GRADED` `N-UNCOUNT` `ADJ-GRADED` `VERB: V` `PHRASE`

5 A number or amount that is just **shy of** another number or amount is just under it. *He died two days shy of his 95th birthday.* `PHR-PREP`

shy away from. If you **shy away from** doing something, you avoid doing it, often because you are afraid or not confident enough. *We frequently shy away from making decisions.* `PHRASAL VB V P -ing/n`

-shy /-ʃaɪ/. **-shy** is added to nouns to form adjectives which indicate that someone does not like a particular thing, and tries to avoid it. *The publicity-shy singer spoke frankly in his first interview in three years.* `COMB`

shy·ster /ˈʃaɪstə/ **shysters.** If you refer to someone, especially a lawyer or politician, as a **shyster**, you mean that they are dishonest and immoral. `N-COUNT AMERICAN, INFORMAL`

Sia·mese cat /ˌsaɪəmiːz ˈkæt/ **Siamese cats.** A **Siamese cat** is a type of cat with short cream and brown fur, blue eyes, dark ears, and a dark tail. `N-COUNT`

Sia·mese twin /ˌsaɪəmiːz ˈtwɪn/ **Siamese twins.** **Siamese twins** are twins who are born joined to each other by a part of their bodies. `N-COUNT`

sibi·lant /ˈsɪbɪlənt/. **Sibilant** sounds are soft, hissing sounds, like the sounds a snake makes. *A sibilant murmuring briefly pervaded the room.* `ADJ FORMAL`

sib·ling /ˈsɪblɪŋ/ **siblings.** Your **siblings** are your brothers and sisters. `◆◇◇◇◇ N-COUNT`

sic. You write **sic** in brackets after a word or expression when you want to indicate to the reader that although the word or expression looks odd or wrong, you intended to write it in that way or the original writer wrote it like that. *The latest school jobs page advertises a 'wide rnage (sic) of 6th form courses.'* `◆◆◇◇◇`

sick /sɪk/ **sicker, sickest. 1** If you are **sick**, you are ill. **Sick** usually means physically ill, but it can sometimes be used to mean mentally ill. *He's very sick. He needs medication... He was not evil, but he was sick.* ► **The sick** are people who are sick. *There were no doctors to treat the sick.* **2** If you are **sick**, the food that you have eaten comes up from your stomach and out of your mouth. If you feel **sick**, you feel as if you are going to be sick. *She got up and was sick in the handbasin.* **3 Sick** is vomit. *I can't leave him lying covered in sick, can I?* **4** If you say that you are **sick of** something or **sick and tired of** it, you are emphasizing that you are very annoyed by it and want it to stop. *I am sick and tired of hearing all these people moaning.* **5** If you describe something such as a joke or story as **sick**, you mean that it deals with death or suffering in an unpleasantly frivolous way; used showing disapproval. *...a sick joke about a cat.* **6** If you say that something or someone **makes** you **sick**, you mean that they make you feel angry or disgusted. *The British press makes me sick.* **7** If you are **off sick**, you are not at work because you are ill. The usual American expression is **out sick. 8** If you say that you are **worried sick**, you are emphasizing that you are extremely worried. *He was worried sick about what our mothers would say.* `◆◆◆◇◇ ADJ-GRADED` `N-PLURAL: the N` `ADJ-GRADED: v-link ADJ` `N-UNCOUNT BRITISH` `ADJ-GRADED: v-link ADJ of n/ -ing` `PRAGMATICS` `ADJ-GRADED` `PRAGMATICS` `PHRASE INFORMAL` `PHRASE BRITISH` `PHRASE PRAGMATICS INFORMAL`

'sick bay, sick bays; also spelled **sick-bay.** A **sick bay** is an area, especially on a ship or in a school or university, where medical treatment is given and where beds are provided for people who are ill. `N-COUNT`

sick·bed /ˈsɪkbed/ **sickbeds;** also spelled **sick-bed.** Your **sickbed** is the bed that you are lying in while you are ill. `N-COUNT`

sick·en /ˈsɪkən/ **sickens, sickening, sickened.** **1** If something **sickens** you, it makes you feel disgusted. *What he saw there sickened him, despite all his years of police work.* **2** If you **sicken**, you become ill. *Many of them sickened and died.* `◆◇◇◇◇ VERB V n` `VERB V DATED`

sick·en·ing /ˈsɪkənɪŋ/. You describe something as **sickening** when it gives you feelings of horror or disgust, or makes you feel sick in your stomach. *...a sickening attack on a pregnant and defenceless woman.* ◆ **sick·en·ing·ly** *The interview was offensive and sickeningly irresponsible.* `◆◇◇◇◇ ADJ-GRADED` `ADV-GRADED`

sick·le /ˈsɪkəl/ **sickles.** A **sickle** is a tool that is used for cutting grass and grain crops. It has a short handle and a long curved blade. `◆◇◇◇◇ N-COUNT`

'sick leave. Sick leave is the time that a person N-UNCOUNT spends away from work because of illness or injury. *I have been on sick leave for seven months.*

,sickle-cell a'naemia; spelled **sickle-cell anemia** N-UNCOUNT in American English. Sickle-cell anaemia is a hereditary disease in which the red blood cells become sickle-shaped, causing jaundice, ulcers, and a high temperature.

sick·ly /'sɪkli/ **sicklier, sickliest. 1** A sickly per- ◆◇◇◇ son or animal is weak, unhealthy, and often ill. *He* ADJ-GRADED *had been a sickly child.* **2** A sickly smell or taste is ADJ-GRADED unpleasant and makes you feel slightly sick, often because it is extremely sweet. *...the sickly smell of rum.*

sick·ness /'sɪknəs/ **sicknesses. 1** Sickness is the ◆◆◇◇ state of being ill or unhealthy. *In fifty-two years of* N-UNCOUNT *working he had one week of sickness.* **2** Sickness is N-UNCOUNT the uncomfortable feeling that you are going to vomit. *He felt a great rush of sickness.* ● See also **morning sickness, travel sickness. 3** A sickness is a N-VAR particular illness. *...radiation sickness.*

'sickness benefit. Sickness benefit is money that N-UNCOUNT you receive regularly from the government when BRITISH you are unable to work because of illness.

'sick pay. When you are ill and unable to work, N-UNCOUNT sick pay is the money that you get from your employer instead of your normal wages.

sick·room /'sɪkruːm/ **sickrooms;** also spelled **sick** N-COUNT **room.** A sickroom is a room in which a sick person is lying in bed.

side /saɪd/ **sides, siding, sided. 1** The side of ◆◆◆◆ something is a position to the left or right of it, ra- N-COUNT ther than in front of it, behind it, or on it. *On one side of the main entrance there's a red plaque. ...the nations on either side of the Pacific. ...both sides of the border... To the side of the large star is a smaller star.* **2** If something moves **from side to side,** it PHRASE moves repeatedly to the left and to the right. *She was shaking her head from side to side.* **3** The **side** N-COUNT of an object, building, or vehicle is any of its flat surfaces which is not considered to be its front, its back, its top, or its bottom. *We put a notice on the side of the box... A carton of milk lay on its side.* **4** The **sides** of a hollow or a container are its inside N-COUNT vertical surfaces. *Line the base of the dish with greaseproof paper and lightly grease the sides. ...narrow valleys with steep sides.* **5** The **sides** of an area N-COUNT or surface are its edges. *Park on the side of the road... Coyne slid his legs over the side of the bed.* **6** The two **sides** of an area, surface, or object are its N-COUNT two halves. *She turned over on her stomach on the other side of the bed. ...the right side of your face.* **7** The N-COUNT two **sides** of something flat, for example a piece of paper, are its two flat surfaces. You can also refer to one side of a piece of paper filled with writing as one **side** of writing. *The new copiers only copy onto one side of the paper... Fry the chops until brown on both sides.* **8** If you talk about the other **side** of a town or of the N-COUNT: world, you mean a part of the town or of the world with supp that is very far from where you are. *He lives the other side of London.* **9** Your **sides** are the parts of your body N-COUNT under your arms from your armpits down to your hips.

10 If someone is **by your side** or **at your side,** they N-COUNT stay near you and give you comfort or support. *He was constantly at his wife's side.* **11** If two people or things PHRASE are **side by side,** they are next to each other. *We sat side by side on two wicker seats.* **12** If people work or PHRASE live **side by side,** they work or live closely and peacefully together. *...areas where different nationalities have lived side by side for centuries.* **13** If you take PHRASE someone **to one side** or **draw** them **to one side,** you speak to them privately, usually in order to give them advice or a warning.

14 One **side** of a tape or record is what you can hear or N-COUNT record if you play the tape or record from beginning to end without turning it over. *We want to hear side A.*

15 A **side of** beef, bacon, or other meat consists of the N-COUNT: meat from half the animal cut along its backbone. N of n

16 Side is used to describe things that are not the ADJ: ADJ n

main or most important ones of their kind. *...a side street. ...a prawn curry with a lentil side dish.*

17 The different **sides** in a war, argument, or negotia- N-COUNT tion are the different groups of people who are fighting, arguing, or negotiating with each other. *Both sides appealed for a new ceasefire.* **18** If you are **on** PHRASE someone's **side,** you are supporting them in an argument or a war. *Some of the younger people seem to be on the side of reform.* **19** The different **sides** of an ar- N-COUNT gument or deal are the different points of view or positions involved in it. *His words drew sharp reactions from people on both sides of the issue.* **20** If you take PHRASE **sides** or **take** someone's **side** in an argument or war, you support one of the sides against the other. *See? You're taking his side again.* **21** If one person or coun- VERB try **sides** with another, they support them in an argu- V with/ ment or a war. If people or countries **side** against an- against n other person or country, they support each other in arguing or fighting against that person or country. *...speculation that America might be siding with the rebels.*

22 In sport, a **side** is a team. *Italy were definitely a bet-* N-COUNT *ter side than West Germany.*

23 A particular **side** of something such as a situation N-COUNT or someone's character is one aspect of it. *It shows that your child can now see the funny side of things... Anxiety has a mental and a physical side.*

24 The **mother's side** and the **father's side** of your N-COUNT family are your mother's relatives and your father's relatives.

25 If you say that someone **has let the side down,** you PHRASE mean that they have embarrassed their family or friends by behaving badly or not doing very well at something. **26** If something is **on** your **side** or if you PHRASE have it **on** your **side,** it helps you when you are trying to achieve something. *The weather is rather on our side... The law is not on their side.* **27** If you get **on the** PHRASE **wrong side of** someone, you do something to annoy them and make them dislike you. If you stay **on the right side of** someone, you try to please them and avoid annoying them. *I wouldn't like to get on the wrong side of him.* **28** If you say that something is, for PHRASE example, **on the** small **side,** you are saying politely PRAGMATICS that you think it is slightly too small. *He's quiet and a bit on the shy side.* **29** If someone does something **on** PHRASE **the side,** they do it in addition to their main work. *...ways of making a little bit of money on the side.* **30** If PHRASE you **put** something **to one side** or **put** it **on one side,** you temporarily ignore it in order to concentrate on something else. *Health and safety regulations are often put to one side.* **31** If you say that something will PHR-PREP not happen **this side of** a date or event, you mean that it will not happen before that date or event. *A race between the two is now unlikely to take place this side of the world championships.*

32 See also **-sided, siding.** ● **look on the bright side:** see **bright.** ● **the other side of the coin:** see **coin.** ● **two sides of the same coin:** see **coin.** ● **to err on the side of** something: see **err.** ● **to be on the safe side:** see **safe.** ● someone's **side of the story:** see **story.**

side·arm /'saɪdɑːm/ **sidearms.** Sidearms are N-COUNT weapons, usually small guns, that some people carry at their side in a holster or belt. *Two guards with sidearms patrolled the wall.*

side·board /'saɪdbɔːd/ **sideboards.** A sideboard is N-COUNT a long cupboard which is about the same height as a table. Sideboards are usually kept in dining rooms to put plates and glasses in.

side·burns /'saɪdbɜːnz/. If a man has **sideburns,** he N-PLURAL has a strip of hair growing down the side of each cheek. *...a young man with long sideburns.*

side·car /'saɪdkɑː/ **sidecars.** A sidecar is a kind of N-COUNT box with wheels which you can attach to the side of a motorcycle so that you can carry a passenger in it.

-sided /-'saɪdɪd/. **-sided** combines with numbers or COMB adjectives to describe how many sides something has, or what kind of sides something has. *...a three-sided pyramid. ...a steep-sided valley.* ● See also **one-sided.**

'side dish, side dishes. A side dish is a portion of food that is served at the same time as and in addition to the main dish. *These mushrooms would make a delicious side dish.* `N-COUNT`

'side-effect, side-effects; also spelled **side effect. 1** The **side-effects** of a drug are the effects, usually bad ones, that the drug has on you in addition to its function of curing illness or pain. *...unpleasant side-effects including weight gain, acne, skin rashes and headaches.* **2** A **side-effect** of a situation is something that is unplanned, and usually unpleasant, that happens in addition to the main results or effects of that situation. *One side effect of modern life is stress.* `N-COUNT`

'side issue, side issues. A side issue is an issue or subject that is not considered to be as important as the main one. `N-COUNT`

side·kick /'saɪdkɪk/ **sidekicks.** Someone's **sidekick** is a companion or colleague who helps them with routine tasks, and who you consider to be inferior, less intelligent, or less important than the other person. `N-COUNT INFORMAL`

side·light /'saɪdlaɪt/ **sidelights. 1** The **sidelights** on a vehicle are the small lights at the front that help other drivers to notice the vehicle and to judge its width. The usual American term is **parking lights. 2** A **sidelight** on a particular situation is a piece of information about that situation which is interesting but which is not particularly important. *The book's interspersed with interesting and often amusing sidelights on his family background.* `N-COUNT BRITISH` `N-COUNT`

side·line /'saɪdlaɪn/ **sidelines, sidelining, sidelined. 1** A sideline is something that you do in addition to your main job in order to earn extra money. *Mr. Means sold computer disks as a sideline.* **2** The **sidelines** are the lines marking the long sides of the playing area, for example on a football pitch or tennis court. **3** In sport, if a player **is sidelined**, he or she is prevented from playing for a period of time, for example because of an injury. **4** If you are on the **sidelines** in a situation, you do not influence events at all, either because you have chosen not to be involved, or because other people have not involved you. *France no longer wants to be on the sidelines when critical decisions are taken.* **5** If someone or something **is sidelined**, they are made to seem unimportant and not included in what people are doing. `◆◇◇◇◇` `N-COUNT` `N-PLURAL` `VERB: be V-ed` `N-PLURAL: the N` `VERB: be V-ed`

side·long /'saɪdlɒŋ, AM -lɔːŋ/. If you give someone a **sidelong** look, you look at them out of the corner of your eyes. `ADJ: ADJ n`

side-'on. A **side-on** collision or view is a collision or view from the side of an object. `◆◇◇◇◇ ADJ`

'side-saddle. When you ride a horse **side-saddle**, you sit on a special saddle with both your legs on one side rather than one leg on each side of the horse. *Naomi was given a pony and taught to ride side-saddle.* `ADV: ADV after v`

side·show /'saɪdʃəʊ/ **sideshows;** also spelled **side-show. 1** A sideshow is a less important or less significant event or situation related to a larger, more important one that is happening at the same time. *The meeting was a sideshow to a political storm that broke Thursday.* **2** At a circus or fair, a sideshow is a performance that you watch or a game of skill that you play, that is provided in addition to the main entertainment. `N-COUNT` `N-COUNT`

'side-splitting. Something that is **side-splitting** is very funny and makes you laugh so much that you ache all over. *...a side-splitting joke.* `ADJ INFORMAL`

side·step /'saɪdstep/ **sidesteps, sidestepping, sidestepped;** also spelled **side-step. 1** If you sidestep a problem, you avoid discussing it or dealing with it. *Rarely, if ever, does he sidestep a question.* **2** If you **sidestep**, you step sideways in order to avoid something or someone that is coming towards you or going to hit you. *He made a grab for her but she sidestepped him and kicked him.* `◆◇◇◇◇` `VERB V n Also V` `VERB: V n`

side·swipe /'saɪdswaɪp/ **sideswipes;** also spelled **side-swipe.** If you take a **sideswipe** at someone or `N-COUNT`

something, you make an unexpected critical remark about them while you are talking about something else.

side-track /'saɪdtræk/ **sidetracks, sidetracking, sidetracked;** also spelled **side-track.** If you **are sidetracked** by something, it makes you forget what you intended to do or say, and start instead doing or talking about a different thing. *The leadership moved to sidetrack the proposal... They have a tendency to try to sidetrack you from your task.* `VERB: be V-ed V n V n from n Also be V-ed into n/-ing`

side·walk /'saɪdwɔːk/ **sidewalks.** A sidewalk is a path with a hard surface by the side of a road. The British word is **pavement.** `◆◇◇◇◇ N-COUNT AMERICAN`

side·ways /'saɪdweɪz/. **1** Sideways means from or towards the side of something or someone. *I took a step sideways.* ▶ Also an adjective. *Alfred shot him a sideways glance.* **2** If you are moved **sideways** at work, you move to another job at the same level as your old job. ▶ Also an adjective. *...her recent sideways move.* `◆◇◇◇◇` `ADV: ADV after v` `ADJ: ADJ n` `ADV: ADV after v` `ADJ: ADJ n`

sid·ing /'saɪdɪŋ/ **sidings.** A siding is a short railway track beside the main tracks, where engines and carriages are left when they are not being used. `N-COUNT`

si·dle /'saɪdəl/ **sidles, sidling, sidled.** If you sidle somewhere, you walk there uncertainly or cautiously, as if you do not want anyone to notice you. *A young man sidled up to me.* `VERB V prep/adv`

siècle. See **fin de siècle.**

siege /siːdʒ/ **sieges. 1** A siege is a military or police operation in which soldiers or police surround a place in order to force the people there to surrender or to come out. *We must do everything possible to lift the siege. ...a city virtually under siege.* ● See also **state of siege. 2** If police, soldiers, or journalists **lay siege** to the place where someone is, they surround it in order to force the people there to surrender or to come out. **3** If someone or something is **under siege**, they are being severely criticized or put under a great deal of pressure. `◆◆◇◇◇` `N-COUNT: also under N` `PHRASE` `PHRASE`

'siege mentality. If someone has a **siege mentality**, they refuse to co-operate with other people, because they think that other people are constantly trying to harm or defeat them. `N-SING: also no det`

si·es·ta /si'estə/ **siestas.** A siesta is a short sleep or rest which you have in the early afternoon, especially in hot countries. `N-COUNT`

sieve /sɪv/ **sieves, sieving, sieved. 1** A sieve is a device used for separating solids from liquids or larger pieces of something from smaller pieces. See picture headed **kitchen utensils. 2** When you **sieve** a liquid or powdery substance, you put it through a sieve. *Cream the margarine in a small bowl, then sieve the icing sugar into it.* `◆◇◇◇◇` `N-COUNT` `VERB V n`

sift /sɪft/ **sifts, sifting, sifted. 1** If you **sift** a loose or powdery substance such as flour or sand, you put it through a sieve in order to remove large pieces or lumps. **2** If you **sift** through something such as evidence, you examine it thoroughly. *Brook has sifted the evidence and summarises it clearly.* `◆◇◇◇◇` `VERB: V n` `V through n V n`

sigh /saɪ/ **sighs, sighing, sighed. 1** When you **sigh**, you let out a deep breath, as a way of expressing feelings such as disappointment, tiredness, or pleasure. *'Everyone forgets,' the girl sighed.* ▶ Also a noun. *She kicked off her shoes with a sigh... Prue heaved a weary sigh.* **2** If the wind **sighs** through a place, it moves through the place with a sound like a sigh. **3** If people breathe a **sigh of relief**, they feel very glad because something unpleasant has not happened or is no longer happening. *There was an audible sigh of relief in Washington when the foreign ministers decided to postpone the meeting.* `◆◆◇◇◇` `VERB: V V with quote` `N-COUNT` `VERB: V prep LITERARY` `PHRASE`

sight /saɪt/ **sights, sighting, sighted. 1** Someone's **sight** is their ability to see. *My sight is failing, and I can't see to read any more.* **2** The **sight** of something is the act of seeing it or an occasion on which you see it. *I faint at the sight of blood.* **3** If you **sight** someone or something, you suddenly see them, often briefly. **4** If you **catch sight of** someone, you suddenly see them, often briefly. *Then he* `◆◆◆◇` `N-UNCOUNT` `N-SING: the N of n` `VERB: V n` `PHRASE`

caught sight of her small black velvet hat in the crowd.

5 If something is **in sight** or **within sight**, you can see it. If it is **out of sight**, you cannot see it. **6** If you **know** someone **by sight**, you can recognize them when you see them, although you have never met them personally. **7** If you say **'out of sight, out of mind'**, you mean that people quickly forget someone if he or she goes away. **8** If someone is ordered to do something **on sight**, they have to do it without delay, as soon as a person or thing is seen. *Troops shot anyone suspicious on sight.* **9** If you say that someone or something is **not a pretty sight**, you mean that it is not pleasant to look at. **10** If you agree to buy something **sight unseen**, you agree to buy it, even though you have not seen it and do not know what condition it is in. **11** A **sight** is something that you see. *...the pathetic sight of a family packing up its home.* **12** The **sights** are the places that are interesting to see and that are visited by tourists. *We'd toured the sights of Paris.* **13** You can use **a sight** to mean a lot. For example, if you say that something is **a sight** worse than it was before, you are emphasizing that it is much worse than it was. **14** If you say that something seems to have certain characteristics **at first sight**, you mean that it appears to have the features you describe when you first see it but later it is found to be different. *It promised to be a more difficult undertaking than might appear at first sight.* **15** If a result or a decision is **in sight** or **within sight**, it is likely to happen within a short time. *An agreement on many aspects of trade policy was in sight.* **16** If you **lose sight of** an important aspect of something, you no longer pay attention to it because you are worrying about less important things. *US industry has lost sight of customer needs in designing products.* **17** If you **set** your **sights on** something, you decide that you want it and try hard to get it. *They have set their sights on the world record.* **18** If you have something **in** your **sights**, you are determined to have it or achieve it. *She already has the world record in her sights.* **19** If you have someone **in** your **sights**, you are determined to catch, defeat, or overcome them. *The chasing group was gaining ground rapidly and had the three leaders in their sights.* **20** See also **sighted, sighting. 21 ● love at first sight**: see **love**.

sight·ed /ˈsaɪtɪd/. **Sighted** people have the ability to see. This word is usually used to contrast people who can see with people who are blind. *Blind children tend to be more passive in this area of motor development than sighted children.* ● See also **far-sighted, long-sighted, near-sighted, short-sighted**.

sight·ing /ˈsaɪtɪŋ/ **sightings**. A **sighting** of something, especially something unusual or unexpected, is an occasion on which it is seen. *...the sighting of a rare sea bird at Lundy island.*

sight·less /ˈsaɪtləs/. Someone who is **sightless** is blind. *He wiped a tear from his sightless eyes.*

sight·see·ing /ˈsaɪtsiːɪŋ/; also spelled **sight-seeing**. If you go **sightseeing** or do some **sightseeing**, you travel around visiting the interesting places that tourists usually visit. ♦ **sight·seer** /ˈsaɪtsiːə/ **sight-seers** *...coachloads of sightseers.*

sign /saɪn/ **signs, signing, signed. 1** A **sign** is a mark or shape that always has a particular meaning, for example in mathematics or music. *Equations are generally written with a two-bar equals sign.* **2** A **sign** is a movement of your arms, hands, or head which is intended to have a particular meaning. *They gave Lavalle the thumbs-up sign.* **3** If you **sign**, you communicate with someone using sign language. If a programme or performance **is signed**, someone uses sign language so that deaf people can understand it. *All programmes will be either 'signed' or subtitled.* ♦ **sign·er, signers** *I'm keen on providing signers for deaf people.* ♦ **sign·ing** *The two deaf actors converse solely in signing.*

4 A **sign** is a piece of wood, metal, or plastic with words or pictures on it. Signs give you information about something, or give you a warning or an instruction. *...a sign saying that the highway was closed.* **5** If there is a **sign** of something, there is something which shows that it exists or is happening. *They are prepared to hand back a hundred prisoners of war a day as a sign of good will.* **6** If you say that there is **no sign of** someone, you mean that they have not yet arrived, although you are expecting them to come. **7** In astrology, a **sign** of the zodiac is one of the twelve areas into which the heavens are divided. **8** See also **call sign**.

sign /saɪn/ **signs signing signed. 1** When you **sign** a document, you write your name on it, usually at the end or in a special space. *Before an operation the patient will be asked to sign a consent form.* ♦ **signing** *Spain's top priority is the signing of an EMU treaty.* **2** If an organization **signs** someone or if someone **signs** for an organization, they sign a contract agreeing to work for that organization for a specified period of time. *The band then signed to Slash Records.* ♦ **sign·ing** *...Aston Villa's signing of the Australian goalkeeper Mark Bosnich.* **3** See also **signing. 4** If you say that an agreement is **signed and sealed**, or **signed, sealed and delivered**, you mean that it is absolutely definite because everybody involved has signed all the legal documents. *A government spokesman said the bill must be signed, sealed and delivered by tomorrow.* **5 ●** to **sign** one's **own death warrant**: see **death warrant**.

sign away. If you **sign** something **away**, you sign official documents that mean that you no longer own it or have a right to it. *The Duke signed away his inheritance.*

sign for. If you **sign for** something, you officially state that you have received it, by signing a form or book.

sign in. If you **sign in**, you officially indicate that you have arrived at a hotel or club by signing a book or form.

sign off. 1 If someone **signs off**, they write a final message at the end of a letter or they say a final message at the end of a telephone conversation. You can say that people such as entertainers **sign off** when they finish a broadcast. *He would sign off each week with the catch-phrase, 'I'll see thee!'.* **2** When someone who has been unemployed **signs off**, they officially inform the authorities that they have found a job, so that they no longer receive money from the government. *If he sold his art he would be breaking the law, but if he signed off the dole he wouldn't.*

sign on. When an unemployed person **signs on**, they officially inform the authorities that they are unemployed, so that they can receive money from the government in order to live. *I had to sign on the dole on Monday.*

sign on for. If you **sign on for** something, you officially agree to work for an organization or do a course of study by signing a contract or form. *He had signed on for a driving course.*

sign over. If you **sign** something **over**, you sign documents that give someone else property, possessions, or rights that were previously yours. *He signed over his art collection to the New York Metropolitan Museum of Art.*

sign up. If you **sign up** for an organization or if an organization **signs** you **up**, you sign a contract officially agreeing to do a job or course of study. *He saw the song's potential, and persuaded the company to sign her up.*

sig·nal /ˈsɪɡnəl/ **signals, signalling, signalled;** spelled **signaling, signaled** in American English. **1** A **signal** is a gesture, sound, or action which is intended to give a particular message to the person who sees or hears it. *They fired three distress signals... You mustn't fire without my signal.* **2** If you **signal** to someone, you make a gesture or sound in order to send them a particular message. *He stood up,*

signalling to the officer that he had finished with his client... She signalled a passing taxi. Also V

3 If an event or action is a **signal** of something, it suggests that this thing exists or is going to happen. *Kurdish leaders saw the visit as an important signal of support.* **4** If someone or something **signals** an event, they suggest that the event is happening or likely to happen. *The outcome of that meeting could signal whether there truly exists a political will to begin negotiating.* N-COUNT: with supp / VERB: V n / V wh

5 A **signal** is a piece of equipment beside a railway, which indicates to train drivers whether they should stop the train or not. N-COUNT

6 A **signal** is a series of radio waves, light waves, or electrical impulses, which carry information. *...high-frequency radio signals.* N-COUNT

7 You use **signal** to describe a triumph, success, or failure when you are emphasizing the fact that it has occurred and indicating that the consequences are significant. *His final round was a signal triumph in a career marked by many sweet moments.* ♦ **sig·nal·ly** *...a demoralised party which its leader signally failed to reassure.* ADJ: ADJ n PRAGMATICS / ADV

'signal box, signal boxes. A **signal box** is a small building near a railway, which contains the switches used to control the signals. N-COUNT

signal·man /'sɪgnəlmæn/ **signalmen.** A **signalman** is a person whose job is to control the signals on a particular section of a railway. N-COUNT

sig·na·tory /'sɪgnətri, AM -tɔːri/ **signatories.** The **signatories** of an official document are the people, organizations, or countries that have signed it. ♦◇◇◇◇ N-COUNT FORMAL

sig·na·ture /'sɪgnətʃə/ **signatures. 1** Your **signature** is your name, written in your own characteristic way, often at the end of a document to indicate that you wrote the document or that you agree with what it says. *...a petition containing 170 signatures.* **2** If you **put** your **signature to** a document, you sign it as a way of officially showing that you agree with what is written. *The two sides met to put their signatures to a formal agreement.* ♦♦◇◇◇ N-COUNT / PHRASE

'signature tune, signature tunes. A **signature tune** is the tune which is always played at the beginning or end of a particular television or radio programme, or which people always associate with a particular performer. *Doesn't that sound like the signature tune from The Late Late Show?* N-COUNT BRITISH

sign·er /'saɪnə/ **signers.** See **sign.**

signet ring /'sɪgnət rɪŋ/ **signet rings.** A **signet ring** is a ring with a flat oval or circular section at the front with a pattern or letters carved into it. N-COUNT

sig·nifi·cance /sɪg'nɪfɪkəns/. The **significance** of something is the importance that it has, usually because it will have an effect on a situation or shows something about a situation. *...the social significance of religion.* ♦♦◇◇◇ N-UNCOUNT

sig·nifi·cant /sɪg'nɪfɪkənt/. **1** A **significant** amount of something is large enough to be important or make a difference. *...foods that offer a significant amount of protein.* ♦ **sig·nifi·cant·ly** The number of MPs now supporting him had increased significantly... America's airlines have significantly higher productivity than European ones. **2** If one thing has a **significant** effect on another, it has an important and fundamental effect on it. *Her upbringing had a significant effect on her adult life and relationships.* ♦ **significantly** The 1990 Clean Air Act will significantly improve the environment. ...the virtues of positive liberty and more significantly humanitarian equality. **3** A **significant** action or gesture is intended to have a special meaning. *Mrs Bycraft gave Rose a significant glance.* ♦ **significantly** She looked up at me significantly, raising an eyebrow. ♦♦♦◇ ADJ-GRADED / ADV-GRADED / ADJ-GRADED / ADV-GRADED / ADJ-GRADED / ADV-GRADED: ADV after v

sig,nificant 'other, significant others. If you refer to your **significant other,** you are referring to your wife, husband, or the person you are having a relationship with. N-COUNT

sig·ni·fy /'sɪgnɪfaɪ/ **signifies, signifying, signified. 1** If an event, a sign, or a symbol **signifies** something, it is a sign of that thing or represents that thing. *A 'Les Routiers' symbol proudly displayed outside a restaurant signifies there's excellent cuisine to be enjoyed inside.* **2** If you **signify** something, you make a sign or gesture in order to convey a particular meaning. *The UN flag was raised at the airport yesterday to signify that control had passed into its hands.* ♦◇◇◇◇ VERB: V n / V that / VERB: V n / V that

sign·ing /'saɪnɪŋ/ **signings. 1** A **signing** is someone who has recently signed a contract agreeing to play for a football club or work for a record company. *...Steve McMahon, Manchester City's recent £900,000 signing from Liverpool.* **2** See also **sign.** ♦♦◇◇◇ N-COUNT

'sign language, sign languages. Sign language is a method of communicating by using movements of your hands and arms. N-VAR

sign·post /'saɪnpəʊst/ **signposts. 1** A **signpost** is a sign by a road junction, telling you which direction to go to reach a particular place. *Turn off at the signpost for Attlebridge.* ♦ **sign·post·ed.** A place or route that is **signposted** has signposts beside the road to show the way. **2** A **signpost** is something that helps you to know how a situation or a course of action will develop. *These events were all signposts pointing toward change.* N-COUNT / ADJ / N-COUNT

Sikh /siːk/ **Sikhs.** A **Sikh** is a member of an Indian religion which separated from Hinduism in the sixteenth century and which teaches that there is only one God. ♦ **Sikh·ism** /'siːkɪzəm/. **Sikhism** is the religion of Sikhs. ♦♦◇◇◇ N-COUNT / N-UNCOUNT

si·lage /'saɪlɪdʒ/. **Silage** is food for cattle that is made by harvesting a crop such as grass or corn when it is green and then partly fermenting it. N-UNCOUNT

si·lence /'saɪləns/ **silences, silencing, silenced. 1** If there is **silence,** nobody is speaking. *They stood in silence... Then he bellowed 'Silence!'* **2** The **silence** of a place is the extreme quietness there. *...the silence of that rainless, all-concealing fog.* **3** Someone's **silence** about something is their failure or refusal to speak to other people about it. *He broke his silence for the first time yesterday about his lovechild.* **4** To **silence** someone or something means to stop them speaking or making a noise. *A ringing phone silenced her.* **5** If someone **silences** you, they stop you expressing opinions that they do not agree with. *He tried to silence anyone who spoke out against him.* **6** To **silence** someone means to kill them in order to stop them revealing something secret. *A hit man had been sent to silence her over the affair.* ♦♦♦◇◇ N-VAR / N-UNCOUNT / N-UNCOUNT / VERB: V n / VERB: V n / VERB: V n

si·lenc·er /'saɪlənsə/ **silencers. 1** A **silencer** is a device that is fitted onto a gun to make it very quiet when it is fired. **2** A **silencer** is a device on a car exhaust that makes it quieter. The American word is **muffler.** N-COUNT / N-COUNT BRITISH

si·lent /'saɪlənt/. **1** Someone who is **silent** is not speaking. *They both fell silent... She offered a silent prayer of thanks.* ♦ **si·lent·ly** She and Ned sat silently for a moment... Most of those attending the funeral stood silently showing little emotion. **2** If you describe someone as a **silent** person, you mean that they do not talk to people very much, and sometimes give the impression of being unfriendly. **3** A place that is **silent** is completely quiet, with no sound at all. Something that is **silent** makes no sound at all. *The heavy guns have again fallen silent.* ♦ **silently** Strange shadows moved silently in the almost permanent darkness. **4** If someone is **silent about** something, they do not tell people anything about it, because they think it is a private matter or because they want to keep the information secret. **5** A **silent** film has pictures usually accompanied by music but does not have the actors' voices or any other sounds. **6** A **silent** letter in a word is written but not pronounced. For example, the 'k' in the word 'know' is silent. ♦♦♦◇◇ ADJ-GRADED / ADV: ADV with v / ADJ-GRADED: ADJ n / ADJ-GRADED / ADV-GRADED: ADV with v / ADJ-GRADED: ADV with v / v-link ADJ: about n / ADJ: ADJ n / ADJ

,silent ma'jority. If you believe that in society or in a particular group the opinions of most people are very different from the opinions that are most often heard in public, you can refer to these people N-COLL-SING

as the **silent majority**. *...arguing that a silent major-ity should never again allow extremists to take con-trol of the country.*

sil·hou·ette /ˌsɪluˈet/ **silhouettes. 1** A **silhouette** is the solid dark shape that you see when someone or something has a bright light or pale background behind them. *The dark silhouette of the castle ruins stood out boldly against the fading light.* ♦ **sil·hou·ett·ed** *Silhouetted against the sun stood the figure of a man.* **2** The **silhouette** of something is the out-line that it has, which often helps you to recognize it. *The shirt's ideal worn loose over leggings or tuck it in for a streamlined silhouette.* **3** If you see some-thing **in silhouette**, you see it as a dark shape with no detail except for the outline. ◇◇◇◇ N-COUNT / N-COUNT / PHRASE

sil·i·ca /ˈsɪlɪkə/ **Silica** is silicon dioxide, a com-pound of silicon which is found in sand, quartz, and flint, and which is used to make glass. N-UNCOUNT

sil·i·cate /ˈsɪlɪkət/ **silicates.** A **silicate** is a com-pound of silica which does not dissolve. *...alumi-num silicate.* N-VAR

sil·i·con /ˈsɪlɪkən/. **Silicon** is a non-metallic element that is found combined with oxygen in sand and in minerals such as quartz and granite. Silicon is used to make parts of computers and other electronic equipment. ◆◇◇◇ N-UNCOUNT

ˌsilicon 'chip, silicon chips. A **silicon chip** is a very small piece of silicon inside a computer. It has electronic circuits on it and can hold large quan-tities of information or perform mathematical or logical operations. N-COUNT

sil·i·cone /ˈsɪlɪkəʊn/. **Silicone** is a tough artificial substance made from silicon, which is used to make things such as lubricants and polishes, and which is also used in cosmetic surgery and plastic surgery. ♦◇◇◇ N-UNCOUNT

silk /sɪlk/ **silks. 1** Silk is a substance produced by silkworms which is made into smooth fine cloth and sewing thread. You can also refer to this cloth or thread as **silk**. **2** You can refer to the substance produced by some creatures such as spiders as **silk**. *...the silk threads of a spider's web.* ♦♦◇◇ N-VAR / N-UNCOUNT

silk·en /ˈsɪlkən/. **1 Silken** is used to describe things that are very pleasantly smooth and soft. *...her long, silken legs.* **2** A **silken** garment, fabric, or rope is made of silk or a material that looks like silk. *...a silken nightshirt.* ADJ LITERARY / ADJ: ADJ n LITERARY

silk·screen /ˈsɪlkskriːn/. **Silkscreen** printing is a method of printing patterns onto cloth by forcing paint or dyes through silk or similar material. *...silkscreen prints.* ADJ: ADJ n

silk·worm /ˈsɪlkwɜːm/ **silkworms.** A **silkworm** is a type of caterpillar that produces silk. N-COUNT

silky /ˈsɪlki/ **silkier, silkiest. 1** If something has a **silky** texture, it is smooth, soft, and shiny, like silk. *...dresses in seductively silky fabrics.* **2** If you de-scribe someone's voice as **silky**, you mean that it sounds confident but gentle and you find it attrac-tive. *...a well-spoken man with a silky voice.* **3** If you describe the way someone or something moves as **silky**, you mean that they move effortlessly and gracefully. *Some people moved in silky, liquid move-ments, others were jerky, probably drunk.* ♦◇◇◇ ADJ-GRADED / ADJ-GRADED / ADJ-GRADED

sill /sɪl/ **sills.** A **sill** is a ledge at the bottom of a window, either inside or outside a building. ♦◇◇◇ N-COUNT

sil·ly /ˈsɪli/ **sillier, silliest. 1** If you say that some-one or something is **silly**, you mean that they are foolish, childish, or ridiculous. *I thought it would be silly to be too rude at that stage.* ♦ **sil·li·ness** *She looked round to make sure there was no giggling or silliness.* **2** If you do something such as laugh or drink yourself **silly**, you do it so much that you are unable to think or behave sensibly. *Poor Donald's been worrying himself silly.* ♦♦◇◇ ADJ-GRADED / N-UNCOUNT / ADJ: v n ADJ INFORMAL

'silly season. The **silly season** is the time of the year, usually around August, when the newspapers are full of trivial or silly news stories because parlia-ment is in recess and there is often very little real news to report. N-PROPER: the N BRITISH

silo /ˈsaɪləʊ/ **silos. 1** A **silo** is a tall round metal tower on a farm, in which silage, grain, or some N-COUNT

other substance is stored. **2** A **silo** is a specially built place underground where a nuclear missile is kept. N-COUNT

silt /sɪlt/ **silts, silting, silted.** Silt is fine sand, soil, or mud which is carried along by a river. ♦◇◇◇ N-UNCOUNT

silt up. If a river or lake **silts up**, it becomes blocked with silt. *The soil washed from the hills is silting up the hydroelectric dams.* PHRASAL VB ERG: V P / V P n

sil·ver /ˈsɪlvə/ **silvers. 1 Silver** is a valuable greyish-white metal that is used for making jewel-lery and ornaments. **2 Silver** consists of coins that are made from silver or that look like silver. *...£150,000 in silver.* **3** You can use **silver** to refer to all the things in a house that are made of silver, es-pecially the cutlery and dishes. *He beat the rugs and polished the silver.* **4 Silver** is used to describe things that are shiny greyish-white in colour or look as if they are made from silver. *He had thick silver hair.* **5** A **silver** is the same as a **silver medal**. **6** ● **born with a silver spoon in** your mouth: see **spoon**. ◆◆◇◇ N-UNCOUNT / N-UNCOUNT / N-UNCOUNT: also the N / COLOUR / N-VAR

ˌsilver 'birch, silver birches; silver birch can also be used as the plural form. A **silver birch** is a tree with a greyish-white trunk and branches. N-COUNT

sil·vered /ˈsɪlvəd/. You can describe something as **silvered** when it has become silver in colour. ADJ LITERARY

ˌsilver 'jubilee, silver jubilees. A **silver jubilee** is the 25th anniversary of an important event, such as a king or queen coming to the throne. N-COUNT

ˌsilver 'lining. 1 If you say that **every cloud has a silver lining**, you mean that every sad or unpleasant situation has a positive side to it. **2** If you talk about a **silver lining**, you are talking about something positive that comes out of a sad or unpleasant situation. *The fall in inflation is the silver lining of the prolonged recession.* PHRASE / N-SING

ˌsilver 'medal, silver medals. If you win a **silver medal**, you come second in a competition, especial-ly a sports contest, and are given a medal made of silver as a prize. ◆◇◇◇ N-COUNT

ˌsilver 'plate. Silver plate is metal that has been coated with a thin layer of silver. ● See also: **plate**. N-UNCOUNT

ˌsilver 'screen. People sometimes refer to the films that are shown in cinemas as the **silver screen**. *We don't see much of dear old Peter O'Toole on the silver screen these days.* N-SING: the N

silver·smith /ˈsɪlvəsmɪθ/ **silversmiths.** A **silver-smith** is a person who makes things out of silver. N-COUNT

ˌsilver-'tongued. A **silver-tongued** person is very skilful at persuading people to believe what they say or to do what they want them to do. ADJ-GRADED

silver·ware /ˈsɪlvəweə/. You can use **silverware** to refer to all the things in a house that are made of silver, especially the cutlery and dishes. N-UNCOUNT

ˌsilver 'wedding, silver weddings. A married couple's **silver wedding** or **silver wedding anniver-sary** is the 25th anniversary of their wedding. N-COUNT

sil·very /ˈsɪlvəri/. **Silvery** things look like silver or are the colour of silver. ♦◇◇◇ ADJ

sim·ian /ˈsɪmiən/. **1** If someone has **simian** features or mannerisms, their features or mannerisms are like those of a monkey or ape. **2 Simian** is used to describe things relating to monkeys or apes. *...a simian virus.* ADJ FORMAL / ADJ TECHNICAL

simi·lar /ˈsɪmɪlə/. If one thing is **similar** to anoth-er, or if two things are **similar**, they have features that are the same. *...the accident was similar to one that happened in 1973. ...a group of similar pictures.* ◆◆◆◇ ADJ-GRADED

simi·lar·ity /ˌsɪmɪˈlærɪti/ **similarities. 1** If there is a **similarity** between two or more things, they are similar to each other. *She is also 25 and a native of Birmingham, but the similarity ends there.* **2** Simi-larities are features that things have which make them similar to each other. *There were significant similarities between mother and son.* ♦♦◇◇ N-UNCOUNT / N-COUNT

simi·lar·ly /ˈsɪmɪləli/. **1** You use **similarly** to say that something is similar to something else. *Most of the men who now gathered round him again were similarly dressed.* **2** You use **similarly** to say that there is a correspondence or similarity between the ♦♦◇◇ ADV-GRADED / ADV: ADV with cl

way two things happen or are done. *A mother some-how memorises the feel of her child's skin from the very first touches and can recognise it even when blindfolded. Similarly a baby's cry is instantly identi-fied by the mother.*

simi·le /'sɪmɪli/ **similes.** A **simile** is an expression N-COUNT which describes a person or thing as being similar to someone or something else. For example, the sentences 'She runs like a deer' and 'He's as white as a sheet' contain similes.

sim·mer /'sɪmə/ **simmers, simmering, sim-** ◆◆◇◇◇ **mered. 1** When you **simmer** food, you cook it by V-ERG: V n keeping it just below boiling point. *Turn the heat* V *down so the sauce simmers gently.* ▸ Also a noun. N-SING *Combine the stock, whole onion and peppercorns in a pan and bring to a simmer.* **2** If a conflict or a VERB: V quarrel **simmers**, it does not actually happen for a V-ing period of time, but eventually builds up to the point where it does. *The province was attacked a month ago after weeks of simmering tension.*

sim·per /'sɪmpə/ **simpers, simpering, sim-** VERB: V **pered.** When someone **simpers**, they smile in a ra-ther silly way. ▸ Also a noun. *'Thank you doctor,'* N-COUNT *said the nurse with a simper.*

sim·ple /'sɪmpəl/ **simpler, simplest. 1** If you de- ◆◆◆◇ scribe something as **simple**, you mean that it is not ADJ-GRADED complicated, and is therefore easy to understand. *...simple pictures and diagrams.* ◆ **simp·ly** When ADV-GRADED: *applying for a visa extension state simply and clearly* ADV with v *the reasons why you need an extension.* **2** If a prob- ADJ-GRADED lem is **simple** or if its solution is **simple**, the prob-lem can be solved easily. *Some puzzles look difficult but once the solution is known are actually quite simple.* **3** A **simple** task is easy to do. *The simplest* ADJ-GRADED *way to install a shower is to fit one over the bath.* ◆ **simply** *Simply dial the number and tell us your* ADV-GRADED: *area.* ADV with v

4 If you describe people or things as **simple**, you ADJ-GRADED mean that they have all the basic or necessary things they require, but nothing extra. *He ate a simple dinner of rice and beans... He lives a very simple life for a man who has become incredibly rich.* ◆ **simply** *He dressed* ADV-GRADED: *simply and led a quiet family life.* **5** You use **simple** to ADJ: ADJ n emphasize that the thing you are referring to is the PRAGMATICS only important or relevant reason for something. *His refusal to talk was simple stubbornness.*

6 If you say that someone is **simple**, you mean that ADJ-GRADED they are not very intelligent or that they are mentally retarded.

7 In English grammar, **simple** tenses are ones which ADJ are not formed using the auxiliary verb 'be', as in 'I dressed and went for a walk' and 'These wines taste awful'. Simple verb groups are used especially to refer to completed actions, habitual actions, and situa-tions. Compare **continuous. 8** In English grammar, a ADJ **simple** sentence consists of one main clause. Com-pare **compound, complex.**

9 See also **simply.**

,simple 'interest. Simple interest is interest that N-UNCOUNT is calculated on an original sum of money and not also on interest which has previously been added to the sum.

,simple-'minded. If you describe someone as ADJ-GRADED **simple-minded,** you believe that they interpret PRAGMATICS things in a way that is too simple and do not under-stand how complicated things are; used showing disapproval.

sim·ple·ton /'sɪmpəltən/ **simpletons.** If you call N-COUNT someone a **simpleton,** you believe they are easily fooled or not very intelligent.

sim·plic·ity /sɪm'plɪsɪti/ **1** The **simplicity** of ◆◇◇◇◇ something is the fact that it is uncomplicated and N-UNCOUNT can be understood or done easily. *Because of its simplicity, this test could be carried out easily by a family doctor.* **2** When you talk about something's N-UNCOUNT **simplicity,** you approve of it because it is natural PRAGMATICS and simple rather than elaborate or ornate. *...fussy details that ruin the simplicity of the design.* **3** If PHRASE you say that doing something is **simplicity itself,**

you mean that it is very easy to do. *Using a credit card to pay for an order is simplicity itself.*

sim·pli·fi·ca·tion /,sɪmplɪfɪ'keɪʃən/ **simplifica-** **tions. 1** You can use **simplification** to refer to the N-COUNT thing that is produced when you make something simpler or when you reduce it to its basic elements. *Like any such diagram, it is a simplification.* **2** Sim- N-UNCOUNT **plification** is the act or process of making some-thing simpler. *Everyone favours the simplification of court procedures.*

sim·pli·fy /'sɪmplɪfaɪ/ **simplifies, simplifying,** ◆◇◇◇◇ **simplified.** If you **simplify** something, you make it VERB easier to understand or you remove the things V n which make it complex. *The aim of the scheme is to simplify the complex social security system.* ◆ **sim-** **·pli·fied** *...a shorter, simplified version of his speech.* ADJ-GRADED

sim·plis·tic /sɪm'plɪstɪk/. A **simplistic** view or in- ◆◇◇◇◇ terpretation of something makes it seem much sim- ADJ-GRADED pler than it really is. ◆ **sim·plis·ti·cal·ly** ADV-GRADED /sɪm'plɪstɪkli/. *The impact of religion on voting has been analysed far too simplistically.*

simp·ly /'sɪmpli/. **1** You use **simply** to emphasize ◆◆◆◇ that something consists of only one thing, happens ADV for only one reason, or is done in only one way. *The table is simply a chipboard circle on a base... Most of the damage that's occurred was simply because of fallen trees... Many people switch on the television simply to stave off boredom.* **2** You use **simply** to ADV emphasize what you are saying. *This sort of increase* PRAGMATICS *simply cannot be justified. ...nine out of ten thought it was simply marvellous.* **3** See also **simple.**

simu·late /'sɪmjʊleɪt/ **simulates, simulating,** ◆◇◇◇◇ **simulated. 1** If you **simulate** an action or a feel- VERB ing, you pretend that you are doing it or feeling it. V n *They rolled about on the Gilligan Road, simulating a* Also V-ed *bloodthirsty fight.* **2** If you **simulate** an object, a VERB substance, or a noise, you produce something that V n looks or sounds like it. *The wood had been painted to simulate stone.* **3** If you **simulate** a set of condi- VERB: V n tions, you reproduce them in some form, for exam- V-ed ple in order to conduct an experiment. *Cars are test-ed to see how much damage they suffer in simulated crashes.*

simu·la·tion /,sɪmjʊ'leɪʃən/ **simulations.** Simula- ◆◇◇◇◇ **tion** is the process of simulating something or the N-VAR result of simulating it. *Training includes realistic simulation of casualty procedures.*

simu·la·tor /'sɪmjʊleɪtə/ **simulators.** A **simulator** N-COUNT is a device which is designed to reproduce actual conditions. Simulators are used in training people such as pilots or astronauts. *...a flight simulator.*

sim·ul·ta·neous /,sɪməl'teɪniəs, AM ,saɪm-/. ◆◆◇◇◇ Things which are **simultaneous** happen or exist at ADJ the same time. *...the simultaneous release of the book and the album.* ◆ **sim·ul·ta·neous·ly** *The* ADV *two guns fired almost simultaneously.*

sin /sɪn/ **sins, sinning, sinned. 1** Sin or a sin is ◆◆◇◇◇ an action or type of behaviour which is believed to N-VAR break the laws of God. *The Vatican's teaching on abortion is clear: it is a sin.* ● See also **cardinal sin.** **2** If you **sin,** you do something that is believed to VERB: V break the laws of God. *The Spanish Inquisition* V against n *charged him with sinning against God and man.* ◆ **sin·ner** /'sɪnə/ **sinners** *I was known that I am a* N-COUNT *sinner, that I needed to repent of my sins.* **3** A **sin** is N-COUNT any action or behaviour that people disapprove of or consider morally wrong. *The ultimate sin was not infidelity, but public mention which led to scandal.* PHRASE **4** If you say that a man and a woman **are living in** DATED **sin,** you mean that they are living together as a cou-ple although they are not married.

'sin-bin; also spelled **sin bin.** In the sports of ice- N-SING hockey or rugby league, if a player is sent to the **sin-bin,** they are ordered to leave the playing area for a short period of time because they have done something wrong such as making an illegal tackle.

since /sɪns/ **1** You use **since** when you are men- ◆◆◆◆◆ tioning a time or event in the past and indicating PREP that a situation has continued from then until now. *Jacques Arnold has been a member of parliament*

since 1987... She had a sort of breakdown some years ago, and since then she has been very shy. ▶ Also an adverb. *When we first met, we had a row, and we have rowed frequently ever since.* ▶ Also a conjunction. *I've earned my own living since I was seven, doing all kinds of jobs.* **2** You use **since** to mention a time or event in the past when you are describing an event or situation that has happened after that time. *The percentage increase in reported crime in England and Wales this year is the highest since the war.* ▶ Also a conjunction. *So much has changed in the sport since I was a teenager.* **3** When you are talking about an event or situation in the past, you use **since** to indicate that another event happened at some point later in time. *About six thousand people were arrested, several hundred of whom have since been released.* **4** If you say that something has **long since** happened, you mean that it happened a long time ago. *Even though her parents have long since died, she still talks about them in the present tense.* **5** You use **since** to introduce reasons or explanations. *I'm forever on a diet, since I put on weight easily.*

ADV:
ADV with v

CONJ

PREP

CONJ

ADV:
ADV with v

PHRASE

CONJ

sin·cere /sɪnˈsɪə/. If you say that someone is **sincere**, you approve of them because they really mean the things they say. You can also describe someone's behaviour and beliefs as **sincere**. *He accepted her apologies as sincere... There was such a sincere expression of friendliness on both their faces that it was a joy to see.* ♦ **sin·cer·ity** /sɪnˈserɪti/. *I was impressed with his deep sincerity.*

◆◆◇◇◇
ADJ-GRADED
PRAGMATICS

N-UNCOUNT

sin·cere·ly /sɪnˈsɪəli/. **1** If you say or feel something **sincerely**, you really mean or feel it, and are not pretending. *'Congratulations,' he said sincerely. ...sincerely held religious beliefs.* **2** People write **Yours sincerely** before their signature at the end of a formal letter when they have addressed it to someone by name. In the United States, people often write **Sincerely yours** before their signature.

◆◇◇◇◇
ADV-GRADED

CONVENTION
BRITISH

si·necure /ˈsɪnɪkjʊə, ˈsaɪn-/ **sinecures.** A sinecure is a job for which you receive payment but which does not involve much work or responsibility.

N-COUNT

sine qua non /ˌsɪni kwɑː ˈnɒn, AM -ˈnɑːn/. A **sine qua non** is something that is essential if you want to achieve a particular result or thing. *Successful agricultural reform is also a sine qua non of Mexico's modernisation.*

N-SING:
a N
FORMAL

sin·ew /ˈsɪnjuː/ **sinews.** A sinew is a cord in your body that connects a muscle to a bone.

N-COUNT

sin·ewy /ˈsɪnjuːi/. Someone who is **sinewy** has a lean body with strong muscles.

ADJ-GRADED

sin·ful /ˈsɪnfʊl/. If you describe someone or something as **sinful**, you mean that they are very wicked or immoral. ♦ **sin·ful·ness** *...the sinfulness of apartheid.*

ADJ-GRADED

N-UNCOUNT

sing /sɪŋ/ **sings, singing, sang, sung. 1** When you **sing**, you make musical sounds with your voice, usually producing words that fit a tune. *I sing about love most of the time... They were all singing the same song... Go on, then, sing us a song!* **2** When birds or insects **sing**, they make pleasant high-pitched sounds. **3** ● to **sing** someone's **praises**: see **praise.** See also **singing.**

◆◆◆◇◇
VERB: V
V about n
V n n

VERB: V

sing along. If you **sing along** with a piece of music, you sing it while you are listening to someone else perform it. *...fifteen hundred people all singing along and dancing.* ● See also **singalong.**

PHRASAL VB
V P with/to n
V P

sing out. If someone **sings out** something, they say it in a loud, cheerful voice. *'See you,' Geoff sang out.*

PHRASAL VB
no cont
V P with quote

sing. Sing. is a written abbreviation for **singular.**

sing·along /ˈsɪnəlɒŋ, AM -lɔːŋ/ **singalongs;** also spelled **sing-along.** A singalong is an occasion when a group of people sing songs together for pleasure.

N-COUNT

singe /sɪndʒ/ **singes, singeing, singed.** If you **singe** something or if it **singes**, it burns very slightly and changes colour but does not catch fire. *The electric fire had begun to singe the bottoms of his trousers... Her hair was singed.*

V-ERG
V n
V-ed
Also V

sing·er /ˈsɪŋə/ **singers.** A **singer** is a person who sings, especially as a job.

◆◆◆◇◇
N-COUNT

,singer-'songwriter,   singer-songwriters. A **singer-songwriter** is someone who writes and performs their own songs, especially popular songs.

◆◇◇◇◇
N-COUNT

sing·ing /ˈsɪŋɪŋ/. **Singing** is the activity of making musical sounds with your voice. *...a people's carnival, with singing and dancing in the streets.*

◆◆◇◇◇
N-UNCOUNT

sin·gle /ˈsɪŋɡəl/ **singles, singling, singled. 1** You use **single** to emphasize that you are referring to one thing, and no more than one thing. *She hadn't uttered a single word.* **2** You use **single** to indicate that you are considering something on its own and separately from other things like it. *Every single house in town had been damaged... The Middle East is the world's single most important source of oil.* **3** Someone who is **single** is not married. You can also use **single** to describe someone who does not have a girlfriend or boyfriend. **4** A **single** room is a room intended for one person to stay or live in. ▶ Also a noun. *It's £65 for a single, £98 for a double.* A **single** bed is wide enough for one person to sleep in. **Single** bedclothes are designed to fit single beds. **6** A **single** ticket is a ticket for a journey from one place to another but not back again. The usual American term is **one-way** ticket. ▶ Also a noun. *...a Club Class single to Los Angeles.* **7** A **single** is a small record which has one short song on each side. You can also refer to the main song on a small record as a **single**. *The collection includes all the band's British and American hit singles.* **8 Singles** is a game of tennis or badminton in which one player plays another. The plural **singles** can be used to refer to one or more of these matches. **9** See also **single-.** ● **in single file:** see **file.**

◆◆◆◆◆
PRAGMATICS

ADJ: det ADJ
PRAGMATICS

ADJ

ADJ
N-COUNT
ADJ: ADJ n

ADJ
BRITISH
N-COUNT
N-COUNT

N-UNCOUNT

single out. If you **single** someone **out** from a group, you choose them and give them special attention or treatment. *His immediate superior has singled him out for a special mention... We wanted to single out the main threat to civilisation.*

PHRASAL VB
V n P
V n P for/as n
V P noun
Also V P noun
for/as n

single- /ˈsɪŋɡəl-/. **Single-** is used to form words which describe something that has one part or feature, rather than having two or more of them. *...a single-sex school. ...a single-track road.*

COMB

,single-'breasted. A **single-breasted** coat, jacket, or suit fastens in the centre of the chest and has only one row of buttons.

ADJ

,single 'cream. **Single cream** is thin cream that does not have a lot of fat in it.

N-UNCOUNT
BRITISH

,single-'decker,   single-deckers. A **single-decker** or a **single-decker bus** is a bus with only one deck.

N-COUNT
BRITISH

,single-'handed. If you do something **single-handed**, you do it on your own, without help from anyone else. *I brought up my seven children single-handed.* ▶ Also an adjective. *...a single-handed yachtsman.* ♦ **single-'handed·ly** *Olga Korbut single-handedly turned gymnastics into a major event.*

◆◇◇◇◇
ADJ:
ADV after v

ADJ

ADV:
ADV with v

,single-'minded. Someone who is **single-minded** has only one aim or purpose and is determined to achieve it. ♦ **single-'minded·ly** *He was single-mindedly devoted to the hastening of freedom for the oppressed.* ♦ **single-'minded·ness** *...the single-mindedness of the athletes as they train.*

◆◇◇◇◇
ADJ-GRADED

ADV-GRADED

N-UNCOUNT

,single 'parent,   single parents. A **single parent** is someone who is bringing up a child on their own, because the other parent is not living with them. *...single-parent families.*

◆◇◇◇◇
N-COUNT

'singles bar,   singles bars. In North America, a **singles bar** is a bar where single people can go in order to drink and meet other single people.

N-COUNT

sin·glet /ˈsɪŋɡlət/ **singlets.** A **singlet** is a sleeveless piece of clothing like a vest, worn as underwear or worn as a sports shirt by athletes and boxers.

N-COUNT

sin·gly /ˈsɪŋɡli/. If people do something **singly**, they each do it on their own, or do it one by one. *Patients went singly into the consulting room.*

ADV:
ADV with v

'sing-song,   sing-songs; also spelled **singsong. 1** A **sing-song** voice repeatedly rises and falls in

ADJ: ADJ n

pitch. **2** A **sing-song** is an occasion on which a group of people sing songs together for pleasure. N-COUNT BRITISH

sin·gu·lar /ˈsɪŋgjʊlə/. **1** The **singular** form of a word is the form that is used when referring to one person or thing. *The word 'you' can be singular or plural.* **2** The **singular** of a noun is the form of it that is used to refer to one person or thing. *The inhabitants of the Arctic are known as the Inuit. The singular is Inuk.* **3** **Singular** means very great and remarkable. *...a smile of singular sweetness.* ♦ **sin·gu·lar·ly** *...a former sales executive singularly unsuited for the job.* **4** If you describe someone or something as **singular**, you mean that they are strange or unusual. *Cardinal Meschia was without doubt a singular character.* ♦ **sin·gu·lar·ity** /ˌsɪŋgjʊˈlærɪtɪ/. *...the singularity of his appearance.* ◆◇◇◇ ADJ N-SING: theN ADJ: ADJ n FORMAL ADV: ADJ adj/adv ADJ-GRADED DATED N-UNCOUNT

singular noun, singular nouns. A **singular noun** is a noun such as 'standstill' or 'vicinity' that does not have a plural form and always has a determiner such as 'a' or 'the' in front of it. N-COUNT

sin·is·ter /ˈsɪnɪstə/. Something that is **sinister** seems evil or harmful. ◆◆◇◇ ADJ-GRADED

sink /sɪŋk/ **sinks, sinking, sank, sunk. 1** A **sink** is a large basin in a kitchen with taps that supply water. It is used for washing dishes. *...the kitchen sink.* **2** A **sink** is the same as a **washbasin**. ◆◆◆◇ N-COUNT N-COUNT

3 If a boat **sinks**, it disappears below the surface of a mass of water. *In a naval battle your aim is to sink the enemy's ship... The lifeboat crashed against the side of the sinking ship.* ♦ **sink·ing, sinkings** *...the sinking of the Titanic.* **4** If something **sinks**, it disappears below the surface of a mass of water. *A fresh egg will sink and an old egg will float.* **5** If you say that someone will have to **sink or swim**, you mean that they will have to succeed through their own efforts, or fail. ● to **sink without trace:** see trace. V-ERG: V V n V-ing N-COUNT VERB V PHRASE

6 If something **sinks**, it moves slowly downwards. *Far off to the west the sun was sinking.* **7** If you **sink**, you move into a lower position, for example by sitting down in a chair or kneeling. *She sank into an armchair and crossed her legs.* **8** If something **sinks** to a lower level or standard, it falls to that level or standard. *Share prices would have sunk - hurting small and big investors... Pay increases have sunk to around seven per cent.* VERB: V VERB V adv/prep WRITTEN VERB V V to/from/at amount/n Also V amount

9 If your voice **sinks**, it becomes quieter. *She heard their voices sink into a confidential whisper.* **10** To **sink** into an unpleasant or undesirable mood, situation, or state means to pass gradually into it. *Bulgaria's economy has sunk into chaos.* **11** If your heart **sinks**, you become depressed or lose hope. VERB: V V to/into n VERB V into n VERB: V

12 If something sharp **sinks** or **is sunk** into something solid, it goes deeply into it. *He sinks the needle into my arm... The spade sank into a clump of overgrown bushes.* **13** If someone **sinks** a well, mine, or other large hole, they make a deep hole in the ground, usually by digging or drilling. V-ERG V n in to n V into n VERB: V n

14 If you **sink** money into a business or project, you spend money on it in the hope of making more money. *He has already sunk $25million into the project.* VERB V n into n

15 If someone **sinks** a number of alcoholic drinks, they drink them quickly. **16** In golf, snooker, and some other games, if you **sink** a ball or a putt, you successfully hit the ball into a hole. **17** See also **sinking, sunk**. VERB: V n BRITISH VERB: V n

sink in. When a statement or fact **sinks in**, you finally understand or realize it fully. PHRASAL VB V P

sink·er /ˈsɪŋkə/. You can use **hook, line, and sinker** to emphasize that someone is tricked or forced into a situation completely. *I was caught hook, line and sinker.* PHRASE PRAGMATICS

sink·ing /ˈsɪŋkɪŋ/. If you have a **sinking** feeling, you suddenly become depressed or lose hope. ● See also **sink**. ADJ: ADJ n

'sinking fund, sinking funds. A **sinking fund** is money that a company or government has invested in order to pay off a long-term debt. N-COUNT

Sino- /ˈsaɪnəʊ-/. **Sino-** is added to adjectives indicating nationality to form adjectives which describe COMB

relations between China and another country. *...Sino-Vietnamese friendship.*

sinu·ous /ˈsɪnjʊəs/. **1** Something that is **sinuous** moves with smooth twists and turns. *...the silent, sinuous approach of a snake through the long grass.* **2** Something that is **sinuous** has many smooth turns and curves. *...sinuous mountain roads.* ADJ-GRADED LITERARY ADJ-GRADED LITERARY

si·nus /ˈsaɪnəs/ **sinuses.** Your **sinuses** are the spaces in the bones of your skull just behind your nose. ◆◇◇◇ N-COUNT

si·nusi·tis /ˌsaɪnəˈsaɪtɪs/. If you have **sinusitis**, the membranes lining your sinuses become swollen and painful, which can cause headaches and a blocked-up nose. N-UNCOUNT

sip /sɪp/ **sips, sipping, sipped.** If you **sip** a drink or **sip at** it, you drink by taking just a small amount at a time. *She sipped from her coffee mug, watching him over the rim.* ▶ Also a noun. *Harry took a sip of bourbon.* ◆◆◇◇ VERB V at/from n also V N-COUNT

si·phon /ˈsaɪfən/ **siphons, siphoning, siphoned;** also spelled **syphon. 1** If you **siphon** liquid from a container, you draw it out of the container through a tube by using atmospheric pressure. *Tell Mac to siphon petrol out of his wagon.* ▶ **Siphon off** means the same as **siphon**. *Surgeons siphoned off fluid from his left lung.* **2** A **siphon** is a tube that you use for siphoning liquid. **3** If you **siphon** money or resources from something, you use them for a purpose for which they were not intended. *He had siphoned thousands of pounds a week from the failing business.* ▶ **Siphon off** means the same as **siphon**. *He had siphoned off a small fortune in aid money from the United Nations.* ◆◇◇◇ VERB V n prep Also V n PHRASAL VB V P noun N-COUNT VERB V n prep PHRASAL VB V P noun Also V n P

sir /sɜː/ **sirs. 1** People sometimes say **sir** as a polite way of addressing a man whose name they do not know or a man of superior rank. For example, a shop assistant might address a male customer as **sir**. *Good afternoon to you, sir.* **2** **Sir** is the title used in front of the name of a knight or baronet. *...Sir Geoffrey Howe.* **3** You use the expression **Dear sir** at the beginning of a formal letter or a business letter when you are writing to a man. You use **Dear sirs** when you are writing to an organization. ◆◆◆◆ N-VOC PRAGMATICS FORMAL N-TITLE CONVENTION

sire /saɪə/ **sires, siring, sired.** When a male animal, especially a horse, **sires** offspring, he makes a female pregnant and she gives birth to a young animal. *Comet also sired the champion foal out of Spinway Harvest.* ▶ Also a noun. *Her sire is the thoroughbred Silver Season.* ◆◇◇◇ VERB V n TECHNICAL N-COUNT

si·ren /ˈsaɪərən/ **sirens. 1** A **siren** is a warning device which makes a long, loud, wailing noise. Most fire engines, ambulances, and police cars have sirens. **2** Some people refer to a woman as a **siren** when they think that she is attractive to men but dangerous in some way. **3** A **siren call** or **siren song** is the appeal that something has although it is harmful or dangerous. *We have to resist any siren song for a partial solution.* ◆◇◇◇ N-COUNT N-COUNT LITERARY PHRASE

sir·loin /ˈsɜːlɔɪn/ **sirloins.** A **sirloin** is a piece of beef which is cut from the bottom and side parts of a cow's back. *...fresh beef sirloin steaks.* N-VAR

si·sal /ˈsaɪzəl/. **Sisal** is the fibre from the leaves of a plant that is grown in the West Indies, South America, and Africa. **Sisal** is used to make rope, cord, and mats. N-UNCOUNT

sis·sy /ˈsɪsɪ/ **sissies;** also spelled **cissy.** If you describe an action or activity as **sissy**, you disapprove of it because you think it is unmanly. *Far from being sissy, it takes a real man to accept that he is not perfect.* ▶ A **sissy** is someone who is sissy. ADJ PRAGMATICS INFORMAL N-COUNT

sis·ter /ˈsɪstə/ **sisters. 1** Your **sister** is a girl or woman who has the same parents as you. *His sister Sarah helped him.* ● See also **half-sister, stepsister. 2** **Sister** is a title given to a woman who belongs to a religious community such as a convent. *...the Hospice of the Sisters of Charity at Lourdes.* **3** In Britain, a **sister** is a senior female nurse who supervises a hospital ward. *Sister Middleton followed the coffee trolley.* **4** You might use **sister** to describe a woman who be- ◆◆◆◆ N-COUNT N-COUNT; N-TITLE; N-VOC N-TITLE; also N-VOC N-COUNT

longs to the same race, religion, country, profession, or trade union as you, or who has ideas that are similar to yours. *...our Jewish brothers and sisters.* **5** You can use **sister** to describe something that is of the same type or is connected in some way to another thing you have mentioned. For example, if a company has a **sister** company, they are connected, perhaps because they are both part of a larger organization. *...Voyager 2 and its sister ship, Voyager 1.*   ADJ: ADJ n

sis·ter·hood /'sɪstəhʊd/. **Sisterhood** is the affection and loyalty that women feel for other women who they have something in common with. *There was a degree of solidarity and sisterhood among the women.*   N-UNCOUNT

'sister-in-law, sisters-in-law. Someone's **sister-in-law** is the sister of their husband or wife, or the woman who is married to their brother.   ◆◇◇◇◇ N-COUNT

sis·ter·ly /'sɪstəli/. A woman's **sisterly** feelings are the feelings of love and loyalty which you expect a sister to show. *We just had a sisterly relationship.*   ADJ-GRADED

sit /sɪt/ **sits, sitting, sat. 1** If you **are sitting** somewhere, for example in a chair, your weight is supported by your buttocks rather than your feet and the upper part of your body is upright. *Mother was sitting in her chair in the kitchen... He was unable to sit still for longer than a few minutes.* **2** When you **sit** somewhere, you lower your body until you are sitting on something. *He set the cases against a wall and sat on them... When you stand, they stand; when you sit, they sit.* ▶ To **sit down** means the same as to **sit.** *Hughes beckoned him to sit down on the sofa.* **3** If you **sit** someone somewhere, you tell them to sit there or put them in a sitting position. *He used to sit me on his lap.* ▶ To **sit** someone down somewhere means to **sit** them there. *They sat me down and had a serious discussion about sex.* **4** If a building or object **sits** in a particular place, it is in that place. *Our new house sat next to a stream.* **5** If you **sit** for an artist or photographer, you place yourself in a sitting position so you can be painted or photographed. **6** If you **sit** an examination, you do it. In American English, you **take** an examination. **7** If you **sit** on a committee or other official group, you are a member of it. *He was asked to sit on numerous committees.* **8** When a parliament, court, or other official body **sits**, it officially carries out its work. **9** See also **sitting. 10** If you **sit tight**, you remain in the same place or situation and do not take any action, usually because you are waiting for something to happen. *Sit tight. I'll be right back.* ● to **sit on the fence**: see **fence.** ● to **sit in judgement**: see **judgement.** ● **sitting pretty**: see **pretty.**   ◆◆◆◆◇ VERB V prep/adv Also V / VERB V prep/adv / PHRASAL VB: V P / VERB V n prep/adv / PHRASAL VB: V n P prep/adv V n P Also V P n noun / VERB WRITTEN / VERB: V n BRITISH / VERB: V n / VB: no cont V on/in n / VERB: V FORMAL / PHRASE

sit around; the form **sit about** is also used in British English. If you **sit around** or **sit about**, you spend time doing nothing useful or interesting. *Eve isn't the type to sit around doing nothing.*   PHRASAL VB V P INFORMAL

sit back. If you **sit back** while something is happening, you relax and do not become involved in it. *American firms handed over technologies to their partners and then sat back to enjoy the cash flow.*   PHRASAL VB V P / V P to-inf

sit down. 1 See **sit** 2, 3. **2** If you **sit down** and do something, you spend time and effort doing it in order to try to achieve something. *Have you both sat down and worked out a budget together?* **3** See also **sit-down.**   PHRASAL VB V P

sit in on. If you **sit in on** a lesson, meeting, or discussion, you are present while it is taking place but do not take part in it. *Will they permit you to sit in on a few classes?*   PHRASAL VB V P P n

sit on. If you say that someone **is sitting on** something, you mean that they are delaying dealing with it. *He had been sitting on the document for at least two months.*   PHRASAL VB V P n

sit out. If you **sit** something **out**, you wait patiently for it to finish, without taking any action. *He can afford to sit out the property slump.*   PHRASAL VB V n P / V P noun

sit through. If you **sit through** something such as a film, lecture, or meeting, you stay until it is finished   PHRASAL VB V n P

although you are not enjoying it. *...movies so bad you can hardly bear to sit through them.*

sit up. 1 If you **sit up**, you move into a sitting position when you have been leaning back or lying down. **2** If you **sit** someone **up**, you move them into a sitting position when they have been leaning back or lying down. *She sat him up and made him comfortable.* **3** If you **sit up**, you do not go to bed although it is very late. *We sat up drinking and talking.* **4** If something makes you **sit up**, it makes you suddenly pay attention to what is happening. *A defeat like that makes you sit up and think.* **5** See also **sit-up.**   PHRASAL VB V P V n P Also V P noun / V P / V P

si·tar /sɪ'tɑː/ **sitars.** A **sitar** is an Indian musical instrument with two layers of strings, a long neck, and a round body. See picture headed **musical instruments.**   N-VAR

sit·com /'sɪtkɒm/ **sitcoms.** A **sitcom** is a television comedy series which shows the same set of characters in each episode, in amusing situations that are similar to everyday life. **Sitcom** is an abbreviation for **situation comedy.** *...the classic '70s TV sitcom 'Rising Damp'.*   ◆◇◇◇◇ N-COUNT

'sit-down. 1 If you have a **sit-down**, you sit down and rest for a short time. *All he wanted was a cup of tea and a sit-down.* **2** A **sit-down** meal is served to people sitting at tables. *A sit-down dinner was followed by a disco.* **3** In a **sit-down** protest, people refuse to leave a place until they get what they want. *A number of university teachers staged a sit-down protest in front of the president's office.*   ◆◇◇◇◇ N-SING: a N INFORMAL ADJ: ADJ n / ADJ: ADJ n

site /saɪt/ **sites, siting, sited. 1** A **site** is a piece of ground that is used for a particular purpose or where a particular thing happens. *...a building site.* **2** The **site** of an important event is the place where it happened. *Scientists have described the Aral sea as the site of the worst ecological disaster on earth.* **3** A **site** is a piece of ground where something such as a statue or monument stands or used to stand. *...the site of Moses' tomb.* **4** If something **is sited** in a particular place or position, it is put there or built there. *He said chemical weapons had never been sited in Germany.* ♦ **sit·ing** *...controls on the siting of gas storage vessels.*   ◆◆◆◆◇ N-COUNT: also on N / N-COUNT / N-COUNT / VB: usu passive be V-ed prep/adv N-SING

'sit-in, sit-ins. A **sit-in** is a protest in which people go to a public place and stay there for a long time. *The campaigners held a sit-in outside the Supreme Court.*   ◆◆◇◇◇ N-COUNT

sit·ter /'sɪtə/ **sitters.** A **sitter** is the same as a **babysitter**: see **babysit.**   ◆◇◇◇◇ N-COUNT

sit·ting /'sɪtɪŋ/ **sittings. 1** A **sitting** is one of the periods when a meal is served when there is not enough space for everyone to eat at the same time. *Dinner was in two sittings.* **2** A **sitting** of a parliament, court, or other official body is one of the occasions when it meets in order to carry out its work. *...the recent emergency sittings of the UN Security Council.* **3** A **sitting** president or member of parliament is a present one, not a future or past one. *...the greatest clash in our history between a sitting president and an ex-president.* **4** See also **sit.** ● **sitting pretty**: see **pretty.**   N-COUNT / N-COUNT / ADJ: ADJ n

,sitting 'duck, sitting ducks. If you say that someone is a **sitting duck**, you mean that they are an obvious target and that it would be easy to attack or cheat them.   N-COUNT INFORMAL

'sitting-room, sitting-rooms. A **sitting-room** is a room in a house where people sit and relax. See picture headed **house and flat.**   ◆◇◇◇◇ N-COUNT BRITISH

situ·ate /'sɪtʃueɪt/ **situates, situating, situated.** If you **situate** something such as an idea or fact in a particular context, you relate it to that context. *How do we situate Christianity in the context of modern physics and psychology?*   VERB V n adv/prep FORMAL

situ·at·ed /'sɪtʃueɪtɪd/. If something is **situated** in a particular place or position, it is in that place or position. *His hotel is situated in one of the loveliest places on the Loire.*   ◆◆◇◇◇ ADJ: v-link ADJ prep, adv ADJ v

situa·tion /ˌsɪtʃu'eɪʃən/ **situations. 1** You use the word **situation** to refer generally to what is happening in a particular place at a particular time, or to   ◆◆◆◆◇ N-COUNT

refer to what is happening to you. *Army officers said the situation was under control... And now for a look at the travel situation.* **2** The **situation** of a building or town is the kind of surroundings that it has. *The garden is in a beautiful situation on top of a fold in the rolling Hampshire landscape.* N-COUNT FORMAL

,situation 'comedy, situation comedies. A **situation comedy** is television comedy series which shows the same set of characters in each episode, in amusing situations that are similar to everyday life. The abbreviation **sitcom** is also used. N-VAR

'sit-up, sit-ups. **Sit-ups** are exercises that you do to strengthen your stomach muscles. They involve sitting up from a lying position while keeping your legs straight on the floor. N-COUNT

six /sɪks/ sixes. **1** **Six** is the number 6. See Appendix headed **Numbers**. **2** In cricket, if a player hits a **six**, they score six runs by hitting the ball so that it crosses the boundary at the edge of the playing area before it touches the ground. **3** If someone or something **is hit for six** or **knocked for six**, they are surprised or overwhelmed by something that has happened to them. *The loss of my wife hit me for six; it took me months to recover.* NUMBER N-COUNT / PHRASE INFORMAL, BRITISH

,six 'footer, six footers. Someone who is six foot tall can be called a **six footer**. *...a strapping six-footer.* N-COUNT INFORMAL

'six-pack, six-packs. A **six-pack** is a pack containing six bottles or cans sold together. N-COUNT

'six·pence /'sɪkspəns/ sixpences. A **sixpence** is a small silver coin which was used in Britain before 1971. It was the equivalent of 2.5 pence. N-COUNT

six·teen /,sɪks'tiːn/ sixteens. **Sixteen** is the number 16. See Appendix headed **Numbers**. NUMBER

six·teenth /,sɪks'tiːnθ/ sixteenths. **1** The **sixteenth** item in a series is the one that you count as number sixteen. See Appendix headed **Numbers**. **2** A **sixteenth** is one of sixteen equal parts of something. ORDINAL FRACTION

sixth /sɪksθ/ sixths. **1** The **sixth** item in a series is the one that you count as number six. See Appendix headed **Numbers**. **2** A **sixth** is one of six equal parts of something. ORDINAL FRACTION

'sixth form, sixth forms; also spelled **sixth-form**. The **sixth form** in a British school consists of the classes that pupils go into at the age of about sixteen, usually in order to study for A levels. *...a sixth form college in Solihull.* ♦ **'sixth former, sixth formers** *By comparison, teaching sixth-formers is a doddle.* N-COUNT / N-COUNT

,sixth 'sense. If you say that someone has a **sixth sense**, you mean that they seem to know things instinctively or intuitively, without any direct evidence of them. N-SING

six·ti·eth /'sɪkstiəθ/ sixtieths. **1** The **sixtieth** item in a series is the one that you count as number sixty. See Appendix headed **Numbers**. **2** A **sixtieth** is one of sixty equal parts of something. ORDINAL FRACTION

six·ty /'sɪksti/ sixties. **Sixty** is the number 60. See Appendix headed **Numbers**. NUMBER

siz·able /'saɪzəbəl/. See sizeable.

size /saɪz/ sizes, sizing, sized. **1** The **size** of something is how big or small it is. Something's size is determined by comparing it to other things, counting it, or measuring it. *...a hoofed grazing animal about the size of a small horse... In 1970 the average size of a French farm was 19 hectares.* ♦ **-size** *...full-size gymnasiums.* ♦ **-sized** *...a medium-sized college. ...golfball-sized lumps of coarse black rock.* **2** The **size** of something is the fact that it is very large. *Jack walked around the hotel and was mesmerized by its sheer size.* **3** A **size** is one of a series of graded measurements, especially for things such as clothes or shoes. *My sister is the same height but only a size 12.* **4** If someone is **cut down to size**, something happens to make them realize that they are not as important as they think they are. **5** If an object **is cut to size**, its size is altered to make it suitable for a particular purpose. *Your timber merchant may cut the wood to size for* N-VAR / COMB / COMB / N-UNCOUNT / N-COUNT / PHRASE INFORMAL / PHRASE

you. **6** If you try something **for size**, you put it on to see if it is the right size for you. *She was trying on an £8,000 jacket for size.* PHRASE

size up. If you **size up** a person or situation, you carefully look at the person or think about the situation, so that you can decide how to act. *He spent the evening sizing me up intellectually.* PHRASAL VB V P noun V n P INFORMAL

size·able /'saɪzəbəl/; also spelled **sizable**. **Sizeable** means fairly large. *...a sizeable chunk of land.* ADJ-GRADED ♦◇◇◇◇

siz·zle /'sɪzəl/ sizzles, sizzling, sizzled. If something **sizzles**, it makes a hissing sound like the sound made by frying food. *The sausages and burgers sizzled on the barbecue.* VERB V ♦◇◇◇◇

skate /skeɪt/ skates, skating, skated. **1** **Skates** are **ice-skates** or **roller-skates**. **2** If you **skate**, you move about wearing ice-skates or roller-skates. *Dan skated up to him.* ♦ **skat·ing** *They all went skating together in the winter.* ♦ **skat·er, skaters** *West Lake, an outdoor ice-skating rink, attracts skaters during the day and night.* **3** If you **skate** over or round a difficult subject, you avoid discussing it. *When pressed, she skates around the subject of those women who he met as a 19-year-old.* **4** A **skate** is a kind of flat sea fish. The plural of **skate** is **skate**. ▶ **Skate** is this fish eaten as food. N-COUNT / VERB: V adv/prep / N-UNCOUNT / N-COUNT / VERB: V over n / V round/ around n / N-COUNT / N-UNCOUNT N-COUNT ♦♦◇◇◇

skate·board /'skeɪtbɔːd/ skateboards. A **skateboard** is a narrow board with wheels at each end, which people stand on and ride for pleasure. ♦ **skate·board·ing.** **Skateboarding** is the activity of riding on a skateboard. N-UNCOUNT

'skating rink, skating rinks. A **skating rink** is the same as a **rink**. N-COUNT

skein /skeɪn/ skeins. A **skein** is a loosely coiled length of thread, especially wool or silk. N-COUNT

skel·etal /'skelɪtəl/. **1** **Skeletal** means relating to skeletons. *...the skeletal remains of seven adults.* **2** A **skeletal** person is so thin that you can see their bones through their skin. **3** Something that is **skeletal** has been reduced to its basic structure. *Passenger services can best be described as skeletal.* ADJ: ADJ n / ADJ-GRADED / ADJ-GRADED ♦◇◇◇◇

skel·eton /'skelɪtən/ skeletons. **1** Your **skeleton** is the framework of bones in your body. *...a human skeleton.* **2** A **skeleton** staff is the smallest number of staff necessary in order to run an organization or service. **3** The **skeleton** of something such as a building or a plan is its basic framework. *...a skeleton of policy guidelines.* **4** If you say that someone has **a skeleton in the closet**, or in British English **a skeleton in the cupboard**, you mean that they are keeping secret something that is scandalous or embarrassing. N-COUNT / ADJ: ADJ n / N-COUNT / PHRASE ♦♦◇◇◇

skep·tic /'skeptɪk/. See sceptic.

skep·ti·cal /'skeptɪkəl/. See sceptical.

skep·ti·cism /'skeptɪsɪzəm/. See scepticism.

sketch /sketʃ/ sketches, sketching, sketched. **1** A **sketch** is a drawing that is done quickly without a lot of details. **2** If you **sketch** something, you make a quick rough drawing of it. *I always sketch with pen and paper... Her hobbies were playing the guitar and sketching.* **3** A **sketch** of a situation, person, or incident is a brief description of it without many details. *...thumbnail sketches of heads of state and political figures.* **4** If you **sketch** a situation or incident, you give a short description of it. *Cross sketched the story briefly, telling the facts just as they had happened.* ▶ **Sketch out** means the same as **sketch**. *Luxembourg sketched out an acceptable compromise between Britain, France and Germany.* **5** A **sketch** is a short humorous piece of acting, usually forming part of a comedy show. *...a five-minute sketch about a folk singer.* N-COUNT / VERB: V n / V -ing / N-COUNT / VERB V n / PHRASAL VB V P noun / N-COUNT ♦♦◇◇◇

sketch in. If you **sketch in** details about something, you tell them to people. *We sat in Lily's sunroom while I sketched in the situation.* PHRASAL VB V P noun

sketch out. See sketch 4. PHRASAL VB

sketch·book /'sketʃbʊk/ sketchbooks; also spelled **sketch-book**. A **sketchbook** is a book of blank pages for drawing on. N-COUNT

sketchy /'sketʃi/ sketchier, sketchiest. A **sketchy** account of something is incomplete and ADJ-GRADED ♦◇◇◇◇

does not contain many details. If your knowledge of something is **sketchy**, you know only a few things about it. *Details of what actually happened are still sketchy.*

skew /skjuː/ **skews, skewing, skewed.** If information or a situation **is skewed**, it is altered or distorted by external factors, so that people do not get an accurate view of it. *Today's election will skew the results in favor of the northern end of the county.* ◆ **skewed** *Policies are definitely more skewed towards economic growth than before.* ADJ-GRADED

◆◇◇◇
VERB:
be V-ed
V n

skew·er /ˈskjuːə/ **skewers, skewering, skewered. 1** A **skewer** is a long metal pin which is used to hold pieces of food together during cooking. **2** If you **skewer** something, you push a long, thin, pointed object through it. *He skewered his victim through the neck.*

◆◇◇◇
N-COUNT
VERB
V n prep

ski /skiː/ **skis, skiing, skied. 1** Skis are long, flat, narrow pieces of wood, metal, or plastic that are fastened to boots so that you can move easily on snow. **2** When people **ski**, they move over snow on skis. *The whole party then skied off.* ◆ **ski·er** /ˈskiːə/ **skiers** *He is an enthusiastic skier.* ◆ **ski·ing** *...a skiing holiday.* **3** You use **ski** to refer to things that are concerned with skiing. *...the Swiss ski resort of Klosters.* **4** See also **water-ski**.

◆◆◇◇
N-COUNT
VERB: V
V adv/prep
N-COUNT
N-UNCOUNT
ADJ: ADJ n

skid /skɪd/ **skids, skidding, skidded. 1** If a vehicle **skids**, it slides sideways or forwards while moving, for example when you are trying to stop suddenly. *The plane skidded off the runway while taking off in a snow storm.* ▶ Also a noun. *I slammed the brakes on and went into a skid.* **2** If you say that something is **on the skids** you believe that it is out of control and certain to fail.

◆◇◇◇
VERB: V
V prep
N-COUNT
PHRASE

skid row /ˌskɪd ˈrəʊ/; also spelled **Skid Row**. You can refer to the poorest part of town where drunks and vagrants live as **skid row**. *He was suspended from his job and actually became a skid row type of drunkard.*

N-UNCOUNT
AMERICAN

skiff /skɪf/ **skiffs.** A **skiff** is a small light rowing-boat or sailing boat, which usually has room for only one person.

N-COUNT

skil·ful /ˈskɪlfʊl/; spelled **skillful** in American English. Someone who is **skilful** at something does it very well. *He is widely regarded as Hungary's most skilful politician.* ◆ **skil·ful·ly** *He had a clear idea of his company's strengths and skilfully exploited them.*

◆◇◇◇
ADJ-GRADED
ADV-GRADED:
ADV with v

'ski lift, ski lifts; also spelled **ski-lift.** A **ski lift** is a machine for taking people to the top of a slope so that they can ski down it.

N-COUNT

skill /skɪl/ **skills. 1** A **skill** is a type of work or activity which requires special training and knowledge. *Most of us will know someone who is always learning new skills, or studying new fields.* **2** Skill is the knowledge and ability that enables you to do something well. *The cut of a diamond depends on the skill of its craftsman.*

◆◆◆◆
N-COUNT

N-UNCOUNT

skilled /skɪld/. **1** Someone who is **skilled** has the knowledge and ability to do something well. *...a network of amateur but highly skilled observers of wildlife.* **2** Skilled work can only be done by people who have had some training. *...skilled workers, such as plumbers and electricians.*

◆◆◇◇
ADJ-GRADED

ADJ

skil·let /ˈskɪlɪt/ **skillets.** A **skillet** is a shallow cast-iron pan which is used for frying.

N-COUNT

skill·ful /ˈskɪlfʊl/. See **skilful**.

skim /skɪm/ **skims, skimming, skimmed. 1** If you **skim** something from the surface of a liquid, you remove it from view. *Rough seas today prevented specially equipped ships from skimming oil off the water's surface... Skim off the fat.* **2** If something **skims** a surface, it moves quickly along just above it. *The little boat was skimming across the sunlit surface of the bay.* **3** If you **skim** a piece of writing, you read through it quickly. *I only had time to skim through the script before I flew over here.*

◆◇◇◇
VERB
V n off/from n
V n with off

VERB: V n
V over/across
n

VERB: V n
V through n

skim off. If someone **skims off** the best part of something, or money which belongs to other people, they take it for themselves. *He has been accused of skimming the cream off the economy.*

PHRASAL VB
V P noun
V n P n

,skimmed 'milk. Skimmed milk is milk from which the cream has been removed. The American term is **skim milk**.

N-UNCOUNT
BRITISH

skimp /skɪmp/ **skimps, skimping, skimped.** If you **skimp on** something, you use less time, money, or material for it than you really need, so that the result is not good enough. *You can't skimp on sunscreen.*

VERB
V on n

skimpy /ˈskɪmpi/ **skimpier, skimpiest.** Something that is **skimpy** is too small in size or quantity. *...skimpy underwear.*

ADJ-GRADED

skin /skɪn/ **skins, skinning, skinned. 1** Your **skin** is the natural covering of your body. *His skin is clear and smooth.* **2** An animal **skin** is skin which has been removed from a dead animal. *...a leopard skin coat.* **3** The **skin** of a fruit or vegetable is its outer layer or covering. *...banana skins.* **4** If a **skin** forms on the surface of a liquid, a thin fairly solid layer forms on it. *Stir the custard occasionally to prevent a skin forming.* **5** If you **skin** a dead animal, you remove its skin. **6** See also **-skinned; banana skin.**
7 If you try to **save** your **own skin** or **save** your **skin**, you try to save yourself from something dangerous or unpleasant; used showing disapproval. **8** If you do something **by the skin of** your **teeth**, you just manage to do it. **9** If you say that someone has **a thick skin**, you mean that they are able to listen to criticism about themselves without becoming offended. **10** ● to **make** your **skin crawl**: see **crawl**.

◆◆◆◆
N-VAR

N-VAR

N-VAR

N-SING

VERB: V n

PHRASE
PRAGMATICS

PHRASE

PHRASE

,skin 'deep; also spelled **skin-deep.** Something that is only **skin deep** is not a major or important feature of something, although initially you may think that it is. *He denies that racism is just skin-deep.*

ADJ

skin·head /ˈskɪnhed/ **skinheads.** A **skinhead** is a young person whose hair is shaved or cut very short. Skinheads are usually regarded as violent, aggressive, and racist.

◆◇◇◇
N-COUNT

skin·less /ˈskɪnləs/. **Skinless** meat has had its skin removed. *...skinless chicken breast fillets.*

ADJ

-skinned /-skɪnd/. **-skinned** is used after adjectives such as 'dark' and 'clear' to form adjectives that indicate what kind of skin someone has. *Dark-skinned people rarely develop skin cancer.*

COMB

skin·ny /ˈskɪni/ **skinnier, skinniest.** A skinny person is extremely thin, in a way that you find unattractive. *She had stringy hair and skinny legs.*

◆◇◇◇
ADJ-GRADED
PRAGMATICS
INFORMAL

skint /skɪnt/. If you say that you are **skint**, you mean that you have no money.

ADJ-GRADED,
INFORMAL,
BRITISH

,skin-'tight; also spelled **skintight.** Skin-tight clothes fit very tightly so that they show the shape of your body.

ADJ

skip /skɪp/ **skips, skipping, skipped. 1** If you **skip** along, you move with a series of little jumps from one foot to the other. *She was skipping to keep up with him.* ▶ Also a noun. *The boxer gave a little skip as he came out of his corner.* **2** When someone **skips**, they jump up and down over a rope which is turning round and round. *Outside a dozen children were skipping and singing a complicated rhyme.* ◆ **skip·ping** *Skipping is one of the most enjoyable aerobic activities.* **3** If you **skip** something that you usually do or something that most people do, you decide not to do it. *It is important not to skip meals.* **4** If you **skip** or **skip over** a part of something you are reading or a story you are telling, you miss it out or pass over it quickly. *She reinvented her own life story, skipping over the war years.* **5** If you **skip** from one subject or activity to another, you move quickly from one to the other although there is no obvious connection between them. *She kept up a continuous chatter, skipping from one subject to the next.*
6 A **skip** is a large, open, metal container which is used to hold and take away rubbish.

◆◆◇◇
VERB:
V adv/prep
N-COUNT

VERB
V

N-UNCOUNT

VERB
V n

VERB: V n
V over/to n

VERB
V from n to n

N-COUNT
BRITISH

skip·per /ˈskɪpə/ **skippers, skippering, skippered. 1** You can use **skipper** to refer to the captain of a ship or boat. **2** You can use **skipper** to

◆◆◇◇
N-COUNT
N-COUNT

refer to the captain of a sports team. **3** To **skipper** a team or a boat means to be the captain of it. *The yacht was skippered by Pierre Mas.*   VERB: V n / beV-ed

'**skipping rope, skipping ropes.** A **skipping rope** is a piece of rope, usually with handles at each end. You exercise with it by turning it round and round and jumping over it.   N-COUNT BRITISH

skir·mish /'skɜːmɪʃ/ **skirmishes, skirmishing, skirmished. 1** A **skirmish** is a minor battle. *One Federal soldier was killed in the skirmish that ensued.* **2** If people **skirmish**, they fight. *Police skirmished with youths on the estate last Friday. ...as Serb and Bosnian forces skirmished around the airport.* ♦ **skir·mish·ing** *On land there was minor skirmishing.* **3** A **skirmish** is a short sharp argument. *This difference in approach has led to several political skirmishes.*   ◆◇◇◇◇ / N-COUNT / V-RECIP V with n pl-n V / N-UNCOUNT / N-COUNT

skirt /skɜːt/ **skirts, skirting, skirted. 1** A **skirt** is a piece of clothing worn by women and girls. It fastens at the waist and hangs down around the legs. See picture headed **clothes**. **2** Something that **skirts** an area is situated around the edge of it. **3** If you **skirt** something, you go around the edge of it. *She skirted round the edge of the room to the door.* **4** If you **skirt** a problem or question, you avoid dealing with it. *He skirted round his main differences with her.*   ◆◆◇◇◇ / N-COUNT / VERB: V n / VERB: V n V round/ around n / VERB: V round/ around n

'**skirting board, skirting boards. Skirting board** or **skirting** is a narrow length of wood which goes along the bottom of a room and makes a border between the walls and the floor.   N-VAR BRITISH

'**ski slope, ski slopes.** A **ski slope** is a sloping surface down which you can ski, either on a snow-covered mountain or on a specially made structure.   N-COUNT

skit /skɪt/ **skits.** A **skit** is a short performance in which the actors make fun of people, events, and types of literature by imitating them.   N-COUNT

skit·ter /'skɪtə/ **skitters, skittering, skittered.** If something **skitters**, it moves about very lightly and quickly. *Pieces of paper were skittering along the sidewalk.*   VERB V adv/prep

skit·tish /'skɪtɪʃ/. **1** If you describe a person or animal as **skittish**, you mean they are excitable and easily frightened. **2** Someone who is **skittish** does not concentrate on anything or take life very seriously.   ADJ-GRADED / ADJ-GRADED

skit·tle /'skɪtəl/ **skittles. 1** A **skittle** is a wooden object used as a target in the game of skittles. **2** Skittles is a game in which players try to knock over as many skittles as they can out of a group of nine by throwing a ball at them.   N-COUNT BRITISH / N-UNCOUNT

skive /skaɪv/ **skives, skiving, skived.** If you **skive**, you avoid working, especially by staying away from the place where you should be working. ▶ **Skive off** means the same as **skive**. *'I absolutely hated school,' Rachel says. 'I skived off all the time.'*   VERB: V INFORMAL, BRITISH / PHRASAL VB V P

skul·dug·gery /skʌl'dʌgəri/. **Skulduggery** is behaviour in which someone acts in a dishonest way in order to achieve their aim. *...accusations of intimidation and political skulduggery.*   N-UNCOUNT DATED

skulk /skʌlk/ **skulks, skulking, skulked.** If you **skulk** somewhere, you hide or move around quietly because you do not want to be seen. *Harry skulked off.*   VERB V prep/adv

skull /skʌl/ **skulls.** Your **skull** is the bony part of your head which encloses your brain.   ◆◆◇◇◇ N-COUNT

,**skull and 'crossbones.** A **skull and crossbones** is a picture of a human skull above a pair of crossed bones which warns of death or danger. It used to appear on the flags flown by pirate ships and is now sometimes found on containers holding poisonous substances.   N-SING

'**skull cap, skull caps;** also spelled **skullcap.** A **skull cap** is a small close-fitting cap.   N-COUNT

skunk /skʌŋk/ **skunks.** A **skunk** is a small black and white animal which releases an unpleasant smelling liquid if it is frightened or attacked. Skunks live in America.   N-COUNT

sky /skaɪ/ **skies. 1** The **sky** is the space around the earth which you can see when you stand outside   ◆◆◆◇◇ N-VAR

and look upwards. *...clear blue skies.* **2** ● **pie in the sky:** see **pie**.

,**sky-'blue.** Something that is **sky-blue** is a very pale blue in colour.   COLOUR

sky·div·ing /'skaɪdaɪvɪŋ/. **Skydiving** is the sport of jumping out of an aeroplane and falling freely through the air before opening your parachute. ♦ **sky·div·er, skydivers** *...a popular base for sky-divers.*   N-UNCOUNT / N-COUNT

,**sky-'high.** If you say that prices or confidence are **sky-high**, you are emphasizing that they are at a very high level. ▶ Also an adverb. *Their prestige went sky high.*   ADJ PRAGMATICS / ADV: ADV after v

sky·lark /'skaɪlɑːk/ **skylarks.** A **skylark** is a small brown bird that sings while hovering high above the ground.   N-COUNT

sky·light /'skaɪlaɪt/ **skylights.** A **skylight** is a window in a roof.   N-COUNT

sky·line /'skaɪlaɪn/ **skylines.** The **skyline** is the line or shape that is formed where the sky meets buildings or the land. *The village church dominates the skyline.*   ◆◇◇◇◇ N-COUNT

sky·rocket /'skaɪrɒkɪt/ **skyrockets, skyrocketing, skyrocketed.** If prices or amounts **sky-rocket**, they go up suddenly and steeply. *...the skyrocketing costs of health care.*   VERB: V / V-ing

sky·scraper /'skaɪskreɪpə/ **skyscrapers.** A **sky-scraper** is a very tall building in a city.   ◆◇◇◇◇ N-COUNT

sky·ward /'skaɪwəd/; also spelled **skywards.** If you look **skyward** or **skywards**, you look up towards the sky.   ADV after v LITERARY

slab /slæb/ **slabs.** A **slab** of something is a thick flat piece of it. *...huge concrete paving slabs.*   N-COUNT: with supp ◆◇◇◇◇

slack /slæk/ **slacker, slackest; slacks, slacking, slacked. 1** Something that is **slack** is loose and not firmly stretched or tightly in position. *The boy's jaw went slack.* **2** A **slack** period is one in which there is not much work or activity. **3** Someone who is **slack** in their work does not do it properly. ♦ **slack·ness** *He accused the government of slackness and complacency.* **4** To **take up the slack** or **pick up the slack** in an organization or system means to reduce its spare capacity so that it works more efficiently.   ADJ-GRADED / ADJ-GRADED / ADJ-GRADED / N-UNCOUNT / PHRASE

slack off. If someone **slacks off**, they are not working as hard as they should.   PHRASAL VB V P

slack·en /'slækən/ **slackens, slackening, slackened. 1** If something **slackens**, it becomes slower, less active, or less intense. *The Conservative government will not slacken the pace of radical reform.* ♦ **slack·en·ing** *There was a slackening of western output during the 1930s.* **2** If a part of your body **slackens** it becomes looser or more relaxed. *Muscles stretch, slacken and relax during child-birth.*   ◆◇◇◇◇ / V-ERG: V V n / N-SING / V-ERG Also V n

slacken off. If something **slackens off**, it becomes slower, less active, or less intense. *At about five o'clock, business slackened off.*   PHRASAL VB no passive V P

slack·er /'slækə/ **slackers.** If you describe someone as a **slacker**, you mean that they are lazy and do less work than they should.   N-COUNT

'**slack-jawed.** If you say that someone is **slack-jawed**, you mean that their mouth is hanging open, often because they are surprised.   ADJ

slacks /slæks/. **Slacks** are casual trousers. *He was dressed in slacks and a short-sleeve shirt.*   ◆◇◇◇◇ N-PLURAL DATED

slag /slæg/ **slags, slagging, slagged.** **Slag** is an offensive word which some people use to refer to a woman who they disapprove of because they think she is sexually immoral.   ◆◇◇◇◇ N-COUNT PRAGMATICS RUDE, BRITISH

slag off. To **slag** someone **off** means to criticize them in an unpleasant way; an informal use. *All bands slag off their record companies.*   PHRASAL VB V n P V P noun BRITISH

'**slag heap, slag heaps;** also spelled **slagheap.** A **slag heap** is a hill made from waste material, such as rock and mud, left over from mining.   N-COUNT

slain /sleɪn/. **Slain** is the past participle of **slay**.

slake /sleɪk/ **slakes, slaking, slaked.** If you **slake** your thirst, you drink something that stops you being thirsty.   VERB: V n LITERARY

sla·lom /'slɑːləm/ **slaloms.** A **slalom** is a race on ◆◇◇◇◇ skis or in canoes in which the competitors have to N-COUNT avoid a series of obstacles in a twisting and difficult course.

slam /slæm/ **slams, slamming, slammed. 1** If ◆◆◇◇◇ you **slam** a door or window, you shut it noisily and V-ERG: V n with great force. *I was relieved to hear the front door* V *slam... He slammed the gate shut behind him.* **2** If V n adj you **slam** something down, you put it there quickly VERB and with great force. *She listened in a mixture of* V n with adv shock and anger before slamming the phone down. **3** If one thing **slams** into or against another, it VERB: crashes into it with great force. *He slammed me* V into/against *against the ground.* **4** To **slam** someone or some- n thing means to criticize them very severely. *Adver-* VERB *tisers have been slammed for portraying men as* V n JOURNALISM *wimps.* **5** See also **Grand Slam**.

slam·mer /'slæmə/ **. The slammer** is prison. N-SING INFORMAL

slan·der /'slɑːndə, 'slæn-/ **slanders, slandering,** **slandered. 1** Slander is an untrue spoken state- N-VAR ment about someone which is intended to damage their reputation. *Korea has been a target of threats* *and slanders from the major western powers.* **2** To VERB: V n **slander** someone means to say untrue things about them in order to damage their reputation.

slan·der·ous /'slɑːndərəs, 'slæn-/ **.** A spoken state- ADJ-GRADED ment that is **slanderous** is untrue and intended to damage the reputation of the person to whom it refers.

slang /slæŋ/ **. Slang** consists of words, expressions, ◆◇◇◇◇ and meanings that are informal and are used by N-UNCOUNT people who know each other very well or who have the same interests.

slang·ing match /'slæŋɪŋ mætʃ/ **slanging** N-COUNT **matches.** A **slanging match** is an angry quarrel in BRITISH which people insult each other.

slant /slɑːnt, slænt/ **slants, slanting, slanted.** ◆◇◇◇◇ **1** Something that **slants** is sloping, rather than hori- VERB zontal or vertical. *The morning sun slanted through* V adv/prep *the glass roof.* **2** If something is on a **slant**, it is in a Also V-ing slanting position. **3** If information or a system is VB: usu **slanted**, it is made to show favour towards a par- passive ticular group or opinion. *The programme was delib-* Also be V-ed *erately slanted to make the home team look good.* Also be V-ed ♦ **slant·ed** *...slanted news coverage.* **4** A particular ADJ-GRADED **slant** on a subject is a particular way of thinking N-SING about it, especially one that is unfair or biased. *They* *give a slant to every single news item that's put on* *the air.*

slap /slæp/ **slaps, slapping, slapped. 1** If you ◆◆◇◇◇ **slap** someone, you hit them with the palm of your VERB: V n hand. *I slapped him hard across the face.* ▶ Also a V n adv/prep noun. *He reached forward and gave her a slap.* **2** If N-COUNT you describe something that someone does as a PHRASE **slap in the face**, you mean that it shocks or upsets you because it shows that they do not support you or respect you. **3** A **slap on the wrist** is a warning or PHRASE a punishment that is not very severe. **4** If you **slap** VERB: someone **on** the back, you hit them in a friendly V on n manner on their back. **5** If you **slap** something onto VERB a surface, you put it there quickly, roughly, or care- V on/onto n lessly. *'Coffee!' bellowed the barman, slapping the* *cup on to the waiting saucer.* **6** If journalists say that VERB the authorities **slap** something such as a tax or a PRAGMATICS ban **on** something, they think that it is unreason- V n on n able or too hasty. *Thankfully the Government still* INFORMAL *hasn't discovered a way of slapping a tax on love,* *sunshine or air.*

slap 'bang; also spelled **slap-bang. Slap bang** is ADV: used in expressions such as **slap bang in the mid-** ADV prep **dle** of somewhere to mean exactly in that place. *Of* INFORMAL *course, slap-bang in the middle of town the rents are* *high.*

slap·dash /'slæpdæʃ/; also spelled **slap-dash.** If you ADJ-GRADED describe someone as **slapdash**, you mean that they do things carelessly without thinking about them or planning them first.

slap·stick /'slæpstɪk/ **. Slapstick** is a simple type of N-UNCOUNT comedy in which the actors behave in a rough and foolish way.

'slap-up. A **slap-up** meal is a large enjoyable meal. ADJ: ADJ n *...a slap-up lunch at a city restaurant.* BRITISH

slash /slæʃ/ **slashes, slashing, slashed. 1** If ◆◆◇◇◇ you **slash** something, you make a long, deep cut in VERB it. *Four cars had their tyres slashed.* ▶ Also a noun. V-n *Make deep slashes in the meat.* **2** If you **slash at** VERB: someone or something, you quickly hit at them with V at n something. **3** To **slash** something such as costs or VERB jobs means to reduce them by a large amount. *Car* V n *makers could be forced to slash prices after being ac-* JOURNALISM *cused of overcharging yesterday.* **4** You use **slash** to refer to a diagonal line that separates letters, words, or numbers. For example, if you are giving the number 340/21/K, you say 'Three four zero, slash two one, slash K.'

,slash and 'burn; also spelled **slash-and-burn.** N-UNCOUNT **Slash and burn** is a method of farming that involves clearing land by destroying and burning all the trees and plants on it, farming there for a short time, and then moving on to a new piece of land.

slat /slæt/ **slats. Slats** are the narrow pieces of N-COUNT wood, metal, or plastic in things such as Venetian blinds or cupboard doors.

slate /sleɪt/ **slates, slating, slated. 1** Slate is a ◆◆◇◇◇ dark grey rock that can be easily split into thin lay- N-UNCOUNT ers. Slate is often used for covering roofs. **2** A **slate** N-COUNT is one of the small flat pieces of slate that are used for covering roofs. **3** A **slate** is a list of candidates for an election, usually N-COUNT from the same party. *The leadership want to present a* *single slate of candidates to be approved in an open* *vote.* **4** If something is **slated** to happen, it is planned V-PASSIVE: to happen at a particular time. *A controversial meas-* be V-ed to-inf *ure designed to set the nation's future energy course is* be V-ed for n *slated for Senate debate within days.* **5** If something is AMERICAN **slated**, it is criticized very severely; used mainly by VB: usu journalists. passive BRITISH **6** If you start with **a clean slate**, you do not take ac- PHRASE count of previous mistakes or failures and make a fresh start. **7** If you **wipe the slate clean**, you decide to PHRASE forget previous mistakes, failures, or debts and to start again.

slat·ted /'slætɪd/ **.** Something that is **slatted** is made ADJ with slats. *...slatted window blinds.*

slaugh·ter /'slɔːtə/ **slaughters, slaughtering,** ◆◆◇◇◇ **slaughtered. 1** If large numbers of people or ani- VB: usu mals **are slaughtered**, they are killed in a way that is passive cruel, unjust, or unnecessary. ▶ Also a noun. *The* N-UNCOUNT *annual slaughter of wildlife in Italy is horrific.* **2** To VERB: V n **slaughter** animals such as cows and sheep means to kill them for their meat. ▶ Also a noun. *More* N-UNCOUNT *than 491,000 sheep were exported to the Continent* *for slaughter last year.* **3** ● **like lambs to the slaugh-** **ter**: see **lamb**.

slaughter·house /'slɔːtəhaʊs/ **slaughterhouses.** N-COUNT A **slaughterhouse** is a place where animals are killed for their meat.

slave /sleɪv/ **slaves, slaving, slaved. 1** A slave ◆◆◇◇◇ is someone who is the property of another person N-COUNT and has to work for that person. **2** You can describe N-COUNT: someone as a **slave** when they are completely under with supp the control of another person or of a powerful influ- ence. *She may no longer be a slave to the studio sys-* *tem, but she still has a duty to her fans.* **3** If you say VERB that someone **is slaving** over something or is **slav-** V over n **ing** for someone, you mean that they work very Also V, hard. *When you're busy all day the last thing you* V prep *want to do is spend hours slaving over a hot stove.* ▶ To **slave away** means the same as to **slave**. *...hun-* PHRASAL VB *dreds of workers slaving away in the intense sun.* V P

,slave 'labour; spelled **slave labor** in American English. **1** Slave labour refers to slaves or to work N-UNCOUNT done by slaves. *The children were used as slave la-* *bour in gold mines.* **2** If people work very hard for N-UNCOUNT long hours for very little money, you can refer to it PRAGMATICS as **slave labour**; used showing disapproval. *He's* *been forced into slave labour at burger bars to earn a* *bit of cash.*

slav·er /'slævə/ **slavers, slavering, slavered.** VERB: V **1** If an animal **slavers**, saliva drips from its mouth. VERB

2 If you say that someone **is slavering**, you mean that they are so excited by something that they cannot control themselves, and that you find this disgusting. *I found myself skipping these passages, though no doubt many readers will slaver over them.* `PRAGMATICS` `V over n` `Also V`

slav·ery /'sleɪvəri/. Slavery is the system by which people are owned by other people as slaves. `◆◇◇◇◇` `N-UNCOUNT`

'slave trade. The **slave trade** is the buying and selling of slaves, especially the sale into slavery of Black Africans from the 16th to the 19th centuries. `N-SING:` `theN`

slav·ish /'sleɪvɪʃ/. **1** You use **slavish** to describe things that copy or imitate something exactly, without any attempt to be original; used showing disapproval. *She is no slavish follower of fashion.* ♦ **slav·ish·ly** *Most have slavishly copied the design of IBM's big mainframe machines.* **2** If you describe someone as **slavish**, you are critical of the fact that they behave like a slave, for example by being completely obedient to another person. `ADJ-GRADED` `PRAGMATICS` `ADV-GRADED` `ADJ-GRADED` `PRAGMATICS`

slay /sleɪ/ **slays, slaying, slew, slayed, slain**. **1** If someone **slays** an animal, they kill it in a violent way. ♦ **slay·ing** *The festival commemorates the slaying of the demon buffalo.* ♦ **slay·er, slayers** *...the story of the Monster Slayer.* **2** Journalists say that someone **has been slain** when they have been murdered. `◆◇◇◇◇` `VERB: V n` `FORMAL` `N-UNCOUNT` `N-COUNT` `V-PASSIVE` `AMERICAN`

slay·ing /'sleɪɪŋ/ **slayings**. Journalists sometimes use the word **slaying** to refer to a murder. *...a trail of motiveless slayings.* `N-COUNT` `AMERICAN`

sleaze /sliːz/. You use **sleaze** to describe activities that you consider immoral, dishonest, or not respectable, especially in politics, business, journalism, or entertainment. *The President denounced the press for engaging in 'sleaze' and called the story a lie.* `N-UNCOUNT` `PRAGMATICS` `INFORMAL`

slea·zy /'sliːzi/ **sleazier, sleaziest. 1** If you describe a place as **sleazy**, you dislike it because it looks dirty and not respectable. *...sleazy bars.* **2** If you describe something or someone as **sleazy**, you disapprove of them because you think they are not respectable and are rather sordid. *...sex shops and sleazy magazines.* `◆◇◇◇◇` `ADJ-GRADED` `INFORMAL` `ADJ-GRADED` `INFORMAL`

sled /sled/ **sleds, sledding, sledded. 1** A **sled** is the same as a **sledge**. *She stood in the deep snow beside the sled.* **2** If you go **sledding**, you ride on a sled. `N-COUNT` `AMERICAN` `VERB: V` `AMERICAN`

sledge /sledʒ/ **sledges, sledging, sledged. 1** A **sledge** is an object used for travelling over snow. It consists of a framework which slides on two strips of wood or metal. **2** If you **sledge** or go **sledging**, you ride on a sledge. `N-COUNT:` `also by N` `BRITISH` `VERB: V` `BRITISH`

sledge·hammer /'sledʒhæmə/ **sledgehammers;** also spelled **sledge-hammer**. A **sledgehammer** is a large heavy hammer with a long handle, used for smashing rocks and concrete. `N-COUNT`

sleek /sliːk/ **sleeker, sleekest. 1** **Sleek** hair or fur is smooth and shiny and looks healthy. **2** If you describe someone as **sleek**, you mean that they look rich and stylish. **3** **Sleek** vehicles, furniture, or other objects look smooth, shiny, and expensive. `◆◇◇◇◇` `ADJ-GRADED` `ADJ-GRADED` `ADJ-GRADED`

sleep /sliːp/ **sleeps, sleeping, slept. 1** Sleep is the natural state of rest in which your eyes are closed, your body is inactive, and your mind does not think. *Try and get some sleep... Be quiet and go to sleep.* **2** When you **sleep**, you rest with your eyes closed and your mind and body inactive. *...a pool surrounded by sleeping sunbathers.* **3** A **sleep** is a period of sleeping. *I think he may be ready for a sleep soon.* **4** If a building or room **sleeps** a particular number of people, it has beds for that number of people. *The villa sleeps 10.* **5** If you cannot **get to sleep**, you are unable to sleep. **6** If you say that you didn't **lose** any **sleep** over something, you mean that you did not worry about it at all. **7** If you are trying to make a decision and you say that you will **sleep on it**, you mean that you will delay making a decision until the following day, so you have time to think about it. **8** If a sick or injured animal **is put to sleep**, it is painlessly killed by a vet. **9** ● **sleep rough**: see **rough**. **10** See also **sleeping**. `◆◆◆◆◇` `N-UNCOUNT` `VERB: V` `V-ing` `N-COUNT` `VB: no cont,` `no passive` `V amount` `PHRASE` `PHRASE` `PHRASE` `PHRASE`

sleep around. If you say that someone **sleeps around**, you disapprove of them because they have sex with a lot of different people. *...a drunken husband who slept around with other women.* `PHRASAL VB` `VP` `PRAGMATICS` `V P with n` `INFORMAL`

sleep off. If you **sleep off** the effects of too much travelling, drink, or food, you recover from it by sleeping. *It's a good idea to spend the first night of your holiday sleeping off the jet lag.* `PHRASAL VB` `V P noun` `Also V n P`

sleep through. If you **sleep through** something, it does not wake you up. *Some children can sleep through any kind of noise.* `PHRASAL VB` `V P n`

sleep together. If two people **are sleeping together**, they are having a sexual relationship, but are not usually married to each other. `PHRASAL VB` `V P`

sleep with. If you **sleep with** someone, you have sex with them. `PHRASAL VB` `V P n`

sleep·er /'sliːpə/ **sleepers. 1** You can use the word **sleeper** to indicate how well someone sleeps. For example, if someone is a light **sleeper**, they are easily woken up. **2** A **sleeper** is a train with beds for passengers on overnight journeys. You can also refer to the beds themselves as **sleepers**. **3** Railway **sleepers** are large heavy beams that support the rails of a railway track. `◆◇◇◇◇` `N-COUNT:` `adj N` `N-COUNT` `BRITISH` `N-COUNT` `BRITISH`

sleep·ing /'sliːpɪŋ/. You use **sleeping** to describe places where people sleep or things concerned with where people sleep. *...sleeping quarters for women and children. ...investigations of people's finances, sleeping arrangements and housekeeping habits.* ● See also **sleep**. `ADJ: ADJ n`

'sleeping bag, sleeping bags. A **sleeping bag** is a large deep bag with a warm lining, used for sleeping in, especially when you are camping. `◆◇◇◇◇` `N-COUNT`

'sleeping pill, sleeping pills. A **sleeping pill** is a pill that you can take to help you sleep. `◆◇◇◇◇` `N-COUNT`

'sleeping sickness. Sleeping sickness is a serious tropical disease which causes great tiredness and often leads to death. `N-UNCOUNT`

'sleeping tablet, sleeping tablets. A **sleeping tablet** is the same as a **sleeping pill**. `N-COUNT`

sleep·less /'sliːpləs/. **1** A **sleepless** night is one during which you do not sleep. *He was said to be worn out after so many sleepless nights.* **2** Someone who is **sleepless** is unable to sleep. ♦ **sleep·less·ness** *Sleeplessness is sometimes the side effect of certain medications.* `◆◇◇◇◇` `ADJ-GRADED` `ADJ` `N-UNCOUNT`

sleep·walk /'sliːpwɔːk/ **sleepwalks, sleepwalking, sleepwalked.** If someone **is sleepwalking**, they are walking around while they are asleep. ♦ **sleep·walk·er, sleepwalkers** *We don't know what makes a sleepwalker.* `VERB: V` `N-COUNT`

sleepy /'sliːpi/ **sleepier, sleepiest. 1** If you are **sleepy**, you are very tired and are almost asleep. ♦ **sleep·i·ly** *Joanna sat up, blinking sleepily.* ♦ **sleep·i·ness** *He tried to fight the sleepiness that overwhelmed him.* **2** A **sleepy** place is quiet and does not have much activity or excitement. `◆◇◇◇◇` `ADJ-GRADED` `ADV-GRADED` `N-UNCOUNT` `ADJ-GRADED`

sleet /sliːt/. Sleet is rain that is partly frozen. `N-UNCOUNT`

sleeve /sliːv/ **sleeves. 1** The **sleeves** of a coat, shirt, or other item of clothing are the parts that cover your arms. **2** If you have something **up your sleeve**, you have an idea or plan which you have not told anyone about. You can also say that someone has **an ace, card**, or **trick up** their **sleeve**. *I'd been doing some quiet investigating in the meantime and had an ace up my sleeve.* **3** ● **wear** your **heart on** your **sleeve**: see **heart**. **4** A record **sleeve** is the stiff envelope in which a record is kept. `◆◆◇◇◇` `N-COUNT` `PHRASE` `PHRASE` `N-COUNT`

-sleeved /-sliːvd/. **-sleeved** is added to adjectives such as 'long' and 'short' to form adjectives which indicate that an item of clothing has long or short sleeves. *...a short-sleeved blue shirt.* `COMB`

sleeve·less /'sliːvləs/. A **sleeveless** T-shirt or dress has no sleeves. `ADJ`

'sleeve note, sleeve notes. On record sleeves, the **sleeve notes** are short pieces of writing that tell you something about the record or the musicians playing on the record. The American term is **liner note**. `N-COUNT` `BRITISH`

sleigh /sleɪ/ **sleighs.** A **sleigh** is a vehicle which can slide over snow. Sleighs are usually pulled by horses. N-COUNT

sleight of hand /ˌslaɪt əv ˈhænd/ **sleights of hand.** Sleight of hand is a skilful piece of deception. *...a financial sleight of hand.* N-VAR

slen·der /ˈslendə/ **1** A **slender** person is attractively thin and graceful. *...a tall, slender man in a denim jumpsuit.* **2** You can use **slender** to describe a situation which exists but only to a very small degree. *...the first slender hope of peace.* ◆◇◇◇ ADJ-GRADED WRITTEN ADJ-GRADED WRITTEN

slept /slept/. **Slept** is the past tense and past participle of **sleep**.

sleuth /sluːθ/ **sleuths.** A **sleuth** is a detective. *...Bob Woodward, the Watergate sleuth who toppled President Nixon.* N-COUNT DATED

sleuth·ing /ˈsluːθɪŋ/. **Sleuthing** is the investigation of a crime or mystery by someone who is not a detective in the police force. N-UNCOUNT LITERARY

slew /sluː/ **slews, slewing, slewed. 1** Slew is the past tense of **slay. 2** If a vehicle **slews** across a road, it slides or skids across it. *The bus slewed sideways... He slewed the car against the side of the building.* V-ERG V adv/prep V n prep/adv

3 A **slew** of things is a large number of them. *They dealt with a slew of other issues.* N-COUNT AMERICAN

slice /slaɪs/ **slices, slicing, sliced. 1** A **slice** of bread, meat, fruit, or other food is a thin piece that has been cut from a larger piece. **2** If you **slice** bread, meat, fruit, or other food, you cut it into thin pieces. *Slice the steak into long thin slices.* ▶ **Slice up** something means the same as **slice**. *I sliced up an onion.* **3** If something **slices** through a substance, it moves through it quickly, like a knife. *The ship sliced through the water.* ◆◇◇◇ N-COUNT VERB: V n V n into n PHRASAL VB V P noun Also V n P VERB V through n Also V n LITERARY

4 You can use **slice** to refer to a part of a situation or activity. *Fiction takes up a large slice of the publishing market.* **5** In tennis, golf, and other sports, if you **slice** a ball, you hit its edge rather than its centre, so that it travels at an angle. *The captain swung his left foot, but sliced the ball wide.* **6** See also **sliced. 7 • slice of the action:** see **action.** N-COUNT VERB V n adv/adj Also V n

sliced /slaɪst/. **Sliced** bread has been cut into slices before being wrapped and sold. ADJ

slick /slɪk/ **slicker, slickest; slicks, slicking, slicked. 1** A **slick** performance, production, or advertisement is attractively and professionally presented. **• slick·ly** *The products had been slickly marketed.* **• slick·ness** *These actors and directors brought a new sophistication and slickness to modern theatre.* **2** A **slick** action is done quickly and smoothly, and without any obvious effort. **3** A **slick** person speaks easily and persuasively but is not sincere; used showing disapproval. *Don't be fooled by slick politicians.* ◆◆◇◇ ADJ-GRADED ADV-GRADED N-UNCOUNT ADJ-GRADED ADJ-GRADED PRAGMATICS

4 A **slick** is the same as an **oil slick**. *There is little chance of the slick reaching the shore.* **5** If someone **slicks** their hair back, they make it flat, smooth, and shiny by putting oil or water on it. *He slicked down his few remaining wisps of gray hair.* N-COUNT VERB V with back/ down Also be V-ed prep

slick·er /ˈslɪkə/ **slickers. 1** A **slicker** is a long loose waterproof coat. The British term is **oilskins. 2** See also **slick.** N-COUNT AMERICAN

slide /slaɪd/ **slides, sliding, slid. 1** When something **slides** somewhere, it moves there smoothly over or against something. *She slid the door open... I slid the wallet into his pocket... Tears were sliding down his cheeks.* **2** A **slide** in a playground is a structure that has a steep slope for children to slide down. **3** If you **slide** somewhere, you move there smoothly and quietly. *He slid into the driver's seat.* ◆◆◇◇ V-ERG V n with adj V n prep/adv Also V N-COUNT VERB V prep/adv

4 To **slide into** a particular mood, attitude, or situation means to gradually start to have that mood, attitude, or situation often without intending to. *She had slid into a depression.* **5** If you **let** something **slide,** you allow it to get into a worse state or condition by not attending to it. **6** If currencies or prices **slide,** they gradually become worse or lower in value. *The upset sent share prices sliding to their lowest level for almost 18 months... Its share slid from 24.24 per cent to 22.17* VERB V into n PHRASE VERB: V V prep/adv V from/to/by amount JOURNALISM

per cent. ▶ Also a noun. *...the dangerous slide in oil prices.* N-COUNT

7 A **slide** is a small piece of photographic film which you project onto a screen so that you can see the picture. **8** A **slide** is a piece of glass on which you put something that you want to examine through a microscope. N-COUNT N-COUNT

slide rule, slide rules. A **slide rule** is an instrument that you use for calculating numbers. It looks like a ruler and has a middle part that slides backwards and forwards. N-COUNT

sliding door, sliding doors. Sliding doors are doors which slide together on runners rather than swinging on hinges. N-COUNT

sliding scale, sliding scales. Payments such as wages or taxes that are calculated on a **sliding scale** are higher or lower depending on various different factors. *Many practitioners have a sliding scale of fees for those who need but can't afford treatment.* N-COUNT

slight /slaɪt/ **slighter, slightest; slights, slighting, slighted. 1** Something that is **slight** is very small in degree or quantity. *Doctors say he has made a slight improvement... He's not the slightest bit worried.* **2** You use **in the slightest** to emphasize a negative statement. *That doesn't interest me in the slightest... 'Do you worry about ageing?' 'Not in the slightest.'* **3** A **slight** person has a slim and delicate body. **• slight·ly** *...a slightly built man with a moustache.* **4** If you are **slighted,** someone does or says something that insults you by treating you as if your views or feelings are not important. *They felt slighted by not being adequately consulted.* ▶ Also a noun. *It's difficult to persuade my husband that it isn't a slight on him that I enjoy my evening class.* **• slight·ing** *...slighting references to her age.* ◆◆◇◇ ADJ-GRADED PHRASE PRAGMATICS ADJ-GRADED ADJ-GRADED: ADV-ed passive feel V-ed N-COUNT ADJ-GRADED

slight·ly /ˈslaɪtli/. **Slightly** means to some degree but not to a very large degree. *His family then moved to a slightly larger house... You can adjust it slightly.* ◆◆◆◇ ADV

slim /slɪm/ **slimmer, slimmest; slims, slimming, slimmed. 1** A **slim** person has an attractively thin and well-shaped body. **2** If you **are slimming,** you are trying to make yourself thinner and lighter by eating less food. *Some people will gain weight, no matter how hard they try to slim.* ▶ **Slim down** means the same as **slim.** *Doctors have told Benny to slim down. ...salon treatments that claim to slim down thighs.* **• slim·mer, slimmers** *...meals for slimmers.* **• slim·ming** *We live in a society which is obsessed with slimming.* **3** If an organization **slims** its products, profits, or workforce, it reduces them. **4** A **slim** book, wallet, or other object is thinner than usual. **5** A **slim** chance or possibility is a very small one. ◆◆◇◇ ADJ-GRADED VERB V Also V n PHRASAL VB V P V P n N-COUNT N-UNCOUNT VERB: V n ADJ-GRADED ADJ-GRADED

slim down. **1** If a company or other organization **slims down,** it employs fewer people, in order to save money or become more efficient. *...the plan to slim down the coal industry.* **2** See **slim** 2. PHRASAL VB ERG: V P V P noun Also V P n

slime /slaɪm/. **Slime** is a thick slippery substance which covers a surface or comes from the bodies of animals such as snails. N-UNCOUNT

slim·line /ˈslɪmlaɪn/. **Slimline** objects are thinner or narrower than normal ones. *The slimline diary fits easily into a handbag.* ADJ

slimy /ˈslaɪmi/ **slimier, slimiest. 1** Slimy substances are thick, slippery, and unpleasant. **Slimy** objects have slippery unpleasant surfaces. *His feet slipped in the slimy mud.* **2** If you describe someone as **slimy,** you dislike them because they are friendly and pleasant in an insincere way. ADJ-GRADED ADJ-GRADED PRAGMATICS BRITISH

sling /slɪŋ/ **slings, slinging, slung. 1** If you **sling** something somewhere, you throw it there carelessly. *I saw him take off his anorak and sling it into the back seat.* **2** If you **sling** something over your shoulder or over something such as a chair, you hang it there loosely. *He had a small green rucksack slung over one shoulder.* **3** If a rope, blanket, or other object **is slung** between two points, someone has hung it loosely between them. *...two long poles with a blanket slung between them.* ◆◇◇◇ VERB V n prep/adv VERB V n prep VB: usu passive be V-ed prep

4 A **sling** is an object made of ropes, straps, or cloth N-COUNT
that is used for carrying things. **5** A **sling** is a piece of N-COUNT
cloth which supports someone's broken or injured
arm and is tied round their neck. **6 Slings and arrows** PHRASE
are unpleasant things that happen to you and that are WRITTEN
not your fault. *She had suffered her own share of slings
and arrows in the quest for publicity.* **7** See also **mud-
slinging**.

sling·shot /'slɪŋʃɒt/ **slingshots.** A slingshot is a N-COUNT
catapult.

slink /slɪŋk/ **slinks, slinking, slunk.** If you **slink** VERB
somewhere, you move there in a slow and secretive V adv/prep
way because you do not want to be seen. *He decided that he couldn't just slink away, so he went and
sat next to his wife.*

slinky /'slɪŋki/ **slinkier, slinkiest. Slinky** clothes ADJ-GRADED
fit very closely to a woman's body in a way that
makes her look sexually attractive.

slip /slɪp/ **slips, slipping, slipped. 1** If you **slip**, ◆◆◆◇
you accidentally slide and lose your balance. *Thou-* VERB
sands of us slip and hurt bits of ourselves when it's V
icy. **2** If something **slips**, it slides out of place or out VERB: V
of your hand. *The hammer slipped out of her grasp.* V prep/adv
3 If you **slip** somewhere, you go there quickly and qui- VERB
etly. *Amy slipped downstairs and out of the house... I* V adv/prep
slipped out of bed. **4** If you **slip** something some- VERB
where, you put it there quickly in a way that does not V n prep
attract attention. *He found a coin in his pocket and* V n with adv
*slipped it into her collecting tin... Just slip in a piece of
paper.* **5** If you **slip** something to someone, you give it VERB:
to them secretly. *Robert had slipped her a note in* V n n
school. V n n

6 To **slip into** a particular state or situation means to VERB
pass gradually into it, in a way that is hardly noticed. V into n
*There was 50-50 chance that the economy could slip
back into recession.* **7** If something **slips** to a lower lev- VERB
el or standard, it falls to that level or standard. *The* V to/from/by
club had slipped to the bottom of Division Four... In amount/n
June, producer prices slipped 0.1% from May. ▶ Also a V amount
noun. *...a slip in consumer confidence.* **8** If you **slip** N-SING
into or out of clothes or shoes, you put them on or VERB:
take them off quickly and easily. *I slipped off my wool-* V into/out of n
len gloves. V n with on/
off
9 A **slip** is a small or unimportant mistake. **10** See also N-COUNT
Freudian slip.

11 A **slip** of paper is a small piece of paper. **12** A **slip** is N-COUNT
a thin piece of clothing that a woman wears under her N-COUNT
dress or skirt. **13** If you refer to someone as a **slip of a** N-COUNT
girl or a **slip of a** boy, you mean they are small, thin, INFORMAL
and young.

14 If you **give** someone **the slip**, you escape from PHRASE
them when they are following you or watching you. INFORMAL
15 If you **let slip** information, you accidentally tell it PHRASE
to someone, when you wanted to keep it secret. **16** If PHRASE
something **slips** your **mind**, you forget about it.
17 ● **slip through** your **fingers**: see **finger**. ● **slip of
the tongue**: see **tongue**.

slip in. If you **slip in** a question or comment, you ask PHRASAL VB
or make it without interrupting the flow of the conver- V P noun
sation. *Skillfully Bush slipped in a reference to his own* Also V n P
military service.

slip through. If something **slips through** a set of PHRASAL VB
checks or rules, it is accepted when in fact it should V P n
not be. *...trouble-makers who have slipped through* Also V P
the security checks.

slip up. If you **slip up**, you make a small or unimpor- PHRASAL VB
tant mistake. ● See also **slip-up.** V P

'**slip-on, slip-ons. Slip-on** shoes have no laces or ADJ: ADJ n
buckles. ▶ Also a noun. *...his brown slip-ons.* N-COUNT

slip·page /'slɪpɪdʒ/ **slippages. Slippage** is a fail- N-VAR
ure to maintain a steady position or rate of progress, so that a particular target or standard is not
achieved. *...a substantial slippage in the value of
sterling.*

'**slipped 'disc, slipped discs.** If you have a N-COUNT
slipped disc, you have a bad back because one of
the discs in your spine has moved out of its proper
position.

slip·per /'slɪpə/ **slippers. Slippers** are loose soft ◆◇◇◇
shoes that you wear in the house. N-COUNT

slip·pery /'slɪpəri/. **1** Something that is **slippery** is ◆◇◇◇
smooth, wet, or greasy and is therefore difficult to ADJ-GRADED
walk on or to hold. *Motorists were warned to beware
of slippery conditions.* **2** You can describe someone ADJ-GRADED
as **slippery** if you think that they are dishonest in a PRAGMATICS
clever way and cannot be trusted. **3** If someone is PHRASE
on a **slippery slope**, they are involved in a course of
action that is difficult to stop and that will eventually lead to failure or trouble. *The company started
down the slippery slope of believing that they knew
better than the customer.*

'**slip road, slip roads.** A **slip road** is a road which N-COUNT
cars use to drive on and off a motorway. The usual BRITISH
American expressions are **entrance ramp** and **exit
ramp**.

slip·shod /'slɪpʃɒd/. If something is **slipshod** it has ADJ-GRADED
been done without care or thoroughness. *The hotel
had always been run in a slipshod way.*

slip·stream /'slɪpstriːm/ **slipstreams.** The **slip-** N-COUNT
stream of a fast-moving object such as a car or
plane is the flow of air directly behind it.

'**slip-up, slip-ups.** A **slip-up** is a small or unimpor- N-COUNT
tant mistake. INFORMAL

slip·way /'slɪpweɪ/ **slipways.** A **slipway** is a large N-COUNT
platform that slopes down into the sea, from which
boats are launched.

slit /slɪt/ **slits, slitting.** The form **slit** is used in the ◆◇◇◇
present tense and is the past tense and past partici-
ple. **1** If you **slit** something, you make a long nar- VERB: V n
row cut in it. *He began to slit open each envelope...* V n with open
She was wearing a white dress slit to the thigh. be V-ed to/
▶ Also a noun. *Make a slit in the stem about half an* from n
inch long.* **2** A **slit** is a long narrow opening in N-COUNT
something. *She watched them through a slit in the
curtains.*

slith·er /'slɪðə/ **slithers, slithering, slithered.** ◆◇◇◇
1 If you **slither** somewhere, you slide along in an VERB
uneven way. *Robert lost his footing and slithered* V prep/adv
down the bank.* **2** If an animal such as a snake **slith-** VERB
ers, it moves along in a twisting way. *The snake* V prep/adv
slithered into the water. Also V

sliv·er /'slɪvə/ **slivers.** A **sliver** of something is a ◆◇◇◇
small thin piece or amount of it.

slob /slɒb/ **slobs.** If you call someone a **slob**, you N-COUNT
think they very lazy and untidy.

slob·ber /'slɒbə/ **slobbers, slobbering, slob-** VERB: V
bered. If a person or an animal **slobbers**, they let
liquid fall from their mouth. *He hated the animals,
the way they slobbered everywhere.*

sloe /sləʊ/ **sloes.** A **sloe** is a small sour fruit that N-VAR
has a dark purple skin. It is often used to flavour
gin.

slog /slɒg/ **slogs, slogging, slogged. 1** If you ◆◇◇◇
slog through something, you work hard and steadily VERB: V prep
through it. *She has slogged her way through ballet* V way through
classes since the age of six... While slogging at work, V
have you neglected your marriage?* **2** If you describe INFORMAL
a task as a **slog**, you mean that it is tiring and re- N-SING
quires a lot of effort. **3** If you **slog** somewhere, you INFORMAL
make a long and tiring journey there. *The men had* VERB
to slog up a steep muddy incline.* ▶ Also a noun. *...a* V prep/adv
slog through heather and bracken to the top of a hill.* INFORMAL
N-SING

slo·gan /'sləʊgən/ **slogans.** A **slogan** is a short ◆◆◇◇
easily-remembered phrase used in advertisements N-COUNT
and by political parties.

sloop /sluːp/ **sloops.** A **sloop** is a small sailing boat N-COUNT
with one mast.

slop /slɒp/ **slops, slopping, slopped. 1** If liquid ◆◇◇◇
slops, it spills over the edge of a container in a V-ERG: V
messy way. *If the cognac slopped over the edge of* V adv/prep
the glass... She slopped some tea into the saucer.* V n adv/prep
2 You can use **slop** or **slops** to refer to liquid waste Also V n
containing the remains of food. N-UNCOUNT:
also N in pl

slope /sləʊp/ **slopes, sloping, sloped. 1** A **slope** ◆◆◇◇
is the side of a mountain, hill, or valley. *...the lower* N-COUNT
slopes of the Himalayas.* **2** A **slope** is a surface that N-COUNT
is at an angle, so that one end is higher than the
other. *The street must have been on a slope.* **3** See
also **ski slope. 4** ● **slippery slope**: see **slippery**.
5 If a surface **slopes**, it is at an angle, so that one end is VERB: V

higher than the other. *The bank sloped down sharply to the river.* ✦ **slop·ing** *...the gently sloping beach.* `V adv/prep` `ADJ-GRADED`

6 If something **slopes**, it leans to the right or to the left rather than being upright. *The writing sloped backwards.* **7** The **slope** of something is the angle at which it slopes. *...a slope of ten degrees.* `VERB` `V adv/prep` `N-COUNT`

8 If someone **slopes** into or out of a place, they enter or leave it quickly and quietly, especially because they are trying to avoid or escape something. `VERB:` `V adv/prep` `INFORMAL,` `BRITISH`

,slopping 'out; also spelled **slopping-out.** In prisons where prisoners have to use buckets as toilets, **slopping out** is the practice in which they empty the buckets. `N-UNCOUNT`

slop·py /ˈslɒpi/ **sloppier, sloppiest.** If you describe someone's work or activities as **sloppy**, you mean they have done them in a careless and lazy way. ✦ **slop·pi·ly** /ˈslɒpɪli/. *They lost because they played sloppily.* ✦ **slop·pi·ness** *Miss Furniss could not abide sloppiness.* `◆◇◇◇◇` `ADJ-GRADED` `ADV-GRADED` `N-UNCOUNT`

slosh /slɒʃ/ **sloshes, sloshing, sloshed.** If a liquid **sloshes** around or if you **slosh** it around, it splashes or moves around in a messy way. *The water sloshed around the bridge.* `V-ERG` `V adv/prep` `Also V,` `V n`

sloshed /slɒʃt/. If someone is **sloshed**, they are drunk. *When Flynn arrived he was sloshed out of his head.* `ADJ-GRADED` `INFORMAL`

slot /slɒt/ **slots, slotting, slotted. 1** A **slot** is a narrow opening in a machine or container, for example a hole that you put coins in to make a machine work. **2** If you **slot** something into something else, or if it **slots** into something else, you put it into a space where it fits. *The car seat belt slotted into place easily.* **3** A **slot** in a schedule or scheme is a place in it where an activity can take place. *The first episode occupies a peak evening viewing slot.* `◆◆◇◇◇` `N-COUNT` `V-ERG:` `V n into/in/` `onto n` `V into/in/` `onto n` `N-COUNT`

sloth /sləʊθ/ **sloths. 1** **Sloth** is laziness, especially with regard to work. **2** A **sloth** is an animal from Central and South America that lives in trees. `N-UNCOUNT` `FORMAL` `N-COUNT`

'slot machine, slot machines. A **slot machine** is a machine from which you can get food or cigarettes or on which you can gamble. `N-COUNT`

slouch /slaʊtʃ/ **slouches, slouching, slouched. 1** If someone **slouches**, they sit or stand with their shoulders and head drooping so they look lazy and unattractive. *She has recently begun to slouch over her typewriter.* ▶ Also a noun. *He straightened himself from a slouch.* ✦ **slouched** *She had been slouched against the counter.* **2** If someone **slouches** somewhere, they walk around slowly with their shoulders and heads drooping looking lazy or bored. `◆◇◇◇◇` `VERB: V` `V prep/adv` `N-SING` `ADJ` `VERB:` `V adv/prep`

3 If you say that someone is **no slouch** at a particular activity, you mean that they are skilful at it or are willing to work hard at it. *The Welsh are no slouches at cooking.* `PHRASE`

slough /slʌf/ **sloughs, sloughing, sloughed.** When a plant **sloughs** its leaves, or an animal such as a snake **sloughs** its skin, the leaves or skin come off naturally. *All reptiles have to slough their skin to grow.* ▶ **Slough off** means the same as **slough**. *Our bodies slough off dead cells.* `◆◇◇◇◇` `VERB: V n` `Also V` `PHRASAL VB` `V P noun` `Also V n P`

slough off. 1 See **slough. 2** If you **slough off** something that you no longer want or need, you get rid of it. *The nation states of Eastern Europe finally sloughed off their totalitarian regimes.* `PHRASAL VB` `V P noun` `Also V n P` `WRITTEN`

slov·en·ly /ˈslʌvənli/. **Slovenly** people are careless, untidy, or inefficient. `ADJ-GRADED`

slow /sləʊ/ **slower, slowest; slows, slowing, slowed. 1** Something that is **slow** moves, happens, or is done without much speed. *The traffic is heavy and slow. ...slow, regular breathing.* ✦ **slow·ly** *Christian backed slowly away.* ✦ **slow·ness** *She lowered the glass with calculated slowness.* **2** In informal English, **slower** is used to mean 'at a slower speed' and **slowest** is used to mean 'at the slowest speed'. In non-standard English, **slow** is used to mean 'with little speed'. *I began to walk slower and slower... We got there by driving slow all the way.* **3** If something **slows**, or if you **slow** it, it starts to move or happen more slowly. *The rate of bombing* `◆◆◆◆◇` `ADJ-GRADED` `ADV-GRADED` `N-UNCOUNT` `ADV-GRADED` `ADV after v` `V-ERG` `V n`

has slowed considerably... She slowed the car and began driving up a narrow road. **4** If someone is **slow** to do something, they do it after a delay. *I've been a bit slow in making up my mind.* `ADJ-GRADED:` `v-link ADJ`

5 Something that is **slow** takes a long time. *The distribution of passports has been a slow process.* ✦ **slowly** *My resentment of her slowly began to fade.* ✦ **slow·ness** *...the slowness of political and economic progress.* **6** If you describe a situation, place, or activity as **slow**, you mean that it is not very exciting. *The island is too slow for her liking.* **7** If a clock or watch is **slow**, it shows a time that is earlier than the correct time. `ADJ-GRADED` `ADV-GRADED:` `ADV with v` `N-UNCOUNT` `ADJ-GRADED` `ADJ-GRADED`

8 Someone who is **slow** is not very clever and takes a long time to understand things. See also **slow-.** **10** ● **slow off the mark:** see **mark.** ● **slowly but surely:** see **surely.** ● **slow on the uptake:** see **uptake.** `ADJ-GRADED`

slow down. 1 If something **slows down**, or if you **slow** it **down**, it starts to move or happen more slowly. *The car slowed down... Damage to the turbine slowed the work down... We want to slow down the process of eating.* **2** If someone **slows down**, or if something **slows** them **down**, they become less active. *He was still taking some medication which slowed him down.* **3** See also **slowdown.** `PHRASAL VB` `ERG:` `V P` `V n P` `V n P` `ERG:` `V P` `V n P`

slow up. Slow up means the same as **slow down** 1. *The introduction of a new code of criminal procedure has also slowed up the system.* `PHRASAL VB` `ERG:` `V P` `V P noun`

slow- /sləʊ-/. **slow-** is used to form words which describe something that happens slowly. *He was stuck in a line of slow-moving traffic.* `COMB`

slow·down /ˈsləʊdaʊn/ **slowdowns. 1** A **slowdown** is a reduction in speed or activity. *There has been a sharp slowdown in economic growth.* **2** A **slowdown** is a protest in which workers deliberately work slowly and cause problems for their employers. The British term is a **go-slow.** `◆◇◇◇◇` `N-COUNT` `N-COUNT` `AMERICAN`

'slow lane, slow lanes. 1 On a motorway, the **slow lane** is the lane for vehicles which are moving more slowly than the other vehicles. **2** If you say that a country or company is in the **slow lane**, you mean that they are not progressing as fast as other countries or companies in a particular area of activity. `N-COUNT` `N-SING`

,slow 'motion. When film or television pictures are shown in **slow motion**, they are shown much more slowly than normal. `◆◇◇◇◇` `N-UNCOUNT`

sludge /slʌdʒ/ **sludges. Sludge** is thick mud, sewage, or industrial waste. `◆◇◇◇◇` `N-VAR`

slug /slʌɡ/ **slugs, slugging, slugged. 1** A **slug** is a small slow-moving creature with a long slimy body, like a snail without a shell. `◆◇◇◇◇` `N-COUNT`

2 If you take a **slug** of an alcoholic drink, you take a large mouthful of it. `N-COUNT` `INFORMAL`

3 A **slug** is a bullet. *Paramedics found a 25 caliber slug indented in the radio.* `N-COUNT` `INFORMAL`

4 If you **slug** someone, you hit them hard. *The chief said someone slugged the jailer and opened the cell they were in.* **5** If two or more people **slug it out**, they work very hard to try to be the one who is successful or has their ideas and wishes accepted. *Four candidates are slugging it out in a dirty campaign.* `VERB` `V n` `INFORMAL` `PHRASE`

slug·ger /ˈslʌɡə/ **sluggers.** In baseball, a **slugger** is a player who hits the ball very hard. `N-COUNT`

slug·gish /ˈslʌɡɪʃ/. You can describe something as **sluggish** if it moves, works, or reacts much slower than is normal. *Circulation is much more sluggish in the feet than in the hands.* ✦ **slug·gish·ly** *The company has responded sluggishly to these changes in technology.* ✦ **slug·gish·ness** *...the sluggishness of Britain's economic recovery.* `◆◇◇◇◇` `ADJ-GRADED` `ADV-GRADED` `N-UNCOUNT`

sluice /sluːs/ **sluices, sluicing, sluiced. 1** A **sluice** is a passage that carries a current of water and has an opening, called a sluice-gate, which can be opened and closed to control the flow of water. **2** If you **sluice** something, you wash it with a stream of water. *Ten minutes later we were sluicing off dust at the fountain.* `N-COUNT` `VERB: V n` `V n with adv`

slum /slʌm/ **slums, slumming, slummed. 1** A **slum** is an area of a city where living conditions are very bad and where the houses are in bad condi- `◆◇◇◇◇` `N-COUNT`

tion. **2** If someone **is slumming it** or **is slumming**, they are spending time in a place or in conditions that are at a much lower social level than they are used to. ...*aristocratic types who enjoyed slumming around in musty old Scottish castles.* `VERB` `V`

slum·ber /'slʌmbə/ **slumbers, slumbering, slumbered.** Someone who **is slumbering** is sleeping. *The older three girls are still slumbering peacefully.* ▶ **Slumber** is sleep. *He roused Charles from his slumbers.* `VERB` `V` `LITERARY` `N-VAR`

slump /slʌmp/ **slumps, slumping, slumped.** **1** If something such as the value of something **slumps**, it falls suddenly and by a large amount. *Net profits slumped by 41%.* ▶ Also a noun. ...*a slump in property prices.* **2** A **slump** is a time when there is a lot of unemployment and poverty in a country. **3** If you **slump** somewhere, you fall or sit down there heavily, for example because you are very tired or you feel ill. *She slumped into a chair.* `VERB` `V prep` `Also V` `N-COUNT` `VERB` `V prep/adv`

slung /slʌŋ/. **Slung** is the past tense and past participle of **sling**.

slunk /slʌŋk/. **Slunk** is the past tense and past participle of **slink**.

slur /slɜː/ **slurs, slurring, slurred.** **1** A **slur** is an insulting remark which could damage someone's reputation. **2** If someone **slurs** their speech, they do not pronounce each word clearly and distinctly, because they are drunk or sleepy. *He repeated himself and slurred his words more than usual... The newscaster's speech began to slur.* ♦ **slurred** *Her speech was so slurred as to be almost incomprehensible.* `N-COUNT` `V-ERG` `V n` `V` `Also V with quote` `ADJ-GRADED`

slurp /slɜːp/ **slurps, slurping, slurped.** **1** If you **slurp** a liquid, you drink it noisily. *He slurped down a cup of sweet, black coffee.* **2** A **slurp** is a noise that you make with your mouth when you drink noisily. It is also the mouthful of liquid that you are drinking noisily. `VERB: V n` `V adv n` `Also V` `N-COUNT`

slur·ry /'slʌri, AM 'slɜːri/ **slurries. Slurry** is a watery mixture of something such as mud, animal waste, or dust. `N-VAR`

slush /slʌʃ/. **Slush** is snow that has begun to melt and is therefore very wet and dirty. `N-UNCOUNT`

'slush fund, slush funds. A **slush fund** is a sum of money collected to pay for an illegal activity, especially in politics or business. `N-COUNT`

slushy /'slʌʃi/. If you describe a story or idea as **slushy**, you mean you dislike it because it is extremely romantic and sentimental. `ADJ-GRADED` `PRAGMATICS` `BRITISH`

slut /slʌt/ **sluts.** People sometimes refer to a woman as a **slut** when they consider her to be immoral in her sexual behaviour; a rude and offensive word. `N-COUNT` `PRAGMATICS` `RUDE`

sly /slaɪ/. **1** A **sly** look, expression, or remark shows that you know something that other people do not know or that was meant to be a secret. ♦ **sly·ly** *Anna grinned slyly.* **2** If you describe someone as **sly**, you disapprove of them because they are secretive and clever at deceiving people. **3** If someone does something **on the sly**, they do it in a secretive way, often because it is something that they should not be doing. *Was she meeting some guy on the sly?* `ADJ-GRADED` `ADV-GRADED` `ADJ-GRADED` `PRAGMATICS` `PHRASE` `INFORMAL`

smack /smæk/ **smacks, smacking, smacked.** **1** If you **smack** someone, you hit them with your hand. ▶ Also a noun. *Sometimes he just doesn't listen and I end up shouting at him or giving him a smack.* **2** If you **smack** something somewhere, you put it or throw it there so that it makes a loud, sharp noise. *Ray Houghton smacked the ball against a post.* **3** If you **smack** your **lips**, you open and close your mouth noisily, especially before or after eating, to show that you are keen to eat or enjoyed eating. **4** Something that is **smack** in a particular place is exactly in that place. *In part that's because industry is smack in the middle of the city.* **5** If one thing **smacks of** another thing that you consider bad, it reminds you of it or is like it. *The engineers' union was unhappy with the motion, saying it smacked of racism.* `VERB: V n` `N-COUNT` `VERB` `V n adv/prep` `PHRASE` `ADV:` `ADV prep` `INFORMAL` `VERB` `V of n`

6 Some people use the word **smack** to refer to **heroin**. `N-UNCOUNT`

small /smɔːl/ **smaller, smallest. 1** A **small** person, thing, or amount of something is not large in `ADJ-GRADED`

physical size. *She is small for her age... The window was far too small for him to get through.* ♦ **small·ness** *Amy had not mentioned the smallness and bareness of Luis's home.* **2** A **small** group or quantity consists of only a few people or things. *Guns continued to be produced in small numbers.* **3** A **small** child is a very young child. *What were you like when you were small?* **4** You use **small** to describe something that is not significant or great in degree. *No detail was too small to escape her attention. ...a relatively small problem.* `N-UNCOUNT` `ADJ-GRADED` `ADJ-GRADED` `ADJ-GRADED`

5 **Small** businesses or companies employ a small number of people and do business with a small number of clients. **6** If someone speaks in a **small** voice, they speak very quietly, because they are frightened or ashamed. **7** If someone makes you look or feel **small**, they make you look or feel stupid, so that you are ashamed or humiliated. **8** **The small of** your back is the bottom part of your back that curves inwards slightly. **9** See also **smalls**. ● **the small hours:** see **hour**. ● **small wonder:** see **wonder**. `ADJ-GRADED` `ADJ-GRADED:` `ADJ n` `ADJ-GRADED:` `v-link ADJ` `N-SING:` `the N of n`

'small ad, small ads. The **small ads** in a newspaper are short advertisements in which you can advertise something such as an object for sale or a room to let. `N-COUNT` `BRITISH`

'small arms. Small arms are guns that are light and easy to carry. *The two sides exchanged small arms fire for about three hours.* `N-PLURAL`

'small 'beer. If you say that something is **small beer**, you mean it is unimportant in comparison with something else. *The arrangement and furnishing of public spaces is small beer compared with saving the rainforests.* `N-UNCOUNT` `BRITISH`

small 'change. Small change refers to coins of low value. `N-UNCOUNT`

'small fry; small fry is both the singular and the plural form. **Small fry** is used to refer to someone or something that is considered to be unimportant. *It's the small fry who are usually the last to get paid.* `N-UNCOUNT:` `also N in pl`

small·holder /'smɔːlhəʊldə/ **smallholders.** A **smallholder** is someone who has a smallholding. `N-COUNT` `BRITISH`

small·holding /'smɔːlhəʊldɪŋ/ **smallholdings.** A **smallholding** is a piece of land used for farming that is smaller than a normal farm. `N-COUNT` `BRITISH`

small 'hours. If something happens in the **small hours**, it happens shortly after midnight, in the very early morning. *They were arrested in the small hours of Saturday morning.* `N-PLURAL`

small·ish /'smɔːlɪʃ/. Something that is **smallish** is fairly small. `ADJ`

small·'minded. If you say that someone is **small-minded**, you are critical of them because they have fixed opinions and are unwilling to change them or to think about more general subjects. ♦ **small-minded·ness** *Helen's small-mindedness bored and disgusted her.* `ADJ-GRADED` `PRAGMATICS` `N-UNCOUNT`

small·pox /'smɔːlpɒks/. **Smallpox** is a serious infectious disease that causes a rash and leaves deep scars on the skin. `N-UNCOUNT`

'small 'print. The **small print** of a contract or agreement is the part of it that is written in very small print. You refer to this part as the **small print** especially when you think that it might include unfavourable conditions which someone might not notice or understand. *Read the small print in your contract to find out exactly what you are insured for.* `N-UNCOUNT`

smalls /smɔːlz/. Some people refer to their underwear as their **smalls**. ...*the sight of her smalls drying over the bath.* `N-PLURAL` `INFORMAL` `BRITISH`

small·'scale. A **small-scale** activity or organization is small in size and limited in extent. ...*the small-scale production of farmhouse cheeses.* `ADJ-GRADED`

small 'screen. When people talk about **the small screen**, they are referring to television, in contrast to films that are made for the cinema. *Live concerts are never quite the same on the small screen.* `N-SING`

'small talk. Small talk is polite conversation about unimportant things that people make, for example, at social occasions. `N-UNCOUNT`

'small-time. If you refer to workers or businesses as **small-time**, you think they are not very important because they work only on a small-scale. `ADJ-GRADED`

small·town /'smɔːltaʊn/. **Smalltown** is used to refer to people or places that have characteristics such as friendliness, honesty, and politeness. A smalltown person can also be considered narrow-minded. *She seemed to be living the dream teenage life in smalltown America.* `ADJ AMERICAN`

smarmy /'smɑːmi/ **smarmier, smarmiest.** If you describe someone as **smarmy**, you dislike them because they are unpleasantly polite and flattering, usually because they want you to like them or to do something for them. `ADJ-GRADED`

smart /smɑːt/ **smarter, smartest; smarts, smarting, smarted. 1** Smart people and things are pleasantly neat and clean in appearance. *...smart new offices.* ♦ **smart·ly** *He dressed very smartly which was important in those days.* ♦ **smart·ness** *The jumper strikes the perfect balance between comfort and smartness.* **2** A **smart** place or event is connected with wealthy and fashionable people. *...smart London dinner parties.* **3** The **smart set** is a group of fashionable and wealthy people. *...the Los Angeles smart set.* ● the **smart money**: see **money. 4** You can describe someone who is clever as **smart.** ● See also **smartly; street smart. 5** Smart bombs and weapons are guided by computers and lasers so that they hit their targets accurately. **6** If a part of your body or a wound **smarts**, you feel a sharp stinging pain in it. **7** If you **are smarting** from something such as criticism or failure, you feel upset about it. *He is still smarting over criticism of his victorious but clumsy performance.* ♦♦♦◇◇ `ADJ-GRADED BRITISH` `ADV-GRADED: ADV with v` `ADJ-UNCOUNT` `ADJ-GRADED` `PHRASE JOURNALISM` `ADJ-GRADED` `ADJ: ADJ n` `VERB: V` `VERB: V from n V prep JOURNALISM`

smart 'alec, smart alecs; also spelled **smart aleck.** If you describe someone as a **smart alec**, you dislike the fact that they think they are very clever and always have an answer for everything. `N-COUNT PRAGMATICS INFORMAL`

smart·arse /'smɑːtɑːs/ **smartarses;** also spelled **smartass.** If you describe someone as a **smartarse**, you dislike the fact that they think they are very clever and like to show everyone this; a word which some people find offensive. `N-COUNT PRAGMATICS INFORMAL`

'smart card, smart cards. A **smart card** is a plastic card which looks like a credit card and can store and process computer data. `N-COUNT`

smart 'drug, smart drugs. Smart drugs are drugs which some people think can improve your memory and intelligence. `N-COUNT`

smart·en /'smɑːtən/ **smartens, smartening, smartened.**

smarten up. If you **smarten** yourself or a place **up**, you make yourself or the place look neater and tidier. *...a 10-year programme to smarten up the London Underground.* `PHRASAL VB V n P V P noun Also V P`

smart·ly /'smɑːtli/. If someone moves or does something **smartly**, they do it quickly and neatly. ● See also **smart.** ♦◇◇◇◇ `ADV-GRADED: ADV with v WRITTEN`

smash /smæʃ/ **smashes, smashing, smashed. 1** If something **smashes**, it breaks into many pieces, for example when it is hit or dropped. *Someone smashed a bottle... Two or three glasses fell off and smashed into pieces.* **2** If you **smash** through a wall, gate, or door, you get through it by hitting and breaking it. *Soldiers smashed their way into his office.* **3** If something **smashes** or **is smashed** against something solid, it moves very fast and with great force against it. *He smashed his fist into Anthony's face.* **4** You can refer to a car crash as a **smash.** *I had a head on smash with another car.* **5** To **smash** a political group or system means to deliberately destroy it. *The President said he would smash the communists.* **6** A **smash** is the same as a **smash hit. 7** See also **smashed, smashing.** ♦♦♦◇◇ `V n V into n` `VERB: V through n V way prep/ adv` `V-ERG: V prep/adv V n prep` `N-COUNT INFORMAL` `VERB V n INFORMAL` `N-COUNT`

smash down. If you **smash down** a door, building, or other large heavy object, you hit it hard and break it until it falls on the ground. *The crowd tried to smash down the door of the police station.* `PHRASAL VB V P noun Also V n P`

smash up. 1 If you **smash** something **up**, you com- `PHRASAL VB`

pletely destroy it by hitting and breaking it into many pieces. *She took revenge on her ex-boyfriend by smashing up his home.* **2** If you **smash up** your car, you damage it by crashing it into something. *All you told me was that he'd smashed up yet another car.* `V n P V P noun` `V P noun Also V n P`

smash-and-'grab, smash-and-grabs; also spelled **smash and grab.** A **smash-and-grab** is a robbery in which a person smashes a shop window, seizes the things that are on display there, and rushes away with them. *...a smash and grab raid.* `N-COUNT`

smashed /smæʃt/. Someone who is **smashed** is extremely drunk. `ADJ INFORMAL`

smash 'hit, smash hits. A **smash hit** or **smash** is a very popular show, play, or song. `N-COUNT`

smash·ing /'smæʃɪŋ/. If you describe something or someone as **smashing**, you mean that you like them very much. `ADJ BRITISH, INFORMAL, DATED`

smat·ter·ing /'smætərɪŋ/. A **smattering** of something is a very small amount of it. `N-SING`

smear /smɪə/ **smears, smearing, smeared. 1** If you **smear** a surface with a greasy or sticky substance or **smear** the substance onto the surface, you spread a layer of the substance over the surface. *My sister smeared herself with suntan oil... Smear a little olive oil over the inside of the salad bowl.* **2** A **smear** is a dirty or greasy mark. ♦ **smeared** *The other child's face was smeared with dirt.* **3** To **smear** someone means to spread unpleasant and untrue rumours or accusations about them in order to damage their reputation. ▶ A **smear** is an unpleasant and untrue rumour or accusation. *...a smear campaign by his political opponents.* **4** A **smear** or a **smear test** is a medical test in which a few cells are taken from a woman's cervix and analysed to see if any cancer cells are present. ♦♦◇◇◇ `VERB V n V n prep` `N-COUNT` `ADJ-GRADED` `VERB: V n JOURNALISM` `N-COUNT` `N-COUNT BRITISH`

smell /smel/ **smells, smelling, smelled, smelt. 1** The **smell** of something is a quality it has which you become aware of when you breathe in through your nose. *...the smell of freshly baked bread.* **2** Your sense of **smell** is the ability that your nose has to detect things. **3** If something **smells** of a particular thing, it has a particular quality which you become aware of through your nose. *The room smelled of lemons... It smells delicious.* **4** If you say that something **smells**, you mean that it smells unpleasant. *Do my feet smell?* **5** If you **smell** something, you become aware of it when you breathe in through your nose. *As soon as we opened the front door we could smell the gas.* **6** If you **smell** something, you put your nose near it and breathe in, so that you can discover its smell. *I took a fresh rose out of the vase on our table, and smelled it.* **7** If you **smell** something, you feel instinctively that it is likely to happen or be true. *He knew virtually nothing about music but he could smell a hit.* **8** ● to **smell a rat:** see **rat.** ♦♦♦◇◇ `N-COUNT` `N-UNCOUNT` `V-LINK V of n V adj Also V as if, V like n VERB V` `VERB V n` `VERB V n` `VERB V n`

-smelling /-smelɪŋ/. **-smelling** combines with adjectives to form adjectives which indicate how something smells. *...a foul-smelling cloud of smoke.* `COMB`

'smelling salts. A bottle of **smelling salts** contains a chemical with a strong smell which is used to help someone recover after they have fainted. `N-PLURAL`

smelly /'smeli/ **smellier, smelliest.** Something that is **smelly** has an unpleasant smell. ♦◇◇◇◇ `ADJ-GRADED`

smelt /smelt/ **smelts, smelting, smelted. 1** Smelt is a past tense and past participle of **smell. 2** To **smelt** a substance containing metal means to process it by heating it until it melts, so that the metal is extracted and changed chemically. `VERB: V n`

smel·ter /'smeltə/ **smelters.** A **smelter** is a furnace for smelting metal. `N-COUNT`

smid·gen /'smɪdʒɪn/ **smidgens;** also spelled **smidgeon** or **smidgin.** A **smidgen** is a small amount of something. `N-COUNT INFORMAL`

smile /smaɪl/ **smiles, smiling, smiled. 1** When you **smile**, the corners of your mouth curve upwards, usually because you are pleased or amused, or because you are being friendly. *He rubbed the back of his neck and smiled ruefully at me.* **2** A **smile** is the expression that you have on ♦♦♦♦◇ `VERB: V V at n` `N-COUNT`

S

your face when you smile. *She had a big smile on her face.* **3** If you **smile** something, you say it with a smile or express it by a smile. *'Aren't we daft?' she smiled.* **4** If you say that something such as fortune **smiles** on someone, you mean that they are lucky or successful. *God is not smiling on our cause.* **5** If you say that someone is **all smiles**, you mean that they look very happy, often when they have previously been worried or upset about something. ● to **wipe the smile off** someone's **face**: see **wipe**. — VERB / V with quote / Also V n / VERB / V on/upon n / LITERARY / PHRASE

smiley /ˈsmaɪli/. A **smiley** person smiles a lot or is smiling. — ADJ-GRADED / INFORMAL

smil·ing·ly /ˈsmaɪlɪŋli/. If someone does something **smilingly**, they smile as they do it. — ADV: ADV with v / WRITTEN

smirk /smɜːk/ **smirks, smirking, smirked.** If you **smirk**, you smile in an unpleasant way, often because you believe that you have gained an advantage over someone else or know something that they do not know. *A dozen people were watching her, smirking at her discomfort.* ▶ Also a noun. *Her mouth was drawn back into a smirk of triumph.* — VERB: V / V at n / N-COUNT

smite /smaɪt/ **smites, smiting, smote, smitten.** To **smite** something means to hit it hard. ● See also **smitten**. — VERB: V n / LITERARY

smith·er·eens /ˌsmɪðəˈriːnz/. If something is smashed or blown to **smithereens**, it breaks into very small pieces. — N-PLURAL

smit·ten /ˈsmɪtən/. **1** If you are **smitten**, you find someone so attractive that you are or seem to be in love with them. *They were totally smitten with each other.* **2** If you are **smitten** by something, you are very impressed by it and enthusiastic about it. **3 Smitten** is the past participle of **smite**. — ADJ-GRADED / ADJ-GRADED

smock /smɒk/ **smocks. 1** A **smock** is a loose garment, rather like a long blouse, usually worn by women. **2** A **smock** is a loose garment worn by people such as artists to protect their clothing. — N-COUNT / N-COUNT

smog /smɒg/ **smogs. Smog** is a mixture of fog and smoke which occurs in some busy industrial cities. — N-VAR

smog·gy /ˈsmɒgi/ **smoggier, smoggiest.** A **smoggy** city or town is badly affected by smog. — ADJ-GRADED

smoke /sməʊk/ **smokes, smoking, smoked. 1 Smoke** consists of gas and small bits of solid material that are sent into the air when something burns. *...cigarette smoke.* **2** If something **is smoking**, smoke is coming from it. *...a pile of smoking rubble.* **3** When someone **smokes** a cigarette, cigar, or pipe, they suck the smoke from it into their mouth and blow it out again. If you **smoke**, you regularly smoke cigarettes, cigars, or a pipe. *Do you smoke?* ▶ Also a noun. *Someone came out for a smoke.* ♦ **smok·ing** *...a no-smoking area.* ♦ **smok·er, smokers** *He was not a heavy smoker.* **4** If fish or meat **is smoked**, it is hung over burning wood so that the smoke preserves it and gives it a special flavour. *...smoked bacon.* **5** If someone says **there's no smoke without fire** or **where there's smoke there's fire**, they mean that there are rumours or signs that something is true so it must be at least partly true. **6** If something **goes up in smoke**, it is destroyed by fire. If something that is very important to you **goes up in smoke**, it fails or ends without anything being achieved. — N-UNCOUNT / VERB: V / V-ing / VERB: V n / V / N-SING: a N / N-UNCOUNT / N-COUNT / VB: usu passive V-ed / PHRASE / PHRASE / PHRASE

smoke out. If you **smoke out** someone who is hiding, you discover them and make them publicly known. *...technology to smoke out tax evaders.* — PHRASAL VB / V P noun / Also V n P

smoked /sməʊkt/. **Smoked** glass has been made darker by being treated with smoke. — ADJ

smoked 'salmon. Smoked salmon is the flesh of a salmon which is smoked and eaten raw. — N-UNCOUNT

smoke-filled 'room, smoke-filled rooms. If you talk about a decision being made in a **smoke-filled room**, you mean that it is made by a small group of people in a private meeting, rather than in a more democratic or open way; used showing disapproval. *The danger is that the professionals in smoke-filled rooms will impose an over-centralised European Union.* — N-COUNT / PRAGMATICS

smoke·less /ˈsməʊkləs/. **Smokeless** fuel burns without producing smoke. — ADJ

smoke·screen /ˈsməʊkskriːn/ **smokescreens;** also spelled **smoke screen.** If something that you do or say is a **smokescreen**, it is intended to hide the truth about your activities or intentions. *He was accused of putting up a smokescreen to hide poor standards in city schools.* — N-COUNT

'smoke signal, smoke signals. If someone such as a politician or businessman sends out **smoke signals**, they give an indication of their views and intentions. — N-COUNT

smoke·stack /ˈsməʊkstæk/ **smokestacks.** A **smokestack** is a very tall chimney that carries smoke away from a factory. — N-COUNT

,smoking 'gun, smoking guns. A **smoking gun** is a piece of evidence that proves that someone is responsible for something or that something is true. — N-COUNT / AMERICAN, JOURNALISM

smoky /ˈsməʊki/ **smokier, smokiest;** also spelled **smokey. 1** A place that is **smoky** has a lot of smoke in the air. **2** You can use **smoky** to describe something that looks like smoke, for example because it is slightly blue or grey or because it appears cloudy. **3** Something that has a **smoky** flavour tastes as if it has been smoked. — ADJ-GRADED / ADJ: ADJ n, ADJ colour / ADJ-GRADED

smol·der /ˈsməʊldə/. See **smoulder**.

smooch /smuːtʃ/ **smooches, smooching, smooched.** If two people **smooch**, they kiss and hold each other closely. *I smooched with him on the dance floor.* ▶ Also a noun. *...a good smooch.* — V-RECIP: pl-n V / V with n / N-SING

smooth /smuːð/ **smoother, smoothest; smooths, smoothing, smoothed. 1** A **smooth** surface has no roughness, lumps, or holes. *The flagstones beneath their feet were smooth by centuries of use.* ♦ **smooth·ness** *...the smoothness of her skin.* **2** A **smooth** liquid or mixture has been mixed well so that it has no lumps. *Blend the cornflour to a smooth paste with a little cold water.* **3** Something that is **smooth** happens or continues evenly and steadily with no sudden changes or breaks. *...the smooth curve of the trunk.* ♦ **smooth·ly** *Make sure that you execute all movements smoothly and without jerking.* ♦ **smoothness** *Sayer was delighted with the smoothness of the engine.* **4** A **smooth** ride, flight, or sea crossing is comfortable because there are no bumps or jolts. ♦ **smoothness** *The smoothness of the flight was memorable.* **5** You use **smooth** to describe something that is going well and is free of problems or trouble. *Political hopes for a swift and smooth transition to democracy have been dashed.* ♦ **smoothly** *So far, talks at GM have gone smoothly.* ♦ **smoothness** *The Albanians deserve a bit of credit, frankly, for the smoothness of the election.* **6** If you describe a drink such as wine, whisky, or coffee as **smooth**, you mean that it is not bitter and is pleasant to drink. **7** If you describe a man as **smooth**, you mean that he is extremely smart, confident, and polite, often in a way that you find rather unpleasant. **8** If you **smooth** something, you move your hands over its surface to make it smooth and flat. *She stood up and smoothed down her frock.* **9** If you **smooth** something somewhere, you use your hands to spread it there. *She smoothed the lotion across his shoulder blades.* **10** If you **smooth the path** or **smooth the way** towards something, you make it easier or more likely to happen. *Their talks were aimed at smoothing the path towards a treaty to limit long-range weapons.* — ADJ-GRADED / N-UNCOUNT / ADJ-GRADED / ADJ-GRADED / ADV-GRADED: ADV with v / N-UNCOUNT / ADJ-GRADED / N-UNCOUNT / ADJ-GRADED / ADV-GRADED: ADV with v / N-UNCOUNT / ADJ-GRADED / ADJ-GRADED / VERB: V n / V n with adv / VERB / V n prep / Also V n with adv / PHRASE

smooth out. If you **smooth out** a problem or difficulty, you solve it, especially by talking to the people concerned. *Baker was smoothing out differences with European allies.* — PHRASAL VB / V P noun / Also V n P

smooth over. If you **smooth over** a problem or difficulty, you make it less serious and easier to deal with, especially by talking to the people concerned. *...an attempt to smooth over the violent splits that have occurred.* — PHRASAL VB / V n P / V P noun

smoothie /ˈsmuːði/ **smoothies.** If you describe a man as a **smoothie**, you mean that he is extremely smart, confident, and polite, often in a way that you find rather unpleasant. — N-COUNT

,**smooth-'talking.** A **smooth-talking** man talks `ADJ`
very confidently and persuasively, but may not be
sincere or honest.

smor·gas·bord /'smɔːgəsbɔːd/. A **smorgasbord** of `N-SING`
things is a number of different things that are com- `JOURNALISM`
bined together as a whole. *...Further Education
colleges with a smorgasbord of academic and
vocational courses.*

smote /sməʊt/. **Smote** is the past tense of **smite.**

smoth·er /'smʌðə/ **smothers, smothering,** ◆◇◇◇◇
smothered. 1 If you **smother** a fire, you cover it `VERB: V n`
with something in order to put it out. **2** To **smother** `VERB: V n`
someone means to kill them by covering their face
with something so that they cannot breathe.
3 Things that **smother** something cover it com- `VERB`
pletely. *Once the shrubs begin to smother the little* `V n`
plants, we have to move them. ♦ **smoth·ered** `ADJ:`
...macaroni smothered in cheese. `v-link ADJ`
4 If you **smother** someone, you show your love for `VERB: V n`
them too much and protect them too much. **5** If you `VERB: V n`
smother an emotion or a reaction, you control it so `V-ed`
that people do not notice it. *...smothered giggles.* **6** If `VERB:`
an activity or process **is smothered**, it is prevented `be V-ed`
from continuing or developing. *The debts of both Po-* `V n`
*land and Hungary are beginning to smother the re-
form process.*

smoul·der /'sməʊldə/ **smoulders, smoulder-** ◆◇◇◇◇
ing, smouldered; spelled **smolder** in American
English. **1** If something **smoulders**, it burns slowly, `VERB: V`
producing smoke but not flames. *Whole blocks had* `V-ing`
been turned into smouldering rubble. **2** If a feeling `VERB`
such as anger or hatred **smoulders** inside you, you `V`
continue to feel it but rarely show it. *That's a lot of* `Also V-ing`
people smouldering with resentment. **3** If you say `VERB`
that someone **smoulders**, you mean that they are `V prep`
sexually attractive, usually in a mysterious or very `Also V-ing`
intense way. *Melanie Griffith seems to smoulder
with sexuality.*

smudge /smʌdʒ/ **smudges, smudging,** ◆◇◇◇◇
smudged. 1 A **smudge** is a dirty mark. **2** If you `N-COUNT`
smudge something, you make it dirty or messy by `VERB: V n`
touching it. *Her lipstick was smudged.* `V-ed`

smug /smʌg/. If you say that someone is **smug,** ◆◇◇◇◇
you are criticizing the fact they seem very pleased `ADJ-GRADED`
with how good, clever, or fortunate they are. `PRAGMATICS`
♦ **smug·ly** *The Major smiled smugly and sat down.* `ADV-GRADED`
♦ **smug·ness** *...a trace of smugness in his voice.* `N-UNCOUNT`

smug·gle /'smʌgəl/ **smuggles, smuggling,** ◆◇◇◇◇
smuggled. If someone **smuggles** things or people `VERB:`
into a place or out of it, they take them there illegal- `V n prep`
ly or secretly. *My message is 'If you try to smuggle* `V n`
drugs you are stupid'... Had it really been impossible `V n with adv`
to find someone who could smuggle out a letter?
♦ **smug·gler, smugglers** *...drug smugglers.* `N-COUNT`
♦ **smug·gling** *An air hostess was arrested and* `N-UNCOUNT`
charged with drug smuggling.

smut /smʌt/. If you refer to words or pictures that `N-UNCOUNT`
are related to nudity or sex as **smut**, you disapprove `PRAGMATICS`
of them because you think that they have been said
or published just to shock or excite people, rather
than for serious reasons.

smut·ty /'smʌti/ **smuttier, smuttiest.** If you de- `ADJ-GRADED`
scribe something such as a joke, book, or film as `PRAGMATICS`
smutty, you disapprove of it because it refers to sex
or features nudity in a way that you think is intended just to shock or excite people.

snack /snæk/ **snacks, snacking, snacked. 1** A ◆◆◇◇◇
snack is a simple meal that is quick to cook and to `N-COUNT`
eat. **2** A **snack** is something such as a chocolate bar `N-COUNT`
that you eat between meals. *Do you eat sweets,
cakes or sugary snacks?* **3** If you **snack**, you eat `VERB: V`
snacks between meals. *Instead of snacking on crisps* `V on n`
and chocolate, nibble on celery or carrot.

'**snack bar, snack bars.** A **snack bar** is a place `N-COUNT`
where you can buy and eat simple meals such as
sandwiches, and also drinks.

snaf·fle /'snæfəl/ **snaffles, snaffling, snaffled.** If `VERB: V n`
you **snaffle** something, you quickly take it for `BRITISH,`
yourself. `INFORMAL`

snag /snæg/ **snags, snagging, snagged. 1** A ◆◇◇◇◇
snag is a small problem or disadvantage. *A police* `N-COUNT`
*clampdown on car thieves hit a snag when villains
stole one of their cars.* **2** If you **snag** part of your `V-ERG:`
clothing on a sharp or rough object, it gets caught `V n on n`
on the object and tears. *Brambles snagged his suit...* `V n`
Local fishermen complained that their nets kept `V on n`
snagging on some underwater objects.

snail /sneɪl/ **snails. 1** A **snail** is a small animal ◆◇◇◇◇
with a long, soft, slimy body and a spiral-shaped `N-COUNT`
shell. Snails move very slowly. **2** If you say that `PHRASE`
someone does something **at a snail's pace**, you are `PRAGMATICS`
emphasizing that they are doing it very slowly,
usually when you think it would be better if they
did it much more quickly.

snake /sneɪk/ **snakes, snaking, snaked. 1** A ◆◆◇◇◇
snake is a long, thin reptile without legs. **2** Some- `N-COUNT`
thing that **snakes** in a particular direction goes in `VERB`
that direction in a line with a lot of bends. *The road* `V prep/adv`
snaked through forested mountains... The three-mile `V way prep/`
procession snaked its way through the richest streets `adv`
of the capital. `LITERARY`

snake·bite /'sneɪkbaɪt/ **snakebites;** also spelled `N-VAR`
snake bite. A **snakebite** is the bite of a snake, especially a poisonous one.

'**snake charmer, snake charmers;** also spelled `N-COUNT`
snake-charmers. A **snake charmer** is a person who
entertains people by controlling the behaviour of a
snake, for example by playing music and causing
the snake to rise out of a basket and drop back in
again.

,**snakes and 'ladders.** **Snakes and ladders** is a `N-UNCOUNT`
British children's game played with a board and
dice.

snap /snæp/ **snaps, snapping, snapped. 1** If ◆◆◆◇◇
something **snaps**, it breaks suddenly, usually with a `V-ERG: V`
sharp cracking noise. *The brake pedal had just* `V adv/prep`
snapped off... She gripped the pipe with both hands, `V n adv/prep`
trying to snap it in half. ▶ Also a noun. *Every min-* `Also V n`
ute or so I could hear a snap, a crack and a crash as `N-SING`
another tree went down. **2** If something **snaps** into a `V-ERG`
particular position, it moves quickly into that posi- `V n adv/prep`
tion, with a sharp sound. *He snapped the cap on his* `V adv`
ballpoint... The bag snapped open. ▶ Also a noun. `N-SING`
He shut the book with a snap and stood up. **3** If you `VERB: V n`
snap your fingers, you make a sharp sound by mov-
ing your middle finger quickly across your thumb,
for example in order to accompany music or to order someone to do something. ▶ Also a noun. *I* `N-SING:`
could obtain with the snap of my fingers anything I `N of n`
chose.
4 If someone **snaps**, if their patience **snaps**, or if `VERB`
something **snaps** inside them, they suddenly stop be- `V`
ing calm and become very angry because the situation has become too tense or too difficult for them. *He
finally snapped when she prevented their children
from visiting him one weekend... For the first and only
time Grant's self-control snapped... Then something
seemed to snap in me. I couldn't endure any more.* **5** If `VERB:`
someone **snaps** at you, they speak to you in a sharp, `V at n`
unfriendly way. *'Of course I don't know her,' Roger* `V with quote`
snapped. **6** If an animal such as a dog **snaps** at you, it `VERB:`
opens and shuts its jaws quickly near you, as if it were `V at n`
going to bite you. *The poodle yapped and snapped.* `V`
7 A **snap** decision or action is one that is taken sud- `ADJ: ADJ n`
denly, without careful thought. *It's important
not to make snap judgments. ...a snap election.*
8 If you **snap** someone or something, you take a `VERB: V n`
photograph of them. ▶ Also a noun. *...holiday snaps.* `INFORMAL`
9 Snap is a simple British card game in which the `N-COUNT`
players take turns to put cards down on a pile, and try `N-UNCOUNT`
to be the first to shout 'snap' when two cards with the
same number or picture are put down. **10** A **snap** is `N-COUNT`
the same as a **snap fastener.** **11** See also **cold snap.** `AMERICAN`

snap out of. If someone who is depressed **snaps out** `PHRASAL VB`
of it, they suddenly become more cheerful, especially `V PP it`
by making an effort.

snap up. If you **snap** something **up**, you buy it `PHRASAL VB`
quickly because it is a bargain or because it is just `V n P`
`V P noun`

what you want. *One eagle-eyed collector snapped up a pair of Schiaparelli earrings for just £6.*

snap·dragon /'snæpdrægən/ **snapdragons.** A snapdragon is a common garden plant with small colourful flowers that can open and shut like a mouth. `N-COUNT`

'snap fastener, snap fasteners. A snap fastener is a small metal fastener for clothes, made up of two parts which can be pressed together. The British term is **press stud** or **popper**. `N-COUNT` `AMERICAN`

snap·per /'snæpə/ **snappers;** snapper can also be used as the plural form. A **snapper** is a fish that has sharp teeth and lives in warm seas. `N-COUNT`

snap·py /'snæpi/ **snappier, snappiest. 1** If someone has a **snappy** style of speaking, they speak in a quick, clever, concise, and often funny way. **2** If someone is a **snappy** dresser or if they wear **snappy** clothes, they wear smart, stylish clothes. ♦ **snap·pi·ly** *...his usual band of snappily dressed friends.* `◆◇◇◇◇` `ADJ-GRADED` `ADJ-GRADED: ADJ n` `ADV-GRADED`

snap·shot /'snæpʃɒt/ **snapshots. 1** A **snapshot** is a photograph that is taken quickly and casually. **2** If something provides you with a **snapshot** of a place or situation, it gives you a brief idea of what that place or situation is like. *The interviews present a remarkable snapshot of Britain in these dark days of recession.* `N-COUNT` `N-COUNT`

snare /sneə/ **snares, snaring, snared. 1** A **snare** is a trap for catching birds or small animals. It consists of a loop of wire or rope which pulls tight around the animal. **2** If someone **snares** an animal, they catch it using a snare. **3** If someone **is snared**, they are caught in a trap. *A motor-cyclist was seriously injured when she was snared by a rope stretched across the road.* **4** If someone **snares** something, they get it by using cleverness and cunning. *Most of all I want to snare a husband.* `◆◇◇◇◇` `N-COUNT` `VERB: V n` `VB: usu passive beV-ed Also V n VERB V n`

'snare drum, snare drums. A **snare drum** is a small cylindrical drum. It has springs stretched across the lower of its two surfaces which allow it to make a continuous sound. Snare drums are usually played with wooden sticks. `N-COUNT`

snarl /snɑːl/ **snarls, snarling, snarled. 1** When an animal **snarls**, it makes a fierce, rough sound in its throat while showing its teeth. *The dogs snarled at the intruders.* ▶ Also a noun. *With a snarl, the second dog made a dive for his heel.* **2** If you **snarl** something, you say it in a fierce, angry way. *'Let go of me,' he snarled.* ▶ Also a noun. *His lips were drawn back in a furious snarl.* **3** A **snarl** is a tangled or disorganized mass of things. *...the snarl of logs and branches where she had gotten entangled.* `◆◇◇◇◇` `VERB: V V at n` `N-COUNT` `V with quote Also V at n N-COUNT N-COUNT`

snatch /snætʃ/ **snatches, snatching, snatched. 1** If you **snatch** something or snatch at something, you take it or pull it away quickly. *Mick snatched the cards from Archie's hand... He snatched up the telephone.* **2** If something **is snatched** from you, it is stolen, usually using force. If a person **is snatched**, they are taken away by force. ♦ **snatch·er, snatchers** *Wealthy tourists are tempting targets for bag snatchers.* **3** If you **snatch** an opportunity, you take it quickly. If you **snatch** something to eat or a rest, you have it quickly in between doing other things. *I snatched a glance at the mirror... You can even snatch a few hours off... He was going out for a run, then snatching a piece of toast and a cup of coffee.* **4** If you **snatch** victory in a competition, you defeat your opponent by a small amount or just before the end of the contest. **5** A **snatch** of a conversation or a song is a very small piece of it. `◆◆◇◇◇` `VERB: V at n V n prep V n prep` `VB: usu passive, beV-ed` `N-COUNT: n N VERB V n` `VERB: V n` `N-COUNT`

snaz·zy /'snæzi/ **snazzier, snazziest.** Something that is **snazzy** is stylish and attractive, often in a rather bright or noticeable way. `ADJ-GRADED` `INFORMAL`

sneak /sniːk/ **sneaks, sneaking, sneaked;** American English sometimes uses the form **snuck** for the past tense and past participle. **1** If you **sneak** somewhere, you go there very quietly on foot, trying to avoid being seen or heard. *Sometimes he would sneak out of his house late at night to be with me.* **2** If you **sneak** something somewhere, you take it there secretly. *He smuggled papers out each day,* `◆◆◇◇◇` `VERB V adv/prep` `VERB V n prep/adv`

photocopied them, and snuck them back. **3** If you **sneak** a look at someone or something, you secretly have a quick look at them. **4** See also **sneaking**. `VERB: V n`

sneak up on. If someone **sneaks up on** you, they try to approach you without being seen or heard, perhaps to surprise you or do you harm. `PHRASAL VB` `V P P n`

sneak·er /'sniːkə/ **sneakers.** Sneakers are casual shoes with rubber soles. The usual British word is **trainers**. `◆◇◇◇◇` `N-COUNT` `AMERICAN`

sneak·ing /'sniːkɪŋ/. A **sneaking** feeling is a slight or vague feeling, especially one that you are unwilling to accept. *I have a sneaking suspicion that they are going to succeed.* `ADJ: ADJ n`

'sneak 'preview, sneak previews. A **sneak preview** of something is an unofficial opportunity to have a look at it before it is officially published or shown to the public. `N-COUNT`

sneaky /'sniːki/ **sneakier, sneakiest.** If you describe someone as **sneaky**, you disapprove of them because they do things secretly rather than openly. `ADJ-GRADED` `PRAGMATICS` `INFORMAL`

sneer /snɪə/ **sneers, sneering, sneered.** If you **sneer** at someone or something, you express your contempt for them by the expression on your face or by what you say. *'Hypocrite,' he sneered... Although some may sneer, working as a secretary is for many the fastest route to career success.* ▶ Also a noun. *...a contemptuous sneer.* `◆◇◇◇◇` `VERB: V n` `V with quote` `Also V that` `N-COUNT`

sneer·ing·ly /'snɪərɪŋli/. If someone refers **sneeringly** to someone or something, they refer to them in a contemptuous way. `ADV-GRADED` `WRITTEN`

sneeze /sniːz/ **sneezes, sneezing, sneezed. 1** When you **sneeze**, you suddenly and involuntarily take in your breath and then blow it down your nose noisily. People sneeze when they have a cold, or if something irritates their nose. *See your doctor now to beat summer sneezing.* ▶ Also a noun. *Coughs and sneezes spread infections.* **2** If you say that something is **not to be sneezed at**, you mean that it is worth having. `◆◇◇◇◇` `VERB: V` `V-ing` `N-COUNT` `PHRASE` `INFORMAL`

snick·er /'snɪkə/ **snickers, snickering, snickered.** If you **snicker**, you laugh quietly and disrespectfully, for example at something rude or at someone's misfortune. *We all snickered at Mrs. Swenson.* ▶ Also a noun. *...a chorus of jeers and snickers.* `VERB: V` `V at n` `N-COUNT`

snide /snaɪd/. A **snide** comment or remark is one which criticizes someone nastily, often in an indirect, sarcastic way. `ADJ-GRADED`

sniff /snɪf/ **sniffs, sniffing, sniffed. 1** When you **sniff**, you breathe in air through your nose hard enough to make a sound, for example when you are trying not to cry, or in order to show disapproval or scorn. *He sniffed back the tears.* ▶ Also a noun. *At last the sobs ceased, to be replaced by sniffs.* **2** If you **sniff** something, you smell it by sniffing. *She sniffed at it suspiciously.* **3** You can use **sniff** to indicate that someone says something disapproving or scornful. *'Tourists!' she sniffed.* **4** If you say that something is **not to be sniffed at**, you mean you think it is very good or worth having. **5** If someone **sniffs** a substance such as glue, they deliberately breathe in the substance or its fumes as a drug. **6** If you get a **sniff** of something, you learn or guess that it might be happening or might be near. *Then, at the first sniff of danger, he was back at his post.* `◆◆◇◇◇` `VERB: V` `V n with adv` `N-COUNT` `VERB: V n` `V at n` `VERB V with quote` `PHRASE` `VERB: V n` `N-SING` `INFORMAL`

sniff around or **sniff round. 1** If someone is **sniffing around** or **sniffing round**, they are trying to find out information about someone or something, especially information that someone else does not want known. *They might have sent a couple of plain-clothes men to sniff round his apartment.* **2** If a person or organization is **sniffing around** someone or **sniffing round** them, they are trying to get them, for example as a lover or employee. `PHRASAL VB` `V P` `V P n` `INFORMAL` `V P n,` `no passive` `INFORMAL`

sniff out. 1 If you **sniff out** something, you discover it after some searching. *...journalists who are trained to sniff out sensation or scandal.* **2** When a dog used by a group such as the police **sniffs out** hidden `PHRASAL VB` `V P noun` `Also V n P` `INFORMAL`

explosives or drugs, it finds them using its sense of smell. ...*a police dog, trained to sniff out explosives.* `V P noun Also V n P`

sniff round. See **sniff around.** `PHRASAL VB`

'sniffer dog, sniffer dogs. A **sniffer dog** is a dog used by the police or army to find explosives or drugs by their smell. `N-COUNT`

snif·fle /'snɪfəl/ **sniffles, sniffling, sniffled. 1** If you **sniffle**, you keep sniffing, usually because you are crying or have a cold. **2** A **sniffle** is a slight cold. You can also say that someone has **the sniffles.** `VERB: V` `N-COUNT`

snif·fy /'snɪfi/ **sniffier, sniffiest.** Someone who is **sniffy** has a scornful and contemptuous attitude towards something. `ADJ-GRADED INFORMAL`

snif·ter /'snɪftə/ **snifters. 1** A **snifter** is a small amount of an alcoholic drink. **2** A **snifter** is a bowl-shaped glass used for drinking brandy. `N-COUNT INFORMAL` `N-COUNT AMERICAN`

snig·ger /'snɪɡə/ **sniggers, sniggering, sniggered.** If someone **sniggers**, they laugh quietly and disrespectfully, for example at something rude. *The tourists snigger at the locals' outdated ways and dress... 'We know what that means,' Robert sniggered.* ► Also a noun. ...*trying to suppress a snigger.* `◆◇◇◇◇` `VERB: V V atn V-ing V with quote Also V adv to n` `N-COUNT`

snip /snɪp/ **snips, snipping, snipped. 1** If you **snip** something, or if you **snip at** or **through** something, you cut it using scissors or shears in a single quick action. *We have begun to snip away at the piece of paper.* **2** If you say that something is **a snip** you mean that it is very good value. *The beautifully made briefcase is a snip at £74.25.* `◆◇◇◇◇` `VERB: V n V adv/prep` `N-SING: a N INFORMAL, BRITISH`

snipe /snaɪp/ **snipes, sniping, sniped; snipe** is both the singular and the plural form of the noun. **1** If someone **snipes** at you, they criticize you. *This leaves him vulnerable to sniping from within his own party.* **2** To **snipe** at someone means to shoot at them from a hidden position. ...*sniping attacks.* **3** A **snipe** is a type of bird with a very long beak which normally lives in marshy areas. `◆◇◇◇◇` `VERB: V Also V V-ing` `VERB: V V-ing` `N-COUNT`

snip·er /'snaɪpə/ **snipers.** A **sniper** is someone who shoots at people from a hidden position. `◆◇◇◇◇` `N-COUNT`

snip·pet /'snɪpɪt/ **snippets.** A **snippet** of something is a small piece of it. ...*snippets of popular classical music.* `◆◇◇◇◇` `N-COUNT`

snitch /snɪtʃ/ **snitches, snitching, snitched. 1** A **snitch** is a person who tells someone in authority that another person has done something naughty or wrong. **2** If you **snitch** something, you steal it quickly and quietly. `N-COUNT INFORMAL` `VERB: V n INFORMAL`

sniv·el /'snɪvəl/ **snivels, snivelling, snivelled;** spelled **sniveling, sniveled** in American English. If someone **is snivelling**, they are crying, sniffing, and whining in a way that irritates you. ► Also a noun. *Carol managed a few proper snivels for the sake of appearance.* `VERB: V` `N-COUNT`

snob /snɒb/ **snobs. 1** If you call someone a **snob**, you disapprove of them because they admire upper-class people and despise lower-class people. **2** If you call someone a **snob**, you disapprove of them because they behave as if they are superior to other people because of their intelligence or taste. *She was an intellectual snob.* `◆◇◇◇◇` `N-COUNT PRAGMATICS` `N-COUNT PRAGMATICS`

snob·bery /'snɒbəri/. **Snobbery** is the attitude of a snob. `◆◇◇◇◇` `N-UNCOUNT`

snob·bish /'snɒbɪʃ/. If you describe someone as **snobbish**, you disapprove of them because they are excessively proud of their social status, intelligence, or taste. *They had a snobbish dislike for their intellectual and social inferiors.* ♦ **snob·bish·ness** ...*his snobbishness and loathing of democracy.* `ADJ-GRADED PRAGMATICS` `N-UNCOUNT`

snob·by /'snɒbi/ **snobbier, snobbiest.** Snobby means the same as snobbish. `ADJ-GRADED`

snog /snɒɡ/ **snogs, snogging, snogged.** If one person **snogs** another, they embrace that person and kiss them for a period of time. *A couple were snogging under a bridge.* ► Also a noun. *They went for a quick snog behind the bike sheds.* `VERB: V-RECIP: V n pl-n V INFORMAL, BRITISH` `N-COUNT`

snook /snuːk/. If you **cock a snook** at someone in authority or at an organization, you do something that they cannot punish you for, but which insults them or expresses your contempt. `PHRASE BRITISH`

snook·er /'snuːkə, AM 'snʊk-/ **snookers, snookering, snookered. 1** Snooker is a game involving balls on a large table. The players use a long stick to hit a white ball, and score points by knocking coloured balls into the pockets at the sides of the table. **2** If you **are snookered** by something, it is difficult or impossible for you to take action or do what you want to do. *The President has been snookered on this issue.* `◆◇◇◇◇` `N-UNCOUNT` `VB: usu passive be V-ed INFORMAL, BRITISH`

snoop /snuːp/ **snoops, snooping, snooped. 1** If someone **snoops** around a place, they secretly look around it in order to find out things. *Ricardo was the one she'd seen snooping around Kim's hotel room.* ► Also a noun. *The second house that Grossman had a snoop around contained 'strong simple furniture'.* ♦ **snoop·er, snoopers** ...*journalistic snoopers.* **2** If someone **snoops on** a person, they watch them secretly in order to find out things about their life. ♦ **snooper** *You bloody snooper! All the time you've been talking to me you've been prying into my family.* **3** A **snoop** is the same as a snooper. `V adv/prep Also V` `N-COUNT` `N-COUNT` `VERB: V on n` `N-COUNT` `N-COUNT`

snooty /'snuːti/ **snootier, snootiest.** If you say that someone is **snooty**, you disapprove of them because they behave as if they are superior to other people. ...*snooty intellectuals.* `ADJ-GRADED PRAGMATICS INFORMAL`

snooze /snuːz/ **snoozes, snoozing, snoozed.** If you **snooze**, you sleep lightly for a short period of time. ► Also a noun. *Dad is having a snooze.* `VERB: V INFORMAL` `N-COUNT`

snore /snɔː/ **snores, snoring, snored.** When someone who is asleep **snores**, they make a loud noise each time they breathe. ► Also a noun. *Uncle Arthur, after a loud snore, woke suddenly.* `◆◇◇◇◇` `VERB: V` `N-COUNT`

snor·kel /'snɔːkəl/ **snorkels, snorkelling, snorkelled;** spelled **snorkeling, snorkeled** in American English. **1** A **snorkel** is a tube through which a person swimming just under the surface of the sea can breathe. **2** When someone **snorkels** they swim under water using a snorkel. `N-COUNT` `VERB: V`

snort /snɔːt/ **snorts, snorting, snorted. 1** When people or animals **snort**, they breathe air noisily out through their noses. People sometimes snort in order to express disapproval or amusement. *Harrell snorted with laughter.* ► Also a noun. ...*snorts of laughter.* **2** If someone **snorts** something, they say it in a way that shows contempt. *'Reports,' he snorted. 'Anyone can write reports.'* **3** To **snort** a drug such as cocaine means to breathe it in quickly through one nostril. `◆◇◇◇◇` `VERB: V V with n` `N-COUNT` `VERB V with quote` `VERB: V n`

snot /snɒt/. **Snot** is the slimy substance that is produced inside your nose; a word which some people find offensive. `N-UNCOUNT INFORMAL`

snot·ty /'snɒti/. **1** Something that is **snotty** is covered in snot; a use which some people find offensive. *He suffered from a snotty nose, runny eyes and a slight cough.* **2** If you describe someone as **snotty**, you disapprove of them because they have a very proud and superior attitude to other people. ...*snotty college kids.* `ADJ: ADJ n INFORMAL` `ADJ-GRADED PRAGMATICS INFORMAL`

snout /snaʊt/ **snouts. 1** The **snout** of an animal such as a pig is its long nose. **2** Writers sometimes refer to the front of a car or the barrel of a gun as its **snout.** *The snout of the Mercedes poked through the gates.* `N-COUNT` `N-COUNT`

snow /snəʊ/ **snows, snowing, snowed. 1** Snow consists of a lot of soft white bits of frozen water that fall from the sky in cold weather. ...*six inches of snow blocked roads.* **2** You can refer to a great deal of snow in an area as the **snows.** ...*the first snows of winter.* **3** When it **snows**, snow falls from the sky. **4** See also **snowed in, snowed under.** `◆◆◇◇` `N-UNCOUNT` `N-PLURAL` `VERB: it V`

snow·ball /'snəʊbɔːl/ **snowballs, snowballing, snowballed. 1** A **snowball** is a ball of snow. Children often throw snowballs at each other. **2** If something such as a project or campaign **snowballs**, it rapidly increases and grows. *From those early days the business has snowballed.* `◆◇◇◇◇` `N-COUNT` `VERB V`

snow·bound /'snəʊbaʊnd/. If people or vehicles are **snowbound**, they cannot go anywhere because of heavy snow. `ADJ`

S

'snow-capped. A **snow-capped** mountain is cov- `ADJ: ADJ n`
ered with snow at the top. `LITERARY`

snow·drift /'snəʊdrɪft/ **snowdrifts.** A **snowdrift** is `N-COUNT`
a deep pile of snow formed by the wind.

snow·drop /'snəʊdrɒp/ **snowdrops.** A **snowdrop** `N-COUNT`
is a small white flower which appears in the early
spring.

,snowed 'in. If you are **snowed in**, you cannot go `ADJ`
anywhere because of heavy snow.

,snowed 'under. If you say that you are **snowed** `ADJ-GRADED:`
under, you are emphasizing that you have a lot of `v-link ADJ`
work or other things to deal with. *Ed was snowed* `INFORMAL`
under with fan mail.

snow·fall /'snəʊfɔːl/ **snowfalls. 1** The **snowfall** in `N-UNCOUNT`
an area or country is the amount of snow that falls
there during a particular period. **2** A **snowfall** is a `N-COUNT`
fall of snow.

snow·field /'snəʊfiːld/ **snowfields.** A **snowfield** is `N-COUNT`
a large area which is always covered in snow.

snow·flake /'snəʊfleɪk/ **snowflakes.** A **snowflake** `N-COUNT`
is one of the soft white bits of frozen water that fall
as snow.

snow·man /'snəʊmæn/ **snowmen.** A **snowman** is `N-COUNT`
a large shape which is made out of snow and is supposed to look like a person.

snow·mobile /'snəʊməbiːl/ **snowmobiles.** A `N-COUNT`
snowmobile is a small vehicle built to move across
snow and ice.

snow·plough /'snəʊplaʊ/ **snowploughs;** spelled `N-COUNT`
snowplow in American English. A **snowplough** is a
vehicle which is used to push snow off roads or railway lines.

snow·storm /'snəʊstɔːm/ **snowstorms.** A **snow-** `N-COUNT`
storm is a very heavy fall of snow, usually when
there is also a strong wind blowing at the same
time.

,snow-'white. Something that is **snow-white** is of ◆◇◇◇◇
a brilliant white colour. `ADJ`

snowy /'snəʊi/ **snowier, snowiest.** A **snowy** ◆◇◇◇◇
place is covered in snow. A **snowy** day is a day `ADJ-GRADED`
when a lot of snow has fallen.

Snr. Snr is the written abbreviation for 'Senior'. It is `BRITISH`
used after someone's name to distinguish them
from a younger member of their family who has the
same name. ...*Robert Trent Jones, Snr.*

snub /snʌb/ **snubs, snubbing, snubbed. 1** If ◆◇◇◇◇
you **snub** someone, you deliberately insult them by `VERB`
ignoring them or by behaving or speaking rudely to- `V n`
wards them. *He snubbed her in public.* ► Also a `N-COUNT`
noun. *Ryan took it as a snub.* **2** Someone who has a `ADJ: ADJ n`
snub nose has a short nose which points slightly
upwards.

snuck /snʌk/. **Snuck** is a past tense and past parti- `AMERICAN`
ciple of **sneak**.

snuff /snʌf/ **snuffs, snuffing, snuffed. 1** Snuff ◆◇◇◇◇
is powdered tobacco which some people take by `N-UNCOUNT`
sniffing it up their nose. **2** If someone **snuffs it**, they `VERB`
die. *Perhaps he thought he was about to snuff it.* `V it`
`INFORMAL`

snuff out. 1 If someone or something **snuffs out** `PHRASAL VB`
something such as a rebellion or disagreement, they `V P noun`
stop it, usually in a forceful or sudden way. *Every time* `V n P`
a new flicker of resistance appeared, the government
snuffed it out. **2** If you **snuff out** a small flame, you `V P noun`
stop it burning, usually by using your fingers or by `Also V n P`
covering it with something for a few seconds. *Tenzin*
snuffed out the candle.

snuf·fle /'snʌfəl/ **snuffles, snuffling, snuffled.** If `VERB: V`
people or animals **snuffle**, they make sniffing
noises, for example because they have a cold or are
trying not to cry.

snug /snʌg/ **snugger, snuggest. 1** If you feel ◆◇◇◇◇
snug or are in a **snug** place, you are very warm and `ADJ-GRADED`
comfortable, especially when you are protected
from cold weather. ...*a snug log cabin.* ♦ **snug·ly** `ADV:`
Wrap your baby snugly in a shawl or blanket. `ADV with v`
2 Something such as a piece of clothing that is **snug** `ADJ-GRADED`
fits very closely or tightly. ♦ **snugly** *His jeans fit* `ADV-GRADED:`
snugly. `ADV with v`

snug·gle /'snʌgəl/ **snuggles, snuggling, snug-** `VERB`
gled. If you **snuggle** somewhere, you settle yourself `V adv/prep`

into a warm, comfortable position, especially by
moving closer to another person. *Jane snuggled up*
against his shoulder.

so /səʊ/. **1** You use **so** to refer back to something ◆◆◆◆◆
that has just been mentioned. *'Do you think that* `ADV:`
made much of a difference to the family?'—'I think `ADV after v`
so.'... Almost all young women who turn to prostitu-
tion do so as a means of survival. **2** You use **so** when `ADV:`
you are saying that something which has just been `ADV cl`
said about one person or thing is also true of another one. *They had a wonderful time and so did I.*
3 You use the structures **as...so** and **just as...so** `CONJ`
when you want to indicate that two events or situations are alike in some way. *Just as John has*
changed, so has his wife.
4 If you say that a state of affairs **is so**, you mean that it `ADV:`
is the way it has been described. *It is strange to think* `v-link ADV`
that he held strong views on many things, but it must
have been so. **5** You can use **so** with actions and ges- `ADV:`
tures to show someone how to do something, or to in- `ADV after v`
dicate the size, height, or length of something. *Clasp*
the chain like so.
6 You use **so** and **so that** to introduce the result of the `CONJ`
situation you have just mentioned. *I was an only*
child, and so had no experience of large families...
There was snow everywhere, so that the shape of things
was difficult to identify. **7** You use **so**, **so that**, and **so** `CONJ`
as to introduce the reason for doing the thing that you
have just mentioned. *Come to my suite so I can tell you*
all about this wonderful play I saw... I was beginning
to feel alarm, but kept it to myself so as not to worry our
two friends. **8** You can use **so** in stories and accounts `ADV:`
to introduce the next event in a series of events or to `ADV cl`
suggest a connection between two events. *He said*
he'd like to meet Sharon. So I said all right... And so
Christmas passed.
9 You can use **so** in conversations to introduce a new `ADV:`
topic, or to introduce a question or comment about `ADV cl`
something that has been said. *So how was your day?...*
So you're a runner, huh?. **10** You can use **so** in conver- `ADV:`
sations to show that you are accepting what someone `ADV cl`
has just said. *'It makes me feel, well, important.'—'And*
so you are.'... 'Why, this is nothing but common vegeta-
ble soup!'—'So it is, madam.'. **11** You say **'So?'** and **'So** `CONVENTION`
what?' to indicate that you think something that `INFORMAL`
someone has said is unimportant. *'My name's*
Bruno.'—'So?'... 'You take a chance on the weather if
you holiday in the UK.'—'So what?'.
12 You can also use **so** in front of adjectives and ad- `ADV:`
verbs to emphasize the quality that they are describ- `ADV adj/adv`
ing. *'I am so afraid,' Francis thought... What is so*
compromising about being an employee of the state?
13 You can use **so...that** and **so...as** to emphasize the `ADV`
degree of something by mentioning the result of consequence of it. *The tears were streaming so fast she*
could not see.
14 You use **and so on** or **and so forth** at the end of a `PHRASE`
list to indicate that there are other items that you
could also mention. *...health, education, tax and so*
on. **15** You use **so much** and **so many** when you are `PHRASE`
saying that there is a definite limit to something but
you are not saying what this limit is. *There is only so*
much time in the day for answering letters... Even the
greatest city can support only so many lawyers. **16** You `PHRASE`
use the structures **not...so much** and **not so**
much...as to say that something is one kind of thing
rather than another kind. *I did not really object to*
Will's behaviour so much as his personality... A good
birth depends not so much on who you are but where
you are and how much you know. **17** You use or **so** `PHRASE`
when you are giving an approximate amount. *They'll*
be here within the next fortnight or so.
18 ● **so much the better**: see **better**. ● **ever so**: see
ever. ● **so far so good**: see **far**. ● **so long**: see **long**.
● **so much for**: see **much**. ● **so much so**: see **much**.
● **every so often**: see **often**. ● **so there**: see **there**.

soak /səʊk/ **soaks, soaking, soaked. 1** If you ◆◆◇◇◇
soak something or leave it to **soak**, you put it into a `VERB: V n`
liquid and leave it there. *He turned off the water and* `V`
left the dishes to soak. **2** If a liquid **soaks** something `VERB: V n`

or if you **soak** something with a liquid, the liquid makes the thing very wet. *Soak the soil around each bush with at least 4 gallons of water.* ♦ **soaked** *We got soaked to the skin.* ♦ **soak·ing** *My face and raincoat were soaking wet.* **3** If a liquid **soaks** through something, it passes through it. **4** If someone **soaks**, they spend a long time in a hot bath, because they enjoy it. ▶ Also a noun. *I was having a long soak in the bath.*

> V n with n

> ADJ
> ADJ

> VERB:
> V prep/adv
> VERB: V

> N-COUNT

soak up. 1 If a soft or dry material **soaks up** a liquid, the liquid goes into the substance. *The cells will promptly start to soak up moisture.* **2** If you **soak up** the sun, you sit or lie in the sun, because you enjoy it. **3** If you **soak up** the atmosphere in a place that you are visiting, you observe or get involved in the way of life there, because you enjoy it or are interested in it. *Keaton comes here once or twice a year to soak up the atmosphere.* **4** If something **soaks up** something such as money or other resources, it uses a great deal of money or other resources. *Defence soaks up forty per cent of the budget.*

> PHRASAL VB
> V P noun
> Also V n P
> V P noun
> INFORMAL

> V P noun
> Also V n P
> INFORMAL

> V P noun
> Also V n P

-soaked /-səʊkt/. **1 -soaked** combines with nouns such as 'rain' and 'blood' to form adjectives which describe someone or something that is extremely wet or extremely damp because of the thing mentioned. *...a rain-soaked pitch. ...blood-soaked clothes.* **2 -soaked** combines with nouns such as 'sun' to form adjectives which describe places, times, or events that have a lot of the thing mentioned. *...a sun-soaked Caribbean island. ...the cash-soaked Eighties.*

> COMB

> COMB

'so-and-so, so-and-sos. 1 You use **so-and-so** instead of a word, expression, or name when you are talking generally rather than giving a real example of a particular thing. *If Mrs So-and-so was ill then Mrs So-and-so down the street would go and clean for her.* **2** People sometimes refer to another person as a **so-and-so** when they are annoyed with them or think that they are foolish. People often use **so-and-so** in order to avoid using a swear word. *...the wicked little so-and-so.*

> ◆◇◇◇
> PRON

> N-COUNT
> PRAGMATICS
> INFORMAL

soap /səʊp/ **soaps, soaping, soaped. 1** Soap is a substance that you use with water for washing yourself or sometimes for washing clothes. *...a bar of lavender soap. ...a large packet of soap powder.* **2** If you **soap** yourself, you rub soap on your body in order to wash yourself. **3** A **soap** is the same as a **soap opera**.

> ◆◆◇◇
> N-VAR

> VERB: V n
> N-COUNT
> INFORMAL

soap·box /'səʊpbɒks/ **soapboxes.** If you say that someone is on their **soapbox**, you mean that they are speaking or writing about something they feel passionate about. *We were interested in pushing forward certain issues and getting up on our soapbox about them.*

> N-COUNT

'soap opera, soap operas. A **soap opera** is a popular television drama serial about the daily lives and problems of a group of people.

> ◆◇◇◇
> N-COUNT

soapy /'səʊpi/ **soapier, soapiest.** Something that is **soapy** is full of soap or covered with soap. *...hot soapy water.*

> ADJ-GRADED

soar /sɔː/ **soars, soaring, soared. 1** If the amount, value, level, or volume of something **soars**, it quickly increases by a great deal. *Shares soared on the stock exchange... The temperature in the south will soar into the hundreds.* **2** If something such as a bird **soars** into the air, it goes quickly up into the air. *The two sheets of flame clashed, soaring hundreds of feet high.* **3** Trees or buildings that **soar** upwards are very tall. *The steeple soars skyward.* **4** If music **soars**, it rises greatly in volume or pitch. *The music soared to the rafters, carrying its listeners' hearts.* **5** If your spirits **soar**, you suddenly start to feel very happy.

> ◆◆◇◇
> VERB
> V
> V prep/adv
> JOURNALISM

> VERB:
> V prep/adv
> V n
> LITERARY
> VERB
> V prep/adv
> LITERARY
> VERB: V
> V prep
> LITERARY
> VERB: V
> LITERARY

soar·away /'sɔːrəweɪ/. If you describe something as a **soaraway** success, you mean that its success has suddenly increased.

> ADJ: ADJ n
> BRITISH,
> JOURNALISM

sob /sɒb/ **sobs, sobbing, sobbed.** When someone **sobs**, they cry in a noisy way, breathing in short breaths. *'Everything's my fault,' she sobbed.* ▶ Also a noun. *With a sob, she dropped the bag and went to*

> ◆◇◇◇
> VERB: V
> V with quote
> N-COUNT

sit beside him. ♦ **sob·bing** *The room was silent except for her sobbing.*

> N-UNCOUNT

so·ber /'səʊbə/ **sobers, sobering, sobered. 1** When you are **sober**, you are not drunk. **2** A **sober** person is serious and thoughtful. *We are now far more sober and realistic,' he said soberly.* **3** Sober colours and clothes are plain and rather dull. ♦ **soberly** *She saw Ellis, soberly dressed in a well-cut dark suit.* **4** See also **sobering**. ● **stone-cold sober**: see **stone-cold**.

> ♦♦◇◇
> ADJ-GRADED
> ADJ-GRADED

> ADV-GRADED
> ADV-GRADED: ADV with v

sober up. When someone **sobers up**, they become sober after being drunk. If someone or something **sobers** a person **up**, they make the person sober after he or she has been drunk. *...the idea that a cup of strong black coffee sobers you up.*

> PHRASAL VB
> ERG:
> V P
> V n P

so·ber·ing /'səʊbərɪŋ/. You say that something is a **sobering** thought or has a **sobering** effect when a situation seems serious and makes you become serious and thoughtful.

> ◆◇◇◇
> ADJ-GRADED

so·bri·ety /sə'braɪɪti/. **1** Sobriety is the state of being sober rather than drunk. **2** Sobriety is serious and thoughtful behaviour. *...the values society depends upon, such as honesty, sobriety and trust.*

> N-UNCOUNT
> FORMAL
> N-UNCOUNT
> FORMAL

so·bri·quet /'səʊbrɪkeɪ/ **sobriquets;** also spelled **soubriquet.** A **sobriquet** is a humorous nickname or description that is applied to someone or something. *In 1970, Lawton Chiles walked the length of Florida to win election to the US Senate, earning the sobriquet 'Walkin' Lawton'.*

> N-COUNT
> WRITTEN

'sob story, sob stories. You can describe what someone tells you about their own or someone else's difficulties as a **sob story** when you think that they have told you about it in order to get sympathy.

> N-COUNT
> PRAGMATICS

Soc. /sɒk/. **Soc.** is the written abbreviation for **Society**. *The Folio Soc., 202 Great Suffolk St, London.*

so-'called; also spelled **so called. 1** You use **so-called** to indicate that you think the following word or expression is incorrect or misleading. *...so-called environmentally-friendly products.* **2** You use **so-called** to indicate that something is generally referred to by the name that you are about to use. *She was one of the so-called Gang of Four.*

> ♦♦◇◇
> ADJ: ADJ n
> PRAGMATICS

> ADJ: ADJ n

soc·cer /'sɒkə/. **Soccer** is a game played by two teams of eleven players using a ball. Players kick the ball to each other and try to score goals by kicking the ball into a large net. In Europe and South America, this game is also referred to as **football**.

> ♦♦♦◇
> N-UNCOUNT

so·cia·ble /'səʊʃəbəl/. **Sociable** people are friendly and enjoy talking to other people. ♦ **so·cia·bil·ity** /,səʊʃə'bɪlɪti/. *Enthusiasm, adaptability, sociability, and good health are essential.*

> ◆◇◇◇
> ADJ-GRADED
> N-UNCOUNT

so·cial /'səʊʃəl/ **socials. 1** Social means relating to society or to the way society is organized. *...unemployment, low pay and other social problems.* ♦ **so·cial·ly** *Let's face it – drinking is a socially acceptable habit.* **2** Social means relating to the status or rank that someone has in society. *The guests came from all social backgrounds.* ♦ **socially** *...socially disadvantaged children.* **3** Social means relating to leisure activities that involve meeting other people. *We ought to organize more social events.* ♦ **socially** *We have known each other socially for a long time.* **4** A **social** is a party, dance, or informal gathering that is organized for the members of a club or institution.

> ◆◆◆◆◆
> ADJ: ADJ n

> ADV
> ADJ: ADJ n

> ADV
> ADJ: ADJ n

> ADV
> N-COUNT
> DATED

social 'climber, social climbers. You describe someone as a **social climber** when you disapprove of them because they try to have friends and acquaintances who belong to a higher social class, in order to be regarded as belonging to that class themselves. ♦ **social 'climbing.** You can refer to this type of behaviour as **social climbing**.

> N-COUNT
> PRAGMATICS

> N-UNCOUNT

'social club, social clubs. A **social club** is a club where members go in order to meet and be sociable with each other.

> N-COUNT

social de'mocracy, social democracies. 1 Social democracy is a political system according to which social justice and equality can be achieved

> N-UNCOUNT

S

within the framework of a market economy. ...*western-style social democracy*. **2** A **social democracy** is a country where there is social democracy. N-COUNT

social demo'cratic A **social democratic** party is a political party whose principles are based on social democracy. ...*relations with the social democratic governments in Europe*. ADJ: ADJ n

social 'housing In Britain, **social housing** is housing which is provided for rent or sale at a fairly low cost by organizations such as housing associations and local councils. N-UNCOUNT

so·cial·i·sa·tion /ˌsəʊʃəlaɪˈzeɪʃən/. See **socialize**.

so·cial·ize /ˈsəʊʃəlaɪz/. See **socialize**.

so·cial·ism /ˈsəʊʃəlɪzəm/. **Socialism** is a set of left-wing political principles whose general aim is to create a system in which everyone has an equal opportunity to benefit from a country's wealth. Under socialism, the country's main industries are usually owned by the state. N-UNCOUNT

so·cial·ist /ˈsəʊʃəlɪst/ **socialists**. **1 Socialist** means based on socialism or relating to socialism. ...*members of the ruling Socialist party*. **2** A **socialist** is a person who believes in socialism or who is a member of a socialist party. ADJ / N-COUNT

so·cial·is·tic /ˌsəʊʃəˈlɪstɪk/. If you describe a policy or organization as **socialistic**, you mean that it has some of the features of socialism; often used showing disapproval. *The Conservatives denounce it as socialistic*. ADJ

so·cial·ite /ˈsəʊʃəlaɪt/ **socialites**. A **socialite** is a person who attends many fashionable upper-class social events and who is well known because of this. N-COUNT JOURNALISM

so·cial·ize /ˈsəʊʃəlaɪz/ **socializes, socializing, socialized**; also spelled **socialise** in British English. **1** If you **socialize**, you meet other people socially, for example at parties. *It distressed her that she and Charles no longer socialized with old friends*. ♦ **so·cial·iz·ing** *The hours were terrible, so socialising was difficult*. **2** When people, especially children, **are socialized**, they are made to behave in a way which is acceptable in their culture or society. *From the time you are born you have to be socialised into being a good father*. ♦ **so·cial·i·za·tion** /ˌsəʊʃəlaɪˈzeɪʃən/. *Female socialization emphasizes getting along with others, while male socialization stresses becoming independent*. VERB: V / V with n / VB: usu passive beV-ed TECHNICAL / N-UNCOUNT

social life, social lives. Your **social life** consists of the activities in which you meet your friends and acquaintances, for example at parties or in pubs or bars. N-COUNT: with supp

social 'order, social orders. The **social order** in a place is the way in which society is organized there. ...*the threat to social order posed by right-wing extremists*. N-VAR

social 'science, social sciences. **1 Social science** is the scientific study of society. **2** The **social sciences** are the various branches of social science, for example sociology and politics. N-UNCOUNT / N-COUNT

social 'scientist, social scientists. A **social scientist** is a person who studies or teaches social science. N-COUNT

social se'curity. In Britain, **social security** is money that is paid by the government to people who are unemployed, poor, or ill. The American term is **welfare**. ...*families on social security benefits*. N-UNCOUNT

social 'services. The **social services** in a district are the services provided by the local authority to help people who have serious family problems or financial problems. *I have asked the social services for help, but they have not done anything*. N-PLURAL

social 'studies. Social studies is a subject that is taught in British schools and colleges. It includes sociology, politics, and economics. N-UNCOUNT

social work. Social work is work which involves giving help and advice to people with serious family problems or financial problems. N-UNCOUNT

social worker, social workers. A **social worker** is a person whose job is to do social work. N-COUNT

so·ci·etal /səˈsaɪətəl/. **Societal** means relating to society or to the way society is organized. ...*the soci-* ADJ: ADJ n FORMAL

etal changes that have taken place over the last two decades.

so·ci·ety /səˈsaɪəti/ **societies**. **1 Society** is people in general, thought of as a large organized group. *He maintains Islam must adapt to modern society*. **2** A **society** is the people who live in a country or region, their organizations, and their way of life. *We live in a capitalist society*. ...*the fabric of our society*. **3** A **society** is an organization for people who have the same interest or aim. ...*the North of England Horticultural Society*. **4 Society** is the rich, fashionable people in a particular place who meet on social occasions. *The couple quickly became a fixture of society pages*. ...*society weddings*. **5** See also **building society**. N-UNCOUNT / N-VAR: with supp / N-COUNT / N-UNCOUNT

socio- /ˈsəʊsiəʊ-/. **Socio-** is used to form adjectives and nouns which describe or refer to things relating to or involving social factors. *Sociobiology is the study of how animal behaviour evolves to fit function in the same way that anatomy does*. PREFIX

socio-eco'nomic; also spelled **socioeconomic**. **Socio-economic** circumstances or developments involve a combination of social and economic factors. ...*socio-economic status*. ...*the western European historical model of socio-economic development*. ADJ: ADJ n TECHNICAL

so·ci·ol·ogy /ˌsəʊsiˈɒlədʒi/. **Sociology** is the study of society or of the way society is organized. ♦ **so·ci·o·logi·cal** /ˌsəʊsiəˈlɒdʒɪkəl/. *Psychological and sociological studies were emphasizing the importance of the family*. ♦ **so·ci·olo·gist, sociologists** *By the 1950s some sociologists were confident that they had identified the key characteristics of capitalist society*. N-UNCOUNT / ADJ / N-COUNT

so·cio·path /ˈsəʊsiəpæθ/ **sociopaths**. A **sociopath** is the same as a **psychopath**. N-COUNT

socio-po'litical; also spelled **sociopolitical**. **Socio-political** systems and problems involve a combination of social and political factors. ...*contemporary sociopolitical issues such as ecology, human rights, and nuclear arms*. ADJ: ADJ n TECHNICAL

sock /sɒk/ **socks, socking, socked**. **1 Socks** are pieces of clothing which cover your foot and ankle and are worn inside shoes. See picture headed **clothes**. **2** If you tell someone to **pull their socks up**, you mean that they should start working harder, because they have been lazy or careless recently. **3** If someone **socks it to** another person, they do or say something that makes a big impact on them. *Come on, lads. Sock it to 'em*. N-COUNT / PHRASE PRAGMATICS INFORMAL, BRITISH / PHRASE INFORMAL, JOURNALISM

sock·et /ˈsɒkɪt/ **sockets**. **1** A **socket** is a device on a piece of electrical equipment into which you can put a bulb or plug. **2** A **socket** is a device or point in a wall where you can connect electrical equipment to the power supply. The usual American term is **outlet**. **3** You can refer to any hollow part or opening in a structure which another part fits into as a **socket**. *Her eyes were sunk deep into their sockets*. N-COUNT / N-COUNT BRITISH / N-COUNT

soda /ˈsəʊdə/ **sodas**. **1 Soda** is the same as **soda water**. *Strickland invited me to have another whisky and soda*. **2 Soda** is a sweet fizzy drink. *He went to fetch hot dogs and cans of soda*. ► A **soda** is a bottle or glass of soda. **3** See also **bicarbonate of soda**. N-UNCOUNT / N-VAR AMERICAN N-COUNT

soda pop, soda pops. Soda pop is a sweet fizzy drink. ► A **soda pop** is a bottle or a glass of soda pop. N-UNCOUNT AMERICAN N-COUNT

soda water; also spelled **soda-water**. Soda water is water used for mixing with alcoholic drinks and fruit juice. N-UNCOUNT

sod·den /ˈsɒdən/. Something that is **sodden** is extremely wet. ADJ

-sodden /-sɒdən/. **1 -sodden** is used to form adjectives which describe someone who has drunk too much alcohol. **2 -sodden** is used to form adjectives which describe someone or something that has become extremely wet as a result of the thing that is mentioned. ...*our scruffy rain-sodden luggage*. COMB / COMB

so·dium /ˈsəʊdiəm/. **1 Sodium** is a silvery-white chemical element which combines with other chemicals. **2 Sodium** lighting gives out a strong orange light. ...*sodium streetlamps*. N-UNCOUNT / ADJ: ADJ n

sodo·my /'sɒdəmi/. **Sodomy** is anal sexual inter-course, especially between men. `N-UNCOUNT`

sofa /'səʊfə/ **sofas**. A **sofa** is a long, comfortable seat with a back and usually with arms, which two or three people can sit on. `◆◆◇◇◇` `N-COUNT`

'sofa-bed, sofa-beds. A **sofa-bed** is a sofa with a special seat that folds out so that it can also be used as a bed. `N-COUNT`

soft /sɒft, AM sɔːft/ **softer, softest**. **1** Something that is **soft** is pleasant to touch, and not rough or hard. *Regular use of a body lotion will keep the skin soft and supple.* ♦ **soft·ness** *The sea air robbed her hair of its softness.* **2** Something that is **soft** changes shape or bends easily when you press it. *She lay down on the soft, comfortable bed. ...soft cheese.* **3** Something that has a **soft** appearance has smooth curves rather than sharp or distinct edges. *...the soft curves of her body.* ♦ **soft·ly** *She wore a softly tai-lored suit.* **4** Something that is **soft** is very gentle and has no force. For example, a **soft** sound or voice is quiet and not harsh. A **soft** light or colour is pleasant to look at because it is not bright. *A soft spring rain had fallen all day.* ♦ **softly** *She crossed the softly lit room... She bent forward and kissed him softly.* `◆◆◆◇` `ADJ-GRADED` `N-UNCOUNT` `ADJ-GRADED` `ADJ-GRADED` `ADV-GRADED` `ADJ-GRADED` `ADV-GRADED: ADV with v`

5 If you are **soft** on someone, you do not treat them as strictly or severely as you should do; used showing disapproval. **6** You use **soft** to describe a way of life that is easy and involves very little work. *The regime at Latchmere could be seen as a soft option.* **7** If you have **a soft spot for** someone or something, you feel a great deal of affection for them or like them a lot. `ADJ-GRADED` `PRAGMATICS` `ADJ-GRADED` `PHRASE`

8 Soft drugs are drugs, such as marijuana, which are illegal but which many people do not consider to be strong, harmful, or addictive. **9** A **soft** target is a place or person that can easily be attacked. **10** Soft water does not contain much calcium and so makes bub-bles easily when you use soap to wash things. `ADJ: ADJ n` `ADJ-GRADED` `ADJ-GRADED`

11 ♦ a soft touch: see **touch**.

soft·back /'sɒftbæk/. A **softback** is a book with a thin cardboard, paper, or plastic cover. Compare **hardback** and **paperback**. *This title was a best seller and is now available in softback.* `N-SING: also in N`

soft·ball /'sɒftbɔːl, AM 'sɔːft-/ **softballs**. **1** Softball is a game similar to baseball, but played with a larg-er, softer ball. **2** A **softball** is the ball used in the game of softball. `N-UNCOUNT` `N-COUNT`

,soft-'boiled. A **soft-boiled** egg has been boiled for only a few minutes, so that the yolk is still soft. `ADJ`

'soft-core; also spelled **softcore**. Soft-core pornog-raphy shows or mentions sexual acts or naked bodies, but not in a very explicit or violent way. Compare **hard core**. `ADJ: ADJ n`

,soft 'drink, soft drinks. A **soft drink** is a cold, non-alcoholic drink such as lemonade or fruit juice. `◆◇◇◇◇` `N-COUNT`

sof·ten /'sɒfən, AM 'sɔːf-/ **softens, softening, softened**. **1** If you **soften** something, it becomes less hard, stiff, or firm. *Fry for about 5 minutes, until the onion has softened.* **2** If one thing **softens** the impact or the damaging effect of another thing, it makes the impact or effect seem less severe. **3** If you **soften** your position, you become more sympa-thetic and less hostile or critical. *His party's policy has softened a lot in recent years.* `◆◆◇◇◇` `V-ERG: V n` `V` `VERB: V n` `V-ERG: V`

4 If your voice or expression **softens**, it becomes much more gentle and friendly. *She did not smile or soften her voice.* **5** If you **soften** something such as light, a colour, or a sound, you make it less bright or harsh. **6** Something that **softens** your skin makes it very smooth and pleasant to touch. `V-ERG: V V n` `VERB: V n` `VERB: V n`

soften up. If you **soften** someone **up**, you put them into a good mood before asking them to do some-thing. *If they'd treated you well it was just to soften you up.* `PHRASAL VB V n P Also V P noun INFORMAL`

sof·ten·er /'sɒfənə, AM 'sɔːf-/ **softeners**. **1** A water softener is a device or substance which removes certain minerals, for example calcium, from water, so that it makes bubbles easily when you use soap to wash things. **2** A fabric **softener** is a chemical `N-COUNT` `N-VAR`

substance that you add to water when you wash clothes in order to make the clothes feel softer.

,soft 'focus. If something in a photograph or film is in **soft focus**, it has been made to look slightly blurred to give it a more romantic effect. `N-UNCOUNT`

,soft 'fruit, soft fruits. Soft fruits are small fruits with soft skins, such as strawberries and currants. `N-VAR` `BRITISH`

,soft 'furnishings. Soft furnishings are cushions, curtains, lampshades, and furniture covers. `N-PLURAL` `BRITISH`

soft-'hearted. Someone who is **soft-hearted** has a very sympathetic and kind nature. `ADJ-GRADED`

softie /'sɒfti/ **softies**; also spelled **softy**. If you de-scribe someone as a **softie**, you mean that they are very emotional or that they can easily be made to feel sympathy towards other people. `N-COUNT` `INFORMAL`

,soft 'loan, soft loans. A **soft loan** is a loan with a very low interest rate. `N-COUNT` `BRITISH`

softly-'softly; also spelled **softly, softly**. A **softly-softly** approach to something is cautious and pa-tient and avoids direct action or force. `ADJ: ADJ n` `BRITISH`

,soft-'pedal, soft-pedals, soft-pedalling, soft-pedalled; spelled **soft-pedaling, soft-pedaled** in American English. If you **soft-pedal** something, you deliberately reduce the amount of activity or pressure that you have been using to get something done. *He refused to soft-pedal an investigation into the scandal.* `VERB V n Also V on n`

,soft 'porn. Soft porn is pornography that shows or mentions sexual acts, but not in a very explicit or violent way. `N-UNCOUNT`

,soft 'sell; also spelled **soft-sell**. A **soft sell** is a method of selling or advertising that involves gentle persuasion rather than putting a lot of pressure on people. `N-SING`

,soft-'soap, soft-soaps, soft-soaping, soft-soaped. If you **soft-soap** someone, you flatter them or tell them what you think they want to hear in order to try and persuade them to do something. `VERB: V n`

,soft-'spoken. Someone who is **soft-spoken** has a quiet, gentle voice. `ADJ-GRADED`

,soft 'toy, soft toys. Soft toys are toys that look like animals. They are made of soft material and stuffed. `N-COUNT`

soft·ware /'sɒftweə, AM 'sɔːf-/. Computer pro-grams are referred to as **software**. *...the people who write the software for big computer projects.* `◆◆◆◇◇` `N-UNCOUNT`

soft·wood /'sɒftwʊd, AM 'sɔːft-/ **softwoods**. Soft-wood is the wood from trees such as pines, that grow quickly and can be sawn easily. `N-VAR`

softy /'sɒfti, AM 'sɔːfti/. See **softie**.

sog·gy /'sɒgi/ **soggier, soggiest**. Something that is **soggy** is unpleasantly wet. `◆◇◇◇◇` `ADJ-GRADED`

soil /sɔɪl/ **soils, soiling, soiled**. **1** Soil is the sub-stance on the surface of the earth in which plants grow. *...regions with sandy soils.* **2** You can use **soil** in expressions like '**British soil**' to refer to a country's territory. *The issue of foreign troops on Turkish soil is a sensitive one.* **3** If you **soil** some-thing, you make it dirty. ♦ **soiled** *...a soiled white apron.* `◆◆◇◇◇` `N-VAR` `N-UNCOUNT: with supp` `VERB: V n FORMAL` `ADJ-GRADED`

soi·ree /'swɑːreɪ, AM swɑːˈreɪ/ **soirees**; also spelled **soirée**. A **soiree** is a social gathering held in the evening. `N-COUNT` `FORMAL`

so·journ /'sɒdʒɜːn, AM 'səʊdʒ-/ **sojourns**. A so-journ is a short stay in a place that is not your home. `N-COUNT` `LITERARY`

sol·ace /'sɒlɪs/. **1** Solace is a feeling of comfort that makes you feel less sad. *Henry was inclined to seek solace in drink.* **2** If something is a **solace** to you, it makes you feel less sad. `◆◇◇◇◇` `N-UNCOUNT FORMAL` `N-SING FORMAL`

so·lar /'səʊlə/. **1** Solar is used to describe things relating to the sun. *...a total solar eclipse.* **2** Solar power is obtained from the sun's light and heat. `◆◇◇◇◇` `ADJ` `ADJ`

,solar 'cell, solar cells. A **solar cell** is a device that produces electricity from the sun's rays. `N-COUNT`

so·lar·ium /səʊˈleəriəm/ **solariums**. A **solarium** is a place equipped with sun lamps, where you can go to get an artificial suntan. `N-COUNT`

S

so·lar plex·us /ˌsəʊlə 'pleksəs/. Your **solar plexus** is the part of your stomach, below your ribs, where it is painful if you are hit hard.
N-SING: theN, N with poss

'**solar system, solar systems.** The **solar system** is the sun and all the planets and comets that go round it.
N-COUNT

sold /səʊld/. **Sold** is the past tense and past participle of **sell**.

sol·der /'səʊldə, AM 'sɑːdə/ **solders, soldering, soldered. 1** If you **solder** two pieces of metal together, you join them by melting a small piece of soft metal and putting it between them so that it holds them together after it has cooled. *He then soldered the wire to the telephone terminal.* **2 Solder** is the soft metal used for soldering.
VERB V n adv/prep Also V, V n
N-UNCOUNT

sol·dier /'səʊldʒə/ **soldiers, soldiering, soldiered.** A **soldier** is a person who works in an army, especially a person who is not an officer.
N-COUNT ◆◆◆◆◇

soldier on. If you **soldier on**, you continue to do something although it is difficult or unpleasant.
PHRASAL VB V P

sol·dier·ly /'səʊldʒəli/. If you act in a **soldierly** way, you behave like a good or brave soldier.
ADJ FORMAL

sol·diery /'səʊldʒəri/. **Soldiery** is a group or body of soldiers.
N-UNCOUNT LITERARY

,**sold 'out. 1** If a performance, sports event, or other entertainment is **sold out**, all the tickets for it have been sold. **2** If a shop is **sold out** of something, it has sold all of it that it had.
◆◇◇◇◇ ADJ: v-link ADJ ADJ: v-link ADJ

sole /səʊl/ **soles. 1** The **sole** thing or person of a particular type is the only one of that type. *Their sole aim is to destabilize the Indian government.* ♦ **sole·ly** /'səʊlli/. *Too often we make decisions based solely upon what we see in the magazines.* **2** If you have **sole** charge or ownership of something, you are the only person in charge of it or who owns it. *Many women are left as the sole providers in families.* **3** The **sole** of your foot or of a shoe or sock is the underneath surface of it. See picture headed **human body. 4** A **sole** is a kind of flat fish. ▶ **Sole** is this fish eaten as food.
ADJ: ADJ n
ADV
ADJ: ADJ n
N-COUNT
N-COUNT N-UNCOUNT

-**soled** /-səʊld/. -**soled** combines with adjectives and nouns to form adjectives which describe shoes with a particular kind of sole. *...rubber-soled shoes.*
COMB

sol·emn /'sɒləm/. **1** Someone or something that is **solemn** is very serious rather than cheerful or humorous. ♦ **sol·emn·ly** *Her listeners nodded solemnly.* ♦ **so·lem·nity** /sə'lemnɪti/. *The setting for this morning's signing ceremony matched the solemnity of the occasion.* **2** A **solemn** promise or agreement is one that you make in a very formal, sincere way. ♦ **solemnly** *I do solemnly swear by whatever I hold most sacred, that I will be loyal to the profession of medicine.*
◆◆◇◇◇ ADJ-GRADED
ADV-GRADED
N-UNCOUNT
ADJ-GRADED
ADV-GRADED ADV with v

so·lic·it /sə'lɪsɪt/ **solicits, soliciting, solicited. 1** If you **solicit** money, help, support, or an opinion from someone, you ask them for it. ♦ **so·lici·ta·tion** /sə,lɪsɪ'teɪʃən/ **solicitations** *...the party's solicitation of huge donations from a group of wealthy businessmen.* **2** When prostitutes **solicit**, they offer to have sex with people in return for money. ♦ **so·lic·it·ing** *Girls could get very heavy sentences for soliciting.*
◆◇◇◇◇ VERB: V n FORMAL
N-VAR
VERB: V
N-UNCOUNT

so·lici·tor /sə'lɪsɪtə/ **solicitors.** In Britain, a **solicitor** is a lawyer who gives legal advice, prepares legal documents and cases, and represents clients in the lower courts of law. Compare **barrister.**
◆◆◇◇◇ N-COUNT

So,licitor 'General; also spelled **solicitor-general.** In Britain, the **Solicitor General** is the second most important legal officer, next in rank below the Attorney General.
N-SING

so·lici·tous /sə'lɪsɪtəs/. A person who is **solicitous** shows anxious concern for someone or something. ♦ **so·lici·tous·ly** *He took her hand in greeting and asked solicitously how everything was.* ♦ **so·lici·tude** /sə'lɪsɪtjuːd, AM -tuːd/. *He is full of tender solicitude towards my sister.*
ADJ-GRADED
ADV-GRADED
N-UNCOUNT

sol·id /'sɒlɪd/ **solids. 1** A **solid** substance or object stays the same shape whether it is in a container or
◆◆◆◇◇ ADJ

not. *He did not eat solid food for several weeks.* **2** A **solid** is a substance that stays the same shape whether it is in a container or not. *Solids turn to liquids at certain temperatures.* **3** A substance that is **solid** is very hard or firm. *The concrete will stay as solid as a rock.*
N-COUNT
ADJ-GRADED

4 A **solid** object or mass does not have a space inside it, or holes or gaps in it. *...a tunnel carved through 50ft of solid rock... The car park was absolutely packed solid with people.* **5** If an object is made of **solid** gold or **solid** wood, for example, it is made of gold or wood all the way through, rather than just on the outside. **6** A structure that is **solid** is strong and is not likely to collapse or fall over. *The car feels very solid.* ♦ **sol·id·ly** *Their house, which was solidly built, resisted the main shock.* ♦ **so·lid·ity** /sə'lɪdɪti/. *...the solidity of walls and floors.* **7** See also **rock-solid.**
ADJ
ADJ: ADJ n
ADJ: ADJ n
ADJ-GRADED
ADV-GRADED: ADV with v
N-UNCOUNT

8 If you describe someone as **solid**, you mean that they are very reliable and respectable. *Mr Zuma has a solid reputation as a grass roots organiser.* ♦ **solidly** *Graham is so solidly consistent.* ♦ **solidity** *He had the proverbial solidity of the English.* **9 Solid** evidence or information is reliable because it is based on facts. **10** You use **solid** to describe something such as advice or a piece of work which is useful and reliable. *All I am looking for is a good solid performance.* ♦ **solidly** *She's played solidly throughout the spring.* **11** You use **solid** to describe something such as the basis for a policy or support for an organization when it is strong, because it has been developed carefully and slowly. *...Washington's attempt to build a solid international coalition.* ♦ **solidly** *...a society based solidly on trust and understanding.* ♦ **solidity** *...doubts over the solidity of Chinese backing for the American approach.*
ADJ-GRADED
ADV-GRADED
ADJ-GRADED
ADJ-GRADED
ADJ-GRADED
ADV-GRADED
N-UNCOUNT

12 If you do something for a **solid** period of time, you do it without any pause or interruption throughout that time. *We had worked together for two solid years.* ♦ **solidly** *People who had worked solidly since Christmas enjoyed the chance of a Friday off.*
ADJ: ADJ n, -ed ADJ
ADV-GRADED: ADV with v

soli·dar·ity /ˌsɒlɪ'dærɪti/. If a group of people show **solidarity**, they show complete unity and support for each other, especially in political or international affairs.
◆◆◇◇◇ N-UNCOUNT

,**solid 'fuel, solid fuels. Solid fuel** is fuel such as coal or wood, that is solid rather than liquid or gas.
N-VAR

so·lidi·fy /sə'lɪdɪfaɪ/ **solidifies, solidifying, solidified. 1** When a liquid **solidifies**, it changes into a solid. *The thicker lava would have taken two weeks to solidify... The Energy Department plans to solidify the deadly waste in a high-tech billion-dollar factory.* **2** If something such as a position or opinion **solidifies**, it becomes firmer and more definite and unlikely to change. *Her attitudes solidified through privilege and habit... Her behavior this week has solidified her support within the Department of Justice.*
V-ERG: V V n Also V-ed
V-ERG: V V n Also V n

,**solid-'state. Solid-state** electronic equipment is made using transistors, silicon chips, or other semi-conductors, instead of valves or other mechanical parts.
ADJ: ADJ n TECHNICAL

so·lilo·quy /sə'lɪləkwi/ **soliloquies.** A **soliloquy** is a speech in a play in which an actor or actress speaks to himself or herself and to the audience, rather than to another actor.
N-COUNT

soli·taire /ˌsɒlɪ'teə/ **solitaires. 1 Solitaire** is a game for one person in which you move pegs to different positions on a board, with the aim of having one peg left at the end of the game. **2 Solitaire** is a card game for only one player. The British word is **patience. 3** A **solitaire** is a diamond or other jewel that is set on its own in a ring or other piece of jewellery. *...a very large solitaire diamond ring.*
N-UNCOUNT
N-UNCOUNT AMERICAN
N-COUNT

soli·tary /'sɒlɪtri, AM -teri/. **1** A person or animal that is **solitary** spends a lot of time alone. **2** A **solitary** activity is one that you do alone. *His evenings were spent in solitary drinking.* **3** A **solitary** person or object is alone, with no others nearby. *...the occasional solitary figure making a study of wildflowers or grasses.* **4 Solitary** is the same as **solitary**
◆◇◇◇◇ ADJ-GRADED ADJ: ADJ n
ADJ: ADJ n
N-UNCOUNT

confinement. *Tom was in solitary across the way from me.* *INFORMAL*

soli·tary con'finement. A prisoner who is in **solitary confinement** is being kept alone away from all other prisoners, usually as a punishment. *N-UNCOUNT*

soli·tude /'sɒlɪtjuːd, AM -tuːd/. **Solitude** is the state of being alone, especially when this is peaceful and pleasant. *Imagine long golden beaches where you can wander in solitude.* ◆◇◇◇◇ *N-UNCOUNT*

solo /'səʊləʊ/ **solos.** A **solo** is a performance, especially of a piece of music, done by one person. ▶ Also an adjective. *He had just completed his final solo album.* ▶ Also an adverb. *Charles Lindbergh became the first person to fly solo across the Atlantic.* ◆◆◇◇◇ *N-COUNT* *ADJ* *ADV:* *ADV after v*

so·lo·ist /'səʊləʊɪst/ **soloists.** A **soloist** is a person who performs a solo, usually a piece of music. ◆◇◇◇◇ *N-COUNT*

sol·stice /'sɒlstɪs/ **solstices.** The **summer solstice** and the **winter solstice** are the two times of the year when the sun is farthest away from the equator. In the northern hemisphere, the summer solstice is on June 21 or 22, and the winter solstice is on December 21 or 22. In the southern hemisphere the summer solstice is in December and the winter solstice is in June. ◆◇◇◇◇ *N-COUNT*

sol·uble /'sɒljʊbəl/. **1** A substance that is **soluble** will dissolve in a liquid. *Uranium is soluble in sea water.* **2** If something is **water-soluble** or **fat-soluble**, it will dissolve in water or in fat. ◆◇◇◇◇ *ADJ-GRADED* *COMB*

so·lu·tion /sə'luːʃən/ **solutions. 1** A **solution** to a problem or difficult situation is a way of dealing with it so that the difficulty is removed. *Although he has sought to find a peaceful solution, he is facing pressure to use greater military force.* **2** The **solution** to a riddle or a puzzle is the answer to it. **3** A **solution** is a liquid in which a solid substance has been dissolved. ...*a warm solution of liquid detergent.* ◆◆◆◇ *N-COUNT* *N-COUNT* *N-COUNT:* *also in N*

solve /sɒlv/ **solves, solving, solved.** If you **solve** a problem or a question, you find a solution or an answer to it. *Their dramatic reforms did nothing to solve the problem of unemployment.* ◆◆◇◇ *VERB* *V n*

sol·ven·cy /'sɒlvənsi/. A person or organization's **solvency** is their ability to pay their debts. *N-UNCOUNT*

sol·vent /'sɒlvənt/ **solvents. 1** If a person or a company is **solvent**, they have enough money to pay all their debts. **2** A **solvent** is a liquid that can dissolve other substances. ◆◇◇◇◇ *ADJ* *N-VAR*

'solvent abuse. Solvent abuse is the dangerous practice of breathing in the vapour from solvents such as glue in order to feel as if you are drunk. *N-UNCOUNT* *FORMAL*

som·bre /'sɒmbə/; spelled **somber** in American English. **1** If someone is **sombre**, they are serious, sad, or pessimistic. ♦ **som·bre·ly** *'All the same, I wish he'd come back,' Martha said sombrely.* **2** **Sombre** colours and places are dark and dull. ◆◇◇◇◇ *ADJ-GRADED* *ADV-GRADED* *ADJ-GRADED*

som·brero /sɒm'breərəʊ/ **sombreros.** A **sombrero** is a hat with a very wide brim which is worn especially in Mexico. *N-COUNT*

some /səm, STRONG sʌm/. **1** You use **some** to refer to a quantity of something or to a number of people or things, when you are not stating the quantity or number precisely. *Robin opened some champagne... He went to fetch some books... Some children refuse to eat on time and others overeat.* ▶ Also a pronoun. *This year all the apples are all red. My niece and nephew are going out this morning with stepladders to pick some.* **2** You use **some** to emphasize that a quantity or number is fairly large. For example, if an activity takes **some** time, it takes quite a lot of time. *The question of local government finance has been the subject of debate for some years... I have discussed this topic in some detail.* **3** You use **some** to emphasize that a quantity or number is fairly small. For example, if something happens to **some** extent, it happens a little. *'Isn't there some chance that William might lead a normal life?' asked Jill... Some fishing is still allowed.* **4** If you refer to **some of** the people or things in a group, you mean a few of them but not all of them. If you refer to **some of** a particular thing, you mean a part of it but not all of ◆◆◆◆ *DET* *PRON* *DET* *DET* *QUANT*

it. *Remove the cover and spoon some of the sauce into a bowl... Boats crammed with hot and angry holidaymakers, some of whom had waited for up to two days to cross.* ▶ Also a pronoun. *When the chicken is cooked I'll freeze some.* *PRON*

5 If you refer to **some** person or thing, you are referring to that person or thing vaguely, without stating precisely which one you mean. *If you are worried about some aspect of your child's health, call us... Three years ago there was an incident at the local school when some bloke started shooting the place up.* **6** You can also use **some** in front of a number to indicate that it is approximate. *I have kept birds for some 30 years.* **7** **Some** is used to mean to a small extent or degree. *If Susanne is somewhere, I'll kill time by looking around some... He decided we should spend Christmas in Acapulco. There we could ski some and relax.* **8** You can use **some** in front of a noun in order to express your approval or disapproval of the person or thing you are mentioning. *'Some party!'—'Yep. One hell of a party.'* *DET* *ADV:* *ADV num* *ADV:* *ADV after v* *AMERICAN* *DET* *INFORMAL*

some·body /'sʌmbədi, AM -bɑːdi/. **Somebody** means the same as **someone**. ◆◆◆◇ *PRON-INDEF*

'some day; also spelled **someday. Some day** means at a date in the future that is unknown or that has not yet been decided. *She believed that some day he'd learn to trust her.* ◆◇◇◇◇ *ADV:* *ADV with v,* *ADV with cl*

some·how /'sʌmhaʊ/. **1** You use **somehow** to say that you do not know or cannot say how something was done or will be done. *We'll manage somehow, you and me. I know we will... Somehow I knew he would tell me the truth... This city is somehow different.* **2** ● **somehow or other:** see **other.** ◆◆◇◇ *ADV*

some·one /'sʌmwʌn/. The form **somebody** is also used. **1** You use **someone** or **somebody** to refer to a person without saying exactly who you mean. *I need someone to help me... He noticed a huge crowd gathered outside – someone really famous must be staying there.* **2** If you say that a person is **someone** or **somebody** in a particular kind of work or in a particular place, you mean that they are considered to be important in that kind of work or in that place. *He was somebody in the law division.* ◆◆◆◇ *PRON-INDEF* *PRON-INDEF*

some·place /'sʌmpleɪs/. **Someplace** means the same as **somewhere.** *They lived over around Coyote Canyon someplace.* ◆◇◇◇◇ *ADV:* *ADV after v* *AMERICAN*

som·er·sault /'sʌməsɔːlt/ **somersaults, somersaulting, somersaulted. 1** If someone or something does a **somersault** they turn over completely in the air. **2** If someone or something **somersaults**, they perform one or more somersaults. *I hit him back and he somersaulted down the stairs.* *N-COUNT* *VERB: V* *V prep*

some·thing /'sʌmθɪŋ/. **1** You use **something** to refer to a thing, situation, event, or idea, without saying exactly what it is. *There was something vaguely familiar about him... 'You said there was something you wanted to ask me,' he said politely... People are always out in their cars, watching television or busy doing something else.* **2** You can use **something** to say that the description or amount that you are giving is not exact. *Clive made a noise, something like a grunt... Their membership seems to have risen to something over 10,000.* **3** If you say that a person or thing is **something** or is really **something**, you mean that you are very impressed by them. *The doors here are really something, all made of good wood like mahogany.* **4** You can use **something** in expressions like **'that's something'** when you think that a situation is not very good but is better that it might have been. *Well, at least he was in town. That was something.* **5** If you say that a thing is **something of** a disappointment, you mean that it is quite disappointing. If you say that a person is **something of** an artist, you mean that they are quite good at art. *She received something of a surprise when Robert said that he was coming to New York.* **6** If you say that there is **something in** an idea or suggestion, you mean that it is quite good and should be considered seriously. *Christianity has stood the test of time, so there must be something in it...* ◆◆◆◆ *PRON-INDEF* *PRON-INDEF:* *PRON prep* *PRON-INDEF* *PRON-INDEF* *PRON-INDEF:* *PRON of n* *PRON-INDEF:* *PRON in n*

Could there be something in what he said? **7** You use **something** in expressions such as **'or something'** and **'or something like that'** to indicate that you are referring to something similar to what you have just mentioned when you are not being exact. *This guy, his name was Briarly or Beardly or something... The air fare was about a hundred and ninety-nine pounds or something like that.* **8** ● **something like:** see **like**. `PRON-INDEF` `PRAGMATICS`

-something /-sʌmθɪŋ/ **-somethings.**
1 **-something** is combined with numbers such as twenty and thirty to form adjectives which indicate an approximate amount, especially someone's age. For example, if you say that someone is **thirty-something**, you mean they are between thirty and forty years old. **2** People of a similar age range are sometimes referred to as, for example, **twenty-somethings** or **thirty-somethings.** `COMB` `COMB` `JOURNALISM`

some·time /ˈsʌmtaɪm/. **1** You use **sometime** to refer to a time in the future or the past that is unknown or that has not yet been decided. *The sales figures won't be released until sometime next month... Why don't you come and see me sometime.* **2** You also use **sometime** to describe a job or role that a person used to have. *...sometime boxer Frank Bruno.* ◆◆◇◇◇ `ADV` `ADJ: ADJ n`

some·times /ˈsʌmtaɪmz/. You use **sometimes** to say that something happens on some occasions rather than all the time. *Sometimes I think he dislikes me... You must have noticed how tired he sometimes looks.* ◆◆◆◇ `ADV`

some·what /ˈsʌmwɒt/. You use **somewhat** to indicate that something is the case to a limited extent or degree. *He concluded that Oswald was somewhat abnormal... Conditions in the village had improved somewhat since January.* ◆◆◆◇ `ADV:` `ADV with cl/ group`

some·where /ˈsʌmweə/. **1** You use **somewhere** to refer to a place without saying exactly where you mean. *Somewhere in Ian's room were some of the letters that she had sent him... Don't I know you from somewhere?... I needed somewhere to live in London.* **2** You use **somewhere** when giving an approximate amount, number, or time. *Caray is somewhere between 73 and 80 years of age... The W.H.O. safety standard for ozone levels is somewhere about a hundred.* **3** If you say that you **are getting somewhere**, you mean that you are making progress towards achieving something. *At last they were agreeing, at last they were getting somewhere.* ◆◆◆◇ `ADV` `ADV: ADV prep` `PHRASE`

som·no·lent /ˈsɒmnələnt/. **1** If you are **somnolent** you feel sleepy. **2** If a place is **somnolent** it is very peaceful and quiet. `ADJ` `FORMAL` `ADJ` `LITERARY`

son /sʌn/ **sons. 1** Someone's **son** is their male child. *Sam is the seven-year-old son of Eric Davies.* **2** A man, especially a famous man, can be described as a **son** of the place he comes from. *...New Orleans's most famous son, Louis Armstrong.* **3** Some people use **son** as an affectionate form of address to a boy or a man who is younger than them. *Don't be frightened by failure, son.* ◆◆◆◆ `N-COUNT` `N-COUNT: with poss` `JOURNALISM` `N-VOC` `PRAGMATICS` `INFORMAL`

so·nar /ˈsəʊnɑː/ **sonars.** Sonar is equipment on a ship which can calculate the depth of the sea or the position of an underwater object using sound waves. `N-VAR`

so·na·ta /səˈnɑːtə/ **sonatas.** A sonata is a piece of classical music written either for a single instrument, or for one instrument and a piano. ◆◇◇◇◇ `N-COUNT`

song /sɒŋ, AM sɔːŋ/ **songs. 1** A song is words and music sung together. *...a love song.* **2** Song is the art of singing. *...the history of American popular song.* **3** A bird's **song** is the pleasant, musical sounds that it makes. **4** If someone **bursts into song** or **breaks into song**, they start singing. **5** If you buy something **for a song**, you buy it for much less than its real value. **6** Journalists sometimes describe sportsmen or sportswomen as being **on song** when they are playing really well. **7** See also **birdsong, song and dance, songbird, swan song.** ◆◆◆◆ `N-COUNT` `N-UNCOUNT` `N-COUNT` `PHRASE` `PHRASE` `INFORMAL` `PHRASE` `BRITISH`

,song and 'dance. 1 A song and dance act is a theatrical performance in which a person or group `N-UNCOUNT`

of people both sing and dance. **2** If you say that someone is making a **song and dance** about something, you mean they are making an unnecessary fuss about it; used showing disapproval. `PHRASE` `PRAGMATICS` `INFORMAL,` `BRITISH`

song·bird /ˈsɒŋbɜːd, AM ˈsɔːŋ-/ **songbirds;** also spelled **song bird.** A **songbird** is a bird that produces musical sounds which are like singing. There are many different kinds of songbird. `N-COUNT`

song·stress /ˈsɒŋstrəs, AM ˈsɔːŋ-/ **songstresses.** Journalists sometimes refer to a female popular singer as a **songstress.** `N-COUNT`

song·writer /ˈsɒŋraɪtə, AM ˈsɔːŋ-/ **songwriters.** A **songwriter** is someone who writes the words or the music, or both, for popular songs. ● See also **singer-songwriter.** ◆◇◇◇◇ `N-COUNT`

son·ic /ˈsɒnɪk/. Sonic is used to describe things related to sound. *...the sonic boom of enemy fighter-bombers.* ◆◇◇◇◇ `ADJ: ADJ n` `TECHNICAL`

'son-in-law, sons-in-law. Someone's **son-in-law** is the husband of their daughter. ◆◇◇◇◇ `N-COUNT`

son·net /ˈsɒnɪt/ **sonnets.** A sonnet is a poem that has 14 lines. Each line has 14 syllables, and the poem has a fixed pattern of rhymes. ◆◇◇◇◇ `N-COUNT`

son·ny /ˈsʌni/. Some people address a boy or young man informally as **sonny.** `N-VOC` `PRAGMATICS`

so·nor·ity /səˈnɒrɪti, AM -ˈnɔːr-/ **sonorities.** The **sonority** of a sound is its deep resonance. *The lower strings contribute a splendid richness of sonority.* `N-UNCOUNT: also N in pl` `FORMAL`

so·no·rous /ˈsɒnərəs, AM səˈnɔːrəs/. A **sonorous** sound is deep and rich. *...an even, sonorous voice.* `ADJ-GRADED`

soon /suːn/ **sooner, soonest. 1** If something is going to happen **soon**, it will happen after a short time. If something happened **soon** after a particular time or event, it happened a short time after it. *This chance has come sooner than I expected... You'll find out soon enough... Soon afterwards he separated from his wife.* **2** If you say that something happens **as soon as** something else happens, you mean that it happens immediately after the other thing. *You'll never guess what happened as soon as I left my room.* **3** If you say that you **would just as soon** do something or you'**d just as soon** do it, you mean that you would prefer to do it. *I'd just as soon not have to make this public... I'd just as soon you put that thing away... She'd just as soon throw your plate in your face as serve you.* ◆◆◆◆◆ `ADV-GRADED:` `ADV with v,` `ADV after n/cl` `PHR-CONJ` `PHR-MODAL` `MODAL not inf` `MODAL that` `MODAL inf as` `inf`

soon·er /ˈsuːnə/. **1** Sooner is the comparative of **soon. 2** You say **the sooner the better** when you think something should be done as soon as possible. *Detective Holt said: 'The kidnapper is a man we must catch and the sooner the better.'* **3** If you say that something will happen **sooner or later**, you mean that it will happen at some time in the future, even though it might take a long time. **4** If you say that **no sooner** has one thing happened **than** another thing happens, you mean that the second thing happens immediately after the first thing. *No sooner had he arrived in Rome than he was kidnapped.* **5** If you say that you **would sooner** do something or you'**d sooner** do it, you mean that you would prefer to do it. *I'd sooner not talk about it... I'd sooner he didn't know till I've talked to Pete... I would sooner give up sleep than miss my evening class.* ◆◆◇◇◇ `PHRASE` `PHRASE` `PHR-CONJ` `PHR-MODAL` `MODAL not inf` `MODAL that` `MODAL inf` `than inf`

soot /sʊt/. Soot is black powder which rises in the smoke from a fire and collects on the inside of chimneys. ◆◇◇◇◇ `N-UNCOUNT`

soothe /suːð/ **soothes, soothing, soothed. 1** If you **soothe** someone who is angry or upset, you make them feel calmer. *It did not take long for the central bank to soothe the investors' fears.* ♦ **soothing** *His casual, relaxed manner was very soothing.* ♦ **sooth·ing·ly** *'Now don't you worry,' she said soothingly.* **2** Something that **soothes** a part of your body where there is pain or discomfort makes the pain or discomfort less severe. *...body lotion to soothe dry skin.* ♦ **soothing** *Cold tea is very soothing for burns.* ◆◆◇◇◇ `VERB` `V n` `ADJ-GRADED` `ADV` `VERB` `V n` `ADJ-GRADED`

sooth·say·er /ˈsuːθseɪə/ **soothsayers.** In former times, **soothsayers** were people who believed they `N-COUNT`

could see into the future and say what was going to happen.

sooty /'sʊti/. Something that is **sooty** is covered with soot. *Their uniforms are torn and sooty.* ADJ-GRADED

sop /sɒp/ **sops.** You describe something as a **sop** to someone when they are offered something small or unimportant in order to prevent them from getting angry or causing trouble; used showing disapproval. N-COUNT PRAGMATICS

so·phis·ti·cat·ed /sə'fɪstɪkeɪtɪd/. **1** A **sophisticated** machine, device, or method is more advanced or complex than others. *...a large and sophisticated new British telescope.* **2** Someone who is **sophisticated** is at ease in social situations and knows about culture, fashion, and other matters that are considered socially important. *Recently her tastes have become more sophisticated.* ♦ **so·phis·ti·cate** /sə'fɪstɪkeɪt/ **sophisticates.** Someone who is sophisticated can also be called a **sophisticate**. **3** A **sophisticated** person is intelligent and well-informed, and shows an ability to understand complicated matters. *These people are very sophisticated observers of the foreign policy scene.* ♦♦♦◇ ADJ-GRADED / ADJ-GRADED / N-COUNT / ADJ-GRADED

so·phis·ti·ca·tion /sə,fɪstɪ'keɪʃən/. The **sophistication** of people, places, machines, or methods is their quality of being sophisticated. *...the sophistication of one of the world's richest cities. ...the sophistication of modern machines.* ♦◇◇◇ N-UNCOUNT

soph·ist·ry /'sɒfɪstri/. **Sophistry** is the practice of using clever arguments that sound convincing but are in fact false. ♦ **soph·ist·ries.** These kind of arguments are called **sophistries** N-UNCOUNT FORMAL / N-PLURAL

sopho·more /'sɒfəmɔː/ **sophomores.** In the United States, a **sophomore** is a student in the second year of college or high school. N-COUNT

sopo·rif·ic /,sɒpə'rɪfɪk/. Something that is **soporific** makes you feel sleepy. *A pint of beer at lunchtime has a strongly soporific effect.* ADJ-GRADED

sop·ping /'sɒpɪŋ/. Something that is **sopping** or **sopping wet** is extremely wet. ADJ INFORMAL

sop·py /'sɒpi/ **soppier, soppiest.** If you describe someone or something as **soppy**, you mean that they are foolishly sentimental. *He's constantly on the phone to his girlfriend being soppy.* ADJ-GRADED INFORMAL, BRITISH

so·pra·no /sə'prɑːnəʊ, -'præn/ **sopranos. 1** A so**prano** is a woman, girl, or boy with a high singing voice. **2** A **soprano** saxophone or other musical instrument has a range of notes of high pitch. ♦◇◇◇ N-COUNT / ADJ: ADJ n

sor·bet /'sɔːbeɪ, AM -bɪt/ **sorbets.** Sorbet is water ice that is usually made from fruit. N-VAR

sor·cer·er /'sɔːsərə/ **sorcerers.** In stories and fairy tales, a **sorcerer** is a person who performs magic by using the power of evil spirits. N-COUNT

sor·cer·ess /'sɔːsərɪs/ **sorceresses.** In stories and fairy tales, a **sorceress** is a woman who performs magic by using the power of evil spirits. N-COUNT

sor·cery /'sɔːsəri/. **Sorcery** is the practice of performing magic by using the power of evil spirits. N-UNCOUNT

sor·did /'sɔːdɪd/. **1** If you describe someone's behaviour as **sordid**, you mean that it is immoral or dishonest. *I don't want to hear the sordid details of your relationship with Sandra.* **2** If you describe a place as **sordid**, you mean that it is dirty, unpleasant, or depressing. *...the attic windows of their sordid little rooms.* ♦◇◇◇ ADJ-GRADED / ADJ-GRADED

sore /sɔː/ **sorer, sorest; sores. 1** If part of your body is **sore**, it causes you pain and discomfort. *It's years since I've had a sore throat like I did last night.* ♦ **sore·ness** The soreness lasted for about six weeks. **2** A **sore** is a painful place on the body where the skin is infected. ● See also **cold sore. 3** If you are **sore** about something, you are angry and upset about it. *The result is that they are now all feeling very sore at you.* **4** If something is **a sore point** with someone, it is likely to make them angry or embarrassed if you try to discuss it. ● **to stick out like a sore thumb**: see **thumb**. ♦♦◇◇ ADJ-GRADED / N-COUNT / N-COUNT / ADJ-GRADED: v-link ADJ INFORMAL / PHRASE

sore·ly /'sɔːli/. **Sorely** is used to emphasize that a feeling such as disappointment or need is very strong. *...sorely needed money... He will be sorely missed.* ♦◇◇◇ ADV-GRADED PRAGMATICS

sor·ghum /'sɔːgəm/. **Sorghum** is a type of corn that is grown in warm countries. Its grain can be made into flour or syrup. N-UNCOUNT

so·ror·ity /sə'rɒrɪti/ **sororities.** In the United States, a **sorority** is a society of women students that is formed for social purposes. N-COUNT

sor·rel /'sɒrəl, AM 'sɔːr-/. **Sorrel** is a plant with bitter-tasting arrow-shaped leaves which are sometimes used in salads and sauces. N-UNCOUNT

sor·row /'sɒrəʊ/. **Sorrow** is a feeling of deep sadness or regret. *It was a time of great sorrow.* ♦◇◇◇ N-UNCOUNT

sor·row·ful /'sɒrəʊfʊl/. **Sorrowful** means very sad. *His father's face looked suddenly soft and sorrowful.* ♦ **sor·row·ful·ly** The postmaster shook his head sorrowfully. ADJ-GRADED LITERARY / ADV: ADV with v

sor·rows /'sɒrəʊz/. **Sorrows** are events or situations that cause deep sadness. *...the joys and sorrows of everyday living.* ● **to drown** one's **sorrows**: see **drown**. N-PLURAL

sor·ry /'sɒri/ **sorrier, sorriest. 1** You say '**Sorry**' or '**I'm sorry**' as a way of apologizing to someone for upsetting them or causing them difficulties. *Sorry I took so long... I'm really sorry if I said anything wrong... She came into my room and said she was sorry.* **2** You use **I'm sorry** or **sorry** as an introduction when you are telling someone something that you do not think they will want to hear, for example when you are disagreeing with them, or giving them bad news. *Sorry – no baths after ten o'clock... I'm sorry to have to tell you that Janet West is dead.* **3** If you are **sorry** about a situation, you feel regret, sadness, or disappointment about it. *She was very sorry about all the trouble she'd caused.* **4** You use the expression **I'm sorry to say** to express regret together with disappointment or disapproval. *This, I am sorry to say, is almost entirely wishful thinking.* **5** You say '**I'm sorry**' to express your regret and sadness when you hear sad or unpleasant news. *I've heard about Mollie – I'm so sorry.* **6** If you feel **sorry for** someone who is unhappy or in an unpleasant situation, you feel sympathy and sadness for them. *I am very sorry for the family.* **7** You say that someone is feeling **sorry for** himself or herself when you disapprove of the fact that he or she is miserable and full of self-pity, rather than trying to be cheerful and positive. **8** If someone or something is in a **sorry** state, they are in a bad state, mentally or physically. *She is a sorry sight.* **9** You say '**Sorry?**' when you have not heard something that someone has said and you want them to repeat it. **10** You use **sorry** when you correct yourself and use different words to say what you have just said, especially when what you say the second time does not use the words you would normally choose to use. *...refugees (sorry, economic migrants) who refuse to return to Vietnam.* **11** ● **better safe than sorry**: see **safe**. ♦♦♦♦◇ CONVENTION PRAGMATICS / CONVENTION PRAGMATICS / ADJ-GRADED: v-link ADJ / PHRASE PRAGMATICS / CONVENTION PRAGMATICS / ADJ-GRADED: v-link ADJ for n / ADJ-GRADED: v-link ADJ for pron-refl PRAGMATICS / ADJ-GRADED: ADJ n / CONVENTION PRAGMATICS / CONVENTION PRAGMATICS

sort /sɔːt/ **sorts, sorting, sorted. 1** If you talk about a particular **sort** of something, you are talking about a class of things that have particular features in common and that belong to a larger group of related things. *What sort of school did you go to?... Let's have some more articles of this sort.* **2** You describe someone as a particular **sort** when you are describing their character. *He seemed to be just the right sort for the job... She was a very vigorous sort of person.* **3** If you **sort** things, you separate them into different classes, groups, or places, for example so that you can do different things with them. *The students are sorted into three ability groups... He unlatched the box and sorted through the papers.* **4** If you get a problem or the details of something **sorted**, you do what is necessary to solve the problem or organize the details. *These problems have now been sorted.* **5** **All sorts** of things or people means a large number of different things or people. *...self-help groups of all sorts.* **6** If you describe something as a thing **of sorts** or as a thing **of a sort**, you are suggesting that the thing is of a rather poor quality or standard. *He made* ♦♦♦♦♦ N-COUNT: with supp / N-SING: with supp / VERB: V n, V n into n, V through n / VERB: getn V-ed, be V-ed INFORMAL / PHRASE / PHRASE

a living of sorts selling pancakes from a van. **7** You use PHRASE **sort of** when you want to say that your description of PRAGMATICS something is not very accurate. *In the end, she sort of pushed it... I suppose it sort of made it more exciting.*

8 If you are **out of sorts**, you feel slightly unwell, dis- PHRASE contented, or annoyed.

9 ● **nothing of the sort**: see **nothing**.

sort out. 1 If you **sort out** a group of things, you PHRASAL VB separate them into different classes, groups, or V P noun V P noun *from* places. *Trying to sort out fact from fiction is difficult.* n **2** If you **sort out** a problem or the details of some- Also V n P thing, you do what is necessary to solve the problem V P noun or organize the details. *Have you sorted something out* V n P *for tomorrow night?* **3** If you **sort** someone **out**, you V n P make them realize that they have behaved wrongly, V P noun BRITISH for example by talking to them or by punishing them. *The crucial skill you need to develop is sorting out the parents.* **4** If you **sort** yourself **out**, you organize your- V pron-refl P self or calm yourself so that you can act effectively and reasonably.

sor·tie /'sɔːti/ **sorties. 1** A **sortie** is a brief trip ◆◇◇◇◇ away from your home base, especially a trip to an N-COUNT FORMAL unfamiliar place. *From here we plan several sorties into the countryside.* **2** If a military force makes a N-COUNT FORMAL **sortie**, it makes an attack or raid by leaving its own position and going briefly into enemy territory.

'sorting office, sorting offices. A **sorting office** N-COUNT is a place where letters and parcels are taken after posting and are sorted according to their delivery addresses.

SOS /ˌes əʊ 'es/. An **SOS** is a signal which indicates N-SING to other people that you are in danger and need help quickly. *The ferry did not even have time to send out an SOS.*

,so-'so. If you say that something is **so-so**, you ◆◇◇◇◇ mean that it is average in quality, rather than being ADJ INFORMAL very good or very bad. *Their lunch was only so-so.* ▶ Also an adverb. *'How's it going?'—'So-so.'* ADV

sotto voce /ˌsɒtəʊ 'vəʊtʃeɪ/. If you say something ADV **sotto voce**, you say it in a soft voice. LITERARY

sou·bri·quet /'suːbrɪkeɪ/ **soubriquets.** See **sobriquet.**

souf·flé /'suːfleɪ, AM suːˈfleɪ/ **soufflés;** also spelled ◆◇◇◇◇ **souffle.** A **soufflé** is a light food made from a mix- N-VAR ture of beaten egg whites and other ingredients that is baked in the oven.

sought /sɔːt/. **Sought** is the past tense and past participle of **seek.**

'sought-after. Something that is **sought-after** is ◆◇◇◇◇ in great demand, usually because it is rare or of very ADJ-GRADED good quality. *An Olympic gold medal is the most sought-after prize in world sport.*

souk /suːk/ **souks;** also spelled **suq.** A **souk** is an N-COUNT open-air marketplace in Muslim countries, especial- ly in North Africa and the Middle East.

soul /səʊl/ **souls. 1** Your **soul** is the part of you ◆◆◇◇◇ that consists of your mind, character, thoughts, and N-COUNT feelings. *'I will put my heart and soul into the job,'* he promises. **2** If you say that someone **sells** their PHRASE **soul**, you mean that they give up something very important such as their honesty in exchange for wealth or success. **3** **Soul** or **soul music** is a type of N-UNCOUNT pop music which developed from gospel and blues and is performed mainly by black American musicians.

4 The **soul** of a nation or a political movement is its N-SING basic nature and beliefs. *...a struggle for the soul of the* with poss *Republican Party.* **5** You can refer to someone as a N-COUNT: particular kind of **soul** when you are describing their adj N character or condition. *He's a jolly soul.*

6 You use **soul** in negative statements like **not a soul** N-SING: to mean nobody at all. *I've never harmed a soul in my* with brd-neg *life.* **7** You can refer to the number of people who live N-PLURAL: in a particular place as **souls.** *...a tiny village of only* num N LITERARY *100 souls.*

8 ● **to bare** one's **soul**: see **bare.** ● **body and soul**: see **body.** ● **the life and soul of the party**: see **life.**

'soul-destroying. Situations that are **soul-** ADJ-GRADED **destroying** make you depressed, because they are boring or because there is no hope of improvement.

soul·ful /'səʊlfʊl/. Something that is **soulful** ex- ◆◇◇◇◇ presses deep feelings, especially sadness or love. ADJ-GRADED *...his great, soulful, brown eyes.* ◆ **soul·ful·ly** *She* ADV-GRADED *gazed at him soulfully.*

soul·less /'səʊlləs/. If you describe a thing or per- ADJ-GRADED son as **soulless**, you mean that they lack human qualities and the ability to feel or produce deep feelings. *...a grey and soulless existence.*

'soul mate, soul mates; also spelled **soulmate.** A N-COUNT **soul mate** is someone with whom you share a close friendship and deep personal understanding.

'soul music. See **soul**.

'soul-searching. Soul-searching is a long and N-UNCOUNT careful examination of your thoughts and feelings, especially when you are trying to make a difficult moral decision or thinking about something that has gone wrong.

sound 1 noun and verb uses

sound /saʊnd/ **sounds, sounding, sounded.** ◆◆◆◆◇ **1** A **sound** is something that you hear. *Liza was so* N-COUNT *frightened she couldn't make a sound. ...the sounds of children playing.* **2 Sound** is what you hear as a N-UNCOUNT result of vibrations travelling through air or water. *...twice the speed of sound.* **3** The **sound** on a N-SING: television, radio, or record player is what you hear the N coming from the machine. Its loudness can be con- trolled. *She went and turned the sound down.* **4** A N-COUNT: singer's or band's **sound** is the distinctive quality of with supp their music. *They have started showing a strong soul element in their sound.*

5 If something such as a horn or a bell **sounds** or if you V-ERG: V **sound** it, it makes a noise. *A young man sounds the* V n *bell to start the Sunday service.* **6** When you are de- V-LINK scribing a noise, you can talk about the way it **sounds.** V *like* n *They heard what sounded like a huge explosion... The* V adj creaking of the hinges sounded very loud in that si- Also V as if *lence.* **7** If you **sound** a warning, you publicly give it. If VERB: V n you **sound** a note of caution, scepticism, or optimism, you say publicly that you feel cautious, sceptical, or optimistic.

8 When you talk about the way someone **sounds**, you V-LINK are describing the impression you have of them when V adj they speak. *She sounded a bit worried... Murphy* V *like* n *sounds like a child... She sounded as if she really cared.* V as if Also V n **9** When you are describing your impression or opin- V-LINK ion of something you have heard about or read about, V *like* n you can talk about the way it **sounds.** *It sounds like a* V as if *wonderful idea to me... It sounds as if they might have* Also V adj/n *made a dreadful mistake.* **10** You can describe your N-SING: impression of something you have heard about or the N of n read about by talking about **the sound of** it. *I don't like the sound of Toby Osborne.*

11 See also **-sounding, sounding. 12** ● to **sound the alarm**: see **alarm.** ● to **sound the death knell**: see **death knell.** ● **safe and sound**: see **safe.**

sound off. If someone **sounds off**, they express their PHRASAL VB opinions strongly and rather rudely to everyone with- V P *about/on* n out being asked. *It is surprising how many people start* Also V P *sounding off about something without really deciding* INFORMAL *what they think about it.*

sound out. If you **sound** someone **out**, you question PHRASAL VB them in order to find out what their opinion is about V n P something. *He is sounding out Middle Eastern govern-* V P noun *ments on ways to resolve the conflict.*

sound 2 adjective uses

sound /saʊnd/ **sounder, soundest. 1** If a struc- ◆◆◇◇◇ ture, part of someone's body, or someone's mind is ADJ-GRADED **sound**, it is in good condition or healthy. *His body was still sound.* ◆ **sound·ness** *...the structural* N-UNCOUNT *soundness of the coachwork.* **2 Sound** advice, rea- ADJ-GRADED soning, or evidence is reliable and sensible. *...sound scientific evidence.* ◆ **soundness** *...it is the sound-* N-UNCOUNT *ness of his thought that I question.* **3** If you describe ADJ-GRADED someone's ideas as **sound**, you mean that you ap- PRAGMATICS prove of them and think they are correct. *I am not sure that this is sound democratic practice.*

4 If someone is in a **sound** sleep, they are sleeping ADJ: ADJ n very deeply. ▶ Also an adverb. *He was lying in bed,* ADV: ADV adj *sound asleep.* **5** See also **soundly.**

'sound barrier. If an aircraft breaks the **sound barrier**, it reaches a speed that is faster than the speed of sound. `N-SING`

sound-bite /'saʊndbaɪt/ **soundbites;** also spelled **sound-bite**. A **soundbite** is a short sentence or phrase, usually from a politician's speech, which is broadcast during a news bulletin. `N-COUNT`

'sound effect, sound effects. Sound effects are the sounds that are created artificially to make a play more realistic, especially a radio play. `N-COUNT`

'sound engineer, sound engineers. A **sound engineer** is a person who works in a recording studio or for a radio or television company, whose job is to alter and balance the levels of different sounds as they are recorded. `N-COUNT`

sound·ing /'saʊndɪŋ/ **soundings. 1 The sounding of** a bell or a horn is the act of causing it to make a sound. ...*the sounding of the all-clear signal.* **2** If you take **soundings**, you try to find out people's opinions on a subject. `N-SING` `the N of n` `N-COUNT`

-sounding /-saʊndɪŋ/. **-sounding** combines with adjectives to indicate a quality that a word, phrase, or name seems to have. ...*faraway places with strange-sounding names.* ● See also **high-sounding**. `COMB`

'sounding board, sounding boards. If you use someone as a **sounding board**, you discuss your ideas with them in order to get another opinion. `N-COUNT`

sound·less /'saʊndləs/. Something that is **soundless** does not make a sound. *My bare feet were soundless over the carpet.* ● **sound·less·ly** *Joe's lips moved soundlessly.* `ADJ` `LITERARY` `ADV`

sound·ly /'saʊndli/. **1** If someone is soundly defeated or beaten, they are defeated or beaten thoroughly. **2** If a decision, opinion, or statement is **soundly** based, there are sensible or reliable reasons behind it. **3** If you sleep **soundly**, you sleep deeply and do not wake during your sleep. *She was too soundly asleep to hear Stefano's return.* `ADV-GRADED` `ADV-ed` `ADV-GRADED` `ADV-ed` `ADV-GRADED`

sound·proof /'saʊndpruːf/ **soundproofs, soundproofing, soundproofed;** also spelled **sound-proof.** If you **soundproof** a room, you line it with special materials to stop all sound from getting in or out. *The dog was placed in a soundproofed room.* ● Also an adjective. *The studio isn't soundproof.* ● **sound·proof·ing** *We did make a mistake in not having enough soundproofing upstairs.* `VERB: V n` `V-ed` `ADJ` `N-UNCOUNT`

'sound stage, sound stages; also spelled **sound-stage, soundstage.** A **sound stage** is a stage or set which is suitable for recording sound, especially for a film. `N-COUNT`

'sound system, sound systems. A **sound system** is a set of equipment for playing and amplifying recorded music, or for amplifying live music. `N-COUNT`

sound·track /'saʊndtræk/ **soundtracks;** also spelled **sound track**. The **soundtrack** of a film is its sound, speech, and music. It is used especially to refer to the music. `N-COUNT`

'sound wave, sound waves; also spelled **soundwave**. **Sound waves** are the waves of energy that we hear as sound. `N-COUNT`

soup /suːp/ **soups, souping, souped. 1** Soup is liquid food made by boiling meat, fish, or vegetables in water. ...*home-made chicken soup.* **2** If you say that someone is **in the soup**, you mean they are in trouble. `N-VAR` `PHRASE` `INFORMAL, JOURNALISM`

soup up. To **soup up** something such as a car engine means to make it more powerful. To **soup up** something such as a piece of music or writing means to make it more interesting and exciting. *He had his first car at sixteen, a Mini, which he souped up and crashed.* ● **souped-up** ...*a souped-up Peugeot 205.* `PHRASAL VB` `V P noun` `ADJ: ADJ n`

'soup kitchen, soup kitchens; also spelled **soup-kitchen**. A **soup kitchen** is a place where homeless people or very poor people are provided with free food. `N-COUNT`

'soup plate, soup plates. A **soup plate** is a deep plate with a wide rim in which soup is served. `N-COUNT` `BRITISH`

sour /saʊə/ **sours, souring, soured. 1** Something that is **sour** has a sharp taste like the taste of a lemon or an unripe apple. *The stewed apple was* `ADJ-GRADED`

---

sour even with honey. ● See also **sweet and sour**.

2 Sour milk is milk that has an unpleasant taste because it is no longer fresh. `ADJ`

3 Someone who is **sour** is bad-tempered and unfriendly. *She made a sour face.* ● **sour·ly** *'Leave my mother out of it,' he said sourly.* **4** If a situation or relationship turns **sour** or goes **sour**, it stops being enjoyable or satisfactory. *Even the European dream is beginning to turn sour.* **5** If a friendship, situation, or attitude **sours** or if something **sours** it, it becomes less friendly, enjoyable, or hopeful. *Her mood soured a little.* **6 sour grapes**: see **grape** `ADJ-GRADED` `ADV:` `ADV with v` `ADJ` `V-ERG: V n` `V`

source /sɔːs/ **sources, sourcing, sourced. 1** The **source** of something is the person, place, or thing which you get it from. ...*renewable sources of energy.* ...*tourism, which is a major source of income for the city.* **2** In business, if a person or firm **sources** a product or a raw material, they find someone who will supply it. *About 60 per cent of an average car is sourced from outside of the manufacturer.* ● **sourc·ing** *The union is particularly concerned at the sourcing of products abroad.* **3** A **source** is a person or book that provides information for a news story or for a piece of research. *Military sources say the boat was heading south at high speed.* **4** The **source of** a difficulty is its cause. *This gave me a clue as to the source of the problem.* **5** The **source** of a river or stream is the place where it begins. `N-COUNT` `VERB: V n` `V n` `Also V from n` `N-UNCOUNT` `N-COUNT` `N-COUNT: N of n` `N-COUNT`

,sour 'cream; also spelled **soured cream**. **Sour cream** is cream that has been artificially made sour by being mixed with bacteria. It is used in cooking. `N-UNCOUNT`

south /saʊθ/. **South** is one of the four points of the compass. See Appendix headed **Compass**. `◆◆◆◆◆`

south·bound /'saʊθbaʊnd/. See Appendix headed **Compass**.

,south-'east; also spelled **South-East**. See Appendix headed **Compass**. `◆◆◆◇`

,south-'easterly; also spelled **south easterly**. See Appendix headed **Compass**.

,south-'eastern; also spelled **south eastern**. See Appendix headed **Compass**. `◆◇◇◇◇`

south·er·ly /'sʌðəli/. See Appendix headed **Compass**.

south·ern /'sʌðən/. See Appendix headed **Compass**. `◆◆◆◆◇`

south·ern·er /'sʌðənə/ **southerners**. See Appendix headed **Compass**. `◆◇◇◇◇`

south·ern·most /'sʌðənməʊst/. See Appendix headed **Compass**.

,South 'Pole. The South Pole is the place on the surface of the earth which is farthest towards the south. `N-PROPER:` `the N`

south·ward /'saʊθwəd/; the form **southwards** is also used. See Appendix headed **Compass**.

,south-'west; also spelled **South-West**. See Appendix headed **Compass**. `◆◆◆◇`

,south-'westerly; also spelled **south westerly**. See Appendix headed **Compass**.

,south-'western; also spelled **south western**. See Appendix headed **Compass**. `◆◇◇◇◇`

sou·venir /ˌsuːvə'nɪə, AM 'suːvənɪr/ **souvenirs**. A **souvenir** is something which you buy or keep to remind you of a holiday, place, or event. ...*a souvenir of the summer of 1992.* `◆◇◇◇◇` `N-COUNT`

sou'west·er /ˌsaʊ'westə/ **sou'westers**. A **sou'wester** is a waterproof hat with a wide brim at the back, that is worn especially by sailors in stormy weather. `N-COUNT`

sov·er·eign /'sɒvrɪn/ **sovereigns. 1** A **sovereign** state or country is independent and not under the authority of any other country. **2 Sovereign** is used to describe the person or institution that has the highest power in a particular country. ...*the Armed Forces Ruling Council, Nigeria's sovereign body.* **3** A **sovereign** is a king, queen, or other royal ruler of a country. `◆◆◇◇◇` `ADJ` `ADJ` `N-COUNT`

sov·er·eign·ty /'sɒvrɪnti/. **Sovereignty** is the power that a country has to govern itself or another country or state. `◆◆◇◇◇` `N-UNCOUNT` `also N in pl`

S

sow 1 verb uses

sow /səʊ/ **sows, sowing, sowed, sown. 1** If you **sow** seeds, you plant them in the ground. *Yesterday the field opposite was sown with maize.* **2** If someone **sows** an undesirable feeling or situation, they cause it to begin and develop. *He cleverly sowed doubts into the minds of his rivals.* **3** If one thing **sows the seeds of** another, it starts the process which leads eventually to the other thing. *He may have sown the seeds of renewed conflict.*

sow 2 noun use

sow /saʊ/ **sows.** A **sow** is an adult female pig.

sown /səʊn/. **Sown** is the past participle of **sow**.

soya /ˈsɔɪə/. **Soya** flour, butter, or other food is made from soya beans.

'soya bean, soya beans; spelled **soybean** /ˈsɔɪbiːn/ in American English. **Soya beans** are beans that can be eaten or used to make flour, oil, or soy sauce.

soy sauce /ˌsɔɪ ˈsɔːs/; also spelled **soya sauce. Soy sauce** is a dark brown liquid made from soya beans and used as a flavouring, especially in Chinese cooking.

spa /spɑː/ **spas. 1** A **spa** is a place where water with minerals in it bubbles out of the ground. People drink the water or bathe in it in order to improve their health. **2** A health **spa** is a place where people go to use facilities such as a pool, a gymnasium, and a sauna in order to improve their health.

space /speɪs/ **spaces, spacing, spaced. 1** You use **space** to refer to an area of any size that is empty or available. *...cutting down yet more trees to make space for houses... I had plenty of space to write and sew... List in the spaces below the specific changes you have made.* **2** A particular kind of **space** is the area that is available for a particular activity or for putting a particular kind of thing in. *...the high cost of office space... Finding a parking space in the summer months is still a virtual impossibility.* **3** If you give someone **space** for a topic to be discussed in a document is the number of words, paragraphs, or pages available to discuss the topic. *We can't promise to publish a reply as space is limited.* **4** If you are staring **into space**, you are looking straight in front of you, without actually looking at anything in particular. **5** If you describe someone or something as a **waste of space**, you are indicating that you have a very low opinion of them. **6** Journalists write **'Watch this space'** in order to indicate that they will give more information about something in the future. *Watch this space for details of our next event.* **7** If you give someone **space** to think about something or to develop as a person, you allow them the time and freedom to do this. *He won't give you enough space.* **8** A **space** of time is a period of time. *I have known dramatic changes occur in the space of a few minutes with this method.* **9** If you **space** a series of things, you arrange them so that they are not all together but have gaps or time intervals between them. *Women once again are having fewer children and spacing them further apart.* ► **Space out** means the same as **space**. *I was spacing out the seedlings into divided trays... He talks quite slowly and spaces his words out.* ♦ **spaced** *Its houses are large, well-spaced and surrounded by gardens.* ♦ **spacing** *Generous spacing gives healthier trees and better crops.* **10** Space is the vast area that lies beyond the Earth's atmosphere and surrounds the stars and planets. *...launching satellites into space.* **11** Space is the whole area within which everything exists. *She felt herself transcending time and space.* **12** See also **spacing; airspace, breathing space, personal space.**

'space age; also spelled **space-age. 1 The space age** is the present period in the history of the world, when travel in space has become possible. **2** You use **space-age** to describe something that is very modern and makes you think of the technology of the space age. *...a space-age tower of steel and glass.*

space·craft /ˈspeɪskrɑːft, -kræft/; **spacecraft** is both the singular and the plural form. A **spacecraft** is a rocket or other vehicle that can travel in space.

,spaced-'out; also spelled **spaced out.** Someone who is **spaced-out** feels as if nothing around them is real, usually because they have taken drugs or because they are very tired.

space·man /ˈspeɪsmæn/ **spacemen.** A **spaceman** is a male astronaut; used mainly by children.

'space probe, space probes. A **space probe** is a small unmanned spacecraft that is sent into space in order to transmit information about it.

space·ship /ˈspeɪsʃɪp/ **spaceships.** A **spaceship** is a spacecraft that carries people through space.

'space shuttle, space shuttles. A **space shuttle** is a spacecraft that is designed to travel into space and back to earth several times.

'space station, space stations. A **space station** is an object which is sent into space and then goes around the earth, and is used as a base by astronauts.

'space suit, space suits; also spelled **spacesuit.** A **space suit** is a special protective suit that is worn by astronauts in space.

'space walk, space walks. When an astronaut goes on a **space walk**, he or she leaves the spacecraft and works outside it while floating in space.

spac·ing /ˈspeɪsɪŋ/. **Spacing** refers to the way that typing or printing is arranged on a page, especially in relation to the amount of space that is left between words or lines. ● See also **space.**

spa·cious /ˈspeɪʃəs/. A **spacious** room or other place is large in size or area, so that you can move around freely in it. ♦ **spa·cious·ness** *A high ceiling creates a feeling of spaciousness.*

spade /speɪd/ **spades. 1** A **spade** is a tool used for digging, with a flat metal blade and a long handle. See picture headed **tools.** **2 Spades** is one of the four suits in a pack of playing cards. Each card in the suit is marked with one or more black symbols: ♠. *...the ace of spades.* ► A **spade** is a playing card of this suit.

spade·work /ˈspeɪdwɜːk/. The **spadework** is the uninteresting work that has to be done as preparation before you can start a project or activity.

spa·ghet·ti /spəˈgeti/. **Spaghetti** is a type of pasta. It looks like long pieces of string and is usually served with a sauce.

spa,ghetti 'western, spaghetti westerns. A **spaghetti western** is a film made in Europe by an Italian director about life in the American Wild West.

spake /speɪk/. **Spake** is the very old-fashioned form of the past tense of **speak.**

span /spæn/ **spans, spanning, spanned. 1** A **span** is the period of time between two dates or events during which something exists, functions, or happens. *The batteries had a life span of six hours.* **2** Your concentration **span** or your attention **span** is the length of time you are able to concentrate on something or be interested in it. **3** If something **spans** a long period of time, it lasts throughout that period of time or relates to that whole period of time. *His professional career spanned 16 years.* **4** If something **spans** a range of things, all those things are included in it. *...a remarkable man whose interests spanned almost every aspect of nature.* **5** The **span** of something that extends or is spread out sideways is the total width of it from one end to the other. *It is a very pretty butterfly, with a 2 inch wing span.* **6** A bridge or other structure that **spans** something such as a river stretches right across it. **7** See also **spick and span.**

span·gled /ˈspæŋgəld/. Something that is **spangled** is covered with small shiny objects. *...spangled, backless dresses.*

span·iel /ˈspænjəl/ **spaniels.** A **spaniel** is a type of dog with long ears that hang down.

spank /spæŋk/ **spanks, spanking, spanked.** If someone **spanks** a child, they punish them by

hitting them on the bottom several times. ♦ **spank·ing**, **spankings** *Andrea gave her son a sound spanking.*   N-COUNT

spank·ing /'spæŋkɪŋ/. **1** If you describe something as **spanking** new, **spanking** clean, or **spanking** white, you mean that it is very new, very clean, or very white. **2** If something moves at a **spanking** pace, it moves quickly. **3** See also **spank**.   ADV: ADV adj INFORMAL   ADJ: ADJ n BRITISH

span·ner /'spænə/ **spanners**. **1** A **spanner** is a metal tool with a specially shaped end that fits round a nut so that you can loosen or tighten the nut. The usual American word is **wrench**. See picture headed **tools**. **2** If someone or something **throws a spanner in the works**, they prevent something happening smoothly in the way that it was planned, by causing a problem or difficulty. The usual American expression is to **throw a wrench** into a process.   N-COUNT BRITISH   PHRASE BRITISH

spar /spɑː/ **spars, sparring, sparred. 1** If you **spar** with someone, you box using fairly gentle blows instead of hitting your opponent hard, for example in training. *They sparred for a moment, on the brink of a full fist-fight.* **2** If you **spar** with someone, you argue with them but not in an aggressive or serious way. *Morisot and Manet had always gotten along, even when they sparred.*   ◆◇◇◇◇   V-RECIP: V with n pl-n V   V-RECIP: V with n pl-n V

spare /speə/ **spares, sparing, spared. 1** You use **spare** to describe something that is the same as things that you are already using, and that you are keeping ready in case another one is needed. *Don't forget to take a few spare batteries... He could have taken a spare key.* ► The spare wheel carried by a car or other vehicle can be called a **spare**. **2** You use **spare** to describe something that is not being used by anyone, and is therefore available for someone to use. *They don't have a lot of spare cash... The spare bedroom is on the second floor.* **3** If you have something such as time, money, or space to **spare**, you have some extra time, money, or space that you have not used or which you do not need. *You got here with ninety seconds to spare.* **4** If you **spare** time or another resource for a particular purpose, you make it available for that purpose. *She said that she could only spare 35 minutes for our meeting.* **5** If you **spare a thought for** an unfortunate person, you make an effort to think sympathetically about them and their bad luck. *Spare a thought for the nation's shopkeepers – consumer sales slid again in May.* **6** If a person or a place **is spared**, they are not harmed, although someone or something threatened them or harmed other people or places. *Northern Somalia was largely spared from the famine.* **7** If you **spare** someone an unpleasant experience, you prevent them from suffering it. *She's just trying to spare Shawna's feelings... The policy has not spared the farming community from severe financial pressure.* **8** If you **spare no effort** in doing something, you do it as well as possible, without worrying about the amount of work involved. If you **spare no expense** in doing it, you do it as well as possible, without trying to save money. **9** See also **sparing**; ● to **spare** someone's **blushes**: see **blush**.   ◆◆◇◇◇   ADJ   N-COUNT   ADJ   VB: only to-inf V   VERB V n   PHRASE BRITISH   VERB: beV-ed beV-ed from n LITERARY   VERB: V n n V n from n   PHRASE

,spare 'part, spare parts. **Spare parts** are parts that you can buy separately to replace old or broken parts in a vehicle or piece of equipment.   ◆◇◇◇◇ N-COUNT

,spare 'room, spare rooms. A **spare room** is a bedroom which is kept especially for visitors to sleep in.   N-COUNT

,spare 'time. Your **spare time** is the time during which you do not have to work and you can do whatever you like. *In her spare time she read books on cooking.*   ◆◇◇◇◇ N-UNCOUNT

,spare 'tyre, spare tyres; spelled **spare tire** in American English. **1** A **spare tyre** is the same as a spare wheel. **2** If you describe someone as having a **spare tyre**, you mean that they are fat around their waist.   N-COUNT   N-COUNT

,spare 'wheel, spare wheels. A **spare wheel** is a complete wheel with a tyre already on it that you   N-COUNT BRITISH

keep in your car in case you have a puncture and need to replace one of your wheels.

spar·ing /'speərɪŋ/. Someone who is **sparing** with something uses it or gives it only in very small quantities. *I've not been sparing with the garlic.* ♦ **spar·ing·ly** *Medication is used sparingly.*   ◆◇◇◇◇ ADJ-GRADED   ADV-GRADED

spark /spɑːk/ **sparks, sparking, sparked. 1** A **spark** is a tiny bright piece of burning material that flies up from something that is burning. **2** A **spark** is a flash of light caused by electricity. It often makes a crackling sound. **3** If something **sparks**, sparks of fire or light come from it. **4** If a burning object or electricity **sparks** a fire, it causes a fire. **5** A **spark** of a quality or feeling, especially a desirable one, is a small but noticeable amount of it. *His music lacked that vital spark of imagination.* **6** If one thing **sparks** another, the first thing cause the second thing to start happening. *What was it that sparked your interest in motoring? ...a row sparked by a comment about his sister.* ► **Spark off** means the same as **spark**. *His book, Animal Liberation, sparked off a revolution in the way we think about animals. ...a political crisis sparked off by religious violence.* **7** See also **bright spark**. **8** If **sparks fly** between people, they discuss something in an excited or angry way.   ◆◆◆◇◇ N-COUNT   N-COUNT   VERB: V   VERB: V n   N-COUNT: N of n   VERB V n V-ed   PHRASAL VB: V n P V P noun V-ed   PHRASE

spark off. See **spark** 6.   PHRASAL VB

spar·kle /'spɑːkəl/ **sparkles, sparkling, sparkled. 1** If something **sparkles**, it is clear and bright and shines with a lot of very small points of light. *...the sparkling blue waters of the ocean.* ► Also a noun. *...the sparkle of coloured glass.* **2** **Sparkles** are small points of light caused by light reflecting off a clear bright surface. *There was a sparkle in her eye that could not be hidden.* **3** Someone who **sparkles** is lively, intelligent, and witty. ► Also a noun. *There was little sparkle in their performance.* ♦ **spar·kling** *He is sparkling and versatile in front of the camera.*   ◆◆◇◇◇ VERB: V V-ing   N-UNCOUNT   N-COUNT   VERB: V   N-UNCOUNT   ADJ-GRADED

spar·kling /'spɑːklɪŋ/. **Sparkling** drinks are slightly fizzy. *...a glass of sparkling wine.*   ◆◇◇◇◇ ADJ

spark·ly /'spɑːkli/. **Sparkly** things sparkle. *...a sparkly toy necklace.*   ADJ-GRADED INFORMAL

'spark plug, spark plugs. A **spark plug** is a device in the engine of a motor vehicle, which produces electric sparks to make the petrol burn.   N-COUNT

sparky /'spɑːki/ **sparkier, sparkiest. Sparky** people or events are lively and entertaining. *She's a terrific, sparky girl.*   ADJ-GRADED INFORMAL, BRITISH

'sparring partner, sparring partners. **1** A boxer's **sparring partner** is another boxer who he or she fights regularly in training. **2** Your **sparring partner** is a person with whom you regularly have good-humoured arguments.   N-COUNT   N-COUNT

spar·row /'spærəʊ/ **sparrows**. A **sparrow** is a small brown bird that is very common in Britain.   ◆◇◇◇◇ N-COUNT

sparse /spɑːs/ **sparser, sparsest**. Something that is **sparse** is small in number or amount and spread out over an area. *Many slopes are rock fields with sparse vegetation... Traffic was sparse on the highway.* ♦ **sparse·ly** *...the sparsely populated interior region.*   ◆◇◇◇◇ ADJ-GRADED   ADV-GRADED

spar·tan /'spɑːtən/. A **spartan** lifestyle or existence is very simple or strict, with no luxuries.   ◆◇◇◇◇ ADJ-GRADED

spasm /'spæzəm/ **spasms. 1** A **spasm** is a sudden tightening of your muscles, which you cannot control. *A lack of magnesium causes muscles to go into spasm.* **2** A **spasm** is a sudden strong pain or unpleasant emotion which lasts for a short period of time. *A spasm of pain brought his thoughts back to the present.*   ◇◇◇◇◇ N-VAR   N-COUNT WRITTEN

spas·mod·ic /spæz'mɒdɪk/. Something that is **spasmodic** happens suddenly, for short periods of time, and at irregular intervals. *My husband's work was so spasmodic.* ♦ **spas·mod·i·cal·ly** /spæz'mɒdɪkli/. *Buildings trembled spasmodically for forty-five seconds or so.*   ADJ-GRADED   ADV-GRADED

spas·tic /'spæstɪk/ **spastics**. Someone who is **spastic** is born with a disability which makes it difficult for them to control their muscles, especially in   ADJ

S

their arms and legs. Most people now refer to someone with this disability as having **cerebral palsy**.
▶ A **spastic** is someone who is spastic. N-COUNT

spat /spæt/ **spats. 1 Spat** is the past tense and past participle of **spit**. **2** A **spat** between people, countries, or organizations is a disagreement between them. **3 Spats** are specially shaped pieces of cloth or leather which button down one side and which were worn in former times by men over their ankles and part of their shoes. N-COUNT / N-PLURAL

spate /speɪt/ **spates. 1** A **spate** of things, especially unpleasant things, is a large number of them that happen or appear within a short period of time. *...the recent spate of attacks on horses.* **2** When a river is **in spate** it contains a lot more water than usual and is flowing very fast. ◆◇◇◇ N-COUNT / PHRASE BRITISH

spa·tial /ˈspeɪʃl/. **1 Spatial** is used to describe things relating to size, area, or position. *These images indicate the intensity and spatial distribution of rainfall.* ♦ **spa·tial·ly** The growth of home ownership has been both socially and spatially uneven. **2** Your **spatial** ability is your ability to see and understand the relationships between shapes, spaces, and areas. *His manual dexterity and fine spatial skills were wasted on routine tasks.* ◆◇◇◇ ADJ: ADJ n / ADV / ADJ: ADJ n

spat·ter /ˈspætə/ **spatters, spattering, spattered.** If a liquid **spatters** a surface, drops of it fall on an area of the surface. *He stared at the rain spattering on the glass... Gently turn the fish, being careful not to spatter any hot butter on yourself.* ♦ **-spattered** *...the blood-spattered body.* V-ERG: V n / V prep / V n prep / COMB

spatu·la /ˈspætʃʊlə/ **spatulas.** A **spatula** is a tool like a knife with a wide, flat blade that is used, for example, in cooking. See picture headed **kitchen utensils.** N-COUNT

spawn /spɔːn/ **spawns, spawning, spawned. 1 Spawn** is a soft, jelly-like substance containing the eggs of fish, frogs, or other amphibians. **2** When fish, or frogs or other amphibians **spawn**, they lay their eggs. **3** If something **spawns** something else, it causes it to happen or to be created. *Tyndall's inspired work spawned a whole new branch of science.* ◆◇◇◇ N-UNCOUNT / VERB: V / VERB V n LITERARY

spay /speɪ/ **spays, spaying, spayed.** When a female animal **is spayed**, it has its ovaries removed so that it cannot become pregnant. VERB: be V-ed

speak /spiːk/ **speaks, speaking, spoke, spoken. 1** When you **speak**, you use your voice in order to say something. *He tried to speak, but for once, his voice had left him... I rang the hotel and spoke to Louie... She cried when she spoke of Oliver. ...as I spoke these idiotic words.* ♦ **speak·er, speakers** *From a simple gesture or the speaker's tone of voice, the Japanese listener gleans the whole meaning.* **2** When someone **speaks** to a group of people, they make a speech. *He's determined to speak at the Democratic Convention... The President spoke of the need for territorial compromise.* ♦ **speaker** *Bruce Wyatt will be the guest speaker at next month's meeting.* ♦ **speak·ing** *It would also train women union members in public speaking.* **3** If you **speak for** a group of people, you make their views and demands known, or represent them. *He said it was the job of the Church to speak for the underprivileged.* **4** If you **speak** a foreign language, you know the language and are able to have a conversation in it. *He doesn't speak English.* ♦ **speaker** *...the Ukraine, where a fifth of the population are Russian speakers.* ● See also **native speaker.** ♦ **-speaking** *...the mainly French-speaking province of Quebec.* **5** If two people **are** not **speaking**, they no longer talk to each other because they have quarrelled. *He is not speaking to his mother because of her friendship with his ex-wife.* ● If you are **on speaking terms** with someone, you are quite friendly with them and often talk to them. **6** If you **speak well of** someone or **speak highly of** someone, you say good things about them. If you **speak ill of** someone, you criticize them. **7** People sometimes mention something that has been written by saying what the author **speaks of**. *The text spoke of the late emperor as an enlightened hero.* ♦♦♦♦♦ VERB / V to/with n / V of/about n / V n / N-COUNT / VERB: V / V t on / V of n / N-COUNT / N-UNCOUNT / VERB V for n / VERB V n / N-COUNT / COMB / V-RECIP: with neg, pl-n V / V t on / PHRASE / PHRASE / VERB: V of n / V of n as n

8 If you say that something **speaks** to you of a quality, experience, or feeling, you mean that it is evidence of it or conveys it. *His behaviour spoke of an early maturity.* **9** If you say that something **speaks for** itself, you mean that its meaning or quality is so obvious that it does not need explaining or pointing out. *The figures speak for themselves: six million people will have died of AIDS in Africa by the end of the century.* **10** Nothing **to speak of** means 'hardly anything' or 'only unimportant things'. *They have no weaponry to speak of.* **11** You can use **not to speak of** when adding something about your previous statement also applies to, or applies to even more than other things. *We wonder how housing for so many newcomers can be found, not to speak of employment.* **12** You use **so to speak** to draw attention to the fact that you are describing or referring to something in a metaphorical, colourful, or unusual way. *I ought not to tell you but I will, since you're in the family, so to speak.* **13** ● to **speak** your **mind:** see **mind.** ● to **speak volumes:** see **volume. 14** See also **speaking.** VB: no cont / V ofn / Also V t on / VB: no cont / V for pron-refl / PHRASE / PHRASE PRAGMATICS / PHRASE PRAGMATICS

speak out. If you **speak out** against something or in favour of something, you say publicly that you think it is bad or good. *Even then, she continued to speak out at rallies around the country.* PHRASAL VB / V P prep / V P

speak up. 1 If you **speak up**, you say something, especially to defend someone or protest about something. *Uncle Herbert never argued, never spoke up for himself.* **2** If you ask someone to **speak up**, you are asking them to speak more loudly. PHRASAL VB / V P / V P for/about / V P

-speak /-spiːk/. **-speak** is used to form nouns which refer to the kind of language used by a particular person or by people involved in a particular activity. You use **-speak** when you disapprove of this kind of language because it is difficult for other people to understand. *Unfortunately, the simplicity of this message is almost lost within his constant management-speak.* COMB PRAGMATICS

speak·er /ˈspiːkə/ **speakers. 1** In the parliament of many countries, the **Speaker** is the person who is in charge of the meetings of the parliament. **2** A **speaker** is a piece of equipment, for example part of a radio or hi-fi system, through which sound comes out. **3** See also **speak.** ♦♦♦◇◇ N-PROPER / N-COUNT

speak·ing /ˈspiːkɪŋ/. **1** You can say 'speaking as a parent' or 'speaking as a teacher', for example, to indicate that the opinion you are giving is based on your experience as a parent or as a teacher. **2** You can say **speaking of** something that has just been mentioned as a way of introducing a new topic which has some connection with that thing. *There's plenty of time to drop hints for Christmas presents! And speaking of presents, we have 100 exclusive fragrance collections to give away.* **3** You use **speaking** in expressions such as **generally speaking** and **technically speaking** to indicate the way in which your statement is true or relevant. *Politically speaking, do you think that these moves have been effective?* ◆◆◇◇ PHR-PREP PRAGMATICS / PHR-PREP PRAGMATICS / PHRASE PRAGMATICS

spear /spɪə/ **spears, spearing, speared. 1** A **spear** is a weapon consisting of a long pole with a sharp metal point attached to the end. **2** If you **spear** something, you push or throw a pointed object into it. *A police officer was speared to death.* **3** Asparagus or broccoli **spears** are individual stalks of asparagus or broccoli. ◆◇◇◇ N-COUNT / VERB: V n be V-ed into n / N-COUNT: with supp

spear·head /ˈspɪəhed/ **spearheads, spearheading, spearheaded.** If someone **spearheads** a campaign or an attack, they lead it. *Helicopters can to some extent take the place of tanks by spearheading the airborne attack.* ▶ The **spearhead** of a campaign is the person or group that leads it. ◆◇◇◇ VERB V n JOURNALISM / N-COUNT

spear·mint /ˈspɪəmɪnt/. **Spearmint** is a plant whose leaves have a strong smell and taste. It is often used for flavouring foods, especially sweets. N-UNCOUNT

spec /spek/ **specs. 1** A pair of **specs** is a pair of glasses. *...a well-groomed gent in smart dress and specs.* **2** The **spec** for something, especially a machine or vehicle, is its design and the features included in it. *The standard spec includes stainless steel holding tanks.* ◆◇◇◇ N-PLURAL INFORMAL / N-COUNT INFORMAL

spe·cial /ˈspeʃəl/ **specials. 1** Someone or something that is **special** is better or more important ◆◆◆◆◇ ADJ-GRADED than other people or things. *You're very special to me, darling... My special guest will be comedian Ben Elton.* **2 Special** means different from normal. *So* ADJ: ADJ n *you didn't notice anything special about him? ...a special variety of strawberry.*
3 You use **special** to describe someone who is officially appointed or who has a particular position specially ADJ: ADJ n created for them. *Deford is a special correspondent for Newsweek magazine.* **4 Special** schools or institutions ADJ: ADJ n are for people who have particular problems such as physical or mental handicaps. **5** You use **special** to ADJ: ADJ n describe something that relates to one particular person, group, or place. *Every anxious person will have his or her own special problems or fears.* ◆ **spe·cial·ly** ADV: *...a soap specially designed for those with sensitive* ADV with v *skins.* **6** A **special** is a product, programme, or meal N-COUNT which is not normally available, or which is made for a particular purpose. *Grocery stores have to offer enough specials to bring people into the store.*

'Special Branch. The **Special Branch** is the de ◆◇◇◇◇ partment of the British police that is concerned N-PROPER: with political security.

,special ef'fect, special effects. In film, spe ◆◇◇◇◇ cial effects are unusual pictures or sounds that are N-COUNT created by using special techniques.

spe·cial·ist /ˈspeʃəlɪst/ **specialists.** A specialist ◆◆◆◇◇ is a person who has a particular skill or knows a lot N-COUNT about a particular subject. *...a specialist in diseases of the nervous system.* ◆ **spe·cial·ism** /ˈspeʃəlɪzəm/ N-VAR **specialisms.** A **specialism** is a particular subject or skill of a specialist. *...a teacher with a specialism in mathematics.*

spe·ci·al·ity /ˌspeʃiˈælɪti/ **specialities.** ◆◇◇◇◇ **1** Someone's **speciality** is a particular type of work N-COUNT that they do most or do best, or a subject that they know a lot about. *His speciality was the history of Germany.* **2** A **speciality** of a particular place is a N-COUNT: special food or product that is always very good with supp there. *Buckwheat noodles are a speciality of the Alpine region of Italy.*

spe·cial·ize /ˈspeʃəlaɪz/ **specializes, specializ** ◆◆◆◇◇ **ing, specialized;** also spelled **specialise** in British VERB English. If you **specialize in** a subject of study or a V in n type of work, you know a lot about it and spend a lot of your time and attention on it. *...a University professor who specializes in the history of the Russian empire.* ◆ **spe·cial·i·za·tion** /ˌspeʃəlaɪˈzeɪʃən/ N-VAR **specializations** *This degree offers a major specialisation in Social Policy.*

spe·cial·ized /ˈspeʃəlaɪzd/. Someone or some ◆◆◇◇◇ thing that is **specialized** is trained or developed for ADJ-GRADED a particular purpose or area of knowledge. *Cocaine addicts get specialized support from knowledgeable staff.*

spe·cial·ly /ˈspeʃəli/. **Specially** is used to mean ◆◇◇◇◇ more than usually or more than other things. *What* ADV *was specially enjoyable about that job?* INFORMAL

,special 'needs. **1** People with **special needs** are ◆◇◇◇◇ people who have particular problems, for example N-PLURAL they are physically or mentally handicapped. *...a teacher who's worked with special needs students.* **2** You use **special needs** to refer to things which are ADJ: ADJ n intended for people with special needs. *...special needs housing.*

,special 'offer, special offers. A **special offer** is ◆◇◇◇◇ a product, service, or programme that is offered at N-COUNT reduced prices or rates.

,special 'pleading. If you say that someone is N-UNCOUNT using **special pleading,** you mean that they are trying to persuade you to do something by only telling you the facts that support their case.

'special school, special schools. A **special** N-COUNT **school** is a school for children who have some kind of physical or mental handicap.

spe·cial·ty /ˈspeʃəlti/ **specialties.** A **specialty** is ◆◇◇◇◇ the same as a **speciality**. *His specialty is internation* N-COUNT *al law.* AMERICAN

spe·cies /ˈspiːʃiːz/; **species** is both the singular and ◆◆◆◇◇ the plural form. A **species** is a class of plants or ani N-COUNT mals whose members have the same main characteristics and are able to breed with each other. *Pandas are an endangered species.*

spe·cif·ic /spɪˈsɪfɪk/. **1** You use **specific** to indicate ◆◆◆◇ that you are referring to one or more particular ADJ-GRADED things among others of the same general kind. *Mas* ADJ n *sage may help to increase blood flow to specific areas of the body.* **2** If someone is **specific**, they give a de ADJ-GRADED scription that is precise and exact. You can also use **specific** to describe their description. *This report offered the most specific and accurate description of the problems.* ◆ **spe·cif·ic·ity** /ˌspesɪˈfɪsɪti/. *...the* N-UNCOUNT *kind of extreme specificity normally associated only with computer programmes.* **3** Something that is ADJ **specific** to a particular thing is connected with that thing only. *Send your resume with a cover letter that is specific to that particular job.* ▸ Also after nouns. COMB *Most studies of trade have been country-specific.*

spe·cifi·cal·ly /spɪˈsɪfɪkli/. **1** You use **specifically** ◆◆◆◇◇ to emphasize that something is given special atten ADV: tion and considered separately from other things of ADV with v the same kind. *...the first nursing home designed* PRAGMATICS *specifically for people with AIDS.* **2** You use **specifi** ADV: **cally** to add something more precise or exact to ADV with v what you have already said. *Death frightens me, spe* group *cifically my own death.* **3** You use **specifically** to PRAGMATICS indicate that something has a restricted nature, as ADV: ADV adj opposed to being more general in nature. *...a specifically female audience.* **4** If you state or describe ADV: something **specifically**, you state or describe it pre ADV with v cisely and clearly. *I asked her to repeat specifically the words that Patti had used.*

speci·fi·ca·tion /ˌspesɪfɪˈkeɪʃən/ **specifications.** ◆◇◇◇◇ A **specification** is a requirement which is clearly N-COUNT stated, for example about the necessary features in the design of something. *Handmade jewellery can be produced to your specifications.*

spe·cif·ics /spɪˈsɪfɪks/. The **specifics** of a subject ◆◇◇◇◇ are the details of it that need to be considered. *Of* N-PLURAL *course I don't know the specifics of your problem.*

speci·fy /ˈspesɪfaɪ/ **specifies, specifying,** ◆◆◇◇◇ **specified. 1** If you **specify** something, you give in N-COUNT formation about what is required or should happen V wh in a certain situation. *He has not specified what action he would like them to take.* **2** If you **specify** that VERB something should be done, you tell someone pre V that cisely what you want doing or how something Also V n should be done. *One rule specifies that learner drivers must be supervised by adults.*

speci·men /ˈspesɪmɪn/ **specimens. 1** A **specimen** ◆◆◇◇◇ is a single plant or animal which is an example of a N-COUNT particular species or type and is examined by scientists. *200,000 specimens of fungus are kept at the Komarov Botanical Institute.* **2** A **specimen** of something is an example of it which gives an idea of what the whole of it is like. *Applicants have to submit a specimen of handwriting.*
3 A **specimen** is a small quantity of someone's urine, N-COUNT blood, or other body fluid which is examined in a medical laboratory, in order to find out if they are ill or if they have been drinking alcohol or taking drugs.
4 You can use **specimen** to refer to someone who has N-COUNT: a quality of a particular kind. *What a poor specimen* with supp *that child is!* WRITTEN

spe·cious /ˈspiːʃəs/. Something that is **specious** ADJ-GRADED seems to exist or be true, but is in fact false or an illusion. *It is unlikely that the Duke was convinced by such specious arguments.*

speck /spek/ **specks.** A **speck** is a very small ◆◇◇◇◇ stain, mark, or shape, or a very small piece of some N-COUNT thing. *There is a speck of blood by his ear... He brushed a speck of dust off his shoes.*

speck·led /ˈspekəld/. A **speckled** surface is covered ADJ with small marks, spots, or shapes. *The sky was speckled with stars.*

specs /speks/. See spec.

spec·ta·cle /ˈspektəkəl/ **spectacles. 1** Glasses ◆◆◇◇◇ are sometimes referred to as **spectacles**. *He looked* N-PLURAL: also a pair of N

at me over the tops of his spectacles. **2 ◆ rose-coloured spectacles:** see **rose-coloured.** *FORMAL*

3 A **spectacle** is a strange or interesting sight. *These collectors items always provide an unusual spectacle.* N-COUNT

4 A **spectacle** is a grand and impressive event or performance. *...a director passionate about music and spectacle.* N-VAR

spec·tac·u·lar /spek'tækjʊlə/ **spectaculars.** ◆◇◇◇◇
1 Something that is **spectacular** is very impressive or dramatic. *...spectacular views of the Sugar Loaf Mountain... The results have been spectacular.* ADJ-GRADED
◆ spec·tac·u·lar·ly *Many of her movies had been spectacularly successful.* **2** A **spectacular** is a show or performance which is very grand and impressive. *...one of the world's great sporting spectaculars.* ADV-GRADED / N-COUNT

spec·ta·tor /spek'teɪtə, AM 'spekteɪtər/ **specta-tors.** A **spectator** is someone who watches something, especially a sporting event. ◆◇◇◇ N-COUNT

spec'tator sport, spectator sports. A **spectator sport** is a sport that is interesting and entertaining to watch. N-COUNT

spec·tra /'spektrə/. **Spectra** is a plural form of **spectrum.**

spec·tral /'spektrəl/. If you describe someone or something as **spectral**, you mean that they look like a ghost. ADJ LITERARY

spec·tre /'spektə/ **spectres;** spelled **specter** in American English. If you refer to the **spectre** of something unpleasant, you are referring to something that you are frightened might occur. *This has raised the spectre of a full-scale war.* ◆◇◇◇ N-COUNT

spec·trum /'spektrəm/ **spectra** or **spectrums.** ◆◇◇◇
1 The **spectrum** is the range of different colours which is produced when light passes through a prism or through a drop of water. **2** A **spectrum** is a range of a particular type of thing. *The term 'special needs' covers a wide spectrum of problems.* **3** A **spectrum** is a range of light waves or radio waves within particular frequencies. *...the ultraviolet spectra of hot stars.* N-SING: the N / N-COUNT / N-COUNT

specu·late /'spekjʊleɪt/ **speculates, speculat-ing, speculated.** **1** If you **speculate** about something, you make guesses about its nature or identity, or about what might happen. *The doctors speculate that he died of a cerebral haemorrhage caused by a blow on the head... The reader can speculate what will happen next.* **◆ specu·la·tion** /ˌspekjʊ'leɪʃən/ **speculations** *...speculation over the future of the economy.* **2** If someone **speculates** financially, they buy property, stocks, or shares, in the hope of being able to sell them again at a higher price and make a profit. *They speculated in property whose value has now dropped.* **◆ specu·la·tor** /'spekjʊleɪtə/ **speculators.** A **speculator** is a person who speculates financially. ◆◇◇◇ VERB: V prep / V that / V wh / Also V, / V with quote / N-VAR / VERB: V / V prep/adv / N-COUNT

specu·la·tive /'spekjʊlətɪv, AM -leɪt-/. **1** A **specu-lative** statement or opinion is based on speculation rather than knowledge. *He has written a speculative biography of Christopher Marlowe.* **2** Someone who has a **speculative** expression seems to be trying to guess something about someone or something. *His mother regarded him with a speculative eye.* ◆◇◇◇ ADJ-GRADED / ADJ-GRADED
3 Speculative is used to describe activities which involve buying goods or shares, or buildings and properties in the hope of being able to sell them again at a higher price and make a profit. *Pensioners were persuaded to mortgage their homes to invest in speculative bonds.* ADJ

sped /sped/. **Sped** is a past tense and past participle of **speed.**

speech /spiːtʃ/ **speeches. 1 Speech** is the ability to speak or the act of speaking. *...the development of speech in children.* **2** Your **speech** is the way in which you speak. *His speech became increasingly thick and nasal.* **3 Speech** is spoken language. *...the way common letter clusters are usually pronounced in speech.* ◆◆◆◇ N-UNCOUNT / N-SING / N-UNCOUNT
4 A **speech** is a formal talk which someone gives to an audience. *He delivered his speech in French.* **5** A **speech** is a group of lines spoken by a character in a N-COUNT / N-COUNT

play. *...the hilarious speech from Alan Bennett's 'Forty Years On'.* **6** See also **direct speech, figure of speech, indirect speech, part of speech, reported speech.**

speech·less /'spiːtʃləs/. If you are **speechless**, you are temporarily unable to speak, usually because something has shocked you. *Alex was almost speechless with rage and despair.* ADJ

speech 'therapy. Speech therapy is the treatment of people who have speech and language problems. **◆ 'speech therapist, speech thera-pists.** A **speech therapist** is a person who is trained to give speech therapy. N-UNCOUNT / N-COUNT

speech·writ·er /'spiːtʃraɪtə/ **speechwriters.** A **speechwriter** is a person who writes speeches for important people such as politicians. N-COUNT

speed /spiːd/ **speeds, speeding, sped, speed-ed.** The form of the past tense and past participle is **sped** in meaning 5 but **speeded** for the phrasal verb. ◆◆◆◆◇
1 The **speed** of something is the rate at which it moves or travels. *He drove off at high speed... Wind speeds reached force five.* **2** The **speed** of something is the rate at which it happens or is done. *Each learner can proceed at his own speed.* **3 Speed** is very fast movement or travel. *Speed is the essential ingredient of all athletics.* **4 Speed** is a very fast rate at which something happens or is done. *I was amazed at his speed of working.* **5** If you **speed** somewhere, you move or travel there quickly, usually in a vehicle. *Trains will speed through the Channel Tunnel at 186mph.* N-VAR: with supp / N-COUNT: with supp / N-UNCOUNT / N-UNCOUNT / VERB: V prep/adv
6 Someone who **is speeding** is driving a vehicle faster than the legal speed limit. *This man was not qualified to drive and was speeding.* **◆ speed·ing** *He was fined for speeding last year.* VERB V / N-UNCOUNT
7 Speed is an illegal drug which some people take to increase their energy and excitement and give them unusual sensations in their minds. N-UNCOUNT INFORMAL
8 See also **-speed. ● pick up speed:** see **pick.**

speed up. 1 When something **speeds up** or when you **speed** it **up**, it moves or travels faster. *It would allow scientists to study the structure of atoms by speeding them up.* **2** When a process or activity **speeds up** or when something **speeds** it **up**, it happens at a faster rate. *I had already taken steps to speed up a solution to the problem.* PHRASAL VB ERG: V P / V P / ERG: V P / V P noun / Also V n P

-speed /-spiːd/. **-speed** is used after numbers to form adjectives that indicate that a bicycle or car has a particular number of gears. *...a 12-speed bike.* COMB

speed·boat /'spiːdbəʊt/ **speedboats.** A **speed-boat** is a boat that can go very fast because it has a powerful engine. N-COUNT

'speed limit, speed limits. The **speed limit** on a road is the maximum speed at which you are legally allowed to drive. ◆◇◇◇ N-COUNT

speed·om·eter /spiː'dɒmɪtə/ **speedometers.** A **speedometer** is the instrument in a vehicle which shows how fast the vehicle is moving. See picture headed **car and bicycle.** N-COUNT

speed·way /'spiːdweɪ/. **Speedway** is the sport of racing lightweight motorcycles on special tracks. N-UNCOUNT

speedy /'spiːdi/ **speedier, speediest.** A **speedy** process, event, or action happens or is done very quickly. *We wish Bill a speedy recovery.* **◆ speedi·ly** *The commission often needs to act speedily.* ◆◇◇◇ ADV-GRADED: ADV with v

spell /spel/ **spells, spelling, spelled, spelt.** The form **spelled** is both the past tense and past participle. British English also uses the form **spelt**. **1** When you **spell** a word, you write or speak each letter in the word in the correct order. *He gave his name and then helpfully spelt it... How do you spell 'potato'?* ◆◆◆◇◇ VERB V n
▶ Spell out means the same as **spell**. *He always prints his name next to his signature and spells it out when leaving telephone messages.* **2** Someone who can **spell** knows the correct order of letters in words. *You accused me of inaccuracy yet you can't spell 'Middlesex'.* **●** See also **spelling.** PHRASAL VB V n P / Also V P noun / VERB: no cont V,
3 If something **spells** a particular result, often an unpleasant one, it suggests that this will be the result. *A report has just arrived on government desks which spells more trouble.* VB: no cont V n

4 A **spell** of a particular type of weather or a particular N-COUNT
activity is a short period of time during which this
type of weather or activity occurs. *There has been a
long spell of dry weather.*
5 A **spell** is a situation in which events are controlled N-COUNT
by a magical power. *A witch cast a spell on her.* **6** If you PHRASE
are **under** someone's **spell**, you are so fascinated by
them that you cannot think about anything else. *Even
sensible Frank had fallen under her spell.*

spell out. 1 If you **spell** something **out**, you explain PHRASAL VB
it in detail or in a very clear way. *Be assertive and spell* V P noun
out exactly how you feel. **2** See **spell** 1. Also V n P

spell·bind·ing /ˈspelbaɪndɪŋ/. A **spellbinding** im- ADJ-GRADED
age or sound is one that is so fascinating that you
can think about nothing else. *...the spectacular finale to this enthralling and spellbinding ballet.*

spell·bound /ˈspelbaʊnd/. If you are **spellbound** by ADJ
something or someone, you are so fascinated that
you cannot think about anything else. *His audience
had listened like children, spellbound by his words.*

spell·er /ˈspelə/ **spellers.** If you describe someone N-COUNT:
as a good or bad **speller**, you mean that they find it adj N
easy or difficult to spell words correctly.

spell·ing /ˈspelɪŋ/ **spellings. 1** A **spelling** is the ◆◇◇◇◇
correct order of the letters in a word. **2 Spelling** is N-COUNT
the ability to spell words in the correct way. It is N-UNCOUNT
also an attempt to spell a word in the correct way.
*...basic skills in reading, writing, grammar and spell-
ing.* **3** See also **spelling.**

spelt /spelt/. **Spelt** is a past tense and past partici- BRITISH
ple form of **spell.**

spend /spend/ **spends, spending, spent.** ◆◆◆◆◇
1 When you **spend** money, you pay money for VERB
things that you want. *Businessmen spend enormous* V n -ing
amounts advertising their products... Juventus have V amount/n
spent £23m on new players. **◆ spend·ing** *Has your* Also V n
spending on food increased? **2** If you **spend** time or N-UNCOUNT
energy doing something, you use your time or effort VERB
doing it. *Engineers spend much time and energy de-* V n -ing
veloping brilliant solutions. **3** If you **spend** a period VERB
of time in a place, you stay there for a period of V n adv/prep
time. *We spent the night in a hotel.*

spend·er /ˈspendə/ **spenders.** If a person or or- ◆◇◇◇◇
ganization is a big **spender** or a compulsive **spend-** N-COUNT
er, for example, they spend a lot of money or are
unable to stop themselves spending money. *The
Swiss are Europe's biggest spenders on food.*

'spending money. **Spending money** is money ◆◇◇◇◇
that you have or are given to spend on personal N-UNCOUNT
things for pleasure, especially on holiday.

spend·thrift /ˈspendθrɪft/ **spendthrifts.** If you call N-COUNT
someone a **spendthrift**, you mean that they spend
money in a wasteful or extravagant way. **▶** Also an ADJ-GRADED
adjective. *...his father's spendthrift ways.*

spent /spent/. **1 Spent** is the past tense and past
participle of **spend. 2 Spent** substances or contain- ADJ
ers have been used and cannot be used again.
Radioactive waste is simply spent fuel.

'spent force. If you refer to someone who used to N-SING:
be powerful as a **spent force**, you mean that they no a N
longer have any power or influence.

sperm /spɜːm/ **sperms; sperm** can also be used as ◆◆◇◇◇
the plural form. **1** A **sperm** is a cell which is pro- N-COUNT
duced in the sex organs of a male animal and can
enter a female animal's egg and fertilize it. **2 Sperm** N-UNCOUNT
is used to refer to the liquid that contains sperm
when it is produced.

sper·mi·ci·dal /ˌspɜːmɪˈsaɪdəl/. A **spermicidal** ADJ: ADJ n
cream or jelly contains spermicide.

sper·mi·cide /ˈspɜːmɪsaɪd/ **spermicides.** Spermi- N-VAR
cide is a substance that kills sperm. *Most condoms
contain spermicide.*

'sperm whale, sperm whales. A **sperm whale** is N-COUNT
a large whale that has a cavity in its head that contains a large amount of oil.

spew /spjuː/ **spews, spewing, spewed.** ◆◇◇◇◇
1 When something **spews** out a substance or when V-ERG:
a substance **spews** from something, the substance V n with adv
flows out quickly in large quantities. *Leaking oil* Also V n prep
spewed from the tanker. **2** If someone **spews** or VERB: V

spews up, they vomit. *We were used to Duncan* V adv
spewing up behind the drumkit. INFORMAL

sphere /sfɪə/ **spheres. 1** A **sphere** is an object ◆◆◇◇◇
that is perfectly round in shape like a ball. See pic- N-COUNT
ture headed **shapes.**
2 A **sphere** of activity or interest is a particular area of N-COUNT
activity or interest. *...nurses, working in all spheres of
the health service.* **3** A **sphere** of people is a group of N-COUNT
them who are similar in social status or who have the
same interests. *...the government and academic
spheres of society.* **4** A country's **sphere of influence** is PHRASE
an area of the world where it is the dominant power
and where it can affect events and developments.
*...countries traditionally within the British or Ameri-
can spheres of influence.*

spheri·cal /ˈsferɪkəl, AM ˈsfɪr-/. A **spherical** object ADJ
is round like a ball. *...perfectly spherical pearls.* FORMAL

sphinc·ter /ˈsfɪŋktə/ **sphincters.** A **sphincter** is a N-COUNT
ring of muscle that surrounds an opening to the TECHNICAL
body and that can tighten to close this opening.

sphinx /sfɪŋks/ **sphinxes.** The **Sphinx** is a huge N-COUNT
statue of a monster with a human head and a lion's
body that stands near the pyramids in Egypt. It was
built by the ancient Egyptians.

spice /spaɪs/ **spices, spicing, spiced. 1** A **spice** ◆◆◇◇◇
is a part of a plant, or a powder made from that N-VAR
part, which you put in food to give it flavour. Cinnamon, ginger, and paprika are spices. **2** If you **spice** VERB
something that you say or do, you add excitement V n with n
or interest to it. *They spiced their conversations and
discussions with intrigue.* **▶ Spice up** means the PHRASAL VB
same as **spice.** *Her publisher wants her to spice up* V P noun
her stories with sex. ...a discovery which spiced the V n P
conversation up. **3 Spice** is something which makes N-UNCOUNT
life more exciting. *To add spice to the debate, they
disagreed about method and ideology.*

spice up. See **spice** 2. PHRASAL VB

spiced /spaɪst/. Food that is **spiced** has had spices ◆◇◇◇◇
or other strong-tasting foods added to it. *Every dish* ADJ-GRADED
was served heavily spiced.

spick and span /ˌspɪk ənd ˈspæn/; also spelled ADJ
spick-and-span. A place that is **spick and span** is
very clean and tidy.

spicy /ˈspaɪsi/ **spicier, spiciest.** Spicy food is ◆◇◇◇◇
strongly flavoured with spices. ADJ-GRADED

spi·der /ˈspaɪdə/ **spiders.** A **spider** is a small crea- ◆◆◇◇◇
ture with eight legs. Most types of spider make webs N-COUNT
in which they catch insects for food.

spi·dery /ˈspaɪdəri/. If you describe something such ADJ
as handwriting as **spidery**, you mean that it consists
of thin, dark, pointed lines.

spiel /ʃpiːl, AM spiːl/ **spiels.** Someone's **spiel** is a N-COUNT
well-prepared speech that they make, and that they INFORMAL
have usually made many times before, in order to
persuade you to do something or to buy something.

spig·ot /ˈspɪgət/ **spigots. 1** A **spigot** is a type of N-COUNT
valve that controls the flow of a liquid from one BRITISH
source to another. **2** A **spigot** is a faucet or tap. *It* N-COUNT
looks like I forgot to turn the spigot off. AMERICAN

spike /spaɪk/ **spikes, spiking, spiked. 1** A **spike** ◆◆◇◇◇
is a long piece of metal with a sharp point. *...a 15-* N-COUNT
foot wall topped with iron spikes. **2** Any thin point- N-COUNT
ed object can be referred to as a **spike.** *Her hair
stood out in spikes.* **3 Spikes** are sports shoes with N-PLURAL:
pointed pieces of metal attached to the soles. They also a pair of n
help runners' feet to grip the ground when they are
running. **4** If your drink **is spiked**, someone has VB: usu
added alcohol or drugs to it without telling you. passive
INFORMAL

spiked /spaɪkt/. **1** Something that is **spiked** has ADJ
one or more spikes on it. *...spiked golf shoes.* **2** If ADJ
someone has **spiked** hair, their hair is short and
sticks up all over their head.

spiky /ˈspaɪki/. Something that is **spiky** has one or ◆◇◇◇◇
more sharp points. *...tall, spiky evergreen trees.* ADJ-GRADED

spill /spɪl/ **spills, spilling, spilled, spilt.** The ◆◆◇◇◇
form **spilled** is both the past tense and past participle. British English also uses the form **spilt. 1** If a V-ERG: V
liquid **spills** or if you **spill** it, it accidentally flows V n
over the edge of a container. *He always spilled the* V n adv/prep
drinks... Don't spill water on your suit. **▶** A **spill** is N-COUNT

an amount of liquid that has spilled from a container. **2** If the contents of a bag, box, or other container **spill** or **are spilled**, they come out of the container onto a surface. *A number of bags had split and were spilling their contents.* **3** If people or things **spill** out of a place, they come out of it in large quantities. *Tears began to spill out of the boy's eyes.* **4** To **spill** someone's **blood** means to kill them or wound them. *If blood is spilled the countries will be at war.* **5 ●** to **spill the beans**: see **bean. ● thrills and spills**: see **thrill**.

V-ERG
V n
Also V adv/
prep
VERB
V adv/prep

PHRASE
WRITTEN

spill out. If you **spill out** information or if it **spills out**, you tell someone about it in a hurried way, because you cannot or do not want to keep it secret. *The words spilled out in a rush... He was tempted to spill out his problems to Philip.*

PHRASAL VB
ERG
V P
V P noun
Also V n P

spill·age /ˈspɪlɪdʒ/ **spillages.** If there is a **spillage**, a substance such as crude oil escapes from its container. **Spillage** is also used to refer to the substance that escapes. *...an oil spillage off the coast of Texas.*

N-VAR

spill·over /ˈspɪləʊvə/ **spillovers.** A **spillover** is a situation or feeling that starts in one place but then begins to happen or have an effect somewhere else. *...spillover damage from the building's demolition.*

N-COUNT

spilt /spɪlt/. **Spilt** is a past tense and past participle form of **spill**.

BRITISH

spin /spɪn/ **spins, spinning, spun. 1** If something **spins**, it turns quickly around a central point. *He spun the wheel sharply and made a U turn in the middle of the road... He spun his car round and went after them.* ▶ Also a noun. *...the spin of the earth around its axis.* **2** When you **spin** washing, it is turned round and round quickly in a spin drier or a washing machine to get the water out. ▶ Also a noun. *Set on a cool wash and finish with a short spin.* **3** When people **spin**, they make thread by twisting together pieces of a fibre such as wool or cotton using a device or machine. *Glenis sat in the kitchen and spun some wool.* **♦ spin·ning** *They do their own cooking, spinning, and woodworking.*

♦♦♦◇◇
V-ERG: V
V n round/
around
N-VAR
VERB: V n

N-SING

VERB: V
V n

N-UNCOUNT

4 If someone **spins** a story or **spins** a tale, they give you an account of something that is untrue or only partly true. *I became adept at spinning wonderful tales about my childhood.* **5** If someone puts a certain **spin** on an event or situation, they interpret it and try to present it in a particular way. ● See also **spin doctor**.

VERB
V n
Also V n n

N-SING:
with supp
INFORMAL

6 If you go for **a spin** or take a car for **a spin**, you make a short journey in a car just to enjoy yourself.

N-SING:
a N

7 If a plane goes into **a spin**, it falls very rapidly towards the ground in a spiral movement. **8** In a game such as tennis or cricket, if you put **spin** on a ball, you make it spin rapidly when you hit it or throw it.

N-SING:
a N
N-UNCOUNT

9 If your head **is spinning**, you feel dizzy because you are excited, ill, or confused. **10** If you say that someone is **in a spin** or **in a flat spin**, you mean that they are confused and unable to act sensibly because of something that has happened.

VERB: V
PHRASE
INFORMAL

spin out. If you **spin** something **out**, you make it last longer than it normally would. *The Government will try to spin out the conference into next autumn.*

PHRASAL VB
V n P
V P noun

spi·na bi·fi·da /ˌspaɪnə ˈbɪfɪdə/. **Spina bifida** is a condition of the spine that some people are born with. It often causes paralysis.

N-UNCOUNT

spin·ach /ˈspɪnɪdʒ, -ɪtʃ/. **Spinach** is a vegetable with large dark green leaves.

♦◇◇◇◇
N-UNCOUNT

spi·nal /ˈspaɪnəl/. **Spinal** means relating to your spine. *...spinal injuries.*

♦◇◇◇◇
ADJ: ADJ n

spinal column, spinal columns. Your **spinal column** is your spine.

N-COUNT
TECHNICAL

spinal 'cord, spinal cords. Your **spinal cord** is a thick cord of nerves inside your spine which connects your brain to nerves in all parts of your body.

N-COUNT

spin·dle /ˈspɪndəl/ **spindles. 1** A **spindle** is a rod in a machine, around which another part of the machine turns. **2** A **spindle** is a rod which you use when you are spinning wool into thread by hand.

♦◇◇◇◇
N-COUNT

N-COUNT

spin·dly /ˈspɪndli/ **spindlier, spindliest.** Something that is **spindly** is long and thin and looks very weak. *I did have rather spindly legs.*

ADJ-GRADED

'spin doctor, spin doctors. In politics, a **spin doctor** is someone who is skilled in public relations and who advises political parties on how to present events and policies favourably.

N-COUNT
INFORMAL

spine /spaɪn/ **spines. 1** Your **spine** is the row of bones down your back. **2** The **spine** of a book is the narrow stiff part which the pages and covers are attached to. **3** **Spines** are also long, sharp points on an animal's body or on a plant.

♦♦◇◇◇
N-COUNT
N-COUNT

N-COUNT

spine·less /ˈspaɪnləs/. If you say that someone is **spineless**, you mean they are weak and cowardly.

ADJ-GRADED

'spine-tingling. A **spine-tingling** film or piece of music is enjoyable because it causes you to feel a strong emotion such as excitement or fear.

ADJ-GRADED

spin·na·ker /ˈspɪnəkə/ **spinnakers.** A **spinnaker** is a large, light, triangular sail that is attached to the front mast on a racing yacht.

N-COUNT

spin·ner /ˈspɪnə/ **spinners.** A **spinner** is a person who makes thread by spinning.

N-COUNT

spin·ney /ˈspɪni/ **spinneys.** A **spinney** is a small area covered with trees.

N-COUNT
BRITISH

'spinning wheel, spinning wheels. A **spinning wheel** is a wooden spinning machine used in people's homes, mainly in former times. It has a wheel which makes the spindle turn round.

N-COUNT

'spin-off, spin-offs. 1 A **spin-off** is a useful or valuable result of an activity that was designed to achieve something else. *The company put out a report on commercial spin-offs from its research.* **2** A **spin-off** is a book, film, or television series that is derived from a similar book, film, or television series which has been very successful.

♦◇◇◇◇
N-COUNT

N-COUNT

spin·ster /ˈspɪnstə/ **spinsters.** A **spinster** is a woman who has never been married, especially an old or middle-aged woman.

N-COUNT
DATED

spiny /ˈspaɪni/. A **spiny** plant or animal is covered with long sharp points. *...a spiny cactus.*

ADJ

spi·ral /ˈspaɪərəl/ **spirals, spiralling, spiralled;** spelled **spiraling, spiraled** in American English. **1** A **spiral** is a shape which winds round and round, with each curve above or outside the previous one. ▶ Also an adjective. *Grace ran down the spiral staircase.* **2** If something **spirals** somewhere, it grows or moves in a spiral curve. *A joss stick spiralled smoke.* ▶ Also a noun. *Larks were rising in spirals from the ridge.* **3** If an amount or level **spirals** or **spirals** upwards, it rises quickly and at an increasing rate. If it **spirals** downwards, it falls quickly and at an increasing rate. *House prices will continue to spiral downwards.* ▶ Also a noun. *...an inflationary spiral.*

♦♦◇◇◇
N-COUNT

ADJ-GRADED:
ADJ n
V-ERG:
V adv/prep
V n
N-COUNT
VERB: V
V adv/prep

N-SING

spire /spaɪə/ **spires.** The **spire** of a building such as a church is the tall cone-shaped structure on the top.

♦◇◇◇◇
N-COUNT

spir·it /ˈspɪrɪt/ **spirits, spiriting, spirited. 1** Your **spirit** is the part of you that is not physical and that motivates you. It is connected with your character, behaviour, and feelings. *Marian retains a restless, youthful spirit, in search of new horizons.* ● See also **kindred spirit**. **2** A person's **spirit** is the non-physical part of them that is believed to remain alive after their death. **3** A **spirit** is a ghost or supernatural being. ● See also **Holy Spirit**. **4** **Spirit** is the courage, determination, and energy that someone shows, especially during difficult times. *Everyone who knew her admired her spirit.* **5** Your **spirits** are your feelings at a particular time. *A bit of exercise will help lift his spirits.* **6** The **spirit** in which you do something is the attitude you have when you are doing it. *They approached the talks in a conciliatory spirit.* **7** A particular kind of **spirit** is the set of ideas, beliefs, and aims that are held by a group of people. *...the real spirit of the Labour movement.* **8** The **spirit of** something such as a law or an agreement is the way that it was intended to be interpreted or applied. *The requirement for work permits violates the spirit of the 1950 treaty.* **9** You can refer to a person as a particular kind of **spirit** if they show a certain characteristic or if they show a lot of enthusiasm in what they are doing. *I like to think of myself as a free spirit.*

♦♦♦◇
N-SING

N-COUNT

N-COUNT

N-UNCOUNT

N-PLURAL

N-SING

N-SING

N-SING:
the N of n

N-COUNT

10 If someone or something **is spirited** away, they are taken from a place quickly and secretly without anyone noticing. *His parents had spirited him away to the country.* `VERB: be V-ed prep/adv V n prep/adv`
11 Spirits are strong alcoholic drinks such as whisky and gin. `N-VAR` **12 Spirit** or **spirits** is an alcoholic liquid that is used as a fuel, for cleaning things, or for other purposes. ● See also **surgical spirit, methylated spirits**. `N-UNCOUNT`
13 If you **enter into the spirit** of something, you take part in it in an enthusiastic way. `PHRASE` **14** If you say you are somewhere **in spirit** or with someone **in spirit**, you mean that although you are not with them, you are thinking about them a lot. `PHRASE` **15 The spirit of the age** or **the spirit of the times** is the set of ideas, beliefs, and aims that is typical of a particular period in history. `PHRASE`

spir·it·ed /'spɪrɪtɪd/. **1** A **spirited** action shows great energy and courage. *President Gorbachev made a spirited defence of his reforms.* `ADJ-GRADED` **2** A **spirited** person is very active, lively, and confident. `ADJ-GRADED`

-spirited /-'spɪrɪtɪd/. **-spirited** combines with adjectives to describe the nature of a person's character, attitude, or behaviour. For example, a **mean-spirited** person behaves in a way that is unkind to other people. ● See also **high-spirited; public-spirited**. `COMB`

'spirit level, spirit levels. A **spirit level** is a device for testing to see if a surface is level. It consists of a plastic, wood, or metal frame containing a glass tube of liquid with an air bubble in it. `N-COUNT`

spir·it·u·al /'spɪrɪtʃuəl/ **spirituals. 1 Spiritual** means relating to people's thoughts and beliefs, rather than to their bodies and physical surroundings. `ADJ` ♦ **spir·itu·al·ly** *Our whole programme is spiritually oriented but not religious.* `ADV` ♦ **spir·itu·al·ity** /ˌspɪrɪtʃu'ælɪti/. *...the peaceful spirituality of Japanese culture.* `N-UNCOUNT` **2 Spiritual** means relating to people's religious beliefs. *A man in priestly clothes offered spiritual guidance.* `ADJ` **3** A **spiritual** is a religious song of the type originally sung by Negro slaves in America. `N-COUNT` **4** Your **spiritual home** is the place where you feel you belong, often because your ideas or attitudes are the same as those of the people who live there. `PHRASE`

spir·itu·al·ism /'spɪrɪtʃuəlɪzəm/. **Spiritualism** is the belief that the spirits of people who are dead can communicate with people who are still alive. `N-UNCOUNT` ♦ **spir·itu·al·ist, spiritualists.** `N-COUNT`

spit /spɪt/ **spits, spitting, spat.** In American English, the form **spit** is used as the past tense and past participle. **1 Spit** is the watery liquid produced in your mouth. `N-UNCOUNT` **2** If someone **spits**, they force an amount of liquid out of their mouth, often to show hatred or scorn. *They spat at me and taunted me.* `VERB: V V prep` **3** If you **spit** liquid or food somewhere, you force a small amount of it out of your mouth. *Spit out that gum and pay attention... He felt as if a serpent had spat venom into his eyes.* `VERB V n with out V n prep Also V n` **4** If something such as a machine or food that is cooking **spits**, it makes a series of short, sharp, hissing noises. `VERB: V` **5** If someone **spits** an insult or comment, they say it in an angry or hostile way. *'Wait a damn minute,' Mindy spat.* ► **Spit out** means the same as **spit**. *He spat out 'I don't like the way he looks at me.'... She spat the name out like an insult.* `VERB: V n V with quote WRITTEN PHRASAL VB V P with quote V n P` **6** If it is **spitting**, it is raining very lightly. The American term is **sprinkle**. `VERB: it V BRITISH` **7** A **spit** is a long rod which is pushed through a piece of meat and hung over an open fire to cook the meat. `N-COUNT` **8** A **spit of** land is a long, flat, narrow piece of land that sticks out into the sea. `N-COUNT N of n` **9** If you say that one person is **the spitting image of** another, you mean that they look very similar. `PHRASE`

spit out. See spit 5. `PHRASAL VB`

spite /spaɪt/. **1** You use **in spite of** to introduce a fact which makes the rest of the statement you are making seem surprising. *He hired her in spite of the fact that she had never sung on stage.* `PHR-PREP` **2** If you do something **in spite of** yourself, you do it although you did not really intend to or expect to. `PHR-PREP` **3** If you do something nasty out of **spite**, you do it be- `N-UNCOUNT` cause you want to hurt or upset someone. **4** If you do something nasty to **spite** someone, you do it in order to hurt or upset them. `VERB: V n, only to-inf` **5** ● to **cut off** your **nose to spite** your **face**: see **nose**. `PHRASE`

spite·ful /'spaɪtful/. Someone who is **spiteful** does nasty things to people they dislike. `ADJ-GRADED`

spit·tle /'spɪtəl/. **Spittle** is the watery liquid which is produced in your mouth. `N-UNCOUNT DATED`

spiv /spɪv/ **spivs.** A **spiv** is a man who does not have a regular job and who makes money by business deals which are usually illegal. `N-COUNT INFORMAL, BRITISH`

splash /splæʃ/ **splashes, splashing, splashed. 1** If you **splash** around in water, you hit or disturb the water in a noisy way, causing some of it to fly up into the air. *She could hear the voices of her friends as they splashed in a nearby rock pool... The gliders and their pilots splashed into the lake.* `VERB: V about/around V into n` **2** If you **splash** a liquid somewhere or if it **splashes**, it hits someone or something and scatters in a lot of small drops. *Tears ran down Fran's cheeks and splashed on the satin dressing gown... Beer splashed the carpet.* `V n prep V prep/adv V n Also V n with n` **3** A **splash** is the sound made when something hits water or falls into it. `N-SING` **4** A **splash** of a liquid is a small quantity of it that has been spilt on something or added to something. `N-COUNT` **5** A **splash** of colour is an area of a bright colour which contrasts strongly with the colours around it. `N-COUNT with supp` **6** If a magazine or newspaper **splashes** a story, it prints it in such a way that it is very noticeable. *A picture of his girlfriend Sheryl had been splashed in the previous weekend's tabloids.* `VERB: V n be V-ed` **7** If you **make a splash**, you become noticed or become popular because of something that you have done. `PHRASE`

splash out. If you **splash out** on something, especially on a luxury, you buy it even though it costs a lot of money. *Can you afford to splash out a little?* `PHRASAL VB VP on n V P BRITISH`

splat /splæt/. **Splat** is used to describe the sound of something wet hitting a surface with a lot of force. `N-SING; SOUND`

splat·ter /'splætə/ **splatters, splattering, splattered.** If a thick wet substance **splatters** on something or **is splattered** on it, it drops or is thrown over it. *'Sorry Edward,' I said, splattering the cloth with jam. ...a mud-splattered white shirt.* `V-ERG: V adv/prep V n V-ed`

splay /spleɪ/ **splays, splaying, splayed.** If things **splay** or **are splayed**, their ends are spread out away from each other. *He splayed his fingers across his face... His fingers splay out in a star shape.* `V-ERG V adv/prep`

spleen /spliːn/ **spleens. 1** Your **spleen** is an organ near your stomach that controls the quality of your blood. `N-COUNT` **2 Spleen** is violent and spiteful anger. *There were other targets for Mr Lamont's spleen.* `N-UNCOUNT FORMAL`

splen·did /'splendɪd/. **1** If you say that something is **splendid**, you mean that it is very good. *...a splendid view across towards the Cotswolds... I found him to be splendid company.* `ADJ-GRADED` ♦ **splen·did·ly** *I have heard him tell people that we get along splendidly.* `ADV-GRADED: ADV with v` **2** If you describe a building or work of art as **splendid**, you mean that it is beautiful, impressive, and extremely well made. *...a splendid Victorian mansion.* `ADJ-GRADED` ♦ **splendid·ly** *The young women are splendidly dressed.* `ADV-GRADED` **3** You can say **'splendid'** in a conversation to indicate that you approve of a particular situation or something that someone has said. `EXCLAM PRAGMATICS`

splen·dour /'splendə/ **splendours;** spelled **splendor** in American English. **1** The **splendour** of something is its beautiful and magnificent appearance. `N-UNCOUNT` **2** The **splendours** of a place or way of life are its beautiful and impressive features. *...the splendours of the French court.* `N-PLURAL`

splice /splaɪs/ **splices, splicing, spliced.** If you **splice** two pieces of rope, film, or tape together, you join them neatly at the ends so that they make one continuous piece. *The film will be spliced with footage of Cypress Hill.* `VERB: V n be V-ed`

spliff /splɪf/ **spliffs.** A **spliff** is a cigarette which contains cannabis. `N-COUNT BRITISH`

splint /splɪnt/ **splints.** A **splint** is a long piece of wood or metal that is fastened to a broken arm, leg, or back to keep it still. `N-COUNT`

splinter

splin·ter /ˈsplɪntə/ **splinters, splintering, splintered.** **1** A **splinter** is a very thin, sharp piece of wood, glass, or other hard substance, which has broken off from a larger piece. **2** If something **splinters** or **is splintered**, it breaks into thin, sharp pieces. *The ruler cracked and splintered into pieces... The stone rocketed into the glass, splintering it.*

'splinter group, splinter groups. A **splinter group** or organization is a group of people who break away from a larger group and form a separate organization, usually because they no longer agree with the views of the larger group.

split /splɪt/ **splits, splitting.** The form **split** is used in the present tense and is the past tense and past participle of the verb. **1** If something **splits** or if you **split** it, it is divided into two or more parts. *In a severe gale the ship split in two... If the chicken is fairly small, you may simply split it in half. ...uniting families split by the Korean war.* **2** If an organization **splits** or **is split**, one group of members disagree strongly with the other members, and may form a group of their own. *Women priests are accused of splitting the church.* ▶ Also an adjective. *The Kremlin is deeply split in its approach to foreign policy.* **3** A **split** in an organization is a disagreement between its members. *They accused both radicals and conservatives of trying to provoke a split in the party.* **4** A **split** between two things is a division or difference between them. *...a split between what is thought and what is felt.* **5** If something such as wood or a piece of clothing **splits** or **is split**, a long crack or tear appears in it. *Twist the mixture into individual sausages without splitting the skins... He had a split lip.* ▶ A **split** is a long crack or tear. **6** If two or more people **split** something, they share it between them. *All exhibits are for sale, the proceeds being split between Oxfam and the artist.* ● See also **splitting**.

split off. If people **split off** from a group, they stop being part of the group and become separated from it. *...the Youth Wing which split off the National Liberal party earlier this year.*

split up. 1 If two people **split up**, or if someone or something **splits** them **up**, they end their relationship or marriage. *I was beginning to think that nothing could ever split us up... I split up with my boyfriend last year.* **2** If a group of people **split up** or **are split up**, they go away in different directions. *This situation has split up the family... Touring the 'Lovey' album temporarily split the band up.* **3** If you **split** something up, or if it **splits up**, you divide it so that it is in a number of smaller separate sections. *Any thought of splitting up the company was unthinkable they said... Her company has had to split up and work from two locations.*

,split-'level. A **split-level** house or room has part of the ground floor at a different level from another part.

,split per'sonality, split personalities. If you say that someone has a **split personality**, you mean that their moods can change so much that they seem to have two separate personalities.

,split-'screen, split-screens. 1 **Split-screen** is used to describe the technique in making films and television programmes in which two different pieces of film are shown at the same time. *...split-screen movies.* **2** On a computer terminal, a **split-screen** is a display of two different sets of output in separate windows on the screen.

,split 'second; also spelled split-second. A **split second** is an extremely short period of time. *Soldiers had to make split-second decisions before opening fire, he said.*

split·ting /ˈsplɪtɪŋ/. A **splitting** headache is a very severe and painful one.

splurge /splɜːdʒ/ **splurges, splurging, splurged.** If you **splurge on** something, you spend a lot of money extravagantly, usually on things that you do not need. ▶ Also a noun. *I'm confident that there's enough in the bank for a splurge on a great pair of shoes.*

splut·ter /ˈsplʌtə/ **splutters, spluttering, spluttered. 1** If someone **splutters**, they make spitting sounds and have difficulty speaking clearly, for example because they are embarrassed or angry. *'But it cannot be', he spluttered.* ▶ Also a noun. *He gave a brief splutter of laughter.* **2** If something **splutters**, it makes a series of short, sharp sounds.

spoil /spɔɪl/ **spoils, spoiling, spoiled, spoilt.** The form **spoiled** is both the past tense and past participle. British English also uses the form **spoilt**. **1** If you **spoil** something, you prevent it from being successful or satisfactory. *It's important not to let mistakes spoil your life.* **2** If food **spoils** or if it **is spoilt**, it is no longer fit to be eaten. *Some organisms are responsible for spoiling food and cause food poisoning.* **3** If someone **spoils** their vote, they deface their voting paper, usually as a protest about the election. This makes their vote invalid. *The results showed that 7.2% of the voters cast blank or spoiled ballots.* **4** If you **spoil** children, you give them everything they want or ask for. This is considered to have a bad effect on a child's character. **♦ spoilt, spoiled** *A spoilt child is rarely popular with other children.* **5** If you **spoil** yourself or **spoil** someone you love, you give yourself or them something nice as a treat or do something special for them. *Susan spoils her guests with champagne.* **6** If you say that someone is **spoilt for choice** or **spoiled for choice**, you mean that they have a great many things to choose from. **7** The **spoils** of something are things that people get as a result of winning a battle or of doing something successfully. *True to military tradition, the victors are now treating themselves to the spoils of war.*

spoil for. If you **are spoiling for** a fight, you are very eager for it to happen. *A mob armed with guns was at the border between the two republics, spoiling for a fight.*

spoil·er /ˈspɔɪlə/ **spoilers. 1** If you describe someone or something as a **spoiler**, you mean that they try to spoil the performance of other people or things. *I was a talentless spoiler. If I couldn't be good, why should they?* **2** A **spoiler** is an object which forms part of an aeroplane's wings or part of the body of a car. It redirects the flow of air around the vehicle, allowing an aircraft to change direction or making a car's forward movement more efficient.

spoil·sport /ˈspɔɪlspɔːt/ **spoilsports.** If you say that someone is a **spoilsport**, you mean that they are behaving in a way that ruins other people's pleasure or enjoyment.

spoilt /spɔɪlt/. **Spoilt** is a past participle and past tense of **spoil**.

spoke /spəʊk/ **spokes. 1** **Spoke** is the past tense of **speak**. **2** The **spokes** of a wheel are the bars that connect the outer ring to the centre. See picture headed **car** and **bicycle**.

spo·ken /ˈspəʊkən/. **Spoken** is the past participle of **speak**.

-spoken /-ˈspəʊkən/. **-spoken** combines with adverbs and adjectives to form adjectives which indicate how someone speaks. *The woman was smartly dressed and well-spoken.*

,spoken 'word. The **spoken word** is used to refer to language expressed in speech, for example in contrast to written texts or music.

spokes·man /ˈspəʊksmən/ **spokesmen.** A **spokesman** is a male spokesperson.

spokes·person /ˈspəʊkspɜːsən/ **spokespersons** or **spokespeople.** A **spokesperson** is a person who speaks as the representative of a group or organization.

spokes·woman /ˈspəʊkswʊmən/ **spokeswomen.** A **spokeswoman** is a female spokesperson.

sponge /spʌndʒ/ **sponges, sponging, sponged. 1** **Sponge** is a very light absorbent substance with lots of little holes in it. Sponge can be

sponge

sponge cake

either man-made or natural and is capable of absorbing a lot of water or of acting as an insulating material. *...a sponge mattress.* **2** A **sponge** is a sea animal with a soft round body made of natural sponge. **3** A **sponge** is a piece of sponge that you use for washing yourself or for cleaning things. **4** If you **sponge** something, you clean it by wiping it with a wet sponge. *Fill a bowl with water and gently sponge your face and body.* ▸ **Sponge down** means the same as **sponge**. *If your child's temperature rises, sponge her down gently with tepid water.* **5** A **sponge** is a light cake or pudding made from flour, eggs, sugar, and sometimes fat. **6** If you say that someone **sponges off** other people or **sponges on** them, you mean that they regularly get money from other people when they should be trying to support themselves; used showing disapproval. *He should just get an honest job and stop sponging off the rest of us!* ♦ **spong·er, spongers** *He's not a sponger content to live off the state.*

sponge down. See **sponge** 4.

'sponge cake, sponge cakes. A **sponge cake** is a very light cake made from flour, eggs, and sometimes fat.

spon·gy /'spʌndʒi/. Something that is **spongy** is soft and squashy, like a sponge.

spon·sor /'spɒnsə/ **sponsors, sponsoring, sponsored. 1** If an organization or an individual **sponsors** something such as an event or someone's training, they pay some or all of the expenses connected with it, often in order to get publicity for themselves. *The competition was sponsored by Ruinart Champagne.* **2** If you **sponsor** someone who is doing something to raise money for charity, for example trying to walk a certain distance, you agree to give them a sum of money for the charity if they succeed in doing it. **3** If you **sponsor** a proposal or suggestion, you officially put it forward and support it. *Eight senators sponsored legislation to stop the military funding.* **4** A **sponsor** is a person or organization that sponsors something or someone. *The chief sponsor of the New York law, state Senator Emanuel Gold, says he's not giving up.* **5** When a country or an organization such as the United Nations **sponsors** negotiations between countries, it suggests holding the negotiations and organizes them. *The agreement was reached during peace talks sponsored by the European Community.* **6** If one country accuses another of **sponsoring** terrorism, they mean that the other country does not do anything to prevent it, and may even encourage it.

spon·sored /'spɒnsəd/. In Britain, a **sponsored** event is an event in which participants try to do something such as walk a certain distance in order to raise money for charity.

spon·sor·ship /'spɒnsəʃɪp/. **1 Sponsorship** is financial support given by a sponsor. *Campbell is one of an ever-growing number of skiers in need of sponsorship.* **2 Sponsorship** of something is the act of sponsoring it. *When it is done properly, arts sponsorship can be more effective than advertising.*

spon·ta·neity /ˌspɒntəˈneɪɪti/. **Spontaneity** is spontaneous, natural behaviour. *He had the spontaneity of a child.*

spon·ta·neous /spɒnˈteɪniəs/. **1 Spontaneous** acts are not planned or arranged, but are done because someone suddenly wants to do them. *I joined in the spontaneous applause.* ♦ **spon·ta·neous·ly** *He was never spontaneously warm or friendly towards us.* **2** A **spontaneous** event happens because of processes within something rather than being caused by things outside it. *...a spontaneous explosion.* ♦ **spontaneously** *These images surface spontaneously in dreams.*

spoof /spuːf/ **spoofs.** A **spoof** is something such as an article or television programme that seems to be about a serious matter but is actually a joke.

spook /spuːk/ **spooks, spooking, spooked. 1** A **spook** is a ghost. **2** A **spook** is a spy. *...a US intelligence spook.* **3** If people **are spooked**, something

has scared them or made them nervous. *Was it the wind that spooked her?* ♦ **spooked** *He was so spooked that he, too, began to believe that he heard strange clicks and noises on their telephones.*

spooky /'spuːki/ **spookier, spookiest.** A **spooky** place has a frightening atmosphere, and makes you feel that there are ghosts there.

spool /spuːl/ **spools.** A **spool** is a round object onto which thread, tape, or film can be wound, especially before it is put in a sewing machine, tape recorder, or projector.

spoon /spuːn/ **spoons, spooning, spooned. 1** A **spoon** is an implement used for eating, stirring, and serving food. One end of it is shaped like a shallow bowl and it has a long handle. See picture headed **kitchen utensils. 2** If you **spoon** food somewhere, you put it there with a spoon. *Spoon the sauce over the meat.* **3** See also **greasy spoon**, **wooden spoon. 4** If you think that someone has a lot of advantages because they have a rich or influential family, you can say that they were **born with a silver spoon in** their mouth.

'spoon-feed, spoon-feeds, spoon-feeding, spoon-fed. 1 If you think that someone is being given too much help with something and is not making enough effort themselves, you can say they **are being spoon-fed**; used showing disapproval. *Students are unwilling to really work. They want to be spoon-fed.* **2** If you say that someone **is spoon-fed** ideas or information, you mean that they are told about them and are expected to accept them without questioning them; used showing disapproval. *The children who were spoon-fed consumerism have discovered that the years of excess are over.* **3** If you **spoon-feed** a small child or sick person, you feed them using a spoon.

spoon·ful /'spuːnfʊl/ **spoonfuls.** You can refer to an amount of food resting on a spoon as a **spoonful** of food. *...three spoonfuls of sugar.*

spo·rad·ic /spəˈrædɪk/. **Sporadic** occurrences of something happen at irregular intervals. *...a year of sporadic fighting over northern France.* ♦ **spo·radi·cal·ly** *The distant thunder from the coast continued sporadically.*

spore /spɔː/ **spores. Spores** are cells produced by fungi which can develop into new fungi.

spor·ran /'spɒrən, AM 'spɔːrən/ **sporrans.** In traditional Scottish dress, a **sporran** is a purse made from leather or fur, worn in front of a kilt.

sport /spɔːt/ **sports, sporting, sported. 1 Sports** are games such as football, golf, and other competitive leisure activities which need physical effort and skill. *Football is my favourite sport... She excels at sport. ...the sports news.* **2** If you say that someone is a **sport** or a good **sport**, you mean that they cope with difficulties or teasing in a cheerful way. *He was accused of having no sense of humor, of not being a good sport.* **3** If you say that someone is **sporting** something such as a distinctive item of clothing, you mean that they are wearing it. *He sported a collarless jacket with pleated black panels.*

sport·ing /'spɔːtɪŋ/. **1 Sporting** means relating to sport or used for sport. *...major sporting events, such as Wimbledon.* **2** If you have a **sporting chance** of doing something, it is quite likely that you will do that thing. *There was a sporting chance they would meet, but not necessarily at the party.*

'sports car, sports cars. A **sports car** is a low, fast car, usually with room for only two people.

'sports day, sports days. In British schools, **sports day** is a special day or afternoon when pupils compete in races and other athletics events.

'sports jacket, sports jackets. A **sports jacket** is a man's jacket, usually made of tweed, which is worn on informal occasions.

sports·man /'spɔːtsmən/ **sportsmen.** A **sportsman** is a man who takes part in sports.

sports·man·ship /'spɔːtsmənʃɪp/. **Sportsmanship** is behaviour and attitudes that show respect for the

rules of a game and for the other players. *The team also won praise for sportsmanship and fair play.*

sports·wear /ˈspɔːtsweə/. Sportswear is special clothing worn for playing sports or for informal leisure activities.   N-UNCOUNT

sports·woman /ˈspɔːtswʊmən/ **sportswomen.** A sportswoman is a woman who takes part in sports.   N-COUNT

sporty /ˈspɔːti/. 1 You can describe a car as sporty when it performs like a racing car but can be driven on normal roads. 2 A sporty person likes playing sports.   ◆◇◇◇◇ ADJ-GRADED ADJ-GRADED

spot /spɒt/ **spots, spotting, spotted.** 1 Spots are small, round, coloured areas on a surface. *The swimsuit comes in navy with white spots or blue with green spots.* ◆ **spot·ted** *...hand-painted spotted cups and saucers in green and blue.* 2 Spots on a person's skin are small lumps or marks. 3 A spot of a liquid is a small amount of it. *Spots of rain had begun to fall.* 4 If you have a spot of something, you have a small amount of it. *We've given all the club members tea, coffee and a spot of lunch.*   ◆◆◆◇ N-COUNT ADJ N-COUNT N-COUNT: N of n BRITISH, INFORMAL QUANT BRITISH, INFORMAL

5 You can refer to a place as a spot. *...the island's top tourist spots... They all stood there staring, as if frozen to the spot.* 6 A spot in a television or radio show is a part of it that is regularly reserved for a particular performer or type of entertainment. *He got a spot on a CNN film show.*   N-COUNT N-COUNT

7 If you spot something or someone, you notice them. *He left the party seconds before smoke was spotted coming up the stairs.*   VERB: V n be V-ed

8 If you are on the spot, you are at the actual place where something is happening. *...areas where troops are on the spot and protecting civilians. ...an on-the-spot assessment of the border situation.* 9 If you do something on the spot, you do it immediately. *The surveyor will use a lap-top computer to give on the spot advice.* 10 If you put someone on the spot, you cause them to have to answer a difficult question or make a difficult decision. *He put me on the spot a bit because he invited me right in front of his mum and I didn't particularly want to go.* 11 If you are in a tight spot, you are in a difficult situation.   PHRASE PHRASE PHRASE PHRASE INFORMAL

12 See also **black spot, blind spot.** ● **rooted to the spot**: see rooted. ● **have a soft spot for** someone: see soft.

spot 'check, spot checks. If someone carries out a spot check, they examine a randomly chosen thing from a group in order to make sure that it is satisfactory.   N-COUNT

spot·less /ˈspɒtləs/. Something that is spotless is perfectly clean. *Each morning cleaners make sure everything is spotless.* ◆ **spot·less·ly** *The house had huge, spotlessly clean rooms.*   ADJ-GRADED ADV: ADV adj

spot·light /ˈspɒtlaɪt/ **spotlights, spotlighting, spotlighted.** 1 A spotlight is a powerful light, for example in a theatre, which can be directed so that it lights a small area. 2 To spotlight a particular problem or situation means to make people notice it and think about it. *The budget crisis also spotlighted a weakening American economy.* 3 Someone or something that is in the spotlight is getting a lot of public attention. 4 If someone or something comes under the spotlight, they are thoroughly examined. *The economy will come under the spotlight today at the conference of the Trades Union Congress.*   ◆◆◇◇◇ N-COUNT VERB V n PHRASE PHRASE

spot-'on. Spot-on means exactly correct or accurate. *Schools were told their exam information had to be spot-on.*   ADJ ◇◇◇◇ BRITISH

spot·ter /ˈspɒtə/ **spotters.** A spotter of something such as trains or aeroplanes is someone whose hobby is looking out for them. *I was a devoted train spotter.* ◆ **-spotting** *...bird-spotting.*   ◆◇◇◇◇ N-COUNT: n N COMB

spot·ty /ˈspɒti/. 1 A spotty person has spots or pimples on their face. 2 Something that is spotty does not stay the same but is sometimes good and sometimes bad. *He quit in 1981 – had a spotty political career.*   ADJ-GRADED ADJ-GRADED AMERICAN

spous·al /ˈspaʊzəl/. Spousal rights and duties are ones which you gain when you are married.   ADJ: ADJ n AMERICAN, FORMAL

spouse /spaʊs/ **spouses.** Someone's spouse is the person they are married to.   ◆◆◇◇◇ N-COUNT

spout /spaʊt/ **spouts, spouting, spouted.** 1 If something spouts liquid or fire or if liquid or fire spout out of something, it comes out very quickly with a lot of force. *...a fountain that spouts water 40 feet into the air... Water spouts out of the blowhole just like a whale.* 2 If you say that someone spouts something, you disapprove of them because they say something which you think is wrong or insincere. 3 A spout is a long, hollow part of a container through which liquid is poured out.   ◆◇◇◇◇ V-ERG: V n V n prep V adv/prep VERB: V n PRAGMATICS N-COUNT

sprain /spreɪn/ **sprains, spraining, sprained.** 1 If you sprain a joint such as your ankle or wrist, you injure it by twisting or bending it violently. *...a badly sprained ankle.* 2 A sprain is the injury caused by spraining a joint.   VERB: V n V-ed N-COUNT

sprang /spræŋ/. Sprang is the past tense of spring.

sprat /spræt/ **sprats.** Sprats are very small European sea fish which can be eaten.   N-COUNT

sprawl /sprɔːl/ **sprawls, sprawling, sprawled.** 1 If you sprawl somewhere, you sit or lie with your legs and arms spread out. *They sprawled in lawn chairs, snoozing... Rolando lay sprawled on his stomach, snoring.* ▶ **Sprawl out** means the same as sprawl. *He would take two aspirin and sprawl out on his bed.* 2 If a place sprawls, it covers a large area of land. *The State Recreation Area sprawls over 900 acres... The sprawling city contained some 4m people.* ● Also a noun. *The whole urban sprawl of Ankara contains over 2.6m people.*   ◆◇◇◇◇ VERB V prep/adv V-ed PHRASAL VB V P prep VERB V prep V-ing N-UNCOUNT

spray /spreɪ/ **sprays, spraying, sprayed.** 1 Spray is a lot of small drops of water which are splashed or forced into the air. *...the spray from the waterfall.* 2 If you spray a liquid somewhere or if it sprays somewhere, drops of the liquid cover a place or shower someone. *A sprayer hooked to a tractor can spray five gallons onto ten acres... Inmates hurled slates at prison officers spraying them with a hose... Blood sprayed across the room.* 3 If a lot of small things spray somewhere or if something sprays somewhere, they are scattered somewhere with a lot of force. *A shower of mustard seeds sprayed into the air and fell into the grass... The bullet slammed into the ceiling, spraying them with bits of plaster.* 4 If someone sprays bullets somewhere, they fire a lot of bullets at a group of people or things. *The army lorries were sprayed with machinegun fire.* 5 A spray is a liquid kept under pressure in a can, which you can force out in very small drops. *...a can of insect spray.* 6 If something is sprayed, it is painted using paint from a pressurized container. *The bare metal was sprayed with several coats of primer.* 7 When someone such as a farmer sprays, he or she covers plants or crops with a chemical which prevents insects from feeding on them. *He doesn't spray against pests or diseases... Do not spray plants that are in flower.* 8 A spray of flowers or leaves is a number of them on one stem or branch.   ◆◆◇◇ N-VAR V-ERG V n prep/adv V n with n V prep V-ERG V prep V n with n Also V n prep VERB: V n prep/adv be V-ed with n Also V n N-VAR VERB be V-ed with n Also V n colour VERB: V V against n V n Also V n prep N-COUNT: N of n

'spray can, spray cans. A spray can is a small metal container containing liquid such as paint under pressure so that it can be sprayed.   N-COUNT

spread /spred/ **spreads, spreading, spread.** 1 If you spread something somewhere, you open it out or arrange it over a place or surface, so that all of it can be seen or used easily. *She spread a towel on the sand and lay on it.* ▶ **Spread out** means the same as spread. *Tom was spreading out a map of Scandinavia on the bed.* 2 If you spread your arms, hands, fingers, or legs, you stretch them out until they are far apart. *Sitting on the floor, spread your legs as far as they will go.* ● **spread your wings**: see wing. ▶ **Spread out** means the same as spread. *...a bed that's large enough to let you spread yourself out.* 3 If something such as a liquid, gas, or smoke spreads, it moves outwards in all directions so that it covers a larger area. *Fire spread rapidly after a chemical truck exploded... A dark red stain was*   ◆◆◆◇ VERB V n prep PHRASAL VB V P noun VERB: V n V n adv/adj Also V n PHRASAL VB V n P VERB V V prep

spreading across his shirt. ▶ Also a noun. *...the* N-SING
spread of a serious forest fire.
4 If you **spread** a substance on a surface or **spread** the VERB:
surface with the substance, you put a thin layer of the V n prep
substance over the surface. *A thick layer of wax was* be V-ed prep
spread over the surface... Spread the bread with the V n with n
cheese. **5 Spread** is a soft food which is put on bread. N-VAR
...a wholemeal salad roll with low fat spread.
6 If something **spreads** or **is spread** by people, it V-ERG
gradually reaches or affects a larger and larger area or V prep/adv
more and more people. *The industrial revolution* be V-ed
which started a couple of hundred years ago in Europe Also V,
is now spreading across the world. ...the lies being V n
spread about him. **7** If you **spread** something **over** a VERB:
period of time, it takes place regularly or continuously V n over n
over that period, rather than happening at one time. be V-ed over n
The course is spread over a five week period. **8** If you VERB: V n
spread something such as wealth or work, you dis- be V-ed prep
tribute it evenly or equally. *The loss of jobs has been far*
more evenly spread across the regions than it was dur-
ing the early 1980s. ▶ Also a noun. *There are easier* N-SING
ways to encourage the even spread of wealth. **9** A N-SING
spread of ideas, interests, or other things is a wide variety of them. *...schools with a typical spread of abil-*
ity... We have an enormous spread of industries.
10 A **spread** is a large meal, especially one prepared N-COUNT
for a special occasion.
11 A **spread** is two pages of a book, magazine, or N-COUNT
newspaper that are opposite each other when you
open it at a particular place.
spread out. If people, animals, or vehicles **spread** PHRASAL VB
out they move apart from each other. ● See also V P
spread 1, 2.
spread·eagled /'spredi:gəld/; also spelled **spread-** ADJ
eagled. Someone who is **spreadeagled** is lying with
their arms and legs spread out.
spread 'out. If people or things are **spread out**, ◆◇◇◇◇
they are a long way apart. *The Kurds are spread out* ADJ-GRADED
across five nations.
spread·sheet /'spredʃiːt/ **spreadsheets.** A N-COUNT
spreadsheet is a computer program that is used for
entering and arranging numerical data. **Spread-**
sheets are used mainly for financial planning and
budgeting.
spree /spriː/ **sprees.** If you spend a period of time ◆◇◇◇◇
doing something in an excessive way, you can say N-COUNT
that you are going on a particular kind of **spree**.
Some Americans went on a spending spree in De-
cember to beat the new tax.
sprig /sprɪg/ **sprigs.** A **sprig** is a small twig or stem ◆◇◇◇◇
with leaves on it which has been picked from a N-COUNT
bush or plant.
spright·ly /'spraɪtli/ **sprightlier, sprightliest.** A ADJ-GRADED
sprightly person, especially an old person, is lively
and active. *...the sprightly 85-year-old President.*
spring /sprɪŋ/ **springs, springing, sprang,** ◆◆◆◆◇
sprung. **1 Spring** is the season between winter N-VAR
and summer when the weather becomes warmer
and plants start to grow again. *...migrating birds go-*
ing south in autumn or coming north in spring.
2 A **spring** is a coil of wire which returns to its original N-COUNT
shape after it is pressed or pulled. *The mattress con-*
tains hundreds of springs.
3 A **spring** is a place where water comes up through N-COUNT
the ground. *...the hot springs of Banyas de Sant Loan.*
4 If a person or animal **springs**, they jump upwards or VERB
forwards suddenly or quickly. *He sprang to his feet...* V prep
The lion roared once and sprang. **5** If something V
springs in a particular direction, it moves suddenly VERB
and quickly. *The lid of the boot sprang open.* **6** If things V adj
or people **spring into action** or **spring to life**, they VERB
suddenly start being active or suddenly come to ex- V prep
istence. *When she contacted me at the beginning of*
August to enlist support, Sharon and I sprang into ac-
tion. ● **spring to mind**: see **mind**.
7 If one thing **springs from** another thing, it is the re- VERB
sult of it. *His anger sprang from his suffering at the loss* V from n
of the most important love he had ever known in his
life. **8** If a boat or container **springs a leak**, water or VERB: V n

some other liquid starts coming in or out through a
hole or crack. **9** If you **spring** some news or a surprise VERB:
on someone, you tell them something that they did V n on n
not expect to hear, without warning them. *The two* V n
superpower leaders sprang a surprise at a ceremony in
the White House yesterday by signing a trade deal.
spring up. If something **springs up**, it suddenly ap- PHRASAL VB
pears or comes into existence. *New theatres and arts* V P
centres sprang up all over the country.
spring·board /'sprɪŋbɔːd/ **springboards.** **1** If N-COUNT:
something is a **springboard** for an action or enter- N for/to n
prise, it makes it possible for the action or enterprise to begin. *The 1981 budget was the springboard*
for an economic miracle. **2** A **springboard** is a flex- N-COUNT
ible board which you jump on before performing a
dive into water.
spring 'chicken, spring chickens. If you say PHRASE
that someone is **no spring chicken**, you are saying
in a humorous way that they are not young.
spring-'clean, spring-cleans, spring- VERB: V n
cleaning, spring-cleaned. If you **spring-clean** a
house, you thoroughly clean everything in it. ▶ Also N-SING
a noun. *It needs a thorough spring clean.* ♦ **spring-**
cleaning *The rooms inside were undergoing a* N-SING
spring-cleaning.
spring 'onion, spring onions. Spring onions ◆◇◇◇◇
are small onions with long green leaves. They are N-VAR
often eaten raw in salads. The usual American term BRITISH
is **scallion**.
spring 'roll, spring rolls. A **spring roll** is an item N-COUNT
of Chinese food consisting of a small, fried roll of BRITISH
thin pastry filled with vegetables and sometimes
meat.
'spring tide, spring tides. A **spring tide** is an un- N-COUNT
usually high tide that happens at the time of a new
moon or full moon.
spring-time /'sprɪŋtaɪm/. **Springtime** is the period N-UNCOUNT
of time during which spring lasts.
springy /'sprɪŋi/. If something is **springy**, it returns ADJ-GRADED
quickly to its original shape after you press it. *Steam*
for about 12 mins until the cake is risen and springy
to touch.
sprin·kle /'sprɪŋkəl/ **sprinkles, sprinkling,** ◆◆◇◇◇
sprinkled. **1** If you **sprinkle** a thing with some- VERB:
thing such as a liquid or powder, you scatter the liq- V n with n
uid or powder over it. *At the festival, candles are* be V-ed with n
blessed and sprinkled with holy water... Cheese can be V-ed on n
be sprinkled on egg or vegetable dishes. **2** If it **is** VERB:
sprinkling, it is raining very lightly. The British it V
word is **spit**. AMERICAN
sprin·kled /'sprɪŋkəld/. If something is **sprinkled** ADJ:
with particular things, it has some of them through- v-link ADJ
out it and they are far apart from each other. *The*
text is sprinkled with errors.
sprin·kler /'sprɪŋklə/ **sprinklers.** A **sprinkler** is a N-COUNT
device used to spray water, especially to water
plants or lawns or to put out a fire in a building. See
picture headed **tools**.
sprin·kling /'sprɪŋklɪŋ/. A **sprinkling** of something N-SING
is a small quantity or amount of it, especially if it is
spread over a large area. *Norway has a fair sprin-*
kling of women ministers.
sprint /sprɪnt/ **sprints, sprinting, sprinted. 1** A ◆◆◇◇◇
sprint is a short race in which the competitors run, N-COUNT
drive, ride, or swim very fast. *...the women's 100-*
metres sprint... I knew there were other riders who
could beat me in a sprint. **2** A **sprint** is a fast run N-SING:
that someone does, either at the end of a race or a N
because they are in a hurry. *Gilles Delion, of France,*
won the Tour of Lombardy in a sprint finish... I
broke into a sprint. **3** If you **sprint**, you run or ride VERB
as fast as you can over a short distance. *Sergeant* V adv/prep
Horne sprinted to the car.
sprint·er /'sprɪntə/ **sprinters.** A **sprinter** is a per- ◆◇◇◇◇
son who takes part in short, fast races. N-COUNT
sprite /spraɪt/ **sprites.** In fairy stories and legends, N-COUNT
a **sprite** is a small, magic creature which lives near
water.
spritz·er /'sprɪtsə/ **spritzers.** A **spritzer** is a drink N-COUNT
consisting of white wine and soda water.

sprock·et /ˈsprɒkɪt/ **sprockets.** A **sprocket** is a wheel with teeth around the outer edge that fit into the holes in a chain or a reel of film or tape in order to turn it. `N-COUNT`

sprout /spraʊt/ **sprouts, sprouting, sprouted.** ◆◇◇◇◇ **1** When plants, vegetables, or seeds **sprout**, they produce new shoots or leaves. *It only takes a few days for beans to sprout.* **2** When leaves, shoots, or plants **sprout** somewhere, they grow there. You can also say that a place **sprouts** leaves, shoots, or plants. *Leaf-shoots were beginning to sprout on the hawthorn. ...the garden, which had had time to sprout a shocking collection of weeds.* **3** If you **sprout** beans or seeds, you make them grow small shoots before eating them. You usually do this by soaking them in water. `VERB` `V` `V-ERG` `V prep` `V n` `VERB: V n`

4 If something such as hair **sprouts** from a person or animal, or if they **sprout** it, it grows on them. *As well as sprouting a few grey hairs, Kevin seems to be suffering the occasional memory loss.* **5** If a large number of things have appeared or developed somewhere, you can say that they **have sprouted** there or that the place **has sprouted** them. *More than a million satellite dishes have sprouted on homes across the country.* `V-ERG` `V n` `Also V prep` `V-ERG` `V adv/prep` `Also V, V n`

6 Sprouts are vegetables that look like tiny cabbages. They are also called **brussels sprouts.** `N-COUNT`

spruce /spruːs/ **spruces, sprucing, spruced;** ◆◇◇◇◇ **spruce** is both the singular and the plural of the noun. **1** A **spruce** is a kind of evergreen tree. **2** Someone who is **spruce** is very neat and smart in appearance. *Chris was looking spruce in his stiff-collared black shirt and new short hair cut.* `N-VAR` `ADJ-GRADED`

spruce up. If something **is spruced up**, its appearance is improved. *Many buildings have been spruced up... We spruced ourselves up a bit and went out for dinner.* `PHRASAL VB` `be V-ed P` `V n P`

sprung /sprʌŋ/. **Sprung** is the past participle of **spring.**

spry /spraɪ/. Someone, especially an old person, who is **spry**, is lively and active. `ADJ-GRADED`

spud /spʌd/ **spuds. Spuds** are potatoes. `N-COUNT` `INFORMAL`

spun /spʌn/. **Spun** is the past tense and past participle of **spin.**

spunk /spʌŋk/. **Spunk** is courage. *I admired her independence and her spunk.* `N-UNCOUNT` `INFORMAL`

spunky /ˈspʌŋki/ **spunkier, spunkiest.** A **spunky** person shows courage. `ADJ-GRADED` `INFORMAL`

spur /spɜː/ **spurs, spurring, spurred. 1** If one thing **spurs** you to do another, it encourages you to do it. *It's the money that spurs these fishermen to risk a long ocean journey... His friend's plight had spurred him into taking part.* ▶ **Spur on** means the same as **spur.** *Their attitude, rather than reining him back, only seemed to spur Philip on... Criticism can be of great use; we may not like it at the time, but it can spur us on to greater things.* **2** Something that acts as a **spur** to something else encourages a person or organization to do that thing or makes it happen more quickly. *...a belief in competition as a spur to efficiency.* `◆◆◇◇◇` `VERB` `V n to-inf` `V n to/into n/-ing` `PHRASAL VB` `V n P` `Also V n P to n` `V n P noun,` `V n P to-inf` `N-COUNT`

3 Spurs are small metal wheels with sharp points attached to the heels of a rider's boots. The rider uses them to make a horse go faster. **4** If you **win** or **earn** your **spurs**, you achieve a particular status by proving that you can do something skilfully. *Young conductors earn their spurs in a small orchestra or opera house.* `N-COUNT` `PHRASE`

5 The **spur** of a hill or mountain is a piece of ground which sticks out from its side. `N-COUNT`

6 If you do something **on the spur of the moment**, you do it suddenly, without planning it. *They admitted they had taken a vehicle on the spur of the moment. ...a spur-of-the-moment decision.* `PHRASE`

spur on. See **spur** 1. `PHRASAL VB`

spu·ri·ous /ˈspjʊəriəs/. A **spurious** claim or argument seems to be correct or genuine, but is false or dishonest; used showing disapproval. *He was arrested in 1979 on spurious corruption charges.* ◆ **spu·ri·ous·ly** *...a spuriously scientific book.* `ADJ-GRADED` `PRAGMATICS` `ADV-GRADED`

spurn /spɜːn/ **spurns, spurning, spurned.** If you **spurn** someone or something, you reject them. `◆◇◇◇◇` `VERB` *He spurned the advice of management consultants. ...a spurned lover.* `V n` `V-ed`

spur-of-the-'moment. See **spur.**

spurt /spɜːt/ **spurts, spurting, spurted. 1** If something **spurts** liquid or fire or if liquid or fire **spurts** from somewhere or something, it comes out quickly in a thin, powerful stream. *He hit her on the head, causing her too to spurt blood... I saw flames spurt from the roof.* ▶ **Spurt out** means the same as **spurt.** *When the washing machine spurts out water at least we can mop it up.* **2** A **spurt** of liquid is a stream of it which comes out of something very forcefully. *A spurt of diesel came from one valve and none from the other.* **3** A **spurt** of activity, effort, or emotion is a sudden, brief period of intense activity, effort, or emotion. *A spurt of anger flashed through me. ...the recent spurt in violence... The deals came in spurts: three in 1977, none in 1978, three more in 1979.* **4** If someone or something **spurts** somewhere, they suddenly increase their speed for a short while in order to get there. *The back wheels spun and the van spurted up the last few feet.* ▶ Also a noun. *...at the end when the athlete puts on a spurt.* `◆◇◇◇◇` `V-ERG` `V n` `V prep` `Also V` `PHRASAL VB` `ERG` `V P noun` `N-COUNT` `N-COUNT` `VERB` `V prep/adv` `N-COUNT`

spurt out. See **spurt** 1. `PHRASAL VB`

sput·ter /ˈspʌtə/ **sputters, sputtering, sputtered. 1** If something such as an engine or a flame **sputters**, it works or burns unevenly and makes a series of soft popping sounds. *The truck sputtered and stopped... The flame sputters out. ...the sputtering engine.* **2** If you **sputter**, you speak with difficulty and make soft, spitting sounds, especially because you are agitated or angry. *Stunned, I sputtered, 'What do you mean?'* `VERB` `V` `V prep/adv` `V-ing` `VERB: V` `V with quote` `Also V n`

spu·tum /ˈspjuːtəm/. **Sputum** is mucus coughed up from the chest or lungs. `N-UNCOUNT` `MEDICAL`

spy /spaɪ/ **spies, spying, spied. 1** A **spy** is a person whose job is to find out secret information about another country or organization. **2** A **spy** satellite or **spy** plane obtains secret information about another country by taking aerial photographs of particular areas. **3** Someone who **spies** for a country or organization tries to find out secret information about another country or organization. *Russian intelligence is still spying on Western countries.* ◆ **spy·ing** *...a ten-year sentence for spying.* `◆◆◇◇◇` `N-COUNT` `ADJ: ADJ n` `VERB:` `V for n` `V on n` `Also V against n` `N-UNCOUNT`

4 If you **spy on** someone, you watch them secretly. *He spied on her while pretending to work on the shrubs.* **5** If you **spy** someone or something, you notice them. *He was walking down the street when he spied an old friend.* `VERB` `V on n` `VERB` `V n` `LITERARY`

spy·master /ˈspaɪmɑːstə, -mæs-/ **spymasters.** A **spymaster** is a spy who is in charge of a group of spies. `N-COUNT`

sq. 1 sq is used as a written abbreviation for 'square' when you are giving the measurement of an area. *...25,500 sq ft.* **2 Sq** is used as a written abbreviation for 'Square' in addresses and on maps and signs. *...28 Berkeley Sq, W1.*

squab·ble /ˈskwɒbəl/ **squabbles, squabbling, squabbled.** When people **squabble**, they quarrel about something that is not really important. *The children were squabbling over the remote-control... My four-year-old squabbles with his friends.* ▶ Also a noun. *...minor squabbles about phone bills.* `◆◇◇◇◇` `pl-n V` `pl-n V over/` `pl-n V` `about n` `V with n` `N-COUNT`

squad /skwɒd/ **squads. 1** A **squad** is a section of a police force that is responsible for dealing with a particular type of crime. *The club is under investigation by the fraud squad.* **2** A **squad** is a group of players from which a sports team will be chosen. **3** A **squad** of soldiers is a small group of them. *...a squad of commandos.* ● See also **death squad, firing squad, Flying Squad, vice squad.** `◆◆◆◇◇` `N-COUNT` `N-COUNT` `N-COUNT`

'squad car, squad cars. A **squad car** is a car used by the police. The usual British term is **patrol car.** `N-COUNT` `AMERICAN`

squad·die /ˈskwɒdi/ **squaddies.** A **squaddie** is a soldier of the lowest rank in the army. *They saw the squaddie leaving a disco with a girl.* `N-COUNT` `BRITISH,` `INFORMAL`

squad·ron /'skwɒdrən/ **squadrons.** A squadron ◆◇◇◇◇
is a section of one of the armed forces, especially N-COLL-
the air force. COUNT

,**squadron 'leader, squadron leaders.** A N-COUNT;
squadron leader is an officer in the British air force. N-TITLE

squal·id /'skwɒlɪd/. **1** A **squalid** place is dirty, unti- ◆◇◇◇◇
dy, and in bad condition. ...*living in squalid condi-* ADJ-GRADED
tions. **2** Squalid activities are unpleasant and often ADJ-GRADED
dishonest. ...*the squalid pursuit of profit.*

squall /skwɔːl/ **squalls, squalling, squalled. 1** A N-COUNT
squall is a sudden strong wind which often causes a
brief, violent rain storm or snow storm. **2** If a per- VERB: V
son or animal **squalls**, they make a loud unpleasant
noise like the noise made by a crying baby.

squal·ly /'skwɔːli/. In **squally** weather, there are ADJ
sudden strong winds which often cause brief, violent storms.

squal·or /'skwɒlə/. You can refer to squalid condi- ◆◇◇◇◇
tions or surroundings as **squalor.** *He was out of* N-UNCOUNT
work and living in squalor.

squan·der /'skwɒndə/ **squanders, squander-** ◆◇◇◇◇
ing, squandered. If you **squander** money, re- VERB
sources, or opportunities, you use them in a foolish V n
and wasteful way. *Hooker didn't squander his money*
on flashy cars.

square /skweə/ **squares, squaring, squared.** ◆◆◆◇
1 A **square** is a shape with four sides that are all the N-COUNT
same length and four corners that are all right an-
gles. See picture headed **shapes.** *There was a calen-*
dar on the wall, with large squares around the dates.
2 Something that is **square** has a shape the same as ADJ-GRADED
a square or similar to a square. ...*a square table.*
3 In a town or city, a **square** is a flat open place, of- N-COUNT
ten in the shape of a square. ...*cafe-lined squares.*
4 Square is used before units of length when men- ADJ: ADJ n
tioning the area of something. For example, if a rectangle is three metres long and two metres wide, its
area is six square metres. **5** Square is used after units ADJ:
of length when you are giving the length of each side amount ADJ
of something that is square in shape. ...*a linen cushion*
cover, 45 cm square. **6** To **square** a number means to VERB:
multiply it by itself. For example, **3 squared** is 3 x 3, or V-ed
9. 3 squared is usually written as 3². **7** The **square** of a N-COUNT
number is the number produced when you multiply
that number by itself. For example, the square of 3 is
9. ...*the square of the speed of light, an exceedingly*
large number.
8 If you **square** two different situations or ideas **with** V-ERG
each other or when they **square with** each other, they V with n
can be accepted together or they seem compatible. Also V n with n
That explanation squares with the facts, doesn't it. **9** If VERB
you **square** something **with** someone, you go to them V n with n
to ask their permission or to check with them that
what you are doing is acceptable to them. *She should*
have squared things with Jay before she went into this
business.
10 If you say that someone **squares the circle,** you PHRASE
mean that they bring together two things which are
normally thought to be so different that they cannot
exist together. *He has squared the circle of keeping the*
City happy and doing something to improve business
cash flow. **11** If you are **back to square one,** you have PHRASE
to start dealing with something from the beginning
again because the way you were dealing with it has
failed. *We got a phone call from the lawyers and it was*
back to square one.
12 ● **fair and square:** see **fair.**

square off. If you **square** something **off,** you alter it PHRASAL VB
so that it has the shape of a square. *Peel a thick-* V P noun
skinned orange and square off the ends. Also V P n

square up. If you **square up** to a problem, person, PHRASAL VB
or situation, you accept that you have to deal with it V P to n
and take action to do so. ...*squaring up to the deepest* Also V P
crisis she has yet had to face. BRITISH

squared /skweəd/. Something that is **squared** has ADJ
the shape of a square, or has a pattern of squares on
it.

'**square dance, square dances.** A square dance N-COUNT
is a traditional American dance in which sets of four
couples dance together, beginning the dance in a

square formation. You can also refer to the event
where this takes place as a **square dance.**

square·ly /'skweəli/. **1** Squarely means directly ◆◇◇◇◇
and in the middle, rather than indirectly or at an ADV:
angle. *I kept the gun aimed squarely at his eyes.* **2** If ADV with v
you face something **squarely,** you face it directly, ADV:
without trying to avoid it. *The management commit-* ADV with v
tee have faced the situation squarely.

,**square 'meal, square meals.** A **square meal** is N-COUNT
a meal which is big enough to satisfy you.

,**square 'root, square roots.** The **square root** of N-COUNT
a number is another number which produces the
first number when it is multiplied by itself. For example, the square root of 16 is 4.

squash /skwɒʃ/ **squashes, squashing,** ◆◆◇◇
squashed. 1 If someone or something **is** VERB
squashed, they are pressed or crushed with such be V-ed
force that they become injured or lose their shape. prep/adj
Robert was lucky to escape with just a broken foot Also V n
after being squashed against a fence by a car... She
made clay models and squashed them flat again. **2** If ADJ:
people or things are **squashed into** a place, they are v-link ADJ into
put or pushed into a place where there is not
enough room for them to be. *There were 2000 peo-* N-SING:
ple squashed into her recent show. **3** If you say that a N
getting a number of people into a small space is a INFORMAL,
squash, you mean that it is only just possible for BRITISH
them all to get into it.
4 If you **squash** something that is causing you trouble, VERB: V n
you put a stop to it, often by force.
5 Squash is a game in which two players hit a small N-UNCOUNT
rubber ball against the walls of a court using rackets.
6 Squash is a drink made from fruit juice, sugar, and N-VAR
water. Squash is sold in bottles in a concentrated form BRITISH
to which you add water. **7** A **squash** is any vegetable N-COUNT
belonging to the marrow family.

squashy /'skwɒʃi/. **Squashy** things are soft and ADJ-GRADED
able to be squashed easily. ...*deep, squashy sofas.*

squat /skwɒt/ **squats, squatting, squatted.** ◆◇◇◇◇
1 If you **squat,** you lower yourself towards the VERB: V
ground, balancing on your feet with your legs bent. V on n
He came over and squatted on his heels, looking up
at the boys. ► **Squat down** means the same as PHRASAL VB
squat. *Albert squatted down and examined it.* ► Also V P prep
a noun. *He bent to a squat and gathered the puppies* N-SING:
on his lap. **2** If you describe someone or something a N
as **squat,** you mean they are short and thick, usually ADJ-GRADED
in an unattractive way. ...*squat stone houses.* **3** Peo- VERB: V
ple who **squat** occupy an unused building or uncul- V n
tivated land without having a legal right to do so.
They earn their living by squatting the land and
sharecropping. **4** A **squat** is an empty building that N-COUNT
people are living in illegally, without paying any BRITISH
rent or any property tax.

squat down. See **squat** 1. PHRASAL VB

squat·ter /'skwɒtə/ **squatters.** A **squatter** is ◆◇◇◇◇
someone who lives in an unused building or who N-COUNT
occupies unused land without having a legal right
to do so.

squaw /skwɔː/ **squaws.** In the past, people some- N-COUNT
times referred to North American Indian women
as **squaws;** this word is now considered to be
offensive.

squawk /skwɔːk/ **squawks, squawking,**
squawked. 1 When a bird **squawks,** it makes a VERB: V
loud harsh noise. ► Also a noun. ...*an angry* N-COUNT
squawk. **2** If a person **squawks,** they complain VERB: V
loudly, often in a high-pitched, harsh tone. *'Wait for* V with quote
me!' Melanie squawked. 'I'm not staying here alone.' Also V that
► Also a noun. *She gave a loud squawk when the* N-COUNT
water was poured on her.

squeak /skwiːk/ **squeaks, squeaking,** ◆◇◇◇◇
squeaked. If something or someone **squeaks,** VERB: V
they make a short, high-pitched sound. *The door* V with n
squeaked open... She squeaked with delight. ► Also a N-COUNT
noun. *He gave an outraged squeak.*

squeaky /'skwiːki/. Something that is **squeaky** ADJ-GRADED
makes squeaking noises. ...*squeaky floorboards.*

squ,eaky 'clean; also spelled **squeaky-clean.** If ADJ-GRADED
you say that someone is **squeaky clean,** you mean INFORMAL

that they live a very moral life and that they do not appear to have any vices. *Maybe this guy isn't so squeaky clean after all.*

squeal /skwiːl/ **squeals, squealing, squealed.** ◆◇◇◇◇ If someone or something **squeals**, they make a long, high-pitched sound. *Jennifer squealed with delight and hugged me.* ▶ Also a noun. ...*a squeal of brakes and the angry blowing of a car horn.*
VERB: V
V with n
Also V with quote
N-COUNT

squeam·ish /ˈskwiːmɪʃ/. If you are **squeamish**, you are easily upset by unpleasant sights or situations.
ADJ-GRADED

♦ squeam·ish·ness ...*when you've got over your squeamishness.*
N-UNCOUNT

squeeze /skwiːz/ **squeezes, squeezing, squeezed. 1** If you **squeeze** something, you press it firmly, usually with your hands. *Dip the bread briefly in water, then squeeze it dry.* ▶ Also a noun. ...*a squeeze of the hand.* **2** If you **squeeze** a liquid or a soft substance out of an object, you get the liquid or substance out by pressing the object. *Joe put the plug in the sink and squeezed some detergent over the dishes.*
◆◆◆◇◇
VERB: V n
V n adj
N-COUNT
VERB
V n

3 If you **squeeze** your eyes shut or if your eyes **squeeze** shut, you close them tightly. *Nancy squeezed her eyes shut and prayed... If you keep your eyes squeezed shut, you'll miss the show.* **4** If you **squeeze** someone or something somewhere or if they **squeeze** there, they manage to get through or into a small space. *Somehow they squeezed him in the tight space, and strapped him in. ...youngsters who can squeeze through tiny windows.* **5** If you say that getting a number of people into a small space is **a squeeze**, you mean that it is only just possible for them all to get into it. *It was a squeeze in the car with five of them.*
V-ERG
V n adj
V adj
V-ERG
V n prep/adv
V prep/adv
N-SING
aN
INFORMAL

6 If you **squeeze** something out of someone, you persuade them to give it to you, although they may be uncooperative or unwilling to do this. ...*the difficulties of squeezing information out of residents.* **7** If a government **squeezes** the economy, they put strict controls on people's ability to borrow money or on their own departments' freedom to spend money, in order to control the country's rate of inflation. *If a voluntary agreement is not reached the government will squeeze the economy into a severe recession to force inflation down.* ▶ Also a noun. *The CBI also says the squeeze is slowing down inflation.*
VERB
V n prep
VERB
V n
N-SING

squeeze in. If you **squeeze** something **in**, you manage to find time to do it. *The executives squeezed in a few meetings at the hotel before boarding the buses again.*
PHRASAL VB
V P noun
Also V n P

squeeze out. If someone or something **is squeezed out**, they are no longer included in something they were formerly involved in. *Latin and Greek will be squeezed out of school timetables.*
PHRASAL VB
usu passive
be V-ed P

squelch /skwɛltʃ/ **squelches, squelching, squelched. 1** To **squelch** means to make a wet, sucking sound, like the sound you make when you are walking on wet, muddy ground. *He squelched across the turf.* **2** If you **squelch** something that is causing you trouble, for example rumours or opposition, you firmly put a stop to it.
VERB: V
V prep/adv
VERB: V n
INFORMAL

squib /skwɪb/ **squibs.** You can describe something such as an event or a performance as a **damp squib** when it is expected to be interesting, exciting, or impressive, but fails to be any of these things.
PHRASE
BRITISH

squid /skwɪd/ **squids; squid** can also be used as the plural form. A **squid** is a sea creature with a long soft body and many tentacles. ▶ **Squid** is pieces of this creature eaten as food.
◆◇◇◇◇
N-COUNT
N-UNCOUNT

squidgy /ˈskwɪdʒi/. Something that is **squidgy** is soft and can be squashed easily. ...*the squidgy end of a melon. ...a squidgy sofa.*
ADJ-GRADED
BRITISH,
INFORMAL

squig·gle /ˈskwɪɡəl/ **squiggles.** A **squiggle** is a line that bends and curls in an irregular way.
N-COUNT

squig·gly /ˈskwɪɡəli/. **Squiggly** lines are lines that bend and curl in an irregular way.
ADJ-GRADED

squint /skwɪnt/ **squints, squinting, squinted. 1** If you **squint** at something, you look at it with your eyes partly closed. *The girl squinted at the photograph... He squinted his eyes and looked at the*
◆◇◇◇◇
VERB
V prep/adv
Also V

floor. **2** If someone has a **squint**, their eyes look in different directions from each other.
N-COUNT

squire /skwaɪə/ **squires.** In former times, the **squire** of an English village was the man who owned most of the land in it.
N-COUNT;
N-TITLE

squirm /skwɜːm/ **squirms, squirming, squirmed. 1** If you **squirm**, you move your body from side to side, usually because you are nervous or uncomfortable. *He gave a feeble shrug and tried to squirm free... He squirmed out of the straps of his backpack.* **2** If you **squirm**, you are very embarrassed or ashamed. *Mentioning religion is a sure way to make him squirm. ...the type of awful occasion that makes politicians squirm with embarrassment.*
◆◇◇◇◇
VERB: V
V adj
V adv/prep
VERB: V
V with n

squir·rel /ˈskwɪrəl, AM ˈskwɜːrəl/ **squirrels, squirrelling, squirrelled;** spelled **squirreling, squirreled** in American English. A **squirrel** is a small furry animal with a long bushy tail. Squirrels live mainly in trees.
◆◇◇◇◇
N-COUNT

squirrel away. If you **squirrel** things **away**, you hide or store them so that you can use them in the future. *She says the kid's been squirrelling money away like there's no tomorrow.*
PHRASAL VB
V n P
Also V P noun

squirt /skwɜːt/ **squirts, squirting, squirted.** If you **squirt** a liquid somewhere or if it **squirts** somewhere, the liquid comes out of a narrow opening in a thin fast stream. *Norman cut open his pie and squirted tomato sauce into it.* ▶ Also a noun. *It just needs a little squirt of oil.*
◆◇◇◇◇
V-ERG
V n prep/adv
Also V prep/adv
N-COUNT

Sr. Sr. is a written abbreviation for 'Senior', and is written after a man's name. It is used in order to distinguish a man from his son when they both have the same name. ...*Donald Cunningham, Sr.*

St; the form **SS** is used as the plural for meaning 2. **1 St** is a written abbreviation for 'Street'. ...*116 Princess St.* **2 St** is a written abbreviation for 'Saint'. ...*St Thomas.*

st. st is used as a written abbreviation for 'stone' when you are mentioning someone's weight. *He weighs 11st 8lb.*
BRITISH

stab /stæb/ **stabs, stabbing, stabbed. 1** If someone **stabs** you, they push a knife or sharp object into your body. *Somebody stabbed him in the stomach... Stephen was stabbed to death.* **2** If you **stab** something or **stab at** it, you push at it with your finger or with something pointed that you are holding. *Bess stabbed a slice of cucumber... He stabbed at the omelette with his fork.*
◆◆◇◇◇
VERB
V n
V to n
VERB
V n
V at n
Also V n at n

3 If you have **a stab at** something, you try to do it. *Several tennis stars have had a stab at acting.* **4** You can refer to a sudden, usually unpleasant feeling as **a stab of** that feeling. ...*a stab of pain just above his eye... She felt a stab of pity for him.* **5** If you say that someone has **stabbed** you **in the back**, you mean that they have done something very harmful to you when you thought that you could trust them. You can refer to an action of this kind as **a stab in the back**.
N-SING
INFORMAL
N-SING
LITERARY
PHRASE

stab·bing /ˈstæbɪŋ/ **stabbings. 1** A **stabbing** is an incident in which someone stabs someone else with a knife. **2** A **stabbing** pain is a sudden sharp pain.
◆◇◇◇◇
N-COUNT
ADJ: ADJ n

sta·bil·ity /stəˈbɪlɪti/. See **stable**.

sta·bi·lize /ˈsteɪbɪlaɪz/ **stabilizes, stabilizing, stabilized;** also spelled **stabilise** in British English. If something **stabilizes**, or if someone or something **stabilizes** it, it becomes stable. *Although her illness is serious, her condition is beginning to stabilize... Officials hope the move will stabilize exchange rates.*
◆◆◇◇◇
V-ERG
V n

♦ sta·bi·li·za·tion /ˌsteɪbɪlaɪˈzeɪʃən/. ...*the stabilisation of property prices.*
N-UNCOUNT

sta·bi·liz·er /ˈsteɪbɪlaɪzə/ **stabilizers;** also spelled **stabiliser**. A **stabilizer** is a device, mechanism, or chemical that stabilizes something.
N-COUNT

sta·ble /ˈsteɪbəl/ **stabler, stablest; stables, stabling, stabled. 1** If something is **stable**, it is not likely to change or come to an end suddenly. ...*a stable marriage.* **♦ sta·bil·ity** /stəˈbɪlɪti/. ...*a time of political stability and progress.* **2** If someone has a **stable** personality, they are calm and reasonable and they do not have frequent changes of
◆◆◆◇
ADJ-GRADED
N-UNCOUNT
ADJ-GRADED

mood. **3** You can describe someone who is serious-ly ill as **stable** when their condition has stopped getting worse. **4** Chemical substances are described as **stable** when they tend to remain in the same chemical or atomic state. **5** If an object is **stable**, it is firmly fixed in position and is not likely to move or fall.
6 A **stable** or **stables** is a building in which horses are kept. **7** A **stable** or **stables** is an organization that breeds and trains racehorses. **8** When horses **are sta-bled**, they are put into a stable. *The animals had been fed and stabled.*

ADJ-GRADED

ADJ-GRADED TECHNICAL

ADJ-GRADED

N-COUNT
N-COUNT
VB: usu passive be V-ed

'stable boy, stable boys. A **stable boy** is the same as a **stable lad**.

N-COUNT

'stable lad, stable lads. A **stable lad** is a young man who works in a stable looking after the horses.

N-COUNT

stable·mate /'steɪbəlmeɪt/ **stablemates. 1** Stablemates are race horses that come from the same stables and often compete against each other. **2** A person's **stablemate** is someone who is man-aged by the same organization. A product's **stablemate** is something which is produced by the same company.

N-COUNT

N-COUNT: poss N

'stab wound, stab wounds. A **stab wound** is a wound that someone has when they have been stabbed with a knife.

N-COUNT

stac·ca·to /stə'kɑːtəʊ/. A **staccato** noise consists of a series of short, sharp, separate sounds. *...the stac-cato chattering of several machine-guns.*

ADJ-GRADED

stack /stæk/ **stacks, stacking, stacked. 1** A **stack** of things is a pile of them. *There were stacks of books on the bedside table and floor.* **2** If you **stack** a number of things, you arrange them in neat piles. *Mme Cathiard was stacking the clean bottles in crates.* ► **Stack up** means the same as **stack**. *He or-dered them to stack up pillows behind his back.* **3** If you say that someone has **stacks of** something, you mean that they have a lot of it. *If the job's that good, you'll have stacks of money.* **4** If you say that **the odds are stacked against** someone, or that particu-lar factors **are stacked against** them, you mean that they are unlikely to succeed in what they want to do because the conditions are not favourable. *The odds are stacked against civilians getting a fair trial.* **5** See also **chimney stack**.

◆◆◇◇◇
N-COUNT

VERB
V n

PHRASAL VB
V P noun
Also V n P
N-PLURAL:
N of n
INFORMAL
PHRASE

stacked /stækt/. If a place or surface is **stacked** with objects, it is filled with piles of them.

ADJ

sta·dium /'steɪdiəm/ **stadiums** or **stadia** /'steɪdiə/. A **stadium** is a large sports ground with rows of seats all round it.

◆◆◆◇◇
N-COUNT

staff /stɑːf, stæf/ **staffs, staffing, staffed. 1** The **staff** of an organization are the people who work for it. *The staff were very good... The outpatient program has a staff of six people.* ● See also **Chief of Staff**. **2** People who are part of a particular staff are often referred to as **staff**. *He had the complete support of hospital staff.* **3** If an organization **is staffed** by par-ticular people, they are the people who work for it. *They are staffed by volunteers... The centre is staffed at all times.* ● **staffed** *...poorly staffed hotels.* ● see also **short-staffed**.
4 A **staff** is a strong stick or pole.

◆◆◆◆◇
N-COLL-COUNT

N-PLURAL

VERB
be V-ed by/ with n
be V-ed
ADJ:
adv ADJ
N-COUNT

staff·er /'stɑːfə, 'stæf-/ **staffers.** A **staffer** is a member of staff, especially in political organizations or in journalism. *The Sky News TV station is largely run by ex-BBC news staffers.*

◆◇◇◇◇
N-COUNT
AMERICAN

staff·ing /'stɑːfɪŋ, 'stæf-/. **Staffing** refers to the number of workers employed to work in a particu-lar organization or building. *Staffing levels in pris-ons are too low.*

◆◇◇◇◇
N-UNCOUNT

'staff nurse, staff nurses. A **staff nurse** is a hos-pital nurse whose rank is just below that of a sister or charge nurse.

N-COUNT

'staff officer, staff officers. In the army and air force, a **staff officer** is an officer who works for a commander or in the headquarters.

N-COUNT

'staff sergeant, staff sergeants; also spelled **Staff Sergeant.** In the British and US armies, a **staff sergeant** is a soldier who ranks just above sergeant.

N-COUNT;
N-TITLE

stag /stæg/ **stags.** A **stag** is an adult male deer be-longing to one of the larger species of deer. Stags usually have large branch-like horns called antlers.

◆◇◇◇◇
N-COUNT

stage /steɪdʒ/ **stages, staging, staged. 1** A **stage** of an activity, process, or period is one part of it. *The way children talk about or express their feel-ings depends on their age and stage of development. ...the final stage of a tour which also included Egypt and Israel.* **2** In a theatre, the **stage** is an area where actors or other entertainers perform. *I went on stage and did my show.* **3** You can refer to acting and the production of plays in a theatre as the **stage**. *He was the first comedian I ever saw on the stage.* **4** If someone **stages** a play or other show, they organize and present a performance of it. **5** If you **stage** an event or ceremony, you organize it and usually take part in it. *This year the government staged a huge military parade.* **6** You can refer to a particular area of activity as a particular **stage**, espe-cially when you are talking about politics. *He hoped Mr Shevardnadze would not leave the political stage.* **7** ● **to set the stage:** see **set**.

◆◆◆◆◆
N-COUNT

N-COUNT:
also on N
N-SING:
the N

VERB: V n

VERB
V n

N-SING

stage·coach /'steɪdʒkəʊtʃ/ **stagecoaches;** also spelled **stage-coach.** In former times, **stagecoaches** were large carriages pulled by horses which carried passengers and mail.

N-COUNT:
also by N

stage·craft /'steɪdʒkrɑːft, -kræft/. **Stagecraft** is skill in writing or producing or directing plays in the theatre.

N-UNCOUNT

'stage direction, stage directions. Stage direc-tions are the notes in the text of a play which say what the actors should do.

N-COUNT

,stage 'door, stage doors. The **stage door** of a theatre is the entrance used by actors and actresses and by employees of the theatre.

N-COUNT

'stage fright. **Stage fright** is a feeling of fear or nervousness that some people have just before they appear in front of an audience.

N-COUNT

stage·hand /'steɪdʒhænd/ **stagehands;** also spelled **stage hand.** A **stagehand** is a person whose job is to move the scenery and equipment on the stage in a theatre.

N-COUNT

,stage 'left. **Stage left** is the left-hand side of the stage for an actor standing facing the audience.

ADV

'stage-manage, stage-manages, stage-managing, stage-managed. If someone **stage-manages** an event, they carefully organize and con-trol it, rather than let it happen spontaneously; used showing disapproval. *...the attempt of his supporters to stage manage the congress.*

VERB
PRAGMATICS
V n

'stage manager, stage managers. At a theatre, a **stage manager** is the person who is responsible for the scenery and lights and for the way that ac-tors or other performers move about and use the stage during a performance.

N-COUNT

'stage name, stage names. A **stage name** is a name that an actor or entertainer uses professional-ly instead of his or her real name.

N-COUNT

,stage 'right. **Stage right** is the right-hand side of the stage for an actor standing facing the audience.

ADV

stag·fla·tion /,stæg'fleɪʃən/. If an economy is suf-fering from **stagflation**, inflation is high but there is no corresponding increase in demand for goods or in employment.

N-UNCOUNT
JOURNALISM

stag·ger /'stægə/ **staggers, staggering, stag-gered. 1** If you **stagger**, you walk very unsteadily, for example because you are ill or drunk. *He lost his balance, staggered back against the rail and toppled over.* **2** If you say that someone or something **stag-gers on**, you mean that it is only just succeeds in continuing. *...a government that staggered from cri-sis to crisis.* **3** If something **staggers** you, it sur-prises you very much. *The whole thing staggers me.* ♦ **stag·gered** *I was simply staggered by the heat.* **4** To **stagger** things such as people's holidays or hours of work means to arrange them so that they do not all happen at the same time.

◆◇◇◇◇
VERB: V
V adv/prep

VERB
V adv/prep

VERB
V n
ADJ-GRADED:
v-link ADJ
VERB: V n

stag·ger·ing /'stægərɪŋ/. Something that is **stag-gering** is very surprising. *...a three-year contract re-puted to be worth a staggering £25,000-a-week.*

◆◆◇◇◇
ADJ-GRADED

S

✦ **stag·ger·ing·ly** *The South Pole expedition proved to be staggeringly successful.*   ADV-GRADED ADV adj

'**staging post, staging posts;** also spelled **staging-post. 1** A place that is a **staging post** on a long journey is where people who are making that journey usually stop, for example to rest or to get new supplies. **2** If you describe an action or achievement as a **staging post**, you mean that it helps you reach a particular goal that you have. *Privatisation is a necessary staging post to an open market.*   N-COUNT BRITISH / N-COUNT BRITISH

stag·nant /ˈstægnənt/. **1** If something such as a business or society is **stagnant**, there is little activity or change; used showing disapproval. *He is seeking advice on how to revive the stagnant economy.* **2 Stagnant** water is not flowing, and is therefore often dirty, smelly, and unhealthy.   ◆◇◇◇◇ ADJ-GRADED PRAGMATICS / ADJ

stag·nate /stægˈneɪt, AM ˈstægneɪt/ **stagnates, stagnating, stagnated.** If something such as a business or society **stagnates**, it becomes inactive or unchanging; used showing disapproval. *Industrial production is stagnating... His career had stagnated.*   ◆◇◇◇◇ VERB PRAGMATICS V

✦ **stag·na·tion** /stægˈneɪʃən/. *...the stagnation of the steel industry.*   N-UNCOUNT

'**stag night, stag nights.** A **stag night** is a party for a man who is getting married very soon, to which only men are invited.   N-COUNT

'**stag party, stag parties.** A **stag party** is the same as a **stag night.**   N-COUNT

staid /steɪd/. If you say that someone or something is **staid**, you mean that they are serious, dull, and rather old-fashioned.   ADJ-GRADED

stain /steɪn/ **stains, staining, stained. 1** A stain is a mark on something that is difficult to remove. *Remove stains by soaking in a mild solution of bleach.* **2** If a liquid **stains** something, the thing becomes coloured or marked by the liquid. ✦ **stained** *His clothing was stained with mud.* ✦ **-stained** *...ink-stained fingers.*   ◆◆◇◇◇ N-COUNT / VERB: V n / ADJ-GRADED / COMB

,**stained 'glass.** **Stained glass** consists of pieces of glass of different colours which are fixed together to make decorative windows or other objects.   ◆◇◇◇◇ N-UNCOUNT

stain·less steel /ˌsteɪnləs ˈstiːl/. **Stainless steel** is a metal made from steel and chromium which does not rust.   ◆◇◇◇◇ N-UNCOUNT

stair /steə/ **stairs. 1 Stairs** are a set of steps inside a building which go from one floor to another. *We walked up a flight of stairs.* **2** A **stair** is one of the steps in a flight of stairs.   ◆◆◇◇◇ N-PLURAL / N-COUNT

stair·case /ˈsteəkeɪs/ **staircases.** A **staircase** is a set of stairs inside a building.   ◆◇◇◇◇ N-COUNT

stair·way /ˈsteəweɪ/ **stairways.** A **stairway** is a staircase or a flight of steps, inside or outside a building.   ◆◇◇◇◇ N-COUNT

stair·well /ˈsteəwel/ **stairwells.** The **stairwell** is the part of a building that contains the staircase.   N-COUNT

stake /steɪk/ **stakes, staking, staked. 1** If something is **at stake**, it is being risked and might be lost or damaged if you are not successful. *At stake are more than 20,000 jobs in Britain's aerospace sector.* **2** The **stakes** involved in a contest or a risky action are the things that can be gained or lost. *By arresting the organisation's two top leaders the government and the army have now raised the stakes.* **3** If you **stake** something such as your money or your reputation on the result of something, you risk your money or reputation on it. **4** If you have a **stake in** something such as a business, it matters to you, for example because you own part of it or because its success or failure will affect you. **5** You can use **stakes** to refer to something that is like a contest. For example, you can refer to the choosing of a leader as **the leadership stakes. 6** A **stake** is a pointed wooden post which is pushed into the ground, for example in order to support a young tree. **7** If you **stake a claim**, you say that something is yours or that you have a right to it. *Baguet's success staked his claim for a place in Belgium's world championship team.*   ◆◆◆◇ PHRASE / N-PLURAL / VERB: V n on n / N-COUNT: N in n / N-PLURAL: the supp N / N-COUNT / PHRASE

stake out. If you **stake out** a position or a claim that you are making, you are defending the boundaries or limits of the position or claim.   PHRASAL VB V P noun

stake·holder /ˈsteɪkhəʊldə/ **stakeholders. Stakeholders** are people who have an interest in a company's or organization's affairs.   N-COUNT

'**stake out, stake outs.** If police officers are on a **stake out**, they are secretly watching a building for evidence of criminal activity.   N-COUNT

stal·ac·tite /ˈstæləktaɪt, AM stəˈlæk-/ **stalactites.** A **stalactite** is a long piece of rock which hangs down from the roof of a cave.   N-COUNT

stal·ag·mite /ˈstæləgmaɪt, AM stəˈlæg-/ **stalagmites.** A **stalagmite** is a long piece of rock which sticks up from the floor of a cave.   N-COUNT

stale /steɪl/ **staler, stalest. 1 Stale** food is no longer fresh or good to eat. **2 Stale** air or smells are unpleasant because they are no longer fresh. **3** If you feel **stale**, you are bored because you have no new ideas or enthusiasm for what you are doing. **4** If you say that a place, an activity, or an idea is **stale**, you mean that is has become boring because it is always the same. *Her relationship with Mark has become stale.*   ◆◇◇◇◇ ADJ-GRADED / ADJ-GRADED / ADJ-GRADED: v-link ADJ / ADJ-GRADED

stale·mate /ˈsteɪlmeɪt/ **stalemates. 1 Stalemate** is a situation in which neither side in an argument or contest can win or in which no progress is possible. *The war had reached a stalemate.* **2** In chess, **stalemate** is a position in which a player cannot make any move which is permitted by the rules, so that the game ends and no one wins.   ◆◇◇◇◇ N-VAR / N-VAR

stalk /stɔːk/ **stalks, stalking, stalked. 1** The **stalk** of a flower, leaf, or fruit is the thin part that joins it to the plant or tree. **2** If you **stalk** a person or a wild animal, you follow them quietly in order to kill them, catch them, or observe them carefully. **3** If you **stalk** somewhere, you walk there in a stiff, proud, or angry way. **4** If something bad or dangerous **stalks** a place, it moves menacingly through it, causing death and disaster. *The spectre of neo fascism, as he put it, was stalking the streets of Sofia.*   ◆◆◇◇◇ N-COUNT / VERB: V n / VERB: V adv/prep / VERB V n LITERARY

stalk·er /ˈstɔːkə/ **stalkers.** A **stalker** is someone who has become obsessed with a person, often a famous person or someone they used to have a relationship with, and has begun to pester and harass that person in a frightening way.   N-COUNT

'**stalking horse, stalking horses. 1** If you describe someone or something as a **stalking horse**, you mean that it is being used to obtain a temporary advantage so that someone can get what they really want; used showing disapproval. *The successful applicants will almost certainly use victory as a stalking horse for an altogether more lucrative prize.* **2** In politics, a **stalking horse** is someone who stands against a leader in order to see how strong the opposition is. The stalking horse then withdraws in favour of a stronger challenger.   N-COUNT PRAGMATICS BRITISH / N-COUNT BRITISH

stall /stɔːl/ **stalls, stalling, stalled. 1** If a process **stalls**, or if someone or something **stalls** it, the process stops but may continue at a later time. *The Social Democratic Party has vowed to try to stall the bill until the current session ends.* **2** If you **stall**, you try to avoid doing something until later. *Thomas had spent all week stalling over his decision.* **3** If you **stall** someone, you prevent them from doing something until a later time. *Shop manager Brian Steel stalled the man until the police arrived.* **4** If a vehicle **stalls** or if you accidentally **stall** it, the engine stops suddenly. *Your foot falls off the pedal and you stall the car.* **5** A **stall** is a large table on which you put goods that you want to sell, or information that you want to give people. *...market stalls selling local fruits.* **6** The **stalls** in a theatre or concert hall are the seats on the ground floor directly in front of the stage. **7** A **stall** is a small enclosed area in a room which is used for a particular purpose, for example a shower. **8** If you **set out** your **stall** or **set** your **stall out**, you make all the necessary arrangements to deal with   ◆◆◇◇◇ V-ERG: V V n / VERB: V V over/on n / VERB V n / V-ERG: V V n / N-COUNT / N-PLURAL: the N BRITISH / N-COUNT AMERICAN / PHRASE

something. *The Czechs set out their stall to woo foreign investors.*

stall·holder /'stɔːlhəʊldə/ **stallholders.** A stall-holder is a person who sells goods at a stall in a market. `N-COUNT BRITISH`

stal·lion /'stælɪən/ **stallions.** A stallion is a male horse, especially one kept for breeding. `◆◇◇◇ N-COUNT`

stal·wart /'stɔːlwət/ **stalwarts.** **1** A stalwart is a loyal and hard-working worker or supporter of an organization, especially of a political party. *His free-trade policies aroused suspicion among Tory stalwarts.* ▶ Also an adjective. *The stalwart volunteers marched in this morning ready to go to work.* **2** A stalwart man is strong and sturdy. `◆◇◇◇ N-COUNT` `ADJ-GRADED` `ADJ: ADJ n DATED`

sta·men /'steɪmen/ **stamens.** The stamens of a flower are the small, delicate stalks which grow at the flower's centre and produce pollen. `N-COUNT`

stami·na /'stæmɪnə/. Stamina is the physical or mental energy needed to do a tiring activity for a long time. `◆◇◇◇ N-UNCOUNT`

stam·mer /'stæmə/ **stammers, stammering, stammered.** **1** If you stammer, you speak with difficulty, hesitating and repeating words or sounds. *'Forgive me,' I stammered... People cursed and stammered apologies.* ♦ **stam·mer·ing** *Of all speech impediments stammering is probably the most embarrassing.* **2** Someone who has a stammer tends to stammer when they speak. `◆◇◇◇ VERB: V V with quote V n` `N-UNCOUNT` `N-SING`

stamp /stæmp/ **stamps, stamping, stamped.** **1** A stamp or a postage stamp is a small piece of gummed paper which you stick on an envelope or parcel before you post it to pay for the cost of the postage. ● see also **food stamp.** ♦ **stamped.** A stamped envelope or parcel has a stamp stuck on it. **2** A stamp is a small block of wood or metal which has a pattern or a group of letters on one side. You press it onto a pad of ink and then onto a piece of paper in order to produce a mark on the paper. The mark that you produce is also called a stamp. **3** If you stamp a mark or word on an object, you press the mark or word onto the object using a stamp or other device. **4** If you stamp or stamp your foot, you lift your foot and put it down very hard on the ground, for example because you are angry or because your feet are cold. *His foot stamped down on the accelerator... She stamped her feet on the pavement to keep out the cold.* ▶ Also a noun. *...the stamp of cold feet.* **5** If you stamp somewhere, you walk there putting your feet down very hard on the ground because you are angry. **6** If you stamp on something, you put your foot down on it very hard. **7** If something bears the stamp of a particular quality or person, it clearly has that quality or was done by that person. *Most of us want to make our home a familiar place and put the stamp of our personality on its walls.* **8** A quality, feature, or action that stamps someone or something as a particular thing shows clearly that they are this thing. *Chris Boardman stamped himself as the 4,000m favourite by setting the world's fastest outdoor time.* **9** See also **rubber stamp.** ● stamp of approval: see **approval.** `◆◆◇◇ N-COUNT` `ADJ` `N-COUNT` `VERB: V n prep` `VERB: V V adv/prep V n prep/adv Also V n` `N-COUNT VERB: V prep/adv` `VERB: V on n` `N-SING` `VERB: V n as n V pron-refl as n`

stamp out. If you stamp something out, you put an end to it. *...on-the-spot fines to stamp the problems out.* `PHRASAL VB V n P Also V P noun`

stamp on. If someone stamps on a dishonest or undesirable activity, they act immediately to stop it happening or spreading. `PHRASAL VB V P n BRITISH`

stamp duty. In Britain, stamp duty is a tax that you pay to the government when you buy a house. `◆◇◇◇ N-UNCOUNT`

stamped addressed envelope, stamped addressed envelopes. A stamped addressed envelope is an envelope on which you have stuck a stamp and written your own name and address. You send it to an organization or a person so that they can use it to send you something without having to pay the cost of posting it to you. The abbreviation s.a.e. is also used. `◆◇◇◇ N-COUNT`

stam·pede /stæm'piːd/ **stampedes, stampeding, stampeded.** **1** If a group of animals or people stampede or if something stampedes them, `◆◇◇◇ V-ERG: V V n`

they run in a wild, uncontrolled way. *Countryside robbers are learning the ways of the wild west by stampeding cattle to distract farmers before raiding their homes.* ▶ Also a noun *There was a stampede for the exit.* **2** If a lot of people all do the same thing at the same time, you can describe it as a stampede. *Generous redundancy terms had triggered a stampede of staff wanting to leave.* **3** If people are stampeded into doing something, they are forced into doing it by pressure from other people, even though they do not think it is the right thing to do. *It was widely believed that Powell had stampeded the Government into taking action.* `N-COUNT N-COUNT` `VERB: be V-ed V n into -ing/n`

'stamping ground, stamping grounds. Someone's stamping ground is a place where they like to go often. `N-COUNT`

stance /stæns/ **stances.** **1** Your stance on a particular matter is your attitude to it. *They have maintained a consistently neutral stance.* **2** Your stance is the way that you are standing. `◆◆◇◇ N-COUNT` `N-COUNT FORMAL`

stan·chion /'stæntʃən/ **stanchions.** A stanchion is a pole or bar that stands upright and is used as a support. `N-COUNT FORMAL`

stand /stænd/ **stands, standing, stood.** **1** When you are standing, your body is upright, your legs are straight, and your weight is supported by your feet. *She was standing beside my bed staring down at me... They told me to stand still.* ▶ Stand up means the same as stand. *...a shop assistant who has to stand up all day.* **2** When someone who is sitting stands, they change their position so that they are upright and on their feet. *Becker stood and shook hands with Ben.* ▶ Stand up means the same as stand. *When I walked in, they all stood up and started clapping.* **3** If you stand aside or stand back, you move a short distance sideways or backwards, so that you are standing in a different place. **4** If something such as a building or a piece of furniture stands somewhere, it is in that position, and is upright. *The house stands alone on top of a small hill.* **5** You can say that a building is standing when it remains after other buildings around it have been down or been destroyed. *There are very few buildings left standing.* **6** If you stand something somewhere, you put it there in an upright position. *Stand the plant in the open in a sunny, sheltered place.* **7** If you leave food or a mixture of something to stand, you leave it without disturbing it for some time. **8** If you take or make a stand, you do something or say something in order to make it clear what your attitude to a particular thing is. **9** If you ask someone where or how they stand on a particular issue, you are asking them what their attitude or view is. *So far, the bishop hasn't said where he stands.* **10** If you do not know where you stand with someone, you do not know exactly what their attitude to you is. *All children need discipline, to know where they stand.* **11** You can use stand instead of 'is' when you are describing the present state or condition of something or someone. *The alliance stands ready to do what is necessary... The peace plan as it stands violates basic human rights.* **12** If a decision, law, or offer stands, it still exists and has not been changed or cancelled. **13** If something that can be measured stands at a particular level, it is at that level. *The inflation rate now stands at 3.6 per cent.* **14** You can describe how tall or high someone or something is by saying that they stand a particular height. *The dam will stand 600 feet high.* **15** If something can stand a situation or a test, it is good enough or strong enough to experience it without being damaged, harmed, or shown to be inadequate. **16** If you cannot stand something, you cannot bear it or tolerate it. *I can't stand any more. I'm going to run away.* **17** If you cannot stand someone or something, you dislike them very strongly. *He can't stand me smoking.* **18** If you stand to gain something, you are likely to gain it. If you stand to lose something, you are likely `◆◆◆◆ VERB: V V prep V adj` `PHRASAL VB V P` `VERB V` `PHRASAL VB V P` `VERB: V adv/prep` `VERB V prep/adv WRITTEN` `VERB V` `VERB V n prep/adv` `VERB: V` `N-COUNT` `VERB: where V on n where V` `VERB: where V with n where V` `V-LINK V adj V` `VERB: V` `VERB V at amount` `VERB V amount adj` `VERB: V n` `VERB V n/-ing` `VERB V n/-ing INFORMAL` `V to-inf`

S

to lose it. *The management group would stand to gain millions of dollars if the company were sold.*

19 If you **stand** in an election, you are a candidate in it. The usual American word is **run.** *He has not yet announced whether he will stand in the election... Some ardent supporters were urging him to stand... She is to stand as a Member of the European Parliament.* `VERB` `V inn` `V as/for/ againstn` `BRITISH`

20 If you **stand** someone a meal or a drink, you buy it for them. `VERB: V n n` `INFORMAL`

21 A **stand** is a small shop or stall, outdoors or in a large public building. ● See also **newsstand.** **22** A **stand** at a sports ground is a large structure where spectators sit or stand to watch what is happening. ● See also **grandstand.** `N-COUNT` `N-COUNT`

23 A **stand** is an object or piece of furniture that is designed for supporting or holding a particular kind of thing. *The teapot came with a stand to catch the drips.* `N-COUNT`

24 In a law court, **the stand** is the place where a witness stands to answer questions. *When the father took the stand today, he contradicted his son's testimony.* `N-SING:` `the N`

25 If an idea, claim, or attempt **stands or falls** on something, its truth or success depends on that thing. *Airlines should stand or fall on their ability to attract passengers.* **26** You can describe someone's final attempt to defend themselves before they are defeated as their **last stand. 27** If you say it **stands to reason** that something is true or likely to happen, you mean that it is obvious. **28** If you **stand in the way of** something or **stand in** someone's **way,** you prevent that thing from happening or prevent that person from doing something. `PHRASE` `PHRASE` `PHRASE` `INFORMAL` `PHRASE`

29 See also **standing. 30** ● to **stand a chance:** see **chance.** ● to **stand up and be counted:** see **count.** ● to **stand firm:** see **firm.** ● to **stand on** your **own two feet:** see **foot.** ● to **stand** your **ground:** see **ground.** ● to **stand** someone **in good stead:** see **stead.**

stand aside. 1 If you **stand aside** from something, you allow it to happen without interfering in it or doing anything to prevent it. *The key question was whether they would stand aside or would disrupt the elections.* **2** See also **stand down.** `PHRASAL VB` `VP from n` `VP`

stand back. If you **stand back** and think about a situation, you think about it as if you were not involved in it. `PHRASAL VB` `VP`

stand by. 1 If you **are standing by,** you are ready and waiting to provide help or to take action. *British and American warships are standing by to evacuate their citizens if necessary... We will be holding the auditions from nine o'clock tomorrow night so stand by for details.* ● See also **standby. 2** If you **stand by** and let something bad happen, you do not do anything to stop it; used showing disapproval. *The Secretary of Defence has said that he would not stand by and let democracy be undermined.* **3** If you **stand by** someone, you continue to give them support, especially when they are in trouble; used showing approval. *I wouldn't break the law for a friend, but I would stand by her if she did.* **4** If you **stand by** an earlier decision, promise, or statement, you continue to support it or keep it. `PHRASAL VB` `VP to-inf` `VP forn` `Also VP` `PRAGMATICS` `VP` `PRAGMATICS` `VPn`

stand down. If someone **stands down** or **stands aside,** they resign from an important job or position, often in order to let someone else take their place. *Profits plunged and he stood down as chairman last January.* `PHRASAL VB` `VP` `VP asn`

stand for. 1 If you say that a letter **stands for** a particular word, you mean that it is an abbreviation for that word. *AIDS stands for Acquired Immune Deficiency Syndrome.* **2** The ideas or attitudes that someone or something **stands for** are the ones that they support or represent. *He hates us and everything we stand for.* **3** If you will **not stand for** something, you will not allow it to happen or continue. *It's outrageous, and we won't stand for it any more.* `PHRASAL VB` `VP n` `VP n` `with neg` `VP n`

stand in. If you **stand in** for someone, you take their place or do their job, because they are ill or away. *...the acting president, who's standing in while Franco's out of the country.* ● See also **stand-in.** `PHRASAL VB` `VP forn` `VP`

stand out. 1 If something **stands out,** it is very noticeable. **2** If something **stands out,** it is much better `PHRASAL VB` `VP` `VP`

or much more important than other things of the same kind. *He played the violin, and he stood out from all the other musicians.* **3** If something **stands out** from a surface, it rises up from it. *His tendons stood out like rope beneath his skin.* `VP from n` `VP`

stand up. 1 See **stand** 1, 2. **2** If something such as a claim or a piece of evidence **stands up,** it is accepted as true or satisfactory after being carefully examined. *How well does this thesis stand up to close examination?* **3** If a boyfriend or girlfriend **stands** you **up,** they fail to keep an arrangement to meet you. *We were to have had dinner together yesterday evening, but he stood me up.* `PHRASAL VB` `VP` `VP to n` `V n P` `Also VP noun` `INFORMAL`

stand up for. If you **stand up for** someone or something, you defend them and make your feelings or opinions very clear; used showing approval. `PHRASAL VB` `PRAGMATICS`

stand up to. 1 If something **stands up to** rough treatment, it remains almost undamaged or unharmed. **2** If you **stand up to** someone, especially someone more powerful than you are, you defend yourself against their attacks or demands. *Women are now aware of their rights and are prepared to stand up to their employers.* `PHRASAL VB` `VPP n/-ing` `VPP n`

stand·ard /'stændəd/ **standards. 1** A **standard** is a level of quality or achievement, especially a level that is thought to be acceptable. *...new national standards for hospital cleanliness.* **2** A **standard** is something that you use in order to judge the quality of something else. *...systems that were by later standards absurdly primitive.* **3** Standards are moral principles which affect people's attitudes and behaviour. *My father has always had high moral standards.* ● See also **double standard. 4** You use **standard** to describe things which are usual and normal. *It was standard practice for untrained clerks to advise in serious cases such as murder.* **5** A **standard** work or text on a particular subject is one that is widely read and often recommended. `◆◆◆◇` `N-COUNT:` `with supp` `N-COUNT:` `with supp` `N-PLURAL` `ADJ-GRADED` `ADJ: ADJ n`

'standard-bearer, standard-bearers; also spelled **standard bearer.** If you describe someone as the **standard-bearer** of a group, you mean that they act as the leader or representative of a group of people who have the same aims or interests. `N-COUNT`

stand·ard·ize /'stændədaɪz/ **standardizes, standardizing, standardized;** also spelled **standardise** in British English. To **standardize** things means to change them so that they all have the same features. *There is a drive both to standardise components and to reduce the number of models on offer.* **♦ stand·ard·i·za·tion** /,stændədaɪ'zeɪʃən, AM -dɪ'z-/. *...the standardisation of working hours in Community countries.* `◆◇◇◇` `VERB` `V n` `N-UNCOUNT`

'standard of 'living, standards of living. Your **standard of living** is the level of comfort and wealth which you have. `◆◇◇◇` `N-COUNT`

'standard time. Standard time is the official local time of a region or country. `N-UNCOUNT`

stand·by /'stændbaɪ/ **standbys;** also spelled **stand-by. 1** A **standby** is something or someone that is always ready to be used if they are needed. *Canned varieties of beans and pulses are a good standby.* **2** If someone or something is **on standby,** they are ready to be used if they are needed. *Five ambulances are on standby.* **3** A **standby** ticket for something such as the theatre or a plane journey is a cheap ticket that you buy just before the performance starts or the plane takes off, if there are still some seats left. ▶ Also an adverb. *Magda was going to fly standby.* `◆◇◇◇` `N-COUNT` `PHRASE` `ADJ: ADJ n` `ADV:` `ADV after v`

'stand-in, stand-ins. A **stand-in** is a person who takes someone else's place or does someone else's job for a while, for example because the other person is ill or away. `N-COUNT`

stand·ing /'stændɪŋ/ **standings. 1** Someone's **standing** is their reputation or status. *...an artist of international standing.* **2** A party's or person's **standing** is their popularity, usually according to opinion polls. *There is one thing that Mr Clinton can do to improve his standing with the electorate.* **3** In a contest or competition, the list of competitors `◆◇◇◇` `N-UNCOUNT:` `with supp` `N-UNCOUNT` `N-PLURAL` `JOURNALISM`

which shows their places during the event is called the **standings**. *Britain is 11th in the team standings.* **4** You use **standing** to describe something which is permanently in existence. *Elizabeth had a standing invitation to stay with her. ...the finance standing committee.* **5** You can use the expression **of many years' standing** to say that something has had a particular function or someone has had a particular role for many years. For example, if a place is your home **of ten years' standing**, it has been your home for ten years. **6** See also **free-standing**, **long-standing**.

ADJ: ADJ n

PHRASE
WRITTEN

,standing 'order, standing orders. A **standing order** is an instruction to your bank to pay a fixed amount of money to someone at regular intervals.

N-COUNT:
also by N
BRITISH

,standing o'vation, standing ovations. If a speaker or performer gets a **standing ovation** when they have finished speaking or performing, the audience stands up to applaud them in order to show great admiration or support for them.

◆◇◇◇
N-COUNT

'standing room. **Standing room** is space in a room or bus, where people can stand when all the seats have been occupied.

N-UNCOUNT

'stand-off, stand-offs; also spelled standoff. A **stand-off** is a situation in which neither of two opposing groups or forces will make a move until the other one does something, so nothing can happen until one of them gives way. *...a stand-off between the government and the unions.*

◆◇◇◇
N-COUNT

,stand-'offish; also spelled standoffish. If you say that someone is **stand-offish**, you mean that they behave in a formal and rather unfriendly way.

ADJ-GRADED

stand·point /'stændpɔɪnt/ standpoints. From a particular **standpoint** means looking at an event, situation, or idea in a particular way. *From a military standpoint, the situation is under control.*

◆◇◇◇
N-COUNT:
with supp

stand·still /'stændstɪl/. If movement or activity comes to or is brought to **a standstill**, it stops completely.

◆◇◇◇
N-SING:
a N

'stand-up. A **stand-up** comic or comedian stands alone in front of an audience and tells jokes.

◆◇◇◇
ADJ: ADJ n

stank /stæŋk/. **Stank** is the past tense of **stink**.

Stan·ley knife /'stænli naɪf/ Stanley knives. A **Stanley knife** is a very sharp knife used in crafts such as woodwork. It consists of a small triangular blade on the end of a short plastic handle. **Stanley knife** is a trademark.

N-COUNT

stan·za /'stænzə/ stanzas. A **stanza** is a verse of a poem.

◆◇◇◇
TECHNICAL

sta·ple /'steɪpəl/ staples, stapling, stapled. **1** A **staple** food, product, or activity is one that is basic and important in people's everyday lives. *Rice is the staple food of more than half the world's population.* ▶ Also a noun. *...boutiques selling staples such as jeans and T-shirts.* **2** A **staple** is something that forms an important part of something else. *Political reporting has become a staple of American journalism.* **3** **Staples** are small pieces of wire that are used for holding sheets of paper together firmly. **4** If you **staple** something, you fasten it to something else or fix it in place using staples. *Staple some sheets of paper together into a book.*

◆◇◇◇
ADJ: ADJ n

N-COUNT

N-COUNT

N-COUNT

VERB
V n with adv
Also V n prep

sta·pler /'steɪplə/ staplers. A **stapler** is a special device used for putting staples into sheets of paper.

N-COUNT

star /stɑː/ stars, starring, starred. **1** A **star** is a large ball of burning gas in space. Stars appear to us as small points of light in the sky on clear nights. ● see **morning star**, **shooting star**. **2** You can refer to a shape or an object as a **star** when it has four, five, or more points sticking out of it in a regular pattern. See picture headed **shapes**. **3** **Stars** are star-shaped marks that are printed against the name of something to indicate its quality. The more stars something has, the better it is. *...five star hotels.* **4** Famous actors, musicians, and sports players are often referred to as **stars**. *...Gemma, 41, star of the TV series Pennies From Heaven.* **5** If an actor or actress **stars in** a play or film, he or she has one of the most important parts in it. **6** If a play or film **stars** a famous

◆◆◆◆
N-COUNT

N-COUNT

N-COUNT

N-COUNT

VERB:
V in

VERB: V n

actor or actress, he or she has one of the most important parts in it.

7 The horoscope in a newspaper or magazine is sometimes referred to as the **stars**.

N-PLURAL

8 If you say that someone should **thank** their **lucky stars** that something is the case, you mean that they should be very grateful that it is the case, because otherwise their situation would be a lot worse.

PHRASE

star·board /'stɑːbəd/. The **starboard** side of a ship is the right side when you are on it and facing towards the front. ▶ Also a noun. *I could see the fishing boat to starboard.*

◆◇◇◇
ADJ
TECHNICAL
N-UNCOUNT

starch /stɑːtʃ/ starches, starching, starched. **1** **Starch** is a carbohydrate found in foods such as bread, potatoes, pasta, and rice. ◆ **starchy**, **starchier**, **starchiest**. **Starchy** foods contain a lot of starch. **2** **Starch** is a substance that is used for stiffening cloth, especially cotton and linen. **3** If you **starch** cloth, you stiffen it using starch. ◆ **starched** *...a starched white shirt.*

N-VAR

ADJ-GRADED

N-UNCOUNT

VERB: V n

ADJ

star·dom /'stɑːdəm/. **Stardom** is the state of being very famous, usually as an actor, musician, or sports player. *In 1929 she shot to stardom on Broadway.*

◆◇◇◇
N-UNCOUNT

stare /steə/ stares, staring, stared. **1** If you **stare** at someone or something, you look at them for a long time. *Ben continued to stare out the window... Mahoney tried not to stare.* ▶ Also a noun. *Hlasek gave him a long, cold stare.* **2** If a situation or the answer to a problem **is staring** you **in the face**, it is very obvious, although you may not be immediately aware of it.

◆◆◇◇
VERB
V prep/adv
V

N-COUNT

PHRASE
INFORMAL

stare down or stare out. If you **stare** someone **out** or **stare** them **down**, you look steadily into their eyes for such a long time that they feel that they have to turn their eyes away from you.

PHRASAL VB
V n P

star·fish /'stɑːfɪʃ/; **starfish** is both the singular and plural form. A **starfish** is a flat, star-shaped creature with five arms that lives in the sea.

N-COUNT

'star-gazing; also spelled stargazing. **Star-gazing** is the activity of studying the stars as an astronomer or astrologer. ◆ **star-gazer**, **star-gazers**.

N-UNCOUNT
INFORMAL

N-COUNT

stark /stɑːk/ starker, starkest. **1** **Stark** choices or statements are harsh and unpleasant. *He issued a stark warning to Washington and other Western capitals.* ◆ **stark·ly** *The point is a starkly simple one.* **2** If two things are in **stark** contrast to one another, they are very different from each other in a way that is very obvious. *...secret cooperation between London and Washington that was in stark contrast to official policy.* ◆ **starkly** *The outlook now is starkly different.* **3** Something that is **stark** is very bare and plain in appearance. *...the stark white, characterless fireplace in the drawing room.* ◆ **starkly** *The room was starkly furnished.*

◆◆◇◇
ADJ-GRADED

ADV-GRADED

ADJ-GRADED

ADV-GRADED

ADJ-GRADED

ADV-GRADED

,stark 'naked. Someone who is **stark naked** is completely naked.

ADJ:
ADJ after v,
v-link ADJ

star·let /'stɑːlɪt/ starlets. A **starlet** is a young actress who is expected to become a film star in the future.

N-COUNT
JOURNALISM

star·light /'stɑːlaɪt/. **Starlight** is the light that comes from the stars at night.

N-UNCOUNT

star·ling /'stɑːlɪŋ/ starlings. A **starling** is a very common European bird with greenish-black feathers.

N-COUNT

star·lit /'stɑːlɪt/. **Starlit** means made lighter or brighter by the stars. *...a clear starlit sky.*

ADJ: ADJ n

star·ry /'stɑːri/. A **starry** night or sky is one in which a lot of stars are visible.

ADJ: ADJ n

'starry-eyed. If you say that someone is **starry-eyed**, you mean that they are so full of dreams or idealistic thoughts that they do not see how things really are.

ADJ-GRADED

,Stars and 'Stripes. The **Stars and Stripes** is the name of the national flag of the United States of America.

N-PROPER:
the N

'star sign, star signs. Your **star sign** is the sign of the zodiac under which you were born.

N-COUNT

'star-studded. A **star-studded** show or cast is one that includes a large number of famous performers.

ADJ: ADJ n
JOURNALISM

S

start /staːt/ **starts, starting, started.** 1 If you **start** to do something, you do something that you were not doing before and you continue doing it. *It was 1956 when Susanna started the work on the garden.* ▶ Also a noun. *After several starts, she read the report properly.* 2 See also **head start, false start.** 3 When something **starts**, or when someone **starts** it, it takes place from a particular time. *Trains start at 11.00 and an hourly service will operate until 16.00.* ▶ Also a noun. *She demanded to know why she had not been told from the start.* 4 If you **start** by doing something, or if you **start with** something, you do that first in a series of actions. *I started by asking how many day-care centers were located in the United States.* 5 You use **start** to say what someone's first job was. For example, if their first job was that of a porter, you can say that they **started as** a porter.* ▶ **Start off** means the same as **start.** *Mr. Dambar had started off as an assistant to Mrs. Spear's husband.* 6 You use **for a start** or **to start with** to introduce the first of a number of things or reasons that you want to mention or could mention. *You must get her name and address, and that can be a problem for a start.* 7 If you **get off to a good start**, you are successful in the early stages of doing something. If you **get off to a bad start**, you are not successful in the early stages of doing something. *Mrs Thatcher's war on inflation got off to a bad start. The cost of living rose to 21.9% in May 1980.* 8 '**To start with**' means at the very first stage of an event or process. *Success was assured and, at least to start with, the system operated smoothly.* 9 When someone **starts** something such as a new business, they create it or cause it to begin. ▶ **Start up** means the same as **start.** *He said what a good idea it would be to start a community magazine up.* ● See also **start-up.** 10 If you **start** an engine, car, or machine, or if it **starts**, it begins to work. *We were just passing one of the parking bays when a car's engine started.* ▶ **Start up** means the same as **start.** *Put the key in the ignition and turn it to start the car up... The engine of the seaplane started up... I started up my car and turned on the lights.* 11 If you **start**, your body jerks as a result of surprise or fear. *Rachel started forward on the sofa.—'You mean you've arrested Pete?'* ▶ Also a noun. *Sylvia woke with a start.* 12 ● **in fits and starts:** see **fit.** ● **get off to a flying start:** see **fly.**

start off. 1 If you **start off** by doing something, you do it as the first part of an activity. *She used to start off making pastry and then go on to make the buns and the cakes.* 2 To **start** someone **off** means to cause them to begin doing something. *Her mother started her off acting in children's theatre.* 3 To **start** something **off** means to cause it to begin. *He became more aware of the things that started that tension off.* 4 See also **start** 5.

start on. If you **start on** something that needs to be done, you start dealing with it. *No need for you to start on the washing-up yet.*

start out. 1 If someone or something **starts out as** a particular thing, they are that thing at the beginning although they change later. *What started out as fun quickly became hard work.* 2 If you **start out by** doing something, you do it at the beginning of an activity. *The child'll start out by making relatively few distinctions in the language.*

start over. If you **start over** or **start** something **over**, you begin something again from the beginning. *It's just not enough money to start life over.*

start up. See **start** 9 and 10.

start·er /ˈstaːtə/ **starters. 1** A **starter** is a small quantity of food that is served as the first course of a meal. 2 The **starter** of a car is the device that starts the engine. 3 The **starters** in a race are the people who take part at the beginning even if they do not finish. 4 You use **for starters** when you mention something to indicate that it is the first item or point in a series.

VERB:
V to-inf
Vn/-ing
Also V

N-COUNT

V-ERG: V
V prep
Also V n

N-SING:
the N
VERB
V by-ing
Also V with n
VERB:
V as n

PHRASAL VB
V P as n

PHRASE
PRAGMATICS

PHRASE

PHRASE

VERB: V n
PHRASAL VB
V n P
Also V P noun

V-ERG: V n
V

PHRASAL VB
ERG
V n P
V P
V P noun

VERB: V
V adv
WRITTEN
N-COUNT

PHRASAL VB
V P by-ing
V P-ing

V n P

V n P

PHRASAL VB
V P n

PHRASAL VB
V P as n
Also V P as n n

V P by-ing

PHRASAL VB
V P
V n P
AMERICAN
PHRASAL VB

◆◆◇◇◇
N-COUNT

N-COUNT

N-COUNT

PHRASE

'**starting point, starting points;** also spelled **starting-point. 1** Something that is a **starting point** for a discussion or process can be used to begin it or act as a basis for it. *These proposals represent a realistic starting point for negotiation.* 2 When you make a journey, your **starting point** is the place from which you start.

star·tle /ˈstaːtəl/ **startles, startling, startled.** If something sudden and unexpected **startles** you, it surprises and frightens you slightly. *Sorry, I didn't mean to startle you.* ♦ **star·tled** *Martha gave her a startled look.*

star·tling /ˈstaːtəlɪŋ/. Something that is **startling** is so different, unexpected, or remarkable that people react to it with surprise. ♦ **star·tling·ly** *He was startlingly handsome.*

'**start-up. 1** The **start-up** costs of something such as a new business are the costs of starting to run it. 2 A **start-up** company is a small business that has recently been started by someone.

,star '**turn, star turns.** The **star turn** of a performance or show is the main item, or the one that is considered to be the most interesting or impressive.

star·va·tion /staːˈveɪʃən/. **Starvation** is extreme suffering or death, caused by lack of food.

starve /staːv/ **starves, starving, starved. 1** If people **starve**, they suffer greatly from lack of food which sometimes leads to their death. *In the 1930s, millions of Ukrainians starved to death or were deported.* 2 To **starve** someone means not to give them any food. *Judy decided I was starving myself.* 3 If someone or something **is starved** of something that they need, they are suffering because they are not getting enough of it. *The most damaging thing the West could do is to starve Russia of new foreign capital.*

starv·ing /ˈstaːvɪŋ/. If you say that you are **starving**, you mean that you are very hungry.

stash /stæʃ/ **stashes, stashing, stashed. 1** If you **stash** something valuable in a secret place, you store it there to keep it safe. *...the bottle of whiskey that we had stashed behind the bookcase... Andrews had stashed money away in secret offshore bank accounts.* 2 A **stash** of something valuable is a secret store of it.

sta·sis /ˈsteɪsɪs, AM ˈsteɪ-/. **Stasis** is a state in which something remains the same, and does not change or develop.

state /steɪt/ **states, stating, stated. 1** You can refer to countries as **states**, particularly when you are discussing politics. *...Albania, Europe's only remaining communist state.* 2 A **state** occasion is a formal one involving the head of a country. *...a state visit to India.* 3 Some large countries such as the USA are divided into smaller areas called **states.** 4 The USA is sometimes referred to as **the States.** *...a visit to the States.* 5 You can refer to the government of a country as **the state.** *The state does not collect enough revenue to cover its expenditure.* 6 **State** industries or organizations are financed and organized by the government rather than private companies. *...the state social-security system.* ● See **state school.** 7 See also **head of state, nation state, police state, welfare state.** 8 When you talk about the **state** of someone or something, you are referring to the condition they are in or what they are like at a particular time. *I was in a state of clinical depression.* 9 If you say that someone is **not in a fit state** to do something, you mean that they are too upset or ill to do it. 10 If you are **in a state** or if you get **into a state**, you are very upset or nervous about something. 11 If you **state** something, you say or write it in a formal or definite way. *The police report stated that he was arrested for allegedly assaulting his wife... 'Our relationship is totally platonic,' she stated.* 12 If the dead body of an important person **lies in state**, it is publicly displayed for a few days before it is buried.

◆◇◇◇
N-COUNT

◆◆◇◇◇
VERB
V n

ADJ-GRADED

◆◆◇◇◇
ADJ-GRADED

ADV-GRADED

ADJ: ADJ n

ADJ: ADJ n

N-COUNT
BRITISH

◆◆◇◇◇
N-UNCOUNT

◆◆◇◇◇
VERB: V
V to n

VERB: V n
V pron-refl

VERB:
be V-ed of n
V n of n

ADJ:
v-link ADJ
INFORMAL

◆◇◇◇◇
VERB
V n
V n with adv
Also V n
INFORMAL

N-COUNT:
with supp
INFORMAL

N-UNCOUNT
FORMAL

◆◆◆◆
N-COUNT

ADJ: ADJ n

N-COUNT

N-PROPER
INFORMAL

N-SING:
the N

ADJ: ADJ n

N-COUNT

PHRASE

PHRASE

VERB: V n
V that
V with quote

PHRASE

'State Department. In the United States, the ◆◆◆◇◇
State Department is the government department N-PROPER:
that is concerned with foreign affairs. *the* N

state·hood /'steɪthʊd/. **Statehood** is the condition ◆◇◇◇◇
of being an independent state or nation. N-UNCOUNT

state·house /'steɪthaʊs/ **statehouses.** In the N-COUNT
United States, a **statehouse** is where the governor of
a state has his offices.

state·less /'steɪtləs/. A person who is **stateless** is ADJ
not a citizen of any country and therefore has no
nationality.

state·let /'steɪtlət/ **statelets.** A **statelet** is a small, N-COUNT
independent state which is usually formed by the JOURNALISM
break-up of a larger state.

state·ly /'steɪtli/. Something or someone that is ◆◇◇◇◇
stately is impressive because they look very graceful ADJ-GRADED
and dignified.

,stately 'home, stately homes. A stately home ◆◇◇◇◇
is a large old house which has belonged to an aris- N-COUNT
tocratic family for a long time, especially one that
people can pay to visit.

state·ment /'steɪtmənt/ **statements. 1** A state- ◆◆◆◇◇
ment is something that you say or write which gives N-COUNT
information in a formal or definite way. *'Things are
moving ahead.' – I found that statement vague and
unclear.* **2** A **statement** is an official or formal an- N-COUNT
nouncement that is issued on a particular occasion.
*The statement by the military denied any involve-
ment in last night's attack.* **3** You can refer to the of- N-COUNT
ficial account of events which a suspect or a witness
gives to the police as a **statement. 4** If you describe N-COUNT
an action or thing as a **statement**, you mean that it
clearly expresses a particular opinion or idea that
you have. *The following recipe is a statement of another kind – food is fun!* **5** A printed document N-COUNT
showing how much money has been paid into and
taken out of a bank or building society account is
called a **statement**.

,state of af'fairs. If you refer to a particular **state** ◆◇◇◇◇
of affairs, you mean the general situation and cir- N-SING
cumstances connected with someone or something.
*The nation had a chance to move towards a more
democratic, and modern, state of affairs.*

'state of mind, states of mind. Your **state of** ◆◇◇◇◇
mind is your mood or mental state at a particular N-COUNT
time. *He's in hospital, and in a confused state of
mind.*

'state of siege. A **state of siege** is a situation in N-SING
which a government or other authority puts restrictions on the movement of people into or out of a
country, town, or building.

,state-of-the-'art. If you describe something as ◆◇◇◇◇
state-of-the-art, you mean that it is the best avail- ADJ
able because it has been made using the most modern techniques and technology. *...state-of-the-art
military equipment.*

state·room /'steɪtruːm/ **staterooms. 1** On a pas- N-COUNT
senger ship, a **stateroom** is a private room, especially one that is large and comfortable. **2** In a pal- N-COUNT
ace or other impressive building, a **stateroom** is a BRITISH
large room for use on formal occasions.

'state school, state schools. A **state school** is a ◆◇◇◇◇
school that is controlled and funded by the govern- N-COUNT
ment or a local authority, and which children can BRITISH
attend without having to pay. The usual American
term is **public school**.

state·side /'steɪtsaɪd/; also spelled **Stateside. State-** ADJ
side means in, from, or to the United States; used INFORMAL
mainly in American English and British journalism.
...a well-known Stateside cop show. ▶ Also an ad- ADV:
verb. *His debut album was hugely successful* ADV after v
Stateside.

states·man /'steɪtsmən/ **statesmen.** A states- ◆◆◇◇◇
man is an important and experienced politician, es- N-COUNT
pecially one who is widely known and respected.
● See also **elder statesman.**

states·man·like /'steɪtsmənlaɪk/. If you describe ADJ-GRADED
someone, especially a political leader, as PRAGMATICS
statesmanlike, you approve of them because they
appear to be very able and experienced.

states·man·ship /'steɪtsmənʃɪp/. **Statesmanship** N-UNCOUNT
is the skill and activities of a statesman.

state·wide /,steɪt'waɪd/. **Statewide** means across ◆◇◇◇◇
or throughout the whole of one of the states of the ADJ
United States. *...a prominent statewide bicycle race.*
▶ Also an adverb. *In the weeks since flooding began,* ADV:
16 people have died statewide. ADV after v

stat·ic /'stætɪk/. **1** Something that is **static** does ◆◇◇◇◇
not move or change. *The number of young people* ADJ-GRADED
*obtaining qualifications has remained static or de-
creased.* **2 Static** or **static electricity** is electricity N-UNCOUNT
which is caused by friction and which collects in
things such as your body or metal objects. **3** If there N-UNCOUNT
is **static** on the radio or television, you hear a series
of loud crackling noises.

sta·tion /'steɪʃən/ **stations, stationing, sta-** ◆◆◆◆◇
tioned. 1 A **station** is a building by a railway line N-COUNT
where trains stop so that people can get on or off.
2 A **bus station** or **coach station** is a building where N-COUNT:
buses or coaches start their journey. **3** See also **fire** n N
**station, gas station, petrol station, police station,
power station, service station, space station, way
station.
4** If you talk about a particular radio or television **sta-** N-COUNT
tion, you are referring to the programmes broadcast
by a particular radio or television company. *...an independent local radio station.*
5 If soldiers or officials **are stationed** in a place, they V-PASSIVE:
are sent there to do a job or to work for a period of beV-ed
time. *...United States military personnel stationed in* prep/adv
the Philippines. **6** If you **station** yourself somewhere, VERB:
you go there and wait, usually for a particular V pron-refl
purpose. prep/adv
FORMAL

sta·tion·ary /'steɪʃənri, AM -neri/. Something that ◆◇◇◇◇
is **stationary** is not moving. ADJ

sta·tion·er /'steɪʃənə/ **stationers.** A stationer is a N-COUNT
person who sells paper, envelopes, pens, and other
equipment used for writing.

sta·tion·ery /'steɪʃənri, AM -neri/. **Stationery** is pa- ◆◇◇◇◇
per, envelopes, and other materials or equipment N-UNCOUNT
used for writing.

station·master /'steɪʃənmɑːstə, -mæstə/ **station-** N-COUNT
masters; also spelled **station master.** A station-
master is the official who is in charge of a railway
station.

'station wagon, station wagons. A station N-COUNT
wagon is car with a long body, a door at the rear, AMERICAN
and space behind the back seats. The British term is
estate car.

stat·ist /'steɪtɪst/. When a country has **statist** poli- ADJ-GRADED
cies, the state has a lot of control over the economy.

sta·tis·tic /stə'tɪstɪk/ **statistics. 1 Statistics** are ◆◆◆◇◇
facts which are obtained from analysing informa- N-COUNT
tion expressed in numbers, for example information
about the number of times that something happens. *Official statistics show real wages declining by
24%.* ● See also **vital statistics. 2 Statistics** is a N-UNCOUNT
branch of mathematics concerned with the study of
information that is expressed in numbers.

sta·tis·ti·cal /stə'tɪstɪkəl/. **Statistical** means relat- ◆◆◇◇◇
ing to the use of statistics. *We need to back our suspicion up with statistical proof.* ♦ **sta·tis·ti·cal·ly** ADV
/stə'tɪstɪkli/. *The results are not statistically
significant.*

stat·is·ti·cian /,stætɪ'stɪʃən/ **statisticians.** A ◆◇◇◇◇
statistician is a person who studies statistics or who N-COUNT
works using statistics.

stats /stæts/. **1 Stats** are facts which are obtained N-PLURAL
from analysing information expressed in numbers. INFORMAL
Stats is an abbreviation for **statistics. 2 Stats** is a N-UNCOUNT
branch of mathematics concerned with the study of INFORMAL
information that is expressed in numbers.

statu·ary /'stætʃuəri, AM -ʊeri/. If you talk about N-UNCOUNT
the **statuary** in a place, you are referring to all the FORMAL
statues and sculpture there.

statue /'stætʃuː/ **statues.** A statue is a large sculp- ◆◆◇◇◇
ture of a person or an animal, made of stone, N-COUNT
bronze, or some other hard material.

statu·esque /,stætʃu'esk/. A woman who is **statu-** ADJ-GRADED
esque is big and tall and has good posture. WRITTEN

statu·ette /ˌstætʃuˈet/ **statuettes.** A statuette is a N-COUNT very small sculpture of a person or an animal.

stat·ure /ˈstætʃə/. **1** Someone's **stature** is their ◆◇◇◇◇ height. *She was a little short in stature.* **2** The **stat-** N-UNCOUNT **ure** of a person is the importance and reputation N-UNCOUNT that they have. *Who can deny his stature as the world's greatest cellist?*

sta·tus /ˈsteɪtəs/. **1** Your **status** is your social or ◆◆◆◇◇ professional position. *The status of children in soci-* N-UNCOUNT *ety has long been underestimated.* **2 Status** is the N-UNCOUNT prestige and importance that someone has in the eyes of other people. *He has risen to gain the status of a national hero.* **3** The **status** of something is the N-UNCOUNT importance that people give it. *The fact that the most senior judge of the High Court's Family Divi- sion had taken control of the case was proof of its urgency and status.* **4 Status** is an official classifica- N-UNCOUNT: tion that a person, organization, or country re- with supp ceives, which gives them particular rights or advan- tages. *The personal allowance depends on your age and marital status.* **5** The **status** of something is its N-UNCOUNT: state of affairs at a particular time. *What is your cur-* with supp *rent financial status?*

sta·tus quo /ˌsteɪtəs ˈkwəʊ/. The **status quo** is the ◆◇◇◇◇ state of affairs that exists at a particular time, espe- N-SING cially in contrast to a different possible state of af- fairs. *By 492 votes to 391, the federation voted to maintain the status quo.*

status symbol, status symbols. A status sym- N-COUNT **bol** is something that a person has or owns that shows they have prestige and importance in society.

stat·ute /ˈstætʃuːt/ **statutes.** A statute is a rule or ◆◇◇◇◇ law which has been made by a government or other N-VAR organization and formally written down.

statute book, statute books. The statute book N-COUNT: is a record of all the laws made by the government. the poss N *The Bill could reach the statute book by the summer.* BRITISH

statu·tory /ˈstætʃʊtəri, AM -tɔːri/. **Statutory** means ◆◇◇◇◇ relating to rules or laws which have been formally ADJ written down. *We had a statutory duty to report to* FORMAL *Parliament.* ♦ **statu·to·ri·ly** /ˈstætʃʊtərɪli, AM ADV: -ˈtɔːrɪli/. *Such tenants are statutorily protected.* ADV with v

staunch /stɔːntʃ/ **stauncher, staunchest;** ◆◇◇◇◇ **staunches, staunching, staunched.** **1** A ADJ-GRADED staunch supporter or believer is very loyal to a per- son, organization, or a set of beliefs, and supports them strongly. ♦ **staunch·ly** *He was staunchly op-* ADV-GRADED *posed to a public confession.* **2** To **staunch** the flow VERB of something means to stop it. *The government* V n claims this is the only way to staunch the annual FORMAL flow to Germany of hundreds of thousands of refu- gees. **3** To **staunch** a wound, or to **staunch** the VERB: V n blood from a wound, means to stop the wound FORMAL from bleeding.

stave /steɪv/ **staves, staving, staved.** **1** A stave ◆◇◇◇◇ is a strong stick, usually used as a weapon. N-COUNT **2** A **stave** is the five lines that music is written on. N-COUNT

stave off. If you **stave off** something bad, or if you PHRASAL VB **stave** it **off**, you succeed in stopping it happening for a V P noun while. *Labour chose a new Prime Minister in a last-* Also V n P *minute bid to stave off defeat.*

stay /steɪ/ **stays, staying, stayed.** **1** If you stay ◆◆◆◆◇ where you are, you continue to be there and do not VERB leave. *'Stay here,' Trish said. 'I'll bring the car down* V adv/prep *the drive to take you back.'... In the old days the woman stayed at home and the man earned the money.* **2** If you **stay put**, you remain somewhere. PHRASE *He is very happy to stay put in Lyon.* **3** If you **stay in** VERB: a town, or hotel, or at someone's house, you live V prep/adv there for a short time. *He tried to stay a few months* V n *every year in Scotland.* ▶ Also a noun. *An experi-* N-COUNT *enced Indian guide is provided during your stay.* **4** If PHRASE you **stay the night** in a place, you sleep there for one night.

5 If you **stay** away from a place, you do not go there. VERB: *Every single employee turned up at the meeting, even* V away from n *people who usually stayed away.* **6** If you **stay out of** VERB something, you do not get involved in it. *In the past,* V out of n *the UN has stayed out of the internal affairs of coun- tries unless invited in.*

7 If you say that something is **here to stay**, you mean PHRASE that people have accepted it and it has become a part of everyday life. *Satellite TV is here to stay.* **8** If some- V-LINK one or something **stays** in a particular state or situa- V adv/prep tion, they continue to be in it. *The Republican candi-* V adj *date said he would 'work like crazy to stay ahead'...* Also V n *Nothing stays the same for long.*

stay in. If you **stay in** during the evening, you remain PHRASAL VB at home and do not go out. V P

stay on. If you **stay on** somewhere, you remain PHRASAL VB there after other people have left or after the time V P when you were going to leave. *He had managed to ar- range to stay on in Adelaide.*

stay out. If you **stay out** at night, you remain away PHRASAL VB from home, especially when you are expected to be V P there. *I met some friends and stayed out until eleven or twelve.*

stay up. If you **stay up**, you remain out of bed at a PHRASAL VB time when most people have gone to bed or at a time V P adv/prep when you are normally in bed yourself. *I used to stay up late with my mom and watch movies.*

'stay-at-home, stay-at-homes. If you describe N-COUNT someone as a **stay-at-home**, you mean that they stay at home rather than travelling or going out to work.

'staying power; also spelled **staying-power.** **1** If N-UNCOUNT you have **staying power**, you have the strength and stamina to keep going until you reach the end of what you are doing. **2** If something such as an idea N-UNCOUNT or a product has **staying power**, it remains popular or successful for a long time.

stay of exe'cution, stays of execution. If you N-COUNT are given a **stay of execution**, you are legally per- LEGAL mitted to delay obeying an order of a court of law.

STD /ˌes tiː ˈdiː/ **STDs.** STD is an abbreviation for N-COUNT 'sexually transmitted disease'. *...an STD clinic.* MEDICAL

stead /sted/. **1** If you do something in someone's ◆◇◇◇◇ stead, you replace them and do it instead of them. PHRASE *My grandmother and aunt will be there in my par-* FORMAL *ents' stead.* **2** If you say that something will **stand** PHRASE someone **in good stead**, you mean that it will be very useful to them in the future. *My years of teach- ing stood me in good stead.*

stead·fast /ˈstedfɑːst, -fæst/. If someone is **stead-** ◆◇◇◇◇ **fast** in something that they are doing, they are con- ADJ-GRADED vinced that what they are doing is right and they re- PRAGMATICS fuse to change it or to give up; used showing ap- proval. *He remained steadfast in his belief that he had done the right thing.* ♦ **stead·fast·ly** *She* ADV-GRADED *steadfastly refused to look his way.* ♦ **stead·fast- ·ness** *...the steadfastness and strength of his* N-UNCOUNT *resistance.*

steady /ˈstedi/ **steadier, steadiest; steadies,** ◆◆◆◇◇ **steadying, steadied.** **1** A steady situation con- ADJ-GRADED tinues or develops gradually without any interrup- tions and is not likely to change quickly. *Despite the steady progress of building work, the campaign against it is still going strong.* ♦ **stead·i·ly** /ˈstedɪli/. ADV-GRADED: *Relax as much as possible and keep breathing steadi-* ADV with v *ly.* **2** If an object is **steady**, it is firm and does not ADJ-GRADED shake or move about. *Hold the camera steady.* **3** If V-ERG: V n you **steady** something or if it **steadies**, it stops shak- V ing or moving about. *Lovelock eased back the throt- tles and the ship steadied.*

4 If you look at someone or speak to them in a **steady** ADJ-GRADED way, you look or speak in a calm, controlled way. *'Well, go on,' said Camilla, her voice fairly steady.* ♦ **steadily** *He moved back a little and stared steadily* ADV-GRADED: *at Elaine.* **5** If you **steady** yourself, you control your ADV after v voice or expression, so that people will think that you VERB: are calm and not nervous. *She breathed in to steady* V pron-refl *her voice.* V n

6 If you describe a person as **steady**, you mean that ADJ-GRADED they are sensible and reliable.

7 You say **'steady on'** to someone to tell them to calm EXCLAM down or to be careful about what they are saying. *'What if there's another murder?'—'Steady on!'*

steak /steɪk/ **steaks.** **1** A steak is a large flat piece ◆◆◇◇◇ of beef without much fat on it. You cook it by grill- N-VAR ing or frying it. ● See also **rump steak, T-bone**

steak. **2 Steak** is beef that is used for making stews N-UNCOUNT and casseroles. ...*steak and kidney pie.* **3** A fish N-COUNT **steak** is a large piece of fish that contains few bones. ...*fresh salmon steaks.*

'steak house, steak houses; also spelled **steak-** N-COUNT **house.** A **steak house** is a restaurant where the main food served is steak.

steal /sti:l/ **steals, stealing, stole, stolen. 1** If ◆◆◆◇◇ you **steal** something from someone, you take it VERB: away from them without their permission and with- V n *from* n out intending to return it. *He was accused of stealing* V n *a small boy's bicycle... She has since been jailed for* Also V *six months for stealing from the tills.* ◆ **sto·len** We ADJ *have now found the stolen car.* **2** If you **steal** some- VERB one else's ideas, you pretend that they are your V n own. *His team solved the engineering problem by stealing an idea from nature.* **3** If you describe N-SING: something as **a steal**, you mean that it is very good a N INFORMAL value. *At only £13.50, this champagne is a steal.* **4** If someone **steals** somewhere, they move there qui- VERB etly and cautiously. *They can steal away at night and* V adv/prep *join us.* **5** ● to **steal a march** on someone: see **march.** ● to **steal the show:** see **show.**

stealth /stelθ/. If you use **stealth** when you do ◆◇◇◇◇ something, you do it in such a slow, quiet, and se- N-UNCOUNT cretive way that other people do not notice what you are doing. *Both sides advanced by stealth.*

stealthy /ˈstelθi/ **stealthier, stealthiest.** ADJ-GRADED **Stealthy** actions or movements are performed qui- etly and secretively, so that no one will notice what you are doing. *I would creep in and with stealthy footsteps explore the second-floor.* ◆ **stealthi·ly** ADV-GRADED: /ˈstelθɪli/. *Slowly and stealthily, someone was creep-* ADV with v *ing up the stairs.*

steam /sti:m/ **steams, steaming, steamed.** ◆◆◆◇◇ **1 Steam** is the hot mist that forms when water N-UNCOUNT boils. **Steam** vehicles and machines are operated using steam as a means of power. **2** If something VERB: V **steams**, it gives off steam. **3** If you **steam** food or if V-ERG: V n it **steams**, you cook it in steam rather than in water. V *Leave the vegetables to steam over the rice.* **4** If something such as a plan or a project goes **full** PHRASE **steam ahead**, it proceeds quickly and efficiently so that a lot of progress is made. **5** If you **let off steam**, PHRASE you get rid of your energy, anger, or strong emotions INFORMAL with physical activity or by behaving in a noisy or vio- lent way. **6** If a belief, a plan, or a project **picks up** PHRASE **steam**, it starts to develop and become more impor- tant. **7** If you **run out of steam**, you stop doing some- PHRASE thing because you have no more energy or enthusi- INFORMAL asm left. **8** If you do something **under** your **own** PHRASE **steam**, you do it without any help from anyone else.

steam up. 1 If someone **gets steamed up** about PHRASAL VB something, they are very annoyed about it. *Terry was* PASSIVE *getting really steamed up.* **2** When, for example, a win- get V-ed P dow or mirror, **steams up**, it becomes covered with V P steam or mist. ◆ **steamed up** *The glass is all steamed* ADJ *up still.*

steam·boat /ˈsti:mbəʊt/ **steamboats.** A **steam-** N-COUNT **boat** is a boat or ship that has an engine powered by steam.

steam·er /ˈsti:mə/ **steamers. 1** A **steamer** is a ◆◇◇◇◇ ship that has an engine powered by steam. **2** A N-COUNT **steamer** is a special saucepan used for steaming N-COUNT food such as vegetables and fish.

'steam iron, steam irons. A **steam iron** is an N-COUNT electric iron that produces steam.

steam·roller /ˈsti:mrəʊlə/ **steamrollers, steam-** **rolling, steamrollered. 1** A **steamroller** is a N-COUNT large heavy vehicle with wide solid wheels or rollers, which is used to flatten the surface of a road. **2** If VERB: V n you **steamroller** someone who disagrees with you V n *into* n or opposes you, you defeat them or you force them to do what you want by using your power or by put- ting a lot of pressure on them. ...*the Prime Minister's attempt to steamroller the general into a job he did not want.*

steam·ship /ˈsti:mʃɪp/ **steamships.** A **steamship** N-COUNT is a ship that has an engine powered by steam.

steamy /ˈsti:mi/. **1 Steamy** means erotic or pas- ◆◇◇◇◇ sionate. *He'd had a steamy affair with an office col-* ADJ-GRADED *league.* **2** A **steamy** place is very hot and humid be- INFORMAL cause it is full of steam. ADJ-GRADED

steed /sti:d/ **steeds.** A **steed** is a large strong horse N-COUNT used for riding. LITERARY

steel /sti:l/ **steels, steeling, steeled. 1 Steel** is ◆◆◇◇◇ a very strong metal made mainly from iron. ● See N-VAR also **stainless steel. 2 Steel** is used to refer to the in- N-UNCOUNT dustry that produces steel and items made of steel. ...*a three-month study of European steel.* **3** If you VERB: **steel** yourself for something unpleasant, you pre- V pron-refl pare to deal with it. *I was steeling myself to call* V pron-refl *round when Simon arrived.* to-inf

'steel band, steel bands. A **steel band** is a band N-COUNT of people who play music on special metal drums.

steel·maker /ˈsti:lmeɪkə/ **steelmakers.** A N-COUNT **steelmaker** is a company that makes steel.

,steel 'wool. Steel wool is made of a mass of fine N-UNCOUNT steel threads twisted together into a small ball. It is used for cleaning hard surfaces.

steel·worker /ˈsti:lwɜ:kə/ **steelworkers;** also N-COUNT spelled **steel worker.** A **steelworker** is a person who works in a steelworks.

steel·works /ˈsti:lwɜ:ks/; **steelworks** is both the N-COUNT singular and plural form. A **steelworks** is a factory where steel is made.

steely /ˈsti:li/. **1 Steely** is used to emphasize that a ◆◇◇◇◇ person is hard, strong, and determined. *Their inde-* ADJ-GRADED *cision has been replaced by confidence and steely de-* *termination.* **2** You use **steely** to describe something ADJ that has a hard greyish colour like steel.

steep /sti:p/ **steeper, steepest; steeps, steep-** ◆◆◇◇◇ **ing, steeped. 1** A **steep** slope rises at a very sharp ADJ-GRADED angle and is difficult to go up. ...*a narrow, steep- sided valley.* ◆ **steep·ly** *The road climbs steeply,* ADV-GRADED: *with good views of Orvieto through the trees.* **2** A ADV with v **steep** increase or decrease in something is a very ADJ-GRADED big increase or decrease. *Comsumers are rebelling at steep price increases.* ◆ **steeply** *Unemployment is* ADV-GRADED: *rising steeply.* ADV with v **3** If you say that the price of something is **steep**, you ADJ-GRADED mean that it is expensive. INFORMAL **4** To **steep** food in a particular liquid means to im- VERB merse it in it, so that it becomes soft and absorbs the V n flavour of the liquid. *It's a drink made by steeping pineapple rind in water.*

steeped /sti:pt/. If a place or person is **steeped in** ◆◇◇◇◇ a quality or characteristic, they are surrounded by it ADJ-GRADED: or deeply influenced by it. *The castle is steeped in* v-link ADJ in n *history and legend.*

stee·ple /ˈsti:pəl/ **steeples.** A **steeple** is a tall ◆◇◇◇◇ pointed structure on top of the tower of a church. N-COUNT

steeple·chase /ˈsti:pəltʃeɪs/ **steeplechases.** ◆◇◇◇◇ **1** A **steeplechase** is a long horse race in which the N-COUNT horses have to jump over obstacles such as hedges and water jumps. **2** A **steeplechase** is a race over N-COUNT 3000 metres in which people jump over hurdles and water jumps round an athletics track.

steer /stɪə/ **steers, steering, steered. 1** When ◆◆◇◇◇ you **steer** a car, boat, or plane, you control it so that VERB: V n it goes in the direction that you want. *She would of-* V n prep *ten let me steer the car along our driveway.* **2** If you Also V **steer** people towards a particular course of action VERB or attitude, you try to lead them gently in that direc- V n prep tion. *The new government is seen as one that will steer the country in the right direction.* **3** If you **steer** VERB someone in a particular direction, you guide them V n prep there. *Nick steered them into the nearest seats.* **4** If you **steer** a particular **course**, you take a particular VERB line of action. *Prime Minister Hun Sen has sought to* V n prep *steer a course between the two groups.* **5** If you **steer** PHRASE **clear** of someone or something, you deliberately avoid them. **6** A **steer** is a bull that has been castrated. N-COUNT

steer·ing /ˈstɪərɪŋ/. **1** The **steering** in a vehicle is ◆◇◇◇◇ the mechanical parts of it which make it possible to N-UNCOUNT steer. **2** A **steering** group is a group of people that ADJ: ADJ n manage the early stages of a project, in particular

the order and priority of business, and oversee its progress.

'steering column, steering columns. The steering column in a vehicle is the rod on which the steering wheel is mounted.   N-COUNT

'steering wheel, steering wheels. The steering wheel in a vehicle is the wheel which the driver holds to steer the vehicle. See picture headed **car and bicycle**.   ◆◇◇◇◇ N-COUNT

stel·lar /'stelə/. **1 Stellar** is used to describe anything connected with stars. *A stellar wind streams outward from the star.* **2** A **stellar** person or thing is considered to be excellent. *...a stellar education at Eton and Oxford.*   ADJ: ADJ n / ADJ-GRADED

stem /stem/ **stems, stemming, stemmed. 1** If a condition or problem **stems from** something, it was caused originally by that thing. *All my problems stem from drink.*   ◆◆◇◇◇ VERB V from n

2 If you **stem** something, you stop it spreading, increasing, or continuing. *The authorities seem powerless to stem the rising tide of violence.*   VERB V n FORMAL

3 The **stem** of a plant is the thin upright part on which the flowers and leaves grow. **4** The **stem** of a glass or vase is the long thin part which connects the bowl to the base. **5** The **stem** of a pipe is the long thin part through which smoke is sucked.   N-COUNT

-stemmed /-stemd/. **-stemmed** is added to adjectives to form adjectives which indicate what the stem of something is like. *...long-stemmed roses.*   COMB

stench /stentʃ/ **stenches.** A **stench** is a strong and very unpleasant smell.   ◆◇◇◇◇ N-COUNT

sten·cil /'stensəl/ **stencils, stencilling, stencilled;** spelled **stenciling, stenciled** in American English. **1** A **stencil** is a piece of paper, plastic, or metal which has a design cut out of it. You place the stencil on a surface and use it to create a design, by allowing ink or paint to go through the holes in the stencil onto the surface below. **2** If you **stencil** a design or if you **stencil** a surface with a design, you print a design on a surface using a stencil. *He then stencilled the ceiling with a moon and stars motif.*   ◆◇◇◇◇ N-COUNT / VERB V n with n Also V n

ste·nog·ra·pher /stə'nɒgrəfə/ **stenographers.** A **stenographer** is an office worker who can write shorthand and type.   N-COUNT AMERICAN

sten·to·rian /sten'tɔːriən/. A **stentorian** voice is very loud and strong.   ADJ-GRADED FORMAL

step /step/ **steps, stepping, stepped. 1** If you take a **step**, you lift your foot and put it down in a different place, for example when you are walking. *She walked on a few steps... He heard steps in the corridor.* **2** If you **step** on something or **step** in a particular direction, you put your foot on the thing or move your foot in that direction. *I tried to step back, but he held my upper arms too tightly.* **3** The **steps** of a dance are the sequences of foot movements which make it up. **4** Someone's **step** is the way they walk. *He quickened his step.* **5** If people who are walking or dancing are **in step**, they are moving their feet forward at exactly the same time as each other. If they are **out of step**, their feet are moving forward at different times.   ◆◆◆◆◆ N-COUNT / VERB V prep/adv / N-COUNT / N-SING poss N PHRASE

6 Steps are a series of surfaces at increasing or decreasing heights, on which you put your feet in order to walk up or down to a different level. You can also refer to a single one of these things in front of a door as a **step**. *...a flight of stone steps.* ● See also **doorstep**.   N-COUNT

7 Some people use the word **steps** to refer to a **stepladder**.   N-PLURAL

8 A **step** is one of a series of actions that you take in order to achieve something. *He greeted the agreement as the first step towards peace.*   N-COUNT

9 If you stay **one step ahead of** someone or something, you manage to achieve more than they do or avoid competition or danger from them. **10** If people are **in step** with each other, their ideas or opinions are the same. If they are **out of step** with each other, their ideas or opinions are different. **11** If you tell someone to **step on it**, you are telling them to go faster or hurry up. *We've only got thirty-five minutes so step on it.* **12** If you do something **step by step**, you do it by pro-   PHRASE / PHRASE / PHRASE PRAGMATICS / PHRASE

gressing gradually from one stage to the next. **13** If someone tells you to **watch** your **step**, they are warning you to be careful about how you behave or what you say so that you don't get into trouble.   PHRASE PRAGMATICS

step aside. See **step down**.   PHRASAL VB

step back. If you **step back** and think about a situation, you think about it as if you were not involved in it. *It was necessary to step back from the project and look at it as a whole.*   PHRASAL VB V P V P from n

step down or **step aside.** If someone **steps down** or **steps aside**, they resign from an important job or position, often in order to let someone else take their place. *Mr Orlando was forced to step down as mayor.*   PHRASAL VB V P V P as n

step in. If you **step in**, you get involved in a difficult situation because you think you can or should help with it. *If no agreement was reached, the army would step in.*   PHRASAL VB V P

step up. If you **step up** something, you increase it or increase its intensity. *He urged donors to step up their efforts to send aid to Somalia.*   PHRASAL VB V P noun Also V n P

step·brother /'stepbrʌðə/ **stepbrothers;** also spelled **step-brother.** Someone's **stepbrother** is the son of their stepfather or stepmother.   N-COUNT

,step-by-'step. See **step**.

step·child /'steptʃaɪld/ **stepchildren;** also spelled **step-child.** Someone's **stepchild** is a child that was born to their husband or wife during a previous relationship.   N-COUNT

step·daughter /'stepdɔːtə/ **stepdaughters;** also spelled **step-daughter.** Someone's **stepdaughter** is a daughter that was born to their husband or wife during a previous relationship.   N-COUNT

step·father /'stepfɑːðə/ **stepfathers;** also spelled **step-father.** Someone's **stepfather** is the man who has married their mother after the death or divorce of their father.   ◆◇◇◇◇ N-COUNT

step·ladder /'steplædə/ **stepladders.** A **stepladder** is a portable ladder that is made of two sloping parts that are hinged together at the top so that it will stand up on its own.   N-COUNT

step·mother /'stepmʌðə/ **stepmothers;** also spelled **step-mother.** Someone's **stepmother** is the woman who has married their father after the death or divorce of their mother.   ◆◇◇◇◇ N-COUNT

'step-parent, step-parents; also spelled **stepparent.** Someone's **step-parent** is their stepmother or stepfather.   N-COUNT

steppe /step/ **steppes.** Steppes are large areas of grassland where there are no trees. It is often used to refer to the area that stretches from Eastern Europe across the south of the former Soviet Union to Siberia.   N-UNCOUNT: also N in pl

'stepping stone, stepping stones; also spelled **stepping-stone. 1** You can describe a job or event as a **stepping stone** when it helps you to make progress, especially in your career. *Many students now see university as a stepping stone to a good job.* **2 Stepping stones** are a line of large stones which you can walk on in order to cross a shallow stream or river.   ◆◇◇◇◇ N-COUNT / N-COUNT

step·sister /'stepsɪstə/ **stepsisters;** also spelled **step-sister.** Someone's **stepsister** is the daughter of their stepfather or stepmother.   N-COUNT

step·son /'stepsʌn/ **stepsons;** also spelled **stepson.** Someone's **stepson** is a son born to their husband or wife during a previous relationship.   N-COUNT

ste·reo /'steriəʊ/ **stereos. 1 Stereo** is used to describe a sound system or record in which the sound is played through two speakers. **2** A **stereo** is a record player with two speakers.   ◆◆◇◇◇ ADJ / N-COUNT

ste·reo·type /'steriətaɪp/ **stereotypes, stereotyping, stereotyped. 1** A **stereotype** is a fixed general image or set of characteristics that a lot of people believe represent a particular type of person or thing. *There's always been a stereotype about successful businessmen.* **2** If someone **is stereotyped** as something, people form a fixed general idea or image of them, so that it is assumed that they will behave in a particular way. *...the way women are stereotyped in a lot of mainstream films.*   ◆◆◇◇◇ N-COUNT / VB: usu passive, be V-ed as n be V-ed

ste·reo·typi·cal /ˌsteriəʊ'tɪpɪkəl/. A **stereotypical** ADJ-GRADED idea of a type of person or thing is a fixed general idea that a lot of people have about it, that may be false in many cases. ...*stereotypical images of the unfeeling male.*

ster·ile /'steraɪl, AM -rəl/. **1** Something that is **sterile** is completely clean and free from germs. *Urine is sterile.* ◆ **ster·il·ity** /stə'rɪlɪti/. ...*the antiseptic sterility of the hospital.* **2** A person or animal that is **sterile** is unable to have or produce babies. ◆ **sterility** *This disease causes sterility.* **3** A **sterile** situation is lacking in energy and new ideas. *Too much time has been wasted in sterile debate.* ◆ **sterility** ...*the sterility of Dorothea's life in industry.*
- ◆◇◇◇◇ ADJ
- N-UNCOUNT
- ADJ
- N-UNCOUNT
- ADJ-GRADED
- N-UNCOUNT

ster·i·lize /'sterɪlaɪz/ **sterilizes, sterilizing, sterilized**; also spelled **sterilise** in British English. **1** If you **sterilize** a thing or a place, you make it completely clean and free from germs. ◆ **ster·i·li·za·tion** /ˌsterɪlaɪ'zeɪʃən, AM -lɪ'z-/. ...*the pasteurization and sterilization of milk.* **2** If a person or an animal **is sterilized**, they have a medical operation that makes it impossible for them to have or produce babies. ◆ **ster·i·li·za·tion, sterilizations** *In some cases, a sterilization is performed through the vaginal wall.*
- ◆◇◇◇◇
- VERB: V n
- N-UNCOUNT
- VERB: be V-ed
- N-VAR

ster·ling /'stɜːlɪŋ/. **1** Sterling is the money system of Great Britain. **2** If you describe someone's work or character as **sterling**, you mean it is excellent. *Those are sterling qualities to be admired in anyone.*
- ◆◆◇◇
- N-UNCOUNT
- ADJ FORMAL

stern /stɜːn/ **sterner, sternest; sterns. 1** Someone who is **stern** is very serious and strict. ...*a stern warning.* ◆ **stern·ly** *'We will take the necessary steps,' she said sternly.* **2** The **stern** of a boat is the back part of it.
- ◆◆◇◇
- ADJ-GRADED
- ADV-GRADED
- N-COUNT

ster·num /'stɜːnəm/ **sternums.** Your **sternum** is the long flat bone which goes from your throat to the bottom of your ribs and to which your ribs are attached.
- N-COUNT MEDICAL

ster·oid /'steroɪd, AM 'stɪr-/ **steroids.** A **steroid** is a type of chemical substance found in your body. Steroids can be artificially introduced into the bodies of athletes to improve their strength.
- ◆◇◇◇◇ N-COUNT

stetho·scope /'steθəskəʊp/ **stethoscopes.** A **stethoscope** is an instrument that a doctor uses to listen to your heart and breathing.
- N-COUNT

stet·son /'stetsən/ **stetsons.** A **stetson** is a hat with a wide brim, traditionally worn by cowboys.
- N-COUNT

stew /stjuː, AM stuː/ **stews, stewing, stewed. 1** A **stew** is a meal which you make by cooking meat and vegetables in liquid at a low temperature. **2** When you **stew** meat, vegetables, or fruit, you cook them slowly in liquid in a closed dish. **3** If you **let** someone **stew** or if you **leave** them **to stew**, you deliberately leave them to worry about something for a while, rather than telling them something which would make them feel better.
- ◆◇◇◇◇ N-VAR
- VERB: V n
- PHRASE

stew·ard /'stjuːəd, AM 'stuː-/ **stewards. 1** A **steward** is a man who works on a ship, plane, or train, looking after passengers and serving meals to them. **2** A **steward** is someone who has the responsibility for looking after property. **3** A **steward** is a man or woman who helps to organize a race, march, or other public event. ● See also **shop steward.**
- ◆◆◇◇◇
- N-COUNT
- N-COUNT
- N-COUNT

stew·ard·ess /ˌstjuː'des, ˌstuː-/ **stewardesses.** A **stewardess** is a woman who works on a ship, plane, or train, looking after passengers and serving meals to them.
- N-COUNT

stew·ard·ship /'stjuːədʃɪp, AM 'stuː-/. **Stewardship** is the responsibility of looking after property.
- N-UNCOUNT FORMAL

stick /stɪk/ **sticks. 1** A **stick** is a thin branch which has fallen off a tree. ...*bundles of dried sticks.* **2** A **stick** is a long thin piece of wood which is used for supporting someone's weight or for hitting people or animals. *He looks old, has diabetes and walks with a stick.* ● See also **carrot and stick. 3** A **stick** is a long thin piece of wood which is used for a particular purpose. ...*lolly sticks.* **4** Some long thin objects used when taking part in
- ◆◆◇◇
- N-COUNT
- N-COUNT
- N-COUNT

sports are called **sticks.** ...*hockey sticks.* **5** A **stick** of something is a long thin piece of it. ...*a stick of celery.*
- N-COUNT

6 If you say that something is **a stick to beat** someone **with**, you mean that it is used, or could be used, as a basis for criticism. *Historic American fiction is constantly being used as a stick to beat contemporary British writers with.*
- PHRASE

7 If you give someone some **stick**, you criticize them or tease them roughly. *I get some stick from the lads because of my faith.*
- N-UNCOUNT INFORMAL, BRITISH

8 If you say that someone lives in **the sticks**, you mean that they live a long way from any large cities; used showing disapproval.
- N-PLURAL: the N INFORMAL

9 If someone **gets the wrong end of the stick** or **gets hold of the wrong end of the stick**, they completely misunderstand something.
- PHRASE INFORMAL

stick /stɪk/ **sticks, sticking, stuck. 1** If you **stick** something somewhere, you put it there in a rather casual way. *He folded the papers and stuck them in his desk drawer.* **2** If you **stick** a pointed object in something, or if it **sticks** in something, it pierces it. *They sent in loads of male nurses and stuck a needle in my back.*
- ◆◆◆◇
- VERB V n prep/adv
- V-ERG V n in/into/through n Also V in n

3 If something is **sticking** out from somewhere or **sticking** into something else, it extends away from something or through something. *Something was sticking from the pocket of the little man's grimy shorts.*
- VERB V adv/prep

4 If you **stick** one thing to another, you attach it using glue, sticky tape, or another sticky substance. *He has nowhere to stick up his posters.* **5** If one thing **sticks** to another, it becomes attached to it and is difficult to remove. *If left to stand, cooked pasta sticks together.*
- VERB: V n prep
- V n with adv
- VERB: V to n
- V together

6 If something **sticks** in your mind, you remember it for a long time. **7** If you give someone or something a name and the name **sticks**, it becomes the name which most people use to refer to that person or thing.
- VERB: V inn
- VERB: V

8 If someone manages to make a charge or accusation **stick**, they show that the person accused is guilty of the crime or wrongdoing they are accused of. **9** If something which can usually be moved **sticks**, it becomes fixed in one position.
- VB: no cont, with brd-neg, V
- VERB: V

10 If you are in an unpleasant or difficult situation and can hardly **stick** it, you cannot bear to remain there long.
- VERB: V n INFORMAL, BRITISH

11 If you say that someone **can stick** something, especially a job, or if you tell them where **to stick** it, you are rudely refusing it or emphasizing that you do not want it or like it. Some people find this use offensive. *It's a rotten play, so they can stick it... She then stormed out in a temper telling him to 'stick his job'.*
- PHRASE [PRAGMATICS] INFORMAL

12 See also **stuck.**

stick around. If you **stick around**, you stay where you are, often because you are waiting for something. *I didn't stick around long enough to find out.*
- PHRASAL VB V P Also V P n INFORMAL

stick at. If you **stick at** a task or activity, you continue doing it, even if it is difficult. *You will find it hard at first, but stick at it.*
- PHRASAL VB V P n

stick by. 1 If you **stick by** someone, you continue to give them help or support. ...*friends who stuck by me during the difficult times.* **2** If you **stick by** a promise, agreement, decision, or principle, you do what you said you would do, or do not change your mind. *But I made my decision then and stuck by it.*
- PHRASAL VB V P n
- V P n

stick out. 1 If you **stick out** part of your body, you extend it away from your body. *She made a face and stuck out her tongue at him.* ● to **stick** your **neck out:** see **neck. 2** If something **sticks out**, it is very noticeable because it is unusual. *What had Cutter done to make him stick out from the crowd?* ● to **stick out like a sore thumb:** see **thumb.**
- PHRASAL VB V P Also V n P
- V P
- V P from n

3 If someone in an unpleasant or difficult situation **sticks it out**, they do not leave or give up. *I really didn't like New York, but I wanted to stick it out a little bit longer.* ● to **stick in** your **throat:** see **throat.**
- PHRASE

stick out for. If you **stick out for** something, you keep demanding it and do not accept anything different or less. *I stuck out for a handsome redundancy package.*
- PHRASAL VB V P P n BRITISH

S

stick to. **1** If you **stick to** something or someone when you are travelling, you stay close to them. *Stick to well-lit roads.* **2** If you **stick to** something, you continue doing, using, saying, or talking about it, rather than changing to something else. *Perhaps he should have stuck to writing.* **3** If you **stick to** a promise, agreement, decision, or principle, you do what you said you would do, or do not change your mind. *Immigrant support groups are waiting to see if he sticks to his word.* • to **stick to** your **guns**: see **gun**. **4** If you **stick to** rules, you do what they say you must do. PHRASAL VB / V P n

stick together. If people **stick together**, they stay with each other and support each other. *If we all stick together, we ought to be okay.* PHRASAL VB / V P

stick up for. If you **stick up for** a person or a principle, you support or defend them forcefully. PHRASAL VB / V P P n

stick with. **1** If you **stick with** something, you do not change to something else. *If you're in a job that keeps you busy, stick with it.* **2** If you **stick with** someone, you stay close to them. PHRASAL VB / V P n

stick·er /ˈstɪkə/ **stickers.** A **sticker** is a small piece of paper or plastic, with writing or a picture on one side, which you can stick onto a surface. • See also **bumper sticker**. ◆◇◇◇◇ N-COUNT

'sticking plaster, sticking plasters. Sticking **plaster** is material that you can stick over a cut in order to protect it. A **sticking plaster** is a piece of this. N-VAR BRITISH

'sticking point, sticking points; also spelled **sticking-point**. A **sticking point** in a discussion or series of negotiations is a point on which the people involved cannot agree and which may delay or stop the talks. A **sticking point** is also one aspect of a problem which you have trouble dealing with. ◆◇◇◇◇ N-COUNT

'stick insect, stick insects. A **stick insect** is an insect with a long thin body and legs. See picture headed **insects**. N-COUNT BRITISH

'stick-in-the-mud, stick-in-the-muds. If you describe someone as a **stick-in-the-mud**, you disapprove of them because they do not like doing anything that is new or fun. N-COUNT PRAGMATICS INFORMAL

stick·ler /ˈstɪklə/ **sticklers.** If you are a **stickler** for something, you always insist on it. *I'm a bit of a stickler for accuracy.* N-COUNT

'stick-on. **Stick-on** labels, shapes, and objects have an adhesive material on one side so that they will stick to surfaces. The usual American term is **self-adhesive**. ADJ: ADJ n BRITISH

sticky /ˈstɪki/ **stickier, stickiest.** **1** A **sticky** substance is soft, or thick and liquid, and can stick to other things. **Sticky** things are covered with a sticky substance. *...sticky toffee... Peel away the sticky paper.* ♦ **sticki·ness** *...the stickiness of her hands.* **2** **Sticky** weather is unpleasantly hot and damp. ♦♦◇◇◇ ADJ-GRADED / N-UNCOUNT ADJ-GRADED

3 A **sticky** situation involves problems or is embarrassing. *Her research was going through a sticky patch.* ADJ-GRADED INFORMAL

4 If someone **comes to a sticky end** or **meets a sticky end**, they suffer very badly or die in an unpleasant way. PHRASE INFORMAL, BRITISH

'sticky 'tape. **Sticky tape** is clear sticky tape that is sold in rolls and that you use to stick paper or card together or onto a wall. N-UNCOUNT BRITISH

stiff /stɪf/ **stiffer, stiffest.** **1** Something that is **stiff** is firm or does not bend easily. *His gaberdine trousers were brand new and stiff.* ♦ **stiff·ly** *Moira sat stiffly upright in her straight-backed chair.* ♦♦◇◇◇ ADJ-GRADED / ADV-GRADED

2 Something such as a door or drawer that is **stiff** does not move as easily as it should. *The gears were too stiff.* ADJ-GRADED

3 If you are **stiff**, your muscles or joints ache when you move, because of illness or because of too much exercise. ♦ **stiffly** *He climbed stiffly from the car.* ♦ **stiff·ness** *Stiffness and discomfort can usually be eased with heat or a warm bath.* ADJ-GRADED / ADV-GRADED / N-UNCOUNT

4 **Stiff** behaviour is rather formal and not very friendly or relaxed. *They always seemed a little awkward with each other, a bit stiff and formal.* ♦ **stiffly** *...a stiffly worded letter of complaint to the club.* **5** **Stiff** can be used to mean difficult or severe. *...stiff anti-drugs laws.* ADJ-GRADED / ADV-GRADED / ADJ-GRADED

6 A **stiff** drink is a large amount of a strong alcoholic drink. *...a stiff whisky.* ADJ-GRADED: ADJ n

7 A **stiff** breeze is one that blows quite strongly. *A stiff breeze had sprung up.* ADJ-GRADED

8 If you are bored **stiff**, worried **stiff**, or scared **stiff**, you are extremely bored, worried, or scared. ▶ Also an adjective. *Even if he bores you stiff, it is good manners not to let him know it.* ADV; adj ADV INFORMAL ADJ: v n ADJ

9 • **stiff upper lip**: see **lip**.

stiff·en /ˈstɪfən/ **stiffens, stiffening, stiffened.** **1** If you **stiffen**, you stop moving and stand or sit with muscles that are suddenly tense, for example because you feel afraid or angry. **2** If your muscles or joints **stiffen**, or if something **stiffens** them, they become difficult to bend or move. *The blood supply to the skin is reduced when muscles stiffen.* ▶ **Stiffen up** means the same as **stiffen**. *These clothes restrict your freedom of movement and stiffen up the whole body.* **3** If attitudes or behaviour **stiffen**, or if something **stiffens** them, they become stronger or more severe, and less likely to be changed. *Canada has recently stiffened its immigration rules.* **4** If something such as cloth is **stiffened**, it is made firm so that it does not bend easily. *...soft Sugiwara paper that had been stiffened with a kind of paste.* ◆◇◇◇◇ VERB: V / V-ERG Also V n / PHRASAL VB ERG V P noun Also V n P, V P / V-ERG: V V n / VB: usu passive be V-ed

stiffen up. See **stiffen** 2. PHRASAL VB

sti·fle /ˈstaɪfəl/ **stifles, stifling, stifled.** **1** If someone **stifles** something you consider to be a good thing, they prevent it from continuing. *Critics have accused the US of trying to stifle debate.* **2** If you **stifle** a yawn or laugh, you prevent yourself from yawning or laughing. **3** If you **stifle** your natural feelings or behaviour, you prevent yourself from having those feelings or behaving in that way. *He stifled his temptation to take hold of Ivy and shake her.* ◆◇◇◇◇ VERB V n / VERB: V n / VERB V n

sti·fling /ˈstaɪflɪŋ/. **1** **Stifling** heat is so intense that it makes you feel uncomfortable. You can also use **stifling** to describe a place that is extremely hot. **2** If a situation is **stifling**, it makes you feel uncomfortable because you cannot do what you want. *Life at home with her parents and two sisters was stifling.* **3** See also **stifle**. ◆◇◇◇◇ ADJ-GRADED / ADJ-GRADED

stig·ma /ˈstɪɡmə/ **stigmas.** **1** If something has a **stigma** attached to it, people consider it to be unacceptable or a disgrace. *There is very little stigma attached to crime and criminals.* **2** The **stigma** of a flower is the top of the centre part which takes in pollen. ◆◇◇◇◇ N-VAR / N-COUNT

stig·mata /stɪɡˈmɑːtə/. If marks appear on a person's body in the same places where Christ was wounded when He was crucified, they are called **stigmata**. Some Christians believe that this is a sign of holiness. N-PLURAL

stig·ma·tize /ˈstɪɡmətaɪz/ **stigmatizes, stigmatizing, stigmatized;** also spelled **stigmatise** in British English. If someone or something is **stigmatized**, they are unfairly regarded by many people as unacceptable or disgraceful. *The AIDS epidemic has further stigmatised gays.* ♦ **stig·ma·tized** *It is a stigmatized illness.* VERB: be V-ed V n / ADJ

stile /staɪl/ **stiles.** A **stile** is an entrance to a field or path that consists of a step on either side of a fence or wall. N-COUNT

sti·let·to /stɪˈletəʊ/ **stilettos. Stilettos** are women's shoes that have high, very narrow heels. The usual American expression is **spike heels**. N-COUNT BRITISH

still 1 adverb uses

still /stɪl/. **1** If a situation that used to exist **still** exists, it has continued and exists now. *I still dream of home... Brian's toe is still badly swollen and he cannot put on his shoe.* **2** If something that has not yet happened could **still** happen, it is possible that it will happen. If something that has not yet happened is **still** to happen, it will happen at a later time. *We could still make it, but we won't get there till three... Still to come, the financial news and the weather at a quarter to two.* **3** If you say that there **is still** an amount of something left, you are emphasizing that there is that amount left. *There are still* ♦♦♦♦♦ ADV: ADV before v, ADV group ADV: ADV before v / ADV: be ADV n

some outstanding problems... There's still time to catch up with them. **4** You use **still** to emphasize that something remains the case or is true in spite of what you have just said. *Despite the ruling, Boreham was still found guilty.* ADV: ADV before v

5 You use **still** when you are dismissing a problem or difficulty as not really worth worrying about. *'Any idea who is going to be here this weekend?'—No. Still, who cares?'* **6** You use **still** in expressions such as **still further**, **still another**, and **still more** to show that you find the number or quantity of things you are referring to surprising or excessive. *Why did the bank not conduct its own audit before lending still more?* **7** You use **still** with comparatives to indicate that something has even more of a quality than something else. *Formula One motor car racing is supposed to be dangerous. 'Indycar' racing is supposed to be more dangerous still.* ADV: ADV with cl / ADV: ADV n/adv / ADV: ADV with compar

still 2 not moving or making a noise

still /stɪl/ **stiller, stillest; stills, stilling, stilled.** **1** If you stay **still**, you stay in the same position and do not move. *He played the tape through once, then sat very still for several minutes... He recalled her still face and the hurt in her eyes when he had refused her help.* **2** If air or water is **still**, it is not moving. *The night air was very still.* **3** If a place is **still**, it is quiet and shows no sign of activity. ♦ **still·ness** *...the stillness of the night air.* **4** If a sound **stills** or **is stilled**, it becomes quiet. *The people's voice has been stilled.* **5** A **still** is a photograph taken from a cinema film which is used for publicity purposes. ADJ-GRADED: ADJ after v, v-link ADJ, ADJ n / ADJ-GRADED / ADJ-GRADED / N-UNCOUNT / V-ERG: V be V-ed / N-COUNT

still·birth /'stɪlbɜːθ/ **stillbirths.** A **stillbirth** is the birth of a dead baby. N-VAR

still·born /'stɪlbɔːn/. A **stillborn** baby is dead when it is born. ADJ

still 'life, still lifes. A **still life** is a painting or drawing of an arrangement of objects such as flowers or fruit. It also refers to this type of painting or drawing. N-VAR

stilt /stɪlt/ **stilts.** **1** **Stilts** are long upright pieces of wood or metal which are used to support some buildings, especially when the ground is wet or very soft. **2** **Stilts** are two long pieces of wood with ledges high up on the sides that people such as circus clowns or children stand on in order to walk high up above the ground. N-COUNT / N-COUNT

stilt·ed /'stɪltɪd/. If someone's behaviour or conversation is **stilted**, they behave or speak in a formal, self-conscious, or unnatural way. ADJ-GRADED

stimu·lant /'stɪmjʊlənt/ **stimulants.** A **stimulant** is a drug that makes your body work faster, often increasing your heart rate and making you less likely to sleep. N-COUNT

stimu·late /'stɪmjʊleɪt/ **stimulates, stimulating, stimulated.** **1** To **stimulate** something means to encourage it to begin or develop further. *The Russian health service has stimulated public interest in home cures.* ♦ **stimu·la·tion** /ˌstɪmjʊ'leɪʃən/. *...an economy in need of stimulation.* **2** If you are **stimulated** by something, it makes you feel full of ideas and enthusiasm. *I was stimulated to examine my deepest thoughts.* ♦ **stimu·lat·ing** *It is a complex yet stimulating book.* ♦ **stimulation** *Many enjoy the mental stimulation of a challenging job.* **3** If something **stimulates** a part of a person's body, it causes it to move or function, usually automatically by a natural reflex. *Exercise stimulates the digestive and excretory systems.* ♦ **stimulating** *...the stimulating effect of adrenaline.* ♦ **stimulation** *...the chemical stimulation of drugs.* VERB: V n / N-UNCOUNT / VERB: be V-ed be V-ed to-inf / ADJ-GRADED / N-UNCOUNT / VERB: V n / ADJ-GRADED / N-UNCOUNT

stimu·la·tive /'stɪmjʊlətɪv/. If a government policy has a **stimulative** effect on the economy, it encourages the economy to grow. *It is possible that a tax cut might have some stimulative effect.* ADJ-GRADED

stimu·lus /'stɪmjʊləs/ **stimuli** /'stɪmjʊlaɪ/. A **stimulus** is something that encourages activity in people or things. *In many cases the stimulus is economic.* N-VAR

sting /stɪŋ/ **stings, stinging, stung.** **1** If a plant, animal, or insect **stings** you, it pricks your skin, usually with poison, so that you feel a sharp pain. *This type of bee rarely stings.* **2** The **sting** of an insect or animal is the part that stings you. See picture headed **insects**. **3** If you feel a **sting**, you feel a sharp pain in your skin or other part of your body. **4** If a part of your body **stings**, or if a substance **stings** it, you feel a sharp pain there. *Sprays can sting sensitive skin.* **5** If someone's remarks **sting** you, they make you feel hurt and annoyed. *...some of the criticism has stung him.* ♦ **sting·ing** *...a stinging attack on the government's economic practice.* **6** A **sting** is a clever secret plan by undercover police to catch criminals. *The police ran a sting operation to crack down on illegal guns.* **7** If an announcement or decision has **a sting in the tail** or **a sting in its tail**, it contains a critical and unpleasant part, normally at the end. **8** If something **takes the sting out** of a situation, it makes it less hurtful or unpleasant. ♦♦◇◇◇ VERB: V n V / N-COUNT / N-COUNT / V-ERG: V V n / VB: no cont V n / ADJ-GRADED / N-COUNT AMERICAN / PHRASE BRITISH / PHRASE

sting·ray /'stɪŋreɪ/ **stingrays.** A **stingray** is a type of large flat fish with a long tail which it can use as a weapon. N-COUNT

stin·gy /'stɪndʒi/ **stingier, stingiest.** Someone who is **stingy** is very mean. *The West is stingy with aid.* ADJ-GRADED

stink /stɪŋk/ **stinks, stinking, stank, stunk.** **1** If something **stinks**, it smells extremely unpleasant. *The place stinks of fried onions... The pond stank like a sewer.* ► Also a noun. *...the stink of stale beer on his breath.* ♦ **stink·ing** *They were locked up in a stinking cell.* **2** If you say that something **stinks**, you mean that you disapprove of it because it involves ideas, feelings, or practices that you do not like. *The whole thing stinks of political corruption.* **3** If someone makes a **stink** about something they are angry about, they show their anger in order to make people take notice. *The tabloid press kicked up a stink about his seven-day visit.* ♦◇◇◇◇ VERB: V V of n V like n / N-SING / ADJ-GRADED / VERB: V V of n PRAGMATICS INFORMAL / N-SING: a N INFORMAL

stink·er /'stɪŋkə/ **stinkers.** If you describe someone or something as a **stinker**, you mean that you think they are very unpleasant or bad. *I think he's an absolute stinker to do that to her.* N-COUNT INFORMAL

stink·ing /'stɪŋkɪŋ/. **1** You use **stinking** to describe something that is unpleasant or bad. *I had a stinking cold.* **2** See also **stink**. ADJ: ADJ n INFORMAL

stinky /'stɪŋki/ **stinkier, stinkiest.** **Stinky** means the same as **stinking**. ADJ-GRADED

stint /stɪnt/ **stints.** A **stint** is a period of time which you spend doing a particular job or activity or working in a particular place. *...a five-year stint in Hong Kong.* ♦◇◇◇ N-COUNT: with supp

sti·pend /'staɪpend/ **stipends.** A **stipend** is a sum of money that is paid regularly to a person, especially a magistrate or clergyman, as a salary or as living expenses. N-COUNT

sti·pen·di·ary /staɪ'pendiəri, AM -dieri/. In Britain, a **stipendiary** magistrate or clergyman is one who receives a stipend. ADJ: ADJ n

stip·pled /'stɪpəld/. A surface that is **stippled** is covered with tiny dots. ADJ

stipu·late /'stɪpjʊleɪt/ **stipulates, stipulating, stipulated.** If you **stipulate** a condition or that something must be done, you say clearly that it must be done. *She could have stipulated that she would pay when she collected the computer.* ♦ **stipu·la·tion** /ˌstɪpjʊ'leɪʃən/ **stipulations** *Clifford's only stipulation is that his clients obey his advice.* ♦◇◇◇ VERB: V n V that/wh / N-COUNT

stir /stɜː/ **stirs, stirring, stirred.** **1** If you **stir** a liquid or other substance, you move it around or mix it in a container using something such as a spoon. *There was Mrs Bellingham, stirring sugar into her tea.* **2** If you **stir**, you move slightly, for example because you are uncomfortable or beginning to wake up. *Eileen shook him, and he started to stir.* **3** If you do not ♦♦♦◇◇ VERB: V n V n into n / VERB V WRITTEN / VERB

stir from a place, you do not move from it. *She had not stirred from the house that evening.* **4** If something **stirs** or if the wind **stirs** it, it moves gently in the wind. *Not a breath of fresh air stirred the long white curtains.* V from n WRITTEN V-ERG: V V n WRITTEN

5 If you **stir** yourself, or if something **stirs** you into action, you move in order to start doing something. *You can't even stir yourself to have a drink with them... The sight of them stirred him into action.* VERB: V pron-refl V pron-refl to-inf V n prep

6 If something **stirs** you, it makes you react with a strong emotion. *I was intrigued by him, stirred by his intellect.* **7** If a particular memory, feeling, or mood **stirs** you or **is stirred** in you, you begin to think about it or feel it. *Amy remembered the anger he had stirred in her... Beneath my antipathy a powerful curiosity was stirring.* **8** If an event causes a **stir**, it causes great excitement, shock, or anger among people. *His film has caused a stir in America.* VERB V n WRITTEN V-ERG: V in n V n in n V WRITTEN N-SING

9 See also **stirring**.

stir up. 1 If something **stirs up** dust or **stirs up** mud in water, it causes it to rise up and move around. *They saw first a cloud of dust and then the car that was stirring it up.* **2** If you **stir up** a particular mood or situation, usually a bad one, you cause it. *As usual, Harriet is trying to stir up trouble.* PHRASAL VB V n P Also V P noun V P noun Also V n P

'stir-fry, stir-fries, stir-frying, stir-fried. 1 If you **stir-fry** vegetables, meat, or fish, you cook small pieces of them quickly by stirring them in a small quantity of very hot oil. This method is often used in Chinese cookery. *...stir-fried vegetables.* ► Also a noun *Serve the stir-fry with 'instant' noodles.* **2** **Stir-fry** vegetables, meat, or fish or **stir-fry** dishes are cooked by the stir-fry method. ◆◇◇◇◇ VERB: V n V-ed N-COUNT ADJ: ADJ n

stir·ring /'stɜːrɪŋ/ **stirrings. 1** A **stirring** event, performance, or account of something makes people very excited or enthusiastic. *The Prime Minister made a stirring speech.* **2** A **stirring** of a feeling or thought is the beginning of one. *...the first stirrings of a sense of guilt.* ◆◇◇◇◇ ADJ-GRADED N-COUNT

stir·rup /'stɪrəp, AM 'stɜːr-/ **stirrups. Stirrups** are the two metal loops which are attached to a horse's saddle by long pieces of leather, and which you place your feet in when riding a horse. N-COUNT

stitch /stɪtʃ/ **stitches, stitching, stitched. 1** If you **stitch** cloth, you use a needle and thread to join two pieces together or to make a decoration. *Fold the fabric and stitch the two layers together.* **2** **Stitches** are the short pieces of thread that have been sewn in a piece of cloth. **3** In knitting and crochet, a **stitch** is a loop made by one turn of wool around a knitting needle or crochet hook. **4** If you sew or knit something in a particular **stitch**, you sew or knit in a way that produces a particular pattern. *...a woolly vest knitted in garter stitch.* ◆◆◇◇◇ VERB: V n V n adv/prep Also V N-COUNT N-COUNT N-UNCOUNT

5 When doctors **stitch** a wound, they use a special needle and thread to sew the skin together. ► **Stitch up** means the same as **stitch**. *Dr Armonson stitched up her wrist wounds.* **6** A **stitch** is a piece of thread that has been used to sew the skin of a wound together. *He had six stitches in a head wound.* VERB: V n PHRASAL VB V P noun Also V n P N-COUNT

7 A **stitch** is a sharp pain in your side, usually caused by running or laughing a lot. **8** If you are **in stitches**, you cannot stop laughing. *Here's a book that will have you in stitches.* N-SING PHRASE INFORMAL

stitch up. 1 To **stitch** someone **up** means to trick them so that they are put in a situation where they are at a disadvantage, or where they are blamed for something they have not done. *He claimed that a police officer had threatened to stitch him up and send him to prison.* **2** See **stitch** 5. PHRASAL VB V n P Also V P noun INFORMAL, BRITISH

stitch·ing /'stɪtʃɪŋ/. **Stitching** is a row of stitches that have been sewn in a piece of cloth. *The stitching had begun to fray at the edges.* N-UNCOUNT

'stitch-up, stitch-ups; also spelled **stitch up**. If you describe a situation as a **stitch-up**, you mean that it has been altered in a way that makes it unfair. *The whole messy business has been a stitch-up by the unions.* N-COUNT INFORMAL, BRITISH

stock /stɒk/ **stocks, stocking, stocked.** ◆◆◆◆◆ **1** **Stocks** are shares in the ownership of a company, or investments on which a fixed amount of interest will be paid. *As stock prices have dropped, so too has bank capital.* **2** A company's **stock** is the amount of money which it has through selling shares. *The Fisher family holds 40% of the stock.* N-COUNT N-UNCOUNT

3 If a shop **stocks** particular goods, it keeps a supply of them to sell. *The shop stocks everything from cigarettes to recycled loo paper.* **4** A shop's **stock** is the total amount of goods which it has available to sell. **5** If goods are **in stock**, a shop has them available to sell. If they are **out of stock**, it does not. VB: no cont V n N-UNCOUNT PHRASE

6 If you **stock** something such as a cupboard, shelf, or room, you fill it with food or other things. *Some families stocked their cellars with food and water.* ► **Stock up** means the same as **stock**. *Customers travel from hundreds of miles away to stock up their deep freezes.* VERB: V n V n with n PHRASAL VB V P noun Also V n P

7 If you have a **stock** of things, you have a supply of them stored in a place ready to be used. *Stocks of ammunition were running low.* **8** The **stock** of something is the total amount of it that is available in a particular area. *...the stock of accommodation available to be rented.* N-COUNT: with supp N-SING: with supp

9 If you are from a particular **stock**, you are descended from a particular group of people. *We are both from working class stock.* **10** **Stock** are cattle, sheep, pigs, or other animals which are kept by a farmer, usually ones which have been specially bred. N-UNCOUNT FORMAL N-PLURAL

11 **Stock** is a liquid, usually made by boiling meat, bones, or vegetables in water. Stock is used to give flavour to soups and sauces. N-VAR

12 In former times, the **stocks** were an instrument of punishment. The criminal's hands and legs were locked into holes in a wooden frame while people threw things at them. N-PLURAL

13 A **stock** answer, expression, or way of doing something is one that is very commonly used, especially because people cannot be bothered to think of something new; used showing disapproval. *National security is the stock excuse for keeping things confidential.* ADJ: ADJ n PRAGMATICS

14 If you **take stock**, you pause to think about all the aspects of a situation or event, before deciding what to do next. *It was time to take stock of the situation.* PHRASE

15 See also **stocking**; **laughing stock**, **rolling stock**.

● **lock, stock, and barrel**: see **barrel**.

stock up. 1 If you **stock up** on something, you buy a lot of it, in case you cannot get it later. *The authorities have urged people to stock up on fuel.* **2** See **stock** 6. PHRASAL VB V P on/with n

stock·ade /stɒ'keɪd/ **stockades.** A **stockade** is a wall of large wooden posts built around an area to keep out enemies or wild animals. N-COUNT

stock·broking /'stɒkbrəʊkɪŋ/. **Stockbroking** is the professional activity of buying and selling stocks and shares for clients. *His stockbroking firm was hit by the 1987 crash.* ♦ **stock·broker, stockbrokers** *A stockbroker focuses on tiny changes in the market that others do not register.* N-UNCOUNT N-COUNT

'stock car, stock cars. A **stock car** is an old car which has had changes made to it to make it suitable for races on a small dirt track, in which the cars often collide. N-COUNT

'stock control. Stock control is the management of goods for sale so that a company has exactly the right amount of them at any one time. N-UNCOUNT

'stock cube, stock cubes. A **stock cube** is a solid cube made from dried meat or vegetable juices and other flavourings. Stock cubes are used to add flavour to dishes such as stews and soups. N-COUNT BRITISH

'stock exchange, stock exchanges. A **stock exchange** is a place where people buy and sell stocks and shares. The **stock exchange** is also the trading activity that goes on there and the trading organization itself. *The shortage of good stock has kept some investors away from the stock exchange.* ◆◆◆◇◇ N-COUNT

stock·holder /'stɒkhəʊldə/ **stockholders.** A **stockholder** is a person who owns shares in a company. The usual British word is **shareholder**. ◆◇◇◇◇ N-COUNT AMERICAN

stock·ing /'stɒkɪŋ/ **stockings. Stockings** are items of women's clothing which fit closely over their feet and legs. Stockings are usually made of nylon or silk and are held in place by suspenders. ◆◇◇◇◇ N-COUNT

...*a pair of nylon stockings.* ● See also **stock**; **body stocking**.

stock·inged /'stɒkɪŋd/. If someone is in their **stockinged** feet, they are wearing socks, tights, or stockings, but no shoes. *ADJ: ADJ n*

,stock-in-'trade; also spelled **stock in trade**. If you say that something is someone's **stock-in-trade**, you mean that it is a usual part of their behaviour or work. *Patriotism is every politician's stock-in-trade.* *N-SING: with poss*

stock·ist /'stɒkɪst/ **stockists**. A **stockist** of a particular brand or type of goods is someone who sells this brand or type in their shop. *Take it to your nearest Kodak Photo CD stockist.* *◆◇◇◇◇ N-COUNT BRITISH*

'stock market, stock markets. The stock market consists of the general activity of buying stocks and shares, and the people and institutions that organize it. *He's been studying and playing the stock market since he was 14.* *◆◆◇◇ N-COUNT: the N*

stock·pile /'stɒkpaɪl/ **stockpiles, stockpiling, stockpiled**. If people **stockpile** things such as food or weapons, they store large quantities of them for future use. *People are stockpiling food for the coming winter.* ▶ Also a noun ...*treaties to cut stockpiles of chemical weapons.* *◆◇◇◇◇ VERB V n / N-COUNT*

stock·room /'stɒkruːm/ **stockrooms**; also spelled **stock-room**. A **stockroom** is a room, especially in a shop or a factory, where a stock of goods is kept. *N-COUNT*

,stock-'still. If someone stands or sits **stock-still**, they do not move at all. *The lieutenant stopped and stood stock-still.* *ADJ: ADJ after v*

stock·taking /'stɒkteɪkɪŋ/. **Stocktaking** is the activity of counting and checking all the goods that a shop or business has. *N-UNCOUNT*

stocky /'stɒki/ **stockier, stockiest**. A **stocky** person has a body that is broad, solid, and often short. *◆◇◇◇◇ ADJ-GRADED*

stodgy /'stɒdʒi/ **stodgier, stodgiest**. **1** **Stodgy** food is very solid and heavy. It makes you feel very full, and is difficult to digest. **2** If you describe someone or something as **stodgy**, you dislike them or are bored by them because they are very old-fashioned or serious. *ADJ-GRADED / ADJ-GRADED PRAGMATICS*

sto·ic /'stəʊɪk/ **stoics**. **1** **Stoic** means the same as **stoical**. ...*this noble image of the tall, stoic land-loving peasant.* **2** If you say that someone is a **stoic**, you approve of them because they suffer hardship without showing their emotions. *ADJ-GRADED FORMAL / N-COUNT FORMAL*

stoi·cal /'stəʊɪkəl/. If you say that someone behaves in a **stoical** way, you approve of them because they accept difficulties and suffering without complaining or getting upset. ...*the stoical courage of those in Northern Ireland.* ♦ **stoi·cal·ly** *She put up with it all stoically.* *ADJ-GRADED PRAGMATICS FORMAL / ADV-GRADED*

stoi·cism /'stəʊɪsɪzəm/. **Stoicism** is stoical behaviour. *She liked and admired the stoicism of the Lambeth hospital's mostly working-class patients.* *N-UNCOUNT FORMAL*

stoke /stəʊk/ **stokes, stoking, stoked**. **1** If you **stoke** a fire, you add coal or wood to it to keep it burning. *She was stoking the stove with sticks of maple.* ▶ **Stoke up** means the same as **stoke**. *He stoked up the fire in the hearth.* **2** If you **stoke** something such as a feeling, you cause it to be felt more strongly. *These demands are helping to stoke fears of civil war.* ▶ **Stoke up** means the same as **stoke**. *He has sent his proposals in the hope of stoking up interest for the idea.* *◆◇◇◇◇ VERB V n / PHRASAL VB V P noun / VERB V n / PHRASAL VB V P noun*

stok·er /'stəʊkə/ **stokers**. In former times a **stoker** was a person whose job was to stoke fires, especially on a ship or a steam train. *N-COUNT*

stole /stəʊl/ **stoles**. **1** **Stole** is the past tense of **steal**. **2** A **stole** is a long, wide scarf for women which is worn round the shoulders. *N-COUNT*

sto·len /'stəʊlən/. **Stolen** is the past participle of **steal**.

stol·id /'stɒlɪd/. If you describe someone as **stolid**, you mean that they are rather solemn and conventional in their behaviour, and do not show much emotion. ...*the stolid faces of the two detectives.* *ADJ-GRADED*

stom·ach /'stʌmək/ **stomachs, stomaching, stomached**. **1** Your **stomach** is the organ inside your body where food is digested before it moves into the intestines. **2** You can refer to the front part of your body below your waist as your **stomach**. See picture headed **human body**. *The children lay down on their stomachs.* **3** If the front part of your body below your waist feels uncomfortable because you are feeling worried or frightened, you can refer to it as your **stomach**. *His stomach was in knots.* **4** If you say that someone has a strong **stomach**, you mean that they are not disgusted by things that disgust most other people. **5** If you cannot **stomach** something, you cannot accept it because you dislike it or disapprove of it. *I could never stomach the cruelty involved in the wounding of animals.* **6** If you do something **on an empty stomach**, you do it without having eaten. **7** If you **have no stomach** for something, you do not have the courage to do it. **8** If you say that you feel **sick to your stomach** about something, you mean that you feel very angry or upset about it. **9** If you say that something **turns** your **stomach** or makes your **stomach turn**, you mean that it is so unpleasant or offensive that it makes you feel sick. **10** ● **butterflies in** your **stomach**: see **butterfly**. *◆◆◆◇◇ N-COUNT / N-COUNT / N-COUNT / N-COUNT / VB: with brd-neg V n/-ing / PHRASE / PHRASE / PHRASE / PHRASE*

'stomach ache, stomach aches; also spelled **stomachache**. If you have a **stomach ache**, you have a pain in your stomach. *N-VAR*

'stomach-churning. If you describe something as **stomach-churning**, you mean that it is so unpleasant that it makes you feel physically sick. *ADJ-GRADED*

stomp /stɒmp/ **stomps, stomping, stomped**. If you **stomp** somewhere, you walk there with very heavy steps, often because you are angry. *He stomped out of the room.* *◆◇◇◇◇ VERB V prep/adv*

stone /stəʊn/ **stones, stoning, stoned**. The plural is usually **stone** in meaning 9. **1** **Stone** is a hard solid substance found in the ground and often used for building houses. *He could not tell whether the floor was wood or stone.* **2** A **stone** is a small piece of rock that is found on the ground. *He removed a stone from his shoe.* **3** If people **stone** someone or something, they throw stones at them. *Youths burned cars and stoned police.* **4** A **stone** is a large piece of stone put somewhere in memory of a person or event, or as a religious symbol. *The monument consists of a circle of gigantic stones.* **5** You can refer to a jewel as a **stone**. ...*a diamond ring with three stones.* **6** A **stone** is a small hard ball of minerals and other substances which sometimes forms in a person's kidneys or gall bladder. *He had kidney stones.* **7** The **stone** in a plum, cherry, or other fruit is the large hard seed in the middle of it. The American term is **pit**. **8** If you **stone** a fruit, you remove its stone. **9** A **stone** is a measurement of a person's weight, equal to 14 pounds or 6.35 kilograms. *I weighed around 16 stone.* **10** **Stone** is used in expressions such as **set in stone** and **tablets of stone** to suggest that an idea or rule is firm and fixed, and cannot be changed. *Scientific opinions are not carved on tablets of stone.* **11** If you say that one place is a **stone's throw** from another, you mean that the places are close to each other. **12** If you say that you will **leave no stone unturned**, you are emphasizing that you will try every way you can think of in order to achieve what you want. **13** See also **stoned**; **foundation stone, paving stone, precious stone, stepping stone**. ● **kill two birds with one stone**: see **bird**. *◆◆◆◆◇ N-VAR / N-COUNT / VERB V n / N-COUNT / N-COUNT / N-COUNT / N-COUNT BRITISH / VERB: V n / N-COUNT BRITISH / N-UNCOUNT / PHRASE / PHRASE PRAGMATICS*

'Stone Age. The **Stone Age** is a very early period of human history, when people used tools and weapons made of stone, not metal. *N-PROPER: the N*

,stone-'cold. **1** If something that should be warm is **stone-cold**, it is very cold indeed. *Hillsden took a sip of tea, but it was stone cold.* **2** If someone is **stone-cold sober**, they are completely sober. *ADJ / PHRASE INFORMAL*

S

stoned /stəʊnd/. If someone is **stoned**, their mind is greatly affected by a drug such as cannabis. ● See also **stone**. `ADJ-GRADED INFORMAL`

,stone-'dead. If you **kill** something such as an idea or emotion **stone-dead**, you completely destroy it. *The prospect of having to pay a graduate tax until retirement would kill the students' enthusiasm stone dead.* `PHRASE`

,stone 'deaf; also spelled **stone-deaf.** Someone who is **stone deaf** is completely deaf. `ADJ`

stone·mason /'stəʊnmeɪsən/ **stonemasons.** A **stonemason** is a person who is skilled at cutting and preparing stone so that it can be used for building walls and buildings. `N-COUNT`

stone·wall /'stəʊnwɔːl/ **stonewalls, stonewalling, stonewalled.** If you say that someone **stonewalls**, you disapprove of them because they delay giving a clear answer or making a clear decision, often because there is something that they want to hide or avoid doing. *He did his best this week to stonewall questions and to block even the most modest proposals.* ◆ **stone·wall·ing** *After 18 days of stonewalling, he at last came out and faced the issue.* `VERB: V` `PRAGMATICS` `V n` `N-UNCOUNT`

stone·ware /'stəʊnweə/. **Stoneware** is earthenware pottery which is baked at a high temperature. `N-UNCOUNT`

stone·work /'stəʊnwɜːk/. **Stonework** consists of objects or parts of a building that are made of stone. *...the crumbling stonework of the derelict church.* `N-UNCOUNT`

stony /'stəʊni/ **stonier, stoniest. 1 Stony** ground is rough and contains a lot of stones. *The steep, stony ground is well drained.* **2** A **stony** expression or attitude does not show any sympathy or friendliness. *He drove us home in stony silence.* `◆◇◇◇◇` `ADJ-GRADED` `ADJ-GRADED`

stood /stʊd/. **Stood** is the past tense and past participle of **stand**.

stooge /stuːdʒ/ **stooges.** If you refer to someone as a **stooge**, you are criticizing them because they are used by someone else to do unpleasant or dishonest tasks. `N-COUNT` `PRAGMATICS`

stool /stuːl/ **stools. 1** A **stool** is a seat with legs but no support for your arms or back. **2 Stools** are the pieces of solid waste matter that are passed out of a person's body through their bowels. `◆◇◇◇◇` `N-COUNT` `N-COUNT` `FORMAL`

stoop /stuːp/ **stoops, stooping, stooped. 1** If you **stoop**, you stand or walk with your shoulders bent forwards. ▶ Also a noun. *He was a tall, thin fellow with a slight stoop.* ◆ **stoop·ing** *...a slender slightly stooping American.* **2** If you **stoop**, you bend your body forwards and downwards. ▶ **Stoop down** or **stoop over** means the same as **stoop**. *Stooping down, he picked up a big stone and hurled it.* **3** If you say that someone **stoops** to doing something, you are criticizing them because they do something wrong or immoral that they would not normally do. *He had not, until recently, stooped to personal abuse... How could anyone stoop so low?* **4** A **stoop** is a small platform at the door of a building, with steps leading up to it. `◆◇◇◇◇` `VERB: V` `N-SING` `ADJ-GRADED` `VERB: V` `PHRASAL VB` `V P` `VERB` `PRAGMATICS` `V to n/-ing` `V adj` `N-COUNT` `AMERICAN`

stop /stɒp/ **stops, stopping, stopped. 1** If you have been doing something and then you **stop** doing it, you no longer do it. *He can't stop thinking about it... Does either of the parties want to stop the fighting?* **2** If you **stop** something happening, you prevent it from happening or continuing. *I think she really would have liked to stop us seeing each other... Motherhood won't stop me from pursuing my acting career.* **3** If you **put a stop to** something you do not like or approve of, you prevent it from happening or continuing. *His daughter should have stood up and put a stop to all these rumours.* **4** If an activity or process **stops**, it is no longer happening. *The rain had stopped... The system overheated and filming had to stop.* **5** If you say that someone will **stop at nothing** to get or achieve something, you are emphasizing that they are very determined about it, and are willing to do things that are extreme, wrong, or dangerous in order to get or achieve it. **6** If you say that someone doesn't **know when to stop**, you mean that they do not con- `◆◆◆◆◆` `VERB` `V -ing` `V n` `Also V` `VERB: V n` `V n -ing` `V n from -ing` `PHRASE` `VERB` `V` `PHRASE` `PRAGMATICS` `PHRASE`

trol their own behaviour very well and so they often annoy or upset other people. **7** If something such as a machine **stops**, it is no longer moving or working. *The clock had stopped at 2.12 a.m... Arnold stopped the engine and got out of the car.* **8** When a moving person or vehicle **stops**, they no longer move and they remain in the same place. *The car failed to stop at an army checkpoint... The event literally stopped the traffic.* **9** If something that is moving comes **to a stop**, it slows down and no longer moves. *He slowed the car almost to a stop.* **10** If you **stop** somewhere on a journey, you stay there for a short while. **11** A **stop** is a time or place at which you stop during a journey. *Mack was driving down from Vermont, with a stop in Boston to pick Sarah up.* **12** A **stop** is a place where buses or trains regularly stop so that people can get on and off. *They waited at a bus stop.* **13** If someone does not **stop** to think or to explain, they continue with what they are doing without taking any time to think about or explain it. *People who lead busy lives have no time to stop and reflect.* **14** If you say that a quality or state **stops** somewhere, you mean that it exists or is true up to that point, but no further. *The cafe owner has put up the required 'no smoking' signs, but thinks his responsibility stops there.* **15** If you **pull out all the stops**, you do everything you can to make something happen or succeed. *New Zealand police vowed yesterday to pull out all the stops to find the killer.* **16** ● **to stop dead:** see **dead**. ● **to stop short of:** see **short**. ● **to stop** someone **in** their **tracks:** see **track**. `V-ERG` `V` `V n` `V-ERG` `V` `V n` `N-SING: to a N` `VERB: V prep/adv` `N-COUNT` `N-COUNT` `VERB: V` `VERB V to-inf` `VERB V adv` `PHRASE` `PHRASE`

stop by. If you **stop by** somewhere, you make a short visit to a person or place. *Perhaps I'll stop by the hospital this afternoon.* `PHRASAL VB` `V P n` `Also V P` `INFORMAL`

stop off. If you **stop off** somewhere, you stop for a short time in the middle of a journey. *The president stopped off in Poland on his way to Munich for the economic summit.* `PHRASAL VB` `V P` `V P prep/adv`

stop up. If you **stop** something **up**, you cover or fill a hole or gap in it. *They stopped up leaks with chewing gum.* `PHRASAL VB` `V n P` `V P noun`

stop·cock /'stɒpkɒk/ **stopcocks.** A **stopcock** is a tap on a pipe, which you turn on to allow something to pass through the pipe or to stop it from passing through. `N-COUNT`

stop·gap /'stɒpgæp/ **stopgaps.** A **stopgap** is something that serves a purpose for a short time, but is replaced as soon as possible. *Even if the bill were approved, it would be no more than a stopgap measure.* `N-COUNT`

,stop-'go. Stop-go is used to describe processes in which inactivity and activity alternate. *...stop-go economic cycles.* `ADJ`

stop·light /'stɒplaɪt/ **stoplights;** also spelled **stop light.** A **stoplight** is a set of coloured lights which controls the flow of traffic on a road. The British term is **traffic light**. `N-COUNT` `AMERICAN`

stop·over /'stɒpəʊvə/ **stopovers.** A **stopover** is a short stay in a place in between parts of a journey. *The Sunday flights will make a stopover in Paris.* `N-COUNT`

stop·page /'stɒpɪdʒ/ **stoppages. 1** When there is a **stoppage**, people stop working because of a disagreement with their employers. **2** In football and some other sports, when there is a **stoppage**, the game stops for a short time, for example because a player is injured. `◆◇◇◇◇` `N-COUNT` `N-COUNT`

stop·per /'stɒpə/ **stoppers.** A **stopper** is a piece of glass, plastic, or cork that fits into the top of a bottle or jar to close it. ● See also **show-stopper**. `N-COUNT`

,stop 'press. Stop press is sometimes printed next to an article in a newspaper to indicate that this is very recent news that was inserted after the rest of the newspaper had been printed.

stop·watch /'stɒpwɒtʃ/ **stopwatches;** also spelled **stop-watch.** A **stopwatch** is a watch with buttons which you press at the beginning and end of an event, so that you can measure exactly how long it takes. `N-COUNT`

stor·age /'stɔːrɪdʒ/. **1** If you refer to the **storage** of ◆◆◇◇◇ N-UNCOUNT something, you mean that it is kept in a particular place until it is needed. *Some of the space will at first be used for storage.* **2 Storage** is the process of N-UNCOUNT storing data in a computer. **3** See also **cold storage**.

store /stɔː/ **stores, storing, stored. 1** A **store** is ◆◆◆◆ a shop. In British English, **store** is used mainly to N-COUNT refer to a large shop selling a variety of goods, but in American English, a **store** can be any shop. ● See also **chain store**, **department store**.

2 When you **store** things, you put them in a container VERB: V n or other place and leave them there until they are V n prep/adv needed. *Store the cookies in an airtight tin.* ▶ **Store** PHRASAL VB **away** means the same as **store**. *He simply stored the* V n P Also V P noun *tapes away.* **3** When you **store** information, you keep VERB: V n it in your memory, in a file, or in a computer. **4** A **store** N-COUNT of things is a supply of them that you keep somewhere until you need them. *...my secret store of chocolate biscuits.* **5** A **store** is a place where things are kept while N-COUNT they are not being used. *...a grain store.* **6** If you have a N-COUNT **store** of facts, jokes, or stories, you know a large number of them. *He possessed a vast store of knowledge.* **7** If something is **in store** for you, it is going to happen PHRASE at some time in the future. *Surprises were also in store for me.* **8** If you **set great store** by something, you PHRASE think that it is extremely important or necessary. *...a* FORMAL *retail group which sets great store by traditional values.*

store away. See **store** 2. PHRASAL VB

store up. If you **store** something **up**, you keep it un- PHRASAL VB til you think that the time is right to use it. *Investors* V n P *were storing up a lot of cash in anticipation of disaster.* V P noun

store·card /'stɔːkɑːd/ **storecards;** also spelled N-COUNT **store card.** A **storecard** is a plastic card that you use BRITISH to buy goods on credit from a particular store or group of stores. The more usual American term is **charge card.**

store·front /'stɔːfrʌnt/ **storefronts.** A **storefront** N-COUNT is the outside part of a shop which faces the street, AMERICAN including the door and windows. The British term is **shop front.**

store·house /'stɔːhaʊs/ **storehouses. 1** A **store-** ◆◇◇◇◇ **house** is a building in which things, usually food, N-COUNT are stored. **2** When a lot of things can be found together in one place, you can refer to this place as a **storehouse** of a particular kind. *This book is a veritable storehouse of information.*

store·keeper /'stɔːkiːpə/ **storekeepers.** A **store-** N-COUNT **keeper** is a shopkeeper. AMERICAN

store·room /'stɔːruːm/ **storerooms.** A **storeroom** N-COUNT is a room in which you keep things until they are needed.

sto·rey /'stɔːri/ **storeys;** spelled **story** in American ◆◇◇◇◇ English. A **storey** of a building is one of its different N-COUNT levels, which is situated above or below other levels. ▶ Also a combining form. *...a modern three-storey* COMB building. ◆ **-storeyed** *The narrow streets were* COMB *lined with two-storeyed houses.*

stork /stɔːk/ **storks.** A **stork** is a large bird with a N-COUNT long beak and long legs, which lives near water.

storm /stɔːm/ **storms, storming, stormed. 1** A ◆◆◆◇◇ **storm** is very bad weather, with heavy rain, strong N-COUNT winds, and often thunder and lightning. **2** If something causes a **storm**, it causes an angry or N-COUNT excited reaction from a large number of people. *The announcement provoked an immediate storm of protest.* **3** A **storm** of applause or laughter is a sudden N-COUNT loud burst of applause or laughter from an audience or other group of people. **4** If you **storm** into or out of a place, you enter or leave VERB it quickly and noisily, because you are angry. *After a* V adv/prep *bit of an argument, he stormed out.* **5** If you **storm**, VERB you say something in a very loud voice, because you V with quote are angry. *'It's a fiasco,' he stormed.* WRITTEN **6** If a place that is being defended **is stormed**, a group VERB: of people attack it, usually in order to get inside it. *The* be V-ed *refugees decided to storm the embassy.* ◆ **storm·ing** V n *...the storming of the Bastille.* N-UNCOUNT: N of n **7** See also **firestorm**.

8 If someone or something **takes** a place **by storm**, PHRASE they are extremely successful in that place. *Kenya's long distance runners have taken the athletics world by storm.* **9** If someone **weathers the storm**, they suc- PHRASE ceed in reaching the end of a very difficult period without much harm or damage. *He insists he will not resign and will weather the storm.* **10** ● **the eye of the storm**: see **eye**.

'storm cloud, storm clouds; also spelled stormcloud. **1 Storm clouds** are the dark clouds N-COUNT which are seen before a storm. **2** You can use **storm** N-COUNT **clouds** to refer to a sign that something very un- FORMAL pleasant is going to happen. *Over the past three weeks, the storm clouds have gathered again over the government.*

'storm trooper, storm troopers; also spelled N-COUNT stormtrooper. **Storm troopers** were members of a force of soldiers in Nazi Germany, who were specially trained to be violent and ruthless.

stormy /'stɔːmi/ **stormier, stormiest. 1** If there ◆◇◇◇◇ is **stormy** weather, there are strong winds and ADJ-GRADED heavy rain. **2 Stormy** seas have very large strong ADJ-GRADED waves because there are strong winds. **3** If you de- ADJ-GRADED scribe a situation as **stormy**, you mean it involves a lot of angry argument or criticism. *Their working relationship was stormy at times.*

sto·ry /'stɔːri/ **stories. 1** A **story** is a description of ◆◆◆◆◆ imaginary people and events, which is written or N-COUNT told in order to entertain. *I shall tell you a story about four little rabbits.* **2** A **story** is a description of N-COUNT an event or something that happened to someone, especially a spoken description of it. *The parents all shared interesting stories about their children.* **3** The N-COUNT **story** of something is a description of all the important things that have happened to it since it began. *...the story of the women's movement in Ireland.* **4** If N-COUNT someone invents a **story**, they give a false explanation or account of something. *He invented some story about a cousin.* **5** A news **story** is a piece of news N-COUNT in a newspaper or in a news broadcast. *Those are some of the top stories in the news.*

6 You say **'but that's another story'** when you have PHRASE mentioned a subject that you are not going to talk PRAGMATICS about or explain in detail. *I'd met him at a dance I'd* SPOKEN *gone to on my own. But that's another story.* **7** You use PHRASE **to cut a long story short** to indicate that you are going PRAGMATICS to state the final result of an event and not give any SPOKEN, more details. In American English, you say **to make a** BRITISH **long story short.** *To cut a long story short, I ended up as managing director.* **8** You use **a different story** to PHRASE refer to a situation, usually a bad one, which exists in PRAGMATICS one set of circumstances when you have mentioned that it does not exist in another set of circumstances. *Where Marcella lives, the rents are fairly cheap, but a little further north it's a different story.*

9 If you say it's **the same old story** or **the old story**, PHRASE you mean that something unpleasant or undesirable PRAGMATICS seems to happen again and again. *It's the same old story. They want one person to do three people's jobs.* **10** If you say that something is **only part of the story** PHRASE or is **not the whole story**, you mean that the explana- PRAGMATICS tion or information given is not enough for a situation to be fully understood. *This may be true but it is only part of the story.* **11** If someone tells you their **side of** PHRASE **the story**, they tell you why they behaved in a particular way and why they think they were right, when other people think that person behaved wrongly. *He had already made up his mind before even hearing her side of the story.* **12** See also **cock-and-bull story, short story, sob story, storey, success story, tall story.**

story·book /'stɔːrɪbʊk/ **storybooks. 1** A **story-** N-COUNT **book** is a book of stories for children. **2** A **storybook** ADJ: ADJ n relationship, situation, or life is one that is perfect and ends happily, just as many fairy stories do.

story·line /'stɔːrɪlaɪn/ **storylines.** The **storyline** of ◆◇◇◇◇ a book, film, or play is its story and the way in N-COUNT which it develops. *The surprise twists in the storyline are the film's greatest strength.*

story·teller /'stɔːrɪtelə/ **storytellers;** also spelled ◆◇◇◇◇ **story-teller.** A **storyteller** is someone who tells or N-COUNT

S

writes stories. ◆ **story·telling** ...*mothers with a gift for bedtime storytelling.* N-UNCOUNT

stout /staʊt/ **stouter, stoutest; stouts. 1** A stout person is rather fat. ...*a short, stout man with a thick mustache.* **2** Stout shoes, branches, or other objects are thick and strong. **3** If you use **stout** to describe someone's actions, attitudes, or beliefs, you approve of them because they are strong and determined. *He produced a stout defence of the car business.* ◆ **stout·ly** *She stoutly defended her husband during the trial.* **4** Stout is a strong darkcoloured beer. ◆◇◇◇◇ ADJ-GRADED ADJ-GRADED ADJ-GRADED PRAGMATICS ADV-GRADED N-VAR BRITISH

stove /stəʊv/ **stoves.** A **stove** is an apparatus which provides heat, either for cooking or for heating a room. *She put the kettle on the gas stove.* ◆◇◇◇◇ N-COUNT

stow /stəʊ/ **stows, stowing, stowed.** If you **stow** something somewhere, you carefully put it there until it is needed. *I helped her stow her bags in the boot of the car.* ◆◇◇◇◇ VERB V n prep/adv Also V n

stow away. If someone **stows away,** they hide in a ship, aeroplane, or other vehicle in order to make the journey secretly or without paying the fare. PHRASAL VB V P

stow·age /'stəʊɪdʒ/. **Stowage** is the space that is available for stowing things on a ship or aeroplane. N-UNCOUNT

stow·away /'stəʊəweɪ/ **stowaways.** A **stowaway** is a person who hides in a ship, aeroplane, or other vehicle in order to make a journey secretly or without paying the fare. N-COUNT

strad·dle /'strædəl/ **straddles, straddling, straddled. 1** If you **straddle** something, you put or have one leg on either side of it. *He looked at her with a grin and sat down, straddling the chair.* **2** If something such as a bridge or town **straddles** a river, road, or border, it stretches across it or exists on both sides of it. **3** Someone or something that **straddles** different periods, groups, or fields of activity exists in, belongs to, or takes elements from them all. *He straddles two cultures, having been brought up in Britain and later converted to Islam.* ◆◇◇◇ VERB V n VERB: V n VERB V n

strafe /streɪf/ **strafes, strafing, strafed.** To **strafe** an enemy means to attack them by scattering bombs or bullets on them from a low-flying aircraft. VERB: V n

strag·gle /'strægəl/ **straggles, straggling, straggled. 1** If people **straggle** somewhere, they move there slowly, in small groups with large, irregular gaps between them. *They came straggling up the cliff road.* **2** When things **straggle** over an area, they cover it in an uneven or untidy way. *Her grey hair straggled in wisps about her face.* ◆ **strag·gly** /'strægəli/. *The yard held a few straggly bushes.* VERB V prep/adv VERB V prep ADJ-GRADED

strag·gler /'strægələ/ **stragglers.** The **stragglers** are the people in a group who are moving more slowly or making less progress than the others. N-COUNT

straight /streɪt/ **straighter, straightest; straights. 1** A **straight** line or edge continues in the same direction and does not bend or curve. *Keep the boat in a straight line... His teeth were perfectly straight.* ▶ Also an adverb. *Turn right and just basically walk straight.* **2** Straight hair has no curls or waves in it. **3** You use **straight** to indicate that the way from one place to another is very direct, with no changes of direction. *He finished his conversation and stood up, looking straight at me... Straight ahead were the low cabins of the motel.* **4** On a racetrack, a **straight** is a section of the track that is straight, rather than curved. The usual American word is **stretch**. **5** If you go **straight** to a place, you go there immediately. *We went straight to the experts for advice... We'll go to a meeting in Birmingham and come straight back.* **6** Straight means following one after the other without any interruption. *They'd won 12 straight games before they lost.* ▶ Also an adverb. *He called from Weddington, having been there for 31 hours straight.* **7** A **straight** choice or a **straight** fight involves only two people or things. *It's a straight choice between low-paid jobs and no jobs.* **8** If you give someone a **straight** answer, you speak honestly and frankly to them. *Can't you give me a straight answer, dear?* ▶ Also an adverb. *I lost my tem-* ◆◆◆◇ ADJ-GRADED ADV ADJ-GRADED ADV: ADV prep/adv N-COUNT BRITISH ADV: ADV prep/adv ADJ: ADJ n ADV: n ADV ADJ: ADJ n ADJ-GRADED: ADJ n ADV-GRADED:

per and told him straight that I hadn't been looking for any job. **9** If you **get** something **straight,** you make sure that you understand it properly or that someone else does. *You need to get your facts straight... Let's get things straight. I didn't lunch with her.* ADV after v PHRASE SPOKEN

10 If you describe someone as **straight,** you mean that they are normal and conventional, for example in their opinions and in the way they live. **11** If you describe someone as **straight,** you mean that they are heterosexual rather than homosexual. ▶ Also a noun. *...a standard of sexual conduct that applies equally to gays and straights.* **12** If a criminal **is going straight,** he or she is no longer involved in crime. **13** If something keeps people **on the straight and narrow,** it helps to keep them living an honest or healthy life. **14** See also **home straight.** ● **a straight face:** see **face.** ● **set the record straight:** see **record.** ADJ-GRADED ADJ INFORMAL N-COUNT PHRASE PHRASE

straight a·way; also spelled **straightaway.** If you do something **straight away,** you do it immediately and without delay. ◆◇◇◇ ADV: ADV with v

straight·en /'streɪtən/ **straightens, straightening, straightened. 1** If you **straighten** something, you make it tidy or put it in its proper position. *She sipped her coffee and straightened a picture on the wall.* **2** If you are standing in a relaxed or slightly bent position and then you **straighten,** you make your back or body straight and upright. ▶ **Straighten up** means the same as **straighten.** *He straightened up and slipped his hands in his pockets.* **3** If you **straighten** something, it becomes straight. *Straighten both legs until they are fully extended.* ▶ **Straighten out** means the same as **straighten.** *The road twisted its way up the mountain then straightened out.* ◆◇◇◇ VERB V n VERB: V PHRASAL VB V-ERG Also V PHRASAL VB ERG: V P noun V P

straighten out. 1 If you **straighten out** a confused situation, you succeed in getting it organized and tidied up. *He would make an appointment with him to straighten out a couple of things.* **2** See **straighten** 3. PHRASAL VB V P noun

straighten up. See **straighten** 2. PHRASAL VB

straight-'faced. A **straight-faced** person appears not to be amused in a funny situation. '*Whatever gives you that idea?' she replied straight-faced.* ADJ-GRADED

straight·forward /ˌstreɪt'fɔːwəd/. **1** If something is **straightforward,** it is not complicated to do or understand. *Disposable nappies are fairly straightforward to put on... The question seemed straightforward enough.* ◆ **straight·forward·ly** *Acid rain is not straightforwardly attributable to the burning of coal.* **2** If you use **straightforward** to describe a person or their behaviour, you approve of them because they are honest and direct, and do not try to hide their feelings. ◆ **straightforwardly** *His daughter says straightforwardly that he was not good enough.* ◆◆◇◇ ADJ-GRADED ADV ADJ-GRADED PRAGMATICS ADV-GRADED

strain /streɪn/ **strains, straining, strained. 1** If **strain** is put on an organization or system, it has to do more than it is able to do. *The prison service is already under considerable strain.* **2** To **strain** something means to make it do more than it is able to do. *The volume of scheduled flights is straining the air traffic control system.* **3** Strain is a state of worry and tension caused by a difficult situation. *She was tired and under great strain. ...the stresses and strains of a busy and demanding career.* **4** If you say that a situation is **a strain,** you mean that it makes you worried and tense. *I sometimes find it a strain to be responsible for the mortgage.* **5** Strain is a force that pushes, pulls, or stretches something in a way that may damage it. *You need to learn how to lift things properly with the least strain on your back.* **6** Strain is an injury to a muscle in your body, caused by using it too much or twisting it awkwardly. *Avoid muscle strain by warming up with slow jogging.* **7** If you **strain** a muscle, you injure it by using it too much or twisting it awkwardly. *He strained his back during a practice session.* **8** If you **strain** to do something, you make a great effort to do it when it is difficult to do. *Several thousand supporters strained to catch a glimpse of the new president... They strained their eyes, but saw nothing.* ◆◆◇◇ N-VAR VERB V n N-UNCOUNT: also N in pl N-SING: a N N-UNCOUNT: also a N N-VAR VERB V n VERB V to-inf V n

9 When you **strain** food, you separate the liquid part of it from the solid parts by sieving it. ♦ **strain·er**, **strainers**. A strainer is a small sieve for straining food. ...*a tea strainer.* VERB: V n / N-COUNT

10 You can use **strain** to refer to a particular quality in someone's character, remarks, or work. *There was a strain of bitterness in his voice.* N-SING: with supp **11** A **strain** of a germ, plant, or other organism is a particular type of it. N-COUNT **12** If you hear the **strains** of music, you hear music being played. N-PLURAL: WRITTEN

13 See also **eye strain**, **repetitive strain injury**.

strained /streɪnd/. **1** If someone's appearance, voice, or behaviour is **strained**, they seem worried and nervous. *His laughter seemed a little strained.* ♦◇◇◇ ADJ-GRADED **2** If relations between people are **strained**, their relationship has become difficult because they no longer like or trust each other. ADJ-GRADED

strait /streɪt/ **straits**. **1** You can refer to a narrow strip of sea which joins two large areas of sea as a **strait** or the **straits**. ♦◇◇◇ N-COUNT **2** If someone is in dire or desperate **straits**, they are in a very difficult situation, usually because they do not have much money. *The company's closure has left many small businessmen in desperate financial straits.* N-PLURAL: adj N

strait·ened /ˈstreɪtənd/. If someone is living in **straitened** circumstances, they do not have as much money as they used to, and are finding it very hard to buy or pay for everything that they need. ADJ-GRADED FORMAL

strait·jacket /ˈstreɪtdʒækɪt/ **straitjackets**. **1** A straitjacket is a special jacket used to tie the arms of a violent person tightly around their body. N-COUNT **2** If you describe an idea or a situation as a **straitjacket**, you disapprove of it because you think that it is very limited and restricting. ...*the ideological straitjacket of Marxism-Leninism.* N-COUNT PRAGMATICS

strait-'laced; also spelled **straight-laced** or **straitlaced**. If you describe someone as **strait-laced**, you disapprove of them because they have a very strict or narrow-minded attitude towards questions of morality. ADJ-GRADED PRAGMATICS

strand /strænd/ **strands, stranding, stranded**. **1** A **strand** of something such as hair, wire, or thread is a single thin piece of it. *She tried to blow a gray strand of hair from her eyes.* ♦♦◇◇ N-COUNT **2** A **strand** of a plan or theory is a part of it. *He's trying to bring together various strands of radical philosophic thought.* N-COUNT **3** If you are **stranded**, you are prevented from leaving a place, for example because of bad weather. *The airport had to be closed, stranding tourists.* VERB: be V-ed V n

strange /streɪndʒ/ **stranger, strangest**. **1** Something that is **strange** is unusual or unexpected, and makes you feel slightly uneasy or afraid. *There was something strange about the flickering blue light... It was so strange to see a policeman lying down, without his helmet... It's strange how things turn out.* ♦♦♦◇ ADJ-GRADED ♦ **strange·ly** *The hut suddenly seemed strangely silent... Strangely, the race didn't start until 8.15pm.* ADV-GRADED ♦ **strange·ness** ...*the breathy strangeness of the music.* N-UNCOUNT **2** A **strange** place is one that you have never been to before. A **strange** person is someone you have never met before. *I ended up alone in a strange city.* ADJ: ADJ n **3** If you feel **strange**, you have an unpleasant or uncomfortable feeling, either physical or emotional. ADJ-GRADED **4** See also **stranger**.

strang·er /ˈstreɪndʒə/ **strangers**. **1** A stranger is someone you have never met before or do not know at all. If two people are **strangers**, they have never met or do not know each other at all. *Telling a complete stranger about your life is difficult.* ♦♦◇◇ N-COUNT **2** If you are a **stranger** in a place, you do not know the place at all. N-COUNT **3** If you are a **stranger** to something, you have had no experience of it or do not understand it. *He is no stranger to controversy.* N-COUNT **4** See also **stranger**.

stran·gle /ˈstræŋgəl/ **strangles, strangling, strangled**. **1** To **strangle** someone means to kill them by squeezing their throat tightly so that they are unable to breathe. ♦◇◇◇ VERB: V n ♦ **stran·gu·la·tion** /ˌstræŋgjuˈleɪʃən/. *He is charged with the strangulation of two students.* ♦ **stran·gler** /ˈstræŋglə/ N-UNCOUNT / N-COUNT

stranglers ...*a strangler who's terrorising the town.* **2** To **strangle** something means to prevent it from succeeding or developing. *The country's economic plight is strangling its scientific institutions.* VERB V n

stran·gled /ˈstræŋgəld/. A **strangled** voice or cry sounds unclear and muffled. ADJ: ADJ n

strangle·hold /ˈstræŋgəlhəʊld/. To have a **stranglehold** on something means to have control over it and prevent it from being free or from developing. *To succeed, the new paper will need to break the stranglehold of the printing unions.* ♦◇◇◇ N-SING

stran·gu·la·tion. See **strangle**.

strap /stræp/ **straps, strapping, strapped**. **1** A **strap** is a narrow piece of leather, cloth, or other material. Straps are used to carry things, fasten things together, or to hold a piece of clothing in place. *Nancy gripped the strap of her beach bag... I undid my watch strap.* ♦♦◇◇ N-COUNT **2** If you **strap** something somewhere, you fasten it there with a strap. *I saw him strap on his pink cycling helmet.* VERB: V n prep V n with on/ in/down

strap·less /ˈstræpləs/. A **strapless** dress or bra does not have the usual narrow bands of material over the shoulders. ADJ

strapped /stræpt/. If someone is **strapped** for money, they do not have enough money to buy or pay for the things they want or need. *My husband and I are really strapped for cash.* ● See also **cash-strapped**. ♦◇◇◇ ADJ-GRADED

strap·ping /ˈstræpɪŋ/. If you describe someone as **strapping**, you mean that they are tall, strong, and healthy-looking. ADJ

stra·ta /ˈstrɑːtə, AM ˈstreɪtə/. **Strata** is the plural of **stratum**.

strata·gem /ˈstrætədʒəm/ **stratagems**. A **stratagem** is a plan that is intended to achieve a particular effect, often by deceiving people. N-COUNT FORMAL

stra·tegic /strəˈtiːdʒɪk/. **1** Strategic means relating to the most important, general aspects of something such as a military operation or political policy. ...*a strategic plan for reducing the rate of infant mortality.* ♦◇◇◇ ADJ ♦ **stra·tegi·cal·ly** /strəˈtiːdʒɪkli/. ...*strategically important roads, bridges and buildings.* ADV **2** Strategic weapons are very powerful, long-range weapons, and the decision to use them can be made only by a political leader. ...*strategic nuclear weapons.* ADJ **3** If you put something in a **strategic** position, you place it cleverly in a position where it will be most useful or have the most effect. ♦ **strategically** ...*a strategically placed chair.* ADJ / ADV

strat·egist /ˈstrætədʒɪst/ **strategists**. A strategist is someone who is skilled in planning the best way to gain an advantage or to achieve success, especially in war. ...*a clever political strategist.* ♦◇◇◇ N-COUNT

strat·egy /ˈstrætədʒi/ **strategies**. **1** A strategy is a general plan or set of plans intended to achieve something, especially over a long period. *The Labour Party launched its new strategy for industry.* ♦♦♦◇ N-VAR **2** Strategy is the art of planning the best way to gain an advantage or achieve success, especially in war. N-UNCOUNT

strati·fi·ca·tion /ˌstrætɪfɪˈkeɪʃən/. **Stratification** is the division of something, especially society, into different classes or layers. N-UNCOUNT

strati·fied /ˈstrætɪfaɪd/. A **stratified** society is one that is divided into different classes or social layers. ADJ-GRADED FORMAL

strato·sphere /ˈstrætəsfɪə/. **1** The stratosphere is the layer of the earth's atmosphere which lies between 10 and 50 kilometres above the earth. ♦◇◇◇ N-SING: the N ♦ **strato·spher·ic** /ˌstrætəˈsferɪk, AM -ˈsfɪrɪk/. ...*stratospheric ozone.* ADJ **2** If you say that someone or something climbs or is sent into the **stratosphere**, you mean that they reach a very high level. *This was enough to launch their careers into the stratosphere.* N-SING: the N JOURNALISM

stra·tum /ˈstrɑːtəm, AM ˈstreɪtəm/ **strata**. **1** A **stratum** of society is a group of people in it who are similar in their education, income, or social status. ♦◇◇◇ N-COUNT FORMAL **2** The **strata** in the earth's crust are the different layers of rock. N-COUNT TECHNICAL

straw /strɔː/ **straws. 1 Straw** consists of the dried, yellowish stalks from crops such as wheat or barley. *...a wide-brimmed straw hat.* ◆◆◇◇◇ N-UNCOUNT

2 A **straw** is a thin tube of paper or plastic, which you use to suck a drink into your mouth. N-COUNT

3 If you **are clutching at straws**, you are trying unusual or extreme ideas or methods because other ideas or methods have failed. PHRASE **4** If an event is **the last straw**, it is the latest in a series of unpleasant or undesirable events, and makes you feel that you cannot tolerate a situation any longer. *For him the Church's decision to allow the ordination of women had been the last straw.* PHRASE **5** If you say that an incident or piece of news is a **straw in the wind**, you mean that it gives an indication of what might happen in the future. *The latest straw in the wind is a pick-up in sales among the nation's retail giants.* PHRASE

straw·berry /ˈstrɔːbri, AM -beri/ **strawberries.** A **strawberry** is a small red fruit which is soft and juicy and has tiny yellow seeds on its skin. See picture headed **fruit.** ◆◆◇◇◇ N-COUNT

,**strawberry 'blonde, strawberry blondes;** also spelled **strawberry blond. 1 Strawberry blonde** hair is reddish blonde. ADJ **2** A **strawberry blonde** is a person, especially a woman, who has strawberry blonde hair. N-COUNT

,**straw 'poll, straw polls.** A **straw poll** is the unofficial questioning of a group of people to find out their opinion about something. N-COUNT

stray /streɪ/ **strays, straying, strayed. 1** If someone **strays** somewhere, they wander away from where they are supposed to be. *Tourists often get lost and stray into dangerous areas.* ◆◆◇◇◇ VERB V prep/adv Also V **2** A **stray** dog or cat has wandered away from its owner's home. ► Also a noun. *The dog was a stray which had been adopted.* ADJ: ADJ n N-COUNT **3** If your mind or your eyes **stray**, you do not concentrate on or look at one particular subject, but start thinking about or looking at other things. *She could not keep her eyes from straying towards him.* VERB V **4** You use **stray** to describe something that exists separated from other similar things. *She shrugged a stray lock of hair out of her eyes.* ADJ: ADJ n

streak /striːk/ **streaks, streaking, streaked. 1** A **streak** is a long stripe or mark on a surface which contrasts with the surface because it is a different colour. *There are these dark streaks on the surface of the moon.* ◆◆◇◇◇ N-COUNT **2** If something **streaks** a surface, it makes long stripes or marks on the surface. *Rain had begun to streak the window-panes... His face was pale and streaked with dirt.* ♦ **-streaked** *Her bare feet were dirt-streaked and cracked with cold.* VERB V n be V-ed with n COMB **3** If someone has a **streak** of a particular type of behaviour, they sometimes behave in that way. *We're both alike - there is a streak of madness in us both.* N-COUNT **4** A winning **streak** or a lucky **streak** is a continuous series of successes, for example in gambling or sport. A losing **streak** or an unlucky **streak** is a series of failures or losses. N-COUNT: adj N **5** If something or someone **streaks** somewhere, they move there very quickly. *A meteorite streaked across the sky.* VERB V prep/adv

streaky /ˈstriːki/ **streakier, streakiest.** Something that is **streaky** is marked with long stripes that are a different colour to the rest of it. *She has streaky fair hair and blue eyes.* ADJ-GRADED

'**streaky bacon. Streaky bacon** is bacon which has strips of fat between strips of meat. N-UNCOUNT BRITISH

stream /striːm/ **streams, streaming, streamed. 1** A **stream** is a small narrow river. *...a mountain stream.* ◆◆◆◇◇ N-COUNT **2** A **stream** of things is a large number of them occurring one after another. *...a never-ending stream of jokes... We had a constant stream of visitors.* N-COUNT **3** A **stream** of smoke, air, or liquid is a narrow moving mass of it. *He breathed out a stream of cigarette smoke.* N-COUNT **4** If a liquid **streams** somewhere, it flows or comes out in large amounts. *Tears streamed down their faces.* VERB V prep/adv **5** If your eyes **are streaming**, liquid is coming from them, VERB V

for example because you have a cold. You can also say that your nose **is streaming.** *Her eyes were streaming now from the wind.* **6** If people or vehicles **stream** somewhere, they move there quickly and in large numbers. *Refugees have been streaming into Travnik for months... The traffic streamed past him.* ► A **stream** of vehicles or people is a long moving line of them. VERB V prep/adv N-COUNT **7** When light **streams** into or out of a place, it shines strongly into or out of it. *Sunlight was streaming into the courtyard.* VERB V prep/adv **8** If something such as a flag or someone's hair **streams** in the wind, it is blown so that it is almost horizontal. *She was wearing a flimsy pink dress that streamed out behind her.* VERB V prep/adv Also V **9** In a school, a **stream** is a group of children of the same age and ability who are taught together. *...which pupils are to move into the top streams.* N-COUNT: with supp BRITISH **10** To **stream** pupils means to divide them into groups according to their ability. *He advocates streaming children, and educating them according to their needs.* ♦ **stream·ing** *There's no streaming at St Benedict's school.* VERB V n Also V n BRITISH N-UNCOUNT **11** See also **jet stream.**

stream·er /ˈstriːmə/ **streamers. Streamers** are long rolls of coloured paper used for decorating rooms at parties. N-COUNT

stream·line /ˈstriːmlaɪn/ **streamlines, streamlining, streamlined.** To **streamline** an organization or process means to make it more efficient by removing unnecessary parts of it; used showing approval. *Things should be better now that they have streamlined application procedures.* ♦ **stream·lined** *...streamlined companies using cheap freelance staff.* ◆◇◇◇◇ VERB PRAGMATICS V n ADJ-GRADED

stream·lined /ˈstriːmlaɪnd/. A **streamlined** vehicle, animal, or object has a shape that allows it to move quickly or efficiently through air or water. ◆◇◇◇◇ ADJ-GRADED

,**stream of con'sciousness, streams of consciousness;** also spelled **stream-of-consciousness.** If you describe what someone writes or says as a **stream of consciousness,** you mean that it expresses their thoughts as they occur, rather than in a structured way. N-VAR FORMAL

street /striːt/ **streets. 1** A **street** is a road in a town or village, usually with houses along it. *...a small, quaint town with narrow streets.* ◆◆◆◆◇ N-COUNT **2** You can use **street** or **streets** when talking about activities that happen out of doors in a town rather than inside a building. *Changing money on the street is illegal – always use a bank.* N-COUNT **3** If someone is **streets ahead** of you, they are much better at something than you are. *He was streets ahead of the other contestants.* PHRASE BRITISH **4** If you talk about **the man in the street** or **the man or woman in the street,** you mean ordinary people in general. PHRASE **5** If a job or activity is **up your street,** it is the kind of job or activity that you are very interested in. *She loved it, this was just up her street.* PHRASE **6** See also **back street, Downing Street, Fleet Street, high street, Wall Street.**

street·car /ˈstriːtkɑː/ **streetcars.** A **streetcar** is an electric vehicle for carrying people which travels on rails in the streets of a town. The British word is **tram.** N-COUNT AMERICAN

'**street cred;** also spelled **street-cred.** If someone says that you have **street cred,** they mean that ordinary young people would approve of you and consider you to be part of their culture, usually because you share their sense of fashion or their views. N-UNCOUNT PRAGMATICS INFORMAL, BRITISH

,**street credi'bility. Street credibility** is the same as **street cred.** N-UNCOUNT BRITISH

street·lamp /ˈstriːtlæmp/ **streetlamps;** also spelled **street-lamp.** A **streetlamp** is the same as a **streetlight.** N-COUNT

street·light /ˈstriːtlaɪt/ **streetlights;** also spelled **street light.** A **streetlight** is a tall post with a light at the top, which stands by the side of a road to light it up, usually in a town. N-COUNT

,**street 'smart;** also spelled **street-smart.** Someone who is **street smart** knows how to deal with intimidating people or dangerous situations, especially in ADJ-GRADED AMERICAN, INFORMAL

big cities. *He is street smart and is not afraid of this neighborhood.*

'street value. The **street value** of a drug is the price that is paid for it when it is sold illegally to drug users.   N-SING   JOURNALISM

street·wise /'striːtwaɪz/. Someone who is **street-wise** knows how to deal with difficult or dangerous situations, especially in big cities.   ADJ-GRADED   INFORMAL

strength /streŋθ/ **strengths. 1** Your **strength** is the physical energy that you have, which gives you the ability to perform various actions, such as lifting or moving things. *He threw it forward with all his strength... You don't need strength to take part in this sport.* **2** Someone's **strength** in a difficult situation is their confidence or courage. *Something gave me the strength to overcome the difficulty... You need strength of mind to stand up for yourself.* **3** Someone's **strengths** are the qualities and abilities that they have which are an advantage to them, or which make them successful. *Take into account your own strengths and weaknesses... Organisation is the strength of any good army.* **4** If a person or organization **goes from strength to strength**, they become more and more successful or confident. *A decade later, the company has gone from strength to strength.* **5** The **strength** of an object or material is its ability to be treated roughly, or to support or carry heavy weights, without being damaged or destroyed. *He checked the strength of the cables.* **6** If you refer to the **strength** of a currency, economy, or industry, you mean that its value or productivity is steady or increasing. *...the long-term competitive strength of the American economy.* **7** The **strength** of a person, organization, or country is the power or influence that they have. *...the military, economic, and political strength of the Soviet Union.* **8** If you refer to the **strength** of a feeling, opinion, or belief, you are talking about how deeply it is felt or believed by people, or how much they are influenced by it. *He was surprised at the strength of his own feeling. ...the strength of his public support.* **9** The **strength** of a wind, current, or other force is its power or speed. *A tropical storm is gaining strength in the eastern Atlantic.* **10** The **strength** of a drink, chemical, or drug is the amount of the particular substance in it that gives it its particular effect. *It is very alcoholic, sometimes near the strength of port.* **11** You can talk about the **strength** of a flavour, smell, colour, sound, or light to describe how intense or easily noticed it is. *The wine has lots of strength of flavour.* **12** The **strength** of a group of people is the total number of people in it. *...elite forces, comprising about one-tenth of the strength of the army.* **13** If a team or army is at **full strength**, all the members that it needs or usually has are present. *He needed more time to bring US forces there up to full strength.* **14** If a group turns out **in strength**, they arrive in large numbers. *Security forces have been out in strength.* **15** If an army or team is **under strength** or **below strength**, it does not have all the members that it needs or usually has. **16** If one thing is done **on the strength of** another, it is done because of the influence of that other thing. *On the strength on those grades, he won a scholarship to Syracuse University.*
  ◆◆◆◇   N-UNCOUNT (1)
  N-UNCOUNT: also a N (2)
  N-VAR (3)
  PHRASE (4)
  N-UNCOUNT: also N in pl (5)
  N-UNCOUNT (6)
  N-UNCOUNT: also N in pl (7)
  N-UNCOUNT (8)
  N-UNCOUNT: also N in pl (9)
  N-UNCOUNT: also N in pl (10)
  N-UNCOUNT: also N in pl (11)
  N-UNCOUNT: also N in pl (12)
  PHRASE (13)
  PHRASE (14)
  PHRASE (15)
  PHRASE (16)

strength·en /'streŋθən/ **strengthens, strengthening, strengthened. 1** If something **strengthens** a person or group or if they **strengthen** their position, they become more powerful and secure, or more likely to succeed. *He hoped to strengthen the position of the sciences in the leading universities.* **2** If something **strengthens** a case or argument, it supports it by providing more reasons or evidence for it. *...research which might have strengthened his own arguments.* **3** If a currency, economy, or industry **strengthens**, or if something **strengthens** it, it increases in value or becomes more productive. *If the Government wants to save the Pound it should start by strengthening the British economy.* **4** If a government **strengthens** laws or measures or if they
  ◆◆◇◇   VERB V n (1)
  VERB V n (2)
  V-ERG: V (3)
  V-ERG V n V (4)

strengthen, they are made more severe. *Community leaders want to strengthen controls at external frontiers... Because of the war, security procedures have strengthened.* **5** If something **strengthens** you or **strengthens** your resolve or character, it makes you more confident and determined. *Any experience can teach and strengthen you, but particularly the more difficult ones.* **6** If something **strengthens** a relationship or bond, or if it **strengthens**, it becomes closer and more likely to last for a long time. *His visit is intended to strengthen ties between the two countries.* **7** If something **strengthens** an impression, feeling, or belief, or if it **strengthens**, it affects people more powerfully or affects more people. *His speech strengthens the impression he is the main power in the organization.* **8** If something **strengthens** your body or a part of your body, it makes it healthier, often in such a way that you can move or carry heavier things. *Cycling is good exercise. It strengthens all the muscles of the body.* **9** If something **strengthens** an object or structure, it makes it able to be treated roughly or able to support heavy weights, without being damaged or destroyed. *The builders will have to strengthen the existing joists with additional timber.* **10** If the wind, current, or other force **strengthens**, it becomes faster or more powerful.
  VERB V n (5)
  V-ERG V n Also V (6)
  V-ERG V n Also V (7)
  VERB V n (8)
  VERB V n (9)
  VERB: V (10)

strenu·ous /'strenjʊəs/. A **strenuous** activity or action involves a lot of energy or effort. *Avoid strenuous exercise in the evening... Strenuous efforts had been made to improve conditions in the jail.* ♦ **strenu·ous·ly** *Exercising too much or too strenuously is just as bad as not doing it at all.*
  ◆◇◇◇   ADJ-GRADED
  ADV-GRADED: ADV with v

stress /stres/ **stresses, stressing, stressed. 1** If you **stress** a point in a discussion, you put extra emphasis on it because you think it is important. *The spokesman stressed that the measures did not amount to an overall ban... China's leaders have stressed the need for increased co-operation between Third World countries.* ▶ Also a noun. *Japanese car makers are laying ever more stress on European sales.* **2** If you feel under **stress**, you feel worried and tense because of difficulties in your life. *Katy could think clearly when not under stress. ...a wide range of stress-related problems.* **3** **Stresses** are strong physical pressures applied to an object. *Earthquakes happen when stresses in rock are suddenly released as the rocks fracture.* **4** If you **stress** a word or part of a word when you say it, you put emphasis on it so that it sounds slightly louder. ▶ Also a noun. *...the misplaced stress on the first syllable of this last word.*
  ◆◆◆◇   VERB V that V n Also V with quote (1)
  N-VAR: N on n (1)
  N-VAR (2)
  N-VAR (3)
  VERB: V n (4)
  N-VAR (4)

stressed /strest/. **1** If you are **stressed**, you feel tension and anxiety because of difficulties in your life. *Work out what situations or people make you feel stressed.* **2** A **stressed** object is affected by strong physical pressure which has been applied to it. *...stressed metal.* **3** If a word or part of a word is **stressed**, it is pronounced with emphasis.
  ◆◇◇◇   ADJ-GRADED (1)
  ADJ: ADJ n TECHNICAL (2)
  ADJ (3)

stressed 'out. If someone is **stressed out**, they are very tense and anxious because of difficulties in their lives.
  ADJ-GRADED INFORMAL

stress·ful /'stresfʊl/. If a situation or experience is **stressful**, it causes the person involved to feel stress. *I think I've got one of the most stressful jobs there is.*
  ◆◇◇◇   ADJ-GRADED

stretch /stretʃ/ **stretches, stretching, stretched. 1** Something that **stretches** over an area or distance covers or exists in the whole of that area or distance. *The procession stretched for several miles. ...an artificial reef stretching the length of the coast.* **2** A **stretch** of road, water, or land is a length or area of it. *...a long stretch of beach with fine white sand.* **3** When you **stretch**, you put your arms or legs out straight and tighten your muscles. *He yawned and stretched... Try stretching your legs and pulling your toes upwards.* ▶ Also a noun. *...slow stretches.* ♦ **stretch·ing** *Make sure no awkward stretching is required.* **4** If you are **at full stretch**, your arm is straight and extended as far as possible, usually be-
  ◆◆◆◇◇   VB: no cont V prep/adv (1)
  N-COUNT (2)
  VERB V V n (3)
  N-COUNT (3)
  N-UNCOUNT (3)
  PHRASE (4)

cause you are trying to reach something that is almost too far away. **5** If you **stretch** your **legs**, you go for a short walk, usually after you have been sitting down for a long time. **6** A **stretch** of time is a period of time. *...an 18-month stretch in the army... He would study for eight to ten hours at a stretch.* **7** If an event or activity **stretches** or **is stretched** into a further period of time, it continues into that period, which is later than expected. *...as anti-abortion protests stretched into their second week.* **8** If something **stretches** from one time to another, it begins at the first time and ends at the second, which is longer than expected. *...a working day that stretches from seven in the morning to eight at night.* **9** If a group of things **stretch** from one type of thing to another, the group includes a wide range of things. *...a trading empire, with interests that stretched from chemicals to sugar.* **10** When something soft or elastic **stretches** or **is stretched**, it becomes longer or bigger as well as thinner, usually because it is pulled. *The cables are designed not to stretch.* **11** **Stretch** fabric is soft and elastic and stretches easily. *....stretch cotton swimsuits.* **12** If you **stretch** an amount of something or if it **stretches**, you make it last longer than it usually would by being careful and not wasting any of it. *They're used to stretching their budgets.* **13** If your resources can **stretch** to something, you can just afford to do it. *If your pocket can stretch to it, do get some good advice.* **14** If something **stretches** your money or resources, it uses them up so you have hardly enough for your needs. *The drought there is stretching American resources.* ♦ **stretched** *...the company's stretched finances.* **15** If you say that a job or task **stretches** you, you mean that you like it because it makes you work hard and use all your energy and skills so that you do not become bored or achieve less than you should. **16** If you are **at full stretch**, you are using the maximum amount of effort or energy. *Everyone would be working at full stretch.* **17** If you say that something is not true or possible **by any stretch of the imagination**, you are emphasizing that it is completely untrue or absolutely impossible. *Her husband was not a womaniser by any stretch of the imagination.* **18** If you **stretch a point**, you describe something in a way which is not accurate, although it may be partly true. *It is stretching a point to call this censorship.* **19** • **home stretch**: see **home straight**.

stretch out. 1 If you **stretch out** or **stretch yourself out**, you lie with your legs and body in a straight line. *The jacuzzi was too small to stretch out in.* **2** If you **stretch out** a part of your body, you hold it out straight. *He was about to stretch out his hand to grab me.*

stretch·er /ˈstretʃə/ **stretchers; stretchered.** **1** A **stretcher** is a long piece of canvas with a pole along each side, which is used to carry an injured or sick person. **2** If someone **is stretchered** somewhere, they are carried there on a stretcher. *I was close to by as Lester was quickly stretchered into the ambulance.*

'stretch marks. Stretch marks are lines or marks on someone's skin caused by the skin stretching after the person's weight has changed rapidly.

stretchy /ˈstretʃi/ **stretchier, stretchiest. Stretchy** material is slightly elastic and stretches easily.

strew /struː/ **strews, strewing, strewed, strewn.** To **strew** things somewhere, or to **strew** a place with things, means to scatter them in an untidy way. *The racoons knock over the rubbish bins in search of food, and strew the contents all over the ground.*

strewn /struːn/. **1** If a place is **strewn with** things, they are scattered there untidily. *The front room was strewn with books and clothes.* ▶ Also a com-

bining form. *...a litter-strewn street.* **2 Strewn** is the past participle of **strew**.

strick·en /ˈstrɪkən/. **1 Stricken** is the past participle of some meanings of **strike**. **2** If a person or place is **stricken** by something such as an unpleasant feeling, an illness, or a natural disaster, they are severely affected by it. *...a family stricken by genetically inherited cancer.* ▶ Also a combining form. *...was panic-stricken at the thought he might never play again.*

strict /strɪkt/ **stricter, strictest. 1** A **strict** rule or order is very clear and precise or severe and must be obeyed absolutely. *French privacy laws are very strict... Even if you are on a fairly strict diet you can still go out for a good meal.* ♦ **strict·ly** *The acceptance of new members is strictly controlled.* **2** Someone who is **strict** does not tolerate impolite or disobedient behaviour, especially from children. *My parents were very strict.* ♦ **strictly** *My own mother was brought up very strictly.* ♦ **strict·ness** *She resented her parents' strictness.* **3** If you talk about the **strict** meaning of something, you mean the precise meaning of it. *It's not quite peace in the strictest sense of the word, rather the absence of war.* ♦ **strictly** *Actually, that is not strictly true.* **4** You use **strict** to describe someone who never does things that are against their beliefs. *Four million Britons are now strict vegetarians.*

strict·ly /ˈstrɪktli/. You use **strictly** to emphasize that something is of one particular type, or intended for one particular thing or person, rather than any other. *He seemed fond of her in a strictly professional way.*

stric·ture /ˈstrɪktʃə/ **strictures. 1** You can use **strictures** to refer to severe criticism or disapproval of something. *...Mencken's strictures on the 1920s, with its self-righteous prohibition on alcohol and unconventional ideas.* **2** You can refer to things that limit what you can do as **strictures** of a particular kind. Some people consider this use to be incorrect. *Your goals are hindered by financial strictures.*

stride /straɪd/ **strides, striding, strode. 1** If you **stride** somewhere, you walk there with quick, long steps. *He turned abruptly and strode off down the corridor.* **2** A **stride** is a long step which you take when you are walking or running. **3** Someone's **stride** is their way of walking with long steps. *He lengthened his stride to keep up with her.* **4** If you make **strides** in something that you are doing, you make rapid progress in it. *The country has made enormous strides politically but not economically.* **5** If you **get into** your **stride** or **hit** your **stride**, you start to do something easily and confidently, after being slow and uncertain. *The campaign is just getting into its stride.* **6** If you **take** a problem or difficulty **in** your **stride**, you deal with it calmly and easily. In American English, you can also **take something in stride**.

stri·den·cy /ˈstraɪdənsi/. **Stridency** is the quality of being strident. *Many voters were alarmed by the President's new stridency.*

stri·dent /ˈstraɪdənt/. **1** If you use **strident** to describe someone or the way they express themselves, you mean that they make their feelings or opinions known in a very noticeable or persistent manner. *...the unnecessarily strident tone of the President's remarks.* ♦ **stri·dent·ly** *In the late 1920s the party began to adopt a more stridently nationalistic posture.* **2** If a voice or sound is **strident**, it is loud, harsh, and unpleasant to listen to. *She tried to laugh, and the sound was harsh and strident.*

strife /straɪf/. **Strife** is strong disagreement or fighting. *Money is a major cause of strife in many marriages.*

strike /straɪk/ **strikes, striking, struck, stricken.** The form **struck** is the past tense and past participle. The form **stricken** can also be used as the past participle for meanings 6, 17, and 19. **1** When there is a **strike**, workers stop doing their work for a

period of time, usually in order to try to get better pay or conditions for themselves. *Staff at the hospital went on strike in protest at the incidents. ...a call for strike action.* **2** When workers **strike**, they go on strike. *They shouldn't be striking for more money.* VERB: V / V for/against / n

♦ **strik·er, strikers** *The strikers want higher wages.* N-COUNT

3 If you **strike** someone or something, you deliberately hit them. *She took two quick steps forward and struck him across the mouth.* **4** If something that is falling or moving **strikes** something, it hits it. *His head struck the bottom when he dived into the 6ft end of the pool.* VERB: V n / V n prep/adv FORMAL / VERB / V n FORMAL

5 If you **strike** one thing against another, or if one thing **strikes** against another, the first thing hits the second thing. *My right toe struck against a submerged rock.* V-ERG: V n on/against n / V against n FORMAL

6 If something such as an illness or disaster **strikes**, it suddenly happens. *A powerful earthquake struck the Italian island of Sicily early this morning.* VERB: V / V n

7 To **strike** means to attack someone or something quickly and violently. *The killer says he will strike again.* VERB

8 A military **strike** is a military attack, especially an air attack. *...strategic strikes against Italian air bases.* N-COUNT: with supp

9 If something **strikes at** the heart or foundation of something, it attacks or conflicts with the basic elements or principles of that thing. *The issue strikes at the very foundation of our community.* V at n LITERARY

10 If an idea or thought **strikes** you, it suddenly comes into your mind. *It suddenly struck me that I was wasting my time.* VERB: V n / it V n that/how

11 If something **strikes** you as being a particular thing, it gives you the impression of being that thing. *He struck me as a very serious but friendly person... You've always struck me as being an angry man.* VERB / V n as adj / V n as n/-ing

12 If you **are struck** by something, you think it is very impressive, noticeable, or interesting. *She was struck by his simple, spellbinding eloquence.* be V-ed by/ with n / Also V n

13 If you **strike** a deal or a bargain with someone, you come to an agreement with them. *The two struck a deal in which Rendell took half of what a manager would... He insists he has struck no bargains for their release.* V-RECIP: V n with n / pl-n V n

14 If you **strike** a balance, you do something that is halfway between two extremes. *You have to strike a balance between sleep and homework.* VERB V n

15 If you **strike** a pose or attitude, you put your body and limbs in a particular position, for example when someone is taking your photograph. VERB: V n

16 If something **strikes** fear or terror into people, it makes them very frightened or anxious. **17** If you **are struck** dumb or blind, you suddenly become unable to speak or to see. *I was struck dumb by this and had to think it over for a moment.* VERB: V n into n / VB: usu passive / be V-ed adj WRITTEN

18 When a clock **strikes**, its bells make a sound to indicate what the time is. *The clock struck nine.* VERB: V / V n

19 If you **strike** words from a document or an official record, you delete them. *Strike that from the minutes.* VERB FORMAL

► **Strike out** means the same as **strike**. *The censor struck out the next two lines.* PHRASAL VB V P noun

20 When you **strike** a match, you make it produce a flame by moving it quickly against something rough. VERB: V n

21 If someone **strikes** oil or gold, they discover it in the ground as a result of mining or digging. **22** When a coin or medal **is struck**, it is made. *Another medal was specially struck for him.* VERB: V n / VB: usu passive be V-ed

23 If you are **within striking distance** of something, or if something is **within striking distance**, it is quite near, so it could be reached or achieved quite easily. *I believe we are within striking distance of an agreement.* PHRASE

24 If you **strike gold**, you find, do, or produce something that brings you a lot of money or success. *The company has struck gold with its new holiday development.* PHRASE JOURNALISM

25 If you **strike it rich**, you make a lot of money, especially in a short time. PHRASE INFORMAL

26 See also **hunger strike**, **stricken**, **striking**. ● to **strike a chord**: see **chord**. ● to **strike home**: see **home**. ● to **strike a happy medium**: see **medium**. ● to **strike it lucky**: see **lucky**.

strike back. If you **strike back**, you harm or criticize someone who has harmed or criticized you. *Sometimes, Kappy got angry and struck back at him in whatever way she could.* PHRASAL VB V P / V P at n

strike down. 1 If someone **is struck down**, especially by an illness, they are killed or severely harmed. *Frank had been struck down by a massive heart attack.* PHRASAL VB be V-ed P WRITTEN

2 If a judge or court **strikes down** a law or regulation, they abolish it. *The Supreme Court today struck down a law that prevents criminals from profiting from books or movies about their crimes.* V P n AMERICAN

strike off. If someone such as a doctor or lawyer **is struck off**, their name is removed from the official register and they are not allowed to do medical or legal work any more. *He could be struck off the medical register.* PHRASAL VB be V-ed P / be V-ed P n

strike out. 1 If you **strike out**, you begin to do something different, often because you want to become more independent. *She wanted me to strike out on my own, buy a business.* **2** If you **strike out** at someone, you hit, attack, or speak angrily to them. *Frampton struck out blindly, hitting not Waddington, but an elderly man.* **3** If you **strike out** in a particular direction, you start travelling in that direction. *They left the car and struck out along the muddy track.* **4** In baseball, if a pitcher **strikes out** a batter or if a batter **strikes out**, the batter fails to hit three balls thrown properly by the pitcher, and is out. *Canseco, nursing a back injury, struck out.* **5** See also **strike** 19. PHRASAL VB VP / VP at n / VP / V P prep/adv LITERARY / ERG: V P noun / V P

strike up. 1 When you **strike up** a conversation or friendship with someone, you begin one. **2** When musicians **strike up** a piece of music, or when music **strikes up**, the music begins. *The band struck up, and riders paraded round the ring.* PHRASAL VB V P noun / ERG: V P noun / V P

'**strike-breaker, strike-breakers**; also spelled **strikebreaker**. A **strike-breaker** is a person who continues to work during a strike, or someone who takes over the work of a person who is on strike. N-COUNT

strik·er /ˈstraɪkə/ **strikers. 1** In football and some other team sports, a **striker** is a player whose main function is to attack and score goals, rather than defend. **2** See also **strike**. ◆◆◇◇ N-COUNT

strik·ing /ˈstraɪkɪŋ/. **1** Something that is **striking** is very noticeable or unusual. *The most striking feature of those statistics is the high proportion of suicides.* ◆◆◆◇◇ ADJ-GRADED

♦ **strik·ing·ly** *Most strikingly, the amount consumers spent in the shops grew much more quickly than anyone expected.* ADV-GRADED

2 Someone who is **striking** is very attractive, in a noticeable way. *She was a striking woman with long blonde hair.* **3** See also **strike**. ADJ-GRADED

string /strɪŋ/ **strings, stringing, strung. 1** String is thin rope made of twisted threads, used for tying things together or tying up parcels. *He held out a small bag tied with string.* **2** A **string** of things is a number of them on a piece of string, thread, or wire. *She wore a string of pearls around her neck.* ◆◆◆◇◇ N-VAR / N-COUNT

3 A **string** of places or objects is a number of them that form a line. *The landscape is broken only by a string of villages.* **4** A **string** of similar events is a series of them that happen one after the other. *Between 1940 and 1943 he had a string of 62 consecutive victories.* N-COUNT

5 The **strings** on a musical instrument such as a violin or guitar are thin pieces of tightly-stretched wire or nylon. **6** The **strings** are the section of an orchestra which consists of stringed instruments played with a bow. *There was a 20-member string section.* N-COUNT / N-PLURAL

7 If you **string** something somewhere, you hang it up between two or more objects. *He had strung a banner across the wall.* ► **String up** means the same as **string**. *People were stringing up decorations on the fronts of their homes.* VERB V n prep/adv / PHRASAL VB V P noun / Also V n P

8 If someone has more than one **string to** their **bow**, they have more than one ability or thing they can use if the first one they try is not successful. *I'm never out of work because I have so many strings to my bow.* **9** If something is offered to you with **no strings attached** or with **no strings**, it is offered without any special conditions. *Aid should be given to developing countries with no strings attached.* **10** If you **pull strings**, you use your influence with other people in order to get something done, often unfairly. **11** See also **highly-strung**, **purse strings**, **second string**, **strung out**. ● **apron strings**: see **apron**. PHRASE / PHRASE / PHRASE

string along. If you **string** someone **along**, you de- PHRASAL VB

ceive them by letting them believe that you have the same desires, beliefs, or hopes as them. *She took advantage of him, stringing him along even after they were divorced.* `V n P` `INFORMAL`

string together. If you **string** things **together**, you form something from them by adding them to each other, one at a time. *The speaker strung together a series of jokes.* `PHRASAL VB` `V n P` `V P noun`

string up. 1 See **string 7. 2** To **string** someone **up** means to kill them by hanging them. *Guards rushed into his cell and strung him up.* `PHRASAL VB` `V n P` `Also V P noun` `INFORMAL`

,stringed 'instrument, stringed instruments. A **stringed instrument** is a musical instrument that has strings, such as a violin or a guitar. `N-COUNT`

strin·gen·cy /'strindʒənsi/. Financial **stringency** is a shortage of money, either for spending or for investing. *Despite financial stringency, Britain remained the leading pioneer of mechanization.* `N-UNCOUNT:` `supp N` `TECHNICAL`

strin·gent /'strindʒənt/. **Stringent** laws, rules, or conditions are very severe or are strictly controlled. *Its drug-testing procedures are the most stringent in the world.* ◆ **strin·gent·ly** *He is determined to see the Act enforced more stringently.* `◆◇◇◇◇` `ADJ-GRADED` `FORMAL` `ADV:` `ADV with v`

string·er /'strɪŋə/ **stringers.** A **stringer** is a journalist who is employed part-time by a newspaper or news service in order to report on a particular area. `◆◇◇◇◇` `N-COUNT` `TECHNICAL`

,string quar'tet, string quartets. 1 A **string quartet** is a group of four musicians who play stringed instruments together. The instruments are two violins, a viola, and a cello. **2** A **string quartet** is a musical composition for two violins, a viola, and a cello. *...Dvorak's String Quartet Opus 34.* `N-COUNT` `N-COUNT`

stringy /'strɪŋi/ **stringier, stringiest. 1** Stringy food is unpleasant to eat because it contains long, thin strands that are difficult to chew, or are messy. *Try to pick French and runner beans every day before they get old and stringy.* **2** Stringy hair is thin and unattractive. *...an enormously fat man with long, stringy gray hair.* `ADJ-GRADED` `ADJ-GRADED`

strip /strip/ **strips, stripping, stripped. 1** A **strip** of something such as paper, cloth, or food is a long, narrow piece of it. *The simplest rag-rugs are made with strips of fabric plaited together.* **2** A **strip** of land or water is a long narrow area of it. *...a short boat ride across a narrow strip of water.* **3** A **strip** is a long road, usually just outside a town, where there are a lot of stores, restaurants, and hotels. `◆◆◆◇◇` `N-COUNT` `N-COUNT` `N-COUNT` `AMERICAN`

4 If you **strip**, you take off your clothes. *Women residents stripped naked in protest.* ► **Strip off** means the same as **strip**. *The children were brazenly stripping off and leaping into the sea.* **5** If someone is **stripped**, their clothes are taken off by another person, for example in order to search for hidden or illegal things. `VERB: V` `V adj` `PHRASAL VB` `V P` `VERB:` `be V-ed`

6 To **strip** something means to remove everything that covers it. *I stripped the beds and vacuumed the carpets.* **7** If you **strip** an engine or a piece of equipment, you take it to pieces so that it can be cleaned or repaired. ► **Strip down** means the same as **strip**. *I stripped down the two SU carburettors, cleaned and polished the pieces and rebuilt the units.* `VERB` `V n` `VERB: V n` `PHRASAL VB` `V P down` `Also V n P`

8 To **strip** someone of their property, rights, or titles means to take those things away from them. *The soldiers have stripped the civilians of their passports, and every other type of document.* `VERB` `V n of n`

9 In a newspaper or magazine, a **strip** is a series of drawings which tell a story. The words spoken by the characters are often written on the drawings. *...the Doonesbury strip.* `N-COUNT` `AMERICAN`

10 See also **landing strip, strip-search.**

strip away. 1 To **strip away** something misleading or unnecessary means to remove it completely, so that people can see what is important or true. *Altman strips away the pretence and mythology to expose the film industry as a business like any other.* **2** To **strip away** a layer of something means to remove it completely. *She'd managed to strip the bloodied rags away from Nellie's body.* `PHRASAL VB` `V P noun` `V P noun` `V n P from n`

strip down. See **strip 7.**

strip off. ● See **strip 4.**

'strip club, strip clubs. A **strip club** is a club which people go to in order to see striptease. `N-COUNT`

stripe /straip/ **stripes. 1** A **stripe** is a long line which is a different colour from the areas next to it. See picture headed **patterns.** *The walls in the front bedroom are painted with broad, pale blue and white stripes.* **2** In the armed forces or the police, **stripes** are V-shaped bands of material sewn onto a uniform to indicate the rank of corporal or sergeant. `◆◆◇◇◇` `N-COUNT` `N-COUNT`

striped /straipt/. Something that is **striped** has stripes on it. *...striped wallpaper.* `◆◇◇◇◇` `ADJ`

stripey /'straipi/. See **stripy.**

'strip joint, strip joints. A **strip joint** is the same as a **strip club.** `N-COUNT` `INFORMAL`

strip·per /'stripə/ **strippers.** A **stripper** is a person who earns money by doing striptease. *...a male stripper.* `◆◇◇◇◇` `N-COUNT`

'strip-search, strip-searches, strip-searching, strip-searched; also spelled **strip search.** If a person is **strip-searched**, someone such as a police officer makes them take off all their clothes and searches them, usually to see if they are carrying drugs or weapons. *All 23 of them were strip-searched for drugs.* ► Also a noun. *They suspected that he might be carrying a weapon and ordered a strip search.* `VERB:` `be V-ed` `be V-ed for n` `N-COUNT`

strip·tease /'stripti:z, AM -ti:z/; also spelled **striptease.** **Striptease** is a form of entertainment in which someone takes off their clothes slowly and in a sexy way to music. `N-UNCOUNT`

stripy /'straipi/; also spelled **stripey.** Something that is **stripy** has stripes on it. The usual American word is **striped.** *He was wearing a stripy shirt and baggy blue trousers.* `ADJ` `INFORMAL,` `BRITISH`

strive /straiv/ **strives, striving.** The past tense is either **strove** or **strived**, and the past participle is either **striven** or **strived.** If you **strive** to do something or **strive** for something, you make a great effort to do it or get it. *Mr Calderon said the region must now strive for economic development as well as peace.* ◆ **striv·ing, strivings** *...a politician consumed by his own passionate striving for leadership.* `◆◆◇◇◇` `VERB:` `V to-inf` `V for n` `Also V` `N-UNCOUNT:` `also N in pl`

strobe /strəub/ **strobes.** A **strobe** or a **strobe light** is a very bright light which flashes on and off very quickly. `N-COUNT`

strode /strəud/. **Strode** is the past tense and past participle of **stride.**

stroke /strəuk/ **strokes, stroking, stroked. 1** If you **stroke** someone or something, you move your hand slowly and gently over them. *Carla, curled up on the sofa, was smoking a cigarette and stroking her cat.* `◆◆◆◇◇` `VERB` `V n`

2 If someone has a **stroke**, a blood vessel in their brain bursts or gets blocked, which may kill them or cause one side of their body to be paralysed. `N-COUNT`

3 The **strokes** of a pen or brush are the movements or marks you make with it when you are writing or painting. *Fill in gaps by using short, upward strokes of the pencil.* **4** When you are swimming or rowing, your **strokes** are the repeated movements you make with your arms or the oars. *I turned and swam a few strokes further out to sea.* **5** A swimming **stroke** is a particular style or method of swimming. *She spent hours practising the breast stroke.* **6** In sports such as tennis, cricket, and golf, a **stroke** is the action of hitting the ball. *Compton was sending the ball here, there, and everywhere with each stroke.* `N-COUNT` `N-COUNT` `N-COUNT` `N-COUNT`

7 The **strokes** of a clock are the sounds that indicate each hour. *On the stroke of 12, fireworks suddenly exploded into the night.* `N-COUNT`

8 A **stroke of** luck or good fortune is something lucky that happens. **9** A **stroke of** genius or inspiration is a sudden idea or inspiration. `N-SING` `N-SING`

10 If something happens **at a stroke** or **in one stroke**, it happens suddenly and completely because of one single action. *Myxomatosis wiped out 40 million rabbits at a stroke.* **11** If someone does not **do a stroke of** work, they are very lazy and do no work at all. `PHRASE` `PHRASE` `INFORMAL`

stroll /strəul/ **strolls, strolling, strolled.** If you **stroll** somewhere, you walk there in a slow, relaxed `◆◆◇◇◇` `VERB` `V prep/adv`

way. *Afterwards, we strolled back, put the kettle on and settled down with the newspapers.* ► Also a noun. *After dinner, I took a stroll round the city.* ◆ **stroll·er, strollers** *The foggy streets were virtually empty, except for the occasional evening stroller.* `N-COUNT`

stroll·er /ˈstrəʊlə/ **strollers.** A **stroller** is a small chair on wheels, in which a baby or small child can sit and be wheeled around. The British word is **pushchair.** `N-COUNT` `AMERICAN`

strong /strɒŋ, AM strɔːŋ/ **stronger** /ˈstrɒŋgə, AM ˈstrɔːŋgər/ **strongest** /ˈstrɒŋgɪst, AM ˈstrɔːŋgɪst/. `◆◆◆◆◆`
1 Someone who is **strong** is healthy with good muscles and can move or carry heavy things, or do hard physical work. *I'm not strong enough to carry him... I feared I wouldn't be able to control such a strong horse.* **2 Strong** objects or materials are not easily broken and can support a lot of weight or resist a lot of strain. *The vacuum flask has a strong casing, which won't crack or chip... Glue the mirror in with a strong adhesive.* ◆ **strong·ly** *The fence was very strongly built, with very large posts.* **3** A **strong** wind, current, or other force has a lot of power or speed, and can cause heavy things to move. *A fairly strong current seemed to be moving the whole boat.* ◆ **strongly** *The metal is strongly attracted to the surface.* `ADJ-GRADED` `ADV-GRADED` `ADJ-GRADED` `ADV-GRADED:` `ADV with v`
4 Someone who is **strong** is confident and determined, and is not easily influenced or worried by other people. *He is sharp and manipulative with a strong personality.* **5** If you have **strong** opinions on something or express them using **strong** words, you have extreme or very definite opinions which you are willing to express or defend. *The paper is a strong supporter of President Mandela's reforms.* ◆ **strongly** *We are strongly opposed to the presence of America in this region.* **6** If someone in authority takes **strong** action, they act firmly and severely. *He has also said he will have to become a strong President to put things right.* **7** A **strong** impression or influence has a great effect on someone. *We're glad if our music makes a strong impression, even if it's a negative one.* ◆ **strongly** *He is strongly influenced by Spanish painters such as Goya and El Greco.* **8** If there is a **strong** case or argument for something, it is supported by a lot of evidence. *A strong link was found between parental mental illness and disturbance in their children.* ◆ **strongly** *These are conditions said by doctors to be strongly indicative of heart failure.* **9** If there is a **strong** possibility or likelihood that something is true or will happen, it is very likely to be true or to happen. *There is a strong possibility that the cat contracted the condition by eating contaminated pet food.* `ADJ-GRADED` `ADJ-GRADED` `ADV-GRADED` `ADJ-GRADED` `ADJ-GRADED` `ADV-GRADED` `ADJ-GRADED`
10 Your **strong** points are your best qualities or talents, or the things you are good at. *Discretion is not Jeremy's strong point... Cynics argue that the EC is far stronger on rhetoric than on concrete action.* **11** A **strong** competitor, candidate, or team is talented or likely to succeed. *She was a strong contender for Britain's Olympic team.* `ADJ-GRADED:` `v-link ADJ on` `n` `ADJ-GRADED`
12 If a relationship or bond is **strong**, it is close and likely to last for a long time. *This has tested our marriage, and we have come through it stronger than ever.* `ADJ-GRADED`
13 A **strong** currency, economy, or industry has a high value or is very productive. *The local economy is strong and the population is growing.* `ADJ-GRADED`
14 If something is a **strong** element or part of something else, it is an important or large part of it. *There is a strong element of truth to each of these explanations.* `ADJ-GRADED`
15 You can use **strong** when you are saying how many people there are in a group. For example, if a group is twenty strong, there are twenty people in it. `ADJ:` `num ADJ`
16 A **strong** drink, chemical, or drug contains a lot of the particular substance which makes it effective. *Strong coffee or tea late at night may cause sleeplessness.* **17** A **strong** colour, flavour, smell, sound, or light is intense and easily noticed. *The wine goes with strong and mild cheese alike.* ◆ **strongly** *He leaned over her, smelling strongly of sweat.* `ADJ-GRADED` `ADJ-GRADED` `ADV-GRADED:` `ADV with v`
18 If someone has a **strong** accent, they speak in a distinctive way that shows very clearly what country `ADJ-GRADED`

or region they come from. **19** You can say someone has **strong** features or a **strong** face if they have large and distinctive facial features. *He had a strong Greek nose and olive-black eyes.* `ADJ-GRADED`
20 If someone **comes on strong**, they make their intentions or feelings clear in an excessive or aggressive way. *'I come on strong sometimes. Don't know why.' She was beginning to feel like a bully.* **21** If someone or something is still **going strong**, they are still alive, in good condition, or popular after a long time. `PHRASE` `INFORMAL` `PHRASE` `INFORMAL`

'strong-arm. If you refer to someone's behaviour as **strong-arm** tactics or methods, you disapprove of it because it consists of using threats or force in order to achieve something. *The paper is openly critical of the strong-arm president.* `ADJ: ADJ n` `PRAGMATICS`

strong·hold /ˈstrɒŋhəʊld, AM ˈstrɔːŋ-/ **strongholds.** **1** If you say that a place or region is a **stronghold** of a particular attitude or belief, you mean that most people there share this attitude or belief. *The seat was a stronghold of the Labour party.* **2** If you say that somewhere is a **stronghold** of a particular type of animal, you mean that a relatively large number of that type of animal lives there. *Shetland is the last stronghold of otters in the British Isles.* `◆◇◇◇◇` `N-COUNT` `N-COUNT:` `with poss`

strong·man /ˈstrɒŋmæn, AM ˈstrɔːŋ-/ **strongmen.** If you refer to a male political leader as a **strongman**, you mean that he has great power and control over people and events, although his methods may sometimes be brutal or morally wrong. *He was a military strongman who ruled the country after a coup.* `N-COUNT`

,strong-'minded. If you describe someone, especially a woman, as **strong-minded**, you approve of them because they have their own firm attitudes and opinions, and are not easily influenced by other people. `ADJ-GRADED` `PRAGMATICS`

,strong-'willed. Someone who is **strong-willed** has a lot of determination and always tries to do what they want, even though other people may advise them not to. `ADJ-GRADED`

strop·py /ˈstrɒpi/ **stroppier, stroppiest.** Someone who is **stroppy** is bad-tempered and obstinate. *The gas people haven't called to repair the cooker so I shall have to get stroppy with them.* `ADJ-GRADED` `BRITISH,` `INFORMAL`

strove /strəʊv/. **Strove** is a past tense of **strive.**

struck /strʌk/. **Struck** is the past tense and past participle of **strike.**

struc·tur·al /ˈstrʌktʃərəl/. **Structural** means relating to or affecting the structure of something. *The explosion caused little structural damage to the office towers themselves.* ◆ **struc·tur·al·ly** *When we bought the house, it was structurally sound.* `◆◆◇◇◇` `ADJ` `ADV`

struc·tur·al·ism /ˈstrʌktʃərəlɪzəm/. **Structuralism** is a method of analysis applied to such things as language, literature, or systems of thought. According to structuralism, something such as a language or a literary work can be understood as a structure whose various parts or elements make sense only in relation to the whole. `N-UNCOUNT` `TECHNICAL`

struc·tur·al·ist /ˈstrʌktʃərəlɪst/ **structuralists.** **1** A **structuralist** is someone whose work is based on structuralism. **2 Structuralist** is used to refer to people and things that are connected with structuralism. *There are two main structuralist techniques incorporated into critical social research.* `N-COUNT` `ADJ: ADJ n`

struc·ture /ˈstrʌktʃə/ **structures, structuring, structured.** **1** The **structure** of something is the way in which it is made, built, or organized. *The typical family structure of Freud's patients involved two parents and two children... The chemical structure of this particular molecule is very unusual.* **2** A **structure** is something that consists of parts connected together in an ordered way. *The feet are highly specialised structures made up of 26 small delicate bones.* **3** A **structure** is something that has been built. *The house was a handsome four-story brick structure.* **4** If you **structure** something, you arrange it in a careful, organized pattern or system. *By structuring the course this way, we're forced to* `◆◆◆◆◇` `N-VAR` `N-COUNT` `N-COUNT` `VERB` `V n`

S

produce something the companies think is valuable.
♦ **struc·tured** *We have introduced a much more* ADJ-GRADED
structured training programme. **5** See also **report structure.**

strug·gle /ˈstrʌgəl/ **struggles, struggling,** ♦♦♦♦◇
struggled. 1 If you **struggle** to do something, you VERB:
try hard to do it, even though other people or things V to-inf
may be making it difficult for you to succeed. *They* Also V
had to struggle against all kinds of adversity. **2** A N-VAR
struggle is an attempt to obtain something or to defeat someone who is denying you something, such
as your freedom. *Life became a struggle for surviv-*
al... He is currently locked in a power struggle with
his Prime Minister.
3 If you **struggle** when you are being held, you twist, VERB
kick, and move violently in order to get free. *I strug-* V
gled, but he was a tall man, well-built. **4** If two people V-RECIP:
struggle with each other, they fight. *We were strug-* pl-n V
gling for the gun when it went off.... There were signs pl-n V for n
that she struggled with her attacker. ▶ Also a noun. *He* V with n
died in a struggle with prison officers. **5** If you **struggle** VERB:
to move yourself or to move a heavy object, you try to V to-inf
do it, but it is difficult. *I struggled with my bags, des-* V prep
perately looking for a porter. **6** If you **struggle** to do VERB
something or go somewhere, you succeed in doing it V prep/adv
or in going there but with great difficulty. *Catherine*
struggled to her feet.
7 If a person or organization **is struggling**, they are VERB:
likely to fail in what they are doing, even though they V,
might be trying very hard. *The company is struggling* only one V
to find buyers for its new product... One in five young V to-inf
adults was struggling with everyday mathematics. V prep
8 An action or activity that is **a struggle** is very difficult N-SING:
for you to do. *Losing weight was a terrible struggle.* a N

struggle on. If you **struggle on**, you continue doing PHRASAL VB
something although it is difficult, rather than stop- V P
ping. *The rest of the world struggles on with its perpet-* V P with n
ual problems.

strum /strʌm/ **strums, strumming, strummed.** ♦◇◇◇◇
If you **strum** a stringed instrument such as a guitar, VERB: V n
you play it by moving your fingers backwards and V prep/adv
forwards across the strings. *Vaska strummed away*
on his guitar. ▶ Also a noun. *I heard the strum of* N-SING
my father's guitar.

strung /strʌŋ/. **Strung** is the past tense and past
participle of **string.**

strung 'out. 1 If things are **strung out** some- ADJ
where, they are spread out in a line. *Colleges, tem-*
ples and administrative buildings were strung out on
the north side of the river. **2** If someone is **strung** ADJ-GRADED:
out on drugs, they are heavily affected by drugs. v-link ADJ
INFORMAL

strut /strʌt/ **struts, strutting, strutted. 1** Some- ♦◇◇◇◇
one who **struts** walks in a proud way, with their VERB
head held high and their chest out, as if they are PRAGMATICS
very important; used showing disapproval. *He* V prep/adv
struts around town like he owns the place. ● If you PHRASE
strut your **stuff**, you act in a proud way and show INFORMAL
off. **2** A **strut** is a piece of wood or metal which N-COUNT
holds the weight of other pieces in a building.

strych·nine /ˈstrɪkniːn, AM -naɪn/. **Strychnine** is a N-UNCOUNT
very poisonous drug which is sometimes used in
very small amounts as a medicine.

stub /stʌb/ **stubs, stubbing, stubbed. 1** The ♦◇◇◇◇
stub of a cigarette or a pencil is the last short piece N-COUNT:
of it which remains when the rest has been used. with supp
2 The **stub** of a ticket or cheque is the part that you N-COUNT
keep after the rest of it has been used. **3** If you **stub** VERB: V n
your toe, you hurt it by accidentally kicking some-
thing hard.

stub out. When someone **stubs out** a cigarette, they PHRASAL VB
put it out by pressing it against something hard. *Signs* V P noun
across the entrances warn all visitors to stub out their Also V n P
cigarettes.

stub·ble /ˈstʌbəl/. **1 Stubble** consists of the short N-UNCOUNT
stalks which are left in fields after corn or wheat has
been harvested. **2** The very short hairs on a man's N-UNCOUNT
face when he has not shaved recently are referred to
as **stubble.** ♦ **stub·bly** /ˈstʌbəli/. *...a man with a* ADJ-GRADED
stubbly chin.

stub·born /ˈstʌbən/. **1** Someone who is **stubborn** ♦♦◇◇◇
or who behaves in a **stubborn** way is determined to ADJ-GRADED
do what they want and is very unwilling to change
their mind. ♦ **stub·born·ly** *He stubbornly refused* ADV-GRADED
to tell her how he had come to be in such a state.
♦ **stub·born·ness** *I couldn't tell if his refusal to* N-UNCOUNT
talk was simple stubbornness. **2** A **stubborn** stain or ADJ-GRADED
problem is difficult to remove or to deal with.
♦ **stubbornly** *Some interest rates have remained* ADV-GRADED
stubbornly high.

stub·by /ˈstʌbi/. An object that is **stubby** is shorter ADJ-GRADED
and thicker than usual. *He pointed a stubby finger at*
a wooden chair opposite him.

stuc·co /ˈstʌkəʊ/. **Stucco** is a type of plaster used N-UNCOUNT
for covering walls and decorating ceilings.

stuck /stʌk/. **1 Stuck** is the past tense and past ♦♦◇◇◇
participle of **stick. 2** If something is **stuck** in a par- ADJ:
ticular position, it is fixed tightly in this position v-link ADJ
and is unable to move. **3** If you are **stuck** in a place ADJ:
or unpleasant situation, you want to get away from v-link ADJ
it, but are unable to. *I don't want to get stuck in an-* prep/adv
other job like that.
4 If something is **stuck** at a particular level or stage, it ADJ:
is not progressing or changing. *The economy is still* v-link ADJ
stuck in recession. **5** If you are **stuck with** something prep/adv
that you do not want, you cannot get rid of it. *Many* ADJ:
people are now stuck with expensive fixed-rate mort- with n
gages. **6** If you get **stuck** when you are trying to do ADJ:
something, you are unable to continue doing it be- v-link ADJ
cause it is too difficult. **7** If you **get stuck in**, you start PHRASE
what you are going to do with a lot of enthusiasm and INFORMAL,
determination. BRITISH

stuck-'up. If you say that someone is **stuck-up,** ADJ-GRADED
you mean that you dislike them because they think PRAGMATICS
they are very important and they are proud and INFORMAL
unfriendly.

stud /stʌd/ **studs. 1 Studs** are small pieces of met- ♦◇◇◇◇
al which are attached to a surface for decoration. N-COUNT
2 Studs are earrings which consist of one small N-COUNT
piece of jewellery attached to a bar which goes
through your ear. **3 Studs** are small round objects N-COUNT
attached to the bottom of boots, especially sports
boots, so that the wearer does not slip.
4 Horses or other animals that are kept for **stud** are N-UNCOUNT
kept to be used for breeding. **5** If you refer to a man as N-COUNT
a **stud**, you mean that he is thought to be very active INFORMAL
sexually and good at satisfying women's sexual de-
sires. **6** A **stud** is the same as a **stud farm. 7** See also N-COUNT
press stud.

stud·ded /ˈstʌdɪd/. **1** Something that is **studded** is ♦◇◇◇◇
decorated with studs or things that look like studs. ADJ
...a beautiful gold bracelet studded with diamonds.
▶ Also after nouns. *...a gold and diamond-studded* COMB
trophy. **2** If you say that something is **studded** with ADJ:
another thing, you mean that there are a lot of the v-link ADJ,
second thing in or on the first thing. *...a metal panel* ADJ with n
studded with small microphones. **3** See also **star-**
studded.

stu·dent /ˈstjuːdənt, ˈstuː-/ **students. 1** A student ♦♦♦♦
is a person who is studying at a university or col- N-COUNT
lege. ● See also **mature student. 2** A **student** is a N-COUNT
person who is studying at a secondary school. AMERICAN
3 Someone who is a **student** of a particular subject N-COUNT
is interested in the subject and spends time learning N of n
about it.

students' 'union, students' unions. 1 The stu- N-COUNT
dents' union or the student union is the students'
organization in a university or college which organizes leisure activities, provides welfare services, and
represents students' political interests. **2** The stu- N-SING:
dents' union or the student union is the building the N
where the students' union organization has its offices and which usually has a shop, a coffee bar, and
a meeting place.

stud farm, stud farms. A **stud farm** is a place N-COUNT
where horses are bred.

stud·ied /ˈstʌdɪd/. A **studied** action has been care- ADJ: ADJ n
fully thought about or planned and is not sponta-
neous or natural. ● See also **study.**

stu·dio /ˈstjuːdiəʊ, ˈstuː-/ **studios. 1** A studio is a room where a painter, photographer, or designer works. [N-COUNT] **2** A studio is a room where radio or television programmes are recorded, records are produced, or films are made. [N-COUNT] **3** You can refer to film-making companies as studios. *She wrote to Paramount Studios and asked if they would audition her.* [N-COUNT] **4** A studio, a studio flat, or a studio apartment is a small flat with one room for living and sleeping in, a kitchen, and a bathroom. [N-COUNT]

studio 'audience, studio audiences. A studio audience is a group of people who are in a television or radio studio watching while a programme is being made, so that their clapping, laughter, or questions are recorded on the programme. [N-COLL-COUNT]

stu·di·ous /ˈstjuːdiəs, ˈstuː-/. Someone who is studious spends a lot of time reading and studying books. [ADJ-GRADED]

stu·di·ous·ly /ˈstjuːdiəsli, ˈstuː-/. If you do something studiously, you do it carefully and deliberately. *When I looked at Clive, he studiously avoided my eyes.* [ADV-GRADED]

study /ˈstʌdi/ **studies, studying, studied. 1** If you study, you spend time learning about a particular subject or subjects. *He went to Hull University, where he studied History and Economics... She came to Britain to study for her A levels.* [VERB: V, V n, V for n] **2** Study is the activity of studying. *She gave up her studies to have Alexander.* [N-UNCOUNT: also N in pl] **3** A study of a subject is a piece of research on it. *...the first study of English children's attitudes.* [N-COUNT] **4** You can refer to educational subjects or courses that contain several elements as studies of a particular kind. *She is currently doing a business studies course at Leeds.* [N-PLURAL: supp N] **5** If you study something, you look at it or watch it very carefully, in order to find something out. [VERB: V n] **6** If you study something, you consider it or observe it carefully in order to be able to understand it fully. *I know that you've been studying chimpanzees for thirty years now.* [VERB, V n] **7** A study by an artist is a drawing which is done in preparation for a larger picture. [N-COUNT] **8** A study is a room in a house which is used for reading, writing, and studying. [N-COUNT] **9** See also studied; case study.

stuff /stʌf/ **stuffs, stuffing, stuffed. 1** You can use stuff to refer to things such as a substance, a collection of things, events, or ideas, or the contents of something in a general way without mentioning the thing itself by name. *I'd like some coffee, and I don't object to the powdered stuff if it's all you've got... Don't tell me you still believe in all that stuff?... He pointed to a duffle bag. 'That's my stuff.'* [N-UNCOUNT INFORMAL] **2** If you do your stuff, you perform an activity in the way that people expect. *Once I get on the pitch I know I can do my stuff.* [PHRASE INFORMAL] **3** If you say that someone knows their stuff, you mean that they are good at doing something because they know a lot about it. [PHRASE INFORMAL] **4** ● strut one's stuff: see strut. **5** If you say that one thing is the stuff of another, you mean that the first thing is a very important feature or characteristic of the second thing, or that the second thing can be based or built on the first thing. *The idea that we can be whatever we want has become the stuff of television commercials.* [N-SING: the N of n FORMAL] **6** If you stuff something somewhere, you push it there quickly and roughly. *I stuffed my hands in my pockets.* [VERB V n prep/adv] **7** If you stuff a container or space with something, you fill it with something or with a quantity of things until it is full. *He grabbed my purse, opened it and stuffed it full, then gave it back to me. ...wallets stuffed with dollars.* [VERB: V n with n, V n adj, V-ed] **8** If you stuff yourself, you eat a lot of food. [VERB: V pron-refl] **9** If you stuff a bird such as a chicken or a vegetable such as a pepper, you put a mixture of food inside it before cooking it. *...stuffed tomatoes.* [prep VERB: V n, V-ed] **10** If a dead animal is stuffed, it is filled with a substance so that it can be preserved and displayed. *...stuffed animal heads.* [VB: usu passive V-ed] **11** If you are angry with someone for something that they have said or done, you might say 'Get stuffed!' to them; a rude expression. [EXCLAM PRAGMATICS BRITISH] **12** Stuff is used in front of nouns to emphasize that you do not care about some-[VB: only imper PRAGMATICS]

thing, or do not want to think about it. *Ultimately my attitude was: stuff them.* [V n INFORMAL, BRITISH]

stuff·ing /ˈstʌfɪŋ/ **stuffings. 1** Stuffing is a mixture of food that is put inside a bird such as a chicken, or a vegetable such as a pepper, before it is cooked. [N-VAR] **2** Stuffing is material that is put inside pillows, cushions, or toys, in order to fill them and make them firm. [N-UNCOUNT] **3** If something knocks the stuffing out of you when you are feeling enthusiastic or confident about something, it causes you to lose your enthusiasm or confidence. [PHRASE]

stuffy /ˈstʌfi/ **stuffier, stuffiest. 1** Stuffy people or institutions are formal and old-fashioned. [ADJ-GRADED] **2** If it is stuffy in a place, it is unpleasantly warm and there is not enough fresh air. [ADJ-GRADED] **3** If you have a stuffy nose, your nose is blocked with mucus, usually because of a cold. [ADJ-GRADED] ♦ **stuffi·ness** *Peppermint leaves are believed to relieve tiredness and nasal stuffiness.* [N-UNCOUNT]

stul·ti·fy /ˈstʌltɪfaɪ/ **stultifies, stultifying, stultified.** If something stultifies you, it makes you feel empty or dull in your mind, because it is so boring or repetitive. *Only a uniformed guard stultified with boredom might have overheard them.* ♦ **stul·ti·fy·ing** *A rigid routine can be stultifying and boring.* [VERB: V n, V-ed] [ADJ-GRADED]

stum·ble /ˈstʌmbəl/ **stumbles, stumbling, stumbled. 1** If you stumble, you put your foot down awkwardly while you are walking or running and nearly fall over. *I stumbled into the telephone box and dialed 999.* ► Also a noun. *I make it into the darkness with only one stumble.* [V prep/adv] [N-COUNT] **2** If you stumble while you are reading aloud or speaking, you make a mistake, and have to pause before saying the words properly. *Labour was delighted to see the Premier stumbling over answers to questions on Tory tax plans.* [VERB V overn, Also V]

stumble across or **stumble on.** If you stumble across something or stumble on it, you find it or discover it unexpectedly. [PHRASAL VB V P n]

'stumbling block, stumbling blocks. A stumbling block is a problem which stops you from achieving something. *Perhaps the major stumbling block to reunification is the military presence in South Korea.* [N-COUNT]

stump /stʌmp/ **stumps, stumping, stumped. 1** A stump is a small part of something that remains when the rest of it has been removed or broken off. *If you have a tree stump, check it for fungus.* [N-COUNT] **2** In cricket, the stumps are the three wooden sticks that are placed upright in the ground to form the wicket. [N-COUNT] **3** If you are stumped by a question or problem, you cannot think of any solution or answer to it. *Well, maybe I stumped you on that one.* [VERB: be V-ed V n] **4** If you stump somewhere, you walk there with heavy steps. *The Marshal stepped over the vacuum-cleaner and stumped out of the room.* [VERB V prep/adv] **5** If politicians stump the country or stump for a candidate, they travel around making campaign speeches before an election. *He was in Georgia stumping for Senator Wyche Fowler, a Democrat.* [VERB: V n, V for n AMERICAN] **6** If politicians are on the stump, they are campaigning for an election. [PHRASE AMERICAN]

stump up. If you stump up a sum of money, you pay the money that is required for something, often reluctantly. *Customers do not have to stump up any cash for at least four weeks.* [PHRASAL VB V P noun Also V P INFORMAL, BRITISH]

stumpy /ˈstʌmpi/. Stumpy things are short and thick. [ADJ-GRADED]

stun /stʌn/ **stuns, stunning, stunned. 1** If you are stunned by something, you are very shocked or astonished by it and are therefore unable to speak or do anything. ♦ **stunned** *His announcement did not produce any immediate cheers, only a stunned silence.* **2** If something such as a blow on the head stuns you, it makes you unconscious or confused and unsteady. **3** See also stunning. [VB: usu passive] [ADJ-GRADED] [VERB: V n]

stung /stʌŋ/. Stung is the past tense and past participle of sting.

stunk /stʌŋk/. Stunk is the past participle of stink.

stun·ner /ˈstʌnə/ **stunners. 1** A stunner is an extremely attractive woman. **2** If you say that some-[N-COUNT INFORMAL N-COUNT]

thing is a **stunner**, you mean that it is very surprising or impressive. *Their debut single is a stunner.*   INFORMAL

stun·ning /ˈstʌnɪŋ/. **1** A **stunning** person or thing is extremely beautiful or impressive. *...a stunning display of fireworks.* ♦ **stun·ning·ly** *beautiful countryside.* **2** A **stunning** thing or event is so unusual or unexpected that people are astonished by it. *The minister resigned last night after a stunning defeat in Sunday's vote.* ♦ **stunningly** *Sometimes people were quite stunningly rude to him.*   ◆◆◇◇◇ ADJ-GRADED / ADV-GRADED / ADJ-GRADED / ADV-GRADED

stunt /stʌnt/ **stunts, stunting, stunted. 1** A **stunt** is something interesting that is done in order to attract attention and get publicity for the person or company responsible for it. *In a bold promotional stunt for the movie, he smashed his car into a passing truck.* **2** If someone **pulls a stunt**, they do something silly or risky. **3** A **stunt** is a dangerous and exciting piece of action in a film. *Sean Connery insisted on living dangerously for his new film by performing his own stunts.* **4** If something **stunts** the growth or development of a person or thing, it prevents it from growing or developing as much as it should. *High interest rates have stunted economic growth.* ♦ **stunt·ed** *...low stunted trees.*   ◆◇◇◇◇ N-COUNT / PHRASE / N-COUNT / VERB Vn / ADJ-GRADED

stunt man, stunt men; also spelled **stuntman.** A **stunt man** is a man whose job is to do dangerous things, either for publicity or in a film instead of the actor so that the actor does not risk being injured.   N-COUNT

stu·pefy /ˈstjuːpɪfaɪ, ˈstuː-/ **stupefies, stupefying, stupefied.** If something **stupefies** you, it shocks or surprises you so much that you cannot think properly for a while. ♦ **stu·pefied** *Primrose, stupefied by tiredness, began to wail that she was hungry.*   VERB: Vn / ADJ

stu·pen·dous /stjuːˈpendəs, AM stuː-/. Something that is **stupendous** is surprisingly impressive or large.   ADJ-GRADED

stu·pid /ˈstjuːpɪd, AM ˈstuː-/ **stupider, stupidest. 1** If you say that someone or something is **stupid**, you mean that they show a lack of good judgement or intelligence and are not at all sensible. *I made a stupid mistake.* ♦ **stu·pid·ly** *We had stupidly been looking at the wrong column of figures.* ♦ **stu·pid·ity** /stjuːˈpɪdɪti/ **stupidities** *I stared at him, astonished by his stupidity.* **2** You say that something is **stupid** to indicate that you do not like it or that it annoys you. *Friendship is much more important to me than a stupid old ring!*   ◆◆◆◇◇ ADJ-GRADED PRAGMATICS / ADV-GRADED / N-VAR / ADJ-GRADED PRAGMATICS

stu·por /ˈstjuːpə, AM ˈstuː-/ **stupors.** Someone who is in a **stupor** is almost unconscious and is unable to act or think normally, especially as a result of drink or drugs.   N-COUNT

stur·dy /ˈstɜːdi/ **sturdier, sturdiest.** Someone or something that is **sturdy** looks strong and is unlikely to be easily injured or damaged. ♦ **stur·di·ly** *was a good table too, sturdily constructed of elm.*   ◆◇◇◇◇ ADJ-GRADED / ADV-GRADED

stur·geon /ˈstɜːdʒən/; **sturgeon** is both the singular and the plural form. A **sturgeon** is a fish which lives in the northern hemisphere. Sturgeon are usually caught for their eggs, which are known as caviar.   N-VAR

stut·ter /ˈstʌtə/ **stutters, stuttering, stuttered. 1** If someone **stutters**, they have difficulty speaking because they find it hard to say the first sound of a word. ► Also a noun. *He spoke with a pronounced stutter.* ♦ **stut·ter·ing** *He had to stop talking because if he'd kept on, the stuttering would have started.* **2** If something **stutters** along, it progresses slowly and unevenly. *The political debate stutters on.*   ◆◇◇◇◇ VERB: V / N-COUNT / N-UNCOUNT / VERB V prep/adv BRITISH

sty /staɪ/ **sties.** A **sty** is the same as a **pigsty.**   N-COUNT

stye /staɪ/ **styes.** A **stye** is an infection of the skin at the bottom of an eyelash, which makes the eyelid red and swollen.   N-COUNT

style /staɪl/ **styles, styling, styled. 1** The **style** of something is the general way in which it is done or presented, which often shows the attitudes of the people involved. *Belmont Park is a broad sweeping track which will suit the European style of running.* ♦ **-style** *...the development of a Western-style political system.* **2** If people or places have **style**, they are   ◆◆◆◆◇ N-COUNT: with supp, also in adj N / COMB / N-UNCOUNT

smart and elegant. **3** If you say that something is **not** someone's **style**, you mean that it is not the way in which they usually do things, or does not fit the way they usually see themselves. ● to **cramp** someone's **style**: see **cramp**.   PHRASE

4 The **style** of a product is its design. *Several styles of hat were available.* ♦ **-style** *Guests have been asked to dress 1920s-style.* **5** In the arts, a particular **style** is characteristic of a particular period or group of people. *...six scenes in the style of a classical Greek tragedy.* **6** If something such as a piece of clothing, a vehicle, or someone's hair **is styled** in a particular way, it is designed or shaped in that way. *...classically styled clothes.* **7** See also **old-style, self-styled, styling.**   N-VAR / COMB / N-COUNT / VB: usu passive V-ed

styl·ing /ˈstaɪlɪŋ/. **1** The **styling** of an object is the design and appearance of it. *The car neatly blends classic styling into a smooth modern package.* **2** The **styling** of someone's hair is the way in which it is cut and arranged. *...shampoos and styling products.* **3** See also **style.**   ◆◇◇◇◇ N-UNCOUNT / N-UNCOUNT

styl·ised /ˈstaɪlaɪzd/. See **stylized.**

styl·ish /ˈstaɪlɪʃ/. Someone or something that is **stylish** is smart, elegant, and fashionable. ♦ **styl·ish·ly** *...stylishly dressed middle-aged women.*   ◆◆◇◇◇ ADJ-GRADED / ADV-GRADED

styl·ist /ˈstaɪlɪst/ **stylists. 1** A **stylist** is a hairdresser. **2** A **stylist** is someone whose job is to create the style of something such as an advertisement or the image of people such as pop singers. **3** If you describe someone as a **stylist**, you mean that they pay a lot of attention to the way they write, say, or do something so that it is attractive and elegant.   ◆◇◇◇◇ N-COUNT / N-COUNT / N-COUNT

sty·lis·tic /staɪˈlɪstɪk/. **Stylistic** describes things relating to the methods and techniques used in creating a piece of writing, music, or art. *There are some stylistic elements in the statue that just don't make sense.* ♦ **sty·lis·ti·cal·ly** *While both share some similarities they are stylistically very different.*   ◆◇◇◇◇ ADJ / ADV

styl·ized /ˈstaɪlaɪzd/; also spelled **stylised.** Something that is **stylized** uses various artistic or literary conventions in order to create an effect, instead of being natural or true to life.   ◆◇◇◇◇ ADJ-GRADED

sty·lus /ˈstaɪləs/ **styluses.** The **stylus** on a record player is the small needle that picks up the sound signals on the records.   N-COUNT

sty·mie /ˈstaɪmi/ **stymies, stymieing, stymied.** If you **are stymied** by something, you find it very difficult to take action or to continue what you are doing. *Relief efforts have been stymied in recent weeks by armed gunmen.*   VB: usu passive beV-ed

Styro·foam /ˈstaɪrəfəʊm/. **Styrofoam** is a very light, plastic substance, used especially to make containers or as an insulating material. The usual British word is **polystyrene.**   N-UNCOUNT AMERICAN

suave /swɑːv/ **suaver, suavest.** Someone who is **suave** is charming, polite, and elegant, but may be insincere.   ADJ-GRADED

sub /sʌb/ **subs. 1** In team games such as football, a **sub** is a player who is brought into a match to replace another player. **2** A **sub** is a submarine. *...their new nuclear sub.* **3** A fixed amount of money that you pay regularly in order to be a member of a club or society is called your **subs.**   ◆◆◇◇◇ N-COUNT / N-COUNT INFORMAL / N-PLURAL BRITISH

sub- /sʌb-/. **1** **Sub-** is used at the beginning of words that have 'under' as part of their meaning. *The waters were rising about the rock and would soon submerge it. ...a nuclear-powered submarine.* **2** **Sub-** is added to the beginning of nouns in order to form other nouns that refer to things that are part of a larger thing. *...a subcommittee on family values and individual rights.* **3** **Sub-** is added to the beginning of adjectives in order to form other adjectives that describe someone or something as inferior, for example inferior to normal people or to normal things. *The cold has made already substandard living conditions even worse.*   PREFIX / PREFIX / PREFIX

sub·al·tern /ˈsʌbəltən/ **subalterns.** A **subaltern** is any commissioned officer in the army below the rank of captain.   N-COUNT BRITISH

sub·atom·ic /ˌsʌbə'tɒmɪk/. A subatomic particle is `ADJ: ADJ n` a particle which is part of an atom, for example an `TECHNICAL` electron, a proton, or a neutron.

sub·com·mit·tee /'sʌbkəmɪti/ **subcommittees;** ◆◇◇◇ also spelled **sub-committee**. A subcommittee is a `N-COLL-COUNT` small committee made up of members of a larger committee.

sub·con·scious /ˌsʌb'kɒnʃəs/. **1** Your subcon- ◆◇◇◇ scious is the part of your mind that can influence `N-SING: the N,` you or affect your behaviour even though you are `N with poss` not aware of it. **2** A subconscious feeling or action `ADJ` exists in or is influenced by your subconscious. ...*a subconscious cry for affection.* ♦ **sub·con·scious·ly** *Subconsciously I had known that I would not be* `ADV` *in personal danger.*

sub·con·ti·nent /ˌsʌb'kɒntɪnənt/ **subcontinents;** `N-COUNT` also spelled **sub-continent**. A subcontinent is part of a larger continent, made up of a number of countries that form a large mass of land. 'The subcontinent' is often used to refer to the area that contains India, Pakistan, and Bangladesh.

sub·con·tract, subcontracts, subcontracting, subcontracted. The verb is pronounced /ˌsʌbkən'trækt/. The noun is pronounced /sʌb'kɒntrækt/. **1** If one firm subcontracts part of `VERB:` its work to another firm, it pays the other firm to do `V n to n` part of the work that it has been employed to do. `V n` *The company is subcontracting production of most of the parts.* **2** A subcontract is a contract between a `N-COUNT` firm which is being employed to do a job and another firm which agrees to do part of that job.

sub·con·trac·tor /ˌsʌbkən'træktə, AM -'kɑːntræk-/ `N-COUNT` **subcontractors;** also spelled **sub-contractor**. A subcontractor is a person or firm that has a contract to do part of a job which another firm is responsible for.

sub·cul·ture /'sʌbkʌltʃə/ **subcultures;** also `N-COUNT` spelled **sub-culture**. A subculture is the ideas, art, and way of life of a group of people within a society, which are different from the ideas, art, and way of life of the rest of the society. ...*the violent subculture of London youth gangs.*

sub·cu·ta·neous /ˌsʌbkjuː'teɪnɪəs/. Subcutaneous `ADJ: ADJ n` is used to indicate that something is situated, used, or put under your skin. ...*subcutaneous fat.*

sub·di·vide /ˌsʌbdɪ'vaɪd/ **subdivides, subdividing, subdivided;** also spelled **sub-divide**. If something is subdivided, it is divided into several smaller `be V-ed into n` areas, parts, or groups. *The verbs were subdivided into transitive and intransitive categories.* `VB: usu passive`

sub·di·vi·sion /ˌsʌbdɪ'vɪʒən/ **subdivisions;** also spelled **sub-division**. **1** A subdivision is an area, `N-COUNT` part, or section of something which is itself a part of something larger. *Months are a conventional subdivision of the year.* **2** You can refer to a plot of land `N-COUNT` for building houses as a subdivision. `AMERICAN`

sub·due /səb'djuː, AM -'duː/ **subdues, subduing, subdued.** **1** If soldiers or the police subdue a `VERB: V n` group of people, they defeat them or bring them under control by using force. **2** To subdue feelings `VERB` means to make them less strong. *He forced himself* `V n` *to subdue and overcome his fears.* ◆◇◇◇

sub·dued /səb'djuːd, AM -'duːd/. **1** Someone who ◆◇◇◇ is subdued is very quiet, often because they are sad `ADJ-GRADED` or worried about something. **2** Subdued sounds are `ADJ-GRADED` not very loud. **3** Subdued lights or colours are not `ADJ-GRADED` very bright.

ˌsub-'editor, sub-editors; also spelled **subeditor**. `N-COUNT` A sub-editor is a person whose job is to check and `BRITISH` correct articles in newspapers or magazines before they are printed.

sub·group /'sʌbɡruːp/ **subgroups;** also spelled `N-COUNT` **sub-group**. A subgroup is a group that is part of a larger group.

sub·hu·man /ˌsʌb'hjuːmən/; also spelled **sub-** `ADJ` **human**. If you describe someone's behaviour or situation as subhuman, you mean that it is disgusting and not worthy of a civilized person.

sub·ject, subjects, subjecting, subjected. ◆◆◆◇ The noun and adjective are pronounced /'sʌbdʒɪkt/.

The verb is pronounced /səb'dʒekt/. **1** The subject `N-COUNT` of a conversation, letter, or book is the thing that is being discussed or written about. *It was I who first raised the subject of plastic surgery.* **2** Someone or `N-COUNT: N of n` something that is the subject of criticism, study, or an investigation is being criticized, studied, or investigated. *He's now the subject of an official inquiry.* **3** When someone involved in a conversation `PHRASE` changes the subject, they start talking about something else.

4 A subject is an area of knowledge or study, especial- `N-COUNT` ly one that you study at school, college, or university.

5 In an experiment or piece of research, the subject is `N-COUNT` the person or animal that is being tested or studied. `FORMAL`

6 An artist's subjects are the people, animals, or ob- `N-COUNT: with supp` jects that he or she paints, models, or photographs.

7 In grammar, the subject of a clause is the noun `N-COUNT` group that refers to the person or thing that is doing the action expressed by the verb. For example, in 'My cat keeps catching birds', 'my cat' is the subject.

8 If someone or something is subject to something, `ADJ:` they are affected by it or are likely to be affected by it. `v-link ADJ to n` *Prices may be subject to alteration.* **9** If someone is `ADJ:` subject to a particular set of rules or laws, they have to `v-link ADJ to n` obey those rules or laws. *Mr Jones is not subject to the normal police discipline code.* **10** If an event will take `PHR-PREP` place subject to a condition, it will take place only if that thing happens. *Egypt had agreed to a summit, subject to certain conditions.*

11 If you subject someone to something unpleasant, `VERB` you make them experience it. ...*the man who had sub-* `V n to n` *jected her to four years of beatings.*

12 The people who live in or belong to a particular `N-COUNT: with supp` country, usually one ruled by a monarch, are the subjects of that monarch or country. Compare citizen.

13 Subject peoples and countries are ruled or con- `ADJ: ADJ n` trolled by the government of another country. ...*colonies and other subject territories.* `FORMAL`

sub·jec·tion /səb'dʒekʃən/. Subjection to someone `N-UNCOUNT` involves being controlled and oppressed by them.

sub·jec·tive /səb'dʒektɪv/. Something that is sub- ◆◇◇◇ jective is based on personal opinions and feelings `ADJ-GRADED` rather than on facts. ♦ **sub·jec·tive·ly** *I can choose* `ADV-GRADED` *to see things subjectively of course.* ♦ **sub·jec·tiv·ity** `N-UNCOUNT` /ˌsʌbdʒek'tɪvɪti/. *They accused her of flippancy and subjectivity in her reporting.*

'subject matter; also spelled **subject-matter**. The ◆◇◇◇ subject matter of something such as a book, lec- `N-UNCOUNT` ture, film, or painting is the thing that is being written about, discussed, or shown.

sub ju·di·ce /ˌsʌb 'dʒuːdɪsi/. When something is `ADJ` sub judice, people are not allowed to comment `LEGAL` about it in the media because it is the subject of a trial in a court of law.

sub·ju·gate /'sʌbdʒuɡeɪt/ **subjugates, subjugating, subjugated.** **1** If someone subjugates a `VERB: V n` group of people, they take complete control of them, especially by defeating them in a war. ♦ **sub·ju·ga·tion** /ˌsʌbdʒu'ɡeɪʃən/. ...*the brutal subjuga-* `N-UNCOUNT` *tion of native tribes.* **2** If your wishes or desires are `VERB` subjugated to something, they are treated as less `be V-ed to n` important than that thing. *After having been subju-* `Also be V-ed` *gated to ambition, your maternal instincts are at last starting to assert themselves.*

sub·junc·tive /səb'dʒʌŋktɪv/. In English, a clause `N-SING:` expressing a wish or suggestion can be put in the `the N` subjunctive, or in the subjunctive mood, by using `FORMAL` the base form of a verb or 'were'. An example is 'He asked that they be removed'.

sub·let /ˌsʌb'let/ **sublets, subletting.** The form `VERB: V n` sublet is used in the present tense and is the past tense and past participle of the verb. If you sublet a building or part of a building, you allow someone to use it and you take rent from them, although you are not the owner and pay rent for it yourself.

ˌsub-lieu'tenant, sub-lieutenants. A sub- `N-COUNT` lieutenant is a naval officer of the lowest rank.

sub·li·mate /'sʌblɪmeɪt/ **sublimates, sublimat-** `VERB: V n` **ing, sublimated.** If you sublimate a strong desire `be V-ed into n` or feeling, you express it in a way that is socially ac- `TECHNICAL`

ceptable. *The erotic impulse is sublimated into art.* ♦ **sub·li·ma·tion** /ˌsʌblɪˈmeɪʃən/. *...sublimation of the sexual drive.* [N-UNCOUNT]

sub·lime /səˈblaɪm/. **1** If you describe something as **sublime**, you mean that it has a wonderful quality that affects you deeply. ► You can refer to sublime things as **the sublime**. *She elevated every rare small success to the sublime.* ● If you describe something as going **from the sublime to the ridiculous**, you mean that it changes from being of very high quality to being silly or trivial. **2** If you describe someone's attitude or behaviour as **sublime**, you mean that they seem surprisingly ignorant or unaware of something. *...the administration's sublime incompetence.* ♦ **sub·lime·ly** *Mrs Trollope was sublimely uninterested in what she herself wore.* [◆◇◇◇◇ ADJ-GRADED LITERARY N-SING: the N PHRASE] [ADJ FORMAL] [ADV]

sub·limi·nal /sʌbˈlɪmɪnəl/. **Subliminal** influences or messages affect your mind without you being aware of it. ♦ **sub·limi·nal·ly** *I have read many books, perhaps they influenced me subliminally.* [ADJ] [ADV]

sub-ma·chine gun, sub-machine guns; also spelled **submachine gun**. A **sub-machine gun** is a light portable type of machine gun. [N-COUNT]

sub·ma·rine /ˌsʌbməˈriːn/ **submarines. 1** A **submarine** is a type of ship that can travel both above and below the surface of the sea. ♦ **sub·ma·rin·er** /sʌbˈmærɪnə, AM ˌsʌbməˈriːnə/ **submariners.** A **submariner** is a sailor who works on a submarine. **2 Submarine** means existing below the surface of the sea. *...submarine plants.* [◆◆◇◇◇ N-COUNT] [N-COUNT] [ADJ: ADJ n FORMAL]

sub·merge /səbˈmɜːdʒ/ **submerges, submerging, submerged. 1** If something **submerges**, it goes below the surface of some water or another liquid. *The river burst its banks, submerging an entire village. ...a submerged rock.* **2** If you **submerge** yourself in an activity, you give all your attention to it and do not think about anything else. [◆◇◇◇◇ V-ERG: V V n V-ed] [VERB: V pron-refl in n]

sub·mers·ible /səbˈmɜːsɪbəl/. If something is **submersible**, it can go or operate under water. [ADJ]

sub·mis·sion /səbˈmɪʃən/ **submissions. 1 Submission** is a state in which people accept that they are under the control of someone else, for example because they are not powerful enough to resist them. **2** The **submission** of a proposal, application, or other document is the act of sending it to someone, so that they can decide whether to accept it or not. *...the submission of a dissertation.* **3** A **submission** is a proposal, application, or other document that is sent or presented to someone, so that they can decide whether to accept it or not. [◆◇◇◇◇ N-UNCOUNT] [N-UNCOUNT FORMAL] [N-COUNT]

sub·mis·sive /səbˈmɪsɪv/. If you are **submissive**, you behave in a quiet obedient way. ♦ **sub·mis·sive·ly** *The troops submissively lay down their weapons.* [ADJ-GRADED] [ADV-GRADED]

sub·mit /səbˈmɪt/ **submits, submitting, submitted. 1** If you **submit** to something, you accept it or undergo it reluctantly, for example because you are not powerful enough to resist it. *They demanded $7 million, saying that if I submitted to their demands, they would not press the allegations.* **2** If you **submit** a proposal or application to someone, you send it to them so that they can decide whether to accept it or not. *Head teachers yesterday submitted a claim for a 9 per cent pay rise.* [◆◇◇◇◇ VERB V to n Also V] [VERB: V n to n V n]

sub·nor·mal /ˌsʌbˈnɔːməl/. If someone is **subnormal**, they have less ability or intelligence than a normal person of their age. ► The **subnormal** are people who are subnormal. [ADJ] [N-PLURAL: the N]

sub·or·di·nate, subordinates, subordinating, subordinated. The noun and adjective are pronounced /səˈbɔːdɪnət/. The verb is pronounced /səˈbɔːdɪneɪt/. **1** If someone is your **subordinate**, they have a less important position than you in the organization that you both work for. **2** Someone who is **subordinate** to you has a less important position than you and has to obey you. *Women were regarded as subordinate to free men.* **3** Something that is **subordinate** to something else is less important than the other thing. *...an art in which words* [◆◆◇◇◇ N-COUNT] [ADJ] [ADJ-GRADED]

were subordinate to images. **4** If you **subordinate** something to another thing, you regard it or treat it as less important than the other thing. ♦ **sub·or·di·na·tion** /səˌbɔːdɪˈneɪʃən/. *...economic subordination to Europe.* [VERB: V n to n] [N-UNCOUNT]

sub,ordinate 'clause, subordinate clauses. A **subordinate clause** is a clause in a sentence which adds to or completes the information given in the main clause. It cannot usually stand alone as a sentence. Compare **main clause**. [N-COUNT]

sub,ordinating con'junction, subordinating conjunctions. A **subordinating conjunction** is a word such as 'although', 'because', or 'when' which begins a subordinate clause. Compare **co-ordinating conjunction**. [N-COUNT]

'sub-plot, sub-plots. The **sub-plot** in a play, film, or novel is a story that is separate from and less important than the main story. [N-COUNT]

sub·poe·na /səˈpiːnə/ **subpoenas, subpoenaing, subpoenaed. 1** A **subpoena** is a legal document telling someone that they must give evidence as a witness in a court of law. **2** If someone **subpoenas** someone, they serve them with a subpoena. If someone **subpoenas** evidence, it must be produced in a court of law as evidence. [◆◇◇◇◇ N-COUNT] [VERB: V n]

sub·scribe /səbˈskraɪb/ **subscribes, subscribing, subscribed. 1** If you **subscribe to** an opinion or belief, you are one of a number of people who have this opinion or belief. *I've personally never subscribed to the view that either sex is superior to the other.* **2** If you **subscribe to** a service, magazine, or organization, you pay money regularly to receive the service or magazine, or to belong to or support the organization. ♦ **sub·scrib·er, subscribers** *I have been a subscriber to Railway Magazine for many years.* **3** If you **subscribe** for shares in a company, you apply to buy shares in that company. [◆◇◇◇◇ VERB V to n] [VERB: V to n] [N-COUNT] [VERB: V for n]

sub·scrip·tion /səbˈskrɪpʃən/ **subscriptions.** A **subscription** is an amount of money that you pay regularly in order to receive a service or magazine, or to belong to or support an organization. [◆◇◇◇◇ N-COUNT]

sub·sec·tion /ˈsʌbsekʃən/ **subsections;** also spelled **sub-section**. A **subsection** of a text or a document such as a law is one of the smaller parts into which its main parts are divided. [N-COUNT: also N num]

sub·se·quent /ˈsʌbsɪkwənt/. **1** You use **subsequent** to describe something that happened or existed after the time or event that has just been referred to. *Those concerns were overshadowed by subsequent events.* ♦ **sub·se·quent·ly** *She subsequently became the Faculty's President.* **2** If something happened **subsequent to** something else, it happened after that thing. *They won only one more game subsequent to their Cup semi-final win.* [◆◆◇◇◇ ADJ: ADJ n FORMAL] [ADV] [PHRASE FORMAL]

sub·ser·vi·ent /səbˈsɜːviənt/. **1** If you are **subservient** to someone, you do whatever they want you to do. ♦ **sub·ser·vi·ence** /səbˈsɜːviəns/. *...an austere regime stressing obedience and subservience to authority.* **2** If you treat one thing as **subservient to** another, you treat it as less important than the other thing. *The woman's needs are seen as subservient to the group interest.* [◆◇◇◇◇ ADJ-GRADED] [N-UNCOUNT] [ADJ: v-link ADJ to n]

sub·set /ˈsʌbset/ **subsets.** A **subset** of a group of things is a smaller number of things that belong together within that group. [N-COUNT]

sub·side /səbˈsaɪd/ **subsides, subsiding, subsided. 1** If a feeling or a noise **subsides**, it becomes less strong or loud. *Catherine's sobs finally subsided.* **2** If fighting **subsides**, it becomes less intense or widespread. **3** If the ground or a building **is subsiding**, it is sinking to a lower level. ♦ **sub·sid·ence** /səbˈsaɪdəns, ˈsʌbsɪdəns/. *The problems were caused by subsidence and the house needed to be underpinned.* **4** If the level of water, especially flood water, **subsides**, it goes down. [◆◇◇◇◇ VERB] [VERB: V] [VERB: V] [N-UNCOUNT] [VERB: V]

sub·sidi·ar·ity /səbˌsɪdiˈæriti/. **Subsidiarity** is the principle of allowing the individual members of a large organization to make decisions on issues that affect them, rather than leaving those decisions to be made by the whole group. [◆◇◇◇◇ N-UNCOUNT]

sub·sid·i·ary /səb'sɪdiəri, AM -dieri/ **subsidiaries.** ◆◆◇◇◇
1 A **subsidiary** or a **subsidiary** company is a company which is part of a larger and more important company. ...*British Asia Airways, a subsidiary of British Airways.* **2** If something is **subsidiary**, it is less important than something else with which it is connected. *The economics ministry has increasingly played a subsidiary role to the finance ministry.* N-COUNT ADJ

sub·si·dize /'sʌbsɪdaɪz/ **subsidizes, subsidizing, subsidized;** also spelled **subsidise** in British English. **1** If an authority **subsidizes** something, they pay part of the cost of it. *Governments have subsidized the housing of middle and upper-income groups.* ♦ **sub·si·dized** ...*heavily subsidized prices for housing.* ♦ **sub·si·diz·ing** ...*their heavy subsidising of mortgage rates.* ♦ **sub·si·di·za·tion** /,sʌbsɪdaɪ'zeɪʃən/. ...*the federal government's subsidisation of poorer parts of the country.* **2** If a government **subsidizes** an industry, they provide money in order to enable the industry to continue. ...*a government decision to subsidise coal mining.* ♦ **subsidized** ...*Scotland's subsidised theatre.* ♦ **subsidization** ...*the subsidization of Japanese agriculture.* ◆◆◇◇◇ VERB V n ADJ-GRADED N-UNCOUNT N-UNCOUNT VERB V n ADJ-GRADED N-COUNT

sub·si·dy /'sʌbsɪdi/ **subsidies.** A **subsidy** is money that is paid by an authority in order to help an industry or business, or to pay for a public service. *Farmers are planning a massive demonstration against farm subsidy cuts.* ◆◆◆◇◇ N-COUNT

sub·sist /səb'sɪst/ **subsists, subsisting, subsisted.** If people **subsist**, they are just able to obtain the food or money that they need in order to stay alive. *The prisoners subsisted on one mug of the worst quality porridge three times a day.* VERB: V V on n

sub·sist·ence /səb'sɪstəns/. **1 Subsistence** is the condition of having just enough food or money to stay alive. *The standard of living today is on the edge of subsistence.* **2** In **subsistence** farming or **subsistence** agriculture, farmers produce food to eat themselves rather than to sell. ◆◇◇◇◇ N-UNCOUNT ADJ: ADJ n

sub·soil /'sʌbsɔɪl/. The **subsoil** is a layer of earth that is just below the surface soil but above hard rock. N-UNCOUNT: also a N

sub·son·ic /,sʌb'sɒnɪk/. **Subsonic** speeds or aeroplanes are very fast but slower than the speed of sound. ADJ: ADJ n

'sub-species; also spelled **subspecies. Sub-species** is both the singular and plural form. A **sub-species** of a plant or animal is a subdivision of a species. N-COUNT TECHNICAL

sub·stance /'sʌbstəns/ **substances. 1** A **substance** is a solid, powder, liquid, or gas with particular properties. *The substance that's causing the problem comes from the barley.* **2 Substance** is the quality of being important or significant. *It's questionable whether anything of substance has been achieved.* **3** The **substance** of what someone says or writes is the main thing that they are trying to say. *The substance of his discussions doesn't really matter.* **4** If you say that something has no **substance**, you mean that it is not true. *There is no substance in any of these allegations.* **5** A person **of substance** has a lot of money, power, or influence. ◆◆◆◇◇ N-COUNT N-UNCOUNT FORMAL N-SING: the N of n N-UNCOUNT FORMAL PHRASE FORMAL

,sub-'standard; also spelled **substandard.** A **substandard** service or product is unacceptable because it is below a required standard. ADJ-GRADED

sub·stan·tial /səb'stænʃəl/. **1 Substantial** means large in amount or degree. *That is a very substantial improvement.* **2** A **substantial** building is large and strongly built. ...*those fortunate enough to have a fairly substantial property to sell.* ◆◆◆◇◇ ADJ-GRADED FORMAL ADJ-GRADED FORMAL

sub·stan·tial·ly /səb'stænʃəli/. **1** If something increases or decreases **substantially**, it increases or decreases by a large amount. *The something changes or improves substantially, it changes or improves to a great extent.* **2** If something is **substantially** different from something else, there is a large or basic difference between the two things. **3** If you say that something is **substantially** correct or unchanged, you mean that it is generally correct or unchanged. ◆◆◇◇◇ ADV-GRADED: ADV with v FORMAL ADV-GRADED: ADV adj/prep FORMAL ADV: ADV adj FORMAL

sub·stan·ti·ate /səb'stænʃieɪt/ **substantiates, substantiating, substantiated.** To **substantiate** a statement or a story means to supply evidence which proves that it is true. *There is little scientific evidence to substantiate the claims.* ♦ **sub·stan·tia·tion** /səb,stænʃi'eɪʃən/. ...*alternative methods of substantiation other than written records.* ◆◇◇◇◇ VERB V n FORMAL N-UNCOUNT

sub·stan·tive /səb'stæntɪv/. **1 Substantive** negotiations or talks involve real issues and aim to arrive at a meaningful agreement. **2 Substantive** issues or questions are real and important. ◆◇◇◇◇ ADJ-GRADED FORMAL ADJ-GRADED FORMAL

sub·sta·tion /'sʌbsteɪʃən/ **substations.** A **substation** is a place where high voltage electricity from power plants is converted to lower voltage electricity for homes or factories. N-COUNT

sub·sti·tute /'sʌbstɪtjuːt, AM -tuːt/ **substitutes, substituting, substituted. 1** If you **substitute** one thing for another, or if one thing **substitutes** for another, it takes the place or performs the function of the other thing. *You could always substitute a low-fat soft cheese... Would phone conversations substitute for cosy chats over lunch?* ♦ **sub·sti·tu·tion** /,sʌbstɪ'tjuːʃən, AM -'tuː-/ **substitutions** ...*a straight substitution of carob for chocolate.* **2** A **substitute** is something that you have or use instead of something else. *She is seeking a substitute from the very man whose departure made her cry.* **3** If you say that one thing is no **substitute** for another, you mean that it does not have certain desirable features that the other thing has, and is therefore unsatisfactory. If you say that there is no **substitute** for something, you mean that it is the only thing which is really satisfactory. *The printed word is no substitute for personal discussion.* **4** In team games such as football and rugby, a **substitute** is a player who is brought into a match to replace another player. ◆◆◆◇◇ V-ERG: V n for n V n V for n Also V N-VAR N-COUNT N-COUNT: with neg N-COUNT

sub·stra·tum /'sʌbstrɑːtəm, AM -'streɪt-/ **substrata.** A **substratum** of something is something that exists under the surface of something else, or is less obvious than something else. ...*its deep substratum of chalk.* N-COUNT: with supp FORMAL

sub·sume /səb'sjuːm, AM -'suːm/ **subsumes, subsuming, subsumed.** If something **is subsumed** within a larger group or class, it is included within it, rather than being considered as something separate. *East Germany was subsumed by capitalist West Germany.* VERB: be V-ed prep be V-ed Also V n, V n prep FORMAL

sub·ter·fuge /'sʌbtəfjuːdʒ/ **subterfuges. Subterfuge** is a trick or a dishonest way of getting what you want. *Most people can see right through that type of subterfuge.* N-VAR

sub·ter·ra·nean /,sʌbtə'reɪniən/. A **subterranean** river or tunnel is under the ground. ◆◇◇◇◇ ADJ FORMAL

sub·text /'sʌbtekst/ **subtexts.** The **subtext** is the implied message or subject of something that is said or written. N-VAR

sub·ti·tle /'sʌbtaɪtəl/ **subtitles. 1** The **subtitle** of a piece of writing is a second title which is often longer and explains more than the main title. ♦ **sub·ti·tled** *'Lorna Doone' is subtitled 'a Romance of Exmoor'.* **2 Subtitles** are the printed translation that you can read at the bottom of the screen when you are watching a foreign film. ♦ **subtitled** *Much of the film is subtitled.* N-COUNT V-PASSIVE: be V-ed with quote N-PLURAL ADJ

sub·tle /'sʌtəl/ **subtler, subtlest. 1** Something that is **subtle** is not immediately obvious or noticeable. ...*the slow and subtle changes that take place in all living things.* ♦ **sub·tly** *The truth is subtly different.* **2 Subtle** smells, tastes, sounds, or colours are pleasantly complex and delicate. ...*delightfully subtle scents.* ♦ **subtly** ...*a white sofa teamed with subtly coloured rugs.* ◆◆◇◇◇ ADJ-GRADED ADV-GRADED ADJ-GRADED ADV-GRADED

sub·tle·ty /'sʌtəlti/ **subtleties. 1 Subtleties** are very small details or differences which are not obvious. ...*his fascination with the subtleties of human behaviour.* **2 Subtlety** is the quality of being not immediately obvious or noticeable, and therefore difficult to describe. *African dance is vigorous, but full of subtlety.* **3 Subtlety** is the ability to notice and recognize things which are not obvious, ◆◇◇◇◇ N-COUNT N-UNCOUNT N-UNCOUNT

S

especially small differences between things. *She analyses herself with great subtlety.* **4 Subtlety** is the ability to use indirect methods to achieve something, rather than doing something that is obvious. *They had obviously been hoping to approach the topic with more subtlety.* N-UNCOUNT

sub·to·tal /'sʌbtəʊtəl/ **subtotals.** A **subtotal** is a figure that is the result of adding some numbers together but is not the final total. N-COUNT

sub·tract /səb'trækt/ **subtracts, subtracting, subtracted.** If you **subtract** one number from another, you do a calculation in which you take it away from the other number. *We have subtracted $25 per adult to arrive at a basic room rate.* ♦ **sub·trac·tion** /səb'trækʃən/ **subtractions** *She's ready to learn simple addition and subtraction.* ◆◇◇◇ VERB: V n from n / V n ♦ N-VAR

,sub·'tropical; also spelled **subtropical.** **1 Sub-tropical** places have a climate that is warm and humid, and are often near tropical regions. **2 Sub-tropical** plants and trees grow in places that are warm and humid. ADJ / ADJ

sub·urb /'sʌbɜːb/ **suburbs.** **1 A suburb** of a city or large town is a smaller area which is part of the city or large town but is outside its centre. **2** If you live in the **suburbs**, you live in the mainly residential area outside the centre of a large town or city. ◆◆◇◇ N-COUNT / N-PLURAL

sub·ur·ban /sə'bɜːbən/. **1 Suburban** means relating to a suburb. *...a suburban shopping centre in Sydney.* **2** If you describe something as **suburban**, you mean that it is dull and conventional. *His clothes are conservative and suburban.* ◆◆◇◇ ADJ: ADJ n / ADJ-GRADED

sub·ur·bia /sə'bɜːbiə/. **Suburbia** is sometimes used to refer to the suburbs of cities and large towns considered as a whole. *...images of bright summer mornings in leafy suburbia.* N-UNCOUNT

sub·ver·sive /səb'vɜːsɪv/ **subversives.** **1** Something that is **subversive** is intended to weaken or destroy a political system or government. *The play was promptly banned as subversive.* **2 Subversives** are people who attempt to weaken or destroy a political system or government. ◆◇◇◇ ADJ-GRADED / N-COUNT

sub·vert /səb'vɜːt/ **subverts, subverting, subverted.** To **subvert** something means to destroy its power and influence. *...an alleged plot to subvert the state.* ♦ **sub·ver·sion** /səb'vɜːʃən, AM -ʒən/. *He was arrested in parliament on charges of subversion.* ◆◇◇◇ V n FORMAL ♦ N-UNCOUNT

sub·way /'sʌbweɪ/ **subways.** **1 A subway** is an underground railway. *I don't ride the subway late at night.* **2 A subway** is a passage for pedestrians that goes underneath a busy road or a railway track. N-COUNT AMERICAN / N-COUNT BRITISH

,sub·'zero; also spelled **subzero. Sub-zero** temperatures are below 0° centigrade. ADJ

suc·ceed /sək'siːd/ **succeeds, succeeding, succeeded.** **1** If you **succeed** in doing something, you manage to do it. *We have already succeeded in working out ground rules with the Department of Defense... If they can succeed in America and Europe, then they can succeed here too.* **2** If something **suc-ceeds**, it works in a satisfactory way or has the result that is intended. *If marriage is to succeed in the 1990's, then people have to recognise the new pressures it is facing.* **3** Someone who **succeeds** gains a high position in what they do, for example in business or politics. *...the skills and qualities needed to succeed in small and medium-sized businesses.* **4** If you **succeed** another person, you are the next person to have their job or position. *Prince Rainier III succeeded to the throne on 9 May 1949.* **5** If one thing is **succeeded** by another thing, the other thing happens or comes after it. *A quick divorce can be succeeded by a much longer—and more agonising—period of haggling over the fate of the family.* ◆◆◆◇ VERB: V in -ing/n / V / VERB: V / VERB: V / VERB: V n / V to n / VB: usu passive be V-ed

suc·cess /sək'ses/ **successes.** **1 Success** is the achievement of something that you have been trying to do. *It's important for the long-term success of any diet.* **2 Success** is the achievement of a high position in a particular field, for example in business or politics. *Nearly all of the young people interviewed believed that work was the key to success.* **3** The **success** of something is the fact that it works ◆◆◆◆ N-UNCOUNT / N-UNCOUNT / N-UNCOUNT

in a satisfactory way or has the result that is intended. *Most of the cast was amazed by the play's success.* **4** Someone or something that is a **success** achieves a high position, makes a lot of money, or is admired a great deal. *The jewellery was a great success.* N-COUNT

suc·cess·ful /sək'sesful/. **1** Something that is **suc-cessful** achieves what it was intended to achieve. Someone who is **successful** achieves what they intended to achieve. *How successful will this new treatment be?.* ♦ **suc·cess·ful·ly** *The doctors have successfully concluded preliminary tests.* **2** Something that is **successful** is popular or makes a lot of money. *...the hugely successful movie that brought Robert Redford an Oscar.* **3** Someone who is **suc-cessful** achieves a high position in what they do, for example in business or politics. *She is a successful lawyer.* ◆◆◆◇ ADJ-GRADED / ADV / ADJ-GRADED / ADJ-GRADED

suc·ces·sion /sək'seʃən/ **successions.** **1 A suc-cession** of things of the same kind is a number of them that exist or happen one after the other. *Ad-ams took a succession of jobs. ...scoring three goals in quick succession.* **2 Succession** is the act or right of being the next person to have an important job or position. *She is now seventh in line of succession to the throne.* ◆◆◇◇ N-SING: also in N / N-UNCOUNT: also N in pl

suc·ces·sive /sək'sesɪv/. **Successive** means happening or existing one after another without a break. *Jackson was the winner for a second successive year.* ♦ **suc·ces·sive·ly** *He successively won the British, European and World championships.* ◆◆◇◇ ADJ / ADV

suc·ces·sor /sək'sesə/ **successors.** Someone's **successor** is the person who takes their job after they have left. ◆◆◇◇ N-COUNT

suc·cess story, success stories. Someone or something that is a **success story** is very successful, often unexpectedly or in spite of unfavourable conditions. *Her nationwide chain, Sock Shop, was one of the high-street success stories of the Eighties.* N-COUNT

suc·cinct /sək'sɪŋkt/. Something that is **succinct** expresses facts or ideas clearly and in few words; used showing approval. *The book gives an admirably succinct account of the technology.* ♦ **suc-cinct·ly** *He succinctly summed up his manifesto as 'Work hard, train hard and play hard'.* ◆◇◇◇ ADJ-GRADED / PRAGMATICS / ADV-GRADED: ADV with v

suc·cour /'sʌkə/ **succours, succouring, suc-coured;** spelled **succor** in American English. **1 Succour** is help given to people who are suffering or in difficulties. *...Italy's commitment to give suc-cour to populations involved in an absurd conflict.* **2** If you **succour** someone who is suffering or in difficulties, you help them. *Helicopters fly in appalling weather to succour shipwrecked mariners.* N-UNCOUNT FORMAL / VERB V n FORMAL

suc·cu·lent /'sʌkjʊlənt/ **succulents.** **1 Succulent** food, especially meat or vegetables, is juicy and delicious. **2 Succulents** or **succulent** plants are types of plants which have thick fleshy leaves. ◆◇◇◇ ADJ-GRADED / N-COUNT

suc·cumb /sə'kʌm/ **succumbs, succumbing, succumbed.** **1** If you **succumb** to persuasion or to a desire for something, you are unable to resist it although you feel it might be wrong. *Don't succumb to the temptation to have just one cigarette.* **2** If you **succumb to** an illness, you become affected by it or die from it. ◆◇◇◇ VERB V to n FORMAL / VERB: V to n FORMAL

such /sʌtʃ/. When **such** is used as a predeterminer, it is followed by 'a' and a count noun in the singular. When it is used as a determiner, it is followed by a count noun in the plural or by an uncount noun. **1** You use **such** to refer back to the thing or person that you have just mentioned, or a thing or person like the one that you have just mentioned. You use **such as** and **such...as** to introduce a reference to the person or thing that has just been mentioned. *There have been previous attempts at coups. We regard such methods as entirely unacceptable... There'd be no telling how John would react to such news as this.* ▶ Also a predeterminer. *How can we make sense of such a story as this?* ▶ Also before **be.** *We are scared because we are being watched – such is the atmosphere in Pristina.* ▶ Also **as such.** *Products tested on animals have to be* ◆◆◆◆ DET / PREDET / such be / -ed as such

labelled as such. ► Also **such as.** *Issues such as these* such as pron
were not really his concern.

2 You use **such...as** to link something or someone DET
with a clause in which you give a description of the PRAGMATICS
kind of thing or person that you mean. *Britain is not
enjoying such prosperity as it was in the mid-1980s.*
► Also **such as.** *...special knowledge such as could only* n such as cl
have been known by the killer. **3** You also use DET
such...as to introduce one or more examples of the PRAGMATICS
kind of thing or person that you have just mentioned.
*...such careers as teaching, nursing, hairdressing and
catering.* ► Also **such as.** *...serious offences, such as* such as n
assault.

4 You use **such** before noun groups to emphasize the DET
extent of something or to emphasize that something PRAGMATICS
is remarkable. *One will never be able to understand
why these political issues can acquire such force.*
► Also a predeterminer. *You know the health service is* PREDET
in such a state... It was such a pleasant surprise. **5** You PREDET
use **such...that** in order to emphasize the degree of PRAGMATICS
something by mentioning the result or consequence
of it. *He was in such a hurry that he almost pushed me
over on the stairs.* ► Also a determiner. *She looked at* DET
him in such distress that he had to look away. ► Also be such that
after **be.** *His extravagance was such that he died in
poverty.* **6** You use **such...that** or **such...as** in order to DET
say what the result or consequence of something that PRAGMATICS
you have just mentioned is. *The operation has uncovered such backstreet dealing in stolen property that police might now press for changes in the law.* ► Also a PREDET
predeterminer. *He could put an idea in such a way
that Alan would believe it was his own.* ► Also after **be.** be such that
*OFSTED's brief is such that it can conduct any inquiry
which the Secretary of State requires.*

7 You use **such and such** to refer to a thing or person PHRASE
when you do not want to be exact or precise. *I said,* SPOKEN
*'Well what time'll I get to Leeds?' and he said such and
such a time.* **8** You use **such as it is** or **such as they are** PHRASE
to suggest that the thing you have just mentioned is PRAGMATICS
not very good, important, or useful. *...the British
Women's Movement, such as it is these days.*

9 You use **as such** with a negative to indicate that a PHRASE
word or expression is not a very accurate description
of the actual situation. *I am not a learner as such – I
used to ride a bike years ago.* **10** You use **as such** after a PHRASE
noun to indicate that you are considering that thing
on its own, separately from other things or factors. *Mr
Simon said he was not against taxes as such.* **11 ● no
such thing**: see **thing**.

such·like /ˈsʌtʃlaɪk/. You use **suchlike** to refer to PRON
things like the ones already mentioned. *I suppose
you'd rather be in Chicago, eating waffles and hamburgers, or suchlike?* ► Also a determiner. *The prices* DET
of polymers and suchlike materials will decrease.

suck /sʌk/ **sucks, sucking, sucked.** **1** If you ◆◆◇◇◇
suck something, you hold it in your mouth and pull V on/at n
at it with the muscles in your cheeks and tongue, V
for example in order to get liquid out of it. *He
sucked on his cigarette... Doran was clutching the
bottle with both hands and sucking intently.* **2** If VERB
something **sucks** a liquid, gas, or object in a par- V n with adv
ticular direction, it draws it there with a powerful be V-ed prep
force. *They sucked in deep lungfuls of air. ...the air- Also V n prep
line pilot who was almost sucked from the cockpit of
his plane when a window shattered.* **3** If you **are** V-PASSIVE
sucked into a bad situation, you are unable to pre- be V-ed into n
vent yourself from becoming involved in it. *He
warned that if the President tried to enforce control,
the country would be sucked into a power vacuum.*

4 If someone says that something **sucks**, they are in- VB: no cont
dicating that they think it is very bad; some people V
find this use offensive. *The system sucks.* **5 ● to suck** INFORMAL
something **dry**: see **dry**.

suck up. You say that someone **is sucking up** to a PHRASAL VB
person in authority when you do not like the fact that PRAGMATICS
they are trying to please the person because of his or V P to n
her position. *She kept sucking up to the teachers, espe- Also V P
cially Mrs Clements.* INFORMAL

suck·er /ˈsʌkə/ **suckers.** **1** If you call someone a ◆◇◇◇◇
sucker, you mean that it is very easy to cheat them; N-COUNT;
N-VOC

used showing disapproval. *Keep giving us your mon- INFORMAL
ey, sucker!* **2** If you describe someone as a **sucker** N-COUNT:
for something, you mean that they find it very diffi- N for n
cult to resist it. *I'm such a sucker for romance.* INFORMAL

3 On a plant, a **sucker** is a new growth that is sent out N-COUNT
from the base of the plant or from its root.

suck·le /ˈsʌkəl/ **suckles, suckling, suckled.** V-ERG: V n
When a mother **suckles** her baby, or when the baby V
suckles, the baby sucks milk from her breast. *As the* DATED
baby suckles, a further supply of milk is generated.

su·crose /ˈsuːkrəʊs/. **Sucrose** is a common type of N-UNCOUNT
sugar. *Exclude from the diet simple sugars like su-* TECHNICAL
crose, glucose and fructose.

suc·tion /ˈsʌkʃən/. **1 Suction** is the process by N-UNCOUNT
which liquids, gases, or other substances are drawn
out of somewhere. *The suction of the milking
machine ensures that the teat becomes attached.* N-UNCOUNT
2 Suction is the process by which two surfaces stick
together when the air between them is removed.
*...their pneumatic robot which uses air to move and
sticks to surfaces by suction.*

sud·den /ˈsʌdən/. **1 Sudden** means happening ◆◆◆◇◇
quickly and unexpectedly. *He had been deeply af- ADJ-GRADED
fected by the sudden death of his father-in-law... It
was all very sudden.* **♦ sud·den·ness** *The enemy* N-UNCOUNT
seemed stunned by the suddenness of the attack. **2** If PHRASE
something happens **all of a sudden**, it happens
quickly and unexpectedly. *All of a sudden she didn't
look sleepy any more.*

,**sudden 'death.** **Sudden death** is a way of quick- ◆◇◇◇◇
ly deciding the winner of something such as a foot- N-UNCOUNT
ball match or golf tournament when there are equal
scores at the time when it would normally end. In a
sudden-death situation, the team who next scores a
goal for example is the winner.

sud·den·ly /ˈsʌdənli/. If something happens **sud-** ◆◆◆◇
denly, it happens quickly and unexpectedly. *Her ex- ADV-GRADED
pression suddenly altered.*

suds /sʌdz/. **Suds** are the bubbles that are pro- N-PLURAL
duced when soap or detergent is mixed with water.

sue /suː/ **sues, suing, sued.** If you **sue** someone, ◆◆◇◇◇
you start a legal case against them, usually in order VERB
to claim money from them because they have V n for n
harmed you in some way. *Mr Warren sued him for* Also V n
libel... *One former patient has already indicated his
intention to sue.*

suede /sweɪd/. **Suede** is leather with a soft, slightly ◆◇◇◇◇
rough surface. *Albert wore a brown suede jacket and* N-UNCOUNT
jeans.

suet /ˈsuːɪt/. **Suet** is hard animal fat that is used in N-UNCOUNT
cooking.

suf·fer /ˈsʌfə/ **suffers, suffering, suffered.** **1** If ◆◆◆◆◇
you **suffer** pain, you feel it in your body or in your VERB: V n
mind. *Can you assure me that my father is not suf-* V
fering? **2** If you **suffer from** an illness or from some VERB
other bad condition, you are badly affected by it. *He* V from n
was eventually diagnosed as suffering from terminal
cancer.* **♦ suf·fer·er, sufferers** *Frequently sufferers* N-COUNT
of this kind of allergy are also sufferers of asthma.

3 If you **suffer** something bad, you are in a situation in VERB
which something painful, harmful, or very unpleas- V n
ant happens to you. *Romania suffered another setback
in its efforts to obtain financial support for its reforms.*

4 If you **suffer**, you are badly affected by an unfavour- VERB: V
able event or situation. *It is obvious that Syria will* V from n
suffer most from this change of heart.* **5** If something VERB
suffers, it becomes worse in quality or condition V
because it has been neglected or because of an unfavourable situation. *Investment would suffer badly.*

6 See also **suffering**. **7** If you do not **suffer fools glad-** PHRASE
ly, you do not have much patience with people who
are stupid.

suf·fer·ance /ˈsʌfrəns/. If you are allowed to do N-UNCOUNT
something **on sufferance**, you can do it, although
you know that the person who gave you permission
would prefer that you did not do it.

suf·fer·ing /ˈsʌfrɪŋ/ **sufferings. Suffering** is seri- ◆◆◇◇◇
ous pain which someone feels in their body or their N-UNCOUNT:
mind. *It has caused terrible suffering to animals.* also N in pl

● See also **long-suffering**.

S

suf·fice /səˈfaɪs/ **suffices, sufficing, sufficed.** ◆◇◇◇◇
1 If you say that something will **suffice**, you mean it will be enough to achieve a purpose or to fulfil a need. *A cover letter should never exceed one page; often a far shorter letter will suffice.* **2 Suffice it to say** or **suffice to say** is used at the beginning of a statement to indicate that what you are saying is obvious, or that you will only give a short explanation. *Suffice it to say that afterwards we never met again.*

suf·fi·cien·cy /səˈfɪʃənsi/. **Sufficiency** of something is enough of that thing to achieve a purpose or to fulfil a need. *When foods from different plant sources are eaten together, deficiency in one is compensated for by sufficiency in another.*

suf·fi·cient /səˈfɪʃənt/. **1** If something is **sufficient** for a particular purpose, there is enough of it for the purpose. *Lighting levels should be sufficient for photography without flash.* ♦ **suf·fi·cient·ly** *She recovered sufficiently to accompany Chou on his tour of Africa in 1964.* **2** If something is a **sufficient** cause or condition for something to happen, it can happen. *Discipline is a necessary, but certainly not a sufficient condition for learning to take place.*

suf·fix /ˈsʌfɪks/ **suffixes. 1** A **suffix** is a letter or group of letters, for example '-ly' or '-ness', which is added to the end of a word in order to form a different word, often of a different word class. Compare **affix** and **prefix**. **2** A **suffix** is one or more numbers or letters added to the end of a code number to indicate, for example, what area something belongs to. *These ships were all numbered with the suffix LBK.*

suf·fo·cate /ˈsʌfəkeɪt/ **suffocates, suffocating, suffocated. 1** If someone **suffocates** or is **suffocated**, they die because there is no air for them to breathe. *They were suffocated as they slept.* ♦ **suf·fo·ca·tion** /ˌsʌfəˈkeɪʃən/. *Many of the victims died of suffocation.* **2** If you say that you **are suffocating** or that something **is suffocating** you, you mean that you feel very uncomfortable because there is not enough fresh air and it is difficult to breathe. *The airlessness of the room suffocated her.* **3** You say that someone or something **is suffocating** or that something **is suffocating** them when the situation that they are in does not allow them to act freely or to develop. *The governor's proposals would actually cost millions of jobs and suffocate the economy.*

suf·frage /ˈsʌfrɪdʒ/. **Suffrage** is the right of people to vote for a government or national leader.

suf·fra·gette /ˌsʌfrəˈdʒet/ **suffragettes.** In Britain, in the early twentieth century, a **suffragette** was a woman who was involved in the campaign for women to have the right to vote.

suf·fuse /səˈfjuːz/ **suffuses, suffusing, suffused. 1** If something, especially a colour or feeling, **suffuses** someone or something, it gradually spreads over or through them. *A dull red flush suffused Selby's face.* **2** If something such as a book, film, or piece of music **is suffused** with a quality, it is full of that quality. *Kingdon's broad experience, as writer and scholar, suffuses this important book.*

sug·ar /ˈʃʊɡə/ **sugars. 1 Sugar** is a sweet substance that is used to sweeten food and drink. It is usually in the form of white or brown crystals. *Ice cream is high in fat and sugar.* ● See also **caster sugar, confectioners' sugar, granulated sugar, icing sugar. 2** If someone has one **sugar** in their tea or coffee, they have one small spoon of sugar or one sugar lump in it. *How many sugars do you take?* **3 Sugars** are substances that occur naturally in food. When you eat them, the body converts them into energy. *...the natural sugars found in grape juice.* **4 ●** to **sugar the pill**: see **pill**.

'sugar beet, sugar beets. Sugar beet is a crop with a large round root. It is grown for the sugar which can be obtained from this root.

'sugar bowl, sugar bowls. A **sugar bowl** is a small bowl in which sugar is kept.

'sugar cane; also spelled **sugarcane. Sugar cane** is a tall tropical plant. It is grown for the sugar that can be obtained from its thick stems.

sug·ary /ˈʃʊɡəri/. **1 Sugary** food or drink contains a lot of sugar. **2** If you describe a film or piece of music as **sugary**, you mean that it is sentimental and insincere; used showing disapproval. *The programme seemed false and sugary, and the characters smug.*

sug·gest /səˈdʒest, AM səɡˈdʒ-/ **suggests, suggesting, suggested. 1** If you **suggest** something, you put forward a plan or idea for someone to think about. *I suggest you ask him some specific questions about his past... I suggested to Mike that we go out for a meal with his colleagues... No one has suggested how this might occur.* **2** If you **suggest** the name of a person or place, you recommend them to someone. *They can suggest where to buy one.* **3** If you **suggest** that something is the case, you say something which you believe to be the case. *I'm not suggesting that is what is happening... Their success is conditional, I suggest, on this restriction.* **4** If one thing **suggests** another, it implies it or makes you think that it might be the case. *Earlier reports suggested that a meeting would take place on Sunday.* **5** If one thing **suggests** another, it brings it to your mind through an association of ideas. *This onomatopoeic word suggests to me the sound a mousetrap makes when it snaps shut.*

sug·ges·tion /səˈdʒestʃən, AM səɡˈdʒ-/ **suggestions. 1** If you make a **suggestion**, you put forward an idea or plan for someone to think about. *The dietitian was helpful, making suggestions as to how I could improve my diet... Perhaps he'd followed her suggestion of a stroll to the river.* **2** A **suggestion** is something that someone says which implies that something is the case. *There are suggestions that he might be supported by the Socialists.* **3** If there is no **suggestion** that something is the case, there is no reason to think that it is the case. *There is absolutely no suggestion of any mainstream political party involvement in this.* **4** If there is a **suggestion** of something, there is a slight indication or sign of it. *...that fashionably faint suggestion of a tan.* **5 Suggestion** means giving people a particular idea by associating it with other ideas. *The power of suggestion is very strong.*

sug·ges·tive /səˈdʒestɪv, AM səɡˈdʒ-/. **1** Something that is **suggestive of** something else gives a hint of it or reminds you of it. *The atmosphere is more suggestive of a relaxed lunchtime jazz session than an intense rock gig.* **2 Suggestive** remarks or looks cause people to think about sex, often in a way that makes them feel uncomfortable. *...another former employee who claims Thomas made suggestive remarks to her.* ♦ **sug·ges·tive·ly** *She winked suggestively.*

sui·cid·al /ˌsuːɪˈsaɪdəl/. **1** People who are **suicidal** want to kill themselves. *Her suicidal tendencies continued for several more weeks.* **2** If you describe an action or behaviour as **suicidal**, you mean that it is very dangerous. *It would be suicidal to resist in the face of overwhelming military superiority.*

sui·cide /ˈsuːɪsaɪd/ **suicides. 1** People who commit **suicide** deliberately kill themselves because they do not want to continue living. *...a growing number of suicides in the community.* **2** You say that people commit **suicide** when they deliberately do something which ruins their career or position in society. *They say it would be political suicide for the party to abstain.* **3** The people involved in a **suicide** attack, mission, or bombing do not expect to survive. *...a suicide bomber.*

suit /suːt/ **suits, suiting, suited. 1** A man's **suit** consists of a jacket, trousers, and sometimes a waistcoat, all made from the same fabric. See picture headed **clothes.** *...a smart suit and tie.* **2** A woman's **suit** consists of a jacket and skirt, or sometimes trousers, made from the same fabric. *I was wearing my tweed suit.* **3** A particular type of **suit** is

a piece of clothing that you wear for a particular activity. *The six survivors only lived through their North Sea ordeal because of the special rubber suits they were wearing.* **4** People sometimes refer to **suits** or to the **men in grey suits** when they are referring to the men who have control of an organization or company, and who have a lot of power. *Elsewhere in the system there is a clash between the interests of men in grey suits and those of the general public. ...which is why, just a few days ago, he was to be found among the suits at a cocktail party.*

5 If something **suits** you, it is convenient for you or is the best thing for you in the circumstances. *...the best package to suit your needs.* **6** If something **suits** you, you like it. *I don't think a sedentary life would altogether suit me.* **7** If a piece of clothing or a particular style or colour **suits** you, it makes you look attractive. *Green suits you.* **8** If you **suit** yourself, you do something just because you want to do it, without bothering to consider other people. *He made a dismissive gesture. 'Suit yourself.'*

9 In a court of law, a **suit** is a case in which a person tries to get justice for some wrong that has been done to them. *Up to 2,000 former employees have filed personal injury suits against the company.* ▶ In American English, you can say that someone files or brings **suit** against another person. *One insurance company has already filed suit against the city of Chicago.*

10 A **suit** is one of the four types of card in a set of playing cards. These are hearts, diamonds, clubs, and spades. **11** See also **bathing suit, birthday suit, boiler suit, trouser suit.**

12 If you **follow suit**, they do the same thing that someone else has just done. *Efforts to persuade the remainder to follow suit have continued.* **13 ● suit someone down to the ground:** see **ground.**

suit·able /ˈsuːtəbəl/. Someone or something that is **suitable** for a particular purpose or occasion is right or acceptable for it. *She had no other dress suitable for the occasion... The authority must make suitable accommodation available to the family.* ♦ **suit·abil·ity** /ˌsuːtəˈbɪlɪti/. *...information on the suitability of a product for use in the home.*

suit·ably /ˈsuːtəbli/. **1** You use **suitably** to describe something that you think is right or appropriate for a particular purpose or occasion. *There are problems in recruiting suitably qualified scientific officers for NHS laboratories... Unfortunately I'm not suitably dressed for gardening.* **2** If you say that someone or something is, for example, **suitably** impressed or **suitably** modest, you mean that they show as much of that quality as you would expect in the circumstances.

suit·case /ˈsuːtkeɪs/ **suitcases.** A **suitcase** is a box or bag with a handle and a hard frame in which you carry your clothes when you are travelling.

suite /swiːt/ **suites. 1** A **suite** is a set of rooms in a hotel or other building. *...a new suite of offices.* ● See also **en suite. 2** A **suite** is a set of matching armchairs and a sofa. **3** A bathroom **suite** is a matching bath, basin, and toilet.

suit·ed /ˈsuːtɪd/. **1** If something is well **suited** to a particular purpose, it is right or appropriate for that purpose. If someone is well **suited** to a particular job, they are right or appropriate for that job. *Satellites are uniquely suited to provide this information.* **2** If two people, especially a man and a woman, are **well suited**, they are likely to have a successful relationship because they have similar personalities or interests.

suit·or /ˈsuːtə/ **suitors. 1** A woman's **suitor** is a man who wants to marry her. *Her suitor was attracted to her personality.* **2** A **suitor** is a company or organization that wants to buy another company. *Whatever is offered by the bank is unlikely to be improved on by any rival suitor.*

sul·fate /ˈsʌlfeɪt/. See **sulphate.**
sul·fide /ˈsʌlfaɪd/. See **sulphide.**
sul·fur /ˈsʌlfə/. See **sulphur.**

sul·fu·ric acid /sʌlˌfjʊərɪk ˈæsɪd/. See **sulphuric acid.**

sulk /sʌlk/ **sulks, sulking, sulked.** If you **sulk**, you are silent and bad-tempered for a while because you are annoyed about something; used showing disapproval. *He turned his back and sulked.* ▶ Also a noun. *Now she must be tired of my sulks.*

sulky /ˈsʌlki/. Someone who is **sulky** is sulking or is unwilling to enjoy themselves; used showing disapproval. *a sulky adolescent.*

sul·len /ˈsʌlən/. Someone who is **sullen** is bad-tempered and does not speak much. *The offenders lapsed into a sullen silence.* ♦ **sul·len·ly** *'I've never seen it before,' Harry said sullenly.*

sul·ly /ˈsʌli/ **sullies, sullying, sullied. 1** If something **is sullied** by something else, it is damaged so that it is no longer pure or of such high value. *She claimed they were sullying the Conservative Party's good name.* **2** If someone **sullies** something, they make it dirty or imperfect. *I felt loath to sully the gleaming brass knocker by handling it.*

sul·phate /ˈsʌlfeɪt/ **sulphates;** spelled **sulfate** in American English. A **sulphate** is a salt of sulphuric acid. *...copper sulphate.*

sul·phide /ˈsʌlfaɪd/ **sulphides;** spelled **sulfide** in American English. A **sulphide** is a compound of sulphur with some other chemical elements. *...hydrogen sulphide.*

sul·phur /ˈsʌlfə/; spelled **sulfur** in American English. **Sulphur** is a yellow chemical which has a strong smell. *...measures to reduce emissions of sulphur dioxide.*

sul·phu·ric acid /sʌlˌfjʊərɪk ˈæsɪd/; spelled **sulfuric acid** in American English. **Sulphuric acid** is a colourless, oily, and very powerful acid.

sul·phur·ous /ˈsʌlfərəs/; spelled **sulfurous** in American English. **Sulphurous** air or places contain sulphur or smell of sulphur. *...sulphurous volcanic gases.*

sul·tan /ˈsʌltən/ **sultans.** A **sultan** is a ruler in some Muslim countries.

sul·tana /sʌlˈtɑːnə, -ˈtæn-/ **sultanas. Sultanas** are dried white grapes.

sul·try /ˈsʌltri/. **1 Sultry** weather is hot and humid. **2** Someone who is **sultry** is attractive in a way that suggests hidden passion. *...a dark-haired sultry woman.*

sum /sʌm/ **sums, summing, summed. 1** A **sum** of money is an amount of money. *Even the relatively modest sum of £50,000 now seems beyond his reach.* **2** A **sum** is a simple calculation in arithmetic. *I can't do my sums.* **3** In mathematics, the **sum of** two numbers is the number that is obtained when they are added together. *The sum of all the angles of a triangle is 180 degrees.* **4** The **sum** of something is all of it. You often use 'sum' in this way to indicate that you are disappointed because the extent of something is rather small, or because it is not very good. *The sum of evidence points to the crime resting on them... Has it, in its 30 years, added much to the sum of human happiness?* **5** See also **lump sum.**

6 You use **in sum** to introduce a statement that briefly describes a situation. *It is a situation, in sum, devoid of logic.* **7** If you say that something is **more than the sum of** its **parts** or **greater than the sum of** its **parts,** you mean that it is better than you would expect from the individual parts, because the way they combine adds a different quality. *As individual members' solo careers have proved, each band was greater than the sum of its parts.*

sum up. 1 If you **sum** something **up,** you describe it as briefly as possible. *One voter in Brasilia summed up the mood – 'Politicians have lost credibility,' he complained.* **2** If something **sums** a person or situation **up,** it represents their most typical characteristics. *Sadly, the feud sums up the relationship between Lord Bath and the man who succeeds him.* **3** If you **sum up** after a speech or at the end of a piece of writing, you briefly state the main points again. When a judge

sums up after a trial, he reminds the jury of the evidence and the main arguments of the case they have heard. **4** See also **summing-up**.

sum·ma·rize /ˈsʌməraɪz/ **summarizes, summa-** ◆◇◇◇◇
rizing, summarized; also spelled **summarise** in VERB: V n
British English. If you **summarize** something, you be V-ed
give a summary of it. *Basically, the article can be* prep/adv
summarized in three sentences... To summarise, this V
is a clever approach to a common problem. Also V with quote

sum·mary /ˈsʌməri/ **summaries. 1** A **summary** ◆◆◇◇◇
of something is a short account of it, which gives N-COUNT
the main points but not the details. *What follows is*
a brief summary of the process... Here's a summary
of the day's news. ● You use **in summary** to indi- PHRASE
cate that what you are about to say is a summary of PRAGMATICS
what has just been said. *In summary, it is my opin-*
ion that this complete treatment process was very
successful. **2 Summary** actions are done without de- ADJ: ADJ n
lay, often when something else should have been FORMAL
done first or done instead. *It says torture and sum-*
mary execution are common. ◆ **sum·mari·ly** *Sever-* ADV:
al detainees had been summarily executed. ADV with v

sum·mat /ˈsʌmət/. **Summat** is used in writing to
represent a regional spoken form of the word
'something'. *Are we going to write a story or*
summat?

sum·ma·tion /sʌˈmeɪʃən/ **summations.** A **sum-** N-COUNT
mation is a summary of what someone has said or FORMAL
done. *Her introduction is a model of fairness, a lively*
summation of Irish history.

sum·mer /ˈsʌmə/ **summers. Summer** is the sea- ◆◆◆◇◇
son between spring and autumn. In the summer the N-VAR
weather is usually warm or hot. *I escaped the*
heatwave in London earlier this summer and flew to
Cork... It was a perfect summer's day. ● See also
high summer, Indian summer.

'summer house, summer houses; also spelled
summerhouse. 1 A **summer house** is a small build- N-COUNT
ing in a garden. It contains seats, and people can sit
there in the summer. **2** Someone's **summer house** N-COUNT
is a house in the country or by the sea where they
spend the summer.

'summer school, summer schools. A **summer** N-VAR
school is an educational course on a particular subject that is run during the summer. The students
usually stay at the place where the summer school
is being held.

'summer time; also spelled **summertime** for ◆◇◇◇◇
meaning 1. **1 Summer time** is the period of time N-UNCOUNT
during which the summer lasts. *It's a very beautiful*
place in the summertime. **2 Summer time** is a peri- N-UNCOUNT
od in the spring and summer during which the BRITISH
clocks are put forward, so that people can have an
extra hour of daylight in the evening. The American
expression is **daylight saving time.**

sum·mery /ˈsʌməri/. Something that is **summery** is ADJ-GRADED
suitable for summer or characteristic of summer.
...light summery fruit salads.

,summing-'up, summings-up; also spelled ◆◇◇◇◇
summing up. In a trial, the judge's **summing-up** is N-COUNT
the speech he or she makes to the jury at the end of
a trial to remind them of the evidence and the main
arguments of the case they have heard.

sum·mit /ˈsʌmɪt/ **summits. 1** A **summit** is a meet- ◆◆◆◇◇
ing at which the leaders of two or more countries N-COUNT
discuss important matters. *...the NATO summit*
meeting in Rome. **2** The **summit** of a mountain is N-COUNT
the top of it.

sum·mon /ˈsʌmən/ **summons, summoning,** ◆◆◇◇◇
summoned. 1 If you **summon** someone, you VERB: V n
order them to come to you. *Suddenly we were* be V-ed
summoned to the interview room... He has been prep/adv
summoned to appear in court on charges of incite- be V-ed to-inf
ment to law-breaking. **2** If you **summon** a quality, VERB
you make a great effort to have it on a particular V n
occasion. For example, if you **summon** the strength
to do something, you make a great effort to be
strong, so you will be able to do it. *It took her a full*
month to summon the courage to tell her mother.
▶ **Summon up** means the same as **summon.** *We* PHRASAL VB
couldn't even summon up the energy to open the V P noun
envelope.

summon up. 1 See **summon** 2. **2** If something **sum-** PHRASAL VB
mons up a memory, it causes it to come to your mind. V P n
LITERARY

sum·mons /ˈsʌmənz/ **summonses, summons-** ◆◇◇◇◇
ing, summonsed. 1 A **summons** is an order to N-COUNT
come and see someone. **2** A **summons** is an official N-COUNT
order to appear in court. **3** If someone **is sum-** VB: usu
monsed, they are officially ordered to appear in passive
court. *She has been summonsed to appear at St Al-* be V-ed to-inf
bans magistrates' court.

sumo /ˈsuːməʊ/. **Sumo** is the Japanese style of ◆◇◇◇◇
wrestling. *...a sumo wrestler.* N-UNCOUNT

sump /sʌmp/ **sumps.** The **sump** is the place under N-COUNT
an engine which holds the engine oil.

sump·tu·ous /ˈsʌmptʃuəs/. Something that is ◆◇◇◇◇
sumptuous is magnificent and obviously very ex- ADJ-GRADED
pensive. *...a variety of sumptuous fabrics.* ◆ **sump-**
·tu·ous·ly *...this sumptuously illustrated volume.* ADV-GRADED

,sum 'total. The **sum total** of a number of things N-SING
consists of all the things added or considered together. You often use this expression to indicate
that you are disappointed because the extent of
something is rather small, or because it is not very
good. *That small room contained the sum total of*
the family's possessions.

sun /sʌn/ **suns, sunning, sunned. 1** The **sun** is ◆◆◆◆◇
the ball of fire in the sky that the Earth goes round, N-SING
and that gives us heat and light. **2** You refer to the N-UNCOUNT
light and heat that reach us from the sun as the
sun. *Dena took them into the courtyard to sit in the*
sun. **3** If you **are sunning** yourself, you are sitting VERB:
or lying in a place where the sun is shining on you. V pron-refl
4 A **sun** is any star which has planets revolving N-COUNT
around it. **5** ● **a place in the sun:** see **place.**

Sun. Sun. is a written abbreviation for **Sunday.** ◆◆◇◇◇

'sun-baked. Sun-baked land or earth has been ADJ: ADJ n
made hard and dry by the sun shining on it.

sun·bathe /ˈsʌnbeɪθ/ **sunbathes, sunbathing,** ◆◇◇◇◇
sunbathed. When people **sunbathe,** they sit or lie VERB: V
in a place where the sun shines strongly on them,
so that they get a suntan. ◆ **sun·bather, sun-** N-COUNT
bathers *A week ago Bournemouth beach was*
thronged with sunbathers soaking up the 80 degrees
heat. ◆ **sun·bath·ing** *Nearby there is a stretch of* N-UNCOUNT
white sand beach perfect for sunbathing.

sun·beam /ˈsʌnbiːm/ **sunbeams.** A **sunbeam** is a N-COUNT
ray of sunlight.

sun·bed /ˈsʌnbed/ **sunbeds.** A **sunbed** is a piece of N-COUNT
equipment with ultraviolet lights, that you lie on to BRITISH
get a suntan.

sun·block /ˈsʌnblɒk/ **sunblocks. Sunblock** is a N-VAR
cream which you put on your skin to protect it
completely from the sun.

sun·burn /ˈsʌnbɜːn/ **sunburns.** If someone has N-VAR
sunburn, their skin is bright pink and sore because
they have spent too much time in hot sunshine.

sun·burnt /ˈsʌnbɜːnt/; also spelled **sunburned.**
1 Someone who is **sunburnt** has sore bright pink ADJ-GRADED
skin because they have spent too much time in hot
sunshine. **2** Someone who is **sunburnt** has very ADJ-GRADED
brown skin because they have spent a lot of time in
the sunshine.

sun·burst /ˈsʌnbɜːst/ **sunbursts.** A **sunburst** is a N-COUNT
pattern or design that resembles the sun with rays
coming from it. *She designed a huge sunburst*
window.

sun·dae /ˈsʌndeɪ, -di/ **sundaes.** A **sundae** is a tall N-COUNT
glass of ice cream with whipped cream and nuts or
fruit on top.

Sun·day /ˈsʌndeɪ, -di/ **Sundays. Sunday** is the ◆◆◆◆◇
day after Saturday and before Monday. *I thought we* N-VAR
might go for a drive on Sunday.

,Sunday 'best. If you are in your **Sunday best,** N-SING:
you are wearing your best clothes, which you only poss N
wear for special occasions.

'Sunday school, Sunday schools. Sunday ◆◇◇◇◇
school is a class organized by a church that some N-VAR
children go to on Sundays in order to learn about
Christianity.

sun·der /'sʌndə/ **sunders, sundering, sundered.** If people or things **are sundered**, they are separated by something. *Police moved in to separate the two groups, already sundered by distrust.* `VB: usu passive V-ed LITERARY`

sun·dial /'sʌndaɪəl/ **sundials.** A sundial is a device used for telling the time when the sun is shining. The shadow of a pointer falls onto a flat surface that is marked with the hours, and points to the correct hour. `N-COUNT`

sun·down /'sʌndaʊn/. **Sundown** is the time when the sun sets. The usual British word is **sunset**. `N-UNCOUNT AMERICAN`

'sun-drenched; also spelled **sundrenched. Sun-drenched** places have a lot of hot sunshine. `ADJ-GRADED: ADJ n`

sun·dries /'sʌndriz/. When someone is making a list of things, items that are not important enough to be listed individually are sometimes referred to together as **sundries**. *The inn gift shop stocks quality Indian crafts and sundries.* `N-PLURAL FORMAL`

sun·dry /'sʌndri/. **1** If someone refers to **sundry** people or things, they are referring to several people or things that are all different from each other and which they do not wish to describe individually. *She could ring for food and drink, laundry and sundry services.* **2 All and sundry** means everyone. *I made tea for all and sundry at the office.* `◆◇◇◇ ADJ FORMAL` `PHRASE`

sun·flower /'sʌnflaʊə/ **sunflowers.** A **sunflower** is a very tall plant with large yellow flowers. `◆◇◇◇ N-COUNT`

sung /sʌŋ/. **Sung** is the past participle of **sing**.

sun·glasses /'sʌnɡlɑːsɪz, -glæs-/. **Sunglasses** are spectacles with dark lenses which you wear to protect your eyes from bright sunlight. `◆◇◇◇ N-PLURAL`

'sun hat, sun hats; also spelled **sunhat.** A **sun hat** is a wide-brimmed hat that protects your head from the sun. `N-COUNT`

sunk /sʌŋk/. **Sunk** is the past participle of **sink**.

sunk·en /'sʌŋkən/. **1 Sunken** ships have sunk to the bottom of a sea, ocean, or lake. **2 Sunken** gardens, roads, or other features are below the level of their surrounding area. *The room was dominated by a sunken bath.* **3 Sunken** eyes, cheeks, or other parts of the body curve inwards and make you look thin and unwell. `◆◇◇◇ ADJ: ADJ n ADJ: ADJ n ADJ`

'sun lamp, sun lamps; also spelled **sunlamp.** A **sun lamp** is a lamp that produces ultraviolet rays. People use sun lamps to get a suntan. `N-COUNT`

sun·less /'sʌnləs/. **1** On **sunless** days, the sun does not shine. **2 Sunless** places are not lit by the sun. `ADJ ADJ: ADJ n`

sun·light /'sʌnlaɪt/. **Sunlight** is the light that comes from the sun during the day. `◆◆◇◇ N-UNCOUNT`

sun·lit /'sʌnlɪt/. **Sunlit** places are brightly lit by the sun. `ADJ: ADJ n`

sun·ny /'sʌni/ **sunnier, sunniest. 1** When it is **sunny**, the sun is shining brightly. *There is a chance of sunny spells in the West.* **2 Sunny** places are brightly lit by the sun. **3** Someone who is a **sunny** disposition is usually cheerful and happy. `◆◆◇◇ ADJ-GRADED ADJ-GRADED ADJ-GRADED`

sun·rise /'sʌnraɪz/ **sunrises. 1 Sunrise** is the time in the morning when the sun first appears in the sky. **2** A **sunrise** is the colours and light that you see in the eastern part of the sky when the sun first appears. *There was a spectacular sunrise yesterday.* `◆◇◇◇ N-UNCOUNT N-COUNT`

sun·roof /'sʌnruːf/ **sunroofs.** A **sunroof** is a panel in the roof of a car that opens to let sunshine and air enter the car. `N-COUNT`

sun·screen /'sʌnskriːn/ **sunscreens.** A **sunscreen** is a cream that protects your skin from the sun's rays, especially in hot weather. `◆◇◇◇ N-VAR`

sun·set /'sʌnset/ **sunsets. 1 Sunset** is the time in the evening when the sun disappears out of sight from the sky. **2** A **sunset** is the colours and light that you see in the western part of the sky when the sun disappears in the evening. *There was a red sunset over Paris.* `◆◆◇◇ N-UNCOUNT N-COUNT`

sun·shine /'sʌnʃaɪn/. **Sunshine** is the light and heat that comes from the sun. `◆◆◇◇ N-UNCOUNT`

sun·spot /'sʌnspɒt/ **sunspots. Sunspots** are dark cool patches that appear on the surface of the sun and last for about a week. `N-COUNT`

sun·stroke /'sʌnstrəʊk/. **Sunstroke** is an illness caused by spending too much time in hot sunshine. `N-UNCOUNT`

sun·tan /'sʌntæn/ **suntans;** also spelled **sun-tan. 1** If you have a **suntan**, the sun has turned your skin an attractive brown colour. **2 Suntan** lotion, oil, or cream protects your skin from the sun. `N-COUNT ADJ: ADJ n`

sun·tanned /'sʌntænd/. Someone who is **sun-tanned** has an attractive brown colour from being in the sun. `ADJ-GRADED`

'sun-up; also spelled **sunup. Sun-up** is the time of day when the sun rises. The usual British word is **sunrise**. `N-UNCOUNT AMERICAN`

sup /sʌp/ **sups, supping, supped.** If you **sup** something, you drink it, especially in fairly small sips. `VERB: V n DATED, LITERARY`

su·per /'suːpə/. **1** Some people use **super** to mean very nice or very good; a slightly old-fashioned use. *We had a super time... 'I think I could find you something.'—'That would be super.'* **2 Super** is used before adjectives to indicate that something has a lot of a quality. *...squads of super-fit athletes.* ▶ Also a prefix. *...the development of superfast computers.* **3 Super** is used before nouns to indicate that something is larger, better, or more advanced than similar things. *...a chance to test-drive a stunning Lotus super-car.* ▶ Also a prefix. *...the next generation of superweapons.* `ADJ INFORMAL, BRITISH` `ADV: ADV adj` `PREFIX` `ADJ: ADJ n` `PREFIX`

super- /'suːpə-/. **Super-** is used to form adjectives which indicate that something is at a higher level than something else. *...his superhuman efforts to find work. ...a fragment of crystal with supernormal powers.* `PREFIX`

super·an·nu·at·ed /ˌsuːpər'ænjʊeɪtɪd/. If you describe something as **superannuated**, you mean that it is old and no longer used for its original purpose. *...the superannuated idealism of the Sixties.* `ADJ FORMAL`

super·an·nua·tion /ˌsuːpərænjuː'eɪʃən/. **Superannuation** is money which people pay regularly into a special fund so that when they retire from their job they will receive money regularly as a pension. `N-UNCOUNT BRITISH`

su·perb /suː'pɜːb/. **1** If something is **superb**, its quality is very good indeed. *The waters are crystal clear and offer a superb opportunity for swimming.* ♦ **su·perb·ly** *The orchestra played superbly.* **2** If you say that someone has **superb** confidence, control, or skill, you mean that they have very great confidence, control, or skill. ♦ **superbly** *...his superbly disciplined opponent... The sports complex is huge and superbly well-equipped.* `◆◆◇◇ ADJ-GRADED` `ADV-GRADED ADJ-GRADED` `ADV-GRADED`

super·charged /'suːpətʃɑːdʒd/. If a car engine is **supercharged**, it has more air than normal forced into it so that the petrol burns more quickly and the car has more power. `ADJ`

super·cili·ous /ˌsuːpə'sɪliəs/. If you say that someone is **supercilious**, you disapprove of them because they behave in a scornful way towards other people because they think they are superior to them. `ADJ-GRADED PRAGMATICS`

super·com·put·er /ˌsuːpəkəm'pjuːtə/ **supercomputers.** A **supercomputer** is a powerful computer that can process large amounts of data very quickly. `◆◇◇◇ N-COUNT`

super·con·duc·tiv·ity /ˌsuːpəkɒndʌk'tɪvɪti/. **Superconductivity** is the ability of certain metals to allow electricity to pass through them without any resistance at very low temperatures. `N-UNCOUNT TECHNICAL`

super·con·duc·tor /ˌsuːpəkən'dʌktə/ **superconductors.** A **superconductor** is a metal that allows electricity to pass through it without resistance at very low temperatures. `◆◇◇◇ N-COUNT TECHNICAL`

super-'ego, super-egos; also spelled **superego.** Your **super-ego** is the part of your mind which makes you aware of what is right and wrong, and which causes you to feel guilt when you have done something wrong. `N-COUNT TECHNICAL`

super·fi·cial /ˌsuːpə'fɪʃəl/. **1** If you describe someone as **superficial**, you disapprove of them because they do not think deeply, and have little understanding of anything serious or important. ♦ **super·fi·ci·al·ity** /ˌsuːpəfɪʃi'ælɪti/. *He hated the superficiality, the neon glamour and the cheap prettiness of life in L.A.* **2** If you describe something such as an action, feeling, or relationship as **superficial**, you `◆◆◇◇ ADJ-GRADED PRAGMATICS` `N-UNCOUNT` `ADJ-GRADED`

S

mean that it includes only the simplest and most obvious aspects of that thing, and not those aspects which require more effort to deal with or understand. *His roommate had been pleasant on a superficial level... Father had no more than a superficial knowledge of music.* ♦ **superficiality** *His assessment only serves to demonstrate the superficiality of the judgements we make when we first meet people.* N-UNCOUNT

♦ **super·fi·cial·ly** *The film touches on these difficult questions, but only superficially.* **3 Superficial** is used to describe the appearance of something or the impression that it gives, especially if its real nature is very different. *Spain may well look different but the changes are superficial.* ♦ **superficially** *Many of these killers are frequently glib and superficially charming.* **4 Superficial** injuries are not very serious, and affect only the surface of the body. You can also describe damage to an object as **superficial.** *The explosion caused superficial damage to the fortified house.* ADV-GRADED ADJ-GRADED ADV-GRADED ADJ-GRADED

super·flu·ity /ˌsuːpəˈfluːɪti/ **superfluities.** If there is a **superfluity of** something, there is more of it than is needed. N-COUNT FORMAL

super·flu·ous /suːˈpɜːfluəs/. Something that is **superfluous** is unnecessary or is no longer needed. *My presence at the afternoon's proceedings was superfluous.* ◆◇◇◇◇ ADJ-GRADED

super·grass /ˈsuːpəgrɑːs, -ɡræs/ **supergrasses.** A **supergrass** is a person who gives the police information about a large group of criminals. N-COUNT INFORMAL BRITISH

super·group /ˈsuːpəgruːp/ **supergroups.** A **supergroup** is a pop group that has become very popular and famous. N-COUNT

super·heat·ed /ˌsuːpəˈhiːtəd/. If a liquid is **superheated**, it has been heated to a temperature that is higher than its boiling point without being allowed to boil. ADJ TECHNICAL

super·he·ro /ˌsuːpəˈhɪərəʊ/ **superheroes.** A **superhero** is a fictional character in a cartoon who has superhuman powers and fights against evil. N-COUNT

super·high·way /ˌsuːpəˈhaɪweɪ/ **superhighways.** **1** A **superhighway** is a large fast motorway with several lanes. **2** The information **superhighway** is the network of computer links that enables computer users all over the world to communicate with each other. N-COUNT AMERICAN N-COUNT

super·hu·man /ˌsuːpəˈhjuːmən/. If you describe a quality that someone has as **superhuman**, you mean that it seems to be much greater than that of ordinary people. *They saw their bills rising steadily, in spite of superhuman efforts to save water.* ADJ

super·im·pose /ˌsuːpərɪmˈpəʊz/ **superimposes, superimposing, superimposed. 1** If one image **is superimposed** on another, it is put on top of it so that you can see the second image through it. *The features of different faces were superimposed over one another.* **2** If features or characteristics from one situation **are superimposed** onto another, they are transferred onto or used in the second situation, though they may not fit. *Patterns of public administration and government are superimposed on traditional societies.* ◆◇◇◇◇ VB: usu passive be V-ed on/ overn VB: usu passive be V-ed on n

super·in·tend /ˌsuːpərɪnˈtend/ **superintends, superintending, superintended.** If you **superintend** something, you have responsibility for ensuring that it is carried out properly. *During the interval, Linton superintended a prize draw.* VERB V n FORMAL

super·in·ten·dent /ˌsuːpərɪnˈtendənt/ **superintendents. 1** A **superintendent** is a senior police officer of the rank above an inspector. In the United States, a **superintendent** is the head of a police department. **2** A **superintendent** is a person who is responsible for a particular thing or the work done in a particular department. *He became superintendent of the bank's East African branches.* ◆◆◇◇◇ N-COUNT; N-TITLE BRITISH N-COUNT: N of n

su·pe·ri·or /suːˈpɪəriə/ **superiors. 1** If one thing or person is **superior** to another, the first is better than the second. *...a woman greatly superior to her husband in education and sensitivity... Long-term stock market investments have produced superior returns* ◆◆◇◇◇ ADJ-GRADED

compared with cash deposits.* ♦ **su·peri·or·ity** *The technical superiority of laser discs over tape is well established.* **2** If you describe something as **superior**, you mean that it is good, and better than other things of the same kind. *A few years ago it was virtually impossible to find superior quality coffee in local shops.* **3** A **superior** person or thing has more authority or importance than another person or thing in the same organization or system. *Locally passed laws are of superior authority to those laws passed in Moscow.* **4** Your **superior** in an organization that you work for is a person who has a higher rank than you. N-UNCOUNT ADJ-GRADED ADJ N-COUNT: poss N

5 If you describe someone as **superior**, you disapprove of them because they behave as if they are better, more important, or more intelligent than other people. ♦ **superiority** *...a false sense of his superiority over mere journalists.* **6** If one group of people has **superior** numbers to another group, the first has more people than the second, and therefore has an advantage over it. **7** If you describe someone as your **superior** in a particular activity, you mean that they are better than you at that activity. ADJ-GRADED PRAGMATICS N-UNCOUNT ADJ-GRADED N-COUNT: poss N WRITTEN

su·peri·or·ity /suːˌpɪɒriˈɒriti, AM -ˈɔːriti/. If one side in a war or conflict has **superiority**, it has an advantage over its enemy, for example because it has more soldiers or better equipment. *We have air superiority.* N-UNCOUNT

super·la·tive /suːˈpɜːlətɪv/ **superlatives. 1** If you describe something as **superlative**, you mean that it is extremely good. *Some superlative wines are made in this region.* **2** If someone uses **superlatives** to describe something, they use adjectives and expressions which indicate that it is extremely good. *...a spectacle which has critics world-wide reaching for superlatives.* **3** In grammar, the **superlative** form of an adjective or adverb is the form that indicates that something has more of a quality than anything else. For example, 'biggest' is the superlative form of 'big'. Compare **comparative.** ► Also a noun. *...his tendency towards superlatives and exaggeration.* ◆◇◇◇◇ ADJ N-COUNT ADJ: ADJ n N-COUNT

super·man /ˈsuːpəmæn/ **supermen.** A **superman** is a man who has very great physical or mental powers or who is extremely good at something. N-COUNT

super·mar·ket /ˈsuːpəmɑːkɪt/ **supermarkets.** A **supermarket** is a large shop which sells all kinds of food and some household goods. ◆◆◇◇◇ N-COUNT

super·model /ˈsuːpəmɒdəl/ **supermodels.** A **supermodel** is a world-famous fashion model. ◆◇◇◇◇ N-COUNT

super·natu·ral /ˌsuːpəˈnætʃrəl/. **Supernatural** creatures, forces, and events are believed by some people to exist or happen, although they are impossible according to scientific laws. ► The **supernatural** is things that are supernatural. *He writes short stories with a touch of the supernatural.* ADJ-GRADED N-SING: the N

super·no·va /ˌsuːpəˈnəʊvə/ **supernovas** or **supernovae** /ˌsuːpəˈnəʊviː/. A **supernova** is an exploding star. ◆◇◇◇◇ N-COUNT

super·pow·er /ˈsuːpəpaʊə/ **superpowers.** A **superpower** is a very powerful and influential country, usually one that has nuclear weapons and is economically successful. ◆◆◇◇◇ N-COUNT

super·sede /ˌsuːpəˈsiːd/ **supersedes, superseding, superseded.** If something **is superseded** by something newer, it is replaced because it has become old-fashioned or unacceptable. *Hand tools are relics of the past that have now been superseded by the machine.* ◆◇◇◇◇ VB: usu passive be V-ed

super·son·ic /ˌsuːpəˈsɒnɪk/. **Supersonic** aircraft travel faster than the speed of sound. ◆◇◇◇◇ ADJ: ADJ n

super·star /ˈsuːpəstɑː/ **superstars.** A **superstar** is a very famous entertainer or sports player. ◆◇◇◇◇ INFORMAL N-COUNT

super·state /ˈsuːpəsteɪt/ **superstates.** A **superstate** is a political alliance or union of several nations. *...a European superstate.* N-COUNT

super·sti·tion /ˌsuːpəˈstɪʃən/ **superstitions.** **Superstition** is belief in things that are not real or possible, for example magic. *The phantom of the merry-go-round is just a local superstition.* ◆◇◇◇◇ N-VAR

super·sti·tious /ˌsuːpəˈstɪʃəs/. **1** People who are superstitious believe in things that are not real or possible, for example magic. **2 Superstitious** fears or beliefs are irrational and not based on fact. ◆◇◇◇◇ ADJ-GRADED: ADJ n

super·store /ˈsuːpəstɔː/ **superstores.** Superstores are very large supermarkets or shops selling household goods and equipment. Superstores are usually built outside city centres away from other shops. ◆◇◇◇◇ N-COUNT

super·struc·ture /ˈsuːpəstrʌktʃə/ **superstructures.** The **superstructure** of a ship is the part of it that is above its main deck. N-COUNT

super·tank·er /ˈsuːpətæŋkə/ **supertankers.** A **supertanker** is an extremely large ship that is used for transporting oil. N-COUNT

super·vise /ˈsuːpəvaɪz/ **supervises, supervising, supervised. 1** If you **supervise** an activity or a person, you make sure that the activity is done correctly or that the person is doing a task or behaving correctly. *University teachers have refused to supervise students' examinations.* **2** If you **supervise** a place where work is done, you ensure that the work there is done properly. *He makes the wines and supervises the vineyards.* ◆◆◇◇◇ VERB V n

super·vi·sion /ˌsuːpəˈvɪʒən/. **Supervision** is the supervising of people, activities, or places. *A toddler requires close supervision and firm control at all times.* ◆◆◇◇◇ N-UNCOUNT

super·vi·sor /ˈsuːpəvaɪzə/ **supervisors.** A **supervisor** is a person who supervises activities or people, especially workers or students. ◆◆◇◇◇ N-COUNT

super·vi·sory /ˌsuːpəˈvaɪzəri/. **Supervisory** means concerned with the supervision of people, activities, or places. *...staff with a minor supervisory role.* ◆◇◇◇◇ ADJ: ADJ n

su·pine /ˈsuːpaɪn/. **1** If you are **supine**, you are lying flat on your back. *The book's cover is decorated with a supine woman.* ▶ Also an adverb. *I lay supine on the poolside grass.* **2** If you describe someone as **supine**, you mean that they let events happen because they are too lazy or afraid to influence them. ADJ FORMAL / ADV / ADJ-GRADED FORMAL

sup·per /ˈsʌpə/ **suppers. 1** Some people refer to the main meal eaten in the early part of the evening as **supper. 2 Supper** is a simple meal eaten just before you go to bed at night. ◆◆◇◇◇ N-VAR / N-VAR BRITISH

sup·per·time /ˈsʌpətaɪm/. **Suppertime** is the period of the day when people have their supper. It can be in the early part of the evening or just before they go to bed at night. N-UNCOUNT

sup·plant /səˈplɑːnt, -ˈplænt/ **supplants, supplanting, supplanted.** If a person or thing **is supplanted**, another person or thing takes their place. *By the 1930s the wristwatch had almost completely supplanted the pocket watch.* ◆◇◇◇◇ VERB: be V-ed V n FORMAL

sup·ple /ˈsʌpəl/ **suppler, supplest. 1** A **supple** object or material bends or changes shape easily without cracking or breaking; used showing approval. *The leather is supple and sturdy enough to last for years.* ♦ **sup·ple·ness** *This luxurious talcum lotion restores softness and suppleness to dehydrated skin.* **2** A **supple** person can move and bend their body very easily. ♦ **suppleness** *Exercise in pregnancy can build up your strength and suppleness.* ADJ-GRADED [PRAGMATICS] / N-UNCOUNT / ADJ-GRADED / N-UNCOUNT

sup·ple·ment /ˈsʌplɪmənt/ **supplements, supplementing, supplemented. 1** If you **supplement** something, you add something to it in order to improve it. *I suggest supplementing your diet with vitamins E and A.* ▶ Also a noun. *Business sponsorship must be a supplement to, not a substitute for, public funding.* **2** A **supplement** is a pill that you take or a special kind of food that you eat in order to improve your health or diet. *...a multiple vitamin and mineral supplement.* **3** A **supplement** is a separate part of a magazine or newspaper, often dealing with a particular topic. ● See also **colour supplement. 4** A **supplement** is an extra amount of money that you pay in order to obtain special facilities or services, for example when you are travelling or staying at a hotel. *The single room supplement is £11 a night.* ◆◆◇◇◇ VERB: V n V n with n / N-COUNT / N-COUNT / N-COUNT BRITISH

sup·ple·men·tal /ˌsʌplɪˈmentəl/. **Supplemental** means **supplementary**. *You'll probably be able to buy supplemental insurance at an extra cost.* ADJ: ADJ n FORMAL, usu AMERICAN

sup·ple·men·ta·ry /ˌsʌplɪˈmentri, AM -teri/. **Supplementary** things are added to something in order to improve it. *...the question of whether or not we need to take supplementary vitamins.* ◆◇◇◇◇ ADJ

supple,mentary 'benefit, supplementary benefits. In Britain, **supplementary benefit** is the name that used to be given to money that the government gives regularly to people with no income or very low incomes. The new name for this amount of money is **income support.** N-UNCOUNT: also N in pl

sup·ple·men·ta·tion /ˌsʌplɪmənˈteɪʃən/. **Supplementation** is the use of drugs or special types of food in order to improve your health or diet. N-UNCOUNT MEDICAL

sup·pli·cant /ˈsʌplɪkənt/ **supplicants.** A **supplicant** is a person who asks God or an important person to help them or to give them something that they want very much. N-COUNT FORMAL

sup·pli·ca·tion /ˌsʌplɪˈkeɪʃən/ **supplications.** A **supplication** is a prayer or a request to God or someone in authority for help. *The Tory government has to date resisted all supplications.* N-VAR FORMAL

sup·plied /səˈplaɪd/. If you say that a person or place is well **supplied with** particular things, you mean that they have a large number of them. *France is abundantly supplied with excellent family-run hotels.* ● See also **supply.** ADJ-GRADED: v-link ADJ with n

sup·pli·er /səˈplaɪə/ **suppliers.** A **supplier** is a person, company, or organization that sells or supplies something such as goods or equipment to customers. *...Hillsdown Holdings, one of the UK's biggest food suppliers.* ◆◆◇◇◇ N-COUNT

sup·ply /səˈplaɪ/ **supplies, supplying, supplied. 1** If you **supply** someone with something that they want or need, you give them a quantity of it. *...an agreement not to produce or supply chemical weapons. ...the blood vessels supplying oxygen to the brain.* **2** You can use **supplies** to refer to food, equipment, and other essential things that people need, especially when these are provided in large quantities. *What happens when food and gasoline supplies run low?* **3** A **supply** of something is an amount of it which someone has or which is available for them to use. *The brain requires a constant supply of oxygen.* **4** If something is **in short supply**, there is very little of it available. **5 Supply** is the quantity of goods and services that can be made available for people to buy. *Prices change according to supply and demand.* ◆◆◆◆◇ VERB: V n with n V n V n to n / N-PLURAL / N-VAR: N of n, n N / PHRASE / N-UNCOUNT TECHNICAL

sup'ply line, supply lines. A **supply line** is a route along which goods and equipment are transported to an army during a war. N-COUNT

sup'ply teacher, supply teachers. A **supply teacher** is a teacher whose job is to take the place of other teachers at different schools when they are absent. The usual American term is **substitute teacher.** N-COUNT BRITISH

sup·port /səˈpɔːt/ **supports, supporting, supported. 1** If you **support** someone or their ideas or aims, you agree with them, and perhaps help them because you want them to succeed. *The vice president insisted that he supported the hard-working people of New York.* ▶ Also a noun. *The prime minister gave his full support to the government's reforms.* ♦ **sup·port·er, supporters** *Bradley was a major supporter of the 1986 tax reform plan.* **2** If you give **support** to someone during a difficult or unhappy time, you are kind to them and help them. *It was hard to come to terms with her death after all the support she gave to me and the family.* **3** If a government or person gives someone or something financial **support**, they provide them with money or other things that they need. *...the EC's proposal to cut agricultural support by only about 15%.* **4** If you **support** someone, you provide them with money or some of the things that they need. *She sold everything she'd ever bought in order to support herself through art school.* **5** If a fact **supports** a statement or a theory, ◆◆◆◆◆ VERB V n / N-UNCOUNT / N-COUNT N-COUNT / N-UNCOUNT / N-UNCOUNT / VERB: V n V pron-refl / VERB: V n

it helps to show that it is true or correct. ▶ Also a noun. *History offers some support for this view.* **6** If you **support** a sports team, especially a football team, you want them to win and perhaps go regularly to their games. *Tim, 17, supports Manchester United.* ♦ **supporter** *Football supporters have been gathering for tonight's World Cup semi-final.* [N-UNCOUNT] [VERB] [V n] [N-COUNT]

7 If something **supports** an object, it is underneath the object and holding it up. *...the thick wooden posts that supported the ceiling.* **8** A **support** is a bar or other object that supports something. **9** If something **supports** you, it prevents you from falling because you are holding onto it or leaning on it. *He supported himself by means of a nearby post.* ▶ Also a noun. *Alice was leaning against him as if for support.* [VERB] [V n] [N-COUNT] [VERB: V n] [V pron-refl] [N-UNCOUNT]

sup·port·ing /səˈpɔːtɪŋ/. **1** In a film or play, a **supporting** actor or actress is one who has an important part, but not the most important part. *Kevin Costner has agreed to appear in a supporting role.* **2** See also **support**. [ADJ: ADJ n]

sup·port·ive /səˈpɔːtɪv/. If you are **supportive**, you are kind and helpful to someone at a difficult or unhappy time in their life. *They were always supportive of each other.* ◆◇◇◇ [ADJ-GRADED]

sup·pose /səˈpəʊz/ **supposes, supposing, supposed.** **1** You can use **suppose** or **supposing** before you state a possible situation or action. You usually then go on to consider the effects or results that this situation or action might have. *Suppose someone gave you an egg and asked you to describe exactly what was inside... But supposing it does fail? I'd wind up with a big overdraft.* ♦♦♦♦◇ [VERB] [PRAGMATICS] [V that]

2 If you **suppose** that something is true, you believe that it is probably true, because of other things that you know. *The policy is perfectly clear and I see no reason to suppose that it isn't working... It had been supposed that by then Peter would be married.* **3** You can say **'I suppose'** before stating something that you believe to be true, or something that you think you should do, when you want to express slight uncertainty about it. *I get a bit uptight these days. Hormones, I suppose... I suppose I'd better do some homework... 'Is that the right way up?'—'Yeah. I suppose so.'* **4** You can use **'do you suppose'** to introduce a question when you want someone to give their opinion about something, although you know that they are unlikely to have any more knowledge or information about it than you. *Do you suppose he was telling the truth?... You don't suppose they'd start the trip without us, do you?* **5** You can use **'do you suppose'** as a polite way of suggesting or requesting that someone does something. *Do you suppose we could get together for a little chat sometime soon?* [VERB] [PRAGMATICS] [V that] [it be V-ed that] [Also V n] [PHRASE] [PRAGMATICS] [SPOKEN] [PHRASE] [PRAGMATICS] [SPOKEN] [PHRASE] [PRAGMATICS]

6 You can say **'I suppose'** or **'I don't suppose'** to introduce a clause in which you report someone's thoughts or attitude, when you want to express impatience or slight anger at them. *I suppose you think you're funny... I don't suppose it occurred to you to notify the police.* **7** You can say **'I don't suppose'** as a way of introducing a polite request. *I don't suppose you could tell me where James Street is?* [PHRASE] [PRAGMATICS] [SPOKEN] [PHRASE] [PRAGMATICS] [SPOKEN]

sup·posed. Pronounced /səˈpəʊzd/ or /səˈpəʊst/ for meanings 1 to 4, and /səˈpəʊzɪd/ for meaning 5. **1** If you say that something **is supposed to** happen, you mean that it is planned or expected. Sometimes this use suggests that the thing does not really happen in this way. *Public spending is supposed to fall, not rise, in the next few years.* If something **was supposed to** happen, it was planned or intended to happen, but did not in fact happen. *The first debate was supposed to have been held on Tuesday.* **3** If you say that something **is supposed to** be true, you mean that people say it is true but you do not know for certain that it is true. *'The Whipping Block' has never been published, but it's supposed to be a really good poem.* **4** You can use **'be supposed to'** to express annoyance at someone's ideas, or because something is not happening in the proper way. *You're supposed to be my friend!... What am I supposed to have done wrong now?* **5** You can use **sup-** ♦♦♦♦◇ [PHR-MODAL] [PRAGMATICS] [PHR-MODAL] [PHR-MODAL] [PRAGMATICS] [PHR-MODAL] [ADJ: ADJ n]

posed when you want to suggest that the following word or description is misleading, or when it is not definitely known to be true. *Not all indigenous regimes were willing to accept the supposed benefits of British trade.* ♦ **sup·pos·ed·ly** /səˈpəʊzɪdli/. *He was more of a victim than any of the women he supposedly offended.* [PRAGMATICS] [ADV: ADV with v, ADV with cl/ group]

sup·po·si·tion /sʌpəˈzɪʃən/ **suppositions.** **1** A **supposition** is an idea or statement which someone believes or assumes to be true, although they may have no evidence for it. *There's a popular supposition that we're publicly funded.* **2** You can describe someone's ideas or statements as **supposition** if you disapprove of the fact that they have no evidence to support them. *The report has been rejected by the authorities, who said much of it was based on supposition.* [N-COUNT] [FORMAL] [N-UNCOUNT] [PRAGMATICS]

sup·posi·tory /səˈpɒzɪtri, AM -tɔːri/ **suppositories.** A **suppository** is a solid block of medicine that is put into the rectum or vagina where it dissolves. [N-COUNT]

sup·press /səˈpres/ **suppresses, suppressing, suppressed.** **1** If someone in authority **suppresses** an activity, they prevent it from continuing, by using force or making it illegal. *...drug traffickers, who continue to flourish despite international attempts to suppress them.* ♦ **sup·pres·sion** /səˈpreʃən/. *...the violent suppression of the pro-democracy movement protests.* **2** If a natural function or reaction of your body **is suppressed**, it is stopped, for example by drugs or illness. *Ultraviolet light can suppress human immune responses.* ♦ **suppression** *...suppression of the immune system.* **3** If you **suppress** your feelings or reactions, you do not express them, even though you might want to. *Deep sleep allowed suppressed anxieties to surface.* ♦ **suppression** *A mother's suppression of her own feelings can cause problems.* **4** If someone **suppresses** a piece of information, they prevent other people from learning it. ♦ **suppression** *There has been a miscarriage of justice by reason of suppression of evidence.* ♦♦◇◇ [VERB] [V n] [N-UNCOUNT] [VERB: be V-ed] [V n] [N-UNCOUNT] [VERB: V n] [V-ed] [N-UNCOUNT] [VERB: V n] [N-UNCOUNT: N of n]

sup·pres·sant /səˈpresənt/ **suppressants.** A **suppressant** is a drug which is used to stop one of the natural functions of the body. *She took Dexedrine as an appetite suppressant.* [N-COUNT: n N] [MEDICAL]

sup·pres·sor /səˈpresə/ **suppressors.** **Suppressors** are cells or genes that prevent a cancer from developing or spreading. *...a recently-discovered class of genes called tumour suppressor genes.* [N-COUNT] [MEDICAL]

supra·na·tion·al /ˌsuːprəˈnæʃənəl/; also spelled **supra-national**. A **supranational** organization or authority involves more than one country. [ADJ: ADJ n]

su·prema·cist /suːˈpreməsɪst/ **supremacists.** A **supremacist** is someone who believes that one group of people, usually white people, are superior to any other group and should be more powerful. [N-COUNT]

su·prema·cy /suːˈpreməsi/. **1** If one group of people has **supremacy** over another group, they are more powerful politically or militarily. *The conservative old guard had re-established its political supremacy.* **2** If someone or something has **supremacy** over another person or thing, they are better. *In the United States Open final, Graf has retained overall supremacy.* ♦◇◇◇ [N-UNCOUNT] [N-UNCOUNT]

su·preme /suːˈpriːm/. **1** **Supreme** is used in the title of a person or an official group to indicate that they are at the highest level in a particular organization or system. *MacArthur was Supreme Commander for the allied powers in the Pacific. ...the Supreme Court.* **2** You use **supreme** to emphasize the greatness of a quality or thing. *Her approval was of supreme importance.* ♦ **su·preme·ly** *Mr Kohl is now in a supremely confident position.* ♦♦♦◇ [ADJ: ADJ n] [ADJ] [ADV: ADV adj/ adv]

su·pre·mo /suːˈpriːməʊ/ **supremos.** A **supremo** is someone who is considered to have the most authority or skill in a particular organization or area of activity. *...London's new arts supremo.* [N-COUNT] [BRITISH, INFORMAL]

Supt. Supt is a written abbreviation for **superintendent** when it is part of the title of someone in the police force.

sur·charge /'sɜːtʃɑːdʒ/ **surcharges.** A surcharge is an extra payment for something, added to the usual payment for a specific reason. *The government introduced a 15% surcharge on imports.*　◇◇◇◇ N-COUNT

sure /ʃʊə/ **surer, surest. 1** If you are **sure** that something is true, you are certain that it is true. If you are not **sure** about something, you do not know for certain what the true situation is. *He'd never been in a class before and he was not even sure that he should have been teaching... The president has never been sure which direction he wanted to go in on this issue... It is impossible to be sure about the value of land.* **2** If someone is **sure of** getting something, they will certainly get it. *A lot of people think that it's better to pay for their education so that they can be sure of getting quality.* **3** If you say that something **is sure to** happen, you are emphasizing your belief that it will happen. *Anyone who goes food shopping without a list is sure to forget the things they really need.* **4** If you tell someone to **be sure** to do something, you mean that they must not forget to do it. *Be sure you get your daily quota of calcium and daily vitamins.* **5** You can use **sure** in order to emphasize what you are saying. *It sure is hot, he thought.*
♦♦♦♦
ADJ-GRADED: v-link ADJ, ADJ that/wh, ADJ about n
ADJ: v-link ADJ of
PHR-MODAL PRAGMATICS
ADJ-GRADED: v-link ADJ, ADJ to-inf, ADJ that
PRAGMATICS
ADV: ADV before v
PRAGMATICS

6 You say **sure enough**, especially when telling a story, to confirm that something you thought was true or would happen was really true or actually happened. *I called the hotel and asked them to check the room. Sure enough, they had found the ticket in the blankets.* PHRASE

7 If you say that something is **for sure** or that you know it **for sure**, you mean that it is definitely true. *Even to this day we don't know what happened for sure.* PHRASE **8** If you **make sure** that something is done, you take action so that it is done. *Make sure that you follow the instructions carefully.* PHRASE **9** If you **make sure** that something is the way that you want or expect it to be, you check that it is that way. *He looked in the bathroom to make sure that he was alone.* **10** If you are **sure of yourself**, you are very confident about your own abilities or opinions. PHRASE

11 Sure is used to emphasize that something such as a sign or ability is reliable or accurate. *Sharpe's leg and shoulder began to ache, a sure sign of rain... She has a sure grasp of social issues.* **♦ sure·ness** *...the acuteness of his critical faculties and the sureness of his judgment.* ADJ-GRADED: ADJ n PRAGMATICS
N-UNCOUNT

12 Sure is a way of saying 'yes' or 'all right'. *'He rang you?'—'Sure. Last night.'... 'I'd like to be alone, O.K.?'— 'Sure. O.K.'* CONVENTION PRAGMATICS INFORMAL

13 You use **to be sure** when you are admitting that something is true, although it seems to contradict a more general statement that you are making. *Parents make the rules. To be sure, many of the rules are no longer appropriate today.* PHRASE PRAGMATICS

'sure-fire; also spelled **surefire. A sure-fire** success is certain to succeed. *If something's a sure-fire hit then Radio One will play it.* ADJ: ADJ n INFORMAL

,sure-'footed; also spelled **surefooted. 1** A person or animal that is **sure-footed** can move easily over steep or uneven ground without falling. **2** If someone is **sure-footed**, they are confident in what they are doing and do not make mistakes. *The Labour Party is growing increasingly sure-footed.* ADJ-GRADED
ADJ-GRADED

sure·ly /'ʃʊəli/. **1** You use **surely** to emphasize that you think something should be true, and you would be surprised if it was not true. *You're an intelligent woman, surely you realize by now that I'm helping you... You surely haven't forgotten Dr Walters?* **2** If something will **surely** happen or is **surely** the case, it will definitely happen or is certainly the case. *He killed Willy as surely as if he'd been steering the car.* **3** If you say that something is happening **slowly but surely**, you mean that it is happening gradually but it is definitely happening. ♦♦♦◇◇
ADV: ADV with cl/ group PRAGMATICS
ADV: ADV with cl, ADV before v
PHRASE

sure·ty /'ʃʊərɪti/ **sureties. Surety** is money or something valuable which you give to someone to show that you will do what you have promised. N-VAR

surf /sɜːf/ **surfs, surfing, surfed. 1 Surf** is the mass of white foam that is formed by waves as they fall upon the shore. **2** If you **surf**, you ride on big waves on a special board. *I'm going to be surfing bigger waves when I get to Australia!* **♦ surf·er, surfers** *...this small fishing village, which continues to attract painters and surfers.* **♦ surf·ing** *The best time for surfing in Waikiki is in January.* ♦◇◇◇
N-UNCOUNT
V n
N-COUNT
N-UNCOUNT

sur·face /'sɜːfɪs/ **surfaces, surfacing, surfaced. 1** The **surface** of something is the flat top part of it or the outside of it. *...tiny little waves on the surface of the water... Its total surface area was seven thousand square feet.* **2** A work **surface** is a flat area, for example the top of a table or cupboard, on which you can work. **3 Surface** is used to describe the parts of the armed forces which travel by ship or by land rather than underwater or in the air. **4** If someone or something under water **surfaces**, they come up to the surface of the water. *He surfaced, gasping for air.* **5** When you refer to the **surface** of a situation, you are talking about what can be seen easily rather than what is hidden or not immediately obvious. *Back in Britain, things appear, on the surface, simpler... It's brought to the surface a much wider controversy.* **6** When something such as a piece of news, a feeling, or a problem **surfaces**, it becomes known or becomes obvious. *The evidence, when it surfaces, is certain to cause uproar... The emotions will surface at some point in life.* **7** When someone **surfaces**, they appear after not being seen for some time, for example because they have been asleep.
♦♦♦♦
N-COUNT
N-COUNT
ADJ: ADJ n
VERB V
N-SING
VERB V
VERB: V INFORMAL

'surface mail. Surface mail is the system of sending mail by road, rail, or sea, not by air. N-UNCOUNT

,surface-to-'air. Surface-to-air missiles are fired from the land or sea at aircraft or at other missiles. ADJ: ADJ n

surf·board /'sɜːfbɔːd/ **surfboards.** A **surfboard** is a long narrow board that is used for surfing. N-COUNT

sur·feit /'sɜːfɪt/. A **surfeit** of something is an amount which is too large or larger than is needed. N-SING FORMAL

surge /sɜːdʒ/ **surges, surging, surged. 1** A **surge** is a sudden large increase in something that has previously been steady, or has only increased or developed slowly. *Specialists see various reasons for the recent surge in inflation.* **2** If something **surges**, it increases suddenly and greatly, after being steady or developing only slowly. *The Freedom Party's electoral support surged from just under 10 per cent to nearly 17 per cent.* **3** If people **surge** forward, they move forward suddenly and powerfully, usually in a crowd. **4** A **surge** is a sudden powerful movement of a mass of liquid or gas, such as wind or water. *London Bridge was destroyed by a tidal surge during a storm.* **5** If a physical force such as water or electricity **surges** through something, it moves through it suddenly and powerfully. *Thousands of volts surged through his car.* **6** If you feel a **surge** of a particular emotion or feeling, you experience it suddenly and powerfully. *McKee felt a sudden surge of hope.* **7** If an emotion or sensation **surges** in you, you feel it suddenly and powerfully. **▶ Surge up** means the same as **surge**. *A slow hatred for Hilton began to surge up in him.*
♦♦◇◇◇
N-COUNT
VERB: V V from/to/by amount
VERB: V adv/prep N-COUNT
VERB V adv/prep Also V
N-COUNT
VERB: V in/through n
PHRASAL VB V P prep

sur·geon /'sɜːdʒən/ **surgeons.** A **surgeon** is a doctor who is specially trained to perform surgery. *...a heart surgeon.* ● See also **plastic surgeon.** ♦♦◇◇◇ N-COUNT

sur·gery /'sɜːdʒəri/ **surgeries. 1 Surgery** is medical treatment in which someone's body is cut open so that a doctor can repair or remove a diseased or damaged part. *Mr Clark underwent five hours of emergency surgery.* ● See also **plastic surgeon. 2** A **surgery** is the room or house where a doctor or dentist works. **3** A doctor's or dentist's **surgery** is the period of time each day when he or she sees patients at his or her surgery. *His surgery always ends at eleven.* ♦♦♦◇◇
N-UNCOUNT
N-COUNT BRITISH
N-COUNT BRITISH

S

sur·gi·cal /'sɜːdʒɪkəl/. **1 Surgical** equipment and ◆◆◇◇◇ ADJ: ADJ n clothing is used in surgery. *...an array of surgical instruments.* **2 Surgical** treatment involves surgery. ADJ: ADJ n ♦ **sur·gi·cal·ly** *In very severe cases, bunions may be* ADV *surgically removed.* **3 Surgical** military actions are ADJ: ADJ n designed to attack or destroy a particular target without harming other people or damaging other buildings nearby. *...a surgical strike aimed at a terrorist organization.*

ˌ**surgical ˈspirit. Surgical spirit** is a liquid consist- N-UNCOUNT ing mainly of alcohol which is used to clean and BRITISH sterilize wounds or surgical instruments.

sur·ly /'sɜːli/ **surlier, surliest.** Someone who is ADJ-GRADED **surly** behaves in a rude bad-tempered way. WRITTEN

sur·mise /sə'maɪz/ **surmises, surmising, sur-** VERB: **mised.** If you **surmise** that something is true, you V that guess it from the available evidence, although you V wh do not know for certain. *There's so little to go on, we* FORMAL *can only surmise what happened.* ▶ Also a noun. *His* N-VAR *surmise proved correct.*

sur·mount /sə'maʊnt/ **surmounts, surmount-** ◆◇◇◇◇ **ing, surmounted. 1** If you **surmount** a problem VERB or difficulty, you deal successfully with it. *I realized I* V n *had to surmount the language barrier.* **2** If some- VERB: thing **is surmounted** by a particular thing, that beV-ed thing is on top of it. FORMAL

sur·name /'sɜːneɪm/ **surnames.** Your **surname** is ◆◇◇◇◇ the name that you share with other members of N-COUNT your family. In English speaking countries and many other countries it is your last name.

sur·pass /sə'pɑːs, -'pæs/ **surpasses, surpass-** ◆◇◇◇◇ **ing, surpassed. 1** If one person or thing **sur-** VERB: V n **passes** another, the first is better than, or has more V-ed of a particular quality than, the second. *Warwick Arts Centre is the second largest Arts Centre in Britain, surpassed in size only by London's Barbican.* **2** If something **surpasses** expectations, it is better than it was expected to be. **3** If something **surpasses** VERB: V n understanding, it is too difficult to understand.

sur·plus /'sɜːpləs/ **surpluses. 1** If there is a **sur-** ◆◆◇◇ **plus** of something, there is more than is needed. N-VAR *Germany suffers from a surplus of teachers.* **2 Sur-** ADJ **plus** is used to describe something that is extra or that is more than is needed. *Few people have large sums of surplus cash... The houses are being sold because they are surplus to requirements.* **3** A **surplus** N-COUNT refers to a situation in which a person or organization receives more than it spends. For example, if a country has a trade **surplus**, it exports more than it imports.

sur·prise /sə'praɪz/ **surprises, surprising, sur-** ◆◆◆◆◆ **prised. 1** A **surprise** is an unexpected event, fact, N-COUNT or piece of news. *I have a surprise for you: We are moving to Switzerland!... It may come as a surprise to some that a normal, healthy child is born with many skills.* ▶ Also an adjective. *Baxter arrived here* ADJ: ADJ n *this afternoon, on a surprise visit.* **2 Surprise** is the N-UNCOUNT feeling that you have when something unexpected happens. *The Foreign Office in London has expressed surprise at these allegations... I started working hard for the first time in my life. To my surprise, I found I liked it.* **3** If something **surprises** you, it VERB: V n gives you a feeling of surprise. *It surprised me that a* it V n that/if *driver of Alain's experience should make those mistakes.* ♦ **sur·prised** *This lady was genuinely sur-* ADJ-GRADED *prised at what happened to her pet... Chang seemed surprised to find the big living-room empty.* ♦ **sur·** ·**pris·ing** *It is not surprising that children learn to* ADJ-GRADED *read at different rates... A surprising number of customers order the same sandwich.* ♦ **sur·pris·ing·ly** ADV-GRADED *Not surprisingly, he enjoyed telling tales about his time at the military academy.* **4** If you **surprise** VERB: V n someone, you give them, tell them, or do something V n with n pleasant that they are not expecting. *Surprise a new neighbour with one of your favourite home-made dishes.* **5** A **surprise** is something pleasant that you N-COUNT were not expecting. *My father decided to slip a little extra spending money into my purse as a surprise.* **6** If you **surprise** someone, you attack, capture, or VERB: V n find them when they are not expecting it.

7 You can say **'surprise, surprise'** if you disapprove of PHRASE something because it is not surprising or original, or PRAGMATICS could easily have been predicted. *Everybody starts growing carrots. Next season, surprise, surprise, there is a glut of carrots.* **8** You can say **'surprise, surprise'** if PHRASE you meet someone you know or give them something PRAGMATICS when they are not expecting it. **9** If something **takes** PHRASE you **by surprise**, it happens when you are not expecting it or when you are not prepared for it.

sur·real /sə'riːəl/. If you describe something as ◆◇◇◇◇ **surreal**, you mean that it has a strange dreamlike ADJ-GRADED quality.

sur·real·ist /sə'riːəlɪst/ **surrealists. Surrealist** ◆◇◇◇◇ art is a style of art in which ideas, images, and ob- ADJ-GRADED jects are combined in a strange dreamlike way. ▶ A N-COUNT **surrealist** is an artist whose work is based on surrealist ideas. *...Andre Breton and the French Surrealists.* ♦ **sur·real·ism** *His early work was influenced* N-UNCOUNT *by the European surrealism of the 1930s.*

sur·real·is·tic /sə,riːə'lɪstɪk/. **1 Surrealistic** means ADJ-GRADED the same as **surreal**. **2 Surrealistic** means the same ADJ: ADJ n as **surrealist**.

sur·ren·der /sə'rendə/ **surrenders, surrender-** ◆◆◆◇◇ **ing, surrendered. 1** If you **surrender**, you stop VERB: V fighting or resisting someone or something, and V to n agree that you have been beaten. *He surrendered to American troops.* ▶ Also a noun. *...the government's* N-VAR *apparent surrender to demands made by the religious militants... Depression is a partial surrender to death.* **2** If you **surrender** something you would ra- VERB ther keep, you give it up or let someone else have it, V n often after a struggle. *Nadja had to fill out forms* Also Vo V n to n *surrendering all rights to her property.* ▶ Also a N-UNCOUNT noun. *...the sixteen-day deadline for the surrender of weapons and ammunition.* **3** If you **surrender** VERB: V n something such as a ticket or your passport, you FORMAL give it to someone in authority when they ask you to.

sur·render value, surrender values. The **sur-** N-COUNT **render value** of a life insurance policy is the TECHNICAL amount of money you receive if you decide you no longer wish to continue with the policy.

sur·rep·ti·tious /ˌsʌrəp'tɪʃəs, AM ˌsɜːr-/. A **surrep-** ◆◇◇◇◇ **titious** action is done in a secretive way, because ADJ-GRADED the person doing it does not want anyone to see them. *He made a surreptitious entrance to the club through the little door in the brick wall.* ♦ **sur·rep·** ·**ti·tious·ly** *Surreptitiously Mark looked at his* ADV-GRADED: *watch.* ADV with v

sur·ro·ga·cy /'sʌrəgəsi, AM 'sɜːr-/. **Surrogacy** is an N-UNCOUNT arrangement by which a woman gives birth to a baby on behalf of a woman who cannot have babies herself.

sur·ro·gate /'sʌrəgeɪt, AM 'sɜːr-/ **surrogates.** You ◆◇◇◇◇ use **surrogate** to describe a person or thing that ADJ: ADJ n acts as a substitute for someone or something else. *Martin had become Howard Cosell's surrogate son... Leningrad was the third alien city to offer him a surrogate home.* ▶ Also a noun. *Arms control should* N-COUNT *not be made into a surrogate for peace.*

ˌ**surrogate ˈmother, surrogate mothers.** A N-COUNT **surrogate mother** is a woman who has agreed to give birth to a baby on behalf of another woman.

sur·round /sə'raʊnd/ **surrounds, surrounding,** ◆◆◆◇ **surrounded. 1** If something or someone is **sur-** VERB: **rounded** by something, that thing is situated all beV-ed around them. *...the fluid that surrounds the brain.* V n *...in the surrounding hills.* **2** If you **are surrounded** V-ing by soldiers or police, they spread out so that they VERB: are in positions all the way around you. *He tried to* beV-ed run away but gave up when he found himself sur- V-ed rounded.* **3** The circumstances, feelings, or ideas Also V n which **surround** something are those that are close- VERB ly associated with it. *Controversy surrounds the* V n cause of his death.* **4** If you **surround** yourself with VERB certain people or things, you make sure that you V n with/by n have a lot of them near you all the time. *They love being surrounded by familiar possessions.*

5 The **surround** of something such as a fireplace is N-COUNT the border, wall, or shelves around it. **6** Your N-PLURAL

surrounds are your surroundings. *The entire team enjoyed hot showers in the spacious surrounds of a new, modern village hall.*

sur·round·ings /səˈraʊndɪŋz/. The place where someone or something is can be referred to as their **surroundings.** *...a peaceful holiday home in beautiful surroundings.* ◆◆◇◇◇ N-PLURAL

sur·tax /ˈsɜːtæks/. **Surtax** is an additional tax on incomes higher than the level at which ordinary tax is paid. N-UNCOUNT

sur·veil·lance /səˈveɪləns/. **Surveillance** is the careful watching of someone, especially by an organization such as the police or the army. *He was arrested after being kept under constant surveillance. ...a two-week surveillance operation.* ◆◆◇◇◇ N-UNCOUNT

sur·vey, surveys, surveying, surveyed. The noun is pronounced /ˈsɜːveɪ/. The verb is pronounced /səˈveɪ/, and can also be pronounced /ˈsɜːveɪ/ in meanings 1 and 4. **1** If you **survey** a number of people, companies, or organizations, you try to find out information about their opinions or behaviour, usually by asking them a series of questions. *Business Development Advisers surveyed 211 companies for the report.* ► Also a noun. *The council conducted a survey of the uses to which farm buildings are put.* **2** If you **survey** something, you look at or consider the whole of it carefully. *He pushed himself to his feet and surveyed the room.* **3** If you give something a brief **survey** or a quick **survey,** you look at or consider all of it quickly, but not in detail. *...a brief survey of some important books on astrology.* **4** If someone **surveys** an area of land, they examine it and measure it, usually in order to make a map of it. ► Also a noun. *...the organizer of the geological survey of India.* ♦ **sur·vey·ing** *...surveying equipment.* ♦ **sur·vey·or** /səˈveɪə/ **surveyors** *...the surveyor's maps.* **5** If someone **surveys** a house, they examine it carefully and report on its structure, usually in order to give advice to a person who is thinking of buying it. ► Also a noun. *...a structural survey undertaken by a qualified surveyor.* ♦ **surveyor** *Our surveyor warned us that the house needed totally rebuilding.* ◆◆◆◆◇ VERB / Vn / N-COUNT / VERB Vn / N-SING: with supp / VERB: Vn / N-COUNT / N-UNCOUNT / N-COUNT / VERB: Vn BRITISH / N-COUNT / N-COUNT

sur·viv·al **1** You can use **the survival of the fittest** to refer to a situation in which only the strongest people or things continue to live or be successful, while the others die or fail. **2** See also **survive.** PHRASE

sur·vive /səˈvaɪv/ **survives, surviving, survived.** **1** If a person or living thing **survives** in a dangerous situation, they do not die. *...the sequence of events that left the eight pupils battling to survive in icy seas for over four hours... Drugs that dissolve blood clots can help people survive heart attacks.* ♦ **sur·viv·al** *An animal's sense of smell is still crucial to its survival.* ♦ **sur·vi·vor, survivors** *Officials said there were no survivors of the plane crash.* **2** If you **survive** in difficult circumstances, you manage to live or continue in spite of them and do not let them affect you very much. *Jim Hogg survives on £65 pounds a fortnight after losing his job.* **3** If something **survives,** it continues to exist although there is a risk of it being destroyed or abolished. *When the market economy is introduced, many factories will not survive.* ♦ **survival** *...companies which have been struggling for survival in the advancing recession.* **4** If you **survive** someone, you continue to live after they have died. *Most women will survive their spouses.* ◆◆◆◆◇ VERB V / Vn / N-UNCOUNT / N-COUNT / VERB: V Also V n / VERB V Also V n / N-UNCOUNT / VERB Vn

sur·vi·vor /səˈvaɪvə/ **survivors.** **1** A **survivor** of a very unpleasant experience is a person who has had such an experience, and who is still affected by it. *...survivors of child sexual abuse.* **2** If you describe someone as a **survivor,** you approve of the fact that they are able to carry on with their life even though they experience many difficulties. *Susie is a great survivor.* See also **survive.** ◆◇◇◇◇ N-COUNT / N-COUNT PRAGMATICS

sus·cep·ti·bil·ity /səˌseptɪˈbɪlɪti/ **susceptibilities. 1** If you have a **susceptibility** to something unpleasant, you are likely to be affected by it. *...his* ◆◇◇◇◇ N-VAR

increased susceptibility to infections. **2** A person's **susceptibilities** are their feelings which can be easily hurt. *In saying this I shall outrage a few susceptibilities.* N-PLURAL

sus·cep·ti·ble /səˈseptɪbəl/. **1** If you are **susceptible to** something or someone, you are very likely to be influenced by them. *Young people are the most susceptible to advertisements.* **2** If you are **susceptible to** a disease or injury, you are very likely to be affected by it. **3** A **susceptible** person is very easily influenced emotionally. *Hers was a susceptible nature.* ◆◇◇◇◇ ADJ-GRADED: v-link ADJ to n / ADJ-GRADED / ADJ-GRADED: ADJ n

su·shi /ˈsuːʃi/. **Sushi** is a Japanese dish of rice with sweet vinegar, often served with raw fish. N-UNCOUNT

sus·pect, suspects, suspecting, suspected. The verb is pronounced /səˈspekt/. The noun is pronounced /ˈsʌspekt/. **1** You use **suspect** when you are stating something that you believe is probably true, in order to make it sound less strong or direct. *I suspect they were right... Do women really share such stupid jokes? We suspect not.* **2** If you **suspect** that something dishonest or unpleasant has been done, you believe that it has probably been done. If you **suspect** someone of doing an action of this kind, you believe that they probably did it. *He suspected that the woman staying in the flat above was using heroin... The police had not suspected him of anything.* **3** A **suspect** is a person who the police or authorities think may be guilty of a crime. **4** If something is **suspect,** it cannot be trusted or regarded as genuine. *Delegates evacuated the building when a suspect package was found... The whole affair has been highly suspect.* ◆◆◆◆◇ VERB PRAGMATICS V that V not/so / VERB V that V n of n Also V n/wh / N-COUNT / ADJ-GRADED

sus·pend /səˈspend/ **suspends, suspending, suspended. 1** If you **suspend** something, you delay it or stop it from happening for a while or until a decision is made about it. *The union suspended strike action this week.* ♦ **sus·pen·sion** /səˈspenʃən/ **suspensions.** *...the suspension of flights between London and Manchester.* **2** If someone **is suspended,** they are prevented from holding a particular job or position for a fixed length of time or until a decision is made about them. *Julie was suspended from her job shortly after the incident.* ♦ **suspension** *The athlete received a two-year suspension following a positive drug test.* **3** If something **is suspended** from a high place, it is hanging from that place. *...a mobile of birds or nursery rhyme characters which could be suspended over the cot.* **4** See also **suspension.** ◆◆◆◇◇ VERB Vn / N-UNCOUNT / VERB beV-ed Also V n / VB: usu passive beV-ed

sus·pend·ed ani·ma·tion. 1 Suspended animation is a state in which the important body functions of an animal are slowed down for a period of time. This is done by freezing or because the animal hibernates. **2** If you describe someone as being in a state of suspended animation, you mean that they have become inactive and are doing nothing. N-UNCOUNT / N-UNCOUNT

sus·pend·ed sentence, suspended sentences. If a criminal is given a **suspended sentence,** they are given a prison sentence which they have to serve if they commit another crime within a specified period of time. N-COUNT

sus·pend·er /səˈspendə/ **suspenders. 1** Suspenders are the fastenings which hang down from a suspender belt and hold up a woman's stockings. The American word is **garter. 2** Suspenders are a pair of straps that go over someone's shoulders and are fastened to their trousers at the front and at the back to prevent the trousers from falling down. The British word is **braces.** N-COUNT BRITISH / N-PLURAL: also a pair of N AMERICAN

sus·pend·er belt, suspender belts. A **suspender belt** is a piece of underwear for women that is used for holding up stockings. The American expression is **garter belt.** N-COUNT BRITISH

sus·pense /səˈspens/. **Suspense** is a state of excitement or anxiety about something that is going to happen very soon, for example about some news that you are waiting to hear. *...the suspense over the two remaining hostages... 'Go on, don't leave us in suspense,' Dennis said.* ◆◇◇◇◇ N-UNCOUNT

S

sus·pen·sion /sə'spenʃən/ **suspensions.** A vehi- ◆◆◇◇◇ N-VAR
cle's **suspension** consists of the springs and shock
absorbers attached to the wheels, which give a
smooth ride in spite of bumps in the road. ● See
also **suspend**.

su'spension bridge, suspension bridges. A N-COUNT
suspension bridge is a type of bridge that is supported from above by cables.

sus·pi·cion /sə'spɪʃən/ **suspicions. 1** Suspicion ◆◆◆◇◇
is a belief or feeling that someone has committed a N-VAR
crime or done something wrong. *There was a suspicion that this runner attempted to avoid the procedures for dope testing... An East German has been
arrested in Switzerland on suspicion of spying.* **2** If N-VAR
there is **suspicion** of someone or something, people
do not trust them or consider them to be reliable. *I
was always regarded in the Army with a certain
amount of suspicion.* **3** A **suspicion** is a feeling that N-COUNT
something is probably true or is likely to happen. *I
had a sneaking suspicion she was enjoying herself.*

sus·pi·cious /sə'spɪʃəs/. **1** If you are **suspicious** of ◆◆◇◇◇
someone or something, you do not trust them, and ADJ-GRADED
deal with them cautiously. *He was suspicious of all
journalists by now.* ◆ **sus·pi·cious·ly** *'What's the* ADV-GRADED:
matter with you?' Jake asked suspiciously. **2** If you ADV after v
are **suspicious** of someone or something, you be- ADJ-GRADED
lieve that they are probably involved in a crime or
some dishonest activity. *Two officers on patrol became suspicious of two men in a car.* **3** If you de- ADJ-GRADED
scribe someone or something as **suspicious**, you
mean that there is some aspect of them which
makes you think that they are involved in a crime
or a dishonest activity. *Police last night found
what they described as a suspicious package.*
◆ **suspiciously** *...voters found with suspiciously* ADV-GRADED
large sums of money in their pockets.

sus·pi·cious·ly /sə'spɪʃəsli/. **1** If you say that ◆◇◇◇◇
something looks or sounds **suspiciously** like a par- ADV:
ticular thing, you mean that it probably is that ADV prep
thing, or something very similar to it. *'Yes,' he replied, though it sounded suspiciously like a question.*
2 You can use **suspiciously** when you are describ- ADV:
ing something that you think is slightly strange or ADV adj/adv
not as it should be. *He lives alone in a suspiciously
tidy flat in Notting Hill Gate.* **3** See also **suspicious**.

suss /sʌs/ **susses, sussing, sussed.** If you **suss** VERB
a person or situation, you realize or work out what V n
their real character or nature is. *I think I've sussed* V that
the reason for it... The women began to suss that Also V wh
there was no reason why they should be impressed by BRITISH,
him. ► **Suss out** means the same as **suss**. *They're* INFORMAL
sussing out the area to see how strong the police PHRASAL VB
presence is... He susses his colleagues out and he V P noun
knows who he can trust. Also V P wh

sussed /sʌst/. If someone is **sussed**, they are clever ADJ-GRADED
and knowledgeable, often about a particular thing BRITISH,
such as clothes, pop music, or politics. INFORMAL

sus·tain /sə'steɪn/ **sustains, sustaining, sus-** ◆◆◆◇◇
tained. 1 If you **sustain** something, you continue it VERB
or maintain it for a period of time. *Mandela has to* V n
*be patient if he's to sustain his position as a great in-
ternational figure.* **2** If you **sustain** something such VERB
as a defeat, loss, or injury, it happens to you. *Every* V n
aircraft in there has sustained some damage. **3** If FORMAL
something **sustains** you, it supports you by giving VERB
you help, strength, or encouragement. *The cash* V n
dividends they get from the cash crop would sustain FORMAL
them during the lean season.

sus·tain·able /sə'steɪnəbəl/. **1** You use **sustain-** ◆◇◇◇◇
able to describe the use of natural resources when ADJ-GRADED
this use is kept at a steady level that is not likely to
damage the environment. *...the management, conservation and sustainable development of forests.*
◆ **sus·tain·abil·ity** /sə,steɪnə'bɪliti/ *...concern* N-UNCOUNT
about environmental sustainability. **2** A **sustain-** ADJ-GRADED
able plan, method, or system can be continued at
the same pace or level of activity without harming
its efficiency and the people affected by it. *...an
efficient and sustainable transport system.*

◆ **sustainability** *...doubts about the sustainability* N-UNCOUNT
of the current economic expansion.

sus·te·nance /'sʌstɪnəns/. **Sustenance** is food or N-UNCOUNT
drink which a person, animal, or plant needs to re- FORMAL
main alive and healthy.

su·ture /'suːtʃə/ **sutures.** A **suture** is a stitch made N-COUNT
to join together the open parts of a wound, espe- MEDICAL
cially one made after a patient has been operated
on.

svelte /svelt, sfelt/. A **svelte** person is attractively ADJ-GRADED
slim, elegant, and stylish.

SW. SW is a written abbreviation for **south-west**.

swab /swɒb/ **swabs, swabbing, swabbed. 1** A N-COUNT
swab is a small piece of cotton wool used by a doctor or nurse for cleaning a wound or for applying
ointment or disinfectant. **2** If you **swab** something, VERB: V n
you clean it using a wet cloth or mop.

swad·dle /'swɒdəl/ **swaddles, swaddling,** VERB: V n
swaddled. If you **swaddle** a baby, you wrap cloth DATED
or a shawl around it in order to keep it warm or to
prevent it from moving.

swag /swæg/ **swags. 1** A criminal's **swag** is the N-UNCOUNT
goods or money that they have stolen. INFORMAL
2 A **swag** is a piece of material that is hung above a N-COUNT
window in such a way that the material hangs down
ornamentally.

swag·ger /'swægə/ **swaggers, swaggering,** ◆◇◇◇◇
swaggered. If you **swagger**, you walk in a proud VERB
confident way, holding your body upright and V prep/adv
swinging your hips. *A broad shouldered man wear-* Also V
ing a dinner jacket swaggered confidently up to the
bar. ► Also a noun. *He walked with something of a* N-SING
swagger.

swal·low /'swɒləʊ/ **swallows, swallowing,** ◆◆◇◇◇
swallowed. 1 When you **swallow** something, you VERB
cause it to go from your mouth down into your V n
stomach. *You are asked to swallow a capsule con-* Also V
taining vitamin B. ► Also a noun. *Jan lifted her glass* N-COUNT
and took a quick swallow. **2** If you **swallow**, you VERB
make a movement in your throat as if you are swal- V
lowing something, often because you are nervous or
frightened. *Nancy swallowed hard and shook her
head.* **3** If someone **swallows** a story or statement, VERB
they believe it completely. *I too found this story a* V n
little hard to swallow. **4** If you **swallow** your feel- VERB
ings, you do not express them, although you want V n
to very much. *Gordon has swallowed the anger he
felt.* **5** ● **a bitter pill to swallow:** see **pill.** ● to **swal-**
low one's **pride:** see **pride**.
6 A **swallow** is a small bird with pointed wings and a N-COUNT
forked tail.

swallow up. 1 If one thing **is swallowed up** by an- PHRASAL VB
other, it becomes part of the first thing and no longer V P noun
has a separate identity of its own. *Monster publishing* Also V n P
houses started to swallow up smaller companies. **2** If V P noun
something **swallows up** money or resources, it uses V n P
them entirely while giving very little in return. *A
seven-day TV ad campaign could swallow up the best
part of £50,000.* **3** If someone or something **is swal-** be V-ed P
lowed up by something, they disappear into it so that V P noun
you cannot see them any more. *Weeds had swallowed* Also V n P
up the garden.

swam /swæm/. **Swam** is the past tense of **swim**.

swamp /swɒmp/ **swamps, swamping,** ◆◆◇◇◇
swamped. 1 A **swamp** is an area of very wet land N-VAR
with wild plants growing in it. **2** If something VERB
swamps a place or object, it fills it with water. *The* V n
*Ventura river burst its banks, swamping a mobile
home park.* **3** If you **are swamped** by things or peo- VB: usu
ple, you have more of them than you can deal with. passive
The railway station was swamped with thousands of be V-ed
families.

swamp·land /'swɒmplænd/ **swamplands.** N-VAR
Swampland is an area that is permanently swampy.

swampy /'swɒmpi/. A **swampy** area of land con- ADJ-GRADED
sists mainly of swamps.

swan /swɒn/ **swans, swanning, swanned. 1** A ◆◇◇◇◇
swan is a large bird with a very long neck. Swans N-COUNT
live on rivers and lakes and are usually white. **2** If VERB
you describe someone as **swanning around** or V prep/adv
BRITISH,

swanning off, you mean that they are wandering about or going somewhere in a leisurely and irresponsible manner. *She spends her time swanning around the world.* INFORMAL

swank /swæŋk/. **1 Swank** is boastful talk or behaviour intended to impress other people; used showing disapproval. *There was no swank in Martin.* N-UNCOUNT PRAGMATICS INFORMAL **2 Swank** means the same as **swanky**. *...a swank new shop on the outskirts of Beijing.* ADJ-GRADED INFORMAL

swanky /'swæŋki/ **swankier, swankiest**. If you describe something as **swanky**, you mean that it is glamorous, fashionable, and expensive. *...the swanky hotels that line the Pacific shore at Acapulco.* ADJ-GRADED INFORMAL

swan·song /'swɒnsɒŋ/ also spelled **swan song**. Someone's **swansong** is the last time that they do something for which they are famous, for example the last time that an actor gives a performance in the theatre. N-SING

swap /swɒp/ **swaps, swapping, swapped;** also spelled **swop**. **1** If you **swap** something with someone, you give it to them and receive something else in exchange. *Next week they will swap places... I'd gladly swap places with mummy any day.* ▶ Also a noun. *...if she ever fancies a job swap.* **2** If you **swap** one thing for another, you remove the first thing and replace it with the second, or you stop doing the first thing and start doing the second. *He'd swapped his overalls for a suit and tie.* **3** If you **swap** stories or opinions with someone, you tell each other stories or give each other your opinions. *They all sat together at table, laughing and swapping stories.* ◆◆◇◇◇ V-RECIP V pl-n V pl-n with n Also V n for/ with n N-COUNT V n for n Also V n VERB V pl-n

swarm /swɔːm/ **swarms, swarming, swarmed**. **1** A **swarm** of bees or other insects is a large group of them flying together. **2** When bees or other insects **swarm**, they move or fly in a large group. **3** When people **swarm** somewhere, they move there quickly in a large group. *People swarmed to the shops, buying up everything in sight.* **4** If a place **is swarming** with people, it is full of people moving about in a busy way. *Within minutes the area was swarming with officers.* **5** A **swarm** of people is a large group of them moving about quickly. ◆◇◇◇ N-COLL-COUNT VERB: V VERB V prep/adv Also V n V with n N-COLL-COUNT

swarthy /'swɔːði/. A **swarthy** person has a dark complexion. *He had a broad swarthy face.* ADJ-GRADED

swash·buck·ling /'swɒʃbʌklɪŋ/. If you describe something or someone as **swashbuckling**, you mean that they remind you of the courageous and daring behaviour of pirates. *...a swashbuckling adventure story.* ADJ-GRADED

swas·ti·ka /'swɒstɪkə/ **swastikas**. A **swastika** is a symbol in the shape of a cross with each arm bent at right angles. It was used by the Nazis in Germany as their official symbol. ◆◇◇◇ N-COUNT

swat /swɒt/ **swats, swatting, swatted**. If you **swat** something such as an insect, you hit it with a quick, swinging movement, using your hand or a flat object. *Hundreds of flies buzz around us, and the workman keeps swatting them.* VERB V n

swathe /sweɪð, AM swɑːð/ **swathes, swathing, swathed;** the noun is also spelled **swath**. **1** A **swathe** of land is a long strip of land. *On May 1st the army took over another swathe of territory.* **2** A **swathe** of cloth is a long strip of cloth, especially one that is wrapped round someone or something. **3** To **swathe** someone or something **in** cloth means to wrap them in it completely. *She swathed her enormous body in thin black fabrics.* **4** If someone or something **cuts a swathe** through something, they pass through it causing great destruction or change. *The storm cut a swathe through southern England.* ◆◇◇◇ N-COUNT N-COUNT VERB V n in n PHRASE

SWAT team /'swɒt tiːm/ **SWAT teams**. A SWAT team is a group of policemen who are specially trained to deal with incidents involving violence or terrorism. SWAT is an abbreviation for Special Weapons and Tactics. N-COUNT AMERICAN

sway /sweɪ/ **sways, swaying, swayed**. **1** When people or things **sway**, they lean or swing slowly from one side to the other. *The people swayed back* ◆◆◇◇◇ VERB V V adv/prep

and forth... *The whole boat swayed and tipped.* **2** If you **are swayed** by someone or something, you are influenced by them. *Don't ever be swayed by fashion.* **3** If someone or something **holds sway**, they have great power or influence over a particular place or activity. *The 'families' are the basic units, each holding sway over a recognised territory.* **4** If you are **under the sway** of someone or something, they have great influence over you. VERB be V-ed Also V n PHRASE PHRASE

swear /sweə/ **swears, swearing, swore, sworn**. **1** If someone **swears**, they use language that is considered to be rude or offensive, usually because they are angry. *They swore at them and ran off.* **2** If you **swear** to do something, you solemnly promise that you will do it. *Alan swore that he would do everything in his power to help us... He swore allegiance to the U.S. government.* **3** If you say that you **swear** that something is true or that you can **swear** to it, you are saying very firmly that it is true. *I swear I've told you all I know... I swear on all I hold dear that I had nothing to do with this.* **4** If someone **is sworn to** secrecy or silence, they promise another person that they will not reveal a secret. *She was bursting to announce the news but was sworn to secrecy.* **5** See also **sworn**. ◆◆◇◇◇ VERB: V V at n VERB: V to-inf V that V n VERB V that V on/by n that VB: usu passive be V-ed to n

swear by. If you **swear by** something, you believe that it can be relied on to have a particular effect. *Many people swear by vitamin C's ability to ward off colds.* PHRASAL VB V P n INFORMAL

swear in. When someone **is sworn in**, they make a solemn promise to fulfil the duties of a new job or appointment. ♦ **swearing-'in**. *...the first act of Nicaragua's new president after her swearing-in.* PHRASAL VB be V-ed P N-SING

'swear word, swear words. A **swear word** is a word which is considered to be rude or offensive. N-COUNT

sweat /swet/ **sweats, sweating, sweated**. **1 Sweat** is the salty colourless liquid which comes through your skin when you are hot, ill, or afraid. *He wiped the sweat off his face.* **2** When you **sweat**, sweat comes through your skin. ♦ **sweat·ing** *...symptoms such as sweating, irritability, anxiety and depression.* **3** If someone is in a **sweat**, they are sweating a lot. *Cool down very gradually after working up a sweat.* **4** If someone is **in a cold sweat** or **in a sweat**, they feel frightened or embarrassed. *The very thought brought me out in a cold sweat.* **5** If someone **sweats it out**, they wait anxiously for a situation to improve or be resolved, because they cannot do anything about it. **6** If someone says **no sweat** when you ask them about something or to do something, they mean that it can be done without any problems or effort. *'Many thanks.'—'No sweat. Anything else?'* **7** ● **blood, sweat, and tears**: see **blood**. ● to **sweat blood**: see **blood**. **8** In American English, **sweats** are the same as a **sweatsuit** or **sweatpants**. ◆◆◇◇◇ N-UNCOUNT VERB: V N-UNCOUNT N-COUNT PHRASE PHRASE CONVENTION INFORMAL N-PLURAL INFORMAL

sweat·er /'swetə/ **sweaters**. A **sweater** is a warm knitted piece of clothing which covers the upper part of your body and your arms. ◆◆◇◇◇ N-COUNT

sweat·pants /'swetpænts/. **Sweatpants** are the part of a sweatsuit that covers your legs. The British term is **tracksuit trousers** or **tracksuit bottoms**. N-PLURAL AMERICAN

sweat·shirt /'swetʃɜːt/ **sweatshirts**. A **sweatshirt** is a loose warm piece of casual clothing, usually made of thick stretchy cotton, which covers the upper part of your body and your arms. ◆◇◇◇ N-COUNT

sweat·shop /'swetʃɒp/ **sweatshops;** also spelled **sweat shop**. If you describe a small factory or workshop as a **sweatshop**, you mean that many people work together there in poor conditions for low pay; used showing disapproval. N-COUNT PRAGMATICS

sweat·suit /'swetsuːt/ **sweatsuits**. A **sweatsuit** is a loose, warm, stretchy suit consisting of long pants and a top which people wear to relax and do exercise. The usual British word is **tracksuit**. N-COUNT AMERICAN

sweaty /'sweti/. **1** If parts of your body or your clothes are **sweaty**, they are soaked or covered with sweat. **2** A **sweaty** place or activity makes you sweat because it is hot or tiring. *...a sweaty nightclub.* ◆◇◇◇ ADJ-GRADED ADJ-GRADED

S

swede /swiːd/ **swedes.** A **swede** is a round yellow root vegetable with a brown or purple skin. The usual American word is **rutabaga**. — N-VAR BRITISH

sweep /swiːp/ **sweeps, sweeping, swept. 1** If you **sweep** an area of floor or ground, you push dirt or rubbish off it with a long-handled brush. *She was in the kitchen sweeping crumbs into a dust pan.* **2** If you **sweep** things off something, you push them off with a quick smooth movement of your arm. *With a gesture of frustration, she swept the cards from the table.* **3** If someone with long hair **sweeps** their hair into a particular style, they put it into that style. — VERB: V n; V n prep/adv; Also V; VERB V n prep/adv; VERB V n prep/adv

4 If your arm or hand **sweeps** in a particular direction, or if you **sweep** it there, it moves quickly and smoothly in that direction. *His arm swept around the room... Daniels swept his arm over his friend's shoulder.* ▶ Also a noun. *With one sweep of her hand she threw back the sheets.* — V-ERG V prep/adv; V n prep/adv; N-COUNT

5 If wind, a stormy sea, or another strong force **sweeps** someone or something along, it moves them quickly along. *...landslides that buried homes and swept cars into the sea.* **6** If you **are swept** somewhere, you are taken there very quickly. *The visitors were swept past various monuments.* **7** If someone **sweeps** into a place, they walk into it in a proud confident manner, often when they are angry. *She swept into the conference room.* **8** If something **sweeps** from one place to another, it moves there extremely quickly. *An icy wind swept through the streets.* — VERB V n prep/adv; VERB beV-ed prep/adv; VERB V prep/adv WRITTEN; VERB V prep/adv WRITTEN

9 If events or ideas **sweep** through a place, they spread quickly through it. *A flu epidemic is sweeping through Moscow. ...the wave of patriotism sweeping the country.* — VERB V through/across n; V n

10 If something or someone **sweeps** something away or aside, they remove it quickly and completely. *In times of war, governments often sweep human rights aside.* — VERB V n with adv; Also V n prep

11 If a light or someone's gaze **sweeps** an area, it moves across the area steadily from side to side. *Helicopters with searchlights swept the park which was sealed off.* **12** If land or water **sweeps** somewhere, it stretches out in a long, wide, curved shape. *The land sweeps away from long areas of greenery.* ▶ Also a noun. *...the great sweep of the bay.* — VERB V n; VERB V prep/adv; N-COUNT: with supp

13 If a person or group **sweeps** to victory, for example in an election, or something **sweeps** them to victory, they win easily. *...a wave of acclaim that could well sweep her back to power.* — V-ERG V to n; V n to n

14 If you refer to the **sweep** of something, you are indicating that it includes a large number of different events, qualities, or opinions. *...the whole sweep of German social and political history.* — N-SING: with supp

15 If someone **sweeps** something bad or wrong **under the carpet**, they try to prevent people from hearing about it. **16** If you make **a clean sweep** of something, such as a series of matches or tournaments, you win them all. **17** If someone **sweeps** you **off your feet**, you fall in love with them almost as soon as you see them because you find them very good-looking or exciting. **18** See also **chimney sweep**. ● **sweep the board**: see **board**. — PHRASE; PHRASE; PHRASE

sweep up. When you **sweep up** rubbish or dirt, you push it together with a brush and then remove it. *Get a broom and sweep up that glass will you? ...sweeping up and making the tea.* — PHRASAL VB V P noun; V P; Also V n P

sweep·ing /swiːpɪŋ/ **1** If someone makes a **sweeping** statement or generalization, they make a firm definite statement although they have not considered the relevant facts or details carefully; used showing disapproval. *It is far too early to make sweeping statements about gene therapy.* **2** **Sweeping** changes or reforms are large in scale and have very important or significant results. — ADJ-GRADED PRAGMATICS; ADJ-GRADED

sweep·stake /swiːpsteɪk/ **sweepstakes.** A **sweepstake** is a method of gambling in which each person pays a small amount of money and is given the name of a competitor before a race or contest. Then the person who has the name of the winner receives all the money. — N-COUNT

sweet /swiːt/ **sweeter, sweetest; sweets. 1 Sweet** food and drink contains a lot of sugar. *...a mug of sweet tea. ...the sweet taste of wild strawberries.* ◆ **sweet·ness** *Florida oranges have a natural sweetness.* **2 Sweets** are sweet things such as toffees, chocolates, and mints. The American word is **candy**. **3** A **sweet** is something sweet, such as fruit or a pudding, that you eat at the end of a meal, especially in a restaurant. The American word is **dessert**. — ADJ-GRADED; N-UNCOUNT; N-COUNT BRITISH; N-VAR BRITISH

4 A **sweet** smell is pleasant and fragrant. *...the sweet smell of her shampoo.* **5** If you describe something such as air or water as **sweet**, you mean that it smells or tastes pleasantly fresh and clean. *I gulped a breath of sweet air.* **6** A **sweet** sound is pleasant, smooth, and gentle. *...the sweet sounds of Mozart.* ◆ **sweet·ly** *He sang much more sweetly than he has before.* — ADJ-GRADED; ADJ-GRADED; ADJ-GRADED; ADV-GRADED

7 If you describe something as **sweet**, you mean that it gives you great pleasure and satisfaction. *There are few things quite as sweet as revenge.* — ADJ-GRADED WRITTEN

8 If you describe someone as **sweet**, you mean that they are pleasant, kind, and gentle towards other people. *How sweet of you to think of me!* ◆ **sweetly** *I just smiled sweetly.* **9** If you describe a small person or thing as **sweet**, you mean that they are attractive in an unsophisticated way. *...a sweet little baby girl.* **10** You might address someone as **sweet** or **my sweet** if you are very fond of them. *I am so proud of you, my sweet!* — ADJ-GRADED; ADV-GRADED; ADJ-GRADED INFORMAL; N-VOC DATED

11 If you **keep** someone **sweet**, you do something to please them in order to prevent them from becoming annoyed or dissatisfied. *Where's the money to keep us sweet?* **12** See also **sweetly**. ● **a sweet tooth**: see **tooth**. — PHRASE INFORMAL

sweet and 'sour; also spelled **sweet-and-sour. Sweet and sour** is used to describe Chinese food that contains both a sweet flavour and a sharp or sour one. — ADJ: ADJ n

sweet·bread /swiːtbred/ **sweetbreads. Sweetbreads** are meat obtained from the pancreas of a calf or a lamb. — N-COUNT

sweet·corn /swiːtkɔːn/; also spelled **sweet corn. Sweetcorn** is a long rounded vegetable covered in small yellow seeds. It is part of the maize plant. The seeds themselves can also be referred to as **sweetcorn**. — N-UNCOUNT

sweet·en /swiːtən/ **sweetens, sweetening, sweetened. 1** If you **sweeten** food or drink, you add sugar, honey, or another sweet substance to it. *The Australians fry their bananas and sweeten them with honey.* **2** If you **sweeten** something such as an offer or a business deal, you try to make someone want it more by improving it or by increasing the amount you are willing to pay. *He may yet have to sweeten the deal with a cash alternative.* — VERB: V; V n with n; VERB: V n with n

sweet·en·er /swiːtənə/ **sweeteners. 1** A **sweetener** is an artificial substance that can be used in drinks instead of sugar and is less fattening than sugar. **2** A **sweetener** is something that is given or offered to someone in order to persuade them to accept an offer or business deal. — N-VAR; N-COUNT

sweet·heart /swiːthɑːt/ **sweethearts. 1** You call someone **sweetheart** if you are very fond of them. *Happy birthday, sweetheart.* **2** Your **sweetheart** is your boyfriend or your girlfriend. *I married Shurla, my childhood sweetheart, in Liverpool.* — N-VOC; N-COUNT DATED, JOURNALISM

sweetie /swiːti/ **sweeties. 1** You might call someone **sweetie** if you are fond of them, especially if they are younger than you. **2** If you say that someone is a **sweetie**, you mean that they are kind, pleasant, and lovable. **3** Sweets are sometimes referred to as **sweeties** by children or adults speaking to children. — N-VOC INFORMAL; N-COUNT INFORMAL; N-COUNT PRAGMATICS BRITISH

sweet·ish /swiːtɪʃ/ A **sweetish** smell or taste is fairly sweet. — ADJ

sweet·ly /swiːtli/ **1** If an engine or machine is running **sweetly**, it is working smoothly and efficiently. **2** If you kick or hit a ball **sweetly**, you kick or hit it in the very middle of it so that it goes firmly and accurately to the place you are aiming for. **3** See also **sweet**. — ADV-GRADED: ADV with v; ADV-GRADED: ADV with v

sweet·meat /'swi:tmi:t/ **sweetmeats.** Sweet- N-COUNT
meats are sweet items of food, especially delicacies DATED
that are considered to be rather special.

sweet 'nothings. If someone whispers **sweet** N-PLURAL
nothings in your ear, they quietly say nice, loving,
and flattering things to you.

sweet 'pea, sweet peas; also spelled **sweetpea.** N-COUNT
A **sweet pea** is a climbing plant which has delicate
fragrant flowers.

sweet 'pepper, sweet peppers. A **sweet pep-** N-COUNT
per is a hollow green, red, or yellow vegetable.

sweet po'tato, sweet potatoes. Sweet pota- N-VAR
toes are vegetables that look like large ordinary potatoes but taste sweet.

'sweet shop, sweet shops; also spelled N-COUNT
sweetshop. A **sweet shop** is a small shop that sells BRITISH
sweets and cigarettes, and sometimes newspapers
and magazines. The usual American expression is
candy store.

'sweet talk, sweet talks, sweet talking, VERB: V n
sweet talked; also spelled **sweet-talk.** If you V n into -ing/n
sweet talk someone, you talk to them very nicely so
that they will do what you want. *She could always
sweet-talk Pamela into letting her stay up late.*

swell /swel/ **swells, swelling, swelled, swol-** ◆◆◇◇◇
len; the forms **swelled** and **swollen** are both used
as the past participle. **1** If the amount or size of V-ERG: V
something **swells**, it becomes larger than it was be- V to/by n
fore. *His bank balance has swelled by £222,000... Of-* V n to n
fers from other countries should swell the force to Also V n
35,000. **2** If something such as a part of your body VERB: V
swells, it becomes larger and rounder than normal. V to n
The limbs swell to an enormous size. ▶ **Swell up** PHRASAL VB
means the same as **swell**. *The glands in the neck* V P
swell up.

3 If you **swell** with a feeling, you are suddenly full of VERB
that feeling. *She could see her two sons swell with* V with n
pride. **4** If sounds **swell**, they get louder. *The taped* LITERARY
music swelled. VERB
 V

5 A **swell** is the regular movement of waves up and N-COUNT
down in the open sea.

6 You can describe something as **swell** if you think it is ADJ-GRADED
really nice. **7** See also **swelling, swollen; groundswell.** INFORMAL,
swell up. See **swell** 2. AMERICAN
 PHRASAL VB

swell·ing /'swelɪŋ/ **swellings.** A **swelling** is a ◆◇◇◇◇
raised curved shape on the surface of your body N-VAR
which appears as a result of an injury or an illness.
*There is some swelling and he is being detained for
observation.*

swel·ter /'sweltə/ **swelters, sweltering, swel-** VERB
tered. If you **swelter**, you are very uncomfortable V
because the weather is extremely hot. *They swel-
tered in temperatures rising to a hundred degrees.*
▶ **swel·ter·ing** *...the oppressively sweltering sum-* ADJ-GRADED
mer of 1976.

swept /swept/. **Swept** is the past tense and past
participle of **sweep.**

swerve /swɜ:v/ **swerves, swerving, swerved.** ◆◇◇◇◇
If a vehicle or other moving thing **swerves**, it sud- V-ERG: V
denly changes direction, often in order to avoid col- V prep/adv
liding with something else. *Her car swerved off the* V n
*road... Suddenly Ned swerved the truck, narrowly
missing a blond teenager.* ▶ Also a noun. *He swung* N-COUNT
*the car to the left and that swerve saved Malone's
life.*

swift /swɪft/ **swifter, swiftest; swifts. 1** A swift ◆◆◇◇◇
event or process happens very quickly or without ADJ-GRADED
delay. *The police were swift to act.* ▶ **swift·ly** *He* ADV-GRADED
feared they might be leaked unless he acted swiftly.
▶ **swift·ness** *...the secrecy and swiftness of the in-* N-UNCOUNT
vasion. **2** Something that is **swift** moves very quick- ADJ-GRADED
ly. *With a swift movement, Matthew Jerrold sat
upright.* ▶ **swiftly** *...a swiftly flowing stream.* ADV-GRADED:
▶ **swiftness** *With incredible swiftness she ran* ADV with v
down the passage. N-UNCOUNT

3 A **swift** is a small bird with long curved wings. N-COUNT

swig /swɪg/ **swigs, swigging, swigged.** If you VERB: V n
swig a drink, you drink it from a bottle or cup V n with
quickly and in large amounts. *I swigged down two* down/back

white wines. ▶ Also a noun. *McGuire took a long* N-COUNT
swig from his bottle of bitter lemon.

swill /swɪl/ **swills, swilling, swilled. 1** If you VERB
swill an alcoholic drink, you drink a lot of it. *Edgar* V n
swilled a double scotch. ▶ **-swilling** *...beer-swilling* COMB
louts. **2** If a liquid **swills** around, it moves around V-ERG
the area that it is contained in. *...six inches of water* V around/
swilling around in the bilges... She swilled the whis- n
ky around in her glass. **3** To **swill** out something V n around/
means to clean it by pouring water over it. *He* about
swilled out the mug and left it on the draining V n with out
board. BRITISH

4 Swill is a liquid mixture containing waste food such N-UNCOUNT
as vegetable peelings that is given to pigs to eat.

swim /swɪm/ **swims, swimming, swam,** ◆◆◆◇◇
swum. 1 When you **swim**, you move through wa- VERB: V
ter by making movements with your arms and legs. V adv/prep
He was rescued only when an exhausted friend V amount/n
swam ashore... I swim a mile a day. ▶ Also a noun. N-SING
When can we go for a swim, Mam? ▶ **swim·mer,** N-COUNT
swimmers *I'm a good swimmer.* **2** If you **swim** a VERB
race, you take part in a swimming race. *She swam* V n
the 400 metres medley. **3** If you **swim** a stretch of VERB
water, you keep swimming until you have crossed V n
it. *...the first man to swim the English Channel.*
4 When a fish **swims**, it moves through water by VERB: V
making movements with its tail and fins. *...fish try-* V adv/prep
ing to swim upstream.
5 If objects **swim**, they seem to be moving backwards VERB: V
and forwards, usually because you are ill. **6** If your VERB: V
head **is swimming**, you feel dizzy.
7 If something **is swimming** in liquid or **is swimming** VERB:
with liquid, it is surrounded by and covered with it. V in/with n,
8 ● sink or swim: see sink. only cont

swim·ming /'swɪmɪŋ/. **Swimming** is the activity of ◆◆◇◇◇
swimming, especially as a sport or for pleasure. N-UNCOUNT

'swimming bath, swimming baths. 1 A swim- N-COUNT
ming baths or swimming bath is a building that BRITISH
contains an indoor public swimming pool. The plural **swimming baths** can be used to refer either to
one or to more than one of these places. **2** A swim- N-COUNT
ming bath is a public swimming pool, especially an BRITISH
indoor one.

'swimming costume, swimming costumes. A N-COUNT
swimming costume is the same as a swimsuit. BRITISH

swim·ming·ly /'swɪmɪŋli/. If you say that some- PHRASE
thing **is going swimmingly**, you mean that every- INFORMAL
thing is happening in a satisfactory way, without
any problems.

'swimming pool, swimming pools. A swim- ◆◆◇◇◇
ming pool is a place that has been built for people N-COUNT
to swim in. It consists of a large hole that has been
tiled and filled with water.

'swimming trunks. Swimming trunks are the N-PLURAL:
shorts that a man wears when he goes swimming. also a pair of N
The usual American term is **bathing trunks.**

swim·suit /'swɪmsu:t/ **swimsuits.** A swimsuit is a ◆◇◇◇◇
piece of clothing that is worn for swimming, espe- N-COUNT
cially by women and girls.

swim·wear /'swɪmweə/. **Swimwear** refers to the N-UNCOUNT
things people wear for swimming.

swin·dle /'swɪndəl/ **swindles, swindling, swin-** ◆◇◇◇◇
dled. If someone **swindles** a person or an organiza- VERB
tion, they deceive them in order to get something V n out of n
valuable from them, especially money. *A City
businessman swindled investors out of millions of
pounds.* ▶ Also a noun. *He fled to Switzerland rather* N-COUNT
than face trial for a tax swindle. ▶ **swin·dler,** N-COUNT
swindlers *Swindlers have cheated investors out of
£12 million.*

swine /swaɪn/ **swines.** The form **swines** is used as N-COUNT
the plural for meaning 1; **swine** is used as both the
singular and plural for meaning 2. **1** If you call N-COUNT
someone a **swine**, you dislike them or think that INFORMAL
they are a bad person, usually because they have
behaved unpleasantly towards you.

2 A **swine** is a pig. N-COUNT

swing /swɪŋ/ **swings, swinging, swung. 1** If ◆◆◆◇◇
something **swings**, it moves repeatedly backwards V-ERG
and forwards or from side to side from a fixed point. V adv/prep
 V n

The sail of the little boat swung crazily from one side `Also V`
to the other... She was swinging a bottle of wine by
its neck. ▶ Also a noun. ...a woman in a tight red `N-COUNT`
dress, walking with a slight swing to her hips. **2** If `V-ERG`
something **swings** in a particular direction, it moves `V prep/adv`
in that direction with a smooth curving movement. `V n prep/adv`
The canoe found the current and swung around...
Roy swung his legs carefully off the couch and sat up.
▶ Also a noun. You'll find him practising his golf `N-COUNT`
swing. **3** If a vehicle **swings** in a particular direction, `V-ERG`
the driver turns it suddenly in that direction. Joanna `V prep/adv`
swung back on to the main approach... He swung `V n prep/adv`
the car off the road. **4** If someone **swings** round, `VERB:`
they turn around quickly, usually because they are `V adv`
surprised.

5 If you **swing** at someone or something, you try to hit `VERB`
them with your arm or with something that you are `V at n`
holding. I picked up his baseball bat and swung at the `Also V n at n`
man's head. ▶ Also a noun. I often want to take a `N-COUNT`
swing at someone to relieve my feelings.

6 A **swing** is a seat hanging by two ropes or chains `N-COUNT`
from a metal frame or from the branch of a tree. You
can sit on the seat and move forwards and backwards
through the air.

7 Swing is a style of jazz dance music played by big `N-UNCOUNT`
bands that was popular in the 1930's.

8 If people's opinions, attitudes, or feelings **swing**, `VERB: V`
they change significantly. The mood amongst Tory `V adv/prep`
MPs seems to be swinging away from the Prime Minister. ▶ Also a noun. Dieters suffer from violent mood `N-COUNT`
swings.

9 If something is **in full swing**, it is operating fully and `PHRASE`
is no longer in its early stages. The international rugby
season is in full swing. **10** If you **get into the swing of** `PHRASE`
something, you become very involved in it and enjoy
what you are doing. **11** If you say that something is `PHRASE`
going with a swing, you mean that it is happening in a `BRITISH`
lively and exciting way. **12** If you say that a situation is `PHRASE`
swings and roundabouts, you mean that there are as `BRITISH`
many gains as there are losses.

,swing 'door, swing doors. Swing doors are `N-COUNT`
doors that can open both towards you and away
from you.

swinge·ing /'swɪndʒɪn/. A **swingeing** attack or cut- `ADJ: ADJ n`
back causes serious harm or hardship. `BRITISH,`
`JOURNALISM`

swing·er /'swɪŋə/ **swingers.** A **swinger** is a person `N-COUNT`
who is lively and fashionable. `DATED,`
`INFORMAL`

swing·ing /'swɪŋɪŋ/. If you describe something or `ADJ-GRADED`
someone as **swinging**, you mean that they are lively `DATED,`
and fashionable. `INFORMAL`

swipe /swaɪp/ **swipes, swiping, swiped. 1** If ◆◇◇◇
you **swipe** at a person or thing, you try to hit them `VERB:`
with a stick or other object, making a swinging `V at n`
movement with your arm. He swiped me across the `V n`
shoulder with the poker. ▶ Also a noun. He took a `N-COUNT`
swipe at Andrew. **2** If someone **swipes** something, `VERB: V n`
they steal it quickly. **3** If you take a **swipe at** a per- `INFORMAL`
son or an organization, you attack them, usually in `N-COUNT`
an indirect way.

swirl /swɜːl/ **swirls, swirling, swirled.** If you ◆◇◇◇
swirl something liquid or flowing, it moves round `V-ERG: V n`
and round quickly. The black water swirled around `V prep/adv`
his legs, reaching almost to his knees... She swirled `V n prep`
the ice-cold liquid around her mouth. ▶ Also a `Also V n with`
noun. ...small swirls of chocolate cream. `adv,`
`V`
`N-COUNT`

swish /swɪʃ/ **swishes, swishing, swished;** ◆◇◇◇
swisher, swishest. 1 If something **swishes**, it `V-ERG`
moves quickly through the air, making a soft sound. `V adv/prep`
A car swished by... He swished his cape around his `Also V`
shoulders. ▶ Also a noun. She turned with a swish of `N-COUNT`
her skirt. **2** If you describe something as **swish**, you `ADJ-GRADED`
mean that it is smart and fashionable. ...a swish `BRITISH,`
cocktail bar. `INFORMAL`

,swiss 'roll, swiss rolls; also spelled **swiss-roll.** A `N-VAR`
swiss roll is a cylindrical cake made from a thin flat
sponge which is covered with jam or cream on one
side, then rolled up.

switch /swɪtʃ/ **switches, switching, switched.** ◆◆◆◇◇
1 A **switch** is a small control for an electrical device `N-COUNT`

which you use to turn the device on or off. ...a light
switch.

2 If you **switch** to something different, for example to `VERB:`
a different system, task, or subject of conversation, `V to n`
you change to it from what you were doing or saying `V from n to n`
before. The law would encourage companies to switch `V pl-n`
from coal to cleaner fuels... The encouragement of a `Also V`
friend spurred Chris into switching jobs. ▶ Also a
noun. New technology made a switch to oil possible. `N-COUNT`
▶ **Switch over** means the same as **switch.** Everywhere `PHRASAL VB`
communists are tending to switch over to social de- `V P to n`
mocracy. **3** If you **switch** your attention from one `Also V P`
thing to another, you stop paying attention to the first `V-ERG:`
thing and start paying attention to the second. My `V n to n`
mother's interest had switched to my health. `V to n`

4 If you **switch** two things, you replace one with the `VERB`
other. The ballot boxes have been switched. `V pl-n`

switch off. 1 If you **switch off** a light or other electri- `PHRASAL VB`
cal device, you stop it working by operating a switch. `V P noun`
The driver dipped the headlights and then switched `V n P`
them off. **2** If you **switch off**, you stop paying attention `Also V P`
or stop thinking or worrying about something. You `V P`
may find you've got so many things to think about that `INFORMAL`
it's difficult to switch off.

switch on. If you **switch on** a light or other electrical `PHRASAL VB`
device, you make it start working by operating a `V P noun`
switch. He pointed the light at his feet and tried to `V n P`
switch it on. `Also V P`

switch over. 1 If you **switch over** when you are `PHRASAL VB`
watching television, you change to another channel. `V P`
Let's switch over to Channel 4. **2** See **switch** 2. `V P to n`

switch·back /'swɪtʃbæk/ **switchbacks. 1** A `N-COUNT`
switchback is a road which rises and falls sharply `BRITISH`
many times, or a sharp rise and fall in a road. **2** A `N-COUNT`
switchback is a road which goes up a steep hill in a `AMERICAN`
series of zigzags or sharp bends, or a sharp bend in
a road.

switch·blade /'swɪtʃbleɪd/ **switchblades.** A `N-COUNT`
switchblade is a knife with a blade that is hidden in `AMERICAN`
the handle and that springs out when a button is
pressed. The usual British word is **flick-knife.**

switch·board /'swɪtʃbɔːd/ **switchboards.** A ◆◇◇◇
switchboard is a place in a large office or business `N-COUNT`
where all the telephone calls are connected.

swiv·el /'swɪvəl/ **swivels, swivelling, swiv-** ◆◇◇◇
elled; spelled **swiveling, swiveled** in American
English. **1** If something **swivels**, it turns around a `V-ERG: V`
central point so that it is facing in a different direc- `V n adv/prep`
tion. She swivelled her chair round. **2** If you **swivel** `Also V n`
in a particular direction, you turn suddenly in that `VERB`
direction. He swivelled round to face Sarah. **3** If `V adv/prep`
your head or your eyes **swivel** in a particular direc- `V-ERG:`
tion, you quickly look in that direction. Roger swiv- `V prep/adv`
elled his head to look at her. `Also V`

'swivel chair, swivel chairs. A **swivel chair** is a `N-COUNT`
chair whose seat can be turned around a central
point to face in a different direction without moving
the legs.

swol·len /'swəʊlən/. **1** If a part of your body is ◆◇◇◇
swollen, it is larger and rounder than normal, `ADJ-GRADED`
usually as a result of injury or illness. **2** A **swollen** `ADJ-GRADED`
river has more water in it and flows faster than nor-
mal, usually because of heavy rain. **3 Swollen** is the
past participle of **swell.**

swoon /swuːn/ **swoons, swooning, swooned.** `VERB: V`
If you **swoon**, you are strongly affected by your feel- `V over n`
ings for someone you love or admire very much.
Virtually every woman in the '20s swooned over
Valentino.

swoop /swuːp/ **swoops, swooping, swooped.** ◆◇◇◇
1 If police or soldiers **swoop** on a place, they go `VERB:`
there suddenly and quickly, usually in order to ar- `V on n`
rest someone or to attack the place. The drugs `JOURNALISM`
squad swooped and discovered 240 kilograms of cannabis. ▶ Also a noun. Police held 10 suspected illegal `N-COUNT`
immigrants after a swoop on a German lorry.

2 When a bird or aeroplane **swoops**, it suddenly `VERB: V`
moves downwards through the air in a smooth curv- `V adv/prep`
ing movement. More than 20 helicopters began
swooping in low. **3** If something is done **in one fell** `PHRASE`

swoop or **at one fell swoop**, it is done on a single occasion or by a single action. *In one fell swoop the bank wiped away the tentative benefits of this policy.*

swop /swɒp/. See **swap**.

sword /sɔːd/ **swords.** 1 A **sword** is a weapon with ◆◆◇◇◇ a handle and a long sharp blade. 2 If you **cross** N-COUNT **swords** with someone, you disagree with them and PHRASE argue with them about something. 3 If you say that PHRASE something is a **double-edged sword** or a **two-edged sword**, you mean that its positive effects are balanced or outweighed by its negative effects. 4 ● **Sword of Damocles**: see **Damocles**.

sword·fish /ˈsɔːdfɪʃ/; **swordfish** is both the singular N-VAR and plural form. A **swordfish** is a large sea fish with a very long upper jaw. ▶ **Swordfish** is this fish eaten N-UNCOUNT as food.

swore /swɔː/. **Swore** is the past tense of **swear**.

sworn /swɔːn/. 1 **Sworn** is the past participle of **swear**. 2 If you make a **sworn** statement or declara- ADJ: ADJ n tion, you swear that everything that you have said in it is true. *The allegations against them were made in sworn evidence to the inquiry.* 3 If two people or ADJ: ADJ n two groups of people are **sworn** enemies, they dislike each other very much.

swot /swɒt/ **swots, swotting, swotted.** 1 If you VERB: V swot, you study very hard, especially when you are V forn preparing for an examination. *They swotted for their* BRITISH, INFORMAL *A levels.* ▶ **Swot up** means the same as **swot**. ...*sev-* PHRASAL VB *eral hours spent swotting up on how to be a pop* V P on n *star.* 2 If you call someone a **swot**, you disapprove N-COUNT of the fact that they study extremely hard and are PRAGMATICS not interested in other things. BRITISH, INFORMAL

swot up. See **swot** 1. PHRASAL VB

swum /swʌm/. **Swum** is the past participle of **swim**.

swung /swʌŋ/. **Swung** is the past tense and past participle of **swing**.

syba·rit·ic /ˌsɪbəˈrɪtɪk/. A **sybaritic** person or way of ADJ-GRADED life is lazy, luxurious, and devoted to pleasure.

syca·more /ˈsɪkəmɔː/ **sycamores.** A **sycamore** or N-VAR a **sycamore tree** is a tree that has yellow flowers and large leaves with five points. ▶ **Sycamore** is the N-UNCOUNT wood of this tree.

syco·phant /ˈsɪkəfænt, AM -fənt/ **sycophants.** A N-COUNT **sycophant** is a person who flatters people who are PRAGMATICS more important and powerful than they are in order FORMAL to gain an advantage for themselves; used showing disapproval. ◆ **syco·phan·tic** /ˌsɪkəˈfæntɪk/. ...*all* ADJ-GRADED *those sycophantic press officers offering to buy your drinks.*

syl·la·ble /ˈsɪləbəl/ **syllables.** A **syllable** is a part ◆◇◇◇◇ of a word that contains a single vowel sound and N-COUNT that is pronounced as a unit. So, for example, 'book' has one syllable, and 'reading' has two syllables.

syl·la·bus /ˈsɪləbəs/ **syllabuses.** You can refer to ◆◇◇◇◇ the subjects that are studied in a particular course N-COUNT as the **syllabus**. ...*the GCSE history syllabus.* BRITISH

syl·van /ˈsɪlvən/. **Sylvan** is used to describe things ADJ that have an association with woods and trees. LITERARY

sym·bio·sis /ˌsɪmbiˈəʊsɪs, -baɪ-/. 1 **Symbiosis** is a N-UNCOUNT close relationship between two organisms of differ- TECHNICAL ent kinds which benefits both organisms. 2 **Symbiosis** is any relationship between different things, N-UNCOUNT people, or groups that benefits all the things or people concerned. ...*a symbiosis between monarch and church.*

sym·bi·ot·ic /ˌsɪmbiˈɒtɪk, -baɪ-/. A **symbiotic** rela- ADJ-GRADED tionship is one in which organisms, people, or things exist together in a way that benefits them all. *Racing has always had a symbiotic relationship with betting.*

sym·bol /ˈsɪmbəl/ **symbols.** 1 Something that is a ◆◆◆◇◇ **symbol** of a society or an aspect of life seems to N-COUNT: represent it because it is very typical of it. To them, with supp *the monarchy is the special symbol of nationhood.* 2 A **symbol** of something such as an idea is a shape or N-COUNT: design that is used to represent it. *I frequently use sun-* with supp *flowers as symbols of strength.* 3 A **symbol** for an item N-COUNT in a calculation or formula is a number, letter, or shape that represents the item. *What's the chemical*

symbol *for mercury?* 4 See also **sex symbol**, **status symbol**.

sym·bol·ic /sɪmˈbɒlɪk/. 1 If you describe an event, ◆◆◇◇◇ action, or procedure as **symbolic**, you mean that it ADJ represents an important change, although it has little practical effect. ◆ **sym·boli·cal·ly** /sɪmˈbɒlɪkli/. ADV *It was a simple enough gesture, but symbolically important.* 2 Something that is **symbolic** of someone ADJ-GRADED or something else is regarded or used as a symbol of them. ◆ **symbolically** *Each circle symbolically rep-* ADV: *resents the whole of humanity.* 3 **Symbolic** is used ADV with v to describe things involving or relating to symbols. ADJ: ADJ n ...*symbolic representations of landscape.*

sym·bol·ise /ˈsɪmbəlaɪz/. See **symbolize**.

sym·bol·ism /ˈsɪmbəlɪzəm/. 1 **Symbolism** is the ◆◇◇◇◇ use of symbols in order to represent something. ...*a* N-UNCOUNT *film much praised at the time for its visual symbolism.* 2 You can refer to the **symbolism** of an event N-UNCOUNT or action when it seems to show something important about a situation. *The symbolism of the two events will not be lost on most Albanians.*

sym·bol·ize /ˈsɪmbəlaɪz/ **symbolizes, symboliz-** ◆◇◇◇◇ **ing, symbolized;** also spelled **symbolise** in British VERB: V n English. If one thing **symbolizes** another, it is used V-ed or regarded as a symbol of it. ...*the post-war world order symbolised by the United Nations.*

sym·met·ri·cal /sɪˈmetrɪkəl/. If something is **sym-** ◆◇◇◇◇ **metrical**, it has two halves which are exactly the ADJ same, except that one half is the mirror image of the other. ◆ **sym·met·ri·cal·ly** /sɪˈmetrɪkli/. *The south* ADV: *garden at Sissinghurst was composed symmetrically.* ADV with v

sym·me·try /ˈsɪmɪtri/ **symmetries.** 1 Something ◆◇◇◇◇ that has **symmetry** is symmetrical in shape, design, N-VAR or structure. ...*the incredible beauty and symmetry of a snowflake.* 2 **Symmetry** in a relationship or N-UNCOUNT agreement is the fact of both sides giving and receiving an equal amount. *The superpowers pledged to maintain symmetry in their arms shipments.* 3 You can refer to **symmetry** between countries, in- N-VAR stitutions, or situations if you think that there is a close similarity between them.

sym·pa·thet·ic /ˌsɪmpəˈθetɪk/. 1 If you are **sym-** ◆◆◇◇◇ **pathetic** to someone who has had a misfortune, you ADJ-GRADED are kind to them and show that you understand how they are feeling. ◆ **sym·pa·theti·cal·ly** ADV-GRADED: /ˌsɪmpəˈθetɪkli/. *She nodded sympathetically.* 2 If ADV with v you are **sympathetic** to a proposal or action, you ADJ-GRADED approve of it and are willing to support it. *His speeches against corruption may find a sympathetic hearing among some Trinidadians.* 3 You describe ADJ-GRADED someone as **sympathetic** when you like them and approve of the way that they behave. *She sounds a most sympathetic character.*

sym·pa·thize /ˈsɪmpəθaɪz/ **sympathizes, sym-** ◆◇◇◇◇ **pathizing, sympathized;** also spelled **sympa-** **thise** in British English. 1 If you **sympathize** with VERB: someone who has had a misfortune, you show that V with n you are sorry for them. *He would sympathize but he* V *wouldn't understand.* 2 If you **sympathize** with VERB: someone's feelings, you understand them and are V with n not critical of them. *He liked Max, and sympathized* Also V *with his ambitions.* 3 If you **sympathize** with a pro- VERB posal or action, you approve of it and are willing to V with n support it. *Most of the people living there sympa- thized with the guerrillas.* ◆ **sym·pa·thiz·er, sym-** N-COUNT **pathizers** ...*a group of Nazi sympathizers.*

sym·pa·thy /ˈsɪmpəθi/ **sympathies.** 1 If you have ◆◆◆◇◇ **sympathy** for someone who has had a misfortune, N-UNCOUNT: you are sorry for them, and show this in the way also N in pl you behave towards them. *I have had very little help from doctors and no sympathy whatsoever.* 2 If you N-UNCOUNT: have **sympathy** with someone's ideas or opinions, also N in pl you agree with them. *Lithuania still commands considerable international sympathy for its cause.* 3 If N-COUNT you take some action in **sympathy** with someone else, you do it in order to show that you support them. *Several hundred workers struck in sympathy with their colleagues at KBS.*

sym·pho·ny /ˈsɪmfəni/ **symphonies.** A **sympho-** ◆◆◇◇◇ **ny** is a piece of music written to be played by an N-COUNT

S

orchestra. Symphonies are usually made up of four separate sections called movements. ♦ **sym·phon·ic** /sɪm'fɒnɪk/. ...*symphonic music.* ADJ

'**symphony orchestra, symphony orchestras.** A **symphony orchestra** is a large orchestra that plays classical music. ◆◇◇◇◇ N-COUNT

sym·po·sium /sɪm'pəʊziəm/ **symposia** /sɪm'pəʊziə/ or **symposiums.** A **symposium** is a conference in which experts or scholars discuss a particular subject. ◆◇◇◇◇ N-COUNT

symp·tom /'sɪmptəm/ **symptoms. 1** A **symptom** of an illness is something wrong with your body or mind that is a sign of the illness. ...*patients with flu symptoms.* **2** A **symptom** of a bad situation is something that happens which is considered to be a sign of this situation. *The contradictory statements are symptoms of disarray in the administration.* ◆◆◆◇◇ N-COUNT
N-COUNT

symp·to·mat·ic /ˌsɪmptə'mætɪk/. If something is **symptomatic** of something else, especially something bad, it is a sign of it. *The city's problems are symptomatic of the crisis that is spreading throughout the country.* ◆◇◇◇◇ ADJ: v-link ADJ FORMAL

syna·gogue /'sɪnəgɒg/ **synagogues.** A **synagogue** is a building where Jewish people meet to worship or to study their religion. ◆◇◇◇◇ N-COUNT

syn·apse /'saɪnæps, AM sɪ'næps/ **synapses.** A **synapse** is one of the points in the nervous system at which a nerve signal is passed from one neuron to another. N-COUNT TECHNICAL

sync /sɪŋk/; also spelled **synch.** If two things are **out of sync,** they are badly matched or do not work simultaneously as they should. If two things are **in sync,** they are well-matched or work simultaneously as they should. *Normally, when demand and supply are out of sync, you either increase the supply, or you adjust the price mechanism.* PHRASE INFORMAL

syn·chro·nize /'sɪŋkrənaɪz/ **synchronizes, synchronizing, synchronized;** also spelled **synchronise** in British English. If you **synchronize** two activities, processes, or movements, or **synchronize** one activity, process, or movement with another, you cause them to happen at exactly the same time and speed as each other. *Synchronise the score with the film action.* ♦ **syn·chro·ni·za·tion** /ˌsɪŋkrənaɪ'zeɪʃən/. *With perfect synchronization, two other girls cartwheeled toward the ropes.* ◆◇◇◇◇ V-RECIP-ERG: V pl-n V n with n Also V with n, pl-n V
N-UNCOUNT

,**synchronized 'swimming;** also spelled **synchronised swimming. Synchronized swimming** is a sport in which two or more swimmers perform complicated and carefully planned movements in water in time to music. N-UNCOUNT

syn·co·pat·ed /'sɪŋkəpeɪtɪd/. In **syncopated** music, the weak beats in the bar are stressed instead of the strong beats. ADJ-GRADED

syn·di·cate, syndicates, syndicating, syndicated. 1 A **syndicate** is an association of people or organizations that is formed for business purposes or in order to carry out a project. ...*a major crime syndicate.* **2** When newspaper articles or television programmes **are syndicated,** they are sold to several different newspapers or television stations, who then publish the articles or broadcast the programmes. *Today his programme is syndicated to 500 stations.* ♦ **syn·di·ca·tion** /ˌsɪndɪ'keɪʃən/. *All together, Columbia has 23 sitcoms in syndication.* ◆◆◇◇◇ N-COUNT
VERB: be V-ed be V-ed prep/adv
N-UNCOUNT

syn·drome /'sɪndrəʊm/ **syndromes. 1** A **syndrome** is a medical condition that is characterized by a particular group of signs and symptoms. ● See also **Down's syndrome. 2** You can refer to an undesirable condition that is characterized by a particular type of activity or behaviour as a **syndrome.** *Scientists call this the 'it won't affect me' syndrome.* ◆◆◇◇◇ N-COUNT
N-COUNT

syn·er·gy /'sɪnədʒi/ **synergies.** If someone, especially a business person, says that there is **synergy** between two or more organizations or groups, they mean that when they combine or work together, they are more successful than they are when they are on their own. N-VAR

syn·od /'sɪnɒd/ **synods.** A **synod** is a special council of members of a Church, which meets regularly to discuss religious issues. ◆◇◇◇◇ N-COUNT

syno·nym /'sɪnənɪm/ **synonyms.** A **synonym** is a word or expression which means the same as another word or expression. N-COUNT

syn·ony·mous /sɪ'nɒnɪməs/. If you say that one thing is **synonymous** with another, you mean that the two things are very closely associated with each other so that one suggests the other or one cannot exist without the other. *In politics, power and popularity are not synonymous.* ◆◇◇◇◇ ADJ

syn·op·sis /sɪ'nɒpsɪs/ **synopses** /sɪ'nɒpsiːz/. A **synopsis** is a summary of a longer piece of writing or work. N-COUNT

syn·tax /'sɪntæks/. **Syntax** is the ways that words can be put together, or are put together, in order to make sentences. ♦ **syn·tac·tic** /sɪn'tæktɪk/. *We select dictionary examples to show syntactic behaviour.* N-UNCOUNT TECHNICAL
ADJ

syn·the·sis /'sɪnθɪsɪs/ **syntheses. 1** A **synthesis** of different ideas or styles is a mixture or combination of these ideas or styles. *Her synthesis of feminism and socialism ran counter to all other historical currents.* **2** The **synthesis** of a substance is the production of it by means of chemical or biological reactions. ◆◇◇◇◇ N-COUNT FORMAL
N-VAR TECHNICAL

syn·the·size /'sɪnθɪsaɪz/ **synthesizes, synthesizing, synthesized;** also spelled **synthesise** in British English. **1** To **synthesize** a substance means to produce it by means of chemical or biological reactions. **2** If you **synthesize** different ideas, facts, or experiences, you combine them to form a single idea or impression. ◆◇◇◇◇ VERB: V n TECHNICAL
VERB: V n FORMAL

syn·the·sized /'sɪnθɪsaɪzd/; also spelled **synthesised** in British English. **Synthesized** sounds are produced electronically using a synthesizer. ADJ: ADJ n

syn·the·siz·er /'sɪnθɪsaɪzə/ **synthesizers;** also spelled **synthesiser** in British English. A **synthesizer** is an electronic machine that produces speech, music, or other sounds by using its computer to combine individual syllables or sounds that have been previously recorded and stored. ◆◇◇◇◇ N-COUNT

syn·thet·ic /sɪn'θetɪk/. **Synthetic** products are made from chemicals or artificial substances rather than from natural ones. ♦ **syn·theti·cal·ly** ...*the therapeutic use of natural and synthetically produced hormones.* ◆◇◇◇◇ ADJ
ADV: ADV with v

syn·thet·ics /sɪn'θetɪks/. You can refer to synthetic clothing, fabric, or materials as **synthetics.** N-PLURAL

syphi·lis /'sɪfɪlɪs/. **Syphilis** is a serious disease which is passed on through sexual intercourse. N-UNCOUNT

sy·phon /'saɪfən/ **syphons.** See **siphon.**

sy·ringe /sɪ'rɪndʒ/ **syringes.** A **syringe** is a small tube with a plunger and a fine hollow needle or pointed end. Syringes may be used for injecting drugs or for taking blood from someone's body. ◆◇◇◇◇ N-COUNT

syr·up /'sɪrəp/ **syrups. 1 Syrup** is a sweet liquid made by cooking sugar with water, and sometimes with fruit juice as well. **2 Syrup** is a very sweet thick liquid made from sugar. ● See also **golden syrup, maple syrup.** ♦ **syr·upy.** Liquid that is **syrupy** is sweet or thick like syrup. **3 Syrup** is a medicine in the form of a thick, sweet liquid. ...*cough syrup.* ◆◇◇◇◇ N-VAR
N-UNCOUNT
ADJ-GRADED
N-VAR

sys·tem /'sɪstəm/ **systems. 1** A **system** is a way of working, organizing, or doing something which follows a fixed plan or set of rules. You can use **system** to refer to an organization or institution that is organized in this way. *The present system of funding for higher education is unsatisfactory.* **2** A **system** is a device or set of devices powered by electricity, for example a hi-fi or computers. **3** A system is a set of equipment or parts such as water pipes or electrical wiring, which is used to supply water, heat, or electricity. ...*a central heating system.* **4** A system is a network of things linked together so that people or things can travel from one place to another or communicate. ...*Australia's road and rail system.* **5** Your **system** is your body's organs and other parts that together perform particular functions. ...*the reproductive system.* ◆◆◆◆◆ N-COUNT
N-COUNT
N-COUNT
N-COUNT
N-COUNT

6 A **system** is a particular set of rules, especially in mathematics or science, which is used to count or measure things. ...*the decimal system of metric weights and measures.* N-COUNT
7 People sometimes refer to the government or administration of a country as **the system.** N-SING: theN
8 See also **central nervous system, digestive system, ecosystem, immune system, nervous system, public address system, solar system, sound system.**
9 If you **get** something **out of** your **system**, you take some action so that you no longer want to do it or no longer have strong feelings about it. PHRASE
sys·tem·at·ic /ˌsɪstə'mætɪk/. Something that is done in a **systematic** way is done according to a fixed plan, in a thorough and efficient way. ♦ **sys-** ADJ-GRADED

·tem·ati·cal·ly /ˌsɪstə'mætɪkli/. *The army has systematically violated human rights.* ADV: ADV with v
sys·tema·tize /'sɪstəmətaɪz/ **systematizes, systematizing, systematized;** also spelled **systematise** in British English. If you **systematize** things, you make them systematic or organize them into a system. *Systematize your approach to problem solving.* VERB V n Also V FORMAL
sys·tem·ic /sɪ'stiːmɪk/. **Systemic** means affecting the whole of a system or organism. *The economy is locked in a systemic crisis.* ♦◊◊◊◊ ADJ
,systems 'analyst, systems analysts. A **systems analyst** is someone whose job is to assess a company's computer needs and to provide the equipment and software needed to fulfil them. N-COUNT

T t

T, t /tiː/ **T's, t's;** also spelled **tee** for meaning 3. **1 T** is the twentieth letter of the English alphabet. **2 T** or **t** is a written abbreviation for words beginning with 't', such as 'ton' and 'time'. **3** You can use **to a T** or **to a tee** to mean perfectly or exactly right. For example, if something suits you **to a T**, it suits you perfectly. If you have got an activity or a skill **down to a T**, you have succeeded in doing it exactly right. N-VAR / PHRASE INFORMAL
ta /taː/. **Ta** means thankyou. *Peter got a wad of banknotes folded in half out of his jeans pocket. 'Ta very much,' said Sam.* ♦◊◊◊◊ CONVENTION INFORMAL, BRITISH
tab /tæb/ **tabs. 1** A **tab** is a small piece of cloth or paper that is attached to something, usually with information about that thing written on it. ...*a small red tab sewn on to the left-hand side of the back right pocket.* ♦◊◊◊◊ N-COUNT
2 If someone **keeps tabs on** you, they make sure that they always know where you are and what you are doing, often in order to control you. PHRASE INFORMAL
3 A **tab** is a metal strip that you pull off the top of a can of drink in order to open it. The British term is **ring-pull. 4** A **tab** is a tablet of a drug that is sold illegally. *One tab of Ecstasy costs at least £15.* N-COUNT AMERICAN / N-COUNT
5 A **tab** is a bill or check for goods or services that you have received. *At least one estimate puts the total tab at $7 million.* **6** If you **pick up the tab**, you pay a bill on behalf of a group of people or provide the money that is needed for something. N-COUNT AMERICAN / PHRASE INFORMAL
Ta·bas·co /tə'bæskəʊ/. **Tabasco** is a hot spicy sauce made from peppers. **Tabasco** is a trademark. N-UNCOUNT
tab·by /'tæbi/ **tabbies.** A **tabby** or a **tabby cat** is a cat whose fur has dark stripes or wavy markings on a lighter background. N-COUNT
tab·er·nac·le /'tæbənækəl/ **tabernacles. 1** A **tabernacle** is a church used by certain Christian Protestant groups and by Mormons. **2 The Tabernacle** was a small tent which contained the most sacred writings of the ancient Jews and which they took with them when they were travelling. N-COUNT / N-PROPER: theN
ta·ble /'teɪbəl/ **tables, tabling, tabled. 1** A **table** is a piece of furniture with a flat top that you put things on or sit at. ...*the kitchen table.* **2** If you ask for a **table** in a restaurant, you want to have a meal there. *I booked a table at the Savoy Grill.* ♦♦♦♦◊ N-COUNT / N-COUNT
3 If someone **tables** a proposal, they say formally that they want it to be discussed at a meeting. *They've tabled a motion criticising the Government for doing nothing about the problem.* **4** If someone **tables** a proposal or plan which has been put forward, they decide to discuss it or deal with it at a later date, rather than straight away. *We will table that for later.* If you put something **on the table**, you present it at a meeting for it to be discussed. *It means that all the options are at least on the table.* VERB V n BRITISH / VERB V n AMERICAN / PHRASE
6 A **table** is a written set of facts and figures arranged N-COUNT:

in columns and rows. **7** A **table** or **multiplication table** is a list of the multiplications of numbers between one and twelve, which children learn at school. also N num N-COUNT
8 See also **coffee table, dressing table, negotiating table, round table, tea table.**
9 If you **turn the tables** on someone, you change the situation completely, so that instead of them causing problems for you, you are causing problems for them. PHRASE
10 ● to put your **cards on the table**: see **card.**
tab·leau /'tæbləʊ/ **tableaux. 1** A **tableau** is a scene, for example from the Bible, history, or mythology, portrayed by people in costumes posing silently, sometimes on a float in a procession. ...*a nativity tableau.* **2** A **tableau** is a piece of art such as a sculpture or painting that depicts a scene, especially one from the Bible, history, or mythology. ♦◊◊◊◊ N-COUNT / N-COUNT
table·cloth /'teɪbəlklɒθ, AM -klɔːθ/ **tablecloths.** A **tablecloth** is a cloth used to cover a table. ♦◊◊◊◊ N-COUNT
'table lamp, table lamps. A **table lamp** is a small electric lamp which stands on a table or other piece of furniture. N-COUNT
'table manners. You can use **table manners** to refer to the way you behave when you are eating a meal at a table. ...*decent table manners.* N-PLURAL
table·spoon /'teɪbəlspuːn/ **tablespoons.** A **tablespoon** is a fairly large spoon used for serving food and whilst cooking. ♦◊◊◊◊ N-COUNT
table·spoon·ful /'teɪbəlspuːnfʊl/ **tablespoonsful** or **tablespoonfuls.** You can refer to an amount of food resting on a tablespoon as a **tablespoonful** of food. N-COUNT
tab·let /'tæblət/ **tablets. 1** A **tablet** is a small solid round mass of medicine which you swallow. ...*sleeping tablets.* **2** Clay **tablets** or stone **tablets** are the flat pieces of clay or stone which people used to write on before paper was invented. ♦♦◊◊◊ N-COUNT / N-COUNT
'table tennis. **Table tennis** is a game played indoors by two or four people. The players stand at each end of a long table which has a low net across its middle and hit a small light ball to the other side of the table, using small bats. ♦◊◊◊◊ N-UNCOUNT
'table top, table tops; also spelled **tabletop.** A **table top** is the flat surface on a table. N-COUNT
table·ware /'teɪbəlweə/. **Tableware** consists of the objects used on the table at meals, for example plates, glasses, or cutlery. N-UNCOUNT FORMAL
'table wine, table wines. **Table wine** is fairly cheap wine that is drunk with meals. N-VAR
tab·loid /'tæblɔɪd/ **tabloids.** A **tabloid** is a newspaper that has small pages, short articles, and lots of photographs. Tabloids are often considered to be less serious than other newspapers. *'The British tabloids called me "leggy" and "stunning"',* she recalls. ♦♦◊◊◊ N-COUNT

ta·boo /tæˈbuː/ **taboos.** If there is a **taboo** on a ◆◇◇◇◇ N-COUNT
subject or activity, it is a social custom to avoid do-
ing that activity or talking about that subject, because people find them embarrassing or offensive.
The topic of addiction remains something of a taboo.
▶ Also an adjective. *Cancer is a taboo subject.* ADJ-GRADED

tabu·late /ˈtæbjʊleɪt/ **tabulates, tabulating,** VERB
tabulated. To **tabulate** information means to ar- V n
range it in columns on a page so that it can be analysed. *...tabulating and analysing numerical data.*

tacho·graph /ˈtækəɡrɑːf, -ɡræf/ **tachographs.** A N-COUNT
tachograph is a device that is put in vehicles such BRITISH
as lorries and coaches in order to record information such as how fast the vehicle goes, how far it
travels, and the number of breaks the driver takes.

tac·it /ˈtæsɪt/. If you refer to someone's **tacit** agree- ◆◇◇◇◇
ment or approval, you mean they are agreeing to ADJ
something or approving it without actually saying
so, often because they are unwilling to admit to doing so. *The question was a tacit admission that a
mistake had indeed been made.* ♦ **tac·it·ly** *He tacit-* ADV:
ly admitted that the government had breached ADV with v
regulations.

taci·turn /ˈtæsɪtɜːn/. A **taciturn** person does not ADJ-GRADED
say very much and can seem unfriendly.

tack /tæk/ **tacks, tacking, tacked. 1** A **tack** is a ◆◆◇◇◇
short nail with a broad, flat head, especially one N-COUNT
that is used for fastening carpets to the floor. ● See
also **thumbtack**. **2** If you **tack** something to a sur- VERB
face, you pin it there with tacks or drawing pins. *He* V n to n
had tacked this note to her door. **3** If you **tack** pieces Also V n with
of material together, you sew them together with adv
big, loose stitches in order to hold them firmly or VERB:
check that they fit, before sewing them properly. V pl-n with
Tack the cord around the cushion with raw edges together
level. V n prep/adv
4 If you change **tack** or try a different **tack**, you try a N-SING:
different method for dealing with a situation. *This re-* also no det
*port takes a different tack from the 20 that have come
before.* **5** If a sailing boat **is tacking** or if the crew **tacks** V-ERG: V
it, it is sailing towards a particular point in a series of V adv/prep
diagonal movements rather than in a straight line. V n
*Our last serious trip involved a coastal passage from
Morocoy to Puerto la Cruz, tacking east against wind
and current... The helmsman could tack the boat
singlehanded.*

tack on. If you say that something **is tacked on** to PHRASAL VB
something else, you think that it is added in a hurry be V-ed P to n
and in an unsatisfactory way. *The child-care bill is to* Also V n P
*be tacked on to the budget plan now being worked out
in the Senate.*

tack·le /ˈtækəl/ **tackles, tackling, tackled. 1** If ◆◆◆◇◇
you **tackle** a difficult problem or task, you deal with VERB
it in a very determined or efficient way. *Firemen lat-* V n
er tackled the blaze. **2** If you **tackle** someone in a VERB: V n
game such as hockey or soccer, you try to take the
ball away from them. If you **tackle** someone in rugby or American football, you knock them to the
ground. ▶ Also a noun. *...a tackle by full-back Brian* N-COUNT
Burrows. **3** If you **tackle** someone about a matter, VERB
you speak to them frankly about it, usually in order V n about
to get something changed or done. *I tackled him* wh/n
*about how anyone could live amidst so much pover-
ty.* **4** If you **tackle** someone, you attack them and VERB
fight them. *He claims Pasolini overtook and tackled* V n
him, pushing him into the dirt.
5 Tackle is the equipment that you need for a sport or N-UNCOUNT
activity, especially fishing. **6 Tackle** is the equipment, N-UNCOUNT
usually consisting of ropes and pulleys, needed for
lifting or pulling something.

tacky /ˈtæki/ **tackier, tackiest. 1** If you describe ◆◇◇◇◇
something as **tacky**, you dislike it because it is ADJ-GRADED
cheap and badly made or vulgar. *...a woman in a* PRAGMATICS
fake leopard-skin coat and tacky red sunglasses. **2** If INFORMAL
something such as paint or glue is **tacky**, it is slight- ADJ-GRADED
ly sticky and not yet dry.

tact /tækt/. **Tact** is the ability to avoid upsetting or ◆◇◇◇◇
offending people by being careful not to say or do N-UNCOUNT
things that would hurt their feelings. *...helping to
smooth over problems with great tact and efficiency.*

tact·ful /ˈtæktfʊl/. If you use **tactful** to describe ◆◇◇◇◇
someone, or something they say or do, you approve ADJ-GRADED
of them because they are careful not to say or do PRAGMATICS
something which would offend or upset another
person. *He had been extremely tactful in dealing
with the financial question.* ♦ **tact·ful·ly** *Alex tact-* ADV-GRADED
fully refrained from further comment.

tac·tic /ˈtæktɪk/ **tactics. Tactics** are the methods ◆◆◆◇◇
that you choose to use in order to achieve what you N-COUNT
want in a particular situation. *The terrorists continue to express confidence that their guerrilla tactics
can defeat a conventional force.*

tac·ti·cal /ˈtæktɪkəl/. **1** You can use **tactical** to ◆◆◇◇◇
describe an action or plan which is intended to ADJ
help someone achieve what they want in a particular situation. *The security forces had made a tactical
withdrawal from the area.* ♦ **tac·ti·cal·ly** ADV
/ˈtæktɪkli/. *They cannot actually tell their supporters
to vote tactically against the Conservatives.* **2 Tacti-** ADJ: ADJ n
cal weapons or forces are those which a military
commander can decide to use in a battle, rather
than waiting for a decision by a political leader.
...U.S. tactical air fighter squadrons.

tactical 'voting. Tactical voting is the act of vot- N-UNCOUNT
ing for a particular person or political party in order BRITISH
to prevent someone else from winning, rather than
because you support that person or party.

tac·ti·cian /tækˈtɪʃən/ **tacticians.** If you say that N-COUNT
someone is a good **tactician**, you mean that they
are skilful at choosing the best methods in order to
achieve what they want.

tac·tile /ˈtæktaɪl, AM -təl/. **1** If you describe some- ADJ-GRADED
one as **tactile**, you mean that they tend to touch
other people a lot when talking to them. *I am a very
tactile person.* **2** Something such as fabric which is ADJ-GRADED
tactile is pleasant or interesting to touch. *Tweed is
timeless, tactile and tough.* **3 Tactile** experiences or ADJ
sensations are received or felt by touch. *Heat, cold,* FORMAL
tactile and other sensations contribute to flavour.

tact·less /ˈtæktləs/. If you describe someone as ADJ-GRADED
tactless, you think what they say or do is likely to
offend other people. *He had alienated many people
with his tactless remarks.*

tad /tæd/. You can use a **tad** in expressions such as PHRASE
a tad big or **a tad small** when you mean that some- INFORMAL
thing is slightly too big or slightly too small.

tad·pole /ˈtædpəʊl/ **tadpoles. Tadpoles** are small N-COUNT
water creatures which grow into frogs or toads.

taf·fe·ta /ˈtæfɪtə/. **Taffeta** is shiny stiff material N-UNCOUNT
made of silk or nylon that is used mainly for making
women's clothes.

tag /tæg/ **tags, tagging, tagged. 1** A **tag** is a ◆◆◇◇◇
small piece of card or cloth which is attached to an N-COUNT
object or person and has information about that
object or person on it. *...baggage tags.* ● See also
dog tag, price tag. 2 An electronic **tag** is a device N-COUNT
that is attached to someone or something and sets
off an alarm if that person or thing moves away or is
removed. **3** If you **tag** something, you attach some- VERB
thing to it or mark it so that it can be identified V n
later. *The most important trees were tagged to
protect them from being damaged by construction
machinery.*
4 If you **tag** someone with a particular label, you keep VERB:
describing them using a particular phrase or thinking V n with n
of them as a particular thing. *She has always lived in* be V-ed n
John's house and is still tagged 'Dad's girlfriend' by his Also V n as n,
children. ▶ Also a noun. *In Britain, jazz is losing its* V n
elitist tag and gaining a much broader audience. JOURNALISM
N-COUNT
5 A **tag** is a short quotation or saying. **6 Tag** is a N-COUNT
children's game in which one child chases the others N-UNCOUNT
and tries to touch them.
7 See also **question tag**.

tag along. If someone goes somewhere and you **tag** PHRASAL VB
along, you go with them, especially when they have V P
not asked you to. *She seems quite happy to tag along* V P with n
with them.

tag on. If you **tag** something o·n, you add it. *It is also* PHRASAL VB
worth tagging on an extra day or two to see the capital. V P noun

tail

tail /teɪl/ **tails, tailing, tailed. 1** The **tail** of an animal, bird, or fish is the part extending beyond the end of its body. ♦ **-tailed** ...*white-tailed deer.* **2** You can use **tail** to refer to the end or back of something, especially something long and thin. ...*the horizontal stabilizer bar on the plane's tail.* **3** If a man is wearing **tails**, he is wearing a formal jacket which has two long pieces hanging down at the back. **4** To **tail** someone means to follow close behind them and watch where they go and what they do. *He trusted her so little that he had her tailed.* **5** A **tail** is someone who is paid to watch and to follow another person. **6** If you **turn tail**, you turn and run away. **7** If you toss a coin and it comes down **tails**, you can see the side of it that does not have a picture of a head on it. **8** • **cannot make head or tail of** something: see **head**. • **to top and tail**: see **top**.
(margins: ♦♦♦◇◇ N-COUNT; COMB; N-COUNT; N-PLURAL; VERB: Vn, have n V-ed INFORMAL; N-COUNT INFORMAL; PHRASE ADV; ADV after v)

tail off. When something **tails off**, it gradually becomes less in amount or value, often before coming to an end completely. *Last year, economic growth tailed off to below four percent.* *(PHRASAL VB VP)*

tail·back /ˈteɪlbæk/ **tailbacks.** A **tailback** is a long queue of traffic stretching back along a road, moving very slowly or not at all, for example because of roadworks or an accident. *(N-COUNT BRITISH)*

tail 'end; also spelled **tail-end.** The **tail end** of an event, situation, or period of time is the last part of it. ...*the tail-end of the conversation.* *(N-SING)*

tail·gate /ˈteɪlɡeɪt/ **tailgates.** A **tailgate** is a door at the back of a truck or car, that is hinged at the bottom so that it opens downwards. *(N-COUNT)*

'tail-light, tail-lights; also spelled **taillight.** The **tail-lights** on a car or other vehicle are the two red lights at the back. *(N-COUNT)*

tai·lor /ˈteɪlə/ **tailors, tailoring, tailored. 1** A **tailor** is a person whose job is to make men's clothes. **2** If you **tailor** something such as a plan or system to someone's needs, you make it suitable for a particular person or purpose by changing the details of it. ...*the local forces were trying to tailor their policing style to increase public confidence.* ...*scripts tailored to American comedy audiences.* *(♦♦◇◇◇ N-COUNT; VERB: Vn to n, Vn to-inf V-ed Also Vn)*

tai·lored /ˈteɪləd/. **Tailored** clothes are designed to fit close to the body, rather than being loose and baggy. ...*a white tailored shirt.* *(ADJ-GRADED)*

tailor-'made. 1 If something is **tailor-made**, it has been specially designed for a particular person or purpose. ...*tailor-made itineraries for tourists.* **2** If you say that someone or something is **tailor-made** for a particular task, purpose, or need, you are emphasizing that they are perfectly suitable for it. *These questions were tailor-made for Professor Posner.* **3** **Tailor-made** clothes have been specially made by a tailor to fit a particular person. *(♦◇◇◇◇ ADJ; ADJ PRAGMATICS; ADJ)*

tailor-'make, tailor-makes, tailor-making, tailor-made. If someone **tailor-makes** something for you, they make or design it to suit your requirements. *The company can tailor-make your entire holiday.* • See also **tailor-made**. *(VERB Vn)*

tail·pipe /ˈteɪlpaɪp/ **tailpipes.** A **tailpipe** is the same as an **exhaust** pipe. See picture headed **car and bicycle**. *(N-COUNT AMERICAN)*

tail·spin /ˈteɪlspɪn/. If something goes into a **tailspin**, it starts to deteriorate suddenly and rapidly. *The war sent world tourism into a tailspin.* *(N-SING)*

tail·wind /ˈteɪlwɪnd/ **tailwinds;** also spelled **tail wind.** A **tailwind** is a wind that is blowing from behind an aeroplane, boat, or other vehicle, making it move faster. *(N-COUNT)*

taint /teɪnt/ **taints, tainting, tainted. 1** If you say that something or someone **is tainted** by something undesirable or corrupt, you mean that their status or reputation is harmed because they are associated with it. ...*a series of political scandals that has tainted the political stars of a generation.* ♦ **taint·ed** ...*tainted evidence.* **2** A **taint** is an undesirable quality which spoils the status or reputation of someone or something. *Her government never really shook off the taint of corruption.* **3** If an un- *(♦◇◇◇◇ VERB: be V-ed Vn; ADJ-GRADED N-COUNT; VERB: Vn)*

pleasant substance **taints** food or medicine, the food or medicine is spoiled or damaged by it. ...*blood tainted with the AIDS and hepatitis viruses.* *(V-ed)*

take

take 1 used with nouns describing actions

take /teɪk/ **takes, taking, took, taken.** Take is used in combination with a wide range of nouns, where the meaning of the combination depends mostly on the noun. Many of these combinations are common expressions whose meanings can be found at the appropriate nouns. For example, the expression **take care** is explained at **care**. *(♦♦♦♦♦)*

1 You can use **take** followed by a noun to refer to a particular action, when it would also be possible to use a verb that has a similar form to the noun. For example, you can say **'she took a sip'** instead of 'she sipped'. *She was too tired to take a shower... Betty took a photograph of us.* **2** You can use **take** with a range of nouns when it is clear from the context what it means, often instead of a more specific verb. For example, you can say **'he took control'** or **'she took a positive attitude'** instead of 'he assumed control' or 'she adopted a positive attitude'. *President Collor de Mello took power in March... The constitution requires members of parliament to take an oath of allegiance.* *(VERB Vn; VERB Vn)*

take 2 other verb and noun senses

take /teɪk/ **takes, taking, took, taken. 1** If you **take** something, you reach for it and hold it. *Let me take your coat... Alberg took the portrait down from the wall.* **2** If you **take** something with you when you go somewhere, you carry it or have it with you. *I'll take these papers home and read them... You should take your passport with you when changing money... Don't forget to take your camera.* **3** If you **take** something from a place, you remove it from there. *He took a handkerchief from his pocket... Opening a drawer, she took out a letter.* **4** If you **take** something from its owner, you steal it or go away with it without their permission. *(♦♦♦♦♦ VERB Vn, Vn adv/prep; VERB Vn adv/prep, Vn with n; VERB Vn with prep/adv; VERB: Vn)*

5 If a person, vehicle, or path **takes** someone somewhere, they transport or lead them there. *She took me to a Mexican restaurant.* **6** If something such as a job or interest **takes** you to a place, it is the reason for you going there. *My work takes me abroad a lot.* **7** If you **take** something such as your problems or your business to someone, you go to them to discuss your problems or to do business with them. *You need to take your problems to a trained counsellor.* **8** If one thing **takes** another to a particular level or state, it causes it to reach that level or state. *The managing director had given himself a pay rise of 20%, taking his salary to £220,000.* *(VERB Vn prep/adv; VERB Vn adv/prep; VERB Vn prep/adv; VERB Vn prep/adv)*

9 To **take** something or someone means to win or capture them from an enemy or opponent. *Marines went in, taking 15 prisoners... Labour also took Warrington South from the Conservative Party.* **10** If you **take** a prize, you win it. *Christie took the gold medal.* **11** If a shop, restaurant, cinema, or business **takes** a certain amount of money, it gets that amount from people buying goods or services. *The firm took £100,000 in bookings.* ▶ In American English, the usual expression is **take in.** *The average cabbie takes in about $600 a week.* *(VERB Vn, Vn from n; VERB Vn; VERB V amount BRITISH; PHRASAL VB VP amount)*

12 If you **take** something that is given or offered to you, you accept it. *When I took the job I thought I could change the system... His sons took his advice.* **13** If you **take** the blame, responsibility, or credit for something, you accept it. *His brother Raoul did it, but Leonel took the blame and kept his mouth shut.* **14** If you **take** something from among a number of things, you choose to have or buy it. *'I'll take the grilled tuna,' Mary Ann told the waiter.* **15** If you **take** a road or route, you choose to travel along it. *Take the Chester Road to the outskirts of town.* **16** If you **take** a house or flat, you rent it, usually for a short time. *My wife and I have taken the cottage for a month.* **17** If you **take** a car, train, bus, or plane, you use it to go from one place to another. *It's the other end of the High Street. We'll take the car... She took the train to New York.* **18** If you **take** a particular size in shoes or *(VERB Vn; VERB Vn; VERB Vn; VERB: Vn, Vn prep/adv; VERB Vn; VERB Vn, Vn prep/adv)*

clothes, that size fits you. *47 per cent of women in the UK take a size 16 or above.* `Vn`

19 If someone **takes** a drug or medicine, they use it on themselves, for example by swallowing it. **20** If you **take** food or drink, you eat or drink it. *Does the Queen take sugar in her coffee?* `VERB: Vn` `VERB` `Vn`

21 If you **take** notes, you write down something you want to remember or something someone says. **22** If you **take** a measurement, you find out what it is by measuring. *If he feels hotter than normal, take his temperature.* `VERB: Vn` `VERB` `Vn`

23 You use **take** when you are discussing or explaining a particular matter, in order to introduce an example or to say how the matter is being considered. *There's confusion and resentment, and it's almost never expressed out in the open. Take this office, for example... Taken in isolation these statements can be dangerous fallacies.* `VERB` `PRAGMATICS` `Vn` `V-ed` `Also Vn` `prep/adv`

24 If you **take** a feeling such as pleasure or pride in something that you have or do, it gives you that feeling. *They take great pride in their heritage... The government will take comfort from the latest opinion poll.* `VERB` `Vn inn/-ing` `Vn fromn/-ing`

25 If you **take** an event or a piece of news in a particular way, you react to it in that way. *No one took my messages seriously.* **26** If you **take** someone's meaning or point, you understand and accept what they are saying. *'I'm not saying it's right, I'm just saying that's what happens.'—'I take your point.'* **27** If you **take** someone for something, you believe wrongly that they are that thing. *I naturally took him to be the owner... Do you take me for an idiot?* **28** Someone's **take** on a particular situation or fact is their attitude to it or their interpretation of it. *What's your take on the new government? Do you think it can work?* `VERB` `Vn adv/prep` `VERB` `Vn` `VERB` `Vn to-inf` `Vn forn` `N-SING:` `N onn`

29 If something **takes** a certain amount of time, that amount of time is needed in order to do it. *The journey took us a long time... The sauce takes 25 minutes to prepare and cook... It takes 15 minutes to convert the plane into a car by removing the wings.* **30** If something **takes** a particular quality or thing, that quality or thing is needed in order to do it. *Walking across the room took all her strength... It takes the bark of three whole trees to make enough of the drug to treat a single patient... It takes a pretty bad level of performance before the teachers will criticize the students.* **31** If a place or container **takes** a particular amount or number, there is enough space for that amount or number. *The place could just about take 2,000 people.* `VERB: Vn` `Vnn` `Vn to-inf` `itV n to-inf` `Also Vn n to-inf` `VB: no passive` `itV n to-inf` `itV n before cl` `VB: no passive` `V amount`

32 If you cannot **take** something difficult, painful, or annoying, you cannot experience it without becoming upset, ill, or angry. *Don't ever ask me to look after those kids again. I just can't take it!* **33** If you **take** something such as damage or loss, you suffer it, especially in war or in a battle. *They have taken very heavy casualties.* `VB: no passive` `Vn` `VERB` `Vn`

34 If you **take** a subject or course at school or university, you choose to study it. *Students are allowed to take European history and American history.* **35** If you **take** a test or examination, you do it in order to obtain a qualification. *She took her driving test in Greenford.* **36** The teacher who **takes** a class for a subject teaches the class that subject. **37** If you **take** one number or amount from another, you subtract or deduct it. *Take off the price of the house, that's another five thousand.* **38** If something such as a drug or a dye **takes**, it has the intended result. *If the cortisone doesn't take, I may have to have surgery.* **39** A **take** is a short piece of action which is filmed in one continuous session for a cinema or television film. `VERB` `Vn` `VERB` `Vn` `VERB:` `Vn forn` `BRITISH` `VERB:` `Vn fromn` `Vn with off/away` `VERB` `V` `N-COUNT`

take 3 phrases

take /teɪk/ **takes, taking, took, taken.** **1** You can say **'I take it'** to someone in order to confirm that you have understood their meaning or understood a situation. *I take it that neither of you reads 'The Times'.* **2** You can say **'take it from me'** to tell someone that you are absolutely sure that what you are saying is correct, and that they should believe you. *Take it from me – this is the greatest achieve-* `◆◇◇◇` `PHRASE` `PRAGMATICS` `PHRASE` `PRAGMATICS`

ment by any Formula One driver ever. **3** If you say to someone **'take it or leave it'**, you are telling them that they can accept something or not accept it, but that you are not prepared to discuss any other alternatives. **4** If someone **takes** an insult or attack **lying down**, they accept it without protesting or retaliating. *The government is not taking such criticism lying down.* **5** If something **takes a lot out of** you or **takes it out of** you, it requires a lot of energy or effort and makes you feel very tired and weak afterwards. **6 Take** is used in a large number of expressions which are explained under other words in the dictionary. For example, the expression 'to be taken aback' is explained at 'aback'. `CONVENTION` `PRAGMATICS` `PHRASE` `PHRASE`

take 4 phrasal verbs

take /teɪk/ **takes, taking, took, taken.** `◆◆◆◆`

take after. If you **take after** a member of your family, you resemble them in your appearance, behaviour, or character. *Ted's always been difficult, Mr Kemp – he takes after his dad.* `PHRASAL VB` `no passive` `V P n`

take apart. **1** If you **take** something **apart**, you separate it into its different parts. *When the clock stopped, he took it apart, found what was wrong, and put the whole thing together again.* **2** If you **take apart** something such as an argument or an idea, you discuss it forcefully or thoroughly, often to show that it is wrong. *They will take that problem apart and analyze it in great detail.* `PHRASAL VB` `V P noun` `Also V P noun` `V P n` `V n P`

take away. **1** If you **take** something **away** from someone, you remove it from them, so that they no longer have it. *'Give me the knife,' he said softly, 'or I'll take it away from you.'* **2** If someone in authority **takes** you **away**, they force you to go with them, for example to a police station. *They were taken away in a police bus... Soldiers took away four people one of whom was later released.* **3** To **take** something **away from** an achievement, success, or quality means to make it seem lower in value or worth than it should be. *The victory looks rather hollow. That takes nothing away from the courage and skill of the fighting forces.* **4** See also **takeaway**. `PHRASAL VB` `V P n` `V n P from n` `Also V P noun` `V n P` `be V-ed P` `V P noun` `V n P from n`

take back. **1** If you **take** something **back**, you return it to the place where you bought it or borrowed it from, because it is unsuitable or broken, or because you have finished with it. *I once took back a pair of shoes that fell apart after a week.* **2** If you **take** something **back**, you admit that something that you said or thought is wrong. *Take back what you said about Jeremy!* **3** If you **take** someone **back**, you allow them to come home again, after they have gone away because of a quarrel or other problem. *The government has agreed to take back those people who are considered economic rather than political refugees.* **4** If you say that something **takes** you **back**, you mean that it reminds you of a period of your past life and makes you think about it again. *I enjoyed experimenting with colours – it took me back to being five years old... This takes me back.* `PHRASAL VB` `V P noun` `V P noun` `V n P` `V P noun` `V n P` `V P noun` `V n P ton/-ing` `V n P`

take down. **1** If you **take down** a structure, you get rid of it by removing each piece of it. *The Canadian army took down the barricades.* **2** If you **take down** a piece of information or statement, you write it down. *I took down his comments in shorthand.* `PHRASAL VB` `V P noun` `Also V n P` `V P noun` `Also V n P`

take in. **1** If you **take** someone **in**, you allow them to stay in your house or country, especially when they are homeless or in trouble. *The monastery has taken in 26 refugees.* **2** If the police **take** someone **in**, they remove them from their home in order to question them. *The police have taken him in for questioning.* **3** If you **are taken in** by someone or something, you are deceived or fooled by them. *He is a real charmer who totally took me in.* **4** When people, animals, or plants **take in** air, drink, or food, they allow it to enter their body, usually by breathing or swallowing. **5** If you **take** something **in**, you pay attention to it and understand it when you hear or read it. *Robert took it all in without needing second explanations.* **6** If you **take** something **in**, you see all of it at the same time or with just one look. *The* `PHRASAL VB` `V n P` `V P n` `V n P` `Also V P noun` `be V-ed P` `V n P` `Also V n P` `V P noun` `V n P` `Also V n P` `V P noun` `Also V n P`

eyes behind the lenses were dark and quick-moving, taking in everything at a glance.

7 If you **take in** something such as a film or a museum, you go to see it. *I was wondering if you might want to take in a movie with me this evening.* [no passive] [V P noun] [Also V n P]

8 If one thing **takes in** another, it is big enough to include the other thing within it. *Ethiopia's large territorial area takes in a population of more than 40 million people.* [no passive] [V P noun] [Also V n P]

9 If you **take in** a dress, jacket, or other item of clothing, you make it smaller and tighter by altering its seams. [V P noun] [V n P]

take off. 1 When an aircraft **takes off**, it leaves the ground and starts flying. *We eventually took off at 11 o'clock.* [PHRASAL VB] [V P]

2 If something such as a product, an activity, or someone's career **takes off**, it suddenly becomes very successful. *They need to expand the number of farmers who are involved if the scheme's going to really take off.* [V P]

3 If you **take off** or **take** yourself **off**, you go away, often suddenly and unexpectedly. *He took himself off to Mexico.* [V pron-refl P] [Also V P]

4 When you **take** your clothes **off**, you remove them. *She took off her spectacles.* [V n P]

5 If something such as a service or entertainment **is taken off**, it is withdrawn so that people can no longer use it or watch it. *We would very much deplore it if a popular programme were taken off as a result of political pressure.* [V P noun] [be V-ed P] [Also V n P] [V P noun]

6 If you **take** time **off**, you obtain permission not to go to work for a short period of time. *She took two days off work.* [V n P] [V n P n]

7 See also **takeoff**.

take on. 1 If you **take on** a job or responsibility, especially a difficult one, you accept it. *Don't take on more responsibilities than you can handle.* [PHRASAL VB] [V P noun] [Also V n P]

2 If you **take** someone **on**, especially someone bigger or more powerful than you, you fight or compete against them. *Democrats were reluctant to take on a president whose popularity ratings were historically high.* [V P noun]

3 If you **take** someone **on**, you employ them to do a job. *The party has been taking on staff.* [V n P] [V P noun]

4 If a vehicle such as a bus or ship **takes on** passengers, goods, or fuel, it stops in order to allow them to get on or to be loaded on. [V P noun]

5 If something **takes on** a new appearance or quality, it develops that appearance or quality. *Believing he had only a year to live, his writing took on a feverish intensity.* [no passive] [Also V n P]

take out. 1 If you **take** something **out**, you remove it permanently from its place. *I got an abscess so he took the tooth out... When you edit the tape you can take out the giggles.* [PHRASAL VB] [V n P] [V P noun]

2 If you **take out** something such as a loan or insurance policy, a company agrees to let you have it. *They find a house, agree a price, and take out a mortgage through their building society.* [V P noun] [Also V n P]

3 If you **take** someone **out**, they go to something such as a restaurant or cinema with you after you have invited them, and usually you pay for them. *Reichel took me out to lunch. ...a father taking out his daughter for a celebratory dinner.* [V n P] [V P n to n] [V P noun]

4 To **take** someone **out** means to kill or injure them so badly that they can no longer fight or harm anyone. *In my neighbourhood, the local crack dealers would have taken him out a long time ago.* [V n P] [Also V P noun] [INFORMAL]

5 If you **take** something **out on** someone, you behave in an unpleasant way towards them because you feel angry or upset, even though this is not their fault. *Just because you've had a bad day at work, there's no need to take it out on us.* [V n P on n]

take over. 1 To **take over** a company means to get control of it, for example by buying its shares. *A British newspaper says British Airways plan to take over Trans World Airways.* [PHRASAL VB] [V P noun] [Also V n P]

2 If someone **takes over** a country or building, they get control of it by force, for example with the help of the army. *The republic of Byelarus was taken over by the Soviet Union at the end of World War II.* [be V-ed P] [Also V n P]

3 If you **take over** a job or role, or you **take over**, you become responsible for the job after someone else has stopped doing it. *His widow has taken over the running of his empire, including six London theatres... In 1966, Pastor Albertz took over from him as governing mayor.* [V P noun] [V P from n] [Also V P]

4 If one thing **takes over** from another, it becomes more important, suc- [V P from n] [Also V P]

cessful, or powerful than the other thing, and eventually replaces it. *Cars gradually took over from horses.*

5 See also **takeover**.

take to. 1 If you **take to** someone or something, you like them, especially after knowing them or thinking about them for only a short time. *The first series was really bad. But for some reason the public took to it.* [PHRASAL VB] [V P n]

2 If you **take to** doing something, you begin to do it as a regular habit. *They had taken to wandering through the streets arm-in-arm.* [V P -ing]

take up. 1 If you **take up** a hobby or career, you start doing it. *He left a job in the City to take up farming.* [PHRASAL VB] [V P noun]

2 If you **take up** a job, you start doing it. *He will take up his post as the head of the civil courts at the end of next month.* [V P n]

3 If you **take up** a matter, you start to deal with it or discuss how you are going to deal with it. *Dr Mahathir intends to take up the proposal with the prime minister... If the bank is unhelpful take it up with the Ombudsman.* [V P noun] [V n P with n] [Also V n P]

4 If you **take up** an offer, invitation, or challenge, or you **take** someone **up** on it, you accept it. *Since she'd offered to babysit, I took her up on it.* [V P noun] [V P on n] [Also V n P]

5 If you **take up** something such as a task or a story, you begin doing it after it has been interrupted or after someone else has begun it. *'No, no, no,' says Damon, taking up where Dave left off.* [V P noun] [V P where] [Also V n P]

6 If something **takes up** a particular amount of time, space, or effort, it uses that amount. *A good deal of my time is taken up with reading critical essays... His mind was wholly taken up with the question... The entire memo took up all of two pages.* [be V-ed P with] [-ing/v] [V-ed P] [V P noun]

7 If you **take up** a particular position, you move into that position. *Peacekeeping forces are expected to take up positions along the border.* [V P noun]

8 If one person begins a close relationship with another, and you disapprove of this, you can say that the first person **has taken up with** the second. *Sandy took up with a widow 21 years his junior.* [PRAGMATICS] [V P with n]

9 See also **take-up**.

take upon. If you **take** something **upon** yourself, you decide to do it without asking anyone for permission or approval. *Cassandra took it upon herself to destroy many of Jane's notes... He took upon himself the responsibility for protecting her.* [PHRASAL VB] [V n P pron-refl] [V it P pron-refl to-inf] [V P pron-refl n]

take·a·way /ˈteɪkəweɪ/ **takeaways. 1** A takeaway is a shop or restaurant which sells hot meals that you eat somewhere else. The usual American word is takeout. [N-COUNT] [BRITISH]

2 A takeaway is a hot meal that you buy from a shop or restaurant and eat somewhere else. The usual American word is takeout. *...a Chinese takeaway.* [N-COUNT] [BRITISH]

take-home 'pay. Your take-home pay is the amount of your wages or salary that is left after deductions such as income tax have been made. [N-UNCOUNT]

tak·en /ˈteɪkən/ **1** Taken is the past participle of take. **2** If you are taken with something or someone, you are very interested in them or attracted to them. *She seems very taken with the idea.* [ADJ-GRADED] [v-link ADJ with n] [INFORMAL]

take·off /ˈteɪkɒf, AM -ɔːf/ **takeoffs;** also spelled **take-off. 1** Takeoff is the beginning of a flight, when an aircraft leaves the ground. *The commuter plane was waiting for takeoff.* [N-VAR]

2 A takeoff of someone is a funny imitation of the way they talk or behave. *The programme was worth watching for an inspired take-off of the Collins sisters.* [N-COUNT]

3 Takeoff is the point in the development of something, such as an economy or a business, when it begins to be successful. *The 1950s were the decade of Hong Kong's industrial take-off.* [N-UNCOUNT]

take·out /ˈteɪkaʊt/ **takeouts.** A takeout is the same as a takeaway. [N-COUNT] [AMERICAN]

take·over /ˈteɪkəʊvə/ **takeovers. 1** A takeover is the act of gaining control of a company by buying a majority of its shares. *...the proposed £3.4 billion takeover of Midland Bank by the Hong Kong and Shanghai.* [N-COUNT] ◆◆◆◇◇

2 A takeover is the act of taking control of a country, political party, or movement by force. *There's been a military takeover of some kind.* [N-COUNT]

tak·er /ˈteɪkə/ **takers.** If there are no takers for something such as an investment or a challenge, [N-COUNT] ◆◇◇◇◇

T

nobody is willing to accept it. *He hasn't found any takers for that idea.*

-taker /-teɪkə/ **-takers.** -taker combines with COMB nouns to form other nouns which refer to people who take things, for example decisions or notes. *40% told census-takers they were Muslims... They've got some terrific penalty-takers.*

'take-up. Take-up is the rate at which people ap- N-UNCOUNT ply for or buy something which is offered, for exam- BRITISH ple financial help from the government or shares in a company. *...a major campaign to increase the take-up of welfare benefits.*

tak·ings /'teɪkɪŋz/. The **takings** of a business such N-PLURAL as a shop or cinema consist of the amount of mon- BRITISH ey it gets from selling its goods or tickets during a certain period.

talc /tælk/. Talc is the same as **talcum powder.** N-UNCOUNT

talcum powder /ˌtælkəm 'paʊdə/. Talcum powder N-UNCOUNT is fine, perfumed powder which people put on their bodies after they have had a bath or shower.

tale /teɪl/ **tales. 1** A **tale** is a story, often involving ◆◆◇◇ adventure or magic. *...a collection of stories, poems* N-COUNT *and folk tales.* **2** You can refer to an interesting, ex- N-COUNT citing, or dramatic account of a real event as a **tale**. *The media have been filled with tales of horror and loss resulting from Monday's earthquake.* **3** If some- PHRASE one **tells tales** about you, they tell other people things about you which are untrue or which you wanted to be kept secret. ● See also **tell-tale. 4** See also **fairy tale, old wives' tale, tall tale.**

tal·ent /'tælənt/ **talents.** Talent is the natural abil- ◆◆◆◇ ity to do something well. *Both her children have a* N-VAR *talent for music... The player was given hardly any opportunities to show off his talents.* ♦ **tal·ent·ed** ADJ-GRADED *Howard is a talented pianist.*

'talent contest, talent contests. A talent con- N-COUNT test or talent show is a show where ordinary people perform an act on stage, usually in order to try to win a prize for the best performance.

'talent scout, talent scouts. A talent scout is N-COUNT someone whose job is to find people with talent, for example as footballers or musicians, so that they can be offered work.

tal·is·man /'tælɪzmən/ **talismans.** A talisman is an N-COUNT object which you believe has magic powers to pro- tect you or bring you luck.

talk /tɔːk/ **talks, talking, talked. 1** When you ◆◆◆◆◆ **talk,** you use spoken language to express your VERB thoughts, ideas, or feelings. *A teacher reprimanded a* V *girl for talking in class.* ▶ Also a noun. *That's not the* N-UNCOUNT *kind of talk one usually hears from accountants.* **2** If V-RECIP: you **talk** to someone, you have a conversation with V to/with n them. You can also say that two people **talk.** *We* pl-n V *talked and laughed a great deal... They were talking* pl-n V about n *about American food... Can't you see I'm talking?* V (non-recip) *Don't interrupt.* ▶ Also a noun. *We had a long talk* Also V to n *about her father.* **3** If you **talk** to someone, you tell N-COUNT them about the things that are worrying you. You V-RECIP: can also say that two people **talk.** *Do ring if you* V about n *want to talk about it... I have to sort some things out.* (non-recip) *We really needed to talk.* ▶ Also a noun. *I think it's* V (non-recip) *time we had a talk.* **4** If you **talk** on or about some- N-COUNT thing, you make an informal speech telling people VERB: *what you know or think about it. He intends to talk* V on/about n *to young people about the dangers of AIDS.* ▶ Also a V to n noun. *He then set about campaigning, giving talks* N-COUNT *and fund-raising.*

5 Talks are formal discussions intended to produce N-PLURAL an agreement, usually between different countries or between employers and employees. **6** If one group of V-RECIP: people **talks** to another, or if two groups **talk,** they V with/to n have formal discussions in order to do a deal or prod- V to about n uce an agreement. *We're talking to some people about* n/-ing *opening an office in London... It triggered broad specu-* pl-n V *lation that GM and Jaguar might be talking.* **7** When V-RECIP: different countries or different sides in a dispute **talk,** pl-n V they discuss their differences in order to try and settle V to n the dispute. *The Foreign Minister said he was ready to* V to/with n *talk to any country that had no hostile intentions...* Also V (non-*Croats and Serbs still aren't prepared to talk to each* recip)

other. **8** If people **are talking** about another person or VERB: **are talking,** they are discussing that person and gos- V about/of n siping about them. *People will talk, but you have to get* V *on with your life.* ▶ Also a noun. *There has been a lot of* N-UNCOUNT *talk about me getting married.*

9 If someone **talks** when they are being held by police VERB: V or soldiers, they reveal important or secret informa- tion, usually unwillingly. **10** If you **talk** a particular VB: no language or **talk** with a particular accent, you use that passive, language or have that accent when you speak. *They* V n *were amazed that I was talking in an Irish accent.* **11** If V prep/adv you **talk** something such as politics or sport, you dis- VB: no passive cuss it. *...middle-aged men talking business.* **12** If you V n say that something such as an idea or threat is just N-UNCOUNT **talk,** you mean that it does not mean or matter much, because people are exaggerating about it or do not re- ally intend to do anything about it. *Conditions should be laid down. Otherwise it's all talk.*

13 You can use **talk** to say what you think of the ideas VERB that someone is expressing. For example, if you say V n that someone is **talking sense,** you mean that you think the opinions they are expressing are sensible. *You must admit George, you're talking absolute rub- bish.* **14** In conversations, you can say that you are VB: no passive **talking** a particular thing to draw attention to your PRAGMATICS topic or to point out a characteristic of what you are V n discussing. *We're talking megabucks this time.* **15** You PHRASE can say **talk about** before mentioning a particular ex- PRAGMATICS pression or situation, when you mean that something INFORMAL is a very striking or clear example of that expression or situation. *She threw the cake I'd made on the floor and stood on it. Talk about being humiliated!* **16** You can PHRASE use the expression **talking of** to introduce a new topic PRAGMATICS that you want to discuss, and to link it to something that has already been mentioned. *I'll give a prize to the best idea. Talking of good ideas, here's one to break the ice at a wedding party.* **17** ● to **talk shop:** see **shop.**

talk back. If you **talk back** to someone in authority PHRASAL VB such as a parent or teacher, you answer them in a V P to n rude way. *I talked back and asked questions.* V P

talk down. 1 If someone **talks down** a particular PHRASAL VB thing, they make it less interesting, valuable, or likely V P noun than it originally seemed. *Businessmen are tired of* V n P politicians talking the economy down. **2** To **talk** some- V P noun one **down** in negotiations means to persuade them to BRITISH accept less money than they originally asked for. *This leaves the Prime Minister, like his predecessors, ear- nestly trying to talk down wages.*

talk down to. If you say that someone **talks down** PHRASAL VB **to** you, you disapprove of the way they talk to you, V P P n treating you as if you are not very intelligent or not PRAGMATICS very important.

talk into. 1 If you **talk** someone **into** doing some- PHRASAL VB thing they do not want to do, especially something V n P -ing/n wrong or stupid, you persuade them to do it. **2** If you V pron-refl P n **talk** yourself **into** a particular situation or state, you get yourself into it by talking. *He has talked himself into a position where he will have no option but to go.*

talk out. If you **talk out** something such as a prob- PHRASAL VB lem, you discuss it thoroughly in order to settle it. V P noun *Talking things out with someone else can be helpful.* V n P

talk out of. 1 If you **talk** someone **out of** doing PHRASAL VB something they want or intend to do, you persuade V n P P -ing/n them not to do it. **2** If you **talk** yourself **out of** a par- V pron-refl P P ticular situation or state, you get yourself out of it by n talking. *I tried to talk myself out of a fight.*

talk over. If you **talk** something **over,** you discuss it PHRASAL VB thoroughly and honestly. *He always talked things over* V n P *with his friends.* V P noun Also V P noun

talk round. If you **talk** someone **round,** you per- PHRASAL VB suade them to change their mind so that they agree V n P with you, or agree to do what you want them to do. *It* V P noun *advises salesmen to talk round reluctant customers* BRITISH *over a cup of tea.*

talk through. 1 If you **talk** something **through** with PHRASAL VB someone, you discuss it with them thoroughly. *He* V n P with n *and I have talked through this whole tricky problem.* pl-n V P noun **2** If someone **talks** you **through** something that you V n P n do not know, they explain it to you carefully.

talk up. 1 If someone **talks up** a particular thing, PHRASAL VB

they make it sound more interesting, valuable, or likely than it originally seemed. *Politicians accuse the media of talking up the possibility of a riot.* **2** To **talk** someone or something **up** in negotiations means to persuade someone to pay more money than they originally offered or wanted to. *Allan Clarke kept talking the price up, while Wilkinson kept knocking it down.* `V P noun Also V n P` `V n P Also V P noun BRITISH`

talka·tive /'tɔːkətɪv/. Someone who is **talkative** talks a lot. `ADJ-GRADED`

talk·er /'tɔːkə/ **talkers.** You can use **talker** to refer to someone when you are considering how much they talk, or how good they are at talking to people. *...a fluent talker.* `N-COUNT`

talkie /'tɔːki/ **talkies.** A **talkie** is a cinema film made with sound, as opposed to a silent film. `N-COUNT DATED`

talking 'head, talking heads. Talking heads are people who appear in television discussion programmes and interviews to give their opinions about a topic. `N-COUNT INFORMAL`

'talking point, talking points. A **talking point** is an interesting subject for discussion or argument. `N-COUNT`

'talking shop, talking shops. If you say that a conference or a committee is just a **talking shop,** you disapprove of it because nothing is achieved as a result of what is discussed. `N-COUNT PRAGMATICS BRITISH`

'talk show, talk shows; also spelled **talk-show.** A **talk show** is a television or radio show in which an interviewer and his or her guests talk in an informal way about different topics. `◆◇◇◇◇ N-COUNT`

tall /tɔːl/ **taller, tallest. 1** Someone or something that is **tall** has a greater height than is normal or average. *She was a young woman, fairly tall and fairly slim. ...a lawn of tall waving grass.* **2** You use **tall** to ask or talk about the height of someone or something. *How tall are you?... I'm only 5ft tall... Lucy was tall, nearly as tall as Eleanor, and had the same blue eyes and long, light brown hair.* **3** If something is a **tall order,** it is very difficult. *Financing your studies may seem like a tall order, but there is plenty of help available.* **4** If you say that someone **walks tall,** you mean that they behave in a way that shows that they have pride in themselves and in what they are doing. `◆◆◆◇◇ ADJ-GRADED` `ADJ-GRADED: amount ADJ, as ADJ as, ADJ-compar than PHRASE` `PHRASE`

tal·low /'tæləʊ/. **Tallow** is hard animal fat used for making candles and soap. `N-UNCOUNT`

'tall 'story, tall stories. A **tall story** is the same as a tall tale. `N-COUNT`

'tall 'tale, tall tales. A **tall tale** is a long and complicated story that is very difficult to believe because most of the events it describes seem unlikely or impossible. `N-COUNT`

tal·ly /'tæli/ **tallies, tallying, tallied. 1** A **tally** is a record of amounts or numbers which you keep changing and adding to as the activity which affects it progresses. *The final tally was 817 votes for her and 731 for Mr Lee.* **2** If one number or statement **tallies** with another, they agree with each other or are exactly the same. You can also say that two numbers or statements **tally.** *This description didn't seem to tally with what we saw... The figures didn't seem to tally.* **3** If you **tally** numbers, items, or totals, you count them. ► **Tally up** means the same as **tally.** *Bookkeepers haven't yet tallied up the total cost.* `◆◇◇◇◇ N-COUNT` `V-RECIP V with n pl-n V` `VERB: V n PHRASAL VB V P noun Also V n P`

Tal·mud /'tælmʊd/. **The Talmud** is the collection of ancient Jewish laws which governs the religious and non-religious life of Orthodox Jews. `N-PROPER: the N`

tal·on /'tælən/. **talons.** The **talons** of a bird of prey are its hooked claws. `N-COUNT`

tama·rind /'tæmərɪnd/ **tamarinds.** A **tamarind** is a fruit which grows on a tropical evergreen tree which has pleasant-smelling flowers. `N-VAR`

tam·bou·rine /ˌtæmbə'riːn/ **tambourines.** A **tambourine** is a musical instrument which you shake or hit with your hand. It consists of a drum skin on a circular frame with pieces of metal all around the edge which clash together. See picture headed **musical instruments.** `N-COUNT`

tame /teɪm/ **tames, taming, tamed; tamer, tamest. 1** A **tame** animal or bird is not afraid of humans. **2** If you say that something or someone is **tame,** you are criticizing them for being weak and unadventurous, rather than forceful or shocking. *Some of today's political demonstrations look rather tame.* **♦ tame·ly** *There was no excuse though when Thomas shot tamely from eight yards.* **3** If someone **tames** a wild animal or bird, they train it not to be afraid of humans and to be obedient. **4** If you **tame** someone or something that is dangerous, uncontrolled, or likely to cause trouble, you bring them under control. *Two regiments of cavalry were called out to tame the crowds.* `◆◇◇◇◇ ADJ-GRADED` `ADJ-GRADED PRAGMATICS` `ADV-GRADED` `VERB: V n` `VERB V n`

tamp /tæmp/ **tamps, tamping, tamped.** If you **tamp** something, you press it down by tapping it several times so that it becomes more solid and compact. *Then I tamp down the soil with the back of a rake.* `VERB: V n V n with adv Also V n prep/adv`

tam·per /'tæmpə/ **tampers, tampering, tampered.** If someone **tampers** with something, they interfere with it or try to change it when they have no right to do so. *He found his computer had been tampered with.* **♦ tam·per·ing** *...discovering a motive for a crime like product tampering.* `◆◇◇◇◇ VERB: V with n be V-ed` `N-UNCOUNT`

tam·pon /'tæmpɒn/ **tampons.** A **tampon** is a piece of cotton wool that a woman puts inside her vagina in order to absorb the blood during menstruation. `◆◇◇◇◇ N-COUNT`

tan /tæn/ **tans, tanning, tanned. 1** If you have a **tan,** your skin has become darker than usual because you have been in the sun. **2** If a part of your body **tans,** your skin becomes darker than usual because you spend a lot of time in the sun. *Leigh rolled over on her stomach to tan her back.* **♦ tanned** *Their skin was tanned and glowing.* **3** Something that is **tan** is a light brown colour. **4** To **tan** animal skins means to make them into leather by treating them with tannin or other chemicals. `◆◆◇◇◇ N-SING` `V-ERG: V V n` `ADJ-GRADED` `COLOUR` `VERB: V n`

tan·dem /'tændəm/ **tandems. 1** A **tandem** is a bicycle designed for two riders, on which one rider sits behind the other. **2** If one thing happens or is done **in tandem** with another thing, the two things happen at the same time. *Malcolm's contract will run in tandem with his existing one.* **3** If one person does something **in tandem** with another person, the two people do it by working together. `◆◇◇◇◇ N-COUNT` `PHRASE` `PHRASE`

tan·doori /ˌtæn'dʊəri/. **Tandoori** dishes are Indian meat dishes which are cooked in a clay oven. `ADJ`

tang /tæŋ/. A **tang** is a strong, sharp smell or taste. *She could smell the salty tang of the sea.* `N-SING`

tan·gent /'tændʒənt/ **tangents. 1** A **tangent** is a line that touches the edge of a curve or circle at one point, but does not cross it. **2** If someone **goes off at a tangent,** they start saying or doing something that is not directly connected with what they were saying or doing before. `N-COUNT` `PHRASE`

tan·gen·tial /tæn'dʒenʃəl/. If you describe something as **tangential,** you mean that it has only a slight or indirect connection with the thing you are concerned with. *Too much time was spent discussing tangential issues.* `ADJ-GRADED FORMAL`

tan·ge·rine /ˌtændʒə'riːn/ **tangerines.** A **tangerine** is a small sweet orange. `N-COUNT`

tan·gible /'tændʒɪbəl/. If something is **tangible,** it is clear enough or definite enough to be easily seen, felt, or noticed. *...tangible evidence that the economy is starting to recover.* `◆◇◇◇◇ ADJ-GRADED`

tan·gle /'tæŋgəl/ **tangles, tangling, tangled. 1** A **tangle** of something is a mass of it twisted together in an untidy way. *...a tangle of wires.* **2** If something **is tangled** or **tangles,** it becomes twisted together in an untidy way. *Animals get tangled in fishing nets and drown... Lee and I fell in a tangled heap... Her hair tends to tangle.* **3** You can refer to a confusing or complicated situation as a **tangle.** *...the tangle of domestic politics.* **4** If ideas or situations **are tangled,** they become confused and complicated. *The themes get tangled in Mr. Mahfouz's* `◆◆◇◇◇` `V-ERG get/be V-ed in n V-ed V` `N-SING` `VB: usu passive get/be V-ed Also V-ed`

elliptical storytelling. ♦ **tan·gled** *His personal life has become more tangled than ever.* ADJ-GRADED

tangle up. 1 If something or someone is **tangled up** in something such as a mass of wire or ropes, they are caught or trapped in it. *The teeth are like razors. Once you get tangled up it will never let you go.* **2** If you are **tangled up** in a complicated or unpleasant situation, you are involved in it and cannot get free of it. ♦ **tan·gled up** *For many days now Buddy and Joe had appeared to be more and more tangled up in secrets.* PHRASAL VB usu passive get/be V-ed P / usu passive, get/be V-ed P in/with n / ADJ-GRADED v-link ADJ

tangle with. If you **tangle with** another person, you get involved in a conflict with them. *In the past Clinton has tangled with the teachers' unions.* PHRASAL VB V P n

tan·go /'tæŋgəʊ/ **tangos.** **1** The **tango** is a South American dance for two people. **2** A **tango** is a piece of music intended for tango dancing. **3** ● it takes two to tango: see **two.** ◆◇◇◇◇ N-SING N-VAR

tangy /'tæŋi/ **tangier, tangiest.** A **tangy** flavour or smell is one that is sharp. ◆◇◇◇◇ ADJ-GRADED

tank /tæŋk/ **tanks.** **1** A **tank** is a large container for holding liquid or gas. *...a tank full of goldfish.* ► A **tank** of a liquid or gas is an amount of it contained in a tank. **2** A **tank** is a military vehicle covered with armour and equipped with weapons which moves along on metal tracks fitted over the wheels. **3** See also **septic tank, think-tank.** ◆◆◇◇◇ N-COUNT / N-COUNT / N-COUNT

tank·ard /'tæŋkəd/ **tankards.** A **tankard** is a large metal mug with a handle, which you can drink beer from. ► A **tankard** of beer is an amount of it contained in a tankard. N-COUNT / N-COUNT

tank·er /'tæŋkə/ **tankers.** **1** A **tanker** is a very large ship used for transporting large quantities of gas or liquid, especially oil. **2** A **tanker** is a large truck, railway vehicle, or aircraft used for transporting large quantities of a substance. ◆◆◇◇◇ N-COUNT / N-COUNT

tan·nin /'tænɪn/. **Tannin** is a yellow or brown chemical that is found in plants such as tea. It is used in the process of making leather and in dyeing. N-UNCOUNT

Tan·noy /'tænɔɪ/. A **Tannoy** is a system of loudspeakers used to make public announcements, for example at a sports stadium. **Tannoy** is a trademark. N-SING BRITISH

tan·ta·lize /'tæntəlaɪz/ **tantalizes, tantalizing, tantalized;** also spelled **tantalise** in British English. If someone or something **tantalizes** you, they make you feel hopeful and excited about getting something, usually before disappointing you by not letting you have what they appeared to offer. *...the dreams of democracy that have so tantalized them.* ♦ **tan·ta·liz·ing** *A tantalising aroma of roast beef fills the air.* ♦ **tan·ta·liz·ing·ly** *A political settlement remains tantalisingly out of reach.* ◆◇◇◇◇ VERB V n / Also V / ADJ-GRADED / ADV-GRADED

tan·ta·mount /'tæntəmaʊnt/. If you say that one thing is **tantamount** to a second, more serious thing, you are emphasizing how bad, unacceptable, or unfortunate the first thing is by comparing it to the second. *He said the decision was tantamount to protecting terrorist organisations around the world.* ◆◇◇◇◇ ADJ: v-link ADJ to n/-ing / PRAGMATICS FORMAL

tan·trum /'tæntrəm/ **tantrums.** If a child has a **tantrum**, they suddenly lose their temper in a noisy and uncontrolled way. If you say that an adult is throwing a **tantrum**, you are criticizing them for losing their temper and acting childishly. ◆◇◇◇◇ N-COUNT PRAGMATICS

tap /tæp/ **taps, tapping, tapped.** **1** A **tap** is a device that controls the flow of a liquid or gas from a pipe or container, for example on a sink. The usual American word is **faucet.** **2** If drinks are **on tap**, they come from a barrel rather than from a bottle. **3** If something is **on tap**, you can have as much of it as you want whenever you want. *The advantage of group holidays is company on tap.* **4** If you **tap** something, you hit it with a quick light blow or a series of quick light blows. *To hold the carpet in place, it's a good idea to tap in a few nails temporarily.* ► Also a noun. *A tap on the door interrupted him.* **5** If you **tap** your fingers or feet, you make a rhythmic sound by hitting a surface lightly and repeatedly with them. **6** If you **tap** a resource or situation, you make use of it by getting from it something that you need or want. *The company is tapping share-* ◆◆◆◇◇ N-COUNT BRITISH / PHRASE / PHRASE INFORMAL / VERB: V n V adv/prep / N-COUNT / VERB: V n / VERB: V n V n for n

holders for £15.8 million. **7** If someone **taps** your telephone, they attach a special device to the line so that they can secretly listen to your conversations. ● See also **phone-tapping, wiretap.** ► Also a noun. *He assured MPs that ministers and MPs were not subjected to phone taps.* VERB: V n / N-COUNT

tap out. If you **tap out** a rhythm, a code, or a number, you indicate it by hitting a surface or a machine such as a telephone. *...his eyes on the dance floor, his fingers tapping out a rhythm on the table.* PHRASAL VB V P noun

tapas /'tæpəs/. In Spain, **tapas** are small portions of food that are served with drinks or before a main meal. N-PLURAL

'tap dancer, tap dancers. A **tap dancer** is a dancer who does tap dancing. N-COUNT

'tap dancing; also spelled **tap-dancing.** **Tap dancing** is a style of dancing in which the dancers wear special shoes with pieces of metal on the heels and toes. The shoes make clicking noises as the dancers move their feet. N-UNCOUNT

tape /teɪp/ **tapes, taping, taped.** **1** Tape is a narrow plastic strip covered with a magnetic substance. It is used to record sounds, pictures, and computer information. *Many students declined to be interviewed on tape.* **2** A **tape** is a cassette or spool with magnetic tape wound round it. **3** If you **tape** music, sounds, or television pictures, you record them using a tape recorder or a video recorder. *...taped evidence from prisoners.* ♦ **tap·ing** *...an unauthorized taping.* **4** A **tape** is a strip of cloth used to tie things together or to identify who a piece of clothing belongs to. **5** A **tape** is a ribbon that is stretched across the finishing line of a race. **6** Tape is an adhesive strip of plastic used for sticking things together. **7** If you **tape** one thing to another, you attach it using sticky tape. *The envelope has been tampered with and then taped shut again.* **8** See also **masking tape, red tape, sticky tape, videotape.** ◆◆◆◇ N-UNCOUNT / N-COUNT / VERB: V n V-ed Also V / N-COUNT / N-VAR / N-COUNT supp N / N-UNCOUNT / VERB: V n onto/to n be V-ed adj

tape up. If you **tape** something **up**, you fasten tape around it firmly, in order to protect it or hold it in a fixed position. *Put the bottles into boxes and tape them up... Shopkeepers were taping up their windows.* PHRASAL VB V n P / V P noun

'tape deck, tape decks. A **tape deck** is the machine on which you can play or record tapes. N-COUNT

'tape measure, tape measures. A **tape measure** is a strip of metal, plastic, or cloth which has markings on and which is used for measuring things. N-COUNT

tap·er /'teɪpə/ **tapers, tapering, tapered.** **1** If something **tapers**, it becomes gradually thinner at one end. *...beautiful hands with long, tapering fingers... Taper the shape of your eyebrows towards the outer corners.* ♦ **ta·pered** *...the elegantly tapered legs of the dressing-table.* **2** If something **tapers** or **is tapered**, it gradually becomes reduced in amount, number, or size. *If you take these drugs continuously, withdrawal must be tapered.* ► **Taper off** means the same as **taper.** *Immigration is expected to taper off... I suggested that we start to taper off the counseling sessions.* **3** A **taper** is a long, thin, fast-burning candle or a thin wooden strip that is used for lighting fires. ◆◇◇◇◇ V-ERG: V n V-ing V n Also V prep / VERB: V-ed / ADJ-GRADED / V-ERG: V n be V-ed / PHRASAL VB V P V P noun Also V n P / N-COUNT

'tape-record, tape-records, tape-recording, tape-recorded; also spelled **tape record.** If you **tape-record** speech, music, or another kind of sound, you record it on tape, using a tape recorder or a tape deck. *...a tape-recorded interview.* VERB: V n V-ed

'tape recorder, tape recorders; also spelled **tape-recorder.** A **tape recorder** is a machine used for recording and playing music, speech, or other sounds. ◆◇◇◇◇ N-COUNT

'tape recording, tape recordings. A **tape recording** is a recording of sounds that has been made on tape. N-COUNT

tap·es·try /'tæpɪstri/ **tapestries.** **1** A **tapestry** is a large piece of heavy cloth with a picture sewn on it using coloured threads. **2** You can refer to something as a **tapestry** when it is made up of many varied types of people or things. *Hedgerows and meadows are thick with a tapestry of wild flowers.* ◆◇◇◇◇ N-VAR / N-COUNT: with supp LITERARY

tapeworm

tapeworm /ˈteɪpwɜːm/ **tapeworms.** A tapeworm N-COUNT is a long, flat, parasitic creature which lives in the stomach and intestines of animals or people.

tapioca /ˌtæpiˈəʊkə/. Tapioca is a food consisting N-UNCOUNT of white grains, rather like rice, which come from the cassava plant.

'tap water. Tap water is the water that comes out N-UNCOUNT of a tap in a building such as a house.

tar /tɑː/ **tars, tarring, tarred. 1** Tar is a thick ◆◇◇◇◇ black sticky substance that is used especially for N-UNCOUNT making roads. **2** Tar is one of the poisonous sub- N-UNCOUNT stances contained in tobacco. **3** If some people in a PHRASE group behave badly and if people falsely think that all of the group is equally bad, you can say that the whole group **is tarred with the same brush.** All police were being tarred with the same brush of corruption. **4** See also **tarred.**

tarantula /təˈræntjʊlə/ **tarantulas.** A tarantula N-COUNT is a large hairy spider which has a poisonous bite.

tardy /ˈtɑːdi/ **tardier, tardiest. 1** If you describe ADJ-GRADED something or someone as **tardy,** you think that they LITERARY are later than they should be or later than expected. ◆ **tardiness** His legendary tardiness left audiences N-UNCOUNT waiting for hours. **2** If you describe someone or ADJ-GRADED something as **tardy,** you are criticizing them PRAGMATICS because they are slow to act. ...companies who are tardy in paying bills. ◆ **tardiness** ...England's tardi- N-UNCOUNT ness in giving talented young players greater international experience.

target /ˈtɑːgɪt/ **targets, targeting, targeted;** ◆◆◆◇ also spelled **targetting, targetted. 1** A target is N-COUNT something at which someone is aiming a weapon or other object. **2** A target is a result that you are try- N-COUNT ing to achieve. He's won back his place too late to achieve his target of 20 goals this season. **3** If some- VERB one **targets** someone or something, they decide to V n attack or criticize them. In 23 attacks, the terrorists targeted military bases. ▶ Also a noun. They have N-COUNT been the target of racist abuse.

4 If you **target** a particular group of people, you try to VERB: V n appeal to those people or affect them. ▶ Also a noun. N-COUNT Yuppies are a prime target group for marketing strategies. **5** If someone or something is **on target,** they are PHRASE making good progress and are likely to achieve the result that is wanted.

tariff /ˈtærɪf/ **tariffs. 1** A tariff is a tax that a gov- ◆◆◇◇◇ ernment collects on goods coming into a country. N-COUNT **2** A tariff is the rate at which you are charged for N-COUNT public services such as gas and electricity, or for ac- FORMAL, commodation and services in a hotel. BRITISH

tarmac /ˈtɑːmæk/. **1** Tarmac is a material used for ◆◇◇◇◇ making road surfaces, consisting of crushed stones N-UNCOUNT mixed with tar. The usual American word is **black-** BRITISH **top.** Tarmac is a trademark. **2** The **tarmac** is an N-SING: area that has a surface of tarmac, especially airport theN runways. Standing on the tarmac were two American planes.

tarn /tɑːn/ **tarns.** A tarn is a small lake in an area of N-COUNT mountains.

tarnish /ˈtɑːnɪʃ/ **tarnishes, tarnishing, tar-** ◆◇◇◇◇ **nished. 1** If you say that something **tarnishes** VERB someone's reputation or image, you mean that it V n causes people to have a worse opinion of them than they would otherwise have had. The affair could tarnish the reputation of the prime minister. ◆ **tar- nished** He says he wants to improve the tarnished ADJ-GRADED image of his country. **2** If a metal **tarnishes** or if V-ERG something **tarnishes** it, it becomes stained and V loses its brightness. It never rusts or tarnishes. Also V n ◆ **tarnished** ...its brown surfaces of tarnished brass. ADJ-GRADED

Tarot /ˈtærəʊ/. The Tarot is a pack of cards with ◆◇◇◇◇ pictures on them that is used to predict what will N-UNCOUNT happen to people in the future. Tarot is also used to refer to the system of predicting people's futures using these cards.

tarpaulin /tɑːˈpɔːlɪn/ **tarpaulins. 1** Tarpaulin is N-UNCOUNT a fabric made of canvas or similar material coated with tar, wax, paint, or some other waterproof substance. **2** A tarpaulin is a sheet of heavy waterproof N-COUNT material that is used as a protective cover.

tarragon /ˈtærəgɒn/. Tarragon is a small Euro- N-UNCOUNT pean herb with narrow leaves which are used to add flavour to food.

tarred /tɑːd/. A tarred road or roof has a surface of ADJ tar.

tarry /ˈtæri/ **tarries, tarrying, tarried.** If you VERB: V tarry somewhere, you stay there longer than you DATED meant to and delay leaving.

tart /tɑːt/ **tarts, tarting, tarted. 1** A tart is a shal- ◆◇◇◇◇ low pastry case with a filling of food, especially N-VAR sweet food. ...jam tarts. **2** If something such as fruit ADJ-GRADED is **tart,** it has a sharp taste. **3** A **tart** remark or way ADJ-GRADED of speaking is sharp and unpleasant, often in a way that is rather cruel. The words were more tart than she had intended. ◆ **tartly** 'There are other patients ADV-GRADED on the ward, Lovell,' the staff nurse reminded her tartly. **4** If someone refers to a woman or girl as a N-COUNT **tart,** they are criticizing her behaviour or her ap- PRAGMATICS pearance because they think she is sexually immor- RUDE, al or dresses in a vulgar way in order to attract BRITISH men's sexual interest; an offensive use.

tart up. If someone **tarts up** a room or building, they PHRASAL VB try to improve its appearance, often with the result V P noun that it looks vulgar; used showing disapproval. V-ed P ...schemes to tart up inner-city derelict sites. ...tarted Also V n P up pubs. BRITISH, INFORMAL

tartan /ˈtɑːtən/ **tartans.** Tartan is a design for ◆◇◇◇◇ cloth traditionally associated with Scotland. It is N-VAR composed of lines of different widths and colours crossing each other at right angles. Tartan is also used to refer to cloth which has this pattern. See picture headed **patterns.**

tartar /ˈtɑːtə/. Tartar is a hard yellowish substance N-UNCOUNT that forms on your teeth and causes them to decay if it is not removed.

tartare sauce /ˌtɑːtə ˈsɔːs/; also spelled **tartar** N-UNCOUNT **sauce.** Tartare sauce is a thick cold sauce, usually eaten with fish, consisting of chopped onions and capers mixed with mayonnaise.

tarty /ˈtɑːti/. If you describe a woman or her clothes ADJ-GRADED as **tarty,** you are critical of her because she tries to PRAGMATICS make herself look sexually attractive in a vulgar way; RUDE an offensive use.

task /tɑːsk, tæsk/ **tasks. 1** A task is an activity or ◆◆◆◇ piece of work which you have to do, usually as part N-COUNT of a larger project. Walker had the unenviable task of breaking the bad news to Hill. **2** If you **take** some- PHRASE one **to task,** you criticize them or reprimand them because of something that they have done.

'task force, task forces; also spelled **taskforce.** ◆◆◇◇◇ **1** A task force is a small section of an army, navy, or N-COUNT air force that is sent to a particular place to deal with a military crisis. **2** A task force is a group of N-COUNT people working together on a particular task. ...a task force to look at the question of women returning to work.

taskmaster /ˈtɑːskmɑːstə, ˈtæskmæstə/ **task-** N-COUNT **masters.** If you refer to someone as a hard task- master, you mean that they expect the people they supervise to work very hard.

tassel /ˈtæsəl/ **tassels.** Tassels are bunches of N-COUNT short pieces of wool or other material tied together at one end and attached as decorations to something. ◆ **tasselled** /ˈtæsəld/. ...tasselled cushions. ADJ

taste /teɪst/ **tastes, tasting, tasted. 1** Taste is ◆◆◆◇ one of the five senses that people have. When you N-UNCOUNT have food or drink in your mouth, your sense of taste makes it possible for you to recognize what it is. **2** The **taste** of something is the individual quality N-COUNT which it has when you put it in your mouth and which distinguishes it from other things. I like the taste of wine and enjoy trying different kinds. **3** If VB: no cont food or drink **tastes** of something, it has that par- V of/like n ticular flavour, which you notice when you eat or V adj drink it. I drank a cup of tea that tasted of diesel... The pizza tastes delicious. **4** If you **taste** some food VERB: V n or drink, you eat or drink a small amount of it in order to try its flavour. ▶ Also a noun. Take a taste of N-COUNT the stew. **5** If you can **taste** something that you are VB: no passive eating or drinking, you are aware of its flavour. You V n

taste

can taste the chilli in the dish. **6** When a recipe tells you to add a particular spice or other flavouring **to taste**, it means that you can add as much of that ingredient as you like.   PHRASE

7 If you **taste** something such as a way of life or a pleasure, you experience it for a short period of time. ...*tasting the good life aboard a luxury liner.* ▸ Also a noun. ...*a taste of power.*   VB: no passive / V n / N-COUNT

8 If you have a **taste for** something, you have a liking or preference for it. *That gave me a taste for reading.*   N-SING: N for n/-ing

9 A person's **taste** is their choice in the things that they like or buy, for example their clothes, possessions, or favourite music. If you say that someone has good **taste**, you mean that you approve of their choices. If you say that they have poor **taste**, you disapprove of their choices. *There was music for all ages and all tastes.* **10** If you say that something that is said or done is **in bad taste** or **in poor taste**, you mean that it is offensive, often because it concerns death or sex and is inappropriate for the situation. If you say that something is **in good taste**, you mean that it is not offensive and that it is appropriate for the situation.   N-UNCOUNT: also N in pl / PHRASE

'taste bud, taste buds; also spelled **tastebud**. Your **taste buds** are the little points on the surface of your tongue which enable you to recognize the flavour of a food or drink.   N-COUNT

taste·ful /ˈteɪstfʊl/. If you say that something is **tasteful**, you consider it to be attractive, elegant, and in good taste. ♦ **taste·ful·ly** ...*a large and tastefully decorated home.*   ADJ-GRADED / ADV-GRADED

taste·less /ˈteɪstləs/. **1** If you describe something as **tasteless**, you consider it to be vulgar and unattractive. **2** If you describe something such as a remark or joke as **tasteless**, you mean that it is offensive. **3** If you describe food or drink as **tasteless**, you mean that it has very little or no flavour.   ADJ-GRADED

tast·er /ˈteɪstə/ **tasters**. **1** A **taster** is someone whose job is to taste different wines, teas, or other foods or drinks, in order to test their quality. **2** If you refer to something as a **taster** of something greater, or of something that will come later, you mean that the first thing gives you an idea what the second thing is like, and often makes you interested in it or want more of it. *The book is essentially a taster for those unfamiliar with the subject.*   N-COUNT / N-COUNT BRITISH

tast·ing /ˈteɪstɪŋ/ **tastings**. **Tasting** is used in expressions such as **wine tasting** to refer to an event at which people try different kinds of the specified drink or food in small amounts.   N-COUNT

tasty /ˈteɪsti/ **tastier, tastiest**. **1** If you say that food, especially savoury food, is **tasty**, you mean that it has a pleasant and fairly strong flavour which makes it good to eat. **2** People sometimes use **tasty** to describe something or someone that they find attractive or desirable. ...*tasty profits.*   ADJ-GRADED / ADJ-GRADED BRITISH, INFORMAL

tat /tæt/. You can use **tat** to refer to cheap ornaments, clothes, or other items which you think are of bad quality.   N-UNCOUNT BRITISH, INFORMAL

ta-ta /tæ ˈtɑː/; also spelled **ta ta**. **Ta-ta** is used to say goodbye. *The voice was shy. 'Thanks. Ta-ta.'—'Bye, Stephanie.' Liz put the phone down.*   CONVENTION PRAGMATICS BRITISH, INFORMAL

tat·tered /ˈtætəd/. **1** If something such as clothing or a book is **tattered**, it is damaged, torn, or crumpled, especially because it has been used a lot over a long period of time. **2** If you describe something as **tattered**, you mean that it has been badly damaged or has failed completely. *Stanley's dreams of fame and fortune lie tattered and torn.*   ADJ-GRADED / ADJ-GRADED

tat·ters /ˈtætəz/. **1** Clothes that are in **tatters** are badly torn in several places. **2** If you say that something such as a plan is in **tatters**, you are emphasizing that it is weak and has suffered a lot of damage.   N-PLURAL / N-PLURAL PRAGMATICS

tat·tle /ˈtætəl/. See **tittle-tattle**.

tat·too /tæˈtuː/ **tattoos, tattooing, tattooed. 1** A **tattoo** is a design on someone's skin, made by pricking little holes and filling them with coloured dye. **2** If someone **tattoos** you, they give you a tattoo. *He had the words 'Angie loves Ian' tattooed on his left shin.* **3** In Britain, a military **tattoo** is a pub-   N-COUNT / VERB: V n haven V-ed / N-COUNT

lic display of exercises and music given by members of the armed forces.   PHRASE

tat·ty /ˈtæti/. If you describe something as **tatty**, you think it is untidy, rather dirty, and looks as if it has not been cared for. ...*a very tatty old bathrobe.*   ADJ-GRADED

taught /tɔːt/. **Taught** is the past tense and past participle of **teach**.

taunt /tɔːnt/ **taunts, taunting, taunted.** If someone **taunts** you, they say unkind or insulting things to you. ▸ Also a noun. *For years they suffered racist taunts.*   VERB: V n / N-COUNT

taut /tɔːt/ **tauter, tautest. 1** Something that is **taut** is stretched very tight. *The clothes line is pulled taut.* **2** If a person or their body is **taut**, they are very lean with firm muscles. **3** If someone has a **taut** expression, they look very worried and tense.   ADJ-GRADED / ADJ-GRADED / ADJ-GRADED

tav·ern /ˈtævən/ **taverns.** A **tavern** is a bar or pub. ...*Selly Park Tavern, Pershore Road.*   N-COUNT DATED

taw·dry /ˈtɔːdri/ **tawdrier, tawdriest. 1** If you describe something such as clothes or decorations as **tawdry**, you mean that they look cheap and show a lack of taste. **2** If you describe something such as a story or an event as **tawdry**, you mean that it is unpleasant or immoral. *None of us want another tawdry scandal.*   ADJ-GRADED / ADJ-GRADED

taw·ny /ˈtɔːni/. **Tawny** hair, fur, or skin is pale golden brown.   COLOUR

tax /tæks/ **taxes, taxing, taxed. 1** Tax is an amount of money that you have to pay to the government so that it can pay for public services. *We need to take steps such as higher taxes on tobacco.* **2** When a person or company **is taxed**, they have to pay a part of their income or profits to the government. When goods **are taxed**, a percentage of their price has to be paid to the government. *The Bonn government taxes profits of corporations at a rate that is among the highest in Europe.* **3** If something **taxes** your strength, your patience, or your resources, it uses nearly all of them, so that you have great difficulty in carrying out what you are trying to do. *These dilemmas would tax the best of statesmen.* ● See also **taxing; council tax, income tax, poll tax, value added tax.**   N-VAR / VERB: be V-ed / V n / Also V / VERB V n

tax·able /ˈtæksəbəl/. **Taxable** income is income on which you have to pay tax.   ADJ

taxa·tion /tækˈseɪʃən/. **1 Taxation** is the system by which a government takes money from people and spends it on things such as education, health, and defence. **2 Taxation** is the amount of money that people have to pay in taxes. ...*higher taxation.*   N-UNCOUNT / N-UNCOUNT

'tax avoidance. Tax avoidance is the use of legal methods to pay the smallest possible amount of tax.   N-UNCOUNT

'tax break, tax breaks. If the government gives a **tax break** to a particular group of people or type of organization, it reduces the amount of tax they have to pay or changes the tax system in a way that benefits them.   N-COUNT

,tax-de'ductible. If an expense is **tax-deductible**, it can be paid out of your untaxed income, so that the amount of your income which you pay tax on is reduced.   ADJ

'tax evasion. Tax evasion is the crime of not paying the full amount of tax that you should pay.   N-UNCOUNT

,tax-'free; also spelled **tax free**. **Tax-free** is used to describe income on which you do not have to pay tax. ...*a return of 16.5% tax free.*   ADJ

'tax haven, tax havens. A tax haven is a country or place which has a low rate of taxation, so that people choose to live there or register companies there in order to avoid paying higher tax in their own countries.   N-COUNT

taxi /ˈtæksi/ **taxis, taxiing, taxied. 1** A **taxi** is a car driven by a person whose job is to take people where they want to go in return for money. **2** When an aircraft **taxis** along the ground, it moves slowly along it. *The pilot taxied the plane to the end of the runway.*   N-COUNT: also by N / V-ERG: V prep/adv / V n prep/adv / Also V, / V n

taxi·cab /ˈtæksikæb/ **taxicabs;** also spelled **taxi-cab**. A **taxicab** is the same as a **taxi**.   N-COUNT

taxi·der·mist /'tæksidɜːmɪst/ **taxidermists.** A N-COUNT
taxidermist is a person whose job is to stuff dead
animals and birds so that they look lifelike and can
be displayed.

tax·ing /'tæksɪŋ/. A **taxing** task or problem is one ADJ-GRADED
that needs a lot of mental or physical effort. *It's unlikely that you'll be asked to do anything too taxing.*

'taxi rank taxi ranks. A **taxi rank** is a place where N-COUNT
taxis wait for passengers. The American term is **taxi** BRITISH
stand.

tax·ono·my /tæk'sɒnəmi/ **taxonomies.** Taxono- N-VAR
my is the classification and naming of things such TECHNICAL
as animals in groups within a larger system.

tax·payer /'tækspeɪə/ **taxpayers.** Taxpayers are ◆◆◇◇◇
people who pay a percentage of their income to the N-COUNT
government as tax.

'tax relief. Tax **relief** is a reduction in the amount ◆◇◇◇◇
of tax that a person or company has to pay. N-UNCOUNT

'tax return, tax returns. A **tax return** is an offi- ◆◇◇◇◇
cial form on which you declare your income and N-COUNT
give details about your personal circumstances so
that the authorities can decide how much tax you
should pay.

'tax year, tax years. A **tax year** is a particular N-COUNT
period of twelve months which is used by the government as a basis for calculating taxes and for organizing its own finances and accounts.

TB /,tiː 'biː/. **TB** is a very serious infectious disease ◆◇◇◇◇
that affects someone's lungs and other parts of their N-UNCOUNT
body. **TB** is an abbreviation for **tuberculosis.**

tba. tba is sometimes written in announcements
about events to indicate that something such as a
date or time has not yet been decided. **tba** is an abbreviation for 'to be arranged' or 'to be announced'.

,T-bone 'steak, T-bone steaks. A **T-bone steak** N-VAR
is a thick piece of beef that contains a T-shaped
bone.

tea /tiː/ **teas. 1** Tea is a drink made by adding hot ◆◆◆◆◇
water to tea leaves or tea bags. Many people add N-VAR
milk to the drink and some add sugar. *...a cup of
tea.* ▶ A cup of tea can be referred to as a **tea.** N-COUNT
2 The chopped dried leaves of the plant tea is made N-VAR
from is referred to as **tea.** *...a packet of tea.* **3** Drinks N-VAR
such as mint tea or camomile **tea** are made by
pouring hot water on the dried leaves of the particular plant or flower. **4** Tea is a meal some people N-VAR
eat in the late afternoon, especially in Britain. It
consists of food such as sandwiches and cakes, with
tea to drink. ● See also **afternoon tea**, **high tea.**
5 Some people refer to the main meal that they eat N-VAR
in the early part of the evening as **tea. 6** If you say BRITISH
that someone or something is not your **cup of tea,** PHRASE
you mean that they are not the kind of person or
thing that you like.

'tea bag, tea bags; also spelled **teabag. Tea bags** N-COUNT
are small paper bags with tea leaves in them. You
pour hot water onto them to make tea.

'tea break, tea breaks. If you have a **tea break,** N-COUNT
you stop working and have a cup of tea or coffee. BRITISH
The usual American expression is **coffee break.**

tea·cake /'tiːkeɪk/ **teacakes.** Teacakes are round N-COUNT
flat bread cakes. They usually contain raisins and BRITISH
are often toasted and eaten with butter.

teach /tiːtʃ/ **teaches, teaching, taught. 1** If ◆◆◆◇
you **teach** someone something, you give them in- VERB: V n n
structions so that they know about it or how to do V n wh
it. *George had taught him how to ride a horse... She* V n to-inf
taught Julie to read... The computer has simplified V n to n
the difficult task of teaching reading to the deaf.
2 To **teach** someone something means to show VERB: V n n
them how to think, feel, or act in a new or different V n that
way. *He taught his followers that they could all be* Also V n wh,
members of the kingdom of God... Teach them to V n about n
voice their feelings. **3** If you **teach,** your job is to VERB: V
help students to learn about a subject by explaining V n
it or showing them how to do it. *Ingrid is currently* V n to n
teaching Mathematics at Shimla Public School... She V n n
*taught English to Japanese business people... She
taught children French.* ♦ **teach·er, teachers** *I'm* N-COUNT
a teacher with 21 years' experience. ...her chemistry

teacher. ● See also **supply teacher.** ♦ **teach·ing** N-UNCOUNT
...the teaching of English in schools. **4** See also
teaching. ● to **teach someone a lesson:** see **lesson.**

'tea chest, tea chests. A **tea chest** is a large N-COUNT
wooden box in which tea is packed when it is ex- BRITISH
ported. People also use tea chests for putting things
in when they move from one house to another.

'teach-in, teach-ins. A **teach-in** is an informal N-COUNT
meeting between students and teachers with discussions on important or controversial topics.

'teach·ing /'tiːtʃɪŋ/ **teachings. 1** The **teachings** of ◆◆◆◇◇
a particular person, school of thought, or religion N-COUNT
are all the ideas and principles that they teach.
...their teachings on sexuality and marriage. **2** See
also **teach.**

'teaching hospital, teaching hospitals. A N-COUNT
teaching hospital is a hospital that is linked with a
medical school, where medical students and newly
qualified doctors receive practical training.

'teaching practice. Teaching **practice** is a peri- N-UNCOUNT
od that a student teacher spends at a school doing BRITISH
practical teaching as part of his or her training. The
usual American expression is **practice teaching.**

'tea cosy, tea cosies; also spelled **tea-cosy.** A **tea** N-COUNT
cosy is a soft knitted or fabric cover which you put
over a teapot in order to keep the tea hot.

tea·cup /'tiːkʌp/ **teacups;** also spelled **tea-cup.** A N-COUNT
teacup is a medium-sized cup with a handle. This
type of cup is often used for drinking tea.

teak /tiːk/. Teak is the wood of a tall tree with very ◆◇◇◇◇
hard, light-coloured wood which grows in South- N-UNCOUNT
East Asia.

teal /tiːl/ **teals.** The plural can be either **teal** or N-COUNT
teals. A **teal** is a small duck found in Europe and
Asia.

'tea leaf, tea leaves; also spelled **tea-leaf.** Tea N-COUNT
leaves are the small pieces of dried leaves that are
left in a teapot or a cup after the tea has been
drunk.

team /tiːm/ **teams, teaming, teamed. 1** A team ◆◆◆◆◆
is a group of people who play a particular sport or N-COLL-
game together against other similar groups of peo- COUNT
ple. *He had lost his place in the England team.*
2 You can refer to any group of people who work N-COLL-
together as a **team.** *Each specialist consultant has a* COUNT
team of doctors under him.
3 If something **is teamed** with something else, the two VB: usu
things are made to appear together, often to create a passive
particular effect. *A white sofa teamed with subtly col-* V-ed with n
oured rugs has a soft but unmistakably modern feel.

team up. If you **team up** with someone, you join PHRASAL VB
them in order to work together for a particular pur- RECIP:
pose. *A friend suggested that we team up for a working* V P with n
holiday in Europe. pl-n V

'team-mate, team-mates. In a game or sport, ◆◆◇◇◇
your **team-mates** are the other members of your N-COUNT
team.

,team 'spirit. Team **spirit** is the feeling of pride N-UNCOUNT
and loyalty that exists among the members of a
team.

team·ster /'tiːmstə/ **teamsters.** A **teamster** is a N-COUNT
person who drives a truck. The British expression is AMERICAN
lorry driver.

team·work /'tiːmwɜːk/. Teamwork is the ability a N-UNCOUNT
group of people have to work well together. *Today's
complex buildings require close teamwork between
the architect and the builders.*

'tea party, tea parties; also spelled **tea-party.** A N-COUNT
tea party is a social gathering in the afternoon at DATED
which tea, cakes, and sandwiches are served.

tea·pot /'tiːpɒt/ **teapots;** also spelled **tea pot.** A ◆◇◇◇◇
teapot is a container with a lid, a handle, and a N-COUNT
spout, used for making and serving tea.

tear 1 crying

tear /tɪə/ **tears. 1** Tears are the drops of salty liq- ◆◆◇◇◇
uid that come out of your eyes when you are crying. N-COUNT
2 You can use **tears** in expressions such as **in tears,** N-PLURAL
burst into tears, and **close to tears** to indicate that
someone is crying or is almost crying. *He was in*

T

floods of tears on the phone. **3** See also **crocodile tears.** • **blood, sweat, and tears:** see **blood.**

tear 2 damaging or moving

tear /teə/ **tears, tearing, tore, torn. 1** If you **tear** paper, cloth, or another material, you pull it into two pieces or you pull it so that a hole appears in it. *Mary Ann tore the edge off her napkin... He took a small notebook from his jacket pocket and tore out a page... Nancy quickly tore open the envelope... Too fine a material may tear... Female fans fought their way past bodyguards and tore at his clothes... He went ashore leaving me to start repairing the torn sail.* **2** A **tear** in paper, cloth, or another material is a hole that has been made in it. **3** If something **tears** your flesh or skin, it scratches or cuts it violently. *He had stumbled down and torn the skin from his knees.* **4** If you **tear** one of your muscles or ligaments, you injure it by accidentally moving it in the wrong way. *If the muscle is stretched again it could even tear. ...torn ligaments.* **5** To **tear** something from somewhere means to remove it roughly and violently. *She tore the windscreen wipers from his car... He tore down the girl's photograph, and crumpled it.*
6 If you **tear** somewhere, you move there very quickly, often in an uncontrolled or dangerous way. *The door flew open and Miranda tore into the room.*
7 If you say that a place **is torn** by particular events, you mean that unpleasant events which cause suffering and division among people are happening there. *...a country that has been torn by civil war.* ♦ **-torn** *...the riot-torn areas of Los Angeles.* **8** See also **torn; wear and tear.** • to **tear** someone **to pieces:** see **piece.** • to **tear** someone **to shreds:** see **shred.**

V-ERG: V n / V n prep / V n with adv / V n with adj / V / V at n / V-ed / Also V adv/ prep

N-COUNT
VERB: V n / V n prep
V-ERG: V n / V / V-ed
VERB / V n prep / V n with adv

V prep/adv

V-PASSIVE / be V-ed
COMB

tear apart. 1 If something **tears** people **apart,** it causes them to quarrel or to leave each other. *The quarrel tore the party apart.* **2** If something **tears** you **apart,** it makes you feel very upset, worried, and unhappy.

PHRASAL VB / V n P
V n P

tear away. If you **tear** someone **away** from a place or activity, you force them to leave the place or stop doing the activity, even though they want to remain there or carry on. *She couldn't tear herself away from the radio... I stared at the man, couldn't tear my eyes away.*

PHRASAL VB / V n P from n / V n P

tear down. If you **tear** something **down,** you destroy it or remove it completely. *I imagine they'll be tearing the building down sooner or later.*

PHRASAL VB / V P noun / V n P

tear into. If you **tear into** someone, you criticize them very angrily and strongly. *She had spoken softly, but he knew her body language. She was ready to tear into George with a fury.*

PHRASAL VB / V P n / INFORMAL

tear off. If you **tear off** your clothes, you take them off in a rough and violent way. *He tore his clothes off and fell into bed.*

PHRASAL VB / V P noun / V n P

tear up. 1 If you **tear** something **up,** you tear it into several pieces. *Don't you dare tear up her ticket. ...a torn up photograph.* **2** If something such as a road, railway, or area of land **is torn up,** it is completely removed or destroyed. *The company came under furious attack from environmentalists for tearing up the forests.*

PHRASAL VB / V n P / V P noun / V-ed P / be V-ed P / V P noun

tear·away /ˈteərəweɪ/ **tearaways.** If you refer to a young person as a **tearaway,** you mean that they behave in a wild and uncontrolled way.

N-COUNT / BRITISH

tear·drop /ˈtɪədrɒp/ **teardrops.** A **teardrop** is a large tear that comes from your eye when you are crying quietly.

N-COUNT

tear·ful /ˈtɪəfʊl/. If someone is **tearful,** their face or voice shows signs that they have been crying or that they want to cry. *...a tearful farewell.* ♦ **tear·ful·ly** *Gwendolen smiled tearfully.*

♦◇◇◇◇ / ADJ-GRADED
ADV-GRADED

tear gas /ˈtɪə gæs/; also spelled **tear-gas.** Tear gas is a gas that causes your eyes to sting and fill with tears so that you cannot see. It is sometimes used by the police or army to control crowds.

N-UNCOUNT

tear-jerker /ˈtɪə dʒɜːkə/ **tear-jerkers;** also spelled **tearjerker.** If you refer to a play, film, or book as a **tear-jerker,** you mean that it is very sad or sentimental.

N-COUNT / INFORMAL

'tea room, tea rooms; also spelled **tearoom.** A **tea room** is the same as a **tea shop.**

N-COUNT

tease /tiːz/ **teases, teasing, teased. 1** To tease someone means to laugh at them or make jokes about them in order to embarrass, annoy, or upset them. *He teased me mercilessly about going Hollywood... 'You must be expecting a young man,' she teased.* ► Also a noun. *Calling her by her real name had always been one of his teases.* ♦ **teas·ing** *She tolerated the teasing, until the fourth grade.* **2** If you refer to someone as a **tease,** you mean that they like laughing at people or making jokes about them. **3** If you say that someone **is teasing,** you mean that they are pretending to offer something, especially sex, but then not giving it. *She used to think nothing of teasing her audience by wearing tight suggestive clothes.* **4** If you refer to someone as a **tease,** you disapprove of them because they pretend to offer something, especially sex, but do not give it. **5** See also **teasing; striptease.**

♦♦◇◇◇ / VERB: V n / V n about n/- ing / V with quote
N-COUNT
N-UNCOUNT
N-COUNT
VERB: V / V n
N-COUNT / PRAGMATICS

tease out. If you **tease out** information or a solution, you succeed in obtaining it even though this is difficult. *They try to tease out the answers without appearing to ask.*

PHRASAL VB / V P n / Also V n P

teas·er /ˈtiːzə/ **teasers.** A **teaser** is a difficult question, especially one in a quiz or competition.

N-COUNT / INFORMAL

'tea service, tea services. A **tea service** is the same as a **tea set.**

N-COUNT

'tea set, tea sets. A **tea set** is a set of cups, saucers, and plates, with a milk jug, sugar bowl, and teapot.

N-COUNT

'tea shop, tea shops; also spelled **teashop.** A **tea shop** is a small restaurant or café where tea, coffee, cakes, sandwiches, and light meals are served.

N-COUNT / BRITISH

teas·ing /ˈtiːzɪŋ/. **1** A **teasing** expression or manner shows that the person is not completely serious about what they are saying or doing. ♦ **teas·ing·ly** *'My, what a lot of things you want to know, Sergeant', she said teasingly.* **2** See also **tease.**

ADJ-GRADED
ADV-GRADED

tea·spoon /ˈtiːspuːn/ **teaspoons.** A **teaspoon** is a small spoon that you use to put sugar into tea or coffee. ► You can refer to an amount of food held by a teaspoon as a **teaspoon** of food.

♦♦◇◇◇ / N-COUNT
N-COUNT

tea·spoon·ful /ˈtiːspuːnfʊl/ **teaspoonfuls;** **teaspoonful** can also be used as the plural form. You can refer to an amount of food held by a teaspoon as a **teaspoonful** of food.

N-COUNT

teat /tiːt/ **teats. 1** A **teat** is a pointed part on the body of a female animal which her offspring suck in order to get milk. **2** A **teat** is a piece of rubber or plastic that is shaped like a teat, especially one that is fitted to a bottle so that a baby can suck liquids from it.

N-COUNT
N-COUNT

'tea table; also spelled **tea-table.** You refer to a table as **the tea table** when it is being used for a meal eaten in the late afternoon or early evening.

N-SING: / the N / BRITISH

tea·time /ˈtiːtaɪm/ **teatimes.** In Britain, **teatime** is the period of the day when people usually have their tea, which is the late afternoon or the early part of the evening. *We left at teatime.*

N-VAR

'tea towel, tea towels. A **tea towel** is a cloth used to dry dishes after they have been washed. The usual American term is **dish towel.**

N-COUNT / BRITISH

tech /tek/ **techs.** In Britain, **tech** is the same as a **technical college.** *Even at tech there were no female teachers.*

N-COUNT: / also at N / INFORMAL

tech·ni·cal /ˈteknɪkəl/. **1 Technical** means involving the sorts of machines, processes, and materials that are used in industry, transport, and communications. *A number of technical problems will have to be solved. ...jobs that require technical knowledge.* ♦ **tech·ni·cal·ly** /ˈteknɪkli/. *...the largest and most technically advanced furnace company in the world.* **2** You use **technical** to describe the practical skills and methods used to do an activity such as an art, a craft, or a sport. *Their technical ability is exceptional.* ♦ **technically** *While Sade's voice isn't technically brilliant it has a quality which is unmistakable.* **3 Technical** language involves using special words to describe the details of a specialized activity. *The*

♦♦◇◇ / ADJ
ADV: ADV adj
ADJ
ADV: ADV adj
ADJ-GRADED

technical term for sunburn is erythema. **4** See also **technically**.

'technical college, technical colleges. In Britain, a **technical college** is a college where you can study arts and technical subjects, often as part of the qualifications and training required for a particular job. N-VAR

tech·ni·cal·ity /ˌteknɪˈkælɪti/ **technicalities.** ◆◇◇◇◇ **1** The **technicalities** of a process or activity are the N-PLURAL detailed methods used to do it or to carry it out. *...the technicalities of classroom teaching.* **2** A **tech·** N-COUNT **nicality** is a point that is based on a strict interpretation of the law or of a set of rules. *The earlier verdict was overturned on a legal technicality.*

tech·ni·cal·ly /ˈteknɪkəli/. If something is **techni-** ◆◇◇◇◇ **cally** the case, it is the case according to a strict in- ADV: terpretation of facts, laws, or rules, but may not be ADV adj, important or relevant in a particular situation. *Tech-* ADV with cl *nically, the two sides have been in a state of war ever since 1949.*

tech·ni·cian /tekˈnɪʃən/ **technicians. 1** A techni- ◆◆◇◇◇ cian is someone whose job involves skilled practical N-COUNT work with scientific equipment, for example in a laboratory. **2** A **technician** is someone who is very N-COUNT good at the detailed technical aspects of an activity.

Tech·ni·col·or /ˈteknɪkʌlə/; also spelled **technicol-** **our** in British English for meaning 2. **1** Technicolor N-UNCOUNT is a system of colour photography used in making cinema films. **Technicolor** is a trademark. **2** You N-UNCOUNT can use **technicolour** to describe real or imagined PRAGMATICS scenes when you want to emphasize that they are INFORMAL very colourful. *I was seeing it all in glorious technicolour: mountains, valleys, lakes.*

tech·nique /tekˈniːk/ **techniques. 1** A technique ◆◆◆◆◇ is a particular method of doing an activity, usually a N-COUNT: method that involves practical skills. *...tests per-* with supp *formed using a new technique.* **2** Technique is skill N-UNCOUNT and ability in an artistic, sporting, or other practical activity that you develop through training and practice. *...tunes that emphasize the band's lack of technique.*

techno /ˈteknəʊ/. Techno is a form of modern elec- N-UNCOUNT tronic music with a very fast beat.

techno- /ˈteknəʊ-/. Techno- is used at the begin- PREFIX ning of words that refer to technology. *...a group of futurist technologists.*

tech·no·crat /ˈteknəkræt/ **technocrats.** A tech- ◆◇◇◇◇ nocrat is a scientist, engineer, or other expert who N-COUNT is one of a group of similar people who have political power as well as technical knowledge. ♦ **tech-** **·no·crat·ic.** Technocratic means consisting of or ADJ influenced by technocrats. *...the current technocratic administration.*

tech·no·logi·cal /ˌteknəˈlɒdʒɪkəl/ **Technological** ◆◆◇◇◇ means relating to or associated with technology. ADJ: ADJ n *...an era of very rapid technological change.* ♦ **tech-** **·no·logi·cal·ly** /ˌteknəˈlɒdʒɪkli/. *...technologically* ADV *advanced aircraft.*

tech·nol·ogy /tekˈnɒlədʒi/ **technologies.** Tech- ◆◆◆◆◇ nology refers to methods, systems, and devices N-VAR which are the result of scientific knowledge being used for practical purposes. ♦ **tech·nolo·gist** N-COUNT /tekˈnɒlədʒɪst/ **technologists** *...the scientists and technologists that we will need for the future.*

tec·ton·ic /tekˈtɒnɪk/. Tectonic means relating to ADJ: ADJ n the structure of the earth's surface or crust. *...the* TECHNICAL *tectonic plates of the Pacific region.*

tec·ton·ics /tekˈtɒnɪks/. See **plate tectonics**.

ted·dy /ˈtedi/ **teddies.** A teddy or teddy bear is a ◆◇◇◇◇ children's soft toy which looks like a friendly bear. N-COUNT

'Teddy boy, Teddy boys. A Teddy boy is a man N-COUNT who dresses in a style that became popular in the 1950's. Teddy boys were associated with early rock and roll music.

te·di·ous /ˈtiːdiəs/. If you describe something such ◆◇◇◇◇ as a job, task, or situation as **tedious**, you mean it is ADJ-GRADED boring and rather frustrating. ♦ **te·di·ous·ly** These ADV-GRADED *introductory chapters are tediously repetitive.*

te·dium /ˈtiːdiəm/. If you talk about the **tedium** of a N-UNCOUNT job, task, or situation, you think it is boring and rather frustrating.

tee /tiː/ **tees, teeing, teed. 1** In golf, a **tee** is a ◆◇◇◇◇ small piece of wood or plastic which is used to sup- N-COUNT port the ball before it is hit at the start of each hole. **2** On a golf course, a **tee** is one of the small flat N-COUNT areas of ground from which people hit the ball at the start of each hole. **3** ● **to a tee**: see T.

tee off. In golf, when you **tee off**, you hit the ball PHRASAL VB from a tee at the start of a hole. V P

tee up. In golf, when you **tee up** a ball, you place it on PHRASAL VB a tee so that it is ready for you to hit it. *I never dreamed* V P noun *that I'd tee up with Bob Hope.* V P Also V n P

teem /tiːm/ **teems, teeming, teemed.** If you say ◆◇◇◇◇ that a place **is teeming** with people or animals, you VERB: mean that it is crowded and the people and animals V with n are moving around a lot.

teen /tiːn/ **teens. 1** If you are in your **teens**, you ◆◆◇◇◇ are between thirteen and nineteen years old. *My* N-PLURAL: *late teens and early twenties were really rough years.* with supp **2** Teen is used to describe things such as films, ADJ: ADJ n magazines, bands, or activities that are aimed at or done by teenagers. *...a teen movie starring George Carlin.* **3** A **teen** is someone aged between thirteen N-COUNT and nineteen years old. The usual British word is AMERICAN **teenager**.

teen·age /ˈtiːneɪdʒ/. **1** Teenage children are aged ◆◆◇◇◇ between thirteen and nineteen years old. *Almost* ADJ: ADJ n *one in four teenage girls now smoke.* **2** Teenage is ADJ: ADJ n used to describe things such as films, magazines, bands, or activities that are aimed at or are done by teenage children. *...teenage pregnancies.*

teen·aged /ˈtiːneɪdʒd/. Teenaged people are aged ADJ: ADJ n between thirteen and nineteen.

teen·ager /ˈtiːneɪdʒə/ **teenagers.** A teenager is ◆◆◆◇◇ someone who is between thirteen and nineteen N-COUNT years old.

tee·ny /ˈtiːni/ **teenier, teeniest.** If you describe ADJ-GRADED: something as **teeny**, you are emphasizing that it is ADJ n very small. *...little teeny bugs.* PRAGMATICS INFORMAL

teeny·bopper /ˈtiːnibɒpə/ **teenyboppers;** also N-COUNT spelled **teeny-bopper.** A teenybopper is a teenager, INFORMAL, usually a girl, who is very interested in pop music. DATED

tee·pee /ˈtiːpiː/. See **tepee**.

'tee-shirt. See **T-shirt**.

tee·ter /ˈtiːtə/ **teeters, teetering, teetered.** ◆◇◇◇◇ **1** Teeter is used in expressions such as **teeter on** VERB **the brink** to emphasize that something seems to be PRAGMATICS in a very unstable situation or position. *His voice* V on n *teetered on the edge of hysteria.* **2** If someone or VERB: V something **teeters**, they shake in an unsteady way, V adv/prep and seem to be about to lose their balance and fall over. *He watched the cup teeter on the edge before it fell.*

teeth /tiːθ/. Teeth is the plural of **tooth**.

teeth·ing /ˈtiːðɪŋ/. When babies **are teething**, their VERB: teeth are starting to appear through their gums, of- V, ten causing them pain. *...a remedy for teething* only cont *babies.* ► Also a noun. *Teething can be painful and* V-ing *make your baby irritable.* N-UNCOUNT

'teething problems or **teething troubles.** If a N-PLURAL project or new product has **teething problems** or BRITISH **teething troubles**, it has problems in its early stages or when it first becomes available.

tee·to·tal /tiːˈtəʊtəl, AM ˈtiːtəʊtəl/. Someone who is ADJ **teetotal** never drinks alcohol. ♦ **tee·to·tal·ler, tee-** N-COUNT **totallers** *He is a strict teetotaller.*

TEFL /ˈtefəl/. TEFL is the teaching of English to N-UNCOUNT people whose first language is not English, especially people from a country where English is not spoken. **TEFL** is an abbreviation for 'teaching English as a foreign language'.

Tef·lon /ˈteflɒn/. Teflon is a type of plastic which is N-UNCOUNT often used to coat cooking pans so that food does not stick to them. **Teflon** is a trademark.

tel. Tel. is a written abbreviation for 'telephone number'.

T

tele·cast /'telɪkɑːst, -kæst/ **telecasts.** A telecast is a programme that is broadcast on the television, especially a programme that is broadcast live. N-COUNT AMERICAN

tele·com·mu·ni·ca·tions /ˌtelɪkəmjuːnɪˈkeɪʃənz/; the form **telecommunication** is used as a modifier. Telecommunications is the technology of sending signals and messages over long distances using electronic equipment, for example by radio and telephone. ◆◆◇◇◇ N-UNCOUNT

tele·com·mut·er /ˌtelɪkəˈmjuːtə/ **telecommuters.** A telecommuter is the same as a **teleworker**. N-COUNT BRITISH

tele·gen·ic /ˌtelɪˈdʒenɪk/. Someone who is telegenic looks good on the television. ADJ-GRADED

tele·gram /'telɪɡræm/ **telegrams.** A telegram is a message that is sent by telegraph and then printed and delivered to someone's home or office. *The President received a briefing by telegram.* ◆◇◇◇◇ N-COUNT: also by N

tele·graph /'telɪɡrɑːf, -ɡræf/ **telegraphs, telegraphing, telegraphed. 1** Telegraph is a system of sending messages over long distances, either by means of electricity or by radio signals. Telegraph was more commonly used before the invention of telephones. **2** To telegraph someone means to send them a message by telegraph. *Churchill telegraphed an urgent message to Wavell... 'Please,' he telegraphed, 'just leave it alone.'* **3** If someone telegraphs something that they are planning or intending to do, they make it obvious, either deliberately or accidentally, that they are going to do it. *The commission telegraphed its decision earlier this month by telling an official to prepare the order.* ◆◇◇◇◇ N-UNCOUNT VERB: V n VERB V with quote VERB V n

'telegraph pole, telegraph poles. A telegraph pole is a tall wooden pole with telephone wires attached to it, connecting several different buildings to the telephone system. N-COUNT

te·lepa·thy /tɪˈlepəθi/. Telepathy is the direct communication of thoughts and feelings between people's minds, without the need to use speech or writing. ◆ **tele·path·ic** /ˌtelɪˈpæθɪk/. *The pair of them had a telepathic understanding.* ◆ **tele·pathi·cal·ly** /ˌtelɪˈpæθɪkli/. *I used to communicate with her telepathically.* N-UNCOUNT ADJ ADV: ADV with v

tele·phone /'telɪfəʊn/ **telephones, telephoning, telephoned. 1** The telephone is an electrical system of communication that you use to talk directly to someone else in a different place. You use the telephone by dialling a number on a piece of equipment and speaking into it. *They usually exchanged messages by telephone.* **2** A telephone is the piece of equipment that you use when you talk to someone by telephone. *He got up and answered the telephone... The telephone in Rizzoli's room rang.* **3** If you telephone someone, you dial their telephone number and speak to them by telephone. *They usually telephone first to see if she is at home.* **4** If you are on the telephone, you are speaking to someone by telephone. *Linda remained on the telephone to the police for three hours.* **5** If someone is on the telephone, they have a telephone in their house or office which is connected to the rest of the telephone system. *He's not on the telephone.* ◆◆◆◆◇ N-UNCOUNT N-COUNT VERB: V n V PHRASE PHRASE

'telephone book, telephone books. The telephone book is a book that contains an alphabetical list of the names, addresses, and telephone numbers of the people in a particular area. N-COUNT

'telephone booth, telephone booths. A telephone booth is a place in a public building or in the street where there is a telephone that can be used by the public. N-COUNT FORMAL

'telephone box, telephone boxes. A telephone box is a small shelter in the street in which there is a public telephone. The American term is **phone booth.** N-COUNT BRITISH

'telephone directory, telephone directories. The telephone directory is the same as the **telephone book.** N-COUNT

'telephone exchange, telephone exchanges. A telephone exchange is a place where connections are made between telephone lines. N-COUNT

'telephone number, telephone numbers. Your telephone number is the number that other people dial when they want to talk to you on the telephone. ◆◇◇◇ N-COUNT

te·lepho·nist /tɪˈlefənɪst/ **telephonists.** A telephonist is someone who works at a telephone exchange or whose job is to answer the telephone for a business or other organization. The usual American term is **telephone operator.** N-COUNT BRITISH

te·lepho·ny /tɪˈlefəni/. Telephony is a system of sending voice signals using electronic equipment. N-UNCOUNT

telephoto lens, /ˌtelɪfəʊtəʊ ˈlenz/ **telephoto lenses.** A telephoto lens is a powerful camera lens which allows you to take close-up pictures of something that is far away. N-COUNT

tele·scope /'telɪskəʊp/ **telescopes.** A telescope is a long instrument shaped like a tube. It has lenses inside it that make distant things seem larger and nearer when you look through it. ◆◆◇◇◇ N-COUNT

tele·scop·ic /ˌtelɪˈskɒpɪk/. **1** Telescopic lenses and instruments are used to make things seem larger and nearer, and are usually longer than others of the same type. *...a sporting rifle fitted with a telescopic sight.* **2** A telescopic object is made of cylindrical sections that fit or slide into each other, so that it can be made longer or shorter, for example to save space when it is not being used. *...this new lightweight telescopic ladder.* ADJ ADJ

tele·vise /'telɪvaɪz/ **televises, televising, televised.** If an event or programme is televised, it is broadcast so that it can be seen on television. ◆◆◇◇◇ VERB: be V-ed

tele·vi·sion /'telɪvɪʒən, -ˈvɪʒ-/ **televisions. 1** A television or television set is a piece of electrical equipment consisting of a box with a glass screen on it on which you can watch programmes with pictures and sounds. *She turned the television on.* **2** Television is the system of sending pictures and sounds by electrical signals over a distance so that people can receive them on a television in their home. *Toy manufacturers began promoting some of their products on television.* **3** Television refers to all the programmes that you can watch. *I don't have much time to watch very much television.* **4** Television is the business or industry concerned with making programmes and broadcasting them on television. *...ITN, the company which provides news for commercial television.* ◆◆◆◆◇ N-COUNT N-UNCOUNT N-UNCOUNT N-UNCOUNT

tele·vis·ual /ˌteləˈvɪʒʊəl/. Televisual means broadcast on or related to television. *...a televisual masterpiece.* ADJ: ADJ n BRITISH

tele·worker /'teliwɜːkə/ **teleworkers.** Teleworkers are people who work from home using equipment such as telephones, fax machines, and modems to contact their colleagues and customers. ◆ **tele·work·ing** *Can teleworking become reality for most of us?* N-COUNT N-UNCOUNT

tel·ex /'teleks/ **telexes, telexing, telexed. 1** Telex is an international system of sending written messages by transmitting them as electrical or radio signals, which are printed out by a machine in another place. **2** A telex is a machine that transmits and receives telex messages. **3** A telex is a message that is sent or received by telex. **4** If you telex a message to someone, you send it to them by telex. *They telexed British Airways.* ◆◇◇◇◇ N-UNCOUNT N-COUNT N-COUNT VERB: V n to n V n

tell /tel/ **tells, telling, told. 1** If you tell someone something, you give them information. *In the evening I returned to tell Phyllis our relationship was over... I called Andie to tell her how spectacular the stuff looked... I only told the truth to the press when the single was released... Tell us about your moment on the summit... She told him: 'It doesn't seem fair'.* **2** If you tell something such as a joke, a story, or your personal experiences, you communicate it to other people using speech. *He told his story to The Sunday Times... I told him a joke.* ◆ **tell·ing, tellings** *Herbert sat quietly through the telling of this saga.* **3** If you tell someone to do something, you order, instruct, or advise them to do it. *A passer-by told the driver to move his car.* **4** If you ◆◆◆◆◆ VERB: V n V that V n to n V n about n V n with quote Also V of n VERB: V n V n to n V n N-VAR VERB V n to-inf VERB

tell, you reveal or give away a secret. *Many of the children know who they are but are not telling.* **5** If you **tell** yourself something, you put it into words in your own mind because you need to encourage or persuade yourself about something. *'Come on', she told herself... I told myself I would be satisfied with whatever I could get.* **6** If facts or events **tell** you something, they reveal certain information to you through ways other than speech. *The facts tell us that this is not true... I don't think the unemployment rate ever tells us much about the future... The photographs tell a different story.* **7** You can say **'I can tell you', 'I can tell you'**, or **'I can't tell you'** to add emphasis to what you are saying. *This little letter gave us a few chuckles, I can tell you.* **8** If someone disagrees with you or refuses to do what you suggest and you are eventually proved to be right, you can say **'I told you so'**. **9** You use **I'll tell you what** or **I tell you what** to introduce a suggestion or a new topic of conversation. *I tell you what, I'll bring the water in a separate glass.*
10 If you can **tell** what is happening or what is true, you are able to judge correctly what is happening or what is true. *You can tell he's joking.* **11** If you can **tell** one thing from another, you are able to recognize the difference between it and other similar things. *I can't really tell the difference between their policies and ours... I had to look twice to tell which was Martinez.* **12** You use **as far as I can tell** or **so far as I could tell** to indicate that what you are saying is based on the information you have, but that there may be things you do not know. *So far as anyone can tell, there's evidence that there was a Robin Hood.* **13** If you say **'You never can tell'**, you mean that the future is always uncertain and it is never possible to know exactly what will happen.
14 If an unpleasant or tiring experience begins to **tell**, it begins to have a serious effect. *The strains of office are beginning to tell on the prime minister.*
15 See also **telling; kiss and tell**. **16 ●** to **tell the time**: see **time ● time will tell**: see **time**.

V INFORMAL VERB · *V pron-refl with quote* · *V pron-refl that* · *VERB: V n n · V n that · V n amount · V n* · *CONVENTION PRAGMATICS INFORMAL CONVENTION INFORMAL* · *CONVENTION PRAGMATICS SPOKEN* · *VERB: V wh · V that VERB: V n from n · V n between pl-n · V wh* · *PHRASE PRAGMATICS* · *CONVENTION* · *VERB: V · V on n*

tell against. If a feature or characteristic **tells against** someone, it spoils their chance of success when they are being considered for something, for example a job.   *PHRASAL VB V P n*

tell apart. If you can **tell** people or things **apart**, you are able to recognize the differences between them and can therefore identify them individually.   *PHRASAL VB V pl-n P*

tell off. If you **tell** someone **off**, you speak to them angrily or seriously because they have done something wrong. *I'm always being told off for being so awkward.*   *PHRASAL VB V n P · V n P for n/-ing Also V P noun INFORMAL*

tell on. If you **tell on** someone, you give information about them to someone in authority, especially if they have done something wrong. *I'll tell my mummy on you.*   *PHRASAL VB V P n · V n P n INFORMAL*

tell·er /ˈtelə/ **tellers.** A **teller** is someone who works in a bank and who customers pay money to or get money from.   *◆◇◇◇◇ N-COUNT*

tell·ing /ˈtelɪŋ/. **1** If something is **telling**, it shows the true nature of a person or situation. *How a man shaves may be a telling clue to his age.* **♦ tell·ing·ly** *Most tellingly, Labour's vote was well down on its 1990 performance.* **2** A **telling** argument or criticism is a very effective one. **3** You use **there's no telling** to introduce a statement when you want to say that it is impossible to know what will happen in a situation. *There's no telling how long the talks could drag on.* **4** See also **tell**.   *◆◇◇◇◇ ADJ-GRADED · ADV-GRADED · ADJ-GRADED · PHRASE*

telling-'off; tellings-off; also spelled **telling off.** If you give someone a **telling-off**, you tell them that you are very angry with them about something they have done. *I got a severe telling off for not phoning him.*   *N-COUNT INFORMAL*

'tell-tale; also spelled **telltale.** Something that is described as **tell-tale** gives away information, often about something bad that would otherwise not be noticed. *...the telltale redness around his eyes.*   *ADJ: ADJ n*

tel·ly /ˈteli/ **tellies.** A **telly** is a television. The usual American word is **TV**. *She was desperate to get to a*   *◆◇◇◇◇ N-VAR BRITISH,*

telly. There was something on that she did not want to miss.   *INFORMAL*

te·mer·i·ty /tɪˈmerɪti/. If you say that someone has the **temerity** to do something, you are annoyed about something they have done which you think showed a lack of respect.   *N-UNCOUNT PRAGMATICS*

temp /temp/ **temps, temping. 1** A **temp** is a person, usually a secretary, who is employed by an agency that sends him or her to work in different offices for short periods of time, for example to replace someone who is ill or on holiday. **2** If someone **is temping**, they are working as a temp.   *N-COUNT · VERB: V, only cont*

tem·per /ˈtempə/ **tempers, tempering, tempered. 1** If you refer to someone's **temper** that they have a **temper**, you mean that they become angry very easily. *I hope he can control his temper.* **2** Your **temper** is the way you are feeling at a particular time. If you are in a good **temper**, you feel cheerful. If you are in a bad **temper**, you feel angry and impatient. *Lee stormed off the field in a furious temper.* **3** If someone is **in a temper** or gets **into a temper**, the way that they are behaving shows that they are feeling angry and impatient. *When I try to explain how I feel he just flies into a temper.* **4** If you **lose** your **temper**, you become so angry that you shout at someone or show in some other way that you are no longer in control of yourself. **5** To **temper** something means to make it less extreme. *For others, especially the young and foolish, the state will temper justice with mercy.*   *◆◇◇◇ N-VAR · N-VAR: with supp · PHRASE · PHRASE · VERB: V n · V n with n FORMAL*

tem·pera·ment /ˈtempərəmənt/ **temperaments. 1** Your **temperament** is your basic nature, especially as it is shown in the way that you react to situations or to other people. *She was furtive and vicious by temperament.* **♦ tem·pera·men·tal·ly** /ˌtemprəˈmentəli/. *Temperamentally I am unsuited to tennis.* **2 Temperament** is the tendency to behave in an uncontrolled, bad-tempered, or unreasonable way. *Some of the models were given to fits of temperament.*   *◆◇◇◇ N-VAR · ADV · N-UNCOUNT*

tem·pera·men·tal /ˌtemprəˈmentəl/. **1** If you say that someone is **temperamental**, you are criticizing them for not being calm or quiet by nature, but having moods that change often and suddenly. **2** If you describe something such as a machine or car as **temperamental**, you mean that it often does not work properly.   *ADJ-GRADED PRAGMATICS · ADJ-GRADED*

tem·per·ance /ˈtempərəns/. **1** If you believe in **temperance**, you disapprove of drinking alcohol. **2** A person who shows **temperance** is very self-controlled and does not eat too much, drink too much, or do anything to excess.   *N-UNCOUNT · N-UNCOUNT*

tem·per·ate /ˈtempərɪt/. **1 Temperate** is used to describe a climate or a place which is never extremely hot or extremely cold. **2** If a person's behaviour is **temperate**, it is calm and self-controlled, so that they do not get angry or lose their temper easily.   *◆◇◇◇ ADJ-GRADED · ADJ-GRADED*

tem·pera·ture /ˈtemprətʃə/ **temperatures. 1** The **temperature** of something is a measure of how hot or cold it is. *Winter closes in and the temperature drops below freezing.* ● If something is at **room temperature**, its temperature is neither hot nor cold. **2** Your **temperature** is the temperature of your body. A normal temperature is about 37° centigrade. *His temperature continued to rise.* **3** If you **are running a temperature** or if you **have a temperature**, your temperature is higher than it usually is because you are ill. **4** If you **take** someone's **temperature** you use a thermometer to measure the temperature of their body in order to see if they are ill. **5** You can use **temperature** to talk about the feelings and emotions that people have in particular situations. *There's also been a noticeable rise in the political temperature.*   *◆◆◆◇ N-VAR · PHRASE · N-UNCOUNT · PHRASE · PHRASE · N-COUNT*

tem·pest /ˈtempɪst/ **tempests. 1** A **tempest** is a very violent storm. **2** You can refer to a situation in which people are very angry or excited as a **tempest**. *The takeover provoked a tempest of criticism.*   *N-COUNT LITERARY · N-COUNT*

T

tem·pes·tu·ous /tem'pestʃʊəs/. If you describe a relationship or a situation as **tempestuous**, you mean that very strong and passionate emotions, especially anger, are involved. ADJ-GRADED

tem·pi /'tempi/. **Tempi** is a plural of **tempo**.

tem·plate /'templeɪt, AM -plɪt/ **templates.** **1** A **template** is a thin piece of metal or plastic which is cut into a particular shape. It is used to help you cut wood, paper, metal, or other materials accurately, or to reproduce the same shape many times. **2** If one thing is a **template** for something else, the second thing is based on the first thing. *The template for Adair's novel is not somebody else's fiction, but fact.* N-COUNT

tem·ple /'templ/ **temples.** **1** A **temple** is a building used for the worship of a god or gods, especially in the Buddhist and Hindu religions, and in ancient Greek and Roman times. **2** Your **temples** are the flat parts on each side of the front part of your head, near your forehead. ◆◆◇◇ N-COUNT / N-COUNT

tem·po /'tempəʊ/ **tempos; tempi** can also be used as the plural form. **1** The **tempo** of an event is the speed at which it happens. *He was dissatisfied with the tempo of political change.* **2** The **tempo** of a piece of music is the speed at which it is played. ◆◇◇◇ N-SING / N-VAR

tem·po·ral /'tempərəl/. **1** **Temporal** powers or matters relate to ordinary institutions and activities rather than to religious or spiritual ones. *...the need for the clergy not to become pre-occupied with temporal matters.* **2** In your brain, the **temporal** lobes are the parts near your temples, at the sides of your head. **3** **Temporal** means relating to time. *...units of creative experience that influence one another in temporal sequence.* ♦ **tem·po·ral·ly** /'tempərəli/. *In the last stages of dementia, persons will be spatially and temporally disoriented.* ◆◇◇◇ ADJ: ADJ n FORMAL / ADJ: ADJ n MEDICAL / ADJ: ADJ n FORMAL / ADV

tem·po·rary /'tempərəri, AM -reri/. Something that is **temporary** lasts for only a limited time. *His job here is only temporary. ...a temporary loss of memory.* ♦ **tem·po·rari·ly** /,tempə'reərɪli/. *Checkpoints between the two zones were temporarily closed.* ◆◆◇◇ ADJ / ADV

tem·po·rize /'tempəraɪz/ **temporizes, temporizing, temporized;** also spelled **temporise** in British English. If you say that someone **is temporizing**, you mean that they keep doing something unimportant, in order to delay something important such as making a decision. VERB: V FORMAL

tempt /tempt/ **tempts, tempting, tempted.** **1** Something that **tempts** you attracts you and makes you want it, even though it may be wrong or harmful. *Children not attending schools may be tempted into crime... Can I tempt you with a little puff pastry?... Don't let credit tempt you to buy something you can't afford. ...a million dollar marketing campaign to tempt American tourists back to Britain.* ♦ **tempt·ing** *I turned down Raoul's tempting offer of the Palm Beach trip.* ♦ **tempt·ing·ly** *The good news is that prices are still temptingly low.* **2** If someone says that something they say or do **is tempting fate** or **is tempting providence**, they mean they are worried that it may cause the good luck they have had so far to end. ◆◇◇◇ VERB: V n / V n into n/-ing / V n with n / V n to-inf / V n prep/adv / ADJ-GRADED / ADV-GRADED / PHRASE

temp·ta·tion /temp'teɪʃən/ **temptations.** **Temptation** is the feeling that you want to do or have something, even though you know you really should avoid it. You can also refer to the thing you want to do or have as a **temptation**. *Will they be able to resist the temptation to buy?* ◆◆◇◇ N-VAR

tempt·ed /'temptɪd/. If you say that you are **tempted** to do something, you mean that you would like to do it. *I'm very tempted to sell my house.* ◆◆◇◇ ADJ-GRADED: v-link ADJ

tempt·ress /'temptrəs/ **temptresses.** If you describe a woman as a **temptress**, you mean that she deliberately uses her female charm and sexuality to attract men. N-COUNT

ten /ten/ **tens. Ten** is the number 10. See Appendix headed **Numbers.** ● See also **Number Ten.** ● **ten a penny**: see **penny.** ◆◆◆◆◆ NUMBER

ten·able /'tenəbəl/. If you say that an argument, point of view, or situation is **tenable**, you believe that it is reasonable and could be successfully defended against criticism. ADJ-GRADED

te·na·cious /tɪ'neɪʃəs/. **1** If you are **tenacious**, you are very determined and do not give up easily. ♦ **te·na·cious·ly** *In spite of his illness, he clung tenaciously to his job.* **2** If you describe something such as a mistaken idea or belief as **tenacious**, you mean that it has a strong influence on people and is difficult to change. ◆◇◇◇ ADJ-GRADED / ADV-GRADED / ADJ-GRADED

te·nac·ity /tɪ'næsɪti/. If you have **tenacity**, you are very determined and do not give up easily. N-UNCOUNT

ten·an·cy /'tenənsi/ **tenancies. Tenancy** is the use that you have of land or property belonging to someone else, for which you pay rent. *His father took over the tenancy of the farm 40 years ago.* N-VAR

ten·ant /'tenənt/ **tenants.** A **tenant** is someone who pays rent for the place they live in, or for land or buildings that they use. ◆◆◇◇ N-COUNT

tench /tentʃ/ **tench; tench** is both the singular and the plural form. **Tench** are dark green European fish that live in lakes and rivers. N-VAR

tend /tend/ **tends, tending, tended. 1** If something **tends** to happen, it usually happens or it often happens. *In older age groups women predominate because men tend to die younger.* **2** If you **tend** towards a particular characteristic, you often display that characteristic. *Artistic and intellectual people tend towards left-wing views.* **3** You can say that you **tend** to think something when you want to give your opinion, but do not want it to seem too forceful or definite. *I tend to think that members of parliament by and large do a good job.* **4** If you **tend** someone or something, you do what is necessary to keep them in a good condition or to improve their condition. *He tends the flower beds and evergreens.* **5** If you **tend** to someone or something, you pay attention to them and deal with their problems and needs. *I was upstairs tending to David.* ◆◆◆◆ VERB V to-inf / VERB V towards/to n / VERB PRAGMATICS V to-inf / VERB V n FORMAL / VERB V to n

ten·den·cy /'tendənsi/ **tendencies. 1** A **tendency** is a worrying or unpleasant habit or action that keeps occurring. *...the mounting separatist tendencies of the northern republics.* **2** A **tendency** is a part of your character that makes you behave in an unpleasant or worrying way. *He is spoiled, arrogant and has a tendency towards snobbery.* ◆◆◆◇ N-COUNT: with supp / N-COUNT: with supp

ten·den·tious /ten'denʃəs/. Something that is **tendentious** expresses a particular opinion or point of view very strongly, especially one that many people disagree with. *His analysis was rooted in a somewhat tendentious reading of French history.* ADJ-GRADED FORMAL

tender 1 adjective uses

ten·der /'tendə/ **tenderer, tenderest. 1** Someone or something that is **tender** expresses gentle and caring feelings. *Her voice was tender, full of pity.* ♦ **ten·der·ly** *Mr. White tenderly embraced his wife.* ♦ **ten·der·ness** *She smiled, politely rather than with tenderness or gratitude.* **2** If you say that someone does something at a **tender** age, you mean that they do it when they are still young and inexperienced. **3** Meat or other food that is **tender** is easy to cut or chew. **4** If part of your body is **tender**, it is sensitive and feels painful when it is touched. ♦ **tenderness** *There is still some tenderness in her tummy.* ◆◆◇◇ ADJ-GRADED / ADV-GRADED: ADV with v / N-UNCOUNT / ADJ-GRADED: ADJ n / ADJ-GRADED / ADJ-GRADED / N-UNCOUNT

tender 2 noun and verb uses

ten·der /'tendə/ **tenders, tendering, tendered. 1** A **tender** is a formal offer to supply goods or to do a particular job, and a statement of the price that you or your company will charge. If a contract is **put out to tender**, formal offers are invited. If a company **wins a tender**, their offer is accepted. **2** If a company **tenders for** something, it makes a formal offer to supply goods or do a job for a particular price. ♦ **ten·der·ing** *...competitive tendering for council leisure and recreation services.* **3** If you **tender** something such as a suggestion or money, you formally offer or present it. *She quickly tendered her resignation.* **4** See also **legal tender.** ◆◆◇◇ N-VAR / VERB V for n / N-UNCOUNT / VERB V n

ten·don /'tendən/ **tendons.** A tendon is a strong ◆◇◇◇◇ N-COUNT
cord in a person's or animal's body which joins a
muscle to a bone. ● See also **Achilles tendon.**

ten·dril /'tendrɪl/ **tendrils. 1** A tendril is something N-COUNT
thin and wispy, for example a piece of hair which
hangs loose away from the main part. **2** Tendrils N-COUNT
are thin stems which grow on some plants so that
they can attach themselves to supports such as
walls or other plants.

ten·ement /'tenəmənt/ **tenements. 1** A tenement N-COUNT
is a large old terraced building which is divided into
a number of individual flats. **2** A tenement is one of N-COUNT
the flats in a tenement.

ten·et /'tenɪt/ **tenets.** The tenets of a theory or be- ◆◇◇◇◇
lief are the main principles on which it is based. N-COUNT:
Non-violence and patience are the central tenets of with supp
their faith. FORMAL

ten·ner /'tenə/ **tenners.** A tenner is ten pounds or N-COUNT
a ten-pound note. *Vaska got out a tenner and gave* INFORMAL,
it to the old woman. BRITISH

ten·nis /'tenɪs/. Tennis is a game played by two or ◆◆◆◇◇
four players on a rectangular court. The players use N-UNCOUNT
rackets to hit a ball over a net which is placed
across the middle of the court.

ten·or /'tenə/ **tenors. 1** A tenor is a male singer ◆◇◇◇◇
whose voice is fairly high. **2** A tenor saxophone or N-COUNT
other musical instrument has a range of notes that ADJ
are of a fairly low pitch. **3** The tenor of something is N-SING:
the general meaning or mood that it expresses. *The* with poss
whole tenor of discussions has changed. FORMAL

ten-pin 'bowling; also spelled **tenpin bowling.** N-UNCOUNT
Ten-pin bowling is a game in which you try to BRITISH
knock down ten bottle-shaped objects by rolling a
heavy ball towards them. The usual American word
is **bowling.**

tense /tens/ **tenses, tensing, tensed; tenser,** ◆◆◇◇◇
tensest. 1 A tense situation or period of time is ADJ-GRADED
one that makes people anxious, because they do
not know what is going to happen next. *This gesture
of goodwill did little to improve the tense atmos-
phere at the talks.* **2** If you are tense, you are anx- ADJ-GRADED
ious and nervous and cannot relax. *She* ADV-GRADED
waited tensely for the next bulletin. **3** If your body is ADJ-GRADED
tense, your muscles are tight and not relaxed. **4** If V-ERG: V
your muscles tense, if you tense, or if you tense Vn
your muscles, your muscles become tight and stiff,
often because you are anxious or frightened. *Jane
tensed her muscles to stop them from shaking.*
▶ **Tense up** means the same as **tense.** *The muscles* PHRASAL VB
in her shoulders were tensing up... Tense up the V P
muscles in both of your legs. V P noun
5 The tense of a verb group is its form, which usually N-COUNT
shows whether you are referring to past, present, or
future time.

tense up. See tense 4. PHRASAL VB

ten·sile /'tensaɪl, AM -sɪl/. You use tensile when ADJ: ADJ n
you are talking about the amount of stress that ma- TECHNICAL
terials such as wire, rope, and concrete can take
without breaking. *Certain materials can be manufactured with a high tensile strength.*

ten·sion /'tenʃən/ **tensions. 1** Tension is the feel- ◆◆◆◇◇
ing that is produced in a situation when people are N-UNCOUNT:
anxious and do not trust each other, and when also N in pl
there is a possibility of sudden violence or conflict.
*The tension between the two countries is likely to re-
main.* **2** Tension is a feeling of worry and nervous- N-UNCOUNT:
ness which makes it difficult for you to relax. also N in pl
*Laughing has actually been shown to relieve tension
and stress.* **3** If there is a tension between forces, N-VAR
arguments, or influences, there are differences
between them that cause difficulties. *...the tension
between public duty and personal affections.* **4** The N-UNCOUNT
tension in something such as a rope or wire is the
extent to which it is stretched tight.

tent /tent/ **tents.** A tent is a shelter made of canvas ◆◆◇◇◇
or nylon which is held up by poles and ropes, used N-COUNT
mainly by people who are camping. ◆ **tent·ed.** A ADJ
tented field or a tented camp is an area where a
number of people are living in tents.

ten·ta·cle /'tentəkəl/ **tentacles. 1** The tentacles ◆◇◇◇◇
of an animal such as an octopus are the long thin N-COUNT
parts that are used for feeling and holding things,
for getting food, and for moving. **2** If you talk about N-COUNT
the tentacles of a political, commercial, or social or- PRAGMATICS
ganization, you are referring to the power and influence that it has in the outside community; used
showing disapproval.

ten·ta·tive /'tentətɪv/. **1** Tentative agreements, ◆◆◇◇◇
plans, or arrangements are not definite or certain, ADJ-GRADED
but have been made as a first step. *...a tentative
agreement to hold a preparatory conference next
month.* ◆ **ten·ta·tive·ly** *The next round of talks is* ADV-GRADED:
tentatively scheduled to begin October 21st. **2** If ADV with v
someone is tentative, they are cautious and not ADJ-GRADED
very confident because they are uncertain or afraid.
She did not return his tentative smile. ◆ **tentatively** ADV-GRADED:
Perhaps, he suggested tentatively, they should send ADV with v
for Dr Brand.

tenter·hooks /'tentəhʊks/. If you are on tenter- PHRASE
hooks, you are very nervous and excited because
you are wondering what is going to happen in a
particular situation.

tenth /tenθ/ **tenths. 1** The tenth item in a series is ◆◆◆◇
the one that you count as number ten. See Appen- ORDINAL
dix headed Numbers. **2** A tenth is one of ten equal FRACTION
parts of something.

tenu·ous /'tenjuəs/. If you describe something ◆◇◇◇◇
such as a connection, a reason, or someone's posi- ADJ-GRADED
tion as tenuous, you mean that it is very uncertain
or weak. *The cultural and historical links between
the many provinces were seen to be very tenuous.*
◆ **tenu·ous·ly** *The sub-plots are only tenuously* ADV-GRADED:
interconnected. ADV with v

ten·ure /'tenjə/. **1** Tenure is the legal right to live ◆◇◇◇◇
in a particular building or to use a particular piece N-UNCOUNT
of land during a fixed period of time. **2** Tenure is N-UNCOUNT:
the period of time during which someone holds an with supp
important job. *...during his tenure as foreign minister.* **3** If you have tenure in your job, you have the N-UNCOUNT
right to keep it until you retire.

te·pee /'tiːpiː/ **tepees;** also spelled **teepee.** A tepee N-COUNT
is a cone-shaped tent. Tepees were first made by
Native American peoples from animal skins or bark.

tep·id /'tepɪd/. **1** Water or another liquid that is ◆◇◇◇◇
tepid is slightly warm. **2** If you describe something ADJ
such as a feeling or reaction as tepid, you mean that ADJ-GRADED
it lacks enthusiasm or liveliness. *His strongly
backed by the President, has received
tepid support in the Senate.*

term /tɜːm/ **terms, terming, termed. 1** If you ◆◆◆◆◆
talk about something in terms of something or in PHRASE
particular terms, you are specifying which aspect of
it you are discussing or from what point of view you
are considering it. *Our goods compete in terms of
product quality, reliability and above all variety.*
2 If you say or express something in particular terms, PHRASE
you say or express it using a particular type or level of
language. *The video explains in simple terms how the
new tax works.* **3** A term is a word or expression with a N-COUNT
specific meaning. *Myocardial infarction is the medical term for a heart attack.* **4** If you say that something VERB:
is termed a particular thing, you mean that that is be V-ed n
what people call it or that is their opinion of it. *He* V n n
termed the war a humanitarian nightmare. Also V n as n
5 A term is one of the periods of time that a school, N-VAR
college, or university divides the year into. *...the last
day of term.* **6** A term is a period of time between two N-COUNT:
elections during which a particular party, prime min- with supp
ister, or president is in power. *Felipe Gonzalez won a
fourth term of office.* **7** A term is a period of time that N-COUNT:
someone spends doing a particular job or in a par- with supp
ticular place. *...a seven-year prison term.* **8** A term is N-COUNT:
the period for which a legal contract or insurance with supp
policy is valid. **9** The term of a woman's pregnancy is N-UNCOUNT
the nine month period that it lasts. Term is also used
to refer to the end of the nine month period.
10 The terms of an agreement, treaty, or other ar- N-PLURAL
rangement are the conditions that must be accepted

by the people involved in it. ...*the terms of the Helsinki agreement.*

11 If you **come to terms with** something difficult or unpleasant, you learn to accept and deal with it. **12** If two people or groups compete **on equal terms** or **on the same terms**, neither of them has an advantage over the other. **13** If two people are **on good terms** or **on friendly terms**, they are friendly with each other. **14** You use the expressions **in the long term**, **in the short term**, and **in the medium term** to talk about what will happen over a long period of time, over a short period of time, and over a medium period of time. ● See also **long-term**, **medium-term**, **short-term**. **15** If you do something on your **terms**, you do it under conditions that you decide because you are in a position of power. **16** If you say that you **are thinking in terms** of doing a particular thing, you mean that you are considering it. *United should be thinking in terms of winning the European Cup.* **17** ● a **contradiction in terms**: see **contradiction**. ● **in no uncertain terms**: see **uncertain**. ● **in real terms**: see **real**. ● **on speaking terms**: see **speak**.

ter·mi·nal /ˈtɜːmɪnəl/ **terminals. 1** A **terminal** illness or disease causes death, often slowly, and cannot be cured. ♦ **ter·mi·nal·ly** *The patient is terminally ill.* **2** A **terminal** patient is dying of a terminal illness or disease.

3 A **terminal** is a place where vehicles, passengers, or goods begin or end a journey. **4** A computer **terminal** is a piece of equipment consisting of a keyboard and a screen that is used for putting information into a computer or getting information from it. **5** On a piece of electrical equipment, a **terminal** is one of the points where electricity enters or leaves it.

ter·mi·nate /ˈtɜːmɪneɪt/ **terminates, terminating, terminated. 1** When you **terminate** something or when it **terminates**, it ends completely. *His contract terminates at the season's end.* ♦ **ter·mi·na·tion** /ˌtɜːmɪˈneɪʃən/. ...*the abrupt termination of trade.* **2** To **terminate** a pregnancy means to end it. *About ten per cent of all pregnancies are terminated.* ♦ **ter·mi·na·tion, terminations** ...*a medical check-up after the termination of a pregnancy.* **3** When a train or bus **terminates** somewhere, it ends its journey there. *This train will terminate at Taunton.*

ter·mi·nol·o·gy /ˌtɜːmɪˈnɒlədʒi/ **terminologies.** The **terminology** of a subject is the set of special words and expressions used in connection with it. ...*gastritis, which in medical terminology means an inflammation of the stomach.*

ter·mi·nus /ˈtɜːmɪnəs/ **termini.** On a bus or train route, the **terminus** is the last stop or station, where the bus or train turns round or starts a journey in the opposite direction.

ter·mite /ˈtɜːmaɪt/ **termites. Termites** are small white insects which live in hot countries in nests made of earth. Termites do a lot of damage by eating wood.

terms of 'reference. Terms of reference are the instructions given to someone when they are asked to consider or investigate a particular subject, telling them what to deal with and what to ignore. *The government has announced the terms of reference for its proposed committee of inquiry.*

tern /tɜːn/ **terns.** A **tern** is a small black and white seabird with long wings and a forked tail.

ter·race /ˈterɪs/ **terraces. 1** A **terrace** is a row of similar houses joined together by their side walls. See picture headed **house** and **flat**. ...*3 Queensborough Terrace.* **2** A **terrace** is a flat area of stone or grass next to a building where people can sit. **3 Terraces** are a series of flat areas of ground built like steps on a hillside so that crops can be grown there. ♦ **ter·raced** ...*a terraced hillside.* **4 The terraces** at a football ground are wide steps that people can stand on when they are watching a game.

terraced 'house, terraced houses. A **terraced house** or a **terrace house** is one of a row of similar houses joined together by their side walls. The usual American term is a **row house**. See picture headed **house and flat.**

ter·rac·ing /ˈterəsɪŋ/. At a football stadium, **terracing** is an area of wide steps that people can stand on when they are watching the game.

terra·cotta /ˌterəˈkɒtə/; also spelled **terra-cotta. 1 Terracotta** is a brownish-red clay that has been baked but not glazed and that is used for making things such as flower pots, small statues, and tiles. **2 Terracotta** is used to describe things that are brownish-red in colour.

ter·rain /təˈreɪn/ **terrains.** Terrain is used to refer to an area of land or a type of land when you are considering its physical features. *The terrain changed quickly from arable land to desert.*

ter·res·trial /tɪˈrestriəl/. **1** A **terrestrial** animal or plant lives on land or on the ground rather than in the sea, in trees, or in the air. ...*terrestrial and aquatic fauna.* **2 Terrestrial** means relating to the planet Earth rather than to some other part of the universe. ...*terrestrial life forms.* **3 Terrestrial** television channels are transmitted using equipment situated at ground level, and not by satellite.

ter·ri·ble /ˈterɪbəl/. **1** A **terrible** experience or situation is very serious or very unpleasant. *Tens of thousands more suffered terrible injuries in the world's worst industrial disaster.* ♦ **ter·ri·bly** *My son has suffered terribly. He has lost his best friend.* **2** If you **feel terrible**, you feel extremely ill or unhappy. If you tell someone that they **look terrible**, you mean that they look as if they are extremely ill or unhappy. **3** If something is **terrible**, it is very bad or of very poor quality. *She admits her French is terrible.* **4** You use **terrible** to emphasize the great extent or degree of something. *Her death is a terrible waste.* ♦ **terribly** *I'm terribly sorry to bother you.*

ter·ri·er /ˈteriə/ **terriers.** A **terrier** is a small breed of dog. ● See also **bull terrier**, **pit bull terrier.**

ter·rif·ic /təˈrɪfɪk/. **1** If you describe something or someone as **terrific**, you are very pleased with them or very impressed by them. *You look terrific, Ann.* **2 Terrific** means very great in amount, degree, or intensity. *All of a sudden there was a terrific bang and a flash of smoke.* ♦ **ter·rifi·cal·ly** /təˈrɪfɪkli/. *She really is terrifically pretty.*

ter·ri·fy /ˈterɪfaɪ/ **terrifies, terrifying, terrified.** If something **terrifies** you, it makes you feel extremely frightened. *The thought of dying slowly and painfully terrified me.* ♦ **ter·ri·fied** *He was terrified of heights.*

ter·ri·fy·ing /ˈterɪfaɪɪŋ/. If something is **terrifying**, it makes you very frightened. *Rabies has been described as one of the most terrifying diseases known to man.* ♦ **ter·ri·fy·ing·ly** *Below was a terrifyingly deep crevasse.*

ter·ri·to·ri·al /ˌterɪˈtɔːriəl/ **territorials. 1 Territorial** means concerned with the ownership of a particular area of land or water. ...*the only republic which has no territorial disputes with the others.* **2** In Britain, the **Territorials** are the members of the **Territorial Army**. **3** If you describe an animal or its behaviour as **territorial**, you mean that it has an area which it regards as its own, and which it defends when other animals try to enter it.

Territorial 'Army. The Territorial Army is a British armed force whose members are not professional soldiers but train as soldiers in their spare time.

territorial 'waters. A country's **territorial waters** are the parts of the sea close to its coast which are recognized by international agreement to be under its control.

ter·ri·to·ry /ˈterɪtri, AM -tɔːri/ **territories. 1 Territory** is land which is controlled by a particular country or ruler. *The government denies that any of its territory is under rebel control.* **2** A **territory** is a country or region that is controlled by another country. *They just want to return to their families in the occupied territories.* **3** You can use **territory** to refer to an area of knowledge or experience. *Even*

on their own familiar territory of trade, the EC's 12 member states have failed to reach agreement.
● **virgin territory**: see **virgin**. **4** An animal's **territory** is an area which it regards as its own and which it defends when other animals try to enter it. N-VAR
5 Territory is land with a particular character. N-UNCOUNT: with supp
...mountainous territory. **6** If you say that something **comes with the territory**, you mean that you accept it as a natural result of the situation you are in. *Doing human rights work is risky business. That comes with the territory.* PHRASE

ter·ror /ˈterə/ **terrors. 1 Terror** is very great fear. *I shook with terror whenever I was about to fly in an aeroplane.* **2 Terror** is violence or the threat of violence, especially when it is used for political reasons. *...the start of a pre-election terror campaign.* ◆◆◇◇◇ N-UNCOUNT   N-UNCOUNT
3 A **terror** is something that makes you very frightened. *As a boy, he had a real terror of facing people.* N-COUNT
4 If something **holds no terrors for** you, you are not at all frightened or worried by it. **5** If someone describes a child as a **terror**, they think that he or she is naughty and difficult to control. **6** ● to **live in terror**: see **live**. ● **reign of terror**: see **reign**. PHRASE   N-COUNT INFORMAL

ter·ror·ise /ˈterəraɪz/. See **terrorize**.

ter·ror·ist /ˈterərɪst/ **terrorists.** A **terrorist** is a person who uses violence in order to achieve political aims; used showing disapproval. *Three were wounded in terrorist attacks.* ♦ **ter·ror·ism** *...indiscriminate acts of terrorism.* ◆◆◇◇◇ N-COUNT [PRAGMATICS]   N-UNCOUNT

ter·ror·ize /ˈterəraɪz/ **terrorizes, terrorizing, terrorized;** also spelled **terrorise** in British English. If someone **terrorizes** you, they keep you in a state of fear by making it seem likely that they will attack you. *...pensioners terrorised by anonymous telephone calls.* ◆◇◇◇◇ VERB: V n V-ed

ter·ry /ˈteri/. **Terry** or **terry cloth** is a type of fabric which has a lot of very small loops covering both sides. It is used especially for making things with towels. N-UNCOUNT

terse /tɜːs/ **terser, tersest.** A **terse** statement or comment is brief and unfriendly. *His tone was terse as he asked the question.* ♦ **terse·ly** *'It's too late,' he said tersely.* ◆◇◇◇◇ ADJ-GRADED   ADV-GRADED: ADV with v

ter·tiary /ˈtɜːʃəri, AM -ʃieri/. **1 Tertiary** means third in order, third in importance, or at a third stage of development. *He must have come to know those philosophers through secondary or tertiary sources.* **2 Tertiary** education is education at university or college level. ADJ FORMAL   ADJ: ADJ n

test /test/ **tests, testing, tested. 1** When you **test** something, you try it, for example by touching it or using it for a short time, in order to find out what it is, what condition it is in, or how well it works. *Either measure the temperature with a bath thermometer or test the water with your wrist.* **2** A **test** is a deliberate action or experiment to find out how well something works. *...the banning of nuclear tests.* **3** If you **test** someone, you ask them questions or tell them to perform certain actions in order to find out how much they know about a subject or how well they are able to do something. *She decided to test herself with a training run in London.* ▶ Also a noun. *Only 922 passed the test.* **4** If you **test** someone, you deliberately make things difficult for them in order to see how they react. *Rudolf was testing me, seeing if I would make him tea, bring him a Coke.* **5** If an event or situation is a **test** of a person or thing, it reveals their qualities or effectiveness. *The test of any civilised society is how it treats its minorities.* **6** If you **are tested** for a particular disease or medical condition, you are examined or undergo various procedures in order to find out whether you have that disease or condition. *Girls in an affected family can also be tested to see if they carry the defective gene.* **7** A medical **test** is an examination of a part of your body in order to check that you are healthy or to find out what is wrong with you. **8** A **test** or a **test match** is a sports match between two international sides, usually at cricket, rugby union, or ◆◆◆◆◆ VERB V n   N-COUNT   VERB: V n V pron-refl   N-COUNT   VERB V n   N-COUNT   VERB: be V-ed for n be V-ed   N-COUNT   N-COUNT BRITISH

rugby league. **9** See also **testing, acid test, breath test, means test, litmus test.**
10 If you **put** something **to the test**, you find out how useful or effective it is by using it. *The Liverpool team are now putting their theory to the test.* **11** If new circumstances or events **put** something **to the test**, they put strain on it and indicate how strong or stable it really is. *Sooner or later, life will put the relationship to the test.* **12** If you say that something **will stand the test of time**, you mean that it is strong or effective enough to last for a very long time. **13** ● to **test the waters**: see **water**. PHRASE   PHRASE   PHRASE

tes·ta·ment /ˈtestəmənt/ **testaments. 1** If one thing is a **testament** to another, it shows that the other thing exists or is true. *The fact that these scandals are now public is testament to the relative openness of America's government.* **2** Someone's **last will and testament** is the most recent will that they have made, especially the last will before they die. **3** See also **New Testament, Old Testament.** ◆◇◇◇◇ N-VAR FORMAL   PHRASE LEGAL

test 'case, test cases. A **test case** is a legal case which becomes an example for deciding other similar cases. ◆◇◇◇◇ N-COUNT

test·er /ˈtestə/ **testers. 1** A **tester** is a person who has been asked to test a particular thing. **2** A **tester** is a machine or device that you use to test whether another machine or device is working properly. ◆◇◇◇◇ N-COUNT   N-COUNT

tes·ti·cle /ˈtestɪkəl/ **testicles.** A man's **testicles** are the two sex glands between his legs that produce sperm. ◆◇◇◇◇ N-COUNT

tes·ti·fy /ˈtestɪfaɪ/ **testifies, testifying, testified. 1** When someone **testifies** in a court of law, they give a statement of what they saw someone do or what they know of a situation, after having promised to tell the truth. *Several eyewitnesses testified that they saw the officers hit Miller in the face... Eva testified to having seen Herndon with his gun on the stairs.* **2** If one thing **testifies** to another, it supports the belief that the second thing is true. *Recent excavations testify to the presence of cultivated inhabitants on the hill during the Arthurian period.* ◆◆◇◇◇ VERB: V V that V to-ing/n   VERB V to n FORMAL

tes·ti·mo·nial /ˌtestɪˈməʊniəl/ **testimonials. 1** A **testimonial** is a written statement about a person's character and abilities, often written by their employer. **2** A **testimonial** is a sports match which is specially arranged so that part of the profit from the tickets sold can be given to a particular player or to a particular player's family. ◆◇◇◇◇ N-COUNT   N-COUNT

tes·ti·mo·ny /ˈtestɪməni, AM -məʊni/ **testimonies. 1** In a court of law, someone's **testimony** is a formal statement that they make about what they saw someone do or what they know of a situation, after having promised to tell the truth. **2** If you say that one thing is **testimony** to another, you mean that it shows clearly that the second thing has a particular quality. *Her living room is also her office, filled with desks, books, papers, a testimony to her dedication to her work.* ◆◆◇◇◇ N-VAR   N-UNCOUNT: also a N

test·ing /ˈtestɪŋ/. **1** A **testing** problem or situation is very difficult to deal with and shows a lot about the character of the person who is dealing with it. *The papers in maths and English are very testing.* **2 Testing** is the activity of testing something or someone in order to find out information. *...product testing and labelling.* ◆◆◇◇◇ ADJ-GRADED   N-UNCOUNT

tes·tis /ˈtestɪs/ **testes** /ˈtestiːz/. A man's **testes** are his **testicles.** N-COUNT MEDICAL

'test match, test matches. A **test match** is the same as a **test.** ◆◇◇◇◇ N-COUNT

tes·tos·ter·one /teˈstɒstərəʊn/. **Testosterone** is a hormone found in higher levels in men and male animals than in females. It is thought to be responsible for the male sexual instinct and for aggression. ◆◇◇◇◇ N-UNCOUNT

'test pilot, test pilots. A **test pilot** is a pilot who flies aircraft of a new design in order to test their performance. ◆◇◇◇◇ N-COUNT

test 'run, test runs. If you give a machine or system a **test run**, you try it to see if it will work properly when it is actually in use. *...a set-back after the failure of an engine in a test run.* N-COUNT

T

'test tube, test tubes; also spelled **test-tube.** A ◆◇◇◇◇ N-COUNT
test tube is a small, narrow, glass container used for
chemical experiments.

,test-tube 'baby, test-tube babies; also spelled N-COUNT
test tube baby. A **test-tube baby** is a baby that develops from an egg which has been removed from
the mother's body, fertilized, and then replaced in
her womb.

tes·ty /'testi/. If someone is **testy**, they easily be- ADJ-GRADED
come impatient or angry. *The board members were*
clearly testy. ♦ **tes·ti·ly** *He reacted testily to reports* ADV-GRADED:
that he'd opposed military involvement. ADV with v

teta·nus /'tetənəs/. **Tetanus** is a serious painful N-UNCOUNT
disease caused by bacteria getting into wounds. It
makes your muscles, especially your jaw muscles,
go stiff.

tetchy /'tetʃi/. If someone is **tetchy**, they are irri- ADJ-GRADED
table and likely to get angry suddenly without an BRITISH,
obvious reason. INFORMAL

teth·er /'teðə/ **tethers, tethering, tethered. 1** If ◆◇◇◇◇
you are at **the end of** your **tether**, you are so wor- PHRASE
ried, tired, and unhappy because of your problems
that you feel you cannot cope. **2** A **tether** is a rope N-COUNT
or chain which is used to tie an animal to a post or
fence so that it can only move around within a
small area. **3** If you **tether** an animal or object to VERB:
something, you attach it there with a rope or chain V n to n,
so that it cannot move very far. V n

Teu·ton·ic /tjuː'tɒnɪk, AM tuː-/. **Teutonic** means ADJ
typical of or relating to German people. *...a master-*
piece of Teutonic engineering.

text /tekst/ **texts. 1** The **text** of a book is the main N-SING:
part of it, rather than the introduction, pictures, theN
notes, or index. **2** Text is any written material. A N-UNCOUNT
CD-ROM can store more than 250,000 pages of typed
text. **3** The **text** of a speech, broadcast, or recording N-COUNT
is a written copy of it. **4** A **text** is a book or other N-COUNT
piece of writing, especially one connected with science or education. *His early plays are set texts in*
universities.

text·book /'tekstbʊk/ **textbooks;** also spelled ◆◇◇◇◇
text book. **1** A **textbook** is a book containing facts N-COUNT
about a particular subject that is used by people
studying that subject. **2** If you say that something is ADJ: ADJ n
a **textbook** case or example, you are emphasizing PRAGMATICS
that it is a good or typical example of something.
The house is a textbook example of medieval domes-
tic architecture.

tex·tile /'tekstaɪl/ **textiles. 1** Textiles are types of ◆◆◇◇◇
cloth or fabric. **2** Textiles are the industries con- N-COUNT
cerned with the manufacture of cloth. *75,000 jobs* N-PLURAL:
will be lost in textiles and clothing. no det

tex·tu·al /'tekstʃʊəl/. **Textual** means relating to ADJ: ADJ n
written texts, especially literary texts. *...close textual*
analysis of Shakespeare.

tex·ture /'tekstʃə/ **textures.** The **texture** of some- ◆◆◇◇◇
thing is the way that it feels when you touch it, for N-VAR
example how smooth, rough, firm, or crumbly it is.
Her skin is pale, the texture of fine wax. ♦ **-textured** COMB
This kind of mixer produces light, silky, even-
textured batters.

tex·tured /'tekstʃəd/. A **textured** surface is not ◆◇◇◇◇
smooth, but has a particular texture, for example, ADJ
rough or fluffy.

-th /-θ/. **-th** is found at the end of ordinal numbers, SUFFIX
except those formed from numbers ending in 1, 2,
or 3. *...10th May, 1990. ...my twenty-fifth birthday.*

tha·lido·mide /θəˌlɪdə'maɪd/. **1** Thalidomide is a N-UNCOUNT
tranquilliser drug which used to be given to pregnant women. It is no longer used because it was
found to cause abnormalities in their babies. **2** Tha- ADJ: ADJ n
lidomide is used to describe someone whose body
is deformed because their mother took thalidomide
when she was pregnant. *...thalidomide children.*

than /ðən, STRONG ðæn/. **1** You use **than** after a ◆◆◆◆◆
comparative adjective or adverb in order to link two PREP
parts of a comparison. *The radio only weighs a few*
ounces and is smaller than a cigarette packet... In-
dian skins age far more slowly than American or
Italian ones. ► Also a conjunction. *He could have* CONJ:

helped her more than he did. **2** You use **than** when compar CONJ
you are stating a number, quantity, or value ap- cl
proximately by saying that it is above or below an- PREP
other number, quantity, or value. *They talked on the*
phone for more than an hour... Semi-skimmed milk
contains less than half the fat of whole milk. **3** You CONJ
use **than** in order to link two parts of a contrast, for
example in order to state a preference. *The arrange-*
ment was more a formality than a genuine partner-
ship... I would rather dance than do anything else.
4 ● **easier said than done:** see **easy.** ● **less than:** see
less. ● **more than:** see **more.** ● **more often than**
not: see **often.** ● **other than:** see **other.** ● **rather**
than: see **rather.**

thank /θæŋk/ **thanks, thanking, thanked.** ◆◆◆◆◆
1 You use **thank you** or, informally, **thanks** to ex- CONVENTION
press your gratitude or acknowledgement when PRAGMATICS
someone does something for you or gives you
something. *Thank you very much for your call...*
Thanks for the information. **2** You use **thank you** CONVENTION
or, informally, **thanks** after a negative in order to PRAGMATICS
politely refuse something that has been offered to
you. *'Would you like a cigarette?'—'No thank you.'...*
'A whisky?'—'I'd better not, thanks.' **3** You can use CONVENTION
thank you to say firmly that you do not want PRAGMATICS
someone's help or to tell them that you do not like
the way they are behaving towards you. *I can stir*
my own tea, thank you.

4 When you **thank** someone, you express your grati- VERB: V n
tude to them for something. *I thanked them for their* V n for n
long and loyal service. ► Also a plural noun. *They ac-* N-PLURAL
cepted their certificates with words of thanks. **5** If you PHRASE
say that you **have** someone **to thank** for something,
you mean that you are grateful to them because they
caused it to happen. *I have her to thank for my life.*
6 You say **'Thank God', 'Thank Goodness',** or **'Thank** PHRASE
heavens' when you are very relieved about some- PRAGMATICS
thing. *Thank heavens we have you here.*
7 If something happens **thanks to** someone or some- PHRASE
thing, they are responsible for it or caused it to happen. *Thanks to recent research, effective treatments are*
available. **8** If you say that something happened **no** PHRASE
thanks to someone, you mean that they did not help
it to happen, or that it happened in spite of them. *It is*
no thanks to you people were not killed.
9 See also **thankyou.** ● **to thank** your **lucky stars:** see
star.

thank·ful /'θæŋkful/. When you are **thankful,** you ◆◇◇◇◇
are very happy and relieved that something has ADJ-GRADED
happened. *I'm just thankful that I've got a job.*
♦ **thank·ful·ly** *Simon thankfully slipped off his uni-* ADV-GRADED:
form and relaxed. ADV with v

thank·ful·ly /'θæŋkfuli/. You use **thankfully** to ex- ADV:
press approval or relief about a statement that you ADV with cl/
are making. *Thankfully, she was not injured.* group
PRAGMATICS

thank·less /'θæŋkləs/. If you describe something as ADJ-GRADED
a **thankless** task, you mean that it is hard work and
brings very few rewards.

thanks·giving /ˌθæŋks'gɪvɪŋ/. **1** Thanksgiving is ◆◇◇◇◇
the giving of thanks to God, especially in a religious N-UNCOUNT
ceremony. **2** In the United States, **Thanksgiving** or N-UNCOUNT
Thanksgiving Day is a public holiday on the fourth
Thursday in November. It was originally a day when
people thanked God for the harvest.

thank·you /'θæŋkjuː/ **thankyous;** also spelled N-COUNT
thank-you. A **thankyou** is a gift or message intended to thank someone for something. *...a thank-you*
note. ● See also **thank.**

that /ðæt/. **1** You use **that** to refer to an idea ◆◆◆◆◆
or situation expressed in a previous sentence. *They* PRON
said you particularly wanted to talk to me. Why was PRAGMATICS
that?... I've never been to Paris.'—'That's a pity.'
► Also a determiner. *I try to recreate history as it* DET
was. For that reason, I research collections of old
photos. **2** When you have been talking about a par- DET
ticular period of time, you use **that** to indicate that
you are still referring to the same period. You use
expressions such as **that morning** or **that afternoon**
to indicate that you are referring to an earlier period

of the same day. *She returned to work later that week... He could see them out in the field, doing much the same as they had done that morning.* **3** You use **that is** to indicate that you are about to express the same idea more clearly or precisely. *I am a disappointing, though generally dutiful, student. That is, I do as I'm told.* **4** You use **that's it** to express agreement, approval, or confirmation of what has just been said or done. *'You got married, right?'—'Yeah, that's it.'* **5** You use **that** in expressions such as **that of** and **that which** to introduce information or comparisons relating to a noun already mentioned. *One of the skills you want your children to learn is that of sharing with other people... The situation is much more manageable than that which exists in the Baltic states.* **6** You use **that** to introduce a person or thing which you are going to give information about. *I chose that course which I considered right.* ▶ **That which** is used to introduce a subject in very general terms. *Too much time is spent worrying over that which one can't change.* **7** You use **that** when you are referring to someone or something which is a distance away from you, especially when you indicate or point to them. When there are two things near you, **that** refers to the more distant one. *Where did you get that hat?... You see that man over there, that man who has just walked into the room?* ▶ Also a pronoun. *What's that you're writing?... That looks heavy. May I carry it for you?* **8** You use **that** when you are identifying someone or asking about their identity. *That's John Gibb, operations chief for New York Emergency Management... I answered the phone and this voice went, 'Hello? Is that Alison?'* **9** You can use **that** when you expect your hearer to know what or who you are referring to, without needing to identify the particular person or thing fully. *Did you get that cheque I sent?... That idiot porter again knocked on my door!* ▶ Also a pronoun. *That was a good year, wasn't it?* **10** You use **and all that** to refer generally to everything else which is associated with what you have just mentioned. *You'll be a star. You'll win Oscars, and write your autobiography and all that.* **11** You use **that's it** to indicate that nothing more needs to be done or that the end has been reached. *When he left the office, that was it, the workday was over.* **12** You use **that's that** to say there is nothing more to be done or said about a particular matter. *I'm staying here, and that's that.* **13** You use **just like that** to emphasize that something happens or is done immediately or in a very simple way, often without much thought or discussion. *You mean he sent you back just like that?* **14** If something is not **that** bad, funny, or expensive for example, it is not as bad, funny, or expensive as it might be or as has been suggested. *It isn't that funny... Do I look that stupid?* **15** You use **at that** after a statement which modifies or emphasizes what you have just said. *Success never seems to come but through hard work, often physically demanding work at that.* **16** See also **those**. ● **like that**: see **like**. ● **this and that**: see **this**. ● **this, that, and the other**: see **this**.

PHRASE PRAGMATICS

CONVENTION PRAGMATICS

PRON FORMAL

DET PRAGMATICS FORMAL

PRON

DET

PRON

PRON

DET SPOKEN

PRON

PHRASE INFORMAL

PHRASE

PHRASE SPOKEN

PHRASE INFORMAL

ADV

PHRASE PRAGMATICS

that 2 conjunction and relative pronoun uses

that /ðət, STRONG ðæt/. **1** You can use **that** after many verbs, adjectives, nouns, and expressions to introduce a clause in which you report what someone's words or feelings relate to. *He called her up one day and said that he and his wife were coming to New York... We were worried that she was going to die... I welcome the news that attacks on women on the railways are 19 per cent down.* **2** You use **that** after 'it' and a link verb and an adjective to comment on a situation or fact. *It's obvious that you need more time... It's extraordinary that he left without making a public statement.* **3** You use **that** immediately after a noun to introduce a clause which gives more information about the noun. *...a car that won't start. ...things that don't concern you. ...a man that Maddock has known for nearly 20 years.*

♦♦♦♦♦ CONJ

CONJ: *it*v-link adj CONJ cl

PRON-REL

4 You use **that** after expressions with 'so' and 'such' in order to introduce the result or effect of something. *She came towards me so quickly that she knocked a chair over... It made such a revolting brew that it was worse than drinking no tea at all.*

CONJ: *so/such* group CONJ cl

thatch /θætʃ/ **thatches**. **1** A **thatch** or a **thatch roof** is a roof made from straw or reeds. ♦ **thatched** *...a thatched cottage.* **2** **Thatch** or **thatching** is straw or reeds used to make a roof. **3** You can refer to someone's hair as their **thatch** of hair, especially when it is very thick and untidy.

♦◇◇◇◇ N-COUNT

ADJ N-UNCOUNT

N-SING

that's /ðæts/. **That's** is a spoken form of 'that is'.

thaw /θɔː/ **thaws, thawing, thawed**. **1** When ice, snow, or something frozen **thaws**, it melts. **2** A **thaw** is a period of warmer weather when snow and ice melt, often at the end of winter. **3** When you **thaw** frozen food, you leave it in a place where it can reach room temperature so that it is ready for use. *Always thaw pastry thoroughly.* **4** If something **thaws** relations between people, they become friendly again after a period of tension. *It took up to Christmas for political relations to thaw.* ▶ Also a noun. *...the thaw in relations between East and West.*

♦◇◇◇◇ VERB: V N-COUNT

V n Also V

V-ERG: V n V

N-SING

thaw out. If you are very cold and you **thaw out**, you begin to feel warmer. *Bob and Louise had prepared a sumptuous meal to thaw out our bodies.*

PHRASAL VB ERG: V P V P noun

the. Usually pronounced /ðə/ before a consonant and /ði/ before a vowel, but pronounced /ðiː/ when you are emphasizing it. **The** is the definite article. It is used at the beginning of noun groups.

♦♦♦♦♦

1 You use **the** at the beginning of noun groups to refer to someone or something that you have already mentioned or identified, or when it is clear which particular thing or person you are referring to. *A kerosene lamp stood on a table. At the table sat two men... Six of the 38 people were Soviet citizens.* **2** You use **the** in front of an abstract or uncountable noun followed by 'of' then another noun. *...a slight increase in the consumption of meat.* **3** You use **the** instead of a possessive determiner when you are talking about a part of someone's body. *I patted him on the head.* **4** You use **the** in front of some nouns that refer to something that is part of our general experience of the world. *It's always hard to speculate about the future... Amy sat outside in the sun.* **5** You use **the** in front of nouns that refer to people, things, services, or institutions that are associated with everyday life. *Who was that on the phone?... They have a generator when the electricity fails... Four executive journalists were detained for questioning by the police.* **6** You use **the** in front of a singular noun when you want to make a general statement about things or people of that type. *An area in which the computer has made considerable strides in recent years is in playing chess... After dogs, the horse has had the closest relationship with man.* **7** You use **the** with the name of a musical instrument when you are talking about someone's ability to play the instrument. *Did you play the piano as a child?* **8** You use **the** in front of an adjective when you are referring to a particular thing that is described by that adjective. *He's wishing for the impossible... You might like to read the enclosed.* **9** You use **the** with words such as 'rich', 'poor', and 'unemployed' to refer to all people of a particular type. *...care for the elderly, the mentally handicapped and the disabled.* **10** You use **the** with nationality adjectives and nouns to talk about all the people who live in a country. *The Japanese, Americans, and even the French and Germans, judge economic policies by results.* **11** You use **the** with some titles and place-names. *...the DAILY EXPRESS. ...the Albert Hall. ...the Prime Minister.* **12** If you want to refer to a whole family or a married couple, you can make their surname into a plural and use **the** in front of it. *The Taylors decided that they would employ an architect to do the work.* **13** You use **the** in front of ordinal numbers. *The meeting should take place on the fifth of May... FC Liege have won the Belgian Cup for the first time.* **14** You use **the** in front of numbers when they refer to decades.

DET

DET

DET

DET

DET

DET

DET

DET

DET

DET

DET

DET

DET

T

...how bad things were in the thirties. **15 The** is used in rates, prices, and measurements to refer to a single unit, which is related or compared to a number of units of a different kind. *New Japanese cars averaged 13 km to the litre in 1981... Analysts predicted that the exchange rate would soon be $2 to the pound.* DET

16 You use **the** in front of superlative adjectives and adverbs. *Brisk daily walks are still the best exercise... They competed to agree with their master the most forcefully and laugh at his jokes the loudest.* **17** You use **the** in front of each of two comparative adjectives or adverbs when you are describing how one amount or quality changes in relation to another. *The more confidence you build up in yourself, the greater are your chances of success.* **18** You use **the** to indicate that you have enough of the thing mentioned for a particular purpose. *She may not have the money to maintain or restore her property... Carl couldn't even raise the energy for a smile.* DET

19 You use **the** to emphasize that something or someone is the most famous, important, or best of their kind. You often show this emphasis in the way you say or write the word. *Camden Market is the place to be on a Saturday... Surely you don't mean THE K Records?* DET PRAGMATICS

thea·tre /ˈθiːətə/ **theatres;** spelled **theater** in American English. **1** A **theatre** is a building with a stage in it, in which plays, shows, and other performances take place. *We went to the theatre. ...the Grand Theatre.* **2** You can refer to work in theatres such as acting or writing plays as **the theatre**. *...a career in the theatre.* **3** Theatre is entertainment involving the performance of plays. *Companies across the country are beginning to show a healthy interest in theatre for children.* **4** A **theater** or a **movie theater** is a place where people go to watch films. The British term is **cinema**. **5** In a hospital, a **theatre** is a room where surgeons carry out operations. *She is back from theatre and her condition is comfortable.* **6** A **theatre** of war is an area of the world in which a war is taking place. ◆◆◆◇ N-COUNT / N-SING: theN / N-UNCOUNT / N-COUNT AMERICAN / N-COUNT: also prep N / N-COUNT

'theatre-goer, theatre-goers; spelled **theatergoer** in American English. **Theatre-goers** are people who go to the theatre to see plays. *I'm a keen theatre-goer.* N-COUNT

the·at·ri·cal /θiˈætrɪkəl/ **theatricals. 1** Theatrical means relating to the theatre. *...the most outstanding British theatrical performances of the year.* ◆ **the·at·ri·cal·ly** /θiˈætrɪkli/. *...his ability to animate ideas theatrically.* **2** Theatrical behaviour is deliberately exaggerated and unnatural. *In a theatrical gesture Glass clamped his hand over his eyes.* ◆ **the·at·ri·cal·ity** /θi,ætrɪˈkælti/. *There was no theatricality in her long silence.* ◆ **theatrically** He looked theatrically at his watch. **3** Theatrical can be used to describe something that is grand and dramatic, as if it is part of a performance in a theatre. *Religious architecture from the Romanesque to the Baroque was a highly theatrical artifice.* ◆ **theatricality** *...the theatricality of a wedding.* **4** Theatricals are performances of plays and other entertainments, especially when they are done by amateur actors. ◆◆◇◇ ADJ: ADJ n / ADV / ADJ-GRADED / N-UNCOUNT / ADV / ADJ-GRADED / N-UNCOUNT / N-PLURAL DATED

thee /ðiː/. Thee is an old-fashioned or religious word for 'you' when you are talking to only one person. It is used as the object of a verb or preposition. *I miss thee, beloved father.* PRON

theft /θeft/ **thefts.** Theft is the crime of stealing. *Art theft is now part of organised crime. ...the theft of classified documents from a car.* ◆◆◇◇ N-VAR

their /ðeə/. Their is the third person plural possessive determiner. ◆◆◆◆◆

1 You use **their** to indicate that something belongs or relates to the group of people, animals, or things that you are talking about. *Janis and Kurt have announced their engagement... Horses were poking their heads over their stall doors. ...as the trees shed their leaves.* DET-POSS **2** You use **their** instead of 'his or her' to indicate that something belongs or relates to a person without saying whether that person is a man or a woman. Some DET-POSS

people think this use is incorrect. *...anyone looking for income from their investments.*

theirs /ðeəz/. Theirs is the third person plural possessive pronoun. ◆◆◇◇

1 You use **theirs** to indicate that something belongs or relates to the group of people, animals, or things that you are talking about. *...at the table next to theirs... Theirs had been a happy and satisfactory marriage.* **2** You use **theirs** instead of 'his or hers' to indicate that something belongs or relates to a person without saying whether that person is a man or a woman. Some people think this use is incorrect. *He would leave the trailer unlocked. If there was something inside someone wanted, it would be theirs for the taking.* PRON-POSS / PRON-POSS

them /ðəm, STRONG ðem/. Them is a third person plural pronoun. **Them** is used as the object of a verb or preposition. ◆◆◆◆◆

1 You use **them** to refer to a group of people, animals, or things. *The Beatles – I never get tired of listening to them... She let the dogs into the house and fed them... His dark socks, I could see, had a stripe on them.* **2** You use **them** instead of 'him or her' to refer to a person without saying whether that person is a man or a woman. Some people think this use is incorrect. *It takes great courage to face your child and tell them the truth.* PRON / PRON

the·mat·ic /θiˈmætɪk/. Thematic means concerned with the subject or theme of something, or with themes and topics in general. *...assembling this material into thematic groups.* ◆ **the·mati·cal·ly** /θiˈmætɪkli/. *...a thematically-linked threesome of songs.* ADJ-GRADED FORMAL / ADV

theme /θiːm/ **themes. 1** A **theme** in a piece of writing, a talk, a discussion, or a work of art is an important idea or subject that runs through it. *The novel's central theme is the perennial conflict between men and women... The need to strengthen the family has been a recurrent theme for the Prime Minister.* **2** A **theme** is a short simple tune on which a piece of music is based. *...variations on themes from Mozart's The Magic Flute.* **3** Theme music is played at the beginning and end of a film or of a television or radio programme. *...the theme from Dr Zhivago... The BBC used Vangelis's Chariots of Fire as its Olympic theme tune.* ◆◆◆◇ N-COUNT / N-COUNT / N-COUNT

themed /θiːmd/. A **themed** place or event has been built or created so that it reflects a particular historical time, way of life, or well-known story. *...themed restaurants, bars, and nightclubs.* ADJ BRITISH

'theme park, theme parks. A **theme park** is a large outdoor area where people pay to go to enjoy themselves. All the different attractions in a theme park are usually based on the same idea or theme. ◆◇◇◇ N-COUNT

them·self /ðəmˈself/. Themself is sometimes used instead of 'themselves' when it clearly refers to a singular subject. Some people consider this use to be incorrect. *No one perceived themself to be in a position to hire such a man.* PRON-REFL

them·selves /ðəmˈselvz/. Themselves is the third person plural reflexive pronoun. ◆◆◆◆◆

1 You use **themselves** to refer to people, animals, or things when the object of a verb or preposition refers to the same people or things as the subject of the verb. *They all seemed to be enjoying themselves... The men talked amongst themselves.* **2** You use **themselves** to emphasize the people or things that you are referring to. **Themselves** is also sometimes used instead of 'them' as the object of a verb or preposition. *The waters around the islands have value as fishing grounds, but the islands themselves are largely uninhabitable... Care-givers get a chance to socialize with men and women who are in the same position as themselves.* **3** You use **themselves** instead of 'himself or herself' to refer back to the person who is the subject of sentence without saying whether it is a man or a woman. Some people think this use is incorrect. *What can a patient with emphysema do to help themselves?... After all, what more can anyone be than themselves?* PRON-REFL: v PRON, prep PRON / PRON-REFL PRAGMATICS / PRON-REFL

then /ðen/. **1 Then** means at a particular time in the past or in the future. *He wanted to have a source of income after his retirement; until then, he wouldn't require additional money... I spent years on the dole trying to get bands together and I never worried about money then.* **2 Then** is used when you refer to something which was true at a particular time in the past but is not true now. *...the Race Relations Act of 1976 (enacted by the then Labour Government).* ▶ Also an adverb. *Roberts was then a newly married man.* **3** You use **then** to say that one thing happens after another, or is after another on a list. *New mothers have been observed to touch the feet and hands first, then the body, and then the baby's face.* **4** You use **then** in conversation to indicate that what you are about to say follows logically in some way from what has just been said or implied. *'I got a load of money out of them.'—'So you're okay, then.'* **5** You use **then** at the end of a topic or at the end of a conversation. *He stood up. 'That's settled then.'* **6** You use **then** with words like 'now', 'well', and 'okay', to introduce a new topic or a new point of view. *Well then, I'll put the kettle on.* **7** You use **then** to introduce a summary of what you have said or the conclusions that you are drawing from it. *By 1931, then, France alone in Europe was a country of massive immigration.* **8** You use **then** to introduce the second part of a sentence which begins with 'if'. The first part of the sentence describes a possible situation, and **then** introduces the result of the situation. *If the answer is 'yes', then we must decide on an appropriate course of action.* **9** You use **then** at the beginning of a sentence or after 'and' or 'but' to introduce a comment or an extra piece of information. *He sounded sincere, but then, he always did.* **10** • **now and then**: see **now**. • **there and then**: see **there**.

♦♦♦♦♦   ADV: ADV with cl   ADJ: ADJ n   ADV: ADV group ADV: ADV cl/group, ADV before v   ADV: cl/group ADV   ADV: cl/group ADV   ADV: adv ADV   PRAGMATICS   ADV: ADV with cl PRAGMATICS WRITTEN   ADV: ADV cl   ADV: ADV cl PRAGMATICS

thence /ðens/. **1 Thence** means from a particular place, especially when you are giving directions about how to get somewhere. *The mosaics were sent to Munich, and thence to Geneva.* **2 Thence** is used to say that something changes from one state or condition to another. *...the conversion of sunlight into heat and thence into electricity.*

ADV FORMAL   ADV FORMAL

thence·forth /ˌðensˈfɔːθ/. **Thenceforth** means from a particular time in the past that you have mentioned onwards. *My life was totally different thenceforth.*

ADV: ADV with cl FORMAL

the·oc·ra·cy /θiˈɒkrəsi/ **theocracies.** A **theocracy** is a society which is ruled by priests who represent a god.

N-VAR TECHNICAL

theo·lo·gian /ˌθiːəˈləʊdʒən/ **theologians.** A **theologian** is someone who studies the nature of God, religion, and religious beliefs.

♦◇◇◇◇ N-COUNT

the·ol·ogy /θiˈɒlədʒi/ **theologies. 1 Theology** is the study of the nature of God and of religion and religious beliefs. **♦ theo·logi·cal** /ˌθiːəˈlɒdʒɪkəl/. *...theological books.* **2** A **theology** is a particular set of religious beliefs and ideas.

♦◇◇◇◇ N-UNCOUNT   ADJ   N-COUNT

theo·rem /ˈθiːərəm/ **theorems.** A **theorem** is a statement in mathematics or logic that can be proved to be true by reasoning.

N-COUNT

theo·reti·cal /ˌθiːəˈretɪkəl/. **1** A **theoretical** study or explanation is based on or uses the ideas and abstract principles that relate to a subject, rather than the practical aspects or uses of it. **2** If you describe a situation as **theoretical**, you mean that although it is supposed to be true or to exist in the way stated, it may not in fact be true or exist in that way. *These fears are purely theoretical.* **♦ theo·reti·cal·ly** /ˌθiːəˈretɪkəli/. *Theoretically, the price is supposed to be marked on the shelf.*

♦♦◇◇◇ ADJ   ADJ   ADV: ADV with cl/group

theo·reti·cian /ˌθɪərəˈtɪʃən/ **theoreticians.** A **theoretician** is the same as a **theorist**.

N-COUNT

theo·rist /ˈθiːərɪst/ **theorists.** A **theorist** is someone who develops a set of abstract ideas about a particular subject in order to explain it.

♦◇◇◇◇ N-COUNT

theo·rize /ˈθiːəraɪz/ **theorizes, theorizing, theorized;** also spelled **theorise** in British English. If you **theorize** that something is true or **theorize**

♦◇◇◇◇ VERB: V that V about n

about it, you develop a set of abstract ideas about something in order to explain it. *By studying the way people behave, we can theorize about what is going on in their mind.* **♦ theo·riz·ing** *This was no time for theorizing.*

Also V   N-UNCOUNT

theo·ry /ˈθɪəri/ **theories. 1** A **theory** is a formal idea or set of ideas that is intended to explain something. *Marx produced a new theory about historical change based upon conflict between competing groups.* **2** If you have a **theory** about something, you have your own opinion about it which you cannot prove but which you think is true. *There was a theory that he wanted to marry her.* **3** The **theory** of a particular subject or skill is the set of rules and principles that form the basis of it. *...graduates who are well-trained in both the theory and practice of statistics.* **4** You use **in theory** to say that although something is supposed to be true or to happen in the way stated, it may not in fact be true or happen in that way. *A school dental service exists in theory.*

♦♦♦♦◇ N-VAR   N-COUNT   N-UNCOUNT   PHRASE

thera·peu·tic /ˌθerəˈpjuːtɪk/. **1** If something is **therapeutic**, it helps you to relax or to feel better about things, especially about a situation that made you unhappy. **2 Therapeutic** treatment is designed to treat a disease or to improve a person's health, rather than to prevent a disease or ill-health. *...therapeutic drugs.*

♦◇◇◇◇ ADJ-GRADED   ADJ MEDICAL

thera·pist /ˈθerəpɪst/ **therapists.** A **therapist** is a person who is skilled in a particular type of therapy.

♦♦◇◇◇ N-COUNT

thera·py /ˈθerəpi/ **therapies. 1 Therapy** is the treatment of someone with mental or physical illness without the use of drugs or operations. **2** A **therapy** is a particular treatment of someone with a particular illness. *...conventional drug therapy.*

♦♦◇◇◇ N-UNCOUNT   N-VAR: with supp MEDICAL

there. Pronounced /ðə, STRONG ðeə/ for meanings 1 and 2, and /ðeə/ for meanings 3 to 19. **1 There** is used as the subject of the verb 'be' to say that something exists or does not exist, or to draw attention to it. *Are there some countries that have been able to tackle these problems successfully?... There's no way we can afford to buy a house.* **2** You use **there** in front of certain verbs when you are saying that something exists, develops, or can be seen. Whether the verb is singular or plural depends on the noun which follows the verb. *There remains considerable doubt over when the intended high-speed rail link will be complete... There appeared no imminent danger.* **3** If something is **there**, it exists or is available. *The group of old buildings on the corner by the main road is still there today... The book is there for people to read and make up their own mind.* **4** You use **there** to refer to a place which has already been mentioned. *What if Spain reacts to the similar economic pressures which are appearing over there?* **5** You use **there** to indicate a place that you are pointing to or looking at, in order to draw someone's attention to it. *There she is on the left up there... The toilets are over there, dear.* **6** You use **there** when speaking on the telephone to ask if someone is available to speak to you. *Hello, is Gordon there please?* **7** You use **there** in expressions such as **there he was** or **there we were** to summarize part of a story or to slow a story down for dramatic effect. *So there we were with Amy and she was driving us crazy.* **8** You use **there** to refer to a point that someone has made in a conversation. *I think you're right there John.* **9** You use **there** to refer to a stage that has been reached in an activity or process. *We are making further investigations and will take the matter from there.* **10** You use **there** to indicate that something has reached a point or level which is completely successful. *Life has not yet returned to normal but we are getting there.* **11** You use **there** in expressions such as **there you go** or **there we are** when accepting that an unsatisfactory situation cannot be changed. *It's the wages that count. Not over-generous, but there you are.* **12** You can use **there** in expressions such as **there you go** and **there we are** when emphasizing that something proves that you were right. *'There you are,*

♦♦♦♦♦ PRON   PRON   ADV: be ADV   ADV: be ADV, ADV with v, n ADV   ADV: ADV with be, ADV after v   ADV: ADV with be   ADV: ADV cl PRAGMATICS SPOKEN   ADV: ADV after v   ADV: ADV with cl   ADV: be ADV, ADV after v   ADV: ADV cl SPOKEN   ADV: ADV cl PRAGMATICS SPOKEN

T

you see!' she exclaimed. 'I knew you'd say that!' **13** You use **there again** to introduce an extra piece of information which either contradicts what has been said or gives an alternative to it. *I mean small cars are the answer surely. Or there again a good system of public transport.* **14** Phrases such as **there** you **go again**, are used to show annoyance at someone who is repeating something that has annoyed you in the past. *'There you go again, upsetting the child!' said Shirley.* **15** You can add **so there** to what you are saying to show that you will not change your mind about a decision you have made, even though the person you are talking to disagrees with you. *'Take That' are the best group in the whole world. So there.* **16** If something happens **there and then** or **then and there**, it happens immediately. **17 There** is used after 'hello' or 'hi' when you are greeting someone. *Oh, hi there. You must be Sidney.* **18** You say **there there** to someone who is very upset, especially a small child, in order to comfort them. *'There, there,' said Mum. 'You've been having a really bad dream.'* **19** You say **there you are** or **there you go** when you are offering something to someone. *There you are, Lennie, you take the nice biscuit.*

there·abouts /ˌðeərəˈbaʊts/. You add **or there-abouts** after a number or date to indicate that it is approximate. *Her age was forty-eight or thereabouts.*

there·after /ˌðeərˈɑːftə, -ˈæftə/. **Thereafter** means after the event or date mentioned. *Inflation will fall and thereafter so will interest rates.*

there·by /ˌðeəˈbaɪ/. You use **thereby** to introduce an important result or consequence of the event or action you have just mentioned. *Our bodies can sweat, thereby losing heat by evaporation.*

there·fore /ˈðeəfɔː/. You use **therefore** to introduce a logical result or conclusion. *Muscle cells need lots of fuel and therefore burn lots of calories.*

there·in /ˌðeərˈɪn/. **1 Therein** means contained in the place that has been mentioned. *By burning tree branches, pine needles, and pine cones, many not only warm their houses but improve the smell therein.* **2 Therein** means relating to something that has just been mentioned. *Afternoon groups relate to the specific addictions and problems therein.* **3** When you say **therein lies** a situation or problem, you mean that an existing situation has caused that situation or problem. *Santa Maria di Castellabate is barely mentioned in guidebooks; therein lies its charm.*

there·of /ðeərˈɒv/. **Thereof** is used after a noun to relate that noun to a situation or thing that you have just mentioned. *...a charge of £2 per hour or part thereof.*

there·on /ˌðeərˈɒn/. **1 Thereon** means on the object or surface just mentioned. *There was a card on each door with a guest's name inscribed thereon.* **2 There-on** can be used to refer back to a thing that has previously been mentioned to show that the word just used relates to that thing. *You will, in addition, pay to the Bank any losses, costs, expenses or legal fees (including VAT thereon).*

there·upon /ˌðeərəˈpɒn/. **Thereupon** means happening immediately after something else has happened and usually as a result of it. *Some months ago angry demonstrators mounted a noisy demonstration beneath his window. His neighbours thereupon insisted upon more security.*

therm /θɜːm/ **therms**. A **therm** is a measurement of heat.

ther·mal /ˈθɜːml/ **thermals**. **1 Thermal** means relating to or caused by heat or by changes in temperature. *...thermal power stations.* **2 Thermal** streams or baths contain water which is naturally hot or warm. **3 Thermal** clothes are specially designed to keep you warm in cold weather. ▶ **Thermals** are thermal clothes. **4** A **thermal** is a movement of rising warm air. *Birds use thermals to lift them through the air.*

thermo /ˈθɜːməʊ/. **Thermo** means using or relating to heat. *The main thermo power station in the area*

has been damaged. ▶ Also a combining form. *...the dangers of thermo-nuclear war.* ▶ Also combines to form nouns. *...mineral-reinforced thermo-plastic.*

ther·mo·dy·nam·ics /ˌθɜːməʊdaɪˈnæmɪks/; the form **thermodynamic** is used as a modifier. **Thermodynamics** is the branch of physics that is concerned with the relationship between heat and other forms of energy.

ther·mom·eter /θəˈmɒmɪtə/ **thermometers**. A **thermometer** is an instrument for measuring temperature. It usually consists of a narrow glass tube containing a thin column of mercury which rises and falls as the temperature rises and falls.

ther·mo·nu·clear /ˌθɜːməʊˈnjuːklɪə, AM -ˈnuːk-/; also spelled **thermo-nuclear**. A **thermonuclear** weapon or device is one which uses the high temperatures that are generated in nuclear fission to detonate it.

ther·mo·plas·tic /ˈθɜːməʊplæstɪk/ **thermoplastics**. **Thermoplastic** materials are types of plastic which become soft when they are heated and hard when they cool down.

Ther·mos /ˈθɜːmɒs/ **Thermoses**. A **Thermos** or a **Thermos flask** is a container which is used to keep hot drinks hot or cold drinks cold. It has two thin silvery glass walls with a vacuum between them. **Thermos** is a trademark.

ther·mo·stat /ˈθɜːməstæt/ **thermostats**. A **thermostat** is a device that switches a system or motor on or off according to the temperature.

the·sau·rus /θɪˈsɔːrəs/ **thesauruses**. A **thesaurus** is a reference book in which words with similar meanings are grouped together.

these /ðiːz/. **1** You use **these** at the beginning of noun groups to refer to someone or something that you have already mentioned or identified. *Switch to an interest-paying current account and stay in credit. Most banks and larger building societies now offer these accounts.* ▶ Also a pronoun. *AIDS kills mostly the young population of a nation. These are the people who contribute most to a country's economic development.* **2** You use **these** to introduce people or things that you are going to talk about. *If you're converting your loft, these addresses will be useful.* ▶ Also a pronoun. *Look after yourself properly while you are pregnant. These are some of the things you can do for yourself.* **3** People use **these** to introduce people or things into a story. *I was on my own and these fellows came along towards me.* **4** You use **these** when you are identifying someone or asking about their identity. *These are my children.* **5** You use **these** to refer to people or things that are near you, especially when you touch them or point to them. *These scissors are awfully heavy.* ▶ Also a pronoun. *These are the people who are doing our loft conversion for us.* **6** You use **these** when you refer to something which you expect the hearer to know about or when you are checking that you are both thinking of the same person or thing. *You know these funny cigarettes I smoke?* **7** You use **these** in the expression **these days** to mean 'at the present time'. *Living in Bootham these days can be depressing.*

the·sis /ˈθiːsɪs/ **theses** /ˈθiːsiːz/. **1** A **thesis** is an idea or theory that is expressed as a statement and is discussed in a logical way. *...the thesis that computers can be programmed to do anything which a human mind does.* **2** A **thesis** is a long piece of writing based on your own ideas and research that you do as part of a university degree, especially a PhD.

thes·pian /ˈθespɪən/ **thespians**. A **thespian** is an actor or actress. *...her thespian career.*

they /ðeɪ/. **They** is a third person plural pronoun. **They** is used as the subject of a verb. **1** You use **they** to refer to a group of people, animals, or things. *The two men were far more alike than they would ever admit.* **2** You use **they** instead of 'he or she' to refer to a person without saying whether that person is a man or a woman. Some people think this use is incorrect. *The teacher is not responsible for the*

student's success or failure. They are only there to help the student learn. **3** You also use **they** in expressions such as 'they say' or 'they call it' to refer vaguely to people in general when you are making general statements about what people say, think, or do. *They say there's plenty of opportunities out there.*   PRON

they'd /ðeɪd/. **1 They'd** is a spoken form of 'they had', especially when 'had' is an auxiliary verb. *They'd both lived in this road all their lives.* **2 They'd** is a spoken form of 'they would'. *He agreed that they'd visit her after they stopped at Jan's for coffee.*

they'll /ðeɪəl/. **They'll** is the usual spoken form of 'they will'. *They'll probably be here Monday and Tuesday.*

they're /ðeə, ðeɪə/. **They're** is the usual spoken form of 'they are'. *People eat when they're depressed.*

they've /ðeɪv/. **They've** is the usual spoken form of 'they have', especially when 'have' is an auxiliary verb. *The worst thing is when you call friends and they've gone out.*

thick /θɪk/ **thicker, thickest. 1** Something that is **thick** has a large distance between its two opposite sides. *He wore glasses with thick rims... This material is very thick and this needle is not strong enough to go through it.* ♦ **thick·ly** *Slice the meat thickly.* **2** You can use **thick** to talk or ask about how wide or deep something is. *The folder was two inches thick... How thick are these walls?... It is a perennial plant, with a brown root as thick as a finger.* ► Also a combining form. *His life was saved by a quarter-inch-thick bullet-proof steel screen.* ♦ **thick·ness, thicknesses** *The size of the fish will determine the thickness of the steaks.* **3** If something that consists of several things is **thick**, it has a large number of them very close together. *She inherited our father's thick, wavy hair... They walked through thick forest.* ♦ **thickly** *I rounded a bend where the trees and brush grew thickly.* **4** If something is **thick with** another thing, the first thing is full of or covered with the second. *She ate scones thick with butter.* **5 Thick** clothes are made from heavy cloth, so that they will keep you warm in cold weather. **6 Thick** smoke, fog, or cloud is difficult to see through. **7 Thick** liquids are fairly stiff and solid and do not flow easily. *They had to battle through thick mud.* **8** If someone's voice is **thick**, they are not speaking clearly, for example because they are ill, upset, or drunk. **9** A **thick** accent is very obvious and easy to identify. *'What do you want?' a teenage girl demanded in a thick German accent.* **10** If you describe someone as **thick**, you think they are stupid. **11** If things happen **thick and fast**, they happen very quickly and in large numbers. *The rumours have been coming thick and fast.* **12** If you are **in the thick of** an activity or situation, you are very involved in it. *Peterson suddenly found himself in the thick of desperate fighting.* **13** If you do something **through thick and thin**, you do it although the conditions or circumstances are very bad. *I will go on loving James through thick and thin.* **14** ● **a thick skin**: see **skin**.   ADJ-GRADED · ADV-GRADED · ADJ: n ADJ, how ADJ, amount ADJ, as ADJ as · COMB · N-VAR · ADJ-GRADED · ADV-GRADED · ADJ-GRADED: v-link ADJ with n · ADJ-GRADED · ADJ-GRADED · ADJ-GRADED · ADJ-GRADED · ADJ-GRADED · ADJ-GRADED, INFORMAL, BRITISH · PHRASE · PHRASE · PHRASE · PHRASE

thick·en /ˈθɪkən/ **thickens, thickening, thickened. 1** When a liquid **thickens**, it becomes stiffer and more solid. *Thicken the broth with the cornflour.* **2** If something **thickens**, it becomes more closely grouped together or denser than it was before. *The crowds around him began to thicken... As the ice sheet grows and thickens it chills the nearby air.* **3** People sometimes say **'the plot thickens'** when a situation or series of events is getting more and more complicated and mysterious.   V-ERG: V V n · VERB V · PHRASE

thick·en·er /ˈθɪkənə/ **thickeners.** A **thickener** is a substance that is added to a liquid in order to make it stiffer and more solid.   N-VAR

thick·et /ˈθɪkɪt/ **thickets. 1** A **thicket** is a small group of trees or bushes which are growing closely together. **2** If you refer to a **thicket** of ideas or events, you mean that there a lot of them together, and often that they are confusing or difficult to   N-COUNT · N-COUNT: with supp

identify. *To try to open a foreign-owned business is to enter a thicket of regulations.*

thick·set /ˌθɪkˈset/; also spelled **thick-set**. A man who is **thickset** is broad and heavy, with a solid-looking body.   ADJ-GRADED

thick-ˈskinned. If you say that someone is **thick-skinned**, you mean that they are not easily upset by criticism or unpleasantness.   ADJ-GRADED

thief /θiːf/ **thieves** /θiːvz/. A **thief** is a person who steals something from another person.   ♦♦♦◇◇ N-COUNT

thiev·ing /ˈθiːvɪŋ/. **1 Thieving** is the act of stealing things from people. *...an ex-con who says he's given up thieving.* **2 Thieving** means involved in stealing things or intending to steal something. *...a thieving grocer who put sand in the sugar.*   N-UNCOUNT DATED · ADJ: ADJ n

thigh /θaɪ/ **thighs.** Your **thighs** are the top parts of your legs, between your knees and your hips. See picture headed **human body**.   ♦♦♦◇◇ N-COUNT

thim·ble /ˈθɪmbəl/ **thimbles.** A **thimble** is a small metal or plastic object which you use to protect your finger when you are sewing.   N-COUNT

thin /θɪn/ **thinner, thinnest; thins, thinning, thinned. 1** Something that is **thin** is much narrower than it is long. *A thin cable carries the signal to a computer.* **2** A person or animal that is **thin** has no extra fat on their body. ♦ **thin·ness** *There was something familiar about him, his fawn raincoat, his thinness, the way he moved.* **3** Something such as paper or cloth that is **thin** is flat and has only a very small distance between its two opposite surfaces. *A thin layer of topsoil was swept away.* ♦ **thin·ly** *Peel and thinly slice the onion.* **4 Thin** clothes are made from light cloth and are not warm to wear. **5** Liquids that are **thin** are weak and watery. *Creosote is a very thin liquid.* **6** To **thin** a liquid means to make it weaker and more watery by adding another liquid to it. *Aspirin thins the blood, letting it flow more easily through narrowed blood vessels.* ► **Thin down** means the same as **thin**. *Thin down your mayonnaise with soured cream or natural yoghurt.* **7** A crowd or audience that is **thin** does not have many people in it. ♦ **thinly** *The island is thinly populated.* **8** If something **thins**, or is **thinned**, it becomes less crowded because people or things have been removed from it. *It would have been better to have thinned the trees over several winters rather than all at one time... By midnight the crowd had thinned.* ► **Thin out** means the same as **thin**. *NATO will continue to thin out its forces... When the crowd began to thin out, I realized that most of the food was still there.* **9** A **thin** smile is one that is not genuinely warm or humorous. ♦ **thinly** *Wilson smiled thinly.* **10** If you describe an argument or explanation as **thin**, you mean that it is weak and unconvincing. *However, the evidence is thin and, to some extent, ambiguous.* ♦ **thinly** *Much of the speech was a thinly disguised attack on British Airways.* **11** A voice or sound that is **thin** is high-pitched and not very loud. **12** If someone's hair is **thin**, they do not have a lot of hair. **13** If a man's hair **is thinning** he is beginning to go bald. **14** If someone's patience, for example, is **wearing thin**, they are beginning to become impatient or angry with someone. **15** ● **on thin ice**: see **ice**. ● **into thin air**: see **air**.   ♦♦♦◇◇ ADJ-GRADED · ADJ-GRADED · N-UNCOUNT · ADJ-GRADED · ADV-GRADED: ADV with v · ADJ-GRADED · ADJ-GRADED · VERB V n · PHRASAL VB V P noun · ADJ-GRADED · ADV-GRADED · V-ERG V n V · PHRASAL VB ERG V P noun V P · ADJ-GRADED · ADV-GRADED · ADJ-GRADED · ADV · ADJ-GRADED · ADJ-GRADED · VERB: V · PHRASE

thin down. See **thin** 6   PHRASAL VB

thin out. See **thin** 8   PHRASAL VB

thine /ðaɪn/. **Thine** is an old-fashioned, poetic, or religious word for 'yours' when you are talking to only one person. *I am Thine, O Lord.*   PRON-POSS

thing /θɪŋ/ **things. 1** You can use **thing** as a substitute for another word when you are unable to be more precise, or you do not need or want to be more precise, for example because you have already mentioned the word or are going to give more details later. *What's that thing in the middle of the fountain?... The Earth is made mainly of iron and silicon and things like that... Of course, literacy isn't the same thing as intelligence... The captain of the submarine has got this periscope thing... One thing I*   ♦♦♦♦♦ N-COUNT

am sure of was that she was scared... Getting drunk is a thing all young men do. **2** The word **thing** is often used instead of the pronouns 'anything,' or 'everything' in order to emphasize what you are saying. *It isn't going to solve a single thing... Don't you worry about a thing.* **3** The word **thing** is used in expressions such as **such a thing** or **things like that**, especially in negative statements, in order to emphasize the bad or difficult situation you are referring back to. *'Are you accusing me of being a thief?'—'I have done no such thing, Tony.'* **4** A **thing** is a physical object that is considered as having no life of its own. *It's not a thing, Beauchamp. It's a human being!... This thing's virtually useless.* **5** You can call a person or an animal a particular **thing** when you want to mention a particular quality that they have and express your feelings towards them, usually affectionate feelings. *You really are quite a clever little thing... Oh you lucky thing!* **6** Your **things** are your clothes or possessions. *Sara told him to take all his things and not to return.* **7 Things** can refer to the situation or life in general and the way it is changing or affecting you. *Everyone agrees things are getting better... How are things going?* **8** You can refer to a monster or something else that is too frightening, strange, or horrible to describe clearly as a **thing**. *...John W. Campbell, author of 'The Thing From Another World.'* **9** If you say that something is **the thing** you mean that it is fashionable or popular. *I feel under pressure to go out and get drunk because it's the thing to do.* **10** If you say that someone or something is trying to **be all things to all men** or **to all people**, you are criticizing them because they are trying to behave in a way that will please everybody, and this is impossible. **11** If, for example, you **do the** right **thing** or **do the** decent **thing** in a situation, you do something which is considered correct or socially acceptable in that situation. *Carrington did the honourable thing and resigned.* **12** If something is **a thing of the past**, it no longer exists or happens, or is being replaced by something new. *Cheap computers, faxes and phone calls will make commuting to work a thing of the past.* **13** If you say that someone is **seeing** or **hearing things**, you mean that they believe they are seeing or hearing something that is not really there. **14** You can say there is **no such thing** as something to emphasize that it does not exist or is not possible. *There really is no such thing as a totally risk-free industry.* **15** If you say that someone knows **a thing or two** about something or could teach someone **a thing or two** about it, you mean that they are very knowledgeable about it or good at it. **16** If you say that something is **the done thing**, you mean it is the socially acceptable way to behave. **17** If you **do your own thing**, you live, act, or behave in the way you want to, without paying attention to convention or depending on other people. **18** If you say that something is **just the thing** or is **the very thing**, you are emphasizing that it is exactly what is wanted or needed. *Kiwi fruit are just the thing for a healthy snack.* **19** If you do something **first thing**, you do it at the beginning of the day, before you do anything else. If you do it **last thing**, you do it at the end of the day. *I always do it last thing on a Saturday.* **20** If you **have a thing about** someone or something, you have very strong positive or negative feelings about them. *He's got this thing about ties.* **21** If you **make a thing of** something or **make a thing about** it, you talk about it or do it in an exaggerated way, so that it seems much more important than it really is. *Gossips made a big thing about him going on shopping trips with her.* **22** You can say that the first of two ideas, actions, or situations **is one thing** when you want to contrast it with a second idea, action, or situation and emphasize that the second one is much more difficult, important, or extreme. *It was one thing to talk about leaving; it was another to physically walk out the door.*

(margin labels, left column:) N-SING PRAGMATICS · N-COUNT PRAGMATICS · N-COUNT · N-COUNT: adj N INFORMAL · N-PLURAL: poss N · N-PLURAL · N-COUNT · N-SING: the N · PRAGMATICS · PHRASE · PHRASE · PHRASE · PHRASE · PHRASE · PHRASE · PHRASE PRAGMATICS · PHRASE · PHRASE INFORMAL · PHRASE PRAGMATICS · PHRASE · PHRASE INFORMAL · PHRASE INFORMAL · PHRASE PRAGMATICS

23 You can say **for one thing** when you are explaining a statement or answering a question, to suggest that your explanation or answer is only partial, and that there are other points that you could add to it. *She was unable to sell it, because for one thing its size was awkward.* **24** You can use the expression **one thing and another** to suggest that there are several reasons for something or several items on a list, but you are not going to explain or mention them all. *What with one thing and another, it was fairly late in the day when we returned to Shrewsbury.* **25** If you say **it is just one of those things** you mean that you cannot explain or prevent it happening, because it seems to happen by chance. **26** You say **one thing led to another** when you are explaining how something happened, but you do not really want to give the details or you think people will be able to imagine the details. *He came by on Saturday to see if she was lonely. One thing led to another and he stayed the night.* **27** You say **the thing is** to introduce an explanation, comment, or opinion, that relates to something that has just been said. **The thing is** is often used to identify a problem relating to what has just been said. *I'm getting a grant for a speech therapy course. But the thing is, I don't know whether I want to do it any more.* **28** ● **other things being equal**: see **equal**. ● **first things first**: see **first**. ● **the real thing**: see **real**. ● **the shape of things to come**: see **shape**.

(margin labels:) PHRASE PRAGMATICS · PHRASE SPOKEN · PHRASE · PHRASE · PHRASE PRAGMATICS

thingum·my /ˈθɪŋəmi/ **thingummies.** You refer to something or someone as **thingummy** or **thingummyjig** when you cannot remember or do not know the proper word or name for them, or when you cannot be bothered to use the proper word or name for them.

(margin label:) N-COUNT SPOKEN, INFORMAL

thingy /ˈθɪŋi/ **thingies.** You refer to something or someone as **thingy** when you cannot remember or do not know the proper word or name for them, or when you cannot be bothered to use the proper word or name for them.

(margin label:) N-COUNT SPOKEN, INFORMAL

think /θɪŋk/ **thinks, thinking, thought. 1** If you **think** that something is the case, you have the opinion that it is the case. If you **think** in a particular way, you have those general opinions. *I certainly think there should be a ban on tobacco advertising... Tell me, what do you think of my theory?... Most people thought her charming... 'It ought to be stopped.'—'Yes, I think so.'... You wouldn't think like that if you were in Somalia or Bosnia.* ◆ **think·ing** *Socialist attitudes prevail in his thinking on welfare provisions.* **2** If you say that you **think** that something is true or will happen, you mean that you have the impression that it is true or will happen, although you are not certain of the facts. *Nora thought he was seventeen years old... She's in Napa, I think... The storm is thought to be responsible for as many as four deaths... 'Did Mr Stevens ever mention her to you?'—'No, I don't think so.'* **3** If you **think of** someone or something as having a particular quality or purpose, you regard them as having this quality or purpose. If you **think** a lot of them, you regard them as being very good. *We all thought of him as a father... In China bats are thought of as being very lucky... People at the club think very highly of him.* **4** When you **think** about ideas or problems, you make a mental effort to consider them or solve them. If you **think** in a particular way, you consider or solve things in that way. *She closed her eyes for a moment, trying to think... I have often thought about this problem... Let's think what we can do... We had to think what to do next... The programmer has to think like the machine.* ▶ Also a noun in British English. *I'll have a think about that.* ◆ **thinking** *This is a time of decisive action and quick thinking.* **5** If you **think** of something, it comes into your mind or you remember it. *Nobody could think of anything to say... I was trying to think what else we had to do.* **6** If you **are thinking** something at a particular moment, you have words or ideas in your mind without saying them out loud. *She must be ill, Tatiana thought... I remember thinking how*

(margin labels, right column:) ◆◆◆◆◆ VB: no cont V that V n of/about n V n adj V so/not V like n · N-UNCOUNT · VB: no cont V that be V-ed to-inf V so/not · VB: no cont V of n asn/-ing V amount/adv of n Also V n adj · VERB V V about n V wh V wh-to-inf V prep Also V n · N-SING: a N N-UNCOUNT VB: no cont V of n V wh · VB: no passive V with quote V wh/that V n

lovely he looked... I'm trying to think positive thoughts. VERB | PRAGMATICS
7 You can say that you **are thinking of** a particular as- V of n
pect or subject, in order to introduce an example or
explain more exactly what you are talking about. *I'm* VERB
primarily thinking of the first year.* **8** If you **think of** V of/about n
someone, you show consideration for them and pay
attention to their needs. *I'm only thinking of you...* VERB
You don't have to think about me and Hugh. **9** If you V of-ing/n
are thinking of taking a particular course of action,
you are considering it as a possible course of action.
*Martin was thinking of taking legal action against
Zuckerman.*
10 You use **think** in questions where you are express- VB:
ing your anger or shock at someone's behaviour. *Who* only interrog | PRAGMATICS
does she think she is? Trying to make a fool of me like V of n/-ing
that... What were you thinking of? You shouldn't steal.
11 You use **think** when you are commenting on V: no cont,
something which you did or experienced in the past no passive | PRAGMATICS
and which now seems surprising, foolish, or shocking V that
to you. *To think I left you alone in a place with a mad-* V of n
man at large!... When I think of how you've behaved!
12 You can use **think** in expressions such as **you** VB: no cont
would think or **I would have thought** when you are V that
criticizing someone because they ought to or could be V so
expected to do something, but have not done it. *You'd* Also V
think you'd remember to wash your ears... 'Surely to
God she should have been given some proper help.'—
'Well I would have thought so.' **13** You can use **think** VB: no cont
in expressions such as **anyone would think** and **you** V that
would think to express your surprise or disapproval
at the way someone is behaving, and to suggest that
their behaviour gives a particular wrong impression.
Anyone would think you were in love with the girl.
14 You use expressions such as **come to think of it**, PHRASE
when you think about it, or **thinking about it**, when PRAGMATICS
you mention something that you have suddenly re-
membered or realized. *He was her distant relative, as
was everyone else on the island, come to think of it.*
15 You use **I think** as a way of being polite when you PHRASE
are explaining or suggesting something, expressing PRAGMATICS
your opinion, or accepting or refusing an offer. *I think
I'll go home and have a shower... I think he means 'at'
rather than 'to'... 'Would you like to do that another
time?'—'Yes I think so.'* **16** You say **just think** when PHRASE
you feel excited, fascinated, or shocked by something, PRAGMATICS
and you want the person to whom you are talking to
feel the same. *Just think; tomorrow we shall walk out
of this place and leave it all behind us forever.* **17** If you PHRASE
think again about an action or decision, you consider
it very carefully, often with the result that you change
your mind and decide to do things differently. *He intends to ask the court to think again.* **18** If you **think** PHRASE
nothing of doing something that other people might
consider difficult, strange, or wrong, you do it often or
would be quite willing to do it. *I thought nothing of
betting £1,000 on a horse.* **19** If something happens PHRASE
and you **think nothing of it**, you do not pay much attention to it or do not think of it as strange or important, although later you realize that it is. *When she
went off to see her parents for the weekend I thought
nothing of it.* **20** See also **thinking**, **thought**. • you
can't hear yourself **think**: see **hear**. • to **shudder** to
think: see **shudder**. • to **think big**: see **big**. • to **think**
twice: see **twice**. • to **think the world of**: see **world**.

think back. If you **think back**, you make an effort to PHRASAL VB
remember things that happened to you in the past. *I* V P
thought back to the time in 1975 when my son was des- V P prep
perately ill.

think out. If you **think** something **out**, you consider PHRASAL VB
all the aspects and details of it before doing anything V n P
or making a decision. *I need time alone to think things* V-ed P
out... The book is detailed and well thought out. Also V P noun

think over. If you **think** something **over**, you con- PHRASAL VB
sider it carefully before making a decision. *She said* V n P
she needs time to think it over.* Also V P noun

think through. If you **think** a situation **through**, PHRASAL VB
you consider it thoroughly, together with all its pos- V n P
sible effects or consequences. *I didn't think through* V P noun
the consequences of promotion... The administration* V P wh

*has not really thought through what it plans to do once
the fighting stops.*

think up. If you **think** something **up**, for example an PHRASAL VB
idea or plan, you invent it using mental effort. *Julian* V n P
has been thinking up new ways of raising money.* V P noun

think·er /ˈθɪŋkə/ **thinkers.** A thinker is a person ◆◇◇◇◇
who spends a lot of time thinking deeply about im- N-COUNT
portant things, especially a philosopher who is famous for thinking of new ideas.

think·ing /ˈθɪŋkɪŋ/. **1** If you describe someone as ◆◆◆◇
thinking, you approve of them because you think ADJ: ADJ n | PRAGMATICS
they are intelligent and take an interest in impor-
tant issues. *Thinking people on both sides will applaud this book.* **2** See also **think**; **wishful thinking**.
• to my **way of thinking**: see **way**.

'think-tank, think-tanks. A think-tank is a ◆◇◇◇
group of experts who are gathered together by an N-COLL-COUNT
organization, especially by a government, in order
to consider various problems.

thin-'skinned. If you say that someone is **thin-** ADJ-GRADED
skinned, you mean that they are easily upset by PRAGMATICS
criticism or unpleasantness; used showing disapproval. *Artists are likely to be thin-skinned and
insecure.*

third /θɜːd/ **thirds. 1** The **third** item in a series is ◆◆◆◇
the one that you count as number three. See Ap- ORDINAL
pendix headed **Numbers**. **2** A **third** is one of three FRACTION
equal parts of something. **3** You say **third** when you ADV
want to list a third point or give a third reason for
something. **4** A **third** is the lowest honours degree N-COUNT
that can be obtained from a British university.

third-'class. 1 A **third-class** degree is the lowest ADJ: ADJ n
honours degree that can be obtained from a British
university. **2** In Britain in the past, the **third-class** ADJ
accommodation on a train or ship was the cheapest
and least comfortable accommodation. ▶ Also an ADV:
adverb. *...travelling third class.* ADV after v

third-de'gree. 1 Third-degree burns are very se- ADJ
vere, destroying tissue under the skin. **2** If you say N-SING
that someone has been given the **third degree**, you INFORMAL
mean that they have been questioned or reprimanded extremely severely.

third·ly /ˈθɜːdli/. You use **thirdly** when you want to ◆◇◇◇
list a third point or give a third reason for some- ADV
thing. *First of all, there are not many of them, and
secondly, they have little money and, thirdly, they
have few big businesses.*

third 'party, third parties. 1 A third party is ◆◇◇◇
someone who is not one of the main people in- N-COUNT
volved in a business agreement or legal case, but
who is involved in it in a minor role. *You can instruct your bank to allow a third party to remove
money from your account.* **2** Third-party insurance ADJ
is a type of insurance you have that gives financial
compensation to other people who are hurt or
whose property is damaged as a result of something
you have done.

third 'person. A statement in **the third person** is N-SING:
a statement about another person or thing, and not the N
directly about yourself or about the person you are
talking to. The subject of a statement like this is
'he', 'she', 'it', or a name or noun.

third-'rate. If you describe something as **third-** ADJ-GRADED
rate, you mean that it is of a very poor quality or
standard. *...a third-rate movie.*

Third 'World. The countries of Africa, Asia, and ◆◆◇◇
South America are sometimes referred to collective- N-PROPER:
ly as **the Third World**. the N, N n

thirst /θɜːst/ **thirsts, thirsting, thirsted.** ◆◇◇◇
1 Thirst is the feeling that you need to drink some- N-VAR
thing. *Instead of tea or coffee, drink water to quench
your thirst.* **2** Thirst is the condition of not having N-UNCOUNT
enough to drink. *They died of thirst on the voyage.*
3 A thirst for something is a very strong desire for N-SING
that thing. *Children show a real thirst for learning.*
4 If you say that someone **thirsts** for something, VERB
you mean that they have a strong desire for it. *We* V for/after n
all thirst for the same things. LITERARY

thirsty /ˈθɜːsti/ **thirstier, thirstiest. 1** If you are ◆◇◇◇
thirsty, you feel a need to drink something. ADJ-GRADED

♦ **thirsti·ly** /ˈθɜːstɪli/. *The child nodded, drinking her milk thirstily.* **2** If you are **thirsty for** something, you have a strong desire for it. *People should understand how thirsty for revenge they are.*   ADV / ADJ-GRADED: v-link ADJ for n / LITERARY

thir·teen /ˌθɜːˈtiːn/ **thirteens.** Thirteen is the number 13. See Appendix headed **Numbers**.   NUMBER

thir·teenth /ˌθɜːˈtiːnθ/. The **thirteenth** item in a series is the one that you count as number thirteen. See Appendix headed **Numbers**.   ORDINAL

thir·ti·eth /ˈθɜːtiəθ/. The **thirtieth** item in a series is the one that you count as number thirty. See Appendix headed **Numbers**.   ORDINAL

thir·ty /ˈθɜːti/ **thirties. 1** Thirty is the number 30. See Appendix headed **Numbers**. **2** When you talk about the **thirties**, you are referring to numbers between 30 and 39. For example, if you are **in your thirties**, you are aged between 30 and 39. **3** The **thirties** is the decade between 1930 and 1939.   NUMBER / N-PLURAL / N-PLURAL: the N

this /ðɪs/. **1** You use **this** to refer back to a person, thing, idea, or situation that has been mentioned or implied. *On 1 October the US suspended a proposed $574 million aid package for 1991. Of this amount, $250 million is for military purchases... There have been continual demands for action by the political authorities to put an end to this situation.* ▸ Also a pronoun. *He's had these turns before but he has never had one like this... You feel that it's uneconomic to insist that people work together in groups. Why is this?.* **2** You use **this** to introduce someone or something that you are going to talk about. *This is what I will do. I will telephone Anna and explain.* ▸ Also a determiner. *This report from David Cook of our Science Unit.* **3** You use **this** to refer to a person or thing that is near you now, to the place where you are now, or to the present time. When there are two or more people or things near you, **this** refers to the nearest one. *Is this what you were looking for?... This is my colleague, Mr Arnold Landon... This is the worst place I've come across... This is not the moment to waste a lot of time.* ▸ Also a determiner. *This place is run like a hotel ought to be run... I think coffee is probably the best thing at this point.* **4** You use **this** when you refer to a general situation, activity, or event which is happening or has just happened and which you feel involved in. *Tim, this is awful. I know what you must think, but it's not so... This is what you want to do with the rest of your life?* **5** You use **this** to refer to the next occurrence in the future of a particular day, month, season, or festival. *...this Sunday's 7.45 performance... We're getting married this June.* **6** People use **this** to introduce a person or thing into a story. *I came here by chance and was just watching what was going on, when this girl attacked me.* **7** You use **this** when you are indicating the size or shape of something with your hands. *They'd said the wound was only about this big.* **8** You use **this** in order to say who you are or what organization you are representing, when you are speaking on the telephone, radio, or television. *'Hello, is this Raymond Brown?'—'Yeah, who's this?'... This is NPR, National Public Radio.* **9** You use **this** when you are going to specify how much you know or how much you can tell someone. *I will tell you this much, if it works out, the next seven years will be very interesting.* **10** If you say **this is it**, you are agreeing with what someone else has just said. *'You know, people conveniently forget the things they say.'—'Well this is it.'* **11** If you say that you are doing or talking about **this and that**, or **this, that, and the other** you mean that you are doing or talking about a variety of things that you do not want to specify. **12** See also **these**.   DET / PRAGMATICS / PRON / PRON / DET / PRON / DET / DET / PRAGMATICS SPOKEN / ADV: ADV adj SPOKEN / PRON / ADV: ADV adv / CONVENTION PRAGMATICS / PHRASE

this·tle /ˈθɪsəl/ **thistles.** A **thistle** is a wild plant with prickly leaves and purple flowers.   N-COUNT

thith·er /ˈðɪðə/. **Thither** means to the place that has already been mentioned. ● **hither and thither**: see **hither**.   ADV: ADV after v DATED

tho'; also spelled **tho. Tho'** and **tho** are very informal written forms of **though**.

thong /θɒŋ, AM θɔːŋ/ **thongs. 1** A **thong** is a long thin strip of leather, plastic, or rubber. **2** A **thong** is a narrow band of cloth that is worn between a person's legs to cover his or her sexual organs, and that is held up by a piece of string around the waist. **3** **Thongs** are sandals which are held on your foot by a V-shaped strap that goes between your big toe and the toe next to it. The usual British word is **flip-flops**.   N-COUNT / N-COUNT / N-COUNT AMERICAN

tho·rac·ic /θɔːˈræsɪk/. **Thoracic** means relating to or affecting your thorax.   ADJ: ADJ n MEDICAL

thor·ax /ˈθɔːræks/ **thoraxes** or **thoraces** /ˈθɔːrəsiːz/. **1** Your **thorax** is the part of your body between your neck and your waist. **2** An insect's **thorax** is the central part of its body to which the legs and wings are attached. See picture headed **insects**.   N-COUNT MEDICAL / N-COUNT TECHNICAL

thorn /θɔːn/ **thorns. 1** Thorns are the sharp points on some plants and trees, for example on a rose bush. **2** A **thorn** or a **thorn bush** or a **thorn tree** is a bush or tree such as a hawthorn which has a lot of thorns on it. **3** If you describe someone or something as a **thorn in** your **side** or a **thorn in** your **flesh**, you mean that they are a constant problem or annoyance to you. *The Party was a thorn in the flesh of his coalition.*   N-COUNT / N-VAR / PHRASE

thorny /ˈθɔːni/ **thornier, thorniest. 1** A **thorny** plant or tree is covered with thorns. **2** A **thorny** problem is very complicated and difficult to solve, and people are often unwilling to discuss it. *...the thorny issue of immigration policy.*   ADJ / ADJ-GRADED

thor·ough /ˈθʌrə, AM ˈθɜːrəʊ/. **1** A **thorough** action or activity is one that is done very carefully and methodically so that nothing is forgotten. *We are making a thorough investigation.* ♦ **thor·ough·ly** *...a thoroughly researched and illuminating biography.* ♦ **thor·ough·ness** *The thoroughness of the evaluation process we went through was impressive.* **2** Someone who is **thorough** is always very careful and methodical in their work. ♦ **thoroughness** *His thoroughness and attention to detail is legendary.* **3** **Thorough** is used to emphasize the great degree or extent of something. *The management has got itself into a thorough mess.* ♦ **thoroughly** *I thoroughly enjoy your programme.*   ADJ-GRADED / ADV-GRADED: ADV with v / N-UNCOUNT / ADJ-GRADED / N-UNCOUNT / ADJ: det ADJ PRAGMATICS / ADV-GRADED

thor·ough·bred /ˈθʌrəbred, AM ˈθɜːrəʊ-/ **thoroughbreds.** A **thoroughbred** is a horse that has parents that are of the same high quality breed.   N-COUNT

thor·ough·fare /ˈθʌrəfeə, AM ˈθɜːrəʊ-/ **thoroughfares.** A **thoroughfare** is a main road in a town or city which usually has shops along it and a lot of traffic.   N-COUNT FORMAL

thor·ough·going /ˌθʌrəˈɡəʊɪŋ, AM ˌθɜːrəʊ-/; also spelled **thorough-going**. **1** You use **thoroughgoing** to emphasize that someone or something is fully or completely the type of person or thing specified. *...a thoroughgoing conservative.* **2** If you describe a piece of work as **thoroughgoing**, you approve of it because it has been carefully and thoroughly put together. *He wrote a thoroughgoing review of prison conditions.*   ADJ-GRADED PRAGMATICS / ADJ-GRADED PRAGMATICS

those /ðəʊz/. **1** You use **those** to refer to people, things, or situations which have already been mentioned. *Most of those crimes are committed by boys.* ▸ Also a pronoun. *I understand that there are a number of projects going on. Could you tell us a little bit about those?... The cells of the body, especially those of the brain, can live only minutes without circulating blood.* **2** You use **those** when you are referring to people or things that are a distance away from you in position or time, often when you indicate or point to them. *What are those buildings?... In those days he was, like me, a student.* ▸ Also a pronoun. *Those are nice shoes. Where'd you get them?* **3** You use **those** to refer to someone or something about them. *Those people who took up weapons to defend themselves are political prisoners.* **4** You use **those** to mean 'people'. *A little selfish behaviour is unlikely to cause real damage to those*   DET PRAGMATICS / PRON / DET / PRON / DET / PRON

around us. **5** You use **those** when you refer to DET things that you expect the hearer to know about, or when you are checking that you are both thinking of the same people or things. *He did buy me those daffodils a week or so ago. ...those embarrassing moments we all have.*

thou /ðaʊ/. **Thou** is an old-fashioned, poetic, or re- ◆◇◇◇◇ ligious word for 'you' when you are talking to only PRON one person. It is used as the subject of a verb. ● See also **holier-than-thou**.

though. /ðəʊ/. **1** You use **though** to introduce a ◆◆◆◆◆ statement which contrasts with a statement you CONJ have just made, for example one that makes your PRAGMATICS first statement seem surprising. *Gaelic has been a dying language for many years, though children are nowadays taught it in school.* ▶ Also an adverb. *It* ADV: *might be worth your while to go to court. This is* ADV with cl *tricky, though, and you'll need expert advice... I like him. Though he makes me angry sometimes.* **2** You CONJ use **though** to introduce some information that is PRAGMATICS relevant to a statement you have just made and weakens its force. *I look back on it as the bloodiest (though not literally) winter of the war... His achievements, though hardly exciting, were widely admired.* **3** ● **as though**: see **as**. ● **even though**: see **even**.

thought /θɔːt/ **thoughts.** **1** Thought is the past ◆◆◆◆◆ tense and past participle of **think**.
2 A **thought** is an idea that you have in your mind. *The* N-COUNT *thought of Nick made her throat tighten... I tormented myself with the thought that life was just too comfortable.* **3** A person's **thoughts** are all the ideas or all the N-PLURAL ideas in their mind when they are concentrating on one particular thing. *Usually at this time our thoughts are on Christmas. ...he was always in her thoughts.* **4** A N-PLURAL person's **thoughts** are their opinions on a particular subject. *Many of you have written to us to express your thoughts on the conflict.*
5 A **thought** is an intention, hope, or reason for doing N-COUNT something. *Mansell has now banished all thoughts of retirement.* **6** A **thought** is an act of kindness or an of- N-SING: fer of help; used especially when you are thanking with supp someone, or expressing admiration of someone. *'She* PRAGMATICS *has given them this seven hundred pounds.'—'What a lovely thought.'*
7 Thought is the activity of thinking, especially deep- N-UNCOUNT ly, logically, or with concentration. *He had given some thought to what she had told him... After much thought I decided to end my marriage.* **8** Thought is N-UNCOUNT the group of ideas and beliefs or way of thinking which belongs, for example, to a particular religion, philosopher, political party, or scientist. *This school of thought argues that depression is best treated by drugs.*
9 See also **second thought**.

thought·ful /ˈθɔːtfʊl/. **1** If you are **thoughtful**, you ◆◆◇◇◇ are quiet and serious because you are thinking ADJ-GRADED about something. ♦ **thought·ful·ly** *Daniel nodded* ADV-GRADED *thoughtfully.* **2** If you describe someone as **thought-** ADJ-GRADED **ful**, you approve of them because they remember PRAGMATICS what other people want, need, or feel, and try not to upset them. ♦ **thoughtfully** *...the bottle of wine he* ADV-GRADED: *had thoughtfully purchased for the celebrations.* ADV with v ♦ **thought·ful·ness** *I can't tell you how much I ap-* N-UNCOUNT *preciate your thoughtfulness.* **3** If you describe ADJ-GRADED something such as a book, film, or speech as **thoughtful**, you mean that it is serious and well thought out. ♦ **thoughtfully** *...these thoughtfully* ADV-GRADED *designed machines.* ADV with v

thought·less /ˈθɔːtləs/. If you describe someone as ADJ-GRADED **thoughtless**, you are critical of them because they PRAGMATICS forget or ignore other people's wants, needs, or feelings. ♦ **thought·less·ly** *They thoughtlessly planned* ADV-GRADED *a picnic without him.* ♦ **thought·less·ness** *What* N-UNCOUNT *many women mistake as thoughtlessness is often just diffidence.*

thou·sand /ˈθaʊzənd/ **thousands.** The plural ◆◆◆◆◆ form is **thousand** after a number, or after a word or expression referring to a number, such as 'several' or 'a few'. **1** A **thousand** or one **thousand** is the NUMBER number 1,000. See Appendix headed **Numbers**. **2** If QUANT

you refer to **thousands of** things or people, you are PRAGMATICS emphasizing that there are very many of them. *I must have driven past that place thousands of times.* ▶ Also a pronoun. *Hundreds have been killed in the* PRON *fighting and thousands made homeless.*
3 ● **a thousand and one**: see **one**.

thou·sandth /ˈθaʊzənθ/ **thousandths.** **1** The ORDINAL **thousandth** item in a series is the one that you count as number one thousand. See Appendix headed **Numbers**. **2** A **thousandth** is one of a thou- FRACTION sand equal parts of something.

thrall /θrɔːl/. If you say that someone is in **thrall** to N-UNCOUNT a person or thing, you mean that they are complete- JOURNALISM ly in their power or are greatly influenced by them. *Tomorrow's children will be even more in the thrall of the silicon chip.*

thrash /θræʃ/ **thrashes, thrashing, thrashed.** ◆◇◇◇ **1** If one player or team **thrashes** another in a game VERB or contest, they defeat them easily or by a large V n amount score. *Second-placed Rangers thrashed St Johnstone* Also V n 5-nil. ♦ **thrash·ing, thrashings** *She dropped only* N-COUNT *eight points in the 43-minute thrashing of the former Wimbledon champion.*
2 If you **thrash** someone, you hit them several times VERB: V n as a punishment. ♦ **thrash·ing** *If Sarah caught her,* N-COUNT *she would get a thrashing.* **3** If someone **thrashes** V-ERG: about, they move in a wild or violent way, often hit- V adv/prep ting against something. *Jimmy collapsed on the floor,* V n adv/prep *thrashing his legs about.* **4** If something or someone VERB: **thrashes** at something, they hit it repeatedly in a vio- V at n lent or noisy way. *...a magnificent paddle-steamer on* V n *the mighty Mississippi, her huge wheel thrashing the muddy water.* ▶ Also a noun. *...the thrash of the* N-SING *horses' hooves.*
5 Thrash or **thrash metal** is a type of pop music that N-UNCOUNT consists of loud, fast, simple guitar tunes. **6** A **thrash** JOURNALISM is a party. N-COUNT INFORMAL

thrash out. 1 If people **thrash out** something such PHRASAL VB as a plan or an agreement, they decide on it after a V P noun/wh great deal of discussion. *The foreign ministers have* Also V n P *thrashed out a suitable compromise formula.* **2** If peo- V P noun ple **thrash out** a problem or a dispute, they discuss it Also V n P thoroughly until they reach an agreement. *...a sincere effort by two people to thrash out differences.*

thread /θred/ **threads, threading, threaded.** ◆◆◇◇◇ **1** Thread or a **thread** is a long very thin piece of a N-VAR material such as cotton, nylon, or silk, especially one that is used in sewing. **2** When you **thread** a VERB: V n needle, you put a piece of thread through the hole in the top of the needle in order to sew with it. **3** If VERB you **thread** a long thin object through something, V n through/ you pass it through one or more holes or narrow into n spaces. *...threading the laces through the eyelets of his shoes.* **4** If you **thread** small objects such as VERB: beads onto a string or thread, you join them togeth- V n prep er by pushing the string through them.
5 The **thread** of an argument, a story, or a situation is N-COUNT an aspect of it that connects all the different parts to- gether. *The possible consequences so filled his mind that he lost the thread of Wan Da's narrative.* **6** A N-COUNT **thread** of something such as liquid, light, or colour is a long thin line or piece of it.
7 The **thread** on a screw, or on something such as a lid N-COUNT or a pipe, is the raised spiral line of metal or plastic around it which allows it to be fixed in place by twisting.
8 If you **thread** your way through a group of people or VERB: things, you move through it carefully or slowly, V way prep/ changing direction frequently as you move. *We* adv *threaded through a network of back streets.* V prep
9 If you say that something **is hanging by a thread**, PHRASE you mean that it is in a very uncertain state and is un- likely to survive or succeed. *The fragile peace was hanging by a thread as thousands of communist hard- liners took to the streets.* **10** If you **pick up the threads** PHRASE of an activity, you start it again after an interruption. If you **pick up the threads** of your **life**, you become more active again after a period of failure or bad luck. *Many women have been able to pick up the threads of their former career.*

T

thread·bare /'θredbeə/. **1 Threadbare** clothes, carpets, and other pieces of cloth look old, dull, and very thin, because they have been worn or used too much. **2** If you describe an activity, an idea, or an argument as **threadbare**, you mean that it is very weak, or inadequate, or old and no longer interesting. ...*the government's threadbare domestic policies.* `ADJ-GRADED` `ADJ-GRADED`

threat /θret/ **threats. 1** A **threat** to someone or something is a danger that something unpleasant might happen to them. A **threat** is also the cause of this danger. *Some couples see single women as a threat to their relationships.* **2** A **threat** is a statement by someone that they will do something unpleasant, especially if you do not do what they want. *He may be forced to carry out his threat to resign.* **3** If someone or something is **under threat**, there is a danger that something unpleasant might be done to them, or that they might cease to exist. *His position as leader will be under threat at a party congress due next month.* `N-VAR:` `with supp` `◇` `N-COUNT` `PHRASE`

threat·en /'θretən/ **threatens, threatening, threatened. 1** If someone **threatens** to do something unpleasant to you, or if they **threaten** you, they say or imply that they will do something unpleasant to you, especially if you do not do what they want. *He tied her up and threatened her with a six-inch knife... If you threaten me or use any force, I shall inform the police.* **2** If something or someone **threatens** a person or thing, they are likely to harm that person or thing. *30 percent of reptiles, birds, and fish are currently threatened with extinction.* **3** If something unpleasant **threatens** to happen, it seems likely to happen. *The fighting is threatening to turn into full-scale war.* **4** See also **threatened, threatening**. `◆◆◆◇` `VERB:` `V to-inf` `V n with n` `Also V that` `VERB: V n` `be V-ed with n` `VERB` `V to-inf` `Also V`

threat·ened /'θretənd/. If you feel **threatened**, you feel as if someone is trying to harm you. ● See also **threaten**. `◆◇◇◇` `ADJ-GRADED:` `v-link ADJ`

threat·en·ing /'θretənɪŋ/. You can describe someone's behaviour as **threatening**, when you think that they are trying to harm you. *She said Denny had received a threatening letter.* **♦ threat·en·ing·ly** *'This ain't no affair of yours, boy!' McClosky said threateningly.* ● See also **threaten; life-threatening**. `◆◇◇◇` `ADJ-GRADED` `ADV-GRADED`

three /θriː/ **threes. Three** is the number 3. See Appendix headed **Numbers**. `◆◆◆◇` `NUMBER`

three-'cornered. If you describe something such as a disagreement, competition, or game as **three-cornered**, you mean that it involves three people, groups, or teams. `ADJ`

three-di'mensional. **1** A **three-dimensional** object is solid rather than flat, because it can be measured in three dimensions, usually the height, depth, and width. The abbreviation '3-D' can also be used. *...a three-dimensional model.* **2** A **three-dimensional** picture, image, or film looks as though it is deep or solid rather than flat. The abbreviation '3-D' can also be used. *...three dimensional pictures created by lasers.* **3** If you describe fictional characters as **three-dimensional** you mean that they seem real and lifelike; used showing approval. `◆◇◇◇` `ADJ` `ADJ` `ADJ-GRADED` `PRAGMATICS`

three-'fourths. **Three-fourths** of a particular thing is an amount that is equal to three out of four equal parts of that thing. The more usual American word and the usual British word is **three-quarters**. ▶ Also a pronoun. *He has just under 1,600 delegates, about three-fourths what he needs to win the Democratic presidential nomination.* `QUANT` `AMERICAN` `PRON`

three-'quarter; also spelled **three quarter**. You can use **three-quarter** to describe something which is three fourths of the usual size or three fourths of a standard measurement. *...one and three-quarter hours.* `◆◇◇◇` `ADJ: ADJ n`

three-'quarters; also spelled **three quarters. Three-quarters** is an amount that is three out of four equal parts of something. *Three-quarters of the country's workers took part in the strike.* ▶ Also a pronoun. *Road deaths have increased by three-* `◆◆◇◇` `QUANT` `PRON`

quarters. ▶ Also an adverb. *We were left with an open bottle of champagne three-quarters full.* `ADV:` `ADV adj'-ed`

three 'Rs. When talking about children's education, **the three Rs** are the basic skills of reading, writing, and arithmetic. `N-PLURAL:` `the N`

three·some /'θriːsəm/ **threesomes**. A **threesome** is a group of three people. `N-COUNT`

thresh /θreʃ/ **threshes, threshing, threshed.** When a cereal such as corn, wheat, or rice **is threshed**, it is beaten in order to separate the grains from the rest of the plant. **♦ thresh·ing** *...a threshing machine.* `VERB:` `be V-ed` `N-UNCOUNT`

thresh·old /'θreʃhəʊld/ **thresholds. 1** The **threshold** of a building or room is the floor in the doorway, or the doorway itself. *He stopped at the threshold of the bedroom.* **2** A **threshold** is an amount, level, or limit on a scale. When the **threshold** is reached, something else happens or changes. *Fewer than forty per cent voted – the threshold for results to be valid.* **3** If you are **on the threshold of** something exciting or new, you are about to experience it. *We stand on the threshold of a tremendously exciting period in the history of our country.* `◆◆◇◇` `N-COUNT` `N-COUNT` `PHRASE`

threw /θruː/. **Threw** is the past tense of **throw**.

thrice /θraɪs/. **1** Something that happens **thrice** happens three times. **2** You can use **thrice** to indicate that something is three times the size, value, or intensity of something else. *The metal had been valued at twice or thrice its current price.* `ADV` `DATED` `ADV:` `ADV n` `DATED`

thrift /θrɪft/ **thrifts. 1 Thrift** is the quality and practice of being careful with money and not wasting things; used showing approval. **2** In America, a **thrift** or a **thrift institution** is a kind of savings bank. `◆◇◇◇` `N-UNCOUNT` `PRAGMATICS` `N-COUNT`

'thrift shop, thrift shops. A **thrift shop** or a **thrift store** is a shop that sells second-hand goods cheaply and gives its profits to a charity. The British term is **charity shop**. `N-COUNT` `AMERICAN`

thrifty /'θrɪfti/ **thriftier, thriftiest**. If you say that someone is **thrifty**, you are praising them for saving money, not buying unnecessary things, and not wasting things. `ADJ-GRADED` `PRAGMATICS`

thrill /θrɪl/ **thrills, thrilling, thrilled. 1** If something gives you a **thrill**, it gives you a sudden feeling of great excitement, pleasure, or fear. *I can remember the thrill of not knowing what I would get on Christmas morning.* **2** If something **thrills** you, it gives you a feeling of great pleasure and excitement. *The children will thrill at all their favourite characters.* **3** If you refer to **thrills and spills**, you are referring to an experience which is exciting and full of surprises. **4** See also **thrilled, thrilling**. `◆◆◇◇` `N-COUNT` `V-ERG: V n` `V at/to n` `PHRASE`

thrilled /θrɪld/. **1** If someone is **thrilled**, they are extremely pleased about something. *I was so thrilled to get a good report from him.* ● If you say that someone is **thrilled to bits**, you are emphasizing the fact that they are extremely pleased about something. *I'm thrilled to bits to have won the cash.* **2** See also **thrill**. `◆◇◇◇` `ADJ-GRADED:` `v-link ADJ` `PHRASE` `PRAGMATICS`

thrill·er /'θrɪlə/ **thrillers**. A **thriller** is a book, film, or play that tells an exciting fictional story about something such as criminal activities or spying. `◆◆◇◇` `N-COUNT`

thrill·ing /'θrɪlɪŋ/. **1** Something that is **thrilling** is very exciting and enjoyable. *Our wildlife trips offer a thrilling encounter with wildlife in its natural state.* **♦ thrill·ing·ly** *I have seen them play many times, but never as thrillingly and flawlessly as tonight.* **2** See also **thrill**. `◆◇◇◇` `ADJ-GRADED` `ADV-GRADED`

thrive /θraɪv/ **thrives, thriving, thrived. 1** If someone or something **thrives**, they do well and are successful, healthy, or strong. *Today his company continues to thrive. ...the river's thriving population of kingfishers.* **2** If you say that someone **thrives on** a particular situation, you mean that they enjoy it or that they can deal with it very well, especially when other people find it unpleasant or difficult. *Many people thrive on a stressful lifestyle.* `◆◇◇◇` `VERB` `V` `V-ing` `VERB` `V on n/-ing`

thro'; also spelled **thro. Thro'** is sometimes used as an abbreviation for **through**. `INFORMAL,` `WRITTEN`

throat /θrəʊt/ **throats. 1** Your **throat** is the back N-COUNT of your mouth and the top part of the tubes that go down into your stomach and your lungs. See picture headed **human body**. *She had a sore throat... She felt her throat go dry.* **2** Your **throat** is the front N-COUNT part of your neck. *His striped tie was loosened at his throat.* **3** If you **clear** your **throat**, you cough once PHRASE in order to make it easier to speak or to attract people's attention.
4 If you **ram** something **down** someone's **throat** or PHRASE **force** it **down** their throat, you keep mentioning something such as an idea in order to make them accept it or believe it. *I've always been close to my dad but he's never rammed his career down my throat.* **5** If PHRASE two people or groups are **at each other's throats**, they are quarrelling or fighting violently with each other.
6 If something **sticks in** your **throat**, you find it unac- PHRASE ceptable. *What sticks in my throat is that I wasn't able to win the trophy.* **7 • a lump in** your **throat**: see **lump**.

throaty /ˈθrɔːti/. A **throaty** voice, whisper, or laugh ADJ-GRADED is low and rather rough.

throb /θrɒb/ **throbs, throbbing, throbbed. 1** If ◆◇◇◇◇ part of your body **throbs**, you feel a series of strong VERB: V and usually painful beats there. *Presently George's* V with n ankle began to throb with pain. ...the throbbing* V-ing *tooth whose pain had woken her.* ► Also a noun. N-SING *The bruise on his stomach ached with a steady throb.* **2** If something **throbs**, it vibrates and makes a VERB rhythmical noise. *The music throbbed hypnotically...* V *The gardens blazed with colour and throbbed with* V with n *birdsong.* ► Also a noun. *Jake's head jerked up at the* N-SING *throb of the engine.*

throes /θrəʊz/. **1** If someone is experiencing some- ◆◇◇◇◇ thing very unpleasant or emotionally painful, you FORMAL can say that they are in the **throes** of it, especially when it is in its final stages. ...*when the country was going through the final throes of civil war.* **2** If you PHR-PREP are **in the throes of** doing or experiencing some- FORMAL thing, especially something difficult, you are busy doing it or are deeply involved in it. *The country is in the throes of a general election.* **3** See also **death throes**.

throm·bo·sis /θrɒmˈbəʊsɪs/ **thromboses** N-VAR /θrɒmˈbəʊsiːz/. **Thrombosis** is the formation of a MEDICAL blood clot in a person's heart or in one of their blood vessels, which can cause death. ...*a lady with a thrombosis in her lung.*

throne /θrəʊn/ **thrones. 1** A **throne** is an ornate ◆◆◇◇◇ chair used by a king, queen, or emperor on impor- N-COUNT tant official occasions. **2** You can talk about **the** N-SING: **throne** as a way of referring to the position of being the N king, queen, or emperor. ...*the heir to the throne.*

throng /θrɒŋ/ AM /θrɔːŋ/ **throngs, thronging,** ◆◇◇◇◇ **thronged. 1** A **throng** is a large crowd of people. N-COUNT *An official pushed through the throng.* **2** When peo- LITERARY ple **throng** somewhere, they go there in great num- V to/into/ bers. *Students started emerging from the Inn, talking* around n *noisily, thronging into the cloakroom.* **3** If people LITERARY **throng** a place, they are present there in great num- V n bers. *They throng the beaches between late June and early August.* **♦ thronged** *The streets are thronged* ADJ: *with people.* v-link ADJ with n

throt·tle /ˈθrɒtəl/ **throttles, throttling, throt-** ◆◇◇◇◇ **tled. 1** To **throttle** someone means to kill or injure VERB them by squeezing their throat or tightening some- V n thing around it and preventing them from breath- ing. *He throttled her and hid her body.* **2** If you say VERB that something or someone **is throttling** a process, V n institution, or group, you mean that they are re- stricting it severely or destroying it. *He said the over-valuation of sterling was throttling industry.*
3 The **throttle** of a motor vehicle or aircraft is a device, N-COUNT lever, or pedal that controls the quantity of fuel enter- ing the engine and is used to control the vehicle's speed. *He gently opened the throttle, and the ship be- gan to ease forward.* **4** If something is done **at full** N-UNCOUNT **throttle**, it is done by using a throttle. ...*motor bikes revving at full throttle. ...a little more throttle.* **5** If you say that PHRASE something is done **at full throttle**, you mean that it is

done with great speed and eagerness. *He lived his life at full throttle.*

throttle back. If you **throttle back**, or you **throttle** PHRASAL VB **back** the engine, when driving a motor vehicle or fly- V P noun ing an aircraft, you make it go slower by reducing the V P quantity of fuel entering the engine. *The pilot throttles back slightly to maintain level flight.*

through /θruː/. In addition to the uses shown be- ◆◆◆◆◆ low, **through** is used in phrasal verbs such as 'see through', 'think through', and 'win through'.
1 To move **through** something such as a hole, open- PREP ing, or pipe means to move directly from one side or end of it to the other. ...*rain poured through the roof at the Liverpool Playhouse... Go straight through that door under the EXIT sign.* ► Also an adverb. *He went* ADV: *straight through to the kitchen and took a can of beer* ADV after v *from the fridge.* **2** To cut **through** something means to PREP cut it in two pieces or to make a hole in it. *Use a proper fish knife and fork if possible as they are designed to cut through the flesh but not the bones.* ► Also an adverb. ADV: *Score lightly at first and then repeat, scoring deeper* ADV after v *each time until the board is cut through.* **3** To go PREP **through** a town, area, or country means to travel across it or in it. ...*travelling through pathless woods... President Bush leaves tomorrow for a trip through Asia.* ► Also an adverb. *Few know that the tribe was* ADV *just passing through.* **4** If you move **through** a group PREP of things or a mass of something, it is on either side of you or all around you. *Sybil's fingers ran through the water... He hurried through the rain, to the patrol car.* ► Also an adverb. *He pushed his way through to the* ADV: *edge of the crowd where he waited.* ADV after v
5 To get **through** a barrier or obstruction means to get PREP from one side of it to the other. *Allow twenty-five min- utes to get through Passport Control and Customs.* ► Also an adverb. ...*a maze of concrete and steel barri-* ADV: *ers, designed to prevent vehicles driving straight* ADV after v *through.* **6** If something goes into an object and PREP comes out of the other side, you can say that it passes **through** the object. *Zita was herself unconventional, keeping a safety-pin stuck through her ear lobe.* ► Also ADV: an adverb. *I bored a hole so that the fixing bolt would* ADV after v *pass through.* **7** To go **through** a system means to PREP move around or to pass from one end of it to the other. ...*electric currents travelling through copper wires... What a lot of cards you've got through the post!* ► Also an adverb. *It is also expected to consider a reso-* ADV: *lution which would allow food to go through immedi-* ADV after v *ately with fewer restrictions.* **8** A **through** train goes di- ADJ: ADJ n rectly to a particular place, so that the people who want to go there do not have to change trains. ...*Britain's longest through train journey, 685 miles.*
9 If you see, hear, or feel something **through** a par- PREP ticular thing, that thing is between you and the thing you can see, hear, or feel. *Alice gazed pensively through the wet glass... They could hear music pulsing through the walls of the house.* **10** If something such PREP as a feeling, attitude, or quality, happens or exists **through** an area, organization, or a person's body, it happens or exists everywhere in it or affects all of it. *An atmosphere of anticipation vibrated through the crowd... What was going through his mind when he spoke those amazing words?.*
11 If something happens or exists **through** a period of PREP time, it happens or exists from the beginning until the end. *We're playing in New Zealand, Australia and Ja- pan through November... She kept quiet all through breakfast.* ► Also an adverb. *We've got a tough pro-* ADV *gramme, hard work right through to the summer.* **12** If PREP something happens from a particular period of time AMERICAN **through** another, it starts at the first period and con- tinues until the end of the second period. The usual British word is **to**. *During her busy season (March through June), she often completes as many as fifty paintings a week.*
13 If you go **through** a particular experience or event, PREP you experience it, and if you behave in a particular way **through** it, you behave in that way while it is hap- pening. *Men go through a change of life emotionally just like women... Through it all, Mark was outwardly*

calm. **14** If you are **through** with something or if it is `ADJ: v-link ADJ` **through**, you have finished doing it and will never do it again. If you are **through** with someone, you do not want to have anything to do with them again. _Training as a marriage counsellor would guarantee her some employment once her schooling was through... I'm through with women._ **15** You use **through** in expressions such as **half-way through** and **all the way through** to indicate to what extent an action or task is completed. _A thirty-nine-year-old competitor collapsed half-way through the marathon and died shortly afterwards._ ▶ Also an adverb. `ADV: n ADV` _Stir the pork about until it turns white all the way through._

16 If something happens because of something else, `PREP` you can say that it happens **through** it. _They are understood to have retired through age or ill health._

17 You use **through** when stating the means by which `PREP` a particular thing is achieved. _You simply can't get a ticket through official channels._ **18** If you do something **through** someone else, they take the necessary `PREP` action for you. _Speaking through an interpreter, he called for some new thinking from the West._

19 If something such as a proposal or idea goes `ADV: ADV after v` **through**, it is accepted by people in authority and is made legal or official. _The secretary of state during the Nixon-Ford transition did not wish to push the proposals through._ ▶ Also a preposition. _They want to get_ `PREP` _the plan through Congress as quickly as possible._ **20** If `PREP` someone gets **through** an examination or a round of a competition, they succeed or win. _All the seeded players got through the first round._ ▶ Also an adverb. _Ni-_ `ADV` _geria also go through from that group._ **21** When you `ADV: ADV after v` get **through** while making a telephone call, the call is connected and you can speak to the person you are phoning. _Smith tried to get through to Frank at Warm Springs the next morning._

22 If you look or go **through** a lot of things, you look at `PREP` them or deal with them one after the other. _Let's go through the numbers together and see if a workable deal is possible... David ran through the agreement with Guy, point by point._ **23** If you read **through** `PREP` something, you read it from beginning to end. _She read through pages and pages of the music I had brought her._ ▶ Also an adverb. _The article had been_ `ADV: ADV after v` _authored by Raymond Kennedy. He read it straight through._

24 If you say that someone or something is wet `ADV: adj ADV` **through**, you are emphasizing how wet they are. _I re-_ `PRAGMATICS` _turned to the inn cold and wet, soaked through by the drizzling rain._ **25 Through and through** means com- `PHRASE` pletely and to the greatest extent possible. _People assume they know me through and through the moment we meet._

through·out /θruːˈaʊt/. **1** If you say that some- ◆◆◆◇ thing happens **throughout** a particular period of `PREP` time, you mean that it happens during the whole of that period. _...a single-minded devotion to racing which Gaye has shown throughout her career._ ▶ Also an adverb. _The first song, 'Blue Moon', didn't_ `ADV: ADV with cl` _go too badly except that everyone talked throughout._ **2** If you say that something happens or exists `PREP` **throughout** a place, you mean that it happens or exists in all parts of that place. _'Sight Savers', founded in 1950, now runs projects throughout Africa, the Caribbean and South East Asia._ ▶ Also an adverb. `ADV: ADV with cl` _The route is well sign-posted throughout... Through-out, the walls are white._

through·put /ˈθruːpʊt/. The **throughput** of an or- `N-UNCOUNT` ganization or system is the amount of things it can do or deal with in a particular period of time. _...technologies which will allow us to get much higher throughput._

throw /θrəʊ/ **throws, throwing, threw,** ◆◆◆◇ **thrown**. **1** When you **throw** an object that you are `VERB: V n` holding, you move your hand or arm quickly and let `V n prep/adv` go of the object, so that it moves through the air. _He_ `Also V n with` _spent hours throwing a tennis ball against a wall..._ `V n n` _He threw Brian a rope._ ▶ Also a noun. _One of the_ `N-COUNT` _judges thought it was a foul throw._ ◆ **throw·ing** _He_ `N-UNCOUNT` _didn't really know very much about javelin throw-_

ing. **2** If you **throw** your body or part of your body `VERB: V n prep` into a particular position or place, you move it there `Also V n with` suddenly and with a lot of force. _She threatened to_ `adv` _throw herself in front of a train._ **3** If you **throw** `VERB: V n prep/adv` something into a particular place or position, you put it there in a quick and careless way. _He struggled out of his bulky jacket and threw it on to the back seat._ **4** To **throw** someone into a particular `VERB: V n prep/adv` place or position means to force them roughly into that place or position. _He threw me to the ground and started to kick._ **5** If a horse **throws** its rider, it `VERB: V n` makes him or her fall off, by suddenly jumping or moving violently. **6** If you **throw** a punch, you `VERB: V n` punch someone.

7 If you say that someone **is thrown** into prison, you `VERB: be V-ed in/` mean that they are sent there by the authorities, often `into n` in a brutal way. **8** If a person or thing **is thrown** into an `VERB: be V-ed prep` unpleasant situation or state, something causes them `Also V n prep` to be in that situation or state. _Abidjan was thrown into turmoil because of a protest by taxi drivers._

9 If something **throws** light or a shadow on a surface, `VERB: V n on/onto n` it causes that surface to have light or a shadow on it. **10** If something **throws** doubt or suspicion on a per- `VERB: V n on/upon n` son or thing, it causes people to doubt or suspect them. **11** If you **throw** a look or smile at someone or `VB: no cont,` something, you look or smile at them quickly and `V n at n` suddenly. _Emily turned and threw her a suggestive_ `V n n` _grin._ **12** If you **throw** yourself, your energy, or your `VERB: V n into n` money into a particular job or activity, you become involved in it very actively or enthusiastically.

13 If you **throw** a fit or a tantrum, you suddenly start `VERB: V n` to behave in an uncontrolled way.

14 If something such as a remark or an experience `VERB: V n` **throws** you, it surprises you or confuses you because it is unexpected. _The professor rather threw me by asking if I went in for martial arts._ ▶ **Throw off** means the `PHRASAL VB: V n P` same as **throw**. _I lost my first serve in the first set, it threw me off a bit._ **15** If someone **throws** themselves `PHRASE` **at** you, they make it very obvious that they want to begin a relationship with you, by behaving in a bold and flirtatious way.

16 When someone **throws** a party, they organize one, `VERB: V n` usually in their own home. `INFORMAL`

17 If something cost a particular amount of money **a** `PHRASE` **throw**, they cost that amount each. _Most applications_ `INFORMAL` _software for personal computers cost over $500 a throw._ **18 Throw** is used in a large number of expressions which are explained under other words in this dictionary. For example, the expression to **throw the book at someone** is explained at **book.**

throw around. If you say that someone **throws** `PHRASAL VB: V P noun` **around** a word or name, you disapprove of the fact `PRAGMATICS` that they mention it frequently, often in a silly or irrel- `V P n` evant way in order to impress someone. _Occasionally,_ `INFORMAL` _he throws fancy words around._

throw away or **throw out. 1** When you **throw** `PHRASAL VB: V P noun` **away** or **throw out** something that you do not want, `V P noun` you get rid of it. _I never throw anything away._ **2** If you `V P noun` **throw away** an opportunity, advantage, or benefit, `V n P` you waste it, rather than using it sensibly. _We should have won. We threw it away._ ● See also **throwaway.**

throw back. 1 If you **throw** something **back** at `PHRASAL VB: V n P at n` someone, you remind them of something bad they `Also V P at n n` did in the past, in order to hurt them. _I should never have told you that. I knew you'd throw it back at me._ **2** If someone **is thrown back** on their own powers or `usu passive` resources, they have to use them, because there is nothing else they can use.

throw down. If you **throw down** a challenge to `PHRASAL VB: V P noun` someone, you do something new or unexpected in a bold or forceful manner that will probably cause them to reply or react equally strongly.

throw in. 1 If you **throw in** a remark when having a `PHRASAL VB: V P noun` conversation, you add it in a casual or unexpected `Also V n P` way. _Occasionally Farling threw in a question._ **2** If `V P noun` someone who is selling something **throws** in some- `V-ed P` thing extra, they give you the extra thing and only ask `Also V n P` you to pay for the first thing. _...a weekend break in Paris—with free beer thrown in._

throw off. 1 If you **throw off** something that is re- `PHRASAL VB`

stricting you or making you unhappy, you get rid of it. `V P noun` `V n P`
One day depression descended upon him, and wherever he went after that he could never throw it off. **2** If `V P noun`
something **throws off** a substance, it produces it and
releases it into the air. **3** If you **throw off** people who `V P noun`
are chasing you or trying to find you, you do some- `V n P n.`
thing unexpected that makes them unable to catch `Also V n P`
you or find you. *He tried to throw police off the track of
his lover.* **4** See also **throw** 14.

throw out. 1 See **throw away** 1. **2** If a judge **throws** `PHRASAL VB`
out a case, he or she rejects it and the accused person `Also V P n`
does not have to stand trial. *The defense wants the dis- `Also V n P`
trict Judge to throw out the case.* **3** If you **throw** some- `V n P`
one **out**, you force them to leave a place or group. *He `be/get V-ed P`
was thrown out of the Olympic team after testing posi- `of n`
tive for drugs... I wanted to kill him, but instead I just `Also V P noun`
threw him out of the house.*

throw together. 1 If you **throw** something **togeth-** `PHRASAL VB`
er, for example a meal or a costume, you make it `V n P`
quickly and not very carefully. *Too often, picnic prepa- `V P noun`
ration consists of throwing together some sandwiches.* `INFORMAL`
2 If people **are thrown together** by a situation or `RECIP:`
event, or if one person or group **is thrown together** `be V-ed P`
with another, the situation or event causes them to `V-ed P`
meet and get to know each other, even though they `Also V pl-n P,`
may not want to. *My husband is constantly thrown to- `V P pl-noun,`
gether with young people... If you have men and wom- `V n P with n`
en thrown together in inhospitable surroundings, you
are going to get some sexual tension.*

throw up. 1 When someone **throws up**, they vomit. `PHRASAL VB`
*She said she had thrown up after reading reports of the `V P`
trial.* `INFORMAL`
2 If something **throws up** dust, stones, or water when `V P noun`
it moves or hits the ground, it causes them to rise up `Also V n P`
into the air. *It would have made a crater 100 miles
across and thrown up an immense cloud of dust.*
3 If you say that a building or structure **is thrown up**, `be V-ed P`
you mean that it is built or made very quickly, and is `V P noun`
usually not of very good quality. *Youths threw up bar- `Also V n P`
ricades on the streets.*
4 To **throw up** a particular person or thing means to `V P noun`
produce them or cause them to become noticeable. `Also V n P`
The political struggle threw up a strong leader. `BRITISH`

throw·away /ˈθrəʊəweɪ/ **throwaways. 1** A **throw-** `ADJ: ADJ n`
away product is intended to be used only for a short
time, and then to be thrown away. *...throwaway ra-
zors.* ▶ A **throwaway** is a throwaway product. *...sur-* `N-COUNT`
plus goods and throwaways. **2** If you say that some- `ADJ: ADJ n`
one makes a **throwaway** remark or gesture, you
mean that they make it in a casual way, although it
may be important, or have some serious or humorous effect.

throw·back /ˈθrəʊbæk/ **throwbacks.** If you say `N-COUNT`
that something is a **throwback** to a former time,
you mean that it is like something that existed a
long time ago. *The hall is a throwback to another
era with its old prints and stained-glass.*

ˈthrow-in, ˈthrow-ins. When there is a **throw-in** in `◆◇◇◇◇`
a football or rugby match, the ball is thrown back `N-COUNT`
onto the field after it has been kicked off it.

thrown /θrəʊn/. **Thrown** is the past participle of
throw.

thru. Thru is sometimes used as an abbreviation `WRITTEN,`
for **through**. `usu`
`AMERICAN`
thrum /θrʌm/ **thrums, thrumming, thrummed.** `VERB`
When something such as a machine or engine `V`
thrums, it makes a low beating sound. *The air-
conditioner thrummed.* ▶ Also a noun. *...the thrum* `N-COUNT;`
of refrigeration motors. `SOUND`

thrush /θrʌʃ/ **thrushes. 1** A **thrush** is a fairly `N-COUNT`
small bird with a brown back and a spotted breast.
2 Thrush is a medical condition that most often oc- `N-UNCOUNT`
curs in a baby's mouth or in a woman's vagina.

thrust /θrʌst/ **thrusts, thrusting, thrust. 1** If `◆◆◇◇◇`
you **thrust** something or someone somewhere, you `VERB`
push or move them there quickly with a lot of force. `V n prep/adv`
They thrust him into the back of a jeep. ▶ Also a `N-COUNT`
noun. *Two of the knife thrusts were fatal.* **2 Thrust** `N-UNCOUNT`
is the power or force that is required to make a ve-

hicle move in a particular direction. *...the thrust that
makes the craft move forward.*
3 If something **thrusts** up or out of something else, it `VERB`
sticks up or sticks out in a noticeable way. *A small dish `V adv/prep`
aerial thrust up from the grass verge.* **4** The **thrust** of `LITERARY`
an activity or of an idea is the main or essential things `N-SING`
it expresses. *The main thrust of the research will be the* `adj N`
study of the early Universe.

Thu. See **Thurs.**

thud /θʌd/ **thuds, thudding, thudded. 1** A **thud** `◆◇◇◇◇`
is a dull sound, such as that which a heavy object `N-COUNT`
makes when it hits something soft. *She tripped and
fell with a sickening thud. ...the thud of hammers.*
2 If something **thuds** somewhere, it makes a dull `VERB`
sound, usually when it falls onto something else or `V prep/adv`
hits something else. *She ran up the stairs, her bare `Also V`
feet thudding on the wood.* ♦ **thud·ding** *...the thud-* `N-UNCOUNT`
ding of the bombs beyond the hotel. **3** When your `VERB: V`
heart **thuds**, it beats strongly and quickly, for example because you are very frightened or very happy.

thug /θʌg/ **thugs.** You can refer to a violent person `◆◇◇◇◇`
or criminal as a **thug**; used showing disapproval. `N-COUNT`
...the cowardly thugs who mug old people.
thug·gery /ˈθʌgəri/. **Thuggery** is rough violent `N-UNCOUNT`
behaviour.

thumb /θʌm/ **thumbs, thumbing, thumbed.** `◆◆◇◇◇`
1 Your **thumb** is the short thick digit on the side of `N-COUNT`
your hand next to your first finger. See picture
headed **human body. 2** The **thumb** of a glove or `N-COUNT`
mitten is the part which a person's thumb fits into.
3 If you **thumb** a lift or **thumb** a ride, you stand by `VERB: V n`
the side of the road holding out your thumb until a `V n to n`
driver stops and gives you a lift. *A boy answering
Rory's description thumbed a ride to Howth.* **4** See
also **well-thumbed.**
5 If you say that someone or something **sticks out like** `PHRASE`
a sore thumb or **stands out like a sore thumb**, you `PRAGMATICS`
are emphasizing that they are very noticeable, usually
because they are unusual or inappropriate. *In Japan a
European stands out like a sore thumb.* **6** If you say `PHRASE`
that someone is **twiddling** their **thumbs**, you mean
that they do not have anything to do and are waiting
for something to happen. **7** If you are **under** `PHRASE`
someone's **thumb**, you are under their control, or
very heavily influenced by them.
8 ● **green thumb**: see **green.** ● to **thumb** your **nose at**
someone: see **nose.** ● **rule of thumb**: see **rule.**

thumb through. If you **thumb through** something `PHRASAL VB`
such as a book or magazine, you turn the pages quick- `V P n`
ly and glance at the contents rather than reading each
page carefully. *He thumbed through a couple of pages,
feigning just a slight interest.*

thumb·nail /ˈθʌmneɪl/. A **thumbnail** sketch or ac- `ADJ: ADJ n`
count is a very short description of an event, idea,
or plan which gives only the main details.

ˌthumbs ˈdown; also spelled **thumbs-down.** If you `N-SING`
say that someone gives a plan, idea, or suggestion `INFORMAL`
the **thumbs-down**, you are indicating that they do
not approve of it and refuse to accept it.

ˌthumbs ˈup; also spelled **thumbs up. 1** A `N-SING`
thumbs-up or a **thumbs-up sign** is a sign that you
make by raising up your thumb to show that you agree
with someone, that you are happy with an idea or
situation, or that everything is all right. *She checked
the hall, then gave the others a thumbs-up sign.* **2** If `N-SING:`
you give a plan, idea, or suggestion the **thumbs-up**, `the N`
you indicate that you approve of it and are willing `INFORMAL`
to accept it. *It more or less gets the thumbs up from
everyone.*

thumb·tack /ˈθʌmtæk/ **thumbtacks.** A **thumb-** `N-COUNT`
tack is a short pin with a broad flat top which is `AMERICAN`
used for fastening papers or pictures to a board or
other surface. The usual British term is **drawing
pin.**

thump /θʌmp/ **thumps, thumping, thumped.** `◆◇◇◇◇`
1 If you **thump** something, you hit it hard, usually `VERB: V n`
with your fist. *I heard you thumping on the door.* `V n`
▶ Also a noun. *He felt a thump on his shoulder.* **2** If `N-COUNT`
you **thump** someone, you attack them and hit them `VERB`
with your fist. *Don't say it serves me right or I'll* `V n`
`INFORMAL`

thump you. **3** If you **thump** something somewhere or if it **thumps** there, it makes a loud, dull sound by hitting something else. *Waiters went scurrying down the aisles, thumping down tureens of soup. ...paving stones and bricks which have been thumping down on police shields and helmets... She dashed out through the door, her stockinged feet thumping softly as she ran up the stairs.* ▶ Also a noun. *There was a loud thump as the horse crashed into the van.* **4** When your heart **thumps**, it beats strongly and quickly, usually because you are afraid or excited.
> BRITISH
> V-ERG:
> V n prep
> V n with adv
> V prep/adv
> V
> N-COUNT
> VERB: V

thump·ing /ˈθʌmpɪŋ/. **Thumping** is used to emphasize that something is very great or severe. *The Right has a thumping majority... The gloom deepened after a thumping £145m loss at British Rail.* ▶ Also an adverb. *A thumping good time was had by all.*
> ◆◇◇◇◇
> ADJ: ADJ n
> PRAGMATICS
> BRITISH,
> INFORMAL
> ADV: ADV adj

thun·der /ˈθʌndə/ **thunders, thundering, thundered.** **1 Thunder** is the loud noise that you hear from the sky after a flash of lightning, especially during a storm. *...a distant clap of thunder.* **2** When it **thunders**, a loud noise comes from the sky after a flash of lightning. **3** The **thunder of** something that is moving or making a sound is the loud deep noise it makes. *...the thunder of the sea on the rocks.* **4** If something or someone **thunders** somewhere, they move there quickly and with a lot of noise. *The horses thundered across the valley floor.* **5** If something **thunders**, it makes a very loud noise, usually continuously. *...the sound of the guns thundering in the fog.* **6** If you **thunder** something, you say it loudly and forcefully, especially because you are angry. *'It's your money. Ask for it!' she thundered.*
> ◆◆◇◇◇
> N-UNCOUNT
> VERB: V
> N-UNCOUNT:
> N of n
> VERB
> V prep/adv
> VERB
> V
> VERB: V n
> V with quote
> WRITTEN

thunder·bolt /ˈθʌndəbəʊlt/ **thunderbolts.** A **thunderbolt** is a flash of lightning, accompanied by thunder, which strikes something such as a building or a tree.
> N-COUNT

thunder·clap /ˈθʌndəklæp/ **thunderclaps.** A **thunderclap** is a short loud bang that you hear in the sky just after you see a flash of lightning.
> N-COUNT

thun·der·ous /ˈθʌndərəs/. If you describe a noise as **thunderous**, you mean that it is very loud and deep. *The audience responded with a round of thunderous applause.*
> ◆◇◇◇◇
> ADJ-GRADED

thunder·storm /ˈθʌndəstɔːm/ **thunderstorms.** A **thunderstorm** is a storm in which there is thunder and lightning and a lot of heavy rain.
> ◆◇◇◇◇
> N-COUNT

thunder·struck /ˈθʌndəstrʌk/. If you say that someone is **thunderstruck**, you mean that they are extremely surprised or shocked.
> ADJ
> FORMAL

thun·dery /ˈθʌndəri/. When the weather is **thundery**, there is a lot of thunder, or there are heavy clouds which make you think that there will be thunder soon. *Thundery weather is forecast.*
> ADJ-GRADED

Thurs. Also spelled **Thur.** or **Thu..** **Thurs.** is an abbreviation for **Thursday.**
> ◆◆◇◇◇
> WRITTEN

Thurs·day /ˈθɜːzdeɪ, -di/ **Thursdays.** Thursday is the day after Wednesday and before Friday. *On Thursday Barrett invited me for a drink... We go and do the weekly shopping every Thursday morning.*
> ◆◆◆◇
> N-VAR

thus /ðʌs/. **1** You use **thus** to show that what you are about to mention is the result or consequence of something else that you have just mentioned. *Neither of them thought of turning on the lunchtime news. Thus Caroline didn't hear of John's death until Peter telephoned... Some people will be more capable and thus better paid than others.* **2** If you say that something is **thus** or happens **thus** you mean that it is, or happens, as you have just described or as you are just about to describe. *Joanna was pouring the drink. While she was thus engaged, Charles sat on one of the bar-stools.* **3 ● thus far**: see **far.**
> ◆◆◆◇
> ADV:
> ADV with cl/
> group
> PRAGMATICS
> FORMAL
> ADV
> PRAGMATICS
> FORMAL

thwart /θwɔːt/ **thwarts, thwarting, thwarted.** If you **thwart** someone or **thwart** their plans, you prevent them from doing or getting what they want. *The security forces were doing all they could to thwart terrorists.*
> ◆◇◇◇◇
> VERB
> V n

thy /ðaɪ/. **Thy** is an old-fashioned, poetic, or religious word for 'your' when you are talking to one person. *Honor thy father and thy mother.*
> ◆◇◇◇◇
> DET-POSS

thyme /taɪm/. **Thyme** is a type of herb used in cooking.
> ◆◇◇◇◇
> N-UNCOUNT

thy·roid /ˈθaɪrɔɪd/ **thyroids.** Your **thyroid** or your **thyroid gland** is a gland in your neck that produces chemicals which control the way your body grows and functions.
> ◆◇◇◇◇
> N-COUNT

thy·self /ðaɪˈself/. **Thyself** is an old-fashioned, poetic, or religious word for 'yourself' when you are talking to only one person. *Love thy neighbour as thyself.*
> PRON-REFL

ti·ara /tiˈɑːrə/ **tiaras.** A **tiara** is a semi-circular metal band decorated with jewels which a woman of very high social rank wears on her head at formal social occasions.
> N-COUNT

tibia /ˈtɪbiə/ **tibias.** Your **tibia** is the inner bone of the two bones in the lower part of your leg.
> N-COUNT
> MEDICAL

tic /tɪk/ **tics.** If someone has a **tic**, a part of their face or body keeps making an uncontrollable twitching movement, for example because they are tired or have a nervous illness. *She developed a tic in her left eye.*
> N-COUNT

tick /tɪk/ **ticks, ticking, ticked.** **1** A **tick** is a written mark like a V with the right side extended. It is used to show that something is correct or has been selected or dealt with. The usual American word is **check**. *Place a tick in the appropriate box.* **2** If you **tick** something that is written on a piece of paper, you put a tick next to it. *Please tick this box if you do not wish to receive such mailings.* **3** When a clock or watch **ticks**, it makes a regular series of short sounds as it works. *A wind-up clock ticked busily from the kitchen counter.* ▶ **Tick away** means the same as **tick**. *A grandfather clock ticked away in a corner.* ◆ **tick·ing** *...the endless ticking of clocks.* **4** The **tick** of a clock or watch is the series of short sounds it makes when it is working, or one of those sounds. *...the tick of the grandfather clock.* **5** You can use **tick** to refer to a very short period of time. *Just hang on a tick, we may be able to help... I'll be back in a tick... I shall be with you in two ticks.* **6** If you talk about what makes someone **tick**, you are talking about the beliefs, wishes, and feelings that make them behave in the way that they do. **7** A **tick** is a small creature like a flea which lives on the bodies of people or animals and uses their blood as food. *...chemicals that destroy ticks and mites.*
> ◆◆◇◇◇
> N-COUNT
> BRITISH
> VERB
> V n
> BRITISH
> VERB
> V
> PHRASAL VB
> V P
> N-UNCOUNT
> N-COUNT
> N-COUNT
> BRITISH,
> INFORMAL
> VERB: V
> INFORMAL
> N-COUNT

tick away or **tick by** or **tick on.** If you say that the clock or time is **ticking away, ticking by**, or **ticking on**, you mean that time is passing, especially when there is something urgent that needs to be done or when someone is waiting for something to happen. *The clock ticks away, leaving little time for talks.* ● See also **tick 3.**
> PHRASAL VB
> V P

tick by. See **tick away.**
> PHRASAL VB

tick off. **1** If you **tick off** items on a list, you write a tick or other mark next to them, in order to show that they have been dealt with. *Tick it off in the box.* **2** If you **tick** someone **off**, you speak angrily to them because they have done something wrong. *Abdel felt free to tick him off for smoking too much... Traffic police ticked off a pensioner for jumping a red light.* ◆ **tick·ing off, tickings off** *They got a ticking off from the police.* **3** If you say that something **ticks** you **off**, you mean that it annoys you. *She's still ticked off at him for brushing her off and going out with you instead.*
> PHRASAL VB
> V P noun
> V n P
> V P noun
> INFORMAL
> N-COUNT
> V n P
> V-ed P
> INFORMAL

tick on. See **tick away.**
> PHRASAL VB

tick over. **1** If an engine is **ticking over**, it is running at a low speed or rate, for example when it is switched on but you are not actually using it. **2** If a person, system, or business **is ticking over**, they are working steadily, but not producing very much or making much progress.
> PHRASAL VB
> V P
> BRITISH
> V P
> BRITISH

tick·er /ˈtɪkə/ **tickers.** Your **ticker** is your heart. *He suffers from a bit of a dodgy ticker.*
> N-COUNT
> INFORMAL

'ticker tape. **Ticker tape** consists of long narrow strips of paper on which information such as stock exchange prices is printed by a machine.
> N-UNCOUNT

tick·et /'tɪkɪt/ **tickets. 1** A **ticket** is an official piece of paper or card which shows that you have paid to enter a place of entertainment such as a cinema or a sports ground, or shows that you have paid for a journey. *I queued for two hours to get a ticket to see the football game... Entrance is free, but by ticket only. ...a ticket collector at Waterloo Station.* **2** A **ticket** is an official piece of paper which orders you to pay a fine or to appear in court because you have committed a driving or parking offence. *I want to know at what point I break the speed limit and get a ticket.* **3** A **ticket** for something such as a raffle or a lottery is a piece of paper with a number on it. **4** The particular **ticket** on which a person fights an election is the party they represent or the policies they support. *He first ran for president on a far-left ticket.* **5** If you say that something is **just the ticket**, you mean that it is exactly what is needed. *Young kids need all the energy and protein they can get and whole milk is just the ticket.* **6** See also **ticketing; big-ticket, dream ticket, meal ticket, parking ticket, season ticket.**

N-COUNT: also by N

N-COUNT

N-COUNT

N-SING

PHRASE INFORMAL

tick·et·ing /'tɪkɪtɪŋ/. **1 Ticketing** is the act or activity of selling tickets. *...automatic ticketing machines.* **2** See also **ticket.**

N-UNCOUNT

'ticket office, ticket offices. A **ticket office** is a place where you can buy a ticket, for example at a railway station.

N-COUNT

,ticking 'off. See **tick off.**

tick·le /'tɪkəl/ **tickles, tickling, tickled. 1** When you **tickle** someone, you move your fingers lightly over a sensitive part of their body, often in order to make them laugh. **2** If something **tickles** you or **tickles**, it causes an irritating feeling by lightly touching a part of your body. *A beard doesn't scratch, it just tickles.* **3** If a fact or a situation **tickles** you, it amuses you or gives you pleasure. *It tickles me to see him riled.* **♦ tick·led** *They all sounded just as tickled.*

VERB: V n

VERB: V n V

VERB: V n it V n to-inf

ADJ-GRADED

tick·lish /'tɪkəlɪʃ/. **1** A **ticklish** problem, situation, or task is difficult and needs to be dealt with carefully. *...the ticklish question of the future of the European Community.* **2** Someone who is **ticklish** is sensitive to being tickled, and laughs as soon as you tickle them.

ADJ-GRADED

ADJ-GRADED

tid·al /'taɪdəl/. **Tidal** means relating to or produced by tides. *The tidal stream or current gradually decreases in the shallows.*

ADJ

'tidal wave, tidal waves. 1 A **tidal wave** is a very large wave, often caused by an earthquake, that flows onto the land and destroys things. **2** If you describe a very large number of emotions, things, or people as a **tidal wave**, you mean that they all occur at the same time. *We are now seeing a tidal wave of job losses in all sections of the economy.*

N-COUNT

N-COUNT

tid·bit /'tɪdbɪt/. See **titbit.**

tid·dler /'tɪdlə/ **tiddlers. 1** A **tiddler** is a very small fish of any kind. **2** If you refer to a person or thing as a **tiddler**, you mean that they are very insignificant or small, especially when compared to other people or things of the same type. *Conde Nast's British division is a relative tiddler compared with the giant IPC.*

N-COUNT INFORMAL

N-COUNT INFORMAL, BRITISH

tid·dly /'tɪdəli/. **1** If someone is **tiddly**, they are slightly drunk. *I feel a bit tiddly. I don't know what you must think.* **2** If you describe a thing as **tiddly**, you mean that it is very small. *It's a tiddly little thing.*

ADJ-GRADED INFORMAL, BRITISH

ADJ-GRADED INFORMAL, BRITISH

tiddly·wink /'tɪdəliwɪŋk/ **tiddlywinks. 1 Tiddlywinks** is a game in which the players try to make small round pieces of plastic jump into a container, by pressing their edges with a larger piece of plastic. **2 Tiddlywinks** are the small round piece of plastic used in the game of tiddlywinks.

N-UNCOUNT

N-COUNT

tide /taɪd/ **tides, tiding, tided. 1** The **tide** is the regular change in the level of the sea on the shore. *The tide was at its highest... The tide was going out.* **2** A **tide** is a current in the sea that is caused by the regular and continuous movement of large areas of water towards and away from the shore. *Roman ves-*

N-COUNT

N-COUNT

sels used to sail with the tide from Boulogne to Richborough. • See also **high tide, low tide.** **3** The **tide of** opinion, for example, is what the majority of people think at a particular time. *The tide of opinion seems overwhelmingly in his favour.* **4** People sometimes refer to events or forces that are difficult or impossible to control as **the tide of** history, for example. *The tide of war swept back across their country.* **5** You can talk about a **tide of** something, especially something which is unpleasant, when there is a large and increasing amount of it. *...an ever increasing tide of crime.*

N-SING: N of n

N-SING: the N of n

N-SING: N of n

tide over. If you do something for someone to **tide** them **over**, you help them through a period when they are having difficulties, especially by lending them money. *The banks were prepared to put up 50 million guilders to tide over the company.*

PHRASAL VB V n P V P noun

tid·ings /'taɪdɪŋz/. You can use **tidings** to refer to news that someone tells you. *He hated always to be the bearer of bad tidings.*

N-PLURAL FORMAL, DATED

tidy /'taɪdi/ **tidier, tidiest; tidies, tidying, tidied. 1** Something that is **tidy** is neat and arranged in an orderly way. *Having a tidy desk can seem impossible if you have a busy, demanding job.* **♦ tidi·ly** /'taɪdɪli/. *...books and magazines stacked tidily on shelves.* **♦ tidi·ness** *Employees are expected to maintain a high standard of tidiness in their dress and appearance.* **2** Someone who is **tidy** likes everything to be neat and arranged in an orderly way. *She's obsessively tidy, always hoovering and polishing.* **♦ tidiness** *I'm very impressed by your tidiness.* **3** When you **tidy** a place such as a room or cupboard, you make it neat by putting things in their proper places. *She made her bed, and tidied her room.* **4** A **tidy** amount of money is a large amount. *The opportunities are there to make a tidy profit.*

♦♦♦◇◇◇

ADJ-GRADED

ADV

N-UNCOUNT

ADJ-GRADED

N-UNCOUNT

VERB V n

ADJ-GRADED: ADJ n INFORMAL

tidy away. When you **tidy** something **away**, you put it in something else so that it is not in the way. *When they'd gone, McMinn tidied away the glasses and teacups.*

PHRASAL VB V n P V P noun BRITISH

tidy up. When you **tidy up** or **tidy** a place **up**, you put things back in their proper places so that everything is neat. *I really must start tidying the place up.*

PHRASAL VB V P V n P Also V P noun

tie /taɪ/ **ties, tying, tied. 1** If you **tie** two things together, you fasten them together with a knot. *He tied the ends of the plastic bag together... They tied the ends of the bags securely.* **2** If you **tie** something or someone in a particular place or position, you put them in that place or position and fasten them there using rope or string. *He tied her hands behind her back.* **3** If you **tie** a piece of string or cloth around something, you put a piece of string or cloth around it and fasten the ends together in a knot or bow. *Roll the meat and tie it with string.* **4** If you **tie** something in a knot or bow, you fasten the ends together in a knot or bow. *He took a short length of rope and swiftly tied a slip knot... She tied a knot in a cherry stem.* **5** When you **tie** something, you close or fasten it using a bow or knot. *He pulled on his heavy suede shoes and tied the laces.* **6** A **tie** is a long narrow piece of cloth that is worn round the neck under a shirt collar and tied in a knot at the front. Ties are worn mainly by men. See picture headed **clothes.** **7** If one thing **is tied** to another, the two things have a close connection or link. *My social life and business life are closely tied.* **8 Ties** are the connections you have with people or a place. *Quebec has always had particularly close ties to France.* **9** If you **are tied** to a particular place or situation, you are forced to accept it and cannot change it. *They had children and were consequently tied to the school holidays.* **10** If two people **tie** in a competition or game, they have the same number of points or the same degree of success. *Ronan Rafferty had tied with Frank Nobilo.* ▶ Also a noun. *The first game ended in a tie.* **11** In sport, a **tie** is a match that is part of a competition. The

♦♦♦♦◇

VERB V n adv/prep V n

VERB: V n to n V n prep/adv

VERB: V n prep/adv V n with n

VERB V n V n in n

V-ERG V n Also V

N-COUNT

VERB: be V-ed to n pl-n be V-ed N-COUNT

VB: usu passive be V-ed to n/ -ing

V-RECIP: pl-n V V with n

N-COUNT

N-COUNT

losers are eliminated and the winners go on to the next round.

12 See also **tied**; **black tie**, **bow tie**, **old school tie**. ● your **hands are tied**: see **hand**. ● to **tie the knot**: see **knot**.

tie down. A person or thing that **ties** you **down** re- PHRASAL VB   V n P
stricts your freedom in some way. *We'd agreed from the beginning not to tie each other down.*

tie in with or **tie up with.** If something such as an PHRASAL VB   ERG
idea or fact **ties in with** or **ties up with** something else,   V P P n
it is compatible with it or connected with it. *Our wed-   Also be V-ed P
ding had to tie in with David leaving the army.*   P n

tie up. 1 When you **tie** something **up**, you fasten PHRASAL VB   V P noun
string or rope round it so that it is firm or secure. *He   Also V n P
tied up the bag and took it outside.* **2** If someone **ties**   V n P
another person **up**, they fasten ropes or chains   Also V P noun
around them so that they cannot move or escape.
*Masked robbers broke in, tied him up, and made off
with $8,000.* **3** If you **tie** an animal **up**, you fasten it to   V P noun
a fixed object with a piece of rope so that it cannot run   Also V n P
away. *They dismounted, tied up their horses and gave
them the grain.*
4 If you **tie up** an issue or problem, you deal with it in   V P noun
a way that gives definite conclusions or answers. *It   Also V n P
hopes to tie up a deal within the next two weeks.*
5 See also **tied up**.

tie up with. See **tie in with**. PHRASAL VB

'tie-break, tie-breaks. A **tie-break** is an extra N-COUNT
game which is played in a tennis match when the
score in a set is 6-6. The player who wins the tie-
break wins the set.

'tie-breaker, tie-breakers. A **tie-breaker** is an N-COUNT
extra question or round that decides the winner of a
competition or game when two or more people
have the same score at the end.

tied /taɪd/. **1** A **tied** cottage or house belongs to a ADJ
farmer or other employer and is rented to someone BRITISH
who works for him or her. **2** See also **tie**.

,tied 'up. If someone or something is **tied up**, they ◆◇◇◇◇
are busy or being used, with the result that they are ADJ-GRADED:
not available for anything else. *He's tied up with his* v-link ADJ
new book. INFORMAL

'tie-dye, tie-dyes, tie-dyeing, tie-dyed. 1 If a VERB:
piece of cloth or a garment is **tie-dyed**, it is tied in be V-ed
knots and then put into dye, so that some parts become more deeply coloured than others. **2** A **tie-** N-VAR
dye is a garment or piece of cloth that has been tie-
dyed. *...a hideous tie-dye shirt.*

'tie-pin, tie-pins; also spelled **tiepin.** A **tie-pin** is N-COUNT
narrow brooch used to pin a person's tie to their
shirt.

tier /tɪə/ **tiers. 1** A **tier** is a row or layer of some- ◆◇◇◇◇
thing that has other layers above or below it. *...the* N-COUNT
*auditorium with the tiers of seats around and above
it.* ▶ Also a combining form. *...a three-tier wedding* COMB
cake. **2** A **tier** is a level in an organization or sys- N-COUNT
tem. ▶ Also a combining form. *...the possibility of a* COMB
two-tier system of universities.

tiff /tɪf/ **tiffs.** A **tiff** is a small unimportant quarrel, N-COUNT
especially between two close friends or between a
husband and wife.

ti·ger /'taɪgə/ **tigers.** A **tiger** is a large fierce animal ◆◇◇◇◇
belonging to the cat family. Tigers are orange with N-COUNT
black stripes. See picture headed **animals**. ● See
also **paper tiger**.

tight /taɪt/ **tighter, tightest. 1** **Tight** clothes or ◆◆◆◇◇
shoes are rather small and fit closely to your body. ADJ-GRADED
♦ **tight·ly** *He buttoned his collar tightly round his* ADV-GRADED:
thick neck. ADV with v
2 If you hold someone or something **tight**, you hold ADV-GRADED
them firmly and securely. *Hold on tight!* ▶ Also an ad- ADJ-GRADED
jective. *He kept a tight hold of her arm.* ♦ **tightly** *She* ADV-GRADED:
climbed back into bed and wrapped her arms tightly ADV after v
round her body.
3 **Tight** controls or rules are very strict. *The Govern-* ADJ-GRADED
*ment were prepared to keep a tight hold on public sec-
tor pay rises.* ♦ **tightly** *The internal media is tightly* ADV-GRADED
controlled by the Communist Party.
4 Something that is shut **tight** is shut very firmly. ADV-GRADED
...closing her bedroom door tight behind her.

♦ **tightly** *Pemberton frowned and closed his eyes* ADV-GRADED
tightly.
5 Skin, cloth, or string that is **tight** is stretched or ADJ-GRADED
pulled so that it is smooth or straight. ♦ **tightly** *Her* ADV-GRADED:
sallow skin was drawn tightly across the bones of her ADV with v
face.
6 **Tight** is used to describe a group of things or an ADJ-GRADED
amount of something that is closely packed together.
She curled up in a tight ball. ▶ Also an adverb. *The* ADV
people sleep on sun loungers packed tight. ♦ **tightly** ADV-GRADED:
Many animals travel in tightly packed lorries. ADV after v,
  ADV -ed
7 If a part of your body is **tight**, it feels rather uncom- ADJ-GRADED
fortable and painful, for example because you are ill,
anxious, or angry. *...a tight and angry face.* ♦ **tight-**
·ness *...pain or tightness in the chest.* N-UNCOUNT
8 A **tight** group of people is one whose members are ADJ-GRADED
closely bound by beliefs, feelings, or interests. *...a
small, tight knot of people who have been with Madonna since the beginning.*
9 A **tight** bend or corner is one that changes direction ADJ-GRADED
very quickly so that you cannot see very far round it.
10 A **tight** schedule or budget allows very little time or ADJ-GRADED
money for unexpected events or expenses. *Financial-
ly, things are a bit tight.*
11 A **tight** contest is one where none of the competi- ADJ-GRADED
tors has a clear advantage or looks likely to win, so
that it is difficult to say who the winner will be.
12 If you say that someone is **tight**, you disapprove of ADJ-GRADED
them because they are unwilling to spend money. PRAGMATICS
13 If you are in **a tight corner** or in **a tight spot**, you PHRASE
are in a difficult situation. *That puts the president in a* INFORMAL
tight spot if the vote is not a resounding 'yes.'
14 See also **airtight**, **skin-tight**. ● to **keep a tight rein**
on: see **rein**. ● to **sit tight**: see **sit**.

tight·en /'taɪtən/ **tightens, tightening, tight-** ◆◆◇◇◇
ened. 1 If you **tighten** your grip on something, you V-ERG: V n
hold the thing more firmly or securely. *Stefano's* V
grip tightened and his tone became colder. **2** If you V-ERG
tighten a rope or chain, it is stretched or pulled V n
hard until it is straight. *The anchorman flung his* Also V
whole weight back, tightening the rope. **3** When you VERB: V n
tighten a screw, nut, or other device, you turn it or
move it so that it is more firmly in place or holds
something more firmly. ▶ **Tighten up** means the PHRASAL VB
same as **tighten**. *It's important to tighten up the* V P noun
wheels properly. Also V n P
4 If a part of your body **tightens**, the muscles in it be- VERB: V
come tense and stiff, for example because you are an-
gry or afraid. ♦ **tight·en·ing** *...a tightening of the* N-UNCOUNT
muscles in the neck.
5 If a government or organization **tightens** its grip on V-ERG
a group of people or an activity, it begins to have more V n
control over it. *...his plans to tighten his grip on the* Also V
machinery of central government. **6** If someone in VERB: V n
authority **tightens** a rule, a policy, or a system, they
make it stricter or more efficient. ▶ **Tighten up** PHRASAL VB
means the same as **tighten**. *Every attempt to tighten* V P noun
up the law had failed. ♦ **tightening** *...the tightening* N-UNCOUNT
of state control over press and broadcasting.
7 ● to **tighten** your **belt**: see **belt**. ● to **tighten the**
screw: see **screw**.

tighten up. If a group, team, or organization **tight-** PHRASAL VB
ens up, they make an effort to control what they are V P
doing more closely, in order to become more efficient
and successful. *I want us to be a bit more sensible this
time and tighten up.* ● See also **tighten** 3 and 6.

,tight-'fisted. If you describe someone as **tight-** ADJ-GRADED
fisted, you disapprove of them because they are un- PRAGMATICS
willing to spend money.

,tight-'lipped. 1 If you describe someone as ADJ-GRADED
tight-lipped, you mean that they are unwilling to
give any information about something. *Military officials are still tight-lipped about when or whether
their forces will launch a ground offensive.* **2** Some- ADJ-GRADED
one who is **tight-lipped** has their lips pressed tightly
together, especially because they are angry.

tight·rope /'taɪtrəʊp/ **tightropes. 1** A **tightrope** is ◆◇◇◇◇
a tightly stretched piece of rope on which an acro- N-COUNT
bat balances and performs tricks. **2** You can use N-COUNT
tightrope in expressions such as **walk a tightrope**

and **live on a tightrope** to indicate that someone is in a difficult situation and has to be very careful about what they say or do. *For the past few days Corinne has been living on an emotional tightrope.*

tights /taɪts/. Tights are a piece of clothing made of thin material such as nylon that covers your hips and each of your legs and feet separately. In American English, the usual word is **pantyhose** when referring to the kind of tights worn by women and girls. *...a new pair of tights.*   ◆◇◇◇ N-PLURAL: also a pair of N BRITISH

ti·gress /'taɪgrɪs/ **tigresses**. A tigress is a female tiger.   N-COUNT

til·de /'tɪldə/ **tildes**. A tilde is a symbol that is written over the letter 'n' in Spanish (ñ) and the letters 'o' (õ) and 'a' (ã) in Portuguese to indicate the way in which they should be pronounced.   N-COUNT

tile /taɪl/ **tiles, tiling, tiled**. **1** Tiles are flat, square pieces of baked clay, carpet, cork, or other substance, which are fixed as a covering onto a floor or wall. **2** Tiles are flat pieces of baked clay which are used for covering roofs. See picture headed **house and flat**. **3** When someone **tiles** a surface such as a roof or floor, they cover it with tiles. ♦ **-tiled** *...a slate-tiled floor.* **4** See also **tiling**.   ◆◆◇◇ N-VAR / N-VAR / VERB: V n / COMB

5 If someone has a night **on the tiles** or is out **on the tiles**, they go out in the evening, for example to a bar or a disco, and do not return home until very late.   PHRASE BRITISH, INFORMAL

til·ing /'taɪlɪŋ/. **1** You can refer to a surface that is covered by tiles as **tiling**. **2** See also **tile**.   N-UNCOUNT

till /tɪl/ **tills, tilling, tilled**. **1** Till is often used instead of **until**. *They had to wait till Monday to ring the bank manager.* ► Also a conjunction. *They slept till the alarm bleeper woke them at four.* **2** In a shop or other place of business, a **till** is a counter or cash register where money is kept, and where customers pay for what they have bought. **3** When people **till** land, they prepare the earth and work on it in order to grow crops.   ◆◆◇◇ PREP INFORMAL / CONJ / N-COUNT / VERB: V n LITERARY

till·er /'tɪlə/ **tillers**. The **tiller** of a boat is a handle that is fixed to the rudder. It is used to turn the rudder, which then steers the boat.   N-COUNT

tilt /tɪlt/ **tilts, tilting, tilted**. **1** If you **tilt** an object, it moves into a sloping position with one end or side higher than the other. *Leonard tilted his chair back on two legs and stretched his long body... The boat instantly tilted, filled and sank.* **2** If you **tilt** part of your body, usually your head, you move it slightly upwards or to one side. *Mari tilted her head back so that she could look at him.* ► Also a noun. *...an apologetic tilt of his head.* **3** The **tilt** of something is the fact that it tilts or slopes, or the angle at which it tilts or slopes.   ◆◆◇◇ V-ERG: V n / V n adv/prep / Also V adv/ prep / VERB / V n adv/prep / Also V n / N-COUNT / N-COUNT

4 If something or someone **tilts** towards a particular opinion, they change slightly so that they become more in agreement with that opinion or position. *The paper has done much to tilt American public opinion in favour of military intervention.* ► Also a noun. *The chairman also criticised the plan for its tilt towards higher taxes.*   V-ERG: V prep/adv / V n prep/adv / N-SING

5 A **tilt** at something is an attempt to win or conquer it. *His first tilt at Parliament came in the same year but he failed to win the seat.*   N-COUNT: N at n JOURNALISM

6 If something is moving or happening **full tilt** or at **full tilt**, it is moving or happening with as much speed, energy, or force as possible.   PHRASE

tim·ber /'tɪmbə/ **timbers**. **1** Timber is wood that is used for building houses and making furniture. You can also refer to trees that are grown for this purpose as **timber**. **2** The **timbers** of a ship or house are the large pieces of wood that have been used to build it.   ◆◆◇◇ N-UNCOUNT / N-COUNT

tim·bered /'tɪmbəd/. A **timbered** building has a wooden frame or wooden beams showing on the outside. ● See also **half-timbered**.   ADJ

'timber yard, timber yards. A **timber yard** is a place where timber is stored and sold. The usual American word is **lumberyard**.   N-COUNT BRITISH

tim·bre /'tæmbə/ **timbres**. The **timbre** of someone's voice or of a musical instrument is the   N-COUNT FORMAL

particular quality of sound that it has. *His voice had a deep timbre.*

time /taɪm/ **times, timing, timed**. **1** Time is what we measure in minutes, hours, days, and years. *...a two-week period of time... Time passed, and still Ma did not appear... Religion has changed over time.*   ◆◆◆◆◆ N-UNCOUNT

2 You use **time** to ask or talk about a specific point in the day, which can be stated in hours and minutes and is shown on clocks. *'What time is it?'—'Eight o'clock.'... He asked me the time.* **3** If a child can **tell the time**, they are able to find out what the time is by looking at a clock or watch. **4** The **time** when something happens is the point in the day when it happens or is supposed to happen. *Departure times are 0815 from St Quay, and 1815 from St Helier.* **5** You use **time** to refer to the system of expressing time and counting hours that is used in a particular part of the world. *The incident happened just after ten o'clock local time.*   N-SING: what/the N / PHRASE / N-COUNT / N-UNCOUNT: supp N

6 You use **time** to refer to the period that someone spends doing something or when something has been happening. *Adam spent a lot of time in his grandfather's office... Listen to me, I haven't got much time... Thank you very much for your time.* **7** If you say that something has been happening for **a time** you mean that it has been happening for a fairly long period of time. *He stayed for quite a time.* **8** You use **time** to refer to a period of time or a point in time, when you are describing what is happening then. *We were in the same college, which was male-only at that time... During the time I was married I tried to be the perfect wife... Homes are more affordable than at any time in the past five years.*   N-UNCOUNT: also a N / N-SING: a N / N-COUNT: with supp

9 You use **time** or **times** to talk about a particular period in history or in your life. *We'll be alone together, quite like old times... We are in one of the most severe recessions in modern times.* **10** You can use the **times** to refer to the present time and to modern fashions, tastes, and developments. *He is unafraid to move with the times... Johnny has changed his image to fit the times.* **11** When you describe the **time** that you had on a particular occasion or during a particular part of your life, you are describing the sort of experience that you had then. *Sarah and I had a great time while the kids were away.* **12** Your **time** is the amount of time that you have to live, or to do a particular thing. *Now Martin has begun to suffer the effects of AIDS, and he says his time is running out... I doubt I would change anything if I had my time again.*   N-COUNT: with supp / N-PLURAL: the N / N-COUNT: adj N / N-SING: poss N

13 If you say it is **time** for something, **time** to do something, or **time** someone did something, you mean that this thing ought to happen or be done now. *It was time for him to go to work... This was no time to make a speech.*   N-UNCOUNT

14 When you talk about a **time** when something happens, you are referring to a specific occasion when it happens. *The last time I saw her was about sixteen years ago... Remember that time she picked up my daughter when I was ill?* **15** You use **time** after numbers to say how often something happens. *It was her job to make tea three times a day... How many times has your mother told you never to talk to strangers?*   N-COUNT: with supp / N-COUNT

16 You use **times** after numbers when comparing one thing to another and saying, for example, how much bigger, smaller, better, or worse it is. *Its profits are rising four times faster than the average company. ...an area five times the size of Britain.* **17** You use **times** in arithmetic to link numbers or amounts that are multiplied together to reach a total. *Four times six is 24.*   N-PLURAL: num N compar, num N, num N n, num N as adj/ adv / CONJ

18 Someone's **time** in a race is the amount of time it takes them to finish the race. *He was over a second faster than his previous best time.* **19** The **time** of a piece of music is the number of beats that the piece has in each bar.   N-COUNT: with supp / N-UNCOUNT

20 If you **time** something for a particular time, you plan or decide to do it or cause it to happen at this time. *He timed the election to coincide with new measures to boost the economy... We had timed our visit for March 7... He had timed his intervention well.*   VERB V n to-inf V n for n V n adv Also V n

21 If you **time** an action or activity, you measure how long someone takes to do it or how long it lasts. VERB: V n

22 If you say it is **about time** that something was done, you are saying in an emphatic way that it should happen or be done now, and really should have happened or been done sooner. *'Here she is.'—'About time too.'* PHRASE PRAGMATICS

23 If you say that **it is high time** that something happened or was done, you are saying in an emphatic way that it should happen or be done now, and really should have happened or been done sooner. *It is high time to consider the problem on a global scale.* PHRASE PRAGMATICS

24 If you say **not before time** when a statement is made about something that has been done, you are saying in an emphatic way that you think it should have been done sooner. *Not before time, that is about to change.* PHRASE PRAGMATICS BRITISH

25 If you are **in time** for a particular event, you are not too late for it. *I arrived just in time for my flight to London.* PHRASE

26 If you arrive somewhere **in good time**, you arrive early so that there is time to spare before a particular event. *We always make sure we're home in good time for the programme.* PHRASE

27 If you are **on time**, you are not late. *Their planes usually arrive on time.* PHRASE

28 If you do something **ahead of time**, you do it before a particular event or before you need to, in order to be well prepared. *Find out ahead of time what regulations apply to your situation.* PHRASE

29 If someone is **ahead of** their **time** or **before** their **time**, they have new ideas a long time before other people start to think in the same way. *He was indeed ahead of his time in employing women, ex-convicts, and the handicapped.* PHRASE

30 If someone has reached a particular stage in life **before** their **time**, they have reached it at a younger age than is normal. *There is nothing like a college town to make you feel old before your time.* PHRASE

31 If you say that something was **before** your **time**, you mean that it happened or existed before you were born or before you were able to know about it or remember it. PHRASE

32 When you refer to **our time** or **our times** you are referring to the present period in the history of the world. PHRASE

33 If something happens or is done **all the time**, it happens or is done continually. *We can't be together all the time.* PHRASE

34 You use **at times** to say that something happens or is true on some occasions or at some moments. *The debate was highly emotional at times.* PHRASE

35 If you do something **from time to time**, you do it occasionally but not regularly. *Her daughters visited him from time to time when he was ill.* PHRASE

36 If you say that something is the case **half the time** you mean that it often is the case. *Half the time, I don't have the slightest idea what he's talking about.* PHRASE INFORMAL

37 If something happens **time after time**, it happens in a similar way on many occasions. *Burns had escaped from jail time after time.* PHRASE

38 If you say that something happens or is the case **nine times out of ten** or **ninety-nine times out of a hundred**, you mean that it happens on nearly every occasion or is almost always the case. *When they want something, nine times out of ten they get it.* PHRASE

39 If you say that something will be the case **for all time**, you mean that it will be the case forever. PHRASE

40 If something could happen **at any time**, it is possible that it will happen very soon, though nobody can predict exactly when. *Conditions are still very tense and the fighting could escalate at any time.* PHRASE

41 If you say that something will happen **in time** or **given time**, you mean that it will happen eventually, when a lot of time has passed. *He would sort out his own problems, in time.* PHRASE

42 If you say that something will happen, for example, **in a week's time** or **in two years' time**, you mean that it will happen a week from now or two years from now. *Presidential elections are due to be held in ten days' time.* PHRASE

43 If you tell someone that something will happen **in good time** or **all in good time**, you are telling them to be patient because it will happen eventually. *'I can't wait to be grown up.'—'All in good time.'* PHRASE

44 If something happens **in no time** or **in next to no time**, it happens almost immediately or very quickly. *He expects to be out of prison in next to no time.* PHRASE

45 If you say that it is **only a matter of time** or **only a question of time** before something happens, you mean that it is unavoidable and will definitely happen at some future date. *It now seems only a matter of time before they resign.* PHRASE

46 If you do something to **pass the time**, you do it because you have some time available and not because you really want to do it. PHRASE

47 If you **play for time**, you try to make something happen more slowly, because you do not want it to happen or because you need time to think about what to do if it happens. PHRASE

48 If you say that **time flies**, you mean that it seems to pass very quickly. *Time flies when you're having fun.* PHRASE

49 If you say there is **no time to lose** or **no time to be lost**, you mean you must hurry as fast as you can to do something. PHRASE

50 If you **waste no time** in doing something, you take the opportunity to do it immediately or quickly. *Tom wasted no time in telling me why he had come.* PHRASE

51 If you are playing, singing, or dancing **in time** with a piece of music, you are following the rhythm and speed of the music correctly. If you are **out of time** with it, you are not following the rhythm and speed of the music correctly. PHRASE

52 If you **keep time** to a beat when playing or singing music, you follow or play the beat, without going too fast or too slowly. PHRASE

53 If you do something in your **own time**, you do it at the speed or pace that you choose, rather than allowing anyone to hurry you. *Now, in your own time, tell me what happened.* PHRASE

54 If you do something such as work **in** your **own time**, you do it in your free time rather than, for example, at work or school. The usual American expression is **on** your **own time**. PHRASE BRITISH

55 If you **take** your **time** doing something, you do it quite slowly and do not hurry. *He took his time answering.* PHRASE

56 If you **make time** for a particular activity or person, you arrange to have some free time so that you can do the activity or spend time with the person. *I think you should always make time to see your friends.* PHRASE

57 If someone is **making up for lost time**, they are doing something intensively and with enthusiasm because they have not had the opportunity to do it before or when they were younger. *Five years older than the majority of officers of his same rank, he was determined to make up for lost time.* PHRASE

58 If you **are marking time**, you are doing something that is not particularly useful or interesting while you wait for something more important or interesting to happen. PHRASE

59 If you say that something will **take time**, you mean that it will take a long time. *Change will come, but it will take time.* PHRASE

60 If you say that **time will tell** whether something is true or correct, you mean that it will not be known until some time in the future whether it is true or correct. *I can't see any problems, but time will tell.* PHRASE

61 Someone who **is doing time** is in prison. *He is serving 11 years for robbery, and did time for a similar offence before that.* PHRASE INFORMAL

62 If you say that you **have no time for** someone or something, you mean you do not like them or approve of them, and if you say that you **have a lot of time for** someone or something, you mean you like them or approve of them very much. PHRASE INFORMAL

63 You say **at the best of times** when you are making a negative or critical comment to emphasize that it is true even when the circumstances are as favourable as possible. *His voice is hardly resonant at the best of times. Today he is almost inaudible.* PHRASE PRAGMATICS

64 If you say that something was the case **at one time**, you mean that it was the case during a particular period in the past. *At one time 400 men, women and children lived in the village.* PHRASE

65 At the same time is used to introduce a statement that slightly changes or contradicts the previous statement. *I was afraid of her, but at the same time I really liked her.* PHRASE PRAGMATICS

66 If something is the case or will happen **for the time being**, it is the case or will happen now, but only until something else becomes possible or happens. *The situation is calm for the time being.* PHRASE

67 You say **at a time** after an amount to say how many things or how much of something is involved in one action, place, or group. *Beat in the eggs, one at a time.* PHRASE

68 When you talk about how well a watch or clock **keeps time**, you are talking about how PHRASE

accurately it measures time. **69** If you say that someone or something is, for example, the best writer **of all time**, or the most successful film **of all time**, you mean that they are the best or most successful that there has ever been. **70** If you **pass the time of day** with someone, you have a short friendly conversation with them. **71** If you have **the time of** your **life**, you enjoy yourself very much indeed. [PHRASE] [PHRASE] [PHRASE]

72 See also **opening time, timing**. • time and again: see **again**. • **in the fullness of time**: see **fullness**. • **the time is ripe**: see **ripe**.

'time bomb, time bombs; also spelled **time-bomb**. **1** A time bomb is a bomb with a mechanism that causes it to explode at a particular time. **2** If you describe something as a **time bomb**, you mean that it is likely to cause serious damage to a person or situation at a later date. *Unemployment is building up into a social time bomb.* [N-COUNT] [N-COUNT]

'time-consuming; also spelled **time consuming**. If something is **time-consuming**, it takes a lot of time. [◇◇◇◇◇ ADJ-GRADED]

'time frame, time frames. The **time frame** of an event is the length of time during which it happens or develops. *The time frame within which all this occurred was from September 1985 to March 1986.* [N-COUNT] [FORMAL]

'time-honoured. A **time-honoured** tradition or way of doing something is one that has been used and appreciated for a very long time. [ADJ: ADJ n]

time·keeper /'taɪmkiːpə/ **timekeepers;** also spelled **time-keeper**. **1** A timekeeper is a person or an instrument that records or checks the time. **2** If you say that someone is a good **timekeeper**, you mean that they regularly arrive on time at work. If you say that they are a poor **timekeeper**, you mean that they are often late. [N-COUNT] [N-COUNT: supp N]

'time·keeping /'taɪmkiːpɪŋ/. **1** If you talk about someone's **timekeeping**, you are talking about how good they are at arriving in time for things. *I am trying to improve my timekeeping.* **2 Timekeeping** is the process or activity of timing an event or series of events. *Who did the timekeeping?* [N-UNCOUNT: poss N, adj N] [N-UNCOUNT]

'time lag, time lags; also spelled **time-lag**. A **time lag** is a fairly long interval of time between one event and another related event that happens after it. *...the time-lag between theoretical research and practical applications.* [N-COUNT]

time·less /'taɪmləs/. If you describe something as **timeless**, you mean that it is so good or beautiful that it cannot be affected by changes in society or fashion. *There is a timeless quality to his best work.* ♦ **time·less·ness** *...an atmosphere of mystery and timelessness.* [◇◇◇◇◇ ADJ-GRADED] [N-UNCOUNT]

'time limit, time limits. A **time limit** is a date before which a particular task must be completed. *We have extended the time limit for claims until July 30.* [◇◇◇◇◇ N-COUNT]

time·ly /'taɪmli/. If you describe an event as **timely**, you approve of it because it happens exactly at the moment when it is most useful, effective, or relevant. *The exhibition is timely, since 'self-taught' art is catching on in a big way.* [◇◇◇◇◇ ADJ-GRADED] [PRAGMATICS]

,time 'out, time outs; also spelled **time-out**. **1** In basketball, ice hockey, and some other sports, when a team calls a **time out**, they call a stop to the game for a few minutes in order to rest and discuss tactics. **2** If you take **time out** from a job or activity, you have a break from it and do something different instead. *...women returning to the labour market after time out to raise young families.* [◇◇◇◇◇ N-VAR] [N-UNCOUNT]

time·piece /'taɪmpiːs/ **timepieces;** also spelled **time piece**. A **timepiece** is a clock, watch, or other device that measures and shows time. [N-COUNT] [DATED]

tim·er /'taɪmə/ **timers.** A timer is a device that measures time, especially one that is part of a machine and causes it to start or stop working at specific times. *...electronic timers that automatically switch on the lights when it gets dark.* • See also **egg timer**. [◇◇◇◇◇ N-COUNT]

'time scale, time scales; also spelled **time-scale**. The **time scale** of an event is the length of time during which it happens or develops. *These companies* [N-COUNT]

now will show excellent profits on a two-year time scale.

'time-server, time-servers; also spelled **time-server**. If you refer to someone as a **time-server**, you disapprove of them because they are making very little effort at work and are just waiting until they retire or leave for a new job. [N-COUNT] [PRAGMATICS]

'time-share, time-shares; also spelled **time share**. If you have a **time-share**, you have the right to use a particular property as holiday accommodation for a specific amount of time each year. [N-VAR]

'time signal, time signals. In Britain, the **time signal** is the series of high-pitched sounds that are broadcast at certain times on the radio, for example at exactly one o'clock or exactly six o'clock. [N-COUNT]

'time signature, time signatures. The **time signature** of a piece of music consists of two numbers written at the beginning that show how many beats there are in each bar. [N-COUNT]

'time switch, time switches. A **time switch** is a device that causes a machine to start or stop working at specific times. [N-COUNT]

time·table /'taɪmteɪbl/ **timetables, time-tabling, timetabled**. **1** A timetable is a plan of the times when particular events are to take place. *Don't you realize we're working to a timetable? We have to have results.* **2** In a school or college, a **timetable** is a chart that shows the times in the week at which particular subjects are taught. You can also refer to the range of subjects that a student learns or the classes that a teacher teaches as their **timetable**. *Members of the union will continue to teach their full timetables.* **3** A **timetable** is a list of the times when trains, boats, buses, or aeroplanes are supposed to arrive at or depart from a particular place. **4** If something **is timetabled**, it is scheduled to happen or do something at a particular time. *On both days, three very different trains will be timetabled... Opie is timetabled to work a four-day week.* ♦ **time·tabling** *Timetabling is a nightmare for all schools.* [♦♦◇◇◇] [N-COUNT] [N-COUNT] [N-COUNT] [VERB: be V-ed, be V-ed to-inf, BRITISH] [N-UNCOUNT]

'time trial, time trials. In cycling and some other sports, a **time trial** is a contest in which competitors race along a course individually, in as fast a time as possible, instead of racing directly against each other. [◆◇◇◇◇ N-COUNT]

'time-worn; also spelled **timeworn**. Something that is **time-worn** is old or has been used a lot over a long period of time. *Even in the dim light the equipment looked old and time-worn.* [ADJ-GRADED]

'time zone, time zones; also spelled **time-zone**. A **time zone** is one of the areas into which the world is divided where the time is calculated as being a particular number of hours behind or ahead of GMT. [◆◇◇◇◇ N-COUNT]

tim·id /'tɪmɪd/. **1** Timid people are shy, nervous, and have no courage or self-confidence. *A timid child, Isabella had learned obedience at an early age.* ♦ **ti·mid·ity** /tɪˈmɪdɪti/. *She doesn't ridicule my timidity.* ♦ **tim·id·ly** *The little boy stepped forward timidly and shook Leo's hand.* **2** If you describe someone's attitudes or actions as **timid**, you are criticizing them for being too cautious or slow to act, because they are nervous about the possible consequences of their actions. *The President's critics say he has been too timid in responding to changing international developments.* ♦ **timidity** *...the government's timidity on social reform.* ♦ **timidly** *...moving timidly towards multi-party democracy.* [◆◇◇◇◇ ADJ-GRADED] [N-UNCOUNT] [ADV-GRADED] [ADJ-GRADED] [PRAGMATICS] [N-UNCOUNT] [ADV with v]

tim·ing /'taɪmɪŋ/. **1** Timing is the skill or action of judging the right moment in a situation or activity at which to do something. *His photo is a wonderful happy moment caught with perfect timing.* **2** Timing is used to refer to the time at which something happens or is planned to happen, or to the length of time that something takes. *The timing of the announcement from the Iraqi leader is seen as significant.* **3** See also **time**. [♦♦◇◇◇ N-UNCOUNT] [N-UNCOUNT]

tim·or·ous /'tɪmərəs/. If you describe someone as ADJ-GRADED
timorous, you mean that they are frightened and LITERARY
nervous of other people and situations.

tim·pa·ni /'tɪmpəni/. Timpani are kettledrums that N-PLURAL
are played in an orchestra.

tin /tɪn/ **tins. 1** Tin is a soft silvery-white metal. ◆◆◇◇◇
2 A **tin** is a metal container which is filled with food N-UNCOUNT
and sealed in order to preserve the food for long pe- N-COUNT
riods of time. The usual American word is **can**. ▶ A BRITISH
tin of food is the amount of food contained in a tin. N-COUNT
...*a small tin of fruit.* **3** A **tin** is a metal container N-COUNT
with a lid in which things such as biscuits or cakes
can be kept. ▶ A **tin** of things is the amount of N-COUNT
things contained in a tin. *They emptied out the remains of the tin of paint.* **4** A baking **tin** is a metal N-COUNT
container used for baking things such as cakes and BRITISH
bread in an oven. The usual American word is **pan**.
...*a 2 lb loaf tin.*

tinc·ture /'tɪŋktʃə/ **tinctures.** A tincture is a medi- N-VAR
cine consisting of alcohol and a small amount of a
drug.

tin·der /'tɪndə/. Tinder consists of small pieces of N-UNCOUNT
something dry, especially wood or grass, that burns
easily and can be used for lighting a fire.

tinder·box /'tɪndəbɒks/ **tinderboxes;** also spelled N-COUNT
tinder box. If you say that a situation is a **tinder-
box**, you mean that it is very tense and something
dangerous or unpleasant is likely to happen very
soon.

tin·foil /'tɪnfɔɪl/; also spelled **tin foil.** Tinfoil consists N-UNCOUNT
of shiny metal in the form of a thin sheet which is
used for wrapping food.

tinge /tɪndʒ/ **tinges.** A tinge of a colour, feeling, or ◆◇◇◇◇
quality is a small amount of it. *Could there have* N-COUNT
been a slight tinge of envy in Eva's voice?

tinged /tɪndʒd/. If something is **tinged** with a par- ADJ-GRADED
ticular colour, feeling, or quality, it has a small
amount of that colour, feeling, or quality in it. *Her
homecoming was tinged with sadness.* ▶ Also a com- COMB
bining form. ...*fragrant white, pink-tinged flowers.*

tin·gle /'tɪŋgəl/ **tingles, tingling, tingled.** ◆◇◇◇◇
1 When a part of your body **tingles**, you feel a slight VERB: V
prickling or stinging sensation there. ...*a tingling* V-ing
sensation. ◆ **tin·gling** *Its effects on the nervous sys-* N-UNCOUNT
*tem include weakness, paralysis, and tingling in the
hands and feet.* **2** If you **tingle** with a feeling such as VERB:
excitement or anticipation, you feel it very strongly. V with n
When I look over and see Terry I tingle all over.
▶ Also a noun. *I felt a sudden tingle of excitement.* N-COUNT

tink·er /'tɪŋkə/ **tinkers, tinkering, tinkered.** ◆◇◇◇◇
1 If you **tinker with** something, you make some VERB
small adjustments to it, in an attempt to improve it V with n
or repair it. *They tinkered with the engine.* ◆ **tink-** Also V
·er·ing *No amount of tinkering is going to improve* N-UNCOUNT
matters. **2** In former times, a **tinker** was a person N-COUNT
who did not have a fixed home, but travelled from
place to place mending metal pots and doing other
small repair jobs. **3** Some people refer to any travel- N-COUNT
ler or gipsy, especially one who is Irish, as a **tinker**, BRITISH,
an offensive use. RUDE

tin·kle /'tɪŋkəl/ **tinkles, tinkling, tinkled. 1** If VERB
something **tinkles**, it makes a clear, high-pitched, V prep/adv
ringing noise, especially as small parts of it strike a V-ing
surface. *A fresh cascade of splintered glass tinkled to* Also V
the floor. ...*tinkling fountains and perfumed gardens.* ▶ Also a noun. *There was a tinkle of broken* N-COUNT
glass. **2** If a bell **tinkles**, it makes a quiet ringing V-ERG: V
noise as you shake it. *Miss Peel tinkled her desk bell* V n
and they all sat down again.

tinned /tɪnd/. Tinned food has been preserved by ◆◇◇◇◇
being sealed in a tin; the usual American word is ADJ
canned. ...*tinned salmon.* BRITISH

tin·ny /'tɪni/. If you describe a sound as **tinny**, you ADJ-GRADED
mean that it has an irritating, high-pitched quality.

'tin opener, tin openers; also spelled **tin-opener.** N-COUNT
A **tin opener** is a tool that is used for opening tins BRITISH
of food; the usual American word is **can opener.** See
picture headed **kitchen utensils.**

tin·pot /'tɪnpɒt/; also spelled **tin-pot.** You can use ADJ: ADJ n
tinpot to describe a leader, country, or government PRAGMATICS
BRITISH

that you consider to be unimportant and inferior to
most others.

tin·sel /'tɪnsəl/. Tinsel consists of small strips of N-UNCOUNT
shiny paper attached to long pieces of thread. Peo-
ple use tinsel as a decoration at Christmas.

Tin·sel·town /'tɪnsəltaʊn/. People sometimes refer N-PROPER
to Hollywood as **Tinseltown**, especially when they PRAGMATICS
want to show that they disapprove of it or when
they are making fun of it.

tint /tɪnt/ **tints, tinting, tinted. 1** A tint is a small ◆◇◇◇◇
amount of colour. *Its large leaves often show a deli-* N-COUNT
cate purple tint. **2** If you put a **tint** on your hair, you N-COUNT
dye it a slightly different colour. **3** If something is VB: usu
tinted, it has a small amount of a particular colour passive
or dye in it. *Eyebrows can be tinted with the same* be V-ed
dye. ◆ **-tinted** *He wore green-tinted glasses.* COMB

tin 'whistle, tin whistles. A tin whistle is a sim- N-COUNT
ple musical instrument in the shape of a metal pipe
with holes. Tin whistles make a high sound and are
often used in folk music.

tiny /'taɪni/ **tinier, tiniest.** Something or someone ◆◆◆◇◇
that is **tiny** is extremely small. ADJ-GRADED

-tion /-ʃən/ **-tions.** See -ation.

tip /tɪp/ **tips, tipping, tipped. 1** The **tip** of some- ◆◆◆◇◇
thing long and narrow is the end of it. ...*the tips of* N-COUNT
his fingers. ...*the southern tip of Florida.* **2** If you PHRASE
say that a problem is **the tip of the iceberg**, you
mean that it is one small part of a much larger
problem. **3** If a comment or question is **on the tip** PHRASE
of your **tongue**, you really want to say it or ask it,
but you decide not to say it.

4 If an object or part of your body **tips**, it moves into a V-ERG: V
sloping position with one end or side higher than the V n adv/prep
other. *She had to tip her head back to see him.* **5** If PHRASE
something **tips the scales** or **tips the balance**, it gives
someone a slight advantage. *Today's slightly shorter
race could well help to tip the scales in his favour.* **6** If VERB
you **tip** something somewhere, you pour it there. *Tip* V n prep
the vegetables into a bowl... Tip away the salt and wipe V n with adv
the pan.

7 To **tip** rubbish means to get rid of it by leaving it VERB: V n
somewhere. ...*other strategies like how do you stop* V
people tipping? **8** A **tip** is a place where rubbish is left. BRITISH
I took a load of rubbish and grass cuttings to the tip. N-COUNT
9 If you describe a place as a **tip**, you mean it is very BRITISH
untidy. N-COUNT
BRITISH

10 If you **tip** someone such as a waiter, you give them VERB: V n
some money in order to thank them for their services. V n amount
She tipped the barmen 10 dollars. ▶ Also a noun. *I* Also V
gave the barber a tip. ◆ **tip·ping** *A 10 percent service* N-UNCOUNT
charge is added in lieu of tipping. **11** A **tip** is a useful N-COUNT
piece of advice. *A good tip is to buy the most expensive
lens you can afford.* **12** If a person **is tipped to** do VB: usu
something or **is tipped for** success at something, ex- passive
perts or journalists believe that they will do that thing be V-ed to-inf
or achieve that success. *He is tipped to be the country's* BRITISH
next foreign minister. **13** Someone's **tip** for a race or N-COUNT
competition is their advice on its likely result, especially to someone who wants to bet on the result.

tip off. If someone **tips** you **off**, they give you infor- PHRASAL VB
mation about something that has happened or is go- V n P
ing to happen. *He was arrested two days later after a* V P noun
friend tipped off the FBI.

tip over. If something **tips over**, it falls over or turns PHRASAL VB
over. *He tipped the table over in front of him... We* ERG
grabbed it just as it was about to tip over. V n P
V P

tip up. If something **tips up**, it moves into a sloping PHRASAL VB
position with one end or side higher than the other. ERG
We had to tip up the bed and the model was in grave V P noun
danger of falling off it!... The aircraft leveled out, and V P
tipped up again for its climb to 20,000 feet.

'tip-off, tip-offs. A tip-off is a piece of information ◆◇◇◇◇
or a warning that you give to someone, often pri- N-COUNT
vately or secretly. *The man was arrested at his home
after a tip-off to police from a member of the public.*

-tipped /-tɪpt/. **-tipped** combines with nouns to COMB
form adjectives that describe something as having a
tip made of a particular substance or covered with a
particular material. ...*poison-tipped arrows.*

tip·ple /'tɪpəl/ **tipples.** A person's **tipple** is the al- N-COUNT
coholic drink that they usually drink. *My favourite* BRITISH,
tipple is a glass of port. INFORMAL

tip·ster /'tɪpstə/ **tipsters.** A **tipster** is someone N-COUNT
who tells you, usually in exchange for money, which
horses they think will win particular races, so that
you can bet money on the horses.

tip·sy /'tɪpsi/. If someone is **tipsy**, they are slightly ADJ-GRADED
drunk.

tip·toe /'tɪptəʊ/ **tiptoes, tiptoeing, tiptoed. 1** If ◆◇◇◇◇
you **tiptoe** somewhere, you walk there very quietly V prep/adv
without putting your heels on the floor when you Also V
walk. *She slipped out of bed and tiptoed to the win-*
dow. **2** If you do something **on tiptoe** or **on tiptoes**, PHRASE
you do it standing or walking on the front part of
your foot, without putting your heels on the ground.

tip-'top; also spelled **tiptop**. You can use **tip-top** to ADJ
indicate that something is extremely good. *Her hair* DATED,
was thick, glossy and in tip-top condition. INFORMAL

ti·rade /taɪ'reɪd/ **tirades.** A **tirade** is a long angry N-COUNT
speech in which someone criticizes something or
someone.

tire /taɪə/ **tires, tiring, tired. 1** If something **tires** ◆◇◇◇◇
you or you **tire**, you feel that you have used a lot of V-ERG: V
energy and you want to rest or sleep. *If driving tires* V n
you, take the train. **2** If you **tire** of something, you VERB:
no longer wish to do it, because you have become V of n/-ing,
bored of it or unhappy with it. **3** See **tyre**. no passive

tire out. If something **tires** you **out**, it makes you ex- PHRASAL VB
hausted. *His objective was to tire out the climbers.* V n P
♦ **tired out** *He was obviously tired out.* V P noun
ADJ

tired /taɪəd/. **1** If you are **tired**, you feel that you ◆◆◇◇◇
want to rest or sleep. ♦ **tired·ness** *He had to cancel* ADJ-GRADED
some engagements because of tiredness. **2** You can ADJ-GRADED
describe a part of your body as **tired** if it looks or ADJ-GRADED:
feels as if you need to rest it or to sleep. **3** If you are v-link ADJ of
tired of something, you do not want it to continue n/-ing
because you are bored of it or unhappy with it. *I*
was tired of being a bookkeeper. **4** If you describe ADJ-GRADED
something as **tired**, you are critical of it because you PRAGMATICS
have heard it or seen it many times. *I didn't want to*
hear another one of his tired excuses.

tire·less /'taɪələs/. If you describe someone or ◆◇◇◇◇
their efforts as **tireless**, you approve of the fact that ADJ-GRADED
they put a lot of hard work into something, and ref- PRAGMATICS
use to give up or take a rest. ♦ **tire·less·ly** *He* ADV-GRADED:
worked tirelessly for the cause of health and safety. ADV with v

tire·some /'taɪəsəm/. If you describe someone or ◆◇◇◇◇
something as **tiresome**, you mean that you find ADJ-GRADED
them irritating or boring.

tir·ing /'taɪərɪŋ/. If you describe something as **tir-** ◆◇◇◇◇
ing, you mean that it makes you tired so that you ADJ-GRADED
want to rest or sleep.

tis·sue /'tɪʃuː, 'tɪsjuː/ **tissues. 1** In animals and ◆◆◇◇◇
plants, **tissue** consists of cells that are similar to N-UNCOUNT:
each other in appearance and that have the same also N in pl
function. ...*muscle tissue*... *All the cells and tissues*
in the body benefit from the increased intake of oxy-
gen. **2** **Tissue** or **tissue paper** is thin paper that is N-UNCOUNT
used for wrapping things that are easily damaged,
such as objects made of glass. **3** A **tissue** is a piece N-COUNT
of thin soft paper that you use as a handkerchief.
...*a box of tissues.*

tit /tɪt/ **tits. 1** A **tit** is a small European bird that ◆◇◇◇◇
eats insects and seeds. There are several kinds of tit. N-COUNT
● See also **blue tit. 2** A woman's **tits** are her breasts; N-COUNT
a use which some people find offensive. INFORMAL,
RUDE

ti·tan /'taɪtən/ **titans.** If you describe someone as a N-COUNT
titan of a particular field, you mean that they are
very important and powerful or successful in that
field. ...*the country's two richest business titans.*

ti·tan·ic /taɪ'tænɪk/. If you describe something as ADJ
titanic, you mean that it is very big or important,
and usually that it involves very powerful forces.
The world had witnessed a titanic struggle between
two visions of the future.

ti·ta·nium /taɪ'teɪniəm/. **Titanium** is a strong white ◆◇◇◇◇
metal used in making lightweight alloys. N-UNCOUNT

tit·bit /'tɪtbɪt/ **titbits.** The form **tidbit** is used in
American English. **1** You can refer to a small piece N-COUNT

of information about someone's private affairs as a
titbit, especially when it is interesting and shocking. BRITISH,
INFORMAL
2 A **titbit** is a small delicious piece of food. N-COUNT

tit-for-'tat. A **tit-for-tat** action is one where some- ADJ
one takes revenge on another person for what they
have done by doing something similar to them. *The*
two countries have each expelled another diplomat
following a round of tit-for-tat expulsions.

tithe /taɪð/ **tithes.** A **tithe** is a fixed amount of N-COUNT
money or goods that is given regularly in order to
support a church, a priest, or a charity.

tit·il·late /'tɪtɪleɪt/ **titillates, titillating, titillat-** ◆◇◇◇◇
ed. If something **titillates** someone, it pleases and VERB: V n
excites them, especially in a sexual way. ♦ **tit·il·lat-**
·ing ...*deliberately titillating lyrics.* ♦ **tit·il·la·tion** ADJ-GRADED
/tɪtɪ'leɪʃən/. *People buy sex manuals for titillation.* N-UNCOUNT

ti·tle /'taɪtəl/ **titles, titling, titled. 1** The **title** of a ◆◆◆◆◇
book, play, film, or piece of music is its name. N-COUNT
2 When a writer, composer, or artist **titles** a work, VERB
they give it a title. *Pirandello titled his play 'Six* V n
Characters in Search of an Author'... *The single is ti-* be V-ed n
tled 'White Love'. ♦ **-titled** ...*his aptly titled autobi-* COMB
ography, Life is Meeting. **3** Publishers and N-COUNT
booksellers often refer to books or periodicals as **ti-**
tles. *It has become the biggest publisher of new poet-*
ry in Britain, with 50 new titles a year.
4 Someone's **title** is a word such as 'Lord', 'Mrs', or N-COUNT
'Doctor', that is used before their name in order to
show their status or profession. **5** Someone's **title** is a N-COUNT
name that describes their job or status in an organization. *He was given the title of deputy prime minister.*
6 In sports competitions, a **title** is the position of N-COUNT
champion. Usually a person keeps a title until some-
one else defeats them.

ti·tled /'taɪtəld/. Someone who is **titled** has a name ◆◆◇◇◇
such as 'Lady', 'Sir', or 'Princess' before their name ADJ
showing that they are a member of the aristocracy.

'title-holder, title-holders; also spelled **title** N-COUNT
holder. The **title-holder** is the person who holds the
position of champion in a sports competition that is
held regularly.

title 'role, title roles. The **title role** in a play or N-COUNT:
film is the role referred to in the name of the play or the N
film. *My novel 'The Rector's Wife' is being adapted*
for TV, with Lindsay Duncan in the title role.

'title track, title tracks. The **title track** on a CD, ◆◇◇◇◇
record, or tape is a song or piece of music that has N-COUNT
the same title as the CD, record, or tape.

tit·ter /'tɪtə/ **titters, tittering, tittered.** If some- VERB: V
one **titters**, they give a short nervous laugh, especially when they are embarrassed about something.
▶ Also a noun. *Mollie gave an uneasy little titter.* N-COUNT
♦ **tit·ter·ing** *There was nervous tittering in the stu-* N-UNCOUNT
dio audience.

tittle-tattle /'tɪtəl tætəl/. If you refer to something N-UNCOUNT
that a group of people talk about as **tittle-tattle**, you PRAGMATICS
mean that you disapprove of it because it is trivial
gossip, and there is no real evidence that it is true.

titu·lar /'tɪtʃʊlə/. A **titular** job or position has a ADJ: ADJ n
name that makes it seem important, although the
person who has it is not really important or powerful. *He is titular head, and merely signs laws*
occasionally.

tiz·zy /'tɪzi/. If you get **in a tizzy** or **into a tizzy**, you PHRASE
get excited, worried, or nervous about something, INFORMAL
especially something that is not important.

'T-junction, T-junctions. If you arrive at a N-COUNT
T-junction, the road that you are on ends at right
angles to another road, so that you have to turn
either left or right to continue.

TM /tiː 'em/. **TM** is a written abbreviation for **trade-**
mark.

TNT /tiː en 'tiː/. **TNT** is a powerful explosive sub- N-UNCOUNT
stance; an abbreviation for 'trinitrotoluene'.

to 1 preposition and adverb uses

to. Usually pronounced /tə/ before a consonant ◆◆◆◆◆
and /tʊ/ before a vowel, but pronounced /tuː/ when
you are emphasizing it. In addition to the uses
shown below, **to** is used after some verbs, nouns,
and adjectives in order to introduce extra informa-

tion, and in phrasal verbs such as 'see to' and 'come to'. It is also used with some verbs that have two objects in order to introduce the second object.

1 You use **to** when indicating the place that someone PREP or something visits, moves towards, or points at. *Ramsay made a second visit to Italy... She went to the window and looked out... He pointed to a chair, signalling for her to sit.* **2** If you go **to** an event, you go PREP where it is taking place. *We went to a party at the leisure centre... He came to dinner.* **3** If someone goes PREP from place **to** place or from job **to** job, they go to several places, or work in several jobs, and spend only a short time in each one. **4** If someone moves **to and** PHRASE **fro**, they move repeatedly from one place to another and back again, or from side to side. ● See also **to-ing and fro-ing**.

5 If something is attached **to** something larger or fixed PREP **to** it, the two things are joined together. *There was a piece of cloth tied to the dog's collar.* **6** You use **to** when PREP indicating the position of something. For example, if something is **to** your left, it is nearer your left side than your right side. *Atlanta was only an hour's drive to the north.*

7 When you give something **to** someone, they receive PREP it. *Firms should be allowed to offer jobs to the long-term unemployed at a lower wage.* **8** You use **to** to indicate who or what an action or a feeling is directed towards. *...troops loyal to the government... I have had to pay for repairs to the house.* **9** You use **to** with certain nouns and adjectives to show that a following noun is related to them. *Marriage is not the answer to everything... She was very sympathetic to the problems of adult students.*

10 If you say something **to** someone, you want that PREP person to listen and understand what you are saying. *I'm going to explain to them that I can't pay them.* **11** You use **to** when indicating someone's reaction PREP to something or someone's feelings about a situation or event. For example, if you say that something happens **to** someone's relief, you mean that they are relieved when it happens. *To his surprise, the bedroom door was locked.* **12** You use **to** when indicating the person whose opinion you are stating. *It was clear to me that he respected his boss... Everyone seemed to her to be amazingly kind.* ● See also **according to**.

13 You use **to** when indicating what something or PREP someone is becoming, or the state or situation that they are progressing towards. *...an old ranch house that has been converted to a nature centre. ...a return to active politics.* **14 To** can be used as a way of introducing the person or organization you are employed by, when you perform some service for them. *He was an official interpreter to the government of Nepal.* **15** You use **to** to indicate that something happens until the time or amount mentioned is reached. *From 1977 to 1985 the United States gross national product grew 21 percent... The annual rate of inflation in Britain has risen to its highest level for eight years.* **16** You PREP use **to** when indicating the last thing in a range of things, usually when you are giving two extreme examples. *I read everything from fiction to history and science.* **17** You use **to** when you are stating a time which is PREP less than thirty minutes before an hour. For example, if it is 'five to eight', it is five minutes before eight o'clock. **18** You use **to** when giving ratios and rates. PREP *...engines that can run at 60 miles to the gallon. ...a mixture of one part milk to two parts water.* **19** You PREP use **to** when indicating that two things happen at the same time. For example, if something is done **to** music, it is done at the same time as music is being played. *Romeo left the stage, to enthusiastic applause.* **20** If you say **'There's nothing to it', 'There's not** CONVENTION **much to it'**, or **'That's all there is to it'**, you are emphasizing how simple you think something is. **21** If ADV: you push or shut a door **to**, you close it but may ADV after v not shut it completely. *He slipped out, pulling the door to.*

to 2 used before the base form of a verb

to Pronounced /tə/ before a consonant and /tu/ be- ◆◆◆◆◆ fore a vowel. **1** You use **to** before the base form of a to inf verb to form the 'to-infinitive'. You use the to-infinitive after certain verbs, nouns, and adjectives, and after words such as 'how', 'which', and 'where'. *The management wanted to know what I was doing there... Nuclear plants are expensive to build, though cheap to operate... She did not take the judge's advice about how to do her job... The Foreign Minister is to visit China.* **2** You use **to** before the base form to inf of a verb to indicate the purpose or intention of an action. *...programs set up to save animals... To help provide essential nourishment, we've put together these nutritious drinks.* ● **in order to**: see **order**. **3** You use **to** before the base form of a verb when to inf you are commenting on a statement that you are making, for example when saying that you are being honest or brief, or that you are summing up or giving an example. *I'm disappointed, to be honest... Well, to sum up, what is the message that you are trying to get across?* **4** You use **to** before the base form of a verb in excla- to inf mations when you are emphasizing a very strong emotion, such as a desire or wish, or a regret or disappointment. *Oh, to think of his poor wife, standing there helpless.* **5** You use **to** before the base form of a to inf verb when indicating what situation follows a particular action. *From the garden you walk down to discover a large and beautiful lake.* **6** You use **to** with 'too' and 'enough' in expressions like **too much to** and **old enough to**; see **too** and **enough**.

toad /təʊd/ **toads.** A toad is a creature which is ◆◇◇◇◇ similar to a frog but which has a drier skin and N-COUNT spends less time in water.

toad·stool /ˈtəʊdstuːl/ **toadstools.** A toadstool is N-COUNT a poisonous fungus.

toady /ˈtəʊdi/ **toadies, toadying, toadied. 1** If N-COUNT you refer to someone as a **toady**, you disapprove of PRAGMATICS them because they flatter or are pleasant towards an important or powerful person in the hope of getting some advantage from them. **2** If you say that VERB: someone **is toadying** to an important or powerful V ton person, you disapprove of them because they are PRAGMATICS flattering or being pleasant towards that person in the hope of getting some advantage from them.

toast /təʊst/ **toasts, toasting, toasted. 1** Toast ◆◆◇◇◇ is bread which has been cut into slices and made N-UNCOUNT brown and crisp by cooking at a high temperature. **2** When you **toast** something such as bread, you VERB: V n cook it at a high temperature in a toaster or under a grill so that it becomes brown and crisp. **3** When VERB: V n you **toast** someone or something, you drink some wine or another alcoholic drink as a symbolic gesture, in order to show your appreciation of them or to wish them success. ▶ Also a noun. *Eleanor and I* N-COUNT *drank a toast to Miss Jacobs.* **4** If someone is **the** N-SING: **toast** of a place, they are very popular and greatly the N of n admired there, because they have done something very successfully or well.

toast·er /ˈtəʊstə/ **toasters.** A toaster is a piece of N-COUNT electric equipment used to toast bread.

toast·master /ˈtəʊstmɑːstə, -mæs-/ **toast-** N-COUNT **masters.** At a reception or formal dinner, the **toastmaster** is the person who proposes toasts and introduces the speakers.

to·bac·co /təˈbækəʊ/ **tobaccos. 1** Tobacco is the ◆◆◇◇◇ dried leaves of a plant which people smoke in pipes, N-VAR cigars, and cigarettes. You can also refer to pipes, cigars, and cigarettes collectively as **tobacco**. *It is time to ban tobacco advertising altogether.* **2** Tobac- N-UNCOUNT co is the plant from which tobacco is obtained.

to·bac·co·nist /təˈbækənɪst/ **tobacconists.** A to- N-COUNT **bacconist** is a shopkeeper who sells things such as tobacco, cigarettes, and cigars. You can refer to a shop where these goods are sold as a **tobacconist** or a **tobacconist's**.

to·bog·gan /təˈbɒgən/ **toboggans.** A toboggan is N-COUNT an object that is designed to be used for travelling downhill on snow or ice.

to·day /tə'deɪ/. **1** You use **today** to refer to the day on which you are speaking or writing. *How are you feeling today?* ▶ Also a noun. *Today is Friday, September 14th... The Prime Minister remains the main story in today's newspapers.* **2** You can refer to the present period of history as **today**. *The United States is in a serious recession today.* ▶ Also a noun. *...the Africa of today.*
◆◆◆◆◆ ADV; ADV with cl N-UNCOUNT
ADV
N-UNCOUNT

tod·dle /'tɒdəl/ **toddles, toddling, toddled.** When a child **toddles**, it walks unsteadily with short quick steps. *She fell while toddling around.*
VERB: V V adv/prep

tod·dler /'tɒdlə/ **toddlers.** A **toddler** is a young child who has only just learnt to walk or who still walks unsteadily with small, quick steps.
◆◇◇◇◇ N-COUNT

to-do /tə 'duː/. When there is a **to-do**, people are very excited, confused, or angry about something.
N-SING INFORMAL

toe /təʊ/ **toes, toeing, toed. 1** Your **toes** are the five movable parts at the end of each foot. See picture headed **human body**. **2** The **toe** of a shoe or sock is the part that covers the end of your foot. **3** If you say that someone or something **keeps** you **on** your **toes**, you mean that they cause you to remain alert and ready for anything that might happen. **4** If you **toe the line**, you behave in the way that people in authority expect you to. *He's one of the politicians that wouldn't toe the party line.* **5** If you **tread on** someone's **toes**, you offend them by criticizing the way in which they do something or by interfering in something that is their responsibility.
◆◆◇◇◇ N-COUNT
N-COUNT
PHRASE
PHRASE
PHRASE INFORMAL

toe·cap /'təʊkæp/ **toecaps;** also spelled **toe-cap.** A toecap is a piece of leather or metal which is fitted over the end of a shoe or boot in order to protect or strengthen it.
N-COUNT

TOEFL /'təʊfəl/. **TOEFL** is an English language examination which is often used to evaluate the level of English of students who want to study at universities in English-speaking countries. TOEFL is an abbreviation of 'Test of English as a Foreign Language'.
N-PROPER

toe·hold /'təʊhəʊld/ **toeholds;** also spelled **toehold.** If you have a **toehold** in a situation, you have managed to gain an uncertain position or a small amount of power in it, which you hope will give you the opportunity to get a better or more powerful position. *Mitsubishi Motors were anxious to get a toehold in the European market.*
N-COUNT

toe·nail /'təʊneɪl/ **toenails;** also spelled **toe nail.** Your **toenails** are the thin hard areas at the end of each of your toes. See picture headed **human body**.
N-COUNT

toff /tɒf/ **toffs.** If you refer to someone as a **toff**, you are saying in an unkind way that they come from the upper classes or are very rich.
N-COUNT PRAGMATICS INFORMAL, BRITISH

tof·fee /'tɒfi, AM 'tɔːfi/ **toffees.** A **toffee** is a sticky chewy sweet that is made by boiling sugar and butter together with water.
N-VAR

'toffee-nosed. If you say that someone is **toffee-nosed**, you disapprove of them because they have a high opinion of themselves and a low opinion of other people.
ADJ-GRADED PRAGMATICS INFORMAL, BRITISH

tog /tɒg/ **togs. 1** A **tog** is an official measurement that shows how warm a blanket or quilt is. ▶ Also a combining form. *...a snug 13.5-tog winter duvet.* **2** **Togs** are clothes, especially ones for a particular purpose. *The photograph showed him wearing football togs.*
N-COUNT BRITISH
COMB
N-PLURAL INFORMAL

toga /'təʊgə/ **togas.** A **toga** is a piece of clothing which was worn by the ancient Romans.
N-COUNT

to·geth·er /tə'geðə/. In addition to the uses shown below, **together** is used in phrasal verbs such as '**piece** together' and '**pull** together'.
◆◆◆◆◆

1 If people do something **together**, they do it with each other. *We went on long bicycle rides together... They all live together in a three-bedroom house... Together they swam to the ship.* **2** If things are joined **together**, they are joined with each other so that they touch or form one whole. *Mix the ingredients together thoroughly... She clasped her hands together on her lap.* **3** If things or people are situated **together**, they are in the same place and very near to each other. *The trees grew close together... Ginette and I gathered our things together.* **4** If a group of people are held or kept **together**, they are united with each other in some way. *He has done enough to pull the party together... I want us all to be a happy family together.* ▶ Also an adjective. *We are together in the way we're looking at this situation.* **5** If two things happen or are done **together**, they happen or are done at the same time. *Three horses crossed the finish line together.* **6** You use **together** when you are adding two or more amounts or things to each other in order to consider a total amount or effect. *The two main right-wing opposition parties together won 29.8 per cent... Together they account for less than five per cent of the population.* **7** If two people are **together**, they are married or having a sexual relationship with each other. *We were together for five years.* **8** If you say that two things **go together**, or that one thing **goes together** with another, you mean that they are compatible with each other or cannot be separated from each other. *Some colours go together and some don't... Poverty and illiteracy go together with high birth rates.* **9** You use **together with** to mention someone or something else that is also involved in an action or situation. *Every month we'll deliver the very best articles, together with the latest fashion and beauty news.* **10** If you describe someone as **together**, you admire them because they are very confident, organized, and know what they want. **11** ● to **get** your **act together**: see **act**. ● to **put** your **heads together**: see **head**.
ADV
ADV: ADV after v
ADV: ADV after v
ADJ: v-link ADJ
ADV: ADV after v
ADV
ADJ: v-link ADJ, n ADJ, v n ADJ PHRASE
PHR-PREP
ADJ-GRADED PRAGMATICS INFORMAL

to·geth·er·ness /tə'geðənəs/. **Togetherness** is a happy feeling of affection and closeness to other people, especially your friends and family.
N-UNCOUNT

tog·gle /'tɒgəl/ **toggles.** A **toggle** is a small rod of wood or plastic which is pushed through a loop as a fastener for a coat or bag.
N-COUNT

toil /tɔɪl/ **toils, toiling, toiled. 1** When people **toil**, they work very hard doing unpleasant or tiring tasks. *Workers toiled long hours... Writing all night, she toiled at a huge novel.* ▶ Also a noun. *Their welfare depends exclusively on their own sweat and toil.* **2** If you **toil** somewhere, you move there slowly and with difficulty, usually because you are very tired. *Arnold had his head down, gasping as he toiled up the hill.*
◆◇◇◇◇ VERB: V V n V at/on n LITERARY N-UNCOUNT
VERB V prep/adv LITERARY

toi·let /'tɔɪlət/ **toilets. 1** A **toilet** is a bathroom fixture which you use when you want to get rid of urine or faeces from your body. **2** A **toilet** is a room in a house or public building that contains a toilet. See picture headed **house and flat**. **3** You can say that someone **goes to the toilet** to mean that they urinate or defecate.
◆◆◇◇◇ N-COUNT
N-COUNT
PHRASE

'toilet paper. **Toilet paper** is thin absorbent paper that people use to clean themselves after they have got rid of urine or faeces from their body.
N-UNCOUNT

toi·let·ries /'tɔɪlətriz/. **Toiletries** are things that you use when washing or taking care of your body, for example soap, deodorant, and toothpaste.
N-PLURAL

'toilet roll, toilet rolls. A **toilet roll** is a long narrow strip of toilet paper that is wound around a small cardboard tube.
N-VAR

to-ing and 'fro-ing. If you say that there is a lot of **to-ing and fro-ing**, you mean that the same actions or movements or the same arguments are being repeated many times.
N-UNCOUNT

to·ken /'təʊkən/ **tokens. 1** You use **token** to describe things or actions which are small and insignificant but are meant to show particular intentions or feelings, which may or may not be sincere. *This may seem a token gesture but at least it's a step in the right direction.* **2** A **token** is a piece of paper or card that can be exchanged for goods, either in a particular shop or as part of a special promotional offer. *...£10 book tokens.* **3** A **token** is a round flat piece of metal or plastic that is sometimes used instead of money. *Some of the older telephones still only accept tokens.* **4** If you give something to someone or do something for them as a **token** of your feelings, you give it or do it as a way of expressing those feelings. **5** You use **by the same token** to
◆◆◇◇◇ ADJ: ADJ n
N-COUNT
N-COUNT
N-COUNT
PHRASE

tokenism

tongue

introduce a statement that you think is true for the same reasons that were given for a previous statement. *If you give up exercise, your muscles shrink and fat increases. By the same token, if you expend more energy you will lose fat.*

to·ken·ism /ˈtəʊkənɪzəm/. If you refer to an action as **tokenism**, you disapprove of it because you think it is just done for effect, to show a particular intention or to impress a particular type of person.
N-UNCOUNT PRAGMATICS

told /təʊld/. **1** Told is the past tense and past participle of **tell**. **2** You can use **all told** to introduce or follow a summary, generalization, or total. *All told there were 104 people on the payroll.*
PHRASE PRAGMATICS

tol·er·able /ˈtɒlərəbəl/. **1** If you describe something as **tolerable**, you mean that it is bearable, even though it is unpleasant or painful. ♦ **tol·er·ably** *Their captors treated them tolerably well.* **2** If you describe something as **tolerable**, you mean that it is fairly good and reasonably satisfactory, but not of the highest quality or standard. ♦ **tolerably** *He can see tolerably well and he can read.*
◆◇◇◇ ADJ-GRADED · ADV · ADJ-GRADED FORMAL · ADV-GRADED

tol·er·ance /ˈtɒlərəns/ **tolerances. 1** Tolerance is the quality of allowing other people to say and do as they like, even if you do not agree or approve of it; used showing approval. ♦ **tol·er·ant** *...more tolerant attitudes to unmarried couples having children.* ♦ **tolerantly** *She had listened tolerantly to his jumbled account.* **2** Tolerance is the ability to bear or survive something painful or unpleasant. ♦ **tolerant** *...plants which are more tolerant of dry conditions.* **3** If someone or something has a **tolerance to** a substance, they are exposed to it so often that it does not have very much effect on them. ♦ **tolerant** *Physical dependence occurs when a person's body becomes tolerant to a drug.*
◆◆◇◇ N-UNCOUNT PRAGMATICS · ADJ-GRADED · ADV-GRADED · N-UNCOUNT · ADJ-GRADED · N-VAR with supp · ADJ-GRADED

tol·er·ate /ˈtɒləreɪt/ **tolerates, tolerating, tolerated. 1** If you **tolerate** a situation or person, you accept them although you do not particularly like them. ♦ **tol·era·tion** /ˌtɒləˈreɪʃən/. *...his views on religious toleration, education, and politics.* **2** If you can **tolerate** something unpleasant or painful, you are able to bear it.
◆◆◇◇ VERB: V n · N-UNCOUNT · VERB: V n

toll /təʊl/ **tolls, tolling, tolled. 1** When a bell **tolls**, it rings slowly and repeatedly, often as a sign that someone has died. *The pilgrims tolled the bell.* **2** A **toll** is a small sum of money that you have to pay in order to use a particular bridge or road. **3** A **toll** is a total number of deaths, accidents, or disasters that occur in a particular period of time. *...the second highest annual murder toll in that city's history.* ● See also **death toll**. **4** If you say that something **takes its toll** or **takes a heavy toll**, you mean that it has a bad effect on something or someone, or causes a lot of suffering. *Winter takes its toll on your health.*
◆◆◇◇ V-ERG: V, V n · N-COUNT · N-COUNT JOURNALISM · PHRASE

toll-'free. A **toll-free** telephone number is one which you can dial without having to pay for the call. The usual British word is **freefone**. ▶ Also an adverb. *Call our customer-service staff toll-free.*
ADJ AMERICAN · ADV: ADV after v

'toll road, toll roads. A **toll road** is a road which people have to pay to drive on.
N-COUNT BRITISH

tom /tɒm/ **toms.** A **tom** is a male cat.
N-COUNT

toma·hawk /ˈtɒməhɔːk/ **tomahawks.** A **tomahawk** is a small light axe, traditionally used by Native Americans.
N-COUNT

to·ma·to /təˈmɑːtəʊ, AM -ˈmeɪ-/ **tomatoes.** Tomatoes are small, soft, red fruit that you can eat raw in salads or cooked as a vegetable. See picture headed **vegetables**.
◆◆◇◇ N-VAR

tomb /tuːm/ **tombs.** A **tomb** is a large grave that is above ground and that usually has a sculpture or other decoration on it.
◆◇◇◇ N-COUNT

tom·boy /ˈtɒmbɔɪ/ **tomboys.** If you say that a girl is a **tomboy**, you mean that she likes playing rough or noisy games, or doing things that were traditionally considered to be things that boys enjoy.
N-COUNT

tomb·stone /ˈtuːmstəʊn/ **tombstones.** A **tombstone** is a large stone with words carved into it, which is placed on a grave.
◆◇◇◇ N-COUNT

'tom cat, tomcats; also spelled **tomcat.** A **tom cat** is a male cat.
N-COUNT

tome /təʊm/ **tomes.** A **tome** is a very large, heavy book.
◆◇◇◇ N-COUNT

tom·fool·ery /tɒmˈfuːləri/. **Tomfoolery** is playful behaviour, usually of a rather silly, noisy, or rough kind.
N-UNCOUNT

to·mor·row /təˈmɒrəʊ, AM -ˈmɔːr-/ **tomorrows. 1** You use **tomorrow** to refer to the day after today. *The first official results will be announced tomorrow.* ▶ Also a noun. *Tomorrow is her thirteenth birthday.* **2** You can refer to the future, especially the near future, as **tomorrow**. *What is education going to look like tomorrow?* ▶ Also a noun. *...tomorrow's computer industry.*
◆◆◆◇ ADV: ADV with cl · ADV: ADV with cl · N-UNCOUNT: also N in pl

ton /tʌn/ **tons. 1** A **ton** is a unit of weight that is equal to 2240 pounds in Britain and to 2000 pounds in the United States. **2** A **ton** is the same as a **tonne**. **3** If you say that something **weighs a ton**, you mean that it is extremely heavy.
◆◆◇◇ N-COUNT: num N · N-COUNT · PHRASE INFORMAL

tone /təʊn/ **tones, toning, toned. 1** The **tone** of a sound is its particular quality. *Cross could hear him speaking in low tones to Sarah. ...the clear tone of the bell.* ♦ **to·nal** /ˈtəʊnəl/. *She found it easy to copy a voice, a tonal quality.* ♦ **-toned** *...a beautiful silver-toned voice.* **2** Someone's **tone** is a quality in their voice which shows what they are feeling or thinking. *I still didn't like his tone of voice... Her tone implied that her patience was limited.*
◆◆◆◇ N-COUNT: with supp · ADJ · COMB · N-COUNT

3 The **tone** of a speech or piece of writing is its style and the opinions or ideas expressed in it. *The spokesman said the tone of the letter was very friendly... His comments to reporters were conciliatory in tone.* **4** The **tone** of a place or an event is its general atmosphere. *The service desk at the entrance, with its friendly, helpful and efficient staff, sets the tone for the rest of the store.* **5** If you say that something **lowers the tone** of a place or event, you mean that it is not appropriate and makes the place or event seem less respectable. **6** The **tone** of someone's body, especially their muscles, is its degree of firmness and strength. *...stretch exercises that aim to improve muscle tone.* **7** Something that **tones** your body makes it firm and strong. ▶ **Tone up** means the same as **tone**. *A quick walk round the block would tone you up more.* **8** A **tone** is one of the lighter, darker, or brighter shades of the same colour. ♦ **tonal** *Indigo and violet bring a tonal richness to these outfits.* ♦ **-toned** *...soft, pastel-toned drawings.* **9** A **tone** is one of the sounds that you hear when you are using a telephone. *They phoned at the same time, and got the engaged tone.* **10** A **tone** is a difference in pitch between two musical notes equal to two semitones.
N-SING: also in N · N-SING: the N · PHRASE PRAGMATICS · N-UNCOUNT · VERB: V n · PHRASAL VB: V P noun, V P n · N-COUNT: also in N, ADJ COMB · N-SING · N-COUNT

tone down. 1 If you **tone down** something that you have written or said, you make it less forceful, severe, or offensive. *We have had to ask the agency and their client to tone their ads down.* **2** If you **tone down** a colour or a flavour, you make it less bright or strong. *He was asked to tone down the spices and garlic in his recipes.*
PHRASAL VB V P noun V n P · V P noun Also V n P

tone up. See tone 6.
PHRASAL VB

tone-'deaf. If you say that someone is **tone-deaf**, you mean that they cannot sing in tune or recognize different tunes.
ADJ PRAGMATICS

tone·less /ˈtəʊnləs/. A **toneless** voice is dull and does not express any feeling. ♦ **tone·less·ly** *'That's most kind of him,' Eleanor said tonelessly.*
ADJ-GRADED · ADV-GRADED: ADV after v

ton·er /ˈtəʊnə/ **toners.** A **toner** is a substance which you can put on your skin to make it less oily.
◆◇◇◇ N-VAR

tongs /tɒŋz, AM tɔːŋz/. **Tongs** are a tool that you use to grip and pick up objects that you do not want to touch. They consist of two long narrow pieces of metal joined together at one end.
N-PLURAL: also a pair of N

tongue /tʌŋ/ **tongues. 1** Your **tongue** is the soft movable part inside your mouth which you use for tasting, licking, and speaking. See picture headed **human body**. **2** You can use **tongue** to refer to the kind of things that a person says. *...her sharp wit and quick tongue... She had a nasty tongue, but I*
◆◆◇◇ N-COUNT · N-COUNT

liked her. **3** A **tongue** is a language. *The French feel passionately about their native tongue.* ● See also **mother tongue**. **4** A **tongue-in-cheek** remark or attitude is ironic and not serious, although it may seem to be serious. **5** If you **hold** your **tongue**, you do not say anything even though you might want to or be expected to, because it is the wrong time to say it. **6** If you say that you can not **get** your **tongue round** a word or phrase, you mean that you find it very difficult to pronounce. **7** If you describe something you said as **a slip of the tongue**, you mean that you said it by mistake. **8** ● to **bite** your **tongue**: see **bite**.
N-COUNT LITERARY
PHRASE
PHRASE
PHRASE
PHRASE

9 Tongue is the cooked tongue of an ox or sheep. It is usually eaten cold. **10** The **tongue** of a shoe or boot is the piece of leather which is underneath the laces. **11** A **tongue** of something such as fire or land is a long thin piece of it.
N-VAR
N-COUNT
N-COUNT: N *of* n LITERARY

,tongue-in-'cheek. See **tongue**.

'tongue lashing, tongue lashings. If someone gives you a **tongue lashing**, they shout at you or criticize you in a very forceful way.
N-COUNT INFORMAL

'tongue-tied. If someone is **tongue-tied**, they are unable to say anything because they feel shy or nervous.
ADJ-GRADED

'tongue-twister, tongue-twisters; also spelled **tongue twister.** A **tongue-twister** is a sentence or expression which is very difficult to say properly, especially when you try to say it quickly. An example of a tongue-twister is 'She sells seashells on the seashore'.
N-COUNT

ton·ic /'tɒnɪk/ **tonics. 1 Tonic** or **tonic water** is a colourless fizzy drink that has a slightly bitter flavour and is often mixed with alcoholic drinks, especially gin. ▶ A glass of tonic can be referred to as a **tonic** or a **tonic water**. **2** A **tonic** is a medicine that makes you feel stronger, healthier, and less tired. **3** A **tonic** is anything that makes you feel stronger, more cheerful, or more enthusiastic. *Seeing Marcus at that moment was a great tonic.* **4** Skin **tonic** or hair **tonic** is a liquid that you put on your skin or hair in order to improve it.
N-VAR
N-COUNT
N-VAR
N-COUNT
N-VAR

to·night /tə'naɪt/. **Tonight** is used to refer to the evening of today or the night that follows today. *Tonight, I think he proved to everybody what a great player he was... There they will stay until 11 o'clock tonight.* ▶ Also a noun. *Tonight is the opening night of the opera.*
ADV
N-UNCOUNT

ton·nage /'tʌnɪdʒ/ **tonnages. 1** The **tonnage** of a ship is its size or the amount of space that it has inside for cargo. **2 Tonnage** is the total number of tons that something weighs, or the total amount that there is of it.
N-VAR TECHNICAL
N-VAR

tonne /tʌn/ **tonnes.** A **tonne** is a metric unit of weight that is equal to 1000 kilograms.
N-COUNT: num N

ton·sil·li·tis /,tɒnsɪ'laɪtɪs/. **Tonsillitis** is a painful swelling of your tonsils caused by an infection.
N-UNCOUNT

ton·sils /'tɒnsɪlz/; the form **tonsil** is used as a modifier. Your **tonsils** are the two small soft lumps in your throat at the back of your mouth.
N-PLURAL

too 1 adding something or responding

too /tuː/. **1** You use **too** after mentioning another person, thing, or aspect that a previous statement applies to or includes. *'Nice to talk to you.'—'Nice to talk to you too.'... 'I've got a great feeling about it.'—'Me too.'... Depression may be expressed physically too... He doesn't want to meet me. I, too, have been afraid to talk to him.* **2** You use **too** after adding a piece of information or a comment to a statement, in order to emphasize it. *We did learn to read, and quickly too... 'That money's mine.'—'Of course it is, and quite right too.'... 'Oh excuse me.'—'I should think so too.'* **3** You use **too** in order to emphasize in a humorous or childish way your contradiction of what someone else has said or your refusal to obey them. *'I'm getting a bike for my birthday.'—'You are not.'—'I am too.'*
ADV: cl/group ADV PRAGMATICS
ADV: cl/group ADV PRAGMATICS
ADV: ADV after aux PRAGMATICS INFORMAL

too 2 indicating excess

too /tuː/. **1** You use **too** in order to indicate that there is a greater amount or degree of something
ADV: ADV adj/adv

than is desirable, necessary, or acceptable. *Eggs shouldn't be left in the fridge, it's too cold... She was drinking too much, eating too much, having too many late nights... I know you need your freedom too much to stay with me.* **2** You use **too** with a negative to make what you are saying sound less forceful or more polite or cautious. *Americans are never too keen to leave their beloved country... I wasn't too happy with what I'd written so far.* **3** You use **too** when you want to emphasize your thanks to someone for something that they have done for you. *'I'll try and get you a cake.'—'Oh Ann you're too kind.'* **4** You use **all too** or **only too** to emphasize that something happens to a greater extent or degree than is pleasant or desirable. *She remembered it all too well... The letter spoke only too clearly of his anxiety for her.* **5** If you describe a situation as **too little too late**, you are blaming someone for not doing enough to prevent a problem and for taking action only after the problem had become very bad. **6** ● **too bad**: see **bad**. ● **none too**: see **none**.
ADV PRAGMATICS
ADV: ADV adj PRAGMATICS
PHRASE PRAGMATICS
PHRASE

took /tʊk/. **Took** is the past tense of **take**.

tool /tuːl/ **tools. 1** A **tool** is any instrument or simple piece of equipment that you hold in your hands and use to do a particular kind of work. For example, spades, hammers, and knives are all tools. ● See also **machine tool**. **2** You can refer to anything that you use for a particular purpose as a particular type of **tool**. *Writing is a good tool for discharging overwhelming feelings... The video has become an invaluable teaching tool.* **3** If you describe someone as a **tool** of a particular person, group, or ideology, you mean that they are controlled and used by that person, group, or ideology, especially to do unpleasant or dishonest things; used showing disapproval. *He became the tool of the security services.* **4** If you say that workers **down tools**, you mean that they stop working suddenly in order to strike or to make a protest of some kind. **5 The tools of** your **trade** or **the tools of the trade** are the skills, instruments, and other equipment that you need in order to do your job properly.
N-COUNT
N-COUNT
N-COUNT PRAGMATICS
PHRASE BRITISH
PHRASE

'tool box, tool boxes. A **tool box** is a metal or plastic box which contains general tools that you need at home, for example to do repairs in your house or car.
N-COUNT

'tool kit, tool kits. A **tool kit** is a special set of tools that are kept together and that are often used for a particular purpose.
N-COUNT

toot /tuːt/ **toots, tooting, tooted.** If someone **toots** their car horn, it produces a short sound or series of sounds. *Car horns toot as cyclists dart precariously through the traffic.* ▶ Also a noun. *The driver gave me a wave and a toot.*
V-ERG: V n V
N-SING

tooth /tuːθ/ **teeth. 1** Your **teeth** are the hard white objects in your mouth and which you use for biting and chewing. See picture headed **human body**. **2** The **teeth** of something such as a comb, saw, cog, or zip are the parts that stick out in a row on its edge. **3** If you say that something such as an official group or a law has **teeth**, you mean that it has power and is able to be effective. *The opposition argues that the new council will be unconstitutional and without teeth.* **4** See also **wisdom tooth**. **5** Someone who is **armed to the teeth** is armed with a lot of weapons or with very effective weapons. **6** If you say that someone **cut their teeth** doing a particular thing, at a particular time, or in a particular place, you mean they began their career and learned some of their skills doing that thing, at that time, or in that place. *...director John Glen, who cut his teeth on Bond movies.* **7** If you say that something **sets** your **teeth on edge**, you mean that you find it extremely unpleasant or irritating. **8** If you **fight tooth and nail** to do something, you do everything you can in order to achieve it. If you **fight** something **tooth and nail**, you do everything you can in order to prevent it. **9** If you describe a task or activity as something you can **get your teeth into**, you mean that you like it because it is substantial or complex enough to hold all your interest.
N-COUNT
N-PLURAL
N-PLURAL
PHRASE
PHRASE
PHRASE
PHRASE
PHRASE PRAGMATICS

10 If you do something **in the teeth of** a difficulty or PHRASE
danger, you do it in spite of the difficulty or danger. *I
was battling my way along the promenade in the teeth
of a force ten gale.* **11** If you say that someone **is lying** PHRASE
through their **teeth**, you are emphasizing that they PRAGMATICS
are telling lies. **12** You can describe someone as **long** PHRASE
in the tooth if they are old or getting old. *Aren't I a bit* INFORMAL
long in the tooth to start being an undergraduate?
13 If you have **a sweet tooth**, you like sweet food very PHRASE
much. **14 ●** to **get the bit between** your **teeth**: see **bit**.
● to **gnash** one's **teeth**: see **gnash**. ● to **grit** your
teeth: see **grit**. ● **a kick in the teeth**: see **kick**. ● **by the**
skin of your **teeth**: see **skin**.

tooth·ache /ˈtuːθeɪk/. **Toothache** is pain in one of N-UNCOUNT
your teeth.

tooth·brush /ˈtuːθbrʌʃ/ **toothbrushes.** A tooth- ◆◇◇◇◇
brush is a small brush that you use for cleaning N-COUNT
your teeth.

tooth·less /ˈtuːθləs/. **1** You use **toothless** to de- ADJ
scribe a person or their smile when they have no
teeth. **2** If you describe something such as an offi- ADJ-GRADED
cial group or a law as **toothless**, you mean it has no
real power and is not effective.

tooth·paste /ˈtuːθpeɪst/ **toothpastes. Tooth-** ◆◇◇◇◇
paste is a thick substance which you put on your N-VAR
toothbrush and use to clean your teeth.

tooth·pick /ˈtuːθpɪk/ **toothpicks.** A **toothpick** is a N-COUNT
small stick which you use to remove food from be-
tween your teeth.

toothy /ˈtuːθi/. A **toothy** smile is one in which a ADJ-GRADED:
person shows a lot of teeth. ADJ n

top /tɒp/ **tops, topping, topped. 1** The **top** of ◆◆◆◆◆
something is its highest point or part. *I waited at* N-COUNT
the top of the stairs. ...the top of the page... Bake the
biscuits for 20-25 minutes, until the tops are lightly
browned. **2** The **top** part of something is its highest ADJ: ADJ n
part. The **top** thing in a series of things is the highest one. *...the top shelf... Our new flat was on the*
top floor. **3** If one thing is **on top** of another, it is PHRASE
placed over it or on its highest part. *...the vacuum*
flask that was resting on top of the stove... Place the
sliced pork fillet on top. **4** If something **is topped** VERB:
with something, it has that thing as its highest part. beV-ed with/
Top the fish with the cooked leeks. ◆ **-topped** *...the* byn
glass-topped table. V n with n
COMB

5 The **top** of a place such as a street or garden is the N-SING:
end which is farthest away from where you usually theN
enter it or from where you are. *...a little shop at the top* BRITISH
of the street.

6 The **top** of something such as a bottle or jar is its cap N-COUNT
or lid. **7** A **top** is a piece of clothing that you wear on N-COUNT
the upper half of your body, for example a blouse or
T-shirt.

8 You can use **top** to describe the highest level of a ADJ: ADJ n
scale or measurement. *The vehicles have a top speed of*
80 kilometres per hour. **9** If someone is **top** of a table ADJ
or league, their performance is better than that of all
the other people involved. *He was the top student in*
physics... He stood in the subsequent by-election and
came top of the poll. ▶ Also a noun. *The United States* N-SING
will be at the top of the medal table. **10** You can use ADJ
top to indicate that something is the most important
of a number of things, and therefore it will be dealt
with first. *Cleaning up the water supply is their top pri-*
ority... On arrival, a six-course meal was top of the
agenda.

11 If someone is at the **top** of an organization or ca- N-SING
reer, or if they are **on top**, they are among the most
senior, important, or successful people in it. *...his dra-*
matic rise to the top of the military hierarchy. ▶ Also ADJ: ADJ n
an adjective. *...the top people in this company... So you*
want to be a top model. **12** If you say that someone is PHRASE
at the **top of the tree**, you mean that they have BRITISH
reached the highest level in their career or profession.
13 If someone **comes out on top**, they are more suc- PHRASE
cessful than their rivals in a competition or contest.
14 If someone or something **tops** a list, poll, or chart, VERB: V n
they are mentioned or chosen more times than any- JOURNALISM
one or anything else. **15** To **top** a particular amount VERB
means to be larger than that amount. *Imports topped* V amount

£10 billion last month. **16** If you **top** a story, remark, VERB
or action, you follow it with a better or more impres- V n
sive one. *How are you going to top that?*

17 You can use **tops** after mentioning a quantity, to ADV:
say that it is the maximum possible. *The publisher ex-* num ADV
pected the book to sell 1,500 copies, tops. **18** If you say INFORMAL
that something **is tops** or **is the tops**, you mean that it PHRASE
is better or more successful than anything else. *Ma-* INFORMAL
jorca and Ibiza are tops for holiday bargain-hunters in
June. **19** You describe something as **over the top** PHRASE
when you think that it is exaggerated, and therefore BRITISH,
unacceptable. INFORMAL

20 You can use **on top** or **on top of** to indicate that a PHRASE
particular problem exists in addition to a number of
other problems. *An extra 700 jobs are being cut on top*
of the 2,000 that were lost last year. **21** If work or prob- PHRASE
lems **get on top of** you, they make you feel depressed
and helpless because they are very difficult, worrying,
or excessive. *Things have been getting on top of me*
lately. **22** If you are **on top of** something that you are PHRASE
doing, you are dealing with it successfully. *...the gov-*
ernment's inability to get on top of the situation. **23** If PHRASE
you say that you feel **on top of the world**, you are em- PRAGMATICS
phasizing that you feel extremely happy and healthy.
24 If you say that you clean, tidy, or examine some- PHRASE
thing **from top to bottom**, you are emphasizing that PRAGMATICS
you do it completely and thoroughly. **25** You can use PHRASE
from top to toe to emphasize that the whole of PRAGMATICS
someone's body is covered or dressed in a particular
thing or type of clothing. *They were sensibly dressed*
from top to toe in rain gear.

26 If you shout something **at the top of** your **voice**, PHRASE
you shout it very loudly. **27** If you say something **off** PHRASE
the top of your **head**, you say it without thinking
much before you speak, especially because you do
not have enough time. *It was the best I could think of*
off the top of my head. **28** If someone **blows** their **top**, PHRASE
they become very angry about something. INFORMAL

29 If you **top and tail** vegetables or fruit, you cut off PHRASE
the top and bottom of them when you are preparing BRITISH
them to be eaten.

30 See also **topping**. ● **at the top of the heap**: see
heap.

top off. To **top off** an event or period with a particu- PHRASAL VB
lar thing means to end it in an especially satisfactory, V P noun
dramatic, or annoying way by doing that thing. *He* V n P
topped off his career with an Olympic gold medal... To
top it all off one of the catering staff managed to slice
their finger cutting cheese.

top up. If you **top** something **up**, you make it full PHRASAL VB
again when part of it has been used. *He topped her* V P noun
glass up. ● See also **top-up**. V n P
BRITISH

to·paz /ˈtəʊpæz/ **topazes.** A **topaz** is a precious N-VAR
stone, usually yellowish-brown in colour.

top-class; also spelled **top class. Top-class** ◆◇◇◇◇
means amongst the finest of its kind. ADJ

top·coat /ˈtɒpkəʊt/ **topcoats**; also spelled **top**
coat. 1 A **topcoat** is a thick, warm coat. **2** A **topcoat** N-COUNT
is the final layer of paint that is put on something. N-VAR
Topcoat is the type of paint that you use for this
layer.

top 'dog, top dogs. If someone or something is N-COUNT;
top dog, they are the best within a certain group. also no det
London's been top dog among the musical cities INFORMAL
these last few years.

top-'drawer. If you describe someone or some- ADJ
thing as **top-drawer**, you mean that they are of high DATED,
social class or of very good quality. INFORMAL

top 'hat, top hats. A **top hat** is a man's tall hat N-COUNT
with a narrow brim. Top hats are now worn only on
special occasions, for example at some weddings.

top-'heavy. 1 **Top-heavy** things are larger or ADJ-GRADED
bulkier at the top than at the bottom, and are therefore not stable. *...top-heavy flowers such as sun-*
flowers. **2** If you describe a business or organiza- ADJ-GRADED
tion as **top-heavy**, you mean that it has too many PRAGMATICS
senior managers in relation to the number of junior
people or workers; used showing disapproval.

to·pi·ary /'təʊpiəri, AM -eri/. Topiary is the art of cutting hedges and bushes into different shapes, for example into the shapes of birds or animals. `N-UNCOUNT`

top·ic /'tɒpɪk/ **topics.** A topic is a particular subject that you discuss or write about. *The weather is a constant topic of conversation in Britain.* `◆◆◇◇◇ N-COUNT`

topi·cal /'tɒpɪkəl/. Topical is used to describe something that concerns or relates to events that are happening at the present time. *The sinking of the tanker has made aspects of marine pollution particularly topical.* ♦ **topi·cal·ity** /ˌtɒpɪ'kælɪti/. ...*all the lively topicality of first-rate journalism.* `◆◆◇◇◇ ADJ-GRADED` `N-UNCOUNT`

top·less /'tɒpləs/. **1** If a woman goes topless, she does not wear anything to cover her breasts. *I wouldn't sunbathe topless.* **2** In a topless show or bar, the female entertainers or staff do not wear anything to cover their breasts. `◆◇◇◇◇ ADJ` `ADJ: ADJ n`

top·'level. A top-level discussion or activity involves the people with the greatest amount of power and authority in an organization or country. ...*a top-level meeting of American generals.* `◆◇◇◇◇ ADJ: ADJ n`

top·most /'tɒpməʊst/. The topmost thing in a number of things is the one that is highest or nearest the top. ...*the topmost branches of a gigantic oak tree.* `ADJ: ADJ n`

top·'notch; also spelled top notch. If you describe someone or something as top-notch, you mean that they are of a very high standard or quality. `ADJ DATED, INFORMAL`

to·pog·ra·phy /tə'pɒgrəfi/ **topographies.** The topography of an area is its physical shape, including its hills, valleys, and rivers. ♦ **topo·graphi·cal** /ˌtɒpə'græfɪkəl/. `N-COUNT` `ADJ`

top·ping /'tɒpɪŋ/ **toppings.** A topping is food, such as cream or cheese, that is put on top of other food in order to decorate it or add to its flavour. ● See also top. `◆◇◇◇◇ N-VAR`

top·ple /'tɒpəl/ **topples, toppling, toppled. 1** If someone or something topples somewhere, they become unsteady and fall over. *Winds and rain toppled trees and electricity lines.* ▶ **Topple over** means the same as topple. *We lost our balance and toppled over on to a table.* **2** To topple a government or leader means to cause them to lose power. ...*the revolution which toppled the communist regime.* `◆◆◇◇◇ V-ERG: V adv/prep V n PHRASAL VB V P` `VERB V n JOURNALISM`

top·'ranked. A top-ranked sports player or team is the most successful in a particular sport. `ADJ: ADJ n JOURNALISM`

top·'ranking. A top-ranking person is of very high rank or status in a particular organization or field of activity. ...*400 of Germany's top-ranking military officials.* `ADJ: ADJ n`

top·'rated. A top-rated show or service is the most successful or highly regarded of its kind. ...*the top-rated American television series.* `ADJ: ADJ n JOURNALISM`

top·'secret; also spelled top-secret. Top secret information or activity is intended to be kept completely secret, for example in order to prevent a country's enemies from finding out about it. ...*a top-secret mission.* `◆◇◇◇◇ ADJ`

top·side /'tɒpsaɪd/ **topsides. 1** Topside is a joint of beef that is cut from the upper part of the leg. It is usually cooked by roasting. **2** The topside or topsides of a ship or boat are the top deck or the parts which you can see above the water. `N-UNCOUNT BRITISH` `N-COUNT TECHNICAL`

top·soil /'tɒpsɔɪl/. Topsoil is the layer of soil nearest the surface of the ground. `N-UNCOUNT`

topsy-turvy /ˌtɒpsi 'tɜːvi/. Something that is topsy-turvy is in a confused or disorganized state. *The world has turned topsy-turvy.* `ADJ INFORMAL`

'top-up, top-ups. 1 A top-up is another serving of a drink in the same glass that you have just used. *Anyone ready for a top-up?* **2** A top-up loan or payment is added to an amount of money in order to bring it up to a required level. `◆◇◇◇◇ N-COUNT BRITISH` `ADJ: ADJ n BRITISH`

torch /tɔːtʃ/ **torches, torching, torched. 1** A torch is a small, battery-powered electric light which you can carry in your hand. The usual American word is flashlight. **2** A torch is a long stick with burning material at one end, used to provide light or to set things on fire. ...*a torch-lit march for peace.* **3** A torch is a device that uses a hot flame for a task `◆◆◇◇◇ N-COUNT BRITISH` `N-COUNT` `N-COUNT:`

such as welding or cutting metal. ● See also blow-torch. **4** If you say that someone is carrying the torch of a particular belief or movement, you mean that they are working hard to ensure that it is not forgotten and continues to grow stronger. **5** If someone torches a building or vehicle, they set fire to it deliberately. *Cars and trucks have been torched, bottles and bricks thrown.* `supp N` `PHRASE` `VERB: V n be V-ed`

torch·light /'tɔːtʃlaɪt/. If you do something by torchlight, you do it using the light that is produced by a torch or torches. ...*a torchlight procession.* `N-UNCOUNT`

tore /tɔː/. Tore is the past tense of tear.

tor·ment, torments, tormenting, tormented. The noun is pronounced /'tɔːment/. The verb is pronounced /tɔː'ment/. **1** Torment is extreme suffering, usually mental suffering. *He spent days in torment while the police searched for his stolen car.* **2** If something torments you, it causes you extreme mental suffering. *He had lain awake all night, tormented by jealousy.* ♦ **tor·men·tor** /tɔː'mentə/ **tormentors** ...*cases where women subjected to years of brutality lose control and kill their tormentors.* **3** To torment a person or animal means to annoy them in a playful, rather cruel way, for your own amusement. *My older brother and sister used to torment me by singing it to me.* `◆◆◇◇◇` `N-UNCOUNT: also N in pl` `VERB: V n V-ed` `N-COUNT` `VERB V n`

torn /tɔːn/. **1** Torn is the past participle of tear. **2** If you are torn between two or more things, you cannot decide which to choose, and so you feel anxious or troubled. *Robb is torn between becoming a doctor and a career in athletics.* `◆◇◇◇◇ ADJ-GRADED`

tor·na·do /tɔː'neɪdəʊ/ **tornadoes** or **tornados.** A tornado is a violent wind storm whose centre is a cloud in the shape of a funnel. `◆◇◇◇◇ N-COUNT`

tor·pe·do /tɔː'piːdəʊ/ **torpedoes, torpedoing, torpedoed. 1** A torpedo is bomb shaped like a tube which travels under water. **2** If a ship is torpedoed, it is hit, and usually sunk, by a torpedo or torpedoes. **3** If someone torpedoes negotiations or plans, they deliberately prevent them from being completed or from being successful. `◆◇◇◇◇ N-COUNT` `VB: usu passive` `VERB: V n JOURNALISM`

tor·pid /'tɔːpɪd/. If you are torpid, you are mentally or physically inactive, especially because you are feeling lazy or sleepy. `ADJ-GRADED FORMAL`

tor·por /'tɔːpə/. Torpor is the state of being completely inactive mentally or physically, for example because of illness or laziness. *He had slumped into a state of torpor from which nothing could rouse him.* `N-UNCOUNT: also a N`

torque /tɔːk/. Torque is a force that causes something to spin around a central point or axle. `N-UNCOUNT TECHNICAL`

tor·rent /'tɒrənt, AM 'tɔːr-/ **torrents. 1** A torrent is a lot of water falling or flowing rapidly or violently. *Torrents of water gushed into the reservoir... The rain came down in torrents... The trip involved crossing a raging torrent.* **2** A torrent of abuse or questions is a lot of insults or questions directed continuously at someone. ...*a £45,000 offer which prompted a torrent of criticism in the media.* `◆◇◇◇◇ N-COUNT`

tor·ren·tial /tə'renʃəl, AM tɔːr-/. Torrential rain pours down very rapidly and in great quantities. `◆◇◇◇◇ ADJ`

tor·rid /'tɒrɪd, AM 'tɔːrɪd/. **1** Torrid weather is extremely hot. ...*the torrid heat of a Spanish summer.* **2** A torrid relationship or incident involves very strong emotions connected with love and sex. ...*torrid bedroom scenes.* **3** If someone or something has a torrid time, they experience a lot of difficulties. *He suffered yet another torrid day of criticism.* `ADJ-GRADED` `ADJ-GRADED` `ADJ-GRADED BRITISH, JOURNALISM`

tor·so /'tɔːsəʊ/ **torsos.** Your torso is the main part of your body, excluding your arms, head, and legs. `◆◇◇◇◇ N-COUNT FORMAL`

tort /tɔːt/ **torts.** A tort is something that you do or fail to do which harms someone else and for which you can be sued for damages. `N-COUNT LEGAL`

tor·til·la /tɔː'tiːjə/ **tortillas.** A tortilla is a Mexican pancake. `N-VAR`

tor·toise /'tɔːtəs/ **tortoises.** A tortoise is a slow-moving animal with a shell into which it can pull its head and legs for protection. `◆◇◇◇◇ N-COUNT`

tortoise·shell /'tɔːtəsʃel/. Tortoiseshell is a hard, polished, yellow and brown material that is often `N-UNCOUNT`

used to make jewellery and ornaments. Genuine tortoiseshell is made from the shell of a kind of sea turtle. ...*huge spectacles with thick tortoiseshell frames.*

tor·tu·ous /'tɔːtʃuəs/. **1** A **tortuous** road is full of bends and twists. *It was a tortuous mountain route.* ◆◇◇◇◇ ADJ-GRADED **2** A **tortuous** process or piece of writing is very long and complicated. ...*long and tortuous negotiations.* ADJ-GRADED

tor·ture /'tɔːtʃə/ **tortures, torturing, tortured.** ◆◆◇◇◇ **1** If someone **is tortured**, another person deliberately causes them great pain over a period of time, in order to punish them or make them reveal information. *They never again tortured a prisoner in his presence.* ► Also a noun. *Many died under torture, others committed suicide... I had thought this was a medieval torture that had mercifully disappeared.* VERB: be V-ed V n N-VAR ◆ **tor·tur·er** *The paper described the army officers as 'criminals and torturers'.* N-COUNT **2** To **torture** someone means to cause them to suffer mental pain or anxiety. *She tortured herself with fantasies of Bob and his new girlfriend.* **3** If you say that something is **torture** or a **torture**, you mean that it causes you great mental or physical suffering. *The friction of the sheets against his skin was torture... Learning – something she had always loved – became a torture.* VERB: V n V pron-refl N-UNCOUNT: also a N INFORMAL

tor·tur·ous /'tɔːtʃərəs/. Something that is **torturous** is extremely painful and causes great suffering. *This is a torturous, agonizing way to kill someone.* ADJ-GRADED

Tory /'tɔːri/ **Tories.** In Britain, a **Tory** politician or voter is a member of or votes for the Conservative Party. ...*the constituency with the largest Tory majority in the country.* ► Also a noun. ...*the first budget since the Tories won the 1992 general election.* ◆◆◆◆◇ ADJ N-COUNT

toss /tɒs, AM tɔːs/ **tosses, tossing, tossed. 1** If you **toss** something somewhere, you throw it there lightly, often in a rather careless way. *He tossed his blanket aside and got up... He tossed Malone a can of beer, and took one himself.* **2** If you **toss** your head or your hair, you move your head backwards quickly and suddenly, often as a way of expressing an emotion such as anger or contempt. *'I'm sure I don't know.' Cook tossed her head... She tossed her hair out of her face.* ► Also a noun. *With a toss of his head and a few hard gulps, Bob finished the last of his beer.* **3** If something such as the wind or sea **tosses** an object, it causes it to move from side to side or up and down. *The seas grew turbulent, tossing the small boat like a cork.* **4** If you **toss** food while preparing it, you put pieces of it into a liquid and lightly shake them so that they become covered with the liquid. *Toss the apple slices in the mixture.* ...*a tossed green salad.* **5** If you **toss** and **turn**, you move restlessly in bed and cannot sleep properly, for example because you are ill or worried. ◆◆◇◇◇ VERB V n adv/prep V n n VERB V n V n prep/adv N-COUNT VERB V n LITERARY VERB: V n V n in n V-ed PHRASE

6 In sports and informal situations, if you decide something by **tossing** a coin, you spin a coin into the air and guess which side of the coin will face upwards when it lands. *We tossed a coin to decide who would go out and buy the buns.* ► Also a noun. *It would be better to decide it on the toss of a coin.* **7** The **toss** is a way of deciding something, such as who is going to go first in a game, that consists of spinning a coin into the air and guessing which side of the coin will face upwards when it lands. *Bangladesh won the toss and decided to bat first.* VERB V n N-COUNT N-SING: the N

8 If you say that you do not **give a toss** about someone or something, you are emphasizing that you do not care about them at all. *I don't give a toss what people think.* PHRASE PRAGMATICS BRITISH, INFORMAL

'toss-up, toss-ups. If you say that it is a **toss-up** whether one thing will happen or another thing will happen, you mean that either event seems equally likely. *It's a toss-up whether oil prices will go up or down.* N-COUNT

tot /tɒt/ **tots, totting, totted.** A **tot** is a very young child. ◆◇◇◇◇ N-COUNT INFORMAL **tot up.** To **tot up** a total or a list of numbers means to add up several numbers in order to reach a total. *I finally sat down to tot up the full extent of my debt.* PHRASAL VB V P noun Also V n P BRITISH

to·tal /'təʊtl/ **totals, totalling, totalled. 1** A **total** is the number that you get when you add several numbers together or when you count how many things are in a group. *The companies have a total of 1,776 employees... I was with my husband for eight years in total.* ► Also an adjective. *The total cost of the project would be more than $240 million dollars.* **2** If several numbers or things **total** a certain figure, that figure is the total of all the numbers or things. *They will compete for prizes totalling nearly £300.* **3** You can use **total** to emphasize that something is as great in extent, degree, or amount as it possibly can be. *There was an almost total lack of management control... Why should we trust a total stranger?... I have total confidence that things will change.* ♦ **to·tal·ly** ...*something totally different... The fire totally destroyed the top floor.* ◆◆◆◆◆ N-COUNT: also in N ADJ: ADJ n VERB V amount ADJ PRAGMATICS ADV

to·tali·tar·ian /ˌtəʊtælɪˈteəriən/. In a **totalitarian** political system, there is only one political party which controls everything and does not allow any opposition; used showing disapproval. ♦ **to·tali·tari·an·ism. Totalitarianism** is used to refer to totalitarian political systems or ideologies. ◆◇◇◇◇ ADJ PRAGMATICS N-UNCOUNT

to·tal·ity /təʊˈtælɪti/. The **totality** of something is the whole of it. ...*the totality of human experience... He did not want to reform the criminal justice system in its totality.* N-UNCOUNT FORMAL

tote /təʊt/ **totes, toting, toted. 1** In Britain, the **Tote** is a system of betting money on horses at a racetrack. **2** To **tote** something, especially a gun, means to carry it with you in such a way that people can see it. *The demonstrators fled when soldiers toting machine guns advanced on the crowd.* ♦ **-toting** ...*gun-toting thugs.* ◆◇◇◇◇ N-SING: the N V n COMB

to·tem /'təʊtəm/ **totems.** A **totem** of a person or group of people is a particular object or living thing that they believe to have special cultural or spiritual significance. *The funny little scooter became a tribal totem for generations of youngsters.* ◆◇◇◇◇ N-COUNT

'totem pole, totem poles. In some Native American cultures, a **totem pole** is a long wooden pole with symbols and pictures carved and painted on it. N-COUNT

tot·ter /'tɒtə/ **totters, tottering, tottered. 1** If someone **totters** somewhere, they walk there in an unsteady way, for example because they are ill or drunk. *He tottered to the fridge, got a beer and slumped at the table.* **2** If something such as a market or government **is tottering**, it is weak and likely to collapse or fail completely. *The property market is tottering. ...the tottering government.* ◆◇◇◇◇ VERB V prep/adv VERB V-ing

tou·can /'tuːkən, AM -kæn/ **toucans.** A **toucan** is a South American bird with a large brightly-coloured beak. N-COUNT

touch /tʌtʃ/ **touches, touching, touched. 1** When you **touch** something, you put your hand on it in order to feel it or to make contact with it. *She touched David's desk for the sense of something solid in the dark... The virus is not passed on through touching.* ► Also a noun. *Even a light touch on the face is enough to trigger off this pain.* **2** If two things **are touching**, or if one thing **touches** another, or if you **touch** two things, their surfaces or edges come into contact with each other. *Their knees were touching... As the aeroplane went down the runway the wing touched a pile of rubble... In some countries people stand close enough to touch elbows.* **3** Your sense of **touch** is your ability to tell what something is like when you feel it with your hands. ...*boys and girls who are blind and who want to be able to read and write by touch.* **4** You use expressions such as **at the touch of a button** and **at the touch of a key** to indicate that something is possible by simply touching a switch or one of the keys of a keyboard. *Staff will be able to trace calls at the touch of a button. ...seats that flip out at the touch of a lever.* **5** **Touch** is used to emphasize that someone makes deliberate physical contact with something or someone, often in order to cause harm, to use something wrongly, or to have a particular effect. *Pearce re-* ◆◆◆◇ VERB V n V N-COUNT V-RECIP-ERG pl-n V V n V pl-n N-UNCOUNT PHRASE VERB PRAGMATICS V n

mained adamant, saying 'I didn't touch him'... Don't touch that dial... He scored the first time he touched the ball. **6** You say that you **have** never **touched** something in order to emphasize that you have never used or consumed it. He doesn't drink much and doesn't touch drugs... Jones hasn't touched a trumpet in 10 years. **7** If something **has** not **been touched**, nobody has dealt with it or taken care of it. When John began to restore the house in the 1960, nothing had been touched for 40 years. **8** To **touch** a particular high level, amount, or score means to reach it for a short time. By the third lap Kinkead had touched 289 m.p.h. **9** If you **touch on** a particular subject, you mention it briefly. The film touches on these issues, but only superficially. **10** If something **is touched with** a particular quality, it has a certain amount of that quality. His crinkly hair was touched with grey... The boy was touched with genius. **11** If something that someone says or does **touches** you, it affects you emotionally, often because that person is suffering or is being very kind. It has touched me deeply to see how these people live. ♦ **touched** I'm always touched to discover that such innocence still survives... He was touched that we came. ♦ **touch·ing** ...the touching tale of a wife who stood by the husband she loved. ♦ **touch·ing·ly** He was touchingly naive about sex. **12** If something **touches** you, it involves or affects you. ...a guilt that in some sense touches everyone... Nor had the benefits of the war years touched all sectors of the population.

13 If you say about someone that nobody can **touch** them **for** something, you mean that they are much better at it than anyone else. No one can touch these girls for professionalism. **14** If someone has a particular kind of **touch**, they have a particular kind of talent or style when they do something. For example, if someone such as a politician has **the common touch**, they have a natural ability to be friendly or popular with ordinary people. Used showing approval. The dishes he produces all have a personal touch... The striker was unable to find his scoring touch.

15 A **touch** is a detail that is added to something to improve it. They called the event 'a tribute to heroes', which was a nice touch... Small touches to a room such as flowers can be what gives a house its vitality. **16** A **touch of** something is a very small amount of it. She just had a touch of flu... At university he wrote a bit, did a touch of acting, and indulged in internal college politics. **17** You can use **a touch** to mean 'slightly' or 'to a small extent'. We were all a touch uneasy... I found it a touch distasteful.

18 If you get **in touch** with someone, you contact them by writing to them or telephoning them. If you are, keep, or stay **in touch** with them, you write, phone, or visit each other regularly. I will get in touch with solicitors about this... I was in her class in Canterbury two summers ago and since then we've kept in touch. **19** If you are **in touch** with a subject or situation, or if someone keeps you **in touch** with it, you know the latest news or information about it. If you are **out of touch** with it, you do not know the latest news or information about it. You'll also be kept in touch with local Oxfam events... Mr Cavazos' problem was that he was out of touch. **20** If you **lose touch** with someone, you gradually stop writing, telephoning, or visiting them. We lost touch after that. **21** If you **lose touch** with something, you no longer have the latest news or information about it. Their leaders have lost touch with what is happening in the country.

22 If something is **touch and go**, it is uncertain whether it will happen or succeed. It was touch and go whether we'd go bankrupt.

23 If you **touch** someone **for** money, you ask them to give it to you. Now is the time to touch him for a loan. **24** If you say that someone is **a soft touch**, you mean that they can easily be persuaded to lend you money or to do things for you. Mr Wilson is no soft touch.

25 ● **would not touch** someone or something **with a barge pole**: see **barge pole**. ● **the finishing touch**: see **finish**. ● **touch wood**: see **wood**.

VB: no
passive,
with brd-neg
PRAGMATICS
V n

VB: usu
passive,
with brd-neg
be V-ed

VB: no passive
V n
BRITISH
VERB
V on/upon n

VB: usu
passive
be V-ed with n
WRITTEN

VERB: V n
it V n to-inf

ADJ-GRADED:
v-link ADJ

ADJ-GRADED

ADV-GRADED

VERB
V n

VB with brd-
neg: no cont,
no passive
V n for n
N-SING
PRAGMATICS

N-COUNT:
supp N

QUANT

PHRASE

PHRASE

PHRASE

PHRASE

PHRASE

PHRASE

PHRASE

VERB
V n for n
INFORMAL
PHRASE
INFORMAL

---

touch down. When an aircraft or spacecraft **touches down**, it lands. The first large contingent of troops touches down on American soil today.

PHRASAL VB
V P

touch off. To **touch off** a situation or series of events means to cause it to start happening. Is the massacre likely to touch off a new round of violence?

PHRASAL VB
V P noun
Also V n P

touch·down /ˈtʌtʃdaʊn/ **touchdowns. 1** Touch-down is the landing of an aircraft or spacecraft. ...a perfect touchdown... The astronauts are preparing for touchdown. **2** In American football, a **touch-down** is when a team scores points by carrying the ball over a line on their opponent's end of the pitch.

◆◇◇◇◇
N-VAR

N-COUNT

touch·ing. See touch.

touch·ing·ly. See touch.

touch·line /ˈtʌtʃlaɪn/. In sports such as football and rugby, the **touchline** is one of the two lines marking the sides of the playing area.

◆◇◇◇◇
N-SING

touch·stone /ˈtʌtʃstəʊn/ **touchstones.** If you use one thing as a **touchstone** of another, you use it as a test, standard, or criterion by which you judge and assess the second thing. Job security has become the touchstone of a good job for many employees.

N-COUNT

touchy /ˈtʌtʃi/. **1** If someone is **touchy**, they are easily upset, offended, or irritated. She is very touchy about her past. **2** If you say that something is a **touchy** subject, you mean that it needs to be dealt with carefully and tactfully, because it might upset or offend people. ...the touchy question of political reform.

ADJ-GRADED

ADJ-GRADED

tough /tʌf/ **tougher, toughest; toughs, tough-ing, toughed. 1** A **tough** person has a strong determined character and can tolerate difficulty or hardship. She is tough and ambitious. ♦ **tough-·ness** Mrs Potter has won a reputation for tough-ness and determination. **2** If you describe someone as **tough**, you mean that they are rough and violent. He had shot three people dead earning himself a reputation as a tough guy. ► A **tough** is a tough person. Three burly toughs elbowed their way to the front. **3** A **tough** place or area is considered to have a lot of crime and violence. **4** **Tough** policies or actions are strict and firm. He announced tough measures to limit the money supply. **5** ● a **tough nut**: see **nut**.

◆◆◆◇
ADJ-GRADED

N-UNCOUNT

ADJ-GRADED

N-COUNT

ADJ-GRADED

ADJ-GRADED

6 A **tough** way of life or period of time is difficult or full of hardship. She had a pretty tough childhood. **7** A **tough** task or problem is difficult to do or solve. It may be tough to raise cash. **8** A **tough** substance is strong and difficult to break, cut, or tear. ...dark brown beans with a rather tough outer skin. **9** **Tough** meat is difficult to cut and chew.

ADJ-GRADED

ADJ-GRADED

ADJ-GRADED

ADJ-GRADED

tough out. If you **tough out** a difficult situation, you do not give in or show any weakness in that situation. I think it was very brave of him to tough it out.

PHRASAL VB
V P noun
V n P

tough·en /ˈtʌfən/ **toughens, toughening, toughened. 1** If you **toughen** something or if it **toughens**, you make it stronger so that it will not break easily. ...toughened glass. **2** If a person, institution, or law **toughens** its policies, regulations, or penalties, it makes them firmer or stricter. Talks are under way to toughen trade restrictions. ► **Toughen up** means the same as **toughen**. The new law toughens up penalties for those that misuse guns. **3** If an experience **toughens** you, it makes you stronger and more independent in character. They believe that participating in fights toughens boys. ► **Toughen up** means the same as **toughen**. He thinks boxing is good for kids, that it toughens them up.

◆◇◇◇◇
V-ERG: V n

V-ed

VERB
V n

PHRASAL VB
V P noun

VERB
V n

PHRASAL VB:
V P
V n P
Also V P noun

tou·pee /ˈtuːpeɪ, AM tuːˈpeɪ/ **toupees.** A toupee is a small wig worn by a man to cover a bald patch on his head.

N-COUNT

tour /tʊə/ **tours, touring, toured. 1** A tour is an organized trip that people such as musicians, politicians, or theatre companies go on to several different places, stopping to meet people or perform. ● When people are travelling on a tour, you can say that they are **on tour**. **2** When people such as musicians, politicians, or theatre companies **tour**, they go on a tour, for example in order to perform or to

◆◆◆◇
N-COUNT

PHRASE
VERB: V n
V

meet people. *He toured for nearly two years and played 500 sell-out shows.* **3** A **tour** is a journey during which you visit several places that interest you. *...my tour of the major cities of Europe.* **4** A **tour** is a short trip that you make round a place, for example round a historical building, so that you can look at it. *...a guided tour of a ruined Scottish castle.* **5** If you **tour** a place, you go on a journey or trip round it. *We toured the streets of Milan.*   N-COUNT   N-COUNT   VERB V n

tour de force /ˌtʊə də ˈfɔːs/ **tours de force.** If you call something such as a performance or a creation a **tour de force**, you are emphasizing that it is extremely good or extremely well done or made.   N-COUNT

tour·ism /ˈtʊərɪzəm/. **Tourism** is the business of providing services for people on holiday, for example hotels, restaurants, and sightseeing trips.   ◆◆◇◇ N-UNCOUNT

tour·ist /ˈtʊərɪst/ **tourists.** A **tourist** is a person who is visiting a place for pleasure and interest, especially when they are on holiday. *Blackpool is the top tourist attraction in England.*   ◆◆◇◇ N-COUNT

tour·isty /ˈtʊərɪsti/. If you describe a place as **touristy**, you do not like it because it is full of tourists or full of things for tourists to buy and do.   ADJ-GRADED PRAGMATICS

tour·na·ment /ˈtʊənəmənt/ **tournaments.** A **tournament** is a sports competition in which players who win a match continue to play further matches in the competition until just one person or team is left.   ◆◆◇◇ N-COUNT

tour·ni·quet /ˈtʊənɪkeɪ/ **tourniquets.** A **tourniquet** is a strip of cloth that is tied tightly round an injured arm or leg in order to stop it bleeding.   N-COUNT

'tour operator, tour operators. A **tour operator** is a company that provides holidays in which your travel and accommodation are booked for you.   ◆◇◇◇ N-COUNT

tou·sled /ˈtaʊzəld/. If you have **tousled** hair, your hair is untidy.   ADJ-GRADED

tout /taʊt/ **touts, touting, touted. 1** If someone **touts** something, they try to sell it or convince people that it is good; used showing disapproval. *The product is touted as being completely natural.* **2** If someone **touts for** business or custom, they try to obtain it. **3** If someone **touts** tickets, they sell them outside a sports ground or theatre, usually for more than their original value. The American word is **scalp. 4** A **tout** is someone who sells things such as tickets unofficially, usually at prices which are higher than the official ones. The American word is **scalper.**   ◆◇◇◇ VERB: be V-ed as n/ adj/-ing VERB: V form BRITISH VERB: V n BRITISH N-COUNT BRITISH

tow /təʊ/ **tows, towing, towed. 1** If one vehicle **tows** another, it pulls it along behind it. *There may be supplementary charges if you are towing a caravan... They threatened to tow away my car.* **2** If you have someone **in tow**, they are following you closely because you are looking after them or you are leading them somewhere. *There she was on my doorstep with child in tow.*   ◆◇◇◇ VERB V n V n with adv PHRASE INFORMAL

to·wards /təˈwɔːdz, AM tɔːrdz/. The form **toward** is also used, and is the more usual form in American English. In addition to the uses shown below, **towards** is used in phrasal verbs such as 'count towards'.   ◆◆◆◆◆

1 If you move, look, or point **towards** something or someone, you move, look, or point in their direction. *Caroline leant across the table towards him... When he looked towards me, I smiled and waited... Patterson pointed toward a plain cardboard box.* **2** If things develop **towards** a particular situation, that situation becomes nearer in time or more likely to happen. *The talks made little evident progress towards agreement... She also began moving toward a different life-style.* **3** If you have a particular attitude **towards** something or someone, you have that attitude when you think about them or deal with them. *Not everyone in the world will be kind and caring towards you.* **4** If something happens **towards** a particular time, it happens just before that time. *The Channel tunnel was due to open towards the end of 1993.* **5** If something is **towards** part of a place or thing, it is near that part. *The home of the Morgan family was up Gloucester Road, towards the top of the hill.* **6** If you give money to-   PREP   PREP   PREP   PREP   PREP

wards something, you give it to help pay for that thing. *He gave them £20,000 towards a house.*

tow·el /ˈtaʊəl/ **towels, towelling, towelled;** spelled **towelling, toweled** in American English. **1** A **towel** is a piece of thick soft cloth that you use to dry yourself. **2** If you **towel** something or **towel** it dry, you dry it with a towel. *James came out of his bedroom, toweling his wet hair... He stepped out of the shower and began towelling himself down.* **3** If you **throw in the towel**, you stop trying to do something because you realize that you cannot succeed. **4** See also **sanitary towel, tea towel.**   ◆◆◇◇ N-COUNT VERB: V n adj V n V n down/off PHRASE INFORMAL

tow·el·ling /ˈtaʊəlɪŋ/; spelled **toweling** in American English. **Towelling** is a kind of fairly thick soft cloth that is used especially for making towels.   N-UNCOUNT

tow·er /ˈtaʊə/ **towers, towering, towered. 1** A **tower** is a tall narrow building, that either stands alone or forms part of another building such as a church or castle. *...an eleventh century castle with 120-foot high towers.* **2** Someone or something that **towers** over surrounding people or things is a lot taller than they are. *At school, a girl may tower over most boys her age.* **3** A **tower** is a tall structure that is used for sending radio or television signals. *Troops are still in control of the television and radio tower.* **4** A **tower** is the same as a **tower block.** *...a new office tower in Frankfurt.* **5** See also **clock tower, control tower, ivory tower. 6** If you refer to someone as a **tower of strength**, you appreciate them because they give you a lot of help, support, and encouragement when you have problems or are in a difficult situation.   ◆◆◇◇ N-COUNT VERB V over/above n N-COUNT N-COUNT PHRASE

'tower block, tower blocks. A **tower block** is a tall building divided into flats or offices. *...a 23-storey tower block.*   ◆◇◇◇ N-COUNT BRITISH

tow·er·ing /ˈtaʊərɪŋ/. **1** If you describe something such as a mountain or cliff as **towering**, you mean that it is very tall and therefore impressive. **2** If you describe someone or something as **towering**, you are emphasizing that they are impressive because of their importance, skill, or intensity. *He remains a towering figure in modern British politics.*   ◆◇◇◇ ADJ: ADJ n LITERARY ADJ: ADJ n LITERARY

town /taʊn/ **towns. 1** A **town** is a place with many streets and buildings where people live and work. Towns are larger than villages and smaller than cities. *...the small town of St Augustine, in north-east Florida.* ► You can use **the town** to refer to the people of a town. *The town takes immense pride in recent achievements.* **2** You use **town** in order to refer to the town where you live. *She left town.* **3** You use **town** in order to refer to the central area of a town where most of the shops and offices are. *I caught a bus into town.* **4** If you refer to **the town,** you are referring to town and city areas in general, as opposed to country areas. *More people are going to escape from the town into the country.* **5** See also **ghost town, hometown, new town.**

6 If you say that someone **goes to town** on something or someone, you mean that they deal with them with a lot of enthusiasm or intensity. *We really went to town on it, turning it into a full, three-day show.* **7** If you describe a man as a **man about town,** you mean that he is sophisticated, likes to go out and spend money, and has a busy social life. **8** If you go out **on the town** or go for a night **on the town,** you enjoy yourself by going to a town centre in the evening and spending a long time there visiting several places of entertainment.   ◆◆◆◆ N-COUNT N-COUNT N-UNCOUNT N-UNCOUNT N-SING BRITISH PHRASE PHRASE PHRASE

town 'council, town councils. A **town council** is a group of people who have been elected to govern a town.   N-COLL-COUNT

town 'crier, town criers. In former times, a **town crier** was a man whose job was to walk through the streets of a town shouting out news and official announcements.   N-COUNT

town 'hall, town halls; also spelled **Town Hall.** A **town hall** in a town is a large building owned and used by the town council, often as its headquarters. You can also use **town hall** to refer to the town council that uses this building.   ◆◇◇◇ N-COUNT

'town house, town houses. 1 A **town house** is a N-COUNT
tall narrow house in a town, usually in a row of
similar houses. **2** The **town house** of a wealthy per- N-COUNT:
son is their house in a town or city, rather than an- with poss
other house that they own in the country.

townie /'taʊni/ **townies.** If someone who lives in N-COUNT
the countryside refers to someone from a town or PRAGMATICS
city as a **townie,** they disapprove of that person because they think they have no knowledge of the
countryside or country life.

,town 'planning. Town planning is the planning N-UNCOUNT
and design of all the new buildings, roads, and
parks in a place in order to make them attractive
and convenient for the people who live there.

towns·folk /'taʊnzfəʊk/. The **townsfolk** of a town N-PLURAL
or city are the people who live there. ...some of the DATED
prominent townsfolk of the 1860s.

town·ship /'taʊnʃɪp/ **townships. 1** In South Afri- ◆◆◇◇◇
ca, a **township** was a town where only black people N-COUNT
lived. ...the South African township of Soweto. **2** In N-COUNT
the United States and Canada, a **township** is an
area of land, especially a part of a county which is
organized as a unit of local government.

towns·people /'taʊnzpiːpəl/. The **townspeople** of N-PLURAL
a town or city are the people who live there.

tow·path /'təʊpɑːθ, -pæθ/ **towpaths.** A **towpath** is N-COUNT
a path along the side of a canal or river, which
horses used to walk on when they towed boats.

'tow truck, tow trucks. A **tow truck** is a motor N-COUNT
vehicle which is used to tow away broken or damaged vehicles.

tox·ic /'tɒksɪk/. A **toxic** substance is poisonous. ◆◆◇◇◇
...toxic waste. ♦ **tox·ic·ity** /tɒk'sɪsɪti/ **toxicities** ADJ-GRADED
...data on the toxicity of chemicals. N-VAR

toxi·col·ogy /,tɒksɪ'kɒlədʒi/. **Toxicology** is the N-UNCOUNT
study of poisonous substances. ♦ **toxi·co·logi·cal** TECHNICAL
/,tɒksɪkə'lɒdʒɪkəl/. There were no adverse toxicologi- ADJ: ADJ n
cal effects. ♦ **toxi·colo·gist, toxicologists** Toxi- N-COUNT
cologists attempt to identify and understand toxic
hazards.

tox·in /'tɒksɪn/ **toxins.** A **toxin** is any poisonous ◆◇◇◇◇
substance produced by bacteria, animals, or plants. N-VAR
...a build-up of toxins in the body.

toy /tɔɪ/ **toys, toying, toyed. 1** A **toy** is an object ◆◆◆◇◇
that children play with, for example a doll or a N-COUNT
model car. ...a toy telephone. ● See also **soft toy.**
2 You can refer to objects that adults use for fun ra- N-COUNT
ther than for a serious purpose as **toys.** Computers
have become household toys.

toy with. 1 If you **toy with** an idea, you consider it PHRASAL VB
casually without making any decisions about it. He V P n
toyed with the idea of going to China. **2** If you **toy with** V P n
an object or with your food, you keep moving it
around but do not use it properly or eat it, especially
because you are thinking about something else. He
picked up a pencil and toyed with it idly.

toy·boy /'tɔɪbɔɪ/ **toyboys.** People sometimes refer N-COUNT
humorously to a woman's lover as her **toyboy** when INFORMAL,
he is much younger than she is. BRITISH

toy·town /'tɔɪtaʊn/. You use **toytown** to show that ADJ: ADJ n
you think something is silly, childish, or worthless. PRAGMATICS
Inflation has turned the rouble into a toytown BRITISH
currency.

trace /treɪs/ **traces, tracing, traced. 1** If you ◆◆◆◇◇
trace the origin or development of something, you VERB: V n
find out or describe how it started or developed. V n to n
The psychiatrist successfully traced some of her problems to severe childhood traumas. ▶ **Trace back** PHRASAL VB
means the same as **trace.** Britain's Parliament can V n P to n
trace its history back to the English Parliament of the Also V P noun
13th century.
2 If you **trace** someone or something, you find them VERB: V n
after looking for them. They traced the van to a New V n to n
Jersey car rental agency.
3 If you **trace** something such as a pattern or a shape, VERB
for example with your finger or toe, you mark its out- V n
line on a surface. I traced the course of the river on the
map. **4** If you **trace** a picture you copy it by covering it VERB: V n
with a piece of transparent paper and drawing over
the lines underneath.

5 A **trace** of something is a very small amount of it. N-COUNT
Wash them in cold water to remove all traces of sand.
6 A **trace** is a sign which shows you that someone or N-COUNT
something has been in a place. The local church has
traces of fifteenth-century frescoes... Hoffa disappeared
without trace. **7** If you say that someone or something PHRASE
sinks without trace or **sinks without a trace,** you
mean that they stop existing or stop being successful
very suddenly and completely. The Social Democratic
Party has sunk without trace at these elections.

trace back. See trace 1. PHRASAL VB

trace·able /'treɪsəbəl/. If one thing is **traceable** to ADJ
another, there is evidence to suggest that the first
thing was caused by or is connected to the second
thing. The probable cause of his death is traceable to
an incident in November 1724.

tra·chea /trə'kiːə, AM 'treɪkiə/ **tracheas** or **tra-** N-COUNT
cheae /trə'kiːiː, AM 'treɪkiiː/. Your **trachea** is your MEDICAL
windpipe.

track /træk/ **tracks, tracking, tracked. 1** A ◆◆◆◆◇
track is a narrow road or path. ...a rough mountain N-COUNT
track. **2** A **track** is a piece of ground, often oval- N-COUNT
shaped, that is used for races involving athletes, cyclists, cars, horses, or greyhounds. ...the athletics
track. **3** Railway **tracks** are the rails that a train N-COUNT
travels along. A woman fell on to the tracks.
4 A **track** is one of the songs or pieces of music on a N-COUNT
CD, record, or tape.
5 Tracks are footprints or other marks left in the N-PLURAL
ground by animals or people. **6** If you **track** animals VERB: V n
or people, you try to find them by following their footprints or other signs that they have left behind.
♦ **track·er, trackers** ...the Native American tracker N-COUNT
who uses ancient methods to find drug smugglers.
7 To **track** someone or something means to follow VERB
their movements by means of a special device, such V n
as a satellite or radar. Our radar began tracking the
jets. **8** If you **track** someone or something, you inves- VERB
tigate them, because you are interested in finding out V n
more about them. If it's possible, track the rumour
back to its origin.
9 See also **backtrack, fast track, racetrack, sidetrack,
soundtrack, title track.**
10 If someone **covers** their **tracks,** they hide or de- PHRASE
stroy evidence of their identity or their actions, because they want to keep them secret. The killer may
have returned to the scene of the crime to cover his
tracks. **11** If you **keep track of** a situation or a person, PHRASE
you have accurate and up-to-date information about
them all the time. If you **lose track of** a situation or
person, you no longer know where they are or what is
happening. With eleven thousand employees, it's very
difficult to keep track of them all... You become so
deeply absorbed in an activity that you lose track of
time. **12** If you **make tracks,** you leave the place PHRASE
where you are, especially when you are in a hurry. INFORMAL
We'd better make tracks soon, hadn't we? **13** If some- PHRASE
one or something is **on track,** they are acting or progressing in a way that is likely to result in success. It
may take some time to get the British economy back on
track. **14** If you are **on the right track,** you are acting PHRASE
or progressing in a way that is likely to result in success. If you are **on the wrong track,** you are acting or
progressing in a way that is likely to result in failure.
15 If someone or something **stops** you **in** your **tracks,** PHRASE
or if you **stop dead in** your **tracks,** you suddenly stop
moving or doing something because you are very surprised, impressed, or frightened. This magnificent
church cannot fail to stop you in your tracks. **16** If PHRASE
someone or something **stops** a process or activity **in
its tracks,** or if it **stops dead in its tracks,** they prevent
the process or activity from continuing or developing.
17 ● off the beaten track: see beaten.

track down. If you **track down** someone or some- PHRASAL VB
thing, you find them, or find information about them, V P noun
after a difficult or long search. I don't know where that V n P
old story came from, I've never been able to track it
down.

,track and 'field. Track and field refers to athlet- N-UNCOUNT
ics as opposed to other sports. AMERICAN

track 'record, track records. If you talk about the **track record** of a person, company, or product, you are referring to their past performance, achievements, or failures in it. *The job needs someone with a good track record in investment.* ◆◇◇◇◇ N-COUNT

track·suit /'træksuːt/ **tracksuits;** also spelled **track suit.** A **tracksuit** is a loose warm suit consisting of trousers and a top which people wear to relax and do exercise. The usual American word is **sweatsuit.** ◆◇◇◇◇ N-COUNT BRITISH

tract /trækt/ **tracts. 1** A **tract** of land or **tracts** of land is a very large area of land. **2** A **tract** is a short article expressing a strong opinion on a religious, moral, or political subject in order to try to influence people's attitudes. **3** A **tract** is a system of organs and tubes in an animal's or person's body that has a particular function, especially the function of processing a substance in the body. *...the digestive tract.* ◆◇◇◇◇ N-COUNT N-COUNT / N-COUNT MEDICAL

trac·ta·ble /'træktəbəl/. If you say that a person, problem, or device is **tractable,** you mean that they can be easily controlled or dealt with. *He could easily manage his tractable and worshipping younger brother.* ADJ-GRADED FORMAL

trac·tion /'trækʃən/. **1 Traction** is a form of medical treatment, in which weights and pulleys are used to gently pull or stretch an injured part of the body for a period of time. You say that a person who is having this treatment is **in traction. 2 Traction** is a particular form of power that makes a vehicle move. **3 Traction** is the grip that something has on the ground, especially the wheels of a vehicle. ◆◇◇◇◇ N-UNCOUNT / N-UNCOUNT / N-UNCOUNT

trac·tor /'træktə/ **tractors.** A **tractor** is a farm vehicle that is used to pull farm machinery and to provide the energy needed for the machinery to work. ◆◇◇◇◇ N-COUNT

trad /træd/. **Trad** is a kind of jazz based on the jazz that was played in the 1920s. N-UNCOUNT BRITISH

trade /treɪd/ **trades, trading, traded. 1 Trade** is the activity of buying, selling, or exchanging goods or services between people, firms, or countries. *The ministry had direct control over every aspect of foreign trade... Texas has a long history of trade with Mexico.* **2** When people, firms, or countries **trade,** they buy, sell, or exchange goods or services between themselves. *They had years of experience of trading with the West.* ♦ **trad·ing** *...trading on the stock exchange.* **3** A **trade** is a particular area of business or industry. *...the tourist trade.* **4** Someone's **trade** is the kind of work that they do, especially when they have been trained to do it over a period of time. *He learnt his trade as a diver in the North Sea.* **5** If someone **trades** one thing for another or if two people **trade** things, they agree to exchange one thing for the other thing. *Kids used to trade baseball cards... They suspected that Neville had traded secret information with Mr Foster.* ▶ Also a noun. *I am willing to make a trade with you.* **6** If you **trade** places with someone or the two of you **trade** places, you move into the other person's position or situation, and they move into yours. *Mike asked George to trade places with him so he could ride with Tod... The receiver and the quarterback are going to trade positions.* **7** If two people or groups **trade** something such as blows, insults, or jokes, they hit each other, insult each other, or tell each other jokes. *Children usually settle disputes by trading punches... They traded artillery fire with government forces inside the city.* ◆◆◆◆◆ N-UNCOUNT / VERB: V / V with n / Also V in n / N-UNCOUNT / N-COUNT / N-COUNT / V-RECIP: V n for n (non-recip) pl-n V n / V n with n / V-RECIP V n with n pl-n V n / V-RECIP pl-n V n / V n with n

trade in. If you **trade in** an old car or appliance, you give it to a dealer when you buy a new one so that you get a reduction on the price. *He had a Rolls-Royce, and he traded it in for two matching silver Range Rovers.* ● See also **trade-in.** PHRASAL VB V P noun V n P

trade off. 1 If you **trade off** one thing against another, you exchange all or part of one thing for another, as part of a negotiation or compromise. *There is a possibility of being able to trade off information for a reduced sentence.* ● See also **trade-off. 2** If someone **trades off** or **trades on** something, they make use of it PHRASAL VB V P n for n V P n for n / V P n

for their own advantage, often in an unfair way. *They would be able to trade off their looks and manage on that alone.*

'trade fair, trade fairs. A **trade fair** is an exhibition where manufacturers show their products to other people in industry and try to get business. N-COUNT

'trade gap, trade gaps. If a country imports goods worth more than the value of the goods that it exports, this is referred to as a **trade gap.** N-COUNT

'trade-in, trade-ins. A **trade-in** is an arrangement in which someone buys something such as a new car or washing machine at a reduced price by giving their old one, as well as money, in payment. *...the trade-in value of the car.* ◆◆◇◇◇ N-COUNT

trade·mark /'treɪdmɑːk/ **trademarks;** also spelled **trade mark. 1** A **trademark** is a name or symbol that a company uses on its products and that cannot legally be used by another company. **2** If you say that something is the **trademark** of a particular person or place, you mean that it is characteristic of them or typically associated with them. *...the spiky punk hairdo that became his trademark.* ◆◇◇◇◇ N-COUNT / N-COUNT: with poss

'trade name, trade names. A **trade name** is the name which manufacturers give to a product or to a range of products. *It's marketed under the trade name 'Tattle'.* N-COUNT

'trade-off, trade-offs; also spelled **tradeoff.** A **trade-off** is a situation where you make a compromise between two things, or where you exchange all or part of one thing for another. *...the trade-off between inflation and unemployment.* ◆◇◇◇◇ N-COUNT

trad·er /'treɪdə/ **traders.** A **trader** is a person whose job is to trade in goods or stocks. ◆◆◆◇◇ N-COUNT

'trade route, trade routes. A **trade route** is a route, often covering long distances, that used by traders. N-COUNT

trade 'secret, trade secrets. 1 A **trade secret** is information that is known, used, and kept secret by a particular firm, for example about a method of production or a chemical formula. **2** A **trade secret** is a piece of knowledge that you have, especially about how to do something, that you are not willing to tell other people. *I'd rather not talk about it too much because I don't like giving trade secrets away.* N-COUNT / N-COUNT

trades·man /'treɪdzmən/ **tradesmen.** A **tradesman** is someone, usually a man, who sells goods or services, especially one who owns and runs a shop. N-COUNT

trade 'union, trade unions; also spelled **trades union.** A **trade union** is an organization that has been formed by workers in order to represent their rights and interests to their employers, for example in order to improve working conditions or wages. The American term is **labor union.** ◆◆◇◇◇ N-COUNT BRITISH

trade 'unionist, trade unionists; also spelled **trades unionist.** A **trade unionist** is an active member of a trade union. ◆◇◇◇◇ N-COUNT

'trading estate, trading estates. A **trading estate** is the same as an **industrial estate.** N-COUNT BRITISH

tra·di·tion /trə'dɪʃən/ **traditions. 1** A **tradition** is a custom or belief that has existed for a long time. *...the rich traditions of Afro-Cuban music, and dance.* **2** If you say that something or someone is **in the tradition of** a person or thing from the past, you mean that they have many features that remind you of that person or thing. *...marvellous pictures in the tradition of Gainsborough.* ◆◇◇◇◇ N-VAR / PHR-PREP

tra·di·tion·al /trə'dɪʃənəl/. **1 Traditional** customs, beliefs, or methods are ones that have existed for a long time without changing. *Traditional teaching methods sometimes only succeeded in putting students off learning.* ♦ **tra·di·tion·al·ly** *Married women have traditionally been treated as dependent on their husbands.* **2** A **traditional** organization or person prefers older methods and ideas to modern ones. *...traditional parents, who believed in laying down the law for their children.* ♦ **traditionally** *He is loathed by some of the more traditionally minded officers.* ◆◆◆◆◇ ADJ-GRADED / ADV-GRADED: ADV with cl/ group / ADJ-GRADED / ADV-GRADED

tra·di·tion·al·ism /trə'dɪʃənəlɪzəm/. **Traditional-** N-UNCOUNT
ism is behaviour and ideas that support established
customs and beliefs, rather than modern ones.

tra·di·tion·al·ist /trə'dɪʃənəlɪst/ **traditionalists.** ◆◇◇◇◇
A **traditionalist** is a person who supports the estab- N-COUNT
lished customs and beliefs of his or her society or
group, and does not want to change them. ♦ **tra·di·** N-UNCOUNT
·tion·al·ism.

traf·fic /'træfɪk/ **traffics, trafficking, traf-** ◆◆◆◇◇
ficked. **1 Traffic** refers to all the vehicles that are N-UNCOUNT:
moving along the roads in a particular area. *Traffic* also the N
was unusually light for that time of day. **2 Traffic** N-UNCOUNT:
refers to the movement of ships, trains, or aircraft with supp
between one place and another. **Traffic** also refers
to the people and goods that are being transported.
Air traffic had returned to normal. **3 Traffic** in N-UNCOUNT:
something such as drugs or stolen goods is an il- with supp
legal trade in them. *Traffic in illicit drugs was now*
worth some $500 thousand million a year. **4** Some- VERB:
one who **traffics** in something such as drugs or stol- V in n
en goods buys and sells them even though it is illegal to do so. ♦ **traf·fick·ing** *He was sentenced to* N-UNCOUNT
ten years in prison on charges of drug trafficking.
5 See also **air traffic control, traffic jam.**

'**traffic calming;** also spelled **traffic-calming.** N-UNCOUNT
Traffic calming consists of measures designed to
make roads safer, for example making them narrower, so that drivers are forced to slow down.

'**traffic cone, traffic cones. Traffic cones** are N-COUNT
plastic cones that are placed on a road to prevent
people from driving or parking there.

'**traffic jam, traffic jams.** A **traffic jam** is a long ◆◇◇◇◇
line of vehicles that cannot move forward because N-COUNT
there is too much traffic, or because the road is
blocked by something.

traf·fick·er /'træfɪkə/ **traffickers.** A **trafficker** in ◆◇◇◇◇
particular goods, especially drugs, is a person who N-COUNT
illegally buys or sells these goods.

'**traffic light, traffic lights. Traffic lights** are sets ◆◇◇◇◇
of red, green, and amber lights at a road junction N-COUNT
that control the flow of traffic by signalling when
vehicles have to stop and when they can go.

'**traffic warden, traffic wardens.** A **traffic war-** N-COUNT
den is a person whose job is to make sure that cars BRITISH
are not parked illegally.

trag·edy /'trædʒɪdi/ **tragedies.** **1** A **tragedy** is an ◆◆◇◇◇
extremely sad event or situation. *They have suffered* N-VAR
an enormous personal tragedy... Maskell's life had
not been without tragedy. **2 Tragedy** is a type of lit- N-VAR
erature, especially drama, that is serious and sad,
often ending in the death of the main character.

trag·ic /'trædʒɪk/. **1** A **tragic** event or situation is ◆◆◇◇◇
extremely sad, usually because it involves death or ADJ-GRADED
suffering. *It was just a tragic accident. ...the tragic*
loss of so many lives. ♦ **tragi·cal·ly** /'trædʒɪkli/. ADV-GRADED
Tragically, she never saw the completed building.
2 Tragic is used to refer to literary tragedy. ADJ: ADJ n

tragi-comedy /,trædʒi 'kɒmədi/ **tragi-comedies.** N-COUNT
A **tragi-comedy** is a play or other written work that
is both sad and amusing.

tragi-comic /,trædʒi 'kɒmɪk/. Something that is ADJ
tragi-comic is both sad and amusing at the same
time.

trail /treɪl/ **trails, trailing, trailed.** **1** A **trail** is a ◆◆◇◇◇
rough path across open country or through forests. N-COUNT
2 A **trail** is a route along a series of paths or roads, of- N-COUNT
ten one that has been planned and marked out for a
particular purpose. *The Council has laid out a visitors'*
trail. **3** A **trail** is a series of marks or other signs of N-COUNT
movement or other activities left by someone or
something. *He left a trail of clues at the scenes of his*
crimes. **4** If you are **on the trail of** a person or thing, PHRASE
you are trying hard to find them or find out about
them, often by following clues. **5** If you **trail** someone VERB: V n
or something, you follow them secretly, often by find- V n prep/adv
ing the marks or signs that they have left. *I trailed her*
to a shop in Kensington.
6 You can refer to all the places that a politician visits N-COUNT:
in the period before an election as their campaign n N
trail.

7 If you **trail** something, it hangs down loosely behind V-ERG: V n
you as you move along. *He let his fingers trail in the* V prep
water. **8** If someone **trails** somewhere, they move VERB
there slowly, without any energy or enthusiasm, often V adv/prep
following someone else. *He trailed through the wet*
Manhattan streets. **9** If a person or team **is trailing** VERB: V
during a contest, they have a lower score than their V amount
opponents. *He scored again, leaving Dartford trailing* Also V behind
2-0 at the break. n
10 See also **nature trail, paper trail.** ● **to blaze a trail:**
see **blaze.**

trail off or **trail away.** If a speaker's voice or a PHRASAL VB
speaker **trails off** or **trails away,** their voice becomes V P
quieter and they hesitate until they stop speaking
completely.

trail·blazer /'treɪlbleɪzə/ **trailblazers.** A **trail-** N-COUNT
blazer is a person who is the leader in a particular
field, or who does a particular thing before anybody
else does.

'**trail-blazing.** A **trail-blazing** idea, event, or or- ADJ: ADJ n
ganization is new, exciting, and daring.

trail·er /'treɪlə/ **trailers.** **1** A **trailer** is a container ◆◆◇◇◇
or frame on wheels used for transporting large or N-COUNT
heavy items. It is pulled by a car or van. **2** A **trailer** N-COUNT
is the long rear section of an articulated lorry, in
which the goods are carried. **3** A **trailer** is a long ve- N-COUNT
hicle which people use as a home or office and AMERICAN
which can be pulled behind a car. The British word
is **caravan.** **4** A **trailer** for a film or television pro- N-COUNT
gramme is a set of short extracts which are shown
to advertise it.

train 1 noun uses

train /treɪn/ **trains.** **1** A **train** is a number of car- ◆◆◆◆◇
riages or trucks which are all connected together N-COUNT:
and which are pulled by an engine along a railway. also by N
He arrived in Shenyang by train yesterday.
2 A **train** of vehicles, people, or animals is a long line N-COUNT:
of them travelling slowly in the same direction. with supp
3 A **train** of thought or a **train** of events is a connected N-COUNT
sequence, in which each thought or event seems to
arise naturally or logically as a result of the previous
one. *He lost his train of thought for a moment.* **4** The N-COUNT
train of a woman's formal gown or wedding dress is
the long part at the back of it which flows along the
floor behind her when she is wearing it.
5 If a process or event is **in train** or has been set **in** PHRASE
train, it is happening or starting to happen. *He* BRITISH
praised the economic reforms set in train by the gov-
ernment. **6** If something brings problems or difficul- PHRASE
ties **in** its **train,** the problems or difficulties occur as a
natural or logical result of it.

train 2 verb uses

train /treɪn/ **trains, training, trained.** **1** If some- ◆◆◆◆◇
one **trains** you to do something, they teach you the V-ERG:
skills that you need in order to do it. *Stavros was* V n to-inf
training to be a priest... Psychiatrists initially train V to-inf
as doctors... These courses train you in the basics of V n as/in n
stage craft. ♦ **-trained** *...an American-trained law-* COMB
yer. ♦ **train·er, trainers** *...a book for both teachers* N-COUNT
and teacher trainers. ♦ **train·ing** *Kennedy had no* N-UNCOUNT
formal training as a decorator. **2** To **train** a natural V-ERG: V n
quality or talent that someone has, for example V-ed
their intellect or voice, means to help them to develop it. *Some children come to school with more*
finely trained perceptual skills than others. **3** If you V-ERG:
train for a physical activity such as a race, you pre- V for n
pare for it by doing particular physical exercises. *He* V for n
has spent a year training crews for next month's Also V,
round the world race. ♦ **train·er** *She went to the* N-COUNT
gym with her trainer. ♦ **train·ing** *He will soon be* N-UNCOUNT
back in training for next year's National. **4** If an ani- VERB:
mal or bird **is trained** to do particular things, it is V n to-inf
taught to do them. *...a man who trained hundreds* V n
of dogs... She had brought her trained sheepdog to V-ed
help in the rescue. ♦ **train·er** *The horse made a win-* N-COUNT
ning start for his new trainer. **5** If you **train** a tree, N-COUNT
bush, or plant in a particular direction, you tie it V n prep
and cut it so that it grows in that direction. *You* V n to-inf
could even put a trellis on your walls and train
plants to grow up it.

6 If you **train** something such as a gun, a camera, or a light **on** someone or something, you aim it at them and keep it pointing steadily towards them. *She trained her binoculars on the horizon.* `VERB V n on n`

train up. If someone **trains** you **up**, they teach you new skills or give you the necessary preparation so that you will reach the standard required for a particular job or activity. *The first companies to go in are taking a policy of employing East Germans and training them up.* `PHRASAL VB V n P Also V P noun BRITISH, INFORMAL`

trainee /treɪˈniː/ **trainees.** A **trainee** is someone who is employed at a junior level in a particular job in order to learn the skills needed for that job. `N-COUNT`

train·er /ˈtreɪnə/ **trainers.** **Trainers** are special shoes that people wear for running or jogging. The American word is **sneakers**. See picture headed **clothes**. • See also **train**. `N-COUNT BRITISH`

'training camp, training camps. A **training camp** for soldiers or sports players is an organized period of training at a particular place. `N-COUNT`

'training shoe, training shoes. Training shoes are the same as **trainers**. `N-COUNT`

traipse /treɪps/ **traipses, traipsing, traipsed.** **1** If you **traipse** somewhere, you go there reluctantly, because you are tired or dissatisfied and do not wish to go there. *If traipsing around shops does not appeal to you, perhaps using a catalogue will.* **2** If you talk about people **traipsing** somewhere, you mean that they are going there or moving about there in a way that annoys someone or gets in their way. *You will have to get used to a lot of people traipsing in and out of your home.* `VERB V prep/adv` `VERB PRAGMATICS V prep/adv`

trait /treɪt, treɪ/ **traits.** A **trait** is a particular characteristic, quality, or tendency that someone or something has. *Creativity is a human trait.* `N-COUNT: with supp`

trai·tor /ˈtreɪtə/ **traitors.** **1** If you call someone a **traitor**, you mean that they have betrayed beliefs that they used to hold, or that their friends hold, by their words or actions. *Some say he's a traitor to the working class.* **2** If someone is a **traitor**, they betray their country or a group of which they are a member by helping their enemies, especially during wartime. `N-COUNT` `N-COUNT`

tra·jec·tory /trəˈdʒektəri/ **trajectories.** **1** The **trajectory** of a moving object is the path that it follows as it moves. **2** The **trajectory** of something such as a person's career is the course that it follows over time. *The economy's trajectory is clear enough.* `N-COUNT: with supp` `N-COUNT: with supp`

tram /træm/ **trams.** A **tram** is a public transport vehicle, usually powered by electricity, which travels along rails laid in the surface of a street. The usual American word is **streetcar**. `N-COUNT: also by N BRITISH`

tram·line /ˈtræmlaɪn/ **tramlines.** A **tramline** is one of the rails laid in the surface of a road that trams travel along. The American term is **streetcar line**. `N-COUNT BRITISH`

tramp /træmp/ **tramps, tramping, tramped.** **1** A **tramp** is a person who has no home or job, and who gets food or money by begging or by doing casual work. **2** If you **tramp** somewhere, you walk there slowly and with regular, heavy steps, for a long time. *She spent all day yesterday tramping the streets, gathering evidence.* **3** The **tramp** of people is the sound of their heavy, regular walking. *He heard the slow, heavy tramp of feet on the stairs.* **4** If someone refers to a woman as a **tramp**, they are insulting her, because they think that she is immoral in her sexual behaviour; an offensive word. `N-COUNT` `VERB V prep/adv V n` `N-UNCOUNT` `N-COUNT PRAGMATICS AMERICAN`

tram·ple /ˈtræmpəl/ **tramples, trampling, trampled.** **1** To **trample** on someone's rights or values means to deliberately ignore or disregard them. *Diplomats denounced the leaders for trampling their citizens' civil rights.* **2** If someone **is trampled**, they are injured or killed by being trodden on by animals or by other people. *Thousands of victims perished, trampled underfoot.* **3** If someone **tramples** on something, they tread heavily and carelessly on it and damage it. *They don't want people trampling the grass, pitching tents or building fires.* `VERB: V on n` `VERB: be V-ed V-ed` `VERB: V on n V n`

tram·po·line /ˈtræmpəliːn/ **trampolines.** A **trampoline** is a piece of gymnastic apparatus on which you do acrobatic jumps. It consists of a large piece of strong cloth held by springs in a frame. `N-COUNT`

tram·way /ˈtræmweɪ/ **tramways.** A **tramway** is a set of rails laid in the surface of a road for trams to travel along. `N-COUNT BRITISH`

trance /trɑːns, træns/ **trances.** If someone is in a **trance**, they seem to be asleep and to have no conscious control over their thoughts or actions, but they can respond to things they see and hear. `N-COUNT`

tranche /trɑːnʃ/ **tranches.** **1** In economics, a **tranche** of shares in a company, or a **tranche** of a company, is a number of shares in that company. **2** A **tranche** of something is a piece, section, or part of it. A **tranche** of things is a group of them. *They risk losing the next tranche of funding.* `N-COUNT` `N-COUNT FORMAL`

tran·quil /ˈtræŋkwɪl/. A place that is **tranquil** is calm and peaceful. ♦ **tran·quil·lity** /træŋˈkwɪlɪti/. or **tranquility** *The scene is one of rural tranquility.* `ADJ-GRADED N-UNCOUNT`

tran·quil·lize /ˈtræŋkwɪlaɪz/ **tranquillizes, tranquillizing, tranquillized;** also spelled **tranquillise** in British English, and **tranquilize** in American English. To **tranquillize** a person or an animal means to make them become calm, sleepy, or unconscious by means of a drug. ♦ **tran·quil·liz·er, tranquillizers.** A **tranquillizer** is a drug that is used to tranquillize people or animals. `VERB: V n` `N-COUNT`

trans. **trans.** is a written abbreviation for 'translated by'.

trans- /trænz-/. **1 trans-** is used to form adjectives which indicate that something involves or enables travel from one side of an area to the other. *...the Trans-Siberian railway.* **2 trans-** is used to form words which indicate that someone or something moves from one group, thing, state, or place to another. *...trans-racial adoption.* `PREFIX` `PREFIX`

trans·act /trænˈzækt/ **transacts, transacting, transacted.** If you **transact** business, you enter into a deal with someone, for example by buying or selling something. ♦ **trans·ac·tion** /trænˈzækʃən/, **transactions.** A **transaction** is a piece of business. `VERB: V n FORMAL` `N-COUNT`

trans·at·lan·tic /ˌtrænzətˈlæntɪk/. **1** Transatlantic flights or signals go across the Atlantic Ocean, usually between the United States and Britain. **2** Transatlantic is used to refer to something that happens, exists, or originates in the United States. *...transatlantic fashions.* `ADJ: ADJ n` `ADJ: ADJ n BRITISH`

trans·cend /trænˈsend/ **transcends, transcending, transcended.** Something that **transcends** normal limits or boundaries goes beyond them, because it is more significant than them. *...issues like European union that transcend party loyalty.* ♦ **trans·cend·ence** /trænˈsendəns/. *...the transcendence of class differences.* ♦ **trans·cend·ent** *...the idea of a transcendent God who stood apart from mankind.* `VERB V n` `N-UNCOUNT` `ADJ`

tran·scen·den·tal /ˌtrænsenˈdentəl/. **Transcendental** refers to things that lie beyond the practical experience of ordinary people, and cannot be discovered or understood by ordinary reasoning. *...the transcendental nature of God.* `ADJ`

tran·scribe /trænˈskraɪb/ **transcribes, transcribing, transcribed.** **1** If you **transcribe** a speech or text, you write it out in a different form from the one in which it exists, for example by writing it out in full from notes or from a tape recording. **2** If you **transcribe** a piece of music for an instrument which is not the one for which it was originally written, you rewrite it so that it can be played on that instrument. `VERB: V n` `VERB: V n`

tran·script /ˈtrænskrɪpt/ **transcripts.** A **transcript** of a conversation or speech is a written text of it, based on a recording or notes. `N-COUNT`

tran·scrip·tion /trænˈskrɪpʃən/ **transcriptions.** **1** Transcription of speech or text is the process of transcribing it. **2** A **transcription** is the same as a **transcript**. `N-UNCOUNT` `N-COUNT`

tran·sept /'trænsept/ **transepts.** In a cathedral or N-COUNT
church the **transept** is the part which projects to
the north or south of the main part of the building.

trans·fer, transfers, transferring, trans- ◆◆◆◆◇
ferred. The verb is pronounced /træns'fɜː/. The
noun is pronounced /'trænsfɜː/. **1** If you **transfer** V-ERG
something or someone from one place to another, V n from/to n
they go from the first place to the second. *He wants* V from/to n
to transfer some money to the account of his daugh-
ter... The person can transfer from wheelchair to seat
with relative ease. ▶ Also a noun. *Arrange for the* N-VAR
transfer of medical records to your new doctor. **2** If V-ERG
something **is transferred** from one person or group V n from/to n
of people to another, the second person or group V from/to n
gets it from the first or instead of the first. *On 1 De-*
cember the presidency of the Security Council auto-
matically transfers from the US to Yemen. ▶ Also a N-VAR
noun. *...technology transfer to developing countries.*
♦ trans·fer·able /træns'fɜːrəbəl/. *Use the transfer-* ADJ
able skills acquired from your previous working
background. **♦ trans·fer·ence** /'trænsfərəns/. *It is* N-UNCOUNT
a struggle for a transference of power. **3** When prop- VERB:
erty or land **is transferred**, it stops being owned by beV-ed
one person or institution and becomes owned by V n from/to n
another. *He has already transferred ownership of* LEGAL
most of the works to a British foundation. ▶ Also a N-VAR
noun. *...an outright transfer of property.*

4 In professional sport, especially football, if a player V-ERG:
is transferred from one club to another, they stop beV-ed
playing for the first club and start playing for the sec- from/to n
ond club. The usual American word is **trade**. *...a deal* V from/to n
to allow Diego Maradona to transfer from Napoli to BRITISH
Seville. ▶ Also a noun. *...Gascoigne's transfer to the* N-COUNT
Italian club, Lazio. **5** If you **are transferred** to a differ- V-ERG:
ent job or place, you move to a different job or start beV-ed
working in a different place. *Many personnel depart-* from/to n
ments began to take charge of deciding who should be beV-ed
transferred... Anton was able to transfer from Lavine's V from/to n
to an American company. ▶ Also a noun. *They will be* N-VAR
offered transfers to other locations.

6 When information **is transferred** onto a different VERB
medium, it is copied from one medium to another. beV-ed
Such information is easily transferred onto microfilm. onto/to n
▶ Also a noun. *...data transfer.* N-UNCOUNT

7 If you **transfer** when you are on a journey, you V-ERG:
change from one vehicle to another. *1,654 passengers* V from/to n
were transferred at sea to a Norwegian cruise ship. beV-ed
from/to n

8 Transfers are pieces of paper with a design on one N-COUNT
side. The design can be transferred by heat or pressure onto material, paper, or china for decoration.

trans·fig·ure /træns'fɪɡə, AM -'fɪɡjər/ **transfig-** VERB:
ures, transfiguring, transfigured. If someone beV-ed
or something **is transfigured**, they are completely V n
transformed into something great or beautiful. *He* LITERARY
smiled back, which for an instant transfigured his
unrevealing features.

trans·fix /træns'fɪks/ **transfixes, transfixing,** VERB:
transfixed. If you **are transfixed** by something, it beV-ed
captures all of your interest or attention, so that you
are unable to think of anything else or unable to
act. **♦ trans·fixed** *For hours he stood transfixed.* ADJ-GRADED

trans·form /træns'fɔːm/ **transforms, transform-** ◆◆◆◇◇
ing, transformed. 1 To **transform** something VERB:
into something else means to change or convert it V n into n
into that thing. *Delegates also discussed transform-* V n from n into
ing them from a guerrilla force into a regular army. Also V n
♦ trans·for·ma·tion /,trænsfə'meɪʃən/ **transfor-** N-VAR
mations *Norah made plans for the transformation*
of an attic room into a study. **2** To **transform** some- VERB
thing or someone means to change them complete- V n
ly and suddenly so that they are much better or Also V n
more attractive. *The Minister said the Urban Devel-* from/into n
opment Corporation was now transforming the area.
♦ transformation *In the last five years he's under-* N-VAR
gone a personal transformation.

trans·form·er /træns'fɔːmə/ **transformers.** A N-COUNT
transformer is a piece of electrical equipment
which changes a voltage to a higher or lower
voltage.

trans·fu·sion /træns'fjuːʒən/ **transfusions.** A ◆◇◇◇◇
transfusion is the same as a **blood transfusion.** N-VAR

trans·gress /trænz'gres/ **transgresses, trans-** VERB: V
gressing, transgressed. If someone **trans-** V against n
gresses, they break a moral law or a rule of behav- Also V n
iour. *...a monk who had transgressed against the law*
of celibacy. **♦ trans·gres·sion** /trænz'greʃən/ N-VAR
transgressions *Tales of the candidate's alleged*
past transgressions have been springing up. **♦ trans-**
·gres·sor /,trænz'gresə/ **transgressors.** N-COUNT

tran·si·ent /'trænziənt, AM -nʃənt/ **transients.** ◆◇◇◇◇
1 Transient is used to describe a situation that lasts ADJ-GRADED
only a short time or is constantly changing. **♦ tran-** FORMAL
·si·ence *...the superficiality and transience of the* N-UNCOUNT
club scene. **2** Transients are people who stay in a N-COUNT
place for only a short time and then move, rather FORMAL
than having a fixed home.

tran·sis·tor /træn'zɪstə/ **transistors. 1** A transis- ◆◇◇◇◇
tor is a small electronic component in something N-COUNT
such as a television or radio, which is used for amplification and switching. **2** A **transistor** or a **tran-** N-COUNT
sistor radio is a small portable radio. DATED

trans·it /'trænzɪt/. **1** Transit is the carrying of ◆◇◇◇◇
goods or people by vehicle from one place to anoth- N-UNCOUNT
er. ● If people or things are **in transit**, they are PHRASE
travelling or being taken from one place to another.
We cannot be held responsible for goods lost in tran-
sit. **2** A **transit** area is an area where goods are kept ADJ: ADJ n
where goods are kept between different stages of a
journey. *...a transit lounge at Moscow airport.* **3** A N-UNCOUNT
transit system is a system for moving people or AMERICAN
goods from one place to another, for example on
buses or trains. The usual British word is **transport**.
...the New York City Transit Authority.

tran·si·tion /træn'zɪʃən/ **transitions.** Transition ◆◆◆◇◇
is the process in which something changes from N-VAR
one state to another. *The transition to a multi-party*
democracy is proving to be difficult. **♦ tran·si·tion-**
·al *...a transitional period following more than a* ADJ
decade of civil war.

tran·si·tive /'trænzɪtɪv/. A **transitive** verb has a di- ADJ
rect object.

tran·si·tory /'trænzɪtəri, AM -tɔːri/. If you say that ADJ-GRADED
something is **transitory**, you mean that it lasts only
for a short time. *Her affair with Jim was transitory.*

trans·late /trænz'leɪt/ **translates, translating,** ◆◆◇◇◇
translated. 1 If something that someone has said VERB:
or written **is translated**, it is said or written again in beV-ed into/
a different language. *Martin Luther translated the* from n
Bible into German... The Celtic word 'geis' is usually V into/from
translated as 'taboo'... The girls waited for Mr Esch to beV-ed as n
translate. **♦ trans·la·tion** *The papers have been* N-UNCOUNT
sent to Saudi Arabia for translation. **2** If a word or VERB
expression **translates** as something in a different V as n
language, that is what it means in that language. *His*
family's Cantonese nickname for him translates as
Never Sits Still. **3** If one thing **translates** into anoth- V-ERG:
er, the second happens or is done as a result of the V into n
first. *Your decision must be translated into specific,* beV-ed into n
concrete actions. **4** If you say that a remark, a ges- V-ERG
ture, or an action **translates** as something, you V as n
think this is what its significance is. *'I love him' of-* Also V n as n
ten translates as 'He's better than nothing'. **5** See
also **translation**.

trans·la·tion /trænz'leɪʃən/ **translations. 1** A ◆◆◇◇◇
translation is a piece of writing or speech that has N-COUNT:
been translated from a different language. *I've only* also in N
read Solzhenitsyn in translation. **2** If you say that a PHRASE
quality of something has **been lost in translation**,
or that the thing **loses something in translation**,
you mean that it is not very good as a result of being translated into another language or retold in
another form.

trans·la·tor /trænz'leɪtə/ **translators.** A transla- ◆◆◇◇◇
tor is a person whose job is translating writing or N-COUNT
speech from one language to another.

trans·lu·cent /trænz'luːsənt/. **1** If a material is ◆◇◇◇◇
translucent, some light can pass through it. **2** You ADJ-GRADED
use **translucent** to describe something that has a ADJ-GRADED

glowing appearance, as if light is passing through it. *She had fair hair, blue eyes and translucent skin.*

trans·mis·sion /trænz'mɪʃən/ **transmissions.** ◆◆◇◇◇ N-UNCOUNT
1 The **transmission** of something is the passing or sending of it to a different person or place. *...the fax machine and other forms of electronic data transmission.* **2** The **transmission** of television or radio programmes is the broadcasting of them. **3** A **trans-** N-UNCOUNT **mission** is a television or radio broadcast. **4** The N-VAR **transmission** on a car or other vehicle is the system of gears and shafts by which the power from the engine reaches and turns the wheels.

trans·mit /trænz'mɪt/ **transmits, transmitting,** ◆◆◇◇◇
transmitted. 1 When radio and television pro- VERB: grammes, computer data, or other electronic mes- be V-ed sages **are transmitted**, they are sent from one place V n to another, using wires, radio waves, or satellites. V to n *This is currently the most efficient way to transmit certain types of data like electronic mail... The device is not designed to transmit to satellites.* **2** If one per- VERB: son or animal **transmits** a disease to another, they V n to n have the disease and cause the other person or ani- V n mal to have it. *There was no danger of transmitting* V-ed *the infection through operations. ...the spread of sex-* FORMAL *ually transmitted diseases.* **3** If you **transmit** an VERB: idea or feeling to someone else, you make them V n to n understand and share the idea or feeling. **4** If an LITERARY object or substance **transmits** something such as VERB: V n sound or vibrations, the sound or vibrations are able to pass through it or along it.

trans·mit·ter /trænz'mɪtə/ **transmitters.** A trans- ◆◇◇◇◇
mitter is a piece of apparatus that is used for broad- N-COUNT casting television or radio programmes.

trans·mute /trænz'mjuːt/ **transmutes, trans-** V-ERG **muting, transmuted.** If something **transmutes** V into n or **is transmuted** into a different form, it is changed V n into n into that form. *She ceased to think, as anger trans-* Also V n muted into passion... Scientists transmuted matter FORMAL *into pure energy.* ◆ **trans·mu·ta·tion, transmu-** N-VAR **tations** *...the transmutation of food into energy.*

trans·par·en·cy /træns'pærənsi, AM -'per-/ **trans-** ◆◇◇◇◇
parencies. 1 A **transparency** is a small piece of N-COUNT photographic film with a frame around it which can be projected onto a screen so that you can see the picture. **2 Transparency** is the quality that an ob- N-UNCOUNT ject or substance has when you can see through it. **3** The **transparency** of a process, situation, or state- N-UNCOUNT ment is its quality of being easily understood or recognized, for example because there is no secrecy surrounding it, or because it is expressed in a clear way. *...to promote openness and transparency in the Government's economic decision-making.*

trans·par·ent /træns'pærənt, AM -'per-/. **1** If an ◆◇◇◇◇
object or substance is **transparent**, you can see ADJ-GRADED through it. **2** If a situation, system, or activity is ADJ-GRADED **transparent**, it is easily understood or recognized. *The company has to make its accounts and opera- tions as transparent as possible.* ◆ **trans·par·ent·ly** ADV-GRADED *The system was clearly not functioning smoothly or transparently.* **3** You use **transparent** to describe a ADJ-GRADED statement or action that is obviously dishonest or wrong, and that you think will not deceive people. *He thought he could fool people with transparent de- ceptions.* ◆ **transparently** *Her answers were trans-* ADV-GRADED: parently untruthful.* ADV adj

tran·spire /træn'spaɪə/ **transpires, transpiring,** ◆◇◇◇◇
transpired. 1 When it **transpires** that something VERB is the case, people discover that it is the case. *It* it V that *transpired that Paolo had left his driving licence at* FORMAL *home.* **2** When something **transpires**, it happens. VERB: V *Some people consider this use to be incorrect.*

trans·plant,   **transplants, transplanting,** ◆◆◇◇◇
transplanted. The noun is pronounced /'trænzplɑːnt, -plænt/. The verb is pronounced /træns'plɑːnt, -'plænt/. **1** A **transplant** is a medical N-VAR operation in which a part of a person's body is re- placed because it is diseased. *...a heart transplant operation.* **2** If doctors **transplant** an organ such as VERB: V n a heart, they use it to replace a patient's diseased organ. ◆ **trans·plan·ta·tion** /ˌtrænzplæn'teɪʃən/. N-UNCOUNT

...a shortage of kidneys for transplantation. **3** To VERB: V n **transplant** someone or something means to move V n from/to/ them to a different place. *Marriage had transplant-* into n *ed Rebecca from London to Manchester.*

trans·port,   **transports, transporting, trans-** ◆◆◆◇
ported. The noun is pronounced /'trænspɔːt/. The verb is pronounced /træns'pɔːt/. **1 Transport** refers N-UNCOUNT to any type of vehicle that you can travel in or carry goods in. *Have you got your own transport?* **2 Transport** is a system for taking people or goods N-UNCOUNT from one place to another, for example using buses or trains. *The extra money could be spent on improving public transport.* **3** To **transport** people or goods VERB: V n somewhere means to take them from one place to an- V n prep/adv other in a vehicle. *They use tankers to transport the oil to Los Angeles.* ▶ Also a noun. *Local production virtu-* N-UNCOUNT *ally eliminates transport costs.* **4** A military or troop N-COUNT **transport** is a military vehicle, especially a plane, that is used to carry soldiers or equipment.

trans·por·ta·tion /ˌtrænspɔː'teɪʃən/. **1 Transpor-** ◆◆◇◇◇
tation refers to any type of vehicle that you can N-UNCOUNT travel in or carry goods in. The usual British word is AMERICAN **transport.** *The company will provide transportation.* **2 Transportation** is a system for taking people or N-UNCOUNT goods from one place to another, for example using AMERICAN buses or trains. The usual British word is **transport.** *...our national transportation policy.* **3 Transporta-** N-UNCOUNT **tion** is the activity of taking goods or people from one place to another in a vehicle.

trans·port·er /træns'pɔːtə/ **transporters.** A trans- N-COUNT **porter** is a large vehicle or an aeroplane that is used BRITISH for carrying very large or heavy objects, for example cars.

trans·pose /træns'pəʊz/ **transposes, transpos-** **ing, transposed. 1** If you **transpose** something VERB from one place or situation to another, you move it V n from n to n there. *The director transposes the action from 16th* Also V n to n, Century France to post-Civil War America.* ◆ **trans-** V n **po·si·tion** /ˌtrænspə'zɪʃən/ **transpositions** *...a* N-VAR *transposition of 'Macbeth' to third century BC China.* **2** If you **transpose** two things, you reverse them or put VERB them in each other's place. *Many people inadvertently transpose digits of the ZIP code.* ◆ **transposition** N-VAR *...the transposition of his initials and his middle name.*

trans·sex·ual /ˌtræn'sekʃʊəl/ **transsexuals.** A N-COUNT **transsexual** is a person who has decided that they want to live as a person of the opposite sex, and so has changed their name and appearance in order to do this.

trans·verse /trænz'vɜːs/. **Transverse** is used to de- ADJ scribe something that is at right angles to some- thing else.

trans·ves·tism /trænz'vestɪzəm/. **Transvestism** is N-UNCOUNT the practice of wearing clothes normally worn by a person of the opposite sex, usually for pleasure.

trans·ves·tite /trænz'vestaɪt/ **transvestites.** A ◆◇◇◇◇
transvestite is a person, usually a man, who enjoys N-COUNT wearing clothes normally worn by people of the op- posite sex.

trap /træp/ **traps, trapping, trapped. 1** A trap is ◆◆◆◇◇
a device which is placed somewhere or a hole which N-COUNT is dug somewhere in order to catch animals or birds. **2** If a person **traps** animals or birds, he or she VERB: V n catches them using traps. **3** If you **trap** someone into doing or saying some- VERB thing, you trick them so that they do or say it, al- V n into -ing/n though they did not want to. *Were you just trying to* Also V n *trap her into making some admission?* ▶ A **trap** is a N-COUNT trick that is intended to catch or deceive someone. **4** To **trap** someone, especially a criminal, means to cap- VERB: V n ture them. **5** A **trap** is an unpleasant situation that you JOURNALISM cannot easily escape from. *The Government has found* N-COUNT it's caught in a trap of its own making.* **6** If you **are trapped** somewhere, something falls onto VERB: you or blocks your way and prevents you from mov- be V-ed ing or escaping. *The light aircraft then cartwheeled,* V n *trapping both men.* **7** When something **traps** gas, wa- VERB ter, or energy, it prevents it from escaping. *Wool traps* V n *your body heat, keeping the chill at bay.*

8 A **trap** is a light horse-drawn carriage with two wheels in which people used to travel.   N-COUNT
9 If someone **falls into** the **trap** of doing something, they do something which it would be better for them not to do, especially something which many people make the mistake of doing. *Many people fall into the trap of believing that home decorating must always be done on a large scale.*   PHRASE
10 See also **trapped; booby-trap, death trap, poverty trap.**

trap·door /ˌtræpˈdɔː/ **trapdoors;** also spelled **trap door.** A **trapdoor** is a small horizontal door in a floor, a ceiling, or on a stage.   N-COUNT

tra·peze /trəˈpiːz/ **trapezes.** A **trapeze** is a bar of wood or metal hanging from two ropes on which acrobats and gymnasts swing and perform skilful movements.   N-COUNT

trapped /træpt/. If you feel **trapped**, you are in an unpleasant situation in which you lack freedom, and you feel that you cannot escape from it. ● See also **trap.**   ◆◆◇◇◇ ADJ-GRADED

trap·per /ˈtræpə/ **trappers.** A **trapper** is a person who traps animals, especially for their fur.   N-COUNT

trap·pings /ˈtræpɪŋz/. The **trappings** of power, wealth, or a particular job are the extra things, such as decorations and luxury items, that go with it; used showing disapproval.   ◆◇◇◇◇ N-PLURAL PRAGMATICS

trash /træʃ/ **trashes, trashing, trashed.**
1 **Trash** consists of unwanted things or waste material such as used paper, empty tins and bottles, and waste food. The British word is **rubbish. 2** If you say that something such as a book, painting, or film is **trash** you mean that it is of very poor quality. *Don't read that awful trash.* **3** If someone **trashes** a place or vehicle, they deliberately destroy it or make a great deal of mess in it. *The building had been trashed and its electricity supply cut.* **4** If you **trash** people or their ideas, you criticize them very strongly and say that they are worthless. *People asked why the candidates spent so much time trashing each other.*   ◆◇◇◇◇ N-UNCOUNT: also the N AMERICAN / N-UNCOUNT INFORMAL / VERB: V n beV-ed INFORMAL / VERB V n AMERICAN, INFORMAL

'trash can, trash cans. A **trash can** is a large round container which people put their rubbish in and which is usually kept outside their house. The British word is **dustbin.**   N-COUNT AMERICAN

trashy /ˈtræʃi/ **trashier, trashiest.** If you describe something as **trashy**, you think it is of very poor quality. *I was reading some trashy romance novel.*   ADJ-GRADED INFORMAL

trat·to·ria /ˌtrætəˈriːə/ **trattorias.** A **trattoria** is an Italian restaurant.   N-COUNT

trau·ma /ˈtrɔːmə, AM ˈtraʊmə/ **traumas. Trauma** is a very severe shock or very upsetting experience, which may cause psychological damage. *...the trauma of losing a house.* ♦ **trau·mat·ic** /trɔːˈmætɪk, AM traʊ-/. *Redundancy can be traumatic.*   ◆◆◇◇◇ N-VAR / ADJ-GRADED

trau·ma·tize /ˈtrɔːmətaɪz, AM ˈtraʊ-/ **traumatizes, traumatizing, traumatized;** also spelled **traumatise** in British English. If someone **is traumatized** by an event or situation, it shocks or upsets them very much, and may cause them psychological damage. *Traumatising a child with an abnormal fear of strangers probably won't do much good.* ♦ **trau·ma·tized** *He could not cope alone with two traumatized children.*   ◆◇◇◇◇ VERB: beV-ed V n with n Also V n / ADJ-GRADED

trav·ail /ˈtræveɪl, AM trəˈveɪl/ **travails.** You can refer to unpleasant hard work or difficult problems as **travail.**   N-VAR LITERARY

trav·el /ˈtrævəl/ **travels, travelling, travelled;** spelled **traveling, traveled** in American English. **1** If you **travel**, you go from one place to another, often to a place that is far away. *You had better travel to Helsinki tomorrow... Students often travel hundreds of miles to get here... I had been travelling at 150 kilometres an hour.* ▶ Also a noun. *Information on travel in New Zealand is available at the hotel.* ♦ **trav·el·ling** *...two hours' travelling a day.* **2** If you **travel light**, you travel without taking much luggage. **3** If you **travel** the world, the country, or the area, you go to many different places in the world or in a particular country or area.   ◆◆◆◆◇ VERB: V V prep/adv V amount/n V at amount / N-UNCOUNT / N-UNCOUNT PHRASE / VERB: V n

4 Someone's **travels** are the journeys that they make to places a long way from their home. *He also collects things for the house on his travels abroad.*   N-PLURAL: with poss
5 When light or sound from one place reaches another, you say that it **travels** to the other place. *When sound travels through water, strange things can happen.* **6** When news becomes known by people in different places, you say that it **travels** to them. *News of his work traveled all the way to Asia.* **7** If goods such as food products **travel well**, they can be transported a long way without being damaged or their quality being spoiled.   VERB V prep/adv / VERB V adv/prep / PHRASE
8 See also **travelling, much-travelled, well-travelled.**

'travel agency, travel agencies. A **travel agency** is a business which makes arrangements for people's holidays and journeys.   N-COUNT

'travel agent, travel agents. 1 A **travel agent** or **travel agent's** is a shop where you can go to arrange a holiday or journey. **2** A **travel agent** is a person or business that arranges holidays and journeys.   ◆◇◇◇◇ N-COUNT / N-COUNT

trav·el·ler /ˈtrævələ/ **travellers;** spelled **traveler** in American English. **1** A **traveller** is a person who is making a journey or a person who travels a lot. *Many air travellers suffer puffy ankles and feet during long flights.* **2** A **traveller** is a person who travels from place to place, often living in a van or other vehicle, rather than living in one place. ● See also **New Age Traveller.**   ◆◆◆◇◇ N-COUNT / N-COUNT

'traveller's cheque, traveller's cheques; spelled **traveler's check** in American English. **Traveller's cheques** are cheques that you buy at a bank and take with you when you travel so that you can exchange them for the currency of the country that you are in.   N-COUNT

trav·el·ling /ˈtrævəlɪŋ/; spelled **traveling** in American English. A **travelling** actor or musician, for example, is one who travels around an area or country performing in different places.   ADJ: ADJ n

,travelling 'salesman, travelling salesmen; spelled **traveling salesman** in American English. A **travelling salesman** is a salesman who travels to different places and meets people in order to sell goods or take orders.   N-COUNT

trav·elogue /ˈtrævəlɒg, -lɔːg/ **travelogues.** A **travelogue** is a talk or film about travel or about a particular person's travels.   N-COUNT

'travel sickness. If someone has **travel sickness**, they feel sick as a result of travelling in a vehicle.   N-UNCOUNT

trav·erse /ˈtrævɜːs, trəˈvɜːs/ **traverses, traversing, traversed.** If someone or something **traverses** an area of land or water, they go across it.   ◆◇◇◇◇ VERB: V n LITERARY

trav·es·ty /ˈtrævəsti/ **travesties.** If you describe something as a **travesty** of another thing, you mean that it is a very bad representation of that other thing. *If he couldn't prepare his case properly, the trial would be a travesty.*   N-COUNT

trawl /trɔːl/ **trawls, trawling, trawled. 1** If you **trawl** through a large number of similar things, you search through them looking for something that you want. *A team of officers is trawling through the records of thousands of petty thieves.* ▶ Also a noun. *Any trawl through the band's interviews will reveal statements that are challenging and incisive.* **2** When fishermen **trawl** for fish, they drag a wide net behind their ship in order to catch fish. *They had seen him trawling and therefore knew that there were fish.*   ◆◇◇◇◇ VERB V through n Also V n BRITISH / N-COUNT / VERB: V for n V Also V n

trawl·er /ˈtrɔːlə/ **trawlers.** A **trawler** is a fishing boat that is used for trawling.   ◆◇◇◇◇ N-COUNT

tray /treɪ/ **trays.** A **tray** is a flat piece of wood, plastic, or metal, which usually has raised edges and which is used for carrying things, especially food and drinks.   ◆◆◇◇◇ N-COUNT

treach·er·ous /ˈtretʃərəs/. **1** If you describe someone as **treacherous**, you mean that they are likely to betray you and cannot be trusted. *The President spoke of the treacherous intentions of the enemy.* **2** If you say that something is **treacherous**, you mean that it is very dangerous and unpredictable. *The current of the river is fast flowing and treacherous.*   ◆◇◇◇◇ ADJ-GRADED / ADJ-GRADED

T

treach·ery /'tretʃəri/ **treacheries. Treachery** is behaviour or an action in which someone betrays their country or betrays a person who trusts them. *He was deeply wounded by the treachery of close aides and old friends.*
◆◇◇◇◇
N-UNCOUNT: also N in pl

trea·cle /'triːkəl/. **Treacle** is a thick, sweet, sticky liquid that is obtained when sugar is refined. It is used in making cakes and puddings. The usual American word is **molasses**.
N-UNCOUNT
BRITISH

tread /tred/ **treads, treading, trod, trodden.**
1 If you **tread** on something, you put your foot on it when you are walking or standing. *Oh, sorry, I didn't mean to tread on your foot.* **2** If you **tread** in a particular way, you walk that way. *She trod casually, enjoying the touch of the damp grass on her feet.* **3** A person's **tread** is the sound that they make with their feet as they walk. *We could now very plainly hear their heavy tread and an occasional loud, coarse laugh.*
◆◇◇◇
VERB
V on n

VERB
V adv
LITERARY
N-SING:
supp N
WRITTEN

4 If you **tread** carefully, you behave carefully or with caution.
VERB:
V adv

5 The **tread** of a step or stair is its flat upper surface.
N-COUNT

6 The **tread** of a tyre or shoe is the pattern of grooves on it that stops it slipping.
N-VAR

7 If someone who is in deep water **treads water,** they stay afloat in an upright position by moving their legs slightly. **8** If you say that someone **is treading water,** you mean that they are in an unsatisfactory situation where they are not progressing, but are just continuing doing the same things.
PHRASE

PHRASE

9 • to **tread on** someone's **toes:** see **toe.**

tread·mill /'tredmɪl/ **treadmills. 1** You can refer to a task or a job as a **treadmill** when you have to keep doing it although it is unpleasant and exhausting. *Mr Stocks can expect a gruelling week on the publicity treadmill.* **2** A **treadmill** is a piece of equipment consisting of a wheel with steps around its edge or a continuous moving belt. The weight of a person or animal walking on it causes the wheel or belt to turn.
◆◇◇◇
N-COUNT

N-COUNT

trea·son /'triːzən/. **Treason** is the crime of betraying your country, for example by helping its enemies or by trying to overthrow its government.
◆◇◇◇
N-UNCOUNT

treas·ure /'treʒə/ **treasures, treasuring, treasured. 1** In children's stories, **treasure** is a collection of valuable old objects, such as gold coins and jewels. **2 Treasures** are valuable objects, especially works of art and items of historical value. *...a collection of stolen art treasures.* **3** If you **treasure** something that you have, you keep or preserve it carefully because it gives you great pleasure and you think it is very special. *She treasures her memories of those joyous days.* ► Also a noun. *His greatest treasure is his collection of rock records.* ♦ **treas·ured** *...my most treasured possessions.* **4** If you say that someone is a **treasure,** you mean that they are very helpful and useful to you.
◆◆◇◇
N-UNCOUNT

N-COUNT

VERB
V n

N-COUNT
ADJ-GRADED:
ADJ n
N-COUNT
INFORMAL

treas·ur·er /'treʒərə/ **treasurers.** The **treasurer** of a society or organization is the person who is in charge of its finances.
◆◇◇◇
N-COUNT

'treasure trove, treasure troves. 1 If you describe something or someone as a **treasure trove** of a particular thing, you mean that they are a very good or rich source of that thing. *The dictionary is a vast treasure trove of information.* **2** You can refer to a collection of valuable objects as a **treasure trove.** *Windsor Castle is quite literally an antique treasure trove.*
N-COUNT

N-COUNT

treas·ury /'treʒəri/ **treasuries. 1** In Britain and some other countries, the **Treasury** is the government department that deals with the country's finances. **2** The **treasury** in a building such as a castle or a cathedral is a room where valuable objects are displayed or stored.
◆◆◇◇
N-COLL-
PROPER

N-COUNT

treat /triːt/ **treats, treating, treated. 1** If you **treat** someone or something in a particular way, you behave towards them or deal with them in that way. *Artie treated most women with indifference... Police say they're treating it as a case of attempted murder... She adored Paddy but he didn't treat her*
◆◆◆◇
VERB: V n with
n
V n as/like n
V n adv

well. **2** When a doctor or nurse **treats** a patient or an illness, he or she tries to make the patient well again. *The boy was treated for a minor head wound.*
VERB: V n
V n for n

3 If something **is treated** with a particular substance, the substance is put onto or into it in order to clean it, to protect it, or to give it special properties. *About 70% of the cocoa acreage is treated with insecticide.*
VERB
be V-ed with n
Also V n

4 If you **treat** someone to something special which they will enjoy, you buy it or arrange it for them. *Tomorrow I'll treat myself to a day's gardening.* ► Also a noun. *Lettie had never yet failed to return from town without some special treat for him.* **5** If you say that something is your **treat,** you mean that you are paying for it as a treat for someone else.
VERB: V n to n
V pron-refl to n
Also V n
N-COUNT

N-SING:
poss N
SPOKEN

6 If you say, for example, that something looks or works a **treat,** you mean that it looks very good or works very well. ● to **treat** someone **like dirt:** see **dirt.**
PHRASE
INFORMAL

treat·able /'triːtəbəl/. A **treatable** disease is one which can be cured or controlled, usually by the use of drugs. *Depression is treatable.*
ADJ-GRADED

trea·tise /'triːtɪz, AM -tɪs/ **treatises.** A **treatise** is a long, formal piece of writing about a particular subject. *...Locke's Treatise on Civil Government.*
◆◇◇◇
N-COUNT

treat·ment /'triːtmənt/ **treatments. 1 Treatment** is medical attention given to a sick or injured person or animal. *Many patients are not getting the medical treatment they need.* **2** Your **treatment** of someone is the way you behave towards them or deal with them. *Ginny's initial rage at his treatment of Chris had simmered down.* **3 Treatment** of something involves putting a particular substance onto or into it, in order to clean it, to protect it, or to give it special properties. *As with all oily hair treatments, shampoo needs to be applied first.* **4** If you say that someone is given the **full treatment,** you mean either that they are treated extremely well or that they are treated extremely harshly.
◆◆◆◇
N-VAR

N-UNCOUNT

N-VAR

PHRASE
INFORMAL

trea·ty /'triːti/ **treaties.** A **treaty** is a written agreement between countries in which they agree to do a particular thing or to help each other. *...the Treaty of Rome, which established the European Community.*
◆◆◆◇
N-COUNT

tre·ble /'trebəl/ **trebles, trebling, trebled. 1** If something **trebles** or if you **treble** it, it becomes three times greater in number or amount than it was. *The city has trebled the number of its prisoners to 21,000.* **2** If one thing is **treble** the size or amount of another thing, it is three times greater in size or amount. *...treble the normal daily average.* **3** A **treble** is a boy with a very high singing voice. **4** In sport, a **treble** is three successes one after the other.
◆◇◇◇
V-ERG:
V n

PREDET

N-COUNT
N-COUNT
BRITISH,
JOURNALISM

tree /triː/ **trees. 1** A **tree** is a tall plant that has a hard trunk, branches, and leaves. *I planted those apple trees.* ● See also **Christmas tree, family tree. 2** If you say that someone **is barking up the wrong tree,** you mean that they are following the wrong course of action because their beliefs or ideas about something are incorrect. **3** If you say that someone **can't see the wood for the trees,** you mean that they are so involved in the details of something that they forget or do not realize the real purpose or importance of the thing as a whole. The usual American expression is **can't see the forest for the trees. 4** ● the **top of the tree:** see **top.**
◆◆◆◇
N-COUNT

PHRASE
INFORMAL

PHRASE
BRITISH

tree·less /'triːləs/. A **treeless** area or place has no trees in it.
ADJ-GRADED

'tree-lined. A **tree-lined** road or street has trees on either side.
ADJ

tree·top /'triːtɒp/ **treetops;** also spelled **tree tops.** The **treetops** are the top branches of the trees in a wood or forest.
N-COUNT

'tree trunk, tree trunks. A **tree trunk** is the wide central part of a tree, from which the branches grow.
N-COUNT

trek /trek/ **treks, trekking, trekked. 1** If you **trek** somewhere, you go on a journey across difficult terrain, usually on foot. *...trekking through the jungles.* ► Also a noun. *...a trek through the South Gobi desert.* **2** If you **trek** somewhere, you go there rather slowly and unwillingly, usually because you
◆◆◇◇
VERB
V prep/adv
Also V

N-COUNT

VERB
V prep/adv

are tired. *They trekked from shop to shop in search of white knee-length socks.* ► Also a noun. *The World Trade Centre is a bit of a trek from Soho.* N-COUNT

trel·lis /'trelɪs/ **trellises.** A **trellis** is a frame which supports climbing plants. N-VAR

trem·ble /'trembəl/ **trembles, trembling, trembled.** **1** If you **tremble**, you shake slightly, for example because you are frightened or cold. *Gil was white and trembling with anger.* ► Also a noun. *...the look on the patient's face, the tremble in his hand.* **2** If something **trembles**, it shakes slightly. *He felt the earth tremble under him.* **3** If your voice **trembles**, it sounds unsteady and hesitant, usually because you are upset or nervous. ► Also a noun. *'Please understand this,' she began, a tremble in her voice.* ♦♦◇◇◇ VERB: V V with n N-SING VERB: V VERB: V LITERARY N-SING

tre·men·dous /trɪ'mendəs/. **1** You use **tremendous** to emphasize how strong a feeling or quality is, or how large an amount is. *I felt a tremendous pressure on my chest... That's a tremendous amount of information.* ♦ **tre·men·dous·ly** *I enjoyed it tremendously.* **2** You can describe someone or something as **tremendous** when you think they are very good or impressive. *He was a tremendous person.* ♦♦♦◇◇ ADJ-GRADED PRAGMATICS INFORMAL ADV ADJ-GRADED INFORMAL

trem·or /'tremə/ **tremors.** **1** A **tremor** is a small earthquake. **2** If an event causes a **tremor** in a group or organization, it threatens the stability of that group or organization. *Low market prices for wine caused economic tremors.* **3** A **tremor** is a shaking of your body or voice that you cannot control. *He felt a tremor of apprehension.* ♦◇◇◇◇ N-COUNT N-COUNT N-COUNT

tremu·lous /'tremjʊləs/. If someone's voice, smile, or actions are **tremulous**, they are unsteady because the person is uncertain, afraid, or upset. *She took a deep, tremulous breath.* ADJ-GRADED LITERARY

trench /trentʃ/ **trenches. 1** A **trench** is a long narrow channel that is cut into the ground, for example for drainage or in order to lay pipes. **2** A **trench** is a long narrow channel in the ground used by soldiers as a defensive position. ♦◇◇◇◇ N-COUNT N-COUNT

trench·ant /'trentʃənt/. You can use **trenchant** to describe something such as a criticism or comment that is very clear, effective, and forceful. *He was shattered and bewildered by this trenchant criticism.* ADJ-GRADED FORMAL

'trench coat, trench coats; also spelled **trenchcoat.** A **trench coat** is a type of raincoat with pockets and a belt. Trench coats are often similar in design to military coats. N-COUNT

trend /trend/ **trends. 1** A **trend** is a change or development towards something new or different. *...a trend towards part-time employment. ...the downward trend in gasoline prices.* **2** If someone or something sets a **trend**, they do something that becomes accepted or fashionable. *The record has already proved a success and may well start a trend.* ♦♦♦◇◇ N-COUNT N-COUNT

'trend-setter, trend-setters; also **trendsetter.** A **trend-setter** is a person or institution that starts a new fashion or trend. N-COUNT

trendy /'trendi/ **trendier, trendiest; trendies. 1** If you say that something or someone is **trendy**, you mean that they are very fashionable and modern. *...a trendy London night club.* ► A **trendy** is someone who is **trendy**. **2** You can describe someone who follows new ideas as **trendy** to show that you disapprove of them because they are more interested in being up to date than in thinking seriously about the implications of such ideas. *Trendy teachers are denying children the opportunity to study classic texts.* ♦◇◇◇◇ ADJ-GRADED INFORMAL N-COUNT ADJ-GRADED PRAGMATICS INFORMAL

trepi·da·tion /ˌtrepɪ'deɪʃən/. **Trepidation** is fear or anxiety about something that you are going to do or experience. *It was with some trepidation that I viewed the prospect of cycling across Uganda.* N-UNCOUNT FORMAL

tres·pass /'trespəs/ **trespasses, trespassing, trespassed.** If someone **trespasses**, they go onto someone else's land without their permission. *They were trespassing on private property.* ► **Trespass** is the act of trespassing. ♦ **tres·pass·er, trespassers** *Trespassers will be prosecuted.* ♦◇◇◇◇ VERB: V V prep N-VAR N-COUNT

tress /tres/ **tresses.** A woman's **tresses** are her long flowing hair. N-COUNT LITERARY

tres·tle /'tresəl/ **trestles.** A **trestle** is a wooden or metal structure that is used, for example, as one of the supports for a table. It has two pairs of sloping legs which are joined by a flat piece across the top. N-COUNT

'trestle table, trestle tables. A **trestle table** is a table made of a long board that is supported on trestles. N-COUNT

tri- /traɪ-/. **Tri-** is used at the beginning of nouns and adjectives that have 'three' as part of their meaning. *It was triangular in shape.* PREFIX

tri·ad /'traɪæd/ **triads;** also spelled **Triad** for meaning 1. **1** The **Triads** are Chinese secret societies that are often associated with organized crime. **2** A **triad** is a group of three similar things. ♦◇◇◇◇ N-COUNT N-COUNT FORMAL

tri·al /'traɪəl/ **trials. 1** A **trial** is a formal meeting in a law court, at which a judge and jury listen to evidence and decide whether a person is guilty of a crime. If someone is **on trial** or **is standing trial** they are being tried in a court of law. *New evidence showed the police lied at the trial.* **2** A **trial** is an experiment in which you test something by using it or doing it for a period of time to see how well it works. If something is **on trial**, it is being tested in this way. *They have been treated with this drug in clinical trials.* **3** If someone gives you a **trial** for a job or position, they let you do it for a short period of time to see if you are suitable for it or to see if you will succeed or fail. You can also say that someone is **on trial**. *He had just given a trial to a young woman who said she had previous experience.* **4** If you do something by **trial and error**, you try several different methods of doing it until you find the method that works properly. **5** If you refer to the **trials** of a situation, you mean the unpleasant things that you experience in it. *...the trials of adolescence.* **6** In some sports or outdoor activities, **trials** are a series of contests that test a competitor's skill and ability. ♦♦♦♦◇ N-VAR N-VAR N-COUNT PHRASE N-COUNT N-COUNT

'trial balloon, trial balloons. If you refer to a suggestion or proposal as a **trial balloon**, you mean that it has been put forward in order to find out how people will react to it. *Like many proposals floated in Washington, the $300 tax rebate idea may only be a trial balloon.* N-COUNT

,trial 'run, trial runs. A **trial run** is a first attempt at doing something to make sure you can do it properly. N-COUNT

tri·an·gle /'traɪæŋgəl/ **triangles. 1** A **triangle** is an object, arrangement, or flat shape with three straight sides and three angles. See picture headed **shapes.** *...triangles of fried bread.* ♦ **tri·an·gu·lar** /traɪ'æŋgjʊlə/. *...triangular bandages to make slings.* **2** The **triangle** is a musical instrument that consists of a piece of metal shaped like a triangle. You play it by hitting it with a short metal bar. See picture headed **musical instruments. 3** If you describe a group of three people as a **triangle**, you mean that they are all connected with each other in a particular situation, but often have different interests. *...the classic triangle of husband, wife and mistress.* ♦ **triangular** *One particular triangular relationship became the model of Simone's first novel.* ♦◇◇◇◇ N-COUNT ADJ N-COUNT N-COUNT ADJ

tri·ath·lon /traɪ'æθlən/ **triathlons.** A **triathlon** is an athletics competition in which each competitor takes part in three different events; swimming, cycling, and marathon running. N-COUNT

trib·al·ism /'traɪbəlɪzəm/. **1** **Tribalism** is the state of existing as a tribe. **2** You can use **tribalism** to refer to the loyalties that people feel towards particular social groups and to the way these loyalties affect their behaviour and attitudes towards others; used showing disapproval. *Across Europe, countries are worried about the destructive force of tribalism.* N-UNCOUNT N-UNCOUNT PRAGMATICS

tribe /traɪb/ **tribes. 1** **Tribe** is sometimes used to refer to a group of people of the same race, language, and customs, especially in a developing country. Some people disapprove of this use. *...the Xhosa tribe.* ♦ **trib·al** *They would go back to their* ♦♦◇◇◇ N-COLL-COUNT ADJ

tribal lands. **2** You can use **tribe** to refer to a group N-COLL-COUNT INFORMAL of people who are all doing the same thing or who all behave in the same way. *...the particularly unpleasant tribe who argue over the splitting of restaurant and bar bills.*

tribes·man /'traɪbzmən/ **tribesmen.** A **tribesman** N-COUNT is a man who belongs to a tribe.

tribu·la·tion /,trɪbjʊ'leɪʃən/ **tribulations.** You can N-VAR FORMAL refer to the suffering or difficulty that you experience in a particular situation as **tribulations.** *...the trials and tribulations of everyday life.*

tri·bu·nal /traɪ'bjuːnəl/ **tribunals.** A **tribunal** is a ◆◆◇◇◇ N-COLL-COUNT special court or committee that is appointed to deal with particular problems. *His case comes before an industrial tribunal in March.*

tribu·tary /'trɪbjʊtəri, AM -teri/ **tributaries.** A N-COUNT **tributary** is a stream or river that flows into a larger one.

trib·ute /'trɪbjuːt/ **tributes.** **1** A **tribute** is some- ◆◆◇◇◇ N-VAR thing that you say, do, or make to show your admiration and respect for someone. *The song is a tribute to Roy Orbison... He paid tribute to the organising committee.* **2** If one thing is a **tribute** to another, N-SING: aN the first thing is the result of the second and shows how good it is. *It is a tribute to Mr Chandler's skill that he has fashioned a fascinating book out of such unpromising material.*

tri·ceps /'traɪseps/; **triceps** is both the singular and N-COUNT the plural form. Your **triceps** is the muscle in the back part of your upper arm.

trick /trɪk/ **tricks, tricking, tricked.** **1** A **trick** is ◆◆◆◇◇ N-COUNT an action that is intended to deceive someone. *We are playing a trick on a man who keeps bothering me.* **2** If someone **tricks** you, they deceive you, of- VERB: V n ten in order to make you do something. *His family* V n into-ing/n V way prep/ *tricked him into going to Pakistan... His real purpose* adv *is to trick his way into your home.* **3** A **trick** is a clev- N-COUNT er or skilful action that someone does in order to entertain people. *...card tricks.* **4** A **trick** is a clever N-COUNT way of doing something. *Everything I cooked was a trick of my mother's.* **5** See also **confidence trick, hat-trick.**

6 If something **does the trick**, it achieves what you PHRASE INFORMAL wanted. *Sometimes a few choice words will do the trick.* **7** If someone tries **every trick in the book**, they PHRASE INFORMAL try every possible thing that they can think of in order to achieve something. **8** If you say that someone does PHRASE INFORMAL not **miss a trick**, you mean that they always know what is happening and take advantage of every situation. **9** The **tricks of the trade** are the quick and clever PHRASE ways of doing something that are known by people who regularly do a particular activity. **10** If you say PHRASE PRAGMATICS that someone is **up to** their **tricks** or **up to** their **old** INFORMAL **tricks,** you disapprove of them because they are behaving in the dishonest or deceitful way in which they typically behave.

trick·ery /'trɪkəri/. **Trickery** is the use of dishonest N-UNCOUNT methods in order to achieve something. *They are notorious for resorting to trickery in order to impress their clients.*

trick·le /'trɪkəl/ **trickles, trickling, trickled.** ◆◇◇◇◇ V-ERG: V **1** When a liquid **trickles**, or when you **trickle** it, it V prep/adv flows slowly in very small amounts. *A tear trickled* Also V n *down the old man's cheek.* ▶ Also a noun. *There was* N-COUNT *not so much as a trickle of water.* **2** When people or VERB: V adv/prep things **trickle** in a particular direction, they move there slowly in small groups or amounts, rather than all together. ▶ Also a noun. *The flood of cars* N-COUNT *has now slowed to a trickle.*

'trickle-down. The **trickle-down** theory is the ADJ: ADJ n theory that benefits given to people at the top of a system will eventually be passed on to people lower down the system.

,trick or 'treat. Trick or treat is an activity in N-UNCOUNT which children knock on the doors of houses at Halloween and shout 'trick or treat'. If the person who answers the door does not give the children a treat, such as sweets, they play a trick on him or her.

trick·ster /'trɪkstə/ **tricksters.** A **trickster** is a per- N-COUNT INFORMAL son who deceives or cheats people, often in order to get money from them.

tricky /'trɪki/ **trickier, trickiest.** If you describe a ◆◆◇◇◇ ADJ-GRADED task or problem as **tricky,** you mean that it is difficult to do or deal with. *Parking can be tricky in the town centre.*

tri·col·our /'trɪkələ/ **tricolours;** also spelled **tricol-** N-COUNT **or.** A **tricolour** is a flag which is made up of blocks of three different colours.

tri·cy·cle /'traɪsɪkəl/ **tricycles.** A **tricycle** is a cycle N-COUNT with three wheels.

tried /traɪd/. **Tried** is used in the expressions **tried** ◆◇◇◇◇ **and tested, tried and trusted,** and **tried and true,** ADJ: ADJ and adj which describe a product or method that has already been used and has been found to be successful. *...over 1000 tried-and-tested recipes.* ● See also **try; well-tried.**

tri·er /traɪə/ **triers.** If you say that someone is a **tri-** N-COUNT PRAGMATICS **er,** you approve of them because they try very hard BRITISH at things that they do, although they are not often successful.

tri·fle /'traɪfəl/ **trifles, trifling, trifled. 1** You can ◆◇◇◇◇ PHRASE use **a trifle** to mean slightly or to a small extent, especially in order make something you say seem less extreme. *His uniform made him look a trifle out of place.* **2** A **trifle** is something that is considered to N-COUNT have little importance, value, or significance. *Believe me, it's the least I can do, a mere trifle.* **3** **Trifle** is a cold British dessert made of layers of N-VAR sponge cake, jelly, fruit, and custard, and usually covered with cream.

trifle with. If you say that someone is not a person to PHRASAL VB **be trifled with,** you are indicating to other people that V P n they must treat that person with respect. *No man in Tabriz trifled with the executioner.*

tri·fling /'traɪfəlɪŋ/. A **trifling** matter is small and ADJ-GRADED unimportant. *Outside California these difficulties may seem fairly trifling.*

trig·ger /'trɪgə/ **triggers, triggering, triggered.** ◆◆◆◇◇ **1** The **trigger** of a gun is a small lever which you N-COUNT pull to fire it. **2** The **trigger** of a bomb is the device N-COUNT which causes it to explode. **3** To **trigger** a bomb or VERB system means to cause it to work. *The thieves must* V n *have deliberately triggered the alarm.* **4** If something VERB **triggers** an event or situation, it causes it to begin to V n happen or exist. *...the incident which triggered the outbreak of the First World War.* ▶ **Trigger off** PHRASAL VB V P noun means the same as **trigger.** *It is still not clear what* Also V n P *events triggered off the demonstrations.* **5** If some- N-COUNT thing acts as a **trigger** for another thing such as an illness, event, or situation, the first thing causes the second thing to begin to happen or exist. *Stress may act as a trigger for these illnesses.*

,trigger-'happy. If you describe someone as ADJ-GRADED PRAGMATICS **trigger-happy,** you disapprove of them because INFORMAL they are too ready and willing to use violence and weapons, especially guns. *They were gunned down by members of the trigger-happy National Guard.*

trike /traɪk/ **trikes.** A **trike** is a child's tricycle. *He* N-COUNT INFORMAL *listened from the seat of his trike.*

tril·by /'trɪlbi/ **trilbies.** A **trilby** or a **trilby hat** is a N-COUNT BRITISH man's hat which is made of felt and has a groove along the top from front to back.

trill /trɪl/ **trills, trilling, trilled. 1** If a bird **trills,** it VERB: V sings with short, high-pitched, repeated notes. **2** If VERB: V you say that a woman **trills,** you mean that she talks V with quote or laughs in a high-pitched voice which sounds musical but rather irritating. *'How adorable!' she trills.* **3** A **trill** is the playing of two musical notes repeat- N-COUNT TECHNICAL edly and quickly one after the other.

tril·lion /'trɪljən/ **trillions.** The plural form is **tril-** ◆◆◇◇◇ **lion** after a number, or after a word or expression NUMBER referring to a number, such as 'several' or 'a few'. A **trillion** is the number 1,000,000,000,000. See Appendix headed **Numbers.** *The central bank printed over 2 trillion roubles.*

tril·lionth /'trɪljənθ/ **trillionths.** The **trillionth** item in a series is the one you count as number one trillion. See Appendix headed **Numbers.**

tril·o·gy /'trɪlədʒi/ **trilogies.** A **trilogy** is a series of ◆◇◇◇◇ three books, plays, films, or operas that have the N-COUNT same subject or the same characters.

trim /trɪm/ **trimmer, trimmest; trims, trim-** ◆◆◇◇◇ **ming, trimmed. 1** Something that is **trim** is neat, ADJ-GRADED tidy, and attractive. *The neighbours' gardens were trim and neat.* **2** If you describe someone's figure as ADJ-GRADED **trim**, you mean that it is attractive because there is PRAGMATICS no extra fat on their body. *The driver was a trim young woman of perhaps thirty.* **3** When people are PHRASE **in trim**, they are in good physical condition. *He is already getting in trim for the big day.*
4 If you **trim** something, for example someone's hair, VERB you cut off small amounts of it in order to make it look V n neater and tidier. *Grass shears are specially made to trim grass growing in awkward places.* ► Also a noun. ◆ N-SING *His hair needed a trim.* **5** If a government or other or- VERB ganization **trims** something such as a plan, policy, or V n amount, they reduce it slightly in extent or size. *American companies looked at ways they could trim these costs.*
6 If something such as a piece of clothing **is trimmed** VB: usu with a type of material or design, it is decorated with passive be V-ed with n it, usually along its edges. *...jackets, which are then trimmed with crocheted flowers.* ◆ **-trimmed** ...a COMB *fur-trimmed coat.* **7** The **trim** on something such as a N-VAR piece of clothing is a decoration, for example along its edges, that is in a different colour or material.

trim away or **trim off.** If you **trim away** or **trim off** PHRASAL VB parts of something, you cut them off, because they are V P noun not needed. *Trim the fat off the ham.* V n P
Also V n P

tri·ma·ran /'traɪməræn/ **trimarans.** A trimaran is a N-COUNT fast sailing boat similar to a catamaran, but with three hulls instead of two.

trim·ming /'trɪmɪŋ/ **trimmings. 1** The **trimming** ◆◇◇◇◇ on something such as a piece of clothing is the N-VAR decoration, for example along its edges, that is in a different colour or material. *...the lace trimming on her satin nightgown.* **2 Trimmings** are pieces of N-PLURAL something, usually food, which are left over after you have cut what you need. *Use any pastry trim- mings to decorate the apples.* **3** If you say that some- PHRASE thing comes with **all the trimmings**, you mean that it has many extra things added to it to make it more special. *They were married with all the trimmings, soon after graduation.*

trin·ket /'trɪŋkɪt/ **trinkets.** A trinket is a pretty N-COUNT piece of jewellery or small ornament that is inex- pensive. *She sold trinkets to tourists.*

trio /'triːəʊ/ **trios.** A trio is a group of three people, ◆◆◇◇◇ especially musicians or singers, or a group of three N-COLL- things that have something in common. *...classy* COUNT *American songs from a Texas trio... The trio are part of Sotheby's sale of Works of Art.*

trip /trɪp/ **trips, tripping, tripped. 1** A **trip** is a ◆◆◆◆◇ journey that you make to a place and back again. N-COUNT *On the Thursday we went out on a day trip. ...a busi- ness trip.* ● See also **round trip. 2** A **trip** is an im- N-COUNT aginary experience caused by taking hallucinogenic INFORMAL drugs. *An anxious or depressed person can experi- ence a really bad trip.*
3 If you **trip** when you are walking, you knock your VERB foot against something and fall or nearly fall. *She* V *tripped and fell... The cables are all bright yellow to* V on/over n *prevent you tripping over them.* ► **Trip up** means the PHRASAL VB same as **trip**. *Make sure trailing flexes are kept out of* V P on/over n the way so you don't trip up over them. 4 If you **trip** Also V P someone who is walking, you put your foot or some- VERB: V n thing else in front of them, so that they knock their own foot against it and fall or nearly fall. ► **Trip up** PHRASAL VB means the same as **trip**. *He made a sudden dive for* V n P *Uncle Jim's legs to try to trip him up.* Also be V-ed P

trip up. If someone or something **trips** someone **up** PHRASAL VB or they **trip up**, someone or something causes them ERG: to fail or make a mistake. *He will do all he can* V n P *to trip up the new right-wing government.* ● See also V P noun **trip** 5, 6. Also V P

tri·par·tite /traɪ'pɑːtaɪt/. You can use **tripartite** to ADJ describe something that has three parts or that in- FORMAL volves three groups of people. *...tripartite meetings*

between Government ministers, trades union leaders and industrialists.

tripe /traɪp/. **1 Tripe** is the stomach of a pig, cow, N-UNCOUNT or ox which is eaten as food. **2** You refer to some- N-UNCOUNT thing that someone has said or written as **tripe** INFORMAL when you think that it is silly and worthless. *I've never heard such a load of tripe in all my life.*

tri·ple /'trɪpəl/ **triples, tripling, tripled. 1 Triple** ◆◆◇◇◇ means consisting of three things or parts. *...a triple* ADJ: ADJ n *somersault.* **2** If something **triples** or if you **triple** it, V-ERG: V it becomes three times as large in size or number. V inn *The Exhibition has tripled in size from last year...* V n *The merger puts the firm in a position to triple its earnings.* **3** If something is **triple** the amount or size PREDET of another thing, it is three times as large. *The kitch- en is triple the size it once was.*

'triple jump. The **triple jump** is an athletic event N-SING in which competitors have to jump as far as they can, and are allowed to touch the ground once with each foot in the course of the jump.

tri·plet /'trɪplət/ **triplets. Triplets** are three chil- N-COUNT dren born at the same time to the same mother.

tri·pod /'traɪpɒd/ **tripods.** A **tripod** is a stand with ◆◇◇◇◇ three legs that is used to support something such as N-COUNT a camera or a telescope.

trip·per /'trɪpə/ **trippers.** A **tripper** is a person who N-COUNT is on a trip or on holiday. *...when the shops shut and* INFORMAL, *the trippers go home.* ● See also **day-tripper.** BRITISH

trip·tych /'trɪptɪk/ **triptychs.** A **triptych** is a paint- N-COUNT ing or a carving on three panels that are usually joined together by hinges.

trip·wire /'trɪpwaɪə/ **tripwires; also trip wire.** A N-COUNT **tripwire** is a wire stretched just above the ground, which triggers a trap or an explosion if someone touches it.

trite /traɪt/. If you say that something such as an ADJ-GRADED idea, remark, or story is **trite**, you mean that it is dull and boring because it has been said or told too many times. *The movie is teeming with obvious and trite ideas.*

tri·umph /'traɪʌmf/ **triumphs, triumphing, tri-** ◆◆◆◇◇ **umphed. 1** A **triumph** is a great success or N-VAR achievement, often one that has been gained with a lot of skill or effort. *Cataract operations are a tri- umph of modern surgery.* **2** If someone or some- VERB: V thing **triumphs**, they gain complete success, con- V over n trol, or victory, often after a long or difficult strug- gle. *The whole world looked to her as a symbol of good triumphing over evil.*

tri·um·phal /traɪ'ʌmfəl/. **Triumphal** is used to de- ADJ-GRADED scribe things that are done or made to celebrate a victory or great success. *He made a triumphal entry into the city.*

tri·um·phal·ist /traɪ'ʌmfəlɪst/. **Triumphalist** be- ADJ-GRADED: haviour is behaviour in which politicians or organi- ADJ n zations celebrate a victory or a great success, espe- BRITISH cially when this is intended to upset the people they have defeated. *...a triumphalist celebration of their supremacy.* ◆ **tri·um·phal·ism** *There was a touch* N-UNCOUNT *of triumphalism about the occasion.*

tri·um·phant /traɪ'ʌmfənt/. Someone who is **tri-** ◆◇◇◇◇ **umphant** has gained a victory or succeeded in ADJ-GRADED something and feels very happy about it. *Duncan and his triumphant soldiers celebrate their military victory.* ◆ **tri·um·phant·ly** *They marched trium-* ADV-GRADED: *phantly into the capital.* ADV with v

tri·um·vi·rate /traɪ'ʌmvɪrət/. A **triumvirate** is a N-COLL-SING group of three people who work together, especially FORMAL when they are in charge of something. *...the trium- virate of women who worked together on the TV dramatisation of the novel.*

trivia /'trɪviə/. **1 Trivia** consists of unimportant ◆◇◇◇◇ facts or details that are considered to be amusing N-UNCOUNT rather than serious or useful. *The two men chatted about such trivia as their favourite kinds of fast food.* **2** A **trivia** game or quiz is one where the competitors ADJ: ADJ n are tested on their knowledge of interesting but unim- portant facts on many subjects.

triv·ial /'trɪviəl/. If you describe something as **triv-** ◆◇◇◇◇ **ial**, you think that it is unimportant and not serious. ADJ-GRADED

T

...*trivial details that could be settled later.* ♦ **trivi·al·ity** /ˌtrɪvɪˈælɪti/ **trivialities.** *He accused me of making a great fuss about trivialities.*   N-VAR

trivi·al·ize /ˈtrɪviəlaɪz/ **trivializes, trivializing, trivialized;** also spelled **trivialise** in British English. If you say that someone **trivializes** something important, you disapprove of them because they make it seem less important, serious, and complex than it is. *The business world continues to trivialize the world's environmental problems.*   VERB PRAGMATICS V n

trod /trɒd/. **Trod** is the past tense of **tread.**

trod·den /ˈtrɒdən/. **Trodden** is the past participle of **tread.**

troi·ka /ˈtrɔɪkə/ **troikas.** A group of three powerful politicians or states are sometimes referred to as a **troika.** *The press regard her as merely one of a ruling troika.*   N-COUNT JOURNALISM

Tro·jan horse /ˌtrəʊdʒən ˈhɔːs/ **Trojan horses.** If you describe something or someone as a **Trojan horse,** you mean that they are being used to conceal someone's true purpose or intentions, and you disapprove of this.   N-COUNT PRAGMATICS

troll /trɒl, trəʊl/ **trolls.** In Scandinavian mythology, **trolls** are creatures who look like ugly people.   N-COUNT

trol·ley /ˈtrɒli/ **trolleys.** 1 A **trolley** is an object with wheels that you use to transport heavy things such as shopping or luggage. The American word is **cart.** *...supermarket trolleys.* 2 A **trolley** is a small table on wheels which is used for serving drinks or food. The American word is **wagon.** 3 A **trolley** is an electric vehicle for carrying people which travels on rails in the streets of a town. The British word is **tram.** *He took a northbound trolley on State Street.* 4 If you say that someone is **off their trolley,** you mean that their ideas or behaviour are very strange.   ◆◇◇◇ N-COUNT BRITISH / N-COUNT BRITISH / N-COUNT AMERICAN / PHRASE BRITISH, INFORMAL

trom·bone /trɒmˈbəʊn/ **trombones.** A **trombone** is a large musical instrument of the brass family. It consists of two long oval tubes, one of which can be pushed backwards and forwards to play different notes. See picture headed **musical instruments.** ♦ **trom·bon·ist, trombonists.** A **trombonist** is someone who plays the trombone.   N-VAR / N-COUNT

troop /truːp/ **troops, trooping, trooped.** 1 **Troops** are soldiers, especially when they are in a large organized group and on a particular mission. *...the deployment of more than 35,000 troops from a dozen countries.* 2 A **troop** is a group of soldiers within a cavalry or armoured regiment. 3 A **troop** of scouts or guides is a local group of them that meets regularly. 4 A **troop of** people or animals is a group of them. *Amy was aware of the little troop of travellers watching the two of them.* 5 If people **troop** somewhere, they walk there in a group, often sadly or wearily. *They all trooped back to the house for a rest.*   ◆◆◆◇ N-PLURAL / N-COLL-COUNT / N-COUNT / N-COUNT: N ofn / VERB V adv/prep INFORMAL

troop·er /ˈtruːpə/ **troopers.** 1 A **trooper** is a soldier of low rank in the cavalry or in an armoured regiment in the army. 2 In the United States, a **trooper** is a police officer in a state police force. 3 See also **storm trooper.**   ◆◇◇◇ N-COUNT; N-TITLE / N-COUNT

tro·phy /ˈtrəʊfi/ **trophies.** 1 A **trophy** is a prize, for example a silver cup or shield, that is given to the winner of a competition or race. 2 **Trophy** is used in the names of some competitions and races in which the winner receives a trophy. *He finished third in the Tote Gold Trophy.* 3 A **trophy** is something that you keep in order to show that you have done something very difficult. *His office was lined with animal heads, trophies of his hunting hobby.*   ◆◆◇◇ N-COUNT / N-COUNT

tropi·cal /ˈtrɒpɪkəl/. 1 **Tropical** means belonging to or typical of the tropics. *...tropical diseases. ...a plan to preserve the world's tropical forests.* 2 **Tropical** weather is hot and humid weather that people believe to be typical of the tropics.   ◆◆◇◇ ADJ: ADJ n / ADJ-GRADED

trop·ics /ˈtrɒpɪks/. **The tropics** are the parts of the world that lie between the tropic of Cancer and the tropic of Capricorn.   ◆◇◇◇ N-PLURAL: the N

trot /trɒt/ **trots, trotting, trotted.** 1 If you **trot** somewhere, you move fairly fast at a speed between walking and running, taking small quick steps. *He* was almost trotting, and the supermarket bag flapped against his trouser leg. ▶ Also a noun. *He walked briskly, but without breaking into a trot.* 2 When an animal such as a horse **trots,** it moves fairly fast, taking quick small steps. *Pete got on his horse and started trotting across the field.* ▶ Also a noun. *The horse broke into a brisk trot.* 3 If something happens several times **on the trot,** it happens that number of times without a break. *She lost five games on the trot.*   VERB: V prep/adv V / VERB: V / V prep/adv / N-SING / PHRASE INFORMAL

trot out. If you say that a person **trots out** old ideas or information, you are criticizing him or her for repeating them in a way that is not new or interesting. *It made a good anecdote to trot out at cocktail parties.*   PHRASAL VB PRAGMATICS V P noun Also V n P INFORMAL

Trot·sky·ist /ˈtrɒtskiɪst/ **Trotskyists.** A **Trotskyist** is someone who supports the revolutionary left-wing ideas of Trotsky.   N-COUNT

trot·ter /ˈtrɒtə/ **trotters.** 1 **Trotters** are pig's feet which you can cook and eat. 2 A **trotter** is a horse that has been trained to trot fast and to pull a carriage in races.   N-COUNT BRITISH / N-COUNT

trou·ba·dour /ˈtruːbədɔː/ **troubadours.** 1 **Troubadours** were poets and singers who used to travel around and perform to noble families in Italy and France in the twelfth and thirteenth centuries. 2 People sometimes refer to popular singers as **troubadours,** especially when the words of their songs are an important part of their music.   N-COUNT / N-COUNT

trou·ble /ˈtrʌbəl/ **troubles, troubling, troubled.** 1 You can refer to problems or difficulties as **trouble.** *I had trouble parking... The plane developed engine trouble soon after taking off. ...financial troubles.* 2 If you say that one aspect of a situation is the **trouble,** you mean that it is the aspect which is causing problems. *The trouble is that these restrictions have remained.* 3 If you say that someone or something is **more trouble than they are worth,** you mean that they cause you a lot of problems or take a lot of time and effort and you do not achieve or gain very much in return. 4 If you tell someone that it is no **trouble** to do something for them, you are saying politely that you can or will do it, because it is easy or convenient for you. 5 Your **troubles** are the things that you are worried about. 6 If something **troubles** you, it makes you feel rather worried. ♦ **trou·bling** *But most troubling of all was the simple fact that nobody knew what was going on.* 7 If you have kidney **trouble** or back **trouble,** for example, there is something wrong with your kidneys or your back. 8 If a part of your body **troubles** you, it causes you physical pain or discomfort. 9 If there is **trouble** somewhere, especially in a public place, there is fighting or rioting there. *...fans who make trouble during the World Cup.* 10 If someone is **in trouble,** they are in a situation in which someone in authority is angry with them or is likely to punish them because they have done something which they shouldn't have done. 11 If you say that someone does not **trouble** to do something or does not **trouble** himself or herself to do something, you are critical of them because they do not do something that they should do, and that you think would require very little effort. *He hadn't troubled himself to check his mirrors.* 12 If you **take the trouble** to do something, you do something which requires a small amount of additional effort. *It is worth taking the trouble to sieve the fruit by hand.* 13 You use **trouble** in expressions such as **I'm sorry to trouble you** when you are apologizing to someone for disturbing them in order to ask them something. *I hate to trouble you, but Aunt Lina's birthday is coming up and I would like to buy something nice for her.*   ◆◆◆◇ N-UNCOUNT / N-SING / PHRASE / N-UNCOUNT: with brd-neg PRAGMATICS / N-PLURAL / VERB: V n / ADJ-GRADED / N-UNCOUNT: n N, N with n / N-UNCOUNT: VERB: V n / N-UNCOUNT: also N in pl / PHRASE / VB: with brd-neg, V to-inf PRAGMATICS V pron-refl to-inf / PHRASE / VERB PRAGMATICS V n

trou·bled /ˈtrʌbəld/. 1 Someone who is **troubled** is worried because they have problems. 2 A **troubled** place, situation, organization, or time has many problems or conflicts. 3 ● to **pour oil on troubled waters:** see **oil.**   ◆◆◇◇ ADJ-GRADED / ADJ-GRADED

trouble-'free. Something that is **trouble-free** does not cause any problems or difficulties. *The carnival got off to a virtually trouble-free start.*   ADJ-GRADED

trouble·maker /ˈtrʌbəlmeɪkə/ **troublemakers.** If N-COUNT
you refer to someone as a **troublemaker**, you mean
that they cause unpleasantness, quarrels, or fights,
especially by encouraging people to rebel against
authority.

trouble·shooting /ˈtrʌbəlʃuːtɪŋ/. **Troubleshooting** N-UNCOUNT
is the activity or process of solving major problems
or difficulties that occur in a company or government. ♦ **trouble·shooter, troubleshooters.** N-COUNT

trou·ble·some /ˈtrʌbəlsəm/. **1** You use **trouble-** ♦◇◇◇◇
some to describe something or someone that ADJ-GRADED
causes annoying problems or difficulties. ...*a troublesome back injury.* **2** A **troublesome** situation or ADJ-GRADED
issue is full of complicated problems or difficulties.

'trouble spot, trouble spots; also spelled N-COUNT
trouble-spot. A **trouble spot** is a country or an area
of a country where there is repeated fighting between two or more groups of people.

trough /trɒf, AM trɔːf/ **troughs. 1** A **trough** is a ♦◇◇◇◇
long narrow container from which farm animals N-COUNT
drink or eat. **2** A **trough** is a low area between two N-COUNT
big waves on the sea. **3** A **trough** is a low point in a N-COUNT
pattern that has regular high and low points, for example a period of low productivity in business.
*American bank shares have risen by 60% since their
trough last October.*

trounce /traʊns/ **trounces, trouncing,** VERB: V n
trounced. If you **trounce** someone in a competi- INFORMAL
tion or contest, you defeat them easily.

troupe /truːp/ **troupes.** A **troupe** is a group of ac- ♦◇◇◇◇
tors, singers, or dancers who work together and of- N-COLL-
ten travel around together, performing in different COUNT
places.

troup·er /ˈtruːpə/ **troupers.** You can refer to an ac- N-COUNT
tor or other performer as a **trouper**, especially when
you want to suggest that they have a lot of experience and can deal with difficult situations in a professional way.

trou·sers /ˈtraʊzəz/; the form **trouser** is used as a ♦♦◇◇◇
modifier. **Trousers** are a piece of clothing that you N-PLURAL
wear over your body from the waist downwards, BRITISH
and that cover each leg separately. The usual
American word is **pants**. ● see picture headed
clothes. ♦ **-trousered** *I smoothed his khaki-* COMB
trousered leg. ● to **wear the trousers**: see **wear**.

'trouser suit, trouser suits. A **trouser suit** is a N-COUNT
woman's outfit consisting of a pair of trousers and a BRITISH
jacket which are made from the same material. The
usual American term is **pant suit**.

trous·seau /ˈtruːsəʊ/ **trousseaux.** A **trousseau** is N-COUNT
a collection of clothes, linen, and other possessions DATED
that a bride uses for her marriage.

trout /traʊt/ **trouts.** The plural can be either **trout** ♦◇◇◇◇
or **trouts**. A **trout** is a fairly large fish that lives in N-VAR
rivers and streams. ► **Trout** is this fish eaten as N-UNCOUNT
food.

trove /trəʊv/. See **treasure trove**.

trow·el /ˈtraʊəl/ **trowels. 1** A **trowel** is a garden N-COUNT
tool that is rather like a small rounded spade. You
hold it in one hand and use it for digging small
holes or removing weeds. ● see picture headed **tools**.
2 A **trowel** is a small tool with a flat blade that you N-COUNT
use for spreading things such as cement and plaster
onto surfaces.

tru·ant /ˈtruːənt/ **truants. 1** A **truant** is a pupil who N-COUNT
stays away from school without permission. **2** If a PHRASE
pupil **plays truant**, he or she stays away from
school without permission. ♦ **tru·an·cy** /ˈtruːənsi/. N-UNCOUNT
...*the level of truancy at schools.*

truce /truːs/ **truces.** A **truce** is an agreement be- ♦♦◇◇◇
tween two people or groups of people to stop fight- N-COUNT
ing or quarrelling for a short time.

truck /trʌk/ **trucks, trucking, trucked. 1** A ♦♦♦◇◇
truck is a large vehicle that is used to transport N-COUNT
goods by road; the usual British word is **lorry**. **2** A AMERICAN
truck is an open vehicle used for carrying goods on N-COUNT
a railway. **3** When something or someone **is** BRITISH
trucked somewhere, they are driven there in a lorry. VERB
The liquor was sold legally and trucked out of the be V-ed
state. **4** If you say that you will **have no truck with** prep/adv
                                                                PHRASE

someone or something, you are refusing to be involved with them in any way. *He would have no
truck with deceit.*

truck·er /ˈtrʌkə/ **truckers.** A **trucker** is someone ♦◇◇◇◇
who drives a truck as their job; the usual British N-COUNT
term is **lorry driver**. AMERICAN

truck·ing /ˈtrʌkɪŋ/. **Trucking** is the activity of N-UNCOUNT
transporting goods from one place to another using AMERICAN
trucks; the usual British word is **haulage**.

truck·load /ˈtrʌkləʊd/ **truckloads;** also spelled N-COUNT
truck load. A **truckload** of goods or people is the
amount of them that a truck can carry.

trucu·lent /ˈtrʌkjʊlənt/. If you say that someone is ADJ-GRADED
truculent, you mean that they are bad-tempered
and aggressive. ♦ **trucu·lence** /ˈtrʌkjʊləns/. *'Your* N-UNCOUNT
*secretary said you'd be wanting a cleaner,' she an-
nounced with her usual truculence.*

trudge /trʌdʒ/ **trudges, trudging, trudged.** If ♦◇◇◇◇
you **trudge** somewhere, you walk there slowly and VERB:
with heavy steps, especially because you are tired or V prep/adv
unhappy. ► Also a noun. ...*the long trudge home.* N-SING

true /truː/ **truer, truest. 1** If something is **true**, it ♦♦♦♦◇
is based on facts rather than being invented or im- ADJ-GRADED
agined, and is accurate and reliable. *He said it was
true that a collision had happened... The film tells
the true story of a group who survived in the Andes
in sub-zero temperatures.* **2** If a dream, wish, or pre- PHRASE
diction **comes true**, it actually happens. *Owning a
place of their own is a dream come true for the cou-
ple.* **3** If a general statement **holds true** in particular PHRASE
circumstances, or if your previous statement **holds** FORMAL
true in different circumstances, it is true or valid in
those circumstances. *This law is known to hold true
for galaxies at a distance of at least several billion
light years.* **4** If you say that something seems **too** PHRASE
good to be true, you are suspicious of it because it
seems better than you had expected, and you think
there may something wrong with it that you have
not noticed.
5 You use **true** to emphasize that something or some- ADJ: ADJ n
one is genuine or sincere, often in contrast to some- PRAGMATICS
thing that is pretended or hidden. *The true cost often
differs from that which had first been projected.* **6** If ADJ: ADJ n
you use **true** to describe something or someone, you PRAGMATICS
approve of them because they have all the characteristics or qualities that such a person or thing typically
has. *This country professes to be a true democracy.* **7** If ADJ-GRADED:
you say that a fact is **true** of a particular person or v-link ADJ of/
situation, you mean that it is valid or relevant for for n
them. *Expenditure on health in most of these countries
has gone down, and the same is true for education.*
8 You can use **true** in order to admit that a fact or ADJ-GRADED
opinion is real or valid before indicating that you PRAGMATICS
think that it is not important or relevant in the circumstances. *It's true she gets madly impatient with
him, but what mother doesn't?... 'Things are a bit different in my country.' 'True, true, but we're not in your
country, are we?'*
9 If you are **true to** someone, you remain committed ADJ:
and loyal to them. If you are **true to** an idea or prom- v-link ADJ to n
ise, you remain committed to it and continue to act
according to it. *David was true to his wife... India has
remained true to democracy.* **10** If you say that some- PHRASE
thing such as a story or a film is **true to life**, you ap- PRAGMATICS
prove of it because it seems real. **11** ● **true colours**:
see **colour**. ● **true to form**: see **form**. ● **ring true**: see
ring. ● **tried and true**: see **tried**.

,true-'blue; also spelled **true blue**. If you describe ADJ
someone as **true-blue**, you mean that they are
right-wing in their ideas and opinions.

truf·fle /ˈtrʌfəl/ **truffles. 1** A **truffle** is a soft round ♦◇◇◇◇
sweet made with chocolate and usually flavoured N-COUNT
with rum. **2** A **truffle** is a round mushroom-like fun- N-COUNT
gus which is expensive and very good to eat.

tru·ism /ˈtruːɪzəm/ **truisms.** A **truism** is a state- N-COUNT
ment that is generally accepted as obviously true
and is repeated so often that it has become boring.

tru·ly /ˈtruːli/. **1** You use **truly** to emphasize that ♦♦♦◇◇
something has all the features or qualities of a par- ADV
ticular thing, or is the case to the fullest possible

extent. ...*a truly democratic system... Not all doctors truly understand the reproductive cycle.* **2** You can use **truly** in order to emphasize your description of something. *They were truly appalling.* **3** You use **truly** to emphasize that feelings are genuine and sincere. *Believe me, Susan, I am truly sorry.* **4** You can use **truly** in order to emphasize that what you are saying is true. *I do not expect a war between my country and yours. Truly I do not.* **5** ● **well and truly:** see **well**.

6 You write **Yours truly** before your signature at the end of a letter to someone you do not know very well. *CONVENTION*

7 You can say **yours truly** as a humorous way of referring to yourself. *Yours truly was awoken by a shout!* *PHRASE INFORMAL*

trump /trʌmp/ **trumps, trumping, trumped.** *◆◇◇◇◇*
1 In a game of cards, **trumps** is the suit which is chosen to have the highest value in one particular game. **2** If you **trump** something that someone has said or done, you beat it by saying or doing something else that seems better. *The Hong Kong and Shanghai Bank has trumped Lloyds by raising its offer.* **3** Your **trump card** is something powerful that you can use or do, which gives you an advantage over someone. *Mr Amato's trump card is his colleagues' fear of an early election.* **4** If you say that someone **came up trumps,** you mean that they did something successfully, often when they were not expected to. *N-COLL-UNCOUNT* *VERB V n* *PHRASE* *PHRASE BRITISH*

trumped-'up. **Trumped-up** charges are untrue, and made up in order to punish someone unfairly. *ADJ*

trum·pet /ˈtrʌmpɪt/ **trumpets, trumpeting, trumpeted.** **1** A **trumpet** is a musical instrument of the brass family which plays quite high notes. See picture headed **musical instruments.** ♦ **trum·pet·er, trumpeters.** A **trumpeter** is someone who plays a trumpet. **2** If someone **trumpets** something that they are proud of or that they think is important, they speak about it publicly in a very forceful way. *The Conservative government has been trumpeting tourism as a growth industry... Nobody should be trumpeting about chemical weapons. ...the much trumpeted 'tax cuts' in the 1980s.* **3** If you **blow** your own **trumpet,** you boast about yourself. *N-VAR* *N-COUNT* *VERB V n as n V about n V-ed Also V n* *PHRASE*

trun·cat·ed /trʌŋˈkeɪtɪd, AM ˈtrʌŋkeɪtɪd/. A **truncated** version of something has been shortened. *ADJ-GRADED*

trun·cheon /ˈtrʌntʃən/ **truncheons.** A **truncheon** is a short thick stick that is carried as a weapon by policemen in Britain. *N-COUNT*

trun·dle /ˈtrʌndəl/ **trundles, trundling, trundled.** **1** If a vehicle **trundles** somewhere, it moves there slowly, often with difficulty or an irregular movement. *The train eventually trundled in at 7.54.* **2** If you **trundle** something somewhere, especially a small heavy object with wheels, you move or roll it along slowly. *The old man lifted the barrow and trundled it away.* **3** If you say that someone **is trundling,** you mean that they are walking slowly, often in a tired way or with heavy steps. *Girls trundle in, a book bag on one shoulder, a diaper bag on the other.* *◆◇◇◇◇ VERB V prep/adv* *VERB V n adv/prep* *VERB V adv/prep*

trunk /trʌŋk/ **trunks.** **1** The **trunk** of a tree is the large main stem from which the branches grow. **2** A **trunk** is a large strong case or box used for storing things or for taking on a journey. **3** An elephant's **trunk** is its very long nose that it uses to lift food and water to its mouth. **4** The **trunk** of a car is a covered space at the back or front in which you put luggage or other things. The usual British word is **boot.** See picture headed **car and bicycle.** **5** **Trunks** are shorts that a man wears when he goes swimming. **6** Your **trunk** is the central part of your body, from your neck to your waist. *◆◇◇◇◇ N-COUNT N-COUNT* *N-COUNT* *N-COUNT* *N-COUNT AMERICAN* *N-PLURAL* *N-COUNT FORMAL*

'trunk road, trunk roads. A **trunk road** is a major road that has been specially built for travelling long distances. A trunk road is not as wide or as fast as a motorway. *N-COUNT BRITISH*

truss /trʌs/ **trusses, trussing, trussed.** **1** To **truss** someone means to tie them up very tightly so that they cannot move. ▶ **Truss up** means the same as **truss.** *She was trussed up with yellow nylon rope.* **2** A **truss** is a special belt with a pad that a man *VERB: V n WRITTEN* *PHRASAL VB: usu passive be V-ed* *N-COUNT*

---

wears when he has a hernia in order to prevent it from getting worse.

trust /trʌst/ **trusts, trusting, trusted.** **1** If you **trust** someone, you believe that they are honest and sincere and will not deliberately do anything to harm you. *The president can't be trusted.* ♦ **trust·ed** *...her most trusted advisers.* **2** If you **trust in** someone or something, you believe strongly in them, and do not doubt their powers or their good intentions. *Don't blindly trust in the good faith of any government official.* **3** Your **trust** in someone is your belief that they are honest and sincere and will not deliberately do anything to harm you. *You've betrayed their trust... There's a feeling of warmth and trust here.* *♦♦♦◇ be V-ed* *ADJ-GRADED ADJ n VERB V in n FORMAL* *N-UNCOUNT*

4 If you **trust** someone to do something, you believe that they will do it. **5** If you **trust** someone **with** something important or valuable, you allow them to look after it or deal with it. *I'd trust him with my life.* ▶ Also a noun. *She was organizing and running a large household, a position of trust which was generously paid.* **6** If you **trust** someone's judgement or advice, you believe that it is good or right. **7** If you do not **trust** something, you feel that it is not safe or reliable. *He didn't trust his legs to hold him up... I still can't trust myself to remain composed in their presence.* *VERB: V n to-inf VERB V n with n N-UNCOUNT: also a N* *VERB: V n VERB V n to-inf V pron-refl to-inf*

8 If you say you **trust that** something is true, you mean you hope and expect that it is true. *I trust you will take the earliest opportunity to make a full apology.* **9** If you **take** something **on trust** after having heard or read it, you believe it completely without checking it. *VERB V that FORMAL* *PHRASE*

10 A **trust** is a financial arrangement in which a group of people or an organization keeps and invests money for someone. *The money will be put in trust until she is 18.* **11** A **trust** is a group of people or an organization that has control of an amount of money or property and invests it on behalf of other people or as a charity. *...The National Childbirth Trust.* **12** In Britain, a **trust** or a **trust hospital** is a public hospital that receives its funding directly from the national government. It has its own board of governors and is not controlled by the local health authority. **13** If something valuable is kept **in trust,** it is held and protected by a group of people or an organization on behalf of other people. **14** ● **tried and trusted:** see **tried.** See also **trusting; unit trust.** *N-COUNT: also in N* *N-COUNT: supp N* *N-COUNT: supp N, N n* *PHRASE*

trust to. If you **trust to** luck or instinct, you hope that it will enable you to achieve what you are trying to do, because you have nothing else to help you. *PHRASAL VB V P n, no passive*

trus·tee /trʌˈstiː/ **trustees.** A **trustee** is someone with legal control of money or property that is kept or invested for another person or organization. *♦♦◇◇ N-COUNT*

'trust fund, trust funds. A **trust fund** is an amount of money or property that someone owns, usually after inheriting it, but which is kept and invested for them. *◆◇◇◇ N-COUNT*

trust·ing /ˈtrʌstɪŋ/. A **trusting** person believes that people are honest and sincere and do not intend to harm him or her. *♦◇◇◇ ADJ-GRADED*

trust·worthy /ˈtrʌstwɜːði/. A **trustworthy** person is reliable, responsible, and can be trusted completely. ♦ **trust·worthi·ness** *He wrote a reference for him, describing his reliability and trustworthiness as 'above questioning'.* *♦◇◇◇ ADJ-GRADED N-UNCOUNT*

trusty /ˈtrʌsti/. **Trusty** things, animals, or people are reliable. *ADJ-GRADED: ADJ n*

truth /truːθ/ **truths.** **1** The **truth** about something is all the facts about it, rather than things that are imagined or invented. *The truth of the matter is that we had no other choice... In the town very few know the whole truth.* **2** If you say that there is some **truth** in a statement or story, you mean that it is true, or at least partly true. *Is there any truth to the rumors?... The criticisms have at least an element of truth and validity.* **3** A **truth** is something that is believed to be true. *It is an almost universal truth that the more we are promoted in a job, the less we actually exercise the skills we initially used to perform it.* **4** See also **home truth, moment of truth.** *♦♦♦◇ N-UNCOUNT* *N-UNCOUNT* *N-COUNT*

5 You say **in truth** in order to indicate that you are giving your honest opinion about something. *In truth, we were both unhappy.* **6** You say **to tell you the truth** or **truth to tell** in order to indicate that you are telling someone something in an open and honest way, without trying to hide anything. *Truth to tell, John did not want Veronica at his wedding.* PHRASE

truth·ful /ˈtruːθʊl/. If a person or their comments are **truthful**, they are honest and do not tell any lies. ♦ **truth·ful·ly** *I answered all their questions truthfully.* ♦ **truth·ful·ness** *I can say, with absolute truthfulness, that I did not injure her.* ◆◇◇◇◇ ADJ-GRADED ADV-GRADED ADV with V N-UNCOUNT

try /traɪ/ **tries, trying, tried. 1** If you **try to do** something, you want to do it, and you take action which you hope will help you to do it. *Does it annoy you if others do things less well than you would, or don't seem to try hard enough?... I tried calling him when I got here but he wasn't at home... No matter how bad you feel, keep trying.* ▶ Also a noun. *After a few tries Patrick had given up.* **2** To **try** and do something means to try to do it. *I must try and see him.* **3** If you say that something fails but not **for want of trying**, you mean that everything possible was done to make it succeed. *Not all is perfect, but it isn't for want of trying.* **4** If you **try for** something, you make an effort to get it or achieve it. *My partner and I have been trying for a baby for two years.* ◆◆◆◆ VERB: V to-inf V adv V -ing V N-COUNT VERB V and inf PHRASE VERB V for n

5 If you **try** something new or different, you use it, do it, or experience it in order to discover its qualities or effects. *It's best not to try a new recipe for the first time on such an important occasion.* ▶ Also a noun. *If you're still sceptical about exercising, we can only ask you to trust us and give it a try.* **6** If you **try** a particular place or person, you go to that place or person because you think they may be able to provide you with what you want. *Have you tried the local music shops?* **7** If you **try** a door or window, you try to open it. **8** When a person **is tried**, he or she has to appear in a law court and is found innocent or guilty after the judge and jury have heard the evidence. When a legal case **is tried**, it is considered in a court of law. *He suggested that those responsible should be tried for crimes against humanity... Why does it take 253 days to try a case of fraud?* **9** In the game of rugby, a **try** is the action of scoring by putting the ball down behind the goal line of the opposing team. **10** See also **tried, trying.** ● to **try** your **best**: see **best**. ● to **try** your **hand**: see **hand**. ● to **try** your **luck**: see **luck**. ● to **try** someone's **patience**: see **patience.** VERB V n Also V -ing N-COUNT VERB V n VERB: V n VERB: be V-ed be V-ed for n V n N-COUNT

try on. 1 If you **try on** a piece of clothing, you put it on to see if it fits you or if it looks nice. *Try on clothing and shoes to make sure they fit.* **2** If someone **is trying it on**, they are trying to obtain something or to impress someone, often in a slightly dishonest way or without much hope of success. PHRASAL VB V P noun Also V n P V it P INFORMAL, BRITISH

try out. If you **try** something **out**, you test it in order to find out how useful or effective it is or what it is like. *London Transport hopes to try out the system in September.* PHRASAL VB V n P V P noun

try out for. If you **try out for** a sports team or an acting role, you compete or audition in an attempt to be chosen for it. PHRASAL VB V P P n AMERICAN

try·ing /ˈtraɪɪŋ/. If you describe something or someone as **trying**, you mean that they are difficult to deal with and make you feel impatient or annoyed. *Support from those closest to you is vital in these trying times.* ● See also **try.** ◆◇◇◇◇ ADJ-GRADED

try·out /ˈtraɪaʊt/ **tryouts;** also spelled **try-out.** If an athlete or a performer is given a **tryout**, they are given a test or an audition. N-COUNT

tryst /trɪst/ **trysts.** A **tryst** is a meeting between lovers in a quiet secret place. N-COUNT LITERARY

tsar /zɑː/ **tsars;** also spelled **czar.** In former times, the **tsar** was the king of Russia. ◆◇◇◇◇ N-COUNT; N-TITLE

tsa·ri·na /zɑːˈriːnə/ **tsarinas;** also spelled **czarina.** In former times, a **tsarina** was the queen of Russia or the wife of the tsar. N-COUNT; N-TITLE

tsar·ist /ˈzɑːrɪst/; also spelled **czarist. Tsarist** means belonging to or supporting the system of government by a tsar, especially in Russia before 1917. ADJ

tset·se fly /ˈtsetsi flaɪ/ **tsetse flies.** A **tsetse fly** or a **tsetse** is an African fly that feeds on blood and can cause serious diseases in the people and animals that it bites. N-COUNT

'T-shirt, T-shirts; also spelled **tee-shirt.** A **T-shirt** is a cotton shirt with no collar or buttons. T-shirts usually have short sleeves. See picture headed **clothes.** ◆◆◇◇◇ N-COUNT

tsp., tsps. In a recipe, **tsp.** is a written abbreviation for **teaspoon.**

tub /tʌb/ **tubs. 1** A **tub** is a deep container of any size. ▶ A **tub of** something is the amount of it contained in a tub. *She would eat four tubs of ice cream in one sitting.* **2** A **tub** is the same as a **bathtub.** **3** See also **hot tub.** ◆◇◇◇◇ N-COUNT N-COUNT: N of n N-COUNT AMERICAN

tuba /ˈtjuːbə, AM ˈtuː-/ **tubas.** A **tuba** is a large musical instrument of the brass family which produces very low notes. See picture headed **musical instruments.** N-VAR

tub·by /ˈtʌbi/ **tubbier, tubbiest.** If you describe someone as **tubby**, you mean that they are rather fat. ADJ-GRADED INFORMAL

tube /tjuːb, AM tuːb/ **tubes. 1** A **tube** is a long hollow object that is usually round, like a pipe. *He is fed by a tube that enters his nose.* **2** A **tube** of something such as paste is a long thin container which you squeeze in to order to force the paste out. *...a tube of toothpaste.* **3** Some long, thin, hollow parts in your body are referred to as **tubes.** *The lungs are in fact constructed of thousands of tiny tubes.* **4 The tube** is the underground railway system in London. *I took the tube then the train and came straight here... He travelled by tube.* **5** You can refer to the television as **the tube;** the British word is **the box.** *The only baseball he saw was on the tube.* **6** If a business, economy, or institution **goes down the tubes** or **goes down the tube,** it fails or collapses completely. **7** See also **bronchial tube, cathode-ray tube, fallopian tube, inner tube, test tube.** ◆◆◇◇◇ N-COUNT N-COUNT N-COUNT N-SING the N, also by N N-COUNT: the N AMERICAN, INFORMAL PHRASE

tu·ber /ˈtjuːbə, AM ˈtuː-/ **tubers.** A **tuber** is the swollen underground stem of particular types of plants. ◆◇◇◇◇ N-COUNT

tu·ber·cu·lar /tjuːˈbɜːkjʊlə, AM tuː-/. **Tubercular** means suffering from, relating to, or causing tuberculosis. *...tubercular bacteria.* ADJ

tu·ber·cu·lo·sis /tjuːˌbɜːkjʊˈləʊsɪs, AM tuː-/. **Tuberculosis** is a serious infectious disease that affects someone's lungs and other parts of their body. The abbreviation 'TB' is also used. ◆◇◇◇◇ N-UNCOUNT

tub·ing /ˈtjuːbɪŋ, AM ˈtuː-/. **Tubing** is plastic, rubber, or another material in the shape of a tube. ◆◇◇◇◇ N-UNCOUNT

tubu·lar /ˈtjuːbjʊlə, AM ˈtuː-/. Something that is **tubular** is long, round, and hollow in shape, like a tube. ◆◇◇◇◇ ADJ

tuck /tʌk/ **tucks, tucking, tucked. 1** If you **tuck** something somewhere, you put it there so that it is safe, comfortable, or neat. *He tried to tuck his flapping shirt inside his trousers... She found a rose tucked under the windscreen wiper of her car.* **2 Tuck** is food that children eat as a snack at school. *...the school tuck shop.* **3** You can use **tuck** to refer to a form of plastic surgery which involves reducing the size of a part of someone's body. *She'd undergone 13 operations, including a tummy tuck.* ◆◆◇◇◇ VERB V n prep V-ed N-UNCOUNT BRITISH, INFORMAL N-COUNT

tuck away. 1 If you **tuck away** something such as money, you store it in a safe place. *I tucked the box away in that bottom drawer.* **2** If someone or something **is tucked away,** they are well hidden in a quiet place where very few people go. PHRASAL VB V P noun V n P usu passive

tuck in. 1 If you **tuck in** a piece of material, you secure it in position by placing the edge of it behind or under something else. For example, if you **tuck in** your shirt, you place the bottom part of it inside your trousers. *Tuck the sheets in firmly.* **2** If you **tuck** a child **in** bed or **tuck** them **in,** you make them comfortable by straightening the sheets and blankets and pushing the loose ends under the mattress. *I read Lili a story and tucked her in her own bed.* PHRASAL VB V P noun V n P V n P V n P n

tuck into or **tuck in.** If someone **tucks into** a meal or **tucks in,** they start eating enthusiastically or hun- PHRASAL VB V P n V P

grily. *She tucked into a breakfast of bacon and eggs...* BRITISH
Tuck in, it's the last hot food you'll get for a while.

tuck up. If you **tuck** a child **up** in bed, you tuck them PHRASAL VB
in. *He mostly stayed at home tucking up the children...* V n P
She had gone to work believing Helen was safely V P noun
tucked up in bed. V-ed P
BRITISH

Tues.; also spelled **Tue..** Tues. or Tue. is a written ◆◆◇◇◇
abbreviation for **Tuesday.**

Tues·day /'tjuːzdeɪ, -di, AM 'tuːz-/ **Tuesdays.** ◆◆◆◇
Tuesday is the day after Monday and before N-VAR
Wednesday. *Talks are likely to start next Tuesday.*

tuft /tʌft/ **tufts.** A **tuft** of something such as hair or N-COUNT
grass is a small section of it which has strands that
grow closely together or that are held together at
the bottom. *He had a small tuft of hair on his chin.*
♦ **tuft·ed.** Something that is **tufted** has a tuft or ADJ
tufts on it.

tug /tʌg/ **tugs, tugging, tugged. 1** If you **tug** ◆◆◇◇◇
something or **tug** at it, you give it a quick and VERB: V n
usually strong pull. *A little boy came running up and* V at n
tugged at his sleeve excitedly. ▶ Also a noun. *Bobby* N-COUNT
gave her hair a tug. **2** A **tug** or a **tug boat** is a small N-COUNT
powerful boat which pulls large ships, usually when
they come into a port.

tug-of-'love. A **Tug-of-love** is used to refer to a N-SING
situation in which the parents of a child are di- JOURNALISM
vorced and the parent who does not have custody
tries to get the child, for example by kidnapping it.

tug-of-'war; also spelled **tug of**
war. 1 A **tug-of-war** is a sports event in which two N-VAR
teams test their strength by pulling against each
other on opposite ends of a rope. **2** You can use N-VAR
tug-of-war to refer to a situation in which two people or groups both want the same thing and are
fairly equally matched in their struggle to get it.
...the tug of war between government departments.

tui·tion /tjuˈɪʃən, AM tuˈ-/. **1** If you are given **tui-** ◆◇◇◇◇
tion in a particular subject, you are taught about N-UNCOUNT
that subject. *...personal tuition in all types of out-*
door photography. **2** You can use **tuition** to refer to N-UNCOUNT
the amount of money that you have to pay for being
taught particular subjects, especially in a university
or college. *Angela's $7,000 tuition at University this*
year will be paid for with scholarships.

tu·lip /'tjuːlɪp, AM 'tuː-/ **tulips.** Tulips are flowers ◆◇◇◇◇
that grow in the spring, and have a lot of oval or N-COUNT
pointed petals packed closely together.

tulle /tjuːl, AM tuːl/. **Tulle** is a soft nylon or silk N-UNCOUNT
cloth similar to net.

tum /tʌm/ **tums.** Your **tum** is your stomach. *I've got* N-COUNT
a sore tum! INFORMAL,
BRITISH

tum·ble /'tʌmbəl/ **tumbles, tumbling, tumbled.** ◆◆◇◇◇
1 If someone or something **tumbles** somewhere, VERB
they fall there with a rolling or bouncing movement. V prep/adv
...the gun tumbled out of his hand. ▶ Also a noun. N-COUNT
He injured his ribs in a tumble from his horse. **2** If VERB: V
prices **are tumbling**, they are decreasing rapidly. V by/from/to
House prices have tumbled by almost 30 per cent in amount
real terms since mid-1989. ▶ Also a noun. *Oil prices* N-COUNT
JOURNALISM
took a tumble yesterday. **3** If water **tumbles**, it flows VERB: V
quickly over an uneven surface with a lot of splash- V prep
ing. *Waterfalls crash and tumble over rocks.* **4** If you VERB
say that someone **tumbles** into a situation or place, V into n
you mean that they get into it without being fully in BRITISH
control of themselves or knowing what they are doing. *Many mothers and children tumble into poverty*
after divorce. **5** See also **rough and tumble.**

tumble down. If a building is **tumbling down,** it PHRASAL VB
collapses or parts of it fall off, usually because it is old V P
and neglected.

tumble over. If someone or something **tumbles** PHRASAL VB
over, they fall, often with a rolling or bouncing V P
movement.

tumble-down /'tʌmbəldaʊn/. A **tumbledown** ADJ-GRADED
building is in such a bad condition that it is partly
falling down or has holes in it.

tumble 'dryer, tumble dryers; also spelled N-COUNT
tumble drier. A **tumble dryer** is an electric machine
which dries washing.

tum·bler /'tʌmblə/ **tumblers.** A **tumbler** is a drink- N-COUNT
ing glass with straight sides.

tum·my /'tʌmi/ **tummies.** Your **tummy** is your ◆◇◇◇◇
stomach. *I've got a sore tummy. ...a tummy upset.* N-COUNT
INFORMAL

tu·mour /'tjuːmə, AM 'tuː-/ **tumours;** spelled **tu-** N-COUNT
mor in American English. A **tumour** is a mass of
diseased or abnormal cells that has grown in a person's or animal's body.

tu·mult /'tjuːmʌlt, AM 'tuː-/. **1** A **tumult** is a state of N-SING:
great confusion or excitement. *A tumult of feelings* also no det
inside her fought for supremacy. ♦ **tu·mul·tu·ous** ADJ-GRADED
/tjuːˈmʌltʃuəs, AM tuː-/. *...the tumultuous changes*
in Eastern Europe. **2** A **tumult** is a lot of noise N-SING:
made by a crowd of people. *Round one ends, to a* also no det
tumult of whistles, screams and shouts.
♦ **tumultuous** *Delegates greeted the news with tu-* ADJ
multuous applause.

tuna /'tjuːnə, AM 'tuːnə/ **tunas.** The plural can be ◆◇◇◇◇
either **tuna** or **tunas. Tuna** or **tuna fish** are large N-VAR
fish that live in warm seas and are caught for food.
▶ **Tuna** or **tuna fish** is this fish eaten as food. *...a* N-UNCOUNT
tin of tuna.

tun·dra /'tʌndrə/ **tundras. Tundra** is one of the N-VAR
large flat areas of land in the north of Europe, Asia,
and America. The ground below the top layer of soil
is always frozen and no trees grow there.

tune /tjuːn, AM tuːn/ **tunes, tuning, tuned. 1** A ◆◆◆◇◇
tune is a series of musical notes that is pleasant to N-COUNT
listen to. *...a merry little tune.* **2** You can refer to a N-COUNT
song or a short piece of music as a **tune.** *...your fa-*
vourite pop tunes. **3** When someone **tunes** a musi- VERB: V n
cal instrument, they adjust it so that it produces the
right notes. ▶ **Tune up** means the same as **tune.** PHRASAL VB
Others were quietly tuning up their instruments. V P noun
4 A person or musical instrument that is **in tune** Also V P
produces exactly the right notes but a person or PHRASE
musical instrument that is **out of tune** does not.
5 See also **fine-tune, signature tune.**
6 When an engine or machine is **tuned**, it is adjusted VB: usu
so that it works well. ▶ **Tune up** means the same as passive
tune. *The shop charges up to $500 to tune up a* PHRASAL VB
Porsche. **7** If your radio or television is **tuned** to a par- V P noun
ticular broadcasting station, you are listening to or VB: usu
watching the programmes being broadcast by that passive
station.
8 If you say that a person or organization is **calling the** PHRASE
tune, you mean that they are in a position of power or
control in a particular situation. **9** If you say that PHRASE
someone **has changed** their **tune,** you are criticizing PRAGMATICS
them because they have changed their opinion or way
of doing things. **10** If you say that someone is **dancing** PHRASE
to someone else's **tune,** you mean that they are allow- PRAGMATICS
ing themselves to be controlled by the other person;
used showing disapproval. **11** If you are **in tune with** PHRASE
a group of people, you are in agreement or sympathy
with them but if you are **out of tune with** them, you
are not. **12** To the tune of a particular amount of PHR-PREP
money means to the extent of that amount. *They've*
been sponsoring the World Cup to the tune of a million
and a half pounds.

tune in. 1 If you **tune in** to a particular television or PHRASAL VB
radio station or programme, you watch or listen to it. V P to n
The idea that people plan their radio listening is non- V P
sense; most tune in impulsively. **2** If you **tune in** to V P to n
something such as your own or other people's feel-
ings, you become aware of them.

tune out. If you **tune out,** you stop listening or pay- PHRASAL VB
ing attention to what is being said. *Rose heard the fa-* V P
miliar voice, but tuned out the words. V P noun

tune up. See tune 3, 6. PHRASAL VB

tune·ful /'tjuːnfʊl, AM 'tuːn-/. A piece of music that ADJ-GRADED
is **tuneful** has a pleasant tune.

tune·less /'tjuːnləs, AM 'tuːn-/. **Tuneless** music and ADJ-GRADED
voices do not sound pleasant. ♦ **tune·less·ly** *My* ADV-GRADED:
dad whistled tunelessly. ADV after v

tun·er /'tjuːnə, AM 'tuːn-/ **tuners.** The **tuner** in a N-COUNT
radio or television set is the part which you adjust
to receive the radio signals or television signals at
the right wavelength, so that you can watch or listen
to the programme that you want.

tung·sten /'tʌŋstən/. Tungsten is a greyish-white metal.   N-UNCOUNT

tu·nic /'tjuːnɪk, AM 'tuː-/ **tunics**. A tunic is a sleeveless garment that is worn on the top part of your body.   ◆◇◇◇◇   N-COUNT

'tuning fork, tuning forks. A tuning fork is a small steel instrument used to tune instruments.   N-COUNT

tun·nel /'tʌnəl/ **tunnels, tunnelling, tunnelled**; spelled **tunneling, tunneled** in American English.   ◆◆◇◇◇   N-COUNT
1 A tunnel is a long passage which has been made under the ground, usually through a hill or under the sea. **2** To tunnel somewhere means to make a tunnel there. *The rebels tunnelled out of a maximum security jail*.   VERB   V prep/adv Also V   **3** See also **wind tunnel**. • **light at the end of the tunnel**: see **light**.

,tunnel 'vision. **1** If you suffer from tunnel vision, you are unable to see things that are not straight in front of you. **2** If you say that someone has tunnel vision, you are criticizing them for concentrating completely on achieving one particular aim, and not noticing or considering all the different aspects of what they are doing.   N-UNCOUNT   N-UNCOUNT   PRAGMATICS

tup·pence /'tʌpəns/. In Britain, tuppence was two old pence.   N-UNCOUNT INFORMAL

tur·ban /'tɜːbən/ **turbans**. A turban is a type of headgear worn by Sikh men and by some Hindu and Muslim men. It consists of a long piece of cloth wound round and round the head.   N-COUNT

tur·bine /'tɜːbaɪn, AM -bɪn/ **turbines**. A turbine is a machine or engine which uses a stream of air, gas, water, or steam to turn a wheel and produce power.   ◆◇◇◇◇   N-COUNT

turbo /'tɜːbəʊ/ **turbos**. A turbo is a fan in the engine of a car or plane that improves its performance by using exhaust gases to blow fuel vapour into the engine.   ◆◇◇◇◇   N-COUNT

'turbo-charged; also spelled **turbocharged**. A turbo-charged engine or vehicle is fitted with a turbo.   ADJ

tur·bot /'tɜːbət/; turbot is both the singular and the plural. Turbot are a type of edible flat fish that live in European seas. ► Turbot is this fish eaten as food. *...a fillet of turbot*.   N-VAR   N-UNCOUNT

tur·bu·lent /'tɜːbjʊlənt/. **1** A turbulent time, place, or relationship is one in which there is a lot of change, confusion, and disturbance. *...six turbulent years of rows and reconciliations*. ♦ **tur·bu·lence** *...a region often beset by political turbulence*. **2** Turbulent water or air contains strong currents which change direction suddenly. ♦ **turbulence** *His plane encountered severe turbulence*.   ◆◇◇◇◇ ADJ-GRADED   N-UNCOUNT ADJ-GRADED   N-UNCOUNT

tu·reen /tjʊə'riːn, AM tʊr-/ **tureens**. A tureen is a large bowl with a lid from which you can serve soup or vegetables.   N-COUNT

turf /tɜːf/ **turfs, turfing, turfed**. **1** Turf is short, thick, even grass. **2** A turf is a small rectangular piece of grass which you lay on the ground in order to make a lawn. **3** Someone's turf is the area which is most familiar to them or where they feel most confident. *On its home turf, the combined bank would be unrivalled*.   ◆◇◇◇◇ N-UNCOUNT N-COUNT   N-UNCOUNT

turf out. If someone is turfed out of a place or position, they are forced to leave. *...the right wing landslide which has turfed out the Socialist government*.   PHRASAL VB be V-ed P V P noun INFORMAL

tur·gid /'tɜːdʒɪd/. If you describe something such as a piece of writing or a film as turgid, you think it is pompous, boring, and difficult to understand.   ADJ-GRADED

tur·key /'tɜːki/ **turkeys**. A turkey is a large bird that is kept on a farm for its meat. ► Turkey is the flesh of this bird eaten as food. *It's a proper Christmas dinner, with turkey and bread sauce*. • See also **cold turkey**.   ◆◇◇◇◇ N-COUNT N-UNCOUNT

,Turkish 'bath, Turkish baths. **1** A Turkish bath is a type of bath in which you sit in a very hot steamy room, then wash, have a massage, and finally swim or shower in very cold water. **2** A Turkish bath is a place where you can have a Turkish bath.   N-COUNT   N-COUNT

,Turkish de'light, Turkish delights. Turkish delight is a jelly-like sweet that is covered with powdered sugar or chocolate.   N-VAR

tur·mer·ic /'tɜːmərɪk/. Turmeric is a yellow spice that is used to flavour hot food such as curry.   N-UNCOUNT

tur·moil /'tɜːmɔɪl/ **turmoils**. Turmoil is a state of confusion, disorder, uncertainty, or great anxiety. *...the political turmoil of 1989... Her marriage was in turmoil*.   ◆◆◇◇◇ N-VAR

---

turn 1 to change in direction or nature

turn /tɜːn/ **turns, turning, turned**. **1** When you turn or when you turn part of your body, you move your body or part of your body so that it is facing in a different or opposite direction. *He turned to his publicist and jokingly asked, 'What's next?'... He turned his head left and right*. ► **Turn around** or **turn round** means the same as **turn**. *Turn your upper body round so that your shoulders are facing to the side*. **2** When you turn something, you move it so that it is facing in a different or opposite direction, or is in a very different position. *They turned their telescopes towards other nearby galaxies... She had turned the bedside chair to face the door*. **3** When something such as a wheel turns, or when you turn it, it continually moves around in a particular direction. *The engine turned a propeller*. **4** When you turn in a particular direction or turn a corner, you change the direction in which you are moving or travelling. *Now turn right to follow West Ferry Road*. ► Also a noun. *You can't do a right-hand turn here*. • See also **turning**. **5** When you turn something such as a key, knob, or switch, or when it turns, you hold it and twist your hand, in order to open something or make it start working. *Turn the heat to very low and cook for 20 minutes*. **6** The point where a road, path, or river turns, is the point where it has a bend or curve in it. *...the corner where Tenterfield Road turned into the main road*. ► Also a noun. *...a sharp turn in the road*. **7** When you turn a page of a book or magazine, you move it so that it is flat against the previous page, and you can read the next page. **8** If you turn a weapon or an aggressive feeling on someone, you direct it at them. **9** If you turn to a particular page in a book or magazine, you open it at that page. **10** If you turn your attention or thoughts to a particular person or thing or if you turn to them, you start thinking about them or discussing them. *We turn now to the British news*. **11** If you turn to someone, you ask for their help or advice. *There was no one to turn to*. **12** If you turn to a particular activity, job, or way of doing something, you start doing or using it. *These communities are now turning to recycling in large numbers*. **13** If a business turns a profit, it earns more money than it spends. The usual British word is **make**. *He says the fares are just too low to turn profits*. **14** When something turns into something else or when you turn it into something else, it becomes something different. *The hated dictator had turned his country into one of the poorest police states in Europe*. **15** You can use turn before an adjective to indicate that something or someone changes by acquiring the quality described by the adjective. *She announced that she was going to turn professional*. **16** If something turns a particular colour or if something turns it a particular colour, it becomes that colour. *Her contact lenses turned her eyes green*. **17** If a situation or trend takes a particular kind of turn, it changes so that it starts developing in a different or opposite way. **18** In sport, if a game turns, or if someone or something turns it, something significant happens which changes the way the game is developing. *...the Gareth Edwards try which turned the game between France and Wales*. **19** When someone turns a particular age, they pass that age. When it turns a particular time, it passes that time. *It had just turned twelve o'clock*. **20** Turn is used in expressions such as **the turn of the century** and **the turn of the year** to refer to a period of time when one century or year is ending and the next one is beginning. **21** If someone turns a place **inside out** or **upside down**, they search it thoroughly and usually make it   ◆◆◆◆◇ VERB: V V prep/adv V n prep/adv Also V n   PHRASAL VB: V P V n P   VERB: V n V n prep/adv V n to-inf   V-ERG: V V n   VERB: V n V prep/adv   N-COUNT   V-ERG: V n V n prep/adv Also V   VERB V prep/adv Also V   N-COUNT VERB: V n   VERB: V n on n   VERB: V to n VERB: V n to n   VERB V to n VERB V to/from n/-ing   VB: no passive V n AMERICAN   V-ERG: V into/to n V n into/to n   V-LINK V adj   V-LINK-ERG: V colour V n colour   N-COUNT: with supp   V-ERG: V V n BRITISH, JOURNALISM   VERB V n   N-SING: the N of n   PHRASE

turn

1186

turn

untidy. **22** If something such as a system or way of life **is turned inside out** or **upside down**, it is changed completely, making people confused or upset. PHRASE

23 If a situation **takes a turn for the worse**, it suddenly becomes worse. If a situation **takes a turn for the better**, it suddenly becomes better. **24** Turn is used in a large number of other expressions which are explained under other words in the dictionary. For example, the expression 'turn over a new leaf' is explained at **leaf**. PHRASE

turn 2 your go to do something

turn /tɜːn/ **turns. 1** If it is your **turn** to do something, you now have the duty, chance, or right to do it, when other people have done it before you or will do it after you. *Tonight it's my turn to cook.* N-COUNT
2 You can use **by turns** to indicate that someone has two particular emotions or qualities, one after the other. *His tone was by turns angry and aggrieved.* PHRASE **3** If you **speak out of turn** or **talk out of turn**, you say something that you do not have the right or authority to say. PHRASE
4 You use **in turn** to refer to actions or events that are in a sequence one after the other, for example because one causes the other. *One of the members of the surgical team leaked the story to a fellow physician who, in turn, confided in a reporter.* **5** If each person in a group does something **in turn**, they do it one after the other in a fixed or agreed order. **6** If two or more people **take turns** to do something or **take it in turns** to do it, they do it one after the other several times, rather than do it together. PHRASE
7 If there is a particular **turn of events**, a particular series of things happens. **8** If you say that something happens **at every turn**, you are emphasizing that it happens frequently or all the time, usually so that it prevents you from achieving what you want. **9** If you do someone **a good turn**, you do something that helps or benefits them. PHRASE

turn 3 phrasal verbs

turn /tɜːn/ **turns, turning, turned.**

turn against. If you **turn against** someone or something, or if something **turns** you **against** them, you stop supporting them, trusting them, or liking them. *Working with the police has turned me against the use of violent scenes as entertainment.* PHRASAL VB ERG: V P n V n P n

turn around or **turn round. 1** See turn 1. **2** If you **turn** something **around**, or if it **turns around**, it is moved so that it faces the opposite direction. *There was enough room for a wheelchair to get in but not to turn round.* **3** If something such as a business or economy **turns around**, or if someone **turns** it **around**, it becomes successful, after being unsuccessful for a period of time. *Turning the company around won't be easy.* **4** If you **turn around** a question, sentence, or idea, you change the way in which it is expressed, in order to consider it differently. *Now turn the question around and start looking not for what you did wrong in the past, but for what you can do to make things better in the future.* **5** See also **turnaround.** PHRASAL VB ERG: V P V P n ERG: V n P Also V P noun V P noun V n P

turn away. 1 If you **turn** someone **away**, you do not allow them to enter your country, home, or other place. *Hard times are forcing community colleges to turn away students.* **2** To **turn away** from something such as a method or an idea means to stop using it or to become different from it. PHRASAL VB V n P V P noun V P from n

turn back. 1 If you **turn back** or if someone **turns** you **back** when you are going somewhere, you change direction and go towards where you started from. *She turned back towards the crossroads... Police attempted to turn back protesters.* **2** If you cannot **turn back**, you cannot change your plans and decide not to do something, because the action you have already taken makes it impossible. *The administration has now endorsed the bill and can't turn back.* PHRASAL VB ERG: V P noun V P noun Also V n P with brd-neg V P

turn down. 1 If you **turn down** a person or their request or offer, you refuse their request or offer. *I thanked him for the offer but turned it down.* **2** When you **turn down** a radio, heater, or other piece of equipment, you reduce the amount of sound or heat PHRASAL VB V P noun V P noun V P noun V n P

being produced, by adjusting the controls. *He kept turning the central heating down.* **3** If the rate or level of something **turns down**, it decreases. *The divorce rate turned down in the 1950s.* V P BRITISH, JOURNALISM

turn in. 1 When you **turn in**, you go to bed. *He was obviously about to turn in for the night.* **2** If you **turn** someone **in**, you take them to the police because they are suspected of committing a crime. If you **turn** yourself **in**, you go voluntarily to the police because you are suspected of committing a crime. *I might today hesitate to turn in a burglar.* **3** If you **turn** something **in**, you return it to the place or person you borrowed it from. *The official showed up to tell her to turn in her library books.* PHRASAL VB V P V n P V P noun V n P V P noun AMERICAN

turn off. 1 If you **turn off** the road or path you are going along, you start going along a different road or path which leads away from it. *He turned off only to find he was trapped in a town square.* **2** When you **turn off** a piece of equipment or a supply of something, you stop heat, sound, or water being produced by adjusting the controls. *The light's a bit too harsh. You can turn it off.* **3** If something **turns** you **off** a particular subject or activity, it makes you have no interest in it. *Teaching off a blackboard is boring, and undoubtedly turns people off.* **4** If something or someone **turns** you **off**, you do not find them sexually attractive or they stop you feeling sexually excited. *Aggressive men turn me off completely.* **5** See also **turn-off.** PHRASAL VB V P noun V P V P noun V n P V n P n V n P Also V P noun Also V P noun

turn on. 1 When you **turn on** a piece of equipment or a supply of something, you cause heat, sound, or water to be produced by adjusting the controls. *She asked them why they hadn't turned the lights on.* **2** If someone or something **turns** you **on**, they attract you and make you feel sexually excited. *The body that turns men on doesn't have to be perfect.* ● See also **turn-on. 3** If you say that someone **turns** on a particular way of behaving, you mean that they suddenly start behaving in that way, and you often think that this is insincere. *He could also turn on the style when the occasion demanded.* **4** If someone **turns** on you, they attack you or speak angrily to you. **5** If something **turns** on a particular thing, its success or truth depends on that thing. *The plot turns on whether Ilsa will choose her lover or her husband.* PHRASAL VB V P noun V n P V n P Also V P noun V P noun Also V n P INFORMAL V P n V P n

turn out. 1 If something **turns out** a particular way, it happens in that way or has the result or degree of success indicated. *Sometimes things don't turn out the way we think they're going to... I was positive things were going to turn out fine.* **2** If something **turns out** to be a particular thing, it is discovered to be that thing. *It turned out that I knew the person who got shot.* **3** When you **turn out** something such as a light or gas, you move the switch or knob that controls it so that it stops giving out light or heat. *Turn the lights out.* **4** If a business or other organization **turns out** something, it produces it. *They have been turning out great blades for 400 years.* **5** If you **turn** someone **out** of a place, especially the place where they have been living, you force them to leave that place. *It was previously a small monastery but the authorities turned all the monks out.* **6** If you **turn out** the contents of a container, you empty it by removing them or letting them fall out. *Turn the plants out of their pots.* **7** If people **turn out** for a particular event or activity, they go and take part in it or watch it. **8** See also **turnout, turned out.** PHRASAL VB LINK: V P prep V P n V P adj V P to-inf it V-ed P that V n P Also V P noun V P noun Also V n P V n P of/from n V P Also V P noun V P noun V n P of/from n Also V n P V P for n, V P

turn over. 1 If you **turn** something **over**, or if it **turns over**, it is moved so that the top part is now facing downwards. *I don't suppose you thought to turn over the tape, did you?... The buggy turned over and Nancy was thrown out.* **2** If you **turn over**, for example when you are lying in bed, you move your body so that you are lying in a different position. **3** If you **turn** something **over** in your mind, you think carefully about it. **4** If you **turn** something **over** to someone, you give it to them when they ask for it, because they have a right to it. *The lawyer turned over the release papers.* **5** If you **turn over** a job or responsibility that you have, you give it to someone else, so that you no longer have it. PHRASAL VB ERG: V n P V P noun V P V P n in n V n P to n V P noun Also V n P V P noun Also V n P

Parliamentarians were eager to turn over responsibility for the decision. **6** If you **turn over** when you are watching television, you change to another channel. *Whenever he's on TV, I turn over.* **7** See also **turnover**.   V P

turn over to. If you **turn** something **over to** a different function or use, you change its function or use. *When he first leased the land in the late 1970s, he planned to turn it over to cereal production.*   PHRASAL VB / V n P P n / Also V P noun / P n

turn round. See **turn around**.   PHRASAL VB

turn up. **1** If you say that someone or something **turns up**, you mean that they arrive, often unexpectedly or after you have been waiting a long time. *This is similar to waiting for a bus that never turns up.* **2** If you **turn** something **up** or if it **turns up**, you find, discover, or notice it. *Investigations have never turned up any evidence.* **3** When you **turn up** a radio, heater, or other piece of equipment, you increase the amount of sound, heat, or power being produced. *I turned the volume up... Turn the heat up high.*   PHRASAL VB V P / ERG: V P V P noun Also V n P / V P noun V n P / V n P adj

turn·about /ˈtɜːnəbaʊt/. A **turnabout** is a complete change in opinion, attitude, or method.   N-SING

turn·around /ˈtɜːnəraʊnd/ **turnarounds**. **1** A **turnaround** is a complete change in opinion, attitude, or method. *I don't see any vast turnarounds in the way we do business.* **2** A **turnaround** is a sudden improvement, especially in the success of a business or a country's economy. *...signs of a turnaround in Northern California's housing market.* **3** The **turnaround** or **turnround** time of a task, for example the unloading of an aircraft or ship, is the amount of time that it takes.   ◆◇◇◇◇ N-COUNT / N-COUNT / N-VAR

turn·coat /ˈtɜːnkəʊt/ **turncoats**. If you describe someone as a **turncoat**, you disapprove of them and think they are disloyal or hypocritical, because they have left their party or organization and joined an opposing one.   N-COUNT PRAGMATICS

turned 'out. If you are well **turned out** or smartly **turned out**, you are dressed smartly.   ADJ: adv ADJ

turn·ing /ˈtɜːnɪŋ/ **turnings**. If you take a particular **turning**, you go along a road which leads away from the side of another road. *Take the next turning on the right.* ● See also **turn**.   ◆◇◇◇◇ N-COUNT

'turning point, turning points. A **turning point** is a time at which an important change takes place which affects the future of a person or thing. *Hungary's opening of the border was a turning point for the refugees.*   ◆◇◇◇◇ N-COUNT

tur·nip /ˈtɜːnɪp/ **turnips**. A **turnip** is a round vegetable with a greenish-white skin that is the root of a crop. See picture headed **vegetables**.   ◆◇◇◇◇ N-VAR

'turn-off, turn-offs. **1** A **turn-off** is a road leading away from a major road or a motorway. **2** Something that is a **turn-off** causes you to lose interest or sexual excitement.   N-COUNT N-COUNT

'turn-on, turn-ons. Something or someone that is a **turn-on** is sexually exciting.   N-COUNT

turn·out /ˈtɜːnaʊt/ **turnouts**; also spelled **turn-out**. **1** The **turnout** at an event is the number of people who go to it or take part in it. *It was a marvellous afternoon with a huge turnout of people.* **2** The **turnout** in an election is the number of people who vote in it, as a proportion of the number of people who have the right to vote in it. *Election officials said the turnout of voters was low.*   ◆◇◇◇◇ N-COUNT / N-COUNT

turn·over /ˈtɜːnəʊvə/ **turnovers**. **1** The **turnover** of a company is the value of the goods or services sold during a particular period of time. *Her annual turnover is around £45,000.* **2** The **turnover** of people in an organization or place is the rate at which people leave and are replaced. *Short-term contracts increase staff turnover.*   ◆◆◇◇◇ N-VAR / N-VAR

turn·pike /ˈtɜːnpaɪk/ **turnpikes**. A **turnpike** is a road, especially an expressway, which people have to pay to drive on.   N-COUNT AMERICAN

turn·round /ˈtɜːnraʊnd/. A **turnround** is the same as a **turnaround**.   N-SING

turn·stile /ˈtɜːnstaɪl/ **turnstiles**. A **turnstile** is a mechanical barrier at the entrance to a place such as a zoo or a football ground.   N-COUNT

turn·table /ˈtɜːnteɪbəl/ **turntables**. A **turntable** is the flat round part of a record player on which a record is put when it is played.   N-COUNT

'turn-up, turn-ups. The **turn-ups** on a pair of trousers or pants are the parts at the ends of the legs, which are folded over. The American expression is **cuff**.   N-COUNT BRITISH

tur·pen·tine /ˈtɜːpəntaɪn/. **Turpentine** is a colourless liquid used, for example, for cleaning paint off brushes.   N-UNCOUNT

tur·quoise /ˈtɜːkwɔɪz/ **turquoises**. **1** Turquoise or **turquoise blue** is used to describe things that are of a light greenish-blue colour. **2** Turquoise is a bright blue stone that is often used in jewellery.   ◆◇◇◇◇ COLOUR / N-VAR

tur·ret /ˈtʌrɪt, AM ˈtɜːr-/ **turrets**. **1** A turret is a small narrow tower on top of a building or a larger tower. **2** The **turret** on a tank or warship is the part where the guns are fixed.   ◆◇◇◇◇ N-COUNT / N-COUNT

tur·tle /ˈtɜːtəl/ **turtles**. **1** A turtle is a large reptile which has a thick shell covering its body and which lives in the sea most of the time. The usual American term is **sea turtle**. **2** A **turtle** is any reptile that has a thick shell around its body, for example a tortoise or terrapin.   ◆◇◇◇◇ N-COUNT BRITISH / N-COUNT AMERICAN

turtle·neck /ˈtɜːtəlnek/ **turtlenecks**. A **turtleneck** or **turtleneck sweater** is a sweater with a short round collar that fits closely around your neck.   N-COUNT

tusk /tʌsk/ **tusks**. The **tusks** of an elephant, wild boar, or walrus are its two very long, curved, pointed teeth.   N-COUNT

tus·sle /ˈtʌsəl/ **tussles, tussling, tussled**. **1** If one person **tussles** with another, or if they **tussle**, they grab hold of and struggle with each other. *They ended up ripping down perimeter fencing and tussling with the security staff.* ► Also a noun. *...a tussle with the goalie.* **2** If one person **tussles** with another for something, or if they **tussle** for it, they try to beat each other in order to get it. *Pezzo tussled for fourth place with Orvosova.* ► Also a noun. *...a legal tussle.* **3** If someone **tussles with** a difficult problem or issue, they try hard to solve it. *He is tussling with the problem of what to do about inflation.*   ◆◇◇◇◇ V-RECIP V with n Also pl-n V, pl-n V overn / V-RECIP V for n with n Also pl-n V for/overn JOURNALISM / N-COUNT VERB V with n JOURNALISM

tus·sock /ˈtʌsək/ **tussocks**. A **tussock** is a small clump of grass which is much longer and thicker than the grass around it.   N-COUNT

tut /tʌt/ **tuts, tutting, tutted**. **1** Tut is used in writing to represent a clicking sound that you make with your tongue to indicate disapproval, annoyance, or sympathy. **2** If someone **tuts**, they make a clicking sound with their tongue to indicate disapproval, annoyance, or sympathy.   VERB: V

tu·telage /ˈtjuːtɪlɪdʒ, AM ˈtuːt-/. If one person, group, or country does something **under the tutelage of** another, they do it while they are being taught or guided by them.   N-UNCOUNT FORMAL

tu·tor /ˈtjuːtə, AM ˈtuːt-/ **tutors, tutoring, tutored**. **1** A tutor is a teacher at a British university or college. **2** A **tutor** is someone who gives private lessons to one pupil or a very small group of pupils. **3** If someone **tutors** a person or a subject, they teach that person or subject. *The old man was tutoring her in the stringed instruments.* ♦ **tu·tor·ing** *...a mixture of tutoring and journalism.*   ◆◆◇◇◇ N-COUNT / N-COUNT / VERB: V n V n in n Also V / N-UNCOUNT

tu·to·rial /tjuːˈtɔːriəl, AM tuːt-/ **tutorials**. **1** In a university or college, a **tutorial** is a regular meeting between a tutor and one or several students, for discussion of a subject that is being studied. **2** Tutorial means relating to a tutor or tutors, especially one at a university or college. *Students may decide to seek tutorial guidance.*   ◆◇◇◇◇ N-COUNT / ADJ: ADJ n

tut-'tut, tut-tuts, tut-tutting, tut-tutted; also spelled **tut tut**. **1** Tut-tut is used in writing to represent a clicking sound that you make with your tongue to indicate disapproval, annoyance, or sympathy. **2** If you **tut-tut** about something, you express your disapproval about it, especially by clicking your tongue. *...tut-tutting about Angie and her lifestyle.*   CONVENTION PRAGMATICS / VERB V about n Also V

tutu /ˈtuːtuː/ **tutus**. A **tutu** is a costume worn by female ballet dancers. It has a very short stiff skirt   N-COUNT

made of many layers of material that sticks out from the waist.

tux·edo /tʌkˈsiːdəʊ/ **tuxedos.** A tuxedo is a black or white jacket worn by men for formal social events. The British expression is **dinner jacket.** N-COUNT AMERICAN

TV /ˌtiː ˈviː/ **TVs.** TV means the same as **television.** *I prefer going to the cinema to watching TV.* N-VAR

TV 'dinner, TV dinners. TV dinners are complete meals that are sold in a single package. They can be heated up quickly and eaten from the package they are cooked in. N-COUNT

twad·dle /ˈtwɒdəl/. If you refer to something that someone says as **twaddle**, you mean that it is silly or untrue. N-UNCOUNT INFORMAL

twang /twæŋ/ **twangs, twanging, twanged.** **1** If you **twang** something such as a tight string or elastic band, or if it **twangs**, it makes a fairly loud, resonating sound because it has been pulled and then released. ► Also a noun. *...a loud discordant twang.* **2** A **twang** is a nasal quality in someone's way of speaking. *...her broad Australian twang.* V-ERG: Vn, V / N-COUNT; SOUND / N-COUNT

tweak /twiːk/ **tweaks, tweaking, tweaked. 1** If you **tweak** something, especially part of someone's body, you hold it between your finger and thumb and twist it or pull it. **2** If you **tweak** something such as a system or a design, you improve it by making a slight change. ► Also a noun. *...nothing too radical, just a tweak here and there.* VERB: Vn / VERB: Vn INFORMAL / N-COUNT

twee /twiː/. If you say that something is **twee**, you disapprove of it because it is pretty or sentimental in a way that you think is excessive or tasteless. ADJ-GRADED PRAGMATICS BRITISH

tweed /twiːd/ **tweeds. 1** Tweed is a thick woollen cloth, often woven from different coloured threads. **2** Someone who is wearing **tweeds** is wearing a tweed suit. N-VAR N-PLURAL

tweedy /ˈtwiːdi/. **1** If you describe someone as **tweedy**, you mean that they have an upper-class but plain appearance, and look as if they live in the country. **2** Tweedy clothes are made from tweed. ADJ-GRADED / ADJ-GRADED

twee·zers /ˈtwiːzəz/. **Tweezers** are a small tool that you use for pulling out hairs or splinters and picking up small objects. N-PLURAL

twelfth /twelfθ/ **twelfths. 1** The **twelfth** item in a series is the one that you count as number twelve. See Appendix headed **Numbers.** **2** A **twelfth** is one of twelve equal parts of something. ORDINAL / FRACTION

twelve /twelv/ **twelves.** Twelve is the number 12. See Appendix headed **Numbers.** NUMBER

twen·ti·eth /ˈtwentiəθ/ **twentieths. 1** The **twentieth** item in a series is the one that you count as number twenty. See Appendix headed **Numbers.** **2** A **twentieth** is one of twenty equal parts of something. ORDINAL / FRACTION

twen·ty /ˈtwenti/ **twenties. 1** Twenty is the number 20. See Appendix headed **Numbers.** **2** When you talk about the **twenties**, you are referring to numbers between 20 and 29. If you are **in your twenties**, you are aged between 20 and 29. **3** The **twenties** is the decade between 1920 and 1929. NUMBER N-PLURAL / N-PLURAL: theN

twerp /twɜːp/ **twerps.** If you call someone a **twerp**, you are insulting them and saying that they are silly or stupid. N-COUNT PRAGMATICS INFORMAL

twice /twaɪs/. **1** If something happens **twice**, there are two actions or events of the same kind. *The government has twice declined to back the scheme... Thoroughly brush teeth and gums twice daily.* **2** You use **twice** in expressions such as **twice a day** and **twice a week** to indicate that two events or actions of the same kind happen in each day or week. **3** If one thing is, for example, **twice as** big or old as another, the first thing is bigger or older by an amount equal to the second thing. People sometimes say that one thing is **twice as** good or hard as another when they think that the first thing is much better or harder than the second. ► Also a predeterminer. *Unemployment in Northern Ireland is twice the national average.* **4** If you **think twice** about doing something, you reconsider it and may decide to do it differently or not to do it at all. **5 ● once or twice:** see **once. ● twice over:** see **over.** ADV / ADV: ADV a n / ADV: ADV as adj/ adv / PREDET / PHRASE

twid·dle /ˈtwɪdəl/ **twiddles, twiddling, twiddled. 1** If you **twiddle** something, you twist it or turn it quickly with your fingers. *She had sat there twiddling nervously with the clasp of her handbag.* **2 ● to twiddle** your thumbs: see **thumb.** VERB: Vn / V with n

twig /twɪg/ **twigs, twigging, twigged. 1** A twig is a small thin branch that grows out from a main branch of a tree or bush. **2** If you **twig**, you suddenly realize or understand something. *By the time she'd twigged what it was all about it was too late.* N-COUNT / VERB: V / V wh BRITISH, INFORMAL

twi·light /ˈtwaɪlaɪt/. **1** Twilight is the time just before night when the daylight has almost gone but when it is not completely dark. **2** Twilight is the dim light that there is outside just after sunset. *...the deepening autumn twilight.* **3** The **twilight of** a period of time is the final stages of it, when the most important events have already happened, and there is a state of weakness or decline. *Both men are in the twilight of their careers.* **4** A **twilight** state or a **twilight** zone is a situation of confusion or uncertainty, which seems to exist between two different states or categories. *...that twilight zone between military personnel and civilian employees.* N-UNCOUNT / N-UNCOUNT / N-SING: theN of n, Nn / ADJ: ADJ n

twill /twɪl/. **Twill** is cloth that is woven in a way which produces diagonal lines across it. N-UNCOUNT

twin /twɪn/ **twins, twinning, twinned. 1** If two people are **twins**, they have the same mother and were born on the same day. **●** See also **Siamese twin.** **2** Twin is used to describe a pair of things that look the same and are close together. *...the world's largest twin-engined aircraft.* **3** Twin is used to describe two things or ideas that are similar or connected in some way. *...the twin concepts of liberty and equality.* **4** When a place or organization in one country **is twinned** with a place or organization in another country, a special relationship is formally established between them. **♦ twin·ning** *...the twinning of Leeds and St Mary.* **5** Twin towns or cities are twinned with each other. N-COUNT / ADJ: ADJ n / ADJ: ADJ n / VERB: be V-ed with n / N-UNCOUNT / ADJ: ADJ n

,twin 'bed, twin beds. Twin beds are two single beds in one bedroom. N-COUNT

,twin-'bedded; also spelled **twin bedded.** A **twin-bedded** room, for example in a hotel, has twin beds. ADJ: ADJ n BRITISH

twine /twaɪn/ **twines, twining, twined. 1** Twine is strong string used especially in gardening and farming. **2** If you **twine** one thing around another, or if one thing **twines** around another, the first thing is twisted or wound around the second. *He had twined his chubby arms around Vincent's neck.* N-UNCOUNT / V-ERG: Vn prep Also V prep

twinge /twɪndʒ/ **twinges. 1** A twinge is a sudden sharp feeling or emotion, usually an unpleasant one. *I would have twinges of guilt occasionally.* **2** A twinge is a sudden sharp pain. *...the occasional twinge of indigestion.* N-COUNT / N-COUNT

twin·kle /ˈtwɪŋkəl/ **twinkles, twinkling, twinkled. 1** If a star or a light **twinkles**, it shines with an unsteady light which rapidly and constantly changes. **2** If you say that someone's eyes **twinkle**, you mean that their face expresses good humour, amusement, or mischief. ► Also a noun. *A kindly twinkle came into her eyes.* VERB: V / VERB: V / N-SING

twin·set /ˈtwɪnset/ **twinsets;** also spelled **twin set** or **twin-set.** A **twinset** is a set of women's clothing, consisting of a matching cardigan and sweater of the same colour. N-COUNT BRITISH

twirl /twɜːl/ **twirls, twirling, twirled. 1** If you **twirl** something or if it **twirls**, it turns round and round with a smooth fairly fast movement. *All around me leaves twirl to the ground.* **2** If you **twirl**, you move round and round rapidly, for example when you are dancing. **3** If you **twirl** something such as your hair, you twist it around your finger. V-ERG: Vn V / VERB: V / VERB: Vn

twist /twɪst/ **twists, twisting, twisted. 1** If you **twist** something, you turn it to make a spiral shape, for example by turning the two ends of it in opposite directions. *Her hands began to twist the handles of the bag... She twisted her hair into a bun.* **2** A **twist** is the shape that something has when it has been twisted. *...bunches of violets in twists of paper.* VERB Vn V n adv/prep / N-COUNT

3 If you **twist** something, especially a part of your body, or if it **twists**, it moves into a strange, uncomfortable, or distorted shape or position. *He twisted her arms behind her back.* **4** If you **twist** part of your body such as your head or your shoulders, you turn that part while keeping the rest of your body still. *She twisted her head sideways... Susan twisted round in her seat.* **5** If you **twist** a part of your body such as your ankle or wrist, you injure it by turning it too sharply, or in an unusual direction. V-ERG / V n prep / Also V / VERB / V n adv / V adv/prep / VERB: V n

6 If you **twist** something, you turn it so that it moves around in a circular direction. *He takes out a jar and twists the lid off.* ▶ Also a noun. *The bag is re-sealed with a simple twist of the valve.* **7** If a road or river **twists**, it has a lot of sudden changes of direction in it. *The roads twist round hairpin bends.* ▶ Also a noun. *...the twists and turns of existing track.* VERB: V n / V n with adv / N-COUNT / VERB: V / V prep / N-COUNT

8 If you say that someone **has twisted** something that you have said, you are critical of them because they have repeated it in a way that changes its meaning, in order to harm or benefit themselves. *The media can twist your words and misrepresent you.* VERB / PRAGMATICS / V n

9 A **twist** in something is an unexpected and significant development. *This little story has a twist in the tail.* **10** If something happens by **a twist of fate**, it happens by chance, and it is strange, interesting, or unfortunate in some way. *By a curious twist of fate, cricket was also my favourite sport.* N-COUNT / PHRASE

11 The twist is a dance that was popular in the 1960's, in which you twist your body and move your hips vigorously. N-SING: the N

12 See also **twisted**. ● to **twist** someone's **arm**: see **arm**. ● to **twist the knife**: see **knife**.

twist·ed /'twɪstɪd/. If you describe a person as **twisted**, you dislike them because you think they are strange in an unpleasant way. ADJ-GRADED / PRAGMATICS

twisty /'twɪsti/. A **twisty** road, track, or river has a lot of sharp bends and corners. ADJ-GRADED

twit /twɪt/ **twits**. If you call someone a **twit**, you are insulting them and saying that they are silly or stupid. N-COUNT / PRAGMATICS / BRITISH, / INFORMAL

twitch /twɪtʃ/ **twitches, twitching, twitched.** If something, especially a part of your body, **twitches** or you **twitch** it, it makes a little jerking movement. *His left eyelid twitched involuntarily.* ▶ Also a noun. *He developed a nervous twitch.* V-ERG / V / Also V n / N-COUNT

twitchy /'twɪtʃi/. If you are **twitchy**, you are anxious or uneasy about something and so are behaving in a rather nervous unpredictable way. *The department had suddenly become very twitchy about journalists.* ADJ-GRADED / INFORMAL

twit·ter /'twɪtə/ **twitters, twittering, twittered. 1** When birds **twitter**, they make a lot of short high-pitched sounds. ▶ Also a noun. *...the twitter of birds.* **2** If you say that someone **is twittering** about something, you mean that they are speaking about silly or unimportant things. *She laughs, blushes and twitters: 'Oh, doesn't Giles have just the most charming sense of humour?'* VERB: V / N-UNCOUNT / VERB: V about n / V with quote / Also V

two /tuː/ **twos. 1 Two** is the number 2. See Appendix headed **Numbers**. **2** If you say **it takes two** or **it takes two to tango**, you mean that a situation or argument involves two people and they are both therefore responsible for it. **3** If you **put two and two together**, you work out the truth about something by using the clues available to you. *Putting two and two together, I assume that this was the car he used.* **4** ● to **kill two birds with one stone**: see **bird**. ● two **a penny**: see **penny**. NUMBER / PHRASE / PHRASE

two-di·mensional; also spelled **two dimensional. 1** A **two-dimensional** object or figure is flat rather than solid and can be measured only in the dimensions of length and width. **2** If you describe fictional characters as **two-dimensional**, you are critical of them because they are very simple and not realistic. ADJ / ADJ-GRADED / PRAGMATICS

two-edged. Two-edged means the same as **double-edged**. *Firepower proved a two-edged sword, as it destroyed the country US forces were pledged to protect.* ◆◇◇◇◇ / ADJ

two-'faced. If you describe someone as **two-faced**, you are critical of them because they say they do or believe one thing when their behaviour or words show that they do not. ADJ-GRADED / PRAGMATICS

two·fold /'tuːfəʊld/; also spelled **two-fold**. You can use **twofold** to introduce a topic that has two equally important parts. *The purpose of the ambassador's visit is twofold – to step up pressure on the invaders to withdraw peacefully, and to intensify preparations for war if that pressure fails.* ADJ / PRAGMATICS / FORMAL

two-'handed. A **two-handed** blow or catch is done using both your hands. ADJ

'two-piece, two-pieces; also spelled **two piece. 1** You can use **two-piece** to describe something, especially a set of clothing, that is in two parts. *...a simple light-grey two-piece suit.* **2** A **two-piece** is a woman's suit which consists of a jacket and a skirt or pair of trousers. ◆◇◇◇◇ / ADJ: ADJ n / N-COUNT

two·some /'tuːsəm/ **twosomes.** A **twosome** is a group of two people. N-COUNT

two-'thirds; also spelled **two thirds. Two-thirds** of something is an amount that is two out of three equal parts of it. *Two-thirds of householders in this country live in a mortgaged home.* ▶ Also a pronoun. *...a treaty to cut their nuclear arsenals by two-thirds.* ▶ Also an adverb. *Do not fill the container more than two-thirds full.* ▶ Also an adjective. *...the two thirds majority in parliament.* ◆◇◇◇◇ / QUANT / PRON / ADV: / ADV adj/-ed / ADJ: ADJ n

two-'way. 1 Two-way means moving or working in two opposite directions or allowing something to move or work in two opposite directions. *The bridge is now open to two-way traffic.* **2** A **two-way** radio or transmitter can both send and receive signals. **3** If there is **two-way** co-operation or learning, two people or groups are helping each other or learning from each other. *Education is a two-way process.* ◆◇◇◇◇ / ADJ / ADJ: ADJ n / ADJ: ADJ n

ty·coon /taɪˈkuːn/ **tycoons.** A **tycoon** is a person who is successful in business and so has become rich and powerful. N-COUNT

tyke /taɪk/ **tykes.** You can refer to a child, especially a naughty or mischievous one, as a **tyke** when you want to show affection for them. N-COUNT / PRAGMATICS / INFORMAL

type 1 *sort or kind*

type /taɪp/ **types. 1** A **type** of something is a group of those things that have particular features in common. *...several types of lettuce... There are various types of the disease.* **2** If you refer to a particular thing or person as a **type** of something more general, you are considering that thing or person as an example of that more general group. *Have you done this type of work before?* **3** If you refer to a person as a particular **type**, you mean that they have that particular appearance, character, or type of behaviour. *She was certainly not the type to murder her husband.* **4** If you say that someone is **not your type**, you mean that they are not the sort of person who you usually find attractive. **5** See also **blood type**. ◆◆◆◇ / N-COUNT / N-COUNT: / with supp / N-COUNT / PHRASE / INFORMAL

type 2 *writing and printing*

type /taɪp/ **types, typing, typed. 1** If you **type** something, you use a typewriter or word processor to write it. *I had never really learnt to type properly.* **2 Type** is printed text as it appears in a book or newspaper, or the small pieces of metal that are used to create this. **3** See also **typing**. ◆◆◆◇ / VERB: V n / V / N-UNCOUNT

type in or **type into.** If you **type** information **into** a computer or **type** it **in**, you press keys on the keyboard so that the computer stores or processes the information. *Officials type each passport number into a computer... You have to type in commands, such as 'help' and 'print'.* PHRASAL VB / V n P n / V P noun / Also V n P

type out. If you **type** something **out**, you write it in full using a typewriter or word processor. *The two of us stood by while two typists typed out the whole document again.* PHRASAL VB / V P noun / Also V n P

type up. If you **type up** a handwritten text, you produce a typed copy of it. *They didn't get around to typing up the letter.* PHRASAL VB / V P noun / Also V n P

type·cast /'taɪpkɑːst, -kæst/ **typecasts, typecasting**; the form **typecast** is used in the present tense and is the past tense and past participle. If an VERB: / be V-ed / be V-ed as n

actor **is typecast**, they play the same type of character in every play or film that they are in. *African-Americans were often typecast as servants.* ◆ **type·cast·ing** ...*the early typecasting as the empty-headed sex symbol.* N-UNCOUNT

type·face /ˈtaɪpfeɪs/ **typefaces.** In printing, a **typeface** is a set of alphabetical, numerical, and other characters that share a common design. N-COUNT

type·script /ˈtaɪpskrɪpt/ **typescripts.** A **typescript** is a typed copy of an essay, article, or literary work. N-VAR

type·writ·er /ˈtaɪpraɪtə/ **typewriters.** A **typewriter** is a machine with keys which are pressed in order to print letters, numbers, or other characters onto paper. ◆◇◇◇ N-COUNT

type·writ·ten /ˈtaɪprɪtən/. A **typewritten** document has been typed on a typewriter or word processor. ADJ

ty·phoid /ˈtaɪfɔɪd/. **Typhoid** or **typhoid fever** is a serious infectious disease that produces fever and diarrhoea and can cause death. N-UNCOUNT

ty·phoon /taɪˈfuːn/ **typhoons.** A **typhoon** is a very violent tropical storm. ◆◇◇◇ N-COUNT

ty·phus /ˈtaɪfəs/. **Typhus** is a serious infectious disease that produces a skin rash, a high fever, and a severe headache. N-UNCOUNT

typi·cal /ˈtɪpɪkəl/. **1** You use **typical** to describe someone or something that shows the most usual characteristics of a particular type of person or thing, and is therefore a good example of that type. ...*such typical schoolgirl pastimes as horse-riding and watching old films.* **2** If a particular action or feature is **typical** of someone or something, it shows their usual qualities or characteristics. *This is not typical of Chinese, but is a feature of the Thai language.* **3** If you say that something is **typical** of a person, situation, or thing, you are criticizing or complaining about them and saying that they are just as bad or disappointing as you expected them to be. *She threw her hands into the air. 'That is just typical of you, isn't it?'* ◆◆◇◇ ADJ-GRADED / ADJ-GRADED / ADJ-GRADED PRAGMATICS

typi·cal·ly /ˈtɪpɪkəli/. **1** You use **typically** to say that something usually happens in the way that you are describing. *Female migrants are typically very young.* **2** You use **typically** to say that something shows all the most usual characteristics of a particular type of person or thing. *Philip paced the floor, a typically nervous expectant father.* **3** You use **typically** to indicate that someone has behaved in the way that they normally do. *Robbins is typically cool in his pronouncements about his future.* ◆◆◇◇ ADV-GRADED: ADV with cl/ group / ADV-GRADED: ADV adj / ADV-GRADED

typi·fy /ˈtɪpɪfaɪ/ **typifies, typifying, typified.** If something or someone **typifies** a situation or type of thing or person, they have all the usual characteristics of it and are a typical example of it. *The design* ◆◇◇◇ VERB V n

typifies Ercol's furniture.

typ·ing /ˈtaɪpɪŋ/. **1 Typing** is the work or activity of typing something by means of a typewriter or word processor. **2 Typing** is the skill of using a typewriter or keyboard quickly and accurately. *My typing is quite dreadful.* ◆◇◇◇ N-UNCOUNT / N-UNCOUNT

typ·ist /ˈtaɪpɪst/ **typists.** A **typist** is someone who works in an office typing letters and other documents. *I got a job as a typist.* N-COUNT

ty·pog·ra·phy /taɪˈpɒɡrəfi/. **Typography** is the way in which written material is arranged and prepared for printing. ◆ **ty·po·graphi·cal** /ˌtaɪpəˈɡræfɪkəl/. ...*a typographical error.* N-UNCOUNT / ADJ: ADJ n

ty·pol·ogy /taɪˈpɒlədʒi/ **typologies.** A **typology** is a system for dividing things into different types, especially in science and the social sciences. N-COUNT FORMAL

ty·ran·ni·cal /tɪˈrænɪkəl/. **1** If you describe someone as **tyrannical**, you mean that they are severe or unfair towards the people that they have authority over. *He killed his tyrannical father with a blow to the head.* **2** If you describe a government or organization as **tyrannical**, you mean that it acts without considering the wishes of its people and treats them cruelly or unfairly. ADJ-GRADED / ADJ-GRADED

tyr·an·nize /ˈtɪrənaɪz/ **tyrannizes, tyrannizing, tyrannized;** also spelled **tyrannise** in British English. If you say that one person **tyrannizes** another, you mean that the first person uses their power over the second person in order to treat them very cruelly and unfairly. *Armed groups use their power to tyrannise over civilians.* VERB: V n / V over n / Also V

tyr·an·ny /ˈtɪrəni/ **tyrannies.** **1** A **tyranny** is a cruel, unfair, and oppressive regime in which a person or small group of people have absolute power over everyone else. **2** If you describe someone's behaviour and treatment of others that they have authority over as **tyranny**, you mean that they are severe with them or unfair to them. **3** You can describe something that you have to use or have as a **tyranny** if you think it is undesirable or unpleasant. *The telephone is one of the great tyrannies of modern life.* ◆◇◇◇ N-VAR / N-UNCOUNT / N-COUNT

ty·rant /ˈtaɪərənt/ **tyrants.** You can use **tyrant** to refer to someone who treats the people they have authority over in a cruel and unfair way. *Since 1804 the country has mostly been ruled by tyrants.* ◆◇◇◇ N-COUNT

tyre /taɪə/ **tyres;** spelled **tire** in American English. A **tyre** is a thick piece of rubber which is fitted onto the wheels of vehicles such as cars, buses, and bicycles. See picture headed **car and bicycle**. ● See also **spare tyre**. ◆◆◇◇ N-COUNT

tyro /ˈtaɪrəʊ/ **tyros.** A **tyro** is someone who is just beginning to learn something or who has very little experience of something. ...*a tyro journalist.* N-COUNT JOURNALISM

U u

U, u /juː/ **U's, u's.** **1 U** is the twenty-first letter of the English alphabet. **2 U** or **u** is used as an abbreviation for words beginning with 'u', such as 'unit', 'united', or 'University'. N-VAR

ubiqui·tous /juːˈbɪkwɪtəs/. If you describe something or someone as **ubiquitous**, you mean that they are very widespread or that they seem to be everywhere at the same time. *In the US, the camcorder has become ubiquitous.* ◆ **ubiquity** /juːˈbɪkwɪti/. ...*the ubiquity of television.* ◆◇◇◇ ADJ-GRADED / N-UNCOUNT

ud·der /ˈʌdə/ **udders.** A cow's **udder** is the organ that hangs below its body and produces milk. N-COUNT

UFO /ˌjuː ef ˈəʊ, ˈjuːfəʊ/ **UFOs.** A **UFO** is an object seen in the sky or landing on earth which cannot be identified and which is often believed to be from N-COUNT

another planet. It is an abbreviation for 'unidentified flying object'.

ugh. **Ugh** is used to represent the sound that people make if they think something is unpleasant, horrible, or disgusting. ◆◇◇◇ EXCLAM WRITTEN, INFORMAL

ugly /ˈʌɡli/ **uglier, ugliest.** **1** If you say that someone or something is **ugly**, you mean that they are very unattractive and unpleasant to look at. ...*the raw ugliness of his native city.* **2** If you refer to an event, situation, or issue as **ugly**, you mean that it is very unpleasant, usually because it involves violence or aggression. *There have been some ugly scenes.* ◆ **ugliness** *There is so much ugliness between us.* **3** ● to **rear its ugly head**: see **head**. ◆◆◇◇ ADJ-GRADED / N-UNCOUNT / ADJ-GRADED / N-UNCOUNT

ugly 'duckling, ugly ducklings. If you say that someone, especially a child, is an **ugly duckling,** N-COUNT

you mean that they are unattractive or awkward now, but will probably develop into an attractive and successful person.

UHF /ˌjuː eɪtʃ 'ef/. UHF refers to a range of radio N-UNCOUNT waves which allows a radio or television receiver to produce a good quality of sound. It is an abbreviation for 'ultra-high frequency'.

uh huh; also spelled **uh-huh**. Uh huh is used to ◆◇◇◇ represent a sound that people make when they are CONVENTION agreeing with you, when they want to show that PRAGMATICS they understand what you are saying, or when they WRITTEN, are answering 'yes' to a question. INFORMAL

UHT /ˌjuː eɪtʃ 'tiː/. UHT milk has been treated at a ADJ very high temperature so that it can be kept for a long time if the container is not opened. It is an abbreviation for 'ultra-heat-treated'.

UK /ˌjuː 'keɪ/. The UK consists of Great Britain and ◆◆◆◇ Northern Ireland. It is an abbreviation for 'United N-PROPER: Kingdom'. theN

uku·lele /ˌjuːkə'leɪli/ **ukuleles;** also spelled **uke-** N-COUNT **lele**. A ukulele is a small guitar with four strings.

ul·cer /'ʌlsə/ **ulcers.** An ulcer is a sore area on or ◆◇◇◇ inside a part of your body which is very painful and N-COUNT may bleed, or produce a poisonous substance. ♦ **ul-** **·cer·at·ed** /'ʌlsəreɪtɪd/. If a part of someone's ADJ body is **ulcerated**, ulcers have developed on it.

ul·te·ri·or /ʌl'tɪəriə/. If you say that someone has ADJ: ADJ n **ulterior** motives for doing something, you believe that their real reason for doing it is that it will benefit them in some way.

ul·ti·mate /'ʌltɪmət/. **1** You use ultimate to de- ◆◆◆◇ scribe the final result or aim of a long series of ADJ: ADJ n events. *It is still not possible to predict the ultimate outcome.* **2** You use **ultimate** to describe the origi- ADJ: ADJ n nal source or cause of something. *The ultimate cause of what's happened seems to have been the advertising campaign.* **3** You use **ultimate** to describe ADJ: ADJ n the most important or powerful thing of a particular kind. *The ultimate authority remained the presidency.* **4** You use **ultimate** to describe the most extreme ADJ: ADJ n and unpleasant example of a particular thing. *Bringing back the death penalty would be the ultimate abuse of human rights.* **5** You use **ultimate** to ADJ: ADJ n describe the best possible example of a particular thing. *He is the ultimate English gentleman.* ● **The** PHRASE **ultimate in** something is the best possible example of it. *This hotel is the ultimate in luxury.*

ul·ti·mate·ly /'ʌltɪmətli/. **1** Ultimately means ◆◆◆◇◇ finally, after a long and often complicated series of ADV events. *Whatever the scientists ultimately conclude, all of their data will immediately be disputed.* **2** You ADV: use **ultimately** to indicate that what you are saying ADV with cl is the most important point in a discussion. *Ulti-* PRAGMATICS *mately, Bismarck's revisionism scarcely affected or damaged British interests at all.*

ul·ti·ma·tum /ˌʌltɪ'meɪtəm/ **ultimatums.** An ulti- ◆◇◇◇ **matum** is a warning to someone that unless they N-COUNT act in a particular way within a particular time limit, action will be taken against them. *A campaigning group has issued an ultimatum to the police to rid an area of racist attackers.*

ultra- /'ʌltrə-/. Ultra- is used to form adjectives that PREFIX emphasize that something or someone has a quality PRAGMATICS to an extreme degree. *...ultra-modern equipment.*

ultra·ma·rine /ˌʌltrəmə'riːn/. Ultramarine is used COLOUR to describe things that are very bright blue.

ultra·son·ic /ˌʌltrə'sɒnɪk/. Ultrasonic sounds have ADJ very high frequencies, which humans cannot hear.

ultra·sound /'ʌltrəsaʊnd/ **ultrasounds. 1** Ultra- ◆◇◇◇ **sound** is used to refer to sound waves which travel N-UNCOUNT at such a high frequency that they cannot be heard by humans. **2** An **ultrasound** or an **ultrasound scan** N-COUNT is a medical test in which ultrasound waves are used to form a picture of the inside of someone's body.

ultra·vio·let /ˌʌltrə'vaɪələt/. Ultraviolet light or ra- ◆◇◇◇ diation is what causes your skin to become darker ADJ in colour after you have been in sunlight.

um. Um is used to represent a sound that people ◆◇◇◇◇ make when they are hesitating, usually while decid- PRAGMATICS ing what they want to say next. WRITTEN

um·bili·cal cord /ʌmˌbɪlɪkəl 'kɔːd/ **umbilical** N-COUNT **cords.** The **umbilical cord** is the tube connecting an unborn baby to its mother, through which it receives oxygen and nutrients.

um·brage /'ʌmbrɪdʒ/. If you say that someone PHRASE **takes umbrage,** you mean that they are offended or upset by something that someone says or does, often without sufficient reason.

um·brel·la /ʌm'brelə/ **umbrellas. 1** An umbrella ◆◆◇◇ is an object which you use to protect yourself from N-COUNT the rain or hot sun. It consists of a long stick with a folding frame covered in cloth. **2** Umbrella is used N-SING to refer to a single group or description that includes a lot of different organizations or ideas. *Does coincidence come under the umbrella of the paranormal? ...Socialist International, an umbrella group comprising almost a hundred Social Democrat parties.* **3** Umbrella is used to refer to a system or N-SING: agreement which protects a country or group of N of n, people. *These Cambodians are under the protective* supp N *umbrella of the United Nations.*

um·laut /'ʊmlaʊt/ **umlauts.** An umlaut is a symbol N-COUNT that is written over vowels in German and some other languages to indicate the way in which they should be pronounced. For example, the word 'über' has an umlaut over the 'u'.

um·pire /'ʌmpaɪə/ **umpires, umpiring, um-** ◆◆◇◇ **pired. 1** An umpire is a person whose job is to N-COUNT make sure that a sports match or contest is played fairly and that the rules are not broken. **2** To um- VERB: V **pire** means to be the umpire in a sports match or V n contest. *He umpired baseball games.*

ump·teen /ˌʌmp'tiːn/. Umpteen can be used to re- DET fer to an extremely large number of things or peo- INFORMAL ple. *He was interrupted by applause umpteen times.* ♦ **ump·teenth** He checked his watch for the ump- ORDINAL *teenth time.*

un- /ʌn-/. Un- is added to the beginning of words in PREFIX order to form words that have the opposite meaning. *My father was an unemployed labourer... He had sensed his mothers' unhappiness... She was anxious for me to unwrap the other gifts.*

UN /ˌjuː 'en/. The UN is the same as the United ◆◆◆◇◇ Nations. N-PROPER

un·abashed /ˌʌnə'bæʃt/. If you describe someone ADJ as **unabashed,** you mean that they are not ashamed, embarrassed, or shy about something, especially when you think most people would be. *He seems unabashed by his recent defeat.*

un·abat·ed /ˌʌnə'beɪtɪd/. If something continues ADJ **unabated,** it continues without any reduction in intensity or amount. *...his unabated enthusiasm for cinema.*

un·able /ʌn'eɪbəl/. If you are **unable** to do some- ◆◆◆◇◇ thing, it is impossible for you to do it, for example ADJ: because you do not have the necessary skill or v-link ADJ to- knowledge, or because you do not have enough inf time or money.

un·abridged /ˌʌnə'brɪdʒd/. An unabridged piece of ADJ writing, for example a book or article, is complete and not shortened in any way.

un·ac·cep·table /ˌʌnək'septəbəl/. If you describe ◆◆◇◇ something as **unacceptable,** you strongly disap- ADJ-GRADED prove of it or object to it and feel that it should not be allowed to happen or continue. *It is totally unacceptable for children to swear.* ♦ **un·ac·cept·ably** ADV-GRADED /ˌʌnək'septəbli/. *The reform program has brought unacceptably high unemployment.*

un·ac·com·pa·nied /ˌʌnə'kʌmpənid/. **1** If some- ADJ one is **unaccompanied,** they are alone. *Kelly's too young to go unaccompanied.* **2** Unaccompanied ADJ: ADJ n luggage or goods are being sent or transported separately from their owner. **3** An **unaccompanied** ADJ voice or instrument sings or plays alone, with no other instruments playing at the same time.

un·ac·count·able /ˌʌnə'kaʊntəbəl/. **1** Something ADJ-GRADED that is **unaccountable** does not seem to have any

sensible explanation. *For some unaccountable reason, it struck me as extremely funny.* ♦ **un·ac·count·ably** /ˌʌnəˈkaʊntəbli/. *Leonard felt unaccountably happy.* **2** If you describe a person or organization as **unaccountable**, you are critical of them because they are not responsible to anyone for their actions, or do not feel they have to explain their actions to anyone.

ADV-GRADED
ADJ-GRADED
PRAGMATICS

un·ac·count·ed for /ˌʌnəˈkaʊntɪd fɔː/. If people or things are **unaccounted for**, you do not know where they are or what has happened to them. *5,000 American servicemen who fought in Korea are still unaccounted for.*

ADJ:
v-link ADJ

un·ac·cus·tomed /ˌʌnəˈkʌstəmd/. **1** If you are **unaccustomed to** something, you do not know it very well or have not experienced it very often. *It is a part of Britain as yet largely unaccustomed to tourists.* **2** If you describe someone's behaviour or experiences as **unaccustomed**, you mean that they do not usually behave like this or have experiences of this kind. *He began to comfort me with such unaccustomed gentleness.*

ADJ-GRADED:
v-link ADJ to
n/-ing
WRITTEN

ADJ-GRADED:
ADJ n
WRITTEN

un·ac·knowl·edged /ˌʌnækˈnɒlɪdʒd/. **1** If you describe something or someone as **unacknowledged**, you mean that people ignore their existence or presence, or are not aware of it. *Unresolved or unacknowledged fears can trigger sleepwalking.* **2** If you describe something or someone as **unacknowledged**, you mean that their existence or importance is not recognized officially or publicly. *This tradition goes totally unacknowledged in official guidebooks.*

ADJ

ADJ-GRADED

un·ac·quaint·ed /ˌʌnəˈkweɪntɪd/. If you are **unacquainted with** something, you do not know about it or do not have not any experience of it. *I was then totally unacquainted with his poems.*

ADJ-GRADED:
v-link ADJ
with n

un·adorned /ˌʌnəˈdɔːnd/. Something that is **unadorned** is plain, rather than having decorations or being artistically designed.

ADJ

un·adul·ter·at·ed /ˌʌnəˈdʌltəreɪtɪd/. **1** Something that is **unadulterated** is completely pure and has had nothing added to it. **2** You can also use **unadulterated** to emphasize a particular quality, often a bad quality. *It was pure, unadulterated hell.*

ADJ

ADJ: ADJ n
PRAGMATICS

un·af·fect·ed /ˌʌnəˈfektɪd/. **1** If someone or something is **unaffected** by an event or occurrence, they are not changed by it in any way. *She seemed totally unaffected by what she'd drunk.* **2** If you describe someone as **unaffected**, you approve of them because they are natural and genuine and not pretentious or snobbish. *...this unaffected, charming couple.*

♦◇◇◇◇
ADJ-GRADED:
v-link ADJ

ADJ-GRADED
PRAGMATICS

un·afraid /ˌʌnəˈfreɪd/. If you are **unafraid** to do something, especially something most people would find frightening, you are confident and not at all nervous about doing it. *He is a man with a reputation for being tough and unafraid of unpopular decisions.*

ADJ

un·aid·ed /ˌʌnˈeɪdɪd/. If you do something **unaided**, you do it without help from anyone or anything else. *She brought us up completely unaided.*

ADJ

un·al·loyed /ˌʌnəˈlɔɪd/. If you describe a feeling such as happiness or relief as **unalloyed**, you are emphasizing that it is perfect and complete.

ADJ
PRAGMATICS
LITERARY

un·al·ter·able /ˌʌnˈɔːltərəbəl/. Something that is **unalterable** cannot be changed. *...an unalterable fact of life.*

ADJ

un·al·tered /ˌʌnˈɔːltəd/. Something that remains **unaltered** has not changed or been changed.

ADJ

un·am·bigu·ous /ˌʌnæmˈbɪɡjuəs/. If you describe a message or comment as **unambiguous**, you mean that it is clear and cannot be misunderstood. *...an election result that sent the party an unambiguous message.* ♦ **un·am·bigu·ous·ly** *He has failed to dissociate himself clearly and unambiguously from the attack.*

♦◇◇◇◇
ADJ-GRADED

ADV-GRADED

un·am·bi·tious /ˌʌnæmˈbɪʃəs/. **1** An **unambitious** person is not particularly interested in improving their position in life or in being successful, rich, or powerful. **2** An **unambitious** idea or plan is not very adventurous, and is easy to carry out successfully.

ADJ-GRADED

ADJ-GRADED

una·nim·ity /ˌjuːnəˈnɪmɪti/. When there is **unanimity** among a group of people, they all agree about something or all vote for the same thing. *All decisions would require unanimity.*

♦◇◇◇◇
N-UNCOUNT

unani·mous /juːˈnænɪməs/. When a group of people are **unanimous**, they all agree about something or all vote for the same thing. You can also describe their opinion or vote as **unanimous**. *Editors were unanimous in their condemnation of the proposals. ...the unanimous vote for Hungarian membership.* ♦ **unani·mous·ly** *Today its executive committee voted unanimously to reject the proposals.*

♦♦◇◇◇
ADJ-GRADED

ADV:
ADV with v

un·an·nounced /ˌʌnəˈnaʊnst/. If someone arrives or does something **unannounced**, they do it unexpectedly and without anyone having being told about it beforehand. *He had just arrived unannounced from South America.*

♦◇◇◇◇
ADJ

un·an·swer·able /ʌnˈɑːnsərəbəl, -ˈæns-/. **1** If you describe a question as **unanswerable**, you mean that it has no possible answer or that a particular person cannot possibly answer it. **2** If you describe a case or argument as **unanswerable**, you mean that it is obviously true or correct and that nobody could disagree with it. *He actually became convinced that the nurses had an unanswerable case.*

ADJ

ADJ

un·an·swered /ʌnˈɑːnsəd, -ˈæns-/. Something such as a question or letter that is **unanswered** has not been answered. *Some of the most important questions remain unanswered.*

♦◇◇◇◇
ADJ

un·ap·peal·ing /ˌʌnəˈpiːlɪŋ/. If you describe someone or something as **unappealing**, you find them unpleasant and unattractive.

ADJ-GRADED

un·ap·pe·tiz·ing /ˌʌnˈæpɪtaɪzɪŋ/; also spelled **unappetising** in British English. If you describe food as **unappetizing**, you think it looks unpleasant to eat.

ADJ-GRADED

un·ap·proach·able /ˌʌnəˈprəʊtʃəbəl/. If you describe someone as **unapproachable**, you mean that they seem to be difficult to talk to and not very friendly.

ADJ-GRADED

un·ar·gu·able /ˌʌnˈɑːɡjuəbəl/. If you describe a statement or opinion as **unarguable**, you think that it is obviously true or correct and that nobody could disagree with it. ♦ **un·ar·gu·ably** /ˌʌnˈɑːɡjuəbli/. *He is unarguably an outstanding man.*

ADJ

ADV:
ADV with cl/
group

un·armed /ˌʌnˈɑːmd/. If a person or vehicle is **unarmed**, they are not carrying any weapons.

♦◇◇◇◇
ADJ

un·ashamed /ˌʌnəˈʃeɪmd/. If you describe someone's behaviour or attitude as **unashamed**, you mean that they are open and honest about things that other people might find embarrassing or shocking. ♦ **un·asham·ed·ly** /ˌʌnəˈʃeɪmɪdli/. *...an unashamedly traditional view of geology.*

♦◇◇◇◇
ADJ

ADV

un·asked /ʌnˈɑːskt, -ˈæskt/. **1** An **unasked** question is one that has not been asked, although people are wondering what the answer is. *Significant questions will go unasked.* **2** If someone says or does something **unasked**, they say or do it without being asked to do it. *His advice, offered to her unasked, was to stay home and make the best of things.*

ADJ

ADJ:
ADJ after v

un·as·sail·able /ˌʌnəˈseɪləbəl/. If you describe something or someone as **unassailable**, you mean that nothing can alter, destroy, or challenge them. *That was enough to give Mansell an unassailable lead.*

ADJ-GRADED

un·as·sist·ed /ˌʌnəˈsɪstɪd/. If you do something **unassisted**, you do it on your own and nobody helps you. *He overcame his addictions unassisted.*

ADJ

un·as·sum·ing /ˌʌnəˈsjuːmɪŋ, AM -ˈsuːm-/. If you describe a person or their behaviour as **unassuming**, you approve of them because they have a modest or quiet character.

ADJ-GRADED
PRAGMATICS

un·at·tached /ˌʌnəˈtætʃt/. Someone who is **unattached** is not married or does not have a girlfriend or boyfriend.

ADJ

un·at·tain·able /ˌʌnəˈteɪnəbəl/. If you say that something is **unattainable**, you mean that it cannot be achieved or is not available.

ADJ-GRADED

un·at·tend·ed /ˌʌnəˈtendɪd/. When people or things are left **unattended**, they are not being watched or looked after.

ADJ

un·at·trac·tive /ˌʌnəˈtræktɪv/. **1 Unattractive** ◆◇◇◇
people and things are unpleasant in appearance. ADJ-GRADED
2 If you describe something as **unattractive**, you ADJ-GRADED
mean that people do not like it and do not want to
be involved with it. *The market is still unattractive
to many insurers.*

un·author·ized /ˌʌnˈɔːθəraɪzd/; also spelled **un-** ◆◇◇◇
authorised in British English. If something is **un-** ADJ
authorized, it has been produced or is happening
without official permission. ...*a new unauthorized
biography of the Russian President... The trip was
unauthorised.*

un·avail·able /ˌʌnəˈveɪləbəl/. When things or peo- ◆◇◇◇
ple are **unavailable**, you cannot obtain them, meet ADJ
them, or talk to them. *Mr Icke is out of the country
and so unavailable for comment.*

un·avoid·able /ˌʌnəˈvɔɪdəbəl/. If something is ◆◇◇◇
unavoidable, it cannot be avoided or prevented. ADJ-GRADED
Managers said the job losses were unavoidable.
♦ **un·avoid·ably** /ˌʌnəˈvɔɪdəbli/. *Prince Khalid was* ADV-GRADED
unavoidably detained in Saudi Arabia.

un·aware /ˌʌnəˈweə/. If you are **unaware** of some- ◆◆◇◇
thing, you do not know about it. *She was unaware* ADJ:
that she was being filmed. v-link ADJ

un·awares /ˌʌnəˈweəz/. If something **catches** you PHRASE
unawares or **takes** you **unawares**, it happens when
you are not expecting it. *Dealers were caught completely unawares by the Bundesbank's action.*

un·bal·ance /ˌʌnˈbæləns/ **unbalances, unbal-**
ancing, unbalanced. 1 If something **unbalances** VERB
a relationship, system, or group, it disturbs or V n
upsets it so that it is no longer successful or functioning properly. *The opposition alliance will further
unbalance Mr Kohl's already shaky coalition.* **2** To VERB: V n
unbalance something means to make it unsteady
and likely to tip over.

un·bal·anced /ˌʌnˈbælənst/. **1** If you describe ◆◇◇◇
someone as **unbalanced**, you mean that they ap- ADJ-GRADED
pear disturbed and upset or they seem to be slightly
mad. *He was shown to be mentally unbalanced.* **2** If ADJ-GRADED
you describe something such as a report or argu-
ment as **unbalanced**, you think that it is unfair or
inaccurate because it emphasizes some things and
ignores others.

un·bear·able /ˌʌnˈbeərəbəl/. If you describe some- ◆◇◇◇
thing as **unbearable**, you mean that it is so unpleas- ADJ-GRADED
ant, painful, or upsetting that you feel unable to
accept it or deal with it. *War has made life almost
unbearable for the civilians remaining in the capital.*
♦ **un·bear·ably** /ˌʌnˈbeərəbli/. *By the evening it* ADV-GRADED
had become unbearably hot.

un·beat·able /ˌʌnˈbiːtəbəl/. **1** If you describe ◆◇◇◇
something as **unbeatable**, you mean that it is the ADJ
best thing of its kind. *These resorts, like Magaluf and* PRAGMATICS
Arenal, remain unbeatable in terms of price. **2** In a ADJ
game or competition, if you describe a person or
team as **unbeatable**, or say that they are in an **un-**
beatable position, you mean that they are winning,
succeeding, or performing so well that they are unlikely to lose.

un·beat·en /ˌʌnˈbiːtən/. In sport, if a person or ◆◆◇◇
their performance is **unbeaten**, nobody else has ADJ
performed well enough to beat them. *He's unbeaten
in 20 fights.*

un·be·com·ing /ˌʌnbɪˈkʌmɪŋ/. **1** If you describe ADJ-GRADED
things such as clothes as **unbecoming**, you mean DATED
that they look unattractive. **2** If you describe a per- ADJ-GRADED
son's behaviour or remarks as **unbecoming** to them FORMAL
or of them, you mean that they are shocking and
unsuitable for that person. *His conduct was totally
unbecoming to an officer.*

un·be·known /ˌʌnbɪˈnəʊn/. The form **unbe-** PHR-PREP
knownst /ˌʌnbɪˈnəʊnst/ is also used. If something
happens **unbeknown** to you or **unbeknownst to**
you, you do not know about it. *Unbeknownst to her
father, she began taking dancing lessons.*

un·be·liev·able /ˌʌnbɪˈliːvəbəl/. **1** If you say that ◆◆◇◇
something is **unbelievable**, you are emphasizing ADJ-GRADED
that it is very good, impressive, intense, or extreme. PRAGMATICS
*The pressure they put us under there was unbeliev-

*able... It was an unbelievable moment when Chris
won the gold medal.* ♦ **un·be·liev·ably** ADV-GRADED:
/ˌʌnbɪˈliːvəbli/. *He beamed: 'Unbelievably, we have* ADV with cl/
now made it to the final twice.' **2** You can use **un-** group
believable to emphasize that you think something ADJ
is very bad or shocking. *I find it unbelievable that* PRAGMATICS
people can accept this sort of behaviour.
♦ **unbelievable** *What you did was unbelievably* ADV-GRADED:
stupid... Unbelievably, our Government are now ADV with cl/
planning to close this magnificent institution. **3** If an ADJ
idea or theory is **unbelievable**, it is so unlikely or so
illogical that you cannot believe it. *I know it sounds
unbelievable but I never wanted to cheat.*
♦ **unbelievably** *Lainey was, unbelievably, preg-* ADV-GRADED:
nant again. ADV with cl/
group

un·be·liev·er /ˌʌnbɪˈliːvə/ **unbelievers.** People N-COUNT
who do not believe in a particular religion are
sometimes referred to as **unbelievers**.

un·be·liev·ing /ˌʌnbɪˈliːvɪŋ/. If you describe some- ADJ
one as **unbelieving**, you mean that they do not believe something that they have been told. *He looked
at me with unbelieving eyes.*

un·bend /ˌʌnˈbend/ **unbends, unbending, un-** VERB: V
bent. If someone **unbends**, their attitude becomes
less strict than it was.

un·bend·ing /ˌʌnˈbendɪŋ/. If you describe a person ADJ
or their behaviour as **unbending**, you mean that
they have very strict attitudes and beliefs, which
they are unwilling to change. ...*her unbending opposition to Communist rule.*

un·bi·ased /ˌʌnˈbaɪəst/; also spelled **unbiassed.** If ADJ-GRADED
you describe someone or something as **unbiased**,
you mean they are fair and do not show prejudice
or favouritism.

un·bid·den /ˌʌnˈbɪdən/. If something happens **un-** ADJ
bidden, it happens without you expecting or want- LITERARY
ing it to happen. *The name came unbidden to Cook's
mind – Ashley Stoker.*

un·blem·ished /ˌʌnˈblemɪʃt/. **1** If you describe ADJ
something such as someone's record, reputation, or
character as **unblemished**, you mean it has not
been harmed or spoiled. ...*Lee's unblemished reputation as a man of honor and principle.* **2** If you de- ADJ
scribe something as **unblemished**, you mean that it
has no marks or imperfections on its surface.

un·blink·ing /ˌʌnˈblɪŋkɪŋ/. If you describe ADJ
someone's eyes or expression as **unblinking**, you LITERARY
mean that they are looking steadily at something
without blinking. ♦ **un·blink·ing·ly** *She looked at* ADV
him unblinkingly.

un·born /ˌʌnˈbɔːn/. An **unborn** child is still inside ◆◇◇◇
its mother's womb or is going to be born in the fu- ADJ
ture. *They will affect generations of Britons still unborn.* ▶ **The unborn** are children who are not born N-PLURAL:
yet. the N

un·bound·ed /ˌʌnˈbaʊndɪd/. If you describe some- ADJ
thing as **unbounded**, you mean that it has, or seems
to have, no limits. ...*an unbounded capacity to imitate and adopt the new.*

un·break·able /ˌʌnˈbreɪkəbəl/. **1 Unbreakable** ob- ADJ
jects cannot be broken, usually because they are
made of a very strong material. **2** An **unbreakable** ADJ
rule must be obeyed or adhered to.

un·bridge·able /ˌʌnˈbrɪdʒəbəl/. If there is an ADJ
unbridgeable gap or divide between two sides in an JOURNALISM
argument, it is unlikely that the argument will end
because the two sides will never agree.

un·bri·dled /ˌʌnˈbraɪdəld/. If you describe behav- ADJ
iour or feelings as **unbridled**, you mean that they
are not controlled or limited in any way. ...*the unbridled greed of the 1980s.* ...*unbridled passion.*

un·bro·ken /ˌʌnˈbrəʊkən/. If something is **unbro-** ◆◇◇◇
ken, it is continuous or complete and has not been ADJ
interrupted or broken. ...*an unbroken run of 38
match wins... We've had ten days of almost unbroken sunshine.*

un·buck·le /ˌʌnˈbʌkəl/ **unbuckles, unbuckling,** VERB: V n
unbuckled. If you **unbuckle** something such as a
belt or a shoe, you unfasten it by releasing the
buckle on it.

un·bur·den /ˌʌnˈbɜːdən/ **unburdens, unburden-** VERB: **ing, unburdened.** If you **unburden** yourself to someone, you tell them about something which you have been secretly worrying about. *Some students unburden themselves of emotional problems that faculty members feel ill equipped to handle.*

un·but·ton /ˌʌnˈbʌtən/ **unbuttons, unbuttoning,** VERB: V n **unbuttoned.** If you **unbutton** an item of clothing, you unfasten the buttons on it.

uncalled for /ˌʌnˈkɔːld fɔː/. If you describe a re- ADJ-GRADED mark as **uncalled for**, you feel it should not have been made, because it was unkind or unfair.

un·can·ny /ˌʌnˈkæni/. If you describe something as ◆◇◇◇◇ **uncanny**, you mean that it is strange and difficult to ADJ-GRADED explain. *I had this uncanny feeling that I was seeing the future.* ♦ **un·can·ni·ly** /ˌʌnˈkænɪli/. *They have* ADV-GRADED *uncannily similar voices.*

un·car·ing /ˌʌnˈkeərɪŋ/. If you describe someone as ADJ-GRADED **uncaring**, you are criticizing them for not caring PRAGMATICS about other people's suffering and hardship. *...this uncaring attitude towards the less well off.*

un·ceas·ing /ʌnˈsiːsɪŋ/. If you describe something ADJ as **unceasing**, you are emphasizing that it continues without stopping. *...his unceasing labours.* ♦ **un-** **·ceas·ing·ly** *Paul talked unceasingly.* ADV

un·cer·e·mo·ni·ous·ly /ˌʌnseriˈməʊniəsli/. Some- ADV: thing that is done **unceremoniously** is done in a ADV with v sudden, rude, or rather rough way. *He had to be bundled unceremoniously out of the way.*

un·cer·tain /ʌnˈsɜːtən/. **1** If you are **uncertain** ◆◆◇◇◇ about something, you do not know whether you ADJ-GRADED should do it, whether it will happen, or whether it is true. *He stopped, uncertain how to put the question tactfully.* ♦ **un·cer·tain·ly** *He entered the hallway* ADV-GRADED *and stood uncertainly.* **2** If something is **uncertain**, ADJ-GRADED it is not known or not definite. *It's uncertain wheth- er they will accept the plan.* **3** If you say that some- PHRASE one tells a person something **in no uncertain** PRAGMATICS **terms**, you are emphasizing that they say it strongly and clearly so that there is no doubt about what they mean.

un·cer·tain·ty /ʌnˈsɜːtənti/ **uncertainties.** Un- ◆◆◇◇◇ **certainty** is a state of doubt about the future or N-VAR about what is the right thing to do. *...a period of po- litical uncertainty.*

un·chal·lenged /ˌʌnˈtʃælɪndʒd/. **1** If something ◆◇◇◇◇ goes **unchallenged**, people accept it without asking ADJ questions about whether it is right or wrong. *...the unchallenged principle of parliamentary sovereignty.* **2** If someone's leadership or authority is **unchal-** ADJ **lenged**, it is secure and nobody is able to compete with them. **3** If you do something **unchallenged**, ADJ: nobody stops you and asks you questions, for exam- ADJ after v ple about who you are or why you are doing it.

un·changed /ˌʌnˈtʃeɪndʒd/. If something is **un-** ◆◆◇◇◇ **changed**, it has stayed the same for a particular pe- ADJ riod of time. *For many years prices have remained virtually unchanged.*

un·chang·ing /ˌʌnˈtʃeɪndʒɪŋ/. Something that is ADJ-GRADED **unchanging** always stays the same. *...eternal and unchanging truths.*

un·char·ac·ter·is·tic /ˌʌnkærɪktəˈrɪstɪk/. If an ac- ◆◇◇◇◇ tion or mood is **uncharacteristic** of someone, it is ADJ-GRADED not their usual type of behaviour. *It was uncharac- teristic of her father to disappear like this.* ♦ **un-** **·char·ac·ter·is·ti·cal·ly** /ˌʌnkærɪktəˈrɪstɪkli/. ADV-GRADED *Owen has been uncharacteristically silent.*

un·chari·table /ˌʌnˈtʃærɪtəbəl/. If you describe ADJ-GRADED someone's remarks, thoughts, or behaviour as **un- charitable**, you think they are being unkind or un- fair to someone. *This was an uncharitable assess- ment of the reasons for the failure.*

un·chart·ed /ˌʌnˈtʃɑːtɪd/. If you describe a situa- ADJ tion, experience, or activity as **uncharted** territory or waters, you mean that it is new or unfamiliar. *...a largely uncharted area of medical science.*

un·checked /ˌʌnˈtʃekt/. If something harmful is ◆◇◇◇◇ left **unchecked**, nobody controls it or prevents it ADJ from increasing.

un·civi·lized /ˌʌnˈsɪvɪlaɪzd/; also spelled **uncivilised** ADJ-GRADED in British English. If you describe someone's behav- PRAGMATICS iour as **uncivilized**, you disapprove of it, for exam- ple because it is cruel or rude. *I think any sport in- volving animals where the animals do not have a choice is barbaric and uncivilized.*

un·claimed /ˌʌnˈkleɪmd/. If something is **un-** ADJ **claimed**, nobody has claimed it or said that it be- longs to them. *Her luggage remained unclaimed at Frankfurt Departures.*

un·clas·si·fied /ˌʌnˈklæsɪfaɪd/. If information or a ADJ document is **unclassified**, it is not secret and is available to the general public.

un·cle /ˈʌŋkəl/ **uncles.** Someone's **uncle** is the ◆◆◆◇◇ brother of their mother or father, or the husband of N-FAMILY; their aunt. *My uncle was the mayor of Memphis.* N-TITLE *...Uncle Fred.*

un·clean /ˌʌnˈkliːn/. **1** Something that is **unclean** is ADJ-GRADED dirty and likely to cause disease. *...the Western atti- tude to insects as being dirty and unclean.* **2** If you ADJ describe someone or something as **unclean**, you consider them to be spiritually or morally bad. *...unclean thoughts.*

un·clear /ˌʌnˈklɪə/. **1** If something is **unclear**, it is ◆◆◇◇◇ not known or not certain. *It is unclear how much* ADJ-GRADED *popular support they have.* **2** If you are **unclear** ADJ-GRADED: about something, you do not understand it properly v-link ADJ or are not sure about it. *He is still unclear about his own future.*

Un·cle Sam /ˌʌŋkəl ˈsæm/. The United States of N-PROPER America, or its government, is sometimes referred INFORMAL to as **Uncle Sam**.

Uncle 'Tom, Uncle Toms. In the past, some N-COUNT people referred to a black man as an **Uncle Tom** if PRAGMATICS they disapproved of him because he was always RUDE humble and obedient to white people; an offensive term.

un·clothed /ˌʌnˈkləʊðd/. If someone is **unclothed**, ADJ they are not wearing any clothes. *It's considered im-* FORMAL *proper to be unclothed in public.*

un·clut·tered /ˌʌnˈklʌtəd/. If you use **uncluttered** ADJ-GRADED to describe something such as room or a picture, you mean that it is simple and does not contain a lot of unnecessary things.

un·coil /ˌʌnˈkɔɪl/ **uncoils, uncoiling, uncoiled.** V-ERG If something **uncoils** or if you **uncoil** it, it becomes V straight after being in a coil, twisted, or curled up. V n *Dan played with the tangerine peel, letting it uncoil and then coil again... Robina uncoiled her legs and stood up.*

un·com·fort·able /ˌʌnˈkʌmftəbəl/. **1** If you are ◆◆◇◇◇ **uncomfortable**, you are slightly worried or embar- ADJ-GRADED rassed, and not relaxed and confident. *He says he feels uncomfortable giving interviews.* ♦ **un·com-** **·fort·ably** /ˌʌnˈkʌmftəbli/. *I became uncomfortably* ADV-GRADED *aware that the people at the next table were watch- ing me.* **2** Something that is **uncomfortable** makes ADJ-GRADED you feel slight pain or physical discomfort when you experience it or use it. *Wigs are hot and uncomfort- able to wear constantly... She collapsed in an un- comfortable chair. ...a long, uncomfortable journey.* ♦ **uncomfortably** *The water was uncomfortably* ADV-GRADED *cold. ...sitting in an uncomfortably hot conference room.* **3** If you are **uncomfortable**, you are not ADJ-GRADED physically relaxed, and you feel slight pain or dis- comfort. *I sometimes feel uncomfortable after eating in the evening.* ♦ **uncomfortably** *He awoke to find* ADV-GRADED *himself lying uncomfortably on a pile of firewood.* **4** You can describe a situation or fact as **uncom-** ADJ-GRADED **fortable** when it is difficult to deal with and causes problems and worries. *It is uncomfortable to think of our own death, but we need to... Such questions are uncomfortable to answer.*

un·com·mit·ted /ˌʌnkəˈmɪtɪd/. Someone who is ADJ **uncommitted** is unwilling to show support and loy- alty for a particular belief, group, or person. *...un- committed voters... I was still uncommitted to the venture.*

un·com·mon /ˌʌnˈkɒmən/. **1** If something is **un-** ◆◇◇◇◇ **common**, it does not happen often or is not often ADJ-GRADED

seen. *Cancer of the breast in young women is uncommon... A 15-year lifespan is not uncommon for a dog.* **2** If you describe a good quality as **uncommon**, you mean that it is unusually great in degree or amount. *Both are blessed with uncommon ability.* ◆ **un·com·mon·ly** *Mary Whitehouse was uncommonly good at tennis.* — ADJ: ADJ n LITERARY / ADV

un·com·mu·ni·ca·tive /ˌʌnkə'mjuːnɪkətɪv/. If you describe someone as **uncommunicative**, you are criticizing them because they do not talk to other people very much and are unwilling to say what they know, think, or feel. *My daughter is very difficult, uncommunicative and moody.* — ADJ-GRADED PRAGMATICS

un·com·plain·ing /ˌʌnkəm'pleɪnɪŋ/. If you describe someone as **uncomplaining**, you approve of them because they do difficult or unpleasant things and do not complain about them. *He was a cheerful and uncomplaining travel companion.* — ADJ PRAGMATICS

un·com·pli·cat·ed /ˌʌn'kɒmplɪkeɪtɪd/. If you describe something or someone as **uncomplicated**, you approve of them because they are simple and straightforward. *...good, fresh British cooking with its uncomplicated, direct flavours.* — ◆◇◇◇ ADJ PRAGMATICS

un·com·pre·hend·ing /ˌʌnkɒmprɪ'hendɪŋ/. If you describe someone as **uncomprehending**, you mean that they do not understand what is happening or what someone has said. *He gave the bottle a long, uncomprehending look.* — ADJ

un·com·pro·mis·ing /ˌʌn'kɒmprəmaɪzɪŋ/. **1** If you describe someone as **uncompromising**, you mean that they are determined not to change their opinions or aims in any way. *...a tough and uncompromising politician.* ◆ **un·com·pro·mis·ing·ly** *He states uncompromisingly that he is opposed to any practices which oppress animals.* **2** If you describe something as **uncompromising**, you mean that it does not attempt to make shocking or unpleasant things any more acceptable to people. *...a film of uncompromising brutality.* ◆ **uncompromisingly** *...the uncompromisingly modern decor.* — ◆◇◇◇ ADJ-GRADED / ADV-GRADED / ADJ-GRADED / ADV-GRADED

un·con·cealed /ˌʌnkən'siːld/. An **unconcealed** emotion is one that someone has made no attempt to hide. *...their unconcealed dislike of each other.* — ADJ

un·con·cerned /ˌʌnkən'sɜːnd/. If someone is **unconcerned** about something, usually something that most people would care about, they are not interested in it or worried about it. *Paul was unconcerned about what he had done... He seems totally unconcerned by real dangers.* — ◆◇◇◇ ADJ-GRADED

un·con·di·tion·al /ˌʌnkən'dɪʃənəl/. If you describe something as **unconditional**, you mean that it is done or given to someone freely, without anything being required in return. *Children need unconditional love... The leader of the revolt made an unconditional surrender.* ◆ **un·con·di·tion·al·ly** *The hostages were released unconditionally.* — ◆◆◇◇ ADJ / ADV: ADV with v

un·con·firmed /ˌʌnkən'fɜːmd/. If a report or a rumour is **unconfirmed**, there is no definite proof as to whether it is true or not. *There are unconfirmed reports of several small villages buried by mudslides.* — ◆◇◇◇ ADJ

un·con·gen·ial /ˌʌnkən'dʒiːniəl/. If you describe a person or place as **uncongenial**, you mean that they are unfriendly and unpleasant. *Hollywood was an uncongenial place to work.* — ADJ-GRADED

un·con·nect·ed /ˌʌnkə'nektɪd/. If two things are **unconnected** with each other, they are not related in any way. *I can't believe that those two murders are unconnected.* — ADJ-GRADED

un·con·scion·able /ʌn'kɒnʃənəbəl/. If you describe something as **unconscionable**, you find it very shocking, annoying, or unacceptable. *A nuclear war would be an unconscionable crime against humanity.* — ADJ FORMAL

un·con·scious /ʌn'kɒnʃəs/. **1** Someone who is **unconscious** is in a state similar to sleep, usually as the result of illness or injury. *By the time the ambulancemen arrived he was unconscious... He was dragged from his van and beaten unconscious.* ◆ **un·con·scious·ness** *He knew that he might soon lapse into unconsciousness.* **2** If someone is un- — ◆◆◇◇ ADJ / v-link ADJ, ADJ n, ADJ after v / N-UNCOUNT / ADJ-GRADED

conscious of something, they are unaware of it. If they are unaware of their own feelings or actions, you can describe these as **unconscious**. *Mr Battersby was apparently quite unconscious of their presence.* ◆ **un·con·scious·ly** *'I was very unsure of myself after the divorce,' she says, unconsciously sweeping back the curls from her forehead.* **3** In psychology, the **unconscious** is the part of your mind that contains feelings and ideas that you do not know about or cannot control. — ADV / N-SING: the/poss N

un·con·sti·tu·tion·al /ˌʌnkɒnstɪ'tjuːʃənəl, AM -'tuː-/. An **unconstitutional** action breaks the rules of a political system. *The Moldavian parliament has declared the elections unconstitutional.* — ◆◇◇◇ ADV

un·con·trol·lable /ˌʌnkən'trəʊləbəl/. **1** If a feeling or physical action is **uncontrollable**, you cannot control it or prevent yourself from feeling or doing it. *He was seized with uncontrollable rage... He burst into uncontrollable laughter.* ◆ **un·con·trol·lably** /ˌʌnkən'trəʊləbli/. *I started shaking uncontrollably.* **2** If you describe a person as **uncontrollable**, you mean that their behaviour is bad and that nobody can make them behave more sensibly. *Uncontrollable children grow into young criminals.* **3** If you describe a situation or series of events as **uncontrollable**, you think that nothing can be done to control them or to prevent things from getting worse. *If political and ethnic problems are not resolved the situation could become uncontrollable.* — ◆◇◇◇ ADJ / ADV / ADJ / ADJ

un·con·trolled /ˌʌnkən'trəʊld/. If a situation, activity, or feeling, especially a harmful one, is **uncontrolled**, it is happening freely, and is not being prevented from continuing or growing. *The capital, Nairobi, is choking on uncontrolled immigration. ...a mood of uncontrolled anger.* — ◆◇◇◇ ADJ-GRADED

un·con·ven·tion·al /ˌʌnkən'venʃənəl/. If you describe something such as a method or a person's behaviour as **unconventional**, you mean that they are unusual, and unlike what people generally expect or approve of. *He had rather unconventional work habits, preferring to work through the night.* — ◆◇◇◇ ADJ-GRADED

un·con·vinced /ˌʌnkən'vɪnst/. If you are **unconvinced** that something is true or right, you have strong doubts about it. *Most consumers seem unconvinced that the recession is over.* — ◆◇◇◇ ADJ

un·con·vinc·ing /ˌʌnkən'vɪnsɪŋ/. **1** If you describe a statement, argument, or explanation as **unconvincing**, you do not believe it is true or valid. ◆ **un·con·vinc·ing·ly** *'It is doing me no harm,' he said, unconvincingly.* **2** If you describe a story or a character in a story as **unconvincing**, you think they are not real or believable. *...an unconvincing love story.* — ◆◇◇◇ ADJ-GRADED / ADV-GRADED: ADV with v / ADJ-GRADED

un·cooked /ˌʌn'kʊkt/. **Uncooked** food has not yet been cooked. — ADJ

un·co·op·era·tive /ˌʌnkəʊ'ɒpərətɪv/. If you describe someone as **uncooperative**, you mean that they make no effort at all to help other people or to make other people's lives easier. *She became uncooperative: unwilling to do her homework or help with any household chores.* — ADJ-GRADED

un·co·ordi·nat·ed /ˌʌnkəʊ'ɔːdɪneɪtɪd/. **1** If someone is **uncoordinated**, their movements are jerky and they are not in full control of them. *...an uncoordinated toddler.* **2** If you describe actions or plans as **uncoordinated**, you mean they are not well-organized. *Government action has been half-hearted and uncoordinated.* — ADJ-GRADED / ADJ-GRADED

un·cork /ˌʌn'kɔːk/ **uncorks, uncorking, uncorked.** When you **uncork** a bottle of wine, you open it by pulling the cork out of it. — VERB: V n

un·cor·robo·rat·ed /ˌʌnkə'rɒbəreɪtɪd/. An **uncorroborated** statement or claim is not supported by any evidence or information. *Uncorroborated confessions should no longer be accepted by courts.* — ADJ

un·count·able noun /ˌʌnkaʊntəbəl 'naʊn/ **uncountable nouns.** An **uncountable noun** is the same as an **uncount noun**. — N-COUNT

un·count noun /ˌʌnkaʊnt 'naʊn/ **uncount nouns.** An **uncount noun** is a noun such as 'gold' or 'infor- — N-COUNT

U

mation' which has only one form and can be used without a determiner.

un·couth /ˌʌnˈkuːθ/. If you describe someone as uncouth, you mean that they are bad-mannered, and that their behaviour is unpleasant and totally unacceptable. ADJ-GRADED

un·cov·er /ˌʌnˈkʌvə/ **uncovers, uncovering, uncovered. 1** If you **uncover** facts or secrets, you discover or find out about them. *Auditors said they had uncovered evidence of fraud.* **2** When archaeologists **uncover** something, they find a thing or a place that has been under the ground for a long time. *Archaeologists have uncovered an 11,700-year-old hunting camp in Alaska.* **3** To **uncover** something means to remove something that is covering it. *When the seedlings sprout, uncover the tray.* ◆◆◇◇◇ VERB V n VERB V n VERB V n

un·cov·ered /ˌʌnˈkʌvəd/. Something that is left **uncovered** does not have anything covering it. *The uncovered bucket in the corner stank.* ADJ

un·criti·cal /ˌʌnˈkrɪtɪkəl/. If you describe a person or their behaviour as **uncritical**, you mean that they do not judge whether someone or something is good or bad or right or wrong. ...*the conventional notion of women as uncritical purchasers of heavily advertised products.* ◆ **un·criti·cal·ly** /ˌʌnˈkrɪtɪkli/. *Politicians want a lap-dog press which will uncritically report their propaganda.* ADJ-GRADED ADV-GRADED

unc·tu·ous /ˈʌŋktʃuəs/. If you describe someone as **unctuous**, you are criticizing them because they seem to be full of praise, kindness, or interest, but are obviously insincere. ...*the kind of unctuous tone that I've heard often at diplomatic parties.* ADJ-GRADED PRAGMATICS FORMAL

un·cul·ti·vat·ed /ˌʌnˈkʌltɪveɪtɪd/. **Uncultivated** land has no crops growing on it. ADJ

un·cut /ˌʌnˈkʌt/. **1** Something that is uncut has not been cut. *I suggested that the grass should be left uncut.* **2** An **uncut** book, play, or film has not been shortened or censored. *We saw the uncut version of 'Caligula'.* **3 Uncut** diamonds and gems have not been cut into a regular shape. ADJ ADJ ADJ

un·dam·aged /ˌʌnˈdæmɪdʒd/. Something that is **undamaged** has not been damaged or spoilt at all. ...*stupendous architecture, undamaged by the war.* ADJ-GRADED

un·dat·ed /ˌʌnˈdeɪtɪd/. An **undated** letter, document, or work of art does not have a date written on it. ADJ

un·daunt·ed /ˌʌnˈdɔːntɪd/. If you are **undaunted**, you are confident about dealing with something that would frighten or worry most people. *Undaunted by the scale of the job, Lesley set about planning how each room should look.* ADJ-GRADED

un·de·cid·ed /ˌʌndɪˈsaɪdɪd/. If you are **undecided**, you cannot decide about something or have not yet decided about it. *She was still undecided as to what career she wanted to pursue.* ...*undecided voters.* ◆◇◇◇◇ ADJ-GRADED

un·de·feat·ed /ˌʌndɪˈfiːtɪd/. If a sports player or team is **undefeated**, nobody has beaten them over a particular period of time. *She was undefeated for 12 years... The two London clubs are the only undefeated teams in the division.* ADJ

un·de·mand·ing /ˌʌndɪˈmɑːndɪŋ/. If you describe something such as a job as **undemanding**, you mean that it does not require you to work very hard or to think a great deal about it. *The book is an enjoyable and undemanding read.* ADJ-GRADED

un·demo·crat·ic /ˌʌndeməˈkrætɪk/. An **undemocratic** system, process, or decision is controlled or made by one person or a small number of people, rather than by all the people involved; used showing disapproval. ...*the undemocratic seizure of power by the military.* ◆◇◇◇◇ ADJ-GRADED PRAGMATICS

un·de·mon·stra·tive /ˌʌndɪˈmɒnstrətɪv/. An **undemonstrative** person does not often show affection. ...*an undemonstrative woman who rarely touches even her own son.* ADJ-GRADED

un·de·ni·able /ˌʌndɪˈnaɪəbəl/. If something is **undeniable**, it is definitely true. *Her charm is undeniable.* ...*the undeniable fact that she was driving with almost twice the legal limit of alcohol in her blood.* ◆◇◇◇◇ ADJ

◆ **un·de·ni·ably** /ˌʌndɪˈnaɪəbli/. *Bringing up a baby is undeniably hard work.* ADV

un·der /ˈʌndə/. In addition to the uses shown below, **under** is also used in phrasal verbs such as 'go under' and 'knuckle under'. ◆◆◆◆◆

1 If a person or thing is **under** something, they are at a lower level than that thing, and may be covered by it. ...*a labyrinth of tunnels under the ground... She buried her head under the covers, pretending to be asleep... A path runs under the trees.* **2** In a place such as a sea or swimming pool, if someone or something is **under** the water, they are fully in the water and covered by it. *He'd been held under the water and drowned.* ▶ Also an adverb. *When the water was up to his neck, a hand came from behind and pushed his head under.* **3** If you go **under** something, you move from one side to the other of something that is at a higher level than you. *A river boat passed under the bridge.* **4** Something that is **under** a layer of something, especially clothing, is covered by that layer. *I was wearing two sweaters under the green army jacket... It was hard to see the colours under the layer of dust.* PREP PREP ADV: ADV after v PREP PREP

5 If something or someone is **under** a particular age or amount, they are less than that age or amount. ...*children under five... Expenditure this year should be just under 15 billion pounds.* ▶ Also an adverb. ...*a free childminding service for 5's and under.* PREP ADV: amount and ADV

6 You can use **under** before a noun to indicate that a person or thing is being affected by something or is going through a particular process. *I'm rarely under pressure and my co-workers are always nice to me... The cause of the crash was under investigation.* **7** If something happens **under** particular circumstances, it happens when those circumstances exist. *His best friend was killed by police under extremely questionable circumstances... There would be no new taxes under his leadership.* **8** If something happens **under** a law, agreement, or system, it happens because that law, agreement, or system says that it should happen. ...*a parental rights order under section 4 of the Family Law Reform Act... Under the Constitution, you cannot be tried twice for the same crime.* **9** If a country is **under** a particular person or party, it is being ruled by them. ...*the Baltic Republics, forcibly incorporated into the Soviet Union under Stalin.* **10** If you study or work **under** someone, that person is your teacher or boss. ...*the artists who had studied under Beuys... I am the new manager and you will be working under me.* PREP PREP PREP PREP PREP

11 If you do something **under** a particular name, you use that name instead of your real name. *Were any of your books published under the name Amanda Fairchild?... The patient was registered under a false name.* **12** You use **under** to say which section of a list, book, or system something is classified in. *This study is described under 'General Diseases of the Eye'... 'Where would it be?'—'Filed under C, second drawer down.'* PREP PREP

13 ● **under canvas:** see **canvas. ● under wraps:** see **wrap.**

under- /ˈʌndə-/. **1 Under-** is used to form words that express the idea that an amount or value is too low or not enough. *Make sure that you are not underinsured... The company admits that its shares were underpriced originally.* **2 Under-** is added to the beginning of nouns that refer to a job or rank in order to form nouns that refer to a more junior job or rank. ...*the new undersecretary of education. ...clients who wouldn't deal with an undermanager.* PREFIX PREFIX

under·achieve /ˌʌndərəˈtʃiːv/ **underachieves, underachieving, underachieved.** If someone **underachieves** in something such as school work or a job, they do not perform as well as they could. ◆ **under·achiev·er, underachievers.** An **underachiever** is a worker or student who ought to perform better in their work. VERB: V N-COUNT

under 'age; also spelled **underage.** A person who is **under age** is legally too young to do something, for example to drink alcohol or have sex. You can also describe these activities as **under age** if they ADJ

are done by such a person. *Underage youths can obtain alcohol from their older friends.*

under·arm /ˈʌndɑːrm/. **1** You use **underarm** to refer to your armpits. *...underarm deodorants.* **2** You use **underarm** to describe actions such as throwing a ball, in which you do not stretch your arm over your shoulder. *...an underarm throw.* ▶ Also an adverb. *All the Arsenal goalkeeper could do was fend it off underarm.* ADJ: ADJ n / ADJ: ADJ n / ADV: ADV after v

under·bel·ly /ˈʌndəbeli/. The **underbelly** of something is the part of it that can be most easily attacked or criticized. *They did not see Italy as a soft underbelly through which Europe could be invaded.* N-SING

under·brush /ˈʌndəbrʌʃ/. **Underbrush** consists of bushes and plants growing close together under trees in a forest or jungle. The British word is **undergrowth**. N-UNCOUNT AMERICAN

under·car·riage /ˈʌndəkærɪdʒ/ **undercarriages.** The **undercarriage** of an aeroplane is the part which supports the aeroplane when it is on the ground and when it is landing or taking off. N-COUNT BRITISH

under·class /ˈʌndəklɑːs, -klæs/ **underclasses.** In some societies, the **underclass** consists of those people who are poor, and who have little chance of improving their situation. *The basic problems of the inner-city underclass are inadequate housing and lack of jobs.* ◆◇◇◇◇ N-COUNT

under·clothes /ˈʌndəkləʊðz/. Your **underclothes** are the clothes that you wear next to your skin and under your other clothes. N-PLURAL

under·cloth·ing /ˈʌndəkləʊðɪŋ/. **Underclothing** is the same as **underclothes**. *...a common brand of men's underclothing.* N-UNCOUNT

under·coat /ˈʌndəkəʊt/ **undercoats.** An **undercoat** is a covering of paint put onto a surface as a base for a final covering of paint. N-VAR

under·cov·er /ˌʌndəˈkʌvə/. **Undercover** work involves secretly obtaining information for the government or the police. *...an undercover operation designed to catch drug smugglers.* ▶ Also an adverb. *Swanson persuaded Hubley to work undercover to capture the killer.* ◆◇◇◇◇ ADJ / ADV: ADV after v

under·cur·rent /ˈʌndəkʌrənt, -kɜːr-/ **undercurrents.** If there is an **undercurrent** of a feeling, you are hardly aware of the feeling, but it influences the way you think or behave. *...a deep undercurrent of racism in British society.* ◆◇◇◇◇ N-COUNT

under·cut /ˌʌndəˈkʌt/ **undercuts, undercutting.** The form **undercut** is used in the present tense and is also the past tense and past participle. **1** If a business **undercuts** its competitors or their prices, it sells a product more cheaply than its competitors. *...promises to undercut air fares on some routes by 40 per cent.* **2** If your attempts to achieve something **are undercut** by something, that thing prevents your attempts from being effective. *The appeal in Miller's pictures of Indian women is undercut at times by what the artist writes about them.* ◆◇◇◇◇ / VERB V n / VB: usu passive be V-ed

under·de·vel·oped /ˌʌndədɪˈveləpt/. An **underdeveloped** country or region does not have modern industries and has a low standard of living. Some people dislike this term and prefer to use **developing**. *...public-health problems in the underdeveloped world.* ◆◇◇◇◇ ADJ

under·dog /ˈʌndədɒg, AM -dɔːg/ **underdogs.** The **underdog** in a competition or situation is the person who seems least likely to succeed or win. ◆◇◇◇◇ N-COUNT

under·done /ˌʌndəˈdʌn/. **Underdone** food has been cooked for less time than necessary, and so is not pleasant to eat. ADJ-GRADED

under·em·ployed /ˌʌndərɪmˈplɔɪd/. If someone is **underemployed**, they have not got enough work to do, or their work does not make full use of their skills or abilities. ADJ

under·es·ti·mate /ˌʌndərˈestɪmeɪt/ **underestimates, underestimating, underestimated.** **1** If you **underestimate** something, you do not realize how large or great it is or will be. *None of us should ever underestimate the degree of difficulty* ◆◆◇◇◇ VERB V n Also V wh

women face in career advancement. ◆ **under·es·ti·ma·tion** /ˌʌndərestɪˈmeɪʃən/. *...a serious underestimation of harm to the environment.* **2** If you **underestimate** someone, you do not realize what they are capable of doing. N-UNCOUNT: also a N VERB: V n

under·ex·posed /ˌʌndərɪkˈspəʊzd/. If photographic film is **underexposed**, it has not been exposed to enough light during the developing process, and so the photos are darker than they should be. ADJ-GRADED

under·fed /ˌʌndəˈfed/. People who are **underfed** do not get enough food to eat. ADJ-GRADED

under·foot /ˌʌndəˈfʊt/. **1** You describe something as being **underfoot** when you are standing or walking on it. *It was still wet underfoot.* **2** If you trample or crush something **underfoot**, you spoil or destroy it by treading on it. ADV / ADV: ADV after v

under·fund·ed /ˌʌndəˈfʌndɪd/; also spelled **underfunded.** An organization or institution that is **underfunded** does not have enough money to spend, and so it cannot function properly. ADJ-GRADED

under·gar·ment /ˈʌndəɡɑːmənt/ **undergarments.** **Undergarments** are items of clothing that you wear next to your skin and under your other clothes. N-COUNT DATED

under·go /ˌʌndəˈɡəʊ/ **undergoes, undergoing, underwent, undergone.** If you **undergo** something necessary or unpleasant, it happens to you and you endure it. *He underwent an agonising 48-hour wait for the results of tests.* ◆◆◇◇◇ VERB V n

under·gradu·ate /ˌʌndəˈɡrædʒuət/ **undergraduates.** An **undergraduate** is a student at a university or college who is studying for his or her first degree. ◆◇◇◇◇ N-COUNT

under·ground The adverb is pronounced /ˌʌndəˈɡraʊnd/. The noun and adjective are pronounced /ˈʌndəɡraʊnd/. **1** Something that is **underground** is below the surface of the ground. *The plane hit so hard that one engine was buried 16 feet underground.* ▶ Also an adjective. *...an underground car park.* **2** The **underground** in a city is the railway system in which electric trains travel below the ground in tunnels. The American word is **subway**. **3** In a country which is occupied by another country, or which has a dictatorship, the **underground** is an organized group of people who are involved in illegal activities against the government in power. **4** **Underground** activities are done secretly because they are unofficial and illegal and are usually directed against the government. *...the underground Kashmir Liberation Front.* **5** If you go **underground**, you hide from the authorities or the police because your political ideas or activities are illegal. ◆◆◆◇◇ / ADV: ADV after v / ADJ: ADJ n / N-SING: the N, also by N BRITISH / N-SING: the N / ADJ: ADJ n / ADV: ADV after v

under·growth /ˈʌndəɡrəʊθ/. **Undergrowth** consists of bushes and plants growing together under the trees in a forest or jungle. The American word is **underbrush**. ◆◇◇◇◇ N-UNCOUNT BRITISH

under·hand /ˌʌndəˈhænd/. If an action is **underhand** or if it is done in an **underhand** way, it is done secretly and dishonestly; used showing disapproval. *...a sneaky and underhand way of doing business.* ADJ-GRADED PRAGMATICS

under·lay, underlays. The noun is pronounced /ˈʌndəleɪ/. The verb is pronounced /ˌʌndəˈleɪ/. **1** **Underlay** is a thick material that you place between a carpet and the floor for extra warmth and in order to protect the carpet. **2** **Underlay** is the past tense of **underlie**. N-VAR BRITISH

under·lie /ˌʌndəˈlaɪ/ **underlies, underlying, underlay, underlain.** If something **underlies** a feeling or situation, it is the cause or basis of it. *Try to figure out what feeling underlies your anger.* ● See also **underlying**. ◆◇◇◇◇ VERB V n

under·line /ˌʌndəˈlaɪn/ **underlines, underlining, underlined.** **1** If one thing, for example an action or an event, **underlines** another, it draws attention to it and emphasizes its importance. *All this underlines how important it was for Mr Gorbachev to conclude some sort of agreement with the republics.* **2** If you **underline** something such as a word or a sen- ◆◆◇◇◇ VERB: V n Also V that, V the fact that BRITISH / VERB: V n BRITISH

tence, you draw a line underneath it in order to make people notice it or to give it extra importance.

under·ling /'ʌndəlɪŋ/ **underlings.** You refer to someone as an **underling** when they are inferior in rank or status to someone else and take orders from them.   N-COUNT PRAGMATICS

under·ly·ing /,ʌndə'laɪɪŋ/. **1** The **underlying** features of an object, event, or situation are not obvious, and it may be difficult to discover or reveal them. **2** You describe something as **underlying** when it is below the surface of something else. *...hills with the hard underlying rock poking through the turf.* **3** See also **underlie**.   ADJ: ADJ n

under·mine /,ʌndə'maɪn/ **undermines, undermining, undermined. 1** If you **undermine** something such as a feeling or a system, you make it less strong or less secure than it was before, often by a gradual process or by repeated efforts. *Offering advice on each and every problem will undermine her feeling of being adult.* **2** If you **undermine** someone, or **undermine** their position or authority, you make their authority or position less secure, often by indirect methods. *She undermined him and destroyed his confidence in his own talent.* **3** If you **undermine** someone's efforts, or **undermine** their chances of achieving something, you do something which makes them less likely to succeed. *The continued fighting threatens to undermine efforts to negotiate an agreement.*   VERB V n

under·neath /,ʌndə'niːθ/. **1** If one thing is **underneath** another, it is directly below or beneath it, and may be covered or hidden by it. *The device exploded underneath a van. ...a table for two underneath the olive trees.* ► Also an adverb. *Russell wore his shirt open to reveal a white vest underneath... Pull back a bit of this carpet to see what's underneath.* **2** The part of something which is **underneath** is the part which normally touches the ground or faces towards the ground. *Check the actual construction of the chair by looking underneath.* ► Also an adjective. *...the underneath mechanism of the engine.* ► Also a noun. *...what the underneath of a car looks like.* **3** You use **underneath** when talking about feelings and emotions that people do not show in their behaviour. *Underneath, Sofia was deeply committed to her husband.* ► Also a preposition. *Underneath his outgoing behaviour Luke was shy.*   PREP / ADV / ADV / ADJ: ADJ n / N-SING: the N / ADV: ADV with cl / PREP

under·nour·ished /,ʌndə'nʌrɪʃt, AM -'nɜːr-/. If someone is **undernourished**, they are weak and unhealthy because they have not been eating enough food, or the right kind of food. ♦ **under·nour·ish·ment** /,ʌndə'nʌrɪʃmənt, AM -'nɜːr-/. *Forty per cent of children under five in developing countries are short for their age because of undernourishment.*   ADJ-GRADED / N-UNCOUNT

under·paid /,ʌndə'peɪd/. People who are **underpaid** are not paid enough money for the job that they do.   ADJ-GRADED

under·pants /'ʌndəpænts/. **Underpants** are a piece of underwear which have two holes to put your legs through and elastic around the top to hold them up round your waist or hips. In British English, **underpants** refers to only men's underwear but in American English it refers to both men's and women's.   N-PLURAL: also a pair of N

under·pass /'ʌndəpɑːs, -pæs/ **underpasses.** An **underpass** is a road or footpath that goes underneath a railway or another road.   N-COUNT

under·pin /,ʌndə'pɪn/ **underpins, underpinning, underpinned.** If one thing **underpins** another, it helps the other thing to continue or succeed by supporting and strengthening it. *...mystical themes that underpin all religions.* ♦ **under·pin·ning, underpinnings** *...the economic underpinning of ancient Mexican society.*   VERB V n / N-VAR

under·play /,ʌndə'pleɪ/ **underplays, underplaying, underplayed.** If you **underplay** something, you make it seem less important than it really is. *We often underplay the skills we have.*   VERB V n BRITISH

under·popu·lat·ed /,ʌndə'pɒpjʊleɪtɪd/. You describe a country or region as **underpopulated** when   ADJ

it could support a much larger population than it has.

under·privi·leged /,ʌndə'prɪvɪlɪdʒd/. **Underprivileged** people have less money and fewer possessions and opportunities than other people in their society. *...helping underprivileged children to learn to read.* ► The **underprivileged** are people who are underprivileged.   ADJ / N-PLURAL: the N

under·rate /,ʌndə'reɪt/ **underrates, underrating, underrated.** If you **underrate** someone or something, you do not recognize how clever, important, or significant they are. ♦ **under·rat·ed** *He is a very underrated poet.*   VERB: V n / ADJ-GRADED

under·score /,ʌndə'skɔː/ **underscores, underscoring, underscored. 1** If something such as an action or an event **underscores** another, it draws attention to the other thing and emphasizes its importance. *The rash of accidental shootings underscores how difficult it will be to restore order here.* **2** If you **underscore** something such as a word or a sentence, you draw a line underneath it in order to make people notice it or give it extra importance.   VERB: V n / V wh / Also V that, / V the fact that / AMERICAN / VERB: V n / AMERICAN

under·sea /'ʌndəsiː/. **Undersea** things or activities exist or happen below the surface of the sea. *...an undersea pipeline running to Europe.*   ADJ: ADJ n

under-'secretary, under-secretaries. An **under-secretary** is a senior official with an important post in a government department.   N-COUNT

under·shirt /'ʌndəʃɜːt/ **undershirts.** An **undershirt** is a piece of clothing worn for warmth on the top part of your body next to your skin. The British word is **vest**.   N-COUNT AMERICAN

under·side /'ʌndəsaɪd/ **undersides.** The **underside** of something is the part of it which normally faces towards the ground. *...the underside of the car.*   N-COUNT

under·signed /,ʌndə'saɪnd/. On a legal document, the **undersigned** people are the ones who have signed their names at the bottom of the document. *The undersigned buyers agree to pay a 5,000 pound deposit.* ► The **undersigned** are the people who have signed a legal document.   ADJ: ADJ n / LEGAL / N-PLURAL: the N

under·sized /,ʌndə'saɪzd/. **Undersized** people or things are smaller than usual, or smaller than they should be.   ADJ

under·staffed /,ʌndə'stɑːft, -'stæft/. If an organization is **understaffed**, it does not have enough employees to do its work properly.   ADJ-GRADED

under·stand /,ʌndə'stænd/ **understands, understanding, understood. 1** If you **understand** someone or **understand** what they are saying, you know what they mean. *I don't understand what you are talking about... He was speaking poor English, trying to make himself understood.* **2** If you **understand** a language, you know what someone is saying when they are speaking that language. *I couldn't read or understand a word of Yiddish.* **3** To **understand** someone means to know how they feel and why they behave in the way that they do. *She understands why I get tired and grumpy.* **4** You say that you **understand** something when you know why or how it happens. *They are too young to understand what is going on.*

5 If you **understand** that something is the case, you think it is the case because you have heard or read that it is. You can say that something **is understood** to be the case to mean that people generally think it is the case. *We understand that she's in the studio recording her second album... As I understand it, you came round the corner by the cricket field... The management is understood to be very unwilling to agree to this request.* **6** If someone **is given to understand** that something is the case, it is communicated to them that it is the case, usually without them being told directly. *I am given to understand that he was swearing throughout the game.*   VB: no cont, V n / V wh / make pron- self V-ed / VB: no cont V n / VB: no cont, V n / V wh / VB: no cont, V n / V wh / VB: no cont V that / V it / be V-ed to-inf / Also it be V-ed that/to-inf / PHRASE

7 You can use **understand** in expressions like **do you understand?** or **is that understood?** after you have told someone what you want or told them what to do, to make sure that they have understood you and will   CONVENTION PRAGMATICS

obey you. *I don't want to hear another word about it. Is that understood, Emma?*

under·stand·able /ˌʌndəˈstændəbəl/. **1** If you describe someone's behaviour or feelings as **understandable**, you think that they have reacted to a situation in a natural way or in the way you would expect. *His unhappiness was understandable.* ◆ **under·stand·ably** /ˌʌndəˈstændəbli/. *Most organizations are, quite understandably, suspicious of new ideas.* **2** If you say that something such as a statement or theory is **understandable**, you mean that people can easily understand it. *Roger Neuberg writes in a simple and understandable way.* ♦♦◇◇ ADJ-GRADED ADV-GRADED ADJ-GRADED

under·stand·ing /ˌʌndəˈstændɪŋ/ **understandings. 1** If you have an **understanding** of something, you know how it works or know what it means. *They have to have a basic understanding of computers.* **2** If you are **understanding** towards someone, you are kind and forgiving. *Fortunately for John, he had an understanding wife.* **3** If you show **understanding**, you sympathize with other people's feelings and forgive them if they hurt or disappoint you. *We would like to thank them for their patience and understanding.* **4** If there is **understanding** between people, they are friendly towards each other and trust each other. **5** An **understanding** is an informal agreement about something. *We had not set a date for marriage but there was an understanding between us.* **6** If you say that it is your **understanding** that something is the case, you mean that you believe it to be the case because you have heard or read that it is. *It is my understanding that all of these people have been arrested.* **7** If you agree to do something **on the understanding that** something else will be done, you do it because you have been told that the other thing will definitely be done. ♦♦♦◇◇ N-VAR: N of n ADJ-GRADED N-UNCOUNT N-UNCOUNT N-COUNT: N prep N-SING: poss N PHR-CONJ

under·state /ˌʌndəˈsteɪt/ **understates, understating, understated.** If you **understate** something, you describe it in a way that suggests that it is less important or serious than it really is. *The government chooses deliberately to understate the increase in prices.* ♦◇◇◇◇ VERB V n

under·stat·ed /ˌʌndəˈsteɪtɪd/. If you describe a style, colour, or effect as **understated**, you mean that it is not obvious. *He writes lightly, coolly, with understated humour.* ♦◇◇◇◇ ADJ: ADJ n

under·state·ment /ˈʌndəsteɪtmənt/ **understatements. 1** If you say that a statement is an **understatement**, you mean that it does not fully express the extent to which something is true. *To say I'm disappointed is an understatement.* **2 Understatement** is the practice of suggesting that things have much less of a particular quality than they really have. *...typical British understatement.* ♦◇◇◇◇ N-COUNT N-UNCOUNT

under·stood /ˌʌndəˈstʊd/. **Understood** is the past tense and past participle of **understand**.

under·study /ˈʌndəstʌdi/ **understudies.** An actor's or actress's **understudy** is the person who has learned their part in a play and can act the part if the actor or actress is ill. N-COUNT

under·take /ˌʌndəˈteɪk/ **undertakes, undertaking, undertook, undertaken. 1** When you **undertake** a task or job, you start doing it and accept responsibility for it. *She undertook the arduous task of monitoring the elections.* **2** If you **undertake** to do something, you promise that you will do it. *He undertook to edit the text himself.* ♦♦◇◇◇ VERB V n VERB V to-inf

under·tak·er /ˈʌndəteɪkə/ **undertakers.** An **undertaker** is a person whose job is to deal with the bodies of people who have died and to arrange funerals. The American word is **mortician.** ♦◇◇◇◇ N-COUNT BRITISH

under·tak·ing /ˈʌndəteɪkɪŋ/ **undertakings. 1** An **undertaking** is a task or job, especially a large or difficult one. *Organizing the show has been a massive undertaking.* **2** If you give an **undertaking** to do something, you formally promise to do it. ♦◇◇◇◇ N-COUNT N-COUNT

under·tone /ˈʌndətəʊn/ **undertones. 1** If you say something **in** an **undertone**, you say it very quietly. N-COUNT: in N

'What d'you think?' she asked in an undertone. **2** If something has **undertones** of a particular kind, it suggests ideas or attitudes of this kind without expressing them directly. *...a witty, racy story with surprisingly serious undertones.* N-COUNT: with supp

under·took /ˌʌndəˈtʊk/. **Undertook** is the past tense of **undertake.**

under·tow /ˈʌndətəʊ/ **undertows. 1** If there is an **undertow** of a feeling, that feeling exists in such a weak form that you are hardly aware of it, but it influences the way you think or behave. *The existence of an emotional undertow is an aspect of all politics.* **2** An **undertow** is a strong current of water that is moving below the surface current and in a different direction to it. N-COUNT N-COUNT

under·used /ˌʌndəˈjuːzd/; also spelled **under-used.** Something useful that is **underused** is not used as much as it could be for people's benefit as it could be. *Many schools' sports grounds are grossly underused.* ADJ-GRADED

under·uti·lized /ˌʌndəˈjuːtɪlaɪzd/; also spelled **underutilised** in British English. **Underutilized** is a more formal word for **underused.** ADJ-GRADED

under·value /ˌʌndəˈvæljuː/ **undervalues, undervaluing, undervalued.** If you **undervalue** something or someone, you fail to recognize how valuable or important they are. *We must never undervalue freedom.* ♦ **under·val·ued** *...greatly undervalued German wines.* ♦◇◇◇◇ VERB V n ADJ-GRADED

under·wa·ter /ˌʌndəˈwɔːtə/. **1** Something that exists or happens **underwater** exists or happens below the surface of the sea, a river, or a lake. *Some stretches of beach are completely underwater at high tide.* ► Also an adjective. *...underwater fishing with harpoons.* **2 Underwater** devices are specially made so that they can work in water. ♦◇◇◇◇ ADV ADJ: ADJ n ADJ: ADJ n

under·way /ˌʌndəˈweɪ/. If an activity is **underway**, it has already started. If an activity gets **underway**, it starts. *An investigation is underway to find out how the disaster happened.* ♦♦◇◇◇ ADJ: v-link ADJ

under·wear /ˈʌndəweə/. **Underwear** is clothing which you wear next to your skin under your other clothes. ♦◇◇◇◇ N-UNCOUNT

under·weight /ˌʌndəˈweɪt/. If someone is **underweight**, they are too thin, and therefore not healthy. ADJ-GRADED

under·went /ˌʌndəˈwent/. **Underwent** is the past tense of **undergo.**

under·whelmed /ˌʌndəˈwelmd/. If you are **underwhelmed** by something, you are not impressed or excited by it. *He was underwhelmed by the prospect of meeting the Queen.* ADJ-GRADED INFORMAL

under·whelm·ing /ˌʌndəˈwelmɪŋ/. If you use **underwhelming** to describe the response or reaction to something, you mean that people were not very impressed or excited by it. *He met with underwhelming applause.* ADJ-GRADED INFORMAL

under·world /ˈʌndəwɜːld/. **1** The **underworld** in a city is the organized crime there and the people who are involved in it. *...a wealthy businessman with underworld connections.* **2** In many ancient religions and legends, **the underworld** is a place under the earth's surface where people go after they die. ♦◇◇◇◇ N-SING N-SING: the N

under·write /ˌʌndəˈraɪt/ **underwrites, underwriting, underwrote, underwritten.** If an institution or company **underwrites** an activity or **underwrites** the cost of it, they agree to provide any money that is needed to cover losses or buy special equipment, often for an agreed fee. ♦♦◇◇◇ VERB: V n TECHNICAL

under·writ·er /ˈʌndəraɪtə/ **underwriters. 1** An **underwriter** is someone whose job involves agreeing to provide money for a particular activity or to pay for any losses that are made. **2** In insurance, an **underwriter** is someone whose job is to assess the risks involved in certain activities and decide how much it will cost to insure something or someone. ♦◇◇◇◇ N-COUNT TECHNICAL N-COUNT

un·de·served /ˌʌndɪˈzɜːvd/. If you describe something such as a reaction, treatment, or result as **undeserved**, you mean that the person who experiences it has not earned it and should not really have ADJ

it. *Douglas Hurd has an undeserved reputation for being dull and dry.*

un·de·sir·able /ˌʌndɪˈzaɪərəbəl/ **undesirables.** ◆◇◇◇◇
1 If you describe something or someone as **unde- ADJ-GRADED
sirable**, you think they will have harmful effects. *A
large group of undesirable strangers crashed her party.* **2 Undesirables** are people who a particular gov- N-COUNT
ernment considers to be dangerous or a threat to
society, and therefore wants to get rid of.

un·de·tect·ed /ˌʌndɪˈtektɪd/. If you are **undetected** ADJ
or if you do something **undetected**, people do not
find out where you are or what you are doing. *They
managed to get away from the coast undetected.*

un·de·vel·oped /ˌʌndɪˈveləpt/. **1** An **undeveloped** ADJ-GRADED
country or region does not have modern industries
and usually has a low standard of living. **2 Undevel-** ADJ-GRADED
oped land has not been built on or used for activities such as mining and farming.

un·did /ˌʌnˈdɪd/. **Undid** is the past tense of **undo**.

un·dies /ˈʌndiz/. You can refer to someone's under- N-PLURAL
wear as their **undies**.   INFORMAL

un·dig·ni·fied /ʌnˈdɪɡnɪfaɪd/. If you describe ADJ-GRADED
someone's actions as **undignified**, you mean they
are foolish or embarrassing. *It is sad to see a county
confine its activities to undignified public bickering.*

un·di·lut·ed /ˌʌndaɪˈluːtɪd/. **1** If you describe ADJ
someone's feelings or characteristics as **undiluted**,
you are emphasizing that they are very strong and
not mixed with any other feeling or quality. *Her
Irish accent, after thirty-odd years in London, is undiluted.* **2** A liquid that is **undiluted** has not been ADJ
made weak by mixing it with water.

un·dis·ci·plined /ʌnˈdɪsɪplɪnd/. If you describe ADJ-GRADED
someone as **undisciplined**, you mean that they behave badly or show a lack of self-control. *...a noisy
and undisciplined group of students.*

un·dis·closed /ˌʌndɪsˈkləʊzd/. **Undisclosed** infor- ◆◇◇◇◇
mation is not revealed to the public. *They are now ADJ
in hiding at an undisclosed address.*

un·dis·cov·ered /ˌʌndɪsˈkʌvəd/. Something that is ADJ
undiscovered has not been discovered or noticed.
*This site remained undiscovered, though long
sought, until recent times.*

un·dis·guised /ˌʌndɪsˈɡaɪzd/. If you describe ADJ
someone's feelings as **undisguised**, you mean that
they show them openly and do not make any attempt to hide them. *Hean looked down at Bauer in
undisguised disgust.*

un·dis·mayed /ˌʌndɪsˈmeɪd/. If you say that some- ADJ-GRADED:
one is **undismayed** by something unpleasant or un- v-link ADJ
expected, you mean that they do not feel any fear, FORMAL
worry, or sadness about it. *He was undismayed by
the prospect of failure.*

un·dis·put·ed /ˌʌndɪsˈpjuːtɪd/. **1** If you describe a ◆◇◇◇◇
fact or opinion as **undisputed**, you are trying to per- ADJ
suade someone that it is generally accepted as true
or correct. *...the undisputed fact that he had broken
the law.* **2** If you describe someone as the **undis-** ADJ
puted leader or champion, you mean that everyone
accepts their position as leader or champion. *At 78
years of age, he's still undisputed leader of his
country.*

un·dis·tin·guished /ˌʌndɪsˈtɪŋɡwɪʃt/. If you de- ADJ-GRADED
scribe someone or something as **undistinguished**,
you mean they are not attractive, interesting, or
successful. *...this rather undistinguished, grimy industrial town.*

un·dis·turbed /ˌʌndɪsˈtɜːbd/. **1** Something that re- ◆◇◇◇◇
mains **undisturbed** is not touched, moved, or used ADJ
by anyone. *The desk looked undisturbed.* **2** A place ADJ
that is **undisturbed** is peaceful and has not been affected by changes that have happened in other
places. *The war had not left Bargate undisturbed.*
3 If you are **undisturbed** in something that you are ADJ
doing, you are able to continue doing it and are not
affected by something that is happening. *I can
spend the whole day undisturbed at the warehouse.*
4 If someone is **undisturbed** by something, it does ADJ
not affect, bother, or upset them. *Victoria was

strangely undisturbed by this symptom, even though
her husband and family were frightened.*

un·di·vid·ed /ˌʌndɪˈvaɪdɪd/. **1** If you give someone ADJ
or something your **undivided** attention, you concentrate on them fully and do not think about anything else. *Adults rarely give the television their undivided attention.* **2 Undivided** feelings are ones ADJ
that are very strong and not mixed with other feelings. *He has my undivided loyalty.* **3** An **undivided** ADJ
country or organization is one that is not separated
into smaller parts or groups. *...a united, undivided
South Africa.*

undo /ˌʌnˈduː/ **undoes, undoing, undid, un-** ◆◇◇◇◇
done. 1 If you **undo** something that is closed, tied, VERB
or held together, you unfasten, loosen, or untie it. *I V n
undid the bottom two buttons of my yellow and grey
shirt.* **2** To **undo** something that has been done VERB
means to reverse its effect. *She knew it would be dif- V n
ficult to undo the damage that had been done.* **3** If a VB: usu
person, organization, or plan **is undone by** some- passive
thing, that thing causes their failure. *Macbeth is the be V-ed by n
story of a Scottish soldier who becomes king but is
undone by his own ambition.*

un·do·ing /ʌnˈduːɪŋ/. If something is someone's N-SING:
undoing, it is the cause of their failure. *His lack of with poss
experience may prove to be his undoing.*

un·done /ʌnˈdʌn/. Work that is **undone** has not yet ADJ:
been done. *He left nothing undone that needed ADJ after v
attention.*

un·doubt·ed /ʌnˈdaʊtɪd/. You can use **undoubted** ◆◆◇◇◇
to emphasize that something exists or is true. *The ADJ
event was an undoubted success.* ♦ **un·doubt·ed·ly** PRAGMATICS
*Undoubtedly, political and economic factors have ADV
played their part.*

un·dreamed of /ʌnˈdriːmd ɒv, AM - ʌv/. The form ADJ
undreamt of is also used in British English. If you PRAGMATICS
describe something as **undreamed of**, you are emphasizing that it is much better, worse, or more unusual than you thought was possible. *This new
design will offer undreamed-of levels of comfort.*

un·dress /ˌʌnˈdres/ **undresses, undressing,** ◆◇◇◇◇
undressed. When you **undress** or **undress** some- VERB: V
one, you take off your clothes or someone else's V n
clothes. *She undressed the child before putting her in
the tin bath.* ♦ **un·dressed** *He got undressed in the ADJ
bathroom.*

un·due /ʌnˈdjuː, AM -ˈduː/. If you describe some- ◆◇◇◇◇
thing bad as **undue**, you mean that it is greater or ADJ: ADJ n
more extreme than you think is reasonable or appropriate. *This would help the families to survive the
drought without undue suffering.*

un·du·late /ˈʌndʒʊleɪt/ **undulates, undulating,** ◆◇◇◇◇
undulated. Something that **undulates** has gentle VERB
curves or slopes, or moves gently and slowly up and V
down or from side to side in an attractive manner. Also V n
*The countryside begins to undulate as the rolling LITERARY
hills sweep down to the riverbanks.* ♦ **un·du·lat·ing** ADJ-GRADED
...gently undulating hills.

un·du·ly /ʌnˈdjuːli, AM -ˈduːli/. If you say that ◆◇◇◇◇
something does not happen or is not done **unduly**, ADV
you mean that it does not happen or is not done to
an excessive or unnecessary extent. *This will
achieve greater security without unduly burdening
the consumers or the economy.*

un·dy·ing /ʌnˈdaɪɪŋ/. If you refer to someone's **un-** ADJ
dying feelings, you mean that the feelings are very LITERARY
strong and are unlikely to change. *Dianne declared
her undying love for Sam.*

un·earth /ˌʌnˈɜːθ/ **unearths, unearthing, un-** ◆◇◇◇◇
earthed. 1 If someone **unearths** facts or evidence VERB
about something bad, they discover them with diffi- V n
culty, usually because they were being kept secret
or were being lied about. *Researchers have unearthed documents indicating her responsibility for
the forced adoption of children.* **2** If someone **un-** VERB
earths something that is buried, they find it by dig- V n
ging in the ground. *Fossil hunters have unearthed
the bones of an elephant believed to be 500,000 years
old.* **3** If you say that someone **has unearthed** VERB
something, you mean that they have found it after it V n

had been hidden or lost for some time. *From somewhere, he had unearthed a black silk suit.*

un·earth·ly /ʌnˈɜːθli/. **1** You use **unearthly** to describe something that seems very strange and unnatural. *The sound was so serene that it seemed unearthly.* **2** If you refer to a time as an **unearthly** hour, you are emphasizing that it is unreasonably early. *...the unearthly hour of seven in the morning.* **3** An **unearthly** noise is unpleasant because it sounds menacing and unnatural. *She heard the sirens scream their unearthly wail.*   ADJ; ADJ n PRAGMATICS; ADJ

un·ease /ʌnˈiːz/. **1** If you have a feeling of **unease**, you feel rather anxious or afraid because you think that something is wrong. *Garland tried to appear casual, but he couldn't conquer his unease.* **2** If you say that there is **unease** in a situation, you mean that people are dissatisfied or angry, but have not yet started to take any action. *He faces growing unease among the Democrats about the likelihood of war.*   ◆◇◇◇◇ N-UNCOUNT; N-UNCOUNT

un·easy /ʌnˈiːzi/. **1** If you are **uneasy**, you feel anxious, afraid, or embarrassed, because you think that something is wrong or that there is danger. *He looked uneasy and refused to answer questions.* ♦ **un·eas·i·ly** /ʌnˈiːzɪli/. *Meg shifted uneasily on her chair.* ♦ **un·eas·i·ness** *With a small degree of uneasiness, he pushed it open and stuck his head inside.* **2** If you are **uneasy** about doing something, you are not sure that it is correct or wise. *Richard was uneasy about how best to approach his elderly mother.* **3** If you describe a situation or relationship as **uneasy**, you mean that the situation is not settled and may not last. *An uneasy calm has settled over Los Angeles.* ♦ **un·eas·i·ly** *Democracy and entrepreneurial flair often sit uneasily together.* **4** If you describe a book or music as **uneasy**, you are critical of it because it is difficult to read or listen to.   ♦♦◇◇◇ ADJ-GRADED; ADV-GRADED; N-UNCOUNT; ADJ-GRADED; ADV-GRADED; ADJ PRAGMATICS JOURNALISM

un·eco·nom·ic /ˌʌniːkəˈnɒmɪk, -ek-/. **1** If you describe something such as an industry or business as **uneconomic**, you mean that it does not produce enough profit. *...the closure of uneconomic factories.* **2** If you say that an action or plan is **uneconomic**, you think it will cost a lot of money and not be successful or not be worth the expense. *It would be uneconomic to try and repair it.*   ADJ-GRADED; v-link ADJ

un·eco·nom·i·cal /ˌʌniːkəˈnɒmɪkəl, -ek-/. If you say that an action, a method, or a product is **uneconomical**, you mean that it does not make a profit. *It would be uneconomical to send a brand new tape.*   ADJ-GRADED PRAGMATICS

un·edu·cat·ed /ʌnˈedʒʊkeɪtɪd/. Someone who is **uneducated** has not received much education. ▶ **The uneducated** are people who are uneducated.   ADJ-GRADED; N-PLURAL

un·emo·tion·al /ˌʌnɪˈməʊʃənəl/. If you describe someone as **unemotional**, you mean that they do not show any feelings. *British men are often seen as being reserved and unemotional.* ♦ **un·emo·tion·al·ly** /'I'd like to have their names,' said Johnson unemotionally.*   ADJ-GRADED; ADV-GRADED: ADV after v

un·em·ploy·a·ble /ˌʌnɪmˈplɔɪəbəl/. Someone who is **unemployable** does not have a job and is unlikely to get a job, because they do not have the skills or abilities that an employer might want.   ADJ

un·em·ployed /ˌʌnɪmˈplɔɪd/. Someone who is **unemployed** does not have a job. ▶ **The unemployed** are people who are unemployed.   ♦♦◇◇◇ ADJ N-PLURAL: the N

un·em·ploy·ment /ˌʌnɪmˈplɔɪmənt/. **Unemployment** is the fact that people who want jobs cannot get them. *...an area that had the highest unemployment rate in western Europe.*   ♦♦♦◇◇ N-UNCOUNT

unem·ploy·ment benefit, unemployment benefits. **Unemployment benefit** is money that some people receive from the state when they do not have a job and are unable to find one.   ◆◇◇◇◇ N-UNCOUNT: also N in pl

unem·ploy·ment line, unemployment lines. When people talk about the **unemployment line**, they are talking about the state of being unemployed. The usual British expression is **dole queue**.   N-COUNT AMERICAN

un·end·ing /ʌnˈendɪŋ/. If you describe something as **unending**, you mean that it continues without stopping for a very long time. *I do not recall any formal training, just endless work and an unending stream of people!*   ADJ

un·en·dur·able /ˌʌnɪnˈdjʊərəbəl, AM -ˈdʊr-/. If you describe a bad situation as **unendurable**, you mean that it is so extremely unpleasant that you have to end it. *Isaac had found the work unendurable and walked out of the job.*   ADJ FORMAL

un·en·vi·able /ʌnˈenviəbəl/. If you describe a situation or task as **unenviable**, you mean that nobody would enjoy dealing with it because it is very difficult, dangerous, or unpleasant. *She had the unenviable task of making the first few phone calls.*   ADJ-GRADED

un·equal /ʌnˈiːkwəl/. **1** An **unequal** system or situation is unfair because it gives more power or privileges to one person or group of people than to others. *...a deeply oppressive, unequal and divisive political system.* ♦ **un·equal·ly** *The criteria were far from clear and victims were treated unequally.* **2** If someone is **unequal to** a task, they are incapable of doing it well. **3** **Unequal** means being different in size, strength, or amount. *The Egyptians probably measured their day in twenty-four hours of unequal length.*   ◆◇◇◇◇ ADJ-GRADED; ADV-GRADED: ADV with v; v-link ADJ to n; ADJ

un·equalled /ʌnˈiːkwəld/; spelled **unequaled** in American English. If you describe something as **unequalled**, you mean that it is greater, better, or more extreme than anything else of the same kind. *We offer the very finest properties, and an unequalled level of service.*   ADJ

un·equivo·cal /ˌʌnɪˈkwɪvəkəl/. If you describe someone's attitude as **unequivocal**, you mean that it is completely clear and very firm. *The message to him was unequivocal: 'Get out.'* ♦ **un·equivo·cal·ly** /ˌʌnɪˈkwɪvəkli/. *He stated unequivocally that the French forces were ready to go to war.*   ◆◇◇◇◇ ADJ-GRADED FORMAL; ADV-GRADED

un·err·ing /ʌnˈɜːrɪŋ/. If you describe someone's judgement or ability as **unerring**, you mean that they are always correct and never mistaken. *These designs demonstrate her unerring eye for colour and detail.* ♦ **un·err·ing·ly** *...an unerringly professional team.*   ADJ; ADV

un·escort·ed /ˌʌnɪsˈkɔːtɪd/. If someone or something is **unescorted**, they are not protected or supervised. *Unescorted children are not allowed beyond this point.*   ADJ; ADJ n, ADJ after v, v-link ADJ

un·eth·i·cal /ʌnˈeθɪkəl/. If you describe someone's behaviour as **unethical**, you think it is wrong and unacceptable according to a society's rules or people's beliefs. *It's simply unethical to promote and advertise such a dangerous product.*   ADJ-GRADED FORMAL

un·even /ʌnˈiːvən/. **1** An **uneven** surface or edge is not smooth, flat, or straight. *...the uneven surface of the car park.* *...uneven teeth.* ♦ **un·even·ly** *...wearing dresses that pinched at the armholes, that hung as unevenly as flags.* **2** Something that is **uneven** is not regular or consistent. *He could hear that her breathing was uneven.* ♦ **unevenly** *The steaks were unevenly cooked.* **3** If you describe something as **uneven**, you think it is not very good because it is not consistent in quality. *This was, for him, an oddly uneven performance.* **4** An **uneven** system or situation is unfairly arranged or organized. *Some of the victims are complaining loudly about the uneven distribution of emergency aid.* ♦ **unevenly** *Within a free enterprise capitalist society, resources are very unevenly distributed.*   ♦◇◇◇◇ ADJ-GRADED; ADV-GRADED: ADV with v; ADJ-GRADED; ADV-GRADED: ADV with v; ADJ-GRADED; ADJ-GRADED; ADV-GRADED: ADV with v

un·event·ful /ˌʌnɪˈventfʊl/. If you describe a period of time as **uneventful**, you mean that nothing interesting, exciting, or important happened during it. *...her dull, uneventful life.* ♦ **un·event·ful·ly** *The five years at that school passed fairly uneventfully.*   ADJ-GRADED; ADV-GRADED: ADV after v

un·ex·cep·tion·able /ˌʌnɪkˈsepʃənəbəl/. If you describe someone or something as **unexceptionable**, you mean that it is unlikely to be criticized or objected to, but is not exciting or new. *The school's unexceptionable purpose is to involve parents more closely in the education of their children.*   ADJ FORMAL

un·ex·cep·tion·al /ˌʌnɪkˈsepʃənəl/. If you describe something as **unexceptional**, you mean that it is ordinary, not very interesting, and often disappointing. *Since then, Michael has lived an unexceptional life.* `ADJ-GRADED`

un·ex·cit·ing /ˌʌnɪkˈsaɪtɪŋ/. If you describe someone or something as **unexciting**, you think they are rather boring, and not likely to shock or surprise you in any way. *He is regarded as very capable but unexciting.* `ADJ-GRADED`

un·ex·pec·ted /ˌʌnɪkˈspektɪd/. If an event or someone's behaviour is **unexpected**, it surprises you because you did not think that it was likely to happen. *His death was totally unexpected.* ♦ **un·ex·pect·ed·ly** *Moss had clamped an unexpectedly strong grip on his arm.* `◆◆◇◇` `ADJ-GRADED` `ADV-GRADED`

un·ex·plained /ˌʌnɪkˈspleɪnd/. If you describe something as **unexplained**, you mean that the reason for it or cause of it is unclear or is not known. *The demonstrations were provoked by the unexplained death of an opposition leader.* `◆◇◇◇` `ADJ`

un·fail·ing /ʌnˈfeɪlɪŋ/. If you describe someone's good qualities or behaviour as **unfailing**, you mean that they never change. *He had the unfailing care and support of Erica, his wife.* ♦ **un·fail·ing·ly** *He was unfailingly polite to customers.* `ADJ` `ADV`

un·fair /ˌʌnˈfeə/. **1** An **unfair** action or situation is not right or just. *It was unfair that he should suffer so much.* ♦ **un·fair·ly** *...whether an employee was fairly or unfairly dismissed.* **2** An **unfair** system or situation does not give equal treatment or equal opportunities to everyone involved. *The American plane makers continue to accuse Airbus of unfair competition.* ♦ **un·fair·ness** *...the unfairness of the penalty shoot-out in the FA Cup semi-final.* `◆◆◇◇` `ADJ-GRADED` `ADJ-GRADED` `N-UNCOUNT`

un·faith·ful /ʌnˈfeɪθful/. If someone is **unfaithful** to their lover or to the person they are married to, they have a sexual relationship with someone else. *My husband was unfaithful to me.* `◆◇◇◇` `ADJ-GRADED`

un·fa·mil·iar /ˌʌnfəˈmɪliə/. **1** If something is **unfamiliar** to you, you know nothing or very little about it, because you have not seen or experienced it before. *She grew many wonderful plants that were unfamiliar to me.* ♦ **un·fa·mili·ar·ity** /ˌʌnfəˌmɪliˈærɪti/. *...the newness of the approach and its unfamiliarity to prisoners.* **2** If you are **unfamiliar with** something, it is unfamiliar to you. *She speaks no Japanese and is unfamiliar with Japanese culture.* ♦ **unfamiliarity** *...her unfamiliarity with the politics of the region.* `◆◇◇◇` `ADJ-GRADED` `N-UNCOUNT` `ADJ-GRADED: v-link ADJ with n` `N-UNCOUNT: N with n`

un·fash·ion·able /ʌnˈfæʃənəbəl/. If something is **unfashionable**, it is not approved of or done by most people. *Wearing fur has become deeply unfashionable.* ♦ **un·fash·ion·ably** *He wears his blonde hair unfashionably long.* `◆◇◇◇` `ADJ-GRADED` `ADV-GRADED`

un·fas·ten /ʌnˈfɑːsən, -ˈfæsən/ **unfastens, unfastening, unfastened.** If you **unfasten** something that is holding another thing in place, for example buttons or zips on clothing, you loosen them or separate their parts, for example so that you can remove the clothing. *He needed to know how to fasten and unfasten his seat belt.* `VERB` `V n`

un·fath·om·able /ʌnˈfæðəməbəl/. **1** If you describe something as **unfathomable**, you mean that it cannot be understood or explained, usually because it is very strange or complicated. *An iron gate hung open, with a blue shirt, for some unfathomable reason, jammed between two upright bars.* **2** If you use **unfathomable** to describe a person or the expression on their face, you mean that you cannot tell what they are thinking or what they intend to do. *He was dealing with a strange, unfathomable and unpredictable individual.* `ADJ-GRADED` `ADJ LITERARY`

un·fa·vour·able /ʌnˈfeɪvərəbəl/; spelled **unfavorable** in American English. **1** **Unfavourable** conditions or circumstances cause problems for you and reduce your chances of success. *Unfavourable economic conditions were blocking a recovery of the American insurance market.* **2** If you have an **unfavourable** reaction to something, you do not like it. `◆◇◇◇` `ADJ-GRADED`

President Mubarak was particularly unfavourable to the idea. ♦ **un·fa·vour·ably** /ʌnˈfeɪvərəbli/. *When the body reacts unfavourably to food, the pulse rate will go up.* **3** If you make an **unfavourable** comparison between two things, you say that one thing seems worse than the other. *He makes unfavourable comparisons between British and French cooking.* ♦ **unfavourably** *Childcare facilities in Britain compare unfavourably with other EC countries.* `ADV-GRADED: ADV after v` `ADJ: ADJ n` `ADV-GRADED: ADV with v`

un·feel·ing /ʌnˈfiːlɪŋ/. If you describe someone as **unfeeling**, you are criticizing them for their cruelty or lack of sympathy for other people. *...an unfeeling bully who used his huge size to frighten people.* `ADJ-GRADED` `PRAGMATICS` `WRITTEN`

un·fet·tered /ʌnˈfetəd/. If you describe something as **unfettered**, you mean that it is not controlled or limited by anyone or anything. *Unfettered free trade is an ideal, never achieved.* `ADJ: ADJ n, v-link ADJ, ADJ after v` `FORMAL`

un·fin·ished /ʌnˈfɪnɪʃt/. Something such as a work of art or a piece of work that is **unfinished**, is not complete, for example because there was no time to complete it. *...Jane Austen's unfinished novel.* `◆◇◇◇` `ADJ: ADJ n, v-link ADJ, ADJ after v`

un·fit /ˌʌnˈfɪt/. **1** If you are **unfit**, your body is not in good condition because you have not been taking regular exercise. *Many children are so unfit they are unable to do even basic exercises.* **2** If someone is **unfit** for something, he or she is unable to do it because of injury or illness. *He had a third examination and was declared unfit for duty.* **3** If you say that someone or something is **unfit** for a particular purpose or job, you are criticizing them because they are not good enough for that purpose or job. *Existing houses are becoming totally unfit for human habitation.* `◆◇◇◇` `ADJ-GRADED` `ADJ-GRADED` `ADJ-GRADED` `PRAGMATICS`

un·flag·ging /ʌnˈflægɪŋ/. If you describe something such as support, effort, or enthusiasm as **unflagging**, you mean that it is constant and strong. *He was sustained by the unflagging support of his family.* `ADJ` `PRAGMATICS`

un·flap·pable /ʌnˈflæpəbəl/. Someone who is **unflappable** is always calm and never panics or gets upset or angry. `ADJ-GRADED`

un·flat·ter·ing /ʌnˈflætərɪŋ/. If you describe something as **unflattering**, you mean that it makes someone or something seem less attractive than they really are. *He depicted the town's respectable families in an unflattering light.* `ADJ-GRADED`

un·flinch·ing /ʌnˈflɪntʃɪŋ/. You can use **unflinching** in expressions such as **unflinching honesty** and **unflinching support** to indicate that a good quality which someone has is strong and steady, and never weakens. *...the armed forces, all of whom had pledged their unflinching support and loyalty to the government.* ♦ **un·flinch·ing·ly** *They were unflinchingly loyal to their friends.* `ADJ` `ADV-GRADED`

un·fo·cused /ʌnˈfəʊkəst/; also spelled **unfocussed**. **1** If someone's eyes are **unfocused**, they are open, but not looking at anything. *...his unfocused gaze.* **2** If you describe someone's feelings or plans as **unfocused**, you are criticizing them because they do not seem to be clearly formed or have any clear purpose. *But for now, she is in the grip of a blind, unfocused anger.* `ADJ` `ADJ-GRADED` `PRAGMATICS`

un·fold /ʌnˈfəʊld/ **unfolds, unfolding, unfolded.** **1** If a situation **unfolds**, it develops and becomes known or understood. *The facts started to unfold before them.* **2** If a story unfolds or if it **unfolds** it, it is told to someone else. *Mr Wills unfolds his story with evident enjoyment.* **3** If someone **unfolds** something which has been folded or if it **unfolds**, it is opened out and becomes flat. *When the bird lifts off into flight, its wings unfold to an impressive six-foot span.* `◆◆◇◇` `VERB` `V` `V-ERG: V` `V n` `V-ERG: V n` `V`

un·fore·see·able /ˌʌnfɔːˈsiːəbəl/. An **unforeseeable** problem or unpleasant event is one which you did not expect and could not have predicted. *...severe unforeseeable weather conditions.* `ADJ-GRADED`

un·fore·seen /ˌʌnfɔːˈsiːn/. If something that has happened was **unforeseen**, it was not expected to happen or was not known about beforehand. *Ra-* `◆◇◇◇` `ADJ`

diation may damage cells in a way that was previously unforeseen.

un·for·get·table /ˌʌnfəˈgetəbəl/. If you describe something as **unforgettable**, you mean that it is, for example, extremely beautiful, enjoyable, or unusual, so that you remember it for a long time. You can also describe extremely unpleasant things as **unforgettable**. *A visit to the Museum is an unforgettable experience.* ♦ **un·for·get·tably** /ˌʌnfəˈgetəbli/. *...an unforgettably unique performer.*   ADV-GRADED ◆◇◇◇◇ ADJ-GRADED

un·for·giv·able /ˌʌnfəˈgɪvəbəl/. If you say that something is **unforgivable**, you mean that it is very bad, cruel, or socially unacceptable. *These people are animals and what they did was unforgivable.*   ADJ-GRADED

un·for·giv·ing /ˌʌnfəˈgɪvɪŋ/. **1** If you describe someone as **unforgiving**, you mean that they are unwilling to forgive other people. **2** If you describe a situation or activity as **unforgiving**, you mean that it causes a lot of people to experience great difficulty or failure, even people who deserve to succeed. *Business is a competitive activity. It is very fierce and very unforgiving.*   ADJ FORMAL   ADJ-GRADED

un·formed /ˌʌnˈfɔːmd/. If you describe someone or something as **unformed**, you mean that they are in an early stage of development and not fully formed or matured. *...the unformed minds of children.*   ADJ FORMAL

un·for·tu·nate /ʌnˈfɔːtʃʊnət/ **unfortunates**. **1** If you describe someone as **unfortunate**, you mean that something unpleasant or unlucky has happened to them. You can also describe the unpleasant things that happen to them as **unfortunate**. *Some unfortunate person passing below could all too easily be seriously injured... Through some unfortunate accident, the information reached me a day late.* **2** If you describe something that has happened as **unfortunate**, you think that it is inappropriate, embarrassing, awkward, or undesirable. *It really is desperately unfortunate that this should have happened just now.* **3** You can describe someone as **unfortunate** when they are poor, deprived, or have a difficult life. *...charity days to raise money for unfortunate people.* ▶ An **unfortunate** is someone who is unfortunate. *Dorothy was another of life's poor unfortunates.*   ◆◆◇◇◇ ADJ-GRADED   ADJ-GRADED   ADJ-GRADED   N-COUNT

un·for·tu·nate·ly /ʌnˈfɔːtʃʊnətli/. You can use **unfortunately** to introduce or refer to a statement when you consider that it is sad or disappointing, or when you want to express regret. *Unfortunately, my time is limited... Unfortunately for the Prince, his title brought obligations as well as privileges.*   ◆◆◆◇◇ ADV-GRADED ADV with cl PRAGMATICS

un·found·ed /ˌʌnˈfaʊndɪd/. If you describe a rumour, belief, or feeling as **unfounded**, you mean that it is wrong and is not based on facts or evidence. *There were unfounded rumours of alcohol abuse.*   ◆◇◇◇◇ ADJ

un·friend·ly /ˌʌnˈfrendli/. If you describe a person, organization, or their behaviour as **unfriendly**, you mean that they behave towards you in an unkind or rather hostile way. *People always complain that the big banks are unfriendly and unhelpful.*   ◆◇◇◇◇ ADJ-GRADED

un·ful·filled /ˌʌnfʊlˈfɪld/. **1** If you use **unfulfilled** to describe something such as a promise, ambition, or need, you mean that what was promised, hoped for, or needed has not happened. *Do you have any unfulfilled ambitions?* **2** If you describe someone as **unfulfilled**, you mean that they feel dissatisfied with life or with what they have done. *...the idea that to be single is to be unhappy and unfulfilled.*   ◆◇◇◇◇ ADJ   ADJ-GRADED

un·fun·ny /ˌʌnˈfʌni/. If you describe something or someone as **unfunny**, you mean that they do not make you laugh, although this was their intention or purpose. *We became increasingly fed up with his increasingly unfunny and unintelligent comments.*   ADJ-GRADED

un·furl /ˌʌnˈfɜːl/ **unfurls, unfurling, unfurled**. **1** If you **unfurl** something such as an umbrella, sail, or flag, or if it **unfurls**, you unroll or unfold it so that it is flat or spread out, and can be used or seen. *...two weeks later when the leaves unfurl.* **2** If you say that events, stories, or scenes **unfurl** before you, you mean that you are aware of them or can see   ◆◇◇◇◇ V-ERG: V n V   VERB V

them as they happen or develop. *...as the dramatic changes in Europe continue to unfurl.*

un·fur·nished /ˌʌnˈfɜːnɪʃt/. If you rent an **unfurnished** flat or house, no furniture is provided by the owner.   ADJ

un·gain·ly /ʌnˈgeɪnli/. If you describe a person, animal, or vehicle as **ungainly**, you mean that they look awkward or clumsy, often because they are big. *The dog, an ungainly mongrel pup, was loping about the road.*   ADJ-GRADED

un·gen·er·ous /ʌnˈdʒenərəs/. **1** If you describe someone's remarks, thoughts, or actions as **ungenerous**, you mean that they judge or treat people unfairly or harshly. *This was a typically ungenerous response, even if tinged with truth.* **2** You can use **ungenerous** when you are describing a person or organization that, is selfish or unwilling to give much money to other people. *The company had a good scheme for the salaried employees and an ungenerous scheme for the hourly paid.*   ADJ-GRADED FORMAL   ADJ-GRADED FORMAL

un·god·ly /ʌnˈgɒdli/. **1** If you describe someone or something as **ungodly**, you think they are sinful, wicked, or immoral. *Such a view implies that our bodies and sexual nature are inherently ungodly.* **2** If you refer to a time as an **ungodly** hour, you are emphasizing that it is unreasonably early. *...at the ungodly hour of 4.00am.* **3** If you refer to the amount or volume of something as **ungodly**, you mean that it is excessive or unreasonable. *...a power struggle of ungodly proportions.*   ADJ-GRADED   ADJ: ADJ n PRAGMATICS   ADJ: ADJ n

un·gov·ern·able /ˌʌnˈgʌvənəbəl/. **1** If you describe a country or region as **ungovernable**, you mean that it seems impossible to control or govern it effectively. *Beset by gang murders and kidnappings, the province remains ungovernable.* **2** If you describe feelings as **ungovernable**, you mean that they are so strong that they cannot be controlled. *He was filled with an ungovernable rage.*   ADJ   ADJ

un·gra·cious /ˌʌnˈgreɪʃəs/. If you describe a person or their behaviour as **ungracious**, you mean that they are not polite or friendly in their speech or behaviour. *I was often rude and ungracious in refusing help.*   ADJ-GRADED FORMAL

un·grad·ed /ʌnˈgreɪdɪd/. In this dictionary, an **ungraded** adjective or adverb is one which is not normally with an adverb or phrase indicating degree. 'Absent' is an example of an ungraded adjective.   ADJ

un·grate·ful /ʌnˈgreɪtfʊl/. If you describe someone as **ungrateful**, you are criticizing them for not showing thanks or for being unkind to someone who has given them something or done something for them. *You ungrateful brat.*   ADJ-GRADED PRAGMATICS

un·guard·ed /ˌʌnˈgɑːdɪd/. **1** If something is **unguarded**, nobody is protecting it or looking after it. *I should not leave my briefcase and camera bag unguarded.* **2** If you do or say something in an **unguarded** moment, you do or say it carelessly and without thinking, especially when it is something that you did not want anyone to see or know. *He was ambushed by a reporter into an unguarded comment.*   ADJ: ADJ after v, v-link ADJ, ADJ n   ADJ

un·ham·pered /ˌʌnˈhæmpəd/. If you are **unhampered** by a problem or obstacle, you are free from it, and so you are able to do what you want to. *They are allowed to make money unhampered by any kind of regulations.*   ADJ-GRADED WRITTEN

un·hap·pi·ly /ʌnˈhæpɪli/. You use **unhappily** to introduce or refer to a statement when you consider it is sad and wish that it was different. *On May 23rd, unhappily, the little boy died.*   ADV: ADV with cl PRAGMATICS

un·hap·py /ʌnˈhæpi/ **unhappier, unhappiest**. **1** If you are **unhappy**, you are sad and depressed. *Her marriage is in trouble and she is desperately unhappy.* ♦ **un·hap·pi·ly** *'I don't have your imagination,' King said unhappily.* ♦ **un·hap·pi·ness** *There was a lot of unhappiness in my adolescence.* **2** If you are **unhappy** about something, you are not pleased about it or not satisfied with it. *He has been unhappy with his son's political leanings.* ♦ **unhappiness** *He has, by submitting his resignation, signalled his*   ◆◆◆◇◇ ADJ-GRADED   ADV-GRADED   N-UNCOUNT   v-link ADJ   N-UNCOUNT

unhappiness with the government's decision. **3** An **unhappy** situation or choice is not satisfactory or desirable. *...this unhappy chapter in the history of relations between our two countries.* `ADJ: ADJ n`

un·harmed /ˌʌnˈhɑːmd/. If someone or something is **unharmed** after an accident or violent incident, they are not hurt or damaged in any way. *The car was a write-off, but everyone escaped unharmed.* ◆◇◇◇◇ `ADJ: ADJ after v, v-link ADJ`

un·healthy /ʌnˈhelθi/ **unhealthier, unhealthiest.** **1** Something that is **unhealthy** is likely to cause illness or poor health. *Avoid unhealthy foods such as hamburger and chips.* **2** If you are **unhealthy**, you are not very fit or well. **3** An **unhealthy** economy or company is financially weak and unsuccessful. **4** If you describe someone's behaviour or interests as **unhealthy**, you do not consider them to be normal and think they may be psychologically harmful. *MacGregor believes it is unhealthy to lead a life with no interests beyond politics.* ◆◇◇◇◇ `ADJ-GRADED` `ADJ-GRADED` `ADJ-GRADED` `ADJ-GRADED`

un·heard /ʌnˈhɜːd/. **1** If you say that a person or their words go **unheard**, you are expressing criticism because someone refuses to listen to or consider what is said. *His impassioned pleas went unheard.* **2** If someone's words or cries go **unheard**, nobody can hear them, or a particular person cannot hear them. `ADJ PRAGMATICS WRITTEN` `ADJ WRITTEN`

un·heard of. You can say that an event or situation is **unheard of** when it never happens, or has never happened before. *It's almost unheard of in France for a top politician not to come from the social elite.* ◆◇◇◇◇ `ADJ`

un·heed·ed /ʌnˈhiːdɪd/. If you say that something such as a warning or danger goes **unheeded**, you mean that it has not been taken seriously or dealt with. *The advice of experts went unheeded.* `ADJ WRITTEN`

un·help·ful /ʌnˈhelpfʊl/. If you say that someone or something is **unhelpful**, you mean that they do not help you or improve a situation, and may even make things worse. *The criticism is both unfair and unhelpful.* ◆◇◇◇◇ `ADJ-GRADED`

un·her·ald·ed /ʌnˈherəldɪd/. **1** If you describe an artist or sports player as **unheralded**, you mean that people have not recognized their talent or ability. **2** If you describe something that happens as **unheralded**, you mean that you did not expect it, because nobody mentioned it beforehand. *...Sandi's unheralded arrival on her doorstep.* `ADJ JOURNALISM` `ADJ WRITTEN`

un·hesi·tat·ing·ly /ʌnˈhezɪteɪtɪŋli/. If you say that someone does something **unhesitatingly**, you mean that they do it immediately and confidently, without any doubt or anxiety. *I would unhesitatingly choose the latter option.* `ADV`

un·hinge /ʌnˈhɪndʒ/ **unhinges, unhinging, unhinged.** If you say that an experience **has unhinged** someone, you mean that it has affected them so deeply that they have become mentally ill. ♦ **un·hinged** *...feelings that make you feel completely unhinged and crazy.* `VERB: V n` `ADJ-GRADED`

un·ho·ly /ʌnˈhəʊli/. **1** You use **unholy** to emphasize how unreasonable or unpleasant you think something is. *The economy is still an unholy mess.* **2** If you refer to two or more people or groups that have come together for a common purpose as an **unholy** alliance, you mean that it is very surprising that these people or groups who usually oppose each other are working together, and that you find it worrying or undesirable that they are doing so. **3** If you describe something as **unholy**, you mean that it is wicked or sinful. `ADJ: ADJ n PRAGMATICS` `ADJ: ADJ n` `ADJ-GRADED`

un·hook /ʌnˈhʊk/ **unhooks, unhooking, unhooked.** If you **unhook** something that is fastened or held in place by hooks, you unfasten or remove it by undoing the hooks. `VERB: V n`

un·hur·ried /ʌnˈhʌrid/. If you describe something as **unhurried**, you approve of it because it is relaxed and slow, and is not rushed or anxious. ♦ **un·hur·ried·ly** *She walked unhurriedly away.* `ADJ-GRADED PRAGMATICS` `ADV`

un·hurt /ʌnˈhɜːt/. If someone who has been attacked, or involved in an accident, is **unhurt**, they ◆◇◇◇◇ `ADJ: ADJ after v,`

are not injured. *The lorry driver escaped unhurt, but a pedestrian was injured.* `v-link ADJ`

un·hy·gien·ic /ˌʌnhaɪˈdʒiːnɪk, AM -dʒiˈenɪk/. If you describe something as **unhygienic**, you mean that it is dirty and likely to cause infection or disease. `ADJ-GRADED`

uni·corn /ˈjuːnɪkɔːn/ **unicorns.** In stories and legends, a **unicorn** is an imaginary animal that looks like a white horse and has a horn growing from its forehead. `N-COUNT`

un·iden·ti·fi·able /ˌʌnaɪdentɪˈfaɪəbəl/. If something or someone is **unidentifiable**, you are not able to say exactly what it is or who they are. *All the bodies were totally unidentifiable.* `ADJ-GRADED`

un·iden·ti·fied /ˌʌnaɪˈdentɪfaɪd/. **1** If you describe someone or something as **unidentified**, you mean that nobody knows who or what they are. *He was shot this morning by unidentified intruders at his house.* **2 Unidentified** is used to describe people and organizations whose names are not given. *CNN quoted unidentified sources as saying that the investigation has been expanded.* ◆◆◆◇◇ `ADJ` `ADJ JOURNALISM`

uni·fi·ca·tion /ˌjuːnɪfɪˈkeɪʃən/. **Unification** is the process by which two or more countries join together and become one country. ◆◆◇◇◇ `N-UNCOUNT`

uni·form /ˈjuːnɪfɔːm/ **uniforms.** **1** A **uniform** is a special set of clothes which some people, for example soldiers or the police, wear to work in and which some children wear at school. *The town police wear dark blue uniforms... Philippe was in uniform.* ♦ **uni·formed** /ˈjuːnɪfɔːmd/ *...uniformed policemen.* **2** You can refer to the particular style of clothing which a group of people wear to show they belong to a group or a movement as their **uniform**. *Mark's is the uniform of the young male traveller – green Army trousers, T-shirt and shirt.* **3** If something is **uniform**, it does not vary, but is even and regular throughout. *Chips should be cut into uniform size and thickness.* ♦ **uni·form·ity** /ˌjuːnɪˈfɔːmɪti/. *...the caramel that was used to maintain uniformity of color in the brandy.* ♦ **uni·form·ly** *Microwaves heat water uniformly.* **4** If you describe a number of things as **uniform**, you mean that they are all the same. *Along each wall stretched uniform green metal filing cabinets.* ♦ **uniformity** *...the dull uniformity of the houses.* ♦ **uniformly** *The natives uniformly agreed on this important point.* ◆◆◆◇◇ `N-VAR` `ADJ` `N-COUNT: with supp` `ADJ-GRADED` `N-UNCOUNT` `ADV-GRADED` `ADJ-GRADED` `N-UNCOUNT` `ADV-GRADED`

uni·form·ity /ˌjuːnɪˈfɔːmɪti/. **1** If there is **uniformity** in something such as a system, organization, or group of countries, the same rules, ideas, or methods are applied in all parts of it. *It is unlikely that the Maastricht treaty will produce uniformity of policy.* **2** See also **uniform**. ◆◇◇◇◇ `N-UNCOUNT`

uni·fy /ˈjuːnɪfaɪ/ **unifies, unifying, unified.** If someone **unifies** different things or parts, they are brought together to form one thing. *Mr Major said his main job will be to unify the Conservative Party... His opponents will have a determined and experienced core around which to unify.* ♦ **uni·fied** *...a unified system of taxation.* ◆◆◇◇◇ `V-RECIP-ERG: V pl-n V n pl-n V` `ADJ-GRADED`

uni·lat·er·al /ˌjuːnɪˈlætərəl/. A **unilateral** decision or action is taken by only one of the groups, organizations, or countries that are involved in a particular situation, without the agreement of the others. *...unilateral nuclear disarmament.* ♦ **uni·lat·er·al·ly** *The British Government was careful not to act unilaterally.* ◆◇◇◇◇ `ADJ` `ADV: ADV with v`

un·im·agi·nable /ˌʌnɪˈmædʒɪnəbəl/. If you describe something as **unimaginable**, you are emphasizing that it is difficult to imagine or understand properly, because it is not part of people's normal experience. *The children here have lived through unimaginable horrors.* ♦ **un·im·agi·nably** /ˌʌnɪˈmædʒɪnəbli/. *Conditions in prisons out there are unimaginably bad.* ◆◇◇◇◇ `ADJ-GRADED PRAGMATICS` `ADV-GRADED: ADV adj`

un·im·agi·na·tive /ˌʌnɪˈmædʒɪnətɪv/. **1** If you describe someone as **unimaginative**, you are criticizing them because they are not original or creative in what they do. **2** If you describe something as **unimaginative**, you mean that it is boring or unattractive `ADJ-GRADED PRAGMATICS` `ADJ-GRADED PRAGMATICS`

because very little imagination or effort has been used on it. ...*unimaginative food.*

un·im·paired /ˌʌnɪmˈpeəd/. If something is unim- ADJ: paired after something bad or unpleasant has hap- v-link ADJ, pened to it, it is not damaged or made worse. *His* ADJ after v, *health and vigour were unimpaired by a stroke.* FORMAL

un·im·peach·able /ˌʌnɪmˈpiːtʃəbəl/. If you de- ADJ scribe someone as **unimpeachable**, you mean that FORMAL they are completely honest and reliable. *He said all five were men of unimpeachable character.*

un·im·ped·ed /ˌʌnɪmˈpiːdɪd/. If something moves ADJ: or happens **unimpeded**, it continues without being ADJ after v, stopped or interrupted by anything. *He promised to* ADJ n, *allow justice to run its course unimpeded.* v-link ADJ FORMAL

un·im·por·tant /ˌʌnɪmˈpɔːtənt/. If you describe ◆◇◇◇◇ something or someone as **unimportant**, you mean ADJ-GRADED that they do not have much influence, effect, or value, and are therefore not worth considering.

un·im·pressed /ˌʌnɪmˈprest/. If you are **unim-** ◆◇◇◇◇ **pressed** by something or someone, you do not think ADJ-GRADED: they are particularly good, useful, or important. v-link ADJ

un·im·pres·sive /ˌʌnɪmˈpresɪv/. If you describe ADJ-GRADED someone or something as **unimpressive**, you mean they appear very ordinary, without any special or exciting qualities.

un·in·formed /ˌʌnɪnˈfɔːmd/. If you describe some- ADJ-GRADED one as **uninformed**, you mean that they have very little knowledge or information about a particular situation or subject.

un·in·hab·it·able /ˌʌnɪnˈhæbɪtəbəl/. If a place is ADJ **uninhabitable**, it is impossible for people to live there, for example because it is dangerous or unhealthy.

un·in·hab·it·ed /ˌʌnɪnˈhæbɪtɪd/. An **uninhabited** ADJ place is one where nobody lives. ...*an uninhabited island in the North Pacific.*

un·in·hib·it·ed /ˌʌnɪnˈhɪbɪtɪd/. If you describe a ADJ-GRADED person or their behaviour as **uninhibited**, you mean that they express their opinions and feelings openly, and behave as they want to, without worrying what other people think.

un·ini·ti·at·ed /ˌʌnɪˈnɪʃieɪtɪd/. You can refer to N-PLURAL: people who have no knowledge or experience of a the N particular subject or activity as **the uninitiated**. *For the uninitiated, Western Swing is a fusion of jazz, rhythm & blues, rock & roll and country music.* ▶ Also an adjective. *This may not be visible to the* ADJ *uninitiated eye.*

un·in·spired /ˌʌnɪnˈspaɪəd/. If you describe some- ADJ-GRADED thing or someone as **uninspired**, you are criticizing PRAGMATICS them because they do not seem to have any original or exciting qualities. *Food in the dining car was adequate, if uninspired.*

un·in·spir·ing /ˌʌnɪnˈspaɪərɪŋ/. If you describe ADJ-GRADED something or someone as **uninspiring**, you are PRAGMATICS criticizing them because they have no original or exciting qualities.

un·in·tel·li·gent /ˌʌnɪnˈtelɪdʒənt/. If you describe a ADJ-GRADED person as **unintelligent**, you mean that they are stupid.

un·in·tel·li·gible /ˌʌnɪnˈtelɪdʒɪbəl/. **Unintelligible** ◆◇◇◇◇ speech or writing is impossible to understand, for ADJ-GRADED example because it is not written or pronounced clearly, or because its meaning is confused or complicated. *He muttered something unintelligible.*

un·in·tend·ed /ˌʌnɪnˈtendɪd/. **Unintended** results ADJ or effects were not planned, although they happened. ...*unintended pregnancies resulting from contraceptive failure.*

un·in·ten·tion·al /ˌʌnɪnˈtenʃənəl/. Something that ◆◇◇◇◇ is **unintentional** is not done deliberately, but hap- ADJ pens by accident. ♦ **un·in·ten·tion·al·ly** ...*an over-* ADV *blown and unintentionally funny adaptation of 'Dracula'.*

un·in·ter·est·ed /ʌnˈɪntrəstɪd/. If you are **uninter-** ADJ-GRADED **ested** in something or someone, you do not want to know any more about them.

un·in·ter·est·ing /ʌnˈɪntrəstɪŋ/. If you describe ADJ-GRADED something or someone as **uninteresting**, you mean they have no special or exciting qualities.

un·in·ter·rupt·ed /ˌʌnɪntəˈrʌptɪd/. **1** If something ◆◇◇◇◇ is **uninterrupted**, it is continuous and has no ADJ: breaks or interruptions in it. *This enables the heal-* ADJ after v, *ing process to continue uninterrupted.* **2** An **uninter-** ADJ n, **rupted** view of something is a clear view of it, with- ADJ out any obstacles in the way.

un·in·vit·ed /ˌʌnɪnˈvaɪtɪd/. If someone does some- ADJ: thing or goes somewhere **uninvited**, they do it or go ADJ after v, there without being asked, often when their action v-link ADJ, or presence is not wanted. *He came uninvited to one* ADJ n *of Stein's parties.*

un·ion /ˈjuːnjən/ **unions**. **1** A **union** is a workers' ◆◆◆◆◇ organization which represents its members and N-COUNT which aims to improve things such as their working conditions and pay. **2** When the **union** of two or N-UNCOUNT more things occurs, they are joined together and become one thing. *Britain should move towards closer union with our Community partners.* **3** When N-SING two or more things have been joined together to form one thing, you can refer to them as a **union**. ...*the question of which countries should join the currency union.* **4** The marriage of two people is N-COUNT sometimes referred to as their **union**. **5** **Union** is N-COUNT used in the name of some clubs, societies, and or- FORMAL ganizations. ...*the Mothers' Union.*

un·ion·ism /ˈjuːnjənɪzəm/. **Unionism** is any set of ◆◇◇◇◇ political principles based on the idea that two or N-UNCOUNT more political or national units should be joined or remain together, for example the political belief that Northern Ireland should remain part of the United Kingdom. ♦ **un·ion·ist, unionists** ...*unionists fear-* N-COUNT *ful of home rule.*

un·ioni·za·tion /ˌjuːnjənaɪˈzeɪʃn/; also spelled **un-** N-UNCOUNT **ionisation** in British English. The **unionization** of workers or industries is the process of workers becoming members of trade unions.

un·ion·ized /ˈjuːnjənaɪzd/; also spelled **unionised** ADJ in British English. **Unionized** workers belong to trade unions. If a workplace is **unionized**, most of the workers there belong to trade unions.

Union 'Jack, Union Jacks. The **Union Jack** is ◆◇◇◇◇ the national flag of the United Kingdom. It consists N-COUNT of a blue background with red and white crosses on it.

unique /juːˈniːk/. **1** Something that is **unique** is ◆◆◆◇◇ the only one of its kind. *Each person's signature is* ADJ *unique.* ♦ **unique·ly** *Because of the extreme cold,* ADV *the Antarctic is a uniquely fragile environment.* ♦ **unique·ness** ...*the uniqueness of China's own ex-* N-UNCOUNT *perience.* **2** You can use **unique** to describe things ADJ-GRADED that you admire because they are very unusual and PRAGMATICS special. *Kauffman was a woman of unique talent and determination.* ♦ **uniquely** *There'll never be a* ADV *shortage of people who consider themselves uniquely qualified to be president of the United States.* **3** If ADJ: something is **unique to** one thing, person, group, or v-link ADJ to n place, it concerns or belongs only to that thing, person, group, or place. *This interesting and charming creature is unique to Borneo.* ♦ **uniquely** *The prob-* ADV: ADV adj *lem isn't uniquely American.*

uni·sex /ˈjuːnɪseks/. **Unisex** is used to describe ADJ things, usually clothes or hairdressing salons, which are designed for use by both men and women rather than by only one sex.

uni·son /ˈjuːnɪsən, -zən/. **1** If two or more people ◆◇◇◇◇ do something **in unison**, they do it together at the PHRASE same time. *Michael and the landlady nodded in unison.* **2** If people or organizations act **in unison**, PHRASE they act the same way because they agree with each other or because they want to achieve the same aims. *The international community is ready to work in unison against him.*

unit /ˈjuːnɪt/ **units**. **1** If you consider something as ◆◆◆◆◇ a **unit**, you consider it as a single, complete thing. N-COUNT *Agriculture was based in the past on the family as a unit.* **2** A **unit** is a group of people who work togeth- N-COUNT er at a specific job, often in a particular place. ...*the health services research unit.* **3** A **unit** is a small ma- N-COUNT chine which has a particular function, often part of a larger machine. *The unit plugs into any TV set.*

4 A **unit** of measurement is a fixed standard quantity, length, or weight that is used for measuring things. The litre, the centimetre, and the ounce are all units. **5** A **unit** is one of the parts that a course book is divided into. `N-COUNT` `N-COUNT`

uni·tary /'juːnɪtri, AM -teri/. A **unitary** state or organization is one in which two or more areas or groups in it have joined together, have the same aims, and are controlled by a single government or group of people. ◆◇◇◇◇ `ADJ: ADJ n`

unite /juː'naɪt/ **unites, uniting, united.** If a group of people or things **unite**, they join together and act as a group. *The vast majority of nations have agreed to unite their efforts to bring peace.* ◆◆◇◇◇ `V-ERG: V` `V n`

unit·ed /juː'naɪtɪd/. **1** When people are **united** about something, they agree about it and act together. *Every party is united on the need for parliamentary democracy.* **2 United** is used to describe a country which has been formed from two or more countries or states. *...a united Germany.* ◆◆◆◇◇ `ADJ-GRADED` `ADJ`

U·nited 'Kingdom. The United Kingdom is the official name for the country consisting of Great Britain and Northern Ireland. ◆◆◇◇◇ `N-PROPER:` `the N`

U·nited 'Nations. The United Nations is a worldwide organization which most countries belong to. Its role is to encourage international peace, co-operation, and friendship. ◆◆◆◇ `N-PROPER:` `the N`

,unit 'trust, unit trusts. A **unit trust** is an organization which invests money in many different types of business and which offers units for sale to the public as an investment. You can also refer to an investment of this type as a **unit trust.** The American term is **mutual fund.** ◆◇◇◇◇ `N-COUNT` `BRITISH`

unity /'juːnɪti/. **1 Unity** is the state of different areas or groups being joined together to form a single country or organization. *Senior politicians met today to discuss the future of European economic unity.* **2** When there is **unity**, people are in agreement and act together for a particular purpose. *The choice was meant to create an impression of party unity.* ◆◆◆◇◇ `N-UNCOUNT` `N-UNCOUNT`

Univ. **Univ** is a written abbreviation for 'University' which is used especially in the names of universities. ◆◇◇◇◇

uni·ver·sal /,juːnɪ'vɜːsəl/ **universals. 1** Something that is **universal** relates to everyone in the world or everyone in a particular group or society. *The insurance industry has produced its own proposals for universal health care.* **♦ uni·ver·sal·ity** /,juːnɪvɜː'sælɪti/. *I have been amazed at the universality of all of our experiences, whatever our origins, sex or age.* **♦ uni·ver·sal·ly** *...a universally accepted point of view... The disadvantage is that it is not universally available.* **2** Something that is **universal** affects or relates to every part of the world or the universe. *...universal diseases.* **3** A **universal** is a principle that applies in all cases or a characteristic that is present in all members of a particular group. *There are no economic universals.* ◆◆◇◇◇ `ADJ` `N-UNCOUNT` `ADV` `ADJ` `N-COUNT`

uni·verse /'juːnɪvɜːs/ **universes. 1** The **universe** is the whole of space and all the stars, planets, and other forms of matter and energy in it. **2** If you talk about someone's **universe**, you are referring to the whole of their experience or an important part of it. *He was the center of my universe.* **3** If you say that something is, for example, the best or biggest thing of its kind **in the universe**, you are emphasizing that you think it is bigger or better than anything else of its kind. ◆◆◆◇◇ `N-COUNT` `N-COUNT` `PHRASE` `PRAGMATICS` `INFORMAL`

uni·ver·sity /,juːnɪ'vɜːsɪti/ **universities.** A **university** is an institution where students study for degrees and where academic research is done. *Patrick is now at London University... They want their daughter to go to university.* ◆◆◆◆◆ `N-VAR`

un·just /,ʌn'dʒʌst/. If you describe an action, system, or law as **unjust**, you think that it treats a person or group badly in a way that they do not deserve. **♦ un·just·ly** *She was unjustly accused of stealing money and then given the sack.* ◆◇◇◇◇ `ADJ-GRADED` `ADV-GRADED`

un·jus·ti·fi·able /,ʌndʒʌstɪ'faɪəbəl/. If you describe an action, especially one that harms someone, as **unjustifiable**, you mean there is no good reason for it. **♦ un·jus·ti·fi·ably** *The press invade people's privacy unfairly and unjustifiably every day.* `ADJ-GRADED` `ADV-GRADED`

un·jus·ti·fied /,ʌn'dʒʌstɪfaɪd/. If you describe a belief or action as **unjustified**, you think that there is no good reason for having it or doing it. *...wholly unfounded and totally unjustified allegations.* ◆◇◇◇◇ `ADJ`

un·kempt /,ʌn'kempt/. If you describe something or someone as **unkempt**, you mean that they are untidy, and not looked after carefully or kept neat. `ADJ-GRADED`

un·kind /ʌn'kaɪnd/ **unkinder, unkindest. 1** If someone is **unkind**, they behave in an unpleasant, unfriendly, or slightly cruel way. *All last summer he'd been unkind to her... I think it's a bit unkind to describe the ship in those terms.* **♦ un·kind·ly** *Several viewers commented unkindly on her costumes.* **♦ un·kind·ness** *He realized the unkindness of the remark.* **2** If you describe something bad that happens to someone as **unkind**, you mean that they do not deserve it. *Fate has been unkind to them.* ◆◇◇◇◇ `ADJ-GRADED` `ADV-GRADED` `N-UNCOUNT` `WRITTEN`

un·know·able /,ʌn'nəʊəbəl/. If you describe something as **unknowable**, you mean that it is impossible for human beings to know anything about it. `ADJ` `WRITTEN`

un·know·ing /,ʌn'nəʊɪŋ/. If you describe a person as **unknowing**, you mean that they are not aware of what is happening or of what they are doing. *Some governments have been victims and perhaps unknowing accomplices in the bank's activities.* **♦ un·know·ing·ly** *...if people unknowingly move into more contaminated areas of the river.* `ADJ` `ADV`

un·known /,ʌn'nəʊn/ **unknowns. 1** If something or someone is **unknown** to you, you do not know what or who they are. *An unknown number of demonstrators were arrested... The motive for the killing is unknown... I could not understand how someone with so many awards could be unknown to me.* ▶ An **unknown** is something that is unknown. *The length of the war is one of the biggest unknowns.* **2** An **unknown** person is not famous or publicly recognized. *He was an unknown writer.* ▶ An **unknown** is a person who is unknown. *Within a short space of time a group of complete unknowns had established a wholly original form of humour.* **3** If you say that a particular problem or situation is **unknown**, you mean that it never occurs. *A hundred years ago coronary heart disease was virtually unknown in Europe and America.* **4** The **unknown** refers generally to things or places that people do not know about or understand. *Ignorance of people brings fear, fear of the unknown.* ◆◆◇◇ `ADJ` `N-COUNT` `ADJ-GRADED` `N-COUNT` `ADJ` `N-SING:` `the N`

un·law·ful /,ʌn'lɔːfʊl/. If something is **unlawful**, the law does not allow you to do it. *...employees who believe their dismissal was unlawful.* **♦ un·law·ful·ly** *...the councils' assertion that the government acted unlawfully in imposing the restrictions.* ◆◇◇◇◇ `ADJ` `FORMAL` `ADV:` `ADV with v`

,unlawful 'killing, unlawful killings. Unlawful **killing** is used to refer in a general way to crimes such as murder and manslaughter. `N-VAR` `LEGAL`

un·lead·ed /,ʌn'ledɪd/. **Unleaded** fuels contain a reduced amount of lead in order to reduce the pollution caused when they are burned. ▶ Also a noun. *All its V8 engines will run happily on unleaded.* ◆◇◇◇◇ `ADJ` `N-UNCOUNT`

un·learn /,ʌn'lɜːn/ **unlearns, unlearning, unlearned;** also spelled **unlearnt** in British English. If you **unlearn** something that you have learned, you try to forget it or ignore it, often because it is wrong or it is having a bad influence on you. *It isn't easy to unlearn any habit.* `VERB` `V n`

un·leash /,ʌn'liːʃ/ **unleashes, unleashing, unleashed.** If you say that someone or something **unleashes** a powerful movement, force, or feeling, you mean that it starts suddenly and has an immediate strong effect. *There is a real risk that food rationing will unleash a new stream of refugees. ...the power unleashed by their leg muscles.* ◆◇◇◇◇ `VERB` `V n` `V-ed`

un·leav·ened /,ʌn'levənd/. **Unleavened** bread or dough is made without any yeast. `ADJ`

un·less /ʌn'les/. You use **unless** to introduce the only circumstances in which an event you are mentioning will not take place or in which a statement you are making is not true. *Unless you are trying to lose weight to please yourself, it's going to be tough... I'm not happy unless I ride or drive every day.* ◆◆◆◇ CONJ PRAGMATICS

un·like /ʌn'laɪk/. **1** If one thing is **unlike** another thing, the two things have different qualities or characteristics from each other. *This was a foreign country, so unlike San Jose... She was unlike him in every way except for her coal black eyes.* **2** You can use **unlike** to contrast two people, things, or situations, and show how they are different. *Unlike aerobics, walking entails no expensive fees for classes or clubs.* **3** If you describe something that a particular person has done as being **unlike** them, you mean that you are surprised by it because it is not typical of their character or normal behaviour. *It was so unlike him to say something like that, with such intensity, that I was astonished.* ◆◆◇◇ PREP PREP PREP

un·like·ly /ʌn'laɪkli/ **unlikeliest. 1** If you say that something is **unlikely** to happen or **unlikely** to be true, you believe that it will not happen or that it is not true, although you are not completely sure. *A military coup seems unlikely... As with many technological revolutions, you are unlikely to be aware of it... It's now unlikely that future parliaments will bring back the death penalty... In the unlikely event of anybody phoning, could you just scribble a message down?* **2** If you describe someone or something as **unlikely**, you mean it is surprising that they have a particular role or have done a particular thing. *Bespectacled Potter, a yoga fanatic, looks an unlikely drugs dealer... On the surface they made an unlikely couple.* ◆◆◆◇ ADJ-GRADED ADJ-GRADED: ADJ n

un·lim·it·ed /ʌn'lɪmɪtɪd/. If there is an **unlimited** quantity of something, you can have as much or as many of that thing as you want. *You'll also have unlimited access to the swimming pool.* ◆◇◇◇ ADJ

un·list·ed /ʌn'lɪstɪd/. If a person or his or her telephone number is **unlisted**, the number is not listed in the telephone directory, and the telephone company will refuse to give it to people who ask for it. The usual British word is **ex-directory.** ADJ AMERICAN

un·lit /ʌn'lɪt/. **1** An **unlit** fire or cigarette has not been set alight. **2** An **unlit** street or building is dark because there are no lights switched on in it. ADJ ADJ

un·load /ʌn'ləʊd/ **unloads, unloading, unloaded. 1** If you **unload** goods from a vehicle, or you **unload** a vehicle, you remove the goods from the vehicle. *Unload everything from the boat and clean it thoroughly.* **2** If someone **unloads** investments, they get rid of them or sell them. *Since March, he has unloaded 1.3 million shares.* ◆◇◇◇ VERB V n from V Also V n VERB V n JOURNALISM

un·lock /ʌn'lɒk/ **unlocks, unlocking, unlocked. 1** If you **unlock** something such as a door, a room, or a container that has a lock, you open it using a key. *He unlocked the car and threw the coat on to the back seat.* **2** If you **unlock** the potential or the secrets of something or someone, you release them. *Education and training is the key that will unlock our nation's potential.* ◆◇◇◇ VERB V n VERB V n

un·lov·able /ʌn'lʌvəbəl/. If someone is **unlovable**, they are not likely to be loved by anyone, because they do not have any attractive qualities. ADJ-GRADED

un·loved /ʌn'lʌvd/. If someone feels **unloved**, they feel that nobody loves them. ADJ-GRADED

un·love·ly /ʌn'lʌvli/. If you describe something as **unlovely**, you mean that it is unattractive or unpleasant in some way. *...a small, inexpensive motel on the outskirts of the town; it was barren and unlovely.* ADJ-GRADED

un·lov·ing /ʌn'lʌvɪŋ/. If you describe a person as **unloving**, you believe that they do not love, or show love to, the people they ought to love. ADJ-GRADED

un·luck·i·ly /ʌn'lʌkɪli/. You use **unluckily** as a comment on something bad or unpleasant that happens to someone, in order to suggest sympathy for them or that it was not their fault. *Some people unluckily achieve suicide when they only meant to attempt it.* ADV

un·lucky /ʌn'lʌki/ **unluckier, unluckiest. 1** If someone is **unlucky**, they have bad luck. *Cantona was unlucky not to score on two occasions.* **2** You can use **unlucky** to describe unpleasant things which happen to someone, especially when you feel that the person does not deserve them. *...Argentina's unlucky defeat by Ireland.* **3 Unlucky** is used to describe something that is thought to cause bad luck. *Some people think it is unlucky to look at a new moon through glass.* ◆◇◇◇ ADJ-GRADED ADJ-GRADED ADJ-GRADED

un·made /ʌn'meɪd/. An **unmade** bed has not had the bedclothes neatly arranged after it was last slept in. ADJ

un·man·age·able /ʌn'mænɪdʒəbəl/. **1** If you describe something as **unmanageable**, you mean that is difficult to use, deal with, or control. *...her freckles and unmanageable hair.* **2** If you describe someone, especially a young person, as **unmanageable**, you mean that they behave in an unacceptable way and are difficult to control. ADJ-GRADED ADJ-GRADED

un·man·ly /ʌn'mænli/. If you describe a boy's or man's behaviour as **unmanly**, you are critical of the fact that they are behaving in a way that you think is inappropriate for a man. ADJ-GRADED PRAGMATICS

un·manned /ʌn'mænd/. **1 Unmanned** vehicles such as spacecraft do not have any crew and are operated automatically or by remote control. **2** If a place is **unmanned**, there is nobody working there. *Unmanned post offices meant millions of letters went unsorted.* ADJ ADJ

un·marked /ʌn'mɑːkt/. **1** Something that is **unmarked** has no marks on it. *Her shoes are still white and unmarked.* **2** Something that is **unmarked** has no marking on it which identifies what it is or whose it is. *...an unmarked police car.* **3** In a sport such as football, hockey, or basketball, if a player is **unmarked**, there are no players from the opposing team waiting to challenge them when they have control of the ball. ◆◇◇◇ ADJ ADJ ADJ

un·mar·ried /ʌn'mærɪd/. Someone who is **unmarried** is not married. ◆◇◇◇ ADJ

un·mask /ʌn'mɑːsk, -'mæsk/ **unmasks, unmasking, unmasked.** If you **unmask** someone or something bad, you show or make known their true nature or character, when they had previously been thought to be good. *Elliott unmasked and confronted the master spy and traitor Kim Philby.* VERB V n

un·matched /ʌn'mætʃt/. If you describe something as **unmatched**, you are emphasizing that it is better or greater than all other things of the same kind. *...a landscape of unmatched beauty.* ADJ

un·men·tion·able /ʌn'menʃənəbəl/. If you describe something as **unmentionable**, you mean that it is too embarrassing or unpleasant to talk about. *Has he got some unmentionable disease?* ADJ

un·mer·ci·ful·ly /ʌn'mɜːsɪfʊli/. If you do something **unmercifully**, you do it a lot, showing no mercy or pity. *Uncle Sebastian used to tease Mother and Daddy unmercifully.* ADV

un·met /ʌn'met/. **Unmet** needs or demands are not satisfied. *...the unmet demand for quality family planning services.* ADJ

un·miss·able /ʌn'mɪsəbəl/. When journalists say that something such as an event or a film is **unmissable**, they are emphasizing that it is so good that everyone should try to go to it or see it. ADJ JOURNALISM, INFORMAL

un·mis·tak·able /ˌʌnmɪs'teɪkəbəl/; also spelled **unmistakeable.** If you describe something as **unmistakable**, you mean that it is so obvious that it cannot be mistaken for anything else. *...the unmistakable smell of marijuana drifted down.* ♦ **un·mis·tak·ably** /ˌʌnmɪs'teɪkəbli/. *She's unmistakably Scandinavian.* ◆◇◇◇ ADJ ADV

un·miti·gat·ed /ʌn'mɪtɪgeɪtɪd/. You use **unmitigated** to emphasize how bad a situation or quality is. *She leads a life of unmitigated misery.* ADJ: ADJ n

un·mo·lest·ed /ˌʌnmə'lestɪd/. If someone does something **unmolested**, they do it without being stopped or interfered with. *Like many fugitives, he lived in Argentina unmolested for many years.* ADJ

U

un·moved /ˌʌnˈmuːvd/. If you are **unmoved** by something, you are not emotionally affected by it. *Mr Bird remained unmoved by the corruption allegations.*
◆◇◇◇ ADJ-GRADED: v-link ADJ

un·mu·si·cal /ˌʌnˈmjuːzɪkəl/. **1** An **unmusical** sound is unpleasant to listen to. **2** An **unmusical** person cannot play or appreciate music.
ADJ-GRADED
ADJ-GRADED

un·named /ˌʌnˈneɪmd/. **1 Unnamed** people or things are talked about but their names are not mentioned. *The cash comes from an unnamed source.* **2 Unnamed** things have not been given a name. *...unnamed comets and asteroids.*
◆◇◇◇ ADJ

ADJ

un·natu·ral /ʌnˈnætʃərəl/. **1** If you describe something as **unnatural**, you mean that it is strange and often frightening, because it is different from what you normally expect. *The aircraft rose with unnatural speed on take-off.* ♦ **un·natu·ral·ly** *The house was unnaturally silent.* **2** Behaviour that is **unnatural** seems artificial and not normal or spontaneous. *She gave him a bright, determined smile which seemed unnatural.* ♦ **unnaturally** *Try to avoid shouting or speaking unnaturally.*
◆◇◇◇ ADJ-GRADED

ADV-GRADED: ADV adj ADJ-GRADED

ADV-GRADED: ADV with v

un·natu·ral·ly /ʌnˈnætʃərəli/. You can use **not unnaturally** to indicate that the situation you are describing is exactly as you would expect in the circumstances. *Not unnaturally, Jane greatly resented Harry's interference.* ● See also **unnatural**.
PHRASE

un·nec·es·sary /ʌnˈnesəsri, AM -seri/. If you describe something as **unnecessary**, you mean that it is not needed or does not have to be done, and is undesirable. *He accused Diana of making an unnecessary fuss.* ♦ **un·nec·es·sari·ly** /ˌʌnnesəˈserɪli/. *I didn't want to upset my husband or my daughter unnecessarily.*
◆◆◇◇ ADJ-GRADED

ADV-GRADED

un·nerve /ˌʌnˈnɜːv/ **unnerves, unnerving, unnerved.** If you say that something **unnerves** you, you mean that it worries or troubles you.
◆◇◇◇ VERB: V n

un·nerv·ing /ˌʌnˈnɜːvɪŋ/. If you describe something as **unnerving**, you mean that it is startling or very worrying. *...her unnerving habit of continuously touching people she was speaking to.* ♦ **un·nerv·ing·ly** *...a table decorated, unnervingly, by African fertility symbols.*
◆◇◇◇ ADJ-GRADED

ADV-GRADED

un·no·ticed /ˌʌnˈnəʊtɪst/. If something happens or passes **unnoticed**, it is not seen or noticed by anyone. *I tried to slip up the stairs unnoticed.*
◆◇◇◇ ADJ

un·ob·served /ˌʌnəbˈzɜːvd/. If you do something **unobserved**, you do it without being seen by other people. *John had been sitting, unobserved, in the darkness.*
ADJ

un·ob·tain·able /ˌʌnəbˈteɪnəbəl/. If something or someone is **unobtainable**, you cannot get them. *Fish was unobtainable in certain sections of Tokyo.*
ADJ

un·ob·tru·sive /ˌʌnəbˈtruːsɪv/. If you describe something or someone as **unobtrusive**, you mean that they are not easily noticed or do not draw attention to themselves. *He managed the factory with unobtrusive efficiency.* ♦ **un·ob·tru·sive·ly** *Unobtrusively, the other actors filed into the lounge.*
◆◇◇◇ ADJ-GRADED FORMAL

ADV-GRADED

un·oc·cu·pied /ˌʌnˈɒkjʊpaɪd/. If a building is **unoccupied**, there is nobody in it.
ADJ

un·of·fi·cial /ˌʌnəˈfɪʃəl/. An **unofficial** action or statement is not authorized, approved, or organized by a person in authority. *...an unofficial strike.* ♦ **un·of·fi·cial·ly** *The majority work unofficially with neither health nor wage security.*
◆◆◇◇ ADJ

ADV

un·opened /ˌʌnˈəʊpənd/. If something is **unopened**, it has not been opened yet. *...unopened bottles of olive oil.*
ADJ

un·op·posed /ˌʌnəˈpəʊzd/. In something such as an election or a war, if someone is **unopposed**, there are no opponents competing or fighting against them. *1st Army armoured cars drove unopposed into Tunis.*
ADJ

un·ortho·dox /ˌʌnˈɔːθədɒks/. **1** If you describe someone's behaviour, beliefs, or customs as **unorthodox**, you mean that they are different from what is generally accepted. *She spent an unorthodox girlhood travelling with her father throughout Europe.* **2** If you describe ways of doing things as
◆◇◇◇ ADJ-GRADED

ADJ-GRADED

unorthodox, you are criticizing them because they are illegal or unethical. *The journalists appear to have obtained confidential documents in an unorthodox manner.*
PRAGMATICS

un·pack /ˌʌnˈpæk/ **unpacks, unpacking, unpacked. 1** When you **unpack** a suitcase, box, or similar container, or you **unpack** the things inside it, you take the things out of the container. *Our guide unpacked a picnic of ham sandwiches and offered us tea.* **2** If you **unpack** an idea or problem, you analyse it and consider it in detail.
◆◇◇◇ VERB V n Also V

VERB: V n

un·paid /ˌʌnˈpeɪd/. **1** If you do **unpaid** work or you are an **unpaid** volunteer, you do a job without receiving any money for it. **2 Unpaid** taxes or bills are bills or taxes which have not been paid yet.
◆◇◇◇ ADJ: ADJ n

ADJ

un·pal·at·able /ʌnˈpælɪtəbəl/. **1** If you describe an idea as **unpalatable**, you mean that you find it unpleasant and difficult to accept. *It is an unpalatable fact that rape makes a good news story.* **2** If you describe food as **unpalatable**, you mean that it is so unpleasant that you can hardly eat it.
ADJ-GRADED

ADJ-GRADED

un·par·al·leled /ʌnˈpærəleld/. If you describe something as **unparalleled**, you are emphasizing that it is, for example, bigger, better, or worse than anything else of its kind, or anything that has happened before. *The country is facing a crisis unparalleled since the Second World War.*
◆◇◇◇ ADJ

un·par·don·able /ʌnˈpɑːdənəbəl/. If you say that someone's behaviour is **unpardonable**, you mean that it is very wrong or offensive, and completely unacceptable. *...an unpardonable lack of discipline.*
ADJ

un·pick /ʌnˈpɪk/ **unpicks, unpicking, unpicked. 1** If you **unpick** a piece of sewing, you remove the stitches from it. **2** If someone **unpicks** a plan or policy, they disagree with it and examine it thoroughly in order to find any mistakes that they can use to defeat it.
VERB: V n

VERB: V n BRITISH

un·play·able /ʌnˈpleɪəbəl/. In some sports, if you describe a player as **unplayable**, you mean that they are playing extremely well and are difficult to beat. If you describe a ball as **unplayable**, you mean it is difficult to hit, because it was thrown with great skill or speed, or because of its position.
ADJ-GRADED

un·pleas·ant /ʌnˈplezənt/. **1** If something is **unpleasant**, it gives you bad feelings, for example by making you feel upset or uncomfortable. *It was a very unpleasant and frightening attack.* ♦ **un·pleas·ant·ly** *The smell was unpleasantly strong.* **2** An **unpleasant** person is very unfriendly and rude. ♦ **unpleasantly** *Melissa laughed unpleasantly.* ♦ **un·pleas·ant·ness** *...the unpleasantness some people habitually displayed.*
◆◆◇◇ ADJ-GRADED

ADV ADJ-GRADED

ADV-GRADED N-UNCOUNT

un·plug /ˌʌnˈplʌg/ **unplugs, unplugging, unplugged.** If you **unplug** an electrical device or telephone, you pull a wire out of a socket so that it stops working.
VERB: V n

un·plugged /ˌʌnˈplʌgd/. If a pop group or musician performs **unplugged**, they perform without any electrically amplified instruments.
ADJ JOURNALISM

un·pol·lut·ed /ˌʌnpəˈluːtɪd/. Something that is **unpolluted** is free from pollution.
ADJ

un·popu·lar /ˌʌnˈpɒpjʊlə/. If something or someone is **unpopular**, most people do not like them. *The Chancellor is deeply unpopular with voters.* ♦ **un·popu·lar·ity** /ˌʌnpɒpjʊˈlærɪti/. *...the unpopularity of the new tax.*
◆◆◇◇ ADJ-GRADED

N-UNCOUNT

un·prec·edent·ed /ʌnˈpresɪdentɪd/. **1** If something is **unprecedented**, it has never happened before. *Such a move is rare, but not unprecedented.* **2** If you describe something as **unprecedented**, you are emphasizing that it is very great in quality, amount, or scale. *The scheme has been hailed as an unprecedented success.*
◆◆◇◇ ADJ

ADJ-GRADED

un·pre·dict·able /ˌʌnprɪˈdɪktəbəl/. If you describe someone or something as **unpredictable**, you mean that you cannot tell what they are going to do or how they are going to behave. *...Britain's notoriously unpredictable weather.* ♦ **un·pre·dict·ably** *...her husband's unpredictably violent behavior to others.*
◆◆◇◇ ADJ-GRADED

ADV-GRADED

♦ **un·pre·dict·abil·ity** /ˌʌnprɪˌdɪktəˈbɪlɪti/. ...the N-UNCOUNT unpredictability of the weather.

un·pre·pared /ˌʌnprɪˈpeəd/. **1** If you are **unpre- ◆◇◇◇** **pared** for something, you are not ready for it, and ADJ-GRADED you are therefore surprised or at a disadvantage when it happens. I was totally unprepared for the announcement on the next day. **2** If you are **unpre-** ADJ-GRADED: **pared** to do something, you are not willing to do it. v-link ADJ to-He was unprepared to co-operate. inf

un·pre·pos·sess·ing /ˌʌnpriːpəˈzesɪŋ/. If you de- ADJ-GRADED scribe someone or something as **unprepossessing**, FORMAL you mean that they look rather plain or ordinary, although they may have good or special qualities that are hidden. We found the tastiest and most imaginative paella and tapas in the most unprepossessing bars and cafés.

un·pre·ten·tious /ˌʌnprɪˈtenʃəs/. If you describe a ◆◇◇◇ place, person, or thing as **unpretentious**, you ap- ADJ-GRADED prove of them because they are simple in appear- PRAGMATICS ance or character, rather than sophisticated or luxurious. The Tides Inn hotel is both comfortable and unpretentious.

un·prin·ci·pled /ʌnˈprɪnsɪpəld/. If you describe a ADJ-GRADED person or their actions as **unprincipled**, you are PRAGMATICS criticizing them for their lack of moral principles. It is a market where people can be very unprincipled and unpleasant.

un·print·able /ʌnˈprɪntəbəl/. If you describe some- ADJ thing that someone has said or done as **unprint-able**, you mean that it is so rude or shocking that you do not want to say exactly what it was.

un·pro·duc·tive /ˌʌnprəˈdʌktɪv/. Something that ◆◇◇◇ is **unproductive** does not produce any good results. ADJ-GRADED ...much of their time and effort is unproductive.

un·pro·fes·sion·al /ˌʌnprəˈfeʃənəl/. If you use **un-** ADJ-GRADED **professional** to describe someone's behaviour at PRAGMATICS work, you are criticizing them for not behaving according to the standards that are expected of a person in their profession. What she did was very unprofessional. She left abruptly about 90 minutes into the show.

un·prof·it·able /ˌʌnˈprɒfɪtəbəl/. **1** An industry, ◆◇◇◇ company, or product that is **unprofitable** does not ADJ-GRADED make any profit or does not make enough profit. **2** **Unprofitable** activities or efforts do not produce ADJ any useful or helpful results. ...an endless, unprofitable argument.

un·prom·is·ing /ˌʌnˈprɒmɪsɪŋ/. If you describe ADJ-GRADED something as **unpromising**, you think that it is unlikely to be successful or produce anything good in the future. His business career had distinctly unpromising beginnings.

un·pro·nounce·able /ˌʌnprəˈnaʊnsəbəl/. An **un-** ADJ-GRADED **pronounceable** word or name is too difficult to say.

un·pro·tect·ed /ˌʌnprəˈtektɪd/. **1** An **unprotected** ◆◇◇◇ person or place is not looked after or defended, and ADJ so they may be harmed or attacked. What better target than an unprotected girl, going along that river walkway in the dark. **2** If something is **unprotected**, ADJ it is not covered or treated with anything, and so it may easily be damaged. Exposure of unprotected skin to the sun carries the risk of developing skin cancer. **3** If two people have **unprotected** sex, they ADJ: ADJ n do not use a condom when they have intercourse.

un·pro·voked /ˌʌnprəˈvəʊkt/. If someone makes ADJ an **unprovoked** attack, they attack someone who has not tried to harm them in any way.

un·pub·lished /ˌʌnˈpʌblɪʃt/. An **unpublished** ◆◇◇◇ book, letter, or report has never been published. ADJ

un·pun·ished /ˌʌnˈpʌnɪʃt/. If a criminal or crime ADJ goes **unpunished**, the criminal is not punished.

un·quali·fied /ˌʌnˈkwɒlɪfaɪd/. **1** If you are **un-** ◆◇◇◇ **qualified**, you do not have any qualifications, or ADJ you do not have the right qualifications for a particular job. **2** **Unqualified** means total, unlimited, ADJ and complete. The event was an unqualified success.

un·ques·tion·able /ʌnˈkwestʃənəbəl/. If you de- ◆◇◇◇ scribe something as **unquestionable**, you are em- ADJ phasizing that it is so obviously true or real that nobody can doubt it. There is an unquestionable link

between job losses and deteriorating services. ♦ **un-** **·ques·tion·ably** /ʌnˈkwestʃənəbli/. They have seen ADV-GRADED: the change as unquestionably beneficial to the ADV with cl/ country. group

un·ques·tioned /ʌnˈkwestʃənd/. **1** You use **un-** ADJ **questioned** to emphasize that something is so obvious, real, or great that nobody can doubt it or disagree with it. The play was an immediate and unquestioned success. **2** If something or someone is ADJ **unquestioned**, they are accepted by everyone, without anyone doubting or disagreeing. Stalin was the unquestioned ruler of the Soviet Union. **3** If you de- ADJ: ADJ n scribe someone's belief or attitude as **unques-tioned**, you are emphasizing that they accept something without any doubt or disagreement. Royalty is regarded with unquestioned reverence.

un·ques·tion·ing /ʌnˈkwestʃənɪŋ/. If you describe ADJ-GRADED a person or their beliefs as **unquestioning**, you are emphasizing that they accept something without any doubt or disagreement. Isabella had been taught unquestioning obedience. ♦ **un·quest·ion-** ADV: **·ing·ly** She supported him unquestioningly. ADV with v

un·quote /ˈʌnkwəʊt/. **1** You can say **unquote** to PRAGMATICS mark the end of a quotation, especially one which SPOKEN you have introduced with the word 'quote'. Stalin's history of the Communist Party was, quote, 'full of lies', unquote. **2** You can say **quote, unquote** before PHRASE or after words you are using to show that you are PRAGMATICS quoting someone's words or that the words do not SPOKEN reflect what you believe. We've only had an 'average', quote, unquote, kind of recession.

un·rav·el /ʌnˈrævəl/ **unravels, unravelling,** ◆◇◇◇ **unravelled;** spelled **unraveling, unraveled** in American English. **1** If something such as a plan or VERB system **unravels**, it breaks up or begins to fail. His V government began to unravel because of a banking scandal. **2** If you **unravel** a mystery or puzzle, or it V-ERG **unravels**, it gradually becomes clearer and you can V n work out the answer to it. A young mother has flown Also V to Iceland to unravel the mystery of her husband's disappearance. **3** If you **unravel** something that is V-ERG knotted, twisted, woven, or knitted, or if it **unravels**, V n it separates into its different threads or strands. He Also V was good with his hands and could unravel a knot or untangle yarn.

un·read /ˌʌnˈred/. If a book or other piece of writ- ADJ ing is **unread**, you or other people have not read it, for example because it is boring or because you have no time.

un·read·able /ˌʌnˈriːdəbəl/. **1** If you use **unread-** ADJ-GRADED **able** to describe a book or other piece of writing, PRAGMATICS you are criticizing it because it is very boring, complicated, or difficult to understand. **2** If a piece of ADJ writing is **unreadable**, it is impossible to read because the letters are unclear, especially because it has been damaged in some way. ...if contracts are unreadable because of the microscopic print. **3** If ADJ-GRADED someone's face or expression is **unreadable**, it is LITERARY impossible to tell what they are thinking or feeling.

un·real /ˌʌnˈriːl/. **1** If you say that a situation is **un-** ◆◇◇◇ **real**, you mean that it is so strange that you find it ADJ-GRADED: difficult to believe it is happening. It was unreal. v-link ADJ Like some crazy childhood nightmare. ♦ **un·re·al-** **·ity** /ˌʌnriˈælɪti/. He didn't feel too weak. Light- N-UNCOUNT headed certainly, and with a sense of unreality, but able to walk. **2** If you use **unreal** to describe some- ADJ-GRADED thing that exists or is talked about, you are critical PRAGMATICS of it because you think that is does not correspond to reality or to the truth. ...unreal financial targets.

un·re·al·is·tic /ˌʌnrɪəˈlɪstɪk/. If you say that some- ◆◇◇◇ one is being **unrealistic**, you mean that they do not ADJ-GRADED recognize the truth about a situation, especially about the difficulties involved in something they want to achieve. ...their unrealistic expectations of parenthood. ♦ **un·re·al·is·ti·cal·ly** /ˌʌnrɪəˈlɪstɪkli/. ADV-GRADED Tom spoke unrealistically of getting a full-time job.

un·rea·son·able /ʌnˈriːzənəbəl/. **1** If you say that ◆◇◇◇ someone is being **unreasonable**, you mean that ADJ-GRADED they are behaving in a way that is not fair or sensible. It's unreasonable to expect your child to be-

have in a caring way if you behave selfishly. ♦ **un-rea·son·ably** /ʌnˈriːzənəbli/. *We unreasonably expect near perfect behaviour from our children.* **2** An **unreasonable** decision, action, price, or amount seems unfair and difficult to justify. *...unreasonable increases in the price of petrol.* ♦ **unreasonably** *The banks' charges are unreasonably high.* ADV

un·rec·og·niz·able /ʌnˌrekəɡˈnaɪzəbl/; also spelled **unrecognisable** in British English. If someone or something is **unrecognizable**, they have become impossible to recognize or identify, for example because they have been greatly changed or damaged. *The new town would have been unrecognisable to the original inhabitants.* ADJ

un·rec·og·nized /ʌnˈrekəɡnaɪzd/; also spelled **unrecognised** in British English. **1** If someone does something **unrecognized**, nobody knows or recognizes them while they do it. *He is believed to have worked unrecognised as a doorman at East End clubs.* **2** If something is **unrecognized**, people are not aware of it. *Until comparatively recently, dyslexia remained largely unrecognised.* **3** If you or your achievements or qualities are **unrecognized**, you have not been properly appreciated or acknowledged by other people for what you have done. *She became ill and died with her life's work unrecognised.* **4** An **unrecognized** meeting, agreement, or political party is not formally acknowledged as legal or valid by the authorities. ADJ; ADJ after v, v-link ADJ / ADJ / ADJ / ADJ

un·re·con·struct·ed /ʌnˌriːkənˈstrʌktɪd/. If you describe systems, beliefs, policies, or people as **unreconstructed**, you are critical of them because they have not changed at all, in spite of new ideas and circumstances. ADJ-GRADED PRAGMATICS

un·re·cord·ed /ʌnrɪˈkɔːdɪd/. You use **unrecorded** to describe something that has not been written down or recorded officially, especially when it should have been. *The statistics don't reveal of course unrecorded crime.* ADJ

un·re·fined /ʌnrɪˈfaɪnd/. An **unrefined** food or other substance is in its natural state and has not been processed. ADJ

un·re·hearsed /ʌnrɪˈhɜːst/. **Unrehearsed** activities or performances have not been prepared, planned, or practised beforehand. ADJ

un·re·lat·ed /ʌnrɪˈleɪtɪd/. **1** If one thing is **unrelated** to another, there is no connection between them. You can say that two things are **unrelated**. *Two of them died from apparently unrelated causes.* **2** If one person is **unrelated** to another, they are not members of the same family. You can also say that two people are **unrelated**. ◆◇◇◇ ADJ-GRADED / ADJ WRITTEN

un·re·lent·ing /ʌnrɪˈlentɪŋ/. **1** If you describe someone's behaviour as **unrelenting**, you mean that they are continuing to do something in a very determined way, often without caring whether they hurt or embarrass other people. *She established her authority with unrelenting thoroughness.* **2** If you describe something unpleasant as **unrelenting**, you mean that it is continuing without stopping, and that you have no relief or rest from it. *...an unrelenting downpour of rain.* ◆◇◇◇ ADJ / ADJ-GRADED

un·re·li·able /ʌnrɪˈlaɪəbl/. If you describe a person, machine, or method as **unreliable**, you mean that you cannot trust them to do or provide what you want. *He had an unreliable car.* ♦ **un·re·li·ability** /ʌnrɪlaɪəˈbɪlɪti/. *...his lateness and unreliability.* ◆◇◇◇ ADJ-GRADED / N-UNCOUNT

un·re·lieved /ʌnrɪˈliːvd/. If you describe something unpleasant as **unrelieved**, you mean that it is very severe and is not replaced by anything better, even for a short time. *The sun baked down on the concrete, unrelieved by any breeze.* ADJ

un·re·mark·able /ʌnrɪˈmɑːkəbl/. If you describe someone or something as **unremarkable**, you mean that they are very ordinary, without many exciting, original, or attractive qualities. *...a tall, lean man, with an unremarkable face.* ADJ-GRADED

un·re·marked /ʌnrɪˈmɑːkt/. If something happens or goes **unremarked**, people say nothing about it, ADJ FORMAL because they consider it normal or do not notice it. *His departure, in fact, went almost unremarked.*

un·re·mit·ting /ʌnrɪˈmɪtɪŋ/. Something that is **unremitting** continues without stopping or becoming less intense. *He watched her with unremitting attention.* ♦ **un·re·mit·ting·ly** *The weather was unremittingly awful.* ADJ FORMAL / ADV-GRADED

un·re·pent·ant /ʌnrɪˈpentənt/. If you are **unrepentant**, you are not ashamed of your beliefs or actions. *Pamela was unrepentant about her strong language.* ADJ

un·rep·re·senta·tive /ʌnreprɪˈzentətɪv/. If you describe a group of people as **unrepresentative**, you mean that their views are not typical of the community or society to which they belong. *The President denounced the demonstrators as unrepresentative of the Romanian people.* ADJ-GRADED

un·rep·re·sent·ed /ʌnreprɪˈzentɪd/. If you are **unrepresented** in something such as a parliament, law court, or meeting, there is nobody there speaking or acting for you, for example to give your opinions or instructions. ADJ

un·re·quit·ed /ʌnrɪˈkwaɪtɪd/. If you have **unrequited** love for someone, you love them but they do not love you. ADJ LITERARY

un·re·served /ʌnrɪˈzɜːvd/. An **unreserved** opinion or statement is one that expresses a feeling or opinion completely and without any doubts. *Jones' lawyers are seeking an unreserved apology from the newspaper.* ♦ **un·re·serv·ed·ly** /ʌnrɪˈzɜːvɪdli/. *We apologise unreservedly for any imputation of incorrect behaviour by Mr Taylor.* ADJ / ADV: ADV with v

un·re·solved /ʌnrɪˈzɒlvd/. If a problem or difficulty is **unresolved**, no satisfactory solution has been found to it. ◆◇◇◇ ADJ FORMAL

un·re·spon·sive /ʌnrɪˈspɒnsɪv/. **1** An **unresponsive** person does not react or pay enough attention to something, for example to an urgent situation or to people's needs. *He was totally unresponsive to the pressing social and economic needs of the majority of the population.* **2** If a person or their body is **unresponsive**, they do not react to anything or make any movements, because they are dead or unconscious. ADJ-GRADED FORMAL / ADJ FORMAL

un·rest /ʌnˈrest/. If there is **unrest** in a particular place or society, people are expressing anger and dissatisfaction, often by demonstrating or rioting. *There is growing unrest among students in several major cities.* ◆◆◇◇ N-UNCOUNT JOURNALISM

un·re·strained /ʌnrɪˈstreɪnd/. If you describe someone's behaviour as **unrestrained**, you mean that it is extreme or intense, for example because they are expressing their feelings very strongly. *There was unrestrained joy on the faces of the people.* ADJ

un·re·strict·ed /ʌnrɪˈstrɪktɪd/. **1** If an activity is **unrestricted**, you are free to do it in the way that you want, without being limited by any rules. **2** If you have an **unrestricted** view of something, you can see it fully and clearly, because there is nothing in the way. ◆◇◇◇ ADJ / ADJ

un·re·ward·ed /ʌnrɪˈwɔːdɪd/. You can say that someone goes **unrewarded**, or that their activities go **unrewarded**, when they do not achieve what they are trying to achieve. ADJ

un·re·ward·ing /ʌnrɪˈwɔːdɪŋ/. An **unrewarding** activity does not give you any feelings of achievement or pleasure. ADJ-GRADED

un·ripe /ʌnˈraɪp/. **Unripe** fruit or vegetables are not yet ripe. ADJ

un·ri·valled /ʌnˈraɪvəld/; spelled **unrivaled** in American English. If you describe something as **unrivalled**, you are emphasizing that it is better than anything else of the same kind. *He had an unrivalled knowledge of south Arabian society.* ADJ

un·roll /ʌnˈrəʊl/ **unrolls, unrolling, unrolled**. If you **unroll** something such as a sheet of paper or cloth, or if it **unrolls**, it opens up and becomes flat when it was previously rolled in a cylindrical shape. *...the screen that unrolls from the ceiling.* V-ERG: V n / V

un·ruf·fled /ˌʌnˈrʌfəld/. If you describe someone as unruffled, you mean that they are calm and do not seem to be affected by surprising or frightening events. *Anne had remained unruffled, very cool and controlled.* ADJ-GRADED

un·ru·ly /ʌnˈruːli/. **1** If you describe people, especially children, as unruly, you mean that they behave badly and are difficult to control. **2 Unruly** hair is difficult to keep tidy. ◆◇◇◇◇ ADJ-GRADED

un·safe /ˌʌnˈseɪf/. **1** If a building, machine, activity, or area is unsafe, it is dangerous. *Critics claim the trucks are unsafe.* **2** If you are unsafe, you are in danger of being harmed. *In the larger neighbourhood, I felt very unsafe.* **3** If a criminal conviction is unsafe, it is based on inadequate or false evidence. ◆◇◇◇◇ ADJ-GRADED; v-link ADJ ADJ-GRADED

un·said /ˌʌnˈsed/. If something is left unsaid or goes unsaid in a particular situation, it is not said, although you might have expected it to be said. *Some things, Donald, are better left unsaid.* ADJ

un·sale·able /ˌʌnˈseɪləbəl/; spelled unsalable in American English. If something is unsaleable, it cannot be sold because nobody wants to buy it. ADJ

un·sani·tary /ʌnˈsænɪtri, AM -teri/. Something that is unsanitary is dirty and unhealthy, so that you may catch a disease from it. ADJ-GRADED

un·sat·is·fac·tory /ˌʌnsætɪsˈfæktəri/. If you describe something as unsatisfactory, you mean that it is not as good as it should be, and cannot be considered acceptable. *The inspectors said just under a third of lessons were unsatisfactory.* ◆◇◇◇◇ ADJ-GRADED

un·sat·is·fied /ʌnˈsætɪsfaɪd/. **1** If you are unsatisfied with something, you are disappointed because you have not got what you hoped to get. *...people who are unsatisfied with the solicitors they are given.* **2** If a need or demand is unsatisfied, it is not dealt with. *The strongest unsatisfied appetite for home computers isn't among the richest consumers.* ADJ-GRADED

un·sat·is·fy·ing /ʌnˈsætɪsfaɪɪŋ/. If you find something unsatisfying, you do not get any satisfaction from it. *So far the marriage has been unsatisfying.* ADJ-GRADED

un·sa·voury /ʌnˈseɪvəri/; spelled unsavory in American English. If you describe a person, place, or thing as unsavoury, you mean that you find them unpleasant or morally unacceptable. *The sport has long been associated with illegal wagers and unsavoury characters.* ADJ-GRADED

un·scathed /ʌnˈskeɪðd/. If you are unscathed after a dangerous experience, you have not been injured or harmed by it. ◆◇◇◇◇ ADJ-GRADED

un·sched·uled /ʌnˈʃedjuːld, AM -ˈsked-/. An unscheduled event was not planned to happen, but happens unexpectedly or because someone changes their plans at a late stage. *The ship made an unscheduled stop at Hawaii.* ADJ

un·sci·en·tif·ic /ˌʌnsaɪənˈtɪfɪk/. A method, experiment, or process that is unscientific may be unreliable because it is not based on facts or is not objective. ADJ-GRADED

un·scram·ble /ʌnˈskræmbəl/ unscrambles, unscrambling, unscrambled. To unscramble things that are in a state of confusion or disorder means to arrange them in an orderly way so that you can understand them. VERB: V n

un·screw /ʌnˈskruː/ unscrews, unscrewing, unscrewed. **1** If you unscrew something such as a lid, or if it unscrews, you keep turning it until you can remove it. *A wick soaks up the petrol, and the head of the candle unscrews for refilling.* **2** If you unscrew something which is fastened to something by screws, you remove it by taking out the screws. V-ERG: V n V; VERB: V n

un·script·ed /ʌnˈskrɪptɪd/. An unscripted talk or speech is spoken without a previously prepared script. ADJ

un·scru·pu·lous /ʌnˈskruːpjʊləs/. If you describe a person as unscrupulous, you are critical of the fact that they are prepared to act in a dishonest or immoral way in order to get what they want. ◆◇◇◇◇ ADJ-GRADED PRAGMATICS

un·sea·son·ably /ʌnˈsiːzənəbli/. Unseasonably warm, cold, or mild weather is warmer, colder, or milder than it usually is at the time of year. ADV: ADV adj

un·seat /ʌnˈsiːt/ unseats, unseating, unseated. When people try to unseat a person who is in an important job or position, they try to remove him or her from that job or position. ◆◇◇◇◇ VERB: V n

un·secured /ˌʌnsɪˈkjʊəd/. Unsecured loans or debts are not guaranteed by a particular asset such as a person's home. ◆◇◇◇◇ ADJ

un·seed·ed /ʌnˈsiːdɪd/. In sports competitions such as tennis or badminton, an unseeded player is someone who has not been ranked amongst the top 16 players by the tournament's organizers. ◆◇◇◇◇ ADJ

un·see·ing /ʌnˈsiːɪŋ/. If you describe a person or their eyes as unseeing, you mean that they are not looking at anything, or not noticing something, although their eyes are open. ADJ LITERARY

un·seem·ly /ʌnˈsiːmli/. If you say that someone's behaviour is unseemly, you disapprove of it because it is not polite or is not suitable for a particular situation or occasion. *...unseemly drinking, brawling and gambling.* ADJ-GRADED PRAGMATICS LITERARY

un·seen /ʌnˈsiːn/. **1** If you describe something as unseen, you mean that it has not been seen for a long time. *...a spectacular ballroom, unseen by the public for over 30 years.* **2** You can use unseen to describe things which people cannot see. *There was barely time for the two boys to escape unseen.* ◆◇◇◇◇ ADJ; ADJ

un·self·ish /ʌnˈselfɪʃ/. If you describe someone as unselfish, you approve of the fact that they regard other people's wishes and interests as more important than their own. ADJ-GRADED PRAGMATICS

un·sen·ti·men·tal /ˌʌnsentɪˈmentəl/. If you describe someone as unsentimental, you mean that they do not allow emotions like pity or affection to interfere with their work or decisions. ADJ-GRADED

un·set·tle /ʌnˈsetəl/ unsettles, unsettling, unsettled. If something unsettles you, it causes you to feel restless, dissatisfied, or rather worried. *The presence of the two policemen unsettled her.* ◆◇◇◇◇ VERB V n

un·set·tled /ʌnˈsetəld/. **1** In an unsettled situation, there is a lot of uncertainty about what will happen. *...Britain's unsettled political scene.* **2** If you are unsettled, you cannot concentrate on anything because you are worried. *To tell the truth, I'm a bit unsettled tonight.* **3** An unsettled argument or dispute has not yet been resolved. *There are still unsettled border disputes.* **4** Unsettled places are places where no people have yet lived. **5** Unsettled weather is unpredictable and changes a lot. ◆◇◇◇◇ ADJ-GRADED; ADJ-GRADED: v-link ADJ; ADJ; ADJ; ADJ-GRADED

un·set·tling /ʌnˈsetəlɪŋ/. If you describe something as unsettling, you mean that it causes you to feel restless, dissatisfied, or rather worried. *The prospect of change of this kind has an unsettling effect on any organisation.* ◆◇◇◇◇ ADJ-GRADED

un·shake·able /ʌnˈʃeɪkəbəl/; also spelled unshakable. If you describe someone's beliefs as unshakeable, you are emphasizing that they are so strong that they cannot be destroyed or altered. *William has acquired an unshakeable belief in himself.* ADJ

un·shak·en /ʌnˈʃeɪkən/. **1** If your beliefs are unshaken, you still have those beliefs, although they have been attacked or challenged. **2** If you are unshaken by something, you are not emotionally affected by it. *Mona remains unshaken by her ordeal.* ADJ; ADJ

un·shav·en /ʌnˈʃeɪvən/. If a man is unshaven, he has not shaved recently and there are short hairs on his face or chin. ADJ

un·sight·ly /ʌnˈsaɪtli/. If you describe something as unsightly, you mean that it is unattractive to look at. *My mother has had unsightly varicose veins for years.* ◆◇◇◇◇ ADJ-GRADED

un·signed /ˌʌnˈsaɪnd/. **1** An unsigned document does not have anyone's signature on it. **2** An unsigned band has not signed a contract with a company to produce records. *Fugazi are America's biggest unsigned alternative band.* ADJ; ADJ

un·skilled /ˌʌnˈskɪld/. **1** People who are unskilled do not have any special training for a job. *...work as an unskilled labourer.* **2 Unskilled** work does not require any special training. *In the US, minorities* ◆◇◇◇◇ ADJ; ADJ

U

and immigrants have generally gone into low-paid, unskilled jobs.

un·smil·ing /ˌʌnˈsmaɪlɪŋ/. An **unsmiling** person is not smiling, and looks serious or unfriendly. He was unsmiling and silent. ADJ LITERARY

un·so·cia·ble /ʌnˈsəʊʃəbəl/. Someone who is **unsociable** does not like talking to other people and tries to avoid meeting them. ADJ-GRADED

un·so·cial /ʌnˈsəʊʃəl/. If someone works **unsocial** hours, they work late at night, early in the morning, at weekends, or on public holidays. ADJ

un·sold /ˌʌnˈsəʊld/. **Unsold** goods have been available for people to buy but nobody has bought them. ...piles of unsold books. ◆◇◇◇ ADJ

un·so·lic·it·ed /ˌʌnsəˈlɪsɪtɪd/. Something that is **unsolicited** has been given without being asked for and may not have been wanted. 'If I were you,' she adds by way of some unsolicited advice, 'I'd watch out for that girl of yours.' ADJ

un·solved /ˌʌnˈsɒlvd/. An **unsolved** mystery or problem has never been solved. David's murder remains unsolved. ◆◇◇◇ ADJ

un·so·phis·ti·cat·ed /ˌʌnsəˈfɪstɪkeɪtɪd/. **1 Unsophisticated** people do not have a wide range of experience or knowledge and have simple tastes. It was music of a rather crude kind which unsophisticated audiences enjoyed listening to. **2** An **unsophisticated** method or device is very simple and often not very effective. ...an unsophisticated alarm system. ADJ-GRADED

un·sound /ˌʌnˈsaʊnd/. **1** If a conclusion or method is **unsound**, it is based on ideas that are wrong. The thinking is good-hearted, but muddled and fundamentally unsound. **2** If something or someone is **unsound**, they are unreliable. No sensible person would put his money in a bank he knew to be unsound. **3** If you say that something is **unsound** in some way, you mean that it is damaging in that way or to the thing mentioned. The project is environmentally unsound. **4** If a building or other structure is **unsound**, it is in poor condition and is likely to collapse. ADJ-GRADED ADJ-GRADED ADJ-GRADED ADJ-GRADED

un·speak·able /ʌnˈspiːkəbəl/. If you describe something as **unspeakable**, you are emphasizing that it is extremely unpleasant. ...the unspeakable horrors of chemical weapons. ♦ **un·speak·ably** /ʌnˈspiːkəbli/. The novel was unspeakably boring. ◆◇◇◇ ADJ-GRADED ADV-GRADED

un·speci·fied /ʌnˈspesɪfaɪd/. You say that something is **unspecified** when you are not told exactly what it is. He was arrested on unspecified charges. ◆◇◇◇ ADJ

un·spec·tacu·lar /ˌʌnspekˈtækjʊlə/. If you describe something as **unspectacular**, you mean that it is rather dull and not remarkable in any way. ...pleasant, if largely unspectacular, countryside. ADJ-GRADED

un·spoiled /ˌʌnˈspɔɪld/; also spelled **unspoilt** /ˌʌnˈspɔɪlt/. If you describe a place as **unspoiled**, you think it is beautiful because it has not been changed or built on for a long time. ...the unspoiled island of Cozumel. ADJ-GRADED

un·spo·ken /ˌʌnˈspəʊkən/. **1** If your thoughts, wishes, or feelings are **unspoken**, you do not speak about them. **2** When there is an **unspoken** agreement or understanding between people, their behaviour shows that they agree about something or understand it, even though they have never spoken about it. ◆◇◇◇ ADJ ADJ: ADJ n

un·sport·ing /ˌʌnˈspɔːtɪŋ/. If you describe someone playing a game as **unsporting**, you are critical of them because they have behaved in a selfish way that is unfair to their opponent. ADJ-GRADED PRAGMATICS

un·sta·ble /ˌʌnˈsteɪbəl/. **1** You can describe something as **unstable** if it is likely to change suddenly, especially if this creates difficulty or danger. The situation is unstable and potentially dangerous. **2 Unstable** objects are likely to move or fall. Both clay and sandstone are unstable rock formations. **3** If people are **unstable**, their emotions and behaviour keep changing because their minds are disturbed or upset. He was emotionally unstable. ◆◇◇◇ ADJ-GRADED ADJ-GRADED ADJ-GRADED

un·stat·ed /ʌnˈsteɪtɪd/. If something is **unstated**, it has not been expressed in words. The implication was plain, if left unstated. ADJ

un·steady /ʌnˈstedi/. **1** If you are **unsteady**, you have difficulty doing something, for example walking, because you cannot completely control your legs or your body. The boy was very unsteady and had staggered around when he got up. ♦ **un·steadi·ly** /ʌnˈstedɪli/. She pulled herself unsteadily from the bed to the dresser. **2** If you describe something as **unsteady**, you mean that it is not regular or stable, but unreliable or unpredictable. His voice was unsteady and only just audible. **3 Unsteady** objects are not held, fixed, or balanced securely. ...a slightly unsteady item of furniture. ADJ-GRADED ADV-GRADED: ADV with v ADJ-GRADED ADJ-GRADED

un·stick /ʌnˈstɪk/ **unsticks, unsticking, unstuck.** If you **unstick** something or if it **unsticks**, it becomes separated from the thing that it was stuck to. Mike shook his head, to unstick his hair from his sweating forehead. V-ERG: V V n

un·stint·ing /ʌnˈstɪntɪŋ/. **Unstinting** help, care, or praise is great in amount or degree and is given generously. ADJ

un·stop·pable /ʌnˈstɒpəbəl/. Something that is **unstoppable** cannot be prevented from continuing or developing. The progress of science is unstoppable. ◆◇◇◇ ADJ

un·stressed /ˌʌnˈstrest/. If a word or syllable is **unstressed**, it is pronounced without emphasis. ADJ TECHNICAL

un·struc·tured /ˌʌnˈstrʌktʃəd/. Something such as a meeting, interview, or activity that is **unstructured** is not organized in a complete or detailed way. Our aim was that these meetings be unstructured and informal. ADJ-GRADED

un·stuck /ʌnˈstʌk/. **1** If something **comes unstuck**, it becomes separated from the thing that it was attached to. **2** If a plan or system **comes unstuck**, it fails. **3** If someone **comes unstuck**, they fail badly at something that they are trying to achieve. PHRASE PHRASE INFORMAL PHRASE INFORMAL

un·sub·stan·ti·at·ed /ˌʌnsəbˈstænʃieɪtɪd/. A claim, accusation, or story that is **unsubstantiated** has not been proved to be valid or true. ...unsubstantiated rumours about his private life. ADJ

un·suc·cess·ful /ˌʌnsəkˈsesful/. **1** Something that is **unsuccessful** does not achieve what it was intended to achieve. His efforts were unsuccessful. ...a second unsuccessful operation on his knee. ♦ **un·suc·cess·ful·ly** He has been trying unsuccessfully to sell the business. **2** Someone who is **unsuccessful** does not achieve what they intended to achieve, especially in their career. He and his friend Boris were unsuccessful in getting a job. ◆◆◇◇ ADJ-GRADED ADV-GRADED: ADV with v ADJ-GRADED

un·suit·able /ʌnˈsuːtəbəl/. Someone or something that is **unsuitable** for a particular purpose or situation does not have the right qualities for it. Amy's shoes were unsuitable for walking any distance. ◆◇◇◇ ADJ-GRADED

un·suit·ed /ˌʌnˈsuːtɪd/. **1** If someone or something is **unsuited** to a particular job, situation, or place, they do not have the right qualities or characteristics for it. He's totally unsuited to the job. **2** If two people, especially a man and a woman, are **unsuited** to each other, they have different personalities or interests, and so are unlikely to have a successful relationship. By the end of that first year, I knew how totally unsuited we were to each other. ADJ-GRADED ADJ-GRADED

un·sul·lied /ˌʌnˈsʌlɪd/. If something is **unsullied**, it has not been spoiled or made less pure by the addition of something unpleasant or unacceptable. He smiled, unsullied by doubt. ADJ-GRADED LITERARY

un·sung /ˌʌnˈsʌŋ/. **Unsung** is used to describe people, things, or places that are not appreciated or praised, although you think they deserve to be. They are among the unsung heroes of our time. ADJ

un·sup·port·ed /ˌʌnsəˈpɔːtɪd/. **1** If a statement or theory is **unsupported**, there is no evidence which proves that it is true or correct. It was a theory unsupported by evidence. **2** An **unsupported** person does not have anyone to provide them with money and the things they need. Unsupported mothers are one of the fastest-growing groups of welfare claim- ADJ ADJ

ants. **3** An **unsupported** building or person is not ADJ
being physically supported or held up by anything.
...the child's first unsupported step.

un·sure /ˌʌnˈʃʊə/. **1** If you are **unsure** of yourself, ◆◇◇◇◇
you lack confidence. He made her feel hot, and awk- ADJ-GRADED
ward, and unsure of herself. **2** If you are **unsure** ADJ-GRADED:
about something, you feel uncertain about it. Fifty- v-link ADJ
two per cent were unsure about the idea.

un·sur·passed /ˌʌnsəˈpɑːst, -ˈpæst/. If you de- ADJ
scribe something as **unsurpassed**, you are emphasizing that it is better or greater than anything else
of its kind. The quality of Smallbone furniture is unsurpassed.

un·sur·pris·ing /ˌʌnsəˈpraɪzɪŋ/. If something is ◆◇◇◇◇
unsurprising, you are not surprised by it because ADJ-GRADED
you would expect it to happen or be like it is. It is
unsurprising that he remains so hated. ♦ **un·sur**
·pris·ing·ly Unsurprisingly, not everyone agrees ADV
that things are better.

un·sus·pect·ed /ˌʌnsəˈspektɪd/. If you describe ADJ
something as **unsuspected**, you mean that people
do not realize it or are not aware of it. He died in
1984 of an unsuspected brain tumour.

un·sus·pect·ing /ˌʌnsəˈspektɪŋ/. You can use **un-** ◆◇◇◇◇
suspecting to describe someone who is not at all ADJ
aware of something that is happening or going to
happen. ...his unsuspecting victim.

un·sweet·ened /ˌʌnˈswiːtənd/. **Unsweetened** food ADJ
or drink does not have any sugar or other sweet
substance added to it.

un·swerv·ing /ʌnˈswɜːvɪŋ/. If you describe ADJ
someone's attitude, feeling, or way of behaving as
unswerving, you mean that it is strong and firm
and does not weaken or change. ...her unswerving
belief in her father's innocence.

un·sym·pa·thet·ic /ˌʌnsɪmpəˈθetɪk/. **1** If someone ADJ-GRADED
is **unsympathetic**, they are not kind or helpful to a
person in difficulties. Her husband was unsympathetic and she felt she had no one to turn to. **2** An ADJ-GRADED
unsympathetic person is unpleasant and difficult to
like. ...a very unsympathetic main character. **3** If ADJ-GRADED:
you are **unsympathetic to** a particular idea or aim, v-link ADJ to n
you are not willing to support it. I'm highly unsympathetic to what you are trying to achieve.

un·tamed /ʌnˈteɪmd/. An **untamed** area or place is ADJ
wild or unmanageable because it has not been
greatly changed or influenced by modern things.
The interior of Corsica is high and untamed.

un·tan·gle /ˌʌnˈtæŋgəl/ **untangles, untangling,**
untangled. 1 If you **untangle** something, especial- VERB
ly something that consists of long strands twisted Vn
together, you undo the knots in it or free the twisted
parts. ...desperately trying to untangle several reels of
film. **2** If you **untangle** something complicated or VERB
confusing, you make it understandable or work out Vn
what it means. Lawyers and accountants began trying to untangle the complex affairs of the bank.

un·tapped /ˌʌnˈtæpt/. An **untapped** supply or ADJ
source of something is available but has not yet
been used or exploited. There is enormous, acknowledged and untapped potential in the Indian stock
markets.

un·ten·able /ˌʌnˈtenəbəl/. An argument, theory, or ◆◇◇◇◇
position that is **untenable** cannot be defended suc- ADJ-GRADED
cessfully against criticism or attack. He claimed the
charges against him were untenable.

un·test·ed /ˌʌnˈtestɪd/. **1** If something or someone ADJ
is **untested**, they have not yet been tried out or have
not yet experienced a particular situation, so you do
not know what they will be like. The Egyptian Army
remained an untested force. **2** If you describe some- ADJ
thing such as a drug or chemical as **untested**, you
mean that it has not been subject to scientific tests
to find out if it is safe to use.

un·think·able /ʌnˈθɪŋkəbəl/. **1** If you say that ◆◇◇◇◇
something is **unthinkable**, you mean that it cannot ADJ
possibly be accepted or imagined as a possibility.
Her strong Catholic beliefs made abortion unthinkable. ▶ **The unthinkable** is something that is un- N-SING:
thinkable. Edward VIII had done the unthinkable theN

and abdicated the throne. **2** You can use **unthink-** ADJ
able to describe a situation, event, or action which
is extremely unpleasant to imagine or remember.
This place is going to be unthinkable without you.

un·think·ing /ʌnˈθɪŋkɪŋ/. If you say that someone ADJ-GRADED
is **unthinking**, you are critical of them because they PRAGMATICS
do not think carefully about the effects of their behaviour. Bruce was no unthinking vandal. ♦ **un-**
·think·ing·ly Many motor accidents are the result ADV-GRADED
of unthinkingly mixing speed and alcohol.

un·ti·dy /ʌnˈtaɪdi/. **1** If you describe something as ◆◇◇◇◇
untidy, you mean that it is messy and disordered ADJ-GRADED
and not neat or well arranged. Clothes were thrown
in the luggage in an untidy heap. ♦ **un·ti·di·ly** ADV-GRADED
/ʌnˈtaɪdili/. Her long hair tumbles untidily around
her shoulders. ♦ **un·ti·di·ness** The dust and untidi- N-UNCOUNT
ness in her room no longer bothered her. **2** If you de- ADJ-GRADED
scribe a person as **untidy**, you mean that they do
not care about whether things are neat and well arranged. I'm untidy in most ways.

un·tie /ˌʌnˈtaɪ/ **unties, untying, untied. 1** If you ◆◇◇◇◇
untie something that is tied to another thing or if VERB
you **untie** two things that are tied together, you re- Vn
move the string or rope that holds them or that has
been tied round them. Just untie my hands. **2** If you VERB
untie something such as string or rope, you undo it Vn
so that there is no knot or so that it is no longer tying something. She hurriedly untied the ropes bind-
ing her ankles. **3** When you **untie** your shoelaces or VERB: Vn
your shoes, you loosen or undo the laces of your
shoes.

un·til /ʌnˈtɪl/. **1** If something happens **until** a par- ◆◆◆◆
ticular time, it happens during the period before PREP
that time and stops at that time. Until 1971, he was
a high-ranking official in the Central Communist
Committee. ...consumers who have waited until after
the Christmas holiday to do that holiday shopping.
▶ Also a conjunction. I waited until it got dark... CONJ
Stir with a metal spoon until the sugar has dissolved.
2 You use **until** with a negative to emphasize the PREP
moment in time after which the rest of your statement becomes true, or the condition which would
make it true. The traffic laws don't take effect until
the end of the year... It was not until 1911 that the
first of the vitamins was identified. ▶ Also a con- CONJ:
junction. The EC will not lift its sanctions until that CONJ after
country makes political changes. **3** ● **up until**: see neg
up.

un·time·ly /ʌnˈtaɪmli/. **1** If you describe an event as ADJ
untimely, you mean that it happened earlier than it
should, or sooner than you expected. ...his mother's
untimely death. **2** You can describe something as ADJ
untimely if it happens at an unsuitable time. ...an
untimely visit from the milkman.

un·tir·ing /ʌnˈtaɪərɪŋ/. If you describe a person or ADJ
their efforts as **untiring**, you approve of them be- PRAGMATICS
cause they continue what they are doing without
slowing down or stopping. ...an untiring fighter for
justice, democracy and tolerance.

unto /ˈʌntuː/. **1** **Unto** was used to indicate that ◆◇◇◇◇
something was done or given to someone. And he PREP
said unto him, 'Who is my neighbor?'... I will do LITERARY,
unto others what they did to me. **2** **Unto** was used to DATED
indicate that something continued until a particular PREP
time. Be ye faithful unto the end. LITERARY,
                                     DATED

un·told /ˌʌnˈtəʊld/. **1** You can use **untold** to em- ◆◇◇◇◇
phasize how bad or unpleasant something is. This ADJ: ADJ n
might do untold damage to her health. ...untold misery. **2** You can use **untold** to emphasize that an ADJ: ADJ n
amount or quantity is very large, especially when
you are not sure how large it is. ...the nation's untold millions of anglers.

un·touch·able /ˌʌnˈtʌtʃəbəl/ **untouchables.** ◆◇◇◇◇
1 Some people refer to members of the lowest Hin- N-COUNT
du caste as **untouchables**. **2** If you say that some- ADJ-GRADED
one is **untouchable**, you mean that they cannot be
affected or punished in any way. No one is untouchable in this investigation. ▶ An **untouchable** is N-COUNT
someone who is untouchable. ...a new force of 'untouchables' to deal with narcotics and terrorism.

3 If you describe someone, especially a sports player or entertainer, as **untouchable**, you are emphasizing that they are better than anyone else in what they do. *A lot of the players began to feel they were untouchable.* `ADJ`

un·touched /ˌʌnˈtʌtʃt/. **1** Something that is **untouched** by something else is not affected by it. *Asian airlines remain untouched by the deregulation that has swept America... Vested interests were left untouched.* **2** If something is **untouched**, it is not damaged in any way, although it has been in a situation where it could easily have been damaged. *Michael pointed out to me that amongst the rubble, there was one building that remained untouched.* **3** An **untouched** area or place is thought to be beautiful because it is still in its original state and has not been changed or damaged in any way. *Ducie is one of the world's last untouched islands.* **4** If food or drink is **untouched**, none of it has been eaten or drunk. *The coffee was untouched, the toast had cooled.* `◆◇◇◇ ADJ` `ADJ` `ADJ` `ADJ`

un·to·ward /ˌʌntəˈwɔːd, AM ʌnˈtɔːrd/. If you say that something **untoward** happens, you mean that something happens that is unexpected and causes difficulties. *The surveyor's report didn't highlight anything untoward.* `ADJ FORMAL`

un·trained /ˌʌnˈtreɪnd/. **1** Someone who is **untrained** has not been taught the skills that they need for a particular job, activity, or situation. **2** If you describe a voice or a mind, for example, as **untrained**, you mean that it has not been developed through formal education or training. `ADJ` `ADJ`

un·tram·melled /ˌʌnˈtræməld/; spelled **untrammeled** in American English. Someone who is **untrammelled** is able to act freely in the way they want to, rather than being restricted by rules, conventions, or circumstances. *...a free woman, untrammelled by family relationships.* `ADJ LITERARY`

un·treat·ed /ˌʌnˈtriːtɪd/. **1** If an injury or illness is left **untreated**, it is not given medical treatment. *...the consequences of untreated tuberculosis.* **2 Untreated** materials, water, or chemicals are harmful and have not been made safe. **3 Untreated** materials are in their natural or original state, often before being prepared for use in a particular process. *All the bedding is made of simple, untreated cotton.* `◆◇◇◇ ADJ` `ADJ` `ADJ`

un·tried /ˌʌnˈtraɪd/. If someone or something is **untried**, they have not yet experienced certain situations or have not yet been tried out, so you do not know what they will be like. *...a long legal battle through untried areas of law.* `ADJ`

un·trou·bled /ˌʌnˈtrʌbəld/. If you are **untroubled** by something, you are not affected or worried by it. `ADJ-GRADED`

un·true /ˌʌnˈtruː/. If a statement or idea is **untrue**, it is false and not based on facts. *It was untrue to say that all political prisoners have been released.* `◆◇◇◇ ADJ`

un·trust·wor·thy /ˌʌnˈtrʌstwɜːði/. If you say that someone is **untrustworthy**, you think they are unreliable and cannot be trusted. `ADJ-GRADED`

un·truth /ˌʌnˈtruːθ/ **untruths** /ˌʌnˈtruːðz/. An **untruth** is a lie. *I have never uttered one word of untruth.* `N-VAR FORMAL`

un·truth·ful /ˌʌnˈtruːθful/. If someone is **untruthful** or if they say **untruthful** things, they are dishonest and say things that they know are not true. *Some people may be tempted to give untruthful answers.* `ADJ-GRADED`

un·tu·tored /ˌʌnˈtjuːtəd, AM -ˈtuːt-/. If someone is **untutored**, they have not been formally trained to do something, although they may be skilled at it. `ADJ FORMAL`

un·typi·cal /ˌʌnˈtɪpɪkəl/. If someone or something is **untypical** of a particular type of person or thing, they are not usual and therefore not a good example of the way that type of person or thing normally is. People sometimes say something is **not untypical** to mean that it is quite normal. *I believe our results are not untypical.* ♦ **un·typi·cal·ly** /ˌʌnˈtɪpɪkli/. *I was working untypically hard.* `ADJ-GRADED` `ADV-GRADED`

un·us·able /ˌʌnˈjuːzəbəl/. Something that is **unusable** is not in a good enough state or condition to be used. `ADJ`

un·used. Pronounced /ʌnˈjuːzd/ for meaning 1, and /ʌnˈjuːst/ for meaning 2. **1** Something that is **unused** has not been used or is not being used at the moment. *The insurance on his BMW has run out, and the car stands unused.* **2** If you are **unused** to something, you have not often done it or experienced it before, so it feels unusual and unfamiliar to you. `◆◇◇◇ ADJ` `ADJ` `v-link ADJ to n`

un·usual /ʌnˈjuːʒuəl/. **1** If something is **unusual**, it does not happen very often or you do not see it or hear it very often. *They have re-planted many areas with rare and unusual plants.* **2** If you describe someone as **unusual**, you think that they have extraordinary and remarkable qualities. `◆◆◆◇ ADJ-GRADED` `ADJ-GRADED`

un·usu·al·ly /ʌnˈjuːʒuəli/. **1** You use **unusually** to emphasize that someone or something has more of a particular quality than is usual. *...this year's unusually harsh winter.* **2** You can use **unusually** to suggest that something is not what normally happens. *Unusually among British prime ministers, he was not a man of natural authority.* `◆◆◇◇ ADV-GRADED:` `ADV adj` `PRAGMATICS` `ADV with cl`

un·ut·ter·able /ʌnˈʌtərəbəl/. You can use **unutterable** to emphasize that something, especially a bad quality, is great in degree or intensity. *...unutterable rubbish.* ♦ **un·ut·ter·ably** /ʌnˈʌtərəbli/. *I suddenly felt unutterably depressed.* `ADJ-GRADED:` `ADJ n` `PRAGMATICS` `ADV-GRADED`

un·vary·ing /ʌnˈveəriŋ/. If you describe something as **unvarying**, you mean that it stays the same and never changes. `ADJ`

un·veil /ˌʌnˈveɪl/ **unveils, unveiling, unveiled.** **1** If someone formally **unveils** something such as a new statue or painting, they draw back the curtain which is covering it. ♦ **un·veil·ing** *...the unveiling of a monument to one of the Croatian heroes of the past.* **2** If you **unveil** a plan, new product, or some other thing that has been kept secret, you introduce it to the public. *Companies from across Europe are here to unveil their latest models.* ♦ **unveiling** *...the unveiling of a detailed peace plan.* `◆◆◇◇ VERB: V n` `N-UNCOUNT` `VERB V n` `N-UNCOUNT`

un·waged /ˌʌnˈweɪdʒd/. You can refer to people who do not have a paid job as the **unwaged**. *Individual membership costs £13 (£7 unwaged).* ► Also an adjective. *...the effect on male wage-earners, unwaged females, and children.* `N-PLURAL BRITISH` `ADJ`

un·want·ed /ˌʌnˈwɒntɪd/. If you say that something or someone is **unwanted**, you mean that you do not want them, or that nobody wants them. *...the misery of unwanted pregnancies... Every year thousands of unwanted animals are abandoned.* `◆◆◇◇ ADJ-GRADED`

un·war·rant·ed /ʌnˈwɒrəntɪd, AM -ˈwɔːr-/. If you describe something as **unwarranted**, you are critical of it because it is unnecessary and unjustified. *He accused the police of using unwarranted brutality.* `◇◇◇◇ ADJ` `PRAGMATICS` `FORMAL`

un·wary /ʌnˈweəri/. If you describe someone as **unwary**, you mean that they are not cautious or experienced and are therefore likely to be harmed or deceived. ► The **unwary** are people who are unwary. *Specialist subjects are full of pitfalls for the unwary.* `ADJ-GRADED FORMAL` `N-SING: the N`

un·washed /ˌʌnˈwɒʃt/. **1 Unwashed** people or objects are dirty and need to be washed. **2 The unwashed** or **the great unwashed** is a humorous way of referring to poor or uneducated people. `ADJ` `PHRASE`

un·wa·ver·ing /ʌnˈweɪvəriŋ/. If you describe a feeling or attitude as **unwavering**, you mean that it is strong and firm and does not weaken. *She has been encouraged by the unwavering support of her family.* `ADJ`

un·wel·come /ʌnˈwelkəm/. **1** An **unwelcome** experience is one that you do not like and did not want. *A colleague made unwelcome sexual advances towards her.* **2** If you say that a visitor is **unwelcome**, you mean that you did not want them to come. *She was, quite deliberately, making him feel unwelcome.* `◆◇◇◇ ADJ-GRADED` `ADJ-GRADED`

un·wel·com·ing /ʌnˈwelkəmiŋ/. **1** If someone is **unwelcoming**, or if they behave in an **unwelcoming** way, they are unfriendly or hostile when you visit or approach them. **2** If you describe a place as `ADJ-GRADED` `ADJ-GRADED`

unwelcoming, you mean that it looks unattractive or difficult to live or work in.

un·well /ˌʌnˈwel/. If you are **unwell**, you are ill. *Mrs Potter was too unwell to go with him.* ◇◇◇◇◇ ADJ-GRADED: v-link ADJ

un·whole·some /ˌʌnˈhəʊlsəm/. **1** Unwholesome food or drink is not healthy or good for you. **2** If you describe someone's feelings or behaviour as **unwholesome**, you are critical of it because it is unpleasant or unnatural. ADJ-GRADED [PRAGMATICS]

un·wieldy /ʌnˈwiːldi/. **1** If you describe an object as **unwieldy**, you mean that it is difficult to move or carry because it is so big or heavy. **2** If you describe a system as **unwieldy**, you mean that it does not work very well as a result of it being too large or badly organized. *His firm must contend with the unwieldy Russian bureaucracy.* ◇◇◇◇◇ ADJ-GRADED

un·will·ing /ʌnˈwɪlɪŋ/. **1** If you are **unwilling** to do something, you do not want to do it and will not agree to do it. *Initially the government was unwilling to accept the defeat.* ♦ **un·will·ing·ness** ...*the unwillingness of banks to grant loans.* **2** You can use **unwilling** to describe someone who does not really want to do something so they do it unenthusiastically and often with caution. *A youthful teacher, he finds himself an unwilling participant in school politics.* ♦ **un·will·ing·ly** *Unwillingly, she moved aside.* ◆◇◇◇◇ ADJ-GRADED; N-UNCOUNT; ADJ-GRADED; ADV-GRADED

un·wind /ˌʌnˈwaɪnd/ **unwinds, unwinding, unwound. 1** When you **unwind**, you relax after you have done something that makes you tense or tired. **2** If you **unwind** something that is wrapped round something else or that is in a ball, or if it **unwinds**, you undo it or straighten it out. *I want to try to unwind the ball of wool... The thread unwound a little more.* ◆◇◇◇◇ VERB: V; V-ERG; Vn; V

un·wise /ˌʌnˈwaɪz/. If you describe something as **unwise**, you think that it is foolish and likely to lead to a bad result. *It would be unwise to expect too much.* ♦ **un·wise·ly** *She accepted that she had acted unwisely and mistakenly.* ◆◇◇◇◇ ADJ-GRADED; ADV-GRADED

un·wit·ting /ʌnˈwɪtɪŋ/. If you describe a person or their actions as **unwitting**, you mean that the person does something or is involved in something without realizing it. *It had been an unwitting blunder on Blair's part.* ♦ **un·wit·ting·ly** *He was unwittingly caught up in the confrontation.* ◆◇◇◇◇ ADJ; ADV

un·work·able /ʌnˈwɜːkəbəl/. If you describe something such as a plan, law, or system as **unworkable**, you believe that it cannot be successful. ◆◇◇◇◇ ADJ-GRADED

un·world·ly /ʌnˈwɜːldli/. If you describe someone as **unworldly**, you mean that they have not experienced many things and are therefore innocent and naive. ◇◇◇◇◇ ADJ-GRADED

un·wor·thy /ʌnˈwɜːði/. **1** If someone or something is **unworthy** of something good, they do not deserve it. *He felt unworthy of being married to such an attractive woman.* **2** If you say that an action is **unworthy** of someone, you mean that it is not a nice thing to do and someone with their reputation or position should not do it. *His accusations are unworthy of a prime minister.* ◆◇◇◇◇ ADJ-GRADED LITERARY; ADJ-GRADED LITERARY

un·wound /ˌʌnˈwaʊnd/. **Unwound** is the past tense and past participle of **unwind**.

un·wrap /ˌʌnˈræp/ **unwraps, unwrapping, unwrapped.** When you **unwrap** something, you take off the paper, plastic, or other covering that is around it. ◆◇◇◇◇ VERB: Vn

un·writ·ten /ˌʌnˈrɪtən/. **1** Something such as a book that is **unwritten** has not been printed or written down. *Universal have agreed to pay £2.5 million for Grisham's next, as yet unwritten, novel.* **2** An **unwritten** rule, law, or agreement is one that is understood and accepted by everyone, although it may not have been formally or officially established. ◆◇◇◇◇ ADJ; ADJ

un·yield·ing /ʌnˈjiːldɪŋ/. **1** You describe someone as **unyielding** when they have very strong, fixed ideas about something and are unlikely to change their mind. **2** If a barrier or surface is **unyielding**, it is very solid or hard. ...*the troopers, who had to build roads through those unyielding mountains.* ADJ-GRADED WRITTEN; ADJ-GRADED LITERARY

un·zip /ˌʌnˈzɪp/ **unzips, unzipping, unzipped.** When you **unzip** something which is fastened by a zip or when it **unzips**, you open it by pulling open the zip. *James unzipped his bag.* V-ERG; Vn; Also V

up 1 preposition, adverb, and adjective uses

up. The preposition is pronounced /ʌp/. The adverb and adjective are pronounced /ˌʌp/. **Up** is often used with verbs of movement such as 'jump' and 'pull', and also in phrasal verbs such as 'give up' and 'wash up'. ◆◆◆◆◆

1 If someone or something goes **up** something such as a slope, ladder, or chimney, they move away from the ground or to a higher position. *They move away up a narrow mountain road... I ran up the stairs... The heat disappears straight up the chimney.* ▸ Also an adverb. *Intense balls of flame rose up into the sky... He put his hand up.* **2** If someone or something is **up** something such as a ladder or a mountain, they are near the top of it. *The Newton Hotel is halfway up a steep hill.* ▸ Also an adverb. ...*a research station perched 4000 metres up on the lip of the crater.* **3** You use **up** to indicate that you are looking or facing in a direction that is away from the ground or towards a higher level. *Paul answered, without looking up... Keep your head up, and look around you from time to time.* **4** If someone stands **up**, they move so that they are standing. *He got up and went out into the foyer.* **5** If you go or look **up** something such as a road or river, you go or look along in it. If you are **up** a road or river, you are somewhere along it. *Chinese tanks came up the road from Lhasa... He had a relation who lived up the road.* **6** If you move **up and down** somewhere, you move there repeatedly in one direction and then in the opposite direction. *He continued to jump up and down like a boy at a football match... I strolled up and down thoughtfully before calling a taxi.* **7** If you are travelling to a particular place, you can say that you are going **up** to that place, especially if you are going towards the north or to a higher level of land. If you are already in such a place, you can say that you are **up** there. *I'll be up to see you tomorrow... I live here now, but I've spent all my time up in Swaziland.* **8** If you go **up** to something or someone, you move to the place where they are and stop there. *The girl ran the rest of the way across the street and up to the car... On the way out she put down her ten came up on roller skates.* **9** If you are **up**, you are not in bed. *These days all sorts of people were up at the crack of dawn.* **10** If someone who has been in bed for some time, for example because they have been ill, is **up and about**, they are now out of bed and living their normal life. · **11** If an amount of something goes **up**, it increases. If an amount of something is **up**, it has increased and is at a higher level than it was. *They recently put my rent up... Tourism is up, jobs are up, individual income is up... Western Germany's rate has also risen sharply, up from 3 percent in 1989 to 4.5 percent.* **12** If a period of time is **up**, it has come to an end. *When the six weeks were up, everybody was sad that she had to leave.* **13** You say that a road is **up** when it is being repaired and cannot be used. **14** If you say that **something is up**, you mean that something is wrong or that something worrying is happening. *Mr. Gordon stopped talking, and his friends knew something was up.* **15** If you say to someone 'What's up?', you are asking them what is wrong or what is worrying them. **16** People sometimes say 'Up yours!' as an insult when you have said something to annoy them or make them angry; a expression which some people find offensive. **17** • **up in arms:** see **arm**. **18** If you have **ups and downs**, you experience a mixture of good things and bad things. *Every relationship has a lot of ups and downs.*

PREP; ADV: ADV after v; PREP; ADV: ADV after v; ADV: ADV after v; ADV: ADV after v; PREP; PHRASE; ADV SPOKEN; ADV: ADV after v; ADJ: v-link ADJ; PHRASE; ADV; ADJ: v-link ADJ; ADJ: v-link ADJ BRITISH; PHRASE INFORMAL; PHRASE INFORMAL [PRAGMATICS]; INFORMAL EXCLAM [PRAGMATICS]; INFORMAL, RUDE; PHRASE

up 2 used in combination as a preposition

up /ʌp/. **1** If you feel **up** to doing something, you are well enough to do it. *Those patients who were up to it could move to the adjacent pool... His fellow-directors were not up to running the business without him.* **2** If you say that someone is **up to** some- ◆◆◆◆◆ PHR-PREP; PHR-PREP

thing, you mean that they are secretly doing something that they should not be doing. *They must have known what their father was up to.* **3** If you say that it is **up to** someone to do something, you mean that it is their responsibility to do it. *I'm sure I'd have spotted him if it had been up to me.* `INFORMAL` `PHR-PREP`

4 Up until or **up to** are used to indicate the latest time at which something can happen, or the end of the period of time that you are referring to. *Please feel free to call me any time up until half past nine at night... Up to 1979, the growth of per capita income averaged 1 per cent per year.* **5** You use **up to** to say how large something can be or what level it has reached. *Up to twenty thousand students paid between five and six thousand dollars... It could be up to two years before the process is complete.* **6** If you say that something is **not up to much**, you mean that it is of poor quality. `PHR-PREP` `PHRASE` `INFORMAL,` `BRITISH` `PHR-PREP`

7 If someone or something is **up for** election, review, or examination, they are about to be considered or judged. *A third of the Senate and the entire House are up for re-election.* **8** If you are **up against** something, you have a very difficult situation or problem to deal with. *They were up against a good team but did very well.* **9** ● **up to** your **ears**: see **ear**. ● **up to par**: see **par**. ● **up to scratch**: see **scratch**. `PHR-PREP`

up ③ verb uses

up /ʌp/ **ups, upping, upped. 1** If you **up** something such as the amount of money you are offering for something, you increase it. *We are talking about upping everybody's pay.* **2** If you **up** and leave a place, you go away from it, often suddenly or unexpectedly. *These days people just up and disappear without a word to anybody.* `♦♦◇◇◇` `VERB` `V n` `VERB` `V and v`

,up-and-'coming. Up-and-coming people are likely to be successful in the future. `♦◇◇◇◇` `ADJ: ADJ n`

up·beat /'ʌpbiːt/. If people or their opinions are **upbeat**, they are cheerful and optimistic about a situation. *The Defense Secretary gave an upbeat assessment of the war so far.* `♦◇◇◇◇` `ADJ-GRADED` `INFORMAL`

up·braid /ʌp'breɪd/ **upbraids, upbraiding, upbraided.** If you **upbraid** someone, you tell them that they have done something wrong and criticize them for doing it. *His wife set about upbraiding him for neglecting the children.* `VERB: V n` `V n for n/-ing` `FORMAL`

up·bring·ing /'ʌpbrɪŋɪŋ/. Your **upbringing** is the way that your parents treat you and the things that they teach you when you are growing up. *Her son had a good upbringing and schooling.* `♦◇◇◇◇` `N-UNCOUNT`

up·com·ing /'ʌpkʌmɪŋ/. **Upcoming** events will happen in the near future. `♦◇◇◇◇` `ADJ: ADJ n`

up·country /,ʌp'kʌntri/; also spelled **up-country**. **Upcountry** places are in the more remote or far northern areas of a large country. ▶ Also an adverb. *The Ussuri reserves is 30 miles upcountry from Vlad.* `ADJ: ADJ n` `ADV`

up·date, updates, updating, updated. The verb is pronounced /ʌp'deɪt/. The noun is pronounced /'ʌpdeɪt/. **1** If you **update** something, you make it more modern, usually by adding new parts to it or giving it new information. *Airlines would prefer to update rather than retrain crews. ...an updated edition of the book.* **2** An **update** is a news item which has been rewritten so that it includes the latest developments in a situation. **3** If you **update** someone **on** a situation, you tell them the latest developments in that situation. `♦♦◇◇◇` `VERB: V n` `V` `V-ed` `N-COUNT` `VERB:` `V n on n`

up·end /,ʌp'end/ **upends, upending, upended.** If you **upend** something, you turn it upside down. *...upended flower pots.* `VERB: V n` `V-ed`

,up 'front; also spelled **up-front. 1** If you are **up front** about something, you act openly or publicly so that people know what you are doing or what you believe. *You can't help being biased so you may as well be up front about it.* **2** If a payment is made **up front**, it is made in advance and openly, so that the person being paid can see that the money is there. *Some companies charge a fee up front, but we don't think that's right.* ▶ Also an adjective. *The eleven percent loan has no up-front costs.* `♦◇◇◇◇` `ADJ-GRADED` `INFORMAL` `ADV:` `ADV after v` `ADJ: ADJ n`

up·grade /,ʌp'greɪd/ **upgrades, upgrading, upgraded. 1** If equipment or services **are** `♦♦◇◇◇` `VB: usu`

upgraded, they are improved or made more efficient. *...upgraded catering facilities.* ▶ Also a noun. *...equipment which needs expensive upgrades.* **2** If someone **is upgraded**, their job or status is changed so that they become more important or receive more money. `passive,` `V-ed` `N-COUNT` `VB: usu` `passive,` `be V-ed`

up·heav·al /ʌp'hiːvəl/ **upheavals.** An **upheaval** is a big change which causes a lot of trouble, confusion, and worry. *Algeria has been going through political upheaval for the past two months.* `♦◇◇◇` `N-COUNT`

up·held /ʌp'held/. **Upheld** is the past tense and past participle of **uphold.**

up·hill /,ʌp'hɪl/. **1** If something or someone is **uphill** or is moving **uphill**, they are near the top of a hill or are going up a slope. *The man was no more than ten yards away and slightly uphill. ...trees that ran in a ragged line uphill from the ledge.* ▶ Also an adjective. *...a long, uphill journey.* **2** If you refer to something as an **uphill** struggle or an **uphill** battle, you mean that it requires a great deal of effort and determination, but it should be possible to achieve it. *It's an uphill battle but I think we're going to win.* `♦◇◇◇◇` `ADV` `ADJ` `ADJ: ADJ n`

up·hold /ʌp'həʊld/ **upholds, upholding, upheld. 1** If you **uphold** something such as a law, a principle, or a decision, you support and maintain it. *...upholding the artist's right to creative freedom.* **2** If a court of law **upholds** a legal decision that has already been made, it decides that it was the correct decision. `♦♦◇◇◇` `VERB` `V n` `VERB: V n`

up·hold·er /ʌp'həʊldə/ **upholders.** An **upholder** of a particular tradition or system is someone who believes strongly in it and will support it when it is threatened. `N-COUNT` `FORMAL`

up·hol·stered /ʌp'həʊlstəd/. **Upholstered** chairs and sofas have a soft covering that makes them comfortable to sit on. *All of their furniture was upholstered in flowery materials.* `♦◇◇◇◇` `ADJ`

up·hol·ster·er /ʌp'həʊlstərə/ **upholsterers.** An **upholsterer** is someone whose job is to make and fit the soft covering on chairs and sofas. `N-COUNT`

up·hol·stery /ʌp'həʊlstəri/. **Upholstery** is the soft covering on chairs and sofas that makes them more comfortable to sit on. `♦◇◇◇◇` `N-UNCOUNT`

up·keep /'ʌpkiːp/. **1** The **upkeep** of a building or place is the continual process of keeping it in good condition. *The maintenance department is responsible for the general upkeep of the park.* **2** The **upkeep** of a group of people or services is the process of providing them with the things that they need. *He offered to pay £100 a month towards his son's upkeep.* `♦◇◇◇◇` `N-UNCOUNT` `N-UNCOUNT`

up·land /'ʌplənd/ **uplands. 1 Upland** places are situated on high land. **2 Uplands** are areas of high land. `♦◇◇◇◇` `ADJ: ADJ n` `N-PLURAL`

up·lift, uplifts, uplifting, uplifted. The verb is pronounced /ʌp'lɪft/. The noun is pronounced /'ʌplɪft/. If something **uplifts** people, it helps them to have a better life, for example by making them feel happy or by improving their social conditions. ▶ Also a noun. *...an uplift in the economy.* `VERB: V n` `LITERARY` `N-UNCOUNT`

up·lift·ed /ʌp'lɪftɪd/. **1** If people's faces or arms are **uplifted**, they are pointing them upwards or are holding them up. **2** If something makes you feel **uplifted**, it makes you feel very cheerful and happy. `ADJ` `LITERARY` `ADJ-GRADED:` `v-link ADJ`

up·lift·ing /ʌp'lɪftɪŋ/. You describe something as **uplifting** when it makes you feel very cheerful and happy. `♦◇◇◇◇` `ADJ-GRADED`

up·market /,ʌp'mɑːkɪt/; also spelled **up-market. Upmarket** products or services are expensive, of good quality, and intended to appeal to people in a high social class; the usual American word is **upscale.** *Anne chose an upmarket agency aimed at professional people. He promised a move upmarket and a drive to improve service and quality.* `♦◇◇◇◇` `ADJ-GRADED` `BRITISH` `ADV:` `ADV after v`

upon /ə'pɒn/. In addition to the uses shown below, **upon** is used in phrasal verbs such as 'come upon' and 'look upon', and after some other verbs such as 'decide' and 'depend'. `♦♦♦♦◇`

1 If one thing is **upon** another, it is on it. *He set the tray* `PREP`

upon the table... I imagined the eyes of the others in the FORMAL
room upon me. **2** You use **upon** when mentioning an PREP
event that is followed immediately by another event. FORMAL
The door on the left, upon entering the church, leads to PREP
the Crypt of St Issac. **3** You use **upon** between two occurrences of the same noun in order to say that there
are large numbers of the thing mentioned. *Row upon*
row of women surged forwards. **4** If an event is **upon** PREP
you, it is just about to happen. *They had to conserve*
the candles now with winter upon them.

up·per /ˈʌpə/ **uppers. 1** You use **upper** to describe ◆◆◆◇◇
something that is above something else. *There is a* ADJ-COMPAR:
smart restaurant on the upper floor. **2** You use *the* ADJ n
upper to describe the higher part of something. ADJ-COMPAR:
...the muscles of the upper back and chest. ...the ADJ n
upper rungs of the ladder.
3 If you have **the upper hand** in a situation, you have PHRASE
more power than the other people involved and can
make decisions about what happens. **4** The **upper** of N-COUNT
a shoe is the top part of it, which is attached to the sole
and the heel. *Leather uppers allow the feet to breath.* **5** N-COUNT
Uppers are drugs that make you feel very happy, ex- INFORMAL
cited, and full of energy. **6 • a stiff upper lip:** see **lip**.

upper 'case. Upper case letters are capital let- ADJ
ters.

upper 'class, upper classes; also spelled ◆◇◇◇◇
upper-class. The **upper class** or the **upper classes** N-COLL-COUNT
are the group of people in a society who own the
most property and have the highest social status.
▶ Also an adjective. *All of them came from wealthy,* ADJ
upper class families.

upper 'crust; also spelled **upper-crust.** The **upper** N-COLL-SING
crust are the upper classes. ▶ Also an adjective. *Ser-* INFORMAL
geant Parrott normally spoke with an upper-crust ADJ: ADJ n
accent.

upper·cut /ˈʌpəkʌt/ **uppercuts.** An **uppercut** is a N-COUNT
type of punch used in boxing. It is a hard upward
blow to the opponent's chin.

Upper 'House, Upper Houses. 1 In Britain, the ◆◇◇◇◇
Upper House is the House of Lords. **2** In other N-PROPER
countries where the government is divided into two N-PROPER
debating chambers, the **Upper House** is one of
these chambers, and is often called the Senate.

upper 'lip, upper lips. 1 Your **upper lip** is the ◆◇◇◇◇
part of your face between your mouth and your N-COUNT
nose. *The beginnings of a moustache showed on his*
upper lip. **2** Your **upper lip** is the higher of your two N-COUNT
lips. **• a stiff upper lip:** see **lip**.

upper·most /ˈʌpəmoʊst/. **1** The **uppermost** part ◆◇◇◇◇
of something is the part that is higher than the rest ADJ
of it. The **uppermost** thing is the highest one of a
group of things. *...the uppermost floor of the three-*
storey gatehouse. ▶ Also an adverb. *She placed her* ADV: n ADV
hands palm uppermost in her lap. **2** If something is ADJ
uppermost in a particular situation, it is the most
important thing in that situation. *The economy ap-*
pears to be uppermost in people's minds.

up·pi·ty /ˈʌpɪti/. If you say that someone is **uppity,** ADJ-GRADED
you mean that they are behaving as if they are more INFORMAL
important than they are.

up·raised /ˌʌpˈreɪzd/. If your hand or an object is ADJ
upraised, you are holding it up in the air.

up·right /ˈʌpraɪt/ **uprights. 1** If you are sitting or ◆◆◇◇◇
standing **upright,** you are sitting or standing with ADJ
your back straight, rather than bending or lying
down. *Jerrold pulled himself upright on the bed... He*
moved into an upright position. **2** An **upright** ADJ: ADJ n
vacuum cleaner or freezer stands vertically and is
taller than it is wide. **3** An **upright** chair has a ADJ
straight back and no arms. **4** You can refer to verti- N-COUNT
cal posts or the vertical parts of an object as
uprights. *...the uprights of a four-poster bed.*
5 You can describe people as **upright** when they are ADJ-GRADED
careful to follow acceptable rules of behaviour and
behave in a moral way. *...a very upright, trustworthy*
man.

upright pi'ano, upright pianos. An **upright pia-** N-COUNT
no is a piano in which the strings are laid out vertically rather than horizontally as in a grand piano.
See picture headed **musical instruments**.

up·ris·ing /ˈʌpraɪzɪŋ/ **uprisings.** When there is an ◆◆◇◇◇
uprising, a group of people start fighting against the N-COUNT
people who are in power in their country, because
they want to bring about a political change.

up-'river; also spelled **upriver.** Something that is ADV
moving **up-river** is moving in the direction of the
source of a river. Something that is **up-river** is closer to the source of a river than where you are. *Heavy*
goods could be brought up-river in barges. ▶ Also an ADJ: ADJ n
adjective. *...an upriver trip in Central Africa.*

up·roar /ˈʌprɔː/. **1** If there is **uproar,** there is a lot ◆◇◇◇◇
of shouting and noise because people are very an- N-UNCOUNT:
gry or upset about something. **2** You can also use N-UNCOUNT:
uproar to refer to a lot of public criticism and de- *also a* N
bate about something that has made people angry.
The town is in uproar over the dispute.

up·roari·ous /ʌpˈrɔːriəs/. When events or people ADJ
are **uproarious,** they make people laugh in a very LITERARY
noisy way. *He had spent several uproarious evenings*
at the Embassy Club. **• up·roari·ous·ly** *Bob* ADV
laughed uproariously.

up·root /ˌʌpˈruːt/ **uproots, uprooting,** ◆◇◇◇◇
uprooted. 1 If you **are uprooted,** you leave or are VERB:
made to leave a place where you have lived for a *be* V-ed
long time. *...the trauma of uprooting themselves* V pron-refl
from their homes. **2** If someone **uproots** a tree or VERB: V n
plant, or if the wind **uproots** it, it is pulled out of
the ground.

up·scale /ˌʌpˈskeɪl/. **Upscale** is used to describe ADJ-GRADED
products or services that are expensive, of good AMERICAN
quality, and intended to appeal to people in a high
social class. The British word is **upmarket.** *Vodka*
has acquired an upscale image in the US. ▶ Also an ADV:
adverb. *T-shirts, the epitome of American casualness,* ADV after v
have moved upscale.

up·set, upsets, upsetting. Pronounced /ʌpˈset/ ◆◆◆◇◇
when it is a verb or an adjective, and /ˈʌpset/ when
it is a noun. The form **upset** is used in the present
tense and is also the past tense and past participle
of the verb. **1** If you are **upset,** you are unhappy or ADJ-GRADED
disappointed because something quite unplea-
sant has happened to you. *She sounded upset*
when I said you couldn't give her an appointment.
▶ Also a noun. *...stress and other emotional upsets.* N-COUNT
2 If something **upsets** you, it makes you feel wor- VERB: V n
ried or unhappy. *Don't upset yourself, Ida.* **• up-** V pron-refl
·set·ting *Childhood illness can be upsetting for* ADJ-GRADED
children and parents alike. **3** If events **upset** some- VERB
thing such as a procedure or a state of affairs, they V n
cause it to go wrong. *Political problems could upset*
agreements between Moscow and Kabul. ▶ Also a N-COUNT
noun. *Markets are very sensitive to any upsets in the*
Japanese economic machine. **4** If you **upset** an ob- VERB: V n
ject or container, you accidentally knock it over so
that it scatters or spills over a large area. **5** A stom- N-COUNT:
ach **upset** is a slight illness in your stomach caused *supp* N
by an infection or by something that you have eat-
en. ▶ Also an adjective. *Larry is suffering from an* ADJ: ADJ n
upset stomach. **6 •** to **upset the applecart:** see
applecart.

up·shot /ˈʌpʃɒt/. The **upshot** of a series of events N-SING:
or discussions is the final result of them. *The upshot the* N
is that we have lots of good but not very happy employees.*

up·side down /ˌʌpsaɪd ˈdaʊn/; also spelled ◆◇◇◇◇
upside-down. If something has been moved **upside** ADV
down, it has been turned round so that the part that
is usually lowest is above the part that is usually
highest. *The painting was hung upside down.* **•** to
turn something **upside down:** see **turn.** ▶ Also an ADJ
adjective. *...an upside-down map of Britain.*

up·stage /ˌʌpˈsteɪdʒ/ **upstages, upstaging,** ◆◇◇◇◇
upstaged. 1 When an actor is **upstage** or moves ADV
upstage, he or she is or moves towards the back TECHNICAL
part of the stage. ▶ Also an adjective. *...the large* ADJ: ADJ n
upstage box that Noble used for his 1990 production
of King Lear. **2** If someone **upstages** you, they draw VERB: V n
attention away from you by being more attractive or
interesting.

up·stairs /ˌʌpˈsteəz/. **1** If you go **upstairs** in a ♦♦◇◇◇ building, you go up a staircase towards a higher ADV: floor. **2** If something or someone is **upstairs** in a ADV after v building, they are on a floor that is higher than the be ADV, ground floor. *The restaurant is upstairs and consists* n ADV *of a large, open room.* **3** An **upstairs** room or object ADJ: ADJ n is situated on a floor of a building that is higher than the ground floor. *Marsani moved into the upstairs apartment.* **4** The **upstairs** of a building is N-SING: the floor or floors that are higher than the ground the N floor. *Frances invited them to occupy the upstairs of her home.*

up·stand·ing /ʌpˈstændɪŋ/. **Upstanding** people be- ADJ-GRADED have in a morally acceptable way.

up·start /ˈʌpstɑːt/ **upstarts.** You can refer to ♦◇◇◇◇ someone as an **upstart** when they behave as if they N-COUNT are important, but you think that they are too new PRAGMATICS in a place or job to be treated as important.

up·state /ˌʌpˈsteɪt/. **Upstate** means belonging or ADJ: ADJ n relating to the parts of a state that are furthest to AMERICAN the north or furthest from the centre. *...an idyllic village in upstate New York.* ▶ Also an adverb. ADV *These buses will carry families upstate.*

up·stream /ˌʌpˈstriːm/. Something that is moving ♦◇◇◇◇ **upstream** is moving towards the source of a river, ADV from a point further down the river. Something that is **upstream** is towards the source of a river. *The water rose high enough for them to continue upstream.* ▶ Also an adjective. *Steps lead down to* ADJ: ADJ n *the subway from the upstream side.*

up·surge /ˈʌpsɜːdʒ/, **upsurges.** If there is an ♦◇◇◇◇ **upsurge** in something, there is a sudden, large in- N-COUNT crease in it. *...the upsurge in oil prices.*

up·swing /ˈʌpswɪŋ/ **upswings.** An **upswing** in N-COUNT something is a sudden improvement or increase in it. *...an upswing in the economy.*

up·take /ˈʌpteɪk/. **1** A person's **uptake** of some- N-SING thing is the amount of it that they absorb into their TECHNICAL body. *The drug increases the number of red cells in the blood, enhancing oxygen uptake by 10 percent.* **2** You say that someone is **quick on the uptake** PHRASE when they understand things quickly. You say that someone is **slow on the uptake** when they have dif- ficulty understanding simple or obvious things.

up-'tempo. An **up-tempo** piece of music has a ADJ fast beat.

up·tight /ʌpˈtaɪt/. Someone who is **uptight** is ADJ-GRADED tense, nervous, or annoyed about something. *Penny* INFORMAL *never got uptight about exams.*

up to 'date; also spelled **up-to-date. 1** If some- ♦♦◇◇◇ thing is **up-to-date**, it is the newest thing of its kind. ADJ-GRADED *...Germany's most up to date electric power station.* **2** If you are **up-to-date** with something, you have ADJ-GRADED the latest information about it. *We'll keep you up to date with any news.*

up-to-the-'minute; also spelled **up to the minute.** ADJ-GRADED **Up-to-the-minute** information is the latest infor- mation that you can get about something.

up·town /ˌʌpˈtaʊn/. If you go **uptown**, or go to a ♦◇◇◇◇ place **uptown**, you go away from the centre of a ADV: town or city towards one of its suburbs. *Susan con-* ADV after v *tinued to live uptown... There's a skating rink* AMERICAN *uptown.* ▶ Also an adjective. *...a small uptown radio* ADJ: ADJ n *station. ...uptown New York.*

up·turn /ˈʌptɜːn/ **upturns.** If there is an **upturn** in ♦◇◇◇◇ the economy or in a company or industry, it im- N-COUNT proves or becomes more successful.

up·turned /ˌʌpˈtɜːnd/. **1** Something that is ADJ **upturned** points or faces upwards. *...the rain splashing down on her upturned face.* **2** Something ADJ that is **upturned** is upside down. *He clung to the upturned boat, screaming for help.*

upwardly 'mobile. If you describe someone as ADJ **upwardly mobile**, you mean that they are moving, have moved, or are trying to move to a higher social position. ▶ The **upwardly mobile** are people who N-PLURAL: are upwardly mobile. *...the large detached houses of* the N *the upwardly mobile.*

up·wards /ˈʌpwədz/. In usual British English, ♦♦◇◇◇ **upwards** is an adverb and **upward** is an adjective.

In formal British English and in American English, **upward** is both an adjective and an adverb.
1 If someone moves or looks **upwards**, they move or ADV look up towards a higher place. *They climbed upward along the steep cliffs surrounding the village... Hunter nodded again and gazed upwards in fear... Lie face upwards with a cushion under your head.* ▶ Also an adjective. *She started once again on the steep upward climb.* **2** If an amount or rate moves **upwards**, it in- ADV: creases. *Unemployment will continue upward for* ADV after v *much of this year... The share price is likely to leap upwards.* ▶ Also an adjective. *...the Army's concern* ADJ: ADJ n *that the upward trend in the numbers avoiding mili- tary service may continue.* **3** A quantity that is PHR-PREP **upwards of** a particular number is more than that number. *...projects worth upwards of 200 million pounds.*

up·wind /ˌʌpˈwɪnd/. If something moves **upwind**, it ADV moves in the opposite direction to the wind. If something is **upwind**, the wind is blowing away from it. *The rich went to live in the west of London, upwind of the smell of people and industry.* ▶ Also ADJ: ADJ n an adjective. *...big trees at the forest's upwind edge.*

ura·nium /juˈreɪniəm/. **Uranium** is a naturally oc- ♦♦◇◇◇ curring radioactive metal that is used to produce N-UNCOUNT nuclear energy and weapons.

ur·ban /ˈɜːbən/. **Urban** means belonging to, or re- ♦♦♦◇◇ lating to, a town or city. *Most urban areas are close* ADJ-GRADED *to a park. ...urban planning.*

ur·bane /ɜːˈbeɪn/. Someone who is **urbane** is well- ADJ-GRADED mannered, relaxed, and appears comfortable in so- cial situations. ♦ **ur·ban·ity** /ɜːˈbænɪti/. *Fearey had* N-UNCOUNT *all the charm and urbanity of the trained diplomat.*

ur·bani·za·tion /ˌɜːbənaɪˈzeɪʃən/; also spelled ♦◇◇◇◇ **urbanisation** in British English. **Urbanization** is the N-UNCOUNT process of creating towns in country areas.

ur·ban·ized /ˈɜːbənaɪzd/; also spelled **urbanised** in British English. **1** An **urbanized** country or area has ADJ-GRADED many buildings and a lot of industry and business. **2** An **urbanized** population consists of people who ADJ-GRADED live and work in a town.

ur·chin /ˈɜːtʃɪn/ **urchins.** You can refer to a young N-COUNT child who is dirty and poorly dressed as an **urchin**. DATED
● See also **sea urchin**.

urge /ɜːdʒ/ **urges, urging, urged. 1** If you **urge** ♦♦♦♦◇ someone to do something, you try hard to persuade VERB them to do it. *They urged parliament to approve* V n to-inf *plans for their reform programme.* **2** If you **urge** VERB someone somewhere, you persuade them to go V n prep/adv there by touching them or talking to them firmly. V n with quote *He slipped his arm around her waist and urged her away from the window... 'Come on, Grace,' he was urging her, 'don't wait, hurry up.'* **3** If you **urge** a VERB: V n course of action, you strongly advise that it should V n on n be taken. *He urged restraint on the security forces.* **4** If you have an **urge** to do or have something, you N-COUNT have a strong wish to do or have it.

urge on. If you **urge** someone **on**, you encourage PHRASAL VB them to do something. *Visitors remember a lean,* V n P *cheerful figure on horseback urging on his men.* V P noun

ur·gent /ˈɜːdʒənt/. **1** If something is **urgent**, it ♦♦♦◇◇ needs to be dealt with as soon as possible. *There is* ADJ-GRADED *an urgent need for food and water... He had urgent business in New York.* ♦ **ur·gen·cy** *It is a matter of* N-UNCOUNT *utmost urgency.* ♦ **ur·gent·ly** *Red Cross officials* ADV-GRADED: *said they urgently needed bread and water.* **2** If you ADV with v speak in an **urgent** way, you show that you are anx- ADJ-GRADED ious for people to notice something or to do some- thing. *His voice was low and urgent.* ♦ **urgency** *She* N-UNCOUNT *was surprised at the urgency in his voice.* ♦ **urgently** *They hastened to greet him and asked* ADV-GRADED: *urgently, 'Did you find it?'.* ADV with v

uri·nal /juˈraɪnəl, AM ˈjurɪnəl/ **urinals.** A **urinal** is a N-COUNT bowl or trough fixed to the wall of men's public lavatories for men to urinate in.

uri·nary /ˈjuərɪnəri, AM -neri/. **Urinary** means be- ♦◇◇◇◇ longing to or related to the parts of a person's body ADJ: ADJ n through which urine flows. *...urinary tract* MEDICAL *infections.*

uri·nate /'juərɪneɪt/ **urinates, urinating,** ◆◇◇◇◇
urinated. When someone **urinates**, they get rid of VERB: V
urine from their body.

urine /'juərɪn/. **Urine** is the liquid that you get rid ◆◆◇◇◇
of from your body when you go to the toilet. N-UNCOUNT

urn /ɜːn/ **urns. 1** An **urn** is a container in which ◆◇◇◇◇
the ashes of a cremated person are kept. **2** An **urn** is N-COUNT
a metal container used for making a large quantity N-COUNT
of tea or coffee and keeping it hot.

us /əs, STRONG ʌs/. **Us** is the first person plural pro- ◆◆◆◆◆
noun. **Us** is usually used as the object of a verb or a
preposition.
1 A speaker or writer uses **us** to refer both to himself PRON
or herself and to one or more other people as a group.
In conversation, **us** can also include someone who is
not present. You can use **us** before a noun to make it
clear which group of people you are referring to. *Nei-*
ther of us forgot about it... He showed us aspects of the
game that we had never seen before... Another time of
great excitement for us boys was when war broke out.
2 Us is sometimes used to refer to people in general. PRON
All of us will struggle fairly hard to survive if we are in
danger. **3** A speaker or writer may use **us** instead of 'I' PRON
in order to include the listeners or readers in what he
or she is saying, especially when talking about how
the book or talk is organized. *So that gets us to the end*
of chapter nine. **4** In non-standard English, **us** is PRON
sometimes used instead of 'me'. *I'm not finished yet.* BRITISH,
Give us a chance. SPOKEN

US /ˌjuː 'es/. **US** is an abbreviation for 'United ◆◆◆◆◆
States'. *I arrived in the US in 1956.* N-PROPER:
theN
USA /ˌjuː es 'eɪ/. **The USA** an abbreviation for the ◆◆◇◇◇
'United States of America'. *...Drexel University in the* N-PROPER:
USA. theN

us·able /'juːzəbəl/. If something is **usable**, it is in a ◆◇◇◇◇
good enough state or condition to be used. *Charity* ADJ-GRADED
shops and jumble sales welcome usable clothes.

USAF /ˌjuː es eɪ 'ef/. **USAF** is an abbreviation for N-PROPER
'United States Air Force'.

us·age /'juːsɪdʒ/ **usages. 1 Usage** is the way in ◆◇◇◇◇
which words are used in particular contexts, espe- N-UNCOUNT
cially with regard to their meanings. *The word*
'undertaker' had long been in common usage. **2** A N-COUNT
usage is a meaning that a word has or a way in
which it can be used. *It's very definitely a usage*
which has come over to Britain from America.
3 Usage is the degree to which something is used or N-UNCOUNT
the way in which it is used. *Parts of the motor wore*
out because of constant usage.

use 1 verb uses

use /juːz/ **uses, using, used. 1** If you use some- ◆◆◆◆◆
thing, you do something with it in order to do a job VERB
or to achieve a particular result or effect. *Trim off* V n
the excess pastry using a sharp knife... Officials used V n to-inf
loud-hailers to call for calm... The show uses Zondo's V n prep
trial and execution as its framework. **2** If you use a VERB
supply of something, you finish it so that none of it V n
is left. *You used all the ice cubes and didn't put the*
ice trays back. ► To **use up** something means the PHRASAL VB
same as to **use** it. *It isn't them who use up the* V P noun
world's resources. **3** If someone **uses** drugs, they Also V n P
take drugs regularly, especially illegal ones. **4** You VERB: V n
can say that someone **uses** the toilet or bathroom as VERB: V n
a polite way of saying that they go to the toilet. **5** If PRAGMATICS
you **use** a particular word or expression, you say or VERB
write it, because it has the meaning that you want V n
to express. *The judge liked using the word 'wicked'*
of people he had sent to jail. **6** If you **use** a particu- VERB
lar name, you call yourself by that name, especially V n
when it is not the name that you usually call yourself. *I use a false name if I'm meeting people for the*
first time. **7** If you say that someone **uses** people, VERB: V n
you disapprove of them because they are only inter- PRAGMATICS
ested in other people because they can benefit or
gain some advantage from them, and not because
they care about them. **8** See also **used**.

use 2 noun uses

use /juːs/ **uses. 1** Your **use** of something is the ac- ◆◆◆◆◇
tion or fact of your using it. *The treatment does not* N-UNCOUNT:
involve the use of any artificial drugs. ...research re- also a N

lated to microcomputers and their use in classrooms.
2 If you have **a use for** something, you need it or N-SING:
can find something to do with it. *They both loved* a N for n
the fabric, but couldn't find a use for it. **3** If some- N-VAR:
thing has a particular **use**, it is intended for a par- with supp
ticular purpose. *Infrared detectors have many uses...*
It's an interesting scientific phenomenon, but of no
practical use whatever. **4** If you have the **use** of N-UNCOUNT:
something, you have the permission or ability to also theN
use it. *She will have the use of the car one night a*
week. ...young people who at some point in the past
have lost the use of their limbs... You will have full
use of all the new leisure club facilities. **5** A **use** of a N-COUNT:
word is a particular meaning that it has or a par- with supp
ticular way in which it can be used. *There are new*
uses of words coming in and old uses dying out.
6 Your **use** of a particular name is the fact of your N-UNCOUNT:
calling yourself by it. *Police have been hampered by* N of n
Mr Urquhart's use of bogus names.
7 If something is **for the use of** a particular person or PHRASE
group of people, it is for that person or group to use. *The leisure facilities are there for the use of guests.* **8** If PHRASE
you say that being something or knowing someone INFORMAL
has its **uses**, you mean that it makes it possible for you
to do something you otherwise would not be able to
do. **9** If something such as a technique, building, or PHRASE
machine is **in use**, it is used regularly. If it has gone
out of use, it is no longer used regularly. *...the methods*
of making Champagne which are still in use today.
10 If you **make use of** something, you do something PHRASE
with it in order to do a job or achieve a particular re- WRITTEN
sult or effect. *Not all nursery schools make use of the*
opportunities open to them. **11** You use expressions PHRASE
such as **it's no use, there's no use** and **what's the use**
to indicate that an action is pointless and will not
achieve anything. *It's no use arguing with a drunk.*
12 If you say **it's no use**, you mean that you have PHRASE
failed to do something and realize that it is useless to
continue trying because it is impossible. *It's no use.*
Let's hang up and try for a better line. **13** If something PHRASE
or someone is **of use**, they are useful. If they are **no**
use, they are not at all useful. *The contents of this*
booklet should be of use to all students.

used 1 modal uses and phrases

used /juːst/. **1** If something **used to** be done or ◆◆◆◆◇
used to be the case, it was done regularly in the PHR-MODAL
past or was the case in the past. If something **used**
not to be done or **used not to** be the case, it was
not done in the past or was not the case in the past.
The forms **did not use to** and **did not used to** are
also found, especially in spoken English. *People*
used to come and visit him every day... I feel more
compassion and less anger than I used to... At some
point kids start doing things they didn't use to do.
2 If you **are used** to something, you are familiar PHRASE
with it because you have done it or experienced it
many times before. If you **get used to** something,
you become familiar with it. *I'm used to having my*
sleep interrupted... This is how we do things here.
You'll soon get used to it.

used 2 adjective uses

used /juːzd/. **1** A **used** handkerchief, glass, or other ◆◇◇◇◇
object is dirty or spoiled because it has been used. ADJ
...a used cotton ball stained with makeup. **2** A **used** ADJ
car has already had one or more owners.

use·ful /'juːsfʊl/. **1** If something is **useful**, you can ◆◆◆◆◇
use it to do something or to help you in some way. ADJ-GRADED
Hypnotherapy can be useful in helping you give up
smoking... The police gained a great deal of useful
information about the organization. ♦ **use·ful·ly** ADV-GRADED
...the problems to which computers could be usefully ADV with v
applied. ♦ **use·ful·ness** *His interest lay in the* N-UNCOUNT
usefulness of his work. **2** If an object or skill **comes** PHRASE
in useful, it can help you achieve something in a
particular situation.

use·less /'juːsləs/. **1** If something is **useless**, you ◆◆◇◇◇
cannot use it. *He realised that their money was* ADJ-GRADED
useless in this country. ♦ **use·less·ly** *His right arm* ADV-GRADED
hung rather uselessly. ♦ **use·less·ness** *The car had* N-UNCOUNT
rusted almost to the point of uselessness. **2** If some- ADJ-GRADED

thing is **useless**, it does not achieve anything helpful or beneficial. *She knew it was useless to protest.* ♦ **uselessly** *Uselessly, he checked the same pockets he'd checked before.* ♦ **uselessness** *...the uselessness of their research.* **3** If you say that someone or something is **useless**, you mean that they are no good at all. *He was useless at any game with a ball... Their education system is useless.* **4** If someone feels **useless**, they feel totally worthless and unhelpful to other people. *She sits at home all day, watching TV and feeling useless.* ♦ **uselessness** *...the sense of uselessness and the boredom of empty days.*

ADV-GRADED
N-UNCOUNT
ADJ-GRADED
INFORMAL
ADJ-GRADED
N-UNCOUNT

user /ˈjuːzə/ **users.** A **user** is a person or thing that uses something such as a place, facility, product, or machine. *Beach users have complained that the bikes are noisy. ...a regular user of Holland's health-care system.*

N-COUNT:
with supp

user-'friendly. If you describe something such as a machine or system as **user-friendly**, you mean that it is well designed and easy to use.

ADJ-GRADED

ush·er /ˈʌʃə/ **ushers, ushering, ushered. 1** If you **usher** someone somewhere, you show them where they should go, often by going with them. *I ushered him into the office.* **2** An **usher** is a person who shows people where to sit, for example at a wedding or a concert. **3** An **usher** is a person who organizes people attending a law court.

VERB
V n prep/adv
N-COUNT
N-COUNT

usher in. If one thing **ushers in** another thing, it indicates that the other thing is about to begin. *...a unique opportunity to usher in a new era of stability in Europe.*

PHRASAL VB
V P noun
FORMAL

ush·er·ette /ˌʌʃəˈret/ **usherettes.** An **usherette** is a woman who shows people where to sit in a cinema or theatre and who sells them refreshments or programmes.

N-COUNT
DATED

usu. usu. is a written abbreviation for **usually**.

usu·al /ˈjuːʒʊəl/. **1 Usual** is used to describe what happens or what is done most often in a particular situation. *It is a neighborhood beset by all the usual inner-city problems... After lunch there was a little more clearing up to do than usual... It is usual to tip waiters, porters, guides and drivers.* ▶ You can refer to what most often happens or is done as **the usual**. *I celebrate Thanksgiving the traditional way – with my mom, turkey, the usual.* **2** You use **as usual** to indicate that you are describing something that normally happens or that is normally the case. *The front pages are, as usual, a mixture of domestic and foreign news.* **3** If something happens **as usual**, it happens in the way that it normally does, especially when other things have changed. *When somebody died everything went on as usual, as if it had never happened.* **4** ♦ **business as usual**: see **business**.

ADJ:
det ADJ,
v-link ADJ
N-SING:
the N
PHRASE
PHRASE

usu·al·ly /ˈjuːʒʊəli/. **1** If something **usually** happens, it is the thing that most often happens in a particular situation. *They ate, as they usually did, in the kitchen... Usually, the work is boring... Offering only one loan, usually an installment loan, is part of the plan.* **2** You use **more than usually** to show that something shows even more of a particular quality than it normally does. *She felt more than usually hungry after her excursion.*

ADV
PHRASE

usurp /juːˈzɜːp/ **usurps, usurping, usurped.** If you say that someone **usurps** a job, role, title, or position, they take it from someone when they have no right to do this. ♦ **usurp·er, usurpers** *The usurpers of power were the eight-man 'Emergency Committee'.*

VERB: V n
FORMAL
N-COUNT

usu·ry /ˈjuːʒəri/. **Usury** is the practice of lending money at unacceptably high interest rates; used showing disapproval.

N-UNCOUNT
PRAGMATICS
FORMAL

uten·sil /juːˈtensəl/ **utensils. Utensils** are tools or objects that you use in order to help you to cook or to do other tasks in your home. *...utensils such as bowls, steamers and frying pans... The best carving utensil is a long, sharp, flexible knife.*

N-COUNT

uter·us /ˈjuːtərəs/ **uteruses.** A woman's or female mammal's **uterus** is her womb. ♦ **u·ter·ine** /ˈjuːtəraɪn, AM -rɪn/. *...uterine cancer.*

N-COUNT
TECHNICAL
ADJ

uti·lise /ˈjuːtɪlaɪz/. See **utilize**.

utili·tar·ian /ˌjuːtɪliˈteəriən/ **utilitarians. 1 Utilitarian** views or ideas are based on the notion that the morally correct course of action is one that produces benefit for the greatest number of people. ▶ A **utilitarian** is someone with utilitarian views. ♦ **utili·tari·an·ism. Utilitarianism** is the philosophical theory based on utilitarian principles. **2 Utilitarian** objects and buildings are designed to be useful rather than attractive.

ADJ
TECHNICAL
N-COUNT
N-UNCOUNT
ADJ-GRADED

util·ity /juːˈtɪlɪti/ **utilities. 1** The **utility** of something is its usefulness. **2** A **utility** is an important service such as water, electricity, or gas that is provided for everyone, and that everyone pays for.

N-UNCOUNT:
with supp
FORMAL
N-COUNT

u'tility room, utility rooms. A utility room is a room in a house which is usually connected to the kitchen and which contains things such as a washing machine, sink, and cleaning equipment.

N-COUNT

uti·lize /ˈjuːtɪlaɪz/ **utilizes, utilizing, utilized;** also spelled **utilise** in British English. If you **utilize** something, you use it. *Sound engineers utilize a range of techniques to enhance the quality of the recordings.* ♦ **uti·li·za·tion** /ˌjuːtɪlaɪˈzeɪʃən/. *...the utilisation of human resources.*

VERB
V n
FORMAL
N-UNCOUNT

ut·most /ˈʌtməʊst/. **1** You can use **utmost** to emphasize the importance or seriousness of something or to emphasize the way that it is done. *It is a matter of the utmost urgency to find out what has happened to these people... Utmost care must be taken not to spill any of the contents.* **2** If you say that you are doing your **utmost** to do something, you are emphasizing that you are trying as hard as you can to do it. *He will try his utmost to help them.* **3** If you say that something is done to the **to the utmost**, you are emphasizing that it is done to the greatest extent, amount, or degree possible. *My limited diplomatic skills were tested to the utmost.*

ADJ: ADJ n
PRAGMATICS
FORMAL
N-SING:
poss N
PRAGMATICS
FORMAL
PHRASE

uto·pia /juːˈtəʊpiə/ **utopias.** If you refer to an imaginary situation as a **utopia**, you mean that it is one in which society is perfect and everyone is happy, but which you feel is not possible.

N-VAR

uto·pian /juːˈtəʊpiən/ **utopians. 1** If you describe a plan or idea as **utopian**, you are criticizing it because it is unrealistic and shows a belief that things can be improved much more than is possible. *He was pursuing a utopian dream of world prosperity.* ▶ A **utopian** is someone with utopian ideas. **2 Utopian** is used to describe political or religious philosophies which claim that it is possible to build a new and perfect society in which everyone is happy. ▶ A **utopian** is someone with utopian beliefs.

ADJ-GRADED
PRAGMATICS
N-COUNT
ADJ
FORMAL
N-COUNT

ut·ter /ˈʌtə/ **utters, uttering, uttered. 1** If someone **utters** sounds or words, they say them. *They departed without uttering a word.* **2** You use **utter** to emphasize that something is great in extent, degree, or amount. *This, of course, is utter nonsense. ...this utter lack of responsibility.*

VERB
V n
LITERARY
ADJ: ADJ n
PRAGMATICS

ut·ter·ance /ˈʌtərəns/ **utterances.** Someone's **utterances** are the things that they say. *...the Queen's public utterances.*

N-COUNT
FORMAL

ut·ter·ly /ˈʌtəli/. You use **utterly** when you want to emphasize that something is very great in extent, degree, or amount. *The new laws coming in are utterly ridiculous... Such an allegation is utterly without foundation.*

ADV
PRAGMATICS

'U-turn, U-turns. 1 If you make a **U-turn** when you are driving or cycling, you turn in a half circle in one movement, so that you are then going in the opposite direction. **2** If you describe the change of a politician's policy, plans, or actions as a **U-turn**, you mean that it is a complete change and are suggesting that they made the change because they are weak or were wrong. *...a humiliating U-turn by the Prime Minister.*

N-COUNT
N-COUNT

V v

V, v /viː/ **V's, v's. 1** V is the twenty-second letter of the English alphabet. **2** V or v is an abbreviation for words beginning with v, such as 'verse', 'versus', and 'very'. ...*Newcastle United v Leicester City.*   N-VAR

vac /væk/ **vacs. 1** A **vac** is a period of the year when universities and colleges are officially closed. It is an abbreviation for **vacation. 2** A **vac** is an electric machine which sucks up dust and dirt from carpets. It is an abbreviation for **vacuum cleaner.**   N-COUNT BRITISH, INFORMAL   N-COUNT BRITISH, INFORMAL

va·can·cy /ˈveɪkənsi/ **vacancies. 1** A **vacancy** is a job or position which has not been filled. *They had a short-term vacancy for a person on the foreign desk.* **2** If there are **vacancies** at a building such as a hotel, some of the rooms are available to rent.   ◆◇◇◇◇ N-COUNT   N-COUNT

va·cant /ˈveɪkənt/. **1** If something is **vacant**, it is not being used by anyone. *Half way down the coach was a vacant seat.* **2** If a job or position is **vacant**, no one is doing it or in it at present, and people can apply for it. *The post has been vacant since June.* **3** A **vacant** look or expression is one that suggests that someone does not understand something or that they are not concentrating. ♦ **va·cant·ly** *He looked vacantly out of the window.*   ◆◇◇◇◇ ADJ   ADJ   ADJ-GRADED   ADV: ADV after v

va·cate /vəˈkeɪt, AM ˈveɪkeɪt/ **vacates, vacating, vacated.** If you **vacate** a place or a job, you leave it or give it up, making it available for other people. *He vacated the flat and went to stay with an uncle.*   ◆◇◇◇◇ VERB V n FORMAL

va·ca·tion /vəˈkeɪʃən, AM veɪ-/ **vacations, vacationing, vacationed. 1** A **vacation** is a period of the year when universities or colleges are officially closed. *During his summer vacation he visited Russia.* **2** A **vacation** is a period of time during which you relax and enjoy yourself away from home. The British word is **holiday.** *We went on vacation to Puerto Rico.* **3** If you have a particular number of days' or weeks' **vacation**, you do not have to go to work for that number of days or weeks. The usual British word is **holiday. 4** If you **are vacationing** in a place away from home, you are on vacation there. The British word is **holiday.** *Myles vacationed in Jamaica.* ♦ **va·ca·tion·er, vacationers** ...*sightseers and vacationers traveling by car.*   ◆◆◇◇◇ N-COUNT   N-COUNT: also on/from N   AMERICAN N-UNCOUNT AMERICAN   VERB V prep/adv Also V AMERICAN   N-COUNT

vac·ci·nate /ˈvæksɪneɪt/ **vaccinates, vaccinating, vaccinated.** If a person or animal is **vaccinated**, they are given a vaccine, usually by injection, to prevent them from getting a disease. *Dogs must be vaccinated against distemper... Have you had your child vaccinated against whooping cough?* ♦ **vac·ci·na·tion** /ˌvæksɪˈneɪʃən/ **vaccinations** *Consider getting a vaccination.*   ◆◇◇◇◇ VB: usu passive be V-ed against n have/get n V-ed against n   N-VAR

vac·cine /ˈvæksiːn, AM vækˈsiːn/ **vaccines.** A **vaccine** is a substance containing a harmless form of the germs that cause a particular disease. It is given to people, usually by injection, to prevent them getting that disease. *Anti-malarial vaccines are now undergoing trials.*   ◆◆◇◇◇ N-VAR

vac·il·late /ˈvæsɪleɪt/ **vacillates, vacillating, vacillated.** If you **vacillate** between two alternatives or choices, you keep changing your mind. *She vacillates between men twice her age and men younger than she.* ♦ **vac·il·la·tion** /ˌvæsɪˈleɪʃən/ **vacillations** *He accused President Carter of vacillation and retreat.*   VERB V between pl-n Also V FORMAL   N-VAR

va·cu·ity /væˈkjuːɪti/. If you refer to the **vacuity** of something or someone, you are critical of them because they lack intelligent thought or ideas. *His vacuity was a handicap in these debates.* ♦ **vacu·ous**   N-UNCOUNT PRAGMATICS FORMAL   ADJ-GRADED

/ˈvækjuəs/. *Male models are not always so vacuous as they are made out to be.*

vacuum /ˈvækjuːm, -juːəm/ **vacuums, vacuuming, vacuumed. 1** If someone or something creates a **vacuum**, they leave a place or position which needs to be filled by someone or something else. *The collapse of the army left a vacuum in the area.* **2** If something is done **in a vacuum**, it is done whilst isolated from all the other things which you would normally expect to have an influence on it. *We lived in a vacuum – no life, no news, no books.* **3** A **vacuum** is a space that contains no air or other gas. **4** If you **vacuum** something, you clean it using a vacuum cleaner. *I vacuumed the carpets today... It's important to vacuum regularly.*   ◆◆◇◇◇ N-COUNT   PHRASE   N-COUNT   VERB: V n V

'vacuum cleaner, vacuum cleaners; also spelled **vacuum-cleaner.** A **vacuum cleaner** or a **vacuum** is an electric machine which sucks up dust and dirt from carpets.   ◆◇◇◇◇ N-COUNT

'vacuum flask, vacuum flasks. A **vacuum flask** is a container which is specially designed to keep hot drinks hot or cold drinks cold. The usual American term is **Thermos bottle** or **Thermos.**   N-COUNT BRITISH

,vacuum-'packed. Vacuum-packed food is packed in a container or packet from which most of the air has been removed, in order to keep the food fresh.   ADJ

vaga·bond /ˈvægəbɒnd/ **vagabonds.** A **vagabond** is someone who wanders from place to place and has no home or job.   N-COUNT DATED

va·gary /ˈveɪɡəri/ **vagaries. Vagaries** are unexpected and unpredictable changes in a situation or in someone's behaviour which you have no control over. ...*the perplexing vagaries of politics.*   ◆◇◇◇◇ N-COUNT FORMAL

va·gi·na /vəˈdʒaɪnə/ **vaginas.** A woman's **vagina** is the passage connecting her outer sex organs to her womb. ♦ **vagi·nal** /vəˈdʒaɪnəl/. *The creams have been used to reduce vaginal infections.*   ◆◇◇◇◇ N-COUNT   ADJ: ADJ n

va·gran·cy /ˈveɪɡrənsi/. **Vagrancy** is a way of life in which someone moves a lot from place to place because they have no permanent home or job, and have to beg or steal in order to live. ♦ **va·grant** /ˈveɪɡrənt/ **vagrants** *He had lived on the street as a vagrant.*   N-UNCOUNT   N-COUNT

vague /veɪɡ/ **vaguer, vaguest. 1** If something written or spoken is **vague**, it does not explain or express things clearly. *The description was pretty vague.* ...*vague information.* ♦ **vague·ly** *'I'm not sure,' Liz said vaguely.* ♦ **vague·ness** ...*the vagueness of the language in the text.* **2** If you have a **vague** memory or idea of something, the memory or idea is not clear. ♦ **vaguely** *Judith could vaguely remember her mother lying on the sofa.* **3** If you describe someone as **vague**, you mean that they do not seem to be thinking clearly. ...*a charming but rather vague Englishman.* ♦ **vaguely** *He looked vaguely around the room.* ♦ **vagueness** ...*the blissful vagueness of someone in love.* **4** A **vague** shape or outline is not clear and is therefore not easy to see. **5** If you are **vague** about something, you deliberately do not tell people much about it. *He was vague, however, about just what U.S. forces might actually do.* **6** If something such as a **feeling** is vague, you experience it only slightly. *He was conscious of that vague feeling of irritation again.*   ◆◆◇◇◇ ADJ-GRADED   ADV   N-UNCOUNT   ADJ-GRADED   ADV   ADJ-GRADED   ADV: ADV with v N-UNCOUNT ADJ-GRADED   ADJ-GRADED   ADJ-GRADED

vague·ly /ˈveɪɡli/. **1 Vaguely** means to some degree but not to a very large degree. *The voice on the line was vaguely familiar.* **2** See also **vague.**   ◆◇◇◇◇ ADV-GRADED: ADV adj PRAGMATICS

V

vain /veɪn/ **vainer, vainest.** **1** A **vain** attempt or action is one that fails to achieve what was intended. *I was singing in a vain effort to cheer him up.* ♦ **vain·ly** *He hunted vainly through his pockets for a piece of paper.* **2** If you describe a hope that something will happen as a **vain** hope, you mean that there is no chance of it happening. ♦ **vainly** *...what he vainly hoped would be a peaceful retirement.* **3** If you do something **in vain**, you do not succeed in achieving what you intend. *It became obvious that all her complaints were in vain.* **4** If you say that something such as someone's death, suffering, or effort was **in vain**, you mean that it was pointless because it did not achieve anything. *He wants the world to know his son did not die in vain.* **5** If you describe someone as **vain**, you are critical of their extreme pride in their own beauty, intelligence, or other good qualities.
ADJ: ADJ n
ADV
ADJ: ADJ n
ADV:
ADV with v
PHRASE
PHRASE
ADJ-GRADED
PRAGMATICS

val·ance /ˈvæləns/ **valances.** **1** A **valance** is a decorative frill that hangs down from the sides of a bed. **2** A **valance** is a long narrow piece of wood or fabric which is fitted at the top of a window for decoration and to hide the curtain rail. The British word is **pelmet**.
N-COUNT
N-COUNT
AMERICAN

vale /veɪl/ **vales.** A **vale** is a valley. *...a small vale, sheltering under mist-shrouded hills.*
N-COUNT
LITERARY

val·edic·tory /ˌvælɪˈdɪktəri/. A **valedictory** speech, letter, or performance is one that is intended as a way of saying goodbye when someone leaves another person, a place, or a job.
ADJ
FORMAL

val·et /ˈvæleɪ, -lɪt/ **valets.** A **valet** is a male servant who looks after his employer by doing things such as caring for his clothes and cooking for him.
N-COUNT

val·iant /ˈvæliənt/. A **valiant** action is very brave and determined, though it may lead to failure or defeat. *...a valiant attempt to keep the business going.* ♦ **val·iant·ly** *...heart attacks and strokes, all of which he fought valiantly.*
ADJ-GRADED
ADV-GRADED:
ADV with v

val·id /ˈvælɪd/. **1** A **valid** argument, comment, or idea is based on sensible reasoning. *It is valid to consider memory the oldest mental skill, from which all others derive.* ♦ **va·lid·ity** /væˈlɪdɪti/. *This argument has lost much of its validity.* **2** Something that is **valid** is important or serious enough to make it worth saying or doing. *...the unspoken belief that fashion is a valid form of visual art.* ♦ **validity** *...the validity of making children wear cycle helmets.* **3** If a ticket or other document is **valid**, it can be used and will be accepted by people in authority. *For foreign holidays you will need a valid passport.* **4** See also **validity**.
ADJ-GRADED
N-UNCOUNT
ADJ-GRADED
N-UNCOUNT
ADJ

vali·date /ˈvælɪdeɪt/ **validates, validating, validated.** **1** To **validate** something such as a claim or statement means to prove or confirm that it is true or correct. *This discovery seems to validate the claims of popular astrology.* ♦ **vali·da·tion** /ˌvælɪˈdeɪʃən/ *This validation process ensures that the data conforms to acceptable formats.* **2** To **validate** a person, state, or system means to prove or confirm that they are valuable or worthwhile. *The Academy Awards appear to validate his career.* ♦ **validation** *I think the film is a validation of our lifestyle.*
VERB
V n
FORMAL
N-VAR
VERB
V n
N-VAR

va·lid·ity /vəˈlɪdɪti/. The **validity** of something such as a result or a piece of information is whether it can be trusted or believed. *It raises serious questions about the validity of next month's elections.* ● See also **valid**.
N-UNCOUNT

Va·lium /ˈvæliəm/. **Valium** is both the singular and the plural form. **Valium** is a drug given to people to calm their nerves when they are very depressed or upset. **Valium** is a trademark.
N-VAR

val·ley /ˈvæli/ **valleys.** A **valley** is a low stretch of land between hills, especially one that has a river flowing through it. *...the Loire valley.*
N-COUNT

val·our /ˈvælə/; spelled **valor** in American English. **Valour** is great bravery, especially in battle. *He was himself decorated for valour in the war.* ● **discretion is the better part of valour**: see **discretion**.
N-UNCOUNT
LITERARY

valu·able /ˈvæljuəbəl/. **1** If you describe something or someone as **valuable**, you mean that they are very useful and can help someone a great deal. *Many of our teachers also have valuable academic links with Heidelberg University.* **2 Valuable** objects are objects which are worth a lot of money. *Just because a camera is old does not mean it is valuable.*
ADJ-GRADED
ADJ-GRADED

valu·ables /ˈvæljuəbəlz/. **Valuables** are things that you own that are worth a lot of money, especially small objects such as jewellery.
N-PLURAL

valua·tion /ˌvæljuˈeɪʃən/ **valuations.** A valuation is a judgement that someone makes about how much money something is worth. *...an independent valuation of the company.*
N-VAR

value /ˈvælju/ **values, valuing, valued.** **1** The **value** of something such as a quality, attitude, or method is its importance or usefulness. If you place a particular **value** on something, that is the importance or usefulness you think it has. *The value of this work experience should not be underestimated... Ronnie put a high value on his appearance.* ● If something is **of value**, it is useful or important. If it is **of no value**, it has no usefulness or importance. *This weekend course will be of value to everyone.* **2** If you **value** something or someone, you think that they are important and you appreciate them. *She genuinely values his opinion.* ♦ **valued** *We wish to thank all our valued customers.* **3** The **value** of something is how much money it is worth. *Italy's currency went down in value by 3.5 per cent.* ● If something is **of value**, it is worth a lot of money. If it is **of no value**, it is worth very little money. **4** When experts **value** something, they decide how much money it is worth. *I asked him if he would have my jewellery valued.* **5** You use **value** in certain expressions to say whether something is worth the money that it costs. For example, if something is or gives **good value**, it is worth the money that it costs. *Scottish salmon is excellent value for money.* **6** The **values** of a person or group are the moral principles and beliefs that they think are important. *...a return to traditional family values.* **7 Value** is used after another noun when mentioning an important or noticeable feature about something. *Having a mid-morning party certainly adds novelty value.* **8** In mathematics, a **value** is a particular number or quantity that can replace a general expression such as 'x' or 'y' in a particular case. **9** See also **face value**.
N-UNCOUNT:
also a N
PHRASE
VERB
V n
ADJ-GRADED
N-VAR
PHRASE
VERB: V n
have n V-ed
N-UNCOUNT
N-PLURAL:
with supp
N-UNCOUNT:
n N
N-COUNT
TECHNICAL

value 'added tax. Value added tax is a tax that is added to the price of goods or services. The abbreviation **VAT** is also used.
N-UNCOUNT
BRITISH

'value judgement, value judgements; spelled **value judgment** in American English. If you make a **value judgement** about something, you form an opinion about it based on your principles and beliefs and not on facts which can be checked or proved.
N-COUNT

value·less /ˈvæljuːləs/. If you describe something as **valueless**, you mean that it is not at all useful.
ADJ

valu·er /ˈvæljuːə/ **valuers.** A **valuer** is someone whose job is to estimate the cost or value of something, for example a house, or objects that are going to be sold in an auction. The usual American word is **appraiser**.
N-COUNT
BRITISH

valve /vælv/ **valves.** **1** A **valve** is a device attached to a pipe or a tube which controls the flow of air or liquid through the pipe or tube. **2** A **valve** is a small flap of tissue in your heart or in a vein which controls the flow of blood and keeps it flowing in one direction only. **3** See also **safety valve**.
N-COUNT
N-COUNT

vamp /væmp/ **vamps.** If you describe a woman as a **vamp**, you disapprove of her because she uses her sexual attractiveness to get what she wants from men.
N-COUNT
PRAGMATICS

vam·pire /ˈvæmpaɪə/ **vampires.** A **vampire** is a creature in legends and horror stories. Vampires are said to come out of graves at night and suck the blood of living people.
N-COUNT

vampire 'bat, vampire bats. A **vampire bat** is a N-COUNT
bat from South America which feeds by sucking the
blood of other animals.

van /væn/ **vans. 1** A **van** is a small or medium- ◆◆◇◇◇
sized road vehicle with one row of seats and a space N-COUNT
for carrying goods behind. **2** A **van** is a railway car- N-COUNT
riage, often without windows, which is used to carry BRITISH
luggage, goods, or mail.

van·dal /'vændəl/ **vandals.** A **vandal** is someone ◆◇◇◇◇
who deliberately damages things, especially public N-COUNT
property.

van·dal·ise /'vændəlaɪz/. See **vandalize**.

van·dal·ism /'vændəlɪzəm/. **Vandalism** is the de- ◆◇◇◇◇
liberate damaging of things, especially public prop- N-UNCOUNT
erty. ...*a housing estate with a reputation for violence and vandalism.*

van·dal·ize /'vændəlaɪz/ **vandalizes, vandaliz-** VERB
ing, vandalized; also spelled **vandalise** in British be V-ed
English. If something such as a building or part of a Also V n
building **is vandalized** by someone, it is damaged
on purpose. *The walls had been horribly vandalized
with spray paint.*

vane /veɪn/ **vanes.** A **vane** is a flat blade which N-COUNT
pushes or is pushed by wind or water, and forms
part of a machine such as a fan, a windmill, or a
ship's propeller. ● See also **weather vane**.

van·guard /'vænɡɑːd/. **1** If someone is **in the van-** ◆◇◇◇◇
guard of something such as a revolution or an area N-SING
of research, they are involved in the most advanced
part of it. You can also refer to the people themselves as **the vanguard**. *Students and intellectuals
have been in the vanguard of revolutionary change
in China.* **2 The vanguard** of an army is the part of N-SING:
it that goes into battle first. the N

va·nil·la /və'nɪlə/. **Vanilla** is a flavouring used in N-UNCOUNT
ice cream and other sweet food. ...*vanilla milk-
shakes.*

van·ish /'vænɪʃ/ **vanishes, vanishing, van-** ◆◆◇◇◇
ished. 1 If someone or something **vanishes**, they VERB: V
disappear suddenly or in a way that cannot be ex- V from/into n
plained. *Anne vanished from outside her home last
Wednesday.* **2** If something such as a species of ani- VERB: V
mal or a tradition **vanishes**, it ceases to exist. *In the* V from n
*past two years, one-party rule has vanished from
Eastern Europe.*

'vanishing point, vanishing points. 1 The **van-** N-COUNT
ishing point is the point in the distance where parallel lines seem to meet. **2** If you say that something N-UNCOUNT
has reached **vanishing point**, you mean it has become very small or unimportant. *Everybody accepts
that the threat has now shrunk to vanishing point.*

van·ity /'vænɪti/ **vanities.** If you refer to ◆◇◇◇◇
someone's **vanity**, you are critical of them because N-UNCOUNT:
they take great pride in their appearance or abil- also N in pl
ities. *With my usual vanity, I thought he might be* PRAGMATICS
falling in love with me.

van·quish /'væŋkwɪʃ/ **vanquishes, vanquish-** VERB: V n
ing, vanquished. To **vanquish** someone means LITERARY
to defeat them in a battle or a competition.

van·tage point /'vɑːntɪdʒ pɔɪnt, 'vænt-/ **vantage** ◆◇◇◇◇
points. 1 A **vantage point** is a place from which N-COUNT
you can see a lot of things. *From a concealed van-
tage point, he saw a car arrive.* **2** If you view a situa- N-COUNT
tion from a particular **vantage point**, you have a
clear understanding of it because of the particular
period of time you are in. *The rules of Sparta seem
needlessly cruel from the vantage point of the twentieth century.*

vap·id /'væpɪd/. If you describe someone or some- ADJ-GRADED
thing as **vapid**, you are critical of them because they PRAGMATICS
are dull and uninteresting and contain nothing
stimulating or challenging. *She made a vapid comment about the weather.*

va·por /'veɪpə/. See **vapour**.

va·por·ize /'veɪpəraɪz/ **vaporizes, vaporizing,** V-ERG
vaporized; also spelled **vaporise** in British Eng- V
lish. If a liquid or solid **vaporizes** or if you **vaporize** Also V n
it, it changes into vapour or gas. *The benzene vapor-
ized and formed a huge cloud of gas.*

va·pour /'veɪpə/ **vapours;** spelled **vapor** in Ameri- ◆◇◇◇◇
can English. **Vapour** consists of tiny drops of water N-VAR
or other liquids in the air, which appear as mist.
...*water vapour.*

'vapour trail, vapour trails. A **vapour trail** is a N-COUNT
white trail of water vapour left in the sky by an
aeroplane, a rocket, or a missile.

vari·able /'veəriəbəl/ **variables. 1** Something that ◆◆◇◇◇
is **variable** changes quite often, and there usually ADJ-GRADED
seems to be no fixed pattern to these changes. *The
potassium content of foodstuffs is very variable. ...a
variable rate of interest.* ◆ **vari·abil·ity** N-UNCOUNT
/ˌveəriə'bɪlɪti/. ...*the variability in the climate.* **2** A N-COUNT
variable is a factor, which can change in quality,
quantity, or size, which you have to take into account in a situation. *Too many of the major eco-
nomic variables are not under control.* **3** A **variable** N-COUNT
is a quantity that can have any one of a set of TECHNICAL
values.

vari·ance /'veəriəns/ **variances. 1** If one thing is ◆◇◇◇◇
at variance with another, the two things seem to PHRASE
contradict each other. *Many of his statements were* FORMAL
at variance with the facts. **2** The **variance** between N-VAR
things, is the difference between them. ...*the vari-* FORMAL
ances in the stock price.

vari·ant /'veəriənt/ **variants.** A **variant** of a par- ◆◇◇◇◇
ticular thing is something that has a different form N-COUNT
to that thing, although it is related to it. *There are so
many variant spellings of his name.*

vari·ation /ˌveəri'eɪʃən/ **variations. 1** A **variation** ◆◆◇◇◇
on something is the same thing presented in a N-COUNT
slightly different form. *This delicious variation on
an omelette is quick and easy to prepare.* **2** A **vari-** N-VAR
ation is a change or slight difference in a level,
amount, or quantity. *The survey found a wide variation in the prices charged for canteen food.*

vari·cose vein /ˌværɪkəʊs 'veɪn/ **varicose veins.** N-COUNT
Varicose veins are swollen and painful veins in a
person's legs, which sometimes require a medical
operation.

var·ied /'veərid/. Something that is **varied** consists ◆◆◇◇◇
of things of different types, sizes, or qualities. *It is* ADJ-GRADED
essential that your diet is varied and balanced. ● See
also **vary**.

varie·gat·ed /'veəriəɡeɪtɪd/. **1** A **variegated** leaf or ◆◇◇◇◇
plant has different coloured markings on it. *The
leaves are a variegated red.* **2** If you describe some- ADJ-GRADED
thing as **variegated**, you mean that it is varied and FORMAL
diverse. ...*our variegated dialects.*

va·ri·ety /və'raɪɪti/ **varieties. 1** If something has ◆◆◆◇
variety, it consists of things which are different N-UNCOUNT
from each other. *Susan's idea of freedom was to
have variety in her life style.* **2** A **variety** of things is N-SING
a number of different kinds or examples of the
same thing. *West Hampstead has a variety of good
shops and supermarkets.* **3** A **variety** of something is N-COUNT
a type of it. *She has 12 varieties of old-fashioned
roses.* **4** **Variety** is a type of entertainment which in- N-UNCOUNT
cludes many different kinds of acts in the same
show. ...*a variety show of music, comedy, and magic.*

vari·ous /'veəriəs/. **1** If you say that there are **vari-** ◆◆◆◇
ous things, you mean there are several different ADJ
things of the type mentioned. *The school has received various grants from the education depart-
ment.* **2** If a number of things are described as **vari-** ADJ
ous, they are very different from one another. *The
methods are many and various.*

vari·ous·ly /'veəriəsli/. You can use **variously** to ◆◇◇◇◇
introduce a number of different ways in which ADV
something can be described. *The family was then
described variously as crass, bigoted, racist and plain
boring.*

var·nish /'vɑːnɪʃ/ **varnishes, varnishing, var-** ◆◇◇◇◇
nished. 1 **Varnish** is an oily liquid which is paint- N-VAR
ed onto wood or other material to give it a hard,
clear, shiny surface. **2** If you **varnish** something, VERB: V n
you paint it with varnish. **3** See also **nail varnish**.

var·sity /'vɑːsɪti/. People sometimes use **varsity** to ADJ: ADJ n
describe things that relate to universities, especially JOURNALISM
sports activities.

vary /'veəri/ **varies, varying, varied. 1** If things ◆◆◆◇◇ vary, they are different from each other in size, VERB amount, or degree. *As they're handmade, each one* V from n to n *varies slightly... The amount of sleep we need varies from person to person.* **2** If something **varies** or if V-ERG you **vary** it, it becomes different or changed. *The* V cost of the alcohol duty varies according to the Also V n *amount of wine in the bottle.* **3** See also **varied**.

vas·cu·lar /'væskjʊlə/. **Vascular** is used to describe ADJ: ADJ n the channels and veins through which fluids pass in TECHNICAL the bodies of animals and plants. *...vascular diseases of the legs.*

vase /vɑːz, AM veɪs/ **vases.** A **vase** is a jar, usually ◆◇◇◇◇ made of glass or pottery, used for holding cut flow- N-COUNT ers or as an ornament.

vas·ec·to·my /və'sektəmi/ **vasectomies.** A **vas-** N-VAR **ectomy** is a surgical operation in which the tube that carries sperm to a man's penis is cut, usually as a means of contraception.

Vas·eline /'væsəliːn/. **Vaseline** is a soft clear jelly N-UNCOUNT made from petroleum, which is used as an oint-ment or as grease. **Vaseline** is a trademark.

vas·sal /'væsəl/ **vassals. 1** In feudal society, a **vas-** N-COUNT **sal** was a man who gave military service to a lord in return for which he was protected by the lord and received land to live on. **2** If you say that one coun- N-COUNT try is a **vassal** of another, you mean that it is domi- PRAGMATICS nated by it; used showing disapproval. *Monetary union will turn France into a vassal of Germany.*

vast /vɑːst, væst/ **vaster, vastest.** Something ◆◆◆◇◇ that is **vast** is extremely large. *...Afrikaner farmers* ADJ-GRADED who own vast stretches of land. ◆ **vast·ness** *...the* N-UNCOUNT *vastness of the desert.*

vast·ly /'vɑːstli, 'væst-/. **Vastly** means to an ex- ◆◇◇◇◇ tremely great degree or extent. *...cars that are vastly* ADV *more competitive.*

vat /væt/ **vats.** A **vat** is a large barrel or tank in N-COUNT which liquids can be stored.

VAT /ˌviː eɪ 'tiː, ˈvæt/. **VAT** is a tax that is added to ◆◆◇◇◇ the price of goods or services. **VAT** is an abbrevia- N-UNCOUNT tion for 'value-added tax'. BRITISH

Vati·can /'vætɪkən/. **The Vatican** is the city state in ◆◆◇◇◇ Rome over which the Pope has sovereignty and N-PROPER: where the central administration of the Roman theN Catholic Church has its offices. You can also use **the Vatican** to refer to the Pope or his officials.

vat·man /'vætmæn/; also spelled **VAT man.** In Brit- N-SING: ain, you can refer to the government department theN which advises and checks the accounts of people INFORMAL who have to pay VAT as **the vatman**.

vau·de·ville /'vɔːdəvɪl/. **Vaudeville** is a type of the- N-UNCOUNT atrical entertainment consisting of short acts, such as comedy, acrobatics, singing, and dancing. **Vau-deville** was especially popular in the early part of this century.

vault /vɔːlt/ **vaults, vaulting, vaulted. 1** A **vault** ◆◇◇◇◇ is a secure room where money and other valuable N-COUNT things can be kept safely. *Most of the money was in storage in bank vaults.* **2** A **vault** is a room under- N-COUNT neath a church or in a cemetery where people are buried, usually the members of a single family. **3** A N-COUNT **vault** is an arched roof or ceiling. *...the vault of a great cathedral.*

4 If you **vault** something or **vault** over it, you jump VERB quickly onto or over it, especially by putting a hand on V n top of it to help you balance while you jump. *He could* V prep *easily vault the wall... Ned vaulted over a fallen tree.*

vaunt·ed /'vɔːntɪd/. If something is **vaunted** or ADJ much vaunted, it is described, praised, or displayed FORMAL in a boastful or pompous way. *Its vaunted security procedures hadn't worked.*

vb. Vb is a written abbreviation for **verb**.

VCR /ˌviː siː 'ɑː/ **VCRs.** A **VCR** is a machine that ◆◇◇◇◇ can be used to record television programmes or N-COUNT films onto video tapes, so that people can play them back and watch them later on a television set. **VCR** is an abbreviation for 'video cassette recorder'.

VD /ˌviː 'diː/. **VD** is used to refer to diseases such as N-UNCOUNT syphilis and gonorrhoea which are passed on by

sexual intercourse. It is an abbreviation for **venereal disease**.

VDU /ˌviː diː 'juː/ **VDUs.** A **VDU** is a machine with a N-COUNT screen which is used to display information from a computer. **VDU** is an abbreviation for 'visual dis-play unit'.

veal /viːl/. **Veal** is meat from a calf. *...beef and veal* ◆◇◇◇◇ *exports.* N-UNCOUNT

vec·tor /'vektə/ **vectors. 1** A **vector** is a variable N-COUNT quantity, such as force, that has magnitude and di- TECHNICAL rection. **2** A **vector** is an insect or other organism N-COUNT that causes a disease by carrying a germ or parasite TECHNICAL from one person or animal to another.

veer /vɪə/ **veers, veering, veered. 1** If some- ◆◇◇◇◇ thing **veers** in a certain direction, it suddenly moves VERB in that direction. *The plane veered off the runway* V prep/adv *and careered through the perimeter fence.* **2** If some- VERB one or something **veers** in a certain direction, they V prep/adv change their position or direction in a particular situation. *He is unlikely to veer from his boss's strongly held views.* **3** When the wind **veers**, it VERB changes direction. *The wind had veered from the* V prep/adv *west to north-by-west.* Also V

veg /vedʒ/; **veg** is both the singular and the plural ◆◇◇◇◇ form. **Veg** are plants such as cabbages, potatoes, N-VAR and onions which you can cook and eat. It is an ab-breviation for **vegetables**. *...fruit and veg.*

ve·gan /'viːgən/ **vegans.** Someone who is **vegan** ◇◇◇◇◇ never eats meat or any animal products such as ADJ milk, butter, or cheese. *The menu changes weekly and usually includes a vegan option.* ► A **vegan** is N-COUNT someone who is vegan.

veg·eta·ble /'vedʒtəbəl/ **vegetables. 1** Vegeta- ◆◆◇◇◇ bles are plants such as cabbages, potatoes, and on- N-COUNT ions which you can cook and eat. *A good general diet should include plenty of fresh vegetables. ...veg-etable soup.* **2** Vegetable matter comes from plants. ADJ *...decayed vegetable matter.* **3** If someone refers to a FORMAL very sick or disabled person as a **vegetable**, they N-COUNT mean that they are so severely brain-damaged or physically unwell that they cannot do anything or enjoy anything; an offensive use.

veg·etar·ian /ˌvedʒɪ'teəriən/ **vegetarians.** ◆◆◇◇◇ **1** Someone who is **vegetarian** never eats meat or ADJ fish. *Yasmin sticks to a strict vegetarian diet.* ► A N-COUNT **vegetarian** is someone who is vegetarian. **2** Veg- ADJ **etarian** food does not contain any meat or fish. *...home-cooked vegetarian stew.*

veg·etari·an·ism /ˌvedʒɪ'teəriənɪzəm/. If someone N-UNCOUNT practises **vegetarianism**, they never eat meat or fish. *Vegetarianism is on the increase in Britain.*

veg·etate /'vedʒɪteɪt/ **vegetates, vegetating,** VERB **vegetated.** If someone **vegetates**, they spend their V time doing boring or worthless things, and as a re-sult their mind is not stimulated. *He spends all his free time at home vegetating in front of the TV.*

veg·etat·ed /'vedʒɪteɪtɪd/. If an area is **vegetated**, ADJ it is covered with plants and trees. *That part of Cas-* FORMAL *tle Walk is not thickly vegetated.*

veg·eta·tion /ˌvedʒɪ'teɪʃən/. Plants, trees, and ◆◇◇◇◇ flowers can be referred to as **vegetation**. *The inn* N-UNCOUNT *has a garden of semi-tropical vegetation.* FORMAL

veg·eta·tive /'vedʒɪtətɪv, AM -teɪt-/. **1** If someone ADJ who is in a coma is in a **vegetative** state, they are MEDICAL unable to do anything and their condition is not likely to improve. **2** Vegetative growth or develop- ADJ: ADJ n ment is the growth or development of plants. *The* FORMAL *harshness of the climate makes vegetative growth ex-tremely slow.*

veg·gie /'vedʒi/ **veggies.** If someone is **veggie**, ADJ they never eat meat. *Going veggie can be tasty, easy* INFORMAL *and healthy too.* ► A **veggie** is someone who is veg- N-COUNT etarian. *Many places understand the requirements of a strict veggie.*

ve·he·ment /'viːəmənt/. If a person or their ac- ◆◇◇◇◇ tions or comments are **vehement**, the person has ADJ-GRADED very strong feelings or opinions and expresses them forcefully. *One vehement critic is Michael Howard.* ◆ **ve·he·mence** *He spoke more loudly and with* N-UNCOUNT *much more vehemence than he had intended.*

♦ **ve·he·ment·ly** *Krabbe has always vehemently* ADV
denied using drugs.

ve·hi·cle /'viːɪkəl/ **vehicles. 1** A **vehicle** is a ma- ♦♦♦♦◇
chine with an engine, for example a bus, car, or N-COUNT
truck, that carries people or things from place to
place. *...a vehicle which was somewhere between a
tractor and a truck.* **2** You can use **vehicle** to refer N-COUNT
to something that you use in order to achieve a particular purpose. *Her art became a vehicle for her political beliefs.*

ve·hic·u·lar /vɪ'hɪkjʊlə/. **Vehicular** is used to de- ADJ
scribe something which relates to vehicles and traf- FORMAL
fic. *There is no vehicular access.*

veil /veɪl/ **veils. 1** A **veil** is a piece of thin soft cloth ♦◇◇◇◇
that women sometimes wear over their heads and N-COUNT
which can also cover their face. *She swathes her face
in a veil of decorative muslin.* ♦ **veiled** ADJ
woman gave me a kindly smile. **2** You can refer to N-COUNT
something that hides or partly hides a situation or
activity as a **veil**. *...the chilling facts behind this veil
of silence.* **3** You can refer to something that you N-COUNT
can partly see through, for example a mist, as a **veil**. LITERARY
*He recognized the coast of England through a veil of
mist.*

veiled /veɪld/. A **veiled** comment is expressed in a ♦◇◇◇◇
disguised form rather than directly and openly. *This* ADJ-GRADED:
last clause is a thinly-veiled threat. ADJ n

vein /veɪn/ **veins. 1** Your **veins** are the thin tubes ♦♦◇◇◇
in your body through which your blood flows to- N-COUNT
wards your heart. *Many veins are found just under
the skin.* ● See also **varicose vein**. ♦ **veined** *Helen's* ADJ
hands were thin and veined. ♦ **-veined** *...a man* COMB
who had blue-veined cheeks.
2 Something that is written or spoken in a particular N-COUNT
vein is written or spoken in that style or mood. *The
girl now replies in similar vein.* **3** A **vein** of a particular N-COUNT
quality is evidence of that quality which someone of-
ten shows in their behaviour or work. *...the album's
most abandoned track; venomous, with a vein of humour running right through it.*
4 A **vein** of a particular metal or mineral is a layer of it N-COUNT:
lying in rock. *...a rich and deep vein of limestone.* N of n
5 The **veins** on something such as a leaf are the thin N-COUNT
lines on it. ♦ **veined** *...a bronze ashtray shaped like a* ADJ
veined leaf. ♦ **-veined** *...this distinctive blue-veined* COMB
cheese.

vel·cro /'velkrəʊ/. **Velcro** is a material consisting of N-UNCOUNT
two strips of nylon fabric which press together to
form a strong bond. It is used to open and close
parts of clothes and bags. **Velcro** is a trademark.

veldt /velt/; spelled **veld** in American English. The N-SING
veldt is a high area of flat grassland with very few
trees in southern Africa.

ve·loc·ity /vɪ'lɒsɪti/ **velocities. Velocity** is the ♦◇◇◇◇
speed at which something moves in a particular di- N-VAR
rection. *...the velocity of light.* TECHNICAL

ve·lour /və'lʊə/. **Velour** is a silk or cotton fabric N-UNCOUNT
similar to velvet.

vel·vet /'velvɪt/ **velvets. Velvet** is soft material ♦♦◇◇◇
made from cotton, silk, or nylon, which has a thick N-VAR
layer of short cut threads on one side.

vel·vet·een /ˌvelvɪ'tiːn/. **Velveteen** is a soft fabric N-UNCOUNT
which looks and feels like velvet and is sometimes
used as a cheaper alternative to velvet.

vel·vety /'velvɪti/. If you describe something as **vel-** ADJ-GRADED
vety, you mean that it is pleasantly soft to touch
and has the appearance or quality of velvet. *The
grass grew thick and velvety.*

ve·nal /'viːnəl/. If you describe someone as **venal**, ADJ-GRADED
you disapprove of them because they are prepared PRAGMATICS
to do almost anything in return for money, even
things which are dishonest or immoral. *Ian Trimmer is corrupt and thoroughly venal.*

ven·det·ta /ven'detə/ **vendettas.** If one person ♦◇◇◇◇
has a **vendetta** against another, the first person N-VAR
wants revenge for something the second person did
to them in the past. *A government official has suggested that the football massacre may have been a
vendetta killing by drug traffickers.*

'vending machine, vending machines. A N-COUNT
vending machine is a machine from which you can
get things such as cigarettes, chocolate, or coffee by
putting in money and pressing a button.

ven·dor /'vendə/ **vendors. 1** A **vendor** is someone ♦◇◇◇◇
who sells things such as newspapers, cigarettes, or N-COUNT
hamburgers from a small stall or cart. *...ice-cream
vendors.* **2** The **vendor** of a house or piece of land N-COUNT
is the person who owns it and is selling it. LEGAL

ve·neer /vɪ'nɪə/ **veneers. 1** If you refer to the ♦◇◇◇◇
pleasant way that someone behaves or that some- N-SING
thing appears as a **veneer**, you are critical of them PRAGMATICS
because you believe that their true character or feelings are unpleasant, and are being hidden. *He
was able to fool the world with his veneer of education.* **2** **Veneer** is a thin layer of wood or plastic N-VAR
which is used to improve the appearance of something. *The wood was cut into large sheets of veneer.*

ven·er·able /'venərəbəl/. **1** A **venerable** person ♦◇◇◇◇
deserves respect because they are old and wise. *...a* ADJ-GRADED
venerable old man with white hair. **2** Something
that is **venerable** is impressive because it is old or ADJ-GRADED
important historically. *Venerable dailies such as the
Tokyo Times have shut down.*

ven·er·ate /'venəreɪt/ **venerates, venerating,** ♦◇◇◇◇
venerated. If you **venerate** someone or some- VERB
thing, you value them or feel great respect for them. V n
My father venerated General Eisenhower. ♦ **ven·er-** FORMAL
·at·ed *Jerusalem is Christianity's most venerated* ADJ-GRADED
place. ♦ **ven·era·tion** *Churchill was held in near* N-UNCOUNT
veneration during his lifetime.

ve·nereal dis·ease /vɪˌnɪərɪəl dɪ'ziːz/ **venereal** N-VAR
diseases. Venereal disease is used to refer to diseases such as syphilis and gonorrhoea which are
passed on by sexual intercourse. The abbreviation
VD is also used.

Ve·netian blind /vəˌniːʃən 'blaɪnd/ **Venetian** N-COUNT
blinds. A **Venetian blind** is a window blind made
of thin horizontal strips which can be adjusted to let
in more or less light.

venge·ance /'vendʒəns/. **1 Vengeance** is the act ♦◇◇◇◇
of killing, injuring, or harming someone because N-UNCOUNT
they have harmed you. *He swore vengeance on
everyone involved in the murder.* **2** If you say that PHRASE
something happens **with a vengeance**, you are em- PRAGMATICS
phasizing that it happens to a much greater extent
than was expected. *It began to rain again with a
vengeance.*

venge·ful /'vendʒfʊl/. If you describe someone as ADJ-GRADED
vengeful, you are critical of them because they feel PRAGMATICS
a great desire for revenge. *He was stabbed to death
by his vengeful wife.*

veni·son /'venɪzən/. **Venison** is the meat of a deer. ♦◇◇◇◇
Wild venison has a very distinctive flavor. N-UNCOUNT

ven·om /'venəm/ **venoms. 1** You can use **venom** ♦◇◇◇◇
to refer to someone's feelings of great bitterness N-UNCOUNT
and anger towards someone. *There was no mistaking the venom in his voice.* ♦ **ven·om·ous** ADJ-GRADED
/'venəməs/. *He was surprised by the venomous tone
of the anonymous calls.* **2** The **venom** of a snake, N-VAR
scorpion, or spider is the poison that it injects into
you when it bites or stings you. ♦ **venomous** *The* ADJ
adder is Britain's only venomous snake.

ve·nous /'viːnəs/ is used to describe some- ADJ: ADJ n
thing which is related to veins. *...venous blood.* MEDICAL

vent /vent/ **vents, venting, vented. 1** A **vent** is a ♦◇◇◇◇
hole in something through which air can come in N-COUNT
and smoke, gas, or smells can go out. *There was a
small air vent in the ceiling.* **2** If you **vent** your feel- VERB: V n
ings, you express them forcefully. *The rioters were* V-ed
prevented from venting their anger on the police. **3** If PHRASE
you **give vent to** your feelings, you express them FORMAL
forcefully. *She gave vent to her anger and jealousy.*
4 If you **give vent to** a noise, you make a particular PHRASE
type of noise, especially suddenly or as a reaction to LITERARY
something. *The cabby gave vent to an angry shout.*

ven·ti·late /'ventɪleɪt/ **ventilates, ventilating,** ♦◇◇◇◇
ventilated. 1 If you **ventilate** a room or building, VERB: V n
you allow fresh air to get into it. *...badly ventilated* V-ed
rooms. ♦ **ven·ti·la·tion** /ˌventɪ'leɪʃən/. *The only* N-UNCOUNT

ventilation comes from tiny sliding windows. **2** If
you **ventilate** your ideas or feelings, you talk about
them or express them freely in front of other people. *He did not think it the job of officials to ventilate
their doubts.* VERB / V n / FORMAL

ven·ti·la·tor /'vɛntɪleɪtə/ **ventilators. 1** A ventilator is a machine that helps people breathe when
they cannot breathe naturally, for example because
they are very ill or have been seriously injured. **2** A
ventilator is a device that lets fresh air into a room
or building and lets stale air out. N-COUNT

ven·tri·cle /'vɛntrɪkəl/ **ventricles.** A **ventricle** is a
chamber of the heart that pumps blood from the
heart to the arteries. N-COUNT / TECHNICAL

ven·trilo·quist /vɛn'trɪləkwɪst/ **ventriloquists.** A
ventriloquist is someone who can speak without
moving their lips and who entertains people by
making their words appear to be spoken by a puppet or dummy. N-COUNT

ven·ture /'vɛntʃə/ **ventures, venturing, ventured. 1** A **venture** is a project or activity which is
new, exciting, and difficult because it involves the
risk of failure. *...his latest writing venture.* **2** If you
venture somewhere, you go somewhere that might
be dangerous. *People are afraid to venture out for
fear of sniper attacks.* **3** If you **venture** a question or
statement, you say it in a cautious hesitant manner
because you are afraid it might be stupid or wrong.
*'So you're Leo's girlfriend?' he ventured... He didn't
venture to tell his mother what had happened.* **4** If
you **venture into** an activity, you do something that
involves the risk of failure because it is new and different. *He enjoyed little success when he ventured
into business.* ◆◆◇◇◇ / N-COUNT / VERB / V adv/prep / VERB: V n / V with quote / V to-inf / Also V that / WRITTEN / VERB / V into n

venture 'capital. Venture capital is money
which is lent to someone to start a new business,
especially a risky one, in the hope of making a large
profit. ◆◇◇◇◇ / N-UNCOUNT

venture 'capitalist, venture capitalists. A
venture capitalist is someone who lends money to
people to start new businesses, especially risky
ones, in the hope of making a large profit. N-COUNT

venue /'vɛnjuː/ **venues.** The **venue** for an event
or activity is the place where it will happen.
*Birmingham's International Convention Centre is
the venue for a three-day arts festival.* ◆◆◇◇ / N-COUNT

ve·rac·ity /və'ræsɪti/. **Veracity** is the quality of being true or the habit of telling the truth. *He was
shocked to find his veracity questioned.* N-UNCOUNT / FORMAL

ve·ran·da /və'rændə/ **verandas;** also spelled **ve-
randah.** A **veranda** is a roofed platform along the
outside of a house. N-COUNT

verb /vɜːb/ **verbs.** A **verb** is a word such as 'sing'
or 'feel' which is used with a subject to say what
someone or something does or what happens to
them, or to give information about them. ● See also
phrasal verb. ◆◇◇◇◇ / N-COUNT

ver·bal /'vɜːbəl/. **1** You use **verbal** to indicate that
something is expressed in speech rather than in
writing or action. *We have a verbal agreement with
her.* ♦ **ver·bal·ly** *Twins often have difficulty expressing themselves verbally.* **2** You use **verbal** to indicate that something is connected with words and
the use of words. *Wayne has great verbal dexterity.*
3 In grammar, **verbal** means relating to a verb. *...a
verbal noun.* ◆◆◇◇◇ / ADJ / ADV / ADJ: ADJ n / ADJ

ver·bal·ize /'vɜːbəlaɪz/ **verbalizes, verbalizing,
verbalized;** also spelled **verbalise** in British English. If you **verbalize** your feelings, thoughts, or
ideas, you express them in words. *...his inability to
verbalize his feelings.* VERB / V n / Also V / FORMAL

ver·ba·tim /vɜː'beɪtɪm/. If you repeat something
verbatim, you use exactly the same words as were
used originally. *The President's speeches are regularly reproduced verbatim in the state-run newspapers.*
▶ Also an adjective. *...a verbatim report of every
conversation she's taken part in over the past week.* ADV: ADV after v / ADJ: ADJ n

'verb group, verb groups. A **verb group** or verbal group consists of a verb, or of a main verb fol-
  N-COUNT

lowing a modal or one or more auxiliaries. Examples are 'walked', 'can see', and 'had been waiting'.

ver·bi·age /'vɜːbiɪdʒ/. If you refer to someone's
speech or writing as **verbiage,** you are critical of
them because they use too many words, which
makes their speech or writing difficult to understand. *Stripped of their pretentious verbiage, his
statements come dangerously close to inviting racial
hatred.* N-UNCOUNT / PRAGMATICS / FORMAL

ver·bose /vɜː'bəʊs/. If you describe a person or a
piece of writing as **verbose,** you are critical of them
because they use more words than are necessary,
and so make you feel bored or annoyed. ADJ-GRADED / PRAGMATICS

ver·dant /'vɜːdənt/. If you describe a place as **verdant,** you mean that it is covered with green grass,
trees, and plants. *...a small verdant garden.* ADJ-GRADED / LITERARY

ver·dict /'vɜːdɪkt/ **verdicts. 1** In a court of law,
the **verdict** is the decision that is given by the jury
or judge at the end of a trial. *The jury returned a
unanimous guilty verdict.* **2** Someone's **verdict** on
something is their opinion of it, after thinking about
it or investigating it. *The doctor's verdict was that he
was entirely healthy.* ◆◆◇◇ / N-COUNT / N-COUNT

ver·di·gris /'vɜːdɪgrɪs, -griːs/. **Verdigris** is a
greenish-blue substance that forms on copper,
brass, or bronze after it has been left in wet or
damp conditions. N-UNCOUNT

verge /vɜːdʒ/ **verges, verging, verged. 1** If you
are **on the verge of** something, you are going to do
it very soon or it is likely to happen or begin very
soon. *Carole was on the verge of tears.* **2** The **verge**
of a road is a narrow piece of ground by the side of
a road, usually covered with grass or flowers. ◆◆◇◇ / PHR-PREP / N-COUNT / USU BRITISH

verge on. If someone or something **verges on** a particular state or quality, they are almost the same as
that state or quality. *...a fury that verged on madness.* PHRASAL VB / V P noun

veri·fi·able /'vɛrɪfaɪəbəl/. Something that is **verifiable** can be proved to be true or genuine. *This is not
a romantic notion but verifiable fact.* ADJ

veri·fy /'vɛrɪfaɪ/ **verifies, verifying, verified.
1** If you **verify** something, you check that it is true
by careful examination or investigation. *A clerk
simply verifies that the payment and invoice amount
match.* ♦ **veri·fi·ca·tion** /ˌvɛrɪfɪ'keɪʃən/. *...the
agency's verification procedures.* **2** If you **verify**
something, you state or confirm that it is true. *I can
verify that it takes about thirty seconds.* ◆◇◇◇◇ / VERB: V n / V that / N-UNCOUNT / VB: no cont, V n / V that

veri·ly /'vɛrɪli/. **Verily** is an old-fashioned or religious word meaning 'truly'. It is used to emphasize
a statement or opinion. *Verily she is the best cook in
the parish.* ADV / PRAGMATICS

veri·si·mili·tude /ˌvɛrɪsɪ'mɪlɪtjuːd, AM -tuːd/. **Verisimilitude** is the quality of seeming to be true or
real. *At the required level of visual verisimilitude,
computer animation is costly.* N-UNCOUNT / FORMAL

veri·table /'vɛrɪtəbəl/. You can use **veritable** to
emphasize the size, amount, or nature of some-
thing. *...a veritable feast of pre-match entertainment.* ◆◇◇◇◇ / ADJ / PRAGMATICS

ver·ity /'vɛrɪti/ **verities.** The **verities** of something
are all the things that are believed to be true about
it. *...some verities of human nature.* N-COUNT

ver·mil·ion /və'mɪliən/. **Vermilion** is used to describe things that are bright red in colour. COLOUR / LITERARY

ver·min /'vɜːmɪn/. **Vermin** are small animals such
as rats and mice which cause problems to humans
by carrying disease and damaging crops or food. N-PLURAL

ver·mouth /'vɜːməθ/ **vermouths. Vermouth** is a
strong alcoholic drink made from red or white wine
flavoured with herbs. N-VAR

ver·nacu·lar /və'nækjʊlə/ **vernaculars. 1** The
vernacular is the language or dialect that is most
widely spoken by ordinary people in a region or
country. *...books or plays written in the vernacular.*
2 Vernacular architecture is the style of architecture in which ordinary people's houses are built in a
particular region. N-COUNT / ADJ: ADJ n / FORMAL

ver·ru·ca /və'ruːkə/ **verrucas.** A **verruca** is a kind
of wart which occurs on the sole of the foot. N-COUNT

ver·sa·tile /'vɜːsətaɪl, AM -təl/. **1** If you say that a
person is **versatile,** you approve of them because ◆◆◇◇ / ADJ-GRADED / PRAGMATICS

they have many different skills. *He had been one of the game's most versatile athletes.* ♦ **ver·sa·til·ity** /ˌvɜːsəˈtɪlɪti/. *Aileen stands out for her incredible versatility as an actress.* **2** A tool, machine, or material that is **versatile** can be used for many different purposes. *...a versatile blue chambray skirt.* ♦ **versatility** *Velvet is not known for its versatility.* N-UNCOUNT / ADJ-GRADED / N-UNCOUNT

verse /vɜːs/ **verses. 1 Verse** is writing arranged in lines which have rhythm and which often rhyme at the end. *I have been moved to write a few lines of verse.* ● See also **blank verse. 2 A verse** is one of the parts into which a poem, a song, or a chapter of the Bible or the Koran is divided. **3** ● **chapter and verse:** see **chapter.** ◆◆◇◇◇ N-UNCOUNT / N-COUNT

versed /vɜːst/. If you are **versed in** or **well versed in** something, you know a lot about it. *Page is well versed in many styles of jazz.* ADJ-GRADED: v-link ADJ in n, adv ADJ

ver·sion /ˈvɜːʃən, -ʒən/ **versions. 1 A version** of something is a particular form of it in which some details are different from earlier or later forms. *...an updated version of his book.* **2** Someone's **version** of an event is their own description of it, especially when it is different to other people's. *Yesterday afternoon the White House put out a new version of events.* ◆◆◆◇ N-COUNT / N-COUNT: with supp

ver·sus /ˈvɜːsəs/. **1** You use **versus** to indicate that two figures, ideas, or choices are opposed. *...bottle-feeding versus breastfeeding.* **2 Versus** is used to indicate that two teams or people are competing against each other in a sporting event. *...the Lennox Lewis versus Frank Bruno boxing confrontation.* ◆◆◇◇◇ PREP / PREP

ver·te·bra /ˈvɜːtɪbrə/ **vertebrae** /ˈvɜːtɪbreɪ/. **Vertebrae** are the small circular bones that form the backbone of a human being or animal. ◆◇◇◇◇ N-COUNT

ver·te·brate /ˈvɜːtɪbrɪt/ **vertebrates. A vertebrate** is a creature which has a backbone. N-COUNT

ver·ti·cal /ˈvɜːtɪkəl/ **verticals. 1** Something that is **vertical** stands or points straight upwards. *...a vertical wall of rock.* ♦ **ver·ti·cal·ly** *Cut each bulb in half vertically.* **2 The vertical** is the direction that points straight up, at an angle of 90 degrees to a flat surface. *The seat backs recline up to about 40 degrees from the vertical.* **3 A vertical** is a line or structure that is vertical. *As long as the verticals align, the design will look regular.* ◆◆◇◇◇ ADJ / ADV / N-SING: the N / N-COUNT

ver·tigi·nous /vɜːˈtɪdʒɪnəs/. **Vertiginous** is used to describe a very high cliff or path, from which the ground falls away steeply, and which could cause you to suffer from vertigo. *...vertiginous cliffs that rise out of the Baltic.* ADJ LITERARY

ver·ti·go /ˈvɜːtɪɡəʊ/. **Vertigo** is a feeling of dizziness and sickness caused by looking down from a high place. N-UNCOUNT

verve /vɜːv/. **Verve** is lively and forceful enthusiasm. *...big MGM musicals with their colour and verve.* ◆◇◇◇◇ N-UNCOUNT WRITTEN

very /ˈveri/. **1 Very** is used to give emphasis to an adjective or adverb. *The problem and the answer are very simple... It is very, very strong evidence indeed... They are getting the hang of it very quickly... Thank you very much.* **2 Not very** is used with an adjective or adverb to say that something is not at all true, or that it is true only to a small degree. *She's not very impressed with them... It's obviously not used very much... 'How well do you know her?'—'Not very.'* **3** You use **very** to give emphasis to an adjective that is not usually graded, when you want to say that a quality is very obvious. *Janet looked very pregnant.* **4** You use **very** to give emphasis to a superlative adjective or adverb. For example, if you say that something is **the very best**, you are emphasizing that it is the best. *...the very latest in navigation aids.* **5** You use **very** with certain nouns in order to specify an extreme position or extreme point in time. *I turned to the very end of the book, to read the final words... He was wrong from the very beginning.* **6** You use **very** with nouns to emphasize that something is exactly the right one or exactly the same one. *Everybody says he is the very man for the case... She died in this very house.* **7** You use **very** with nouns to emphasize the ◆◆◆◆◆ ADV: ADV adj/adv [PRAGMATICS] / PHRASE / ADV: ADV adj [PRAGMATICS] / ADV: ADV superl [PRAGMATICS] / ADJ: ADJ n / ADJ: ADJ n [PRAGMATICS] / ADJ: ADJ n

importance or seriousness of what you are saying. *At one stage his very life was in danger... Even the very basis of Indian politics has been transformed.* [PRAGMATICS]

8 Very good is used to tell someone in authority that you agree to carry out a suggestion or order. *'Now give me some account of your voyage.'—'Very good, sir.'* CONVENTION [PRAGMATICS] FORMAL PHRASE

9 The expression **very much so** is an emphatic way of answering 'yes' to something or saying that it is true or correct. *'Are you enjoying your holiday?'—'Very much so.'.* **10 Very well** is used to say that you agree to do something or you accept someone's answer, even though you might not be completely satisfied with it. *'We need proof, sir.' Another pause. Then, 'Very well.'.* [PRAGMATICS] / CONVENTION [PRAGMATICS]

11 If you say that you **cannot very well** do something, you mean that it would not be right or possible to do it. *I said yes. I can't very well say no.* PHRASE

ves·sel /ˈvesəl/ **vessels. 1 A vessel** is a ship or large boat. *...a New Zealand navy vessel. ...the two royal naval vessels in the West African area at the moment.* **2 A vessel** is a bowl or other container in which liquid is kept. *...storage vessels.* **3** See also **blood vessel.** ◆◆◆◇◇ N-COUNT FORMAL / N-COUNT FORMAL

vest /vest/ **vests, vesting, vested. 1 A vest** is a piece of underwear which you can wear on the top half of your body in order to keep warm. The American word is **undershirt.** See picture headed **clothes. 2 A vest** is a sleeveless piece of clothing with buttons which people usually wear over a shirt. The British word is **waistcoat. 3** If something **is vested** in you, or if you **are vested** with it, it is given to you as a right or responsibility. *The mass media have been vested with significant power.* ◆◆◇◇◇ N-COUNT BRITISH / N-COUNT AMERICAN / VB: usu passive, be V-ed in n, be V-ed with n FORMAL

vested 'interest, vested interests. If you have a **vested interest** in something, you have a very strong reason for acting in a particular way, for example to protect your money, power, or reputation. *The administration has no vested interest in proving public schools good or bad.* ◆◇◇◇◇ N-VAR

ves·ti·bule /ˈvestɪbjuːl/ **vestibules. A vestibule** is an enclosed area between the outside door of a building and the inner door. N-COUNT FORMAL

ves·tige /ˈvestɪdʒ/ **vestiges. A vestige** of something is a very small part that still remains of something that was once much larger or more important. *We represent the last vestige of what made this nation great – hard work.* ◆◇◇◇◇ N-COUNT FORMAL

ves·tig·ial /veˈstɪdʒiəl/. **Vestigial** is used to describe the small amounts of something that still remain of a larger or more important thing. *Vestigial remains of these plays are now seen in the Christmas pantomime.* ADJ FORMAL

vest·ments /ˈvestmənts/. **Vestments** are the special clothes that are worn by priests during church ceremonies. N-PLURAL

ves·try /ˈvestri/ **vestries. A vestry** is a room in a church which the clergy use as an office or where they change into their ceremonial clothes for church services. N-COUNT

vet /vet/ **vets, vetting, vetted. 1 A vet** is someone who is qualified to treat sick or injured animals. **2 A vet** is someone who has served in the armed forces of their country, especially during a war. *All three are Vietnam vets.* **3** If something **is vetted**, it is checked carefully to make sure that it is acceptable to people in authority. *He had not been allowed to read any book until his mother had vetted it.* **4** If someone **is vetted**, they are investigated fully before being given a particular job, role, or position, especially one which involves military or political secrets. ♦ **vet·ting** *...the procedure for carrying out security vetting.* ◆◆◇◇◇ N-COUNT / N-COUNT AMERICAN, INFORMAL / VERB: be V-ed V n BRITISH / VB: usu passive BRITISH / N-UNCOUNT

vet·er·an /ˈvetərən/ **veterans. 1 A veteran** is someone who has served in the armed forces of their country, especially during a war. *...veterans of the Persian Gulf War.* **2** You use **veteran** to refer to someone who has been involved in a particular activity for a long time. *...the veteran television campaigner Mary Whitehouse.* ◆◆◆◇◇ N-COUNT / N-COUNT

vet·eri·nar·ian /ˌvetərɪˈneəriən/ **veterinarians. A veterinarian** is a person who is qualified to treat N-COUNT AMERICAN

sick or injured animals. The usual British word is **vet**.

vet·eri·nary /'vetərənəri, AM -neri/. **Veterinary** is used to describe the work of a person whose job is to treat sick or injured animals, or to describe the medical treatment of animals. *...veterinary screening of horses at events.* ◆◇◇◇ ADJ: ADJ n

'veterinary surgeon, veterinary surgeons. A **veterinary surgeon** is someone who is qualified to treat sick or injured animals. The usual American word is **veterinarian**. N-COUNT FORMAL, BRITISH

veto /'viːtəʊ/ **vetoes, vetoing, vetoed. 1** If someone in authority **vetoes** something, they forbid it, or stop it being put into action. *The President vetoed the economic package passed by Congress.* ► Also a noun. *...the veto was a calculated political risk.* **2** Veto is the right that someone in authority has to forbid something. *...the President's power of veto.* ◆◆◇◇ VERB V n ► N-COUNT N-UNCOUNT

vex /veks/ **vexes, vexing, vexed.** If someone or something **vexes** you, they make you feel annoyed, puzzled, and frustrated. *Everything about her vexed him.* ♦ **vexed** *Exporters, farmers and industrialists alike are vexed and blame the government.* ♦ **vex·ing** *There remains, however, another and more vexing problem.* ● See also **vexed**. VERB V n ADJ-GRADED ADJ-GRADED

vexed /vekst/. A **vexed** problem or question is very difficult and causes people a lot of trouble. *Later Mr Moi raised the vexed question of refugees.* ● See also **vex**. ADJ-GRADED

VHF /ˌviː eɪtʃ 'ef/. **VHF** is used to refer to a range of frequencies that is often used for transmitting radio broadcasts in stereo. **VHF** is an abbreviation for 'very high frequency'. N-UNCOUNT

via /vaɪə, 'viːə/. **1** If you go somewhere **via** a particular place, you go through that place on the way to your destination. *Mr Baker will return home via Britain and France.* **2** If you do something **via** a particular means or person, you do it by making use of that means or person. *...the technology to allow relief workers to contact the outside world via satellite.* ◆◆◇◇ PREP PREP

vi·able /'vaɪəbl/. **1** Something that is viable is capable of doing what it is intended to do. *Cash alone will not make Eastern Europe's banks viable.* ♦ **vi·abil·ity** /ˌvaɪə'bɪlɪti/. *...the shaky financial viability of the nuclear industry.* **2** Foetuses, seeds, or eggs are described as **viable** if they are capable of developing into living beings without outside help. *Five viable pregnancies were established.* ◆◇◇◇ ADJ-GRADED N-UNCOUNT ADJ TECHNICAL

via·duct /'vaɪədʌkt/ **viaducts.** A **viaduct** is a long high bridge that carries a road or a railway across a valley. N-COUNT

vial /vaɪəl/ **vials.** A **vial** is a very small bottle which is used to hold something such as perfume. N-COUNT FORMAL

vibe /vaɪb/ **vibes.** **Vibes** are the good or bad atmosphere that you sense with a person or in a place. *I have bad vibes about this guy.* N-COUNT INFORMAL

vi·brant /'vaɪbrənt/. **1** Someone or something that is **vibrant** is full of life, energy, and enthusiasm. *Tom felt himself being drawn towards her vibrant personality.* ♦ **vi·bran·cy** /'vaɪbrənsi/. *She was a woman with extraordinary vibrancy and extraordinary knowledge.* **2** Vibrant colours are very bright and clear. *The grass was a vibrant green.* ♦ **vi·brant·ly** *...a selection of vibrantly coloured French cast-iron saucepans.* ◆◇◇◇ ADJ-GRADED N-UNCOUNT ADJ-GRADED ADV: ADV adj

vi·brate /vaɪ'breɪt, AM 'vaɪbreɪt/ **vibrates, vibrating, vibrated.** If something **vibrates** or if you **vibrate** it, it shakes with repeated small, quick movements. *The noise vibrated the table.... Car alarms aren't intelligent. They just go off whenever a car vibrates.* ♦ **vi·bra·tion** /vaɪ'breɪʃən/ **vibrations** *The vibrations of the vehicles rattled the shop windows.* V-ERG V n N-VAR

vi·bra·tor /vaɪ'breɪtə, AM 'vaɪbreɪtər/ **vibrators.** A **vibrator** is an electric device which vibrates. It is used in massage to give relief from pain, or to give sexual pleasure. N-COUNT

vic·ar /'vɪkə/ **vicars.** In most parishes of the Church of England, the **vicar** is the priest who is in charge of the church and the parish. ◆◆◇◇ N-COUNT N-VOC

vic·ar·age /'vɪkərɪdʒ/ **vicarages.** A **vicarage** is a house in which a vicar lives. ◆◇◇◇ N-COUNT

vi·cari·ous /vɪ'keəriəs, AM vaɪ'kær-/. A **vicarious** pleasure or feeling is experienced by watching, listening to, or reading about other people doing something, rather than by doing it yourself. *She invents fantasy lives for her own vicarious pleasure.* ♦ **vi·cari·ous·ly** *...a father who lived vicariously through his sons' success.* ADJ: ADJ n ADV

vice /vaɪs/ **vices;** spelled **vise** in American English for meaning 3. **1** A **vice** is a habit which is regarded as a weakness in someone's character, but not usually as a serious fault. *Intellectual pretension was never one of his vices.* **2** Vice refers to criminal activities, especially those connected with pornography or prostitution. *...allegations of how she worked in a 'seedy vice den'.* **3** A **vice** or **vise** is a tool with a pair of jaws that hold an object tightly while you do work on it. ◆◆◆◇ N-COUNT N-UNCOUNT N-COUNT

vice- /vaɪs-/. **Vice-** is used before a rank or title to indicate that someone is next in importance to the person who holds the rank or title mentioned. *...the new vice-captain.* PREFIX

vice-'chancellor, vice-chancellors. In a British university, the **vice-chancellor** is the head of academic and administrative matters. ◆◇◇◇ N-COUNT

vice·roy /'vaɪsrɔɪ/ **viceroys.** In former times, a **viceroy** was the person who ruled a colony on behalf of his king, queen, or government. N-COUNT

'vice squad, vice squads. The **vice squad** is the section of a police force that deals with crime relating to pornography, prostitution, and gambling. N-COUNT

vice ver·sa /ˌvaɪsə 'vɜːsə/. **Vice versa** is used to indicate that the reverse of what you have said is true. For example 'women may bring their husbands with them, and vice versa' means that men may also bring their wives with them. ◆◇◇◇ PHRASE

vi·cin·ity /vɪ'sɪnɪti/. If something is in **the vicinity** of a place, it is in the nearby area. *The immediate vicinity of the house remains cordoned off.* ◆◇◇◇ N-SING: the N

vi·cious /'vɪʃəs/. **1** A **vicious** person is violent and cruel. *The blow was so sudden and vicious that he dropped to his knees.* ♦ **vi·cious·ly** *She had been viciously attacked with a hammer.* ♦ **vi·cious·ness** *...the intensity and viciousness of these attacks.* **2** A **vicious** remark is cruel and intended to upset someone. *She never believed he would launch such a vicious personal attack on her and her state of mind.* ♦ **viciously** *'He deserved to die,' said Penelope viciously.* ◆◆◇◇ ADJ-GRADED ADV-GRADED N-UNCOUNT ADJ-GRADED ADV-GRADED: ADV with v

vicious 'circle, vicious circles. A vicious circle is a problem or difficult situation that has the effect of creating new problems which then cause the original problem or situation to occur again. N-COUNT

vi·cis·si·tudes /vɪ'sɪsɪtjuːdz, AM -tuːdz/. You use **vicissitudes** to refer to changes, especially unpleasant ones, that happen to someone or something at different times in their life or development. N-PLURAL FORMAL

vic·tim /'vɪktɪm/ **victims. 1** A **victim** is someone who has been hurt or killed by someone or something. *Our chances of being the victims of violent crime are remote.* **2** A **victim** is someone who has suffered as a result of someone else's actions or beliefs, or as a result of unpleasant circumstances. *Infectious diseases are spreading among many of the flood victims.* **3** If you **fall victim to** something or someone, you suffer as a result of them, or you are killed by them. *He fell victim to pickpockets who pinched his wallet.* ◆◆◆◇ N-COUNT N-COUNT PHRASE

vic·tim·ize /'vɪktɪmaɪz/ **victimizes, victimizing, victimized;** also spelled **victimise** in British English. If someone is **victimized**, they are deliberately treated unfairly. *He felt the students had been victimized because they'd voiced opposition to the government.* ♦ **vic·tim·iza·tion** /ˌvɪktɪmaɪ'zeɪʃən/. *...society's cruel victimization of women.* ◆◇◇◇ VERB be V-ed Also V n N-UNCOUNT

vic·tor /'vɪktə/ **victors.** A **victor** in a battle or contest is the person who wins. ◆◇◇◇ N-COUNT LITERARY

Vic·to·rian /vɪk'tɔːriən/ **Victorians. 1** Victorian means belonging to, connected with, or typical of ◆◇◇◇ ADJ

Britain in the middle and last parts of the 19th century, when Victoria was Queen. *We have a lovely old Victorian house.* **2** You can use **Victorian** to describe people who have old-fashioned qualities, especially in relation to discipline and morals. *Victorian values are much misunderstood.* **3** The **Victorians** were the people who lived in the reign of Queen Victoria. ADJ-GRADED / N-COUNT

Vic·to·ri·ana /vɪkˌtɔːriˈɑːnə/. Interesting or valuable objects made during the reign of Queen Victoria are sometimes referred to as **Victoriana**. N-UNCOUNT

vic·to·ri·ous /vɪkˈtɔːriəs/. You use **victorious** to describe someone who has won a victory in a struggle, war, or competition. *In 1978 he played for the victorious Argentinian side in the World Cup.* ◆◇◇◇◇ ADJ

vic·to·ry /ˈvɪktəri/ **victories. 1** A **victory** is a success in a struggle, war, or competition. *...the former Welsh rugby union skipper who led Great Britain to victory over France.* **2** If you say that someone has won a **moral victory**, you mean that although they have officially lost a contest or dispute, they have succeeded in showing they are right about something. ◆◆◆◇◇ N-VAR / PHRASE

video /ˈvɪdiəʊ/ **videos, videoing, videoed. 1** A **video** is a film or television programme recorded on video tape for people to watch on a television set. **2** **Video** is the recording and showing of films and events, using a video recorder, videotapes, and a television set. *She has watched the race on video.* **3** A **video** is a machine that you can use to record and play videotapes on a television set. **4** If you **video** something, you record it on magnetic tape using a video recorder or camera, in order to watch it later. ◆◆◆◆◇ N-COUNT / N-UNCOUNT / N-COUNT / VERB: V n

video cas'sette, video cassettes. A **video cassette** is a cassette on which you can record or watch films and television programmes. N-COUNT

video con·fer·enc·ing /ˈvɪdiəʊ ˈkɒnfrənsɪŋ/; also spelled **video-conferencing**. **Video conferencing** is a system that enables people in various places around the world to have a meeting by seeing and hearing each other on a screen. N-UNCOUNT

video 'nasty, video nasties. A **video nasty** is an extremely violent or horrific film which has been released on video. N-COUNT BRITISH

video·phone /ˈvɪdiəʊfəʊn/ **videophones;** also spelled **video phone**. A **videophone** is a telephone with a camera and screen so that each caller can see video images of the other. N-COUNT

'video recorder, video recorders. A **video recorder** or a **video cassette recorder** is the same as a **VCR**. N-COUNT

video·tape /ˈvɪdiəʊteɪp/ **videotapes, videotaping, videotaped;** also spelled **video tape**. **1** **Videotape** is magnetic tape that is used to record pictures and sounds to be shown on television. **2** A **videotape** is the same as a **video cassette**. **3** If you **videotape** something, you record it on magnetic tape using a video recorder or camera, in order to watch or show it on television later. ◆◆◇◇◇ N-UNCOUNT / N-COUNT / VERB: V n

vie /vaɪ/ **vies, vying, vied.** If one person **vies** with another to do something, or if they **vie** to do it, they both try hard to do it sooner or better than the other person. *Four rescue plans are vying to save the zoo... He will vie with Mr Clinton for the votes of the young.* ◆◇◇◇◇ V-RECIP: V with to-inf pl-n V to-inf V with n for n Also pl-n V for n FORMAL

view /vjuː/ **views, viewing, viewed. 1** Your **views** on something are the beliefs or opinions that you have about it, for example whether you think it is good, bad, right, or wrong. *I take the view that she should be stopped as soon as possible... You should also make your views known to your local MP.* **2** You use **in my view** when you want to indicate that you are stating a personal opinion, which other people might not agree with. *In my view things won't change.* **3** If you take **a dim view** of someone or something, you disapprove of them or have a low opinion of them. **4** Your **view** of a particular subject is the way that you understand and think about it. *The whole point was to* ◆◆◆◆◇ N-COUNT / PHRASE PRAGMATICS / PHRASE / N-SING: with supp

get away from a Christian-centred view of religion. **5** If you **view** something in a particular way, you think of it in that way. *First-generation Americans view the United States as a land of golden opportunity... We would view favourably any sensible suggestion for maintaining the business.* **6** You use **in view of** when you are taking into consideration facts that have just been mentioned or are just about to be mentioned. *In view of the fact that Hobson was not a trained economist his achievements were remarkable.* **7** If you have something **in view**, you are aware of it and your actions are aimed towards it. *They have very clear career aims in view.* VERB: V n with/in n V n as n/-ing V n with adv / PHR-PREP PRAGMATICS / PHRASE

8 If you **take the long view**, you consider what is likely to happen in the future over a long period, rather than thinking only about the immediate effects of something. *Taking a long view of the project, I began to think in terms of the rehearsal schedules required.* **9** If you do something **with a view to** doing something else, you do it because you hope it will result in that other thing being done. *He has called a meeting of all parties tomorrow, with a view to forming a national reconciliation government.* PHRASE / PHRASE

10 The **view** from a window or high place is everything which can be seen from that place, especially when it is considered to be beautiful. **11** If you have a **view** of something, you can see it. *He stopped in the doorway, blocking her view.* **12** You use **view** in expressions to do with being able to see something. For example, if something is **in view**, you can see it. If something is **in full view of everyone**, everyone can see it. *A group of riders came into view.* **13** If you **view** something, you inspect it or look at it for a particular purpose. *They came back to view the house again.* **14** If something such as a work of art is **on view**, it is shown in public for people to look at. **15** If you **view** a television programme, video, or film, you watch it. *'Elizabeth R', a TV portrait of the Queen, had record viewing figures.* N-COUNT / N-SING: with supp / N-UNCOUNT: in/into N / VERB: V n FORMAL / PHRASE / VERB: V n V-ing FORMAL

view·er /ˈvjuːə/ **viewers. 1** Viewers are people who watch television, or who are watching a particular programme on television. **2** A **viewer** is someone who is looking carefully at a picture, antique, or other interesting object. *...the relationship between the art object and the viewer.* ◆◆◇◇◇ N-COUNT / N-COUNT

view·finder /ˈvjuːfaɪndə/ **viewfinders.** A **viewfinder** is a small square of glass in a camera that you look through in order to see what you are going to photograph. ◆◇◇◇◇ N-COUNT

view·point /ˈvjuːpɔɪnt/ **viewpoints. 1** Someone's **viewpoint** is the way that they think about things in general, or the way they think about a particular thing. *The novel is shown from the girl's viewpoint.* **2** A **viewpoint** is a place from which you can get a good view of something. ◆◆◇◇◇ N-COUNT / N-COUNT: with supp

vig·il /ˈvɪdʒɪl/ **vigils.** A **vigil** is a period of time when people remain quietly in a place, especially at night, for example because they are praying or are making a political protest. *Protesters are holding a twenty-four hour vigil outside the socialist party headquarters.* ● If people remain quietly in a place for a period of time, you can say that they are **keeping a vigil** or **keeping vigil** there. ◆◇◇◇◇ N-COUNT / PHRASE

vigi·lant /ˈvɪdʒɪlənt/. Someone who is **vigilant** gives careful attention to a particular problem or situation and concentrates on noticing any danger or trouble that there might be. *He warned the public to be vigilant and report anything suspicious.* ◆ **vigi·lance** *Drugs are a problem that requires constant vigilance.* ◆◇◇◇◇ ADJ-GRADED / N-UNCOUNT

vigi·lan·te /ˌvɪdʒɪˈlænti/ **vigilantes.** Vigilantes are people who organize themselves into an unofficial group to protect their community and to catch and punish criminals. ◆◇◇◇◇ N-COUNT

vi·gnette /vɪˈnjet/ **vignettes.** A **vignette** is a short description, an illustration, or piece of acting, which expresses very clearly and neatly the typical characteristics of the thing that it represents. *The book is an excellent vignette of some of the major debates in science.* N-COUNT FORMAL

V

vig·or·ous /'vɪɡərəs/. **1 Vigorous** physical activities involve using a lot of energy, usually to do short and repeated actions. ♦ **vig·or·ous·ly** He shook his head vigorously. **2** You use **vigorous** to describe people who take part in a campaign or activity with great energy or enthusiasm, or to describe the campaign or activity. Sir Robert was a strong and vigorous politician... They will take vigorous action to recover the debts. ♦ **vigorously** The police vigorously denied that excessive force had been used. **3** A **vigorous** person is strong and healthy and full of energy. ◆◆◇◇◇ ADJ-GRADED

vig·our /'vɪɡə/; spelled **vigor** in American English. **Vigour** is physical or mental energy and enthusiasm. The election was fought with vigour. ◆◇◇◇◇ N-UNCOUNT

Vi·king /'vaɪkɪŋ/ **Vikings**. The **Vikings** were groups of seamen from Scandinavia who attacked villages in most parts of north-western Europe from the 8th to the 11th centuries. ◆◇◇◇◇ N-COUNT

vile /vaɪl/ **viler, vilest**. If you say that someone or something is **vile**, you mean that they are extremely unpleasant. ◆◇◇◇◇ ADJ-GRADED

vili·fy /'vɪlɪfaɪ/ **vilifies, vilifying, vilified**. If you are vilified by someone, they say or write very unpleasant things about you, so that people will have a low opinion of you. The agency has been vilified by some doctors for being unnecessarily slow to approve life-saving drugs... He was vilified, hounded, and forced into exile by the FBI. ♦ **vili·fi·ca·tion** /ˌvɪlɪfɪ'keɪʃən/. Clare did not deserve the vilification she had been subjected to. VERB FORMAL N-UNCOUNT

vil·la /'vɪlə/ **villas**. A **villa** is a fairly large house, especially one that is used for holidays in Mediterranean countries. ◆◆◇◇◇ N-COUNT

vil·lage /'vɪlɪdʒ/ **villages**. A **village** consists of a group of houses, together with other buildings such as a church and a school, in a country area. ◆◆◆◇◇ N-COUNT

vil·lag·er /'vɪlɪdʒə/ **villagers**. You refer to the people who live in a village, especially the people who have lived there for most or all of their lives, as the **villagers**. ◆◆◇◇◇ N-COUNT

vil·lain /'vɪlən/ **villains**. **1** A **villain** is someone who deliberately harms other people or breaks the law in order to get what he or she wants. **2** The **villain** in a novel, film, or play is the main bad character. **3** If you say that someone is **the villain of the piece**, you are saying in a slightly humorous way that they are seen by some people as the cause of all trouble in a particular situation. ◆◇◇◇◇ N-COUNT N-COUNT PHRASE PRAGMATICS

vil·lain·ous /'vɪlənəs/. A **villainous** person is very bad and willing to harm other people or break the law in order to get what he or she wants. ADJ-GRADED

vil·lainy /'vɪləni/. **Villainy** is very bad or criminal behaviour. N-UNCOUNT FORMAL

vinai·grette /ˌvɪnɪ'ɡret/ **vinaigrettes**. **Vinaigrette** is a dressing made by mixing oil, vinegar, salt, pepper, and herbs, which is put on salad. N-VAR

vin·di·cate /'vɪndɪkeɪt/ **vindicates, vindicating, vindicated**. If a person or their decisions, actions, or ideas are **vindicated**, they are proved to be correct, after people have said that they were wrong. The director said he had been vindicated by the experts' report. ♦ **vin·di·ca·tion** /ˌvɪndɪ'keɪʃən/. He called the success a vindication of his party's free-market economic policy. VERB be V-ed Also V n FORMAL N-UNCOUNT: also a N

vin·dic·tive /vɪn'dɪktɪv/. If you say that someone is **vindictive**, you are critical of them because they deliberately try to upset or cause trouble for someone who they think has done them harm. ♦ **vin·dic·tive·ness** ...a dishonest person who is operating completely out of vindictiveness. ◆◇◇◇◇ ADJ-GRADED PRAGMATICS N-UNCOUNT

vine /vaɪn/ **vines**. A **vine** is a climbing or trailing plant, especially one which produces grapes. ◆◆◇◇◇ N-VAR

vin·egar /'vɪnɪɡə/ **vinegars**. **Vinegar** is a sharp-tasting liquid, usually made from sour wine or malt, which is used to make things such as salad dressing. ◆◇◇◇◇ N-VAR

vin·egary /'vɪnɪɡəri/. If something has a **vinegary** taste or smell, it tastes or smells of vinegar. ADJ-GRADED

vine·yard /'vɪnjəd/ **vineyards**. A **vineyard** is an area of land where grape vines are grown in order ◆◆◇◇◇ N-COUNT to produce wine. You can also use **vineyard** to refer to the buildings in which the wine is produced.

vin·tage /'vɪntɪdʒ/ **vintages**. **1** The **vintage** of a good quality wine is the year and place that it was made before being stored to improve it. You can also use **vintage** to refer to the wine that was made in a certain year. The 1985 vintage has a stronger bouquet. **2 Vintage** wine is good quality wine that has been stored for several years in order to improve its quality. **3 Vintage** cars or aeroplanes are old but are admired because they are considered to be the best of their kind. **4** You can use **vintage** to describe something which is the best and most typical of its kind. This is vintage comedy at its best. ◆◆◇◇◇ N-COUNT ADJ: ADJ n ADJ: ADJ n ADJ

vint·ner /'vɪntnə/ **vintners**. A **vintner** is someone whose job is to make or buy and sell wine. N-COUNT FORMAL

vi·nyl /'vaɪnɪl/ **vinyls**. **1 Vinyl** is a strong plastic used for making things such as floor coverings and furniture. **2** You can use **vinyl** to refer to records, especially in contrast to cassettes or compact discs. This compilation was first issued on vinyl in 1984. N-VAR N-UNCOUNT

vio·la /vi'əʊlə/ **violas**. **1** A **viola** is a musical instrument with four strings that is played with a bow. It is like a violin, but is slightly larger and can play lower notes. **2 Violas** are small plants with white, yellow, or purple flowers. ◆◇◇◇◇ N-VAR N-COUNT

vio·late /'vaɪəleɪt/ **violates, violating, violated**. **1** If someone **violates** an agreement, law, or promise, they break it. They violated the ceasefire agreement. ♦ **vio·la·tion** /ˌvaɪə'leɪʃən/ **violations** To deprive the boy of his education is a violation of state law. ♦ **vio·la·tor, violators** ...a government which is a known violator of human rights. **2** If you **violate** someone's privacy or peace, you disturb it. **3** If someone **violates** a special place, for example a tomb, they damage it or treat it with disrespect. ♦ **violation** The violation of the graves is not the first such incident. ◆◆◇◇◇ VERB V n FORMAL N-VAR N-COUNT VERB: V n FORMAL VERB: V n N-UNCOUNT

vio·lence /'vaɪələns/. **1 Violence** is behaviour which is intended to hurt, injure, or kill people. Twenty people were killed in the violence. ...domestic violence between husband and wife. **2** If you do or say something with **violence**, you use a lot of force and energy in doing or saying it, often because you are angry. The violence in her tone gave Alistair a shock. ◆◆◆◇ N-UNCOUNT N-UNCOUNT LITERARY

vio·lent /'vaɪələnt/. **1** If someone is **violent**, or if they do something which is **violent**, they use physical force or weapons to hurt, injure, or kill other people. A quarter of current inmates have committed violent crimes. ♦ **vio·lent·ly** Some opposition activists have been violently attacked. **2** A **violent** death is painful and unexpected, usually because the person who dies has been murdered. ♦ **violently** ...a girl who had died violently nine years earlier. **3** A **violent** film or television programme contains a lot of scenes which show violence. **4** A **violent** event happens suddenly and with great force. A violent impact hurtled her forward. ♦ **violently** A nearby volcano erupted violently. **5** If you describe something as **violent**, you mean that it is said, done, or felt very strongly. Violent opposition to the plan continues... He had violent stomach pains. ♦ **violently** He was violently scolded by a left-wing lady friend. **6 Violent** weather is extremely stormy and windy. ◆◆◆◇ ADJ-GRADED ADV-GRADED ADJ-GRADED ADV-GRADED ADJ-GRADED ADJ-GRADED ADV-GRADED ADJ-GRADED ADV-GRADED ADJ-GRADED

vio·let /'vaɪələt/ **violets**. **1** A **violet** is a small purple or white flower that blooms in spring. **2** Something that is **violet** is a bluish-purple colour. **3** If you say that someone is no **shrinking violet**, you mean that they are not shy or timid at all. ◆◇◇◇◇ N-COUNT COLOUR PHRASE

vio·lin /ˌvaɪə'lɪn/ **violins**. A **violin** is a musical instrument made of wood and with four strings. You play the violin by holding it under your chin and moving a bow across the strings. See picture headed **musical instruments**. ♦ **vio·lin·ist, violinists**. A **violinist** is someone who plays the violin. ◆◇◇◇◇ N-VAR N-COUNT

VIP /ˌviː aɪ 'piː/ **VIPs**. A **VIP** is someone who is given better treatment than ordinary people because ◆◇◇◇◇ N-COUNT

they are famous or important. **VIP** is an abbreviation for 'very important person'.

vi·per /ˈvaɪpə/, **vipers**. A **viper** is a small poisonous snake found mainly in Europe.   N-COUNT

vi·ral /ˈvaɪərəl/. A **viral** disease or infection is caused by a virus. *...severe viral pneumonia.*   ◆◇◇◇◇ ADJ

vir·gin /ˈvɜːdʒɪn/, **virgins**. **1** A **virgin** is someone, especially a woman or girl, who has never had sex. ◆ **vir·gin·ity** /vəˈdʒɪnɪti/. *She lost her virginity when she was 20.* **2** You use **virgin** to describe something such as land that has never been used or spoiled. *...a sloping field of virgin snow.* **3** If you say that a situation is **virgin territory**, you mean that you have no experience of it and it is completely new for you.   ◆◆◇◇◇ N-COUNT / N-UNCOUNT / ADJ / PHRASE

vir·gin·al /ˈvɜːdʒɪnəl/. If you describe someone as **virginal**, you mean that they look young and innocent, as if they have had no experience of sex.   ADJ-GRADED

vir·ile /ˈvɪraɪl, AM -rəl/. **1** If you describe a man as **virile**, you mean that he has the qualities that a man is traditionally expected to have, such as strength and sexuality. ◆ **vi·ril·ity** /vɪˈrɪlɪti/. *Children are also considered proof of a man's virility.* **2** Something that is described as **virile** is considered to be very strong and forceful. *...a virile approach to difficulties.* ◆ **virility** *The strength of national electronics industries has become the new test of industrial virility.*   ◆◇◇◇◇ ADJ-GRADED / N-UNCOUNT / ADJ-GRADED / N-UNCOUNT

vir·tual /ˈvɜːtʃʊəl/. You can use **virtual** to indicate that something is so nearly true that for most purposes it can be regarded as being true. *The Communist take-over culminated in the virtual banning of religion.*   ◆◆◇◇◇ ADJ: ADJ n

vir·tu·al·ly /ˈvɜːtʃʊəli/. You can use **virtually** to indicate that something is so nearly true that for most purposes it can be regarded as being true. *Virtually all cooking was done over coal-fired ranges.*   ◆◆◇◇◇ ADV / ADV with group

virtual re·ality. **Virtual reality** is an environment which is produced by a computer and seems very like reality to the person experiencing it.   ◆◇◇◇◇ N-UNCOUNT

vir·tue /ˈvɜːtʃuː/, **virtues**. **1** Virtue is thinking and doing what is right and avoiding what is wrong. **2** A **virtue** is a good quality or way of behaving. *Humility is considered a virtue.* **3** The **virtue** of something is an advantage or benefit that it has, especially in comparison with something else. *Its other great virtue, of course, is its hard-wearing quality.* **4** You use **by virtue of** to explain why something happens or is true. *Mr Olaechea has British residency by virtue of his marriage.* **5** If you **make a virtue of** something, you pretend that you did it out of goodness or choice, although in fact you did it because you had to. *The movie makes a virtue out of its economy.*   ◆◆◇◇◇ N-UNCOUNT / N-COUNT / N-COUNT / PHR-PREP FORMAL / PHRASE

vir·tu·os·ity /ˌvɜːtʃuˈɒsɪti/. The **virtuosity** of someone such as an artist or sportsman is their exceptional skill. The **virtuosity** of a performance or creation is the exceptional skill with which it has been done. *At that time, his virtuosity on the trumpet had no parallel in jazz.*   N-UNCOUNT

vir·tuo·so /ˌvɜːtʃuˈəʊzəʊ/, **virtuosos** or **virtuosi** /ˌvɜːtʃuˈəʊzi/. **1** A **virtuoso** is someone who is exceptionally good at something, especially at playing a musical instrument. **2** A **virtuoso** performance or display shows exceptional skill.   ◆◇◇◇◇ N-COUNT / ADJ

vir·tu·ous /ˈvɜːtʃuəs/. **1** A **virtuous** person behaves in a moral and correct way. *...virtuous people who obey the rules and are nice to others.* **2** If you describe someone as **virtuous**, you mean that they feel very pleased with their own good behaviour; often used showing disapproval. *I cleaned the flat, which left me feeling virtuous.* ◆ **vir·tu·ous·ly** *'I've already done that,' said Ronnie virtuously.*   ◆◇◇◇◇ ADJ-GRADED / ADJ-GRADED / ADV-GRADED

virtuous 'circle. If you describe a situation as a **virtuous circle**, you mean that once one good thing starts happening, other good things happen, which cause the first thing to continue happening.   N-SING

viru·lent /ˈvɪrʊlənt/. **1** Virulent feelings or actions are extremely bitter and hostile. *Now he faces virulent attacks from the Italian media.* ◆ **viru·lent·ly** *The talk was virulently hostile to the leadership.*   ◆◇◇◇◇ ADJ-GRADED / ADV

◆ **viru·lence** *The virulence of the café owner's anger had appalled her.* **2** A **virulent** disease or poison is extremely powerful and dangerous. ◆ **virulence** *Medical authorities were baffled, both as to its causes and its virulence.*   N-UNCOUNT / ADJ-GRADED / N-UNCOUNT

vi·rus /ˈvaɪərəs/, **viruses**. **1** A **virus** is a kind of germ that can cause disease. *There are many different strains of flu virus.* **2** In computer technology, a **virus** is a program that introduces itself into a system, altering or destroying the information stored there.   ◆◆◇◇ N-COUNT / N-COUNT

visa /ˈviːzə/, **visas**. A **visa** is an official document, or a stamp put in your passport, which allows you to enter or leave a particular country.   ◆◆◇◇ N-COUNT

vis·age /ˈvɪzɪdʒ/, **visages**. Someone's **visage** is their face.   N-COUNT LITERARY

vis-à-vis /ˌviːz ɑː ˈviː/. You use **vis-à-vis** when you are considering a relationship or comparison between two things or quantities. *...Poland's economic weakness vis-à-vis Germany.*   PREP FORMAL

vis·cera /ˈvɪsərə/. **Viscera** are the large organs inside the body, such as the heart, liver, and stomach.   N-PLURAL MEDICAL

vis·cer·al /ˈvɪsərəl/. **Visceral** feelings and emotions are deep and instinctive rather than rational and carefully thought out.   ADJ-GRADED LITERARY

vis·cose /ˈvɪskəʊs/. **Viscose** is a smooth man-made fabric that is made from cellulose. The usual American word is **rayon**.   N-UNCOUNT BRITISH

vis·count /ˈvaɪkaʊnt/, **viscounts**. A **viscount** is a British nobleman who is below an earl and above a baron in rank.   ◆◇◇◇◇ N-COUNT; N-TITLE

vis·count·ess /ˈvaɪkaʊntɪs/, **viscountesses**. A **viscountess** is either the wife of a viscount or a woman who holds the same position as a viscount.   N-COUNT; N-TITLE

vis·cous /ˈvɪskəs/. A **viscous** liquid is thick and sticky. ◆ **vis·cos·ity** /vɪsˈkɒsɪti/. *...the viscosity of the paint.*   ADJ-GRADED / N-UNCOUNT

vise /vaɪs/. See **vice**.

vis·ibil·ity /ˌvɪzɪˈbɪlɪti/. **1** Visibility means how far or how clearly you can see in particular weather conditions. *Visibility was poor.* **2** If you refer to the **visibility** of something such as a situation or problem, you mean how much it is seen or noticed by other people. *The plight of the Kurds gained global visibility.*   ◆◇◇◇◇ N-UNCOUNT / N-UNCOUNT

vis·ible /ˈvɪzɪbəl/. **1** If something is **visible**, it can be seen. *They found a bacterium visible to the human eye.* **2** You use **visible** to describe something or someone that people notice or recognize. *He was making a visible effort to control himself.* ◆ **vis·ibly** *They emerged visibly distressed.*   ◆◆◇◇ ADJ-GRADED / ADJ-GRADED / ADV-GRADED

vi·sion /ˈvɪʒən/, **visions**. **1** Your **vision** of a future situation or society is what you imagine or hope it would be like, if things were very different from the way they are now. *I have a vision of a society that is free of exploitation and injustice.* **2** If you have a **vision** of someone in a particular situation, you imagine them in that situation, for example because you are worried that it might happen, or hope that it will happen. *Maybe you had visions of being surrounded by happy, smiling children.* **3** A **vision** is an unusual experience that you have, in which you see things that other people cannot see, as a result of divine inspiration, madness, or taking drugs. *It was on 24th June 1981 that young villagers first reported seeing the Virgin Mary in a vision.* **4** Your **vision** is your ability to see clearly with your eyes. *It causes blindness or serious loss of vision.* **5** Your **vision** is everything that you can see from a particular position. *Jane blocked Cross's vision and he could see nothing.* **6** See also **tunnel vision**.   ◆◆◇◇ N-COUNT / N-COUNT / N-COUNT / N-UNCOUNT / N-UNCOUNT

vi·sion·ary /ˈvɪʒənri, AM -neri/, **visionaries**. **1** If you refer to someone as a **visionary**, you mean that they have strong original ideas about how things might be different in the future, especially about how things might be improved. **2** You use **visionary** to describe the strong original ideas of a visionary. *...the visionary architecture of Etienne Boullée.*   ◆◇◇◇◇ N-COUNT / ADJ-GRADED

vis·it /ˈvɪzɪt/, **visits, visiting, visited**. **1** If you **visit** someone, you go to see them and spend time   ◆◆◆◆ VERB: V n

with them. *Bill would visit on weekends.* ► Also a N-COUNT
noun. *Helen had recently paid him a visit.* **2** If you VERB: V n
visit a place, you go there for a short time. ...*a visit-* V-ing
ing truck driver. ► Also a noun. ...*the Pope's visit to* N-COUNT
Canada. **3** If you **visit** a professional person such as VERB: V n
a doctor or solicitor, you go and see them in order BRITISH
to get professional advice. If they **visit** you, they
come to see you in order to give you professional
advice. ► Also a noun. *You may have regular home* N-COUNT
visits from a neonatal nurse. **4** If something very un- V-PASSIVE
pleasant **is visited** upon you, it happens to you. FORMAL

visit with. 1 If you **visit with** someone, you go to see PHRASAL VB
them and spend time with them. *I visited with him in* V P n
San Francisco. **2** If you **visit with** someone, you have a AMERICAN
conversation or discussion with them. *The more I* V P n
come to visit with people about their lives, the less clear AMERICAN
I am about that.

vis·i·ta·tion /ˌvɪzɪˈteɪʃən/ **visitations. 1** A **visita-** N-COUNT
tion is an event which is thought to be a message
from God, an angel, or some other divine force. *The*
young people have claimed almost daily visitations
from the Virgin Mary. **2** People sometimes refer hu- N-COUNT
morously to a visit from someone, especially from
someone in authority, as a **visitation**. *They had an-*
other visitation from Essex police. **3 Visitation** is the N-COUNT
act of officially visiting someone. *I had visitation*
rights.

visi·tor /ˈvɪzɪtə/ **visitors.** A **visitor** is someone ◆◇◇◇
who is visiting a person or place. N-COUNT

vi·sor /ˈvaɪzə/ **visors. 1** A **visor** is a movable part of N-COUNT
a helmet which can be pulled down to protect a
person's eyes or face. **2** A **visor** is a piece of plastic N-COUNT
or other material fixed above the windscreen inside
a car, which can be turned down to protect the
driver's eyes from bright sunshine. *I put down the*
sun visor to shade my eyes.

vis·ta /ˈvɪstə/ **vistas. 1** A **vista** is a wide or beauti- ◆◇◇◇
ful view, especially from a high place. *I looked out* N-COUNT
on a crowded vista of hills and rooftops. **2** A **vista** is WRITTEN
a vision of a situation or of a range or possibilities. N-COUNT
...*a vista of a future without hope.*

vis·ual /ˈvɪʒuəl/ **visuals. 1 Visual** means relating ◆◆◇◇
to sight, or to things that you can see. ...*the visual* ADJ
arts. ...*visual jokes.* ♦ **visu·al·ly** ...*visually handi-* ADV
capped boys and girls. **2** A **visual** is a piece of dis- N-COUNT
play material, such as a photograph or film, that is
used to illustrate or explain something.

visual 'aid, visual aids. Visual aids are things N-COUNT
that you can look at, such as a film, model, map, or
slides, to help you understand something or to remember information.

visu·al·ize /ˈvɪʒuəlaɪz/ **visualizes, visualizing,** ◆◆◇◇
visualized; also spelled **visualise** in British Eng- VERB: V n
lish. If you **visualize** something, you imagine what it V n prep
is like by forming a mental picture of it. *He could* V wh
not visualize her as old... It was hard to visualize
how it could have been done. ♦ **visu·ali·za·tion** N-VAR
/ˌvɪʒuəlaɪˈzeɪʃən/ **visualizations** ...*a vivid visuali-*
zation of a glorious future.

vi·tal /ˈvaɪtəl/ **1** If something is **vital**, it is neces- ◆◆◇◇
sary or very important. *Nick Wileman is a school* ADJ-GRADED
caretaker so it is vital that he gets on well with young
people. ...*vital information.* ♦ **vi·tal·ly** *Lesley's ca-* ADV-GRADED
reer in the church is vitally important to her. **2** If ADJ-GRADED
you describe someone or something as **vital**, you
mean that they are very energetic and full of life.
They have something important to say and vital and
radical ways of saying it.

vi·tal·ity /vaɪˈtælɪti/. If someone or something has ◆◇◇◇
vitality, they have great energy and liveliness. *With-* N-UNCOUNT
out continued learning, graduates will lose their in-
tellectual vitality.

vital sta'tistics. 1 The **vital statistics** of a popu- N-PLURAL
lation are statistics such as the number of births,
deaths, or marriages which take place in it. **2** A N-PLURAL
woman's **vital statistics** are the measurements of DATED
her body around her bust, waist, and hips.

vita·min /ˈvɪtəmɪn, AM ˈvaɪt-/ **vitamins. Vitamins** ◆◆◇◇
are organic substances in food which you need in N-COUNT
order to remain healthy. You can also refer to tab-

lets or medicines containing these substances as
vitamins. ...*vitamin D... Healthy people do not need*
vitamin supplements.

vi·ti·ate /ˈvɪʃieɪt/ **vitiates, vitiating, vitiated.** If VERB
something **is vitiated**, its effectiveness is spoiled or be V-ed
weakened. *Strategic policy during the War was viti-* Also V n
ated because of a sharp division between 'easterners' FORMAL
and 'westerners'.

vit·ri·ol /ˈvɪtriəʊl/. If you refer to what someone ◆◇◇◇
says or writes as **vitriol**, you disapprove of it be- N-UNCOUNT
cause it is full of bitterness and hate. ...*the vitriol he* PRAGMATICS
hurled at members of the press. ♦ **vit·ri·ol·ic** ADJ-GRADED
/ˌvɪtriˈɒlɪk/. ...*a vicious and vitriolic attack on him*
in one of the Sunday newspapers.

vi·tro /ˈviːtrəʊ/. See **in vitro**.

vi·tu·pera·tive /vɪˈtjuːpərətɪv, AM vaɪˈtuːp-/. **Vitu-** ADJ-GRADED:
perative remarks are full of hate, anger, or insults. ADJ n
...*one of journalism's most vituperative critics.* PRAGMATICS
FORMAL

viva, vivas. Pronounced /ˈvaɪvə/ for meaning 1, ◆◇◇◇
and /ˈviːvə/ for meaning 2. **1** A **viva** is an oral ex- N-COUNT
amination, especially at a university. BRITISH
2 People in crowds sometimes shout **'Viva!'** before EXCLAM
the name of a person or thing as a way of showing
their support for them. *Viva Gorbachev!*

vi·va·cious /vɪˈveɪʃəs/. If you describe someone as ADJ-GRADED
vivacious, you mean that they are lively, exciting, WRITTEN
and attractive. *She's beautiful, vivacious, and*
charming. ♦ **vi·vac·ity** /vɪˈvæsɪti/. ...*her exceptional* N-UNCOUNT
vitality, vivacity and wit.

viv·id /ˈvɪvɪd/. **1** If you describe memories and de- ◆◆◇◇
scriptions as **vivid**, you mean that they are very ADJ-GRADED
clear and detailed. ...*a very vivid dream.* ♦ **viv·id·ly** ADV-GRADED
He vividly remembers seeing his first match at the
Baseball Ground. ♦ **viv·id·ness** *The vividness of the* N-UNCOUNT
characterisation came as a complete surprise.
2 Something that is **vivid** is very bright in colour. ADJ-GRADED
...*a vivid blue sky.* ♦ **viv·id·ly** ...*vividly coloured* ADV-GRADED:
birds. ADV -ed/adj

vivi·sec·tion /ˌvɪvɪˈsekʃən/. **Vivisection** is the prac- N-UNCOUNT
tice of using live animals for scientific experiments.

vix·en /ˈvɪksən/ **vixens.** A **vixen** is a female fox. N-COUNT

viz. viz. is used to introduce a list of specific items WRITTEN
or examples. ...*two modules in Teaching English as a*
Foreign Language, viz. Principles and Methods of
Language Teaching and Applied Linguistics.

'V-neck, V-necks. A **V-neck** or a **V-neck** sweater is N-COUNT
a sweater with a neck that is in the shape of the
letter V.

vo·cabu·lary /vəʊˈkæbjʊləri, AM -leri/ **vocabu-** ◆◇◇◇
laries. 1 Your **vocabulary** is the total number of N-VAR
words you know in a particular language. *His speech*
is immature, his vocabulary limited. **2** The **vocabu-** N-SING
lary of a language consists of all the words in it.
3 The **vocabulary** of a subject consists of the words N-VAR:
that are typically used when discussing it. ...*the vo-* with supp
cabulary of natural science.

vo·cal /ˈvəʊkəl/. **1** You say that people are **vocal** ◆◆◇◇
when they speak forcefully about something that ADJ-GRADED
they feel strongly about. *He has been very vocal in*
his displeasure over the results. ♦ **vo·cal·ly** *These* ADV-GRADED
proposals were resisted by the developed countries,
most vocally by the United States. **2 Vocal** means in- ADJ: ADJ n
volving the use of the human voice, especially in
singing. ...*a wider range of vocal styles.* ♦ **vocally** *I* ADV
then begin to improvise melodies vocally.

vocal 'cords; also spelled **vocal chords.** Your **vo-** N-PLURAL
cal cords are the part of your throat that vibrates
when you speak.

vo·cal·ist /ˈvəʊkəlɪst/ **vocalists.** A **vocalist** is a ◆◇◇◇
singer who sings with a pop group. ...*the band's lead* N-COUNT
vocalist.

vo·cals /ˈvəʊkəlz/. In a pop song, the **vocals** are ◆◆◇◇
the singing, in contrast to the playing of instru- N-PLURAL
ments. *Johnson now sings backing vocals for Mica*
Paris.

vo·ca·tion /vəʊˈkeɪʃən/ **vocations.** If you have a ◆◇◇◇
vocation, you have a strong feeling that you are es- N-VAR
pecially suited to a particular job or role in life, especially one which involves serving other people.

You can also refer to this job or role as your **voca-tion**. *Her vocation is her work as an actress.*

vo·ca·tion·al /vəʊˈkeɪʃənəl/. **Vocational** training and skills are the training and skills needed for a particular job, particularly skilled manual work. *...vocational training in engineering.* ◆◇◇◇◇ ADJ

voca·tive /ˈvɒkətɪv/ **vocatives.** A **vocative** is a word such as a 'darling' or 'madam' which is used to address someone or attract their attention. N-COUNT

vo·cif·er·ous /vəˈsɪfərəs, AM vəʊs-/. If you describe someone as **vociferous**, you mean that they speak with great energy and determination, because they want their views to be heard. *He was a vociferous opponent of communism.* ♦ **vo·cif·er·ous·ly** *He vociferously opposed the state of emergency imposed by the government.* ◆◇◇◇◇ ADJ-GRADED ♦ ADV-GRADED

vod·ka /ˈvɒdkə/ **vodkas. Vodka** is a strong, clear, alcoholic drink. ◆◇◇◇◇ N-VAR

vogue /vəʊɡ/. **1** If there is a **vogue** for something, it is very popular and fashionable. *...the vogue for so-called health teas.* **2** If something is **in vogue**, it is very popular and fashionable. If it comes **into vogue**, it becomes very popular and fashionable. *...the hippie-ethnic look which came into vogue in the late 60s.* ◆◆◇◇◇ N-SING / PHRASE

voice /vɔɪs/ **voices, voicing, voiced. 1** When someone speaks or sings, you hear their **voice**. *'The police are here,' she said in a low voice.* **2** You can use **voice** to refer to someone's opinion or their right to express an opinion. *...when a government simply refuses to listen to the voice of the opposition... There were no dissenting voices.* **3** If you **voice** an opinion or feeling, you say what you think or feel. *Some scientists have voiced concern that the disease could be passed on to humans.* **4** In grammar, if a verb is in **the active voice**, the person who performs the action is the subject of the verb. If a verb is in **the passive voice**, the thing or person affected by the action is the subject of the verb. **5** If you **give voice** to an opinion, need, or desire, you express it aloud. *...a community radio run by the Catholic Church which gave voice to the protests of the slum-dwellers.* **6** If someone **finds** their **voice**, they are able to say or write what they really think or feel, often in spite of difficulty. *The poems which he wrote in the trenches are generally agreed to be those in which he found his true voice.* **7** If you **lose** your **voice**, you cannot speak for a while because of illness. *I had to be careful not to get a sore throat and lose my voice.* **8** If a number of people say something **with one voice**, they all express the same opinion about something. **9** ● **at the top of** your **voice**: see **top**. ◆◆◆◇◇ N-COUNT / N-COUNT / VERB Vn / N-SING the adj N / PHRASE FORMAL / PHRASE / PHRASE

'voice box, voice boxes. Your **voice box** is the top part of the passage that leads from your throat to your lungs and contains your vocal cords. N-COUNT

voiced /vɔɪst/. A **voiced** speech sound is produced with vibration of the vocal cords. ADJ TECHNICAL

voice·less /ˈvɔɪsləs/. A **voiceless** speech sound is produced without vibration of the vocal cords. *...the voiceless 'th'.* ADJ TECHNICAL

'voice mail. Voice mail is a system of sending messages over the telephone. Calls are answered by a machine which connects you to the person you want to leave a message for, and they can listen to their messages later. N-UNCOUNT

'voice-over, voice-overs; also spelled **voiceover.** A **voice-over** is a commentary or explanation in a film or television programme which is spoken by someone who is not seen. N-COUNT

void /vɔɪd/ **voids. 1** If you describe a situation or a feeling as a **void**, you mean that it seems empty because there is nothing interesting or worthwhile about it. *His death has left a void in the cricketing world. ...an aching void of loneliness.* **2** You can describe a large or frightening space as a **void**. *The ship moved silently through the black void.* **3** Something that is **void** is officially considered to have no value or authority. *The original elections were declared void by the former military ruler.* ● **null and void**: see **null**. ◆◇◇◇◇ N-COUNT / N-COUNT / ADJ v-link ADJ

voile /vɔɪl/. **Voile** is thin material which is used for making women's clothes, for example dresses, blouses, and scarves. N-UNCOUNT

vol., vols. Vol. is used as an abbreviation for **volume** when you are referring to one or more books in a series of books. ◆◆◆◇◇ WRITTEN

vola·tile /ˈvɒlətaɪl, AM -təl/. **1** A **volatile** situation is likely to change suddenly and unexpectedly. *The international oil markets have been highly volatile since the early 1970s... Armed soldiers guard the streets in this volatile atmosphere.* ♦ **vola·til·ity** /ˌvɒləˈtɪlɪti/. *He is keen to see a general reduction in arms sales given the volatility of the region.* **2** A **volatile** person is someone whose moods or attitudes change quickly and frequently. *Their relationship was always volatile... He has a volatile temper.* **3** A **volatile** substance quickly changes its state, for example from a liquid to a gas, and may be dangerous or explosive. ◆◆◇◇◇ ADJ-GRADED ♦ N-UNCOUNT / ADJ-GRADED / ADJ-GRADED TECHNICAL

vol·can·ic /vɒlˈkænɪk/. **Volcanic** means coming from or created by volcanoes. *...volcanic eruptions. ...volcanic ash... St Vincent is a lush, volcanic island.* ◆◇◇◇◇ ADJ

vol·ca·no /vɒlˈkeɪnəʊ/ **volcanoes.** A **volcano** is a mountain from which hot melted rock, gas, and ash from inside the earth sometimes burst. *The volcano erupted last year killing about 600 people... Etna is Europe's most active volcano.* ◆◆◇◇◇ N-COUNT

vole /vəʊl/ **voles.** A **vole** is a small animal that looks like a mouse but has very small ears and a short tail. Voles usually live in fields or near rivers. ● See also **water vole**. N-COUNT

vo·li·tion /vəˈlɪʃən, AM vəʊl-/. **1** If you do something **of** your **own volition**, you do it because you have decided for yourself that you will do it and not because someone else has told you to do it. *Coombes had gone to the police of his own volition.* **2** Your **volition** is the power you have to decide something for yourself. *We like to think that everything we do and everything we think is a product of our volition.* PHRASE / N-UNCOUNT FORMAL

vol·ley /ˈvɒli/ **volleys, volleying, volleyed. 1** In sports such as tennis and football, if someone **volleys**, they hit or kick the ball before it touches the ground. *He volleyed the ball spectacularly into the far corner of the net.* ► Also a noun. *She hit most of the winning volleys.* **2** A **volley** of gunfire is a lot of bullets that travel through the air at the same time. ◆◇◇◇◇ VERB: V / V n prep/adv / Also V n, V prep/adv / N-COUNT / N-COUNT

volley·ball /ˈvɒlibɔːl/. **Volleyball** is a sport in which two teams use their hands to hit a large ball over a high net. If you allow the ball to touch the ground, the other team wins a point. ◆◇◇◇◇ N-UNCOUNT

volt /vəʊlt/ **volts.** A **volt** is a unit used to measure the force of an electric current. ◆◇◇◇◇ N-COUNT

volt·age /ˈvəʊltɪdʒ/ **voltages.** The **voltage** of an electrical current is its force measured in volts. *The systems are getting smaller and using lower voltages. ...high-voltage power lines.* ◆◇◇◇◇ N-VAR

volte-face /ˌvɒlt ˈfɑːs/ **volte-faces.** If you say that someone's behaviour is a **volte-face**, you mean that they have changed their opinion or decision completely, so that it is the opposite of what it used to be. N-COUNT FORMAL

vol·uble /ˈvɒljʊbəl/. If someone is **voluble**, they talk a lot with great energy and enthusiasm. *She was voluble with excitement... Bert is a voluble, gregarious man.* ADJ-GRADED FORMAL

vol·ume /ˈvɒljuːm/ **volumes. 1** The **volume** of something is the amount of it that there is. *...an increase of around 0.6 per cent in the volume of sales during the month. ...the sheer volume of traffic.* **2** The **volume** of an object is the amount of space that it contains or occupies. *When egg whites are beaten they can rise to seven or eight times their original volume.* **3** A **volume** is one book in a series of books. *...the first volume of his autobiography.* **4** A **volume** is a book. *...a 125-page volume.* **5** If you say that something **speaks volumes** about someone or something, you mean that it gives you a lot of information about them. *What you wear speaks volumes about you.* ◆◆◆◇◇ N-COUNT / N-COUNT / N-COUNT / N-COUNT FORMAL / PHRASE

6 The **volume** of a radio or TV is the amount of sound it produces. *He turned down the volume.* N-UNCOUNT

vo·lu·mi·nous /və'lu:mɪnəs/. If you describe something as **voluminous**, you mean that it is very large in size or quantity. *...a voluminous trench coat... The FBI kept a voluminous file on Pablo Picasso.* ADJ-GRADED FORMAL

vol·un·tary /'vɒləntri, AM -teri/. **1** Voluntary actions or activities are done because someone chooses to do them and not because they have been forced to do them. *Motivation is usually high in classes where attendance is voluntary.* ♦ **vol·un·tar·i·ly** /'vɒləntrəli, AM -terɪli/. *He asked people to surrender their firearms voluntarily.* **2** Voluntary workers do work without being paid for it, because they want to do it. You describe the work they do as **voluntary** work. *He'd been working at the local hostel for the handicapped on a voluntary basis.* **3** A **voluntary** organization, for example a charity, is controlled by the people who have chosen to work for it, often without being paid, and is not officially organized by the government. *Some local authorities and voluntary organizations also run workshops for disabled people... It has been largely through the voluntary sector that the needs of victims have been met.* ◆◆◆◇◇ ADJ / ADV ADJ / ADJ: ADJ n

vol·un·teer /,vɒlən'tɪə/ **volunteers, volunteering, volunteered. 1** A **volunteer** is someone who does work without being paid for it, because they want to do it. *She now helps in a local school as a volunteer.* **2** A **volunteer** is someone who offers to do a particular task without being forced to do it. *What I want now is two volunteers to come down to the front.* **3** A **volunteer** is someone who chooses to join the armed forces, especially in wartime, as opposed to someone who is forced to join by law. *They fought as volunteers with the Afghan guerrillas. ...a mainly volunteer army.* **4** If you **volunteer** to do something, you offer to do it without being forced to do it. *Aunt Mary volunteered to clean up the kitchen... He volunteered for the army in 1939... She volunteered as a nurse in a soldiers' rest-home... He's volunteered his services as a chauffeur.* **5** If you **volunteer** information, you tell someone something without being asked. *The room was quiet; no one volunteered any further information... 'They were both great supporters of Franco,' Ryle volunteered... The next week, Phillida volunteered that they were getting on better.* ◆◆◆◇◇ N-COUNT / N-COUNT / N-COUNT / VERB V to-inf V for n V as n Also V / VERB V n V with quote V that FORMAL

vo·lup·tu·ous /və'lʌptʃuəs/. **1** If you describe a woman as **voluptuous**, you mean that she has large breasts and hips and is considered attractive in a sexual way. **2** Something such as a smell or taste that is **voluptuous** gives you a great deal of pleasure. *'Opium' is a provocative, sensual, and voluptuous fragrance which makes all your senses vibrate.* ♦ **vo·lup·tu·ous·ness** *...a magnificent wine with a soft voluptuousness more reminiscent of old-fashioned burgundy.* ◆◇◇◇◇ ADJ-GRADED / ADJ-GRADED / N-UNCOUNT

vom·it /'vɒmɪt/ **vomits, vomiting, vomited. 1** If you **vomit**, food and drink comes back up from your stomach and out through your mouth. *I thought I was going to vomit.* ♦ **vom·it·ing** Nausea, diarrhoea, and vomiting may accompany migraine. **2** Vomit is partly digested food that comes out of someone's mouth when they vomit. ◆◇◇◇◇ VERB: V n / N-UNCOUNT / N-UNCOUNT

voo·doo /'vu:du:/. Voodoo is a form of religion or witchcraft practised by some people in the West Indies, especially Haiti. N-UNCOUNT

vo·ra·cious /və'reɪʃəs, AM vɔːr-/. If you describe a person or their appetite for something as **voracious**, you mean that they want a lot of it. *Smith was a voracious book collector. ...the band's voracious appetite for fun.* ♦ **vo·ra·cious·ly** He read voraciously. ADJ-GRADED LITERARY / ADV-GRADED

vor·tex /'vɔːteks/ **vortices** /'vɔːtɪsiːz/. **1** A **vortex** is a mass of wind or water spinning round so fast that it pulls objects down into its centre. **2** If you refer to a situation as a **vortex**, you feel that you are being forced into it without being able to prevent it. ◆◇◇◇◇ N-COUNT / N-COUNT

When marriages break down children are swept into the vortex of their parents' embittered emotions.

vote /vəʊt/ **votes, voting, voted. 1** A **vote** is a choice made by a particular person or group in a meeting or an election. *He walked to the local polling centre to cast his vote... Mr Reynolds was re-elected by 102 votes to 60.* ● **One man one vote** or **one person one vote** is a system of voting in which every person in a group or country has the right to vote, and in which each individual's vote has equal value. **2** A **vote** is an occasion when a group of people make a decision by each person indicating his or her choice. The choice that most people support is accepted by the group. *They took a vote and decided not to do it.* **3** The **vote** is the total number of votes or voters in an election, or the number of votes received or cast by a particular group. *The vote was overwhelmingly in favour of the Democratic Party. ...a huge majority of the white male vote.* **4** If you have the **vote** in an election, or have a **vote** in a meeting, you have the legal right to indicate your choice. *In Italy women did not get the vote until 1945.* **5** See also **block vote**. **6** When you **vote**, you indicate your choice officially at a meeting or in an election, for example by raising your hand or writing on a piece of paper. *Are they going to vote for George Bush?... 52.5% of those questioned said they'd vote Labour... Both chambers plan to vote on that policy before January 15th... The parliament has voted by an overwhelming majority to suspend its declaration of independence... The Bridgeport Common Council voted 9:8 for a five percent tax increase.* ♦ **vot·ing** Voting began about two hours ago. **7** If a government or other organization **votes** money for something, they decide to spend the money in that way. *The Parliament voted more funds to help maintain American forces.* **8** If people **vote** someone a particular title, they choose that person to have that title. *Michael has been voted Player of the Year.* **9** If you **vote with your feet**, you show that you do not support something by leaving the place where it is happening or leaving the organization that is supporting it. *Thousands of citizens are already voting with their feet, and leaving the country.* ◆◆◆◆◆ N-COUNT / PHRASE / N-COUNT / N-SING / N-SING / VERB V for/against n V n V prep V by n to-inf/ prep V num prep/ to-inf Also V, V to-inf / N-UNCOUNT / VERB: V n for n Also V n n / VERB: V n n be V-ed n / PHRASE

vote down. If people **vote down** a proposal, they reject it, usually as a result of a formal vote. *The Congress voted down a motion to change the union's structure.* PHRASAL VB V P noun Also V n P

vote in. If people **vote in** a person or political party, they give enough votes to that person or party in an official election for them to hold power. *If he fails, then he will have little excuse in the eyes of those who voted him in.* PHRASAL VB V P noun V n P

vote out. If people **vote out** a governing party or leader, they give that person or party so few votes in an official election that they no longer hold power. *...Nicaragua, whose people voted out the pro-Soviet Sandinista government... They cannot join forces to vote her out of office.* PHRASAL VB V P noun V n P of n Also V n P

vote of 'confidence, votes of confidence. 1 A **vote of confidence** is a vote in which members of a group are asked to indicate that they still support the person or group in power, usually the government. **2** A **vote of confidence** is something that you say or do which shows that you approve of or support a person or a group. *The ten-year deal is a vote of confidence in a coal-fired station at a time when such plants face a loss of the market share to gas-fired ones.* ◆◇◇◇◇ N-COUNT / N-COUNT

vote of no 'confidence, votes of no confidence. A **vote of no confidence** is a vote in which members of a group are asked to indicate that they do not support the person or group in power, usually the government. *The opposition has called for a vote of no confidence in the government.* ◆◇◇◇◇ N-COUNT

vote of 'thanks, votes of thanks. A **vote of thanks** is a speech in which the speaker formally thanks someone for doing something. N-COUNT

vot·er /'vəʊtə/ **voters.** Voters are people who have the legal right to vote in elections, or people who are voting in a particular election. *Nearly a third of* ◆◆◆◆◇ N-COUNT

the voters were either still undecided or said they would abstain.

vouch /vaʊtʃ/ **vouches, vouching, vouched.**

vouch for. 1 If you say that you can or will **vouch for** someone, you mean that you can guarantee their good behaviour. *Kim's mother agreed to vouch for Maria and get her a job.* **2** If you say that you can **vouch for** something, you mean that you have evidence from your own personal experience that it is true or correct. *He cannot vouch for the accuracy of the story.* [PHRASAL VB / VP n / VP n]

vouch·er /ˈvaʊtʃə/ **vouchers.** A **voucher** is a ticket or piece of paper that can be used instead of money to pay for something. *The winners will each receive a voucher for a pair of cinema tickets. ...gift vouchers.* [◆◆◇◇◇ / N-COUNT]

vouch·safe /ˌvaʊtʃˈseɪf/ **vouchsafes, vouchsafing, vouchsafed.** If you **are vouchsafed** something, or if it **is vouchsafed** to you, you are given or granted it. *As we approached the summit we were vouchsafed a rare vision... Eric gritted his teeth and vouchsafed them a few more drops of brandy... 'He drives like a madman,' was all the information he vouchsafed.* [VERB / be V-ed n / V n n / V n / Also V n to n / FORMAL]

vow /vaʊ/ **vows, vowing, vowed. 1** If you **vow** to do something, you make a solemn promise or decision that you will do it. *I solemnly vowed that some day I would return to live in Europe... 'I'll kill him,' she vowed.* ▶ Also a noun. *I made a silent vow to be more careful in the future.* **2 Vows** are a particular set of solemn promises and decisions, for example those made by a couple at their wedding, or by monks and nuns. *I took my marriage vows and kept them... He had broken his vow of poverty.* [◆◆◇◇◇ / VERB: / V to-inf / V with quote / N-COUNT / N-COUNT]

vow·el /ˈvaʊəl/ **vowels.** A **vowel** is a sound such as the ones represented in writing by the letters 'a', 'e' 'i', 'o' and 'u', which you pronounce with your mouth open, allowing the air to flow through it. Compare **consonant**. *...the vowel in words like 'my' and 'thigh'. ...English vowel sounds.* [◆◇◇◇◇ / N-COUNT]

vox pop /ˌvɒks ˈpɒp/ **vox pops.** In a radio or television programme, a **vox pop** is an item consisting of a series of short interviews with ordinary members of the public. [N-VAR / BRITISH, / JOURNALISM]

voy·age /ˈvɔɪɪdʒ/ **voyages, voyaging, voyaged. 1** A **voyage** is a long journey on a ship or in a spacecraft. *...Columbus's voyage to the West Indies. ...the first space shuttle voyage.* **2** To **voyage** to a place means to travel there, especially by sea. *The Greenpeace flagship is voyaging through the Arctic cold of the Barents Sea.* ♦ **voy·ag·er, voyagers** *...fifteenth-century voyagers to the lands now called America and the Caribbean.* [◆◆◇◇◇ / N-COUNT / VERB / V prep/adv / N-COUNT]

vo·yeur /vwaɪˈɜː, AM vɔɪ-/ **voyeurs. 1** A **voyeur** is someone who gets sexual pleasure from secretly watching other people having sex or from watching them undress. **2** If you describe someone as a **voyeur**, you disapprove of them because you think they enjoy watching other people's sufferings or [N-COUNT / N-COUNT / PRAGMATICS]

problems. *The media has made unfeeling voyeurs of all of us.*

vo·yeur·ism /ˈvwaɪərɪzəm, AM vɔɪˈɜːr-/. **1 Voyeurism** is the practice of obtaining sexual pleasure by secretly watching other people having sex or undressing. ♦ **vo·yeur·is·tic** /ˌvwaɪəˈrɪstɪk, AM ˌvɔɪ-/. *...steamy, sexy slides and voyeuristic videos.* **2** If you describe someone's behaviour as **voyeurism**, you disapprove of them because you think they enjoy watching other people's sufferings or problems. *The BBC yesterday defended a series featuring dramatic crime reconstructions against suggestions of voyeurism.* ♦ **voyeuristic** *We as a society are growing more commercial and voyeuristic all the time.* [N-UNCOUNT / ADJ-GRADED / N-UNCOUNT / PRAGMATICS / ADJ-GRADED]

vs. vs. is an abbreviation for **versus**. *...England vs. Brazil.* [◆◆◇◇◇ / WRITTEN]

'V-sign, V-signs. In Britain, a **V-sign** is a rude gesture which is made by sticking up your first two fingers in a V shape, with the palm of your hand facing you. [N-COUNT]

VSO /ˌviː es ˈəʊ/. **VSO** is a British organization that sends skilled people to developing countries to work on projects that help the local community. **VSO** is an abbreviation for 'Voluntary Service Overseas'. [N-PROPER]

vul·gar /ˈvʌlgə/. **1** If you describe something as **vulgar**, you think it is in bad taste or of poor artistic quality. *I think it's a very vulgar house... It's vulgar to be famous.* ♦ **vul·gar·ity** /vʌlˈgærɪti/. *I hate the vulgarity of this room.* **2** If you describe someone or something as **vulgar**, you dislike them because they use bad language, or because they refer to sex or the body in an unpleasant way. *'Don't be vulgar,' she reprimanded. ...vulgar jokes.* ♦ **vulgarity** *It's his vulgarity that I can't take.* [◆◇◇◇◇ / ADJ-GRADED / PRAGMATICS / N-UNCOUNT / ADJ-GRADED / PRAGMATICS / N-UNCOUNT]

vul·ner·able /ˈvʌlnərəbəl/. **1** If someone or something is **vulnerable** to something, they have some weakness or disadvantage which makes them more likely to be harmed or affected by that thing. *People with high blood pressure are especially vulnerable to diabetes... Hotels and restaurants are acutely vulnerable to recession. ...attacks on vulnerable targets.* ♦ **vul·ner·abil·ity** /ˌvʌlnərəˈbɪlɪti/. *...anxieties about the country's vulnerability to invasion.* **2** Someone who is **vulnerable** is weak and without protection, with the result that they are easily hurt physically or emotionally. *Old people are particularly vulnerable members of our society.* ♦ **vulnerability, vulnerabilities** *...the special emotional vulnerability of childhood.* [◆◆◇◇◇ / ADJ-GRADED / N-UNCOUNT / ADJ-GRADED / N-VAR]

vul·ture /ˈvʌltʃə/ **vultures.** A **vulture** is a large bird which lives in hot countries and eats the flesh of dead animals. [◆◇◇◇◇ / N-COUNT]

vul·va /ˈvʌlvə/ **vulvas.** The **vulva** is the outer part of a woman's sexual organs. [N-COUNT / TECHNICAL]

vy·ing /ˈvaɪɪŋ/. **Vying** is the present participle of **vie.**

W w

W, w /ˈdʌbəljuː/ **W's, w's. 1 W** is the twenty-third letter of the English alphabet. **2 W** or **w** is an abbreviation for words beginning with w, such as 'west' or 'watt'. [N-VAR]

wacko /ˈwækəʊ/. If you say that someone is **wacko**, you are saying in an unkind way that you think they are strange and eccentric. [ADJ / PRAGMATICS / INFORMAL]

wacky /ˈwæki/ **wackier, wackiest;** also spelled **whacky**. If you describe something or someone as **wacky**, you mean that they are eccentric, unusual, [◆◇◇◇◇ / ADJ-GRADED / INFORMAL]

and often funny. *...a wacky new television comedy series.*

wad /wɒd/ **wads.** A **wad** of something such as paper, cloth, or money is a thick, tightly packed bundle or ball of it. *...a wad of banknotes.* [◆◇◇◇◇ / N-COUNT]

wad·dle /ˈwɒdl/ **waddles, waddling, waddled.** To **waddle** means to walk with short quick steps, swaying slightly from side to side. A person or animal that waddles usually has short legs and a fat body. *Ducks waddle up to the front door to be fed.* [VERB: V / V prep/adv]

wade /weɪd/ **wades, wading, waded. 1** If you
wade through something that makes it difficult to
walk, usually water or mud, you walk through it. *We
had to wade the river Genal.* **2** To **wade through** a
lot of information or correspondence means to
spend a lot of time and effort reading it or dealing
with it.

wade in or **wade into.** If someone **wades in** or
wades into something, they intervene in something
in a very determined and forceful way, often without
thinking about the consequences. *They don't just listen sympathetically, they wade in with remarks like, 'If
I were you ..'*

wad·er /ˈweɪdə/ **waders. 1** A **wader** is a bird with
long legs and a long neck, which lives near water
and feeds on fish. **2 Waders** are long rubber boots
which cover all of the legs and are worn by fishermen when they are standing in water.

wa·fer /ˈweɪfə/ **wafers.** A **wafer** is a thin crisp biscuit which is usually eaten with ice cream.

wafer-thin. 1 Wafer-thin means extremely thin
and flat. *Cut the fennel into wafer-thin slices. ...how
to slice radishes wafer-thin.* **2** If you succeed by a
wafer-thin margin, you succeed by a very small
amount.

waf·fle /ˈwɒfəl/ **waffles, waffling, waffled. 1** If
you say that someone **waffles**, you are critical of
them because they talk or write a lot without actually making any clear or important points. *There was
some bloke waffling about an airline ticket on the
phone.* ► **Waffle on** means the same as **waffle.**
*Whenever I open my mouth I don't half waffle on...
We don't want to waffle on about it all day.* ► Also a
noun. *He writes smug, sanctimonious waffle.*
2 A **waffle** is a thick crisp pancake with squares
marked on it.

waft /wɒft, wæft/ **wafts, wafting, wafted.** If
sounds, scents, or smoke **waft** through the air, or if
something **wafts** them, they move gently through
the air. *A slight breeze rose, wafting the heavy scent
of flowers past her.* ► Also a noun. *A waft of perfume
drifted into Ingrid's nostrils.*

wag /wæg/ **wags, wagging, wagged. 1** When a
dog **wags** its tail, it repeatedly waves its tail from
side to side. **2** If you **wag** your finger, you shake it
repeatedly and quickly from side to side, usually because you are annoyed with someone.
3 A **wag** is someone who makes jokes. *He's a bit of a
wag, his dad.*

wage /weɪdʒ/ **wages, waging, waged.**
1 Someone's **wages** are the amount of money that
is regularly paid to them for the work that they do.
His wages have gone up.
2 If a person, group, or country **wages** a campaign or a
war, they start it and continue it over a period of time.

wage packet, wage packets. People's wages
can be referred to as their **wage packet**. *They work
long hours in order to take home a fat wage packet.*

wa·ger /ˈweɪdʒə/ **wagers, wagering, wagered.**
1 If you **wager** on the result of a horse race, football
match, or other event, you give someone a sum of
money which they give you back with extra money
if the result is what you predicted, or which they
keep if it is not. *Golfers had wagered a good deal of
money on Nick Faldo winning.* ► Also a noun. *He
won his wager by building a 40-foot-high pyramid.*
2 If you say that you will **wager** that something is
the case, you mean that you are confident that it is the
case. *I'll wager she'll still make the same impact
when she's 70.*

wag·gle /ˈwægəl/ **waggles, waggling, waggled.**
If you **waggle** something, or if something **waggles**, it
moves up and down or from side to side with short
quick movements. *He was waggling his toes in his
socks.*

wag·on /ˈwægən/ **wagons;** also spelled **waggon** in
British English. **1** A **wagon** is a strong vehicle with
four wheels, usually pulled by horses or oxen and
used for carrying heavy loads. **2** A **wagon** is a large

container on wheels which is pulled by a train.
3 See also **station wagon.**

waif /weɪf/ **waifs.** If you refer to a child or young
woman as a **waif**, you mean that they are very thin
and look neglected.

wail /weɪl/ **wails, wailing, wailed. 1** If someone
wails, they make long, loud, high-pitched cries
which express sorrow or pain. *A mother wailing for
her lost child.* ► Also a noun. *There will be wails of
anguish from investors.* ♦ **wail·ing** *...the pitiful
wailing of the trapped and the wounded.* **2** If you
wail something, you say it in a loud high-pitched
voice that shows that you are unhappy or in pain.
*'Now look what you've done!' Shirley wailed... Prim-
rose, stupefied by tiredness, began to wail that she
was hungry.* **3** If something such as a siren or an
alarm **wails**, it makes long, high-pitched, piercing
sounds. ► Also a noun. *The wail of the bagpipe
could be heard in the distance.* ♦ **wailing** *We heard
a fearful wailing and screeching.*

waist /weɪst/ **waists. 1** Your **waist** is the middle
part of your body where it narrows slightly above
your hips. See picture headed **human body.** *Ricky
kept his arm round her waist.* ♦ **-waisted** *Sarah
looked slender-waisted, fragile and very beautiful.*
2 The **waist** of a garment such as a dress, coat, or
pair of trousers is the part of it which covers the
middle part of your body. ♦ **-waisted** *...high-
waisted dresses.*

waist·band /ˈweɪstbænd/ **waistbands.** A **waistband** is a narrow piece of material which is sewn on
to a pair of trousers, a skirt, or other item of clothing at the waist in order to strengthen it.

waist·coat /ˈweɪstkəʊt, ˈweɪskət/ **waistcoats.** A
waistcoat is a sleeveless piece of clothing with buttons, which people wear over a shirt. The American
word is **vest.** See picture headed **clothes.**

waist·line /ˈweɪstlaɪn/ **waistlines.** Your **waistline**
is your waist measurement. *A passion for cooking
does not necessarily have to be bad for your
waistline.*

wait /weɪt/ **waits, waiting, waited. 1** When you
wait for something or someone, you spend some
time, usually doing very little, because you cannot
act until that thing happens or that person arrives.
*Stop waiting for things to happen. Make them hap-
pen... I waited to see how she responded... We will
have to wait a week or so before we know whether
the operation is a success.* ♦ **wait·ing** *The waiting
became almost unbearable.* **2** A **wait** is a period of
time in which you do very little, before something
happens or before you can do something or see
someone. *...the four-hour wait for the organizers to
declare the result.* **3** If something **is waiting** for you,
it is ready for you to use, have, or do. *When we
came home we had a meal waiting for us... Ships
with unfurled sails wait to take them aboard... He
had a taxi waiting to take him to the train.* **4** If you
say that something can **wait**, you mean that it is not
important or urgent and so you will deal with it or
do it later. *I want to talk to you, but it can wait.*
5 You can use **wait** when you are telling someone
something that you expect them to find exciting, reassuring, or threatening. *If you think this all sounds
very exciting, just wait until you read the book.* **6** Wait
is used in expressions such as **wait a minute**, **wait a
second**, and **wait a moment** to interrupt someone
when they are speaking, for example because you object to what they are saying or because you want them
to repeat something.
7 If an employee **waits** on you, for example in a restaurant or hotel, they take orders from you and bring
you what you want. *Each student is expected to wait at
table for one week each semester.*
8 If you say that you **can't wait** to do something or **can
hardly wait** to do it, you are emphasizing that you are
very excited about it and eager to do it. **9** You say **'wait
for it'** to stop someone from doing something too
soon because you have not yet given them the command to do it. *Arms bend. Arms upward. Wait for it.*

Stretch. **10** You can use **'wait for it'** to indicate that you are about to say something that is amusing or surprising. *...a new 'ice cream' made from, wait for it, potatoes.* **11** If you tell someone to **wait and see**, you tell them that they must be patient or that they must not worry about what is going to happen in the future because they have no control over it. **12** • **ready and waiting:** see **ready**.   PHRASE / PRAGMATICS / BRITISH, INFORMAL / PHRASE

wait around; the form **wait about** is also used in British English. If you **wait around** or **wait about**, you stay in the same place, usually doing very little, because you cannot act before something happens or before someone arrives. *The attacker may have been waiting around for an opportunity to strike.*   PHRASAL VB / V P / V P for n / Also V P to-inf

wait in. If you **wait in**, you deliberately stay at home and do not go out, for example because someone is coming to see you. *If I'd waited in for you, I could have waited all day.*   PHRASAL VB / V P / V P for n

wait on. If you **are waiting on** something, you are waiting for it to happen, for example before you do or decide anything. *We cannot wait on the government to make changes at its own pace.*   PHRASAL VB / V P n / AMERICAN, INFORMAL

wait up. 1 If you **wait up**, you deliberately do not go to bed, especially because you are expecting someone to return home late at night. *I hope he doesn't expect you to wait up for him.* **2** If you ask someone to **wait up**, you are asking them to go more slowly or to stop and wait for you. *I was running down the hill shouting, 'Michael, Michael, man, wait up'.*   PHRASAL VB / V P / V P for n / V P / AMERICAN, INFORMAL

wait·er /ˈweɪtə/ **waiters.** A **waiter** is a man who works in a restaurant, serving people with food and drink.   ♦♦◇◇◇ / N-COUNT

waiting 'game, waiting games. If you play a **waiting game**, you deal with a situation by deliberately not doing anything, because you believe you will gain an advantage by acting later, or because you are waiting to see how the other people involved are going to act.   N-COUNT

'waiting list, waiting lists. A **waiting list** is a list of people who have asked for something which cannot be given to them immediately, for example medical treatment, housing, or training, and who must therefore wait until it is available. *There were 20,000 people on the waiting list for a home.*   ♦◇◇◇◇ / N-COUNT

'waiting room, waiting rooms; also spelled **waiting-room.** A **waiting room** is a room in a place such as a railway station or a doctor's surgery, where people can sit down while they wait.   ♦◇◇◇◇ / N-COUNT

wait·ress /ˈweɪtrəs/ **waitresses, waitressing, waitressed. 1** A **waitress** is a woman who works in a restaurant, serving people with food and drink. **2** A woman who **waitresses** works in a restaurant serving food and drink. ♦ **wait·ress·ing** *She does a bit of waitressing as a part-time job.*   ♦◇◇◇◇ / N-COUNT / VERB: V / N-UNCOUNT

waive /weɪv/ **waives, waiving, waived. 1** If you **waive** your right to something, for example legal representation, or if someone else **waives** it, you no longer have the right to receive it. **2** If someone **waives** a rule, they decide not to enforce it in a particular situation. *The art gallery waives admission charges on Sundays.*   ♦◇◇◇◇ / VERB: V n / VERB / V n

waiv·er /ˈweɪvə/ **waivers.** A **waiver** is when a person, government, or organization agrees to give up a right or claim or decides not to enforce a particular rule or law. *Non-members do not qualify for the tax waiver.*   ♦◇◇◇◇ / N-COUNT

wake /weɪk/ **wakes, waking, woke, woken;** the form **waked** is used in American English for the past tense. **1** When you **wake** or when someone or something **wakes** you, you become conscious again after being asleep. *Bob woke slowly to sunshine pouring in his window... She woke to find her dark room lit by flashing lights.* ▶ **Wake up** means the same as **wake.** *One morning I woke up and felt something was wrong... At dawn I woke him up and said we were leaving.* **2** Your **waking** hours are the times when you are awake rather than asleep. **3** A **wake** is a gathering of people who have collected together to mourn someone's death. **4** The **wake** of a boat or other object moving in water   ♦♦♦◇◇ / V-ERG: V / V n to-inf / Also V P / PHRASAL VB / ERG / V P / V n P / PHRASE / N-COUNT

is the track of waves that it makes behind it as it moves through the water. **5** If one thing follows **in the wake of** another, it happens after the other thing is over, often as a result of it. *The governor has enjoyed a huge surge in the polls in the wake of last week's convention.* **6** If you leave something or someone **in** your **wake**, you leave them behind you as you go. *Adam stumbles on, leaving a trail of devastation in his wake.*   PHR-PREP / PHRASE

wake up. If something such as an activity **wakes** you **up**, it makes you more alert and ready to do things after you have been lazy or inactive. *A cool shower wakes up the body and boosts circulation.* • See also **wake 1.**   PHRASAL VB / V P / V P noun

wake up to. If you **wake up to** something, you become aware of it. *People should wake up to the fact that people with disabilities have got a vote as well.*   PHRASAL VB / V P P n

wake·ful /ˈweɪkfʊl/. Someone who is **wakeful** finds it difficult to get to sleep and wakes up very often when they should be sleeping. ♦ **wake·ful·ness**   ADJ-GRADED / N-UNCOUNT

wak·en /ˈweɪkən/ **wakens, wakening, wakened.** When you **waken**, or when someone or something **wakens** you, you wake from sleep. *The noise of a door slamming wakened her.* ▶ **Waken up** means the same as **waken.** *Drink this coffee – it will waken you up.*   V-ERG: V / V n / LITERARY / PHRASAL VB / ERG / V n P / Also V P

walk /wɔːk/ **walks, walking, walked. 1** When you **walk**, you move forward by putting one foot in front of the other on the ground at a regular fairly slow pace. *They would stop the car and walk a few steps... When I was your age I walked five miles to school.* ▶ Also a noun. *She slowed to a steady walk.* **2** If you go for a **walk**, you walk somewhere, usually for pleasure. *He often took long walks in the hills.* **3** A **walk** of a particular distance is the distance which a person has to walk to get somewhere. *The church is a short walk from Piazza Dante.* **4** A **walk** is a route suitable for walking along for pleasure. *...a 2 mile coastal walk.* **5** If you **walk** someone somewhere, you walk there with them in order to show politeness or to make sure that they get there safely. **6** If you **walk** your dog, you take it for a walk in order to keep it healthy. **7** • to be **walking on air:** see **air.** • to **walk tall:** see **tall.**   ♦♦♦♦ / VERB: V / V n / V n to n / N-SING / N-COUNT / N-SING: supp N, N of n / N-COUNT / VERB: V n prep/adv / VERB: V n

walk away. If you **walk away** from a problem or a difficult situation, you do nothing about it or do not face any bad consequences from it. *No one knows you're a part of this. You can just walk away.*   PHRASAL VB / V P from n / V P

walk away with. If you **walk away with** something such as a prize, you win it or achieve it very easily.   PHRASAL VB / JOURNALISM

walk in on. If you **walk in on** someone, you enter the room that they are in while they are doing something private, and this causes an embarrassing situation. *His wife walked in on him making love.*   PHRASAL VB / V P P n

walk into. 1 If you **walk into** an unpleasant situation, you become involved in it without expecting to, especially because you have been careless. **2** If you **walk into** a job, you manage to get it very easily.   PHRASAL VB / V P n / V P n / INFORMAL

walk off with. 1 If someone **walks off with** something that does not belong to them, they take it without permission. **2** If you **walk off with** something such as a prize, you win it or achieve it very easily.   PHRASAL VB / V P P n / V P P n / JOURNALISM

walk out. 1 If you **walk out** of a meeting, a performance, or an unpleasant situation, you leave it suddenly, in order to show that you are angry or bored. *Mr. Mason walked out during the performance.* **2** If someone **walks out** on their family or their partner, they leave them suddenly and go to live somewhere else. *She had walked out and gone to live in Bath with her granny.* **3** If workers **walk out**, they stop doing their work for a period of time, usually in order to try to get more pay or conditions for themselves.   PHRASAL VB / V P of n / V P / V P on n / V P / V P

walk over. If someone **walks over** you, they treat you very badly. *You let your children walk all over you.*   PHRASAL VB / V P

walk·about /ˈwɔːkəbaʊt/ **walkabouts.** A **walkabout** is a walk by a king, queen, or other important person through a public place in order to meet people in an informal way.   N-COUNT / USU BRITISH

walk·er /ˈwɔːkə/ **walkers. 1** A **walker** is a person who walks, especially in the countryside for pleasure or in order to keep healthy. **2** A **walker** is a   ♦◇◇◇◇ / N-COUNT / N-COUNT

special kind of frame which is designed to help babies or disabled or ill people to walk.

walkie-talkie /ˌwɔːki ˈtɔːki/ **walkie-talkies.** A walkie-talkie is a small portable radio which you can talk into and hear messages through so that you can communicate with someone far away. N-COUNT

walk·ing /ˈwɔːkɪŋ/. **1** Walking is the activity of taking walks for exercise or pleasure, especially in the country. *I've started to do a lot of walking and cycling.* **2** You can use walking in expressions like a **walking disaster** or a **walking dictionary** in order to emphasize in a humorous way a particular attribute that someone has, for example the fact that they cause a lot of disasters or that they know a lot of difficult words. ◆◇◇◇ N-UNCOUNT ADJ: ADJ n PRAGMATICS

'walking stick, walking sticks. A walking stick is a long wooden stick which a person can lean on while walking. N-COUNT

Walk·man /ˈwɔːkmən/ **Walkmans.** A Walkman is a small cassette player with very light headphones which people carry around so that they can listen to music while they are doing something. **Walkman** is a trademark. ◆◇◇◇ N-COUNT

,walk of 'life, walks of life. The walk of life that you come from is the position that you have in society and the kind of job you have. *...meeting people from all walks of life.* ◆◇◇◇ N-COUNT

'walk-on. A walk-on part in a play or film is a very small part which usually does not involve any speaking. ◆◇◇◇ ADJ: ADJ n

walk·out /ˈwɔːkaʊt/ **walkouts.** **1** A walkout is a strike. **2** If there is a walkout during a meeting, some or all of the people attending it leave in order to show their disapproval of something that has happened at the meeting. N-COUNT N-COUNT

walk·over /ˈwɔːkəʊvə/ **walkovers.** If you say that a competition or contest is a walkover, you mean that it is won very easily. N-COUNT

'walk-up, walk-ups. A walk-up is a tall apartment block which has no lift. You can also refer to an apartment in such a block as a walk-up. *...a tiny fifth floor walk-up in New York's East Village.* ◆◇◇◇ N-COUNT AMERICAN

walk·way /ˈwɔːkweɪ/ **walkways.** A walkway is a passage or pathway for pedestrians to use. Walkways are often raised above the ground. ◆◇◇◇ N-COUNT

wall /wɔːl/ **walls, walling, walled.** **1** A wall is one of the vertical sides of a building or room. See picture headed **house and flat.** *...the wall of the church. ...the bedroom walls.* ◆ **-walled** *...a glass-walled elevator.* **2** A wall is a long narrow vertical structure made of stone or brick that surrounds or divides an area of land. *The well is surrounded by a wall only 12 inches high.* ◆ **walled** *...a walled rose garden.* **3** The wall of something that is hollow is its side. *He ran his fingers along the inside walls of the box.* **4** A wall of something is a large amount of it forming a high vertical barrier. *She gazed at the wall of books.* **5** You can describe something as a wall of a particular kind when it acts as a barrier preventing people from understanding something or someone. *The police say they met the usual wall of silence.* **6** See also **cavity wall, dry-stone wall, fly-on-the-wall, hole-in-the-wall, off-the-wall, retaining wall, sea wall, wall-to-wall.** **7** If you say that you **are banging your head against a wall,** you are emphasizing that you are frustrated because someone is stopping you from making progress in something. **8** If you have your **back to the wall,** you are in a very difficult situation and can see no way out of it. **9** If you say that you **are climbing the walls,** you are emphasizing that you feel very frustrated, nervous, or anxious. **10** If you say that something or someone **is driving** you **up the wall,** you are emphasizing that they annoy and irritate you. **11** If a person or company **goes to the wall,** they lose all their money and their business fails. **12** ◆ **fly on the wall:** see **fly.** ● **the writing is on the wall:** see **writing.** ◆◆◆◆ N-COUNT COMB N-COUNT ADJ N-COUNT: with supp N-COUNT: with supp N-COUNT: with supp PHRASE PRAGMATICS INFORMAL PHRASE INFORMAL PHRASE PRAGMATICS PHRASE PRAGMATICS INFORMAL PHRASE INFORMAL

wall in. If someone or something **is walled in,** they are surrounded or enclosed by a wall or barrier. PHRASAL VB usu passive

wall off. If part of a place **is walled off,** it is separated PHRASAL VB

from the rest of the place by a wall. *The side alley was walled off from the back garden. ...a ring of cliffs that walled off the surrounding wilderness.* be V-ed P from n V P noun

wall up. If someone **walls up** a room, or if someone **is walled up** in it, every exit to the room is blocked by walls so that nobody can get in or out. *They had walled up her room because of the fear that things might be infected.* PHRASAL VB V P noun Also V n P

wal·la·by /ˈwɒləbi/ **wallabies.** A wallaby is an animal similar to a small kangaroo that is found in Australia and New Guinea. N-COUNT

wall·covering /ˈwɔːlkʌvərɪŋ/ **wallcoverings;** also spelled **wall covering.** Wallcovering is material such as wallpaper that is used to decorate the walls on the inside of a building. N-VAR

wal·let /ˈwɒlɪt/ **wallets.** A wallet is a small flat folded case where you can keep banknotes and credit cards. ◆◇◇◇ N-COUNT

wall·flower /ˈwɔːlflaʊə/ **wallflowers.** **1** A wallflower is a plant that is grown in gardens and has sweet-smelling flowers. N-COUNT

2 If you say that someone is a wallflower, you mean that they are shy and do not get involved in dancing or talking to people at social events. N-COUNT

wal·lop /ˈwɒləp/ **wallops, walloping, walloped.** To wallop someone or something means to hit them very hard. *Once, she walloped me over the head with a frying pan.* ▶ Also a noun. *With one brutal wallop, Clarke flattened him.* VERB: V n V n prep INFORMAL N-COUNT

wal·low /ˈwɒləʊ/ **wallows, wallowing, wallowed.** **1** If you say that someone is wallowing in an unpleasant situation, you are criticizing them for being deliberately unhappy. *His tired mind continued to wallow in self-pity.* **2** If a person or animal **wallows** in water or mud, they lie or roll about in it slowly for pleasure. ◆◇◇◇ VERB PRAGMATICS V in n VERB: V in n

wall·paper /ˈwɔːlpeɪpə/ **wallpapers, wallpapering, wallpapered.** **1** Wallpaper is thick coloured or patterned paper that is used for covering and decorating the walls of rooms. **2** If someone **wallpapers** a room, they cover the walls with wallpaper. **3** If you describe music, television, or art as **wallpaper,** you are critical of it because there is nothing interesting or difficult to understand about it, so that people find it pleasant and soothing but do not pay any attention to it. *...bland, wallpaper music.* ◆◆◇◇ N-VAR VERB: V n N-UNCOUNT PRAGMATICS

'Wall Street. Wall Street is a street in New York where the Stock Exchange and important banks are. Wall Street is often used to refer to the financial business carried out there and to the people who work there. ◆◆◆◇ N-PROPER

,wall-to-'wall. **1** A wall-to-wall carpet covers the floor of a room completely. **2** You can use wall-to-wall to describe something that fills or seems to fill all the available time or space. *...television's wall-to-wall soccer coverage.* ADJ ADJ

wal·ly /ˈwɒli/ **wallies.** If you refer to someone as a wally, you think that they are stupid or foolish. N-COUNT BRITISH, INFORMAL ◆◇◇◇

wal·nut /ˈwɔːlnʌt/ **walnuts.** **1** Walnuts are edible nuts which have a wrinkled shape and a very hard round shell that is light brown in colour. **2** A walnut tree or a walnut is a tree on which walnuts grow. ▶ Walnut is the wood of this tree. N-VAR N-VAR N-UNCOUNT

wal·rus /ˈwɔːlrəs/ **walruses.** A walrus is an animal which lives in the sea. It has long whiskers and two tusks pointing downwards. N-COUNT

waltz /wɔːlts/ **waltzes, waltzing, waltzed.** **1** A waltz is a piece of music with a rhythm of three beats in each bar, which people can dance to. **2** A waltz is a dance in which two people hold each other and move around the floor doing special steps in time to waltz music. **3** If you waltz with someone, you dance a waltz with them. *Couples are waltzing round the wooden floor... He learnt to waltz and foxtrot.* ◆◇◇◇ N-COUNT N-COUNT V-RECIP V with n pl-n V adv/ prep V

4 If you say that someone waltzes somewhere, you mean that they do something in a relaxed and confident way. *She's probably got herself a new man and gone waltzing off with him.* VERB V adv/prep INFORMAL

wan /wɒn/. If you describe someone as **wan**, you mean that they look pale and tired. ♦ **wan·ly** Marcia smiled wanly and shook her head.

ADJ-GRADED
LITERARY
ADV-GRADED

wand /wɒnd/ **wands.** A **wand** is the same as a **magic wand**. You can't simply wave a wand and get rid of nuclear weapons.

N-COUNT

wan·der /'wɒndə/ **wanders, wandering, wandered.** 1 If you **wander** in a place, you walk around there in a casual way, often without intending to go in any particular direction. Those who do not have relatives to return to are left to wander the streets. ▶ Also a noun. A wander around any market will reveal stalls piled high with vegetables. 2 If a person or animal **wanders** from a place where they are supposed to stay, they move away from the place without going in a particular direction. To keep their bees from wandering, beekeepers feed them sugar solutions. 3 If your mind **wanders** or your thoughts **wander**, you stop concentrating on something and start thinking about other things. Grace allowed her mind to wander to other things. 4 If your eyes **wander**, you stop looking at one thing and start looking around at other things. His eyes wandered restlessly around the room.

VERB:
V prep/adv
V n

N-SING:
a N
VERB:
V adv/prep
V

VERB:
V prep/adv

VERB: V
V prep/adv

wan·der·er /'wɒndərə/ **wanderers.** A **wanderer** is a person who travels around rather than settling in one place.

N-COUNT

wan·der·ing /'wɒndərɪŋ/. **Wandering** is used to describe people who travel around rather than staying in one place for a long time. ...a band of wandering musicians.

ADJ: ADJ n
LITERARY

wan·der·ings /'wɒndərɪŋz/. Someone's **wanderings** are journeys that they make from place to place without staying in one place for a long time. On his wanderings he's picked up Spanish, Italian, French and a smattering of Russian.

N-PLURAL

wane /weɪn/ **wanes, waning, waned.** 1 If a condition, attitude, or emotion **wanes**, it becomes gradually weaker, often so that it eventually disappears. His interest in these sports began to wane. ...her mother's waning strength. ● **wax and wane** see **wax**. 2 If a condition, attitude, or emotion is **on the wane**, it is becoming weaker. The influence of the Communist Party was clearly on the wane. 3 When the moon is **waning**, it is showing a smaller area of brightness each day as it changes from a full moon to a new moon.

♦◇◇◇◇
VERB
V
V-ing

PHRASE

VERB: V

wan·gle /'wæŋgəl/ **wangles, wangling, wangled.** If you **wangle** something that you want, you manage to get it by being clever or persuasive. He had wangled his way into the country without a visa... I asked the Captain to wangle us three tickets to Athens... Amanda had wangled a job for Robyn.

VERB: V n
V way prep/
adv
V n n
V n for n
INFORMAL

wan·na /'wɒnə/. **Wanna** is used to represent the words **want to** when they are pronounced informally. I wanna be married to you. Do you wanna be married to me?

WRITTEN

wanna·be /'wɒnəbiː/ **wannabes;** also spelled **wannabee.** If you call someone a **wannabe**, you are saying in an unkind way that they are trying very hard to be like another person or group of people. ...a feeble James Dean wannabe.

N-COUNT
PRAGMATICS
INFORMAL

want /wɒnt/ **wants, wanting, wanted.** 1 If you **want** something, you feel a desire or a need for it. I want a drink... People wanted to know who this talented designer was... They began to want their father to be the same as other daddies... They didn't want people staring at them... He wanted his power recognised. 2 You can say that you **want** to say something to indicate that you are about to say it. I want to say how really delighted I am that you're having a baby. 3 If you ask someone if they **want** something, you are offering them something or inviting them to do something. Do you want another cup of coffee?... Do you want to leave your bike here? 4 If you say to someone that you **want** something or ask them if they **want** to do it, you are firmly telling them what to do. I want an explanation from you, Jeremy... Do you want to tell me what all this is about?... If you

♦♦♦♦
VB: no cont,
no passive
V n
V to-inf
V n to-inf
V n -ing/ed

VB: no cont,
no passive
PRAGMATICS
V to-inf

VB: no cont,
no passive
PRAGMATICS
V n to-inf

VB: no cont,
no passive
PRAGMATICS
V n to-inf
V n to-inf

have a problem with that, I want you to tell me right now.

5 You say **if you want** when you are making or agreeing to an offer or suggestion in a casual way. Mary says you're welcome to stay the night if you want. 6 People sometimes say '**I don't want** to be rude', for example, or '**without wanting** to be rude' as a way of apologizing or warning you in advance when they are going to say something which they think might upset, annoy, or worry you. Without wanting to sound mean about it, these things all have to come from a budget. 7 If you say to someone '**what do you want?**', you are asking them in a rather rude or angry way why they have come to the place where you are or why they want to speak to you.

PHRASE
PRAGMATICS
PHRASE
PRAGMATICS

PHRASE
PRAGMATICS

8 If you say that something **wants** doing, you think that it needs to be done. The windows wanted cleaning. 9 If you tell someone that they **want** to do a particular thing, you are advising them to do it. You want to be careful what you say. 10 If someone is **wanted** by the police, the police are searching for them because they are thought to have committed a crime. He was wanted for the murder of a magistrate. ♦ **want·ed** He is one of the most wanted criminals in Europe. 11 If you **want** someone, you have a great desire to have sex with them. 12 If a child is **wanted**, its mother or another person loves it and is willing to look after it. I want this baby very much. 13 If someone **wants** you in a particular place or role, they desire you to be in that place or role. Albie wants you in his office... I want you out of here.

VB: no cont,
no passive
V -ing
INFORMAL

VB: no cont,
no passive
V to-inf
INFORMAL

VERB:
be V-ed
be V-ed for n

ADJ-GRADED:
ADJ n

VERB: V n

VERB:
be V-ed
V n

VB: no cont
V n prep/adv

14 A **want of** something is a lack of it. The men were daily becoming weaker from want of rest. ● If you do something **for want of** something else, you do it because the other thing is not available or not possible. Many of them had gone into teaching for want of anything better to do. 15 **Want** is the same as poverty. He said they were fighting for freedom of speech, freedom of worship, and freedom from want. 16 Your **wants** are your wishes or the things that you want. You have to respect their wants.

N-SING
FORMAL
PHRASE

N-UNCOUNT
FORMAL

N-PLURAL

want out. If you **want out**, you no longer want to be involved in a plan, project, or situation that you are part of. I just want out of the relationship.

PHRASAL VB
V P
V P of n
INFORMAL

want·ing /'wɒntɪŋ/. If you find something or someone **wanting**, they are not of as high a standard as you think they should be. He analysed his game and found it wanting.

ADJ-GRADED

wan·ton /'wɒntən/. 1 A **wanton** action deliberately causes harm, damage, or waste without there being any reason for it. ...this unnecessary and wanton destruction of our environment. ♦ **wan·ton·ly** His diaries were wantonly destroyed. 2 If someone describes a woman as **wanton**, they disapprove of her because they think she behaves in an immoral or immodest way.

♦◇◇◇◇
ADJ

ADV-GRADED
ADJ-GRADED
PRAGMATICS
DATED

war /wɔː/ **wars.** 1 A **war** is a period of fighting or conflict between countries or states. They've been at war for the last fifteen years. ● If a country **goes to war**, it starts fighting a war. 2 **War** is intense economic competition between countries or organizations. ...a trade war. 3 If you make **war** on someone or something that you are opposed to, you do things to stop them succeeding. She has been involved in the war against organised crime. 4 If two people, countries, or organizations have a **war of words**, they criticize each other because they strongly disagree about something. 5 See also **war-ring, civil war, Cold War, council of war**.

♦♦♦♦
N-VAR

PHRASE
N-VAR

N-VAR

PHRASE
JOURNALISM

war·ble /'wɔːbəl/ **warbles, warbling, warbled.** 1 When a bird **warbles**, it sings pleasantly. A flock of birds was already warbling a cheerful morning chorus. 2 If someone **warbles**, they sing, often with a high-pitched or quavering voice. ...singers warbling 'Over the Rainbow'. ▶ Also a noun. ...the soft warble of her speaking voice. 3 When machines such as telephones **warble**, they make a soft, low sound on two alternating notes.

VERB: V
V n

VERB: V
V n

N-SING

VERB: V

war·bler /ˈwɔːblə/ **warblers.** Warblers are a family N-COUNT
of small birds that have a pleasant song.

'war chest, war chests. A war chest is a fund to N-COUNT
finance a project such as a political campaign.

ward /wɔːd/ **wards, warding, warded. 1** A **ward** ◆◆◇◇◇
is a room in a hospital which has beds for many N-COUNT
people, often people who need similar treatment.
2 A **ward** is a district which forms part of a political N-COUNT
constituency or local council. **3** Someone's **ward** is N-COUNT
a child who they are responsible for as their ap- LEGAL
pointed guardian. If a child is made a **ward of
court**, a court of law decides that they will be responsible for the child.

ward off. To **ward off** a danger or illness means to PHRASAL VB
prevent it from affecting you or harming you. *She may* V P noun
have put up a fight to try to ward off her assailant. Also V n P

war·den /ˈwɔːdən/ **wardens. 1** A **warden** is a per- ◆◇◇◇
son who is responsible for a particular place or N-COUNT
thing, and for making sure that the laws or regulations that relate to it are obeyed. *Game wardens
were appointed to enforce hunting laws.* ● See also
traffic warden. 2 A **warden** is someone who works N-COUNT
in a prison supervising the prisoners. The American BRITISH
word is **guard. 3** The **warden** of a prison is the per- N-COUNT
son in charge of it. The British word is **governor.** AMERICAN

war·der /ˈwɔːdə/ **warders.** A **warder** is a person N-COUNT
who works in a prison and is in charge of prisoners. BRITISH
The American word is **guard.**

ward·robe /ˈwɔːdrəub/ **wardrobes. 1** A **wardrobe** ◆◆◇◇◇
is a tall cupboard in which you can hang your N-COUNT
clothes. **2** Someone's **wardrobe** is the total collec- N-COUNT
tion of clothes that they have. **3** The **wardrobe** in a N-COUNT:
theatre company consists of the actors' and ac- also the N
tresses' costumes.

ware /weə/ **wares. 1** -**ware** is used to form nouns ◆◇◇◇◇
that refer to objects that are made of a particular COMB
material, or that are used for a particular purpose.
...porcelain cooking ware. **2** Someone's **wares** are N-PLURAL
the things that they sell, usually in the street or in a DATED
market.

ware·house /ˈweəhaus/ **warehouses.** A ware- ◆◆◇◇◇
house is a large building where raw materials or N-COUNT
manufactured goods are stored until they are exported to other countries or distributed to shops to
be sold. ♦ **ware·hous·ing** /ˈweəhauzɪŋ/. **Ware-** N-UNCOUNT
housing is the act or process of storing goods in a
warehouse.

war·fare /ˈwɔːfeə/. **1** Warfare is the activity of ◆◆◇◇◇
fighting a war. *...the threat of chemical warfare.* N-UNCOUNT
2 Warfare is sometimes used to refer to any violent N-UNCOUNT
struggle or conflict. *Much of the violence is related to
drugs and gang warfare.*

war·head /ˈwɔːhed/ **warheads.** A **warhead** is the ◆◇◇◇◇
front part of a bomb or missile where the explosives N-COUNT
are carried.

war·horse /ˈwɔːhɔːs/ **warhorses.** You can refer to N-COUNT
someone such as an old soldier or politician who is
still active and aggressive as a **warhorse.**

war·like /ˈwɔːlaik/. **Warlike** people seem aggressive ADJ-GRADED
and eager to start a war. *...increased warlike rhetoric
from both sides.*

war·lord /ˈwɔːlɔːd/ **warlords.** If you describe a ◆◇◇◇◇
leader of a country or organization as a **warlord**, N-COUNT
you are critical of them because they have achieved PRAGMATICS
power by behaving in an aggressive and violent
way.

warm /wɔːm/ **warmer, warmest; warms,** ◆◆◆◇
warming, warmed. 1 Something that is **warm** ADJ-GRADED
has some heat but not enough to be hot. *Because it
was warm, David wore only a white cotton shirt.
...warm water.* **2** Warm clothes and blankets are ADJ-GRADED
made of a material such as wool which protects you
from the cold. ♦ **warm·ly** *Remember to wrap up* ADV-GRADED
warmly on cold days. **3** Warm colours have red or ADJ-GRADED
yellow in them rather than blue or green, and make
you feel comfortable and relaxed. **4** A **warm** person ADJ-GRADED
is friendly and shows a lot of affection or enthusi-
asm in their behaviour. ♦ **warmly** *New members* ADV-GRADED:
are warmly welcomed... He greeted me warmly. **5** If ADV with v
you **warm** a part of your body, or if something hot VERB: V n

warms it, it stops feeling cold and starts to feel hotter. **6** If you **warm** to a person or an idea, you be- VERB
come fonder of the person or more interested in the V to n
idea. *Those who got to know him better warmed to
his openness and honesty.*

warm up. 1 If you **warm** something **up**, or if it PHRASAL VB
warms up, it gets hotter. *Have you warmed the potato* ERG
up, Mum?... All that she would have to do was warm V n P
up the pudding... The weather had warmed up. **2** If V P
you **warm up** for an event such as a race, you prepare V P
yourself for it by doing exercises or by practising just
before it starts. ● See also **warm-up. 3** When a ma- ERG:
chine or engine **warms up**, or someone **warms** it **up**, V P
it becomes ready for use a little while after being V P noun
switched on or started. *We spent a frustrating five* Also V n P
minutes while the pilot warmed up the engines. **4** If a ERG:
comedian or speaker **warms up** an audience, or the V P
audience **warms up**, the audience is prepared for the V P noun
main act or speaker by being told jokes or funny stories, so that they are in a good mood. *The crowd began
to warm up.*

warm-'blooded. A **warm-blooded** animal has a ADJ
relatively high body temperature which remains
constant and is not affected by the surrounding
temperature.

warm-'hearted. A **warm-hearted** person is ADJ-GRADED
friendly and affectionate.

war·monger /ˈwɔːmʌŋgə/ **warmongers.** If you N-COUNT
describe a politician or leader as a **warmonger**, you PRAGMATICS
disapprove of them because you think they are encouraging people to start or join a war.

warmth /wɔːmθ/. **1** The **warmth** of something is ◆◇◇◇◇
the heat that it has or produces. *...the warmth of the* N-UNCOUNT
fire. **2** The **warmth** of something such as a garment N-UNCOUNT
or blanket is the protection that it gives you against
the cold. **3** Someone who has **warmth** is friendly N-UNCOUNT
and enthusiastic in their behaviour towards other
people.

'warm-up, warm-ups. A **warm-up** is something ◆◇◇◇◇
that prepares you for an activity or event, usually N-COUNT
because it is a short practice or example of what the
activity or event will involve. *The exercises can be
fun and a good warm-up for the latter part of the
programme.*

warn /wɔːn/ **warns, warning, warned. 1** If you ◆◆◆◆◇
warn someone about something such as a possible VERB:
danger or problem, you tell them about it so that V n of/about n
they are aware of it. *Friends warned me that chil-* V n that
dren were expensive... Analysts warned that Europe's V that
most powerful economy may be facing trouble. **2** If VERB:
you **warn** someone not to do something, you advise V n to-inf
them not to do it so that they can avoid possible V with quote
danger or punishment. *'Don't do anything yet,' he* V n against n/
warned. 'Too risky.'... 'Keep quiet, or they'll all come -ing
out,' they warned him... Officials warned people n/-ing
against eating or picking mushrooms. **3** If someone CONVENTION
says to you **'be warned'**, they are advising you to be PRAGMATICS
cautious, because there are risks that you may not
have thought about. *But be warned: this is not a
cheap option.*

warn away or **warn off.** If you **warn** someone PHRASAL VB
away or **warn** them **off**, you tell them to go away or to V n P
stop doing something because of possible danger or V n P from n/
punishment. *Analysts warn us away from drawing* -ing
any conclusions... He spends his spare time visiting V n P n/-ing
schools to warn pupils off drugs. Also V P noun

warn·ing /ˈwɔːnɪŋ/ **warnings. 1** A **warning** is ◆◆◆◇◇
something which is said or written to tell people of N-COUNT
a possible danger, problem, or other unpleasant
thing that might happen. **2** A **warning** is an ad- N-VAR
vance notice of something that will happen, often
something unpleasant or dangerous. *The soldiers
opened fire without warning.* **3** Warning actions or ADJ: ADJ n
signs give a warning. *The driver apparently ignored
warning signals.*

'war of 'nerves. A **war of nerves** is a conflict in N-SING
which the opposing sides try to weaken each other
psychologically, for example by making each other
frightened or telling lies about each other.

warp /wɔːp/ **warps, warping, warped. 1** If something **warps** or **is warped**, it becomes damaged by bending or curving, often because of the effect of heat or water. *It should have prevented rain water warping the door trim.* ► Also an adjective. *The key was fractionally warped.* **2** If something **warps** someone's character or mind, it damages them or it influences them in a bad way. ► Also an adjective. *...the sort of appalling deed which is committed by the warped mind.* **3** A time **warp** or space **warp** is an imaginary break or sudden change in the normal experience of time or space. **4** In weaving, **the warp** in a piece of woven material is the threads which are held along a loom while other threads are passed across them.

◆◇◇◇◇
V-ERG: V
V n

ADJ-GRADED
VERB: V n

ADJ-GRADED

N-COUNT:
n N

N-SING:
the N

'**war paint**; also spelled **warpaint**. War paint is the paint which some tribal people use to decorate their faces and bodies before they fight a battle.

N-UNCOUNT

war·path /'wɔːpɑːθ, -pæθ/. If you say that someone is **on the warpath**, you mean that they are angry and getting ready for a fight or conflict.

PHRASE
INFORMAL

war·plane /'wɔːpleɪn/ **warplanes**; also spelled **war plane**. A **warplane** is an aeroplane that is specially designed to be used in warfare.

◆◇◇◇◇
N-COUNT

war·rant /'wɒrənt, AM 'wɔːr-/ **warrants, warranting, warranted. 1** If something **warrants** a particular action, it makes the action seem necessary or appropriate for the circumstances. *The allegations are serious enough to warrant an investigation.* ♦ **war·rant·ed** *Do you think this fear is warranted?* **2** A **warrant** is a legal document that allows or orders someone to do something, especially one that is signed by a judge or magistrate and gives the police permission to arrest someone or search their house. ● See also **death warrant**.

◆◆◇◇◇
VERB
V n

ADJ-GRADED
N-COUNT

'**warrant officer, warrant officers**. A **warrant officer** is a person in the army, the air force, or the marines, who is above the rank of sergeant and below the rank of lieutenant.

N-COUNT

war·ran·ty /'wɒrənti, AM 'wɔːr-/ **warranties**. A **warranty** is a written promise by a company that, if you find faults or defects in something that they have sold you within a certain time, they will repair it or replace it free of charge. *The equipment is still under warranty.*

◆◇◇◇◇
N-COUNT:
also under N

war·ren /'wɒrən, AM 'wɔːr-/ **warrens. 1** A **warren** is a group of holes in the ground which are connected by tunnels and which rabbits live in. **2** If you describe a building or an area of a city as a **warren**, you mean that the conditions are crowded and that there are many narrow passages, corridors, or streets.

N-COUNT

N-COUNT

war·ring /'wɔːrɪŋ/. **Warring** is used to describe groups of people who are involved in a conflict or quarrel with each other. *The warring factions have not yet turned in all their heavy weapons.*

◆◆◇◇◇
ADJ: ADJ n

war·ri·or /'wɒrɪə, AM 'wɔːr-/ **warriors**. A **warrior** is a fighter or soldier, especially one in former times who was very brave and experienced in fighting.

◆◆◇◇◇
N-COUNT

war·ship /'wɔːʃɪp/ **warships**. A **warship** is a ship with guns that is used for fighting in wars.

◆◇◇◇◇
N-COUNT

wart /wɔːt/ **warts. 1** A **wart** is a small lump which grows on your skin and which is usually caused by a virus. **2** If you describe someone or accept them **warts and all**, you describe or accept them as they are, including all their faults.

◆◇◇◇◇
N-COUNT

PHRASE

wart·hog /'wɔːthɒg, AM -hɔːg/ **warthogs**. A **warthog** is a wild pig with two small tusks. Warthogs live in Africa.

N-COUNT

war·time /'wɔːtaɪm/; also spelled **war-time**. **Wartime** is a period of time when a war is being fought. *...his wartime experiences in France.*

◆◆◇◇◇
N-UNCOUNT

'**war widow, war widows**. A **war widow** is a woman whose husband was killed while he was in the armed forces during a war.

N-COUNT

wary /'weəri/ **warier, wariest**. If you are **wary of** something or someone, you are cautious because you do not know much about them and you believe they may be dangerous or cause problems. *They*

◆◆◇◇◇
ADJ-GRADED

were very wary about giving him a contract. ♦ **war·i·ly**. *She studied me warily.*

ADV-GRADED

was /wəz, STRONG wɒz, AM wʌz/. **Was** is the first and third person singular of the past tense of **be**.

wash /wɒʃ/ **washes, washing, washed. 1** If you **wash** something, you clean it, usually with water and soap or detergent. *It took a long time to wash the mud out of his hair... Rub down the door and wash off the dust.* ► Also a noun. *That coat could do with a wash.* **2** If you **wash**, you clean part of your body using soap and water. *She washed her face with cold water... You are going to have your dinner, get washed, and go to bed.* ► Also a noun. *She had a wash and changed her clothes.* **3** If you say that something such as an item of clothing is in **the wash**, you mean that it is being washed, waiting to be washed, or has just been washed and can therefore not be worn or used.

◆◆◆◇◇
VERB: V n
V n prep
V n with adv

N-COUNT
VERB: V
V n
get V-ed

N-COUNT
PHRASE
INFORMAL

4 If a sea or river or something carried by a sea or river **washes** somewhere or **is washed** there, it flows there gently. *The force of the water washed him back into the cave.* **5 The wash** in a sea or river is water which has a lot of waves and froth, for example because a boat has just passed. **6** If a feeling **washes** over you, you suddenly feel it very strongly and cannot control it. *Waves of horror and disgust washed over her.* **7** A **wash** of something such as light or colour is a thin layer of it. **8** If you say that an excuse or idea will not **wash**, you mean that people will not accept or believe it. *He said her policies didn't work and the excuses didn't wash.* **9** See also **washing**. ● to **wash** your **dirty linen in public**: see **dirty**. ● to **wash** your **hands of** something: see **hand**.

V-ERG:
V prep/adv
V n with adv
Also V n prep

N-SING:
the N

VERB
V over/
through n
N-COUNT
WRITTEN

VERB
V
Also V with n
INFORMAL

wash away. If rain or floods **wash away** something, they destroy it and carry it away. *Flood waters washed away one of the main bridges.*

PHRASAL VB
V P noun
Also V n P

wash down. 1 If you **wash** something **down** with a drink, you swallow it and then drink the drink, for example to make it easier to swallow or digest. *...a massive beef sandwich washed down by a bottle of beer.* **2** If you **wash down** an object, you wash it all, from top to bottom. *The prisoner started to wash down the walls of his cell.*

PHRASAL VB
V n P
V-ed P
Also V P noun

V P noun
Also V n P

wash out. 1 If you **wash out** a container, you wash the inside of it. *It was my job to wash out the fish tank.* **2** If dye or dirt **washes out**, it can be removed by washing. **3** If rain **washes out** a sports match or other event, it spoils it or prevents it from continuing. **4** See also **washed-out, washout**.

PHRASAL VB
V P noun
Also V n P
V P
V P noun

wash over. If something someone does or says **washes over** you, you do not notice it or it does not affect you in any way.

PHRASAL VB
V P noun

wash up. 1 If you **wash up**, you wash the plates, cups, knives, forks, and other utensils which have been used in cooking and eating a meal. *I bet you make breakfast and wash up their plates, too.* **2** If you **wash up**, you clean part of your body with soap and water, especially your hands and face. **3** If something **is washed up** on a piece of land, it is carried by a river or sea and left there. *The fossils appear to be an early form of seaweed washed up on a beach.* **4** See also **washed up, washing-up**.

PHRASAL VB
V P
V P noun
BRITISH

V P
AMERICAN

be V-ed P
prep/adv
V-ed P

wash·able /'wɒʃəbəl/. **Washable** clothes or materials can be washed in water without being damaged.

ADJ

wash·basin /'wɒʃbeɪsən/ **washbasins**; also spelled **wash basin**. A **washbasin** is a large bowl, usually with taps for hot and cold water, for washing your hands and face.

N-COUNT

wash·cloth /'wɒʃklɒθ, AM -klɔːθ/ **washcloths**. A **washcloth** is a small cloth that you use for washing yourself. The British word is **flannel**.

N-COUNT
AMERICAN

,**washed-'out**; also spelled **washed out. 1** If **washed-out** colours are pale and dull rather than vivid. **2** If someone looks **washed-out**, they look very tired and lacking in energy.

ADJ-GRADED

ADJ-GRADED

,**washed 'up**; also spelled **washed-up**. If you say that someone is **washed up**, you mean that they are at the end of their career with no prospects for the future.

ADJ-GRADED
INFORMAL

W

wash·er /'wɒʃə/ **washers. 1** A **washer** is a thin flat ring of metal, plastic, or other substance, which is placed over a bolt before the nut is screwed on. ◆◇◇◇◇ N-COUNT
2 A **washer** is the same as a **washing machine**. N-COUNT

wash·ing /'wɒʃɪŋ/. **Washing** is a collection of clothes, sheets, and other things which are waiting to be washed, are being washed, or have just been washed. ◆◇◇◇◇ N-UNCOUNT

'washing machine, washing machines. A **washing machine** is a machine that you use to wash clothes in. ◆◇◇◇◇ N-COUNT

'washing powder, washing powders. Washing powder is powdered detergent that you use to wash clothes. The usual American term is **soap powder**. N-VAR BRITISH

,washing-'up. 1 To do the **washing-up** means to wash the plates, cups, cutlery, and pans which have been used in cooking and eating a meal. The usual American expression is to do the **dishes**. ◆◇◇◇◇ N-UNCOUNT BRITISH
2 **Washing-up** consists of the plates, cups, cutlery, and pans which you have to wash after a meal. N-UNCOUNT BRITISH

,washing-'up liquid, washing-up liquids. **Washing-up liquid** is a thick soapy liquid which you add to hot water to clean dirty dishes. N-VAR BRITISH

wash·out /'wɒʃaʊt/ **washouts.** If an event or plan is a **washout**, it fails completely. N-COUNT INFORMAL

wash·room /'wɒʃruːm/ **washrooms.** A **washroom** is a room with toilets and washing facilities, situated in a large building such as a factory or an office block. N-COUNT

wash·stand /'wɒʃstænd/ **washstands.** A **washstand** is a piece of furniture designed to hold a basin and other things for washing your face and hands, especially one that was used in former times, before wash basins were connected to water pipes. N-COUNT

wasn't /'wɒzənt, AM 'wʌz-/. In informal English, **was not** is usually said or written as **wasn't**.

wasp /wɒsp/ **wasps.** A **wasp** is an insect with wings and yellow and black stripes across its body. Wasps have a painful sting like a bee but do not produce honey. See picture headed **insects**. ◆◇◇◇◇ N-COUNT

wasp·ish /'wɒspɪʃ/. A **waspish** remark or sense of humour is sharp and critical. ADJ-GRADED

wast·age /'weɪstɪdʒ/. **1** **Wastage** of something is the act of wasting it or the amount of it that is wasted. *...a series of measures to prevent the wastage of water.* **2** **Wastage** is the process of deterioration and weakening that takes place in the body of someone who is very ill or starving. *...muscle wastage.* **3** **Wastage** refers to a number of people who leave a job or an educational establishment, especially before they have completed their education or training. *Wages are low and the wastage rate of staff is high.* ● See also **natural wastage**. N-UNCOUNT

waste /weɪst/ **wastes, wasting, wasted. 1** If you **waste** time, money, or energy, you use too much of it doing something that is not important or necessary, or is unlikely to succeed. *There could be many reasons and he was not going to waste time speculating on them... I resolved not to waste money on a hotel.* ▶ Also a noun. *I think that is a total waste of money.* **2** **Waste** is the use of money or other resources on things that do not need it. *The packets are measured to reduce waste.* **3** If you **waste** an opportunity for something, you do not take advantage of it when it is available. ◆◆◆◇◇ VERB: V n-ing V n onn N-SING: a N ofn N-UNCOUNT VERB: V n

4 **Waste** is material which has been used and is no longer wanted, for example because the valuable or useful part of it has been taken out. *Up to 10 million tonnes of toxic wastes are produced every year in the UK.* **5** **Waste** land is land, especially in or near a city, which is not used or looked after by anyone. **6** **Wastes** are a large area of land, for example a desert, in which there are very few people, plants, or animals. *...the barren wastes of the Sahara.* N-UNCOUNT: also N in pl ADJ N-PLURAL: adj N, N ofn

7 If you say that something **is wasted on** someone, you mean that there is no point giving it or telling it to them as they will not appreciate, understand, or pay any attention to it. VERB: be V-ed on n

8 If something **goes to waste** it remains unused or has to be thrown away. *Mexican cookery is economical,* PHRASE

she says. Nothing goes to waste. **9** If something or someone **lays waste** an area or town or **lays waste to** it, they completely destroy it. *The war has laid waste large regions of the countryside.* PHRASE

10 See also **wasted. 11** ● to **waste no time**: see **time**. ●

waste away. If someone **wastes away**, they become extremely thin or weak because they are ill or worried and they are not eating properly. PHRASAL VB V P

waste·basket /'weɪstbɑːskɪt, -bæsk-/ **wastebaskets.** A **wastebasket** is the same as a **wastepaper basket**. N-COUNT AMERICAN

wast·ed /'weɪstɪd/. **1** A **wasted** action is one that is unnecessary. *I'm sorry you had a wasted journey.* **2** Someone who is **wasted** is very thin and weak, often because of an illness. ADJ ADJ-GRADED

waste·ful /'weɪstfʊl/. Action that is **wasteful** uses too much of something valuable such as time, money, or energy. *This kind of training is ineffective, and wasteful of scarce resources.* ● **waste·ful·ly** *...companies that use energy wastefully.* ◆◇◇◇◇ ADJ-GRADED ADV-GRADED: ADV with v

waste·land /'weɪstlænd/ **wastelands.** A **wasteland** is an area of land which cannot be used, for example because it is infertile or because it has been misused by people. ◆◇◇◇◇ N-VAR

'wastepaper basket, wastepaper baskets. A **wastepaper basket** is a container for rubbish, especially paper. N-COUNT

wast·ing /'weɪstɪŋ/. A **wasting** disease is one which makes you gradually become thinner and weaker. ADJ: ADJ n

wast·rel /'weɪstrəl/ **wastrels.** If you describe someone as a **wastrel** you mean that they are lazy and spend their time and money on foolish things. N-COUNT LITERARY

watch 1 looking and paying attention

watch /wɒtʃ/ **watches, watching, watched. 1** If you **watch** someone or something, you look at them, usually for a period of time, and pay attention to what is happening. *He watched the barman prepare the beer he had ordered... Chris watched him sipping his brandy.* **2** If you **watch** something on television or an event such as a sports match, you spend time looking at it. **3** If you **watch** people, especially children or animals, you are responsible for them, and make sure that they are safe. *Parents can't be expected to watch their children 24 hours a day.* **4** If you **watch** someone, you follow them secretly or spy on them. ◆◆◆◆◆ VERB: V n V n inf V n -ing Also V VERB: V n VERB V n VERB: V n

5 If you **watch** a situation or event, you pay attention to it or you are aware of it, but you are not participating in it. *Human rights groups have been closely watching the case.* **6** If you **keep watch** on events or a situation, you pay attention to what is happening, so that you can take action at the right moment. **7** If you tell someone to **watch** a particular person or thing, you are warning them to be careful that the person or thing does not get out of control or do something unpleasant. *If you're watching the calories, don't have mayonnaise.* VERB V n Also V PHRASE VERB [PRAGMATICS] V n

8 The **watch** is the job of carefully looking around, usually when other people are asleep, so that you can warn them of danger or an attack. **9** If someone **keeps watch**, or if they are **on watch**, they look around all the time, usually when other people are asleep, so that they can warn the others of danger or an attack. N-COUNT PHRASE

10 If someone is being kept **under watch**, they are being guarded or observed all the time. PHRASE

11 You say **'watch it'** in order to warn someone to be careful. **12** You say to someone **'you watch'** or **'just watch'** when you are predicting that something will happen, and you are very confident that it will happen as you say. *You watch. Things will get worse before they get better.* **13** ● **watch this space**: see **space**. ● **watch your step**: see **step**. PHRASE [PRAGMATICS] PHRASE

watch for or **watch out for.** If you **watch for** something or **watch out for** it, you pay attention so that you notice it, either because you do not want to miss it or because you want to avoid it. *He called out to them to watch out for the unexploded mine.* PHRASAL VB V P n V P P n

watch out. If you tell someone to **watch out**, you are warning them to be careful, because something PHRASAL VB V P [PRAGMATICS]

unpleasant might happen to them or they might get into difficulties.

watch out for. See **watch for.** PHRASAL VB

watch over. If you **watch over** someone or something, you pay attention to them to make sure that nothing bad happens to them. PHRASAL VB / V P n

watch 2 instrument that tells the time

watch /wɒtʃ/ **watches.** A **watch** is a small clock which you wear on a strap on your wrist or on a chain. N-COUNT ◆◆◆◇◇

watch·dog /'wɒtʃdɒg, AM -dɔːg/ **watchdogs.** A **watchdog** is a person or committee whose job is to make sure that companies do not act illegally or irresponsibly. ...the Parliamentary watchdog Finance Committee. N-COUNT

watch·ful /'wɒtʃfʊl/. **1** Someone who is **watchful** notices everything that is happening. The police are watchful of all foreigners. **2** If you do something **under the watchful eye** of someone who has authority over you, they watch you carefully to make sure there are no problems. **3** If you **keep a watchful eye on** someone or something, you watch carefully to make sure there are no problems. ◆◇◇◇◇ ADJ-GRADED / PHRASE / PHRASE

-watching /-wɒtʃɪŋ/. **-watching** combines with nouns to form other nouns which refer to the activity of looking at a group of animals or people and studying them because they interest you. ...the sport of celebrity-watching. ◆ **-watcher** /-wɒtʃə/ **-watchers** The bird-watchers crept about in the bushes. COMB / COMB

watch·man /'wɒtʃmən/ **watchmen.** A **watchman** is a person whose job is to guard a building or area. ● See also **nightwatchman.** N-COUNT

watch·tower /'wɒtʃtaʊə/ **watchtowers.** A **watchtower** is a high building which gives a sentry a good view of an area which is being guarded. N-COUNT

watch·word /'wɒtʃwɜːd/ **watchwords.** Someone's **watchword** is a word or phrase that sums up their attitude or approach to a particular subject or to things in general. Caution has been one of Mr Allan's watchwords. N-COUNT

wa·ter /'wɔːtə/ **waters, watering, watered. 1** Water is a clear thin liquid that has no colour or taste when it is pure. It falls from clouds as rain. **2** You use **waters** to refer to a large area of sea, especially the area of sea which is near to a country and which is regarded as belonging to it. ...Chinese territorial waters. **3** If you **water** plants, you pour water over them in order to help them to grow. **4** If your eyes **water**, tears build up in them because they are sore or because you are upset. **5** If you say that your mouth **is watering**, you mean that you can smell or see some appetizing food and you might mean that your mouth is actually producing saliva. ● See also **mouth-watering.** ◆◆◆◆◆ N-UNCOUNT / N-PLURAL: with supp / VERB: V n / VERB: V / VERB: V

6 When a pregnant woman's **waters** break, the fluid in her womb that surrounds the baby passes out of her body, showing that the baby is ready to be born. A midwife can **break** a woman's **waters** so that the birth can begin. PHRASE

7 You sometimes use **waters** to refer to a situation which is very complex or difficult. The British Government may be in stormy economic waters. **8** If you are in **deep water**, you are in a difficult or awkward situation. **9** If you are in **hot water**, you are in trouble. The company has already been in hot water over high prices this year. N-PLURAL: adj N / PHRASE / PHRASE INFORMAL

10 If you say that an event or incident is **water under the bridge**, you mean that it has happened and cannot now be changed, so there is no point in worrying about it any more. **11** If an argument or theory does not **hold water**, it does not seem to be reasonable or be in accordance with the facts. **12** If you **pour cold water on** an idea or suggestion, you show that you have a low opinion of it. **13** If you **test the water** or **test the waters**, you try to find out what reaction an action or idea will get before you do it or tell it to people. Test the water before committing yourself. PHRASE / PHRASE / PHRASE / PHRASE

14 ● like a fish out of **water**: see **fish.** ● to **keep your**

head above **water**: see **head.** ● to **pour oil on troubled waters**: see **oil.**

water down. 1 If you **water down** a substance, for example food or drink, you add water to it to make it weaker. You can water down a glass of wine and make it last twice as long. **2** If something, especially a proposal, speech, or statement **is watered down**, it is made much weaker and less forceful or less controversial. Proposed European Community legislation affecting bird-keepers has been watered down. ● See also **watered-down.** PHRASAL VB / V P noun / Also V n P / VERB / be V-ed P

water·bed /'wɔːtəbed/ **waterbeds;** also spelled **water bed.** A **waterbed** is a bed whose mattress consists of a plastic case filled with water. N-COUNT

'water-borne; also spelled **waterborne. 1** Water-borne disease or infection is passed on through contact with infected water. **2** Something that is **water-borne** travels or is transported on water. ...a waterborne safari down the Nile. ADJ: ADJ n / ADJ: ADJ n

'water bottle, water bottles. A **water bottle** is a small container for carrying water to drink on a long journey. ● See also **hot-water bottle.** N-COUNT

'water butt, water butts. A **water butt** is a large barrel for collecting rain as it flows off a roof. The usual American word is **rain barrel.** N-COUNT BRITISH

'water cannon, water cannons. A **water cannon** can also be used as the plural form. A **water cannon** is a machine which shoots out a large powerful jet of water. It is used by police to break up crowds of people who are demonstrating. N-COUNT

'water chestnut, water chestnuts. A **water chestnut** is the thick bottom part of the stem of a plant which grows in China. It is frequently used in Chinese cookery. N-COUNT

water·colour /'wɔːtəkʌlə/ **watercolours;** spelled **watercolor** in American English. **Watercolours** are coloured paints, used for painting pictures, which you apply with a wet brush or dissolve in water first. A **watercolour** is also a picture which has been painted with watercolours. ◆◇◇◇◇ N-VAR

water·course /'wɔːtəkɔːs/ **watercourses;** also spelled **water course.** A **watercourse** is a stream or river, or the channel that it flows along. N-COUNT FORMAL

water·cress /'wɔːtəkres/. **Watercress** is a small plant with white flowers which grows in streams and pools. Its leaves taste hot and are eaten raw in salads. ◆◇◇◇◇ N-UNCOUNT

,watered-'down; also spelled **watered down.** If you describe something such as a proposal, speech, or statement as **watered down**, you mean that it is weaker or less forceful or controversial than its original form. ● See also **water.** ◆◇◇◇◇ ADJ-GRADED

water·fall /'wɔːtəfɔːl/ **waterfalls.** A **waterfall** is a place where water flows over the edge of a steep, high cliff in hills or mountains, and falls into a pool below. ◆◇◇◇◇ N-COUNT

water·fowl /'wɔːtəfaʊl/; **waterfowl** is both the singular and the plural form. **Waterfowl** are birds that swim in water, especially ducks, geese, and swans. N-COUNT

water·front /'wɔːtəfrʌnt/ **waterfronts.** A **waterfront** is a street or piece of land which is next to an area of water, for example a harbour or the sea. ◆◇◇◇◇ N-COUNT

'water hole, water holes; also spelled **waterhole.** In a desert or other dry area, a **water hole** is a pond or pool where animals can find water to drink. N-COUNT

'watering can, watering cans. A **watering can** is a container with a long spout which is used to water plants. See picture headed **tools.** N-COUNT

'watering hole, watering holes. You can refer to a pub or bar where people go to drink and meet their friends as a **watering hole.** N-COUNT

'water lily, water lilies; also spelled **waterlily.** A **water lily** is a plant with large flat leaves and colourful flowers which floats on the surface of lakes and rivers. N-COUNT

water·line /'wɔːtəlaɪn/ **waterlines;** also spelled **water line.** The **waterline** is a line, either real or imaginary, on the side of a ship representing the level the water reaches when the ship is at sea. N-COUNT

wa·ter·logged /ˈwɔːtəlɒgd, AM -lɔːgd/; also spelled **water-logged**. Something such as soil or land that is **waterlogged** is so wet that it cannot absorb any more water, so that a layer of water remains on its surface. ADJ-GRADED

'water main, water mains. A **water main** is a very large underground pipe used for supplying water to houses and factories. N-COUNT

water·mark /ˈwɔːtəmɑːk/ **watermarks.** A **watermark** is a design which is put into paper by the people who make it, and which you can only see if you hold the paper up to the light. ● See also **high-water mark**. N-COUNT

'water meadow, water meadows. Water **meadows** are wet fields of grass near a river, which are often flooded. N-COUNT BRITISH

water·melon /ˈwɔːtəmelən/ **watermelons.** A **watermelon** is a large round fruit with green skin, pink flesh, and black seeds. N-VAR

water·mill /ˈwɔːtəmɪl/ **watermills;** also spelled **water mill.** A **watermill** is a mill powered by a water wheel. N-COUNT

'water pistol, water pistols. A **water pistol** is a small toy gun which shoots out water. N-COUNT

'water polo. Water polo is a game played in a swimming pool in which two teams of swimmers try to score goals with a ball. N-UNCOUNT

water·proof /ˈwɔːtəpruːf/ **waterproofs, waterproofing, waterproofed.** 1 Something which is **waterproof** does not let water pass through it. *Take waterproof clothing – Orkney weather is unpredictable.* 2 **Waterproofs** are items of clothing which do not let water in. 3 If something **is waterproofed**, it is treated so that water cannot pass through it or damage it. ◆◇◇◇◇ ADJ / N-COUNT BRITISH / VERB: be V-ed

'water rate, water rates. In Britain, the charges made for the use of water from the public water supply are known as the **water rates**. N-COUNT

'water-resistant. Something that is **water-resistant** does not allow water to pass through it easily, or is not easily damaged by water. ADJ-GRADED

water·shed /ˈwɔːtəʃed/ **watersheds.** 1 If something such as an event is a **watershed** in the history or development of something, it is very important because it represents the beginning of a new stage in it. *Tonight could prove to be a watershed for the international career of Barnes.* 2 In Britain, the **watershed** is a time before which television broadcasters have agreed not to show programmes unsuitable for children. *The advert should only be shown after the 9pm watershed.* 3 A **watershed** is an area of high ground which divides two or more river systems. ◆◇◇◇◇ N-COUNT / N-COUNT / N-COUNT TECHNICAL

water·side /ˈwɔːtəsaɪd/. The **waterside** is the area beside a stretch of water such as a river or lake. *...pretty waterside hotels.* N-SING

'water-ski, water-skis, water-skiing, water-skied; also spelled **waterski.** If you **water-ski**, you stand on skis in the water while being pulled along by a boat. ♦ **water-skiing** *He offered to teach them water-skiing.* VERB: V / N-UNCOUNT

,water-'soluble; also spelled **water soluble.** Something that is **water-soluble** dissolves in water. ADJ

'water supply, water supplies. The **water supply** in an area is the water which is collected and passed through pipes to buildings for people to use. ◆◇◇◇◇ N-COUNT

'water table, water tables. The **water table** is the level below the surface of the ground where water can be found. N-COUNT

water·tight /ˈwɔːtətaɪt/; also spelled **water-tight.** 1 Something that is **watertight** does not allow water to pass through it, for example because it is tightly sealed. *The batteries are safely enclosed in a watertight compartment.* 2 A **watertight** case, argument, or agreement is one that has been so carefully put together that nobody will be able to find a fault in it. *The police had a watertight case.* ADJ / ADJ-GRADED

'water tower, water towers. A **water tower** is a large tank of water which is placed on a high metal N-COUNT structure so that water can be supplied at a steady pressure to surrounding buildings.

'water vole, water voles. A **water vole** is a small rat-like animal that can swim. Water voles live in holes in the banks of rivers. N-COUNT

water·way /ˈwɔːtəweɪ/ **waterways.** A **waterway** is a canal, river, or narrow channel of sea which ships or boats can sail along. ◆◇◇◇◇ N-COUNT

'water wheel, water wheels; also spelled **waterwheel.** A **water wheel** is a large wheel which is turned by water flowing through it. Water wheels are used to provide power to drive machinery. N-COUNT

water·works /ˈwɔːtəwɜːks/; **waterworks** is both the singular and the plural form. A **waterworks** is a building where a supply of water is stored and cleaned before being distributed to the public. N-COUNT

wa·tery /ˈwɔːtəri/. 1 Something that is **watery** is weak or pale. *A watery light began to show through the branches.* 2 If you describe food or drink as **watery**, you dislike it because it contains too much water or is thin or tasteless like water. *...a plateful of watery soup.* 3 Something that is **watery** contains, resembles, or consists of water. *Diana's eyes went red and watery.* ◆◇◇◇◇ ADJ-GRADED / ADJ-GRADED PRAGMATICS / ADJ-GRADED

watt /wɒt/ **watts.** A **watt** is a unit of measurement of electrical power. *...a 100-watt lightbulb.* ◆◇◇◇◇ N-COUNT

watt·age /ˈwɒtɪdʒ/. The **wattage** of a piece of electrical equipment is the amount of electrical power, expressed in watts, which it generates or uses. N-UNCOUNT

wat·tle /ˈwɒtəl/. **Wattle** is a framework made by weaving thin sticks and twigs over thick sticks, which are used for making fences and walls. N-UNCOUNT

wave /weɪv/ **waves, waving, waved.** 1 If you **wave** or **wave** your hand, you move your hand from side to side in the air, usually in order to say hello or goodbye to someone. *Jessica caught sight of Lois and waved to her.* ▶ Also a noun. *...a cheery wave.* 2 If you **wave** someone away or **wave** them on, you make a movement with your hand to indicate that they should move in a particular direction. *Leshka waved him away with a show of irritation.* 3 If you **wave** something, you hold it up and move it rapidly from side to side. *...waving flags and applauding.* ♦ **-waving** *There will be marching bands and plenty of flag-waving.* 4 If a crowd of people do a **wave**, each person in the crowd stands up and puts their arms in the air after the person to one side of them, creating a continuous rolling motion through the crowd. The British term is **Mexican wave.** 5 If something **waves**, it moves gently from side to side or up and down. *...flowers waving in the wind.* 6 A **wave** is a raised mass of water on the surface of water, especially the sea. 7 If someone's hair has **waves**, it curves slightly instead of being straight. 8 A **wave** is a sudden increase in heat or energy that spreads out from an earthquake, eruption, or explosion. *The shock waves of the earthquake were felt in Teheran.* 9 A **wave** is a sudden increase in a particular feeling, activity, or type of behaviour, especially an undesirable or unpleasant one. *...the current wave of violence... The loneliness and grief comes in waves.* 10 A **wave** is a sudden increase in the number of people moving somewhere. *A wave of immigrants is washing over Western Europe.* 11 **Wave** is used to refer to the way in which things such as sound, light, and radio signals travel. *Radio waves have a certain frequency.* 12 See also **long wave, medium wave, new wave, short-wave, tidal wave.** ◆◆◆◇ VERB: V V to/at n Also V n / N-COUNT / VERB V n adv/prep / VERB V n / COMB / N-COUNT AMERICAN / VERB V / N-COUNT / N-COUNT / N-COUNT: with supp / N-COUNT / N-COUNT / N-COUNT

wave aside. If you **wave aside** something such as a suggestion, explanation, or idea, you decide that it is not important enough to consider seriously. *Rachel waved aside the explanation.* PHRASAL VB V P noun Also V n P

wave down. If someone **waves down** a vehicle, they wave their hand as a signal to the driver to stop the vehicle. *He was frustrated by his inability to wave down a taxi.* PHRASAL VB V P noun Also V n P

wave·band /ˈweɪvbænd/ **wavebands.** A **waveband** is a group of radio waves of similar length N-COUNT

which are used for particular types of radio transmission.

wave·length /ˈweɪvleŋθ/ **wavelengths.** 1 A ◆◇◇◇ wavelength is the distance between the same point N-COUNT on consecutive cycles of a wave of energy such as light or sound. *Blue light has a shorter wavelength than red.* 2 A wavelength is the size of radio wave N-COUNT: which a particular radio station uses to broadcast its with supp programmes. 3 If two people are **on the same** PHRASE **wavelength**, they find it easy to understand each other and they tend to agree, because they share similar interests or opinions.

wa·ver /ˈweɪvə/ **wavers, wavering, wavered.** ◆◇◇◇ 1 If you **waver**, you are uncertain or indecisive VERB about something. *Some military commanders wa-* V *vered over whether to support the coup.* 2 If some- VERB thing **wavers**, it shakes with very slight movements V or changes. *The shadows of the dancers wavered continually.*

wavy /ˈweɪvi/ **wavier, waviest.** 1 Wavy hair is not ADJ-GRADED straight or curly, but curves slightly. 2 A wavy line ADJ-GRADED has a series of regular curves along it. *The boxes were decorated with a wavy gold line.*

wax /wæks/ **waxes, waxing, waxed.** 1 Wax is a ◆◆◇◇ solid, slightly shiny substance made of fat or oil N-VAR which is used to make candles and polish. It melts when it is heated. 2 If you **wax** a surface, you put a VERB: V n thin layer of wax onto it, especially in order to pol- ish it. 3 If you have your legs waxed, you have the VERB hair removed from your legs by having wax put on *haven V-ed* them and then pulled off quickly. *She has just had* Also V n *her legs waxed at the local beauty parlour.* 4 Wax is N-UNCOUNT the sticky yellow substance found in your ears. 5 If you say that someone, for example, **waxes** lyrical VERB or **waxes** indignant about a subject, you mean that V adj they talk a lot in a lyrical or indignant way about it. *My* LITERARY *mother waxed eloquent on the theme of wifely duty.* 6 If something **waxes and wanes**, it first increases and PHRASE then decreases over a period of time. *Portugal and Spain had possessed vast empires that waxed and waned.*

,**waxed 'paper.** Waxed paper is the same as **wax** N-UNCOUNT **paper**.

wax·en /ˈwæksən/. A **waxen** face is very pale and ADJ looks very unhealthy. LITERARY

'**wax paper.** Wax paper is paper that has been N-UNCOUNT covered with a thin layer of wax in order to make it waterproof.

wax·work /ˈwækswɜːk/ **waxworks.** 1 A waxwork N-COUNT is a model of a person, especially a famous person, made out of wax. 2 A waxworks is a place where N-COUNT waxworks are displayed for the public to look at. Waxworks is both the singular and the plural form.

waxy /ˈwæksi/. Something that is **waxy** looks or ADJ-GRADED feels like wax. *...the waxy coating on the insect's body.*

way /weɪ/ **ways.** 1 If you refer to a **way** of doing ◆◆◆◆◆ something, you are referring to how you can do it, N-COUNT for example the method you can use to achieve it. *Another way of making new friends is to go to an evening class... I can't think of a worse way to spend my time.* 2 If you talk about the **way** someone does N-COUNT something, you are talking about the qualities their action has. *She smiled in a friendly way.* 3 If a gen- N-COUNT: eral statement or description is true in a particular with supp **way**, that is a particular manner or form that it takes in a specific case. *Computerized reservation systems help airline profits in several ways... She was afraid in a way that was quite new to her.* 4 You use N-COUNT: **way** in expressions such as **in some ways** and **in** *in N with supp* **many ways** to indicate the degree or extent to which a statement is true. *In some ways, the official opening is a formality.* 5 The **ways** of a particular N-PLURAL: person or group of people are their customs or their with supp usual behaviour. 6 If you refer to someone's **way**, you are referring to N-SING: their usual or preferred type of behaviour. *Direct con-* with poss *frontation was not his way.* 7 You use **way** to refer to N-COUNT: one particular opinion or interpretation of some- with supp thing, when others are possible. *I suppose that's one*

way of looking at it. 8 You use **way** when mentioning N-COUNT: one of a number of possible alternative results or de- with supp cisions. *There is no indication which way the vote could go.* 9 The **way** you feel about something is your N-SING: attitude to it or your opinion about it. *I'm terribly sor-* with supp *ry, I had no idea you felt that way.* 10 If you mention N-SING: the **way** that something happens, you are mentioning *the N that* the fact that it happens. *I hate the way he manipulates people.* 11 You use **way** in expressions such as **push your way** N-SING: or **eat your way**, followed by a prepositional phrase, poss N in order to suggest an idea of movement, progress, or force as well as the action described by the verb. *She thrust her way into the crowd... He thought we were trying to buy our way into his company.* 12 The **way** N-COUNT somewhere consists of the different places that you go through or the route that you take in order to get there. *Does anybody know the way to the bathroom?... We'll go out the back way.* 13 If you go or look a par- N-SING: ticular **way**, you go or look in that direction. *As he* with supp *strode into the kitchen, he passed Pop coming the other way.* 14 You can refer to the direction you are travel- N-SING: ling in as your **way**. *She would say she was going my* poss N *way and offer me a lift.* 15 If you find your **way**, you N-SING: manage to get to the place that you want to go to. poss N 16 You talk about people going their different **ways** N-COUNT: when their lives develop differently and they have less poss N contact with each other. 17 If something comes your N-SING: **way**, you get it or receive it. 18 If someone or some- poss N thing is in the **way**, they prevent you from moving for- N-SING: ward or seeing clearly. *Get out of my way!* 19 Way is *the/poss N,* used in the names of some roads, and also in the *in/out ofN* names of some long-distance walking paths in the countryside. *...the well-trodden 250-mile Pennine Way.* 20 You can use **way** to refer to the area near N-UNCOUNT: where someone lives or near a specified place. supp N *...somebody from Newcastle way.* INFORMAL 21 You use **way** in expressions like **the right way up** N-SING: and **the other way round** to refer to one of two or with supp more possible positions or arrangements that some- thing can have. *It's important to fit it the right way round.* 22 You can use **way** to emphasize, for exam- ADV: ple, that something is a great distance away or is very ADV adv/prep much below or above a particular level or amount. *Way down in the valley to the west is the town of Frei- burg... I have to decide my plan way in advance.* 23 If N-PLURAL: you split something a number of **ways**, you divide it num N into a number of different parts or quantities, usually fairly equal in size. ▶ Also a combining form. *...a sim-* COMB *ple three-way division.* 24 Way is used in expressions N-SING: such as **a little way** and **quite a way**, to say how far *a N* away something is or how far you have travelled. *We've a fair way to go yet.* 25 Way is used in expres- N-SING: sions such as **a long way** and **a little way** to say how *a N* far away in time something is. *August is still an awful- ly long way away.* 26 You use **way** in expressions such as **all the way**, N-SING: **most of the way** and **half the way** to refer to the extent predet/quant to which an action has been completed. *When was the* the N *last time you listened to an album all the way through?* 27 If something is **across the way**, it is nearby, espe- PHRASE cially on the opposite side of a road or area. 28 You INFORMAL use **all the way** to emphasize how long a distance is. PHRASE *That dress came all the way from New York.* 29 You PHRASE can use **all the way** to emphasize that your remark ap- plies to every part of a situation, activity, or period of time. *Having started a revolution we must go all the way.* 30 If someone or something is **in a bad way**, they PHRASE are in a bad condition or situation. INFORMAL 31 If something is happening **in a big way**, it is hap- PHRASE pening on a large scale. *Soccer in the States has never* INFORMAL *taken off in a big way.* 32 If someone says that you PHRASE **can't have it both ways**, they are telling you that you have to choose between two things and cannot do or have them both. 33 You say **by the way** when you add PHRASE something to what you are saying, especially some- PRAGMATICS thing that you have just thought of. *By the way, how* SPOKEN *did your seminar go?* 34 You use **by way of** when you PHR-PREP are explaining the purpose of something that you PRAGMATICS have said or are about to say. For example, if you say

something **by way of an introduction**, you say it as an introduction. **35** If you do something **by way of** a particular method, you use that method to do it. *I teach psychology by way of a range of traditional lectures.* **36** If you go somewhere **by way of** a particular place, you go through that place in order to get to where you want. *The path goes under the river by way of the tunnel.* **37** If someone **changes** their **ways** or **mends** their **ways**, they permanently improve their behaviour or their way of doing something. **38** If you **clear the way**, **open the way**, or **prepare the way** for something, you create an opportunity for it to happen. **39** If you say that someone takes **the easy way out**, you disapprove of them because they do what is easiest for them in a difficult situation, rather than dealing with it properly. **40** You use **either way** in order to introduce a statement which is true in each of the two possible or alternative cases that you have just mentioned. *The sea may rise or the land may fall; either way the sand dunes will be gone in a short time.* **41** If you say that a particular type of action or development is **the way forward**, you approve of it or recommend it because it is likely to lead to success. **42** If someone **gets** their **way** or **has** their **way**, nobody stops them doing what they want to do. You can also say that someone **gets** their **own way** or **has** their **own way**. **43** If one thing **gives way to** another, the first thing is replaced by the second. *The last houses give way to soybean fields.* **44** If an object that is supporting something **gives way**, it breaks or collapses, so that it can no longer support that thing. *The hook in the ceiling had given way and the lamp had fallen blazing on to the table.* **45** If you **give way** to someone or something that you have been resisting, you stop resisting and allow yourself to be persuaded or controlled by them. *The President has given way to pressure from the hardliners.* **46** If a moving person or a vehicle or its driver **gives way**, they slow down or stop in order to allow other people or vehicles to pass in front of them. The usual American word is **yield**. **47** If you say that someone or something **has a way of** doing a particular thing, you mean that they often do it. *Bosses have a way of always finding out about such things.* **48** If you say that a person **has a way with** something or someone, you mean that that person seems to have a natural skill or instinct for dealing with them; used showing approval. *Constance doesn't have a way with words the way you do.* **49** You use **in no way** or **not in any way** to emphasize that a statement is not at all true. *In no way am I going to adopt any of his methods.* **50** If you say that something is true **in a way**, you mean that although a statement is not completely true, it is true to a limited extent or in certain respects. You use **in a way** to reduce the force of a statement. *In a way, I suppose I'm frightened of failing.* **51** If you say that someone does something or contributes to something **in a small way**, you mean that although they do not do very much, their actions are useful or significant. *By doing this you will, in a small way, help win the victory.* **52** If you say that someone **gets in the way**, or **is in the way**, you are annoyed because their presence or their actions stop you doing something properly. **53** To **get in the way** of something means to make it difficult for it to happen, continue, or be appreciated properly. *...a job which never got in the way of her leisure interests.* **54** If you **know** your **way around** a particular subject, system, or job, you know all the procedures and facts about it. **55** If you say that someone **is laughing all the way to the bank**, you mean that they are making a lot of money very easily. **56** If you **lead the way** along a particular route, you go along in front of someone in order to show them where to go. **57** If a person or group **leads the way** in a particular activity, they are the first person or group to do it or they make the most new developments in it. *Sony has also led the way in shrinking the size of compact-disc players.* **58** If you say that someone or something **has come a long way**, you mean that they

PHR-PREP
WRITTEN

PHR-PREP

PHRASE

PHRASE

PHRASE
PRAGMATICS

PHRASE

PHRASE

PHRASE

PHRASE

PHRASE

PHRASE
WRITTEN

PHRASE
BRITISH

PHRASE

PHRASE
PRAGMATICS
SPOKEN

PHRASE

PHRASE
PRAGMATICS

PHRASE

PHRASE

PHRASE

PHRASE
INFORMAL

PHRASE

PHRASE

have developed, progressed, or become very successful. **59** You can use **by a long way** to emphasize that something is, for example, much better, worse, or bigger than any other thing of that kind. *It was, by a long way, the worst meeting I have ever attended.* **60** If you say that something is **a long way from** being true, you are emphasizing that it is definitely not true. **61** If you say that something **goes a long way** towards doing a particular thing, you mean that it is an important factor in achieving that thing. *A sale would go a long way towards easing the council's financial problems.* **62** If you say that someone has **lost** their **way**, you are criticizing them because they do not have any good ideas any more, or seem to have become unsure about what to do. **63** If you **lose** your **way**, you become lost when you are trying to go somewhere. **64** When you **make** your **way** somewhere, you walk or travel there. **65** If one person or thing **makes way** for another, the first is replaced by the second. *He said he was prepared to make way for younger people in the party.* **66** If you say **there's no way** that something will happen, you are emphasizing that you think it will definitely not happen. *There was absolutely no way that we were going to be able to retrieve it.* **67** You can say **no way** as an emphatic way of saying no. *Mike, no way am I playing cards with you for money.* **68** You use **in the way of** or **by way of** in order to specify the kind of thing you are talking about. *Meetings held today produced little in the way of an agreement... The man with whom she maintains a relationship provides nothing by way of support.* **69** If you **are on** your **way**, you have started your journey somewhere. **70** If you **go on** your **way**, you continue with your journey. **71** If something happens **on the way** or **along the way**, it happens during the course of a particular event or process. *You may have to learn a few new skills along the way.* **72** If you are **on** your **way** or **well on** your **way** to something, you have made so much progress that you are almost certain to achieve that thing. *I am now out of hospital and well on the way to recovery.* **73** If something is **on the way**, it is due to come in the near future. *The forecasters say more snow is on the way.* **74** You can use **one way or another** or **one way or the other** when you want to say that something definitely happens, but without giving any details about how it happens. *...those who had entered Germany one way or another during the war.* **75** You use **one way or the other** or **one way or another** to refer to two possible decisions or conclusions that have previously been mentioned, without stating which one is reached or preferred. *I didn't really care one way or another.* **76** You say **in more ways than one** to indicate that what you have said is intended to have more than one meaning. *These local elections may prove a turning point in more ways than one.* **77** You use **the other way around** or **the other way round** to refer to the opposite of what you have just said. *You'd think you were the one who did me the favor, and not the other way around.* **78** If something or someone is **on the way out**, or **on their way out**, they are likely to disappear or to be replaced very soon. *The ban on Sunday shopping could be on its way out before Christmas.* **79** If you **go out of** your **way** to do something, for example to help someone, you make a special effort to do it. **80** If you **keep out of** someone's **way** or **stay out of** their **way**, you avoid them or do not get involved with them. **81** When something is **out of the way**, it has finished or you have dealt with it. *The plan has to remain confidential at least until the local elections are out of the way.* **82** If you **go** your **own way**, you do what you want rather than what everyone else does or expects. **83** You use **in the same way** to introduce a situation that you are comparing with one that you have just mentioned, because there is a strong similarity between them. *There is no reason why a gifted aircraft designer should also be a capable pilot. In the same way, a brilliant pilot can be a menace behind the wheel of a car.* **84** If you say that someone is **set in** their **ways**, you

PHRASE
PRAGMATICS

PHRASE
PRAGMATICS

PHRASE

PHRASE

PHRASE

PHRASE

PHRASE

PHRASE
PRAGMATICS

PHRASE
PRAGMATICS
INFORMAL
PHRASE

PHRASE

PHRASE

PHRASE

PHRASE

PHRASE

PHRASE

PHRASE

PHRASE

PHRASE

PHRASE

PHRASE
PRAGMATICS

PHRASE

mean that they have been behaving in the same way for many years and do not want to change. **85** You can use **that way** and **this way** to refer to a statement or comment that you have just made. *We have a beautiful city and we pray it stays that way... I've never found it hard to make friends so I suppose I was lucky that way.* **86** You can use **that way** or **this way** to refer to PHRASE an action or situation that you have just mentioned, PRAGMATICS when you go on to mention the likely consequence or effect of it. *Keep the soil moist. That way, the seedling will flourish.* **87** You can use **the way things are going** to indicate PHRASE that you expect something to happen because of the way the present situation is developing. *The way things are going, perhaps he won't come at all.* **88** You PHRASE use **to** my **way of thinking** when you are giving your PRAGMATICS opinion. *To my way of thinking, it didn't seem as if it ought to be so terribly complicated.* **89** If you say that PHRASE there are **no two ways about it**, you are emphasizing PRAGMATICS that there is no doubt at all about the situation or how SPOKEN it should be interpreted. **90** If an activity or plan is **un-** PHRASE **der way**, it has begun and is now taking place. **91** Every which way is used to emphasize that some- PHRASE thing happens, or might happen, in a lot of different PRAGMATICS ways, or using a lot of different methods. *He re-ran the* INFORMAL *experiment every which way he could.* **92** Every which way is used to emphasize that things PHRASE move in a lot of different directions or are arranged in PRAGMATICS a lot of different positions. *...cars parked every which* INFORMAL *way.* **93** ● to see the error of your ways: see error.   ● to look the other way: see look.

-way /-weɪ/. **-way** combines with numbers to form COMB adjectives that describe a means of communication that functions or takes place between the stated number of people. *...a two-way radio.* ● See also **one-way, two-way.**

way·lay /weɪˈleɪ/ **waylays, waylaying, waylaid.** VERB: V n If someone **waylays** you, they stop you when you are going somewhere, for example in order to talk to you or to attack you.

,way of 'life, ways of life. 1 A **way of life** is the ◆◆◇◇◇ behaviour and habits that are typical of a particular N-COUNT person or group, or that are chosen by them. *...the traditional way of life of the Yanomami Indians.* **2** If you describe a particular activity as a **way of life** N-COUNT for someone, you mean that it has become a very important and regular thing in their life, rather than something they do or experience occasionally. *...cities where violence is a way of life.*

,way-'out. If you describe someone or something ADJ-GRADED as a **way-out**, you are critical of them because they PRAGMATICS are very different from other things or people, espe- INFORMAL cially if they are very modern or fashionable.

way·side /ˈweɪsaɪd/ **waysides. 1** The **wayside** is N-COUNT the side of the road. **2** If a person or plan **falls by** LITERARY **the wayside**, they fail or stop before they complete PHRASE what they set out to do. *In the mid 70s, Morrison planned a comedy album. The project fell by the wayside.*

'way station, way stations. A **way station** is a N-COUNT place where people stop to eat and rest when they are on a long journey.

way·ward /ˈweɪwəd/. If you describe a person or ◆◇◇◇◇ their behaviour as **wayward**, you mean that they are ADJ-GRADED likely to change suddenly, are often selfish or stubborn, and are therefore difficult to control. ◆ **way·ward·ness** *...the curiosity, caprice and way-* N-UNCOUNT *wardness of children.*

WC /ˌdʌbəlju: ˈsiː/ **WCs.** A toilet is sometimes re- N-COUNT ferred to as a **WC**, especially on signs or in adver- BRITISH tisements for houses, flats, or hotels.

we /wɪ, STRONG wiː/. **We** is the first person plural ◆◆◆◆◆ pronoun. **We** is used as the subject of a verb. **1** A speaker or writer uses **we** to refer both to himself PRON or herself and to one or more other people as a group. In conversation, **we** can also include someone who is not present. You can use **we** before a noun to make it clear which group of people you are referring to. *We ordered another bottle of champagne... Don't you think we should ask this young man some technical questions?... We students outnumbered our teachers.* **2 We** is sometimes used to refer to people in gener- PRON al. *We need to take care of our bodies.* **3** A speaker or PRON writer may use **we** instead of 'I' in order to include FORMAL the listeners or readers in what he or she is saying. *We will now consider the raw materials from which the body derives energy.*

weak /wiːk/ **weaker, weakest. 1** If someone is ◆◆◆◆◇ **weak**, they are not healthy or do not have good ADJ-GRADED muscles, so that they cannot move quickly or carry heavy things. ◆ **weak·ly** *He weakly pressed his arms* ADV-GRADED: *against her sides.* ◆ **weak·ness** *Symptoms of* ADV with v *anaemia include weakness, fatigue and iron defi-* N-UNCOUNT *ciency.* **2** If someone has an organ or sense that is ADJ-GRADED **weak**, it is not very effective or powerful, or is likely to fail. *Until the beating, Cantanco's eyesight had been weak, but adequate... She tired easily and had a weak heart.* **3** If you describe someone as **weak**, you ADJ-GRADED mean that they are not very confident or determined, so that they are often frightened or worried, or easily influenced by other people. ◆ **weakness** N-UNCOUNT *Many people felt that admitting to stress was a sign of weakness.* **4** If you describe someone's voice or ADJ-GRADED smile as **weak**, you mean that it is not very loud or big, suggesting that the person lacks confidence, enthusiasm, or physical strength. ◆ **weakly** *He* ADV-GRADED: *smiled weakly at reporters.* ADV after v **5** If an object or surface is **weak**, it breaks easily and ADJ-GRADED cannot support a lot of weight or resist a lot of strain. *The bird may have escaped through a weak spot in the aviary.* **6** A **weak** physical force does not have much ADV-GRADED power or intensity. *...the weak winter sun.* ◆ **weakly** ADV-GRADED *The mineral is weakly magnetic.* **7** A **weak** drink, ADJ-GRADED chemical, or drug contains very little of a particular substance, for example because it has been diluted with a lot of water. *...a cup of weak tea.* **8** If individuals or groups are **weak**, they do not have ADJ-GRADED any power or influence. *The council was too weak to do anything about it.* ▶ **The weak** are people who are N-PLURAL: **weak**. ◆ **weakness** *It made me feel patronised, in a* theN *position of weakness.* **9** A **weak** government or leader ADJ-GRADED does not have much control, and is not prepared or able to act firmly or severely. ◆ **weakly** *...the* ADV-GRADED *weakly-led movement for reform.* ◆ **weakness** *Offi-* N-UNCOUNT *cials fear that he might interpret the emphasis on diplomacy as a sign of weakness.* **10** If a country's currency, economy, industry, or government is **weak**, it is ADJ-GRADED not successful, and may collapse. *The weak dollar means American goods are relative bargains for foreigners.* ◆ **weakness** *The weakness of his regime is* N-UNCOUNT *showing more and more.* **11** If something such as an argument or case is **weak**, ADJ-GRADED it is not convincing or there is little evidence to support it. *The evidence against him was weak and insufficient.* ◆ **weakly** *The doctor also rather weakly puts* ADV-GRADED: *the case that the mother-to-be has many relatives.* ADV before v ◆ **weak·ness, weaknesses** *The law recognises the* N-VAR *weakness of claims based on retrospective knowledge.* **12** Your **weak** points are the qualities or talents you ADJ-GRADED do not possess, or the things you are not very good at. *Geography was my weak subject.* ◆ **weakness** *His* N-VAR *only weakness is his temperament.* **13** See also **weakness**.

weak·en /ˈwiːkən/ **weakens, weakening,** ◆◆◆◇◇ **weakened. 1** If you **weaken** something or if it V-ERG **weakens**, it becomes less strong or less powerful. V n *The recession has weakened so many firms that* V many can no longer survive... Family structures are weakening and breaking up. **2** If your resolve **weak-** V-ERG **ens** or if something **weakens** it, you become less de- V termined or less certain about taking a particular V n course of action that you had previously decided to take. *Jennie weakened, and finally relented... The verdict hasn't weakened his resolve to fight the charges against him.* **3** If something **weakens** you, it VERB: V n causes you to lose some of your physical strength. **4** If something **weakens** an object, it does some- VERB thing to it which causes it to become less firm and V n more likely to break. *Never dry underwear over direct heat; it will weaken the fabric.*

,weak-'kneed. If you describe someone as **weak-kneed**, you mean that they are unable or unwilling to do something because they are influenced by a strong emotion such as fear.   ADJ-GRADED INFORMAL

weak·ling /'wiːklɪŋ/ **weaklings. 1** If you describe a person or an animal as a **weakling**, you mean that they are physically weak; used showing disapproval. **2** If you describe someone as a **weakling**, you mean that they are weak or cowardly in character; used showing disapproval.   N-COUNT PRAGMATICS / N-COUNT PRAGMATICS

weak·ness /'wiːknəs/ **weaknesses.** If you have a **weakness** for something, you like it very much, although this is perhaps surprising or undesirable. *Stephen himself had a weakness for cats.* ● See also **weak.**   ◆◆◇◇◇ N-COUNT

weal /wiːl/ **weals.** A **weal** is a swelling made on someone's skin by a blow, especially from something such as a sword or whip.   N-COUNT BRITISH

wealth /welθ/. **1 Wealth** is the possession of a large amount of money, property, or other valuable things. You can also refer to a particular person's money or property as their **wealth.** *His own wealth grew.* **2** If you say that someone or something has a **wealth of** good qualities or attributes, you are emphasizing that they have a very large number or amount of them. *The city boasts a wealth of beautiful churches.*   ◆◆◆◇◇ N-UNCOUNT / N-SING aN of n PRAGMATICS LITERARY

wealthy /'welθi/ **wealthier, wealthiest.** Someone who is **wealthy** has a large amount of money, property, or valuable possessions. ▶ **The wealthy** are people who are wealthy.   ◆◆◇◇◇ ADJ-GRADED / N-PLURAL: theN

wean /wiːn/ **weans, weaning, weaned. 1** When a baby or baby animal **is weaned,** its mother stops feeding it milk and starts giving it other food, especially solid food. *Phil took the labrador home and is weaning him off milk on to meat.* ◆ **wean·ing** *Weaning should be a gradual process.* **2** If you **wean** someone off a habit or something they like, you gradually make them stop doing it or liking it, especially when you think it is bad for them. *It's two years since I've seen Iain. I'm still trying to wean myself off him but it's hard.*   ◆◇◇◇◇ VERB: be V-ed V n off/from n Also V-ed / N-UNCOUNT / VERB: V n off/from n V pron-refl off/from n

weap·on /'wepən/ **weapons. 1** A **weapon** is an object such as a gun, a knife, or a missile, which is used to kill or hurt people in a fight or a war. **2** If you refer to something such as a piece of knowledge as a **weapon,** you mean that you can use it to protect yourself or to get what you want in a difficult situation. *I attack politicians with the one weapon they don't have, a sense of humor.*   ◆◆◆◇◇ N-COUNT / N-COUNT

wea·pon·ry /'wepənri/. **Weaponry** is all the weapons that a group or country has or that are available to it.   ◆◇◇◇◇ N-UNCOUNT

wear /weə/ **wears, wearing, wore, worn. 1** When you **wear** something such as clothes, shoes, or jewellery, you have them on your body. *He was wearing a brown uniform.* ◆ **wear·er, wearers** *The mascara is suitable for contact lens wearers.* **2** If you **wear** your hair or beard in a particular way, you have it cut or styled in that way. *She wore her hair in a long braid.* **3** If you **wear** a particular expression, that expression is on your face and shows the emotions that you are feeling. *When we drove through the gates, she wore a look of amazement.* **4** You use **wear** to refer to clothes that are suitable for a certain time or place. For example, **evening wear** is clothes suitable for the evening. **5** If you say that one person in a married couple **wears the trousers,** especially the wife, you mean that they are the one who makes all the decisions. The American expression is **wear the pants.** **6 Wear** is the amount or type of use that something has over a period of time. *You'll get more wear out of a hat if you choose one in a neutral colour.* **7 Wear** is the damage or change that is caused by something being used a lot or for a long time. *...a large, well-upholstered armchair which showed signs of wear.* **8** If something **wears,** it becomes thinner or weaker because it is constantly being used over a long period of time. *Your horse needs new shoes if the shoe has*   ◆◆◆◆◇ VERB V n / N-COUNT / VERB V n prep/adv / VERB V n / N-UNCOUNT supp N / PHRASE BRITISH, INFORMAL / N-UNCOUNT / N-UNCOUNT / VERB: V V adj

worn thin or smooth. **9** You can use **wear** to talk about how well something lasts over a period of time. For example, if something **wears well,** it still seems quite new or useful after a long time or a lot of use. **10** If your patience or temper **is wearing thin,** you are beginning to lose patience or lose your temper, and are likely to become angry soon. **11** If you say that something **is wearing thin,** you mean that people do not find it funny or interesting any more and are becoming annoyed with it, because they have seen or heard it so many times. *Some of Wilson's eccentricities are beginning to wear thin.* **12** If you say that someone is **the worse for wear,** you mean that they are tired, ill, or in a bad state because they have been very active, been through a difficult experience, or have drunk too much alcohol.   VERB: V adv / PHRASE / PHRASE / PHRASE INFORMAL

wear away. If you **wear** something **away,** it becomes thin and eventually disappears because it is used a lot or rubbed a lot. *The softer rock wears away.*   PHRASAL VB ERG: V n P V P

wear down. 1 If you **wear** something **down,** it becomes flatter or smoother as a result of constantly rubbing against something else. *The machines start to wear down.* **2** If you **wear** someone **down,** you make them gradually weaker or less determined until they eventually do what you want, by being more persistent than they are. *...your sheer will-power and persistence in wearing down the opposition.*   PHRASAL VB ERG: V n P V P / V n P V P noun

wear off. If a sensation or feeling **wears off,** it disappears slowly until it no longer exists or has any effect. *For many the philosophy was merely a fashion, and the novelty soon wore off.*   PHRASAL VB V P

wear on. If you say that time **wears on,** you mean that it passes, especially when it seems to pass slowly. *As the day wore on Brand found himself increasingly impressed.*   PHRASAL VB V P

wear out. 1 When something **wears out,** it is used so much that it becomes thin or weak and unable to be used any more. *Horses used for long-distance riding tend to wear their shoes out more quickly.* **2** If something **wears** you **out,** it makes you feel extremely tired. *The young people run around kicking a ball, wearing themselves out.* **3** If someone **wears out** their welcome with you, they spend a lot of time with you and you are no longer happy that they are with you. You can also say that a feeling **wears out** or **is worn out.** *His stubborn resistance to anything new eventually wore out the patience of his superiors... No matter how often they turn up, their welcome never wears out.* **4** See also **worn out.**   PHRASAL VB ERG: V P V n P / V P V pron-refl P INFORMAL / ERG: V P noun V P

wear·able /'weərəbəl/. **Wearable** clothes are practical, comfortable, and suitable for ordinary people to wear, rather than being very unusual or extreme.   ADJ-GRADED

wear and tear /,weər ən 'teə/. **Wear and tear** is the damage or change that is caused to something when it is being used normally.   N-UNCOUNT

wear·ing /'weərɪŋ/. If you say that a situation or activity is **wearing,** you mean that it requires a lot of energy and makes you feel mentally or physically tired.   ADJ-GRADED

wea·ri·some /'wɪərɪsəm/. If you describe something as **wearisome,** you mean that it is very tiring and boring or frustrating.   ADJ-GRADED FORMAL

wea·ry /'wɪəri/ **wearier, weariest; wearies, wearying, wearied. 1** If you are **weary,** you are very tired. ◆ **wea·ri·ly** /'wɪərɪli/. *I sighed wearily.* ◆ **wea·ri·ness** *Despite his weariness, Brand mustered a wan smile.* **2** If you are **weary of** something, you have become tired of it and want it to end. *She was weary of being alone.* ◆ **wearily** *'I'm not Mrs Reynolds,' she said wearily.* **3** If you **weary of** something, you become tired of it and want it to end. *He had wearied of teaching in state universities... The political hysteria soon wearied him.*   ◆◆◇◇◇ ADJ-GRADED / ADV-GRADED / N-UNCOUNT / ADJ-GRADED v-link ADJ of n/-ing / ADV-GRADED / VERB V of n/-ing V n FORMAL

wea·sel /'wiːzəl/ **weasels.** A **weasel** is a small wild animal with a long thin body, a tail, short legs, and reddish-brown fur.   ◆◇◇◇◇ N-COUNT

weath·er /'weðə/ **weathers, weathering, weathered. 1** The **weather** is the condition of the atmosphere in one area at a particular time, for example if it is raining, hot, or windy. *The weather was*   ◆◆◆◆◇ N-UNCOUNT

bad... I like cold weather. ● If you say that someone does something **in all weathers**, you mean that they do it regularly whether the weather is good or bad. **2** If something such as wood or rock **weathers**, it changes colour or shape as a result of the wind, sun, rain, or frost. *This rock has been weathered and eroded.* ♦ **weath·ered** *The building was a little weathered.* **3** If you **weather** a difficult time or a difficult situation, you survive it and are able to continue normally after it has passed or ended. *The company has weathered the recession.* ● **to weather the storm**: see **storm**. **4** If you say that you are **under the weather**, you mean that you feel slightly ill. [PHRASE]

'**weather-beaten**; also spelled **weatherbeaten**. If an object or a person's skin is **weather-beaten**, it has become roughened and perhaps changed colour as a result of being out in bad weather for a long time. *...a ruddy, weather-beaten face.* [ADJ-GRADED]

'**weather forecast, weather forecasts.** A **weather forecast** is a statement saying what the weather will be like the next day or for the next few days. ♦ '**weather forecaster, weather forecasters.** A **weather forecaster** is a person whose job is to make weather forecasts. [N-COUNT] [N-COUNT]

weather·man /ˈweðəmæn/ **weathermen.** A **weatherman** is a man who makes weather forecasts at regular times on television or radio. [N-COUNT]

weather·proof /ˈweðəpruːf/. Something that is **weatherproof** is made of material which protects it from the weather or keeps out wind and rain. [ADJ]

'**weather station, weather stations.** A **weather station** is a building that is used for studying and recording facts about the weather, so that weather forecasts can be made. [N-COUNT]

'**weather vane, weather vanes.** A **weather vane** is a metal object on the roof of a building which turns round as the wind blows. It is used to show the direction of the wind. [N-COUNT]

weave /wiːv/ **weaves, weaving, wove, woven.** The form **weaved** is used for the past tense and past participle for meaning 4. **1** If you **weave** cloth, you make it by crossing the threads over and under each other using a machine called a loom. *In one room, young mothers weave while babies doze in their laps.* ♦ **weav·er, weavers** *She was a linen weaver from Ireland.* ♦ **weav·ing** *I studied weaving.* **2** A particular **weave** is the way in which the threads are arranged in a cloth or carpet. *Fabrics with a close weave are ideal for painting.* **3** If you **weave** something such as a basket, you make it by crossing long plant stems or fibres over and under each other. ♦ **wo·ven** *The floors are covered with woven straw mats.* ♦ **weav·er** *...basket weavers in Wiltshire.* **4** If you **weave** your way somewhere, you move between and around things as you go there. *He weaves his way through a crowd.* **5** If a writer or speaker **weaves** a story, they tell it. [VERB: V n] [V] [N-COUNT] [N-UNCOUNT] [N-COUNT] [VERB: V n] [ADJ] [N-COUNT] [VERB] [V way prep/adv] [VERB: V n] [WRITTEN]

web /web/ **webs.** **1** A spider's **web** is the thin net which it makes from the sticky substance it produces in its body. **2** A **web** is a complicated pattern of connections or relationships, sometimes considered as an obstacle or a danger. *They accused him of weaving a web of lies and deceit.* ● See also **World-Wide Web.** [N-COUNT] [N-COUNT]

webbed /webd/. **1** Webbed feet or toes have a piece of skin between the toes. Water birds such as ducks have webbed feet. **2** If a computer is **webbed**, it has the necessary connections and software to be able to access the World-Wide Web. *We've been fully webbed for the last 18 months.* [ADJ: ADJ n] [ADJ]

web·bing /ˈwebɪŋ/. Webbing is strong material which is woven in strips and used to make belts or straps, or used in seats to support the springs. [N-UNCOUNT]

wed /wed/ **weds, wedded.** The form **wed** is used in the present tense and is the past tense. The past participle can be either **wed** or **wedded**. If one person **weds** another or if two people **wed**, they get married. *In 1952 she wed film director Roger Vadim... The couple wed late at night in front of just* [V-RECIP-ERG: no cont V n] [pl-n V] [be V-ed] [Also V] [DATED or]

nine guests... They were wed at Amiens last August. ● See also **newlywed, wedded.** [JOURNALISM]

Wed.; also spelled **Weds.. Wed.** or **Weds.** is a written abbreviation for **Wednesday.**

we'd /wɪd, wiːd/. **We'd** is the usual spoken form of 'we would' or 'we had', especially when 'had' is an auxiliary verb. *I don't know how we'd have managed without her!*

wed·ded /ˈwedɪd/. **1** If you are **wedded to** something such as an idea, you support it so strongly or like it so much that you are unable to give it up. *Conservationists are mostly wedded to preserving diversity in nature.* **2** **Wedded** means the same as **married.** *...a romantic fantasy of wedded bliss.* [ADJ-GRADED: v-link ADJ to n] [FORMAL] [ADJ: ADJ n] [FORMAL]

wed·ding /ˈwedɪŋ/ **weddings.** A **wedding** is a marriage ceremony and the party or special meal that often takes place after the ceremony. [N-COUNT]

'**wedding band, wedding bands.** A **wedding band** is the same as a **wedding ring.** [N-COUNT]

'**wedding ring, wedding rings.** A **wedding ring** is a plain ring that you wear to show that you are married. [N-COUNT]

wedge /wedʒ/ **wedges, wedging, wedged.** **1** If you **wedge** something, you force it to remain in a particular position by holding it there tightly or by fixing something next to it to prevent it from moving. *We slammed the gate after them, wedging it shut with planks.* **2** If you **wedge** something somewhere, you fit it there tightly. *Wedge the plug into the hole.* **3** A **wedge** is an object with one pointed edge and one thick edge, which you put under a door to keep it firmly in position. **4** A **wedge** of something such as fruit or cheese is a piece of it that has a thick triangular shape. **5** If someone **drives a wedge** between two people who are close, they cause ill feelings between them in order to weaken their relationship. [VERB: V n] [V n adj] [VERB] [V n prep] [N-COUNT] [N-COUNT] [PHRASE]

wed·lock /ˈwedlɒk/. **1** Wedlock is the state of being married. **2** If a baby is born **in wedlock**, it is born while its parents are married. If it is born **out of wedlock**, it is born at a time when its parents are not married. [N-UNCOUNT] [DATED] [PHRASE] [FORMAL]

Wednes·day /ˈwenzdeɪ, -di/ **Wednesdays.** Wednesday is the day after Tuesday and before Thursday. *Come and have supper with us on Wednesday, if you're free... Did you happen to see her leave last Wednesday?* [N-VAR]

wee /wiː/ **wees, weeing, weed.** **1** Wee means small in size or extent; used especially in Scotland. *He just needs to calm down a wee bit.* **2** To **wee** means to urinate; used especially by children. ▶ Also a noun. *The baby has done a wee in his potty.* [ADJ: ADJ n] [INFORMAL] [VERB: V] [INFORMAL] [N-VAR]

weed /wiːd/ **weeds, weeding, weeded.** **1** A **weed** is a wild plant that grows in gardens or fields of crops and prevents the cultivated plants from growing properly. **2** Weed is any of several kinds of plant that grow in water and usually form a thick floating mass. **3** If you **weed** an area, you remove the weeds from it. *The Hodges are busy weeding and planting.* ♦ **weed·ing** *She taught me to do the weeding.* **4** People sometimes refer to tobacco or marijuana as **weed.** [N-COUNT] [N-VAR] [VERB: V n] [V] [N-UNCOUNT] [N-COUNT: also the N] [INFORMAL]

weed out. If you **weed out** things or people that are useless or unwanted in a group, you find them and get rid of them. *He is keen to weed out the many applicants he believes may be frauds.* [PHRASAL VB] [V P noun] [Also V n P]

weed·killer /ˈwiːdkɪlə/ **weedkillers.** Weedkiller is a substance that you put on your garden to kill weeds. [N-VAR]

weedy /ˈwiːdi/ **weedier, weediest.** **1** A **weedy** place is full of weeds. **2** If you describe someone as **weedy**, you are criticizing them or laughing at them because they are thin and physically weak. [ADJ-GRADED] [ADJ-GRADED] [PRAGMATICS] [BRITISH, INFORMAL]

week /wiːk/ **weeks.** **1** A **week** is a period of seven days, which is often considered to start on Monday and end on Sunday. A **week** can also be used to refer to any period of approximately seven days. *I had a letter from my mother last week... Her mother stayed for another two weeks.* **2** Your working **week** is the hours that you spend at work during a week. *It is not unusual for women to work a 40-hour week.* [N-COUNT] [N-COUNT]

...workers on a three-day week because of the sales slump. **3 The week** is the part of the week that does not include Saturday and Sunday. ...the hard work of looking after the children during the week. **4** You use **week** in expressions such as 'a week on Monday', 'a week next Tuesday', and 'tomorrow week' to mean exactly one week after the day that you mention. You use **week** in expressions such as 'a week last Monday' to mean exactly one week before the day that you mention. That was a week ago yesterday. **5** If you say that something happens **week in week out**, you do not like it because it happens all the time, and never seems to change. `N-SING: theN` `N-COUNT` `PHRASE PRAGMATICS`

week·day /'wi:kdeɪ/ **weekdays.** A **weekday** is any of the days of the week except Saturday and Sunday. If you want to avoid the crowds, it's best to come on a weekday. `◆◇◇◇◇ N-COUNT`

week·end /ˌwiːk'end/ **weekends.** A **weekend** is Saturday and Sunday. He told me to give you a call over the weekend. `◆◆◆◇ N-COUNT`

week·end·er /wiːk'endə/ **weekenders.** A **weekender** is someone who goes to a place or lives at a place only at weekends. He converted his barns into cottages for weekenders. `N-COUNT`

week·ly /'wi:kli/ **weeklies. 1** A **weekly** event or publication happens or appears once a week or every week. We go and do the weekly shopping every Thursday... His story was published in a weekly newspaper. ▶ Also an adverb. The group meets weekly. **2 Weekly** quantities or rates relate to a period of one week. Working wives get an average weekly wage of £153. **3** A **weekly** is a newspaper or magazine that is published once a week. `◆◆◆◇◇ ADJ: ADJ n` `ADV` `ADJ: ADJ n` `N-COUNT`

weep /wiːp/ **weeps, weeping, wept. 1** If someone **weeps**, they cry. The weeping family hugged and comforted each other... She wept tears of joy. ▶ Also a noun. There are times when I sit down and have a good weep. **2** If a wound **weeps**, pus or blood comes from it because it is not healing properly. ...little blisters which develop into weeping sores. `◆◆◇◇◇ VERB: V V-ing V n` `N-SING` `VERB: V V-ing`

weeping willow, **weeping willows.** A **weeping willow** is a type of willow tree. It has long thin branches that hang down to the ground. `N-COUNT`

weepy /'wi:pi/ **weepies. 1** Someone who is **weepy** is sad and likely to cry easily. **2** A **weepy** is a film or a story which is sentimental and makes you cry. `ADJ-GRADED` `N-COUNT INFORMAL`

wee·vil /'wiːvɪl/ **weevils.** A **weevil** is a small beetle which feeds on grain and seeds, and destroys crops. `N-COUNT`

weft /weft/. The **weft** of a piece of woven material is the threads which are passed sideways in and out of the threads held in the loom. `N-SING`

weigh /weɪ/ **weighs, weighing, weighed. 1** If someone or something **weighs** a particular amount, this amount is how heavy they are. I weighed 22 stone at the time... You always weigh less in the morning. **2** If you **weigh** something or someone, you measure how heavy they are. **3** If you **weigh** the facts about a situation or **weigh** your words, you consider them very carefully before you decide or say anything. She weighed her options... She spoke very slowly, weighing what she would say. ▶ **Weigh up** means the same as **weigh**. Nirex will be able to weigh up the environmental pros and cons of each site... You have to weigh up whether a human life is more important than an animal's life. **4** If a problem **weighs** on you, it makes you worried or unhappy. The separation weighed on both of them. **5** Something that **weighs** heavily in a situation has a strong influence or important effect on it. Current economic hardships weigh heavily in young women's decisions to find salaried work... There are many factors weighing against the meeting happening. `◆◆◇◇◇ VB: no cont V amount` `VERB: V n` `VERB V n V wh` `PHRASAL VB V P n V P wh Also V n P` `VERB V on/upon n` `VERB V adv prep V against n/-ing`

weigh down. 1 If something that you are wearing or carrying **weighs** you **down**, it stops you moving easily by making you heavier. He wrenched off his sneakers. If they had to swim, he didn't want anything weighing him down. ...soldiers weighed down by their heavy packs. **2** If you **are weighed down** by something, it makes you extremely worried or causes you great problems. The merchant bank is being weighed `PHRASAL VB V n P V-ed P Also V P noun` `be V-ed by/ with n Also V n P`

down by a £1.3 billion book of bad debts. ♦ **weighed down** I was too weighed down by guilt to eat. `ADJ-GRADED: v-link ADJ`

weigh in. 1 If you **weigh in** on a plan, decision, or discussion, you make a significant or important contribution to it. Clinton's political advisers also weighed in on the plan. **2** If someone **weighs in at** a particular weight, for example before competing in a sports competition, their weight is measured at that amount. ● See also **weigh-in**. `PHRASAL VB V P on n JOURNALISM` `V P at amount`

weigh out. If you **weigh** something **out**, you measure a certain weight of it so that you get the correct amount. I learned how to weigh out packages of seed. `PHRASAL VB V n P V P noun`

weigh up. 1 See **weigh 3**. **2** If you **weigh** someone **up**, you try to find out what they are like and form an opinion of them, especially when you are suspicious of them. She weighed him up now with professional eyes. `PHRASAL VB V n P Also V P noun BRITISH`

weigh-in, weigh-ins. When there is a **weigh-in** on the day of a boxing match or a horse race, each competitor is weighed to check their weight shortly before the event. `N-COUNT`

weight /weɪt/ **weights, weighting, weighted. 1** The **weight** of a person or thing is how heavy they are, measured in units such as kilos, pounds, or tons. What is your height and weight?... This reduced the weight of the load. ● If someone **loses weight**, they become lighter. If they **gain weight** or **put on weight**, they become heavier. **2** A person's or thing's **weight** is the fact that they are very heavy. His weight was harming his health. **3** If you move your **weight**, you change position so that most of the pressure of your body is on a particular part of your body. He shifted his weight from one foot to the other. **4 Weights** are objects which weigh a known amount. Small weights are used with scales to weigh other things, and larger ones are lifted as a form of fitness training. **5** You can refer to a heavy object as a **weight**, especially when you have to lift it. Straining to lift heavy weights can lead to a rise in blood pressure. **6** If you **weight** something, you make it heavier by adding something to it, for example in order to stop it from moving easily. ▶ **Weight down** means the same as **weight**. Put some tins on top to weight it down. **7** If you **weight** things, you give them different values according to how important or significant they are. The index includes 24 commodities, weighted according to the imports of the various countries. **8** If something is given a particular **weight**, it is given a particular value according to how important or significant it is. The scientists involved put different weight on the conclusions of different models. **9** If you talk about the **weight** of something, you think it is large in amount or has great power, which means that it is difficult to contradict or fight against. Companies found themselves collapsing under the weight of debts. **10** If you feel a **weight** on you, you have a problem or a responsibility that is worrying and difficult for you to deal with. It was freedom after years of slavery. A great weight lifted from me. **11** See also **weighting; dead weight.** **12** If a person or their opinion **carries weight**, they are respected and are able to influence people. Senator Kerry carries considerable weight in Washington. **13** If you say that someone or something is **worth their weight in gold**, you are emphasizing that they are so useful, helpful, or valuable that you feel you could not manage without them. **14** If someone is not **pulling** their **weight**, they are not working as hard as everyone else who is involved in the same task. **15** If someone **throws** their **weight around** or **throws** their **weight about**, they act aggressively and use their authority over other people more than they need to. **16** If you **throw your weight behind** a person, plan, or campaign, you use all your influence and do everything you can to support them. The administration is throwing its full weight behind the UN plan. `◆◆◆◇ N-VAR` `PHRASE` `N-UNCOUNT: with poss` `N-SING: poss/the N` `N-COUNT` `N-COUNT` `VERB: V n` `PHRASAL VB V n P` `VERB: V n V-ed` `N-VAR` `N-UNCOUNT: the N of n` `N-SING` `PHRASE` `PHRASE PRAGMATICS` `PHRASE` `PHRASE` `PHRASE`

weight down. See **weight 6**. `PHRASAL VB`

weight·ed /'weɪtɪd/. A system that is **weighted** in favour of a particular person or group is organized `ADJ-GRADED`

so that this person or group has an advantage. *The peace process is so heavily weighted against them that it will never achieve results.*

weight·ing /'weɪtɪŋ/ **weightings. 1** A **weighting** is a value which is given to something according to how important or significant it is. *Each country's currency is given a weighting in the ECU.* **2** A **weighting** is an advantage that a particular group of people receives in a system, especially an extra sum of money that people receive if they work in a city where the cost of living is very high. *I get an extra £2,700-a-year London weighting.* **3** See also **weight**. N-COUNT

weight·less /'weɪtləs/. **1** Something that is **weightless** weighs or seems to weigh nothing. **2** A person or object is **weightless** when they are in space and the earth's gravity does not affect them. ♦ **weight·less·ness** ...*the human body's response to weightlessness.* ADJ-GRADED / ADJ / N-UNCOUNT

weight·lifting /'weɪtlɪftɪŋ/; also spelled **weight-lifting**. **Weightlifting** is a sport in which the competitor who can lift the heaviest weight wins. ♦ **weight·lifter, weightlifters.** A **weightlifter** is a person who does weightlifting. N-UNCOUNT / N-COUNT

weighty /'weɪti/ **weightier, weightiest. 1** Something such as an issue or a concept that is **weighty** seems serious or important. *Surely such weighty matters merit a higher level of debate?* **2** You use **weighty** to describe something that is heavy or heavier than you would expect. ADJ-GRADED FORMAL / ADJ-GRADED FORMAL

weir /wɪə/ **weirs. 1** A **weir** is a low dam which is built across a river in order to control or direct the flow of water. **2** A **weir** is a wooden fence which is built across a stream in order to create a pool for catching fish. N-COUNT / N-COUNT

weird /wɪəd/ **weirder, weirdest.** If you describe something or someone as **weird**, you mean that they are strange and peculiar. *That first day was weird... It must be really weird to be rich.* ♦ **weird·ly** ...*men who dressed weirdly.* ♦ **weird·ness** *The weirdness of Hollywood suits him well.* ADJ-GRADED / ADV-GRADED / N-UNCOUNT

weir·do /'wɪədəʊ/ **weirdos.** If you describe someone as a **weirdo**, you disapprove of them because they behave in an unusual way which you find difficult to understand or to accept as normal. N-COUNT INFORMAL

wel·come /'welkəm/ **welcomes, welcoming, welcomed. 1** If you **welcome** someone, you greet them in a friendly way when they arrive somewhere. *She was there to welcome him home from war. ...a welcoming speech by the President.* ► Also a noun. *There would be a fantastic welcome awaiting him.* **2** You use **welcome** in expressions such as **welcome home, welcome to London,** and **welcome back** when you are greeting someone who has just arrived somewhere. **3** If you say that someone is **welcome** in a particular place, you are encouraging them to go there by assuring them that they will be accepted. *New members are always welcome... I told him he wasn't welcome in my home.* **4** If you **make** someone **welcome** or **make** them **feel** welcome, you make them feel happy and accepted in a new place. **5** If you say that someone **outstays** their **welcome** or **overstays** their **welcome**, you mean that they stay somewhere longer than they are wanted or expected to. **6** If you **welcome** an action, decision, or situation, you approve of it and are pleased that it has occurred. *She welcomed this move but said that overall the changes didn't go far enough.* ► Also a noun. *Environmental groups have given a guarded welcome to the Prime Minister's proposal.* **7** If you describe something as **welcome**, you mean that people wanted it and are happy that it has occurred. *This was certainly a welcome change of fortune.* **8** If you say that you **welcome** certain people or actions, you are inviting and encouraging people to do something. *We would welcome your views about the survey.* **9** If you tell someone that they are **welcome** to do something, you are encouraging them to do it by assuring them that they are allowed to do it. ...*a conservatory which guests are welcome to use.* **10** If you say that someone is **welcome to** VERB: V n / V n adv/prep / V-ing / N-COUNT / CONVENTION PRAGMATICS / ADJ-GRADED / PHRASE / PHRASE / VERB V n / N-COUNT / ADJ-GRADED / VERB PRAGMATICS V n / ADJ-GRADED: v-link ADJ PRAGMATICS / ADJ-GRADED:

come to something, you mean that you do not want it yourself and you are very willing for them to have it. *If women want to take on the business world they are welcome to it as far as I'm concerned.* **11** You say **'You're welcome'** to someone who has thanked you for something in order to acknowledge their thanks in a polite way. v-link ADJ to n / CONVENTION PRAGMATICS

wel·com·ing /'welkəmɪŋ/. **1** If someone is **welcoming**, they are friendly to you when you arrive somewhere, so that you feel happy and accepted. *Her face spread in a welcoming smile.* **2** A **welcoming** building or room is pleasantly decorated and furnished and you feel as though you would be happy spending time there. ADJ-GRADED / ADJ-GRADED

weld /weld/ **welds, welding, welded. 1** To **weld** one piece of metal to another means to join them by heating the edges and putting them together so that they cool and harden into one piece. *They will also be used on factory floors to weld things together... Where did you learn to weld?* ♦ **weld·ing** *All the welding had been done from inside the car.* ♦ **weld·er, welders.** A **welder** is a person whose job is welding metal. **2** A **weld** is a join where two pieces of metal have been welded together. **3** If you **weld** people together, you join them together to form a united organization. *The miracle was that Rose had welded them into a team.* ◇◇◇◇◇ VERB: V n to n / V n with / together / V / Also V n / N-UNCOUNT / N-COUNT / VERB: V n with / together / V n into n / FORMAL

wel·fare /'welfeə/. **1** The **welfare** of a person or group is their health, comfort, and prosperity. *I do not think he is considering Emma's welfare.* **2** **Welfare** services are provided to help with people's living conditions and financial problems. **3** In the United States, **welfare** is money that is paid by the government to people who are unemployed, poor, or ill. The British term is **social security**. ♦♦♦◇◇ N-UNCOUNT / ADJ / N-UNCOUNT

welfare 'state. In Britain and some other countries, the **welfare state** is a system in which the government provides free social services such as health and education and gives money to people when they are unable to work, for example because they are old, unemployed, or sick. ◇◇◇◇◇ N-SING

well 1 discourse uses

well /wel/. **Well** is used mainly in spoken English. ♦♦♦♦♦ **1** You say **well** to indicate that you intend to say something or to carry on speaking. *Well, I don't like the look of that... The trouble with City is that they do not have enough quality players. Well, that can easily be rectified.* **2** You say **well** to indicate that you are changing the topic, and are going back to something that was being discussed earlier or are going on to something new. *Well, let's press on.* **3** You say **well** to indicate that you have reached the end of a conversation. *'I'm sure you will be an asset,' she finally added. 'Well, I see it's just about time for lunch.'... Well, thank you for speaking with us.* **4** You say **well** to make a suggestion, criticism, or correction seem less definite or rude. *Well, I thought she was a bit unfair about me.* **5** You say **well** just before or after you pause, especially to give yourself time to think about what you are going to say, or because you want to rephrase something that you have just said. *Look, I'm really sorry I woke you, and, well, I just wanted to tell you I was all right.* **6** You say **well** when you are modifying or correcting something that you have just said. *There was a note. Well, not really a note.* **7** You say **well** to express your doubt about something that someone has said. *'Go on, Dennis.'—'Well, if you're sure.'* **8** You say **well** to express your surprise or anger at something that someone has just said or done. *Well, honestly! They're like an old married couple at times.* **9** You say **well** to indicate that you are waiting for someone to say something or explain something, and often to express your irritation with them. *'Well?' asked Barry, 'what does it tell us?'* **10** You use **well** to indicate that you are amused by something you have heard or seen, and often to introduce a comment on it. *Bob peered at it. 'Well, well!' he said, 'I haven't seen Spam since the war!' and laughed.* **11** You say **oh well** to indicate that you accept a situation or that someone else should accept ADV cl / ADV cl PRAGMATICS / ADV cl / ADV cl PRAGMATICS / ADV: ADV cl PRAGMATICS / ADV: ADV cl PRAGMATICS / ADV: ADV cl PRAGMATICS / ADV: ADV cl/group PRAGMATICS / ADV: ADV cl PRAGMATICS / EXCLAM PRAGMATICS / CONVENTION PRAGMATICS / CONVENTION PRAGMATICS / CONVENTION PRAGMATICS

it, even though you or they are not very happy about it. *Oh well, it could be worse.* **12 • very well:** see **very**.

well 2 adverb uses

well /wel/ **better, best. 1** If you do something **well**, you do it to a high standard or to a great extent. *All the Indian batsmen played well... He speaks English better than I do... It is a formula that worked very well indeed.* **2** If you do something **well**, you do it thoroughly and completely. *Mix all the ingredients well.* **3** Well is used in front of past participles to indicate that something is done to a high standard or to a great extent. Many of the commonest combinations are treated as separate headwords in this dictionary. *Helen is a very well-known novelist in Australia... People live longer nowadays, and they are better educated.* **4** You use **well** to ask or talk about the extent or standard of something. *How well do you remember your mother, Franzi?... He wasn't dressed any better than me.*
5 If you speak or think **well** of someone, you say or think favourable things about them. *It might help people think better of him.*
6 You use **well** in front of a prepositional phrase to emphasize it. For example, if you say that one thing happened **well before** another, you mean that it happened a long time before it. *Franklin did not turn up until well after midnight... We often plan our meals well in advance.* **7** You use **well** before certain adjectives to emphasize them. *Men are generally better able to express anger... The show is well worth a visit.*
8 You use **well** after adverbs such as 'perfectly', 'jolly', or 'damn' in order to emphasize an opinion or the truth of what you are saying. *You know perfectly well I can't be blamed for the failure of that mission.*
9 You use **well** after verbs such as 'may' and 'could' when you are saying what you think is likely to happen. *The murderer may well come from the estate.*

◆◆◆◆
ADV-GRADED:
ADV after v

ADV-GRADED:
ADV after v
COMB

ADV-GRADED

ADV-GRADED:
ADV after v

ADV:
ADV prep
PRAGMATICS

ADV-GRADED:
ADV adj
PRAGMATICS

ADV
PRAGMATICS

ADV:
modal ADV

well 3 phrases

well /wel/. **1** You use **as well** when mentioning something which happens in the same way as something else already mentioned, or which should be considered at the same time as something else already mentioned. *It is most often diagnosed in women in their thirties and forties, although I've seen it in many younger women, as well.* **2** You use **as well as** when you want to mention another item connected with the subject you are discussing. *It is in his best interests as well as yours.*
3 If you say, after stating that something has happened or is the case, **as well it might** or **as well it may**, you mean that this is not at all surprising or is quite appropriate. *This caused a few gasps, as well it might.*
4 If you say that something that has happened **is just as well**, you mean that it is fortunate that it happened in the way it did. *Judging from everything she said, it was just as well she wasn't there.* **5** You say **it is as well to** think or do something when you are advising someone to think in a particular way or to take a particular action. *It is as well to bear in mind that laughter is a great releaser of tension.* **6** If you say that someone **would do well to** do something, you mean that you advise or recommend that they do it. *Investors would do well to take a look at the Swiss economy.* **7** If you say that something, usually something bad, **might as well** be true or **may as well** be true, you mean that the situation is the same or almost the same as if it were true. *The couple might as well have been strangers.* **8** If you say that you **might as well** do something, or that you **may as well** do it, you mean that you will do it although you do not have a strong desire to do it and may even feel slightly reluctant about it. *Anyway, you're here; you might as well stay.*
9 If you say that something is **all well and good**, you are suggesting that it has faults or disadvantages, although it may appear to be correct or reasonable. *It's all well and good for him to say he's sorry for dropping you, but has he told you why he did it?* **10** You say **well and good** or **all well and good** to indicate that if something is true or happens you will be pleased in general, but you think that it probably is not true or will not

◆◆◆◆
PHRASE

PHR-PREP

PHRASE
PRAGMATICS

PHRASE

PHRASE
PRAGMATICS

PHR-MODAL
PRAGMATICS

PHRASE

PHRASE
PRAGMATICS

PHRASE
PRAGMATICS

happen, or you are aware of disadvantages. *If they arrive before I leave, well and good. If not, the responsibility will be mine.*
11 If you say that something is **well and truly** finished, gone, or done, you are emphasizing that it is completely finished or gone, or thoroughly done. *The war is well and truly over.*
12 If you say that you like something or someone **well enough**, you mean that you quite like them or find them reasonably acceptable. *Nancy liked it well enough, but complained about the color.*
13 • all very well: see **all. • to know full well:** see **full. • to leave well alone:** see **leave. • to mean well:** see **mean. • pretty well:** see **pretty.**

PHRASE
PRAGMATICS
BRITISH

PHRASE

well 4 adjective use

well /wel/. If you are **well**, you are healthy and not ill. *I'm not very well today, I can't come in.*

◆◆◆◆◆
ADJ-GRADED

well 5 noun uses

well /wel/ **wells. 1** A **well** is a hole in the ground from which a supply of water is extracted. **2** A **well** is an oil well.

◆◆◇◇◇
N-COUNT
N-COUNT

well 6 verb uses

well /wel/ **wells, welling, welled. 1** If liquids, for example tears, **well**, they come to the surface and form a pool. ▶ **Well up** means the same as **well.** *Tears welled up in Anni's eyes.* **2** If an emotion **wells** in you, it suddenly becomes stronger, to the point where you have to express it. *Her love for him welled stronger than ever.* ▶ **Well up** means the same as **well.** *He could feel the anger welling up inside him.*

◆◇◇◇◇
VERB: V

PHRASAL VB
V P
VERB:
V in/inside n
V

PHRASAL VB
V P in/inside n
Also V P

we'll /wɪl, STRONG wiːl/. **We'll** is the usual spoken form of 'we shall' or 'we will'. *Whatever you want to chat about, we'll do it tonight.*

well-ad'justed; also spelled **well adjusted**. A **well-adjusted** person has a mature personality and can control their emotions and deal with problems without becoming anxious.

ADJ-GRADED

well ad'vised. If someone says that you would be **well advised** to do a particular thing, they are advising you to do it. *The party would be well advised to talk to the government.*

ADJ-GRADED:
v-link ADJ to-inf
PRAGMATICS

well-ap'pointed. A **well-appointed** room or building is equipped or furnished to a very high standard.

ADJ-GRADED
FORMAL

well-'balanced; also spelled **well balanced. 1** If you describe someone as **well-balanced**, you mean that they are sensible and do not have many emotional problems. **2** If you describe something that is made up of several elements or parts as **well-balanced**, you mean that the way that the different elements or parts are put together is good, because there is not too much or too little of any one element or part. *...a well balanced diet.*

◆◆◇◇◇
ADJ-GRADED

ADJ-GRADED

well-be'haved; also spelled **well behaved**. If you describe someone, especially a child, as **well-behaved**, you mean that they behave in a way that adults generally like and think is correct.

ADJ-GRADED

well-being; also spelled **wellbeing**. Someone's **well-being** is their health and happiness. *Singing can create a sense of wellbeing.*

◆◆◇◇◇
N-UNCOUNT

well-'born. Someone who is **well-born** belongs to an upper-class family.

ADJ-GRADED

well-'bred. A **well-bred** person is very polite and has good manners.

ADJ-GRADED

well-brought-'up; also spelled **well brought up**. If you say that someone, especially a child, is **well-brought-up**, you mean that they are very polite because they have been taught good manners.

ADJ-GRADED

well-'built; also spelled **well built**. A **well-built** person, especially a man, is strong and muscular.

ADJ-GRADED

well-con'nected; also spelled **well connected**. Someone who is **well-connected** has important or influential relatives or friends.

ADJ-GRADED

well-de'fined; also spelled **well defined**. Something that is **well-defined** is clear and precise and therefore easy to recognize or understand. *...well-defined financial regulations.*

◆◇◇◇◇
ADJ-GRADED

well dis'posed. If you are **well disposed** to a person, plan, or activity, you are likely to agree with them or support them. ADJ-GRADED

well 'done. 1 You say '**Well done**' to indicate that you are pleased that someone has got something right or done something good. *'Daddy! I came second in history'—'Well done, sweetheart!'* **2** If something that you have cooked, especially meat, is **well done**, it has been cooked thoroughly. CONVENTION PRAGMATICS ◆◇◇◇◇ ADJ-GRADED

well-'dressed; also spelled **well dressed**. Someone who is **well-dressed** is wearing smart or elegant clothes. ◆◇◇◇◇ ADJ-GRADED

well-'earned. You can use **well-earned** to indicate that you think something is deserved, usually because the person who gets it has been working very hard. *...his well-earned win in Sunday's race.* ADJ-GRADED

well-es'tablished; also spelled **well established**. If you say that something is **well-established**, you mean that it has been in existence for quite a long time and is successful. *...well-established companies.* ◆◇◇◇◇ ADJ-GRADED

well-'fed; also spelled **well fed**. If you say that someone is **well-fed**, you mean they get good food regularly. ADJ-GRADED

well-'founded; also spelled **well founded**. If you say that a report, opinion, or feeling is **well-founded**, you mean that it is based on facts and can therefore be justified. *We must respond to well-founded criticism with a willingness to change.* ADJ-GRADED

well-'groomed; also spelled **well groomed**. A **well-groomed** person is very neat and tidy, and has taken care over their appearance. ADJ-GRADED

well-'heeled. Someone who is **well-heeled** is wealthy. ADJ-GRADED

well-in'formed, better-informed; also spelled **well informed**. If you say that someone is **well-informed**, you mean that they know a lot about many different subjects or about one particular subject. *...a lending library to encourage members to become as well informed as possible.* ◆◇◇◇◇ ADJ-GRADED

wel·ling·ton /ˈwelɪŋtən/ **wellingtons. Wellingtons** or **wellington boots** are long rubber boots which you wear to keep your feet dry. The usual American term is **rubber boots**. N-COUNT BRITISH

well-in'tentioned; also spelled **well intentioned**. If you say that a person or their actions or remarks are **well-intentioned**, you mean that they intend to be helpful or kind but they are unsuccessful or cause unfortunate results. ADJ-GRADED

well-'kept; also spelled **well kept. 1** A **well-kept** building, street, garden, or other place is always neat and tidy because it is carefully looked after. **2** A **well-kept** secret has not been made known to anyone, or has been made known to only a small number of people. ADJ-GRADED ADJ-GRADED

well-'known; also spelled **well known. 1** A **well-known** person or thing is known about by a lot of people and is therefore famous or familiar. If someone is **well-known** for a particular activity, a lot of people know about them because of their involvement with that activity. *He is well-known to the local police.* **2** A **well-known** fact is a fact that is known by people in general. ◆◆◆◇◇ ADJ-GRADED ADJ-GRADED

well-'mannered. Someone who is **well-mannered** is polite and has good manners. ADJ-GRADED

well-'meaning; also spelled **well meaning**. If you say that a person or their actions or remarks are **well-meaning**, you mean that they intend to be helpful or kind but they are unsuccessful or cause unfortunate results. *He is a well-meaning but ineffectual leader... Even well-meaning attempts at conservation can bring problems.* ◆◇◇◇◇ ADJ-GRADED

well-'meant; also spelled **well meant**. A **well-meant** decision, action, or comment is intended to be helpful or kind but is unsuccessful or causes unfortunate results. *...a well-meant experiment gone wrong.* ADJ-GRADED

well-'nigh; also spelled **well nigh. Well-nigh** means almost, but not completely or exactly. *...a hierarchical structure that was well-nigh unassailable.* ADV: ADV adj

well-'off; also spelled **well off**. Someone who is **well-off** is rich enough to be able to do and buy most of the things that they want. ▶ The **well-off** are people who are well-off. ◆◇◇◇◇ ADJ-GRADED INFORMAL N-PLURAL: the N

well-'oiled. A system or organization that is operating very efficiently can be referred to as a **well-oiled** machine. ADJ: ADJ n JOURNALISM

well-'paid; also spelled **well paid**. If you say that a person or their job is **well-paid**, you mean that they receive a lot of money for the work that they do. ◆◇◇◇◇ ADJ-GRADED

well-pre'served; also spelled **well preserved. 1** If you describe a middle-aged or old person as **well-preserved**, you mean that they look good for their age. **2** A **well-preserved** object or building does not show any signs of its age. *...well-preserved fossils.* ADJ-GRADED ADJ-GRADED

well-read /ˌwel ˈred/; also spelled **well read**. A **well-read** person has read a lot of books and has learnt a lot from them. ADJ-GRADED

well-'spoken; also spelled **well spoken**. A **well-spoken** person speaks in a polite correct way and with an accent which is considered socially acceptable. ADJ-GRADED

well-'thumbed. A book or magazine that is **well-thumbed** is creased and marked because it has been read so often. ADJ-GRADED

well-'timed. A **well-timed** action or comment is done or made at the most appropriate or suitable time. ADJ-GRADED

well-to-'do. A **well-to-do** person is rich enough to be able to do and buy most of the things that they want. *...a rather well-to-do family of diamond cutters.* ▶ The **well-to-do** are people who are well-to-do. ◆◇◇◇◇ ADJ-GRADED N-PLURAL: the N

well-'travelled; spelled **well-traveled** in American English. A **well-travelled** person has travelled a lot in foreign countries. ADJ-GRADED

well-'tried; also spelled **well tried**. A **well-tried** treatment, product, or method is one that has been used many times before and so is known to work well or to be successful. *...a number of well-tried remedies which are perfectly safe to take.* ADJ-GRADED

well-'trodden. 1 A **well-trodden** path is used regularly by a large number of people, and therefore looks worn and is easy to see. **2** You can use **well-trodden**, especially in expressions such as a **well-trodden path** and **well-trodden ground**, to indicate that a plan or course of action has been tried or done by a lot of people and so the result of it is easy to predict. *Political power has long been a well-trodden path to personal wealth.* ADJ-GRADED ADJ-GRADED

well 'versed; also spelled **well-versed**. If someone is **well versed** in a particular subject, they know a lot about it. ADJ-GRADED

'well-wisher, well-wishers. Well-wishers are people who hope that a particular person or thing will be successful, and who show this by their behaviour. *The street was lined with well-wishers.* N-COUNT

well-'worn. 1 A **well-worn** expression, remark, or idea has been used so often that it no longer seems to have much meaning or to be interesting. *To use a well-worn cliche, it is packed with information.* **2** A **well-worn** object or piece of clothing has been worn or used so frequently that it looks rather old. ADJ-GRADED ADJ-GRADED

wel·ly /ˈweli/ **wellies. Wellies** are long rubber boots which you wear to keep your feet dry. N-COUNT BRITISH, INFORMAL

welt /welt/ **welts.** A **welt** is a mark which is made on someone's skin, usually by a blow from something such as a whip or sword. N-COUNT

wel·ter /ˈweltə/. A **welter** of something is a large quantity of it which occurs suddenly or in a confusing way. *...patients with a welter of symptoms.* QUANT WRITTEN

wench /wentʃ/ **wenches.** A **wench** was a girl or young woman who worked as a servant or waitress. N-COUNT DATED

wend /wend/ **wends, wending, wended.** If you **wend** your **way** in a particular direction, you walk, especially slowly, casually, or carefully, in that direction. *...sleepy-eyed commuters were wending their way to work.* PHRASE LITERARY

went /went/. **Went** is the past tense of **go**.

wept /wept/. **Wept** is the past tense and past participle of **weep**.

were /wə, STRONG wɜː/. **1 Were** is the plural and the second person singular of the past tense of **be**. **2 Were** is sometimes used instead of 'was' in certain structures, for example in conditional clauses or after the verb 'wish'. *He believes in atheism as though it were a new religion.* **3 ● as it were:** see as. FORMAL

we're /wɪə/. **We're** is the usual spoken form of 'we are'. *I'm married, but we're separated.*

weren't /wɜːnt/. **Were not** is usually said or written as **weren't**. INFORMAL

were·wolf /'weəwʊlf/ **werewolves.** In folklore, horror stories, and films, a **werewolf** is a person who changes into a wolf. N-COUNT

west /west/. **West** is one of the four points of the compass. See Appendix headed **Compass**. ◆◆◆◆◆

west·bound /'westbaʊnd/. See Appendix headed **Compass**.

west·er·ly /'westəli/. See Appendix headed **Compass**.

west·ern /'westən/ **westerns. 1** See Appendix headed **Compass**.
2 A **western** is a film or book about life in the west of America in the nineteenth century, especially the life of cowboys. N-COUNT

west·ern·er /'westənə/ **westerners.** See Appendix headed **Compass**. ◆◇◇◇◇

west·ern·i·za·tion /ˌwestənaɪ'zeɪʃn/; also spelled **westernisation** in British English. The **westernization** of a country, place, or person is the process of them adopting ideas and behaviour that are typical of Europe and North America, rather than preserving the ideas and behaviour traditional in their culture. *...the westernization of Afghan culture.* N-UNCOUNT

west·ern·ized /'westənaɪzd/; also spelled **westernised.** A **westernized** country, place, or person has adopted ideas and behaviour typical of Europe and North America, rather than preserving the ideas and behaviour that are traditional in their culture. *We must stop our country becoming Westernized.* ADJ-GRADED

west·ern·most /'westənməʊst/. See Appendix headed **Compass**.

west·ward /'westwəd/. the form **westwards** is also used. See Appendix headed **Compass**.

wet /wet/ **wetter, wettest; wets, wetting, wetted.** The forms **wet** and **wetted** are both used as the past tense and past participle of the verb. **1** If something is **wet**, it is covered in water, rain, sweat, tears, or another liquid. *He towelled his wet hair... My gloves were soaking wet... His face was wet with tears.* ◆ **wet·ly** *Her hair clung wetly to her head.* ◆ **wet·ness** *Anti-perspirants stop wetness, deodorants stop odour.* **2** To **wet** something means to get water or some other liquid over it. *When assembling the pie, wet the edges where the two crusts join.* **3** If the weather is **wet**, it is raining. ► **The wet** is used to mean wet weather. *They had come in from the cold and the wet.* **4** If something such as paint, ink, or cement is **wet**, it is not yet dry or solid. **5** If a child or its nappy or clothing is **wet**, its nappy or clothing is soaked in urine. **6** If people, especially children, **wet** their beds or clothes or **wet** themselves, they urinate in their beds or clothes because they cannot control their bladder.
7 If you say that someone is **wet**, you have a low opinion of them because you think they are weak and lacking in enthusiasm, energy, or confidence. *Don't be so wet, Charles.* **8** A **wet** is a Conservative politician who supports moderate political policies and opposes extreme ones. ◆◆◆◇◇ ADJ-GRADED ADV-GRADED N-UNCOUNT VERB V n ADJ-GRADED N-SING: theN ADJ ADJ-GRADED VERB: V n, V pron-refl ADJ-GRADED PRAGMATICS BRITISH, INFORMAL N-COUNT BRITISH

wet 'blanket, wet blankets. If you say that someone is a **wet blanket**, you are criticizing them because they refuse to join other people in an enjoyable activity or because they want to stop other people enjoying themselves. N-COUNT PRAGMATICS INFORMAL

wet·land /'wetlænd/ **wetlands.** A **wetland** is an area of very wet muddy land with wild plants growing in it. You can also refer to a wetland as **wet·** ◆◇◇◇◇ N-VAR

lands. *...a scheme that aims to protect the wilderness of the wetlands.*

'wet suit, wet suits; also spelled **wetsuit.** A **wet suit** is a close-fitting rubber suit which a diver or underwater swimmer wears in order to keep his or her body warm. N-COUNT

we've /wɪv, STRONG wiːv/. **We've** is the usual spoken form of 'we have', especially when 'have' is an auxiliary verb. *'Hello, I don't think we've met,' Robert introduced himself.*

whack /wæk/ **whacks, whacking, whacked. 1** If you **whack** someone or something, you hit them hard. *Someone whacked him on the head.* ► Also a noun. *He gave the donkey a whack across the back with his stick.* **2** Your **whack** of something is your share of it. *The majority of people in this country pay their whack.* **3** If something is **out of whack**, it is not working properly, often because its natural balance has been upset. *The ecosystem will be thrown out of whack.* ◆◇◇◇◇ VERB: V n V n prep INFORMAL SOUND N-SING INFORMAL PHRASE INFORMAL

whack·ing /'wækɪŋ/. You can use **whacking** to emphasize how big something is. *The supermarkets may be making whacking profits.* ► Also an adverb. *...a whacking great hole.* ADJ: ADJ n BRITISH, INFORMAL ADV: ADV adj

whacky /'wæki/. See **wacky**.

whale /weɪl/ **whales. 1 Whales** are very large mammals that live in the sea. ● See also **killer whale, sperm whale. 2** If you say that someone is **having a whale of a time**, you mean that they are enjoying themselves very much. ◆◆◇◇◇ N-COUNT PHRASE INFORMAL

whal·er /'weɪlə/ **whalers. 1** A **whaler** is a ship which is used in hunting whales. **2** A **whaler** is someone who works on a ship which is used in hunting whales. N-COUNT N-COUNT

whal·ing /'weɪlɪŋ/. **Whaling** is the activity of hunting and killing whales. *...commercial whaling.* ◆◇◇◇◇ N-UNCOUNT

wham /wæm/. You use **wham** to indicate that something happens suddenly or forcefully. *There you are driving along and wham! You hit a pothole.* EXCLAM INFORMAL

wham·my /'wæmi/. Journalists use **whammy** in expressions such as **double whammy** and **triple whammy** to indicate that two or three unpleasant or difficult situations occur at the same time, or occur one after the other. *This is a double whammy for public sector workers.* N-SING: adj N

wharf /wɔːf/ **wharves** or **wharfs.** A **wharf** is a platform by a river or the sea where ships can be tied up. ◆◆◇◇◇ N-COUNT

what /wɒt/. **1** You use **what** in questions when you ask for specific information about something that you do not know. *What do you want?... 'Has something happened?'—'Indeed it has.'—'What?'... Hey! What are you doing?* ► Also a determiner. *What kind of poetry does he like?* **2** You use **what** after certain words, especially verbs and adjectives, when you are referring to a situation that is unknown or has not been specified. *I want to know what happened to Norman... She turned scarlet from embarrassment, once she realized what she had done.* ► Also a determiner. *I didn't know what else to say.* **3** You use **what** at the beginning of a clause in structures where you are changing the order of the information to give special emphasis to something. *What she does possess is the ability to get straight to the core of a problem.* **4** You use **what** in expressions such as **what is called** and **what amounts to** when you are giving a possible description or identification of something. *She had been in what doctors described as an irreversible vegetative state for five years.* **5** You use **what** to indicate that you are talking about the whole of an amount that is available to you. *He drinks what is left in his glass as if it were water.* ► Also a determiner. *They had had to use what money they had.* **6** You say **'What?'** to tell someone who has indicated that they want to speak to you that you have heard them and are inviting them to continue. *'Dad?'—'What?'—'Can I have the car tonight?'* **7** You say **'What?'** when you ask someone to repeat the thing that they have just said because you did not hear or ◆◆◆◆◆ QUESTION DET-QUEST CONJ DET CONJ PRAGMATICS CONJ CONJ DET CONVENTION PRAGMATICS CONVENTION PRAGMATICS

understand it properly. 'What?' is more informal and less polite than expressions such as 'Pardon?' and 'Excuse me?'. *'They could paint this place,' she said. 'What?' he asked.* **8** You say **'What'** to express surprise or disbelief. *'We've got the car that killed Myra Moss.'—'What!'* **9** You use **what** in exclamations to emphasize an opinion or reaction. *What a horrible thing to do.* ▶ Also a determiner. *What ugly things; throw them away.* **10** You use **what** to indicate that you are making a guess about something such as an amount or value. *It's, what, eleven years or more since he's seen him.* CONVENTION PRAGMATICS / PREDET PRAGMATICS / DET / ADV: ADV n

11 You say **guess what** or **do you know what** to introduce a piece of information which is surprising, which is not generally known, or which you want to emphasize. *Guess what? I'm going to dinner at Mrs. Combley's tonight.* **12** In conversation, you say **or what?** after a question as a way of stating an opinion forcefully and showing that you expect other people to agree. *Look at that moon. Is that beautiful or what?* **13** You say **so what?** or **what of it?** to indicate that the previous remark seems unimportant, uninteresting, or irrelevant to you. *'I skipped off school today,'—'So what?'* **14** You say **'Tell you what'** to introduce a suggestion or offer. *Tell you what, let's stay another day.* **15** You use **what about** at the beginning of a question when you make a suggestion, offer, or request. *'What about Sunday evening at Frank's?'—'Sure. What time?'* **16** You use **what about** or **what of** when you introduce a new topic or a point which seems relevant to a previous remark. *Now you've talked about work on daffodils, what about other commercially important flowers, like roses?* **17** You say **what about** a particular person or thing when you ask someone to explain why they have asked you about that person or thing. *'This thing with the Corbett woman.'—'Oh, yeah. What about her?'* **18** You say **what have you** at the end of a list in order to refer generally to other things of the same kind. *My great-grandfather, who had the forge in town, made horseshoes and nails and what have you.* **19** You say **what if** at the beginning of a question when you ask about the consequences of something happening, especially something undesirable. *What if this doesn't work out?* **20** If you know **what's what**, you know the important things that need to be known about a situation. *He is massively self-confident. He knows what's what.* **21** You say **what with** in order to introduce the reasons for a particular situation, especially an undesirable one. *Maybe they are tired, what with all the sleep they're losing.* **22** In informal conversation, people say **you what?** to indicate that they do not believe or accept the remark that someone has just made, or that they have not heard or understood it properly. *'What are you doing here?'—'Oh I work here now.'—'You what?'* **23** ● **what's more**: see **more**. CONVENTION PRAGMATICS / PHRASE PRAGMATICS / CONVENTION PRA.MATICS / PHRASE PRAGMATICS / PHRASE PRAGMATICS / PHRASE PRAGMATICS / PHRASE PRAGMATICS / PHRASE / PHRASE PRAGMATICS / PHRASE / PHR-PREP PRAGMATICS / CONVENTION PRAGMATICS

what·ev·er /ˈwɒtˈevə/. **1** You use **whatever** to refer to anything or everything of a particular type. *Franklin was free to do pretty much whatever he pleased.* ▶ Also a determiner. *Whatever doubts he might have had about Ingrid were all over now.* **2** You use **whatever** to say that something is the case in all circumstances. *We shall love you whatever happens, Diana... People will judge you whatever you do.* **3** You use **whatever** after a noun group in order to emphasize a negative statement. *I have nothing whatever to say.* **4** You use **whatever** to ask in an emphatic way about something which you are very surprised about. *Whatever is the matter with you both?* **5** You use **whatever** when you are indicating that you do not know the precise identity, meaning, or value of the thing just mentioned. *'I love you,' he said.—'Whatever that means,' she said.* **6** You say **whatever** to refer generally to something else of the same kind as the thing or things that you have just mentioned. *You may like a Malt whisky that is peatier, or smokier, or sweeter, or whatever.* **7** You say **'whatever you say'** to indicate that you accept what someone has said, even though you do not CONJ / DET / CONJ / ADV: with brd-neg, n ADV / QUESTION PRAGMATICS / CONJ / PHRASE INFORMAL / CONVENTION PRAGMATICS

really believe them or do not think it is a good idea. *'We'll go in your car, Billy.'—'Whatever you say.'* **8** You say **whatever** you **do** when giving advice or warning someone about something. *Whatever you do, don't upset the woman.* PHRASE PRAGMATICS

what·not /ˈwɒtnɒt/. People sometimes say **'and whatnot'** or **'or whatnot'** after mentioning one or more things, to refer in a vague way to other things which are similar. *The women were there in their jeans and T-shirts and overalls and whatnot.* PHRASE INFORMAL, SPOKEN

what's /wɒts/. **What's** is the usual spoken form of 'what is' or 'what has', especially when 'has' is an auxiliary verb.

whats·her·name /ˈwɒtsəneɪm/; also spelled **whatsername**. You say **whatshername** instead of a woman's name when you cannot remember it or are trying to remember it. PRON INFORMAL

whats·his·name /ˈwɒtsɪzneɪm/; also spelled **whatsisname**. You say **whatshisname** instead of a man's name when you cannot remember it or are trying to remember it. *...the new junior minister, whatsisname, Donald Sinclair.* PRON INFORMAL

whats·it /ˈwɒtsɪt/ **whatsits.** You use **whatsit** instead of a noun or name which you cannot remember or which you do not want to say because it is rude. *He's got that fiery temper which scares the whatsit out of everybody.* N-VAR INFORMAL

what·so·ev·er /ˌwɒtsəʊˈevə/. You use **whatsoever** after a noun group in order to emphasize a negative statement. *My school did nothing whatsoever in the way of athletics.* ◆◆◇◇◇ ADV PRAGMATICS

wheat /wiːt/ **wheats.** Wheat is a cereal crop grown for food. Wheat is also used to refer to the grain of this crop, which is usually ground into flour and used to make bread. *...farmers growing wheat, corn, or other crops.* ◆◆◇◇◇ N-VAR

wheat·germ /ˈwiːtdʒɜːm/; also spelled **wheat germ**. Wheatgerm is the middle part of a grain of wheat which is rich in vitamins and is often added to other food. N-UNCOUNT

whee·dle /ˈwiːdəl/ **wheedles, wheedling, wheedled.** If you say that someone **wheedles**, you mean they try to persuade someone to do or give them what they want, for example by saying nice things that they do not mean; used showing disapproval. *He managed to wheedle his way into the offices. ...an opportunity to wheedle more money out of Wilson.* VERB: V V way prep V n out of/ from n Also V n, V with quote

wheel /wiːl/ **wheels, wheeling, wheeled.** **1** The **wheels** of a vehicle are the circular objects which are fixed underneath it and which enable it to move along the ground. *The car wheels spun and slipped on some oil on the road.* ● Something **on wheels** has wheels attached to the bottom. *...a trolley on wheels.* **2** If you **wheel** an object that has wheels somewhere, you push it along. *He wheeled his bike into the alley at the side of the house.* **3** A **wheel** is a circular object which forms a part of a machine, usually a moving part. **4** The **wheel** of a car or other vehicle is the circular object that is used to steer it. **5** People sometimes refer to a car as **wheels**. *'Do you own a house?'—'No. But I have wheels.'* **6** If something such as a group of animals or birds **wheels**, it moves in a circle. *A flock of crows wheeled overhead.* **7** If you **wheel** round, you turn round suddenly on the place where you are standing, often because you are surprised, shocked, or angry. *He wheeled around to face her.* **8** People talk about **the wheels of** an organization or system to mean the way in which it operates. *He knows the wheels of administration turn slowly.* ● to **oil the wheels**: see **oil**. **9** See also: **meals on wheels, spare wheel, spinning wheel, steering wheel, water wheel.** ◆◆◆◇◇ N-COUNT / PHRASE / VERB V n prep/adv / N-COUNT / N-COUNT / N-PLURAL INFORMAL / VERB LITERARY / VERB V adv Also V / N-PLURAL: the N of n

wheel and 'deal, wheels and deals, wheeling and dealing, wheeled and dealed. If you say that someone **wheels and deals**, you mean that they use a lot of different methods and contacts to achieve what they want in business or politics, often VERB: V

in a way which you consider dishonest.
♦ **'wheeler-dealer, wheeler-dealers** *...a modern political wheeler-dealer.* ♦ **wheel·ing and deal·ing** *He hates the wheeling and dealing associated with conventional political life.* N-COUNT / N-UNCOUNT

wheel·barrow /'wiːlbærəʊ/ **wheelbarrows.** A wheelbarrow is a small open cart with one wheel and handles that is used for carrying things, for example in the garden. N-COUNT

wheel·chair /'wiːltʃeə/ **wheelchairs.** A wheelchair is a chair with wheels that you use in order to move about in if you cannot walk properly, for example because you are disabled or ill. ♦♦◇◇◇ N-COUNT

wheel·house /'wiːlhaʊs/ **wheelhouses.** A wheelhouse is a small room or shelter on a ship or boat, where the steering wheel used is situated. N-COUNT

wheel·wright /'wiːlraɪt/ **wheelwrights.** A wheelwright is someone who makes and repairs wooden wheels and other wooden things such as carts, carriages, and gates. N-COUNT

wheeze /wiːz/ **wheezes, wheezing, wheezed.** 1 If someone **wheezes**, they breathe with difficulty, making a hissing or whistling sound. *He had quite serious problems with his chest and wheezed and coughed all the time.* 2 A **wheeze** is a clever idea, joke, or trick. *...the temptation to boost profits through accounting wheezes.* ♦◇◇◇ VERB / V Also V with quote / N-COUNT BRITISH, DATED, INFORMAL

wheezy /'wiːzi/. A **wheezy** cough or laugh comes from someone who has difficulty in breathing, so it has hissing or whistling in it. ADJ-GRADED

whelk /welk/ **whelks.** A **whelk** is a creature like a snail that is found in the sea near the shore. N-COUNT

when /wen/. 1 You use **when** to ask questions about the time at which things happen. *When did you get married?... 'I'll be there this afternoon.'— 'When?'* 2 You use **when** to introduce a clause where you mention the time at which something happens. *I asked him when he'd be back to pick me up... I don't know when the decision was made.* 3 You use **when** to introduce a clause which specifies or refers to the time at which something happens. *She remembered clearly that day when she'd gone exploring the rockpools.* 4 If something happens **when** something else is happening, the two things are happening at the same time. *When eating a whole cooked fish, you should never turn it over to get at the flesh on the other side.* 5 You use **when** to introduce a clause in which you mention something which happens at some point during an activity, event, or situation. *When I met the Gills, I had been gardening for nearly ten years.* 6 You use **when** to introduce a clause where you mention the circumstances under which the event in the main clause happened or will happen. *When he brought Imelda her drink she gave him a genuine sweet smile.* 7 You use **when** to introduce the reason for an opinion, comment, or question. *How can I love myself when I look like this?* 8 You use **when** in order to introduce a fact or comment which makes the other part of the sentence rather surprising or unlikely. *The temperature sensor is making the computer think the engine is cold when, in fact, it's hot.* ♦♦♦♦♦ QUESTION / CONJ / PRON-REL / CONJ / CONJ / CONJ / CONJ PRAGMATICS / CONJ PRAGMATICS

whence /wens/. **Whence** means from where. *We looked down to the river whence we'd climbed., and nobody complained of the effort.* ▶ Also a question. *Whence then come the lofty Olympian ideals of fair play?* ▶ Also a conjunction. *Asked whence he had come, he said in the broadest of accents, 'Lancashire'.* ♦◇◇◇ PRON-REL DATED QUESTION / CONJ

when·ever /wen'evə/. 1 You use **whenever** to refer to any time or every time that something happens or is true. *She always called at the vicarage whenever she was in the area... Avoid processed foods whenever possible.* 2 You use **whenever** to mean an unspecified time. *He married Miss Vancouver in 1963, or whenever it was.* ♦♦♦◇ CONJ / CONJ

where /weə/. 1 You use **where** to ask questions about the place something is in, or is coming from or going to. *Where did you meet him?... 'You'll never believe where Julie and I are going.'—'Where?'* 2 You use **where** to introduce a clause in which you men- ♦♦♦♦♦ QUESTION / CONJ

tion the place in which something is situated or happens. *People began looking across to see where the noise was coming from... He knew where Henry Carter had gone.* ▶ Also a relative pronoun. *Conditions which apply to your flight are available at the travel agency where you book your holiday.* 3 You use **where** to ask questions about a situation, a stage in something, or an aspect of something. *Where will it all end?... They'll have to let the draft board know, and then where will we be?* 4 You use **where** to introduce a clause in which you mention a situation, a stage in something, or an aspect of something. *It's not hard to see where she got her feelings about herself... I didn't know where to start.* ▶ Also a relative pronoun. *The government is at a stage where it is willing to talk.* 5 You use **where** to introduce a clause that contrasts with the other parts of the sentence. *Sometimes a teacher will be listened to, where a parent might not.* PRON-REL / QUESTION / CONJ / PRON-REL / CONJ

where·abouts. Pronounced /'weərəbaʊts/ for meaning 1, and /ˌweərə'baʊts/ for meanings 2 and 3. 1 If you refer to the **whereabouts** of a particular person or thing, you mean the place where that person or thing may be found. *The police are anxious to hear from anyone who may know the whereabouts of the firearms.* 2 You use **whereabouts** in questions when you are asking precisely where something is. *Whereabouts in Liverpool are you from?... 'I actually live near Chester.'—'Whereabouts?'* 3 You use **whereabouts** to introduce a clause in which you mention precisely where something is situated or happens. *I live in a village near to Germaine Greer and know whereabouts she lives.* ♦◇◇◇◇ N-COLL-SING: with poss / QUESTION / CONJ

where·as /weər'æz/. You use **whereas** to introduce a comment which contrasts with what is said in the main clause. *These fixed-price menus for two or three courses can cost as little as 50f, whereas the à la carte is always more expensive.* ♦♦♦◇◇ CONJ PRAGMATICS

where·by /weə'baɪ/. A system or action **whereby** something happens is one that makes that thing happen. *They voted to accept a deal whereby the union will receive nearly three-quarters of a million pounds.* ♦♦◇◇◇ PRON-REL FORMAL

where·fores /'weəfɔːz/. **The whys and wherefores** of something are the reasons for it. *Even successful bosses need to be queried about the whys and wherefores of their actions.* PHRASE

where·in /weər'ɪn/. 1 **Wherein** means in which place or thing. *...a riding school wherein we could learn the art of horsemanship.* 2 **Wherein** means in which part or respect. *Wherein lies the truth?* ▶ Also a conjunction. *It is difficult to know wherein Mr Ritchie hoped to find salvation for his country.* ♦◇◇◇◇ PRON-REL FORMAL / QUESTION FORMAL / CONJ

where·upon /ˌweərə'pɒn/. You use **whereupon** to say that one thing happens immediately after another thing, and usually as a result of it. *'Well, get on with it then,' said Dobson, whereupon Davies started to explain.* ♦◇◇◇◇ CONJ FORMAL

wher·ever /weər'evə/. 1 You use **wherever** to indicate that something happens or is true in any place or situation. *Some people enjoy themselves wherever they are.* 2 You use **wherever** when you indicate that you do not know where a person or place is. *'Till we meet again, wherever that is,' said the chairman.* 3 You use **or wherever** to say that something might happen in a place other than the place you have mentioned, but that you are not able to specify where. *The next day she was gone to Lusaka, Kampala, or wherever.* 4 You use **wherever** in questions as an emphatic form of 'where', usually when you are surprised about something. *Wherever did you get that idea?* ♦♦◇◇◇ CONJ / CONJ / PHRASE INFORMAL / QUESTION PRAGMATICS

where·with·al /'weəwɪðɔːl/. If you have the **wherewithal** for something, you have the means, especially the money, that you need for it. *She didn't have the financial wherewithal to do it.* N-SING: the N

whet /wet/ **whets, whetting, whetted.** If someone or something **whets** your **appetite** for a particular thing, they increase your desire to have it or know about it, especially by giving you an idea of PHRASE

what it is like. ...*lectures he hopes might whet the appetite and keep students' enthusiasm.*

wheth·er /'weðə/. **1** You use **whether** when you are talking about a choice or doubt between two or more alternatives. *To this day, it's unclear whether he shot himself or was murdered... They now have two weeks to decide whether or not to buy.* **2** You use **whether** to say that something is true in any of the circumstances that you mention. *Whether they say it aloud or not, most men expect their wives to be faithful. ...beers and lagers of all kinds, whether bottled or draught.* ◆◆◆◆◆ CONJ / CONJ

whet·stone /'wetstəʊn/ **whetstones.** A **whetstone** is a stone which is used for sharpening knives, chisels, or other tools. N-COUNT

whew. Whew is used in writing to represent a sound that you make when you breathe out quickly, for example because you are very hot, very relieved, or very surprised. *'Whew,' he said. 'It's hot.'* EXCLAM / PRAGMATICS

whey /weɪ/. Whey is the watery liquid that is separated from the curds in sour milk, for example when you are making cheese. N-UNCOUNT

which /wɪtʃ/. **1** You use **which** in questions when there are two or more possible answers or alternatives. *Which are the ones you really like? Which are the good adverts for you?* ▶ Also a determiner. *Which woman or man do you most admire?* **2** You use **which** to refer to a choice between two or more possible answers or alternatives. *I wanted to know which school it was you went to.* ▶ Also a conjunction. *There are so many diets on the market, how do you know which to choose?* **3** You use **which** at the beginning of a relative clause when specifying the thing that you are talking about or when giving more information about it. *Soldiers opened fire on a car which failed to stop at an army checkpoint.* **4** You use **which** to refer back to an idea or situation expressed in a previous sentence or sentences, especially when you want to give your opinion about it. *They ran out of drink. Which actually didn't bother me because I wasn't drinking.* ▶ Also a determiner. *You haven't fully decided what you want from your career at the moment, in which case you're definitely not cut out to be a boss yet!* **5** If you cannot tell the difference between two things, you can say that you do not know **which is which**. *They all look so alike to me that I'm never sure which is which.* **6 ● every which way:** see **way.** ◆◆◆◆◆ QUESTION / DET-QUEST / DET / CONJ / PRON-REL / PRON-REL / DET / PHRASE

which·ever /wɪtʃ'evə/. **1** You use **whichever** in order to indicate that it does not matter which of the possible alternatives happens or is chosen. *Whichever way you look at it, nuclear power is the energy of the future.* ▶ Also a conjunction. *We will gladly exchange your goods, or refund your money, whichever you prefer.* **2** You use **whichever** to specify which of a number of possibilities is the right one or the one you mean. *...learning to relax by whichever method suits you best.* ▶ Also a conjunction. *Fishing is from 6 am to dusk or 10.30pm, whichever is sooner.* ◆◇◇◇◇ DET / CONJ / DET / CONJ

whiff /wɪf/ **whiffs. 1** If there is a **whiff** of a particular smell, you smell it faintly or for only a brief period of time. *He caught a whiff of her perfume.* **2** A **whiff** of something bad or harmful is a slight sign of it. *Not a whiff of scandal has ever tainted his private life.* ◆◇◇◇◇ N-COUNT / N-COUNT

Whig /wɪg/ **Whigs.** A **Whig** was a member of an English political party that in the 18th and 19th centuries was in favour of political and social reforms. ◆◇◇◇◇ N-COUNT

while 1 conjunction uses

while /waɪl/. The form **whilst** is also used in formal or literary English, especially British English. **1** If something happens **while** something else is happening, the two things are happening at the same time. *I sat on the settee to unwrap the package while he stood by... Her parents could help with child care while she works.* **2** If something happens **while** something else happens, the first thing happens at some point during the time that the second thing is ◆◆◆◆◆ CONJ / CONJ

happening. *The two ministers have yet to meet, but may do so while in New York.* **3** You use **while** at the beginning of a clause to introduce information which contrasts with information in the main clause. *The first two services are free, while the third costs £35.00.* **4** You use **while** when you admit in the clause that something is the case but say that it does not affect the truth of the other part of the sentence, although the two statements partly conflict. *While the news, so far, has been good, there may be days ahead while when it is bad.* CONJ / PRAGMATICS / CONJ / PRAGMATICS

while 2 noun and verb uses

while /waɪl/ **whiles, whiling, whiled. 1** A **while** is a period of time. *They walked on in silence for a while... He was married a little while ago.* **2** You use **all the while** in order to say that something happens continually or that it happens throughout the time when something else is happening. *All the while the people at the next table watched me eat.* **3 ● once in a while:** see **once. ● worth your while:** see **worth.** ◆◆◆◆◇ N-SING: aN / PHRASE

while away. If you **while away** the time in a particular way, you spend time in that way, because you are waiting for something, or because you have nothing else to do. *Miss Bennett whiled away the hours playing old films on her video-recorder.* PHRASAL VB / V P noun / Also V n P

whilst /waɪlst/. Whilst means the same as **while** when it is a conjunction. *The girls met four years ago whilst singing backing vocals for local Birmingham bands.* ◆◆◇◇◇ CONJ / BRITISH

whim /wɪm/ **whims.** A **whim** is a sudden wish to do or have something which seems to have no serious reason or purpose behind it. *We decided, more or less on a whim, to sail to Morocco.* ◆◇◇◇◇ N-VAR

whim·per /'wɪmpə/ **whimpers, whimpering, whimpered. 1** If someone **whimpers**, they make quiet unhappy or frightened sounds, as if they are about to start crying. *She lay at the bottom of the stairs, whimpering in pain.* ▶ Also a noun. *David's crying subsided to a whimper.* **2** If you say that something happens **not with a bang but a whimper**, you mean that it is less effective or exciting than was expected or intended. *The festival started with a whimper rather than a bang.* ◆◇◇◇◇ VERB / Also V with quote / N-COUNT / PHRASE

whim·si·cal /'wɪmzɪkəl/. A **whimsical** person or idea is unusual, playful, and unpredictable, rather than serious and practical. *His graphic art became slighter and more whimsical.* ◆◇◇◇◇ ADJ-GRADED

whim·sy /'wɪmzi/. Whimsy is behaviour which is unusual, playful, and unpredictable, rather than having any serious reason or purpose behind it. N-UNCOUNT

whine /waɪn/ **whines, whining, whined. 1** If something or someone **whines**, they make a long, high-pitched noise, especially one which sounds sad or unpleasant. *He could hear her dog barking and whining in the background.* ▶ Also a noun. *...the whine of air-raid sirens.* **2** If you say that someone **is whining** about something, you mean they are complaining in an annoying way about something unimportant. *...children who whine that they are bored... 'Why can't you tell me?' I whined.* ◆◇◇◇◇ VERB / V / N-COUNT / VERB: V aboutn/-ing / V that / V with quote / Also V

whinge /wɪndʒ/ **whinges, whingeing, whinged.** If you say that someone **is whingeing** about something, you think that they are complaining in an annoying way about something unimportant. *Stop whingeing and get on with it.* ▶ Also a noun. *...listening to everybody's whinges.* ♦ **whinger, whingers** *Shut up, you moaning whinger.* ◆◇◇◇◇ VERB: V aboutn / PRAGMATICS / V / INFORMAL / N-COUNT / N-COUNT

whin·ny /'wɪni/ **whinnies, whinnying, whinnied.** When a horse **whinnies**, it makes a sound rather like a laugh. VERB: V

whip /wɪp/ **whips, whipping, whipped. 1** A **whip** is a long thin piece of leather or rope fastened to a handle. It is used for hitting animals or people. **● a fair crack of the whip:** see **crack. 2** If someone **whips** an animal or person, they beat them or hit them with a whip or something like a whip. *He was whipped with a studded belt.* ♦ **whip·ping, whippings** *He threatened to give her a whipping.* ◆◆◇◇◇ N-COUNT / VERB: V n / be V-ed / N-COUNT

3 If you have **the whip hand**, you have power over someone else in a particular situation. *These days the shopper has the whip hand, and will not buy if stores fail to lower their prices.* PHRASE

4 If someone **whips** something out or **whips** it off, they take it out or take it off very quickly and suddenly. *Bob whipped out his notebook... My waitress whipped the plate away and put down my bill.* VERB V n with adv **5** If something or someone **whips** somewhere, they move there or go there very quickly. *I whipped into a parking space.* VERB V adv/prep

6 When you **whip** something liquid such as cream or an egg, you stir it very fast until it is thick and frothy or stiff. *Whip the eggs, oils and honey together.* VERB: V n V n adv/prep

7 If a speaker **whips** people **into** an emotional state, he or she deliberately causes and encourages them to be in that state. *He could whip a crowd into hysteria.* VERB V n into n

8 A **whip** is a member of a particular party in a parliament, who is responsible for making sure that party members are present to vote on important issues in the appropriate way. **9** In Britain, a **whip** is a notice telling the members of a particular party in parliament that it is important for them to vote in a particular way on an important issue. N-COUNT N-COUNT

whip up. 1 If someone **whips up** an emotion, especially a dangerous one such as hatred, or if they **whip** people **up** into a state of hatred, they deliberately cause and encourage people to feel that emotion. *He accused politicians of whipping up anti-foreign sentiments... Joe McCarthy whipped up Americans into a frenzy of anti-Communist activity.* **2** If a force such as the wind **whips up** dust or water, it makes it rise up. *...clouds of smoke and sand whipped up by a strong wind.* **3** If you **whip up** something, especially a meal, you make it quickly. *I can still whip up a fairly decent dinner party.* PHRASAL VB V P noun V P noun into n Also V n P into n V P noun V-ed P Also V n P V P noun Also V n P INFORMAL

whip·lash /ˈwɪplæʃ/. **Whiplash**, or a **whiplash** injury, is a neck injury caused by the head suddenly jerking forwards and then back again, for example in a car accident. N-UNCOUNT

whip·pet /ˈwɪpɪt/ **whippets**. A **whippet** is a small thin dog which looks like a greyhound. N-COUNT

'whipping boy, whipping boys. If someone or something is a **whipping boy** for a particular situation, they get all the blame for it. *He has become a convenient whipping boy for the failures of the communist regime.* N-COUNT

'whip-round. When a group of people have a **whip-round**, money is collected from each person so that it can be used to buy something for all of them or for someone they all know. N-SING INFORMAL

whir /wɜː/. See **whirr**.

whirl /wɜːl/ **whirls, whirling, whirled. 1** If something or someone **whirls** round or if you **whirl** them round, they move round or turn round very quickly. *The smoke began to whirl and grew into a monstrous column... He was whirling Anne around the floor.* ▶ Also a noun. *...the barely audible whirl of wheels.* **2** You can refer to a lot of intense activity as a **whirl** of activity. You can refer to someone's active social life as a **social whirl. 3** If a person or their mind is **in a whirl**, they are very confused or excited. ◆◇◇◇◇ V-ERG V V n adv/prep Also V n, V adv/prep N-COUNT N-COUNT PHRASE

whirl·pool /ˈwɜːlpuːl/ **whirlpools. 1** A **whirlpool** is a small area in a river or the sea where the water is moving quickly round and round, so that objects near it are pulled into its centre. **2** A **whirlpool bath** or a **whirlpool** is a bath that is specially designed so that the water moves round and round. ◆◇◇◇◇ N-COUNT N-COUNT

whirl·wind /ˈwɜːlwɪnd/ **whirlwinds. 1** A **whirlwind** is a tall column of air which spins round and round very fast and moves across the land or sea. **2** You can describe a situation in which a lot of things happen very quickly and are very difficult for someone to control as a **whirlwind**. *I had been running around southern England in a whirlwind of activity.* **3** A **whirlwind** event or action happens or is done much more quickly than normal. *He got married after a whirlwind romance.* ◆◇◇◇◇ N-COUNT N-COUNT ADJ: ADJ n

whirr /wɜː/ **whirrs, whirring, whirred;** also spelled **whir**. If something such as a machine or an insect's wing **whirrs**, it makes a series of low sounds so quickly that they seem like one continuous sound. *The camera whirred and clicked.* ▶ Also a noun. *He could hear the whirr of a vacuum cleaner.* ♦ **whir·ring** *...the whirring of a helicopter.* VERB V N-COUNT N-UNCOUNT

whisk /wɪsk/ **whisks, whisking, whisked. 1** If you **whisk** someone or something somewhere, you take them or move them there quickly. *I was whisked away in a police car.* **2** If you **whisk** something such as eggs or cream, you stir it very fast, often with an electric device, so that it becomes light and fluffy. *Whisk together the remaining sugar and the yolks.* **3** A **whisk** is a kitchen tool used for whisking eggs or cream. See picture headed **kitchen utensils.** ◆◆◇◇◇ VERB: V n adv/prep be V-ed adv/ prep VERB: V n V pl-n with together N-COUNT

whisk·er /ˈwɪskə/ **whiskers. 1** The **whiskers** of an animal such as a cat or mouse are the long stiff hairs that grow near its mouth. **2** You can refer to the hair on a man's face as his **whiskers. 3** You can use **whisker** in expressions such as **by a whisker** or **within a whisker of** to indicate that something happened or is true, but only by a very small amount or degree. *She came within a whisker of taking a gold medal.* ◆◇◇◇◇ N-COUNT N-PLURAL N-SING

whis·key /ˈwɪski/ **whiskeys. Whiskey** is whisky made in Ireland or the United States. ◆◇◇◇◇ N-VAR

whis·ky /ˈwɪski/ **whiskies. Whisky** is a strong alcoholic drink made, especially in Scotland, from grain such as barley or rye. ▶ A **whisky** is a glass of whisky. ◆◆◇◇◇ N-VAR N-COUNT

whis·per /ˈwɪspə/ **whispers, whispering, whispered. 1** When you **whisper**, you say something very quietly so that only one person can hear you. *'Keep your voice down,' I whispered... He whispered the message to David.* ▶ Also a noun. *Men were talking in whispers in every office.* **2** If people **whisper** about a piece of information, they talk about it, although it might not be true or accurate, or might be a secret. *It is whispered that he intended to resign... But don't whisper a word of that.* ▶ Also a noun. *There have been whispers about her.* **3** If something **whispers**, it makes a low quiet sound which can only just be heard. *The cold breeze moved through the bushes around him, whispering just loud enough to obscure the chanting.* ▶ Also a noun. *They heard the whisper of leaves.* ◆◆◆◇◇ VERB: V V with quote V prep V n prep N-COUNT VERB: V about wh/n it be V-ed that V n N-COUNT VERB V LITERARY N-COUNT

whist /wɪst/. **Whist** is a card game in which people play in pairs against each other. N-UNCOUNT

whis·tle /ˈwɪsəl/ **whistles, whistling, whistled. 1** If you **whistle**, you make a series of musical sounds by forcing your breath out between your lips or teeth. *As he washed he whistled a tune.* **2** If you **whistle**, you make a sound by forcing your breath out between your lips or teeth. People whistle, for example, when they are surprised or impressed, or when they want to attract someone's attention. *In New York, she'd put her fingers in her mouth and whistle for a cab.* ● See also **wolf-whistle.** ▶ Also a noun. *Jackson gave a low whistle.* **3** If something such as a train or a kettle **whistles**, it makes a loud, high sound. ▶ Also a noun. *...a shrill whistle from the boiling kettle.* **4** If something such as the wind or a bullet **whistles** somewhere, it moves, making a loud, high sound. *A bullet whistled past my back.* ♦ **whis·tling** *...the whistling of the wind.* **5** A **whistle** is a small metal tube which you blow in order to produce a loud sound and attract someone's attention. *The referee blew his whistle for a penalty.* **6** A **whistle** is a simple musical instrument in the shape of a metal pipe with holes. ● See also **tin whistle. 7** If you **blow the whistle** on someone, or on something secret or illegal, you tell another person, especially someone in authority, what is happening. *Companies should protect employees who blow the whistle on dishonest workmates and work practices.* ◆◆◇◇◇ VERB: V V n VERB: V V prep N-COUNT VERB: V N-COUNT VERB V prep N-SING N-COUNT N-COUNT PHRASE

'whistle-blower, whistle-blowers; also spelled **whistleblower**. A **whistle-blower** is someone who N-COUNT JOURNALISM

finds out that the organization they are working for is doing something immoral or illegal and tells the authorities or the public about it.

'whistle-stop. If someone such as a politician goes on a **whistle-stop** tour, they visit a lot of different places in a short time. *...the next leg on her whistle-stop tour of eight countries in nine days.* `ADJ: ADJ n`

whit /wɪt/. You say **not a whit** or **not one whit** to emphasize that something is not the case at all. *It does not matter one whit to the customer.* `PHRASE` `PRAGMATICS` `DATED`

white /waɪt/ **whites, whiter, whitest. 1** Something that is **white** is the colour of snow or milk. *He was dressed in white.* ◆ **white·ness** *Her scarlet lipstick emphasized the whiteness of her teeth.* `◆◆◆◆◆` `COLOUR` `N-UNCOUNT`

2 A **white** person has a pale skin and belongs to a race of European origin. *He was white, with brown shoulder-length hair.* ► **Whites** are white people. *...a school that's brought blacks and whites and Hispanics together.* `ADJ` `N-COUNT`

3 If someone goes **white**, the skin on their face becomes very pale, for example because of fear, shock, or illness. *He turned white and began to stammer.* `ADJ-GRADED`

4 The **white** of someone's eye is the white part of their eyeball. `N-COUNT`

5 In your body, **white** blood cells are those which fight infection. `ADJ: ADJ n`

6 White wine is clear and light in colour. ► You can refer to white wine as white. *...a bottle of Californian white.* `ADJ` `N-VAR`

7 White coffee has had milk or cream added to it. `ADJ` `BRITISH`

8 The **white** of an egg, especially a hen's egg, is the transparent liquid that surrounds the yolk. `N-VAR`

white·board /'waɪtbɔːd/ **whiteboards.** A **whiteboard** is a shiny white board on which people such as teachers or speakers can draw or write using special pens. `N-COUNT`

,white 'Christmas, white Christmases. A **white Christmas** is a Christmas when it snows. `N-COUNT`

,white-'collar; also spelled **white collar. 1 White-collar** workers work in offices rather than doing manual work in industry. **2 White-collar** crime is committed by people who work in offices, and involves stealing from companies by fraud. `◆◇◇◇◇` `ADJ: ADJ n` `ADJ: ADJ n`

,white 'elephant, white elephants. If you describe something as a **white elephant**, you mean that it is a waste of money because it is completely useless. `N-COUNT`

'white goods. People in business sometimes refer to fridges, washing machines, and other large pieces of electrical household equipment as **white goods**. `N-PLURAL`

White·hall /'waɪthɔːl/. **Whitehall** is the name of a street in London in which there are many government offices. **Whitehall** is often used to mean the British government or civil service. `◆◆◇◇◇` `N-PROPER`

,white-'hot. If something is **white-hot**, it is extremely hot. *It is important to get the coals white-hot before you start.* `ADJ`

'White House. The **White House** is the official home in Washington DC of the President of the United States. You can also use **the White House** to refer to the President of the United States and his or her officials. *The White House has not participated in any talks.* `◆◆◆◇◇` `N-PROPER: the N, N n`

,white 'lie, white lies. If you refer to an untrue statement as a **white lie**, you mean that it is made to avoid hurting someone's feelings or to avoid trouble, and not for an evil purpose. `N-COUNT`

,white 'meat, white meats. White meat is meat such as chicken and pork, which is pale in colour after it has been cooked. `N-COUNT: also N in pl`

whit·en /'waɪtən/ **whitens, whitening, whitened.** If something **whitens** or if you **whiten** it, it becomes whiter or paler in colour. *...toothpastes that whiten teeth.* `V-ERG: V, V n`

,white 'noise. White noise is sound, especially loud, continuous, or unpleasant sound, that seems to have no pattern or rhythm. `N-UNCOUNT`

,White 'Paper, White Papers. In Britain and some other countries, a **White Paper** is an official report which gives the policy of the Government on a particular subject. `◆◆◇◇◇` `N-COUNT`

,white 'sauce, white sauces. White sauce is a thick, white-coloured sauce, usually made from milk, flour, and butter. `N-VAR`

,white 'spirit. White spirit is a colourless liquid that is made from petrol and is used, for example, to make paint thinner or to clean surfaces. `N-UNCOUNT` `BRITISH`

white·wash /'waɪtwɒʃ/ **whitewashes, whitewashing, whitewashed. 1** Whitewash is a mixture of lime or chalk and water that is used for painting walls white. **2** If a wall or building **has been whitewashed**, it has been painted white with whitewash. *...picturesque whitewashed cottages.* **3** If you say that people **whitewash** something, you are accusing them of hiding the unpleasant facts or truth about it in order to make it acceptable. *Without whitewashing the King, Ziegler tries, not altogether persuasively, to absolve him of pro-Nazi sympathies.* ► Also a noun. *He pledged that there would be no whitewash and that the police would carry out a full investigation.* **4** In sport, if a player or team **whitewashes** an opponent, they win very easily, and the opponent does not get any points at all. `◆◇◇◇◇` `N-UNCOUNT` `VERB: be V-ed, V-ed` `VERB` `PRAGMATICS V n` `N-UNCOUNT: also a N` `VERB: V n` `INFORMAL`

,white 'wedding, white weddings. A **white wedding** is a wedding where the bride wears white and the ceremony takes place in a church. `N-COUNT`

whith·er /'wɪðə/. **Whither** means 'to where'. *Who are you and whither are you bound?* `QUESTION` `DATED`

whit·ing /'waɪtɪŋ/ **whitings.** The plural can be either **whitings** or **whiting**. A **whiting** is a black and silver fish that lives in the sea. ► **Whiting** is this fish eaten as food. *He ordered stuffed whiting.* `N-VAR` `N-UNCOUNT`

whit·ish /'waɪtɪʃ/. **Whitish** means very pale and almost white in colour. *...a whitish dust.* `COLOUR`

whit·tle /'wɪtəl/ **whittles, whittling, whittled.** If you **whittle** an object from a piece of wood, or you **whittle** the wood, you carve the object by cutting or shaving parts off it with a small knife or other tool. *He whittled a new handle for his ax.* `◆◇◇◇◇` `VERB` `V n`

whittle away. To **whittle away** at something means to gradually make it smaller, weaker, or less effective. *Their approach is to whittle away at the evidence to show reasonable doubt.* `PHRASAL VB` `V P at n` `Also V P noun`

whittle down. To **whittle** something **down** means to gradually make it smaller or less extensive. *He had whittled eight interviewees down to two.* `PHRASAL VB` `V n P` `V n P to/from num/n`

whizz /wɪz/ **whizzes, whizzing, whizzed. 1** If something **whizzes** somewhere, it moves there very fast. *Stewart felt a bottle whizz past his head.* **2** If you are a **whizz** at something, you are very good at it. *Simon's a whizz at card games.* `◆◇◇◇◇` `VERB` `V prep/adv` `INFORMAL` `N-COUNT` `INFORMAL`

'whizz-kid, whizz-kids; also spelled **whizz kid.** If you refer to a young person as a **whizz-kid**, you mean that they have achieved success at a young age because they are very clever and very good at something. *...a financial whizz kid.* `N-COUNT` `INFORMAL`

who /huː/. **Who** is used as the subject or object of a verb. See entries at **whom** and **whose**. `◆◆◆◆◆`

1 You use **who** in questions when you ask about the name or identity of a person or group of people. *Who's there?... Who do you work for?... 'You reminded me of somebody.'—'Who?'* **2** You use **who** after certain words, especially verbs and adjectives, to introduce a clause where you talk about the identity of a person or a group of people. *Police have not been able to find out who was responsible for the forgeries... I went over to start up a conversation, asking her who she knew at the party.* **3** You use **who** at the beginning of a relative clause when specifying the person or group of people you are talking about or when giving more information about them. *The woman, who needs constant attention, is cared for by relatives... The hijacker gave himself up to police, who are now questioning him.* `QUESTION` `CONJ` `PRON-REL`

whoa /wəʊ/. **1** Whoa is a command that you give to a horse to slow down or stop. **2** You can say **whoa** to someone who is talking to you, to indicate that you think they are going too fast or assuming things that may not be true. *Slow down! Whoa!* `EXCLAM` `EXCLAM` `PRAGMATICS` `INFORMAL`

who'd /huːd/. **1** Who'd is the usual spoken form of 'who had', especially when 'had' is an auxiliary verb. **2** Who'd is a spoken form of 'who would'.

who·dun·nit /huːˈdʌnɪt/ **whodunnits;** also spelled **whodunit.** A **whodunnit** is a novel, film, or play about a murder. The identity of the murderer is kept a mystery until the end. `N-COUNT INFORMAL`

who·ever /huːˈevə/ **1** You use **whoever** to refer to someone when their identity is not yet known. *Whoever did this will sooner or later be caught and will be punished... Whoever wins the election is going to have a tough job getting the economy back on its feet.* **2** You use **whoever** to indicate that the actual identity of the person who does something will not affect a situation. *You can have whoever you like to visit you... Everybody who goes into this region, whoever they are, is at risk of being taken hostage.* **3** You use **whoever** in questions as an emphatic way of saying 'who', usually when you are surprised about something. *Ridiculous! Whoever suggested such a thing?* **4** You can say **or whoever** to refer vaguely to someone when their exact identity is not important. *We're not just some big business like Mobil or IBM or whoever.* `◆◆◇◇◇ CONJ` `CONJ` `QUESTION PRAGMATICS` `PHRASE INFORMAL`

whole /həʊl/ **wholes. 1** If you refer to **the whole** of something, you mean all of it. *I was cold throughout the whole of my body. ...the whole of August.* ▶ Also an adjective. *We spent the whole summer in Italy.* **2** A **whole** is a single thing which contains several different parts. *An atom itself is a complete whole, with its electrons, protons and neutrons and other elements... Taken as a percentage of the whole, the mouth has to be a fairly minor body part.* **3** If something is **whole**, it is in one piece and is not broken or damaged. *Much of the temple was ruined, but the front was whole... Small bones should be avoided as the dog may swallow them whole and risk internal injury.* **4** You use **whole** to emphasize what you are saying. *...a whole new way of doing business... There's a whole group of friends he doesn't want you to meet.* **5** If you refer to something **as a whole**, you are referring to it generally and as a single unit. *He described the move as a victory for the people of South Africa as a whole.* **6** You use **on the whole** to indicate that what you are saying is true in general and may not be true in every case, or that you are giving a general opinion or summary of something. *The wines they make are, on the whole, of a high standard.* `◆◆◆◆◇ QUANT` `ADJ:ADJ n` `N-COUNT` `ADJ: v-link ADJ, v n ADJ` `ADJ: ADJ n PRAGMATICS INFORMAL` `PHRASE` `PHRASE PRAGMATICS`

whole·food /ˈhəʊlfuːd/ **wholefoods. Wholefoods** are foods which have had very little refining or processing and which do not contain additives or artificial ingredients. Wholefoods are generally considered to be healthier than ordinary foods. `N-VAR BRITISH`

whole·grains /ˈhəʊlɡreɪnz/; the form **wholegrain** is used as a modifier. **Wholegrains** are the whole unprocessed grains of cereals such as wheat and maize. *Wholegrains are rich in potassium. ...crusty wholegrain bread.* `N-PLURAL`

whole·hearted /ˌhəʊlˈhɑːtɪd/; also spelled **wholehearted.** If you support or agree to something in a **wholehearted** way, you support or agree to it enthusiastically and completely. *The Government deserves our wholehearted support for having taken a step in this direction.* ♦ **whole·heart·ed·ly** *I agree wholeheartedly with you.* `◆◇◇◇◇ ADJ-GRADED` `ADV-GRADED`

whole·meal /ˈhəʊlmiːl/. **1 Wholemeal** flour is made from the complete grain of the wheat plant, including the husk. **Wholemeal** bread or pasta is made from wholemeal flour. The American word is **wholewheat. 2 Wholemeal** means wholemeal bread or wholemeal flour. *...one slice of white and one of wholemeal.* `◆◇◇◇◇ ADJ BRITISH` `N-UNCOUNT BRITISH`

whole·ness /ˈhəʊlnəs/. **Wholeness** is the quality of being complete or a single unit and not broken or divided into parts. *...the need for wholeness and harmony in mind, body and spirit.* `N-UNCOUNT`

whole 'number, whole numbers. A **whole number** is an exact number such as 1, 7, and 24, as opposed to a number with fractions or decimals. `N-COUNT`

whole·sale /ˈhəʊlseɪl/. **1 Wholesale** is the activity of buying and selling goods in large quantities and therefore at cheaper prices, usually to shopkeepers `◆◆◇◇◇ N-UNCOUNT`

who then sell them to the public. Compare **retail.** *Warehouse clubs allow members to buy goods at wholesale prices.* ▶ Also an adverb. *The fabrics are sold wholesale to retailers, fashion houses, and other manufacturers.* **2** If you describe a change, for example, as a **wholesale** change, you are emphasizing the completeness or the severity of it. *...doing what is necessary to prevent wholesale destruction of vegetation.* ▶ Also an adverb. *...a government which kills wholesale and guerrillas who kill selectively.* `ADV: ADV after v` `ADJ: ADJ n PRAGMATICS` `ADV: ADV after v`

whole·sal·er /ˈhəʊlseɪlə/ **wholesalers.** A **wholesaler** is a person whose business is buying large quantities of goods and selling them in smaller amounts, for example to shops. ♦ **whole·sal·ing** *...jobs in wholesaling and retailing.* `◆◇◇◇◇ N-COUNT` `N-UNCOUNT`

whole·some /ˈhəʊlsəm/. **1** If you describe something as **wholesome**, you approve of it because you think it is likely to have a positive influence on people, especially because it does not involve anything sexually immoral. *...good, wholesome fun. ...a very decent and wholesome bunch of lads.* **2** If you describe food as **wholesome**, you approve of it because you think it is good for your health. `◆◇◇◇◇ ADJ-GRADED PRAGMATICS` `ADJ-GRADED PRAGMATICS`

whole·wheat /ˈhəʊlwiːt/; also spelled **whole wheat. 1 Wholewheat** flour is made from the complete grain of the wheat plant, including the husk. **Wholewheat** bread or pasta is made from wholewheat flour. **2 Wholewheat** means wholewheat bread or wholewheat flour. *...a chicken salad sandwich on whole wheat.* `ADJ` `N-UNCOUNT`

who'll /huːl/. **Who'll** is a spoken form of 'who will'.

whol·ly /ˈhəʊlli/. You use **wholly** to emphasize how great or extreme something is. *While the two are only days apart in age they seem to belong to wholly different generations... The accusation is wholly without foundation.* `◆◆◇◇◇ ADV PRAGMATICS`

whom /huːm/. **Whom** is used in formal or written English instead of 'who' when it is the object of a verb or preposition. **1** You use **whom** in questions when you ask about the name or identity of a person or group of people. *'I want to send a telegram.' 'Fine, to whom?'... Whom did he expect to answer his phone?* **2** You use **whom** after certain words, especially verbs and adjectives, to introduce a clause where you talk about the name or identity of a person or a group of people. *He asked whom I'd told about his having been away... They have a free hand to appoint whom they like.* **3** You use **whom** at the beginning of a relative clause when specifying the person or people you are talking about, or when giving more information about them. *One writer in whom I had taken an interest was Immanuel Velikovsky... The Homewood residents whom I knew had little money and little free time.* `◆◆◆◆◇` `QUESTION` `CONJ` `PRON-REL`

whom·ever /huːmˈevə/. **Whomever** is a formal word for **whoever** when it is the object of a verb or preposition. `CONJ`

whoop /wuːp, AM huːp/ **whoops, whooping, whooped. 1** If you **whoop**, you shout loudly in a very happy or excited way. *She whoops with delight at a promise of money.* ▶ Also a noun. *Scattered groans and whoops broke out in the crowd.* **2** See also **whoops.** `◆◇◇◇◇ V WRITTEN N-COUNT`

whoo·pee /wʊˈpiː/. People sometimes shout **'whoopee'** when they are very happy or excited. *I can have a lie in tomorrow. Whoopee!* `EXCLAM PRAGMATICS INFORMAL`

whoop·ing cough /ˈhuːpɪŋ kɒf, AM - kɔːf/. **Whooping cough** is a serious infectious disease which causes people to cough and make a loud noise when they breathe in. `N-UNCOUNT`

whoops /wʊps/. People say **'whoops'** when they have had a slight accident or made a mistake. *Whoops, it's past 11, I'd better be off home.* `EXCLAM PRAGMATICS SPOKEN`

whoosh /wuːʃ, AM hwuːʃ/ **whooshes, whooshing, whooshed. 1** People sometimes say **'whoosh'** when they are emphasizing the fact that something happens very suddenly or very fast. *Then came the riders amid even louder cheers and whoosh! It was all over.* **2** If something **whooshes**, it makes a loud hissing sound, often because it is `EXCLAM PRAGMATICS` `VERB V adv/prep INFORMAL`

moving quickly. *Cool air whooshes up through the grates on the street.* ▶ Also a noun. *...the whoosh and murmur of the wind through the trees.* N-SING; SOUND

whop·per /ˈwɒpə/ **whoppers. 1** If you describe a lie as a **whopper**, you mean that it is very far from the truth. *...the biggest whopper the president told.* N-COUNT INFORMAL **2** If you refer to something as a **whopper**, you mean N-COUNT that it is an unusually large example of the thing INFORMAL mentioned. *As comets go, it is a whopper.*

whop·ping /ˈwɒpɪŋ/. If you describe something as **whopping**, you are emphasizing that it is large. *...whopping great, studded boots... Planned spending amounts to a whopping $31.4 billion.* ADJ; ADJ n, a ADJ amount PRAGMATICS INFORMAL

whore /hɔː/ **whores.** A **whore** is the same as a **prostitute.** ◆◇◇◇◇ N-COUNT

who're /ˈhuːə/. **Who're** is a spoken form of 'who are'.

whore·house /ˈhɔːhaʊs/ **whorehouses.** A **whorehouse** is the same as a **brothel.** N-COUNT

whorl /wɜːl, AM hwɔːl/ **whorls.** A **whorl** is a spiral shape. N-COUNT LITERARY

who's /huːz/. **Who's** is the usual spoken form of 'who is' or 'who has', especially when 'has' is an auxiliary verb.

whose /huːz/. **1** You use **whose** at the beginning of a relative clause where you mention something that belongs to or is associated with the person or thing mentioned in the previous clause. *I saw a man shouting at a driver whose car was blocking the street. ...tourists whose vacations included an unexpected adventure.* **2** You use **whose** in questions to QUESTION ask about the person or thing that something belongs to or is associated with. *Whose was the better performance?... Whose is this?* ▶ Also a determiner. DET-QUEST *Whose daughter is she?* **3** You use **whose** after certain words to introduce a clause where you talk about the person or thing that something belongs to or is associated with. *I can't remember whose idea it was for us to meet again.* ▶ Also a conjunction. *It* CONJ *doesn't matter whose it is.* ◆◆◆◇ PRON-REL

who·so·ever /ˌhuːsəʊˈevə/. **Whosoever** means the CONJ same as **whoever.** DATED, LITERARY

who've /huːv/. **Who've** is the usual spoken form of 'who have,' especially when 'have' is an auxiliary verb.

why /waɪ/. **1** You use **why** in questions when you ask about the reason for something. *Why hasn't he brought the whisky?... 'I just want to see him.'—'Why?'... Why should I leave?* **2** You use **why** at the CONJ beginning of a clause in which you talk about the reasons for something. *Experts wonder why the US government is not taking similarly strong actions.* ▶ Also an adverb. *I don't know why... Here's why.* ADV **3** You use **why** to introduce a clause after the word PRON-REL 'reason'. *There's a reason why women don't read this stuff; it's not funny.* ▶ Also an adverb. *He confirmed* ADV: n ADV *that the city had been closed to foreigners, but gave no reason why.* **4** You use **why** with 'not' in ques- QUESTION tions in order to introduce a suggestion. *Why not* PRAGMATICS *give Claire a call?... Why don't we talk it through?* **5** You use **why** with 'not' in questions in order to ex- QUESTION press your annoyance or anger. *Why don't you watch* PRAGMATICS *where you're going?* **6** You say **why not** in order to CONVENTION agree with what someone has suggested. *'Want to* PRAGMATICS *spend the afternoon with me?'—'Why not?'* **7** People EXCLAM say **'Why!'** to indicate their surprise, shock, or indig- PRAGMATICS nation. *Why hello, Tom... Why, this is nothing but common vegetable soup.* ◆◆◆◆ QUESTION

8 ● **the whys and wherefores**: see **wherefores.**

wick /wɪk/ **wicks. 1** The **wick** of a candle is the N-COUNT piece of string in it which burns when it is lit. **2** The N-COUNT **wick** of a paraffin lamp or cigarette lighter is the part which supplies the fuel to the flame when it is lit.

wick·ed /ˈwɪkɪd/. **1** You use **wicked** to describe someone or something that is very bad in a way that is deliberately harmful to people. *She described the shooting as a wicked attack.* ◆ **wick·ed·ness** N-UNCOUNT *...moral arguments about the wickedness of nuclear weapons.* **2** If you describe someone or something ADJ-GRADED ◆◆◇◇◇ ADJ-GRADED

as **wicked**, you mean that they are naughty or mischievous, but in a way that you find enjoyable. *She had a wicked sense of humour.* ◆ **wick·ed·ly** *...a* ADV *wickedly funny parody.*

wick·er /ˈwɪkə/. **Wicker** is material made by weaving canes, twigs, or reeds together, which is used to make baskets and furniture. ◆◇◇◇◇ N-UNCOUNT

wick·et /ˈwɪkɪt/ **wickets. 1** In cricket, a **wicket** is a set of three upright sticks with two small sticks on top of them at which the ball is bowled. **2** In cricket, a **wicket** is the area of grass in between the two wickets on the pitch. **3** In cricket, when a **wicket** falls or is taken, a batsman is out. ◆◆◇◇◇ N-COUNT N-COUNT N-COUNT

'wicket-keeper, wicket-keepers; also spelled N-COUNT **wicket keeper.** A **wicket-keeper** is the player in a cricket team who stands behind the wicket in order to catch the ball there.

wide /waɪd/ **wider, widest. 1** Something that is **wide** measures a large distance from one side or edge to the other. *...a wide-brimmed sunhat.* **2** A **wide** smile is one in which your mouth is stretched because you are very pleased or amused. ◆ **wide·ly** *He was grinning widely.* **3** If you open or spread something **wide**, you open or spread it as far as possible or to the fullest extent. *Open your mouth wide... 'It was huge,' he announced, spreading his arms wide.* **4** You use **wide** to talk or ask about how much something measures from one side or edge to the other. *The road is only one track wide. ...a desk that was almost as wide as the room.* ◆◆◆◆ ADJ-GRADED ADJ-GRADED ADV-GRADED: ADV after v ADJ ADJ

5 You use **wide** to describe something that includes a large number of different things or people. *...a wide choice of hotels... The proposed constitution gives him much wider powers than his predecessor.* ◆ **widely** *He published widely in scientific journals.* **6** You use **wide** to say that something is found, believed, known, or supported by many people or throughout a large area. *The case has attracted wide publicity... I suspect this book will have the widest appeal.* ◆ **widely** *...the group which is widely blamed for having planted the bomb.* **7** A **wide** difference or gap between two things, ideas, or qualities is a large difference or gap. *There are wide variations caused by different academic programme structures.* ◆ **widely** *...children from widely different backgrounds.* **8 Wider** is used to describe something which relates to the most important or general parts of a situation, rather than to the smaller parts or to details. *He emphasised the wider issue of superpower cooperation.* ADJ-GRADED ADV-GRADED ADV-GRADED ADV-GRADED: ADV with v ADJ-GRADED ADV-GRADED ADJ-GRADED: ADJ n

9 If something such as a shot or punch is **wide**, it does ADJ-GRADED not hit its target but lands to the right or left of it. *Nearly half the missiles landed wide.*

10 ● **wide awake**: see **awake.** ● **far and wide**: see **far.** ● **wide of the mark**: see **mark.** ● **wide open**: see **open.**

-wide /-waɪd/. **-wide** combines with nouns to form COMB adjectives which indicate that something exists or happens throughout the place or area that the noun refers to. *...a Europe-wide conference on security and cooperation.* ▶ Also combines to form adverbs. *Country-wide, a total of 22 political parties are competing for the voters' allegiance.* COMB

,wide-'angle 'lens, wide-angle lenses. A **wide- angle lens** is a lens which allows you to photograph a wider view than a normal lens. N-COUNT

,wide a'wake. If you are **wide awake**, you are completely awake. ADJ

'wide-eyed. 1 If you describe someone as **wide- eyed**, you mean that they seem inexperienced, and may be rather naive and easily impressed. *Her wide-eyed innocence soon exposes the pretensions of the art world.* **2** If you describe someone as **wide- eyed**, you mean that their eyes are more open than usual, especially because they are surprised or frightened. ▶ Also an adverb. *Trevor was staring wide-eyed at me.* ◆◇◇◇◇ ADJ ADJ ADV-GRADED: ADV after v

wid·en /ˈwaɪdən/ **widens, widening, widened. 1** If you **widen** something or if it **widens**, it becomes greater in measurement from one side or edge to the other. *The river widens considerably as it begins to turn east.* ◆ **wid·en·ing** *They have ordered* ◆◇◇◇◇ V-ERG: V n V N-UNCOUNT

the widening of the road where the incident took place. **2** If you **widen** something, it becomes greater in range or variety or includes or affects a larger number of people or things. *The search for my brother widened... Newspapers enjoyed a widening circle of readers.* **3** If your eyes **widen**, they open more. **4** If a difference or gap **widens**, it becomes greater. *The US trade deficit widened to $7.59 billion in November. ...policies that widen the gap between the rich and the poor.*
V-ERG: V n / V / V-ing

VERB: V

V-ERG: V / V to/from/by amount / V n

,wide-'ranging. If you describe something as **wide-ranging**, you mean it deals with or affects a great variety of different things. *...a wide-ranging debate about the party's goals.*
◆◇◇◇◇ ADJ-GRADED

wide·spread /ˈwaɪdspred/. Something that is **widespread** exists or happens over a large area, or to a great extent. *Mr Pasqua's proposals have attracted widespread support.*
◆◆◆◇◇ ADJ-GRADED

widg·et /ˈwɪdʒɪt/ **widgets.** You can refer to any small device as a **widget** when you do not know exactly what it is or how it works.
N-COUNT INFORMAL

wid·ow /ˈwɪdəʊ/ **widows.** A **widow** is a woman whose husband has died and who has not married again.
◆◆◇◇◇ N-COUNT

wid·owed /ˈwɪdəʊd/. If someone **is widowed**, their husband or wife has died and they have not married again. *Imogen stayed with her widowed sister.*
◆◇◇◇◇ V-PASSIVE: be V-ed / V-ed

wid·ow·er /ˈwɪdəʊə/ **widowers.** A **widower** is a man whose wife has died and who has not married again.
N-COUNT

wid·ow·hood /ˈwɪdəʊhʊd/. **Widowhood** is the state of being a widow or widower, or the period of time during which someone is a widow or widower.
N-UNCOUNT

width /wɪdθ/ **widths. 1** The **width** of something is the distance it measures from one side or edge to the other. *Measure the full width of the window... The road was reduced to 18ft in width by adding parking bays.* **2** The **width** of something is its quality of being wide. **3** A **width** is the distance from one side of a swimming pool to the other. *We swam several widths.*
◆◇◇◇◇ N-VAR

N-UNCOUNT
N-COUNT

wield /wiːld/ **wields, wielding, wielded. 1** If you **wield** a weapon, tool, or piece of equipment, you carry and use it. **2** If someone **wields** power, they have it and are able to use it. *He remains chairman, but wields little power at the company.*
◆◇◇◇◇ VERB: V n

VERB V n

wife /waɪf/ **wives.** A man's **wife** is the woman he is married to. • See also **old wives' tale**.
◆◆◆◆◆ N-COUNT

wife·ly /ˈwaɪfli/. **Wifely** is used to describe things that are supposed to be typical of a good wife. *...wifely duty.*
ADJ

wig /wɪg/ **wigs.** A **wig** is a mass of false hair which you wear on your head, for example because you are bald or because you want to cover up your own hair.
◆◆◇◇◇ N-COUNT

wig·gle /ˈwɪgəl/ **wiggles, wiggling, wiggled.** If you **wiggle** something such as a part of your body or if it **wiggles**, it moves up and down or from side to side in small quick movements. *His ears wiggled if you scratched his chin... Your baby will try to shuffle or wiggle along the floor.* ▸ Also a noun. *...a wiggle of the hips.*
◆◇◇◇◇ V-ERG: V n / V prep/adv

N-COUNT

wig·wam /ˈwɪgwæm/, AM -wɑːm/ **wigwams.** A **wigwam** is the same as a **tepee**.
N-COUNT

wild /waɪld/ **wilds; wilder, wildest. 1** Wild animals or plants live or grow in natural surroundings and are not looked after by people. **2** Wild land is natural and not cultivated. ◆ **wild·ness** *...the wildness of the mountains.* **3** The **wilds** are remote areas, far away from towns.
◆◆◆◆◇ ADJ

ADJ-GRADED
N-UNCOUNT
N-PLURAL: the N

4 Wild is used to describe the weather or the sea when it is very windy or stormy. **5** Wild behaviour is uncontrolled and excited or energetic. *As George himself came on stage they went wild. ...a wild party.* ◆ **wild·ly** *The crowd clapped wildly.* ◆ **wildness** *He had come to love the danger and the wildness of his life.* **6** If someone is **wild**, they are very angry. *At this Peter went wild, spitting curses.* **7** If you say that someone has **wild** eyes, you mean that their eyes are wide open and staring because they are frightened, angry, or in-
ADJ-GRADED
ADJ-GRADED
ADV-GRADED
N-UNCOUNT
ADJ-GRADED INFORMAL
ADJ-GRADED

sane. *I could not forget the wild look in his eyes.* ◆ **wild·ness** *She stared at him with wildness in her eyes.* **8** A **wild** idea or guess is unusual and made without much thought. ◆ **wild·ly** *'Thirteen?' he guessed wildly.*
N-UNCOUNT
ADJ-GRADED: ADJ n
ADV-GRADED

9 See also **wildly**.

10 If you **are wild about** someone or something, you like them very much. **11** Animals that live **in the wild** live in a free and natural state and are not looked after by people. **12** If something or someone, especially a child, **runs wild**, they behave in a natural, free, or uncontrolled way. **13** • **beyond** your **wildest dreams**: see **dream**. • **in** your **wildest dreams**: see **dream**. • **to sow** your **wild oats**: see **oats**.
PHRASE
INFORMAL PHRASE
PHRASE

wild 'boar, wild boars. The plural can be either **wild boar** or **wild boars**. A **wild boar** is a large fierce pig which has tusks and a lot of hair and which lives in forests.
N-COUNT

'wild card, wild cards. 1 If you refer to someone or something as a **wild card** in a particular situation, you mean that they cause uncertainty because you do not know how they will behave. *The wild card in the picture is eastern Europe.* **2** If a sports player is given a **wild card** for a particular competition, they are allowed to play in it, although they have not qualified for it in the usual way.
N-COUNT
N-COUNT

wild·cat /ˈwaɪldkæt/ **wildcats. 1** A **wildcat** is a cat which is very fierce and lives especially in mountains and forests. **2** A **wildcat** strike happens suddenly, as a result of a decision by a group of workers, and is not officially approved by a trade union. *...wildcat stoppages on public transport.*
N-COUNT
ADJ: ADJ n

wil·de·beest /ˈwɪldɪbiːst, 'vɪl-/; **wildebeest** is both the singular and the plural form. A **wildebeest** is a large African antelope which has short curved horns and hair under its neck that looks like a beard.
N-COUNT

wil·der·ness /ˈwɪldənəs/ **wildernesses. 1** A **wilderness** is a desert or other area of natural land which is not cultivated. *...one of the largest wilderness areas in North America.* **2** If politicians or other well-known people spend time **in the wilderness**, they are not in an influential position or very active in their profession for that time.
◆◆◇◇◇ N-COUNT
PHRASE JOURNALISM

wild·fire /ˈwaɪldfaɪə/ **wildfires. 1** A **wildfire** is a fire that starts in a wild area such as a forest, and spreads rapidly, causing great damage. **2** If something, especially news or a rumour, **spreads like wildfire**, it spreads extremely quickly. *These stories are spreading like wildfire through the city.*
N-COUNT
PHRASE

'wild flower, wild flowers. Wild **flowers** are plants and their flowers which grow naturally, for example in the countryside, rather than being cultivated in gardens or nurseries.
◆◇◇◇◇ N-COUNT

wild·fowl /ˈwaɪldfaʊl/. **Wildfowl** are birds such as ducks, pheasants, and quails which some people hunt and shoot.
N-PLURAL

,wild 'goose chase, wild goose chases. If you are on a **wild goose chase**, you waste a lot of time searching for something that you have little chance of finding, because you have been given misleading information. *Harry wondered if Potts had deliberately sent him on a wild goose chase.*
N-COUNT

wild·life /ˈwaɪldlaɪf/. You can use **wildlife** to refer to the animals and other living things that live in the wild. *Pets or wildlife could be affected by the pesticides.*
◆◆◇◇◇ N-UNCOUNT

wild·ly /ˈwaɪldli/. You use **wildly** to emphasize the degree, amount, or intensity of something. *The community and police have wildly different stories of what happened... The island's hotels vary wildly.* • See also **wild**.
◆◇◇◇◇ ADV-GRADED
PRAGMATICS

,Wild 'West. The **Wild West** is used to refer to the western part of the United States during the time when Europeans were first settling there.
N-SING: the N

wiles /waɪlz/. **Wiles** are clever tricks that people, especially women, use to persuade other people to do something. *She claimed that women 'use their feminine wiles to get on.'*
N-PLURAL

wil·ful /ˈwɪlful/; spelled **willful** in American English. **1** If you describe actions or attitudes as **wilful**, you
◆◇◇◇◇ ADJ: ADJ n
PRAGMATICS

are critical of them because they are done or expressed deliberately, especially with the intention of causing someone harm. *Wilful neglect of our manufacturing industry has caused this problem. ...wilful misconduct.* ♦ **wil·ful·ly** *There were claims that the Front has wilfully perverted democracy.* **2** If you describe someone as **wilful**, you mean that they are stubborn and determined to have their own way. ♦ **wil·ful·ness** *...her reputation for wilfulness.*   ADV-GRADED / ADJ-GRADED / N-UNCOUNT

will 1 modal verb uses

will /wɪl/. **Will** is a modal verb. It is used with the base form of a verb. In spoken English and informal written English, the form **won't** is often used in negative statements.   ♦♦♦♦♦

1 You use **will** to indicate that you hope, think, or have evidence that something is going to happen or be the case in the future. *It has been estimated that 70 per cent of airports in the Far East will have to be upgraded... Will you ever feel at home here?* **2** You use **will** in order to make statements about official arrangements in the future. *The show will be open to the public at 2pm... When will I be released, sir?* **3** You use **will** in order to make promises and threats about what is going to happen or be the case in the future. *I'll call you tonight... Price quotes on selected product categories will be sent on request... If she refuses to follow rules about car safety, she won't be allowed to use the car.* **4** You use **will** to indicate someone's intention to do something. *'Dinner's ready.'—'Thanks, Carrie, but we'll have a drink first.'... What will you do next?... Will you be remaining in the city?* **5** You use **will** to say that someone or something is able to do something in the future. *How the country will defend itself in the future has become increasingly important... How will I recognize you?* **6** You use **will** in questions in order to make polite invitations or offers. *Will you stay for supper?... Won't you sit down?* **7** You use **will** in questions in order to ask or tell someone to do something. *Will you drive me home?... Wipe the jam off my mouth, will you?* **8** You use **will** in statements to give an order to someone. *You will do as I request, if you please... You will not discuss this matter with anyone.* **9** You use **will** to say that someone is willing to do something. You use **will not** or **won't** to indicate that someone refuses to do something. *All right, I'll forgive you... I'll answer the phone... If you won't let me pay for a taxi, then at least allow me to lend you something.* **10** You use **will** to indicate that an action usually happens in the particular way mentioned. *Art thieves often hide an important work for years.* **11** You use **will** in the main clause of some 'if' and 'unless' sentences to indicate something that you consider to be likely to happen. *If you overcook the pancakes they will be difficult to roll.* **12** You use **will have** with a past participle when you are saying that you are fairly certain that something will be true by a particular time in the future. *He will have left by January the fifteenth.* **13** You use **will have** with a past participle to indicate that you are fairly sure that something is the case. *The holiday will have done him the world of good.* **14** You use **will** to say that someone insists on behaving or doing something in a particular way and you cannot change them. You emphasize the word **will** when you use it in this way. *He will leave his socks lying all over the place and it drives me mad.*   MODAL (etc.) / PRAGMATICS / FORMAL

will 2 wanting something to happen

will /wɪl/ **wills, willing, willed. 1 Will** is the determination to do something. *He was said to have lost his will to live... It's a constant battle of wills with your children.* ● See also **free will. 2** If something is the **will** of a person or group of people with authority, they want it to happen. *He has submitted himself to the will of God... Democracy responds and adjusts to the will of the people.* **3** If you **will** something to happen, you try to make it happen by using mental effort rather than physical effort. *I looked at the telephone, willing it to ring.* **4** If something is done **against** your **will**, it is done even though you   N-VAR / N-SING: with poss / VERB V n to-inf / PHRASE

do not want it to be done. **5** If you can do something **at will**, you can do it when you want and as much as you want. *...scientists who can adjust their experiments at will.* **6** If you do something **with a will**, you do it with a lot of enthusiasm and energy. *Set to work with a will and be pleased with the amount you get done.*   PHRASE / PHRASE

7 A **will** is a document in which you declare what you want to happen to your money and property when you die. **8** If you **will** something to someone, you say in your will that they should have it when you die. **9** See also **willing**.   N-COUNT / VERB: V n to n

will·ful. See **wilful**.
wil·lie /'wɪli/. See **willy**.

will·ing /'wɪlɪŋ/. **1** If someone is **willing** to do something, they do not mind doing it or have no objection to it. *There are, of course, questions which she will not be willing to answer.* ♦ **will·ing·ly** *I am glad you have come here so willingly.* ♦ **will·ing·ness** *I had to prove my willingness to work hard.* **2 Willing** is used to describe someone who does something enthusiastically and because they want to do it, rather than because they are forced to do it. *He was a natural and willing pupil.* ♦ **will·ing·ly** *Most companies willingly correct what went wrong.* ♦ **will·ing·ness** *Self-discipline, willingness, enthusiasm, that's what you must depend on.* **3** ● **God willing:** see **god**.   ADJ-GRADED: v-link ADJ to-inf / ADV-GRADED / N-UNCOUNT / ADJ-GRADED / ADV-GRADED / N-UNCOUNT

wil·low /'wɪləʊ/ **willows.** A **willow** or a **willow tree** is a type of tree with long branches and long narrow leaves that grows near water. ▶ **Willow** is the wood of this tree.   N-COUNT / N-UNCOUNT

wil·lowy /'wɪləʊi/. A person who is **willowy** is tall, thin, and graceful.   ADJ-GRADED

will·power /'wɪlpaʊə/; also spelled **will-power** or **will power. Willpower** is a very strong determination to do something. *His attempts to stop smoking by willpower alone failed.*   N-UNCOUNT

wil·ly /'wɪli/ **willies;** also spelled **willie. 1** A boy's or man's **willy** is his penis; a word used mainly by children. *...the first time he noticed his willy.* **2** If someone or something **gives** you **the willies** they make you feel nervous or frightened.   N-COUNT BRITISH, INFORMAL PHRASE / INFORMAL

willy-nilly /,wɪli 'nɪli/; also spelled **willy nilly. 1** If something happens to you **willy-nilly**, it happens whether you like it or not. *The government were dragged willy-nilly into the confrontation.* **2** If someone does something **willy-nilly**, they do it in a careless and haphazard way, without planning or choosing things in advance. *Clerks bundled papers into files willy-nilly.*   ADV / ADV

wilt /wɪlt/ **wilts, wilting, wilted. 1** If a plant **wilts**, it gradually bends downwards and becomes weak because it needs more water or is dying. **2** If someone **wilts**, they become weak or tired, or lose confidence. *The government wilted in the face of such powerful pressure.*   VERB: V / VERB V

wily /'waɪli/ **wilier, wiliest.** If you describe someone or someone's behaviour as **wily**, you mean that they are clever and cunning, especially in ways that involve deceiving people.   ADJ-GRADED

wimp /wɪmp/ **wimps.** If you call someone a **wimp**, you disapprove of them because they lack confidence or determination, or because they are often afraid of things. ♦ **wimp·ish** or **wimpy** *...a wimpy unpopular schoolboy.*   N-COUNT PRAGMATICS INFORMAL / ADJ-GRADED

win /wɪn/ **wins, winning, won. 1** If you win something such as a competition, battle, or argument, you defeat those people you are competing or fighting against, or you do better than everyone else involved. *He does not have any realistic chance of winning the election... The top four teams all won... Sanchez Vicario won 2-6, 6-4, 6-3.* ▶ Also a noun. *...Arsenal's dismal league run of eight games without a win.* **2** If you **win** something such as a prize or medal, you get it because you have defeated everyone else in something such as an election, competition, battle, or argument, or have done very well in it. **3** If you **win** something that you want or need, you succeed in getting it. *British Aerospace*   VERB V / V n / V amount / Also V n amount / N-COUNT / VERB: V n / VERB V n

has won an order worth 340 million dollars. **4** If VERB
something **wins** you something like a contest or V n n
election, it causes you to defeat the other people involved. If something wins you a prize or something
that you want, it causes you to get it. *They believed
that better economic news, by itself would win Mr
Bush the election.*

5 If you say that someone **can't win** in a particular PHRASE
situation, you mean that they are certain to fail or to INFORMAL
suffer whatever they do. *It seems that the banking consumer just can't win!* **6** You say **'you win'** when you CONVENTION
have been having a slight argument with someone PRAGMATICS
and you are indicating that you agree to do what they
want or that you accept their suggestion, even though
you do not really want to.

7 See also **winning.** • to **lose the battle but win the
war:** see **battle.** • to **win the day:** see **day.** • to **win
hands down:** see **hand.**

win back. If you **win back** something that you have PHRASAL VB
lost, you get it again, especially as a result of a great ef- V P noun
fort. *The Government will have to work hard to win Also V n P
back the confidence of the people.*

win out or **win through.** If something or someone PHRASAL VB
wins out or **wins through,** they are successful or gain V P
an advantage over others, after a competition or V P over/
struggle. *Here is a chance for greengrocers to win out against n
over the supermarkets by selling local produce.*

win over or **win round.** If you **win** someone **over** or PHRASAL VB
win them **round,** you persuade them to support you V n P
or agree with you. *By the end of the day President V P noun
Gorbachev had won over the crowd.*

win through. See **win out.** PHRASAL VB

win through to. If you **win through to** a particular PHRASAL VB
position or stage of a competition, you succeed in V P P n
achieving it after a great effort or by defeating
opponents.

wince /wɪns/ **winces, wincing, winced.** If you ◆◇◇◇◇
wince, the muscles of your face tighten suddenly VERB: V
because you have felt a pain or because you have V with quote
just seen, heard, or remembered something unpleasant. *'Shh!' Sunny winced.* ▶ Also a noun. *He N-COUNT
suppressed a wince as motion renewed the pain.*

winch /wɪntʃ/ **winches, winching, winched.** ◆◇◇◇
1 A winch is a machine which is used to lift heavy N-COUNT
objects or people who need to be rescued. It consists of a drum around which a rope or chain is
wound. **2** If you **winch** an object or person some- VERB:
where, you lift or lower them using a winch. V n with adv/
prep

wind 1 air

wind /wɪnd/ **winds, winding, winded.** **1** A wind ◆◆◆◇
is a current of air that is moving across the earth's N-VAR
surface. *There was a strong wind blowing... During
the night a gust of wind had blown the pot over.*
2 Journalists often refer to a trend or factor that in- N-COUNT:
fluences events as a **wind** of some kind. *The winds N of n
of change are blowing across the country.*
3 If you **are winded** by something such as a blow, the VERB:
air is suddenly knocked out of your lungs so that you be V-ed
have difficulty breathing for a short time. *The cow V n
stamped on his side, winding him.* **4** **Wind** is the air N-UNCOUNT
that you sometimes swallow with food or drink, or gas
that is produced in your intestines, which causes an
uncomfortable feeling. **5** If you **wind** a baby, you pat it VERB: V n
on the back in order to help it to release air from its
stomach.

6 The **wind** section of an orchestra or band is the ADJ: ADJ n
group of people who produce musical sounds by
blowing into their instruments.

7 If you **get wind of** something, you hear about it, es- PHRASE
pecially when someone else did not want you to know INFORMAL
about it. **8** If something is **in the wind,** it is likely to PHRASE
happen. *By the mid-1980s, change was in the wind
again.* **9** • to **throw caution to the wind:** see **caution.**

wind 2 turning or wrapping

wind /waɪnd/ **winds, winding, wound.** **1** If a ◆◆◆◇
road, river, or line of people **winds** in a particular VERB:
direction, it goes in that direction with a lot of V prep/adv
bends or twists in it. *The convoy wound its way V way prep/
through the West Bank.* **2** When you **wind** some- adv
thing flexible round something else, you wrap it VERB
V n prep/adv

around it several times. *The horse jumped forwards
and round her, winding the rope round her waist.*
3 When you **wind** a mechanical device, for example VERB: V n
a watch or a clock, you turn a knob, key, or handle
on it round and round in order to make it operate.
▶ **Wind up** means the same as **wind.** *Frances took* PHRASAL VB
the tiny music box from her trunk and wound it up. V n P
4 To **wind** a tape or film **back** or **forward** is to make VERB:
it move nearer to its starting or ending position V n adv
using a device such as a tape recorder or camera.

wind down. **1** When you **wind down** something PHRASAL VB
such as the window of a car, you make it move down- V n P
wards by turning a handle. *If a stranger stops you, just* Also V P noun
wind the window down a fraction. **2** If you **wind** V P
down, you relax after doing something that has made INFORMAL
you feel tired or tense. **3** If someone **winds down** a ERG
business or activity, they gradually reduce the V P noun
amount of work that is done or the number of people Also V P,
that are involved. *Foreign aid workers have already V n P
begun winding down their operation.*

wind up. **1** When you **wind up** an activity, you finish PHRASAL VB
it or stop doing it. *Winding up the debate, she said: 'It* V P noun
would immediately put up interest rates.' **2** When V P noun
someone **winds up** a business or other organization, Also V n P
they stop running it and close it down completely.
*The Bank of England seems determined to wind up the
company.*

3 If you **wind up** in a particular place, situation, or V P prep/adv
state, you are in it at the end of a series of actions, V P adj/n
events, or experiences, even though you did not origi- Also V P -ing
nally intend to be. *Both partners of the marriage
wound up unhappy.* **4** When you **wind up** something V n P
such as the window of a car, you make it move Also V P noun
upwards by turning a handle. *He started winding the
window up but I grabbed the door and opened it.* **5** If V n P
you **wind** someone **up,** you deliberately say things BRITISH,
which annoy them. *This woman really wound me up.* INFORMAL
She kept talking over me. **6** If you **wind** someone **up,** V n P
you say untrue things in order to trick them. *You're* BRITISH,
joking. Come on, you're winding me up. **7** See also INFORMAL
wind 3, **wind-up, wound up.**

wind-bag /wɪndbæg/ **windbags.** If you call some- N-COUNT
one a **windbag,** you are saying in a fairly rude way INFORMAL
that you think they talk a great deal in a boring way.

wind-blown /wɪnd bləʊn/; also spelled **windblown.** ADJ
You can use **wind-blown** to indicate that something WRITTEN
has been blown about by the wind. *...characteristic
shapes of wind-blown trees.*

wind-break /wɪndbreɪk/ **windbreaks.** A **wind-** N-COUNT
break is something such as a line of trees or a fence
which gives protection against the wind.

wind-fall /wɪndfɔːl/ **windfalls.** **1** A **windfall** is a ◆◇◇◇
sum of money that you receive unexpectedly or by N-COUNT
luck. **2** A **windfall** is a fruit, especially an apple, that N-COUNT
has fallen from a tree.

wind farm /wɪnd fɑːm/ **wind farms.** A **wind farm** N-COUNT
is a kind of power station where windmills are used
to convert the power of the wind into electricity.

wind instrument /wɪnd ɪnstrəmənts/ **wind in-** N-COUNT
struments. A **wind instrument** is any musical instrument that you blow into in order to produce
sounds.

wind-lass /wɪndləs/ **windlasses.** A **windlass** is a N-COUNT
mechanical device for lifting heavy objects, which
uses a motor to pull a rope around a cylinder.

wind-less /wɪndləs/. If the air is **windless,** or if it is ADJ
a **windless** day, it is very calm and still.

wind-mill /wɪndmɪl/ **windmills.** A **windmill** is a ◆◇◇◇
structure with large sails on the outside which turn N-COUNT
round as the wind blows to provides energy.

win-dow /wɪndəʊ/ **windows.** **1** A **window** is a ◆◆◆◆
space in the wall of a building or in the side of a ve- N-COUNT
hicle, which has glass in it so that light can come in
and you can see out. See picture headed **house and
flat.** *The room felt very hot and she wondered why
someone did not open a window.* **2** A **window** is a N-COUNT
large piece of glass along the front of a shop, behind
which some of the goods that the shop sells are displayed. *I stood for a few moments in front of the
nearest shop window.* **3** A **window** is a glass-covered N-COUNT

opening above a counter, for example in a bank or post office, which the person serving you sits behind. **4** On a computer screen, a **window** is one of the work areas that the screen can be divided into. **5** See also **French window, picture window, rose window**. N-COUNT

6 If you say that something such as a plan, or a particular way of thinking or behaving **has gone out of the window** or **has flown out of the window**, you mean that it has disappeared completely. *By now all logic had gone out of the window.* **7** If you say that there is a **window of opportunity** for something, you mean that there is an opportunity to do something but that this opportunity will only last for a short time. PHRASE / PHRASE JOURNALISM

'window box, window boxes. A window box is a long narrow container on a windowsill in which plants are grown. N-COUNT

'window-dressing; also spelled **window dressing**. **1** Window-dressing is the skill of arranging objects attractively in a shop window. **2** If you refer to something as **window-dressing**, you are critical of it because it is done in order to create a good impression and to prevent people from realizing the real or more unpleasant nature of someone's activities. N-UNCOUNT / N-UNCOUNT PRAGMATICS

'window frame, window frames. A window frame is a frame round the edges of a window, which glass is fixed into. N-COUNT

window·pane /'wɪndəʊpeɪn/ **windowpanes;** also spelled **window pane.** A windowpane is a piece of glass in the window of a building. N-COUNT

'window seat, window seats. 1 A window seat is a seat which is fixed to the wall underneath a window in a room. **2** On a train, bus, or aeroplane, a **window seat** is a seat next to a window. N-COUNT / N-COUNT

'window shopping; also spelled **window-shopping**. If you do some **window shopping**, you spend time looking at the goods in the windows of shops without intending to buy anything. N-UNCOUNT

window·sill /'wɪndəʊsɪl/ **windowsills;** also spelled **window sill.** A windowsill is a ledge along the bottom of a window, either inside or outside a building. See picture headed **house and flat**. N-COUNT

wind·pipe /'wɪndpaɪp/ **windpipes.** Your windpipe is the tube in your body that carries air into your lungs when you breathe. N-COUNT

wind·screen /'wɪndskriːn/ **windscreens.** The windscreen of a car or other vehicle is the glass window at the front through which the driver looks. The usual American word is **windshield**. See picture headed **car and bicycle**. ◆◇◇◇ N-COUNT BRITISH

'windscreen wiper, windscreen wipers. A windscreen wiper is a device that wipes rain from a vehicle's windscreen. The usual American word is **windshield wiper**. See picture headed **car and bicycle**. N-COUNT BRITISH

wind·shield /'wɪndʃiːld/ **windshields.** See windscreen.

'windshield wiper, windshield wipers. See windscreen wiper.

wind·surf·er /'wɪndsɜːfə/ **windsurfers. 1** A windsurfer is a long narrow board with a sail attached to it. You stand on a windsurfer in the sea or on a lake and are blown along by the wind. **2** A windsurfer is a person who rides on a windsurfer. N-COUNT / N-COUNT

wind·surfing /'wɪndsɜːfɪŋ/. Windsurfing is a sport in which you move along the surface of the sea or a lake on a long narrow board with a sail on it. N-UNCOUNT

wind·swept /'wɪndswept/. A windswept place has no shelter and is not protected against strong winds. *...the remote and windswept hillside.* ADJ

wind tunnel /'wɪnd tʌnəl/ **wind tunnels.** A wind tunnel is a room or passage which is designed so that air can be made to flow through it at controlled speeds. Wind tunnels are used to test new or experimental equipment or machinery. N-COUNT

wind-up /'waɪnd ʌp/. A **wind-up** device has a mechanism that is operated by clockwork. ◆◇◇◇ ADJ: ADJ n

wind·ward /'wɪndwəd/. **1** Windward is used to describe the side of something, especially a ship, which is facing the wind. **2** If a ship sails **to wind-** ADJ: ADJ n / PHRASE

ward, it sails towards the place from which the wind is blowing. TECHNICAL

windy /'wɪndi/ **windier, windiest.** If it is **windy**, the wind is blowing a lot. ◆◇◇◇ ADJ-GRADED

wine /waɪn/ **wines. 1** Wine is an alcoholic drink which is made from grapes. You can also refer to alcoholic drinks made from other fruits or vegetables as **wine**. *...a bottle of white wine. ...homemade parsnip wine.* **2** Wine is used to describe things that are very dark red in colour. *...an olive and wine wool sweater.* ◆◆◆◇ N-VAR / COLOUR

'wine bar, wine bars. A wine bar is a place where people can buy and drink wine, and sometimes eat food as well. ◆◇◇◇ N-COUNT

'wine glass, wine glasses. A wine glass is a glass, usually with a narrow stem, which you use for drinking wine. N-COUNT

win·ery /'waɪnəri/ **wineries.** A winery is a place where wine is made. The British word is **vineyard**. N-COUNT AMERICAN

wing /wɪŋ/ **wings, winging, winged. 1** The wings of a bird or insect are the two parts of its body that it uses for flying. See picture headed **insects**. ♦ **-winged** *...black-winged birds.* **2** The wings of an aeroplane are the long flat parts sticking out of its side which support it while it is flying. ♦ **-winged** *...a wide-winged plane.* **3** A wing of a building is a part of it which sticks out from the main part. *We were given an office in the empty west wing.* **4** A wing of an organization, especially a political organization, is a group within it which has a particular function or particular beliefs. *...the military wing of the African National Congress.* ● See also **left-wing, right-wing. 5** In a game such as football or hockey, the **left wing** and the **right wing** are the areas on the far left and the far right of the pitch. You can also refer to the players who play in these positions as the **left wing** and the **right wing. 6** A wing of a car is the part of its bodywork which is over a wheel. The American word is **fender**. See picture headed **car and bicycle. 7** In a theatre, **the wings** are the sides of the stage which are hidden from the audience by curtains or scenery. **8** If you say that someone is waiting **in the wings**, you mean that they are ready and waiting for the opportunity to take action. **9** If you say that something or someone **wings their way** somewhere or **wings** somewhere, you mean they go there quickly, especially by plane. *A few moments later they were airborne and winging their way south.* **10** If you say that something or someone **clips** your **wings**, you mean that they restrict your freedom to do what you want. *...legislation aimed at clipping the president's political wings.* **11** If you **spread** your **wings**, you do something new because you feel more confident in your abilities than you used to. **12** If you **take** someone **under** your **wing**, you look after them, help them, and protect them. *Her boss took her under his wing after fully realising her potential.* ◆◆◆◇ N-COUNT / COMB / N-COUNT / COMB / N-COUNT / N-COUNT: with supp / N-COUNT / N-COUNT BRITISH / N-PLURAL: the N / PHRASE / VERB V way adv/ prep / PHRASE / PHRASE / PHRASE

'wing com'mander, wing commanders. A wing commander is a senior officer in the air force. N-COUNT; N-TITLE

winged /wɪŋd/. A **winged** insect or other creature has wings. ◆◇◇◇ ADJ

wing·er /'wɪŋə/ **wingers.** In a game such as football or hockey, a **winger** is an attacking player who plays mainly on the far left or the far right of the pitch. ◆◆◇◇ N-COUNT

wing·span /'wɪŋspæn/ **wingspans;** also spelled **wing span.** The wingspan of a bird, insect, or aeroplane is the distance from the end of one wing to the end of the other wing. N-COUNT

wink /wɪŋk/ **winks, winking, winked.** When you **wink** at someone, you look towards them and close one eye very briefly, usually as a signal that something is a joke or a secret. *Brian winked at his bride-to-be.* ▶ Also a noun. *I gave her a wink.* ◆◇◇◇ VERB V at n Also V / N-COUNT

win·kle /'wɪŋkəl/ **winkles.** A winkle is a small sea snail with a hard shell and a soft body which you can eat. N-COUNT BRITISH

win·ner /'wɪnə/ **winners. 1** The **winner** of a prize, race, or competition is the person, animal, or thing ◆◆◆◇ N-COUNT

that wins it. *She will present the trophies to the award winners.* **2** If you say that something or someone is **a winner**, you mean that they are popular and successful, or that they are likely to be popular and successful. *Selling was my game and I intended to be a winner.* **3** The **winners** in a particular situation are the people who have benefited from it and are in a better position than they previously were because of it. *The real winners of the election, he said, were the Hungarian people.* [N-COUNT INFORMAL] [N-COUNT]

win·ning /ˈwɪnɪŋ/. **1** You can use **winning** to describe a person or thing that wins something such as a competition, game, or election. *Donovan scored the winning goal.* **2** You can use **winning** to describe actions or qualities that please other people and make them feel friendly towards you. *He had much charm and a winning personality.* ♦ **win·ning·ly** *Livingstone smiled again, winningly.* **3** See also **win**. [◆◆◇◇ ADJ: ADJ n] [ADJ: ADJ n] [ADV-GRADED]

win·nings /ˈwɪnɪŋz/. You can use **winnings** to refer to the money that someone wins in a competition or by gambling. [◆◇◇◇ N-PLURAL]

win·now /ˈwɪnəʊ/ **winnows, winnowing, winnowed.** If you **winnow** a group of things or people, you reduce its size by separating the ones that are useful or relevant from those that are not. ▶ **Winnow out** means the same as **winnow.** *The committee will need to winnow out the nonsense and produce more practical proposals.* [VERB: V n] [PHRASAL VB V P noun]

wino /ˈwaɪnəʊ/ **winos.** Some people refer to alcoholics as **winos**, especially if the alcoholics are poor or homeless; some people find this word offensive. [N-COUNT INFORMAL]

win·some /ˈwɪnsəm/. If you describe someone as **winsome**, you mean that they are attractive and charming. *...a winsome young screen star.* [ADJ-GRADED]

win·ter /ˈwɪntə/ **winters, wintering, wintered.** **1** **Winter** is the season between autumn and spring. In the winter the weather is usually cold. *...the winter months. ...the late winter of 1941.* **2** If an animal or plant **winters** somewhere or **is wintered** there, it spends the winter there. *Once fully acclimatised the birds will winter outside in an aviary.* **3** If you **winter** somewhere, you spend the winter there. *The family decided to winter in Nice again.* [◆◆◇◇ N-VAR] [V-ERG V adv/prep Also be V-ed prep/adv] [VERB V prep/adv FORMAL]

'winter sports. Winter sports are sports that take place on ice or snow. [N-PLURAL]

winter·time /ˈwɪntətaɪm/; also spelled **winter time. Wintertime** is the period of time during which winter lasts. [N-UNCOUNT]

win·try /ˈwɪntri/. **1** **Wintry** weather is cold and has features that are typical of winter. *A wintry wind was blowing.* **2** If you describe someone's attitude or behaviour as **wintry**, you mean that they seem very unfriendly. [ADJ-GRADED] [ADJ-GRADED]

wipe /waɪp/ **wipes, wiping, wiped. 1** If you **wipe** something, you rub its surface to remove dirt or liquid from it. *When he had finished washing he began to wipe the basin clean... Lainey wiped her hands on the towel.* ▶ Also a noun. *Tomorrow I'm going to give the toys a good wipe.* **2** If you **wipe** dirt or liquid from something, you remove it, for example by using a cloth or your hand. *Gleb wiped the sweat from his face.* **3** If you say that something **wipes the smile** or the **grin off** someone's **face**, you mean that it suddenly spoils their enjoyment or removes an advantage that they had and that you are pleased about it. *Tony Holmes wiped the smile off the faces of his rivals with a solo 30-second win.* **4** ● to **wipe the floor with** someone: see **floor.** ● to **wipe the slate clean:** see **slate.** [◆◆◇◇ VERB: V n V n with adj V n on n] [N-COUNT] [VERB V n prep Also V n] [PHRASE PRAGMATICS INFORMAL]

wipe away or **wipe off.** If you **wipe away** or **wipe off** dirt or liquid from something, you remove it, for example by using a cloth or your hand. *He wiped away the blood with a paper napkin.* [PHRASAL VB V P noun]

wipe down. If you **wipe down** something, you wash or dry its surface completely. *The girls took it in turn to wipe down the tables after meals.* [PHRASAL VB V P noun Also V n P]

wipe off. See **wipe away.** [PHRASAL VB]

wipe out. To **wipe out** something such as a place or a group of people or animals means to destroy them [PHRASAL VB V P noun Also V n P]

completely. *If the island is not protected, the oil spill could wipe out the Gulf's turtle population.*

wipe up. If you **wipe up** dirt or liquid from something, you remove it using a cloth. *I spilled my coffee all over the table and Mom leaned across to wipe it up.* [PHRASAL VB V n P Also V n P noun]

wip·er /ˈwaɪpə/ **wipers.** A wiper is the same as a windscreen wiper. [N-COUNT]

wire /waɪə/ **wires, wiring, wired. 1** A **wire** is a long thin piece of metal that is used to fasten things or to carry electric current. *...fine copper wire.* **2** A **wire** is a cable which carries power or signals from one place to another. *I ripped out the telephone wire that ran through to his office.* **3** If you **wire** something such as a building or piece of equipment, you install or connect wires inside it so that electricity or signals can pass into or through it. *...learning to wire and plumb the house herself... 95% of all American households will be wired for cable in the year 2000.* ▶ **Wire up** means the same as **wire.** *Wire the thermometers up to trigger off an alarm bell if the temperature drops.* **4** A **wire** is the same as a **telegram.** *He sent a rather unusual wire to his sisters.* **5** If you **wire** a person, you send them a telegram. **6** If you **wire** an amount of money to a person or place, you instruct a bank to send it to the person or place by a telegram message. *I'm wiring you some money... They arranged to wire the money from the United States.* **7** See also **barbed wire, high wire, hot wire, live wire.** [◆◆◇◇ N-VAR] [N-COUNT] [VERB V n be V-ed for n] [PHRASAL VB V n P Also V P noun] [N-COUNT VERB: V n AMERICAN] [VERB V n n V n prep Also V n AMERICAN]

wire up. See **wire** 3. [PHRASAL VB]

wired /waɪəd/. If someone is **wired**, they are tense, nervous, and unable to relax. *Tonight he is manic, wired and uptight.* [ADJ-GRADED AMERICAN. INFORMAL]

wire·less /ˈwaɪələs/ **wirelesses. 1** **Wireless** is a system by which messages are sent over a distance by radio signals. **2** A **wireless** or **wireless set** is a radio. *On top of the cabinet stood a wireless.* [◆◇◇◇ N-UNCOUNT DATED] [N-COUNT DATED]

wire·tap /ˈwaɪətæp/ **wiretaps, wiretapping, wiretapped;** also spelled **wire-tap.** If someone **wiretaps** your telephone, they attach a special device to the line so that they can secretly listen to your conversations. The usual British word is **tap.** ▶ Also a noun. *...illegal wiretaps.* ♦ **wire·tapping** *...allegations of wiretapping.* [VERB: V n AMERICAN] [N-COUNT] [N-UNCOUNT]

wire wool. Wire wool consists of very thin pieces of wire twisted together, often in the form of small pads. These are used to clean wooden and metal objects. The American term is **steel wool.** [N-UNCOUNT BRITISH]

wir·ing /ˈwaɪərɪŋ/. The **wiring** in a building or machine is the system of wires that supply electricity to the different parts of it. [◆◇◇◇ N-UNCOUNT]

wiry /ˈwaɪəri/. **1** Someone who is **wiry** is rather thin but is also strong. *His body is wiry and athletic.* **2** Something such as hair or grass that is **wiry** is stiff and rough to touch. [ADJ] [ADJ]

wis·dom /ˈwɪzdəm/ **wisdoms. 1** **Wisdom** is the ability to use your experience and knowledge in order to make sensible decisions or judgements. *...the patience and wisdom that comes from old age.* **2** **Wisdom** is the store of knowledge that a society or culture has collected over a long period of time. *...a more humane approach, based on ancient wisdoms.* **3** If you talk about **the wisdom of** a particular decision or action, you are talking about how sensible it is. *Many Lithuanians have expressed doubts about the wisdom of the decision.* **4** You can use **wisdom** to refer to ideas that are accepted by a large number of people. *Unchallenged wisdoms flow swiftly among the middle classes.* [◆◆◇◇ N-UNCOUNT] [N-VAR] [N-SING: the N of n/-ing] [N-VAR: supp N]

'wisdom tooth, wisdom teeth. Your **wisdom teeth** are the four large teeth at the back of your mouth. [N-COUNT]

wise /waɪz/ **wiser, wisest; wises, wising, wised. 1** A **wise** person is able to use their experience and knowledge in order to make sensible decisions and judgements. *You're a wise old man: tell me what to do.* ♦ **wise·ly** *The three of us stood around the machine nodding wisely.* **2** A **wise** action or decision is sensible. *It is wise to seek help and counsel as soon as possible.* ♦ **wisely** *They've invest-* [◆◆◇◇ ADJ-GRADED] [ADV-GRADED] [ADJ-GRADED] [ADV-GRADED]

ed their money wisely. **3** If you **get wise to** some- PHRASE
thing, you find out about it, especially when some- INFORMAL
one has been trying to keep it secret. **4** If you say PHRASE
that someone is **none the wiser** after an event or an
explanation, or that nobody is **any the wiser** after it,
you mean that they have failed to understand it, or
are not fully aware of what happened. *The brewers
are still none the wiser about the shape the Government envisages for the industry.*

wise up. If someone **wises up** to a situation or state ◇PHRASAL VB
of affairs, they become aware of it and take appropri- V P to n
ate action. *Some insurers have wised up to the fact that* Also V P
their clients were getting very cheap insurance. INFORMAL

-wise /-waɪz/. **1** **-wise** is added to nouns to form COMB
adverbs indicating that something is the case when
considering the particular thing mentioned. *It was a
much better day weather-wise.* **2** **-wise** is added to COMB
nouns to form adverbs indicating that someone behaves in the same way as the person or thing that is
mentioned. *We were housed student-wise in dormitory rooms.*

wise·crack /ˈwaɪzkræk/ **wisecracks.** A wisecrack N-COUNT
is a clever remark that is intended to be amusing,
but is often rather unkind.

wise·crack·ing /ˈwaɪzkrækɪŋ/; also spelled **wise-** ADJ
cracking. You can use **wisecracking** to describe
someone who keeps making wisecracks.

'wise guy, wise guys; also spelled **wiseguy.** If N-COUNT
you say that someone is a **wise guy**, you dislike the PRAGMATICS
fact that they think they are very clever and always INFORMAL
have an answer for everything.

wish /wɪʃ/ **wishes, wishing, wished. 1** A wish ◆◆◆◇
is a desire or strong feeling that you want to have N-COUNT
something or do something. *Clearly she had no wish
for conversation... She wanted to go everywhere in
the world. She soon got her wish.* ● See also **death
wish. 2** If you **wish** to do something or to have it VERB
done for you, you want to do it or have it done. *If* V to-inf
you wish to go away for the weekend, our office will Also V for n
be delighted to make hotel reservations. **3** If you VB: no cont
wish something were true, you would like it to be V that
true, even though you know that it is impossible or V n to-inf
unlikely. *I wish I could do that... The world is not always what we wish it to be.* **4** If you **wish for** some- VERB
thing, you express the desire silently to yourself. In V for n
fairy stories, when someone wishes for something,
it often happens by magic. *We have all wished for
men who are more like women.* ▶ Also a noun. N-COUNT
Make a wish.

5 Wish is used in sentences such as **I could not wish** VB: no cont
for anything better to indicate that you are very V for n
pleased with what you have and could not imagine
anything better. *I really could not have wished for a
better teacher.* **6** If you say that you would not **wish** VB: no cont,
something **on** someone, you mean that it is so un- with brd-neg
pleasant that you would not want them to be forced to V n on n
experience or deal with it. *It's a horrid experience and I
wouldn't wish it on my worst enemy.* **7 Wish** is used in VB: no cont,
expressions such as **I don't wish to be rude** or **with-** with brd-neg
out wishing to be rude as a way of apologizing or PRAGMATICS
warning someone in advance when you are going to V to-inf
say something which might upset, annoy, or worry
them. *Without wishing to be unkind, she's not the
most interesting company.*

8 If you **wish** someone something such as luck or VERB
happiness, you express the hope that they will be V n n
lucky or happy. *I wish you both a very good journey... I* V n adv
wish you well. **9** If you express your good **wishes** to- N-PLURAL:
wards someone, you are politely expressing your adj N
friendly feelings towards them and your hope that PRAGMATICS
they will be successful or happy. *Western leaders sent
good wishes to the new American president.*

wish·bone /ˈwɪʃbəʊn/ **wishbones.** A wishbone is N-COUNT
a V-shaped bone in chickens, turkeys, and other
birds.

wishful 'thinking. If you say that an idea, wish, ◆◇◇◇◇
or hope is **wishful thinking**, you mean that it has N-UNCOUNT
failed to come true or is unlikely to come true. *It is
wishful thinking to expect deeper change under his
leadership.*

'wish list, wish lists. If you refer to someone's N-COUNT
wish list, you mean the things which they would INFORMAL
ideally like to happen or be given to them. *...one
special toy that tops the wish list of every child.*

wishy-washy /ˈwɪʃi wɒʃi/. If you say that someone ADJ-GRADED
is **wishy-washy**, you are critical of them because PRAGMATICS
their ideas are not firm or clear. INFORMAL

wisp /wɪsp/ **wisps. 1** A **wisp** of hair is a small, ◆◇◇◇◇
thin, untidy bunch of it. *She smoothed away a wisp* N-COUNT
of hair from her eyes. **2** A **wisp** of something such as N-COUNT
smoke or cloud is an amount of it in a long thin
shape. *...an occasional wisp of white cloud.*

wispy /ˈwɪspi/. **1** If someone has **wispy** hair, their ADJ-GRADED
hair is thin and grows in fine strands. **2** A **wispy** ADJ-GRADED
cloud is thin or faint. *The half moon is hidden behind some wispy clouds.*

wis·te·ria /wɪˈstɪəriə/. **Wisteria** is a type of climb- N-UNCOUNT
ing plant, usually with mauve or white flowers.

wist·ful /ˈwɪstfʊl/. Someone who is **wistful** is ra- ◆◇◇◇◇
ther sad because they want something and know ADJ-GRADED
that they cannot have it. *He has a wistful look.*
◆ **wist·ful·ly** *'I wish I had a little brother,' said* ADV-GRADED
Daphne wistfully. ◆ **wist·ful·ness** *...her wistfulness* N-UNCOUNT
when she talked about vacations her relatives took.

wit /wɪt/ **wits. 1 Wit** is the ability to use words or ◆◆◇◇
ideas in an amusing, clever, and imaginative way. N-UNCOUNT
Boulding was known for his biting wit. ▶ A **wit** is N-COUNT
someone who has wit. *Holmes was gregarious, a
great wit, a man of wide interests.* **2** If you say that N-SING:
someone has **the wit** to do something, you mean the N to-inf
they have the intelligence and understanding to
make the right decision or take the right action in a
particular situation. *The information is there and
waiting to be accessed by anyone with the wit to use
it.* **3** You can refer to your ability to think quickly N-PLURAL
and cleverly in a difficult situation as your **wits**. *She
has used her wits to progress to the position she
holds today.*

4 You can use **wits** in expressions such as **frighten** N-PLURAL
someone out of their wits and **scare the wits out of** PRAGMATICS
someone to emphasize that someone or something
worries or frightens someone very much. **5** If you PHRASE
have your **wits about** you or **keep** your **wits about**
you, you are alert and ready to act in a difficult situation. **6** If you say that you are **at** your **wits' end**, you PHRASE
are emphasizing that you are so worried and exhaust- PRAGMATICS
ed by problems or difficulties that you do not know
what to do next. **7 To wit** is used to indicate that you PHRASE
are about to state or describe something more pre- PRAGMATICS
cisely. *Our total loss in killed and wounded is 30, to* LITERARY
wit, 9 killed and 21 wounded. **8** ● **battle of wits:** see
battle.

witch /wɪtʃ/ **witches.** A witch is a woman who ◆◆◇◇
has evil magic powers. N-COUNT

witch·craft /ˈwɪtʃkrɑːft, -kræft/. **Witchcraft** is the ◆◇◇◇◇
use of magic powers, especially evil ones. N-UNCOUNT

'witch doctor, witch doctors. A witch doctor is N-COUNT
a person in some societies who is thought to have
magic powers which can be used to heal people.

'witch-hunt, witch-hunts. A witch-hunt is an at- N-COUNT
tempt to find and punish a particular group of peo- PRAGMATICS
ple who are being blamed for something, often
simply because of their opinions and not because
they have actually done anything wrong; used
showing disapproval.

with /wɪð, wɪθ/. In addition to the uses shown be- ◆◆◆◆◆
low, **with** is used after some verbs, nouns and adjectives in order to introduce extra information.
With is also used in most reciprocal verbs, such as
'agree' or 'fight', and in some phrasal verbs, such as
'deal with' and 'dispense with'.

1 If one person is **with** another, they are together in PREP
one place. *With her were her son and daughter-in-
law.* **2** If something is put **with** or is **with** something PREP
else, they are used at the same time. *Serve hot, with
pasta or rice and French beans.* **3** If someone stands or PREP
goes somewhere **with** something, they are carrying it.
*A man came round with a tray of chocolates... A young
woman came in with a cup of coffee.*

4 If you do something **with** someone else, you both do PREP

it together or are both involved in it. *He walked with PREP
her to the front door.* **5** If you fight, argue, or compete PREP
with someone, you oppose them. **6** If you do something **with** a particular tool, object, or substance, you
do it using that tool, object, or substance.
7 Someone or something **with** a particular feature or PREP
possession has that feature or possession. *He was in
his early forties, tall and blond with bright blue eyes.*
8 Someone **with** an illness has that illness. *I spent a PREP
week in bed with flu.* **9** If something is filled or covered PREP
with a substance or with things, it has that substance
or those things in it or on it. *His legs were caked with
dried mud.*
10 If you are, for example, pleased or cross **with** PREP
someone or something, you have that feeling towards
them. **11** You use **with** to indicate what a state, qual- PREP
ity, or action relates to, involves, or affects. *He still has
a serious problem with money... Depression lowers the
human ability to cope with disease.*
12 You use **with** when indicating the way something PREP
is done or the feeling that someone has when they do
something. *He agreed, but with reluctance.* **13** You PREP
use **with** when indicating a sound, gesture, or facial
expression that is made at the same time as an action.
*With a sigh, she leant back and closed her eyes... The
front door closed with a crash.* **14** You use **with** to indi- PREP
cate the feeling that makes someone have a particular
appearance or type of behaviour. *Gil was white and
trembling with anger.* **15** You use **with** when men- PREP
tioning the position or appearance of someone or
something at the time that they do something, or
what someone else is doing at that time. *Joanne stood
with her hands on the sink, staring out the window...
She walked back to the bus stop, with him following.*
16 You use **with** to introduce a current situation that PREP
is a factor affecting another situation. *With the win,* PRAGMATICS
the US reclaimed the cup for the first time since 1985.
17 You use **with** when making a comparison or con- PREP
trast between the situations of different people or PRAGMATICS
things. *We're not like them. It's different with us.* **18** If PREP
something increases or decreases **with** a factor, it
changes as that factor changes. *Blood pressure decreases with exercise.* **19** If something moves **with** a PREP
wind or current, it moves in the same direction as the
wind or current.
20 If someone says that they are **with** you, they mean PREP
that they understand what you are saying. *I'm not* INFORMAL
with you. Tell me what you mean. **21** If someone says PREP
that they are **with** you, they mean that they support or
approve of what you are doing. *'I'm with you all the
way.'—'Thank you.'*

with·draw /wɪðˈdrɔː/ **withdraws, withdrawing,** ◆◆◆◇
withdrew, withdrawn. 1 If you **withdraw** some- VERB:
thing from a place, you remove it or take it away. *He* V n from n
reached into his pocket and withdrew a sheet of FORMAL
notepaper. **2** When groups of people such as troops V-ERG: V
withdraw or when someone **withdraws** them, they V n from n
leave the place where they are fighting or where Also V to n
they are based and return nearer home. *It is to
withdraw forty-thousand troops from Western
Europe in the next year... Troops withdrew from the
north east of the country last March.* **3** If you **with-** VERB:
draw money from a bank account, you take it out of V n from n
that account. *...a savings account that does not charge ridiculous fees to withdraw money.* **4** If you **with-** VERB: V
draw to another room, you go there. *He poured the* Also V to/into
wine and then withdrew again. n FORMAL
5 If you **withdraw** from an activity or organization, VERB
you stop taking take part in it. *The African National* V n from n
Congress threatened to withdraw from the talks. **6** If Also V
you **withdraw** a remark or statement that you have VERB: V n
made, you say that you want people to ignore it. FORMAL

with·draw·al /wɪðˈdrɔːəl/ **withdrawals. 1** The ◆◆◇◇
withdrawal of something is the act or process of re- N-VAR
moving it, or ending it. *...withdrawal of friendship.* FORMAL
*...allied troop withdrawal from the north of the
country.* **2** Someone's **withdrawal** from an activity N-UNCOUNT
or an organization is their decision to stop taking
part in it. *...his withdrawal from government in
1946.* **3** A **withdrawal** is an amount of money that N-COUNT

you take from your bank account. **4** The **withdraw-** N-SING:
al of a remark or statement that you have made is N of n
the act of saying that you want people to ignore it.
*The charity says it wants a withdrawal of the
comments.*
5 Withdrawal is the period during which someone N-UNCOUNT
feels ill after they have stopped taking a drug which
they were addicted to. *Withdrawal from heroin is actually like a severe attack of gastric flu.* **6 Withdrawal** N-UNCOUNT
is behaviour in which someone prefers to be alone
and does not want to talk to other people.

with·drawal symptoms. When someone has N-PLURAL
withdrawal symptoms, they feel ill after they have
stopped taking a drug which they were addicted to.

with·drawn /wɪðˈdrɔːn/. **1 Withdrawn** is the past ◆◇◇◇
participle of **withdraw**. **2** Someone who is **with-** ADJ-GRADED:
drawn is very quiet, and does not want to talk to v-link ADJ
other people.

with·drew /wɪðˈdruː/. **Withdrew** is the past tense
of **withdraw**.

with·er /ˈwɪðə/ **withers, withering, withered.** ◆◇◇◇
1 If someone or something **withers**, they become VERB
very weak. *When he went into retirement, he visibly V
withered.* ▶ **Wither away** means the same as **wither**. PHRASAL VB
To see my body literally wither away before my eyes V P
was exasperating. **2** If a flower or plant **withers**, it VERB: V
shrinks, dries up, and dies. ♦ **with·ered** *...a mound* ADJ-GRADED
of withered leaves.

wither away. See wither 1. PHRASAL VB

with·ered /ˈwɪðəd/. **1** If you describe a person or a ADJ-GRADED
part of their body as **withered**, you mean that their
skin is very wrinkled and dry, and looks old. **2 With-** ADJ
ered is used to describe someone's leg, arm, or
other part of their body when it is thin and weak
because of disease or paralysis.

with·er·ing /ˈwɪðərɪŋ/. A **withering** look or remark ADJ-GRADED
is very angry or scornful, and is often intended to
make someone feel ashamed or stupid.

with·hold /wɪðˈhəʊld/ **withholds, withholding,** ◆◆◇◇
withheld /wɪðˈheld/. If you **withhold** something VERB
that someone wants, you do not let them have it. V n
Police withheld the dead boy's name yesterday until V n from n
relatives could be told... The captain decided to with- Also V from
hold the terrible news even from his officers. ♦ **with-** n /-ing
·hold·ing *...the withholding of property from the* N-UNCOUNT FORMAL
market.

with·in /wɪˈðɪn/. **1** If something is **within** a place, ◆◆◆◆◆
area, or object, it is inside it or surrounded by it. *An* PREP
olive-coloured tent stood within a thicket of trees. ...a FORMAL
*1987 agreement which would recognise Quebec as a
distinct society within Canada.* ▶ Also an adverb. *A* ADV
small voice called from within. 'Yes, just coming.'
2 Something that happens or exists **within** a soci- PREP
ety, organization, or system, happens or exists inside it or to something that is part of it. *Within
criminal law almost anything could be defined as
'crime'.* ▶ Also an adverb. *...the Church of England,* ADV
with threats of split from within. **3** If you experi- PREP
ence a particular feeling, you can say that it is **with-** LITERARY
in you. *He's coping much better within himself.*
▶ Also an adverb. *'God!' cried Dennis from within.* ADV
'Oh, my God!' **4** If something is **within** a particular PREP
limit or set of rules, it does not go beyond it or is
not more than what is allowed. *Troops have agreed
to stay within specific boundaries.*
5 If you are **within** a particular distance of a place, you PREP
are less than that distance from it. *It was within easy
walking distance of the hotel.* **6 Within** a particular PREP
length of time means before that length of time has
passed. *About 40% of all students entering as freshmen
graduate within 4 years.*
7 If something is **within sight**, **within earshot**, or PREP
within reach, you can see it, hear it, or reach it.
8 ● **within reason**: see **reason**.

with·out /wɪˈðaʊt/. In addition to the uses shown ◆◆◆◆◆
below, **without** is used in the phrasal verbs 'do
without', 'go without', and 'reckon without'.
1 You use **without** to indicate that someone or some- PREP
thing does not have or use the thing mentioned. *I
don't like myself without a beard. ...a meal without*

barbecue sauce. **2** If one thing happens **without** another thing, or if you do something **without** doing something else, the second thing does not happen or occur. *They worked without a break until about eight in the evening... Alex had done this without consulting her.* **3** If you do something **without** a particular feeling, you do not have that feeling when you do it. *'Hello, Swanson,' he said without surprise.* **4** If you do something **without** someone else, they are not with you when you do it. *We would never go anywhere without you.* [PREP] [PREP] [PREP]

with·stand /wɪð'stænd/ **withstands, withstanding, withstood** /wɪð'stʊd/. If something or someone **withstands** a force or action, they survive it or do not give in to it. *...armoured vehicles designed to withstand chemical attack.* ◆◇◇◇◇ [VERB] [V n] [FORMAL]

wit·less /'wɪtləs/. If you describe something or someone as **witless**, you think they are very foolish or stupid. [ADJ] [PRAGMATICS]

wit·ness /'wɪtnəs/ **witnesses, witnessing, witnessed.** **1** A **witness** to an event such as an accident or crime is a person who saw it. **2** If you **witness** something, you see it happen. *Anyone who witnessed the attack should call the police.* **3** A **witness** is someone who appears in a court of law to say what they know about a crime or other event. *Eleven witnesses will be called to testify.* **4** A **witness** is someone who writes their name on a document that you have signed, to confirm that it really is your signature. **5** If someone **witnesses** your signature on a document, they write their name after it, to confirm that it really is your signature. **6** If you say that a place or period of time **witnessed** a particular event or change, you mean that it happened in that place or during that period of time. You can also say that a person **witnessed** an event or change. *India has witnessed many political changes in recent years.* **7** You use **witness** to introduce an example of what you have just been talking about. *Americans are a generous people: witness the increase in charitable giving, even during the recession.* **8** If you **are witness to** something, you see it happen. **9** If something or someone **bears witness to** something else, they show or say that it exists or happened. *Many of these poems bear witness to his years spent in India.* ◆◆◆◇◇ [N-COUNT] [VERB] [V n] [N-COUNT] [N-COUNT] [VERB: V n] [VERB] [V n] [VB: only imper] [PRAGMATICS] [V n] [WRITTEN] [PHRASE] [FORMAL] [PHRASE] [FORMAL]

'witness box. The **witness box** in a court of law is the place where people stand or sit when they are giving evidence. The usual American expression is **witness stand.** [N-SING:] [the N] [BRITISH]

wit·ter /'wɪtə/ **witters, wittering, wittered.** If you say that someone **is wittering** about something, you mean that they are talking a lot about things that you think are silly and boring. *They just sat there wittering about what lectures they had tomorrow.* ► **Witter on** means the same as **witter**. *They started wittering on about their last trip to Provence.* [VERB] [PRAGMATICS] [V about n] [Also V] [INFORMAL,] [BRITISH] [PHRASAL VB] [V P about n] [Also V P]

wit·ti·cism /'wɪtɪsɪzəm/ **witticisms.** A **witticism** is a witty remark or joke. [N-COUNT] [FORMAL]

wit·ty /'wɪti/ **wittier, wittiest.** Someone or something that is **witty** is amusing in a clever way. *His plays were very good, very witty.* ► **wit·ti·ly** *'Count Dracula, I presume,' I said wittily.* ◆◆◇◇◇ [ADJ-GRADED] [ADV-GRADED]

wives /waɪvz/. **Wives** is the plural of **wife.**

wiz·ard /'wɪzəd/ **wizards.** **1** In legends and fairy stories, a **wizard** is a man who has magic powers. **2** If you admire someone because they are very good at doing a particular thing, you can say they are a **wizard.** *...a financial wizard.* ◆◇◇◇◇ [N-COUNT] [N-COUNT:] [with supp] [PRAGMATICS]

wiz·ard·ry /'wɪzədri/. You can refer to a very clever achievement or piece of work as **wizardry**, especially when you do not understand how it is done. *...a piece of technical wizardry.* [N-UNCOUNT]

wiz·ened /'wɪzənd/. A **wizened** person is old and has very wrinkled skin. [ADJ-GRADED]

wk, wks. wk is a written abbreviation for **week.**

wob·ble /'wɒbəl/ **wobbles, wobbling, wobbled.** If something or someone **wobbles**, they make small movements from side to side, for example because they are unsteady. *...a cyclist who wobbled* ◆◇◇◇◇ [VERB: V] [V prep/adv]

into my path. ► Also a noun. *We might look for a tiny wobble in the position of a star.* [N-VAR]

wob·bly /'wɒbli/. **1** Something that is **wobbly** moves unsteadily from side to side. *...a wobbly green jelly. ...wobbly teeth.* **2** If you feel **wobbly** or if your legs feel **wobbly**, you feel weak and have difficulty standing up, especially because you are afraid, ill, or exhausted. *Ryan was exhausted by the flight and walked off with wobbly legs to find Clark.* **3** If a person's voice is **wobbly**, it sounds weak and keeps varying in pitch, for example because the person is about to cry. ◆◇◇◇◇ [ADJ-GRADED] [ADJ-GRADED] [ADJ-GRADED]

wodge /wɒdʒ/ **wodges.** A **wodge** of something is a large amount of it or a large piece of it. *...a wodge of syrupy sponge.* [N-COUNT] [BRITISH,] [INFORMAL]

woe /wəʊ/ **woes.** **1** Woe is very great sadness. *A fellow recently told me his business's tale of woe. Sales were markedly down.* **2** You can refer to someone's problems or misfortunes as their **woes.** *He did not tell his relatives and friends about his woes.* **3** ● **woe betide**: see **betide**. ◆◇◇◇◇ [N-UNCOUNT] [LITERARY] [N-PLURAL] [WRITTEN]

woe·be·gone /'wəʊbɪgɒn/. Someone who is **woebegone** is very sad. *She sniffed and looked very woebegone.* [ADJ-GRADED] [WRITTEN]

woe·ful /'wəʊfʊl/. **1** If someone or something is **woeful**, they are very sad. *...a woeful ballad.* ♦ **woe·ful·ly** *He said woefully: 'I love my country, but it does not give a damn about me.'* **2** You can use **woeful** to emphasize that something is very bad or undesirable. *...the woeful state of the economy.* ♦ **woefully** *Public expenditure on the arts is woefully inadequate.* ◆◇◇◇◇ [ADJ-GRADED] [ADV-GRADED] [ADJ-GRADED] [PRAGMATICS] [ADV-GRADED]

wok /wɒk/ **woks.** A **wok** is a large bowl-shaped pan which is used for Chinese-style cooking. [N-COUNT]

woke /wəʊk/. **Woke** is the past tense of **wake.**

woken /'wəʊkən/. **Woken** is the past participle of **wake.**

wolf /wʊlf/ **wolves; wolfs, wolfing, wolfed.** **1** A **wolf** is a wild animal that looks like a large dog. **2** If someone **wolfs** their food, they eat it all very quickly and greedily. ► **Wolf down** means the same as **wolf.** *He wolfed down the rest of the biscuit and cheese.* **3** If someone **cries wolf**, they say that there is a problem when there is not, with the result that people do not believe them when there really is a problem. ◆◇◇◇◇ [N-COUNT] [VERB: V n] [INFORMAL] [PHRASAL VB] [V P noun] [Also V n P] [PHRASE]

wolf down. See **wolf** 2. [PHRASAL VB]

wolf·hound /'wʊlfhaʊnd/ **wolfhounds.** A **wolfhound** is a type of very large dog. [N-COUNT]

'wolf-whistle, wolf-whistles, wolf-whistling, wolf-whistled. If someone **wolf-whistles**, they make a whistling sound with a short rising note and a longer falling note. ► Also a noun. *Her dancing brought loud cheers, wolf whistles and applause.* [VERB: V] [N-COUNT]

wolves /wʊlvz/. **Wolves** is the plural of **wolf.**

wom·an /'wʊmən/ **women.** **1** A **woman** is an adult female human being. *...a young Lithuanian woman named Dayva.* ♦ **-woman.** **-woman** combines with numbers to indicate that something involves the number of women mentioned. *The Squash Association yesterday selected Sue Wright for its four-woman squad.* **2** You can refer to women in general as **woman.** *...the oppression of woman.* **3** Some people refer to a man's wife, lover, or girlfriend as his **woman.** *I know my woman will never leave me.* **4** If you say that a woman is, for example, a gambling **woman** or an outdoors **woman**, you mean that she likes gambling or outdoor activities. **5** If you say that a woman is, for example, a London **woman** or an Oxford **woman**, you mean that she comes from London or Oxford, or went to university there. **6** You can refer to a female representative of a company or organization as that company or organization's **woman.** *That's Judith Croft, the CND woman.* **7** If you say that a woman an **is her own woman**, you approve of the fact that she makes her plans and decisions herself, and does not depend on other people. **8** People sometimes address a woman as **woman** when they are ordering her to do something or when they are angry or impatient with her. *Do you realize,* ◆◆◆◆◇ [N-COUNT] [COMB] [N-UNCOUNT] [N-COUNT:] [poss N] [INFORMAL] [N-COUNT:] [supp N] [N-COUNT:] [n-proper N] [N-COUNT:] [with supp] [PHRASE] [PRAGMATICS] [N-VOC] [PRAGMATICS] [RUDE]

woman, the scandal and publicity that will be involved?

9 See also **career woman**. ● **woman of the world**: see **world**.

wom·an·hood /'wʊmənhʊd/. **1** Womanhood is the state of being a woman rather than a girl, or the period of a woman's adult life. **2** You can refer to women in general or the women of a particular country or community as **womanhood**. *She symbolised for me the best of Indian womanhood.* `N-UNCOUNT`

wom·an·iz·er /'wʊmənaɪzə/ **womanizers;** also spelled **womaniser**. If you describe a man as a **womanizer**, you disapprove of him because he has many short sexual relationships with women. `N-COUNT PRAGMATICS`

wom·an·iz·ing /'wʊmənaɪzɪŋ/; also spelled **womanising**. If you talk about a man's **womanizing**, you disapprove of him because he has many short sexual relationships with women. `N-UNCOUNT PRAGMATICS`

wom·an·kind /,wʊmən'kaɪnd/. You can refer to all women as **womankind** when considering them as a group. `N-UNCOUNT FORMAL`

wom·an·ly /'wʊmənli/. People describe a woman's behaviour, character, or appearance as **womanly** when they like it because they think it is typical of, or suitable for, a woman rather than a man or girl. *She had a classical, womanly shape.* `ADJ-GRADED PRAGMATICS`

,woman-to-'woman; also spelled **woman to woman**. If you talk about a **woman-to-woman** conversation, you are talking about an honest and open discussion between two women. *She had had a woman-to-woman chat with Mrs Hardie.* ► Also an adverb. *Maybe she would talk to her mother one day, woman to woman.* `ADJ: ADJ n` `ADV: ADV after v`

womb /wuːm/ **wombs.** A woman's **womb** is the part inside her body where a baby grows before it is born. `N-COUNT`

wom·en /'wɪmɪn/. **Women** is the plural of **woman**.

wom·en·folk /'wɪmɪnfəʊk/. Some people refer to the women of a particular community as its **womenfolk**. `N-PLURAL`

,Women's Libe'ration. Women's Liberation is the ideal that women should have the same social and economic rights and privileges as men. `N-UNCOUNT DATED`

'women's movement. The women's movement is a social and political movement which aims to achieve equality for women by organizing groups and campaigns, and by causing individuals to change their attitudes. `N-SING`

won /wʌn/. **Won** is the past tense and past participle of **win**.

won·der /'wʌndə/ **wonders, wondering, wondered. 1** If you **wonder** about something, you think about it, either because it interests you and you want to know more about it, or because you are worried or suspicious about it. *I wondered what that noise was... 'Why does she want to get in there?' Pete wondered.* **2** If you **wonder** at something, you are surprised and amazed about it. *He liked to sit and wonder at all that had happened... We all wonder you're still alive.* **3** If you say that it is a **wonder** that something happened, you mean that it is very surprising and unexpected. *The wonder is that Olivier was not seriously hurt.* **4** Wonder is a feeling of surprise, pleasure, or amusement that you have, for example when something happens that you thought was impossible. *I was expressing some amazement and wonder at her good fortune.* **5** The **wonder** of something is a quality in it that causes people to feel astonishment or great admiration. *...the wonders of space and space exploration.* **6** If you refer, for example, to a young man as a **wonder** boy, or to a new product as a **wonder** drug, you mean that other people admire or praise them for their qualities, although you yourself may not yet be convinced that they are very good. **7** You can say **'I wonder'** if you want to be very polite when you are asking someone to do something, or when you are asking someone to give you information or their opinion about something. *I was just wondering if you could help me.* **8** If you say **'no wonder'**, `VERB: V about n / V with quote / Also V` `VERB V at n / V that` `N-SING` `N-UNCOUNT` `N-COUNT` `ADJ: ADJ n` `PHRASE PRAGMATICS` `PHRASE`

'little wonder', or **'small wonder'**, you mean that you are not surprised by something that has happened. *No wonder my brother wasn't feeling well.* **9** You can say **'No wonder'** to express your satisfaction when you find out the answer to something that has been puzzling you for some time. *Brad was Jane's brother! No wonder he reminded me so much of her!* **10** If you say that something or someone **works wonders** or **does wonders**, you mean that they have a very good effect on something. *A few moments of relaxation can work wonders.* `PRAGMATICS` `PHRASE PRAGMATICS` `PHRASE`

won·der·ful /'wʌndəfʊl/. If you describe something or someone as **wonderful**, you think they are extremely good. *The cold, misty air felt wonderful on his face... It's wonderful to see you.* ♦ **won·der·ful·ly** *It's a system that works wonderfully well... The weather was wonderfully warm.* `♦♦♦♦◇ ADJ-GRADED` `ADV-GRADED`

wonder·land /'wʌndəlænd/ **wonderlands. 1** Wonderland is an imaginary world that exists in fairy tales. **2** You can refer to a place as a **wonderland** when it is strange and very beautiful or exciting. *Children find Lake George Village a wonderland of amusement parks.* `♦◇◇◇◇` `N-UNCOUNT` `N-COUNT`

won·der·ment /'wʌndəmənt/. **Wonderment** is a feeling of pleasant amazement. *His big blue eyes opened wide in wonderment.* `N-UNCOUNT`

won·drous /'wʌndrəs/. If you describe something as **wondrous**, you mean it is strange and beautiful or impressive. *We were driven across this wondrous vast land of lakes and forests.* `♦◇◇◇◇ ADJ-GRADED LITERARY`

won·ky /'wɒŋki/. If something is **wonky**, it is not steady, not straight, or not evenly balanced. *The wheels keep going wonky.* `ADJ-GRADED BRITISH, INFORMAL`

wont /wəʊnt, AM wɔːnt/. **1** If someone is **wont to** do something, they often or regularly do it. *Both have committed their indiscretions, as human beings are wont to do.* **2** If you say that someone does something **as is** their **wont**, you mean that it is something that they often or regularly do. *Paul woke early, as was his wont.* `ADJ: v-link ADJ to-inf WRITTEN` `PHRASE WRITTEN`

won't /wəʊnt/. **Won't** is the usual spoken form of 'will not'. *The space shuttle Discovery won't lift off the launch pad until Sunday.*

woo /wuː/ **woos, wooing, wooed. 1** If you **woo** people, you try to encourage them to help you, support you, or vote for you, for example by promising them things which they would like. *They are trying to woo back electoral support.* **2** If a man **woos** a woman, he spends time with her and tries to persuade her to marry him. `♦♦◇◇◇ VERB: V n / V n with adv` `VERB: V n DATED`

wood /wʊd/ **woods. 1** Wood is the material which forms the trunks and branches of trees. *Their dishes were made of wood.* **2** A **wood** is a fairly large area of trees growing near each other. You can refer to one or several of these areas as **woods**. *...a walk in the woods.* **3** If something or someone is **not out of the woods** yet, they are still having difficulties or problems, although they may have improved. **4** You can say **'touch wood'** to indicate that you hope to have good luck in something you are doing and that nothing will go wrong, usually after saying that so far you have not had bad luck with it. The American expression is **knock on wood**. *She's never even been to the doctor's, touch wood.* **5** See also **dead wood**. ● your **neck of the woods**: see **neck**. ● **can't see the wood for the trees**: see **tree**. `♦♦♦♦◇ N-VAR` `N-COUNT` `PHRASE INFORMAL` `CONVENTION BRITISH`

wood·cock /'wʊdkɒk/ **woodcocks.** The plural can be either **woodcocks** or **woodcock**. A woodcock is a small brown bird with a long beak. Woodcock are sometimes shot for sport or food. `N-COUNT`

wood·ed /'wʊdɪd/. A **wooded** area is covered in trees. *...a wooded valley.* `♦◇◇◇◇ ADJ-GRADED`

wood·en /'wʊdən/. **1** Wooden objects are made of wood. *...faded wooden floorboards.* **2** If you describe an actor as **wooden**, you are critical of them because their performance is not lively or natural. `♦♦♦◇◇ ADJ: ADJ n` `ADJ-GRADED PRAGMATICS`

,wooden 'spoon, wooden spoons. 1 A wooden spoon is a spoon that is used for stirring sauces and for mixing ingredients in cooking. It is made of `N-COUNT`

wood and has a long handle. **2** In British English, if someone gets the **wooden spoon**, they come last in a race or competition. *Jarvis took the wooden spoon in the first tournament.*   N-COUNT

wood·land /'wʊdlənd/ **woodlands. Woodland** is land which is mostly covered with trees.   ◆◆◇◇◇ N-VAR

wood·louse /'wʊdlaʊs/ **woodlice** /'wʊdlaɪs/. A **woodlouse** is a very small grey creature with a hard shell and fourteen legs.   N-COUNT

wood·pecker /'wʊdpekə/ **woodpeckers.** A **woodpecker** is a type of bird with a long sharp beak which it uses to make holes in trees.   N-COUNT

wood·pile /'wʊdpaɪl/ **woodpiles.** A **woodpile** is a pile of firewood.   N-COUNT

'wood pulp. Wood pulp is wood that has been cut up into small pieces and crushed, so that it can be used to make paper.   N-UNCOUNT

wood·shed /'wʊdʃed/ **woodsheds.** A **woodshed** is a small building which is used for storing firewood.   N-COUNT

wood·wind /'wʊdwɪnd/ **woodwinds. Woodwind** instruments are musical instruments such as flutes and clarinets, that are played by blowing into them.   N-VAR

wood·work /'wʊdwɜːk/. **1** You can refer to the doors and other wooden parts of a house as the **woodwork.** *...fresh paint on the woodwork.*   ◆◇◇◇◇ N-UNCOUNT
2 Woodwork is the activity or skill of making things out of wood. **3** If you say that people **are coming out of the woodwork,** you are criticizing them for suddenly appearing in public or revealing their opinions when previously they did not make themselves known. *Politicians have been coming out of the woodwork to condemn the treaty.*   N-UNCOUNT   PHRASE   PRAGMATICS

wood·worm /'wʊdwɜːm/ **woodworms.** The plural can be either **woodworms** or **woodworm. 1 Woodworm** are the larvae of certain types of beetle which make holes in wood by feeding on it. **2 Woodworm** is damage caused to wood by woodworm, especially to the wooden parts of a house or to furniture.   N-COUNT   N-UNCOUNT

woody /'wʊdi/. **1 Woody** plants have very hard stems. **2** A **woody** area has a lot of trees in it. **3** Something that smells **woody** smells like wood.   ADJ-GRADED   ADJ-GRADED   ADJ

woof /wʊf/. A **woof** is the sound that a dog makes when it barks; a word used especially by children.   N-SING   INFORMAL

wool /wʊl/ **wools. 1 Wool** is the hair that grows on sheep and on some other animals. **2 Wool** is a material made from animal's wool that is used to make things such as clothes, blankets, and carpets. **3** If you say that someone is **pulling the wool over** your **eyes,** you mean that they are trying to deceive you, in order to have an advantage over you. **4** See also **cotton wool, steel wool, wire wool.**   ◆◆◇◇◇ N-UNCOUNT N-VAR   PHRASE

wool·len /'wʊlən/ **woollens;** spelled **woolen** in American English. **1 Woollen** clothes or materials are made from wool or from a mixture of wool and artificial fibres. **2 Woollens** are clothes, especially sweaters, that are made of wool.   ◆◇◇◇◇ ADJ   N-PLURAL

wool·ly /'wʊli/ **woollies;** spelled **wooly** in American English. **1** Something that is **woolly** is made of wool or looks like wool. *...a woolly hat.* **2** A **woolly** is a woollen piece of clothing, especially a pullover. **3** If you describe a person or their aims or ideas as **woolly,** you are criticizing them for being inconsistent or confused.   ◆◇◇◇◇ ADJ   N-COUNT BRITISH, INFORMAL ADJ-GRADED PRAGMATICS

woozy /'wuːzi/. If you feel **woozy** you feel rather weak and unsteady and cannot think clearly.   ADJ-GRADED INFORMAL

word /wɜːd/ **words, wording, worded. 1** A **word** is a single unit of language that can be represented in writing or speech. In English, a word has a space on either side of it when it is written. *The word 'ginseng' comes from the Chinese word 'Shenseng'.* **2** Someone's **words** are what they say or write. *I was devastated when her words came true.* **3** The **words** of a song consist of the text that is sung, in contrast to the music that is played. **4** You can use **word** after a letter of the alphabet to refer politely or humorously to a word beginning with that letter which people find offensive or are embarrassed to use. *Politicians began to use the dreaded R-word: recession.* **5** If you say that someone   ◆◆◆◆◆ N-COUNT   N-PLURAL   N-PLURAL   N-COUNT   N-SING:

does not hear, understand, or say **a word,** you are emphasizing that they hear, understand, or say nothing at all. *Not a word was spoken.*   a N, with brd-neg PRAGMATICS

6 If you have **a word** with someone, you have a short conversation with them, usually in private. *James, could I have a quiet word?* **7** If you offer someone a **word of** warning, advice, or praise, you warn, advise, or praise them. *May I also say a word of thanks to all the people who sent letters.* **8** If there is **word** of something, people receive news or information about it. *There is no word from the authorities on the reported attack.* ● If you **spread the word,** you tell people about something. **9** If someone gives **the word** to do something, they give an order or signal to start doing it. *When I say the word, follow me down.*   N-SING: a N SPOKEN N-COUNT: N of n   N-UNCOUNT   PHRASE   N-SING: the N

10 If you give your **word,** you make a sincere promise to someone. *...an adult who gave his word the boy would be supervised.* ● If you are **true to** your **word** or **as good as** your **word,** you do what you say you will do.   N-SING: poss N   PHRASE

11 To **word** something in a particular way means to choose or use particular words to express it. *If I had written the letter, I might have worded it differently.* ♦ **-worded** *...a strongly-worded statement. ...a carefully-worded speech.*   VERB V n adv/prep   COMB

12 If you say that people consider something to be a **dirty word,** you mean that they disapprove of it. *So many people think feminism is a dirty word.* **13** If you do something **from the word go,** you do it from the very beginning of a period of time or situation. **14** You use **in a word** to indicate that you are summarizing what you have just been saying. *Victor, in a word, got increasingly fed up.* **15** If you say that someone has said something, but not **in so many words,** you mean that they said it or expressed it, but in an indirect way. *'And has she agreed to go with you?'—'Not in so many words. But I read her thoughts.'* **16** You say **in other words** in order to introduce a different, and usually simpler, explanation or interpretation of something that has just been said. *The mobile library services have been reorganised – in other words, they visit fewer places.* **17** If you repeat something **word for word,** you repeat it exactly as it was originally said or written. *I don't try to memorize speeches word for word.* **18** You can use expressions such as **too silly for words,** or **too awful for words** to emphasize that someone or something is extremely silly or awful. *I feel simply too devastated for words.* **19** If you say that someone has to **eat** their **words,** you mean that they have to admit that they were wrong about something they said in the past, especially when this makes them look foolish. **20** A person **of few words** says very little, especially about their opinions or feelings. *He's a man of few words, very polite.* **21** If you **hang on** someone's **every word,** you listen very intently to what they have to say, because you admire or respect them. **22** You can use expressions such as **never have a good word to say** or **never have a bad word to say** to emphasize that someone always criticizes someone or something or that they never criticize them. *The press never has a good word to say about them.* **23** You can use **in** someone's **words** or **in** someone's **own words** to indicate that you are reporting something someone said using the exact words that they used. *Previous policy did not, in his words, produce results.* **24** If you say something **in** your **own words,** you express it in your own way, without copying or repeating someone else's description.   PHRASE   PHRASE   PHRASE PRAGMATICS   PHRASE   PHRASE PRAGMATICS   PHRASE   PHRASE PRAGMATICS   PHRASE   PHRASE   PHRASE PRAGMATICS   PHRASE   PHRASE

25 If someone is **lost for words,** they cannot think of anything to say, especially because they are very surprised or impressed. **26** If you say **'mark my words'** to someone, you are emphasizing that they should listen to your warning or prediction about what will happen. *That's what you'll end up with, you mark my words.* **27** If you say that someone **is putting words into** your **mouth** or **is putting words in** your **mouth,** you mean that they are suggesting that you mean one thing when you really mean something different. **28** If news or information is passed on by **word of**   PHRASE   PHRASE PRAGMATICS   PHRASE   PHRASE

mouth, people tell it to each other rather than it being printed in written form.

29 If one person **has words with** another, they have a serious discussion or argument, especially because one has complained about the other's behaviour. *We had words and she stormed out.* **30** If someone has **the last word** or the **final word** in a discussion, argument, or disagreement, they are the one who wins it or who makes the final decision. **31** If you say that something is **the last word in** luxury, comfort, or some other quality, you are emphasizing that it has a great deal of this quality. *'Venezia' perfume is the last word in languid Italian glamour.* PHRASE · PHRASE · PHRASE PRAGMATICS

32 If you refer to someone as **a man of his word** or a **woman of her word**, you mean that they always keep their promises and can be relied on. **33** If you **take** someone **at their word**, you believe what they say, often when they did not really mean it or when they meant something slightly different. *You have said you wish to be helpful, and I am taking you at your word.* PHRASE · PHRASE

34 If you say to someone **'take my word for it'**, you mean that they should believe you because you are telling the truth. *You'll buy nothing but trouble if you buy that house, take my word for it.* PHRASE

35 See also **wording, code word, four-letter word, play on words, printed word, spoken word, written word.** ● not get a word in edgeways: see **edgeways**. ● not mince your words: see **mince**. ● the operative word: see **operative**. ● war of words: see **war**.

'word class, word classes. A word class is a group of words that have the same basic behaviour, for example nouns, adjectives, or verbs. N-COUNT

word·ing /'wɜːdɪŋ/. The **wording** of a piece of writing or a speech are the words used in it, especially when these are chosen to have a particular effect. *The wording is so vague that no one actually knows what it means.* ◆◇◇◇◇ N-UNCOUNT: also a N

word·less /'wɜːdləs/. **1** You say that someone is **wordless** when they do not say anything, especially at a time when they are expected to say something. ADJ LITERARY

♦ **word·less·ly** *Gil downed his food wordlessly.* **2** If someone makes a **wordless** sound, they make a sound that does not seem to contain any words. *...a wordless chant.* ADV · ADJ LITERARY

word·play /'wɜːdpleɪ/; also spelled **word play.** Wordplay involves making jokes by using the meanings of words in an amusing or clever way. N-UNCOUNT

,word 'processing; also spelled **word-processing.** Word processing is the work or skill of producing printed material using a word processor. N-UNCOUNT

,word 'processor, word processors. A word processor is a computer which is used to produce printed material such as documents, letters, and books. ◆◇◇◇◇ N-COUNT

wordy /'wɜːdi/. If you describe a person's speech or something that they write as **wordy**, you disapprove of the fact that they use too many words, especially words which are very long, formal, or literary. ADJ-GRADED PRAGMATICS

wore /wɔː/. **Wore** is the past tense of **wear**.

work /wɜːk/ **works, working, worked. 1** People who **work** have a job, usually one which they are paid to do. *Weiner works for the US Department of Transport... I started working in a recording studio... He worked as a bricklayer's mate.* **2** People who have **work** or who are in **work** have a job, usually one which they are paid to do. *I was out of work at the time... What kind of work do you do?* **3** When you **work**, you do the things that you are paid or required to do in your job. *I can't talk to you right now – I'm working... Some firms expect the guards to work twelve hours a day.* **4** Your **work** consists of the things you are paid or required to do in your job. *I've got work to do... I used to take work home, but I don't do it any more... There have been days when I have finished work at 2pm.* **5** Work is the place where you do your job. *Many people travel to work by car... She told her friends at work that she was trying to lose weight.* ◆◆◆◆◆ VERB: V · V prep/adv · V as n · N-UNCOUNT · VERB V · V n · N-UNCOUNT · N-UNCOUNT

6 When you **work**, you spend time and effort doing a task that needs to be done or trying to achieve some- VERB V prep

thing. *Linda spends all her time working on the garden... The government expressed hope that all the sides will work towards a political solution... She spent a period of time working with people dying of cancer.* ► Also a noun. *There was a lot of work to do on their house... The peace plan would be rejected because it needed more work... She became involved in social and relief work among the refugees.* **7** Work is something which you produce as a result of an activity or as a result of doing your job. *It can help to have an impartial third party look over your work... That's a beautiful piece of work.* **8** If a researcher **is working on** a particular subject or question, they are studying or researching it. ► Also a noun. *Their work shows that one-year-olds are much more likely to have allergies if either parent smokes.* **9** If you **work on** an assumption or idea, you act as if it were true or base other ideas on it, until you have more information. *We are working on the assumption that it was a gas explosion.* N-UNCOUNT · N-UNCOUNT · VERB: V on n · N-UNCOUNT · VERB V on n

10 A **works** is a place where something is manufactured or where an industrial process is carried out. **Works** is used to refer to one or to more than one of these places. *...a recycling works. ...the works canteen.* **11** Works are activities such as digging the ground or building on a large scale. *...six years of disruptive building works.* **12** If you **work** a particular area or type of place, you travel around that area or work in those places as part of your job, for example trying to sell something there. *Brand has been working the clubs and the pubs since 1986, developing her comedy act.* **13** If you **work** someone, you make them spend time and effort doing a particular activity or job. *They're working me too hard.* **14** If you **work** the land, you cultivate it and do all the various tasks involved in growing and harvesting crops. **15** When a mine or quarry **is worked**, it is in use, and minerals such as coal are removed from it. *Only an agreed number of men was allowed to work any given seam.* **16** If you **work** a machine or piece of equipment, you use or control it. *Many adults still depend on their children to work the video.* N-COLL-COUNT BRITISH · N-PLURAL · VERB V n · VERB V n adv/prep Also V n · VERB: V n · VERB: be V-ed · VERB V n

17 A **work** is something such as a painting, book, or piece of music, produced by an artist, writer, or composer. *The church has several valuable works of art.* **18** If you **work** a material, you make something with it or make it have a particular form, for example by pressing, moulding, or cutting it. *Work the dough with the palm of your hand until it is very smooth... Remove rind from the cheese and work it to a firm paste, with a fork... He studied sculpture because he enjoyed working with clay. ...a long, cool tunnel of worked stone.* **19** If a machine or piece of equipment **works**, it operates and performs a particular function. *The pump doesn't work and we have no running water... How does the gun work?* **20** If an idea, system, or way of doing something **works**, it is successful, effective, or satisfactory. *95 per cent of these diets do not work... The drug works by increasing levels of serotonin in the brain... A methodical approach works best.* **21** If something **works** in your favour, it helps you in some way. If something **works** to your disadvantage, it causes problems for you in some way. *This obviously works against the interests of the child.* **22** If something or someone **works** their magic or **works** their charms on someone, they have a powerful positive effect on them. N-COUNT · VERB V n · V n prep/adv · V with/in n · V-ed · VERB V · V prep/adv · VERB V · V prep/adv · VERB V prep · VERB: V n

23 If your mind or brain **is working**, you are thinking about something or trying to solve a problem. **24** If you **work** a part of your body, you move it. *Each position will work the muscles in a different way... Her mouth was working in her sleep.* **25** If something **works** into a particular state or condition, it gradually moves so that it is in that state or condition. *It's important to put a locking washer on that last nut, or it can work loose.* **26** See also **working**. VERB: V · V-ERG V · V n · VERB V adj

27 If someone is **at work** they are doing their job or are busy doing a particular activity. *He is currently at work on a novel.* **28** If a force or process is **at work**, it is having a particular influence or effect. *The report suggested that the same trend was at work in politics.* **29** If PHRASE · PHRASE · PHRASE

you say that you will **have your work cut out** to do something, you mean that it will be a very difficult task. **30** You can use **work** to talk about how easily or quickly a particular task is done. For example, if someone or something **makes** short **work of** doing something or **makes** light **work of** it, they do it quickly and easily. *Australia made hard work of beating them.* **31** If you **put** someone **to work** or **set** them **to work**, you give them a job or task to do. *Instead of sending them to prison, we have set them to work helping the lemon growers.* **32** If you **get to work**, **go to work**, or **set to work** on a job, task, or problem, you start doing it or dealing with it. *He promised to get to work on the state's massive deficit.* **33** You can say to someone **'nice work'** or **'good work'** in order to thank or congratulate them for doing something well or quickly. **34** If you **work** your **way** somewhere, you move or progress there slowly, and with a lot of effort or work. *Many personnel managers started as secretaries or personnel assistants and worked their way up.* **35 • a nasty piece of work:** see **piece. •** to **throw a spanner in the works:** see **spanner**. **36** You can say the **works** after listing things such as someone's possessions or requirements, to emphasize that they possess or require everything you can think of in a particular category. *Amazing place he's got there – squash courts, swimming pool, jacuzzi, the works.*

PHRASE

PHRASE

PHRASE

CONVENTION
PRAGMATICS

PHRASE

N-SING:
the N
PRAGMATICS
INFORMAL

work in or **work into.** If you **work** one substance **into** another, you add it to the other substance and mix the two together thoroughly. *Gradually pour the liquid into the flour, working it in carefully with a wooden spoon.*

PHRASAL VB
V n P n
V n P
Also V P noun

work off. 1 If you **work off** energy, aggression, or anger, you get rid of it by doing something that requires a lot of physical effort. *If I've had a bad day I'll work it off by cooking.* **2** If you **work off** a debt, you repay it by working. *The report proposes that students be allowed to work off their debt through community service.*

PHRASAL VB
V P noun
V n P
Also V n P

work out. 1 If you **work out** a solution to a problem or mystery, you manage to find the solution by thinking or talking about it. *Negotiators are due to meet later today to work out a compromise... It took me some time to work out what was causing this. •* If you **have** something **all worked out**, you have thought about it carefully, and know exactly what you are going to do or exactly what you want. *I had the ideal man all worked out in my mind.* **2** If you **work out** the answer to a mathematical problem, you calculate it. *It is proving hard to work out the value of bankrupt firms' assets.* **3** If something **works out** at a particular amount, it is calculated to be that amount after all the facts and figures have been considered. *It will probably work out cheaper to hire a van and move your own things.* **4** If a situation **works out** well or **works out**, it happens or progresses in a satisfactory way. *Things just didn't work out as planned... The deal just isn't working out the way we were promised... I'm sure it will work itself out.* **5** If you **work out** your notice or your service, you continue to work at your job until you have completed a specified period of time. **6** If you **work out**, you do physical exercises in order to make yourself fit and strong. **7** See also **workout.**

PHRASAL VB
V P noun
V P wh
Also V n P

V P noun
Also V n P

V P at amount
V P adj

V P prep/adv
V P noun
V pron-refl P
Also V P

V P noun

VP

work up. 1 If you **work** yourself **up**, you make yourself feel very upset or angry about something. *She worked herself up into a bit of a state. •* See also **worked up. 2** If you **work up** the enthusiasm or courage to do something, you succeed in making yourself feel it. If you **work up** a sweat or an appetite, you make yourself sweaty or hungry. *She had never worked up the nerve to tell anyone... Every member of the platoon had worked up a good sweat.* **3** If you **work up** something such as a piece of writing, you spend time and effort preparing it. *They asked me to work up some sample drawings.*

PHRASAL VB
V pron-refl P

V P noun

V P noun

work·able /'wɜːkəbəl/. A **workable** idea or system is realistic and practical, and likely to be effective.

◆◇◇◇◇
ADJ-GRADED

worka·day /'wɜːkədeɪ/. **Workaday** means ordinary and not especially interesting or unusual. *Enough of fantasy, the workaday world awaited him.*

ADJ

worka·hol·ic /ˌwɜːkə'hɒlɪk, AM -'hɔːl-/ **workaholics.** A **workaholic** is a person who works most of the time and finds it difficult to stop working in order to do other things.

◆◇◇◇◇
N-COUNT
INFORMAL

work·bench /'wɜːkbentʃ/ **workbenches.** A **workbench** is a heavy wooden table on which people use tools such as a hammer and nails to make or repair things.

N-COUNT

work·book /'wɜːkbʊk/ **workbooks.** A **workbook** is a textbook that has questions in it with spaces for the answers.

N-COUNT

work·day /'wɜːkdeɪ/ **workdays. 1** A **workday** is the amount of time during a day which you spend doing your job. *His workday starts at 3.30 a.m. and lasts 12 hours.* **2** A **workday** is a day on which people go to work. *What's he doing home on a workday?*

N-COUNT

N-COUNT

,worked 'up. If someone is **worked up**, they are angry or upset.

ADJ-GRADED:
v-link ADJ

work·er /'wɜːkə/ **workers. 1** A particular kind of **worker** does the kind of work mentioned. *She ate her sandwich alongside several other office workers. ...aid workers in Somalia.* **2 Workers** are people who are employed in industry or business and who are not managers. **3** You can use **worker** to say how well or badly someone works. *He is a hard worker.* **4** See also **care worker, casework, social worker, teleworker, youth worker.**

◆◆◆◆◆
N-COUNT
with supp

N-COUNT

N-COUNT

work·force /'wɜːkfɔːs/ **workforces. 1** The **workforce** is the total number of people in a country or region who are physically able to do a job and are available for work. **2** The **workforce** is the total number of people who are employed by a particular company.

◆◆◇◇◇
N-COUNT

N-COUNT

work·horse /'wɜːkhɔːs/ **workhorses.** If you describe a person or a machine as a **workhorse**, you mean that they can be relied upon to do a large amount of work, especially work that is dull.

N-COUNT

work·house /'wɜːkhaʊs/ **workhouses.** A **workhouse** was a place where, in the seventeenth to nineteenth centuries in Britain, very poor people who had no money and nowhere to live did unpleasant jobs in return for food and shelter. People also say **the workhouse** when they are referring to these places in general.

N-COUNT

work·ing /'wɜːkɪŋ/ **workings. 1 Working** people have jobs which they are paid to do. *Like working women anywhere, Asian women are buying convenience foods.* **2 Working** people are ordinary people who do not have professional or very highly paid jobs. *...a working men's club.* **3** A **working** day or week is the number of hours that you work during a day or a week. *...a shorter, more flexible working week.* **4** A **working** day is a day on which people normally have to do their job. **5** Your **working** life is the period of your life in which you have a job or are of a suitable age to have a job. **6** The **working** population of an area consists of all the people in that area who have a job or who are of a suitable age to have a job. **7 Working** conditions or practices are ones which you have in your job. **8 Working** clothes are designed for doing work in, and are intended to be practical rather than attractive. **9** If you have a **working** relationship with someone, you work well together, though you may not know each other personally. *The vice-president seems to have a good working relationship with the president.* **10** A **working** farm or business exists to do normal work and make a profit, and not only for tourists or as someone's hobby. **11** The **working** parts of a machine are the parts which move and operate the machine, in contrast to the outer case or container in which they are enclosed. **12** A **working** model is one that has parts that move. **13** A **working** knowledge or majority is not very great, but is enough to be useful. **14** A **working** title or definition is one which you use as the basis for a particular job or piece of research, but which you are likely to change or improve. **15** The **workings** of a piece of equipment, an organization, or a system are the ways in which it operates and the processes which are involved in it. *Neural*

◆◆◆◆◆
ADJ: ADJ n

ADJ: ADJ n

ADJ: ADJ n

ADJ: ADJ n
ADJ: ADJ n

ADJ: ADJ n

ADJ: ADJ n
ADJ: ADJ n

ADJ: ADJ n

ADJ: ADJ n

ADJ: ADJ n

ADJ: ADJ n
ADJ: ADJ n

ADJ: ADJ n

N-PLURAL

networks are computer systems which mimic the *workings of the brain.* **16** You can use **workings** to refer to a mine or quarry. *...housing which was built above old mine workings.* **17** • in working order: see **order.**

working 'capital. Working capital is money ◆◇◇◇ which is available for use immediately, rather than N-UNCOUNT money which is invested in land or equipment. TECHNICAL

working 'class, working classes. The work- ◆◇◇◇ **ing class** or the **working classes** are the group of N-COLL: people in a society who do not own much property, *the N* who have low social status, and who do jobs which involve using physical skills rather than intellectual skills. *A quarter of the working class voted for him.* ▶ Also an adjective. *...a self-educated man from a* ADJ *working class background.*

'working group, working groups. A **working** ◆◇◇◇ group is the same as a **working party.** N-COLL-COUNT

'working party, working parties. A **working** ◆◇◇◇ party is a committee which is established to investi- N-COLL-gate a particular situation or problem and to COUNT produce a report containing its opinions and rec- BRITISH ommendations about what should be done. The usual American term is **working group.** *They set up a working party to look into the issue.*

work·load /'wɜːkləʊd/ **workloads;** also spelled ◆◇◇◇ **work load.** The **workload** of a person or organiza- N-COUNT tion is the amount of work that has to be done by them. *The sudden cancellation of Mr Major's trip was due to his heavy workload.*

work·man /'wɜːkmən/ **workmen.** A **workman** is a ◆◇◇◇ man who works with his hands, for example a N-COUNT builder or plumber.

work·man·like /'wɜːkmənlaɪk/. If you describe ADJ-GRADED something as **workmanlike,** you mean that it has been done quite well and sensibly, but not in a particularly imaginative or original way. *The script was workmanlike at best.*

work·man·ship /'wɜːkmənʃɪp/. **Workmanship** is N-UNCOUNT the skill with which something is made and which affects the quality of the finished object. *The problem may be due to poor workmanship.*

work·mate /'wɜːkmeɪt/ **workmates.** Your **work-** N-COUNT **mates** are the people you work with. INFORMAL

work of 'art, works of art. 1 A **work of art** is a ◆◇◇◇ painting or piece of sculpture which is of high qual- N-COUNT ity. **2** A **work of art** is something which is very com- N-COUNT plex or which has been skilfully made or produced. *The actual nest is a work of art.*

work·out /'wɜːkaʊt/ **workouts.** A **workout** is a ◆◇◇◇ period of physical exercise or training. *...a 35-* N-COUNT *minute aerobic workout.*

work·place /'wɜːkpleɪs/ **workplaces;** also ◆◆◇◇ spelled **work place.** Your **workplace** is the place N-COUNT where you work. *...the difficulties facing women in the workplace.*

work·room /'wɜːkruːm/ **workrooms.** A person's N-COUNT **workroom** is a room where they work, especially when their work involves making things.

work·sheet /'wɜːkʃiːt/ **worksheets.** A **worksheet** N-COUNT is a specially prepared page of exercises designed to improve your knowledge or understanding of a particular subject.

work·shop /'wɜːkʃɒp/ **workshops. 1** A **work-** ◆◆◇◇ shop is a period of discussion or practical work on a N-COUNT particular subject in which a group of people share their knowledge or experience. *...a jazz workshop for young artists.* **2** A **workshop** is a room or build- N-COUNT ing which contains tools or machinery for making or repairing things, especially using wood or metal.

'work-shy; also spelled **workshy.** If you describe ADJ-GRADED someone as **work-shy,** you disapprove of them be- PRAGMATICS cause you think they are lazy and do not want to work. *He is a morose, work-shy layabout.*

work·sta·tion /'wɜːksteɪʃən/ **workstations;** also ◆◇◇◇ spelled **work station.** A **workstation** is a part of a N-COUNT computerized office system consisting of a display screen and a keyboard.

'work surface, work surfaces; also spelled N-COUNT **worksurface.** A **work surface** is the same as a **work-top.**

work·top /'wɜːktɒp/ **worktops.** A **worktop** is a flat N-COUNT surface in a kitchen which is easily cleaned and on which you can prepare food.

world /wɜːld/ **worlds. 1** The **world** is the planet ◆◆◆◆ that we live on. *It's a beautiful part of the world...* N-SING: *More than anything, I'd like to drive around the* *the N* *world.* **2** If you say that something happens or exists PHRASE the **world over,** you mean that it happens or exists in every part of the world. *Some problems are the same the world over.* **3** A **world** is a planet. *He* N-COUNT looked at something from another world. **4** The N-SING: **world** refers to all the people who live on this plan- *the N,* et, and our societies, institutions, and ways of life. *N n* *The world was, and remains, shocked. ...his personal contribution to world history.* **5** You can use **world** ADJ: ADJ n to describe someone or something that is one of the most important or significant of its kind on earth. *Like Japan, China has emerged as a world power. ...a world authority on heart-diseases.*

6 You can use **world** in expressions such as **the Arab** N-SING: **world, the western world,** and **the ancient world** to *the supp N* refer to a particular group of countries or a particular period in history. **7** You can use **world** to refer to a N-SING: particular field of activity, and the people involved in *the N,* it. *...the latest news from the world of finance.* **8** You N-COUNT: can use **world** to refer to a place or way of life by de- *with supp* scribing its strongest features. *The patient must re-enter a world full of problems and stresses.* **9** You can N-SING: use **world** to refer to a particular group of living *the N* things, for example **the animal world, the plant world,** and **the insect world.**

10 Someone's **world** is the life they lead, the people N-COUNT they have contact with, and the things they experience. *I lost my job and it was like my world collapsed.*

11 You can use **world** in expressions such as **this** N-SING: **world, the next world,** and **the world to come** to refer *with supp* to the state of being alive or a state of existence after death. *Good fortune will follow you, both in this world and the next.* **12** See also **New World, real world, Third World.**

13 If you say that someone is **in a world of** their **own,** PHRASE you mean that they seem not to notice other people or the things going on around them. **14** If you say that PHRASE two people or things are **worlds apart,** they are em- PRAGMATICS phasizing that they are very different from each other. *Intellectually, this man and I are worlds apart.* **15** If PHRASE you say that someone has **the best of both worlds,** you mean that they have the benefits of two things and none of the disadvantages. *Her living room provides the best of both worlds, with an office at one end and comfortable sofas at the other.* **16** If you say that PHRASE there is **a world of difference** between one thing and PRAGMATICS another, you are emphasizing that they are very different from each other. *There's a world of difference between an amateur video and a slick Hollywood production.* **17** If you **think the world of** someone, you PHRASE like them or care about them very much.

18 If you say that you would not do something **for the** PHRASE **world,** you are emphasizing that you definitely would PRAGMATICS not do it. *I wouldn't have missed this for the world.*

19 If you say that something **has done** someone the PHRASE **world of good** or **a world of good,** you mean that it INFORMAL has made them feel better or improved their life. *A sleep will do you the world of good.* **20** You can use **in** PHRASE **the world** in expressions such as **what in the world** PRAGMATICS and **who in the world** to emphasize a question, especially when expressing surprise, anger, or despair. *What in the world is he doing?* **21** If you say that some- PHRASE thing is **out of this world,** you are emphasizing that it PRAGMATICS is extremely good or impressive. *These new trains are* INFORMAL *out of this world.*

22 You can use **in an ideal world** or **in a perfect world** PHRASE when you are talking about things that you would like to happen, although you realize that they are not likely to happen. *In a perfect world, there would be the facilities and money to treat every sick person.* **23** If you PHRASE say that someone is **a man of the world** or **a woman of**

the world, you mean that they are experienced and knowledgeable about life, and are not easily shocked, for example by immoral or dishonest things. **24** You can use **the outside world** to refer to all the people who do not live in a particular place or who are not involved in a particular situation. *For many, the post-office is the only link with the outside world.* **25 • not be the end of the world:** see **end. • the world is your oyster:** see **oyster. • on top of the world:** see **top.**   PHRASE

world beater, world beaters; also spelled   N-COUNT **world-beater.** In British English, if you describe a person or thing as a **world beater**, you mean that they are better than most other people or things of their kind.

world-'class. A **world-class** sportsperson or ◆◇◇◇◇
competitor is one of the best in the world at what   ADJ
they do.   JOURNALISM

world-'famous. Someone or something that is ◆◇◇◇◇
world-famous is known about by people all over   ADJ
the world. *...the world-famous Hollywood Bowl.*

world·ly /'wɜːldli/. **1 Worldly** is used to describe ◆◇◇◇◇
things relating to the ordinary activities of life, ra-   ADJ-GRADED
ther than to spiritual things. *He has repeatedly criti-*   LITERARY
cized Western churches as too worldly. **2** Someone   ADJ-GRADED
who is **worldly** is experienced and knowledgeable
about the practical aspects of life rather than about
spiritual things. **♦ world·li·ness** *To Betty, Joe had*   N-UNCOUNT
an air of worldliness. **3 Worldly** is used to describe   ADJ: ADJ n
things relating to success, wealth, and possessions.   LITERARY
...the view that the important thing is to gain world-
ly success. **4** You can refer to someone's posses-   ADJ: ADJ n
sions as their **worldly** goods or possessions.   LITERARY

worldly-'wise. If you describe someone as   ADJ-GRADED
worldly-wise, you mean they are experienced and
knowledgeable about life, and are not easily
shocked or impressed.

world view, world views; also spelled **world-** ◆◇◇◇◇
view. A person's **world view** is the way they see and   N-COUNT:
understand the world, especially regarding issues   with supp
such as politics, philosophy, and religion. *Many art-*
ists express their world view in their work.

world 'war, world wars. A **world war** is a war ◆◆◇◇◇
that involves countries all over the world.   N-VAR

world-'weary. A **world-weary** person no longer   ADJ-GRADED
feels excited or enthusiastic about anything.

world·wide /ˌwɜːldˈwaɪd/; also spelled **world-wide.** ◆◆◆◇◇
If something exists or happens **worldwide**, it exists   ADV
or happens throughout the world. *His books have*
sold more than 20 million copies worldwide. ▶ Also   ADJ
an adjective. *Today, doctors are fearing a worldwide*
epidemic.

World-Wide 'Web. The World-Wide Web is a   N-PROPER:
system which links documents and pictures into an   the N
information database that is stored in computers in
many different parts of the world and which can be
accessed with a single program. **World-Wide Web** is
often abbreviated to **WWW, W3,** or **the Web.**

worm /wɜːm/ **worms, worming, wormed. 1** A ◆◆◇◇◇
worm is a small animal with a long thin body, no   N-COUNT
bones and no legs. **2** If animals or people have   N-PLURAL
worms, worms are living as parasites in their intestines. **3** If you **worm** an animal, you give it medi-   VERB: V n
cine in order to kill the worms that are living in its
intestines.
4 If you **worm** your **way** somewhere, you move there   VERB
slowly and with difficulty. *The kitten wormed its way*   V way adv/
through the just-open door. **5** If you say that someone   prep
is worming their **way** to success, or **is worming** their   VERB
way into someone else's affection, you disapprove of   V way prep/
the way that they are gradually making someone trust   adv
them or like them, often in order to deceive them or   PRAGMATICS
gain some advantage. *She never misses a chance to*
worm her way into the public's hearts.
6 If you say that someone or something is opening **a**   PHRASE
can of worms, you are warning them that they are   PRAGMATICS
planning to do or talk about something which is more
complicated, unpleasant, and difficult than they realize and which might be better left alone.

worm out of. If you **worm** information **out of** some-   PHRASAL VB
one, you gradually find it out by constantly asking   V n P P n
  Also V P P n n

them about it. *It took me weeks to worm the facts out of*
him.

worn /wɔːn/. **1 Worn** is the past participle of **wear.** ◆◇◇◇◇
2 Worn is used to describe something that is dam-   ADJ-GRADED
aged or thin because it is old and has been used a
lot. *Most of the trek is along worn paths.* **3** If some-   ADJ-GRADED:
one looks **worn**, they look tired and old. *She was*   v-link ADJ
looking very haggard and worn. **4** See also **well-**
worn.

worn 'out; also spelled **worn-out. 1** Something ◆◇◇◇◇
that is **worn out** is so old, damaged, or thin from   ADJ
use that it cannot be used any more. *...faded bits of*
worn-out clothing. **2** Someone who is **worn out** is   ADJ-GRADED
extremely tired after hard work or a difficult or unpleasant experience. **3** If you describe something   ADJ: ADJ n
such as an idea as **worn out**, you mean that it is no   PRAGMATICS
longer relevant or interesting because it is old and
has been repeated often; used showing disapproval.

wor·ried, /'wʌrid, AM 'wɜːrid/. When you are **wor-** ◆◆◆◇◇
ried, you are unhappy because you keep thinking   ADJ-GRADED
about problems that you have or about unpleasant
things that might happen in the future. *He seemed*
very worried... If you're at all worried about his pro-
gress, do discuss it with one of his teachers. **♦ wor-**
·ried·ly *'You don't have to go, you know,' she said*   ADV-GRADED
worriedly.

wor·rier /'wʌriə, AM 'wɜːriər/ **worriers.** If you de-   N-COUNT
scribe someone as a **worrier**, you mean that they
spend a lot of time thinking about problems that
they have or unpleasant things that might happen.

wor·ri·some /'wʌrisəm, AM 'wɜːr-/. Something that   ADJ-GRADED
is **worrisome** causes people to worry or should   AMERICAN
cause them to worry.

wor·ry /'wʌri, AM 'wɜːri/ **worries, worrying,** ◆◆◆◆◇
worried. 1 If you **worry**, you keep thinking about   VERB
problems that you have or about unpleasant things   V
that might happen. *Don't worry, your luggage will*   V about n/-ing
come on afterwards by taxi... I worry about her con-   Also V that
stantly. **2** If someone or something **worries** you,   VERB
they make you anxious because you keep thinking   V n
about problems or unpleasant things that might be   it V n that/to-
connected with them. *'Why didn't you tell us?'—'I*   inf
didn't want to worry you.'... Does it worry you that
the Americans are discussing this? **3 Worry** is the   N-UNCOUNT
state or feeling of anxiety and unhappiness caused
by the problems that you have or by thinking about
unpleasant things that might happen. *His last years*
were overshadowed by financial worry. **4** A **worry** is   N-COUNT
a problem that you keep thinking about and that
makes you unhappy. *My main worry was that Mad-*
eleine Johnson would still be there.
5 If someone or something does not **worry** you, you   VERB
do not dislike them or you are not annoyed by them.   V n
The cold doesn't worry me... It wouldn't worry me if he   it V n if
came to my house. **6** You say **not to worry** to someone   SPOKEN
to indicate that you are not upset or angry when   CONVENTION
something has gone wrong. *'Not to worry, Baby,' he*   PRAGMATICS
said, and kissed her tenderly.   INFORMAL

wor·ry·ing /'wʌriɪŋ, AM 'wɜːriɪŋ/. If something is ◆◆◇◇◇
worrying, it causes people to worry. *It is very worry-*   ADJ-GRADED
ing that petrol bombs have been brought into a fight
between two secondary schools. **♦ wor·ry·ing·ly** *The*   ADV-GRADED
rate of assaults was worryingly high.

worse /wɜːs/. **1 Worse** is the comparative of **bad.** ◆◇◇◇◇
2 Worse is the comparative of **badly. 3 Worse** is
used to form the comparative of compound adjectives beginning with 'bad' and 'badly.' For example,
the comparative of 'badly off' is 'worse off'.
4 If a situation **goes from bad to worse**, it becomes   PHRASE
even more unpleasant or unsatisfactory. **5** If a situa-   PHRASE
tion changes **for the worse**, it becomes more unpleasant or more difficult. **6** If someone or something is **the**   PHRASE
worse for something, they have been harmed or bad-
ly affected by it. If they are **none the worse** for it, they
have not been harmed or badly affected by it. *Father*
came home from the pub very much the worse for
drink. **7** If you tell someone that they **could do worse**   PHRASE
than do a particular thing, you are advising them that   PRAGMATICS
it would be quite a good thing to do. *Scientists in*
search of a challenging career could do worse than

consider forensic science. **8 •** **for better or worse**: see **better.**

wors·en /'wɜːsən/ **worsens, worsening, worsened.** If a bad situation **worsens** or if something **worsens** it, it becomes more difficult, unpleasant, or unacceptable. *The security forces had to intervene to prevent the situation worsening... These options would actually worsen the economy.* ♦ **wors·en·ing** *...a further worsening of relations between the two countries.* ◆◆◇◇◇ V-ERG V n N-SING

wor·ship /'wɜːʃɪp/ **worships, worshipping, worshipped;** spelled **worshiping, worshiped** in American English. **1** If you **worship** a god, you show your respect to the god, for example by saying prayers. *...Jews worshipping at the Wailing Wall.* ► Also a noun. *...the worship of the ancient Roman gods.* ♦ **wor·ship·per, worshippers** *Scores of worshippers streamed down to the altar.* **2** If you **worship** someone or something, you love them or admire them very much. ◆◆◇◇◇ VERB: V n N-UNCOUNT N-COUNT VERB: V n

wor·ship·ful /'wɜːʃɪpfʊl/. If someone has a **worshipful** attitude to someone or something, they show a very great amount of respect and admiration for them. ADJ: ADJ n

worst /wɜːst/. **1 Worst** is the superlative of **bad.** **2 Worst** is the superlative of **badly.** **3 The worst** is the most unpleasant or unfavourable thing that could happen or does happen. *The country had come through the worst of the recession.* **4 Worst** is used to form the superlative of compound adjectives beginning with 'bad' and 'badly'. For example, the superlative of 'badly-affected' is 'worst-affected'. **5** You say **worst of all** to indicate that what you are about to mention is the most unpleasant or has the most disadvantages out of all the things you are mentioning. *The people most closely affected are the passengers who were injured and, worst of all, those who lost relatives.* **6** You use **at worst** or **at the worst** to indicate that you are considering a situation in the most unfavourable or most pessimistic way. *At best Nella would be an invalid; at worst she would die.* **7** If someone is **at their worst**, they are behaving as unpleasantly or doing something as unsuccessfully as it is possible for them to do. *This was their mother at her worst.* **8** If you say that you might do something **if the worst comes to the worst**, you mean that you might do it if the situation develops in the most unfavourable way. *He was asked whether he would walk out if the worst came to the worst.* **9** If someone **does** their **worst**, they do everything unpleasant that they can possibly do. You can say **'do your worst'** to show someone that you are not frightened even if they do everything unpleasant that they can possibly do. *I think it was dangerous to say: look, we've got an army now – do your worst.* ◆◇◇◇◇ N-SING the N V PHRASE PRAGMATICS PHRASE PHRASE PHRASE PHRASE PRAGMATICS

worst·ed /'wʊstɪd/ **worsteds. Worsted** is a kind of woollen cloth. N-VAR

worth /wɜːθ/. **1** If something is **worth** a particular amount of money, it can be sold for that amount or is considered to have that value. *These books might be worth £50 or £60 or more to a collector.* **2 Worth** combines with amounts of money, so that when you talk about a particular amount of money's **worth of** something, you mean the quantity of it that you can buy for that amount of money. *I went and bought about six dollars' worth of potato chips.* ► Also a pronoun. *'How many do you want?'—'I'll have a pound's worth.'* **3 Worth** combines with time expressions, so you can use **worth** when you are saying how long an amount of something will last. For example, a week's **worth** of food is the amount of food that will last you for a week. ► Also a pronoun. *There's really not very much food down there. About two weeks' worth.* **4** If you say that something is **worth** having, you mean that it is pleasant or useful, and therefore a good thing to have. *He's decided to get a look at the house and see if it might be worth buying.* **5** If something is **worth** a particular action, or if an action is **worth** doing, it is considered to be important enough for that action. ◆◆◆◇ v-link worth amount COMB PRON COMB PRON v-link worth -ing v-link worth n/-ing

This restaurant is well worth a visit... It is worth pausing to consider these statements from Mr Wigley. **6** If an action or activity is **worth** someone's **while**, it will be helpful, useful, or enjoyable for them if they do it, even though it requires some effort. *It might be worth your while to go to court and ask for the agreement to be changed.* PHRASE

7 Someone's **worth** is the value, usefulness, or importance that they are considered to have. *He had never met a woman like her, nor had he ever had a woman of her worth as a friend.* N-UNCOUNT FORMAL

8 If you do something **for all** you **are worth**, you do it with a lot of energy and enthusiasm. *We both began waving to the crowd for all we were worth.* **9** If someone does something **for all it is worth**, they do it as much as possible and for as long as they can get benefit from it. *...taking an idea and exploiting it for all it's worth.* **10** If you add **for what it's worth** to something that you say, you are suggesting that what you are saying or referring to may not be very valuable or helpful, especially because you do not want to appear arrogant. *I've brought my notes, for what it's worth.* **11 •** **worth your weight in gold**: see **weight.** PHRASE PHRASE PHRASE

worth·less /'wɜːθləs/. **1** Something that is **worthless** is of no real value or use. *The guarantee could be worthless if the firm goes out of business. ...a worthless piece of old junk.* **2** Someone who is described as **worthless** is considered to have no good qualities or skills. *You feel you really are completely worthless and unlovable.* ♦ **worth·less·ness** *...feelings of worthlessness.* ◆◇◇◇◇ ADJ-GRADED ADJ-GRADED N-UNCOUNT

worth·while /,wɜːθ'waɪl/. If something is **worthwhile**, it is enjoyable or useful, and worth the time, money, or effort that is spent on it. *...a worthwhile movie that was compelling enough to watch again... It might be worthwhile to consider your attitude to an insurance policy.* ◆◇◇◇ ADJ-GRADED

wor·thy /'wɜːði/ **worthier, worthiest; worthies.** **1** If someone or something is **worthy** of something, they deserve it because they have the qualities or abilities required. *The bank might think you're worthy of a loan... I hope he was worthy of her.* ♦ **wor·thi·ly** *...chief constable, a rank I know I could have worthily held.* ♦ **wor·thi·ness** *Their belief in their own worthiness is so low.* **2** A **worthy** person or thing is approved of by most people in society and considered to be morally respectable or correct. *...worthy members of the community.* ► You can refer to worthy people as **worthies.** ◆◆◇◇ ADJ-GRADED FORMAL ADV N-UNCOUNT ADJ-GRADED N-COUNT

-worthy /-wɜːði/. **-worthy** can be added to words to form adjectives which indicate that someone or something deserves or merits a particular thing or action. For example, if a remark or person is **quote-worthy**, they are worth quoting. **•** See also **airworthy, creditworthy, newsworthy, noteworthy, praiseworthy, seaworthy, trustworthy.** COMB

wot. Wot is sometimes used in writing to represent **what,** to show that someone is speaking very informally or that they are being humorous. *'Cor, wot brilliant prizes!'* BRITISH

would /wəd STRONG wʊd/. **Would** is a modal verb. It is used with the base form of a verb. In spoken English, **would** is often abbreviated to **'d.** **1** You use **would** when you are saying what someone believed, hoped, or expected to happen or be the case. *No one believed the soldiers stationed at the border would actually open fire... Would he always be like this?... A report yesterday that said British unemployment would continue to rise.* **2** You use **would** when saying what someone intended to do. *George decided it was such a rare car that he would only use it for a few shows... He did not think he would marry Beth.* **3** You use **would** when you are referring to the result of a possible situation. *Ordinarily it would be fun to be taken to fabulous restaurants... It would cost very much more for the four of us to go from Italy.* **4** You use **would,** or **would have** with a past participle, to indicate that you are assuming or guessing that something is true, because you have good reasons for thinking it. *You wouldn't know him... That would* ◆◆◆◆ MODAL MODAL MODAL MODAL

have been Della's car... Her mother would be annoyed because he was so late.

5 You use **would** in the main clause of some 'if' and 'unless' sentences to indicate something you consider to be fairly unlikely to happen. *If only I could get some sleep, I would be able to cope... the targets would not be achieved unless other departments showed equal commitment.* **6** You use **would** to say that someone was willing to do something. You use **would not** to indicate that someone refused to do something. *She indicated that she would help her husband... He wouldn't say where he was picked up the information.* **7** You use **would not** to indicate that something did not happen, often in spite of a lot of effort. *He kicked, pushed, and hurled his shoulder at the door. It wouldn't open... The paint wouldn't stick to the wallpaper.* **8** You use **would**, especially with verbs such as 'like', 'love', and 'wish' when saying that someone wants to do or have something or wants something to happen. *She asked me what I would like to do... Ideally, she would love to become pregnant again... Anne wouldn't mind going to Italy or France to live.* ● **would rather**: see **rather**.

9 You use **would** with 'if' clauses in questions when you are asking for permission to do something. *Do you think it would be all right if I smoked?* **10** You use **would**, usually in questions, when you are politely offering someone something or inviting someone to do something. *Would you like a drink?... Perhaps you would like to pay a visit to London.* **11** You use **would**, usually in questions, when you are politely asking someone to do something. *Would you come in here a moment, please?... Oh dear, there's the doorbell. See who it is, would you, darling.*

12 You say that someone **would** do something when it is typical of them and you are critical of it. You emphasize the word **would** when you use it in this way. *I was amazed, during a 'Women In Rock' debate, to be told, 'Well, you would say that: you're a man.'* **13** You use **would**, or sometimes **would have** with a past participle, when you are expressing your opinion about something or seeing if people agree with you. *I think you'd agree he's a very respected columnist... I would have thought it a proper job for the Army to fight rebellion.* **14** You use **I would** when you are giving someone advice in an informal way. *If I were you, Mrs Gretchen, I just wouldn't worry about it.* **15** You use **you would** in negative sentences with verbs such as 'guess' and 'know' when you want to say that something is not obvious, especially something surprising. *You'd never think she was the daughter of a banker.* **16** You use **would** to talk about something which happened regularly in the past but which no longer happens. *Sunday mornings my mother would bake. I'd stand by the fridge and help.*

17 You use **would have** with a past participle when you are saying what was likely to have happened by a particular time. *Within ten weeks of the introduction, 34 million people would have been reached by our television commercials.* **18** You use **would have** with a past participle when you are referring to the result or effect of a possible event in the past. *My daughter would have been 17 this week if she had lived.* **19** If you say that someone **would have** liked or preferred something, you mean that they wanted to do it or have it but were unable to. *I would have liked a life in politics.* **20** You use **would**, usually in negative sentences, to criticize something that someone has done and to express your disapproval of it. *I would never have done what they did.* **21** If you say **'would that'** something were the case, you are saying that you wish it were the case. *Would that he could have listened to his father.*

'**would-be.** You can use **would-be** to describe someone who wants or attempts to do a particular thing. For example, a **would-be** writer is someone who wants to be a writer.

wouldn't /'wʊdənt/. **Wouldn't** is written to represent the usual spoken form of 'would not'.

would've /'wʊdəv/. **Would've** is written to represent a spoken form of 'would have', when 'have' is an auxiliary verb.

wound 1 verb form of 'wind'

wound /waʊnd/. **Wound** is the past tense and past participle of **wind** 2.

wound 2 injury

wound /wuːnd/ **wounds, wounding, wounded.** **1** A **wound** is damage to part of your body, especially a cut or a hole in your flesh, which is caused by a gun, knife, or other weapon. *Six soldiers are reported to have died from their wounds.* **2** If a weapon or something sharp **wounds** you, it damages your body. *A bomb exploded in a hotel, killing six people and wounding another five.* ◆ **wound·ed.** **The wounded** are people who are wounded. **3** A **wound** is a lasting bad effect on someone's mind or feelings caused by a very upsetting experience. *She has been so deeply hurt it may take forever for the wounds to heal.* **4** If you **are wounded** by what someone says or does, your feelings are deeply hurt. ◆ **wound·ed** *She feels desperately wounded and unloved.* **5** Something that **opens old wounds** or **reopens old wounds** reminds someone about an upsetting experience in the past which they would prefer to forget. **6** ● to **rub salt into the wound**: see **salt**.

wound up /ˌwaʊnd 'ʌp/. If someone is **wound up**, they are very tense and nervous or angry.

wove /wəʊv/. **Wove** is the past tense of **weave**.

wo·ven /'wəʊvən/. **Woven** is a past participle of **weave**.

wow /waʊ/ **wows, wowing, wowed.** **1** You can say **'wow'** when you are very impressed, surprised, or pleased. *I thought, 'Wow, what a good idea'.* **2** You say that someone **wows** you when they give an impressive performance and fill you with enthusiasm and admiration. *Ben Tankard wowed the crowd with his jazz.*

WPC /ˌdʌbljuː piː 'siː/ **WPCs.** In Britain, a **WPC** is a female police officer of the lowest rank. **WPC** is an abbreviation for 'woman police constable'.

wraith /reɪθ/ **wraiths.** A **wraith** is a ghost. *That child flits about like a wraith.*

wran·gle /'ræŋgəl/ **wrangles, wrangling, wrangled.** If you say that someone **is wrangling** with someone over something, you mean that they are arguing angrily for quite a long time about it. *The two sides have spent most of their time wrangling over procedural problems.* ▶ Also a noun. *The party was torn apart by wrangles over fiscal policy.* ◆ **wran·gling, wranglings** *There was some wrangling between creditors.*

wrap /ræp/ **wraps, wrapping, wrapped.** **1** When you **wrap** something, you fold paper or cloth tightly round it to cover it completely, for example in order to protect it or so that you can give it to someone as a present. *Mexican Indians used to wrap tough meat in leaves from the papaya tree.* ▶ **Wrap up** means the same as **wrap**. *Diana is taking the opportunity to wrap up the family presents... He could buy the paper to wrap the gifts up.* **2** **Wrap** is the material that something is wrapped in. *...gift wrap.* ● See also **plastic wrap**. **3** When you **wrap** something such as a piece of paper or cloth round another thing, you put it around it. *She wrapped a handkerchief around her bleeding palm.* **4** If someone **wraps** their arms, fingers, or legs around something, they put them firmly around it. **5** See also **wrapping**. **6** If you keep something **under wraps**, you keep it secret, often until you are ready to announce it at some time in the future.

wrap up. **1** If you **wrap up**, you put warm clothes on. *Markus has wrapped up warmly in a woolly hat... Thousands of people wrapped up against the icy cold to watch the parade.* **2** If you **wrap up** something such as a job or an agreement, you complete it in a satisfactory way. *NATO defense ministers wrap up their meeting in Brussels today.* **3** See also **wrap** 1; **wrapped up**.

,wrapped 'up. If someone is **wrapped up** in ◆◇◇◇
something or someone, they spend nearly all their ADJ-GRADED:
time thinking about them, so that they forget about v-link ADJ in/
other things which may be important. *He's too seri- with n
ous and dedicated, wrapped up in his career.*

wrap·per /'ræpə/ **wrappers.** A **wrapper** is a piece N-COUNT
of paper, plastic, or foil which covers and protects
something that you buy, especially something perishable such as food. *...sweet wrappers.*

wrap·ping /'ræpɪŋ/ **wrappings.** Wrapping is ◆◇◇◇
something such as paper or plastic which is used to N-VAR
cover and protect something. *Nick asked for the tile
to be delivered in waterproof wrapping.*

'wrapping paper, wrapping papers. Wrapping N-VAR
paper is special paper which is used for wrapping
presents.

wrath /rɒθ, AM ræθ/. **Wrath** means the same as an- ◆◇◇◇
ger. *He incurred the wrath of the authorities in N-UNCOUNT
speaking out against government injustices.*

wreak /riːk/ **wreaks, wreaking, wreaked;** ◆◇◇◇
wrought can also be used as the past participle.
1 Something or someone that **wreaks** havoc or de- VERB
struction causes a great amount of disorder or dam- V n
age. *Violent storms wreaked havoc on the French JOURNALISM
Riviera.* **2** If you **wreak** revenge or vengeance on VERB: V n
someone, you do something that will harm them USU
very much to punish them for the harm they have LITERARY
done to you. **3** See also **wrought**.

wreath /riːθ/ **wreaths. 1** A **wreath** is an arrange- ◆◇◇◇
ment of flowers and leaves, usually in the shape of a N-COUNT
circle, which is put onto a grave or by a statue as a
sign of remembrance for the dead. **2** A **wreath** is a N-COUNT
circle of leaves or flowers which someone wears
around their head. **3** A **wreath** is a circle of leaves N-COUNT
and flowers which some people hang on the front
door of their house at Christmas.

wreathe /riːð/ **wreathes, wreathing,
wreathed. 1** If something **is wreathed** in smoke or VERB
mist, it is surrounded by it. *The National Park is of- be V-ed in n
ten wreathed in cloud... Fog wreathes the temples.* V n
2 If something **is wreathed** with flowers or leaves, it LITERARY
has a circle or chain of flowers or leaves put round VB: usu
it. passive

wreck /rek/ **wrecks, wrecking, wrecked. 1** If ◆◆◇◇
someone or something **wrecks** something, they VERB
completely destroy or ruin it. *A coalition could have V n
defeated the government and wrecked the treaty.*
◆ **wreck·er, wreckers** *They may be remembered N-COUNT
as the wreckers of a fine company.* **2** If a ship **is VB: usu
wrecked,** it is damaged so much that it sinks or can passive
no longer sail. **3** A **wreck** is something such as a N-COUNT
ship, car, plane, or building which has been destroyed, usually in an accident. *...the wreck of a
sailing ship.* **4** A **wreck** is an accident in which a N-COUNT
moving vehicle hits something and is damaged or AMERICAN
destroyed. The British word is **crash.** *He was killed
in a car wreck.* **5** If you say that someone is a **wreck,** N-COUNT
you mean that they are very exhausted or un- INFORMAL
healthy. *You look a wreck.* ● See also **nervous
wreck.**

wreck·age /'rekɪdʒ/. **1** When something such as a ◆◇◇◇
plane, car, or building has been destroyed, you can N-UNCOUNT
refer to what remains as **wreckage** or **the wreckage.**
*Mark was dragged from the burning wreckage of his
car.* **2** If something such as a plan has failed or been N-SING:
spoilt completely, you can refer to what remains as the N
the wreckage of it. *New states were born out of the
wreckage of old colonial empires.*

wren /ren/ **wrens.** A **wren** is a very small brown ◆◇◇◇
bird. N-COUNT

wrench /rentʃ/ **wrenches, wrenching,
wrenched. 1** If you **wrench** something that is VERB
fixed in a particular position, you pull or twist it vio- V n prep
lently, in order to move or remove it. *He felt two V n with adv/
men wrench the suitcase from his hand... He adj
wrenched off his sneakers.* **2** If you **wrench** yourself VERB:
free from someone who is holding you, you get V n adj
away from them by suddenly twisting the part of V pron-refl
your body that is being held. *She wrenched herself prep
from his grasp... She tore at one man's face as she V adj
                                                       Also V n adv

tried to wrench free.* **3** If you **wrench** a limb or one VERB: V n
of your joints, you twist it and injure it. **4** If you say N-SING
that leaving someone or something is a **wrench,**
you feel very sad about it. *I always knew it would be
a wrench to leave Essex after all these years.*

5 A **wrench** or **monkey wrench** is an adjustable metal N-COUNT
tool used for tightening or loosening nuts and bolts.
See picture headed **tools. 6** If someone **throws a** PHRASE
wrench or **throws a monkey wrench** into a process, AMERICAN
they prevent something happening smoothly in the
way that it was planned, by causing a problem or difficulty. The British expression is to **throw a spanner in
the works.**

wrest /rest/ **wrests, wresting, wrested. 1** If ◆◇◇◇
you **wrest** something from someone else, you take it VERB
from them with effort or unlawfully. *He has been V n from n
trying to wrest control from the central government... V n with
The men had returned to wrest back power.* **2** If you away/back
wrest something from someone who is holding it, LITERARY
you take it from them by pulling or twisting it vio- V n from n
lently. *He was attacked by a security man who tried V n with away
to wrest away a gas cartridge.* LITERARY

wres·tle /'resəl/ **wrestles, wrestling, wres-** ◆◇◇◇
tled. 1 When you **wrestle** with a difficult problem, VERB
you try to deal with it. *What he liked to do was to V with n
take an idea and wrestle it by finding every possible V n
consequence.* **2** If you **wrestle** with someone, you VERB:
fight them by forcing them into painful positions or V with n
throwing them to the ground, rather than by hitting V
them. Some people wrestle as a sport. *They taught
me to wrestle.* ◆ **wres·tler, wrestlers** *...a wrestler N-COUNT
waiting to begin a fight.* ◆ **wres·tling** *...a champi- N-UNCOUNT
onship wrestling match.* **3** If you **wrestle** someone VERB
or something somewhere, you move them there V n prep
using a lot of force, for example by twisting a part of
someone's body into painful positions. *We had to
physically wrestle the child from the man's arms.*

wretch /retʃ/ **wretches. 1** You can refer to some- N-COUNT
one as a **wretch** when you feel sorry for them be- LITERARY
cause they are unhappy or unfortunate. *Before the
poor wretch had time to speak, he was shot.* **2** You N-COUNT
can refer to someone as a **wretch** when you think LITERARY
that they are wicked or if they have done something
you are angry about. *Oh, what have you done, you
wretch!*

wretch·ed /'retʃɪd/. **1** You describe someone as ◆◇◇◇
wretched when you feel sorry for them because ADJ-GRADED
they are in an unpleasant situation or have suffered FORMAL
unpleasant experiences. *You have built up a huge
property empire by buying from wretched people
who had to sell or starve.* ◆ **wretch·ed·ly** *...prison- ADV
ers living in wretchedly overcrowded conditions.*
◆ **wretch·ed·ness** *He does deserve some good luck N-UNCOUNT
after so much wretchedness.* **2** Someone who feels ADJ-GRADED
wretched feels very unhappy. *I feel really confused FORMAL
and wretched.* ◆ **wretch·ed·ly** *His marriage was ADV-GRADED
wretchedly unhappy.* ◆ **wretch·ed·ness** *...their N-UNCOUNT
shared wretchedness at Werner's death.* **3** If you de- ADJ-GRADED
scribe something as **wretched,** you are emphasizing FORMAL
that it is very bad or of very poor quality. *The pay PRAGMATICS
has always been wretched.* **4** You use **wretched** to ADJ: ADJ n
describe someone or something that you dislike or PRAGMATICS
feel angry with. *Wretched woman, he thought, why INFORMAL
the hell can't she wait?*

wrig·gle /'rɪgəl/ **wriggles, wriggling, wriggled.** ◆◇◇◇
1 If you **wriggle** or **wriggle** part of your body, you VERB: V
twist and turn with quick movements, for example V n
because you are uncomfortable. *She pulled off her
shoes and stockings and wriggled her toes.* **2** If you VERB
wriggle somewhere, for example through a small V adv/prep
gap, you move there by twisting and turning your
body. *Bauman wriggled into the damp coverall.*

wriggle out of. If you say that someone has **wrig-** PHRASAL VB
gled out of doing something, you disapprove of the PRAGMATICS
fact that they have managed to avoid doing it, al- V P P n/-ing
though they should have done it. *The Government has
tried to wriggle out of any responsibility for providing
childcare for working parents.*

wring /rɪŋ/ **wrings, wringing, wrung. 1** If you ◆◇◇◇
wring something out of someone, you manage to VERB
                                                       V n out of/

make them give it to you even though they do not want to. *Buyers use different ruses to wring free credit out of their suppliers.* **2** If someone **wrings** their **hands**, they hold them together and twist and turn them, usually because they are very worried or upset about something. You can also say that someone is **wringing** their **hands** when they are expressing sorrow that a situation is so bad but are saying that they are powerless to change it.

wring out. When you **wring out** a wet cloth or a wet piece of clothing, you squeeze the water out of it by twisting it strongly. *Soak a small towel in the liquid, wring it out, then apply to the abdomen.*

wrin·kle /ˈrɪŋkəl/ **wrinkles, wrinkling, wrinkled. 1** Wrinkles are lines which form on someone's face as they grow old. **2** When someone's skin **wrinkles** or when something **wrinkles** it, lines start to form in it because the skin is getting old or damaged. *...protection against the sun's rays that age and wrinkle the skin.* ♦ **wrinkled** *I did indeed look older and more wrinkled than ever.* **3** A wrinkle is a raised fold in something such as a piece of cloth or thin paper, usually one made unintentionally. *He noticed a wrinkle in her stocking.* **4** If something such as cloth **wrinkles**, or if someone or something **wrinkles** it, it gets folds or lines in it. *I wrinkled the velvet.* ♦ **wrinkled** *His suit was wrinkled and he looked very tired.* **5** When you **wrinkle** your nose or forehead, or when it **wrinkles**, you tighten the muscles in your face so that the skin folds. *Ellen's face wrinkles as if she is about to sneeze.*

wrin·kly /ˈrɪŋkli/ **wrinklies. 1** A wrinkly surface has a lot of wrinkles on it. *...wrinkly cotton and wool stockings.* **2** Young people sometimes refer to older people as **wrinklies**, especially when they are teasing them or making fun of the way they behave.

wrist /rɪst/ **wrists.** Your wrist is the part of your body between your hand and your arm which bends when you move your hand. See picture headed **human body.**

wrist·watch /ˈrɪstwɒtʃ/ **wristwatches.** A wristwatch is a watch with a strap which you wear round your wrist.

writ /rɪt/ **writs. 1** A writ is a legal document that orders a person to do a particular thing. *He issued a writ against one of his accusers.* **2** If you say that something is **writ large**, you mean that it is very obvious. *They now have to cope with the legacy of their past incompetence writ large on their balance sheets.* **3** If you say that one thing is another thing **writ large**, you mean that the first thing is a larger or more exaggerated version of the second thing. *Her life was her personality writ large.*

write /raɪt/ **writes, writing, wrote, written. 1** When you **write** something on a surface, you use something such as a pen or pencil to produce words, letters, or numbers on it. *They were still trying to teach her to read and write... He wrote the word 'fingerprints'.* **2** If you **write** something such as a book, a poem, an essay, or a piece of music, you create it and record it on paper or perhaps on a computer. *She wrote articles for papers and magazines in Paris... Jung Lu wrote me a poem once.* ♦ **writ·er, writers** *No-one is to see the document without the permission of the writer of the report.* **3** Someone who **writes** creates books, stories, or articles, usually for publication. *She writes for many papers, including the Sunday Times... He now works in industry and writes on science in his spare time.* ♦ **writer** *...detective stories by American writers.* **4** When you **write** to someone or **write** them a letter, you give them information, ask them something, or express your feelings in a letter. In American English, you can also **write** someone. *She had written him a note a couple of weeks earlier... I wrote a letter to the car rental agency, explaining what had happened... Why didn't you write, call, anything?.* **5** If someone **writes** that something is the case, they say it in a letter, book, or article. *'Some six months*

later,' Freud writes, 'Hans had got over his jealousy.'. **6** When someone **writes** something such as a cheque, receipt, or prescription, they put the necessary information on it and usually sign it. *I'll write you a cheque in a moment.* ▸ **Write out** means the same as **write**. *We went straight to the estate agent and wrote out a cheque... Get my wife to write you out a receipt before you leave.* **7** See also **writing, written.**

write back. If you **write back** to someone who has sent you a letter, you write them a letter in reply.

write down. When you **write** something **down**, you record it on a piece of paper using a pen or pencil. *On the morning before starting the fast, write down your starting weight.*

write in. 1 If you **write in** to an organization, you send them a letter. *What's the point in writing in when you only print half the letter anyway?* **2** If someone who is voting in an election **writes in** a person whose name is not on the list of candidates, they write that person's name on the voting paper and vote for him or her. *I'm going to write him in on my ballot next year.*

write into. If a rule or detail **is written into** a contract, law, or agreement, it is included in it when the contract, law, or agreement is made. *The President has encouraged companies to allow unpaid leave for workers with family emergencies, but has opposed writing it into the law.*

write off. 1 If you **write off** to a company or organization, you send them a letter, usually asking for something. *He wrote off to the New Zealand Government for these pamphlets.* **2** If someone **writes off** a debt or an amount of money that has been spent on a project, they accept that they are never going to get the money back. *He had long since written off the money.* **3** If you **write** someone or something **off**, you decide that they are unimportant or useless and that they are not worth further serious attention. *His critics write him off as too cautious to succeed... These people are difficult to write off as malingering employees.* **4** If you **write off** a plan or project, you accept that it is not going to be successful and do not continue with it. *The prices were much higher. So we decided to write that off... It's too soon to write off the whole consultation process as a failure.* **5** If someone **writes off** a vehicle, they have a crash in it and it is so badly damaged that it is not worth repairing. *One of Pete's friends wrote his car off there.* **6** See also **write-off.**

write out. 1 When you **write out** something fairly long such as a report or a list, you write it on paper. *If there's a particularly good recipe, write it out.* **2** If a character in a drama series **is written out**, he or she is taken out of the series. *When Angie was written out of 'Eastenders' her character went to Spain to open a bar... Maybe soon the scriptwriters will have to write her out of the series.* **3** See **write 6.**

write up. If you **write up** something that has been done or said, you record it on paper in a neat and complete form, usually using notes that you have made. *Mr Sadler conducted interviews, and his girlfriend wrote them up.* ● See also **write-up.**

write-off, write-offs. 1 Something such as a vehicle that is a **write-off** has been so badly damaged in an accident that it is not worth repairing. **2** A **write-off** is the decision by a company or government to accept that they will never recover a debt or an amount of money that has been spent on something. *...a large write-off of debt.* **3** If you describe a plan or period of time as a **write-off**, you mean that it has been a failure and you have achieved nothing. *Today was really a bit of a write-off for me.*

write-up, write-ups. A **write-up** is an article in a newspaper or magazine, in which someone gives their opinion of something such as a film, restaurant, or new product.

writhe /raɪð/ **writhes, writhing, writhed.** If you **writhe**, your body twists and turns violently backwards and forwards, usually because you are in

great pain or discomfort. *The shark was writhing around wildly, trying to get free.*

writ·ing /ˈraɪtɪŋ/ **writings. 1 Writing** is something ◆◆◆◆ that has been written or printed. *'It's from a note- N-UNCOUNT book,' the sheriff said, 'And there's writing on it.'... If you have a complaint about your holiday, please in- form us in writing.* **2** You can refer to any piece of N-UNCOUNT written work as **writing,** especially when you are considering the style of language used in it. *It was such a brilliant piece of writing.* **3 Writing** is the ac- N-UNCOUNT tivity of writing, especially of writing books for money. *She had begun to be a little bored with novel writing.* **4** Your **writing** is the way that you write N-UNCOUNT with a pen or pencil, which can usually be recog- nized as belonging to you. *It was a little difficult to read your writing.* **5** An author's **writings** are all the N-PLURAL things that he or she has written, especially on a particular subject. *Althusser's writings are focused mainly on France.* **6** If you say that **the writing is on** PHRASE **the wall,** you mean that there are clear signs that a situation is going to become very difficult or unpleasant.

writing paper, writing papers. Writing paper is N-VAR paper for writing letters on.

writ·ten /ˈrɪtən/. **1 Written** is the past participle of ◆◆◆◇◇ **write. 2** A **written** test or piece of work is one which ADJ involves writing rather than doing something prac- tical or giving spoken answers. **3** A **written** agree- ADJ: ADJ n ment, rule, or law has been officially written down. **4** ● **be written all over** someone's **face:** see **face.**

written 'word. You use the **written word** to refer N-SING to language expressed in writing.

wrong /rɒŋ, AM rɔːŋ/ **wrongs, wronging,** ◆◆◆◆ **wronged. 1** If you say there is something **wrong,** ADJ-GRADED: you mean there is something unsatisfactory about v-link ADJ the situation, person, or thing you are talking about. *Pain is the body's way of telling us that something is wrong. ... What's wrong with him?* **2** If something is ADJ: **wrong** or goes **wrong** with a machine or piece of v-link ADJ equipment, it stops working properly. *We think there's something wrong with the computer.* **3** If a PHRASE situation **goes wrong,** it stops progressing in the way that you expected or intended, and becomes much worse. *It all went horribly wrong.*

4 If you choose the **wrong** thing, person, or method, ADJ you make a mistake and do not choose the one that you really want. *The wrong man had been punished... There is no right or wrong way to do these exercises.* ▶ Also an adverb. *You've done it wrong... I must have* ADV: *dialed wrong.* **5** If something such as a decision, ADV after v choice, or action is the **wrong** one, it is not the best or ADJ: ADJ n most suitable one. *I really made the wrong decision there... We got married when I was 30 for all the wrong reasons.* **6** If something is **wrong,** it is incorrect and ADJ not in accordance with the facts. *20 per cent of the cal- culations are wrong. ...a clock which showed the wrong time.* ▶ Also an adverb. *I must have added it up* ADV: *wrong, then... It looks like it's spelled wrong.* ♦ **wrong-** ADV after v **·ly** *A child was wrongly diagnosed as having a bone tu-* ADV *mour.* **7** If you are **wrong** about something, what you ADJ: say or think about it is not correct. *I was wrong about* v-link ADJ *it being a casual meeting... Am I wrong in thinking that?* **8** You can use **wrong** in expressions such as **you** ADV: **thought wrong** and **you heard wrong** to tell someone ADV after v that what they thought or were told is incorrect, PRAGMATICS usually when you are annoyed. **9** You say **'Don't get** PHRASE **me wrong'** when you want to make sure that some- PRAGMATICS one does not misunderstand what you are doing or saying, or why you are doing or saying it. *I mean, don't*

get me wrong. Joanie's my best friend, but she can be kind of a pain sometimes.

10 If you think that someone was **wrong** to do some- ADJ-GRADED: thing, you think that they should not have done it be- ADJ to-inf cause it was bad or immoral. *She was wrong to leave her child alone... We don't consider we did anything wrong.* ▶ Also a noun. *...a man who believes that he* N-UNCOUNT *has done no wrong.* **11 Wrong** is used to refer to activ- ADJ-GRADED: ities or actions that are considered to be morally bad v-link ADJ and unacceptable. *Is it wrong to try to save the life of someone you love?... There is nothing wrong with jour- nalists commenting on the attractiveness of artists.* ▶ Also a noun. *Johnson didn't seem to be able to tell* N-UNCOUNT *the difference between right and wrong.* **12** A **wrong** is N-COUNT an unfair or immoral action. *I intend to right that wrong.* **13** If someone **wrongs** you, they treat you in VERB an unfair way. *You have wronged my mother.* **14** If V n someone who is involved in an argument or dispute PHRASE has behaved in a way which is morally or legally wrong, you can say that they are **in the wrong. 15** You ADJ: ADJ n use **wrong** to describe something which is not thought to be socially acceptable or desirable. *If you went to the wrong school, you won't get the job.* **16** ● **not far wrong:** see **far.** ● to not **put a foot wrong:** see **foot.** ● to **get the wrong end of the stick:** see **stick.** ● to **be barking up the wrong tree:** see **tree.**

wrong·doing /ˈrɒŋduːɪŋ, AM ˈrɔːŋ-/ **wrong-** ◆◇◇◇◇ **doings. Wrongdoing** is behaviour that is illegal or N-VAR immoral. *The city attorney's office hasn't found any evidence of criminal wrongdoing.* ♦ **wrong·doer,** N-COUNT **wrongdoers** *...a way to punish the wrongdoer.*

wrong-'foot, wrong-foots, wrong-footing, VERB **wrong-footed;** also spelled **wrong foot.** If you V n **wrong-foot** someone, you surprise them by putting BRITISH them into an unexpected or difficult situation. *He has surprised his supporters and wrong-footed his opponents with his latest announcement.* ● to not **put a foot wrong:** see **foot.**

wrong·ful /ˈrɒŋfʊl, AM ˈrɔːŋ-/. A **wrongful** act is ◆◇◇◇◇ one that is illegal, immoral, or unjust. *One of her* ADJ *employees sued her for wrongful dismissal.* ♦ **wrong·ful·ly** *...urgent reform to prevent more* ADV: *people being wrongfully imprisoned.* ADV with v

wrong-'headed. If you describe someone as ADJ-GRADED **wrong-headed,** you mean that although they act in a determined way, their actions and ideas are based on wrong judgements.

wrote /rəʊt/. **Wrote** is the past tense of **write.**

wrought /rɔːt/. **1** If something has **wrought** a VERB: change, it has made it happen. *Events in Paris* V n, *wrought a change in British opinion towards France.* only past **2** If something is **wrought** in a particular material LITERARY or in a particular way, it has been created in that ADJ material or way. *...finely wrought ironwork.* **3** See LITERARY also **wreak.**

wrought 'iron. Wrought iron is a pure type of ◆◇◇◇◇ iron that is formed into decorative shapes and used N-UNCOUNT especially for making gates and railings.

wrung /rʌŋ/. **Wrung** is the past tense of **wring.**

wry /raɪ/. **1** If someone has a **wry** expression, it ◆◇◇◇◇ shows that they find a bad or difficult situation ADJ-GRADED slightly amusing or ironic. ♦ **wry·ly** *She studied him* ADV-GRADED *for the longest time, looking wryly amused.* **2** A **wry** ADJ-GRADED remark or piece of writing refers to a bad or difficult situation in an amusing or ironic way. *There is a wry sense of humour in his work.* ♦ **wryly** *When asked if* ADV-GRADED *he would be visiting his family, Becker said wryly: 'I hope I don't have time.'*

wt. Wt is a written abbreviation for **weight.**

XYZ xyz

X, x /eks/ **X's, x's. 1** X is the twenty-fourth letter of N-VAR
the English alphabet. **2** When writing down the size
of something, you can use **x** in between the measurements to mean 'by'. *The conservatory measures
approximately 13ft x 16ft.* **3** X can be used to represent the name of a person or a number or amount
which is not known or is not important. *...Dr. X...
You can only make X amount of dollars a year.* **4** X
is used to represent a kiss at the end of a letter or
written message.

'X chromosome, X chromosomes. An X chro- N-COUNT
mosome is one of an identical pair of chromosomes
found in a woman's cells, or one of a non-identical
pair found in a man's cells. X chromosomes are associated with female characteristics. Compare **Y
chromosome.**

xeno·pho·bia /ˌzenəˈfəʊbiə/. Xenophobia is strong N-UNCOUNT
and unreasonable dislike or fear of people from oth-
er countries. ♦ **xeno·pho·bic** *Stalin was obsessively* ADJ-GRADED
xenophobic.

Xer·ox /ˈzɪərɒks/ **Xeroxes, Xeroxing, Xeroxed.** ◆◇◇◇◇
1 A Xerox is a machine that can make copies of N-COUNT
pieces of paper which have writing or other marks
on them. Xerox is a trademark. **2** If you **Xerox** a VERB: V n
document, you make a copy of it using a Xerox machine. ▶ Also a noun. *I had to make Xerox copies of* N-COUNT
the letters.

Xmas. Xmas is used in written English to represent INFORMAL
the word **Christmas.**

'X-ray, X-rays, X-raying, X-rayed. 1 An X-ray is ◆◆◇◇◇
a type of radiation that can pass through most solid N-COUNT
materials. X-rays are commonly used by doctors to
examine the bones or organs inside your body, and
at airports to see inside people's luggage. **2** An X- N-COUNT
ray is a picture made by sending X-rays through
something, usually someone's body. **3** If someone VERB:
or something **is X-rayed,** an x-ray picture is taken of beV-ed
them. *They took my pulse, took my blood pressure,* V n
and X-rayed my jaw.

xy·lo·phone /ˈzaɪləfəʊn/ **xylophones.** A xylo- N-COUNT
phone is a musical instrument which consists of a
row of wooden bars of different lengths. You play it
by hitting the bars with special hammers.

Y, y /waɪ/ **Y's, y's. 1** Y is the twenty-fifth letter of N-VAR
the English alphabet. **2** In American English, a N-SING:
YMCA or YWCA hostel is sometimes referred to as theN
the Y. INFORMAL

-y /-i/ **-ies, -ier, -iest. 1** -y is added to nouns in or- SUFFIX
der to form adjectives that describe something or
someone as having the characteristics of what the
noun refers to. *...a smoky pub... The process results
in a much fruitier wine.* **2** -y is added to colours in SUFFIX
order to form adjectives that describe something as
being roughly that colour or having some of that
colour in it. *Her eyes were the bluey-green colour
that often went with red hair.*

yacht /jɒt/ **yachts.** A yacht is a large boat with ◆◆◆◇◇
sails or a motor, used for racing or pleasure trips. N-COUNT

yacht·ing /ˈjɒtɪŋ/. Yachting is the sport or activity ◆◇◇◇◇
of sailing a yacht. N-UNCOUNT

yachts·man /ˈjɒtsmən/ **yachtsmen.** A yachts- ◆◇◇◇◇
man is a man who sails a yacht. N-COUNT

yachts·woman /ˈjɒtswʊmən/ **yachtswomen.** A N-COUNT
yachtswoman is a woman who sails a yacht.

yak /jæk/ ♦**yaks.** The plural can be either **yaks** or N-COUNT
yak. A yak is a type of cattle that has long hair and
long horns. Yaks live mainly in the Himalayan
mountains and in Tibet.

yam /jæm/ **yams.** A yam is a root vegetable which N-VAR
grows in tropical regions. It is similar to a potato in
appearance and texture.

yank /jæŋk/ **yanks, yanking, yanked.** If you ◆◇◇◇◇
yank someone or something somewhere, you pull VERB:
them there suddenly and with a lot of force. *She* V n prep
yanked open the drawer... A quick-thinking ticket in- V n with adj/
spector yanked an emergency cord. ▶ Also a noun. adv
Grabbing his ponytail, Shirley gave it a yank. V n
　　　　　　　　　　　　　　　　　　　　 Also V at n
　　　　　　　　　　　　　　　　　　　　 N-COUNT

Yank, Yanks. Some people refer to people from ◆◇◇◇◇
the United States of America as **Yanks;** a use which N-COUNT
many people find offensive. INFORMAL

Yan·kee /ˈjæŋki/ **Yankees. 1** A Yankee is a per- ◆◇◇◇◇
son from a northern or north-eastern state of the N-COUNT
United States. **2** Some people refer to anyone from AMERICAN
the United States as a **Yankee;** a use which many N-COUNT
people find offensive. INFORMAL

yap /jæp/ **yaps, yapping, yapped. 1** If a small VERB: V
dog **yaps,** it barks a lot with a high-pitched sound.
2 If you say that someone **yaps,** you mean that they VERB: V
talk continuously in an annoying way. *She keeps yap-* V at/about n
ping at me about Joe. INFORMAL

yard /jɑːd/ **yards. 1** A yard is a unit of length ◆◆◆◇◇
equal to thirty-six inches or approximately 91.4 cen- N-COUNT:
timetres. **2** A yard is a flat area of concrete or stone num N
that is next to a building and often has a wall N-COUNT
around it. **3** You can refer to a large open area N-COUNT
where a particular type of work is done as a **yard.**
...a ship repair yard. **4** A yard is a piece of land next N-COUNT
to someone's house where they grow flowers, veg- AMERICAN
etables, or other plants, and may have a lawn. The
usual British word is **garden.**

Yar·die /ˈjɑːdi/ **Yardies.** A Yardie is a member of a N-COUNT
secret criminal organization, based in Jamaica, BRITISH
which is especially associated with drug dealing.

'yard sale, yard sales. A yard sale is a sale where N-COUNT
people sell things they own and do not want from a AMERICAN
little stall or from the back of their car. The usual
British word is **car boot sale.**

yard·stick /ˈjɑːdstɪk/ **yardsticks.** If you use ◆◇◇◇◇
someone or something as a **yardstick,** you use them N-COUNT
as a standard for comparison when you are judging
other people or things. *The best yardstick was to
measure traffic against the 1990 figures.*

yarn /jɑːn/ **yarns. 1** Yarn is thread used for knit- ◆◇◇◇◇
ting or making cloth. N-VAR
2 A yarn is a story that someone tells, often a true sto- N-COUNT
ry with invented details which make it more interest-
ing. *Doug has a yarn or two to tell me about his trips
into the bush.* ● If you say that someone **spins a yarn,** PHRASE
you mean that they tell a story that is not true, often in
an interesting or inventive way.

yaw /jɔː/ **yaws, yawing, yawed.** If an aircraft or VERB: V
a ship **yaws,** it turns to one side so that it changes V prep/adv
the direction in which it is moving. *He spun the* TECHNICAL
steering-wheel so that we yawed from side to side.

yawn /jɔːn/ **yawns, yawning, yawned. 1** If you ◆◇◇◇◇
yawn, you open your mouth very wide and breathe VERB: V
in more air than usual, often when you are tired or
when you are not interested in something. ▶ Also a N-COUNT
noun. *Rosanna stifled a huge yawn.* **2** A gap or VERB: V
opening that **yawns** is large and wide, and often V adj
frightening. *Liddie's doorway yawned blackly open* LITERARY
at the end of the hall.

'Y chromosome, Y chromosomes. A Y chro- N-COUNT
mosome is the single chromosome in a man's cells
which will produce a male baby if it joins with an X
chromosome during the reproductive process. Y

chromosomes are associated with male characteristics. Compare **X chromosome**.

yd, yds. yd is a written abbreviation for **yard**. ...*200 yds further on.*

ye /jiː/. **1 Ye** is an old-fashioned or poetic word for **you** when you are talking to more than one person. **2 Ye** is sometimes used in imitation of an old written form of the word 'the'. ◆◇◇◇◇ PRON DET

yea /jeɪ/. **1 Yea** is an old-fashioned or poetic word for 'yes'. **2 Yea** is sometimes used to mean 'yes' when people are talking about voting for or giving their consent for something. *The House of Commons can merely say yea or nay to the executive judgment.* CONVENTION CONVENTION

yeah /jeə/. **Yeah** is used in written English to represent the way **yes** is pronounced in informal speech. *'Bring us something to drink.'—'Yeah, yeah.'* ◆◆◆◆◆ CONVENTION

year /jɪə/ **years. 1** A **year** is a period of twelve months or 365 or 366 days, beginning on the first of January and ending on the thirty-first of December. **2** A **year** is any period of twelve months. *The museums attract more than two and a half million visitors a year.* **3 Year** is used to refer to the age of a person. For example, if someone or something is twenty **years** old or twenty **years** of age, they have lived or existed for twenty years. **4** A school **year** is the period of time in each twelve months when the school is open and students are studying there. ...*the 1990/91 academic year.* **5** You can refer to someone who is, for example, in their first year at school or university as a first **year**. **6** A financial or business **year** is an exact period of twelve months which businesses or institutions use as a basis for organizing their finances. **7** See also **calendar year, fiscal year. 8** You can use **years** to emphasize that you are referring to a long time. *I haven't laughed so much in years.* **9** • **donkey's years**: see **donkey**. **10** You can refer to the time you spend in a place or doing an activity as your **years** there or your **years** of doing that activity. ...*his years as Director of the Manchester City Art Gallery.* **11** If something happens **year after year**, it happens regularly every year. **12** If something changes **year by year**, it changes gradually each year. **13** If something happens **year in, year out**, it happens every year without changing and is often boring. **14** If you do something happens **all year round** or **all the year round**, it happens continually throughout the year. ◆◆◆◆◆ N-COUNT N-COUNT N-COUNT: num N adj/ prep N-COUNT N-COUNT: ord N BRITISH N-COUNT: with supp N-PLURAL PRAGMATICS N-PLURAL: poss N PHRASE PHRASE PHRASE PHRASE

year·book /'jɪəbʊk/ **yearbooks.** A **yearbook** is a book that is published once a year and that contains information about the events and achievements of the previous year, usually concerning a particular place or organization. N-COUNT

year-'long. Year-long is used to describe something that lasts for a year. *The miners ended their year-long strike in March 1985.* ◆◇◇◇◇ ADJ: ADJ n

year·ly /'jɪəli/. **1** A **yearly** event happens once a year or every year. ▶ Also an adverb. *Clients normally pay fees in advance, monthly, quarterly, or yearly.* **2** You use **yearly** to describe something such as an amount that relates to a period of one year. ...*a yearly budget for health care.* ▶ Also an adverb. *Novello says college students will spend $4.2 billion yearly on alcoholic beverages.* ◆◇◇◇◇ ADJ: ADJ n ADV: ADV after v ADJ: ADJ n ADV: ADV after v

yearn /jɜːn/ **yearns, yearning, yearned.** If someone **yearns** for something that they are unlikely to get, they want it very much. *I yearned to be a movie actor.* VERB: V for n V to-inf

yearn·ing /'jɜːnɪŋ/ **yearnings.** A **yearning** for something is a very strong desire for it. N-VAR

-year-old -year-olds. -year-old combines with numbers to describe the age of people or things. *She has a six-year-old daughter.* ▶ Also combines to form nouns. ...*a ski school for 3- to 6-year-olds.* COMB COMB

year-'round. Year-round is used to describe something that happens, exists, or is done throughout the year. ...*a tropical climate with year-round sunshine.* ▶ Also an adverb. *They work 7 days a week year-round.* ◆◇◇◇◇ ADJ: ADJ n ADV: ADV with cl

yeast /jiːst/ **yeasts. Yeast** is a kind of fungus which is used to make bread rise, and in making alcoholic drinks such as beer. N-VAR

yeast 'extract, yeast extracts. Yeast extract is a brown sticky food that is obtained from yeast. It can be used in cooking or spread on bread. N-VAR

yell /jel/ **yells, yelling, yelled.** If you **yell**, you shout loudly, usually because you are excited, angry, or in pain. *'Eva!' he yelled... I'm sorry I yelled at you last night.* ▶ Also a noun. *He let out a yell.* ▶ **Yell out** means the same as **yell**. *'Are you coming or not?' they yelled out after him.* ◆◆◇◇◇ VERB: V with quote V at n N-COUNT PHRASAL VB V P

yel·low /'jeləʊ/ **yellows, yellowing, yellowed. 1** Something that is **yellow** is the colour of lemons or egg yolks. **2** If something **yellows**, it becomes yellow in colour, often because it is old. ◆◆◆◇◇ COLOUR VERB: V

yellow 'fever. Yellow fever is a serious infectious disease that people can catch in tropical countries. N-UNCOUNT

yel·low·ish /'jeləʊɪʃ/. Something that is **yellowish** is slightly yellow in colour. ▶ Also a combining form. ...*the yellowish brown smoke.* ADJ COMB

yellow 'pages. The **Yellow Pages** are a telephone directory or part of a directory, in which companies and people are listed and grouped according to the kind of business they are involved in. **Yellow Pages** is a trademark. N-PLURAL

yelp /jelp/ **yelps, yelping, yelped.** If a person or dog **yelps**, they give a sudden short cry, often because of fear or pain. ▶ Also a noun. ...*a yelp of pain.* VERB: V N-COUNT

yen /jen/; **yen** is both the singular and the plural form. **1** The **yen** is the unit of currency used in Japan. ▶ **The yen** is also used to refer to the Japanese currency system. **2** If you have a **yen** to do something, you have a strong desire to do it. *Mike had a yen to try cycling.* ◆◆◆◇◇ N-COUNT N-SING: the N N-SING

yeo·man /'jəʊmən/ **yeomen.** In former times, a **yeoman** was a man who was free and not a servant, and who cultivated his own land. N-COUNT

yes /jes/ **yeses. Yes** is used mainly in spoken English. In informal English, **yes** is often pronounced in a casual way that is usually written as **yeah**. **1** You use **yes** to give a positive response to a question. *'Are you a friend of Nick's?'—'Yes.'.* **2** You use **yes** to accept an offer or request, or to give permission. *'Can I ask you something?'—'Yes, of course.'* **3** You use **yes** to tell someone that what they have said is correct. *'That's a type of whitefly, is it?'—'Yes, it is a whitefly.'* **4** You use **yes** to show that you are ready or willing to speak to the person who wants to speak to you, for example when you are answering a telephone or doorbell. *Yes, can I help you?* **5** You use **yes** to indicate that you agree with, accept, or understand what the previous speaker has said. *'This is outrageous.'—'Yes, isn't it?'... 'It's a fabulous opportunity.'—'Yeah. I know.'* **6** You use **yes** to encourage someone to continue speaking. *'I remembered something funny today.'—'Yeah?'* **7** You use **yes** to indicate that you had forgotten something and have just remembered it. *What were we talking about. Oh yes, the number of people.* **8** You use **yes** as a polite way of introducing an objection to what the previous speaker has just said. *'She is entitled to her personal allowance which is three thousand pounds of income.'—'Yes, but she doesn't earn any money.'.* **9** You use **yes** to say that a negative statement or question that the previous speaker has made is wrong or untrue. *'I don't know what you're talking about.'—'Yes, you do.'* **10** You can use **yes** to suggest that you do not believe or agree with what the previous speaker has said, especially when you want to express your annoyance about it. *'There was no way to stop it.'—'Oh yes? Well, here's something else you won't be able to stop.'* **11** You use **yes** to emphasize and confirm a statement that you are making. *He collected the £10,000 first prize. Yes, £10,000.* **12** You say **yes and no** in reply to a question when you cannot give a definite answer, because in some ways the answer is yes and in other ways the answer is no. **13** A **yes** is a person who has ◆◆◆◆◆ CONVENTION PRAGMATICS CONVENTION PRAGMATICS CONVENTION PRAGMATICS CONVENTION CONVENTION PRAGMATICS CONVENTION PRAGMATICS CONVENTION PRAGMATICS CONVENTION CONVENTION PRAGMATICS CONVENTION PRAGMATICS CONVENTION PRAGMATICS CONVENTION PRAGMATICS CONVENTION PRAGMATICS N-COUNT

yes-man

answered 'yes' to a question or who has voted in favour of something, or the answer or vote they have made. *The no-votes are leading the yeses.*

'yes-man, yes-men. If you describe a man as a yes-man, you dislike the fact that he seems always to agree with people who have authority over him, in order to gain favour.

yes·ter·day /'jestədeɪ, -di/ **yesterdays.** **1** You use **yesterday** to refer to the day before today. ▶ Also a noun. *In yesterday's games, Switzerland beat the United States two-one.* **2** You can refer to the past, especially the recent past, as **yesterday**. *The worker of today is different from the worker of yesterday.*

yes·ter·year /'jestəjɪə/. You use **yesteryear** to refer to the past, often a period in the past with a set of values or a way of life that no longer exists. *...the old-fashioned hero of yesteryear.*

yet /jet/. **1** You use **yet** in negative statements to indicate that something has not happened up to the present time, although it probably will happen. You can also use **yet** in questions to ask if something has happened up to the present time. In British English the simple past tense is not normally used in this sense. *No decision has yet been made... 'Has the murderer been caught?' – 'Not yet.'.* **2** You use **yet** with a negative statement when you are talking about the past, to report something that was not the case then, although it became the case later. *He had asked around and learned that Billy was not yet here.* **3** If you say that something should not or cannot be done **yet**, you mean that it should not or cannot be done now, although it will have to be done at a later time. *Don't get up yet... We should not yet abandon this option.* **4** You use **yet** after a superlative to indicate, for example, that something is the worst or the best of its kind up to the present time. *...the BBC's worst idea yet. ...one of the toughest warnings yet delivered.* **5** You can use **yet** to say that there is still a possibility that something will happen. *A negotiated settlement might yet be possible.* **6** You can use **yet** after expressions which refer to a period of time, when you want to say how much longer a situation will continue for. *Unemployment will go on rising for some time yet.* **7** If you say that you have **yet** to do something, you mean that you have never done it, especially when this is surprising or bad. **8** You can use **yet** to introduce a fact which is rather surprising after the previous fact you have just mentioned. *I don't eat much, yet I am a size 16.* **9** You can use **yet** to emphasize a word, especially when you are saying that something is surprising because it is more extreme than previous things of its kind, or a further case of them. *I saw yet another doctor... They would criticize me, or worse yet, pay me no attention.* **10** You use **as yet** with negative statements to describe a situation that has existed up until the present time. *As yet it is not known whether the crash was the result of an accident.*

yew /juː/ **yews.** A **yew** or a **yew tree** is an evergreen tree which has sharp, broad, flat leaves. ▶ **Yew** is the wood of this tree.

'Y-fronts. **Y-fronts** are men's or boys' underpants which have an opening at the front. **Y-fronts** is a trademark.

yield /jiːld/ **yields, yielding, yielded.** **1** If you **yield** to someone or something, you stop resisting them. *I yielded to an impulse... Gessler was the first to yield, announcing his resignation in January.* **2** If you **yield** something that you have control of or responsibility for, you allow someone else to have control or responsibility for it. *The President is now under pressure to yield power to the republics.* ▶ **Yield up** means the same as **yield**. *Giulio Andreotti yielded up the prime ministership last summer.* **3** If one thing **yields** to another thing, it is replaced by this other thing. *Boston's traditional drab brick was slow to yield to the modern glass palaces of so many American urban areas.*

4 If a moving person or a vehicle or its driver **yields**, they slow down or stop in order to allow other people or vehicles to pass in front of them. The usual British expression is **give way**. *When entering a trail or starting a descent, yield to other skiers.* **5** If something **yields**, it breaks or moves position because force or pressure has been put on it. *He reached the massive door of the barn and pushed. It yielded.* **6** If an area of land or a number of animals **yields** a particular amount of food or plants, this amount of food or plants is produced by the land or animals. ▶ **Yield up** means the same as **yield**. *The shallow sea bed yields up an abundance of food.* **7** A **yield** is the amount of food produced on an area of land or by a number of animals. *Polluted water lessens crop yields.* **8** If a tax or investment **yields** an amount of money or profit, this money or profit is obtained from it. *It yielded a profit of at least $36 million.* **9** A **yield** is the amount of money or profit produced by an investment. *...a yield of 4%.* **10** If something **yields** a result or piece of information, it produces it. *His trip to Melbourne had yielded a lot of information.*

yield up. See **yield** 2, 6.

yield·ing /'jiːldɪŋ/. A **yielding** surface or object is quite soft and will move or bend rather than staying stiff if you put pressure on it.

YMCA /ˌwaɪ em siː 'eɪ/ **YMCAs.** A **YMCA** is a hostel where men can stay, run by the YMCA organization. YMCA is an abbreviation for 'Young Men's Christian Association'.

yob /jɒb/ **yobs.** If you call a boy or a man a **yob**, you disapprove of him because he behaves in a noisy, bad-mannered, and perhaps violent way in public.

yob·bo /'jɒbəʊ/ **yobbos.** A **yobbo** is the same as a **yob**.

yo·del /'jəʊdəl/ **yodels, yodelling, yodelled;** spelled **yodeling, yodeled** in American English. When someone **yodels**, they sing normal notes with very high quick notes in between. ◆ **yo·del·ling** *Switzerland isn't all cow bells and yodelling.*

yoga /'jəʊgə/. **1** Yoga is a type of exercise in which you move your body into various positions in order to become more fit or flexible. **2** Yoga is a philosophy which first developed in India, in which physical exercises and meditation are believed to help people to become calmer and gradually united in spirit with a Supreme Being.

yo·gurt /'jɒgət, AM 'jəʊ-/ **yogurts;** also spelled **yoghurt.** Yogurt is a food in the form of a thick, slightly sour liquid that is made by adding bacteria to milk. A **yogurt** is a small pot of yogurt.

yoke /jəʊk/ **yokes, yoking, yoked.** **1** If you say that people are under the **yoke** of a bad thing or person, you mean they are forced to live in a difficult or unhappy state because of that thing or person. *People are still suffering under the yoke of slavery.* **2** If two or more people or things **are yoked** together, they are forced to be closely linked with each other. *The Auto Pact signed in 1965 yoked Ontario into the United States economy.*

yo·kel /'jəʊkəl/ **yokels.** If you refer to someone as a **yokel**, you think they are uneducated and stupid because they come from the countryside.

yolk /jəʊk/ **yolks.** The **yolk** of an egg is the yellow part in the middle.

Yom Kip·pur /ˌjɒm kɪ'pʊə/. Yom Kippur is a Jewish holiday which is a day of fasting and prayers of repentance. It is in September or October.

yon /jɒn/. **Yon** means 'that' or 'those'; an old-fashioned word or a word that is used in some dialects of English.

yon·der /'jɒndə/. **Yonder** means over there; an old-fashioned word or a word which is used in some dialects of English. *Now look yonder, just beyond the wooden post there.* ▶ Also a determiner. *His wife, Claudia, lies under yonder tree.*

yonks /jɒŋks/. You can use **yonks** to mean a very long time. *He's been here for yonks. Everyone knows him.*

yore /jɔː/. Of yore is used to refer to a period of time in the past. *The images provoked strong surges of nostalgia for the days of yore.* PHRASE JOURNALISM, LITERARY

York·shire pud·ding /ˌjɔːkʃə 'pʊdɪŋ/ **Yorkshire puddings.** Yorkshire pudding is a British food which is made by baking a thick mixture of flour, milk, and eggs. It is often eaten with roast beef. N-VAR

you /juː/ **yous.** You is the second person pronoun. You can refer to one or more people and is used as the subject of a verb or the object of a verb or preposition. ◆◆◆◆◆

1 A speaker or writer uses **you** to refer to the person or people that he or she is talking or writing to. You can use **you** before a noun to make it clear which group of people you are referring to. *When I saw you across the room I knew I'd met you before... What you kids need is more exercise.* **2** A speaker or writer sometimes uses **you** to refer to people in general. *'I didn't want to go into nursing,' she said, 'but my dad told me to, and in those days you did what you were told.'* **3** In some dialects of English, **yous** is sometimes used instead of 'you' when talking to two or more people. *'Yous two are no' gettin' paid,' he said. 'Ye're too lazy!'* PRON / PRON / PRON

you'd /juːd/. **1** You'd is the usual spoken form of 'you had', especially when 'had' is an auxiliary verb. **2** You'd is the usual spoken form of 'you would'.

you'll /juːl/. You'll is the usual spoken form of 'you will'.

young /jʌŋ/ **younger** /ˈjʌŋɡə/ **youngest** /ˈjʌŋɡəst/. **1** A young person, animal, or plant has not lived or existed for very long and is not yet mature. *In Scotland, young people can marry at 16... He played with his younger brother.* ► The young are people who are young. **2** You use **young** to describe a time when a person or thing was young. *In her younger days my mother had been a successful fashionwear saleswoman.* **3** Someone who is **young** in appearance or behaviour looks or behaves as if they are young. *I was twenty-three, I suppose, and young for my age.* **4** The **young** of an animal are its babies. *The hen may not be able to feed its young.* ◆◆◆◆◆ ADJ-GRADED / N-PLURAL: the N / ADJ-GRADED: ADJ n / ADJ-GRADED / N-PLURAL

young·ish /ˈjʌŋɪʃ/. If you describe someone as **youngish**, you mean they are fairly young. *...a smart, dark-haired, youngish man.* ADJ

young·ster /ˈjʌŋstə/ **youngsters.** Young people, especially children, are sometimes referred to as **youngsters**. ◆◆◆◇◇ N-COUNT

your /jɔː, jʊə/. Your is the second person possessive determiner. Your can be used to refer to one or more people. ◆◆◆◆◆

1 A speaker or writer uses **your** to indicate that something belongs or relates to the person or people that he or she is talking or writing to. *Emma, I trust your opinion a great deal... I left all of your messages on your desk.* **2** A speaker or writer sometimes uses **your** to indicate that something belongs to or relates to people in general. *Pain-killers are very useful in small amounts to bring your temperature down.* **3** A speaker sometimes uses **your** before an adjective such as 'typical' or 'normal' to indicate that the thing referred to is a typical example of its type. *Stan Reilly is not really one of your typical Brighton Boys.* DET-POSS / DET-POSS / DET-POSS SPOKEN

you're /jɔː, jʊə/. You're is the usual spoken form of 'you are'.

yours /jɔːz, jʊəz/. Yours is the second person possessive pronoun. Yours can refer to one or more people. ◆◆◆◇◇

1 A speaker or writer uses **yours** to refer to something that belongs or relates to the person or people that he or she is talking or writing to. *I'll take my coat upstairs. Shall I take yours, Roberta?... I believe Paul was a friend of yours.* **2** People write **yours**, **yours sincerely**, or **yours faithfully** at the end of a letter before they sign their name. *With best regards, Yours, George... Yours faithfully, Michael Moore, London Business School.* • **yours truly** see **truly**. PRON-POSS / CONVENTION

your·self /jɔːˈself, jʊə-/ **yourselves.** Yourself is the second person reflexive pronoun. ◆◆◆◇

1 A speaker or writer uses **yourself** to refer to the person that he or she is talking or writing to. Yourself is PRON-REFL: v PRON, prep PRON

used when the object of a verb or preposition refers to the same person as the subject of the verb. *Have the courage to be honest with yourself... Treat yourselves to a glass of wine to help you relax.* **2** You use **yourself** to emphasize the person that you are referring to. *They mean to share the business between them, after you yourself are gone.* **3** You use **yourself** instead of 'you' for emphasis or in order to be more polite when 'you' is the object of a verb or preposition. *A wealthy man like yourself is bound to make an enemy or two along the way.* • **by yourself:** see **by**. PRON-REFL PRAGMATICS / PRON-REFL: v PRON, prep PRON PRAGMATICS

youth /juːθ/ **youths** /juːðz/. **1** Someone's **youth** is the period of their life during which they are a child, before they are a fully mature adult. *In my youth my ambition had been to be an inventor.* **2** Youth is the quality or state of being young and perhaps immature and inexperienced. *The team is now a good mixture of experience and youth.* **3** Journalists often refer to young men as **youths**, especially when they are reporting that the young men have caused trouble. *...gangs of youths who broke windows and looted shops.* **4** The **youth** are young people considered as a group. *He represents the opinions of the youth of today.* ◆◆◆◇ N-UNCOUNT / N-UNCOUNT / N-COUNT / N-PLURAL

youth club, youth clubs. A youth club is a club, often run by a church or local authority, where young people can go to meet and take part in various activities. N-COUNT

youth·ful /ˈjuːθfʊl/. Someone who is **youthful** behaves as if they are young or younger than they really are. *I'm a very youthful 50. ...youthful enthusiasm and high spirits.* ♦ **youth·ful·ness** *His youthfulness was as striking as hers.* ◆◇◇◇◇ ADJ-GRADED / N-UNCOUNT

youth hostel, youth hostels. A youth hostel is a place where young people can stay cheaply when they are travelling. N-COUNT

youth worker, youth workers. A youth worker is a person whose job involves providing support and social activities for young people, especially young people from underprivileged backgrounds. N-COUNT BRITISH

you've /juːv/. You've is the usual spoken form of 'you have', especially when 'have' is an auxiliary verb.

yowl /jaʊl/ **yowls, yowling, yowled.** If a person or an animal **yowls**, they make a loud wailing noise. ► Also a noun. *Patsy could hardly be heard above the baby's yowls.* ♦ **yowl·ing** *I couldn't stand that yowling.* VERB: V / N-COUNT / N-UNCOUNT

yo-yo /ˈjəʊ jəʊ/ **yo-yos.** A yo-yo is a toy made of a round piece of wood or plastic attached to a piece of string. You play with the yo-yo by letting it rise and fall on the string. ◆◇◇◇◇ N-COUNT

yr, yrs. yr is a written abbreviation for **year**.

yuan /juːˈæn, AM -ˈɑːn/. Yuan is both the singular and the plural form. The **yuan** is the unit of money used in the People's Republic of China. ► The yuan is also used to refer to the Chinese currency system. *The yuan recovered a little; it now hovers around 8.2 to the dollar.* N-COUNT / num N / N-SING: the N

yuk /jʌk/. Some people say **'yuk'** when they think something is very unpleasant or disgusting. EXCLAM INFORMAL

Yule /juːl/. Yule is an old-fashioned word for **Christmas**. N-UNCOUNT

Yule·tide /ˈjuːltaɪd/. Yuletide is the period of several days around and including Christmas Day. N-UNCOUNT

yum /jʌm/. People sometimes say **'yum'** or **'yum yum'** to show that they think something tastes or smells very good. EXCLAM INFORMAL

yum·my /ˈjʌmi/. Yummy means delicious. *It smells yummy.* ADJ-GRADED INFORMAL

yup·pie /ˈjʌpi/ **yuppies.** A yuppie is a young middle-class person with a well-paid job, who likes to show that they have a lot of money by buying expensive things and doing expensive activities; used showing disapproval. ◆◇◇◇◇ N-COUNT PRAGMATICS

YWCA /ˌwaɪ dʌbəljuː siː 'eɪ/ **YWCAs.** A YWCA is a hostel where women can stay run by the YWCA organization. YWCA is an abbreviation for 'Young Women's Christian Association'. N-COUNT

Z, z /zed, AM ziː/ **Z's, z's.** Z is the twenty-sixth and last letter of the English alphabet. N-VAR

zany /ˈzeɪni/ **zanier, zaniest. Zany** humour or a ADJ-GRADED
zany person is odd or eccentric in an amusing way. INFORMAL

zap /zæp/ **zaps, zapping, zapped. 1** To **zap** ◆◇◇◇
someone or something means to kill, destroy, or hit VERB
them, usually using a gun, spray, or laser. *A guard* V n
zapped him with the stun gun. **2** If you **zap** chan- INFORMAL
nels while watching television, you change channels VERB: V n
using the remote control. INFORMAL

zeal /ziːl/. **Zeal** is great enthusiasm, especially in ◆◇◇◇
connection with work, religion, or politics. *Mr Lopez* N-UNCOUNT
approached his task with a religious zeal.

zeal·ot /ˈzelət/ **zealots.** If you describe someone as N-COUNT
a **zealot**, you think that their views and actions are PRAGMATICS
extreme or fanatical, especially in following a political or religious ideal.

zeal·ous /ˈzeləs/. Someone who is **zealous** spends ◆◇◇◇
a lot of time or energy in supporting something that ADJ-GRADED
they believe in very strongly, especially a political or
religious ideal. ♦ **zeal·ous·ly** *Details of its past ac-* ADV-GRADED
tivities were zealously guarded.

zeb·ra /ˈzebrə, ˈziː-/ **zebras.** The plural can be ◆◇◇◇
either **zebras** or **zebra**. A **zebra** is an African wild N-COUNT
horse which has black and white stripes. See picture
headed **animals**.

zebra 'crossing, zebra crossings. In Britain, a N-COUNT
zebra crossing is a place on the road that is marked
with black and white stripes, where vehicles are
supposed to stop so that people can walk across.

zeit·geist /ˈzaɪtgaɪst/. The **zeitgeist** of a particular N-SING
place during a particular period in history is the attitudes and ideas that are generally common there
at that time, especially the attitudes and ideas
shown in literature, philosophy, and politics.

Zen /zen/. **Zen** or **Zen Buddhism** is a form of the ◆◇◇◇
Buddhist religion that concentrates on meditation N-UNCOUNT
rather than on studying religious writings.

zen·ith /ˈzenɪθ, AM ˈziː-/. The **zenith** of something is N-SING
the time when it is most successful or powerful. *His*
career is now at its zenith.

zero /ˈzɪərəʊ/ **zeros** or **zeroes, zeroing, ze-** ◆◆◇◇
roed. 1 Zero is the number 0. See Appendix Num- NUMBER
bered **Numbers. 2 Zero** is freezing point on the Centi- N-UNCOUNT
grade scale. It is often written as 0°C. *That night the*
mercury fell to thirty degrees below zero. **3** You can ADJ
use **zero** to say that there is none at all of the thing
mentioned. *...zero inflation... His chances are zero.*

zero in on. 1 To **zero in on** a target means to aim at PHRASAL VB
it or move towards it. *The bees were zeroing in on those* V P P n
pears. **2** If you **zero in on** a problem or subject, you V P P n
give it your full attention.

zero-'sum game. If you refer to a situation as a N-SING
zero-sum game, you mean that if one person gains
an advantage from it, someone else involved must
suffer an equivalent disadvantage.

zest /zest/ **zests. 1 Zest** is a feeling of pleasure ◆◇◇◇
and enthusiasm. *...a lovable girl with a zest for life.* N-UNCOUNT:
2 Zest is a quality in an activity or situation which also a N
you find exciting. *Live interviews add zest and a* N-UNCOUNT
touch of the unexpected to any piece of research.
3 The **zest** of a lemon, orange, or lime is the rind when N-UNCOUNT:
it is grated to give flavour to something. also N in pl

zig·zag /ˈzɪɡzæɡ/ **zigzags, zigzagging, zig-**
zagged; also spelled **zig-zag. 1** A **zigzag** is a line N-COUNT
which has a series of angles in it like a continuous
series of 'W's. *They staggered in a zigzag across the*
tarmac. **2** If you **zigzag**, you move forward by going VERB: V
at an angle first to one side then to the other. *I zig-* V prep
zagged down a labyrinth of alleys... Expertly he zig- V way prep
zagged his way across the field.

zilch /zɪltʃ/. **Zilch** means nothing. *At the moment* PRON-INDEF
these shares are worth zilch.

zil·lion /ˈzɪljən/ **zillions.** If you talk about a **zillion** NUMBER
people or things you are emphasizing that there is PRAGMATICS
an extremely large number of them. ▶ Also a quan- INFORMAL
tifier. *There are zillions of things to look at or try out.* QUANT

Zim·mer frame /ˈzɪmə freɪm/ **Zimmer frames.** A N-COUNT
Zimmer frame or a **Zimmer** is a frame that old or ill BRITISH
people sometimes use to help them walk. **Zimmer**
is a trademark.

zinc /zɪŋk/. **Zinc** is a bluish-white metal which is ◆◆◇◇
used to make other metals such as brass or to cover N-UNCOUNT
other metals such as iron to stop them rusting.

zing /zɪŋ/. If you refer to the **zing** in someone or N-UNCOUNT:
something, you mean the quality that makes them also a N
lively or interesting. *He just lacked that extra zing.* INFORMAL

zip /zɪp/ **zips, zipping, zipped. 1** A **zip** or **zip fas-** ◆◇◇◇
tener is a device used to open and close parts of N-COUNT
clothes and bags. It consists of two rows of metal or BRITISH
plastic teeth which separate or fasten together as
you pull a small tag along them. The usual Ameri-
can word is **zipper. 2** When you **zip** something, you VERB: V n
fasten it using a zip. ▶ **Zip up** means the same as PHRASAL VB
zip. *He zipped up his jeans.* Also V n P
3 If you say that something or someone **zips** some- VERB
where, you mean that they move there very quickly. V prep/adv
My craft zipped across the bay. **4** If you say that some- INFORMAL
one or something has **zip**, you mean that they show a N-UNCOUNT
lot of energy and enthusiasm. *Tommy Tune gives the* INFORMAL
choreography his usual class and zip.

zip up. See **zip** 2. PHRASAL VB

'zip code, zip codes. Your **zip code** is a short se- N-COUNT
quence of letters and numbers at the end of your AMERICAN
address, which helps the post office to sort your mail.
The British term is **postcode.**

zip·per /ˈzɪpə/ **zippers.** A **zipper** is the same as a N-COUNT
zip. AMERICAN

'zip-up. A **zip-up** bag or jacket, for example, is fas- ADJ: ADJ n
tened by a zip. *...a brown leather zip-up jacket.*

zit /zɪt/ **zits.** Zits are spots or pimples on the skin. N-COUNT

zo·di·ac /ˈzəʊdiæk/. The **zodiac** is a diagram used ◆◇◇◇
by astrologers to represent the positions of the N-SING:
planets and stars and to calculate their influence. It the N
is divided into twelve sections, each with a special
name and symbol.

zom·bie /ˈzɒmbi/ **zombies. 1** You can describe N-COUNT
someone as a **zombie** if their face or behaviour
shows no feeling, understanding, or interest in what
is going on around them. *Without sleep you will be-*
come a zombie at work. **2** In horror stories and N-COUNT
some religions, a **zombie** is a dead person who has
been brought back to life.

zone /zəʊn/ **zones, zoning, zoned. 1** A **zone** is ◆◆◇◇
an area that has particular features or characteris- N-COUNT
tics. *Many people have stayed behind in the poten-*
tial war zone... The area has been declared a disaster
zone. **2** If an area of land **is zoned**, it is formally set VB: usu
aside for a particular purpose. *The land was not* passive
zoned for commercial purposes. ♦ **zon·ing** *...the use* be V-ed
of zoning to preserve agricultural land. N-UNCOUNT

zonked /zɒŋkt/. If someone is **zonked** or **zonked** ADJ-GRADED
out, they are not capable of doing anything because INFORMAL
they are very tired, drunk, or drugged.

zoo /zuː/ **zoos.** A **zoo** is a park where live animals ◆◆◇◇
are kept so that people can look at them. N-COUNT

zo·ol·ogy /zuːˈɒlədʒi, zəʊ-/. **Zoology** is the N-UNCOUNT
scientific study of animals. *...the Cambridge Mu-*
seum of Zoology. ♦ **zoo·logi·cal** *...zoological speci-* ADJ: ADJ n
mens. ♦ **zo·olo·gist** /zuːˈɒlədʒɪst, zəʊ-/ **zoolo-** N-COUNT
gists *...a renowned zoologist and writer.*

zoom /zuːm/ **zooms, zooming, zoomed. 1** If ◆◆◇◇
you **zoom** somewhere, you go there very quickly. V prep/adv
We zoomed through the gallery. **2** If prices or sales VERB: V
zoom, they increase greatly in a very short time.
3 A **zoom** is the same as a **zoom lens.**

zoom in. If a camera **zooms in** on something that is PHRASAL VB
being filmed or photographed, it gives a close-up pic- V P on n
ture of it. *...a tracking system which can follow a bur-* Also V P
glar round a building and zoom in on his face.

zoom off. If you **zoom off**, you leave very quickly. PHRASAL VB
The bikers zoomed off. V P
INFORMAL

'zoom lens, zoom lenses. A **zoom lens** is a lens N-COUNT
that you can attach to a camera, which allows you
to make the details larger or smaller while always
keeping the picture clear.

zuc·chi·ni /zuːˈkiːni/ **zucchinis.** The plural can be N-VAR
either **zucchini** or **zucchinis. Zucchini** are long thin AMERICAN
green vegetables of the marrow family. The British
word is **courgette.** See picture headed **vegetables.**

X

Human Body

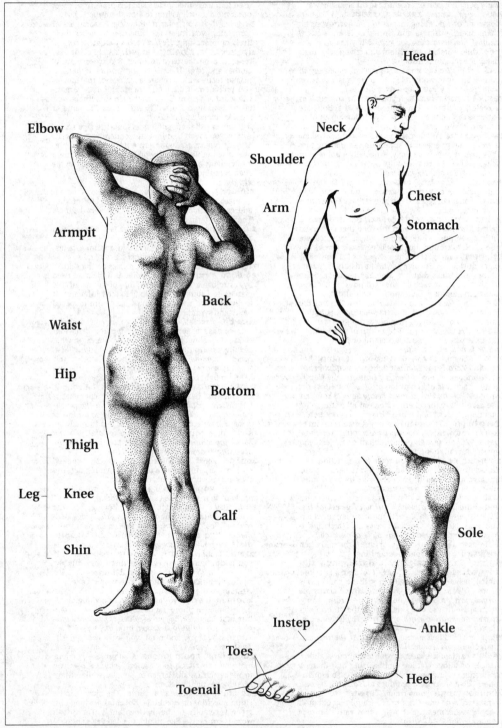

Head

Neck

Shoulder

Arm

Chest

Stomach

Elbow

Armpit

Waist

Hip

Back

Bottom

Thigh

Leg — Knee

Calf

Shin

Sole

Instep

Ankle

Toes

Heel

Toenail

Human Body

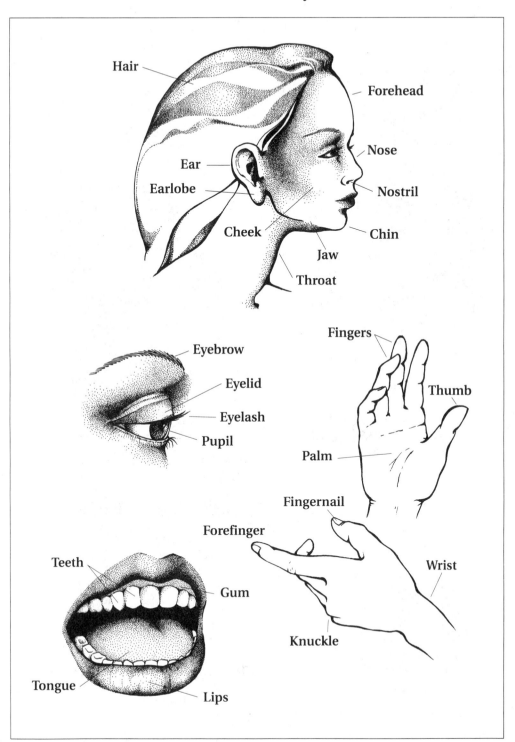

Clothes

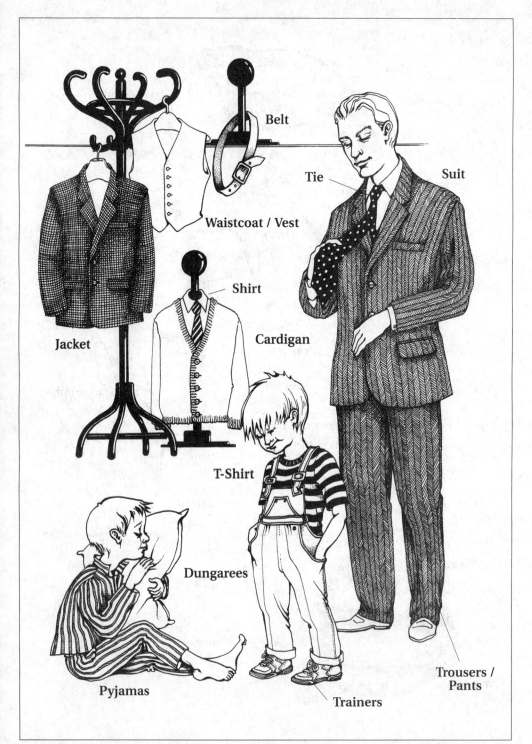

Belt

Tie

Suit

Waistcoat / Vest

Shirt

Jacket

Cardigan

T-Shirt

Dungarees

Trousers / Pants

Pyjamas

Trainers

Clothes

Hat

Beret

Gloves

Scarf

Coat

Blouse

Pullover

Pinafore / Jumper

Skirt

Bra

Dress

Pants / Panties

Boots

Shoes

Socks

Vest

House and Flat

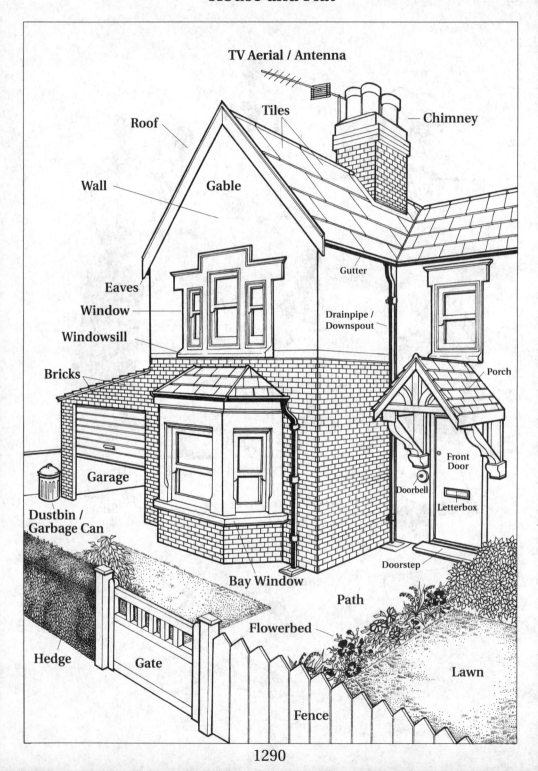

TV Aerial / Antenna

Tiles

Chimney

Roof

Wall

Gable

Eaves

Window

Windowsill

Bricks

Gutter

Drainpipe / Downspout

Porch

Front Door

Doorbell

Letterbox

Garage

Dustbin / Garbage Can

Bay Window

Doorstep

Path

Flowerbed

Lawn

Hedge

Gate

Fence

House and Flat

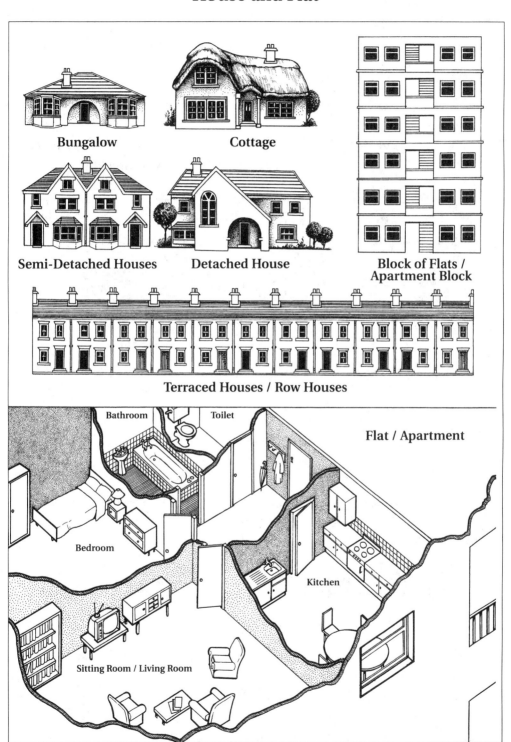

Bungalow

Cottage

Semi-Detached Houses

Detached House

Block of Flats / Apartment Block

Terraced Houses / Row Houses

Flat / Apartment

Bathroom

Toilet

Bedroom

Kitchen

Sitting Room / Living Room

Car and Bicycle

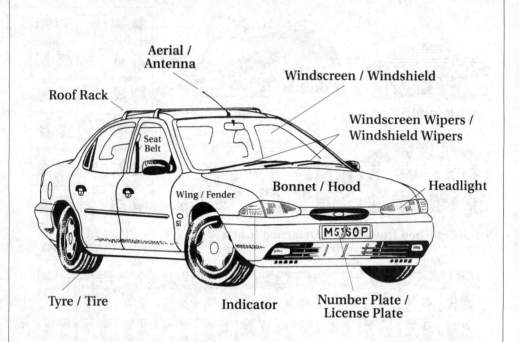

Aerial / Antenna

Windscreen / Windshield

Roof Rack

Windscreen Wipers / Windshield Wipers

Seat Belt

Bonnet / Hood

Headlight

Wing / Fender

Tyre / Tire

Indicator

Number Plate / License Plate

M5 SOP

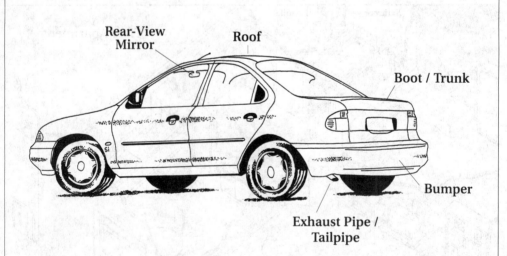

Rear-View Mirror

Roof

Boot / Trunk

Bumper

Exhaust Pipe / Tailpipe

1292

Car and Bicycle

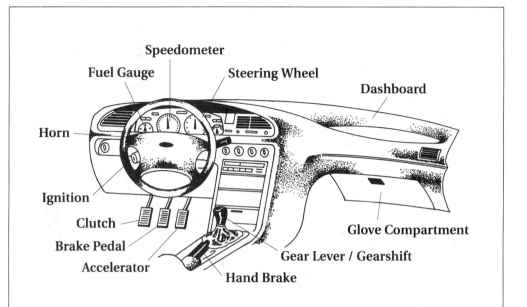

Speedometer

Fuel Gauge

Steering Wheel

Dashboard

Horn

Ignition

Clutch

Brake Pedal

Accelerator

Hand Brake

Gear Lever / Gearshift

Glove Compartment

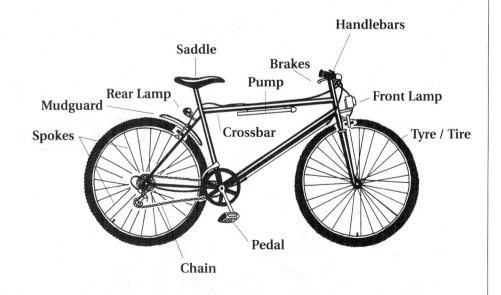

Handlebars

Saddle

Brakes

Pump

Rear Lamp

Mudguard

Front Lamp

Spokes

Crossbar

Tyre / Tire

Pedal

Chain

Tools

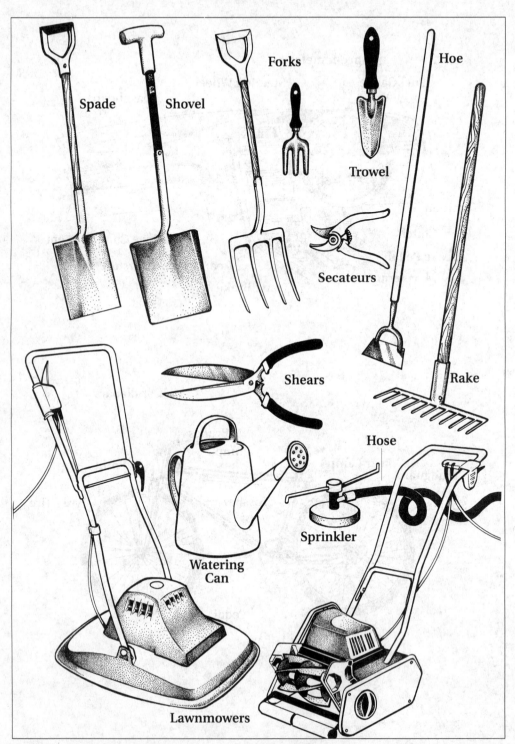

Spade

Shovel

Forks

Trowel

Hoe

Secateurs

Shears

Rake

Hose

Watering Can

Sprinkler

Lawnmowers

Tools

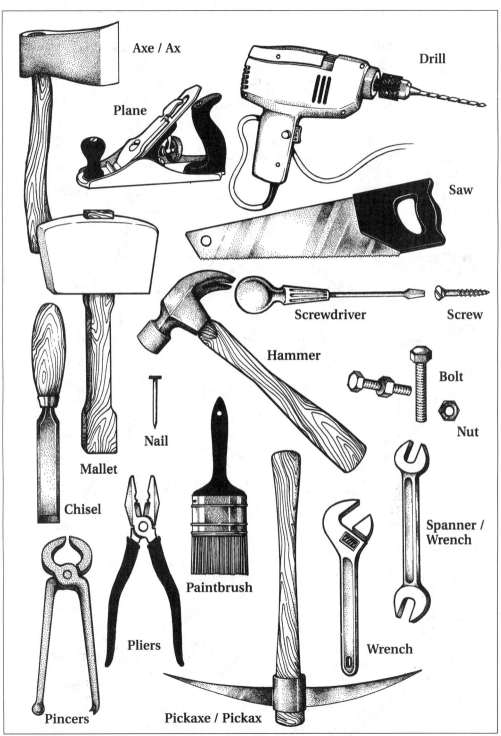

Axe / Ax

Plane

Drill

Saw

Screwdriver

Screw

Hammer

Bolt

Nut

Nail

Mallet

Chisel

Pliers

Paintbrush

Spanner / Wrench

Wrench

Pincers

Pickaxe / Pickax

Kitchen Utensils

Whisk

Spatula

Fork

Spoon

Funnel

Corkscrew

Potato Peeler

Ladle

Saucepan

Pressure Cooker

Frying Pan

Sieve

Bowl

Fish Slice

Grater

Knives

Tin Opener

Scissors

Insects

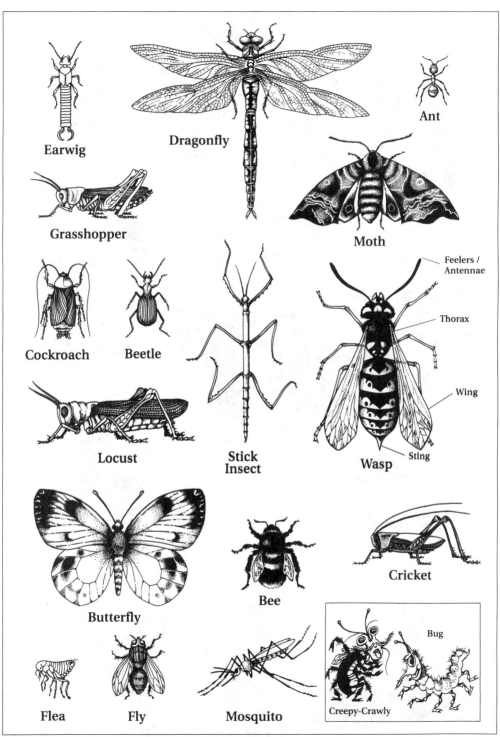

Earwig

Dragonfly

Ant

Grasshopper

Moth

Cockroach

Beetle

Locust

Stick Insect

Feelers / Antennae

Thorax

Wing

Sting

Wasp

Butterfly

Bee

Cricket

Flea

Fly

Mosquito

Bug

Creepy-Crawly

Animals

Donkey

Goat

Goose

Duck

Pig

Horse

Bull

Cow

Sheep

Dogs

Cats

Chicken

Rooster

Animals

Buffalo

Bear

Zebra

Camel

Elephant

Cheetah

Lion

Panther

Lioness

Leopard

Tiger

Gorilla

Giraffe

Chimpanzee

Rhinoceros

Anteater

Hippopotamus

Fruit

Pineapple

Pear

Melon

Banana

Plums

Apple

Strawberries

Peach

Grapes

Raspberries

Lemon

Kiwi Fruit

Cherries

Orange

Segment

Nectarine

Vegetables

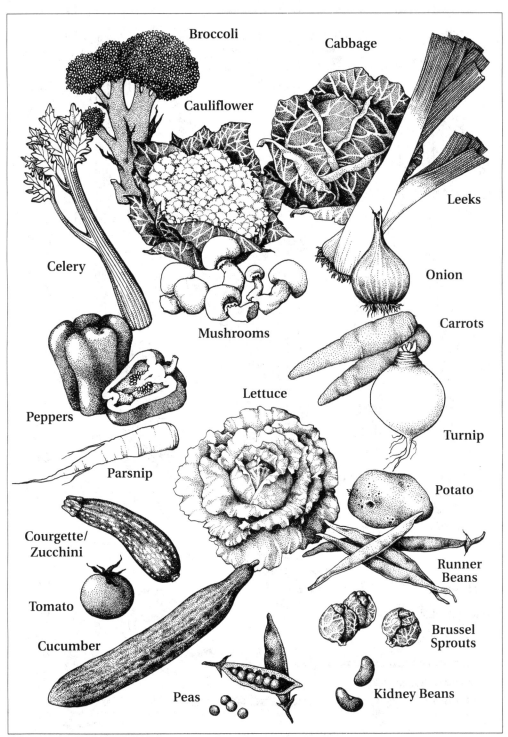

Broccoli

Cabbage

Cauliflower

Celery

Leeks

Mushrooms

Onion

Peppers

Carrots

Lettuce

Turnip

Parsnip

Potato

Courgette/
Zucchini

Runner
Beans

Tomato

Cucumber

Brussel
Sprouts

Peas

Kidney Beans

Musical Instruments

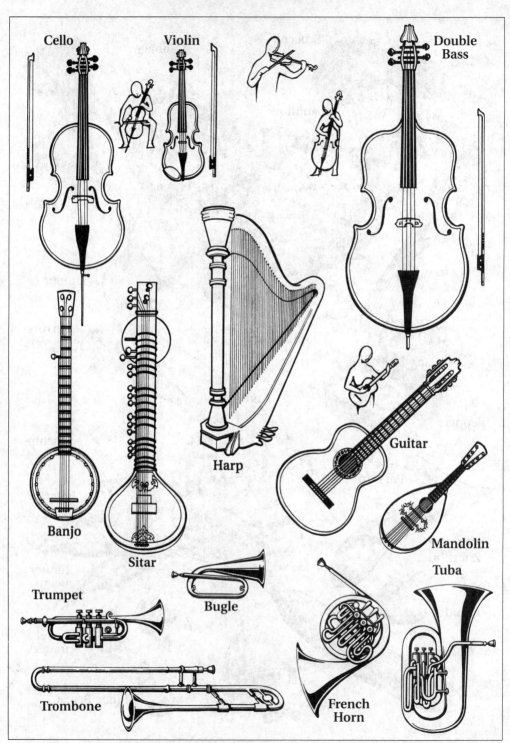

Cello

Violin

Double Bass

Harp

Guitar

Banjo

Sitar

Mandolin

Tuba

Trumpet

Bugle

French Horn

Trombone

Musical Instruments

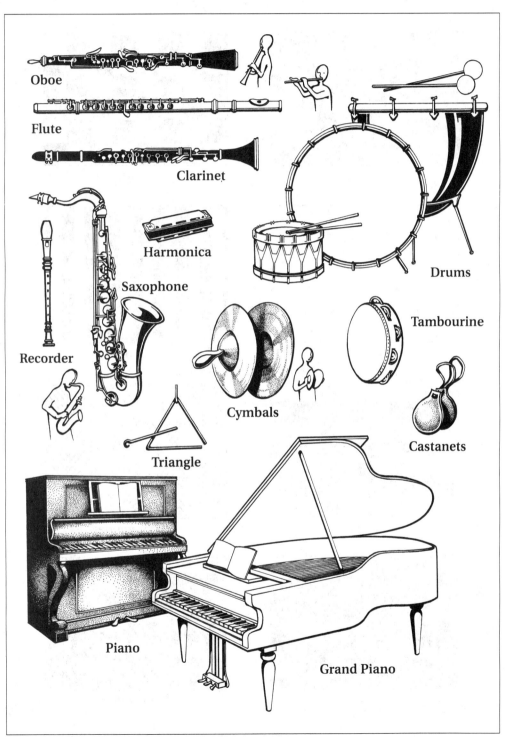

Oboe

Flute

Clarinet

Harmonica

Saxophone

Recorder

Drums

Tambourine

Cymbals

Castanets

Triangle

Piano

Grand Piano

Patterns

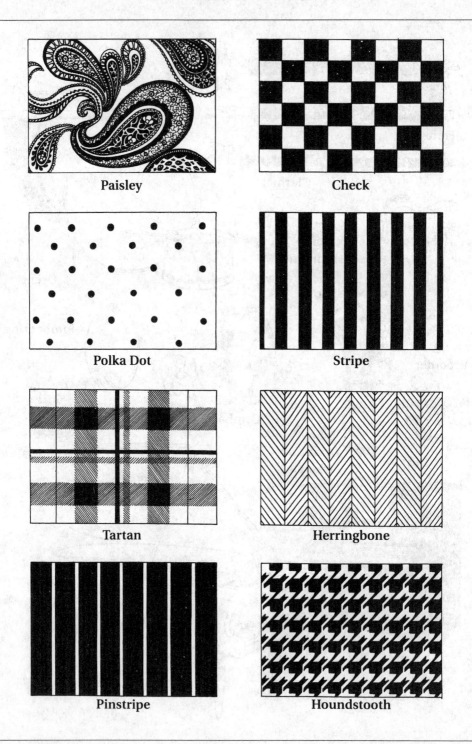

Paisley

Check

Polka Dot

Stripe

Tartan

Herringbone

Pinstripe

Houndstooth

Shapes

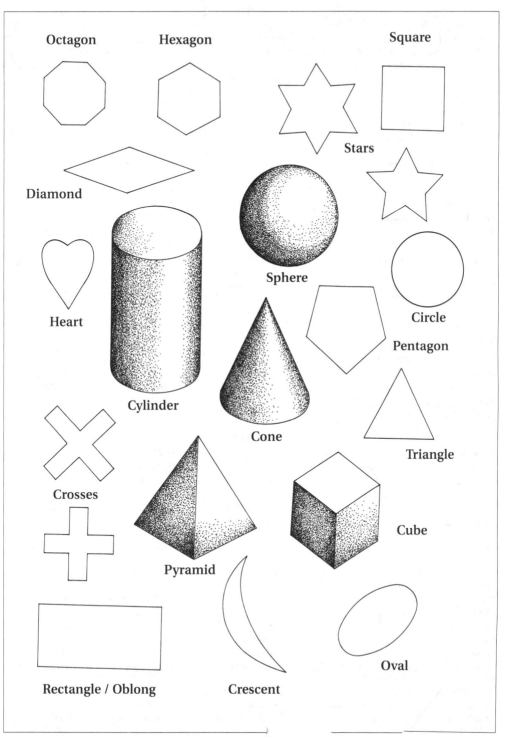

Octagon

Hexagon

Square

Stars

Diamond

Sphere

Circle

Heart

Pentagon

Cylinder

Cone

Triangle

Crosses

Pyramid

Cube

Rectangle / Oblong

Crescent

Oval

1305

Geographical Names

This list gives the names of most countries in the world which have a population greater than 750,000. Entries in the adjective column tell you which word to use when referring to things that come from or relate to that country. Entries in the people column tell you what word refers to the people of that country. Very often, this word is the same as the nationality adjective, in which case it is not repeated. For example, you would refer to the *Afghan* capital, Kabul; and someone who comes from Afganistan is an *Afghan*.

Country	Adjective	People	Language	Currency	Capital
Afghanistan	Afghan		Pashtu, Dari	afghani	Kabul
Albania	Albanian		Albanian	lek	Tirana
Algeria	Algerian		Arabic, French	Algerian dinar	Algiers
Angola	Angolan		Portuguese	new kwanza	Luanda
Argentina	Argentine, Argentinian		Spanish	nuevo peso argentino	Buenos Aires
Armenia	Armenian		Armenian	dram	Yerevan
Australia	Australian		English	Australian dollar	Canberra
Austria	Austrian		German	Austrian schilling	Vienna
Azerbaijan	Azeri, Azerbaijani		Azeri	manat	Baku
Bangladesh	Bangladeshi		Bengali	taka	Dhaka
Belgium	Belgian		Dutch, French	Belgian franc	Brussels
Benin	Beninese, Beninois		French, Fon	CFA franc	Porto-Novo
Bhutan	Bhutanese		Dzongkha, Nepali	ngultrum	Thimphu
Bolivia	Bolivian		Spanish, Quechua, Aymará	boliviano	La Paz, Sucre
Bosnia and Herzegovina	Bosnian, Herzegovinian		Serbo-Croat	dinar	Sarajevo
Botswana	Botswanan		English, Setswana	pula	Gaborone
Brazil	Brazilian		Portuguese	real	Brasília
Bulgaria	Bulgarian		Bulgarian	lev	Sofia
Burkina Faso	Burkinabé		French, Mossi	CFA franc	Ouagadougou
Burma	Burmese, Myanmar		Burmese, Myanmar	kyat	Rangoon
Burundi	Burundi	Burundian	Kirundi, French	Burundi franc	Bujumbura
Byelorussia	Byelorussian		Byelorussian, Russian	Byelorussian rubel	Minsk
Cambodia	Cambodian		Khmer	new riel	Phnom Penh
Cameroon	Cameroonian		French, English	CFA franc	Yaoundé
Canada	Canadian		English, French	Canadian dollar	Ottawa
Central African Republic	Central African		French, Sango	CFA franc	Bangui
Chad	Chadian		French, Arabic, Sara and Sango	CFA franc	N'Djaména
Chile	Chilean		Spanish	Chilean peso	Santiago
China	Chinese		Mandarin	yuan	Beijing
Colombia	Colombian		Spanish	Colombian peso	Bogotá
Congo	Congolese		French	CFA franc	Brazzaville
Costa Rica	Costa Rican		Spanish	colón	San José
Croatia	Croat, Croatian		Croatian	Croatian kuna	Zagreb
Cuba	Cuban		Spanish	Cuban peso	Havana
Cyprus	Greek Cypriot, Turkish Cypriot		Greek, Turkish	Cypriot pound, Turkish lira	Nicosia, Lefkosa
Czech Republic	Czech		Czech, Slovak	koruna	Prague
Denmark	Danish	Dane	Danish	Danish krone	Copenhagen
Dominican Republic	Dominican		Spanish	Dominican peso	Santo Domingo

Country	Adjective	People	Language	Currency	Capital
Ecuador	Ecuadorean		Spanish, Quechua	sucre	Quito
Egypt	Egyptian		Arabic	Egyptian pound	Cairo
El Salvador	Salvadoran, Salvadorean		Spanish	Salvadoran colón	San Salvador
England	English	Englishman, Englishwoman, The English	English	pound sterling	London
Eritrea	Eritrean		Tigre, Kunama	birr	Asmara
Estonia	Estonian		Estonian	kroon	Tallinn
Ethiopia	Ethiopian		Amharic	birr	Addis Ababa
Finland	Finnish	Finn	Finnish, Swedish	markka	Helsinki
France	French	Frenchman, Frenchwoman, The French	French	French franc	Paris
Gabon	Gabonese		French, Fang	CFA franc	Libreville
Gambia, The	Gambian		English	dalasi	Banjul
Georgia	Georgian		Georgian, Russian	lari	Tbilisi
Germany	German		German	Deutsche mark	Berlin
Ghana	Ghanaian		English, Akan	new cedi	Accra
Greece	Greek		Greek	drachma	Athens
Guatemala	Guatemalan		Spanish	quetzal	Guatemala City
Guinea	Guinean		French	Guinean franc	Conakry
Guinea-Bissau	Guinea Bissauan		Portuguese, Creole	Guinea-Bissauan peso	Bissau
Guyana	Guyanese, Guyanan		English	Guyanese dollar	Georgetown
Haiti	Haitian		French, Creole	gourde	Port-au-Prince
Honduras	Honduran		Spanish	lempira	Tegucigalpa
Hong Kong	Hong Kong	Hong Kong Chinese	English, Cantonese	Hong Kong dollar	Victoria
Hungary	Hungarian		Hungarian	forint	Budapest
India	Indian		Hindi, English	Indian rupee	New Delhi
Indonesia	Indonesian		Bahasa Indonesia	Indonesian rupiah	Jakarta
Iran	Iranian		Farsi	Iranian rial	Tehran
Iraq	Iraqi		Arabic, Kurdish	Iraqi dinar	Baghdad
Irish Republic	Irish	Irishman, Irishwoman, The Irish	Irish, English	punt	Dublin
Israel	Israeli		Hebrew, Arabic	new Israeli shekel	Jerusalem, Tel Aviv
Italy	Italian		Italian	Italian lira	Rome
Ivory Coast	Ivorian		French	CFA franc	Yamoussoukro, Abidjan
Jamaica	Jamaican		English	Jamaican dollar	Kingston
Japan	Japanese	The Japanese	Japanese	yen	Tokyo
Jordan	Jordanian		Arabic	Jordanian dinar	Amman
Kazakhstan	Kazakh, Kazakhstani		Kazak, Russian	tenge	Alma Ata
Kenya	Kenyan		Kiswahili, English	Kenyan shilling	Nairobi
Kuwait	Kuwaiti		Arabic	Kuwaiti dinar	Kuwait City
Kyrgyzstan	Kyrgyzstani, Kyrgyz		Kyrgyz	som	Bishkek
Laos	Lao, Laotian		Lao, Laotian	new kip	Vientiane
Latvia	Latvian		Latvian	lats	Riga
Lebanon	Lebanese		Arabic, French	Lebanese pound	Beirut
Lesotho	Lesothan, Basotho	Mosotho, Basotho	Sesotho, English	loti	Maseru

Country	Adjective	People	Language	Currency	Capital
Liberia	Liberian		English	Liberian dollar	Monrovia
Libya	Libyan		Arabic	Libyan dinar	Tripoli
Lithuania	Lithuanian		Lithuanian	litas	Vilnius
Macedonia,The Former Yugoslav Republic of	Macedonian		Macedonian	denar	Skopje
Madagascar	Malagasy		French, Malagasy	Malagasy franc	Antananarivo
Malawi	Malawian		English, Chichewa	Malawian kwacha	Lilongwe
Malaysia	Malaysian		Bahasa Malaysia	ringgit	Kuala Lumpur
Maldives	Maldivian		Divehi	rufiyaa	Malé
Mali	Malian		French, Bambara	CFA franc	Bamako
Mauritania	Mauritanian		French, Arabic	ouguiya	Nouakchott
Mauritius	Mauritian		English, Creole	Mauritian rupee	Port Louis
Mexico	Mexican		Spanish	New Mexican peso	Mexico City
Moldova	Moldovan		Moldovan, Romanian, Russian	leu	Chisinau
Mongolia	Mongol, Mongolian		Khalkha, Mongolian	tughrik	Ulaanbaatar
Morocco	Moroccan		Arabic, Berber	Moroccan dirham	Rabat
Mozambique	Mozambican		Portuguese	metical	Maputo
Namibia	Namibian		Afrikaans, English	South African rand	Windhoek
Nepal	Nepalese		Nepali	Nepalese rupee	Kathmandu
Netherlands	Dutch	Dutchman, Dutchwoman, The Dutch	Dutch	Netherlands guilder	Amsterdam, The Hague
New Zealand	New Zealand	New Zealander	English, Maori	New Zealand dollar	Wellington
Nicaragua	Nicaraguan		Spanish	córdoba	Managua
Niger	Nigerien		French	CFA franc	Niamey
Nigeria	Nigerian		English, Hausa, Yoruba, Ibo	naira	Abuja
North Korea	North Korean		Korean	North Korean won	Pyŏngyang
Norway	Norwegian		Norwegian	Norwegian krone	Oslo
Oman	Omani		Arabic	Omani rial	Muscat
Pakistan	Pakistani		Urdu, English, Punjabi	Pakistani rupee	Islamabad
Panama	Panamanian		Spanish	balboa	Panama City
Papua New Guinea	Papua New Guinean		Pidgin, English, Motu	kina	Port Moresby
Paraguay	Paraguayan		Spanish, Guaraní	guaraní	Asunción
Peru	Peruvian		Spanish, Quechua	nuevo sol	Lima
Philippines	Filipino, Philippine	Filipino, Filipina, Philippine	Filipino, English	Philippine peso	Manila
Poland	Polish	Pole	Polish	zloty	Warsaw
Portugal	Portuguese		Portuguese	Portuguese escudo	Lisbon
Puerto Rico	Puerto Rican		Spanish, English	US dollar	San Juan
Romania	Romanian		Romanian	leu	Bucharest
Russia	Russian		Russian	rouble	Moscow
Rwanda	Rwandan		Kinyarwanda, French	Rwandan franc	Kigali
Saudi Arabia	Saudi, Saudi Arabian		Arabic	Saudi riyal	Riyadh
Scotland	Scottish, Scots	Scot, Scotsman, Scotswoman, The Scots	English, Gaelic	pound sterling	Edinburgh
Senegal	Senegalese		French	CFA franc	Dakar

Country	Adjective	People	Language	Currency	Capital
Serbia and Montenegro	Serb, Serbian or Montenegrin	Serb, Montenegrin	SerbianYugoslav	new dinar	Belgrade
Sierra Leone	Sierra Leonean		English	leone	Freetown
Singapore	Singapore, Singaporean	Singaporean	Malay, Chinese, Tamil, English	Singapore dollar	Singapore
Slovakia	Slovak		Slovak	koruna	Bratislava
Slovenia	Slovenian, Slovene		Slovenian	tolar	Ljubljana
Somalia	Somali		Somali, Arabic	Somali shilling	Mogadishu
South Africa	South African		Afrikaans, English	rand	Cape Town, Pretoria, Bloemfontein
South Korea	South Korean		Korean	South Korean won	Seoul
Spain	Spanish	Spaniard, The Spanish	Castilian Spanish	peseta	Madrid
Sri Lanka	Sri Lankan		Sinhala, Tamil, English	Sri Lankan rupee	Colombo, Sri Jayewardenepura
Sudan	Sudanese		Arabic	Sudanese pound	Khartoum
Swaziland	Swazi		English, Siswati	lilangeni	Mbabane, Lobamba
Sweden	Swede, Swedish	Swede	Swedish	Swedish krona	Stockholm
Switzerland	Swiss		German, French, Italian	Swiss franc	Berne
Syria	Syrian		Arabic	Syrian pound	Damascus
Taiwan	Taiwanese, Chinese		Mandarin Chinese	New Taiwan dollar	Taipei
Tajikistan	Tajik		Tajik, Russian	Tajik rouble	Dushanbe
Tanzania	Tanzanian		Swahili, English	Tanzanian shilling	Dar es Salaam
Thailand	Thai		Thai	baht	Bangkok
Togo	Togolese		French, Ewe	CFA franc	Lomé
Trinidad and Tobago	Trinidadian, Tobagoan		English	Trinidad and Tobago dollar	Port of Spain
Tunisia	Tunisian		Arabic, French	Tunisian dinar	Tunis
Turkey	Turkish	Turk	Turkish, Kurdish, Arabic	Turkish lira	Ankara
Turkmenistan	Turkmen		Turkmen, Russian	manat	Ashkhabad
Uganda	Ugandan		English, Luganda, Swahili, Luo	Ugandan shilling	Kampala
Ukraine	Ukrainian		Ukrainian, Russian	karbovanets	Kiev
United Arab Emirates	Emirian		Arabic	Emirian dirham	Abu Dhabi
United Kingdom	British	Briton, The British	English	pound sterling	London
United States Of America	American		English	US dollar	Washington, DC
Uruguay	Uruguayan		Spanish	Uruguayan peso	Montevideo
Uzbekistan	Uzbek		Uzbek, Russian	sum	Tashkent
Venezuela	Venezuelan		Spanish	bolívar	Caracas
Vietnam	Vietnamese		Vietnamese	new dông	Hanoi
Wales	Welsh	Welshman, Welshwoman, The Welsh	Welsh, English	pound sterling	Cardiff
Yemen	Yemeni		Arabic	yemeni rial	San'aa
Zaire	Zairean		French	zaire	Kinshasa
Zambia	Zambian		English	Zambian kwacha	Lusaka
Zimbabwe	Zimbabwean		English, Shona	Zimbabwean dollar	Harare

Points of the Compass

In the diagram below, you can substitute any one of the eight compass points into any of the definitions. For example, in the definition for 'north' you could substitute the word 'south east' giving 'The south east of a place, country, or region is the part which is in the south east'.

However, in the boxes surrounded by broken lines, you can only substitute north, south, east, and west into the definitions, and not the other compass points.

The definitions in boxes surrounded by unbroken lines are special cases and no compass point other than the one mentioned can be used in them.

The **north** of a place, country, or region is the part which is in the north. *The scheme mostly benefits people in the North and Midlands where rateable values were lowest...a tiny house in the village in the north of France.*

If you add '**ern**' to the word '**north**', you form an adjective that means in or from the north of a region or country.

North

---

northerner If you add '**er**' to the word '**northern**', you form a noun that refers to a person who was born or who lives in the north of a place or country.

A north-**east** wind is a wind that blows from the north-east. *By 9.15 a bitter north-east wind was blowing.*

North East

The **East** is used to refer to the southern and eastern part of Asia, including India, China, and Japan. *Every so often, a new martial art arrives from the East.*

If you go **east**, you travel towards the east. *To drive, go east on Route 9.*

eastbound If you add '**bound**' to the word '**east**', you form an adjective that is used to describe roads, cars, trains, or flights that lead to or are travelling towards the east; a formal word.

East

If you add '**erly**' to the word '**south east**', you form an adjective that is used to describe points, areas, or directions that are to the south-east or towards the south-east.

South East

---

southernmost If you add '**most**' to the word '**southern**', you form an adjective that is used to describe parts of areas or places that are further towards the south than any other.

Something that is **south** of a place is positioned to the south of it. They now own and operate a farm 50 miles south of Rochester...I was living in a house just south of Market Street.

South

If you add '**erly**' to the word '**south west**', you form an adjective that describes winds that blow from the south west.

South West

The **West** is used to refer to the United States, Canada, and the countries of Western, Northern, and Southern Europe. *Gorbachev was never as popular in the Soviet Union as he was in the West.*

The **west** part of a place, country, or region is the part which is towards the west...*a small island off the west coast of South Korea.*

westward If you add 'ward' or 'wards' to the word '**west**', you form an adverb that means towards the west.

West

If you add '**ern**' to the word '**north west**', you form an adjective that means in or from the north west of a region or country.

North West

Numbers

The following table shows the names of numbers. On the left hand side of the table are the **cardinal numbers**. If you want to identify or describe something by indicating where it comes in a series or sequence, you use an **ordinal number**.

Quietly they took their seats in the first three rows.
Flora's flat is on the fourth floor of this five-storey building

The ordinal numbers are shown on the right hand side of the table.

Numbers and ordinals can be written in figures or in words. You can see from the numbers in this table how to form all the other numbers.

0	zero, nought, nothing, oh	1st	first
1	one	2nd	second
2	two	3rd	third
3	three	4th	fourth
4	four	5th	fifth
5	five	6th	sixth
6	six	7th	seventh
7	seven	8th	eighth
8	eight	9th	ninth
9	nine	10th	tenth
10	ten	11th	eleventh
11	eleven	12th	twelfth
12	twelve	13th	thirteenth
13	thirteen	14th	fourteenth
14	fourteen	15th	fifteenth
15	fifteen	16th	sixteenth
16	sixteen	17th	seventeenth
17	seventeen	18th	eighteenth
18	eighteen	19th	nineteenth
19	nineteen	20th	twentieth
20	twenty	21st	twenty-first
21	twenty-one	22nd	twenty-second
22	twenty-two	23rd	twenty-third
23	twenty-three	24th	twenty-fourth
24	twenty-four	25th	twenty-fifth
25	twenty-five	26th	twenty-sixth
26	twenty-six	27th	twenty-seventh
27	twenty-seven	28th	twenty-eighth
28	twenty-eight	29th	twenty-ninth
29	twenty-nine	30th	thirtieth
30	thirty	40th	fortieth
40	forty	50th	fiftieth
50	fifty	60th	sixtieth
60	sixty	70th	seventieth
70	seventy	80th	eightieth
80	eighty	90th	ninetieth
90	ninety	100th	a hundredth
100	a hundred	101st	a hundred and first
101	a hundred and one	110th	a hundred and tenth
110	a hundred and ten	120th	a hundred and twentieth
120	a hundred and twenty	200th	two hundredth
200	two hundred	1000th	a thousandth
1000	a thousand		
1001	a thousand and one	etc.	
1010	a thousand and ten		
2000	two thousand		
10,000	ten thousand		
1,00,000	a hundred thousand		
1,000,000	a million		
2,000,000	two million		
1,000,000,000	a billion		
1,000,000,000,000	a trillion		

Numbers over 100 are usually expressed in figures but if you want to say them aloud or write them in words, you put the word 'and' in front of the number expressed by the last two figures. For example, 345 is said or written as **three hundred and forty five** and 2871 as **two thousand eight hundred and seventy one**. Note that in American English the 'and' is usually omitted so 345 is said or written as **three hundred forty five**.

There are several ways of saying or writing numbers between 1000 and 1,000,000. For example, the number 3456 is usually said or written as **three thousand four hundred and fifty six** when it is being used to refer to a quantity of things. Four figure numbers ending in 00 can also be said or written as a number of hundreds. For example, 1700 can be said or written as **seventeen hundred**.

In telephone numbers, you say each figure separately.
For example, 6727 is said **six seven two seven**.

If you are mentioning the year 1872, you usually say **eighteen seventy two**. See DATES.

Ordinals are often used in their abbreviated forms, especially in dates. For example,

January 7th.
See DATES.
Numbers are used in sentences in a number of different ways. Here are some examples.

Around eight thousand people were killed.
They would need several hundred million dollars.
An oak tree may live for hundreds of years.
... the two women.
... all five sons.
... two small children.
Fifteen people were arrested.
Ten pounds is a negligible sum.
Thirty demonstrators were arrested and ten injured.
Five of the children came with their father.
... a 7,000-word essay.
She's about 35.
... an a la carte menu from 20 pounds.

In addition to these uses, you can also use expressions such as **in the 30's** and **in your sixties** to refer to a temperature, score, age etc that is between 30 and 39 or 60 and 69. For example,

The temperature was in the high eighties.
... a retired headmaster in his seventies.

Dates

Days of the Week

MONDAY
TUESDAY
WEDNESDAY
THURSDAY
FRIDAY
SATURDAY
SUNDAY

Note the way that days are used, and the prepositions that are used with them:

Why didn't you come to the meeting on Wednesday?
Alice has asked us round on Friday afternoon.
I'm usually here on Mondays and Fridays.
They meet here every Tuesday morning.
The attack took place last Thursday.
Talks are likely to start next Tuesday.
It usually arrives on a Wednesday.
He last saw her on the Saturday before her death.
On the Sunday after the election I went for a long run.

Seasons

SPRING
SUMMER
AUTUMN
WINTER

Note the way that seasons are used, and the prepositions you use with them:

In winter the nights are long and cold.
The final report is due out next autumn.
It was a perfect summer's day.
We met again in the spring of 1977.
A few winters ago I was in England attending a conference.
It was here the author spent his summers.
(In American English, 'fall' is used instead of 'autumn').

Months of the Year

JANUARY
FEBRUARY
MARCH
APRIL
MAY
JUNE
JULY
AUGUST
SEPTEMBER
OCTOBER
NOVEMBER
DECEMBER

Note the way that months are used, and the prepositions you use with them:

We always have snow in January.
His exhibition opens on 5 February.
I flew to Milan in early March.
Worcestershire had its wettest April day since records began in 1889.
Since it was late May, there were apple trees in bloom.
Staff have been on strike since last June.
He spent two weeks with us in July 1993.
The trial will resume on August the twenty-second.
They returned to Moscow on 22 September 1930.
There's no telling what the voters will do next November.
...a bright morning in mid-December.

Writing Dates:

There are several different ways of writing a date:

20 April	April 20	the twentieth of April
20th April	April 20th	

If you want to give the year, you put it last.
I was born on December 15th, 1933.
You can write a date entirely in figures.
The date above would be:

15/12/33	15.12.33

Note that Americans put the month in front of the day when writing the date in figures, i.e.:

12/15/33	12.15.33

Dates within a piece of writing are not usually written entirely in figures. However, this way of writing dates is often used for the date at the top of a letter, and for dates on forms.

Saying Dates:

You say the day as an ordinal number, even when it is written in figures as a cardinal number. For example, 'April 20' is said as April the twentieth or the twentieth of April. Speakers of American English usually say April twentieth.

You can omit the month when it is clear which month you are referring to.
So Monday will be the seventeenth.
What's the date? It's the twelfth.
You normally say a year in two parts. For example, '1970' is said as nineteen seventy, and '1826' is said as eighteen twenty-six. In the case of years ending in '00', you say the second part as hundred. For example, '1900' is said as nineteen hundred. There are two ways of saying years ending in '01' to '09'. For example, '1901' can be said as nineteen oh one or nineteen hundred and one.

Decades:

Decades are usually thought of as starting with a year ending in zero and finishing with a year ending in nine. For example, the decade from 1960 to 1969 can be referred to as the nineteen sixties. This is usually written as the 1960s.
In the 1950s, synthetic hair was invented.
When you are talking about a decade in the twentieth century, you do not have to indicate the century. For example, you can refer to the 1920s as the twenties. This can be written as the '20's, the 20s, or the Twenties.

Time

four o'clock four 4.00		nine o'clock nine 9.00		twelve o'clock twelve 12.00	

four in the morning   `04:00`   nine in the morning   `09:00`   twelve in the morning   `12:00`
4.00 a.m.   9.00 a.m.   12.00 a.m.
                                                    midday
                                                    noon

four in the afternoon   `16:00`   nine in the evening   `21:00`   twelve at night   `00:00`
4.00 p.m.   9.00 p.m.   00.00 p.m.
                                                    midnight

half past eleven (British)
half eleven (British)
eleven thirty
11.30

a quarter past twelve (British)
quarter past twelve (British)
twelve fifteen
12.15
quarter after twelve (American)

twenty-five past two (British)
twenty-five minutes past two (British)
two twenty-five
2.25
twenty five after two (American)

a quarter to one (British)
quarter to one (British)
twelve forty-five
12.45
(a) quarter of one (American)

ten to eight (British)
ten minutes to eight (British)
seven-fifty
7.50
ten of eight (American)

Note that if the number of minutes past the hour is less than 10, many people say '0' as 'oh' before the number of minutes. For example, 7.05 can be said as 'seven oh five' or 'seven five'.

The following examples show some of the uses of time;

What time is it? Four o'clock.
What time did you finally leave? About eight-thirty.
What's the time now? Three thirty.

It was quarter of seven in the morning.
It's nearly ten after twelve.

She said to tell you to be sure to watch Channel Nine tomorrow at two o'clock.
Mary left at three and caught the bus.

The students were ordered to vacate their halls of residence by nine o'clock this morning.
He was home by six for dinner.

She was free until three o'clock, when she had to meet her parents back at their suite.

I'd been awake since four.
Have you had anything to eat? Not since one o'clock yesterday.

I'll be watching the eleven-o'clock news.
I caught the eight o'clock bus to the Northern Isles with five minutes to spare.

The flight to Cardiff takes exactly half an hour.
It took her a quarter of an hour to find a parking space.

Note that if it is clear what hour you are talking about, you do not need to add the hour after 'past' or 'to'.

What time is it? Twenty-five past.
What time's the morning break? I think it's twenty-five to or twenty to.

Weights and Measures

Length

METRIC		
1 kilometre (km)	= 1000 metres	=0.6214 miles
1 metre (m)	= 100 centimetres	=1.094 yards
1 centimetre(cm)	= 10 millimetres	=0.394 inches

NON-METRIC		
1 mile	= 1760 yards	= 1.609 kilometres
1 yard (yd)	= 3 feet	= 0.914 metres
1 foot (ft)	= 12 inches	= 30.48 centimetres
1 inch (in)		= 25.4 millimetres

Area

METRIC		
1 square kilometre (km)	= 100 hectares	= 0.386 square miles
1 hectare (ha)	= 100 ares	= 2.471 acres
1 are (a)	= 100 square metres	= 119.6 square yards
1 square metre (m)		= 1.196 square yards

NON-METRIC		
1 square mile	= 640 acres	= 2.59 square kilometres
1 acre	= 4840 square yards	= 0.405 hectares
1 square yard	= 9 square feet	= 0.836 square metres
1 square foot	= 144 square inches	= 929.30 square centimetres
1 square inch		= 6.452 square centimetres

Weight

METRIC		
1 tonne	= 1000 kilograms	= 19.688 hundredweight
1 kilogram (kg)	= 1000 grams	= 2.205 pounds
1 gram (g)	= 1000 milligrams	

NON-METRIC		
1 ton	= 20 hundredweight	= 1.016 tonnes
1 hundredweight (cwt)	= 8 stone	= 50.8 kilograms
1 stone (st)	= 14 pounds	= 6.356 kilograms
1 pound (lb)	= 16 ounces	= 454 grams
1 ounce (oz)		= 28.35 grams

Capacity

METRIC		
1 decalitre (dal)	= 10 litres	= 2.2 gallons (2.63 US gallons)
1 litre (l)	= 100 centilitres	= 1.76 pints (2.1 US pints)
1 centilitre (cl)	= 10 millilitres	= 0.018 pints (0.021 US pints)

NON-METRIC		
1 gallon (gal)	= 4 quarts	= 4.546 litres
1 quart (qt)	= 2 pints	= 1.136 litres
1 pint (pt)	= 20 fluid ounces	= 56.8 centilitres
1 fluid ounce (fl oz)		= 28.4 millilitres

Note that American non-metric measurements are different from British measurements. One US pint is equivalent to 0.833 UK pints, and contains 16 US fluid ounces.

Wordlist

Throughout the dictionary, entries are given markers to indicate how frequently words occur in the language. For example, at the entry for *say*, you will see the marker ◆◆◆◆◆ in the extra column. This means that the word *say* is one of the most frequent words in the English language. (Note that the entry for *say* covers the forms *says*, *saying*, and *said* as well, and that the ◆◆◆◆◆ is an indication of frequency for all these forms taken together.)

The markers are on a scale from 1 to 5, (◆◆◆◆◆ for the most frequent words, ◆◇◇◇◇ for less frequent words.) About half the entries in the dictionary have no frequency markers.

◆◆◆◆◆

Entries in this band are the most frequent words - the 'grammar' words, such as *of, the, as*, and so on, as well as very frequent vocabulary items such as *seem, arm*, and *interest*.

There are nearly 700 entries in this band, representing over 1,500 different forms.

◆◆◆◆◇

In the next band of just over 1,000 entries are words such as *arrive, measure*, and *promise*. These account for a total of nearly 2,500 forms, and together with the top band, represent 75% of all English usage. These two bands, then, represent the essential core of English.

◆◆◆◇◇, ◆◆◇◇◇

The next two bands, (3 black diamonds and 2 black diamonds) cover a further 4,400 entries. These words will extend the range of topics which you can talk about, but you will read them or hear them rather less often than the words in the top two bands.

◆◇◇◇◇

Entries with one black diamond or with no diamonds at all are still important, but some might be slightly restricted in their contexts of use, while others might be rather literary or specialized.

The following lists contain the **headwords** that are represented in each of the top three frequency bands. There are over 3,000 entries, and taken with their inflected forms and derived words, they account for nearly 10,000 forms.

◆◆◆◆◆

a	ask	can	create	election	forty
able	at	can't	cup	eleven	four
about	attack	capital	current	else	fourteen
accept	attempt	car	cut	end	free
accord	authority	care	daughter	enough	friend
according to	available	carry	day	even	from
account	away	case	deal	event	front
across	back	cause	decide	ever	full
act	bad	central	decision	every	fund
action	bank	centre	demand	everything	further
actually	base	century	department	example	future
add	based	chance	describe	expect	game
after	be	change	design	experience	general
again	beat	charge	develop	eye	get
against	because	chief	development	face	girl
age	become	child	didn't	fact	give
ago	before	city	die	fail	go
agree	begin	claim	different	fall	going
aid	behind	class	difficult	family	good
air	believe	clear	direct	far	got
all	better	close	director	father	government
allow	between	club	do	fear	great
almost	big	colour	doesn't	feel	green
along	billion	come	dollar	few	grey
already	bit	coming	don't	fifteen	ground
also	bite	committee	door	fifty	group
although	black	common	down	fight	grow
always	blue	community	draw	figure	half
among	body	company	drive	film	hand
and	book	complete	drug	final	happen
announce	both	concern	during	financial	hard
another	boy	condition	each	find	have
answer	break	conference	early	firm	he
any	bring	consider	east	first	head
anything	brother	continue	easy	five	health
appear	brown	control	economic	fly	hear
area	build	cost	economy	follow	help
arm	building	could	education	food	her
army	business	couldn't	effect	foot	here
around	but	council	effort	for	herself
art	buy	country	eight	force	he's
as	by	course	eighteen	foreign	high
	call	court	eighty	form	him
	campaign	cover	either	former	himself

his
history
hit
hold
home
hope
hospital
host
hour
house
how
however
human
hundred
I
I'd
idea
if
I'll
I'm
important
in
include
including
increase
independent
industry
information
interest
international
into
isn't
issue
it
its
it's
itself
I've
job
join
just
keep
kill
kind
know
labour
land
large
last
late
later
laugh
law
lead
leader
learn
least
leave
left
less
let
letter
level
life
like
likely
line
list
little
live
local
long
look
lose
lot
love
low
main
major
make
man
many
market
match
matter
may
me
mean

meet
meeting
member
middle
might
military
million
mind
mine
minister
minute
moment
money
month
more
morning
most
mother
move
Mr
Mrs
Ms
much
music
must
my
name
nation
national
near
need
never
new
news
next
night
nine
nineteen
ninety
no
north
not
nothing
now
number
of
of course
off
offer
office
officer
official
often
oh
oil
old
on
once
one
only
open
operate
operation
or
order
other
our
out
outside
over
own
page
paper
parent
part
party
pass
past
pay
peace
people
per cent
perhaps
person
photo
place
plan
plant

play
player
point
police
policy
political
position
possible
pound
power
president
press
pressure
price
probably
problem
process
produce
product
programme
provide
public
put
question
quick
quite
race
radio
raise
rate
rather
reach
read
real
really
reason
receive
recent
record
red
release
remain
remember
report
research
result
return
right
rise
road
role
room
rule
run
sale
same
save
say
school
season
second
secretary
security
see
seek
seem
sell
send
sense
serious
service
set
seven
seventeen
seventy
several
share
she
short
should
show
side
sign
since
single
sir
sister
sit

situation
six
sixteen
sixty
small
so
social
society
some
something
son
soon
sort
sound
south
speak
special
spend
staff
stage
stand
star
start
state
stay
step
still
stock
stop
story
street
strong
student
study
such
suggest
support
sure
surprise
system
take
talk
tax
team
tell
ten
term
test
than
thank
that
that's
the
their
them
themselves
then
there
these
they
they're
thing
think
thirteen
thirty
this
those
though
thought
thousand
three
through
time
to
today
together
too
top
total
towards
town
trade
try
turn
twelve
twenty
twice
two

under
understand
union
university
until
up
us
use
value
very
view
visit
vote
wait
walk
wall
want
war
wasn't
watch
water
way
we
week
well
we're
west
we've
what
when
where
whether
which
while
white
who
whole
whose
why
wide
wife
will
win
with
within
without
woman
won't
word
work
worker
working
world
would
wouldn't
write
year
yes
yesterday
yet
you
young
your
you're
you've
◆◆◆◇
ability
above
absolutely
abuse
accepted
accuse
achieve
active
activity
addition
address
administration
admit
adopt
adult
advance
advantage
advice
affair
affect
afternoon

agency
agent
agreement
ahead
AIDS
aim
aircraft
airline
airport
album
allege
all right
ally
alone
alternative
amount
analyst
animal
annual
anyone
anyway
apart
apparently
appeal
appearance
apply
approach
approve
April
aren't
argue
argument
armed
arrange
arrest
arrive
article
artist
aspect
assess
asset
association
assume
attend
attention
attitude
attract
audience
August
aunt
author
average
avoid
award
aware
baby
bag
balance
ball
ban
band
bar
basic
basis
battle
bear
beautiful
bed
behaviour
below
benefit
beyond
bid
bill
bird
blame
block
blood
blow
board
boat
bomb
bond
border
born
boss
bottle
bottom

box
brain
bridge
brief
bright
broad
budget
burn
cabinet
camera
camp
cancer
candidate
captain
caption
card
career
careful
cash
cast
catch
cell
certain
certainly
chair
chairman
challenge
champion
championship
channel
chapter
character
cheap
check
chemical
choice
choose
Christian
Christmas
church
circle
citizen
City
civil
classic
clean
clothes
coach
coast
cold
collapse
colleague
collect
collection
college
comment
commercial
commission
commit
communist
compared
competition
complain
complex
computer
conduct
confidence
confirm
conflict
conservative
considerable
constant
consumer
contact
contain
contract
cook
cool
copy
corner
correct
correspondent
count
county
couple
cousin
crash
credit

crime
criminal
crisis
critic
critical
criticism
cross
crowd
cry
culture
currency
customer
daily
damage
dance
danger
dangerous
dark
data
date
dead
death
debate
debt
decade
December
declare
decline
deep
defeat
defence
defend
deficit
degree
delay
deliver
democracy
democrat
democratic
deny
depend
deputy
desire
desk
despite
destroy
detail
determine
diet
difference
difficulty
dinner
direction
discover
discuss
discussion
disease
dismiss
display
dispute
distance
district
divide
division
doctor
document
dog
domestic
dominate
double
doubt
dozen
dramatic
dream
dress
drink
drop
dry
due
duty
earlier
earn
earth
eastern
eat
economics
edge
edition

editor
effective
egg
eighteenth
eighth
eightieth
elect
element
eleventh
emerge
emergency
employee
encourage
energy
engine
enjoy
ensure
enter
entire
entry
environment
environmental
equal
equipment
escape
especially
essential
establish
estate
estimate
evening
eventually
everybody
everyone
evidence
exact
examine
excellent
except
exchange
executive
exercise
exist
expensive
expert
explain
export
express
extend
extra
extremely
facility
factor
factory
failure
fair
famous
fan
farm
farmer
fashion
fast
fat
favour
favourite
feature
February
federal
fee
feed
feeling
fellow
female
festival
field
fifteenth
fifth
fiftieth
file
fill
finally
finance
fine
finger
finish
fire
fish
fit

flat
flight
floor
flow
flower
focus
following
football
forget
form
formal
fortieth
forward
found
fourteenth
fourth
freedom
frequent
fresh
Friday
fruit
fuel
fully
fun
function
gain
garden
gas
gather
gay
generally
generation
glass
goal
god
gold
gone
goods
governor
grand
grant
growth
guarantee
guard
guess
guest
guide
gun
guy
hadn't
hair
hand
handle
hang
happy
hardly
hasn't
haven't
heart
heat
heavy
he'd
highly
hold
hole
holiday
horse
hostage
hot
hotel
housing
huge
hurt
husband
ice
ideal
identify
ignore
ill
image
imagine
immediate
immediately
impact
import
impose
impossible
improve

incident
income
increasingly
indeed
indicate
individual
industrial
inflation
influence
injury
inside
insist
inspire
instance
instead
institute
institution
insurance
intend
interested
interview
introduce
investigate
investment
investor
invite
involve
involved
island
item
January
joint
journal
journalist
judge
July
jump
June
justice
key
kick
kid
king
kitchen
knowledge
lack
lady
language
largely
last
latest
launch
lawyer
lay
leadership
leading
league
leg
legal
length
let's
liberal
lie
lift
light
limit
link
listen
loan
long-term
lord
loss
lunch
machine
magazine
mainly
maintain
majority
maker
male
manage
management
manager
March
mark
marriage
marry
mass

master
material
May
maybe
means
meanwhile
measure
media
medical
memory
mention
message
method
mile
millionth
ministry
minority
Miss
miss
mission
mistake
mix
model
modern
Monday
mortgage
motor
mountain
mouth
movement
movie
murder
museum
Muslim
myself
narrow
nationalist
natural
nature
nearly
necessary
negotiate
negotiation
neither
network
newspaper
nice
nineteenth
ninetieth
ninth
nobody
none
no one
nor
normal
north-east
north-west
note
notice
novel
November
nuclear
object
obvious
obviously
occasion
occupy
occur
October
odd
okay
opinion
opportunity
opposition
option
order
organization
organize
original
otherwise
overall
owner
pack
package
pain
paint
painting
pair

park	rebel	settlement	suffer	variety	agricultural
parliament	recall	set-up	suit	various	agriculture
particular	recently	seventeenth	summer	vehicle	ahead of
particularly	recession	seventh	summit	version	air force
partner	recognize	seventieth	sun	victim	alarm
patient	recommend	severe	Sunday	victory	alcohol
pattern	reduce	sex	supply	video	alert
payment	refer	sexual	suppose	village	alive
perfect	reflect	shake	supposed	violence	allegation
perform	reform	shall	supreme	voice	alliance
performance	refugee	shape	surface	volume	allied
period	refuse	sharp	surround	voter	alongside
personal	regard	she'd	survey	warm	alter
phone	region	she's	survive	warn	altogether
photograph	regional	ship	suspect	waste	amateur
physical	regular	shock	table	wave	amazing
pick	reject	shoot	talent	weak	ambassador
picture	relation	shop	tape	weapon	ambition
piece	relationship	shot	target	wear	amendment
plane	relief	shoulder	task	weather	amid
please	religious	sight	taste	Wednesday	analysis
plus	remove	significant	tea	weekend	ancient
politician	repeat	similar	teach	weight	anger
politics	replace	simple	tear	welcome	angle
poll	reply	simply	technique	we'll	angry
poor	reporter	sing	technology	weren't	anniversary
popular	reporting	site	telephone	whatever	announcement
population	represent	sixth	television	what's	antique
positive	representative	sixtieth	tend	while	anxiety
possibility	republic	size	tenth	whom	anxious
possibly	republican	skill	terrible	who's	anybody
post	request	skin	territory	wild	anywhere
potential	require	sleep	theatre	will	apart
powerful	reserve	slightly	theory	willing	apartment
practice	resident	slip	therefore	wind	appal
prefer	resolution	slow	they'd	window	apparent
prepare	resource	smile	they'll	wine	apple
prepared	respect	smoke	they've	wing	application
presence	respond	soft	thinking	winner	appoint
present	response	soldier	third	wish	appointment
pretty	responsibility	solution	thirteenth	withdraw	appreciate
prevent	responsible	somebody	thirtieth	wonder	appropriate
previous	rest	someone	threat	wonderful	approval
prince	restaurant	sometimes	threaten	wood	arise
princess	reveal	song	throughout	worry	armed forces
principle	review	sorry	throw	worth	arrangement
print	rich	source	Thursday	wound	arrival
prison	ride	south-east	thus	writing	aside
prisoner	right	southern	ticket	wrong	assault
private	ring	south-west	tie	yard	assembly
prize	risk	space	title	yourself	assist
production	rival	specific	tomorrow	youth	assistance
professional	river	speech	tonight		assistant
professor	rock	speed	touch	◆◆◆◇◇	associate
profit	roll	spirit	tough		associated
program	round	split	tour	abandon	assumption
progress	route	spokesman	track	abandoned	assured
project	royal	sport	traditional	abortion	athlete
promise	running	spot	train	abroad	atmosphere
promote	sad	spread	transfer	absence	attach
proper	safe	spring	transport	absolute	attorney
property	safety	square	travel	academic	attractive
proposal	sanction	stable	treat	acceptable	auction
propose	Saturday	stake	treatment	access	auto
prospect	scale	standard	treaty	accident	automatic
protect	scene	statement	tree	accompany	autumn
protection	schedule	station	trial	accurate	await
protest	scheme	status	trip	acid	awful
prove	science	sterling	troop	acknowledge	background
publish	scientist	stick	trouble	acquire	backing
pull	score	stone	true	acquisition	badly
purchase	screen	store	trust	acre	bake
purpose	sea	straight	truth	activism	ballot
push	search	strange	Tuesday	actor	banker
quality	seat	strategy	TV	actress	banking
quarter	secret	strength	twelfth	actual	bare
queen	section	stress	twentieth	adequate	barely
quiet	sector	strike	type	adjust	bargain
quote	secure	structure	unit	admire	barrel
radical	seed	struggle	unless	advanced	barrier
rain	senior	studio	unlikely	advertise	baseball
range	sentence	stuff	upon	advise	basically
rapid	separate	style	urge	adviser	bat
reaction	September	subject	use	advocate	bath
reader	series	succeed	used	afford	bathroom
ready	serve	success	useful	afraid	bay
reality	session	successful	usual	afterwards	beach
realize	settle	suddenly	usually	agenda	bean
				aggressive	

beaten
beauty
bedroom
beer
beginning
behalf
behave
being
belief
bell
belong
belt
bend
beneath
beside
besides
bet
bike
birth
birthday
bitter
blast
blind
bloody
blow
boil
bone
boom
boost
boot
bore
borrow
bother
bound
bowl
branch
brand
brave
bread
breakfast
breast
breath
breathe
breed
brilliant
broadcast
broadcasting
broker
brush
bunch
burden
burst
bury
bus
businessman
busy
butter
button
bye
cable
cake
calculated
calm
cancel
cap
capable
capacity
capture
carbon
caring
carrier
castle
casualty
cat
category
Catholic
cautious
cave
CD
cease
ceasefire
celebrate
celebration
ceremony
certain
chain
chamber
chaos

characteristic
charity
chart
charter
chase
chat
cheer
cheese
chest
chicken
childhood
chip
chocolate
chop
cigarette
cinema
circuit
circumstance
cite
civilian
civil war
clash
classical
clever
client
climate
climb
clinic
clock
close
clothing
cloud
coal
coalition
coat
code
coffee
collective
colonel
coloured
column
combat
combination
combine
comedy
comfort
comfortable
command
commander
commentator
commerce
commissioner
communicate
communication
compare
comparison
compensation
compete
competitive
competitor
complaint
complicated
component
compose
comprehensive
compromise
concede
concentrate
concentration
concept
concerned
concert
concession
conclude
conclusion
concrete
condemn
confident
confront
confrontation
congressional
connection
conscious
consciousness
consequence
considering
consist
consistent

constitution
construct
construction
consult
consultant
contemporary
content
contest
context
continent
contrast
contribute
controversial
controversy
convention
conventional
conversation
convert
convict
conviction
convince
cooking
co-operate
cope
core
corporate
corporation
corruption
cottage
cotton
cough
counsel
counter
counterpart
countryside
coup
courage
coverage
cow
crack
craft
crazy
cream
creative
crew
cricket
criticize
crop
crown
crucial
cruise
crystal
cue
cultural
cure
curious
curtain
cutting
cycle
dad
dare
deadline
deal
dealer
dear
debut
deck
declaration
decorate
define
definitely
definition
delegate
delegation
deliberate
delight
delighted
delivery
demonstrate
demonstration
deposit
depression
depth
description
desert
deserve
designer
desperate

detailed
detective
determined
device
dialogue
diary
dig
diplomat
diplomatic
dirty
disappear
disappointed
disaster
discipline
disclose
discount
discovery
dish
distribution
dividend
divorce
dominant
done
draft
drag
drain
drama
drift
drum
dump
dust
eager
ear
earnings
ease
easily
echo
edit
editorial
efficient
elderly
electoral
electric
electricity
electronic
elegant
eliminate
elsewhere
embassy
emotion
emotional
emphasis
emphasize
empire
employ
employer
employment
empty
enable
encounter
enemy
engage
engineer
engineering
enhance
enormous
enterprise
entertain
entertainment
enthusiasm
entirely
entitle
entrance
equity
equivalent
era
error
essentially
establishment
etc.
ethnic
everywhere
evil
exactly
examination
exception
excerpt
excess

exchange rate
exciting
excuse
execute
exhaust
exhibition
exile
existing
expand
expectation
expense
experiment
explanation
explode
exploit
explore
explosion
expose
exposure
expression
extensive
extent
extraordinary
extreme
fabric
faction
fade
fairly
faith
false
familiar
fancy
fantasy
fare
fate
fault
federation
fence
fierce
fighter
fine
fiscal
fishing
fit
fix
fixed
flag
flash
flavour
flee
fleet
flexible
float
flood
fold
folk
fool
forecast
foreigner
forest
form
formula
forth
fortune
foundation
frame
fraud
freeze
friendly
friendship
frustrate
fry
fulfil
fundamental
funny
furniture
gallery
gamble
gang
gap
gate
gear
gene
general election
generate
generous
gentle
gentleman

genuine
gesture
giant
gift
given
glad
glance
global
golden
golf
govern
grab
grade
gradual
graduate
grain
grass
grave
grip
gross
guerrilla
guilty
guitar
habit
hall
halt
harass
harbour
harm
hat
hate
headline
headquarters
heal
healthy
hearing
heaven
height
helicopter
hell
he'll
hello
hero
hi
hide
highlight
hill
hint
hip
hire
historic
historical
HIV
holy
homeless
homosexual
honest
honour
hook
horror
household
human rights
humour
hunt
hunter
identity
illegal
illness
illustrate
imagination
immigrant
immigration
immune
implement
implication
imply
impress
impression
impressive
improvement
inch
incredible
index
inevitable
infect
infection
inform
ingredient

initial	live-in	mystery	penalty	proud	revolutionary
initially	living	myth	penny	province	reward
initiative	load	native	pension	provision	rhythm
injured	lobby	naturally	pepper	provoke	rice
inner	local authority	naval	percentage	psychological	rid
innocent	location	navy	perfectly	psychology	rider
inquiry	lock	nearby	permanent	pub	right-wing
inspect	lonely	neat	permission	publication	ring
inspector	long-time	necessarily	permit	publicity	riot
install	loose	neck	personality	publisher	roach
instant	lost	negative	personally	publishing	rocket
instruct	loud	neighbour	personnel	pump	romantic
instrument	lovely	nerve	perspective	punch	roof
integrate	lover	nervous	persuade	pupil	root
intellectual	lower	net	pet	pure	rose
intelligence	luck	nevertheless	phase	pursue	rouge
intelligent	lucky	newly	philosophy	qualified	rough
intense	luxury	nightmare	phrase	qualify	routine
intention	mad	nod	pick-up	quantity	row
interesting	made-up	noise	pile	racial	rugby
interim	magic	normally	pill	racing	ruin
interior	mail	nose	pilot	rage	ruling
internal	make-up	noted	pin	raid	rumour
invasion	manner	notion	pink	rail	runner
invest	manufacture	nowhere	pipe	railway	rural
invitation	manufacturer	numerous	pit	rally	rush
involvement	map	nurse	pitch	rank	sack
iron	march	objective	plain	rape	sacrifice
Islam	margin	observe	planet	rare	sail
Islamic	marine	observer	planning	rarely	saint
it'll	marked	obtain	plastic	rating	sake
jacket	married	occasional	plate	raw	salary
jail	mask	occupation	platform	ray	salt
jazz	massive	ocean	pleasant	react	sample
jersey	mate	o'clock	pleased	reading	sand
jet	maximum	offence	pleasure	rear	satellite
Jew	mayor	offensive	pledge	reasonable	satisfied
joke	meal	offering	plenty	reckon	sauce
journey	meaning	one's	plot	recognition	savings
joy	meat	onto	plunge	recording	scandal
judgment	mechanism	opening	pocket	recover	scientific
juice	medal	opera	poem	recovery	scream
junior	medicine	operator	poet	recruit	script
jury	medium	opponent	poetry	reduction	seal
justify	membership	oppose	point of view	reel	secretary-general
keen	mental	opposed	pole	reference	segment
killer	merchant	opposite	policeman	referendum	seize
killing	mere	opt	police officer	regime	select
kilometre	merely	orange	pollution	register	selection
kiss	merger	ordinary	pool	regret	self
knee	mess	organized	pop	regulation	senator
knife	metal	origin	port	regulator	sensible
knock	metre	originally	portrait	relate	sensitive
know-how	middle class	ought	pose	related	seriously
label	midnight	ourselves	pot	relative	servant
laboratory	mild	outcome	potato	relax	set-to
lad	militant	outline	pour	relevant	shade
lake	milk	output	poverty	reliable	shadow
landscape	mill	outstanding	practical	religion	shame
lane	mind	overcome	praise	reluctant	shaped
lap	miner	overnight	precisely	rely	shareholder
last	minimum	overseas	predict	remaining	shed
latter	minor	overwhelming	pregnant	remark	sheet
laughter	mirror	owe	premier	remarkable	shell
layer	missile	ownership	premium	remind	shelter
leaf	missing	pace	preparation	remote	shift
leak	mixed	pact	preserve	renew	shirt
lean	mixture	painful	presidency	rent	shoe
leap	mobile	palace	presumably	repair	shopping
lease	moderate	pale	previously	reputation	shore
leather	modest	pan	pride	requirement	shortage
lecture	molecule	panel	priest	rescue	shortly
left	monetary	panic	primary	resign	short-term
legislation	monitor	parliamentary	prime	resignation	shouldn't
lend	monthly	part	principal	resist	shout
lens	mood	participate	prior	resistance	shut
lesson	moon	partly	priority	resolve	sick
liberate	moral	partnership	privatize	resort	sigh
liberty	moreover	passage	procedure	restore	signal
library	mostly	passenger	proceed	resume	silence
licence	motion	passion	profession	retail	silent
lie	motivate	path	profile	retain	silver
light	mount	pause	prominent	retire	singer
limited	mum	peaceful	prompt	retirement	sink
lip	muscle	peak	proof	retreat	ski
literary	musical	peer	proportion	revenue	sky
literature	musician	peg	prosecute	reverse	slice
live	mutual	pen	protein	revolution	slide

1321

slight	steal	sweep	ton	unhappy	wash
slim	steam	sweet	tone	unidentified	watch
smart	steel	swim	tool	uniform	weaken
smash	stem	swing	tooth	unique	wealth
smell	stick	switch	torture	united	we'd
smooth	stimulate	symbol	tourist	unity	wedding
snap	stir	sympathy	tournament	universe	weekly
snow	stock exchange	symptom	tower	unknown	weigh
so-called	stock market	tackle	toy	unlike	welfare
soccer	stomach	tactic	trace	unusual	well-known
socialist	storm	tail	trader	upper	wet
software	strain	takeover	tradition	upset	wheel
soil	strategic	tale	traffic	urban	whenever
solicitor	stream	tall	tragedy	urgent	whereas
solid	strengthen	tank	trail	user	whilst
solve	stretch	tap	transform	valley	whip
somehow	strict	teaching	transition	valuable	whisper
somewhat	striking	tear	trap	van	wicket
somewhere	string	technical	traveller	vary	widespread
sophisticated	strip	teenager	treasury	vast	winning
soul	stroke	temperature	tremendous	vegetable	winter
spare	stupid	temple	trend	venture	wipe
spark	subsequent	temporary	trick	venue	wire
speaker	subsidy	tendency	trigger	verdict	wise
specialist	substance	tennis	triumph	vessel	withdrawal
specialize	substantial	tension	truck	veteran	witness
species	substitute	terrorist	truly	via	wooden
specifically	sudden	testing	tube	vice	world war
spectacular	sufficient	text	tune	victimize	worldwide
speculate	sugar	theme	tunnel	violate	worried
spell	suggestion	therapy	twin	violent	wrap
spin	suicide	thick	twist	virtually	written
spiritual	suitable	thin	typical	virus	yacht
spite	sum	Third World	ultimate	visible	yellow
sponsor	super	thorough	ultimately	vision	yen
spray	superb	threatening	unable	visitor	yield
spur	superior	throat	uncle	vital	youngster
squad	surely	tide	underground	vitamin	yours
squeeze	surgery	tight	undermine	voluntary	zone
stadium	surplus	till	understanding	volunteer	
stamp	surrender	tiny	unemployment	vulnerable	
stare	suspend	tip	unexpected	wage	
statistic	suspicion	tired	unfair	wake	
steady	sustain	tissue	unfortunately	warning	